C000144559

MDL marinas - helping you take it easy

SOUTH WEST

QUEEN ANNE'S BATTERY PLYMOUTH
(01752) 671142

DARTSIDE QUAY * BRIXHAM
(01803) 845445 * (boat storage yard only)

BRIXHAM MARINA BRIXHAM
(01803) 882929

TORQUAY MARINA TORQUAY
(01803) 200210

SOUTH COAST

COBB'S QUAY POOLE
(01202) 674299

HYTHE MARINA VILLAGE SOUTHAMPTON
(023) 8020 7073

OCEAN VILLAGE MARINA SOUTHAMPTON
(023) 8022 9385

SHAMROCK QUAY SOUTHAMPTON
(023) 8022 9461

SAXON WHARF SOUTHAMPTON
(023) 8033 9490

HAMBLE POINT MARINA SOUTHAMPTON
(023) 8045 2464

PORT HAMBLE MARINA SOUTHAMPTON
(023) 8045 2741

MERCURY YACHT HARBOUR SOUTHAMPTON
(023) 8045 5994

NORTHNEY MARINA HAYLING ISLAND
(023) 9246 6321

THAMES

BRAY MARINA BRAY
(01628) 623654

WINDSOR MARINA WINDSOR
(01753) 853911

PENTON HOOK MARINA CHERTSEY
(01932) 568681

EAST COAST

CHATHAM MARITIME MARINA CHATHAM
(01634) 899200

WOOLVERSTONE MARINA IPSWICH
(01473) 780206

Quote ref: AL

www.marinas.co.uk email: enquiries@mdlmarinas.co.uk

MDL

Marina Developments Limited

THE MACMILLAN REEDS NAUTICAL ALMANAC 2002

Bound & Looseleaf editions

EDITORS

Basil D'Oliveira, Brian Goulder, Edward Lee-Elliott

First published 1980
This edition published 2001

IMPORTANT NOTE
This Almanac is intended as an aid to navigation only. The information contained within should not be relied on for navigational use, rather it should be used in conjunction with official hydrographic data. Whilst every care has been taken in compiling the information contained in this Almanac, the publishers, editors and their agents accept no responsibility for any errors or omissions, or for any accidents or mishaps which may arise from its use.

CORRESPONDENCE
Letters on nautical and commercial matters should be addressed to:

The Editors, Macmillan Reeds Nautical Almanac,
Nautical Data Ltd, The Book Barn,
Westbourne, Hampshire, PO10 8RS, UK
Tel: +44 (0)1243 389352 *Fax: +44 (0)1243 379136*
editorial@nauticaldata.com

Production control
Chris Stevens

Cartography & production
Jamie Russell, Chris Stevens, Garold West

Design & production consultants
Seb Gardner, John Johnson, Derek Slatter

Advertisement sales
Angie Cross, Kirsten Filby, Kerry White
Moira Baldock – *Production*
Tony Phelps – *Sales director*

Cover design
Slatter-Anderson

Cover photography
The Moody 54 courtesy of
Moody Marketing & Development Ltd

Nautical Data Limited
The Book Barn, Westbourne,
Hampshire, PO10 8RS, UK
Tel: +44 (0)1243 389352
Fax: +44 (0)1243 379136
info@nauticaldata.com

ISBN 0 333 90821 X
ISBN 0 333 90824 4 - Looseleaf UK Edition
ISBN 0 333 90823 6 - Looseleaf Europe Edition
A CIP catalogue record for this book is available from the British Library
Printed in Great Britain by Bath Press

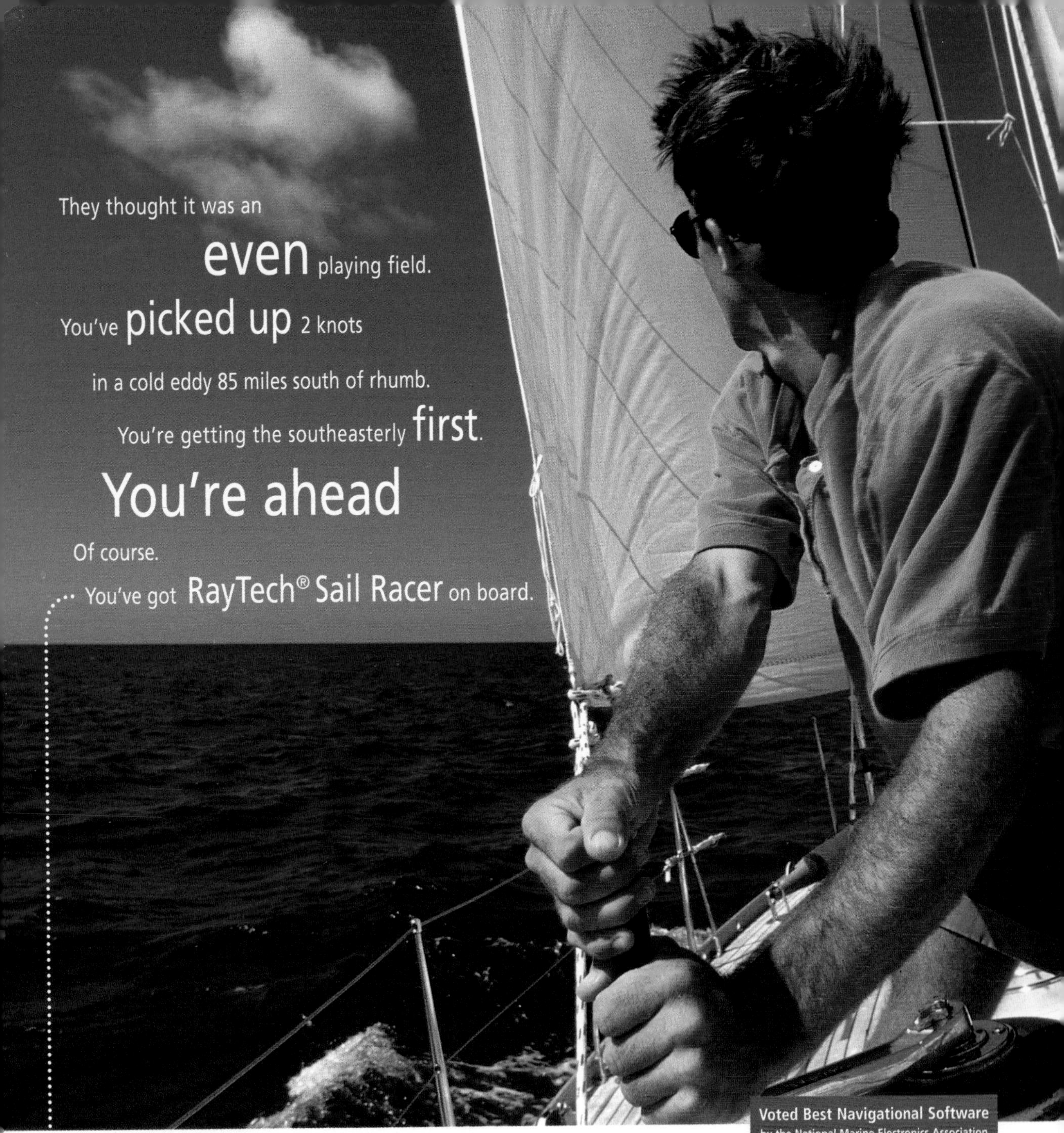
They thought it was an
even playing field.
You've picked up 2 knots
in a cold eddy 85 miles south of rhumb.
You're getting the southeasterly first.
You're ahead
Of course.
You've got RayTech® Sail Racer on board.
Voted Best Navigational Software
by the National Marine Electronics Association

RayTech® Sail Racer is the world's most powerful navigation PC software for racers and serious cruisers. Plot a course, plan a route, and display your vessel on electronic charts. That's just the beginning. Overlay weather forecasts and tides and currents. Collect and analyse polar data. Track vessel and environmental data on time-base graphs. Calibrate your instruments, analyse layline and start strategies. And identify your optimum route based on currents, wind and vessel performance characteristics. If you want to be first over the finish line, visit your Raymarine dealer or go online at www.raytechonline.com

Tides and Currents

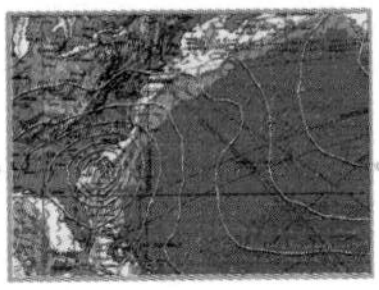

Weather Overlay

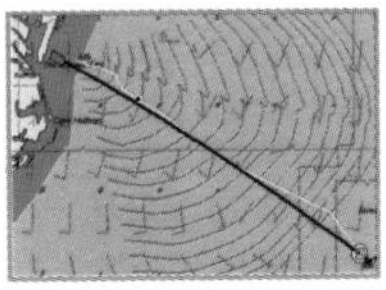

Route Optimisation

So advanced, it's easy.

Raymarine
ON BOARD

Contents

CONTENTS V

BEAUFORT SCALE SEA STATES IX

INTRODUCTION .... Page 1
Numbering system, index, acknowledgments, suggestions for improvements, supplements, abbreviations and symbols.

CHAPTER 1 17
GENERAL INFORMATION
Rules of the road, documentation of yachts, HM Customs, useful addresses.

CHAPTER 2 31
COASTAL NAVIGATION
Definitions and terms, IALA buoyage, light characteristics, passage planning. Tables giving: distance off by Vertical Sextant Angle; distance/speed/time; distance of horizon; distance of lights when rising/dipping; true bearing of Sun at sunrise/set; Sun's declination; phases of the Moon; eclipse notes; sunrise/set, twilights; moonrise/set; conversion tables.

CHAPTER 3 49
RADIO NAVIGATIONAL AIDS
GPS, DGPS, Loran-C, Waypoints, Racons.

CHAPTER 4 63
COMMUNICATIONS
International Code, radio procedures, port operations, VTS, Inmarsat, navigational warnings, time, coast radio stations, link calls, Internet.

CHAPTER 5 81
WEATHER
Shipping forecast, Beaufort scale, conversion scales, weather terms, radio broadcasts, Navtex, Marinecall, MetFax, SMS, forecasters, Coastguard, HF Fax, coast radio stations.

CHAPTER 6 115
SAFETY
Safety equipment, emergency signals, GMDSS, EPIRBs, UK SAR procedures, HM Coastguard, VHF DF, Subfacts and Gunfacts, SAR organisation on the Continent.

CHAPTER 7 149
TIDES
Explanation, definitions, calculating times and heights of HW and LW, intermediate times and heights of tide, factors, rule of twelfths, Standard ports, clearance under bridges, tidal prediction by computer, meteorological conditions, tidal streams.

CHAPTER 8 165
VTS AND TSS
VTS explanation, Listening Watch details and individual area diagrams. TSS explanation, Key to symbols and individual charts with zone sizes and positions.

CHAPTER 9 193
HARBOURS, COASTS AND TIDES
Contents, map of areas, general and harbour information, holidays, high speed craft, ferries, distance tables, harbours, tide tables, lights and waypoints, passage information.

Area 1 **South West England, including Isles of Scilly** 209*
2 **Central Southern England** 255*
3 **South East England** 321*
4 **East England** 345*
5 **North East England** 401*
6 **South East Scotland** 433*
7 **North East Scotland** 461*
8 **North West Scotland** 493*
9 **South West Scotland** 531*
10 **North West England, Isle of Man and North Wales** 561*
11 **South Wales and Bristol Channel** 593*
12 **South Ireland** 629*
13 **North Ireland** 669*
14 **Channel Islands** 703*
15 **Central North France** 737**
16 **North Brittany** 767**
17 **South Brittany** 799**
18 **South Biscay** 829**
19 **North Spain** 863**
20 **Portugal** 887**
21 **SW Spain and Gibraltar** 907**
22 **North East France** 923**
23 **Belgium and Netherlands** 961**
24 **Germany** 1003**
25 **Denmark** 1041**

INDEX 1057***

* *Included in the UK & Ireland Looseleaf edition.*

** *Included in the Continental Europe Looseleaf edition.*

*** *Included in the Combined Looseleaf edition.*

THE NEW MOODY 54
Inspired by passion.
Born out of a deep love of sailing,
the new 54 is a yacht to set the pulse racing.
The British Nautical Awards
Winner 'Offshore' 2000
Moody 54 'Sailboat of the Year' Award
Moody
SHARE THE EXPERIENCE
38 42 47 54 64
www.moody.co.uk

Beaufort Scale Sea States

In enclosed waters or near land with an offshore wind, wave heights will be less but possibly steeper – particularly with wind against tide. Wave height for a given wind strength depends upon the distance it has travelled and the length of time for which the wind has been blowing.

Photography
© Crown – Force 0, 11
© G.J.Simpson – Force 1, 2, 7
© I.G. MacNeil – Force 3, 4, 5, 6
© W.A.E. Smith – Force 8
© J.P. Laycock – Force 9
© G. Allen – Force 10
© J.F.Thomson – Force 12

Force 0 0-1 Kts Calm Wave Ht 0m

Force 1 1-3 Kts Light Air Wave Ht 0m

Force 2 4-6 Kts Light Breeze
Wave Ht 0.1m

Force 3 7-10 Kts Gentle Breeze
Wave Ht 0.4m

Force 4 11-16 Kts Moderate Breeze
Wave Ht 1m

Force 5 17-21 Kts Fresh Breeze
Wave Ht 2m

Force 6 22-27 Kts Strong Breeze
Wave Ht 3m

Force 7 28-33 Kts Near Gale
Wave Ht 4m

Force 8 34-40 Kts Gale
Wave Ht 5.5m

Force 9 41-47 Kts Severe Gale
Wave Ht 7m

Force 10 48-55 Kts Storm
Wave Ht 9m

Force 11 56-63 Kts Violent Storm
Wave Ht 11m

Force 12 64 plus Kts Hurricane
Wave Ht 14m

RYA

The Almanac

The 2002 Macmillan Reeds Almanac contains in one volume all the nautical information needed by yachtsmen navigating the waters around the United Kingdom, Ireland and the coast of Europe from North Denmark to Gibraltar.

A Supplement is issued each year in April to update the Almanac.

Associated publications & navigational products

Macmillan Reeds Looseleaf Almanac is an updateable looseleaf version of this Almanac. Available in two editions, covering the continental European coast, and the UK and Ireland. Supplied in a stout binder, navigators can add and remove information to suit their need.

PBO Small Craft Almanac produced by Macmillan Reeds for Practical Boat Owner magazine. This handy volume contains all the essential facts and figures needed to take a boat from Denmark, round the UK and all the way to Gibraltar.

Three wire-bound Almanacs in a concise, yet detailed format with more localised coverage:

Macmillan Reeds Channel Almanac covers both sides of the English Channel.

Macmillan Reeds Western Almanac covers the West UK and Irish coasts.

Macmillan Reeds Eastern Almanac covers the East UK and adjacent continental coasts.

The Cruising Companions combine traditional pilotage with in-depth information on shore-side facilities and places of interest: West France, North Brittany & Channel Islands, East Coast Rivers, West Country, Northeast France and Belgium, Southwest Spain & Portugal and Northwest Spain.

The Macmillan Reeds Yachtsman's Handbook is the ultimate reference book to provide the boat owner with in-depth information on all aspects of yachting.

Weather to Go - Visit **www.nauticaldata.com** to register for a free, weekly email weather report sent direct to your email inbox.

Seafinder - Your guide to services, supplies, harbours, marinas, emergency services, nationally and area by area. Included FREE of charge with this almanac.

Contact the publishers for details of the availability of these publications.

THE ALMANAC

Numbering system

There are nine chapters. For ease of reference each chapter is divided into numbered sections, prefaced by the number of the chapter. Thus the sections in Chapter 7, for example, are numbered 7.1, 7.2, etc.

Within each section the key paragraphs are numbered. Thus in section 7.2 (say) the main paragraphs are numbered 7.2.1, 7.2.2, 7.2.3, etc.

Diagrams carry the chapter number and a figure in brackets, thus: Fig. 7 (1), Fig. 7 (2), Fig. 7 (3), etc.

Tables carry the chapter number and a figure in brackets, thus: Table 3 (1), Table 3(2), etc.

Chapter 9 is divided into 25 geographical areas. In the Looseleaf editions, only the relevant areas are included.

Contents and Index

The main paragraph headings and the page numbers of each section are listed on the contents page at the start of each chapter and geographical area. A full index for the bound Almanac is located at the back.

General acknowledgments

The Editors would like to thank the many individuals and official bodies who have kindly provided essential information and much advice in the preparation of this Almanac. They include the UK Hydrographic Office, Trinity House, Northern Lighthouse Board, Irish Lights, HM Nautical Almanac Office, HM Stationery Office, HM Customs & Excise, Meteorological Office, British Telecom, BBC and IBA, Maritime and Coastguard Agency, Royal National Lifeboat Institution, Koninklijke Nederlandse Redding Maatschappij (KNRM), Deutsche Gesellschaft zur Rettung Schiffbrüchiger (DGzRS), Port of London Authority, Associated British Ports, countless Harbour Masters and our many individual agents.

Chartlets, tidal stream diagrams and tidal curves are reproduced from Admiralty Charts and Publications with permission of the UK Hydrographic Office (Licence No HO 313/961001/01) and the Controller of HMSO.

The tidal stream arrows on the S and W coasts of Ireland are printed in 9.12.3 and 9.13.3 by kind permission of the Irish Cruising Club and the RCC for the tidal stream diagrams printed in 9.1.5.

Information from the Admiralty List of Lights, Admiralty Sailing Directions, Admiralty Tide Tables, and the Admiralty List of Radio Signals is reproduced with the permission of the UK Hydrographic Office and the Controller of HMSO.

WARNING: No National Hydrographic Office has verified the information in this product and none accepts liability for the accuracy of reproduction or any modifications made thereafter. No National Hydrographic Office warrants that this product satisfies national or international regulations regarding the use of the appropriate products for navigation.

Chartlets are only intended for reference and should not be used for navigation. Always consult fully updated navigational charts for the latest information.

Extracts from the following are published by permission of the Controller of HM Stationery Office: *International Code of Signals, 1969; Meteorological Office Weather Services for Shipping.*

Phases of the Moon and Sun/Moon rising and setting times are derived from the current edition of the Nautical Almanac, and are included by permission of HM Nautical Almanac Office and of the Council for the Central Laboratory of the Research Councils.

Acknowledgments – tidal predictions

UK and Foreign tidal predictions are supplied by the UK Hydrographic Office, Taunton TA1 2DN, and the Proudman Laboratory, Birkenhead, L43 7RA.

Acknowledgment is also made to the following authorities for permission to use tidal predictions stated:

SHOM, France: Dunkerque, Dieppe, Le Havre, Cherbourg, St Malo, Brest, Pointe de Grave, authorisation (No. 769/99).

Rijkswaterstaat, The Netherlands: Vlissingen (Flushing), and Hoek van Holland.

BSH, Hamburg and Rostock: Helgoland, Wilhelmshaven and Cuxhaven (BSH 8095-02/99-Z1102).

Marina Institute Hidrográfico, Portugal: Lisboa.

IMPROVING THE ALMANAC

Suggestions for improvements

The Editors always welcome suggestions for improving the content or layout. Ideas based on experience and practical use afloat are especially welcome. It is not always feasible to implement suggestions received, but all will be carefully considered. Even minor ideas are welcome. Please write your comments on the Supplement application card, or send them by letter, fax or e-mail direct to the appropriate Editor.

The Editor, The MRNA, Nautical Data Limited, The Book Barn, Westbourne, Hants PO10 8RS.
☎: 01243 377977. 📠: 01243 379136.
e-mail: editorial@nauticaldata.com.

Notification of errors

Although great care has been taken in compiling the information from innumerable sources, it is recognised that some errors may occur. The Editors would be grateful if their attention could be called to any such lapses.

KEEPING IT UP TO DATE

Sources of amendments

It is most important that charts and other navigational publications – such as this Almanac – are kept up to date. Corrections to Admiralty charts and publications are issued weekly in *Admiralty Notices to Mariners,* obtainable from Admiralty Chart Agents, or they can be sighted at Customs Houses or Mercantile Marine Offices.

Our update Supplement

This Almanac contains corrections up to Notices to Mariners, Edition No. 23/2001. Corrections up to March 2002 are contained in the free Supplement, published in April 2002.

As information contained in this Almanac is subject to constant change throughout the year, it is essential that users should **immediately** apply for the correcting Supplement in order to bring the Almanac fully up to date before using it for planning or at sea. The correcting supplement will be available both in printed form and online at the Macmillan Reeds website (address below). To register for this free updating service simply complete the online registration form at **www.nauticaldata.com.** If you prefer, you may complete and return the enclosed registration card to: *Nautical Data Limited, The Book Barn, Westbourne, Hants PO10 8RS* **enclosing a stamped (for 100 grammes) self-addressed C4 size envelope or enclose £1.50 for postage and packing.**

Record of amendments

Tick the box when the appropriate amendments have been made.

2001 Weekly Notices to Mariners

1	☐	**14**	☐	**27**	☐	**40**	☐
2	☐	**15**	☐	**28**	☐	**41**	☐
3	☐	**16**	☐	**29**	☐	**42**	☐
4	☐	**17**	☐	**30**	☐	**43**	☐
5	☐	**18**	☐	**31**	☐	**44**	☐
6	☐	**19**	☐	**32**	☐	**45**	☐
7	☐	**20**	☐	**33**	☐	**46**	☐
8	☐	**21**	☐	**34**	☐	**47**	☐
9	☐	**22**	☐	**35**	☐	**48**	☐
10	☐	**23**	☐	**36**	☐	**49**	☐
11	☐	**24**	☐	**37**	☐	**50**	☐
12	☐	**25**	☐	**38**	☐	**51**	☐
13	☐	**26**	☐	**39**	☐	**52**	☐

Abbreviations and symbols

The following selected abbreviations and symbols may be encountered in this Almanac, or in Almanac Supplements, Admiralty Publications and Admiralty Charts.

AB	Alongside berth
Abm	Abeam
ABP	Associated British Ports
abt	About
AC	220-250v AC electrical supplies
AC, ACA	Admiralty Chart, Admiralty Chart Agent
✈	Airport
Aff Mar	Affaires Maritimes
ALL	Admiralty List of Lights
ALRS	Admiralty List of Radio Signals
Alt	Altitude
Al	Alternating Lt
AM	Amplitude Modulation
anch, ⚓	Anchorage
annly	Annually
ANWB	Dutch Tourist Association of Road & Waterway Users
AOR-E or W	Atlantic Ocean Region (Inmarsat)
Appr.	Approaches
ARCC	Aeronautical Rescue Co-ordination Centre
ATT	Admiralty Tide Tables
Auto	Météo Répondeur Automatique
Az	Azimuth
B.	Bay
B	Black
Ⓑ	Bank (£)
Bar, [symbol]	Licensed bar
Bcst	Broadcast
BH	Boat Hoist (tons)
Bk.	Bank (shoal)
bk	Broken
Bkwtr	Breakwater
Bldg	Building
Bn(s)	Beacon, beacon(s)
Bol	Bollard
brg	Bearing
BS	British Standard
BSH	German Hydrographic chart(s)
BST	British Summer Time
BT	British Telecom
Bu	Blue
BWB	British Waterways Board
By(s)	Buoy, buoys
BY	Boatyard
C.	Cape, Cabo, Cap
C	Crane (tons)
c	Coarse
ca	Cable
Cas	Castle
CD	Chart datum
CEVNI	Code Européen de Voies de la Navigation Intérieure
CG, [CGR symbol]	Coastguard, Coastguard radio
[CG symbol], [symbol]	Coastguard MRCC, MRSC
CH, [symbol]	Chandlery
Ch	Channel (VHF)
Ch, ✠	Church, chapel
chan.	Channel (navigational)
Chy	Chimney
cm	Centimetre(s)
Col, ▌	Column, pillar, obelisk
conspic	Conspicuous
const	Construction
cont	Continuous
Corr	Correction
cov	Covers
Cr.	Creek
CROSS	Centre Régional Opérationnel de Surveillance et Sauvetage (French equivalent of MRCC)
CRS, [CRS symbol]	Coast Radio Station
Cup	Cupola
⊖	Customs (see HMC)
Cy	Clay
[D symbol]	Diesel by cans
Dec	Declination
decrg	Decreasing
dest	Destroyed
DGPS	Differential GPS
Dia	Diaphone
♦ ◊	Diamond
D	Diesel from pump
Dir Lt	Directional light
discont	Discontinued
dist	Distance, Distant
Dk	Dock
DLR	Dockland Light Railway
dm	Decimetre(s)
Dn(s)	Dolphin(s)
Dr	Doctor
dr	Dries
DR	Dead Reckoning
DSC	Digital Selective Calling
DST	Daylight Saving Time
DW	Deep Water, Deep-draught Route
DYC	Dutch Yacht Chart(s)
DZ	Danger Zone (buoy)
E	East
EC	Early closing
ECM [symbols]	East Cardinal Mark
ECM	Éditions Cartographiques Maritimes
ED	Existence doubtful, European datum
El	Electrical repairs

Elev	Elevation
Ⓔ	Electronics repairs
Ent.	Entrance
EP	Estimated position
Est.	Estuary
ETA	Estimated Time of Arrival
ETD	Estimated Time of Departure
exper	Experimental
explos	Explosive
ext	Extension
F&A	Fore and aft berth
FAX, Fax	Facsimile
)))	Fog signal
F	Fixed Light
f	Fine
Fcst	Forecast
FFL	Fixed and Flashing light
Fl	Flashing light
FM	Frequency Modulation
Fog Det Lt	Fog Detector Light
Freq, Fx	Frequency
FS	Flagstaff, Flagpole
ft	Foot, feet
Ft	Fort
FV(s)	Fishing vessel(s)
FW	Fresh water supply
G	Gravel
G, Ⓖ	Green, Green Fixed light
Gas	Calor Gas
Gaz	Camping Gaz
GC	Great-circle
GDOP (GPS)	Geometrical Dilution of Precision
GHA	Greenwich Hour Angle
GMDSS	Global Maritime Distress and Safety System
GPS	Global Positioning System
grt	Gross Registered Tonnage
Gt	Great
Gy	Grey
	Hearing-impaired facilities
h	Hard, Hour
H+, H–	Minutes past/before each hour
H24	Continuous
HAT	Highest Astronomical Tide
Hd.	Head, Headland
HF	High Frequency
HFP	High Focal Plane Buoy
HIE	Highlands & Islands Enterprise
HJ	Day Service only, Sunrise to Sunset
HMC, ⊖	HM Customs
HMSO	Her Majesty's Stationery Office
HN	Night Service only, Sunset to Sunrise
Hn.	Haven
Ho	House
HO	Office hours, Hydrographic Office
	Holding tank pumpout
(hor)	Horizontally disposed
🄷 ⊕	Hospital
Hbr	Harbour
Hrs	Hours
Hr Mr, ⓗ	Harbour Master
ht	Height
HW	High Water
HX	No fixed hrs
Hz	Hertz
🄸	Harbour information/tidal data
I	Island, islet
IALA	International Association of Lighthouse Authorities
Ident	Identification signal
IDM	Isolated Danger Mark
IHO	International Hydrographic Organisation
(illum)	Illuminated
IMO	International Maritime Organisation
incrg	Increasing
info	Information
INMARSAT	International Maritime Satellite Organisation
inop	Inoperative
INT	International
intens	Intensified
IPTS	International Port Traffic Signals
IQ	Interrupted quick flashing light
IRPCS	International Regulations for Prevention of Collision at Sea
Iso	Isophase light
ITU	International Telecommunications Union
ITZ	Inshore Traffic Zone
IUQ	Interrupted ultra quick flashing light
IVQ	Interrupted very quick flashing light
kHz	Kilohertz
km	Kilometre(s)
kn	knot(s)
Kos	Kosangas
kW	Kilowatts
L	Lake, Loch, Lough
L, Lndg	Landing place
	Launderette
Lat	Latitude
LAT	Lowest Astronomical Tide
Lanby	Large Automatic Navigational Buoy
LB, 🄻🄱	Lifeboat, inshore lifeboat
Ldg	Leading
L Fl	Long-flashing light
Le.	Ledge
LF	Low frequency
LHA	Local Hour Angle
LH	Left hand

LL	List of Lights
Lndg,	Landing place
LOA	Length overall
Long	Longitude
LT	Local time
Lt(s), ☆	Light(s)
Lt By	Light buoy
Lt F	Light float
Lt Ho	Lighthouse
Lt V	Light vessel
LW	Low Water
	Moorings available
M	Sea mile(s)
M	Mud
m	Metre(s)
mm	Millimetre(s)
Mag	Magnetic, magnitude (of Star)
,	Marina, Yacht harbour, Marina Radio
MCA	Maritime and Coastguard Agency
ME	Marine engineering repairs
Météo	Météorologie/Weather
MF	Medium Frequency
MHWN	Mean High Water Neaps
MHWS	Mean High Water Springs
MHz	Megahertz
min(s)	Minute(s) of time
Mk	Mark
ML	Mean Level
MLWN	Mean Low Water Neaps
MLWS	Mean Low Water Springs
MMSI	Maritime Mobile Service Call Identity Code
Mo	Morse
Mon	Monument, Monday
MRCC, CG	Maritime Rescue Co-ordination Centre
MRSC,	Maritime Rescue Sub-Centre
ms	Millisecond(s); minutes, seconds
MSI	Marine Safety Information
MSL	Mean Sea Level
Mt.	Mountain, Mount
N	North
NB	Notice Board
NCM	North Cardinal Mark
NGS	Naval Gunfire Support
NM	Notice(s) to Mariners
No	Number
NON	Unmodulated continuous wave emission
np	Neap tides
NP	Naval Publication
NRT	Net registered tonnage
NT	National Trust
Obscd	Obscured
Obstn	Obstruction
Oc	Occulting light
(occas)	Occasional
ODAS	Ocean Data Acquisition System
Off	Office
Or	Orange
OSGB	Ordnance Survey GB Datum (1936)
OT	Other times
	Partial-sighted facilities
P	Petrol from pump
	Petrol by cans
P.	Port (harbour)
P	Pebbles
(P)	Preliminary (NM)
PA	Position approximate
Pass.	Passage
Pax	Passengers
	Pilot boarding place
PC	Portuguese chart
PD	Position doubtful
PHM	Port-hand Mark
Pk.	Peak
	Perch, Stake (PHM & SHM)
PLA	Port of London Authority
PO, ✉	Post Office
PR	Port Radio
pos	Position
⚠	Precautionary Area
(priv)	Private
Prog	Prognosis (weather charts)
prohib	Prohibited
proj	Projected
prom	Prominent
Pt.	Point
Pta	Punta
PV	Pilot Vessel
Pyl	Pylon
Q	Quick flashing light
QHM	Queen's Harbour Master
R, Ⓡ	Red, Red Fixed light, Rock
R.	River
R, ✕	Restaurant
R	Rock
Ra	Coast Radar Station
Racon	Radar Transponder Beacon
	Radio reporting point
Radome	Radar dome
Ramark	Radar Beacon
RCC	Rescue Co-ordination Centre
Rds.	Roads, Roadstead
Rep	Reported
Rf.	Reef
RG, ◎RG	Radio Direction-Finding Station

RH	Right hand
⇄	Railway station
Rk, Rky	Rock, Rocky
RNLI	Royal National Lifeboat Institution
Ro-Ro	Roll-on Roll-off (ferry terminal)
● ○	Round, circular; Ball
RT	Radiotelephony
Ru	Ruins
S	South
S	Sand
S, St, Ste	Saint(s)
SAR	Search and Rescue
	SAR helicopter base
SBM,	Single buoy mooring
SC	Sailing Club, Spanish chart
Sch	School
SCM,	South Cardinal Mark
Sd.	Sound
SD	Sailing Directions, Semi-Diameter
SD	Sounding of doubtful depth
sec(s)	Second(s) (of time)
Sem	Semaphore
Seq	Sequence
sf	Stiff
Sh	Shells, Shoal
Sh	Shipwright, hull repairs, etc
SHM,	Starboard-hand Mark
SHOM	French Hydrographic Charts
Si	Silt
Sig	Signal
SIGNI	Signalisation de Navigation Intérieure (Dutch inland buoyage)
SM	Sailmaker
	Slip for launching, scrubbing
SNSM	Société Nationale de Sauvetage en Mer (Lifeboats)
so	Soft
SOLAS	Safety of Life at Sea (IMO Convention)
sous-CROSS	French equivalent to MRSC
Sp	Spire
sp	Spring tides
SPM	Special Mark, Single Point Mooring
SPS	Standard Positioning Service (GPS)
■ □	Square
SR	Sunrise
SS	Sunset, Signal Station
SSB	Single Sideband (Radio)
St	Stones
Stbd	Starboard
Sta	Station
Str.	Strait
subm	Submerged
SWM	Safe Water Mark
sy	Sticky
sync	Synchronised
(T), (temp)	Temporary (NM)
t	Ton, tonne
tbn	To be notified
TD	Fog signal temp discontinued
TE	Light temp extinguished
☎, Tel	Telephone
Tfc	Traffic
Tr	Tower
▲▼△▽	Triangle, cone
TSS,	Traffic Separation Scheme, TSS Radio In transit with
ufn	Until further notice
uncov	Uncovers
Unintens	Unintensified
unexam	Unexamined
UQ	Ultra quick flashing light
UTC	Universal Time (Co-ordinated)
V	Victuals, food stores, etc
Ⓥ,	Visitors berth/mooring
Var	Variation
Vel	Velocity
(vert)	Vertically disposed
VHF	Very High Frequency
Vi	Violet
vis	Visibility, visible
VLCC	Very large crude carrier
Volmet	Weather broadcasts for aviation
VTM	Vessel Traffic Management
VTS,	Vessel Traffic Service, VTS Radio
VQ	Very quick flashing light
W	West
W, Ⓦ	White, White Fixed light
WCM	West Cardinal Mark
Wd	Weed
wef	With effect from
WGS	World Geodetic System (datum)
	Wheelchair access
Whis	Whistle
WIP	Work in progress
	Withy (SHM & PHM)
Wk,	Wreck
WMO	World Meteorological Organisation
WPT, ⊕	Waypoint
, Wx	Weather (☎, frequency or times)
Y, Ⓨ	Yellow, Amber, Orange, Fixed light
YC,	Yacht Club
	Yacht harbour, Marina, Marina Radio
, Ⓥ	Yacht berth, Visitors mooring

SYMBOLS

- Yacht harbour, Marina
- Yacht berths without facilities
- Visitor's berth, Visitor's mooring
- Coastguard Radio, Coast Radio Station
- Port Radio, Marina Radio
- Vessel Traffic Service Radio
- Traffic Separation Scheme Radio
- Coastguard MRCC/MRSC
- Weather information
- Harbour Masters Office
- Anchoring prohibited
- Recommended anchorage
- Hospital
- Visitor's information
- Laundrette
- Post Office
- Airport
- Water tap
- Public toilets
- Search & Rescue helicopter
- Railway station
- Waypoint
- Parking for boats or trailers
- Chandlery
- Alongside berth
- Major light
- Minor light
- Rock awash at chart datum
- Underwater rock, depth unknown
- Dangerous Wreck, depth unknown,
- Rock which covers and uncovers
- Foul area
- Church
- Radio tower or mast
- Yacht Club, Sailing Club
- Public slipway
- Customs
- Precautionary area
- Public landing, steps, ladder
- Fuel station
- Petrol by can
- Diesel by can
- Refuse bin
- Holding tank pumpout
- Lifeboat station
- Fishing harbour
- Radio or Radar aid
- Fog signal
- Direction of buoyage
- Marine farm, Fish haven

BUOYS AND BEACONS

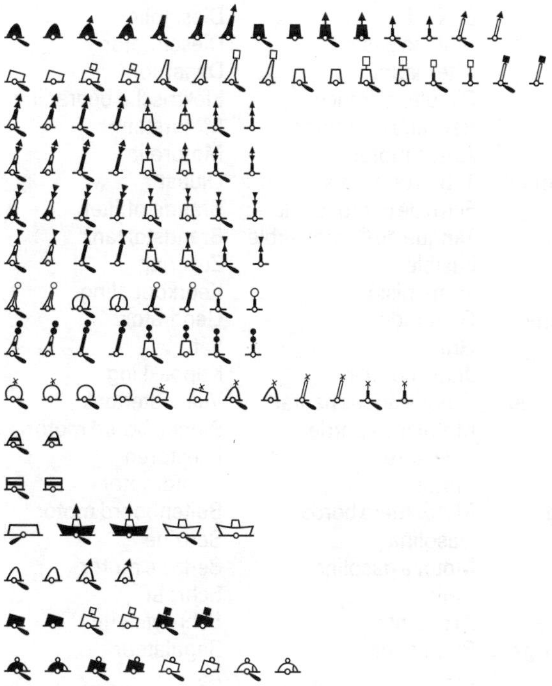

Starboard Hand Mark (SHM) (lit & unlit)

Port Hand Mark (PHM) (lit & unlit)

North Cardinal Mark (NCM) (lit & unlit)

East Cardinal Mark (ECM) (lit & unlit)

South Cardinal Mark (SCM) (lit & unlit)

West Cardinal Mark (WCM) (lit & unlit)

Safe Water Mark (SWM) (lit & unlit)

Isolated Danger Mark (IDM) (lit & unlit)

Special Marks (lit and unlit)

Preferred channels to port (lit and unlit)

Preferred channels to starboard (lit and unlit)

Light Vessel, Light Float, Lanby

Single colour other than green or black

Single colour other than red or black

Mooring buoy (lit & unlit)

English	German	French	Spanish	Dutch
Ashore				
Ashore	An Land	A terre	A tierra	Aan land
Airport	Flughafen	Aéroport	Aeropuerto	Vliegveld
Bank	Bank	Banque	Banco	Bank
Boathoist	Bootskran	Travelift	Travelift	Botenlift
Boatyard	Bootswerft	Chantier naval	Astilleros	Jachtwerf
Bureau de change	Wechselstelle	Bureau de change	Cambio	Geldwisselkantoor
Bus	Bus	Autobus	Autobús	Bus
Chandlery	Yachtausrüster	Shipchandler	Efectos navales	Scheepswinkel
Chemist	Apotheke	Pharmacie	Farmacia	Apotheek
Dentist	Zahnarzt	Dentiste	Dentista	Tandarts
Doctor	Arzt	Médecin	Médico	Dokter
Engineer	Motorenservice	Mécanicien	Mecánico	Monteur
Ferry	Fähre	Ferry/transbordeur	Ferry	Veer/Pont
Garage	Autowerkstatt	Station service	Garage	Garage
Harbour	Hafen	Port	Puerto	Haven
Hospital	Krankenhaus	Hôpital	Hospital	Ziekenhuis
Mast crane	Mastenkran	Grue	Grúa	Masten kraan
Post office	Postamt	Bureau de poste/PTT	Correos	Postkantoor
Railway station	Bahnhof	Gare de chemin de fer	Estación de ferrocanil	Station
Sailmaker	Segelmacher	Voilier	Velero	Zeilmaker
Shops	Geschäfte	Boutiques	Tiendas	Winkels
Slip	Slip	Cale	Varadero	Helling
Supermarket	Supermarkt	Supermarché	Supermercado	Supermarkt
Taxi	Taxi	Taxi	Taxis	Taxi
Village	Ort	Village	Pueblo	Dorp
Yacht club	Yachtclub	Club nautique	Club náutico	Jacht club
Engine and machinery				
Air filter	Luftfilter	Filtre à air	Filtro a aire	Lucht filter
Battery	Batterie	Batterie/accumulateur	Baterías	Accu
Bilge pump	Bilgepumpe	Pompe de cale	Bomba de achique	Bilge pomp
Carburettor	Vergaser	Carburateur	Carburador	Carburateur
Charging	Laden	Charger	Cargador	Opladen
Compression	Kompression	Compression	Compresión	Compressie
Cooling water	Kühlwasser	Eau de refroidissement	Agua refrigerado	Koelwater
Diesel	Diesel	Gas-oil	Gas-oil	Dieselolie
Diesel engine	Dieselmotor	Moteur diésel	Motor a gas-oil	Dieselmotor
Dynamo	Lichtmaschine	Alternateur	Alternador	Dynamo
Electrical wiring	Elektrik	Réseau électrique	Circuito eléctrico	Elektrische bedrading
Engine mount	Motorenfundament	Support moteur	Bancada del motor	Motorsteun
Engine oil	Maschinenöl	Huile de moteur	Aceite motor	Motorolie
Exhaust pipe	Auspuff	Tuyau d'échappement	Tubos de escape	Uitlaat
Fuel filter	Kraftstoffilter	Filtre de fuel	Filtro de combustible	Brandstoffilter
Fuel tank	Tank, Kraftstofftank	Réservoir à fuel	Tanque de Combustible	Brandstof tank
Fuse	Sicherung	Fusible	Fusible	Zekering
Gearbox	Getriebe	Transmission	Transmisión	Keerkoppeling
Generator	Generator	Groupe électrogène	Generador	Generator
Grease	Fett	Graisse	Grasa	Vet
Head gasket	Zylinderkopfdichtung	Joint de culasse	Junta de culata	Koppakking
Holding tank	Schmutzwassertank	Réservoir à eaux usées	Tanque aguas negras	Vuil-watertank
Inboard engine	Einbaumotor	Moteur in-bord	Motor intraborda	Binnen boord motor
Injectors	Einspritzdüsen	Injecteurs	Inyectores	Injectoren
Main engine	Hauptmaschine	Moteur principal	Motor	Hoofdmotor
Outboard engine	Außenborder	Moteur hors-bord	Motor fuera borda	Buitenboord motor
Petrol	Benzin	Essence	Gasolina	Benzine
Petrol engine	Benzinmotor	Moteur à essence	Motor a gasolina	Benzine motor
Propeller	Propeller	Hélice	Hélice	Schroef
Propeller bracket	Propeller-Halterung	Chaise	Arbotante	Schroefsteun
Regulator	Regler	Régulateur de charge	Regulador	Regulateur
Shaft	Welle	Arbre d'hélice	Eje	As

English	German	French	Spanish	Dutch
Spark plug	Zündkerze	Bougie	Bujia	Bougie
Starter	Starter	Démarreur	Arranque	Start motor
Stern gland	Stopfbuchse	Presse étoupe	Bocina	Schroefasdoorvoer
Throttle	Gas	Accélérateur	Acelerador	Gashendel
Water tank	Wassertank	Réservoir à eau	Tanque de agua	Water tank
Water pump	Wasserpumpe	Pompe à eau	Bomba de agua	Water pomp
General yachting terms				
One	Ein	Un	Uno	Een
Two	Zwei	Deux	Duo	Twee
Three	Drei	Trois	Tres	Drie
Four	Vier	Quatre	Cuatro	Vier
Five	Fünf	Cinq	Cinco	Vijf
Six	Sechs	Six	Seis	Zes
Seven	Sieben	Sept	Siete	Zeven
Eight	Acht	Huit	Ocho	Acht
Nine	Neun	Neuf	Nueve	Negen
Ten	Zehn	Dix	Diez	Tien
Aft	Achtern, achteraus	En arriere	Atrás	Achter; achteruit
Ahead	Voraus	Par l'avant	Avante	Vooruit
Anchor	Anker	Ancre	Ancia	Anker
Anchor chain	Ankerkette	Chaîne d'ancre	Cadena	Ankerketting
Anchor warp	Ankerleine	Orin	Cabo	Ankerlijn
Anchor winch	Ankerwinsch	Guindeau	Molinete	Anker lier
Astern	achtern	Par L'arrière	Hacia atrás	Achteruit, slaan
Babystay	Babystag	Babystay	Babystay	Baby stag
Backstay	Achterstag	Pataras	Estay de popa	Achterstag
Beating	Kreuzen	Louvoyer	Ciñendo a rabier	Kruisen
Bilge	Bilge	Galbord	Sentina	Bilge
Bilge keel	Kimmkiel	Bi-quilles	Quillas de balance	Kimkiel
Block	Block	Poulie	Motón	Blok
Boat	Boot	Bateau	Barco	Boot
Boom	Baum	Bôme	Botavara	Giek
Bow	Bug	Etrave	Proa	Boeg
Bridgedeck	Brückendeck	Bridgedeck	Bridgedeck	Brug dek
Cabin	Kajüte	Cabine	Cabina	Kajuit
Cap shrouds	Oberwanten	Gal haubans	Obenques altos	Hoofdwanten
Centreboard	Schwert	Dérive	Orza	Midzwaard
Cockpit	Cockpit	Cockpit	Bañera	Cockpit
Companionway	Niedergang	Descente	Entrada cámera	Opgang
Cruising chute	Cruising chute	Spi asymétrique	MPS	Halfwinder
Cutter stay	Kutterstag	Etai intermédiaire	Estay de tringqueta	Kotter stag
Deck	Deck	Pont	Cubierta	Dek
Dinghy	Jolle	You-you	Chinchorro	Bijboot
Fender	Fender	Défense	Defensa	Stootwil
Ferry	Fähre	Ferry	Ferry	Veerboot
Fin keel	Kurzkiel	Quille courte	Quilla de aleta	Fin kiel
Foresail	Vorsegel	Voile avant/foc	Foque	Fok
Forestay	Vorstag	Etai	Estay	Voorstag
Genoa	Genua	Génois	Génova	Genua
Halyard	Fall	Drisse	Driza	Val
Hull	Rumpf	Coque	Carena	Romp
Inflatable	Schlauchboot	Gonflable	Bote Hinchable	Opblaasbare boot
Jumper	Jumpstag	Guignol	Violín	Diamanstag
Keel	Kiel	Quille	Quilla	Kiel
Long keel	Langkiel	Quille longue	Quilla corrida	Langkiel
Lower shrouds	Unterwanten	Bas haubans	Obenques bajos	Onderwanten
Mainsail	Großsegel	Grand' voile	Mayor	Grootzeil
Mast	Mast	Mât	Mast	Mast
Mizzen	Besan	Artimon	Mesana	Bezaan
Motoring	Motoren	Naviguer au moteur	Navegar a motor	Met motor aan

English	German	French	Spanish	Dutch
Navigate	Navigieren	Naviguer	Navegar	Navigeren
Port	Backbord	Bâbord	Babor	Bakboord
Pulpit	Bugkorb	Balcon arrière	Púlpito	Preekstoel
Pushpit	Heckkorb	Balcon avant	Balcón de popa	Hekrailing
Railing	Reling	Rambarde	Guardamencebos	Railing
Reaching	Raumschodts	Au portant	Viento a través	Ruime wind
Rigging	Rigg	Gréement	Jarcia	Verstaging
Rope	Tauwerk	Cordage	Cabo	Touw
Rudder	Ruder	Safran/gouvernail	Pala de Timón	Roer
Running	Vorm Wind	Vent arrière	Viento a favor	Voor de wind
Running backstay	Backstag	Bastaque	Burde volanto	Bakstag
Sail batten	Segellatte	Latte	Sables	Zeillat
Sailing	Segeln	Naviguer à la voile	Navegar a velas	Zeilen
Shackle	Schäkel	Manille	Grillete	Harp
Sheet	Schoot	Ecoute	Escota	Schoot
Ship	Schiff	Navire	Buque	Schip
Shrouds	Wanten	Haubans	Obenques	Wanten
Spinnaker	Spinnaker	Spi	Spi	Spinnaker
Spinnaker boom	Spinnakerbaum	Tangon de spi	Tangon	Spinnaker boom
Spreader	Oberwantspreiz	Barre de Flèche	encapilladura	Zaling
Stanchion	Seerelingsstütze	Chandelier	Candelero	Scepter
Starboard	Steuerbord	Tribord	Estribor	Stuurboord
Staysail	Stagsegel	Trinquette	Trinquete	Stagzeil
Steamer	Dampfer	Vapeur	Buque de vapor	Stoomschip
Stern	Heck	Arrière	Popa	Spiegel
Storm jib	Sturmfock	Tourmentin	Tormentin	Storm fok
Storm trysail	Trysegel	Voile de cape	Vela de capa	Trysail
Superstructure	Aufbau	Superstructure	Superestructura	Bovenbouw
Tender	Beiboot	Annexe	Anexo (bote)	Bijboot
Tiller	Pinne	Barre franche	Caña	Helmstok
Toe rail	Fußleiste	Rail de fargue	Regala	Voetrail
Topsides	Rumpfseiten	Oeuvres mortes	Obra muerta	Romp
Underwater hull	Unterwasserschiff	Oeuvres vives	Obra viva	Onderwaterschip
Upwind	Am Wind	Au vent	Vienta en contra	Aan de wind
Wheel	Rad	Barre à roue	Rueda	Stuurwiel
Winch	Winsch	Winch	Winche	Lier
Working jib	Arbeitsfock	Foc de route	Foque	Werk fok
Yacht	Yacht	Yacht	Yate	Jacht
Navigation				
Abeam	Querab	Par le Traversé	Por el través	Dwarsscheeps
Ahead	Voraus	Par l'avant	Avante	Voor
Astern	Achteraus	Par l'arrière	Atrás	Achter
Bearing	Peilung	Relèvement	Maración	Peiling
Buoy	Tonne	Bouée	Boya	Boei/ton
Binoculars	Fernglas	Jumelles	Prismáticos	Verrekijker
Channel	Kanal	Chenal	Canal	Kanaal g eul
Chart	Seekarte	Carte	Carta náutica	Zeekaart
Compass	Kompass	Compas	Compás	Kompas
Compass course	Kompass Kurs	Cap du compas	Rumbo de aguja	Kompas koers
Current	Strömung	Courant	Coriente	Stroom
Dead reckoning	Koppelnavigation	Estime	Estimación	Gegist bestek
Degree	Grad	Degré	Grado	Graad
Deviation	Deviation	Déviation	Desvio	Deviatie
Distance	Entfernung	Distance	Distancia	Afstand, verheid
Downstream	Flußabwärts	En aval	Río abajo	Stroomafwaarts
East	Ost	Est	Este	Oost
Ebb	Ebbe	Jusant	Marea menguante	Eb
Echosounder	Echolot	Sondeur	Sonda	Dieptemeter
Estimated position	Gegißte Position	Point estimé	Posición estimado	Gegiste positie
Fathom	Faden	Une brasse	Braza	Vadem

English	German	French	Spanish	Dutch
Feet	Fuß	Pieds	Pie	Voet
Flood	Flut	Flot	Flujo de marea	Vloed
GPS	GPS	GPS	GPS	GPS
Handbearing compass	Handpeilkompass	Compas de relèvement	Compás de marcaciones	Handpeil kompas
Harbour guide	Hafenhandbuch	Guide du port	Guia del Puerto	Havengids
High water	Hochwasser	Pleine mer	Altamer	Hoog water
Latitude	Geographische Breite	Latitude	Latitud	Breedte
Leading lights	Feuer in Linie	Alignement	Luz de enfilación	Geleide lichten
Leeway	Abdrift	Dérive du au vent	Hacia sotavento	Drift
Lighthouse	Leuchtturm	Phare	Faro	Vuurtoren
List of lights	Leuchtfeuer Verzeichnis	Liste des feux	Listude de Luces	Lichtenlijst
Log	Logge	Loch	Corredera	Log
Longitude	Geographische Länge	Longitude	Longitud	Lengte
Low water	Niedrigwasser	Basse mer	Bajamar	Laag water
Metre	Meter	Mètre	Metro	Meter
Minute	Minute	Minute	Minuto	Minuut
Nautical almanac	Nautischer Almanach	Almanach nautique	Almanaque náutico	Almanak
Nautical mile	Seemeile	Mille nautique	Milla marina	Zeemijl
Neap tide	Nipptide	Morte-eau	Marea muerta	Dood tij
North	Nord	Nord	Norte	Noord
Pilot	Lotse	Pilote	Práctico	Loods/Gids
Pilotage book	Handbuch	Instructions nautiques	Derrotero	Vaarwijzer
RDF	Funkpeiler	Radio gonio	Radio-gonió	Radio richtingzoeker
Radar	Radar	Radar	Radar	Radar
Radio receiver	Radio, Empfänger	Réceptor radio	Receptor de radio	Radio ontvanger
Radio transmitter	Sender	Emetteur radio	Radio-transmisor	Radio zender
River outlet	Flußmündung	Embouchure	Embocadura	Riviermond
South	Süd	Sud	Sud, Sur	Zuid
Spring tide	Springtide	Vive-eau	Marea viva	Springtij/springvloed
Tide	Tide, Gezeit	Marée	Marea	Getijde
Tide tables	Tidenkalender	Annuaire des marées	Anuario de mareas	Getijdetafel
True course	Wahrer Kurs	Vrai cap	Rumbo	Ware Koers
Upstream	Flußaufwärts	En amont	Río arriba	Stroomopwaarts
VHF	UKW	VHF	VHF	Marifoon
Variation	Variation	Déclinaison magnétique	Variación	Variatie
Waypoint	Wegpunkt	Point de rapport	Waypoint	Waypoint/Route punt
West	West	Ouest	Oeste	West
Officialdom				
Certificate of registry	Schiffszertifikat	Acte de franchisation	Documentos de matrícuia	Zeebrief
Check in	Einklarieren	Enregistrement	Registrar	Check-in
Customs	Zoll	Douanes	Aduana	Douane
Declare	Verzollen	Déclarer	Declarar	Aangeven
Harbour master	Hafenmeister	Capitaine du port	Capitán del puerto	Havenmeester
Insurance	Versicherung	Assurance	Seguro	Verzekering
Insurance certificate	Versicherungspolice	Certificat d'assurance	Certificado deseguro	Verzekeringsbewijs
Passport	Paß	Passeport	Pasaporte	Paspoort
Police	Polizei	Police	Policía	Politie
Pratique	Verkehrserlaubnis	Pratique	Prático	Verlof tot ontscheping
Register	Register	Liste de passagers	Lista de tripulantes/rol	Register
Ship's log	Logbuch	Livre de bord	Cuaderno de bitácora	Logboek
Ship's papers	Schiffspapiere	Papiers de bateau	Documentos del barco	Scheepspapieren
Surveyor	Gutachter	Expert maritime	Inspector	Opzichter, expert
Safety/Distress				
Assistance	Hilfeleistung	Assistance	Asistencia	Assistentie
Bandage	Verband	Pansement	Vendas	Verband
Burns	Verbrennung	Brûlures	Quemadura	Brand wond
Capsize	Kentern	Sancir, chavirer	Volcó	Omslaan
Coastguard	Küstenwache	Garde de côte	Guarda costas	Kust wacht
Dismasted	Mastbruch	Démâtè	Desarbolar	Mastbreuk
Distress	Seenot	Détresse	Pena	Nood

English	German	French	Spanish	Dutch
Distress flares	Signalraketen	Fusées de détresse	Bengalas	Nood signaal
Doctor	Doktor	Médecin	Médico	Dokter/Arts
EPIRB	EPIRB	Balise de detresse	Baliza	EPIRB
Emergency	Notfall	Urgence	Emergencias	Noodgeval
Exhaustion	Erschöpfung	Epuisement	Agotamiento	Uitputting
Fever	Fieber	Fièvre	Fiebre	Koorts
Fire extinguisher	Feuerlöscher	Extincteur	Extintor	Brand blusser
First aid	Erste Hilfe	Premier secours	Primeros auxillos	Eerste hulp
Fracture	Fraktur	Cassure	Fractura	Breuk
Grounded	Aufgelaufen	Echoué	Encallado	Vastgelopen
Harness	Lifebelt	Harnais	Arnés de seguridad	Harnas/Tuig
Headache	Kopfschmerz	Mal à la tête	Dolor de cabeza	Hoofdpijn
Heart attack	Herzanfall	Crise cardiaque	Ataque corazón	Hartaanval
Helicopter	Hubschrauber	Hélicoptère	Helicóptero	Helikopter
Hospital	Krankenhaus	Hôpital	Hospital	Ziekenhuis
Illness	Krankheit, Übelkeit	Maladie	Enfermo	Ziekte
Injury	Verletzung	Blessure	Lesión	Verwonding
Jackstay	Strecktau	Contre-étai	Violín	Veiligheidstag
Lifeboat	Rettungsboot	Canot de sauvetage	Lancha de salvamento	Reddingsboot
Liferaft	Rettungsinsel	Radeau de sauvetage	Balsa salvavidas	Reddingsvlot
Lifejacket	Schwimmweste	Gilet de sauvetage	Chaleco salvavidas	Reddingsvest
Man overboard	Mann über Bord	Homme à la mer	Hombre al agua	Man over boord
Pulse	Puls	Pouls	Pulso	Hartslag
Rest	Ruhen	Repos	Reposo	Rust
Seacock	Seeventil	Vanne	Grifos de fondo	Afsluiter
Seasickness	Seekrankheit	Mal de mer	Mareo	Zeeziekte
Seaworthy	Seetüchtig	Marin	Marinero	Zeewaardig
Shock	Schock	Choc	Choque	Shock
Sinking	Sinken	En train de couler	Hundiendo	Zinken
Sleep	Schlaf	Sommeil	Sueño	Slaap
Tow line	Schleppleine	Filin de remorque	Cabo	Sleeplijn
Unconscious	Bewußtlos	Inconscient	Inconsciente	Buiten bewustzijn
Wound	Wunde	Blessure	Herida	Wond
Signs and warnings				
Anchoring	Ankern	Mouiller l'ancre	Fondear	Ankeren
Breakwater	Außenmole	Brise-lame	Escolera	Pier
Cable	Kabel	Encablure	Cadena	Kabel
Catwalk	Schlengel	Passerelle	Pasarela	Loopplank
Commercial port	Handelshafen	Port de commerce	Puerto comercial	Commerciele haven
Customs office	Zollamt	Bureau de douane	Aduanas	Douanekantoor
Depth	Wassertiefe	Profondeur	Profundidad	Diepte
Dries	Trockenfallend	Estran	Descubierto	Droogvallen
Drying port	Trockenfallender Hafen	Port d'échouage	Puerto secarse	Droogvallende haven
Ferry terminal	Fährterminal	Gare maritime	Terminal marítmo	Veerboot steiger
Firing range	Schießgebiet	Zone de tir	Zona de tiro	Schietoefeningen
Fishing harbour	Fischereihafen	Port de pêche	Puerto de pesca	Vissershaven
Foul ground	unreiner Grund	Fond malsain	Fondo sucio	Slechte grond
Guest berths	Gastliegeplätze	Place visiteurs	Amarradero visitantes	Gasten plaatsen
Harbour entrance	Hafeneinfahrt	Entrée du port	Entradas	Haveningang
Harbourmaster's office	Hafenmeisterei	Capitainerie	Capitania	Havenkantoor Kantoor
Hazard	Hindernis	Danger	Peligro	Gevaar
Height	Höhe	Hauteur	Alturas	Hoogte
Jetty	Steg	Jetée	Malecón	Steiger
Landing place	Anlegeplatz	Point d'accostage	Embarcadero	Plaats om aan land te gaan
Lock	Schleuse	Ecluse	Esclusa	Sluis
Marina	Marina	Marina	Marina	Marina
Mooring	Anlegen	Mouillage	Fondeadero	Meerplaats
Permitted	Erlaubt	Autorisé	Permitido	Toegestaan
Pier	Pier, Mole	Appontement/quai	Muelle	Pier
Prohibited	Verboten	Interdit	Prohibido	Verboden

English	German	French	Spanish	Dutch
Prohibited area	Sperrgebiet	Zone interdite	Zona de prohibida	Verboden gebied
Swell	Schwell	Houle	Mar de fondo	Golfslag/deining
Swing bridge	Drehbrücke	Pont tournant	Puente giratorio	Draaibrug
Underwater	Unterwasser	Sous-marin	Debajo del agua	Onderwater
Wreck	Wrack	Epave	Naufrago	Wrak
Yacht club	Yachtclub	Club nautique	Club náutico	Jachtclub
Yacht harbour	Yachthafen	Port de plaisance	Puerto deportive	Jachthaven
Weather				
Air mass	Luftmasse	Masse d'air	Massa de aire	Luchtmassa
Anticyclone	Antizyklonisch/hoch	Anticyclone	Anticiclón	Hogedrukgebied
Area	Gebiet	Zone	Zona	Gebied
Backing wind	Rückdrehender Wind	Vent revenant	Rolar el viento	Krimpende wind
Barometer	Barometer	Baromètre	Barómetro	Barometer
Breeze	Brise	Brise	Brisa	Bries
Calm	Flaute	Calme	Calma	Kalmte
Centre	Zentrum	Centre	Centro	Centrum
Clouds	Wolken	Nuages	Nube	Wolken
Cold	Kalt	Froid	Frio	Koud
Cold front	Kaltfront	Front froid	Frente frio	Kou front
Cyclonic	Zyklonisch	Cyclonique	Ciclonica	Cycloonachtig
Decrease	Abnahme	Affaiblissement	Disminución	Afnemen
Deep	Tief	Profond	Profundo	Diep
Deepening	Vertiefend	Se Creusant	Ahondamiento	Verdiepend
Depression	Sturmtief	Dépression	Depresión	Depressie
Direction	Richtung	Direction	Direción	Richting
Dispersing	Auflösend	Se dispersant	Disipación	Oplossend
Disturbance	Störung	Perturbation	Perturbación	Verstoring
Drizzle	Niesel	Bruine	Lioviena	Motregen
East	Ost	Est	Este	Oost
Extending	Ausdehnung	S'étendant	Extension	Uitstrekkend
Extensive	Ausgedehnt	Etendu	General	Uitgebreid
Falling	Fallend	Descendant	Bajando	Dalend
Filling	Auffüllend	Secomblant	Relleno	Vullend
Fog	Nebel	Brouillard	Niebla	Nevel
Fog bank	Nebelbank	Banque de brouillard	Banco de niebla	Mist bank
Forecast	Vorhersage	Prévision	Previsión	Vooruitzicht
Frequent	Häufig	Fréquent	Frecuenta	Veelvuldig
Fresh	Frisch	Frais	Fresco	Fris
Front	Front	Front	Frente	Front
Gale	Sturm	Coup de vent	Temporal	Storm
Gale warning	Sturmwarnung	Avis de coup de vent	Aviso de temporal	Stormwaarschuwing
Good	Gut	Bon	Bueno	Goed
Gradient	Druckunterschied	Gradient	Gradiente	Gradient
Gust, squall	Bö	Rafale	Ráfaga	Windvlaag/bui
Hail	Hagel	Grêle	Granizo	Hagel
Haze	Diesig	Brume	Calina	Nevel
Heavy	Schwer	Abondant	Abunante	Zwaar
High	Hoch	Anticyclone	Alta presión	Hoog
Increasing	Zunehmend	Augmentant	Aumentar	Toenemend
Isobar	Isobar	Isobare	Isobara	Isobar
Isolated	Vereinzelt	Isolé	Aislado	Verspreid
Lightning	Blitze	Eclair de foudre	Relampago	Bliksem
Local	Örtlich	Local	Local	Plaatselijk
Low	Tief	Dépression	Baja presión	Laag
Mist	Dunst	Brume légere	Nablina	Nevel
Moderate	Mäßig	Modéré	Moderado	Matig
Moderating	Abnehmend	Se modérant	Medianente	Matigend
Moving	Bewegend	Se déplacant	Movimiento	Bewegend
North	Nord	Nord	Septentrional	Noorden
Occluded	Okklusion	Occlus	Okklusie	Occlusie

English	German	French	Spanish	Dutch
Poor	Schlecht	Mauvais	Mal	Slecht
Precipitation	Niederschlag	Précipitation	Precipitación	Neerslag
Pressure	Druck	Pression	Presión	Druk
Rain	Regen	Pluie	Iluvia	Regen
Ridge	Hochdruckbrücke	Dorsale	Cresta	Rug
Rising	Ansteigend	Montant	Subiendo	Stijgen
Rough	Rauh	Agitée	Bravo o alborotado	Ruw
Sea	See	Mer	Mar	Zee
Seaway	Seegang	Haute mer	Alta mar	Zeegang
Scattered	Vereinzelt	Sporadiques	Difuso	Verspreid
Shower	Schauer	Averse	Aguacero	Bui
Slight	Leicht	Legère	Leicht	Licht
Slow	Langsam	Lent	Lent	Langzaam
Snow	Schnee	Neige	Nieve	Sneeuw
South	Süd	Sud	Sur	Zuiden
Storm	Sturm	Tempête	Temporal	Storm
Sun	Sonne	Soleil	Sol	Zon
Swell	Schwell	Houle	Mar de fondo	Deining
Thunder	Donner	Tonnerre	Tormenta	Donder
Thunderstorm	Gewitter	Orage	Tronada	Onweer
Trough	Trog, Tiefausläufer	Thalweg	Seno	Trog
Variable	Umlaufend	Variable	Variable	Veranderlijk
Veering	Rechtdrehend	Tournant a l' (Ouest/Est)	Dextrogiro	Ruimende wind
Warm front	Warmfront	Front chaud	Frente calido	Warmte front
Weather	Wetter	Temps	Tiempo	Weer
Wind	Wind	Vent	Viento	Wind
Weather report	Wetterbericht	Bulletin Météo	Previsión meteorologica	Weerbericht

PORTUGUESE GLOSSARY

Navigation	Navegación
Alternating (Al)	luz alternada
Anchorage	fundeadouro
Basin	doca, bacia
Bar	barra
Bay	baía
Beacon (Bn)	baliza
Bell	sino
Black (B)	preto
Breakwater, mole	quebra-mar, molhe
Bridge	ponte
Buoy	bóia
Can (PHM)	cilíndrica
Chart Datum (CD)	zero hidrográfico
Cone, conical (SHM)	cónica
Conspicuous (conspic)	conspicuo
East (E)	este
Fixed (F)	luz fixa
Flashing	luz relâmpagos
Flood/ebb stream	corrente enchente/vasante
Green (G)	verde
High Water (HW)	preia mar (PM)
Height, headroom, clearance	altura
Island	ilha
Isolated danger (IDM)	perigo isolado
Knot (kn)	nó
Landfall (SWM)	aterragem
Leading light	farol de enfiamento
Leading line, transit	enfiamento
Lighthouse	farol
Lightship	barco-farol
Low Water (LW)	baixa mar (BM)
Mussel beds/rafts	viveiros
Neaps (np)	águas mortas
North (N)	norte
Obscured	obscurecido
Occulting (Oc)	ocultações
Point, headland	ponta
Port (side)	bombordo
Quick flashing (Q)	relâmpagos rápidos
Range	amplitude de maré
Rate/set (tide)	força/direcção
Red, (R)	vermelho
River	rio
Rock	rocha
Reef	recife
Sandhill, dunes	dunas de areia

Shoal	baixo
Slack water, stand	águas paradas
South (S)	sul
Special mark (SPM)	marca especiá
Springs (sp)	águas vivas
Starboard	estibordo
Strait(s)	estreito
Stripe/band	faixas verticais/horizontais
Tide tables	Tabela de marés
Tidal stream atlas	Atlas de marés
Topmark	alvo
West (W)	oeste
Whistle	apito
White (W)	branco
Wreck	naufrágio
Yellow (Y)	amarelo

Facilities **Facillidados**

Beam	boca
Boat hoist (BH)	portico elevador
Boatyard (BY)	estaleiro
Chandlery (CH)	aprestos
Coastguard (CG)	policia marítima
Crane (C)	guindaste
Customs (n)	alfândega
Diesel (D)	gasóleo
Draught	calado
Dredged	dragado
Engineer (ME)	engenheiro
Fresh water (FW)	aguada
Harbour Master	capitanía
Insurance certificate	certificado de seguro
Jetty	molhe
Length overall (LOA)	comprimento
Lifeboat (LB)	barco salva-vidas
Lock	eclusa
Methylated spirits	alcool metílico
Mooring buoy	bólia de atracação
Petrol (P)	gasolina
Paraffin	petróleo
Registration number	número do registoSlipway
(slip)	rampa
Sailmaker (SM)	veleir
Yacht harbour, marina	doca de recreio

Meteorology **Meteorologia**

High (anticyclone)	anticiclone
Breakers	arrebentação
Calm (F0)	calma
Choppy	mareta
Cloudy	nublado
Drizzle	chuvisco
Front, warm/cold	frente, quente/fria
Fog	nevoeiro
Fresh breeze (F5)	vento frêsco
Gale (F8)	vento muito forte
Gentle breeze (F3)	vento bonançoso
Gust	rajada
Hail	saraiva
Haze	cerração
Light airs (F1)	aragem
Light breeze (F2)	vento fraco
Low (depression)	depressão
Mist	neblina
Moderate breeze (F4)	vento moderado
Near gale (F7)	vento forte
Overfalls (tide race)	bailadeiras
Pressure, rise/fall	pressão, subida/descida
Rain	chuva
Ridge (high)	crista
Rough sea	mar bravo
Severe gale (F9)	vento tempestuoso
Short/steep (sea state)	mar cavado
Shower	aguaceiro
Squall	borrasca
Slight sea	mar chão
Storm (F10)	temporal
Strong breeze (F6)	vento muito frêsco
Swell	ondulação
Thunderstorm	trovoada
Trough	linha de baixa pressão
Visibility, poor; good	fraca, má; bôa

First aid **Primeiros socorros**

Antibiotic	antibiótico
Bandage	ligadura
Bleeding	sangrar
Burn	queimadura
Chemist	farmácia
Dehydration	desidratação
Dentist	dentista
Drown, to	afogar-se
Fever	febre
Heart attack	ataque de coração
Pain	dôr
Painkiller	analgésico
Poisoning	envenenamento
Shock	choque
Splint	colocar em talas
Sticking plaster	adesivo
Stomach upset	cólicas
Stretcher	maca
Sunburn	queimadura des
Swelling	inchação
Toothache	dôr dos dentes
Unconscious	sem sentidos

Ashore **A Terra**

Bakery	padaria, pastelaria
Beach	praia
Bus station	estação de camionetas
Butcher shop	açougue
Ironmonger	ferreiroa
Launderette	lavanderia
Market	mercad
Post Office	correio (CTT)
Railway station	estação de comboios
Stamps	sellos

The logo of the CHART AND NAUTICAL INSTRUMENT TRADE ASSOCIATION, founded in 1918. With the full support of the Hydrographer of the Navy and leading manufacturers of nautical instruments, members of the Association are able to place their experience and service at the disposal of the shipping industry and all navigators

CHART SUPPLY AND CORRECTION SERVICES

The CNITA counts among its members many of the leading Admiralty Chart Agents who can supply your requirements from a single chart or publication to a world-wide outfit and special folio requirements from comprehensive stocks in all the major ports. Carefully trained chart correctors are available to examine and correct all Admiralty charts.

THE CNITA TRACING SERVICE

Although tracings have been in use by the Royal Navy and Admiralty Chart Agents for many years, it was the Chart Committee of the Chart and Nautical Instrument Trade Association that successfully negotiated with the Hydrographer of the Navy for them to become available to the merchant navigator and private user.

The CNITA tracing overlay correction service is available from all Admiralty Chart Agents who are members of the Association, and is now supplied to more than 5,000 vessels each week. Each tracing wallet contains the weekly "Notices to Mariners" and tracings printed with the relevant details of the area surrounding the correction, making the correction of each chart a simpler operation. All that the user has to do is match the tracing to the chart, pierce through the small circle showing the exact position of the correction and, in conjunction with the "Notices to Mariners", transfer the information onto the chart. Navigating Officers welcome the tracings system for its accuracy and speed. Onboard chart correction time can be cut by 80% and Masters can now rest assured that their charts are kept continually up to date. Reasonably priced, these tracings are economical and an invaluable contribution to safety at sea.

COMPASS ADJUSTING AND NAUTICAL INSTRUMENTS

CNITA Members who provide Compass Adjusting services use Compass Adjusters having professional qualifications recognised in the locality in which they operate. The relevant qualification for the United Kingdom is the Certificate of Competency as Compass Adjuster, the examination for which is conducted by the Maritime and Coastguard Agency with the assistance of the CNITA in assessing the evidence of practical adjusting skills submitted by the Candidate. CNITA Members can provide Compass Adjusters, who are available day and night to "swing" ships, in most major ports and elsewhere by arrangement.

Members of the CNITA, many with life long experience in this field, can advise you when buying all your nautical instruments. Most suppliers provide an instrument repair service combining traditional craftsmanship with modern methods to ensure that instruments are serviced and tested to a high standard.

ARE YOU COMPLYING WITH THE LATEST INTERNATIONAL REGULATIONS?

Chart and Nautical Instrument Trade Association members established in most U.K. ports and overseas are able to advise you. For full details of the Association, its activities and its services to the Navigator, write to:- The Secretaries, CHART AND NAUTICAL INSTRUMENT TRADE ASSOCIATION, Dalmore House, 310 St. Vincent Street, Glasgow G2 5QR, United Kingdom, Email: cnita@biggartbaillie.co.uk, Web: www.cnita.com

PORTS WHERE SHIPS' COMPASSES ARE ADJUSTED AND BRITISH ADMIRALTY CHARTS ARE AVAILABLE

AMI-GFV Marine Ltd, 18 Canute Road, SOUTHAMPTON, Hants SO14 3FJ Tel: 0238 048 0450, Fax: 0238 048 0451, Email: ami-gfv.marine@dial.pipex.com
A/S Navicharts, Industriveien 28, 1483 SKYTTA, NORWAY, Tel: 00 47 6 7062020, Fax: 00 47 6 7060015,
Bade & Hornig GmbH, Herrengraben 31, 20459, HAMBURG, Tel: 00 49 40 3748110, Fax: 00 49 40 366400
Bogerd NV, Oude Leeuwenrui 37, ANTWERP 2000, BELGIUM Tel: 00 32 3 2328532 Fax: 00 32 3 2272959, Email: Sales@martin.be
Brown Son & Ferguson Ltd, 4-10 Darnley Street, GLASGOW, G41 2SD Tel: 0141-429 1234, Fax: 0141-420 1694,
Carmichael & Clarke Co Ltd, 1202 Unicorn Trade Centre, 131 Des Voeux Road, Central, HONG KONG Tel: 00 852 2581 2678, Fax: 00 852 2582 2722, Email: carmi@hkstar.com
B Cooke & Son Ltd*, Kingston Observatory, 58/59 Market Place, HULL HU1 1RH Tel: 01482 224412/223454, Fax: 01482 219793,
D.P.M. Singapore Pte Ltd, 1 Maritime Square #13-03, World Trade Centre, SINGAPORE 099253 Tel: 00 65 2704060, Fax: 00 65 2763858, Email: dpmspore@mbox3.singnet.com.sg
DPM (UK) Ltd, Mersey Chambers, Covent Garden, LIVERPOOL L2 8UF Tel: 0151 236 2776 Fax: 0151 236 4577, Email: iaca@dpm.co.uk
George Falconer (Nautical) Ltd, 1/Floor, Hong Kong Jewellery Bldg, 178-180 Queen's Road, Central, HONG KONG Tel: 00 852 28542882 Fax: 00 852 28158056
J Garraio & Co Lda, Avenida 24 De Julho, 2-1 D.1200 LISBON, PORTUGAL Tel: 00 3511 3473081, Fax: 00 3511 3428950
Thomas Gunn Navigation Services Ltd*, Anchor House, 62 Regents Quay, ABERDEEN AB11 5AR Tel: 01224 595045, Fax: 01224 584702, Email: tgns@globalnet.co.uk, www.thomasgunn.globalnet.co.uk
Hong Kong Ships Supplies Co, Room 1614, Melbourne Plaza, 33 Queen's Road, Central, HONG KONG Tel: 00 852 25225963, 00 852 25231205, Fax: 00 852 28681748
Kelvin Hughes Charts & Maritime Supplies*, New North Road, Hainault, ILFORD, Essex IG6 2UR Tel: 0208 500 1020 Fax: 0208 559 8535,
Kelvin Hughes Observator bv*, Nieuwe Langeweg 41, 3194 DC, HOOGVLIET, The Netherlands Tel: 00 31 10 4167622, Fax: 00 31 10 4167218, Email: kelvin.hughes@wxs.nl
Captain L N Jordanov, 13-A Han Omurtag Str., P.O.B. 14, VARNA 9001, BULGARIA Tel: 00 359 52 242018 Fax: 00 359 52 242018
John Lilley & Gillie Ltd* Clive Street NORTH SHIELDS, Tyne & Wear NE29 6LF Tel: 0191 257 2217, Fax: 0191-257 1521, Email: sales@lilleyandgillie.co.uk
"Magnetico" D.A. Dedegikas 100 Colocotroni Str. PIRAEUS 185 35, GREECE Tel: 00 30 1 4178976, Fax: 00 30 1 4178206
Marine Instruments* The Wheelhouse,, Upton Slip, FALMOUTH, Cornwall TR11 3DQ Tel: 01326 312414, Fax: 01326 211414, Email: info@marineinstruments.co.uk
Maritime Services, 3440 Bridgeway Street VANCOUVER, BC V5K 1B6, CANADA Tel: 00 1 604 294444, Fax: 00 1 604 2945879
Martin & Company* Oude Leeuwenrui 37, ANTWERP 2000, BELGIUM Tel: 00 32 3 2134170, Fax: 00 32 3 2326167 Email: sales@martin.be
Motion Smith 78 Shenton Way #01-03, SINGAPORE 079120 Tel: 00 65 2205098 Fax: 00 65 2254902
R J Muir Esq* 22 Seymour Close, Chandlers Ford, EASTLEIGH, Hants SO53 2JE Tel: 0238 026 1042, Fax: 0238 026 1042
Nautisk Forlag A/S Drammensveien 130 PO Box 321 Sköyen, N-0212, OSLO, NORWAY Tel: 00 47 22 547650 Fax: 00 47 22 562385, Email: sales@nautisk.com, www.nautisk.com
Captain Stephan Nedelchev Soc. Co. J.C. Gomez 1445, esc.301, 11000 MONTEVIDEO, URUGUAY Tel: 00 5982 9167988 Fax: 00 5982 9167990
W F Price & Co Ltd Wapping Wharf, BRISTOL BS1 6UD Tel: 0117 9292229, Fax: 0117 9304403
Riviera-Charts Galerie du Port, 26-30 Rue Lacan, 06600 ANTIBES, France Tel: 00 33 493 344566, Fax: 00 33 493 344336, Email: admiralty@riviera.fr, www.riviera-charts.com
Rule (ITT Industries) Bingley Road, HODDESDON, Herts EN11 0BU Tel: 01992 450145, Fax: 01992 451079
Seath Instruments (1992) Ltd* Unit 30, Colville Rd Works, Colville Road, LOWESTOFT, Suffolk NR33 9QS Tel: 01502 573811, Fax: 01502 514173
S.I.R.S. Navigation Ltd* 186a Milton Road, SWANSCOMBE, Kent DA10 0LX Tel: 01322 383672, Fax: 01322 382418
Small Craft Deliveries Ltd Navigation House, 4 Wilford Bridge Road, MELTON, Woodbridge IP12 1RJ Tel: 01394 382600, Fax: 01394 387672, Telex: 51 317210, Email: sales@scd-charts.co.uk
A M Smith (Marine) Ltd 33 Epping Way, Chingford, LONDON E4 7PB Tel: 0208-529 6988 Fax: 0208-524 4498
Tai Seng Trading Co Ltd 198-1 Ta Tong 1st Road, Kaohsiung 800, TAIWAN, R.O.C. Tel: 00 86 7 2217367, Fax: 00 86 7 2818180, Email: taisengt@ms22.hinet.net
The Tyneside Shop 5 John Ross House, 22 Victoria Embankment, DURBAN 4001, SOUTH AFRICA Tel: 00 27 31 3377005, Fax: 00 27 31 3328139, Email: tyneside@global.co.za
Todd Chart Agency Ltd 4 Seacliff Road, The Harbour, BANGOR, County Down, Northern Ireland BT20 5EY Tel: 028 9146 6640, Fax: 028 9147 1070, Email: admiralty@toddchart.co.uk www.nautical-charts.com
G Undery & Son* PO Box 235 - Unit 31, The New Harbours, GIBRALTAR Tel: 00 350 40402 (B), 00 350 73107, Fax: 00 350 46489
Vanos S.A. 90 Dim. Moutsopoulou Str., 184 41 PIRAEUS, GREECE Tel: 00 30 1 4829911, Fax: 00 30 1 4812313/4817607
Iver C Weilbach & Co A/S, 35 Toldbodgade, Postbox 1560, DK-1253, COPENHAGEN K, DENMARK Tel: 00 45 33 135927, Fax: 00 45 33 935927
Wessex Marine Equipment Ltd, Logistics House, 1 Park Road, Freemantle, Southampton SO15 3US Tel: 0238 063 5215, Fax: 0238 063 6216, Email: wesmarine@aol.com
Zervoudakis Marine Supplies Ltd 31 Milou Str. 185 45 PIRAEUS GREECE Tel: 00 30 1 4623700, Fax: 00 30 1 4627900

NM1 **Those marked * have U.K. Maritime, & Coastguard Agency certificated, Compass Adjusters**

Chapter 1

General Information

C1

Contents

1.1 **INTERNATIONAL REGULATIONS FOR PREVENTING COLLISIONS AT SEA** ..... Page 18

1.1.1 General 18

1.1.2 Traffic Separation Schemes 18

1.1.3 Vessels in sight of one another 19

1.1.4 Restricted visibility 20

1.1.5 Lights and shapes 20

1.1.6 Sound signals 21

1.1.7 Annexes to IRPCS 22

1.1.8 Distress signals 22

1.2 **DOCUMENTATION** 22

1.2.1 Cruising formalities 22

1.2.2 Registration 22

1.2.3 Insurance 22

1.2.4 International Certificate of Competence 23

1.3 **HM CUSTOMS** 23

1.3.1 The European Union 23

1.3.2 Regulations 23

1.3.3 Stores 23

1.3.4 Notice of departure 23

1.3.5 Arrival from an EU country 23

1.3.6 Arrival from a non-EU country 23

1.3.7 Immigration 24

1.3.8 Customs offices – telephone numbers 24

1.3.9 Drug smuggling 24

1.4 **FOREIGN CUSTOMS PROCEDURES** 24

1.4.1 General 24

1.5 **VAT AND THE SINGLE MARKET** 24

1.5.1 General 24

1.5.2 Temporary importation 24

1.6 **USEFUL ADDRESSES** 24

1.7 **INTERNET: WEBSITES AND E-MAIL** 27

1.8 **CONVERSION TABLES** 28

1.8.1 Conversion factors 28

1.8.2 Feet to metres, metres to feet 28

1.9 **CALENDAR, 2002** 29

1.9.1 UK Public Holidays 2002 29

1.9.2 Phases of the Moon, 2002 29

1.9.3 Eclipse Notes, 2002 29

1.9.4 Standard Times 29

1.1 INTERNATIONAL REGULATIONS FOR PREVENTING COLLISIONS AT SEA

1.1.1 General

a. The 1972 International Regulations for Preventing Collisions at Sea (IRPCS), also referred to as Colregs or Rule of the Road, are given in full in The Macmillan Reeds Yachtsman's Handbook, together with supporting diagrams and explanatory notes; also in RYA booklet G2. The exact wording of the IRPCS is important. The following notes on some of the provisions of special interest to yachtsmen are only to be used to help understand the Rules and should only be used in conjunction with the complete IRPCS and not in isolation. The numbers of the rules quoted are given for reference.

b. The rules must be interpreted in a seaman-like way if collisions are to be avoided (Rule 2). The rules do not give any vessel right of way over another regardless of special circumstances – e.g. such as other vessels under way or at anchor, shallow water, poor visibility, traffic separation schemes, fishing fleets, etc. – or the handling characteristics of the vessels concerned in the prevailing conditions. Sometimes vessels may need to depart from the rules to avoid immediate danger (Rule 2b).

c. A sailing vessel is so defined (Rule 3) when she is under sail only. When under power she must show the lights for a power-driven vessel, and when under sail and power a cone, point-down, forward (Rule 25).

d. Keep a good lookout at all times (Rule 5: the most important rule), using eyes and ears as well as radar and VHF, particularly at night or in poor visibility.

e. Safe speed (Rule 6) is dictated by visibility, traffic density, including concentrations of fishing or other vessels, depth of water, the state of wind, sea and current, proximity of navigational dangers, and the manoeuvrability of the boat with special reference to stopping distance and turning ability in the prevailing conditions. Excessive speed gives less time to appreciate the situation, less time to take avoiding action, and produces a worse collision if such action fails.

f. When faced with converging vessel(s), a skipper/crew must always answer the following three questions and take action if required.

1. Is there a risk of collision?
2. If there is, am I the give-way vessel?
3. If I am, what action must I take?

g. If there is any doubt, assume that there is a risk (Rule 7). A yacht should take a series of compass bearings on a converging ship – see Fig. 1 (1). Unless the bearings change appreciably, there is risk of collision. Radar offers early warning of risk of collision.

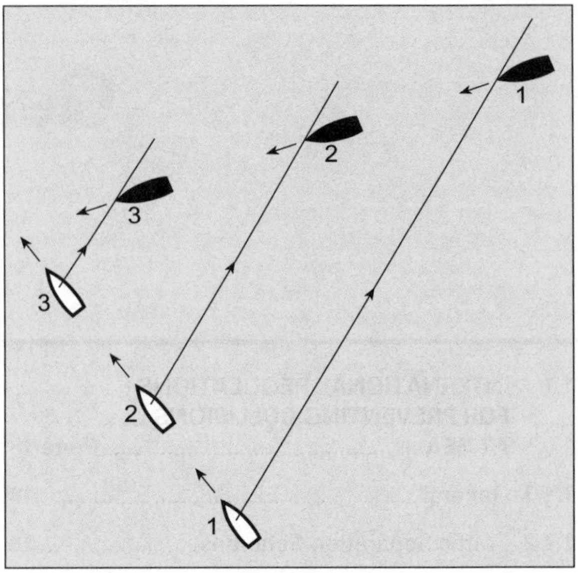

Fig. 1(1) Rule 7. The bearing of black from white is steady. Before position 2 white should have altered to starboard by at least 45° to pass under black's stern.

h. Take early, positive and seamanlike action to avoid collision (Rule 8). Large alterations of course and/or speed are more evident to the other skipper, particularly at night or on radar. Slow down, stop (or even go astern, under power). While keeping clear of one vessel, watch out for others.

i. In narrow channels (Rule 9), keep to starboard and as near to the outer limit of the channel or fairway as is safe and practical whether under power or sail. A yacht under 20m in length shall not impede larger vessels confined to a channel. A yacht should not cross a narrow channel if such crossing would impede a vessel which can only safely navigate within the channel. Avoid anchoring in the channel as well.

1.1.2 Traffic Separation Schemes (TSS)

TSS (Rule 10) are essential to the safety of larger vessels and, whilst inconvenient for yachtsmen, must be accepted as another element of passage planning, or be avoided where possible. TSS are shown on most charts and are covered in detail in Chapter 8.

All vessels, including yachts, must conform to TSS. However, when two vessels meet or converge in a TSS with a risk of collision, Rule 10 does not modify any other provisions of the IRPCS. But note that craft <20m LOA, and any sailing yacht, shall not impede a power vessel using a traffic lane (Rule10j). They should preferably use inshore traffic zones (ITZ) – often the most sensible action for a yacht, rather than using the main lanes. If, unusually, obliged to join or leave a lane, do so at its extremity; if joining or leaving at the side, do so at as shallow an angle as possible. Follow the general direction of traffic in the correct lane.

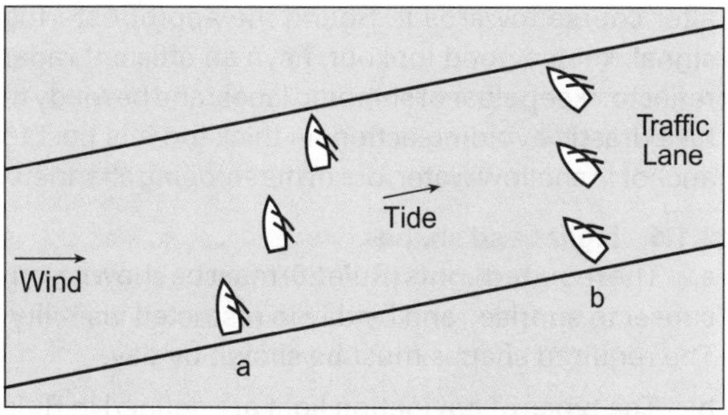

Fig. 1(2) Rule 10. When crossing a traffic lane, the heading heading of a yacht must be at right angles to the traffic flow as shown in (a) above, regardless of the course made good when affected by tidal streams. The yacht at (b) above is not heading at right angles and is therefore on an incorrect course.

1.1.3 Vessels in sight of one another

a. When two sailing vessels (Rule 12) are at risk of collision and on opposite tacks, the one on the port tack keeps clear. If on the same tack, the windward yacht keeps clear. If a yacht A on port tack sees yacht B to windward and cannot be sure whether yacht B is on port or starboard tack, then A must keep out of the way of B. For the purpose of this rule the windward side is deemed to be the side opposite to that on which the mainsail is carried. Rule 12 does not apply when either yacht is motor sailing. Fig. 1 (3) illustrates the practical application of the rules in the three cases mentioned above.

There are two other practical situations which might cause doubt about the application of Rule 12.

i. When running downwind under spinnaker alone. windward would be the side on which the spinnaker boom is set (normally opposite to the mainsail).

ii. When hove-to. This would depend on the most likely position of the mainsail if it were set.

b. Using the arcs of visibility of the sidelights and sternlight to illustrate the rules, Fig. 1 (4) allots names to each arc. The arc of the sternlight is called the 'overtaking sector'; the arc of the starboard (Green) sidelight is called the 'give-way sector'; and the arc of the port (Red) sidelight is called the 'stand-on sector'.

c. Any overtaking vessel, whether power or sail, shall keep out of the way of the vessel being overtaken (Rule 13). Overtaking means approaching the other vessel from a direction more than $22\frac{1}{2}°$ abaft her beam.

d. When two power-driven vessels approach head-on, each must alter course to starboard, to pass port to port (Rule 14). A substantial alteration may be needed, with the appropriate sound signal (Rule 34), to make intentions clear.

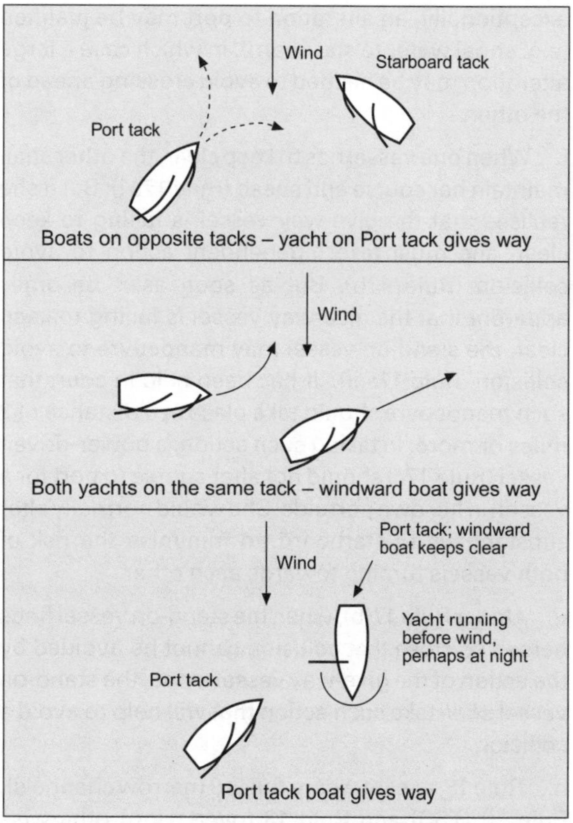

Fig. 1 (3) Rule 12. Conduct between sailing vessels. In all cases the yacht on the port tack keeps clear; if both yachts are on the same tack the windward boat keeps clear. If in doubt, always keep clear.

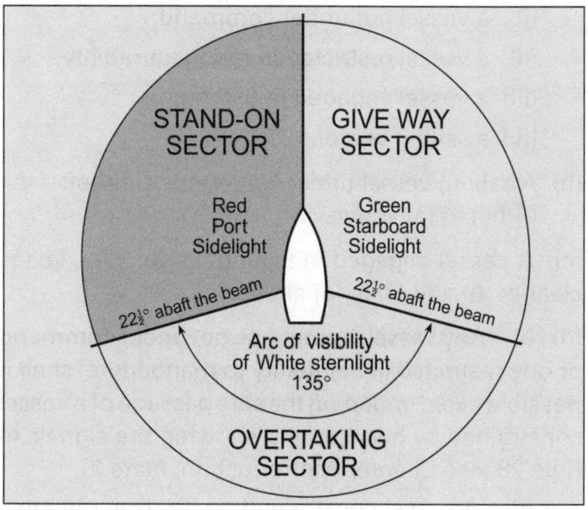

Fig 1(4) Rules 11 to 17. These rules apply only to vessels in sight of one another and do not apply when vessels can only see each other on radar.

e. When two power-driven vessels are crossing and in risk of collision, the one with the other on her starboard side must keep clear and, if possible, avoid passing ahead of the other (Rule 15). The give-way vessel should normally alter to starboard. Very exceptionally, an alteration to port may be justified (e.g. shoal water to starboard), in which case a large alteration may be needed to avoid crossing ahead of the other.

f. When one vessel has to keep clear, the other shall maintain her course and speed (Rule 17a i). But if she realises that the give-way vessel is failing to keep clear, she must take independent action to avoid collision (Rule 17b). But as soon as it becomes apparent that the give-way vessel is failing to keep clear, the stand-on vessel may manoeuvre to avoid collision (Rule 17a ii). It has been held in court that such manoeuvre should take place at a distance of 2 miles or more. In taking such action, a power-driven vessel (Rule 17c) should not alter course to port for a vessel on her own port side. She would normally alter substantially to starboard, to minimise the risk of both vessels turning towards each other.

g. Under Rule 17(b), when the stand-on vessel finds herself so close that collision cannot be avoided by the action of the give-way vessel alone, the stand-on vessel *shall* take such action that will help to avoid a collision.

h. Rule 18, except where Rules 9 (narrow channels), Rule 10 (TSS) and Rule 13 (overtaking) otherwise require, lays down priorities according to manoeuvrability:

(a) A power-driven vessel under way keeps clear of:
- (i) a vessel not under command;
- (ii) a vessel restricted in manoeuvrability;
- (iii) a vessel engaged in fishing;
- (iv) a sailing vessel.

(b) A sailing vessel under way keeps clear of:
(i)-(iii) in (a) above.

(c) A vessel engaged in fishing, under way, keeps clear of: (i) and (ii) in (a) above.

(d) (i) Any vessel, except one not under command or one restricted in her ability to manoeuvre, shall if possible avoid impeding the safe passage of a vessel constrained by her draught, showing the signals in Rule 28 (see Chapter 9 Introduction, Plate 2).

(ii) A vessel constrained by her draught shall navigate with particular caution.

1.1.4 Restricted visibility

In poor visibility vessels must proceed at a safe speed (Rules 19 and 6). On hearing a fog signal ahead of the beam, be prepared to reduce speed or stop. If a vessel is detected by radar, take early action to avoid collision. If the other vessel is ahead of the beam, avoid altering course to port, unless the other vessel is being overtaken. If the other vessel is abaft the beam, do not alter course towards it. Sound the appropriate fog signal; keep a good lookout; have an efficient radar reflector; keep clear of shipping lanes; and be ready to take drastic avoiding action. In thick fog it is best to anchor in shallow water, out of the shipping channels.

1.1.5 Lights and shapes

a. The required lights (Rule 20) must be shown from sunset to sunrise, and by day in restricted visibility. The required shapes must be shown by day.

b. The types of navigation light are defined in Rule 21, and are shown in Chapter 9, Plate 1, together with illustrations of the lights to be shown by power-driven vessels and sailing vessels under way. A summary of further lights and shapes to be shown by various classes of vessel is given in Chapter 9, Plate 2.

c. A power-driven vessel under 12m in length may combine her masthead light and sternlight in one all-round white light (Rule 23).

d. Lights required for vessels towing and being towed (Rule 24) include a special yellow towing light above the sternlight of the towing vessel. But this is not required by a yacht or other small craft not normally used for towing.

e. In a sailing yacht < 20m LOA, the sidelights and sternlight may be combined in one tricolour lantern at the masthead (Rule 25b). This gives excellent visibility for the lights, and maximum brightness for minimum battery drain. A tricolour light should not be switched on at the same time as the normal sidelights and sternlight, and must not be used when under power.

f. A yacht, even with sails set, which is also being driven by engine must show the lights of a power-driven vessel, and by day, a cone, point-down, forward (Rule 25).

g. A sailing vessel under way may, in addition to her normal sidelights and sternlight, show near the masthead two all-round lights in a vertical line, red over green (Rule 25 c). These lights must not be shown in conjunction with the tricolour lantern described in the paragraph g above.

h. In broad terms coloured lights indicate hampered vessels. Commonly encountered all-round lights, displayed vertically, include fishing vessels – red over white; trawlers – green over white; vessels which cannot manoeuvre – red, over white, over red; a vessel constrained by her draught – three red lights. A hovercraft shows an all-round flashing yellow light.

i. Rule 27 (vessels not under command, or restricted in their ability to manoeuvre), does not apply to vessels <12m LOA, except for flying flag 'A' when engaged in diving operations.

j. A yacht <7m LOA, when at anchor not in or near a narrow channel, fairway or anchorage, or where other vessels normally navigate, is not required to show an anchor light or ball (Rule 30e). Apart from this minor exemption, yachts at anchor, like other vessels, shall show an anchor light or ball. This requirement has safety and insurance implications, assists other mariners and is often enforced abroad. A vessel <12m LOA, when aground, is not required to show the lights or shapes prescribed by Rule 30 f.

1.1.6 Sound signals

Sound signals (Rules 34 and 35) are summarised in the table below. Vessels >12m LOA must be provided with a whistle (foghorn) and a bell. A boat <12m LOA is not obliged to carry these sound-signalling appliances, but must have some means of making an efficient sound signal. The effectiveness of a yacht's sound signal should be judged against its audibility from the bridge of a large ship, with conflicting noises from other sources. Note that a short blast is about one second, and a prolonged blast four to six seconds duration.

A sailing vessel under way in fog sounds one prolonged blast, followed by two short blasts (i.e. Morse 'D'). The maximum interval between sound

SUMMARY OF IMPORTANT SOUND SIGNALS – RULES 34 AND 35

Note: • indicates a short blast of foghorn, of about one seconds duration.
— indicates a prolonged blast of foghorn, of four to six seconds duration.

Vessels in sight of each other (Rule 34)

•	I am altering course to starboard (power-driven vessel).
••	I am altering course to port (power-driven vessel).
•••	I am operating astern propulsion (power-driven vessel).
— — •	(In a narrow channel) I intend to overtake you on your starboard side.
— — ••	(In a narrow channel) I intend to overtake you on your port side.
— • — •	Agreement with the overtaking signal above.
•••••	I fail to understand your intentions or actions/I doubt if you are taking sufficient action to avoid collision.
—	Warning signal by vessel(s) approaching a bend in channel.

Sound signals in restricted visibility (Rule 35, a-f)

—	Power-driven vessel making way through the water.
— —	Power-driven vessel under way, but stopped and not making way through the water.
— ••	Vessel not under command, or restricted in her ability to manoeuvre, or constrained by her draught, or engaged in fishing, or towing or pushing, or a sailing vessel.
— •••	Vessel being towed, or if more than one vessel is towed, the last vessel in the tow.
••••	Pilot vessel engaged on pilotage duties.

The maximum intervals between sound signals for vessels under way in restricted visibility is two minutes but they should be sounded more frequently if other craft are near.

Sound signals by vessels at anchor or aground in restricted visibility (Rule 35, g-h)

Bell rung rapidly for about 5 seconds, every minute.	Vessel at anchor.
Gong rung rapidly for about 5 seconds following above signal, every minute.	Vessel of 100m or more in length at anchor: the bell being sounded in the fore part of the vessel and the gong aft.
• — •	Vessel at anchor (optional additional signal).
Bell rung rapidly for about 5 seconds, with three separate and distinct strokes before and after.	Vessel aground.

signals for vessels under way in restricted visibility is two minutes, but they should be sounded more frequently if other craft are near.

1.1.7 Annexes to IRPCS

Annexes I and III give technical details of lights, shapes and sound signals. Annex II gives additional lights which may be shown by fishing vessels working in close proximity to one another.

1.1.8 Distress signals

Annex IV of the IRPCS gives details of all the signals which may be used either together or separately to indicate distress and need of assistance. Those most suited to use by yachts are described in more detail in Chapter 6. For those flag and sound signals having a special meaning under IRPCS, see also Chapter 9, Plate 5. For lesser emergencies use 'V' International Code = 'I require assistance'.

Distress signals must only be used when a vessel or person is in serious and immediate danger and urgent help is needed.

1.2 DOCUMENTATION

1.2.1 Cruising formalities

Before, or while cruising abroad, certain formalities are necessary, as summarised below. It creates a favourable impression, especially abroad, and saves time if ship's and owner's documents are smartly presented in a readily available file.

(1) Yacht documents

Registration certificate (1.2.2). Proof of VAT status (1.5.1). Marine insurance covering the intended cruising area, including third-party cover (1.2.3).

Ship's radio licence (4.2.3). Ship's Log and yacht's itinerary.

(2) Personal documents

Valid passports and Forms E.111. Crew list.

Certificate of Competence, e.g. ICC or Yachtmaster (1.2.4). Radio Operator's certificate of competence and authority to operate (4.2.3).

(3) Health regulations

Comply with health regulations (e.g. report any infectious disease); exceptionally, vaccination certificates may be needed.

(4) National ensign

The yacht should wear the national ensign and fly a courtesy ensign of the country visited at starboard crosstree. Carry flag 'Q'.

(5) Customs regulations

Conform to HM Customs regulations (1.3) and any foreign. Customs regulations in countries visited (1.4). If in doubt about specific items or procedures, ask. All countries are sensitive to the importation (including carriage on board) of illegal quantities of alcohol and tobacco, and any drugs.

(7) Commercial use

In most countries it is illegal to use a visiting cruising yacht for a commercial purpose (e.g. charter).

1.2.2 Registration

British-owned yachts can be registered under the Merchant Shipping Act 1995 and the Merchant Shipping (Registration of Ships) Regulations 1993.

The Register is in four parts:

Part I	for merchant ships and pleasure vessels
Part II	for fishing vessels
Part III	for small ships (Small Ships Register)
Part IV	for bareboat charter ships

The procedures for all types of registration are fully described in a booklet ***Registering British Ships in the United Kingdom*** issued by the RSS/MCA/DoT, and obtainable from:

Registry of Shipping and Seamen (RSS), PO Box 165, Cardiff CF4 5FU. ☎ 029 2074 7333; 📠 029 2074 7877. There is a ☎ help line available on 0891 615353.

a. Registration under Part I is a relatively complex and expensive business (£115), since a yacht has to follow the same procedure as a large merchant vessel. The certificate establishes the ship's nationality and tonnage. It does **not** prove ownership nor show mortgages. It costs £46 to renew for 5 years.

b. Part III, commonly called ***The Small Ships Register (SSR)***, is for ships which only want a simple registration. This is sufficient for most purposes. A small ship is deemed to be <24 metres LOA. It satisfies the law that a British yacht proceeding abroad must be registered, and it also meets the registration requirement for a privileged ensign. Part III registration registers neither 'Title' nor mortgages. The cost is £10 for a five-year period, and measurement is a simple matter of taking the LOA of the boat. An application form is obtainable from: The RSS, PO Box 508, Cardiff CF14 5FH. ☎: 029 2076 8206 or 029 2074 7333 ext 289; 📠: 029 2074 7877.

1.2.3 Insurance

Any cruising boat represents a large capital investment, which should be protected against possible loss or damage by adequate insurance. It is also essential to insure against third-party risks, and cover for at least £1,000,000 is now normal.

The value for which a boat is insured should be the replacement cost of the boat and all equipment. Abide by the nominated period in commission and cruising area. Note the various warranties which are implied or expressed in the policy. For example, the owner is required to keep the boat in a seaworthy condition; theft is only covered if forcible entry or removal can be shown; engines and other mechanical items are only covered in exceptional circumstances; charter and loss of personal effects are not covered, unless specially arranged.

1.2.4 International Certificate of Competence

The International Certificate of Competence (ICC) (Pleasure Craft) replaces the former Helmsman's Overseas Certificate of Competence (HOCC) and is valid for five years. If a suitable RYA Certificate (e.g. Yachtmaster offshore) is not held, the ICC will be issued by the RYA to British Citizens or bonafide UK residents who either:

(a) pass a test at an RYA recognised sea school or participating Club; or

(b) already hold a HOCC, or a professional or military seagoing qualification.

1.3 HM CUSTOMS

1.3.1 The European Union (EU)

EU yachtsmen can move freely within the EU, provided that all taxes due, such as Customs duty, VAT, or any other Customs charges, have been paid in one of the EU countries. But most nations still carry out random checks on yachts to stop illegal goods, especially drugs, from entering their country.

EU and EEA countries are: Austria, Belgium, Denmark, Finland, France, Germany, Greece, Holland, Iceland, Italy, Luxembourg, Norway, Portugal (including the Azores and Madeira), Republic of Ireland, Spain (including the Balearic Islands, but not the Canary Islands), Sweden, and the UK (including Gibraltar, but not the Isle of Man and the Channel Islands).

The Channel Islands and the Canary Islands do not operate a VAT system under EU rules, and are therefore treated as being outside the EU single market.

1.3.2 Regulations

All yachts sailing beyond UK Territorial Waters must comply with Customs Notice No 8 (April 1996), *Sailing your pleasure craft to/from the UK* which is summarised below. This Notice and further information may be obtained from any Customs and Excise Advice Centre.

Advice centre phone numbers for the regions are:

Area	*Telephone*	*Location*	*Manned*
SW England	01752 234600	Plymouth	
SE England	01304 215639	Dover	H24
London	01474 537115	Gravesend	
Anglia	01473 235705	Ipswich	
N England	01482 782107	Hull	
Scotland	0141 887 9369	Glasgow	H24
Wales	02920 76700	Cardiff	
N Ireland	02890 358251	Belfast	H24

Yachtsmen are warned that a boat may be searched at any time. There are severe penalties for non-declaration of prohibited or restricted goods, and the carriage and non-declaration of prohibited drugs and firearms will incur the forfeiture of your boat and all its equipment. It is a good idea to have a copy of Notice No 8 aboard.

1.3.3 Stores

Duty-free stores may be allowed on vessels going south of Brest (France) or north of the north bank of the Eider (Germany), by prior application to a Customs office, and subject to certain conditions. Duty-free stores cannot be taken to the Republic of Ireland or the Channel Islands. Details on how to ship stores, or re-ship previously landed surplus duty-free stores, can be obtained from any Customs office. Stores being shipped under bond, or on which repayment of Customs charges is being claimed, are normally placed under a Customs seal on board. Such goods cannot be used in UK waters without paying duty, and duty may be liable if the voyage is abandoned or interrupted.

1.3.4 Notice of departure

a. To another EU country: No report is needed, unless requested by a Customs Officer.

b. To a place outside the EU: Each intended departure must be notified to HM Customs on Part 1 of Form C1331, copies of which are available at local Customs Advice Centres and from most marinas and yacht clubs. Failure to give notice of departure may result in delay and inconvenience on return, and possible prosecution.

The completed Part I should be handed to a Customs Officer, taken to the Customs office nearest the place of departure, or put in a Customs post box, so that the form arrives before departure. Form C1331 is valid for up to 48 hours from the stated time of departure. Retain Part 2 on board for use on your return. If the voyage is abandoned, Part 2 should be delivered to the same office marked 'voyage abandoned'.

1.3.5 Arrival from an EU country

If arriving directly from another EU country there is no need to fly flag 'Q', complete any paperwork, or contact Customs. You must, however, contact Customs if you have goods to declare, or have non-EU nationals on board. You must declare any animals or birds; any prohibited or restricted goods such as controlled drugs, firearms, or radio transmitters not approved for use in UK; counterfeit goods; any duty-free stores; or the boat itself if duty and VAT are owed on it. Further details on which goods are classified as prohibited or restricted are given in Notice 8.

1.3.6 Arrival from a non-EU country

If arriving directly from a country outside the EU (including the Channel Islands), yachts are subject to Customs control. As soon as UK Territorial Waters are entered, ie the 12-mile limit, complete Part 2 of Form C1331 and fly the flag 'Q' where it can easily be seen until formalities are complete. On arrival contact a Customs Officer in person or by telephone. If an officer boards your vessel, you must hand Form C1331 to him.

You must declare any tobacco goods, alcoholic drinks, perfumes and toilet waters in excess of your duty-free allowance; animals or birds; prohibited or restricted goods;

duty-free stores; or the boat itself if duty and VAT are owed on it. You must also declare any goods that are to be left in the UK. You must not land any persons or goods, or transfer them to another vessel until a Customs Officer says that you may.

1.3.7 Immigration

In most yachting centres the Customs Officer also acts as the Immigration Officer. Anyone aboard who is not an EU national must get an Immigration Officer's permission to enter the UK from any country other than the Isle of Man, the Channel Islands, or Eire. The skipper is responsible for ensuring that this is done.

1.3.8 Customs offices – telephone numbers

The telephone number of the appropriate Customs office (☎) is given under the heading 'Telephone' for each British harbour in Chapter 9.

1.3.9 Drug smuggling

The prevention of drug smuggling is a key role for HM Customs. Public support is very important. If you see a suspicious incident or know of suspicious activity, telephone 0800 595000. This is a 24 hours, free and confidential Action line. There may be a reward.

1.4 FOREIGN CUSTOMS

1.4.1 General

Other EU countries should follow the same regulations as described in 1.3.1 to 1.3.6 above, and any Customs formalities are likely to be minimal. Before departure, skippers are recommended to check the procedures in force in their destination country. Currently, both the Netherlands and Belgium require a vessel to report on arrival even if coming from another EU country.

1.5. VAT AND THE SINGLE MARKET

1.5.1 General

An EU resident can move a yacht between member states without restriction, providing VAT has been paid.

Enquiries concerning VAT on pleasure craft or on any other procedural matters on imported boats should be addressed to the Collection Coordination Unit for each region. The RYA may also be able to provide useful advice.

1.5.2 Temporary importation (TI)

A boat can only be permitted into an EU country under temporary import arrangements if:

(1) The owner is not an EU resident (i.e. lives outside the EU for at least 185 days in any 12-month period), and

(2) The owner does not keep the boat in the EU for more than six months in a continuous 12-month period, within the EU as a whole. The period of TI cannot be extended by moving the boat to another EU member state. It may, however, be extended by written application to the member state where the yacht is at present. For the UK, this is the National Unit for Personal Transport; see next page for address.

1.6 USEFUL ADDRESSES

British Marine Industries Federation (BMIF).
Marine House, Thorpe Lea Road, Egham, Surrey TW20 8BF.
☎: 01784 473377. 📠: 01784 439678.

British Sub-Aqua Club.
Telford's Quay, Ellesmere Port, South Wirral, Cheshire CH65 4FL.
☎: 0151 350 6200. 📠: 0151 350 6215.

British Telecom Maritime Radio Services.
43 Bartholomew Close, London EC1A 7HP.
☎: 020 7583 9416. 📠: 020 7726 8123.

British Waterways Board.
Willow Grange, Church Rd, Watford, Herts WD1 3QA.
☎: 01923 226422. 📠: 01923 226081.

British Waterways (Caledonian Canal).
Seaport Marina, Canal Office, Muirtown Wharf, Inverness IV3 5LS.
☎: 01463 233140. 📠: 01463 710942.

British Waterways (Crinan Canal).
Pier Square, Canal Office, Ardrishaig, Lochgilphead, Argyll PA30 8DZ.
☎: 01546 603210. 📠: 01546 603941.
www.british waterways.co.uk

British Waterways (Scotland).
Regional Office, Canal House, Applecross Street, Glasgow G4 9SP.
☎: 0141 332 6936. 📠: 0141 331 1688.

Clyde Cruising Club.
Suite 408, The Pentagon Centre, 36 Washington Street, Glasgow G3 8AZ.
☎: 0141 221 2774. 📠: 0141 221 2775.

Cowes Combined Clubs.
Secretary, 18 Bath Road, Cowes,
Isle of Wight PO31 7QN.
☎: 01983 295744. 📠: 01983 295329.

Cruising Association (CA).
CA House, 1 Northey Street, Limehouse Basin, London E14 8BT.
☎: 020 7537 2828. 📠: 020 7537 2266.

HM Customs and Excise.
OAS, 5th Floor East, New King's Beam House,
22 Upper Ground, London SE1 9PJ.
☎: 020 7865 5784. 📠: 020 7865 4744.

Hydrographic Office.
Admiralty Way, Taunton, Somerset TA1 2DN.
☎: 01823 337900. 📠: 01823 284077.

Inland Waterways Association.
PO Box 114, Rickmansworth WD3 1ZY.
☎: 01923 711114. 📠: 01923 897000.

IMES (Coastguard Republic of Ireland).
Irish Marine Emergency Services,
Department of the Marine, Leeson Lane, Dublin 2
☎: 00 353 1 678 5444. 📠: 00 353 1 676 2666.

International Maritime Organisation (IMO).
4 Albert Embankment, London SE1 7SR.
☎: 020 7735 7611. 📠: 020 7587 3210.
International Maritime Satellite Org. (Inmarsat).
99 City Road, London EC1Y 1AX.
☎: 020 7728 1000. 📠: 020 7728 1044.
Irish Lights, Commissions of
16 Lower Pembroke Street, Dublin 2.
☎: 00 353 1 662 4525. 📠: 00 353 1 661 8094.
Irish Sailing Association.
3 Park Road, Dun Laoghaire, Co Dublin.
☎: 00 353 1 280 0239. 📠: 00 353 1 280 7558.
Irish Tourist Board (Eire).
150 New Bond Street, London W1Y OAQ.
☎: 0207 518 0800. 📠: 0207 493 9065.
Jersey Tourist Office.
Liberation Square, St Helier,
Jersey JE1 1BB, Channel Isles.
☎: 01534 500700. 📠: 01534 500808.
Junior Offshore Group.
28 Nodes Road, Cowes, Isle of Wight PO31 8AB.
☎: 01983 291192. 📠: 01983 291192.
Little Ship Club.
Bell Wharf Lane, Upper Thames St, London EC4R 3TB.
☎: 020 7236 7729. 📠: 020 7236 9100.
Maritime and Coastguard Agency (MCA).
Spring Place, 105 Commercial Road,
Southampton SO15 1EG.
☎: 023 8032 9100. 📠: 023 8032 9105.
Maritime Trust.
2 Greenwich Church Street, London SE10 9BG.
☎: 020 8858 2698. 📠: 020 8858 6976.
Medway Yachting Association.
Joyce Hall, Betsham, Gravesend, Kent DA13 9PB.
☎: 01474 832308.
Meteorological Office.
London Road, Bracknell, Berks RG12 2SZ.
☎: 01344 420242. 📠: 01344 855921.
National Unit for Personal Transport.
HM Customs & Excise, PO Box 242, Dover, CT17 9GP.
☎: 01304 224556. 📠: 01304 224567.
Nautical Data Limited.
The Book Barn, Westbourne, Hants PO10 8RS.
☎: 01243 377977. 📠: 01243 379136.
Northern Lighthouse Board.
84 George Street, Edinburgh EH2 3DA.
☎: 0131 226 7051. 📠: 0131 220 2093.
Port of London Authority.
Devon House, 58-60 St Katherine's Way, London E1 9LB.
☎: 020 7265 2656. 📠: 020 7265 2699.
Radiocommunications Agency.
Aeronautical & Maritime Section, Wyndham House,
189 Marsh Wall, London E14 9SX.
☎: 020 7211 0215. 📠: 020 7211 0228.

Registry of Shipping and Seamen (RSS).
Anchor Hse, Cheviot Close, Llanishen,
Cardiff CF4 5JA.
☎: 029 2074 7333 Extn 289. 📠: 029 2074 7877.
☎: RSS Helpline 0891 615353.
Royal Cruising Club (RCC).
At the Royal Thames Yacht Club (see below).
Royal Institute of Navigation.
At the Royal Geographical Society,
1 Kensington Gore, London SW7 2AT.
☎: 020 7591 3130. 📠: 020 7591 3131.
Royal National Lifeboat Institution (RNLI).
West Quay Road, Poole, Dorset BH15 1HZ.
☎: 01202 663000. 📠: 01202 663167.
Royal Naval Sailing Association (RNSA).
17 Pembroke Road, Portsmouth, Hants PO1 2NT.
☎: 023 9282 3524. 📠: 023 9287 0654.
Royal Ocean Racing Club (RORC).
20 St James's Place, London SW1A 1NN.
☎: 020 7493 2248. 📠: 020 7493 5252.
Royal Thames Yacht Club (RTYC).
60 Knightsbridge, London SW1 7LF.
☎: 020 7235 2121. 📠: 020 7235 5672.
Royal Yachting Association (RYA).
RYA House, Romsey Rd, Eastleigh, Hants SO50 9YA.
☎: 0023 8062 7400. 📠: 023 8062 9924.
Royal Yachting Association (Scotland).
Caledonia House, South Gyle, Edinburgh EH12 9DQ.
☎: 0131 317 7388. 📠: 0131 317 8566.
Small Ships Register.
Small Ships Section, Registry of Shipping and
Seamen, PO Box 165, Cardiff CF4 5FU.
☎: 029 2074 7333. 📠: 029 2074 7877.
Solent Cruising and Racing Association.
18 Bath Road, Cowes, Isle of Wight PO31 7QN.
☎: 01983 295744. 📠: 01983 295329.
States of Guernsey Tourist Board.
PO Box 23, North Esplanade, St Peter Port, Guernsey,
Channel Isles GY1 3AN.
☎: 01481 726611. 📠: 01481 721246.
The Radio Licensing Centre.
Post Office Customer Management (POCM) Unit,
PO Box 1495, Bristol, BS99 3QS.
☎: 0870 243 4433 📠: 0117 975 8911.
Trinity House.
Tower Hill, London EC3N 4DH.
☎: 020 7481 6900 📠: 020 7480 7662.
Yacht Harbour Association.
Evegate Park Barn, Smeeth, Ashford,
Kent TN25 6SX.
☎: 01303 814434. 📠: 01303 814364.

FRANCE
British Embassy.
35 rue du Faubourg St, Honoré 75008 Paris, Cedex 08
☎: 00 33 1 44 51 31 00. 📠: 00 33 1 44 51 31 27.

Chambre Nationale des Experts Professionnels du Nautisme (CNEPN).
(Professional surveyors' association)
BP 11, 66751 St Cyprien.
☎: 00 33 4 68 21 37 85. 📠: 00 33 4 68 21 91 77.
Comité d'Etudes et de Services des Assureurs Maritimes (CESAM).
(Insurance companies' surveyors group)
20 rue Vivienne, 75002 Paris.
☎: 00 33 1 42 96 12 13. 📠: 00 33 1 42 96 34 59.
CROSS Gris Nez.
62179 Audinghen.
☎: 03·21·87·21·87. 📠: 03·21· 87·78·55.
CROSS Jobourg.
BP 218, 50440 Jobourg.
☎: 02·33·52·72·13. 📠: 02·33· 52·71·72.
CROSS CORSEN.
Pointe de Corsen, 29810 Plouarzel.
☎: 02·98·89·31·31. 📠: 02·98·89·65·75.
CROSSA (ETEL).
Centre Principal, Av Louis. Bougo, 56410 Etel.
☎: 02·97·55·35·35. 📠: 02·97·55·49·34.
S/CROSS SOULAC.
Centre secondaire, Route de l'Amélie BP. 35, 33780 SOULAC-S/Mer.
☎: 05·56·73·31·31 . 📠: 05·56·09·79·73.
Douanes - Bureau d'Information.
(Customs, Office of Information)
23 bis, rue de l'Université, 75700 Paris.
☎: 00 33 1 44 74 49 91. 📠: 00 33 1 44 74 49 37.
Service Hydrographique et Océanographique de la Marine (SHOM).
(French Hydrographic Service)
BP 426, 29275 Brest.
☎: 00 33 2 98 03 09 17. 📠: 00 33 2 98 47 11 42.
Société Nationale de Sauvetage en Mer (SNSM).
(Semi-private Lifeboat Society)
9 rue de Chaillot, 75116 Paris.
☎: 00 33 1 47 23 98 26. 📠: 00 33 1 47 23 64 60.
Yacht Club de France.
(The senior French Yacht Club)
41 avenue Foch, 75116 Paris.
☎: 00 33 1 47 04 10 00. 📠: 00 33 1 47 04 10 01.

GERMANY

Bundesamt für Seeschiffahrt und Hydrographie BSH.
(German hydrographer)
Bernhard-Nocht-Str 78, 20359 Hamburg.
☎: 00 49 40 31 900. 📠: 00 49 40 3190 5000.
Deutscher Segler Verband.
(German yachting association)
Gründgensstr 18, 22309 Hamburg.
☎: 00 49 40 632 0090. 📠: 00 49 40 6320 0928
Deutscher Wetterdienst - Zentralamt.
Frankfurter Str 135, 63067 Offenbach.
☎: 00 49 69 80 620. 📠: 00 49 69 8236 7283.
DGzRS - Deutsche Gesellschaft zur Rettung Schiffbrüchiger. (Rescue service),
Hauptverwaltung, Hermann-Helms-Haus,
Werderstr 2, 28199 Bremen.
☎: 00 49 421 53 70 70. 📠: 00 49 421 537 0743.

THE NETHERLANDS

ANWB Hoofdkantoor.
PO Box 93200, 2509 BA Den Haag.
☎: 00 31 70 314 71 47. 📠: 00 31 70 314 69 69.
Stichting Classificatie Waterrecreatiebedrijven.
(Classification of Marinas etc)
PO Box 93380, 2509 A Den Haag.
☎: 00 31 70 328 3807.
Koninklijk Nederlands Watersport Verbond.
(Royal Netherlands Watersport Association)
PO Box 87, 3980 CB Bunnik,
☎: 00 31 30 656 6550. 📠: 00 31 30 656 4783.
Koninklijke Nederlandse Motorboot Club.
(Royal Netherlands Motorboat Club)
Zoorstede 7, 3431 HK Nieuwegein.
☎: 00 31 30 603 9935. 📠: 00 31 30 605 3834.

DENMARK

Dansk Sejlunion.
(Danish sailing association)
Idraettens Hus, Brøndby Stadion 20,
Brøndby 2605 .
☎: 0045 43 26 26 26. 📠: 0045 43 26 21 91.
DMU Danske Fritidssejlere.
(Motorsport)
Tjørnelund 32, 2635 Ishøj.
☎: 0045 43 53 66 67. 📠: 0045 43 53 66 67
Søfartsstyrelsen.
(Danish Maritime Authority)
Vermundsgade 38C, 2100 Copenhagen.
☎: 0045 39 17 44 00. 📠: 0045 39 17 44 01.
Skov & Naturstryrelsen.
(The National Forest and Nature Agency)
Haraldsgade 53, 2100 Copenhagen.
☎: 0045 39 47 20 00. 📠: 0045 39 47 98 99.

PORTUGAL

British Embassy.
Rua de Sao Bernardo 33, 1200 Lisbon.
☎: 00 351 1 392 4000. 📠: 00 351 1 392 4185.

SPAIN

British Embassy.
Calle de Fernando el Santo 16, 28010 Madrid.
☎: 00 34 91 700 8200. 📠: 00 34 91 700 8311.
Spanish Hydrographic Office.
Instituto Hidrografico de la Marina, Tolosa Latour 1, 11007 CADIZ.
☎: 00 34 95 659 9412. 📠: 00 34 95 627 5358.

1.7 INTERNET: WEB SITES AND E-MAIL

The following is a selected list of useful Web sites and e-mail addresses amongst the thousands available which offer nautical information and interest.

The Macmillan Reeds Nautical Almanac

Nautical Data Ltd www.nauticaldata.com

Editorials editorial@nauticaldata.com

Other Useful addresses:

BBC www.bbc.co.uk
Weather Centre www.bbc.co.uk/weather/index.htm
British Marine Industries Federation (BMIF). www.@bsac.com
British Sub-Aqua Club. www.@bsac.com
British Waterways www.british waterways.co.uk
BT Global Challenge www.btchallenge.com/
Caledonian McBrayne www.calmac.co.uk
Captain O.M. Watts sales@captainwatts.co.uk
Clyde Cruising Club www.clydecruising.demon.co.uk
Commissioners of Irish Lights cil@aol.iol.ie
Cowes Combined Clubs ccc@cowesweek.co.uk
Crest Nicholson www.aboard.co.uk
Cruising Association
General Website www.cruising.org.uk
office @cruising.org.uk
Danish Met Institute www.dmi.dk
Dover Harbour Board www.doverport.co.uk
France Telecom www.francetelecom.fr
German Hydrographic Office (BSH) www.bsh.de
Guernsey Tourist Board www.guernseytourism.gov.ss
Hydrographic Office (UK)
General Website www.hydro.gov.uk
UK Notices to Mariners www.nms.ukho.gov.uk
HM Coastguard www.coastguard.gov.uk
hdc&hdc.hydro.gov.uk
ImrayLaurie Norie & Wilson
General Website www.imray.com
Charts & Books ilnw@imray.com
International Maritime Organisation (IMO).
www.imo.org or info@imo.org
International Maritime Satellite Org. (Inmarsat).
www.inmarsat.com
Irish Sailing Association www.sailing.ie
Irish Tourist Board (Eire) www.ireland.travel.ie
Irish Wx Forecasts from RTE www.rte.ie/aertel/p160.htm
Jersey Tourist Office. www.jersey.com
Junior Offshore Group www.jog.org.uk
Kelvin Hughes cams@kelvinhughes.co.uk
Book Harbour www.bookharbour.com
Little Ship Club www.little-ship-club.co.uk
Marine Accident Investigation Board
maib.detr@gtnet.gov.uk
Marine Data Ltd www.marinedata.co.uk
uk.rec.sailing
www.sailingindex.com
Marina Developments Ltd www.marinas.co.uk
Maritime & Coastguard Agency www.mcagency.org.uk
Maritime Trust www.cuttysark.org.uk
info@cuttysark.org.uk

Meteostat www.nottingham.ac.uk/meteosat
MetFAX Helpline metfax@meto.gov.uk
Meteo France (in French) www.meteo.fr/e_index.html
Meteorological Office UK
General Website www.met-office.gov.uk
www.meto.gov.uk/home.html
MetRoute metroute@meteo.gov.uk
MetWEB metweb@meto.gov.uk
MOAA (Weatherbuoys) www.nws.fsu.edu/buoy
Motor Boat and Yachting www.mby.com
Meteo France www.meteo.fr
National Coastwatch Institution (NCI) info@nci.org.uk
http://www.nci.org.uk
Port of London Authority marketing@portoflondon.co.uk
Portuguese Met Institute www.meteo.pt
Practical Boat Owner www.pbo.co.uk
Radiocommunications Agency arms@ra-gtnet.gov.uk
Registry of Shipping and Seamen (RSS).
www.mcagency.org.uk
RNLI www.rnli.org.uk
RNN - Dutch HO www.hydro.nl
RORC www.rorc.org
rorc@compuserve.com
Royal Cork YC www.iol.ie/royalcork
office@royalcork.iol.ie
Royal Danish Administration of Navigation & Hydrography
pbn@fomfrv.dk
Royal Institute of Navigation www.rin.org.uk
rindir@atlas.co.uk
Royal Northumberland YC www.rnyc.org.uk
hon.sec@rnyc.org.uk
Royal Yachting Association www.rya.org.uk
admin@rya.org.uk
Sail Scotland www.sailscotland.co.uk
SHOM (French HO) www.shom.fr
Small Ships Register, Small Ships Section
www.mcagency.org.uk
Solent Cruising and Racing Association
www.scra.org.uk

Southern Sailing www.southern.co.uk
SMD Schiffsmeldendienst (Hamburg/Cuxhaven) info@smd.de
www.smd.de
Spanish Met Office www.inm.es
www.infomet.fcr.es
Trinity House www.trinityhouse.co.uk
UK Hbrs directory (Solent & South Coast)
www.harbours.co.uk
UK Weather page www.cwp.co.uk/weather/index.html
US Coast Guard Navigation Centre
www.navcen.uscg.mil
ftp//ftp.navcen.usch.mil
Yachtlink www.vossnet.co.uk/yacht/
Yachting Monthly www.yachting monthly.com
Yachting World www.yachting-world.com

1.8 CONVERSION TABLES

1.8.1 Conversion factors

To convert	Multiply by	To convert	Multiply by
Area			
sq in to sq mm	645·16	sq mm to sq in	0·00155
sq ft to sq m	0·0929	sq m to sq ft	10·76
Length			
in to mm	25·40	mm to in	0·0394
yds to m	0·914	m to yds	1·094
fathoms to m	1·8288	m to fathoms	0·5468
nautical miles (M) to kilometres	1·852	kilometres to nautical miles	0·539957
nautical miles to statute miles	1·1515	statute miles to nautical miles	0·8684
(1 cable equals 0·1 M, approx 185m)			
Velocity (See Ch 5 for knots to m/sec)			
ft/sec to m/sec	0·3048	m/sec to ft/sec	3·281
ft/sec to miles/hr	0·682	miles/hr to ft/sec	1·467
ft/min to m/sec	0·0051	m/sec to ft/min	196·8
knots to miles/hr	1·1515	miles/hr to knots	0·868
knots to km/hr	1·852	km/hr to knots	0·54
Mass			
lb to kg	0·4536	kg to lb	2·205
tons to tonnes (1000 kg)	1·016	tonnes to tons (2240 lb)	0·9842
Energy			
hp to kw	0·7457	kw to hp	1·341
Pressure (See Ch 5 for °C to °F)			
inches of mercury to millibars	33·86	millibars to inches of mercury	0·0295
lb/sq in to kg/sq cm	0·0703	kg/sq cm to lb/sq in	14·22
lb/sq in to atmospheres	0·068	atmospheres to lb/sq in	14·7
Volume			
cu ft to galls	6·25	galls to cu ft	0·16
cu ft to litres	28·33	litres to cu ft	0·035
Capacity			
pints to litres	0·568	litres to pints	1·76
galls to litres	4·546	litres to galls	0·22
Imp galls to US galls	1·2	US galls to Imp galls	0·833

1.8.2 Feet to metres, metres to feet

Explanation: The central columns of figures in bold type can be referenced to the left to convert metres into feet, or to the right to convert feet into metres, e.g. five lines down: 5 metres = 16·40 feet, or 5 feet = 1·52 metres. Alternatively multiply feet by 0·3048 for metres, or multiply metres by 3·2808 for feet.

Feet		Metres	Feet		Metres	Feet		Metres	Feet		Metres
3·28	**1**	0·30	45·93	**14**	4·27	88·58	**27**	8·23	131·23	**40**	12·19
6·56	**2**	0·61	49·21	**15**	4·57	91·86	**28**	8·53	134·51	**41**	12·50
9·84	**3**	0·91	52·49	**16**	4·88	95·14	**29**	8·84	137·80	**42**	12·80
13·12	**4**	1·22	55·77	**17**	5·18	98·43	**30**	9·14	141·08	**43**	13·11
16·40	**5**	1·52	59·06	**18**	5·49	101·71	**31**	9·45	144·36	**44**	13·41
19·69	**6**	1·83	62·34	**19**	5·79	104·99	**32**	9·75	147·64	**45**	13·72
22·97	**7**	2·13	65·62	**20**	6·10	108·27	**33**	10·06	150·92	**46**	14·02
26·25	**8**	2·44	68·90	**21**	6·40	111·55	**34**	10·36	154·20	**47**	14·33
29·53	**9**	2·74	72·18	**22**	6·71	114·83	**35**	10·67	157·48	**48**	14·63
32·81	**10**	3·05	75·46	**23**	7·01	118·11	**36**	10·97	160·76	**49**	14·94
36·09	**11**	3·35	78·74	**24**	7·32	121·39	**37**	11·28	164·04	**50**	15·24
39·37	**12**	3·66	82·02	**25**	7·62	124·67	**38**	11·58			
42·65	**13**	3·96	85·30	**26**	7·92	127·95	**39**	11·89			

1.9 CALENDAR, 2002

1.9.1 UK PUBLIC HOLIDAYS 2002

ENGLAND & WALES: Jan 1, Mar 29, Apr 01, May 06, May 27, Aug 26, Dec 25, Dec 26

NORTHERN IRELAND: Jan 1, Mar 18, Mar 29, Apr 01, May 06, May 27, Jul 17, Aug 26, Dec 25, Dec 26

SCOTLAND: Jan 1, Jan 2, Mar 29, May 06, May 27, Aug 05, Dec 25, Dec 26

* Subject to confirmation

1.9.2 PHASES OF THE MOON 2002 (All times UTC)

New Moon ●	d	h	m	First Quarter ◐	d	h	m	Full Moon ○	d	h	m	Last Quarter ◑	d	h	m
												Jan	06	03	55
Jan	13	13	29	Jan	21	17	46	Jan	28	22	50	Feb	04	13	33
Feb	12	07	41	Feb	20	12	02	Feb	27	09	17	Mar	06	01	24
Mar	14	02	02	Mar	22	02	28	Mar	28	18	25	Apr	04	15	29
Apr	12	19	21	Apr	20	12	48	Apr	27	03	00	May	04	07	16
May	12	10	45	May	19	19	42	May	26	11	51	Jun	03	00	05
Jun	10	23	46	Jun	18	00	29	Jun	24	21	42	Jul	02	17	19
Jul	10	10	26	Jul	17	04	47	Jul	24	09	07	Aug	01	10	22
Aug	08	19	15	Aug	15	10	12	Aug	22	22	29	Aug	31	02	31
Sept	07	03	10	Sept	13	18	08	Sep	21	13	59	Sep	29	17	03
Oct	06	11	18	Oct	13	05	33	Oct	21	07	20	Oct	29	05	28
Nov	04	20	34	Nov	11	20	52	Nov	20	01	34	Nov	27	15	46
Dec	04	07	34	Dec	11	15	49	Dec	19	19	10	Dec	27	00	31

1.9.3 ECLIPSE NOTES 2002

1. An annular eclipse of the Sun, 10 -11 December — Not visible from Europe
2. Total Eclipse of the Sun, 04 December — Not visible from Europe

1.9.4 STANDARD TIMES (Corrected to March 2001)

In 2002, Summer time or DST (BST in the UK), which is one hour in advance of Standard Time, is kept in the UK and Channel Islands from Mar 31 0100 UTC until October 27 0100 UTC.

PLACES NORMALLY KEEPING UTC

Canary Islands	Great Britain	Irish Republic
Channel Islands**	Iceland*	Morocco*
Faeroes**	Ireland, Northern**	Portugal

PLACES FAST ON UTC

Algeria	01	Germany	01	Norway	01
Balearic Islands	01	Gibraltar	01	Poland**	01
Belgium	01	Italy	01	Russia, W of 40°**	03
Corsica	01	Latvia	02	Sardinia	01
Denmark	01	Lithuania	02	Spain	01
Estonia	02	Malta	01	Sweden	01
Finland	02	Monaco	01	Switzerland	01
France	01	Netherlands	01	Tunisia*	01

The times given should be added to UTC to give Standard Time, or subtracted from Standard Time to give UTC. * Summertime is not kept in these places. ** Summer time may be kept.

Chapter 2

Coastal Navigation

Contents

2.1 **DEFINITIONS AND TERMS** .... **Page 30**

2.1.1 General 30

2.1.2 Position 30

2.1.3 Direction 30

2.1.4 Compass variation and deviation 30

2.1.5 Distance 30

2.1.6 Speed 30

2.1.7 Depth 31

2.2 **IALA Buoyage** .... **Page 31**

2.2.1 IALA Buoyage System (Region A) 31

2.3 **LIGHTS** .... **Page 32**

2.3.1 Light characteristics 32

2.3.2 Light sectors, arcs of visibility 32

2.4 **PASSAGE PLANNING** .... **Page 34**

2.4.1 General 34

2.4.2 Passage planning check list 34

2.5 **NAVIGATION TABLES** .... **Page 34**

2.5.1 Explanation of the following tables: 34

Tables:

2(1) Distance of horizon 35

2(2) Lights: distance off when rising or dipping 35

2(3) Distance off by vertical sextant angle 36

2(4) Distance for a given speed and time 38

2(5) True bearing of Sun at sunrise/sunset 40

2(6) Sun's declination 41

2.6 **SUN AND MOON TABLES** .... **Page 42**

2.6.1 Rising and setting – phenomena 42

2.6.2 Contents of Tables 2(7), 2(8) and 2(9) 42

2.6.3 Examples 42

Tables:

2(7) Sunrise/Sunset and Twilights 43

2(8) Sun: latitude corrections 44

2(9) Moonrise and Moonset 45

2.1 DEFINITIONS AND TERMS

2.1.1 General

The information given here covers a few of the more important aspects of basic coastal navigation in simplified form, together with useful tables.

The Macmillan Reeds Yachtsman's Handbook provides a more extensive reference on coastal navigation covering terms and definitions, charts, chartwork and pilotage.

2.1.2 Position

Position on the Earth's surface can be expressed in two ways. By Latitude and Longitude, or by a bearing and distance from a known position.

The latitude of a place is its angular distance measured in degrees (°), minutes (') and decimals of a minute from 0° to 90° north or south of the equator.

The longitude of a place is measured in degrees (°), minutes ('), and decimals of a minute from 0° to 180° east or west from the Greenwich meridian.

2.1.3 Direction

Direction is measured clockwise from north in a three-figure group, i.e. 000° to 359°. Thus east is written as 090°, and west 270°.

Direction may be referenced to three different norths namely:

(1) **True North** as measured from the Geographic North Pole.

(2) **Magnetic North** as measured from the Magnetic North Pole, which does not coincide with the Geographic Pole.

(3) **Compass North** as measured from the north-seeking end of the compass needle.

Bearings and tracks as given on charts, or quoted in publications, are normally True bearings.

Wind direction is normally given in points of the compass clockwise from a cardinal or quadrantal point rather than in degrees, i.e. N, NNE, NE by N, etc. There are 32 points of the compass, with each point equal to $11\frac{1}{4}$°.

Tidal streams are always expressed in the direction towards which they are running.

2.1.4 Compass variation and deviation

The magnetic compass is the most vital navigational instrument in a cruising boat. It is affected by: **variation** (the angular difference between True and Magnetic North), which alters from place to place, and year to year, and is shown on the chart, normally at the compass rose; and by **deviation** (the angular difference between Magnetic and Compass North which is caused by the boat's own magnetic field. Deviation varies according to the boat's heading. Following a compass swing and adjustment of the compass, any residual deviation is shown, for different headings on a deviation card. With a properly adjusted compass, deviation should not be more than about 2° on any heading – in which case it can often be ignored except on long passages.

When converting a True course or a True bearing to Magnetic: add westerly (+) variation or deviation and subtract easterly (–).

When converting a Magnetic course or bearing to True: subtract westerly (–) variation or deviation, and add easterly (+).

2.1.5 Distance

Distance at sea is measured in nautical miles (M). A nautical mile is defined as the length of one minute of latitude. The length of a nautical mile varies with latitude and measures 6,108 feet at the Pole and 6,046 feet at the Equator. The International nautical mile is taken as being 6,076 feet or 1,852 metres.

Short distances are measured in cables. A cable is one tenth of a nautical mile, which for practical purposes approximates to 200 yards, 600 feet or 100 fathoms in length and is always used for navigational purposes irrespective of the latitude.

Distances must always be measured from the latitude scale of a chart, never from the longitude scale because the length of one minute of longitude on the earth varies from being roughly equal to a minute of latitude at the Equator, to zero length at the Pole. The longitude scale is therefore of no value as a measure of distance.

2.1.6 Speed

Speed at sea is measured in knots. A knot is one nautical mile per hour. There is an important relationship between speed, time and distance. The relationship is expressed in the formula:

$$\text{Speed} = \frac{\text{Distance (miles)}}{\text{Sailing time (hours)}}$$

from which

$$\text{Distance} = \text{Speed} \times \text{sailing time}$$

or

$$\text{Sailing time} = \frac{\text{Distance}}{\text{Speed}}$$

Whenever possible sailing times should be in units of six minutes i.e. 6 mins = 0·1 hrs, 12 mins = 0·2 hrs and 18 mins = 3 hrs etc. A convenient time, speed and distance table is given in Table 2 (4).

A log measures distance run through the water and most logs today also incorporate a speed indicator. Course and speed made good over the ground can be obtained from the read-out obtained from position-fixing receivers such as GPS, or Loran-C.

2.1.7 Depth

Depths and heights are given in metres (m). The depth of water is usually important and is measured by echo sounder (or lead line). It is important to know whether a echo sounder indicates depth below the water level, the transducer, or the base of the keel.

Chart Datum (CD) is the level below which the tide never, or very rarely, falls. Charted depths and drying heights shown on charts are always referenced to CD. The height of tide is the height of the sea surface above Chart Datum at any instant. Tidal height calculations are fully covered in Chapter 7.

2.2 IALA BUOYAGE

2.2.1 IALA Buoyage System (Region A)

International buoyage is harmonised into a single system which, applied to Regions A and B, differs only in the use of red and green lateral marks. In Region A (which includes all Europe) lateral marks are red on the port hand, and in Region B red on the starboard hand, related to direction of buoyage. Five types of marks are used, as illustrated in Chapter 9 Plate 3.

(1) Lateral marks: are used in conjunction with a direction of buoyage, shown by a special arrow ⇧ on the chart. Around the British Isles the general direction is from SW to NE in open waters, but from seaward when approaching a harbour, river or estuary. Where port or starboard lateral marks do not rely on can or conical buoy shapes for identification, they carry, where practicable, the appropriate topmarks. Any numbering or lettering follows the direction of buoyage, evens to port and odds to starboard.

In Region A, port-hand marks are coloured red, and port-hand buoys are can or spar shaped. Any topmark fitted is a single red can. Any light fitted is red, any rhythm. Starboard-hand marks are coloured green, and starboard-hand buoys are conical or spar shaped. Any topmark fitted is a single green cone, point up. Any light fitted is green, any rhythm. In exceptional cases starboard-hand marks may be coloured black.

At a division, the preferred channel may be shown by lateral marks with red or green bands:

Preferred channel	Indicated by	Light (if any)
To starboard	Port lateral mark with green band	Flashing red (2 + 1)
To port	Starboard lateral mark with red band	Flashing green (2 + 1)

(2) Cardinal marks: are named after the quadrant in which the mark is placed, in relation to the danger or point indicated. The four quadrants (north, east, south and west) are bounded by the True bearings NW-NE, NE-SE, SE-SW and SW-NW, taken from the point of interest. The name of a cardinal mark indicates that it should be passed on the named side. For example, a NCM (situated in the quadrant between NW and NE from the point of interest) should be passed on its north side; an ECM on its East side, and so on.

A cardinal mark may indicate the safe side on which to pass a danger, or that the deepest water is on the named side of the mark, or it may draw attention to a feature in a channel such as a bend, junction or fork, or the end of a shoal.

Cardinal marks are pillar or spar shaped, painted black and yellow, and always carry black double cone topmarks, one cone above the other. Their lights are white, and are either VQ or Q. VQ lights flash at a rate of 80 to 159 flashes per minute, usually either 100 or 120, and Q flash at a rate of between 50 to 79 flashes per minute, usually either 50 or 60. A long flash is one of not less than two seconds' duration.

North cardinal mark

Two black cones	—	Points up
Colour	—	Black above yellow
Light (if fitted)	—	White; Q or VQ

East cardinal mark

Two black cones	—	Base to base
Colour	—	Black, with horizontal yellow band
Light (if fitted)	—	White; Q (3) 10 sec or VQ (3) 5 sec

South cardinal mark

Two black cones	—	Points down
Colour	—	Yellow above black
Light (if fitted)	—	White; VQ (6) plus long flash 10 sec or Q (6) plus long flash 15 sec

West cardinal mark

Two black cones	—	Point to point
Colour	—	Yellow, with horizontal black band
Light (if fitted)	—	White; VQ (9) 10 sec or Q (9) 15 sec

(3) Isolated danger marks: are placed on or above an isolated danger such as a rock or a wreck which has navigable water all around it. The marks are black, with one or more broad horizontal red bands. Buoys are pillar or spar shaped. Any light is white, flashing twice. Topmark – two black spheres.

(4) Safe water marks: indicate that there is navigable water all round the mark, and are used for mid-channel or landfall marks. Buoys are spherical, pillar with spherical topmark, or spar shaped, and are coloured with red and white vertical stripes. Any topmark fitted is a single red sphere. When lit, any light is white – either occulting, isophase, or Morse code (A), or showing a single long-flash every 10 seconds.

(5) Special marks: do not primarily assist navigation, but indicate a special area or feature (e.g. spoil grounds, exercise areas, water-ski areas, cable or pipeline marks, outfalls, Ocean Data Acquisition Systems (ODAS), or traffic separation marks where conventional channel marks may cause confusion). Special marks are yellow, and any shape not conflicting with lateral or safe water marks. If can, spherical or conical are used they indicate the side on which to pass. Any topmark fitted is a yellow X. Any light fitted is yellow, and may have any rhythm not used for white lights.

New dangers (which may be natural obstructions such as a sandbank, or a wreck) are marked in accordance with the rules above, and lit accordingly. For a very grave danger one of the marks may be duplicated.

2.3 LIGHTS

2.3.1 Light characteristics

The abbreviations for, and characteristics of, marine lights are shown in Fig. 2.3.1 opposite, or in **Admiralty Chart 5011** (an A4 booklet).

2.3.2 Light sectors, arcs of visibility

The limits of light sectors and arcs of visibility, and the alignment of directional and leading lights, are always given as seen from seaward by an observer aboard ship looking towards the light. All bearings are given in True, starting from 000°, and going clockwise to 359°. For example, the sector of a white light listed as W090°-180° would be seen over an arc of 90° by any vessel between due West and due North of that light.

Coloured sector lights are often used to guide vessels up narrow channels or warn of a dangerous area. The navigable portion of a channel may be covered by a white pencil beam, flanked by red and green sectors. If you stray to port you see red; if to starboard you see green.

Example (1): Ouistreham main light is a simple sectored light, listed as Oc WR 4s 37m **W17M**, R13M, vis W151°-115°, R115°-151°. This is depicted in Fig. 2 (1).

Bold type indicates a light with a nominal range of >15M which is 37 metres above the level of MHWS, occulting every 4s and has white and red sectors.

The white sector of the light is visible from 151° clockwise right round to 115°, an angular coverage of the remaining 324°; the white sector has a nominal range of **17M**. The red sector of the light has a nominal range of 13M; it is visible over an arc of 36°, i.e. between 115° (WNW of the light) and 151° (NW of the light).

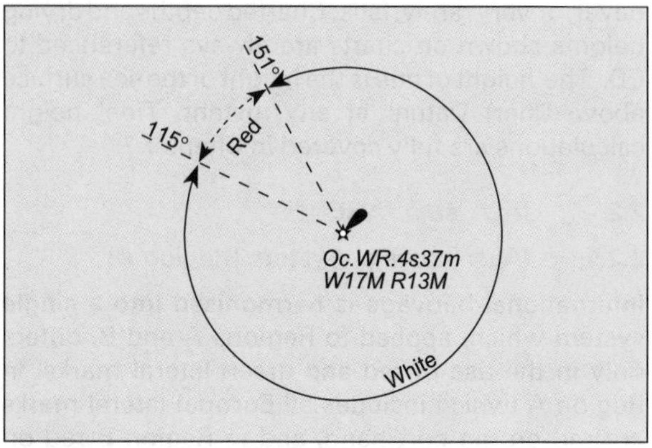

Fig. 2(1)

Example (2): A slightly more complex sectored light is shown below in Fig 2 (2). It is listed as:
Q WRG 9m 10M, vis: G015°-058°(43°), W058°-065°(7°), R065°-103°(38°), G103°-143·5°(40·5°), W143·5°-146·5°(3°), R146·5°-015° (228·5°).

It is a quick flashing light, with an elevation of 9 metres above MHWS, and a nominal range of 10M. It has white, red and green sectors – in fact two sectors of each colour. After plotting these sectors, it will be seen that there are two sets of WRG directional sectors, such that in each case a narrow white sector is flanked by a red sector to port and a green sector to starboard. These sectors provide the guidance described in paragraph 2 of the text of 2.3.2.

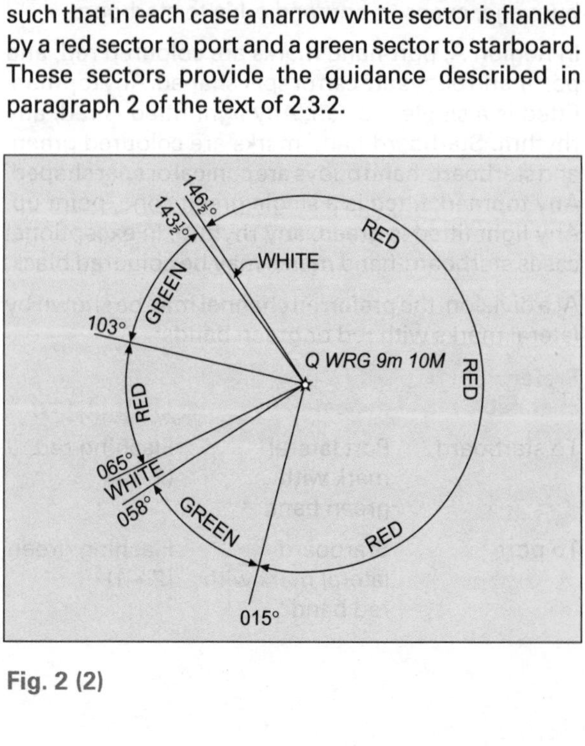

Fig. 2 (2)

Fig. 2.3.1 Light characteristics (Metric and Fathoms charts)

CLASS OF LIGHT		International abbreviations	National abbreviations	Illustration Period shown
FIXED		F		
OCCULTING *(total duration of light longer than dark)*				
Single-occulting		Oc	Occ	
Group-occulting	eg	Oc(2)	Gp Occ(2)	
Composite group-occulting	eg	Oc(2+3)	Gp Occ(2+3)	
ISOPHASE *(light and dark equal)*		Iso		
FLASHING *(total duration of light shorter than dark)*				
Single-flashing		Fl		
Long-flashing *(flash 2s or longer)*		L Fl		
Group-flashing	eg	Fl(3)	Gp Fl(3)	
Composite group-flashing	eg	Fl(2+1)	Gp Fl(2+1)	
QUICK *(50 to 79, usually either 50 or 60, flashes per minute)*				
Continuous quick		Q	Qk Fl	
Group quick	eg	Q(3)	Qk Fl(3)	
Interrupted quick		IQ	Int Qk Fl	
VERY QUICK *(80 to 159, usually either 100 or 120, flashes per minute)*				
Continuous very quick		VQ	V Qk Fl	
Group very quick	eg	VQ(3)	V Qk Fl(3)	
Interrupted very quick		IVQ	Int V Qk Fl	
ULTRA QUICK *(160 or more, usually 240 to 300, flashes per minute)*				
Continuous ultra quick		UQ		
Interrupted ultra quick		IUQ		
MORSE CODE	eg	Mo(K)		
FIXED AND FLASHING		F Fl		
ALTERNATING	eg	Al. WR	Alt. WR	

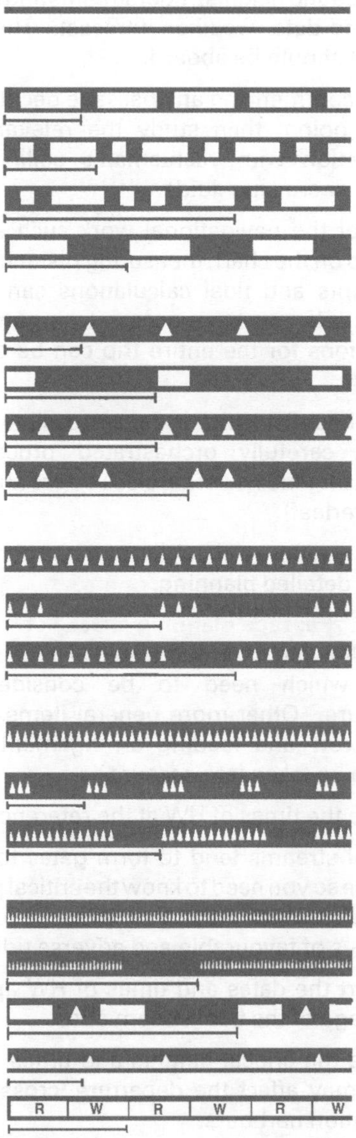

COLOUR	International abbreviations	NOMINAL RANGE in miles		International abbreviations
White	W *(may be omitted)*	Light with single range	eg	15M
Red	R	Light with two different ranges	eg	15/10M
Green	G	Light with three or more ranges	eg	15-7M
Blue	Bu			
Violet	Vi	**PERIOD** is given in seconds	eg	90s
Yellow	Y	**DISPOSITION** horizontally disposed		(hor)
Orange	Y	vertically disposed		(vert)
Amber	Y	**ELEVATION** is given in metres (m) or feet (ft) above MHWS		

2.4 PASSAGE PLANNING

2.4.1 General

Any passage, however short, must be pre-planned. Even in very familiar waters you should at the very least know the state of the tide (springs/neaps; HW/LW times and heights), tidal streams and have studied an up-to-date weather forecast. The necessary chart(s) should be aboard.

Before commencing any passage decide where you intend going, then study the relevant charts in conjunction with yachtsman's sailing directions (Pilots) or cruising guides.

Much of the navigational work such as laying-off courses on the chart, measuring distances, selecting waypoints and tidal calculations can be done in advance. If you have access to a computer, tidal predictions for the entire trip can be done well in advance.

Use a check list which as far as possible schools you into a carefully orchestrated procedure, thus minimising the risk of careless errors and omissions (see overleaf).

Finally, prepare a check list of those items that need further detailed planning.

2.4.2 Passage planning check list

The following is a suggested list of navigational items which need to be considered before departure. Other more general items such as the boat, crew and feeding arrangements may also need to be taken into account.

- Note the times of HW at the reference port(s).
- Tidal streams tend to form gates to a yacht on passage so you need to know the critical points of any tidal gates which affect your passage together with the times of favourable and adverse tides.
- Insert the dates and times of HW applicable on each page of the tidal stream atlas.
- Note the critical heights and times of any tides which may affect the departure, crossing bars, or destination harbours.
- Note potential dangers en route: clearing lines, distances off dangers, Traffic Separation Schemes, busy shipping lanes, etc.
- Consider visual and radio aids to be used.
- Prepare a detailed pilotage plan for entry to any unfamiliar harbour, final destination or refuge port.
- Consider the entry criteria for alternative harbours which might be required during the planned passage.
- Ensure that charts covering the intended route and alternative harbours that might be used are up to date and on board together with a copy of the current Almanac, Yachtsman's Handbook, and correcting Supplement, or the relevant lists of lights, radio and communication aids, and pilotage information.

Having completed all the necessary planning the weather is a major factor which is likely to have considerable impact and may well cause you to alter your original plans.

2.5 NAVIGATION TABLES

2.5.1 Tables – Explanations

Brief explanations are given below, where necessary, on the use of the tables on pages 35-41.

Table 2 (1) – Distance of horizon

Enter with height of eye (in metres), and extract distance of horizon (miles). The actual distance may be affected by abnormal refraction

Table 2 (2) – Lights – rising or dipping distance

Enter with height of eye and height of light to extract the range of a light when rising or dipping above/below the horizon.

Table 2 (3) – Distance off by Vertical Sextant Angle

Enter with the height of the object (in metres) and read across the page until the required sextant angle (corrected for index error) is met. Extract the distance of the object (miles) at the head of the column. Caution is needed when the base of the object (e.g. a lighthouse) is below the horizon. For precise ranges the distance that sea level is below MHWS must be added to the height of the object (above MHWS) before entering the table.

Table 2 (4) – Distance for a given speed and time

Enter with time (in decimals of an hour, or in minutes) and speed (in knots) to determine distance run (in M).

Table 2 (5) – True bearing of Sun at sunrise and sunset

A compass can be checked against the azimuth of the Sun when rising or setting. To do so you only require to know the approximate latitude and the Sun's declination.

Enter with the approximate latitude and declination (obtained from Table 2 (6). The tabulated figure is the True bearing, measured from north if declination is north or from south if declination is south, towards the east if rising or towards the west if setting. Having extracted the True bearing, apply variation before comparing with the compass to determine deviation on course steered. The bearing of the Sun should be taken when its lower limb is a little over half a diameter above the horizon.

Table 2 (6) – Sun's declination

Enter with the appropriate date band and read across to the centre column. Extract declination (bold type) noting whether it is North or South.

TABLE 2 (1) Distance of horizon for various heights of eye

Height of eye		Horizon distance	Height of eye		Horizon distance	Height of eye		Horizon distance
metres	feet	M	metres	feet	M	metres	feet	M
1	3·3	2·1	21	68·9	9·5	41	134·5	13·3
2	6·6	2·9	22	72·2	9·8	42	137·8	13·5
3	9·8	3·6	23	75·5	10·0	43	141·1	13·7
4	13·1	4·1	24	78·7	10·2	44	144·4	13·8
5	16·4	4·7	25	82·0	10·4	45	147·6	14·0
6	19·7	5·1	26	85·3	10·6	46	150·9	14·1
7	23·0	5·5	27	88·6	10·8	47	154·2	14·3
8	26·2	5·9	28	91·9	11·0	48	157·5	14·4
9	29·6	6·2	29	95·1	11·2	49	160·8	14·6
10	32·8	6·6	30	98·4	11·4	50	164·0	14·7
11	36·1	6·9	31	101·7	11·6	51	167·3	14·9
12	39·4	7·2	32	105·0	11·8	52	170·6	15·0
13	42·7	7·5	33	108·3	12·0	53	173·9	15·2
14	45·9	7·8	34	111·6	12·1	54	177·2	15·3
15	49·2	8·1	35	114·8	12·3	55	180·4	15·4
16	52·5	8·3	36	118·1	12·5	56	183·7	15·6
17	55·8	8·6	37	121·4	12·7	57	187·0	15·7
18	59·1	8·8	38	124·7	12·8	58	190·3	15·9
19	62·3	9·1	39	128·0	13·0	59	193·6	16·0
20	65·6	9·3	40	131·2	13·2	60	196·9	16·1

TABLE 2 (2) Lights – distance off when rising or dipping (M)

Height of light		Height of eye									
		metres	1	2	3	4	5	6	7	8	9	10
metres	feet	feet	3	7	10	13	16	20	23	26	30	33
10	33		8·7	9·5	10·2	10·8	11·3	11·7	12·1	12·5	12·8	13·2
12	39		9·3	10·1	10·8	11·4	11·9	12·3	12·7	13·1	13·4	13·8
14	46		9·9	10·7	11·4	12·0	12·5	12·9	13·3	13·7	14·0	14·4
16	53		10·4	11·2	11·9	12·5	13·0	13·4	13·8	14·2	14·5	14·9
18	59		10·9	11·7	12·4	13·0	13·5	13·9	14·3	14·7	15·0	15·4
20	66		11·4	12·2	12·9	13·5	14·0	14·4	14·8	15·2	15·5	15·9
22	72		11·9	12·7	13·4	14·0	14·5	14·9	15·3	15·7	16·0	16·4
24	79		12·3	13·1	13·8	14·4	14·9	15·3	15·7	16·1	16·4	17·0
26	85		12·7	13·5	14·2	14·8	15·3	15·7	16·1	16·5	16·8	17·2
28	92		13·1	13·9	14·6	15·2	15·7	16·1	16·5	16·9	17·2	17·6
30	98		13·5	14·3	15·0	15·6	16·1	16·5	16·9	17·3	17·6	18·0
32	105		13·9	14·7	15·4	16·0	16·5	16·9	17·3	17·7	18·0	18·4
34	112		14·2	15·0	15·7	16·3	16·8	17·2	17·6	18·0	18·3	18·7
36	118		14·6	15·4	16·1	16·7	17·2	17·6	18·0	18·4	18·7	19·1
38	125		14·9	15·7	16·4	17·0	17·5	17·9	18·3	18·7	19·0	19·4
40	131		15·3	16·1	16·8	17·4	17·9	18·3	18·7	19·1	19·4	19·8
42	138		15·6	16·4	17·1	17·7	18·2	18·6	19·0	19·4	19·7	20·1
44	144		15·9	16·7	17·4	18·0	18·5	18·9	19·3	19·7	20·0	20·4
46	151		16·2	17·0	17·7	18·3	18·8	19·2	19·6	20·0	20·3	20·7
48	157		16·5	17·3	18·0	18·6	19·1	19·5	19·9	20·3	20·6	21·0
50	164		16·8	17·6	18·3	18·9	19·4	19·8	20·2	20·6	20·9	21·3
55	180		17·5	18·3	19·0	19·6	20·1	20·5	20·9	21·3	21·6	22·0
60	197		18·2	19·0	19·7	20·3	20·8	21·2	21·6	22·0	22·3	22·7
65	213		18·9	19·7	20·4	21·0	21·5	21·9	22·3	22·7	23·0	23·4
70	230		19·5	20·3	21·0	21·6	22·1	22·5	22·9	23·2	23·6	24·0
75	246		20·1	20·9	21·6	22·2	22·7	23·1	23·5	23·9	24·2	24·6
80	262		20·7	21·5	22·2	22·8	23·3	23·7	24·1	24·5	24·8	25·2
85	279		21·3	22·1	22·8	23·4	23·9	24·3	24·7	25·1	25·4	25·8
90	295		21·8	22·6	23·3	23·9	24·4	24·8	25·2	25·6	25·9	26·3
95	312		22·4	23·2	23·9	24·5	25·0	25·4	25·8	26·2	26·5	26·9
metres	feet	metres	1	2	3	4	5	6	7	8	9	10
Height of light		feet	3	7	10	13	16	20	23	26	30	33
		Height of eye										

TABLE 2 (3) Distance off by Vertical Sextant Angle

Height of object ft	m	Distance of object (nautical miles) 0·1	0·2	0·3	0·4	0·5	0·6	0·7	0·8	0·9	1·0	1·1	1·2	1·3	1·4	1·5	1·6
		° ′	° ′	° ′	° ′	° ′	° ′	° ′	° ′	° ′	° ′	° ′	° ′	° ′	° ′	° ′	° ′
33	**10**	3 05	1 33	1 02	0 46	0 37	0 31	0 27	0 23	0 21	0 19	0 17	0 15	0 14	0 13	0 12	0 12
39	**12**	3 42	1 51	1 14	0 56	0 45	0 37	0 32	0 28	0 25	0 22	0 20	0 19	0 17	0 16	0 15	0 14
46	**14**	4 19	2 10	1 27	1 05	0 52	0 43	0 37	0 32	0 29	0 26	0 24	0 22	0 20	0 19	0 17	0 16
53	**16**	4 56	2 28	1 39	1 14	0 59	0 49	0 42	0 37	0 33	0 30	0 27	0 25	0 23	0 21	0 20	0 19
59	**18**	5 33	2 47	1 51	1 24	1 07	0 56	0 48	0 42	0 37	0 33	0 30	0 28	0 26	0 24	0 22	0 21
66	**20**	6 10	3 05	2 04	1 33	1 14	1 02	0 53	0 46	0 41	0 37	0 34	0 31	0 29	0 27	0 25	0 23
72	**22**	6 46	3 24	2 16	1 42	1 22	1 08	0 58	0 51	0 45	0 41	0 37	0 34	0 31	0 29	0 27	0 26
79	**24**	7 23	3 42	2 28	1 51	1 29	1 14	1 04	0 56	0 49	0 45	0 40	0 37	0 34	0 32	0 30	0 28
85	**26**	7 59	4 01	2 41	2 01	1 36	1 20	1 09	1 00	0 54	0 48	0 44	0 40	0 37	0 34	0 32	0 30
92	**28**	8 36	4 19	2 53	2 10	1 44	1 27	1 14	1 05	0 58	0 52	0 47	0 43	0 40	0 37	0 35	0 32
98	**30**	9 12	4 38	3 05	2 19	1 51	1 33	1 20	1 10	1 02	0 56	0 51	0 46	0 43	0 40	0 37	0 35
105	**32**	9 48	4 56	3 18	2 28	1 58	1 39	1 25	1 14	1 06	0 59	0 54	0 49	0 46	0 42	0 40	0 37
112	**34**	10 24	5 15	3 30	2 38	2 06	1 45	1 30	1 19	1 10	1 03	0 57	0 53	0 49	0 45	0 42	0 39
118	**36**	11 00	5 33	3 42	2 47	2 14	1 51	1 35	1 24	1 14	1 07	1 01	0 56	0 51	0 48	0 45	0 42
125	**38**	11 36	5 41	3 55	2 56	2 21	1 58	1 41	1 28	1 18	1 11	1 04	0 59	0 54	0 50	0 47	0 44
131	**40**	12 11	6 10	4 07	3 05	2 28	2 04	1 46	1 33	1 22	1 14	1 07	1 02	0 57	0 53	0 49	0 46
138	**42**	12 47	6 28	4 19	3 15	2 36	2 10	1 51	1 37	1 27	1 18	1 11	1 05	1 00	0 56	0 52	0 49
144	**44**	13 22	6 46	4 32	3 24	2 43	2 16	1 57	1 42	1 31	1 22	1 14	1 08	1 03	0 58	0 54	0 51
151	**46**	13 57	7 05	4 44	3 33	2 51	2 22	2 02	1 47	1 35	1 25	1 18	1 11	1 06	1 01	0 57	0 53
157	**48**	14 32	7 23	4 56	3 42	2 58	2 28	2 07	1 51	1 39	1 29	1 21	1 14	1 09	1 04	0 59	0 56
164	**50**	15 07	7 41	5 09	3 52	3 05	2 35	2 13	1 56	1 43	1 33	1 24	1 17	1 11	1 06	1 02	0 58
171	**52**	15 41	7 59	5 21	4 01	3 13	2 41	2 18	2 01	1 47	1 36	1 28	1 20	1 14	1 09	1 04	1 00
177	**54**	16 15	8 18	5 33	4 10	3 20	2 47	2 23	2 05	1 51	1 40	1 31	1 23	1 17	1 12	1 07	1 03
184	**56**	16 49	8 36	5 45	4 19	3 28	2 53	2 28	2 10	1 55	1 44	1 34	1 27	1 20	1 14	1 09	1 05
190	**58**	17 23	8 54	5 58	4 29	3 35	2 59	2 34	2 15	2 00	1 48	1 38	1 30	1 23	1 17	1 12	1 07
197	**60**	17 57	9 12	6 10	4 38	3 42	3 05	2 39	2 19	2 04	1 51	1 41	1 33	1 26	1 20	1 14	1 10
203	**62**	18 31	9 30	6 22	4 47	3 50	3 12	2 44	2 24	2 08	1 55	1 45	1 36	1 29	1 22	1 17	1 12
210	**64**	19 04	9 48	6 34	4 56	3 57	3 18	2 50	2 28	2 12	1 59	1 48	1 39	1 31	1 25	1 19	1 14
217	**66**	19 37	10 06	6 46	5 05	4 05	3 24	2 53	2 33	2 16	2 02	1 51	1 42	1 34	1 27	1 22	1 17
223	**68**	20 10	10 24	6 59	5 15	4 12	3 30	3 00	2 38	2 20	2 06	1 55	1 45	1 37	1 30	1 24	1 19
230	**70**	20 42	10 42	7 11	5 24	4 19	3 36	3 05	2 42	2 24	2 09	1 58	1 48	1 40	1 33	1 27	1 21
236	**72**	21 15	11 00	7 23	5 33	4 27	3 42	3 11	2 47	2 48	2 14	2 01	1 51	1 43	1 35	1 29	1 24
246	**75**	22 03	11 27	7 41	5 47	4 38	3 52	3 19	2 54	2 35	2 19	2 07	1 56	1 47	1 39	1 33	1 27
256	**78**	22 50	11 54	7 59	6 01	4 49	4 01	3 27	3 01	2 41	2 24	2 12	2 01	1 51	1 43	1 36	1 30
266	**81**	23 37	12 20	8 18	6 14	5 00	4 10	3 35	3 08	2 47	2 30	2 17	2 05	1 56	1 47	1 40	1 34
276	**84**	24 24	12 47	8 36	6 28	5 11	4 19	3 42	3 15	2 53	2 36	2 22	2 10	2 00	1 51	1 44	1 37
289	**88**	25 25	13 22	9 00	6 46	5 26	4 32	3 53	3 24	3 01	2 43	2 28	2 16	2 06	1 57	1 49	1 42
302	**92**	26 25	13 57	9 24	7 05	5 40	4 44	4 04	3 33	3 10	2 51	2 35	2 22	2 11	2 02	1 54	1 47
315	**96**	27 24	14 32	9 48	7 23	5 55	4 56	4 14	3 42	3 18	2 58	2 42	2 28	2 17	2 07	1 59	1 51
328	**100**	28 22	15 07	10 12	7 41	6 10	5 09	4 25	3 52	3 26	3 05	2 49	2 35	2 23	2 13	2 04	1 56
341	**104**	29 19	15 41	10 36	7 59	6 24	5 21	4 35	4 01	3 34	3 13	2 55	2 41	2 28	2 18	2 09	2 01
358	**109**	30 29	16 24	11 06	8 22	6 43	5 36	4 48	4 12	3 44	3 22	3 04	2 48	2 36	2 24	2 15	2 06
374	**114**	31 37	17 06	11 36	8 45	7 01	5 51	5 02	4 24	3 55	3 31	3 12	2 56	2 43	2 31	2 21	2 12
394	**120**	32 56	17 57	12 11	9 12	7 23	6 10	5 17	4 38	4 07	3 42	3 22	3 05	2 51	2 39	2 28	2 19
427	**130**	35 04	19 20	13 10	9 57	8 00	6 40	5 44	5 01	4 28	4 01	3 39	3 21	3 05	2 52	2 41	2 31
459	**140**	37 05	20 42	14 09	10 42	8 36	7 11	6 10	5 24	4 48	4 19	3 56	3 36	3 20	3 05	2 53	2 42
492	**150**	39 00	22 03	15 07	11 27	9 12	7 41	6 36	5 47	5 09	4 38	4 13	3 52	3 34	3 19	3 05	2 54
574	**175**		25 17	17 29	13 17	10 42	8 57	7 41	6 44	6 00	5 24	4 55	4 30	4 09	3 52	3 36	3 23
656	**200**		28 22	19 48	15 07	12 11	10 12	8 46	7 41	6 51	6 10	5 36	5 09	4 45	4 25	4 07	3 52
738	**225**			22 03	16 54	13 39	11 27	9 51	8 38	7 41	6 56	6 18	5 47	5 20	4 58	4 38	4 21
820	**250**			24 14	18 39	15 07	12 41	10 55	9 35	8 32	7 41	7 00	6 25	5 56	5 30	5 09	4 49
902	**275**			26 20	20 22	16 32	13 54	11 59	10 31	9 22	8 27	7 41	7 03	6 31	6 03	5 39	5 18
984	**300**				22 03	17 57	15 07	13 02	11 27	10 12	9 12	8 23	7 41	7 06	6 36	6 10	5 47
1148	**350**					20 42	17 29	15 07	13 17	11 51	10 42	9 45	8 57	8 16	7 41	7 11	6 44
1312	**400**						19 48	17 09	15 07	13 30	12 11	11 07	10 12	9 26	8 46	8 12	7 41
ft Height of object	m	0·1	0·2	0·3	0·4	0·5	0·6	0·7	0·8	0·9	1·0	1·1	1·2	1·3	1·4	1·5	1·6
		Distance of object (nautical miles)															

TABLE 2 (3) Distance off by Vertical Sextant Angle (continued)

Height of object ft	m	1·8	2·0	2·2	2·4	2·6	2·8	3·0	3·2	3·4	3·6	3·8	4·0	4·2	4·4	4·6	5·0
		Distance of object (nautical miles)															
		° ′	° ′	° ′	° ′	° ′	° ′	° ′	° ′	° ′	° ′	° ′	° ′	° ′	° ′	° ′	° ′
33	**10**	0 10															
39	**12**	0 12	0 11	0 10	0 10												
46	**14**	0 14	0 13	0 12	0 11	0 10											
53	**16**	0 16	0 15	0 13	0 12	0 11	0 11	0 10									
59	**18**	0 19	0 17	0 15	0 14	0 13	0 12	0 11	0 10	0 10							
66	**20**	0 21	0 19	0 17	0 15	0 14	0 13	0 12	0 12	0 11	0 10	0 10					
72	**22**	0 23	0 20	0 19	0 17	0 16	0 15	0 14	0 13	0 12	0 11	0 11	0 10				
79	**24**	0 25	0 22	0 20	0 19	0 17	0 16	0 15	0 14	0 13	0 12	0 12	0 11	0 11	0 10		
85	**26**	0 27	0 24	0 22	0 20	0 19	0 17	0 16	0 15	0 14	0 13	0 13	0 12	0 11	0 11	0 10	
92	**28**	0 29	0 26	0 24	0 22	0 20	0 19	0 17	0 16	0 15	0 14	0 14	0 13	0 12	0 12	0 11	0 10
98	**30**	0 31	0 28	0 25	0 23	0 21	0 20	0 19	0 17	0 16	0 15	0 15	0 14	0 13	0 13	0 12	0 11
105	**32**	0 33	0 30	0 27	0 25	0 23	0 21	0 20	0 19	0 17	0 16	0 16	0 15	0 14	0 13	0 13	0 12
112	**34**	0 35	0 31	0 29	0 26	0 24	0 23	0 21	0 20	0 19	0 17	0 17	0 16	0 15	0 14	0 14	0 13
118	**36**	0 37	0 33	0 30	0 28	0 26	0 24	0 22	0 21	0 20	0 19	0 18	0 17	0 16	0 15	0 14	0 13
125	**38**	0 39	0 35	0 32	0 29	0 27	0 25	0 24	0 22	0 21	0 20	0 19	0 18	0 17	0 16	0 15	0 14
131	**40**	0 41	0 37	0 34	0 31	0 29	0 27	0 25	0 23	0 22	0 21	0 20	0 19	0 18	0 17	0 16	0 15
138	**42**	0 43	0 40	0 35	0 32	0 30	0 28	0 26	0 24	0 23	0 22	0 21	0 19	0 19	0 18	0 17	0 16
144	**44**	0 45	0 41	0 37	0 34	0 31	0 29	0 27	0 25	0 24	0 23	0 22	0 20	0 19	0 19	0 18	0 16
151	**46**	0 47	0 43	0 39	0 36	0 33	0 30	0 28	0 27	0 25	0 24	0 22	0 21	0 20	0 19	0 19	0 17
157	**48**	0 49	0 45	0 40	0 37	0 34	0 32	0 30	0 28	0 26	0 25	0 23	0 22	0 21	0 20	0 19	0 18
164	**50**	0 52	0 46	0 42	0 39	0 36	0 33	0 31	0 29	0 27	0 26	0 24	0 23	0 22	0 21	0 20	0 19
171	**52**	0 54	0 48	0 44	0 40	0 37	0 34	0 32	0 30	0 28	0 27	0 25	0 24	0 23	0 22	0 21	0 19
177	**54**	0 56	0 50	0 46	0 42	0 39	0 36	0 33	0 31	0 29	0 28	0 26	0 25	0 24	0 23	0 22	0 20
184	**56**	0 58	0 52	0 47	0 43	0 40	0 37	0 35	0 32	0 31	0 29	0 27	0 26	0 25	0 24	0 23	0 21
190	**58**	1 00	0 54	0 49	0 45	0 41	0 38	0 36	0 34	0 32	0 30	0 28	0 27	0 26	0 24	0 23	0 21
197	**60**	1 02	0 56	0 51	0 46	0 43	0 40	0 37	0 35	0 33	0 31	0 29	0 28	0 26	0 25	0 24	0 22
203	**62**	1 04	0 58	0 52	0 48	0 44	0 41	0 38	0 36	0 34	0 32	0 30	0 29	0 27	0 26	0 25	0 23
210	**64**	1 06	0 59	0 54	0 49	0 46	0 42	0 40	0 37	0 35	0 33	0 31	0 30	0 28	0 27	0 26	0 24
217	**66**	1 08	1 01	0 56	0 51	0 47	0 44	0 41	0 38	0 36	0 34	0 32	0 31	0 29	0 28	0 27	0 25
223	**68**	1 10	1 03	0 57	0 53	0 49	0 45	0 42	0 39	0 37	0 35	0 33	0 32	0 30	0 29	0 27	0 25
230	**70**	1 12	1 05	0 59	0 54	0 50	0 46	0 43	0 41	0 38	0 36	0 34	0 32	0 31	0 29	0 28	0 26
236	**72**	1 14	1 07	1 01	0 56	0 51	0 48	0 45	0 42	0 39	0 37	0 35	0 33	0 32	0 30	0 29	0 27
246	**75**	1 17	1 10	1 03	0 58	0 54	0 50	0 46	0 44	0 41	0 39	0 37	0 35	0 33	0 32	0 30	0 28
256	**78**	1 20	1 12	1 06	1 00	0 56	0 52	0 48	0 45	0 43	0 40	0 38	0 36	0 34	0 33	0 31	0 29
266	**81**	1 23	1 15	1 08	1 03	0 58	0 54	0 50	0 47	0 44	0 42	0 40	0 38	0 36	0 34	0 33	0 30
276	**84**	1 27	1 18	1 11	1 05	1 00	0 56	0 52	0 49	0 46	0 43	0 41	0 39	0 37	0 35	0 34	0 31
289	**88**	1 31	1 22	1 14	1 08	1 03	0 58	0 54	0 51	0 48	0 45	0 43	0 41	0 39	0 37	0 36	0 33
302	**92**	1 35	1 25	1 18	1 11	1 06	1 01	0 57	0 53	0 50	0 47	0 45	0 43	0 41	0 39	0 37	0 34
315	**96**	1 39	1 29	1 21	1 14	1 09	1 04	0 59	0 56	0 52	0 49	0 47	0 45	0 42	0 41	0 39	0 36
328	**100**	1 43	1 33	1 24	1 17	1 11	1 06	1 02	0 58	0 55	0 52	0 49	0 46	0 44	0 42	0 40	0 37
341	**104**	1 47	1 36	1 28	1 20	1 14	1 09	1 04	1 00	0 57	0 54	0 51	0 48	0 46	0 44	0 42	0 39
358	**109**	1 52	1 41	1 32	1 24	1 18	1 12	1 07	1 03	1 00	0 56	0 53	0 51	0 48	0 46	0 44	0 40
374	**114**	1 58	1 46	1 36	1 28	1 21	1 16	1 11	1 06	1 02	0 59	0 56	0 53	0 50	0 48	0 46	0 42
394	**120**	2 04	1 51	1 41	1 33	1 26	1 20	1 14	1 10	1 06	1 02	0 59	0 56	0 53	0 51	0 48	0 45
427	**130**	2 14	2 01	1 50	1 41	1 33	1 26	1 20	1 15	1 11	1 07	1 03	1 00	0 57	0 55	0 52	0 48
459	**140**	2 24	2 10	1 58	1 48	1 40	1 33	1 27	1 21	1 16	1 12	1 08	1 05	1 02	0 59	0 56	0 52
492	**150**	2 35	2 19	2 07	1 56	1 47	1 39	1 33	1 27	1 22	1 17	1 13	1 10	1 06	1 03	1 01	0 56
574	**175**	3 00	2 42	2 28	2 15	2 05	1 56	1 48	1 41	1 36	1 30	1 25	1 21	1 17	1 14	1 11	1 05
656	**200**	3 26	3 05	2 49	2 35	2 23	2 13	2 04	1 56	1 49	1 43	1 38	1 33	1 28	1 24	1 21	1 14
738	**225**	3 52	3 29	3 10	2 54	2 41	2 29	2 19	2 10	2 03	1 56	1 50	1 44	1 39	1 35	1 31	1 24
820	**250**	4 17	3 52	3 31	3 13	2 58	2 46	2 35	2 25	2 16	2 09	2 02	1 56	1 50	1 45	1 41	1 33
902	**275**	4 43	4 15	3 52	3 32	3 16	3 02	2 50	2 39	2 30	2 22	2 14	2 08	2 01	1 56	1 51	1 42
984	**300**	5 09	4 38	4 13	3 52	3 34	3 19	3 05	2 54	2 44	2 35	2 26	2 19	2 13	2 07	2 01	1 51
1148	**350**	6 00	5 24	4 55	4 30	4 09	3 52	3 36	3 23	3 11	3 00	2 51	2 42	2 35	2 28	2 21	2 10
1312	**400**	6 51	6 10	5 36	5 09	4 45	4 25	4 07	3 52	3 38	3 26	3 15	3 05	2 57	2 49	2 41	2 28
ft	m	1·8	2·0	2·2	2·4	2·6	2·8	3·0	3·2	3·4	3·6	3·8	4·0	4·2	4·4	4·6	5·0
Height of object		Distance of object (nautical miles)															

Table 2 (4) Distance for a given speed and time

Time: Decimal of hr	Time: Mins	Speed in knots: 2·5	3·0	3·5	4·0	4·5	5·0	5·5	6·0	6·5	7·0	7·5	8·0	8·5	9·0	9·5	10·0	Time: Mins	Time: Decimal of hr
·0167	**1**				0·1	0·1	0·1	0·1	0·1	0·1	0·1	0·1	0·1	0·1	0·2	0·2	0·2	**1**	·0167
·0333	**2**	0·1	0·1	0·1	0·1	0·1	0·2	0·2	0·2	0·2	0·2	0·2	0·3	0·3	0·3	0·3	0·3	**2**	·0333
·0500	**3**	0·1	0·1	0·2	0·2	0·2	0·2	0·3	0·3	0·3	0·3	0·4	0·4	0·4	0·4	0·5	0·5	**3**	·0500
·0667	**4**	0·1	0·2	0·2	0·3	0·3	0·3	0·4	0·4	0·4	0·5	0·5	0·5	0·6	0·6	0·6	0·7	**4**	·0667
·0833	**5**	0·2	0·2	0·3	0·3	0·4	0·4	0·5	0·5	0·5	0·6	0·6	0·7	0·7	0·7	0·8	0·8	**5**	·0833
·1000	**6**	0·2	0·3	0·3	0·4	0·4	0·5	0·5	0·6	0·6	0·7	0·7	0·8	0·8	0·9	0·9	1·0	**6**	·1000
·1167	**7**	0·3	0·4	0·4	0·5	0·5	0·6	0·6	0·7	0·8	0·8	0·9	0·9	1·0	1·1	1·1	1·2	**7**	·1167
·1333	**8**	0·3	0·4	0·5	0·5	0·6	0·7	0·7	0·8	0·9	0·9	1·0	1·1	1·1	1·2	1·3	1·3	**8**	·1333
·1500	**9**	0·4	0·4	0·5	0·6	0·7	0·7	0·8	0·9	1·0	1·0	1·1	1·2	1·3	1·3	1·4	1·5	**9**	·1500
·1667	**10**	0·4	0·5	0·6	0·7	0·8	0·8	0·9	1·0	1·1	1·2	1·3	1·3	1·4	1·5	1·6	1·7	**10**	·1667
·1833	**11**	0·5	0·5	0·6	0·7	0·8	0·9	1·0	1·1	1·2	1·3	1·4	1·5	1·6	1·6	1·7	1·8	**11**	·1833
·2000	**12**	0·5	0·6	0·7	0·8	0·9	1·0	1·1	1·2	1·3	1·4	1·5	1·6	1·7	1·8	1·9	2·0	**12**	·2000
·2167	**13**	0·5	0·6	0·8	0·9	1·0	1·1	1·2	1·3	1·4	1·5	1·6	1·7	1·8	2·0	2·0	2·2	**13**	·2167
·2333	**14**	0·6	0·7	0·8	0·9	1·0	1·2	1·3	1·4	1·5	1·6	1·7	1·9	2·0	2·1	2·2	2·3	**14**	·2333
·2500	**15**	0·6	0·7	0·9	1·0	1·1	1·2	1·4	1·5	1·6	1·8	1·9	2·0	2·1	2·2	2·4	2·5	**15**	·2500
·2667	**16**	0·7	0·8	0·9	1·1	1·2	1·3	1·5	1·6	1·7	1·9	2·0	2·1	2·3	2·4	2·5	2·7	**16**	·2667
·2833	**17**	0·7	0·8	1·0	1·1	1·3	1·4	1·6	1·7	1·8	2·0	2·1	2·3	2·4	2·5	2·7	2·8	**17**	·2833
·3000	**18**	0·7	0·9	1·0	1·2	1·3	1·5	1·6	1·8	1·9	2·1	2·2	2·4	2·5	2·7	2·8	3·0	**18**	·3000
·3167	**19**	0·8	1·0	1·1	1·3	1·4	1·6	1·7	1·9	2·1	2·1	2·4	2·5	2·7	2·9	3·0	3·2	**19**	·3167
·3333	**20**	0·8	1·0	1·2	1·3	1·5	1·7	1·8	2·0	2·2	2·3	2·5	2·7	2·8	3·0	3·2	3·3	**20**	·3333
·3500	**21**	0·9	1·0	1·2	1·4	1·6	1·7	1·9	2·1	2·3	2·4	2·6	2·8	3·0	3·1	3·3	3·5	**21**	·3500
·3667	**22**	0·9	1·1	1·3	1·5	1·7	1·8	2·1	2·2	2·4	2·6	2·8	2·9	3·1	3·3	3·5	3·7	**22**	·3667
·3833	**23**	1·0	1·1	1·3	1·5	1·7	1·9	2·1	2·3	2·5	2·7	2·9	3·1	3·3	3·4	3·6	3·8	**23**	·3833
·4000	**24**	1·0	1·2	1·4	1·6	1·8	2·0	2·2	2·4	2·6	2·8	3·0	3·2	3·4	3·6	3·8	4·0	**24**	·4000
·4167	**25**	1·0	1·3	1·5	1·7	1·9	2·1	2·3	2·5	2·7	2·9	3·1	3·3	3·5	3·8	4·0	4·2	**25**	·4167
·4333	**26**	1·1	1·3	1·5	1·7	1·9	2·2	2·4	2·6	2·8	3·0	3·2	3·5	3·7	3·9	4·1	4·3	**26**	·4333
·4500	**27**	1·1	1·3	1·6	1·8	2·0	2·2	2·5	2·7	2·9	3·1	3·4	3·6	3·8	4·0	4·3	4·5	**27**	·4500
·4667	**28**	1·2	1·4	1·6	1·9	2·1	2·3	2·6	2·8	3·0	3·3	3·5	3·7	4·0	4·2	4·4	4·7	**28**	·4667
·4833	**29**	1·2	1·5	1·7	1·9	2·2	2·4	2·7	2·9	3·1	3·4	3·6	3·9	4·1	4·3	4·6	4·8	**29**	·4833
·5000	**30**	1·2	1·5	1·7	2·0	2·2	2·5	2·7	3·0	3·2	3·5	3·7	4·0	4·2	4·5	4·7	5·0	**30**	·5000
·5167	**31**	1·3	1·6	1·8	2·1	2·3	2·6	2·8	3·1	3·4	3·6	3·9	4·1	4·4	4·7	4·9	5·2	**31**	·5167
·5333	**32**	1·3	1·6	1·9	2·1	2·4	2·7	2·9	3·2	3·5	3·7	4·0	4·3	4·5	4·8	5·1	5·3	**32**	·5333
·5500	**33**	1·4	1·6	1·9	2·2	2·5	2·7	3·0	3·3	3·6	3·8	4·1	4·4	4·7	4·9	5·2	5·5	**33**	·5500
·5667	**34**	1·4	1·7	2·0	2·3	2·6	2·8	3·1	3·4	3·7	4·0	4·3	4·5	4·8	5·1	5·4	5·7	**34**	·5667
·5833	**35**	1·5	1·7	2·0	2·3	2·6	2·9	3·2	3·5	3·8	4·1	4·4	4·7	5·0	5·2	5·5	5·8	**35**	·5833
·6000	**36**	1·5	1·8	2·1	2·4	2·7	3·0	3·3	3·6	3·9	4·2	4·5	4·8	5·1	5·4	5·7	6·0	**36**	·6000
·6117	**37**	1·6	1·8	2·1	2·4	2·8	3·1	3·4	3·7	4·0	4·3	4·6	4·9	5·2	5·5	5·8	6·1	**37**	·6117
·6333	**38**	1·6	1·9	2·2	2·5	2·8	3·2	3·5	3·8	4·1	4·4	4·7	5·1	5·4	5·7	6·0	6·3	**38**	·6333
·6500	**39**	1·6	1·9	2·3	2·6	2·9	3·2	3·6	3·9	4·2	4·5	4·9	5·2	5·5	5·8	6·2	6·5	**39**	·6500
·6667	**40**	1·7	2·0	2·3	2·7	3·0	3·3	3·7	4·0	4·3	4·7	5·0	5·3	5·7	6·0	6·3	6·7	**40**	·6667
·6833	**41**	1·7	2·0	2·4	2·7	3·1	3·4	3·8	4·1	4·4	4·8	5·1	5·5	5·8	6·1	6·5	6·8	**41**	·6833
·7000	**42**	1·7	2·1	2·4	2·8	3·1	3·5	3·8	4·2	4·5	4·9	5·2	5·6	5·9	6·3	6·6	7·0	**42**	·7000
·7167	**43**	1·8	2·2	2·5	2·9	3·2	3·6	3·9	4·3	4·7	5·0	5·4	5·7	6·1	6·5	6·8	7·2	**43**	·7167
·7333	**44**	1·8	2·2	2·6	2·9	3·3	3·7	4·0	4·4	4·8	5·1	5·5	5·9	6·2	6·6	7·0	7·3	**44**	·7333
·7500	**45**	1·9	2·2	2·6	3·0	3·4	3·7	4·1	4·5	4·9	5·2	5·6	6·0	6·4	6·7	7·1	7·5	**45**	·7500
·7667	**46**	1·9	2·3	2·7	3·1	3·5	3·8	4·2	4·6	5·0	5·4	5·8	6·1	6·5	6·9	7·3	7·7	**46**	·7667
·7833	**47**	2·0	2·3	2·7	3·1	3·5	3·9	4·3	4·7	5·1	5·5	5·9	6·3	6·7	7·0	7·4	7·8	**47**	·7833
·8000	**48**	2·0	2·4	2·8	3·2	3·6	4·0	4·4	4·8	5·2	5·6	6·0	6·4	6·8	7·2	7·6	8·0	**48**	·8000
·8167	**49**	2·0	2·5	2·9	3·3	3·7	4·1	4·5	4·9	5·3	5·7	6·1	6·5	6·9	7·4	7·8	8·2	**49**	·8167
·8333	**50**	2·1	2·5	2·9	3·3	3·7	4·2	4·6	5·0	5·4	5·8	6·2	6·7	7·1	7·5	7·9	8·3	**50**	·8333
·8500	**51**	2·1	2·5	3·0	3·4	3·8	4·2	4·7	5·1	5·5	5·9	6·4	6·8	7·2	7·6	8·1	8·5	**51**	·8500
·8667	**52**	2·2	2·6	3·0	3·5	3·9	4·3	4·8	5·2	5·6	6·1	6·5	6·9	7·4	7·8	8·2	8·7	**52**	·8667
·8833	**53**	2·2	2·6	3·1	3·5	4·0	4·4	4·9	5·3	5·7	6·2	6·6	7·1	7·5	7·9	8·4	8·8	**53**	·8833
·9000	**54**	2·2	2·7	3·1	3·6	4·0	4·5	4·9	5·4	5·8	6·3	6·7	7·2	7·6	8·1	8·5	9·0	**54**	·9000
·9167	**55**	2·3	2·8	3·2	3·7	4·1	4·6	5·0	5·5	6·0	6·4	6·9	7·3	7·8	8·3	8·7	9·2	**55**	·9167
·9333	**56**	2·3	2·8	3·3	3·7	4·2	4·7	5·1	5·6	6·1	6·5	7·0	7·5	7·9	8·4	8·9	9·3	**56**	·9333
·9500	**57**	2·4	2·8	3·3	3·8	4·3	4·7	5·2	5·7	6·2	6·6	7·1	7·6	8·1	8·5	9·0	9·5	**57**	·9500
·9667	**58**	2·4	2·9	3·4	3·9	4·4	4·8	5·3	5·8	6·3	6·8	7·3	7·7	8·2	8·7	9·2	9·7	**58**	·9667
·9833	**59**	2·5	2·9	3·4	3·9	4·4	4·9	5·4	5·9	6·4	6·9	7·4	7·9	8·4	8·8	9·3	9·8	**59**	·9833
1·0000	**60**	2·5	3·0	3·5	4·0	4·5	5·0	5·5	6·0	6·5	7·0	7·5	8·0	8·5	9·0	9·5	10·0	**60**	1·0000
Decimal of hr	**Mins**	**2·5**	**3·0**	**3·5**	**4·0**	**4·5**	**5·0**	**5·5**	**6·0**	**6·5**	**7·0**	**7·5**	**8·0**	**8·5**	**9·0**	**9·5**	**10·0**	**Mins**	**Decimal of hr**
Time		**Speed in knots**																**Time**	

Table 2 (4) Distance for a given speed and time (continued)

Time: Decimal of hr	Time: Mins	10·5	11·0	11·5	12·0	12·5	13·0	13·5	14·0	14·5	15·0	15·5	16·0	17·0	18·0	19·0	20·0	Time: Mins	Time: Decimal of hr
		Speed in knots																	
·0167	**1**	0·2	0·2	0·2	0·2	0·2	0·2	0·2	0·2	0·2	0·3	0·3	0·3	0·3	0·3	0·3	0·3	**1**	·0167
·0333	**2**	0·3	0·4	0·4	0·4	0·4	0·4	0·4	0·5	0·5	0·5	0·5	0·5	0·6	0·6	0·6	0·7	**2**	·0333
·0500	**3**	0·5	0·5	0·6	0·6	0·6	0·6	0·7	0·7	0·7	0·7	0·8	0·8	0·8	0·8	0·9	1·0	**3**	·0500
·0667	4	0·7	0·7	0·8	0·8	0·8	0·9	0·9	0·9	1·0	1·0	1·0	1·1	1·1	1·2	1·3	1·3	**4**	·0667
·0833	**5**	0·9	0·9	1·0	1·0	1·0	1·1	1·1	1·2	1·2	1·2	1·3	1·3	1·4	1·5	1·6	1·7	**5**	·0833
·1000	**6**	1·0	1·1	1·1	1·2	1·2	1·3	1·3	1·4	1·4	1·5	1·5	1·6	1·7	1·8	1·9	2·0	**6**	·1000
·1167	**7**	1·2	1·3	1·3	1·4	1·5	1·5	1·6	1·6	1·7	1·8	1·8	1·9	2·0	2·1	2·2	2·3	**7**	·1167
·1333	**8**	1·4	1·5	1·5	1·6	1·7	1·7	1·8	1·9	1·9	2·0	2·1	2·1	2·3	2·4	2·5	2·7	**8**	·1333
·1500	**9**	1·6	1·6	1·7	1·8	1·9	1·9	2·0	2·1	2·1	2·2	2·3	2·4	2·5	2·7	2·8	3·0	**9**	·1500
·1667	**10**	1·8	1·8	1·9	2·0	2·1	2·2	2·3	2·3	2·4	2·5	2·6	2·7	2·8	3·0	3·2	3·3	**10**	·1667
·1833	**11**	1·9	2·0	2·1	2·2	2·3	2·4	2·5	2·6	2·7	2·7	2·8	2·9	3·1	3·3	3·5	3·7	**11**	·1833
·2000	**12**	2·1	2·2	2·3	2·4	2·5	2·6	2·7	2·8	2·9	3·0	3·1	3·2	3·4	3·6	3·8	4·0	**12**	·2000
·2167	**13**	2·3	2·4	2·5	2·6	2·7	2·8	2·9	3·0	3·1	3·2	3·3	3·5	3·7	3·9	4·1	4·3	**13**	·2167
·2333	**14**	2·4	2·6	2·7	2·8	2·9	3·0	3·1	3·3	3·4	3·5	3·6	3·7	4·0	4·2	4·4	4·7	**14**	·2333
·2500	**15**	2·6	2·7	2·9	3·0	3·1	3·2	3·4	3·5	3·6	3·7	3·9	4·0	4·2	4·5	4·7	5·0	**15**	·2500
·2667	**16**	2·8	2·9	3·1	3·2	3·3	3·5	3·6	3·7	3·9	4·0	4·1	4·3	4·5	4·8	5·1	5·3	**16**	·2667
·2833	**17**	3·0	3·1	3·3	3·4	3·5	3·7	3·8	4·0	4·1	4·2	4·4	4·5	4·8	5·1	5·4	5·7	**17**	·2833
·3000	**18**	3·1	3·3	3·4	3·6	3·7	3·9	4·0	4·2	4·3	4·5	4·6	4·8	5·1	5·4	5·7	6·0	**18**	·3000
·3167	**19**	3·3	3·5	3·6	3·8	4·0	4·1	4·3	4·4	4·6	4·8	4·9	5·1	5·4	5·7	6·0	6·3	**19**	·3167
·3333	**20**	3·5	3·7	3·8	4·0	4·2	4·3	4·5	4·7	4·8	5·0	5·2	5·3	5·7	6·0	6·3	6·7	**20**	·3333
·3500	**21**	3·7	3·8	4·0	4·2	4·4	4·5	4·7	4·9	5·1	5·2	5·4	5·6	5·9	6·3	6·6	7·0	**21**	·3500
·3667	**22**	3·9	4·0	4·2	4·4	4·6	4·8	5·0	5·1	5·3	5·5	5·7	5·9	6·2	6·6	7·0	7·3	**22**	·3667
·3833	**23**	4·0	4·2	4·4	4·6	4·8	5·0	5·2	5·4	5·6	5·7	5·9	6·1	6·5	6·9	7·3	7·7	**23**	·3833
·4000	**24**	4·2	4·4	4·6	4·8	5·0	5·2	5·4	5·6	5·8	6·0	6·2	6·4	6·8	7·2	7·6	8·0	**24**	·4000
·4167	**25**	4·4	4·6	4·8	5·0	5·2	5·4	5·6	5·8	6·0	6·3	6·5	6·7	7·1	7·5	7·9	8·3	**25**	·4167
·4333	**26**	4·5	4·8	5·0	5·2	5·4	5·6	5·8	6·1	6·3	6·5	6·7	6·9	7·4	7·8	8·2	8·7	**26**	·4333
·4500	**27**	4·7	4·9	5·2	5·4	5·6	5·8	6·1	6·3	6·5	6·7	7·0	7·2	7·6	8·1	8·5	9·0	**27**	·4500
·4667	**28**	4·9	5·1	5·4	5·6	5·8	6·1	6·3	6·5	6·8	7·0	7·2	7·5	7·9	8·4	8·9	9·3	**28**	·4667
·4833	**29**	5·1	5·3	5·6	5·8	6·0	6·3	6·5	6·8	7·0	7·2	7·5	7·7	8·2	8·7	9·2	9·7	**29**	·4833
·5000	**30**	5·2	5·5	5·7	6·0	6·2	6·5	6·7	7·0	7·2	7·5	7·7	8·0	8·5	9·0	9·5	10·0	**30**	·5000
·5167	**31**	5·4	5·7	5·9	6·2	6·5	6·7	7·0	7·2	7·5	7·8	8·0	8·3	8·8	9·3	9·8	10·3	**31**	·5167
·5333	**32**	5·6	5·9	6·1	6·4	6·7	6·9	7·2	7·5	7·7	8·0	8·3	8·5	9·1	9·6	10·1	10·7	**32**	·5333
·5500	**33**	5·8	6·0	6·3	6·6	6·9	7·1	7·4	7·7	8·0	8·2	8·5	8·8	9·3	9·9	10·4	11·0	**33**	·5500
·5667	**34**	6·0	6·2	6·5	6·8	7·1	7·4	7·7	7·9	8·2	8·5	8·8	9·1	9·6	10·2	10·8	11·3	**34**	·5667
·5833	**35**	6·1	6·4	6·7	7·0	7·3	7·6	7·9	8·2	8·5	8·7	9·0	9·3	9·9	10·5	11·1	11·7	**35**	·5833
·6000	**36**	6·3	6·6	6·9	7·2	7·5	7·8	8·1	8·4	8·7	9·0	9·3	9·6	10·2	10·8	11·4	12·0	**36**	·6000
·6117	**37**	6·4	6·7	7·0	7·3	7·6	8·0	8·3	8·6	8·9	9·2	9·5	9·8	10·4	11·0	11·6	12·2	**37**	·6117
·6333	**38**	6·6	7·0	7·3	7·6	7·9	8·2	8·5	8·9	9·2	9·5	9·8	10·1	10·8	11·4	12·0	12·7	**38**	·6333
·6500	**39**	6·8	7·1	7·5	7·8	8·1	8·4	8·8	9·1	9·4	9·7	10·1	10·4	11·0	11·7	12·3	13·0	**39**	·6500
·6667	**40**	7·0	7·3	7·7	8·0	8·3	8·7	9·0	9·3	9·7	10·0	10·3	10·7	11·3	12·0	12·7	13·3	**40**	·6667
·6833	**41**	7·2	7·5	7·9	8·2	8·5	8·9	9·2	9·6	9·9	10·2	10·6	10·9	11·6	12·3	13·0	13·7	**41**	·6833
·7000	**42**	7·3	7·7	8·0	8·4	8·7	9·1	9·4	9·8	10·1	10·5	10·8	11·2	11·9	12·6	13·3	14·0	**42**	·7000
·7167	**43**	7·5	7·9	8·2	8·6	9·0	9·3	9·7	10·0	10·4	10·8	11·1	11·5	12·2	12·9	13·6	14·3	**43**	·7167
·7333	**44**	7·7	8·1	8·4	8·8	9·2	9·5	10·0	10·3	10·6	11·0	11·4	11·7	12·5	13·2	13·9	14·7	**44**	·7333
·7500	**45**	7·9	8·2	8·6	9·0	9·4	9·7	10·1	10·5	10·9	11·2	11·6	12·0	12·7	13·5	14·2	15·0	**45**	·7500
·7667	**46**	8·1	8·4	8·8	9·2	9·6	10·0	10·4	10·7	11·1	11·5	11·9	12·3	13·0	13·8	14·6	15·3	**46**	·7667
·7833	**47**	8·2	8·6	9·0	9·4	9·8	10·2	10·6	11·0	11·4	11·7	12·1	12·5	13·3	14·1	14·9	15·7	**47**	·7833
·8000	**48**	8·4	8·8	9·2	9·6	10·0	10·4	10·8	11·2	11·6	12·0	12·4	12·8	13·6	14·4	15·2	16·0	**48**	·8000
·8167	**49**	8·6	9·0	9·4	9·8	10·2	10·6	11·0	11·4	11·8	12·2	12·7	13·1	13·9	14·7	15·5	16·3	**49**	·8167
·8333	**50**	8·7	9·2	9·6	10·0	10·4	10·8	11·2	11·7	12·1	12·5	12·9	13·3	14·2	15·0	15·8	16·7	**50**	·8333
·8500	**51**	8·9	9·3	9·8	10·2	10·6	11·0	11·5	11·9	12·3	12·7	13·2	13·6	14·4	15·3	16·1	17·0	**51**	·8500
·8667	**52**	9·1	9·5	10·0	10·4	10·8	11·3	11·7	12·1	12·6	13·0	13·4	13·9	14·7	15·6	16·5	17·3	**52**	·8667
·8833	**53**	9·3	9·7	10·2	10·6	11·0	11·5	11·9	12·4	12·8	13·2	13·7	14·1	15·0	15·9	16·8	17·7	**53**	·8833
·9000	**54**	9·4	9·9	10·3	10·8	11·2	11·7	12·1	12·6	13·0	13·5	13·9	14·4	15·3	16·2	17·1	18·0	**54**	·9000
·9167	**55**	9·6	10·1	10·5	11·0	11·5	11·9	12·4	12·8	13·3	13·8	14·2	14·7	15·6	16·5	17·4	18·3	**55**	·9167
·9333	**56**	9·8	10·3	10·7	11·2	11·7	12·1	12·6	13·1	13·5	14·0	14·5	14·9	15·9	16·8	17·7	18·7	**56**	·9333
·9500	**57**	10·0	10·4	10·9	11·4	11·9	12·3	12·8	13·3	13·8	14·2	14·7	15·2	16·1	17·1	18·0	19·0	**57**	·9500
·9667	**58**	10·2	10·6	11·1	11·6	12·1	12·6	13·1	13·5	14·0	14·5	15·0	15·5	16·4	17·4	18·4	19·3	**58**	·9667
·9833	**59**	10·3	10·8	11·3	11·8	12·3	12·8	13·3	13·8	14·3	14·7	15·2	15·7	16·7	17·7	18·7	19·7	**59**	·9833
1·0000	**60**	10·5	11·0	11·5	12·0	12·5	13·0	13·5	14·0	14·5	15·0	15·5	16·0	17·0	18·0	19·0	20·0	**60**	1·0000
Decimal of hr	**Mins**	**10·5**	**11·0**	**11·5**	**12·0**	**12·5**	**13·0**	**13·5**	**14·0**	**14·5**	**15·0**	**15·5**	**16·0**	**17·0**	**18·0**	**19·0**	**20·0**	**Mins**	**Decimal of hr**
Time		**Speed in knots**																**Time**	

TABLE 2 (5) True bearing of Sun at sunrise and sunset

	DECLINATION												
LAT	0°	1°	2°	3°	4°	5°	6°	7°	8°	9°	10°	11°	LAT
	°	°	°	°	°	°	°	°	°	°	°	°	
30°	90	88·8	87·7	86·5	85·4	84·2	83·1	81·9	80·7	79·6	78·4	77·3	30°
31°	90	88·8	87·7	86·5	85·3	84·2	83·0	81·9	80·6	79·5	78·3	77·1	31°
32°	90	88·8	87·6	86·5	85·3	84·1	82·9	81·7	80·5	79·4	78·2	77·0	32°
33°	90	88·8	87·6	86·4	85·2	84·0	82·8	81·6	80·4	79·2	78·0	76·8	33°
34°	90	88·8	87·6	86·4	85·2	84·0	82·7	81·5	80·3	79·1	77·9	76·7	34°
35°	90	88·8	87·5	86·3	85·1	83·9	82·7	81·4	80·2	79·0	77·8	76·5	35°
36°	90	88·8	87·5	86·3	85·0	83·8	82·6	81·3	80·1	78·8	77·6	76·3	36°
37°	90	88·7	87·5	86·2	85·0	83·7	82·5	81·2	80·0	78·7	77·4	76·2	37°
38°	90	88·7	87·5	86·2	84·9	83·6	82·4	81·1	79·8	78·5	77·3	76·0	38°
39°	90	88·7	87·4	86·1	84·8	83·6	82·3	81·0	79·7	78·4	77·1	75·8	39°
40°	90	88·7	87·4	86·1	84·8	83·5	82·1	80·8	79·5	78·2	76·9	75·6	40°
41°	90	88·7	87·3	86·0	84·7	83·4	82·0	80·7	79·4	78·0	76·7	75·3	41°
42°	90	88·6	87·3	86·0	84·6	83·3	81·9	80·6	79·2	77·8	76·5	75·1	42°
43°	90	88·6	87·3	85·9	84·5	83·1	81·8	80·4	79·0	77·6	76·3	74·9	43°
44°	90	88·6	87·2	85·8	84·4	83·0	81·6	80·2	78·8	77·4	76·0	74·6	44°
45°	90	88·6	87·2	85·7	84·3	82·9	81·5	80·1	78·6	77·2	75·8	74·3	45°
46°	90	88·6	87·1	85·7	84·2	82·8	81·3	79·9	78·4	77·0	75·5	74·0	46°
47°	90	88·5	87·1	85·6	84·1	82·6	81·2	79·7	78·2	76·7	75·2	73·7	47°
48°	90	88·5	87·0	85·5	84·0	82·5	81·0	79·5	78·0	76·5	75·0	73·4	48°
49°	90	88·5	86·9	85·4	83·9	82·4	80·8	79·3	77·7	76·2	74·6	73·1	49°
50°	90	88·4	86·9	85·3	83·8	82·2	80·6	79·1	77·5	75·9	74·3	72·7	50°
51°	90	88·4	86·8	85·2	83·6	82·0	80·4	78·8	77·2	75·6	74·0	72·4	51°
52°	90	88·4	86·7	85·1	83·5	81·9	80·2	78·6	76·9	75·3	73·6	71·9	52°
53°	90	88·3	86·7	85·0	83·3	81·7	80·0	78·3	76·6	74·9	73·2	71·5	53°
54°	90	88·3	86·6	84·9	83·2	81·5	79·8	78·0	76·3	74·6	72·8	71·1	54°
55°	90	88·2	86·5	84·8	83·0	81·3	79·5	77·7	76·0	74·2	72·4	70·6	55°
56°	90	88·2	86·4	84·6	82·8	81·0	79·2	77·4	75·6	73·8	71·9	70·0	56°
57°	90	88·2	86·3	84·5	82·6	80·8	78·9	77·0	75·2	73·3	71·4	69·5	57°
58°	90	88·1	86·2	84·3	82·4	80·5	78·6	76·7	74·8	72·8	70·9	68·9	58°
59°	90	88·1	86·1	84·2	82·2	80·3	78·3	76·3	74·3	72·3	70·3	68·3	59°
60°	90	88·0	86·0	84·0	82·0	80·0	77·9	75·9	73·8	71·8	69·7	67·6	60°

	DECLINATION												
LAT	12°	13°	14°	15°	16°	17°	18°	19°	20°	21°	22°	23°	LAT
	°	°	°	°	°	°	°	°	°	°	°	°	
30°	76·1	74·9	73·8	72·6	71·4	70·3	69·1	67·9	66·7	65·5	64·4	63·2	30°
31°	76·0	74·8	73·6	72·4	71·2	70·0	68·9	67·7	66·5	65·3	64·1	62·9	31°
32°	75·8	74·6	73·4	72·2	71·0	69·8	68·6	67·4	66·2	65·0	63·8	62·6	32°
33°	75·6	74·4	73·2	72·1	70·8	69·6	68·4	67·1	65·9	64·7	63·5	62·2	33°
34°	75·5	74·2	73·0	71·8	70·6	69·3	68·1	66·9	65·6	64·4	63·1	61·9	34°
35°	75·3	74·1	72·8	71·6	70·3	69·1	67·8	66·6	65·3	64·1	62·8	61·5	35°
36°	75·1	73·8	72·6	71·3	70·1	68·8	67·5	66·3	65·0	63·7	62·4	61·1	36°
37°	74·9	73·6	72·4	71·1	69·8	68·5	67·2	65·9	64·6	63·3	62·0	60·7	37°
38°	74·7	73·4	72·0	70·8	69·5	68·2	66·9	65·6	64·3	62·9	61·6	60·3	38°
39°	74·5	73·2	71·9	70·5	69·2	67·9	66·6	65·2	63·9	62·5	61·2	59·8	39°
40°	74·2	72·9	71·6	70·2	68·9	67·6	66·2	64·8	63·5	62·1	60·7	59·3	40°
41°	74·0	72·7	71·3	69·9	68·6	67·2	65·8	64·4	63·0	61·6	60·2	58·8	41°
42°	73·7	72·4	71·0	69·6	68·2	66·8	65·4	64·0	62·6	61·2	59·7	58·3	42°
43°	73·5	72·1	70·7	69·3	67·9	66·4	65·0	63·6	62·1	60·7	59·2	57·7	43°
44°	73·2	71·8	70·3	68·9	67·5	66·0	64·6	63·1	61·6	60·1	58·6	57·1	44°
45°	72·9	71·4	70·0	68·5	67·0	65·6	64·1	62·6	61·1	59·5	58·0	56·4	45°
46°	72·6	71·1	69·6	68·1	66·6	65·1	63·6	62·0	60·5	58·9	57·4	55·8	46°
47°	72·2	70·7	69·2	67·7	66·2	64·6	63·1	61·5	59·9	58·3	56·7	55·0	47°
48°	71·9	70·3	68·8	67·2	65·7	64·1	62·5	60·9	59·3	57·6	55·9	54·3	48°
49°	71·5	69·9	68·4	66·8	65·1	63·5	61·9	60·2	58·6	56·9	55·2	53·4	49°
50°	71·1	69·5	67·9	66·2	64·6	62·9	61·3	59·6	57·8	56·1	54·3	52·6	50°
51°	70·7	69·1	67·4	65·7	64·0	62·3	60·6	58·8	57·1	55·3	53·5	51·6	51°
52°	70·3	68·6	66·9	65·1	63·4	61·6	59·9	58·1	56·3	54·4	52·5	50·6	52°
53°	69·8	68·1	66·3	64·5	62·7	60·9	59·1	57·3	55·4	53·5	51·5	49·5	53°
54°	69·3	67·5	65·7	63·9	62·0	60·2	58·3	56·4	54·4	52·4	50·4	48·3	54°
55°	68·7	66·9	65·1	63·2	61·3	59·4	57·4	55·4	53·4	51·3	49·2	47·1	55°
56°	68·2	66·3	64·4	62·4	60·5	58·5	56·5	54·4	52·3	50·1	47·9	45·7	56°
57°	67·6	65·6	63·6	61·6	59·6	57·5	55·4	53·3	51·1	48·9	46·5	44·2	57°
58°	66·9	64·9	62·8	60·8	58·7	56·5	54·3	52·1	49·8	47·4	45·0	42·5	58°
59°	66·2	64·1	62·0	59·8	57·6	55·4	53·1	50·8	48·4	45·9	43·3	40·7	59°
60°	65·4	63·3	61·1	58·8	56·5	54·2	51·8	49·4	46·8	44·2	41·5	38·6	60°

Table 2 (6) Sun's declination

South		Declination	North	
Dec 07 – Jan 05		23°	Jun 05 – Jul 07	
Jan 06 – Jan 12	Nov 30 – Dec 06	22°	May 29 – Jun 04	Jul 08 – Jul 15
Jan 13 – Jan 18	Nov 24 – Nov 29	21°	May 23 – May 28	Jul 16 – Jul 20
Jan 19 – Jan 22	Nov 20 – Nov 23	20°	May 18 – May 22	Jul 21 – Jul 25
Jan 23 – Jan 26	Nov 16 – Nov 19	19°	May 14 – May 17	Jul 26 – Jul 30
Jan 27 – Jan 30	Nov 12 – Nov 15	18°	May 10 – May 13	Jul 31 – Aug 03
Jan 31 – Feb 03	Nov 08 – Nov 11	17°	May 06 – May 09	Aug 04 – Aug 06
Feb 04 – Feb 06	Nov 05 – Nov 07	16°	May 03 – May 05	Aug 07 – Aug 10
Feb 07 – Feb 09	Nov 02 – Nov 04	15°	Apr 30 – May 02	Aug 11 – Aug 13
Feb 10 – Feb 12	Oct 30 – Nov 01	14°	Apr 27 – Apr 29	Aug 14 – Aug 16
Feb 13 – Feb 15	Oct 27 – Oct 29	13°	Apr 23 – Apr 26	Aug 17 – Aug 19
Feb 16 – Feb 18	Oct 24 – Oct 26	12°	Apr 21 – Apr 22	Aug 20 – Aug 22
Feb 19 – Feb 21	Oct 21 – Oct 23	11°	Apr 18 – Apr 20	Aug 23 – Aug 25
Feb 22 – Feb 23	Oct 18 – Oct 20	10°	Apr 15 – Apr 17	Aug 26 – Aug 28
Feb 24 – Feb 26	Oct 16 – Oct 17	9°	Apr 12 – Apr 14	Aug 29 – Aug 31
Feb 27 – Mar 01	Oct 13 – Oct 15	8°	Apr 09 – Apr 11	Sep 01 – Sep 03
Mar 02 – Mar 03	Oct 10 – Oct 12	7°	Apr 07 – Apr 08	Sep 04 – Sep 05
Mar 04 – Mar 06	Oct 08 – Oct 09	6°	Apr 04 – Apr 06	Sep 06 – Sep 08
Mar 07 – Mar 09	Oct 05 – Oct 07	5°	Apr 01 – Apr 03	Sep 09 – Sep 11
Mar 10 – Mar 11	Oct 02 – Oct 04	4°	Mar 30 – Mar 31	Sep 12 – Sep 13
Mar 12 – Mar 14	Sep 30 – Oct 01	3°	Mar 27 – Mar 29	Sep 14 – Sep 16
Mar 15 – Mar 16	Sep 27 – Sep 29	2°	Mar 25 – Mar 26	Sep 17 – Sep 19
Mar 17 – Mar 19	Sep 25 – Sep 26	1°	Mar 22 – Mar 24	Sep 20 – Sep 21
Mar 20 – Mar 21	Sep 22 – Sep 24	0°	Mar 20 – Mar 21	Sep 22 – Sep 24

2.6 SUN AND MOON TABLES – RISING, SETTING AND TWILIGHTS

2.6.1 Rising and Setting Phenomena

The tables of Sunrise, Sunset and Twilights, Moonrise and Moonset enable the degree of darkness around twilight and throughout the night to be estimated.

2.6.2 Contents of Tables 2(7), 2(8) and 2(9)

Table 2 (7) provides Local Mean Times (LMT) for every third day of the year, of morning Nautical Twilight, Sunrise, Sunset and evening Civil Twilight for latitude 50°N and latitude variations (*v*). Use the left-hand sign in the tabular entry for *v* for Sunrise, and the right-hand sign for Sunset. The latitude corrections in Table 2 (8) for Sunrise, Sunset and Twilights, enable the LMT for latitudes in the range 30°N to 60°N to be found.

Table 2 (9) gives times of Moonrise and Moonset for each day for latitude 50°N and latitude variations (v). The latitude correction table enables the LMT for latitudes in the range 30°N to 60°N to be found. The tabular values are for the Greenwich Meridian, and are approximately the LMT of the corresponding phenomena for the other meridians. Expressing the longitude in time, the UTC is obtained from:

$$\text{UTC} = \text{LMT} \begin{matrix} +\text{west} \\ -\text{east} \end{matrix} \text{longitude}$$

For Moonrise and Moonset a further small correction of one minute for every seven degrees of longitude is also required, which is added to the LMT if west, subtracted if east.

At Sunrise and Sunset the upper limb of the Sun is on the horizon at sea level. The Sun's zenith distance is 96° for Civil Twilight and 102° for Nautical Twilight. At Civil Twilight the brightest stars are visible and the horizon is clearly defined. At Nautical Twilight the horizon is not visible.

At Moonrise and Moonset the Moon's upper limb is on the horizon at sea level.

2.6.3 Example (a): The Sun – rising, setting and twilights

Find the UTC of the beginning of morning Nautical Twilight, Sunrise, Sunset and the end of evening Civil Twilight on 22 January 2002 for latitude 36°07'N, longitude 18°20'E.

From table 2(7), for 22 January, *v* = + 30 for the beginning of Nautical Twilight, *v* = + 51 for Sunrise; *v* = – 51 for Sunset and v = – 41 for the end of Civil Twilight. From table 2 (8) the latitude corrections for Nautical Twilight, Sunrise, Sunset and Civil Twilight are – 21 mins, – 38 mins, + 38 mins and + 31 mins respectively. Note that for Sunset, the sign of the correction has to be reversed because v is minus.

Convert longitude from degrees and minutes of arc to whole minutes of time, by multiplying the degrees of longitude by 4 and adding a further correction of 0 mins, 1 min, 2 mins, 3 mins or 4 mins when the minutes of longitude are in the range 0' to 7', 8' to 22', 23' to 37', 38' to 52' or 53' to 59', respectively.

The longitude equivalent in time of 18°20'E is – (18 x 4 + 1) = – 73m.

Remarks	Naut Twilight		Sunrise		Sunset		Civil Twilight	
Tabular value, 22 Jan	06h	31m	07h	46m	16h	37m	17h	13m
Corr'n for latitude		– 21m		– 38m		+ 38m		+ 31m
LMT	06h	10m	07h	08m	17h	15m	17h	44m
Corr'n for longitude	– 1h	13m	– 1h	13m	– 1h	13m	– 1h	13m
UTC of phenomenon	04h	57m	05h	55m	16h	02m	16h	31m

2.6.4 Example (b): The Moon – rising and setting

Find the UTC of Moonrise and Moonset on 24 January 2002 for latitude 36°07'N, longitude 06°30'W.

From Table 2(9) for 24 January, *v* = – 54 for Moonrise and *v* = + 51 for Moonset. The latitude correction for Moonrise and Moonset is + 41 mins and – 38 mins, respectively. Note the reversal of the sign of the correction for Moonset, because *v* is minus.

Using the method in example (a), the longitude equivalent in time of 06°30'W is + 26mins.

Remarks	Moonrise		Moonset	
Tabular value, 24 Jan	12h	25m	03h	18m
Corr'n for latitude		+ 41m		– 38m
LMT	13h	06m	02h	40m
Corr'n for longitude		+ 26m		+ 26m
UTC of phenomenon	13h	32m	03h	06m

These times can be increased by +1min to allow for the effect of longitude on the LMT of the phenomenon. See text at end of Table 2 (9) for the instructions.

TABLE 2 (7) 2001 – SUNRISE, SUNSET and TWILIGHTS

Date	Naut Twi	v	Sun–rise	v	Sun–set	Civil Twi	v
	h m		h m		h m	h m	
Jan 1	06 39	+39	07 59	+63 −	16 09	16 47	− 51
4	06 39	38	07 58	62	16 12	16 50	50
7	06 39	37	07 57	60	16 15	16 53	49
10	06 38	36	07 56	59	16 19	16 57	47
13	06 37	35	07 54	57	16 23	17 01	46
16	06 35	+34	07 52	+56 −	16 28	17 05	− 44
19	06 33	32	07 49	54	16 32	17 09	42
22	06 31	30	07 46	51	16 37	17 13	41
25	06 28	28	07 43	49	16 42	17 18	39
28	06 25	26	07 39	47	16 47	17 22	36
31	06 21	+24	07 35	+44 −	16 52	17 27	− 34
Feb 3	06 18	22	07 31	42	16 57	17 32	32
6	06 14	20	07 26	39	17 02	17 37	29
9	06 09	17	07 21	36	17 08	17 42	27
12	06 05	15	07 16	34	17 13	17 47	24
15	06 00	+12	07 11	+31 −	17 18	17 51	− 22
18	05 55	10	07 05	28	17 23	17 56	19
21	05 49	7	07 00	25	17 28	18 01	16
24	05 44	4	06 54	22	17 33	18 06	13
27	05 38	+ 2	06 48	20	17 38	18 11	11
Mar 2	05 32	− 1	06 42	+17 −	17 43	18 16	− 8
5	05 26	4	06 36	14	17 48	18 21	5
8	05 20	7	06 29	11	17 53	18 25	− 2
11	05 13	10	06 23	8	17 58	18 30	+ 1
14	05 07	13	06 16	5	18 03	18 35	4
17	05 00	−16	06 10	+ 2 −	18 08	18 40	+ 7
20	04 53	19	06 03	− 1 +	18 13	18 45	10
23	04 46	22	05 57	4	18 17	18 50	13
26	04 39	26	05 50	7	18 22	18 55	16
29	04 32	29	05 44	10	18 27	18 59	19
Apr 1	04 25	−32	05 37	−12 +	18 31	19 04	+22
4	04 18	36	05 31	15	18 36	19 09	25
7	04 11	39	05 24	18	18 41	19 14	28
10	04 04	42	05 18	21	18 46	19 19	31
13	03 57	46	05 12	24	18 50	19 24	34
16	03 49	−50	05 06	−27 +	18 55	19 29	+37
19	03 42	53	05 00	30	19 00	19 34	40
22	03 35	57	04 54	32	19 04	19 40	43
25	03 28	61	04 48	35	19 09	19 45	46
28	03 21	64	04 42	38	19 14	19 50	49
May 1	03 14	−68	04 37	−41 +	19 18	19 55	+53
4	03 07	72	04 32	43	19 23	20 00	56
7	03 00	76	04 27	46	19 27	20 05	59
10	02 53	80	04 22	48	19 32	20 10	61
13	02 47	84	04 17	51	19 36	20 15	64
16	02 41	−88	04 13	−53 +	19 40	20 20	+67
19	02 35	92	04 09	55	19 45	20 25	70
22	02 29	95	04 06	57	19 49	20 29	72
25	02 24	99	04 02	59	19 52	20 34	75
28	02 19	102	03 59	61	19 56	20 38	77
31	02 14	−106	03 57	−63 +	19 59	20 42	+79
Jun 3	02 10	109	03 55	64	20 02	20 45	81
6	02 07	111	03 53	66	20 05	20 48	82
9	02 04	114	03 52	67	20 07	20 51	84
12	02 02	116	03 51	68	20 09	20 53	85
15	02 01	−117	03 50	−68 +	20 11	20 55	+85
18	02 00	118	03 50	69	20 12	20 57	86
21	02 00	118	03 51	69	20 13	20 58	86
24	02 01	118	03 51	69	20 13	20 58	86
27	02 03	117	03 53	68	20 13	20 58	85
30	02 05	−116	03 54	−68 +	20 13	20 57	+84
Jul 3	02 08	−114	03 56	−67 +	20 12	20 56	+83

Date	Naut Twi	v	Sun–rise	v	Sun–set	Civil Twi	v
	h m		h m		h m	h m	
Jul 3	02 08	−114	03 56	− 67 +	20 12	20 56	+83
6	02 12	112	03 58	66	20 11	20 54	82
9	02 16	110	04 01	65	20 09	20 52	80
12	02 21	107	04 04	63	20 07	20 49	79
15	02 26	104	04 07	62	20 04	20 46	76
18	02 31	−100	04 11	− 60 +	20 01	20 42	+74
21	02 37	97	04 14	58	19 58	20 39	72
24	02 43	93	04 18	56	19 54	20 34	69
27	02 49	89	04 22	54	19 50	20 30	67
30	02 55	85	04 26	52	19 46	20 25	64
Aug 2	03 01	− 81	04 30	− 49 +	19 41	20 20	+61
5	03 07	78	04 35	47	19 36	20 14	58
8	03 13	74	04 39	44	19 31	20 09	55
11	03 19	70	04 43	42	19 26	20 03	52
14	03 25	66	04 48	39	19 21	19 57	49
17	03 31	− 62	04 52	− 36 +	19 15	19 51	+46
20	03 37	58	04 57	33	19 09	19 44	43
23	03 43	55	05 01	31	19 03	19 38	40
26	03 49	51	05 06	28	18 57	19 31	37
29	03 54	48	05 10	25	18 51	19 25	34
Sep 1	04 00	− 44	05 15	− 22 +	18 45	19 18	+31
4	04 05	41	05 19	19	18 38	19 11	28
7	04 10	37	05 23	17	18 32	19 05	25
10	04 15	34	05 28	14	18 25	18 58	22
13	04 21	31	05 32	11	18 19	18 51	19
16	04 26	− 27	05 37	− 8 +	18 12	18 44	+16
19	04 31	24	05 41	5	18 05	18 38	13
22	04 35	21	05 46	− 2 +	17 59	18 31	10
25	04 40	18	05 50	+ 1 −	17 52	18 24	7
28	04 45	15	05 55	3	17 46	18 18	4
Oct 1	04 50	− 12	06 00	+ 6 −	17 39	18 11	+ 1
4	04 54	9	06 04	9	17 32	18 05	− 1
7	04 59	6	06 09	12	17 26	17 58	4
10	05 04	− 3	06 14	15	17 20	17 52	7
13	05 08	0	06 18	18	17 13	17 46	10
16	05 13	+ 3	06 23	+ 21 −	17 07	17 40	−13
19	05 17	5	06 28	24	17 01	17 34	15
22	05 22	8	06 33	26	16 56	17 29	18
25	05 27	11	06 38	29	16 50	17 23	21
28	05 31	13	06 43	32	16 44	17 18	23
31	05 36	+ 16	06 48	+ 35 −	16 39	17 13	−26
Nov 3	05 40	18	06 53	37	16 34	17 08	28
6	05 45	20	06 58	40	16 29	17 04	31
9	05 49	23	07 03	43	16 24	16 59	33
12	05 53	25	07 07	45	16 20	16 55	35
15	05 58	+ 27	07 12	+ 48 −	16 16	16 52	−38
18	06 02	29	07 17	50	16 13	16 48	40
21	06 06	31	07 22	52	16 09	16 46	42
24	06 10	32	07 26	54	16 06	16 43	43
27	06 13	34	07 31	56	16 04	16 41	45
30	06 17	+ 35	07 35	+ 58 −	16 02	16 39	−47
Dec 3	06 21	37	07 39	59	16 00	16 38	48
6	06 24	38	07 43	61	15 59	16 37	49
9	06 27	39	07 46	62	15 58	16 36	50
12	06 29	39	07 49	63	15 58	16 36	51
15	06 32	+ 40	07 52	+ 64 −	15 58	16 37	−52
18	06 34	40	07 54	64	15 59	16 38	52
21	06 36	40	07 56	64	16 00	16 39	52
24	06 37	40	07 57	64	16 02	16 40	52
27	06 38	40	07 58	64	16 04	16 42	52
30	06 39	+ 40	07 59	+ 63 −	16 07	16 45	−51
Jan 2	06 39	+ 39	07 59	+ 62 −	16 09	16 48	−50

TABLE 2 (8) 2001 – SUNRISE, SUNSET and TWILIGHTS

Corrections to Sunrise and Sunset

N. Lat	30°	35°	40°	45°	50°	52°	54°	56°	58°	60°
v	m	m	m	m	m	m	m	m	m	m
0	0	0	0	0	0	0	0	0	0	0
2	− 2	− 2	− 1	− 1	0	0	+ 1	+ 1	+ 2	+ 2
4	4	3	2	1	0	+ 1	1	2	3	4
6	6	5	4	2	0	1	2	3	4	6
8	8	6	5	3	0	1	2	4	6	7
10	−10	− 8	− 6	− 3	0	+ 1	+ 3	+ 5	+ 7	+ 9
12	12	10	7	4	0	2	4	6	8	11
14	14	11	8	4	0	2	4	7	10	13
16	16	13	9	5	0	2	5	8	11	15
18	18	14	10	6	0	3	6	9	12	16
20	−20	−16	−12	− 6	0	+ 3	+6	+10	+14	+18
22	22	18	13	7	0	3	7	11	15	20
24	24	19	14	8	0	4	7	12	16	22
26	26	21	15	8	0	4	8	13	18	24
28	28	22	16	9	0	4	9	14	19	26
30	−30	−24	−17	−10	0	+ 4	+ 9	+15	+21	+28
32	32	26	19	10	0	5	10	16	22	30
34	34	27	20	11	0	5	11	17	24	32
36	36	29	21	11	0	5	11	18	25	34
38	38	31	22	12	0	6	12	19	27	36
40	−40	−32	−23	−13	0	+ 6	+13	+20	+28	+38
42	42	34	24	13	0	6	13	21	30	40
44	44	35	26	14	0	7	14	22	31	42
46	46	37	27	15	0	7	15	23	33	44
48	48	39	28	15	0	7	15	24	35	47
50	−50	−40	−29	−16	0	+ 8	+16	+26	+36	+49
52	52	42	30	17	0	8	17	27	38	51
54	54	44	32	17	0	8	17	28	40	54
56	56	45	33	18	0	9	18	29	42	56
58	58	47	34	19	0	9	19	30	43	59
60	−60	−49	−35	−19	0	+ 9	+20	+32	+45	+62
62	62	50	36	20	0	10	20	33	47	64
64	64	52	38	21	0	10	21	34	49	67
66	66	53	39	22	0	10	22	36	51	70
68	68	55	40	22	0	11	23	37	54	74
70	−70	−57	−41	−23	0	+11	+24	+38	+56	+77

If *v* is negative reverse the sign of the correction

Corrections to Nautical Twilight

N. Lat	30°	35°	40°	45°	50°	52°	54°	56°	58°	60°
v	m	m	m	m	m	m	m	m	m	m
+40	−40	−31	−22	−12	0	+ 5	+11	+17	+24	+31
30	30	23	16	9	0	4	8	12	17	22
20	20	15	10	5	0	2	5	7	10	13
+10	−10	− 7	− 5	− 2	0	+ 1	+ 2	+ 3	+ 3	+ 4
0	0	+ 1	+ 1	+ 1	0	− 1	− 1	− 2	− 3	− 4
−10	+10	+ 9	+ 7	+ 4	0	− 2	− 4	− 7	−10	−13
20	20	17	13	7	0	3	7	12	17	23
30	30	25	18	10	0	5	11	17	24	33
40	40	33	24	14	0	7	14	23	33	44
50	50	41	30	17	0	− 8	18	29	42	57
−60	+60	+49	+37	+21	0	−10	−22	−36	−52	−73
70	70	58	43	24	0	12	27	44	65	95
80	80	66	49	28	0	15	32	54	83	−136
90	90	75	56	32	0	17	39	67	−116	TAN
100	100	83	63	37	0	20	47	−88	TAN	TAN
−110	+110	+92	+70	+42	0	−24	−59	TAN	TAN	TAN
−120	+120	+101	+78	+47	0	−29	−81	TAN	TAN	TAN

Corrections to Civil Twilight

N. Lat	30°	35°	40°	45°	50°	52°	54°	56°	58°	60°
v	m	m	m	m	m	m	m	m	m	m
−50	+50	+40	+28	+15	0	− 7	−15	−24	−33	−44
40	40	32	23	12	0	6	12	18	26	34
30	30	24	17	9	0	4	8	13	19	25
20	20	16	11	6	0	3	5	8	12	15
−10	+10	+ 8	+ 5	+ 3	0	−1	− 2	− 4	− 5	− 7
0	0	0	0	0	0	0	+ 1	+ 1	+ 2	+ 2
+10	−10	− 8	− 6	− 4	0	+ 2	4	6	8	11
20	20	16	12	7	0	3	7	11	15	20
30	30	24	18	10	0	5	10	16	22	30
40	40	33	24	13	0	6	13	21	30	41
+50	−50	−41	−30	−17	0	+ 8	+17	+27	+39	+52
60	60	49	36	20	0	10	21	33	48	66
70	70	57	42	24	0	12	25	41	60	84
80	80	66	49	27	0	14	30	49	74	110
83	83	68	50	29	0	14	32	52	80	121
+86	−86	−71	−52	−30	0	+15	+33	+56	+86	+137

The times on the previous page are the local mean times (LMT) of morning nautical twilight, sunrise, sunset and evening civil twilight for latitude 50°N, together with their variations *v*. The variations are the differences in minutes of time between the time of the phenomenon for latitudes 50°N and 30°N. The sign on the left-handside of v (between sunrise and sunset) applies to sunrise, and the sign on the right-hand side applies to sunset. The LMT of the phenomenon for latitudes between 30°N and 60°N is found by applying the corrections in the tables above to the tabulated times as follows:

Sunrise and sunset: To determine the LMT of sunrise or sunset, take out the tabulated time and *v* corresponding to the required date. Using *v* and latitude as arguments in the table of "Corrections to Sunrise and Sunset", extract the correction. This table is for positive *v*. If *v* is minus, reverse the sign of the correction. Apply the correction to the tabulated time.

Nautical twilight: To determine the LMT of morning nautical twilight, follow the same method as for sunrise and sunset, but use the table of "Corrections to Nautical Twilight". This table includes both positive and negative values of *v*. The entry TAN stands for Twilight All Night, because the Sun does not reach an altitude of −12°.

Civil twilight: To determine the LMT of evening civil twilight follow the same method as for nautical twilight, but use the table of "Corrections to Civil Twilight". This table includes both positive and negative values of *v*.

Convert LMT to UTC by adding the longitude in time if west (+), or subtracting if east (–).

Examples of the use of these tables are given in 2.6.3

TABLE 2 (9) 2001 – MOONRISE and MOONSET

Day	JANUARY Rise	v	Set	v	MARCH Rise	v	Set	v	MAY Rise	v	Set	v	JULY Rise	v	Set	v
	h m		h m		h m		h m		h m		h m		h m		h m	
1	18 33	− 59	09 51	+ 62	20 41	+ 6	08 07	+ 3	24 43	+ 75	07 34	− 75	23 55	+ 10	10 42	− 17
2	19 56	45	10 27	50	22 04	22	08 28	− 13	00 43	75	08 31	75	24 10	− 3	11 48	− 4
3	21 18	30	10 56	35	23 26	38	08 51	29	01 29	70	09 35	68	00 10	3	12 54	+ 10
4	22 40	− 14	11 20	21	24 45	52	09 16	43	02 04	61	10 43	58	00 26	16	14 01	23
5	23 59	+ 2	11 41	+ 6	00 45	52	09 45	56	02 31	50	11 51	46	00 43	29	15 10	37
6	25 17	+ 17	12 01	− 9	01 59	+ 64	10 20	− 66	02 53	+ 38	12 58	− 33	01 03	− 41	16 21	+ 50
7	01 17	17	12 22	23	03 06	71	11 04	72	03 11	25	14 04	20	01 28	54	17 32	62
8	02 35	32	12 45	37	04 03	73	11 56	73	03 27	+ 12	15 10	− 6	02 00	65	18 42	71
9	03 51	46	13 11	51	04 50	70	12 55	68	03 43	0	1616	+ 7	02 42	73	19 46	75
10	05 05	59	13 43	62	05 27	63	13 59	60	03 58	− 13	17 23	21	03 37	75	20 41	72
11	06 15	+ 68	14 23	− 70	05 56	+ 52	15 06	− 49	04 15	− 26	18 32	+ 34	04 45	− 70	21 24	+ 63
12	07 16	72	15 12	72	06 19	41	16 13	36	04 35	39	19 43	48	06 02	60	21 57	50
13	08 08	71	16 10	70	06 39	28	17 19	23	04 58	52	20 54	60	07 24	45	22 24	35
14	08 49	65	17 13	63	06 56	16	18 25	− 10	05 28	63	22 03	70	08 47	29	22 46	20
15	09 21	56	18 20	52	07 12	+ 4	19 30	+ 3	06 07	72	23 07	75	10 09	− 13	23 06	+ 4
16	09 47	+ 44	19 27	− 40	07 28	− 9	20 36	+ 16	06 57	− 75	24 02	+ 74	11 30	+ 4	23 25	− 11
17	10 09	33	20 33	28	07 45	22	21 43	29	07 59	72	00 02	74	12 51	20	23 45	26
18	10 27	20	21 39	15	08 03	34	22 52	42	09 11	64	00 47	66	14 11	36	24 08	41
19	10 44	+ 8	22 44	− 2	08 25	47	24 01	55	10 30	51	01 22	55	15 31	51	00 08	41
20	11 00	− 4	23 50	+ 11	08 53	58	00 01	55	11 51	35	01 50	41	16 49	64	00 35	55
21	11 17	− 17	24 57	+ 24	09 28	− 68	01 11	+ 65	13 13	− 19	02 13	+ 26	18 01	+ 73	01 10	− 67
22	11 36	29	00 57	24	10 15	73	02 17	72	14 35	− 3	02 34	+ 10	19 03	76	01 53	74
23	11 58	42	02 07	38	11 14	73	03 16	73	15 58	+ 14	02 53	− 5	19 53	73	02 48	76
24	12 25	54	03 18	51	12 25	66	04 05	68	17 22	31	03 14	21	20 31	64	03 51	71
25	13 01	65	04 31	62	13 46	53	04 45	57	18 46	47	03 37	37	21 01	53	05 00	61
26	13 49	− 71	05 42	+ 70	15 12	− 38	05 17	+ 43	20 08	+ 62	04 04	− 52	21 24	+ 40	06 10	− 49
27	14 51	71	06 46	72	16 39	21	05 44	27	21 24	72	04 38	65	21 44	27	07 20	36
28	16 05	64	07 40	67	18 07	− 3	06 07	+ 11	22 30	76	05 21	74	22 00	15	08 28	22
29	17 28	52	08 22	56	19 33	+ 14	06 28	− 5	23 22	74	06 15	76	22 16	+ 2	09 35	− 9
30	18 55	36	08 55	42	20 59	31	06 50	21	24 03	66	07 17	72	22 31	− 11	10 40	+ 5
31	20 20	− 20	09 22	+ 27	22 23	+ 47	07 14	− 37	00 03	+ 66	08 25	− 63	22 47	− 24	11 46	+ 18

Day	FEBRUARY Rise	v	Set	v	APRIL Rise	v	Set	v	JUNE Rise	v	Set	v	AUGUST Rise	v	Set	v
1	21 44	− 3	09 45	+ 11	23 43	+ 61	07 41	− 52	00 33	+ 55	09 34	− 51	23 05	− 36	12 54	+ 32
2	23 05	+ 13	10 06	− 4	24 56	70	08 15	64	00 57	43	10 43	38	23 27	49	14 03	45
3	24 24	28	10 27	19	00 56	70	08 57	72	01 17	30	11 51	25	23 55	61	15 13	58
4	00 24	28	10 49	34	01 58	75	09 47	75	01 34	17	12 57	− 12	24 32	70	16 23	68
5	01 42	43	11 14	47	02 50	73	10 45	72	01 49	+ 5	14 03	+ 2	00 32	70	17 30	75
6	02 57	+ 56	11 45	− 59	03 30	+ 66	11 49	− 64	02 05	− 8	15 09	+ 15	01 21	− 75	18 29	+ 75
7	04 07	66	12 22	68	04 01	56	12 56	53	02 21	21	16 17	29	02 23	74	19 17	68
8	05 11	72	13 08	72	04 26	45	14 03	41	02 39	34	17 27	42	03 38	65	19 55	56
9	06 05	72	14 02	71	04 46	33	15 10	28	03 01	47	18 39	56	05 01	52	20 25	41
10	06 48	68	15 03	66	05 03	20	16 16	15	03 28	59	19 51	67	06 26	36	20 49	25
11	07 23	+ 59	16 08	− 56	05 20	+ 8	17 21	− 1	04 04	− 69	20 58	+ 74	07 51	− 19	21 10	+ 9
12	07 51	48	17 15	45	05 35	− 5	18 28	+ 12	04 51	75	21 58	75	09 15	− 2	21 30	− 6
13	08 13	37	18 22	32	05 51	18	19 35	25	05 50	74	22 47	69	10 38	+ 15	21 50	22
14	08 32	24	19 28	19	06 09	31	20 43	39	07 01	67	23 25	59	12 00	32	22 12	37
15	08 49	+	12 20 33	− 6	06 30	43	21 53	52	08 18	55	23 55	45	13 21	47	22 38	52
16	09 06	0	21 39	+ 7	06 55	− 55	23 03	+ 63	09 39	− 40	24 19	+ 30	14 40	+ 61	23 10	− 64
17	09 22	− 13	22 45	20	07 27	66	24 10	72	11 00	24	00 19	30	15 53	71	23 50	73
18	09 39	25	23 52	33	08 09	73	00 10	72	12 21	− 8	00 40	+ 15	16 57	76	24 41	76
19	09 59	38	25 02	46	09 03	74	01 11	75	13 41	+ 8	01 00	0	17 50	75	00 41	76
20	10 24	50	01 02	46	10 09	70	02 03	72	15 03	25	01 19	− 16	18 32	68	01 41	73
21	10 54	− 61	02 12	+ 58	11 24	− 59	02 45	+ 63	16 24	+ 41	01 40	− 31	19 04	+ 57	02 47	− 65
22	11 35	69	03 22	68	12 45	45	03 18	50	17 45	56	02 04	46	19 28	45	03 57	54
23	12 28	73	04 28	72	14 09	29	03 45	35	19 03	68	02 34	60	19 49	32	05 07	40
24	13 35	69	05 26	71	15 34	− 12	04 08	19	20 13	75	03 13	70	20 06	19	06 16	27
25	14 54	59	06 13	63	17 00	+ 5	04 29	+ 3	21 12	75	04 01	76	20 21	+ 6	07 23	− 13
26	16 20	− 45	06 50	+ 50	18 25	+ 22	04 50	− 13	21 58	+ 70	05 00	− 75	20 36	− 7	08 29	0
27	17 48	− 28	07 20	+ 35	19 51	39	05 12	29	22 33	60	06 06	68	20 52	19	09 35	+ 14
28	19 15	− 11	07 45	+ 19	21 15	55	05 38	45	23 00	48	07 16	57	21 09	32	10 41	27
29					22 35	67	06 08	59	23 21	35	08 27	44	21 29	45	11 49	40
30					23 45	+ 74	06 47	− 70	23 39	+ 23	09 35	− 30	21 53	57	12 58	53
31													22 25	− 67	14 07	+ 65

C2

TABLE 2 (9) *continued* 2001 – MOONRISE and MOONSET

Day	SEPTEMBER Rise	*v*	Set	*v*	NOVEMBER Rise	*v*	Set	*v*
	h m		h m		h m		h m	
1	23 07	−75	15 14	+73	01 44	−27	15 35	+18
2	24 02	76	16 15	76	03 08	−10	15 55	+1
3	00 02	76	17 08	73	04 35	+8	16 15	−16
4	01 11	71	17 50	63	06 02	26	16 36	33
5	02 30	59	18 23	49	07 31	44	17 02	49
6	03 55	−44	18 49	+33	08 59	+60	17 34	−64
7	05 22	27	19 12	+17	10 22	73	18 16	75
8	06 49	−9	19 32	0	11 33	79	19 08	79
9	08 16	+9	19 53	−16	12 30	78	20 12	76
10	09 41	26	20 14	32	13 13	70	21 21	67
11	11 06	+43	20 39	−48	13 45	+59	22 33	−55
12	12 28	58	21 09	62	14 09	46	23 44	41
13	13 45	70	21 47	72	14 28	33	24 52	27
14	14 53	76	22 35	77	14 44	20	00 52	27
15	15 50	77	23 33	76	14 59	+6	02 00	−14
16	16 34	+71	24 38	−69	15 13	−7	03 06	0
17	17 08	61	00 38	69	15 28	20	04 12	+14
18	17 34	49	01 47	58	15 44	33	05 19	28
19	17 55	36	02 56	45	16 04	46	06 28	41
20	18 13	23	04 05	31	16 28	58	07 37	55
21	18 28	+10	05 13	−18	16 59	−69	08 47	+67
22	18 43	−2	06 19	−4	17 39	76	09 53	75
23	18 58	15	07 25	+9	18 31	78	10 53	78
24	19 14	28	08 32	23	19 34	74	11 43	75
25	19 32	41	09 39	36	20 46	64	12 23	67
26	19 55	−54	10 47	+50	22 04	−50	12 54	+54
27	20 23	65	11 56	62	23 24	34	13 19	40
28	21 00	73	13 03	72	24 45	17	13 40	24
29	21 48	77	14 06	77	00 45	17	13 59	+9
30	22 49	75	15 00	76	02 07	1	14 18	−8

Day	OCTOBER Rise	*v*	Set	*v*	DECEMBER Rise	*v*	Set	*v*
1	24 02	−66	15 45	+69	03 31	+17	14 37	−24
2	00 02	66	16 20	57	04 57	34	15 00	41
3	01 23	52	16 49	42	06 25	52	15 28	56
4	02 48	36	17 12	26	07 51	67	16 04	70
5	04 15	18	17 33	+9	09 09	77	16 51	78
6	05 42	−1	17 53	−8	10 15	+79	17 51	−79
7	07 10	+18	18 14	25	11 06	74	19 00	72
8	08 38	35	18 38	41	11 44	64	20 13	61
9	10 05	52	19 06	57	12 12	52	21 27	47
10	11 29	66	19 42	69	12 33	38	22 38	33
11	12 43	+76	20 27	−77	12 51	+25	23 46	−19
12	13 46	78	21 23	78	13 06	+11	24 53	5
13	14 35	74	22 27	73	13 20	−2	00 53	−5
14	15 12	65	23 36	62	13 35	15	01 59	+9
15	15 40	54	24 46	50	13 50	28	03 06	22
16	16 02	+41	00 46	−50	14 08	−41	04 14	+36
17	16 20	28	01 56	36	14 30	54	05 23	50
18	16 36	15	03 03	22	14 59	65	06 33	62
19	16 51	+2	04 10	−9	15 36	74	07 42	73
20	17 05	−11	05 16	+5	16 24	78	08 46	78
21	17 21	−24	06 22	+19	17 25	−76	09 40	+77
22	17 38	37	07 30	32	18 36	67	10 24	70
23	17 59	50	08 38	46	19 53	54	10 58	58
24	18 25	62	09 47	59	21 13	39	11 25	44
25	18 58	72	10 56	70	22 33	23	11 46	29
26	19 41	−77	12 00	+77	23 53	−6	12 05	+13
27	20 37	77	12 56	78	25 13	+11	12 23	−2
28	21 44	71	13 43	73	01 13	11	12 42	18
29	22 59	59	14 21	63	02 35	28	13 02	34
30	24 20	44	14 50	49	03 59	44	13 26	50
31	00 20	−44	15 15	+34	05 23	+60	13 57	−64

Corrections to Moonrise and Moonset

N Lat	30°	35°	40°	45°	50°	52°	54°	56°	58°	60°
v	m	m	m	m	m	m	m	m	m	m
0	0	0	0	0	0	0	0	0	0	0
2	−2	−2	−1	−1	0	0	+1	+1	+1	+2
4	4	3	2	1	0	+1	1	2	3	4
6	6	5	3	2	0	1	2	3	4	5
8	8	6	5	3	0	1	2	4	5	7
10	−10	−8	−6	−3	0	+1	+3	+5	+7	+9
12	12	10	7	4	0	2	4	6	8	11
14	14	11	8	4	0	2	4	7	9	12
16	16	13	9	5	0	2	5	8	11	14
18	18	14	10	6	0	3	5	9	12	16
20	−20	−16	−12	−6	0	+3	+6	+10	+14	+18
22	22	18	13	7	0	3	7	11	15	20
24	24	19	14	8	0	3	7	12	16	22
26	26	21	15	8	0	4	8	13	18	23
28	28	22	16	9	0	4	9	14	19	25
30	−30	−24	−17	−9	0	+4	+9	+15	+21	+27
32	32	26	18	10	0	5	10	16	22	29
34	34	27	20	11	0	5	10	17	23	31
36	36	29	21	11	0	5	11	18	25	33
38	38	31	22	12	0	6	12	19	26	35
40	−40	−32	−23	−13	0	+6	+12	+20	+28	+37
42	42	34	24	13	0	6	13	21	30	39
44	44	35	26	14	0	7	14	22	31	42
46	46	37	27	15	0	7	15	23	33	44
48	48	39	28	15	0	7	15	24	34	46
50	−50	−40	−29	−16	0	+8	+16	+25	+36	+48
52	52	42	30	17	0	8	17	26	38	51
54	54	44	32	17	0	8	17	28	39	53
56	56	45	33	18	0	9	18	29	41	56
58	58	47	34	19	0	9	19	30	43	58
60	−60	−48	−35	−19	0	+9	+20	+31	+45	+61
62	62	50	36	20	0	10	20	33	47	64
64	64	52	38	21	0	10	21	34	49	67
66	66	53	39	22	0	10	22	35	51	70
68	68	55	40	22	0	11	23	37	53	73
70	−70	−57	−41	−23	0	+11	+24	+38	+55	+76
72	72	58	43	24	0	11	24	40	58	80
74	74	60	44	24	0	12	25	41	60	83
76	76	62	45	25	0	12	26	43	62	87
78	78	63	46	26	0	13	27	44	65	91
80	−80	−65	−48	−27	0	+13	+28	+46	+68	+96
82	82	67	49	27	0	13	29	48	70	101
84	84	68	50	28	0	14	30	49	73	106
86	86	70	51	29	0	14	31	51	77	112
88	88	72	53	30	0	15	32	53	80	119
90	−90	−73	−54	−30	0	+15	+33	+55	+84	+127

If *v* is minus reverse the sign of the correction

The daily times of moonrise and moonset given above are the local mean times (LMT) of the phenomena for latitude 50°N, together with their variations *v*. The variations are the differences in minutes between the time of the phenomenon for latitudes 50N° and 30°N. The LMT of the phenomenon for latitudes between 30°N and 60°N is found as follows:

Take out the tabulated time and v corresponding to the required date. Using *v* and latitude as arguments in the table above of "Corrections to Moonrise and Moonset", extract the correction. This table is for positive *v*. If *v* is minus, reverse the sign of the correction. Apply the correction to the tabulated time.

Add a small extra correction of 1m for every 7° of longitude if west. Subtract if east.

Convert LMT to UTC by adding the longitude in time if west, or subtracting if east.

Examples of the use of these tables are given in 2.6.4

Chapter 3

Radio Navigational Aids

Contents

3.1	**INTRODUCTION**	**Page 48**
3.1.1	Types of systems	48
3.2	**SATELLITE SYSTEMS**	**Page 48**
3.2.1	Global Positioning System (GPS)	48
3.2.2	Dilution of precision	49
3.2.3	Horizontal chart datum	49
3.2.4	Differential GPS	49
3.2.5	GPS integrity monitoring	49
3.2.6	Differential GPS beacons	50
3.3	**HYPERBOLIC SYSTEMS**	**Page 52**
3.3.1	Loran-C	52
3.3.2	Navigational displays	52
3.4	**WAYPOINTS**	**Page 52**
3.4.1	Waypoint navigation	52
3.4.3	Loading waypoints	52
3.5	**RADAR**	**Page 54**
3.5.1	Radar in yachts	54
3.5.2	Radar for collision avoidance	54
3.5.3	Radar as a navigation aid	54
3.6	**PROTECTION OF OFFSHORE INSTALLATIONS**	**Page 54**
3.6.1	Safety Zones	54
3.7	**RACONS (RADAR BEACONS)**	**Page 54**
3.7.1	Description	54
3.7.2	Radar beacon listing	55
Table		
3(1)	Racons - Europe	56

C3

3.1 INTRODUCTION

3.1.1 Types of systems

Two fixing systems are presently available. Satellite navigation is provided by the Global Positioning System (GPS), and a hyperbolic area navigation system by Loran-C. Each aid has its own merits for particular applications and coverage.

The choice of aids largely depends on the boat use, the owner's requirements and interests, and the waters sailed. Depending on the receiver used, GPS provides global fixes with an accuracy of better than 50m in any weather. Loran-C provides fixes within coverage areas with but with less accuracy.

3.2 SATELLITE SYSTEMS

3.2.1 Global Positioning System (GPS)

GPS provides highly accurate, worldwide, continuous three-dimensional position fixing (latitude, longitude and altitude), together with velocity and time data in all weather conditions.

The GPS constellation, shown in Fig. 3(1), consists of 24 operational satellites configured in six orbital planes with an inclination of 55° to the Equator. Three further satellites operate as active spares, giving 27 satellites in use. The satellites circle the earth in approximately 12 hour orbits at a height of about 10,900M.

GPS provides two levels of service. These are:

(1) Standard Positioning Service (SPS)

(2) Precise Positioning Service (PPS)

SPS is available to all civil users at no cost. PPS is reserved strictly for military purposes.

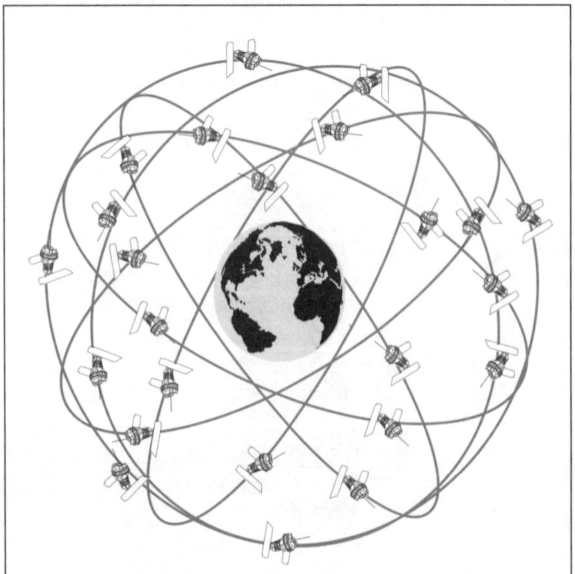

Fig. 3 (1) The GPS constellation consists of 27 satellites (24 operational plus 3 active spares). Satellite spacing is arranged to ensure that at least 4 satellites are in view from anywhere on earth.

The principle on which GPS works is the accurate measurement of the range, or distance, from the receiver to a number of satellites transmitting accurately timed signals together with information on their accurate position in space. In very simplistic terms each satellite transmits a PPS and SPS code saying 'this is my position and this is the time'.

By accurately knowing the times of transmission and reception of the signal you can establish the transit time. Multiply the transit time by the speed of light (161,829 nautical miles per second) to get the range to the satellite. If similar measurements are made on three satellites, three intersecting range circles, each centred on the satellite's position at the time of transmission, are obtained. If no other errors are present, the intersection of the three range circles represents the yacht's position.

Selective Availability (SA) was turned off on 01 May 2000 and resulted in improved accuracy becoming available. GPS basic system errors are relatively small. For SPS they are about 19-20m. Any remaining system errors are due to signal propagation delays in the ionosphere and atmosphere. To eliminate such errors a dual-frequency receiver is required plus a second civil satellite frequency. The latter will not become available until 2005.

With SA switched off, accuracy will to some extent depend on the quality of the receiver coupled with improved technology on the latest satellites. A 12-channel receiver is likely to be more accurate than an 8 Channel. 20 metres accuracy is likely to be normal, but up to 10 metres may be achievable with a quality receiver.

GPS receivers vary from single-channel to multi-channel. Better quality fixing is obtained by tracking more than the minimum three satellites required to produce a two-dimensional fix (i.e. latitude and longitude). A receiver having a minimum of six dedicated channels is the most suitable for use on a yacht. The more channels available the better.

In conventional coastal navigation it is generally recommended to avoid using any visual position lines where the angle of cut is less than 30°. The accuracy of GPS fixes equally depends on the angle of cut of its position lines, but this is more difficult to appreciate because the geometry of the satellites is constantly changing. The receiver, rather than the navigator, selects those satellites which offer the best fix geometry.

3.2.2 Dilution of precision

The efficiency of the satellite geometry is indicated by the Dilution of Precision (DOP) factor which is computed from the angular separation between various satellites. The greater the separation the better the fix geometry is, and the lower the DOP value.

Performance is most likely to be degraded when there are less than 5 satellites visible, or when DOP is greater than 5. Since high DOP is caused by poor satellite geometry, these events usually coincide.

The potential inaccuracy of a 2D GPS fix resulting from poor geometry is expressed by a factor called the Horizontal Dilution of Precision (HDOP). The accuracy of a GPS fix varies with the capability of the user's receiver and receiver-to-satellite geometry. Receivers are programmed to select satellites which give the lowest HDOP value. Should the HDOP value exceed a certain figure, usually 4 or 5, then receivers give a warning, or cease computing fixes until satellite geometry improves.

3.2.3 Horizontal chart datum

GPS fixes are referenced to the World Geodetic System 84 (WGS 84) datum. This means that satellite fixes cannot be directly plotted on many Admiralty charts, which are still referenced to a local datum. Corrections need to be applied to achieve the full benefit of GPS accuracy.

Admiralty charts of the UK are mostly based on the Ordnance Survey Great Britain 1936 (OSGB 36) datum. Charts covering the European Coastline are generally based on the European 1950 Datum (ED 50).

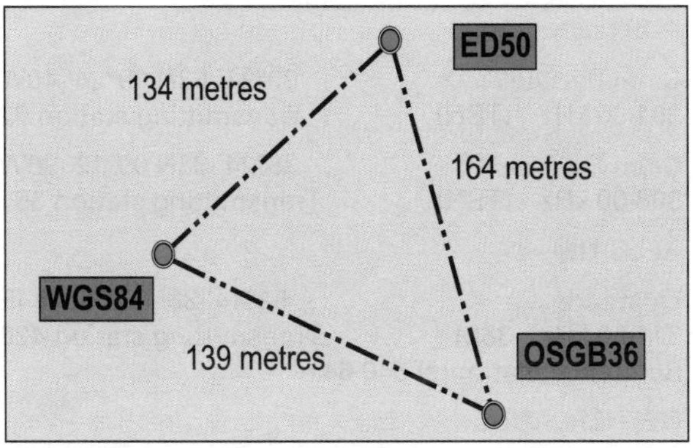

Fig. 3 (2) Chart datum differences in the Dover Strait

On 01 Jan 2000 the HO started to convert all 331 UK charts to the WGS84/ETRS89 datum over a three year period. Charts always state which datum is used in a note on 'Satellite-Derived Positions' printed under the main title. The note shows the amount of correction required between satellite and chart positions.

The approximate difference between WGS 84, OSGB 36 and ED 50 horizontal chart datums in the Dover Strait are shown in Fig.3 (2). The amount of the error will vary at each location but can be substantial in some parts of the world such as the Pacific.

Good receivers allow users a choice of many chart datums. Ensure that the chart datum set on the receiver is the same as the datum stated on the chart.

There are two ways of handling chart datums:

1. Set the receiver to WGS 84 and manually apply the datum shifts given on the chart before plotting position.
2. Alternatively, set the receiver datum to the same datum as the chart in use. In practical terms, this means that a yacht leaving the UK on an OSGB 36 chart **must** change to ED 50 before using any chart of the continental coast which is based on ED 50.

Whilst charts are being changed over to WGS 84, it should no longer be assumed that a UK chart is based on OSGB 36. Neither can you assume that an adjacent chart will be to the same datum. Extreme caution is therefore required and procedure (1) above may be the best course of action to adopt.

3.2.4 Differential GPS

Differential GPS (dGPS) is a method of locally improving the basic accuracy of GPS. The removal of SA, coupled with the increased accuracy of basic GPS, makes it unlikely that dGPS will now appeal to the average yachtsman.

The basic principle of dGPS is that a reference station compares observed GPS satellite pseudo-ranges with calculated pseudo-ranges, for all satellites in view, derived by knowing the reference station position very precisely. Observed differences in pseudo-ranges are then re-transmitted by the reference station to the users' GPS receiver via a data-link. A set capable of receiving selected marine radio beacons, and equipped with a suitable demodulator for the dGPS messages is required and is interfaced to the GPS receiver. It will then automatically apply the transmitted corrections to the navigational data. Once the errors at a particular time and place have been established, differential corrections can be applied to achieve an accuracy of better than ± 10m for a limited period of time DGPS positions are referenced to the WGS 84 datum.

The UK dGPS system is operating on a trial basis. After system validation, the UK Lighthouse Authorities will provide a free public maritime dGPS service for vessels navigating around the coasts of UK and Ireland. dGPS is expected to become fully operational in 2002.

3.2.5 GPS integrity monitoring

Urgent information on GPS is given in HMCG navigation warning broadcasts on VHF or MF, and by any Navtex station under message category J.

Information is also obtainable from the US Coast Guard GPS Information Centre (GPSIC) on ☎ 00 1 703 313 5907 which gives a prerecorded daily status message. GPSIC duty personnel can be contacted on ☎: 00 1 703 313 5900 (fax: 00 1 703 313 5931/5932).

C3

3.2.6 Differential GPS beacons

UNITED KINGDOM

S. Catherine's Point Lt 50°34'·54N 01°17'·87W
307·50 kHz 100M Transmitting station 440 441
Reference station(s) 680

Lizard Lt 49°57'·60N 05°12'·13W
306·00 kHz 150M Transmitting station 441
Reference station(s) 681

Nash Point Lt 51°24'·06N 03°33'·13W
309·50 kHz 100M Transmitting station 449
Reference station(s) 689

Point Lynas Lt 53°24'·98N 04°17'·35W
297·50 kHz 150M Transmitting station 442
Reference station(s) 682

Butt of Lewis Lt 58°30'·94N 06°15'·65W
295·50 kHz 200M Transmitting station 444
Reference station(s) 684

Sumburgh 59°51'·25N 01°16'·49W
291·50 kHz 200M Transmitting station 445
Reference station(s) 685

Girdle Ness Lt 57°08'·34N 02°02'·91W
297·00kHz 150M Transmitting station 446
Reference station(s) 686

Flamborough Head Lt 54°06'·98N 00°04'·96W
290·50kHz 150M Transmitting station 447
Reference station(s) 687

North Foreland 51°22'·49N 01°26'·71E
299·50 kHz 100M Transmitting station 448
Reference station(s) 688

Wormleighton DGPS 52°11'·8N 01°21'·9E
291·00 kHz 172M Transmitting station 439
Reference station(s) 691

IRELAND

Tory Island Lt 55°16'·36N 08°14'·97W
288·50 kHz 200M Transmitting station 435
Reference station(s) 670 694

Loop Head Lt 52°33'·68N 09°55'·96W
293·00 kHz 150M Transmitting station 432
Reference station(s) 665

Mizen Head 51°27'·00N 09°49'·24W
284·00 kHz 150M Transmitting station 430
Reference station(s) 660 661

FRANCE

Pointe de Barfleur 49°41'·87N 01°15'·87E
297·50 kHz 90M Transmitting station 330
Reference station(s) 460

Pointe S. Mathieu 48°19'·85N 04°46'·17W
291·50 kHz 90M Transmitting station 332
Reference station(s) 462

Pen Men, Île de Groix 47°38'·97N 03°30'·36W
298·00 kHz 90M Transmitting station (TBN)
Reference station(s) 463

Les Baleines Lt, Île de Ré 46°14'·70N 01°33'·60W
299·50 kHz 90M Transmitting station 334
Reference station(s) 464

Pointe de la Coubre Lt 45°41'·87N 01°13'·93W
1655 & 3328·8 kHz 330M
Note: Specialist equipment needed to use this aid.

Cap Ferret Lt 44°38'·77N 01°14'·81W
287·00 kHz 90M Transmitting station 336
Reference station(s) 466

SPAIN (North and North-West Coast)

Punta Estaca de Bares Lt 43°47'·17N 07°41'·07W
310·00 kHz (TBN) Transmitting station (TBN)
Reference station(s) (TBN)

Cabo Finisterre Lt 42°53'·00N 09°16'·23W
289·00 kHz 60M Transmitting station 353
Reference station(s) 506 507

PORTUGAL

Cabo Carvoeiro Lt 39°21'·53N 09°24'·40W
301·00 kHz (TBN) Transmitting station 62

Cabo Espichel Lt 38°24'·83N 09°12'·90W
306·00 kHz (TBN) Transmitting station 351

BELGIUM

Oostende 51°14'·36N 02°55'·94E
311·50 kHz 38M Transmitting station 420
Reference station(s) 640 641

NETHERLANDS

Ameland Lt 53°27'·02N 05°37'·60E
299·50 kHz 120M Transmitting station 428
Reference station(s) 655 656

Hoek van Holland 51°58'·90N 04°06'·83E
287·50 kHz 120M Transmitting station 425
Reference station(s) 650 651

GERMANY

Düne 54°11'·20N 07°54'·38E
313·00 kHz 70M Transmitting station 491
Reference station(s) 822 823

DENMARK

Blåvandshuk Lt 55°33'·52N 08°05'·07E
296·50 kHz 120±M Transmitting station 452
Reference station(s) 705 706

Skagen W Lt 57°44'·98N 10°35'·78E
298·50 kHz 100M Transmitting station 453
Reference station(s) 710 711

Hammerodde Lt, Bornholm 55°17'·97N 14°46'·43E
289·00 kHz 120±M Transmitting station 451
Reference station(s) 700 701

Fig. 3 (3) DGPS Station locations

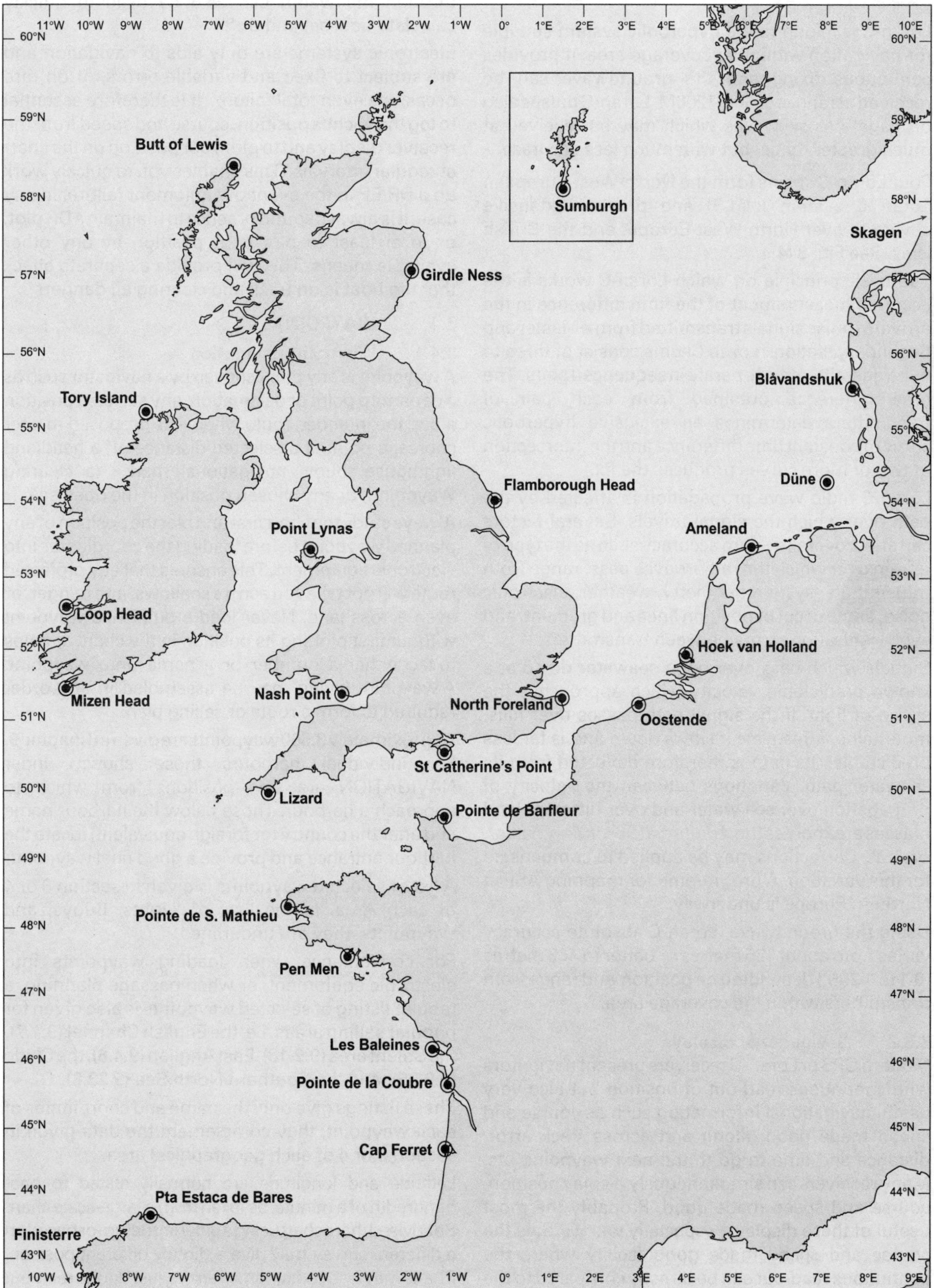

3.3 HYPERBOLIC SYSTEMS

3.3.1 Loran-C

Loran-C is a long-range hyperbolic system suitable for navigation within the coverage area. It provides continuous fixing and the groundwave can be received at ranges of 800-1200M. Loran-C pulses also propagate as skywaves which may be received at much greater range, but with much less accuracy.

Four Loran-C chains form the **North-West European Loran C system (NELS)** and provide extensive coverage over North-West Europe, and the British Isles. See Fig. 3 (4).

The basic principle on which Loran-C works is the accurate measurement of the time difference in the arrival of pulse signals transmitted from a Master and Secondary station. Loran Chains consist of three to five transmitters and operate in sequenced pairs. The time difference obtained from each pair of transmitters determines an exclusive hyperbolic curve of constant time difference and the intersection of two or more curves produces the fix.

Loran-C radio wave propagation is affected by the path over which the signal travels. Several factors can affect overall system accuracy such as the type of terrain over which the radio waves pass, range from transmitters, system geometry, weather, electronic noise, angle of cut of position lines and gradient, and synchronisation errors between transmitters.

Signals which pass over open seawater do so at a known predictable velocity which approaches the speed of light. If the signal path passes over hills, mountains, forests etc it slows down and is far less predictable. Its path is therefore deflected from its seawater path. Variations between the velocity of propagation over sea water and over different land masses are know as the *Additional Secondary Factor, or ASF*. Corrections may be applied to compensate for this variation. A programme for mapping ASF in Northern Europe is underway.

Using the groundwave, Loran-C absolute accuracy varies from about 185 metres or better to 463 metres (0·1 to 0·25M) depending on position and range from transmitters within the coverage area.

3.3.2 Navigational displays

Modern GPS or Loran-C receivers present navigators with continuous read-out of position but also very useful navigational information such as course and speed made good, along and across track error, distance and time to go to the next waypoint, etc. Many receivers can simultaneously display position, course and speed made good. Probably the most useful of these displays, especially with GPS, is the course and speed made good facility where the continuous read-out can be directly compared to the required track.

The same data, if compared with course and speed through the water, can also be used to quickly calculate tidal set and drift.

Electronic systems are only aids to navigation and are subject to fixed and variable errors, or on rare occasions even total failure. It is therefore essential to log the yacht's position, course and speed from the receiver display and to plot your position on the chart at regular intervals. This enables you to quickly work up a DR/EP in the event of equipment failure. In any case, it is always sound practice to maintain a DR plot, or to at least to plot your position by any other available means. This will provide a separate check that the boat is on track and clearing all dangers.

3.4 WAYPOINTS

3.4.1 Waypoint navigation

A waypoint is any point chosen by a navigator such as a departure point or destination, any selected position along the intended route where it is proposed to alter course, a point at a selected distance off a headland lighthouse, buoy, navigational mark (a clearing Waypoint), or any chosen position in the open sea.

Always study the chart first and plot the position of any planned waypoint before loading the coordinates into electronic equipment. This ensures that any projected route will not take you across shallows, into danger, or even across land. Never load a published waypoint without first plotting its position in the chart. It helps to tag either a number or a name onto waypoint. A waypoint listing may be assembled in any order required to form a route or sailing plan.

Approximately 3,600 waypoints are given in Chapter 9. For individual harbours those shown under NAVIGATION are safe positions from which to approach a harbour. Those below the harbour name and after the country (or foreign equivalent) locate the harbour entrance and provide a good final waypoint.

A list of selected waypoints is given in section 3 or 4 of each Area. In the lists of 'Lights, Buoys, and Waypoints' they are underlined.

For convenience when loading waypoints into electronic equipment, or when passage planning, a tabular listing of selected waypoints is also given for popular sailing areas, i.e. the English Channel (9.1.7), the Solent area (9.2.18), East Anglian (9.4.6), the Clyde (9.9.25), and the Southern North Sea (9.23.8).

These listings give only the name and coordinates of each waypoint; they complement the data given in section 3 or 4 of each geographical area.

Latitude and longitude are normally stated to one-hundredth of a minute, as taken from a large-scale chart. Be advised that a chart using a different datum or based on a different survey may give a slightly different position. Charts may also contain small errors, just like the read-out from an electronic instrument.

Fig. 3 (4) – NW European Loran-C chains (NELS)

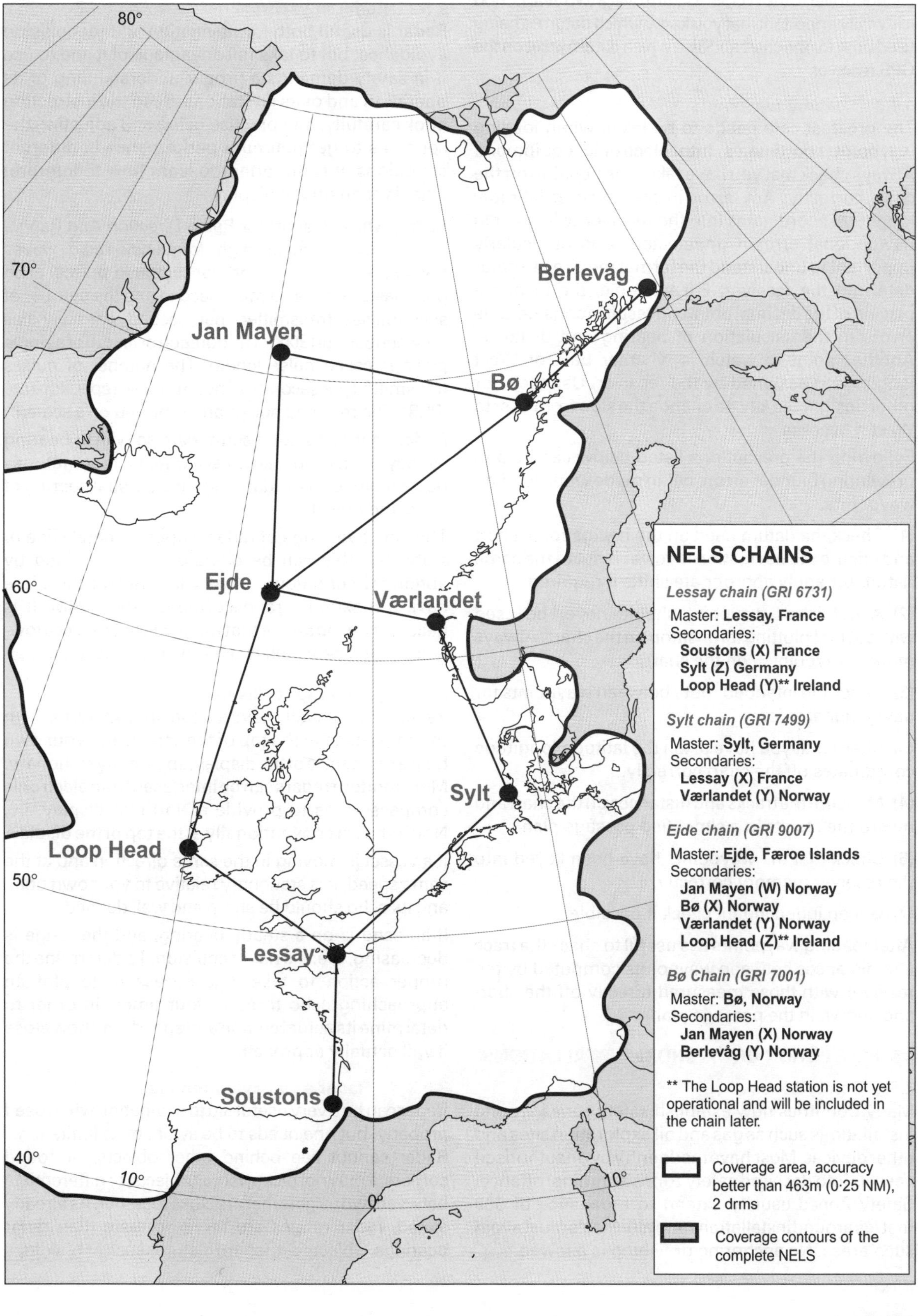

NELS CHAINS

Lessay chain (GRI 6731)

Master: **Lessay, France**
Secondaries:
Soustons (X) France
Sylt (Z) Germany
Loop Head (Y) Ireland**

Sylt chain (GRI 7499)

Master: **Sylt, Germany**
Secondaries:
Lessay (X) France
Værlandet (Y) Norway

Ejde chain (GRI 9007)

Master: **Ejde, Færoe Islands**
Secondaries:
Jan Mayen (W) Norway
Bø (X) Norway
Værlandet (Y) Norway
Loop Head (Z) Ireland**

Bø Chain (GRI 7001)

Master: **Bø, Norway**
Secondaries:
Jan Mayen (X) Norway
Berlevåg (Y) Norway

** The Loop Head station is not yet operational and will be included in the chain later.

Coverage area, accuracy better than 463m (0·25 NM), 2 drms

Coverage contours of the complete NELS

As Admiralty charts of the UK are progressively being changed over to the WGS84 Datum over a two year period it is vitally important that you know which datum is being used both for the chart and also which datum is set on the GPS receiver.

3.4.3 Loading waypoints

The greatest care needs to be taken when loading waypoint coordinates into electronic equipment. Always check that you have taken the position off the chart correctly. Any error in the entry of latitude/longitude coordinates into the receiver will result in navigational error if undetected. It is particularly important to understand the format required to enter data into the receiver. For example, the incorrect placing of the decimal point can result in considerable errors in the calculation of bearing and distance. Another point to watch is whether East or West longitude is assumed by the receiver. Use the ±, or other designated key, to change the sign from East to West if necessary.

Following the precautions listed below can help in preventing blunder errors being made when loading waypoints:

(1) Check the datum used on the navigational chart and ensure the navigation receiver is set to the same datum (or apply appropriate shifts if required)

(2) A published waypoint should never be used without first plotting its position on the chart. Always mark a waypoint ⊕ on the chart.

(3) Check the intended route between waypoints for navigational safety.

(3) Check that you have taken the latitude/longitude coordinates off the chart correctly.

(4) Measure the tracks and distances on the chart and record the results in a simplified passage plan.

(6) Check that the waypoints have been keyed into the receiver memory correctly.

(7) Get an independent check if possible.

After loading waypoints it is useful to check the track and distances between waypoints computed by the receiver with those measured directly off the chart and shown in the passage plan.

3.5 PROTECTION OF OFFSHORE INSTALLATIONS

3.5.1 Safety Zones

Many Countries now establish safety zones around installations such as gas and oil exploration sites and other devices. Most have made entry by unauthorised vessels into declared safety zones a criminal offence. Safety Zones usually extend to a distance of 500 metres around installations and all vessels must avoid such areas. No anchoring or fishing is allowed.

3.6 RADAR

3.6.1 Radar in yachts

Radar is useful both for navigation and for collision avoidance, but to take full advantage of it and to use it in safety demands a proper understanding of its operation and of its limitations. Read the instruction book carefully, and practise using and adjusting the set so as to get optimum performance in different conditions. It is important to learn how to interpret what is seen on the display

Radar, which is short for Radio Direction And Range, makes use of super high frequency radio waves transmitted in very short concentrated pulses. Each pulse lasts less than a microsecond and the number of such pulses transmitted per second normally lies between 800 and 3000. The duration or length of a single pulse is called pulse length. The number of pulses transmitted per second defines the pulse repetition rate (PRR). The returned pulses are displayed on a screen.

Radar beams do not discriminate so well in bearing as they do in range, so an accurate fix is sometimes best obtained by a radar range and a visual bearing of the same object.

The effective range of radar is approximately line of sight, but this can be decreased or increased by abnormal conditions. Most yacht radars therefore have a maximum range of about 16 to 24M. It is necessary to be aware that radar will not detect a low-lying coastline which is over the radar horizon.

3.6.2 Radar for collision avoidance

Yacht radars usually have a head up display, i.e. with the ships head at the top of the screen and your own boat at the centre of the display, apparently stationary. More modern radars can be interfaced to an electronic compass so as to provide a North-up display, i.e. North shown conventionally at the top of the display.

If a vessel is moving in the same direction and at the same speed, it is stationary relative to your own boat, and its echo should be sharp and well defined.

If an echo is on a steady bearing, and the range is decreasing, there is risk of collision. To determine the proper action to take it is necessary to plot an approaching echo three or four times, in order to determine its actual course and speed, and how close it will actually approach.

3.6.3 Radar as a navigation aid

Radar can be a very useful aid to navigation when used properly, but one needs to be aware of its limitations. Radar cannot see behind other objects, or round corners; it may not pick up small objects, or differentiate between two targets that are close together. As already stated, radar ranges are more accurate than radar bearings. Objects with sharp features such as buildings

Fig. 3 (5) – Radar beacon responses

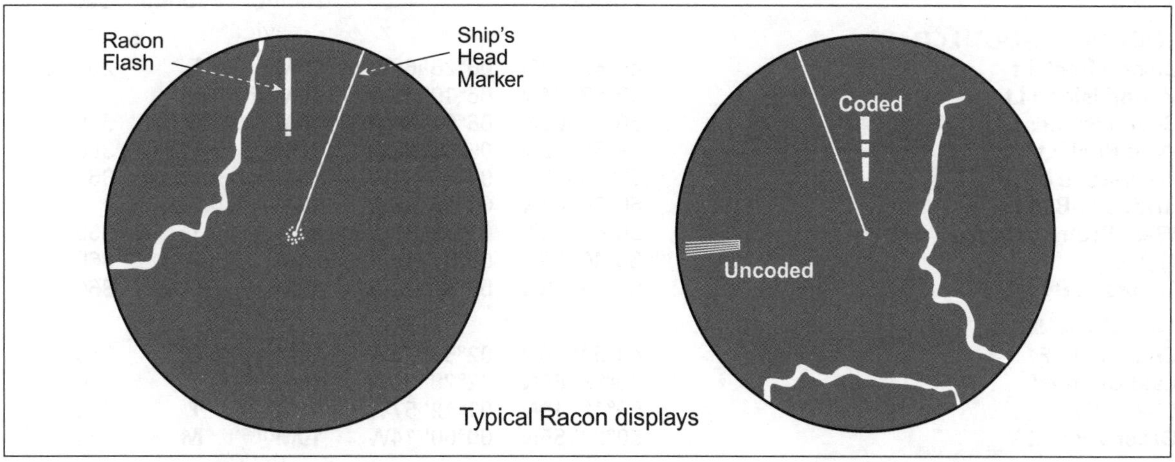

give a better reflection than those with curved or sloping surfaces. High or rocky cliffs make a good target, but chalk cliffs give a poor response, especially when dry. Low coastlines should be approached with extreme caution as the first thing to show on radar may be hills some distance inland.

3.7 RACONS (RADAR BEACONS)

3.7.1 Description

A Racon is a transponder beacon which, when triggered by a transmission from a vessel's radar, sends back a distinctive signal which appears on the vessel's radar display. Racons are often fitted to major light-vessels, lighthouses and buoys. They are shown on charts by a magenta circle and the word Racon.

In most cases the Racon flash on the radar display is a line extending radially outward from a point slightly beyond the actual position of the Racon, due to the slight delay in the response of the Racon apparatus. Thus the distance to the spot of the Racon flash is a little more than the vessels real distance from the Racon. Some Racons give a flash composed of a Morse identification signal, often with a tail to it, the length of the tail depending on the number of Morse characters.

The typical maximum range of a Racon is 10M, but may be as much as 25M. In practice, picking up a Racon at greater ranges depends on the power and elevation of both the Racon and the boat's radar. With abnormal radio propagation, a spurious Racon flash may be seen at much greater distances than the beacon's normal range, appearing at any random position along the correct bearing on the display. Only rely on a Racon flash if it appears to be consistent, and the boat is believed to be within its quoted range. At short range a Racon sometimes causes unwanted interference on the radar display, and this may be reduced by adjusting the rain clutter control on the radar receiver.

3.7.2 Radar beacon listing

Radar beacons within the coverage area of this Almanac are listed in Table 3 (1). They are also indicated on the Lights, Buoys and Waypoint pages for each geographic area.

Details given in Table 3 (1) are:

a. The name of the beacon.

b. Latitude and longitude.

c. Approximate range in nautical miles (M). This to some extent depends on the effective range of the yacht's radar set.

c. The Morse identification signal. Racons coded 'D' are used to mark new dangers such as wrecks.

d. The sector within which signals may be received, if not 360°.

Most Racons respond throughout 360°. A few respond only within an angular sector, bearings quoted always being towards the beacon, clockwise from 000° to 359°.

The majority of Racons sweep the frequency range of marine 3cm (X-band) radar emissions. The older type of Racon (swept frequency) take 30 to 90 seconds to sweep the band.

The newer type of Racon (frequency agile) responds immediately to both 3cm and 10cm (S-band) emissions. In order that the Racon response should not obscure wanted echoes, the agile response is switched 'on' and 'off' at a predetermined rate to suit the installation.

TABLE 3 (1) RACONS – EUROPE

Name	Position		Range	Ident	Sector
ENGLAND – SOUTH COAST					
Bishop Rock Lt	49°52'·33N	06°26'·68W	**18M**	**T**	254°-215°
Round Island Lt	49°58'·74N	06°19'·40W	**10M**	**M**	
Seven Stones Lt F	50°03'·62N	06°04'·34W	**15M**	**O**	360°
Wolf Rock Lt	49°56'·72N	05°48'·58W	**10M**	**T**	360°
Eddystone Lt	50°10'·85N	04°15'·94W	**10M**	**T**	360°
Bridge Lt By	50°39'·63N	01°36'·88W	**10M**	**T**	
West Bramble Lt By	50°47'·20N	01°18'·65W	**3M**	**T**	360°
Nab Lt	50°40'·08N	00°57'·16W	**10M**	**T**	360°
Owers Lt By	50°38'·63N	00°41'·22W	**10M**	**O**	360°
MID CHANNEL					
Channel Lt F	49°54'·36N	02°53'·77W	**15M**	**O**	360°
East Channel	49°58'·66N	02°28'·98W	**10M**	**T**	360°
EC2 Lt By	50°12'·16N	01°12'·57W	**10M**	**T**	360°
Greenwich Lt V	50°24'·55N	00°00'·14W	**10M**	**M**	360°
CHANNEL ISLANDS					
East Goodwin Lt F	51°13'·25N	01°36'·38E	**10M**	**T**	360°
Sandettié Lt F	51°09'·36N	01°47'·12E	**10M**	**T**	360°
Varne Lt V	51°01'·29N	01°23'·90E	**10M**	**T**	360°
East Channel Lt By	49°58'·71N	02°28'·95W	**10M**	**T**	360°
Channel Lt F	49°54'·46N	02°53'·74W	**15M**	**O**	360°
Casquets Lt	49°43'·32N	02°22'·62W	**25M**	**T**	360°
Platte Fougère Lt	49°30'·82N	02°29'·17W		**P**	
St Helier Demi de Pas Lt	49°09'·00N	02°06'·15W	**10M**	**T**	360°
ENGLAND – EAST COAST					
Inter Bank Lt By	51°16'·47N	01°52'·23E	**10M**	**M**	
North East Goodwin Lt By	51°20'·30N	01°34'·18E	**10M**	**M**	360°
Dover Strait TSS Foxtrot 3 Lt V	51°23'·85N	02°00'·51E	**10M**	**T**	360
Thames Reach Lt By No. 1	51°29'·45N	00°52'·57E	**10M**	**T**	360
Thames Reach Lt By No. 7	51°30'·10N	00°37'·05E	**10M**	**T**	360°
Thames Barrier Pier No. 4 E end*	51°29'·90N	00°02'·24E		**T**	
Thames Barrier Pier No. 4 W end*	51°29'·89N	00°02'·18E		**T**	
Thames Barrier Pier No. 5 E end*	51°29'·86N	00°02'·25E		**T**	
Thames Barrier Pier No. 5 W end*	51°29'·86N	00°02'·19E		**T**	
Thames Barrier Pier No. 6 E end*	51°29'·82N	00°02'·25E		**T**	
Thames Barrier Pier No. 6 W end*	51°29'·82N	00°02°19E		**T**	
Thames Barrier Pier No. 7 E end*	51°29'·78N	00°02'·26E		**T**	
Thames Barrier Pier No. 7 W end*	51°29'·78N	00°02'·19E		**T**	
Thames Barrier Pier No. 8 W end*	51°29'·74N	00°02'·26E		**T**	
Thames Barrier Pier No. 8 W end*	51°29'·74N	00°02'·20E		**T**	
NOTE*: Operational only when the visibility in Woolwich Reach is reduced to 1M or less, or upon request by a vessel for test purposes or training. Information relating to Racon operation will be included in routine broadcasts on VHF Ch 14.					
Outer Tongue Lt By	51°30'·69N	01°26'·40E	**10M**	**T**	360°
Barrow Lt By No. 3	51°42'·02N	01°20'·24E	**10M**	**M**	360°
South Galloper Lt By	51°43'·98N	01°56'·439E	**10M**	**T**	360
Sunk Lt F	51°51'·03N	01°34'·89E	**10M**	**T**	360°
Harwich Channel No 1 Lt By	51°56'·14N	01°27'·05E	**10M**	**T**	360°
Outer Gabbard Lt By	51°57'·83N	02°04'·19E	**10M**	**O**	360
North Shipwash Lt By	52°01'·73N	01°38'·27E	**10M**	**M**	360°
Orfordness Lt	52°05'·03N	01°34'·44E	**18M**	**T**	360°
Cross Sand Lt By	52°37'·03N	01°59'·14E	**10M**	**T**	360°
Winterton Old Lt	52°42'·77N	01°41'·70E	**10M**	**T**	360°
Smiths Knoll Lt By	52°43'·52N	02°17'·88E	**10M**	**T**	360
Newarp Lt V	52°48'·37N	01°56'·69E	**10M**	**O**	360°
Cromer Lt	52°55'·48N	01°18'·99E	**25M**	**O**	360°
North Haisbro Lt By	53°00'·22N	01°32'·29E	**10M**	**T**	360°
North Well Lt By	53°03'·02N	00°27'·90E	**10M**	**T**	360°

Name	Position		Range	Ident	Sector
Dudgeon Lt By	53°16'·62N	01°16'·89E	10M	O	360°
Anglia Field Platform A48/19-B	53°22'·04N	01°38'·97E	15M	Q	360°
Inner Dowsing Lt V	53°19'·52N	00°33'·85E	10M	T	360°
Dowsing Platform B1D	53°33'·68N	00°52'·63E	10M	T	360°
Spurn Lt F	53°33'·56N	00°14'·20E	5M	M	360°
Humber Lt By	53°39'·06N	00°19'·98E	7M	T	360°
Tees Fairway By	54°40'·94N	01°06'·47W		B	360°
SCOTLAND – EAST AND NORTH COAST					
St Abb's Head Lt	55°54'·96N	02°08'·29W	18M	T	360°
Inchkeith Fairway By	56°03'·49N	03°00'·10W	5M	T	360°
Firth of Forth N Channel Lt By	56°02'·80N	03°10'·96W	5M	T	360°
Bell Rock Lt	56°26'·05N	02°23'·07W	18M	M	360
Abertay Lt By	56°27'·39N	02°40'·36W	8M	T	360°
Scurdie Ness Lt	56°42'·10N	02°26'·24W	14-16M	T	360
Girdle Ness Lt	57°08'·34N	02°02'·91W	25M	G	360°
Aberdeen Fairway By	57°09'·31N	02°01'·94W	7M	T	360°
Buchan Ness Lt	57°28'·23N	01°46'·51W	14-16M	O	360°
Rattray Head Lt	57°36'·61N	01°49'·03W	15M	M	360°
Kessock Bridge Centre Mark	57°29'·97N	04°13'·81W	6M	K	
Cromarty Firth Fairway By	57°39'·96N	03°54'·19W	5M	M	360°
Tarbat Ness Lt	57°51'·88N	03°46'·76W	14-16M	T	360
Alba Oil Field, Platform Chevron Alba	58°03'·52N	01°04'·88E		C	360°
Saltire Oil Field Platform Saltire Alpha	58°25'·01N	00°19'·93E		Z	360°
Piper Oilfield, Platform Piper Bravo	58°27'·66N	00°14'·98E		N	360°
Duncansby Head Lt	58°38'·65N	03°01'·58W	16M	T	360°
Lother Rock Lt	58°43'·80N	02°58'·68W	10M	M	360°
North Ronaldsay Lt	59°23'·37N	02°23'·03W	14-17M	T	360°
Rumble Rock Bn	60°28'·17N	01°07'·25W	8-10M	O	360°
Gruney Island Lt	60°39'·15N	01°18'·16W	14M	T	360
Ve Skerries Lt	60°22'·36N	01°48'·79W	15M	T	360°
Foinaven Oil Field 204/24	60°18'·90N	04°16'·60W		X	360°
Sule Skerry Lt	59°05'·09N	04°24'·38W	20M	T	360°
SCOTLAND – WEST COAST					
Eilean Glas Lt	57°51'·40N	06°38'·55W	16-18M	T	360°
Ardivachar Pt	57°22'·92N	07°25'·54W	16M	T	360°
Carrach Rocks Lt By	57°17'·20N	05°45'·30W	5M	T	360°
Hyskeir Lt	56°58'·14N	06°40'·87W	14-17M	T	360°
Castlebay South By	56°56'·09N	07°27'·21W	7M	T	360°
Bo Vich Chuan Lt By	56°56'·15N	07°23'·31W	5M	M	360°
Skerryvore Lt	56°19'·36N	07°06'·88W	18M	M	360°
Dubh Sgeir Lt	56°14'·76N	05°40'·20W	5M	M	360
ENGLAND – WEST COAST					
Point of Ayre Lt	54°24'·94N	04°22'·13W	13-15M	M	360°
Halfway Shoal Lt Bn	54°01'·46N	03°11'·88W	10M	B	360°
Lune Deep Lt By	53°55'·81N	03°11'·08W	10M	B	360°
Bar Lt F	53°32'·02N	03°20'·98W	10M	T	360°
West Constable Lt By	53°23'·15N	03°49'·25W	10M	M	
The Skerries Lt	53°25'·27N	04°36'·50W	25M	T	360°
South Bishop Lt	51°51'·14N	05°24'·74W	10M	O	
The Smalls Lt	51°43'·28N	05°40'·19W	25M	T	360°
Watwick Pt Rear Ldg Lt Bn	51°41'·78N	05°09'·25W		Y	On trial
West Blockhouse Front Middle Ldg Lt Bn	51°41'·31N	05°09'·56W		Q	010°-230°
S. Gowan Lt By	51°31'·93N	04°59'·77W	10M	T	360°
West Helwick Lt By W.HWK	51°31'·40N	04°23'·65W	10M	T	360°
Swansea Bar Lt By W. Scar	51°28'·31N	03°55'·57W	10M	T	360°
Cabenda Lt By	51°33'·36N	03°52'·23W		C	
English & Welsh Grounds Lt By	51°27'·13N	02°59'·94W	7M	T	360°
Second Severn Crossing Centre Lt SW	51°34'·45N	02°42'·03W		O	
Breaksea Lt F	51°19'·88N	03°19'·08W	10M	T	360°

C3

Name	Position		Range	Ident	Sector
NORTHERN IRELAND					
Hellyhunter Lt By	54°00'·35N	06°02'·06W	**5-14M**	**K**	
South Rock Lt F	54°24'·49N	05°22'·02W	**13M**	**T**	360°
Mew Island Lt	54°41'·91N	05°30'·81W	**14M**	**O**	360°
Belfast Fairway Lt By	54°41'·70N	05°46'·23N		**G**	
East Maiden Lt	54°55'·73N	05°43'·67W	**11-21M**	**M**	360°
Rathlin East Lt	55°18'·06N	06°10'·30W	**15-27M**	**G**	089°-003°
IRELAND					
Bull Rock Lt	51°35'·51N	10°18'·07W	**16-27M**	**N**	360°
Fastnet Lt	51°23'·35N	09°36'·19W	**18M**	**G**	360°
Cork Lt By	51°42'·92N	08°15'·60W	**7M**	**T**	360°
Hook Head Lt	52°07'·32N	06°55'·85W	**10M**	**K**	237°-177°
Coningbeg Lt F	52°02'·40N	06°39'·49W	**13M**	**M**	360°
Tuskar Rock Lt	52°12'·19N	06°12'·46W	**18M**	**T**	360°
Arklow Lanby	52°39'·52N	05°58'·16W	**10M**	**O**	360°
Codling Lanby	53°03'·02N	05°40'·76W	**10M**	**G**	360°
Dublin Bay Lt By	53°19'·92N	06°04'·64W		**M**	
Kish Bank Lt	53°18'·70N	05°55'·44W	**15M**	**T**	360°
FRANCE					
Dyck (Dunkerque Approach) Lt By	51°02'·98N	01°51'·76E		**B**	360°
Vergoyer Lt By N	50°39'·64N	01°22'·18E	**5-8M**	**C**	360°
Bassurelle Lt By	50°32'·74N	00°57'·69E	**5-8M**	**B**	360°
Antifer Approach Lt By A5	49°45'·77N	00°17'·50W		**K**	360°
Le Havre LHA Lanby	49°31'·38N	00°09'·88W	**8-10M**		360°
Ouessant NE Lt By	48°45'·78N	05°11'·76W	**20M**	**B**	360°
Ouessant SW Lanby	48°31'·15N	05°49'·24W	**10M**	**M**	360°
Pointe de Créac'h Lt (Ile Ouessant)	48°27'·55N	05°07'·76W	**20M**	**C**	030°-248°
Chausée de Sein Lt By	48°03'·75N	05°07'·79W	**10M**	**O**	360°
S. Nazaire Lt By SN1	47°00'·07N	02°39'·84W	**3-8M**	**Z**	360°
S. Nazaire La Couronnée	47°07'·59N	02°20'·05W	**3-5M**		360°
BXA Lanby	45°37'·53N	01°28'·69W		**B**	360°
NORTH SPAIN					
Puerto de Pasajes Pilot Look-out	43°20'·10N	01°55'·47W	**20M**	**K**	
Punta Barracomuturra Lt Ondarroa	43°19'·53N	02°24'·94W	**12M**	**X**	360°
Bilbao Digue de Punta de Lucero Lt	42°22'·67N	03°05'·04W	**20M**	**X**	360°
Punta Rabiosa Front Ldg Lt	43°27'·51N	03°46'·43W	**10M**	**K**	360°
Punta Mera Front Lt	43°23'·08N	08°21'·17W	**18M**	**M**	020°-196
Punta Fiaiteira Lt	43°20'·59N	08°22'·25W	**11-21M**	**X**	
Cabo Villano Lt	43°09'·60N	09°12'·70W	**35M**	**M**	360°
Toriñana Monte Xastas	43°01'·74N	09°16'·52W	**35M**	**T**	360°
Cabo Finisterre Lt	42°52'·93N	09°16'·29W	**35M**	**O**	360°
Cap Corrubedo Lt	42°34'·59N	09°05'·39W	**8-17M**	**K**	360°
Isla Rua Lt	42°32'·96N	08°56'·38W	**10-20M**	**G**	211°-121°
Cabo Estay Front Leg Lt	42°11'·12N	08°48'·89W	**22M**	**B**	
PORTUGAL					
Esteiro Lt	38°41'·95N	09°15'·98W	**15M**	**Q**	
Canal do Barreiro Lt By No. 13B IS	38°39'·30N	09°05'·83W	**15M**	**Q**	360°
Porto de Setúbal Bn No. 2	38°27'·21N	08°58'·45W	**15M**	**B**	360°
SOUTH-WEST SPAIN					
Huelva (Dique)	37°06'·47N	06°49'·94W	**12M**	**K**	360°
Broa de Sanlucar Lt By No. 1	36°45'·82N	06°26'·95W	**10M**	**M**	360°
Bajo Salmedina Lt	36°44'·27N	06°28'·64W	**10M**	**M**	
Tarifa Lt	36°00'·06N	05°36'·58W	**20M**	**C**	360°
BELGIUM					
West Hinder Lt	51°23'·31N	02°26'·27E		**W**	
West Hinder Route Lt By KB	51°21'·03N	02°42'·83E		**K**	
Wandelaar Lt MOW 0	51°23'·73N	03°02'·83E	**10M**	**S**	360°
Bol Van Heist MOW 3	51°23'·37N	03°11'·89E	**10M**	**H**	360°

Name	Position		Range	Ident	Sector
NETHERLANDS					
Keeten B Lt By	51°36'·35N	03°58'·05E		**K**	360°
Zuid Vlije Lt By ZV11/SRK 4	51°38'·18N	04°14'·38E		**K**	360°
Noord Hinder Lt By NHR-SE	51°45'·42N	02°39'·92E	**10M**	**N**	360°
Noord Hinder Lt By	52°00'·04N	02°51'·03E		**T**	
Noord Hinder Noord NHR-N Lt By	52°10'·82N	03°04'·69E		**K**	
Schouwenbank Lt By	51°44'·94N	03°14'·31E	**10M**	**O**	360°
Goeree Lt	51°55'·42N	03°40'·03E	**12-15M**	**T**	360°
Maas Centre Lt By (MC)	52°01'·12N	03°53'·46E	**10M**	**M**	360°
Scheveningen Approach R&W Lt By	52°09'·00N	04°05'·50E		**Z**	On trial
Scheveningen Approach Red Lt By	52°10'·80N	04°07'·15E		**Q**	On trial
Rijn Field Platform P15B	52°18'·37N	03°46'·60E	**12-15M**	**B**	030°-270°
IJmuiden (IJM) Lt By	52°28'·44N	04°23'·78E	**10M**	**Y**	360°
Horizon P9-6 Platform	52°33'·13N	03°44'·45E		**Q**	
Helm Veld A Platform	52°52·28N	04°08'·42E		**T**	
Schulpengat Fairway Lt By SG	52°52'·90N	04°37'·90E		**Z**	
DW Route Lt By BR/S	52°54'·89N	03°18'·06E		**G**	
Logger Platform	53°00'·80N	04°12'·91E	**12-15M**	**X**	060°-270°
NAM Field Platform K14-FA-1	53°16'·14N	03°37'·58E		**7**	360°
Vlieland Lanby VL-CENTER	53°26'·93N	04°39'·85E	**12-15M**	**C**	360°
Wintershall Platform L8-G	53°34'·85N	04°36'·12E	**12-15M**	**G**	000°-340°
Botney Ground BG/S Lt By	53°35'·72N	03°00'·90E		**T**	
Placid Field Platform PL-K9C-PA	53°39'·14N	03°52'·37E		**8**	360°
Markham Field Platform J6-A	53°49'·37N	02°56'·65E		**M**	000°-180°
West Friesland Platform L2-FA-1	53°57'·55N	04°29'·70E		**9**	
Western Mud Hole, North Platform K4-A	53°45'·05N	03°18'·58E		**T**	
DW Route Lt By FR/A	54°00'·28N	04°21'·30E		**T**	
Elf Petroland Platform F15-A	54°12'·91N	04°49'·65E		**U**	360°
DW Route Lt By EF	54°03'·27N	04°59'·70E		**T**	
DW Route Lt By EF/B	54°06'·59N	05°39'·85E		**M**	
DW Route Lt By EF/C	54°08'·24N	05°59'·89E		**O**	
NAM Field Platform F2-A Hanze	54°56'·69N	04°34'·12E		**D**	
NAM Field Platform F3-OLT	54°51'·19N	04°43'·38E		**D**	360°
GERMANY					
Westerems Lt By	53°36'·88N	06°19'·38E	**8M**	**T**	360°
Borkumriff Lt By	53°47'·44N	06°22'·05E	**8M**	**T**	360°
GW/EMS Lt F	54°09'·96N	06°20'·72E	**8M**	**T**	360°
Platform GNSC-H-7	54°30'·47N	06°02'·07E		**D**	
Platform GNSC-B-11	55°27'·72N	04°33'·16E		**D**	
German Bight Lt V	54°10'·72N	07°27'·53E	**8M**	**T**	360°
Weser Lt By	53°54'·25N	07°50'·00E	**8M**	**T**	360
Weser 1/Jade 2 Lt By	53°52'·12N	07°47'·35E	**8M**	**T**	360
Elbe Lt By	53°59'·95N	08°06'·49E	**8M**	**T**	360°
DENMARK					
Skagens Rev, Route 'T' Lt By No.1	57°47'·08N	10°45'·93E	**10M**	**T**	360°
Skagen Lt	57°44'·11N	10°37'·75E	**20M**	**G**	360°
Skagens Rev, Route 'T' Lt By 1A	57°43'·42N	10°53'·51E		**N**	
Thyboron Approach Lt By	56°42'·54N	08°08'·69E	**10M**	**T**	360°
Dan Oil Field Platform DUC-DF-C	55°28'·79N	05°06'·45E		**U**	
Dagmar Oil Field Platform 'A'	55°34'·48N	04°36'·95E		**U**	360°
Rolf Oil Field Platform 'A'	55°36'·26N	04°29'·47E		**U**	
Valdema Oil Field Platform 'A'	55°50'·05N	04°33'·65E		**U**	
Svend Gas Plaform 'A'	56°10'·66N	04°10'·67E		**U**	
Harald Gas Field Platform West 'B'	56°20'·59N	04°16'·36E		**U**	
Gradyb Approach Lt By	55°24'·63N	08°11'·59E	**10M**	**G**	360°

Are you **keeping up to date?**

It is most important that any navigational publications are kept up to date.

The best way is to make use of our FREE supplement which gives all up dating information in a clearly referenced form.

This Almanac contains corrections up to Notices to Mariners, Edition No. 23/2001. Corrections are contained in the FREE Supplement, published in April 2002.

How to get it

As information contained in this Almanac is subject to constant change throughout the year, it is essential that users should **immediately** apply for the correcting Supplement in order to bring the Almanac fully up to date before using it for planning or at sea. Please fill in the registration card supplied, with your correct details so we can speed the process and send your Supplement as soon as possible.

On-line >>

The supplement will be available online at the Macmillan Reeds website. To register for this FREE updating service simply complete the online registration form at **www.nauticaldata.com.**

By Post

Fill in and return the enclosed registration card *complete with self-addressed C4 envelope (230x320mm) stamped (for 100 grammes)* to:
Nautical Data Limited, The Book Barn, Westbourne, Hants PO10 8RS.
The supplements can also be supplied on request upon receipt of a postage and packing fee of £1.50.

Corrections to Admiralty charts and publications are issued weekly in ***Admiralty Notices to Mariners,*** obtainable from Admiralty Chart Agents, or they can be seen at Customs Houses or Mercantile Marine Offices.

www.nauticaldata.com
Nautical Data Limited • The Book Barn • Westbourne • Hampshire PO10 8RS • UK
tel: +44 (0)1243 389352 • fax: +44 (0)1243 379136
• email: sales@nauticaldata.com • web: www.nauticaldata.com

Chapter 4

Communications

Contents

4.1 **INTERNATIONAL CODE** .... Page 64
4.2 **RADIO COMMUNICATIONS** .... Page 64
4.2.1 Radio telephony (R/T) 64
4.2.2 Regulations 64
4.2.3 Licences 64
4.2.4 R/T procedures 64
4.2.5 Prowords 64
4.3 **VHF, MF and HF RADIO** .... Page 65
4.4 **COAST RADIO STATIONS** .... Page 65
4.5 **LINK CALLS** .... Page 66
4.5.1 VHF calls to Coast Radio Stations 66
4.5.2 Making a call 66
4.5.3 Paying for a link call 66
4.5.4 MF call to Coast Radio Stations 66
4.5.5 Autolink RT 66
4.6 **SATELLITE COMMUNICATIONS** ..... Page 66
4.7 **NAVIGATIONAL WARNINGS** .... Page 67
4.7.1 General 67
4.7.2 United Kingdom 67
4.7.3 France 67
4.7.4 Belgium 67
4.7.5 The Netherlands 67
4.7.6 Germany 67
4.7.7 Spain and Portugal 67
4.7.8 Denmark 67
4.8 **CROSS REFERENCES** .... Page 67
4.9 **FLAG ETIQUETTE** .... Page 68
4.10 **TIME SIGNALS** .... Page 69
4.10.1 BBC Radio 4 69
4.10.2 BBC Radio 1 69
4.10.3 BBC Radio 2 69
4.10.4 BBC Radio 3 69
4.10.5 BBC World Service 69
4.10.6 USA Boulder and Hawaii 69
4.11 **UK RADIO STATIONS** .... Page 70
4.11.1 Coastguard MSI broadcasts 70
4.11.2 Channel Islands CRS 70
4.12 **IRISH CRS** .... Page 72
4.13 **BELGIAN CRS** .... Page 73
4.14 **NETHERLANDS COASTGUARD** ...... Page 74
4.15 **GERMAN MRCC** .... Page 74
4.15.1 **GERMAN CRS** .... Page 75
4.16 **SPANISH CRS** .... Page 76
4.17 **PORTUGUESE CRS** .... Page 76
4.18 **DANISH CRS** .... Page 78

C4

4.1 INTERNATIONAL CODE

4.1.1 Description

Marine communication is based on the International Code of Signals (1987 edition) published by IMO, which provides for safety of navigation and of persons, especially where there are language problems. The present Code came into force in 1969 and is available in nine languages: English, French, Italian, German, Japanese, Spanish, Norwegian, Russian and Greek. Ships, aircraft and shore stations can communicate with each other in these languages without knowing a foreign tongue, provided they have a copy of the appropriate Code. The English language edition is published by HMSO.

4.1.2 Using the International Code

The Code can be used by: alphabetical flags and numeral pendants; flashing light and Morse sound signalling; voice, using radiotelephony or loud-hailer; or by hand flags.

Signals consist of: single-letter signals which are important or common; two-letter signals in the General Section; and three-letter signals starting with 'M' in the Medical Section.

Plate 5 in Chapter 9 Introduction shows the Code flags for the alphabet and for numerals, the phonetic alphabet, the phonetic figure-spelling table, the Morse code for letters and numerals, and the meanings of important or common single-letter signals.

The following important two-letters signals may also be encountered:

RY You should proceed at slow speed when passing me (or vessels making signals)

NC I am in distress and require immediate assistance

YG You appear to be contravening the rules of a Traffic Separation Scheme

NE2 You should proceed with great caution; submarines are exercising in this area

4.2 RADIO COMMUNICATIONS

4.2.1 Radio Telephony (R/T)

Most small craft communicate using a VHF radio telephone. VHF gives a range about 30-40M depending on the aerial heights involved.

Medium Frequency (MF) gives much greater ranges (typically 100-300M), but must be Single Sideband (SSB). Double sideband (DSB) transmissions are prohibited except for emergency transmissions on 2182 kHz, the international MF Distress frequency.

High Frequency (HF) radio, which is more powerful and gives a much longer range than MF, is needed for ocean passages. The alternative to HF radio is satellite communications (see 4.6).

4.2.2 Regulations

The regulations for using RT communications are in the ***Handbook for Marine Radio Communication*** (Lloyds of London Press). They are lengthy and form part of the syllabus and examination.

Some of the more important stipulations are: operators must not divulge the contents of messages heard; Distress calls have priority; Coast Radio Stations (CRS), or Coastguard radio stations (CGR), as appropriate control communications in their respective areas. Check that the channel is free before transmitting; unnecessary or superfluous messages are prohibited, as is bad language; in harbour a yacht may not use inter-ship channels except for safety; a log must be kept, recording all transmissions, etc.

4.2.3 Radio Licences

a. The **vessel** requires a Ship Radio Licence for any VHF, UHF, MF, HF, satellite or EPIRB equipment on board. It is obtained from: The Radio Licensing Centre, Post Office Customer Management Unit, PO Box 1495, Bristol, BS99 3QS. ☎ 0870 243 4433. Fax 0117 975 8911. This allows the use of international maritime channels, Ch M for communications between yachts, marinas and clubs, and M2 for race control.

b. The **person** in charge of a set requires a Certificate of Competence (Pt 1) and Authority to Operate (Pt 2). For most yachtsmen this will be the Certificate of Competence, Restricted VHF only. The RYA is responsible for the conduct of an examination. The syllabus and examination are detailed in RYA booklet G26. A new Short Range radiotelephone Certificate (SRC), incorporating GMDSS procedures, will eventually supersede the present certificate.

c. Citizens Band and Amateur (Ham) Radio are not substitutes for proper maritime radio on VHF, MF or HF, but they can be a useful means of communication for other than safety matters. CB and Amateur Radio licences are issued by: The Radio Licensing Centre, Post Office Customer Management Unit, PO Box 1495, Bristol, BS99 3QS. ☎ 0870 243 4433. Fax 0117 975 8911.

4.2.4 RT procedures

Communications between a ship and a Coast radio station are controlled by the latter, except for Distress, Urgency or Safety messages. Between two ships, the ship called chooses a working channel.

Before making a call, decide exactly what needs to be said; writing the message down may help. Speak clearly and distinctly. Names or important words can be repeated or spelt phonetically.

Give your position as Lat/Long or the yacht's bearing and distance from a charted object, e.g. My position 225° Isle of May 4M means you are 4M SW of the Isle of May. Use the 360° True bearing notation and the 24 hours clock, specifying UTC, LT, etc.

4.2.5 Prowords

The following prowords should be used to simplify and expedite communications:

ACKNOWLEDGE	Have you received and understood?
CONFIRM	My version is ... is that correct?
CORRECTION	An error has been made; the correct version is ...
I SAY AGAIN	I repeat ... (e.g. important words).
I SPELL	What follows is spelt phonetically.
OUT	End of work.
OVER	I have completed this part of my message, and am inviting you to reply.
RECEIVED	Receipt acknowledged.
SAY AGAIN	Repeat your message (or part indicated).
STATION CALLING	Used when a station is uncertain of the identity of a station which is calling.

4.3 VHF, MF and HF RADIO

4.3.1 VHF radio

VHF is used by most vessels, coastguard stations, coast radio stations, ports, and other rescue services. Its range is slightly better than the line of sight between the transmitting and receiving aerials. It pays to fit a good aerial, as high as possible.

VHF sets may be Simplex, i.e. transmit and receive on the same frequency, so that only one person can talk at a time; Semi-Duplex, i.e. transmit and receive on different frequencies; or Duplex, i.e. simultaneous semi-duplex, so that conversation is normal.

Marine VHF frequencies are in the band 156·00 – 174·00 MHz. Frequencies are known by their international channel number (Ch), as shown below:

There are three main groups of frequencies, but certain channels can be used for more than one purpose. They are shown in order of preference.

(1) *Public correspondence:* (via Coast Radio Stations). Ch 26, 27, 25, 24, 23, 28, 04, 01, 03, 02, 07, 05, 84, 87, 86, 83, 85, 88, 61, 64, 65, 62, 66, 63, 60, 82. All channels can be used for duplex.

(2) *Inter-ship:* Ch 06, 08, 10, 13, 09, 72, 73, 69, 67, 77, 15, 17. These are all simplex channels.

(3) *Port Operations:*
Simplex: Ch 12, 14, 11, 13, 09, 68, 71, 74, 10, 67, 69, 73, 17, 15.
Duplex: Ch 20, 22, 18, 19, 21, 05, 07, 02, 03, 01, 04, 78, 82, 79, 81, 80, 60, 63, 66, 62, 65, 64, 61, 84.

Ch 0 (156·00 MHz) is used by SAR agencies and requires special authorisation to be fitted to a yacht.

Ch 13 (156·650 MHz) is used for bridge to bridge communications relating to the safety of navigation and should be monitored at sea whenever possible.

Ch 16 (156·80 MHz) is used for initial calling and answering. Once contact has been made, the stations concerned **must** switch to a working channel, except for Safety matters. Ch 16 will be monitored by ships, Coastguard radio stations and, in some areas, any remaining Coast radio stations for Distress and Safety until at least 2005, in parallel with GMDSS Ch 70. Yachts should monitor Ch 16.

Ch 67 (156·375 MHz) is used by all UK Coastguard Stations as the Small Craft Safety Channel, accessed via Ch 16.

Ch 70 (156·525 MHz) is used exclusively for digital selective calling for Distress and Safety purposes.

Ch 80 (157·025 MHz) is the primary working channel between yachts and marinas.

Ch M (157·85 MHz), is the secondary working channel.

Ch M2 (161·425 MHz) is for race control, with Ch M as stand-by. YCs may apply to use Ch M2.

4.3.2 MF radio

MF radiotelephones operate in the 1605-4200 kHz wavebands. Unlike VHF and HF, MF transmissions tend to follow the curve of the earth, which makes them suitable for direction-finding equipment. For this reason, and because of their good range, the marine Distress radiotelephone frequency is in the MF band (2182 kHz).

4.3.3 HF radio

HF radiotelephones use frequencies in the 4, 8, 12, 16 and 22 MHz bands (short wave) that are chosen to suit propagation conditions. HF is more expensive than MF and requires more power, but can provide worldwide coverage – but a good installation and correct operation are essential for satisfactory results.

Whereas MF transmissions follow the curve of the earth, HF waves travel upwards and bounce off the ionosphere back to earth. Reception is better at night when the ionosphere is denser. The directional properties of HF transmissions are poor, and there is no radiotelephone HF Distress frequency.

4.4 COAST RADIO STATIONS

4.4.1 Introduction

Foreign Coast Radio Stations (CRS) (CRS) control communications and link vessels with the telephone network ashore. CRS operate on nominated VHF, MF or HF frequencies.

CRS also transmit traffic lists, navigation warnings, and weather bulletins at scheduled times, and gale warnings as required.

The Coastguard, or similar organisations, have taken over responsibility for monitoring Distress, Urgency and Safety calls on Ch 70 DSC, Ch 16 or MF 2182 kHz. Coastguard radio stations, shown with the symbol (CGR), do not handle any commercial link calls.

4.4.2 CRS availability

Many European countries have already closed, or plan to shut-down, coast radio stations (CRS). The following summarises the latest position in each country covered by this Almanac.

a. **United Kingdom** no CRS remain in operation.

b. **Ireland** all CRS remain in operation.

c. **France** no CRS remain in operation.

d. **Spain and Portugal** all CRS remain in operation.

e. **Belgium** all CRS remain in operation.

f. **The Netherlands** no CRS remain in operation.

g. **Germany** A limited public correspondence service is available through Schiffsmeldedienst (SMD) which is Germany's new CRS service.

h. **Denmark** all CRS remain in operation

4.5 LINK CALLS

4.5.1 VHF calls to Coast radio stations

Within range (about 40M), contact a Coast Radio Station (CRS). You can make ordinary telephone calls, reverse-charge calls, YTD calls (see below), or send telegrams.

Except in emergency, call on a working channel related to the position of the yacht. For a Distress or Urgency call (only) use Ch 16. VHF calls should last several seconds and state the calling channel. A four-tone signal or pips indicate a temporary delay, but you will be answered when an operator is free. Do not use a designated broadcast channel at about the time of a scheduled broadcast.

4.5.2 Making a call

(1) Listen for a 'clear' channel, with no transmission at all. A busy channel will have either carrier noise, speech or the engaged signal (a series of pips).

(2) The initial call must last at least 6 seconds in order to activate the Coast radio station's ship-call latch equipment. For example:

Bilbao Radio, this is Yacht Seabird, Seabird, Golf Oscar Romeo India, Channel 27 Over.

(3) When the call is accepted you will hear pips, indicating that you have engaged the channel. Wait for the operator to speak. If no response, do not change channel since you may lose your turn. If you do not hear the pips you have not activated the station's transmitter or may be out of range. Try another station or call again when closer.

(4) When asked by the Radio Officer give the following: Ship's call sign (phonetics), ship's name, type of call and billing details (see below), and for a link call the telephone number required (and the name of the person in the case of a personal call).

4.5.3 Paying for a link call

Worldwide accounting for calls is achieved by quoting an 'Accounting Authority Indicator Code' (AAIC); this must be pre-arranged with an ITU-recognised authority such as BT, who use GB14 as the AAIC.

4.5.4 MF calls to Coast Radio Stations

Calls should be made on 2182 kHz. The Coast station will answer on 2182 kHz, allocate a working channel, and queue you into the system.

The Radio Officer will request the following information: Vessel's call sign, name, accounting code (AAIC – see 4.5.3), and category of traffic (e.g. telegram, telephone call).

4.5.5 Autolink RT

Autolink RT gives direct dialling from ship to shore into national and international telephone networks without going through a Coast radio station operator. It functions through an on-board unit which is easily connected to the radio, and which does not interfere with normal manual operation.

This service on VHF, MF and HF gives quicker access, cheaper calls, call scrambling on some units where privacy is required, and simplified accounting. Last number redial and a ten-number memory store are available.

Do not use Autolink for Distress, Urgency and Safety (including medical) calls, but use the normal manual procedure on VHF Ch 16 or 2182 kHz.

4.6 SATELLITE COMMUNICATIONS

4.6.1 Inmarsat

The International Maritime Satellite Organisation (Inmarsat) provides satellite communication (Satcom) worldwide via satellites in geostationary orbits above the equator over the Atlantic, Pacific and Indian Oceans. Satcom is more reliable and gives better reception than HF SSB radio. The satellites are the link between Coast Earth Stations (CES) ashore, operated by organisations such as BT, and the ship-board terminals called Ship Earth Stations (SES).

For a shore-ship call, a CES connects the land-based communication network with the satellite system. The message originated on land is transmitted to a ship by one of the satellites. Conversely a ship-shore call is received, via the satellite, by the CES, which transmits it onwards over land-based networks.

Onboard ship (SES) there are several standards of terminal:

Standard 'A' terminals, with a big antenna only suitable for larger vessels, have direct dialling telephone, Telex, data and fax facilities.

Standard 'C' transmit/receive data or text (but not voice). Both 'A' and 'C' offer speedy connection to HM Coastguard's MRCC at Falmouth for Distress, Safety, etc.

More recently, Inmarsat 'B' was launched as an improved successor to Inmarsat 'A', while Standard 'M' now makes satellite telephone, fax and data services available to a wider range of yachts, using smaller and less expensive equipment.

4.7 NAVIGATIONAL WARNINGS

4.7.1 General

The world is divided into 16 sea areas (Navareas I to XVI). Each Navarea has a Co-ordinating country responsible for issuing Long-range nav warnings. These are transmitted in English and other languages at scheduled times by RT, radiotelex and fax. Warnings cover navigational aids, wrecks, dangers of all kinds, SAR operations, cable laying, naval exercises, etc.

Coastal and Local warnings may also be issued. Coastal warnings, up to 100 or 200 miles offshore, are broadcast in English and their national language by Coast radio stations. Local warnings are issued by harbour authorities in the national language.

4.7.2 United Kingdom

The UK is the Area Co-ordinator for Navarea I. Long-range Navigational warnings are broadcast by Coastguard Coordination Centres after an initial announcement on Ch 16 and by Navtex Safetynet. They are also published in weekly *Notices to Mariners,* together with a list of warnings still in force.

WZ (Coastal) warnings are broadcast by Coastguard Coordination Centres every four hours. An initial announcement will be made on Ch 16 indicating which working channel (10, 24, 73, 84 or 86) the broadcast will be made on at the times indicated in 4.10.1 for the Sea Regions lettered A to N in Fig. 4 (1). Coastal Warnings are also transmitted on Navtex. Important warnings are broadcast on VHF Ch 16 and/ or 2182 kHz at any time required.

Vessels which encounter dangers to navigation should notify other craft and the nearest Coastguard radio station, prefacing the message by the Safety signal (see Chapter 6).

4.7.3 France

See Chapter 6 for details of French MSI navigational warning broadcasts.

4.7.4 Belgium

Navigational warnings are broadcast by Oostende Radio (CRS) on MF 2761 kHz and VHF Ch 27 on receipt and at scheduled times after an initial announcement on MF DSC 2187·5 kHz, VHF DSC Ch 70 or VHF Ch 16, and on Navtex.

Navigational warnings for the Schelde are broadcast by Antwerpen on Ch 24 on receipt and every H+03 and H+48.

4.7.5 Netherlands

Navigational warnings are broadcast by Netherlands Coastguard (CGR) (IJmuiden) on MF 3673 kHz, VHF Ch 23 and/or Ch 83, on receipt and at scheduled times, after an initial announcement on MF DSC 2187·5 kHz, VHF DSC Ch 70 or VHF Ch 16, and on Navtex (P).

4.7.6 Germany

Navigational warnings *(Nautische Warnnachricht)* are no longer broadcast by Norddeich Radio. Broadcasts for the North Sea coast are contained in IJmuiden Navtex (P) transmissions. Dangers to navigation should be reported to *Seewarn Cuxhaven.*

4.7.7 Spain and Portugal

Navigational warnings are broadcast by Spanish and Portuguese Coast Radio Stations (CRS) and MRCCs/ MRSCs (CGR) on MF 2182 kHz or VHF Ch 16 before being broadcast on the scheduled frequency or Channel number.

4.7.8 Denmark

Navigational warnings are broadcast by Lyngby Radio (CRS) on MF 1704 kHz, 1734 kHz, 1738 kHz, or 2586 kHz, and on various VHF channels (see Fig. 4 (7)) on receipt and at scheduled times, after an initial announcement on MF 2182 kHz or VHF Ch 16 kHz.

4.8 CROSS REFERENCES

4.8.1. Weather information

See Chapter 5

4.8.2 Safety

Emergency messages, medical help by R/T, GMDSS and SAR are all fully described in Chapter 6.

4.8.3 Navtex

A Navtex receiver prints or displays navigational and meteorological warnings and other Marine Safety Information (MSI). Navtex is the MSI component of GMDSS (see Chapter 6). Navtex is well used by yachtsmen for obtaining weather information; details are therefore to be found in Chapter 5.

4.8.4 Distress signals and emergencies

Details of Distress signals, visual signals between shore and ships in distress, signals used by SAR aircraft, and directing signals used by aircraft are given in Chapter 6.

4.8.5 Port Traffic signals

Traffic signals etc. for individual harbours are shown in Chapter 9. On the Continent Traffic signals are to some extent standardised – see 9.15.7 for France, 9.23.7 for Belgium and the Netherlands, and 9.24.7 for Germany.

International Port Traffic Signals are shown in 9.0.4. These are being increasingly used. Local variations are shown under individual harbours in Chapter 9.

4.8.6 Distress, Urgency and Safety traffic by radiotelephone

There are agreed international procedures for passing radiotelephone messages concerning vessels in Distress–or for lesser emergencies or situations where Urgency or Safety messages are appropriate. These are fully described in Chapter 6. For the Global Maritime Distress and Safety System (GMDSS) see Chapter 6.

If you hear a Distress call, you must cease all transmissions that might interfere with it or other Distress traffic, and continue listening on the frequency concerned. Write down what you hear. You may have responsibilities for assisting the casualty or for relaying the Distress messages. This, and the general control of Distress traffic, are discussed in Chapter 6.

4.8.7 Other maritime radio services

Apart from Coast Radio Stations, Port Operations and Vessel Traffic Services, some countries operate other radio services connected with Search and Rescue (SAR) and Maritime Safety Information (MSI).

These are described in Chapter 6. In most cases these stations also broadcast strong wind warnings together with scheduled weather bulletins and local Navigational Warnings.

4.9 FLAG ETIQUETTE

For many years flags were the only way to pass messages at sea, and although this function has now been largely superseded by radio, flags remain a useful way of expressing identity – by national ensigns, club burgees, etc. Here is brief guidance on how they should be used.

4.9.1 Ensign

A yacht's ensign is the national maritime flag corresponding to the nationality of her owner. Thus a British yacht should wear the Red Ensign, unless she qualifies for a special ensign (see 4.9.2). It goes without saying that the national ensign should be kept clean and in good repair. At sea the ensign must be worn when meeting other vessels, when entering or leaving foreign ports, or when approaching forts, Signal and Coastguard Stations, etc. Increasingly it has become the practice to leave the ensign (and burgee) flying at all times in foreign waters – even at night in harbour, assuming that the boat is not unattended. In British harbours it is the custom for the ensign to be hoisted at 0800 (0900 between 1 November and 14 February) or as soon after that time as people come on board; and lowered at sunset (or 2100 local time if earlier) or before that time if the crew is leaving the boat.

The ensign should normally be worn at the stern, but if this is not possible the nearest position should be used, e.g. at the peak in a gaff-rigged boat, at the mizzen masthead in a ketch or yawl, or about two-thirds up the leech of the mainsail. In harbour or at anchor the proper position is at the stern.

The ensign should not be worn when racing (after the five minute gun). It should be hoisted on finishing or when retiring.

4.9.2 Special ensigns

Members of certain clubs may apply for permission to wear a special ensign (e.g. Blue Ensign, defaced Blue Ensign, or defaced Red Ensign). For this purpose the yacht must either be a registered ship under Part I of the Merchant Shipping Act 1894 and of at least 2 tons gross tonnage, or be registered under the Merchant Shipping Act 1983 (Small Ships Register) and of at least 7 metres overall length. The owner or owners must be British subjects, and the yacht must not be used for any professional, business or commercial purpose. Full details can be obtained from the Secretaries of clubs concerned.

A special ensign must only be worn when the owner is on board or ashore in the vicinity, and only when the yacht is flying the burgee (or a Flag Officer's flag) of the club concerned. The permit must be carried on board. When the yacht is sold, or the owner ceases to be a member of the club, the permit must be returned to the Secretary of the club.

4.9.3 Burgee

A burgee shows that a yacht is in the charge of a member of the club indicated, and does not necessarily indicate ownership. It should be flown at the masthead.

Should this be impossible due to wind sensors, radio antenna, etc. the burgee may be flown at the starboard crosstrees, but this should be avoided unless absolutely necessary. A yacht should not fly more than one burgee. A burgee is not flown when a yacht is racing. If the yacht is on loan, or is chartered, it is correct to use the burgee of the skipper or charterer – not that of the absent owner. Normal practice has been to lower the burgee at night, at the same time as the ensign, but nowadays many owners leave the burgee flying if they are on board or ashore in the vicinity.

4.9.4 Flag Officer's flag

Clubs authorise their Flag Officers to fly special swallow-tailed flags, with the same design as the club burgee and in place of it. The flags of a vice-commodore and a rear-commodore carry one and two balls respectively. A Flag Officer's flag is flown day and night while he is on board, or ashore nearby. A Flag Officer should fly his flag with the Red Ensign (or special ensign, where authorised) in preference to the burgee of some other club.

4.9.5 Choice of burgee

An owner who is not a Flag Officer, and who belongs to more than one club, should normally fly the burgee (and if authorised the special ensign) of the senior club in the harbour where the yacht is lying. An exception may be if another club is staging a regatta or similar function.

4.9.6 Courtesy ensign

It is customary when abroad to fly a small maritime ensign of the country concerned at the starboard spreader. A courtesy ensign must not be worn below any other flag on the same halyard. Thus a club burgee, if usually flown at the starboard spreader, must be shifted to the port spreader when abroad, permitting the courtesy ensign to be close up at the starboard spreader. The correct courtesy flag for a foreign yacht in British waters is the Red Ensign. British yachts do not fly a courtesy flag in the Channel Islands since these are part of the British Isles.

4.9.7 House flag

An owner may fly his personal flag when he is on board in harbour, provided it does not conflict with the design of some existing flag. A house flag is normally rectangular, and is flown at the crosstrees in a sloop or cutter, at the mizzen masthead in a ketch or yawl, or at the foremast head in a schooner.

4.9.8 Salutes

Yachts should salute all Royal Yachts, and all warships of whatever nationality. A salute is made by dipping the ensign (only). The vessel saluted responds by dipping her ensign, and then re-hoisting it, whereupon the vessel saluting re-hoists hers. It is customary for a Flag Officer to be saluted (not more than once a day) by a yacht flying the burgee of that club

4.9.9 Dressing ship

Dressing overall (as opposed to dressing with masthead flags) is normally only done in harbour and marks national festivals. The international code flags and Pennants (see Plate 5) are flown in the following order from stem to masthead(s) to stern: E, Q, p 3, G, p 8, Z, p 4, W, p 6, P, p 1, Code, T, Y, B, X, 1st Sub, H, 3rd Sub, D. F, 2nd Sub, U, A, O, M, R, p 2, J, p 0, N, p 9,K, p 7, V, p 5, L, C, S.

4.10 RADIO TIME SIGNALS

4.10.1 BBC Radio 4 198 kHz

92·4 – 94·6 MHz 94·8 MHz (Channel Islands
603 kHz (Tyneside)720 kHz (London)
756 kHz (Redruth 774 kHz (Plymouth)
1449 kHz (Aberdeen) 1485 kHz (Carlisle)

Mon-Fri:	0600 0700 0800 0900 1000 1100 1200 1300 1400 1500 1600 1700 1900 2200
Sat:	0700 0800 0900 1000 1100 1300 1400 1600
Sun:	0600 0700 0800 0900 1300 1700 2100

4.10.2 BBC Radio 1 97·6 – 99·8 MHz

97·1 MHz (Channel Islands)
1053 kHz, 1089 kHz

Mon-Fri: 0700 0800
Sat: 1300 *Sun:* Nil

4.10.3 BBC Radio 2 88 – 90·2 MHz

89·6 MHz (Channel Islands)

Mon-Fri:	0000 0700 0800 1300 1700
Sat:	0000 0700 0800
Sun:	0000 0800 0900 1900

4.10.4 BBC Radio 3 90·2 – 92·4 MHz

91·1 MHZ (Channel Islands)

Mon-Fri:	0700 0800
Sat:	0600 0700
Sun:	Nil

4.10.5 BBC World service

A: 198 kHz	F: 7150 kHz	K: 9760 kHz	P: 17640 kHz
B: 648 kHz	G: 7230 kHz	L: 9915 kHz	Q: 17705 kHz
C: 1296 kHz	H: 7325 kHz	M: 12095 kHz	
D: 3955 kHz	I: 9410 kHz	N: 15070 kHz	
E: 8195 kHz	J: 9750 kHz	O: 15340 kHz	

Time	*A*	*B*	*C*	*D*	*E*	*F*	*G*	*H*	*I*	*J*	*K*	*L*	*M*	*N*	*O*	*P*	*Q*
0000	♦	♦						♦				♦	♦	♦			
0200	♦	♦	♦		♦			♦	♦			♦	♦				
0300	♦	♦	♦		♦		♦	♦	♦			♦	♦				
0400	♦			♦	♦		♦		♦				♦				
0500	♦			♦	♦				♦				♦	♦			
0600		♦	♦	♦	♦	♦			♦				♦	♦			
0700		♦			♦	♦		♦	♦		♦		♦	♦		♦	
0800		♦				♦		♦	♦		♦		♦	♦		♦	♦
0900		♦						♦	♦	♦	♦		♦	♦		♦	♦
1100		♦							♦	♦	♦		♦	♦		♦	♦
1200		♦							♦	♦	♦		♦	♦		♦	♦
1300		♦							♦	♦	♦		♦	♦		♦	♦
1500		♦			♦				♦	♦	♦		♦	♦		♦	♦
1600		♦			♦				♦		♦		♦	♦			♦
1700		♦			♦				♦				♦	♦			
1800					♦				♦				♦	♦			
1900		♦			♦				♦				♦	♦			
2000		♦			♦			♦	♦				♦	♦			
2200		♦	♦		♦			♦	♦			♦	♦	♦	♦		
2300		♦	♦					♦	♦			♦	♦	♦	♦		

4.10.6 USA Boulder (WWV) and Hawaii (WWVH)

Colorado (WWV) and (Honolulu)WWVH continuously broadcast on frequencies 2500, 5000, 10000, 15000, and 20000 MHz Co-ordinated Universal Time (UTC) signals.

The station identification is made by a voice announcement in English every thirty minutes, approximately on the hour and half-hour.

Semi silent periods with no audio tone or special announcements, whilst the carrier seconds occur from H+45 to 50 at WWV, and H+15 to 20 at WWVH.

Additional information is also broadcast as follows: At H+08 and H+09 WWV broadcasts Atlantic weather in two parts and Pacific weather at H+10.

C4

4.11 UK NAVIGATION WARNINGS BROADCASTS

4.11.1 Coastguard MSI navigation warning broadcasts

HM Coastguard are responsible for broadcasting Navigational warnings and other Marine Safety Information (MSI). Details and times of Weather broadcasts of gale Warnings, shipping forecasts and inshore waters forecasts are given in Chapter 5.

VHF Channels 10, 24, 73, 84 and 86 will be used for all MSI broadcasts in UK. An initial announcement will be made on VHF Ch 16 (and MF 2182 kHz) indicating the VHF Channel and MF frequency to listen to. Dedicated MF SSB frequencies are also allocated to specific Coastguard Coordination Centres.

Station	Region	VHF Ch	MF Freq	Broadcast times (all times UTC)
SOUTH COAST				
Falmouth CGR	D and F	16	2226 Khz	0140 0540 0940 1340 1740 and 2140
Brixham CGR	D and G	16		0050 0450 0850 1250 1650 and 2050
Portland CGR	D, G and H	16		0220 0620 1020 1420 1820 and 2220
Solent CGR	G, H and I	16	1641 kHz	0040 0440 0840 1240 1640 and 2040
Dover CGR	I and J	16		0105 0505 0905 1305 1705 and 2105
EAST COAST				
Thames CGR	I	16		0010 0410 0810 1210 1610 and 2010
Yarmouth CGR	J and K	16	1869 kHz	0040 0440 0840 1240 1640 and 2040
Humber CGR	K and L	16	2226 kHz	0340 0740 1140 1540 1940 and 2340
Forth CGR	L and M	16		0205 0605 1005 1405 1805 and 2205
Aberdeen CGR	M and N	16	2226 kHz	0320 0720 1120 1520 1920 and 2320
Shetland CGR	N	16	1770 kHz	0105 0505 0905 1305 1705 and 2105
WEST COAST				
Stornoway CGR	A, B and N	16	1743 kHz	0110 0510 0910 1310 1710 and 2110
Clyde CGR	B and C	16	1883 kHz	0020 0420 0820 1220 1620 and 2020
Belfast CGR	C and E	16		0305 0705 1105 1505 1905 and 2305
Liverpool CGR	C and E	16		0210 0610 1010 1410 1810 and 2210
Holyhead CGR	E	16	1880 kHz	0235 0635 1035 1435 1835 and 2235
Milford Haven CGR	E and F	16	1767 kHz	0335 0735 1135 1535 1935 and 2335
Swansea CGR	F	16		0005 0405 0805 1205 1605 and 2005

4.11.2 Channel Islands Coast Radio Stations

St Peter Port and Jersey Radio Stations are operated by the States of Guernsey and of Jersey respectively.

St Peter Port CRS 49°27'N 02°32'W	**20 62** 67 16	1764 kHz	VHF **20**; 62 (link calls only) Ch 67 on request for yacht safety calls.

Traffic List Broadcasts on Ch 20, 62 and 1764 kHz at 0133 0533 0933 1333 1733 and 2133 UT.

Jersey CRS 49°11'N 02°14'W	**25** 82 67 16	1659 kHz	VHF **82** (Ch 25 link calls only) Ch 67 on request for yacht safety calls.

MMSI 00230060; DSC Ch 70

Broadcasts on Ch 25, 82 and 1659 kHz at 0645 0745 1245 1845 and 2245 UTC include weather messages, navigation warnings and Traffic Lists.

Fig. 4 (1) HM Coastguard Co-ordination Centres and Navarea Sea Regions

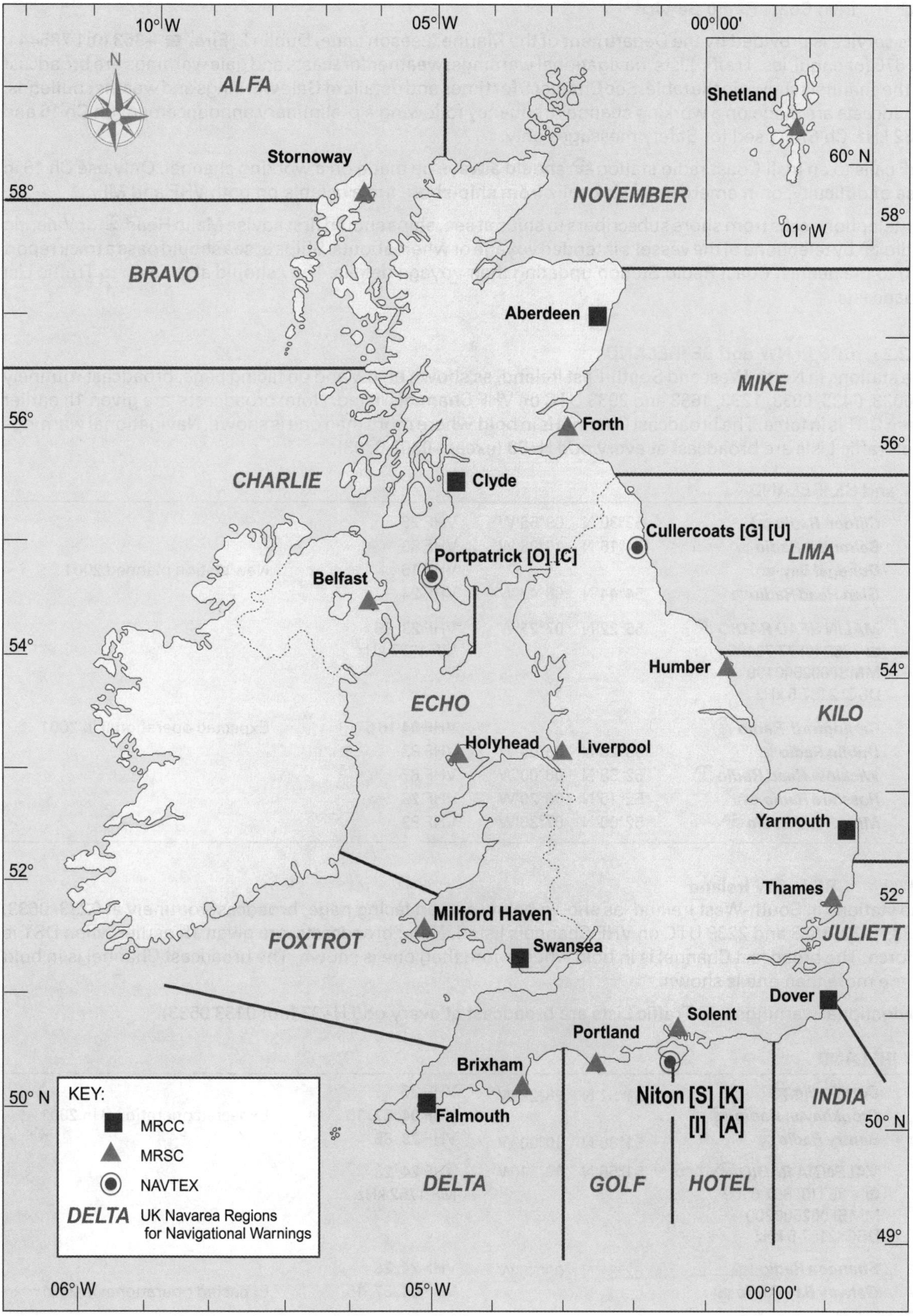

C4

4.12 IRISH COAST RADIO STATIONS

4.12.1 Irish Coast Radio Service

This service is provided by the Department of the Marine, Leeson Lane, Dublin 2, Eire. ☎ +353 (0)1 785444; ext 670 for enquiries. Traffic Lists, navigational warnings, weather forecasts and gale warnings are broadcast on the channels shown in the table. See Chapter 5 for times and details of Gale warnings and weather bulletins. Broadcasts are made on a working channel/frequency following a preliminary announcement on Ch 16 and 2182 kHz. Ch 67 is used for Safety messages only.

VHF calls to an Irish Coast radio station (CRS) should always be made on a working channel. Only use Ch 16 in case of difficulty, or in emergency. Link calls from ship-shore are available on both VHF and MF.

For telephone calls from shore subscribers to ships at sea, ships should first advise Malin Head (CRS) or Valentia Radio (CRS) by telephone of the vessel's intended voyage or whereabouts. Ships at sea should pass a track report (TR) to the nearest Coast Radio Station updating their voyage details. They should also listen to Traffic List broadcasts.

4.12.2 CRS in NW and SE IRELAND

The stations in North-West and South-East Ireland, as shown below and on facing page, broadcast routinely at 0033, 0433, 0833, 1233, 1633 and 2033 UTC on VHF Channels listed. Note: broadcasts are given 1h earlier when DST is in force. The broadcast Channel is in bold where more than one is shown. Navigational warnings and Traffic Lists are broadcast at every odd H+03 (except 0303 0703).

NW and SE IRELAND

Clifden Radio (CRS)	53°30'N	09°56'W	VHF 26	
Belmullet Radio (CRS)	54°16'N	10°03'W	VHF 83	
Donegal Bay (CRS)			VHF 16	New station planned 2001
Glen Head Radio (CRS)	54°44'N	08°43'W	VHF 24	
MALIN HEAD RADIO (CRS)	55°22'N	07°21'W	VHF **23**, 85	
☎ +353 (0) 77 70103			MF 1677 kHz	
MMSI 002500100				
DSC: 2187·5 kHz				
Carlingford Radio (CRS)			VHF **04** 16 67	Expected operational in 2001
Dublin Radio (CRS)	53°23'N	06°04'W	VHF 83	
Wicklow Head Radio (CRS)	52°58'N	06°00'W	VHF 87	
Rosslare Radio (CRS)	52°15'N	06°20'W	VHF 23	
Mine Head Radio (CRS)	52°00'N	07°35'W	VHF 83	

4.12.3 CRS in SW Ireland

The stations in South-West Ireland, as shown below and on facing page, broadcast routinely at 0233, 0633, 1033, 1433, 1833 and 2233 UTC on VHF Channels listed. Note: broadcasts are given 1h earlier when DST is in force. The broadcast Channel is in bold where more than one is shown. The broadcast Channel is in bold where more than one is shown.

Navigational warnings and Traffic Lists are broadcast at every odd H+33 (not 0133 0533).

SW IRELAND

Cork Radio (CRS)	51°51'N	08°29'W	VHF 26	
Crookhaven Radio (CRS)			VHF **04**, 67, 16	Expected operational in 2001
Bantry Radio (CRS)	51°38'N	10°00'W	VHF **23**, 85	
VALENTIA RADIO (CRS)	51°56'N	10°21'W	VHF **24**, 28	
☎ + 353 (0) 667 6109			MF 1752 kHz	
MMSI 002500200				
DSC: 2187·5 kHz				
Shannon Radio (CRS)	52°31'N	09°36'W	VHF 24, **28**	
Galway Bay Radio (CRS)			VHF **04**, 67, 16	Expected operational in 2001

Fig. 4 (2) Irish Coast Radio Stations

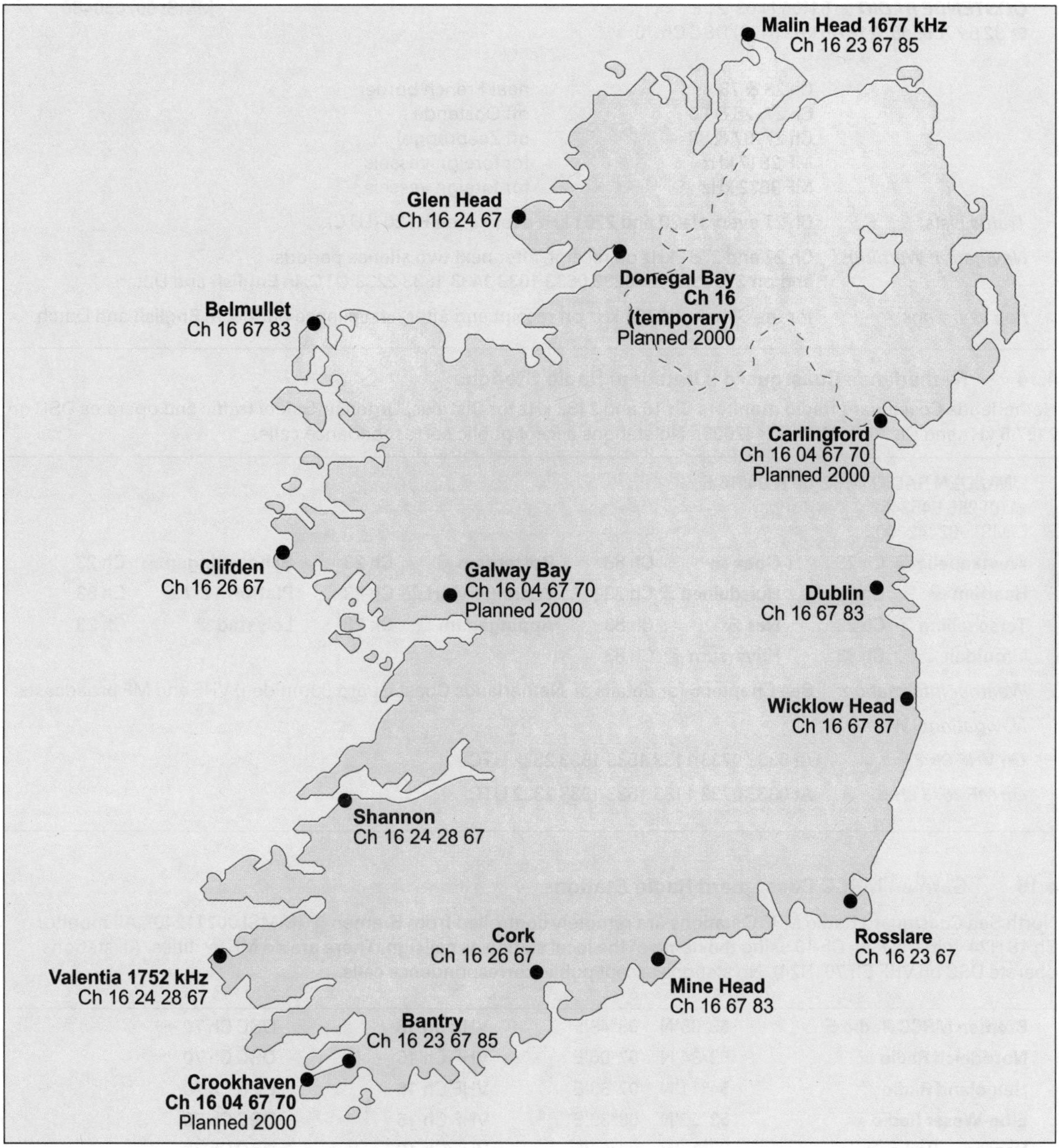
Malin Head 1677 kHz
Ch 16 23 67 85
Glen Head
Ch 16 24 67
Donegal Bay
Ch 16
(temporary)
Planned 2000
Belmullet
Ch 16 67 83
Carlingford
Ch 16 04 67 70
Planned 2000
Clifden
Ch 16 26 67
Galway Bay
Ch 16 04 67 70
Planned 2000
Dublin
Ch 16 67 83
Wicklow Head
Ch 16 67 87
Shannon
Ch 16 24 28 67
Rosslare
Ch 16 23 67
Cork
Ch 16 26 67
Valentia 1752 kHz
Ch 16 24 28 67
Mine Head
Ch 16 67 83
Bantry
Ch 16 23 67 85
Crookhaven
Ch 16 04 67 70
Planned 2000

4.13 Belgian Coast Radio Stations

ANTWERPEN Radio (CRS) 51°17'N 04°20'E — MMSI 002050485
DSC Ch 70

On VHF:	VHF 24 87
Traffic Lists:	Ch 24 every H+05.
Navigation Warnings:	Ch 24 on receipt and every H+03 and H+48, in English and Dutch for the Schelde.

C4

4.13 Belgian Coast Radio Stations – continued

OOSTENDE RADIO (CGR) 51°06'N 03°21'E MMSI 002050480
☎ *32 59 706565*. 2187·5 kHz (H24) DSC Ch 70

	Ch 28 & 78	near French border
	Ch 27, 28 & 85	off Oostende
	Ch 27, 87 & 88	off Zeebrugge)
	MF 2817 kHz	for foreign vessels
	MF 3632 kHz	for foreign vessels
Traffic Lists:	Ch 27 every H+20 and 2761 kHz every even H+20 (UTC).	
Navigation Warnings:	Ch 27 and 2761 kHz on receipt, after next two silence periods and on 2761 kHz at: 0233 0633 1033 1433 1833 2233 UTC, **in English** and Dutch.	
Fog Warnings:	for the Schelde: 2761 kHz on receipt and after next silence period, **in English** and Dutch.	

4.14 Netherlands Coastguard (IJmuiden) Radio Stations

Netherlands Coastguard Radio monitors Ch 16 and 2182 kHz for Distress, Urgency, Safety traffic and operates DSC on 2187·5 kHz and Ch 70 (MMSI 002442000). No stations accept public correspondence calls.

IJMUIDEN RADIO (CGR) 52°06'N 04°16'E
☎ (0) 255 545345
MMSI 002442000

Westkapelle (CGR)	Ch 23	**Goes** (CGR)	Ch 83	**Rotterdam** (CGR)	Ch 23	**Scheveningen** (CGR)	Ch 23
Haarlem (CGR)	Ch 83	**Huisduinen** (CGR)	Ch 23	**Wieringerwerf** (CGR)	Ch 83	**Platform L-7** (CGR)	Ch 83
Terschelling (CGR)	Ch 23	**Nes** (CGR)	Ch 83	**Appingedam** (CGR)	Ch 23	**Lelystad** (CGR)	Ch 23
IJmuiden (CGR)	Ch 83	**Hilversum** (CGR)	Ch 83				

Weather information: See Chapter 5 for details of Netherlands Coast Guard (IJmuiden) VHF and MF broadcasts.

Navigational Warnings:

On VHF Ch 23: At 0333 0733 1133 1533 1933 2322 UTC

On MF 2673 kHz: At 0333 0733 1133 1533 1933 2322 UTC

4.15 German MRCC Coastguard Radio Stations

North Sea Coastguard Radio MRCC stations are remotely controlled from Bremen (CGR) (MMSI 00211240). All monitor Ch 16 H24. Initial call on Ch 16 using the name of the local station as callsign. There are no MF facilities. All stations operate DSC on VHF Ch 70 (H24). No stations accept public correspondence calls.

Bremen MRCC Radio (CGR)	53°05'N	08°48'E	VHF Ch 16	DSC Ch 70
Norddeich Radio (CGR)	53°34'N	07°06'E	VHF Ch 16	DSC Ch 70
Helgoland Radio (CGR)	54°11'N	07°53'E	VHF Ch 16	DSC Ch 70
Elbe-Weser Radio (CGR)	53°50'N	08°39'E	VHF Ch 16	DSC Ch 70
Hamburg Radio (CGR)	53°33'N	09°58'E	VHF Ch 16	DSC Ch 70
Eiderstedt Radio (CGR)	54°20'N	08°47'E	VHF Ch 16	DSC Ch 70
Nordfriesland Radio (CGR)	54°55'N	08°18'E	VHF Ch 16	DSC Ch 70

Navigation Warnings: On VHF Ch 16.
Vital warnings for the North Sea and Baltic.On receipt and repeated at every H+00 and H+30 until cancelled.

Fig. 4 (3) Netherlands Coastguard radio stations

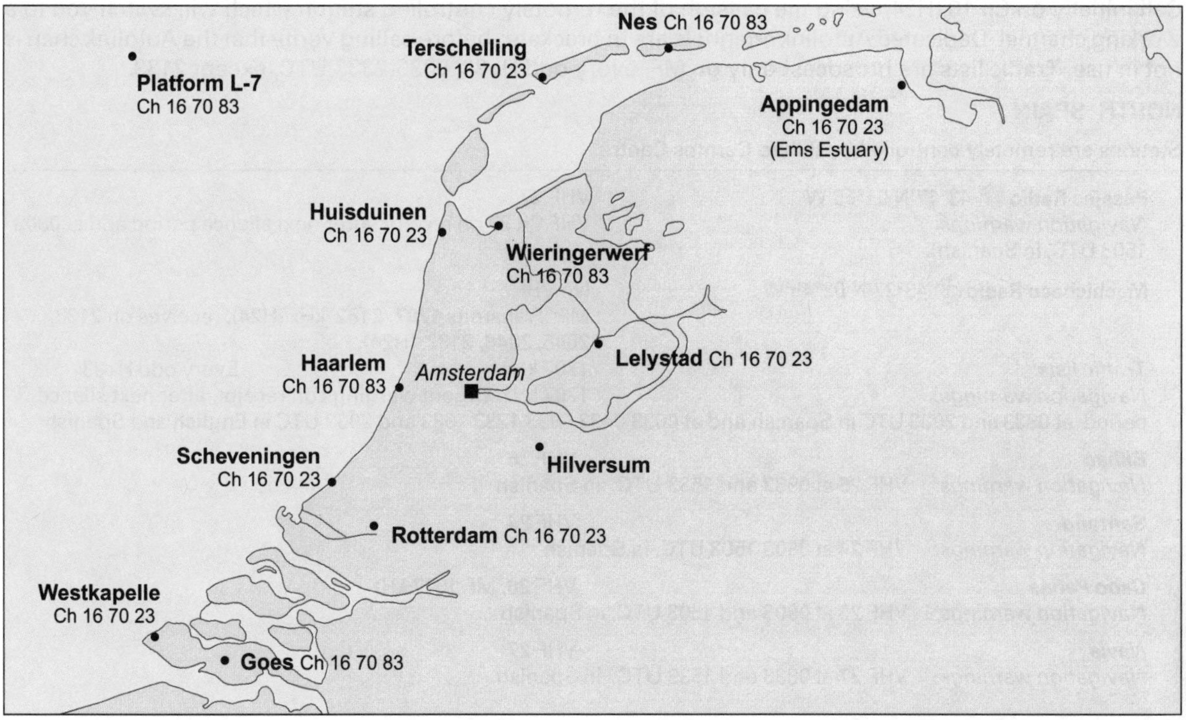

Fig. 4 (4) German Coastguard radio stations

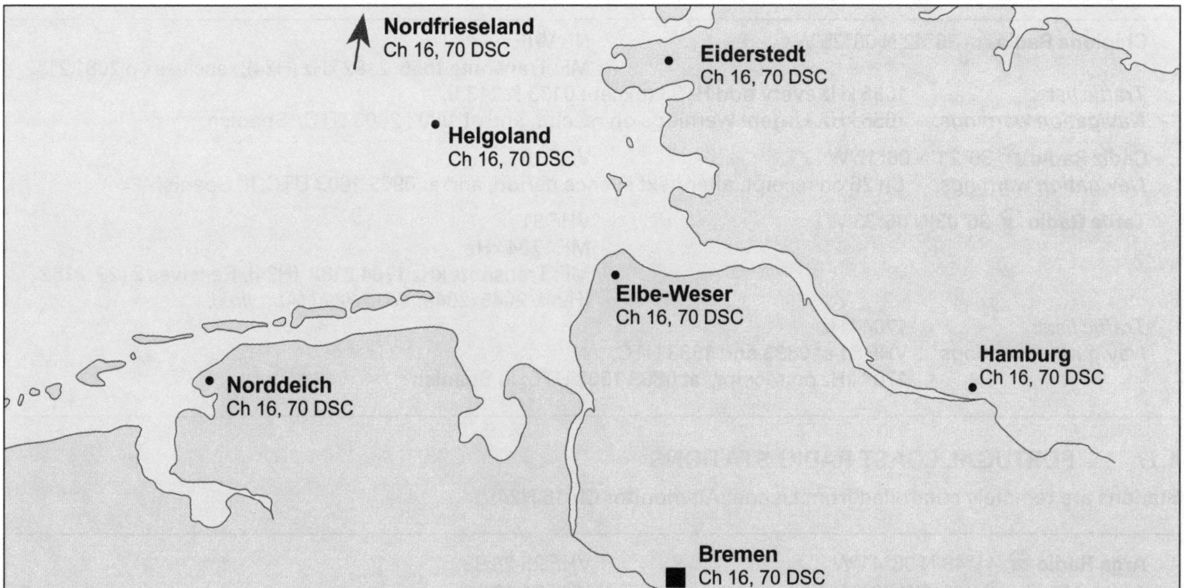

4.15.1 German Coast Radio Stations DPO7 – Seefunk (Hamburg) [MMSI 002113100]

The Coast Radio Stations provided by Seefunk are:

Hamburg (CRS)	53°33'N	09°58'E	VHF Ch 16 27	DSC Ch 70
Borkum (CRS)	53°35'N	06°40'E	VHF Ch 16 28	DSC Ch 70
Elbe Weser (CRS)	53°50'N	08°39'E	VHF Ch 16 01 24	DSC Ch 70
Helgoland (CRS)	54°11'N	07°53'E	VHF Ch 16 86	DSC Ch 70
Traffic Lists:	Ch 16 every H+30			

4.16 SPANISH COAST RADIO STATIONS

Call initially on Ch 16 (H24) using the callsign of the remotely controlled station which will switch you to a working channel. Dedicated Autolink channels are in brackets; before calling verify that the Autolink chan is not in use. Traffic lists are broadcast only on MF, every odd H+33, 0333-2333 UTC, except 2133.

NORTH SPAIN

Stations are remotely controlled by Bilbao Comms Centre.

Pasajes Radio (CRS) 43°17'N 01°55'W — VHF 27
Navigation warnings: VHF Ch 27 on receipt, after next silence period and at 0803 1503 UTC, in Spanish.

Machichaco Radio (CRS) 43°27'N 02°45'W — No VHF
MF: Transmits **1707**, 2182 kHz (H24); receives on 2132, 2045, 2048, 2182 (H24).
Traffic lists: 1707 kHz. Every odd H+33
Navigation warnings: 1707 kHz. Urgent warnings on receipt, after next silence period at 0833 and 2033 UTC in Spanish and at 0033 0433 0833 1233 1633 and 2033 UTC **in English** and Spanish

Bilbao — VHF 26
Navigation warnings: VHF 26 at 0933 and 1533 UTC, in Spanish

Santander — VHF 24
Navigation warnings: VHF 24 at 0803 1503 UTC, in Spanish

Cabo Peñas — VHF 26, MF 1677 kHz
Navigation warnings: VHF 26 at 0903 and 1603 UTC, in Spanish

Navia — VHF 27
Navigation warnings: VHF 27 at 0833 and 1533 UTC, in Spanish

SOUTH WEST SPAIN

Stations are remotely controlled from Malaga. All monitor Ch 16 H24

Chipiona Radio (CRS) 36°42'N 06°25'W — No VHF
MF: Transmits 1656, 2182 kHz (H24); receives on 2081 2182
Traffic lists: 1656 kHz every odd H+33 (except 0133 & 2133).
Navigation warnings: 1656 kHz. Urgent warnings on receipt, and at 0803 2003 UTC. Spanish.

Cádiz Radio (CRS) 36°21'N 06°17'W — VHF 26
Navigation warnings: Ch 26 on receipt, after next silence period, and at 0903 1603 UTC, in Spanish .

Tarifa Radio (CRS) 36°03'N 05°33'W — VHF 81
MF 1704 kHz
MF: Transmits kHz **1704** 2182 (H24). Receives 2129 2182 (H24), 2045 2048. *2610 3290 (Autolink).*
Traffic lists: 1704 kHz.
Navigation warnings: VHF 81 at 0833 and 1533 UTC.
1704 kHz on receipt, at 0803 1503 UTC, in Spanish

4.17 PORTUGAL COAST RADIO STATIONS

Stations are remotely controlled from Lisboa. All monitor Ch 16 H24)

Arga Radio (CRS) 41°48'N 08°41'W — VHF 25 28 83
Arestal Radio (CRS) 40°46'N 08°21'W — VHF 24 26 85
Montejunto Radio (CRS) 39°10'N 09°03'W — VHF 23 27 87
LISBOA RADIO (CRS) 38°44'N 09°14'W — VHF 23 25 26 27 28
MF: Transmits on 2182, 2578, 2640, 2691, 2781, 3607, 2778, 2693 kHz. Receives on 2182 (kHz) (H24)
Traffic lists: 2693 kHz every even H+05, following announcement on 2182 kHz.

Atalaia Radio (CRS) 38°10'N 08°38'W — VHF 24 26 85
Picos Radio (CRS) 37°18'N 08°39'W — VHF 23 27 85
Estoi Radio (CRS) 37°10'N 07°50'W — VHF 24 28 86

Fig. 4 (5) Spanish and Portuguese coast radio stations

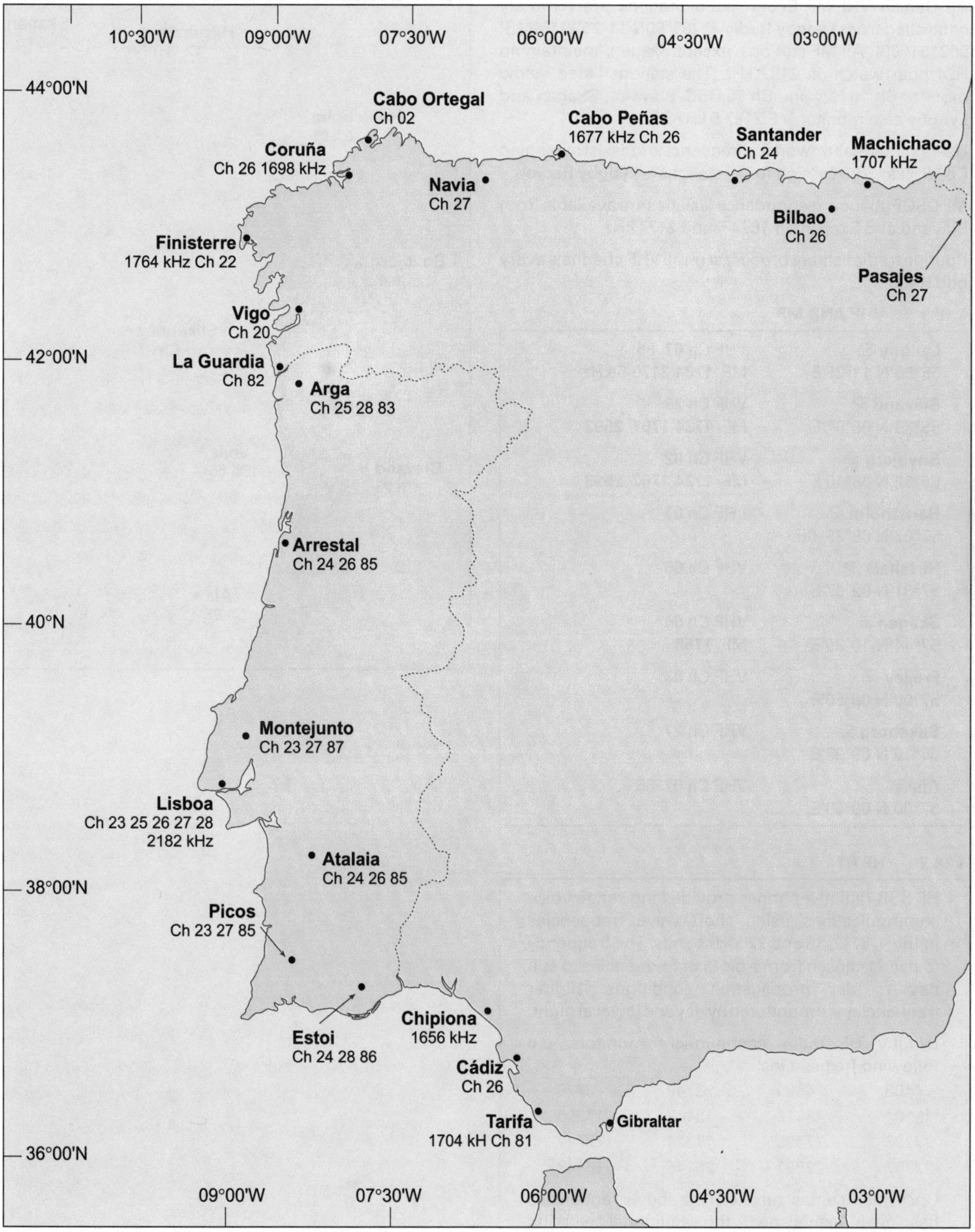

C4

4.18 DANISH COAST RADIO STATIONS

All Danish VHF/MF Coast Radio Stations are remotely controlled from **Lyngby Radio** (55°50N 11°25'E) (MMSI 002191000). All MF stations, except Skagen, maintain an H24 hour watch on 2182 kHz. The stations listed below monitor Ch 16 H24 and Ch 70 DSC. **Blåvand, Skagen and Lyngby** also monitor MF 2187·5 kHz DSC

Users should call on working frequencies to assist in keeping Ch 16 clear. The callsign for all stations is **Lyngby Radio**

MF DSC Public correspondence facilities are available from Blåvand and Skagen on 1624·5 and 2177 kHz

Routine traffic lists are broadcast on all VHF channels every odd H+05.

4.18.1 VHF AND MF

Lyngby 55°50'N 11°25'E	VHF Ch **07** 85 MF **1704** 2170·5 kHz
Blåvand 55°33'N 08°07'E	VHF Ch **23** MF **1734** 1767 **2593**
Bovbjerg 56°32'N 08°10'E	VHF Ch **02** MF **1734** 1767 **2593**
Hanstholm 57°07'N 08°39'·0E	VHF Ch **01**
Hirtshals 57°31'N 09°57'E	VHF Ch **66**
Skagen 57°44'N 10°35'E	VHF Ch **04** MF **1758**
Frejlev 57°00'N 09°50'E	VHF Ch **03**
Silkeborg 56°10'N 09°32'E	VHF Ch **27**
Ais 57°00'N 09°50'E	VHF Ch **07** 85

4.18.2 HF RT

HF SSB radiotelephones provide long range voice communications using short wave frequencies in the 4, 8, 12, 16 and 22 MHz bands. The frequency to use is chosen from a block of frequencies to suit day to day propagation conditions. Higher frequencies are monitored by day and lower at night.

Lyngby HF radio continuously monitors the following frequencies:

4408	4429	8740	8770
13104	13116	13143	17290
17293	17305	17344	22741
22747	22801	26145	16148

Once initial contact on one of the above frequencies has been established, the additional working frequencies available are:

4357	4399	4414	4426
6507	6513	8785	8791
8797	13131	13152	17254
17281	22726	22732	22777

Fig. 4 (6) Danish coast radio stations

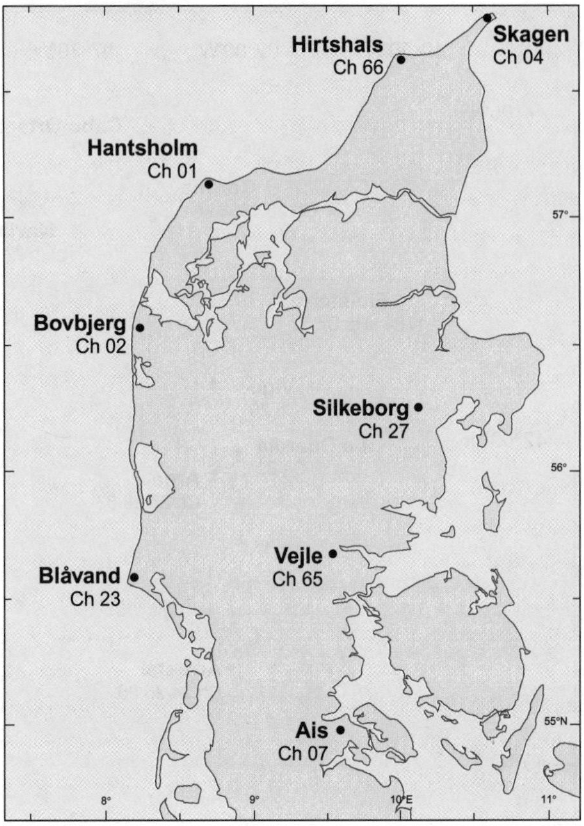

Plain sailing

Met Office

For marine weather services, visit

www.metoffice.com/
leisure marine

or call 0845 300 0300

Chapter 5

Weather

Contents

5.1 **GENERAL WEATHER INFORMATION** Page 82
5.1.1 Map of Shipping forecast areas ... 82
5.1.2 Shipping forecast record ... 83
5.1.3 Beaufort wind scale ... 84
5.1.4 Barometer and temperature scales ... 85
5.1.5 Terms used in weather bulletins ... 85
5.2 **SOURCES OF WEATHER INFORMATION** ... 86
5.2.1 BBC Radio 4 Shipping forecast ... 86
5.2.2 Contents of shipping forecast ... 86
5.2.3 Inshore waters forecast ... 86
5.2.4 BBC general (land) forecasts ... 86
5.2.5 Selected UK local radio stations ... 87
5.3 **NAVTEX** ... 88
5.3.1 Introduction ... 88
5.3.2 Messages ... 88
5.3.3 Message categories ... 89
5.3.4 Stations ... 89
5.4 **TELEPHONE AND FAX** ... 89
5.4.1 Marinecall ... 89
5.4.2 Coastal reports (Marinecall Select) ... 90
5.4.3 Weather by FAX (MetFAX marine) ... 90
5.4.4 Short message service (SMS) ... 91
5.4.5 How to use SMS ... 91
5.4.6 SMS forecast areas ... 91
5.4.7 Shipping forecast sea areas ... 92
5.4.8 Coastal Station reports ... 92
5.4.9 Charging information ... 92
5.5 **WEATHER FORECASTERS** ... 93
5.5.1 Weather centres ... 93
5.5.2 Forecaster direct (MetCALL direct) ... 93
5.6 **HF RADIO FACSIMILE BROADCASTS** ... 93
5.6.1 Introduction ... 93
5.6.2 UK HF Fax stations ... 93
5.6.3 Schedule of UK Fax broadcasts ... 93
5.7 **MISCELLANEOUS SOURCES** ... 94
5.7.1 HM Coastguard ... 94
5.7.2 Internet (MetWEB) ... 94
5.7.3 Press forecasts ... 94
5.7.4 Television forecasts ... 94
5.7.5 Aviation Volmet ... 94
WEATHER BROADCASTS:
5.8 **UK COASTGUARD** ... 95
5.9 **CHANNEL ISLANDS: CRS** ... 96
5.10 **EIRE: CRS AND COAST GUARD** ... 98
5.11 **METAREAS I & II – UK AND FRANCE** ... 100
5.12 **FRANCE: CROSS** ... 101
5.13 **N AND NW: SPAIN CRS** ... 105
5.14 **PORTUGAL: CRS** ... 108
5.15 **SW SPAIN: CRS** ... 109
5.16 **GIBRALTAR: RADIO STATIONS** ... 109
5.17 **BELGIUM: CRS** ... 110
5.18 **NETHERLANDS COASTGUARD** ... 110
5.19 **GERMANY: CRS AND COASTGUARD** ... 111
5.20 **DENMARK: CRS** ... 113

5.1 GENERAL WEATHER INFORMATION

5.1.1 Map of UK shipping forecast areas

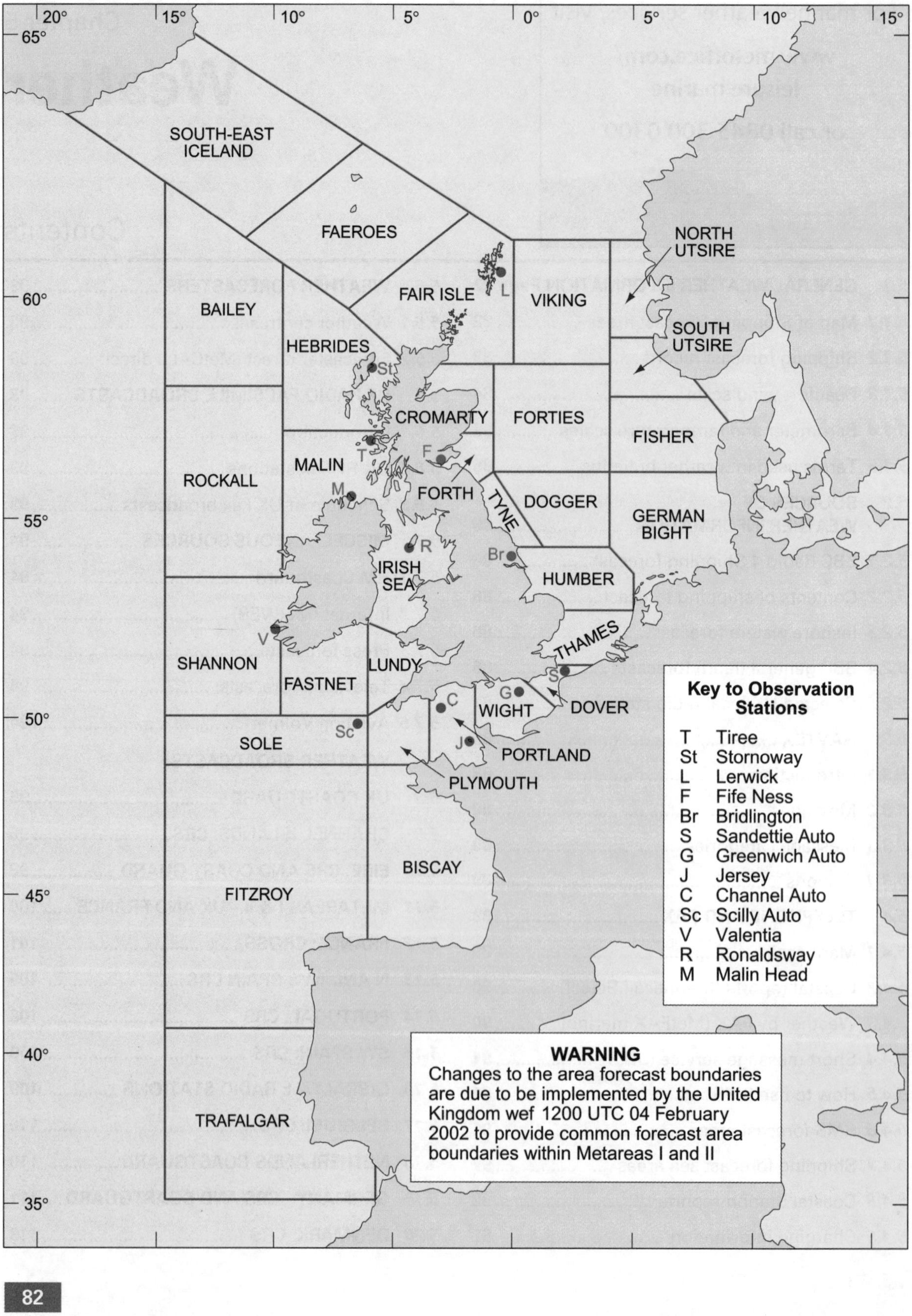
20°
15°
10°
5°
0°
5°
10°
15°
65°
60°
55°
50°
45°
40°
35°
SOUTH-EAST ICELAND
FAEROES
FAIR ISLE
VIKING
NORTH UTSIRE
SOUTH UTSIRE
BAILEY
HEBRIDES
CROMARTY
FORTIES
FISHER
ROCKALL
MALIN
FORTH
TYNE
DOGGER
GERMAN BIGHT
IRISH SEA
HUMBER
THAMES
SHANNON
FASTNET
LUNDY
WIGHT
DOVER
SOLE
PORTLAND
PLYMOUTH
BISCAY
FITZROY
TRAFALGAR
St
L
T
F
M
R
Br
V
S
G
C
Sc
J
Key to Observation Stations
T Tiree
St Stornoway
L Lerwick
F Fife Ness
Br Bridlington
S Sandettie Auto
G Greenwich Auto
J Jersey
C Channel Auto
Sc Scilly Auto
V Valentia
R Ronaldsway
M Malin Head
WARNING
Changes to the area forecast boundaries are due to be implemented by the United Kingdom wef 1200 UTC 04 February 2002 to provide common forecast area boundaries within Metareas I and II

5.1.2 Shipping Forecast Record

Shipping Forecast Record

Time/Day/Date ....

GENERAL SYNOPSIS at .... UT/BST

System	Present position	Movement	Forecast position	at

Gales	SEA AREA FORECAST	Wind (At first)	Wind (Later)	Weather	Visibility
	VIKING				
	NORTH UTSIRE				
	SOUTH UTSIRE				
	FORTIES				
	CROMARTY				
	FORTH				
	TYNE				
	DOGGER				
	FISHER				
	GERMAN BIGHT				
	HUMBER				
	THAMES				
	DOVER				
	WIGHT				
	PORTLAND				
	PLYMOUTH				
	BISCAY				
	FITZROY				
	SOLE				
	LUNDY				
	FASTNET				
	IRISH SEA				
	SHANNON				
	ROCKALL				
	MALIN				
	HEBRIDES				
	BAILEY				
	FAIR ISLE				
	FAEROES				
	S E ICELAND				

COASTAL REPORTS at .... BST UT	Wind Direction	Wind Force	Weather	Visibility	Pressure	Change
Tiree (T)						
Stornoway (St)						
Lerwick (L)						
Fife Ness (F)						
Bridlington (Br)						
Sandettie auto (S)						

COASTAL REPORTS	Wind Direction	Wind Force	Weather	Visibility	Pressure	Change
Greenwich Lt V (G)						
Jersey (J)						
Channel auto (C)						
Scilly auto (Sc)						
Valentia (V)						
Ronaldsway (R)						
Malin Head (M)						

C5

5.1.3 Beaufort scale

Force	Wind speed (knots)	(km/h)	(m/sec)	Description	State of sea	Probable wave ht(m)
0	0–1	0–2	0–0·5	Calm	Like a mirror	0
1	1–3	2–6	0·5–1·5	Light air	Ripples like scales are formed	0
2	4–6	7–11	2–3	Light breeze	Small wavelets, still short but more pronounced, not breaking	0·1
3	7–10	13–19	4–5	Gentle breeze	Large wavelets, crests begin to break; a few white horses	0·4
4	11–16	20–30	6–8	Moderate breeze	Small waves growing longer; fairly frequent white horses	1
5	17–21	31–39	8–11	Fresh breeze	Moderate waves, taking more pronounced form; many white horses, perhaps some spray	2
6	22–27	41–50	11–14	Strong breeze	Large waves forming; white foam crests more extensive; probably some spray	3
7	28–33	52–61	14–17	Near gale	Sea heaps up; white foam from breaking waves begins to blow in streaks	4
8	34–40	63–74	17–21	Gale	Moderately high waves of greater length; edge of crests break into spindrift; foam blown in well-marked streaks	5·5
9	41–47	76–87	21–24	Severe gale	High waves with tumbling crests; dense streaks of foam; spray may affect visibility	7
10	48–55	89–102	25–28	Storm	Very high waves with long overhanging crests; dense streams of foam make surface of sea white. Heavy tumbling sea; visibility affected	9
11	56–63	104–117	29–33	Violent storm	Exceptionally high waves; sea completely covered with long white patches of foam; edges of wave crests blown into froth. Visibility affected	11
12	64 plus	118 plus	33 plus	Hurricane	Air filled with foam and spray; sea completely white with driving spray; visibility very seriously affected	14

Notes: (1) The state of sea and probable wave heights are a guide to what may be expected in the open sea, away from land. In enclosed waters, or near land with an offshore wind, wave heights will be less but possibly steeper – particularly with wind against tide.

(2) It should be remembered that the height of sea for a given wind strength depends upon the fetch and length of time for which the wind has been blowing.

5.1.4 Barometer and temperature conversion scales

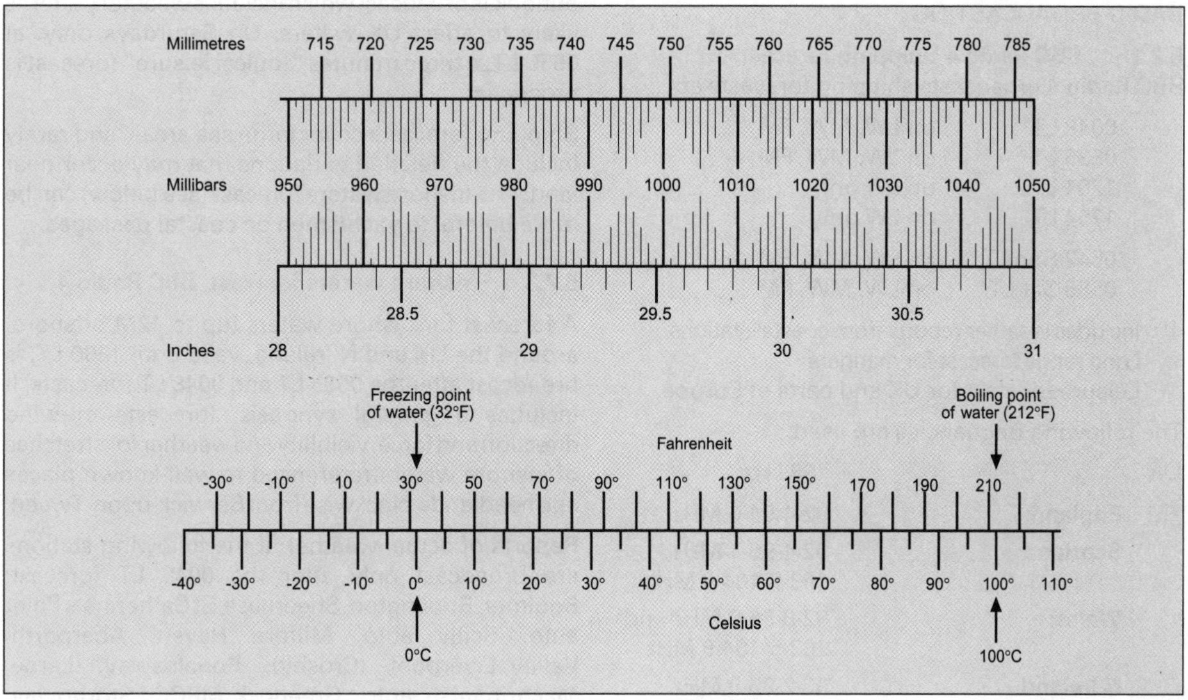

5.1.5 Terms used in weather bulletins

a. Speed of movement of pressure systems

Slowly:	Moving at less than 15 knots
Steadily:	Moving at 15 to 25 knots
Rather quickly:	Moving at 25 to 35 knots
Rapidly:	Moving at 35 to 45 knots
Very rapidly:	Moving at more than 45 knots

b. Visibility

Good:	More than 5 miles
Moderate:	2 – 5 miles
Poor:	1000 metres – 2 miles
Fog:	Less than 1000 metres

c. Barometric pressure changes (tendency)

Rising or falling slowly: Pressure change of 0·1 to 1·5 millibars in the preceding 3 hours.

Rising or falling: Pressure change of 1·6 to 3·5 millibars in the preceding 3 hours.

Rising or falling quickly: Pressure change of 3·6 to 6 millibars in the preceding 3 hours.

Rising or falling very rapidly: Pressure change of more than 6 millibars in the preceding 3 hours.

Now rising (or falling): Pressure has been falling (rising) or steady in the preceding 3 hours, but at the time of observation was definitely rising (falling).

d. Gale warnings

A *'Gale'* warning means that winds of at least force 8 (34-40 knots) or gusts reaching 43-51 knots are expected somewhere within the area, but not necessarily over the whole area. *'Severe Gale'* means winds of at least force 9 (41-47 knots) or gusts reaching 52-60 knots. *'Storm'* means winds of force 10 (48-55 knots) or gusts of 61-68 knots. *'Violent Storm'* means winds of force 11 (56-63 kn) or gusts of 69 kn or more; and *'Hurricane Force'* means winds of force 12 (64 knots or more).

Gale warnings remain in force until amended or cancelled ('gales now ceased'). If a gale persists for more than 24 hours the warning is re-issued.

e. Timing of gale warnings

Imminent	Within 6 hrs of time of issue
Soon	Within 6 – 12 hrs of time of issue
Later	More than 12 hrs from time of issue

f. Strong wind warnings

Issued, if possible 6 hrs in advance, when winds F6 or more are expected up to 5M offshore; valid for 12 hrs.

g. Wind

Wind direction: Indicates the direction from which the wind is blowing.

Winds becoming cyclonic: Indicates that there will be considerable changes in wind direction across the path of a depression within the forecast area.

Veering: The changing of the wind in a clockwise direction, i.e. SW to W.

Backing: The changing of the wind in an anti-clockwise direction, i.e. W to SW.

5.2 SOURCES OF WEATHER INFORMATION

RADIO BROADCASTING

5.2.1 BBC Radio 4 Shipping forecast

BBC Radio 4 broadcasts shipping forecasts at:

0048 LT①	on LW, MW, FM
0535 LT①	on LW, MW, FM
1201 LT	on LW only
1754 LT	on LW only
0542 Sun LT②	on LW, MW, FM
0556 Sat LT③	on LW, MW, FM

① Includes weather reports from coastal stations
② Long range forecast for mariners
③ Leisure forecast for UK and parts of Europe

The following frequencies are used:

LW		198 kHz
FM	**England:**	92·4-94·6 MHz
	Scotland:	92·4-96·1 MHz 103·5-104·9 MHz
	Wales:	92·8-96·0 MHz and 103·5-104·9 MHz
	N Ireland	93·2-96·0 MHz 103·5-104·9 MHz
	Channel Islands:	92·4, 94·6 MHz
MW	**Tyneside:**	603 kHz
	London and N Ireland:	720 kHz
	Redruth:	756 kHz
	Enniskillen & Plymouth:	774 kHz;
	Aberdeen:	1449 kHz
	Carlisle:	1485 kHz

5.2.2 Contents of shipping forecast

The bulletin contains a summary of gale warnings in force; a general synopsis of weather patterns for the next 24 hours with changes expected during that period; and a forecast for each sea area for the next 24 hours, giving wind direction and force, weather and visibility. Sea area **Trafalgar** is included only in the 0048 forecast. Gale warnings are also broadcast at the earliest juncture in Radio 4 programmes after receipt, as well as after the next news bulletin.

The 0048 and 0535 forecast is followed by weather reports from coastal stations. The stations used, and identification letters are shown on pages 82 and 83. as marked by their initial letters on the chart on page 82. These reports of actual weather include wind direction and Beaufort force, present weather, visibility, and (if available) sea-level pressure and tendency.

The 1201 and 1754 LT forecasts do not include reports from coastal stations.

On Sundays only, at 0542 LT, a seven day planning outlook is broadcast which includes weather patterns likely to affect UK waters. On Saturdays only, at 0556 LT, a three minutes "topical leisure" forecast is broadcast.

Shipping forecasts cover large sea areas, and rarely include the detailed variations that may occur near land. The Inshore waters forecast (see below) can be more helpful to yachtsmen on coastal passages.

5.2.3 Inshore waters forecast, BBC Radio 4

A forecast for inshore waters (up to 12M offshore) around the UK and N Ireland, valid until 1800 LT, is broadcast after the 0535 LT and 0048 LT forecasts. It includes a general synopsis, forecasts of wind direction and force, visibility and weather for stretches of inshore waters referenced to well-known places and headlands, clockwise from Berwick-upon-Tweed.

Reports of actual weather at the following stations are broadcast only after the 0048 LT forecast: Boulmer, Bridlington, Sheerness, St Catherine's Point auto, Scilly auto, Milford Haven, Aberporth, Valley, Liverpool (Crosby), Ronaldsway, Larne, Machrihanish auto, Greenock MRCC, Stornoway, Lerwick, Wick auto, Aberdeen and Leuchars. These stations are shown on page 95. See also 5.7.5.

5.2.4 BBC general (land) forecasts

Land area forecasts may include an outlook period up to 48 hours beyond the shipping forecast, more details of frontal systems and weather along the coasts. The most comprehensive land area forecasts are broadcast by BBC Radio 4 on the frequencies in 5.2.1.

Land area forecasts – Wind strength

Wind descriptions used in land forecasts, with their Beaufort scale equivalents, are:

Calm:	0	Fresh:	5
Light:	1–3	Strong:	6 – 7
Moderate:	4	Gale:	8

Land area forecasts – Visibility

The following definitions apply to land forecasts:

Mist:	Visibility between 2000m and 1000m
Fog:	Visibility less than 1000m
Dense fog:	Less than 50m

Weather systems

To obtain the best value from weather forecasts and reports, it is desirable to have some basic understanding of the characteristics and behaviour of different weather which can be expected from the passage of any particular type of weather system.

5.2.5 Selected UK Local Radio Stations

Local radio stations (both BBC and commercial) sometimes broadcast marine weather forecasts and small craft warnings. The scope and quality of these forecasts vary considerably. Broadcast times constantly change. Local radio stations often only provide land forecasts covering large areas but without giving wind direction and speed.

Gale warnings and Strong Wind warnings (winds of Force 6 or more expected within the next 12 hrs, up to 5M offshore) are usually broadcast at the first programme juncture or after the first news bulletin following receipt. The latest broadcast schedule can be obtained by ringing the phone number given.

BBC RADIO CORNWALL 103·9 MHz 630 kHz, 95·2 MHz 657 kHz, 96·0 MHz **☎: 01872 275421**
Mon-Fri: 0608 0725 0825 1225 1325 1725 1825 1925 2210 LT
Sat: 0725 0825 1315 LT
Sun: 0710 0925 1310 LT

BBC RADIO DEVON 95·8 MHz 990 kHz, 103·4 MHz 855 kHz, 94·8 MHz 801 kHz, 103·4 MHz 1458 kHz **☎: 01752 260323**
Mon-Fri: 0530 0605 0833 1330 1550 LT
Sat: 0605 0833 1305 LT
Sun: 0605 0833 1307 LT

BBC RADIO SOLENT 96·1 MHz 999 kHz, 103·8 kHz 1359 kHz **☎: 023 8033 1311**
Mon-Fri: 0735 0835 1130 1230 1325 1425 1525 1625 1735 1835 2305 LT
Sat: 0635 0735 0835 0935 1035 1235 1310 1757 LT
Sun: 0735 0905 1505 2305 LT

BBC RADIO KENT **96·7 MHz, 104·2 MHz 774 kHz, 97·6 MHz 1602 kHz** **☎: 01634 830505**
Mon-Fri: 0530 0630 0730 0830 1730 LT
Sat: 0630 0730 0830 1305 LT
Sun: 0830 0930 1305 LT

BBC ESSEX **103·5 MHz 729 kHz, 95·3 MHz 1530 kHz, 765 kHz** **☎: 01245 262393**
Mon-Sun: 0640 0740 1740 1840 LT

BBC RADIO SUFFOLK **103·9 MHz, 95·5 MHz, 104·6 MHz** **☎:01473 250000**
Mon-Fri: 0617 0717 0817 1305 1717 1805 LT
Sat: 0705 0805 1305 LT
Sun: 0705 0805 1305 LT
* Forecasts direct from Norwich Weather Centre on Mon-Fri: at0650 0750 1250 1750 1850 LT
Sat at: 0650 0750 1250 Ly. Sundays at: 0750 1150 LT

BBC RADIO HUMBERSIDE 95·9 MHz 1485 kHz **☎: 01482 323232**
Mon-Fri: 0632 0732 0832 1332 1632 1732 1832 LT
Sat-Sun: 0732 0832 1309 LT

BBC RADIO CLEVELAND **95·0 MHz 95·8 MHz** **☎: 01642 225211**
Mon-Fri: 0645 0745 0845 1345 1645 1715 1815 LT
Sat: 0645 0745 0945 1245 1345 LT
Sun: 0745 0845 0945 LT

BBC RADIO NEWCASTLE **95·4 MHz 1458 kHz, 96·0 MHz 103·7 MHz 104·4 MHz** **☎: 0191 232 4141**
Mon-Fri: 0655 0755 0855 1155 1655 1755 LT
Sat-Sun: 0755 0855 0955 LT

NEVIS RADIO **96·6 MHz 102·3 MHz**
Mon-Sun: **0710 0730 0810 0830 0910 0930 LT, then every H+06 (1000-2400) 1750 LT.**

BBC RADIO CUMBRIA **756 kHz 837 kHz 1458 kHz 96·1 MHz 104·1 MHz** **☎: 01228 592444**
Mon-Fri: 0632 0732 0832 1632 1732 LT
Sat-Sun: 0732 0832 1132 LT

BBC RADIO MERSEYSIDE **95·8 MHz 1485 kHz** **☎: 0151 708 5500**
Mon-Fri: 0705 0805 1208 1310 1605 1716 1746 LT
Sat: 0742 LT

BBC RADIO GUERNSEY **93·3 MHz 1116 kHz** **☎: 01481 728977**
Mon-Fri: 0807 1235 1710 LT
Sat-Sun: 0810 LT

BBC RADIO JERSEY **88·8 MHz 1026 kHz** **☎: 01534 870000**
Mon-Fri: 0635 1800 LT
Sat-Sun: 0735 LT

RADIO FOYLE **93·1 MHz 792 kHz** **☎: 02871 378600**
Mon-Sun: Every H+00 (0900-1200 LT) then 1230 1400 1500 1600 1730 LT

C5

5.3 NAVTEX

5.3.1 Introduction

Navtex prints or displays navigational warnings, weather forecasts and other MSI by means of a dedicated aerial and receiver with built-in printer or screen. Navtex is a component of GMDSS.

All messages are in English on a single frequency of 518 kHz, with excellent coverage of Europe. A second frequency, 490 kHz is rapidly becoming available for local language broadcasts. 490 kHz is available from all three UK Navtex transmitters. Interference between stations is avoided by time sharing and by limiting the range of transmitters to about 300M. Three stations cover the UK.

The user programmes the receiver for the station(s) and message category(s) required. Navwarnings (A), Gale warnings (B) and SAR (D) are alway s printed.

5.3.2 Messages

Each message is prefixed by a four-character group. The first character is the code letter of the transmitting station (e.g: S for Niton). The second character is the message category, see 5.3.3. The third and fourth are message serial numbers, from 01 to 99. The serial number 00 denotes urgent messages which are always printed. Messages which are corrupt or have already been printed are rejected.

Navtex information applies only to the area for which the transmitting station is responsible, Fig 5 (1).

Weather information accounts for about 75% of all messages and is particularly valuable when out of range of other sources or if there is a language problem. The areas covered by the 3 UK stations are:

Cullercoats (G) (U)	Faeroes clockwise to Wight
Niton (S) (I)	Thames clockwise to Malin
Niton (K) (A)	The French coast from Cap Gris Nez to Île de Bréhat
Portpatrick (O) (C)	Lundy clockwise to Fair Isle

Inshore forecasts on Navtex will be standardised to cover Inshore Waters out to 12M from the coast for the whole of UK, including Shetland. VHF and MF RT broadcasts will cover waters out to 60M of Shetland.

NAVAREA I (Co-ordinator – UK)		**Transmission times (UTC)**					
O	– **Portpatrick**, UK	0220Ⓐ	**0620**	1020	1420	**1820**	2220
C	– **Portpatrick**, UK (490 kHz)		**0820Ⓐ**			**2020Ⓐ**	
G	– **Cullercoats**, UK	0100Ⓐ	0500	**0900**	1300	**1700**	**2100**
U	– **Cullercoats**, UK (490 kHz)		**0720Ⓐ**			**1920Ⓐ**	
S	– **Niton**, UK	0300	**0700**	1100	1500	**1900**	2300Ⓐ
K	– **Niton**, UK (Note 1)	0140	0540	**0940**	1340	1740	**2140**
I	– **Niton**, UK (490 kHz)		**0520Ⓐ**			**1720Ⓐ**	
A	– **Niton**, UK (490 kHz) (Note 2)	0000	0400	0800	1200	1600	2000
W	– **Valentia**, Eire	0340	**0740**	1140	1540	**1940**	2340
Q	– **Malin Head,** Eire	0240	0640	**1040**	1440	1840	**2240**
P	– **Netherlands CG**, IJmuiden	0230	0630	1030	1430	1830	2230
M	– **Oostende**, Belgium	0200	0600	1000	1400	1800	2200
T	– **Oostende**, Belgium	0310	**0710**	1110	1510	**1910**	2310
L	– **Rogaland**, Norway	**0150**	0550	0950	**1350**	1750	2150
NAVAREA II (Co-ordinator – France)							
A	– **Corsen**, Le Stiff, France	**0000**	0400	0800	**1200**	1600	2000
E	– **Corsen,** Le Stiff, France (490 kHz)	0040	0440	**0840**	1240	1640	**2040**
D	– **Coruña**, Spain	**0030**	0430	0830	**1230**	1630	2230
R	– **Lisbon/Monsanto,**Portugal	0250	0650	1050	1450	1850	2250
	– **Lisbon/Monsanto**, Portugal (490 kHz)			Planned			
G	– **Tarifa,** Spain	0100	0500	**0900**	1300	1700	**2100**
I	– **Las Palmas**, Islas Canarias	0120	0520	**0920**	**1320**	**1720**	2120
NAVAREA III (Co-ordinator – Spain)							
X	– **Valencia**, Spain	0350	**0750**	1150	1550	**1950**	2350
W	– **La Garde,** (Toulon), France	0340	0740	**1140**	1540	1940	**2340**
S	– **Fort Ste Marguerite,** France (490 kHz)	0300	**0700**	1100	1500	**1900**	2300

Note: 1 In English, for Areas Golf, Hotel and India, south of the Channel median to the French Coast.
2 In French, for Areas Golf, Hotel and India, south of the Channel median to the French Coast.
Ⓐ Extended outlook three to four days or inshore waters national three-day outlook.

5.3.3 Message categories

- A Navigational warnings
- B Gale warnings
- C Ice reports (unlikely to apply in UK)
- D SAR information and pirate attack warnings
- E Weather forecasts
- F Pilot service messages
- H Loran-C messages
- J Satnav messages
- K Other electronic navaid messages
- L Subfacts and Gunfacts for the UK
- V Amplifying details of nav warnings initially sent under A; plus the weekly oil rig list.
- Z No messages on hand at scheduled time

5.3.4 Stations

The table on p 88 shows Navtex stations in Navareas I to III, and their identity codes and transmission times (UTC). Times of weather messages are shown in **bold**.

Notes: **Oostende (M)** transmits nav warnings for the area bounded by North Foreland and Lowestoft on the UK coast, longitude 03°E and the Belgian/French coasts to Calais. **Oostende (T)** provides nav info for the Belgian coast and weather for sea areas Thames and Dover.

5.4 TELEPHONE & FAX

5.4.1 Marinecall

Provides recorded telephone forecasts for 16 inshore areas around the UK. Dial **09068-500 + Area number** shown on the Marinecall map (see Fig. 5 (2). Calls cost 50p per minute at all times.

Forecasts cover the inshore waters out to 12M offshore for up to 48 hrs and include: General situation, any strong wind or gale warnings in force, wind, weather, visibility, sea state, maximum air temperature and sea temperature. The two-day forecasts are followed by forecasts for days three to five. Forecasts are updated at 0700 and 1900 daily. Area 432 (Channel Islands), is updated at 0700, 1300 and 1900 daily.

The local inshore forecast for Shetland is not given by Marinecall, but is available from Lerwick CG on ☎ 01595 692976. Or dial ☎ 09068 500 426 for a Weathercall general land forecast for Caithness, Orkney and Shetland.

Planning forecasts for the following areas are updated at 0800 daily.

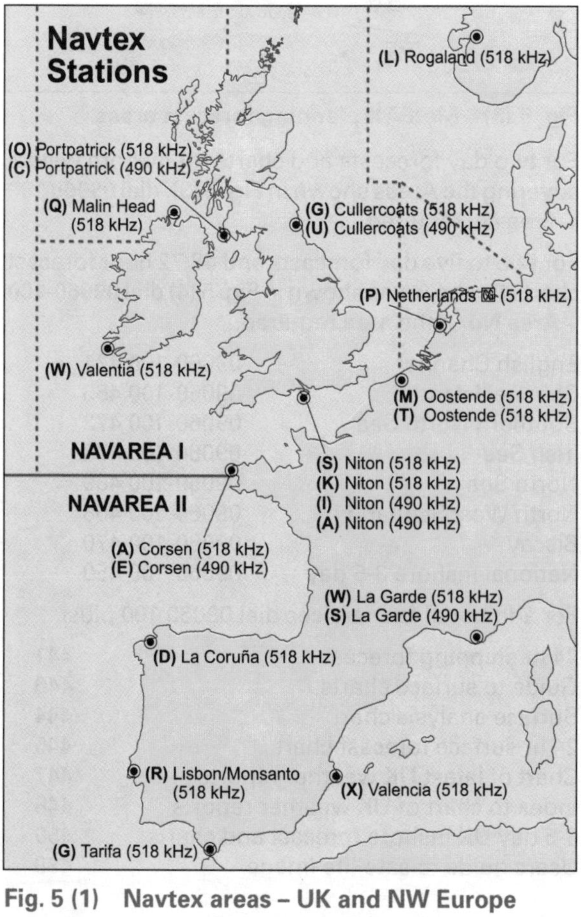

Fig. 5 (1) Navtex areas – UK and NW Europe

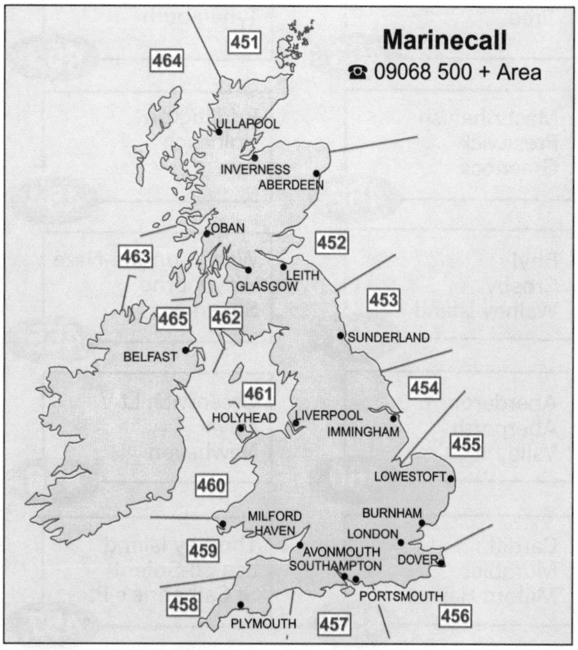

Fig 5 (2) Marinecall and MetFAX areas

National inshore 3 to 5-day **450**	English Channel 2 to 5-day **992**
Southern North Sea 2 to 5-day **991**	Irish Sea 2 to-5 day **954**

5.4.2 Coastal reports (Marinecall Select)

For latest weather reports and forecasts from 47 coastal stations dial ☎ 09068 110 010 and follow instructions, keying in the three-digit area number shown in Fig 5 (2), when requested.

Each of the 16 Marinecall areas contains two to four actual weather reports, which are updated hourly.

The reports include details of wind/gusts, visibility, weather, cloud, temperature, pressure and tendency. After these reports a two day or three – five day forecast for that area is available.

Reports	*Area No*	*Reports*	*Area No*
Ballycastle Bangor Harbour Malin Head	465	Cape Wrath Wick Lossiemouth	451
Benbecula Aultbea Butt of Lewis	464	Peterhead Aberdeen Fife Ness	452
Oban Tiree	463	Boulmer Tynemouth	453
Machrihanish Prestwick Greenock	462	Bridlington Holbeach	454
Rhyl Crosby Walney Island	461	Walton-on-the-Naze Weybourne Sheerness	455
Aberdaron Aberporth Valley	460	Greenwich Lt V Dover Newhaven	456
Cardiff Mumbles Milford Haven	459	Thorney Island Lee-on-Solent St Catherine's Pt	457
Channel Lt V Guernsey Jersey Bréhat	432	Brixham Plymouth Falmouth St Mary's, Scilly	458

5.4.3 Weather by FAX (MetFAX marine)

MetFAX Marine provides printed weather forecasts and charts by dialling 09060 100 + the area number shown in Figs 5(3) and 5(4). Calls cost £1 per minute and the length of call is about three minutes. Do not forget to press the 'Start' button on you fax machine when a connection is made.

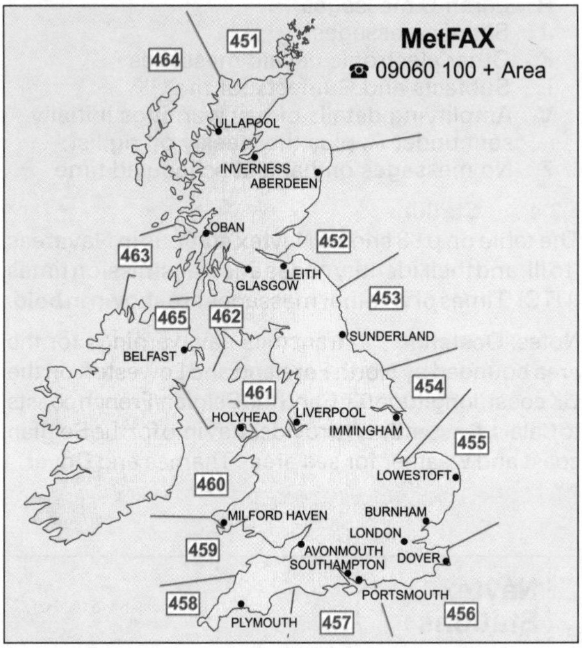

Fig. 5 (3) MetFAX planning forecast areas

For two day forecasts and charts for inshore waters covering the Areas shown in Fig. 5 (3), dial **09060 100 + Area No** required

For two to five day forecasts and 48/72 hour forecast charts for the Areas shown in Fig. 5 (4) dial **09060-100 + Area No** of the area required.

English Channel	09060-100 471
Channel Islands	09060-100 466
Southern North Sea	09060-100 472
Irish Sea	09060-100 473
North Sea	09060-100 469
North West Scotland	09060-100 468
Biscay	09060-100 470
National inshore 3-5 day	09060-100 450

For additional fax services dial 09060 100 plus:

24 hr shipping forecast	441
Guide to surface charts	446
Surface analysis chart	444
24 hr surface forecast chart	445
Chart of latest UK weather reports	447
Index to chart of UK weather reports	448
3-5 day UK inshore forecast and charts	450
Users guide to satellite image	498

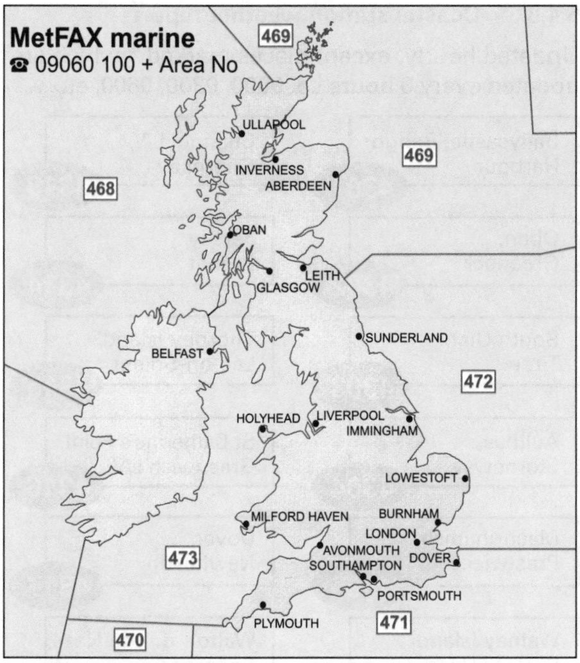

Fig. 5 (4) **MetFAX area planners**

Satellite image	499
Mediterranean plotted weather reports	474
South Coast tide tables	497
Marine index	401

Note: MetFAX, MetCALL, MetWEB, Marinecall Select and MetFAX Marine are registered trademarks of the Meteorological Office.

5.4.4 Short Message Service (SMS) – introduction

By means of the SMS, the following weather information can be obtained from the Met Office via digital mobile telephones which utilise the Vodafone network:

a. Inshore waters forecasts for seven new areas along the South coast of the UK.

b. Shipping forecasts for sea areas

c. Coastal station weather reports

It is likely that the service will be extended to cover other geographical areas in due course.

5.4.5 How to use SMS

Dial 08700 767 838 on your Vodafone Mobile and follow the recorded main menu. It will prompt you to press:

Key 1	for service information
Key 2	to receive index of products on fax
Key 3	to order a product
Key 4	to connect to customer helpline
Key 0	to return to the main menu

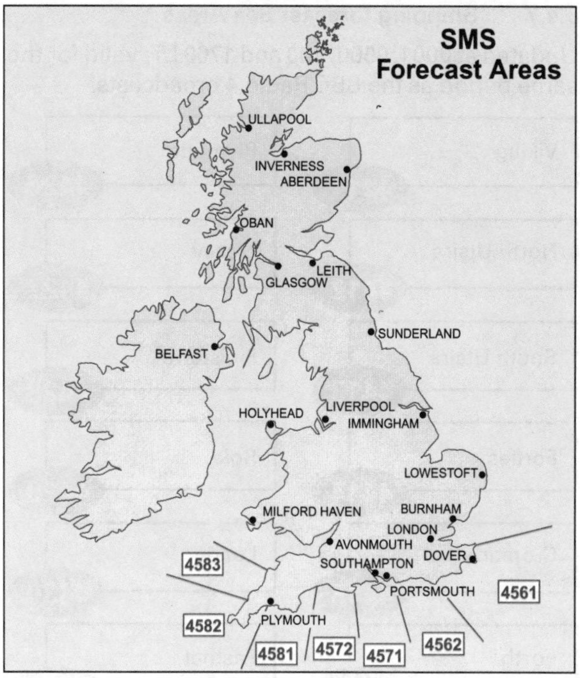

Fig. 5 (5) **SMS areas**

After pressing Key 3, press key 1 for a one-off order or key 2 for a regular order. A regular order ensures that a product, e.g. shipping forecast for sea area around Tyne, is automatically sent to your mobile as it is updated four times during the day.

Then order the product by keying in the appropriate 4 digit code from the list below. The information will duly appear on the screen of your mobile. It can then be read, stored in memory or deleted.

5.4.6 SMS Inshore waters forecast areas

Updated at 0530 for the period 0600 to 1200, 1130 for the period 1200 to 1800 and 1630 for the period 1700 to 2300.

Area	Code
North Foreland to Beachy Head	4561
Beachy Head to Selsey Bill	4562
Selsey Bill to Durlston Head	4571
Durlston Head to Lyme Regis	4572
Lyme Regis to Looe	4581
Looe to Padstow	4582
Padstow to Hartland Point	4583

5.4.7 Shipping forecast Sea Areas

Updated at 0001, 0500, 100 and 1700 LT; valid for the same period as the BBC Radio 4 broadcasts.

Viking	4411	Plymouth	4426
North Utsira	4412	Biscay	4427
South Utsira	4413	Finisterre	4428
Forties	4414	Sole	4429
Cromarty	4415	Lundy	4430
Forth	4416	Fastnet	4431
Tyne	4417	Irish Sea	4432
Dogger	4418	Shannon	4433
Fisher	4419	Rockall	4434
German Bight	4420	Malin	4435
Humber	4421	Hebrides	4436
Thames	4422	Bailey	4437
Dover	4423	Fair Isle	4438
Wight	4424	Faeroes	4439
Portland	4425	South East Iceland	4440

5.4.8 Coastal station weather reports

Updated hourly, except places marked * which are updated every 3 hours i.e. 0000, 0300, 0600, etc...

Ballycastle, Bangor Harbour	4301	Channel L/V, Guernsey	4313
Oban, Greenock	4302	Jersey, Brehat	4314
South Uist, Tiree	4303	Thorney Island, Lee-on-Solent	4315
Aultbea, Stornoway	4304	St Catherine's Point, Greenwich L/V	4316
Machrihanish, Prestwick	4305	Dover, Newhaven	4317
Walney Island, St Bees Head	4306	Walton-on-the-Naze, Sheerness	4318
Rhyl, Crosby	4307	Weybourne Holbeach	4319
Aberdaren, Valley	4308	Bridlington, Donna Nook	4320
Aberporth, Milford Haven	4309	Boulner, Tynemouth	4321
Cardiff Mumbles	4310	Aberdeen, Fife Ness	4322
Falmouth, Scilly-St Mary's	4311	Peterhead, Lossiemouth	4323
Brixham, Plymouth	4312	Sule Skerry, Wick	4324

5.4.9 Charging information and Notes

Charges vary according to the service provided and range from 20p per message on a regular basis to 50p for one-off requests and alerts. Inshore forecasts are charged at 50p per message. Coastal reports and Shipping forecasts are charged at 30p per message. Charges are only made for those messages received.

Registration and pre-set up for these services is via the internet and payment is online via credit card. There is a **MINIMUM** credit card payment of £10.

5.5 FORECASTERS

5.5.1 Weather Centres

Forecasts for port areas can be obtained at a charge from the Weather Centres listed below:

United Kingdom

London	020 7696 0573
	020 7405 4356
Birmingham	0121 717 0572
Norwich	01603 763898
Newcastle	0191 232 3808
Aberdeen Airport	01224 210575
Kirkwall Airport, Orkney	01856 873802
Sella Ness, Shetland	01806 242069
Glasgow	0141 248 7272
Manchester	0161 4771017
Leeds	0113 2440186
Cardiff	029 2022 5746
Bristol	0117 927 6265
Belfast International Airport	028 9031 2353
Jersey	01534 745550

Republic of Ireland

Central Forecast Office, Dublin (H24)	(01) 424655
Dublin Airport Met	(01) 379900 ext 4531
Cork Airport Met (0900–2000)	(021) 965974
Shannon Airport Met (H24)	(061) 61333

European continent

The ☎ Nos of forecast offices and recorded weather messages are shown under 'Telephone' for individual harbours in Areas 15–25 of Chapter 9.

5.5.2 Forecaster direct (MetCALL Direct)

A Met Office forecaster can be consulted by direct telephone line H24 for detailed discussion of, for example, the synoptic situation, specific weather windows or the longer term outlook. The consultancy would normally include a briefing and answers to any questions. A Fax forecast service is also available

To talk to a forecaster in the UK call ☎ 08700 767 888; from the Continent call ☎ + 44 8700 767 888. To talk to a forecaster in Gibraltar about weather in the Mediterranean or Canary Islands call ☎ 08700 767 818: from the Continent call + 44 8700 767 818. Payment of £15·00 is by credit card; there is no specified time limit, but 5-10 minutes is average. A Helpline is available on ☎ 08700 750 075.

Note: MetCALL is a trade mark of the Met Office.

5.6 HF RADIO FACSIMILE BROADCASTS

5.6.1 Introduction

Facsimile recorders that receive pictorial images such as weatherfax charts are now available for use in yachts and at marinas. Not all the meteorological information provided is relevant to the average yachtsman, but among items of direct interest are: Isobaric charts (actual and forecast), Sea and swell charts, Satellite cloud images, Sea temperature charts, Wind charts.

Map areas and comprehensive worldwide schedules are published in the *Admiralty List of Radio Signals, Vol 3* (NP 283).

5.6.2 UK HF Fax stations

Internationally exchanged data is processed and transmitted from various centres. In the UK these are:

Northwood (GYA) (GYZ) (GZZ) (England)

2618·5 4610 8040 11086·5kHz (all H24)

5.6.3 Schedule of selected UK Fax broadcasts

0100	72h Fronts Centres Winds
0200	72h Fronts Centres Winds
0236	Schedule
0300	Surface analysis
0348	Gale summary
0400	Surface analysis
0500	Surface analysis
0524	24h Surface prognosis
0600	Gale summary
0700	Gale summary
0748	24h Significant wind areas
0800	24h Surface prognosis
0812	48 h Significant wind areas
0824	72h Significant wind areas
0836	96h Significant wind areas
0848	48h Fronts Centres Winds
0900	Surface analysis
0912	72h Fronts Centres Winds
0924	24h Sea swell
1000	24h Surface prognosis
1100	Surface analysis
1124	96h Fronts Centres Winds
1136	120h Fronts Centres Winds
1148	Gale summary
1200	Surface analysis
1300	24h Surface prognosis
1324	24h Poor visibility
1400	72h Fronts Centres Winds
1436	Schedule
1500	Surface analysis
1536	Frontal positions (Thursday)
1548	Gale summary
1600	48h Fronts Centres Winds
1700	48h Fronts Centres Winds
1736	24h Surface prognosis
1800	Surface analysis
1900	Gale Summary
1912	24h Sea swell
2000	48h Fronts Centres Winds
2012	72h Fronts Centres Winds
2024	96h Fronts Centres Winds
2036	120h Fronts Centres Winds
2100	Surface analysis
2112	24h Significant wind areas
2124	48h Significant wind areas
2136	72h Significant wind areas
2148	96h Significant wind areas
2200	24h Surface prognosis
2300	Surface analysis

The quality of reception depends on the frequency used and the terrain between transmitter and receiver.

Additional frequencies to those above are also available for limited periods during any 24-hour period. Transmission frequencies and schedules are published in ALRS, Vol 3 (NP 283).

5.7 MISCELLANEOUS SOURCES

5.7.1 HM Coastguard

If requested the following MRCC/MRSCs may be prepared to supply reports of the present weather in their immediate vicinity. Such information only applies to reports of the present weather and do not include forecasts or information concerning other regions.

Falmouth:	☎ 01326 317575	📠 01326 318342
Brixham:	☎ 01803 882704	📠 01803 882780
Portland:	☎ 01305 760439	📠 01305 760452
Solent:	☎ 023 9255 2100	📠 023 9255 1763
Dover:	☎ 01304 210008	📠 01304 210302
Thames:	☎ 01255 675518	📠 01255 675249
Yarmouth:	☎ 01493 851338	📠 01493 852307
Humber:	☎ 01262 672317	📠 01262 606915
Forth:	☎ 01333 450666	📠 01333 450725
Aberdeen:	☎ 01224 592334	📠 01224 575920
Shetland:	☎ 01595 692976	📠 01595 694810
Stornoway:	☎ 01851 702013	📠 01851 704387
Clyde:	☎ 01475 729988	📠 01475 786988
Belfast:	☎ 028 9056 3933	📠 028 9056 5886
Liverpool:	☎ 0151 931 3341	📠 0151 931 3347
Holyhead:	☎ 01407 762051	📠 01497 764373
Milford Haven:	☎ 01646 690909	📠 01646 692176
Swansea:	☎ 01792 366534	📠 01792 369005

5.7.2 Internet (MetWEB)

A range of meteorological information is available over the Internet including MetFAX marine services, 2 and 3 to 5 day inshore forecasts, shipping forecasts, gale warnings; coastal reports charts and satellite images. Visit the Meteorological Office site at:

www.met-office.gov.uk

More information is available from the MetWEB Helpline ☎ 0845 300 0300 or e-mail:

sales@meto.gov.uk

5.7.3 Press forecasts

The interval between the time of issue and the time at which they are available next day make press forecasts of only limited value to yachtsmen. However, the better papers include a synoptic chart which, in the absence of any other chart, can help to interpret the shipping forecast.

5.7.4 Television forecasts

Some TV forecasts show a synoptic chart which, with the satellite pictures, can be a useful guide to the weather situation.

In the UK Ceefax (BBC) gives the weather index on page 400. inshore waters forecasts on p.409 and 5 day forecasts on p.405. Teletext (ITN) has the weather index on page 151, shipping forecasts on page 157 and inshore waters forecasts on page 158.

Antiope is the equivalent French system. In some remote areas abroad a TV forecast in a bar, cafe or even shop window may be the best or only source of weather information.

5.7.5 Volmet

Volmet is a meteorological service provided for aviation which continuously transmits reports of actual weather conditions and/or weather forecasts for selected airfields on HF SSB and/or VHF.

It is possible to receive HF SSB Volmet broadcasts using a suitable portable radio (such as the Sony 7600), provided it is fitted with a SSB function. Reception can often be improved by using a short wire aerial instead of the built-in extendable whip aerial.

Yachtsman wishing to monitor closely the weather situation may find the Volmet reports useful as they are now the only available source of continual weather broadcasts. The continuously updated reports of actual weather conditions can be particularly valuable when drawing your own weather map see Fig. 5 (7) for airfield locations. Reports contain: airport name, wind direction and speed, visibility, cloud amount and height, temperature and dew point, sea level pressure (QNH) and any significant weather.

The RAF Volmet continuously broadcasts actual weather reports for military and civil airports on:

5450 kHz H24 **11253** kHz H24.

Broadcasts of airfields are made twice per hour in the slot times (in minutes past the hour) allocated below:

Slot 1 H+00/30 Aldergrove;Manchester;Prestwick; Stansted; Bardufoss (Norway); Bodo (Norway); Oslo (Norway); Gibraltar; Porto (Portugal).

Slot 2 H+06/36 Benson; Brize Norton; Bruggen; Geilenkirchen; Hannover; Lyneham; Northolt; Odiham; Lyneham.

Slot 3 H+12/42 Coltishall; Cranwell, Leeming; Leuchars; Lossiemouth; Marham; St Mawgan; Waddington; Kinloss

Slot 4 H+18/48 Ascension; Bahrain; Brize Norton; Dakar (Senegal); Keflavik (Iceland); Nairobi (Kenya); Mombasa (Kenya); Montevideo; Rio de Janeiro (Brazil).

Slot 5 H+24/54 Adana (Turkey), Akrotiri (Cyprus), Ancona (Italy), Aviano (Italy); Gioia (Italy), Rimini (Italy), Rome (Italy) (Portugal); Skopje (Macedonia); Split (Croatia); Brindisi (Italy); Waddington (UK).

Shannon Volmet broadcasts on 3413 kHz (HN) and H24 on 5505 kHz, 8957 kHz and 13264 kHz (HJ). Groups of airports are broadcast every 5 mins fromH+00. Coastal airports covered by this Almanac include: Shannon, Prestwick, Dublin, Amsterdam and Hamburg; Lisbon; Santa Maria (Azores).

Fig. 5 (6) Reports of present weather

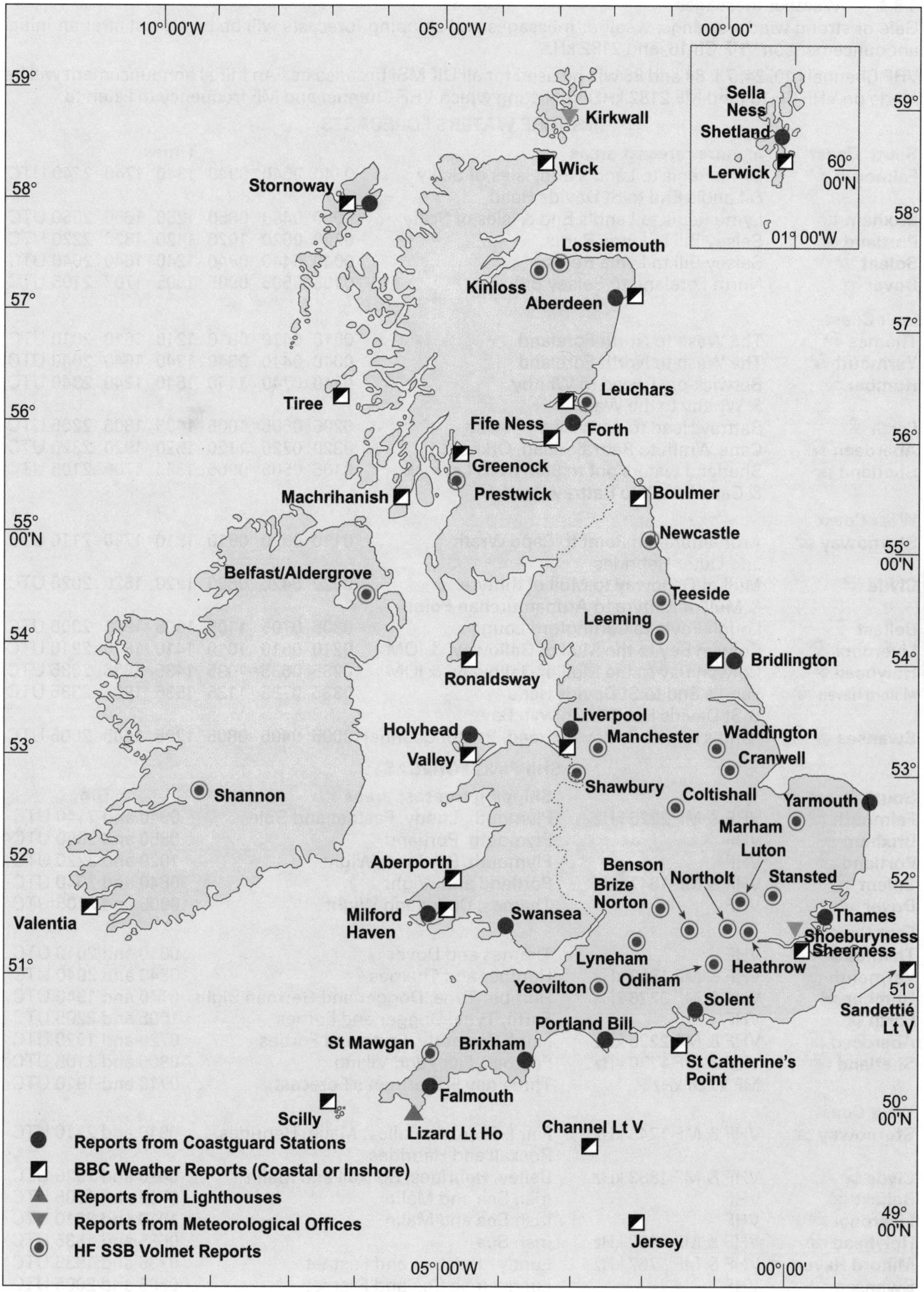

5.8 UK COASTGUARD COORDINATION CENTRES

5.8.1 Weather messages

Gale or strong wind warnings, weather messages and shipping forecasts will be broadcast after an initial announcement on VHF Ch 16, and 2182 kHz.

VHF Channels 10, 24, 73, 84 and 86 will be used for all UK MSI broadcasts. An initial announcement will be made on VHF Ch 16 (and MF 2182 kHz) indicating which VHF Channel and MF frequency to listen to.

INSHORE WATERS FORECASTS

South Coast	**Inshore forecast areas**	**Times**					
Falmouth	Lyme Regis to Land's End, Isles of Scilly & Land's End to St Davids Head	0140	0540	0940	1340	1740	2140 UTC
Brixham	Lyme Regis to Land's End & Isles of Scilly	0050	0450	0850	1250	1650	2050 UTC
Portland	Selsey Bill to Lyme Regis	0220	0620	1020	1420	1820	2220 UTC
Solent	Selsey Bill to Lyme Regis	0040	0440	0840	1240	1640	2040 UTC
Dover	North Foreland to Selsey Bill	0105	0505	0905	1305	1707	2105 UTC
East Coast							
Thames	The Wash to North Foreland	0010	0410	0810	1210	1610	2010 UTC
Yarmouth	The Wash to North Foreland	0040	0440	0840	1240	1640	2040 UTC
Humber	Berwick-on-Tweed to Whitby & Whitby to the Wash	0340	0740	1140	1540	1940	2340 UTC
Forth	Rattray Head to Berwick on Tweed	0205	0605	1005	1405	1805	2205 UTC
Aberdeen	Cape Wrath to Rattray Head, Orkney	0320	0720	1120	1520	1920	2320 UTC
Shetland	Shetland waters out to 60M from Lerwick & Cape Wrath to Rattray Head	0105	0505	0905	1305	1705	2105 UTC
West Coast							
Stornoway	Ardnamurchan Point to Cape Wrath and Outer Hebrides	0110	0510	0910	1310	1710	2110 UTC
Clyde	Mull of Galloway to Mull of Kintyre & Mull of Kintyre to Ardnamurchan Point	0020	0420	0820	1220	1620	2020 UTC
Belfast	Lough Foyle to Carlingford Lough	0305	0705	1105	1505	1905	2305 UTC
Liverpool	Colwyn Bay to the Mull of Galloway, & IOM	0210	0610	1010	1410	1810	2210 UTC
Holyhead	Colwyn Bay to the Mull of Galloway, & IOM	0235	0635	1035	1435	1835	2235 UTC
Milford Haven	Land's End to St Davids Head & St Davids Head to Colwyn Bay	0335	0735	1135	1535	1935	2335 UTC
Swansea	Land's End to St Davids Head, Bristol Channel	0005	0405	0805	1205	1605	2005 UTC

SHIPPING FORECASTS

South Coast		**Shipping forecast areas**	**Times**
Falmouth	VHF & MF 2226 kHz	Plymouth, Lundy, Fastnet and Sole	0940 and 2140 UTC
Brixham	VHF	Plymouth, Portland	0850 and 2050 UTC
Portland	VHF	Plymouth, Portland, Wight	1020 and 2220 UTC
Solent	VHF & MF 1641 kHz	Portland and Wight	0840 and 2040 UTC
Dover	VHF	Thames, Dover and Wight	0905 and 2105 UTC
East Coast			
Thames	VHF	Thames and Dover	0810 and 2010 UTC
Yarmouth	VHF & MF 1869 kHz	Humber and Thames	0840 and 2040 UTC
Humber	VHF & MF 2226 kHz	Humber,Tyne, Dogger and German Bight	0740 and 1940 UTC
Forth	VHF	Forth, Tyne, Dogger and Forties	1005 and 2205 UTC
Aberdeen	VHF & MF 2226 kHz	Fair I, Cromarty, Forth and Forties	0720 and 1920 UTC
Shetland	VHF & MF 1770 kHz	Faeroes, Fair I and Viking	0905 and 2105 UTC
	MF 2226 kHz	Three day Fisherman's Forecast	0710 and 1910 UTC
West Coast			
Stornoway	VHF & MF 1743 kHz	Fair I, Faeroes, Bailey, Malin, Hebrides, Rockall and Hebrides	0910 and 2110 UTC
Clyde	VHF & MF 1883 kHz	Bailey, Hebrides, Rockall and Malin	0820 and 2020 UTC
Belfast	VHF	Irish Sea and Malin	0705 and 1905 UTC
Liverpool	VHF	Irish Sea and Malin	1010 and 2210 UTC
Holyhead	VHF & MF 1880 kHz	Irish Sea	0635 and 1835 UTC
Milford Haven	VHF & MF 1767 kHz	Lundy, Irish Sea and Fastnet	0735 and 1935 UTC
Swansea	VHF	Lundy, Irish Sea and Fastnet	0805 and 2005 UTC

Fig. 5 (7) Coastguard weather forecasts

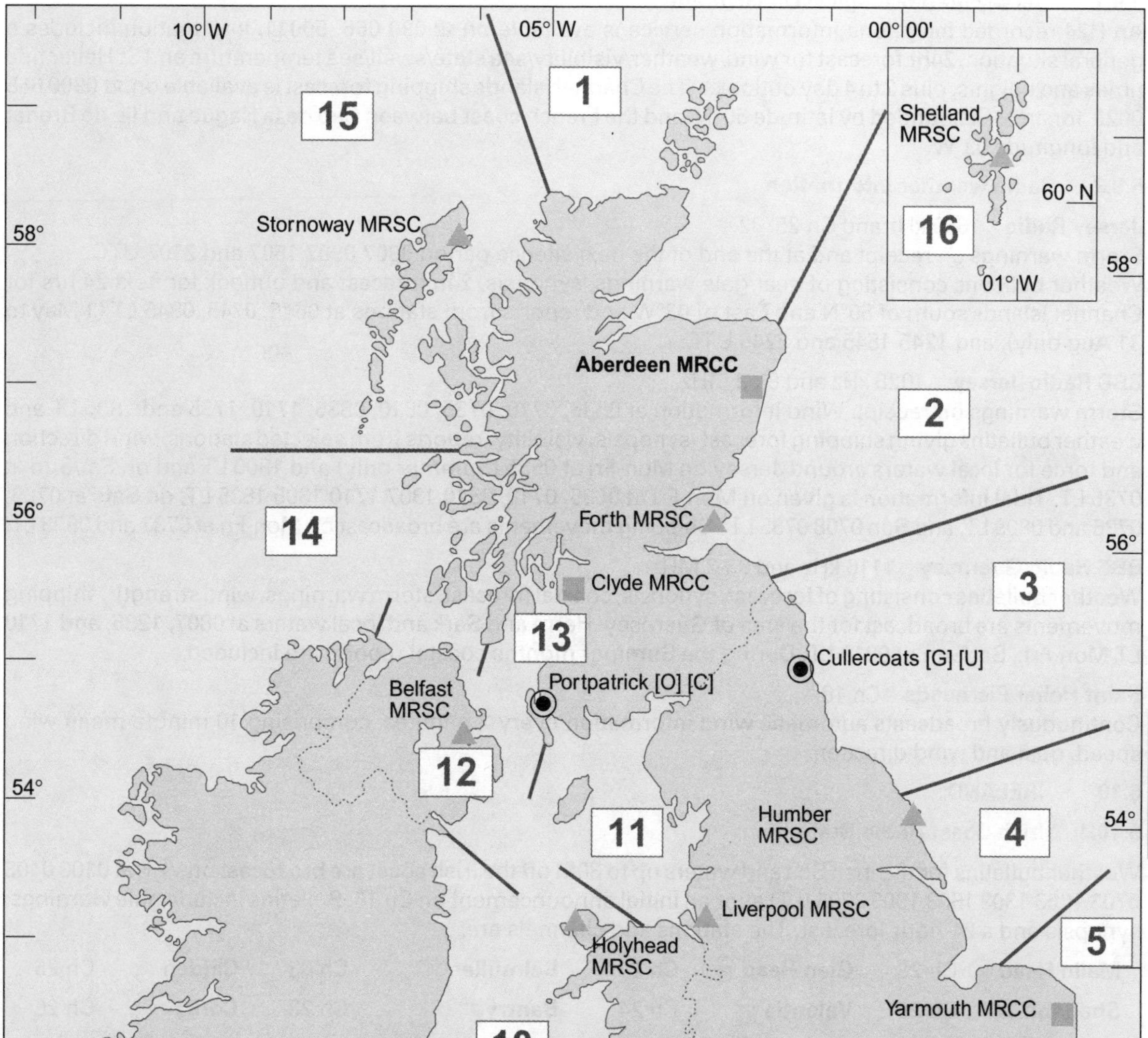

C5

5.9 CHANNEL ISLANDS

5.9.1 Jersey Meteorological Department

An H24 recorded telephone information service is available on ☎ 090 066 50011. Information includes a general situation, 24hr forecast for wind/weather/visibility/sea state/swell/sea temperature and St Helier tide times and heights, plus 2 to 4 day outlooks. The Channel Islands shipping forecast is available on ☎ 0900 665 0022 for an area bounded by latitude 50°N, and the French coast between Cap de la Hague and Ile de Brehat and longitude 03°W.

5.9.2 Radio weather information

Jersey Radio 1659 kHz and Ch 25 82
Storm warnings on receipt and at the end of the next silence period 0307 0907 1507 and 2107 UTC. Weather bulletins consisting of near gale warnings, synopsis, 24h forecast and outlook for next 24 hrs for Channel Islands south of 50°N and East of 03°W and reports from stations at 0645, 0745, 0845 LT (1 May to 31 Aug only), and 1245 1845 and 2245 UTC.

BBC Radio Jersey 1026 kHz and 88·8 MHz
Storm warnings on receipt. Wind information at 0635, 0710, 0735, 0810, 0835, 1710, 1735 and 1835 LT and weather bulletins giving shipping forecast, synopsis, visibility, reports from selected stations, wind direction and force for local waters around Jersey on Mon-Fri at 0635 (Summer only) and 1800 LT and on Sat/Sun at 0735 LT. Tidal information is given on Mon-Fri at 0635, 0710, 0810 1307 1710 1805 1835 LT; on Sats at 0709, 0735 and 0809 LT, and Sun 0708 0735 LT. Shipping movements are broadcast on Mon-Fri at 0733 and 0833 LT.

BBC Radio Guernsey 1116 kHz and 93·2 MHz
Weather bulletins consisting of forecast, synopsis, coastal forecast, storm warnings, wind strength, shipping movements are broadcast for the area of Guernsey, Herm and Sark and local waters at 0807, 1235, and 1710 LT Mon-Fri. Sat/Sun at 0810 LT. During the Summer months coastal reports are included.

Saint Helier Pierheads Ch 18
Continuously broadcasts automatic wind information every 2 minutes, comprising 10 minute mean wind speed, gust and wind direction.

5.10 IRELAND

5.10.1 Irish Coast Radio Stations

Weather bulletins for the Irish Sea and waters up to 30M off the Irish coast are broadcast on VHF at 0103 0403 0703 1003 1303 1603 1903 2203 (LT) after an initial announcement on Ch 16. Bulletins include gale warnings, synopsis and a 24-hour forecast. The stations and channels are:

Malin Head CRS	Ch 23	**Glen Head** CRS	Ch 24	**Belmullet** CRS	Ch 83	**Clifden** CRS	Ch 26
Shannon CRS	Ch 28	**Valentia** CRS	Ch 24	**Bantry** CRS	Ch 23	**Cork** CRS	Ch 26
Mine Head CRS	Ch 83	**Rosslare** CRS	Ch 23	**Wicklow Head** CRS	Ch 87	**Dublin** CRS	Ch 83
Greenore CRS	TBN	**Crookhaven** CRS	TBN	**Donegal Bay** CRS	TBN		

Valentia Radio broadcasts on MF 1752 kHz forecasts for sea areas Shannon and Fastnet at 0833, 2033 UTC, and on request. Broadcasts are given 1h earlier when DST is in force.

Gale warnings are broadcast on above VHF channels on receipt and repeated at 0033 0633 1233 1833 (LT), after an initial announcement on Ch 16. They are also broadcast by Valentia Radio on 1752 kHz at the end of the next silence period after receipt and at 0303, 0903, 1503 and 2103 (UTC) after an initial announcement on 2182 kHz. Broadcasts are given 1h earlier when DST is in force.

5.10.2 Radio Telefís Éireann (RTE Radio 1) Broadcasting coastal forecasts and gale warnings

RTE Radio 1 on 567 kHz broadcasts a synopsis, detailed forecast and current gale warnings for Irish coastal waters up to 30M offshore and the Irish Sea, a 24 hour outlook, and coastal station reports at 0602, 1253, 1823 (Sat, Sun and Public Holidays) and 1824 (Mon-Fri) 2355 UTC. Broadcasts are given 1 hour earlier when DST is in force.

The main transmitters and FM frequencies are:

East Coast Radio: Kippure 94·9 MHz, Bray Head 96·2 MHz, Wicklow Head 102·9 MHz, Arklow 104·4 MHz.
At: Every H+06 (0700-1800 LT) after the news bulletin. Broadcasts a general forecast, storm warnings and wind strength for area from Dublin Bay to Arklow Head.

Fig. 5 (8) Irish CRS and Coast Guard weather forecasts

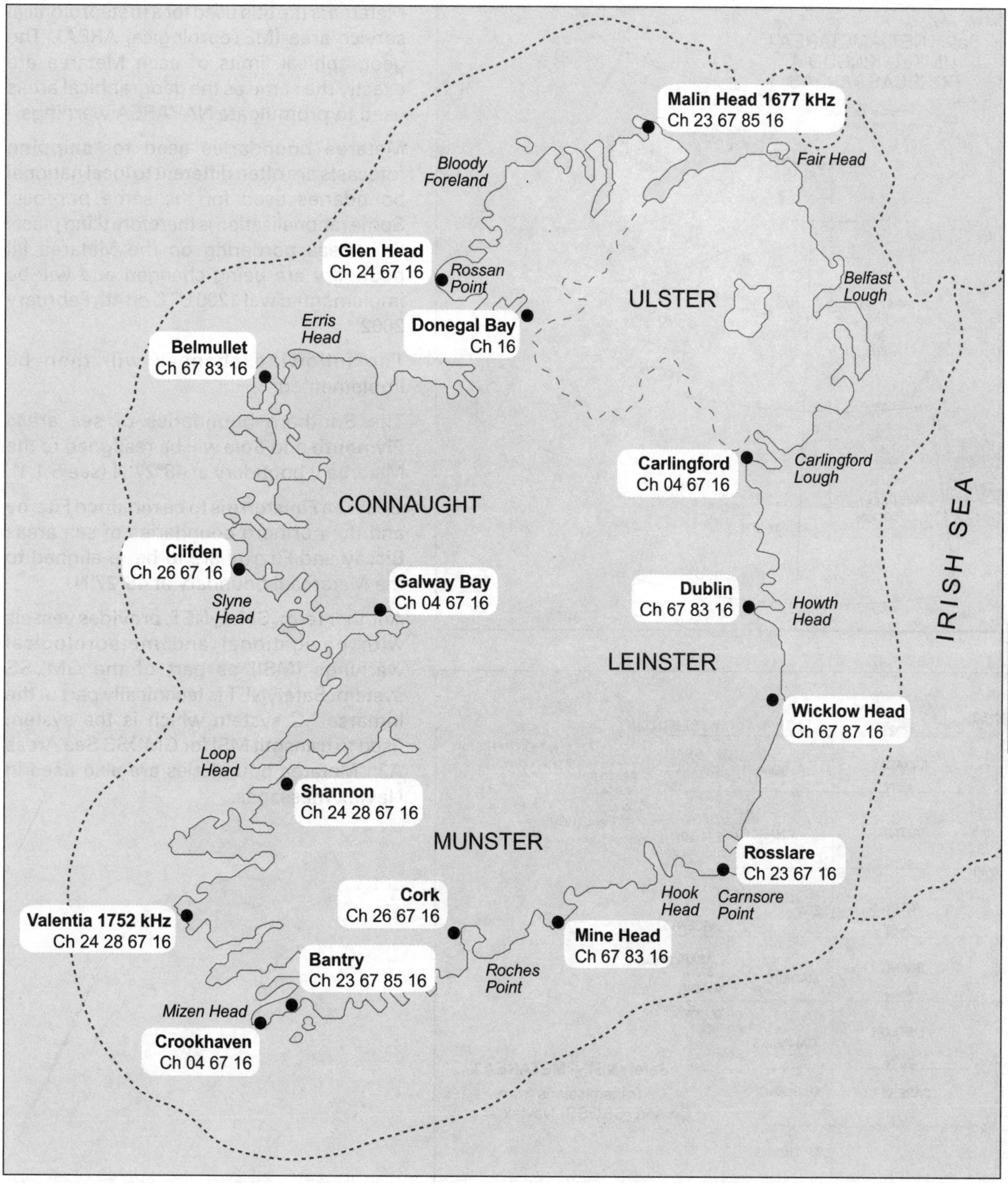

Fig. 5 (8) shows Provinces, headlands sea areas and coastal stations referred to in weather broadcasts. Forecasts for coastal waters cover areas within 30M of the shore. The Irish Sea covers the open waters of the area shown.

C5

Fig. 5 (9) UK – SafetyNET forecast areas Metarea I

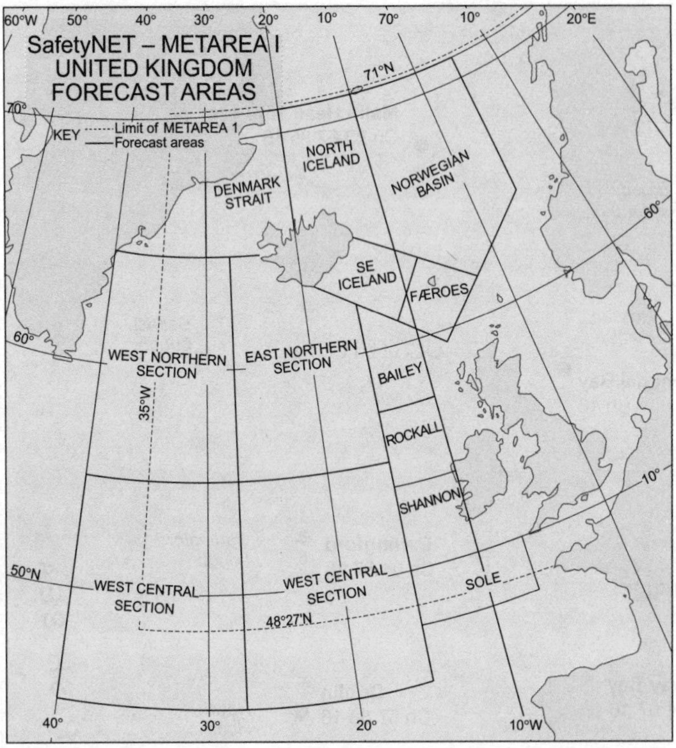

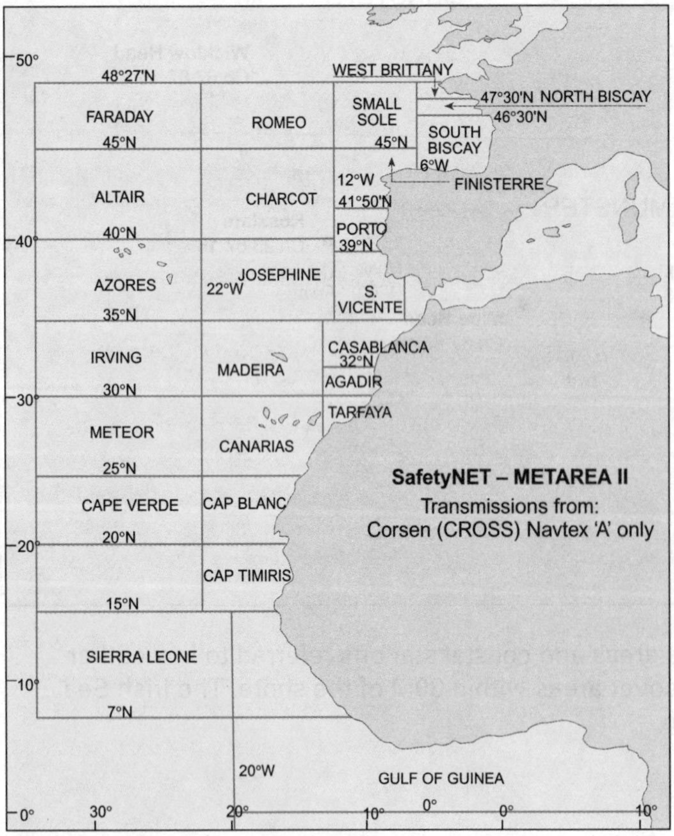

Fig. 5 (10) France – SafetyNET forecast areas Metarea II

5.11 METAREAS

Metarea is the title used for a meteorological service area (METeorological AREA). The geographical limits of each Metarea are exactly the same as the geographical areas used to promulgate NAVAREA warnings.

Metarea boundaries used for shipping forecasts are often different to local national boundaries used for the same purpose. Some rationalisation is therefore tking place. Sea areas bordering on the Metarea I/II boundary are being changed and will be implemented wef 1200 UTC on 4th February 2002.

The following changes will then be implemented:

The Southern boundaries of sea areas **Plymouth** and **Sole** will be realigned to the Metarea II boundary at 48°27'N (see 5.1.1).

Sea area **Finisterre** is to be renamed **Fitzroy** and the northern boundaries of sea areas **Biscay** and **Fitzroy** are to be re-aligned to the Metarea II boundary at 48°27'N.

Another term, SafetyNET, provides vessels with navigational and meteorological warnings (MSI) as part of the GMDSS system. SafetyNET is technically part of the Inmarsat -C system which is the system used to transmit MSI for GMDSS Sea Areas A3. Metarea boundaries are also used in Navtex messages.

South East Radio: Mount Leinster 95·6 MHz, Gorey 96·2 MHz, Wexford 96·4 MHz.
At: 0712 LT (Mon-Fri) and every H+30 (0700-1800 LT) H24 after commercial break. Broadcasts a detailed general forecast and synopsis for coastal waters, including storm warnings if adverse weather conditions are forecast.
WLR FM: Faha Ring 95·1 MHz, Carrickpherish 97·5 MHz.
At every H+03 and 1315 1815 LT broadcasts a general forecast, gale warnings, wind strength for area from Youghal to Kilmore Quay. Tidal information included from Jun-Sep.

Radio Kerry: Mullaghanish 97·0 MHz, Knockanure 97·6 MHz, Kilkieveragh 96·2MHz, Tralee 96·2 MHz.

At: 0004 0104 0704 0804 0835 0910 1004 1107 1204 1330 1404 1507 1607 1704 1740 1904 2204 2104 and 2304, and at 0755 and 1155 LT. Broadcasts a general forecast, synopsis, gale warnings and wind strength for the coastal area from Cork to Shannon.

At: 0755 and 1155 LT a fcst is broadcast including synopsis, visibility, sea state and wind strength for sea areas Fastnet and Shannon. Three Rock 88·5 MHz, Kippure 89·1 MHz, Mount Leinster 89·6 MHz, Mullaghanish 90·0 MHz, Maghera 88·8 MHz, Truskmore 88·2 MHz, Holywell Hill 89·2 MHz, Clermont Carn 95·2 MHz. MW .

5.10.3 Storm warnings

Gale warnings are broadcast by RTE Radio 1 on 567 kHz at the first programme juncture after receipt and with news bulletins; also by RTE 2FM from Athlone 612 kHz, Dublin 1278 kHz and Cork 1278 kHz.

5.10.4 Telephone and Fax

The latest Sea area forecast and gale warnings can be obtained through Weatherdial ☎ on 1550 123 855. The same information, plus isobaric, swell and wave charts are available by Fax 📠 on 1570 131 838 (H24).

5.12 FRANCE

5.12.1 Radio broadcasting

FRANCE INTER (LW) 162 kHz
For all areas: storm warnings, synopsis, 24h fcst and outlook, broadcast in French for Areas 1 to 25, 515, 516, 521-523 and 531-537 (see 5 (13) at 2003 daily. On Sat/Sun at 0654, 2003 LT.

RADIO INTERNATIONALE (RFI) 6175, 15300, 15515, 17570, and 21645 kHz
RFI broadcasts weather messages in French on HF at 1130 UTC daily. Frequencies are: 6175 kHz for North Sea, English Channel and Bay of Biscay; other frequencies are: 15300 kHz, 15515 and 21645 kHz for the North Atlantic, E of 50°W.

RADIO BLEUE (MW)
Essentially a music programme, but with Forecasts in French at 0655 LT covering:

English Channel and North Sea	–	**Paris**	864 kHz	**Lille**	1377 kHz
English Channel and East Atlantic	–	**Rennes**	711 kHz	**Brest**	1404 kHz
Bay of Biscay and East Atlantic	–	**Bordeaux**	1206 kHz	**Bayonne**	1494 kHz

LOCAL RADIO (FM)

Radio France Cherbourg 100·7 MHz
Coastal forecast, storm warnings, visibility, wind strength, tidal information, small craft warnings, in French, for the Cherbourg peninsula, broadcast at 0829 LT by:

Cherbourg	100·7 MHz	**St Vaast-la-Hougue**	85·0 MHz;
La Hague	99·8 MHz	**Barneville Carteret**	99·9 MHz.

5.12.2 Recorded forecasts by telephone

a. MÉTÉO (Weather). The BQR (Bulletin Quotidien des Renseignements) is a very informative daily bulletin displayed in Hr Mr offices and YC's. For each French port, under TELEPHONE, Météo is the ☎ of a local Met Office. Auto gives the ☎ for recorded inshore and Coastal forecasts; dial 08·36·68·08·dd (dd is the Département No, shown under each port). To select the inshore (rivage) or Coastal (Côte; out to 20M offshore) bulletin, say "STOP" as your choice is spoken. Inshore bulletins contain 5 day forecasts, local tides, signals, sea temperature, surf conditions, etc. strong wind/gale warnings, general synopsis, 24hrs forecast and outlook.

b. For Offshore bulletins (zones du large) for Channel and North Sea, Atlantic or Mediterranean, dial ☎ 08·36·68·08·08. To select desired offshore area say "STOP" as it is named. Offshore bulletins contain strong wind/gale warnings, the general synopsis and forecast, and the 5 day outlook.

C5

5.12.3 CROSS VHF broadcasts

CROSS broadcasts in French, after an announcement on Ch 16: Gale warnings, synopsis, a 12 hrs forecast, 48 hrs outlook for coastal waters. VHF channels, coastal areas covered and local times are shown below. In the English Channel broadcasts can also be given in English, on request Ch 16. Gale warnings are broadcast in French and **English** by all stations on VHF channels listed below at H+03 and at other times as shown.

CROSS GRIS-NEZ Ch 79 Belgian border to Baie de Somme

Dunkerque	0720, 1603, 1920 LT	
Gris-Nez	0710, 1545, 1910 LT	

Gale warnings on receipt, on request and at H+03 and H+10, in French and **English.**

CROSS JOBOURG Ch 80 Baie de Somme to Cap de la Hague

Ailly	0703, 1533, 1903 LT	
Antifer	0803, 1633, 2003 LT	
Port-en-Bessin	0745, 1615, 1945 LT	
Jobourg	0733, 1603, 1933 LT	
Jobourg Traffic	H+20 and H+50	Cap de la Hague to Pte de Penmarc'h
Jobourg	0715, 1545, 1915 LT	
Granville	0703, 1533, 1903 LT	

Gale warnings in French and **English** on receipt, on request and at H+03. Also by Jobourg at H+20 & +50.

CROSS CORSEN Ch 79 Cap de la Hague to Pte de Penmarc'h (Times in **bold** = 1 May to 30 Sep).

Cap Fréhel	0545, 0803, **1203**, 1633, 2003 LT
Bodic	0533, 0745, **1145**, 1615, 1945 LT
Ile de Batz	0515, 0733, **1133**, 1603, 1933 LT
Le Stiff	0503, 0715, **1115**, 1545, 1915 LT
Pte du Raz	0445, 0703, **1103**, 1533, 1903 LT

Gale warnings in French and **English** on receipt, on request and at H+03.
Le Stiff broadcasts gale warnings at H+10 and H+40; also weather bulletins in French and **English** every 3 hrs from 0150 UTC. All stations broadcast fog warnings in French and **English** when visibility requires.

CROSS ÉTEL Ch 80 Pte de Penmarc'h to L'anse de l'Aiguillon (46°17'N 01°10'W)

Penmarc'h	0703, 1533, 1903 LT
Groix	0715, 1545, 1915 LT
Belle Ile	0733, 1603, 1933 LT
St Nazaire	0745, 1615, 1945 LT
Ile d'Yeu	0803, 1633, 2003 LT
Les Sables d'Olonne	0815, 1645, 2015 LT

Gale warnings on receipt, on request and at H+03; in French, plus **English** in summer.

Sous-CROSS SOULAC Ch 79 L'Anse de l'Aiguillon to Spanish border

Chassiron	0703, 1533, 1903 LT
Soulac	0715, 1545, 1915 LT
Cap Ferret	0733, 1603, 1933 LT
Contis	0745, 1615, 1945 LT
Biarritz	0803, 1633, 2003 LT

Gale warnings on receipt, on request and at H+03; in French, plus **English** in summer.

5.12.4 CROSS MF broadcasts

CROSS Gris Nez and CROSS Corsen both broadcast routine weather bulletins and gale warnings on 1650 kHz and 2677kHz in French, as follows:

CROSS	Routine bulletins	Areas covered (see Fig. 5(13))	Gale warnings
Gris Nez	0833, 2033 LT	Humber, Thames, French areas 12-14	On receipt, and at every odd H+03.
Corsen	0815, 2015 LT	French areas 12-24	On receipt, and at every even H+03.

Fig. 5 (11) French weather forecasts

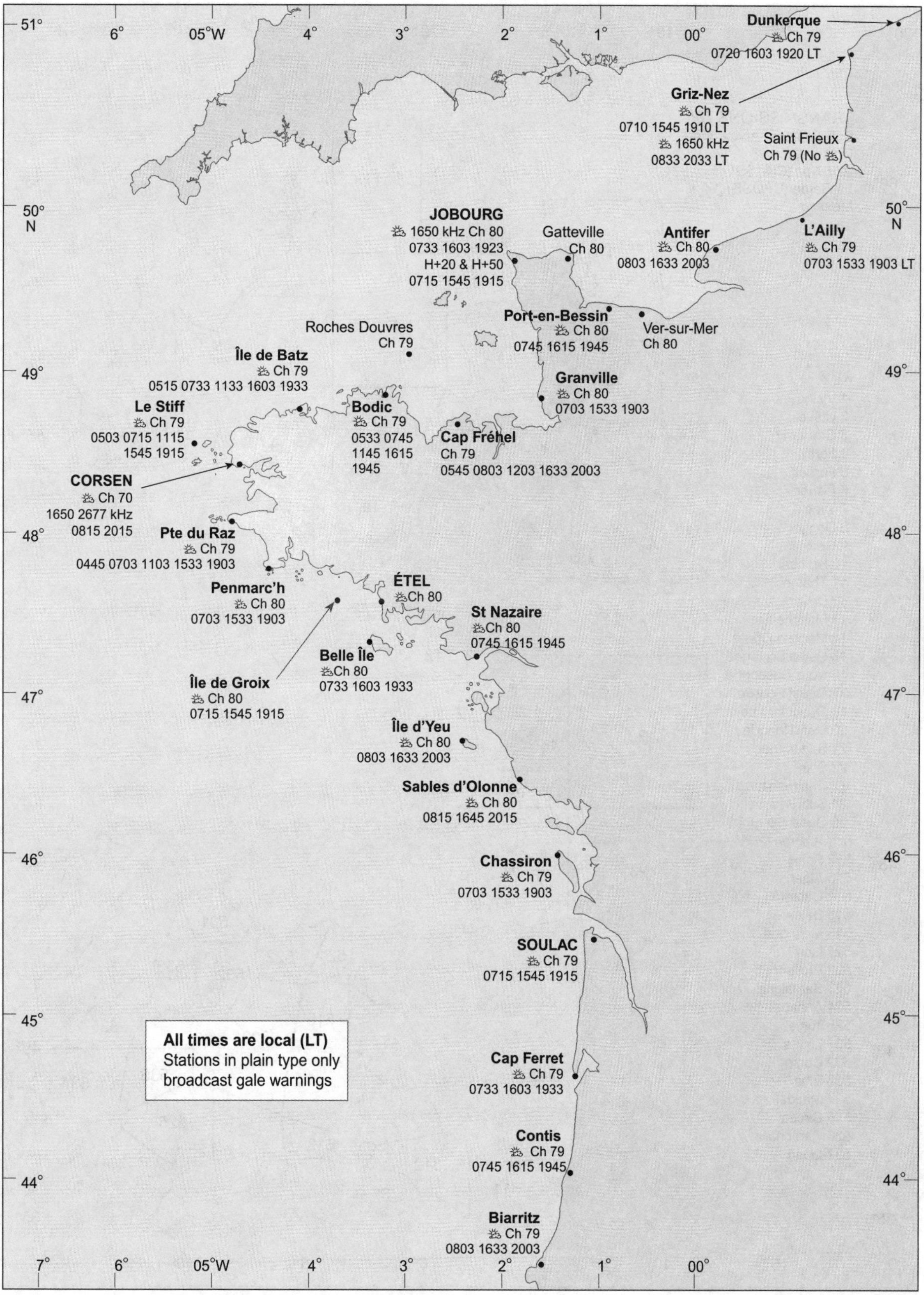

C5

Fig. 5 (12) France – Forecast areas

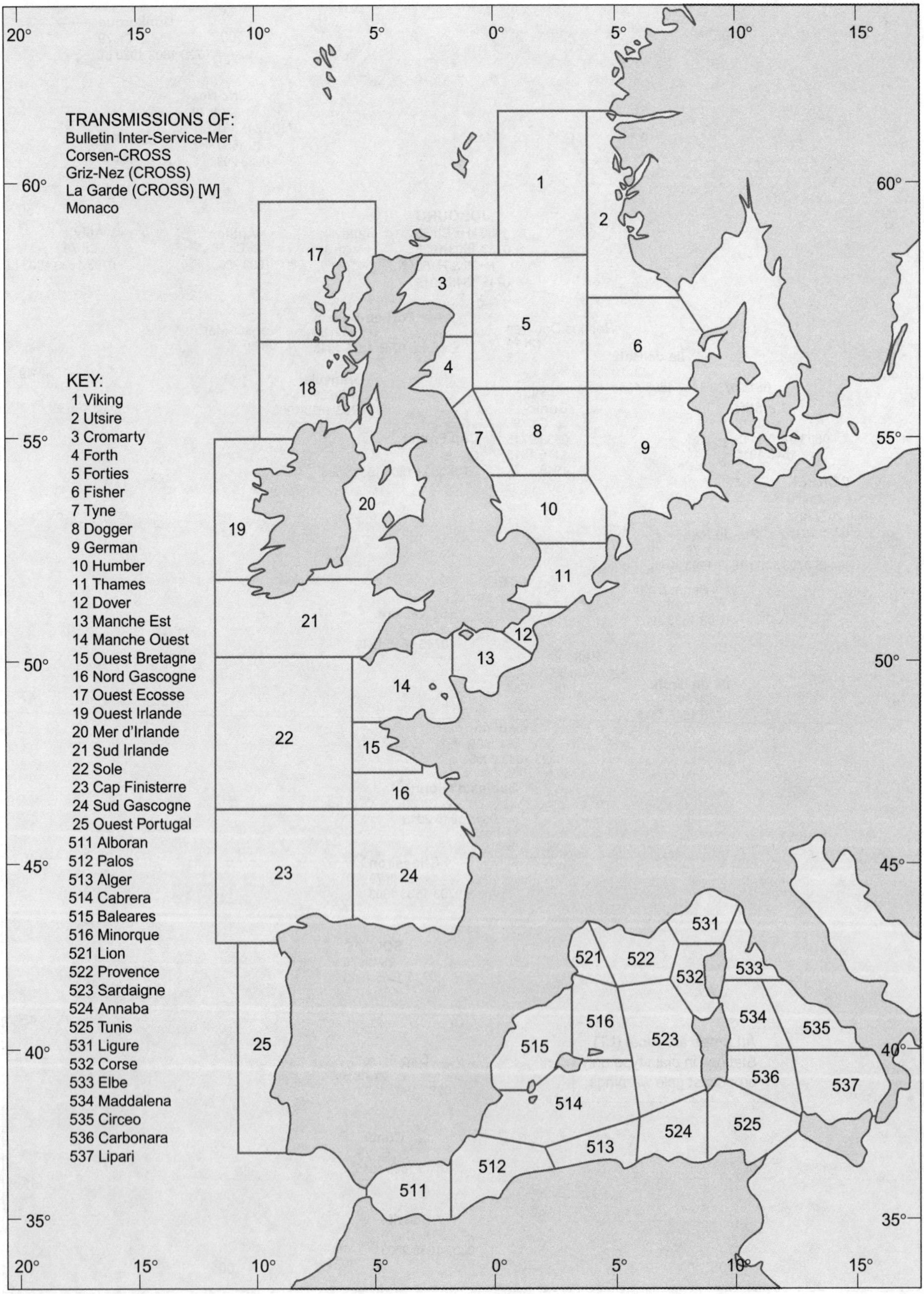
20° 15° 10° 5° 0° 5° 10° 15°
TRANSMISSIONS OF:
Bulletin Inter-Service-Mer
Corsen-CROSS
Griz-Nez (CROSS)
La Garde (CROSS) [W]
Monaco
KEY:
1 Viking
2 Utsire
3 Cromarty
4 Forth
5 Forties
6 Fisher
7 Tyne
8 Dogger
9 German
10 Humber
11 Thames
12 Dover
13 Manche Est
14 Manche Ouest
15 Ouest Bretagne
16 Nord Gascogne
17 Ouest Ecosse
19 Ouest Irlande
20 Mer d'Irlande
21 Sud Irlande
22 Sole
23 Cap Finisterre
24 Sud Gascogne
25 Ouest Portugal
511 Alboran
512 Palos
513 Alger
514 Cabrera
515 Baleares
516 Minorque
521 Lion
522 Provence
523 Sardaigne
524 Annaba
525 Tunis
531 Ligure
532 Corse
533 Elbe
534 Maddalena
535 Circeo
536 Carbonara
537 Lipari
60° 55° 50° 45° 40° 35°
1 2 3 4 5 6 7 8 9 10 11 12 13 14 15 16 17 18 19 20 21 22 23 24 25
511 512 513 514 515 516 521 522 523 524 525 531 532 533 534 535 536 537

5.13 SPAIN

NORTH AND NORTH WEST SPAIN

Coast Radio Stations

The following CRS broadcast in Spanish gale warnings, synopsis and forecasts for Areas 1-9 at the times and on the VHF or MF frequencies shown below:

Pasages	VHF Ch 27	at 0940 1140 2140 UTC
Machichaco	1707 kHz	at 0903 1233 1733 UTC
Bilbao	VHF Ch 26	at 0940 1140 2140 UTC
Santander	VHF Ch 24	at 0940 1140 2140 UTC
Cabo Peñas	VHF Ch 26	at 0940 1140 2140 UTC
	1677 kHz	at 0803 1203 1703 UTC
Navia	VHF Ch 27	at 0940 1140 2140 UTC
Cabo Ortegal	VHF Ch 02	at 0950 1150 2150 UTC
La Coruña	VHF Ch 26	at 0950 1150 2150 UTC
	1698 kHz	at 0833 1233 1733 UTC
Finisterre	VHF Ch 26	at 0950 1150 2150 UTC
	1764 kHz	at 0803 1203 1703 UTC
Vigo	VHF Ch 20	at 0950 1150 2150 UTC
La Guardia	VHF Ch 82	at 0950 1150 2150 UTC
Tarifa	VHF Ch 81	at 0940 1140 2140 UTC
	1704 kHz	at 0803 1233 1703 UTC

Coastguard MRCC/MRSC

Broadcast in Spanish and English gale warnings on receipt, plus synopsis and forecasts for the Areas, times (UTC) and VHF channels listed below:

Bilbao MRCC	VHF Ch 10	every 4h from 0033 for Areas 2-4.
Santander MRSC	VHF Ch 11	every 4h from 0245 for Areas 2-4.
Gijón MRCC	VHF Ch 10 16	every even H+15 from 0015 to 2215 for Areas 3 & 4.
Coruña MRSC	VHF Ch 12 13 14	every 4h from 0005 for Areas 1-5.
Finisterre MRCC	VHF Ch 11	every 4h from 0233 for Areas 1-5.
Vigo MRSC	VHF Ch 10	every 4h from 0015 for Areas 3-6.

C5

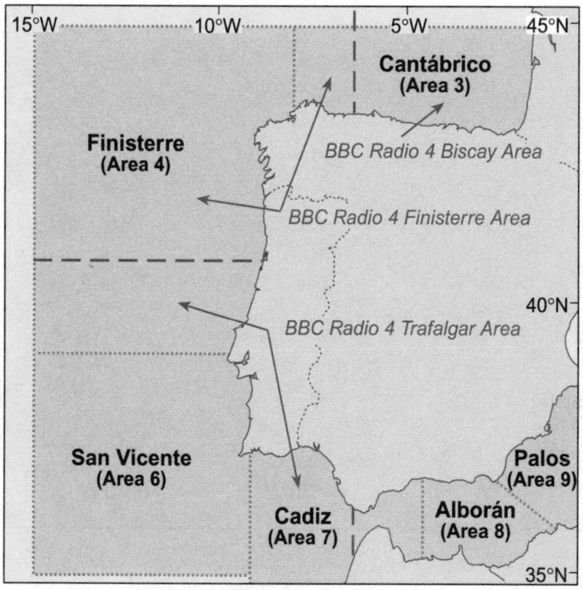

.... Spanish Forecast Areas

– – – – UK Forecast Areas (BBC)

Fig. 5 (13) Spanish forecast areas

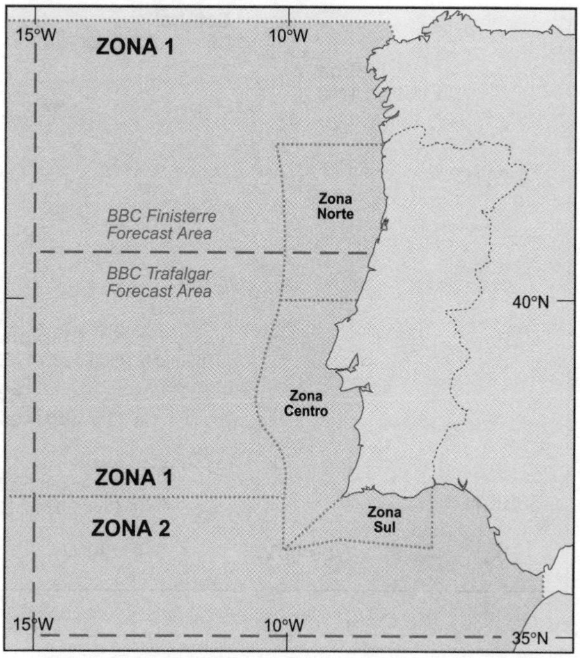

.... Portuguese Forecast Areas

– – – UK Forecast Areas (BBC)

Fig. 5 (14) Portuguese forecast areas

Fig. 5 (15) Spanish and Portuguese CRS MSI broadcasts (All times UTC)

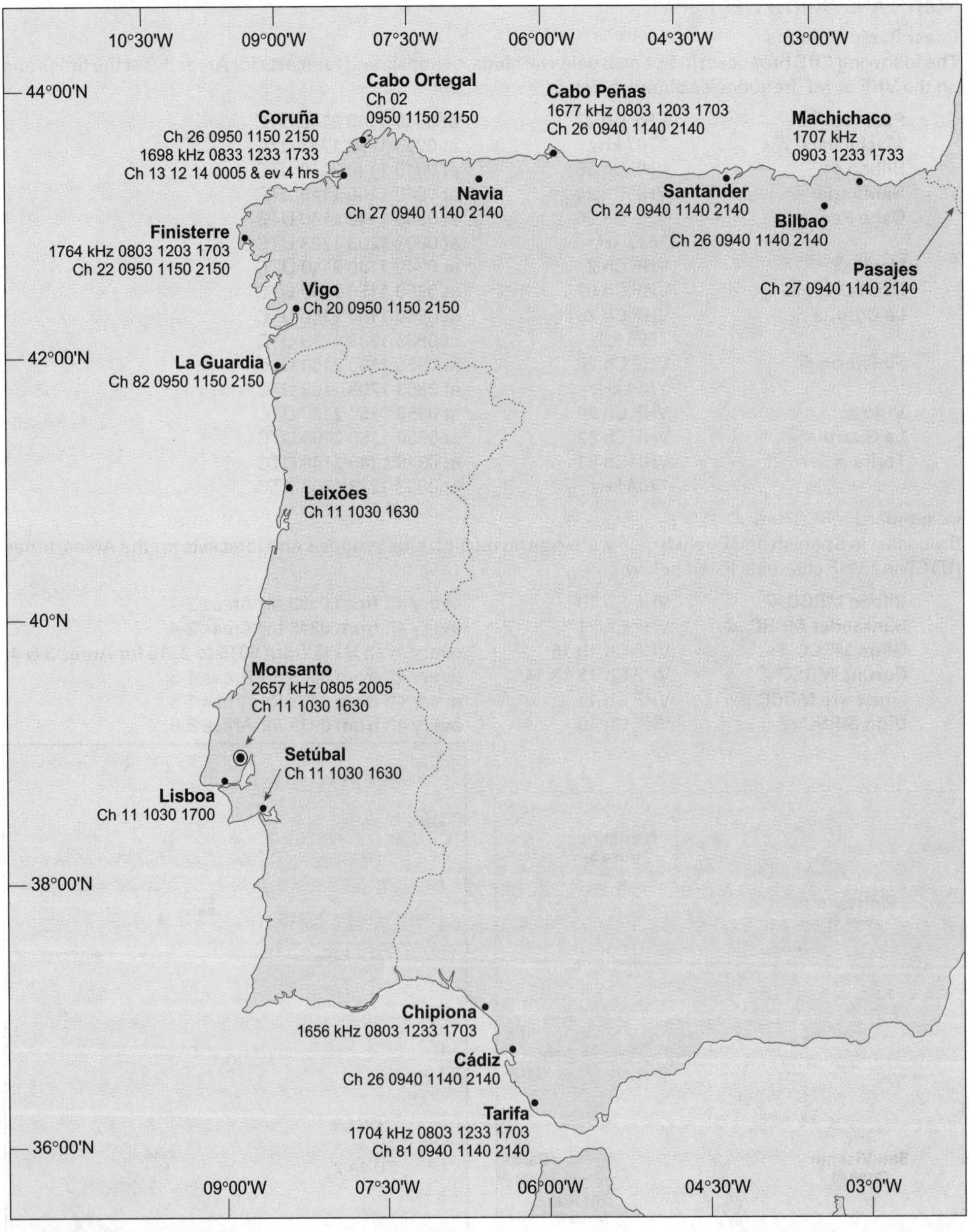
10°30'W
09°00'W
07°30'W
06°00'W
04°30'W
03°00'W
44°00'N
42°00'N
40°N
38°00'N
36°00'N
Cabo Ortegal
Ch 02
0950 1150 2150
Cabo Peñas
1677 kHz 0803 1203 1703
Ch 26 0940 1140 2140
Machichaco
1707 kHz
0903 1233 1733
Coruña
Ch 26 0950 1150 2150
1698 kHz 0833 1233 1733
Ch 13 12 14 0005 & ev 4 hrs
Navia
Ch 27 0940 1140 2140
Santander
Ch 24 0940 1140 2140
Bilbao
Ch 26 0940 1140 2140
Finisterre
1764 kHz 0803 1203 1703
Ch 22 0950 1150 2150
Pasajes
Ch 27 0940 1140 2140
Vigo
Ch 20 0950 1150 2150
La Guardia
Ch 82 0950 1150 2150
Leixões
Ch 11 1030 1630
Monsanto
2657 kHz 0805 2005
Ch 11 1030 1630
Setúbal
Ch 11 1030 1630
Lisboa
Ch 11 1030 1700
Chipiona
1656 kHz 0803 1233 1703
Cádiz
Ch 26 0940 1140 2140
Tarifa
1704 kHz 0803 1233 1703
Ch 81 0940 1140 2140
09°00'W
07°30'W
06°00'W
04°30'W
03°0'W

Fig. 5 (16) Spanish forecast areas

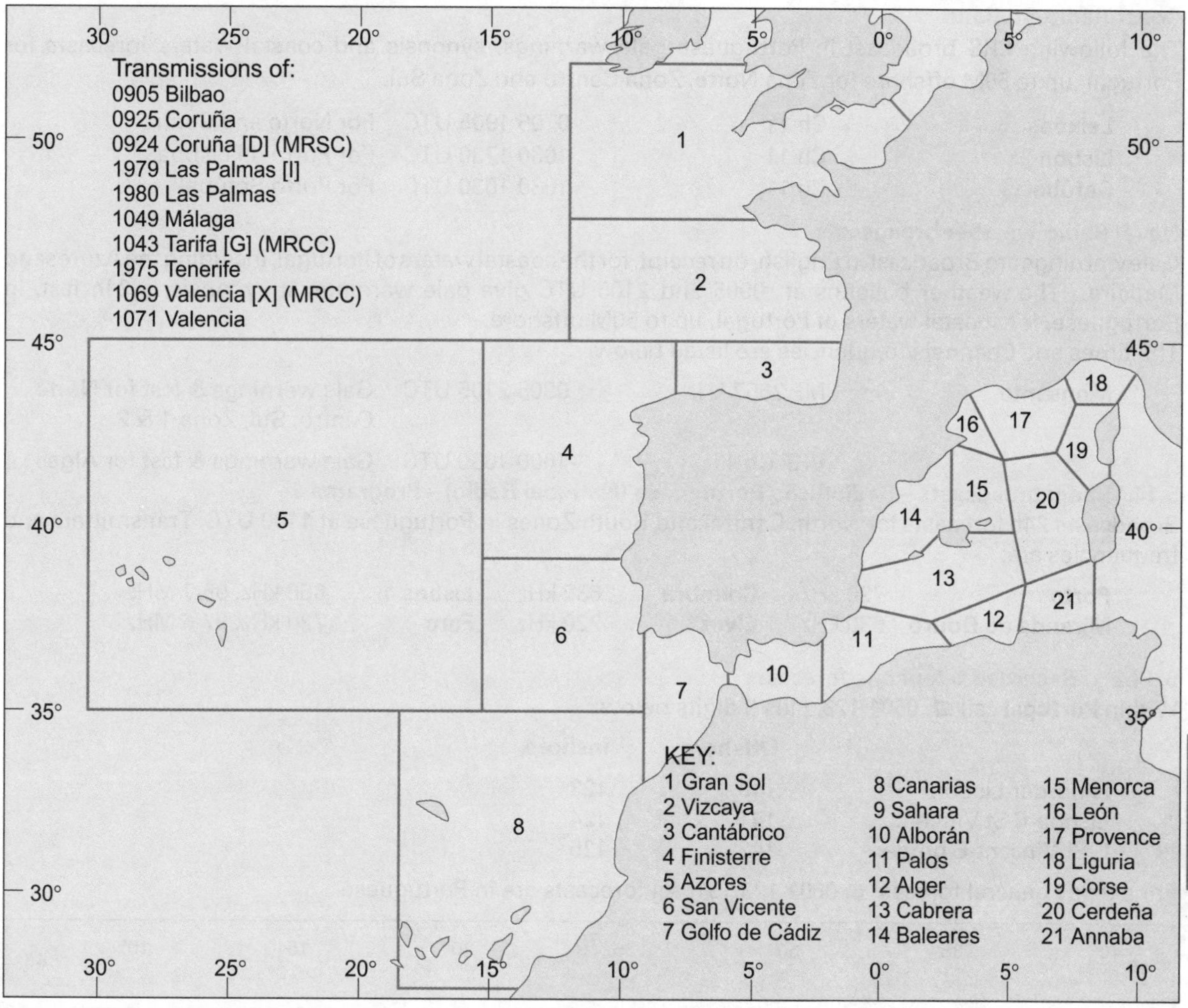

5.13.1 Radio broadcasts – Radio Nacional de España (National Radio)

Broadcasts in Spanish storm warnings, synopsis and 12h or 18h forecasts for Spanish Areas 3 & 4 at 1100, 1400, 1800 and 2200 LT. Stations and frequencies are:

San Sebastián	774 kHz	**Bilbao**	639 kHz	**Santander**	855 kHz
Oviedo	729 kHz	**La Coruña**	639 kHz		

5.13.2 Recorded telephone forecasts

A recorded telephone marine weather information service in Spanish is available for the Spanish forecast areas 1 to 4, i.e. Gran Sol, Vizcaya (North Biscay), Cantábrico and Finisterre. The service also provides forecasts for Coastal waters from the French to Portuguese borders i.e. Guipuzcoa, Vizcaya, Cantabria, Austurias, Lugo, Coruña and Pontevedra. This service is only available within Spain or for Autolink equipped vessels. Dial ☎ 906 365 372.

5.14 PORTUGAL

Coast Radio Stations

The following CRS broadcast in Portuguese gale warnings, synopsis and coastal waters forecasts for Portugal, up to 50M offshore for Zona Norte, Zona Centro and Zona Sul.

Leixões (CRS)	Ch 11	0705 1905 UTC	For Norte and Centro
Lisboa (CRS)	Ch 11	1030 1730 UTC	For Porto de Lisboa
Setúbal (CRS)	Ch 11	1030 1630 UTC	For Porto Setúbal

Naval Radio weather broadcasts

Gale warnings are Broadcast in English, on receipt, for the coastal waters of Portugal, including the Azores and Madeira. The weather bulletins at 0905 and 2105 UTC give gale warnings, a synopsis, a 24h fcst, in Portuguese, for coastal waters of Portugal, up to 50M offshore.
The times and Channels/frequencies are listed below.

Monsanto	MF 2657 kHz	0905 2105 UTC	Gale warnings & fcst for Norte, Centro, Sul, Zona 1 & 2
	VHF Ch 11	1000 1630 UTC	Gale warnings & fcst for Alges

5.14.1 Radio broadcasts – Radiofusão Portuguesa (National Radio) – Programa 1

Broadcasts 24h forecasts for North, Central and South Zones in Portuguese at 1100 UTC. Transmitters and frequencies are:

Porto	720 kHz	**Coimbra**	630 kHz	**Lisboa 1**	666 kHz, 95·7 MHz
Miranda do Douro	630 kHz	**Elvas**	720 kHz	**Faro**	720 kHz, 97·6 MHz

5.14.2 Recorded telephone forecasts

Within **Portugal** call ☎ 0601 123, plus 3 digits below:

	Offshore	Inshore
N border-Lisboa	140	123
Lisboa-C St Vincent	141	124
C St Vincent-E border	142	125

For a 9 day general forecast ☎ 0601 123 131. All forecasts are in Portuguese.

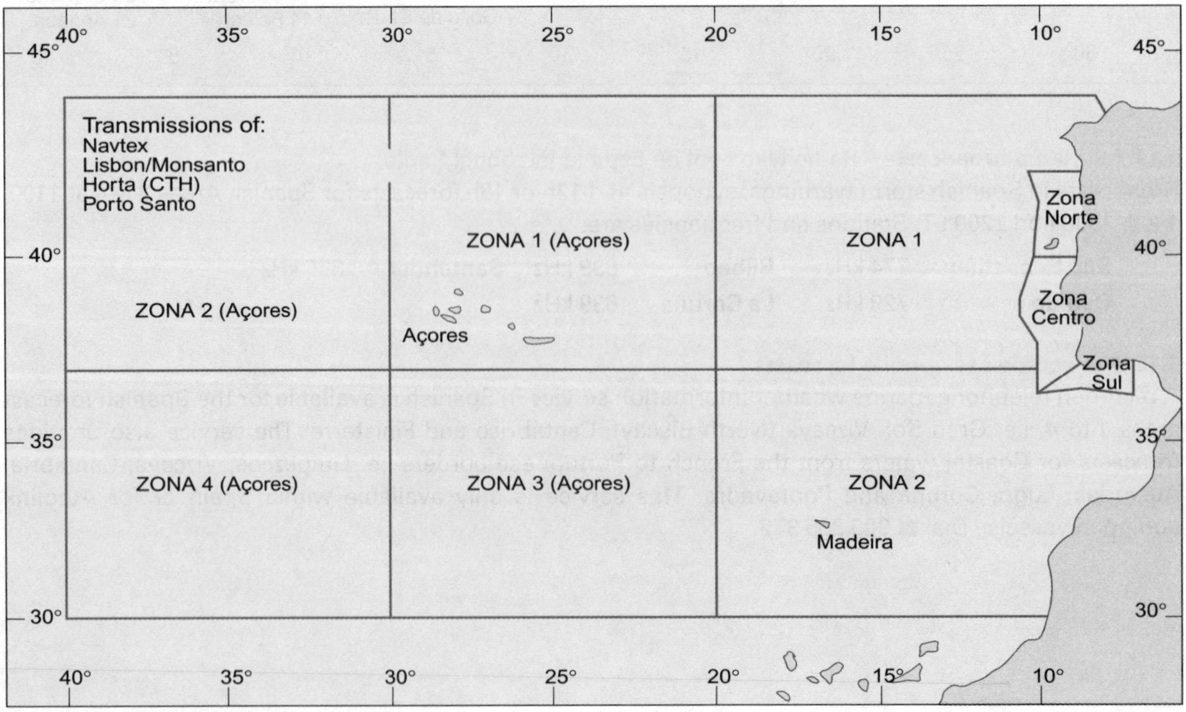

Fig. 5 (17) Portuguese forecast areas

5.15 SOUTH WEST SPAIN

The following CRS broadcast in Spanish gale warnings, synopsis and forecasts for Areas 1-21, in Spanish, at the times and on the VHF or MF frequencies shown below:

Chipiona (CRS)	1656 kHz	at 0803 1233 1703 UTC
Tarifa (CRS)	VHF Ch 81	at 0940 1140 2140 UTC
	1704kHz	at 0803 1233 1703 UTC
Cadiz (CRS)	VHF Ch 26	at 0940 1140 2140 UTC

Coastguard MRCC/MRSC

Broadcast in Spanish and **English** gale warnings on receipt, plus synopsis and forecasts for the Areas, times (UTC) and VHF channels listed below:

5.15.1	**Tarifa MRCC** (CGR)	VHF Ch 10 74	every even H+15 for actual wind and visibility at Tarifa, followed by a forecast for Strait of Gibraltar, Cádiz Bay and Alborán, **in English** and Spanish. Fog (visibility) warnings are broadcast every even H+15, and more frequently when the visibility falls below 2M.
	Algeciras MRSC (CGR)	VHF Ch 15, 74	At 0315 0515 0715 1115 1515 1915 2315 UTC

5.15.2 Recorded telephone forecasts

In SW Spain ☎ 906 365 372 for offshore bulletins for forecast areas San Vicente, Cádiz, Alborán, Azores and Canaries; also coastal bulletins from Portugal to Gibraltar, and Canaries. All forecasts are in Spanish. The service is only available within Spain and to Autolink-equipped vessels.

5.16 GIBRALTAR

a. Radio Gibraltar (Gibraltar Broadcasting Corporation)

Broadcasts in **English**: General synopsis, situation, wind direction and strength, visibility and sea state for area up to 50M from Gibraltar. Frequencies are 1458 kHz, 91·3 MHz, 92·6 MHz and 100·5 MHz. Times are:

Mon-Fri: 0610 0930 1030 1230 1300 1530 1715 UTC
Sat: 0930, 1030 1230 1300 UTC
Sun: 1030 1230 UTC

General synopsis, situation, wind direction and strength, sea state, visibility and Sailing forecast, for area up to 50M from Gibraltar.

Mon-Fri: 0630 0730 0830 1130 1740-1755 LT
Sat: 0630 0730 0830 1130 LT
Sun: 0730 0830 1130 LT

b. British Forces Broadcasting Service (BFBS) Gibraltar

Broadcasts in **English**: Shipping forecast, wind, weather, visbility, sea state, swell, HW & LW times for local waters within 5M of Gibraltar.

Frequencies are: **BFBS 1** – 93·5 and 97·8 MHz FM and **BFBS 2** 89·4 and 99·5 MHGz FM.

BFBS 1 times are:

Mon-Fri: 0745 0845 1130 1715 2345 LT
Sat/Sun: 0845 0945 1230 LT

Mon-Fri: Every H+06 (0700-2400) LT
Sat-Sun: Every H+06 (0700-1000, 1200-1400) LT
Fcst for Gibraltar area; general synopsis, situation, wind direction and strength, sea state, visibility together with HW/LW times.

BFBS 2 times are:

Monday-Fri: 1200 UTC

5.17 BELGIUM

5.17.1 Coast Radio Stations

Oostende Radio (CRS) broadcasts in English and Dutch strong breeze warnings and a forecast on 2761 kHz and VHF Ch 27 at 0820 and 1720 UTC, valid for sea areas Thames and Dover. Gale warnings are issued **in English** and Dutch on receipt and at the end of the next two silent periods.

Antwerpen Radio (CRS), on VHF Ch 24, broadcasts gale warnings on receipt at the end of the next two silent periods and every H+03 and H+48.. Also strong wind warnings (F6+) on receipt and at every H+05 for the Schelde estuary in English and Dutch

5.17.2 Radio broadcasting

VRT Radio 1 (Viaamse Radio en Televisie) broadcasts weather messages in Dutch after the news at 0600 0700 0800 0900 1700 2200 LT. The frequencies are 927 kHz, 91·7 MHz, 94·2 MHz, 95·7 MHz and 98·5 MHz. The weather messages include the present situation, forecast for 24 hrs, outlook for the next few days and windspeed; valid for sea areas Humber, Thames, Dover, Wight and Portland.

5.18 NETHERLANDS

5.18.1 Netherlands Coastguard (IJmuiden) (CGR)

a. VHF weather broadcasts

Weather messages are broadcast in **English** and Dutch at 0805, 1305, 2305 LT on the VHF channels shown below. Messages include a forecast for Netherlands coastal waters up to 30M offshore (including IJsselmeer). Forecasts are broadcast are announced through DSC 2187·5 kHz and VHF Ch 70 before being broadcast on the scheduled frequency or channel. Gale warnings are broadcast on receipt, and at 0333, 0733, 1133, 1533, 1933 and 2333 UTC.

Goes (CGR)	Ch 83	**Westkapelle** (CGR)	Ch 23	**Rotterdam** (CGR)	Ch 23
Scheveningen (CGR)	Ch 23	**Hilversum** (CGR)	Ch 83	**IJmuiden** (CGR)	Ch 83
Lelystad (CGR)	Ch 23	**Huisduinen** (CGR)	Ch 23	**Wieringerwerf** (CGR)	Ch 83
Platform L7 (CGR)	Ch 83	**Terschelling** (CGR)	Ch 23	**Nes** (CGR)	Ch 83
Appingedam (CGR)	Ch 23				

b. MF weather broadcasts

Netherlands Coastguard (IJmuiden) (CGR) broadcasts weather messages in **English** daily at 0940 and 2140 UTC on 2673 kHz. The messages include a forecast for Netherlands coastal waters up to 30M offshore (including IJsselmeer) and areas Dover, Thames, Humber, German Bight, Dogger, Fisher, Forties and Viking.

Gale warnings are broadcast on receipt, and at 0333, 0733, 1133, 1533, 1933 and 2333 UTC.

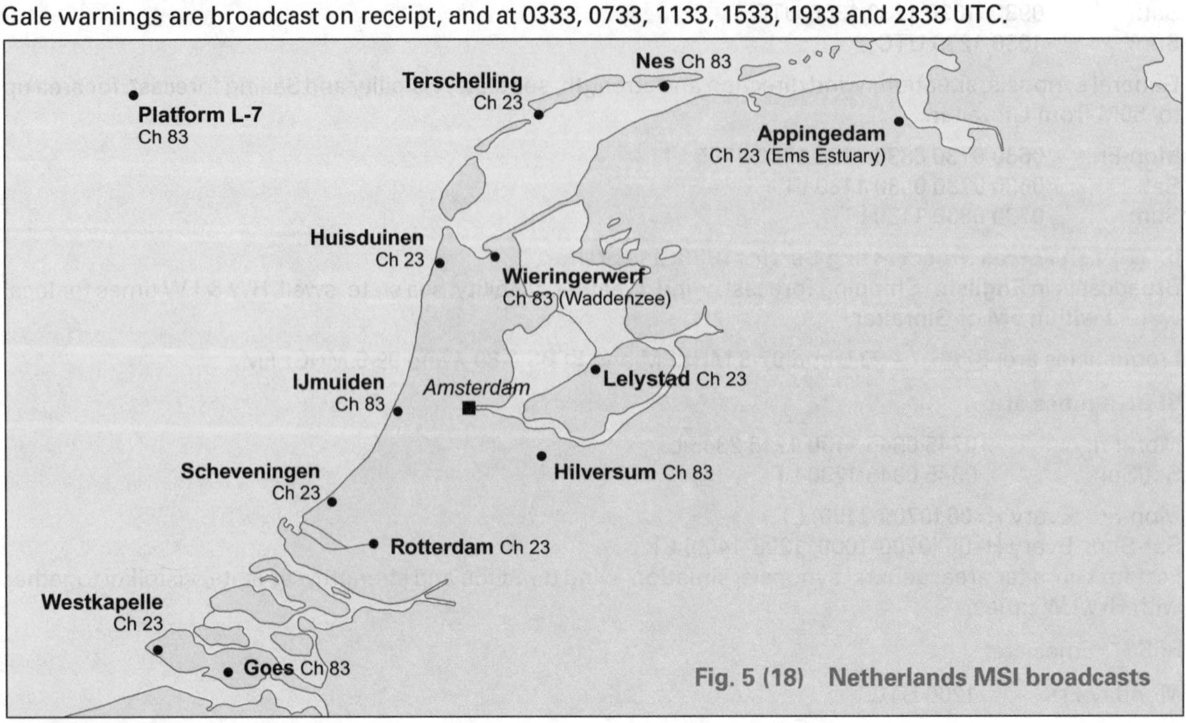

Fig. 5 (18) Netherlands MSI broadcasts

Fig. 5 (19) German MSI broadcasts

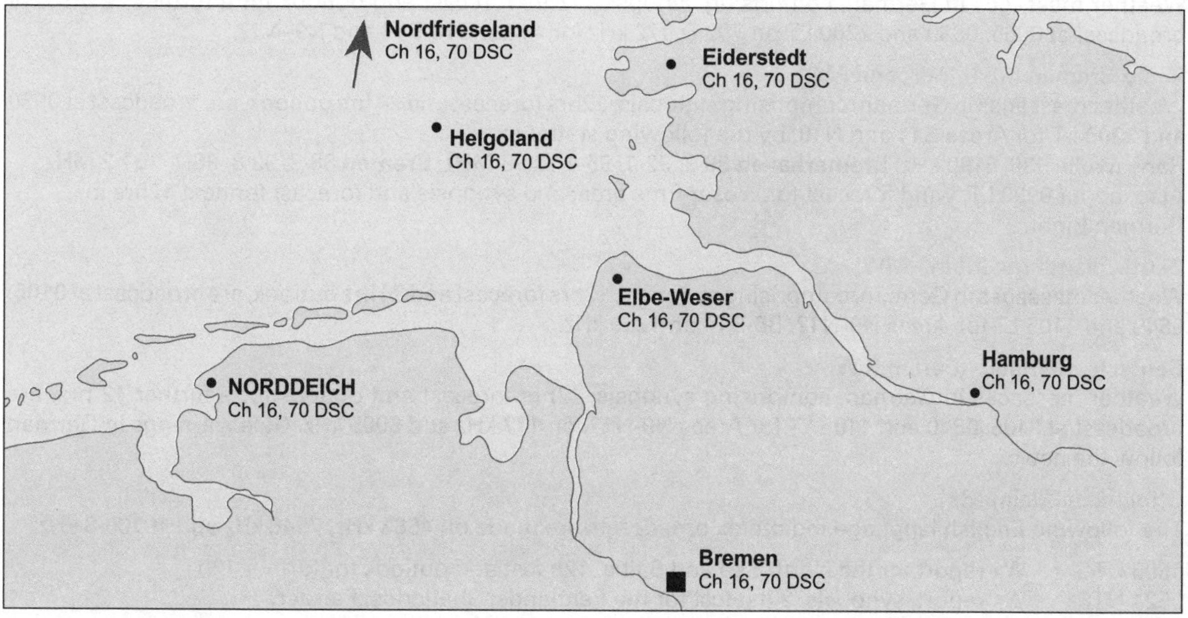

5.19 GERMANY

5.19.1 Coast Radio stations – Seefunk Hamburg (DPO7)

Seefunk broadcast a weather report, synopsis, 12h forecast and outlook for a further 12h, in German, for Areas B10-B12, N9-N10 and Eastern Boddenwässer at 0645, 0845, 1145, 1545 and 1845 UTC. Broadcasts are given 1 hr earlier when DST is in force. Broadcasts are first announced on Ch 16 before being broadcast on the channel below:

Hamburg (CRS)	53°33'N 09°58'E	Ch 16 27
Borkumn (CRS)	53°35'N 06°40'E	Ch 16 18
Elber-Weser (CRS)	53°50'N 08°39'E	Ch 16 01 24
Helgoland (CRS)	54°11'N 07°53'E	Ch 16 86

5.19.2 Traffic Centres

Traffic Centres broadcast in German local storm warnings, weather messages, visibility and ice reports (when appropriate). (E) = in **English** and German.

German Bight Traffic (E)	Ch 80	Every H+00
Ems Traffic	Ch 15, 18, 20, 21	Every H+50
Jade Traffic	Ch 20, 63	Every H+10
Bremerhaven Weser	Ch 02, 04, 05, 07, 21, 22, 82	Every H+20
Bremen Weser Traffic	Ch 19, 78, 81	Every H+30
Hunte Traffic	Ch 63	Every H+30
Cuxhaven Elbe Traffic (E)	Ch 71 (outer Elbe)	Every H+35
Brunsbüttel Elbe Traffic (E)	Ch 68 (lower Elbe)	Every H+05
Kiel Kanal II	Ch 02 (For East going traffic)	H+15 and H+45
KielKanal III	Ch 03 (For West going traffic)	Every H+20 and H+50

The German weather service (*Der Deutsche Wetterdienst*) provides weather information through a databank which is updated twice daily; more often for weather reports and textual forecasts. SEEWIS (Marine weather information system) allows data to be accessed by telephone/modem and fed into an onboard computer. The address is: German Weather Service, PO Box 30 11 90, 20304 Hamburg. ☎ + 49 (0) 40 31 90 88 11; 📠 + 49 (0) 40 31 90 88 03.

5.19.3 Radio broadcasting

Norddeutscher Rundfunk (NDR)

a. NDR 1 Welle Nord (FM)

Weather messages in German, comprising synopsis, 12hrs forecast and 24 hrs outlook, are broadcast at 0730 LT (1 May – 30 Sept) for Helgoland, Elbe and North Frisian coast, by the following stations: **Helgoland** 88·9 MHz; **Hamburg** 89·5, 90·3 MHz; **Flensburg** 89·6 MHz; **Heide** 90·5 MHz; **Sylt** 90·9 MHz; Kiel 91·3 MHz; Cuxhaven 98·4 MHz.

b. NDR 4 Hamburg (MW)
Weather messages in German, comprising synopsis, 12hrs forecast and outlook for a further 12 hrs, are broadcast at 0005, 0830 and 2200 LT on 702 & 972 kHz for Areas B10-B14 and N9–N12.

Radio Bremen (RB1) (MW and FM)
Weather messages in German, comprising synopsis, 12hrs forecast and 24 hrs outlook, are broadcast at 0930 and 2300 LT for Areas B11 and N10, by the following stations:
Hansawelle 936, 6190 kHz; **Bremerhaven** 89·3, 92·1, 95·4 100·8 MHz; **Bremen** 88·3, 93·8, 96·7, 101·2 MHz. Also, about 0930 LT, wind forecast for Weser-Ems area; and synopsis and forecast for next 12hrs in German Bight.

Deutschlandfunk (Köln) (MW)
Weather messages in German, comprising synopsis, 12hrs forecast and 24 hrs outlook, are broadcast at 0105, 0640 and 1105 LT for Areas N9-N12, B6-B14 on 1269 kHz.

Deutschland Radio (Berlin) (LW)
Weather messages in German, comprising synopsis, 12hrs forecast and outlook for a further 12 hrs, are broadcast at 0105, 0640 and 1105 LT for Areas N9-N12, on 177 kHz and 6005 kHz. Gale warnings in German follow the news.

Offenbach (Main) (HF)
The following **English** language radiotelex broadcasts are made on 4583 kHz, 7646 kHz and 10100·8 kHz:

0505 UTC	Wx report for the North Sea and Baltic, 12h fcst and outlook for further 12h
0521 UTC	Wx report, synopsis, 2 dat fcst for the Pentlands, Shetlands, Færøer.
1034 UTC	Wx report, synopsis, 2 day fcst for the North Sea.
1059 UTC	Wx report for next few days, synopsis and 2 day fcst for the North Sea and Baltic Sea.
1122 UTC	Wx report, synopsis, 2 dat fcst for the Pentlands, Shetlands, Færøer.
1136 UTC	Wx report, synopsis and 5 day fcst for the Baltic Sea.
1202 UTC	Wx report for the next few days, synopsis, 5 day fcst for the North Sea and Baltic Sea.
1438 UTC	Coastal Wx report, synopsis, 2 day fcst for Nordcap to West Gibraltar
1740 UTC	Synopsis, 12 hrs forecast, 24 hrs outlook for Viking, Forties, Dogger, Fisher and German Bight including station reports for the North Sea and Baltic
2048 UTC	Wx report, synopsis, 2 day fcst for the North Sea.
2113 UTC	Wx report, synopsis, 2 day fcst for the North Sea
2136 UTC	Wx report, synopsis, 2 dat fcst for the Pentlands, Shetlands, Færøer.

In addition to the English language broadcasts there are radio telex broadcasts in German at different times on 147·3 kHz, 11039 kHz and 14467·3 kHz. Details are listed in NP283(1) The ALRS Vol. 3(1).

5.19.4 German Telephone Forecasts

Similar to the British Marinecall; from 1 April – 30 Sept, forecast and outlook are available by dialling 01901160 plus two digits for the following areas:

- – 40 = Inland pleasure craft
- – 45 = North Frisian Islands and Helgoland
- – 46 = R Elbe from Elbe 1/Cuxhaven to Hamburg
- – 47 = Weser Estuary and Jade Bay
- – 48 = East Frisian Islands and Ems Estuary
- – 53 = For inland pleasure craft
- – 54 = Denmark
- – 55 = Netherlands, IJsselmeer, Schelde, Maas

For year round weather synopsis, forecast and outlook, dial 0190 1169 plus two digits as follows:

- – 20 = General information
- – 21 = North Sea and Baltic
- – 22 = German Bight and SW North Sea
- – 31 = 5 day bulletin for North Sea and Baltic**

**Containing an outlook and forecasts of wind, sea state, air and water temperature, plus warnings of fog, thunderstorms etc.

The latest wind and storm warnings for individual areas of the North Sea coasts are obtainable by dialling +49·40·3·19·66·28 (H24). If no warning is in operation, a wind forecast for the German Bight is given.

Marineweather is available all year round by telephone as follows (Not available from outside Germany):

01·90·11·69·21	North Sea & Baltic Sea
01·90·11·69·22	German Bight and SW North Sea
01·90·11·69·31	Marineweather reports for North Sea and Baltic Sea
01·90·11·69·59	Current wind strength for the North Sea and Baltic Sea coasts

5.20 DENMARK

The following CRS broadcast in Danish and English gale warnings, synopsis and forecasts on the VHF and MF frequencies shown below.

Blåvand (CRS)	Ch 23, 1734 kHz	On request
Bovbjerg (CRS)	Ch 02	On request
Hanstholm (CRS)	Ch 01	On request
Hirtshals (CRS)	Ch 66	On request
Skagen (CRS)	Ch 04, 1758 kHz	On request
Als (CRS)	Ch 07	On request

5.20.1 Radio broadcasts – Danmarks Radio (National Radio)

Broadcasts in Danish storm warnings, synopsis and 12h or 18h forecasts for all Danish Areas (Areas 16 to 20 from 1 Jan to 30 Apr only) and Jylland, Øerne and Bornholm, plus reports from coastal stations at , 0445, 0745 1045 1645 and 2145 UTC. Stations and frequencies are:

Kalundborg	243 kHz
West Jutland	92·9 MHz
Kalundborg	1062 kHz
SW Jutland	92·3 MHz
North Jutland	96·6 MHz
South Jutland	97·2 MHz

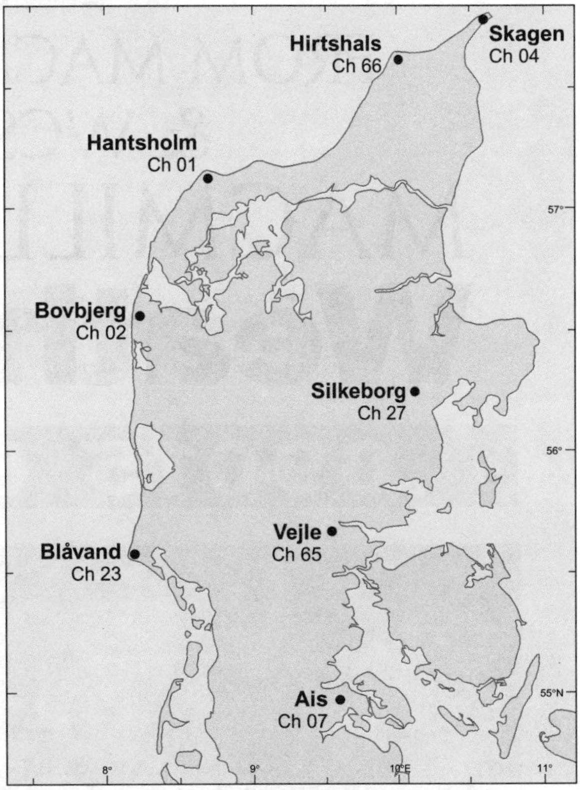
Skagen
Ch 04
Hirtshals
Ch 66
Hantsholm
Ch 01
57°
Bovbjerg
Ch 02
Silkeborg
Ch 27
56°
Vejle
Ch 65
Blåvand
Ch 23
Ais
Ch 07
55°N
8°
9°
10°E
11°

Fig. 5 (20) Danish MSI broadcasts

Fig. 5 (21) Danish forecast areas

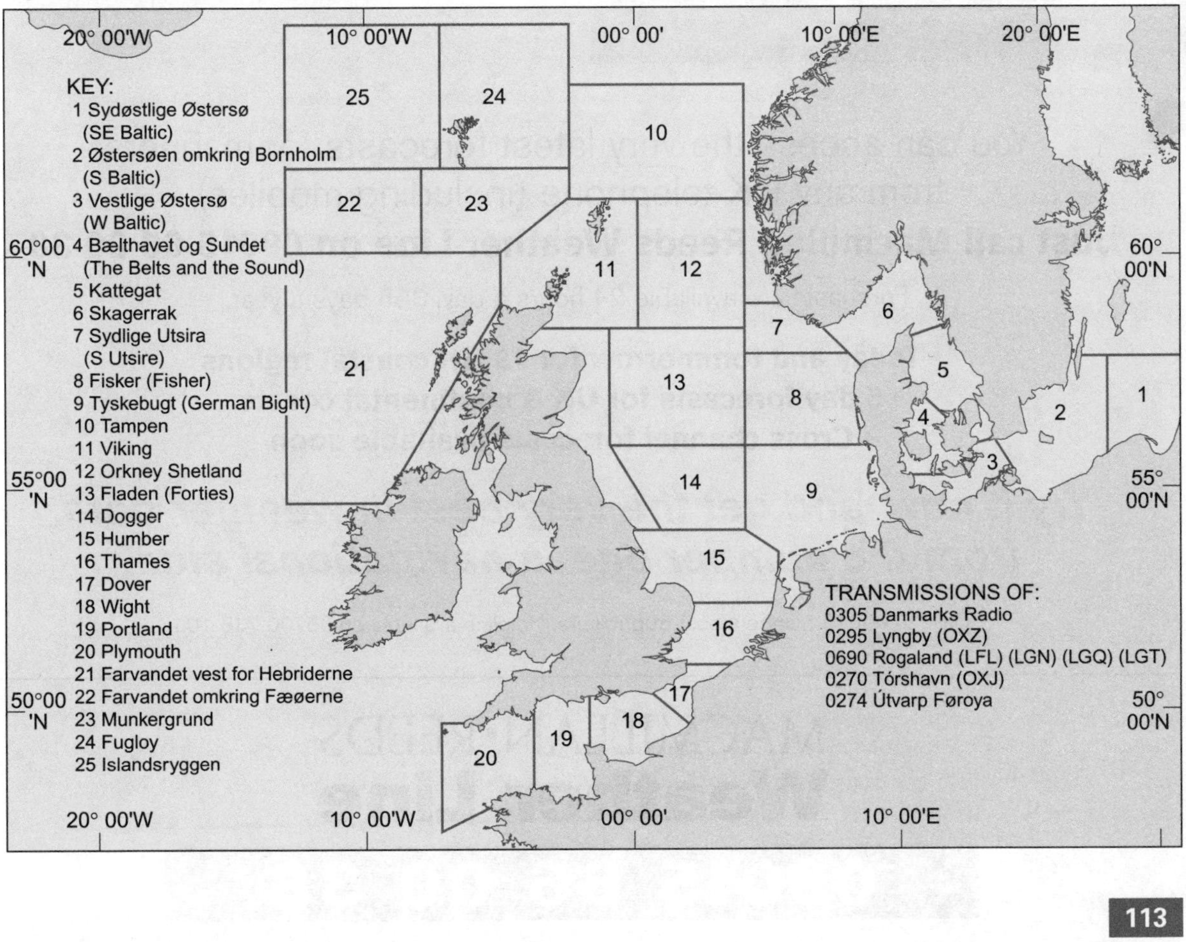
20° 00'W
10° 00'W
00° 00'
10° 00'E
20° 00'E
KEY:
1 Sydøstlige Østersø (SE Baltic)
2 Østersøen omkring Bornholm (S Baltic)
3 Vestlige Østersø (W Baltic)
4 Bælthavet og Sundet (The Belts and the Sound)
5 Kattegat
6 Skagerrak
7 Sydlige Utsira (S Utsire)
8 Fisker (Fisher)
9 Tyskebugt (German Bight)
10 Tampen
11 Viking
12 Orkney Shetland
13 Fladen (Forties)
14 Dogger
15 Humber
16 Thames
17 Dover
18 Wight
19 Portland
20 Plymouth
21 Farvandet vest for Hebriderne
22 Farvandet omkring Fæøerne
23 Munkergrund
24 Fugloy
25 Islandsryggen
60°00 'N
55°00 'N
50°00 'N
60° 00'N
55° 00'N
50° 00'N
TRANSMISSIONS OF:
0305 Danmarks Radio
0295 Lyngby (OXZ)
0690 Rogaland (LFL) (LGN) (LGQ) (LGT)
0270 Tórshavn (OXJ)
0274 Útvarp Føroya
20° 00'W
10° 00'W
00° 00'
10° 00'E

Chapter 6

Safety

Contents

6.1 **SAFETY EQUIPMENT** .... Page 116
6.1.2 Safety equipment - legal requirements. 116
6.1.3 Recommended Safety equipment for sea going yachts 5·5 to 13·7m LOA 116
6.2 **DEFINITIONS OF EMERGENCY** 117
6.2.1 Distress 117
6.2.2 Urgency 117
6.2.3 Safety 117
6.3 **DISTRESS SIGNALS** 117
6.3.1 Authority 117
6.3.2 Mobile telephones 117
6.3.3 Visual and audible distress signals 117
6.4 **MAYDAY CALLS** 118
6.4.1 Sending a MAYDAY call 118
6.4.2 MAYDAY acknowledgement 118
6.4.3 MAYDAY relay 118
6.4.4 Control of MAYDAY traffic 118
6.4.5 Relaxing radio silence 118
6.4.6 Cancelling radio silence 119
6.5 **URGENCY AND SAFETY** 119
6.5.1 Pan-Pan – Urgency signal 119
6.5.2 Medical help by RT 119
6.5.3 Sécurité – Safety signal 119
6.6 **GMDSS** 120
6.6.1 Introduction 120
6.6.2 Objective 120
6.6.3 Distress Alerting 120
6.6.4 Communications 120
6.6.5 Digital Selective Calling 120
6.6.6 Inmarsat 121
6.6.7 Transmitting Distress Alerts 121
6.6.8 Cospas/Sarsat 121
6.6.9 Sea Areas 121
6.6.10 Maritime Safety Information (MSI) 122
6.7 **EPIRB's** 122
6.7.1 Types and installation 122
6.7.2 Operation 122
6.7.3 Registration and false alerts 122
6.7.4 SART 122
6.8 **SEARCH AND RESCUE (SAR) – UK** 123
6.8.1 Introduction 123
6.8.2 Raising the alarm 123
6.8.3 Royal National Lifeboat Institution 123
6.9 **HM COASTGUARD** 123
6.9.1 Organisation 123
6.9.2 Functions 123
6.10 **MARITIME SAR REGIONS** 124
6.10.1 Search & Rescue Regions 124
6.10.1 Search & Rescue Regions 124
6.10.2 Emergency VHF DF 126
6.10.3 Emergency VHF DF 126
6.10.2 Yacht and Boat Safety Scheme 126
6.10.4 National Coastwatch Institution 12
6.11 **OTHER SIGNALS USED IN DISTRESS** .. 127
6.12 **HELICOPTER RESCUE** 127
6.13 **ABANDON SHIP** 128
6.14 **HAZARDS – Subfacts/Gunfacts** 128
6.15 **IRELAND** 129
6.16 **FRANCE** 134
6.17 **BELGIUM** 136
6.18 **NETHERLANDS** 138
6.19 **GERMANY** 138
6.20 **SPAIN AND PORTUGAL** 138
6.21 **FIRST AID AT SEA** 142

6.1 SAFETY EQUIPMENT

6.1.1 A Safety philosophy

The sea demands definite qualities in the mariner – certain attitudes of mind and character: Humility, prudence and a recognition that there is no end to learning and to the acquisition of experience. Humility first because who would dare to be other than humble in the presence of the two great elements – sea and sky – and all the uncertainties which they hold for us?

Prudence second – it is the ingrained characteristic of the professional seaman – the ability to distinguish between the risk which can reasonably be accepted, having regard to prevailing conditions, and the risk which must be rejected as unacceptable. Lastly learn by your own experience and by the experience of others, so that there is never an end to your learning.

The skipper is responsible for the safety of the boat and all on board. He must ensure that:

(1) The boat is suitable in design and in construction for her intended purpose.

(2) The boat is maintained in good condition.

(3) The crew is competent and sufficiently strong.

(4) The necessary safety and emergency equipment is carried, is in good condition, and the crew know how to use it.

Safety guidelines for recreational boat users can be found in a useful booklet Safety on the Sea published jointly by the RNLI, HM Coastguard and the RYA.

Simple precautions can eliminate accidents. Be particularly careful with bottled gas and petrol. Fit a gas detector. Turn off the gas at the bottle after use. If gas or petrol is smelt – no naked lights, and do not run electrical equipment.

Test systems regularly. Carry adequate spares. Insist that crew wear life jackets and harnesses when necessary, and that they do clip on. Make sure a good lookout is maintained at all times.

Listen to every forecast. Double-check all navigational calculations. Take nothing for granted.

Crew members are responsible for their personal gear. Nonslip shoes or boots are essential. So is foul-weather clothing with close fastenings at neck, wrists and ankles. At least two changes of sailing clothing should be carried, including warm sweaters and towelling strips as neck scarves.

Other personal items include a seaman's knife and spike on a lanyard, a waterproof torch, and anti-seasick pills. Life jacket and safety harnesses are usually supplied on board, but if individuals bring their own, the skipper should make certain they are up to standard.

6.1.2 Safety equipment – legal requirements

Yachts > 45ft (13·7m) LOA are required by law to carry certain safety equipment. All yachts must carry navigation lights and sound signals which comply with the IRPCS. Racing yachts must carry the safety equipment specified for the class/event concerned.

6.1.3 Recommended Safety equipment for seagoing yachts 5·5 – 13·7m LOA

The minimum equipment which should be carried for (a) coastal and (b) offshore cruising is listed below.

Safety equipment list

	Coastal	Offshore
Personal safety		
Life jackets, BS3595 or CE equivalent, per person	1	1
Harnesses, BS4224 or CE equivalent, per person	1	1
Navigation		
Charts, almanac, pilot	Yes	Yes
Compass with deviation card	1	1
Hand bearing compass	1	1
Chart table instruments	Yes	Yes
Watch/clock	1	2
Echo sounder	1	1
Lead line	1	1
GPS/Loran	1	1
Radio receiver (forecasts)	1	1
Barometer	1	1
Navigation lights	Yes	Yes
Radar reflector	1	1
Foghorn	1	1
Powerful waterproof torch	1	1
Anchor with warp or chain	2	2
Towline	1	1
Man overboard		
Life buoy, with drogue and light	2	2
Buoyant heaving line	1	1
Dan buoy	–	1
Rope (or boarding) ladder	1	1
Fire		
Fire-extinguishers	2	3
Fire blanket	1	1
Flooding		
Bilge pumps	2	2
Buckets with lanyards	2	2
Leak stopping gear	Yes	Yes
Distress signals		
Hand flares, red	2	4
Hand flares, white (warning)	4	4
Red parachute rockets	2	4
Buoyant orange smoke signals	2	2
Emergency radio transmitter	–	1

Abandon ship

Life raft for whole crew	1	1
or		
Dinghy with buoyancy, or inflated inflatable	1	–
Panic bag, extra water, etc.	–	1

Miscellaneous

First-aid kit	1	1
Engine toolkit	1	1
Name/number prominently displayed	Yes	Yes
Storm canvas	Yes	Yes
Emergency steering arrangements	Yes	Yes

6.2 DEFINITIONS OF EMERGENCY

6.2.1 Distress

Distress is the most serious degree of emergency. It applies to any situation where a boat or person is threatened by grave and imminent danger and requires immediate assistance. The RT prefix to Distress message is MAYDAY – see 6.4. A Distress call has priority over all other transmissions.

6.2.2 Urgency

Urgency is a lesser degree of emergency concerning the safety of a boat or person. Examples include, a vessel disabled but not sinking; medical problems (see also 6.5.2). The RT prefix to an Urgency message is PAN PAN – see 6.5.1.

6.2.3 Safety

Safety is the least serious degree of emergency, usually associated with a warning of hazardous navigational or meteorological circumstances. The RT prefix to a Safety message is SÉCURITÉ – see 6.5.3.

6.3 DISTRESS SIGNALS

6.3.1 Authority

Distress signals must only be made with the authority of the skipper, and only if the boat or a person is in grave and imminent danger, and help is urgently required; or on behalf of another vessel in distress, which for some reason is unable to make a Distress signal. When the problem is resolved, the Distress call must be cancelled by the co-ordinating station using the prowords SEELONCE FEENEE - see 6.4.4/6.

6.3.2 Mobile telephones

Using a mobile telephone to call the Coastguard on 999 (or 112) is NOT considered an adequate substitute for radio communication on VHF Ch 16 or 2182 kHz, when a vessel is in a distress or other emergency situation.

Mobile telephones are one more link in the chain of communication, but should at best be regarded as complementary to VHF radio. They have limited coverage, even in coastal waters, and are not monitored in any way; unlike Ch 16, which continues to be monitored by HM CG.

A mobile telephone call cannot be heard by vessels nearby which might be able to help. Other vessels can only be called by mobile telephone if so fitted and the number is known. On-scene SAR communications may be hampered. Mobile telephones are therefore very strongly discouraged.

6.3.3 Visual and audible distress signals

A full list of the recognised distress signals is given in Annex IV of the IRPCS. The following are those most appropriate to yachts and small craft, together with notes on their use.

(a) Continuous sounding of any fog signalling apparatus.

In order to avoid confusion, this is best done by a succession of letters SOS in Morse (••• ——— •••).

(b) An SOS signal made by any method.

For a yacht the most likely methods are by sound signal or flashing light, as in (a) above.

(c) The International Code signal 'NC'.

This can made by international code flag hoist, see Chapter 9, Plate 5.

(d) A square flag with a ball, or anything resembling a ball, above or below it.

This is not too difficult to contrive from any square flag, and a round fender or anchor ball.

(e) A rocket parachute flare or a hand-held flare showing a red light.

A red flare is the most effective distress signal at night. Flares serve two purposes: first to raise the alarm, and then to pinpoint the boat's position. Within about three miles from land a hand flare will do both. At greater distances a red parachute rocket (which projects a suspended flare to a height of more than 1,000ft, or 300m, and which burns for more than 40 seconds) is needed to raise the alarm, but hand flares are useful to indicate the boat's position.

Hold hand flares firmly, downwind of yourself. Rockets turn into wind; fire them vertically in normal conditions, or aim about 15° downwind in strong winds. Do not aim them into wind, or they will not gain altitude. If there is low cloud, fire rockets at 45° downwind, so that the flare burns under the cloud.

Note: White flares are not distress signals, but are used to indicate your presence to another vessel on a collision course; or to acknowledge the sighting of a red flare. An outfit of at least four is suggested for boats which make night passages. When using them, shield your eyes to protect night vision.

(f) An orange-coloured smoke signal.

By day orange smoke signals are more effective than flares, although the smoke disperses quickly in a strong wind.

(g) Slow and repeated raising/lowering of arms outstretched to each side.

The arms should be raised and lowered together, above and below the horizontal.

6.4 MAYDAY CALLS

6.4.1. Sending a MAYDAY call

This should normally be transmitted on VHF Ch 16 or 2182 kHz, but any frequency may be used if help may thereby be obtained more quickly.

Distress, Urgency and Safety messages from vessels at sea are free of charge. A distress call has priority over all other transmissions. If heard, cease all transmissions that may interfere with the distress call or messages, and listen on the frequency concerned.

Train your crew, as necessary, so that everybody can send a distress message. It is very helpful to display the MAYDAY message format close to the radio. Before making the call, first:

- Check main battery switch ON
- Switch radio ON, and select HIGH power (25 watts)
- Select VHF Ch 16 (or 2182 kHz for MF)
- Press and hold down the transmit button, and say slowly and distinctly:
- **MAYDAY MAYDAY MAYDAY**
- **THIS IS** .... (name of boat, spoken three times)
- **MAYDAY** ...... (name of boat spoken once)
- **MY POSITION IS** .... (latitude and longitude, or true bearing and distance from a known point)
- Nature of distress ..... (sinking, on fire, etc.)
- Aid required .... (immediate assistance)
- Number of persons on board ....
- Any other important, helpful information (eg if the yacht is drifting, whether distress rockets are being fired)
- **OVER.**

On completion of the distress message, release the transmit button and listen. The yacht's position is of vital importance, and should be repeated if time allows.

Vessels fitted with GMDSS equipment should make a DSC distress alert on VHF Channel 70, or MF 2187·5 kHz before sending a distress message on RT. (see 6.6.5).

6.4.2 MAYDAY acknowledgement

In coastal waters an immediate acknowledgment should be expected, as follows:

> **MAYDAY** .... (name of station sending the distress message, spoken three times)
>
> **THIS IS** .... (name of station acknowledging, spoken three times)
>
> **RECEIVED MAYDAY.**

If an acknowledgment is not received, check the set and repeat the distress call.

If you hear a distress message, write down the details, and if you can help you should acknowledge accordingly, but only after giving an opportunity for the nearest coastguard station or some larger vessel to do so.

6.4.3 MAYDAY relay

If you hear a distress message from a vessel, and it is not acknowledged, you should pass on the message as follows:

> **MAYDAY RELAY** .... (spoken three times)
>
> **THIS IS** .... (name of vessel re-transmitting the distress message, spoken three times), followed by the intercepted message.

6.4.4 Control of MAYDAY traffic

A MAYDAY call imposes general radio silence, until the vessel concerned or some other authority (e.g. the nearest Coastguard) cancels the distress. If necessary the station controlling distress traffic may impose radio silence as follows:

> **SEELONCE MAYDAY**, followed by its name or other identification, on the distress frequency.
>
> If some other station nearby believes it necessary to do likewise, it may transmit:
>
> **SEELONCE DISTRESS**, followed by its name or other identification.

6.4.5 Relaxing radio silence

When appropriate the station controlling distress traffic may relax radio silence so that normal working is resumed with caution on the distress frequency, with subsequent communications from the casualty prefixed by the Urgency signal (below).

When complete radio silence is no longer necessary on a frequency being used for distress traffic, the controlling station may relax radio silence as follows, indicating that restricted working may be resumed:

MAYDAY

ALL STATIONS (spoken three times)

THIS IS .... (name or callsign)

The time ....

The name of the vessel in distress ....

PRUDONCE

If distress working continues on other frequencies these will be identified. For example, PRUDONCE on 2182 kHz, but SEELONCE on VHF Ch 16.

6.4.6 Cancelling radio silence

When all distress traffic has ceased, normal working is authorised as follows:

MAYDAY

ALL STATIONS (spoken three times)

THIS IS .... (name or callsign)

The time ....

The name of the vessel in distress

SEELONCE FEENEE.

6.5 URGENCY AND SAFETY

6.5.1 Pan-Pan – Urgency signal

The R/T Urgency signal, consisting of the words PAN-PAN spoken three times, indicates that a vessel, or station, has a very urgent message concerning the safety of a ship or person.

Messages prefixed by PAN PAN take priority over all traffic except distress, and are sent on VHF Ch 16 or on 2182 kHz. The Urgency signal is appropriate when someone is lost overboard or urgent medical advice or attention is needed. It should be cancelled when the urgency is over.

Here is an example of an Urgency call and message from the yacht Seabird, disabled off the Needles.

PAN-PAN, PAN-PAN, PAN-PAN

ALL STATIONS (spoken three times)

THIS IS THE YACHT SEABIRD, SEABIRD, SEABIRD

Two nine zero degrees two miles from Needles lighthouse
Dismasted and propeller fouled

Anchor dragging and drifting east north east towards Shingles Bank

Require urgent tow

OVER.

If the message itself is long or is a medical call, or communications traffic is heavy, it should be passed on a working frequency after an initial call on Ch 16 or 2182 kHz. Where necessary this should be indicated at the end of the initial call.

If you hear an Urgency call you should respond in the same way as for a Distress call.

If help is needed, but the boat is in no immediate danger, the proper signal is 'V' (Victor) International Code, meaning 'I require assistance'. This can be sent as a flag signal (see Chapter 9 Plate 5), or by light or sound in Morse code (•••–).

6.5.2 Medical help by RT

Medical advice can be obtained through any UK HM Coastguard MRCC/MRSC by calling on a working channel and asking for a Medico call. Medico calls are free. A **PAN PAN MEDICO** message should contain:

(1) Yacht's name, call sign and nationality.
(2) Yacht's position, next port of call (with ETA) and nearest harbour if required to divert.
(3) Patient's details: name, age, sex, medical history.
(4) Present symptoms and advice required.
(5) What medication is carried on board.

Urgent requests for medical advice should be made on Ch 16 (or 2182 kHz if out of VHF range) direct to HM Coastguard who will arrange a dedicated channel so that your call is connected to a doctor.

Calls for medical assistance (e.g. the presence of a doctor or a casualty to be off-lifted) should be made direct to HM Coastguard on Ch 16, or on 2182 kHz.

In emergency call PAN PAN MEDICO on Ch 16. PAN PAN Medico applies in other countries. For France call: PAN PAN Radiomédical (name of station) in French.

For Belgium call: Radiomédical Oostende, in French, Dutch, English or German.

For Netherlands call: PAN PAN Medico, in Dutch, English, French or German and expect response from Netherlands CG.

For Germany call: PAN PAN Medico with details in German or English; this type of call is more widely used by Germans than Funkarzt (plus name of station).

The International Code signal 'W' (Whiskey •––), means 'I require medical assistance' and can be made by a number of means; see 4.1.2.

6.5.3 Sécurité – Safety signal

This consists of the word **SÉCURITÉ** (pronounced SAY-CURE-E-TAY) spoken three times, and indicates that the station is about to transmit an important navigational or meteorological warning. Such messages usually originate from a Coastguard Radio Station or a Coast Radio Station, and are transmitted on a working frequency after an announcement on the distress frequency.

Safety messages are usually addressed to 'All stations', and are often transmitted at the end of the

C6

first available silence period. An example of a "Securite" message would be:

> **SAYCUREETAY......** (spoken three times)
>
> **ALL STATIONS......** (spoken three times)
>
> **THIS IS......** (spoken three times)
>
> followed by Coastguard Radio Station (or Coast Radio Station) identification, instructions to move to another channel etc and the message.

6.6 GMDSS

6.6.1 Introduction

The Global Maritime Distress and Safety System (GMDSS) is an improved maritime distress and safety communications system adopted by the International Maritime Organisation (IMO).

Before the advent of GMDSS, maritime distress and safety relied heavily on ships and Coast radio stations keeping continuous watch on the three main international distress frequencies: 500 kHz (Morse) and R/T on 2182 kHz and VHF Ch 16. When out of range of Coast radio stations, only ships in the vicinity of a distress incident could render assistance.

GMDSS was introduced in Feb 1992 and became operational in most respects on 1 Feb 1999. The speed with which the various elements of GMDSS are put in place varies from sea area to sea area according to national policies. The Coastguard will cease its dedicated headset VHF Distress Watch on 31 Jan 2005.

It is important to note that ceasing the dedicated distress watch does not dispense with the capability to monitor the VHF Distress Channel since the channel is still needed to talk to a distressed vessel after the GMDSS DSC electronic alert. It is also still required to maintain communications with other ships assisting in the distress situation. Therefore, after 31 January 2005 HM Coastguard will keep a loudspeaker watch on the VHF Distress Channel.

Recommended reading:

ALRS, Vol 5. (UK Hydrographic Office).
GMDSS for small craft. (Clemmetsen/Fernhurst).
VHF DSC Handbook. (Fletcher/Reed's Publications).

6.6.2 Objective

The objective of GMDSS is to alert SAR authorities ashore and ships in the vicinity to a distress incident by means of a combination of satellite and terrestrial communication, and navigation systems. As a result a coordinated SAR operation can be mounted rapidly and reliably anywhere in the world. GMDSS also provides urgency and safety communications, and promulgates Marine Safety Information (MSI); see 6.6.9.

Regardless of the sea areas in which they operate, vessels complying with GMDSS must be able to perform certain functions:

- transmit ship-to-shore distress alerts by two independent means;
- transmit ship-to-ship distress alerts;
- transmit and receive safety information, e.g. navigation and weather warnings;
- transmit signals for locating incidents;
- receive shore-to-ship distress alerts;
- receive ship-to-ship distress alerts;
- transmit and receive communications for SAR co-ordination.

GMDSS regulations apply to all ships over 300 tons engaged in international voyages, but they affect all seagoing craft. Although not obligatory for yachts, some features of GMDSS are already of interest and, as equipment becomes more affordable, yachtsmen may decide to fit GMDSS voluntarily. This will become an increasing necessity as the present system for sending and receiving distress calls is run down.

6.6.3 Distress alerting

GMDSS requires participating ships to be able to send distress alerts by two out of three independent means. These are:

1 Digital selective calling (DSC) using VHF Ch 70, MF 2187·5 kHz, or HF distress and alerting frequencies in the 4, 6, 8,12 and 16 MHz bands.

2 EPIRBs (406 MHz/121·5MHz; float-free or manually operated) using the Cospas/Sarsat satellite system; or the Inmarsat system in the 1·6 GHz band. Both types transmit distress messages which include the position and identification of the vessel in distress. See 6.7 for further details of EPIRBs.

3 Inmarsat, via ship terminals.

6.6.4 Communications

GMDSS uses both terrestrial and satellite-based communications. Terrestrial communications, ie VHF, MF and HF, are employed in Digital Selective Calling (see below). Satellite communications come in the form of INMARSAT and Cospas/Sarsat.

6.6.5 Digital Selective Calling

DSC is a fundamental part of GMDSS. It is so called because information is sent by a burst of digital code; selective because it is addressed to another DSC radio-telephone.

Under GMDSS, every vessel and relevant shore stations has a 9-digit identification number, known as an MMSI (Maritime Mobile Service Identity) that is used for identification in all DSC messages.

DSC is used to transmit distress alerts from ships, and to receive distress acknowledgments from ships or shore stations. DSC can also be used for relay purposes and for Urgency, Safety and routine calling and answering.

In practice, a DSC distress call sent on VHF might work roughly as follows:

Yachtsman presses the distress button; the set automatically switches to Ch 70 and transmits a coded distress message before reverting to Ch l6.

Any ship will reply directly by voice on Ch 16. but a CRS would send a distress acknowledgment on Ch 70 (automatically turning off the distress transmission), before replying on Ch 16. If a distress acknowledgment is not received from a CRS, the call will automatically be repeated about every four minutes.

6.6.6 Inmarsat

Inmarsat (International Maritime Satellite system), through four geostationary satellites positioned over each of the four ocean areas, provides near-global communications except in the polar regions above about Latitudes 70°N and 70°S.

Additionally, 1·6 GHz satellite L-band EPIRBs, provide global distress alerting through Inmarsat satellites operating through Inmarsat. This is referred to as Inmarsat 'E' which provides an alternative alerting system to 406 MHz EPIRBs which utilise the Cospas/ Sarsat satellite system. Inmarsat 'E' EPIRBs can also be equipped with an optional 121·5 MHz locator beacon for homing purposes and/or optional Search and Rescue Radar Transponder (SART).

6.6.7 Transmitting Distress Alerts

A Distress call using DSC is known as a Distress Alert. It is transmitted on Ch 70 and is automatically repeated five times. Whenever possible, a DSC Distress Alert should always include the last known position and time in UTC. Position information is normally entered automatically from an interfaced GPS, but can be entered manually if required. The nature of the distress can also be selected from the receiver menu. The vessels identity (MMSI number) is automatically included. Subsequent communication will be carried out on a notified channel, normally Ch 16.

Understand and follow the procedures for your VHF/ DSC equipment. The Distress Alert is transmitted as follows:

(a) Tune the transmitter to the DSC Distress channel (VHF Ch 70 or 2187·5 kHz).

(b) If time permits, key in or select on the DSC equipment the nature of the distress; the vessel's last known position and time and the type of distress communication subsequently required (RT).

(c) Hold down the SOS button for 5 seconds and the alert will be transmitted.

Once a DSC Distress acknowledgement has been received, or after waiting for about 15 seconds, the vessel in distress should immediately transmit the Distress Message by voice on Ch 16. (see 6.4).

In the event of inadvertently transmitting a Distress alert it is important to cancel the false Distress Alert immediately by making an all stations call and cancelling the false alert sent at (date and time).

6.6.8 Cospas/Sarsat

The US/Russian Cospas/Sarsat satellites complement the various other Satcom systems. They not only detect an emergency signal transmitted by an EPIRB, but also locate it to a high degree of accuracy.

There are four Cospas/Sarsat satellites operating in low polar orbits. In addition to these, there are six Geolut experimental ground receiving stations and four Geosar geostationary satellites capable of receiving alerts from 406 MHz beacons. Geosar satellites have the capability to provide almost immediate distress alerts using existing 406 MHz beacons, although currently without providing distress location because there is no Doppler shift on the uplink frequency. However, this is not a problem if the EPIRB is provided with an inbuilt GPS receiver to provide location directly.

Currently, IMO is planning to terminate 121·5 MHz alerting services sometime after the year 2009. All Cospas/Sarsat satellites launched up to 2006 will be equipped with 121·5 MHz alerting systems.

6.6.9 Sea Areas

For the purposes of GMDSS, the world's sea area are divided into four categories in each of which ships must carry certain types of radio equipment. The UK has declared its coastal waters to be an A1 area, but intends to continue guarding VHF Channel 16 until 01 Feb 2005. VHF DSC is fully operational at all UK Coastguard Co-ordination Centres.

France has declared the English Channel to be an A1 area. As most UK yachtsmen will operate in an A1 area, a VHF radio and a Navtex receiver will initially meet GMDSS requirements. As suitable VHF DSC sets become available (and affordable) it will make sense to re-equip with DSC equipment.

The types of areas are:

A1	an area within RT coverage of at least one VHF Coast or Coastguard radio station in which continuous alerting via DSC is available. Range: roughly 40 miles from the CRS/CG.
A2	an area, excluding sea area A1, within RT coverage of at least one MF CRS/CG in which continuous DSC alerting is available. Range: roughly 100-150 miles from the CRS/CG.
A3	an area, excluding sea areas A1 and A2, within coverage of an Inmarsat satellite between 70°N and 70°S in which continuous alerting is available.
A4	an area outside sea areas A1, A2 and A3. In practice this means the polar regions.

6.6.10 Maritime Safety Information (MSI)

MSI refers to the vital meteorological, navigational and SAR messages which, traditionally, have been broadcast to vessels at sea by CRSs in Morse and by RT on VHF and MF.

GMDSS broadcasts MSI in English by two independent but complementary means, Navtex and SafetyNet:

Navtex on MF (518 kHz and 490 kHz) covers coastal/offshore waters out to about 300 miles from transmitters. SafetyNet uses the Inmarsat satellites to cover beyond MF range. The Enhanced Group Call (EGC) service is a part of SafetyNet which enables MSI to be sent selectively by Inmarsat-C satellites to groups of users in any of the 4 oceans.

MSI is prepared/coordinated by the nations which control the 16 Navareas used for Nav and Met warnings; see 4.7. The UK controls Navarea I, which covers the Atlantic between 48°27'N and 71°N, out to 35°W.

6.7 EPIRBs

6.7.1 Types and installation

There are two types of approved Emergency Position Indicating Radio Beacons (EPIRB), those transmitting on the emergency frequencies of 121·5 MHz (civilian aeronautical distress) or 406 MHz, or on both frequencies.

A third type transmits on 243·0 MHz (military aeronautical distress). 121·5 MHz and 243·0 MHz are monitored by Air Traffic Control and many aircraft; survivors should switch on an EPIRB without delay.

Dependent on type, they must be installed in a proper location so they can float free and automatically activate if the yacht sinks. Many EPIRBs have lanyards intended to secure the EPIRB to a life raft or person in the water and lanyards must not be used for securing the EPIRB to the yacht. This would clearly prevent a float-free type from activating and the EPIRB would be lost with the yacht should it sink.

6.7.2 Operation

All three frequencies can be picked up by the Cospas/Sarsat (C-S) system which uses four near-polar orbital satellites to detect and localise the signals. The processed positions are passed automatically to a Mission Control Centre (MCC) for assessment of any SAR action required; the UK MCC is co-located with ARCC Kinloss.

C-S location accuracy is normally better than 5 km on 406 MHz and better than 20 km on 121·5 and 243·0 MHz. Dedicated SAR aircraft can home on 121·5 MHz and 243·0 MHz, but not on 406 MHz. Typically a helicopter at 1,000 feet can receive homing signals from about 30M range whilst a fixed-wing aircraft at higher altitudes is capable of homing from about 60M.

Airliners flying on commercial air routes often receive and relay information on alerts on 121·5 MHz EPIRBs at up to 200M range. Best results will invariably be obtained from those 406 MHz EPIRBs which also transmit a 121·5 MHz signal for homing purposes.

6.7.3 Registration and false alerts

406 MHz EPIRBs transmit data with a unique code which identifies the individual beacon. It is therefore **essential** that all 406 MHz EPIRBs are registered.

Send to: The EPIRB Register, HM Coastguard, Southern Region, Pendennis Point, Castle Drive, Falmouth TR11 4WZ, Cornwall, ☎ +44 (0) 1326 211569 Fax +44 (0) 1326 319264

Changes of ownership of a 406 MHz EPIRB, or its disposal, should also be notified.

False alerts caused by inadvertent or incorrect use of EPIRBs puts a significant burden on SAR resources. The likelihood of a false alert coinciding with a genuine distress situation is real; in consequence SAR forces could be delayed in responding to a genuine distress – with tragic results.

If an EPIRB is activated, whether accidentally or intentionally, make every reasonable effort to advise the SAR authorities as soon as possible.

6.7.4 SART

A SART (SAR transponder) is not an EPIRB; it is more akin to a small portable Racon (section 3.5). When interrogated by a search radar a SART responds with a series of easily identifiable blips visible on the radar screen. It is often carried in life rafts to assist searching ships and aircraft in finding survivors; it should be mounted at least 1m above sea level. It operates on 9GHz and has a range of about 5M from a ship's radar, and up to 40M from an aircraft

For maximum range, a mounting as high as possible should be chosen. A SART lying flat on the floor of a liferaft will give a range of about 1·8M; when standing upright on the floor, about 2·5M and floating in the water about 2·0M.

Warning Note: A SART will only respond to an X-Band (3cm) radar and will not be seen on a S-Band (10cm) radar.

6.8 SEARCH AND RESCUE (SAR) – UK

6.8.1 Introduction

Around the United Kingdom, the lead authority is HM Coastguard, which initiates and co-ordinates all civil maritime SAR. To assist; the RNLI provide lifeboats; the Ministry of Defence provide declared fixed wing aircraft and helicopters, together with other aircraft and ships which may be available. HM Coastguard also provides SAR helicopters, and Emergency Towing Vessels at selected sites, and Rescue Teams to assist with coastal searches and other coastal incidents, including cliff and mud rescue.

The ARCC at Kinloss also mans the UK Cospas/Sarsat Mission Control Centre (MCC) which receives satellite data from emergency distress beacons on 121·5 MHz, 243·0 MHz and 406 MHz (6.6.4).

6.8.2 Raising the alarm

If an incident afloat is seen from shore, dial 999 and ask for the Coastguard. You will be asked to report on the incident, and possibly to stay near the telephone for further communications. If at sea you receive a distress signal and you are in a position to give assistance, you are obliged to do so with all speed, unless, or until, you are specifically released.

When alerted the Coastguard summons the most appropriate help, i.e. they may direct vessels in the vicinity of the distress; request the launch of an RNLI lifeboat; scramble a military or Coastguard SAR helicopter; other vessels may be alerted through Coastguard Coordination Centres, Coast Radio Stations abroad, or by satellite communications.

6.8.3 Royal National Lifeboat Institution (RNLI)

The RNLI is a registered charity which exists to save life at sea. It provides, on call, a 24-hour lifeboat service up to 50M out from the coasts of the UK and Irish Republic.

There are 215 lifeboat stations, at which are stationed 289 lifeboats ranging from 4·9 to 17·0m in length. These consist of 123 all-weather, 3 intermediate and 163 inshore lifeboats. There are over 100 lifeboats in the reserve fleet.

All are capable of at least 15 knots, and new lifeboats capable of 25 knots are being introduced.

When launched on service, lifeboats over 10m keep watch on 2182 kHz and Ch 16. They can also use alternative frequencies to contact other vessels, SAR aircraft, HM Coastguard or Coast radio stations or other SAR agencies. All lifeboats are fitted with VHF and show a quick-flashing blue light.

A pamphlet Safety on the Sea, produced by the RNLI in co-operation with the RYA, Maritime and Coastguard Agency, BMIF and the Royal Life Saving Society, offers education and guidelines on safety related topics.

Support the RNLI by becoming a member, contact: RNLI, West Quay Road, Poole, Dorset BH15 1HZ. ☎ 01202 663000. 📠 01202 663167.

6.9 HM Coastguard

6.9.1 Organisation

HM Coastguard combined with the Marine Safety Agency in April 1998 to form the Maritime and Coastguard Agency (MCA). The locations of HM Coastguard Coordination Centres are shown in Table 6(1) and Fig. 6(2).

HM Coastguard initiates and co-ordinates civil maritime SAR around the UK and over a large part of the eastern Atlantic. Its domain is divided into three Maritime Search and Rescue Regions (SRRs), with Maritime Rescue Co-ordination Centres (MRCCs) at Falmouth, Dover, Great Yarmouth, Aberdeen, the Clyde and Swansea.

Each SRR is divided into districts, each under a Maritime Rescue Sub-Centre (MRSC). Their boundaries are stated in Table 6 (1) and shown on the maps at the start of Areas 1–11 in Chapter 9. The telephone number of the nearest MRCC/MRSC (or other national equivalent) is shown for each harbour.

Within each of the eighteen districts thus formed there is an organisation of Auxiliary Coastguard Rescue Teams, grouped within sectors under the management of regular Coastguard Officers.

There are about 560 regular Coastguard Officers, with more than 3,100 Auxiliary Coastguard Rescue Teams on call for emergencies. The Coastguard is also responsible for persons in distress or missing on the coastline and has search, cliff and mud rescue (at selected locations) capabilities.

6.9.2 Functions

HM Coastguard is responsible for:

(1) Maintaining a continuous listening radio watch on 156·8 MHz the VHF Distress, Urgency, Safety and calling frequency (VHF Ch 16) to a range of at least 30M offshore.

(2) Maintaining a continuous listening radio watch on 2182 kHz, the MF Distress, Urgency, Safety and Calling frequency from selected rescue centres, providing 150M ground wave cover for all parts of the UK coastline.

C6

(3) Maintaining an electronic radio watch on VHF DSC Channel 70 around the whole of the UK coastline, effectively, within sight of land, 0-30M offshore. The UK has been declared fully operational for GMDSS Sea Area A1.

(4) Maintaining an electronic radio watch on MF DSC on 2187·5 kHz at selected stations, effectively, within 30M - 150M offshore.

Note: The UKCG have no plans to designate any shore based station for HF DSC. An agreement with Denmark, allows Lyngby radio to forward any HF DSC alert messages to the UK, via the liaison station at MRCC Yarmouth.

(5) Broadcasting MSI to set schedules on VHF and MF RT, including Negative Tidal Surge Warnings, Subfacts and Gunfacts, ice warnings (when appropriate) and interruption to electronic navigational aids.

For Distress, Urgency and Safety calls covering UK waters, all rescue centres keep watch on VHF DSC Ch 70, VHF RT Channel 16, and, at selected stations, on MF DSC 2187·5 kHz and MF RT 2182 kHz.

VHF Channels 10, 24, 67, 73, 44 and 86 are working channels; Ch 67 is the Small Craft Safety channel, accessed via Channel 16. Details of VHF or MF working frequencies will be given after an initial announcement on VHF Ch 16 or MF 2182kHz.

Coastguard MRCC/MRSC's are also responsible for responding to PAN PAN MEDICO calls and providing telephone link calls to a doctor for medical advice. Initial call should be made on MF or VHF DSC, Ch 16, or 2182 kHz. The caller will be advised of an appropriate working channel/frequency.

NOTE: HM Coastguard does not provide a commercial telephone link call service.

The Radiotelephone call sign of an MRCC or MRSC is its geographical name, followed by 'Coastguard' e.g, SOLENT COASTGUARD.

In the Dover Strait the Channel Navigation Information Service (CNIS) provides a 24 hrs radar watch and a radio safety service for all shipping. See Table 6 (1).

All Coastguard Rescue Centres provide Maritime Safety Information broadcasts at four hourly intervals. Information will include WZ Navigational Warnings, Gale Warnings, Local Inshore Forecasts, Tidal Surge Warnings, and local navigation warnings. Each rescue centre follows a separate broadcast schedule. Skippers/Owners should listen to these scheduled broadcasts and avoid requesting individual forecasts.

Gale warnings and WZ Navigation Warnings are broadcast on receipt then at 4 hourly intervals in accordance with the MSI Broadcast Schedule. A brochure HM Coastguard Broadcast Times for Maritime Safety Information – MCA/064 is available from MCA HQ, Southampton – (See page 25).

6.10 MARITIME SEARCH AND RESCUE REGIONS

6.10.1 Search and Rescue Regions

One of the most important aspects of GMDSS is the establishment of a Global Search and Rescue Plan.

The IMO and ICAO, the two agencies of the United Nations devoted to maritime and aeronautical safety are both working towards this aim.

As party to SOLAS, and the IMO/ICAO conventions a State is obliged to provide certain maritime or aeronautical SAR coordination and services.

A Search and Rescue Region (SRR) is an area of defined dimensions associated with a Rescue Coordination Centre within which SAR services are provided. The purpose of having an SRR is to clearly define who has primary responsibility for coordinating responses to distress situations in every area of the world and to enable rapid distribution of the distress alerts to the appropriate RCC.

The delimitation of an SRR is not related to, and shall not prejudice, the delimitation of any boundary between States. Such areas are established to ensure that primary responsibility for coordinating SAR services for that geographical area is assumed by some state.

In practice, SAR services may not necessarily be provided by their designated state. In such cases, SAR facilities are likely to be provided by the nearest country having the most appropriate SAR assets. Very few SSRs around the world have been totally agreed between all neighbouring states, however, those in the British Isles and North-West Europe which have are shown as a tint on the diagram opposite. By far the majority of SSRs have either been unilaterally declared, and are operated by the responsible state, according to a tacit acceptance by neighbouring states, or are awaiting formal approval between neighbouring states.

Fig. 6 (1) Maritime search and rescue regions (to be issued later)

INTENTIONALLY BLANK

For map of British Isles and NE Europe
Maritime Search and Rescue Regions

6.10.2 Emergency VHF DF

A number of HM Coastguard MRCC/MRSC's can provide VHF DF bearings to yachts in distress. The stations operate direction finding antenna around the coast of UK from which the bearings of vessels within range, and transmitting on VHF, can be determined.

On request from a vessel in distress the Coastguard station will transmit from the direction-finding site the bearing of the vessel from the direction finding antenna.

This service is only available for emergency use. Call on VHF Ch 16. Bearings will be passed on Ch 16 or 67 by the CG Centre as the yacht's true bearing from the DF site. Direction finding sites are shown on Admiralty charts by the symbol ◎RG .

In the Channel Islands a yacht should transmit on Ch 16 in distress or Ch 67 for Guernsey or Ch 82 for Jersey.

France operates a similar VHF Direction Finding Service which is remotely controlled by CROSS, a signal station or a Naval lookout station. CROSS stations keep watch on Ch 16, 11 and 67. Signal stations and Lookout stations keep watch on Ch 16

6.10.3 Yacht and Boat Safety Scheme

This free scheme provides useful information about your boat and its equipment which will assist the Coastguard toward a successful SAR operation. Complete a Form CG66, obtainable from the local Coastguard station, harbour master or marina. The completed cards should be returned to your nearest Coastguard Coordination Centre where they will be logged into a data file. You should inform the Coastguard if the ownership, name of the craft, or any address given on Form CG66 changes. A tear-off section can be given to a friend or relative so that they know which Coastguard station to contact if they are concerned for the boat's safety. A CG66 is valid for two years. If it is not renewed within that time, the old CG66 data will be removed from the CG records.

It is not the function of HM Coastguard to maintain watch for boats on passage, but they will record information by phone before departure or from intermediate ports, or while on passage by visual signals or VHF Ch 67 (the Small Craft Safety Channel).

When using Ch 67 for safety messages, skippers should give the name of the MRCC/MRSC holding the boat's CG66. In these circumstances the Coastguard must be told of any change to the planned movements of the boat, and it is important that they are informed of the boat's safe arrival at her ultimate destination – so as to avoid needless overdue action being taken.

6.10.4 National Coastwatch Institution (NCI)

The NCI, a registered charity, was founded in 1994 to re-establish a visual watch around the UK coast.

Many former CG lookout stations are manned in daylight hours by trained volunteers. VHF Ch 16 is monitored, but NCI stations are not at present licenced to transmit on VHF. In poor visibility some stations keep a radar watch to 20M offshore. All NCI stations have telephones; see below. They are able to report the actual local weather on request.

Any incident seen at sea, or on coastal footpaths, is passed to the nearest CG Centre for the CG to take the appropriate action. Most NCI stations can warn a yacht by light signal of an apparently dangerous course, eg 'U' ••— = You are standing into danger.

For further information contact:
NCI Head Office,
4a Trafalgar Square, Fowey, Cornwall PL23 1AZ.
☎ 0870 787 2147; 📠 0870 164 1893;
e-mail: info@nci.org.uk
web: http://www.nci.org.uk

The following NCI stations were operating in 2001:

St Ives	01736 799398
Cape Cornwall (Land's End) Ⓡ	01736 787890
Gwennap Head (Land's End) Ⓡ	01736 871351
Bass Point (Lizard) Ⓡ	01326 290212
Polruan (Fowey)	01726 870291
Rame Head (Plymouth)	01752 823706
Prawle Point Ⓡ	01548 511259
Exmouth	01395 222492
Portland Bill Ⓡ	01305 860178
St Alban's Head Ⓡ	01929 439220
Peverill Pt, Swanage Ⓡ	01929 422596
Folkestone	01303 227132
Canvey Island	01268 696971
Felixstowe	01394 670808
Lowestoft	01502 584400
Gorleston (Great Yarmouth)	01493 440384
North Denes (Great Yarmouth)	01493 332192
Mundesley (Norfolk) Ⓡ	01263 722399
Sheringham (Norfolk)	01263 823470
Redcar (Teesside) Ⓡ	01642 491606
Hartlepool Ⓡ	01429 274931
Wylfa Head (Anglesey)	01407 711152

Ⓡ = Radar equipped.

Stations which were due to open in 2000 included: Needles, Herne Bay, Lowestoft, Wells-next-the-sea, Barry and St Ives.

6.11 SIGNALS USED IN DISTRESS SITUATIONS

6.11.1 Visual signals, shore to ships

If no radio link is possible, the following may be used to a vessel in distress or stranded off the UK coast.

(a) Acknowledgment of distress signal.
By day: Orange smoke signal, or combined light and sound signal consisting of three signals fired at about one-minute intervals.

By night: White star rocket consisting of three single signals at about one-minute intervals.

(b) Landing signals for small boats.

Vertical motion of a white flag or arms (white light or flare by night), or signalling K (–•–) by light or sound = This is the best place to land.

Direction may be given by placing a steady white light or flare at a lower level.

Horizontal motion of a white flag or arms extended horizontally (white light or flare by night), or signalling S (•••) = Landing here is highly dangerous.

In addition, a better landing place may be signalled by carrying a white flag (flare or light), or by firing a white star signal in the direction indicated; or by signalling R (•–•) if a better landing is to the right of the direction of approach, or L (•–••) if it is to the left.

(c) Signals for shore life-saving apparatus.

Vertical motion of a white flag or the arms (or of a white light or flare) = Affirmative; or specifically, Rocket line is held; Tail block is made fast; Hawser is made fast; Man is in breeches buoy; or Haul away.

Horizontal motion of a white flag or the arms (or of a white light or flare) = Negative; or specifically, Slack away or Avast (stop) hauling.

NB: Rocket rescue equipment is no longer used by HM CG. Some larger vessels carry a line-throwing appliance requiring on-shore liaison before use.

(d) Warning signal.

International Code signal U (••–) or NF (–••–•) = You are running into danger. A white flare, white star rocket, or explosive signal may be used to draw attention to the above signals.

6.11.2 Signals used by SAR aircraft

A searching aircraft normally flies at about 3,000–5,000ft, or below cloud, firing a green Very light every five or ten minutes and at each turning point.

On seeing a green flare, a yacht in distress should take the following action:

(1) Wait for the green flare to die out.

(2) Fire one red flare.

(3) Fire another red flare after about 20 seconds. (This allows the aircraft to line up on the bearing.)

(4) Fire a third red flare when the aircraft is overhead, or if it appears to be going badly off course.

6.11.3 Directing signals by aircraft

(1) To direct a yacht towards a ship or aircraft in distress, the aircraft circles the yacht at least once. It then crosses low, ahead of the yacht, opening and closing the throttle or changing the propeller pitch. Finally it heads in the direction of the casualty.

(2) To indicate that assistance by the yacht is no longer required, the aircraft passes low, astern of the yacht, opening and closing the throttle or changing the propeller pitch.

6.12 HELICOPTER RESCUE

6.12.1 Capability:

SAR helicopters in the UK are based at Culdrose, Portland, Lee-on-Solent, Wattisham, Leconfield, Boulmer, Lossiemouth, Sumburgh, Stornoway, Prestwick, Valley and Chivenor.

Sea King SAR helicopters can operate to a range of 300 miles and can rescue up to 18 survivors. The Sea King's automatic hover control system permits rescues at night and in fog.

6.12.2 Communications:

SAR helicopters are generally fitted with VHF, FM and AM, UHF and HF SSB RT and can communicate with lifeboats etc on VHF FM. Communications between ship and helicopter should normally be on VHF Ch 16 or 67; 2182 kHz SSB may also be available. If contact is difficult, communication can often be achieved through a Nimrod aircraft if on scene, or through a lifeboat or HM Coastguard.

When the helicopter is sighted by a boat in distress, a flare (fired away from, not at, the helicopter), an orange smoke signal, dye marker or an Aldis lamp (not pointed directly at the helicopter) will assist recognition – very important if other vessels are in the vicinity. Dodgers with the boat's name or sail number are useful aids to identification.

6.12.3 On the yacht

Survivors from a yacht with a mast may need to be picked up from a dinghy or life raft streamed at least 100ft (30m) away. In a small yacht with no dinghy, survivors (wearing life jackets) may need to be picked up from the water, at the end of a long warp. It is very important that no survivor boards a life raft or jumps into the sea until instructed to do so by the helicopter (either by VHF Ch 16 or 67) or by the winchman (by word of mouth). Sails should be lowered and lashed and it is helpful if the drift of the boat is reduced by a sea anchor.

If a crewman descends from the helicopter, he will take charge. Obey his instructions quickly. Never secure the winch wire to the yacht, and beware that it may carry a lethal static charge if it is not dipped (earthed) in the sea before handling.

6.12.4 Double lift

Survivors may be lifted by double lift in a strop, accompanied by the crewman in a canvas seat. Or it may be necessary, with no crewman, for a survivor to position himself in the strop. Put your head and shoulders through the strop so that the padded part is in the small of the back and the toggle is in front of the face. Pull the toggle down, as close to the chest as possible. When ready, give a thumbs-up sign with an extended arm, and place both arms close down by the side of the body (resist the temptation to hang on to the strop). On reaching the helicopter, do exactly as instructed by the crew. Injured persons can be lifted strapped into a special stretcher carried in the helicopter.

6.12.5 Hi-line

In some circumstances a 'Hi-line technique' may be used. This is a rope tail, attached to the helicopter winch wire by a weak link, and weighted at its lower end. When it is lowered to the yacht do not make it fast, but coil it down carefully. The helicopter pays out the winch wire and then moves to one side of the yacht and descends, while the yacht takes in the slack (keeping it outboard and clear of all obstructions) until the winch hook and strop are on board.

One of the helicopter crew may be lowered with the strop. When ready to lift, the helicopter ascends and takes in the wire. Pay out the tail, keeping enough weight on it to keep it taut until the end is reached, then cast it off well clear of the yacht. But if a further lift is to be made the tail should be retained on board (not made fast) to facilitate recovery of the strop for the next lift.

When alighting from a helicopter, beware of the tail rotor which can be difficult to see. Obey all instructions given by the helicopter crew.

6.13 ABANDON SHIP

Do not abandon a yacht until she is definitely sinking. A yacht is easier to find than a liferaft and provides better shelter. While she is still afloat use her resources (such as R/T, for distress calls) and put extra equipment in the liferaft or lash into the dinghy (which should also be taken, if possible). Make all preparations.

Before entering the liferaft, and cutting it adrift:

(a) Send a MAYDAY call, saying that yacht is being abandoned, with position and number of people on board.

(b) Dress warmly with sweaters etc under oilskins, and life jacket on top. Take extra clothes.

(c) Fill any available containers with fresh water to about ¾ full, so that they will float.

(d) Collect additional food, tins and tin-opener.

(e) Collect navigational gear, EPIRB, SART, handheld VHF, torch, extra flares, bucket, length of line, First-aid kit, knife, fenders etc. Some of items (c) – (e) should already be in a survival bag, essential when a yacht is abandoned in a hurry.

Launch the liferaft on the lee side of the yacht, having first checked that the painter is secured to a strongpoint. The painter may be up to 10m long; after about 3-4m give a sharp tug to activate the CO_2 bottle. If the liferaft inflates upside down, try to right it from the yacht. Keep the liferaft close alongside and try to board it without getting into the water.

Once in the liferaft, plan for the worst, ie a long period before rescue. Protection, Location, Water, Food are your priorities – in that order. Always believe that you will survive.

(a) Keep the inside of the raft as dry as possible. Huddle together for warmth. Close the openings as necessary, but keep a good lookout for shipping and aircraft.

(b) Stream the drogue if necessary for stability, or so as to stay near the original position.

(c) Take anti-seasick pills.

(d) Ration fresh water to ½ litre per person per day; none in the first 24 hours. Do not drink sea water or urine. Collect rain water.

(e) Use flares sparingly, on the skipper's orders.

6.14 HAZARDS

6.14.1 Submarines

Fishing vessels and occasionally yachts have been snagged or hit by submarines operating just below the surface. The best advice available to yachtsmen is:

(a) Listen to Subfacts (6.13.2).

(b) Avoid charted submarine exercise areas.

(c) Keep clear of any vessel flying the Code Flags 'NE2' meaning that submarines are in the vicinity.

(d) Run your engine or generator even when under sail.

(e) Operate your echo sounder.

(f) At night show deck-level navigation lights, ie on pulpit and stern.

The risk is greatest in the English Channel, the Irish Sea, the Firth of Clyde, North Channel, off W Scotland and especially at night. Submarine exercise areas are shown by name/number in 9.1.18, 9.2.33, 9.8.23 and 9.9.24.

6.14.2 Subfacts

These are broadcast warnings of planned or known submarine activity. Subfacts (South Coast) give details relevant to the English Channel; see 9.1.18 & 9.2.33. They are broadcast by **Falmouth MRCC** (CRR) on VHF Channels 10, 24, 73, 84 or 86 after an initial announcement on VHF Ch 16 indicating which VHF

Channel will be used for the broadcast at 0140 UTC and every 4 hours thereafter, and by **Brixham MRSC** on Ch 16 at 0050 and every 4 hours thereafter. See Fig. 6 (1).

Subfacts (Clyde) give details relevant to the W coast of Scotland (see 9.8.23 and 9.9.24). They are broadcast by **Stornoway MRCC** on VHF Channels 10, 24, 73, 84 or 86 after an initial announcement on VHF Ch 16 indicating which VHF Channel will be used for the broadcast at 0110 UTC and every 4 hours thereafter, by **Clyde MRCC** on VHF Channels 10, 24, 73, 84 or 86 after an initial announcement on VHF Ch 16 indicating which VHF Channel will be used for the broadcastUTC and every 4 hours thereafter, and by **Belfast MRSC** on VHF Channels 10, 24, 73, 84 or 86 after an initial announcement on VHF Ch 16 indicating which VHF Channel will be used for the broadcast at 0305 UTC and every 4 hours thereafter.

6.14.3 Gunfacts

Gunfacts are warnings of intended naval firing practice broadcast to mariners. They do not restrict the passage of any vessel. The onus for safety lies with the naval unit concerned. The broadcasts include:

(a) Time (LT) and approximate location of firings, with a declared safe distance in M.

(b) Whether illuminants are to be fired.

Gunfacts include underwater explosions, gunnery and missile firings. For underwater explosions only broadcasts will be made on Ch 16 at 1 hr, 30 mins, and immediately prior to detonation.

Gunfacts (S Coast) are issued by FOST, Plymouth for English Channel exercise areas (9.1.18 and 9.2.33). Gunfacts are broadcast by Falmouth MRCC on on VHF Channels 10, 24, 73, 84 or 86 after an initial announcement on VHF Ch 16 indicating which VHF Channel will be used for the broadcast at 0140 UTC and every 4 hours thereafter, and by Brixham MRSC on VHF Channels 10, 24, 73, 84 or 86 after an initial announcement on VHF Ch 16 indicating which VHF Channel will be used for the broadcast at 0050 and every 4 hours thereafter. See Fig 6 (2).

Gunfacts (Ship) are issued by a nominated warship and cover activity in all UK areas except the English Channel. Broadcasts are made daily at 0800 and 1400 LT on Ch 06 or 67 after an announcement on Ch 16.

6.15 IRISH COAST GUARD

The Irish Coast Guard is part of the Department of Marine, Leeson Lane, Dublin 2. ☎ (01) 6620922; 📠 (01) 662 0795.

The Coast Guard co-ordinates all SAR operations around the coast of Ireland through Dublin MRCC, Malin Head MRSC and Valentia MRSC. It liaises with UK and France during any rescue operation within 100M of the Irish coast.

The MRCC/MRSCs are co-located with the Coast radio stations of the same name and manned by the same staff. All stations maintain H24 listening watch on VHF Ch 16. In emergency dial 999 and ask for Marine Rescue.

Details of the MRCC/MRSCs are as follows:

Dublin (MRCC)

53°20'N 06°15W.
☎ 01 6620922; 📠 01 6620795.
Covers Carlingford Lough to Youghal.
DSC MMSI (to be notified).

Valentia (MRSC)

51°56'N 10°21'W.
☎ 066 76109; 📠 066 76289.
Covers Youghal to Slyne Head.
DSC A2 MMSI 002500200 MF 2187·5 kHz.

Malin Head (MRSC)

55°22'N 07°20W.
☎ 077 70103; 📠 077 70221.
Covers Slyne Head to Lough Foyle.
DSC A2 MMSI 002500100 MF 2187·5 kHz.

6.15.1 SAR resources

The Irish Coast Guard provides some 50 units around the coast and is on call 24 hours a day. Some of these units have a specialist cliff climbing capability.

A dedicated Coast Guard Sikorsky S61N SAR helicopter, based at Shannon, can respond within 15 to 45 minutes and operate to a radius of 200M. It is equipped with infrared search equipment and can uplift 14 survivors. Dauphin SA 365F helicopters (based at Finner Camp in Donegal and at Baldonnel, Dublin) can operate to 150 miles by day and 70 miles at night.

Other military and civilian aircraft and vessels, together with the Garda and lighthouse service can be called upon.

The RNLI maintains four RNLI stations around the coast and some 26 lifeboats. Additionally, six individually community-run inshore rescue boats are available.

6.14.2 Coast and cliff rescue services

This comprises about 50 stations manned by volunteers, who are trained in first aid and equipped with inflatables, breeches buoys, cliff ladders etc. Their ☎ numbers (the Leader's residence) are given, where appropriate, under each port.

C6

TABLE 6 (1) HM Coastguard MRCCs and MRSCs

All Centres have operational A1 DSC. All A2 DSC stations are operational, as indicated by 2187·5 kHz. WZ (Coastal) Navigation Warnings, Gale Warnings and Inshore Forecasts are broadcast as follows:

Stations additionally broadcasting Gunfacts and Subfacts are indicated by *.

FALMOUTH COASTGUARD (CGR) (MRCC) 50°09′N 05°03′W.

Pendennis Point, Castle Drive, Falmouth TR11 4WZ. ☎ 01326 317575. Fax 01326 318342.

Area from Marsland Mouth to Dodman Point.

DSC MMSI 002320014 2187·5 kHz, Ch 70.

On VHF Ch 16*, MF 2226 kHz Navigation Warnings at: 0140 0540 0940 1340 1740 and 2140 UTC.

BRIXHAM COASTGUARD (CGR) (MRSC) 50°24′N 03°31′W.

King's Quay, Brixham TQ59 9TW. ☎ 01803 882704. Fax 01803 882780.

Area from Dodman Point to Topsham.

DSC MMSI 002320013, Ch 70.

On VHF Ch 16* Navigation Warnings at: 0050 0450 0850 1250 1650 2050 UTC

PORTLAND COASTGUARD (CGR) (MRSC) 50°36′N 02°27′W.

Custom House Quay, Weymouth DT4 8BE. ☎ 01305 760439. Fax 01305 760452.

Area from Topsham to Chewton Bunney.

DSC MMSI 002320012, Ch 70.

On VHF Ch 16* Navigation Warnings at: 0220 0620 1020 1420 1820 and 2220 UTC

SOLENT COASTGUARD (CGR) (MRSC) 50°48′N 01°12′W.

44A Marine Parade West, Lee-on-Solent, Gosport PO13 9NR. ☎ 023 9255 2100. Fax 023 9251 1763.

Area from Chewton Bunney to Beachy Head.

Call Ch 67 (H24) for safety traffic.

DSC MMSI 002320011, Ch 70.

On VHF Ch 16*, MF 1641 kHz Navigation Warnings at: 0040 0440 0840 1240 1640 1840 and 2240 UTC

DOVER COASTGUARD (CGR) (MRCC) 50°08′N 01°12′E.

Langdon Battery, Swingate, Dover CT15 5NA. ☎ 01304 210008. Fax 01304 210302.

Area from Beachy Head to Reculver Towers.

DSC MMSI 002320010, Ch 70.

Operates Channel Navigation Information Service (CNIS) which broadcasts nav and tfc info on Ch 11 every H+40 (and at H+55 in bad vis). Monitor Ch 69 for safety info.

THAMES COASTGUARD (CGR) (MRSC) 51°51′N 01°17′E.

East Terrace, Walton-on-the-Naze CO14 8PY. ☎ 01255 675518. Fax 01255 675249.

Area from Reculver Towers to Southwold.

DSC MMSI 002320009, Ch 70.

On VHF Ch 16 Navigation Warnings at: 0010 0410 08105 1210 1610 and 2010 UTC

Fig. 6 (2) Coastguard co-ordination centres

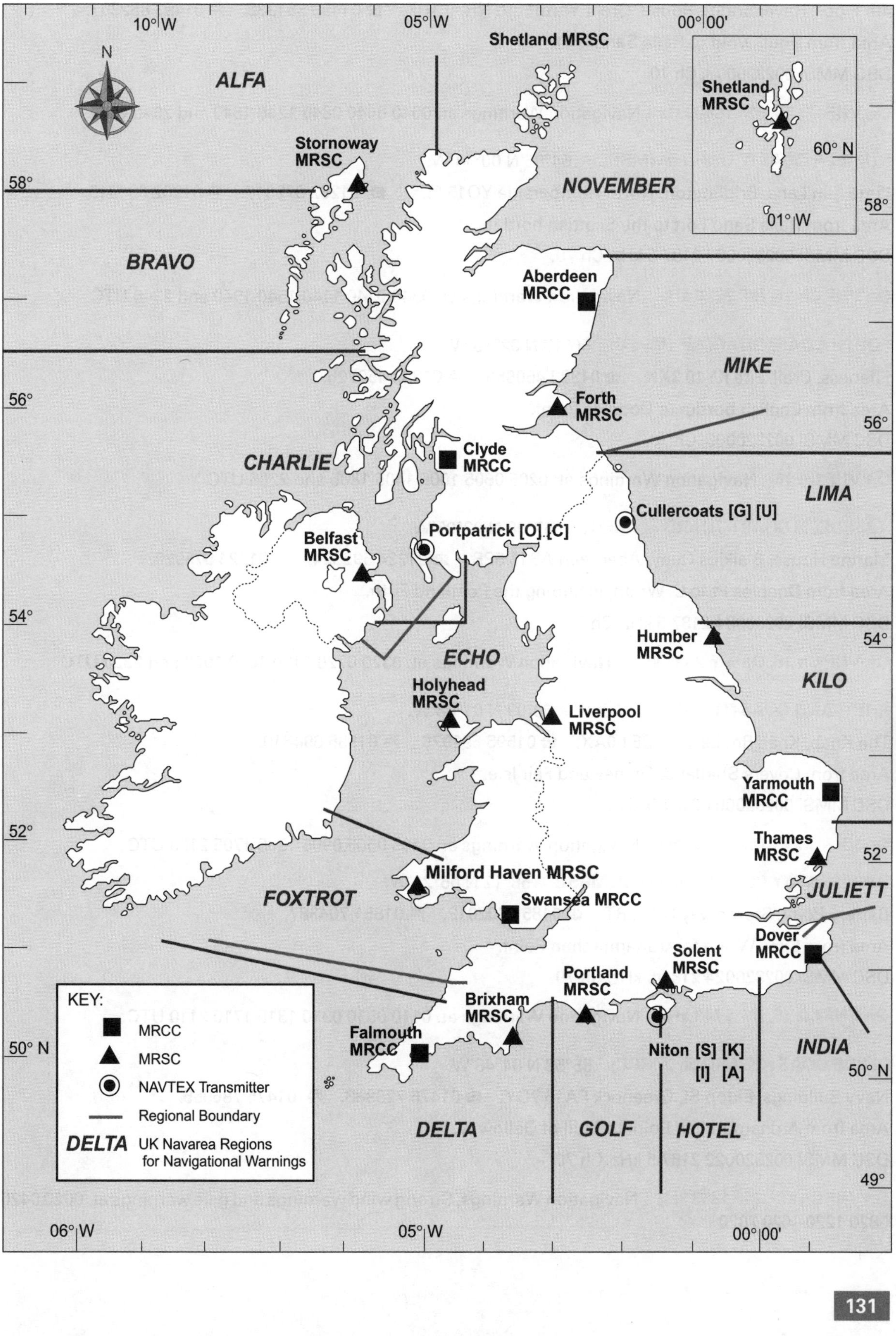

C6

YARMOUTH COASTGUARD (CGR) (MRCC) 52°37'N 01°43'E.

4th Floor, Havenbridge House, Great Yarmouth NR30 1HZ. ☎ 01493 851338. Fax 01493 852307.

Area from Southwold to Haile Sand Fort.

DSC MMSI 002320008, Ch 70.

On VHF Ch 16, MF 1869 kHz Navigation Warnings at: 0040 0440 0840 1240 1640 and 2040 UTC

HUMBER COASTGUARD (CGR) (MRSC) 54°06'N 00°11'W.

Lime Kiln Lane, Bridlington, North Humberside YO15 2LX. ☎ 01262 672317. Fax 01262 606915.

Area from Haile Sand Fort to the Scottish border.

DSC MMSI 002320007 2187·5 kHz, Ch 70.

On VHF Ch 16, MF 2226 kHz Navigation Warnings at: 0340 0740 1140 1540 1940 and 2340 UTC

FORTH COASTGUARD (CGR) (MRSC) 56°17'N 02°35'W.

Fifeness, Crail, Fife KY10 3XN. ☎ 01333 450666. Fax 01333 450725.

Area from English border to Doonies Point.

DSC MMSI 002320005, Ch 70.

On VHF Ch 16 Navigation Warnings at: 0205 0605 1005 1405 1805 and 2205 UTC

ABERDEEN COASTGUARD (CGR) (MRCC) 57°08'N 02°05'W.

Marine House, Blaikies Quay, Aberdeen AB11 5PB. ☎ 01224 592334. Fax 01224 575920.

Area from Doonies Pt to C. Wrath, including the Pentland Firth.

DSC MMSI 00230004 2187·5 kHz, Ch 70.

On VHF Ch 16, On MF 2691 kHz Navigation Warnings at: 0320 0720 1120 1520 1920 and 2320 UTC

SHETLAND COASTGUARD (CGR) (MRSC) 60°09'N 01°08'W.

The Knab, Knab Rd, Lerwick ZE1 0AX. ☎ 01595 692976. Fax 01595 694810.

Area from Covers Shetland, Orkney and Fair Isle.

DSC MMSI 002320001 2187·5 kHz.

On VHF Ch 16, MF 1770 kHz Navigation Warnings at: 0105 0505 0905 1305 1705 2105 UTC

STORNOWAY COASTGUARD (CGR) (MRSC) 58°12'N 06°22'W.

Battery Point, Stornoway HS1 2RT. ☎ 01851 702013. Fax 01851 704387.

Area from Cape Wrath to Ardnamurchan Point.

DSC MMSI 002320024 2187·5 kHz, Ch 70

On VHF Ch 16, MF 1743 kHz Navigation Warnings at: 0110 0510 0910 1310 1710 2110 UTC

CLYDE COASTGUARD (CGR) (MRCC) 55°58'N 04°48'W.

Navy Buildings, Eldon St, Greenock PA16 7QY. ☎ 01475 729988. Fax 01475 786955.

Area from Ardnamurchan Point to Mull of Galloway.

DSC MMSI 002320022 2187·5 kHz, Ch 70.

On VHF Ch 16*, MF 1883 kHz Navigation Warnings, Strong wind warnings and gale warnings at: 0020 0420 0820 1220 1620 2020

BELFAST COASTGUARD (CGR) **(MRSC)** 54°40′N 05°40′W.

Bregenz House, Quay St, Bangor, Co Down BT20 5ED. ☎ 02891 463933. Fax 02891 465886.

Area covers Northern Ireland.

DSC MMSI 002320021, Ch 70.

On VHF Ch 16* Navigation Warnings at: 0305 0705 1105 1505 1905 and 2305 UTC

LIVERPOOL COASTGUARD (CGR) **(MRSC)** 53°30′N 03°03′W.

Hall Road West, Crosby, Liverpool L23 8SY ☎ 0151 931 3341 Fax 0151 931 3347

Area from Mull of Galloway to Queensferry.

DSC MMSI 002320019 Ch 70

On VHF Ch 16 Navigation Warnings at 0210 0610 1010 1410 1810 and 2210 UT

HOLYHEAD COASTGUARD (CGR) **(MRSC)** 53°19′N 04°38′W.

Holyhead, Anglesea, Gwynedd LL65 1ET ☎ 01407 762051 Fax 01407 764373

Area from Queensferry to Friog

DSC MMSI 002320018 Ch 70 2187·5 kHz

On VHF Ch 16 Navigation Warnings at: 0235 0635 1035 1435 1835 and 2235 UTC

MILFORD HAVEN COASTGUARD (CGR) **(MRSC)** 51°41′N 05°10′W.

Gorsewood Drive, Hakin, Milford Haven, Dyfed SA73 3ER. ☎ 01646 690909. Fax 01646 692176.

Area from Friog to River Towy.

DSC MMSI 002320017 2187·5 kHz, Ch 70.

On VHF Ch 16, MF 1767 kHz Navigation Warnings at: 0335 0735 1135 1535 1935 and 2335 UTC

SWANSEA COASTGUARD (CGR) **(MRCC)** 51°34′N 03°58′W.

Tutt Head, Mumbles, Swansea SA3 4EX. ☎ 01792 366534. Fax 01792 369005.

Area from River Towy to Marsland Mouth.

DSC MMSI 002320016, Ch 70.

On VHF Ch 16 Navigation Warnings at: 0005 0405 0805 1205 1605 and 2005 UTC

CHANNEL ISLANDS

ST PETER PORT RADIO (CRS) **(CRS)** 49°27′·00N 02°32′00W.

☎: 01481 720672. Fax: 01534 714177

Are covers the Channel Islands Northern area; Alderney Radio keeps watch Ch 16 HJ.

DSC MMSI 002320064 Ch 70

On VHF Ch 20, MF 1764 kHz Navigation Warnings at: 0133 0533 0933 1333 1733 and 2133 UTC

JERSEY RADIO (CRS) **(CRS)** 49°10′·85N 02°14′30W.

☎: 01534 741121. Fax: 01534 499089

Area covers the Channel Islands Southern area.

DSC MMSI 002320060 Ch 70

On VHF Ch 25 82, MF 1658 kHz Navigation Warnings at: 0645 0433 0745 0845 1245 1633 1845 2033 2245 2033 UTC

C6

6.16 FRANCE – CROSS

Five Centres Régionaux Opérationnels de Surveillance et de Sauvetage (CROSS) cover the Channel and Atlantic coasts; see Fig. 6 (3). A CROSS is an MRCC and a sous-CROSS an MRSC. CROSS provides a permanent, H24, all weather operational presence along the French coast and liaises with foreign CGs. CROSS' main functions include:

(1) Co-ordinating Search and Rescue.
(2) Navigational surveillance.
(3) Broadcasting navigational warnings.
(4) Broadcasting weather information.
(5) Anti-pollution control.
(6) Marine and fishery surveillance.

All centres keep watch on VHF Ch 16 and Ch 70 (DSC), and broadcast gale warnings and weather forecasts and local navigational warnings; see Chapter 5.

CROSS Étel specialises in providing medical advice and responds to alerts from Cospas/Sarsat satellites.

CROSS can be contacted by R/T, by ☎, through Coast radio stations, via the National Gendarmerie or Affaires Maritimes, or via a Semaphore station. Call *Semaphore* stations on Ch 16 (working Ch 10) or by ☎ as listed opposite.

In addition to their safety and SAR functions, CROSS stations using, for example, the call sign *Corsen Traffic* monitor Traffic Separation Schemes in the Dover Strait, off Casquets and off Ouessant, they also broadcast navigational warnings and weather forecasts. See Chapter 5 for times and VHF channels used.

6.16.1 CROSS stations

All stations co-ordinate SAR on VHF Ch 15 67 68 73. DSC Ch 70

CROSS Gris-Nez 50°52'N 01°35'E Belgian Border to Cap d'Antifer **MMSI 002275100**
☎ 03·21·87·21·87 📠 03·21·87·76·55 DSC Ch 70 MF 2187·5 kHz
Navigation Warnings
On VHF Ch 79:
From: **Dunkerque, Gris-Nez, Saint-Frieux,** and **L'Ailly** every H+10
On MF 1659 kHz:
Gris-Nez at 0833 2033 UTC

CROSS Jobourg 49°41'N 01°54'W Cap de la Hague to the Pointe Penmarc'h **MMSI 002275200**
☎ 02·33·52·72·13 📠 02·33·52·71·72
Navigation Warnings
On VHF Ch 80:
From: **Antifer, Ver-sur-Mer, Gatteville, Jobourg, Granville and Roche Douvres every H+20/H+50.**
On MF 1650 kHz:
Gris-Nez at 0915 2115 LT

CROSS Corsen 48°24'N 04°47'W Mont St Michel to Pointe de Penmarc'h **MMSI 002275300**
☎ 02·96·89·31·31 📠 02·96·89·65·75
Navigation Warnings
On MF 2677 kHz:
From **CROSS Corsen** at 0735 1935 LT

CROSS Étel 47°39'N 03°12'W Pointe de Penmarc'h to l'Anse de l'Aiguillon **MMSI 002275000**
☎ 02·97·55·35·35 📠 02·97·55·49·34
Navigation Warnings
On VHF Ch 80:
From: **Penmarc'h** 0703 1533 1903 LT, **Ile de Groix** at 0715 1545 1915 LT.
Belle-Ile at 0733 1603 1933 LT, **Saint-Nazaire** at 0745 1615 1945 LT, **Ile d'Yeu** at 0803 1633 2003 LT, **and Les Sable d'Olonne** at 0815 1645 2015 LT.

CROSS Soulac 45°31'N 01°07'W L'Anse de l'Aguillon to the French border **MMSI 002275010**
From: 0700 to 2200 LT. Night service is provided by CROSS Etel MRCC.
☎ 05·56·09·82·00 📠 05·56·09·79·73
Navigation Warnings
On VHF Ch 79
From: **Chassiron** at 0703 1903 LT, **Soulac** at 0715 1915 LT, **Cap Ferrat** at 0733 1933 LT, **Contis** at 0745 1945 LT, and **Biarritz** at 0803 2003 LT.

Fig. 6 (3) CROSS and sous-Cross centres

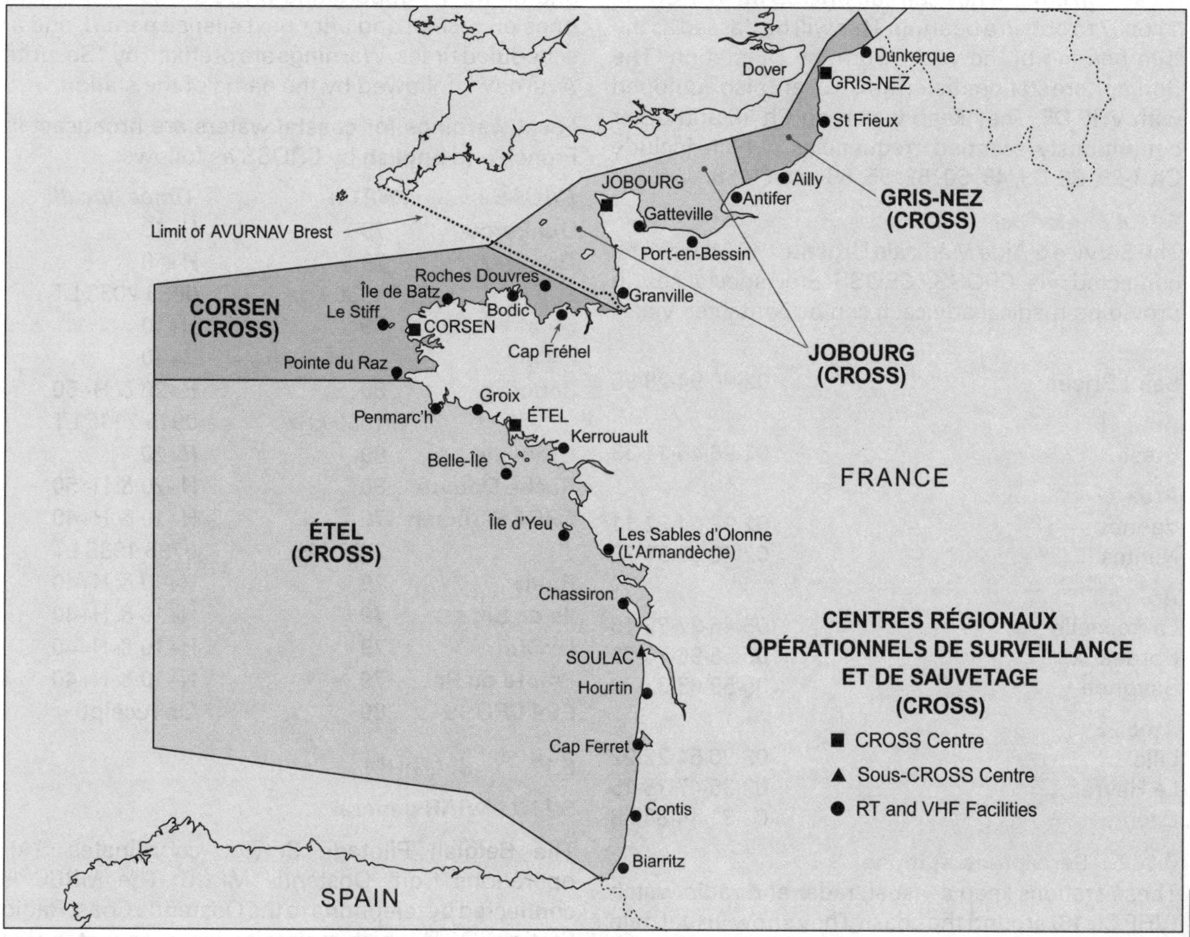

6.16.2 Semaphore (Signal) stations

* Dunkerque	03·28·66·86·18
Boulogne	03·21·31·32·10
Ault	03·22·60·47·33
Dieppe	02·35·84·23·82
* Fécamp	02·35·28·00·91
* La Hève	02·35·46·07·81
* Le Havre (Ch 12)	02·35·21·74·39
Villerville	02·31·88·11·13
* Port-en-Bessin	02·31·21·81·51
St-Vaast	02·33·54·44·50
* Barfleur	02·33·54·04·37
Lévy	02·33·54·31·17
* Le Homet	02·33·92·60·08
La Hague	02·33·52·71·07
Carteret	02·33·53·85·08
Le Roc	02·33·50·05·85
Le Grouin	02·99·89·60·12
St-Cast	02·96·41·85·30
* St Quay-Portrieux	02·96·70·42·18
Bréhat	02·96·20·00·12
* Ploumanac'h	02·96·91·46·51
Batz	02·98·61·76·06
* Brignogan	02·98·83·50·84
* Ouessant Stiff	02·98·48·81·50
Ouessant Creac'h	02·96·46.80.49
* St-Mathieu	02·98·89·01·59
* Portzic (Ch 08)	02·98·22·90·01
Toulinguet	02·98·27·90·02
Cap-de-la-Chèvre	02·98·27·09·55
* Pointe-du-Raz	02·98·70·66·57
* Penmarc'h	02·98·58·61·00
Beg Meil	02·98·94·98·92
* Port-Louis	02·97·82·52·10
Étel	02·97·55·35·59
Beg Melen (Groix)	02·97·86·80·13
Taillefer (Belle-Île)	02·97·31·83·18
Talut (Belle-Île)	02·97·31·85·07
St-Julien	02·97·50·09·35
Piriac-sur-Mer	02·40·23·59·87
* Chemoulin	02·40·91·99·00
St-Sauveur (Yeu)	02·51·58·31·01
Les Baleines (Ré)	05·46·29·42·06
Chassiron (Oléron)	05·46·47·85·43
* La Coubre	05·46·22·41·73
Pointe-de-Grave	05·56·09·60·03
Cap Ferret	05·56·60·60·03
Messanges	05·58·48·94·10
* Socoa	05·59·47·18·54

* H24. Remainder sunrise to sunset.

C6

6.16.3 Emergency VHF DF service

A yacht in emergency can call CROSS on VHF Ch 16, 11 or 67 to obtain a bearing. This will be passed as the true bearing of the yacht *from* the DF station. The Semaphore stations listed in 6.16.2 are also equipped with VHF DF. They keep watch on Ch 16 and other continuously scanned frequencies, which include Ch 1-29, 36, 39, 48, 50, 52, 55, 56 and 60-88.

6.16.4 Medical

The Service d'Aide Médicale Urgente (SAMU) can be contacted via CROSS. CROSS Étel specialises in providing medical advice. It can be contacted via:

Area 15	
Saint Brieuc	02·96·94·28·95
Area 16	
Brest	02·98·46·11·33
Area 17	
Vannes	02·97·54·22·11
Nantes	02·40·08·37·77
Area 18	
La Rochelle	05·46·27·32·15
Bordeaux	05·56·96·70·70
Bayonne	05·59·63·33·33
Area 22	
Lille	03·20·54·22·22
Le Havre	02·35·47·15·15
Caen	02·31·44·88·88

6.16.5 Semaphore stations

These stations keep a visual, radar and radio watch (VHF Ch 16) around the coast. They show visual gale warning signals, will repeat forecasts and offer local weather reports. They relay emergency calls to CROSS and are equipped with VHF DF; see 6.16.2.

6.16.6 Lifeboats

The lifeboat service Société National de Sauvetage en Mer (SNSM) comes under CROSS, but ashore it is best to contact local lifeboat stations direct; Telephone numbers are given in Chapter 9 for each port under SNSM. A substantial charge (approx £160/hr) may be levied if a SNSM lifeboat attends a vessel not in distress.

6.16.7 Navigation warnings

Long-range warnings are broadcast by Inmarsat SafetyNet for Navarea II, which includes the west coast of France. The north coast lies in Navarea I.

Avurnavs (AVis URgents aux NAVigateurs) are regional Coastal and Local warnings issued by two regional authorities:

(1) **Brest** – for the west coast of France and the western Channel to Mont St Michel; and

(2) **Cherbourg** – for the eastern Channel from Mont St Michel to the Belgian frontier.

Avurnavs are broadcast by Niton and Brest on Navtex, and on MF by Joberg and CROSS Gris Nez; urgent ones on receipt and after next silence period, and at scheduled times. Warnings are prefixed by "Sécurité Avurnav", followed by the name of the station.

Local warnings for coastal waters are broadcast in French and **English** by CROSS as follows:

CROSS	*VHF Ch*	*Times (local)*
Dunkerque	79	H+10
Gris Nez	79	H+10
	1650 kHz	0833 2033 LT
Saint Frieux	79	H+10
L'Ailly	79	H+10
Jobourg	80	H+20 & H+50
	1650 kHz	0915 2115 LT
Granville	80	H+20
Roche Douvre	80	H+20 & H+50
CROSS Corsen	79	H+10 & H+40
	2677 kHz	0735 1935 LT
Bodic	79	H+10 & H+40
Ile de Batz	79	H+10 & H+40
Le Stiff	79	H+10 & H=40
Pointe du Raz	79	H+10 & H+40
Étel CROSS	80	On receipt

6.17 BELGIUM

6.17.1 SAR general

The Belgian Pilotage Service coordinates SAR operations from Oostende MRCC. The MRCC is connected by telephone to the Oostende Coast Radio Station (OST) which maintains listening watch H24 on Ch 16, 2182kHz and DSC Ch 70 and 2187·5kHz. MMSI 002050480. ☎ 059 706565; 📠 059 701339. Antwerpen CRS, remotely controlled by Oostende CRS, has MMSI 002050485. DSC Ch 70. See 5.12.1.

Telephone and Fax numbers are:

MRCC Oostende ☎ 059 70 10 00; 📠 059 703605.

MRSC Nieuwpoort ☎ 058 233000.

MRSC Zeebrugge ☎ 050 545072.

RCC Brussels (Point of contact for Cospas/Sarsat):

☎ 02 720 0338; 📠 02 752 4201.

Offshore and inshore lifeboats are based at Nieuwpoort, Oostende and Zeebrugge.

The Belgian Air Force provides helicopters from Koksijde near the French border. The Belgian Navy also cooperates in SAR operations.

Navigational warnings are broadcast by Oostende Radio on receipt and at scheduled times on 2761 kHz and VHF Ch 27 (see 5.11.1). Also by Oostende Navtex (M) at: 0200, 0600, 1000, 1400, 1800, 2200UT for the SW part of the North Sea.

Fig. 6 (4) French MSI navigational warning broadcasts

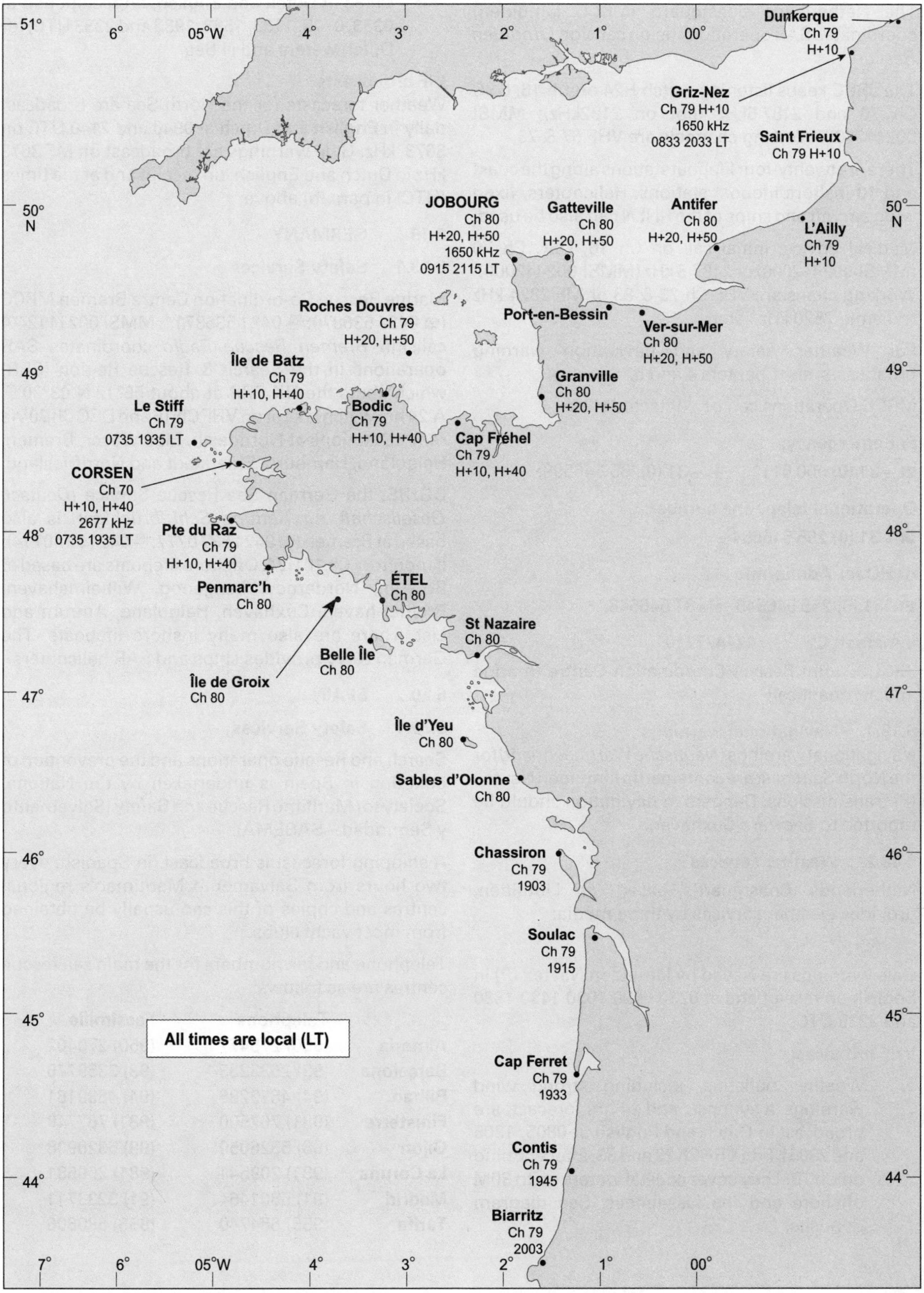

6.18 NETHERLANDS

The Netherlands Coastguard (MRCC IJmuiden) coordinates SAR operations using callsign *IJmuiden Rescue*.

The JRCC keeps listening watch H24 on Ch 16, DSC Ch 70 and 2187·5kHz (not on 2182kHz); MMSI 002442000. Working channels are VHF 67 & 73.

There are twenty-four lifeboat stations along the coast and 10 inshore lifeboat stations. Helicopters, fixed wing aircraft and ships of the RNLN can also be used.

Medical advice: initial call on Ch 16, DSC Ch 70 (MMSI 002442000) or 2187·5 kHz (MMSI 002442000). Working chans are VHF Ch 23 & 83 or MF 2824 kHz transmit, 2520 kHz listen.

For Weather, safety and navigation warning broadcasts: see Chapters 4 and 5.

MRCC Operations can be contacted H24:

For emergency:

☎ + 31 (0) 900 0111. FAX + 31 (0)255 546599;

Operational telephone number:

☎ + 31 (0) 255 546654

or HO for Admin/info

☎+ 31 (0) 255 546546. FAX+31 546548.

Inmarsat 'C': 424477710

JRCC = Joint Rescue Coordination Centre (marine and aeronautical)

6.18.1 Navigational warnings

Navigational warnings (*Nautische Warnnachricht)* for the North Sea coast are contained in IJmuiden Navtex (P) transmissions. Dangers to navigation should be reported to Seewarn Cuxhaven.

6.18.2 Weather services

Netherlands Coastguard, based at IJmuiden, provides weather services by three media:

Navtex

Gale warnings are issued by IJmuiden Navtex (P) in **English** on receipt and at 0230 0630 1030 1430 1830 and 2230 UTC.

VHF broadcasts

a. Weather bulletins, including strong wind warnings, a synopsis and 24 hrs forecast, are broadcast in Dutch **and English** at 0805, 1305 and 2305 LT on VHF Ch 23 and 83, after warning on Ch 70. They cover coastal waters up to 30M offshore and the IJsselmeer. See diagram opposite.

b. Gale warnings are broadcast on VHF Ch 23 and Ch 83 in Dutch and **English,** on receipt and at 0333, 0733, 1133, 1533, 1933 and 2333 UTC; for Dutch waters and N Sea.

MF broadcasts

Weather forecasts for the North Sea are broadcast daily in **English** and Dutch at 0940 and 2140 UTC on 3673 kHz. Gale warnings are broadcast on MF 3673 kHz in Dutch and **English,** on receipt and at the times (UTC) in para (b) above.

6.19 GERMANY

6.19.1 Safety Services

Marine Rescue Co-ordination Centre Bremen MRCC (☎ 0421 536870; FAX 0421 5368714; MMSI 002111240) callsign *Bremen Rescue Radio* coordinates SAR operations in the Search & Rescue Region (SRR) which abuts the UK SRR at about 55°12'N 03°30'E. A 24 hrs watch is kept on VHF Ch 16 and DSC Ch 70 via remote stations at Norddeich, Elbe Weser, Bremen, Helgoland, Hamburg, Eiderstedt and Nordfriesland.

DGzRS, the German Sea Rescue Service *(Deutsch Gesellschaft zur Rettung Schiffbrüchiger)* is also based at Bremen (☎ 0421 537 0777; FAX 0421 537 0714). It monitors Ch 16 H24. Offshore lifeboats are based at Borkum, Norderney, Langeoog, Wilhelmshaven, Bremer-haven, Cuxhaven, Helgoland, Amrum and List. There are also many inshore lifeboats. The German Navy provides ships and SAR helicopters.

6.20 SPAIN

6.20.1 Safety Services

Search and Rescue operations and the prevention of pollution in Spain is undertaken by the National Society for Maritime Rescue and Safety (Salvamento y Seguridad – SASEMA).

A shipping forecast is broadcast, in Spanish, every two hours from Salvamento Marítimao's regional centres and copies of this can usually be obtained from most yacht clubs.

Telephone and fax numbers for the main sea rescue centres are as follows:

	Telephone	Facsimilie
Almeria	(950) 275477	(950) 270402
Barcelona	(93) 2633233	(93) 3359775
Bilbao	(94) 4839286	(94) 4839161
Finisterre	(981) 767500	(981) 767740
Gijon	(98) 5326050	(98) 5320908
La Coruña	(981) 209541	(981) 209581
Madrid	(91) 5801464	(91) 3233711
Tarifa	(956) 684740	(956) 680606

Fig. 6 (5) Netherlands Coastguard radio stations

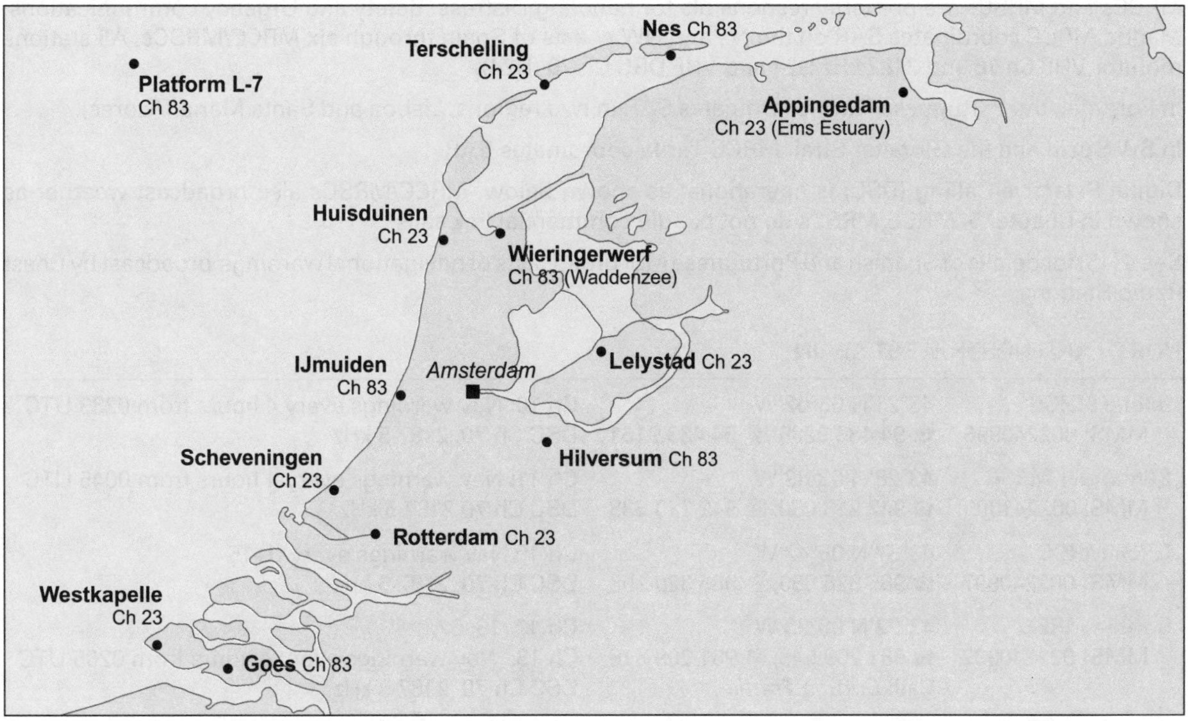

Fig. 6 (6) German Coastguard radio stations

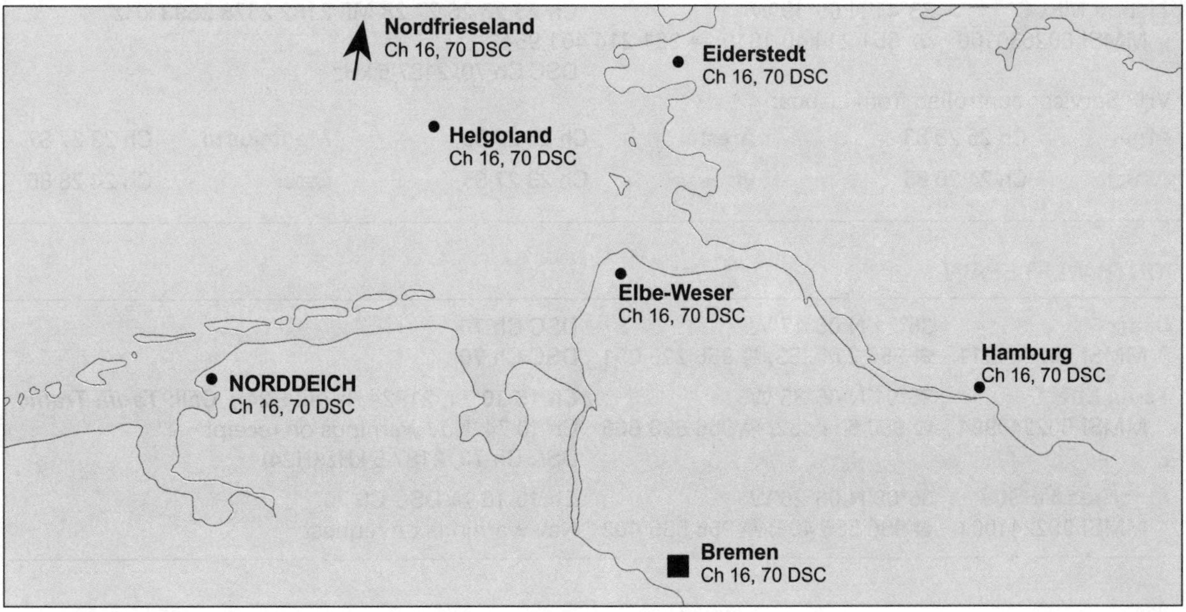

6.20.2 Spain and Portugal – MRCC/MRSC

MRCCs and MRSCs are primarily responsible for handling Distress, Safety and Urgency communications. Madrid MRCC coordinates SAR on the N , and NW coasts of Spain through six MRCC/MRSCs. All stations monitor VHF Ch 16 and 2182 kHz H24 and VHF DSC Ch 70 (H24).

In Portugal, the Portuguese Navy coordinates SAR in two regions, Lisboa and Santa Maria (Azores).

In SW Spain and the Gibraltar Strait MRCC Tarifa coordinates SAR.

Digital Selective Calling (DSC) is operational as shown below. MRCC/MRSCs also broadcast weather as shown in Chapter 5. MRCC/MRSCs do not handle commercial link calls.

See 4 (15) for details of Spanish and Portuguese MSI broadcasts of navigational warnings broadcast by Coast Radio Stations.

NORTH AND NORTH-WEST SPAIN

Bilbao MRCC MMSI 002240996	43°21'N 03°02'W ☎ 94 483 9286; 📠 94 483 9161	Ch 10: Nav warnings every 4 hours from 0233 UTC DSC Ch 70, 2187·5 kHz
Santander MRSC MMSI 002241009	43°28'N 03°43'W ☎ 942 213 030; 📠 942 213 638	Ch 11: Nav warnings every 4 hours from 0045 UTC DSC Ch 70 2187·5 kHz
Gijón MRCC MMSI 002240997	43°37'N 05°42'W ☎ 985 326 050; 📠 985 320 908	Ch 10 Nav warnings every H+15 DSC Ch 70, 2187·5 kHz
Coruña MRSC MMSI 002240992	43°22'N 08°23'W ☎ 981 209 548; 📠 981 209 518 Call: *Coruña Traffic*	Ch 13, 16, 67, Ch 13: Nav warnings every 4 hours from 0205 UTC DSC Ch 70, 2187·5 kHz
Finisterre MRCC MMSI 002240993	42°42'N 08°59'W ☎ 981 767 320; 📠 981 767 740 Call: *Finisterre Traffic*	Ch 11 16 2182 kHz. Ch 11: Nav warnings every 4 hours from 0033 UTC DSC Ch 70, 2187·5 kHz
Vigo MRSC MMSI 002240998	42°10'N 08°41'W ☎ 986 297 403; 📠 986 290 455	Ch 11 16 2182 kHz. DSC Ch 70, 2187·5 kHz Ch 10: Nav warnings every 4 hours from 0215 UTC Call: *Vigo Traffic*

PORTUGAL

Lisbon MRCC MMSI 002630100	38°41'N 09°19'W ☎ 351 214 40 1919; 📠 351 214 401 954	Ch 23 25 26 27 28 MF 2182 2578 2693 kHz DSC Ch 70; 2187·5 kHz

VHF Services controlled from Lisboa:

Arga	Ch 25 28 83	**Arestal**	Ch 24 26 85	**Montejunto**	Ch 23 27 87
Atalaia	Ch 24 26 85	**Picos**	Ch 23 27 85	**Estoi**	Ch 24 28 86

SOUTH WEST SPAIN

Cádiz MMSI 002241011	36°21'N 06°17'W ☎ 956 214 253; 📠 956 226 091	DSC Ch 70 DSC Ch 70
Tarifa MRCC MMSI 002240994	36°01'N 05°35'W ☎ 956 681 452; 📠 956 680 606	Ch 16 10 74, 2182 kHz (all H24); Call: *Tarifa Traffic* Ch 10 74: Nav warnings on receipt DSC Ch 70, 2187·5 kHz (H24)
Algeciras MRSC MMSI 002241001	36°08'N 05°26'W ☎ 956 585 404; 📠 956 585 402	Ch 15 16 74 DSC Ch 70 Nav warnings on request

Fig. 6 (7) Spanish and Portuguese Coastguard radio stations

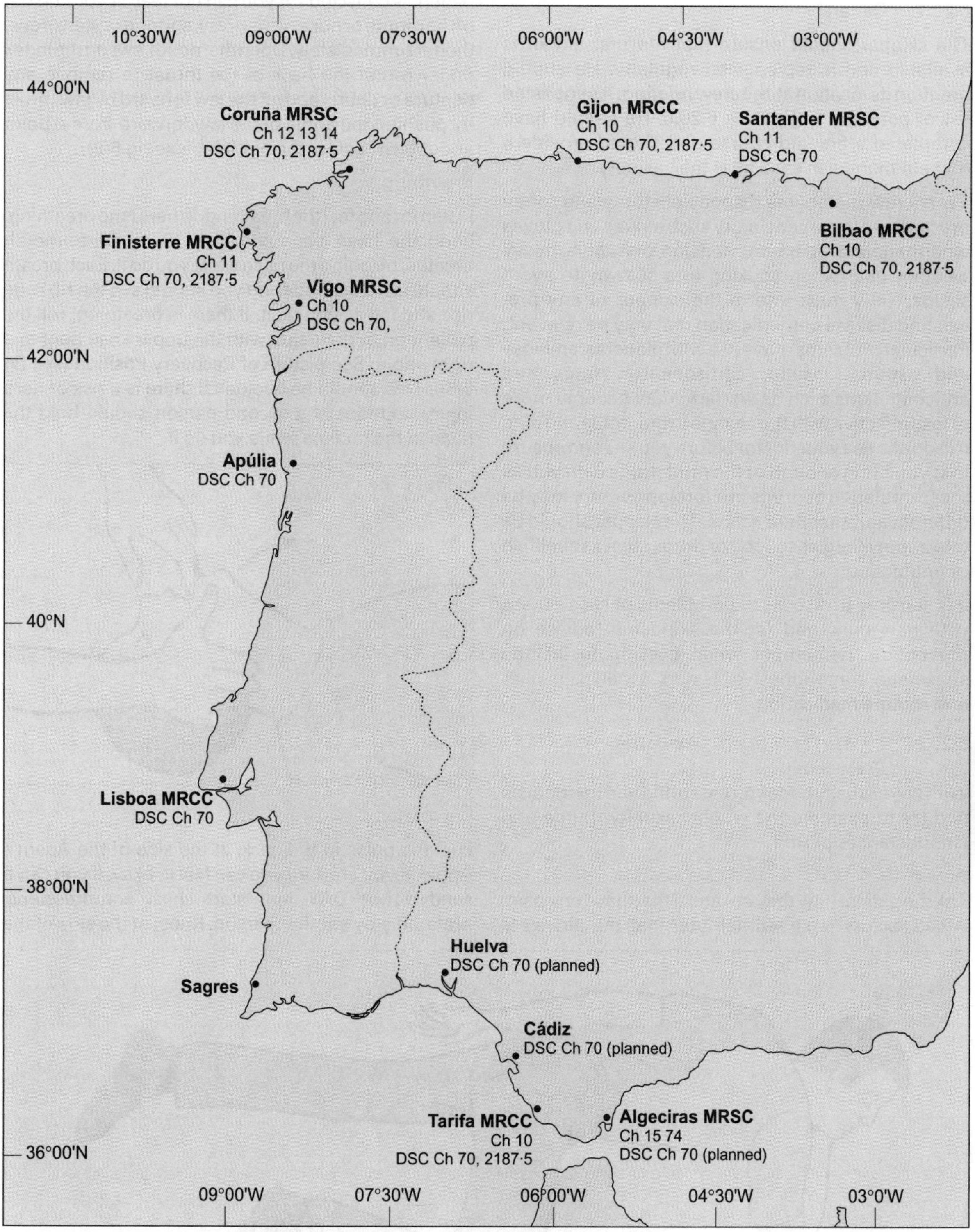

6.20 FIRST AID AT SEA

6.20.1 General

The skipper should ensure that the first aid kit is available and is replenished regularly. He should mention its location at the crew briefing. A suggested list of contents is given at 6.20.6. He should have completed a first-aid course and should provide a first aid manual in case he is the casualty.

Every crew member is responsible for taking safety precautions to prevent injury such as wearing gloves when handling ropes under tension, or wearing heavy weather gear when cooking in a seaway to avoid scalds. They must inform the skipper of any pre-existing disease or medication that may be relevant. Particular problems may arise with diabetes, epilepsy and asthma. Insulin, cortisone-like drugs and anticoagulants such as warfarin may become more or less effective with the change in timetable and diet. If in doubt, see your doctor before you sail and ensure that you bring enough of the right drugs with you as the formulation of drugs in a foreign country may be different and alter their action. The skipper should be told about allergies to food or drugs such as shellfish or antibiotics.

It is sensible to discuss the problems of seasickness with new crew and for the skipper to advise on prevention. Remember when packing to include sunscreen, some adhesive plasters, a mild pain-killer and routine medication.

6.20.2 Airway, Breathing, Circulation (Resuscitation)

With any casualty be calm, reassuring and methodical and try to examine the whole casualty if time and circumstances permit.

Airway

Ask the patient how they are and if they have any pain. A satisfactory reply will tell you that the airway is functioning, the lungs are moving air well and the patient is conscious. If you can not feel air coming out of the mouth or nose or it is noisy, snoring or stertorous, then act immediately. Open the mouth, sweep the index finger round the back of the throat to remove any denture or debris and lift the jaw forward by jaw thrust by pushing the angle of the jaw forward from a point about 3 cm below the ear lobe (see fig 6(8)).

Breathing

Listen for and feel the breathing. If there is no breathing, bend the head back and give 10 mouth-to-mouth breaths, pinching the nose while you do it. Each breath should last 2 seconds and you should see the rib cage rise and fall as you do it. If there is breathing, roll the patient on to their side with the upper knee bent to a right angle. See picture of Recovery Position (see fig 6(9)). This should be avoided if there is a risk of neck injury and ideally a second person should hold the head in the midline while you do it.

Fig. 6 (8)

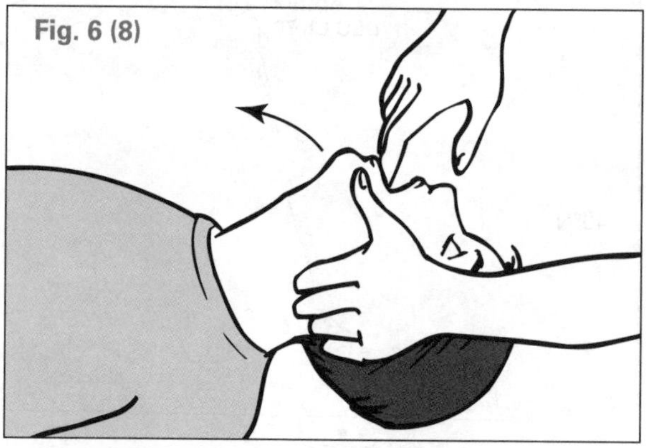

Circulation

Feel the pulse in the neck, at the side of the Adam's Apple. If you are sure you can feel it, okay. If you can't, send a MAYDAY and start chest compressions, preferably by another person. Kneel at the side of the

Fig. 6 (9)

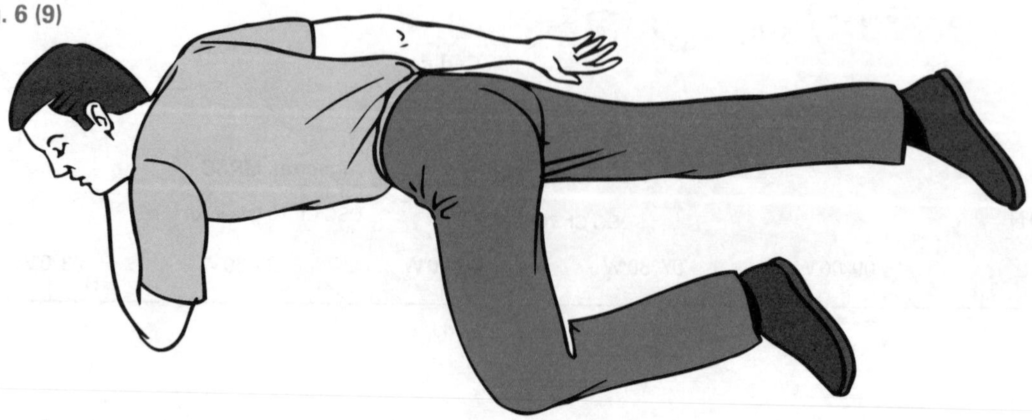

chest, place one hand on the other on the midpoint of the breast bone and swing forward with straight arms so that your weight depresses the breast bone about 5 cm. If you are alone give 15 compressions to 2 breaths. If you have assistance, 1 breath to 5 compressions is the correct ratio. By counting 'one and two, and three' you will be compressing at 100 beats a minute.

State of Consciousness

It may help the rescue services or the hospital accident services to know whether the state of the patient is improving or deteriorating, and whether there is evidence of spinal injury. Start at the top of the head, looking for injuries, or fluid coming from the ears. Are the pupils equal and do they contract when a light is shone in them? What is the level of consciousness, if it is other than normal, record your findings on the chart at the end of this section. Can the casualty move all four limbs? Does anything hurt? Does the back or neck hurt? If you feel round the back, is there localised tenderness or a step in the vertebrae?

Fig. 6 (10)

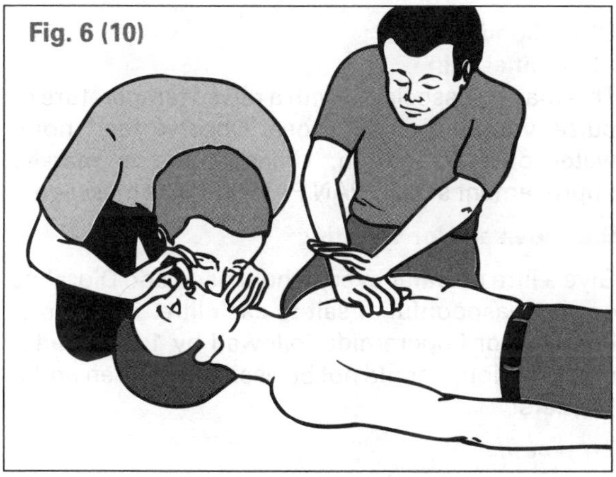

6.20.3 Life Threatening Conditions

If life is at stake, or the conditions of the casualty is getting worse send a MAYDAY call. If you want advice or reassurance use PAN PAN MEDICO. Serious injuries will nearly always need transferring to hospital sooner rather than later.

Common Injuries

Head injuries from the boom must always be regarded seriously. Momentary unconsciousness may occur. Normal consciousness should return immediately, with some headache. KEEP THE AIRWAY CLEAR. Rapid sustained recovery may be disregarded (concussion). Lack of response to voice after 5 minutes, a clouding of consciousness, weakness in any limb, a bloody or clear discharge from nose or ears, visual disturbance or pupils which are unequal in size are all bad signs and the patient will require urgent evacuation.

Falls from a height such as from a quayside, from the mast or down the companionway are a common cause of multiple injury, which may involve the head, neck, spine, ribs, pelvis and limbs. Limb fractures are conspicuous but the others may be lethal unless suspected and treated. The diagnosis may require X-rays and the treatment consists of immobilisation and intravenous fluids. If possible let the casualty move himself with assistance. If there is unconsciousness try to move him in the position that he landed, supporting the head in the midline. Splint limbs before moving. Internal bleeding is the main risk and if the pulse rate is over 100/minute consider urgent evacutaion.

Heavy falls on the chest may break one or more ribs. Usually the only problem is pain on breathing, coughing or laughing. Treat the pain. If there is severe shortness of breath or if there is pallor, pulse rate more than 100/minute suspect internal injury to lung, spleen or liver. Evacuate the patient.

Bleeding from a major artery, vein or the scalp should be controlled by firm pressure with pads and bandages, if necessary applying another layer on top of the first. Observe the circulation in the fingers or toes by pressing the nail bed and registering the flush beyond the bandage and slacken it every 30 minutes if the limb is cold, white or blue. Evacuate the patient.

Bleeding from the nose or a toothsocket, should be controlled by pinching the nose or getting the patient to bite on a pad. If it continues after two hours, send a PAN PAN MEDICO message.

6.20.4 Common medical conditions

Heart attack casualties have severe constricting chest pain sometimes extending to the neck, left arm or jaw sometimes following exertion, not relieved by rest. They tend to be cold, blue and clammy to the touch. Make them comfortable, sitting up, give one aspirin tablet and send a MAYDAY message. If circumstances permit, count pulse and be prepared for external cardiac massage if the heart stops. See Section 6.20.2

Unconsciousness. Consider hypothermia, drugs, alcohol, diabetes, epilepsy and cerebral haemorrhage or thrombosis. Manage the AIRWAY. Put the hypothermic casualty in a dry sleeping bag. If the diabetic patient has injected insulin and is rousable, give sugar by mouth. Known epileptics tend to recover consciousness spontaneously. As unconscious casualties tend to be unmanageable on a small craft - evacuate the patient.

Internal bleeding in the gut. This will declare itself by vomiting blood (may resemble coffee grounds) or by passing black malaena stool resembling tar. If the bleeding is fast, the patient will be shocked with rapid, weak pulse, cold, sweaty, restless, anxious and blue. If the bleeding is slower, the patient will become pale and breathless. Evacuate the patient.

6.20.5 Common Fractures

On a small craft it will be necessary to improvise. When a bone is broken, there may be a snapping sound, it will hurt, there is local tenderness with swelling, the limb may look deformed and movements will be painful or impossible. The aim of first aid is to reduce pain, damage to nerves and vessels and reduce internal bleeding.

Hands and Fingers

Often damaged with a mixture of crush, fractures and lacerations. Clean gently with mild antiseptic or previously boiled water. Replace any skin flaps and fix with steristrip or stitch. Individual fingers may be bandaged or small lacerations covered with elastoplast but, if the whole hand is involved, put it in a plastic bag and tie loosely round the wrist. This will prevent further damage and will help to prevent the fingers stiffening.

Arm

Traction If the fracture is angulated, pull gently by the wrist or fingers along the line of the limb to overcome muscle spasm until the limb is straight.

Splint the Limb

Use a triangular bandage to make a sling if you have one, otherwise fold the bottom of a shirt or jersey worn by the casualty up over the arm and fix with safety pins being careful to support behind the elbow. Complete the support by binding the arm to the chest. Leave the tips of the fingers exposed so that you can check that the blood is circulating by pressing the fingernail and then releasing it. Check every 30 minutes. Send a PAN PAN MEDICO message.

Collar bone

Support the arm on that side as for a broken arm.

Ribs

Send a PAN PAN MEDICO stating ribs extremely painful. It is nowadays not considered helpful, to strap a patient's chest, however some patients find some pain relief if 10 cm strapping is taken from the mid-line at the front to the midline at the back, this will do no harm. Casualty can usually continue with help from regular pain killers. NB Be aware that breathlessness, abdominal pain, pain on the tip of the shoulder or blood in the urine are signs of internal damage which justify a MAYDAY.

Spine, Pelvis, Thighs

These all lead to massive internal bleeding and warrant a MAYDAY message. While waiting for rescue services to arrive it will be helpful to bandage the legs and feet together with padding between the knees and ankles possibly incorporating a sail batten as a splint. If the pelvis is thought to be damaged, male casualties should avoid passing urine as urethral rupture is common.

Lower leg and ankle

Apply gentle sustained traction to the heel to overcome muscle spasm and allow the leg to regain its normal shape. Pad between knees and ankles and bandage the legs together preferably with a sail batten as a splint. Observe the circulation in the feet every 30 minutes and keep the leg up to reduce swelling. It may be necessary to slacken the bandages or reapply traction if the foot becomes cold and white. Send a PAN PAN MEDICO message.

Dislocated shoulders

The shoulder has an angular pointed look and is very painful. There is intense muscle spasm. Lie the casualty down, face up, with the injured arm hanging over the side of the bunk. This will relieve the pain and the weight of the arm will overcome the spasm. Wait for half-an-hour – the dislocation may reduce on its own or may respond to gentle traction on the hand with internal rotation. Apply sling. Seek medical help within 48 hours.

Other Conditions

Abdominal pain

This may be associated with a raised temperature or pulse, vomiting or diarrhoea. Observe for 1 hour, water only by mouth. Unless there is marked improvement send a PAN PAN MEDICO message.

Diarrhoea and/or vomiting

Give a litre of water every 6 hours and add Dioralyte or one teaspoonful of salt to each litre. 2 tablets of Imodium or Loperamide followed by 1 tablet after every motion. Should not be used for children under 12 years.

Drowning

During rescue ensure your own safety first. Don a life jacket, harness and line. Lift casualty horizontally. Carry out ABC – see 6.20.2. If casualty is breathing - place in Recovery Position. If casualty is not breathing - mouth to mouth respiration, check pulse, no pulse start chest compression. Once pulse and respiration are established, place in Recovery Position. Remove wet clothing and put in sleeping bag with a warm hat to treat hypothermia. Many patients develop a delayed collapse of the lungs some hours after rescue. Evacuate to a medical facility within 2 hours.

Burns, Scalds, Friction Burns

Immediately place burned part in cold water for 10 minutes. Cover with cling film or dry dressing and keep dry. Do not burst blisters. If hand or face is more than reddened and is weeping or blackened, send a MAYDAY message. Facial burns are often associated with the inhalation of smoke, carbon monoxide or cyanide from burning cushions, lung complications may kill. Give clear fluids with Diarolyte or a teaspoon of salt in a litre and an antibiotic if the area of burn or scald exceeds two hands in size. Send MAYDAY message.

Eyes

On a boat, ultraviolet light is reflected up from the water under hat brims and round sun spectacles. This tends to cause 'sunburn' of the eye akin to snow blindness and contact lenses may become very uncomfortable after a few days. (Contact lens wearers should note the difficulty of maintaining a good standard of hygiene on a small boat.) There is no treatment and a spare pair of glasses may be required. A wide variety of paints, varnishes and cleaning agents are used on boats, unless wearing goggles, splashes may get in the eye. Wash open eye with copious water for 10 minutes. Apply pad and bandage over eye until next morning.

Fishhooks

Push the hook round until the point and barb appear. Cut off the point and barb and withdraw the hook. Dress the holes and give an antibiotic (Augmentin 4 x daily for 3 days).

Seasickness

This may occur in nearly anybody and can be prevented in most people and nearly everybody develops sealegs with time. It is worse on the first few trips of the season, after a night of drinking, when you are cold and frightened and it sometimes doesn't happen until you have been afloat for a couple of hours. It is made worse in enclosed spaces, by the smell of diesel and with a following wind and sea. It is made much better by fresh air, a job to do and a long hard look at the horizon. Drugs such as Stugeron, Scopolamine, Avomine or dramamine are helpful if taken several hours before symptoms start but may cause drowsiness particularly if taken to excess. Scopolamine skin patches (Scopoderm) are available in the UK on prescription. Seasickness can be of no consequence to some and deeply incapacitating to others, so that they may enter a comatose-like state and become severely dehydrated. A skipper should probably insist that everyone turns out for their watch on deck.

Sunburn

With a cooling breeze the sun can be deceptive. The neck, ears, back and thighs can be painful, red and angry within 4 hours of exposure, they can proceed to blistering and become a weeping mess by the following morning. The casualty feels ill, shivery, may faint or vomit. The skin should be managed as if for superficial burns. Do not prick blisters. Apply calamine lotion cover with dry, clean dressing or cling film. Encourage casualty to drink water or fruit juice or Diarolyte solution. Next day cover up and apply sun block, avoid exposure from noon –2 hours to +2 hours.

Teeth

Tooth-ache arising from the exposed dentine of a broken tooth, caries or a lost filling is eased by taking aspirin or paracetamol. A drop of oil of cloves on a cloth held against the painful area will be effective. A pulp abscess in a dead tooth causes a deep throbbing pain, temporary relief can be obtained by administering antibiotics. The abscess will require drainage on return to land. Teeth which have been knocked out should be placed in a clean container with milk or moist gauze and taken to a dentist at the first opportunity for re-implantation. It is not practical to reimplant and splint on a boat.

Crew Medical Notes

Name	Age	Sex	Blood GP	Medication

6.21.6 First aid equipment

Suggestions

Sterile gloves disposable, thermometer, sharp scissors, needle and forceps for splinters, large safety pins, assorted sterile dressings and plasters, sachets of a mild antiseptic such as betadine, adhesive sterile strips 'Steristrip', triangular bandage for slings. Your chemist will have some of these already made up in a 'First Aid Kit'.

MEDICINES

Allergy, Hayfever, Urticaria	Antihistamine 'Zirtec' cetirizine	10mg tablet daily
Anaphylaxis (bee stings, jelly fish)	adrenaline minijet or Epi-Pen + antihistamine	1 deep intramuscular injection
Constipation	bisacdodyl 'Senokot'	2 tablets at night 2 tablets at night
Fever, Pain relief	paracetamol aspirin	2 tablets 4 hourly 2 tablets 4 hourly
Infections, wounds, burns and abscesses (inc dental abscess)	'Augmentin' NOT if allergic to penicillin erythromycin ONLY if allergic to penicillin	1 tablet 8 hourly 2 tablets 6 hourly
Insect bites, Sun-burn	Calamine lotion	
Indigestion	Gaviscon	chew before bed + after meals
Sprains, muscle pain, gout	'Brufen' ibuprofen	200mg tablet 6 hourly
Heat stroke, burns, diarrhoea	WHO oral rehydration salts 'Rehydrat' or 'Diaoralyte'	1 sachet in 1 litre Dilute in water
Seasickness	'Stugeron' cinnarizine 'Kwells' hyoscine 'Scopoderm TTS patch'	1-2 tablets 2 hours before 1-2 tablets 2 hour before not available in UK
Toothache (exposed dentine)	Oil of cloves or 'Eugenol'	apply on pad

Most of the above are over-the-counter medicines, antibiotics are only available on prescription from your doctor. Alternative proprietary preparations are sometimes available

Checklist

Information you will need to aid communication ashore:

Name, age and sex of the person

Name and type of craft; call sign; present location

Details of the current problem:

Accidents - At what time; Any loss of consciousness; How much blood lost? Details of each injury.

Illnesses - When and how did it begin, any previous episodes? How have symptoms progressed? Type and site of pain - any relieving or exacerbating factors?

General - Does the person have any known medical problems or take regular medication? Are there known drug allergies?

Current level of consciousness, pulse and breathing rate, temperature.

What has been done on board? What medication do you have? Estimated time of arrival at nearest port?

Please note

Care has been taken to present information which is considered correct by current medical standards. *However neither the author nor the publishers can or shall be liable to the user in respect of any liability, loss or damage caused or alleged to have been caused directly or indirectly by this work.*

6.21.7 Condition of Casualty – monitoring chart

Detail a member of crew to fill in the scores below every ten to fifteen minutes.

This scoring system will allow a shore-based doctor to assess the condition of your casualty, and if necessary transfer them ashore. If they are transferred make sure that this chart accompanies them – place in something waterproof and pin firmly to their clothing.

Nature of Injury

Try to record as much as you can to assist a medical team treat the casualty.

....

....

....

....

....

Time - fill in score every 15 minutes

			Time - fill in score every 15 minutes
Eyes Open	Spontaneously	4	
	To speech only	3	
	To pain only	2	
	None	1	
Speech	Orientated	5	
	Confused	4	
	Words only	3	
	Sounds only	2	
	None	1	
Movements	Obeys commands	5	
	Localise to pain	4	
	Withdraws to pain	3	
	Extends to pain	2	
	None	1	
	Totals		
Pupil sizes	Right - small or large		
	Left - small or large		
Pulse rate			
Breathing rate	F = fast S = slow		

C6

FREE

FREE

MACMILLAN•REEDS
Weather Summary

Macmillan Reeds recognises that, as well as detailed tidal and navigational information, mariners need reliable weather information to enjoy comfortable and safe sailing. Therefore, to complement the wealth of navigational information found in our almanacs, we offer a weekly weather forecast summary.

to register and receive a

FREE Weekend Weather Summary direct to your desktop

prepared by WCS Marine contact:

www.nauticaldata.com

Throughout the sailing season we will send you a forecast summary for weather around the UK and Ireland for the coming Friday, Saturday and Sunday, together with a map for each of those days. Each map will provide wind, sea state and weather information for each of 4 geographical areas around UK shores.

Example:

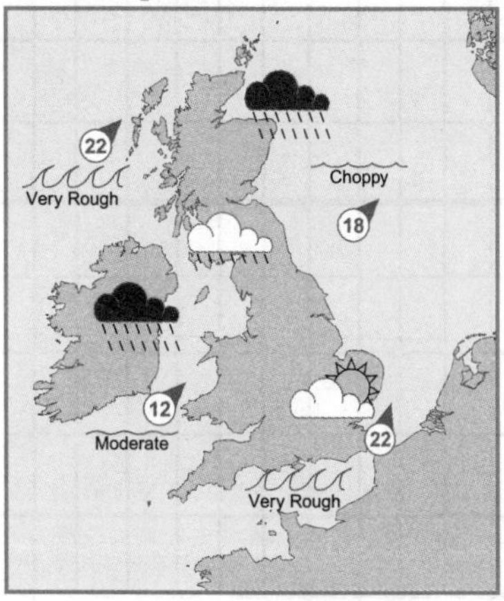

FRIDAY 27th APRIL

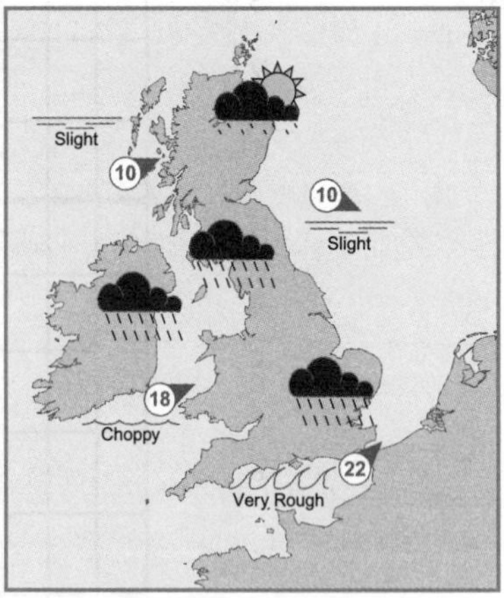

SATURDAY 28th APRIL

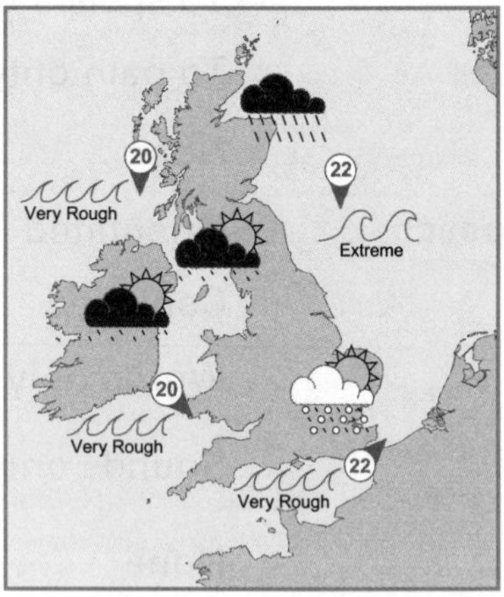

SUNDAY 29th APRIL

WEEKEND WEATHER FORECAST FOR 27-29TH APRIL 2001

FRIDAY: An area of low pressure in the vicinity of the Brest Peninsula early on Friday morning will weaken as it moves across Northern parts of France and by midnight will be a minor feature over the Netherlands. Low pressure and a weak occluded front off Northeast Scotland will also move Northeastward in Norway through the afternoon. An active occluded front will push into Northern Ireland in the afternoon and will lie from Scotland to Southwest England by the end of the day.

Any early residual rain across the far Southeastern parts of England is going to clear away quite quickly then for much of England and Wales there should be some fine, dry weather with sunny spells and a few showers. Thickening cloud and rain already across Northern Ireland will move into Scotland and Northwestern England in the afternoon. Fog will become extensive around the coasts. This rain is expected to spread into most parts in the evening and through the night - always heaviest in the Northwest.

Winds will be increasing to SW F4-5 across Northern Ireland, SW F3-4 in Scotland, SW F2-3 across England becoming SW F3-5 later, initially S F3-4 in Channel.

For a more comprehensive weather forecast call our paid for service at

MACMILLAN•REEDS
Weather Line

09015 66 00 38

Calls to 09015 numbers cost 60p/minute. Helpline available on 08700 738 100

Chapter 7

Tides

Contents

7.1 **GENERAL** .... Page 150
7.1.1 Explanation 150
7.1.2 Times 150
7.1.3 Predicted heights 150
7.2 **DEFINITIONS** 150
7.2.1 Chart datum 150
7.2.2 Charted depth 150
7.2.3 Drying height 150
7.2.4 Heights of lights, bridges, etc 150
7.2.5 Height of tide 150
7.2.6 Rise/Fall of tide 150
7.2.7 Duration 150
7.2.8 Interval 150
7.2.9 Mean High Water and Low Water Springs/Neaps 150
7.2.10 Mean Level 150
7.2.11 Range 151
7.2.12 Tidal coefficients 151
7.3 **CALCULATIONS OF TIMES AND HEIGHTS OF HIGH AND LOW WATER** .. 151
7.3.1 Standard Ports 151
7.3.2 Secondary Ports – times of HW and LW 151
7.3.3 Secondary Ports – heights of HW and LW 151
7.3.4 Graphical method for interpolating 152
7.4 **CALCULATING INTERMEDIATES** 152
7.4.1 Standard Ports 153
7.4.2 Secondary Ports 153
7.4.3 The use of factors 153
7.4.4 The 'Twelfths' rule 154
7.5 **CALCULATIONS OF CLEARANCES UNDER BRIDGES** 154
7.6 **TIDAL PREDICTION BY COMPUTER** 154
7.6.1 TotalTide 154
7.6.2 SHM for Windows 155
7.6.3 Commercial programs 155
7.7 **TIDAL STREAMS** 155
7.7.1 General 155
7.7.2 Tidal stream Atlases 155
7.7.3 Computation of tidal stream rates 156
7.7.4 Tidal streams in rivers 156
7.8 **METEOROLOGICAL CONDITIONS** 156
7.8.1 Storm Tide Warning Service 158
7.9 **STANDARD PORTS** 158
7.9.1 Secondary Spanish Ports 158
7.9.2 Portsmouth hourly height predictions 158

Table

Fig. 7(1) Portsmouth height predictions 159

C7

7.1 GENERAL

7.1.1 Explanation

This chapter explains how to use the tidal information contained in Chapter 9, where the daily times and heights of High Water (HW) and Low Water (LW) for Standard Ports are given, together with time and height differences for many Secondary Ports. Tidal predictions are for average meteorological conditions. In abnormal weather the times and heights of HW and LW may vary considerably. (See 7.8.)

7.1.2 Times

The times of Standard Port predictions in Chapter 9 are given in the Standard, or Zone, Time indicated at the top left-hand corner of each page, i.e. in UTC (Zone 0) as kept in the UK, Channel Islands, Eire and Portugal. In France, Belgium, Netherlands, Germany and Spain Standard Time is UTC +1 (Zone –1). To convert these Zone –1 times to UTC, subtract 1 hour.

When DST (BST in UK) is in force during the summer months, as indicated by the absence of pale yellow tinting, one hour must be added to the predicted times to obtain DST (= LT).

Under each Secondary Port listed in Chapter 9 are its Zone Time, and the time differences required to calculate the times of HW and LW at the Secondary Port in the Zone Time of that Port. If DST is required, then one hour is added *after* the Secondary Port time difference has been applied, but not before.

7.1.3 Predicted heights

Predicted heights are given in metres and tenths of a metre above chart datum (CD) (see 7.2.1). Care must be taken when using charts showing depths in fathoms/feet. A table for converting feet to metres and metres to feet is given in Chapter 1.

7.2 DEFINITIONS

Certain definitions are given below and in Fig. 7 (1). For further details see *The Macmillan Reeds Yachtsman's Handbook.*

7.2.1 Chart datum

Chart datum (CD) is the reference level above which heights of tide are predicted, and below which charted depths are measured. Hence the actual depth of water is the charted depth (at that place) plus the height of tide (at that time).

Tidal predictions for most British ports use as their datum Lowest Astronomical Tide (LAT), which is the lowest sea level predicted under average meteorological conditions. All Admiralty Charts of the British Isles use LAT as chart datum, but others, particularly fathom charts, do not. Where tidal predictions and charted depths are not referenced to the same datum (e.g. LAT), errors resulting in an over-estimation of depth by as much as 0·5m can occur.

7.2.2 Charted depth

Charted depth is the distance of the sea bed below chart datum, and is shown in metres and tenths of a metre on metric charts, or in fathoms and/or feet on older charts. Make sure you know which units are used.

7.2.3 Drying height

Drying height is the height above chart datum of the top of any feature at times covered by water. The figures are underlined on the chart, in metres and tenths of a metre on metric charts, and in fathoms and feet on older charts. The depth of water is the height of tide (at the time) minus the drying height. If the result is negative, then that feature is above water level.

7.2.4 Heights of lights, bridges, etc

Charted heights of land objects such as lights, bridges are measured above the level of MHWS. See 7.5. On French charts these charted elevations are measured above ML rather than MHWS.

7.2.5 Height of tide

The height of the tide is the vertical distance of sea level above (or very occasionally below) chart datum, as defined in 7.2.1.

7.2.6 Rise/Fall of tide

The Rise of the tide is the amount the tide has risen since the earlier Low Water. The Fall of a tide is the amount the tide has fallen since the last High Water.

7.2.7 Duration

Duration is the time between LW and the next HW, normally slightly more than six hours, and can be used to calculate the approximate time of LW when only the time of HW is known.

7.2.8 Interval

The interval is a period of time either side of the time of HW, expressed in hours and minutes before (–) or after (+) HW. Intervals are printed in increments of one hour (–1hr and +1hr) along the bottom of each tidal curve in Chapter 9.

7.2.9 Mean High Water and Low Water Springs/Neaps

Mean High Water Springs (MHWS) and Mean High Water Neaps (MHWN) are the averages of the predicted heights of the Spring or Neap tides at HW over a period of 18·6 years. Similarly, Mean Low Water Springs (MLWS) and Neaps (MLWN) are the average heights of low water for the Spring and Neap tides respectively.

7.2.10 Mean Level

Mean Level (ML) is the average of the heights of Mean High Water Springs (MHWS), Mean High Water Neaps (MHWN), Mean Low Water Springs (MLWS) and Mean Low Water Neaps (MLWN).

Fig. 7(1) Tidal definitions shown pictorially

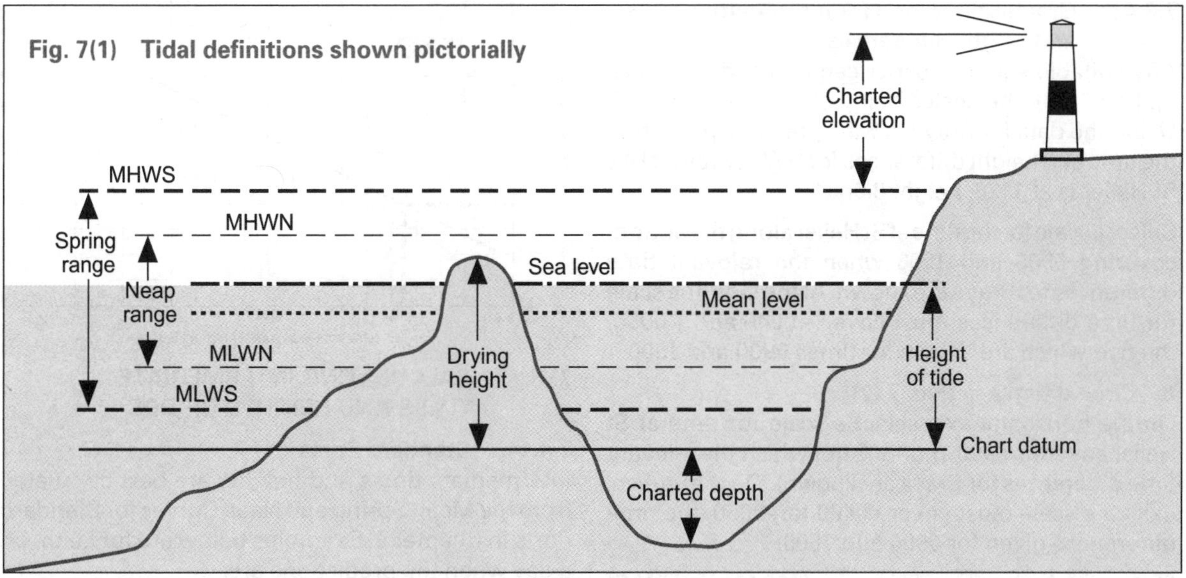

7.2.11 Range

The range of a tide is the difference between the heights of successive High and Low Waters. Spring range is the difference between MHWS and MLWS, and Neap range is the difference between MHWN and MLWN.

7.2.12 Tidal Coefficients

In France the size (range) of a tide and its proximity to Springs/Neaps is quantified by Tidal Coefficients which are listed and explained in 9.16.24

7.3 CALCULATIONS OF TIMES AND HEIGHTS OF HIGH AND LOW WATER

7.3.1 Standard Ports

The predicted times and heights of HW and LW are tabulated for each Standard Port in Chapter 9. (see 7.9 for Standard Port listing). It is stressed that these are predictions only and take no account of the effects of wind and barometric pressure (see 7.8). Daylight Saving Time (DST) is dealt with in 7.1.2.

7.3.2 Secondary Ports – times of HW and LW

Each Secondary Port listed in Chapter 9 has a data block for calculating times of HW and LW. The following example is for Braye (Alderney):

TIDES –0400 Dover; ML 3·5; Duration 0545; Zone 0 (UT)

Standard Port ST HELIER (⟶)

Times				**Height (metres)**			
High Water		Low Water		MHWS	MHWN	MLWN	MLWS
0300	0900	0200	0900	11·0	8·1	4·0	1·4
1500	2100	1400	2100				
Differences BRAYE							
+0050	+0040	+0025	+0105	–4·8	–3·4	–1·5	–0·5

Thus – 0400 Dover indicates that, on average, HW Braye occurs 4 hours 00 minutes before HW Dover (the times of HW Dover, in UTC, can be found on the bookmark). Duration 0545 indicates that LW Braye occurs 5 hours and 45 minutes before its HW. This is a very rough and ready method.

A more accurate and reliable method uses the Standard Port and Time Differences in the table. Thus When HW at St Helier occurs at 0300 and 1500, the Difference is + 0050, and HW at Braye then occurs at 0350 and 1550. When HW at St Helier occurs at 0900 and 2100, the Difference is + 0040, and HW at Braye occurs at 0940 and 2140.

If, as is likely, HW St Helier occurs at some other time, then the Difference for Braye must be found by interpolation: by eye, by the graphical method, or by calculator. Thus, by eye, when HW St Helier occurs at 1200, the Difference is + 0045, and HW Braye occurs at 1245. The same method is used for calculating the times of LW.

The times thus obtained are in the Zone Time of the Secondary Port.

7.3.3 Secondary Ports – heights of HW and LW

The Secondary Port data block also contains height Differences which are applied to the heights of HW and LW at the Standard Port. Thus when the height of HW at St Helier is 11·0m (MHWS), the Difference is – 4·8m, and the height of HW at Braye is 6·2m (MHWS). When the height of HW at St Helier is 8·1m (MHWN), the Difference is – 3·4m, and the height of HW at Braye is 4·7m (MHWN).

If, as is likely, the height of tide at the Standard Port differs from the Mean Spring or Neap level, then the height Difference also must be interpolated: by eye, by graph or by calculator. Thus, by eye, if the height of HW at St Helier is 9·55m (midway between MHWS and MHWN), the Difference is – 4·1m, and the height of HW at Braye is 5·45m (9·55–4·1m).

7.3.4 Graphical method for interpolating time and height differences

Any suitable squared paper can be used, see Figs. 7(2) and 7(3), the scales being chosen as required. Using the data for Braye in 7.3.2 previous page, find the time and height differences for HW at Braye if HW St Helier is at 1126, height 8·9m.

Select a scale for the time at St Helier along the bottom covering 0900 and 1500 when the relevant time differences for Braye are known. At the side, the scale for time differences must cover + 0040 and + 0050, the two which are shown for times 0900 and 1500.

a. Time difference (Fig. 7 (2))
On the horizontal axis select a scale for time at St Helier covering 0900 and 1500 (for which the relevant time differences for Braye are known). On the vertical axis, the scale must cover +0400 to +0050, the time differences given for 0900 and 1500.

Plot point A, the time difference (+0040) for HW St Helier at 0900; and point B, the time difference (+0050) for HW St Helier at 1500. Join AB. Enter the graph at time 1126 (HW St Helier); intersect AB at C then go horizontally to read +0044 on the vertical axis. On that morning HW Braye is 44 minutes after HW St Helier, i.e. 1210.

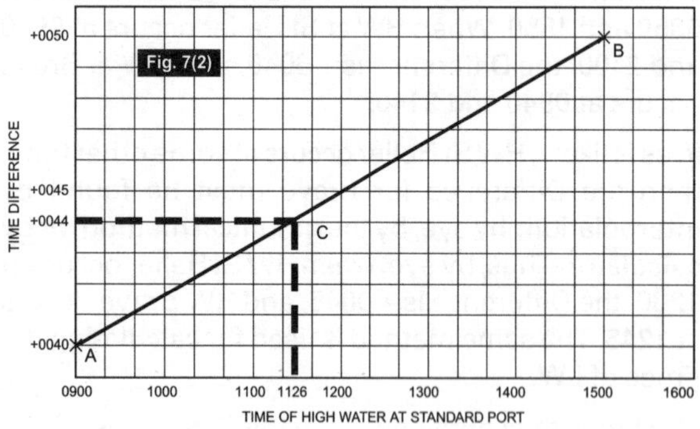

b. Height difference (Fig. 7 (3))
In Fig. 7 (3), the horizontal axis covers the height of HW at St Helier (i.e. 8·1 to 11·0m) and the vertical axis shows the relevant height differences (– 3·4 to – 4·8m). Plot point D, the height difference (– 3·4m) at Neaps when the height of HW St Helier is 8·1m; and E, the height difference (– 4·8m) at Springs when the height of HW St Helier is 11·0m. Join DE. Enter the graph at 8·9m (the height of HW St Helier that morning) and mark F where that height meets DE. From F follow the horizontal line to read off the corresponding height difference: – 3·8m. So that morning the height of HW Braye is 5·1m.

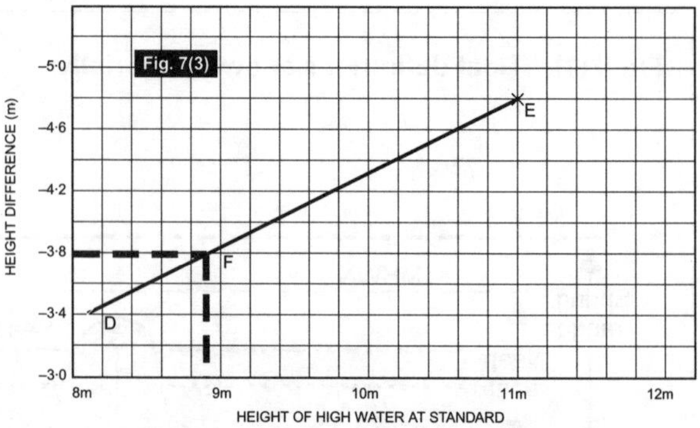

7.4 CALCULATING INTERMEDIATE TIMES AND HEIGHTS OF TIDE

7.4.1 Standard Ports

Intermediate times and heights are best calculated from the Mean Spring and Neap Curves for Standard Ports in Chapter 9. Examples below are for Leith, on a day when the predictions are:

	UTC	Ht (m)
22	0202	5·3
	0752	1·0
	1417	5·4
Tu	2025	0·5

Example: Find the height of tide at Leith at 1200.

(1) On the Leith tidal diagram plot the heights of HW and LW each side of the required time, and join them by a sloping line, Fig. 7 (4).
(2) Enter the HW time and other times as necessary in the boxes below the curves.
(3) From the required time, proceed vertically to the curves. The Spring Curve is a solid line, and the Neap curve (where it differs) is pecked. Interpolate between the curves by comparing the actual range, in this example 4·4m, with the Mean Ranges printed beside the curves. Never extrapolate. Here the Spring Curve applies.
(4) Proceed horizontally to the sloping line plotted in (1), and thence vertically to the height scale, to give 4·2m.

Example: To find the time at which the afternoon height of tide falls to 3·7m.

(1) On the Leith tidal diagram, plot the heights of HW and LW each side of the required event, and join them by a sloping line, Fig. 7 (5).
(2) Enter the HW time and others to cover the required event, in the boxes below.
(3) From the required height, proceed vertically to the sloping line and thence horizontally to the curves. Interpolate between them as in the previous example and do not extrapolate. Here the actual range is 4·9m,

Fig. 7(4)

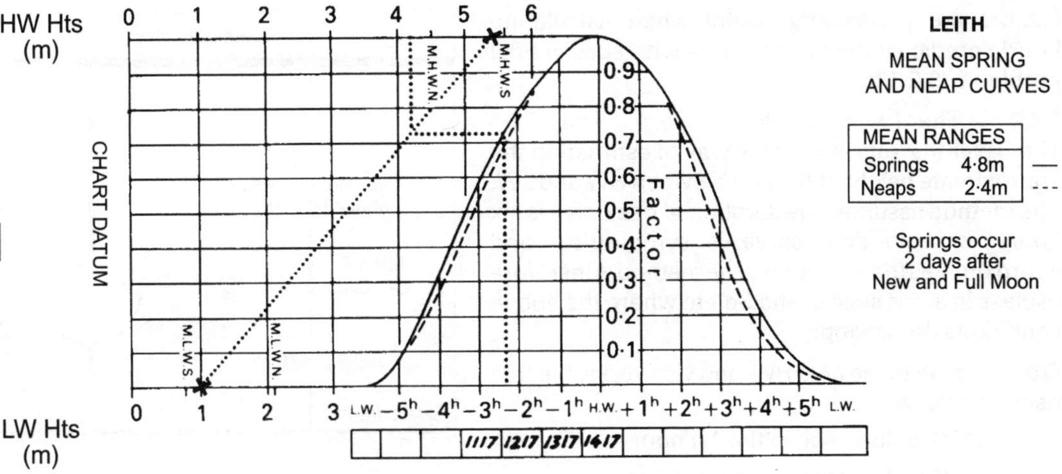

Fig. 7(5)

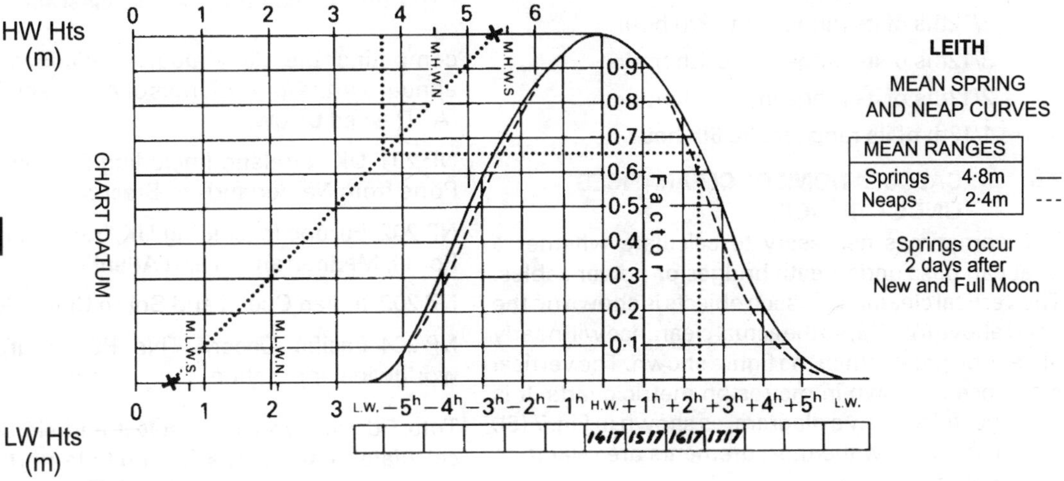

and the Spring Curve applies.

(4) Proceed vertically to the time scale, and read off the time required, 1637.

7.4.2 Secondary Ports

On coasts where there is little change of shape between tidal curves for adjacent Standard Ports, and where the duration of rise or fall at the Secondary Port is like that of the appropriate Standard Port (i.e. where HW and LW time differences are nearly the same), intermediate times and heights may be calculated from the tidal curves for the Standard Port in a similar manner to 7.4.1. The curves are entered with the times and heights of HW and LW at the Secondary Port, calculated as in 7.3.2 and 7.3.3.

Interpolation between the curves can be made by eye, using the range at the Standard Port as argument. Do not extrapolate, use the Spring Curve for Spring ranges or greater, and the Neap Curve for Neap ranges or less. With a large change in duration between Springs and Neaps the results may have a slight error, greater near LW.

Special curves for places between Swanage and Selsey (where the tide is very complex) are given in 9.2.12.

7.4.3 The use of factors

An alternative to the tidal curve method of tidal prediction is the use of factors which remains popular with those brought up on this method. Tidal curves show the factor of the range attained at times before and after HW. By definition a factor of 1 = HW, and 0 = LW. So the factor represents the percentage of the mean range (for the day in question) which has been reached at that particular time.

Range × factor = Rise above LW

and Factor = Rise above LW ÷ range

In determining or using the factor it may be necessary to interpolate between the Spring and Neap curves as described in 7.4.2.

C7

Factors are particularly useful when calculating hourly predicted heights for ports with special tidal problems (9.2.12).

7.4.4 The 'Twelfths' rule

The 'Twelfths' rule is a simple way of estimating the approximate height of the tide between HW and LW. The method assumes the duration of rise or fall is six hours and the tidal curve is symmetrical and approximates to a sine curve. The method is therefore useless in areas such as the Solent where the above conditions do not apply.

From one LW to the next HW, and vice versa, the tide rises or falls by:

1/12th of its range in the 1st hour
2/12ths of its range in the 2nd hour
3/12ths of its range in the 3rd hour
3/12ths of its range in the 4th hour
2/12ths of its range in the 5th hour
1/12th of its range in the 6th hour

7.5 CALCULATIONS OF CLEARANCES UNDER BRIDGES

It is sometimes necessary to calculate whether a boat can pass underneath bridges or power cables. The vertical clearance of such objects is shown on the chart above MHWS, so the actual clearance will nearly always be greater than the figure shown. The vertical clearance is shown in metres on metric charts. It is often useful to draw a diagram, as shown in Fig. 7 (6), which shows how the measurements are related to chart datum.

Clearance = (Vertical clearance of object + height of MHWS) minus (height of tide at the time + height of mast above water).

7.6 TIDAL PREDICTION BY COMPUTER

By virtue of its simplicity, accuracy and speed, tidal prediction by computer or calculator is something no seaman – professional or amateur – with access to a computer can afford to ignore because it can do the job better and quicker than by conventional means. A navigator with access to a PC or lap-top computer, can choose between two tidal prediction programs issued by the Hydrographic Office (HO).

7.6.1 TotalTide

Total Tide (DP 550) is the new digital tidal prediction program produced by the UKHO to meet the requirements of the worldwide SOLAS shipping market. It provides instant tidal height and tidal stream rates for the world's commercial shipping routes.

The program utilises the same harmonic constants and prediction algorithms used by the HO for

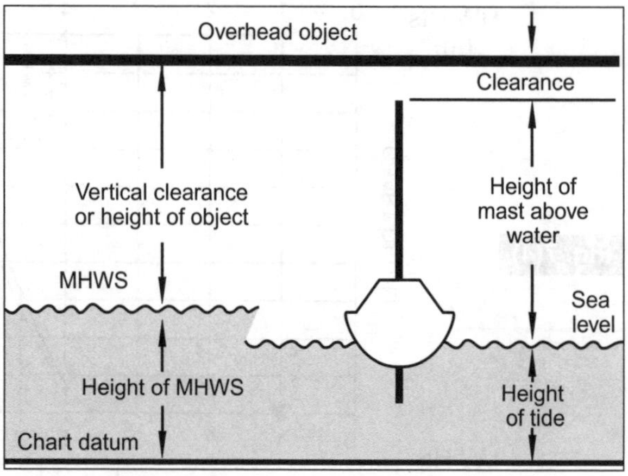

Fig. 7 (6) Calculating vertical clearance

computing the daily tidal predictions published annually in the four volumes of Admiralty Tide Tables (ATT) listed below:

NP 201 UK & Ireland (including European Channel Ports from Netherlands to Brest);

NP 202 Europe (excluding UK, Ireland and Channel Ports), Mediterranean and Atlantic;

NP 203 Indian Ocean and South China Sea;

NP 204 Pacific Ocean. This PC program has a worldwide application.

TotalTide allows you to select and simultaneously calculate tidal heights for multiple ports for up to seven consecutive days ahead. Tidal heights for the world's Standard and Secondary Ports are displayed in both graphical and tabular format.

Other useful facilities provided include periods of daylight and nautical twilight, Moon phases and a Springs and Neaps indicator. Under keel and overhead clearances can be calculated and displayed as a simple graphic to ensure safe passage making and port entry.

The basic tidal curve can be set to show varied time intervals from about 3 hours to seven days. If using the tidal height table, you can to set the time interval required between predictions to 5 mins, 10 mins, 20 mins, 30 mins and one hour intervals.

Tidal stream rates for more than 3,000 positions worldwide are presented on a simple chart based diagram with coloured arrows showing the direction and strength of tidal streams and whether the tide is falling or rising.

TotalTide comes on one CD which includes the calculation program itself and seven Area Data Sets (ADS) which provides worldwide coverage. A permit system gives you access to the Area of the world you require. Most yachtsmen would only require the Data Set for Area 1 (UK, Europe and the Mediterranean).

Whilst TotalTide will continue to predict tidal height and streams indefinitely, the UKHO recommends users should update the ADS annually in order to maintain accuracy. Data updates will be available from Admiralty Chart Agents each January.

TotalTide is designed to run on a PC with a 200 MHz processor or better, with a minimum of 64 Mb RAM and a CD-ROM drive, running Windows 95, 98, NT or 2000. TotalTide also runs on a Macintosh G3, Powerbook G3 , or a Macintosh G4 using Virtual PC.

The previous Tidecalc (NP 158) has already been withdrawn from sale. The associated Tidecalc area discs NP158-A1 to NP 158-A13 will be supported until 30 Nov 2001 and will then be withdrawn from sale.

7.6.2 SHM for Windows 2001 (DP 560)

An alternative computer program issued by the UKHO is SHM for Windows (DP 560) which uses the NP 159 Simplified Harmonic Method of Tidal Prediction and is supplied on a CD-ROM. The user needs to input harmonic constants found in Table VII in all four volumes of ATTs. The Port Harmonic Constant, and where appropriate Shallow Water Corrections and Seasonal Changes in Mean Level, are keyed in manually from data listed in Part III of ATTs, or from ***NP 160 Tidal Harmonic Constants (European Waters) Edition 3 2000***. NP 160 will be updated approximately every five years.

As changes in Port Harmonic Constants are made from time to time, for the best results, it is recommended that only those constants listed in Part 3 of the latest edition of the Admiralty Tide Tables should be used.

Whichever method of tidal prediction is used, the basic accuracy will depend on the accuracy of the tidal observations made, the length of time over which the observations were undertaken, and whether the prediction method chosen is suitable for a particular port or area.

In some geographical areas better tide predictions may be obtained by using non-harmonic methods of prediction. Such areas include the upper reaches of many rivers like the Medway above Chatham; the Forth above Grangemouth; the Severn above Avonmouth, and the Crouch above Burnham. Other areas where non-harmonic methods result in more accurate predictions include many German ports.

7.6.3 Commercial programs

A number of commercial firms offer tidal prediction programs for use on computers or calculators. Most of the commercial programs are usually based on the Admiralty NP 159 method of tidal prediction.

7.7 TIDAL STREAMS

7.7.1 General

Tidal streams are the horizontal movement of water caused by the vertical rise and fall of the tide. They normally change direction about every six hours. They are quite different from ocean currents, such as the Gulf Stream, which run for long periods in the same direction. Tidal streams are always expressed as the direction towards which they are running.

Tidal streams are important to yachtsmen around the British Isles because they often run at about two knots, and much more strongly in a few areas, and at Spring tides. There are a few places where they can attain rates of six to eight knots.

7.7.2 Tidal stream Atlases

The strength and direction of the tidal stream in the more important areas is shown in ***Admiralty Tidal Stream Atlases***, as follows:

NP 209	4th Ed	Orkney and Shetland Islands, 1986
218	5th Ed	North Coast of Ireland, West Coast of Scotland, 1995
219	2nd Ed	Portsmouth Hbr and Appr, 1991
220	2nd Ed	Rosyth Hbr and Appr, 1991
221	2nd Ed	Plymouth Hbr and Appr, 1991
222	1st Ed	Firth of Clyde and Appr, 1992
233	3rd Ed	Dover Strait, 1995
249	2nd Ed	Thames Estuary, 1985 (with Co-Tidal charts)
250	4th Ed	English Channel, 1992
251	3rd Ed	North Sea, S Part, 1976
252	3rd Ed	North Sea, NW Part, 1975
253	1st Ed	North Sea, E Part, 1978
256	4th Ed	Irish Sea and Bristol Channel, 1992
257	3rd Ed	Appr to Portland, 1973
264	5th Ed	The Channel Islands and Adjacent Coasts of France, 1993
26	1st Ed	France, West Coast, 1978
337	4th Ed	Solent and Adjacent Waters, 1993

Extracts from the above (by permission of the Hydrographer and HMSO) are given in Chapter 9 for each area in the Almanac.

The directions of the streams are shown by arrows which are graded in weight and, where possible, in length to indicate the strength of the tidal stream. Thus ⟶ indicates a weak stream and ➞ indicates a strong stream. The figures against the arrows give the Mean Neap and Spring rates in tenths of a knot, thus 19,34 indicates a Mean Neap rate of 1·9 knots and a mean Spring rate of 3·4 knots. The position of the comma on the Atlas indicates the approximate position at which the observations were taken.

It should be remembered that tidal atlases rarely show the details of inshore eddies, and the tide often sets towards the coast in bays. Along open coasts the turn of the tidal stream does not necessarily occur at HW and LW. It often occurs at about half tide. The tidal stream usually turns earlier inshore than offshore. On modern charts lettered diamonds give information on the tidal streams by reference to a table showing Set, Spring Rate and Neap Rate at hourly intervals before and after HW at a Standard Port. Where appropriate, normal river currents are included. Information on tidal streams and current streams is also included in ***Admiralty Sailing Directions.***

7.7.3 Computation of tidal stream rates

Using Fig. 7 (7) it is possible to predict the rate of a tidal stream at intermediate times, assuming that it varies with the range of tide at Dover.

Example:

It is required to predict the rate of the tidal stream off the northerly point of the Isle of Skye at 0420 UTC on a day when the heights of tide at Dover are:

UTC	Ht(m)
LW 0328	1·4
HW 0819	6·3
LW 1602	1·1
HW 2054	6·4

The Mean Range at Dover is therefore:

$$\frac{(4{\cdot}9 + 5{\cdot}2 + 5{\cdot}3)}{3} = 5{\cdot}1$$

When using either the Tidal Stream Atlas NP 218, or the Tidal Stream charts for Area 8 in Chapter 9, the appropriate chart to use is that for '4 hours before HW Dover' and this gives a mean Neap and Spring rate of 08 and 18 respectively (0·8 and 1·8 kn). On Fig. 7 (7), Computation of Rates, on the horizontal line marked Neaps, mark the dot above 08 on the horizontal scale; likewise on the line marked Springs, mark the dot below the figure 18 on the horizontal scale. Join these two dots with a straight line. On the vertical scale, 'Mean Range Dover', find the range 5·1. From this point follow across horizontally until the pencil line just drawn is cut; from this intersection follow the vertical line to the scale of Tidal Stream Rates, either top or bottom, and read off the predicted rate. In this example it is 15 or 1·5 knots.

A perspex sheet, or a sheet of tracing paper can be used on top of Fig. 7 (7), so as to preserve it for future use.

7.7.4 Tidal streams in rivers

Tidal streams in rivers are influenced by the local topography of the river bed as well as by the phases of the Moon. At or near Springs, in a river which is obstructed, for example, by sandbanks at the entrance, the time of HW gets later going up the river; the time of LW also gets later, but more rapidly so the duration of the flood becomes shorter, and duration of ebb becomes longer. At the entrance the flood stream starts at an interval after LW which increases with the degree of obstruction of the channel; this interval between local LW and the start of the flood increases with the distance up river. The ebb begins soon after local HW along the length of the river. Hence the duration of flood is less than that of the ebb and the difference increases with distance up river.

The flood stream is normally stronger than the ebb, and runs harder during the first half of the rise of tide.

At Neaps the flood and ebb both start soon after local LW and HW respectively, and their durations and rates are roughly equal.

7.8 METEOROLOGICAL CONDITIONS

Meteorological conditions can have a significant effect on tides and tidal streams.

a. Wind

The effect of wind on tidal heights and times is exceedingly variable and depends on the topography of the local area in question. Broadly speaking sea level tends to rise in the direction towards which the wind is blowing and lowered in the opposite direction. A strong onshore wind will pile up the water and cause high waters to be higher than predicted, while winds blowing off the land will have the reverse effect. Strong winds blowing along a coast or the sudden onset of a gale can also set up a wave or 'storm surge' which travels along the coast. Under exceptional conditions this can raise the height of the tide by two or three metres, or in the case of a 'negative' surge, can lower the height of LW by one or two metres which may be more serious for the yachtsman.

In practical terms there is no need to consider winds of less than Force 5.

A good example of how localised meteorological effects on water levels can differ from the more general rules occurs in Southampton Water where strong winds between N and NE can significantly reduce tide levels. The longer and stronger the wind blows, the greater the effect. NE winds of Force 5 can be expected to reduce predicted levels by about – 0·2m, but winds of Force 8 to 10 will almost double the effect to – 0·5m.

Strong winds can also be associated with high-pressure systems so the total correction required to counter the combined effects of a strong wind and higher than average pressure can easily reach – 0·6m below predicted levels. Water levels at the entrances to the Newtown or Beaulieu Rivers are significantly lowered when strong N to NW winds combine with high pressure.

b. Barometric pressure

Severe conditions giving rise to a storm surge as described above are likely to be caused by a deep

Fig. 7 (7) Calculating tidal stream rates

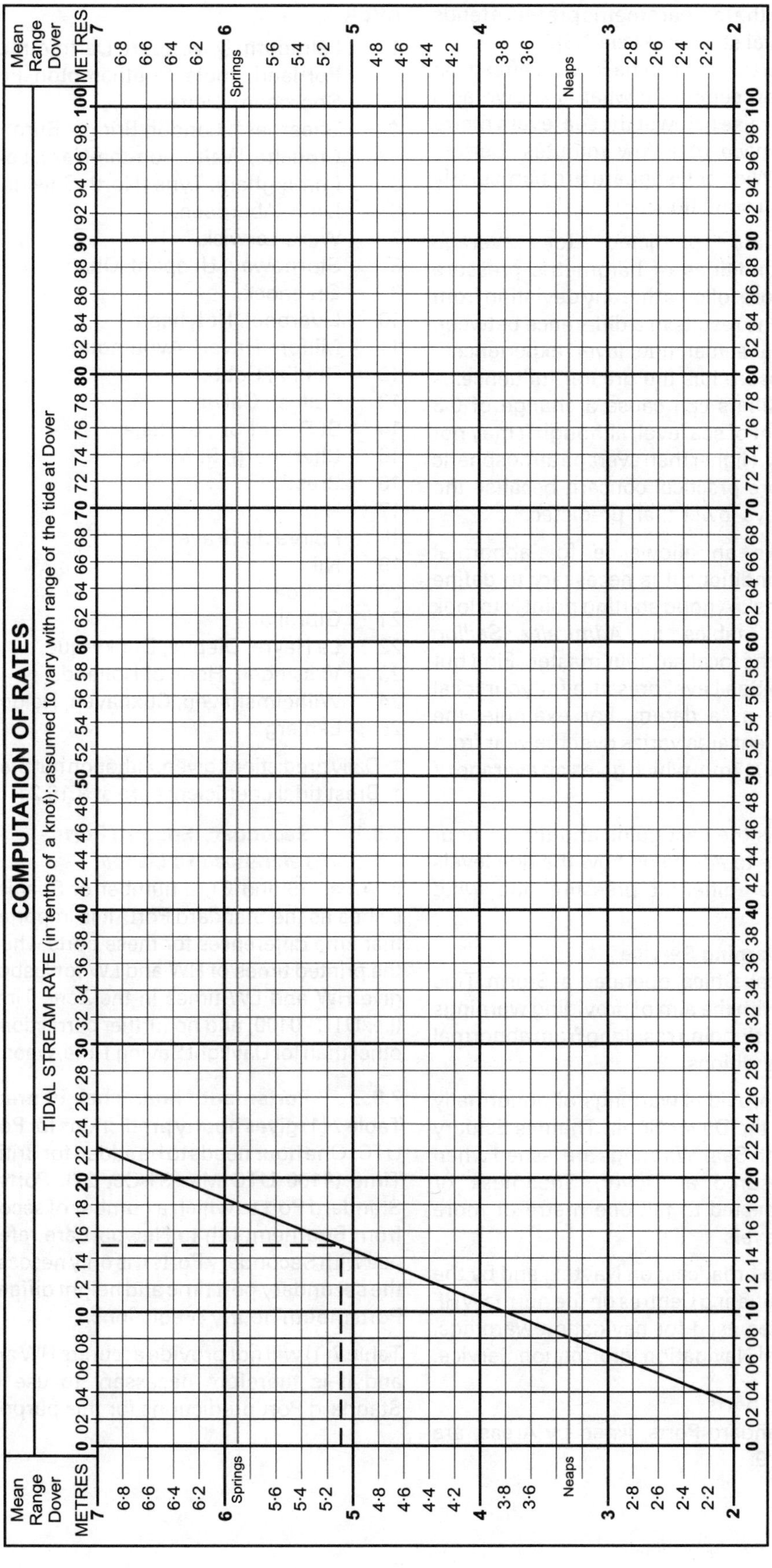

depression, where the low barometric pressure tends to raise the sea level still more (see 7.8).
Intense minor depressions can have local effects on the height of water, setting up what is known as a '*seiche*' which can raise or lower the sea level a metre or more in the space of a few minutes. Certain harbours such as Wick or Fishguard are particularly susceptible to such conditions.

Tidal heights are predicted for average meteorological conditions of barometric pressure and wind. It therefore follows that any deviation from 'average' conditions results in a difference between the predicted and actual tide level experienced. Atmospheric pressure has the greater influence. A change of 34 millibars can cause a change of 0·3 metres in the height of sea level, although it may not be felt immediately. Higher than average atmospheric pressure is of more practical concern because the water level is always lower than predicted.

In order to make an allowance for abnormal meteorological conditions it is necessary to define 'average conditions'. A good starting point is to look at the statistical tables in *Admiralty Sailing Directions*, or ask the local harbour master. Find out the average Mean Sea Level pressure for your local port and use this as a datum. For example, the pressure in the Solent area varies over the year from about 1014mb to 1017mb, which gives an average of 1016mb.

Local knowledge is the best guide and the harbour master will be able to advise on how the tide levels are affected under different pressure and wind conditions.

7.8 Storm Tide Warning Service

The Meteorological Office operates a Storm Tide Warning Service with the aim of providing warnings of potential coastal flooding resulting from abnormal meteorological conditions.

This service also provides warnings of abnormally low tidal levels in the Dover Strait, Thames Estuary and Southern North Sea. Warnings are issued when tidal levels measured at Dover, Sheerness or Lowestoft are expected to fall one metre or more below predicted levels.

Such warnings are broadcast on Navtex, and by the Coastguard Coordinating Centres on the normal VHF and MF frequencies used for navigation warnings, and by the Channel Navigation Information Service.

7.9 Standard ports

The following Standard Ports, listed by Areas, are shown in Chapter 9:

AREA	
1	Falmouth, Devonport, Dartmouth.
2	Portland, Poole, Southampton, Portsmouth.
3	Shoreham, Dover.
4	Sheerness, London Bridge, Burnham-on-Crouch*, Walton-on-the-Naze, Lowestoft.
5	Immingham, Tyne (North Shields).
6	Leith, Aberdeen.
7	Wick, Lerwick.
8	Stornoway, Ullapool, Oban.
9	Greenock.
10	Liverpool, Holyhead.
11	Milford Haven, Avonmouth.
12	Dublin, Cobh.
13	Belfast, Galway.
14	St Peter Port, St Helier.
15	Cherbourg, St Malo.
16	Brest†.
17	Nil.
18	Pointe de Grave.
19	Nil
20	Lisboa
21	Gibraltar
22	Le Havre, Dieppe, Dunkerque
23	Vlissingen, Hook of Holland.
24	Wilhelmshaven, Cuxhaven, Helgoland.
25	Esbjerg

* Daily predictions given, although not Standard Ports.
† Brest tidal coefficients are at 9.16.24

7.9.1. Secondary Spanish Ports referenced to Lisboa

In Areas 19 and 21, a number of Spanish ports use Lisboa as the Standard Port. It is important to realise that time differences for these ports when applied to the printed times of HW and LW for Lisboa (UTC) will give HW and LW times in the Zone Time for Spain (i.e. UTC –0100) and no further correction is required, other than for Daylight Saving Time, when this applies.

7.9.2 Portsmouth hourly height predictions

Table 7 (1) gives hourly predictions for Portsmouth in UTC. One hour needs to be added for British Summer Time (0100 UTC Mar 31-Oct 27). Portsmouth is a Standard Port to which a number of secondary ports from Bournemouth to Newport are referenced. For use with Secondary Ports it is only necessary to apply the secondary port time and height differences to the Portsmouth hourly predictions.

Table 7(1) will not provide accurate HW and LW times and it is therefore necessary to use Portsmouth Standard Port predictions for this purpose.

Table 7 (1) Portsmouth hourly height predictions

ENGLAND – PORTSMOUTH

Lat 50°48'N Long 01°07'W

TIME ZONE **UTC** UNITS **METRES**

JANUARY 2002

DATE	0000	0100	0200	0300	0400	0500	0600	0700	0800	0900	1000	1100	1200	1300	1400	1500	1600	1700	1800	1900	2000	2100	2200	2300
1 TU	4.68	4.60	4.35	3.65	2.25	1.07	1.03	1.71	2.18	2.45	3.12	4.10	4.70	4.67	4.39	3.88	2.66	1.20	0.66	1.17	1.80	2.10	2.59	3.58
2 W	4.46	4.72	4.58	4.29	3.42	1.90	0.94	1.18	1.85	2.20	2.52	3.34	4.29	4.69	4.56	4.27	3.65	2.27	0.95	0.74	1.34	1.85	2.13	2.77
3 TH	3.81	4.54	4.68	4.53	4.19	3.12	1.64	0.98	1.38	1.94	2.20	2.63	3.53	4.34	4.59	4.43	4.14	3.36	1.94	0.90	0.93	1.48	1.87	2.21
4 F	2.97	3.93	4.50	4.61	4.47	4.02	2.84	1.54	1.15	1.57	1.97	2.22	2.75	3.62	4.26	4.44	4.30	3.97	3.08	1.77	1.02	1.15	1.58	1.91
5 SA	2.32	3.10	3.93	4.42	4.53	4.37	3.82	2.66	1.60	1.37	1.68	1.98	2.26	2.83	3.58	4.12	4.30	4.17	3.79	2.90	1.79	1.23	1.33	1.66
6 SU	1.97	2.42	3.14	3.85	4.32	4.44	4.25	3.67	2.64	1.77	1.54	1.73	1.99	2.28	2.81	3.46	3.96	4.18	4.05	3.66	2.86	1.93	1.44	1.45
7 M	1.73	2.04	2.46	3.10	3.75	4.24	4.36	4.16	3.62	2.72	1.94	1.64	1.74	1.97	2.26	2.74	3.31	3.83	4.09	3.98	3.64	2.94	2.13	1.60
8 TU	1.53	1.77	2.07	2.45	3.02	3.66	4.20	4.31	4.14	3.66	2.84	2.05	1.64	1.70	1.93	2.20	2.63	3.18	3.77	4.06	3.98	3.70	3.09	2.30
9 W	1.68	1.55	1.80	2.07	2.42	2.96	3.64	4.20	4.32	4.17	3.73	2.94	2.06	1.57	1.63	1.88	2.13	2.53	3.11	3.78	4.10	4.05	3.82	3.24
10 TH	2.38	1.66	1.53	1.80	2.07	2.40	2.95	3.69	4.26	4.36	4.22	3.79	2.95	1.95	1.43	1.55	1.83	2.08	2.50	3.14	3.88	4.19	4.15	3.95
11 F	3.33	2.35	1.56	1.49	1.81	2.08	2.42	3.01	3.81	4.36	4.41	4.27	3.80	2.83	1.73	1.27	1.49	1.81	2.08	2.54	3.27	4.02	4.30	4.26
12 SA	4.03	3.31	2.18	1.42	1.46	1.84	2.12	2.50	3.17	3.98	4.45	4.44	4.27	3.69	2.58	1.46	1.14	1.48	1.85	2.15	2.67	3.47	4.20	4.40
13 SU ●	4.34	4.02	3.14	1.92	1.27	1.47	1.92	2.22	2.65	3.38	4.17	4.51	4.43	4.18	3.45	2.22	1.19	1.09	1.56	1.94	2.27	2.88	3.73	4.37
14 M	4.47	4.35	3.88	2.82	1.61	1.19	1.56	2.04	2.35	2.85	3.64	4.34	4.51	4.36	3.99	3.09	1.79	1.00	1.15	1.70	2.06	2.45	3.17	4.00
15 TU	4.48	4.47	4.26	3.60	2.39	1.34	1.22	1.74	2.18	2.50	3.11	3.91	4.44	4.44	4.21	3.69	2.60	1.40	0.96	1.33	1.86	2.19	2.69	3.51
16 W	4.23	4.50	4.41	4.06	3.17	1.93	1.22	1.40	1.93	2.30	2.69	3.42	4.14	4.43	4.30	4.00	3.26	2.07	1.15	1.10	1.58	2.00	2.36	3.02
17 TH	3.84	4.36	4.45	4.28	3.72	2.63	1.57	1.29	1.65	2.09	2.41	2.95	3.72	4.25	4.33	4.12	3.68	2.73	1.62	1.12	1.37	1.80	2.13	2.60
18 F	3.37	4.07	4.37	4.34	4.05	3.25	2.13	1.42	1.51	1.89	2.20	2.58	3.23	3.92	4.23	4.17	3.90	3.26	2.22	1.38	1.29	1.65	1.97	2.29
19 SA	2.89	3.65	4.18	4.31	4.17	3.72	2.76	1.79	1.50	1.78	2.07	2.31	2.78	3.45	4.00	4.14	3.98	3.61	2.82	1.86	1.37	1.55	1.89	2.12
20 SU	2.49	3.15	3.82	4.19	4.18	3.94	3.35	2.39	1.69	1.69	1.99	2.19	2.43	2.96	3.57	3.97	3.99	3.76	3.31	2.49	1.72	1.52	1.79	2.07
21 M	2.27	2.69	3.32	3.87	4.12	4.01	3.71	3.06	2.21	1.75	1.88	2.13	2.28	2.53	3.05	3.58	3.88	3.83	3.57	3.09	2.34	1.77	1.70	1.96
22 TU	2.20	2.40	2.82	3.38	3.85	4.02	3.86	3.55	2.92	2.21	1.87	1.99	2.19	2.32	2.58	3.06	3.52	3.77	3.70	3.47	3.02	2.37	1.89	1.83
23 W	2.05	2.28	2.47	2.86	3.37	3.79	3.94	3.79	3.51	2.94	2.29	1.94	1.99	2.16	2.30	2.56	3.01	3.45	3.71	3.66	3.50	3.10	2.49	2.00
24 TH	1.87	2.05	2.28	2.47	2.84	3.32	3.77	3.93	3.84	3.59	3.04	2.35	1.91	1.88	2.07	2.23	2.50	2.94	3.42	3.73	3.75	3.64	3.26	2.62
25 F	2.02	1.80	1.98	2.23	2.43	2.79	3.31	3.82	4.04	3.99	3.73	3.14	2.33	1.76	1.69	1.92	2.13	2.42	2.90	3.47	3.86	3.95	3.85	3.43
26 SA	2.69	1.93	1.63	1.85	2.14	2.37	2.77	3.38	3.98	4.22	4.17	3.86	3.17	2.20	1.49	1.44	1.77	2.05	2.37	2.94	3.63	4.09	4.19	4.04
27 SU	3.56	2.66	1.73	1.40	1.70	2.07	2.35	2.81	3.54	4.20	4.43	4.32	3.94	3.11	1.94	1.16	1.21	1.65	2.00	2.38	3.05	3.86	4.35	4.40
28 M ○	4.19	3.62	2.51	1.43	1.16	1.60	2.04	2.36	2.91	3.76	4.45	4.60	4.39	3.94	2.94	1.60	0.82	1.04	1.62	2.01	2.43	3.24	4.14	4.59
29 TU	4.55	4.28	3.58	2.25	1.10	0.99	1.59	2.07	2.40	3.06	4.03	4.67	4.68	4.39	3.88	2.67	1.19	0.55	1.00	1.67	2.03	2.52	3.50	4.43
30 W	4.75	4.61	4.33	3.44	1.88	0.79	0.95	1.67	2.11	2.45	3.27	4.29	4.79	4.66	4.37	3.74	2.29	0.79	0.44	1.11	1.73	2.04	2.68	3.79
31 TH	4.64	4.81	4.64	4.31	3.16	1.47	0.63	1.07	1.79	2.11	2.54	3.52	4.49	4.79	4.59	4.31	3.49	1.84	0.53	0.53	1.28	1.77	2.10	2.92

FEBRUARY 2002

DATE	0000	0100	0200	0300	0400	0500	0600	0700	0800	0900	1000	1100	1200	1300	1400	1500	1600	1700	1800	1900	2000	2100	2200	2300
1 F	4.06	4.73	4.79	4.64	4.17	2.76	1.14	0.67	1.29	1.86	2.11	2.70	3.76	4.56	4.70	4.51	4.18	3.11	1.43	0.49	0.78	1.45	1.81	2.24
2 SA	3.20	4.22	4.72	4.74	4.56	3.87	2.33	1.01	0.89	1.49	1.89	2.18	2.91	3.89	4.50	4.57	4.39	3.93	2.69	1.23	0.68	1.07	1.58	1.89
3 SU	2.46	3.41	4.25	4.64	4.64	4.37	3.49	2.04	1.10	1.18	1.64	1.94	2.31	3.07	3.89	4.36	4.42	4.21	3.61	2.39	1.27	0.99	1.33	1.71
4 M	2.05	2.66	3.50	4.18	4.51	4.47	4.09	3.17	1.98	1.35	1.43	1.75	2.02	2.43	3.11	3.77	4.18	4.23	3.97	3.34	2.31	1.50	1.31	1.55
5 TU	1.87	2.21	2.78	3.46	4.04	4.34	4.25	3.84	3.03	2.11	1.62	1.61	1.85	2.10	2.48	3.04	3.59	3.99	4.04	3.78	3.23	2.43	1.80	1.58
6 W	1.72	2.00	2.31	2.77	3.34	3.88	4.16	4.06	3.70	3.06	2.32	1.83	1.71	1.89	2.11	2.43	2.89	3.40	3.82	3.90	3.71	3.30	2.67	2.08
7 TH	1.76	1.83	2.06	2.31	2.69	3.19	3.74	4.04	3.98	3.72	3.20	2.52	1.92	1.72	1.86	2.06	2.33	2.73	3.25	3.74	3.89	3.77	3.48	2.92
8 F	2.24	1.81	1.83	2.04	2.25	2.59	3.09	3.69	4.03	4.01	3.82	3.36	2.61	1.87	1.61	1.77	1.97	2.22	2.62	3.21	3.79	3.99	3.93	3.69
9 SA	3.08	2.24	1.72	1.75	1.98	2.19	2.54	3.09	3.76	4.12	4.10	3.94	3.44	2.54	1.68	1.44	1.66	1.90	2.17	2.62	3.31	3.95	4.14	4.10
10 SU	3.83	3.08	2.07	1.52	1.64	1.94	2.18	2.57	3.20	3.93	4.24	4.19	4.00	3.37	2.29	1.39	1.26	1.61	1.90	2.21	2.74	3.54	4.17	4.29
11 M	4.21	3.83	2.87	1.75	1.31	1.59	1.97	2.25	2.70	3.43	4.14	4.34	4.23	3.94	3.14	1.89	1.09	1.18	1.66	1.98	2.34	2.99	3.84	4.37
12 TU ●	4.38	4.22	3.65	2.48	1.38	1.18	1.65	2.07	2.38	2.92	3.72	4.33	4.36	4.19	3.75	2.72	1.44	0.90	1.25	1.79	2.11	2.56	3.33	4.15
13 W	4.47	4.38	4.10	3.28	1.96	1.10	1.23	1.81	2.19	2.56	3.24	4.03	4.42	4.31	4.05	3.40	2.17	1.06	0.91	1.45	1.94	2.27	2.88	3.72
14 TH	4.37	4.47	4.30	3.81	2.71	1.46	1.02	1.43	1.99	2.32	2.82	3.61	4.25	4.40	4.20	3.80	2.87	1.59	0.88	1.12	1.69	2.07	2.52	3.29
15 F	4.07	4.46	4.40	4.12	3.32	2.06	1.15	1.19	1.71	2.12	2.49	3.18	3.95	4.35	4.29	4.03	3.38	2.22	1.16	0.98	1.45	1.88	2.23	2.87
16 SA	3.71	4.30	4.43	4.26	3.77	2.67	1.51	1.12	1.50	1.93	2.23	2.76	3.56	4.17	4.31	4.14	3.76	2.81	1.63	1.02	1.29	1.75	2.04	2.48
17 SU	3.28	4.03	4.37	4.31	4.03	3.26	2.03	1.22	1.35	1.82	2.09	2.40	3.09	3.86	4.24	4.19	3.93	3.35	2.22	1.27	1.16	1.65	1.99	2.22
18 M	2.81	3.63	4.18	4.31	4.11	3.69	2.71	1.60	1.24	1.67	2.07	2.23	2.63	3.38	4.00	4.18	4.00	3.64	2.89	1.79	1.22	1.46	1.95	2.19
19 TU	2.45	3.11	3.81	4.18	4.16	3.85	3.30	2.29	1.47	1.46	1.95	2.23	2.38	2.84	3.53	3.97	4.03	3.76	3.35	2.55	1.66	1.39	1.76	2.17
20 W	2.36	2.66	3.27	3.82	4.07	3.95	3.60	3.02	2.13	1.58	1.71	2.12	2.32	2.49	2.94	3.51	3.85	3.84	3.56	3.17	2.44	1.77	1.65	1.98
21 TH	2.29	2.46	2.76	3.28	3.72	3.91	3.77	3.46	2.95	2.22	1.79	1.89	2.16	2.33	2.50	2.91	3.39	3.69	3.69	3.48	3.17	2.56	2.01	1.87
22 F	2.07	2.30	2.46	2.73	3.17	3.57	3.79	3.71	3.50	3.06	2.42	1.97	1.92	2.07	2.22	2.40	2.78	3.23	3.57	3.67	3.59	3.35	2.81	2.25
23 SA	1.96	2.00	2.18	2.35	2.62	3.03	3.48	3.80	3.83	3.69	3.27	2.62	2.04	1.77	1.84	2.02	2.26	2.63	3.12	3.58	3.82	3.83	3.61	3.08
24 SU	2.39	1.89	1.77	1.96	2.19	2.49	2.94	3.51	3.95	4.07	3.92	3.48	2.74	1.93	1.47	1.53	1.81	2.13	2.53	3.12	3.75	4.10	4.12	3.87
25 M	3.27	2.38	1.63	1.45	1.74	2.07	2.42	2.94	3.67	4.22	4.33	4.12	3.63	2.72	1.66	1.07	1.23	1.68	2.06	2.51	3.25	4.03	4.42	4.37
26 TU	4.07	3.36	2.20	1.25	1.14	1.59	2.03	2.41	3.05	3.93	4.51	4.53	4.24	3.69	2.55	1.25	0.68	1.06	1.65	2.06	2.57	3.48	4.36	4.67
27 W ○	4.53	4.20	3.30	1.85	0.83	0.94	1.58	2.05	2.44	3.24	4.24	4.74	4.61	4.30	3.64	2.23	0.78	0.42	1.06	1.70	2.07	2.71	3.80	4.65
28 TH	4.82	4.62	4.25	3.07	1.39	0.51	0.93	1.68	2.07	2.52	3.51	4.53	4.84	4.62	4.33	3.47	1.77	0.39	0.39	1.21	1.77	2.12	2.95	4.13

Table 7 (1) Portsmouth hourly height predictions – continued

ENGLAND – PORTSMOUTH

Lat 50°48'N Long 01°07'W

TIME ZONE **UTC** UNITS **METRES**

MARCH 2002

DATE	0000	0100	0200	0300	0400	0500	0600	0700	0800	0900	1000	1100	1200	1300	1400	1500	1600	1700	1800	1900	2000	2100	2200	2300
1 F	4.85	4.86	4.67	4.17	2.65	0.92	0.41	1.11	1.78	2.08	2.68	3.82	4.71	4.82	4.60	4.28	3.10	1.26	0.21	0.58	1.40	1.80	2.24	3.27
2 SA	4.41	4.90	4.84	4.66	3.88	2.12	0.62	0.56	1.35	1.83	2.13	2.94	4.09	4.75	4.74	4.56	4.07	2.60	0.88	0.32	0.91	1.55	1.87	2.49
3 SU	3.61	4.55	4.85	4.78	4.49	3.40	1.63	0.60	0.88	1.55	1.87	2.29	3.23	4.22	4.67	4.62	4.42	3.67	2.11	0.79	0.65	1.24	1.69	2.04
4 M	2.81	3.83	4.54	4.72	4.62	4.13	2.86	1.39	0.85	1.22	1.70	1.97	2.52	3.43	4.20	4.50	4.46	4.14	3.21	1.82	0.98	1.06	1.51	1.86
5 TU	2.29	3.06	3.88	4.40	4.52	4.33	3.68	2.49	1.44	1.21	1.51	1.84	2.14	2.72	3.46	4.04	4.29	4.21	3.78	2.88	1.84	1.35	1.44	1.76
6 W	2.08	2.51	3.16	3.78	4.18	4.25	3.98	3.32	2.40	1.71	1.55	1.72	1.99	2.29	2.78	3.34	3.81	4.03	3.93	3.50	2.81	2.10	1.75	1.74
7 TH	1.97	2.25	2.60	3.09	3.57	3.92	3.97	3.70	3.19	2.55	2.03	1.80	1.86	2.08	2.32	2.69	3.14	3.56	3.80	3.74	3.44	2.98	2.45	2.06
8 F	1.93	2.08	2.29	2.54	2.91	3.34	3.70	3.78	3.61	3.29	2.81	2.29	1.92	1.89	2.05	2.23	2.53	2.92	3.36	3.69	3.72	3.57	3.27	2.75
9 SA	2.21	1.96	2.05	2.21	2.40	2.73	3.17	3.60	3.77	3.69	3.50	3.04	2.39	1.86	1.78	1.93	2.10	2.37	2.77	3.32	3.77	3.86	3.81	3.53
10 SU	2.89	2.15	1.81	1.91	2.08	2.27	2.61	3.14	3.69	3.90	3.87	3.70	3.14	2.27	1.64	1.58	1.80	2.00	2.29	2.77	3.46	3.97	4.07	4.03
11 M	3.66	2.81	1.89	1.57	1.76	1.99	2.21	2.63	3.28	3.91	4.07	4.02	3.79	3.04	1.96	1.32	1.41	1.74	1.99	2.33	2.94	3.75	4.21	4.24
12 TU	4.14	3.59	2.48	1.51	1.34	1.70	1.99	2.27	2.79	3.57	4.15	4.20	4.10	3.72	2.71	1.52	1.05	1.36	1.79	2.08	2.51	3.26	4.08	4.38
13 W	4.33	4.09	3.28	1.98	1.14	1.25	1.77	2.08	2.44	3.09	3.91	4.32	4.24	4.06	3.45	2.20	1.09	0.95	1.47	1.92	2.24	2.81	3.66	4.35
14 TH ●	4.45	4.30	3.85	2.75	1.44	0.95	1.36	1.91	2.23	2.70	3.48	4.20	4.38	4.20	3.87	2.97	1.62	0.83	1.07	1.68	2.07	2.49	3.21	4.05
15 F	4.49	4.41	4.15	3.39	2.09	1.03	1.01	1.60	2.07	2.42	3.07	3.87	4.38	4.34	4.09	3.50	2.33	1.12	0.85	1.36	1.89	2.24	2.84	3.67
16 SA	4.33	4.49	4.30	3.82	2.73	1.45	0.91	1.29	1.85	2.20	2.70	3.51	4.19	4.41	4.23	3.86	2.93	1.66	0.88	1.12	1.68	2.05	2.49	3.29
17 SU	4.07	4.46	4.38	4.10	3.29	1.98	1.04	1.10	1.65	2.03	2.37	3.09	3.92	4.35	4.32	4.07	3.46	2.24	1.15	0.97	1.51	1.94	2.22	2.86
18 M	3.74	4.32	4.42	4.20	3.74	2.61	1.37	0.97	1.46	1.94	2.17	2.65	3.51	4.19	4.35	4.16	3.81	2.90	1.62	0.98	1.31	1.87	2.13	2.47
19 TU	3.27	4.05	4.37	4.27	3.94	3.25	1.97	1.07	1.21	1.83	2.14	2.35	2.98	3.81	4.26	4.23	3.94	3.44	2.35	1.28	1.13	1.70	2.14	2.32
20 W	2.78	3.58	4.15	4.26	4.04	3.60	2.75	1.59	1.13	1.56	2.09	2.28	2.56	3.24	3.91	4.16	4.03	3.67	3.07	2.01	1.30	1.46	2.01	2.31
21 TH	2.51	3.02	3.68	4.05	4.06	3.76	3.28	2.43	1.55	1.40	1.85	2.23	2.38	2.71	3.32	3.82	3.97	3.80	3.44	2.85	1.99	1.55	1.79	2.20
22 F	2.41	2.62	3.08	3.59	3.86	3.84	3.55	3.13	2.41	1.77	1.70	2.00	2.24	2.39	2.71	3.22	3.63	3.77	3.64	3.37	2.89	2.22	1.88	2.00
23 SA	2.22	2.38	2.59	2.98	3.39	3.66	3.70	3.52	3.20	2.62	2.07	1.89	1.97	2.11	2.28	2.59	3.02	3.42	3.66	3.66	3.52	3.14	2.55	2.14
24 SU	2.03	2.08	2.22	2.44	2.79	3.19	3.55	3.74	3.69	3.43	2.91	2.31	1.91	1.75	1.85	2.07	2.41	2.83	3.31	3.71	3.88	3.81	3.45	2.85
25 M	2.24	1.84	1.78	1.97	2.25	2.61	3.08	3.61	3.96	3.97	3.71	3.17	2.42	1.72	1.39	1.54	1.88	2.27	2.73	3.35	3.94	4.20	4.11	3.74
26 TU	3.03	2.14	1.48	1.43	1.75	2.12	2.51	3.11	3.84	4.28	4.24	3.94	3.33	2.34	1.36	0.98	1.30	1.78	2.20	2.73	3.55	4.28	4.51	4.35
27 W	3.94	3.04	1.82	1.03	1.14	1.64	2.08	2.51	3.28	4.16	4.56	4.42	4.09	3.36	2.08	0.90	0.65	1.21	1.79	2.20	2.86	3.86	4.61	4.72
28 TH ○	4.50	4.04	2.86	1.37	0.64	1.02	1.67	2.09	2.59	3.55	4.49	4.74	4.51	4.18	3.25	1.67	0.47	0.53	1.29	1.84	2.25	3.08	4.21	4.85
29 F	4.81	4.60	3.99	2.48	0.87	0.44	1.10	1.76	2.12	2.75	3.87	4.73	4.79	4.56	4.18	2.96	1.19	0.22	0.64	1.46	1.90	2.37	3.40	4.52
30 SA	4.95	4.83	4.61	3.75	1.96	0.50	0.49	1.31	1.83	2.17	3.00	4.18	4.84	4.77	4.58	4.05	2.51	0.77	0.24	0.93	1.63	1.96	2.60	3.75
31 SU	4.72	4.93	4.81	4.50	3.29	1.41	0.37	0.76	1.52	1.87	2.31	3.32	4.41	4.82	4.71	4.53	3.71	1.98	0.57	0.52	1.26	1.75	2.09	2.93

APRIL 2002

DATE	0000	0100	0200	0300	0400	0500	0600	0700	0800	0900	1000	1100	1200	1300	1400	1500	1600	1700	1800	1900	2000	2100	2200	2300
1 M	4.06	4.76	4.83	4.71	4.17	2.70	1.05	0.54	1.11	1.68	1.95	2.56	3.62	4.48	4.71	4.62	4.31	3.21	1.57	0.67	0.93	1.53	1.88	2.35
2 TU	3.27	4.21	4.67	4.67	4.46	3.65	2.17	0.98	0.90	1.42	1.81	2.12	2.85	3.78	4.40	4.54	4.43	3.92	2.73	1.44	1.02	1.34	1.77	2.09
3 W	2.65	3.48	4.18	4.46	4.41	4.05	3.13	1.90	1.21	1.29	1.67	1.97	2.35	3.05	3.77	4.22	4.31	4.13	3.50	2.48	1.62	1.45	1.67	2.00
4 TH	2.33	2.85	3.49	3.99	4.18	4.07	3.61	2.81	1.96	1.56	1.62	1.87	2.15	2.51	3.06	3.61	3.97	4.04	3.80	3.25	2.52	1.97	1.82	1.93
5 F	2.20	2.49	2.87	3.34	3.72	3.87	3.73	3.33	2.78	2.22	1.90	1.83	2.01	2.25	2.52	2.94	3.38	3.71	3.80	3.61	3.26	2.78	2.32	2.06
6 SA	2.08	2.29	2.47	2.73	3.11	3.45	3.62	3.55	3.31	2.98	2.51	2.11	1.92	2.04	2.21	2.40	2.75	3.17	3.53	3.71	3.64	3.47	3.08	2.55
7 SU	2.13	2.07	2.22	2.33	2.53	2.89	3.28	3.55	3.57	3.48	3.24	2.72	2.14	1.85	1.94	2.08	2.25	2.60	3.05	3.53	3.81	3.83	3.73	3.29
8 M	2.58	2.00	1.90	2.05	2.15	2.38	2.78	3.29	3.68	3.74	3.72	3.43	2.73	1.96	1.64	1.76	1.95	2.16	2.55	3.11	3.73	4.02	4.05	3.91
9 TU	3.31	2.36	1.71	1.67	1.89	2.05	2.33	2.85	3.49	3.91	3.94	3.89	3.45	2.52	1.63	1.39	1.65	1.91	2.18	2.65	3.35	4.02	4.23	4.21
10 W	3.93	3.08	1.95	1.37	1.50	1.84	2.06	2.44	3.08	3.81	4.13	4.08	3.93	3.28	2.11	1.25	1.24	1.65	1.97	2.31	2.90	3.71	4.29	4.35
11 TH	4.24	3.74	2.63	1.46	1.12	1.49	1.90	2.18	2.68	3.44	4.12	4.26	4.13	3.81	2.88	1.60	0.99	1.26	1.78	2.12	2.55	3.27	4.07	4.45
12 F ●	4.37	4.12	3.34	2.04	1.06	1.09	1.63	2.04	2.39	3.03	3.83	4.33	4.29	4.07	3.50	2.33	1.15	0.94	1.46	1.96	2.31	2.88	3.68	4.35
13 SA	4.49	4.30	3.82	2.74	1.44	0.89	1.27	1.84	2.19	2.67	3.44	4.16	4.41	4.24	3.89	3.00	1.72	0.90	1.14	1.73	2.14	2.56	3.29	4.08
14 SU	4.50	4.42	4.11	3.32	2.04	1.01	1.00	1.57	2.02	2.38	3.05	3.87	4.37	4.38	4.14	3.54	2.36	1.21	0.93	1.48	1.98	2.30	2.90	3.74
15 M	4.36	4.49	4.27	3.79	2.66	1.39	0.88	1.32	1.86	2.16	2.64	3.49	4.20	4.43	4.28	3.94	3.02	1.72	0.96	1.22	1.83	2.15	2.52	3.31
16 TU	4.11	4.46	4.36	4.05	3.31	1.96	0.99	1.05	1.69	2.05	2.31	2.99	3.88	4.37	4.36	4.12	3.61	2.41	1.26	1.04	1.61	2.08	2.30	2.83
17 W	3.70	4.30	4.40	4.16	3.72	2.73	1.43	0.93	1.40	1.97	2.19	2.54	3.34	4.10	4.35	4.21	3.89	3.18	1.91	1.12	1.34	1.95	2.24	2.49
18 TH	3.15	3.92	4.28	4.22	3.89	3.34	2.23	1.21	1.15	1.74	2.13	2.31	2.78	3.56	4.12	4.21	4.01	3.62	2.80	1.70	1.29	1.70	2.16	2.36
19 F	2.68	3.34	3.92	4.12	3.99	3.62	3.01	2.01	1.33	1.47	1.94	2.20	2.42	2.92	3.57	3.97	4.03	3.81	3.41	2.64	1.80	1.61	1.95	2.24
20 SA	2.43	2.78	3.32	3.75	3.90	3.78	3.44	2.89	2.08	1.61	1.72	1.99	2.18	2.43	2.89	3.42	3.78	3.86	3.71	3.37	2.74	2.09	1.90	2.04
21 SU	2.20	2.38	2.71	3.15	3.52	3.72	3.69	3.45	3.00	2.34	1.89	1.81	1.89	2.06	2.33	2.75	3.22	3.62	3.82	3.78	3.55	3.02	2.40	2.05
22 M	1.95	2.02	2.22	2.53	2.93	3.34	3.68	3.78	3.64	3.26	2.63	2.06	1.72	1.65	1.85	2.16	2.57	3.06	3.58	3.94	4.02	3.82	3.32	2.62
23 TU	2.02	1.69	1.74	2.00	2.35	2.76	3.29	3.81	4.02	3.90	3.53	2.85	2.06	1.46	1.33	1.63	2.02	2.45	3.01	3.70	4.22	4.30	4.09	3.55
24 W	2.68	1.78	1.32	1.46	1.84	2.23	2.69	3.39	4.08	4.31	4.13	3.73	2.94	1.89	1.08	1.04	1.50	1.96	2.41	3.09	3.96	4.52	4.54	4.28
25 TH	3.67	2.55	1.39	0.95	1.29	1.78	2.18	2.74	3.63	4.39	4.52	4.29	3.86	2.89	1.56	0.72	0.89	1.50	1.98	2.46	3.30	4.29	4.76	4.67
26 F	4.40	3.65	2.24	0.95	0.72	1.27	1.81	2.21	2.89	3.93	4.63	4.62	4.39	3.90	2.68	1.16	0.48	0.93	1.61	2.04	2.59	3.58	4.57	4.88
27 SA ○	4.73	4.43	3.46	1.80	0.59	0.68	1.39	1.87	2.28	3.12	4.22	4.76	4.66	4.46	3.83	2.34	0.80	0.45	1.12	1.75	2.12	2.78	3.89	4.77
28 SU	4.89	4.73	4.34	3.09	1.32	0.43	0.84	1.56	1.92	2.40	3.40	4.45	4.79	4.66	4.46	3.59	1.90	0.59	0.63	1.38	1.87	2.24	3.06	4.19
29 M	4.83	4.82	4.68	4.08	2.58	0.94	0.50	1.12	1.71	1.99	2.61	3.70	4.58	4.74	4.65	4.34	3.19	1.50	0.61	0.96	1.63	1.97	2.44	3.39
30 TU	4.39	4.78	4.71	4.50	3.64	2.04	0.79	0.77	1.40	1.81	2.12	2.90	3.94	4.58	4.65	4.56	4.04	2.71	1.27	0.86	1.32	1.83	2.13	2.72

Table 7 (1) Portsmouth hourly height predictions – continued

ENGLAND – PORTSMOUTH

Lat 50°48'N Long 01°07'W

TIME ZONE **UTC** UNITS **METRES**

MAY 2002

DATE	0000	0100	0200	0300	0400	0500	0600	0700	0800	0900	1000	1100	1200	1300	1400	1500	1600	1700	1800	1900	2000	2100	2200	2300
1 W	3.67	4.43	4.62	4.52	4.16	3.09	1.65	0.90	1.12	1.63	1.94	2.35	3.18	4.04	4.47	4.51	4.34	3.61	2.33	1.31	1.23	1.64	2.01	2.35
2 TH	3.00	3.80	4.32	4.39	4.23	3.70	2.63	1.55	1.19	1.45	1.82	2.12	2.59	3.33	4.00	4.30	4.30	4.01	3.22	2.19	1.56	1.59	1.89	2.21
3 F	2.58	3.14	3.75	4.10	4.10	3.86	3.27	2.41	1.69	1.52	1.70	2.00	2.30	2.72	3.33	3.85	4.08	4.04	3.69	3.03	2.29	1.88	1.86	2.08
4 SA	2.38	2.68	3.10	3.57	3.83	3.80	3.54	3.06	2.46	1.96	1.78	1.88	2.14	2.39	2.72	3.22	3.66	3.87	3.82	3.53	3.08	2.52	2.13	2.02
5 SU	2.20	2.43	2.62	2.94	3.35	3.58	3.59	3.38	3.10	2.65	2.18	1.91	1.96	2.18	2.35	2.62	3.09	3.50	3.74	3.75	3.58	3.27	2.73	2.24
6 M	2.05	2.18	2.34	2.45	2.77	3.17	3.45	3.54	3.44	3.28	2.85	2.28	1.91	1.92	2.10	2.24	2.52	3.00	3.45	3.77	3.84	3.76	3.44	2.80
7 TU	2.17	1.93	2.03	2.17	2.30	2.66	3.12	3.51	3.66	3.62	3.47	2.93	2.21	1.76	1.79	1.98	2.15	2.49	3.01	3.56	3.94	4.01	3.92	3.49
8 W	2.69	1.93	1.70	1.86	2.04	2.24	2.67	3.23	3.71	3.85	3.80	3.56	2.85	1.96	1.53	1.65	1.92	2.16	2.56	3.17	3.80	4.16	4.16	3.99
9 TH	3.37	2.37	1.59	1.49	1.76	2.01	2.29	2.83	3.49	3.97	4.02	3.91	3.50	2.57	1.60	1.33	1.61	1.96	2.26	2.75	3.45	4.09	4.33	4.23
10 F	3.91	3.06	1.92	1.27	1.39	1.78	2.08	2.46	3.12	3.82	4.18	4.12	3.90	3.27	2.16	1.27	1.26	1.70	2.08	2.43	3.04	3.79	4.33	4.40
11 SA	4.20	3.66	2.57	1.44	1.09	1.45	1.90	2.22	2.73	3.47	4.11	4.30	4.14	3.77	2.88	1.68	1.06	1.36	1.88	2.23	2.68	3.38	4.12	4.47
12 SU ●	4.38	4.05	3.24	2.00	1.07	1.12	1.64	2.04	2.41	3.06	3.84	4.32	4.33	4.09	3.50	2.37	1.27	1.06	1.59	2.06	2.40	2.97	3.76	4.37
13 M	4.49	4.28	3.78	2.69	1.44	0.92	1.32	1.85	2.18	2.65	3.44	4.15	4.42	4.30	3.96	3.08	1.83	1.03	1.25	1.85	2.21	2.59	3.32	4.10
14 TU	4.49	4.41	4.11	3.37	2.07	1.03	1.00	1.60	2.02	2.31	2.96	3.82	4.36	4.42	4.22	3.72	2.56	1.37	1.03	1.55	2.07	2.33	2.85	3.69
15 W	4.34	4.48	4.27	3.85	2.84	1.51	0.88	1.25	1.84	2.13	2.49	3.30	4.11	4.44	4.34	4.08	3.36	2.05	1.13	1.23	1.85	2.20	2.47	3.15
16 TH	3.99	4.41	4.36	4.06	3.51	2.31	1.16	0.98	1.55	2.00	2.22	2.72	3.60	4.24	4.38	4.21	3.87	2.95	1.69	1.15	1.53	2.05	2.29	2.66
17 F	3.42	4.11	4.33	4.17	3.83	3.13	1.92	1.09	1.23	1.76	2.07	2.33	2.95	3.75	4.22	4.27	4.07	3.63	2.64	1.59	1.36	1.78	2.14	2.37
18 SA	2.82	3.54	4.05	4.16	3.98	3.60	2.85	1.79	1.25	1.47	1.85	2.10	2.43	3.06	3.73	4.10	4.14	3.93	3.45	2.54	1.72	1.61	1.91	2.16
19 SU	2.42	2.88	3.48	3.88	3.98	3.83	3.45	2.76	1.89	1.49	1.61	1.84	2.10	2.46	3.02	3.60	3.96	4.05	3.87	3.43	2.65	1.95	1.78	1.91
20 M	2.11	2.38	2.80	3.30	3.69	3.87	3.77	3.46	2.87	2.10	1.66	1.61	1.76	2.03	2.39	2.91	3.46	3.89	4.06	3.94	3.57	2.86	2.15	1.81
21 TU	1.79	1.98	2.25	2.64	3.12	3.58	3.88	3.86	3.61	3.07	2.30	1.73	1.49	1.61	1.91	2.28	2.79	3.38	3.92	4.19	4.12	3.77	3.06	2.24
22 W	1.70	1.58	1.79	2.10	2.49	3.00	3.59	4.02	4.05	3.81	3.26	2.43	1.66	1.28	1.43	1.80	2.20	2.72	3.39	4.08	4.40	4.31	3.95	3.18
23 TH	2.19	1.45	1.33	1.62	1.98	2.39	2.98	3.73	4.24	4.24	3.99	3.40	2.44	1.47	1.05	1.31	1.76	2.18	2.73	3.53	4.32	4.59	4.45	4.07
24 F	3.20	2.00	1.14	1.12	1.54	1.94	2.37	3.07	3.96	4.45	4.37	4.11	3.48	2.34	1.21	0.88	1.30	1.80	2.21	2.82	3.75	4.54	4.70	4.53
25 SA	4.11	3.08	1.68	0.86	1.04	1.56	1.95	2.42	3.25	4.20	4.57	4.45	4.20	3.46	2.13	0.96	0.83	1.40	1.89	2.29	2.99	4.00	4.70	4.73
26 SU ○	4.56	4.05	2.82	1.33	0.69	1.09	1.65	2.00	2.53	3.47	4.39	4.63	4.50	4.24	3.34	1.84	0.80	0.92	1.56	1.99	2.40	3.21	4.23	4.76
27 M	4.71	4.53	3.87	2.45	1.01	0.68	1.24	1.75	2.07	2.69	3.71	4.51	4.63	4.54	4.19	3.08	1.53	0.77	1.12	1.75	2.09	2.56	3.47	4.41
28 TU	4.74	4.65	4.41	3.55	2.01	0.82	0.82	1.44	1.85	2.17	2.92	3.94	4.57	4.61	4.53	4.02	2.72	1.29	0.88	1.39	1.91	2.21	2.79	3.74
29 W	4.50	4.65	4.53	4.17	3.10	1.61	0.81	1.06	1.64	1.94	2.34	3.19	4.11	4.55	4.56	4.42	3.70	2.32	1.20	1.12	1.65	2.05	2.37	3.05
30 TH	3.94	4.47	4.49	4.33	3.79	2.62	1.37	0.97	1.34	1.80	2.07	2.57	3.44	4.18	4.47	4.45	4.18	3.29	2.02	1.29	1.42	1.87	2.20	2.58
31 F	3.28	4.01	4.33	4.27	4.03	3.35	2.23	1.34	1.23	1.59	1.95	2.25	2.80	3.59	4.15	4.34	4.27	3.85	2.93	1.92	1.50	1.68	2.05	2.37

JUNE 2002

DATE	0000	0100	0200	0300	0400	0500	0600	0700	0800	0900	1000	1100	1200	1300	1400	1500	1600	1700	1800	1900	2000	2100	2200	2300
1 SA	2.77	3.39	3.94	4.13	4.02	3.68	2.98	2.05	1.48	1.49	1.79	2.10	2.42	2.95	3.62	4.06	4.18	4.03	3.54	2.73	1.98	1.74	1.89	2.20
2 SU	2.50	2.86	3.37	3.79	3.91	3.76	3.38	2.78	2.07	1.68	1.70	1.95	2.23	2.52	3.00	3.58	3.94	4.01	3.81	3.36	2.70	2.12	1.91	2.02
3 M	2.29	2.54	2.82	3.27	3.63	3.71	3.56	3.23	2.77	2.19	1.84	1.82	2.05	2.28	2.54	2.99	3.53	3.84	3.89	3.70	3.34	2.77	2.23	1.98
4 TU	2.06	2.28	2.47	2.73	3.17	3.51	3.61	3.49	3.25	2.85	2.28	1.89	1.87	2.06	2.26	2.51	2.98	3.50	3.80	3.87	3.73	3.41	2.81	2.23
5 W	1.94	2.01	2.19	2.36	2.65	3.12	3.48	3.63	3.56	3.36	2.93	2.29	1.84	1.83	2.02	2.22	2.51	3.01	3.54	3.87	3.96	3.82	3.46	2.76
6 TH	2.10	1.80	1.89	2.08	2.29	2.65	3.16	3.58	3.77	3.69	3.47	2.92	2.17	1.70	1.75	1.98	2.22	2.56	3.11	3.68	4.03	4.08	3.89	3.42
7 F	2.59	1.84	1.62	1.79	2.03	2.29	2.73	3.32	3.77	3.94	3.81	3.51	2.80	1.94	1.52	1.70	1.99	2.27	2.68	3.30	3.89	4.20	4.17	3.91
8 SA	3.26	2.28	1.54	1.47	1.76	2.04	2.37	2.91	3.56	3.99	4.08	3.89	3.45	2.56	1.65	1.39	1.72	2.06	2.37	2.86	3.55	4.13	4.33	4.21
9 SU	3.82	2.96	1.87	1.27	1.43	1.80	2.11	2.51	3.16	3.83	4.18	4.17	3.91	3.27	2.21	1.37	1.36	1.81	2.16	2.51	3.10	3.83	4.32	4.40
10 M ●	4.18	3.63	2.56	1.46	1.11	1.48	1.90	2.21	2.72	3.46	4.09	4.32	4.22	3.85	2.98	1.83	1.17	1.43	1.95	2.27	2.68	3.38	4.10	4.46
11 TU	4.39	4.08	3.32	2.09	1.12	1.09	1.61	2.01	2.33	2.96	3.76	4.30	4.39	4.21	3.70	2.61	1.46	1.11	1.58	2.08	2.38	2.88	3.68	4.33
12 W	4.51	4.32	3.89	2.92	1.62	0.90	1.18	1.76	2.10	2.47	3.24	4.05	4.44	4.40	4.15	3.46	2.20	1.18	1.17	1.77	2.19	2.48	3.13	3.96
13 TH	4.47	4.46	4.19	3.64	2.47	1.23	0.86	1.36	1.89	2.16	2.65	3.53	4.27	4.48	4.35	4.04	3.14	1.81	1.06	1.34	1.93	2.26	2.61	3.39
14 F	4.18	4.48	4.34	4.02	3.33	2.04	0.99	0.97	1.54	1.96	2.23	2.87	3.78	4.36	4.45	4.28	3.87	2.80	1.53	1.11	1.55	2.03	2.30	2.77
15 SA	3.61	4.25	4.39	4.19	3.84	3.00	1.72	0.96	1.15	1.67	1.99	2.33	3.07	3.91	4.35	4.38	4.19	3.67	2.52	1.44	1.27	1.71	2.07	2.36
16 SU	2.92	3.70	4.19	4.26	4.05	3.65	2.74	1.58	1.07	1.32	1.72	2.02	2.44	3.19	3.92	4.29	4.32	4.09	3.49	2.38	1.51	1.44	1.78	2.09
17 M	2.41	2.98	3.66	4.06	4.14	3.94	3.50	2.61	1.62	1.24	1.41	1.74	2.05	2.51	3.21	3.85	4.22	4.27	4.02	3.41	2.39	1.65	1.55	1.79
18 TU	2.07	2.40	2.94	3.53	3.94	4.07	3.88	3.46	2.63	1.75	1.36	1.44	1.73	2.06	2.51	3.16	3.78	4.20	4.25	4.02	3.43	2.49	1.77	1.57
19 W	1.74	2.01	2.34	2.83	3.40	3.87	4.05	3.89	3.51	2.73	1.89	1.42	1.42	1.70	2.04	2.48	3.10	3.74	4.22	4.29	4.08	3.51	2.60	1.82
20 TH	1.51	1.64	1.92	2.24	2.72	3.31	3.88	4.11	3.98	3.61	2.86	1.99	1.41	1.36	1.67	2.01	2.45	3.06	3.77	4.31	4.38	4.16	3.60	2.67
21 F	1.78	1.38	1.52	1.83	2.16	2.64	3.29	3.96	4.22	4.08	3.73	2.98	2.02	1.33	1.30	1.65	2.01	2.44	3.07	3.87	4.42	4.45	4.23	3.66
22 SA	2.67	1.64	1.22	1.43	1.78	2.11	2.61	3.36	4.10	4.32	4.18	3.84	3.05	1.97	1.22	1.27	1.68	2.03	2.47	3.16	4.02	4.52	4.50	4.28
23 SU	3.66	2.56	1.43	1.07	1.39	1.77	2.10	2.65	3.49	4.23	4.39	4.27	3.92	3.05	1.83	1.12	1.28	1.74	2.09	2.54	3.30	4.18	4.59	4.52
24 M ○	4.28	3.58	2.34	1.20	0.99	1.42	1.81	2.15	2.76	3.66	4.35	4.45	4.34	3.95	2.94	1.64	1.05	1.35	1.84	2.18	2.67	3.49	4.32	4.60
25 TU	4.50	4.22	3.39	2.03	1.01	0.99	1.51	1.88	2.23	2.92	3.85	4.44	4.49	4.38	3.88	2.71	1.43	1.05	1.48	1.97	2.29	2.83	3.70	4.43
26 W	4.57	4.44	4.07	3.09	1.69	0.88	1.09	1.64	1.97	2.36	3.14	4.04	4.49	4.50	4.35	3.69	2.39	1.25	1.13	1.66	2.10	2.41	3.05	3.91
27 TH	4.47	4.48	4.31	3.82	2.68	1.38	0.88	1.27	1.79	2.07	2.55	3.40	4.19	4.50	4.46	4.22	3.36	2.02	1.17	1.31	1.86	2.22	2.58	3.29
28 F	4.07	4.43	4.34	4.12	3.45	2.24	1.18	1.03	1.50	1.92	2.21	2.80	3.65	4.28	4.45	4.37	3.96	2.94	1.73	1.24	1.54	2.03	2.34	2.79
29 SA	3.53	4.14	4.30	4.16	3.83	3.02	1.86	1.16	1.27	1.71	2.05	2.40	3.07	3.84	4.28	4.36	4.19	3.60	2.52	1.59	1.42	1.77	2.16	2.49
30 SU	3.00	3.67	4.10	4.14	3.94	3.49	2.60	1.65	1.30	1.52	1.88	2.19	2.61	3.29	3.93	4.23	4.22	3.93	3.21	2.23	1.62	1.64	1.95	2.28

Table 7 (1) Portsmouth hourly height predictions – continued

ENGLAND – PORTSMOUTH

Lat 50°48'N Long 01°07'W

TIME ZONE **UTC**

UNITS **METRES**

JULY 2002

DATE	0000	0100	0200	0300	0400	0500	0600	0700	0800	0900	1000	1100	1200	1300	1400	1500	1600	1700	1800	1900	2000	2100	2200	2300
1 M	2.63	3.14	3.71	3.99	3.96	3.69	3.14	2.31	1.62	1.50	1.73	2.03	2.34	2.80	3.44	3.95	4.14	4.04	3.64	2.91	2.10	1.74	1.83	2.09
2 TU	2.37	2.73	3.20	3.68	3.87	3.77	3.46	2.90	2.20	1.71	1.68	1.90	2.15	2.46	2.92	3.51	3.93	4.03	3.86	3.43	2.75	2.10	1.86	1.95
3 W	2.16	2.41	2.75	3.20	3.62	3.75	3.63	3.31	2.81	2.20	1.81	1.80	2.01	2.23	2.54	2.99	3.54	3.89	3.93	3.75	3.33	2.71	2.13	1.92
4 TH	2.00	2.18	2.40	2.73	3.17	3.56	3.67	3.58	3.29	2.82	2.24	1.87	1.86	2.07	2.27	2.57	3.03	3.56	3.87	3.89	3.73	3.32	2.70	2.11
5 F	1.89	1.98	2.14	2.36	2.70	3.17	3.56	3.69	3.63	3.35	2.88	2.25	1.85	1.86	2.09	2.28	2.60	3.07	3.60	3.91	3.94	3.78	3.35	2.66
6 SA	2.02	1.78	1.91	2.08	2.32	2.70	3.21	3.63	3.79	3.74	3.45	2.91	2.19	1.75	1.82	2.08	2.29	2.63	3.14	3.71	4.01	4.05	3.85	3.36
7 SU	2.54	1.82	1.62	1.82	2.03	2.30	2.74	3.32	3.78	3.95	3.89	3.54	2.87	2.04	1.60	1.76	2.07	2.30	2.69	3.27	3.87	4.16	4.17	3.91
8 M	3.29	2.32	1.56	1.46	1.75	2.01	2.32	2.86	3.51	3.98	4.13	4.01	3.58	2.74	1.82	1.44	1.72	2.07	2.34	2.80	3.46	4.07	4.32	4.25
9 TU	3.90	3.12	2.02	1.28	1.33	1.72	2.03	2.40	3.03	3.74	4.19	4.28	4.09	3.54	2.52	1.55	1.31	1.71	2.11	2.41	2.95	3.69	4.28	4.44
10 W ●	4.27	3.81	2.86	1.66	1.02	1.25	1.74	2.08	2.51	3.24	4.00	4.39	4.38	4.11	3.42	2.23	1.27	1.22	1.75	2.17	2.51	3.14	3.94	4.47
11 TH	4.49	4.22	3.66	2.53	1.29	0.84	1.27	1.82	2.14	2.64	3.49	4.25	4.53	4.42	4.09	3.22	1.89	1.03	1.23	1.84	2.24	2.61	3.36	4.19
12 F	4.57	4.45	4.13	3.45	2.14	0.95	0.77	1.37	1.90	2.20	2.82	3.76	4.45	4.58	4.41	4.01	2.93	1.52	0.90	1.33	1.95	2.28	2.73	3.61
13 SA	4.37	4.58	4.36	4.02	3.17	1.74	0.73	0.85	1.51	1.94	2.26	3.04	4.01	4.54	4.57	4.38	3.87	2.57	1.23	0.93	1.50	2.02	2.31	2.90
14 SU	3.82	4.44	4.50	4.26	3.87	2.83	1.40	0.69	1.02	1.62	1.96	2.38	3.28	4.16	4.56	4.54	4.32	3.63	2.22	1.11	1.08	1.64	2.04	2.37
15 M	3.08	3.94	4.40	4.40	4.16	3.67	2.50	1.22	0.81	1.21	1.69	2.01	2.55	3.45	4.20	4.52	4.49	4.20	3.35	1.99	1.15	1.27	1.73	2.06
16 TU	2.46	3.19	3.93	4.30	4.29	4.04	3.45	2.27	1.23	1.01	1.36	1.75	2.09	2.70	3.53	4.17	4.47	4.40	4.04	3.12	1.93	1.30	1.42	1.79
17 W	2.09	2.53	3.21	3.83	4.19	4.19	3.91	3.28	2.21	1.38	1.21	1.48	1.82	2.19	2.78	3.51	4.10	4.40	4.30	3.89	3.02	2.00	1.47	1.52
18 TH	1.82	2.11	2.53	3.13	3.70	4.08	4.10	3.82	3.22	2.30	1.58	1.37	1.57	1.90	2.25	2.79	3.45	4.03	4.32	4.21	3.82	3.04	2.14	1.60
19 F	1.57	1.82	2.09	2.47	3.01	3.58	4.01	4.04	3.80	3.27	2.47	1.77	1.48	1.64	1.94	2.26	2.75	3.37	3.98	4.28	4.17	3.83	3.13	2.27
20 SA	1.65	1.55	1.78	2.03	2.38	2.89	3.50	3.99	4.06	3.87	3.41	2.66	1.89	1.52	1.66	1.95	2.25	2.70	3.32	3.98	4.28	4.20	3.89	3.23
21 SU	2.33	1.61	1.47	1.70	1.96	2.29	2.81	3.49	4.04	4.13	3.98	3.57	2.80	1.91	1.49	1.64	1.94	2.23	2.68	3.34	4.04	4.33	4.25	3.96
22 M	3.29	2.28	1.47	1.36	1.63	1.91	2.25	2.80	3.57	4.14	4.23	4.11	3.70	2.84	1.82	1.40	1.61	1.94	2.25	2.72	3.43	4.15	4.39	4.29
23 TU	3.99	3.24	2.10	1.27	1.25	1.61	1.92	2.28	2.89	3.72	4.27	4.33	4.21	3.75	2.73	1.63	1.29	1.61	2.00	2.32	2.82	3.59	4.28	4.43
24 W ○	4.30	3.95	3.07	1.82	1.07	1.20	1.66	1.99	2.37	3.06	3.92	4.40	4.40	4.25	3.66	2.48	1.39	1.22	1.69	2.10	2.43	2.99	3.80	4.39
25 TH	4.42	4.24	3.80	2.76	1.48	0.92	1.26	1.78	2.09	2.53	3.30	4.14	4.47	4.42	4.20	3.42	2.10	1.17	1.26	1.84	2.23	2.57	3.22	4.02
26 F	4.43	4.34	4.12	3.53	2.32	1.16	0.92	1.44	1.93	2.22	2.76	3.61	4.31	4.48	4.38	4.01	3.01	1.69	1.09	1.43	2.01	2.35	2.77	3.51
27 SA	4.19	4.39	4.22	3.92	3.11	1.84	0.98	1.09	1.66	2.05	2.39	3.08	3.90	4.39	4.43	4.27	3.66	2.47	1.38	1.19	1.67	2.15	2.48	3.04
28 SU	3.78	4.26	4.27	4.07	3.60	2.59	1.44	1.03	1.37	1.85	2.17	2.65	3.43	4.11	4.39	4.34	4.02	3.16	1.97	1.28	1.43	1.89	2.26	2.67
29 M	3.33	3.97	4.22	4.13	3.84	3.15	2.07	1.26	1.25	1.65	2.00	2.36	2.98	3.73	4.21	4.32	4.17	3.64	2.61	1.64	1.40	1.70	2.06	2.39
30 TU	2.91	3.57	4.04	4.12	3.95	3.53	2.68	1.72	1.32	1.54	1.88	2.15	2.60	3.27	3.91	4.22	4.19	3.91	3.19	2.19	1.56	1.62	1.93	2.19
31 W	2.55	3.12	3.69	4.01	3.98	3.73	3.18	2.31	1.61	1.51	1.80	2.06	2.33	2.83	3.47	3.98	4.15	4.00	3.61	2.82	1.99	1.65	1.84	2.09

AUGUST 2002

DATE	0000	0100	0200	0300	0400	0500	0600	0700	0800	0900	1000	1100	1200	1300	1400	1500	1600	1700	1800	1900	2000	2100	2200	2300
1 TH	2.31	2.69	3.23	3.71	3.92	3.80	3.50	2.90	2.15	1.68	1.73	2.00	2.22	2.49	2.99	3.55	3.96	4.02	3.80	3.36	2.63	1.98	1.80	2.00
2 F	2.20	2.39	2.76	3.25	3.66	3.80	3.64	3.35	2.79	2.17	1.83	1.90	2.14	2.33	2.59	3.05	3.55	3.89	3.88	3.67	3.26	2.62	2.06	1.91
3 SA	2.06	2.24	2.40	2.74	3.19	3.57	3.69	3.58	3.34	2.85	2.30	1.96	1.98	2.20	2.37	2.61	3.04	3.50	3.82	3.82	3.67	3.30	2.71	2.13
4 SU	1.92	2.02	2.18	2.34	2.67	3.12	3.53	3.68	3.65	3.47	3.00	2.42	2.00	1.96	2.17	2.33	2.57	2.99	3.48	3.83	3.88	3.79	3.42	2.79
5 M	2.12	1.81	1.88	2.06	2.24	2.59	3.09	3.56	3.79	3.84	3.66	3.16	2.47	1.93	1.83	2.05	2.25	2.52	2.98	3.53	3.94	4.05	3.95	3.54
6 TU	2.79	1.98	1.58	1.68	1.91	2.16	2.56	3.14	3.71	4.01	4.07	3.84	3.26	2.40	1.73	1.63	1.91	2.18	2.51	3.04	3.69	4.15	4.26	4.09
7 W	3.59	2.69	1.72	1.27	1.46	1.81	2.14	2.61	3.29	3.94	4.28	4.27	3.97	3.26	2.22	1.44	1.41	1.81	2.18	2.56	3.18	3.91	4.39	4.42
8 TH ●	4.14	3.54	2.47	1.37	0.97	1.32	1.80	2.18	2.71	3.51	4.23	4.51	4.40	4.02	3.16	1.91	1.11	1.25	1.81	2.23	2.65	3.38	4.19	4.59
9 F	4.49	4.13	3.42	2.15	0.97	0.74	1.31	1.87	2.24	2.87	3.79	4.50	4.65	4.45	4.02	2.93	1.52	0.83	1.23	1.89	2.29	2.76	3.63	4.45
10 SA	4.70	4.46	4.08	3.21	1.73	0.61	0.68	1.42	1.94	2.30	3.08	4.10	4.70	4.70	4.47	3.94	2.58	1.11	0.71	1.35	1.99	2.33	2.92	3.91
11 SU	4.63	4.68	4.40	4.00	2.88	1.28	0.42	0.81	1.57	1.98	2.41	3.37	4.35	4.78	4.69	4.47	3.71	2.12	0.81	0.80	1.54	2.04	2.38	3.15
12 M	4.15	4.68	4.60	4.34	3.82	2.45	0.93	0.47	1.06	1.69	2.01	2.61	3.66	4.50	4.77	4.66	4.37	3.34	1.69	0.74	1.03	1.70	2.06	2.49
13 TU	3.39	4.27	4.61	4.50	4.24	3.52	2.03	0.81	0.71	1.30	1.77	2.12	2.86	3.86	4.52	4.71	4.58	4.13	2.90	1.45	0.90	1.29	1.80	2.11
14 W	2.67	3.55	4.25	4.49	4.39	4.05	3.16	1.78	0.94	1.03	1.50	1.87	2.30	3.08	3.93	4.45	4.60	4.41	3.79	2.58	1.45	1.17	1.51	1.88
15 TH	2.22	2.81	3.56	4.12	4.34	4.22	3.80	2.89	1.78	1.23	1.33	1.68	2.01	2.48	3.18	3.86	4.33	4.42	4.16	3.50	2.47	1.65	1.44	1.67
16 F	1.98	2.31	2.84	3.45	3.93	4.16	4.03	3.60	2.83	1.99	1.56	1.57	1.84	2.15	2.57	3.15	3.72	4.15	4.22	3.95	3.38	2.57	1.91	1.65
17 SA	1.77	2.03	2.32	2.75	3.26	3.73	3.99	3.89	3.55	2.96	2.29	1.83	1.74	1.95	2.22	2.56	3.03	3.55	3.99	4.07	3.86	3.43	2.78	2.13
18 SU	1.76	1.80	2.01	2.24	2.60	3.06	3.58	3.90	3.88	3.66	3.21	2.58	2.00	1.81	1.97	2.19	2.47	2.88	3.41	3.90	4.04	3.90	3.58	2.98
19 M	2.24	1.74	1.72	1.91	2.12	2.45	2.92	3.53	3.94	3.99	3.86	3.46	2.76	2.02	1.75	1.90	2.11	2.38	2.78	3.38	3.94	4.11	4.02	3.74
20 TU	3.09	2.19	1.58	1.57	1.79	2.02	2.36	2.89	3.62	4.09	4.16	4.06	3.63	2.76	1.86	1.59	1.80	2.06	2.34	2.79	3.47	4.08	4.22	4.13
21 W	3.82	3.04	1.96	1.33	1.41	1.74	2.01	2.38	3.01	3.83	4.28	4.31	4.19	3.65	2.55	1.58	1.41	1.76	2.09	2.39	2.90	3.68	4.26	4.30
22 TH ○	4.18	3.78	2.80	1.60	1.08	1.36	1.79	2.09	2.51	3.25	4.09	4.43	4.39	4.20	3.46	2.18	1.27	1.32	1.83	2.19	2.52	3.13	3.94	4.39
23 F	4.31	4.13	3.58	2.39	1.22	0.96	1.45	1.92	2.23	2.74	3.57	4.33	4.49	4.40	4.06	3.07	1.71	1.05	1.40	1.99	2.32	2.73	3.44	4.19
24 SA	4.42	4.25	3.98	3.20	1.87	0.93	1.03	1.66	2.08	2.42	3.07	3.92	4.47	4.47	4.30	3.73	2.51	1.29	1.05	1.61	2.16	2.48	3.02	3.78
25 SU	4.35	4.36	4.14	3.70	2.66	1.38	0.88	1.28	1.88	2.23	2.70	3.47	4.21	4.50	4.40	4.08	3.19	1.89	1.09	1.26	1.86	2.29	2.70	3.38
26 M	4.07	4.38	4.24	3.95	3.23	2.04	1.09	1.08	1.60	2.04	2.42	3.08	3.86	4.38	4.44	4.25	3.66	2.52	1.43	1.16	1.58	2.06	2.43	3.01
27 TU	3.75	4.24	4.30	4.09	3.63	2.63	1.52	1.09	1.43	1.87	2.19	2.71	3.49	4.14	4.40	4.31	3.98	3.08	1.90	1.25	1.45	1.88	2.20	2.64
28 W	3.36	4.01	4.27	4.16	3.87	3.16	2.05	1.28	1.34	1.78	2.07	2.40	3.07	3.82	4.27	4.32	4.10	3.56	2.47	1.53	1.38	1.79	2.10	2.35
29 TH	2.91	3.63	4.11	4.18	3.97	3.55	2.65	1.68	1.35	1.69	2.06	2.26	2.66	3.38	3.98	4.24	4.14	3.80	3.09	2.05	1.47	1.65	2.06	2.27
30 F	2.54	3.14	3.75	4.06	4.01	3.72	3.21	2.31	1.62	1.60	2.00	2.27	2.45	2.90	3.53	3.98	4.11	3.90	3.50	2.76	1.93	1.63	1.92	2.24
31 SA	2.39	2.68	3.22	3.71	3.92	3.80	3.49	2.99	2.24	1.79	1.89	2.20	2.41	2.59	3.01	3.52	3.86	3.93	3.68	3.31	2.67	2.05	1.87	2.09

Table 7 (1) Portsmouth hourly height predictions – continued

ENGLAND – PORTSMOUTH

Lat 50°48'N Long 01°07'W

TIME ZONE **UTC** UNITS **METRES**

SEPTEMBER 2002

DATE	0000	0100	0200	0300	0400	0500	0600	0700	0800	0900	1000	1100	1200	1300	1400	1500	1600	1700	1800	1900	2000	2100	2200	2300
1 SU	2.30	2.44	2.71	3.16	3.57	3.75	3.64	3.41	2.99	2.40	2.05	2.09	2.28	2.45	2.61	2.97	3.40	3.72	3.78	3.60	3.32	2.79	2.26	2.03
2 M	2.10	2.24	2.36	2.61	3.02	3.42	3.64	3.62	3.51	3.18	2.66	2.26	2.14	2.22	2.36	2.52	2.85	3.26	3.62	3.77	3.71	3.50	3.02	2.44
3 TU	2.04	1.94	2.05	2.20	2.46	2.87	3.33	3.67	3.79	3.77	3.45	2.90	2.34	2.01	2.01	2.17	2.39	2.73	3.19	3.66	3.93	3.95	3.73	3.21
4 W	2.49	1.87	1.63	1.77	2.02	2.34	2.81	3.38	3.86	4.09	4.05	3.70	3.03	2.24	1.71	1.71	1.98	2.29	2.68	3.25	3.86	4.21	4.21	3.92
5 TH	3.30	2.37	1.53	1.25	1.53	1.91	2.30	2.85	3.57	4.18	4.41	4.28	3.86	3.00	1.95	1.32	1.44	1.87	2.28	2.72	3.42	4.15	4.50	4.39
6 F	4.02	3.26	2.09	1.08	0.91	1.41	1.92	2.34	2.99	3.87	4.52	4.64	4.42	3.91	2.82	1.53	0.93	1.29	1.89	2.32	2.84	3.69	4.47	4.70
7 SA ●	4.46	4.03	3.10	1.68	0.65	0.74	1.45	1.99	2.43	3.22	4.21	4.79	4.76	4.48	3.86	2.48	1.06	0.69	1.33	1.99	2.39	3.01	4.01	4.73
8 SU	4.77	4.46	3.99	2.80	1.20	0.35	0.79	1.60	2.06	2.55	3.52	4.53	4.93	4.78	4.50	3.65	2.00	0.66	0.69	1.50	2.08	2.45	3.25	4.32
9 M	4.86	4.73	4.43	3.84	2.37	0.77	0.31	1.02	1.75	2.12	2.75	3.85	4.75	4.95	4.76	4.43	3.27	1.48	0.49	0.90	1.70	2.11	2.57	3.55
10 TU	4.53	4.85	4.66	4.38	3.55	1.88	0.54	0.53	1.32	1.85	2.21	3.04	4.15	4.82	4.88	4.71	4.19	2.75	1.11	0.61	1.21	1.83	2.16	2.78
11 W	3.81	4.60	4.74	4.56	4.21	3.12	1.49	0.61	0.91	1.57	1.94	2.41	3.35	4.30	4.76	4.77	4.55	3.77	2.26	1.02	0.92	1.49	1.92	2.28
12 TH	3.03	3.94	4.51	4.59	4.42	3.90	2.69	1.37	0.94	1.30	1.76	2.09	2.68	3.55	4.28	4.61	4.58	4.23	3.31	2.00	1.21	1.29	1.71	2.04
13 F	2.46	3.18	3.90	4.32	4.39	4.18	3.55	2.47	1.56	1.36	1.61	1.94	2.29	2.88	3.58	4.13	4.39	4.31	3.86	3.00	2.04	1.56	1.60	1.87
14 SA	2.17	2.59	3.17	3.71	4.07	4.15	3.90	3.33	2.53	1.92	1.74	1.86	2.13	2.45	2.92	3.44	3.89	4.12	4.01	3.59	2.96	2.29	1.90	1.81
15 SU	2.00	2.26	2.58	3.01	3.45	3.82	3.93	3.74	3.35	2.81	2.31	2.01	2.01	2.24	2.48	2.81	3.22	3.64	3.88	3.82	3.55	3.14	2.61	2.13
16 M	1.91	2.03	2.22	2.44	2.78	3.21	3.64	3.84	3.77	3.57	3.16	2.60	2.13	2.04	2.21	2.37	2.62	3.00	3.45	3.78	3.82	3.69	3.40	2.84
17 TU	2.19	1.85	1.93	2.08	2.26	2.59	3.06	3.61	3.92	3.95	3.86	3.44	2.70	2.05	1.92	2.08	2.22	2.47	2.86	3.43	3.86	3.95	3.90	3.61
18 W	2.91	2.06	1.65	1.75	1.93	2.14	2.50	3.08	3.77	4.13	4.19	4.09	3.54	2.56	1.80	1.71	1.94	2.13	2.41	2.89	3.58	4.06	4.12	4.07
19 TH	3.68	2.75	1.75	1.39	1.60	1.87	2.13	2.56	3.28	4.05	4.34	4.37	4.18	3.41	2.21	1.47	1.54	1.90	2.14	2.48	3.08	3.87	4.26	4.25
20 F	4.13	3.55	2.38	1.35	1.18	1.59	1.93	2.24	2.77	3.62	4.33	4.48	4.43	4.07	3.04	1.73	1.18	1.50	1.97	2.26	2.68	3.40	4.16	4.38
21 SA ○	4.28	4.03	3.21	1.88	1.02	1.16	1.71	2.08	2.46	3.11	3.99	4.52	4.51	4.36	3.75	2.48	1.28	1.08	1.63	2.12	2.45	2.99	3.78	4.38
22 SU	4.39	4.21	3.77	2.69	1.37	0.90	1.33	1.92	2.27	2.76	3.52	4.31	4.58	4.46	4.13	3.22	1.86	1.01	1.21	1.86	2.29	2.70	3.38	4.12
23 M	4.47	4.32	4.04	3.32	2.07	1.03	1.03	1.63	2.12	2.50	3.14	3.94	4.50	4.53	4.31	3.70	2.54	1.34	1.03	1.52	2.08	2.47	3.04	3.79
24 TU	4.35	4.43	4.20	3.72	2.70	1.50	0.99	1.37	1.91	2.29	2.81	3.59	4.27	4.54	4.40	4.03	3.09	1.85	1.11	1.31	1.84	2.24	2.70	3.45
25 W	4.14	4.43	4.31	4.00	3.23	2.04	1.18	1.24	1.76	2.12	2.50	3.21	3.99	4.44	4.45	4.20	3.58	2.38	1.36	1.21	1.70	2.09	2.40	3.03
26 TH	3.84	4.33	4.37	4.14	3.68	2.62	1.53	1.20	1.64	2.07	2.30	2.79	3.61	4.24	4.43	4.26	3.89	3.00	1.78	1.22	1.55	2.04	2.26	2.62
27 F	3.37	4.08	4.33	4.21	3.89	3.23	2.08	1.34	1.49	2.03	2.29	2.50	3.12	3.88	4.28	4.28	4.00	3.49	2.45	1.49	1.39	1.91	2.26	2.42
28 SA	2.87	3.61	4.11	4.20	3.98	3.59	2.82	1.82	1.49	1.87	2.30	2.45	2.73	3.36	3.93	4.16	4.06	3.70	3.11	2.16	1.55	1.71	2.17	2.38
29 SU	2.56	3.03	3.64	3.98	3.99	3.74	3.34	2.61	1.89	1.81	2.17	2.43	2.56	2.87	3.40	3.81	3.96	3.82	3.46	2.93	2.18	1.82	1.99	2.27
30 M	2.41	2.60	3.03	3.50	3.78	3.80	3.59	3.27	2.69	2.18	2.12	2.31	2.44	2.57	2.85	3.27	3.61	3.77	3.67	3.42	3.00	2.43	2.11	2.11

OCTOBER 2002

DATE	0000	0100	0200	0300	0400	0500	0600	0700	0800	0900	1000	1100	1200	1300	1400	1500	1600	1700	1800	1900	2000	2100	2200	2300
1 TU	2.20	2.32	2.52	2.88	3.29	3.60	3.71	3.63	3.43	2.97	2.51	2.30	2.25	2.30	2.44	2.71	3.08	3.44	3.68	3.71	3.59	3.25	2.72	2.27
2 W	2.02	1.97	2.10	2.34	2.69	3.13	3.55	3.80	3.87	3.73	3.30	2.74	2.27	2.00	2.04	2.24	2.54	2.92	3.38	3.79	3.95	3.88	3.53	2.93
3 TH	2.25	1.74	1.62	1.85	2.17	2.56	3.08	3.66	4.09	4.21	4.04	3.55	2.79	2.02	1.62	1.73	2.06	2.43	2.87	3.49	4.06	4.28	4.15	3.74
4 F	2.98	2.03	1.31	1.26	1.66	2.09	2.53	3.18	3.94	4.45	4.51	4.26	3.67	2.64	1.61	1.20	1.52	1.99	2.41	2.95	3.75	4.41	4.56	4.32
5 SA	3.83	2.87	1.64	0.85	1.02	1.62	2.11	2.60	3.41	4.31	4.77	4.70	4.39	3.63	2.31	1.12	0.90	1.46	2.03	2.47	3.14	4.09	4.72	4.71
6 SU ●	4.40	3.82	2.60	1.16	0.52	0.99	1.71	2.18	2.75	3.72	4.65	4.96	4.78	4.42	3.44	1.84	0.69	0.81	1.56	2.11	2.56	3.40	4.43	4.91
7 M	4.74	4.42	3.70	2.21	0.73	0.41	1.15	1.85	2.27	2.96	4.07	4.90	5.01	4.79	4.35	3.08	1.33	0.46	0.94	1.74	2.18	2.70	3.70	4.69
8 TU	4.95	4.71	4.39	3.45	1.74	0.46	0.57	1.42	1.97	2.38	3.24	4.38	5.01	4.97	4.75	4.13	2.58	0.92	0.50	1.22	1.89	2.23	2.90	4.00
9 W	4.82	4.88	4.67	4.27	3.05	1.33	0.47	0.92	1.68	2.06	2.56	3.57	4.59	4.97	4.87	4.62	3.74	2.05	0.75	0.78	1.51	1.97	2.34	3.17
10 TH	4.22	4.79	4.76	4.58	4.00	2.59	1.12	0.75	1.32	1.86	2.17	2.83	3.84	4.63	4.82	4.72	4.33	3.22	1.68	0.88	1.16	1.74	2.06	2.53
11 F	3.41	4.27	4.64	4.60	4.38	3.61	2.25	1.21	1.18	1.65	2.02	2.37	3.10	3.95	4.50	4.61	4.46	3.91	2.77	1.60	1.22	1.51	1.90	2.21
12 SA	2.75	3.52	4.15	4.42	4.39	4.07	3.25	2.17	1.55	1.61	1.90	2.20	2.60	3.24	3.87	4.26	4.33	4.11	3.49	2.57	1.81	1.61	1.77	2.06
13 SU	2.37	2.85	3.44	3.92	4.16	4.13	3.77	3.11	2.38	1.97	1.92	2.10	2.38	2.72	3.19	3.65	3.97	4.02	3.78	3.28	2.66	2.14	1.91	1.94
14 M	2.19	2.45	2.79	3.24	3.66	3.92	3.91	3.64	3.24	2.73	2.31	2.11	2.22	2.45	2.67	3.00	3.38	3.70	3.78	3.61	3.33	2.93	2.45	2.07
15 TU	2.01	2.21	2.38	2.62	3.00	3.44	3.77	3.84	3.74	3.52	3.05	2.48	2.15	2.22	2.37	2.50	2.77	3.16	3.53	3.70	3.66	3.56	3.21	2.60
16 W	2.06	1.95	2.11	2.22	2.44	2.84	3.34	3.79	3.96	3.98	3.80	3.21	2.45	2.02	2.07	2.20	2.31	2.61	3.06	3.56	3.82	3.86	3.81	3.36
17 TH	2.55	1.88	1.77	1.95	2.08	2.34	2.80	3.44	3.99	4.18	4.23	3.96	3.16	2.20	1.76	1.88	2.06	2.22	2.58	3.16	3.77	4.03	4.07	3.96
18 F	3.31	2.28	1.58	1.57	1.84	2.04	2.37	2.95	3.71	4.26	4.38	4.37	3.90	2.85	1.80	1.48	1.75	2.01	2.25	2.72	3.43	4.07	4.22	4.21
19 SA	3.93	3.04	1.86	1.29	1.47	1.85	2.12	2.55	3.25	4.07	4.48	4.49	4.33	3.62	2.36	1.38	1.32	1.76	2.09	2.42	3.01	3.79	4.32	4.33
20 SU	4.21	3.72	2.58	1.42	1.13	1.54	1.98	2.31	2.85	3.64	4.38	4.58	4.48	4.12	3.13	1.79	1.11	1.35	1.90	2.25	2.69	3.39	4.14	4.46
21 M ○	4.34	4.07	3.30	2.02	1.10	1.18	1.74	2.17	2.57	3.23	4.04	4.57	4.57	4.35	3.70	2.50	1.32	1.07	1.55	2.09	2.46	3.03	3.80	4.39
22 TU	4.48	4.26	3.78	2.74	1.51	1.03	1.43	1.99	2.37	2.89	3.65	4.36	4.62	4.47	4.07	3.12	1.85	1.07	1.27	1.83	2.27	2.72	3.44	4.16
23 W	4.51	4.41	4.09	3.31	2.12	1.18	1.22	1.77	2.20	2.59	3.27	4.05	4.54	4.55	4.28	3.63	2.43	1.35	1.12	1.61	2.07	2.43	3.04	3.85
24 TH	4.40	4.49	4.28	3.79	2.72	1.58	1.15	1.58	2.08	2.37	2.87	3.68	4.34	4.55	4.38	3.99	3.04	1.78	1.13	1.42	1.95	2.24	2.64	3.42
25 F	4.18	4.48	4.37	4.08	3.36	2.12	1.29	1.40	1.98	2.28	2.54	3.21	4.02	4.45	4.42	4.14	3.59	2.42	1.36	1.24	1.80	2.18	2.38	2.92
26 SA	3.76	4.33	4.40	4.18	3.79	2.86	1.70	1.33	1.79	2.26	2.42	2.77	3.53	4.19	4.38	4.21	3.85	3.12	1.94	1.28	1.55	2.10	2.32	2.55
27 SU	3.18	3.93	4.28	4.22	3.96	3.47	2.47	1.61	1.62	2.13	2.42	2.55	3.00	3.70	4.14	4.19	3.96	3.54	2.75	1.78	1.48	1.87	2.25	2.39
28 M	2.70	3.32	3.89	4.11	4.03	3.74	3.23	2.35	1.80	1.96	2.32	2.47	2.64	3.11	3.65	3.96	3.97	3.73	3.32	2.62	1.91	1.78	2.06	2.26
29 TU	2.41	2.74	3.27	3.72	3.92	3.87	3.63	3.19	2.51	2.11	2.18	2.33	2.43	2.64	3.05	3.48	3.75	3.81	3.64	3.31	2.75	2.19	2.01	2.06
30 W	2.15	2.33	2.66	3.11	3.53	3.80	3.85	3.72	3.38	2.81	2.37	2.22	2.19	2.28	2.51	2.88	3.28	3.62	3.79	3.73	3.50	3.02	2.44	2.06
31 TH	1.88	1.93	2.16	2.50	2.94	3.42	3.82	4.01	3.96	3.67	3.09	2.48	2.06	1.91	2.05	2.34	2.71	3.15	3.63	3.95	3.98	3.77	3.27	2.56

C7

Table 7 (1) Portsmouth hourly height predictions – continued

ENGLAND – PORTSMOUTH

Lat 50°48'N Long 01°07'W

TIME ZONE **UTC** UNITS **METRES**

NOVEMBER 2002

DATE	0000	0100	0200	0300	0400	0500	0600	0700	0800	0900	1000	1100	1200	1300	1400	1500	1600	1700	1800	1900	2000	2100	2200	2300
1 F	1.92	1.56	1.66	1.98	2.37	2.84	3.44	4.02	4.31	4.26	3.94	3.25	2.40	1.72	1.56	1.83	2.20	2.61	3.15	3.81	4.25	4.27	4.01	3.43
2 SA	2.52	1.62	1.19	1.43	1.88	2.31	2.85	3.61	4.34	4.62	4.50	4.11	3.26	2.12	1.30	1.26	1.70	2.15	2.60	3.29	4.11	4.56	4.48	4.16
3 SU	3.48	2.33	1.22	0.88	1.34	1.89	2.34	2.97	3.90	4.67	4.84	4.64	4.17	3.11	1.72	0.90	1.11	1.71	2.17	2.68	3.53	4.44	4.77	4.59
4 M ●	4.24	3.40	2.00	0.84	0.75	1.41	1.97	2.42	3.18	4.23	4.92	4.94	4.69	4.12	2.80	1.27	0.66	1.15	1.80	2.23	2.82	3.81	4.70	4.87
5 TU	4.64	4.25	3.21	1.62	0.59	0.83	1.59	2.08	2.55	3.45	4.53	5.04	4.94	4.68	3.93	2.38	0.89	0.63	1.32	1.92	2.30	3.01	4.10	4.85
6 W	4.86	4.64	4.18	2.90	1.26	0.56	1.07	1.79	2.17	2.72	3.74	4.73	5.03	4.88	4.58	3.60	1.91	0.68	0.80	1.55	2.01	2.39	3.25	4.33
7 TH	4.88	4.80	4.61	3.98	2.51	1.03	0.74	1.40	1.96	2.27	2.95	4.02	4.81	4.92	4.77	4.35	3.15	1.51	0.72	1.10	1.75	2.07	2.55	3.51
8 F	4.46	4.80	4.71	4.50	3.66	2.14	1.02	1.08	1.70	2.09	2.43	3.22	4.20	4.74	4.74	4.57	3.98	2.67	1.32	0.96	1.43	1.90	2.18	2.77
9 SA	3.71	4.45	4.65	4.58	4.26	3.28	1.94	1.25	1.47	1.93	2.22	2.64	3.44	4.21	4.56	4.51	4.27	3.53	2.32	1.38	1.31	1.69	2.04	2.35
10 SU	2.98	3.77	4.31	4.46	4.38	3.93	2.98	1.97	1.60	1.79	2.11	2.39	2.84	3.51	4.07	4.30	4.23	3.90	3.17	2.22	1.64	1.63	1.89	2.19
11 M	2.52	3.06	3.68	4.11	4.24	4.12	3.65	2.91	2.20	1.94	2.01	2.26	2.54	2.90	3.41	3.84	4.02	3.92	3.58	3.02	2.36	1.94	1.85	2.03
12 TU	2.31	2.58	3.01	3.52	3.90	4.04	3.91	3.56	3.04	2.48	2.16	2.14	2.36	2.57	2.82	3.22	3.60	3.78	3.70	3.45	3.11	2.59	2.15	1.96
13 W	2.11	2.34	2.52	2.87	3.35	3.74	3.92	3.85	3.67	3.25	2.68	2.23	2.15	2.34	2.47	2.65	3.03	3.42	3.65	3.64	3.54	3.31	2.78	2.21
14 TH	1.96	2.08	2.25	2.39	2.76	3.26	3.70	3.94	3.96	3.86	3.41	2.71	2.14	2.05	2.21	2.31	2.51	2.92	3.38	3.69	3.75	3.73	3.47	2.82
15 F	2.11	1.84	1.97	2.14	2.31	2.73	3.29	3.82	4.10	4.14	4.01	3.42	2.55	1.92	1.86	2.06	2.19	2.46	2.95	3.50	3.88	3.93	3.90	3.52
16 SA	2.68	1.87	1.66	1.86	2.08	2.33	2.83	3.48	4.06	4.29	4.29	4.03	3.24	2.21	1.62	1.69	1.97	2.17	2.54	3.13	3.77	4.10	4.10	3.98
17 SU	3.39	2.36	1.57	1.53	1.84	2.12	2.45	3.05	3.78	4.32	4.43	4.34	3.87	2.86	1.78	1.39	1.63	1.99	2.26	2.74	3.44	4.06	4.28	4.19
18 M	3.91	3.08	1.94	1.33	1.52	1.92	2.24	2.67	3.37	4.10	4.51	4.48	4.25	3.54	2.35	1.39	1.30	1.70	2.09	2.44	3.05	3.79	4.31	4.37
19 TU	4.19	3.68	2.64	1.53	1.25	1.64	2.07	2.42	2.97	3.73	4.38	4.59	4.44	4.02	3.04	1.81	1.16	1.38	1.86	2.24	2.70	3.41	4.11	4.46
20 W ○	4.39	4.08	3.30	2.12	1.26	1.35	1.86	2.25	2.64	3.31	4.08	4.55	4.57	4.30	3.63	2.45	1.37	1.14	1.59	2.05	2.41	3.00	3.78	4.36
21 TH	4.51	4.33	3.84	2.81	1.66	1.19	1.59	2.09	2.40	2.90	3.67	4.35	4.60	4.46	4.06	3.12	1.87	1.12	1.32	1.85	2.20	2.60	3.35	4.12
22 F	4.50	4.46	4.20	3.47	2.27	1.34	1.34	1.89	2.27	2.56	3.20	4.01	4.51	4.53	4.27	3.70	2.54	1.40	1.12	1.61	2.06	2.32	2.85	3.70
23 SA	4.35	4.51	4.35	3.98	3.02	1.80	1.26	1.63	2.15	2.39	2.75	3.53	4.25	4.51	4.36	4.03	3.26	2.00	1.17	1.32	1.88	2.19	2.45	3.13
24 SU	3.98	4.42	4.41	4.18	3.68	2.57	1.53	1.41	1.94	2.31	2.49	2.98	3.79	4.33	4.38	4.14	3.73	2.81	1.65	1.21	1.60	2.06	2.27	2.62
25 M	3.38	4.10	4.36	4.26	3.99	3.37	2.25	1.52	1.68	2.16	2.38	2.60	3.18	3.89	4.24	4.20	3.92	3.44	2.49	1.55	1.41	1.82	2.13	2.34
26 TU	2.77	3.50	4.06	4.23	4.12	3.82	3.15	2.17	1.70	1.92	2.24	2.40	2.68	3.26	3.83	4.08	4.02	3.75	3.25	2.38	1.68	1.63	1.91	2.12
27 W	2.37	2.83	3.47	3.94	4.11	4.02	3.73	3.11	2.30	1.93	2.04	2.20	2.37	2.68	3.20	3.68	3.93	3.91	3.67	3.23	2.48	1.88	1.76	1.87
28 TH	2.06	2.34	2.79	3.36	3.82	4.06	4.03	3.79	3.25	2.51	2.07	1.99	2.07	2.27	2.60	3.07	3.53	3.85	3.92	3.74	3.36	2.66	2.03	1.74
29 F	1.72	1.94	2.26	2.69	3.25	3.77	4.12	4.16	3.96	3.44	2.68	2.08	1.81	1.87	2.12	2.47	2.93	3.45	3.90	4.06	3.92	3.55	2.84	2.08
30 SA	1.59	1.52	1.80	2.17	2.61	3.20	3.84	4.30	4.37	4.17	3.61	2.74	1.93	1.54	1.65	1.99	2.37	2.85	3.48	4.07	4.27	4.12	3.72	2.94

DECEMBER 2002

DATE	0000	0100	0200	0300	0400	0500	0600	0700	0800	0900	1000	1100	1200	1300	1400	1500	1600	1700	1800	1900	2000	2100	2200	2300
1 SU	2.01	1.35	1.32	1.71	2.12	2.58	3.24	4.02	4.55	4.57	4.32	3.71	2.68	1.66	1.25	1.50	1.92	2.31	2.85	3.62	4.31	4.47	4.28	3.85
2 M	2.96	1.82	1.10	1.21	1.71	2.13	2.61	3.38	4.28	4.76	4.70	4.42	3.71	2.49	1.33	1.03	1.44	1.91	2.31	2.93	3.83	4.53	4.60	4.39
3 TU	3.92	2.87	1.57	0.91	1.21	1.78	2.18	2.70	3.59	4.52	4.88	4.75	4.45	3.60	2.18	1.02	0.93	1.49	1.94	2.34	3.07	4.07	4.69	4.67
4 W ●	4.46	3.92	2.69	1.31	0.84	1.32	1.89	2.25	2.85	3.83	4.70	4.91	4.75	4.40	3.38	1.83	0.82	0.97	1.60	2.00	2.42	3.26	4.28	4.76
5 TH	4.69	4.50	3.83	2.43	1.11	0.91	1.51	2.01	2.34	3.03	4.06	4.80	4.87	4.70	4.24	3.04	1.48	0.75	1.12	1.73	2.06	2.54	3.48	4.43
6 F	4.77	4.69	4.46	3.62	2.13	1.02	1.10	1.73	2.12	2.46	3.25	4.25	4.80	4.76	4.58	3.98	2.63	1.22	0.83	1.35	1.86	2.14	2.72	3.71
7 SA	4.51	4.72	4.64	4.33	3.31	1.85	1.08	1.36	1.93	2.22	2.63	3.48	4.36	4.69	4.60	4.37	3.60	2.23	1.12	1.05	1.58	1.97	2.26	2.95
8 SU	3.89	4.50	4.61	4.53	4.08	2.96	1.70	1.28	1.64	2.08	2.34	2.83	3.66	4.34	4.51	4.39	4.06	3.18	1.94	1.21	1.33	1.78	2.09	2.44
9 M	3.16	3.96	4.41	4.48	4.34	3.75	2.67	1.72	1.55	1.88	2.21	2.49	3.01	3.73	4.20	4.28	4.13	3.70	2.83	1.84	1.42	1.59	1.94	2.23
10 TU	2.62	3.29	3.94	4.27	4.31	4.08	3.46	2.53	1.88	1.80	2.05	2.33	2.61	3.09	3.67	4.02	4.05	3.85	3.39	2.64	1.92	1.66	1.79	2.08
11 W	2.36	2.73	3.32	3.85	4.13	4.12	3.85	3.30	2.56	2.07	1.98	2.16	2.41	2.66	3.06	3.55	3.83	3.84	3.62	3.23	2.64	2.07	1.84	1.93
12 TH	2.18	2.42	2.76	3.29	3.77	4.01	3.98	3.73	3.28	2.65	2.20	2.05	2.19	2.41	2.61	2.98	3.42	3.69	3.70	3.52	3.23	2.72	2.19	1.92
13 F	1.99	2.21	2.42	2.74	3.26	3.72	3.95	3.93	3.74	3.33	2.70	2.20	2.03	2.15	2.33	2.53	2.91	3.35	3.64	3.69	3.56	3.32	2.79	2.21
14 SA	1.90	1.99	2.18	2.39	2.74	3.28	3.75	3.99	3.99	3.81	3.36	2.66	2.09	1.92	2.05	2.25	2.47	2.90	3.38	3.71	3.79	3.67	3.41	2.79
15 SU	2.11	1.81	1.94	2.15	2.38	2.79	3.37	3.86	4.11	4.09	3.88	3.30	2.48	1.87	1.78	1.96	2.19	2.48	2.97	3.51	3.87	3.93	3.80	3.43
16 M	2.66	1.91	1.70	1.90	2.15	2.43	2.90	3.54	4.05	4.26	4.18	3.87	3.11	2.18	1.62	1.67	1.93	2.19	2.56	3.14	3.73	4.06	4.08	3.87
17 TU	3.33	2.41	1.67	1.62	1.92	2.20	2.52	3.09	3.78	4.25	4.37	4.21	3.74	2.79	1.81	1.43	1.64	1.95	2.25	2.72	3.39	3.98	4.24	4.18
18 W	3.86	3.10	2.07	1.47	1.63	1.99	2.28	2.68	3.35	4.04	4.42	4.43	4.17	3.48	2.37	1.46	1.33	1.68	2.02	2.37	2.96	3.69	4.21	4.37
19 TH ○	4.22	3.73	2.76	1.72	1.36	1.71	2.10	2.39	2.89	3.63	4.28	4.52	4.42	4.01	3.10	1.91	1.20	1.35	1.79	2.12	2.54	3.24	3.98	4.39
20 F	4.43	4.18	3.49	2.35	1.42	1.37	1.85	2.22	2.53	3.14	3.93	4.46	4.54	4.32	3.75	2.64	1.48	1.08	1.46	1.92	2.23	2.74	3.55	4.24
21 SA	4.50	4.42	4.05	3.15	1.93	1.24	1.49	2.02	2.32	2.68	3.43	4.20	4.55	4.46	4.14	3.40	2.15	1.16	1.10	1.64	2.04	2.33	2.99	3.86
22 SU	4.43	4.51	4.33	3.85	2.74	1.57	1.21	1.68	2.17	2.41	2.88	3.72	4.38	4.52	4.31	3.92	2.99	1.70	0.99	1.25	1.81	2.12	2.47	3.27
23 M	4.11	4.50	4.45	4.21	3.58	2.34	1.34	1.33	1.89	2.26	2.49	3.10	3.95	4.43	4.41	4.14	3.66	2.58	1.38	1.01	1.45	1.92	2.18	2.65
24 TU	3.52	4.24	4.46	4.35	4.06	3.28	2.02	1.30	1.53	2.03	2.29	2.59	3.31	4.07	4.37	4.26	3.97	3.39	2.23	1.25	1.16	1.62	1.98	2.25
25 W	2.83	3.68	4.25	4.39	4.26	3.90	3.02	1.87	1.41	1.71	2.08	2.31	2.70	3.42	4.04	4.25	4.13	3.81	3.15	2.05	1.30	1.33	1.70	2.00
26 TH	2.33	2.96	3.72	4.19	4.32	4.17	3.77	2.87	1.89	1.57	1.80	2.07	2.31	2.75	3.42	3.94	4.14	4.03	3.70	3.03	2.04	1.44	1.45	1.72
27 F	2.02	2.39	3.00	3.68	4.12	4.29	4.13	3.71	2.87	2.01	1.69	1.80	2.02	2.29	2.74	3.34	3.83	4.07	3.99	3.67	3.03	2.14	1.58	1.50
28 SA	1.71	2.02	2.40	2.98	3.61	4.09	4.30	4.15	3.75	2.95	2.13	1.71	1.72	1.93	2.23	2.67	3.23	3.74	4.07	4.02	3.73	3.13	2.29	1.67
29 SU	1.48	1.67	2.00	2.39	2.93	3.56	4.12	4.36	4.23	3.83	3.06	2.20	1.65	1.59	1.83	2.15	2.57	3.13	3.72	4.13	4.11	3.84	3.27	2.43
30 M	1.69	1.40	1.62	1.98	2.36	2.88	3.56	4.22	4.46	4.32	3.94	3.15	2.19	1.50	1.44	1.75	2.08	2.49	3.07	3.79	4.25	4.22	3.98	3.42
31 TU	2.51	1.62	1.31	1.59	1.97	2.33	2.87	3.64	4.36	4.56	4.41	4.02	3.18	2.07	1.30	1.32	1.69	2.02	2.43	3.10	3.91	4.37	4.34	4.12

Chapter 8

VTS and TSS

Contents

8.1 **VESSEL TRAFFIC SERVICES** .... Page 166
8.1.1 Vessel Traffic Services (VTS)
Fig 8(1) 166
8.1.2 UK Ports VTS listening watch 166
8.1.3 European Ports VTS listening watch 167
8.2 **VTS SCHEMES** 168
Fig 8 (2) VTS - Thames Estuary 168
Fig 8 (3) VTS - Thames & Medway 169
Fig 8 (4) - River Humber VTS/TSS..........170
Fig 8 (5) VTS - Netherlands - Scheldemond (VTS-SM) 171
Fig 8 (6) VTS - Approaches to Nieuwe Waterweg 172
Fig 8 (7) VTS - Nieuwe Waterweg including Oude Maas 173
Fig 8 (8) VTS - Noordseekanaal 174
Fig 8 (9) VTS - Den Helder 174
Fig 8 (10) VTS - Terschelling 175
Fig 8 (11) VTS - Germany - Die Ems 176
Fig 8 (12) VTS - German Bight 176
Fig 8 (13) VTS - Die Jade 177
Fig 8 (14) VTS - Die Weser & Die Hunte 177
Fig 8 (15) VTS - Die Weser & Die Hunte 178
Fig 8 (16) VTS - Die Elbe 178
Fig 8 (17)VTS - Die Elbe 179
Fig 8 (18)VTS - Die Elbe 179
Fig 8 (19)VTS - Kiel Canal West 180
Fig 8 (20) VTS - Kiel Canal East/ Kieler Förde 180
8.3 **TRAFFIC SEPARATION SCHEMES**......... 181
8.3.1 Traffic Separation Schemes (TSS)......... 181
Fig 8 (21) Example 181
Fig 8 (22) Key to TSS Symbols 182
Fig 8 (23) Off Smalls TSS 182
Fig 8 (24) Fastnet Rock TSS 182
Fig 8 (25) Off Skerries TSS 183
Fig 8 (26) Tuskar Rock TSS 183
Fig 8 (27) North Channel 183
Fig 8 (28) TSS Western Approaches 184
Fig 8 (29) Off Casquets TSS 185
Fig 8 (30) Dover Strait TSS 186
Fig 8 (31) Southern North Sea TSS 187
Fig 8 (32) Netherlands TSS 188
Fig 8 (33) German TSS 189
Fig 8 (34) Off Finisterre 190
Fig 8 (35) Off Ilha da Berlenga 190
Fig 8 (36) Off Cape Roca TSS 190
Fig 8 (37) Off Cape St Vincent TSS 190
Fig 8 (38) Straits of Gibraltar 191

8.1 VESSEL TRAFFIC SERVICES

8.1.1 Vessel Traffic Services (VTS)

An increasing number of ports are implementing Vessel Traffic Services (VTS) schemes, to improve the safety and efficiency of traffic management, and protect the environment. Every harbour is different and has its own specific problems.

VTS may range from the provision of information messages about shipping movements to the extensive management of traffic within a port or waterway. Most VTS schemes are aimed at commercial vessels which must comply with the laid down procedures.

Yachts are not normally required to comply with port VTS radio and reporting procedures, but at some ports larger yachts may fall within the stipulated minimum length or tonnage. When available, always use the recommended yacht tracks in preference to the main shipping channels.

When sailing in VTS areas valuable information about other shipping movements can be obtained by listening continuously to the VTS frequency and by having an understanding of where such vessels make their reports, especially in conditions of reduced visibility. Yachts should seldom need to transmit on a VTS or port operations channel. A possible exception to this rule might occur in fog, when it may be advisable to keep port operations informed before starting to cross a busy shipping channel.

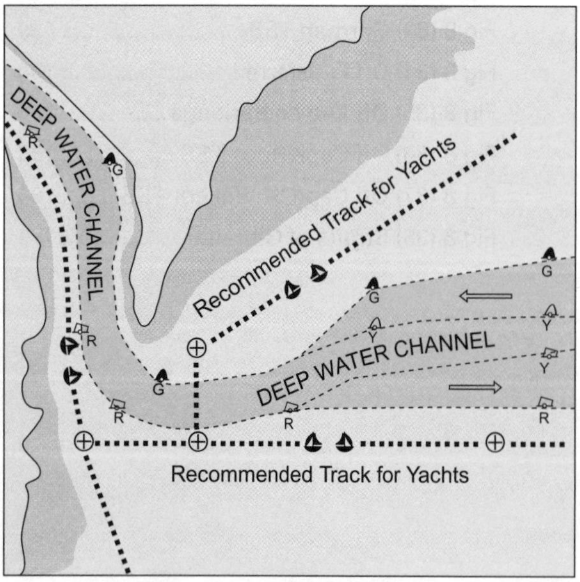

Fig. 8 (1) Yachts should keep well clear of the main shipping channels and whenever possible use any recommended yacht tracks. When the main channels have to be crossed, do so at right angles. Avoid crossing the bows of oncoming commercial traffic.

Many of the larger ports operate VTS Traffic Information broadcasts which provide information about shipping movements, expected times of arrival or departure, and routes they will follow, in addition to weather and tidal information.

In some ports, such as Southampton, a launch is sent ahead of large ships to clear the channel. Obey any instructions given.

VTS radio channels are shown in Chapter 9 under RADIO TELEPHONE in port entries, on Area Maps and on VTS/TSS diagrams.

8.1.2 UK Ports VTS listening watch

Regulations, relevant to yachts, may be in force in respect of maintaining a continuous listening watch. The list below summarises the requirements for UK ports. Although the application of the regulations varies from port to port it is common sense to maintain a listening watch in VTS waters, even though many regulations do not specifically cover small craft.

Port	*VHF Ch*	*Advice*
Falmouth	16	*should*
Fowey	09	*should*
Plymouth	13 14 16	*must*
Portland & Weymouth	74 12	*should*
The Solent	12	*should*
Portsmouth	11 13	*should*
Shoreham	14	*should*
Dover	74	*should*
Ramsgate	14	*should*
River Medway	74	*should*
Port of London	14 12 68	*should*
Colchester	68	*should*
Harwich	71	*should*
Lowestoft	14	*should*
Humber	14 12	*should*
Tees	14	*should*
Sunderland	16	*should*
Tyne	12	*should*
Forth Estuary	71	*should*
Peterhead	14 16	*should*
Shetland Waters	14 16	*should*
Orkney Harbours	16	*should*
Kyle of Lochalsh	16	*should*
Douglas, IOM	12	*should*
Fleetwood	12 16	*should*
Liverpool	12	*should*
Manchester	14	*should*
Holyhead	14	*should*
Milford Haven	12	*must*
Londonderry	14	*should*
Belfast	12 16	*should*

8.1.3 European Ports VTS listening watch

Note that many of these are compulsory and heavy 'on the spot' fines may be levied if a yacht is found not to be complying

Port	*VHF Ch*	*Advice*
Republic of Ireland		
Cork	12	*should*
Belgium and Netherlands		
Scheldemond (see 8.2.3)		
Wandelaar	65	*must*
Zeebrugge	69	*must*
Steenbank	64	*must*
Vlissingen	14	*must*
Terneuzen	03	*must*
Hansweert	65	*must*
Antwerpen	12	*must*
Netherlands		
Nieuwe Waterweg and Oude Maas (see 8.2.4/5)		
Maasaanloop/Maas		
Approach	01	*should*
Pilot Maas	02	*should*
Maasmond/Maas		
Entrance	03	*should*
Maasluis	80	*should*
Rozenburg	65	*should*
Europort	66	*should*
Botlek	61	*should*
Oude Maas	62	*should*
Hartel (not yet in use)	05	*should*
Eemhaven	63	*should*
Waalhaven	60	*should*
Maasbruggen	81	*should*
Brienenoord	21	should
Heerjansdam	04	should
Dordrecht		
Dordrecht	19	must
Heerjansdam	04	must
Noordzeekanaal (see 8.2.6)		
IJmuiden	61	should
Noordzeesluizen	22	should
Noordzeekanaal	03	should
Zijkanaal C Sluice	68	should
Amsterdam	04	should
Den Helder (see 8.2.7)		
As limits on 8.2.7	12	should
Terschelling (see 8.2.8)		
As limits on 8.2.8	02	*must*
Delfzijl - see Die Ems, below		
Germany		
Die Ems (see 8.2.9)		
Lt buoy No 1 to Lt buoy No 35	18	*must*
Lt buoy No 35 to buoy No 57	20	*must*
Buoy No 57 to Lt buoy No 86	21	*must*
Lt buoy No 86 to Papenburg	15	*must*
German Bight (see 8.2.10)		
Eastern Part	80	*must*
Western Part	79	*must*
Die Jade (see 8.2.11)		
Lt buoy 1b/Jade 1 to Lt buoys Nos 33/34	63	*must*
Lt buoys Nos 33/34 to Lt buoy No 58	20	*must*
Weser and Hunte (see 8.2.12/13)		
Lt buoy No 3a to Lt buoy No A2	22	*must*
Lt buoy No 19 to Lt buoy No 37	02	*must*
Lt buoy No 37 to buoy No 53	04	*must*
Buoy No 53 to Lt buoy No 63	07	*must*
Lt buoy No 63 to Lt buoy No 58	05	*must*
Lt buoy No 58 to Lt buoy No 79	82	*must*
Lt buoy No 79 to No 93	21	*must*
BremenWeser (see 8.2.13)		
Buoy No 93 to buoy No 113	19	*must*
Hunte entr to Elsfleth (km 24.3)	19	*must*
Buoy No 113 to Lemwerder Airfield (km 15)	78	*must*
Lemwerder Airfield to Bremen Railway br (km 1·5)	81	*must*
Die Elbe (see 8.2.14/15/16)		
Cuxhaven Elbe	71 or 16	*must*
Brunsbüttel Elbe	68 or 16	*must*
Hamburg Port	74	*must*
Kiel Canal West (see 8.12.17)		
Brunsbüttel appr (inward)	13	*must*
Brunsbüttel appr (outward)	68	*must*
Brunsbüttel Locks	13	*must*
Brunsbüttel to Breiholz	02	*must*
Kiel Canal East (see 8.2.18)		
Kieler Förde	22	*must*
Kieler Holtenau Locks appr	12	*must*
Breiholz to Kiel-Holtenau	03	*must*
France		
R Seine: Rade de la Carosse and Rouen	73	*should*
La Loire	12 & 16	*should*

C8

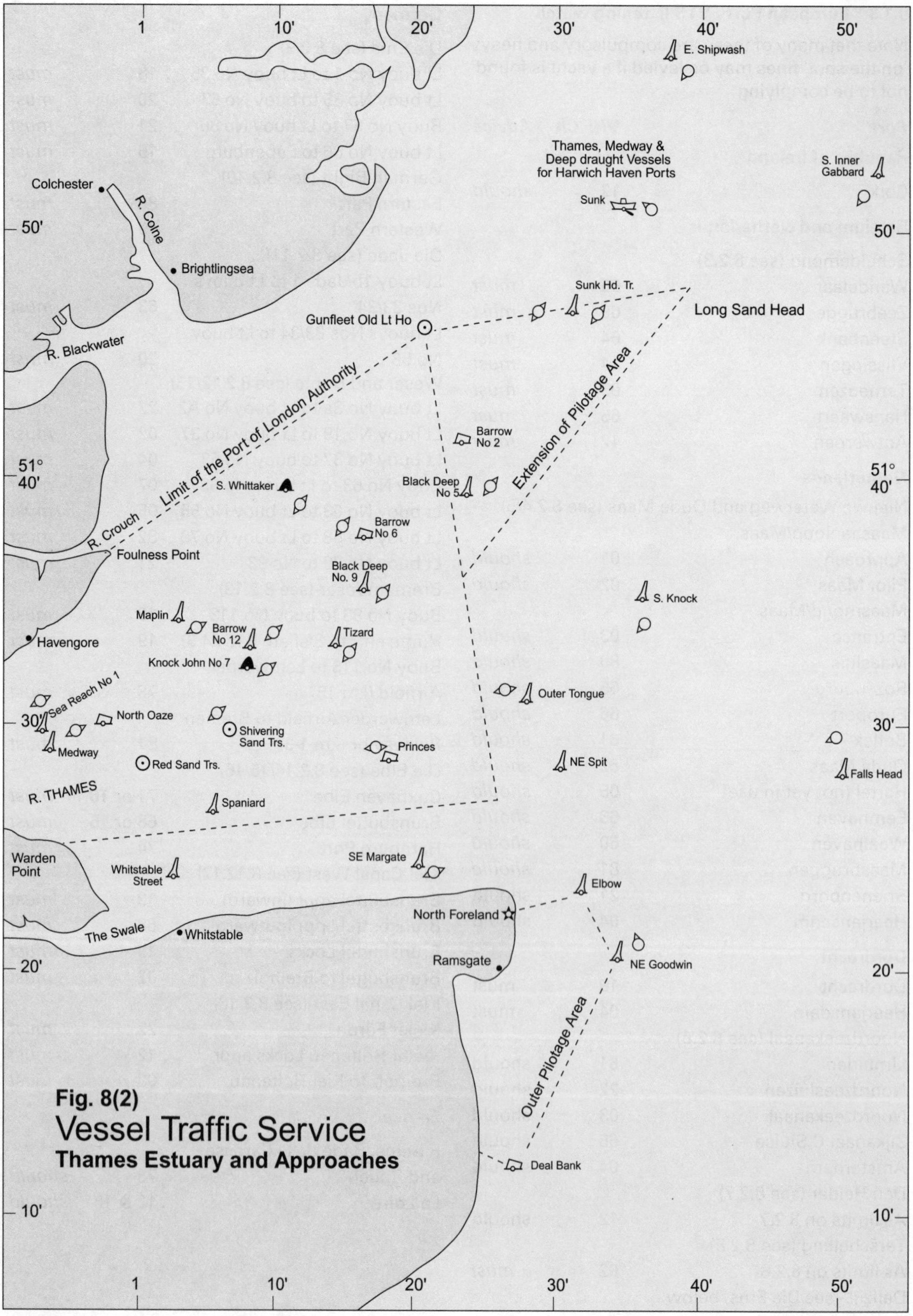
E. Shipwash
Thames, Medway & Deep draught Vessels for Harwich Haven Ports
S. Inner Gabbard
Sunk
Colchester
R. Colne
Brightlingsea
Sunk Hd. Tr.
Long Sand Head
Gunfleet Old Lt Ho
R. Blackwater
Limit of the Port of London Authority
Extension of Pilotage Area
Barrow No 2
S. Whittaker
Black Deep No 5
Barrow No 6
R. Crouch
Foulness Point
Black Deep No. 9
S. Knock
Maplin
Barrow No 12
Tizard
Havengore
Knock John No 7
Sea Reach No 1
Outer Tongue
North Oaze
Shivering Sand Trs.
Medway
Princes
Red Sand Trs.
NE Spit
Falls Head
R. THAMES
Spaniard
Warden Point
Whitstable Street
SE Margate
Elbow
North Foreland
The Swale
Whitstable
Ramsgate
NE Goodwin
Outer Pilotage Area
Deal Bank
1
10'
20'
30'
40'
50'
51° 40'

Fig. 8(2)
Vessel Traffic Service
Thames Estuary and Approaches

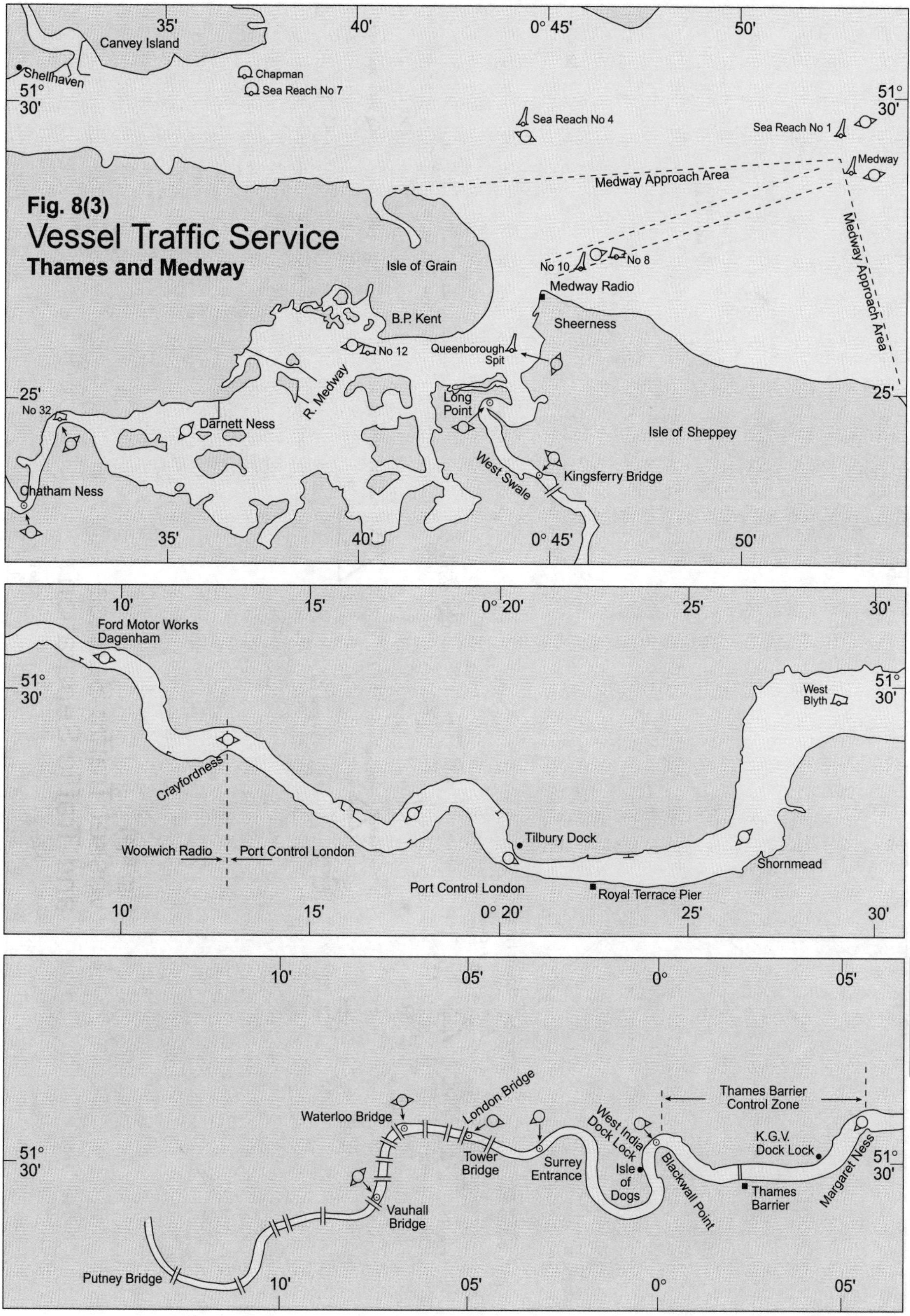

Fig. 8(3)
Vessel Traffic Service
Thames and Medway

C8

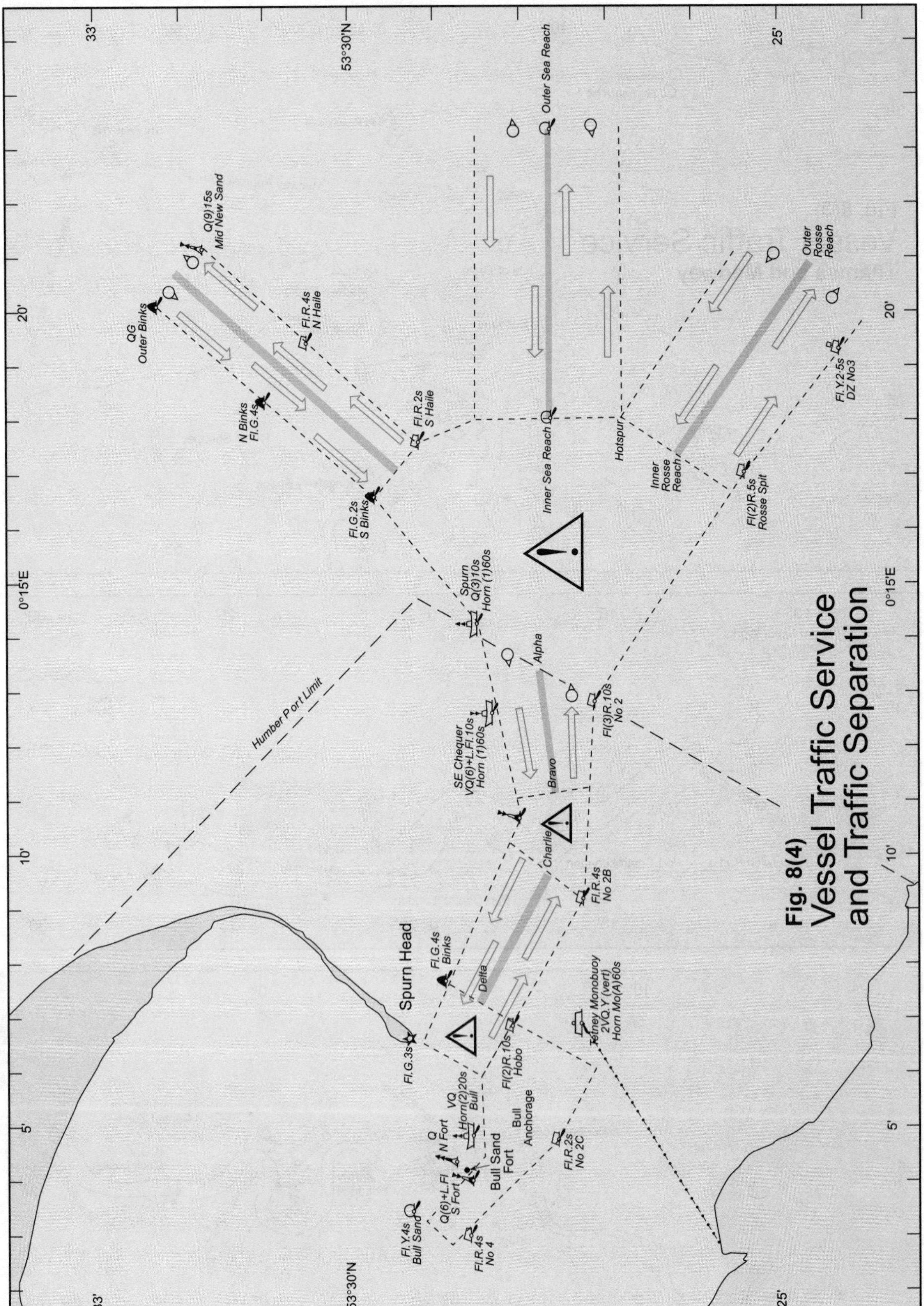

Fig. 8(4)
Vessel Traffic Service and Traffic Separation

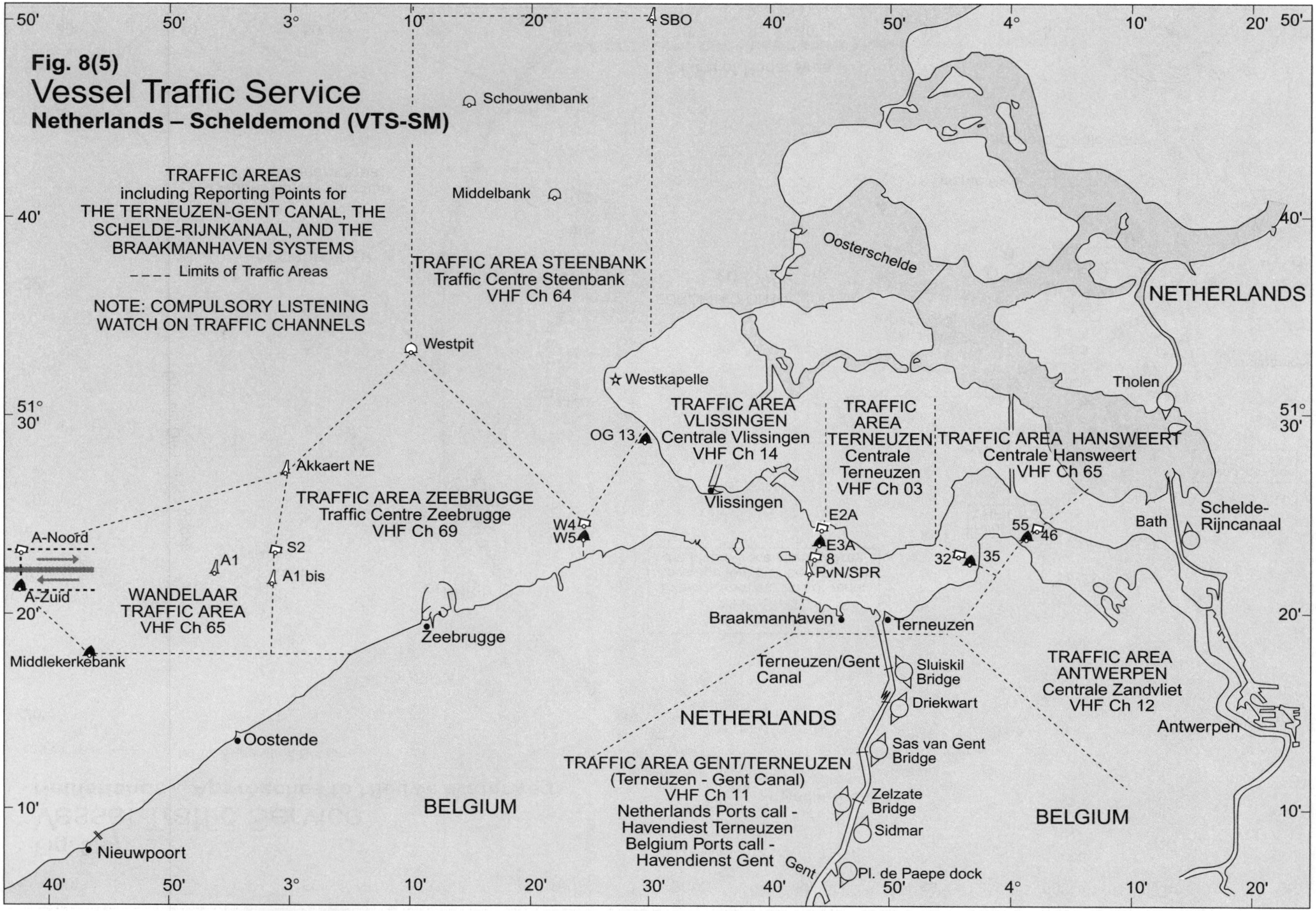
TRAFFIC AREAS
including Reporting Points for
THE TERNEUZEN-GENT CANAL, THE
SCHELDE-RIJNKANAAL, AND THE
BRAAKMANHAVEN SYSTEMS
Limits of Traffic Areas
NOTE: COMPULSORY LISTENING
WATCH ON TRAFFIC CHANNELS
Schouwenbank
Middelbank
SBO
Westpit
TRAFFIC AREA STEENBANK
Traffic Centre Steenbank
VHF Ch 64
Oosterschelde
NETHERLANDS
Tholen
Westkapelle
TRAFFIC AREA
VLISSINGEN
Centrale Vlissingen
VHF Ch 14
TRAFFIC
AREA
TERNEUZEN
Centrale
Terneuzen
VHF Ch 03
TRAFFIC AREA HANSWEERT
Centrale Hansweert
VHF Ch 65
OG 13
Akkaert NE
TRAFFIC AREA ZEEBRUGGE
Traffic Centre Zeebrugge
VHF Ch 69
Vlissingen
E2A
E3A
8
PvN/SPR
W4
W5
32
35
55
46
Bath
Schelde-
Rijncanaal
A-Noord
A-Zuid
S2
A1
A1 bis
WANDELAAR
TRAFFIC AREA
VHF Ch 65
Middlekerkebank
Zeebrugge
Braakmanhaven
Terneuzen
Terneuzen/Gent
Canal
Sluiskil
Bridge
Driekwart
TRAFFIC AREA
ANTWERPEN
Centrale Zandvliet
VHF Ch 12
Antwerpen
NETHERLANDS
Oostende
Sas van Gent
Bridge
TRAFFIC AREA GENT/TERNEUZEN
(Terneuzen - Gent Canal)
VHF Ch 11
Netherlands Ports call -
Havendiest Terneuzen
Belgium Ports call -
Havendienst Gent
Zelzate
Bridge
Sidmar
Pl. de Paepe dock
Gent
BELGIUM
BELGIUM
Nieuwpoort
50'
3°
10'
20'
30'
40'
4°
51° 30'

Fig. 8(5)
Vessel Traffic Service
Netherlands – Scheldemond (VTS-SM)

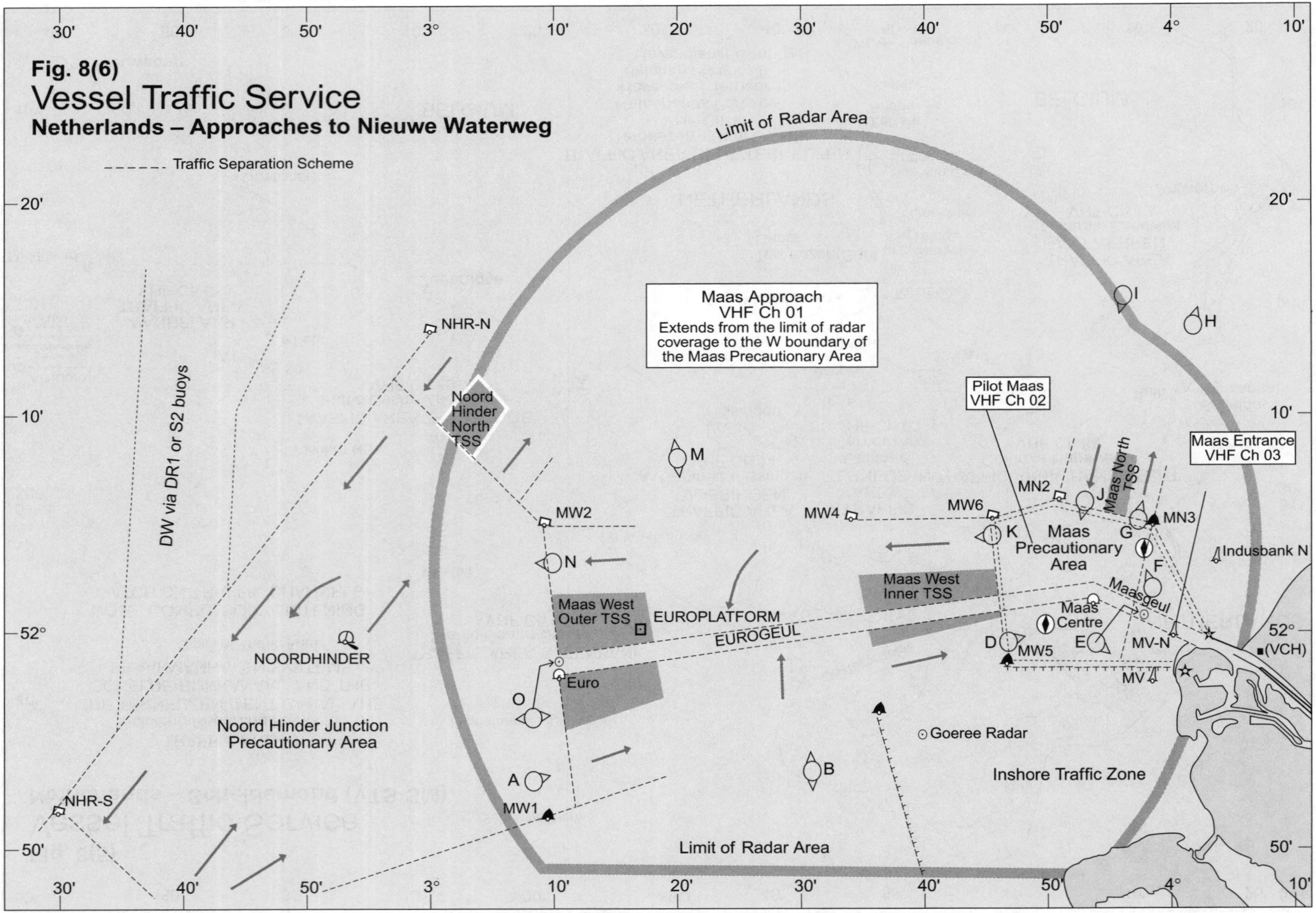
Fig. 8(6)
Vessel Traffic Service
Netherlands – Approaches to Nieuwe Waterweg
Traffic Separation Scheme
Limit of Radar Area
Maas Approach
VHF Ch 01
Extends from the limit of radar coverage to the W boundary of the Maas Precautionary Area
Pilot Maas
VHF Ch 02
Maas Entrance
VHF Ch 03
DW via DR1 or S2 buoys
NHR-N
NHR-S
Noord Hinder North TSS
NOORDHINDER
Noord Hinder Junction Precautionary Area
MW1
MW2
MW4
MW6
MN2
MN3
MW5
MV-N
MV
Maas West Outer TSS
Maas West Inner TSS
Maas North TSS
EUROPLATFORM
EUROGEUL
Euro
Maas Precautionary Area
Maasgeul
Maas Centre
Indusbank N
(VCH)
Goeree Radar
Inshore Traffic Zone
A
B
D
E
F
G
H
I
J
K
M
N
O
30'
40'
50'
3°
10'
20'
4°
52°

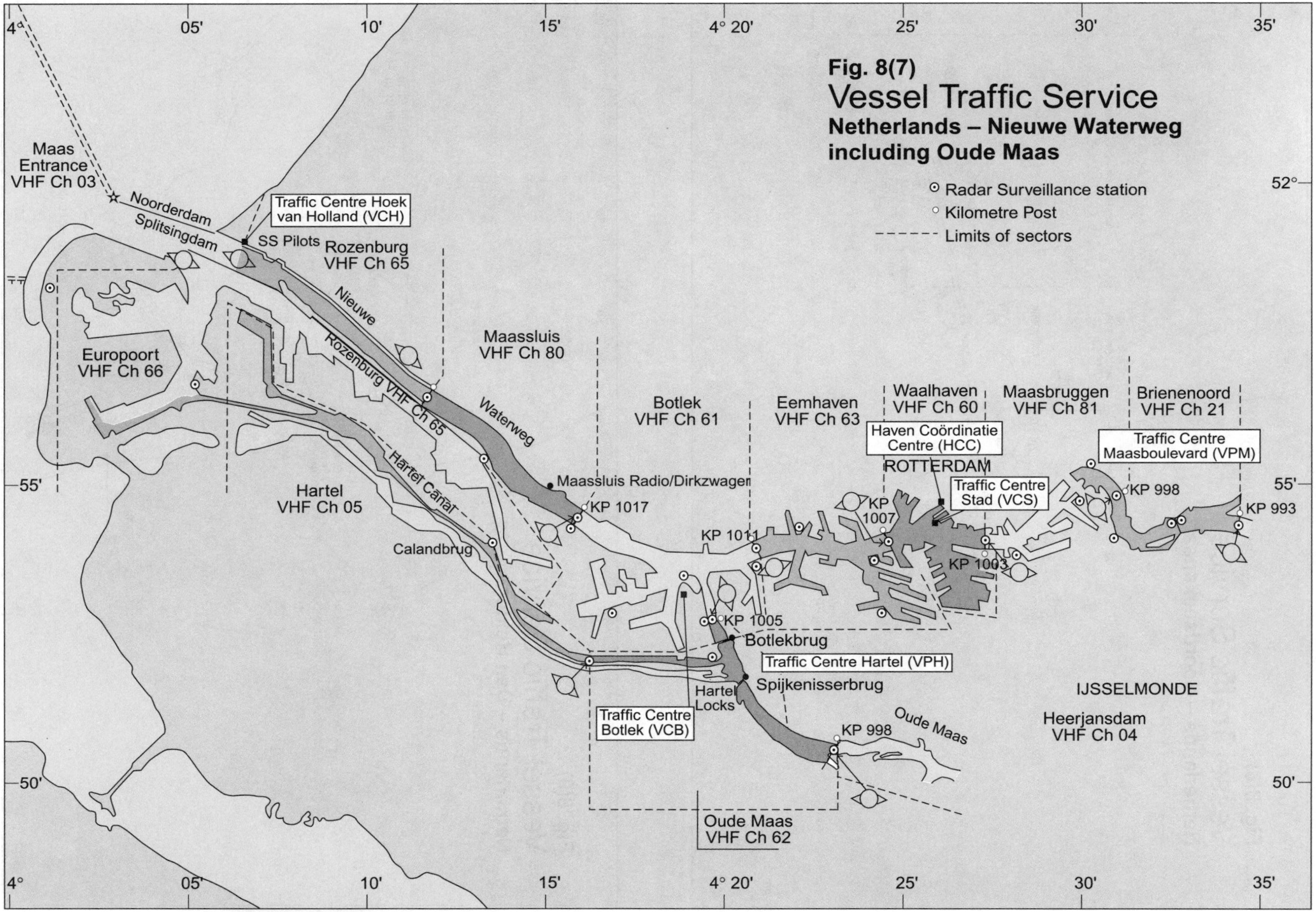

Fig. 8(7)
Vessel Traffic Service
Netherlands – Nieuwe Waterweg including Oude Maas
Radar Surveillance station
Kilometre Post
Limits of sectors
4°
05'
10'
15'
4° 20'
25'
30'
35'
52°
55'
50'
Maas Entrance VHF Ch 03
Noorderdam
Splitsingdam
Traffic Centre Hoek van Holland (VCH)
SS Pilots
Rozenburg VHF Ch 65
Nieuwe
Waterweg
Rozenburg VHF Ch 65
Europoort VHF Ch 66
Maassluis VHF Ch 80
Hartel VHF Ch 05
Hartel Canal
Calandbrug
Maassluis Radio/Dirkzwager
KP 1017
Botlek VHF Ch 61
Eemhaven VHF Ch 63
Waalhaven VHF Ch 60
Haven Coördinatie Centre (HCC)
ROTTERDAM
Traffic Centre Stad (VCS)
Maasbruggen VHF Ch 81
Brienenoord VHF Ch 21
Traffic Centre Maasboulevard (VPM)
KP 998
KP 993
KP 1007
KP 1011
KP 1003
KP 1005
Botlekbrug
Traffic Centre Hartel (VPH)
Spijkenisserbrug
Hartel Locks
Traffic Centre Botlek (VCB)
KP 998
Oude Maas
Oude Maas VHF Ch 62
IJSSELMONDE
Heerjansdam VHF Ch 04

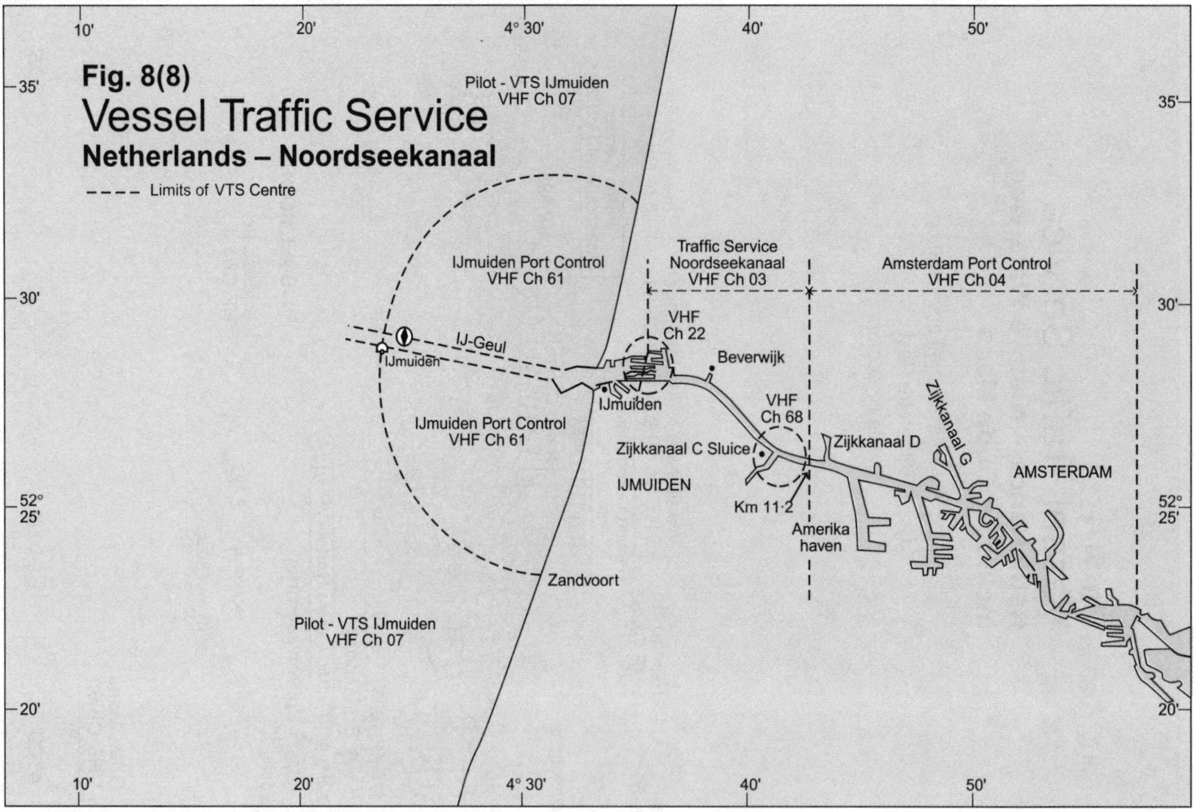
Fig. 8(8)
Vessel Traffic Service
Netherlands – Noordseekanaal
Limits of VTS Centre
Pilot - VTS IJmuiden
VHF Ch 07
IJmuiden Port Control
VHF Ch 61
Traffic Service
Noordseekanaal
VHF Ch 03
Amsterdam Port Control
VHF Ch 04
VHF
Ch 22
IJ-Geul
IJmuiden
Beverwijk
IJmuiden
VHF
Ch 68
IJmuiden Port Control
VHF Ch 61
Zijkkanaal C Sluice
Zijkkanaal D
Zijkkanaal G
AMSTERDAM
IJMUIDEN
Km 11·2
Amerika
haven
Zandvoort
Pilot - VTS IJmuiden
VHF Ch 07
10'
20'
4° 30'
40'
50'
35'
30'
52°
25'
20'

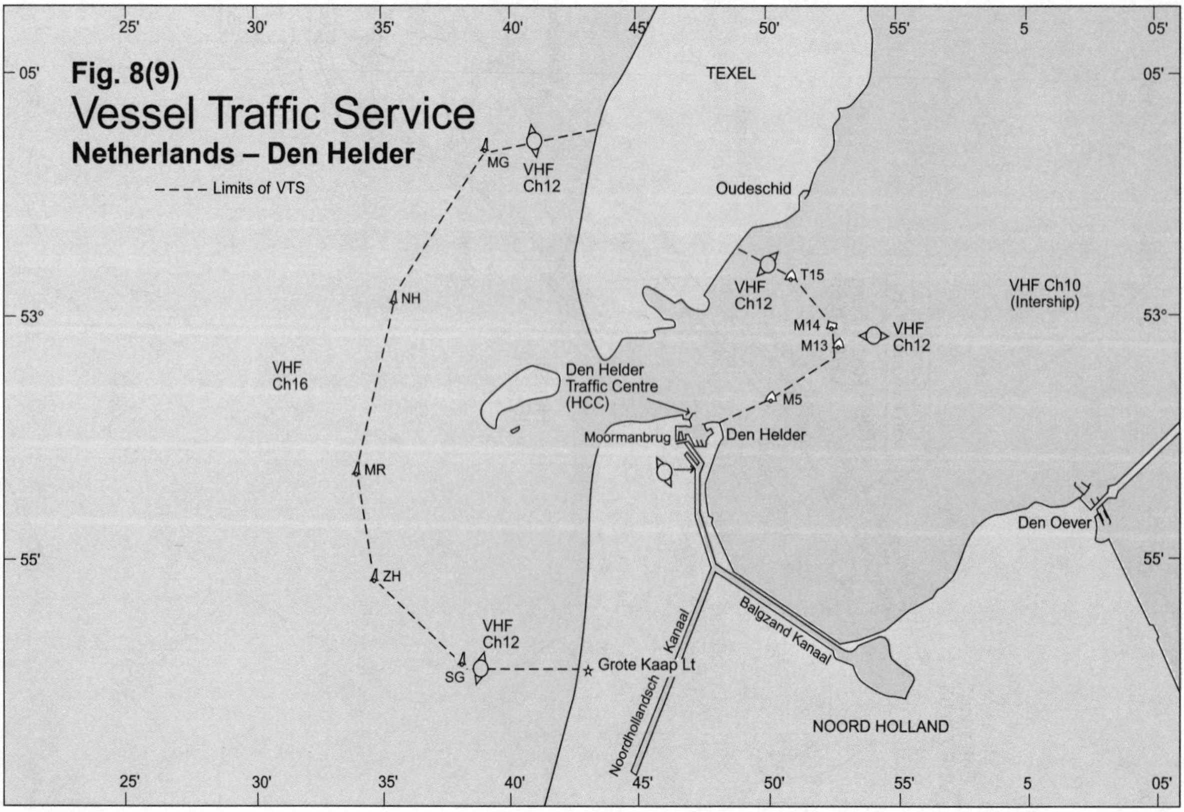
Fig. 8(9)
Vessel Traffic Service
Netherlands – Den Helder
Limits of VTS
TEXEL
MG
VHF
Ch12
Oudeschid
VHF
Ch12
T15
VHF Ch10
(Intership)
NH
M14
M13
VHF
Ch12
VHF
Ch16
Den Helder
Traffic Centre
(HCC)
M5
Moormanbrug
Den Helder
MR
Den Oever
ZH
Balgzand Kanaal
VHF
Ch12
SG
Grote Kaap Lt
Noordhollandsch Kanaal
NOORD HOLLAND
25'
30'
35'
40'
45'
50'
55'
5
05'
53°

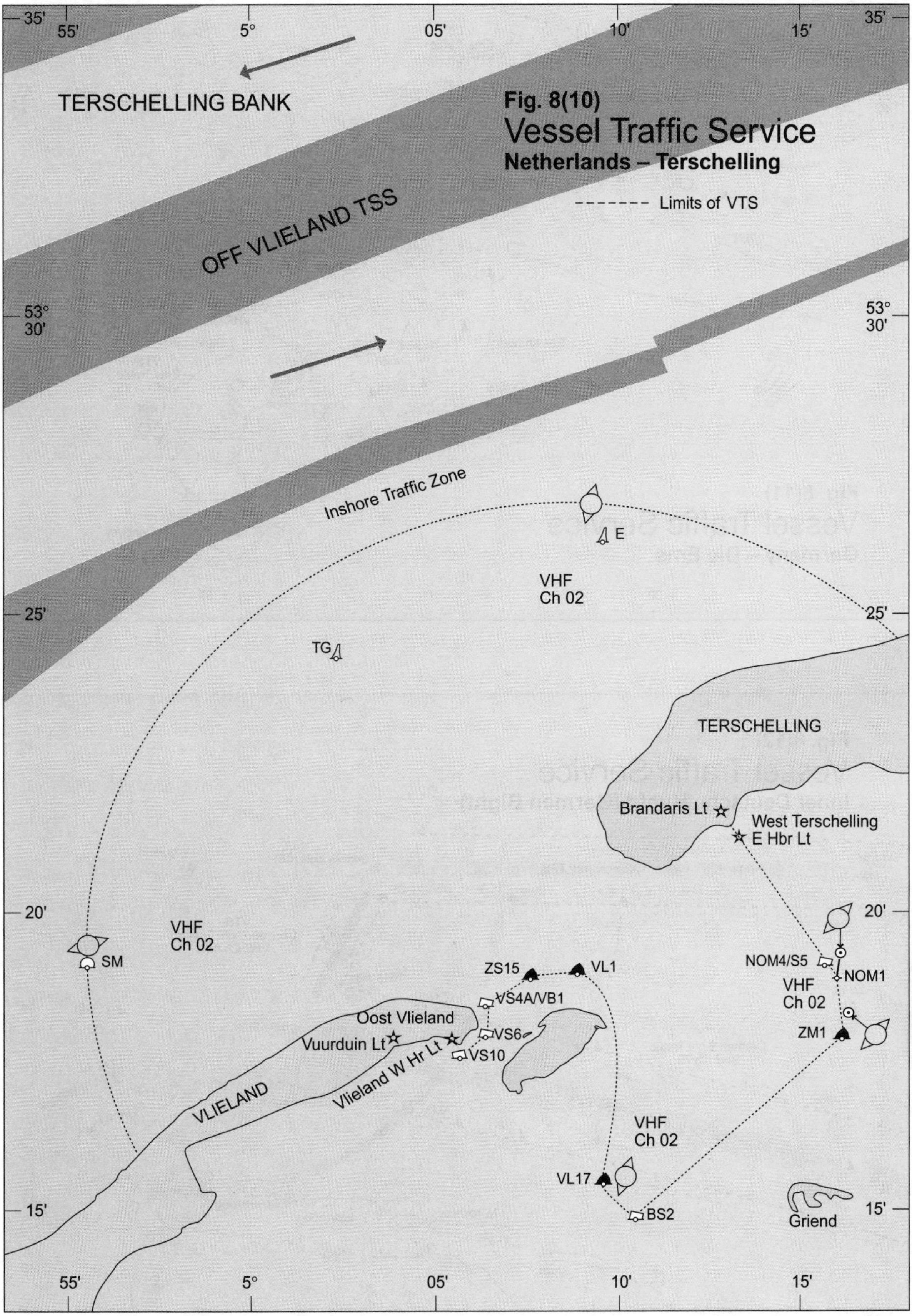
Fig. 8(10)
Vessel Traffic Service
Netherlands – Terschelling
Limits of VTS
35'
55'
5°
05'
10'
15'
53°
30'
25'
20'
TERSCHELLING BANK
OFF VLIELAND TSS
Inshore Traffic Zone
E
VHF
Ch 02
TG
TERSCHELLING
Brandaris Lt
West Terschelling
E Hbr Lt
SM
ZS15
VL1
NOM4/S5
NOM1
VS4A/VB1
Oost Vlieland
Vuurduin Lt
Vlieland W Hr Lt
VS6
VS10
ZM1
VLIELAND
VL17
BS2
Griend

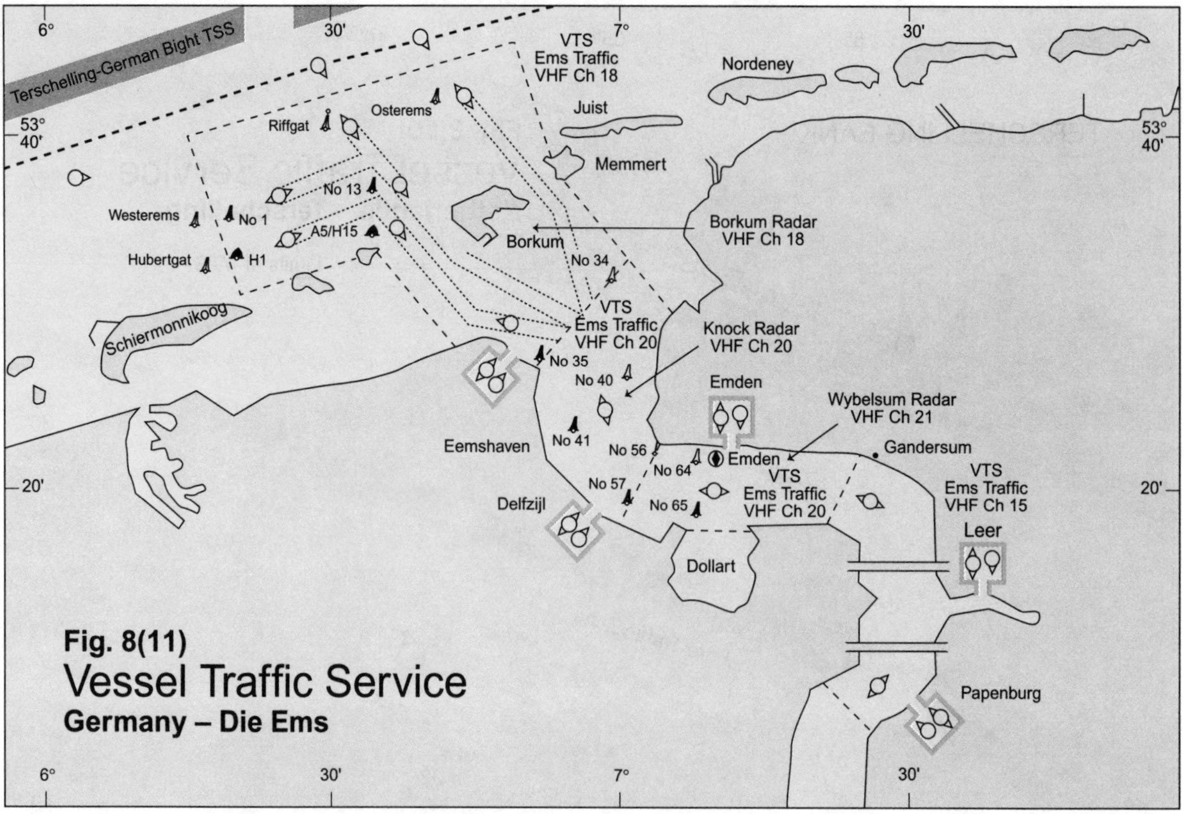
6°
30'
7°
30'
Terschelling-German Bight TSS
VTS
Ems Traffic
VHF Ch 18
Nordeney
Juist
Osterems
Riffgat
53°
40'
Memmert
No 13
Westerems
No 1
A5/H15
Borkum
Borkum Radar
VHF Ch 18
Hubertgat
H1
No 34
Schiermonnikoog
VTS
Ems Traffic
VHF Ch 20
Knock Radar
VHF Ch 20
No 35
No 40
Emden
Wybelsum Radar
VHF Ch 21
No 41
Eemshaven
No 56
Gandersum
No 64
Emden
VTS
Ems Traffic
VHF Ch 20
VTS
Ems Traffic
VHF Ch 15
20'
No 57
Delfzijl
No 65
Leer
Dollart
Papenburg
Fig. 8(11)
Vessel Traffic Service
Germany – Die Ems

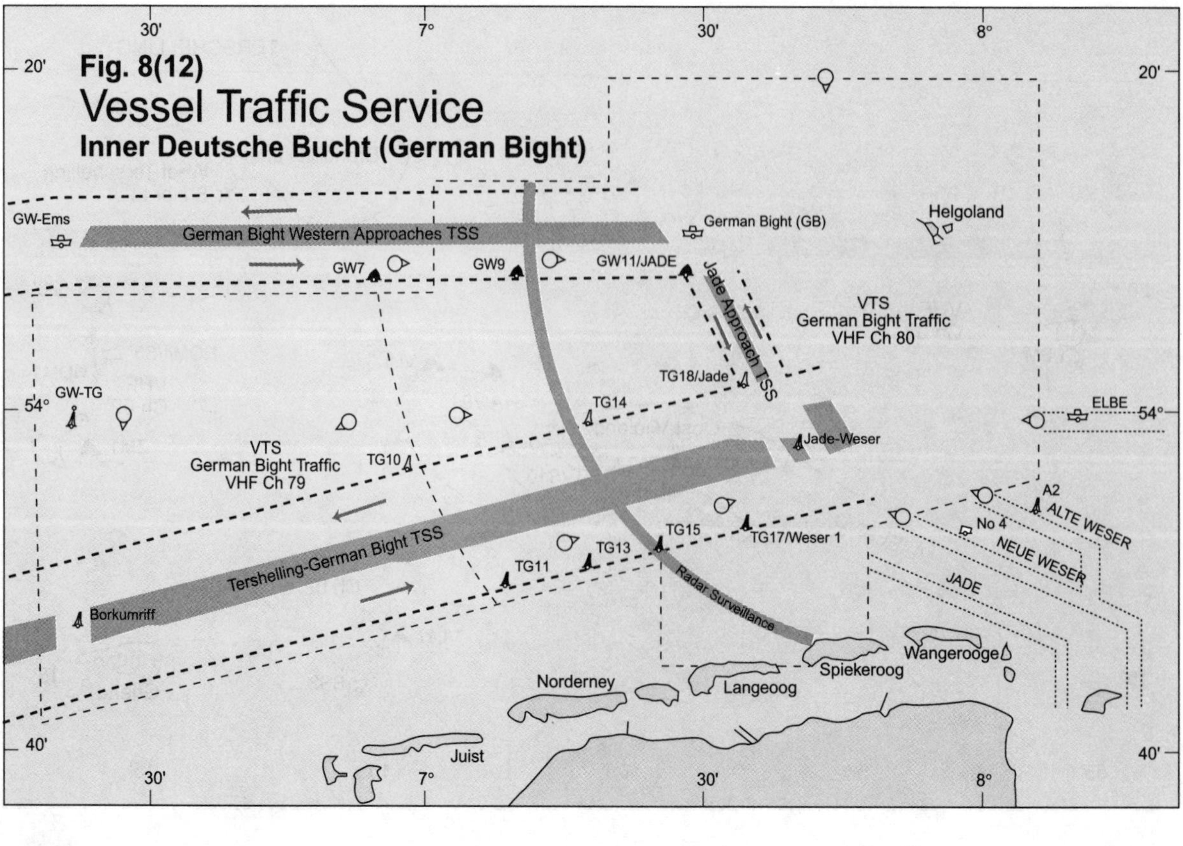
30'
7°
30'
8°
20'
GW-Ems
German Bight Western Approaches TSS
German Bight (GB)
Helgoland
GW7
GW9
GW11/JADE
Jade Approach TSS
VTS
German Bight Traffic
VHF Ch 80
TG18/Jade
GW-TG
54°
TG14
ELBE
Jade-Weser
VTS
German Bight Traffic
VHF Ch 79
TG10
A2
ALTE WESER
TG15
TG17/Weser 1
No 4
NEUE WESER
Tershelling-German Bight TSS
TG13
TG11
JADE
Radar Surveillance
Borkumriff
Wangerooge
Spiekeroog
Norderney
Langeoog
Juist
40'
Fig. 8(12)
Vessel Traffic Service
Inner Deutsche Bucht (German Bight)

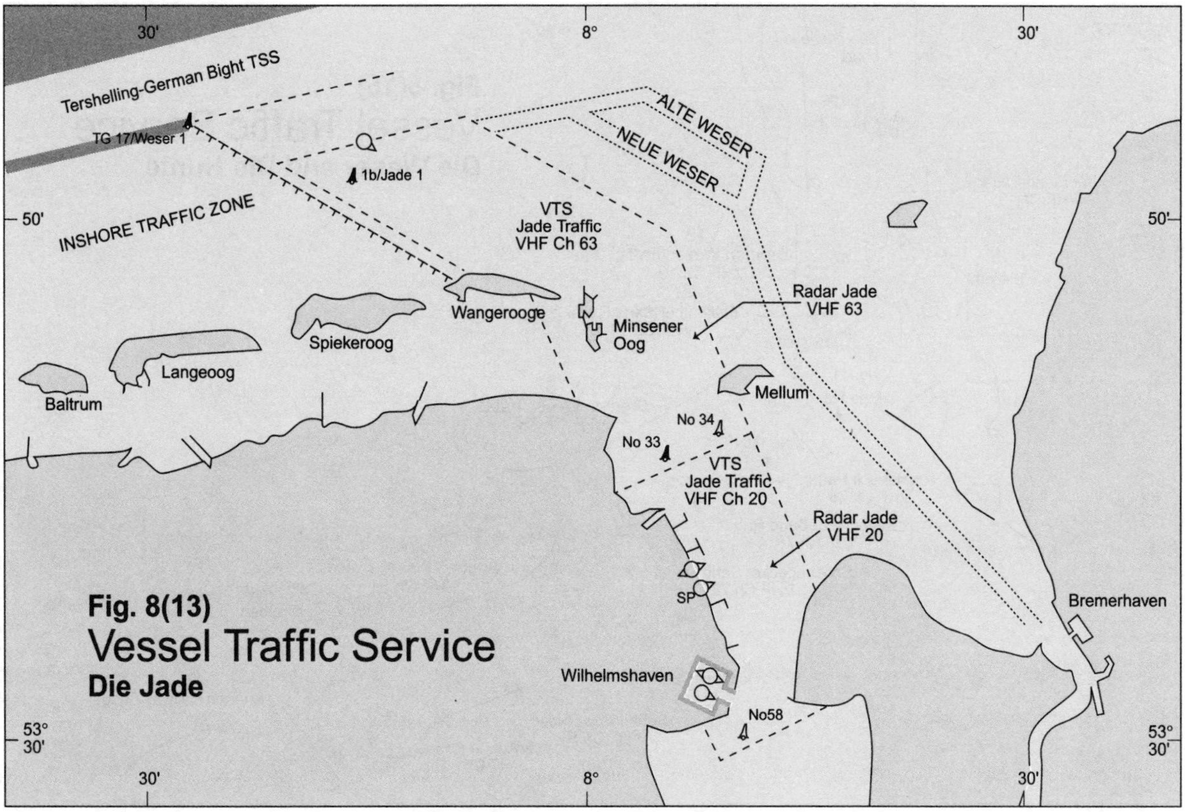
30'
8°
30'
Tershelling-German Bight TSS
TG 17/Weser 1
1b/Jade 1
ALTE WESER
NEUE WESER
50'
INSHORE TRAFFIC ZONE
VTS
Jade Traffic
VHF Ch 63
Radar Jade
VHF 63
Wangerooge
Minsener
Oog
Spiekeroog
Langeoog
Baltrum
Mellum
No 34
No 33
VTS
Jade Traffic
VHF Ch 20
Radar Jade
VHF 20
SP
Bremerhaven
Wilhelmshaven
No58
53°
30'
30'
8°
30'

Fig. 8(13)

Vessel Traffic Service

Die Jade

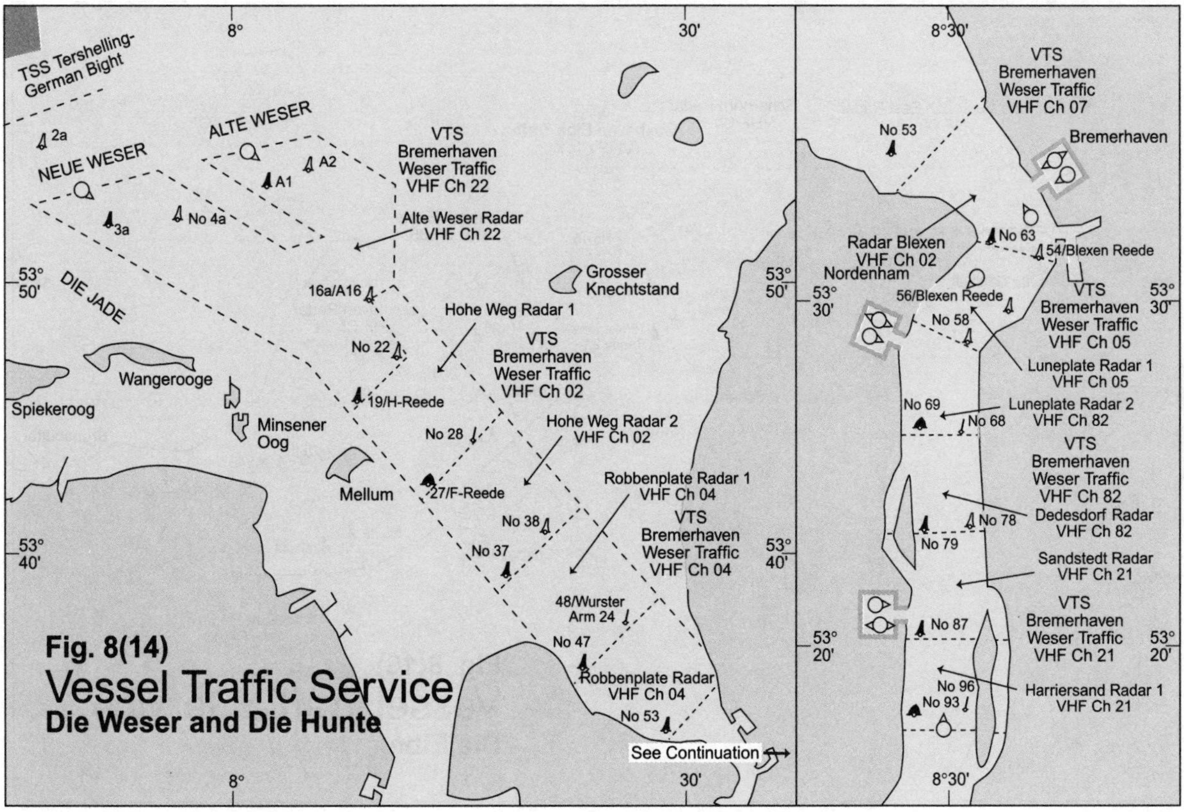
8°
30'
TSS Tershelling-German Bight
ALTE WESER
2a
NEUE WESER
A2
A1
3a
No 4a
VTS
Bremerhaven
Weser Traffic
VHF Ch 22
Alte Weser Radar
VHF Ch 22
53°
50'
DIE JADE
16a/A16
Grosser
Knechtstand
Hohe Weg Radar 1
No 22
VTS
Bremerhaven
Weser Traffic
VHF Ch 02
Wangerooge
Spiekeroog
19/H-Reede
Minsener
Oog
No 28
Hohe Weg Radar 2
VHF Ch 02
Mellum
27/F-Reede
Robbenplate Radar 1
VHF Ch 04
No 38
VTS
Bremerhaven
Weser Traffic
VHF Ch 04
No 37
53°
40'
48/Wurster
Arm 24
No 47
Robbenplate Radar
VHF Ch 04
No 53
See Continuation
8°
30'
8°30'
VTS
Bremerhaven
Weser Traffic
VHF Ch 07
No 53
Bremerhaven
No 63
Radar Blexen
VHF Ch 02
54/Blexen Reede
Nordenham
56/Blexen Reede
VTS
Bremerhaven
Weser Traffic
VHF Ch 05
No 58
Luneplate Radar 1
VHF Ch 05
No 69
No 68
Luneplate Radar 2
VHF Ch 82
VTS
Bremerhaven
Weser Traffic
VHF Ch 82
Dedesdorf Radar
VHF Ch 82
No 78
No 79
Sandstedt Radar
VHF Ch 21
VTS
Bremerhaven
Weser Traffic
VHF Ch 21
No 87
Harriersand Radar 1
VHF Ch 21
No 96
No 93
53°
30'
53°
20'
8°30'

Fig. 8(14)

Vessel Traffic Service

Die Weser and Die Hunte

C8

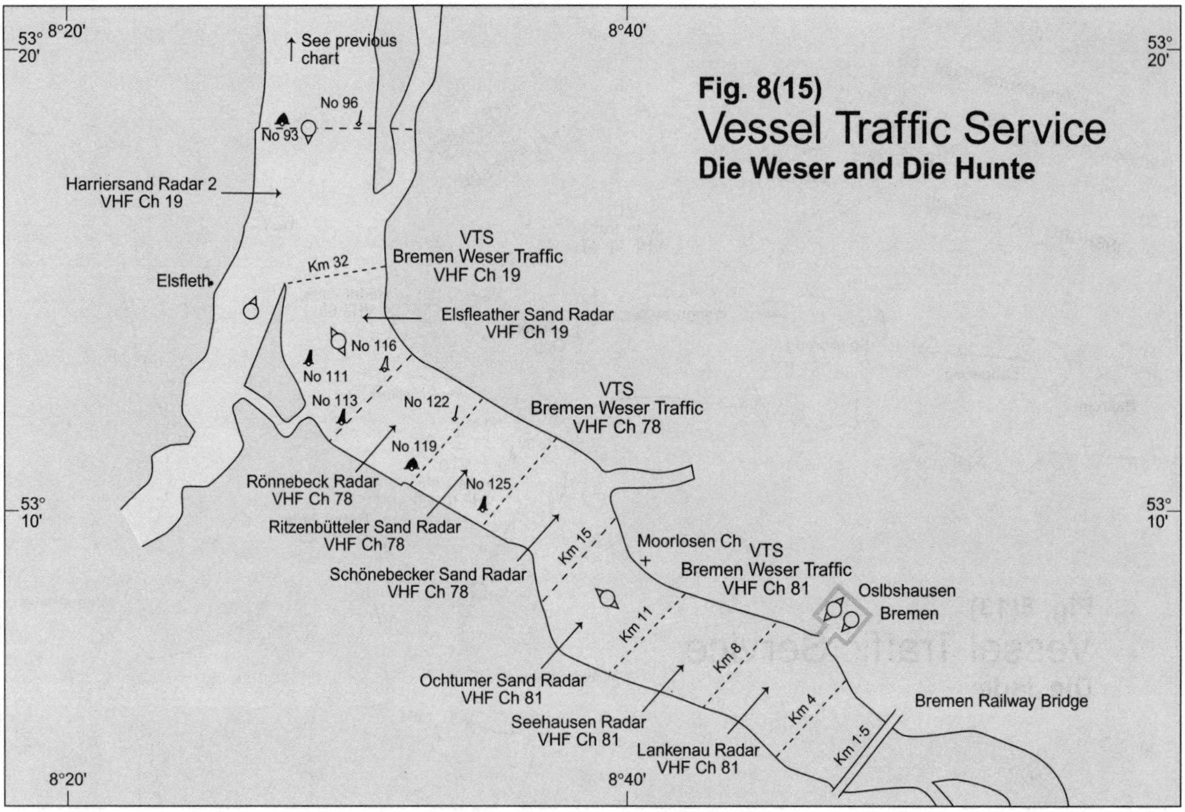
53° 20'
8°20'
See previous chart
8°40'
53° 20'
No 96
No 93
Harriersand Radar 2
VHF Ch 19
Km 32
VTS
Bremen Weser Traffic
VHF Ch 19
Elsfleth
Elsfleather Sand Radar
VHF Ch 19
No 116
No 111
No 113
No 122
VTS
Bremen Weser Traffic
VHF Ch 78
No 119
Rönnebeck Radar
VHF Ch 78
No 125
53° 10'
53° 10'
Ritzenbütteler Sand Radar
VHF Ch 78
Km 15
Moorlosen Ch
VTS
Bremen Weser Traffic
VHF Ch 81
Schönebecker Sand Radar
VHF Ch 78
Oslbshausen
Bremen
Km 11
Km 8
Ochtumer Sand Radar
VHF Ch 81
Seehausen Radar
VHF Ch 81
Km 4
Bremen Railway Bridge
Km 1·5
Lankenau Radar
VHF Ch 81
8°20'
8°40'

Fig. 8(15)
Vessel Traffic Service
Die Weser and Die Hunte

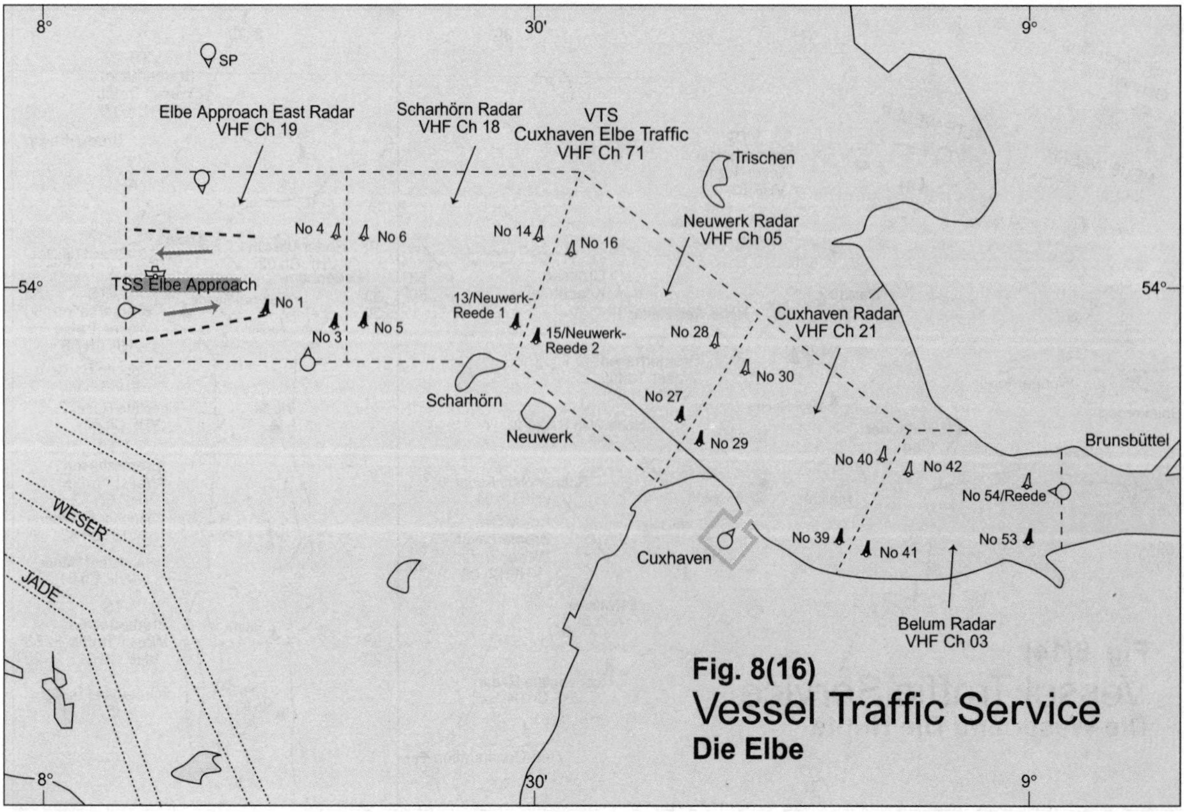
8°
30'
9°
SP
Elbe Approach East Radar
VHF Ch 19
Scharhörn Radar
VHF Ch 18
VTS
Cuxhaven Elbe Traffic
VHF Ch 71
Trischen
No 4
No 6
No 14
No 16
Neuwerk Radar
VHF Ch 05
54°
54°
TSS Elbe Approach
No 1
No 3
No 5
13/Neuwerk-Reede 1
15/Neuwerk-Reede 2
No 28
Cuxhaven Radar
VHF Ch 21
No 30
Scharhörn
No 27
Neuwerk
No 29
Brunsbüttel
No 40
No 42
No 54/Reede
WESER
No 39
No 41
No 53
Cuxhaven
JADE
Belum Radar
VHF Ch 03
8°
30'
9°

Fig. 8(16)
Vessel Traffic Service
Die Elbe

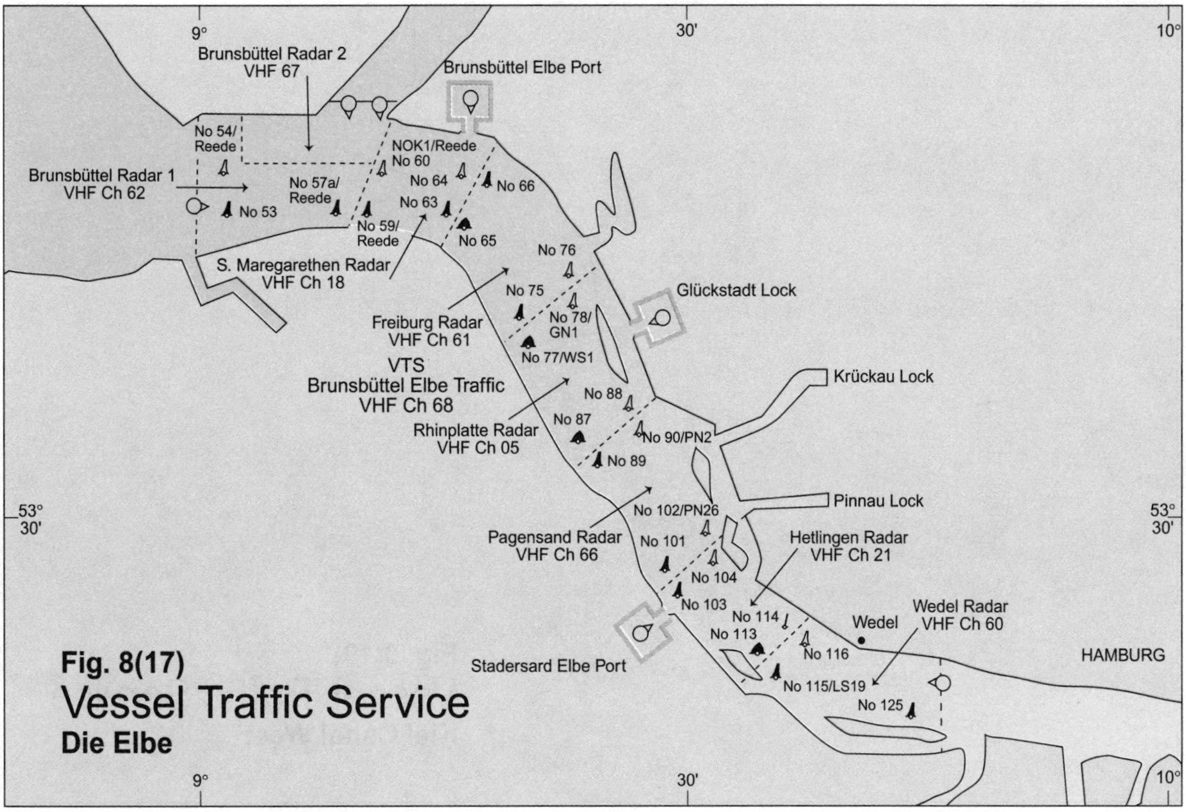
9°
30'
10°
Brunsbüttel Radar 2
VHF 67
Brunsbüttel Elbe Port
No 54/
Reede
NOK1/Reede
No 60
Brunsbüttel Radar 1
VHF Ch 62
No 57a/
Reede
No 64
No 66
No 53
No 63
No 59/
Reede
No 65
S. Maregarethen Radar
VHF Ch 18
No 76
No 75
Glückstadt Lock
Freiburg Radar
VHF Ch 61
No 78/
GN1
No 77/WS1
VTS
Brunsbüttel Elbe Traffic
VHF Ch 68
Krückau Lock
No 88
No 87
Rhinplatte Radar
VHF Ch 05
No 90/PN2
No 89
Pinnau Lock
53°
30'
No 102/PN26
Pagensand Radar
VHF Ch 66
No 101
Hetlingen Radar
VHF Ch 21
No 104
No 103
No 114
Wedel
Wedel Radar
VHF Ch 60
No 113
No 116
HAMBURG
Stadersand Elbe Port
No 115/LS19
No 125

Fig. 8(17)
Vessel Traffic Service
Die Elbe

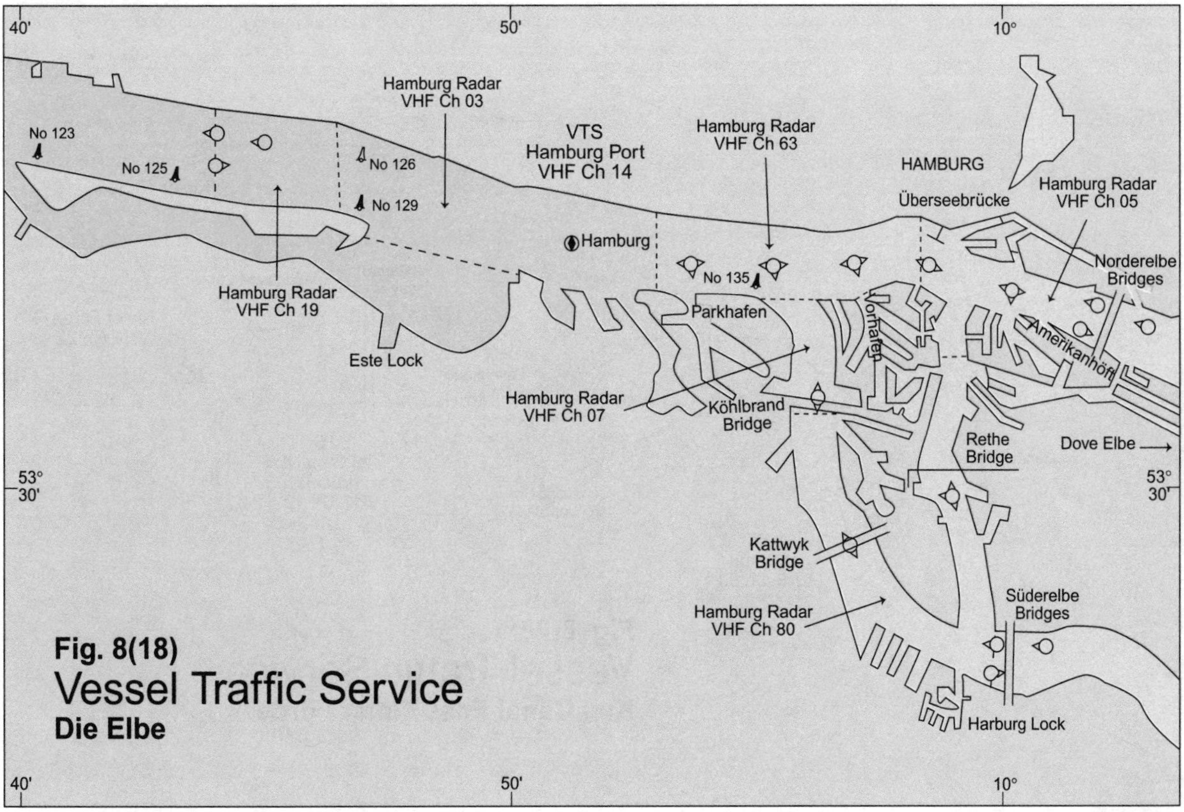
40'
50'
10°
Hamburg Radar
VHF Ch 03
No 123
VTS
Hamburg Port
VHF Ch 14
Hamburg Radar
VHF Ch 63
No 125
No 126
HAMBURG
No 129
Überseebrücke
Hamburg Radar
VHF Ch 05
Hamburg
No 135
Norderelbe
Bridges
Hamburg Radar
VHF Ch 19
Parkhafen
Vorhafen
Amerikanhöft
Este Lock
Hamburg Radar
VHF Ch 07
Köhlbrand
Bridge
Rethe
Bridge
Dove Elbe
53°
30'
Kattwyk
Bridge
Hamburg Radar
VHF Ch 80
Süderelbe
Bridges
Harburg Lock

Fig. 8(18)
Vessel Traffic Service
Die Elbe

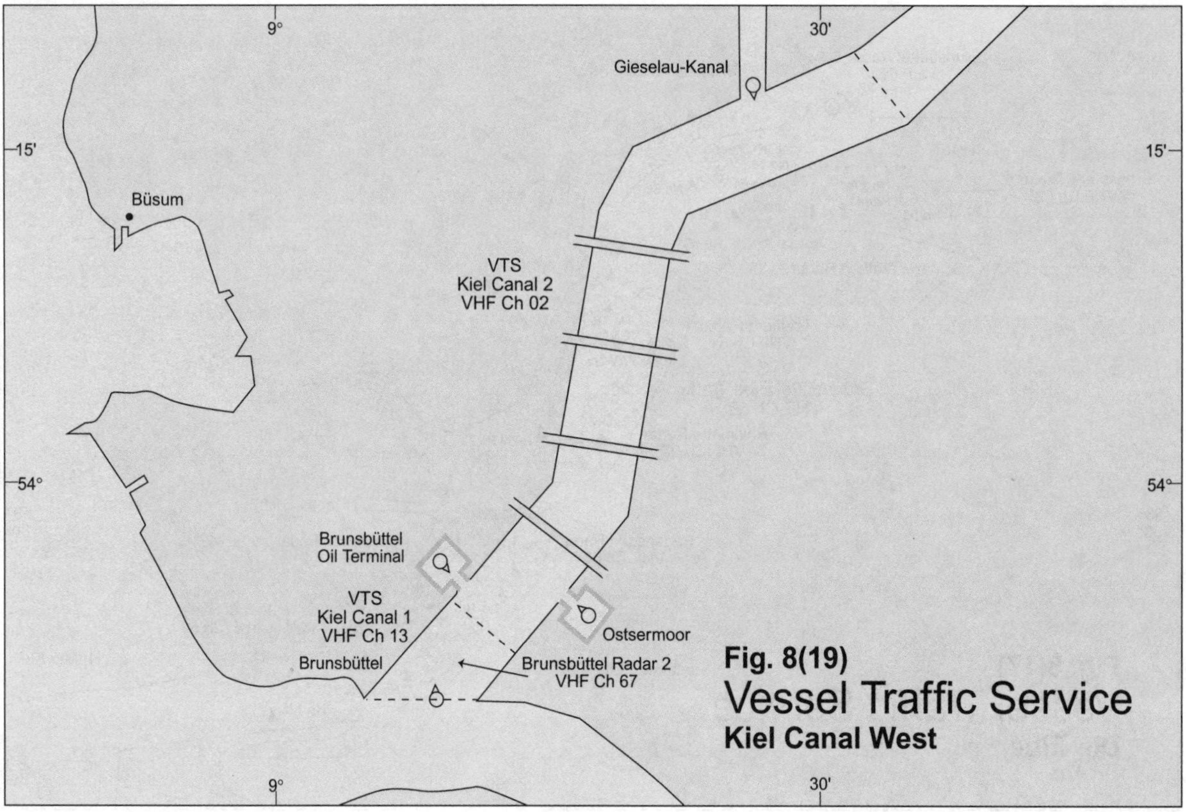

9°
30'
Gieselau-Kanal
15'
15'
Büsum
VTS
Kiel Canal 2
VHF Ch 02
54°
54°
Brunsbüttel
Oil Terminal
VTS
Kiel Canal 1
VHF Ch 13
Ostsermoor
Brunsbüttel
Brunsbüttel Radar 2
VHF Ch 67
9°
30'

Fig. 8(19)
Vessel Traffic Service
Kiel Canal West

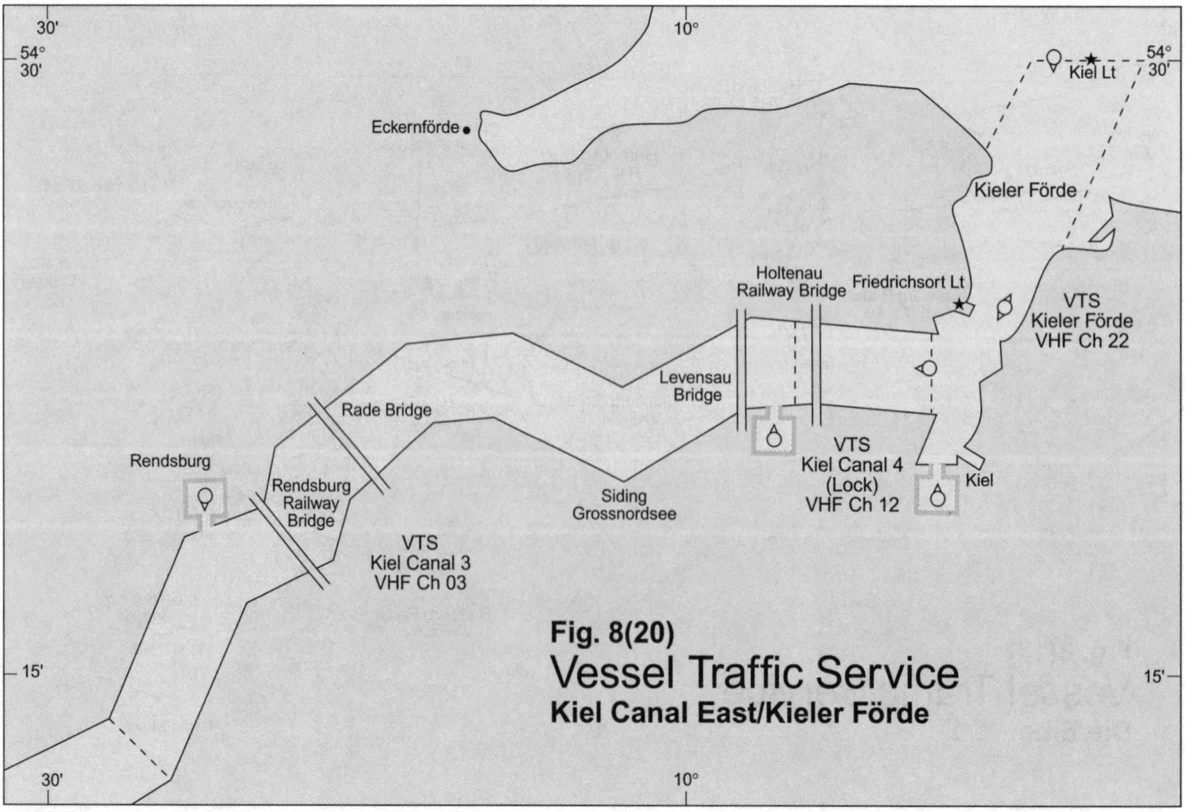

30'
10°
54° 30'
54° 30'
Kiel Lt
Eckernförde
Kieler Förde
Holtenau
Railway Bridge
Friedrichsort Lt
VTS
Kieler Förde
VHF Ch 22
Levensau
Bridge
Rade Bridge
VTS
Kiel Canal 4
(Lock)
VHF Ch 12
Kiel
Rendsburg
Rendsburg
Railway
Bridge
Siding
Grossnordsee
VTS
Kiel Canal 3
VHF Ch 03
15'
15'
30'
10°

Fig. 8(20)
Vessel Traffic Service
Kiel Canal East/Kieler Förde

8.3 TRAFFIC SEPARATION SCHEMES

8.3.1 Traffic Separation Schemes (TSS)

Yachts, like other vessels, must conform to Traffic Separation Schemes (Rule 10 next column). Rule 10 does not however modify the IRPCS when two vessels meet or converge in a TSS with a risk of collision. TSS must be accepted as another element of passage planning, or be avoided where possible. They are shown on Admiralty charts and those around the British Isles and the continental seaboard are depicted in Figs. 8 (22) to 8 (36).

Craft <20m LOA, and any sailing yacht, should consider using inshore traffic zones – often the most sensible action for a yacht, rather than using the main lanes. Otherwise, join or leave a lane at its extremity, but if joining or leaving at the side, do so at as shallow an angle as possible. Proceed in the general direction of traffic.

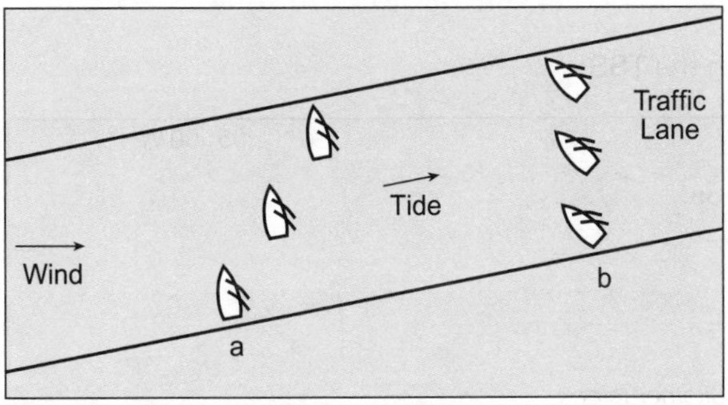

Fig. 8 (21) When crossing a traffic lane, your heading must be at right angles to the traffic flow, see (a) above, regardless of the course made good which is affected by tidal streams. The yacht at (b) above is not heading at right angles and is therefore on an incorrect course. If under sail, start motoring if speed over the ground falls below about 3 kn or if a reasonable course cannot be maintained.

Some TSS are under surveillance by radar, aircraft or patrol vessels. There are heavy penalties for breaking the rules. 'YG' in the International Code means 'You appear not to be complying with the traffic separation scheme'. See Chapter 9, Plate 5.

In summary, the best advice for yachtsmen is:

- Listen out on TSS frequencies, and to TSS information broadcasts.
- Cross TSS schemes as quickly as possible on a heading at right angles to the lane, and use the engine if the speed falls below 3 kn.
- Have a good radar reflector.
- Keep a sharp lookout.
- Bear in mind that you might not easily be seen from the bridge of a big vessel, especially in a steep sea or poor visibility.

Rule 10 *Traffic Separation Scheme*

(a) This Rule applies to traffic separation schemes adopted by the Organization and does not relieve any vessel of their obligation under any other Rule.

(b) A vessel using a traffic separation scheme shall:
(i) proceed in the appropriate traffic lane in the general direction of traffic flow for that lane;
(ii) so far as practicable keep clear of a traffic separation line or separation zone;
(iii) normally join or leave a traffic lane at the termination of the lane, but when joining or leaving from either sizde shall do so at as small an angle to the general direction of traffic flow as practicable.

(c) A vessel shall so far as practicable avoid crossing traffic lanes, but if obliged to do so shall cross on a heading as nearly as practicable at right angles to the general direction of traffic flow.

(d) (i) A vessel shall not use an inshore traffic zone when she can safely use the appropriate traffic lane within the adjacent traffic separation scheme. However, vessels of less than 20 metres in length, sailing vessels and vessels engaged in fishing may use the inshore traffic zone.
(ii) Notwithstanding sub-paragraph (d)(i) a vessel may use an inshore traffic zone when en route to or from a port, offshore installation or structure, pilot station or any other place situated within the traffic zone, or to avoid immediate danger.

(e) A vessel other than a crossing vessel or a vessel joining or leaving a lane shall not normally enter a separation zone or cross a separation line except:
(i) in cases of emergency to avoid immediate danger;
(ii) to engage in fishing within a separation zone.

(f) A vessel navigating in areas near the terminations of traffic separation schemes shall do so with particular caution.

(g) A vessel shall so far as practicable avoid anchoring in a traffic separation scheme or in areas near its terminations.

(h) A vessel not using a traffic separation scheme shall avoid it by as wide a margin as is practicable.

(i) A vessel engaged in fishing shall not impede the passage of any vessel following a traffic lane.

(j) A vessel of less than 20 metres in length or a sailing vessel shall not impede the safe passage of a power-driven vessel following a traffic lane.

(k) A vessel restricted in her ability to manoeuvre when engaged in an operation for the maintenance of safety of navigation in a traffic separation scheme is exempted from complying with this Rule to the extent necessary to carry out the operation.

(l) A vessel restricted in her ability to manoeuvre when engaged in an operation for the laying, servicing or picking up of a submarine cable, within a traffic separation scheme, is exempted from complying with this Rule to the extent necessary to carry out the operation.

Fig. 8 (22) Traffic Separation Schemes (TSS) and Routeing Measures

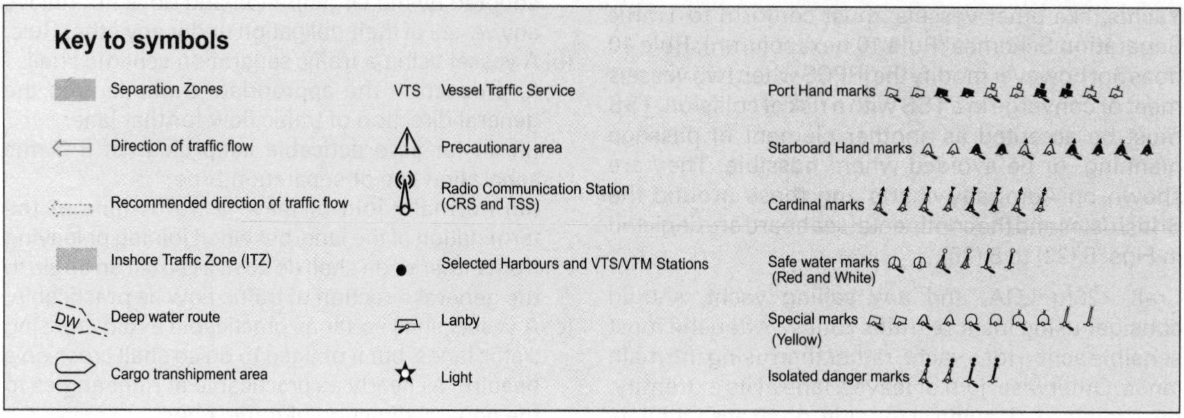
Key to symbols
Separation Zones
Direction of traffic flow
Recommended direction of traffic flow
Inshore Traffic Zone (ITZ)
DW
Deep water route
Cargo transhipment area
VTS
Vessel Traffic Service
Precautionary area
Radio Communication Station (CRS and TSS)
Selected Harbours and VTS/VTM Stations
Lanby
Light
Port Hand marks
Starboard Hand marks
Cardinal marks
Safe water marks (Red and White)
Special marks (Yellow)
Isolated danger marks

Fig. 8 (23) OFF SMALLS TSS

The TSS is located at approximately 51°46'N 05°52'W. The separation zone is 2M wide and the N- and S-bound traffic lanes are 3M wide and orientated 016°-196°.

Yachts are advised to listen out on Ch 16 when crossing the TSS.

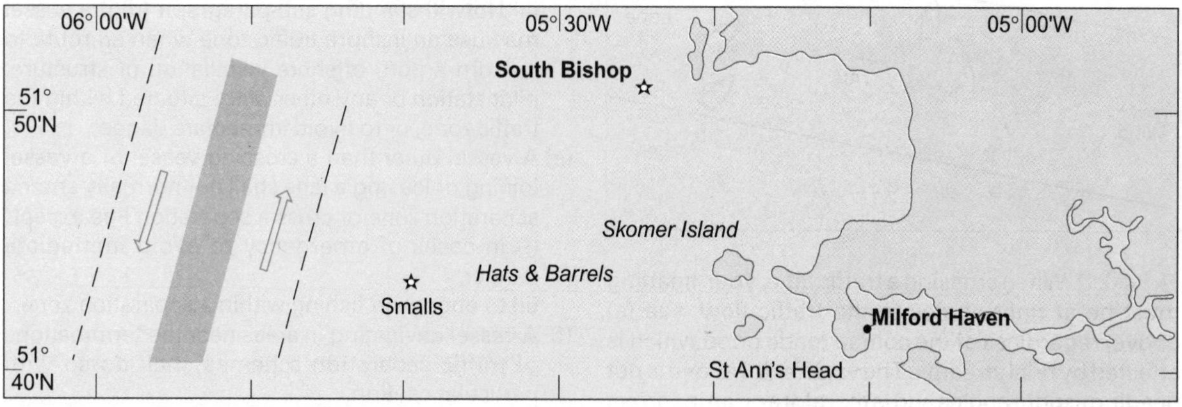
06° 00'W
05° 30'W
05° 00'W
51° 50'N
51° 40'N
South Bishop
Skomer Island
Hats & Barrels
Smalls
Milford Haven
St Ann's Head

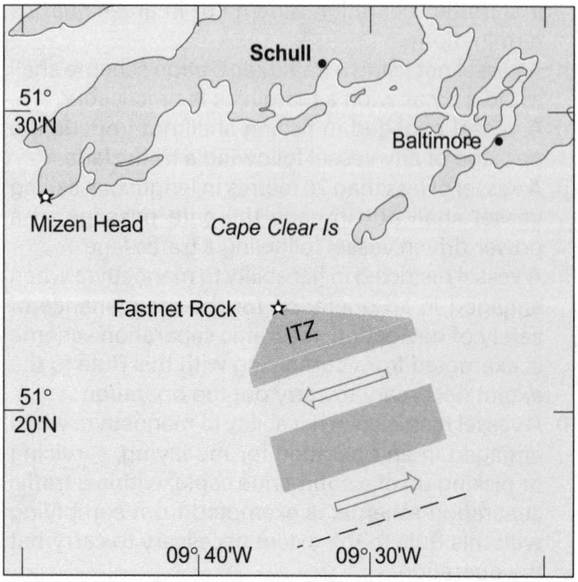
Schull
51° 30'N
Baltimore
Mizen Head
Cape Clear Is
Fastnet Rock
ITZ
51° 20'N
09° 40'W
09° 30'W

Fig. 8 (24) FASTNET ROCK TSS

The TSS is located at approximately 51°19'N 09°31'W. The separation zone and the E- and W-bound traffic lanes are all 2M wide and orientated 073°-253°. The ITZ extends between Fastnet Rock and the North boundary of the TSS which is about 2M SE of the Fastnet Rk and approx 3·5M from Cape Clear.

Yachts are advised to listen out on Ch 16 when crossing the TSS or when navigating in the ITZ.

Fig. 8 (25) OFF SKERRIES TSS

The TSS is centred upon the following positions: 53°22·8'N 04°52·0'W, 53°31'·3N 04°41'·7W and 53°32'·1N 04°31'·6W. The separation zone and the N and S-bound traffic lanes are all 2M wide and orientated 263°-083° and 216°-036°.

The passage outside the Skerries is preferable to the inside passage, except in strong offshore winds. The inside passage should not be used at night. When passing outside the Skerries allow a distance off of at least 1M to avoid the worst of the strong tidal stream.

Yachts are advised to listen out on Ch 16 when crossing the TSS.

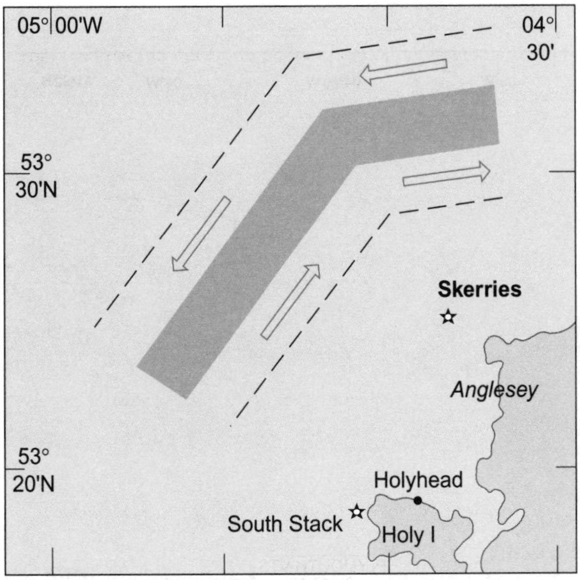

Fig. 8 (26) TUSKAR ROCK TSS

The TSS is centred upon the following positions: 52°14'·0N 06°00'·8W, 52°08'·5N 06°03'·8W and 52°04'·7N 06°11'·5W. The separation zone is 2M wide, and the the N- and S-bound traffic lanes each side of the separation zone are 3M wide and orientated 199°/011° and 232°/052°. The designated ITZ extends between Tuskar Rock and the landward boundary of the TSS.

Yachts are advised to listen out on Ch 16 when crossing the TSS or when navigating in the ITZ.

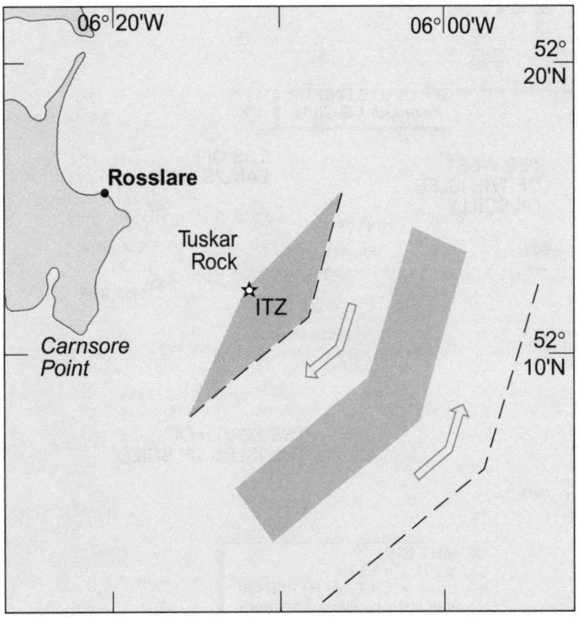

Fig. 8 (27) NORTH CHANNEL TSS

The TSS is centred on the following positions: 55°15'·3N 05°55'·4W, 55°22'·8'N 06°04·6W and 55°24'·0N 06°15'·0W. The lanes, and separation zone are all 2M wide, and the ITZ about 2·5M. The traffic lanes are orientated 325°/145° and 282°/102°. The NW-bound lane is only 2M from the Mull of Kintyre and its race. A strong tidal race, with overfalls, may be encountered S and SW of Mull of Kintyre. Similarly, the SE-bound lane is only 2M north of Rathlin Island where tidal streams are strong on both sides of the island.

Yachts are advised to listen out on Ch 16 when crossing the TSS.

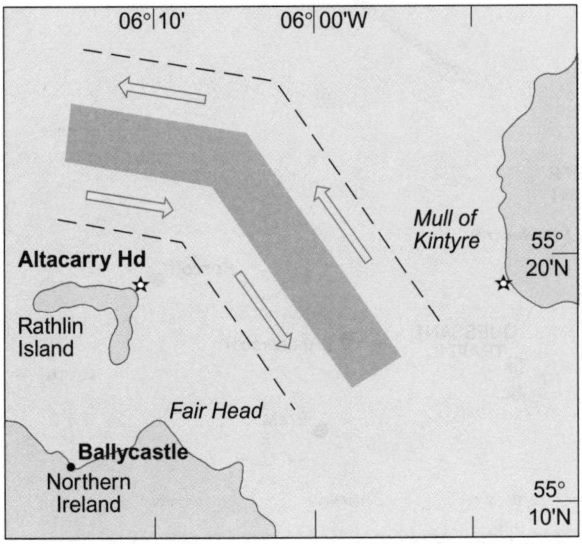

C8

Fig. 8 (28) TSS Western Approaches

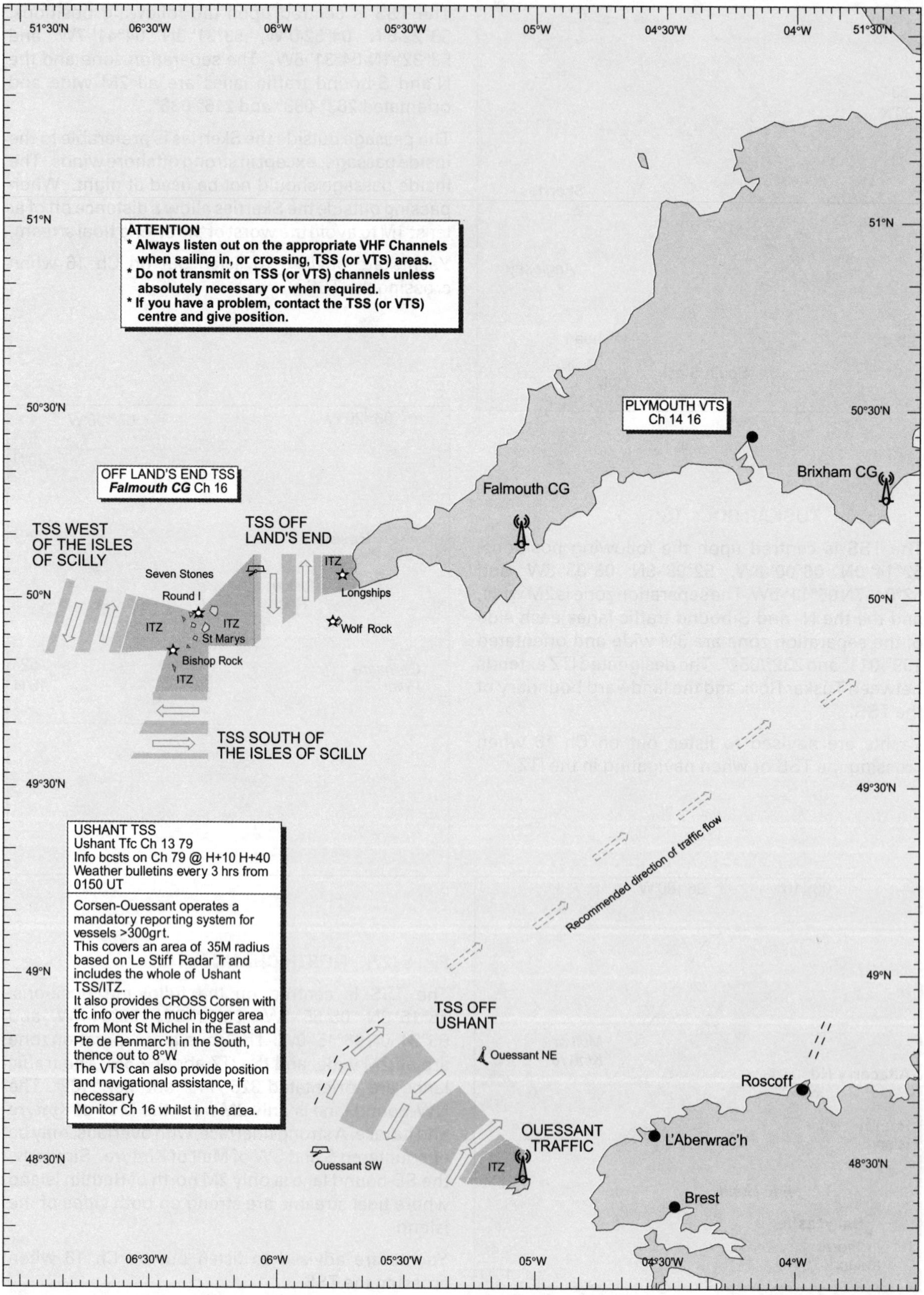
51°30'N
06°30'W
06°W
05°30'W
05°W
04°30'W
04°W
51°30'N
51°N
ATTENTION
* Always listen out on the appropriate VHF Channels when sailing in, or crossing, TSS (or VTS) areas.
* Do not transmit on TSS (or VTS) channels unless absolutely necessary or when required.
* If you have a problem, contact the TSS (or VTS) centre and give position.
51°N
50°30'N
PLYMOUTH VTS
Ch 14 16
50°30'N
OFF LAND'S END TSS
Falmouth CG Ch 16
Brixham CG
Falmouth CG
TSS WEST
OF THE ISLES
OF SCILLY
TSS OFF
LAND'S END
ITZ
Seven Stones
Longships
50°N
Round I
ITZ
ITZ
St Marys
Wolf Rock
50°N
Bishop Rock
ITZ
TSS SOUTH OF
THE ISLES OF SCILLY
49°30'N
49°30'N
USHANT TSS
Ushant Tfc Ch 13 79
Info bcsts on Ch 79 @ H+10 H+40
Weather bulletins every 3 hrs from
0150 UT
Recommended direction of traffic flow
Corsen-Ouessant operates a
mandatory reporting system for
vessels >300grt.
This covers an area of 35M radius
based on Le Stiff Radar Tr and
includes the whole of Ushant
TSS/ITZ.
It also provides CROSS Corsen with
tfc info over the much bigger area
from Mont St Michel in the East and
Pte de Penmarc'h in the South,
thence out to 8°W
The VTS can also provide position
and navigational assistance, if
necessary
Monitor Ch 16 whilst in the area.
49°N
49°N
TSS OFF
USHANT
Ouessant NE
Roscoff
OUESSANT
TRAFFIC
L'Aberwrac'h
48°30'N
Ouessant SW
ITZ
48°30'N
Brest
06°30'W
06°W
05°30'W
05°W
04°30'W
04°W

Fig. 8 (29) Off Casquets TSS

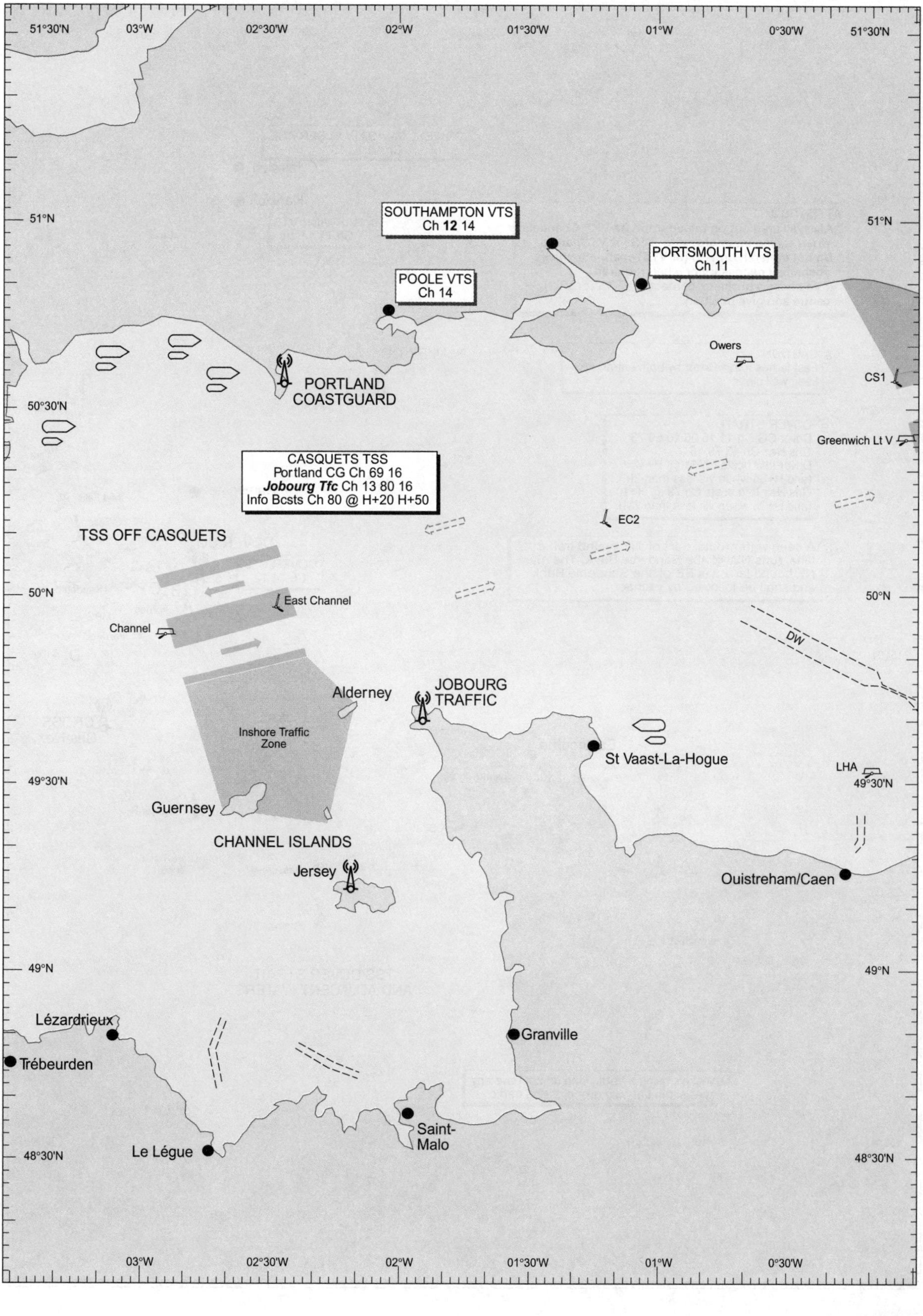

Fig. 8 (30) Dover Strait TSS

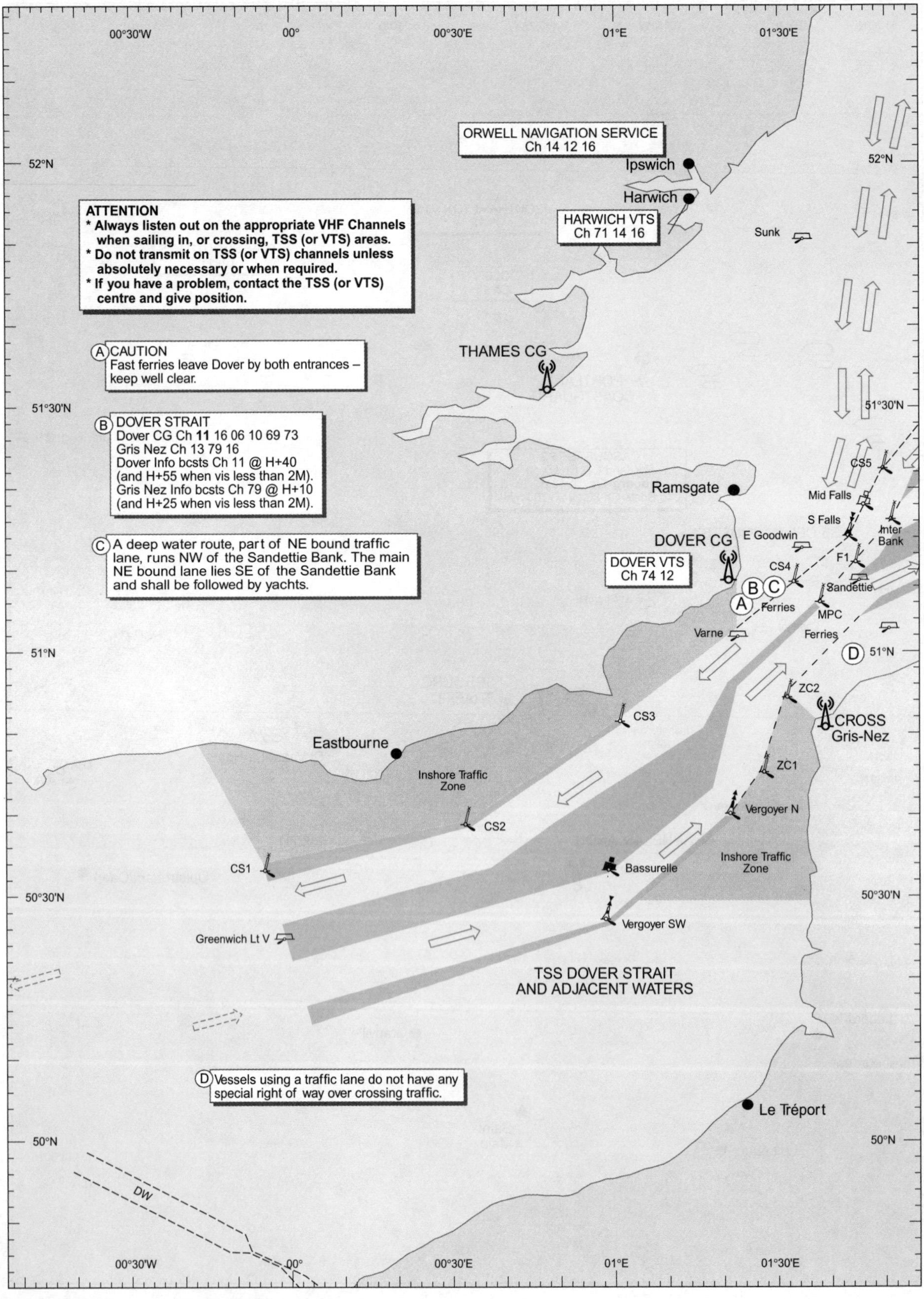
00°30'W
00°
00°30'E
01°E
01°30'E
52°N
51°30'N
51°N
50°30'N
50°N
ORWELL NAVIGATION SERVICE
Ch 14 12 16
Ipswich
Harwich
HARWICH VTS
Ch 71 14 16
Sunk
ATTENTION
* Always listen out on the appropriate VHF Channels when sailing in, or crossing, TSS (or VTS) areas.
* Do not transmit on TSS (or VTS) channels unless absolutely necessary or when required.
* If you have a problem, contact the TSS (or VTS) centre and give position.
A CAUTION
Fast ferries leave Dover by both entrances – keep well clear.
THAMES CG
B DOVER STRAIT
Dover CG Ch 11 16 06 10 69 73
Gris Nez Ch 13 79 16
Dover Info bcsts Ch 11 @ H+40
(and H+55 when vis less than 2M).
Gris Nez Info bcsts Ch 79 @ H+10
(and H+25 when vis less than 2M).
C A deep water route, part of NE bound traffic lane, runs NW of the Sandettie Bank. The main NE bound lane lies SE of the Sandettie Bank and shall be followed by yachts.
Ramsgate
DOVER CG
DOVER VTS
Ch 74 12
E Goodwin
CS5
Mid Falls
S Falls
Inter Bank
F1
CS4
Sandettie
B C
A
Ferries
MPC
Varne
Ferries
D
ZC2
CS3
CROSS
Gris-Nez
Eastbourne
ZC1
Inshore Traffic Zone
Vergoyer N
CS2
CS1
Bassurelle
Inshore Traffic Zone
Vergoyer SW
Greenwich Lt V
TSS DOVER STRAIT
AND ADJACENT WATERS
D Vessels using a traffic lane do not have any special right of way over crossing traffic.
Le Tréport
DW

Fig. 8 (31) Southern North Sea TSS

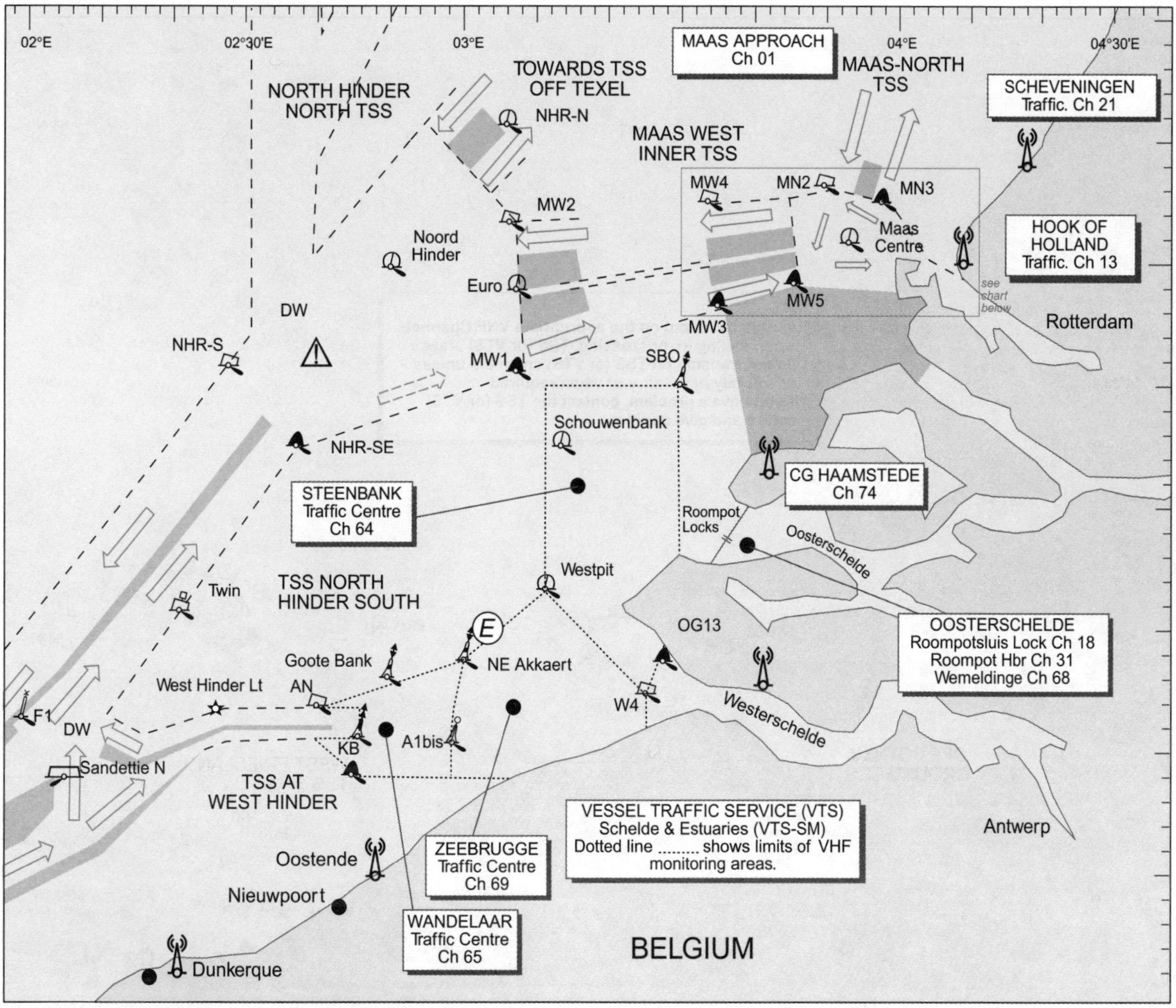

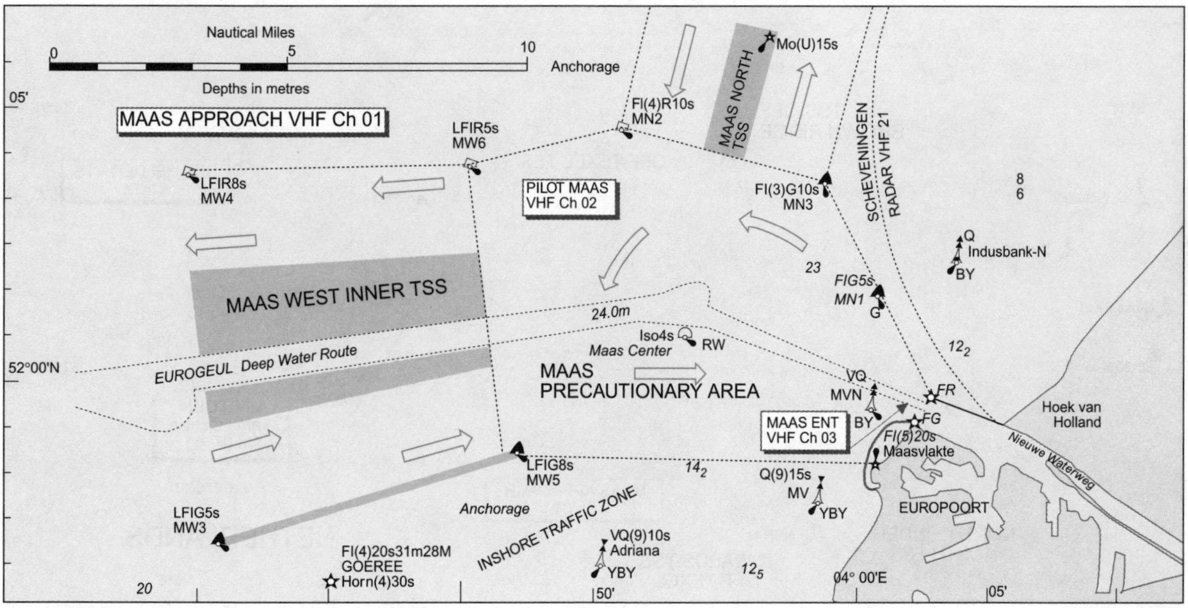

C8

Fig. 8 (32) Netherlands TSS

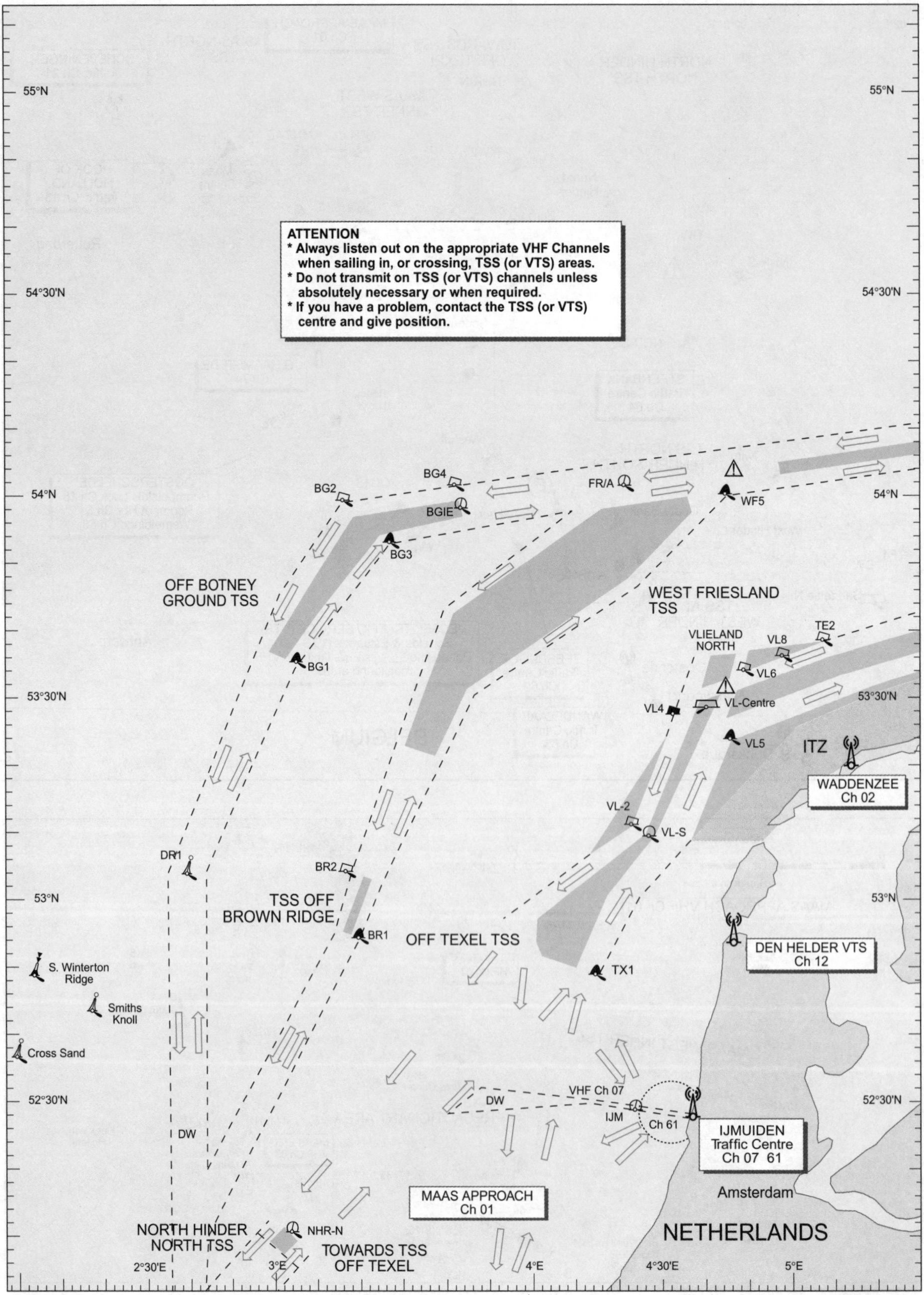
55°N
54°30'N
54°N
53°30'N
53°N
52°30'N
2°30'E
3°E
4°E
4°30'E
5°E
ATTENTION
* Always listen out on the appropriate VHF Channels when sailing in, or crossing, TSS (or VTS) areas.
* Do not transmit on TSS (or VTS) channels unless absolutely necessary or when required.
* If you have a problem, contact the TSS (or VTS) centre and give position.
BG4
BG2
BGIE
BG3
BG1
FR/A
WF5
OFF BOTNEY GROUND TSS
WEST FRIESLAND TSS
VLIELAND NORTH
VL8
TE2
VL6
VL-Centre
VL4
VL5
ITZ
WADDENZEE Ch 02
VL-2
VL-S
DR1
BR2
TSS OFF BROWN RIDGE
BR1
OFF TEXEL TSS
TX1
DEN HELDER VTS Ch 12
S. Winterton Ridge
Smiths Knoll
Cross Sand
VHF Ch 07
DW
IJM
Ch 61
IJMUIDEN Traffic Centre Ch 07 61
Amsterdam
MAAS APPROACH Ch 01
NORTH HINDER NORTH TSS
NHR-N
TOWARDS TSS OFF TEXEL
NETHERLANDS

Fig. 8 (33) German TSS

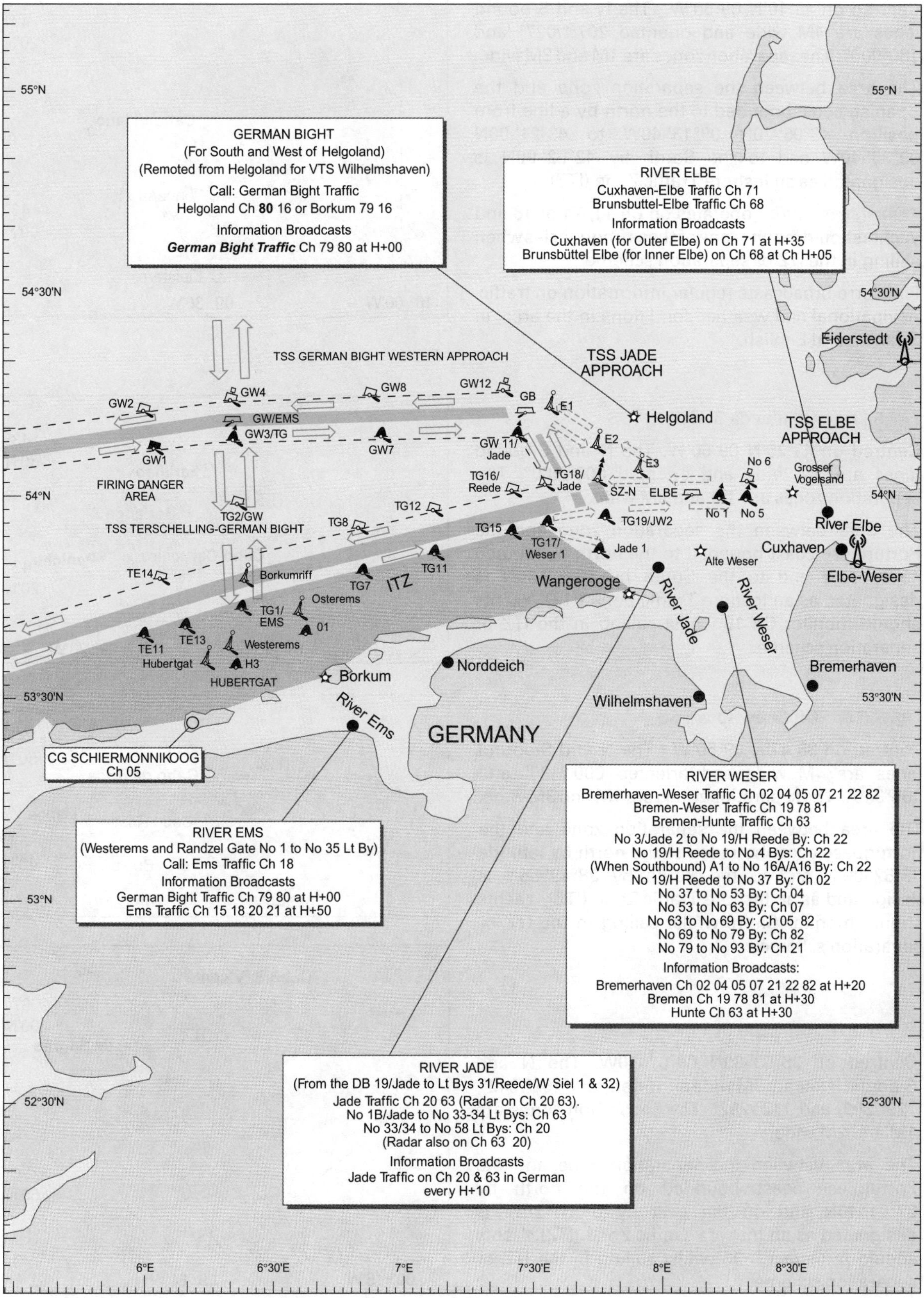

Fig. 8 (34) Off Finisterre TSS

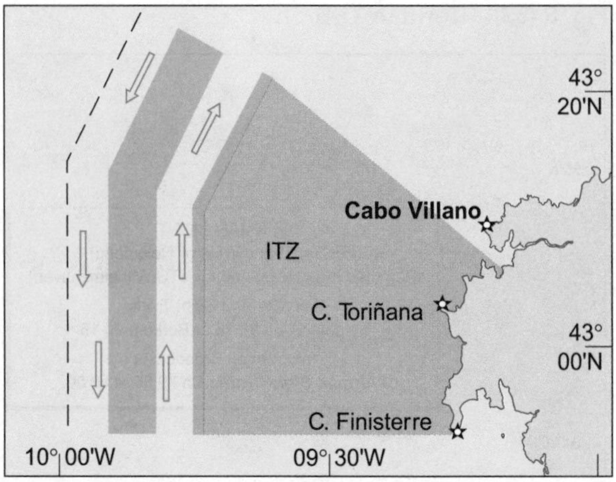

Centred on 43°10'N 09°50'W. The N and S-bound lanes are 4M wide and oriented 207°°/027° and 180°000°. The separation zones are 1M and 3M wide.

The area between the separation zone and the Spanish coast bounded to the north by a line from position 43°06'·70N 09°13'·40W to 43°21'·00N 09°36'·40W and to the South by 42°52'·90N is designated as an Inshore Traffic Zone (ITZ).

"Finisterre Traffic" operates on Ch 11, 74 or 16 and yachts should monitor one of these frequencies when sailing in the ITZ or separation scheme.

Finisterre broadcasts regular information on traffic, navigational and weather conditions in the area, in Spanish and English.

Fig. 8 (35) Off Ilha da Berlenga TSS

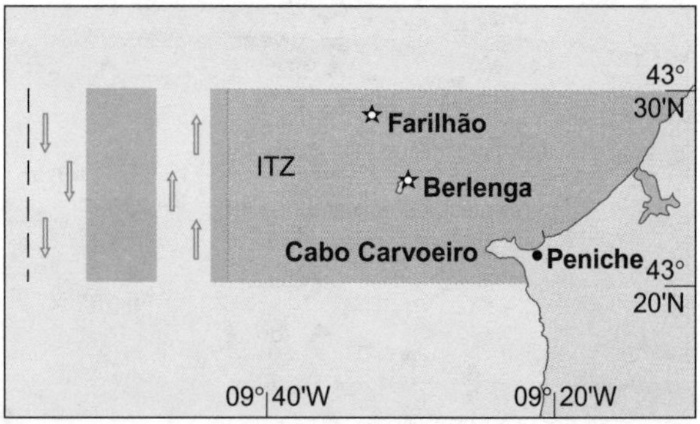

Centred on 43°25'N 09°50'W. The N and S-bound lanes are 3M wide and oriented 000°/180°. The separation zones are 1M and 3M wide.

The area between the separation zone and the Portuguese coast bounded to the north by latitude 43°30'·00'N and to the South by 43°20'·00N is designated as an Inshore Traffic Zone (ITZ). Yachts should monitor Ch 16 whilst sailing in the ITZ or separation scheme.

Fig. 8 (36) Off Cape Roca TSS

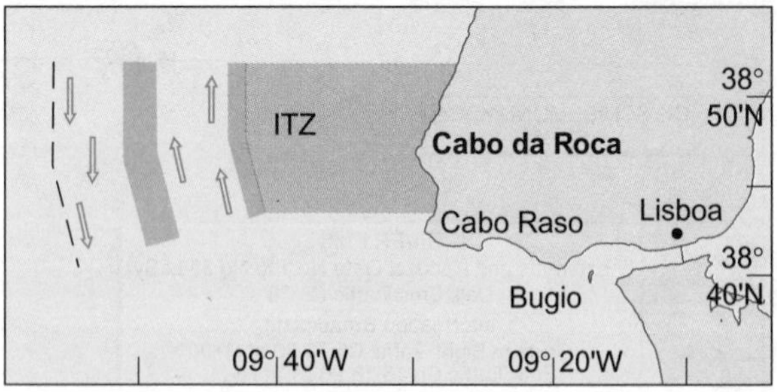

Centred on 38°47'N 09°50'W. The N and S-bound lanes are 4M wide and oriented 000°/180° and 165°345°. The separation zones are 1M and 3M wide.

The area between the separation zone and the Portuguese coast bounded to the north by latitude 38°52'·00'N and to the South by 38°43'·55N is designated as an Inshore Traffic Zone (ITZ). Yachts should monitor Ch 16 whilst sailing in the ITZ or separation scheme.

Fig. 8 (37) Off Cape St Vincent TSS

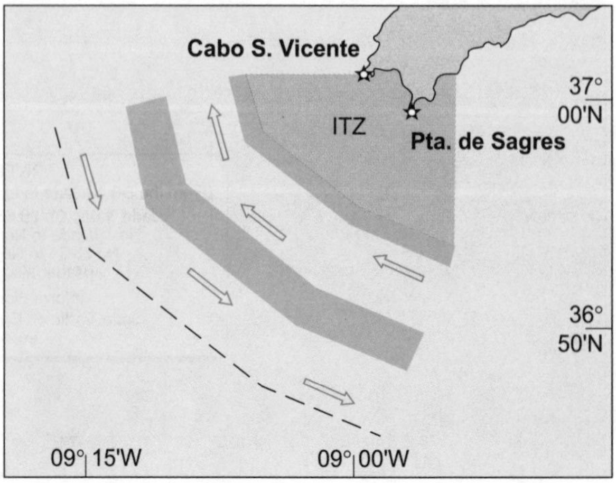

Centred on 36°53'·80N 09°07'·10W. The N and S bound lanes are 3M wide and orientated 162°/342°, 129°/309, and 112°/292°. The separation zones are 1M and 2M wide.

The area between the separation zone and the Portuguese coast bounded on the north by 37°01'·40N and on the east by 08°54'·20W is designated as an Inshore Traffic Zone (ITZ).Yachts should monitor Ch 16 whilst sailing in the ITZ or separation scheme.

Fig. 8(38) Straits of Gibraltar TSS

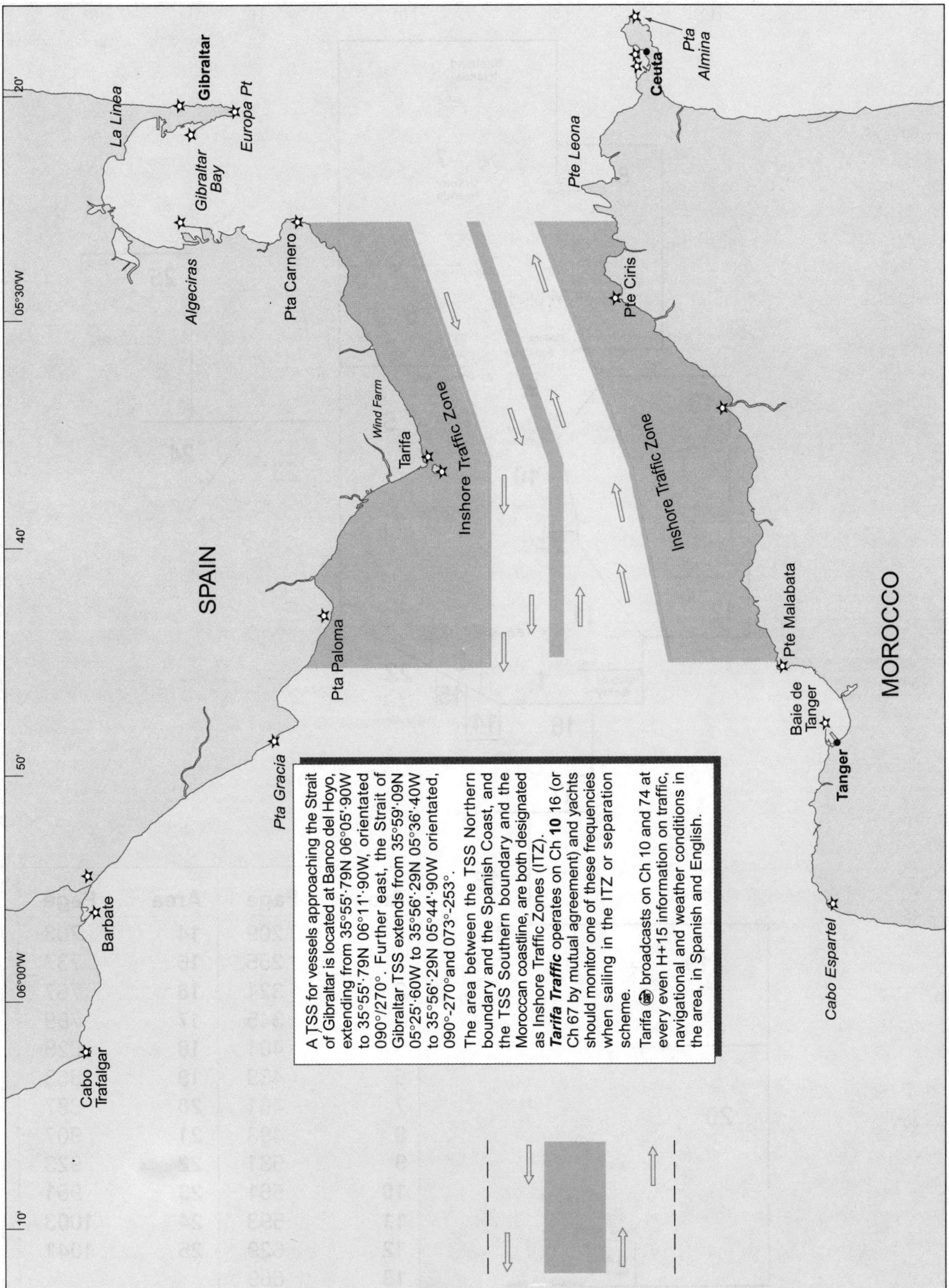
SPAIN
MOROCCO
Cabo Trafalgar
Barbate
Pta Gracia
Pta Paloma
Tarifa
Wind Farm
Inshore Traffic Zone
Pta Carnero
Algeciras
Gibraltar Bay
La Linea
Gibraltar
Europa Pt
Cabo Espartel
Tanger
Baie de Tanger
Pte Malabata
Inshore Traffic Zone
Pte Ciris
Pte Leona
Ceuta
Pta Almina
10'
06°00'W
50'
40'
05°30'W
20'
10'
05'
36° 00'N
55'
50'
45'
A TSS for vessels approaching the Strait of Gibraltar is located at Banco del Hoyo, extending from 35°55'·79N 06°05'·90W to 35°55'·79N 06°11'·90W, orientated 090°/270°. Further east, the Strait of Gibraltar TSS extends from 35°59'·09N 05°25'·60W to 35°56'·29N 05°36'·40W to 35°56'·29N 05°44'·90W orientated, 090°-270°and 073°-253°.
The area between the TSS Northern boundary and the Spanish Coast, and the TSS Southern boundary and the Moroccan coastline, are both designated as Inshore Traffic Zones (ITZ).
Tarifa Traffic operates on Ch 10 16 (or Ch 67 by mutual agreement) and yachts should monitor one of these frequencies when sailing in the ITZ or separation scheme.
Tarifa broadcasts on Ch 10 and 74 at every even H+15 information on traffic, navigational and weather conditions in the area, in Spanish and English.

C8

9.0.1 MAP OF AREAS

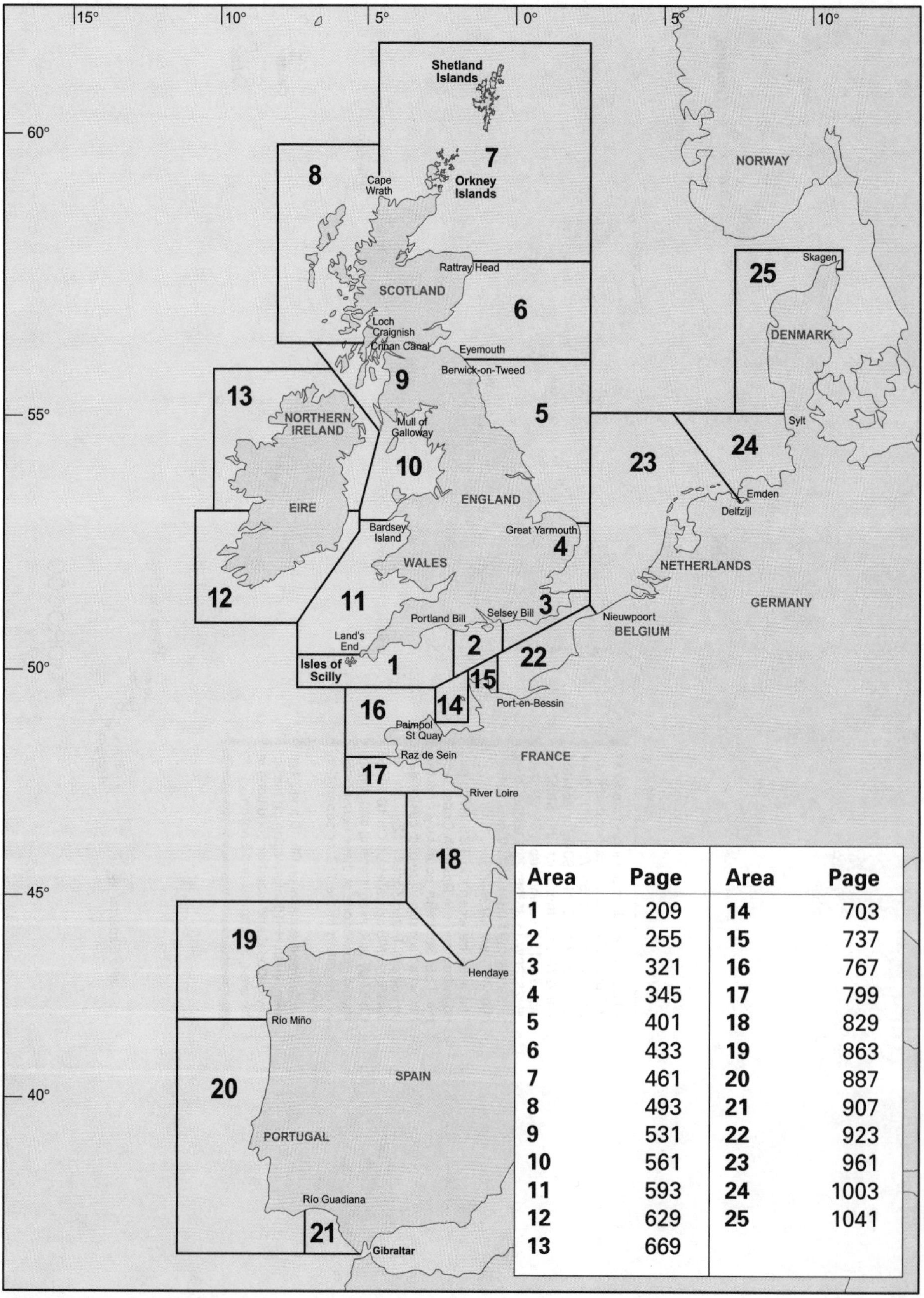

Area	Page	Area	Page
1	209	14	703
2	255	15	737
3	321	16	767
4	345	17	799
5	401	18	829
6	433	19	863
7	461	20	887
8	493	21	907
9	531	22	923
10	561	23	961
11	593	24	1003
12	629	25	1041
13	669		

Chapter 9

Harbours, Coasts and Tides

Contents

9.0 **INTRODUCTION** .... **Page 193**
9.0.1 Map of areas 192
9.0.2 General information 195
9.0.3 Harbour information 195
9.0.4 International Port Traffic Signals 198
9.0.5 Ferry services 199
9.0.6 Distance Tables: Across Channel 200
9.0.7 Across Irish Sea 201
9.0.8 Across North Sea 202
PLATE 1 Navigation Lights 203
PLATE 2 Principal Navigation Lights & Shape 204
PLATE 3 IALA 205
PLATE 4 BuoyageAdmiralty Symbols 206
PLATE 5 International Code Flags 207
PLATE 6 National Ensigns 208
9.1 AREA 1 209
SW England. Isles of Scilly to Portland Bill
9.2 AREA 2 255
Central S England. Portland Bill to Selsey Bill
9.3 AREA 3 321
SE England. Selsey Bill to North Foreland
9.4 AREA 4 345
E England. North Foreland to Winterton
9.5 AREA 5 401
NE England. Winterton to Berwick-upon-Tweed
9.6 AREA 6 433
SE Scotland. Eyemouth to Rattray Head
9.7 AREA 7 461
NE Scotland. Rattray Head to Cape Wrath including Orkney and Shetland Islands
9.8 AREA 8 493
NW Scotland. Cape Wrath to Crinan Canal
9.9 AREA 9 531
SW Scotland. Crinan Canal to Mull of Galloway
9.10 AREA 10 561
NW England, Isle of Man and N Wales. Mull of Galloway to Bardsey Island
9.11 AREA 11 593
S Wales and Bristol Channel. Bardsey Island to Land's End
9.12 AREA 12 629
S Ireland. Malahide clockwise to Liscanor Bay
9.13 AREA 13 669
N Ireland. Lambay Island anti-clockwise to Liscanor Bay
9.14 AREA 14 703
Channel Islands. Alderney to Jersey
Figs 9 (1)-(8) Marina maps and contact data in the UK & Ireland 729
9.15 AREA 15 737
Central N France. Cherbourg to St Quay-Portrieux
9.16 AREA 16 767
N Brittany. Paimpol to Raz de Sein
9.17 AREA 17 799
S Brittany. Raz de Sein to River Loire
9.18 AREA 18 829
S Biscay. River Loire to Spanish Border
Fig 9 (9) Marina map and contact data in France 862
9.19 **AREA 19** **863**
N and NW Spain. Pasajes to Bayona
9.20 AREA 20 887
Portugal.
9.21 AREA 21 907
SW Spain. Ayamonte to Gibraltar
Fig 9 (10) Marina map and contact data in Spain, Portugal & Gibraltar 922
9.22 AREA 22 923
NE France. Barfleur to Dunkerque
9.23 AREA 23 961
Belgium and the Netherlands. Nieuwpoort to Delfzijl
Fig 9 (11) Marina map and contact data in Belgium, Netherlands & Germany 1002
9.24 AREA 24 1003
Germany. Emden to Danish Border
9.25 AREA 25 1041
Denmark. Rømø to Skagen

9.0.2 GENERAL INFORMATION

Harbour, coastal and tidal information is given for each of the 25 Areas shown on the map at 9.0.1, with detailed text and chartlets of 428 harbours and notes on 465 lesser harbours and anchorages. The information provided enables a skipper to assess whether he can get into a harbour (tidal height, depth, wind direction etc), and whether he wants to enter the harbour (shelter, facilities available, early closing days etc). Abbreviations and symbols are in Introduction pp 3-7. Language glossaries are on pp 8-15.

Each Area is arranged as follows:

Index of the harbours covered in that area.

A diagram of the area showing the positions and characteristics of the harbours covered, principal lights, coast, coastguard, port and marina radio, weather information and CG Centres with their boundaries.

Tidal stream chartlets for the area, based on Admiralty tidal stream atlases (by kind permission of the Hydrographer of the Navy and the Controller, HM Stationery Office), showing the rates and directions of tidal streams for each hour referenced to HW Dover and to HW at the relevant Standard Port. For how to use tidal stream charts see 7.7.2.

A list of principal coastal lights, fog signals and useful waypoints in the area. More powerful lights (range 15M or more) are in **bold** type ☆; light-vessels and Lanbys are in *CAPITAL ITALICS*; fog signals are in *italics*. Latitude and longitude are shown for a selection of lights and marks, some of which are underlined as useful waypoints. Unless otherwise stated, lights are white. Elevations are in metres (m) above MHWS, and nominal ranges in nautical miles (M). Where appropriate, a brief description is given of the lighthouse or tower. Arcs of visibility, sector limits, and alignment of leading lights etc are true bearings as seen from seaward measured in a clockwise direction. Where a longitude is given (e.g. 04°12'·05W) W stands for West; W can also mean white. To avoid ambiguity, the words white or West may be written in full, except for longitude.

Passage information briefly calls attention in note form to some of the principal features of the coast, recommended routes, offlying dangers, tide races, better anchorages etc.

Table of distances in nautical miles by the most direct route, avoiding dangers, between selected places in that area and in adjacent areas. See also Tables of distances across the English Channel, Irish and North Seas in this Introduction.

Special notes in certain Areas give information specific to that country or Area.

9.0.3 HARBOUR INFORMATION

a. Below the **harbour name**, the County or Unitary Council (or equivalent abroad) is given, followed by the lat/long of the hbr entrance, or equivalent. This lat/long may be used as a final waypoint after the approach WPT ⊕ given under Navigation. NB: A published waypoint should never be used without first plotting its position on the chart.

b. A **harbour rating** is given after the lat/long. It grades a port for ease of access, facilities available and its attractiveness as a place. Although inevitably subjective, it offers a useful shorthand as to what a yachtsman may expect to find. The rating, shown below the port name as 3 symbols is based on the following criteria:

Ease of access (❁):

❁❁❁ This port can be entered in *gales from most directions and at all states of tide, by day or night.*

❁❁ Accessible in *strong winds* from most quarters; *possible tidal or pilotage constraints.*

❁ Only accessible in *calm, settled* conditions by day with *no swell; there may be a bar and difficult pilotage.*

Facilities available (♨):

♨♨♨ *Most facilities* for yacht and crew.

♨♨ *All domestic facilities,* but probably only a boatyard.

♨ *Usual domestic needs*; possibly some basic marine facilities.

Attractiveness (✿):

✿✿✿ An attractive place; visit, if necessary *going a little out of your way* to do so.

✿✿ Normal for this part of the coast; *if convenient* visit the port concerned.

✿ Visit only if alternatives are unavailable. *Expect to be disappointed* and subject to inconvenience.

This rating system, modified for harbours in this Almanac, was originated by the late Robin Brandon and used in successive editions of his *South Biscay Pilot,* published by Adlard Coles Nautical, to whom grateful ackowledgement is made.

c. **Chart numbers** for Admiralty (AC), Imray Laurie Norie & Wilson (Imray), Stanfords or foreign charts are listed, largest scale first. The *numbers* of Admiralty Small Craft editions and folios are shown in *italics*. The Ordnance Survey (OS. 1:50,000) Map numbers are given for UK and Eire.

d. **Chartlets** are based on British Admiralty, French, Dutch, German, Danish, Spanish and Portuguese charts (as acknowledged in the Introduction).

It is emphasised that these chartlets are not designed or intended for pilotage or navigation, although every effort has been made to ensure that they accurately portray the harbour concerned. The publishers and editors disclaim any responsibility for resultant accidents or damage if they are so used. The largest scale official chart, properly corrected, should always be used.

Due to limitations of scale, chartlets do not always cover the whole area referred to in the text nor do they always contain the approach waypoint ⊕. Not every depth, mark or feature can be shown. Depths and drying heights are shown in metres below/above Chart Datum; elevations (m) are above MHWS. Drying areas and the 5m depth contour are shown as follows.

Dries

<5m

>5m

e. **Tidal predictions** are all provided by the UK Hydrographic Office, with permissions from the French, Dutch, German, Danish and Portuguese Hydrographic Offices.

For each Standard Port daily predictions of times and heights of HW/LW are given. Zone times are given, but no account is taken of BST or other daylight saving times (DST). In UK, Eire and Portugal times are in UT.

At the foot of each page of tidal predictions is given the height difference between Chart Datum at the port in question and Ordnance Datum (Newlyn), for UK ports. For foreign ports the height difference is referenced to the relevant national land survey datum. This enables tidal levels along a stretch of coast to be referred to a common horizontal plane. Further notes are contained in the Admiralty Tide Tables where the height differences are also tabulated.

Time and height differences for Secondary Ports are referenced to the most suitable (not always the nearest) Standard Port. The average time difference between local HW and HW Dover is given, so that the UT (±15 minutes) of local HW can be quickly found. Times of HW Dover are in 9.3.14 and, for quick reference, on a bookmark which also lists Range together with a visual indication of the state of the tide (Springs or Neaps). Duration (quoted for most ports), if deducted from time of HW, gives the approx time of the previous LW.

Mean Level (ML) is also quoted. Given ML and the height of HW, the range and therefore height of LW can also be calculated; see also Chapter 7.

Tidal Coefficients for Brest are listed and explained under Brest and are applicable to all French ports on the Channel and Atlantic coasts. They indicate not only whether Springs or Neaps apply, but also quantify the size of a tide without resort to calculating range. They can be used to specify access hours to tidally-limited harbours.

f. **Tidal curves** are given for Standard Ports and those other ports for which full predictions are shown. Use the appropriate (np/sp) curve for tidal calculations (ie finding the height of tide at a given time, or the time for a given height). See Chapter 7 for tidal calculations.

HW–3 means 3 hrs before local HW; HW+2 means 2 hrs after. Secondary curves are given in 9.2.12 for ports between Swanage and Selsey Bill where special tidal conditions exist.

g. **Shelter** assesses the degree of shelter and advises on access, berths (for charges see under Facilities), moorings and anchorages. Access times, if quoted, are approx figures relative to mean HW. They are purely a guide for a nominal 1·5m draft, plus safety clearance, and take no account of hull form, springs/neaps, flood/ebb, swell or nature of the bottom. Their purpose is to alert a skipper to possible tidal problems. Times of lock and bridge openings etc are local (LT), unless otherwise stated.

h. **Navigation** gives the lat/long of a waypoint (⊕) suitable for starting the approach, with its bearing/distance from/to the hbr ent or next significant feature; some ⊕s may be off the harbour chartlet. **NB: A published waypoint should never be used without first plotting its position on the chart.** Approach chans, buoyage, speed limits and hazards are also described.

Wrecks around the UK which are of historic or archaeological interest are protected under the Protection of Wrecks Act 1973. About 40 sites, as detailed in Annual Notice to Mariners No 16 and depicted on the larger scale Admiralty charts, are listed in this almanac under the nearest harbour or in Passage Information. Unauthorised interference, including anchoring and diving on such sites, may lead to a substantial fine.

j. **Lights and Marks** includes as much detail as space permits; some data may also be shown on the chartlet and/or in Coastal lights, fog signals and waypoints for that Area. Traffic signals for individual harbours are shown in each area: French (9.15.7), Belgian, Dutch (9.23.7) and German (9.24.7). International Port Traffic Signals are shown in 9.0.4.

k. **Radio Telephone** quotes VHF Channels related to each port, marina or VTS. If not obvious, the callsign of a station is shown in *italics*. Frequencies are indicated by their International Maritime Services Channel (Ch) designator. UK Marina Channels are 80 (161·625MHz) and M (157·85MHz; also known as M1 and formerly as Ch 37). M2 (161·425MHz) is allocated to some YCs for race control. MF frequencies, if shown, are in kHz. Initial contact should be made on the listed working Ch, rather than on Ch 16.

Where known, preferred channels are shown in bold type, thus **14**. If there is a choice of calling channel, always indicate which channel you are using; eg, *'Dover Port Control, this is NONSUCH, NONSUCH on Channel 74, over'*. This avoids confusion if the station being called is working more than one channel.

Where local times are stated, the letters LT are added. H24 means continuous watch. Times of scheduled broadcasts are shown (for example) as H +20, ie 20 minutes past the hour.

l. **Telephone** is followed by the dialling code in brackets, which is not repeated for individual ☎ numbers. But it may be repeated or augmented under **Facilities** if different or additional codes also apply. Eg, Portsmouth and Gosport numbers are both on (023 92) as listed; but Fareham's different code (01329) is quoted separately.

In the UK the ☎s of the relevant Coastguard MRCC/MRSC are given under each port, but in an emergency dial 999 and ask for the Coastguard.

The procedures for international calls from/to the UK are given in the relevant sections which also give ☎s for marine emergencies abroad. All EU countries use ☎ 112 for emergency calls to Fire, Police, Ambulance, in addition to their national emergency ☎s.

m. **Facilities** available at the harbour, marinas and yacht clubs are listed first, followed by an abbreviated summary of those marine services provided commercially (for abbreviations see the Introduction and the bookmark). See also the Seafinder guide to marine services and supplies provided free with the Almanac for commercial listings. Note: Facilities at Yacht Clubs are usually available to crews who arrive by sea and belong to a recognised YC.

Town facilities are also listed, including Post Office (✉), Bank (Ⓑ), Railway Station (⇌), or airport (✈). Abroad, the nearest port with a UK ferry link is given (see also 9.0.5).

n. **The overnight cost of a visitors alongside berth** (AB) is shown per metre LOA in local currency usually as a guide only. The figure given is for high season (usually June to Sept), unavoidably at the previous year's rates. Where rates are quoted in LOA bands, averaging has been applied to produce a mean figure. Harbour dues, if applicable, and VAT are included; in the UK the cost of mains electricity is usually extra. The cost of pile moorings, 🅾s or ⚓ where these are the norm, may be given, if no AB is provided. Note: The cost of berthing does not influence the attractiveness of a port, as rated under 9.0.3b.

FACILITIES FOR DISABLED PEOPLE

RYA Sailability is an organisation operating in the UK under the auspices of the RYA to open up sailing and its related facilities to disabled sailors.

Facilities include car parking; ramps for wheel chair access to buildings and pontoons; purpose-built toilets and showers; and at Largs (Ayrshire) a special pontoon and sailing championships. Facilities for those with sight or hearing disabilities are not widely available. Symbols used in the text of Chapter 9 are self explanatory: ♿, 👁 and 🦻, 🦻.

ENVIRONMENTAL GUIDANCE

The following notes are adapted, by kind permission of the RYA, from an RYA leaflet *Tidelines*. This leaflet offers guidance, mainly directed at newcomers to sailing, on waste disposal and the protection of the natural environment. The following points are relevant:

a. In principle never ditch rubbish at sea.
b. Keep it onboard and dispose of it ashore in proper receptacles. These are available in all marinas; elsewhere, eg Helford River, the 🗑 symbol is used in this almanac to indicate waste bins are provided.
c. Readily degradable foodstuffs may be ditched at sea when more than 3M offshore (12M in the English Channel and North Sea).
d. Foodstuffs which are not readily degradable, eg skins and peelings, should not be ditched at sea.
e. Other rubbish, eg packaging of plastic, glass, metal, paper and cardboard; fabrics; ropelines and netting, should never be ditched at sea.
f. Do not discharge anything except 'washing-up' water into a marina, a popular ⚓ or moorings.
g. Oils and oily waste are particularly harmful to the water, fish and wildlife. Take old engine oil ashore in a well-sealed container or bottle. Do not pump oily bilge water overboard.
h. Avoid fuel spillage when topping up outboards.
j. Rowing ashore provides better exercise, less noise and no pollution compared with a 2-stroke outboard!
k. Sewage. If possible use shoreside toilets; and only use the onboard heads in tidal waters.
l. Consider fitting and using a holding tank. These are already compulsory in some countries. This almanac indicates where pump-out facilities (⛽) are known to exist. If there are none, do not pump out your tanks until you are at least 3M offshore.
m. Toxic waste, eg some antifoulings, cleaning chemicals, old batteries, should be disposed of ashore at a proper facility.
n. Wild birds, plants, fish and marine animals are usually abundant along coastlines. Respect protected sites; keep away from nesting sites and breeding colonies. Minimise noise, wash and disturbance.
o. Go ashore at recognised landing places. Do not anchor or dry out where important and vulnerable seabed species exist, eg soft corals, eel grass.

No	Lights	Main message
1	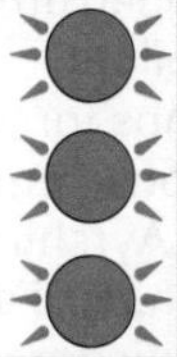 Flashing	Serious emergency – all vessels to stop or divert according to instructions
2	 Fixed or Slow Occulting	Vessels shall not proceed (*Note:* Some ports may use an exemption signal, as in 2a below)
3	 Fixed or Slow Occulting	Vessels may proceed. One-way traffic
4	 Fixed or Slow Occulting	Vessels may proceed. Two-way traffic
5	 Fixed or Slow Occulting	A vessel may proceed only when she has received specific orders to do so. (*Note:* Some ports may use an exemption signal, as in 5a below)
		Exemption signals and messages
2a	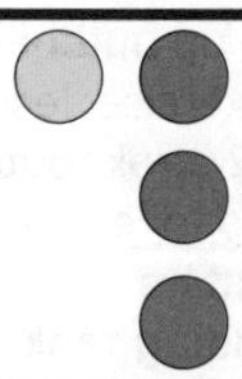 Fixed or Slow Occulting	Vessels shall not proceed, except that vessels which navigate outside the main channel need not comply with the main message
5a	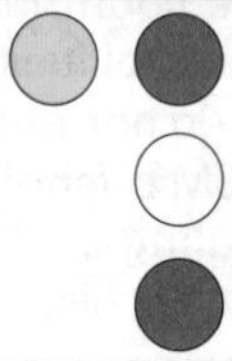 Fixed or Slow Occulting	A vessel may proceed when she has received specific orders to do so, except that vessels which navigate outside the main channel need not comply with the main message
		Auxiliary signals and messages
	White and/or yellow lights, displayed to the right of the main lights	Local meanings, as promulgated in local port orders

9.0.4 INTERNATIONAL PORT TRAFFIC SIGNALS

The international system is gradually being introduced, but its general adoption is likely to take many years.

(a) The main movement message given by a port traffic signal always comprises three lights, disposed vertically. No additional light shall be added to the column carrying the main message. (The fact that the main message always consists of three vertical lights allows the mariner to recognise it as a traffic signal, and not lights of navigational significance.) The signals may also be used to control traffic at locks and bridges.

(b) Red lights indicate 'Do not proceed'.

(c) Green lights indicate 'Proceed, subject to the conditions stipulated'. Note that, to avoid confusion, red and green lights are never displayed together.

(d) Some signals may be omni-directional – i.e. exhibited to all vessels simultaneously: others must be directional, and be shown either to vessels entering or to vessels leaving harbour.

(e) The 'Serious Emergency' signal must be flashing, at least 60 flashes per minute. All other signals must be either fixed or slow occulting (the latter useful when background glare is a problem). A mixture of fixed and occulting lights must not be used.

(f) Signal No 5 is based on the assumption that another means of communication such as VHF radio, signal lamp, loud-hailer, or auxiliary signal will be used to inform a vessel that she may specifically proceed.

(g) A single yellow light, displayed to the left of the column carrying main messages Nos 2 or 5, at the level of the upper light, may be used to indicate that 'Vessels which can safely navigate outside the main channel need not comply with the main message'. This signal, as shown at Nos 2a and 5a, is of obvious significance to yachtsmen.

(h) Signals which are auxiliary to the main message may be devised by local authorities. Such auxiliary signals should employ only white and/or yellow lights, and should be displayed to the right of the column carrying the main message. Ports with complex entrances and much traffic may need many auxiliary signals, which will have to be documented. Smaller harbours with less traffic may only need one or two of the basic signals, such as Nos 2 and 4.

9.0.5 FERRIES AROUND UK AND TO/FROM THE CONTINENT

This Table is a condensed version of many detailed schedules. It is intended to show broadly what is available and to help when cruise plans and/or crew movements are subject to change at short notice.

NOTES: 1. **Hours** = approx duration of day crossing. 2. **Frequency** = number of one-way sailings per day in summer. Specific day(s) of the week may be shown, if non-daily. 3. ☎ **Bookings** may be via a centralised number applicable to all routes.

From	To	Hours	Frequency	Company	☎ Bookings
A.	CROSS CHANNEL (France, Belgium; and to Spain)				
Plymouth (Mar-Nov)	Santander	24	M,W	Brittany Ferries	0870 5360360
Plymouth	Roscoff	6	1-3	Brittany Ferries	0870 5360360
Poole	Cherbourg	4¼	1-2	Brittany Ferries	0870 5360360
Poole	Cherbourg	4¼	1-2	Brittany Ferries (Truckline)	0870 5360360
Portsmouth	St Malo	8¾	1	Brittany Ferries	0870 5360360
Portsmouth	Ouistreham (Caen)	6	3	Brittany Ferries	0870 5360360
Portsmouth	Le Havre	5½	3	P&O European Ferries	0870 5980555
Portsmouth	Bilbao	35	S,Tu	P&O European Ferries	0870 5980555
Portsmouth	Cherbourg	5	3-4	P&O European Ferries	0870 5980555
Portsmouth	Cherbourg	2¾ (Cat)	2	P&O European Ferries	0870 5980555
Newhaven	Dieppe	2 (Cat)	3	Hoverspeed	0870 5240241
Dover	Calais	55 mins. (Cat)	14	Hoverspeed	0870 5240241
Dover	Calais	1½	15	Sea France	0870 5711711
Dover	Calais	1¼	35	P&O Stena Ferries	0870 5980980
Dover	Dunkerque	2	6	Norfolkline	01304 218410
Dover	Ostend	2 (Cat)	3-6	Hoverspeed	0870 5240241
B.	NORTH SEA				
Harwich	Hook of Holland	3¾ (HSS)	2	Stena Line	0870 5707070
Harwich	Hamburg	19	Alternate days.	DFDF Seaways	0870 5333000
Harwich	Esbjerg (Via Amsterdam)	22	4 wkly	DFDF Seaways	0870 5333000
Hull	Rotterdam	14	1	P&O N. Sea Ferries	0870 1296002
Hull	Zeebrugge	14	1	P&O N. Sea Ferries	0870 1296002
Newcastle	Ijmuiden	14	1	DFDF Seaways	0870 5333000
Newcastle	Gothenburg	26	F,M	DFDF Seaways	0870 5333000
Newcastle	Kristiensand	18	F,M	DFDF Seaways	0870 5333000
Newcastle	Stavanger/Bergen	19/26	M,W,S	Fjord Line	0191 296 1313
C.	SCOTLAND				
Aberdeen	Lerwick	14	M,W,T,F/M	P &O Scottish Ferries	01224 572615
Lerwick	Bergen	10-11	M	Smyril Line	00298 315900
Scrabster	Stromness	2	2-3	P&O Scottish Ferries	01856 850655
Stromness	Lerwick	8	Su,Tu	P&O Scottish Ferries	01856 850655
Ullapool	Stornoway	2¾	2-3	Caledonian MacBrayne	08705 650000
Caledonian MacBrayne run ferries to 23 West Scottish islands and many mainland ports; see 9.8.24 for details, inc other companies.					
D.	IRISH SEA (and Eire-France)				
Cork	Roscoff	14	S	Brittany Ferries	+353 214277801
Cork	Swansea	10	1 (not Tu)	Swansea/Cork Ferries	01792 456116
Rosslare	Cherbourg	16	Alternate days.	Irish Ferries	+353 16383333
Rosslare	Roscoff	18	Alternate days.	Irish Ferries	+353 16383333
Rosslare	Pembroke Dock	3¾	2	Irish Ferries	0870 5171717
Rosslare	Fishguard	3½/1¾ (Cat)	2/4	Stena Line	0870 5707070
Dun Laoghaire	Holyhead	3¾/1¾ (HSS)	2/4	Stena Line	0870 5707070
Dublin	Holyhead	3¼/1¾ (FF)	2/3	Irish Ferries	0870 5171717
Belfast	Stranraer	3¼/1½ (HSS)	1/4	SeaCat	0870 5523523
Belfast	Stranraer	3¼/1¾ (HSS)	7	Stena Line	0870 5707070
Belfast	Liverpool	8½	1	Norse Irish Ferries	02890 779090
Larne	Cairnryan	1¾	3	P&O Stena Ferries	0870 2424666
Douglas, IOM*	Heysham	3¾	2	IOM Steam Packet Co.	01624 661661
Douglas, IOM	Liverpool	4/2¼ (Cat)	Wint.moths only/2	IOM Steam Packet Co.	01624 661661
*Also less frequent sailings from Douglas to Belfast (4¾), Dublin (4¾), Fleetwood (3¼) and Ardrossan (8).					
E.	CHANNEL ISLANDS				
Guernsey/Jersey	Portsmouth	6½/10½	1 (not Su)	Condor Ferries	01305 761551
Jersey	Poole	3¾ (Cat)	1	Condor Ferries	01305 761551
Jersey	Weymouth	3¼ (Cat)	1	Condor Ferries	01305 761551
Guernsey	Poole	2½ (Cat)	1	Condor Ferries	01305 761551
Guernsey	Weymouth	2 (Cat)	1	Condor Ferries	01305 761551
Jersey†	St Malo	1¼ (Cat)	2	Condor Ferries	01305 761551
Guernsey	St Malo	1¾ (Cat)	M,W,F	Condor Ferries	01305 761551

†Also Jersey (St Helier) to Guernsey, Sark, Granville; and Jersey (Gorey) to Portbail and Carteret.

9.0.6 DISTANCES (M) ACROSS THE ENGLISH CHANNEL

France/CI \ England	Longships	Falmouth	Fowey	Plymouth bkwtr	Salcombe	Dartmouth	Torbay	Exmouth	Weymouth	Poole Hbr Ent	Needles Lt Ho	Nab Tower	Littlehampton	Shoreham	Brighton	Newhaven	Eastbourne	Rye	Folkestone	Dover
Le Conquet	112	112	123	125	125	137	144	155	172	188	194	212	230	240	245	249	261	278	295	301
L'Aberwrac'h	102	97	106	107	105	117	124	135	153	168	174	192	211	219	224	228	239	257	275	280
Roscoff	110	97	101	97	91	100	107	117	130	144	149	165	184	193	197	200	211	229	246	252
Trébeurden	120	105	106	102	94	102	109	120	129	142	147	164	181	190	194	197	208	226	244	249
Tréguier	132	112	110	101	94	98	102	112	116	128	132	147	162	170	174	177	188	206	224	229
Lézardrieux	142	121	118	107	94	100	105	114	115	126	130	140	157	165	169	172	184	201	219	224
St Quay-Portrieux	159	137	135	124	111	115	121	129	127	135	135	146	162	171	174	178	189	207	225	230
St Malo	172	149	146	133	118	120	124	132	125	130	130	143	157	166	170	173	184	202	220	225
St Helier	155	130	123	108	93	95	100	108	99	104	104	115	132	140	144	147	158	176	194	199
St Peter Port	139	113	104	89	73	70	75	81	71	79	83	97	112	120	124	127	135	156	174	179
Braye (Alderney)	146	116	106	89	72	69	71	75	54	60	62	73	91	100	103	106	114	136	153	159
Cherbourg	168	138	125	107	92	87	88	93	66	64	63	68	81	90	92	96	102	122	140	145
St Vaast-la-Hougue	194	164	150	132	116	111	112	116	83	76	72	71	80	87	88	90	96	115	132	138
Ouistreham	229	198	185	167	151	146	147	147	117	107	100	86	91	92	91	90	92	106	125	130
Deauville	236	205	192	174	158	153	154	154	122	111	104	88	89	88	87	85	87	101	120	125
Le Havre	231	200	187	169	153	148	148	148	118	105	97	82	82	83	82	79	80	94	115	120
Fécamp	242	212	197	179	163	157	157	157	120	105	96	75	71	68	65	62	62	72	90	95
Dieppe	268	237	222	204	188	180	180	180	142	125	117	91	80	75	70	64	63	60	70	75
Boulogne	290	258	242	224	208	198	195	191	153	135	127	97	81	71	66	59	47	33	28	25
Calais	305	272	257	239	223	213	210	209	168	150	141	111	96	86	81	74	62	43	26	22

NOTES

1. This Table applies to Areas 1 – 3, 14 – 16 and 22, each of which also contains its own internal Distance Table. Approximate distances in nautical miles are by the most direct route, while avoiding dangers and allowing for Traffic Separation Schemes.
2. For ports within the Solent, add the appropriate distances given in 9.2.6 to those shown above under either Needles light house or Nab Tower.

9.0.7 DISTANCES (M) ACROSS THE IRISH SEA

Ireland \ Scotland England Wales	Port Ellen (Islay)	Campbeltown	Troon	Portpatrick	Mull of Galloway	Kirkcudbright	Maryport	Fleetwood	Pt of Ayre (IOM)	Port St Mary (IOM)	Liverpool	Holyhead	Pwllheli	Fishguard	Milford Haven	Swansea	Avonmouth	Ilfracombe	Padstow	Longships
Tory Island	75	107	132	119	134	170	185	215	156	171	238	207	260	279	307	360	406	355	372	399
Malin Head	45	76	101	88	103	139	154	184	125	140	207	176	229	248	276	329	375	324	341	368
Lough Foyle	38	61	86	73	88	124	139	169	110	125	192	161	214	233	261	314	360	309	326	353
Portrush	31	50	76	64	80	116	131	161	102	117	184	153	206	225	253	306	352	301	318	345
Carnlough	42	35	57	32	45	81	96	126	67	78	149	115	168	187	215	268	314	363	280	307
Larne	51	39	58	24	37	72	88	118	58	70	141	106	159	178	206	259	305	254	271	298
Carrickfergus	64	48	65	26	34	69	85	115	55	66	138	101	154	173	201	254	300	249	266	293
Bangor	63	48	64	22	30	65	81	111	51	62	134	97	150	169	197	250	296	245	262	289
Strangford Lough	89	72	84	36	30	63	76	97	41	37	107	69	121	141	167	219	265	214	231	258
Carlingford Lough	117	100	112	64	60	90	103	112	70	51	118	67	111	124	149	202	248	197	214	241
Dun Laoghaire	153	136	148	100	93	119	126	120	93	69	119	56	82	94	109	162	208	157	174	201
Wicklow	170	153	165	117	108	133	140	127	108	83	123	56	67	71	90	143	189	138	155	182
Arklow	182	165	177	129	120	144	149	133	117	93	131	64	71	65	79	132	179	128	144	167
Rosslare	215	202	208	161	154	179	180	164	152	125	156	90	83	55	58	109	157	110	119	137
Tuskar Rock	216	203	209	162	155	179	182	165	152	126	152	91	82	48	51	105	150	103	112	130
Dunmore East	250	237	243	196	189	213	216	199	186	160	189	127	116	79	76	130	177	124	127	136
Youghal	281	268	274	227	220	244	247	230	217	191	220	158	147	110	103	156	200	148	139	138
Crosshaven	300	287	293	246	239	263	266	249	236	210	239	177	166	131	118	170	216	163	151	144
Baltimore	346	333	339	292	285	309	312	295	282	256	285	223	212	172	160	209	254	198	178	161
Fastnet Rock	354	341	347	300	293	317	320	303	290	264	293	231	220	181	169	216	260	207	185	170

NOTES

This Table applies to Areas 9 – 13, each of which also contains its own internal Distance Table. Approximate distances in nautical miles are by the most direct route, whilst avoiding dangers and Traffic Separation Schemes.

9.0.8 DISTANCES (M) ACROSS THE NORTH SEA

Norway to France / UK	Bergen	Stavanger	Lindesnes	Skagen	Esjberg	Sylt (List)	Brunsbüttel	Helgoland	Bremerhaven	Willhelmshaven	Delfzijl	Den Helder	IJmuiden	Scheveningen	Roompotsluis	Vlissingen	Zeebrugge	Oostende	Nieuwpoort	Dunkerque
Lerwick	210	226	288	403	428	442	517	470	510	500	493	486	497	505	551	550	552	555	562	588
Kirkwall	278	275	323	438	439	452	516	467	507	497	481	460	473	481	515	514	516	519	526	545
Wick	292	283	323	437	428	440	498	449	489	479	458	433	444	451	485	484	486	489	496	514
Inverness	356	339	381	485	461	462	529	479	519	509	487	460	471	478	513	512	514	517	524	542
Fraserburgh	288	266	296	410	383	384	451	404	444	434	412	385	396	403	430	429	431	434	441	456
Aberdeen	308	279	298	411	371	378	433	382	432	412	386	353	363	369	401	400	402	405	412	426
Dundee	362	329	339	451	394	401	448	396	436	426	395	352	359	364	390	389	385	388	395	412
Port Edgar	391	355	362	472	409	413	457	405	445	435	401	355	361	366	391	390	386	389	396	413
Berwick-on-Tweed	374	325	320	431	356	361	408	355	395	385	355	310	315	320	342	341	337	340	347	364
Hartlepool	409	353	340	440	340	331	367	312	352	342	302	241	243	247	266	265	261	264	271	288
Grimsby	463	395	362	452	324	318	342	291	332	325	288	187	182	185	199	198	190	191	201	198
Kings Lynn	485	416	379	466	330	333	343	292	344	336	283	184	183	183	197	195	187	188	198	195
Lowestoft	508	431	380	453	308	300	295	262	284	271	218	118	104	98	95	99	87	87	89	106
Harwich	540	461	410	483	330	331	320	287	309	296	243	147	126	114	94	100	84	77	80	80
Brightlingsea	558	479	428	501	348	349	338	305	327	314	261	165	144	105	108	106	92	88	86	87
Burnham-on-Crouch	567	488	437	510	357	358	347	314	336	323	270	174	151	112	109	115	99	92	93	95
London Bridge	620	543	490	560	400	408	395	361	382	374	320	222	199	149	153	149	134	125	126	114
Sheerness	580	503	450	520	360	367	353	319	340	334	280	180	157	109	113	109	94	85	86	74
Ramsgate	575	498	446	516	368	346	339	305	323	315	262	161	144	121	89	85	77	65	58	42
Dover	588	511	459	529	378	359	352	328	336	328	275	174	155	132	101	92	79	65	58	44

NOTES This Table applies to Areas 3 – 7 and 22 – 25, each of which also contains its own internal Distance Table. Approximate distances in nautical miles are by the most direct route, while avoiding dangers and allowing for Traffic Separation Schemes.

PLATE 1 NAVIGATION LIGHTS

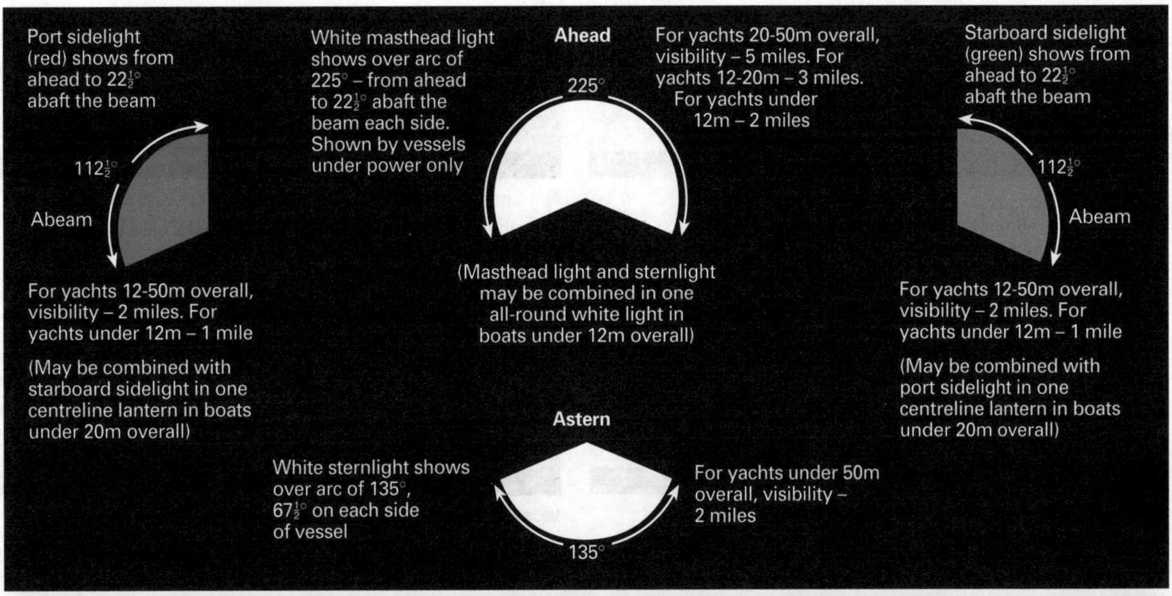
Port sidelight (red) shows from ahead to 22½° abaft the beam
112½°
Abeam
For yachts 12-50m overall, visibility – 2 miles. For yachts under 12m – 1 mile
(May be combined with starboard sidelight in one centreline lantern in boats under 20m overall)
White masthead light shows over arc of 225° – from ahead to 22½° abaft the beam each side. Shown by vessels under power only
Ahead
225°
For yachts 20-50m overall, visibility – 5 miles. For yachts 12-20m – 3 miles. For yachts under 12m – 2 miles
(Masthead light and sternlight may be combined in one all-round white light in boats under 12m overall)
Starboard sidelight (green) shows from ahead to 22½° abaft the beam
112½°
Abeam
For yachts 12-50m overall, visibility – 2 miles. For yachts under 12m – 1 mile
(May be combined with port sidelight in one centreline lantern in boats under 20m overall)
Astern
White sternlight shows over arc of 135°, 67½° on each side of vessel
135°
For yachts under 50m overall, visibility – 2 miles

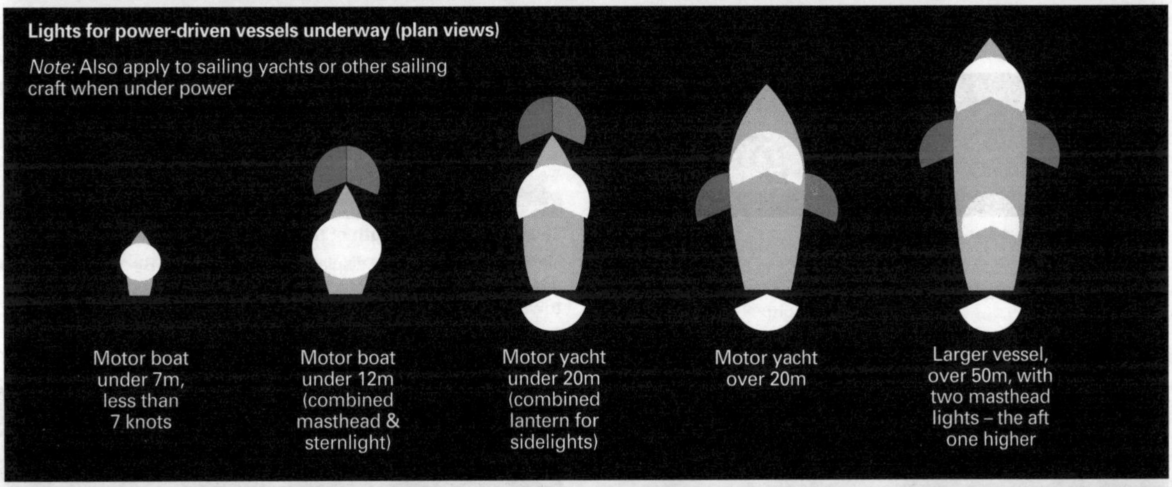
Lights for power-driven vessels underway (plan views)
Note: Also apply to sailing yachts or other sailing craft when under power
Motor boat under 7m, less than 7 knots
Motor boat under 12m (combined masthead & sternlight)
Motor yacht under 20m (combined lantern for sidelights)
Motor yacht over 20m
Larger vessel, over 50m, with two masthead lights – the aft one higher

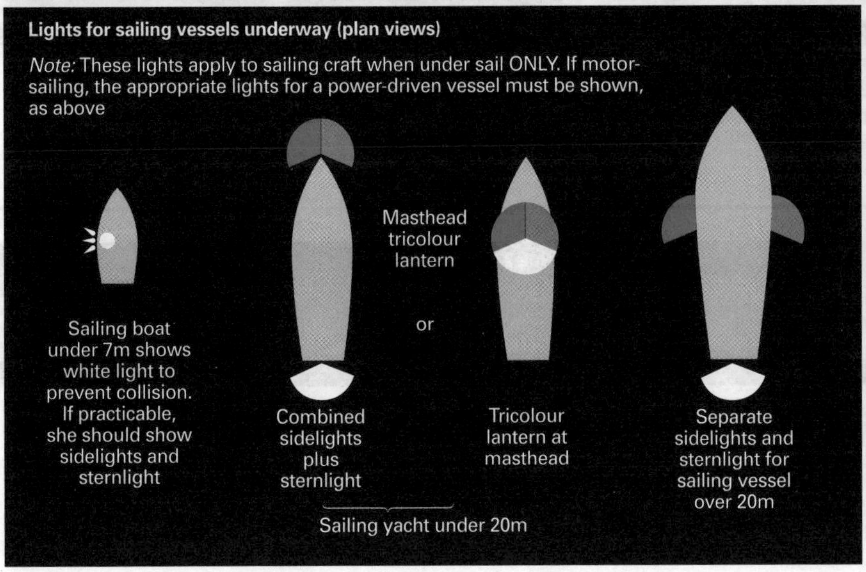
Lights for sailing vessels underway (plan views)
Note: These lights apply to sailing craft when under sail ONLY. If motor-sailing, the appropriate lights for a power-driven vessel must be shown, as above
Sailing boat under 7m shows white light to prevent collision. If practicable, she should show sidelights and sternlight
Combined sidelights plus sternlight
Masthead tricolour lantern
or
Tricolour lantern at masthead
Sailing yacht under 20m
Separate sidelights and sternlight for sailing vessel over 20m

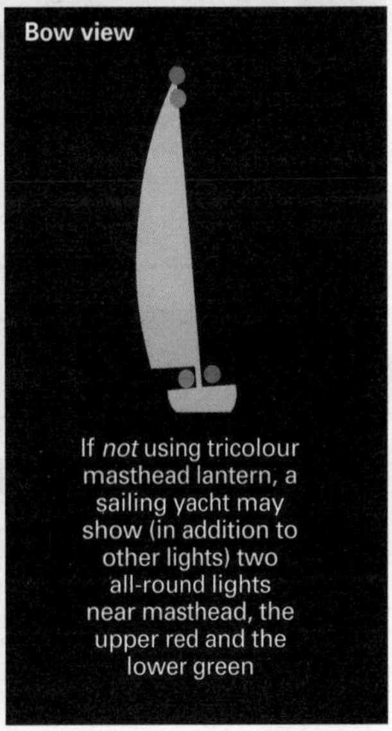
Bow view
If not using tricolour masthead lantern, a sailing yacht may show (in addition to other lights) two all-round lights near masthead, the upper red and the lower green

PLATE 2 PRINCIPAL NAVIGATION LIGHTS AND SHAPES

(*Note:* All vessels seen from starboard side)

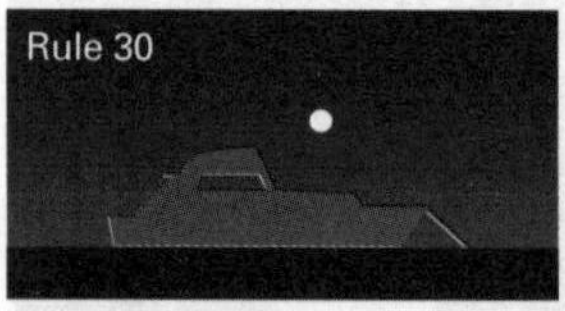

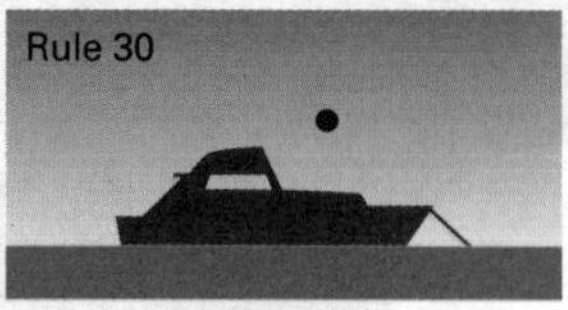

Vessel at anchor

All-round white light; if over 50m, a second light aft and lower

Black ball forward

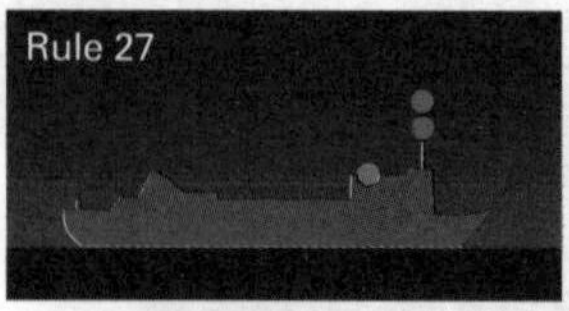

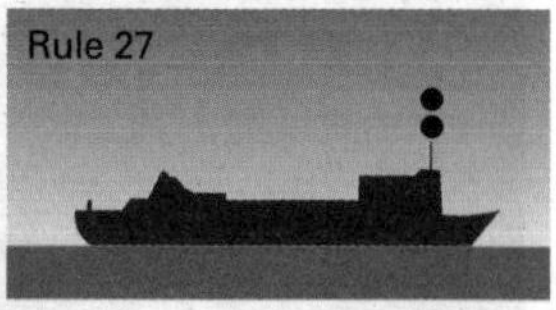

Not under command

Two all-round red lights, plus sidelights and sternlight when making way

Two black balls vertically

Motor sailing

Cone point down, forward

Divers down

Letter 'A' International Code

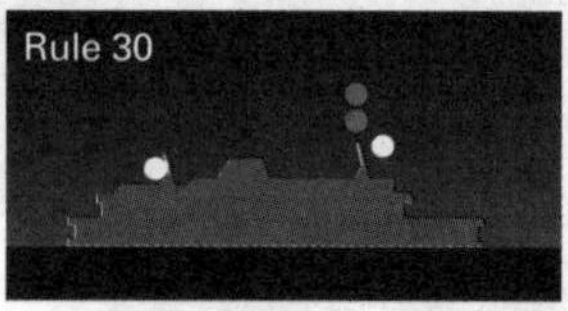

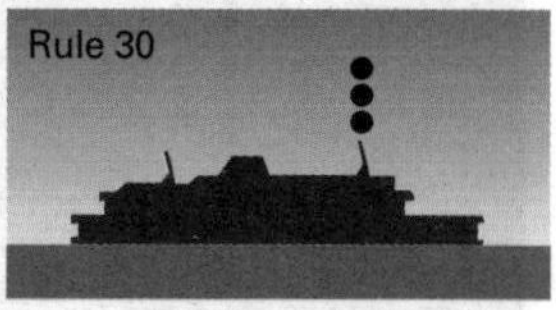

Vessel aground

Anchor light(s), plus two all-round red lights in a vertical line

Three black balls in a vertical line

Vessels being towed and towing

Vessel towed shows sidelights (forward) and sternlight

Tug shows two masthead lights, sidelights, sternlight, yellow towing light

Towing by day – Length of tow more than 200m

Towing vessel and tow display diamond shapes. By night, the towing vessel shows three masthead lights instead of two as for shorter tows

---

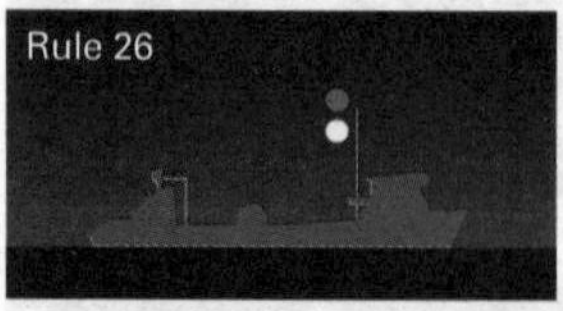

Vessel fishing

All-round red light over all-round white, plus sidelights and sternlight when underway

Fishing/Trawling

A shape consisting of two cones point to point in a vertical line one above the other

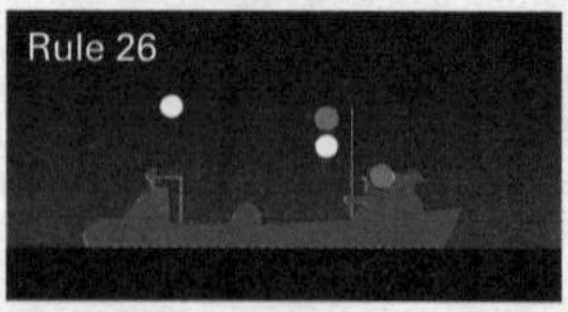

Vessel trawling

All-round green light over all-round white, plus sidelights and sternlight when underway

Pilot boat

All-round white light over all-round red, plus sidelights and sternlight when underway, or anchor light

---

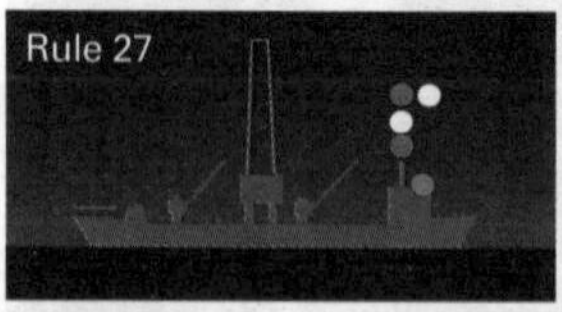

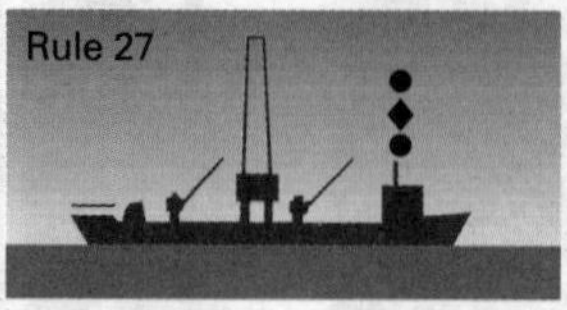

Vessel restricted in her ability to manoeuvre

All-round red, white, red lights vertically, plus normal steaming lights when underway

Three shapes in a vertical line – ball, diamond, ball

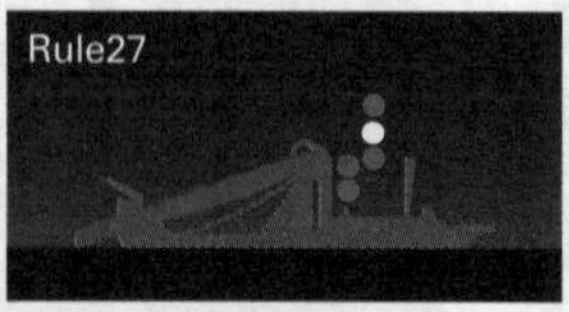

Dredger

As left, plus two all-round red lights (or two balls) on foul side, and two all-round green (or two diamonds) on clear side

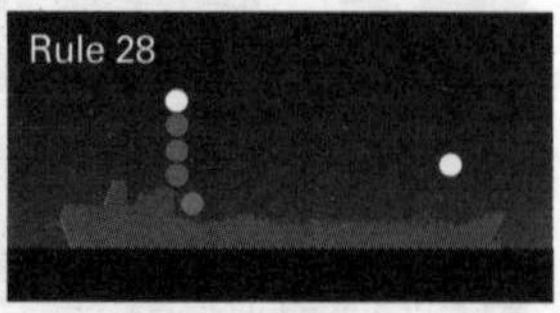

Constrained by draught

Three all-round red lights in a vertical line, plus normal steaming lights. By day – a cylinder

PLATE 3 IALA BUOYAGE

Lateral Marks

Used to mark the sides of well-defined navigable channels

Port Hand marks
Light: red
Rhythm: any

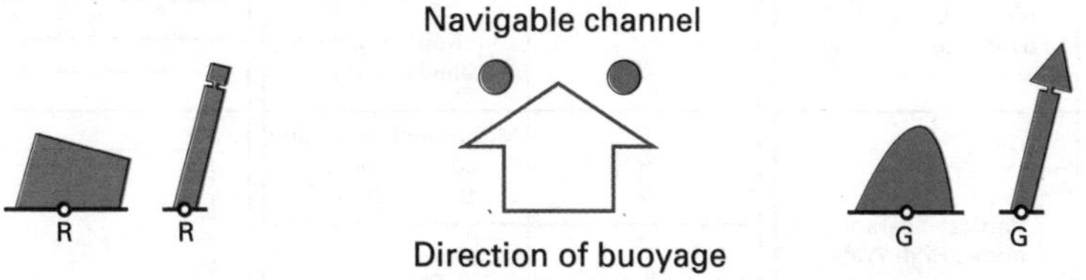
R
R
Navigable channel
Direction of buoyage
G
G

Starboard Hand marks
Light: green
Rhythm: any

Cardinal Marks

Indicate that navigable water lies to the named side of the mark, or draw attention to a bend, junction or fork in a channel, or mark the end of a shoal.

Lights: always white
Rhythm: as shown

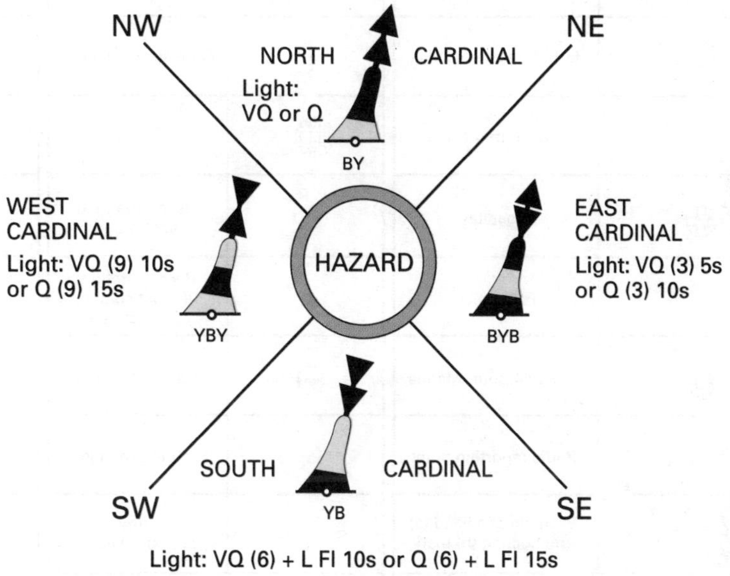
NW
NE
NORTH CARDINAL
Light: VQ or Q
BY
WEST CARDINAL
Light: VQ (9) 10s or Q (9) 15s
YBY
HAZARD
EAST CARDINAL
Light: VQ (3) 5s or Q (3) 10s
BYB
SOUTH CARDINAL
YB
SW
SE
Light: VQ (6) + L Fl 10s or Q (6) + L Fl 15s

Other Marks

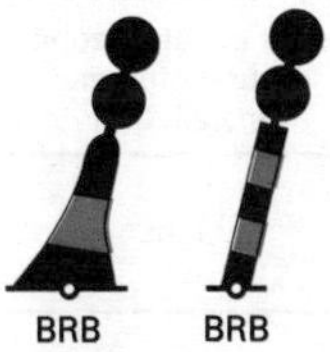
BRB
BRB

Isolated danger marks
Mark an isolated danger with navigable water all round it.
Light: white
Rhythm: Fl (2)

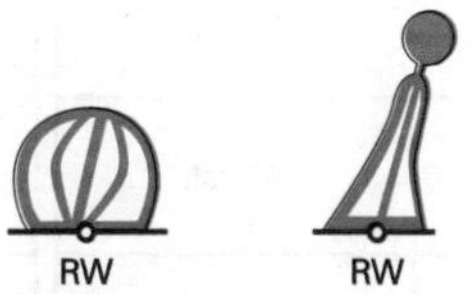
RW
RW

Safe water marks
Use: Landfall, fairway or mid-channel
Light: white
Rhythm: Isophase, occulting or L Fl 10s or Morse A

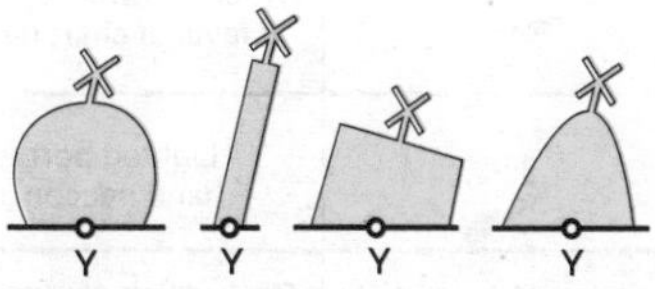
Y
Y
Y
Y

Special marks
Define the limits of special areas or features. Any shape not conflicting with lateral or safe water marks.
Light: yellow
Rhythm: any not used for lights on other buoys

Preferred Channels

Where a channel divides, the preferred channel is indicated by a Port or Starboard mark modified as follows:

Preferred channel to Starboard
Light: red
Rhythm: Fl (2+1)

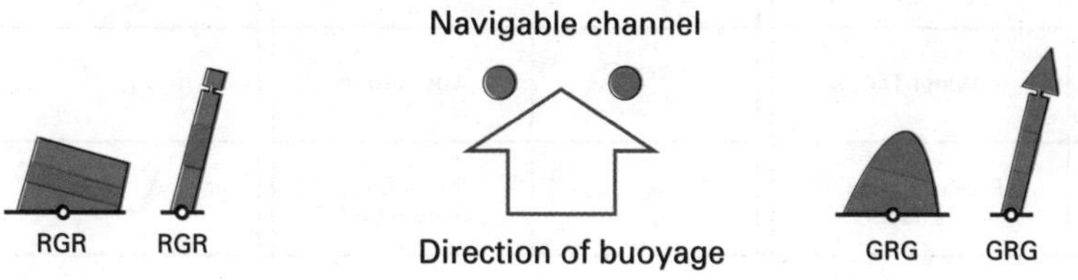
RGR
RGR
Navigable channel
Direction of buoyage
GRG
GRG

Preferred channel to Port
Light: green
Rhythm: Fl (2+1)

C9

PLATE 4 ADMIRALTY SYMBOLS

Symbol	Meaning
	Power transmission line with pylons and safe overhead clearance
	Vertical clearance above High Water
	Harbourmaster's Office
	Custom office
	Hospital
	Post office
	Yacht harbour, Marina
	Radio reporting point
	Example of a fixed (a) and floating (b) mark
	Mooring buoy
	Wreck showing any part at level of chart datum
	Lighted port hand beacon
	Rock which covers and uncovers, height above chart datum
	Rock awash at level of chart datum
	Visitors' Berth
	Fuel Station (Petrol, Diesel)
	Public Slipway
	Water Tap
	Public landing, steps, ladder

Symbol	Meaning
	Church
	Radio mast, television mast
	Monument (including column, pillar, obelisk, statue)
	Chimney
	Flare stack (on land)
	Tanks
	Recommended anchorage
	Rescue station, lifeboat station, rocket station
	Fishing harbour
	Fishing prohibited
	Withy - starboard hand
	Withy - port hand
	Floodlit
	Marsh
	Kelp
	Crane
	Inn and Restaurant
WC	Public Toilets
P	Public Car Park
	Laundrette
	Yacht Club, Sailing Club

Symbol	Meaning
	Drying contour LW line, Chart Datum Below 5m blue ribbon or differing blue tints may be shown
	Anchoring prohibited
	Marine Farm
	Wreck, depth unknown, danger to navigation
	Wreck, depth unknown, no danger to navigation
Wk	Wreck, depth obtained by sounding
Wk	Wreck, swept by wire to the depth shown
	Submarine cable
	Buried pipeline
	Overfalls, tide rips and races
	Limit of safety zone around offshore installation
	Light
	Dangerous underwater rock of unknown depth
	Dangerous underwater rock of known depth
	Caravan Site Camping Site
	Public Telephone
	Bird Sanctuary
CG	Coastguard Station
	Woods in general

PLATE 5 INTERNATIONAL CODE OF SIGNALS, CODE FLAGS, PHONETIC ALPHABET, MORSE SYMBOLS AND SINGLE-LETTER SIGNALS

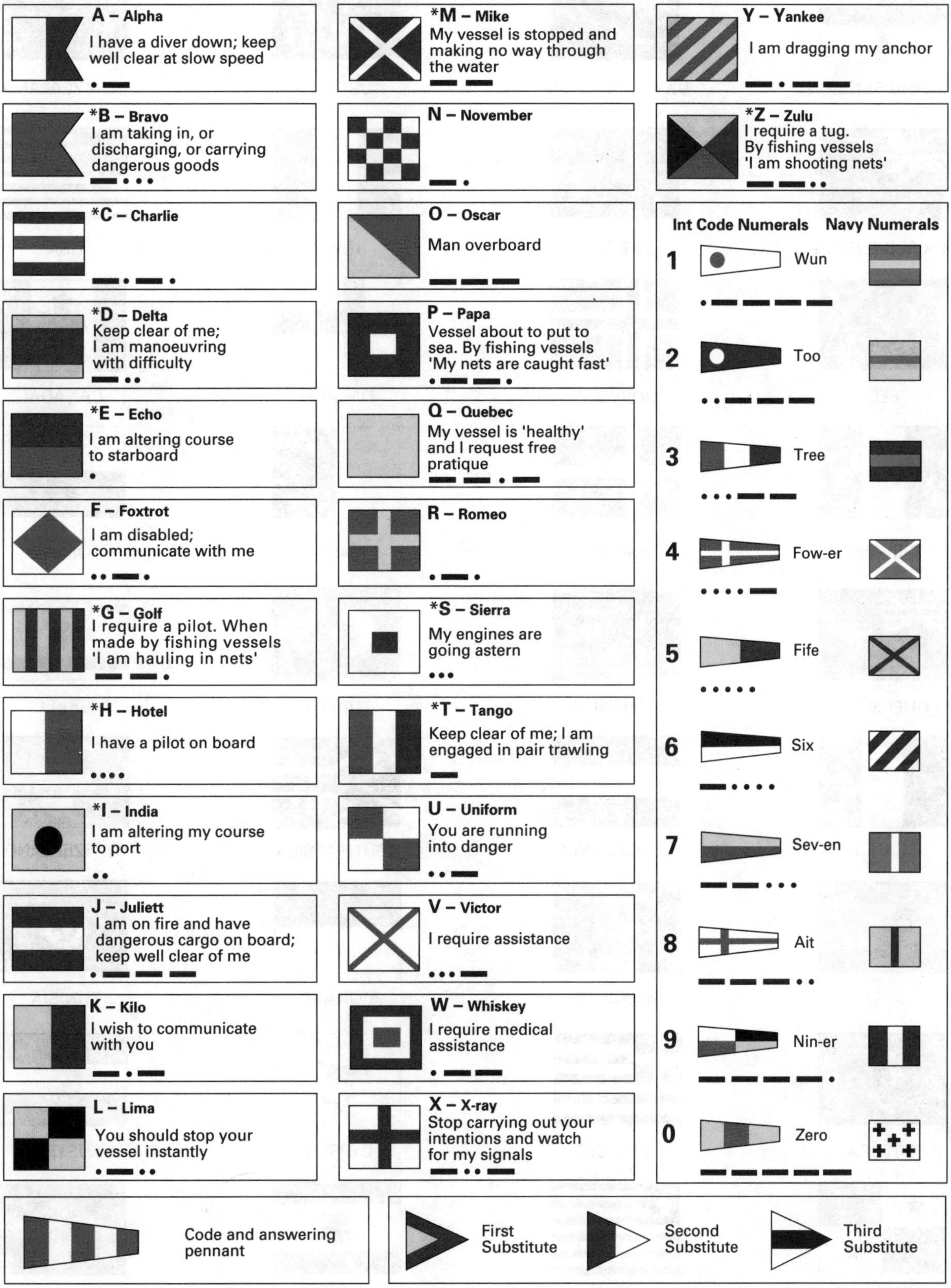
A – Alpha
I have a diver down; keep well clear at slow speed
· —
*B – Bravo
I am taking in, or discharging, or carrying dangerous goods
— · · ·
*C – Charlie
— · — ·
*D – Delta
Keep clear of me; I am manoeuvring with difficulty
— · ·
*E – Echo
I am altering course to starboard
·
F – Foxtrot
I am disabled; communicate with me
· · — ·
*G – Golf
I require a pilot. When made by fishing vessels 'I am hauling in nets'
— — ·
*H – Hotel
I have a pilot on board
· · · ·
*I – India
I am altering my course to port
· ·
J – Juliett
I am on fire and have dangerous cargo on board; keep well clear of me
· — — —
K – Kilo
I wish to communicate with you
— · —
L – Lima
You should stop your vessel instantly
· — · ·
*M – Mike
My vessel is stopped and making no way through the water
— —
N – November
— ·
O – Oscar
Man overboard
— — —
P – Papa
Vessel about to put to sea. By fishing vessels 'My nets are caught fast'
· — — ·
Q – Quebec
My vessel is 'healthy' and I request free pratique
— — · —
R – Romeo
· — ·
*S – Sierra
My engines are going astern
· · ·
*T – Tango
Keep clear of me; I am engaged in pair trawling
—
U – Uniform
You are running into danger
· · —
V – Victor
I require assistance
· · · —
W – Whiskey
I require medical assistance
· — —
X – X-ray
Stop carrying out your intentions and watch for my signals
— · · —
Y – Yankee
I am dragging my anchor
— · — —
*Z – Zulu
I require a tug. By fishing vessels 'I am shooting nets'
— — · ·
Int Code Numerals
Navy Numerals
1 Wun
· — — — —
2 Too
· · — — —
3 Tree
· · · — —
4 Fow-er
· · · · —
5 Fife
· · · · ·
6 Six
— · · · ·
7 Sev-en
— — · · ·
8 Ait
— — — · ·
9 Nin-er
— — — — ·
0 Zero
— — — — —
Code and answering pennant
First Substitute
Second Substitute
Third Substitute

Signals marked * when made by sound may only by used in compliance with the Collision Regulations, Rules 34 and 35

C9

PLATE 6 NATIONAL ENSIGNS

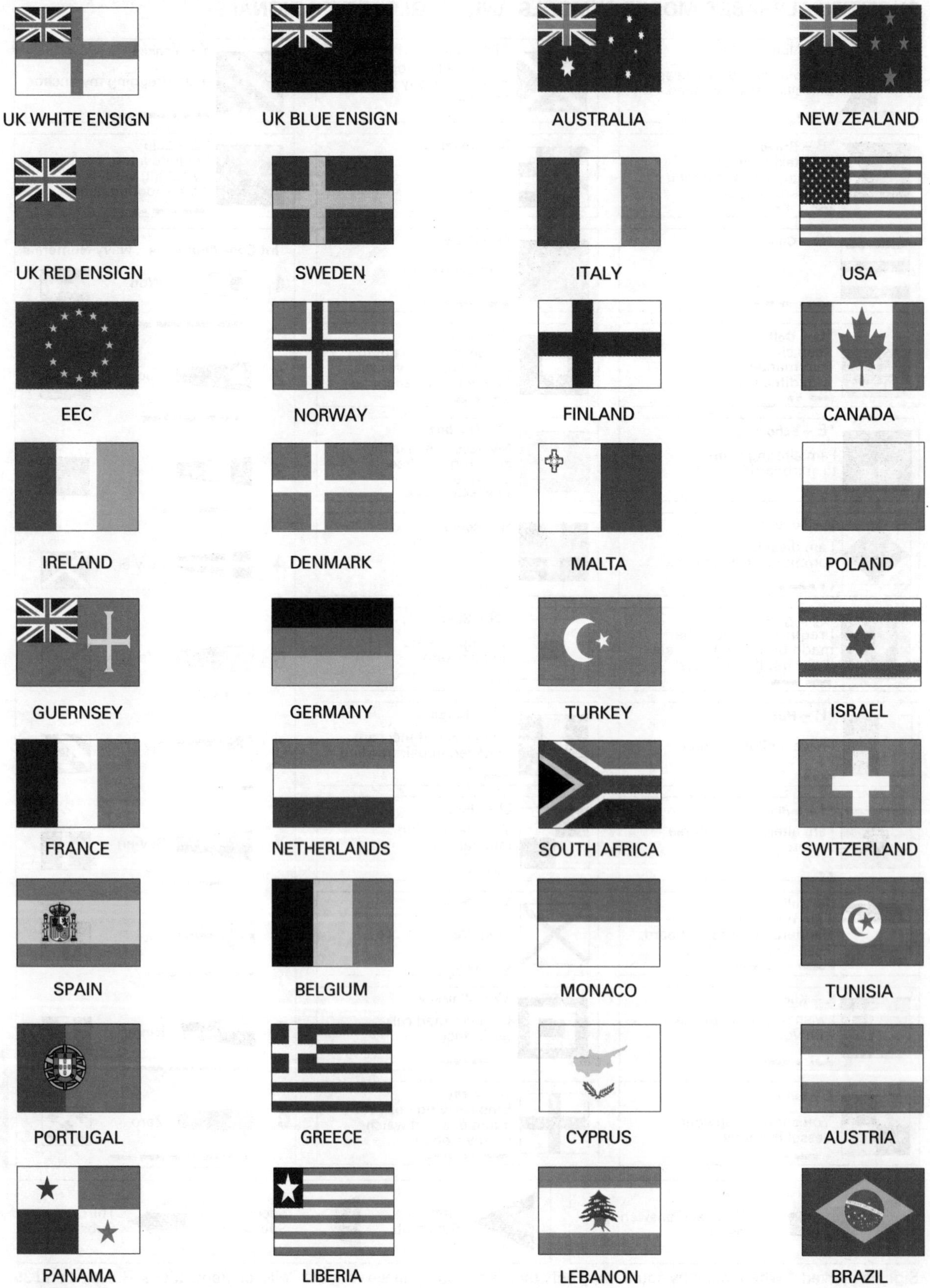
UK WHITE ENSIGN
UK BLUE ENSIGN
AUSTRALIA
NEW ZEALAND
UK RED ENSIGN
SWEDEN
ITALY
USA
EEC
NORWAY
FINLAND
CANADA
IRELAND
DENMARK
MALTA
POLAND
GUERNSEY
GERMANY
TURKEY
ISRAEL
FRANCE
NETHERLANDS
SOUTH AFRICA
SWITZERLAND
SPAIN
BELGIUM
MONACO
TUNISIA
PORTUGAL
GREECE
CYPRUS
AUSTRIA
PANAMA
LIBERIA
LEBANON
BRAZIL

MAPTECH®
Leading the world in digital navigation
Maptech UK Ltd • +44 (0)1243 389352 • sales@maptech.co.uk

Sales and distribution centres in Area 1

Cornwall: *Sea-Com Electronics Ltd*, 01326 376565, The Praze, Penryn TR10 8AA. *Marine Instruments*, 01326 312414, The Bosuns Locker, Upton Slip, Falmouth, Cornwall, TR11 3DQ.
Devon: *Waypoint 1*, 01752 661913, Unit 3, Lynher Building, Queen Anne's Battery, Plymouth PL4 0LP.
Yacht Parts, 01752 252489, Victoria Building, Queen Anne's Battery Marina, Plymouth, PL4 0LP.

www.maptech.co.uk

Area 1

South-West England
Isles of Scilly to Portland Bill

9.1.1 Index .... Page 209

9.1.2 Area map 210

9.1.3 Tidal stream charts 212

9.1.4 Lights, buoys & waypoints 214

9.1.5 Passage information 217

9.1.6 Distance table 219

9.1.7 English Channel Waypoints 220

9.1.8 Isles of Scilly 224

9.1.9 St Mary's (Scilly) 225

9.1.10 Newlyn 226
Mousehole

9.1.11 Penzance 226
St Michael's Mount

9.1.12 Helford River 227
Porthleven
Mullion Cove
Cadgwith
Coverack

9.1.13 River Fal (Tidal predictions and curves) 228

9.1.14 Mevagissey 233
Porthscatho
Gorran Haven
Portmellon

9.1.15 Fowey 234
Dodman Pt gunnery range
Charlestown
Par
Polperro

9.1.16 Looe 235

9.1.17 Plymouth (Devonport), Standard Port, tidal curves 236
River Tamar
River Lynher

9.1.18 Submarine exercise areas 242

9.1.19 River Yealm 243
River Erme
River Avon
Hope Cove

9.1.20 Salcombe 244
Kingsbridge

9.1.21 Dartmouth, (Tidal predictions and curves) 248
Dittisham
Totnes

9.1.22 Brixham 250
Paignton

9.1.23 Torquay 250

9.1.24 Teignmouth 251

9.1.25 River Exe 252
Axmouth/Beer

9.1.26 Lyme Regis 254

9.1.27 Bridport 254

Register for your FREE weekly weather email service from Macmillan Reeds
» at www.nauticaldata.com – NOW! «
weekend weather reports sent to your email address, every Thursday

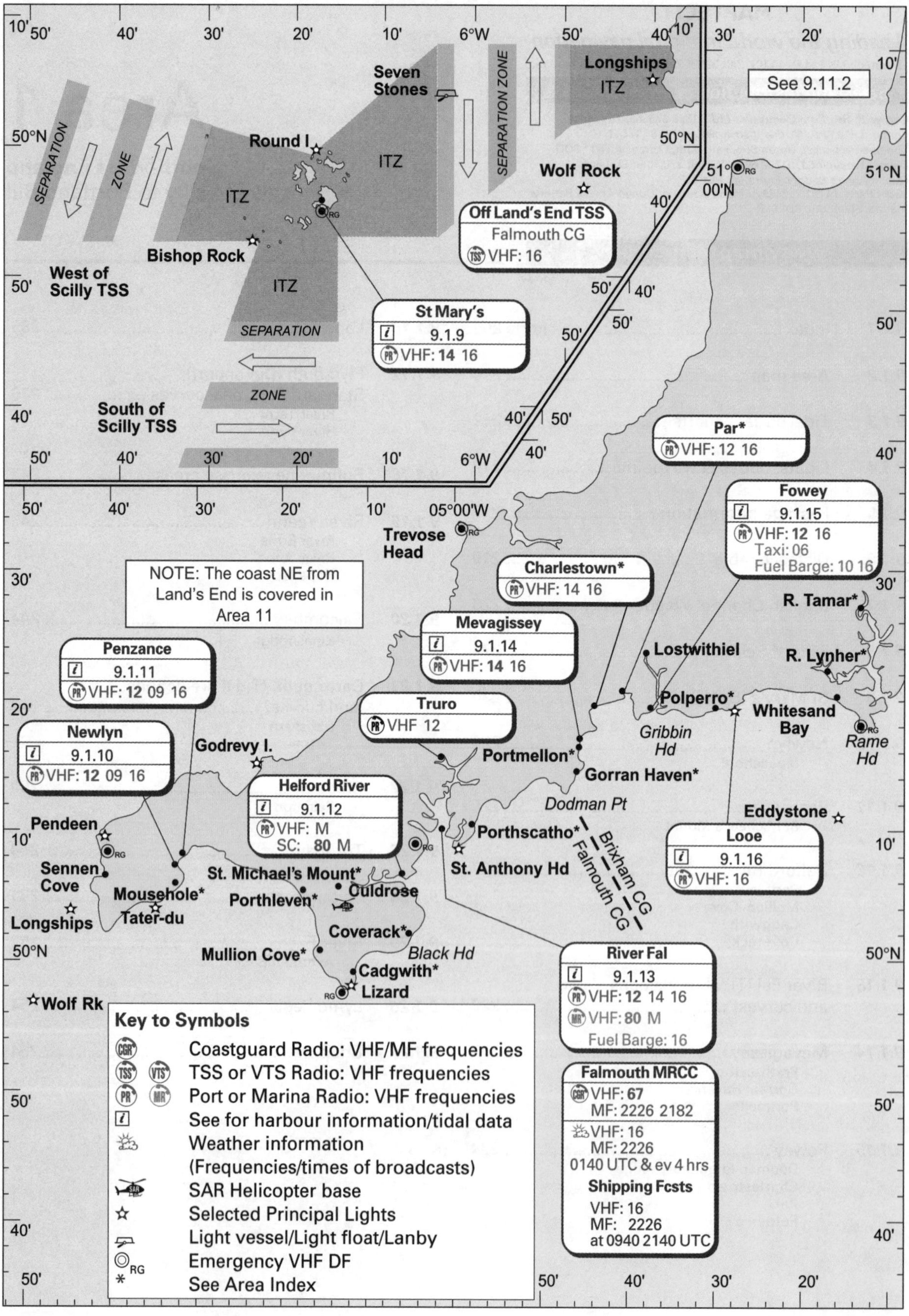
Seven Stones
Longships
ITZ
See 9.11.2
SEPARATION ZONE
Round I
ITZ
Wolf Rock
51° 00'N
51°N
SEPARATION
ZONE
ITZ
Off Land's End TSS
Falmouth CG
VHF: 16
Bishop Rock
West of Scilly TSS
ITZ
St Mary's
9.1.9
VHF: 14 16
SEPARATION
ZONE
South of Scilly TSS
Par*
VHF: 12 16
Fowey
9.1.15
VHF: 12 16
Taxi: 06
Fuel Barge: 10 16
05°00'W
Trevose Head
Charlestown*
VHF: 14 16
NOTE: The coast NE from Land's End is covered in Area 11
R. Tamar*
Mevagissey
9.1.14
VHF: 14 16
Lostwithiel
R. Lynher*
Penzance
9.1.11
VHF: 12 09 16
Truro
VHF 12
Polperro*
Whitesand Bay
Gribbin Hd
Rame Hd
Newlyn
9.1.10
VHF: 12 09 16
Godrevy I.
Portmellon*
Gorran Haven*
Helford River
9.1.12
VHF: M
SC: 80 M
Dodman Pt
Eddystone
Pendeen
Porthscatho*
Brixham CG
Falmouth CG
Looe
9.1.16
VHF: 16
St. Anthony Hd
Sennen Cove
St. Michael's Mount*
Culdrose
Mousehole*
Porthleven*
Longships
Tater-du
Coverack*
Mullion Cove*
Black Hd
Cadgwith*
Lizard
River Fal
9.1.13
VHF: 12 14 16
VHF: 80 M
Fuel Barge: 16
Wolf Rk
Key to Symbols
Coastguard Radio: VHF/MF frequencies
TSS or VTS Radio: VHF frequencies
Port or Marina Radio: VHF frequencies
See for harbour information/tidal data
Weather information (Frequencies/times of broadcasts)
SAR Helicopter base
Selected Principal Lights
Light vessel/Light float/Lanby
Emergency VHF DF
See Area Index
Falmouth MRCC
VHF: 67
MF: 2226 2182
VHF: 16
MF: 2226
0140 UTC & ev 4 hrs
Shipping Fcsts
VHF: 16
MF: 2226
at 0940 2140 UTC

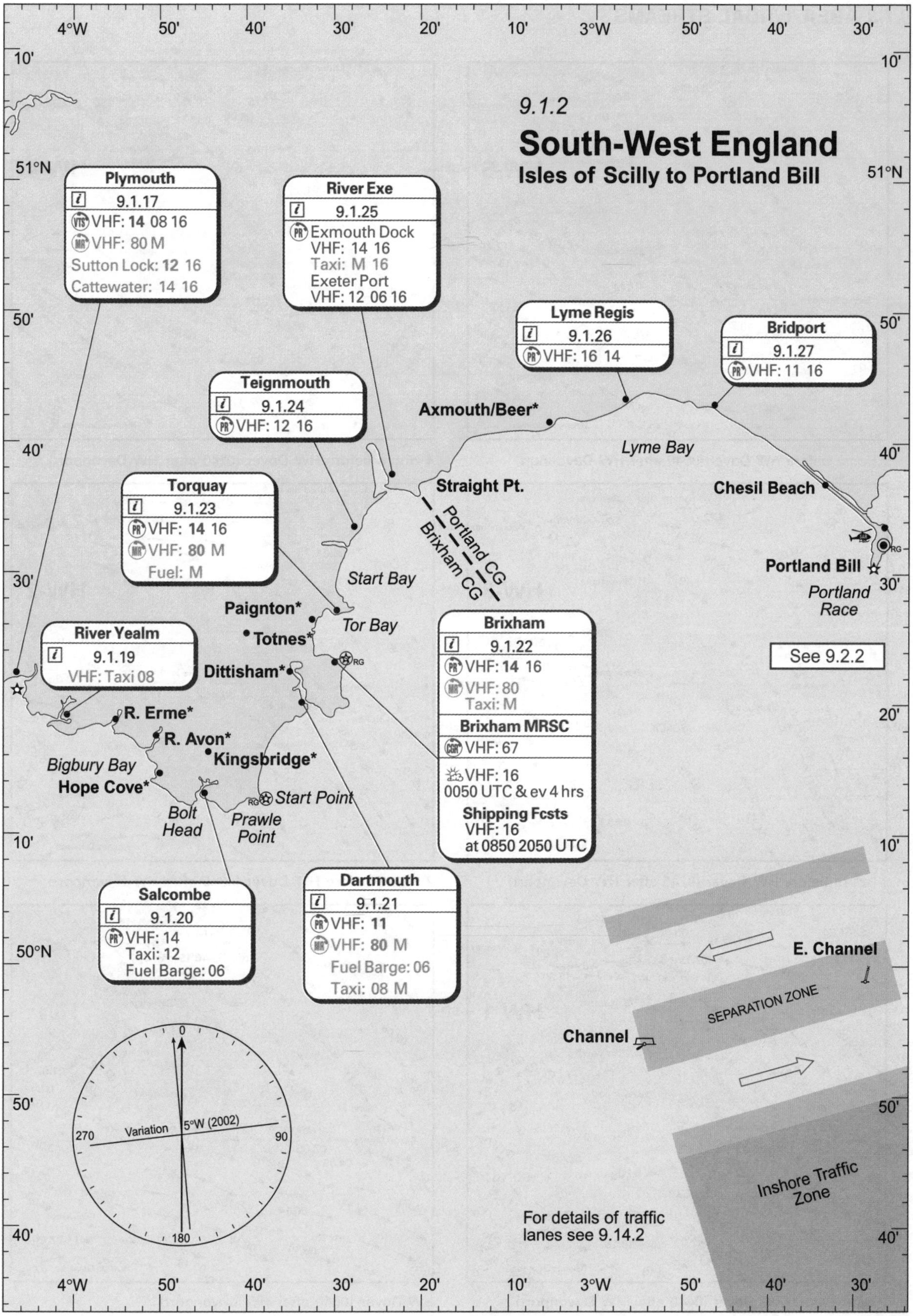
9.1.2
South-West England
Isles of Scilly to Portland Bill
Plymouth
9.1.17
VTS VHF: 14 08 16
MR VHF: 80 M
Sutton Lock: 12 16
Cattewater: 14 16
River Exe
9.1.25
PR Exmouth Dock
VHF: 14 16
Taxi: M 16
Exeter Port
VHF: 12 06 16
Lyme Regis
9.1.26
PR VHF: 16 14
Bridport
9.1.27
PR VHF: 11 16
Teignmouth
9.1.24
PR VHF: 12 16
Axmouth/Beer*
Lyme Bay
Torquay
9.1.23
PR VHF: 14 16
MR VHF: 80 M
Fuel: M
Straight Pt.
Chesil Beach
Portland CG
Brixham CG
Start Bay
Portland Bill
Portland Race
Paignton*
Tor Bay
Totnes*
River Yealm
9.1.19
VHF: Taxi 08
Dittisham*
See 9.2.2
Brixham
9.1.22
PR VHF: 14 16
MR VHF: 80
Taxi: M
Brixham MRSC
CGR VHF: 67
VHF: 16
0050 UTC & ev 4 hrs
Shipping Fcsts
VHF: 16
at 0850 2050 UTC
R. Erme*
R. Avon*
Kingsbridge*
Bigbury Bay
Hope Cove*
Start Point
Bolt Head
Prawle Point
Salcombe
9.1.20
PR VHF: 14
Taxi: 12
Fuel Barge: 06
Dartmouth
9.1.21
PR VHF: 11
MR VHF: 80 M
Fuel Barge: 06
Taxi: 08 M
E. Channel
SEPARATION ZONE
Channel
Variation 5°W (2002)
0
90
180
270
Inshore Traffic Zone
For details of traffic lanes see 9.14.2
4°W
50'
40'
30'
20'
10'
3°W
51°N
50°N
RG

9.1.3 AREA 1 TIDAL STREAMS

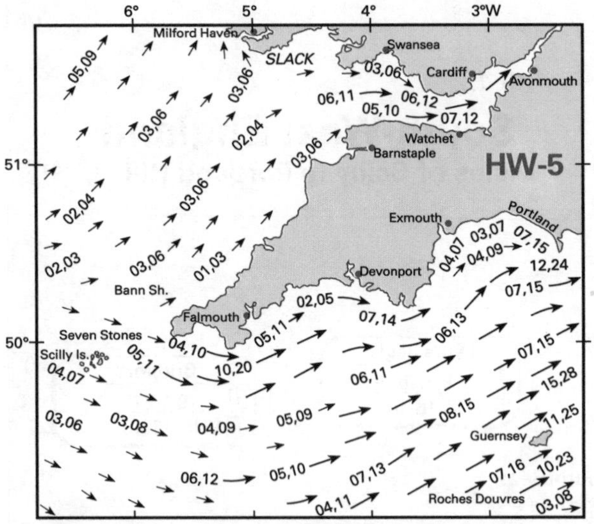

5 Hours before HW Dover (0040 after HW Devonport)

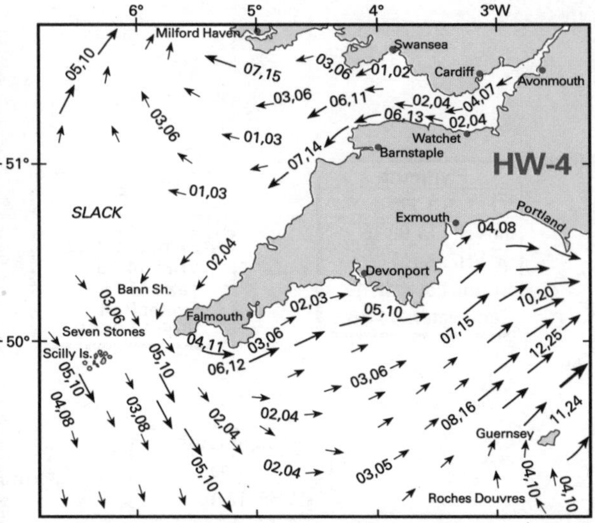

4 Hours before HW Dover (0140 after HW Devonport)

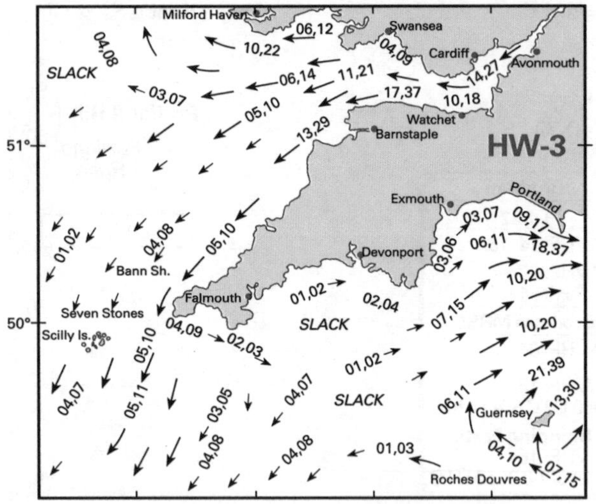

3 Hours before HW Dover (0240 after HW Devonport)

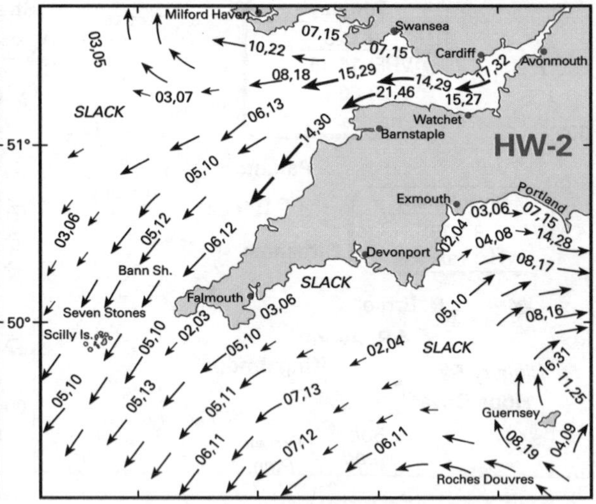

2 Hours before HW Dover (0340 after HW Devonport)

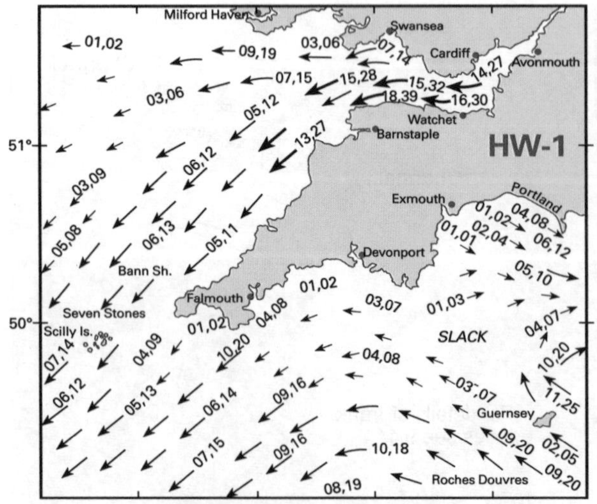

1 Hour before HW Dover (0440 after HW Devonport)

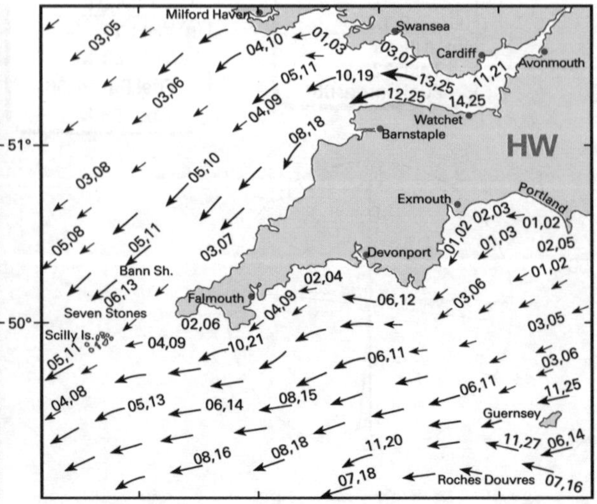

HW Dover (0540 after HW Devonport)

Eastward 9.2.3 Portland 9.2.8 Isle of Wight 9.2.24 Northward 9.11.3 Southward 9.16.3 Channel Is 9.14.3

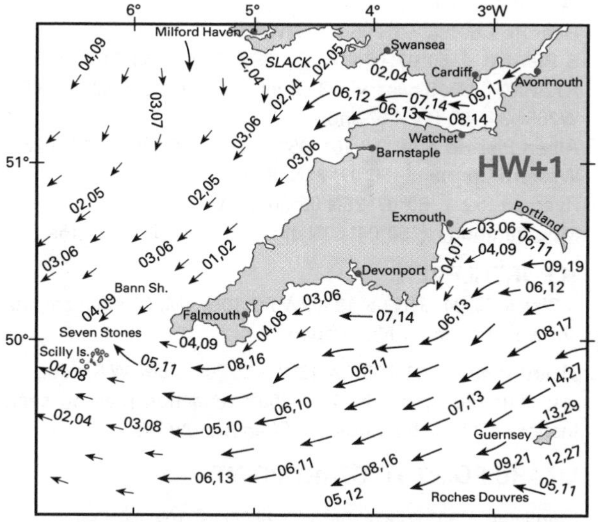

1 Hour after HW Dover (0545 before HW Devonport)

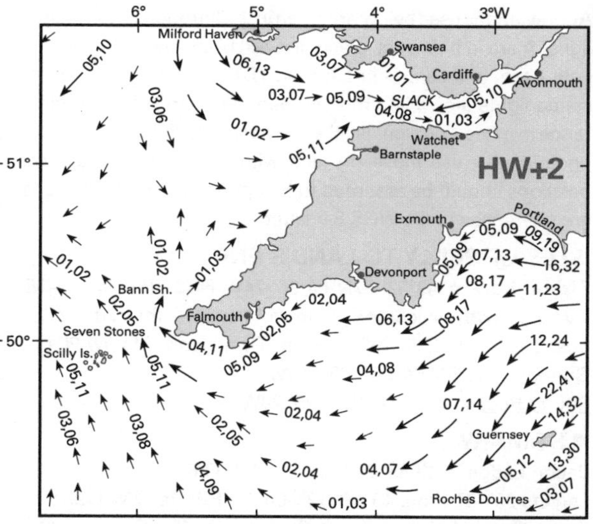

2 Hours after HW Dover (0445 before HW Devonport)

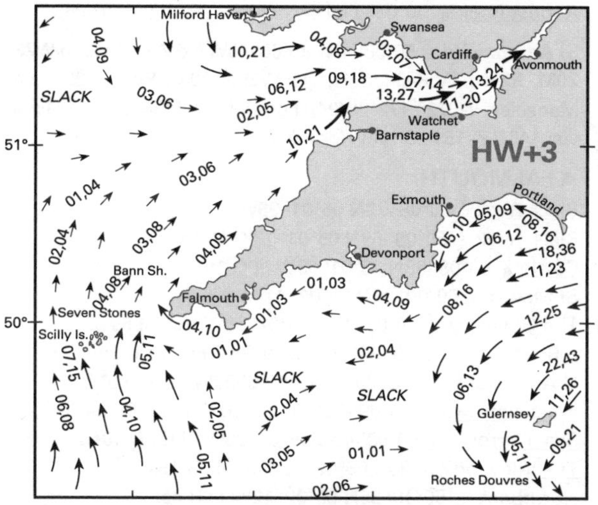

3 Hours after HW Dover (0345 before HW Devonport)

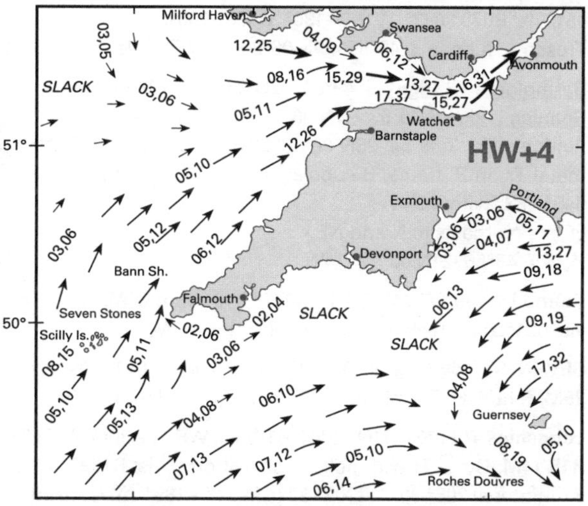

4 Hours after HW Dover (0245 before HW Devonport)

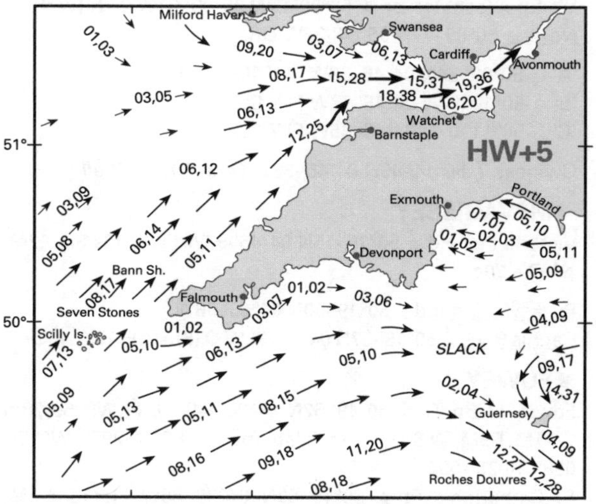

5 Hours after HW Dover (0145 before HW Devonport)

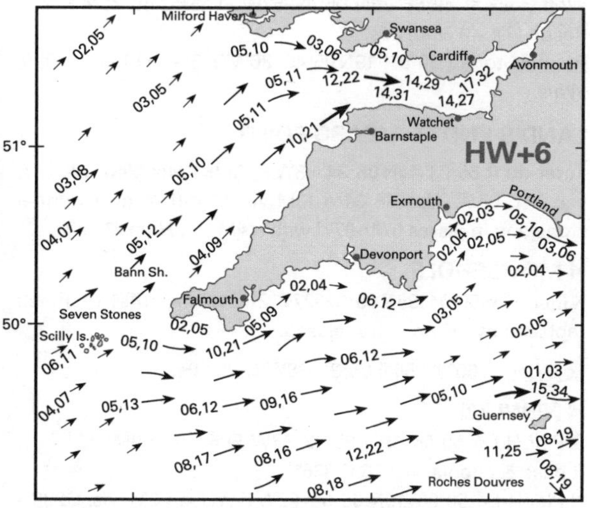

6 Hours after HW Dover (0045 before HW Devonport)

9.1.4 LIGHTS, BUOYS AND WAYPOINTS

Abbreviations used below are given in the Introduction. Principal lights ☆ are in **bold** print, places in CAPITALS, and light-vessels, light floats and Lanbys in *CAPITAL ITALICS.* Unless otherwise stated lights are white. m – elevation in metres; M – nominal range in miles. Fog signals ◦))) are in *italics.* Useful waypoints are underlined – use those on land with care. All geographical positions should be assumed to be approximate. All positions are referenced to the WGS 84 datum.

ISLES OF SCILLY TO LAND'S END

Bishop Rock ☆ 49°52'·37N 06°26'·74W Fl (2) 15s 44m **24M**; Gy ○ Tr with helicopter platform; vis: part obsc 204°-211°, obsc 211°-233°, 236°-259°; Racon (T); ◦))) *Horn Mo (N) 90s.*
Gunner 49°53'·64N 06°25'·09W.
Round Rock 49°53'·10N 06°25'·20W.

◄ ST MARY'S

Bacon Ledge 49°55'·22N 06°19'·27W Fl R 5s.
Ldg Lts 097·3°. Front 49°55'·12N 06°18'·52W Iso RW (vert) 2s; Or △. Rear, 110m from front, Oc WR (vert) 10s; Or x on W Bn.
St Mary's Pool Pier Hd ☆ 49°55'·11N 06°19'·00W Fl WRG 2s 5m 4M; vis: R070°-099°, W100°-130°, G099°-000°.
Tresco – Hulman 49°56'·29N 06°20'·31W Fl G 4s.

Bartholomew Ledges 49°54'·42N 06°19'·86W; Fl R 5s.
Spanish Ledge 49°53'·94N 06°18'·86W; ◦))) *Bell.*
Peninnis Hd ☆ 49°54'·28N 06°18'·22W Fl 20s 36m **17M**; W ○ metal Tr on B frame, B cupola; vis: 231°-117° but part obsc 048°-083° within 5M.
FR Lts on masts to N and NE.
Hats 49°56'·21N 06°17'·14W.

Round I ☆ 49°58'·74N 06°19'·40W Fl 10s 55m **24M**; W ○ Tr; vis: 021°-288°; H24; ◦))) *Horn (4) 60s*; Racon (M).

SEVEN STONES 50°03'·62N 06°04'·34W Fl (3) 30s 12m **25M**; R hull, Lt Tr amidships; Racon (O); ◦))) *Horn (3) 60s.*

Longships ☆ 50°04'·01N 05°44'·81W Iso WR 10s 35m **W18M**, **R15**/14M; Gy ○ Tr with helicopter platform; vis: R189°-208°, R (unintens) 208°-307°, R307°-327°, W327°- 189°; ◦))) *Horn 10s.*
FR on radio mast 4·9M NE.
Wolf Rock ☆ 49°56'·72N 05°48'·57W Fl 15s 34m **23M** (H24); Racon (T); ◦))) *Horn 30s.*
Runnel Stone 50°01'·19N 05°40'·36W Q (6) + L Fl 15s; ◦))) *Bell, Whis.*

LAND'S END TO LIZARD POINT

Tater-du ☆ 50°03'·14N 05°34'·68W Fl (3) 15s 34m **20M**; W ○ Tr; vis: 241°-074°. Also FR 31m 13M vis: 060°-074° over Runnel stone and in places 074°-077° within 4M; ◦))) *Horn (2) 30s.*

◄ MOUSEHOLE

N Pier Hd ☆ 50°04'·98N 05°32'·27W 2 FG (vert) 8m 4M; Gy mast; replaced by FR when hbr closed.

Low Lee 50°05'·56N 05°31'·38W Q (3) 10s.

◄ NEWLYN

S Pier Hd ☆ 50°06'·19N 05°32'·57W Fl 5s 10m 9M; W ○ Tr, R base & cupola; vis: 253°-336°.
N Pier Hd ☆ 50°06'·19N 05°32'·62W F WG 4m 2M; vis: G238°-248°, W over hbr.

The Gear 50°06'·59N 05°31'·56W.

◄ PENZANCE

Gear Rk 50°06'·63N 05°31'·62W.
S Pier Hd ☆ 50°07'·07N 05°31'·69W Fl WR 5s 11m **W17M**, R12M; W ○ Tr, B base; vis: R (unintens) 159°-224°, R224°-268°, W268°-344·5°, R344·5°-shore.
Albert Pier Hd ☆ 50°07'·10N 05°31'·80W 2 FG (vert) 11m 2M.
Western Cressar 50°07'·21N 05°31'·13W.
Ryeman Rks 50°07'·25N 05°30'·33W.
Mountamopus 50°04'·62N 05°26'·27W Q (6) + L Fl 15s.

◄ PORTHLEVEN

S Pier ☆ 50°04'·91N 05°19'·09W FG 10m 4M; G metal col, Lts shown when inner hbr is open.

Lizard ☆ 49°57'·61N 05°12'·13W Fl 3s 70m **26M**; W 8-sided Tr; vis: 250°-120°, part vis: 235°-250°; reflection may be seen inshore of these bearings; ◦))) *Siren Mo (N) 60s.*

LIZARD POINT TO START POINT

Manacles 50°02'·81N 05°01'·92W Q (3) 10s; ◦))) *Bell.*
Helston 50°04'·96N 05°00'·82W Fl Y 2·5s.
August Rock 50°06'·11N 05°04'·93W (PA); (seasonal).

St Anthony Hd ☆ 50°08'·47N 05°00'·96W Iso WR 15s 22m **W22/20M, R20M**; W 8-sided Tr; vis: W295°-004°, R004°-022° over Manacles, W022°-172°; (H24); Fog Det Lt L Fl 5s 18m **16M** min vis: 148·75°-151·25°; ◦))) *Horn 30s.*

◄ FALMOUTH

Black Rock 50°08'·72N 05°01'·99W.
Black Rock 50°08'·68N 05°01'·73W Q (3) 10s.
Castle 50°08'·98N 05°01'·63W Fl G 10s.
St Mawes 50°09'·09N 05°01'·41W.
The Governor 50°09'·15N 05°02'·38W VQ (3) 5s.
E Bkwtr Hd ☆ 50°09'·34N 05°02'·96W 2 FR (vert) 2m.
N Arm East Hd ☆ 50°09'·41N 05°03'·20W Q 19m 3M.
West Narrows 50°09'·38N 05°02'·07W Fl (2) R 10s.
East Narrows 50°09'·43N 05°01'·90W Fl (2) G 10s.
The Vilt 50°09'·98N 05°02'·28W Fl (4) G 15s.
Northbank 50°10'·35N 05°02'·12W Fl R 4s.
St Just 50°10'·42N 05°01'·72W QR.
Visitors Yacht Haven ☆ 50°09'·27N 05°03'·91W 2 FR (vert)
No. 1 50°09'·77N 05°04'·36W QR.

'A' 50°08'·54N 04°46'·38W Fl Y 10s.
'B' 50°10'·94N 04°45'·57W Fl Y 5s.
'C' 50°11'·07N 04°46'·46W Fl Y 2s.

Gwineas 50°14'·49N 04°45'·39W Q (3) 10s; ◦))) *Bell.*

◄ MEVAGISSEY

Victoria Pier Hd ☆ 50°16'·15N 04°46'·93W Fl (2) 10s 9m 12M; ◦))) *Dia 30s.*

Puckey's Ground 50°19'·50N 04°43'·08W.
Cannis Rock 50°18'·37N 04°39'·95W Q (6) + L Fl 15s; ◦))) *Bell.*

◄ FOWEY

Fowey Lt Bn Tr ☆ 50°19'·62N 04°38'·84W L Fl WR 5s 28m W11M, R9M; W 8-sided Tr, R lantern; vis: R284°-295°, W295°-028°, R028°-054°.
St Catherine's Pt ☆ 50°19'·69N 04°38'·66W FR 15m 2M; vis: 150°-295°.

Lamp Rock ☆ 50°19'·70N 04°38'·38W Fl G 5s 7m 2M; vis: 088°-205°.
Whitehouse Pt ☆ 50°19'·98N 04°38'·24W Iso WRG 3s 11m W11M, R8M, G8M; vis: G017°-022°, W022°-032°, R032°-037°.
Udder Rock 50°18'·92N 04°33'·86W; Q (6) + L Fl 15s; *Bell.*

◀ POLPERRO

Tidal basin, W Pier Hd ☆ 50°19'·86N 04°30·96W F or FR 4m 4M; R when hbr closed in bad weather.
Spy House Pt ☆ 50°19'·81N 04°30'·70W Iso WR 6s 30m 7M; vis: W288°-060°, R060°-288°.

◀ LOOE

Mid Main 50°20'·55N 04°26'·94W Q (3) 10s 2M.
Banjo Pier Hd ☆ 50°21'·05N 04°27'·06W Oc WR 3s 8m **W15M**, R12M; vis: W013°-207°, R207°-267°, W267°-313°, R313°-332°.

Eddystone ☆ 50°10'·85N 04°15'·94W Fl (2) 10s 41m **17M**; Gy Tr, R lantern. Same structure, Iso R 10s 28m 8M; vis: 110·5°-130·5° over Hand Deeps; helicopter platform, Racon (T); *Horn 30s.*
Hand Deeps 50°12'·69N 04°21'·11W Q (9) 15s.

◀ PLYMOUTH SOUND, WESTERN CHANNEL

Rame Hd, S end 50°18'·67N 04°13'·37W (unlit).
Draystone 50°18'·85N 04°11'·07W Fl (2) R 5s.
Knap 50°19'·56N 04°10'·02W Fl G 5s.
OSR South 50°18'·86N 04°10'·11W Fl Y 2s.
OSR North 50°19'·00N 04°09'·93WFl Y 2s.
Plymouth Bkwtr W Hd ☆ 50°20'·07N 04°09'·53W Fl WR 10s 19m W12M, R9M; W ○ Tr; vis: W262°-208°, R208°-262°. Iso 4s (same Tr) 12m 10M; vis: 033°-037°; *Horn (1) 15s.*
Mount Wise Pier Root ☆ 50°21'·96N 04°10'·33W Dir Lt 343°. Dir WRG 7m W13M, R5M, G5M; vis: FG331°-338, Al WG 338°-342° W phase increasing with Brg, F W 342°-344°, Al WR344°-348° R phase increasing with bearing, F R348°-351°. H24.
In fog, F; vis: 341·5°-344·5°.
Devils Pt ☆ 50°21'·59N 04°10'·04W QG 5m 3M; in fog Fl 5s.
Queens Gnd 50°20'·29N 04°10'·08W Fl (2) R 10s.
New Gnd 50°20'·47N 04°09'·44W Fl R 2s.
Melampus 50°21'·15N 04°08'·73W Fl R 4s.
S Winter 50°21'·40N 04°08'·56W Q (6) + L Fl 15s.
S Mallard 50°21'·51N 04°08'·30W VQ (6) + L Fl 10s.
W Mallard 50°21'·57N 04°08'·36W QG.
NE Winter 50°21'·54N 04°08'·50W QR.
NW Winter 50°21'·54N 04°08'·70W VQ (9) 10s.
Mount Batten Breakwater Hd ☆ 50°21'·56N 04°08'·13W 2 FG (vert).
Fishers Nose ☆ 50°21'·80N 04°08'·02W Fl (3) R 10s 6m 4M.
Queen Anne's Marina Bkwtr knuckle ☆ 50°21'·85N 04°08'·02W Oc G 8s 5m 2M.

Ldg Lts 349°. Front, Mallard Shoal 50°21'·60N 04°08'·33W Q WRG 5m W10M, R3M, G3M; W △ Or bands; vis: G233°-043°, R043°-067°, G067°-087°, W087°-099°. Ldg sector R099°-108°. Rear, 396m from front, West Hoe Dir WRG 9m W13M, R5M, G5M; vis: FG 309°-311° F 314°-317°, FR 320°-329°; shown H24. In fog Fl 5s; vis: 232°-110°.
Millbay Marina, Military Pier Hd ☆ 50°21'·75N 04°09'·17W QG 10m 2M.
Asia 50°21'·56N 04°08'·88W Fl (2) R 5s.
N Drakes Is 50°21'·52N 04°09'·38W Fl R 4s.

E Vanguard 50°21'·47N 04°10'·70W QG.
W Vanguard 50°21'49N 04°09'·98W Fl G 3s.
Battery 50°21'·52N 04°10'·21W Fl R 2s.
Devils Point 50°21'·59N 04°10'·04W QG 5m 3M; Fl 5s in fog.

◀ PLYMOUTH SOUND, EASTERN CHANNEL

Duke Rk 50°20'·32N 04°08'·23W VQ (9) 10s.
Bovisand Pier 50°20'·24N 04°07·72W 2 FG (vert) 4m 3M.
West Staddon 50°20'·17N 04°07'·84W Q (9) 15s 6m 3M.
Bkwtr E Hd 50°20'·01N 04°08'·25W L Fl WR 10s 9m W8M, R6M; vis: R190°-353°, W353°-001°, R001°-018°, W018°-190°.
Staddon Pt 50°20'·17N 04°07'·54W Oc WRG 10s 15m W8M, R5M, G5M; W structure, R bands. vis: G348°-038°, G038°-050°, R050°-090°; H24.
Whidbey 50°19'·53N 04°07'·27W Oc (2) WRG 10s 29m W8M, R6M, G6M; Or and W col; vis: G000°-137·5°, W137·5°-139·5°, R139·5°-159°; shown H24.
West Tinker 50°19'·25N 04°08'·64W Q (9) 15s.
East Tinker 50°19'·20N 04°08'·30W Q (3) 10s.
Wembury Pt ☆ 50°19'·01N 04°06'·63W Oc Y 10s 45m; occas.

NGS W 50°11'·13N 04°00'·85W Fl Y 5s.
NGS E 50°11'·24N 03°59'·07W Fl Y 10s.

◀ WEMBURY BAY/RIVER YEALM

Range C 50°18'·50N 04°07'·65W Fl Y 5s.
Range B 50°18'·30N 04°07'·07W Fl Y 10s.
Range A 50°18'·10N 04°06'·53W Fl Y 5s.
The Sand Bar 50°18'·59N 04°04'·12W Fl R 5s (Apr-Oct).
East Sand Bar 50°18'·60N 04°04'·06W (Apr-Oct).
Spit 50°18'·64N 04°03'·25W.

◀ SALCOMBE

Sandhill Pt Dir Lt 000° 50°13'·77N 03°46'·67W Dir Fl WRG 2s 27m W10M, R7M, G7M; R&W ♦ on W mast; vis: R002·5°-182·5°, G182·5°-357·5°, W357·5°-002·5°.
Wolf Rk 50°13'·537N 03°46'·58W QG.
Pound Stone 50°13'·64N 03°46'·67W.
Blackstone Rk 50°13'·61N 03°46'·51W Q (2) G 8s 4m 2M.
Ldg Lts 042°5·. Front 50°14'·53N 03°45'·31W Q 5m 8M. Rear, 180m from front, Q 45m 8M.
Old Harry 50°13'·69N 03°46'·59W.
Castle 50°13'·73N 03°46'·52W.
Landing Stage ☆ 50°14'·17N 03°45'·97W FR 4m 3M.

Starehole 50°12'·53N 03°46'·87W; (Apr-Sep).
Gara 50°12'·83N 03°45'·27W; (Apr-Sep).
Gammon 50°12'·03N 03°45'·57W; (Apr-Sep).
Prawle 50°12'·13N 03°43'·87W; (Apr-Sep).

Start Pt ☆ 50°13'·33N 03°38'·54W Fl (3) 10s 62m **25M**; vis: 184°-068°. FR 55m 12M (same Tr) vis: 210°-255° over Skerries bank; *Horn 60s.*
Skerries Bank 50°16'·31N 03°33'·76W; *Bell.*

START POINT TO PORTLAND BILL

◀ DARTMOUTH

Homestone 50°19'·60N 03°33'·56W QR.
Castle Ledge 50°19'·99N 03°33'·11W Fl G 5s.
Checkstone 50°20'·45N 03°33'·81W Fl (2) R 5s.
Kingswear ☆ 50°20'·81N 03°34'·09W Iso WRG 3s 9m 8M; W ○

Tr; vis: G318°-325°, W325°-331°, R331°-340°.
Bayards Cove 50°20'·85N 03°34'·64W Fl WRG 2s 5m 6M; vis: G280°-289°, W289°-297°, R297°-shore.
Kingswear Marina "A" 50°21'·00N 03°34'·39W 2 FG (vert).
Dart Marina S end 50°21'·45N 03°34'·58W 2 FR (vert).
Anchor Stone 50°22'·78N 03°35'·30W Fl (2) R 5s 1M.
RDYC 1 50°18'·83N 03°35'·32W; (Apr-Oct).
RDYC 2 50°18'·71N 03°33'·37W; (Apr-Oct).
RDYC 3 50°20'·10N 03°31'·49W; (Apr-Oct).

Berry Hd ☆ 50°23'·97N 03°29'·01W Fl (2) 15s 58m 14M; W Tr; vis: 100°-023°. R Lts on radio mast 5·7M NW.

◀ BRIXHAM

Victoria Bkwtr Hd 50°24'·33N 03°30'·78W Oc R 15s 9m 6M.
No. 1 50°24'·31N 03°30'·83W Fl R.
No. 2 50°24'·30N 03°30'·89W Fl G.
Fairway Dir Lt 159° 50°23'·83N 03°30'·57W Dir Iso WRG 5s 4m 6M; vis: G145°-157°, W157°-161°, R161°-173°.
No. 3 50°24'·13N 03°30'·72W L Fl R.
No. 4 50°24'·11N 03°30'·77W L Fl G.
New Pier Hd 50°23'·86N 03°30'·65W QG 6m 3M.
Prince William Marina SW end 50°23'·96N 03°30'·60W 2 Fl R 5s (vert) 4m 2M.
Prince William Marina E end 50°24'·07N 03°30'·44W 2 Fl G 5s (vert) 4m 2M.

◀ PAIGNTON

Black Rock Outfall 50°25'·95N 03°33'·15W Q (3) 10s 5m 3M.
E Quay 50°25'·96N 03°33'·35W QR 7m 3M.

◀ TORQUAY

50°27'·42N 03°31'·80W QG (May-Sept).
Princess Pier Hd 50°27'·46N 03°31'·73W QR 9m 6M.
Haldon Pier Hd 50°27'·43N 03°31'·73W QG 9m 6M.
Marina Pontoon SE end 50°27'·50N 03°31'·69W 2 FR (vert) 2m.

◀ TEIGNMOUTH

Outfall 50°31'·95N 03°27'·78W Fl Y 5s.
Trg Wall Middle 50°32'·33N 03°29'·93W Oc R 5·5s 4m 2M.
Den Point 50°32'·42N 03°30'·05W Oc G 5·5s FG (vert).
50°32'·50N 03°30'·11W Fl R 5s.
50°32'·53N 03°30'·00W Fl G 5s.
Powderham Terrace 50°32'·58N 03°29'·81W FR 11m 3M.
The Den 50°32'·55N 03°29'·84W FR 10m 6M.
50°32'·63N 03°30'·03W Fl R 5s.

Pontoon 50°32'·80N 03°29'·20W Fl Y 10s (Jun-Sep)

◀ EXMOUTH

E Exe 50°36'·01N 03°22'·25W Q (3) 10s.
No. 1 51°36'·17N 03°22'·75W QG.
No. 2 50°36'·11N 02°22'·81W.
No. 3 50°36'·29N 02°23'·40W Fl G 2s.
No. 4 50°36'·23N 02°23'·40W.
No. 7 50°36'·39N 02°23'·97W QG.
No. 8 50°36'·36N 02°24'·00W QR.
Ldg Lts 305°. Front, 50°36'·99N 03°25'·34W Iso 2s 6m 7M. Rear, 57m from front, Q 12m 7M.
Pier, S corner 50°36'·98N 03°25'·43W 2 FG (vert) 7m 3M.
Straight Point 50°36'·49N 03°21'·76W Fl R 10s 34m 7M; vis: 246°-071°.
Outfall 50°36'·25N 02°21'·50W Fl Y 5s.

DZS 50°36'·12N 03°19'·42W Fl Y 3s.
DZN 50°36'·82N 03°19'·30W Fl Y 3s.

◀ SIDMOUTH/AXMOUTH

Sidmouth ☆ 50°40'·49'N 03°14'·45W Fl R 5s 2M.
R Sid Outfall 50°40'·52N 03°14'·78W.
Axmouth Pier Hd 50°42'·12N 03°03'·31W Fl G 4s 7m 2M.

◀ LYME REGIS

Ldg Lts 296°. Front, Victoria Pier Hd 50°43'·19N 02°56'·17W Oc WR 8s 6m W9M. R7M; Bu col; vis: R296°-116°, W116°-296°. Rear, 240m from front, FG 8m 9M.

◀ BRIDPORT

West Bay Outfall 50°41'·96N 02°46'·38W Fl Y 5s.
W Pier Hd 50°42'·56N 02°45'·85W FR 3m 2M; (occas).
E Pier Hd 50°42'·56N 02°45'·83W FG 3m 2M; (occas).
W Pier Root 50°42'·64N 02°45'·84W Iso R 2s 9m 5M.
ODAS 50°37'·43N 02°43'·68W Fl (5) Y 10s.

DZ 50°36'·50N 02°42'·00W Fl Y 3s.

◀ OFFSHORE

Channel 49°54'·46N 02°53'·94W Fl 15s 12m **25M**; *Horn 20s*; Racon (O).
E Channel 49°58'·71N 02°28'·95W Fl Y 5s; Racon (T).
Wk Marker 49°53'·34N 02°24'·29W VQ; Racon (D).
Wk Marker 49°52'·04N 02°25'·70W Q (9) 15s; Racon (D).
Wk Marker 49°51'·09N 02°24'·13W Q (6) + L Fl 15s.
Wk Marker 49°52'·11N 02°22'·55W Q (3) 10s.

Note: For English Channel Waypoints see 9.1.7.

9.1.5 PASSAGE INFORMATION

Refer to *West Country Cruising* (Macmillan Reeds/Fishwick); *Shell Channel Pilot* (Imray/Cunliffe); *Isles of Scilly Pilot* (Imray/Brandon) and Admiralty *Channel Pilot* (NP 27). See 9.0.6 for distances across the Channel, and 9.3.5 for cross-Channel passages. Admiralty Small Craft Folio SC5602 (11 charts) covers Falmouth to Fowey and SC5601 (10 charts) Start Point to the Needles. Each contains A2 size charts in a clear plastic wallet and costs £35.00 (2000).

NORTH CORNWALL (charts *1149, 1156*) For the coast of North Cornwall see 9.11.5. For St Ives, Hayle, Newquay, Padstow and Port Issac, see 9.11.27. Certain information is repeated below for continuity and convenience.

The approaches to the Bristol Chan along N coast of Cornwall are very exposed, with little shelter in bad weather. From Land's End to St Ives the coast is rugged with high cliffs. Padstow is a refuge, except in strong NW winds. In these waters yachts need to be sturdy and well equipped, since if bad weather develops no shelter may be at hand. Streams are moderate W of Lundy, but strong around the island, and much stronger towards the Bristol Channel proper.

ISLES OF SCILLY (9.1.8 and charts *34, 883*) There are 50 islands, extending 21-31M WSW of Land's End, with many rky outcrops and offlying dangers. Although they are all well charted, care is needed particularly in poor vis. See 9.1.8 and .9 for details of this rewarding cruising ground.

Several approach transits are shown on chart 34, and these should be followed, because the tidal streams around the islands are difficult to predict with accuracy. They run harder off points and over rks, where overfalls may occur. Yachts must expect to lie to their anchors. No one anch gives shelter from all winds and swell, so be ready to move at short notice.

Conspic landmarks are Bishop Rk lt ho, Round Island lt ho, the disused lt ho on St Agnes, the daymark at the E end of St Martin's, Penninis lt ho at the S end of St Mary's, and the TV mast and CG sig stn (at the old telegraph tower) both in the NW corner of St Mary's.

ISLES OF SCILLY TO LAND'S END (chart *1148*) The Seven Stones (rks) lie 7M NE of the Isles of Scilly and 15M W of Land's End; many of them dry, with ledges in between. They are marked by lt F (fog sig) on E side. Wolf Rk (lt, fog sig) is 8M SW of Land's End, and is steep-to. The N/S lanes of Land's End TSS lie between Seven Stones and Wolf Rk. The ITZ, W of Longships, is 3M wide; see 9.1.2.

Between Scilly and Land's End (chart 1148) streams are rotatory, clockwise. Relative to HW Dover (sp rates about 1kn), they set W from HWD; N from HW + 2; NE from HW + 4; E from HW –6; SSE from HW – 4; and SW from HW – 2.

For the 5-6hrs passage to Scilly leave the Runnel Stone at HWD–2; a fair W-going tide lasts for only 3hrs, with cross tides setting SW then NW to N. Consider arriving at dawn. For the return passage tidal streams are a little less critical.

LAND'S END (charts *1148, 1149, 777* and *2345*) Land's End peninsula (30M Penzance to St Ives) is often a dangerous lee shore and always a critical tidal gate. There are many inshore and offlying rks and no ports of refuge. From S to N the main features are:

Gwennap Head, with the Runnel Stone (buoyed) 1M to the S; Land's End and Longships reef 1M to the W; Cape Cornwall and The Brisons; Pendeen Head and The Wra. The coast of N Cornwall further to the E is described in 9.11.5.

The Runnel Stone (0·5m) lies 7ca S of Gwennap Hd, with rks and uncharted wrecks closer inshore. These dangers are in the R sectors of Longships and Tater-du lts. Passage between the Runnel Stone and Gwennap is not advised even in calm weather and at HW. From Gwennap Hd to Land's End, 2M NW, rks extend up to $1\frac{1}{2}$ca offshore, and depths are irregular to seaward causing a bad sea in strong W winds over a W-going tide.

4 cables S of Land's End Armed Knight, a jagged 27m high rock, overlooks Longships. This is an extensive and very dangerous reef made up of Carn Bras, on which the lt ho stands, and other rky islets. About 5ca to the E and NE are Kettle's Bottom 5m and Shark's Fin 3·4m, both isolated and very dangerous drying rks. The $\frac{1}{2}$M wide passage between Land's End and Kettle's Bottom is safe in calm, settled weather, but never at night. To clear Kettle's Bottom and Shark's Fin, keep the Brisons High summit just open W of Low summit brg 001°. Local streams exceed 4kn at Sp and are unpredictable. In adverse weather navigate in the ITZ, well W of Longships.

Whitesand Bay (chart 2345) is 1M NNE of Land's End. After rounding Cowloe Rks and its drying offliers, Little Bo 3·4m and Bo Cowloe 6m, the transit 150° of two bns on the cliffs E of Sennen Cove leads to a fair weather ⚓ in about 2mon the S side of the bay, only safe in offshore winds. Sennen Ch tr (110m) is conspic, almost on this transit.

Cape Cornwall (conspic ruined chy) is about 3M further N. It overlooks The Brisons, two rky islets (27 and 22m, High and Low summits) about 5ca to SW. There is no passage inside The Brisons. The Vyneck is a rk drying 1·8m 3ca NW of Cape Cornwall.

3M to NNE is Pendeen Hd (lt ho) and the Wra (or Three Stone Oar), drying rks, close N. Between C Cornwall and Pendeen overfalls and a race extend up to $1\frac{1}{2}$M offshore; avoid except in calm weather and at slack water. Midway between Cape Cornwall and Pendeen a conspic TV mast is 1M inland.

Tidal Strategy Streams run hard round Land's End, setting N/S and E/W past it. It is truly a tidal gate, and one which favours a N-bound passage – with careful timing nearly $9\frac{1}{2}$ hrs of fair tide

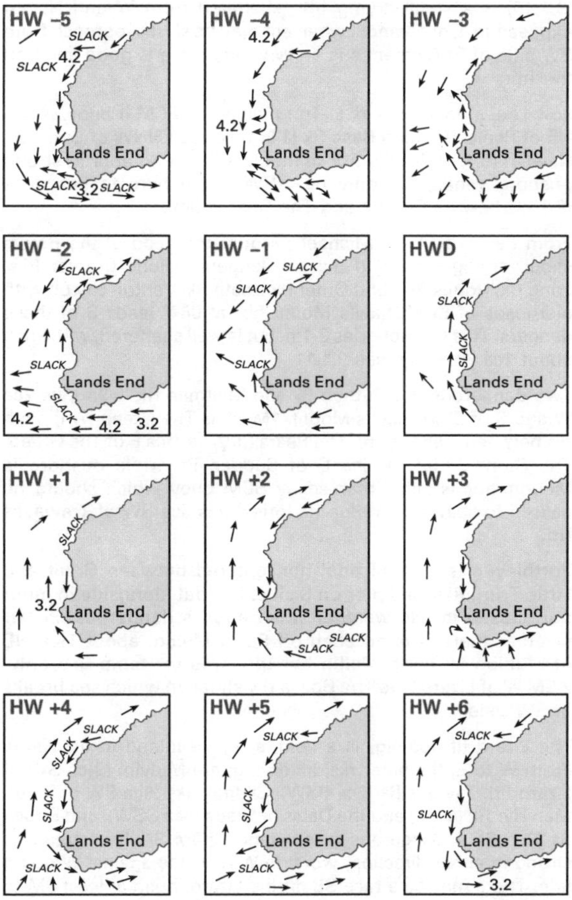

can be carried, from HWD–3 to HWD+5. Stay close inshore to use currents running counter to the tidal streams. The chartlets referenced to HW Dover, illustrate tidal streams and inshore currents.

Example N-bound: At HWD+1 the N-going flood starts off Gwennap and does not turn NE along the N Cornish coast until HWD+3, but as early as HWD–3 an inshore current is beginning to run N'ly. So, N-bound, use this by arriving off Runnel Stone at HWD–2 and then keep within ¼M of the shore. If abeam Brisons at HWD, the tide and current should serve for the next 6 or 7 hrs to make good St Ives, or even Newquay and Padstow.

Example S-bound: If S-bound from St Ives to Newlyn, aim to reach the Runnel Stone by HWD+5, ie with 2 hrs of E-going tide in hand for the remaining 9M to Newlyn. This would entail leaving St Ives 5 hrs earlier, at HWD, to make the 20M passage; buck a foul tide for the first 3 hrs but use an inshore S-going current, keeping as close inshore as prudent, but having to move offshore to clear the Wra and the Brisons. This timing would suit passage from S Wales and Bristol Chan, going inshore of Longships if the weather suits.

From Ireland, ie Cork or further W, the inshore passage would not benefit. But plan to be off the Runnel Stone at HWD+5 if bound for Newlyn; or at HWD+3 if bound for Helford/Falmouth, with the W-going stream slackening and 5 hrs of fair tide to cover the remaining 20M past the Lizard.

GWENNAP HEAD TO LIZARD POINT (chart *777*) Close E of Gwennap there is no anch off Porth Curno, due to cables. Approaching Mount's Bay, the Bucks (3·3m) are 2ca ESE of Tater-du lt ho. Gull Rk (24m) is 9ca NE of Tater-du, close off the E point of Lamorna Cove. Little Heaver (dries) is 100m SW of Gull Rk, and Kemyel Rk (dries) is 1¾ca ENE. Mousehole (9.1.10) is a small drying hbr, sheltered from W and N, but exposed to E or S winds, when ent may be shut. Approach from SW side of St Clement's Is. In W winds there is good anch off the hbr.

Low Lee, a dangerous rk (1·1m) marked by ECM lt buoy, is 4ca NE of Penlee Pt. Carn Base Rk (1·8m) lies 3ca NNW of Low Lee. Newlyn (9.1.10) is only hbr in Mount's B safe to appr in strong onshore winds, but only near HW. From here to Penzance (9.1.11) beware Dog Rk and The Gear (1·9m).

From Penzance to St Michael's Mount the head of the Bay is shoal, drying 4ca off in places. Dangers include Cressar Rks, Long Rk, Hogus Rks, and Outer Penzeath Rk. Venton chy on with pierheads of St Michael's Mount hbr at 084° leads S of these dangers. This tiny hbr dries 2·1m, but is well sheltered, with anch about 1ca W of ent, see 9.1.11.

Two dangerous rks, Guthen Rk and Maltman Rk (0·9m), lie 2ca W and S of St Michael's Mount. 1M SE is The Greeb (7m), with rks between it and shore. The Bears (dry) lie 1¾ca E of The Greeb. The Stone (dries) is 5ca S of Cudden Pt, while offshore is Mountamopus shoal marked by SCM buoy which should be passed to seaward. Welloe Rk (dries) lies 5ca SW of Trewavas Hd.

Porthleven is a small tidal hbr, entered between Great and Little Trigg Rks and pier on S side. Dry out alongside in inner hbr, closed in bad weather when appr is dangerous. In fair weather there is good anch off Porth Mellin, about 1½ca NE of Mullion Is; Porth Mellin hbr (dries) is for temp use only. 2·5M W of Lizard Pt is The Boa, a rky shoal on which sea breaks in SW gales.

The Lizard (lt, fog sig) is a bold, steep headland (chart 2345). From W to E, the outer rks, all drying, are Mulvin, (2½ca SW of Lizard Pt), Taylor's Rk (2ca SSW); Clidgas Rks (5ca SW of lt ho), Men Hyr Rk (4·1m) and the Dales or Stags (5ca SSW), and Enoch Rk (3ca S). A dangerous race extends 2-3M S when stream is strong in either direction, worst in W'ly winds against W-going tide. There may be a race SE off the Lizard. Keep at least 3M to seaward if going outside the race where slack water occurs at about HW Devonport –3 and +3. Closer inshore the stream turns E at HW Devonport –5, and W at HW +2, rates up to 3kn at sp. An inshore passage is shorter, but is never free of rough water. Either side of local LW (½hr before LW Devonport = HW Dover) the drying rks above will be visible, but beware Vrogue, a dangerous sunken rk (1·8m), 1M E of the Lizard lt ho, and Craggan Rks (1·5m) 1M N of Vrogue Rk. If awaiting slack water, there are, from W to E, ⚓s at Kynance Cove, Housel Cove (NE of the lt ho and below conspic hotel), Church Cove, Cadgwith and Coverack.

LIZARD POINT TO GRIBBIN HEAD (chart *1267*) N of Black Head rks extend at least 1ca offshore; a rk drying 1·6m lies off Chynhalls Pt. Coverack gives good anch in W winds, see 9.1.12. From Dolor Pt to E of Lowland Pt are drying rks 2½ca offshore. The Manacles (dry), 7½ca E and SE of Manacle Pt, are marked by ECM lt buoy and are in R sector of St Anthony Hd lt. Off the Manacles the stream runs NE from HW Devonport – 0345, and SW from HW+ 0200, sp rates 1·25kn. From E of the Manacles there are no offshore dangers on courses NNW to Helford River ent (9.1.12) or N to River Fal (9.1.13).

3M NNE from St Anthony Hd, Porthscatho offers safe anch in W'lies (9.1.14). Gull Rk (38m high) lies 6ca E of Nare Hd, at W side of Veryan B. The Whelps (dry) are 5ca SW of Gull Rk. There is a passage between Gull Rk and the shore. In Veryan B beware Lath Rk (2·1m) 1M SE of Portloe.

On E side of Veryan B, Dodman Pt is a 110m flat-topped cliff, with a conspic stone cross. Depths are irregular for 1M S, with heavy overfalls in strong winds over sp tide, when it is best to pass 2M off. 3 SPM lt buoys (targets) lie 2·3 to 4·8M SSE of Dodman Pt. For details of naval gunnery practice between Dodman Pt and Gribbin Head, see 9.1.15. Gorran Haven, a sandy cove with L-shaped pier which dries at sp, is a good anch in offshore winds. 2·1M NE of Dodman Pt, and 1M ENE of Gorran Haven, is Gwineas Rk (8m high) and Yaw Rk (0·9m), marked by ECM lt buoy. Passage inside Gwineas Rk is possible, but not advised in strong onshore winds or poor vis. Portmellon and Mevagissey B, (9.1.14) are good anchs in offshore winds. For Charlestown and Par, see 9.1.15.

GRIBBIN HEAD TO START POINT (charts *1267, 1613*) Gribbin Hd has a conspic daymark, a □ tr 25m high with R & W bands. In bad weather the sea breaks on rocks round Head. Cannis Rk (4·3m) is 2½ca SE, marked by SCM lt buoy. 3M E of Fowey (9.1.15) is Udder Rk (0·6m) marked by a SCM, 5ca offshore in E part of Lantivet Bay. Larrick Rk (4·3m) is 1½ca off Nealand Pt.

Polperro hbr dries, but the inlet gives good anch in offshore winds, see 9.1.15. Beware E Polca Rk roughly in mid-chan. E of Polperro shoals lie 2½ca off Downend Pt, (memorial). The chan between Hannafore Pt and Looe (or St George's) Island nearly dries. The Ranneys (dry) are rks extending 2½ca E and SE of the Island, see 9.1.16. There are overfalls S of Looe Island in bad weather.

Eddystone rks (chart 1613) lie 8M S of Rame Hd. Shoals extend 3ca E. Close NW of the lt ho (lt, fog sig) is the stump of old lt ho. The sea can break on Hand Deeps, sunken rks 3·5M NW of Eddystone, marked by SPM light buoy.

Rame Hd, on W side of ent to Plymouth Sound (9.1.17), is conspic cone shaped, with small chapel on top; rks extend about 1ca off and wind-over-tide overfalls may be met 1·5M to seaward. Approaching Plymouth from the W, clear Rame Hd and Penlee Point by about 8ca, then steer NNE for W end of the Breakwater. At the SE ent to Plymouth Sound, Great Mewstone (59m) is a conspic rky islet 4ca off Wembury Pt (naval gunnery range). Approaching from the E keep at least 1M offshore until clear of the drying Mewstone Ledge, 2½ca SW of Great Mewstone. The Slimers, which dry, lie 2ca E of Mewstone. E and W Ebb Rks (awash) lie 2½ca off Gara Pt (chart 30). Wembury Bay gives access to R. Yealm (9.1.19).

See 9.1.18 for submarine exercise areas from the Isles of Scilly to Start Point. These areas are also used by warships, especially near Plymouth. Yachts should try to stay clear.

Between Gara Pt and Stoke Pt, 2·5M to E, dangers extend about 4ca offshore in places. In Bigbury Bay beware Wells Rk and other dangers 5ca S of Erme Hd. From Bolt Tail to Bolt Hd keep 5ca offshore to clear Greystone Ledge, sunken rks near Ham Stone (11m), and Gregory Rks 5ca SE of Ham Stone. The Little Mew Stone and Mew Stone lie below dramatic Bolt Head. Keep approx 7½ca SE of the Mewstones before turning N for Salcombe (9.1.20).

START POINT TO STRAIGHT POINT (charts *1613, 3315*) Start Pt (lt, horn) is 3M ENE of Prawle Pt; it is a long headland with conspic radio masts, distinctive cock's comb spine and W lt ho near end. Black Stone rk is visible (6m high) 2½ca SSE of the lt ho, with Cherrick Rks (1m) a cable further S; other drying rks lie closer inshore. The stream runs 4kn at sp, causing a race extending 1½M to the E and 1M to the S. In fair weather the overfalls can be avoided by passing close to seaward of rks; there is no clear-cut inshore passage as such. In bad weather keep at least 2M off. 1M off Start the stream sets SW from HW Devonport +4 to HW –3, and NE from HW –2 to HW +3; thus slack water is about HW –2½ and HW +3½. Inshore it turns 30 minutes earlier.

Skerries Bank, on which sea breaks in bad weather, is 6ca NNE of Start Point (chart 1634). It has least depth of 2·1m at the S end, only 9ca from Start Pt. In offshore winds there is good anch in 3m 1ca off Hallsands (1M NW of Start). Between Dartmouth (9.1.21) and Brixham (9.1.22) rks extend 5ca offshore.

Berry Head (lt) is a steep, flat-topped headland (55m). Here the stream turns N at HW Devonport – 0105, and S at HW + 0440, sp rates 1·5kn. In Torbay (chart 26) the more obvious dangers are steep-to, but beware the Sunker 100m SW of Ore Stone, and Morris Rogue 5ca W of Thatcher Rk.

There are good anchs in Babbacombe B and in Anstey's cove in W winds; beware the Three Brothers (drying rks), S side of Anstey's cove. From Long Quarry Pt for 4M N to Teignmouth (9.1.24) there are no offlying dangers. Off Teignmouth the NNE-going stream begins at HW Devonport – 0135, and the SSW-going at HW+ 0510. In the ent the flood begins at HW Devonport – 0535, and the ebb at HW +0040. The stream runs hard off Ferry Pt; the ent is dangerous in onshore winds.

Between Teignmouth and Dawlish rks extend 1ca offshore. Beware Dawlish Rk (depth 2·1m) about 5ca off N end of town. Warren Sands and Pole Sands lie W of ent to the River Exe (9.1.25), and are liable to shift. Along the NE (Exmouth) side of the chan, towards Orcomb Pt and Straight Pt (lt), drying rks and shoals extend up to 2½ca from shore. There is a firing range off Straight Point.

The Editor thanks most warmly the Royal Cruising Club Pilotage Foundation for their kind permission to use material written by Hugh Davies and first published in Yachting Monthly magazine. This includes the unique tidal stream chartlets on the previous page which are of major assistance in rounding Land's End.

LYME BAY (chart 3315) Start Pt is W end of Lyme B (chart 3315), which stretches 50M ENE to Portland Bill. Tides are weak, rarely more than 0·75kn. From Start Pt to Portland Bill the tidal curve becomes progressively more distorted, especially on the rising tide. The rise is relatively fast for the 1st hr after LW; then slackens noticeably for the next 1½ hrs, before resuming the rapid rate of rise. There is often a stand at HW, not very noticeable at Start Point but lasting about 1½ hrs at Lyme Regis.

Between Torbay and Portland there is no hbr accessible in onshore winds, and yachtsmen must take care not to be caught on a lee shore. There are no dangers offshore. In offshore winds there is a good anch NE of Beer Hd, the western-most chalk cliff in England. 3·5M E of Lyme Regis (9.1.26) is Golden Cap (186m and conspic). High Ground and Pollock are rks 7ca offshore, 2M and 3M ESE of Golden Cap.

From 6M E of Bridport (9.1.27), Chesil Beach runs SE for about 8M to the N end of the Portland peninsula. From a distance The Isle of Portland does indeed look like an island, with its distinctive wedge-shaped profile sloping down from 144m at the N to the Bill at the S tip. It is mostly steep-to, but rks extend 2½ca from the Bill which is marked by a stone bn (18m) and conspic lt ho.

If heading up-Channel from Start Point, Dartmouth or Torbay time your departure to pass Portland Bill with a fair tide at all costs, especially at springs. If late, there is temp'y anchorage close inshore at Chesil Cove, abeam the highest part of Portland. See 9.2.5 for passage round the Bill either by the inshore or offshore routes.

9.1.6 DISTANCE TABLE

Approximate distances in nautical miles are by the most direct route while avoiding dangers and allowing for Traffic Separation Schemes. Places in italics are in adjoining areas; places in **bold** are in 9.0.6, Cross-Channel Distances.

1. *Milford Haven*	**1**																			
2. *Lundy Island*	28	**2**																		
3. *Padstow*	67	40	**3**																	
4. **Longships**	100	80	47	**4**																
5. St Mary's (Scilly)	120	102	69	22	**5**															
6. Penzance	115	95	62	15	37	**6**														
7. Lizard Point	123	103	72	23	40	16	**7**													
8. **Falmouth**	139	119	88	39	60	32	16	**8**												
9. Mevagissey	152	132	99	52	69	46	28	17	**9**											
10. **Fowey**	157	137	106	57	76	49	34	22	7	**10**										
11. Looe	163	143	110	63	80	57	39	29	16	11	**11**									
12. **Plymouth** (bkwtr)	170	150	117	70	92	64	49	39	25	22	11	**12**								
13. R. Yealm (ent)	172	152	119	72	89	66	49	39	28	23	16	4	**13**							
14. **Salcombe**	181	161	128	81	102	74	59	50	40	36	29	22	17	**14**						
15. Start Point	186	166	135	86	103	80	63	55	45	40	33	24	22	7	**15**					
16. Dartmouth	195	175	142	95	116	88	72	63	54	48	42	35	31	14	9	**16**				
17. Torbay	201	181	150	101	118	96	78	70	62	55	50	39	38	24	15	11	**17**			
18. **Exmouth**	213	193	162	113	131	107	90	82	73	67	61	51	49	33	27	24	12	**18**		
19. Lyme Regis	226	206	173	126	144	120	104	96	86	81	74	63	62	48	41	35	30	21	**19**	
20. *Portland Bill*	235	215	184	135	151	128	112	104	93	89	81	73	70	55	49	45	42	36	22	**20**

9.1.7 ENGLISH CHANNEL WAYPOINTS

Selected waypoints for use in crossing the English Channel, are listed in order from West to East. Additional waypoints in coastal waters are given in section 4 of each area (i.e. 9.1.4 to 9.3.4 on the English coast, and 9.14.4 to 9.16.4 and 9.22.4 for the North French coast and the Channel Islands). **All positions are referenced to the WGS 84/ETRS89 datum.**

ENGLISH COAST

AREA 1 (WGS 84 coordinates)

Wpt	*Name*	*Position*	
01	Bartholomew Ledge Lt By	49°54'·42N	06°19'·86W
02	Seven Stones Lt F	50°03'·62N	06°04'·36W
03	Runnel Stone Lt By	50°01'·19N	05°40'·36W
04	Low Lee Lt By	50°05'·56N	05°31'·38W
05	Mountamopus By	50°04'·62N	05°26'·27W
06	Lizard Pt Lt	49°57'·61N	05°12'·13W
07	August Rk By (seasonal)	50°06'·11N	05°04'·93W
08	Manacles Lt By	50°02'·81N	05°01'·92W
09	Black Rk Lt By	50°08'·68N	05°01'·73W
10	Castle Lt By	50°08'·98N	05°01'·63W
11	Helston Lt By	50°04'·96N	05°00'·82W
12	Gwineas Lt By	50°14'·49N	04°45'·39W
13	Cannis Rk Lt By	50°18'·37N	04°39'·95W
14	Udder Rk By	50°18'·92N	04°33'·86W
15	Hands Deep Lt By	50°12'·69N	04°21'·11W
16	West Tinker Lt By	50°19'·25N	04°08'·64W
17	East Tinker Lt By	50°19'·20N	04°08'·30W
18	Royal Dart YC No. 1 By*	50°18'·83N	03°35'·32W
19	Checkstone Lt By	50°20'·45N	03°33'·81W
20	Royal Dart YC No. 2 By*	50°18'·71N	03°33'·37W
21	Castle Ledge Lt By	50°19'·99N	03°33'·11W
22	Royal Dart YC No. 3 By*	50°20'·10N	03°31'·49W
23	East Exe Lt By	50°36'·00N	03°22'·38W
24	DZ Lt By	50°36'·50N	02°42'·00W

AREA 2 (WGS84 coordinates)

Wpt	*Name*	*Position*	
30	W Shambles Lt By	50°29'·78N	02°24'·41W
31	E Shambles Lt By	50°30'·78N	02°20'·08W
32	Peverill Ledge Lt By	50°36'·41N	01°56'·10W
33	Poole Bar No. 1 Lt By	50°39'·31N	01°55'·16W
34	Needles Fairway Lt By	50°38'·24N	01°38'·98W
35	SW Shingles Lt By	50°39'·35N	01°37'·39W
36	N Head Lt By	50°42'·69N	01°35'·52W
37	NE Shingles Lt By	50°41'·96N	01°33'·41W
38	W Princessa Lt By	50°40'·16N	01°03'·65W
39	Bembridge Ledge Lt By	50°41'·15N	01°02'·81W
40	New Grounds Lt By	50°42'·00N	00°58'·63W

AREA 3 (WGS84 coordinates)

Wpt	*Name*	*Position*	
45	Boulder Lt By	50°41'·55N	00°49'·11W
46	S Pullar Lt By	50°38'·82N	00°41'·18W
47	Owers Lt By	50°37'·63N	00°41'·19W
48	E Borough Hd Lt By	50°41'·52N	00°39'·11W
49	Littlehampton Outfall Lt By	50°46'·26N	00°30'·55W
50	Beacham Outfall Lt By	50°48'·45N	00°19'·50W
51	Shoreham Outfall Lt By	50°47'·88N	00°13'·72W
52	Sovereign Hbr Lt By	50°47'·41N	00°20'·72E
53	St Leonard's Outfall Lt By	50°49'·31N	00°31'·95E
54	Rye Fairway Lt By	50°54'·04N	00°48'·04E
55	Dungeness Outfall Lt By	50°54'·45N	00°58'·21E
56	Bullock Bank Lt By	50°46'·94N	01°07'·60E
57	S Varne Lt By	50°55'·63N	01°17'·27E
58	Varne Mid Lt By	50°58'·94N	01°19'·88E
59	E Varne Lt By	50°58'·22N	01°20'·87E
60	Varne Lanby	51°01'·29N	01°23'·90E
61	W Quern Lt By	51°18'·98N	01°25'·39E
62	Downs Lt By	51°14'·50N	01°26'·44E
63	Deal Bank Lt By	51°12'·92N	01°25'·57E
64	S Brake Lt By	51°15'·77N	01°26'·82E
65	Goodwin Fork Lt By	51°14'·33N	01°26'·84E
66	W Goodwin Lt By	51°15'·60N	01°27'·36E
67	Brake Lt By	51°16'·98N	01°28'·19E
68	S Goodwin Lt F	51°07'·97N	01°28'·49E
69	NW Goodwin Lt By	51°16'·56N	01°28'·56E
70	SW Goodwin Lt By	51°08'·58N	01°28'·68E
71	E Brake Lt By	51°19'·47N	01°29'·20E
72	Broadstairs Knoll Lt By	51°20'·88N	01°29'·48E
73	Gull Stream Lt By	51°18'·26N	01°29'·69E
74	Ramsgate (RA) Lt By	51°19'·60N	01°30'·13E
75	N Goodwin Lt By	51°17'·90N	01°30'·20E
76	Gull Lt By	51°19'·57N	01°31'·00E
77	Elbow Lt By	51°23'·23N	01°31'·59E
78	Goodwin Knoll Lt By	51°19'·57N	01°32'·20E
79	S Goodwin Lt By	51°10'·58N	01°32'·26E
80	NE Goodwin Lt By	51°20'·30N	01°34'·18E
81	SE Goodwin Lt By	51°12'·97N	01°34'·44E
82	E Goodwin Lt By	51°15'·67N	01°35'·69E
83	E Goodwin Lt F	51°13'·25N	01°36'·38E

OFFSHORE (WGS84 coordinates)

Wpt	*Name*	*Position*	
85	Channel Lt F	49°54'·46N	02°53'·74W
86	E Channel Lt By	49°58'·64N	02°29'·07W
87	EC2 Lt By	50°12'·14N	01°12'·49W
88	CS1 Lt By	50°33'·70N	00°03'·92W
89	Greenwich Lt V	50°24'·54N	00°00'·10W
90	CS2 Lt By	50°39'·12N	00°32'·62E
91	CS3 Lt By	50°52'·04N	01°02'·18E
92	Bullock Bank Lt By	50°46'·94N	01°07'·60E
93	N Colbart Lt By	50°57'·47N	01°23'·30E
94	CS4 Lt By	51°08'·60N	01°33'·94E
95	MPC Lt By	51°06'·13N	01°38'·25E
96	S Falls Lt By	51°13'·84N	01°43'·93E
97	F1 Lt By	51°11'·21N	01°44'·91E
98	Mid Falls Lt By	51°18'·63N	01°47'·00E
99	CS 5 Lt By	51°23'·02N	01°49'·90E
100	Inter Bank Lt By	51°16'·47N	01°52'·23E
101	F2 Lt By	51°20'·41N	01°56'·19E
102	Foxtrot 3 Lt F	51°23'·85N	02°00'·51E

CHANNEL ISLANDS

AREA 14 (WGS84 coordinates)

Wpt	*Name*	*Position*	
105	Reffée Lt By	49°27'·74N	02°31'·27W
106	Petite Canupe Lt Bn	49°30'·18N	02°29'·14W
107	Desormes Lt By	49°18'·94N	02°18'·02W
108	Passage Rk Lt By	49°09'·53N	02°12'·27W
109	Diamond Rk Lt By	49°10'·11N	02°08'·64W
110	Canger Rk Lt By	49°07'·34N	02°00'·38W
111	Frouquier Aubert Lt By	49°06'·09N	

111	Frouquier Aubert Lt By	49°06'·09N 01°58'·84W
112	Violet Lt By	49°07'·81N 01°57'·14W
113	NW Minquiers Lt By	48°59'·64N 02°20'·60W
114	N Minquiers Lt By	49°01'·63N 02°00'·60W
115	NE Minquiers Lt By	49°00'·84N 01°55'·31W
116	SE Minquiers Lt By	48°53'·43N 02°00'·10W
117	S Minquiers Lt By	48°53'·07N 02°10'·11W
118	SW Minquiers Lt By	48°54'·34N 02°19'·41W

FRENCH COAST

Selected waypoints in Area 15 and 16 are listed clockwise around the French coast from East to West, and Area 22 from West to East. **All positions are referenced to the WGS84/ETRS89 datum.**

AREA 15 (WGS84 coordinates)

Wpt	*Name*	*Position*
120	Les Équets Lt By	49°43'·61N 01°18'·36W
121	Basse du Rénier Lt By	49°44'·84N 01°22'·11W
122	La Pierre Noire Lt By	49°43'·53N 01°29'·09W
123	CH1 Lt By	49°43'·24N 01°42'·09W
124	Basse Bréfort Lt By	49°43'·76N 01°51'·10W
125	Flamanville Lt By	49°32'·56N 01°54'·03W
126	Les Trois-Grunes Lt By	49°21'·82N 01°55'·21W
127	Basses de Portbail (PB) By	49°18'·39N 01°44'·75W
128	Écrevière Lt By	49°15'·25N 01°52'·17W
129	Basse Jourdan Lt By	49°06'·83N 01°44'·16W
130	La Catheue Lt By	48°57'·82N 01°42'·06W
131	Les Ardentes Lt By	48°57'·77N 01°51'·64W
132	Anvers Wk Lt By	48°53'·85N 01°40'·95W
133	Le Videcoq Lt By	48°49'·60N 01°42'·12W
134	Pierre d'Herpin Lt Bn	48°43'·77N 01°48'·92W
135	Le Brunel Lt By	48°40'·84N 02°05'·28W
136	Buharats Ouest No. 2 Lt By	48°40'·22N 02°07'·49W
137	St Malo Fairway Lt By	48°41'·38N 02°07'·28W
138	Le Sou Lt By	48°40'·11N 02°05'·30W
139	Bassé NE Lt By	48°42'·43N 02°09'·15W
140	Banchenou Lt By	48°40'·44N 02°11'·48W
141	Le Rohein Lt Bn	48°38'·80N 02°37'·77W
142	Le Légué Lt By	48°34'·32N 02°41'·16W
143	Caffa Lt By	48°37'·81N 02°43'·09W
144	La Roselière Lt By	48°37'·45N 02°46'·43W
145	Roc du Nord-Est By	48°39'·60N 02°44'·04W

AREA 16 (WGS84 coordinates)

Wpt	*Name*	*Position*
150	Roche Gautier Lt By	49°00'·38N 02°53'·01W
151	Les Echaudés By	48°53'·36N 02°57'·34W
152	La Jument des Héaux Lt By	48°55'·36N 03°08'·05W
153	Méloine By	48°45'·56N 03°50'·69W
154	Stolvezen By	48°42'·64N 03°53'·41W
155	Pot de Fer By	48°44'·24N 03°54'·02W
156	Bassee de Bloscon Lt By	48°43'·72N 03°57'·55W
157	Astan Lt By	48°44'·91N 03°57'·67W
158	Aman-ar-Ross Lt By	48°41'·83N 04°27'·09W
159	Lizen Van Ouest Lt By	48°40'·47N 04°33'·73W
160	Trépied By	48°37'·29N 04°37'·56W
161	Libenter Lt By	48°37'·50N 04°38'·45W
162	Rusven Est By	48°36'·30N 04°38'·64W
163	Petite Fourche By	48°36'·98N 04°38'·75W
164	Ruzven Ouest By	48°36'·07N 04°39'·44W
165	Le Relec By	48°35'·99N 04°40'·86W
166	Grande Basse Portsall Lt By	48°36'·70N 04°46'·14W
167	Basse Paupian By	48°35'·31N 04°46'·28W
168	La Valbelle	48°26'·43N 04°50'·04W
169	Ouessant NE Lt By	48°45'·78N 05°11'·76W
170	Ouessant SW Lanby	48°31'·20N 05°49'·10W

AREA 22 (WGS84 coordinates)

Wpt	*Name*	*Position*
180	Dives D1 Lt By	49°18'·85N 00°05'·83W
181	Norfalk Lt By	49°28'·74N 01°03'·69W
182	Est du Cardonnet Lt By	49°26'·83N 01°01'·10W
183	Broadsword Lt By	49°25'·34N 00°52'·98W
184	Cussy Lt By	49°29'·45N 00°43'·04W
185	Ouistreham Lt By	49°20'·42N 00°14'·82W
186	LHA Lanby	49°31'·38N 00°09'·88W
187	A17 Lt By	49°41'·52N 00°01'·74E
188	A18 Lt By	49°42'·01N 00°02'·17E
189	Ratier NW Lt By	49°26'·82N 00°02'·50E
190	Bassurelle Lt By	50°32'·74N 00°57'·69E
191	Vergoyer SW Lt By	50°26'·98N 01°00'·00E
192	Daffodils Lt By	50°02'·46N 01°04'·01E
193	Colbart SW Lt By	50°48'·84N 01°16'·29E
194	Ridens SE Lt By	50°43'·47N 01°18'·88E
195	ZC1 Lt By	50°44'·99N 01°27'·21E
196	AT-SO Lt By	50°14'·23N 01°28'·55E
197	Ophélie Lt By	50°43'·85N 01°30'·84E
198	ZC2 Lt By	50°53'·53N 01°30'·88E
199	Abbeville Lt By	50°56'·05N 01°37'·56E
200	CA3 Lt By	50°56'·82N 01°41'·12E
201	CA4 Lt By	50°58'·89N 01°45'·11E
202	CA6 Lt By	50°58'·24N 01°45'·63E
203	SW Sandettié Lt By	51°09'·72N 01°45'·60E
204	CA5 Lt By	50°57'·64N 01°46'·10E
205	SW Ruytingen Lt By	51°04'·87N 01°46'·83E
206	Sandettié Lt F	51°09'·36N 01°47'·12E
207	CA8 Lt By	50°58'·38N 01°48'·65E
208	CA2 Lt By	51°00'·87N 01°48'·69E
209	CA10 Lt By	50°58'·63N 01°49'·92E
210	Ruytingen W Lt By	51°06'·91N 01°50'·43E
211	Sandettié WSW Lt By	51°12'·34N 01°51'·10E
212	Dyck Lt By	51°02'·98N 01°51'·76E
213	RCE Lt By	51°02'·44N 01°53'·22E
214	DKA Lt By	51°02'·54N 01°56'·95E
215	NW Ruytingen Lt By	51°09'·08N 01°57'·29E
216	DW5 Lt By	51°02'·19N 02°00'·91E
217	N Sandettié Lt By	51°18'·35N 02°04'·73E
218	Haut-fond de Gravelines	51°04'·03N 02°05'·03E
219	E Dyck Lt By	51°05'·62N 02°05'·63E
220	SE Ruytingen Lt By	51°09'·17N 02°08'·93E
221	DKB Lt By	51°02'·95N 02°09'·26E
222	N Ruytingen Lt By	51°13'·10N 02°10'·28E
223	Hinder 1 Lt By	51°20'·79N 02°10'·94E
224	DW23 Lt By	51°03'·54N 02°15'·18E
225	S Fairy Lt By	51°21'·19N 02°17'·30E
226	Bergues Lt By	51°17'·15N 02°18'·62E
227	S Bergues Lt By	51°15'·08N 02°19'·42E
228	DW29 Lt By	51°03'·85N 02°20'·21E

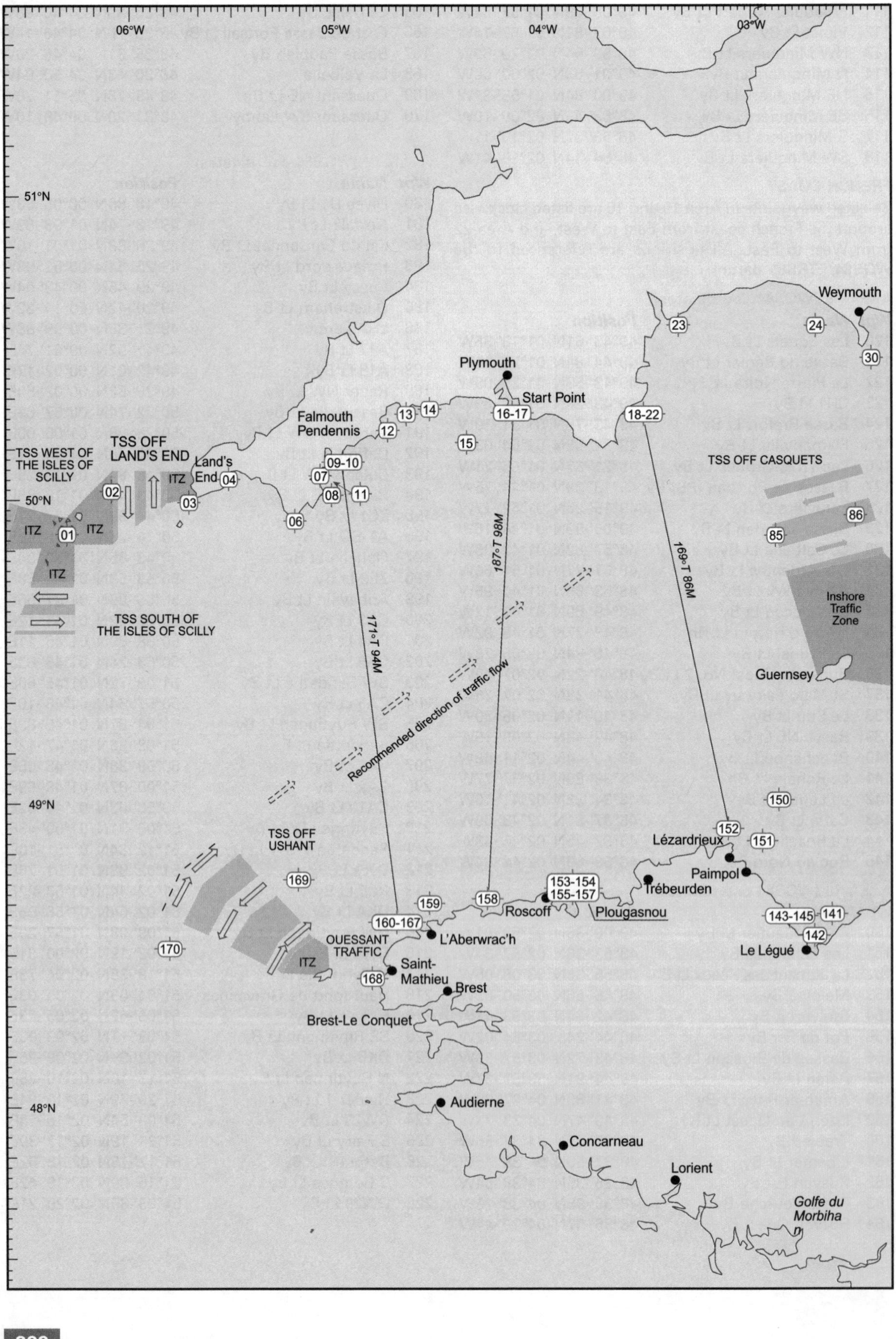
06°W
05°W
04°W
03°W
51°N
50°N
49°N
48°N
Weymouth
23
24
30
Plymouth
Start Point
13
14
16-17
18-22
Falmouth
Pendennis
12
15
TSS WEST OF THE ISLES OF SCILLY
TSS OFF LAND'S END
Land's End
ITZ
04
09-10
07
08
11
02
03
06
01
ITZ
ITZ
ITZ
TSS OFF CASQUETS
86
85
Inshore Traffic Zone
Guernsey
171°T 94M
187°T 98M
169°T 86M
TSS SOUTH OF THE ISLES OF SCILLY
Recommended direction of traffic flow
150
152
151
Lézardrieux
Paimpol
Trébeurden
TSS OFF USHANT
169
153-154
155-157
158
159
Roscoff
Plougasnou
160-167
L'Aberwrac'h
143-145
141
142
Le Légué
OUESSANT TRAFFIC
170
ITZ
Saint-Mathieu
168
Brest
Brest-Le Conquet
Audierne
Concarneau
Lorient
Golfe du Morbihan

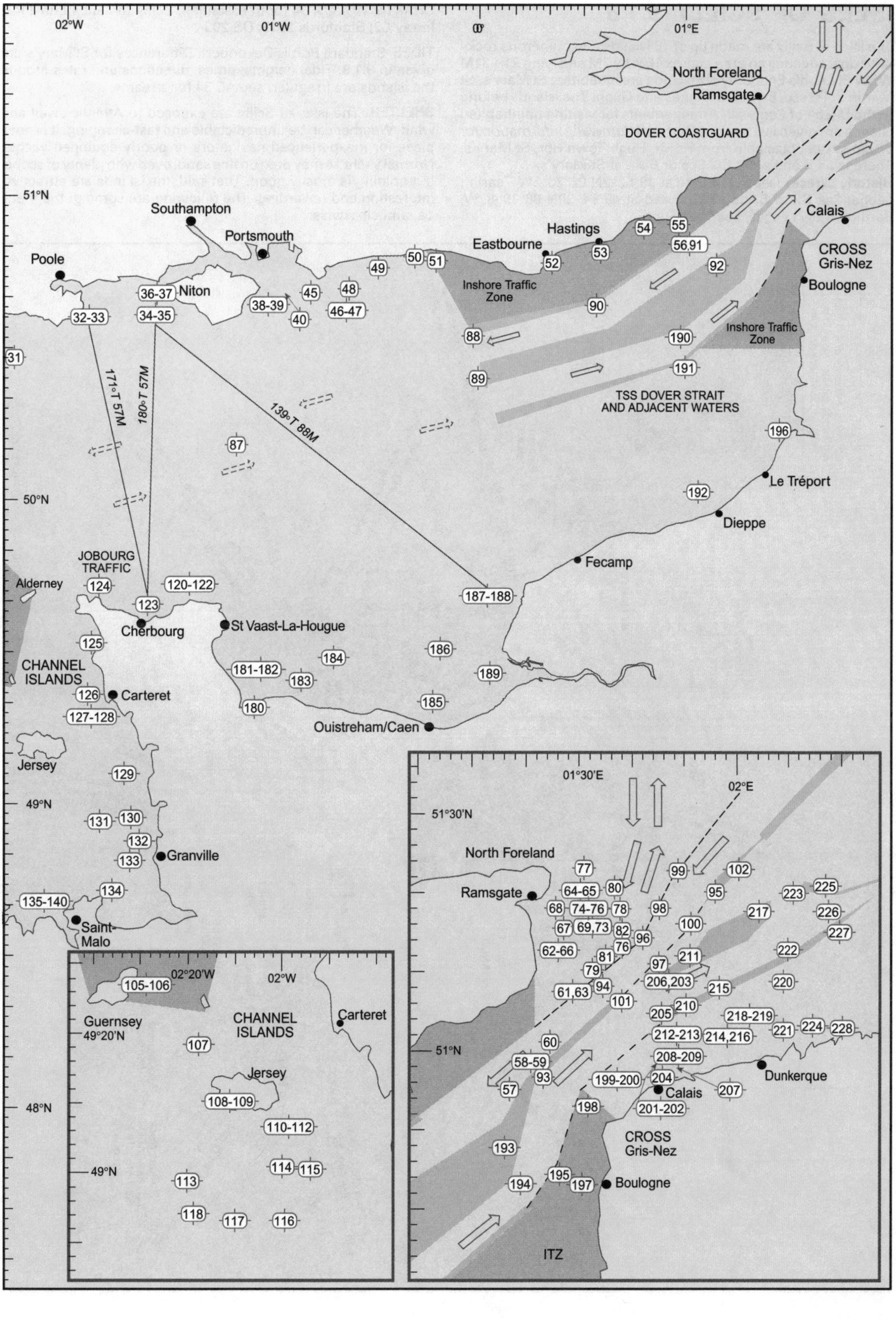
02°W
01°W
0°
01°E
51°N
50°N
49°N
48°N
North Foreland
Ramsgate
DOVER COASTGUARD
Calais
CROSS
Gris-Nez
Boulogne
Inshore Traffic
Zone
Southampton
Portsmouth
Poole
Niton
Eastbourne
Hastings
TSS DOVER STRAIT
AND ADJACENT WATERS
171°T 57M
180°T 57M
139°T 88M
Le Tréport
Dieppe
Fecamp
JOBOURG
TRAFFIC
Alderney
Cherbourg
St Vaast-La-Hougue
CHANNEL
ISLANDS
Carteret
Ouistreham/Caen
Jersey
Granville
Saint-
Malo
02°20'W
02°W
Guernsey
49°20'N
Jersey
01°30'E
02°E
51°30'N
51°N
Dunkerque
ITZ

ISLES OF SCILLY *9.1.8*

The Isles of Scilly are made up of 48 islands and numerous rocky outcrops, covering an area approx 10M by 7M and lying 21 – 31M WSW of Land's End. Only six islands are inhabited: St Mary's, St Martin's, Tresco, Bryher, St Agnes and Gugh. The islands belong to the Duchy of Cornwall. Arrangements for visiting uninhabited islands are given in a booklet *Duchy of Cornwall - Information for visiting craft* obtainable from Hr Mr, Hugh Town Hbr, St Mary's. There is a LB and a HM CG Sector Base at St Mary's.

Historic Wrecks (see 9.0.3h) are at 49°52'·2N 06°26'·5W Tearing Ledge, 2ca SE of Bishop Rk Lt; and at 49°54'·30N 06°19'·89W, Bartholomew Ledges, 5ca N of Gugh.

CHARTS AC *883, 34* (both essential); Scilly to Lands End 1148; Imray C7; Stanfords 2, 13; OS 203

TIDES Standard Port is Devonport. Differences for St Mary's are given in 9.1.9. Tidal heights, times, directions and rates around the islands are irregular; see AC 34 for streams.

SHELTER The Isles of Scilly are exposed to Atlantic swell and wind. Weather can be unpredictable and fast-changing. It is not a place for inexperienced navigators or poorly equipped yachts. Normal yacht ⚓s may drag on fine sand, even with plenty of scope, but holding is mostly good. That said, the islands are attractive, interesting and rewarding. The following are some of the many ⚓s, anti-clockwise:

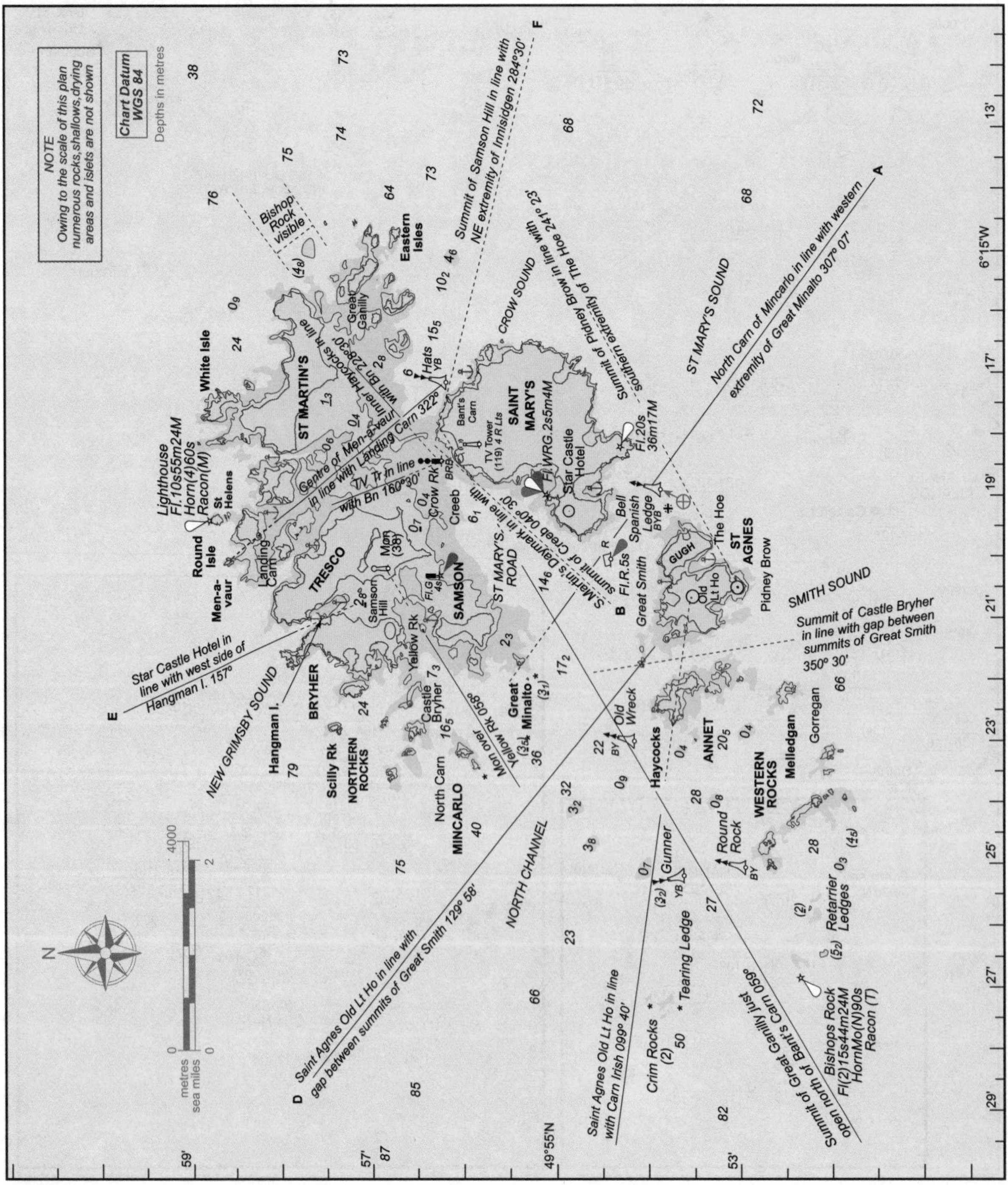

HUGH TOWN HBR (St Mary's). See 9.1.9.
PORTH CRESSA (St Mary's, S of Hugh Town). Beware of dangers on each side of ent and submarine cables. Good ⚓ (2m) in W/NW'lies, but exposed to swell from SE to SW.
WATERMILL COVE (NE corner of St Mary's). Excellent shelter in winds S to NW. ⚓ in approx 5m.
TEAN SOUND (St Martin's, W end). Needs careful pilotage, but attractive ⚓ in better weather. More suitable for shoal draught boats which can ⚓ or take the ground out of main tidal stream in chan. **St Martin's Hotel** ☎ 422092, D, FW, 7 Ⓥs £10 inc showers, V, R, Bar. There are several other ⚓s which can be used in settled weather.
ST HELEN'S POOL (S of St Helen's Is). Ent via St Helen's Gap to ⚓ in 1·5m - 7m. Secure, but may be swell near HW.
OLD GRIMSBY (NE side of Tresco). Green Porth & Raven's Porth, divided by a quay, form the Old Grimsby Hbr; both dry 2·3m. Beware cable in Green Porth. ⚓s 1½ca NE of quay in 2·5m; access more difficult than New Grimsby. Well sheltered in SW'lies but open to swell if wind veers N of W. Facilities: 6 Ⓥs (R cans) £10, L (quay), hotel, slip.
NEW GRIMSBY (between Tresco and Bryher). Appr (line E) through New Grimsby Sound, or with adequate rise of tide across Tresco Flats. Good shelter except in NW'lies. Popular ⚓ between Hangman Is and the quay in 1·5 - 4·5m. Beware cables. 22 Ⓥs £10 via Tresco Estate ☎ 22849, 📠 22807; VHF Ch 08 for R, Bar, FW, V, ✉. Ferry to St Mary's.
THE COVE (St Agnes/Gugh). Well sheltered from W and N winds, except when the sand bar between the islands covers near HWS with a strong NW wind. Beware cables.
PORTH CONGER (St Agnes/Gugh). On the N side of the sandbar, sheltered in winds from E through S to W. May be uncomfortable when the bar is covered. Facilities: L (two quays), ferry to St Mary's; in Middle Town (¾M), St Agnes, V, ✉, R, Bar.

NAVIGATION For TSS to the E, S and W, see 9.1.2. If unable to identify approach ldg lines/marks, then it is best to lie off. Pilotage is compulsory for all vessels, except HM Ships, trawlers <47·5m LOA and yachts <30m LOA, navigating within a radius of 6M from S tip of Samson Is excluding St Mary's Hbr. Many chans between islands have dangerous shallows, often with rky ledges. Beware lobster pots. **Line A**, via St Mary's Sound, is the normal ent to St Mary's Road. Appr from the E or SE to avoid Gilstone Rk (dries 4m) 3ca E of Peninnis Hd. Spanish Ledges, off Gugh, are marked by an unlit ECM By; thence past Woolpack SCM bn and PHM By Fl R 5s (Bartholomew Ledges) to ent St Mary's Rd on 040°. **Line B**, which clears Woodcock Ledge (breaks in bad wx). **Line C**, from SW: Broad Sound is entered between Bishops Rk lt ho and Flemming's Ledge about 7ca to the N, then between Round Rk NCM and Gunner SCM buoys to Old Wreck NCM buoy; beware Jeffrey Rk, close to port. Ldg marks are more than 7M off and at first not easy to see. Smith Sound, 350° between St Agnes and Annet may also be used. **Line D**, from NW: North Chan is about 7ca wide, and of easy access with good ldg marks, but beware cross tide and Steeple Rk (0·1m, 2ca to port). Intercept Line C for St Mary's Road. **Line E**, from the N, leads between Bryher and Tresco, into New Grimsby Hbr (see SHELTER); thence it winds across Tresco Flats (with adequate rise of tide and good vis). **Line F**, from the E & NE: Crow Sound is not difficult, with sufficient rise of tide but can be rough in strong E or S winds. From NE a yacht can pass close to Menawethan and Biggal Rk, avoiding Trinity Rk and the Ridge, which break in bad weather. Hats SCM buoy marks a shoal with an old boiler, drying 0·6m, on it. Track 284° between Bar Pt and Crow Bar (dries 0·7m), passing Crow Rk IDM bn on its N side (for best water) before altering SSW for St Mary's.

LIGHTS AND MARKS See 9.1.4 for lts, including Seven Stones lt float, Wolf Rock lt ho and Longships lt ho. A working knowledge of the following daymarks and conspic features will greatly aid pilotage (from NE to SW):
St Martin's E end: Conical bn tr (56m) with RW bands.
Round Is: conical shaped Is with W lt ho 19/55m high.
Tresco: Abbey & FS, best seen from S. Cromwell's Castle and Hangman Is from the NW.
Bryher: Watch Hill, stone bn (43m); rounded Samson Hill.
St Mary's: TV & radio masts at N end; all with R lts. Crow Rk IDM bn, 11m on rk drying 4·6m, at N.
St Agnes: Old lt ho, ○ W tr, visible from all directions.
Bishop Rk lt ho: Grey ○ tr, 44m; helo pad above lamp.

ST MARY'S *9.1.9*

Isles of Scilly **49°55'·14N 06°18'·71W** ✿✿✿◊◊✿✿✿

CHARTS AC *883, 34*; Imray C7; Stanfords 2; OS 203

TIDES +0607 Dover; ML 3·2; Duration 0600; Zone 0 (UT)

Standard Port DEVONPORT (→)

Times				**Height (metres)**			
High Water		Low Water		MHWS	MHWN	MLWN	MLWS
0000	0600	0000	0600	5·5	4·4	2·2	0·8
1200	1800	1200	1800				
Differences ST MARY'S							
−0035	−0100	−0040	−0025	+0·2	−0·1	−0·2	−0·1

SHELTER Good in St Mary's Pool where 38 Y Ⓥs lie in 5 trots close E of the LB ⌂ in at least 2m. ⚓ is prohib S of a line from the pier hd to the LB slip; to seaward of the LB ⌂; off the pier hd where the ferry turns, and in the apprs. Holding in the Pool is poor and in W/NW gales it is notorious for yachts dragging ⚓, when Porth Cressa (see 9.1.8) is safer. Hbr speed limit 3kn. NB: do not impede *Scillonian III* the ferry which arrives about 1200 and sails at 1630 Mon-Fri; Sat times vary with month. Also cargo ship thrice weekly.

NAVIGATION WPT via St Mary's Sound: Spanish Ledge unlit ECM buoy, 49°53'·94N 06°18'·86W, 128°/308° from/to transit line B (040°), 1·2M. See also 9.1.4 & 9.1.8. The 097° transit leads S of Bacon Ledge (0·3m) marked by PHM buoy (Apr-Oct); the 151° transit leads into the Pool between Bacon Ledge and the Cow & Calf (drying 0·6 and 1·8m) to the E.

LIGHTS AND MARKS Pier hd lt, Fl RWG 2s, R070°-100° (30°), W100°-130° (30°), G130°-070° (300°). 2 ldg lights. Buzza Hill tr and power stn chy (48m) are conspic.

RADIO TELEPHONE *St Mary's Hbr* VHF Ch 14 16 (0800-1700LT). Pilot Ch 69 16. *Falmouth CG* gives radio cover Ch 16 of the TSS/ITZ off Land's End. Do not hesitate to call the CG Ch 16 if in emergency/gales/dragging ⚓.

TELEPHONE (Dial code 01720) Hr Mr 422768 (also 📠); MRCC (01326) 317575; Marinecall 09068 500458; ⊖ 0345 231110, locally 422571; 🄷 422392; Dr 422628; Police 422444; Pilot 422066; Tourist Info 422536.

FACILITIES **Hbr** Ⓥ dues: £10 <18m LOA, D & FW at pier outer berth 0930-1100 & 1630-1800 Mon-Fri; OT see Hr Mr for FW (nil or limited quantity in summer); for D ☎ Sibleys 422431. P (cans) via Hr Mr, Gas, Gaz, Slip. Hbr Office will hold mail for visiting yachts if addressed c/o Hr Mr, Hugh Town. **Hugh Town** EC Wed; limited shopping facilities, ACA, Sh, CH, ME, SM, El, ✉, Ⓑ, ⊡. Ferry sails 0915 Mon-Fri (not Sun) from Penzance and 1630 from St Mary; (Sat varies); about 2¾hrs crossing, booking ☎ 0345-105555 (see also 9.0.4); helicopter (☎ 422646) to Penzance (⇌) and fixed wing ✈ to St Just (Land's End), Exeter, Newquay, Bristol, Plymouth and Southampton, ☎ 0345 105555. There are ✉, R, V, Bar at Tresco, Bryher, St Martins and St Agnes.

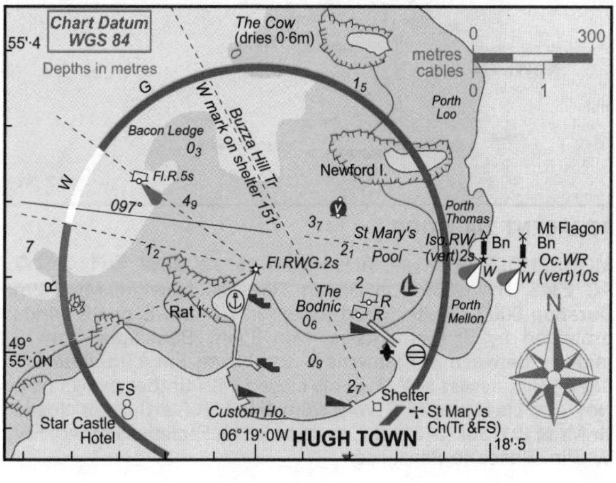

NEWLYN *9.1.10*

Cornwall **50°06′·19N 05°32′.58W** ❁❁◊◊◊✿✿

CHARTS AC 2345, *777*; Imray C7; Stanfords 13, 23; OS 203

TIDES +0600 Dover; ML 3·2; Duration 0555; Zone 0 (UT)

Standard Port DEVONPORT (⟶)

Times				Height (metres)			
High Water		Low Water		MHWS	MHWN	MLWN	MLWS
0000	0600	0000	0600	5·5	4·4	2·2	0·8
1200	1800	1200	1800				
Differences NEWLYN							
−0040	−0110	−0035	−0025	+0·1	0·0	−0·2	0·0

SHELTER Good, except in SE winds when heavy swell enters hbr; access at all tides. FVs take priority. Yachts berth on SW side of Mary Williams Pier, usually on a FV. No ⚓s, no ⚓ in hbr. Good ⚓ in Gwavas Lake in offshore winds.

NAVIGATION WPT 50°06′·19N 05°31′·80W, 090°/270° from/to S pier, 0·5M. From NE, beware The Gear and Dog Rk 3½ca NE of hbr ent; from S beware Low Lee ECM Q(3)10s and Carn Base.

LIGHTS AND MARKS S pier hd, Fl 5s 10m 9M; vis 253°-336°, W tr, R base and cupola; Siren 60s. N pier hd, F WG 4m 2M; vis G238°-248°, W over hbr. Old Quay hd, FR 3m 1M.

RADIO TELEPHONE Call: *Newlyn Hbr* VHF Ch 09 **12** 16 (Mon-Fri 0800-1700, Sat 0800-1200LT).

TELEPHONE (Dial code 01736) Hr Mr 362523, outside office hrs 361017, 🕮 351614; MRCC, ⊖, Marinecall, Police, 🄷, Dr: as for Penzance.

FACILITIES Mary Williams Pier £4–£9 (every 3rd night free). **N Pier** Slip, D (cans), FW, C (6 ton); **Services:** ME, Sh, SM, Gas, El, Ⓔ, CH. **Town** EC Wed; ◙, V, R, Bar, ✉, Ⓑ (AM only), bus to Penzance for ⇌, ✈.

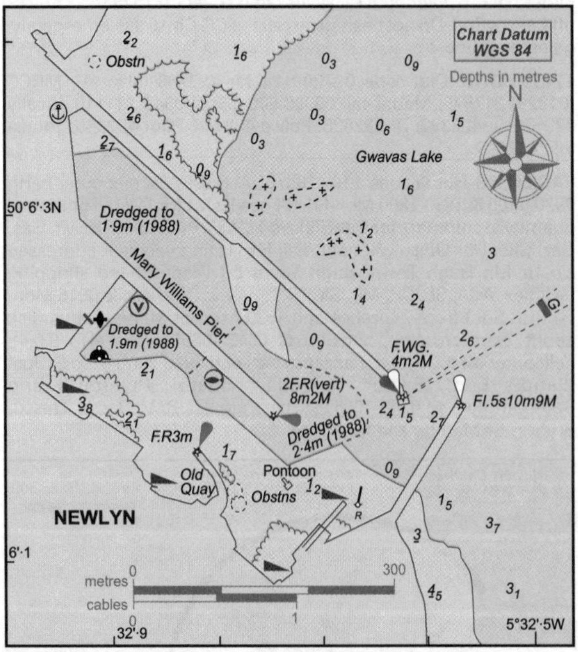

ADJACENT HARBOUR

MOUSEHOLE, Cornwall, **50°04′·97N 05°32′·26W.** ❁❁◊✿✿✿. AC 2345. HW +0550 on Dover; Tides as Newlyn; ML 3·2m; Duration 0600. Shelter good except in NE and S or SE winds; protected by St Clements Is from E'lies. Best appr from S, midway between St Clements Is and bkwtr. Ent 11m wide; hbr dries 1·8m, access HW±3. Ent is closed with timber baulks from Nov-Apl. Lts N pier 2 FG (vert) 8/6m 4M; 2 FR (vert) = hbr closed. Hr Mr ☎ (01736) 731511. £7, multi hull £10. Facilities limited: FW, V, Slip. Buses to Penzance.

PENZANCE *9.1.11*

Cornwall **50°07′·09N 05°31′·68W** ❁❁◊◊◊✿✿✿

CHARTS AC 2345, *777*; Imray C7; Stanfords 13, 23; OS 203

TIDES −0635 Dover; ML 3·2; Duration 0550; Zone 0 (UT)

Standard Port DEVONPORT (⟶)

Times				Height (metres)			
High Water		Low Water		MHWS	MHWN	MLWN	MLWS
0000	0600	0000	0600	5·5	4·4	2·2	0·8
1200	1800	1200	1800				
Differences PENZANCE							
−0040	−0110	−0035	−0025	+0·1	0·0	−0·2	0·0
PORTHLEVEN							
−0045	−0105	−0030	−0025	0·0	−0·1	−0·2	0·0
LIZARD POINT							
−0045	−0100	−0030	−0030	−0·2	−0·2	−0·3	−0·2

SHELTER Excellent in the wet dock (gates open HW −2 to +1), or dry out against Albert pier. 15 waiting buoys are laid S of the lt ho on S pier. Or ⚓ E of hbr, but Mounts Bay is an unsafe ⚓ in S or SE winds, which, if strong, also render the hbr ent dangerous. Hbr speed limit 5kn.

NAVIGATION WPT 50°06′·74N 05°31′·16W, 135°/315° from/to S pier hd, 0·48M. Beware Gear Rk 0·4M S. Cressar (5ca NE of ent) and Long Rks are marked by SCM bns.

LIGHTS AND MARKS There are no ldg lts/marks. Dock ent sigs, shown from FS at N side of Dock gate (may not be given for yachts).
2B ● (hor) (3FG (vert) by night) = Dock gates open.
2B ● (vert) (3FR by night) = Dock gates shut.

RADIO TELEPHONE VHF Ch 09 **12** 16 (HW −2 to HW +1, and office hrs).

TELEPHONE (Dial code 01736) Hr Mr 366113, outside office hrs 365029, 🕮 366114; MRCC (01326) 317575; ⊖ 0345 231110 (H24); Marinecall 09068 500458; Police 362395; Dr 363866; 🄷 362382.

FACILITIES Wet Dock (50 Ⓥ) ☎ 366113, 🕮 366114, £1.04 every 3rd night free), M, D, FW, AC, C (3 ton); **S Pier** D, FW; **Penzance YC** ☎ 364989, Bar, L, FW, R; **Services:** Slip (dry dock), ME, El, CH, SM, Sh, Gas, Gaz. **Town** EC Wed (winter only); P cans, ◙, V, R, Bar, ✉, Ⓑ, ⇌, ✈.

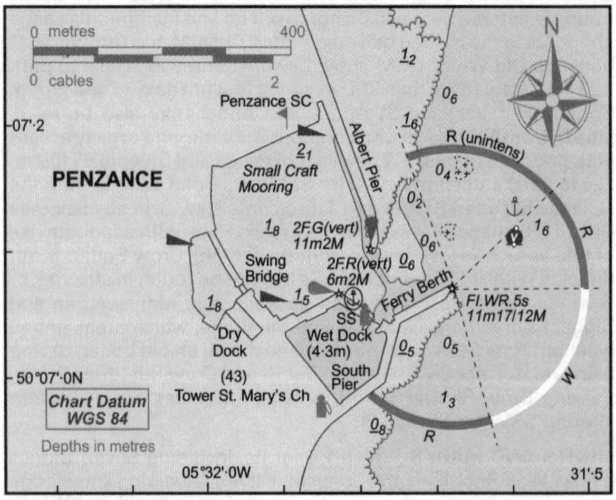

ADJACENT HARBOUR

ST MICHAEL'S MOUNT, Cornwall, **50°07′·14N 05°28′·61W.** AC 2345, *777*. HW +0550 on Dover; Tides as Penzance; ML 3·2m; Duration 0550. Shelter good from N to SE, but only in fair wx. Hbr dries; it has approx 3·3m at MHWS and 1·4m at MHWN. Beware Hogus Rks to NW of hbr and Outer Penzeath Rk about 3ca WSW of Hogus Rks. Also beware Maltman Rk 1ca SSW of the Mount. There are no lts. Ent between piers is 30m wide. Room for 6 to ⚓ W of the pier. Call ☎ 710265 (HO). Facilities: FW, R, café; more facilities at Marazion, 3ca to N. EC Wed.

ADJACENT HARBOURS ON THE LIZARD PENINSULA

PORTHLEVEN, Cornwall, **50°04′·92N 05°19′·13W.** ❁❁✿✿✿. AC 2345, *777.* HW +0551 on Dover; ML 3·1m; Duration 0545. See 9.1.11. Hbr dries 2m above the old LB ho but has approx 2·3m in centre of ent; access HW±3. It is open to W and SW. Beware rks round pier hd and Deazle Rks to W. Lt on S pier FG 10m 4M = inner hbr open. Inside hbr FG vis 033°-067° when required for vessels entering. Visitors go alongside the Quay on E side. Hr Mr ☎ (01326) 574270. Facilities: **Inner Hbr** AB £8, FW, L, ME, P & D(cans). **Village** EC Wed; ⊠, 🄱, R, Ⓑ, V, Bar.

MULLION COVE, Cornwall, **50°00′·90N, 05°15′·54W.** AC 2345, 777. Lizard HW +0552 on Dover, –0050 and –0·2m on HW Devonport; ML 3·0m; Duration 0545. Porth Mellin hbr dries 2·4m and is open to W'lies. ⚓ in Mullion Cove is safer especially in lee of Mullion Island where there is approx 3·5m, but local knowledge advised. NT owns the island and the hbr. Due to lack of space, visiting boats may only stay in hbr briefly to load/unload. No lts. There is a slip on E side of hbr. Hr Mr ☎ (01326) 240222. Only facilities at Mullion village (1M) EC Wed; Bar, V.

Historic Wrecks (see 9.0.3h) are located at:
50°03′·44N 05°17′·16W (*St Anthony*), 2M SE of Porthleven.
50°02′·37N 05°16′·46W (*Schiedam*), 1·5M N of Mullion Is.
49°58′·54N 05°14′·51W, Rill Cove, 1·4M NW of Lizard Pt.
49°57′·49N 05°12′·98W, (*Royal Anne*) The Stags, Lizard Pt.

CADGWITH, Cornwall, **49°59′·22N 05°10′·68W.** AC 2345, *154, 777*; HW +0555 on Dover; –0030 on Devonport; –0·2m on Devonport; ML 3·0m. See Differences Lizard Pt under 9.1.11. Hbr dries; it is divided by a rky outcrop, The Todden. Beware the extension of this, rks called The Mare; also beware The Boa rks to ESE which cover at quarter tide. ⚓ off The Mare in about 2–3m, but not recommended in on-shore winds. There are no lts. Many local FVs operate from here and are hauled up on the shingle beach. Facilities: ⊠, Bar, R, V (1M at Ruan Minor).

COVERACK, Cornwall, **50°01′·44N 05°05′·66W.** AC *154, 777.* HW +0605 on Dover; ML 3·0m; Duration 0550. See 9.1.12. Hbr dries but has 3·3m at MHWS and 2·2m at MHWN. In good weather and off-shore winds it is better to ⚓ outside. Hbr is very small and full of FVs. From the S beware the Guthens, off Chynhalls Pt; from the N, the Dava and other rks off Lowland Pt, and Manacle Rks to the NE (ECM, Q(3) 10s bell). There are no lts. Hr Mr ☎ (01326) 280545. Facilities: EC Tues; FW (hotel) D, P (cans) from garage (2M uphill), V, ⊠.

HELFORD RIVER *9.1.12*

Cornwall **50°05′·79N 05·06′·06W** (Ent) ❁❁❁✿✿✿✿✿

CHARTS AC *5602,* 147, *154*; Imray C6, Y57; Stanfords 13, 23; OS 204

TIDES –0613 Dover; ML 3·0; Duration 0550; Zone 0 (UT)

Reference Port DEVONPORT (⟶)

Times				Height (metres)			
High Water		Low Water		MHWS	MHWN	MLWN	MLWS
0000	0600	0000	0600	5·5	4·4	2·2	0·8
1200	1800	1200	1800				
Differences HELFORD RIVER (Ent)							
–0030	–0035	–0015	–0010	–0·2	–0·2	–0·3	–0·2
COVERACK							
–0030	–0050	–0020	–0015	–0·2	–0·2	–0·3	–0·2

SHELTER Excellent, except in E'lies. 🅐s marked 'Visitors' on G can buoys or G pick-up buoys are administered by Moorings Officer. Ferry will collect people from yachts, if requested during normal ferry operating hrs. ⚓s only where marked on plan. Note: A local bye-law states that yachts must not ⚓ in the river and creeks W of Port Navas Creek due to oyster beds.

NAVIGATION WPT 50°05′·74N 05°04′·56W, 093°/273° from/to The Voose NCM bn, 1·5M. From N beware August Rock (alias the Gedges), marked by SHM (seasonal). From SE keep well clear of Nare Pt and Dennis Hd. Speed limit 6kn in river. Keep Helford Pt open of Bosahan Pt to clear The Voose, a rky reef E of Bosahan Pt, marked by NCM (seasonal). On N side of river opposite Helford Creek avoid mud bank marked by Bar buoy SHM (seasonal). PHM & SHM buoys mark chan from Mawgan Creek to Gweek.

LIGHTS AND MARKS Bosahan Pt on with Mawnan Shear (259°) clears August Rk (The Gedges), dangerous rks marked by unlit SHM By.

RADIO TELEPHONE Moorings Officer VHF Ch M. Helford River SC Ch **80** M.

TELEPHONE (Dial code 01326) Moorings Officer 250749; MRCC 317575; ⊖ 0345 231110 (H24); Marinecall 09068 500458; Police 72231; 🄷 572151.

FACILITIES Moorings ☎ 250770 £8.00. Please ditch rubbish only at the Helford River SC, the Shipwright's Arms or the Ferryboat Inn; protect the wild life of this beautiful river. **Helford River SC** ☎ 231460, Slip, FW, R, Bar, 🄱; **Port Navas YC** ☎ 340419/340065 (Bar), C (3 ton), M*, AC, R, FW; **Helford Passage** Slip, L, FW, V; **Gweek Quay** ☎ 221657, 📠 221685, e mail info@gweek-quay.com M*, FW, CH, El, Sh, ME, C (100 ton), BH; **Village** P, D, Gas, Gaz, bus service. **Gillan Creek** CH, FW, M*; **Services:** Water taxi VHF Ch M or ☎ 250770, Gas, Gaz, Slip, L, Sh, CH, 🄱, D (cans). EC Wed; ⊠ (Helford, Gweek, Mawnan-Smith, Mawgan); Mawnan-Smith (Jan-Sept Mon, Wed, Fri AM only. Oct-May Tues, Fri AM only); ⥬ (bus to Falmouth); ✈ (Penzance or Newquay).

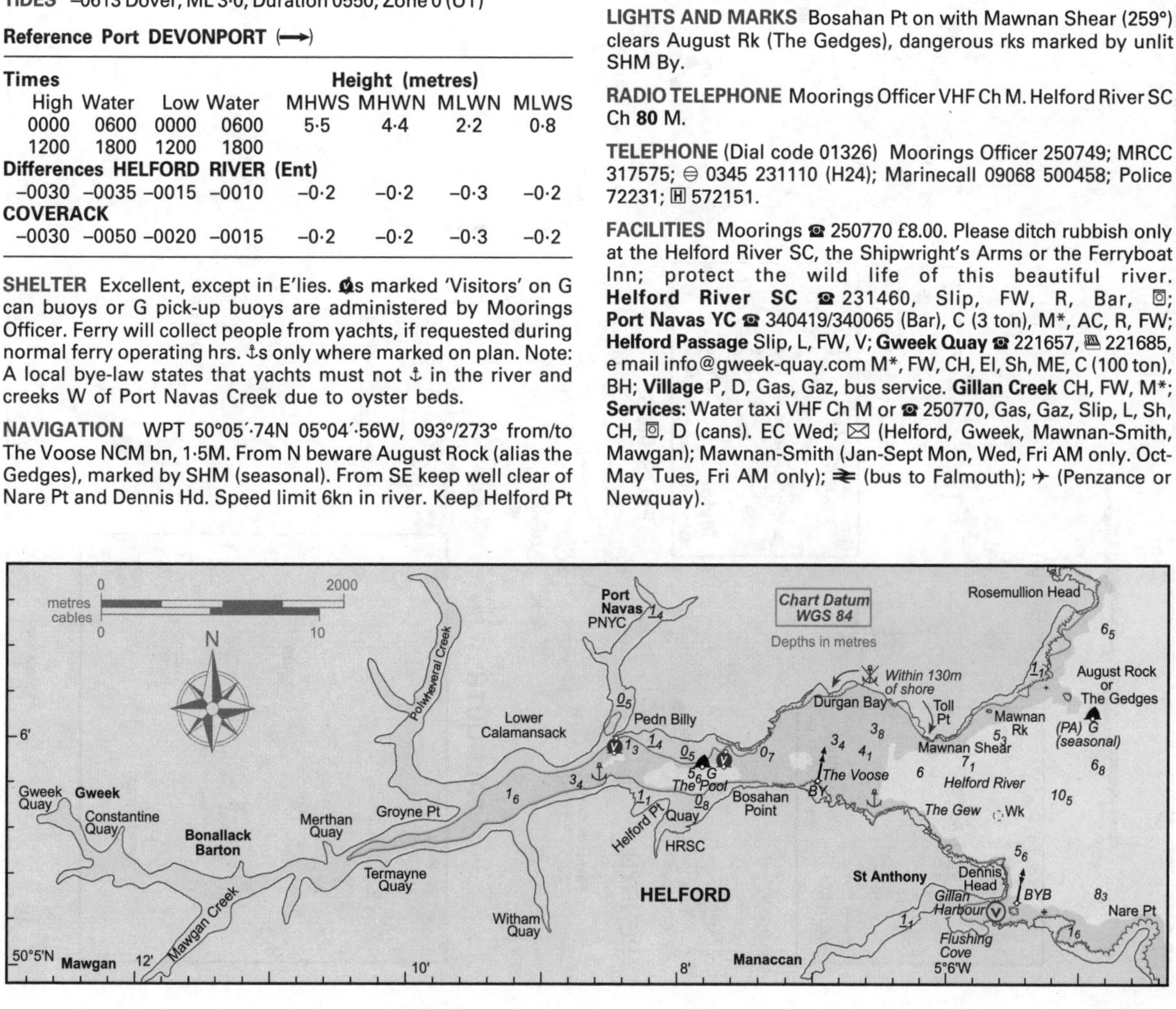

RIVER FAL *9.1.13*

Cornwall **50°08'·61N 05°01'·48W** (Ent) ❁❁❁◊◊◊✿✿✿

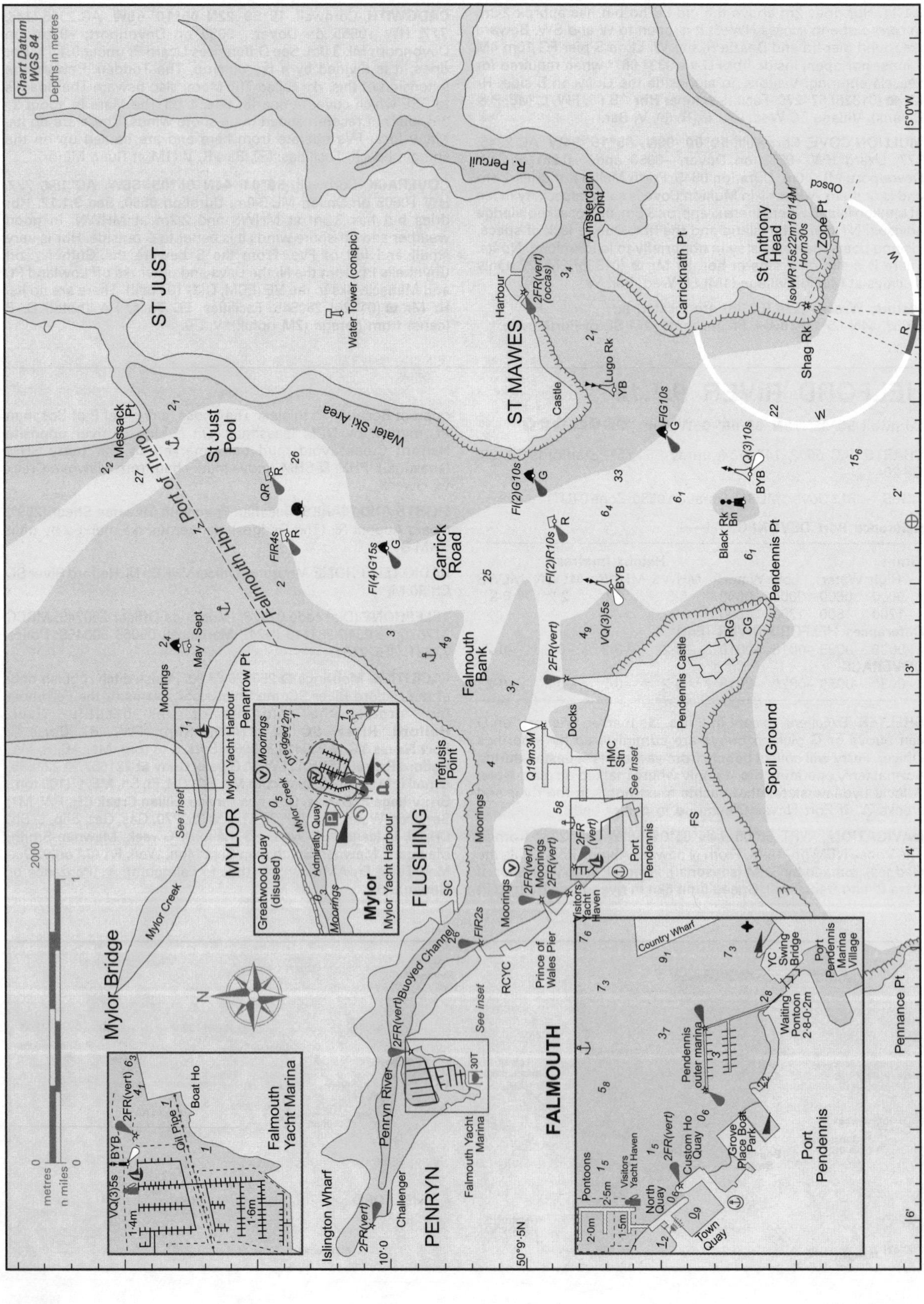

CHARTS AC *5602, 32*, 18, *154*; Imray C6, Y58; Stanfords 13, 23; OS 204

TIDES –0558 Dover; ML 3·0; Duration 0550; Zone 0 (UT). Daily Predictions and Tidal Curve are given below. HW Truro is approx HW Falmouth +0008 and –1·8m.

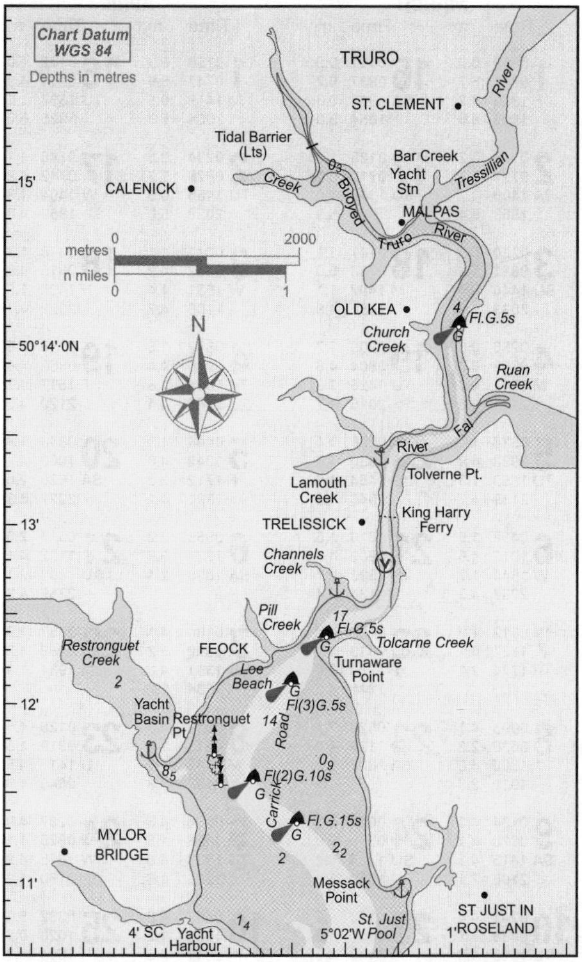
Chart Datum
WGS 84
Depths in metres
TRURO
ST. CLEMENT
Tidal Barrier
(Lts)
Creek
03 Buoyed
Bar Creek
Yacht
Stn
Tressillian
River
MALPAS
Truro
River
CALENICK
metres
0
2000
n miles
0
1
OLD KEA
Fl.G.5s
G
4
Church
Creek
Ruan
Creek
N
River
Fal
Tolverne Pt.
Lamouth
Creek
King Harry
Ferry
TRELISSICK
Channels
Creek
V
Pill
Creek
17
Fl.G.5s
G
Tolcarne Creek
Restronguet
Creek
2
FEOCK
Loe
Beach
Turnaware
Point
G
Fl(3)G.5s
Yacht
Basin
Restronguet
Pt
14
Road
85
09
Fl(2)G.10s
G
Carrick
Fl.G.15s
G
MYLOR
BRIDGE
2
22
Messack
Point
4' SC
Yacht
Harbour
14
St. Just
5°02'W Pool
ST JUST IN
ROSELAND
1
15'
50°14'·0N
13'
12'
11'

SHELTER Excellent. There are many Ⓥ berths, see below; also 18 G 🅥s clearly marked, on SW side of the fairway, owned by Falmouth Hbr Commissioners or the Royal Cornwall YC.
Visitors Yacht Haven, pontoons (100 AB) linked to North Quay are dredged 2 - 2.5m; max draft 2m.
Port Pendennis Marina, access HW±3 via lock with tfc lts. Outer marina (45 + 20 Ⓥ) in about 3m has H24 access.
Falmouth Marina, 6ca beyond RCYC up the Penryn R, is accessible at all times min depth 2m. On near appr pass within 20m of outside pontoon, 2FR (vert), and leave ECM lt bn, VQ (3) 5s (hard to see), close to stbd to keep in narrow ent chan. An unlit PHM and SHM buoy, close NE of ECM bn, mark the Penryn R; speed limit is 8kn.
Mylor Yacht Hbr, on the W bank of Carrick Road, is well sheltered from W'lies but uncomfortable in strong E'lies. **Restronguet Creek**, further up the W bank has good ⚓ in pool (12·4m max depth), but most of the creek dries.
St Mawes Hbr, on E bank, offers excellent shelter except from SW winds, when ⚓ above Amsterdam Pt. 9 G 🅥s (contact SC). Good ⚓ off St Just, but uncomfortable in strong W/SW'lies. Up **River Fal** are pontoons & 🅥s N of Tolcarne Creek; good ⚓s in Tolcarne Creek, Channals Creek, Tolverne, Ruan Creek (Ⓥ pontoon), Church Creek, Mopus Reach (Ⓥ pontoon) & Malpas (Bar Creek Yacht Stn ¼M up Tresillian R has 🅥s). **Truro**, drying AB behind Tesco; showers, AC. 5kn speed limit in upper reaches and creeks.

NAVIGATION WPT 50°08'·03N 05°02'·06W, 183°/003° from/to Black Rock IDM bn, 0·68M. Ent is 1M wide and deep. Hbr accessible in any weather or tide although fresh on-shore winds over an ebb tide make it a bit rough. The only hazard is Black Rk, dries 2·1m almost in the middle of the ent; pass either side, but at night the E chan is advised keeping E of the ECM By, Q (3) 10s. Outside the buoyed chans large areas are quite shallow and care is needed below half tide.
Falmouth is a deep water port, taking ships up to 90,000 tons; appropriate facilities are available. Take care not to impede shipping or ⚓ in prohib areas. Beware oyster beds, especially in Penryn and Percuil Rivers.
Mylor Creek dries or is shoal, <1m, but Mylor Pool has many moorings in up to 2·4m, and some pontoon berths. A PHM and SHM buoy mark the ent to the fairway. **Restronguet Creek** has a 12m deep pool at its ent, but dries above Pandora Inn. Beware Carrick Carlys Rk 0·8m, 3ca E of ent, marked by a NCM and SCM post.
River Fal proper flows into the N end of Carrick Roads at Turnaware Pt; beware strong tides and rips. There are ⚓s off the various creeks. 8ca NW of Malpas a flood barrage, lit by 2 FR/FG (vert), is usually open; 3 Fl R lts show when it is closed. Truro dries to soft mud, but access HW±2½.
St Mawes Hbr In ent keep S of the SCM buoy marking Lugo Rk, 0·6m, which is always covered. The river dries above Percuil.

LIGHTS AND MARKS St Anthony Hd lt (H24), R sector covers the Manacles Rks.

RADIO TELEPHONE Call: *Falmouth Hbr Radio*, VHF Ch **12** 14 16 (Mon-Fri 0800-1700LT); Hbr launch *Killigrew* Ch 12. Customs launch *Curlew* Ch 12 16. Port Pendennis Marina, Royal Cornwall YC, Falmouth Marina and Mylor Yacht Hbr: Ch **80**, M (H24). Visitors Yacht Haven Ch 12 16. Malpas Marine and St Mawes SC: Ch M (HO). Falmouth CG Ch 16 67 provides radio coverage of the TSS/ITZ off Land's End; see 9.1.2. Water taxi Ch 16 06.

TELEPHONE (Dial code Falmouth 01326; Truro 01872) Hr Mr Falmouth 312285/314379, ℻ 211352; Hr Mr Penryn 373352; Hr Mr St Mawes 270553; Hr Mr Truro 224231; MRCC 317575; ⊜ 0345 231110 (H24); Marinecall 09068 500458; Weather 42534; Police 0990 700400; Dr 434800; Ⓗ Truro 274242.

FACILITIES
FALMOUTH **Port Pendennis Marina** ☎ 311113, ℻ 313344, www.portpendennis.com, £2.00, access H24 to outer pontoons (45 + 20 Ⓥ); AC, FW, 🅥s, YC (R, ▣, CH, tennis court); Inner marina access HW±3.
Visitors Yacht Haven (100) ☎ 312285 (Apr-Sept inc), ℻ 211352, AB, £1.55, P, D, FW, Access H24. About 300m E of Yacht Haven in 6m is a Visitors' ⚓age, £5. Max draft 2m.
Falmouth Marina (280+20 Ⓥ), ☎ 316620, ℻ 313939, £2.00; AC, FW, CH, V, D, ME, El, Sh, ▣, BH (30 ton), C (25 ton), Gas, Gaz, SM, Bar, R, ♿; access H24. A pipe-line/sill drying 1·8m bisects the marina E/W. **Services**: Slip, BH (60 ton), C (48 ton), ME, Sh, El, M, SM, Gaz, CH, ACA, FW. Fuel Barge, D only, as chartlet, Ch 16. **Town** V, R, Bar, ✉, Ⓑ, ≷, ✈ (Plymouth or Newquay).

PENRYN/FLUSHING (01326) **Challenger Marine** ☎ 377222, ℻ 377800; M, FW, El, P & D (cans, 500m), Slip, ME, C (12 ton), Sh, SM, ACA, BY, CH. (45 AB (drying), 240 moorings 2m) £1.33.

MYLOR (01326) **Mylor Yacht Hbr** (45 AB(drying) + 240M, 2m) £1.70 ☎ 372121, ℻ 372120, Access HW±1, AC, FW, D, Slip, BH (25 ton), CH, Gas, Gaz, Sh, ME, El, Ⓔ, C (4 ton), V, R, Bar, ▣. Marina enlarged during 2001.

RESTRONGUET (01326) **Yacht Basin** ☎ 373613, Slip, M, Sh, Ⓔ, CH, Gas, Gaz; **Pandora Inn** ☎ 372678, V, R, Bar, pontoon dries 1·9m.

ST MAWES (01326) 270553 **Inner Hbr** FW, Slip. **Services:** M, 🅥s (contact SC), BY, ME, Sh, El, SM, Gas.

MALPAS/TRURO (01872) **Bar Creek Yacht Stn** ☎ 273919, M;
Malpas Marine ☎ 271260, M, CH, ME, El, Sh, access H24 except LWS±1.
Truro ☎ 272130, AB or Ⓥ pontoon or 🅥 = £6, £2.75 for ⚓, access HW ±2½ via tidal barrage gates, FW, AC. **City** V, R, Bar, ✉, Ⓑ, ≷, CH, Gas.
YACHT CLUBS Port of Falmouth Sailing Ass'n ☎ 211555; Royal Cornwall YC (RCYC) ☎ 311105/312126 (Sec'y), M, Slip, FW, R, Bar; Falmouth Town SC ☎ 377061; Falmouth Watersports Ass'n ☎ 211223; Flushing SC ☎ 374043; Mylor YC ☎ 374391, Bar; Restronguet SC ☎ 374536; St Mawes SC ☎ 270686.

TIME ZONE (UTC)
For Summer Time add ONE hour in **non-shaded areas**

ENGLAND – FALMOUTH

LAT 50°09′N LONG 5°03′W

TIMES AND HEIGHTS OF HIGH AND LOW WATERS

SPRING & NEAP TIDES
Dates in red are **SPRINGS**
Dates in blue are **NEAPS**

YEAR **2002**

JANUARY

Date	Day	Time	m	Time	m	Time	m	Time	m
1	TU	0035	0.9	0621	5.4	1302	0.9	1849	5.2
2	W	0120	0.9	0708	5.5	1348	0.9	1936	5.1
3	TH	0205	1.0	0755	5.4	1434	0.9	2025	5.1
4	F	0250	1.1	0842	5.3	1521	1.1	2114	4.9
5	SA	0337	1.3	0933	5.1	1609	1.3	2208	4.7
6	SU	0428	1.5	1028	4.9	1704	1.5	2308	4.6
7	M	0527	1.7	1133	4.7	1809	1.7		
8	TU	0016	4.5	0639	1.8	1242	4.6	1923	1.7
9	W	0124	4.5	0757	1.8	1350	4.6	2036	1.7
10	TH	0227	4.6	0906	1.6	1452	4.7	2138	1.5
11	F	0322	4.8	1004	1.5	1547	4.8	2230	1.4
12	SA	0411	5.0	1055	1.3	1635	4.9	2316	1.3
13	SU	0454	5.1	1140	1.2	1716	5.0	● 2358	1.2
14	M	0531	5.2	1222	1.1	1755	5.0		
15	TU	0037	1.1	0608	5.2	1300	1.1	1831	4.9
16	W	0112	1.2	0643	5.2	1335	1.2	1905	4.9
17	TH	0144	1.3	0717	5.1	1406	1.3	1938	4.8
18	F	0212	1.4	0753	5.0	1434	1.4	2013	4.7
19	SA	0239	1.5	0828	4.9	1502	1.5	2050	4.6
20	SU	0307	1.6	0905	4.7	1533	1.7	2128	4.4
21	M	0341	1.8	0944	4.5	1612	1.8	2213	4.3
22	TU	0428	2.0	1033	4.4	1709	2.0	2311	4.2
23	W	0540	2.2	1137	4.3	1826	2.1		
24	TH	0022	4.2	0704	2.1	1252	4.3	1940	1.9
25	F	0141	4.4	0817	1.9	1412	4.4	2048	1.7
26	SA	0248	4.6	0922	1.6	1516	4.6	2149	1.5
27	SU	0344	4.9	1021	1.3	1611	4.9	2245	1.2
28	M	0434	5.2	1115	1.0	1702	5.1	○ 2337	0.9
29	TU	0520	5.4	1206	0.7	1751	5.2		
30	W	0026	0.7	0608	5.5	1255	0.5	1840	5.3
31	TH	0113	0.6	0658	5.6	1341	0.4	1928	5.3

FEBRUARY

Date	Day	Time	m	Time	m	Time	m	Time	m
1	F	0157	0.6	0746	5.6	1425	0.5	2013	5.3
2	SA	0239	0.7	0831	5.5	1506	0.7	2058	5.1
3	SU	0320	0.9	0917	5.3	1547	1.0	2142	4.9
4	M	0402	1.2	1003	5.0	1631	1.4	2231	4.6
5	TU	0450	1.5	1056	4.6	1722	1.6	2332	4.4
6	W	0550	1.8	1204	4.4	1829	1.9		
7	TH	0045	4.3	0712	2.0	1321	4.3	2001	2.0
8	F	0159	4.3	0844	1.9	1432	4.3	2120	1.8
9	SA	0301	4.5	0952	1.6	1531	4.5	2218	1.6
10	SU	0354	4.8	1044	1.4	1620	4.7	2304	1.4
11	M	0437	5.0	1128	1.2	1701	4.8	2346	1.2
12	TU	0514	5.1	1208	1.0	1737	4.9	●	
13	W	0023	1.0	0550	5.2	1245	0.9	1813	5.0
14	TH	0057	1.0	0626	5.2	1317	0.9	1846	5.0
15	F	0126	1.0	0700	5.2	1345	1.0	1919	4.9
16	SA	0151	1.1	0733	5.1	1409	1.1	1951	4.8
17	SU	0213	1.3	0805	4.9	1431	1.3	2021	4.7
18	M	0236	1.4	0833	4.8	1455	1.4	2049	4.6
19	TU	0303	1.5	0901	4.6	1526	1.6	2121	4.4
20	W	0340	1.7	0940	4.4	1608	1.8	2211	4.3
21	TH	0433	2.0	1041	4.2	1715	2.0	2323	4.2
22	F	0607	2.1	1202	4.1	1856	2.1		
23	SA	0049	4.2	0743	2.0	1337	4.2	2019	1.9
24	SU	0217	4.5	0859	1.6	1457	4.5	2130	1.5
25	M	0322	4.9	1005	1.3	1556	4.8	2231	1.1
26	TU	0415	5.2	1102	0.8	1646	5.1	2324	0.7
27	W	0504	5.5	1153	0.4	1734	5.3	○	
28	TH	0013	0.4	0552	5.7	1240	0.2	1823	5.4

MARCH

Date	Day	Time	m	Time	m	Time	m	Time	m
1	F	0059	0.2	0641	5.7	1325	0.2	1909	5.5
2	SA	0141	0.2	0727	5.7	1406	0.2	1953	5.4
3	SU	0220	0.3	0811	5.6	1444	0.4	2033	5.3
4	M	0258	0.6	0853	5.3	1521	0.8	2111	5.0
5	TU	0336	1.1	0933	4.9	1559	1.3	2149	4.7
6	W	0418	1.5	1017	4.5	1644	1.7	2237	4.3
7	TH	0512	1.9	1127	4.1	1744	2.1		
8	F	0005	4.1	0630	2.2	1300	4.0	1919	2.3
9	SA	0134	4.1	0828	2.1	1415	4.1	2105	2.1
10	SU	0241	4.4	0938	1.7	1513	4.3	2201	1.7
11	M	0332	4.7	1027	1.5	1601	4.6	2246	1.4
12	TU	0415	4.9	1109	1.1	1640	4.8	2325	1.1
13	W	0452	5.1	1147	0.9	1714	4.9		
14	TH	0001	0.9	0526	5.2	1222	0.8	● 1749	5.0
15	F	0034	0.9	0602	5.2	1252	0.8	1822	5.0
16	SA	0101	0.9	0637	5.2	1317	0.9	1854	5.0
17	SU	0125	1.0	0710	5.1	1340	1.0	1924	5.0
18	M	0147	1.1	0738	5.0	1402	1.1	1951	4.8
19	TU	0209	1.2	0804	4.8	1426	1.3	2016	4.7
20	W	0236	1.4	0830	4.6	1454	1.5	2046	4.6
21	TH	0310	1.5	0909	4.4	1533	1.7	2134	4.4
22	F	0400	1.8	1013	4.2	1633	2.0	2246	4.2
23	SA	0528	2.1	1136	4.0	1822	2.2		
24	SU	0015	4.2	0718	2.0	1314	4.2	1956	1.9
25	M	0150	4.5	0841	1.6	1440	4.5	2112	1.5
26	TU	0301	4.9	0948	1.2	1538	4.9	2214	1.1
27	W	0356	5.2	1044	0.7	1628	5.2	2306	0.6
28	TH	0444	5.5	1133	0.3	1713	5.4	○ 2353	0.3
29	F	0530	5.7	1220	0.2	1800	5.5		
30	SA	0038	0.2	0619	5.8	1302	0.1	1845	5.6
31	SU	0119	0.2	0705	5.7	1342	0.2	1926	5.5

APRIL

Date	Day	Time	m	Time	m	Time	m	Time	m
1	M	0158	0.3	0747	5.5	1419	0.5	2004	5.3
2	TU	0234	0.6	0826	5.2	1455	0.9	2038	5.0
3	W	0311	1.1	0902	4.8	1531	1.4	2108	4.7
4	TH	0352	1.5	0940	4.4	1614	1.8	2146	4.4
5	F	0444	1.9	1042	4.0	1712	2.2	2301	4.1
6	SA	0558	2.2	1237	3.9	1838	2.4		
7	SU	0104	4.1	0800	2.2	1351	4.0	2034	2.2
8	M	0213	4.3	0911	1.8	1448	4.3	2132	1.8
9	TU	0304	4.6	0958	1.5	1533	4.6	2216	1.5
10	W	0346	4.8	1039	1.2	1611	4.8	2255	1.2
11	TH	0424	5.0	1116	1.0	1646	5.0	2331	1.0
12	F	0459	5.1	1149	0.9	1719	5.0	●	
13	SA	0002	0.9	0534	5.1	1219	0.8	1754	5.1
14	SU	0031	0.9	0610	5.1	1246	0.9	1827	5.1
15	M	0057	0.9	0644	5.1	1312	1.0	1858	5.0
16	TU	0122	1.0	0714	4.9	1337	1.1	1925	5.0
17	W	0148	1.1	0742	4.8	1404	1.3	1953	4.8
18	TH	0218	1.3	0815	4.6	1435	1.5	2029	4.7
19	F	0255	1.5	0859	4.4	1517	1.7	2120	4.5
20	SA	0348	1.8	1000	4.2	1620	2.0	2227	4.3
21	SU	0517	2.0	1122	4.1	1802	2.1	2352	4.3
22	M	0657	1.9	1258	4.2	1934	1.9		
23	TU	0126	4.5	0819	1.5	1417	4.5	2049	1.5
24	W	0237	4.9	0925	1.1	1515	4.9	2150	1.1
25	TH	0332	5.2	1020	0.7	1604	5.2	2243	0.7
26	F	0422	5.5	1109	0.3	1650	5.4	2330	0.4
27	SA	0509	5.6	1155	0.2	1734	5.5	○	
28	SU	0014	0.2	0555	5.6	1238	0.2	1819	5.5
29	M	0056	0.3	0640	5.5	1318	0.4	1900	5.5
30	TU	0135	0.5	0722	5.3	1355	0.7	1936	5.3

Chart Datum: 2·91 metres below Ordnance Datum (Newlyn)

TIME ZONE (UTC)
For Summer Time add ONE hour in **non-shaded areas**

ENGLAND – FALMOUTH

LAT 50°09′N LONG 5°03′W

TIMES AND HEIGHTS OF HIGH AND LOW WATERS

SPRING & NEAP TIDES
Dates in red are SPRINGS
Dates in blue are NEAPS

YEAR **2002**

MAY

Date	Day	Time	m	Time	m	Time	m	Time	m
1	W	0213	0.8	0801	5.0	1432	1.1	2007	5.0
2	TH	0251	1.2	0836	4.7	1509	1.5	2037	4.7
3	F	0332	1.5	0912	4.3	1552	1.9	2115	4.4
4	SA	0423	1.9	1008	4.0	1647	2.2	2215	4.2
5	SU	0529	2.2	1200	3.9	1759	2.3		
6	M	0017	4.1	0656	2.1	1314	4.0	1929	2.2
7	TU	0131	4.3	0820	1.9	1410	4.2	2042	1.9
8	W	0224	4.5	0913	1.6	1455	4.5	2132	1.6
9	TH	0309	4.7	0956	1.4	1534	4.7	2214	1.4
10	F	0349	4.9	1035	1.2	1612	4.9	2252	1.2
11	SA	0428	5.0	1110	1.0	1648	5.0	2326	1.0
12	SU	0506	5.0	1143	1.0	1724	5.1	● 2359	1.0
13	M	0543	5.0	1216	1.0	1800	5.1		
14	TU	0031	1.0	0621	5.0	1248	1.0	1834	5.1
15	W	0103	1.0	0655	4.9	1319	1.1	1906	5.0
16	TH	0136	1.1	0730	4.8	1353	1.3	1940	5.0
17	F	0213	1.3	0809	4.7	1430	1.5	2022	4.8
18	SA	0256	1.5	0857	4.5	1518	1.6	2113	4.7
19	SU	0353	1.6	0956	4.3	1623	1.8	2216	4.5
20	M	0510	1.7	1111	4.3	1745	1.9	2335	4.5
21	TU	0634	1.6	1236	4.4	1907	1.7		
22	W	0058	4.6	0750	1.5	1348	4.6	2020	1.5
23	TH	0208	4.9	0856	1.2	1447	4.9	2122	1.2
24	F	0306	5.1	0953	0.9	1539	5.1	2216	0.9
25	SA	0357	5.3	1044	0.6	1626	5.3	2306	0.6
26	SU	0446	5.4	1131	0.5	1710	5.4	○ 2351	0.5
27	M	0532	5.4	1215	0.6	1754	5.4		
28	TU	0035	0.6	0618	5.3	1256	0.7	1835	5.3
29	W	0116	0.7	0702	5.1	1335	0.9	1912	5.2
30	TH	0156	1.0	0740	4.9	1413	1.2	1945	5.0
31	F	0235	1.3	0817	4.6	1451	1.5	2017	4.8

JUNE

Date	Day	Time	m	Time	m	Time	m	Time	m
1	SA	0315	1.5	0854	4.4	1532	1.8	2056	4.6
2	SU	0401	1.8	0941	4.2	1620	2.0	2147	4.4
3	M	0455	2.0	1050	4.0	1718	2.2	2255	4.2
4	TU	0558	2.0	1210	4.0	1824	2.2		
5	W	0019	4.2	0703	1.9	1313	4.2	1930	2.0
6	TH	0127	4.3	0805	1.7	1405	4.4	2030	1.8
7	F	0221	4.5	0858	1.5	1451	4.6	2122	1.5
8	SA	0309	4.7	0945	1.4	1535	4.8	2208	1.4
9	SU	0355	4.8	1028	1.2	1617	4.9	2250	1.2
10	M	0438	4.9	1109	1.1	1657	5.0	● 2330	1.1
11	TU	0518	4.9	1149	1.1	1736	5.1		
12	W	0010	1.0	0600	5.0	1229	1.1	1816	5.1
13	TH	0051	1.0	0642	4.9	1309	1.1	1854	5.1
14	F	0132	1.0	0724	4.9	1350	1.2	1935	5.1
15	SA	0215	1.1	0809	4.8	1434	1.3	2020	5.0
16	SU	0302	1.2	0858	4.7	1522	1.5	2109	4.9
17	M	0355	1.4	0952	4.6	1617	1.5	2207	4.8
18	TU	0455	1.5	1057	4.5	1722	1.6	2314	4.7
19	W	0604	1.5	1207	4.5	1833	1.6		
20	TH	0027	4.7	0715	1.5	1315	4.6	1945	1.5
21	F	0138	4.7	0824	1.4	1416	4.7	2052	1.4
22	SA	0240	4.8	0926	1.2	1513	4.9	2152	1.2
23	SU	0336	5.0	1021	1.0	1603	5.1	2245	1.0
24	M	0427	5.0	1110	0.9	1650	5.2	○ 2333	0.9
25	TU	0514	5.1	1156	0.9	1733	5.2		
26	W	0019	0.9	0600	5.0	1240	0.9	1815	5.2
27	TH	0102	0.9	0643	4.9	1320	1.1	1852	5.2
28	F	0142	1.0	0723	4.8	1358	1.2	1927	5.0
29	SA	0220	1.2	0759	4.7	1434	1.4	2001	4.9
30	SU	0257	1.4	0834	4.5	1510	1.5	2038	4.7

JULY

Date	Day	Time	m	Time	m	Time	m	Time	m
1	M	0333	1.5	0913	4.4	1547	1.8	2120	4.6
2	TU	0414	1.7	0959	4.2	1630	1.9	2208	4.4
3	W	0502	1.9	1055	4.1	1724	2.0	2306	4.3
4	TH	0559	1.9	1159	4.1	1827	2.1		
5	F	0014	4.3	0700	1.9	1304	4.2	1930	2.0
6	SA	0125	4.3	0801	1.7	1405	4.4	2030	1.8
7	SU	0228	4.4	0858	1.6	1459	4.6	2127	1.5
8	M	0322	4.6	0951	1.4	1548	4.8	2219	1.4
9	TU	0412	4.8	1041	1.3	1633	5.0	2308	1.2
10	W	0459	4.9	1129	1.1	1716	5.1	● 2355	1.0
11	TH	0544	5.0	1217	1.0	1800	5.2		
12	F	0042	0.9	0632	5.0	1303	0.9	1845	5.3
13	SA	0128	0.8	0719	5.0	1347	0.9	1930	5.3
14	SU	0213	0.8	0805	5.0	1431	1.0	2016	5.3
15	M	0258	0.9	0852	4.9	1515	1.1	2103	5.2
16	TU	0343	1.0	0940	4.8	1601	1.3	2152	5.0
17	W	0432	1.2	1033	4.7	1653	1.5	2249	4.8
18	TH	0529	1.5	1135	4.5	1755	1.6	2355	4.6
19	F	0636	1.6	1242	4.5	1908	1.7		
20	SA	0108	4.5	0751	1.6	1349	4.5	2025	1.6
21	SU	0218	4.5	0903	1.5	1451	4.7	2134	1.5
22	M	0319	4.6	1005	1.4	1546	4.9	2232	1.3
23	TU	0413	4.8	1057	1.2	1635	5.0	2322	1.1
24	W	0500	4.9	1144	1.1	1716	5.1	○	
25	TH	0007	1.0	0544	4.9	1227	1.0	1757	5.2
26	F	0050	0.9	0625	4.9	1306	1.0	1834	5.2
27	SA	0128	1.0	0702	4.8	1341	1.1	1908	5.1
28	SU	0201	1.1	0735	4.8	1413	1.2	1941	5.0
29	M	0232	1.2	0808	4.7	1441	1.4	2016	4.9
30	TU	0259	1.4	0842	4.6	1508	1.5	2050	4.7
31	W	0327	1.5	0919	4.4	1536	1.7	2126	4.5

AUGUST

Date	Day	Time	m	Time	m	Time	m	Time	m
1	TH	0400	1.7	0959	4.3	1613	1.9	2208	4.4
2	F	0447	1.9	1051	4.2	1713	2.1	2304	4.2
3	SA	0557	2.0	1157	4.1	1835	2.1		
4	SU	0018	4.1	0712	2.0	1314	4.2	1949	2.0
5	M	0146	4.2	0821	1.8	1425	4.5	2055	1.7
6	TU	0256	4.5	0923	1.5	1522	4.7	2155	1.5
7	W	0352	4.7	1021	1.3	1612	5.0	2251	1.1
8	TH	0441	4.9	1114	1.1	1658	5.2	● 2342	0.8
9	F	0528	5.1	1204	0.8	1745	5.4		
10	SA	0031	0.6	0617	5.2	1252	0.6	1832	5.5
11	SU	0117	0.5	0705	5.2	1336	0.6	1918	5.6
12	M	0201	0.4	0750	5.2	1418	0.6	2003	5.5
13	TU	0242	0.6	0834	5.2	1458	0.8	2047	5.3
14	W	0322	0.8	0918	5.0	1538	1.0	2131	5.1
15	TH	0404	1.2	1004	4.8	1623	1.4	2219	4.8
16	F	0452	1.5	1059	4.5	1719	1.7	2324	4.4
17	SA	0555	1.8	1211	4.3	1834	2.0		
18	SU	0046	4.2	0722	2.0	1328	4.3	2009	2.0
19	M	0206	4.3	0852	1.9	1437	4.5	2126	1.7
20	TU	0311	4.4	0956	1.6	1533	4.7	2223	1.5
21	W	0402	4.6	1046	1.4	1620	5.0	2311	1.2
22	TH	0446	4.8	1130	1.1	1700	5.1	○ 2353	1.0
23	F	0524	4.9	1211	1.0	1735	5.2		
24	SA	0032	0.9	0601	5.0	1247	0.9	1810	5.2
25	SU	0106	0.9	0635	5.0	1318	1.0	1844	5.2
26	M	0135	1.0	0707	4.9	1345	1.1	1916	5.1
27	TU	0200	1.1	0737	4.9	1408	1.3	1948	5.0
28	W	0221	1.3	0808	4.7	1427	1.4	2017	4.8
29	TH	0242	1.5	0838	4.6	1449	1.5	2044	4.6
30	F	0307	1.6	0910	4.4	1519	1.8	2119	4.4
31	SA	0342	1.8	0953	4.3	1604	2.0	2211	4.2

Chart Datum: 2·91 metres below Ordnance Datum (Newlyn)

TIME ZONE (UTC)
For Summer Time add ONE hour in **non-shaded areas**

ENGLAND – FALMOUTH

LAT 50°09′N LONG 5°03′W

TIMES AND HEIGHTS OF HIGH AND LOW WATERS

SPRING & NEAP TIDES
Dates in **red** are **SPRINGS**
Dates in **blue** are **NEAPS**

YEAR **2002**

SEPTEMBER

Date	Time	m	Time	m	Time	m	Time	m
1 SU	0439	2.1	1058	4.1	1732	2.3	2328	4.1
2 M	0628	2.2	1221	4.2	1916	2.2		
3 TU	0107	4.1	0753	2.0	1354	4.4	2032	1.8
4 W	0238	4.4	0903	1.7	1501	4.8	2138	1.5
5 TH	0335	4.7	1004	1.3	1552	5.1	2235	1.0
6 F	0424	5.0	1058	0.9	1639	5.4	2326	0.6
7 SA ●	0510	5.3	1147	0.6	1724	5.6		
8 SU	0013	0.4	0556	5.4	1234	0.4	1812	5.7
9 M	0058	0.2	0642	5.5	1317	0.3	1858	5.7
10 TU	0140	0.3	0726	5.5	1357	0.4	1941	5.6
11 W	0219	0.5	0808	5.3	1435	0.7	2024	5.4
12 TH	0257	0.8	0850	5.1	1513	1.0	2105	5.1
13 F	0335	1.3	0931	4.8	1555	1.5	2148	4.6
14 SA	0419	1.7	1020	4.5	1648	1.9	2251	4.2
15 SU	0519	2.1	1141	4.2	1806	2.2		
16 M	0033	4.0	0700	2.3	1311	4.2	2004	2.2
17 TU	0157	4.1	0844	2.1	1422	4.4	2118	1.8
18 W	0300	4.4	0942	1.7	1517	4.7	2208	1.5
19 TH	0348	4.7	1028	1.4	1600	5.0	2251	1.2
20 F	0427	4.9	1109	1.2	1638	5.2	2330	1.0
21 SA ○	0501	5.0	1146	1.0	1711	5.3		
22 SU	0005	0.9	0532	5.1	1220	0.9	1744	5.3
23 M	0037	0.9	0605	5.1	1249	1.0	1817	5.3
24 TU	0103	1.0	0636	5.1	1313	1.1	1848	5.2
25 W	0125	1.1	0707	5.0	1334	1.2	1918	5.0
26 TH	0145	1.2	0735	4.9	1353	1.4	1946	4.9
27 F	0206	1.4	0802	4.8	1416	1.5	2010	4.7
28 SA	0230	1.6	0831	4.6	1446	1.7	2044	4.5
29 SU	0304	1.8	0915	4.4	1529	2.0	2140	4.2
30 M	0355	2.2	1021	4.2	1644	2.3	2259	4.1

OCTOBER

Date	Time	m	Time	m	Time	m	Time	m
1 TU	0547	2.4	1145	4.2	1850	2.3		
2 W	0040	4.1	0729	2.2	1323	4.4	2012	1.9
3 TH	0218	4.4	0844	1.7	1437	4.8	2119	1.4
4 F	0315	4.8	0945	1.3	1530	5.2	2214	0.9
5 SA	0403	5.2	1038	0.9	1617	5.5	2304	0.5
6 SU	0447	5.4	1126	0.5	1703	5.7	● 2350	0.3
7 M	0530	5.6	1211	0.3	1748	5.8		
8 TU	0034	0.2	0617	5.6	1253	0.3	1834	5.8
9 W	0115	0.3	0700	5.6	1333	0.4	1918	5.6
10 TH	0154	0.6	0741	5.5	1412	0.7	2000	5.3
11 F	0231	1.0	0820	5.2	1450	1.2	2039	5.0
12 SA	0308	1.5	0858	4.9	1532	1.6	2120	4.5
13 SU	0352	1.9	0941	4.5	1625	2.0	2221	4.1
14 M	0452	2.3	1104	4.2	1742	2.4		
15 TU	0018	4.0	0631	2.5	1249	4.2	1945	2.3
16 W	0138	4.1	0819	2.3	1358	4.4	2053	1.9
17 TH	0237	4.4	0915	1.9	1450	4.7	2141	1.5
18 F	0321	4.7	0959	1.5	1533	5.0	2221	1.3
19 SA	0358	4.9	1038	1.3	1609	5.1	2258	1.1
20 SU	0432	5.1	1114	1.1	1642	5.2	2332	1.0
21 M ○	0503	5.2	1147	1.0	1715	5.3		
22 TU	0002	1.0	0534	5.2	1216	1.0	1749	5.2
23 W	0028	1.0	0607	5.2	1242	1.1	1822	5.2
24 TH	0053	1.1	0639	5.2	1305	1.2	1852	5.1
25 F	0116	1.3	0708	5.1	1329	1.4	1921	4.9
26 SA	0140	1.5	0736	4.9	1356	1.5	1951	4.7
27 SU	0208	1.6	0809	4.8	1429	1.7	2030	4.5
28 M	0245	1.9	0856	4.6	1514	2.0	2127	4.3
29 TU	0338	2.2	0959	4.4	1631	2.2	2240	4.1
30 W	0519	2.4	1118	4.4	1823	2.2		
31 TH	0016	4.2	0702	2.2	1250	4.5	1946	1.8

NOVEMBER

Date	Time	m	Time	m	Time	m	Time	m
1 F	0149	4.5	0818	1.8	1407	4.9	2053	1.4
2 SA	0249	4.9	0920	1.4	1504	5.2	2149	1.0
3 SU	0338	5.2	1013	1.0	1554	5.5	2239	0.6
4 M	0423	5.5	1101	0.6	1641	5.7	● 2326	0.4
5 TU	0508	5.6	1147	0.5	1725	5.7		
6 W	0009	0.4	0551	5.7	1231	0.5	1812	5.7
7 TH	0051	0.5	0635	5.6	1312	0.6	1856	5.5
8 F	0131	0.8	0716	5.5	1352	0.9	1938	5.2
9 SA	0209	1.2	0755	5.2	1432	1.3	2019	4.9
10 SU	0248	1.5	0832	4.9	1515	1.6	2100	4.5
11 M	0332	2.0	0913	4.6	1606	2.0	2155	4.2
12 TU	0427	2.3	1016	4.4	1713	2.3	2342	4.0
13 W	0543	2.5	1205	4.3	1846	2.3		
14 TH	0059	4.1	0722	2.4	1316	4.4	2006	2.1
15 F	0157	4.3	0829	2.1	1411	4.6	2058	1.7
16 SA	0243	4.6	0918	1.7	1455	4.8	2141	1.5
17 SU	0322	4.8	0959	1.5	1534	5.0	2219	1.3
18 M	0357	5.0	1037	1.4	1611	5.1	2254	1.2
19 TU	0433	5.1	1112	1.2	1647	5.1	2326	1.2
20 W	0507	5.2	1144	1.2	1723	5.2	○ 2356	1.2
21 TH	0542	5.2	1215	1.2	1759	5.1		
22 F	0027	1.2	0616	5.2	1245	1.3	1834	5.0
23 SA	0057	1.3	0648	5.1	1316	1.4	1907	4.9
24 SU	0128	1.5	0722	5.1	1350	1.5	1942	4.8
25 M	0202	1.5	0800	4.9	1429	1.6	2026	4.6
26 TU	0244	1.8	0848	4.8	1518	1.8	2120	4.4
27 W	0339	2.0	0945	4.7	1626	1.9	2226	4.3
28 TH	0457	2.1	1056	4.6	1751	1.9	2348	4.3
29 F	0625	2.1	1215	4.7	1911	1.7		
30 SA	0109	4.5	0743	1.8	1330	4.8	2021	1.5

DECEMBER

Date	Time	m	Time	m	Time	m	Time	m
1 SU	0215	4.8	0849	1.5	1434	5.1	2121	1.2
2 M	0310	5.1	0946	1.2	1528	5.3	2214	0.9
3 TU	0359	5.3	1038	0.9	1619	5.4	2303	0.8
4 W	0445	5.5	1126	0.8	1707	5.5	● 2349	0.7
5 TH	0530	5.6	1211	0.7	1754	5.4		
6 F	0032	0.8	0615	5.5	1256	0.8	1839	5.3
7 SA	0114	1.0	0658	5.4	1338	1.0	1923	5.1
8 SU	0154	1.3	0737	5.2	1420	1.3	2004	4.8
9 M	0234	1.5	0815	5.0	1502	1.5	2043	4.6
10 TU	0315	1.8	0854	4.8	1546	1.8	2128	4.3
11 W	0401	2.1	0941	4.6	1636	2.0	2226	4.2
12 TH	0456	2.3	1042	4.4	1736	2.2	2344	4.1
13 F	0601	2.3	1200	4.3	1843	2.2		
14 SA	0052	4.2	0712	2.2	1307	4.4	1948	2.0
15 SU	0148	4.4	0816	2.0	1403	4.5	2044	1.8
16 M	0237	4.6	0909	1.8	1452	4.7	2131	1.6
17 TU	0320	4.8	0955	1.6	1538	4.8	2213	1.5
18 W	0402	5.0	1036	1.5	1621	4.9	2252	1.4
19 TH	0442	5.1	1115	1.3	1702	5.0	○ 2331	1.3
20 F	0520	5.2	1154	1.2	1743	5.0		
21 SA	0009	1.2	0559	5.2	1233	1.2	1822	5.0
22 SU	0047	1.2	0638	5.2	1312	1.2	1902	5.0
23 M	0125	1.3	0717	5.2	1352	1.3	1941	4.9
24 TU	0205	1.4	0758	5.1	1434	1.4	2026	4.8
25 W	0248	1.5	0843	5.0	1520	1.5	2114	4.7
26 TH	0336	1.6	0934	4.9	1613	1.5	2210	4.6
27 F	0433	1.7	1032	4.8	1715	1.6	2315	4.5
28 SA	0542	1.8	1141	4.7	1827	1.7		
29 SU	0026	4.5	0700	1.8	1253	4.7	1942	1.6
30 M	0138	4.6	0815	1.6	1403	4.8	2051	1.5
31 TU	0242	4.8	0921	1.5	1507	4.9	2152	1.3

Chart Datum: 2·91 metres below Ordnance Datum (Newlyn)

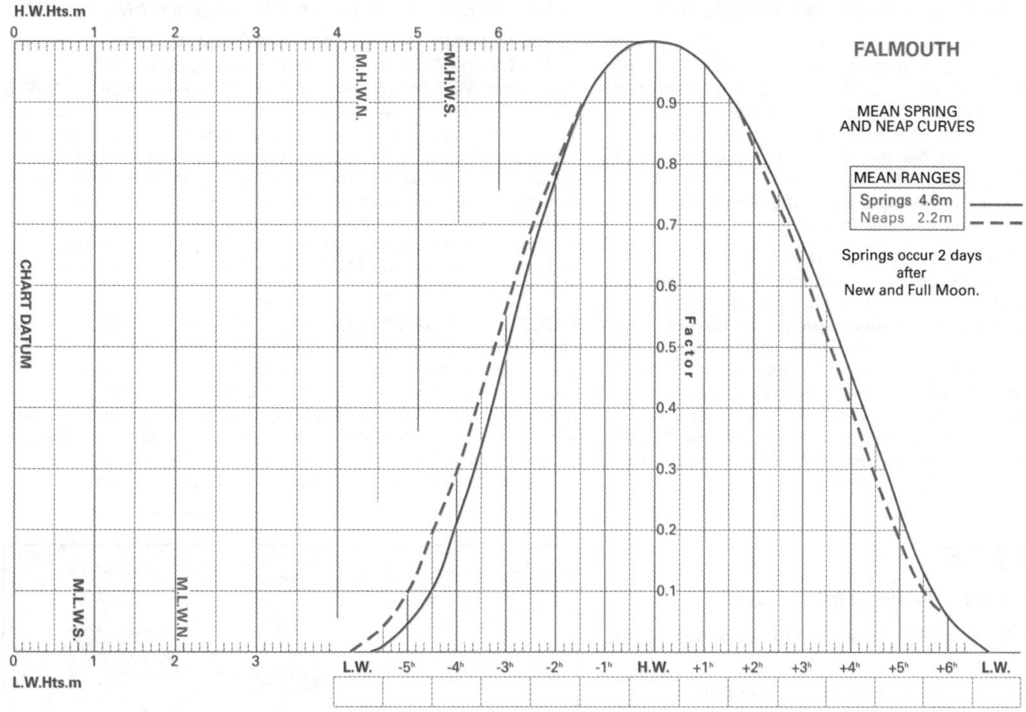

OTHER HARBOURS AND ANCHORAGES BETWEEN ST ANTHONY HEAD AND MEVAGISSEY

PORTSCATHO, Cornwall, **50°10′·84N 04°58′·32W**. AC *154*. HW –0600 on Dover, HW –0025 and –0·2m on Devonport; ML 3·0m; Duration 0550. Small drying hbr, but in settled weather and off-shore winds ⚓ outside moorings in good holding. No lts. Hr Mr ☎ (01872) 580616. Facilities: V, FW, R, Bar, Slip, P & D (cans), Ⓑ 1000-1230 Mon, Wed, Fri, ✉.

GORRAN HAVEN, Cornwall, **50°14′·49N 04°47′·16W**. AC 148, *1267*. HW –0600 on Dover, HW –0010 and –0·1m on Devonport. Shelter good with flat sand beach for drying out in off-shore wind; good ⚓ 100 to 500m E of harbour. Beware Gwineas Rk and Yaw Rk marked by ECM. Beware pot markers on appr. Not suitable ⚓ when wind is in E. Fin keelers without legs should not ⚓ closer than 300m from hbr wall where depth is 1·8m at MLWS. Facilities: ✉, V, Bar, P & D (cans, 1M), R.

PORTMELLON, Cornwall, **50°15′·74N 04°46′·98W**. AC 148, *1267*. HW –0600 on Dover, HW –0010 and –0·1m on Devonport; ML 3·1m; Duration 0600. Shelter good but only suitable as a temp ⚓ in settled weather and off-shore winds. There are no lts and few facilities.

MEVAGISSEY *9.1.14*

Cornwall **50°16′·16N 04°46′·93W** ❁❁◊◊✿✿✿

CHARTS AC *5602*, 147, 148, *1267*; Imray C6; Stanfords 13, 23; OS 204

TIDES –0600 Dover; ML 3·1; Duration 0600; Zone 0 (UT)

Standard Port DEVONPORT (⟶)

Times				Height (metres)			
High Water		Low Water		MHWS	MHWN	MLWN	MLWS
0000	0600	0000	0600	5·5	4·4	2·2	0·8
1200	1800	1200	1800				
Differences MEVAGISSEY							
–0015	–0020	–0010	–0005	–0·1	–0·1	–0·2	–0·1

(MEVAGISSEY *continued)*

SHELTER Exposed only to E'lies, if >F3, go to Fowey. Appr in strong SE'lies is dangerous. Access all tides. Ⓥ berth on S Quay in about 2m (D hose). 2 AB on seaward side of S Pier, but beware lip projecting 71cm, fendered in season. One 🅥 in Outer hbr on request to Hr Mr. Bilge keelers/cats can dry out on sandy beach, SE side of W Quay. No ⚓ inside the hbr due to over-crowding and many FVs. ⚓ off is only advised in settled weather with no E in the wind. Inner hbr (dries 1·5m) is reserved for FVs, unless taking on FW.

NAVIGATION WPT 50°16′·15N 04°46′·61W, 090°/270° from/to pier hd lt, 0·20M. Beware rky ledges off N Quay. Speed limit 3kn.

LIGHTS AND MARKS S Quay Fl (2) 10s 9m 12M, Dia 30s (fishing).

RADIO TELEPHONE Hr Mr VHF Ch 16 14 (Summer 0900-2100LT. Winter 0900-1700LT); call on 16 for berth.

TELEPHONE (Dial code 01726) Hr Mr 843305, (home 842496); MRSC (01803) 882704; ⊜ 0345 231110 (H24); Marinecall 09068 500458; Police 0990 777444; Dr 843701.

FACILITIES Outer Hbr AB (S Quay) £0.67, M, FW, D; **Inner Hbr** Slip, FW, C (1 ton). **Services:** BY, Sh (wood), CH, ♿. **Village** EC Thurs; V, R, ⊡, Gas, Bar, Ice, ✉, Ⓑ (Jun-Sep 1000-1430, Oct-Jun 1000-1300), ⇌ (bus to St Austell), ✈ Newquay.

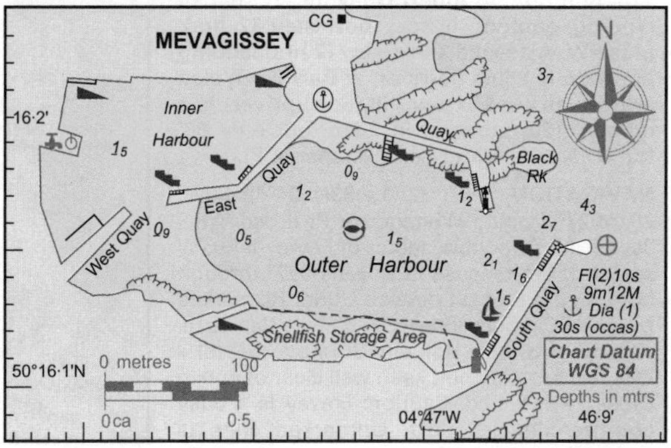

GUNNERY RANGE OFF DODMAN PT AND GRIBBIN HEAD

Naval gunnery practice takes place to seaward of Dodman Pt and Gribbin Hd, under the control of Flag Officer Sea Training (FOST), HMS Drake, Plymouth PL2 2BG. Firing is by day only, approx 1-2 times per week, in a 2 hrs block, although actual firing only lasts about 15 mins. Planned firings are broadcast in Gunfacts (see 6.13.3) and Navtex. Advance details are also printed in local newspapers and are available from Hr Mrs at Fowey, Looe, Polperro and Mevagissey. Firings are not planned for two weeks over Christmas and four weeks in August.

The range is in danger areas D.006A and D.007A & B (see 9.1.18). Warships, between 2·5 and 9M SSE of Gribbin Hd, fire WSW at 3 SPM target buoys, Fl Y, which lie from 2·4 to 4·8M SSE of Dodman Pt. The RN will ensure that safety requirements can be met; if not possible, ie due to vessels in the range area, then firing will not take place. A helicopter conducts range safety surveillance. A range safety boat will advise other craft of firings and may suggest a slight course alteration to clear the area. Yachts are legally entitled to transit through the range area. For info ☎ (01752) 5557550 (H24) or call *FOST OPS* on VHF Ch 74, which is monitored by all warships in the areas S of Plymouth.

MINOR HARBOURS BETWEEN MEVAGISSEY AND FOWEY

CHARLESTOWN, Cornwall, **50°19´·84N 04°45´·35W**. AC 31, 148, *1267*. HW –0555 on Dover, –0010 on Devonport; HW –0·1m on Devonport; ML 3·1m; Duration 0605. Hr Mr ☎ 01726 70241, 🖷 61839, VHF Ch 12 16. A china clay port; yachts should berth in the outer hbr (dries), but only in W'lies. Ent dries and should only be attempted by day and in off-shore winds with calm weather. Hbr is closed in SE winds. Waiting buoys 2ca S of hbr. N bkwtr 2FG (vert) 5m 1M; S bkwtr 2FR (vert) 5m 1M. Ent sig: ● (night) = hbr shut. VHF Ch14 16 (HW –2, only when vessel expected). Yachts should pre-arrange via Hr Mr on Ch 14 or ☎ (01726) 67526. Facilities: www.square-sail.com, EC Thurs; AB, FW, P & D (cans or pre-arranged tanker), R, Bar, V at ✉, ME, Sh.

PAR, Cornwall, **50°20´·61N 04°42´·07W**. AC 31, 148, *1267*. HW –0555 on Dover; ML 3·1m; Duration 0605. See 9.1.15. A china clay port, only in emergency for yachts; dries 1·2m. 4 chys are conspic 2½ca W of ent. Beware Killyvarder Rk (dries 2·4m) 3ca SE of ent, marked by a SHM bn. Only attempt ent by day, in calm weather with off-shore winds. Ent sigs: R shape (day) or ● lt (night) = port closed or vessel leaving. VHF Ch 12 16 (by day, HW –2 to HW +1). Hr Mr ☎ (01726) 817300. Facilities: EC Thurs; Bar, FW.

FOWEY *9.1.15*

Cornwall **50°19'·65N 04°38'·54W** ❁❁❁◊◊◊✿✿✿

CHARTS AC *5602*, 31, 148, *1267*; Imray C6, Y52; Stanfords 13, 23; OS 204

TIDES –0540 Dover; ML 2·9; Duration 0605; Zone 0 (UT)

Standard Port DEVONPORT (→ 163-165)

Times				Height (metres)			
High Water		Low Water		MHWS	MHWN	MLWN	MLWS
0000	0600	0000	0600	5·5	4·4	2·2	0·8
1200	1800	1200	1800				
Differences FOWEY							
–0010	–0015	–0010	–0005	–0·1	–0·1	–0·2	–0·2
LOSTWITHIEL							
+0005	–0010	Dries		–4·1	–4·1	Dries	
PAR							
–0010	–0015	–0010	–0005	–0·4	–0·4	–0·4	–0·2

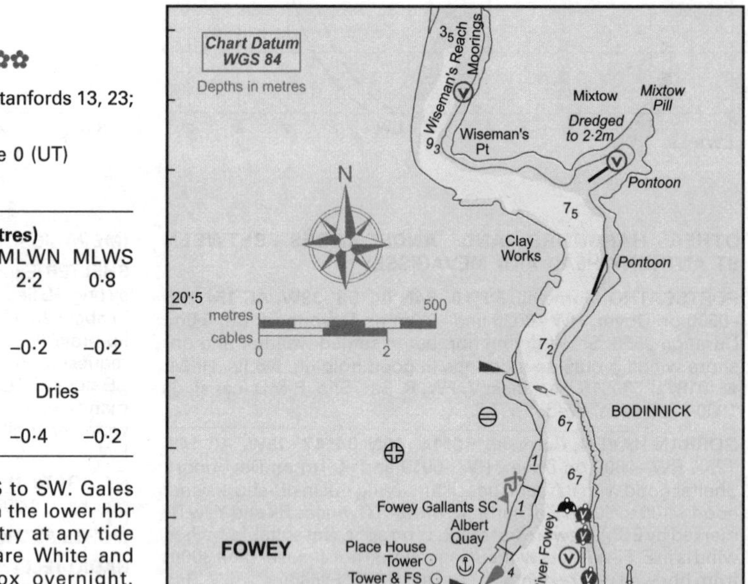

SHELTER Good, but exposed to winds from S to SW. Gales from these directions can cause heavy swell in the lower hbr and confused seas, especially on the ebb. Entry at any tide in any conditions. Speed limit 6kn. All 🅥s are White and marked 'FHC VISITORS'. Dues £1.15 approx overnight. Pontoons are in situ May-Oct. Craft >12 5m LOA should berth/moor as directed by Hr Mr. **Pont Pill**, on the E side, offers double-berth fore and aft 🅥s and AB in 2m on a 120´ floating pontoon; there is also a refuse barge, fuel barge and RNSA members' buoy. Opposite Albert Quay, on the E side of the chan there is a trot of single swinging 🅥s and another 120´ pontoon. At **Albert Quay** the 'T' shaped landing pontoon is for short stay (2 hrs), plus FW. A second short stay (2 hrs) landing pontoon is 250m up-river, at Berrills BYalso at Polruan. At **Mixtow Pill** (5ca upriver) is a quieter 120' pontoon in 2·2m, but only 60' for Ⓥ. A 🅥 is 30m N of Wiseman's Pt.

NAVIGATION WPT 50°19´·33N 04°38´·80W, 207°/027° from/to Whitehouse Pt lt, Iso WRG 3s, 0·72M. Appr in W sector of Fowey lt ho. W sector of Whitehouse Pt lt leads 027° through hbr ent. 3M E of ent beware Udder Rk marked by unlit SCM buoy. From SW beware Cannis Rk (4ca SE of Gribbin Hd) with SCM buoy, Q (6) + L Fl 15s. Entering hbr, keep well clear of Punch Cross Rks to stbd. Caution: Fowey is a busy commercial clay port. Unmarked chan is

FOWEY *continued*

navigable up to Golant, but moorings restrict ⚓ space. Lerryn (1·6M) and Lostwithiel (3M) (5.3m electr cables) are accessible on the tide by shoal draft.

LIGHTS AND MARKS An unlit RW tr 33m on Gribbin Hd (1 3M WSW of hbr ent) is conspic from all sea directions, as is a white house 3ca E of hbr ent. Lt ho is conspic, L Fl WR 5s 28m 11/9M, R284°-295°, W295°-028°, R028°-054°. Whitehouse Pt Iso WRG 3s 11m 11/8M, G017°-022°, W022°-032°, R032°-037°. Ent is marked by Lamp Rk SHM bn Fl G 5s 7m 2M, vis 088°-205°, and St Catherine's Pt FR 15m 2M, vis 150°-295°.

RADIO TELEPHONE Call *Fowey Hbr Radio* Ch **12** 16 (HO). Hbr Patrol (0900-2000LT) Ch 12. Water taxi Ch 06. Pilots & Tugs Ch 09, 12.

TELEPHONE (Dial code 01726) Hr Mr 832471, 🖷 833738; MRSC (01803) 882704; Marinecall 09068 500458; ⊖ 0345 231110 (H24); Police (0990) 777444; 🅷 832241; Dr 832451.

FACILITIES **Albert Quay** L, FW; **Royal Fowey YC** ☎ 832245, FW, R, Bar, Showers; **Fowey Gallants SC** ☎ 832335, Showers, Bar, R. **Services:** M, FW, D, (cans) by arrgt with Hr Mr, Gas, Gaz, CH, ACA, Ⓔ, BY, Slip, ME, El, Sh, C (7 ton); FW, ⛽, oils disposal and ♿ access at Berrills BY pontoon, 250m N of Albert Quay. **Polruan Quay** Pontoon, Slip, L, FW, C (3 ton). **Town** EC Wed & Sat; ✉, Ⓑ, ⇌ (bus to Par), ✈ (Newquay).

MINOR HARBOUR BETWEEN FOWEY AND LOOE

POLPERRO, Cornwall, **50°19′·78N 04°30′·79W**. AC 148, *1267*. HW –0554 on Dover; HW –0007 and –0·2m on Devonport; ML 3·1m; Duration 0610. Shelter good, but hbr dries about 2m. There is 3·3m at MHWS and 2·5m at MHWN. The ent is 9·8m wide (closed by gate in bad weather). AB on N quay or pick up a buoy; also 4 temp buoys at hbr ent. Beware The Ranney to W of ent, and the rks to E. Lights: Iso WR 6s 30m 7M at Spy House Pt CG Stn, vis W288°-060°, R060°-288°. Tidal Basin, W pier hd FW 4m 4M on post; shows FR when hbr closed. Dir FW (occas) shown from measured distance bns 1M and 2·2M to ENE. Hr Mr on Fish Quay, AB £1.25; FW on quays. EC Sat.

LOOE *9.1.16*

Cornwall **50°21′·04N 04°27′·03W** ❀❀◊◊✿✿

CHARTS AC *5602*, 147, 148, *1267*; Imray C6; Stanfords 13, 23; OS 201

TIDES –0538 Dover; ML 3·0; Duration 0610; Zone 0 (UT)

Standard Port DEVONPORT (⟶)

Times				Height (metres)			
High Water		Low Water		MHWS	MHWN	MLWN	MLWS
0000	0600	0000	0600	5·5	4·4	2·2	0·8
1200	1800	1200	1800				
Differences LOOE							
–0010	–0010	–0005	–0005	–0·1	–0·2	–0·2	–0·2
WHITSAND BAY							
0000	0000	0000	0000	0·0	+0·1	–0·1	+0·2

SHELTER Good, but uncomfortable in strong SE winds. ⚓ in 2m E of the pier hd; access approx HW ±1½. Ⓥ berth, above ferry, is marked in Y on W side of hbr which dries 2·4m to the ent. The W bank has rky outcrops to S of ferry.

NAVIGATION WPT 50°19′·77N 04°24′·67W, 130°/310° from/to pier hd lt, 2·0M. Ent dangerous in strong SE'lies, when seas break heavily on the bar. From W, beware The Ranney, rks 2ca SE of Looe Is. Do not attempt the rky passage between Looe Is and mainland except with local knowledge and at HW. From E, beware Longstone Rks extending 1½ca from shore NE of hbr ent. At sp, ebb tide runs up to 5kn.

LIGHTS AND MARKS Looe Island (or St George's Is) is conspic (44m), 8ca S of the ent. Mid Main bn (off Hannafore Pt, halfway between pier hd and Looe Is) Q (3) 10s 2M; ECM. At night appr in W sector (267°-313°) of pier hd lt Oc WR 3s 8m 15/12M; vis W013°-207°, R207°-267°, W267°-313°, R313°-332°. Siren (2) 30s (fishing) at Nailzee Pt. No lts inside hbr.

RADIO TELEPHONE VHF Ch 16 (occas).

TELEPHONE (Dial code 01503) Hr Mr 262839; CG 262138; MRSC (01803) 882704; Marinecall 09068 500458; ⊖ 0345 231110; Police 262233; Dr 263195.

FACILITIES **W Looe Quay** AB £1.20, Slip, M, P & D (cans), L, FW, ME, El, CH; **E Looe Quay** Access HW ±3, Slip, P & D (cans), L, FW, ME, El, C (2½ ton); **Looe SC** ☎ 262559, L, R, Bar. **Services:** Sh (Wood), Ⓔ, Sh, Gas. **Town** EC Thurs (winter only); P, FW, V, R, Bar, ♿, 🅳, ✉, Ⓑ, ⇌, ✈ (Plymouth).

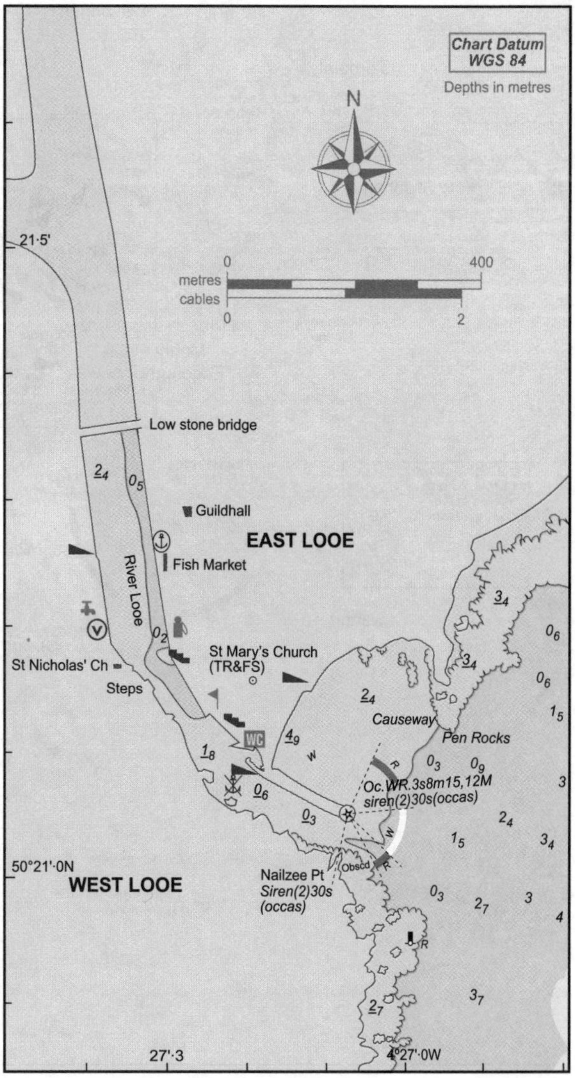

PLYMOUTH (DEVONPORT) *9.1.17*

Devon **50°20'·04N 04°10'·07W** (W Chan) ❁❁❁⛵⛵⛵✿✿✿
50°20'·04N 04°08'·07W (E Chan)

CHARTS AC *5602*, *871*, 1902, 1901, *30*, 1967, 1900, *1267*, *1613*; Imray C14, C6; Stanfords 13, 22; OS 201

TIDES –0540 Dover; ML 3·3; Duration 0610; Zone 0 (UT)

Standard Port DEVONPORT (⟶)

Times				**Height (metres)**			
High Water		Low Water		MHWS	MHWN	MLWN	MLWS
0000	0600	0000	0600	5·5	4·4	2·2	0·8
1200	1800	1200	1800				
Differences BOVISAND PIER							
0000	–0020	0000	–0010	–0·2	–0·1	0·0	+0·1
TURNCHAPEL (Cattewater)							
0000	0000	+0010	–0015	0·0	+0·1	+0·2	+0·1
JUPITER POINT (R. Lynher)							
+0010	+0005	0000	–0005	0·0	0·0	+0·1	0·0
ST GERMANS (R. Lynher)							
0000	0000	+0020	+0020	–0·3	–0·1	0·0	+0·2
SALTASH (R. Tamar)							
0000	+0010	0000	–0005	+0·1	+0·1	+0·1	+0·1
CARGREEN (R. Tamar)							
0000	+0010	+0020	+0020	0·0	0·0	–0·1	0·0
COTEHELE QUAY (R. Tamar)							
0000	+0020	+0045	+0045	–0·9	–0·9	–0·8	–0·4

NOTE: Winds from SE to W increase the flood and retard the ebb; vice versa in winds from the NW to E.

SHELTER Excellent. Plymouth is a Naval Base, a busy commercial/ferry port principally using Mill Bay Docks, and an active fishing port based mainly on Sutton Harbour which is entered via a lock (see Facilities). There are marinas to E and W of the city centre,

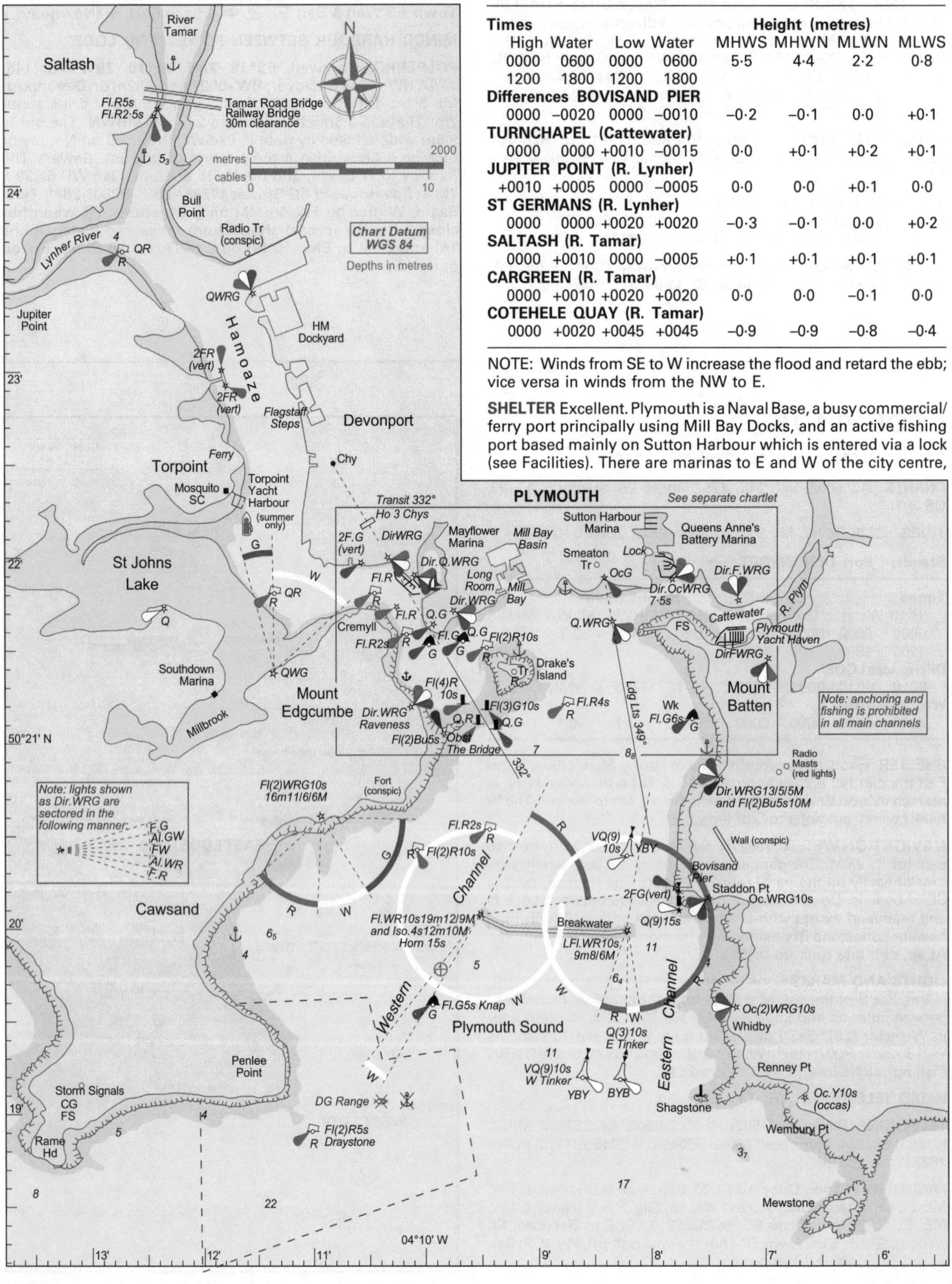

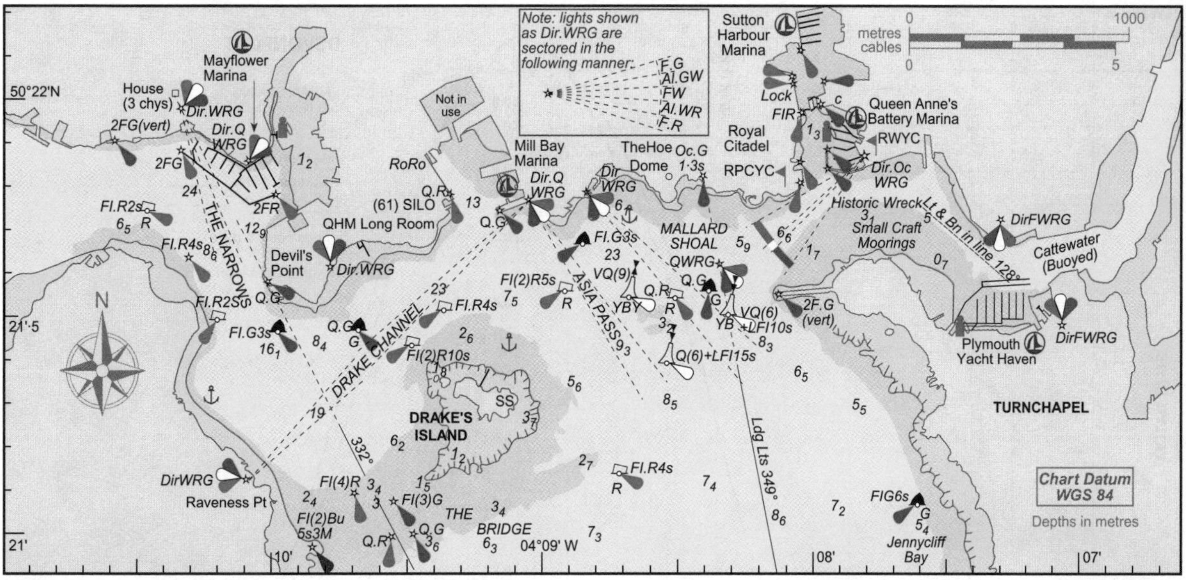

as well as in the Cattewater, off Torpoint and in Millbrook Lake. Around the Sound there are ⚓s, sheltered according to the wind, in Cawsand Bay, in Barn Pool (below Mt Edgcumbe), N of Drake's Island, below The Hoe and in Jennycliff Bay to the E. Also good shelter W of Cremyll and off the Hamoaze in the R Lynher and in the R Tamar/Tavy above Saltash (see overleaf).

NAVIGATION WPT 50°19′·74N 04°09′·87W, 213°/033° from/to W bkwtr lt, 0·40M. The Sound can be entered via the W or E Chans which are well lit/buoyed with no real hazards. There are no shoal patches with less than 3·7m at MLWS. Yachts need not keep to the deep water chans. The short cut to the Hamoaze via The Bridge (channel between Drake's Is and Mt Edgcumbe) is lit by 2 PHM and 2 SHM bns; the seaward pair show QR and QG, the inner pair Fl (4) R 10s and Fl (3) G 10s. The QR bn and the Fl (4) R 10s bn both have tide gauges calibrated to show height of tide above CD; charted depth is 2·1m. The E'ly of 3 conspic high-rise blocks brg 331° leads through The Bridge chan. Caution: a charted depth 1·9m is close SW of No 3 SHM bn, Fl (3) G 10s.

Speed limits: 10kn N of The Breakwater, 8kn in Cattewater (where outbound vessels have right of way), 4kn in Sutton Chan and 5kn in Sutton Hbr.

Historic Wrecks (see 9.0.3h) are at:

Cattewater, 50°21′·73N 04°07′·70W, 1ca N of Mount Batten.

Penlee Pt, 2ca W and 7ca SW of: two sites at 50°19′·00N 04°11′·64W and 50°18′·61N 04°12′·05W.

LIGHTS AND MARKS See 9.1.4 for more detail. Bkwtr W hd, Fl WR 10s 19m 12/9M (vis W262°-208°, R208°-262°) and Iso 4s 12m 10M (vis 033°-037°). Bkwtr E hd, L Fl WR 10s 9m 8/6M (R190°-353°, W353°-001°, R001°-018°, W018°-190°). Mallard Shoal ldg lts 349°: Front Q WRG 10/3M (vis G233°-043°, R043°-067°, G067°-087°, W087°-099°, R099°-108°); rear 396m from front (on Hoe) Oc G 1·3s (vis 310°-040°).

There are Dir WRG lts, all lit H24 except **, at Whidbey (138·5°), Staddon Pt (044°), Withyhedge (070°), W Hoe bn (315°), Western King (271°), Mill Bay** (048·5°), Ravenness (225°), Mount Wise (343°), and Ocean Court** (085°).

In fog the following Dir W lts operate: Mallard (front) Fl 5s (vis 232°-110°); West Hoe bn F (vis 313°-317°); Eastern King Fl 5s (vis 259°-062°); Ravenness Fl (2) 15s (vis 160°-305°;) Mount Wise F (vis 341°-345°); Ocean Court Fl 5s (vis 270°-100°).

Notes: Principal lts in Plymouth Sound show QY if mains power fails. N of The Bkwtr, four large mooring buoys (C, D, E & F) have Fl Y lts.

RADIO TELEPHONE Call: *Long Room Port Control* VHF Ch 08 12 **14** 16 (H24).

Mill Bay Docks Ch 12 14 16 (only during ferry ops).

Sutton Lock, for lock opening and marina, Ch **12** 16 (H24).

Cattewater Hbr Ch 14 16 (Mon-Fri, 0900-1700LT). Call Ch **80** M for Mayflower, Queen Anne's Battery, Sutton Hbr & Plymouth Yacht Haven marinas and Torpoint Yacht Hbr.

TELEPHONE (Dial code 01752) QHM 836952; DQHM 836485; Flagstaff Port Control 552413; Longroom Control 836528, 📠 836401; Cattewater Hr Mr 665934; ABP at Mill Bay 662191; MRSC (01803) 882704; ⊜ 0345 231110 (H24); Marinecall 09068 500458; Police 701188; Dr 663138; Ⓗ 668080.

FACILITIES Marinas (W to E)

Torpoint Yacht Hbr (60+20 Ⓥ) ☎/📠 813658, £1.56, access H24, dredged 2m. FW, AC, BY, C, ME, El, Sh, Diver, SM. Fuel barge ☎ 07803 029237 0830-1600, all week except Wed.

Southdown Marina (35 inc Ⓥ) ☎/📠 823084, £1.17, access HW±4; AB on pontoon (2m) or on drying quay; FW, AC, D, C(5ton).

Mayflower Marina (300+50 Ⓥ) ☎ 556633, 📠 606896, £2.04 inc AC, P, D, FW, ME, El, Sh, C (2 ton), BH (25 ton), CH, Slip, Gas, Gaz, LPG, Divers, SM, BY, YC, V, R, Bar, ⊡.

Mill Bay Village Marina ☎ 226785, 📠 226785, VHF Ch M. NO VISITORS. Ent lts = Oc R 4s & Oc G 4s, not on chartlet.

Queen Anne's Battery Marina (240+60 Ⓥ) ☎ 671142, 📠 266297, £1.80, AC, P, D, ME, El, Sh, FW, BH (20 ton), C (50 ton), CH, Gas, Gaz, ⊡, SM, Slip, V, Bar, YC.

Sutton Hbr Marina (310) ☎ 664186, 📠 223521, £1.91, P, D, FW, AC, El, ME, Sh, CH, C, BH (25 ton), Slip. Enter via lock (Barbican flood protection scheme), which maintains 3m CD in the marina. Lock (floating fenders) operates H24, free; call *Sutton Lock* VHF Ch 12 16. When tide rises to 3m above CD, gates stay open for free-flow. Tfc lts (vert): 3 ● = Stop; 3 ● = Go; 3 Fl ● = Serious hazard, wait.

Plymouth Yacht Haven (450 inc Ⓥ) ☎ 404231, 07721 498422 (1900-0800), 📠 484177, £1.35, dredged 2·25m, D (H24), FW, AC foc, CH, ME, El, Gas, mobile C (12 ton), BH (65 ton), V, ⊡, ♿, Bar, R. Water taxi: daily 0700-2300, 5 mins to Barbican, Ch M or ☎.

YACHT CLUBS **Royal Western YC of England** ☎ 660077, M, Bar, R; **Royal Plymouth Corinthian YC** ☎ 664327, VHF Ch M, M, R, Bar, Slip; **Plym YC** ☎ 404991; **RNSA** ☎ 557679; **Mayflower SC** ☎ 492566; **Torpoint Mosquito SC** ☎ 812508, R, Bar visitors welcome; **Saltash SC** ☎ 845988.

Services All facilities available, inc ACA; consult marina/Hr Mr for details. A *Water Sports and Events Diary* contains much useful information. **City** all facilities, ⇌, ✈.

BYE LAWS/NAVAL ACTIVITY The whole Port is under the jurisdiction of the QHM, but certain areas are locally controlled, i.e. by Cattewater Commissioners and by ABP who operate Mill Bay Docks. Beware frequent movements of naval vessels, which have right of way in the chans. Obey MOD Police orders. Info on Naval activities may be obtained from Naval Ops.

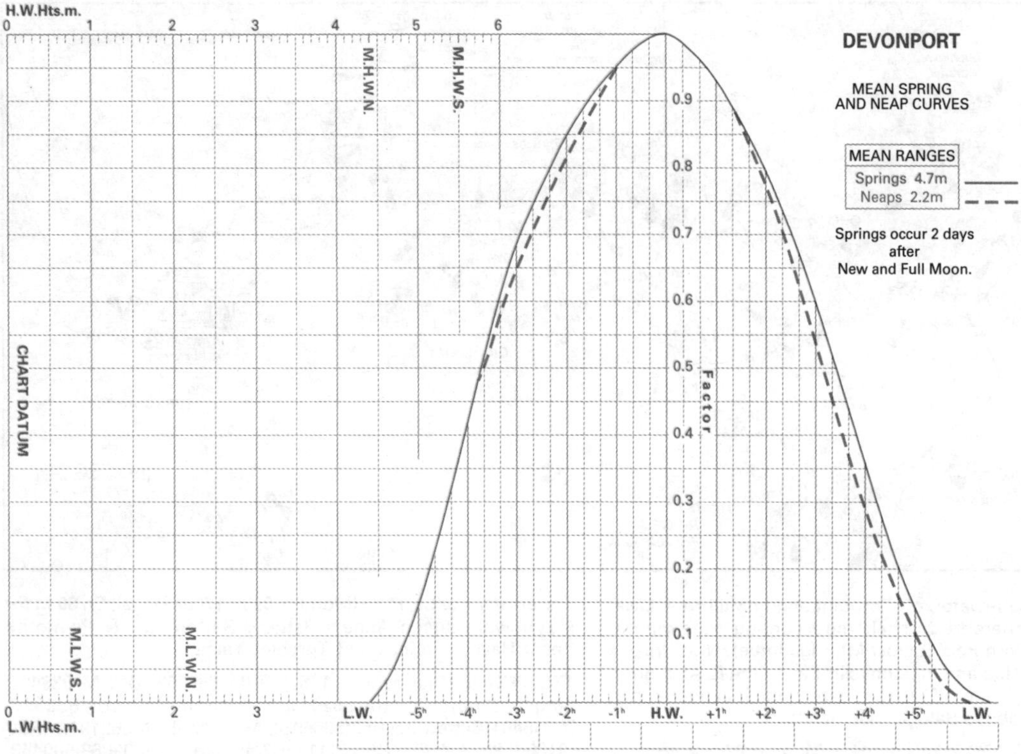
H.W.Hts.m.
0 1 2 3 4 5 6
M.H.W.N.
M.H.W.S.
CHART DATUM
M.L.W.S.
M.L.W.N.
0 1 2 3
L.W.Hts.m.
0.9
0.8
0.7
0.6
0.5
0.4
0.3
0.2
0.1
Factor
L.W. -5h -4h -3h -2h -1h H.W. +1h +2h +3h +4h +5h L.W.
DEVONPORT
MEAN SPRING AND NEAP CURVES
MEAN RANGES
Springs 4.7m
Neaps 2.2m
Springs occur 2 days after New and Full Moon.

☎ 501182 (H24) or Devonport Ops Room ☎ 563777 Ext 2182/3. Submarines may secure to a buoy close N of the Breakwater; they will show a Fl Y anti-collision lt.
For Subfacts in the W English Channel see 9.1.18.
The Cattewater: speed limit 4 knots above Fisher's Nose. All vessels <20m keep clear of vessels >20m

TRAFFIC SIGNALS Traffic is controlled H24 by the following combinations of 3 lts WRG (vert), Fl or Oc, shown from Drake's Island and at Flagstaff Port Control Station in the Dockyard. These signals and any hoisted by HM Ships apply to the waters off the dockyard port and 125m either side of the deep water chan out to the W Ent. The Cattewater, Mill Bay Docks and Sutton Hbr are excluded.

Signal	Meaning
Unlit	No restrictions, unless passed on VHF
● ● ● All Fl	Serious Emergency All traffic suspended
● ● ● All Oc	Outgoing traffic only may proceed on the recommended track. Crossing traffic to seek approval from Port Control*
● ● ● All Oc	Incoming traffic only may proceed on the recommended track. Crossing traffic to seek approval from Port Control*
● ● Ⓦ All Oc	Vessels may proceed in either direction, but shall give a wide berth to HM Ships using the recommended track

*Call Port Control Ch 13 or 14, but craft <20m LOA may proceed in the contrary direction, with care and not impeding the passage of vessels for which the signal is intended.

Wind Strength Warning Flags and Lights
Wind flags (R & W vert stripes) are flown at Queen Anne's Battery, Mayflower Marina and The Camber (HO only) to warn of excessive winds as follows:
1 wind flag (1 Oc Ⓦ lt) = Rough weather, Force 5 - 6.
2 wind flags (2 Oc Ⓦ lts, vert) = Very rough weather, > F 6.
Note: These flags are supplemented by Oc Ⓦ lt(s) shown from Drake's Island, HJ when no traffic signal is in force.
Wembury Firing Range ceased activity on 30 Mar 2001
Diving: Keep clear of regular diving off Bovisand Pier, The Breakwater Fort and Ravenness Point. Diving signals (Flag A) are displayed. Flag N flown from pier indicates steps temporarily occupied.
Submarine operations: do not pass within 200m or cross astern within 800m of any submarine under way.

RIVER TAMAR (and TAVY) The Tamar is navigable on the flood for 15M to Morwhellan. R Tavy flows into the Tamar 1¼M above the bridges, but due to power lines (8m) and a bridge (7·6m) at its mouth, is only accessible to un-masted craft up to Bere Ferrers. Cargreen village is 0·7M beyond the Tavy, on the W bank, with many local moorings and ⚓ in 2m. Weir Quay on E bank has a SC, BY, M and fuel. The river S-bends, narrowing and drying, passes Cothele Quay and then turns 90° stbd to Calstock; possible AB, M, or ⚓ above the viaduct in 2m. **Tamar River SC** ☎ 362741; **Weir Quay SC** ☎ (01822) 840960, M, CH, ME; **Calstock BY** ☎ (01822) 832502, access HW ±3, M, ME, SH, C (8 ton), BH (10 ton). Facilities: P, D, V, Bar, Ⓑ (Mon a.m.), ⇌.

RIVER LYNHER (or ST GERMANS) This river which flows into The Hamoaze about 0·8M S of the Tamar Bridge, dries extensively but is navigable on the tide for 4M up to St Germans Quay (private); but temp AB possible by prior arrangement with Quay SC. The chan, ent at Wearde Quay, is buoyed and partly lit for the first 2M. There are ⚓s, amid local moorings, at the ent to Forder Lake (N bank); SE of Ince Pt and Castle in about 3m; and at Dandy Hole, a pool with 3m, where the river bends NW and dries almost completely. Facilities: V, Bar, ✉, (½M). **Quay SC** Moorings ☎ (01503) 250370.

TIME ZONE (UTC)
For Summer Time add ONE hour in **non-shaded areas**

ENGLAND – PLYMOUTH

LAT 50°22′N LONG 4°11′W

TIMES AND HEIGHTS OF HIGH AND LOW WATERS

SPRING & NEAP TIDES
Dates in red are SPRINGS
Dates in blue are NEAPS

YEAR **2002**

JANUARY

Date	Day	Time	m	Time	m	Time	m	Time	m
1	TU	0045	0.9	0654	5.5	1312	0.8	1922	5.3
2	W	0130	0.9	0740	5.6	1358	0.8	2008	5.2
3	TH	0215	1.0	0826	5.5	1444	0.9	2055	5.2
4	F	0300	1.1	0912	5.4	1531	1.1	2143	5.0
5	SA	0347	1.3	1001	5.2	1619	1.3	2235	4.8
6	SU	0438	1.5	1055	5.0	1714	1.5	2334	4.7
7	M	0537	1.8	1158	4.8	1819	1.7		
8	TU	0042	4.6	0649	1.9	1309	4.7	1933	1.8
9	W	0152	4.6	0807	1.9	1419	4.7	2046	1.8
10	TH	0257	4.7	0916	1.7	1523	4.8	2148	1.6
11	F	0354	4.9	1014	1.5	1619	4.9	2240	1.4
12	SA	0444	5.1	1105	1.3	1708	5.0	2326	1.2
13	SU ●	0528	5.2	1150	1.1	1751	5.1		
14	M	0008	1.2	0606	5.3	1232	1.1	1829	5.1
15	TU	0047	1.1	0642	5.3	1310	1.1	1904	5.0
16	W	0122	1.2	0716	5.3	1345	1.2	1937	5.0
17	TH	0154	1.3	0749	5.2	1416	1.3	2010	4.9
18	F	0222	1.4	0824	5.1	1444	1.4	2044	4.8
19	SA	0249	1.6	0858	5.0	1512	1.6	2119	4.6
20	SU	0317	1.7	0934	4.8	1543	1.8	2156	4.5
21	M	0351	1.9	1012	4.6	1622	1.9	2240	4.4
22	TU	0438	2.1	1100	4.5	1719	2.1	2337	4.3
23	W	0550	2.2	1202	4.4	1836	2.1		
24	TH	0049	4.3	0714	2.2	1319	4.4	1950	2.0
25	F	0209	4.4	0827	2.0	1441	4.5	2058	1.8
26	SA	0319	4.7	0932	1.7	1548	4.7	2159	1.5
27	SU	0416	5.0	1031	1.3	1644	5.0	2255	1.2
28	M	0507	5.3	1125	1.0	1736	5.2	○ 2347	0.9
29	TU	0555	5.5	1216	0.7	1825	5.3		
30	W	0036	0.7	0642	5.6	1305	0.5	1913	5.4
31	TH	0123	0.6	0730	5.7	1351	0.4	2000	5.4

FEBRUARY

Date	Day	Time	m	Time	m	Time	m	Time	m
1	F	0207	0.6	0817	5.7	1435	0.5	2044	5.4
2	SA	0249	0.7	0901	5.6	1516	0.7	2127	5.2
3	SU	0330	0.9	0945	5.4	1557	1.0	2210	5.0
4	M	0412	1.2	1030	5.1	1641	1.3	2258	4.7
5	TU	0500	1.6	1122	4.7	1732	1.7	2357	4.5
6	W	0600	1.9	1230	4.5	1839	2.0		
7	TH	0112	4.4	0722	2.1	1349	4.3	2011	2.1
8	F	0228	4.4	0854	2.0	1502	4.4	2130	1.9
9	SA	0332	4.6	1002	1.7	1603	4.6	2228	1.6
10	SU	0426	4.9	1054	1.4	1653	4.8	2314	1.4
11	M	0510	5.1	1138	1.2	1735	4.9	2356	1.2
12	TU ●	0549	5.2	1218	1.0	1812	5.0		
13	W	0033	1.0	0624	5.3	1255	0.9	1846	5.1
14	TH	0107	1.0	0659	5.3	1327	0.9	1919	5.1
15	F	0136	1.0	0732	5.3	1355	1.0	1951	5.0
16	SA	0201	1.1	0805	5.2	1419	1.1	2022	4.9
17	SU	0223	1.2	0836	5.0	1441	1.3	2051	4.8
18	M	0246	1.4	0903	4.9	1505	1.4	2118	4.7
19	TU	0313	1.6	0930	4.7	1536	1.6	2149	4.5
20	W	0350	1.8	1008	4.5	1618	1.9	2238	4.4
21	TH	0443	2.1	1108	4.3	1725	2.1	2348	4.2
22	F	0617	2.2	1228	4.2	1906	2.2		
23	SA	0116	4.3	0753	2.1	1405	4.3	2029	2.0
24	SU	0247	4.6	0909	1.7	1528	4.6	2140	1.6
25	M	0354	4.9	1015	1.3	1628	4.9	2241	1.1
26	TU	0448	5.3	1112	0.8	1720	5.2	2334	0.7
27	W ○	0538	5.6	1203	0.4	1809	5.4		
28	TH	0023	0.4	0626	5.8	1250	0.2	1856	5.5

MARCH

Date	Day	Time	m	Time	m	Time	m	Time	m
1	F	0109	0.2	0714	5.8	1335	0.1	1941	5.6
2	SA	0151	0.2	0759	5.8	1416	0.2	2024	5.5
3	SU	0230	0.3	0842	5.7	1454	0.4	2103	5.4
4	M	0308	0.6	0922	5.4	1531	0.8	2140	5.1
5	TU	0346	1.0	1001	5.0	1609	1.3	2217	4.8
6	W	0428	1.5	1044	4.6	1654	1.8	2304	4.4
7	TH	0522	2.0	1152	4.2	1754	2.2		
8	F	0031	4.2	0640	2.3	1327	4.1	1929	2.4
9	SA	0202	4.2	0838	2.2	1444	4.2	2115	2.2
10	SU	0311	4.5	0948	1.8	1545	4.4	2211	1.8
11	M	0404	4.8	1037	1.4	1634	4.7	2256	1.4
12	TU	0448	5.0	1119	1.1	1713	4.9	2335	1.1
13	W	0526	5.2	1157	0.9	1749	5.0		
14	TH	0011	0.9	0601	5.3	1232	0.8	● 1823	5.1
15	F	0044	0.9	0636	5.3	1302	0.8	1855	5.1
16	SA	0111	0.9	0710	5.3	1327	0.9	1927	5.1
17	SU	0135	1.0	0742	5.2	1350	1.0	1956	5.0
18	M	0157	1.1	0810	5.1	1412	1.1	2022	4.9
19	TU	0219	1.2	0835	4.9	1436	1.3	2046	4.8
20	W	0246	1.4	0900	4.7	1504	1.5	2115	4.7
21	TH	0320	1.6	0938	4.5	1543	1.8	2202	4.5
22	F	0410	1.9	1040	4.3	1643	2.1	2313	4.3
23	SA	0538	2.2	1201	4.1	1832	2.3		
24	SU	0041	4.3	0728	2.1	1342	4.2	2006	2.0
25	M	0219	4.6	0851	1.7	1510	4.6	2122	1.6
26	TU	0332	5.0	0958	1.1	1610	5.0	2224	1.1
27	W	0428	5.3	1054	0.7	1701	5.3	2316	0.6
28	TH ○	0518	5.6	1143	0.3	1748	5.5		
29	F	0003	0.3	0605	5.8	1230	0.1	1834	5.6
30	SA	0048	0.1	0652	5.8	1312	0.0	1918	5.7
31	SU	0129	0.1	0737	5.8	1352	0.2	1958	5.6

APRIL

Date	Day	Time	m	Time	m	Time	m	Time	m
1	M	0208	0.3	0818	5.6	1429	0.5	2035	5.4
2	TU	0244	0.6	0856	5.3	1505	0.9	2108	5.1
3	W	0321	1.1	0931	4.9	1541	1.4	2137	4.8
4	TH	0402	1.6	1008	4.5	1624	1.9	2214	4.5
5	F	0454	2.0	1109	4.1	1722	2.3	2327	4.2
6	SA	0608	2.3	1304	4.0	1848	2.5		
7	SU	0132	4.2	0810	2.3	1420	4.1	2044	2.3
8	M	0242	4.4	0921	1.9	1519	4.4	2142	1.9
9	TU	0335	4.7	1008	1.5	1605	4.7	2226	1.5
10	W	0418	4.9	1049	1.2	1644	4.9	2305	1.2
11	TH	0457	5.1	1126	1.0	1720	5.0	2341	1.0
12	F ●	0533	5.2	1159	0.8	1754	5.1		
13	SA	0012	0.9	0609	5.2	1229	0.8	1828	5.2
14	SU	0041	0.9	0644	5.2	1256	0.9	1900	5.2
15	M	0107	0.9	0717	5.2	1322	1.0	1930	5.1
16	TU	0132	1.0	0746	5.0	1347	1.1	1957	5.1
17	W	0158	1.1	0814	4.9	1414	1.3	2024	4.9
18	TH	0228	1.3	0845	4.7	1445	1.5	2059	4.8
19	F	0305	1.6	0928	4.5	1527	1.8	2148	4.6
20	SA	0358	1.9	1028	4.3	1630	2.1	2254	4.4
21	SU	0527	2.1	1147	4.2	1812	2.2		
22	M	0018	4.4	0707	1.9	1325	4.3	1944	2.0
23	TU	0154	4.6	0829	1.6	1447	4.6	2059	1.5
24	W	0307	5.0	0935	1.1	1547	5.0	2200	1.1
25	TH	0404	5.3	1030	0.7	1637	5.3	2253	0.6
26	F	0455	5.6	1119	0.3	1724	5.5	2340	0.4
27	SA ○	0543	5.7	1205	0.2	1809	5.6		
28	SU	0024	0.2	0629	5.7	1248	0.2	1852	5.6
29	M	0106	0.3	0713	5.6	1328	0.4	1932	5.5
30	TU	0145	0.5	0754	5.4	1405	0.7	2008	5.4

Chart Datum: 3·22 metres below Ordnance Datum (Newlyn)

TIME ZONE (UTC)
For Summer Time add ONE hour in **non-shaded areas**

ENGLAND – PLYMOUTH

LAT 50°22′N LONG 4°11′W

TIMES AND HEIGHTS OF HIGH AND LOW WATERS

SPRING & NEAP TIDES
Dates in red are SPRINGS
Dates in blue are NEAPS

YEAR **2002**

MAY

Date	Day	Time	m	Time	m	Time	m	Time	m
1	W	0223	0.8	0832	5.1	1442	1.1	2038	5.1
2	TH	0301	1.2	0906	4.8	1519	1.5	2107	4.8
3	F	0342	1.6	0941	4.4	1602	2.0	2144	4.5
4	SA	0433	2.0	1035	4.1	1657	2.3	2242	4.3
5	SU	0539	2.2	1226	4.0	1809	2.4		
6	M	0043	4.2	0706	2.2	1342	4.1	1939	2.3
7	TU	0159	4.3	0830	2.0	1439	4.3	2052	2.0
8	W	0254	4.6	0923	1.6	1526	4.6	2142	1.7
9	TH	0340	4.8	1006	1.4	1606	4.8	2224	1.4
10	F	0421	5.0	1045	1.1	1645	5.0	2302	1.2
11	SA	0501	5.1	1120	1.0	1722	5.1	2336	1.0
12	SU ●	0540	5.1	1153	1.0	1759	5.2		
13	M	0009	1.0	0617	5.1	1226	1.0	1834	5.2
14	TU	0041	1.0	0654	5.1	1258	1.0	1907	5.2
15	W	0113	1.0	0728	5.0	1329	1.1	1938	5.1
16	TH	0146	1.1	0802	4.9	1403	1.3	2012	5.1
17	F	0223	1.3	0840	4.8	1440	1.5	2052	4.9
18	SA	0306	1.5	0926	4.6	1528	1.7	2142	4.8
19	SU	0403	1.7	1024	4.4	1633	1.9	2243	4.6
20	M	0520	1.8	1137	4.4	1755	2.0		
21	TU	0000	4.6	0644	1.7	1303	4.4	1917	1.8
22	W	0125	4.7	0800	1.5	1417	4.7	2030	1.5
23	TH	0237	5.0	0906	1.2	1518	5.0	2132	1.2
24	F	0337	5.2	1003	0.8	1611	5.2	2226	0.9
25	SA	0430	5.4	1054	0.6	1659	5.4	2316	0.6
26	SU ○	0520	5.5	1141	0.5	1745	5.5		
27	M	0001	0.5	0607	5.4	1225	0.5	1828	5.5
28	TU	0045	0.6	0651	5.4	1306	0.7	1908	5.4
29	W	0126	0.7	0734	5.2	1345	0.9	1944	5.3
30	TH	0206	1.0	0812	5.0	1423	1.2	2016	5.1
31	F	0245	1.3	0847	4.7	1501	1.6	2047	4.9

JUNE

Date	Day	Time	m	Time	m	Time	m	Time	m
1	SA	0325	1.6	0923	4.5	1542	1.9	2125	4.7
2	SU	0411	1.9	1009	4.2	1630	2.1	2215	4.5
3	M	0505	2.1	1116	4.1	1728	2.3	2321	4.3
4	TU	0608	2.1	1236	4.1	1834	2.3		
5	W	0046	4.3	0713	2.0	1341	4.3	1940	2.1
6	TH	0155	4.4	0815	1.8	1434	4.5	2040	1.9
7	F	0251	4.6	0908	1.6	1522	4.7	2132	1.6
8	SA	0340	4.8	0955	1.4	1607	4.9	2218	1.4
9	SU	0427	4.9	1038	1.2	1650	5.0	2300	1.2
10	M	0511	5.0	1119	1.1	1731	5.1	● 2340	1.1
11	TU	0553	5.0	1159	1.1	1811	5.2		
12	W	0020	1.0	0634	5.0	1239	1.1	1849	5.2
13	TH	0101	1.0	0715	5.0	1319	1.1	1927	5.2
14	F	0142	1.0	0756	5.0	1400	1.2	2007	5.2
15	SA	0225	1.1	0840	4.9	1444	1.3	2050	5.1
16	SU	0312	1.2	0927	4.8	1532	1.4	2138	5.0
17	M	0405	1.4	1020	4.7	1627	1.6	2234	4.9
18	TU	0505	1.5	1123	4.6	1732	1.7	2340	4.8
19	W	0614	1.5	1233	4.6	1843	1.7		
20	TH	0054	4.8	0725	1.5	1343	4.7	1955	1.6
21	F	0206	4.8	0834	1.4	1446	4.8	2102	1.4
22	SA	0310	4.9	0936	1.2	1544	5.0	2202	1.2
23	SU	0408	5.1	1031	1.0	1636	5.2	2255	1.0
24	M	0500	5.1	1120	0.9	1724	5.3	○ 2343	0.9
25	TU	0549	5.2	1206	0.9	1808	5.3		
26	W	0029	0.8	0634	5.1	1250	0.9	1848	5.3
27	TH	0112	0.9	0716	5.0	1330	1.1	1925	5.2
28	F	0152	1.0	0755	4.9	1408	1.2	1959	5.1
29	SA	0230	1.2	0830	4.7	1444	1.4	2032	5.0
30	SU	0307	1.4	0904	4.6	1520	1.6	2108	4.8

JULY

Date	Day	Time	m	Time	m	Time	m	Time	m
1	M	0343	1.6	0942	4.5	1557	1.8	2148	4.7
2	TU	0424	1.8	1027	4.3	1640	2.0	2235	4.5
3	W	0512	2.0	1121	4.2	1734	2.1	2332	4.4
4	TH	0609	2.0	1225	4.2	1837	2.2		
5	F	0040	4.3	0710	2.0	1332	4.3	1940	2.1
6	SA	0153	4.4	0811	1.8	1434	4.5	2040	1.9
7	SU	0258	4.5	0908	1.7	1530	4.7	2137	1.6
8	M	0354	4.7	1001	1.4	1620	4.9	2229	1.4
9	TU	0445	4.9	1051	1.3	1706	5.1	2318	1.2
10	W ●	0533	5.0	1139	1.1	1751	5.2		
11	TH	0005	1.0	0618	5.1	1227	1.0	1834	5.3
12	F	0052	0.8	0705	5.1	1313	0.9	1918	5.4
13	SA	0138	0.8	0751	5.1	1357	0.9	2002	5.4
14	SU	0223	0.8	0836	5.1	1441	0.9	2046	5.4
15	M	0308	0.9	0921	5.0	1525	1.1	2132	5.3
16	TU	0353	1.0	1008	4.9	1611	1.2	2220	5.1
17	W	0442	1.2	1100	4.7	1703	1.5	2315	4.9
18	TH	0539	1.5	1200	4.6	1805	1.7		
19	F	0021	4.7	0646	1.7	1309	4.6	1918	1.8
20	SA	0136	4.6	0801	1.7	1418	4.6	2035	1.7
21	SU	0248	4.6	0913	1.6	1522	4.8	2144	1.6
22	M	0351	4.7	1015	1.4	1618	5.0	2242	1.3
23	TU	0446	4.9	1107	1.2	1708	5.1	2332	1.1
24	W ○	0534	5.0	1154	1.1	1751	5.2		
25	TH	0017	1.0	0618	5.0	1237	1.0	1831	5.3
26	F	0100	0.9	0658	5.0	1316	1.0	1907	5.3
27	SA	0138	1.0	0734	4.9	1351	1.1	1940	5.2
28	SU	0211	1.1	0807	4.9	1423	1.2	2013	5.1
29	M	0242	1.2	0839	4.8	1451	1.4	2046	5.0
30	TU	0309	1.4	0912	4.7	1518	1.6	2119	4.8
31	W	0337	1.6	0947	4.5	1546	1.8	2154	4.6

AUGUST

Date	Day	Time	m	Time	m	Time	m	Time	m
1	TH	0410	1.8	1027	4.4	1623	2.0	2235	4.5
2	F	0457	2.0	1117	4.3	1723	2.2	2330	4.3
3	SA	0607	2.1	1223	4.2	1845	2.2		
4	SU	0045	4.2	0722	2.1	1342	4.3	1959	2.1
5	M	0215	4.3	0831	1.9	1455	4.6	2105	1.8
6	TU	0327	4.6	0933	1.6	1554	4.8	2205	1.5
7	W	0424	4.8	1031	1.3	1645	5.1	2301	1.1
8	TH	0515	5.0	1124	1.0	1732	5.3	● 2352	0.8
9	F	0603	5.2	1214	0.8	1819	5.5		
10	SA	0041	0.6	0650	5.3	1302	0.6	1905	5.6
11	SU	0127	0.5	0737	5.3	1346	0.6	1950	5.6
12	M	0211	0.4	0821	5.3	1428	0.6	2034	5.6
13	TU	0252	0.6	0904	5.3	1508	0.8	2116	5.4
14	W	0332	0.8	0946	5.1	1548	1.0	2159	5.2
15	TH	0414	1.2	1031	4.9	1633	1.4	2246	4.8
16	F	0502	1.6	1125	4.6	1729	1.8	2349	4.5
17	SA	0605	1.9	1237	4.4	1844	2.1		
18	SU	0113	4.3	0732	2.1	1356	4.4	2019	2.1
19	M	0235	4.4	0902	2.0	1507	4.6	2136	1.8
20	TU	0342	4.5	1006	1.7	1605	4.8	2233	1.5
21	W	0435	4.7	1056	1.4	1653	5.1	2321	1.2
22	TH ○	0520	4.9	1140	1.1	1734	5.2		
23	F	0003	1.0	0559	5.0	1221	1.0	1810	5.3
24	SA	0042	0.9	0635	5.1	1257	0.9	1844	5.3
25	SU	0116	0.9	0708	5.1	1328	1.0	1917	5.3
26	M	0145	1.0	0739	5.0	1355	1.1	1948	5.2
27	TU	0210	1.1	0809	5.0	1418	1.3	2019	5.1
28	W	0231	1.3	0839	4.8	1437	1.4	2047	4.9
29	TH	0252	1.5	0908	4.7	1459	1.6	2114	4.7
30	F	0317	1.7	0939	4.5	1529	1.9	2147	4.5
31	SA	0352	1.9	1021	4.4	1614	2.1	2238	4.3

Chart Datum: 3·22 metres below Ordnance Datum (Newlyn)

TIME ZONE (UTC)
For Summer Time add ONE hour in **non-shaded areas**

ENGLAND – PLYMOUTH

LAT 50°22′N LONG 4°11′W

TIMES AND HEIGHTS OF HIGH AND LOW WATERS

SPRING & NEAP TIDES
Dates in red are **SPRINGS**
Dates in blue are NEAPS

YEAR **2002**

SEPTEMBER

Date	Time	m	Time	m	Time	m	Time	m	
1 SU	0449	2.2	1124	4.2	1742	2.4	2353	4.2	
2 M	0638	2.3	1248	4.3	1926	2.3			
3 TU	0135	4.2	0803	2.1	1423	4.5	2042	1.9	
4 W	0308	4.5	0913	1.8	1532	4.9	2148	1.5	
5 TH	0407	4.8	1014	1.3	1624	5.2	2245	1.0	
6 F	0457	5.1	1108	0.9	1712	5.5	2336	0.6	
7 SA	0544	5.4	1157	0.6	1759	5.7			●
8 SU	0023	0.4	0630	5.5	1244	0.4	1845	5.8	
9 M	0108	0.2	0715	5.6	1327	0.3	1930	5.8	
10 TU	0150	0.3	0758	5.6	1407	0.4	2013	5.7	
11 W	0229	0.5	0839	5.4	1445	0.7	2054	5.5	
12 TH	0307	0.8	0919	5.2	1523	1.0	2134	5.1	
13 F	0345	1.3	0959	4.9	1605	1.5	2216	4.7	
14 SA	0429	1.8	1047	4.6	1658	2.0	2317	4.3	
15 SU	0529	2.2	1206	4.3	1816	2.3			
16 M	0100	4.1	0710	2.4	1339	4.3	2014	2.3	
17 TU	0226	4.2	0854	2.2	1452	4.5	2128	1.9	
18 W	0331	4.5	0952	1.8	1549	4.8	2218	1.5	
19 TH	0420	4.8	1038	1.4	1633	5.1	2301	1.2	
20 F	0500	5.0	1119	1.1	1711	5.3	2340	1.0	
21 SA	0535	5.1	1156	1.0	1746	5.4			○
22 SU	0015	0.8	0607	5.2	1230	0.9	1818	5.4	
23 M	0047	0.9	0639	5.2	1259	1.0	1850	5.4	
24 TU	0113	0.9	0709	5.2	1323	1.1	1921	5.3	
25 W	0135	1.1	0739	5.1	1344	1.2	1950	5.1	
26 TH	0155	1.2	0807	5.0	1403	1.4	2017	5.0	
27 F	0216	1.4	0833	4.9	1426	1.6	2041	4.8	
28 SA	0240	1.6	0901	4.7	1456	1.8	2114	4.6	
29 SU	0314	1.9	0944	4.5	1539	2.1	2208	4.3	
30 M	0405	2.3	1048	4.3	1654	2.4	2325	4.1	

OCTOBER

Date	Time	m	Time	m	Time	m	Time	m	
1 TU	0557	2.5	1210	4.3	1900	2.4			
2 W	0107	4.2	0739	2.3	1351	4.5	2022	1.9	
3 TH	0248	4.5	0854	1.8	1507	4.9	2129	1.4	
4 F	0347	4.9	0955	1.3	1602	5.3	2224	0.9	
5 SA	0436	5.3	1048	0.9	1650	5.6	2314	0.5	
6 SU	0521	5.5	1136	0.5	1737	5.8			●
7 M	0000	0.3	0605	5.7	1221	0.3	1822	5.9	
8 TU	0044	0.2	0650	5.7	1303	0.3	1907	5.9	
9 W	0125	0.3	0732	5.7	1343	0.4	1950	5.7	
10 TH	0204	0.6	0813	5.5	1422	0.7	2031	5.4	
11 F	0241	1.0	0850	5.3	1500	1.2	2109	5.0	
12 SA	0318	1.5	0927	5.0	1542	1.7	2148	4.6	
13 SU	0402	2.0	1009	4.6	1635	2.1	2248	4.2	
14 M	0502	2.4	1130	4.3	1752	2.5			
15 TU	0044	4.1	0641	2.6	1316	4.3	1955	2.4	
16 W	0206	4.2	0829	2.4	1427	4.5	2103	2.0	
17 TH	0307	4.5	0925	2.0	1521	4.8	2151	1.6	
18 F	0353	4.8	1009	1.6	1605	5.1	2231	1.3	
19 SA	0431	5.0	1048	1.3	1642	5.2	2308	1.1	
20 SU	0505	5.2	1124	1.1	1716	5.3	2342	1.0	
21 M	0537	5.3	1157	1.0	1750	5.4			○
22 TU	0012	1.0	0609	5.3	1226	1.0	1823	5.3	
23 W	0038	1.0	0641	5.3	1252	1.1	1855	5.3	
24 TH	0103	1.1	0712	5.3	1315	1.2	1925	5.2	
25 F	0126	1.3	0740	5.1	1339	1.4	1953	5.0	
26 SA	0150	1.5	0808	5.0	1406	1.6	2022	4.8	
27 SU	0218	1.7	0840	4.9	1439	1.8	2100	4.6	
28 M	0255	2.0	0925	4.7	1524	2.1	2155	4.4	
29 TU	0348	2.3	1027	4.5	1641	2.3	2307	4.2	
30 W	0529	2.5	1144	4.5	1833	2.3			
31 TH	0042	4.3	0712	2.3	1317	4.6	1956	1.9	

NOVEMBER

Date	Time	m	Time	m	Time	m	Time	m	
1 F	0218	4.6	0828	1.9	1436	5.0	2103	1.4	
2 SA	0320	5.0	0930	1.4	1535	5.3	2159	1.0	
3 SU	0410	5.3	1023	1.0	1626	5.6	2249	0.6	
4 M	0456	5.6	1111	0.6	1714	5.8	2336	0.4	●
5 TU	0542	5.7	1157	0.5	1800	5.8			
6 W	0019	0.4	0625	5.8	1241	0.5	1845	5.7	
7 TH	0101	0.5	0708	5.7	1322	0.6	1929	5.6	
8 F	0141	0.8	0748	5.6	1402	0.9	2010	5.3	
9 SA	0219	1.2	0826	5.3	1442	1.3	2049	5.0	
10 SU	0258	1.6	0902	5.0	1525	1.7	2129	4.6	
11 M	0342	2.1	0942	4.7	1616	2.1	2223	4.3	
12 TU	0437	2.4	1043	4.5	1723	2.4			
13 W	0007	4.1	0553	2.6	1231	4.4	1856	2.4	
14 TH	0126	4.2	0732	2.5	1344	4.5	2016	2.2	
15 F	0226	4.4	0839	2.2	1440	4.7	2108	1.8	
16 SA	0313	4.7	0928	1.8	1526	4.9	2151	1.6	
17 SU	0354	4.9	1009	1.5	1606	5.1	2229	1.3	
18 M	0430	5.1	1047	1.3	1644	5.2	2304	1.2	
19 TU	0506	5.2	1122	1.2	1721	5.2	2336	1.1	
20 W	0541	5.3	1154	1.2	1758	5.2			○
21 TH	0006	1.2	0616	5.3	1225	1.2	1833	5.2	
22 F	0037	1.2	0649	5.3	1255	1.3	1907	5.1	
23 SA	0107	1.3	0721	5.2	1326	1.4	1939	5.0	
24 SU	0138	1.4	0754	5.1	1400	1.5	2014	4.9	
25 M	0212	1.6	0831	5.0	1439	1.7	2056	4.7	
26 TU	0254	1.9	0917	4.9	1528	1.9	2148	4.5	
27 W	0349	2.1	1013	4.8	1636	2.0	2253	4.4	
28 TH	0507	2.2	1122	4.7	1801	2.0			
29 F	0013	4.4	0635	2.1	1241	4.8	1921	1.8	
30 SA	0137	4.6	0753	1.9	1358	4.9	2031	1.5	

DECEMBER

Date	Time	m	Time	m	Time	m	Time	m	
1 SU	0244	4.9	0859	1.5	1504	5.2	2131	1.2	
2 M	0341	5.2	0956	1.2	1600	5.4	2224	0.9	
3 TU	0432	5.4	1048	0.9	1652	5.5	2313	0.8	
4 W	0519	5.6	1136	0.7	1741	5.6	2359	0.7	●
5 TH	0605	5.6	1221	0.7	1828	5.5			
6 F	0042	0.8	0648	5.6	1306	0.8	1912	5.4	
7 SA	0124	1.0	0730	5.5	1348	1.0	1955	5.2	
8 SU	0204	1.3	0809	5.3	1430	1.3	2035	4.9	
9 M	0244	1.6	0845	5.1	1512	1.6	2113	4.7	
10 TU	0325	1.9	0923	4.9	1556	1.9	2156	4.4	
11 W	0411	2.2	1009	4.7	1646	2.1	2253	4.3	
12 TH	0506	2.4	1109	4.5	1746	2.3			
13 F	0009	4.2	0611	2.4	1226	4.4	1853	2.2	
14 SA	0119	4.3	0722	2.3	1335	4.5	1958	2.1	
15 SU	0217	4.5	0826	2.1	1432	4.6	2054	1.9	
16 M	0307	4.7	0919	1.9	1523	4.8	2141	1.7	
17 TU	0352	4.9	1005	1.7	1610	4.9	2223	1.5	
18 W	0435	5.1	1046	1.5	1654	5.0	2302	1.3	
19 TH	0516	5.2	1125	1.3	1736	5.1	2341	1.3	○
20 F	0555	5.3	1204	1.2	1817	5.1			
21 SA	0019	1.2	0633	5.3	1243	1.2	1855	5.1	
22 SU	0057	1.2	0711	5.3	1322	1.2	1934	5.0	
23 M	0135	1.3	0749	5.3	1402	1.3	2013	5.0	
24 TU	0215	1.4	0829	5.2	1444	1.4	2056	4.9	
25 W	0258	1.5	0913	5.1	1530	1.5	2143	4.8	
26 TH	0346	1.7	1002	5.0	1623	1.6	2237	4.7	
27 F	0443	1.8	1059	4.9	1725	1.7	2341	4.6	
28 SA	0552	1.9	1206	4.8	1837	1.8			
29 SU	0053	4.6	0710	1.9	1320	4.8	1952	1.7	
30 M	0206	4.7	0825	1.7	1432	4.9	2101	1.5	
31 TU	0312	4.9	0931	1.5	1538	5.0	2202	1.3	

Chart Datum: 3·22 metres below Ordnance Datum (Newlyn)

NAVAL EXERCISE AREAS (SUBFACTS & GUNFACTS) *9.1.18*

Submarines and warships use the areas below and others eastwards to Nab Tr (see 9.2.33). Areas where submarines are planned to operate during all or part of the ensuing 24 hrs are broadcast daily by the Coastguard as shown below. Subfacts and Gunfacts are mentioned on Navtex by Niton at 0700 and 1900 UTC daily. Further information may be obtained from Naval Ops, Plymouth ☎ (01752) 501182.

See 6.10.1 for general advice on submarine activity which also occurs in other sea areas. Submarines on the surface and at periscope depth will maintain constant listening watch on VHF Ch 16. The former will comply strictly with IRPCS; the latter will not close to within 1500 yds of a FV without express permission from the FV.

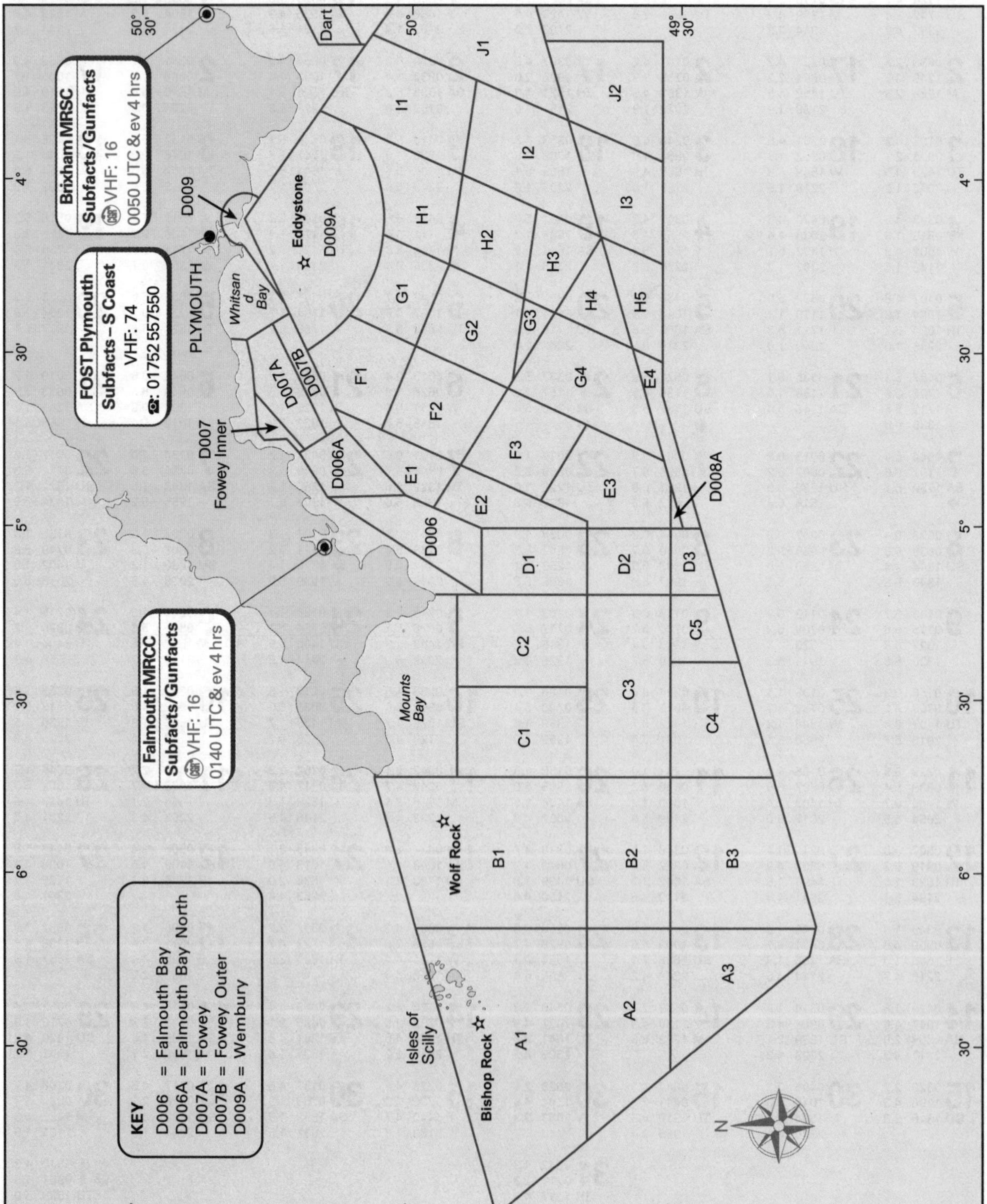

RIVER YEALM *9.1.19*

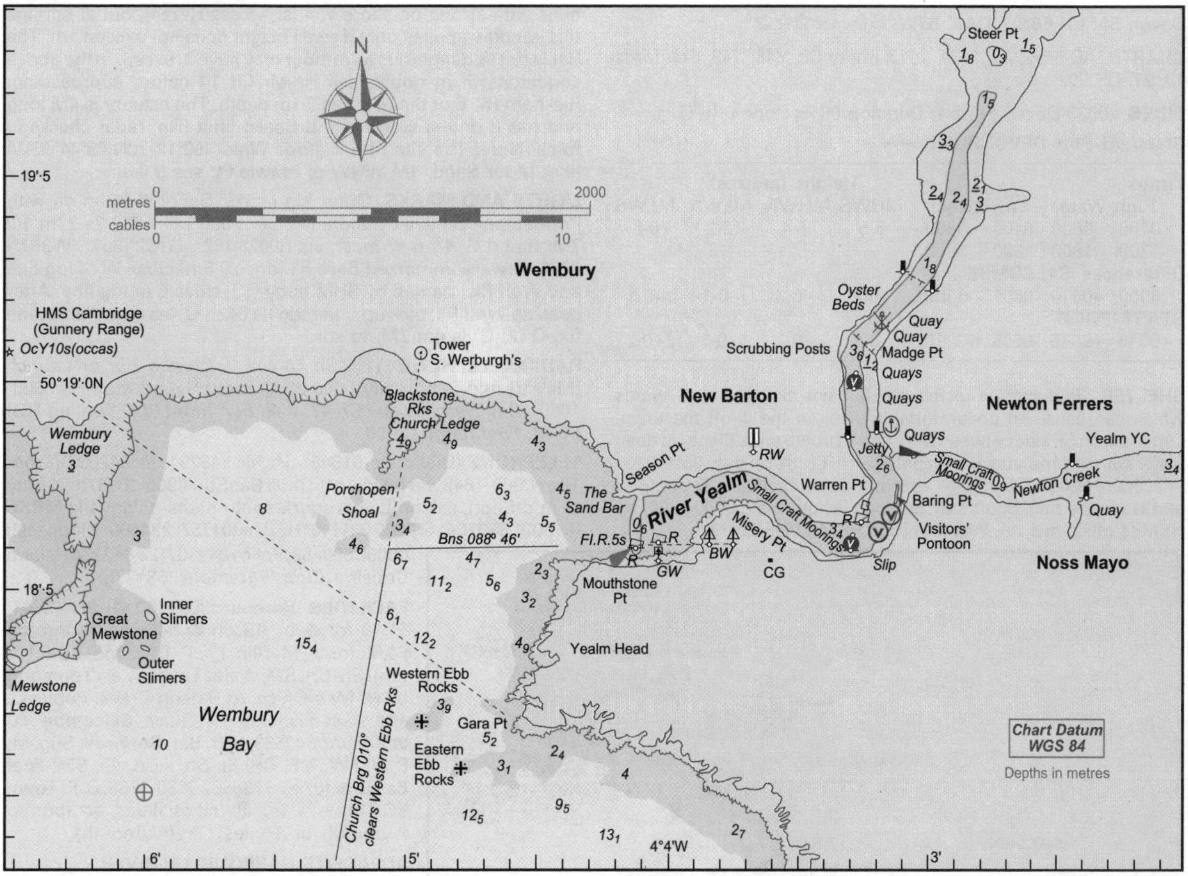

Devon **50°18'·58N 04°04'·13W** (Ent) ❀❀⚓⚓✿✿✿

CHARTS AC *30*,1900,*1613*; Imray C6, C14; Stanfords 13, 22, 23; OS 201

TIDES 0522 Dover; ML 3·2; Duration 0615; Zone 0 (UT)

Standard Port DEVONPORT (⟵)

Times				Height (metres)			
High Water		Low Water		MHWS	MHWN	MLWN	MLWS
0000	0600	0000	0600	5·5	4·4	2·2	0·8
1200	1800	1200	1800				
Differences RIVER YEALM ENTRANCE							
+0006	+0006	+0002	+0002	–0·1	–0·1	–0·1	–0·1

Note: Strong SW winds hold up the ebb and raise levels, as does the river if in spate.

SHELTER Very good. Ent easy except in strong SW or W'lies. ⚓ in Cellar B is open to SW'lies to NW'lies. Ⓥ pontoons in The Pool and up-river. 1 ⛵ off Misery Pt and 2 off Warren Pt. No ⚓ in river.

NAVIGATION WPT 50°18'·03N 04°06'·07W, 240°/060° from/to Season Pt, 1·4M. The W & E Ebb rks and the Inner & Outer Slimers are dangerous, lying awash on E and W sides of Wembury Bay. Ldg bns (W △, B stripe) in line at 089° clear Mouthstone Ledge, but **not** the sand bar. Two PHM buoys (Apr-Oct) mark end of sand bar and **must** be left to port on entry; the seaward buoy is Fl R 5s. When abeam, **but not before**, bn (G ▲ on W □) on S shore, turn NE toward bn (W □, R stripe) on N shore. From sand bar to Misery Pt, river carries only 1·2m at MLWS. Leave Spit PHM buoy off Warren Pt to port. It is impossible to beat in against an ebb tide; the river is very crowded and in wind over tide conditions moored yachts lie athwart the stream. Speed limit 6kn.

LIGHTS AND MARKS Great Mewstone (57m) is conspic 1·5M to W of river ent. Bns as above. Only light is outer PHM buoy Fl R 5s at ent.

TELEPHONE (Dial code 01752) Hr Mr 872533; MRSC (01803) 882704; ⊖ 0345 231110 (H24); Marinecall 09068 500458; Police (0990) 777444; Dr 880392.

RADIO TELEPHONE Water taxi Ch 08.

FACILITIES R Yealm/Pool pontoon, ⛵ £1.07, M, L, FW; **Yealm YC** ☎ 872291, FW, Bar; **Newton Ferrers** L, Slip, FW, Gas, Gaz, SM, V, R, Bar, ✉; **Noss Mayo** L, Slip, FW, R, Bar; Nearest fuel 3M at Yealmpton. ⇄ ✈ (Plymouth).

ADJACENT ANCHORAGES IN BIGBURY BAY

RIVER ERME, Devon, **50°18'·15N 03°57'·67W**. AC*1613*. HW –0525 on Dover; +0015 and –0·6m on HW Devonport. Temp day ⚓ in 3m at mouth of drying river, open to SW. Access near HW, but only in offshore winds and settled wx. Beware Wells Rk (1m) 1M SE of ent. Appr from SW, clear of Edwards Rk. Ent between Battisborough Is and W. Mary's Rk (dries 1·1m) keeping to the W. No facilities. Two Historic Wrecks are at 50°18'·15N 03°57'·41W and 50°18'·41N 03°57'·19W on W side of the ent; see 9.0.3h.

RIVER AVON, Devon, **50°16'·64N 03°53'·67W**. AC*1613*. Tides as R Erme, above. Enter drying river HW –1, only in offshore winds and settled wx. Appr close E of conspic Burgh Is & Murray's Rks, marked by bn. Narrow chan hugs cliffy NW shore, then turns SE and N off Bantham. A recce at LW or local knowledge would assist. Streams run hard, but able to dry out in good shelter clear of moorings. V, ✉, Bar at Bantham. Aveton Gifford accessible by dinghy, 2·5M.

HOPE COVE, Devon, **50°14'·65N 03°51'·78W**. AC *1613*. Tides as R Erme, above; ML 2·6m; Duration 0615. Popular day ⚓ in centre of cove, but poor holding ground and only safe in offshore winds. Appr with old LB ho brg 110° and ⚓ SW of pier hd. Beware rk, drying 2·5m, ½ca offshore and 3ca E of Bolt Tail. No lts. Facilities: very limited in village, EC Thurs; but good at Kingsbridge (6M bus), or Salcombe, (4M bus).

SALCOMBE *9.1.20*

Devon **50°13′·58N 03°46′·67W** ❁❁◊◊◊✿✿✿

CHARTS AC *5602, 28, 1634, 1613*; Imray C6, Y48, Y43; Stanfords 13, 22; OS 202

TIDES –0523 Dover; ML 3·1; Duration 0615; Zone 0 (UT)

Standard Port DEVONPORT (⟵)

Times				Height (metres)			
High Water		Low Water		MHWS	MHWN	MLWN	MLWS
0100	0600	0100	0600	5·5	4·4	2·2	0·8
1300	1800	1300	1800				
Differences SALCOMBE							
0000	+0010	+0005	–0005	–0·2	–0·3	–0·1	–0·1
START POINT							
+0015	+0015	+0005	+0010	–0·1	–0·2	+0·1	+0·2

SHELTER Perfectly protected hbr but ent exposed to S winds which can cause an uncomfortable swell in the ⚓ off the town. Limited ⚓ on SE side between ferry and ⚓ prohib area. Plenty of deep water Ⓜs. (Hr Mr's launch will contact VHF Ch 14, on duty 0600-2100 in season; 0600-2200 in peak season). Good shelter at Ⓥ pontoon and Ⓜs in the Bag. Short stay pontoon (½ hour max, 0700-1900) by Hr Mr's office has 1m. Water taxi via Hr Mr, VHF Ch 12.

NAVIGATION WPT 50°12′·43N 03°46′·67W, 180°/000° from/to Sandhill Pt lt, 1·3M. The bar (0·7m) can be dangerous at sp ebb tides with strong on-shore winds. Access HW±4½, but at springs this window applies only if swell height does not exceed 1m. The Bar is not as dangerous as rumour may have it, except in the above conditions; if in doubt, call Hr Mr Ch 14 before approaching. Rickham Rk, E of the Bar, has 3·1m depth. The estuary is 4M long and has 8 drying creeks off it. Speed limit 8kn; radar checks in force. Note: The site of a Historic Wreck (50°12′·70N 03°44′·33W) is at Moor Sand, 1M WNW of Prawle Pt; see 9.0.3h.

LIGHTS AND MARKS Outer ldg marks: Sandhill Pt bn on with Poundstone bn 000°. Sandhill Pt Dir lt 000°, Fl WRG 2s 27m 10/7M; R and W ♦ on W mast: vis R002°-182°, G182°-357°, W357°-002°. Beware unmarked Bass Rk (dries 0·8m) close W of ldg line and Wolf Rk, marked by SHM buoy QG, close E of ldg line. After passing Wolf Rk, pick up inner ldg lts 042°, Q, leaving Blackstone Rk, Q (2) G 8s 4m 2M, to stbd.

RADIO TELEPHONE VHF Ch 14 call *Salcombe Hbr* or *Launch* (May to mid-Sept: daily 0600-2200; rest of year: Mon-Fri 0900-1600). Call *Harbour taxi* Ch 12. Call: *Egremont* (ICC floating HQ) Ch M. *Fuel Barge* Ch 06.

TELEPHONE (Dial code 01548) Hr Mr 843791, 📠 842033 (Mon-Thur 0900-1645, Fri 0900-1615; plus Sat/Sun 0900-1615, mid-May to mid-Sept), salcombe.harbour@south-hams-dc.gov.uk; MRSC (01803) 882704; ⊖ 0345 231110 (H24) or (01752) 234600; Marinecall 09068 500458; Police 842107; Dr 842284; Island Cruising Club 'Egremont' 531775.

FACILITIES Harbour (300+150 Ⓥ) ☎ 843791, £1.10 for Ⓜ or AB on Ⓥ detached pontoon; £0.55 for ⚓. M, Slip, Ⓔ, P, D, L, ME, El, C (15 ton), Sh, CH, SM, Water Taxi; FW at Ⓥ pontoon by Hr Mr's Office. At Batson Creek: Public ▬ and ⛽ at Fisherman's Quay. **Salcombe YC** ☎ 842872/842593, L, R, Bar; **Services:** Slip, M, P, D, FW, ME, CH, El, Sh, ACA, Ⓔ, SM; **Fuel Barge** ☎ (07801) 798862 0830-1730, D, P. **Town** EC Thurs; ▣, ✉, Ⓑ, all facilities, ⇌ (bus to Plymouth or Totnes), ✈ (Plymouth).

ADJACENT HARBOUR UP-RIVER

KINGSBRIDGE, Devon, **50°16′·88N 03°46′·52W**. AC *28*. HW=HW Salcombe+0005. Access HW±2½ for <2m draft/bilge keelers, max LOA 11m. The 3M chan to Kingsbridge is marked beyond Salt Stone SHM perch by R/W PHM poles with R can topmarks. 6ca N of Salt Stone a secondary chan marked by PHM buoys gradually diverges E into Balcombe Creek. There is a private ferry pontoon at New Quay, 3ca before the drying Kingsbridge basin. Berth at Ⓥ pontoon (outside of seaward end) on E side of basin or on wall at W side, marked 'visitors' and drying 3·4m to soft mud. Best to pre-check berth availability with Salcombe Hr Mr; berthing fees and Hbr dues are payable. Facilities: Slip, SM. **Town** EC Thurs; V, R, Bar, ✉, Ⓑ, ▣.

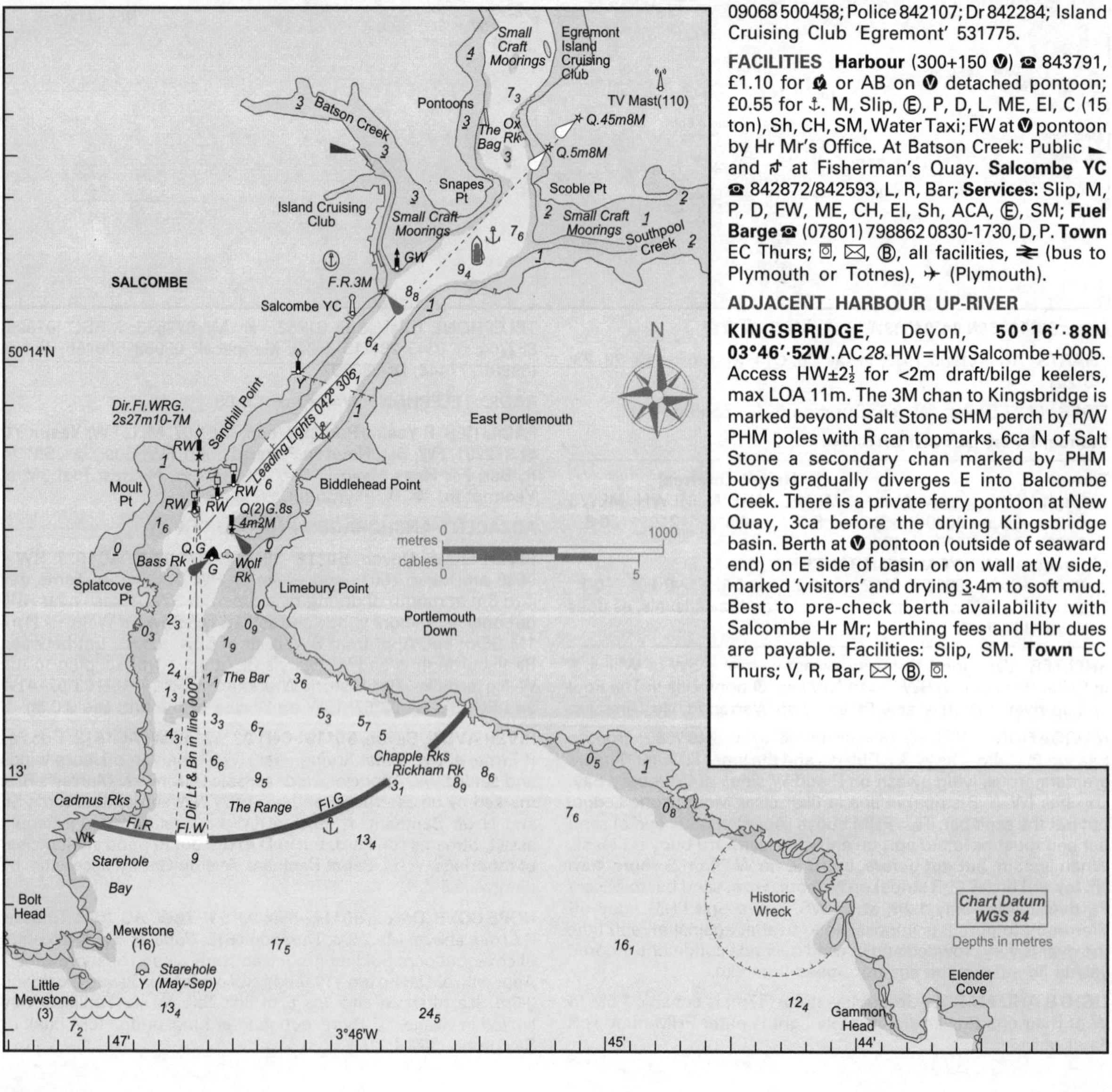

TIME ZONE (UTC)
For Summer Time add ONE hour in **non-shaded areas**

ENGLAND – DARTMOUTH

LAT 50°21′N LONG 3°34′W

TIMES AND HEIGHTS OF HIGH AND LOW WATERS

SPRING & NEAP TIDES
Dates in red are SPRINGS
Dates in blue are NEAPS

YEAR **2002**

JANUARY

Day		Time	m	Time	m	Time	m	Time	m	Moon
1	TU	0045	0.7	0718	4.9	1312	0.7	1945	4.7	
2	W	0129	0.7	0803	5.0	1357	0.7	2030	4.6	
3	TH	0214	0.8	0848	4.9	1442	0.7	2116	4.6	
4	F	0258	0.9	0933	4.8	1528	0.9	2203	4.4	
5	SA	0344	1.1	1020	4.6	1616	1.1	2253	4.2	
6	SU	0434	1.4	1113	4.4	1710	1.4	2351	4.1	
7	M	0532	1.6	1214	4.2	1814	1.6			
8	TU	0057	4.0	0645	1.7	1324	4.1	1929	1.6	
9	W	0209	4.0	0803	1.7	1437	4.1	2043	1.6	
10	TH	0316	4.1	0913	1.5	1543	4.2	2146	1.4	
11	F	0415	4.3	1012	1.3	1641	4.3	2239	1.2	
12	SA	0506	4.5	1104	1.1	1731	4.4	2325	1.1	
13	SU	0552	4.6	1149	1.0	1816	4.5			●
14	M	0007	1.0	0631	4.7	1232	0.9	1854	4.5	
15	TU	0047	0.9	0706	4.7	1310	0.9	1928	4.4	
16	W	0122	1.0	0739	4.7	1344	1.0	2000	4.4	
17	TH	0153	1.1	0811	4.6	1415	1.1	2032	4.3	
18	F	0221	1.2	0846	4.5	1442	1.2	2105	4.2	
19	SA	0247	1.4	0919	4.4	1510	1.4	2139	4.1	
20	SU	0315	1.5	0954	4.2	1540	1.6	2215	3.9	
21	M	0348	1.7	1031	4.0	1619	1.7	2258	3.8	
22	TU	0434	1.9	1118	3.9	1715	1.9	2354	3.7	
23	W	0545	2.1	1218	3.8	1832	2.0			
24	TH	0104	3.7	0710	2.0	1335	3.8	1946	1.8	
25	F	0226	3.9	0823	1.8	1459	3.9	2055	1.6	
26	SA	0339	4.1	0930	1.5	1609	4.1	2157	1.3	
27	SU	0438	4.4	1030	1.1	1706	4.4	2254	1.0	
28	M	0530	4.7	1124	0.8	1800	4.6	2346	0.7	○
29	TU	0620	4.9	1215	0.5	1850	4.7			
30	W	0036	0.5	0706	5.0	1305	0.3	1937	4.8	
31	TH	0123	0.4	0753	5.1	1350	0.2	2022	4.8	

FEBRUARY

Day		Time	m	Time	m	Time	m	Time	m	Moon
1	F	0206	0.4	0839	5.1	1433	0.3	2105	4.8	
2	SA	0247	0.5	0922	5.0	1514	0.5	2147	4.6	
3	SU	0327	0.7	1004	4.8	1554	0.8	2229	4.4	
4	M	0409	1.0	1048	4.5	1637	1.2	2316	4.1	
5	TU	0456	1.4	1139	4.1	1727	1.5			
6	W	0013	3.9	0555	1.7	1245	3.9	1835	1.8	
7	TH	0127	3.8	0718	1.9	1406	3.8	2007	1.9	
8	F	0246	3.8	0851	1.8	1521	3.8	2128	1.7	
9	SA	0352	4.0	1000	1.5	1624	4.0	2226	1.5	
10	SU	0448	4.3	1053	1.2	1716	4.2	2313	1.2	
11	M	0533	4.5	1137	1.0	1759	4.3	2355	1.0	
12	TU	0614	4.6	1217	0.8	1837	4.4			●
13	W	0033	0.8	0649	4.7	1255	0.7	1910	4.5	
14	TH	0107	0.8	0723	4.7	1327	0.7	1942	4.5	
15	F	0135	0.8	0755	4.7	1354	0.8	2013	4.4	
16	SA	0200	0.9	0827	4.6	1418	0.9	2044	4.3	
17	SU	0222	1.1	0857	4.4	1439	1.1	2112	4.2	
18	M	0244	1.2	0924	4.3	1503	1.2	2138	4.1	
19	TU	0311	1.4	0950	4.1	1533	1.5	2208	3.9	
20	W	0347	1.6	1027	3.9	1615	1.7	2256	3.8	
21	TH	0439	1.9	1126	3.7	1721	1.9			
22	F	0004	3.7	0612	2.0	1244	3.6	1902	2.0	
23	SA	0132	3.7	0749	1.9	1422	3.7	2025	1.8	
24	SU	0306	4.0	0906	1.5	1548	4.0	2138	1.4	
25	M	0415	4.4	1013	1.1	1650	4.3	2240	0.9	
26	TU	0511	4.7	1111	0.6	1744	4.6	2333	0.5	
27	W	0602	5.0	1202	0.2	1834	4.8			○
28	TH	0022	0.2	0651	5.2	1250	0.0	1920	4.9	

MARCH

Day		Time	m	Time	m	Time	m	Time	m	Moon
1	F	0109	0.0	0738	5.2	1334	-0.1	2004	5.0	
2	SA	0150	0.0	0821	5.2	1415	0.0	2046	4.9	
3	SU	0228	0.1	0903	5.1	1452	0.2	2124	4.8	
4	M	0306	0.4	0942	4.8	1528	0.6	2200	4.5	
5	TU	0343	0.9	1020	4.4	1606	1.1	2236	4.2	
6	W	0425	1.3	1102	4.0	1650	1.6	2322	3.8	
7	TH	0518	1.8	1208	3.6	1749	2.0			
8	F	0046	3.6	0636	2.1	1343	3.5	1925	2.2	
9	SA	0219	3.6	0835	2.0	1502	3.6	2112	2.0	
10	SU	0330	3.9	0946	1.6	1606	3.8	2209	1.6	
11	M	0425	4.2	1036	1.3	1656	4.1	2255	1.2	
12	TU	0511	4.4	1118	0.9	1736	4.3	2334	0.9	
13	W	0550	4.6	1156	0.7	1814	4.4			
14	TH	0010	0.7	0626	4.7	1232	0.6	1848	4.5	●
15	F	0044	0.7	0700	4.7	1302	0.6	1919	4.5	
16	SA	0111	0.7	0734	4.7	1327	0.7	1950	4.5	
17	SU	0134	0.8	0805	4.6	1349	0.8	2018	4.5	
18	M	0156	0.9	0832	4.5	1411	0.9	2044	4.3	
19	TU	0218	1.0	0856	4.3	1434	1.1	2107	4.2	
20	W	0244	1.2	0921	4.1	1502	1.3	2135	4.1	
21	TH	0318	1.4	0958	3.9	1540	1.6	2221	3.9	
22	F	0407	1.7	1058	3.7	1639	1.9	2331	3.7	
23	SA	0533	2.0	1217	3.5	1828	2.1			
24	SU	0056	3.7	0724	1.9	1358	3.7	2002	1.8	
25	M	0237	4.0	0848	1.5	1529	4.0	2119	1.4	
26	TU	0352	4.4	0956	1.0	1631	4.4	2222	0.9	
27	W	0450	4.7	1053	0.5	1724	4.7	2315	0.4	
28	TH	0542	5.0	1142	0.1	1813	4.9			○
29	F	0002	0.1	0630	5.2	1230	-0.1	1858	5.0	
30	SA	0048	-0.1	0716	5.3	1312	-0.2	1941	5.1	
31	SU	0129	-0.1	0800	5.2	1351	0.0	2020	5.0	

APRIL

Day		Time	m	Time	m	Time	m	Time	m	Moon
1	M	0207	0.1	0840	5.0	1428	0.3	2056	4.8	
2	TU	0242	0.4	0917	4.7	1503	0.7	2129	4.5	
3	W	0319	0.9	0951	4.3	1538	1.2	2157	4.2	
4	TH	0359	1.4	1027	3.9	1621	1.7	2233	3.9	
5	F	0450	1.8	1127	3.5	1718	2.1	2344	3.6	
6	SA	0603	2.1	1319	3.4	1844	2.3			
7	SU	0148	3.6	0806	2.1	1438	3.5	2041	2.1	
8	M	0300	3.8	0918	1.7	1539	3.8	2140	1.7	
9	TU	0355	4.1	1006	1.3	1626	4.1	2224	1.3	
10	W	0440	4.3	1048	1.0	1706	4.3	2304	1.0	
11	TH	0520	4.5	1125	0.8	1744	4.5	2340	0.8	
12	F	0557	4.6	1158	0.7	1819	4.5			●
13	SA	0011	0.7	0634	4.6	1228	0.6	1853	4.6	
14	SU	0041	0.7	0708	4.6	1256	0.7	1924	4.6	
15	M	0107	0.7	0740	4.6	1322	0.8	1953	4.5	
16	TU	0131	0.8	0808	4.4	1346	0.9	2019	4.5	
17	W	0157	0.9	0836	4.3	1413	1.1	2046	4.3	
18	TH	0227	1.1	0906	4.1	1443	1.3	2120	4.2	
19	F	0303	1.4	0948	3.9	1525	1.6	2207	4.0	
20	SA	0355	1.7	1047	3.7	1626	1.9	2312	3.8	
21	SU	0523	1.9	1203	3.6	1807	2.0			
22	M	0034	3.8	0703	1.8	1341	3.7	1940	1.8	
23	TU	0211	4.0	0825	1.4	1506	4.0	2056	1.3	
24	W	0326	4.4	0933	0.9	1608	4.4	2158	0.9	
25	TH	0425	4.7	1029	0.5	1659	4.7	2252	0.5	
26	F	0518	5.0	1118	0.1	1748	4.9	2339	0.2	
27	SA	0607	5.1	1204	0.0	1834	5.0			○
28	SU	0023	0.0	0654	5.1	1248	0.0	1916	5.0	
29	M	0106	0.1	0737	5.0	1328	0.2	1955	5.0	
30	TU	0144	0.3	0816	4.8	1404	0.5	2030	4.8	

Chart Datum: 2·62 metres below Ordnance Datum (Newlyn)

TIME ZONE (UTC)
For Summer Time add ONE hour in **non-shaded areas**

ENGLAND – DARTMOUTH

LAT 50°21′N LONG 3°34′W

TIMES AND HEIGHTS OF HIGH AND LOW WATERS

SPRING & NEAP TIDES
Dates in red are **SPRINGS**
Dates in blue are **NEAPS**

YEAR **2002**

MAY

Date	Day	Time	m	Time	m	Time	m	Time	m
1	W	0222	0.6	0853	4.5	1440	0.9	2059	4.5
2	TH	0259	1.0	0927	4.2	1517	1.3	2128	4.2
3	F	0339	1.4	1001	3.8	1559	1.8	2204	3.9
4	SA	0429	1.8	1053	3.5	1653	2.1	2300	3.7
5	SU	0534	2.1	1242	3.4	1804	2.2		
6	M	0058	3.6	0702	2.0	1358	3.5	1935	2.1
7	TU	0216	3.8	0827	1.8	1457	3.7	2049	1.8
8	W	0313	4.0	0920	1.5	1546	4.0	2140	1.5
9	TH	0400	4.2	1004	1.2	1627	4.2	2222	1.2
10	F	0443	4.4	1044	1.0	1708	4.4	2301	1.0
11	SA	0524	4.5	1119	0.8	1746	4.5	2335	0.8
12	SU ●	0604	4.5	1152	0.8	1824	4.6		
13	M	0008	0.8	0642	4.5	1225	0.8	1858	4.6
14	TU	0041	0.8	0718	4.5	1258	0.8	1931	4.6
15	W	0113	0.8	0751	4.4	1329	0.9	2001	4.5
16	TH	0145	0.9	0824	4.3	1402	1.1	2034	4.5
17	F	0222	1.1	0901	4.2	1438	1.3	2113	4.3
18	SA	0304	1.3	0946	4.0	1526	1.5	2202	4.2
19	SU	0400	1.5	1043	3.8	1629	1.7	2301	4.0
20	M	0516	1.6	1154	3.8	1750	1.8		
21	TU	0016	4.0	0640	1.5	1318	3.9	1913	1.6
22	W	0141	4.1	0756	1.3	1435	4.1	2027	1.3
23	TH	0255	4.4	0903	1.0	1538	4.4	2130	1.0
24	F	0357	4.6	1001	0.7	1632	4.6	2224	0.7
25	SA	0452	4.8	1053	0.4	1722	4.8	2315	0.4
26	SU ○	0544	4.9	1140	0.3	1810	4.9		
27	M	0000	0.3	0632	4.9	1224	0.4	1853	4.9
28	TU	0045	0.4	0715	4.8	1306	0.5	1932	4.8
29	W	0126	0.5	0757	4.6	1344	0.7	2007	4.7
30	TH	0205	0.8	0834	4.4	1422	1.0	2038	4.5
31	F	0243	1.1	0908	4.1	1459	1.4	2108	4.3

JUNE

Date	Day	Time	m	Time	m	Time	m	Time	m
1	SA	0323	1.4	0943	3.9	1539	1.7	2145	4.1
2	SU	0408	1.7	1028	3.7	1626	1.9	2234	3.9
3	M	0501	1.9	1133	3.5	1724	2.1	2338	3.7
4	TU	0603	1.9	1251	3.5	1830	2.1		
5	W	0101	3.7	0709	1.8	1357	3.7	1936	1.9
6	TH	0212	3.8	0811	1.6	1452	3.9	2037	1.7
7	F	0310	4.0	0905	1.4	1542	4.1	2130	1.4
8	SA	0400	4.2	0953	1.2	1628	4.3	2216	1.2
9	SU	0449	4.3	1037	1.0	1713	4.4	2259	1.0
10	M	0534	4.4	1118	0.9	1755	4.5	● 2339	0.9
11	TU	0618	4.4	1158	0.9	1836	4.6		
12	W	0019	0.8	0658	4.5	1239	0.9	1913	4.6
13	TH	0101	0.8	0738	4.4	1319	0.9	1950	4.6
14	F	0141	0.8	0818	4.4	1359	1.0	2029	4.6
15	SA	0224	0.9	0901	4.3	1442	1.1	2111	4.5
16	SU	0310	1.0	0947	4.2	1529	1.3	2158	4.4
17	M	0402	1.2	1039	4.1	1624	1.4	2252	4.3
18	TU	0501	1.3	1140	4.0	1727	1.5	2357	4.2
19	W	0609	1.4	1248	4.0	1839	1.5		
20	TH	0109	4.2	0721	1.3	1359	4.1	1951	1.4
21	F	0223	4.2	0831	1.2	1505	4.2	2059	1.2
22	SA	0329	4.3	0934	1.0	1604	4.4	2200	1.0
23	SU	0429	4.5	1030	0.8	1658	4.6	2254	0.8
24	M	0523	4.5	1119	0.7	1748	4.7	○ 2342	0.7
25	TU	0614	4.6	1205	0.7	1833	4.7		
26	W	0028	0.7	0658	4.5	1250	0.7	1912	4.7
27	TH	0112	0.7	0739	4.4	1329	0.9	1948	4.7
28	F	0151	0.8	0817	4.3	1407	1.0	2021	4.5
29	SA	0228	1.0	0851	4.2	1442	1.2	2053	4.4
30	SU	0305	1.2	0925	4.0	1518	1.4	2129	4.2

JULY

Date	Day	Time	m	Time	m	Time	m	Time	m
1	M	0340	1.4	1002	3.9	1554	1.7	2207	4.1
2	TU	0421	1.6	1046	3.7	1636	1.8	2253	3.9
3	W	0508	1.8	1138	3.6	1729	1.9	2349	3.8
4	TH	0604	1.8	1241	3.6	1833	2.0		
5	F	0055	3.8	0706	1.8	1348	3.7	1936	1.9
6	SA	0210	3.8	0807	1.6	1452	3.9	2037	1.7
7	SU	0317	3.9	0905	1.5	1550	4.1	2135	1.4
8	M	0415	4.1	0959	1.2	1642	4.3	2227	1.2
9	TU	0508	4.3	1050	1.1	1729	4.5	2317	1.0
10	W ●	0557	4.4	1138	0.9	1816	4.6		
11	TH	0004	0.8	0643	4.5	1226	0.8	1858	4.7
12	F	0052	0.7	0729	4.5	1313	0.7	1941	4.8
13	SA	0137	0.6	0813	4.5	1356	0.7	2024	4.8
14	SU	0222	0.6	0857	4.5	1439	0.8	2107	4.8
15	M	0306	0.7	0941	4.4	1523	0.9	2152	4.7
16	TU	0350	0.8	1027	4.3	1608	1.1	2239	4.5
17	W	0438	1.0	1118	4.2	1659	1.3	2332	4.3
18	TH	0534	1.3	1216	4.0	1800	1.5		
19	F	0037	4.1	0642	1.5	1324	4.0	1914	1.6
20	SA	0152	4.0	0757	1.5	1436	4.0	2032	1.5
21	SU	0307	4.0	0910	1.4	1542	4.2	2142	1.4
22	M	0412	4.1	1013	1.2	1640	4.4	2241	1.1
23	TU	0509	4.3	1106	1.0	1731	4.5	2331	0.9
24	W ○	0558	4.4	1153	0.9	1816	4.6		
25	TH	0016	0.8	0643	4.4	1237	0.8	1855	4.7
26	F	0100	0.7	0722	4.4	1316	0.8	1931	4.7
27	SA	0137	0.8	0757	4.3	1350	0.9	2003	4.6
28	SU	0210	0.9	0829	4.3	1422	1.0	2035	4.5
29	M	0240	1.0	0900	4.2	1449	1.2	2107	4.4
30	TU	0307	1.2	0933	4.1	1516	1.4	2139	4.2
31	W	0334	1.4	1006	3.9	1543	1.6	2213	4.0

AUGUST

Date	Day	Time	m	Time	m	Time	m	Time	m
1	TH	0407	1.6	1046	3.8	1620	1.8	2253	3.9
2	F	0453	1.8	1134	3.7	1719	2.0	2347	3.7
3	SA	0602	1.9	1239	3.6	1841	2.0		
4	SU	0100	3.6	0718	1.9	1358	3.7	1955	1.9
5	M	0233	3.7	0828	1.7	1514	4.0	2102	1.6
6	TU	0347	4.0	0931	1.4	1615	4.2	2203	1.3
7	W	0446	4.2	1030	1.1	1708	4.5	2300	0.9
8	TH	0539	4.4	1123	0.9	1756	4.7	● 2351	0.6
9	F	0628	4.6	1213	0.6	1844	4.9		
10	SA	0041	0.4	0714	4.7	1302	0.4	1929	5.0
11	SU	0127	0.3	0800	4.7	1345	0.4	2012	5.1
12	M	0210	0.2	0843	4.7	1427	0.4	2055	5.0
13	TU	0250	0.4	0925	4.7	1506	0.6	2136	4.8
14	W	0329	0.6	1005	4.5	1545	0.8	2218	4.6
15	TH	0411	1.0	1049	4.3	1629	1.2	2304	4.3
16	F	0458	1.4	1142	4.0	1725	1.6		
17	SA	0005	3.9	0600	1.7	1252	3.8	1840	1.9
18	SU	0128	3.7	0728	1.9	1413	3.8	2015	1.9
19	M	0253	3.8	0859	1.8	1526	4.0	2134	1.6
20	TU	0402	3.9	1004	1.5	1626	4.2	2232	1.3
21	W	0457	4.1	1055	1.2	1716	4.5	2320	1.0
22	TH ○	0544	4.3	1139	0.9	1758	4.6		
23	F	0002	0.8	0624	4.4	1220	0.8	1835	4.7
24	SA	0042	0.7	0659	4.5	1257	0.7	1908	4.7
25	SU	0116	0.7	0732	4.5	1328	0.8	1940	4.7
26	M	0144	0.8	0802	4.4	1354	0.9	2010	4.6
27	TU	0209	0.9	0831	4.4	1417	1.1	2041	4.5
28	W	0229	1.1	0900	4.2	1435	1.2	2108	4.3
29	TH	0250	1.3	0929	4.1	1457	1.4	2135	4.1
30	F	0315	1.5	0959	3.9	1527	1.7	2206	3.9
31	SA	0349	1.7	1040	3.8	1611	1.9	2256	3.7

Chart Datum: 2·62 metres below Ordnance Datum (Newlyn)

TIME ZONE (UTC)
For Summer Time add ONE hour in **non-shaded areas**

ENGLAND – DARTMOUTH

LAT 50°21′N LONG 3°34′W

TIMES AND HEIGHTS OF HIGH AND LOW WATERS

SPRING & NEAP TIDES
Dates in red are SPRINGS
Dates in blue are NEAPS

YEAR **2002**

SEPTEMBER

Day	Time	m	Day	Time	m
1 SU	0445 1141 1737	2.0 3.6 2.2	16 M	0115 0706 1355 2010	3.5 2.2 3.7 2.1
2 M	0009 0634 1303 1922	3.6 2.1 3.7 2.1	17 TU	0244 0851 1511 2125	3.6 2.0 3.9 1.7
3 TU	0151 0759 1441 2039	3.6 1.9 3.9 1.7	18 W	0351 0950 1610 2216	3.9 1.6 4.2 1.3
4 W	0327 0910 1552 2146	3.9 1.6 4.3 1.3	19 TH	0442 1037 1655 2300	4.2 1.2 4.5 1.0
5 TH	0428 1012 1646 2244	4.2 1.1 4.6 0.8	20 F	0523 1118 1734 2339	4.4 1.0 4.7 0.8
6 F	0520 1107 1735 2335	4.5 0.7 4.9 0.4	21 SA ○	0559 1155 1811	4.5 0.8 4.8
7 SA ●	0608 1156 1824	4.8 0.4 5.1	22 SU	0014 0632 1230 1843	0.7 4.6 0.7 4.8
8 SU	0022 0654 1244 1909	0.2 4.9 0.2 5.2	23 M	0047 0703 1259 1914	0.7 4.6 0.8 4.8
9 M	0108 0738 1327 1953	0.0 5.0 0.1 5.2	24 TU	0113 0733 1323 1944	0.8 4.6 0.9 4.7
10 TU	0149 0820 1406 2035	0.1 5.0 0.2 5.1	25 W	0134 0802 1343 2012	0.9 4.5 1.0 4.5
11 W	0228 0900 1443 2115	0.3 4.8 0.5 4.9	26 TH	0154 0829 1402 2039	1.0 4.4 1.2 4.4
12 TH	0305 0939 1521 2154	0.6 4.6 0.8 4.6	27 F	0215 0854 1425 2102	1.2 4.3 1.4 4.2
13 F	0342 1018 1602 2235	1.1 4.3 1.3 4.1	28 SA	0238 0922 1454 2135	1.5 4.1 1.6 4.0
14 SA	0426 1105 1654 2334	1.6 4.0 1.8 3.7	29 SU	0312 1004 1536 2227	1.7 3.9 1.9 3.7
15 SU	0525 1222 1811	2.0 3.7 2.1	30 M	0402 1106 1650 2342	2.1 3.7 2.2 3.6

OCTOBER

Day	Time	m	Day	Time	m
1 TU	0552 1226 1856	2.3 3.7 2.2	16 W	0223 0825 1445 2100	3.6 2.2 3.9 1.8
2 W	0122 0735 1408 2018	3.6 2.1 3.9 1.8	17 TH	0326 0922 1541 2149	3.9 1.8 4.2 1.4
3 TH	0307 0851 1526 2126	3.9 1.6 4.3 1.2	18 F	0414 1007 1626 2230	4.2 1.4 4.5 1.1
4 F	0408 0953 1623 2222	4.3 1.1 4.7 0.7	19 SA	0453 1047 1704 2307	4.4 1.1 4.6 0.9
5 SA	0458 1047 1713 2313	4.7 0.7 5.0 0.3	20 SU	0528 1123 1740 2341	4.6 0.9 4.7 0.8
6 SU ●	0545 1135 1801 2359	4.9 0.3 5.2 0.1	21 M ○	0601 1156 1815	4.7 0.8 4.8
7 M	0630 1220 1847	5.1 0.1 5.3	22 TU	0011 0634 1225 1848	0.8 4.7 0.8 4.7
8 TU	0044 0714 1303 1931	0.0 5.1 0.1 5.3	23 W	0038 0705 1252 1919	0.8 4.7 0.9 4.7
9 W	0125 0755 1342 2012	0.1 5.1 0.2 5.1	24 TH	0103 0736 1315 1948	0.9 4.7 1.0 4.6
10 TH	0203 0835 1421 2052	0.4 5.0 0.5 4.8	25 F	0126 0803 1338 2015	1.1 4.6 1.2 4.4
11 F	0239 0911 1458 2130	0.8 4.7 1.0 4.5	26 SA	0149 0830 1405 2044	1.3 4.4 1.4 4.2
12 SA	0316 0947 1539 2207	1.3 4.4 1.5 4.0	27 SU	0217 0901 1437 2121	1.5 4.3 1.6 4.0
13 SU	0359 1028 1631 2306	1.8 4.0 1.9 3.6	28 M	0253 0945 1522 2214	1.8 4.1 1.9 3.8
14 M	0458 1147 1747	2.2 3.7 2.3	29 TU	0345 1046 1637 2325	2.1 3.9 2.1 3.6
15 TU	0059 0637 1332 1951	3.5 2.4 3.7 2.2	30 W	0525 1201 1829	2.3 3.9 2.1
			31 TH	0057 0708 1333 1952	3.7 2.1 4.0 1.7

NOVEMBER

Day	Time	m	Day	Time	m
1 F	0236 0824 1454 2100	4.0 1.7 4.4 1.2	16 SA	0332 0925 1546 2149	4.1 1.6 4.3 1.4
2 SA	0340 0928 1555 2157	4.4 1.2 4.7 0.8	17 SU	0415 1007 1627 2227	4.3 1.4 4.5 1.1
3 SU	0431 1021 1648 2248	4.7 0.8 5.0 0.4	18 M	0452 1046 1706 2303	4.5 1.2 4.6 1.0
4 M ●	0519 1110 1737 2335	5.0 0.4 5.2 0.2	19 TU	0529 1121 1745 2335	4.6 1.0 4.6 1.0
5 TU	0606 1156 1825	5.1 0.3 5.2	20 W ○	0605 1153 1823	4.7 1.0 4.7
6 W	0018 0650 1241 1909	0.2 5.2 0.3 5.2	21 TH	0005 0641 1224 1857	1.0 4.7 1.0 4.6
7 TH	0101 0732 1322 1952	0.3 5.1 0.4 5.0	22 F	0037 0713 1255 1931	1.0 4.7 1.1 4.5
8 F	0140 0810 1401 2032	0.6 5.0 0.7 4.7	23 SA	0107 0744 1326 2002	1.1 4.6 1.2 4.4
9 SA	0218 0848 1440 2110	1.0 4.7 1.1 4.4	24 SU	0137 0816 1359 2036	1.3 4.6 1.3 4.3
10 SU	0256 0923 1523 2149	1.4 4.4 1.5 4.0	25 M	0211 0852 1437 2117	1.4 4.4 1.5 4.1
11 M	0339 1002 1613 2242	1.9 4.1 1.9 3.7	26 TU	0252 0937 1526 2207	1.7 4.3 1.7 3.9
12 TU	0433 1101 1719	2.2 3.9 2.2	27 W	0346 1032 1632 2311	1.9 4.2 1.8 3.8
13 W	0023 0548 1246 1852	3.5 2.4 3.8 2.2	28 TH	0503 1139 1756	2.0 4.1 1.8
14 TH	0142 0728 1400 2012	3.6 2.3 3.9 2.0	29 F	0029 0631 1256 1917	3.8 2.0 4.2 1.6
15 F	0244 0836 1458 2105	3.8 2.0 4.1 1.6	30 SA	0153 0749 1415 2028	4.0 1.7 4.3 1.3

DECEMBER

Day	Time	m	Day	Time	m
1 SU	0302 0856 1523 2129	4.3 1.3 4.6 1.0	16 M	0326 0916 1543 2139	4.1 1.7 4.2 1.5
2 M	0401 0954 1621 2222	4.6 1.0 4.8 0.7	17 TU	0413 1003 1631 2221	4.3 1.5 4.3 1.3
3 TU	0454 1047 1715 2312	4.8 0.7 4.9 0.6	18 W	0457 1045 1717 2301	4.5 1.3 4.4 1.2
4 W ●	0543 1135 1805 2358	5.0 0.6 5.0 0.5	19 TH ○	0540 1124 1800 2340	4.6 1.1 4.5 1.1
5 TH	0630 1220 1853	5.1 0.5 4.9	20 F	0620 1203 1842	4.7 1.0 4.5
6 F	0042 0712 1306 1936	0.6 5.0 0.6 4.8	21 SA	0018 0657 1243 1919	1.0 4.7 1.0 4.5
7 SA	0124 0753 1347 2017	0.8 4.9 0.8 4.6	22 SU	0057 0735 1322 1957	1.0 4.7 1.0 4.5
8 SU	0203 0831 1428 2056	1.1 4.7 1.1 4.3	23 M	0134 0811 1401 2035	1.1 4.7 1.1 4.4
9 M	0242 0906 1510 2134	1.4 4.5 1.4 4.1	24 TU	0214 0851 1442 2117	1.2 4.6 1.2 4.3
10 TU	0323 0943 1553 2215	1.7 4.3 1.7 3.8	25 W	0256 0934 1527 2203	1.3 4.5 1.3 4.2
11 W	0408 1028 1642 2311	2.0 4.1 1.9 3.7	26 TH	0343 1021 1620 2255	1.5 4.4 1.4 4.1
12 TH	0502 1127 1741	2.2 3.9 2.1	27 F	0439 1117 1721 2358	1.6 4.3 1.5 4.0
13 F	0025 0606 1242 1849	3.6 2.2 3.8 2.1	28 SA	0547 1222 1833	1.7 4.2 1.6
14 SA	0135 0718 1351 1954	3.7 2.1 3.9 1.9	29 SU	0108 0706 1336 1948	4.0 1.7 4.2 1.5
15 SU	0235 0822 1450 2051	3.9 1.9 4.0 1.7	30 M	0223 0821 1450 2058	4.1 1.5 4.3 1.3
			31 TU	0331 0929 1558 2200	4.3 1.3 4.4 1.1

Chart Datum: 2·62 metres below Ordnance Datum (Newlyn)

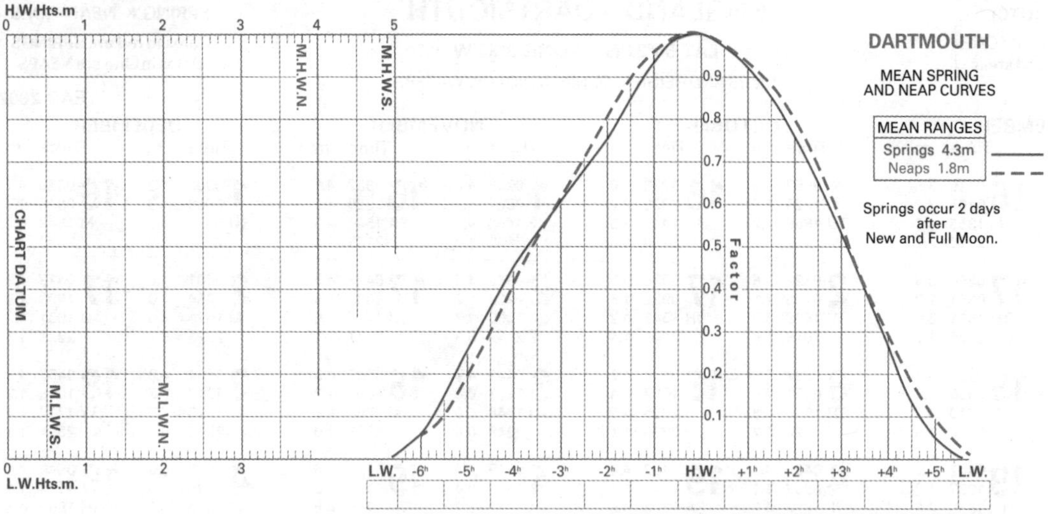

DARTMOUTH *9.1.21*

Devon **50°20'·66N 03°33'·96W** ❀❀❀⚓⚓⚓✿✿✿

CHARTS AC *5602, 2253, 1634, 1613*; Imray C5, Y47, Y43; Stanfords 12, 22; OS 202

TIDES –0510 Dover; ML 2·8; Duration 0630; Zone 0 (UT)

DARTMOUTH (⟵)

Times				Height (metres)			
High Water		Low Water		MHWS	MHWN	MLWN	MLWS
0100	0600	0100	0600	4·9	3·8	2·0	0·6
1300	1800	1300	1800				
Differences GREENWAY QUAY (DITTISHAM)							
+0015	+0020	+0025	+0010	0·0	0·0	0·0	0·0
TOTNES							
+0015	+0015	+0115	+0035	–1·4	–1·5	Dries	Dries

SHELTER Excellent inside hbr, but ent can be difficult in strong SE to SW winds. In mid-stream there are 8 big unlit mooring buoys for commercial vessels/FVs; do not ⚓ over their ground chains, as shown on AC 2253. Only space to ⚓ is E of fairway, from abeam Nos 3 to 5 buoys. The 3 marinas (Darthaven, Dart and Noss-on-Dart) have Ⓥ berths. Apart from the pontoons off the Royal Dart YC, the extensive pontoons and mooring trots elsewhere in the hbr are run by the Hr Mr, who should be contacted by VHF/☎. The most likely Ⓥ berths/Ⓥs from S to N are:

W bank: pontoon off Dartmouth YC (May-Sep); Town jetty (W side only) near Boat Camber; N end of pontoon just S of Dart marina (26'/8m max LOA).

E of fairway: (NB six sets of pontoons N of Darthaven marina are for berth holders only). The 2 pontoons N of Fuel barge are for visitors. Visitors' berths are marked by light blue flags.

NAVIGATION WPT 50°19'·53N 03°32'·88W, 148°/328° from/to Kingswear lt, Iso WRG, 1·5M. To the E of ent, on Inner Froward Pt (153m) is a conspic daymark, obelisk (24·5m). There is no bar and the hbr is always accessible. Speed limit 6kn from Castle Ledge buoy inwards

LIGHTS AND MARKS Kingswear Main lt 328°, Iso WRG 3s 9m 8M, W 325°-331°. Bayard's Cove lt 293°, Fl WRG 2s 5m 6M, W 289°-297°. Entry buoys as on chartlet. Within hbr, all jetty/ pontoon lts to the W are 2FR (vert); and 2FG (vert) to the E.

RADIO TELEPHONE Hr Mr call *Dartnav* VHF Ch 11 16 (Mon-Fri 0830-1800; Sat 0900-1200). Darthaven marina, Ch **80** M; Dart marina, Noss-on-Dart marina and Dart Sailing Centre, Ch 80. Fuel barge Ch 06. Water taxi: Ch 08.

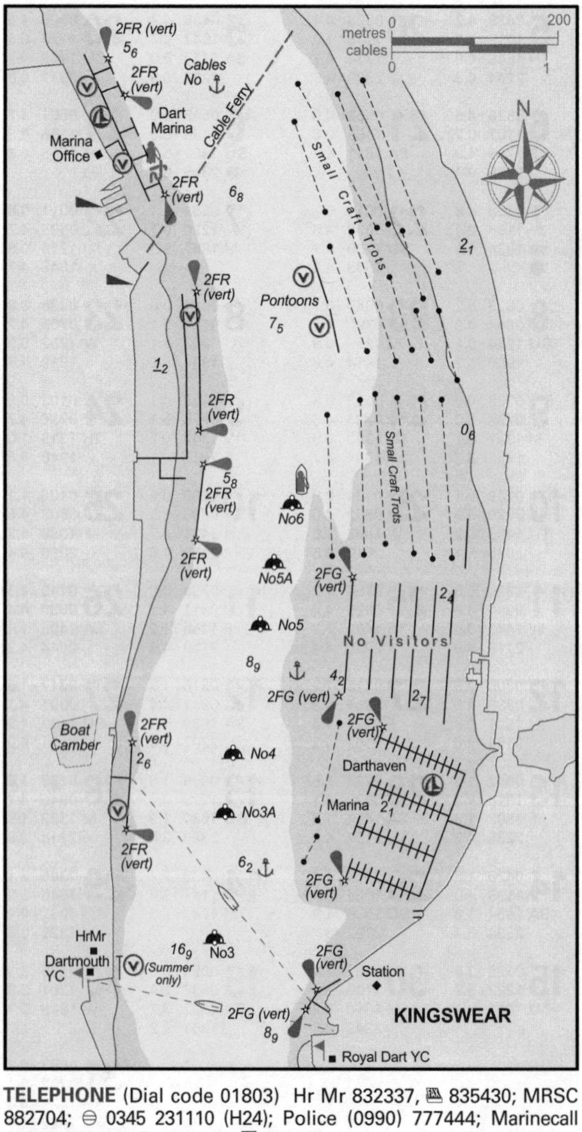

TELEPHONE (Dial code 01803) Hr Mr 832337, 📠 835430; MRSC 882704; ⊜ 0345 231110 (H24); Police (0990) 777444; Marinecall 09068 500458; Dr 832212; Ⓗ 832255, water taxi 07770 628967.

DARTMOUTH *continued*

FACILITIES

HARBOUR/MARINAS **Hbr Authority** (450+90 Ⓥ), ☎ 832337, 📠 833631; £1.47 approx (W bank pontoons), M, FW, Slip, V, R, ♿.

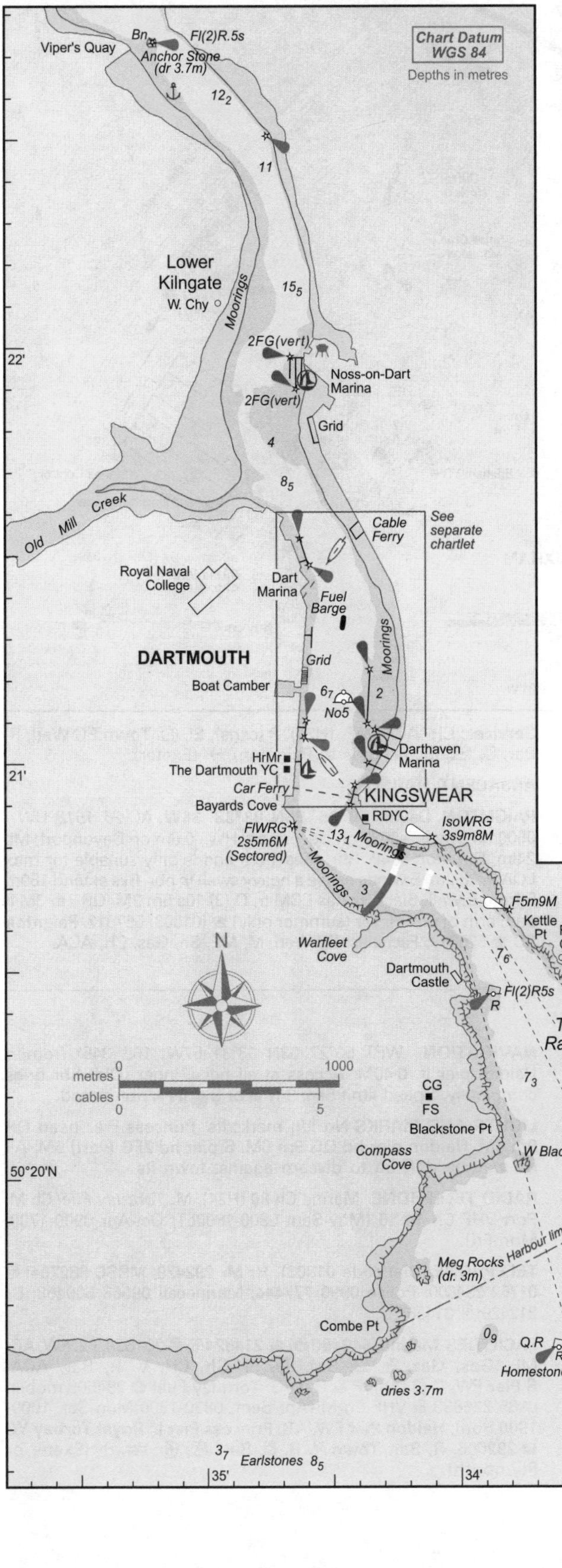
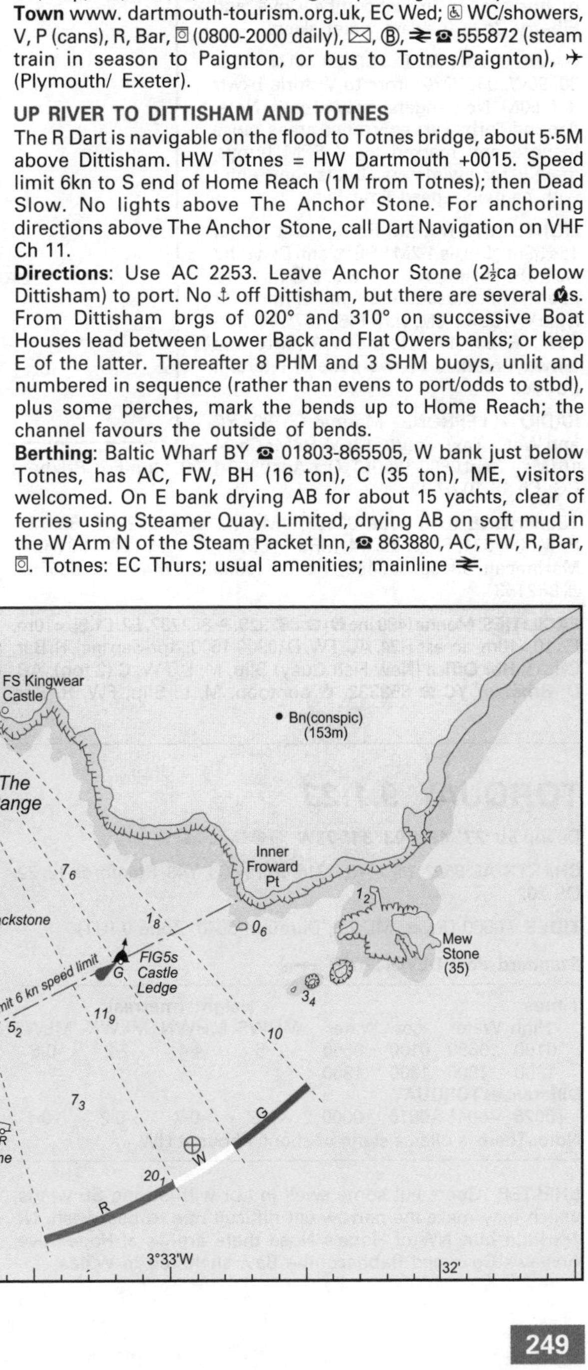

Darthaven Marina (230+12 Ⓥ) ☎ 752242, 📠 752722, £1.10, FW, ME, El, Gas, Gaz, ⊡, Sh, CH, Bar, R, BH (30 ton), AC, Ⓔ;

Dart Marina (110, inc up to 30 Ⓥs) ☎ 833351, 📠 832307, www.ybw.com/web/philipleisure/, £2.50, D, FW, AC, ME, El, Sh, C (9 ton), 2 Slips, ⛽ at fuel berth, Gas, Gaz, CH, Bar, R, ⊡;

Noss-on-Dart Marina (150) ☎ 833351, 📠 835150, £1.10, FW, AC, ME, El, Sh, C (18 ton), CH, Gas, Gaz, ⊡;

Dart Sailing Centre ☎ 752702, AB, AC, Bar, R;

Creekside BY (Old Mill Creek) ☎ 832649, Slip, dry dock, M, ME, Sh, El, C (1 ton), CH, AB, Res Nova Inn moored close downstream of fuel barge: Bar, R, AB (customer only) FW.

YACHT CLUBS **Royal Dart YC** ☎ 752272, M, L, pontoon (short stay), FW, Bar, R, visitors welcome; **Dartmouth YC** ☎ 832305, L, FW, Bar, R. **Royal Regatta**, last week August.

Services M, ME, El, Sh, BH, CH, SM, rigging, masts, Ⓔ; **Water Taxi** ☎ 833727, (VHF Ch 16 06 08); **Fuel Barge** ☎ 07801 798861 summer: 0800-1800; winter: telephone to check, VHF Ch 06, D; next to No 6 buoy. Galmpton Creek: CH, D, FW, L, M, C (6 ton), ME, Sh, SM, BY, Slip, AC, BH (53, 16 ton), El, Ⓔ; Slip at Higher Ferry.

Town www. dartmouth-tourism.org.uk, EC Wed; ♿ WC/showers, V, P (cans), R, Bar, ⊡ (0800-2000 daily), ✉, Ⓑ, ⇌ ☎ 555872 (steam train in season to Paignton, or bus to Totnes/Paignton), ✈ (Plymouth/ Exeter).

UP RIVER TO DITTISHAM AND TOTNES

The R Dart is navigable on the flood to Totnes bridge, about 5·5M above Dittisham. HW Totnes = HW Dartmouth +0015. Speed limit 6kn to S end of Home Reach (1M from Totnes); then Dead Slow. No lights above The Anchor Stone. For anchoring directions above The Anchor Stone, call Dart Navigation on VHF Ch 11.

Directions: Use AC 2253. Leave Anchor Stone (2½ca below Dittisham) to port. No ⚓ off Dittisham, but there are several 🅐s. From Dittisham brgs of 020° and 310° on successive Boat Houses lead between Lower Back and Flat Owers banks; or keep E of the latter. Thereafter 8 PHM and 3 SHM buoys, unlit and numbered in sequence (rather than evens to port/odds to stbd), plus some perches, mark the bends up to Home Reach; the channel favours the outside of bends.

Berthing: Baltic Wharf BY ☎ 01803-865505, W bank just below Totnes, has AC, FW, BH (16 ton), C (35 ton), ME, visitors welcomed. On E bank drying AB for about 15 yachts, clear of ferries using Steamer Quay. Limited, drying AB on soft mud in the W Arm N of the Steam Packet Inn, ☎ 863880, AC, FW, R, Bar, ⊡. Totnes: EC Thurs; usual amenities; mainline ⇌.

BRIXHAM 9.1.22

Devon 50°24′·31N 03°30′·86W
❀❀❀◊◊◊✿✿

CHARTS AC *5602, 26, 1613, 1634, 3315*; Imray C5, Y43; Stanfords 12, 22; OS 202

TIDES –0505 Dover; ML 2·9; Duration 0635; Zone 0 (UT)

Standard Port DEVONPORT (⟵)

Differences BRIXHAM are the same as **TORQUAY** (⟶)

SHELTER Very good in marina; also at YC pontoon in SW corner of hbr, but outer hbr is dangerous in NW winds. Ⓥs (W) to E of main fairway. Inner hbr dries. To W of hbr are ⚓s in Fishcombe Cove and Elberry Cove (beware water skiers).

NAVIGATION WPT 50°24′·41N 03° 30′·90W, 050°/230° from/to Victoria bkwtr lt, 0·60M. No dangers; easy access. Note: Around Torbay are controlled areas, close inshore and marked by Y SPM buoys, mainly for swimmers; boats may enter with caution, speed limit 5kn.

LIGHTS AND MARKS Berry Hd lt, Fl (2) 15s 58m 15M, is 1·2M ESE of ent. Bkwtr hd Oc R 15s 9m 6M, W tr. 3 R ● or 3 ● lts (vert) at ent = hbr closed. At SE end of hbr a Dir lt Iso WR 5s 4m 6M, vis R145°-157°, W157°-161°, R161°-173° leads 159° into the fairway, marked by two pairs of lateral lt buoys.

RADIO TELEPHONE Marina: Ch 80. YC and Water Taxi: *Shuttle* Ch M. Hr Mr Ch 14 16 (May-Sept 0800-1800LT; Oct-Apr 0900-1700, Mon-Fri). Brixham CG: Ch 16 10 67 73.

TELEPHONE (Dial code 01803) Marina ☎ 882929 📠 882737; Hr Mr 853321; Pilot 882214; MRSC 882704; ⊖ 01952 234600 (H24); Marinecall 09068 500458; Police (0990) 777444; Dr 855897; Ⓗ 882153.

FACILITIES **Marina** (480 inc Ⓥ) ☎ 882929, 📠 882737, £2, £1.85<10m, £2.10>10m, access H24, AC, FW, D (0900-1800, Apr-Sep inc), R, Bar, CH, ▣; **Hbr Office** (New Fish Quay) Slip, M, L, FW, C (2 ton), AB, D; **Brixham YC** ☎ 853332, Ⓥ pontoon, M, L, Slip, FW, R, Bar;

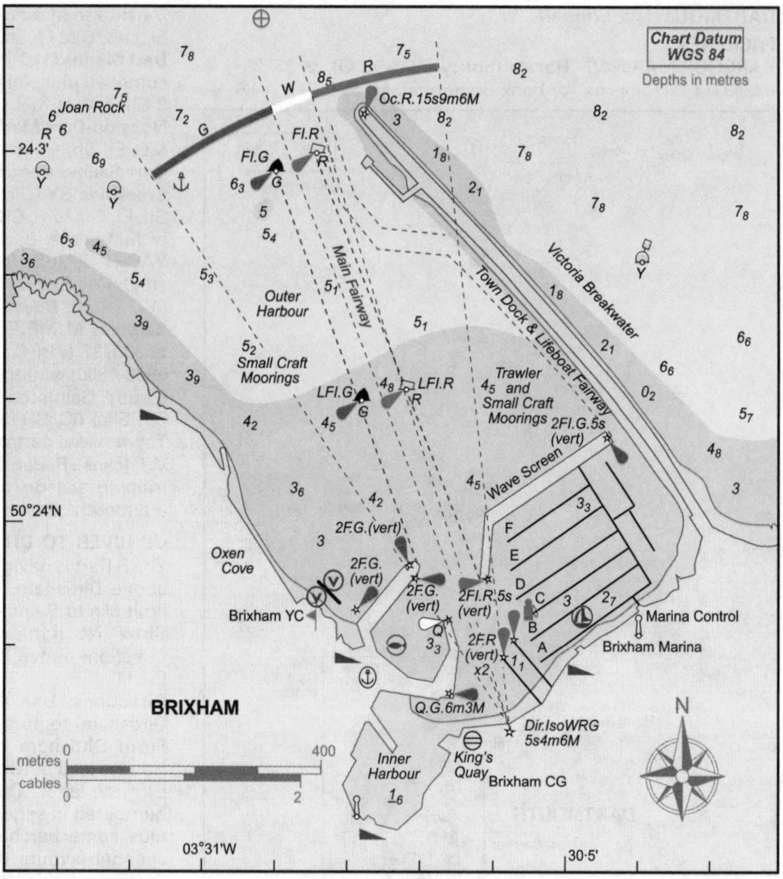

Services: CH, ACA, ME, (H24), P (cans), El, Ⓔ. **Town** EC Wed; R, Bar, ▣, ✉, Ⓑ, ⇌ (bus to Paignton), ✈ (Exeter).

ADJACENT HARBOUR

PAIGNTON, Devon, **50°25′·96N 03°33′·36W**. AC *26, 1613*. HW –0500 on Dover, +0035 on Devonport; HW –0·6m on Devonport; ML 2·9m; Duration 0640. Hbr dries 1·3m and is only suitable for max LOA 27'/8·2m. E winds cause a heavy swell in hbr. Rks extend 180m E from E wall. Black Rk has ECM tr, Q (3) 10s 5m 3M. QR 7m 3M lt on E arm of ent. Hr Mr (summer only) ☎ (01803) 557812. **Paignton SC** ☎ 525817; Facilities: EC Wed, M, ME, Sh, Gas, CH, ACA.

TORQUAY 9.1.23

Devon **50°27′·45N 03°31′·73W** ❀❀❀◊◊◊✿✿

CHARTS AC *5602, 26, 1613, 3315*; Imray C5, Y43; Stanfords 12, 22; OS 202

TIDES –0500 Dover; ML 2·9; Duration 0640; Zone 0 (UT)

Standard Port DEVONPORT (⟵)

Times				Height (metres)			
High Water		Low Water		MHWS	MHWN	MLWN	MLWS
0100	0600	0100	0600	5·5	4·4	2·2	0·8
1300	1800	1300	1800				
Differences TORQUAY							
+0025	+0045	+0010	0000	–0·6	–0·7	–0·2	–0·1

Note: There is often a stand of about 1 hour at HW

SHELTER Good, but some swell in hbr with strong SE winds, which may make the narrow ent difficult due to backwash. No ⚓ within hbr. NW of Hope's Nose there are ⚓s at Hope Cove, Anstey's Cove and Babbacombe Bay, sheltered in W'lies.

NAVIGATION WPT 50°27′·03N 03°31′·57W, 165°/345° from/to Haldon pier lt, 0·40M. Access at all tides. Inner (Old) hbr dries completely. Speed limit 5kn. 3 R ● or 3 ● lts = hbr closed.

LIGHTS AND MARKS No ldg marks/lts. Princess Pier head QR 9m 6M. Haldon pier hd QG 9m 6M. S pier hd 2FG (vert) 5M. All lts may be difficult to discern against town lts.

RADIO TELEPHONE Marina Ch **80** (H24), M. *Torquay Fuel* Ch M. Port VHF Ch 14 16 (May-Sept 0800-1800LT; Oct-Apr 0900-1700, Mon-Fri).

TELEPHONE (Dial code 01803) Hr Mr 292429; MRSC 882704; ⊖ 01752 234600; Police 0990 777444; Marinecall 09068 500458; Dr 212429; Ⓗ 614567.

FACILITIES **Marina** (440+60 Ⓥ) ☎ 214624/5, 📠 291634, £2, FW, AC, ME, Gas, Gaz, ♿, ▣, SM, Ⓔ, El, Sh, CH, V, R, Bar, ACA. **S Pier** FW, C (6 ton), P & D, LPG: Torquay Fuel ☎ 294509/mobile 0385 226839 & VHF Ch M (Apr-Sept, 0830-1900 Mon-Sat, 1000-1900 Sun); **Haldon Pier** FW, AB; **Princess Pier** L; **Royal Torbay YC** ☎ 292006, R, Bar. **Town** V, R, ▣, Bar, ✉, Ⓑ, ⇌, ✈ (Exeter or Plymouth).

TORQUAY *continued*

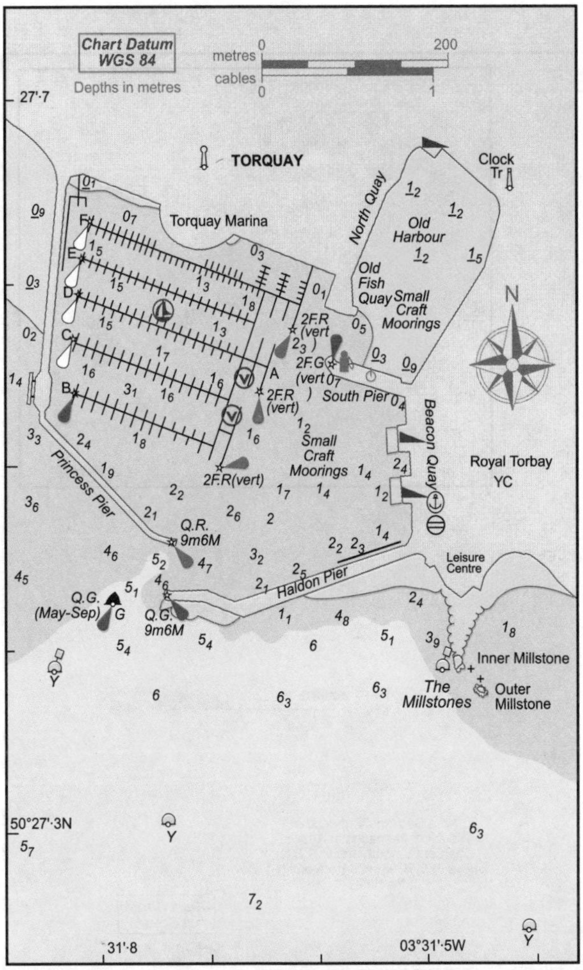

TEIGNMOUTH *9.1.24*

Devon **50°32'·39N 03°30'·07W** (Abeam The Point) ❀❀◊◊✿✿

CHARTS AC *5602, 26, 3315*; Imray C5, Y43; Stanfords 12; OS 192

TIDES –0450 Dover; ML 2·7; Duration 0625; Zone 0 (UT)

Standard Port DEVONPORT (⟵)

Times				**Height (metres)**			
High Water		Low Water		MHWS	MHWN	MLWN	MLWS
0100	0600	0100	0600	5·5	4·4	2·2	0·8
1300	1800	1300	1800				
Differences TEIGNMOUTH (Approaches)							
+0025	+0040	0000	0000	–0·7	–0·8	–0·3	–0·2
SHALDON BRIDGE							
+0035	+0050	+0020	+0020	–0·9	–0·9	–0·2	0·0

SHELTER Hbr completely sheltered, but difficult to enter especially with strong winds from NE to S when surf forms on the bar. Access HW±3. Appr chan is not buoyed so local advice is recommended. No AB, but two ⚓s just N of SHM lt buoy, Fl G 5s. Speed limit is 8kn.

NAVIGATION WPT 50°32'·43N 03°29'·19W, 076°/256° from/to training wall lt, 0·43M. Bar shifts very frequently. Beware rks off the Ness; and variable extent of Salty flats. Clearance under Shaldon bridge is 4·2m at MHWS (AC 26), but it is reported locally to be at most 2·9m at MHWS and approx 5·8m at MLWS. Avoid a Historic wreck site (50°32'·95N 03°29'·24W; just off chartlet), close inshore by Church Rks to ENE of Ch Tr (see 9.0.3h).

LIGHTS AND MARKS The Ness, high red sandstone headland, and church tower are both conspic from afar; close NE of the latter, just off N edge of chartlet, Teign Corinthian YC bldg (cream colour) is also conspic. At seaward end of outfall, 105° The Ness 1 25M, is a Y buoy, Fl Y 5s, at 50°31' 96N 03°27' 88W. Y buoy, Fl Y 2s, marks S edge of Spratt Sand. Once round The Point, Oc G 5·5s and FG (vert), two F Bu lts on quay align 022°, but are not official ldg lts.

RADIO TELEPHONE VHF Ch 12 16 (Mon-Fri: 0800-1700; Sat 0900-1200 LT).

TELEPHONE (Dial code 01626) Hr Mr 774044 or outside office hrs 772892/776530, 🏛 778417; MRSC (01803) 882704; ⊖ 0345 231110 (H24); Marinecall 09068 500458; Police 772433; Dr 774355; 🏥 772161.

FACILITIES **E Quay Polly Steps** Slip (up to 10m); **Teign Corinthian YC** ☎ 772734, ⚓ £8.00, M, Bar; **Services:** ME, CH, El, Slip, BY, Sh, C (8 ton), Gas, Gaz, FW, CH, Ⓔ. **Town** EC Thurs; P & D (cans, 1M), L, FW, V, R, ⊡, Bar, ✉, Ⓑ, ⇌, ✈ (Exeter).

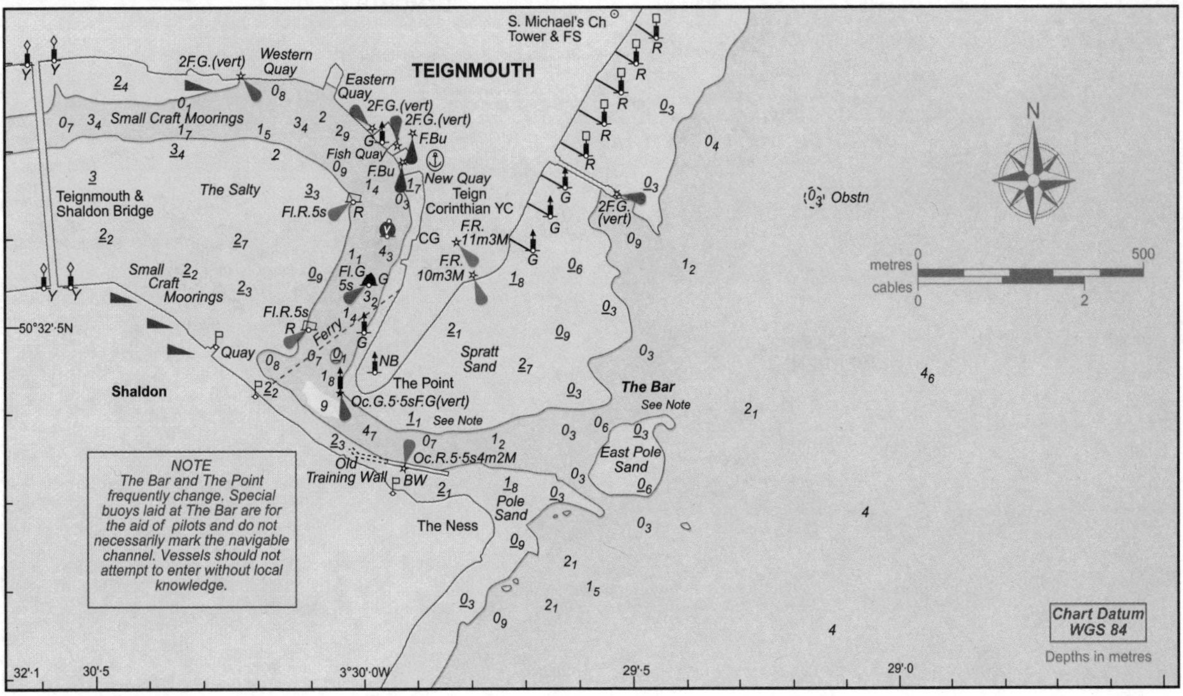

RIVER EXE *9.1.25*

Devon **50°36'·94N 03°25'·40W** (Abeam Exmouth) ❁❁❁◊◊◊✿✿

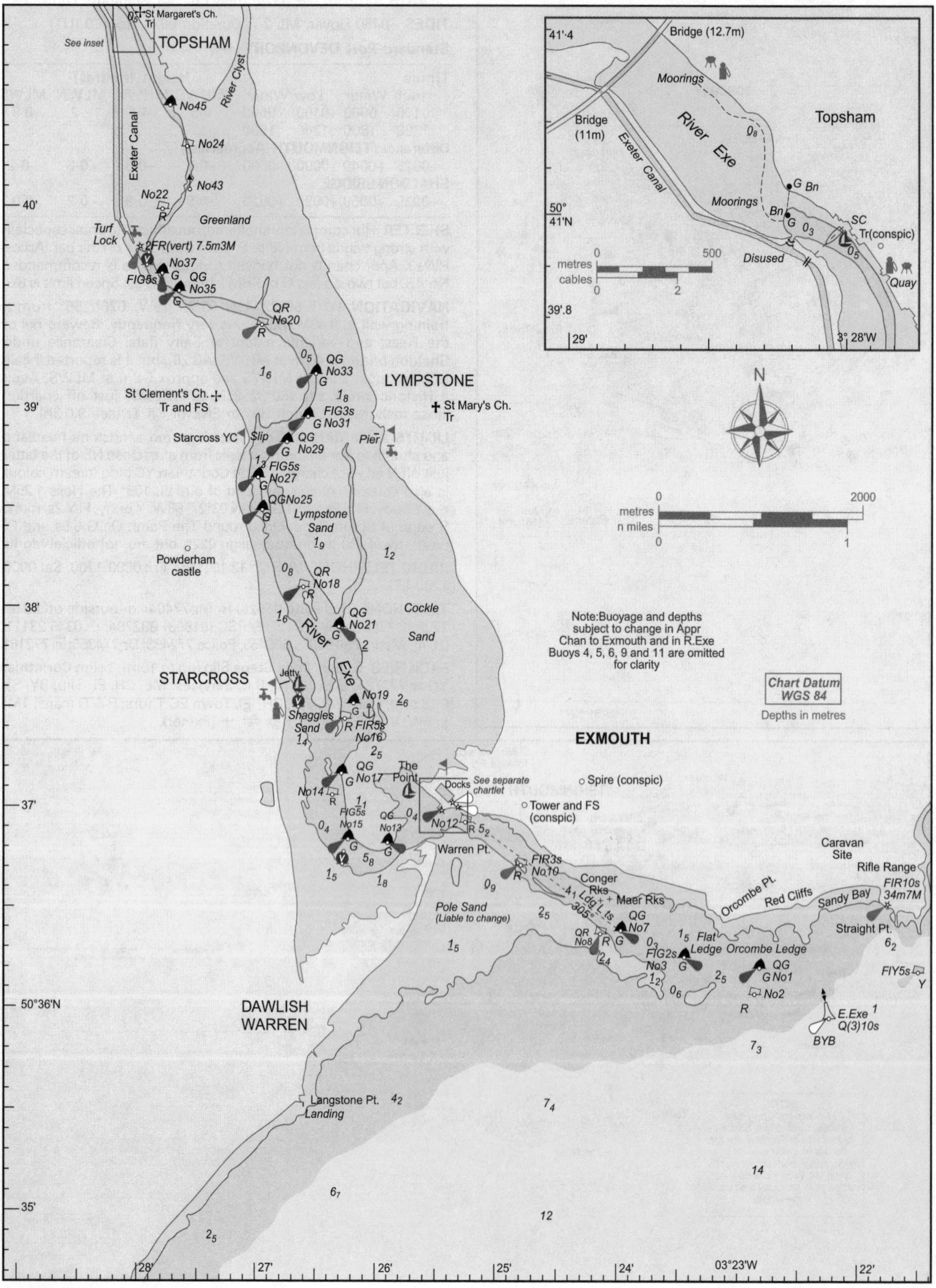

RIVER EXE *continued*

CHARTS AC *5601*, 2290, *3315*; Imray C5, Y45, Y43; Stanfords 12, 22; OS 192

TIDES –0445 Dover; ML 2·1; Duration 0625; Zone 0 (UT)

Standard Port DEVONPORT (⟵)

Times				Height (metres)			
High Water		Low Water		MHWS	MHWN	MLWN	MLWS
0100	0600	0100	0600	5·5	4·4	2·2	0·8
1300	1800	1300	1800				
Differences EXMOUTH (Approaches)							
+0030	+0050	+0015	+0005	–0·9	–1·0	–0·5	–0·3
EXMOUTH DOCK							
+0035	+0055	+0050	+0020	–1·5	–1·6	–0·9	–0·6
STARCROSS							
+0040	+0110	+0055	+0025	–1·4	–1·5	–0·8	–0·1
TOPSHAM							
+0045	+0105	No data		–1·5	–1·6	No data	

SHELTER Good inside R Exe, but ent difficult in fresh winds from E and S. Caution: strong tidal streams, see below.
Exmouth Dock is a yacht basin, 2m depth, usually full of local boats. Call Dock Mr VHF Ch 14 for possible berth. In dock ent the pontoon is much used by local ferries/water taxi. Swing bridge opens on request; stays open HN. Strong cross tides at entr.
Estuary. Ⓥs are in The Bight (2ca SW of No 13 SHM lt buoy, near ship's mooring buoy), off Starcross, Turf Lock and Topsham SC; water taxi will advise (VHF Ch M). ⚓ may be found E of Starcross clear of chan, ie 1ca SSE of No 19 buoy in 2·1m. At **Topsham** the river carries about 0·4m. Options: ⚓ in appr's, dry out at the Quay, find a mooring or berth at BY pontoon (1m at LW).

NAVIGATION WPT East Exe ECM buoy Q (3)10s, 50°35'·99N 03°21'·43W, 111°/291° from/to No 7 SHM buoy, QG, 1·03M.
Caution: Royal Marine firing range at Straight Pt, just E of East Exe buoy, has a danger area to SE, marked by 2 DZ SPM lt buoys (not to be confused with the sewer outfall SPM can buoy, Fl Y 5s, shown on chartlet). R flags are flown when the range is in use (likely times 0800-1600, Mon-Fri); call *Straight Pt Range* VHF Ch 08 16. From the E, check also with safety launch.
Approach is best started at approx LW+2 when hazards can be seen and some shelter obtained. In the appr chan tide runs up to 3·3kn on sp ebb; with wind against tide a confused, breaking sea quickly builds. In the narrows off Warren Pt the flood stream runs at 3-4kn and the ebb can exceed 4½kn when the banks uncover.
Ent chan is well marked/lit, but night entry is not advised. There are drying rky ledges to the N of chan; to the south Pole Sands dry up to 2·8m. Least depths of 0·5m & 1·0m occur in the chan between Nos 3 and 7 buoys, best water to stbd. Note: Approach buoys 2, 4, 5, 6, 9 & 11 are unlit, plus some others up-river, some not shown on chartlet due to small scale. The chan narrows to about 100m between Nos 11 and 10 buoys. After No 10 buoy it is important not to cut the corner round Warren Pt; stand on for 0·5M toward Exmouth Dock and well past No 12 PHM buoy, before altering to the SW. Up-to-date AC 2290 essential. The ch is subject to movement.
The estuary bed is sand/mud, free of rks. Follow the curve of the chan, rather than a straight line between buoys. Some bends are marked on the outside only. The estuary is an international conservation area. 10kn speed limit.
Exeter Ship Canal (3·0m depth). Contact Hr Mr ☎ (01392) 274306 or Ch 12 for non-tidal berth in Turf Basin for visitors and lay-ups; the latter also in Exeter Basin.

LIGHTS AND MARKS Straight Pt has conspic caravan site close W and red cliffs to W and NNE. Exmouth ⛪ tr and FS are conspic, about 2M WNW of the East Exe buoy. Ldg lts 305° at Exmouth: front Iso 2s 6m 7M; rear Q 12m 7M; do not use seaward of No 8 PHM buoy.

RADIO TELEPHONE Exmouth Dock Mr VHF Ch 14 16; Water Taxi at Exmouth, call *Conveyance* Ch M 16. Port of Exeter Ch 12 16 (Mon-Fri: 0730-1730LT).

TELEPHONE (Dial code 01395) Dock Mr 269314; Exeter Hr Mr (01392) 274306; MRSC (01803) 882704; ⊖ 0345 231110 (H24); Marinecall 09068 500458; Police 264651; Dr 273001; Ⓗ 279684.

FACILITIES
EXMOUTH (01395) **Yacht Basin,** ☎ 269314, £1.75, FW, D, No Ⓥ berths as such; showers/WC to be provided. **Exe SC** ☎ 264607. **Town** EC Wed; P, Sh, CH, El, Ⓔ, ACA, SM, Gas, Gaz, V, R, ⓘ, Bar, ⊠, Ⓑ, ≷.

STARCROSS (01626) **Starcross Fishing & Cruising Club** ☎ 890582; **Starcross YC** ☎ 890470; **Starcross Garage** ☎ 890225, P & D (cans), ME, Gas. **Village** V, Bar, ⊠, Ⓑ, ≷.

TOPSHAM (01392) **Topsham SC** ☎ 877524, Slip, L, FW, Bar; **Trouts BY** ☎ 873044, AB, M, D, Gas, Gaz, C, FW, Sh.
Retreat BY ☎ 874270 📠 876182, (access HW±2), M, D, FW, ME, C, CH, Sh.
Town P, CH, SM, ACA, R, V, ⓘ, Bar, ⊠, Ⓑ, ≷.

EXETER (01392) Hr Mr, River & Canal Office, Haven Rd, Exeter EX2 8DU, ☎ 274306: canal berths, £8.75 for 2 days minimum, and laying up. **City** all amenities; CH, ME, ACA, ≷, ✈.

EXMOUTH DOCK 50°37'·00N 03°25'·37W

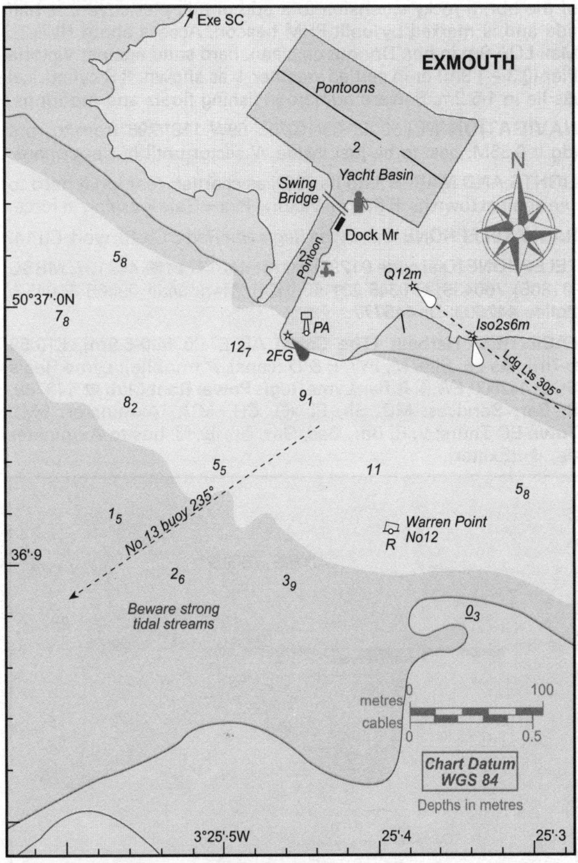

HARBOUR WEST OF LYME REGIS

AXMOUTH/BEER, Devon, **50°42'·13N 03°03'·27W.** AC 3315. HW –0455 on Dover, +0045 and –1·1m on Devonport; ML 2·3m; Duration 0640. MHWS 4·1m, MHWN 3·1m. A small drying hbr on R Axe for boats max draft 1·2m, LOA 8·5m, able to dry out. Appr chan to bar (dries 0·5m) is unmarked and often shifts; prior knowledge from YC is essential. Enter at HW, only in settled weather, via 7m wide ent. Pier hd SHM bn, Fl G 4s 7m 2M; turn hard port inside. Bridge (2m clearance) crosses the river 2ca from ent. Facilities: **Axe YC** ☎ (01297) 20043, Slip, pontoon, M, BH, Bar; **Services:** ME, CH, D (cans).

Beer Roads, 1M WSW, is ⚓ sheltered from prevailing W'ly, but open to S/SE winds. Landing on open beach. **Beer & Seaton:** EC Thurs; R, V, P & D (cans), Bar, Gas, ⊠.

LYME REGIS *9.1.26*

Dorset **50°43'·20N 02°56'·19W** ❀❀◊◊✿✿

CHARTS AC *5601, 3315*; Imray C5; Stanfords 12; OS 193

TIDES –0455 Dover; ML 2·4; Duration 0700; Zone 0 (UT)

Standard Port DEVONPORT (⟵)

Times				Height (metres)			
High Water		Low Water		MHWS	MHWN	MLWN	MLWS
0100	0600	0100	0600	5·5	4·4	2·2	0·8
1300	1800	1300	1800				
Differences LYME REGIS							
+0040	+0100	+0005	–0005	–1·2	–1·3	–0·5	–0·2

NOTE: Rise is relatively fast for the 1st hour after LW, but slackens for the next 1½ hrs, after which the rapid rate is resumed. There is often a stand of about 1½ hours at HW.

SHELTER Good in the hbr (dries up to 2.1m), except in strong E or SE winds when swell enters and it may be best to dry inside the North Wall. A stone pier, The Cobb, protects the W and S sides of the hbr; a rocky extension to E end of this pier covers at half tide and is marked by unlit PHM beacon. Access about HW±2½. Max LOA 9m in hbr. Dry out on clean, hard sand against Victoria Pier (0.3 – 1.3m) or in settled weather ⚓ as shown. 8 R cylindrical ⓥs lie in 1·5-2m. Beware numerous fishing floats and moorings.

NAVIGATION WPT 50°43'·03N 02°55'·69W, 116°/296° from/to front ldg lt 0·35M; best to be just inside W sector until hbr ent opens.

LIGHTS AND MARKS Ldg lts 296°, as chartlet; rear ldg lt hard to see against town lts. R flag on Victoria Pier = Gale warning in force.

RADIO TELEPHONE Call *Lyme Regis Hbr Radio* Ch 16; work Ch 14.

TELEPHONE (Dial code 01297) Hr Mr 442137 ☎/℻ 442137; MRSC (01305) 760439; ⊜ 0345 231110 (H24); Marinecall 09068 500457; Police 442603; Dr 445777.

FACILITIES **Harbour (The Cobb)** AB £7.00 (4.0-6.9m), £10.50 (>7m), ⓥs £5, Slip, M, FW, P & D (cans), ⛽ (mobile); **Lyme Regis SC** ☎ 442800, FW, Ⓢ, R, Bar; **Lyme Regis Power Boat Club** ☎ 443788, R, Bar; **Services:** ME, Sh, El, Ⓔ, CH, ACA (Axminster, 5M). **Town** EC Thurs; V, R, Bar, Gas, Gaz, ✉, Ⓑ, ▣, bus to Axminster ⇌, ✈ (Exeter).

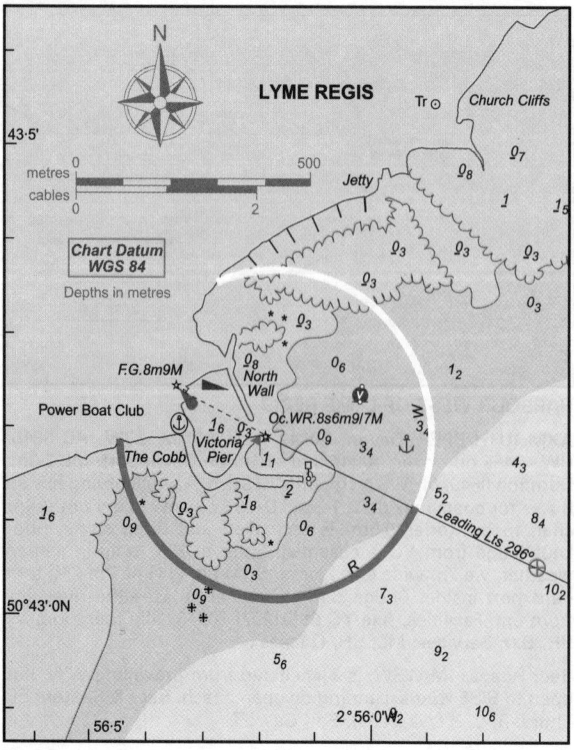

BRIDPORT *9.1.27*

Dorset **50°42'·55N 02°45'·86W** ❀◊◊✿✿✿

CHARTS AC *5601, 3315*; Imray C5; Stanfords 12; OS 193

TIDES –0500 Dover; ML 2·3; Duration 0650; Zone 0 (UT)

Standard Port DEVONPORT (⟵)

Times				Height (metres)			
High Water		Low Water		MHWS	MHWN	MLWN	MLWS
0100	0600	0100	0600	5·5	4·4	2·2	0·8
1300	1800	1300	1800				
Differences BRIDPORT (West Bay)							
+0025	+0040	0000	0000	–1·4	–1·4	–0·6	–0·2
CHESIL BEACH							
+0040	+0055	–0005	+0010	–1·6	–1·5	–0·5	0·0
CHESIL COVE							
+0035	+0050	–0010	+0005	–1·5	–1·6	–0·5	–0·2

NOTE: Rise is relatively fast for first hr after LW, thence a slackening for the next 1½ hrs, after which the rapid rise is resumed. There is often a stand of about 1½ hrs at HW.

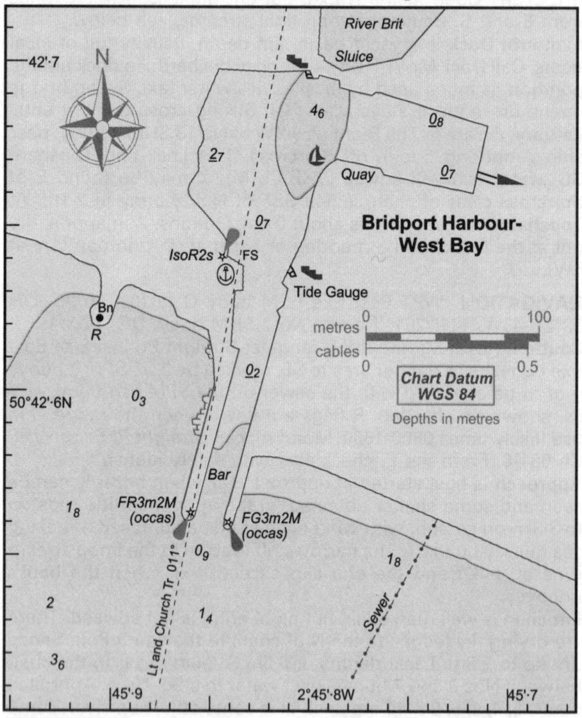

SHELTER Good in hbr, but the narrow (12m), 180m long drying ent, is dangerous in even moderate on-shore winds; access HW±2, in favourable weather. Do not attempt entry in >F4/5 S'lies. Hbr dries apart from pool and former coaster berths scoured 2·1m by sluice water. There is little space; call Hr Mr Ch 11 for berth or dry out at E end of Quay.

NAVIGATION WPT 50°41'·58N 02°46'·09W, 191°/011° from/to ent, 0·75M. No offshore dangers. SPM buoy, Fl, Y 5s, marks sewer outfall 5ca SSW of ent.

LIGHTS AND MARKS Ldg marks 011°, church tr on with W pier hd. At night Iso R 2s 9m 5M on Hr Mr's office in line 011° with FR 3m 2M on W pier. Entry sig: B ● = hbr closed.

RADIO TELEPHONE Call: *Bridport Radio* VHF Ch 11 16.

TELEPHONE (Dial code 01308) Hr Mr ☎ 423222, ℻ 251481; MRSC (01305) 760439; ⊜ 0345 231110 (H24); Marinecall 09068 500457; Police 422266; Dr 421109.

FACILITIES **Quay** AB £7 (4.0-6.9m), £10.50 (>7m), M, FW, Slip, P & D (cans), ▣, Sh, ME, V, R. **Town** CH, V, R, Bar, ✉, Ⓑ, ⇌ (bus to Axminster), ✈ (Exeter). Bridport town is 1½M N of hbr, known locally as West Bay. A new 230m west pier and extensive improvements should start in 2002.

Area 2

Central Southern England
Portland Bill to Selsey Bill

9.2.1	Index	Page 255
9.2.2	Area map	256
9.2.3	Channel: Tidal stream charts	258
9.2.4	Lights, buoys & waypoints	260
9.2.5	Passage information	266
9.2.6	Distance table	267
9.2.7	Portland Harbour, Standard Port, tidal curves	268
9.2.8	Portland: Tidal stream charts	272
9.2.9	Weymouth	274
9.2.10	Lulworth ranges Church Ope Cove Ringstead Bay Durdle Door Lulworth Cove Worbarrow Bay Chapman's Pool	275
9.2.11	Swanage Studland Bay	276
9.2.12	Special tidal problems between Swanage and Selsey Bill: Tidal curves	276
9.2.13	Poole Harbour: Times and heights of LW; heights of HW Wareham	280
9.2.14	Christchurch	287
9.2.15	Keyhaven	287
9.2.16	Needles Channel Alum Bay Totland Bay Freshwater Bay	288
9.2.17	The Solent	289
9.2.18	Solent Waypoints	292
9.2.19	Yarmouth	294
9.2.20	Lymington	295
9.2.21	Newtown River	296
9.2.22	Beaulieu River	297
9.2.23	Cowes and R Medina Folly Reach Newport	298
9.2.24	IoW: Tidal stream charts	300
9.2.25	Southampton, Standard Port, tidal curves	302
9.2.26	River Hamble Ashlett Creek Hill Head	304
9.2.27	Wootton Creek	309
9.2.28	Ryde	309
9.2.29	Bembridge	310
9.2.30	Portsmouth, Standard Port, tidal curves	314
9.2.31	Langstone Harbour	317
9.2.32	Chichester Harbour	318
9.2.33	Subfacts and Gunfacts diagram	320

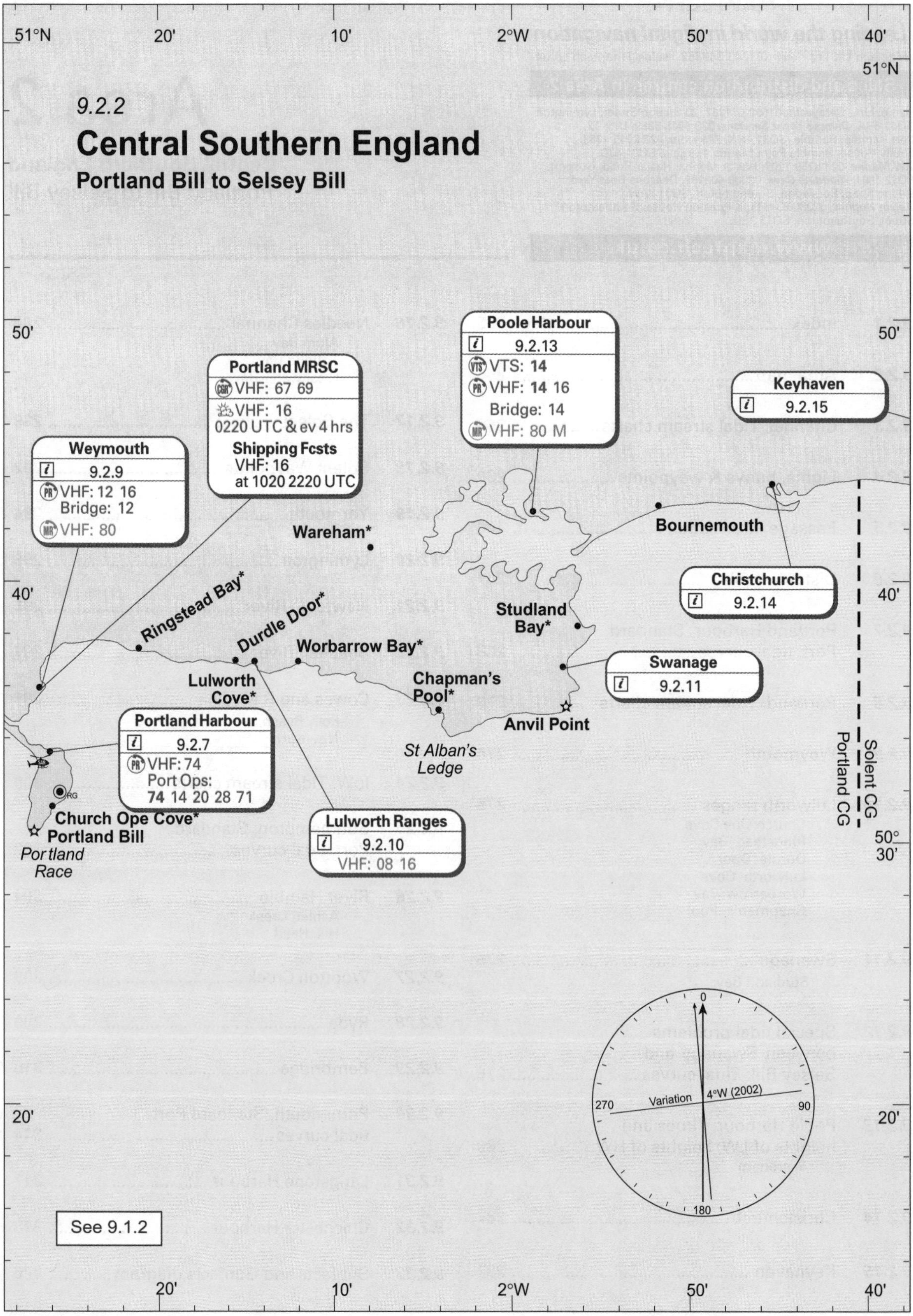
9.2.2
Central Southern England
Portland Bill to Selsey Bill
51°N
20'
10'
2°W
50'
40'
51°N
50'
40'
50° 30'
20'
Portland MRSC
VHF: 67 69
VHF: 16
0220 UTC & ev 4 hrs
Shipping Fcsts
VHF: 16
at 1020 2220 UTC
Poole Harbour
9.2.13
VTS: 14
VHF: 14 16
Bridge: 14
VHF: 80 M
Keyhaven
9.2.15
Weymouth
9.2.9
VHF: 12 16
Bridge: 12
VHF: 80
Wareham*
Bournemouth
Christchurch
9.2.14
Ringstead Bay*
Durdle Door*
Worbarrow Bay*
Studland Bay*
Lulworth Cove*
Chapman's Pool*
Swanage
9.2.11
Anvil Point
Portland Harbour
9.2.7
VHF: 74
Port Ops:
74 14 20 28 71
St Alban's Ledge
RG
Church Ope Cove*
Portland Bill
Portland Race
Lulworth Ranges
9.2.10
VHF: 08 16
Solent CG
Portland CG
0
270
90
180
Variation 4°W (2002)
See 9.1.2

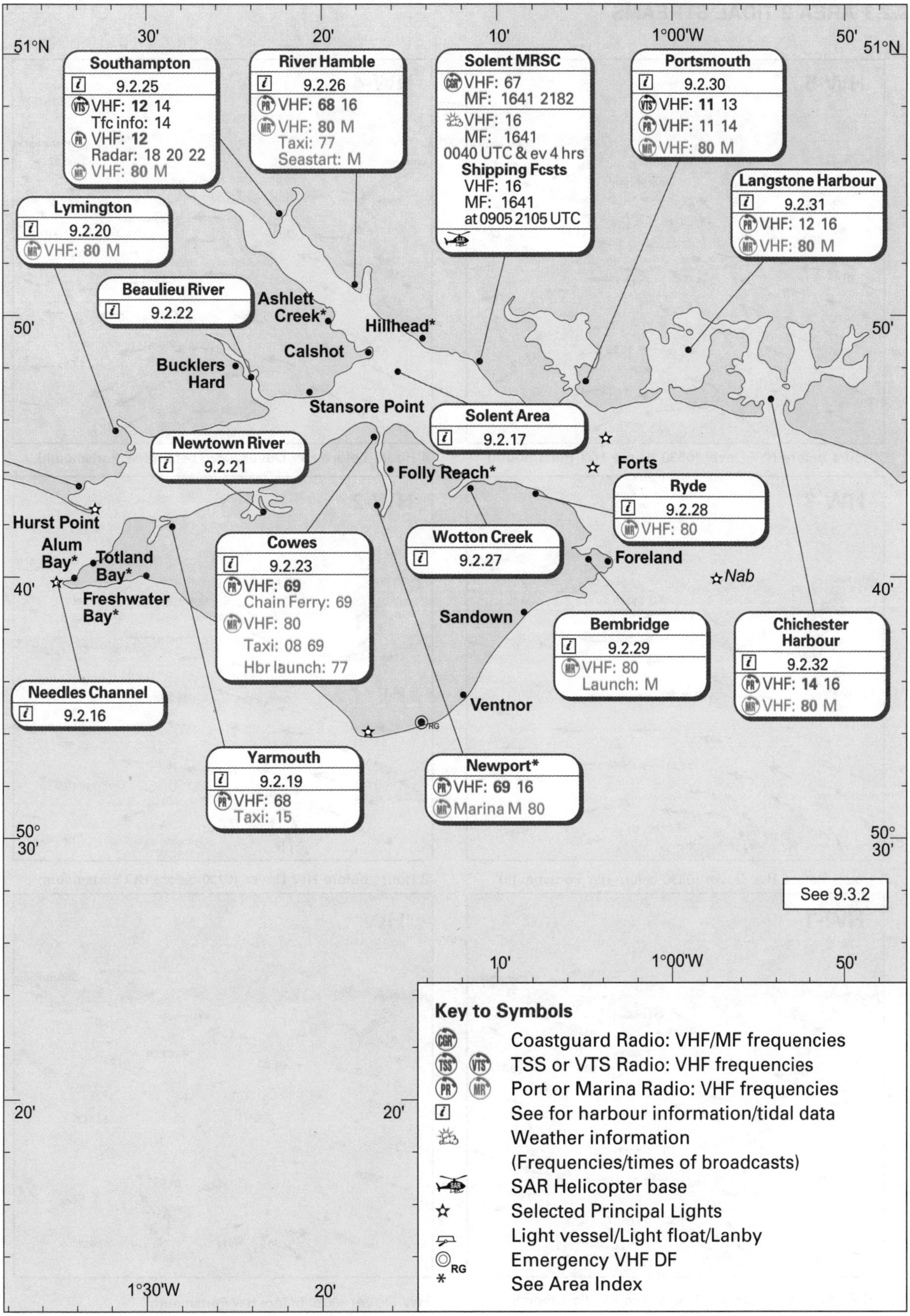
51°N
30'
20'
10'
1°00'W
50'
51°N
Southampton
9.2.25
VHF: 12 14
Tfc info: 14
VHF: 12
Radar: 18 20 22
VHF: 80 M
River Hamble
9.2.26
VHF: 68 16
VHF: 80 M
Taxi: 77
Seastart: M
Solent MRSC
VHF: 67
MF: 1641 2182
VHF: 16
MF: 1641
0040 UTC & ev 4 hrs
Shipping Fcsts
VHF: 16
MF: 1641
at 0905 2105 UTC
Portsmouth
9.2.30
VHF: 11 13
VHF: 11 14
VHF: 80 M
Langstone Harbour
9.2.31
VHF: 12 16
VHF: 80 M
Lymington
9.2.20
VHF: 80 M
Beaulieu River
9.2.22
Ashlett Creek*
Hillhead*
Calshot
Bucklers Hard
Stansore Point
Solent Area
9.2.17
Forts
Newtown River
9.2.21
Folly Reach*
Ryde
9.2.28
VHF: 80
Hurst Point
Alum Bay*
Totland Bay*
Freshwater Bay*
Cowes
9.2.23
VHF: 69
Chain Ferry: 69
VHF: 80
Taxi: 08 69
Hbr launch: 77
Wotton Creek
9.2.27
Foreland
Nab
Sandown
Bembridge
9.2.29
VHF: 80
Launch: M
Chichester Harbour
9.2.32
VHF: 14 16
VHF: 80 M
Needles Channel
9.2.16
Ventnor
RG
Yarmouth
9.2.19
VHF: 68
Taxi: 15
Newport*
VHF: 69 16
Marina M 80
50' 40'
50° 30'
See 9.3.2
20'
1°30'W
40'

Key to Symbols

- (CGR) Coastguard Radio: VHF/MF frequencies
- (TSS) (VTS) TSS or VTS Radio: VHF frequencies
- (PR) (MR) Port or Marina Radio: VHF frequencies
- [i] See for harbour information/tidal data
- Weather information (Frequencies/times of broadcasts)
- SAR Helicopter base
- ☆ Selected Principal Lights
- Light vessel/Light float/Lanby
- ◎RG Emergency VHF DF
- * See Area Index

9.2.3 AREA 2 TIDAL STREAMS

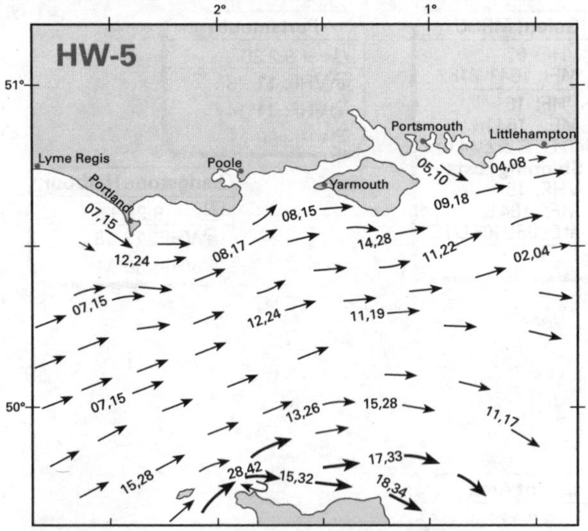

5 Hours before HW Dover (0530 before HW Portsmouth)

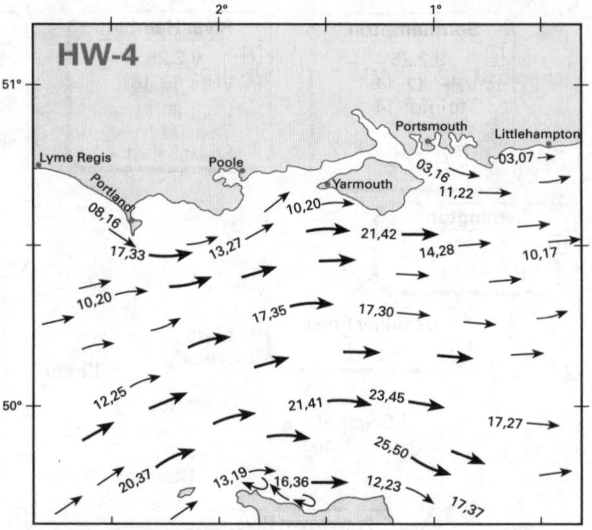

4 Hours before HW Dover (0430 before HW Portsmouth)

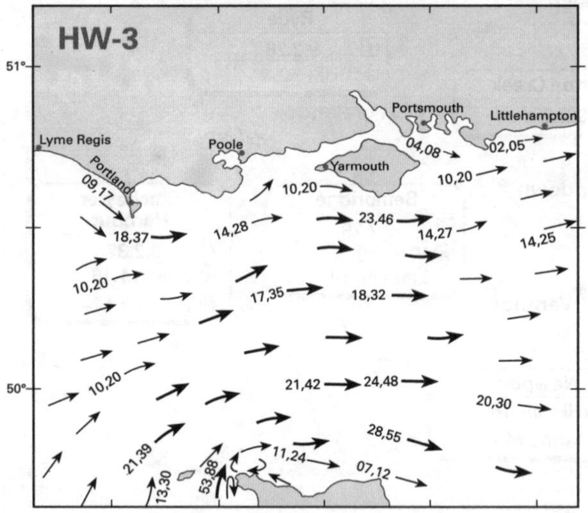

3 Hours before HW Dover (0330 before HW Portsmouth)

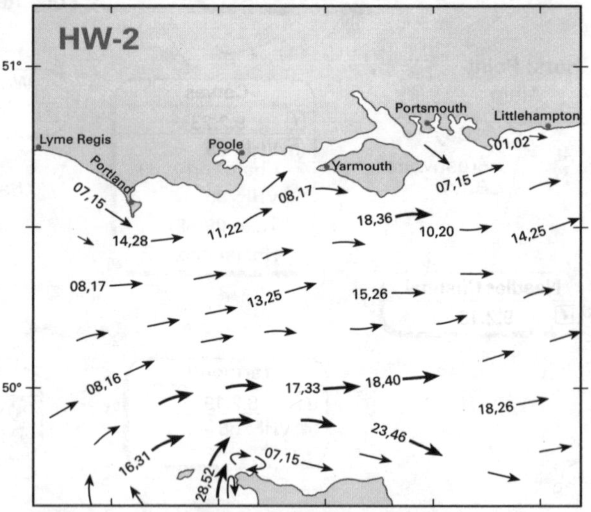

2 Hours before HW Dover (0230 before HW Portsmouth)

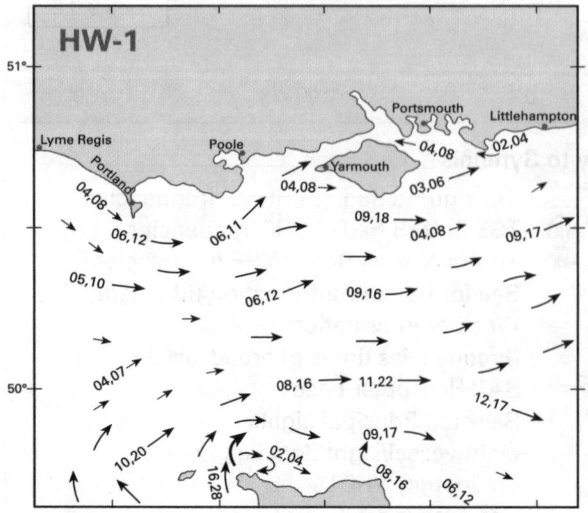

1 Hour before HW Dover (0130 before HW Portsmouth)

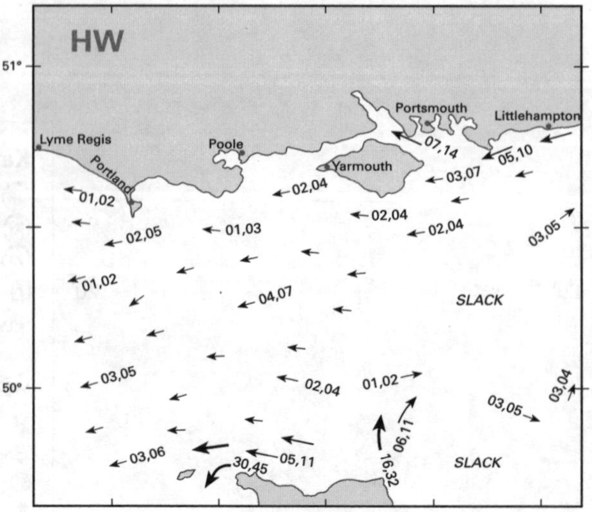

HW Dover (0030 before HW Portsmouth)

Westward 9.1.3 Portland 9.2.8 Isle of Wight 9.2.24 Eastward 9.3.3 Southward 9.16.3 Channel Is 9.14.3

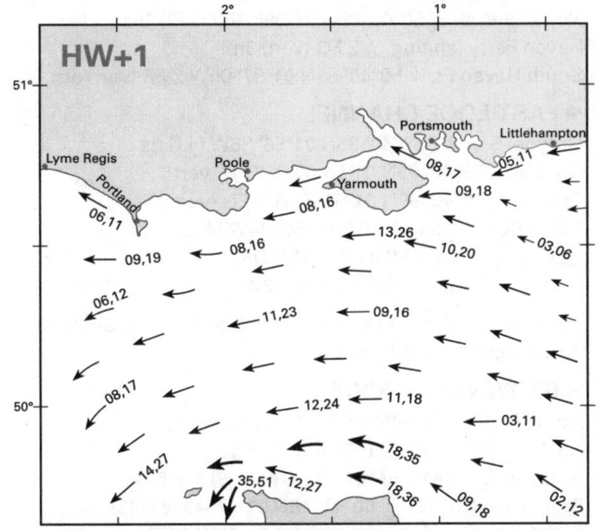

1 Hour after HW Dover (0030 after HW Portsmouth)

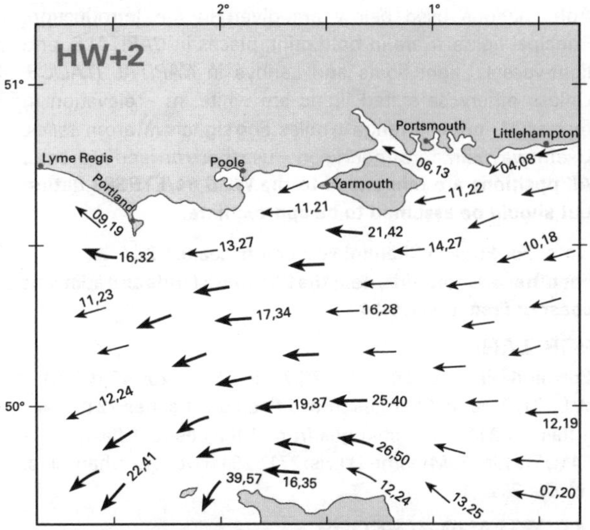

2 Hours after HW Dover (0130 after HW Portsmouth)

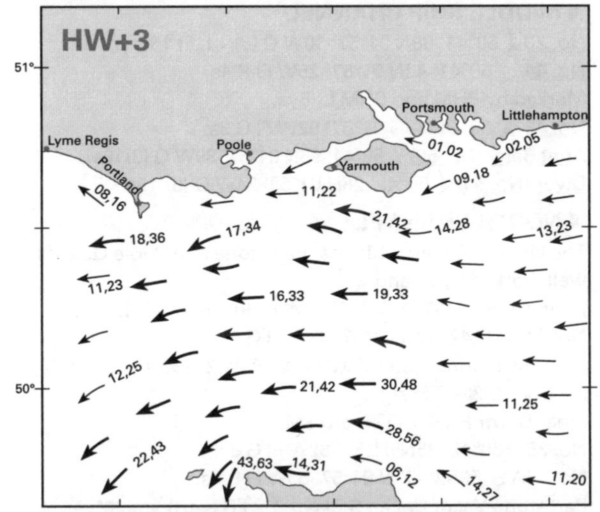

3 Hours after HW Dover (0230 after HW Portsmouth)

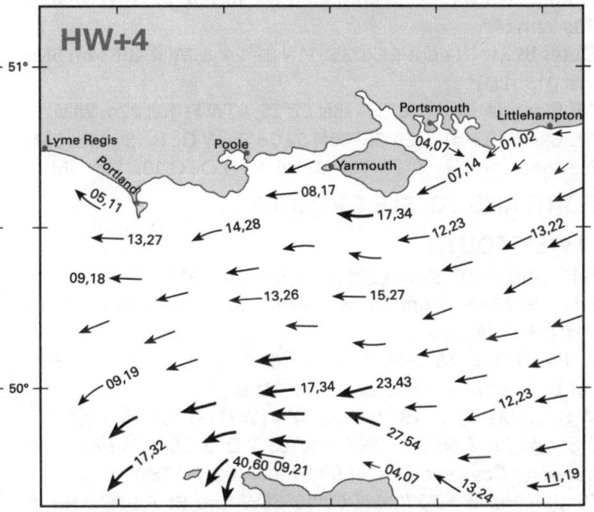

4 Hours after HW Dover (0330 after HW Portsmouth)

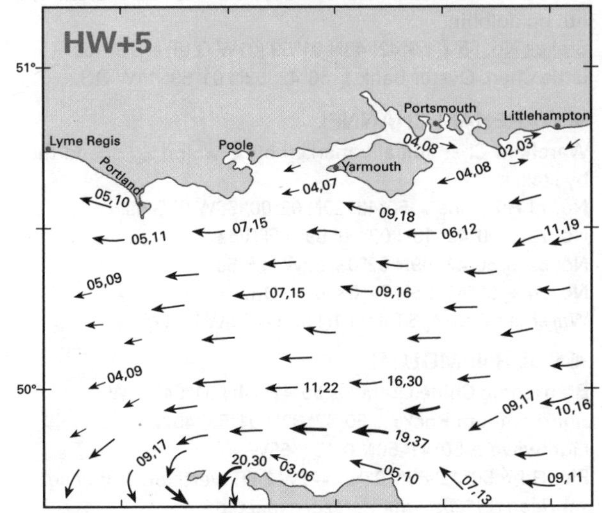

5 Hours after HW Dover (0430 after HW Portsmouth)

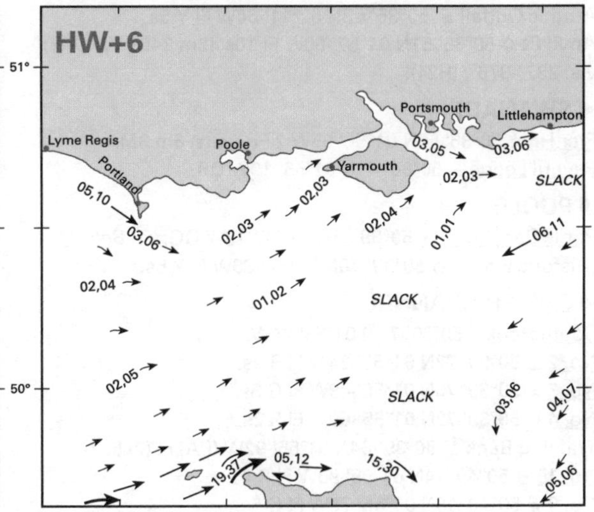

6 Hours after HW Dover (0530 after HW Portsmouth)

9.2.4 LIGHTS, BUOYS AND WAYPOINTS

Abbreviations used below are given in the Introduction. Principal lights ☆ are in **bold** print, places in CAPITALS, and light-vessels, light floats and Lanbys in *CAPITAL ITALICS*. Unless otherwise stated lights are white. m – elevation in metres; M – nominal range in miles. Fog signals are in *italics*. Useful waypoints are underlined – use those on land with care. **All positions are referenced to the WGS 84/ETRS89 datum but should be assumed to be approximate.**

Note: For English Channel Waypoints see 9.1.7.
For other offshore aids, near the Channel Islands and adjacent coast of France, see 9.14.4.

PORTLAND

Portland Bill ☆ 50°30'·85N 02°27'·38W Fl (4) 20s 43m **25M**; W ○ Tr, R band. Changes from 1 flash to 4 flashes 221°-244°, 4 flashes 244°-117°, changes from 4 flashes to 1 flash 117°-141°; FR 19m 13M (same Tr) vis: 271°-291° over The Shambles. *Dia 30s.*

◄ PORTLAND HARBOUR

Outer Bkwtr D Head (S end) ☆ 50°34'·18N 02°25'·23W ☆ Oc R 30s 12m 5M.
Outer Bkwtr (N end) ☆ 50°35'·11N 02°24'·87W ☆ QR 14m 5M; vis: 013°-268°.
NE Bkwtr (A Hd) ☆ 50°35'·16N 02°25'·07W Fl 10s 22m 20M.
NE Bkwtr (B Hd) ☆ 50°35'·65N 02°25'·88W Oc R 15s 11m 5M.
Northern Arm ☆ 50°35'·78N 02°25'·96W Oc G 10s 11m 5M.

PORTLAND TO ISLE OF WIGHT

◄ WEYMOUTH

S Pier Hd ☆ 50°36'·57N 02°26'·49W Q 10m 9M.
Ldg Lts 239·6° Front 50°36'·46N 02°26'·87W, both FR 5/7m 4M; R ♦ on W post.
N Pier Hd ☆ 50°36'·59N 02°26'·63W 2 FG (vert) 9m 6M; *Bell* (when vessels expected); tfc sigs.
W Shambles 50°29'·78N 02°24'·41W Q (9) 15s; *Bell.*
E Shambles 50°30'·78N 02°20'·08W Q (3) 10s; *Bell.*
Lulworth Cove ent, E Point 50°37'·00N 02°14'·78W.
Bindon Hill ☆ 50°37'·33N 02°13'·65W and St Alban's Hd ☆ 50°34'·75N 02°03'·40W Iso R 2s (when firing taking place).
Atomic Outfall 50°35'·03N 02°11'·64W Fl Y 5s.
Anvil Pt ☆ 50°35'·51N 01°57'·60W Fl 10s 45m **24M**; W ○ Tr; vis: 237°-076°; (H24).

◄ SWANAGE

Pier Hd ☆ 50°36'·56N 01°56'·95W 2 FR (vert) 6m 3M.
Peveril Ledge 50°36'·41N 01°56'·10W QR.

◄ POOLE

Poole Bar (No. 1) 50°39'·31N 01°55'·16W QG; *Bell.*
(Historic wreck) 50°39'·70N 01°54'·86W Fl Y 5s.

◄ SWASH CHANNEL

South Hook 50°39'·78N 01°55'·24W.
No. 2 50°39'·22N 01°55'·24W Fl R 2s.
No. 3 50°39'·76N 01°55'·49W Fl G 3s.
No. 4 50°39'·72N 01°55'·60W Fl R 2s.
Training Bank 50°39'·84N 01°55'·92W (PA) Fl (2) 5s o
No. 10 50°40'·14N 01°55'·90W Fl R 4s.
No. 9 50°40'·19N 01°55'·78W Fl G 5s.
No. 11 (Hook Sand) 50°40'·50N 01°56'·13W Fl G 3s.
No. 12 (Channel) 50°40'·45N 01°56'·26W Fl R 2s.
No. 14 50°40'·82N 01°56'·82W Fl R 4s.
No. 13 Swash 50°48'·88N 01°56'·70W Q (9) 15s.
Haven Ferry landing, ☆ 2 FG (vert) 3m.
South Haven Pt, ☆ 50°40'·81N 01°57'·00W 2 FR (vert) 5m.

◄ EAST LOOE CHANNEL

Groyne, S end 50°40'·95N 01°56'·86W Fl G 3s.
Groyne 50°40'·95N 01°56'·73W 2 FG (vert).
Groyne 50°40'·99N 01°56'·59W 2 FG (vert).
North Hook 50°41'·01N 01°56'·44W Fl (2) R 5s.
E Looe 50°41'·25N 01°55'·97W QR.
East Hook 50°40'·58W 01°55'·23W.

South Deep. Marked by lit and unlit Bns from ent South of Brownsea Castle to Furzey Is.

◄ BROWNSEA ROADS

No. 18A 50°40'·94N 01°57'·17W Fl R 4s.
No.18 50°41'·06N 01°57'·40W Fl R 5s.
N Haven 50°41'·15N 01°57'·17W Q (9) 15s 5m.
Brownsea (No. 42) 50°41'·16N 01°57'·41W Q (3) 10s.
RMYC Pier Hds ☆ 50°41'·35N 01°56'·83W 2 FG (vert) 2M.

◄ MIDDLE SHIP CHANNEL

No. 20 50°41'·38N 01°57'·10W Q (6) + L Fl 15s; *Bell.*
No. 44 50°41'·43N 01°57'·25W Fl R 4s
Marked by PHM and SHM Lt Bys.
No. 43 50°41'·68N 01°57'·02W Fl G 3s.
Aunt Betty (No. 50) 50°41'·96N 01°57'·39W Q (3)10s.
Diver (No. 51) 50°42'·28N 01°58'·34W Q (9) 15s.

◄ NORTH CHANNEL

The chan to Salterns Marina, Parkstone and Poole Quay is well marked by and
Bullpit 50°41'·72N 01°56'·71W Q (9) 15s 7m 4M.
No. 31 50°42'·17N 01°57'·07W Fl G 5s.
Salterns Marina Outer Bkwtr Hd ☆ 50°42'·23N 01°57'·10W 2 FR (vert) 2M; Tfc sigs.
Inner Bkwtr Hd ☆ 2 FG (vert) 3M.
No. 35 50°42'·35N 01°57'·62W Fl G 5s.
No. 38A 50°42'·30N 01°57'·63W Fl R 4s.
Parkstone Yacht Haven S Bkwtr ☆ 2 FR (vert) 4m 2M.
Parkstone YC platform ☆ 50°42'·37N 01°58'·08W Q 8m 1M; hut on dolphin.
Stakes No. 55 50°42'·43N 01°59'·01W Q (6) + L Fl 15s.
Little Chan, Oyster Bank 50°42'·63N 01°59'·11W QG.

◄ WAREHAM CHANNEL

Wareham Chan initially marked by and , and then by stakes.
No. 71 Hutchins 50°42'·20N 02°00'·56W Fl G 5s.
No. 72 50°42'·16N 02°00'·59W Fl R 5s.
No. 82 50°42'·09N 02°03'·22W Fl R 5s.
No. 84 50°41'·95N 02°03'·64W QR.
Wareham R Bn 50°41'·61N 02°04'·58W Fl R 4s.

◄ BOURNEMOUTH

Branksome Chine Outfall 50°42'·24N 01°54'·31W.
Bournemouth Rocks 50°42'·32N 01°53'·40W.
Lightwave 50°41'·50N 01°51'·68W.
Pier Hd ☆ 50°42'·83N 01°52'·47W 2 FR (vert) 9m 1M; W col; *Reed (2)120s* when vessel expected.
Dorset Yacht Mark 50°40'·31N 01°52'·45W.

Boscombe Pier Hd 50°43'·08W 01°50'·57W 2 FR (vert) 7m 1M.
Boscombe Outfall 50°42'·89N 01°50'·40W.
Portman Rayine Outfall 50°42'·92N 01°49'·11W.
Hengistbury Head, groyne 50°42'·66N 01°44'·94W.
Christchurch Ledge 50°41'·53N 01°41'·69W (Apr-Oct).

NOTE: **For waypoints of navigational buoys and racing marks in Solent area, see 9.2.18.**

WESTERN APPROACHES TO THE SOLENT

◀ NEEDLES CHANNEL

Needles Fairway 50°38'·24N 01°38'·98W L Fl 10s; *Whis.*
SW Shingles 50°39'·35N 01°37'·39W Fl R 2·5s.
Bridge 50°39'·63N 01°36'·88W VQ (9) 10s; Racon (T).
Needles 50°39'·73N 01°35'·50W Oc (2) WRG 20s 24m **W17M**, R14M, R13M G14M; ○ Tr, R band and lantern; vis: Rshore-300°, W300°-083°; R (unintens) 083°-212°, W212°-217°, G217°-224°. *Horn (2) 30s;* H24.
Shingles Elbow 50°40'·32N 01°36'·06W Fl (2) R 5s.
Mid Shingles 50°41'·20N 01°34'·71W; Fl (3) R 10s.
Totland Pier Hd 50°41'·00N 01°32'·75W 2 FG (vert) 6m 2M.
Warden 50°41'·46N 01°33'·61W Fl G 2·5s; *Bell.*
NE Shingles 50°41'·96N 01°33'·41W Q (3) 10s.
Hurst Point Ldg Lts 042°. Front 50°42'·48N 01°33'·03W FL (4) WR 15s 23m W13M, R11M; W ○ Tr; vis: W(unintens) 080°-104°, W234°-244°, R244°-250°, W250°-053°.
Same Tr, Iso WRG 4s 19m **W21M, R18M, G17M**; vis: G038·6°-040·6°, W040·6°-041·6°, R041·6°-043·6°; By day W7M, R5M, G5M.

◀ NORTH CHANNEL

North Head 50°42'·69N 01°35'·52W Fl (3) G 10s.

◀ THE WEST SOLENT

Sconce 50°42'·53N 01°31'·43W Q; *Bell.*
Fort Victoria Pier 50°42'·45N 01°31'·16W 2 FG (vert) 4M.
Black Rock 50°42'·58N 01°30'·63W Fl G 5s.

◀ YARMOUTH

West Fairway 50°42'·57N 01°30'·17W Fl G 2s.
East Fairway 50°42'·57N 01°29'·93W Fl R 2s.
Yarmouth Road 50°42'·53N 01°30'·17W Fl Y 4s.
Pier Head, centre, 50°42'·51N 01°29'·97W 2 FR (vert) 2M; G col. High intensity FW (occas).
Ldg Lts 187·6° Front 50°42'·36N 01°30'·06 W FG 5m 2M, Rear, 63m from front, FG 9m 2M; both W ◊.
Yarmouth 2 50°42'·89N 01°29'·49W Fl Y 2·5s; (Apr-Oct).
Yarmouth 4 50°42'·88N 01°28'·50W Fl Y 2·5s; (Apr-Oct).

◀ LYMINGTON

Jack in the Basket 50°44'·27N 01°30'·57W Fl R 2s 9m.
Ldg Lts 319·5°. Front, 50°45'·19N 01°31'·65W FR 12m 8M; vis: 309·5°-329·5°. Rear, 363m from front, FR 17m 8M.
Cross Boom No. 2 50°44'·36N 01°30'·58W Fl R 2s 4m 3M; R □ on pile.
No. 1 50°44'·41N 01°30'·48W Fl G 2s 2m 3M; G △ on pile.
Lymington Yacht Haven Ldg Lts 244°. Front 50°45'·09N 01°31'·53W FY 4m; R △. Rear, 22m from front, FY 6m; R ▽.

◀ SOLENT MARKS

Berthon 50°44'·20N 01°29'·22W Fl 4s; (Mar-Dec).
Durn's Pt obstn posts, S end 50°45'·40N 01°27'·06W QR; dolphin.
Hamstead Ledge 50°43'·87N 01°26'18W Fl (2) G 5s.
Newtown River 50°43'·75N 01°24'·91W Fl R 4s.
W Lepe 50°45'·24N 01°24'·09W Fl R 5s.
Salt Mead 50°44'·52N 01°23'·04W Fl (3) G 10s.
Gurnard Ledge 50°45'·52N 01°20'·59W Fl (4) G 15s.
E Lepe 50°46'·12N 01°20'·90W Fl (2) R 5s; *Bell.*
Lepe Spit 50°46'·78N 01°20'·64W Q (6) + L Fl 15s.
Gurnard 50°46'·22N 01°18'·84W Q.

◀ BEAULIEU RIVER

Millenium Dir Lt 334°. 50°47'·12N 01°21'·90W Dir Q WRG 4s 13m W4M, R3M, G3M; vis: G321°-331°, W331°-337°, R337°-347°.
Beaulieu Spit, E end 50°46'·85N 01°21'·76W Fl R 5s 3M; R dolphin; vis: 277°-037°.
No. 1 50°46'·91N 01°21'·70W.
No 2 50°46'·92N 01°21'·78W.
Ent Chan Bn Nos. 5, 9, 19, and 21, all Fl G 4s; Bn Nos 12 and 20, both Fl R 4s.
Bucklers Hard Marina 50°48'·04N 01°25'·37W. 2 FR (vert).

CENTRAL SOLENT AND SOUTHAMPTON WATER

◀ SOLENT MARKS

Lepe Spit 50°46'·78N 01°20'·64W Q (6) + L Fl 15s.
NE Gurnard 50°47'·06N 01°19'·42W Fl (3) R 10s.
W Bramble 50°47'·20N 01°18'·65W VQ (9) 10s; *Bell;* Racon (T).
Thorn Knoll 50°47'·50N 01°18'·44W Fl G 5s.
Bourne Gap 50°47'·83N 01°18'·34W Fl R 3s.
West Knoll 50°47'·55N 01°17'·77W.
North Thorn 50°47'·91N 01°17'·84W QG.
Stanswood Outfall 50°48'·26N 01°18'·82W Iso R 10s 6m 5M; 4 FR Lts; *Horn (1) 20s.*

◀ CALSHOT REACH

East Knoll 50°47'·96N 01°16'·83W.
CALSHOT SPIT 50°48'·35N 01°17'·64W Fl 5s 12m 11M; R hull, Lt Tr amidships; *Horn (2) 60s.*
Calshot 50°48'·44N 01°17'·03W VQ; *Bell (1) 30s.*
Castle Point 50°48'·71N 01°17'·67W IQ R 10s.
Reach 50°49'·05N 01°17'·65W Fl (3) G 10s.
Black Jack 50°49'·13N 01°18'·09W Fl (2) R 4s.
Hook 50°49'·52N 01°18'·30W QG; *Horn (1) 15s.*
Coronation 50°49'·55N 01°17'·62W Fl Y 5s.
Fawley Chan No. 2 50°49'·49N 01°18'·84W Fl R 3s.
Bald Head 50°49'·90N 01°18'·25W.

◀ RIVER HAMBLE

Hamble Pt 50°50'·15N 01°18'·66W Q (6) + L Fl 15s.
No. 1 50°50'·34N 01°18'·65W QG 2m 2M.
No. 2 50°50'·39N 01°18'·77W Q (3) 10s 2m 2M.
No. 3 50°50'·45N 01°18'·65W Fl G 4s 2m 2M.
No. 4 50°50'·49N 01°18'·83W Fl R 4s 2m 2M.
No. 6 50°50'·63N 01°18'·83W QR 2m 2M.
Hamble Common Dir Lt 352°, 50°51'·00N 01°18'·84W Oc (2) WRG 12s 5m W4M; R4M; G4M; vis: G349°-351°, W351°-353°, R353°-355°.
Pile 50°51'·01N 01°18'·44W Fl (2+1) R 10s 2M.
Sailing Club Dir Lt 028·9° 50°51'·10N 01°18'·34W Iso WRG 6s 5m W4M, R4M, G4M: vis: G025·9°-027·9°, W027·9°-029·9°, R029·9°-031·9°.
Hamble Pt Quay 50°51'·02N 01°18'·56W 2 FR.
RSYC offshore pontoon 50°51'·50N 01°18'·70W Fl R 4s.

◀ SOUTHAMPTON WATER

Esso Marine terminal, SE end ☆ 50°50'·06N 01°19'·42W 2 FR (vert) 9m 10M.
BP Hamble Jetty ☆ 50°50'·92N 01°19'·42W 2 FG (vert) 5/3m 2M (on each side of the 4 dolphins).
Greenland 50°51'·11N 01°20'·38W IQ G 10s.
Cadland 50°51'·02N 01°20'·54W Fl R 3s.
After Barn 50°51'·53N 01°20'·82W.
Deans Lake 50°51'·40N 01°21'·59W.
Lains Lake 50°51'·59N 01°21'·65W Fl (2) R 4s.
Hound 50°51'·68N 01°21'·52W Fl (3) G 10s.
Netley 50°52'·03N 01°21'·81W Fl G 3s.
Deans Elbow 50°52'·16N 01°22'·76W Oc R 4s.
NW Netley 50°52'·31N 01°22'·73W Fl G 7s.
Moorhead 50°52'·55N 01°22'·90W.
Weston Shelf 50°52'·71N 01°23'·26W Fl (3) G 15s.

◀ ASHLETT CREEK

Ashlett No. 2 50°49'·97N 01°19'·62W.
Ashlett No. 4 50°49'·93N 01°19'·76W.

◀ HYTHE

Hythe Pier Hd ☆ 50°52'·49N 01°23'·61W 2 FR (vert) 12m 5M.
Hythe Marina Ent 50°52'·63N 01°23'·88W Q (3) 10s.
Hythe Pile 50°52'·62N 01°23'·867W Fl (2) R 5s.
Hythe Lock ent 50°52'·55N 01°23'·98W FG.
Hythe Lock ent 50°52'·54N 01°23'·96W FR; SS Tfc.
Hythe Knock 50°52'·83N 01°23'·81W Fl R 3s.

◀ SOUTHAMPTON/RIVER ITCHEN

Swinging Ground No. 1 50°53'·00N 01°23'·44W Oc G 4s.
E side. No. 1 50°53'·15N 01°23'·40W QG.
No. 2 50°53'·29N 01°23'·38W Fl G 5s 2M.
No. 3 50°53'·48N 01°23'·28W Fl G 7s.
No. 4 50°53'·62N 01°23'·16W QG 4m 2M.
Ocean Village Marina ☆ 50°53'·70N 01°23'·36W 2 FR (vert).
Itchen Bridge. FW on bridge span each side marks main chan. 2 FG (vert) 2M each side on E pier. 2 FR (vert) 2M each side on W pier.
Crosshouse 50°54'·04N 01°23'·20W Oc R 5s 5m 2M.
Chapel 50°54'·14N 01°23'·22W Fl G 3s 5m 3M.
Shamrock Quay SW end ☆ 50°54'·49N 01°22'·93W 2 FR (vert) 4m, and NE end 2 FR (vert) 4m.
No. 5 50°54'·50N 01°22'·76W Fl G 3s.
No. 6 50°54'·58N 01°22'·63W Fl R 3s.
No. 7 50°54'·60N 01°22'·49W Fl (2) G 5s.
No. 9 50°54'·73N 01°22'·48W Fl (4) G 10s.
Kemps Marina Jetty Hd ☆ 50°54'·82N 01°22'·66W 2 FG (vert) 5m 1M.

◀ SOUTHAMPTON/RIVER TEST

Queen Elizabeth II terminal, S end ☆ 50°53'·00N 01°23'·71W 4 FG (vert) 16m 3M.
Gymp 50°53'·17N 01°24'·30W QR.
Lower Foul Gnd 50°53'·26N 01°24'·55W Fl (2) R 10s.
Town Quay Ldg Lts 329°, both FY 12/22m 3/2M (occas).
Town Quay 50°53'·55N 01°24'·33W 2 FG (vert) & FY (occas).
Town Quay Marina Ent ☆ 50°53'·64N 01°24'·24W 2 FG (vert).
Gymp Elbow 50°53'·50N 01°24'·68W Oc R 4s.
Upper Foul Gnd 50°53'·53N 01°24'·89W Fl (2) R 10s.
Pier Hd 50°53'·67N 01°24'·66W QG.
Dibden Bay 50°53'·70N 01°24'·92W Q.
Swinging Gnd No. 2 50°53'·82N 01°25'·12W Fl (2) R 10s.
Cracknore 50°53'·94N 01°25'·20W Oc R 8s.
Marchwood 50°53'·98N 01°25'·57W Fl Y 2·5s.
Swinging Gnd No. 6 50°54'·22N 01°26'·14W Fl R 3s.
Millbrook 50°54'·12N 01°26'·82W QR.
Bury 50°54'·14N 01°27'·12W Fl R 5s.
Eling 50°54'·47N 01°27'·85W Q (3) 10s.

THE EAST SOLENT

◀ NORTH CHANNEL/HILLHEAD

Calshot 50°48'·44N 01°17'·03W VQ; *Bell (1) 30s.*
Hillhead 50°48'·07N 01°16'·00W Fl R 2·5s.
Hillhead 50°49'·06N 01°14'·78W; Or Bn.
E Bramble 50°47'·23N 01°13'·64W VQ (3) 5s; *Bell.*

◀ COWES

South Bramble 50°46'·98N 01°17'·72W Fl G 2·5s.
Prince Consort 50°46'·42N 01°17'·55W VQ.
Prince Consort Shoal 50°46'·29N 01°17'·71W Fl (4) Y 10s.
No. 1 50°46'·07N 01°18'·03W Fl G 3s.
No. 2 50°46'·07N 01°17'·87W QR.
Trinity House 50°46'·13N 01°17'·23W Fl Y 5s.
E Bkwtr Hd ☆ 50°45'·88N 01°17'·52W Fl R 3s 3M.
No. 4 50°45'·85N 01°17'·72W Fl (3) R 5s.
Cowes Yachthaven, North end ☆ 50°45'·72N 01°17'·69W 2 FG (vert) 6m.
No. 6 50°45'·66N 01°17'·56W Fl (2) R 5s.
E Cowes Marina N end ☆ 50°45'·11N 01°17'·51W 2 FR (vert).

◀ EASTERN SOLENT MARKS

West Ryde Mid 50°46'·48N 01°15'·79W Q (9) 15s.
Norris 50°45'·97N 01°15'·51W Fl (3) R 10s.
North Ryde Mid 50°46'·61N 01°14'·31W Fl (4) R 20s.
South Ryde Mid 50°46'·13N 01°14'·16W Fl G 5s.
Peel Bank 50°45'·49N 01°13'·35W Fl (2) R 5s.
Peel Wreck 50°44'·90N 01°13'·41W.
SE Ryde Mid 50°45'·93N 01°12'·10W VQ (6)+L Fl 10s.
NE Ryde Mid 50°46'·21N 01°11'·88W Fl (2) R 10s.

◀ WOOTTON

Wotton Beacon 50°44'·53N 01°12'·13W Q 1M; (NB).
Dir Lt 50°44'·03N 01°12'·86W Oc WRG 10s vis: G220·8°-224·3°, W224°-225·8°, R225·8°-230·8°.
No. 1 50°44'·40N 01°12'·34W Fl (2) G 5s.
No. 2 50°44'·25N 01°12'·47W Fl R 5s.
No. 3 50°44'·28N 01°12'·52W Fl G 3s.

◀ EASTERN SOLENT MARKS

Mother Bank 50°45'·49N 01°11'·21W Fl R 3s.
Browndown 50°46'·57N 01°10'·95W Fl G 15s.
Ft Gilkicker ☆ 50°46'·43N 01°08'·47W Oc G 10s 7M.

◀ RYDE

Ryde Pier ☆, 50°44'·34N 01°09'·72W NW corner, N and E corner marked by 2 FR (vert). In fog FY from N corner, vis: 045°-165°, 200°-320°.
Leisure Hbr E side ☆ 50°43'·99N 01°09'·29W 2 FR (vert) 7m 1M. FY 6m shown when depth of water in Hbr greater than 1m; 2 FY 6m when depth exceeds 1·5m, and 2 FY when depth of water greater than 1·5m.
Hbr W side ☆ 50°43'·97N 01°09'·33W Fl G 3s 7m 1M.

◀ EASTERN SOLENT MARKS

N Sturbridge 50°45'·33N 01°08'·23W VQ.

SW Mining Gnd 50°44'·66N 01°08'·04W.
NE Mining Gnd 50°44'·74N 01°06'·39W Fl Y 10s.

◀ PORTSMOUTH APPROACHES

Horse Sand Ft 50°45'·01N 01°04'·34W Iso G 2s 21m 8M.
Saddle 50°45'·20N 01°04'·98W VQ (3) G 10s.
Horse Sand 50°45'·53N 01°05'·27W Fl G 2·5s.
Outer Spit 50°45'·58N 01°05'·50W Q (6) + L Fl 15s.
Boyne 50°46'·15N 01°05'·26W Fl G 5s.
Spit Refuge 50°46'·15N 01°05'·46W Fl R 5s.
Spit Sand Fort ☆ 50°46'·24N 01°05'·94W Fl R 5s 18m 7M.
Castle (NB) 50°46'·45N 01°05'·38W Fl (2) G 6s.
Southsea Castle N corner 50°46'·69N 01°05'·33W Iso 2s 16m 11M, W stone Tr, B band; vis: 337°-071°.
Southsea Castle Dir Lt 001·5° 50°46'·69N 01°05'·33W Dir WRG 11m W13M, R5M, G5M; same structure; vis: FG 351·5°-357·5°, Al WG 357·5°-000° (W phase incr with brg), FW 000°-003°, AlWR 003°-005·5° (R phase incr with brg), FR 005·5°-011·5°.
Ridge 50°46'·44N 01°05'·65W Fl (2) R 6s.
No. 1 Bar (NB) 50°46'·77N 01°05'·81W Fl (3) G 10s.
No. 2 50°46'·69N 01°05'·97W Fl (3) R 10s.
No. 3 50°47'·08N 01°06'·24W QG.
No. 4 50°47'·01N 01°06'·36W QR.
Victoria Pile 50°47'·35N 01°06'·49W Oc G 15s 1M.

◀ PORTSMOUTH HARBOUR

Fort Blockhouse 50°47'·37N 01°06'·74W Dir Lt 320°; Dir WRG 6m W13M, R5M, G5M; vis: Oc G 310°-316°, Al WG 316°-318·5° (W phase incr with brg), Oc 318·5°-321·5°, Al WR 321·5°-324° (R phase incr with brg), Oc R 324°-330°. 2 FR (vert) 20m E.
Haslar Marina NE end 50°47'·56N 01°06'·92W QG.
The Point 50°47'·57N 01°06'·57W QG 2M.
Ballast 50°47'·62N 01°06'·84W Fl R 2·5s.
Gosport Marina SE end 50°47'·79N 01°06'·96W 2 FR (vert).
Hbr Ent Dir Lt (NB)(Fuel Jetty) 50°47'·85N 01°06'·98W Dir WRG 2m 1M; vis: Iso G 2s 322·5°-330°, Al WG 330°-332·5°, Iso 2s 332·5°-335° (main chan), Al WR 335°-337·5°, Iso R 2s 337·5°-345° (Small Boat Chan).
Port Solent Lock ent 50°50'·61N 01°06'·37W Fl (4) G 10s.

EASTERN APPROACHES TO THE SOLENT

Nab Tower ☆ 50°40'·08N 00°57'·16W Fl 10s 27m **16M**, vis: 300°-120°, *Horn (2) 30s*; Racon (T).
Outer Nab 50°41'·04N 00°56'·74W Fl R 2·5s.
Nab 1 50°41'·26N 00°56'·52W VQ (9) 10s.
Nab 2 50°41'·74N 00°56'·82W Fl Y 2·5.
Nab 3 50°42'·20N 00°57'·12W Fl Y 2·5.
New Grounds 50°42'·00N 00°58'·63W VQ (3) 5s.
Nab End 50°42'·63N 00°59'·49W Fl R 5s; *Whis.*
Dean Tail 50°42'·99N 00°59'·17W Fl G 5s.
Dean Tail S 50°43'·04N 00°59'·57W Q (6) + L Fl 10s.
Dean Tail N 50°43'·13N 00°59'·57W Q.
Horse Tail 50°43'·23N 01°00'·23W Fl (2) G 10s.
Nab East 50°42'·86N 01°00'·80W Fl (2) R 10s.
Dean Elbow 50°43'·69N 01°01'·88W Fl (3) G 15s.
St Helens 50°43'·36N 01°02'·41W Fl (3) R 15s.
Horse Elbow 50°44'·26N 01°03'·88W QG.
Horse Elbow Wreck 50°44'·43N 01°03'·43W.
Warner 50°43'·87N 01°03'·99W QR; *Whis.*
No Man's Land Ft 50°44'·40N 01°05'·70W Iso R 2s 21m 8M.

◀ BEMBRIDGE

St Helen's Fort ☆ (IOW) 50°42'·30N 01°05'·05W Fl (3) 10s 16m 8M; large ○ stone structure.
Bembridge Tide Gauge 50°42'·46N 01°05'·02W Fl Y 2s 1M.

SOUTH EAST COAST OF THE ISLE OF WIGHT

St Catherine's Point ☆ 50°34'·54N 01°17'·87W Fl 5s 41m **27M**; vis: 257°-117°; FR 35m **17M** (same Tr) vis: 099°-116°.
Sandown Pier Hd 50°39'·05N 01°09'·18W 2 FR (vert) 7m 2M.
W Princessa 50°40'·16N 01°03'·65W Q (9) 15s.
Bembridge Ledge 50°41'·15N 01°02'·81W Q (3) 10s.

2

◀ LANGSTONE AND APPROACHES

Eastney Pt Fraser Trials Range 50°47'·19N 01°02'·22W FR, Oc (2) Y 10s, and FY Lts (occas) when firing taking place.
Winner 50°45'·10N 01°00'·10W.
Roway Wk 50°46'·11N 01°02'·28W Fl (2) 5s.
Langstone Fairway 50°46'·32N 01°01'·36W L Fl 10s.
Eastney Pt Outfall 50°47'·23N 01°01'·68W QR 2m 2M.
Eastney landing stage 50°47'·79N 01°01'·78W Fl R 20s.
East Milton 50°48'·14N 01°01'·71W Fl (4) R 10s.
NW Sinah 50°48'·14N 01°01'·58W Fl G 5s.
S Lake 50°49'·49N 00°59'·88W Fl G 3s 3m 2M.
Binness 50°49'·63N 00°59'·95W Fl R 3s 3m 2M.

◀ CHICHESTER ENTRANCE

West Pole 50°45'·71N 00°56'·50W Fl WR 5s W7M, R5M; vis: W321°-081°. R081°-321°.
Chichester Bar 50°45'·92N 00°56'·46W Fl (2) R 10s 14m 2M; Tide gauge.
Eastoke 50°46'·66N 00°56'·16W QR 2m 3M.
West Winner 50°46'·88N 00°55'·98W QG; Tide gauge.

◀ EMSWORTH CHANNEL

Fishery 50°47'·40N 00°56'·00W Q (6) + L Fl 15s.
NW Pilsey 50°47'·50N 00°56'·20W Fl G 5s.
Verner 50°48'·20N 00°56'·63W Fl R 10s.
Marker Pt 50°48'·91N 00°56'·72W Fl (2) G 10s 8m.
Emsworth 50°49'·66N 00°56'·76W Q (6) + L Fl 15s; tide gauge.
Fishermans 50°50'·14N 00°56'·42W Fl (3) R 10s.
Echo 50°50'·55N 00°56'·19W Fl (3) G 10s.
NE Hayling 50°49'·64N 00°56'·85W Fl (2) R 10s 8m.
Sweare Deep 50°49'·99N 00°57'·47W Fl (3) R 10s.
Northney 50°50'·11N 00°57'·79W Fl (4) R 10s, tide gauge.

◀ CHICHESTER CHANNEL

NW Winner 50°47'·19N 00°55'·92W Fl G 10s.
N Winner 50°47'·31N 00°55'·83W Fl (2) G 10s.
Mid Winner 50°47'·38N 00°55'·69W Fl (3) G 10s.
Stocker 50°47'·45N 00°55'·43W Fl (3) R 10s.
East Head Spit 50°47'·37N 00°54'·95W Fl (4) G 10s.
Sandhead 50°47'·49N 00°54'·59W Fl (4) R 10s.
NE Sandhead 57°47'·60N 00°54'·34W Fl R 10s.
Camber 50°47'·87N 00°54'·06W Q (6) + L Fl 15s.
Chalkdock 50°48'·49N 00°53'·30W Fl (2) G 10s.
Fairway 50°48'·63N 00°52'·37W Fl (3) G 10s.
Itchenor Jetty 50°48'·48N 00°51'·97W 2 FG (vert); tide gauge.
Birdham 50°48'·34N 00°50'·26W Fl (4) G 10s; depth gauge.
Chichester Marina (CM) 50°48'·44N 00°49'·98W Fl G 5s 6m; tide gauge.

List below any other waypoints that you use regularly

Description	Latitude	Longitude	Description	Latitude	Longitude

NOTES

9.2.5 PASSAGE INFORMATION

Reference books include: Admiralty *Channel Pilot*; *South Coast Cruising* (YM/Fishwick); *Shell Channel Pilot* (Imray/Cunliffe); and *Creeks and Harbours of the Solent* (Adlard Coles). See 9.0.6 for distances across the Channel, and 9.3.5 and 9.15.5 for notes on cross-Channel passages. Admiralty Small Craft Folio 5601 covers Portland to the Needles, contains 10 A2 size charts in a clear plastic wallet and costs £35.00 (2000). Encapsulated Solent and Chichester Hbr Racing Charts (Macmillan Reeds).

THE PORTLAND RACE (chart *2255*) South of the Bill lies Portland Race in which severe and very dangerous sea states occur. Even in settled weather it should be carefully avoided by small craft, although at neaps it may be barely perceptible.

The Race occurs at the confluence of two strong S-going tidal streams which run down each side of Portland for almost 10 hours out of 12 at springs. These streams meet the main E-W stream of the Channel, producing large eddies on either side of Portland and a highly confused sea state with heavy overfalls in the Race. The irregular contours of the sea-bed, which shoals abruptly from depths of over 100m some 2M south of the Bill to as little as 9m on Portland Ledge 1M further N, greatly contribute to the violence of the Race. Portland Ledge strongly deflects the flow of water upwards, so that on the flood the Race lies SE of the Bill and vice versa on the ebb. Conditions deteriorate with wind-against-tide, especially at springs; in an E'ly gale against the flood stream the Race may spread eastward to The Shambles bank. The Race normally extends about 2M S of the Bill, but further S in bad weather.

The Tidal Stream chartlets at 9.2.8 show the approx hourly positions of the Race. They are referenced to HW Portland, for the convenience of those leaving or making for Portland/Weymouth; and to HW Dover for those on passage S of the Bill. The smaller scale chartlets at 9.2.3 show the English Chan streams referenced to HW at Dover and Portsmouth.

Small craft may avoid the Race either by passing clear to seaward of it, between 3 and 5M S of the Bill; or by using the inshore passage if conditions suit. This passage is a stretch of relatively smooth water between 1ca and 3ca off the Bill (depending on wind), which should not however be used at night under power due to lobster pots. Timing is important to catch "slackish" water around the Bill, i.e:

Westbound = from HW Dover – 1 to HW + 2
(HW Portland + 4 to HW – 6).
Eastbound = from HW Dover + 5 to HW – 4
(HW Portland – 3 to HW + 1).

From either direction, close Portland at least 2M N of the Bill to utilise the S-going stream; once round the Bill, the N-going stream will set a yacht away from the Race area.

PORTLAND TO CHRISTCHURCH BAY (chart *2615*) The Shambles bank is about 3M E of Portland Bill, and should be avoided at all times. In bad weather the sea breaks heavily on it. It is marked by buoys on its E side and at SW end. E of Weymouth are rky ledges extending 3ca offshore as far as Lulworth Cove, which provides a reasonable anch in fine, settled weather and offshore winds; as do Worbarrow Bay and Chapman's Pool (9.2.10).

A firing range extends 5M offshore between Lulworth and St Alban's Hd. Yachts must pass through this area as quickly as possible, when the range is in use, see 9.2.10. Beware Kimmeridge Ledges, which extend over 5ca seaward.

St Alban's Head (107m and conspic) is steep-to and has a dangerous race off it which may extend 3M seaward. The race lies to the E on the flood and to the W on the ebb; the latter is the more dangerous. A narrow passage, at most 5ca wide and very close inshore, avoids the worst of the overfalls. There is an eddy on W side of St Alban's Head, where the stream runs almost continuously SE. 1M S of St Alban's Head the ESE stream begins at HW Portsmouth + 0520, and the WNW stream at HW –0030, with sp rates of 4·75kn.

There is deep water quite close inshore between St Alban's Hd and Anvil Pt (lt). 1M NE of Durlston Hd, Peveril Ledge runs 2½ca seaward, causing quite a bad race which extends nearly 1M eastwards, particularly on W-going stream against a SW wind. Proceeding towards the excellent shelter of Poole Harbour (9.2.13), overfalls may be met off Ballard Pt and Old Harry on the W-going stream. Studland Bay (9.2.11 and chart 2172) is a good anch especially in NW to S winds. Anch about 4ca WNW of Handfast Pt. Avoid foul areas on chart.

Poole Bay offers good sailing in waters sheltered from W and N winds, with no dangers to worry the average yacht. Tidal streams are weak N of a line between Handfast Pt and Hengistbury Hd and within Christchurch Bay. Hengistbury Hd is a dark headland, S of Christchurch hbr (9.2.14), with a groyne extending 1ca S and Beerpan Rks a further 100m E of groyne. Beware lobster pots in this area. Christchurch Ledge extends 2·75M SE from Hengistbury Hd. The tide runs hard over the ledge at sp, and there may be overfalls.

WESTERN APPROACHES TO SOLENT (charts *2219, 2050*) The Needles (see 9.2.16) are distinctive rks at the W end of the Isle of Wight. The adjacent chalk cliffs of High Down are conspic from afar, but the lt ho may not be seen by day until relatively close. Goose Rk, dries, is about 50m WNW of the lt ho, 100-150m WSW of which is a drying wreck. It is hoped that this will be marked in 2001 by a cardinal bn.The NW side of Needles Chan is defined by the Shingles bank, parts of which dry and on which the sea breaks violently in the least swell. The SE side of the bank is fairly steep-to, the NW side shelves more gradually. On the ebb the stream sets very strongly (3·4kn) WSW across the Shingles. The Needles Channel is well lit and buoyed and in fair weather presents no significant problems. But even a SW F4 over the ebb will cause breaking seas near Bridge and SW Shingles buoys.

In bad weather broken water and overfalls extend along The Bridge, a reef which runs 8ca W of the lt ho with extremity marked by WCM lt buoy. S to W gales against the ebb raise very dangerous breaking seas in the Needles Chan, here only 250m wide. The sea state can be at its worst shortly after LW when the flood has just begun. There is then no wind-over-tide situation, but a substantial swell is raised as a result of the recently turned stream. In such conditions use the E route to the Solent, S of the IOW and via Nab Tower; or find shelter at Poole or Studland.

In strong winds the North Channel, N of the Shingles, is preferable to the Needles Channel. The two join S of Hurst Pt, where overfalls and tide rips may be met. Beware The Trap, a shoal spit 150m SE of Hurst Castle.

In E winds Alum B, close NE of the Needles, is an attractive daytime anch with its coloured cliffs, but beware Long Rk (dries) in middle of B, and Five Fingers Rk 1½ca SW of Hatherwood Pt on N side. Totland Bay is good anch in settled weather, but avoid Warden Ledge.

THE SOLENT (charts *2040, 394*) Within the Solent there are few dangers in mid-chan. The most significant is Bramble bank (dries) between Cowes and Calshot. The main shipping chan (buoyed) passes S and W of the Brambles, but yachts can use the North Chan to the NE of the Brambles at any state of tide. Tidal streams are strong at sp, but principally follow the direction of the main chan. An Area of Concern between Cowes and Calshot provides added safety for larger ships; see 9.2.17 for details.

Several inshore spits, banks, rocks and ledges, which a yachtsman should know, include: Pennington and Lymington Spits on the N shore; Black Rk 4ca W of entrance to Yarmouth (9.2.19); Hamstead Ledge 8ca W of entrance to Newtown River

(9.2.21) and Saltmead Ledge 1·5M to E; Gurnard Ledge 1·5M W of Cowes; Lepe, Middle and Beaulieu Spit, S and W of the ent to Beaulieu R. (9.2.22); the shoals off Stone Pt, marked by Lepe Spit SCM buoy and where a bn marks cable area; Shrape Mud, which extends N from the breakwater of Cowes hbr (9.2.23) and along to Old Castle Pt; the shoals and isolated rks which fringe the island shore from Old Castle Pt to Ryde (9.2.28), including either side of the ent to Wootton Creek (9.2.27); and Calshot Spit which extends almost to the lt F which marks the turn of chan into Southampton Water.

Southampton Water is a busy commercial waterway with large tankers, containerships, lesser craft and high speed ferries. Yachts should monitor VHF Ch 12 to ascertain shipping movements. Between the Esso jetty off Fawley and the BP jetty on the E side the channel is narrow for large vessels; yachts can easily stay clear by seeking shoal water. N of this area there is adequate water for yachts close outboard of the main buoyed channel; the banks are of gently shelving soft mud, apart from foul ground between Hythe and Marchwood. Unlit marks and large mooring buoys may however be hard to see against the many shore lights. Except in strong N'lies, Southampton Water and the R Test and Itchen provide sheltered sailing. The River Hamble is convenient, but somewhat crowded.

Depending on the wind direction, there are many good anchs: For example, in W winds there is anch on E side of Hurst, as close inshore as depth permits, NE of Hurst lt. In S winds, or in good weather, anch W of Yarmouth hbr ent, as near shore as possible, but reasonably close to town, see 9.2.19. In winds between W and N there is good anch in Stanswood Bay, about 1M NE of Stansore Pt. Just N of Calshot Spit there is shelter from SW and W. Osborne Bay, 2M E of Cowes, is sheltered from winds between S and W; in E winds Gurnard Bay, to the W of Cowes, is preferable. In N winds anch in Stokes Bay. At E end of IOW there is good anch off Bembridge in winds from S, SW or W; but clear out if wind goes into E.

There are also places which a shoal-draught boat can explore at the top of the tide, such as Ashlett Creek (9.2.26) between Fawley and Calshot, Eling up the R Test, and the upper reaches of the R Medina (9.2.23).

ISLE OF WIGHT – SOUTH COAST (chart *2045*) From the Needles eastward to Freshwater Bay the cliffs can be approached to within 1ca, but beyond the E end of chalk cliffs there are ledges off Brook and Atherfield which require at least 5ca offing. The E-going stream sets towards these dangers. 4M SSW of the Needles the stream turns E x N at HW Portsmouth + 0530, and W at HW – 0030, sp rate 2kn.

St Catherine's lt ho (lt, RC) is conspic. It is safe to pass 2ca off, but a race occurs off the Point and can be very dangerous at or near sp with a strong opposing wind; particularly SE of the Pt on a W-going stream in a W gale, when St Catherine's should be given a berth of at least 2M. 1·25M SE of the Pt the stream turns E x N at HW Portsmouth + 0520, and W x S at HW – 0055, sp rate 3·75kn.

2

Rocks extend about 2½ca either side of Dunnose where a race occurs. In Sandown Bay anch off Shanklin or Sandown where the streams are weak inshore. Off the centre of the Bay they turn NE x E at HW Portsmouth + 0500, and SW x W at HW – 0100, sp rates 2 kn. The Yarborough Monument is conspic above Culver Cliff. Whitecliff Bay provides an anch in winds between W and N. From here to Foreland (Bembridge Pt) the coast is fringed by a ledge of rks (dry) extending up to 3ca offshore, and it is advisable to keep to seaward (E) of Bembridge Ledge ECM lt buoy.

EASTERN APPROACHES TO SOLENT (charts *2050, 2045*) 4·5M E of Foreland is Nab Tr (lt, fog sig), a conspic steel and concrete structure (28m), marking Nab Shoal for larger vessels and of no direct significance to yachtsmen. NW of Nab Tr, the E approach to the Solent via Spithead, presents few problems and is far safer in SW/W gales than the Needles Channel.

The main chan is well buoyed and easy to follow, but there is plenty of water for the normal yacht to the S of it when approaching No Man's Land Fort and Horse Sand Fort, . A submerged barrier lies N of the latter, but the barrier to SW of the former is reported demolished and therefore yachts may pass SW of No Man's Land Fort with caution; a racing mark is planned to mark a possible passage. Ryde Sand dries extensively and is a trap for the unwary; so too is Hamilton Bank on the W side of the chan to Portsmouth (9.2.30).

Nab Tr is also a most useful landmark when approaching the E end of Isle of Wight, or when making for the hbrs of Langstone (9.2.31) or Chichester (9.2.32). Both these hbrs, with offlying sands, are on a dangerous lee shore in strong S'ly winds. East and West Winner flank the ent to Langstone Hbr. Similarly, E and W Pole Sands, drying 1m, lie either side of the ent chan from Chichester Bar bn. SE from Chichester Bar the whole of Bracklesham Bay is shallow, with a pronounced inshore set at certain states of the tide; yachts should keep at least 2M offshore. Further along a low-lying coast is Selsey Bill with extensive offshore rocks and shoals. Pass these to seaward of the Owers SCM lt buoy, or via the Looe Chan (see 9.3.5) in suitable conditions. Boulder SHM lt buoy is at the W ent to this chan, about 6M SE of Chichester Bar bn. Medmery Bank, 3·7m, is 1M WNW of Boulder.

9.2.6 DISTANCE TABLE

Approximate distances in nautical miles are by the most direct route, whilst avoiding dangers and allowing for Traffic Separation Schemes. Places in italics are in adjoining areas; places in **bold** are also in 9.0.6, Cross-Channel Distances.

1.	***Exmouth***	1																			
2.	*Lyme Regis*	21	**2**																		
3.	Portland Bill	36	22	**3**																	
4.	**Weymouth**	46	32	8	**4**																
5.	Swanage	58	44	22	22	**5**															
6.	**Poole Hbr ent**	65	51	28	26	6	**6**														
7.	**Needles Lt Ho**	73	58	35	34	14	14	**7**													
8.	Lymington	79	64	42	40	20	24	6	**8**												
9.	Yarmouth (IOW)	77	63	40	39	18	22	4	2	**9**											
10.	Beaulieu R. ent	84	69	46	45	25	29	11	7	7	**10**										
11.	Cowes	86	71	49	46	28	27	14	10	9	2	**11**									
12.	Southampton	93	78	55	54	34	34	20	16	16	9	9	**12**								
13.	R. Hamble (ent)	90	75	53	51	32	34	18	12	13	6	6	5	**13**							
14.	Portsmouth	96	81	58	57	37	35	23	19	19	12	10	18	13	**14**						
15.	Langstone Hbr	98	84	61	59	39	39	25	21	21	14	12	21	18	5	**15**					
16.	Chichester Bar	101	86	63	62	42	42	28	23	24	17	15	23	18	8	5	**16**				
17.	Bembridge	97	81	59	58	38	39	24	18	19	13	10	18	15	5	6	8	**17**			
18.	**Nab Tower**	102	86	64	63	43	44	29	23	24	18	15	24	19	10	7	6	6	**18**		
19.	St Catherine's Pt	82	68	45	44	25	25	12	19	21	27	15	36	29	20	20	19	17	15	**19**	
20.	***Littlehampton***	117	102	79	79	60	61	46	44	45	38	36	45	42	31	28	25	28	22	35	**20**

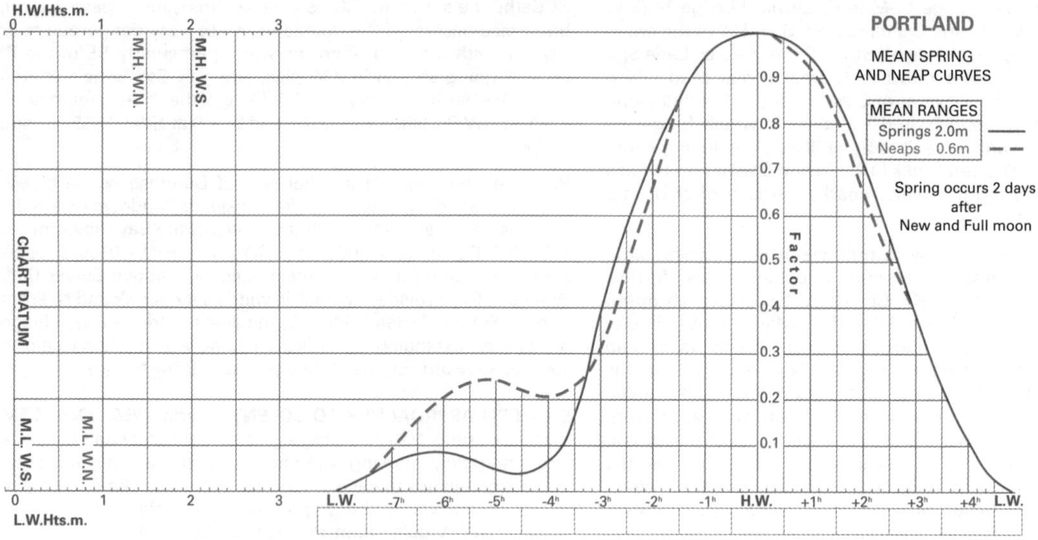

PORTLAND HARBOUR *9.2.7*

Dorset **50°35'·14N 02°24'·98W** (E Ship Chan) ❀❀❀◊◊✿

CHARTS AC *5601*, 2268, 2255, *2610*; Imray C4, C5; Stanfords 7,12; OS 194

TIDES –0430 Dover; ML 1·0; Zone 0 (UT)

Standard Port PORTLAND (⟶)

Times				Height (metres)			
High Water		Low Water		MHWS	MHWN	MLWN	MLWS
0100	0700	0100	0700	2·1	1·4	0·8	0·1
1300	1900	1300	1900				
LULWORTH COVE and MUPE BAY (Worbarrow Bay)							
+0005	+0015	–0005	0000	+0·1	+0·1	+0·2	+0·1

NOTE: Double LWs occur. Predictions are for the first LW. The second LW occurs from 3 to 4 hrs later and may, at Springs, occasionally be lower than the first.

SHELTER Poor, due to lack of wind breaks. ⚓ on W side of hbr in about 3m between ☆ Fl (4) 10s and ☆ L Fl 10s. E Fleet is only suitable for small craft with lowering masts. Better options for yachts are Weymouth hbr or marina.

NAVIGATION WPT 50°35'·10N 02°24'·08W, 090°/270° from/to E Ship Chan, Fort Hd, 0·50M. The S Chan is permanently closed. Speed limit in the hbr is 6kn in the areas defined or within 150m of any breakwater or hbr premises. Vessels under 10m may exceed 12kn in the undefined areas. Beware rky reef extending 1ca off between Castle Cove SC and the Sailing Centre, shoals E of Small Mouth and fast catamarans ex-Weymouth. 4 noise range lt buoys Fl.Y are 7ca SE of D Head and 3 degaussing buoys (1 lit) are 400m SE of Weymouth S Pier head. Portland Race (see 9.2.5 and 9.2.8) is extremely dangerous. Avoid the Shambles bank.

LIGHTS AND MARKS Bill of Portland (S end) Fl (4) 20s 43m 25M; W tr, R band. The number of flashes gradually changes from 4 to 1 in arc 221°-244°, and from 1 to 4 in arc 117°-141°. FR 19m 13M, same tr, vis 271°-291° (20°) over The Shambles, Dia 30s. Other lts as on chartlet.

RADIO TELEPHONE Monitor VHF Ch 74 for commercial ship movements. Port Ops Ch 14, 20, 28, 71, **74**.

TELEPHONE (Dial code 01305) Port Control 824044, 🖷 824055; Ⓗ 824055; ⊖ 0345 231110 (H24); MRSC 760439; Marinecall 09068 500457; Police 821205; Dr (GP) 820422; Ⓗ (Emergency) 820341.

FACILITIES Hbr dues apply to yachts: £3.60 daily for 6 – 9.15m LOA. **Castle Cove SC** ☎ 783708, M, L, FW; **Services:** Slip, M, L, FW, ME, Sh, C, CH, El (mobile workshop). **Town** www.portland-port.co.uk, ✉, Ⓑ, ⇌ (bus to Weymouth), ✈ (Bournemouth).

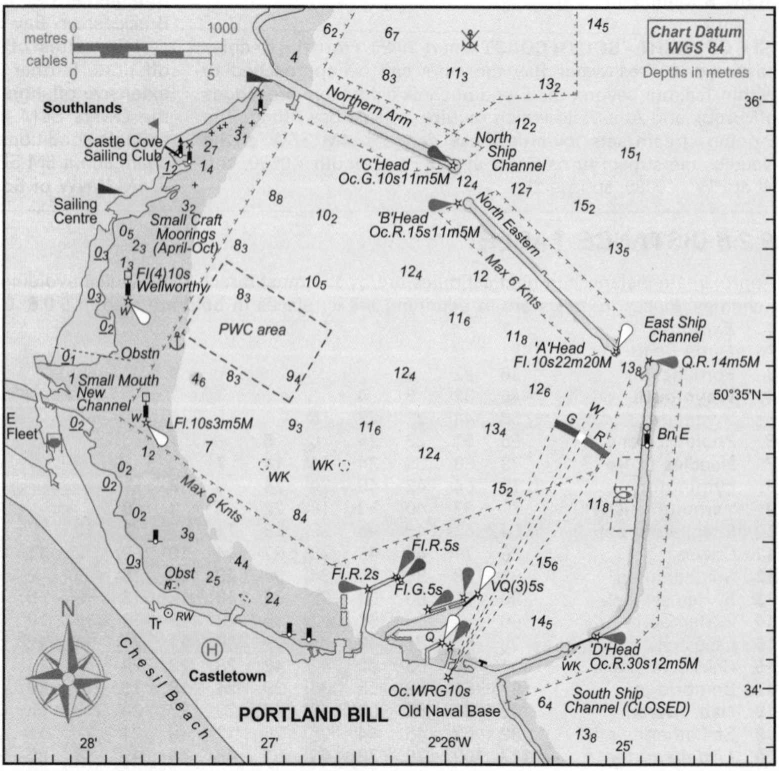

Note - Double LWs occur at Portland. The predictions are for the first LW. The second LW occurs from 3 to 4 Hrs later and may, at Springs, on occasions be lower than the first.

TIME ZONE (UTC)
For Summer Time add ONE hour in **non-shaded areas**

ENGLAND – PORTLAND

LAT 50°34′N LONG 2°26′W

TIMES AND HEIGHTS OF HIGH AND LOW WATERS

SPRING & NEAP TIDES
Dates in red are SPRINGS
Dates in blue are NEAPS

YEAR **2002**

JANUARY

Day	Time	m	Time	m	Time	m	Time	m
1 TU	0026	0.2	0750	2.2	1251	0.3	2022	2.0
2 W	0112	0.2	0833	2.2	1338	0.3	2105	1.9
3 TH	0158	0.3	0915	2.1	1425	0.3	2148	1.9
4 F	0244	0.4	0958	2.0	1515	0.4	2232	1.8
5 SA	0333	0.5	1043	1.9	1610	0.4	2321	1.7
6 SU	0428	0.6	1134	1.8	1710	0.5		
7 M	0019	1.6	0531	0.7	1234	1.7	1816	0.6
8 TU	0128	1.6	0644	0.7	1345	1.6	1925	0.6
9 W	0243	1.6	0800	0.7	1501	1.6	2031	0.6
10 TH	0351	1.7	0909	0.7	1611	1.6	2130	0.5
11 F	0450	1.8	1006	0.6	1711	1.7	2222	0.5
12 SA	0541	1.9	1054	0.5	1804	1.7	2307	0.4
13 SU	0627	2.0	1137	0.4	1851	1.8	● 2349	0.4
14 M	0708	2.0	1218	0.4	1932	1.8		
15 TU	0029	0.3	0743	2.1	1258	0.3	2005	1.8
16 W	0107	0.3	0814	2.0	1336	0.3	2034	1.8
17 TH	0142	0.3	0843	2.0	1411	0.3	2102	1.7
18 F	0212	0.4	0911	1.8	1441	0.4	2131	1.6
19 SA	0235	0.4	0940	1.7	1502	0.4	2201	1.5
20 SU	0256	0.5	1009	1.6	1526	0.5	2234	1.4
21 M	0325	0.6	1040	1.5	1601	0.5	2315	1.3
22 TU	0408	0.6	1123	1.4	1654	0.6		
23 W	0014	1.3	0514	0.7	1233	1.3	1808	0.6
24 TH	0138	1.4	0644	0.7	1408	1.3	1928	0.6
25 F	0303	1.5	0811	0.7	1534	1.4	2041	0.5
26 SA	0412	1.7	0920	0.6	1643	1.6	2143	0.4
27 SU	0511	1.8	1017	0.5	1744	1.7	2239	0.3
28 M	0606	2.0	1109	0.3	1840	1.9	○ 2330	0.2
29 TU	0658	2.2	1158	0.2	1931	2.0		
30 W	0018	0.1	0746	2.3	1246	0.1	2018	2.1
31 TH	0105	0.1	0831	2.3	1331	0.1	2101	2.1

FEBRUARY

Day	Time	m	Time	m	Time	m	Time	m
1 F	0149	0.1	0912	2.3	1416	0.1	2140	2.0
2 SA	0233	0.1	0952	2.2	1501	0.1	2218	1.9
3 SU	0315	0.2	1030	2.0	1547	0.2	2257	1.8
4 M	0400	0.4	1110	1.8	1635	0.4	2340	1.6
5 TU	0451	0.5	1155	1.6	1731	0.5		
6 W	0033	1.5	0554	0.7	1253	1.5	1838	0.6
7 TH	0150	1.4	0720	0.8	1418	1.4	1959	0.7
8 F	0320	1.5	0857	0.7	1551	1.4	2114	0.7
9 SA	0430	1.6	1000	0.6	1701	1.5	2208	0.6
10 SU	0525	1.7	1045	0.5	1755	1.6	2253	0.5
11 M	0613	1.9	1124	0.4	1841	1.7	2333	0.4
12 TU	0654	2.0	1203	0.3	1921	1.8	●	
13 W	0013	0.3	0730	2.0	1241	0.2	1954	1.8
14 TH	0051	0.2	0802	2.1	1318	0.1	2023	1.8
15 F	0126	0.2	0831	2.0	1351	0.1	2049	1.8
16 SA	0156	0.2	0859	1.9	1417	0.2	2116	1.7
17 SU	0218	0.2	0926	1.8	1435	0.2	2140	1.6
18 M	0236	0.3	0951	1.6	1454	0.3	2203	1.5
19 TU	0259	0.4	1014	1.5	1521	0.4	2232	1.4
20 W	0330	0.5	1044	1.4	1600	0.4	2313	1.4
21 TH	0418	0.6	1133	1.3	1701	0.6		
22 F	0019	1.3	0538	0.7	1259	1.2	1837	0.6
23 SA	0157	1.4	0735	0.7	1458	1.3	2018	0.6
24 SU	0337	1.5	0908	0.6	1627	1.5	2132	0.5
25 M	0450	1.8	1009	0.4	1733	1.7	2229	0.3
26 TU	0552	2.0	1101	0.2	1830	1.9	2319	0.1
27 W	0646	2.2	1148	0.1	1920	2.1	○	
28 TH	0006	0.0	0733	2.3	1234	-0.1	2004	2.2

MARCH

Day	Time	m	Time	m	Time	m	Time	m
1 F	0051	-0.1	0817	2.4	1317	-0.1	2044	2.2
2 SA	0133	-0.1	0857	2.4	1359	-0.1	2122	2.1
3 SU	0214	-0.1	0934	2.2	1440	0.0	2156	2.0
4 M	0253	0.1	1009	2.0	1520	0.1	2230	1.8
5 TU	0332	0.3	1044	1.8	1600	0.3	2305	1.6
6 W	0416	0.5	1122	1.5	1647	0.6	2348	1.5
7 TH	0514	0.7	1211	1.3	1751	0.7		
8 F	0054	1.4	0649	0.8	1338	1.2	1926	0.8
9 SA	0250	1.4	0856	0.7	1545	1.3	2057	0.7
10 SU	0411	1.5	0951	0.6	1652	1.4	2150	0.6
11 M	0506	1.7	1028	0.5	1741	1.6	2231	0.5
12 TU	0552	1.8	1103	0.3	1823	1.7	2310	0.3
13 W	0632	1.9	1139	0.2	1900	1.8	2349	0.2
14 TH	0709	2.0	1216	0.1	1933	1.9	●	
15 F	0027	0.1	0741	2.1	1252	0.0	2002	1.9
16 SA	0103	0.1	0811	2.0	1325	0.0	2029	1.9
17 SU	0133	0.1	0840	2.0	1350	0.1	2055	1.8
18 M	0155	0.1	0907	1.8	1409	0.2	2117	1.7
19 TU	0214	0.2	0930	1.7	1428	0.2	2137	1.6
20 W	0235	0.3	0952	1.5	1451	0.3	2202	1.5
21 TH	0303	0.4	1020	1.4	1524	0.4	2238	1.4
22 F	0345	0.5	1106	1.3	1616	0.6	2336	1.4
23 SA	0502	0.7	1228	1.2	1808	0.7		
24 SU	0109	1.4	0721	0.7	1436	1.3	2006	0.7
25 M	0304	1.5	0857	0.5	1613	1.5	2119	0.5
26 TU	0428	1.7	0956	0.3	1718	1.7	2214	0.3
27 W	0531	2.0	1045	0.1	1812	2.0	2303	0.1
28 TH	0625	2.2	1131	-0.1	1859	2.2	○ 2348	0.0
29 F	0713	2.4	1215	-0.2	1942	2.3		
30 SA	0031	-0.1	0756	2.4	1257	-0.2	2022	2.3
31 SU	0113	-0.1	0836	2.4	1337	-0.2	2058	2.2

APRIL

Day	Time	m	Time	m	Time	m	Time	m
1 M	0152	-0.1	0912	2.2	1416	0.0	2132	2.1
2 TU	0229	0.1	0946	2.0	1452	0.2	2204	1.9
3 W	0307	0.3	1018	1.7	1528	0.4	2235	1.6
4 TH	0348	0.5	1054	1.5	1607	0.6	2312	1.5
5 F	0444	0.7	1142	1.3	1706	0.8		
6 SA	0008	1.4	0620	0.8	1313	1.2	1846	0.9
7 SU	0210	1.3	0838	0.7	1532	1.3	2026	0.8
8 M	0340	1.5	0925	0.6	1629	1.4	2119	0.7
9 TU	0433	1.6	0958	0.5	1712	1.6	2201	0.5
10 W	0518	1.8	1032	0.3	1751	1.7	2241	0.4
11 TH	0559	1.9	1108	0.2	1828	1.9	2320	0.2
12 F	0637	2.0	1145	0.1	1902	2.0	● 2358	0.2
13 SA	0713	2.0	1220	0.1	1934	2.0		
14 SU	0033	0.1	0746	2.0	1253	0.1	2003	2.0
15 M	0104	0.1	0817	2.0	1319	0.1	2030	1.9
16 TU	0129	0.2	0845	1.8	1342	0.2	2053	1.8
17 W	0152	0.2	0910	1.7	1406	0.3	2115	1.7
18 TH	0217	0.3	0935	1.6	1432	0.4	2141	1.6
19 F	0249	0.4	1008	1.4	1507	0.5	2218	1.5
20 SA	0335	0.5	1059	1.3	1603	0.7	2317	1.5
21 SU	0501	0.7	1223	1.3	1803	0.8		
22 M	0047	1.4	0707	0.7	1422	1.4	1948	0.7
23 TU	0237	1.6	0833	0.5	1549	1.6	2058	0.5
24 W	0400	1.8	0932	0.3	1651	1.8	2152	0.3
25 TH	0503	2.0	1022	0.1	1744	2.0	2241	0.2
26 F	0558	2.2	1108	0.0	1832	2.2	2326	0.0
27 SA	0648	2.3	1152	-0.1	1916	2.3	○	
28 SU	0009	0.0	0732	2.3	1234	-0.1	1956	2.3
29 M	0051	0.0	0813	2.3	1314	0.0	2034	2.2
30 TU	0130	0.1	0851	2.1	1352	0.1	2109	2.1

Chart Datum: 0·93 metres below Ordnance Datum (Newlyn)

Note - Double LWs occur at Portland. The predictions are for the first LW. The second LW occurs from 3 to 4 Hrs later and may, at Springs, on occasions be lower than the first.

TIME ZONE (UTC)
For Summer Time add ONE hour in **non-shaded areas**

ENGLAND – PORTLAND

LAT 50°34′N LONG 2°26′W

TIMES AND HEIGHTS OF HIGH AND LOW WATERS

SPRING & NEAP TIDES
Dates in red are SPRINGS
Dates in blue are NEAPS

YEAR **2002**

MAY

Day	Time	m	Day	Time	m
1	0208	0.2	16	0136	0.3
	0925	1.9		0856	1.8
W	1427	0.3	TH	1354	0.3
	2139	1.9		2102	1.8
2	0247	0.3	17	0210	0.3
	0957	1.7		0928	1.6
TH	1502	0.5	F	1429	0.4
	2208	1.7		2133	1.7
3	0329	0.5	18	0250	0.4
	1031	1.4		1007	1.5
F	1539	0.7	SA	1514	0.6
	2241	1.5		2215	1.6
4	0423	0.7	19	0346	0.5
	1118	1.3		1103	1.4
SA	1630	0.8	SU	1621	0.7
	2330	1.4		2314	1.6
5	0544	0.8	20	0506	0.6
	1236	1.2		1223	1.4
SU	1801	0.9	M	1752	0.7
6	0050	1.4	21	0036	1.5
	0728	0.7		0639	0.6
M	1448	1.3	TU	1358	1.5
	1932	0.9		1919	0.7
7	0240	1.4	22	0209	1.6
	0832	0.6		0759	0.5
TU	1546	1.4	W	1515	1.6
	2036	0.8		2029	0.6
8	0342	1.5	23	0327	1.8
	0913	0.5		0901	0.3
W	1628	1.6	TH	1618	1.8
	2123	0.6		2126	0.4
9	0430	1.7	24	0432	1.9
	0952	0.4		0954	0.2
TH	1708	1.7	F	1713	2.0
	2206	0.5		2216	0.3
10	0515	1.8	25	0530	2.0
	1030	0.3		1043	0.1
F	1746	1.9	SA	1804	2.1
	2247	0.3		2304	0.2
11	0558	1.9	26	0622	2.1
	1108	0.2		1129	0.1
SA	1824	2.0	SU	1850	2.2
	2325	0.3		○ 2349	0.2
12	0639	2.0	27	0710	2.1
	1144	0.2		1212	0.1
SU	1901	2.0	M	1934	2.2
●					
13	0001	0.2	28	0032	0.2
	0718	2.0		0753	2.1
M	1218	0.2	TU	1254	0.2
	1935	2.0		2013	2.2
14	0034	0.2	29	0113	0.2
	0754	1.9		0833	2.0
TU	1250	0.2	W	1332	0.3
	2007	2.0		2049	2.1
15	0104	0.2	30	0153	0.3
	0826	1.9		0908	1.8
W	1321	0.3	TH	1409	0.4
	2034	1.9		2120	1.9
			31	0233	0.4
				0940	1.6
			F	1445	0.5
				2148	1.7

JUNE

Day	Time	m	Day	Time	m
1	0315	0.5	16	0257	0.4
	1013	1.5		1015	1.7
SA	1521	0.7	SU	1524	0.5
	2218	1.6		2223	1.8
2	0401	0.6	17	0351	0.4
	1054	1.3		1107	1.6
SU	1604	0.8	M	1621	0.6
	2259	1.5		2316	1.7
3	0501	0.7	18	0455	0.5
	1150	1.3		1210	1.5
M	1708	0.9	TU	1728	0.6
	2356	1.4			
4	0615	0.7	19	0021	1.6
	1305	1.3		0607	0.5
TU	1832	0.9	W	1323	1.6
				1841	0.7
5	0111	1.4	20	0136	1.6
	0725	0.6		0720	0.5
W	1426	1.4	TH	1437	1.6
	1943	0.8		1952	0.6
6	0227	1.4	21	0251	1.7
	0820	0.6		0827	0.4
TH	1527	1.5	F	1544	1.7
	2039	0.7		2057	0.6
7	0332	1.5	22	0401	1.7
	0906	0.5		0928	0.4
F	1617	1.6	SA	1644	1.9
	2127	0.6		2154	0.5
8	0428	1.6	23	0504	1.8
	0949	0.4		1022	0.3
SA	1703	1.8	SU	1739	2.0
	2210	0.5		2246	0.4
9	0519	1.8	24	0602	1.9
	1029	0.3		1111	0.3
SU	1748	1.9	M	1830	2.1
	2250	0.4		○ 2334	0.3
10	0607	1.8	25	0654	1.9
	1108	0.3		1156	0.3
M	1831	2.0	TU	1916	2.1
	● 2329	0.3			
11	0652	1.9	26	0019	0.3
	1148	0.2		0740	1.9
TU	1911	2.0	W	1239	0.3
				1957	2.1
12	0008	0.3	27	0102	0.3
	0735	1.9		0821	1.9
W	1228	0.3	TH	1319	0.3
	1949	2.0		2034	2.0
13	0047	0.3	28	0142	0.3
	0815	1.9		0856	1.8
TH	1309	0.3	F	1356	0.4
	2026	2.0		2105	1.9
14	0127	0.3	29	0221	0.3
	0853	1.8		0926	1.7
F	1351	0.3	SA	1432	0.5
	2101	1.9		2132	1.8
15	0210	0.3	30	0259	0.4
	0931	1.7		0954	1.6
SA	1435	0.4	SU	1505	0.5
	2139	1.9		2201	1.7

JULY

Day	Time	m	Day	Time	m
1	0336	0.5	16	0342	0.3
	1027	1.4		1057	1.7
M	1537	0.6	TU	1605	0.4
	2233	1.6		2308	1.8
2	0413	0.5	17	0435	0.4
	1108	1.4		1145	1.6
TU	1611	0.7	W	1659	0.5
	2313	1.5		2358	1.7
3	0457	0.6	18	0534	0.5
	1200	1.3		1244	1.6
W	1704	0.8	TH	1803	0.6
4	0006	1.4	19	0058	1.6
	0557	0.6		0642	0.5
TH	1306	1.3	F	1356	1.5
	1823	0.8		1915	0.7
5	0117	1.4	20	0214	1.5
	0706	0.6		0756	0.6
F	1418	1.4	SA	1514	1.6
	1939	0.8		2033	0.7
6	0234	1.4	21	0336	1.6
	0808	0.6		0909	0.5
SA	1525	1.5	SU	1623	1.7
	2040	0.7		2143	0.6
7	0343	1.5	22	0448	1.6
	0902	0.5		1009	0.5
SU	1623	1.7	M	1723	1.8
	2132	0.6		2238	0.5
8	0444	1.6	23	0551	1.7
	0952	0.4		1059	0.4
M	1716	1.8	TU	1816	1.9
	2220	0.5		2325	0.4
9	0540	1.7	24	0644	1.8
	1041	0.3		1144	0.4
TU	1806	1.9	W	1903	2.0
	2306	0.4	○		
10	0633	1.8	25	0008	0.3
	1128	0.3		0730	1.8
W	1854	2.0	TH	1225	0.3
	● 2352	0.3		1944	2.1
11	0723	1.9	26	0048	0.3
	1215	0.2		0809	1.9
TH	1940	2.1	F	1303	0.3
				2020	2.1
12	0037	0.3	27	0127	0.2
	0809	1.9		0842	1.8
F	1301	0.2	SA	1340	0.3
	2023	2.1		2049	2.0
13	0122	0.2	28	0204	0.2
	0853	1.9		0908	1.8
SA	1346	0.2	SU	1414	0.3
	2104	2.1		2114	1.9
14	0207	0.2	29	0238	0.3
	0934	1.9		0932	1.7
SU	1431	0.3	M	1444	0.4
	2144	2.0		2141	1.8
15	0254	0.2	30	0306	0.3
	1014	1.8		0959	1.6
M	1517	0.3	TU	1507	0.5
	2224	1.9		2208	1.6
			31	0327	0.4
				1029	1.5
			W	1527	0.5
				2235	1.5

AUGUST

Day	Time	m	Day	Time	m
1	0351	0.5	16	0501	0.5
	1104	1.4		1205	1.6
TH	1558	0.6	F	1728	0.6
	2306	1.4			
2	0429	0.5	17	0022	1.5
	1152	1.3		0606	0.6
F	1650	0.7	SA	1316	1.5
	2355	1.3		1847	0.8
3	0529	0.6	18	0142	1.4
	1302	1.3		0734	0.7
SA	1810	0.8	SU	1452	1.5
				2030	0.8
4	0120	1.3	19	0328	1.4
	0652	0.6		0902	0.7
SU	1430	1.4	M	1612	1.6
	1946	0.8		2143	0.7
5	0301	1.4	20	0447	1.5
	0819	0.6		1001	0.6
M	1547	1.6	TU	1713	1.8
	2104	0.7		2232	0.6
6	0418	1.5	21	0545	1.6
	0928	0.5		1046	0.5
TU	1650	1.7	W	1803	1.9
	2202	0.5		2312	0.4
7	0522	1.7	22	0633	1.8
	1024	0.4		1126	0.4
W	1747	1.9	TH	1847	2.0
	2253	0.4		○ 2350	0.3
8	0620	1.8	23	0714	1.9
	1115	0.3		1203	0.3
TH	1840	2.1	F	1926	2.1
	● 2341	0.3			
9	0713	2.0	24	0027	0.2
	1203	0.2		0749	1.9
F	1929	2.2	SA	1241	0.2
				1958	2.1
10	0027	0.1	25	0104	0.2
	0800	2.1		0818	1.9
SA	1249	0.1	SU	1317	0.2
	2014	2.3		2026	2.1
11	0112	0.1	26	0139	0.1
	0842	2.1		0842	1.9
SU	1333	0.1	M	1350	0.2
	2055	2.3		2051	2.0
12	0156	0.0	27	0210	0.2
	0921	2.1		0905	1.8
M	1416	0.1	TU	1417	0.3
	2134	2.2		2116	1.9
13	0239	0.1	28	0232	0.3
	0958	2.0		0929	1.7
TU	1458	0.2	W	1435	0.4
	2211	2.1		2140	1.7
14	0323	0.2	29	0246	0.3
	1035	1.9		0952	1.6
W	1542	0.3	TH	1451	0.5
	2248	1.9		2201	1.5
15	0409	0.3	30	0305	0.4
	1116	1.7		1017	1.5
TH	1629	0.5	F	1514	0.5
	2330	1.7		2224	1.4
			31	0335	0.5
				1052	1.4
			SA	1553	0.6
				2301	1.3

Chart Datum: 0·93 metres below Ordnance Datum (Newlyn)

Note - Double LWs occur at Portland. The predictions are for the first LW. The second LW occurs from 3 to 4 Hrs later and may, at Springs, on occasions be lower than the first.

TIME ZONE (UTC)
For Summer Time add ONE hour in **non-shaded areas**

ENGLAND – PORTLAND

LAT 50°34′N LONG 2°26′W

TIMES AND HEIGHTS OF HIGH AND LOW WATERS

SPRING & NEAP TIDES
Dates in red are SPRINGS
Dates in blue are NEAPS

YEAR **2002**

SEPTEMBER

Date	Day	Time	m	Time	m	Time	m	Time	m
1	SU	0423	0.6	1149	1.3	1705	0.8		
2	M	0012	1.2	0554	0.7	1322	1.4	1911	0.8
3	TU	0224	1.3	0756	0.7	1511	1.5	2050	0.7
4	W	0403	1.5	0915	0.6	1627	1.7	2150	0.5
5	TH	0509	1.7	1011	0.4	1728	2.0	2239	0.3
6	F	0605	1.9	1100	0.3	1822	2.2	2325	0.2
7	SA ●	0655	2.1	1146	0.1	1911	2.3		
8	SU	0010	0.0	0740	2.2	1230	0.0	1955	2.4
9	M	0053	-0.1	0821	2.3	1313	0.0	2035	2.4
10	TU	0136	-0.1	0859	2.2	1354	0.0	2113	2.3
11	W	0217	0.0	0934	2.1	1435	0.1	2148	2.1
12	TH	0257	0.2	1009	1.9	1515	0.3	2224	1.9
13	F	0338	0.4	1045	1.7	1600	0.5	2302	1.6
14	SA	0425	0.6	1129	1.6	1659	0.7	2352	1.4
15	SU	0530	0.8	1238	1.4	1834	0.9		
16	M	0132	1.3	0717	0.9	1441	1.5	2040	0.8
17	TU	0341	1.4	0857	0.8	1601	1.6	2138	0.7
18	W	0444	1.5	0947	0.7	1654	1.8	2215	0.6
19	TH	0529	1.7	1024	0.6	1739	1.9	2247	0.4
20	F	0609	1.8	1059	0.5	1819	2.0	2322	0.3
21	SA	0646	1.9	1135	0.3	1856	2.1	○ 2357	0.2
22	SU	0718	2.0	1212	0.2	1928	2.1		
23	M	0033	0.1	0746	2.0	1249	0.2	1956	2.1
24	TU	0107	0.1	0811	2.0	1321	0.2	2023	2.0
25	W	0135	0.2	0835	1.9	1347	0.3	2049	1.9
26	TH	0155	0.3	0858	1.8	1403	0.4	2112	1.7
27	F	0209	0.4	0918	1.7	1419	0.4	2132	1.6
28	SA	0227	0.4	0940	1.6	1440	0.5	2155	1.4
29	SU	0251	0.5	1012	1.5	1514	0.6	2231	1.3
30	M	0331	0.7	1104	1.4	1621	0.8	2344	1.3

OCTOBER

Date	Day	Time	m	Time	m	Time	m	Time	m
1	TU	0508	0.9	1231	1.4	1900	0.8		
2	W	0206	1.3	0744	0.8	1435	1.5	2035	0.7
3	TH	0350	1.5	0859	0.7	1601	1.8	2130	0.5
4	F	0451	1.8	0952	0.5	1702	2.0	2218	0.3
5	SA	0543	2.0	1039	0.3	1756	2.2	2303	0.1
6	SU	0630	2.2	1124	0.1	1844	2.4	● 2346	0.0
7	M	0713	2.3	1207	0.0	1929	2.4		
8	TU	0029	-0.1	0754	2.4	1249	0.0	2010	2.4
9	W	0110	0.0	0832	2.3	1330	0.1	2048	2.3
10	TH	0150	0.1	0907	2.2	1409	0.2	2124	2.1
11	F	0228	0.3	0941	2.0	1449	0.4	2159	1.8
12	SA	0305	0.5	1015	1.8	1535	0.6	2236	1.6
13	SU	0346	0.7	1054	1.6	1636	0.8	2327	1.4
14	M	0448	0.9	1157	1.5	1822	0.9		
15	TU	0150	1.3	0640	1.0	1419	1.5	2028	0.8
16	W	0334	1.4	0834	1.0	1533	1.6	2113	0.7
17	TH	0421	1.6	0918	0.8	1621	1.7	2142	0.6
18	F	0459	1.7	0952	0.7	1702	1.9	2212	0.4
19	SA	0534	1.9	1026	0.5	1741	2.0	2246	0.3
20	SU	0608	2.0	1103	0.4	1816	2.0	2322	0.2
21	M	0640	2.1	1141	0.3	1850	2.1	○ 2358	0.2
22	TU	0710	2.1	1217	0.3	1922	2.1		
23	W	0030	0.2	0738	2.1	1249	0.3	1953	2.0
24	TH	0058	0.2	0805	2.0	1314	0.3	2022	1.9
25	F	0120	0.3	0829	2.0	1334	0.4	2046	1.8
26	SA	0139	0.4	0851	1.8	1354	0.5	2110	1.6
27	SU	0200	0.5	0915	1.7	1420	0.6	2138	1.5
28	M	0227	0.6	0947	1.6	1459	0.7	2221	1.4
29	TU	0308	0.8	1038	1.5	1616	0.8	2337	1.3
30	W	0458	0.9	1202	1.5	1839	0.8		
31	TH	0150	1.4	0719	0.9	1400	1.6	2005	0.7

NOVEMBER

Date	Day	Time	m	Time	m	Time	m	Time	m
1	F	0324	1.6	0833	0.7	1528	1.8	2102	0.5
2	SA	0422	1.8	0926	0.5	1630	2.0	2150	0.3
3	SU	0513	2.1	1014	0.4	1725	2.2	2236	0.1
4	M	0600	2.2	1059	0.2	1815	2.3	● 2320	0.0
5	TU	0644	2.3	1142	0.1	1902	2.3		
6	W	0003	0.0	0726	2.4	1225	0.1	1945	2.3
7	TH	0044	0.1	0805	2.3	1307	0.2	2025	2.2
8	F	0124	0.2	0843	2.2	1347	0.3	2103	2.0
9	SA	0201	0.4	0917	2.0	1429	0.5	2138	1.8
10	SU	0238	0.6	0949	1.8	1515	0.6	2215	1.5
11	M	0317	0.8	1024	1.7	1615	0.8	2304	1.4
12	TU	0410	1.0	1113	1.5	1738	0.9		
13	W	0101	1.3	0539	1.1	1252	1.5	1922	0.8
14	TH	0250	1.4	0721	1.0	1440	1.5	2018	0.7
15	F	0339	1.5	0826	0.9	1532	1.6	2054	0.6
16	SA	0416	1.7	0910	0.8	1614	1.7	2130	0.5
17	SU	0450	1.8	0949	0.6	1653	1.8	2207	0.4
18	M	0524	1.9	1029	0.5	1733	1.9	2244	0.3
19	TU	0559	2.0	1107	0.4	1812	2.0	2320	0.3
20	W	0634	2.1	1143	0.4	1851	2.0	○ 2354	0.3
21	TH	0708	2.1	1215	0.4	1927	1.9		
22	F	0025	0.3	0740	2.1	1245	0.4	2000	1.9
23	SA	0054	0.4	0809	2.0	1314	0.4	2030	1.8
24	SU	0124	0.5	0835	1.9	1344	0.5	2059	1.7
25	M	0155	0.5	0905	1.8	1420	0.6	2134	1.6
26	TU	0231	0.7	0942	1.7	1509	0.6	2222	1.5
27	W	0323	0.8	1033	1.6	1625	0.7	2333	1.4
28	TH	0456	0.9	1147	1.6	1802	0.7		
29	F	0113	1.5	0637	0.9	1322	1.6	1922	0.6
30	SA	0241	1.6	0754	0.7	1448	1.7	2025	0.5

DECEMBER

Date	Day	Time	m	Time	m	Time	m	Time	m
1	SU	0345	1.8	0854	0.6	1556	1.9	2119	0.4
2	M	0440	2.0	0946	0.5	1654	2.0	2208	0.3
3	TU	0530	2.1	1035	0.4	1748	2.1	2256	0.2
4	W	0618	2.2	1122	0.3	1839	2.1	● 2341	0.2
5	TH	0703	2.3	1207	0.3	1926	2.1		
6	F	0024	0.2	0745	2.3	1251	0.3	2009	2.0
7	SA	0105	0.3	0825	2.2	1334	0.4	2049	1.9
8	SU	0144	0.4	0901	2.1	1416	0.5	2125	1.7
9	M	0222	0.6	0932	1.9	1500	0.6	2159	1.6
10	TU	0300	0.7	1003	1.7	1549	0.7	2237	1.4
11	W	0341	0.8	1041	1.6	1648	0.7	2328	1.3
12	TH	0439	0.9	1133	1.5	1756	0.8		
13	F	0039	1.3	0601	1.0	1243	1.4	1901	0.7
14	SA	0206	1.4	0718	0.9	1400	1.5	1956	0.6
15	SU	0308	1.5	0820	0.8	1507	1.5	2043	0.6
16	M	0356	1.6	0909	0.7	1603	1.6	2126	0.5
17	TU	0439	1.8	0954	0.6	1653	1.7	2206	0.4
18	W	0522	1.9	1034	0.5	1740	1.8	2246	0.4
19	TH	0604	2.0	1113	0.5	1826	1.9	○ 2325	0.3
20	F	0645	2.1	1150	0.4	1910	1.9		
21	SA	0003	0.3	0724	2.1	1228	0.4	1950	1.9
22	SU	0043	0.4	0800	2.1	1306	0.4	2028	1.8
23	M	0122	0.4	0835	2.0	1345	0.4	2104	1.8
24	TU	0202	0.4	0910	1.9	1428	0.4	2142	1.7
25	W	0245	0.5	0950	1.8	1517	0.5	2226	1.6
26	TH	0335	0.6	1036	1.7	1615	0.5	2320	1.5
27	F	0436	0.7	1134	1.7	1724	0.6		
28	SA	0028	1.5	0549	0.7	1243	1.6	1835	0.6
29	SU	0146	1.6	0706	0.7	1402	1.6	1944	0.5
30	M	0302	1.7	0818	0.7	1519	1.7	2048	0.5
31	TU	0409	1.8	0922	0.6	1628	1.8	2147	0.4

Chart Datum: 0·93 metres below Ordnance Datum (Newlyn)

PORTLAND TIDAL STREAMS *9.2.8*

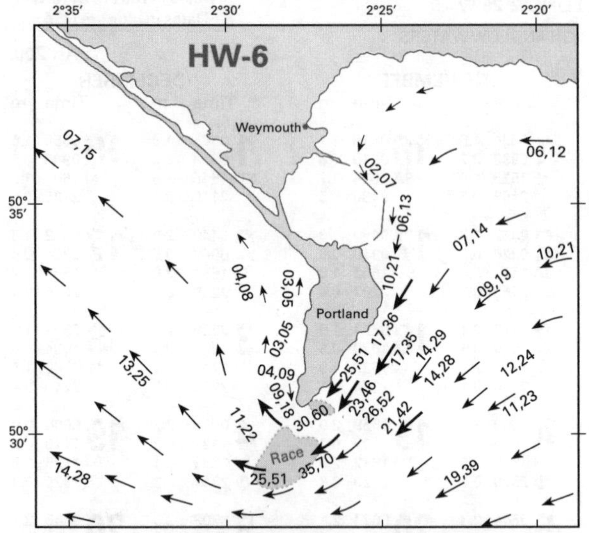

6 Hours before HW Portland (0145 after HW Dover)

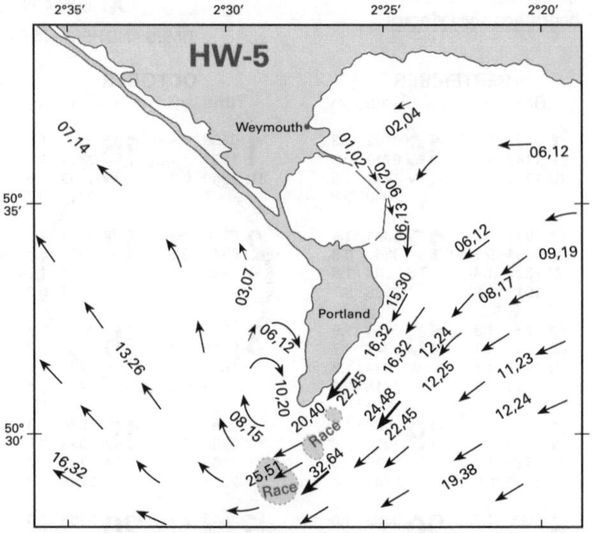

5 Hours before HW Portland (0245 after HW Dover)

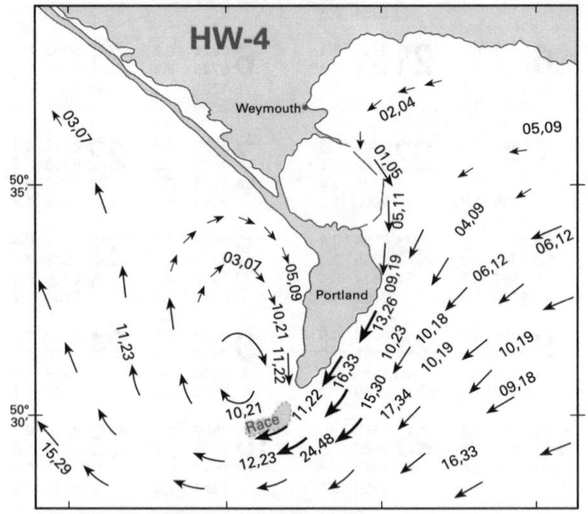

4 Hours before HW Portland (0345 after HW Dover)

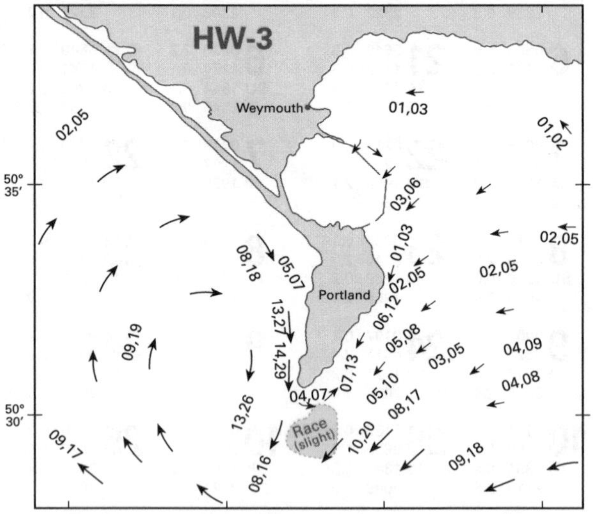

3 Hours before HW Portland (0445 after HW Dover)

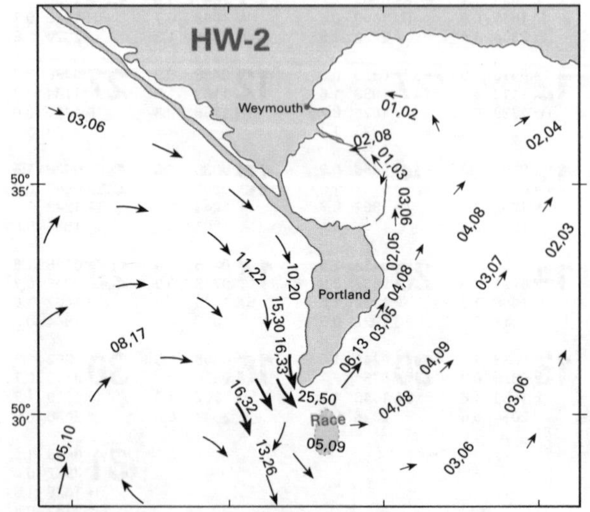

2 Hours before HW Portland (0545 after HW Dover)

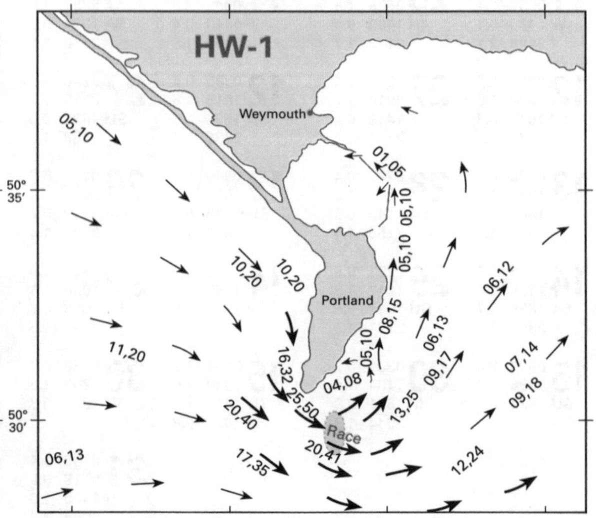

1 Hour before HW Portland (0540 before HW Dover)

General Area 2 9.2.3

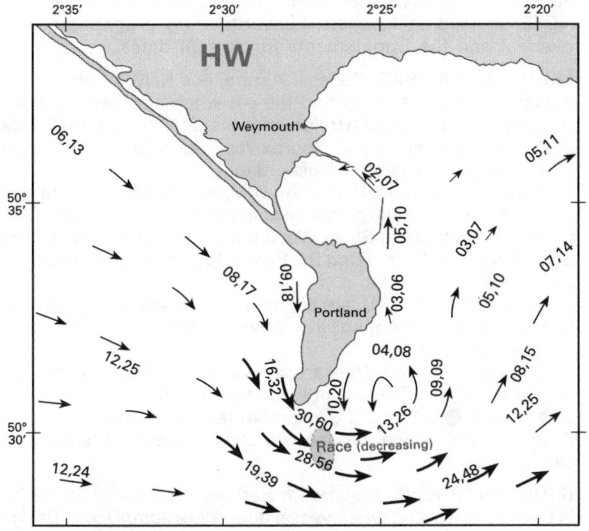

HW Portland (0440 before HW Dover)

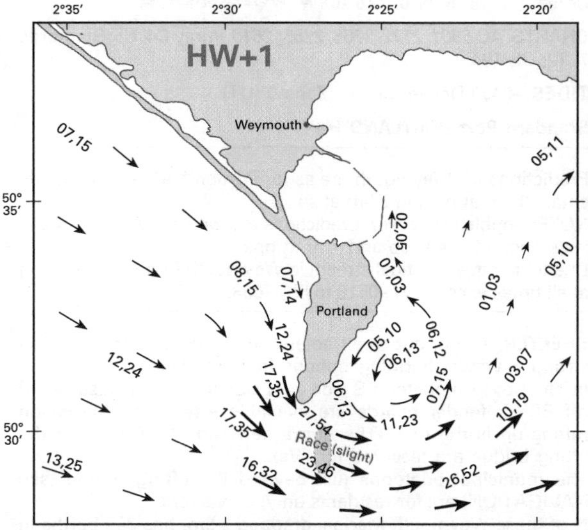

1 Hour after HW Portland (0340 before HW Dover)

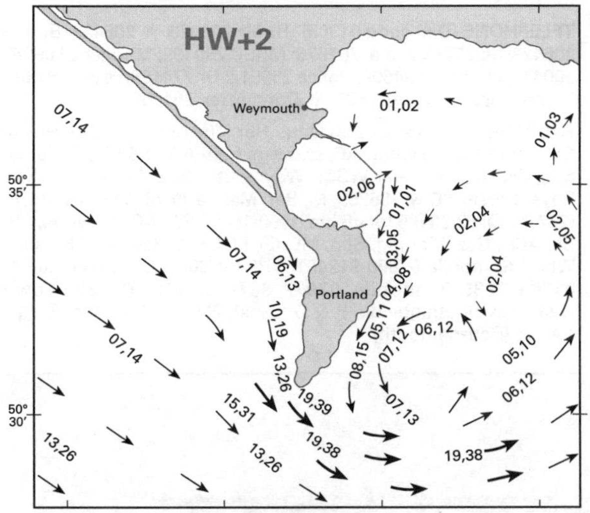

2 Hours after HW Portland (0240 before HW Dover)

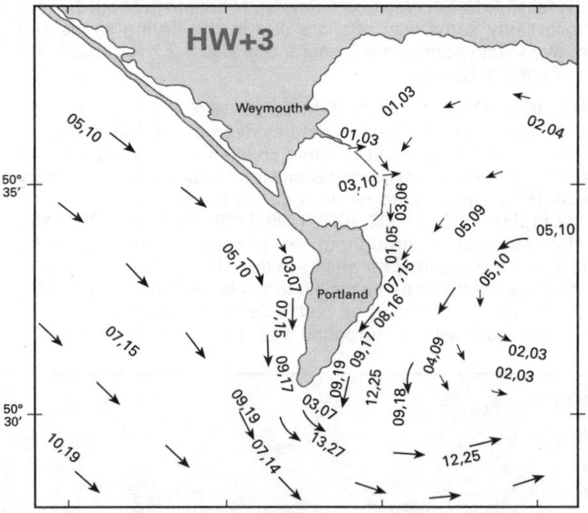

3 Hours after HW Portland (0140 before HW Dover)

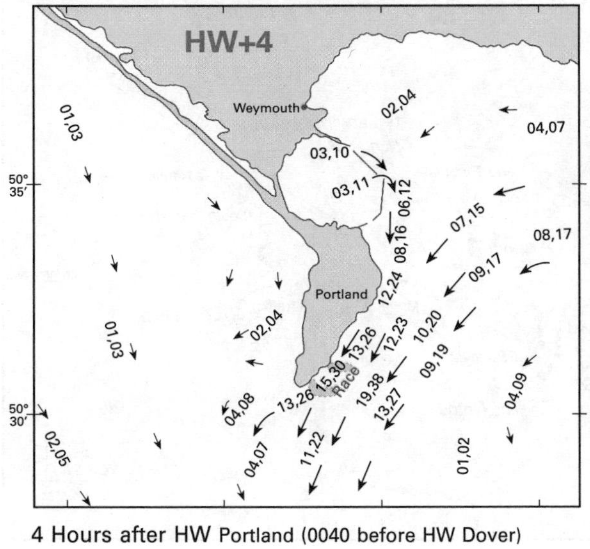

4 Hours after HW Portland (0040 before HW Dover)

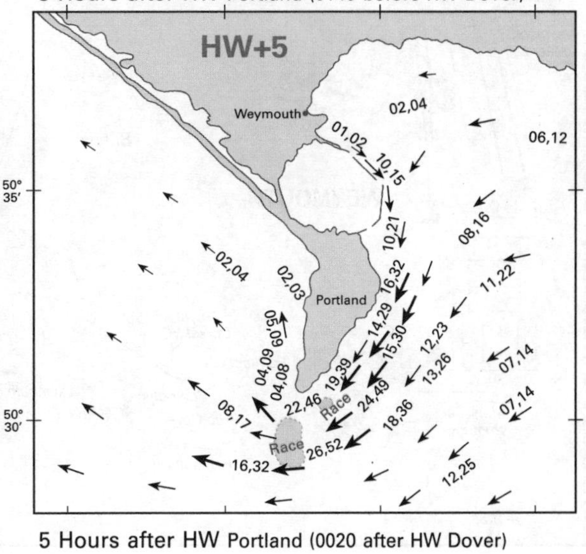

5 Hours after HW Portland (0020 after HW Dover)

WEYMOUTH *9.2.9*

Dorset **50°36'·57N 02°26'·58W** ❁❁❁⛵⛵⛵✿✿✿

CHARTS AC *5601, 2172,* 2268, 2255, *2610*; Imray C4, C5; Stanfords 7, 12; OS 194

TIDES –0438 Dover; ML 1·1; Zone 0 (UT)

Standard Port PORTLAND (⟵)

Predictions for Weymouth are as for Portland. Mean ranges are small: 0·6m at np and 2·0m at sp.
NOTE: Double LWs occur; predictions are for first LW. A LW stand lasts about 4 hrs at sp and 1 hr at nps.
Due to an eddy, the tidal stream in Weymouth Roads is W-going at all times except HW –0510 to HW –038.

SHELTER Good, but swell enters outer hbr and The Cove in strong E winds. Berthing options from seaward:
In The Cove on pontoon S side or N side (Custom House Quay) off RDYC; fender boards are available elsewhere. In season rafting-up is the rule. (The quays between The Cove and the lifting bridge are reserved for FVs).
The municipal pontoons just beyond the lifting bridge (see NAVIGATION) are for residents only; no visitors.
N of these Weymouth Marina, dredged 2·5m, has 300 berths in complete shelter.
It is feasible to ⚓ in Weymouth Bay, NE of hbr ent in about 3m, but necessarily some way offshore due to the drying sands and buoyed watersport areas inshore. See also 9.2.7 for possible ⚓ in Portland Harbour.

NAVIGATION WPT 50°36'·71N, 02°26'·18W 060°/240° from/to front ldg lt, 0·50M. The hbr ent lies deep in the NW corner of Weymouth Bay; it could in some conditions be confused with the N ent to Portland Hbr. Hbr speed limit is 'Dead Slow'. Comply with IPTS. High Speed Ferries operate in the area.
The **bridge** lifts (LT) 0800, 1000, 1200, 1400, 1600, 1800, 2000 and 2100 on request throughout the summer. 1 hr's notice by telephone is required for all lifts in the winter. Five mins before lift times, craft should be visible to the br, and listening on VHF Ch 12. 3FR or 3FG (vert) on both sides of the bridge are tfc lts, not navigational lts; outbound vessels usually take priority. Waiting pontoons are close E of bridge on S side and also on the marina side. Clearances when the bridge is down are approx 2·7m MHWS, 3·8m MHWN, 4·6m MLWN, 5·2m MLWS.
NOTE: If heading E, check Lulworth firing programme; see overleaf and the Supplements for current dates.

LIGHTS AND MARKS Conspic ⊕ spire, 6ca NNW of hbr ent, is a useful daymark to help find the ent when approaching from SE past the Portland bkwtrs or from the E. Note: On the E side of Portland Hbr (see 9.2.7), approx 7ca ESE of 'D' Head lt, are 4 SPM lt buoys (marking a Noise range).
Portland 'A' Head lt ho, Fl 10s 22m 20M, is 1·7M SE of hbr ent and provides the best initial guidance at night; it is also a conspic W tr.
Caution: About 500m SE of Weymouth S Pier there are 3 SPM buoys (one Fl Y 2s) marking DG Range. Pierhead lts may be hard to see against shore lts.
Ldg lts 240°, 2 FR (H24), are 500m inside the pierhds; daymarks (same position) are R open ◊s on W poles; they are not visible until the hbr ent is opened.
IPTS must be obeyed. They are shown from a RW mast near the root of the S pier. There is one additional signal:
2 ● over 1 ● = Ent and dep prohib (ent obstructed).
If no sigs are shown, vessels are clear to enter or leave with caution.

RADIO TELEPHONE *Weymouth Harbour* VHF Ch 12 16 (0800-2000 in summer and when vessel due); *Weymouth Town Bridge* also on 12 (at opening times). *Weymouth Marina* Ch 80. Ch 60 for diesel.

TELEPHONE (Dial code 01305) Hr Mr 206423, 🖷 206422; Bridge 206423/789357; Marina 767576; MRSC 760439; Marinecall 09068 500457; ⊜ 01202 634500; Police 250512; Dr 774466; Ⓗ Weymouth (minor injuries only) 760022, Dorchester 251150.

FACILITIES (From seaward) Outer Hbr, The Cove, Custom House Quay (only at the latter: AC, showers free) AB £1.60 (£5.50 for <4 hrs), FW, M, Slip near WSC; Weymouth SC ☎ 785481, M, Bar; **Royal Dorset YC** ☎ 786258, M, Bar; **Marina** ☎ 767576, 🖷 767575; (237 inc Ⓥ) £2.20 (£5 for <5 hrs, 1000-1600), FW, AC; **Services:** CH, Sh, ACA, Gaz, Rigging, Slip, ME, Ⓔ, El, CH. D Raybar at Nelsons Wharf ☎ mobile 07860 912401, VHF Ch 60 or Quayside Fuel ☎ 01305 783567, mobile 07977 337620, VHF Ch 60. **Town** www.weymouth.gov.uk, P & D (cans), FW, ⓖ, V, R, Bar, ✉, Ⓑ, ⇌, ✈ (Bournemouth).

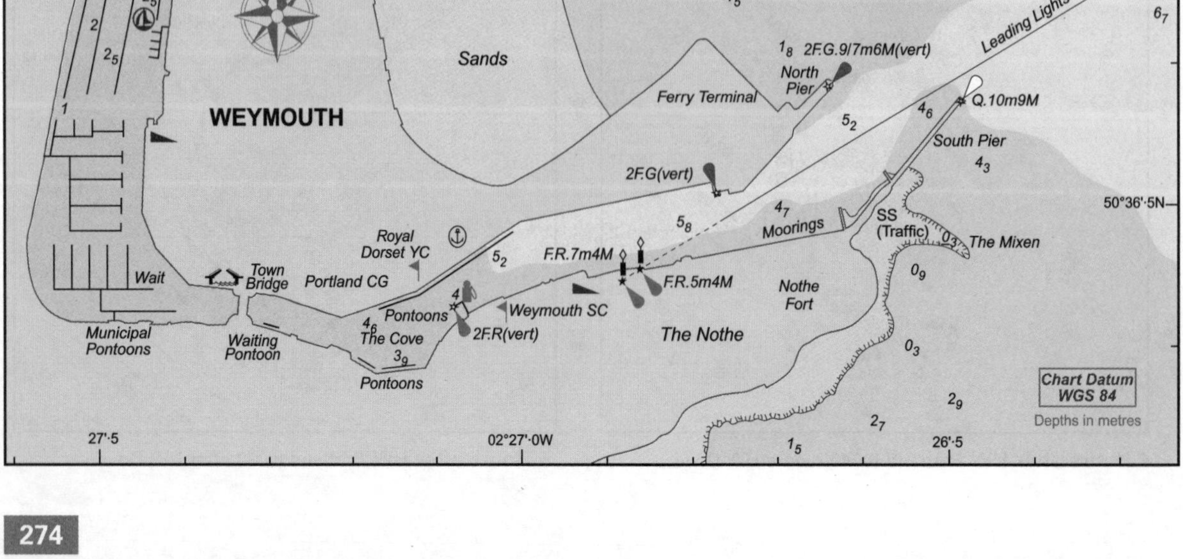

LULWORTH FIRING RANGES *9.2.10*

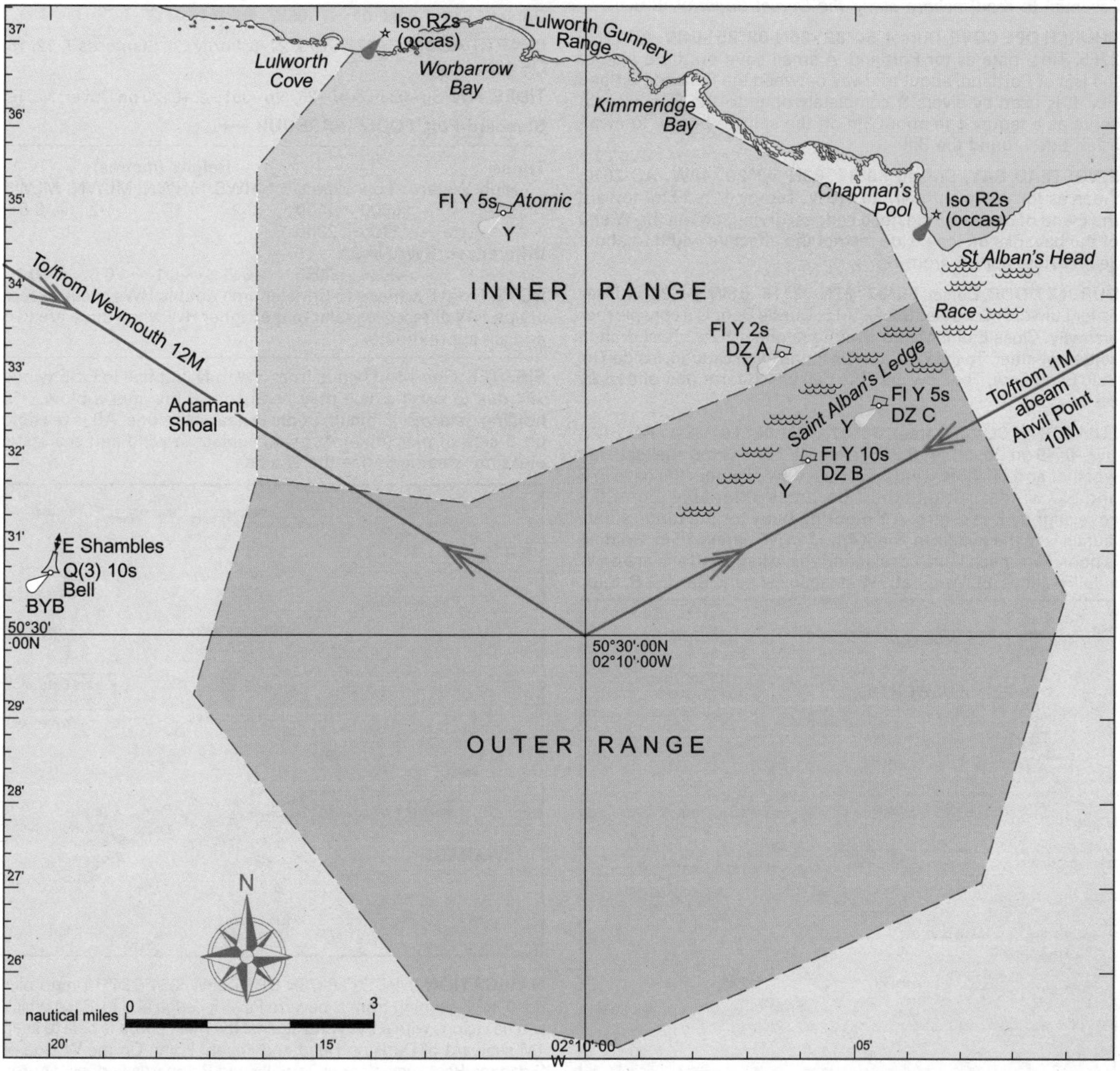
Iso R2s
(occas)
Lulworth Gunnery Range
Lulworth Cove
Worbarrow Bay
Kimmeridge Bay
Chapman's Pool
Iso R2s
(occas)
St Alban's Head
Race
Fl Y 5s Atomic
Y
INNER RANGE
To/from Weymouth 12M
Fl Y 2s
DZ A
Y
Saint Alban's Ledge
Fl Y 5s
DZ C
Y
Fl Y 10s
DZ B
Y
To/from 1M abeam Anvil Point 10M
Adamant Shoal
E Shambles
Q(3) 10s
Bell
BYB
50°30'
·00N
50°30'·00N
02°10'·00W
OUTER RANGE
N
nautical miles
0
3
20'
15'
02°10'·00W
05'
37'
36'
35'
34'
33'
32'
31'
29'
28'
27'
26'

Lulworth Firing Ranges comprise an inner and an outer sea danger area; the former is of most concern to yachts. See chartlet above and AC 2610.

Range boundaries: The inner area extends 5·5M offshore. It runs from 50°36'·96N 02°14'·44W (just E of Lulworth Cove) coastwise to 50°36'·73N 02°08'·23W (Kimmeridge Bay) then seaward, clockwise via: 50°36'·29N 02°08'·23W – 50°35'·03N 02°04'·68W – 50°34'·23N 02°03'·23W Ⓐ – 50°33'·17N 02°06'·43W – 50°31'·63N 02°12'·28W – 50°31'·93N 02°16'·18W Ⓑ – 50°35'·59N 02°16'·19W – just E of Lulworth Cove. The outer area extends 12M offshore and adjoins the seaward boundary of the inner between points Ⓐ and Ⓑ above. Its seaward limits are: 50°30'·53N 02°01'·08W – 50°27'·14N 02°02'·68W – 50°25'·23N 02°09'·48W – 50°25'·63N 02°12'·88W – 50°29'·33N 02°17'·38W – 50°31'·93N 02°16'·19W. It is used about 10 days per annum and is rarely active at night or weekends.

Naval firing: Warships may use the inner and outer areas, firing eastward from Adamant Shoal (50°33'N 02°19'W) at the 3 DZ target buoys, (up to 3M SW of St Alban's Head) which should be avoided by at least 1M. Warships fly R flags and other vessels/helicopters may patrol the area.

Army firing: on the inner range occurs most weekdays from 0930-1700 (1200 on Fri), often on Tues and Thurs nights for 3-4 hrs and for up to six weekends per year. There is NO firing in August. When firing is in progress R flags (Fl R lts at night) are flown from St Alban's Head and Bindon Hill. However some R flags are flown whether or not firing is taking place; these mark the boundary of the range land area.

Information: Times of firing are printed in local papers, sent to local Hr Mrs and YCs and are obtainable from the Range Officer ☎ (01929) 462721 ext. 4700/4859, 📠 4912, during office hours and from the guardroom ext 4819 at other times. Firing times are broadcast daily by Radio Solent (1359kHz, 999kHz or 96·1MHz FM on Mon-Fri at 0533, 0645, 0845, 1745 LT and on Sat-Sun at 0633, 0745 LT. Times can also be obtained from Portland CG (Ch 16), Range Control or Range Safety Boats (Ch 08). The annual firing weekends and No Firing periods are printed in the updating Supplements to this Almanac.

Regulations: When the ranges are active the Range Safety boats will intercept yachts in the area and firmly, but politely, invite them (Ch 08) to clear the area as quickly as possible. However all the land danger area and the inner sea danger area are subject to the regulations laid down in *The Lulworth Ranges Byelaws 1978 operative from 10 Nov 1978 - Statutory Instruments 1978 No 1663.* A key passage states: *The Byelaws shall not apply to any vessel in the ordinary course of navigation, not being used for fishing, in the Sea Area and remaining in the Sea Area no longer than is reasonably necessary to pass through the Sea Area.*

Yachts should make every reasonable effort to keep clear when firing is in progress. If on passage between Weymouth and Anvil Point, a track via 50°30'N 02°10'W just clips the SW corner of the inner range, avoids St Alban's Race and is only 3·3M longer than a direct track.

ANCHORAGES BETWEEN PORTLAND AND SWANAGE

Essential to read *Inshore along the Dorset Coast* (P. Bruce).

CHURCH OPE COVE, Dorset, **50°32′·26N 02°25′·64W**. AC 2268, 2255. Tidal data as for Portland. A small cove on the E side of the Isle of Portland, about midway between the Bill and Portland Hbr. It is used by divers & completely open to the E, but could serve as a tempy ⚓ in about 3m off the shingle beach, to await a fair tide around the Bill.

RINGSTEAD BAY, Dorset, **50°37′·83N 02°20′·48W**. AC 2610. Tides as for Weymouth, 4M to WSW. Tempy ⚓ in 3-5m toward the E end of the bay. Ringstead Ledges, drying, define the W end of the bay. Rks on the E side restrict the effective width to about 3ca; easiest appr is from SE.

DURDLE DOOR, Dorset, **50°37′·27N 02°16′·58W**. AC 2610. Tides as for Lulworth Cove (see 9.2.7), 1M E. Durdle Door is a conspic rock archway. Close E of it Man o' War Cove offers ⚓ for shoal draft in settled weather. To the W, ⚓ may be found, with caution, inside The Bull, Blind Cow, The Cow and The Calf which form part of a rocky reef.

LULWORTH COVE, Dorset, **50°37′·00N 02°14′·82W**. AC *2172*. HW –0449 on Dover, see 9.2.7. Tides; ML 1·2m. Good shelter in fair weather and offshore winds, but heavy swell enters the cove in S and SW winds; if strong the ⚓ becomes untenable. Enter the cove slightly E of centre. A Y mooring buoy for the range safety launch is in the middle in about 4m. ⚓ in NE part in 2·5m. Holding is poor. 8kn speed limit. Local moorings, village and slip are on W side. Facilities: EC Wed/Sat; FW at tap in car park, Bar, ⊠, R, Slip.

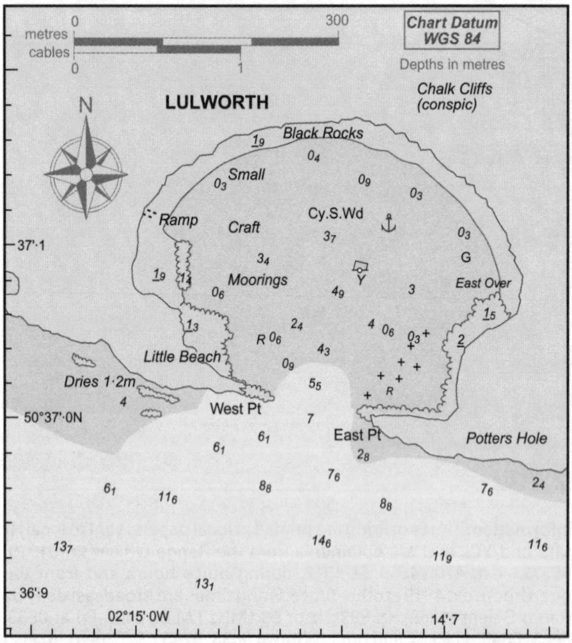

WORBARROW BAY, Dorset, **50°37′·03N 02°12′·08W**. AC *2172*. Tides as Lulworth Cove/Mupe Bay, see 9.2.7. Worbarrow is a 1½M wide bay, close E of Lulworth Cove. It is easily identified from seaward by the V-shaped gap in the hills at Arish Mell, centre of bay just E of Bindon Hill. Bindon Hill also has a white chalk scar due to cliff falls. Caution: Mupe Rks at W end and other rks 1ca off NW side. ⚓s in about 3m sheltered from W or E winds at appropriate end. The bay lies within Lulworth Ranges (see above); landing prohib at Arish Mell. No lights/facilities.

CHAPMAN'S POOL, Dorset, **50°35′·53N 02°03′·93W**. AC *2172*. Tidal data: interpolate between Mupe Bay (9.2.7) and Swanage (9. 2.11). Chapman's Pool, like Worbarrow Bay, Brandy Bay and Kimmeridge Bay, is picturesque and convenient when the wind is off-shore. ⚓ in depths of about 3m in centre of bay to avoid tidal swirl, but beware large unlit Y buoy (for Range Safety boat). From here to St Alban's Hd the stream runs SSE almost continuously due to a back eddy. No lights or facilities.

SWANAGE *9.2.11*

Dorset **50°36′·81N 01°57′·05W** ❀❀❀✿✿✿✿

CHARTS AC *5601, 2172, 2610, 2175*; Imray C4; Stanfords 7, 12, 15; OS 195

TIDES HW Sp –0235 & +0125, Np –0515 & +0120 on Dover; ML 1·5

Standard Port POOLE HARBOUR (⟶)

Times				Height (metres)			
High Water		Low Water		MHWS	MHWN	MLWN	MLWS
–	–	0500	1100	2·2	1·7	1·2	0·6
–	–	1700	2300				
Differences SWANAGE							
–	–	–0045	–0055	–0·2	–0·1	0·0	–0·1

NOTE: From Swanage to Christchurch double HWs occur except at nps. HW differences refer to the higher HW when there are two and are approximate.

SHELTER Good ⚓ in winds from SW to N, but bad in E/SE winds >F4 due to swell which may persist for 6 hrs after a blow. >F6 holding gets very difficult; Poole is nearest refuge. AB is feasible on S side of pier (open Apr-Oct) subject to wind and sea state; pleasure 'steamers' use the N side.

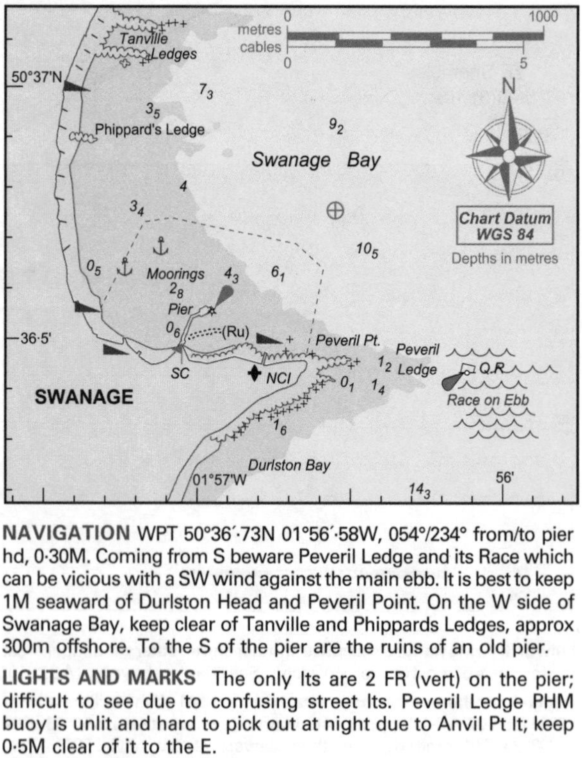

NAVIGATION WPT 50°36′·73N 01°56′·58W, 054°/234° from/to pier hd, 0·30M. Coming from S beware Peveril Ledge and its Race which can be vicious with a SW wind against the main ebb. It is best to keep 1M seaward of Durlston Head and Peveril Point. On the W side of Swanage Bay, keep clear of Tanville and Phippards Ledges, approx 300m offshore. To the S of the pier are the ruins of an old pier.

LIGHTS AND MARKS The only lts are 2 FR (vert) on the pier; difficult to see due to confusing street lts. Peveril Ledge PHM buoy is unlit and hard to pick out at night due to Anvil Pt lt; keep 0·5M clear of it to the E.

RADIO TELEPHONE None.

TELEPHONE (Dial code 01929) Pier 427058, mobile 0780 1616216; MRSC (01305) 760439; ⊜ 0345 231110 (H24) or (01202) 685157; Marinecall 09068 500457; Police 422004; Dr 422231; Ⓗ 422202.

FACILITIES Pier, L*, FW, AB* £1, £3 for <3hrs; after 2100 gain access to pier from ashore via **Swanage SC** ☎ 422987, Slip, L, FW, Bar, ♿; **Boat Park** (Peveril Pt), Slip, FW, L; **Services:** Diving. **Town** P & D (cans, 1½M), FW, V, R, Bar, ⊠, Ⓑ, ⇌ (bus connection to Wareham), ✈ (Hurn).

ADJACENT ANCHORAGE

STUDLAND BAY, Dorset, **50°38′·73N 01°55′·90W**. AC*2172*, 2175. Tides approx as for Swanage (9.2.11). Shelter is good except in N/E winds. Beware Redend Rocks off S shore. Best ⚓ in about 3m, 3ca NW of The Yards (three strange projections on the chalk cliffs near Handfast Pt). **Village**: EC Thurs; FW, V, R, ⊠, hotel, P&D (cans), No marine facilities. A Historic Wreck (see 9.0.3h) is at 50°39′·70N 01°54′·87W, 4·5ca NNE of Poole Bar Buoy.

SPECIAL TIDAL PROBLEMS FROM BOURNEMOUTH TO SELSEY *9.2.12*

Due to the complex tidal variations between Bournemouth and Selsey Bill, applying the usual secondary port time & height differences gives only approximate predictions. More accurate values are obtained by using the individual curves discussed below. **Individual curves,** as shown on the following two pages, are given for each port to cater for the rapidly changing tidal characteristics and distorted tidal curves in this area. Because their low water (LW) points are more sharply defined than high water (HW), *the times on these curves are referenced to LW,* but in all other respects they are used as described in Chapter 7.

Critical curve. Since the curves at hbrs from Bournemouth to Yarmouth, IOW differ considerably in shape and duration between Springs and Neaps, the tide cannot adequately be defined by only Sp and Np curves. A third, "critical", curve is therefore shown for that Portsmouth range (as indicated in the lower right of the graph) at which the heights of the two HWs are equal for the port concerned. Interpolation should be between this critical curve and either the Sp or Np curve, as appropriate.

Note that whilst the critical curve extends throughout the tidal cycle, the spring and neap curves stop at the higher HW. Thus, for example, at 7hrs after LW Lymington, with a Portsmouth range of 3·8m (near Sp), the factor should be referenced to the next LW; whereas if the Portsmouth range had been 2·0m (near Np), it should be referenced to the previous LW.

The procedure is shown step-by-step in the following example using the **Differences BOURNEMOUTH** and the special curves for Bournemouth below.

Example: Find the height of tide at Bournemouth at 0220 on a day when the tidal predictions for Portsmouth are:

November

18 SA

	0110	4·6
	0613	1·1
	1318	4·6
	1833	1·0

Standard Port PORTSMOUTH

Times				**Height (metres)**			
High Water		Low Water		MHWS	MHWN	MLWN	MLWS
0000	0600	0500	1100	4·7	3·8	1·9	0·8
1200	1800	1700	2300				
Differences BOURNEMOUTH							
−0240	+0055	−0050	−0030	−2·7	−2·2	−0·8	−0·3

(a) Complete the upper part of the tidal prediction form (next Col), the contents of boxes 8*, 9* and 10* are obtained by interpolation.

(b) On the left of the Bournemouth tidal curve diagram, plot the Secondary Port HW and LW heights [1·9m and 0·7m from (a) above], and join these points with a sloping line.

(c) The time required (0220) is 3hr 7min before the time of LW at the Secondary Port, so from this point draw a line vertically up towards the curves.

(d) It is necessary to interpolate for the day's range at Portsmouth (3·5m), which is about mid-way between the spring curve (3·9m) and the critical curve (2·8m). (This incidentally gives a point level with a factor of 0·84).

STANDARD PORT Portsmouth TIME/HEIGHT REQUIRED 0220

SECONDARY PORT Bournemouth DATE 18 Nov TIMEZONE 0 (GMT)

	TIME		HEIGHT		
STANDARD PORT	HW	LW	HW	LW	RANGE
	1	2 0613	3 4.6	4 1.1	5 3.5
Seasonal change	Standard Port		6	6	
DIFFERENCES	7*	8* −0046	9* −2.7	10* −0.4	
Seasonal change	Standard Port		11	11	
SECONDARY PORT	12	13 0527	14 1.9	15 0.7	
Duration	16				

STANDARD PORT .... TIME/HEIGHT REQUIRED ....

SECONDARY PORT .... DATE .... TIMEZONE ....

	TIME		HEIGHT		
STANDARD PORT	HW	LW	HW	LW	RANGE
	1	2	3	4	5
Seasonal change	Standard Port		6	6	
DIFFERENCES	7*	8*	9*	10*	
Seasonal change	Standard Port		11	11	
SECONDARY PORT	12	13	14	15	
Duration	16				

(e) From this point draw a horizontal line to intersect the sloping line constructed in (b) above.

(f) From the intersection of the horizontal line and the sloping line, proceed vertically to the height scale at the top, and read off the height of tide at 0220 = 1·7m.

Note: From Bournemouth to Christchurch double HWs occur, except at nps. HW height differences, as given for each secondary port, always apply to the higher HW (that which reaches a factor of 1·0 on the curves). This higher HW should be used to obtain the range at the Secondary Port. HW time differences, which are not needed for this example, also refer to the higher HW.

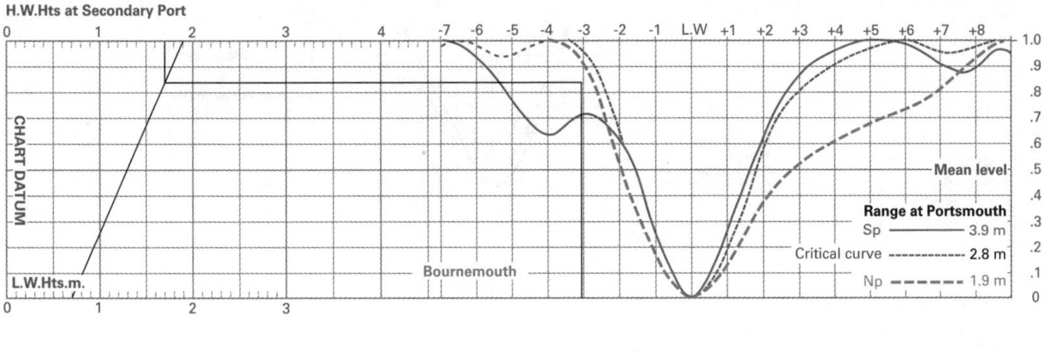

TIDAL CURVES: SWANAGE TO SELSEY BILL Individual tidal curves for places between Swanage and Selsey Bill are given below; their use is explained above. In this area the times of LW are much more sharply defined than the times of HW; the curves are therefore drawn with their times related to LW instead of HW. Apart from referencing the times to LW, the procedure for obtaining intermediate times and heights of tide is the same as for normal Secondary Ports (see 7.4.2). For places between Bournemouth and Yarmouth IOW a third curve is shown, for the range at Portsmouth at which the two HWs are equal at the port concerned; for interpolation between these curves see the previous page

Note 1.* Due to the constriction of the R Medina, Newport requires special treatment since the hbr dries 1·4m. The calculation should be made using the LW time and height differences for Cowes, and the HW height differences for Newport. Any calculated heights which fall below 1·4m should be treated as 1·4m.
Note 2.*** Wareham and Tuckton LWs do not fall below 0·7m except under very low river flow conditions.

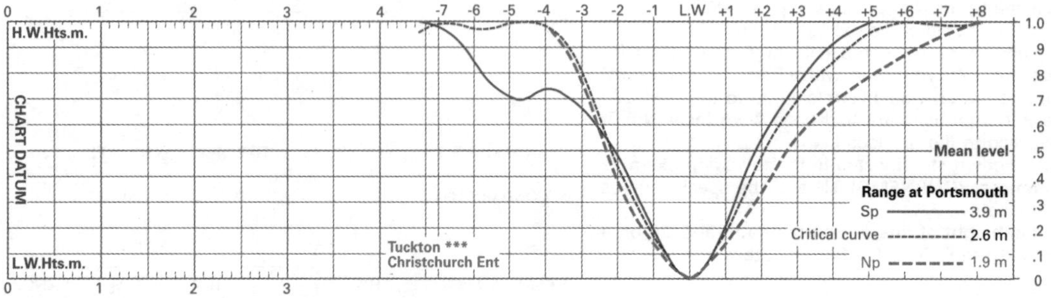
H.W.Hts.m.
L.W.Hts.m.
CHART DATUM
Tuckton ***
Christchurch Ent
L.W
Mean level
Range at Portsmouth
Sp 3.9 m
Critical curve 2.6 m
Np 1.9 m

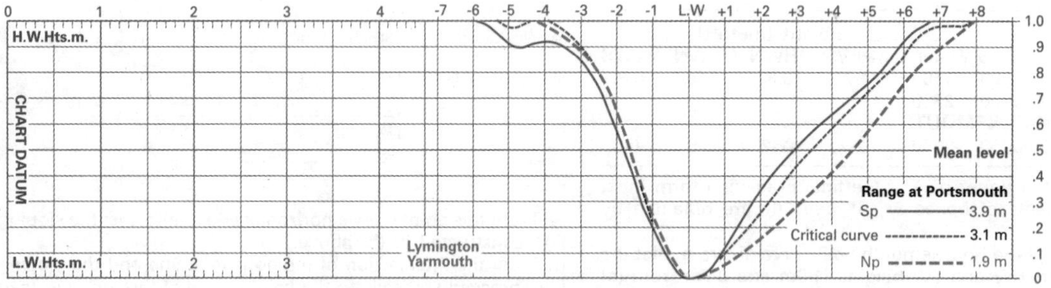
H.W.Hts.m.
L.W.Hts.m.
CHART DATUM
Lymington
Yarmouth
L.W
Mean level
Range at Portsmouth
Sp 3.9 m
Critical curve 3.1 m
Np 1.9 m

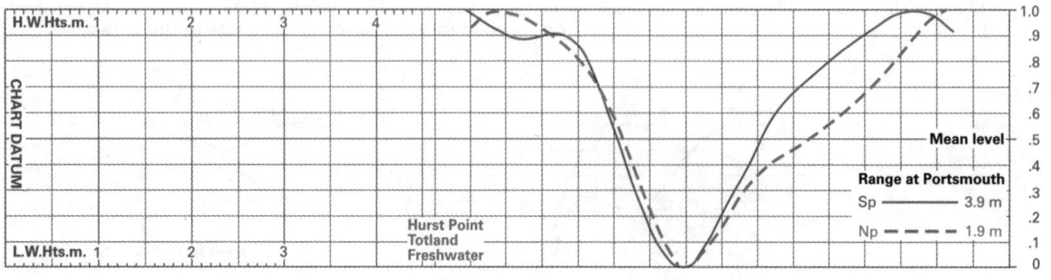
H.W.Hts.m.
L.W.Hts.m.
CHART DATUM
Hurst Point
Totland
Freshwater
Mean level
Range at Portsmouth
Sp 3.9 m
Np 1.9 m

H.W.Hts at Secondary Ports

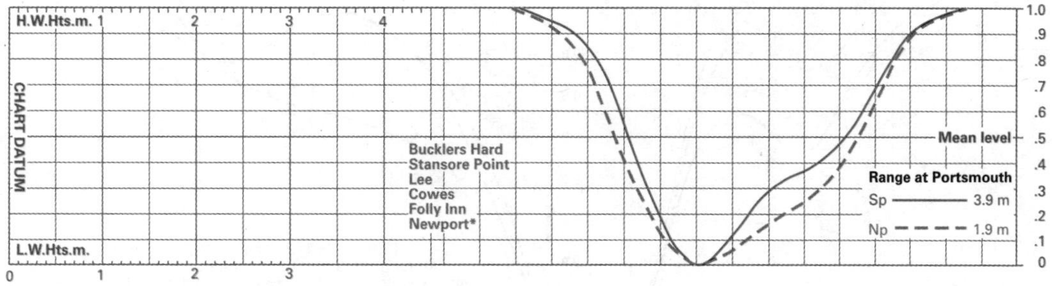
H.W.Hts.m. 1 2 3 4
CHART DATUM
L.W.Hts.m.
0 1 2 3
Bucklers Hard
Stansore Point
Lee
Cowes
Folly Inn
Newport*
Mean level
Range at Portsmouth
Sp 3.9 m
Np 1.9 m
1.0 .9 .8 .7 .6 .5 .4 .3 .2 .1 0

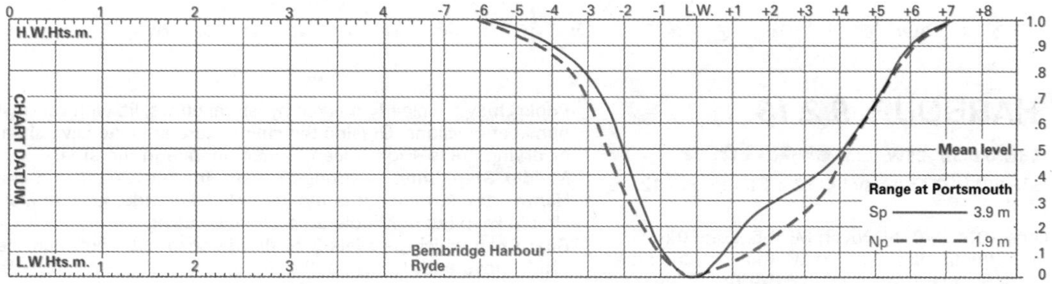
0 1 2 3 4
-7 -6 -5 -4 -3 -2 -1 L.W. +1 +2 +3 +4 +5 +6 +7 +8
H.W.Hts.m.
CHART DATUM
L.W.Hts.m. 1 2 3
Bembridge Harbour
Ryde
Mean level
Range at Portsmouth
Sp 3.9 m
Np 1.9 m
1.0 .9 .8 .7 .6 .5 .4 .3 .2 .1 0

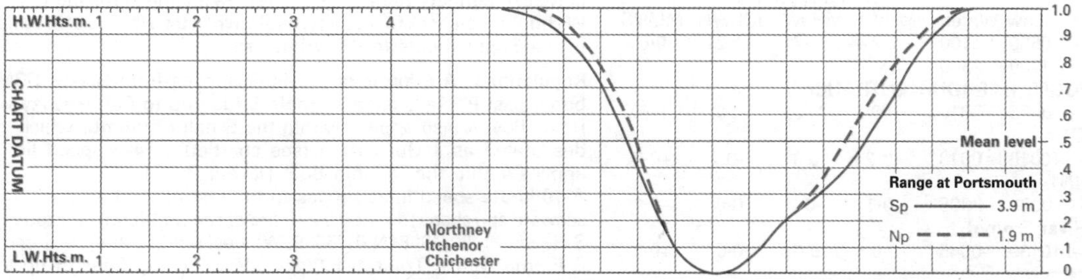
H.W.Hts.m. 1 2 3 4
CHART DATUM
L.W.Hts.m. 1 2 3
Northney
Itchenor
Chichester
Mean level
Range at Portsmouth
Sp 3.9 m
Np 1.9 m
1.0 .9 .8 .7 .6 .5 .4 .3 .2 .1 0

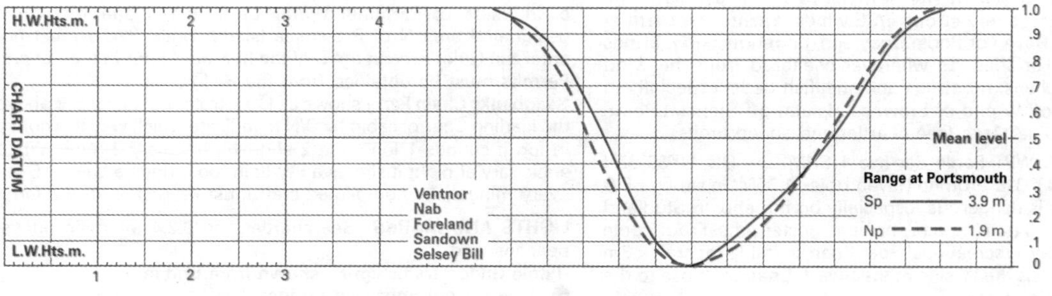
H.W.Hts.m. 1 2 3 4
CHART DATUM
L.W.Hts.m.
1 2 3
Ventnor
Nab
Foreland
Sandown
Selsey Bill
Mean level
Range at Portsmouth
Sp 3.9 m
Np 1.9 m
1.0 .9 .8 .7 .6 .5 .4 .3 .2 .1 0

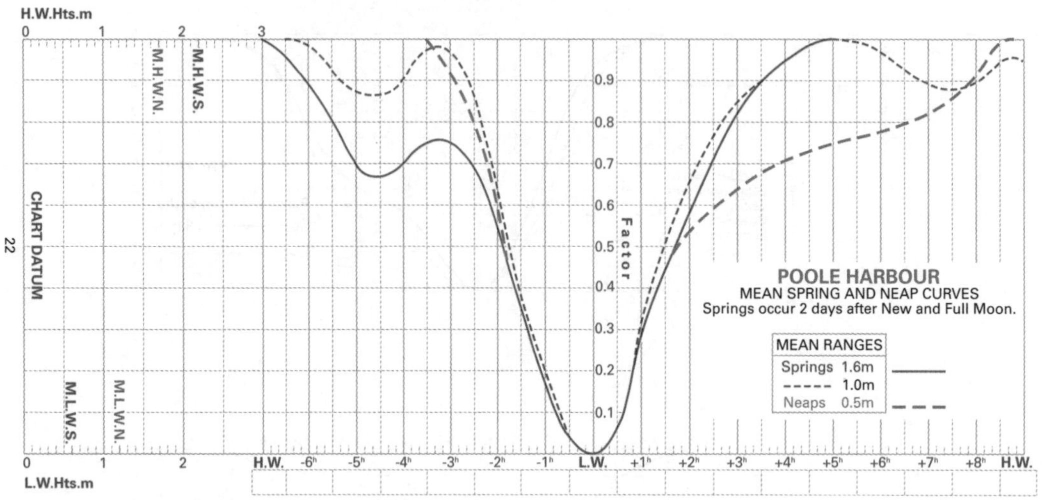
H.W.Hts.m
M.H.W.N.
M.H.W.S.
CHART DATUM
22
M.L.W.S.
M.L.W.N.
L.W.Hts.m
Factor
H.W. -6h -5h -4h -3h -2h -1h L.W. +1h +2h +3h +4h +5h +6h +7h +8h H.W.
POOLE HARBOUR
MEAN SPRING AND NEAP CURVES
Springs occur 2 days after New and Full Moon.
MEAN RANGES
Springs 1.6m
1.0m
Neaps 0.5m

POOLE HARBOUR *9.2.13*

Dorset **50°40'·93N 01°56'·96W** (Ent) ❀❀❀◊◊◊✿✿✿

CHARTS AC *5601, 2611, 2175*; Imray C4, Y23; Stanfords 7,12, 15; OS 195

TIDES Town Quay –0141, +0114 Dover; ML 1·6; Zone 0 (UT)
Daily predictions of the times and hts of LW (but only the hts of HW) are (⟶) for the Standard Port of **POOLE HARBOUR** (near the Ro-Ro terminal); sp and neap curves are above. (The tidal curves (⟵) simplify intermediate calculations.) Secondary Port differences are given below.

Standard Port POOLE HARBOUR (⟶)

Times				Height (metres)			
High Water		Low Water		MHWS	MHWN	MLWN	MLWS
–	–	0500	1100	2·2	1·7	1·2	0·6
–	–	1700	2300				
Differences POOLE HARBOUR ENTRANCE							
–	–	–0025	–0010	0·0	0·0	0·0	0·0
POTTERY PIER							
–	–	+0010	+0010	–0·2	0·0	+0·1	+0·2
CLEAVEL POINT							
–	–	–0005	–0005	–0·1	–0·2	0·0	–0·1
WAREHAM (River Frome)							
–	–	+0130	+0045	0·0	0·0	0·0	+0·3

Double HWs occur, except at nps. The ht of the 2nd HW is always about 1·8m; only the ht of the 1st HW varies from sp to nps. The tide is above Mean Level (1·6m) from about LW+2 to next LW–2. Strong and continuous winds from E to SW may raise sea levels by as much as 0·2m; W to NE winds may lower levels by 0·1m. Barometric pressure effects are also appreciable, see Chapter 7.

SHELTER An excellent hbr with narrow ent; access in all conditions except very strong E/SE winds. Yachts can berth at Dolphin Boat Haven or Poole Quay and, on request, in marinas listed under Facilities. ⚓s wherever sheltered from the wind and clear of chans, moorings and shellfish beds; especially in South Deep, off W end of Brownsea Is and off Shipstal Point, all within a Quiet Area (see chartlet and speed limits).

NAVIGATION WPT Poole Bar (No 1 SHM) By, QG, 50°39'·32N 01°55'·16W, 148°/328° from/to Haven Hotel, 1·95M. In strong SE-S winds the Bar is dangerous especially on the ebb. In Studland Bay and close to training bank beware lobster pots. From Poole Bar to Shell Bay a recreational **Boat Chan**, suitable for craft < 3m draught, parallels the W side of the Swash Channel, close to the E of the Training Bank.

East Looe Chan (buoyed) is liable to shift and may have less water than charted; only 1m was reported 1ca ENE of East Looe PHM buoy. 5 groynes to the N are marked by SHM bns, the two most W'ly are lit, 2 FG (vert).

Within the hbr the two chans (Middle Ship and North) up to Poole Quay are clearly marked by lateral buoys, lit, with cardinal buoys at divisions. Outside the chans there are extensive shoal or drying areas. High Speed Ferries operate in the area.

Middle Ship Chan is dredged 6·0m for ferries to/from the Hamworthy terminal; it is mostly only 80m wide. Leisure craft should keep out of Middle Ship Chan, by using a

Boat Chan which parallels S of the dredged chan between the PHM buoys and, further outboard, stakes with PHM topmarks marking the edge of the bank. Depth is 2·0m in this chan, but 1·5m closer to the stakes. Caution: When large ferries pass, a temporary, but significant reduction in depth may be remedied by closing the PHM buoys.

North Channel, the other option remains usable for yachts/leisure craft; best water is on the outside of chan bends.

Lulworth gunnery range (see 9.2.10). Yachtsmen cruising to the W should pre-check for activity, as shown in the Hr Mr's office and in the Supplements to this Almanac.

Regulations **A 6 knots** speed limit applies from Stakes SCM buoy, past Poole Quay and Poole Bridge up to Cobbs Quay in Holes Bay. It also applies within the S half of the hbr which is designated as a Quiet Area (see chartlet). A 4kn speed limit applies within the Dolphin Boat Haven.

A 10 knots speed limit applies to the rest of the hbr, from the seaward app chans (defined by an arc of radius 1400m centred on S Haven Pt, 50°40'·81N 01°56'·99W) westward to the junction of R Frome with R Trent at 02°04'·60W. Speeding fines of up to £1000 can be imposed.

Exemptions. The 10kn speed limit does not apply:

a. From 1 Oct to 31 Mar to vessels in the North, Middle Ship and Wareham Chans.

b. to water-skiers within the water-ski area between Gold Pt and No 82 PHM buoy (Wareham Chan; see chartlet). Permits must be obtained from the Hr Mr.

c. to users of Personal Water Craft (PWC) operating in a designated area N of Brownsea Island. Note: PWCs must not enter the Quiet Area in the S of the hbr, nor linger in the hbr ent. Permits must be obtained from the Hr Mr.

Sandbanks Chain Ferry shows a Fl W lt (rotating) and a B ● above the leading Control cabin by D/N to indicate which way it is going. In fog it sounds 1 long and 2 short blasts every 2 mins. When stationary at night it shows a FW lt; in fog it rings a bell for 5 sec every minute. All non-piloted craft must keep clear of the ferry.

LIGHTS AND MARKS See chartlet and 9.2.4 for main buoys, beacons and lts.

Poole Bridge traffic lights, shown from bridge tr:

● = Do not approach bridge;

Fl ● = Bridge lifting, proceed with caution; ● = Proceed.

Bridge lifts routinely for small craft at: Mon-Fri 0930, 1030, 1230, 1430, 1630, 1830, 2130; Sat, Sun & Bank hols = as Mon-Fri, plus 0730; at 2345 daily bridge will also lift if any vessels are waiting. Each lift only permits one cycle of traffic in each direction.

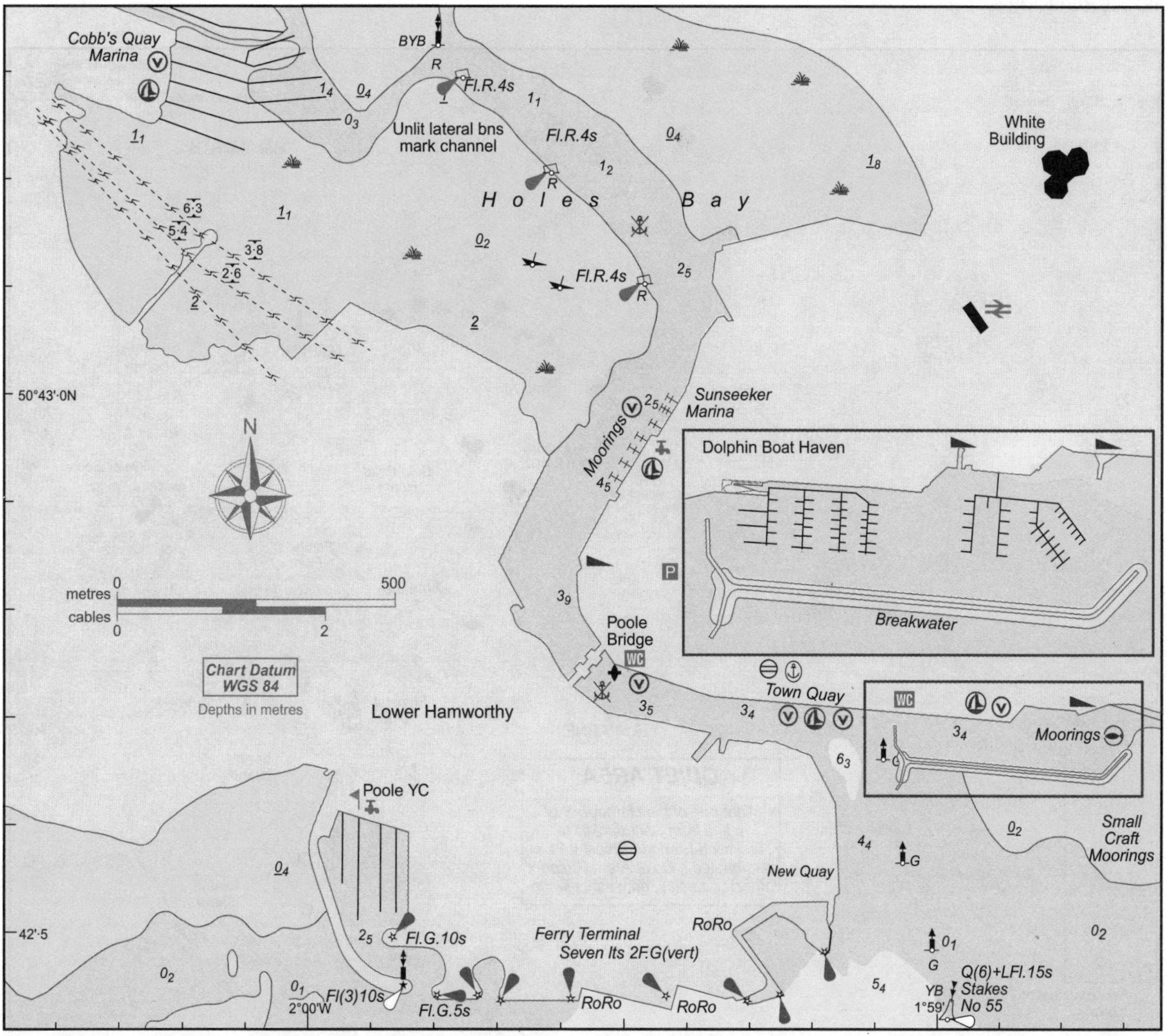

Pleasure craft may pass when the bridge lifts on request for a commercial vessel; monitor Ch 14. Bridge will not usually lift during weekday road traffic Rush Hours 0730-0930 and 1630-1830.

RADIO TELEPHONE Call: *Poole Hbr Control* VHF Ch 14 16 (H24). Dolphin Boat Haven Ch 80; Salterns Marina Ch M 80; Parkstone Haven Ch M; Poole YC Haven, call *Pike* Ch M; Poole Bridge, call *PB* Ch 14. Cobbs Quay, call *CQ Base* Ch 80.

TELEPHONE (Dial code 01202) Hr Mr 440233, 📠 440231; Dolphin Boat Haven 649488; Bridge 674115; MRSC (01305) 760439; ⊜ 01752 234600 (H24); Met (02392) 228844; Marinecall 09068 500457; Police 223954; Ⓗ 665511.

FACILITIES The following are some of the many facilities:
Marinas (from seaward)
Salterns Marina (300, few visitors) ☎ 709971, 📠 700398, ≤10m £23, max draft 2·5m, AC, FW, P & D (H24), ME, El, Ⓔ, Sh, CH, Gas, Gaz, C (5 ton), BH (45 ton), Bar, R, ⊡. Appr from No 31 SHM buoy, Fl G 5s.
Parkstone Haven, (Parkstone YC ☎ 743610), some Ⓥ berths, £16; dredged 2m. Access from North Chan near No 35 SHM buoy, Fl G 5s. Appr chan, dredged 2·5m, is marked by SHM buoy (Fl G 3s), 2 PHM and 3 SHM unlit buoys. Ldg daymarks 006°, both Y ◇s; ldg lts, front Iso Y 4s, rear FY. 2 FG and 2FR (vert) on bkwtr hds.
Poole Quay-Dolphin Boat Haven (100 Ⓥ) ☎/📠 649488, max draft 2.5m, £2.82, AC, FW, Haven Office open 0700-2200 Apr-Sep.
Dorset Yacht Co (56 AB + 6 Ⓥ; 90M + 6Ⓥ) ☎ 674531, 📠 677518, £1.50, P, D, AC, FW, CH, Slip, Gas/Gaz, ME, El, Sh, C (5 ton), BH (50 ton), Club bar/food; ent marked by 2FR (vert) and two 2FG (vert). Water taxi, weekends 1/4 to 1/10.

Beyond Poole Bridge:
Sunseeker International Marina (50) ☎ 685335, AC, Sh, D, BH (30 ton), C (36 ton), FW, ME, El, CH, V, R, Bar;
Cobbs Quay Marina (850, some visitors) ☎ 674299, 📠 665217, £2, Slip, P, D, Gas, LPG, ⊡, SM, FW, AC, ME, El, Ⓔ, Sh, C (10 ton), CH, R, Bar;
Public Landing Places: On Poole Quay, in Holes Bay and by ferry hards at Sandbanks. **Fuel** Poole Bay Fuels barge (May-Sep 0900-1800; moored near Aunt Betty buoy, No 50) P, D, Gas, Gaz, V, Off licence. **Corrals** (S side of Poole Quay adjacent bridge) P & D; **Salterns marina** P & D. **Yacht Clubs: Royal Motor YC** ☎ 707227, M, Bar, R; **Poole Bay YC; Parkstone YC** ☎ 743610 (Parkstone Haven); **Poole YC** ☎ 672687. **Services** A complete range of marine services is available; consult marina/Hr Mr for exact locations. **Town** EC Wed; ✉, Ⓑ, ≹, ✈. Ferry to Cherbourg and Channel Islands (all year).

WAREHAM, Dorset, **50°41′·03N 02°06′·56W.** AC *2611*. HW –0030 (Np), +0320 (Sp) on Dover (see 9.2.12 & .13). Shelter very good. Access approx HW±2, via narrow and winding chan and R Frome, but well marked by buoys and posts at ent; keep to the outside of all bends. Passage is unlit beyond No 82 PHM buoy, FIR 5s. There is a water-ski area between this buoy and Gold Pt on the N side of the Arne peninsula. Beware prohib ⚓s (salmon holes) marked on the chart; also many moored boats. Max draft 1·2m to Wareham Quay.
Facilities: **Ridge Wharf Yacht Centre** (180+6 visitors) (½M upstream of R Frome ent) ☎ (01929) 552650, £14, Access HW±2 approx AB, M, FW, P, D, ME, El, Gas, AC, BH (20 ton), Slip, Sh, CH; **Redclyffe YC** ☎ 551227 (½M below bridge); **Wareham Quay** AB, FW, R. **Town** EC Wed, P & D (cans), V, Gas, R, Bar, ✉, Ⓑ, ≹, Dr ☎ 3444.

POOLE HARBOUR *continued*

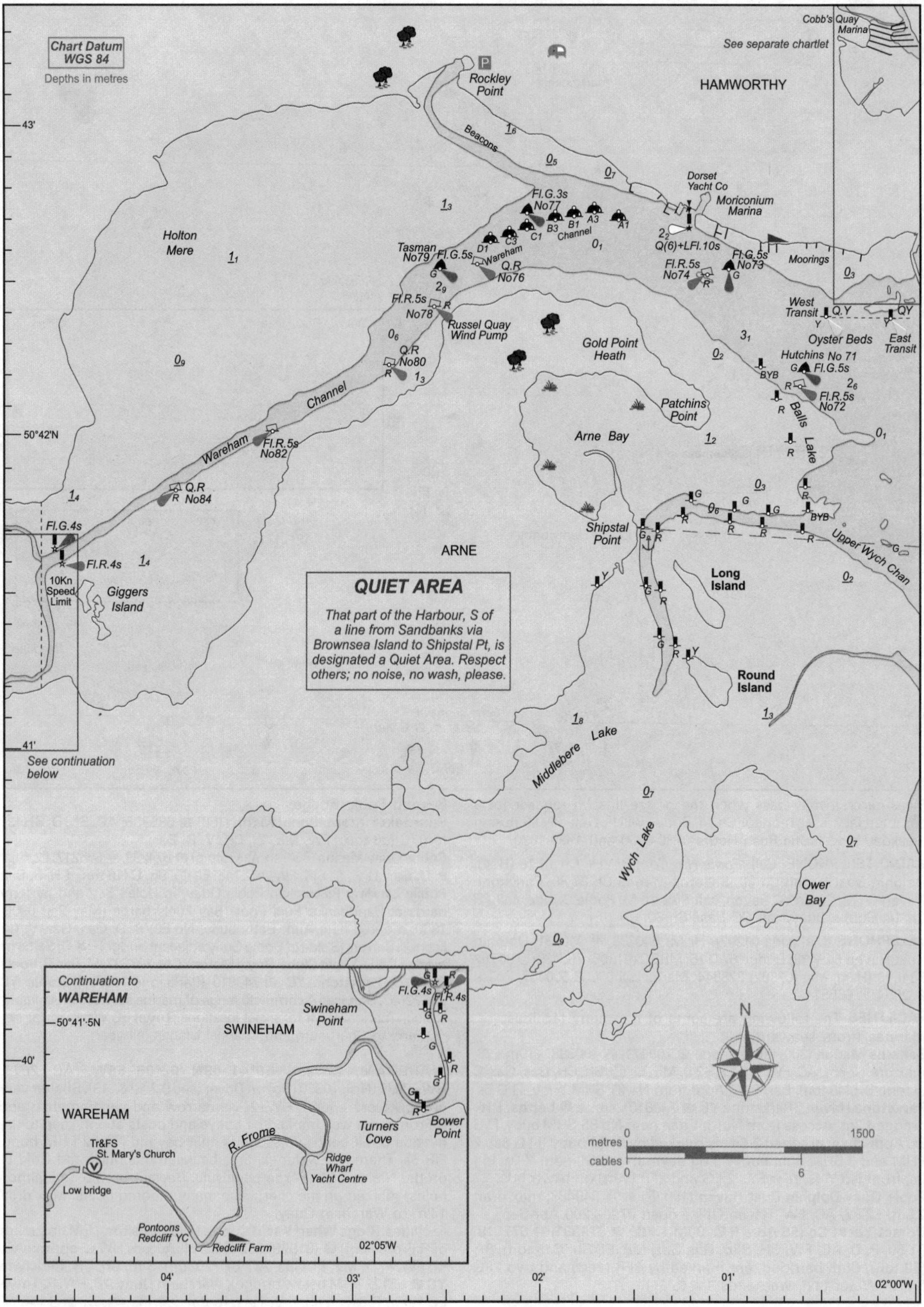
Chart Datum WGS 84
Depths in metres
Rockley Point
HAMWORTHY
Cobb's Quay Marina
See separate chartlet
Beacons
Dorset Yacht Co
Moriconium Marina
Fl.G.3s No77
Wareham Channel
Tasman No79
Fl.G.5s
Q.R No76
Q(6)+LFl.10s
Fl.G.5s No73
Fl.R.5s No74
Moorings
Holton Mere
Fl.R.5s No78
Russel Quay Wind Pump
Q.R No80
Gold Point Heath
West Transit
East Transit
Oyster Beds
Hutchins No 71
Fl.G.5s
Fl.R.5s No72
Balls Lake
Patchins Point
Arne Bay
Fl.R.5s No82
Q.R No84
Fl.G.4s
Fl.R.4s
10Kn Speed Limit
Giggers Island
ARNE
Shipstal Point
Upper Wych Chan
Long Island
Round Island
QUIET AREA
That part of the Harbour, S of a line from Sandbanks via Brownsea Island to Shipstal Pt, is designated a Quiet Area. Respect others; no noise, no wash, please.
50°42'N
43'
41'
See continuation below
Middlebere Lake
Wych Lake
Ower Bay
Continuation to WAREHAM
50°41'·5N
40'
SWINEHAM
Swineham Point
WAREHAM
R. Frome
Tr&FS St. Mary's Church
Low bridge
Turners Cove
Bower Point
Ridge Wharf Yacht Centre
Pontoons Redcliff YC
Redcliff Farm
02°05'W
04'
03'
02'
01'
02°00'W
N
metres 0 1500
cables 0 6

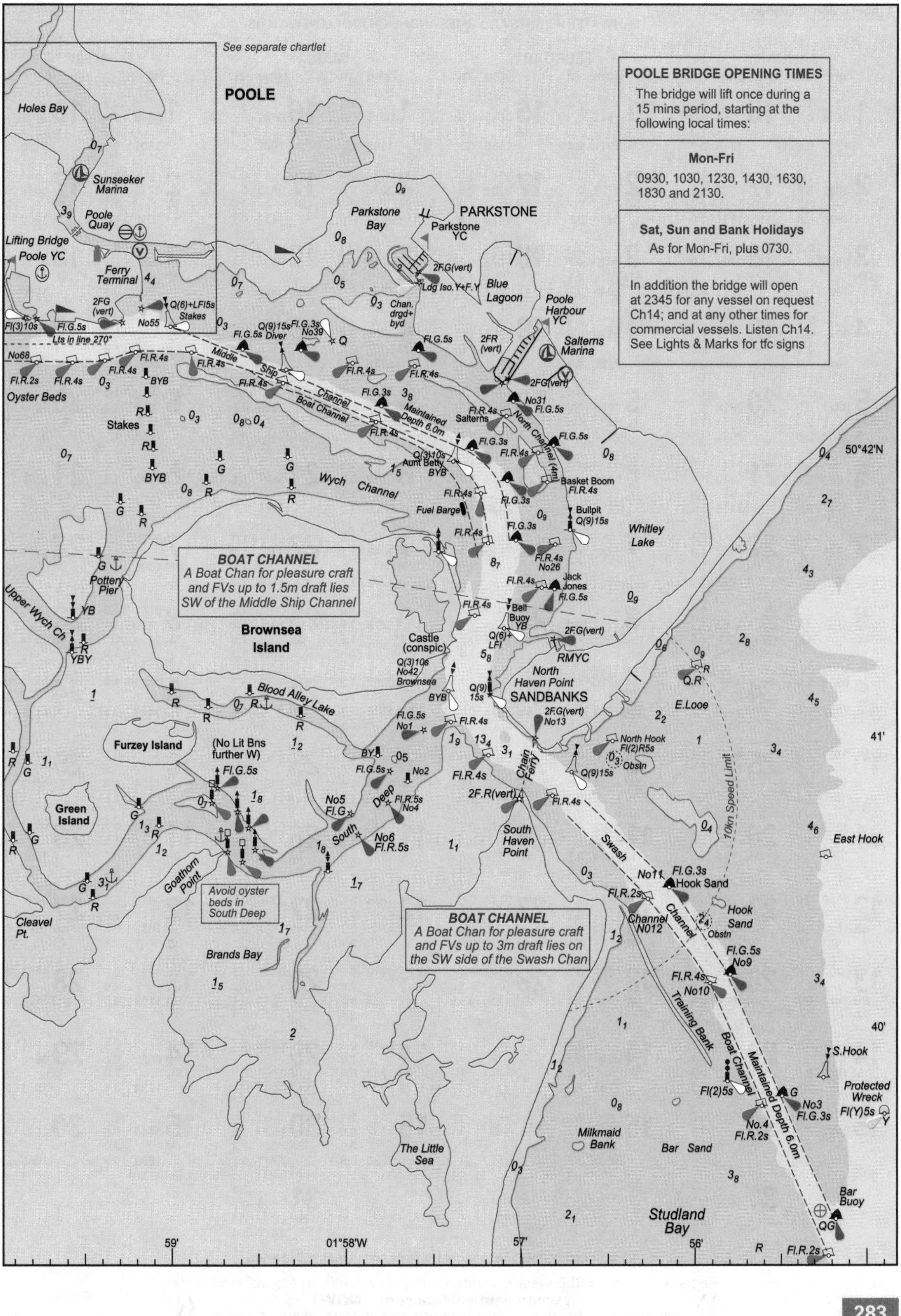
See separate chartlet
POOLE
Holes Bay
Sunseeker Marina
Poole Quay
Lifting Bridge
Poole YC
Ferry Terminal
2FG (vert)
Q(6)+LFl15s Stakes
No55
Fl(3)10s
Fl.G.5s
Lts in line 270°
Parkstone Bay
PARKSTONE
Parkstone YC
2F.G(vert)
Ldg Iso.Y+F.Y
Chan. drgd+ byd
Blue Lagoon
Poole Harbour YC
Salterns Marina
2FR (vert)
2FG(vert)
Q(9)15s Diver
Fl.G.3s No39
Fl.G.5s
Middle Ship Channel
Boat Channel
Maintained Depth 6.0m
No68
Fl.R.2s
Fl.R.4s
Oyster Beds
BYB
Stakes
Salterns
North Channel (4m)
No31 Fl.G.5s
Aunt Betty
Q(3)10s
Wych Channel
Fuel Barge
Basket Boom Fl.R.4s
Bullpit Q(9)15s
Whitley Lake
No26
Jack Jones Fl.G.5s
Bell Buoy YB
Q(6)+LFl
BOAT CHANNEL
A Boat Chan for pleasure craft and FVs up to 1.5m draft lies SW of the Middle Ship Channel
Pottery Pier
Upper Wych Ch
YBY
Brownsea Island
Castle (conspic)
Q(3)10s No42 Brownsea
RMYC
North Haven Point
SANDBANKS
Q(9) 15s
Blood Alley Lake
Q.R
E.Looe
2F.G(vert) No13
Furzey Island
(No Lit Bns further W)
No1
No2
North Hook Fl(2)R5s
Obstn
Q(9)15s
Chain Ferry
Green Island
No5 Fl.G
South Deep
Fl.R.5s No4
No6 Fl.R.5s
2F.R(vert)
South Haven Point
10kn Speed Limit
Swash Channel
East Hook
No11 Fl.G.3s
Hook Sand
Goathorn Point
Avoid oyster beds in South Deep
Cleavel Pt.
Channel No012
BOAT CHANNEL
A Boat Chan for pleasure craft and FVs up to 3m draft lies on the SW side of the Swash Chan
Brands Bay
Fl.G.5s No9
Fl.R.4s No10
Training Bank
Boat Channel
Maintained Depth 6.0m
S.Hook
Fl(2)5s
No3 Fl.G.3s
Protected Wreck Fl(Y)5s
No.4 Fl.R.2s
Milkmaid Bank
Bar Sand
The Little Sea
Bar Buoy
QG
Studland Bay
50°42'N
41'
40'
59'
01°58'W
57'
56'
Fl.R.2s
POOLE BRIDGE OPENING TIMES
The bridge will lift once during a 15 mins period, starting at the following local times:
Mon-Fri
0930, 1030, 1230, 1430, 1630, 1830 and 2130.
Sat, Sun and Bank Holidays
As for Mon-Fri, plus 0730.
In addition the bridge will open at 2345 for any vessel on request Ch14; and at any other times for commercial vessels. Listen Ch14. See Lights & Marks for tfc signs

Note - HW times are not shown because they cannot be predicted with reasonable accuracy. Approximate times can be gained using LW times and the Tidal Curves at the start of this section.

TIME ZONE (UTC)
For Summer Time add ONE hour in **non-shaded areas**

ENGLAND – POOLE HARBOUR

LAT 50°42'N LONG 1°59'W

HIGH WATER HEIGHTS AND TIMES AND HEIGHTS OF LOW WATERS

SPRING & NEAP TIDES
Dates in red are SPRINGS
Dates in blue are NEAPS

YEAR **2002**

JANUARY

Date	Day	Time m	Time m	Time m	Time m
1	TU	2.2	0519 0.7	2.2	1747 0.6
2	W	2.3	0607 0.7	2.2	1834 0.6
3	TH	2.2	0656 0.7	2.1	1923 0.6
4	F	2.2	0747 0.8	2.1	2014 0.7
5	SA	2.1	0841 0.9	2.0	2108 0.8
6	SU	2.1	0941 0.9	1.9	2207 0.9
7	M	2.0	1046 1.0	1.9	2313 1.0
8	TU	2.0	1157 1.0	1.8	
9	W	0023 1.0	2.0	1307 1.0	1.9
10	TH	0131 1.0	2.0	1408 0.9	1.9
11	F	0229 0.9	2.1	1501 0.9	2.0
12	SA	0319 0.9	2.1	1547 0.8	2.0
13	SU ●	0403 0.8	2.1	1630 0.7	2.1
14	M	0444 0.8	2.1	1709 0.7	
15	TU	2.1	0522 0.8	2.1	1745 0.7
16	W	2.1	0558 0.8	2.0	1819 0.7
17	TH	2.1	0632 0.9	2.0	1851 0.8
18	F	2.0	0705 0.9	2.0	1922 0.8
19	SA	2.0	0738 1.0	1.9	1955 0.9
20	SU	1.9	0813 1.1	1.8	2031 1.0
21	M	1.9	0856 1.2	1.8	2116 1.1
22	TU	1.8	0950 1.3	1.7	2215 1.2
23	W	1.8	1100 1.3	1.6	2329 1.2
24	TH	1.8	1221 1.2	1.7	
25	F	0047 1.2	1.9	1330 1.1	1.8
26	SA	0151 1.0	2.0	1425 0.9	1.9
27	SU	0245 0.9	2.1	1515 0.8	2.1
28	M ○	0335 0.8	2.1	1604 0.6	2.2
29	TU	0424 0.7	2.2	1652 0.5	2.3
30	W	0512 0.6	2.3	1739 0.4	
31	TH	2.3	0559 0.6	2.3	1825 0.4

FEBRUARY

Date	Day	Time m	Time m	Time m	Time m
1	F	2.3	0645 0.6	2.2	1911 0.4
2	SA	2.3	0732 0.6	2.1	1956 0.6
3	SU	2.2	0820 0.7	2.1	2043 0.7
4	M	2.1	0910 0.8	1.9	2135 0.8
5	TU	2.0	1009 1.0	1.8	2236 1.0
6	W	1.9	1120 1.1	1.7	2350 1.1
7	TH	1.8	1240 1.1	1.7	
8	F	0110 1.2	1.8	1351 1.0	1.8
9	SA	0216 1.0	1.9	1448 0.9	1.9
10	SU	0309 0.9	2.0	1534 0.8	2.0
11	M	0352 0.8	2.0	1614 0.7	2.1
12	TU ●	0431 0.8	2.0	1652 0.7	2.1
13	W	0507 0.7	2.0	1727 0.7	
14	TH	2.1	0540 0.7	2.0	1759 0.7
15	F	2.1	0611 0.7	2.0	1828 0.7
16	SA	2.1	0640 0.8	2.0	1855 0.7
17	SU	2.0	0706 0.8	2.0	1922 0.8
18	M	2.0	0736 0.9	1.9	1953 0.9
19	TU	1.9	0811 1.0	1.8	2031 1.0
20	W	1.8	0856 1.1	1.8	2122 1.2
21	TH	1.8	0958 1.2	1.6	2236 1.3
22	F	1.7	1129 1.3	1.6	
23	SA	0014 1.3	1.8	1304 1.2	1.8
24	SU	0135 1.1	1.9	1409 0.9	1.9
25	M	0234 0.9	2.0	1502 0.7	2.1
26	TU	0325 0.7	2.1	1551 0.6	2.2
27	W ○	0413 0.6	2.2	1638 0.4	2.3
28	TH	0500 0.4	2.3	1724 0.3	

MARCH

Date	Day	Time m	Time m	Time m	Time m
1	F	2.4	0545 0.4	2.3	1809 0.3
2	SA	2.4	0629 0.4	2.3	1852 0.4
3	SU	2.3	0711 0.4	2.2	1934 0.4
4	M	2.2	0754 0.6	2.1	2016 0.6
5	TU	2.1	0839 0.7	2.0	2103 0.8
6	W	1.9	0932 0.9	1.8	2203 1.0
7	TH	1.8	1043 1.2	1.7	2323 1.2
8	F	1.6	1213 1.2	1.6	
9	SA	0052 1.2	1.6	1333 1.2	1.8
10	SU	0205 1.1	1.8	1431 1.0	1.9
11	M	0255 1.0	1.9	1515 0.9	2.0
12	TU	0336 0.8	2.0	1553 0.7	2.0
13	W	0412 0.7	2.0	1629 0.7	2.1
14	TH ●	0446 0.7	2.0	1703 0.6	
15	F	2.1	0518 0.6	2.0	1734 0.6
16	SA	2.1	0547 0.6	2.0	1802 0.6
17	SU	2.1	0613 0.7	2.0	1827 0.7
18	M	2.0	0638 0.7	2.0	1853 0.7
19	TU	2.0	0705 0.8	2.0	1923 0.8
20	W	1.9	0739 0.8	1.9	1959 0.9
21	TH	1.9	0821 1.0	1.8	2049 1.1
22	F	1.8	0920 1.2	1.7	2204 1.3
23	SA	1.6	1055 1.2	1.6	2354 1.3
24	SU	1.7	1243 1.2	1.8	
25	M	0121 1.1	1.8	1352 0.9	1.9
26	TU	0220 0.9	2.0	1446 0.7	2.1
27	W	0310 0.7	2.1	1533 0.5	2.3
28	TH ○	0357 0.5	2.2	1619 0.4	2.3
29	F	0442 0.4	2.3	1704 0.3	
30	SA	2.4	0525 0.3	2.3	1747 0.3
31	SU	2.4	0608 0.3	2.3	1828 0.4

APRIL

Date	Day	Time m	Time m	Time m	Time m
1	M	2.3	0649 0.4	2.3	1909 0.5
2	TU	2.2	0729 0.6	2.1	1949 0.7
3	W	2.1	0811 0.7	2.0	2035 0.9
4	TH	1.9	0900 0.9	1.8	2133 1.1
5	F	1.7	1009 1.2	1.7	2255 1.3
6	SA	1.6	1142 1.2	1.6	
7	SU	0027 1.3	1.6	1306 1.2	1.8
8	M	0140 1.2	1.7	1404 1.0	1.9
9	TU	0230 1.0	1.8	1446 0.9	2.0
10	W	0309 0.8	1.9	1524 0.8	2.0
11	TH	0344 0.7	1.9	1559 0.7	2.1
12	F ●	0418 0.7	2.0	1633 0.6	2.1
13	SA	0451 0.6	2.0	1705 0.6	
14	SU	2.1	0520 0.6	2.0	1733 0.6
15	M	2.1	0546 0.6	2.0	1800 0.7
16	TU	2.1	0612 0.7	2.0	1828 0.7
17	W	2.0	0642 0.7	2.0	1900 0.8
18	TH	2.0	0718 0.8	1.9	1940 0.9
19	F	1.9	0802 0.9	1.8	2033 1.1
20	SA	1.8	0904 1.1	1.8	2151 1.2
21	SU	1.7	1037 1.2	1.7	2332 1.2
22	M	1.7	1216 1.0	1.8	
23	TU	0056 1.1	1.8	1327 0.9	2.0
24	W	0157 0.9	2.0	1421 0.7	2.1
25	TH	0248 0.7	2.1	1509 0.6	2.3
26	F	0335 0.5	2.2	1555 0.4	2.3
27	SA ○	0420 0.4	2.3	1640 0.4	2.4
28	SU	0504 0.4	2.3	1723 0.4	
29	M	2.3	0546 0.4	2.3	1804 0.4
30	TU	2.3	0627 0.4	2.2	1845 0.6

Chart Datum: 1·40 metres below Ordnance Datum (Newlyn)

Note - HW times are not shown because they cannot be predicted with reasonable accuracy. Approximate times can be gained using LW times and the Tidal Curves at the start of this section.

TIME ZONE (UTC)
For Summer Time add ONE hour in **non-shaded areas**

ENGLAND – POOLE HARBOUR

LAT 50°42'N LONG 1°59'W

HIGH WATER HEIGHTS AND TIMES AND HEIGHTS OF LOW WATERS

SPRING & NEAP TIDES
Dates in red are SPRINGS
Dates in blue are NEAPS

YEAR **2002**

MAY

Date	Day	Time m	Time m	Time m	Time m
1	W	2.2	0707 0.6	2.1	1926 0.8
2	TH	2.0	0748 0.8	2.0	2011 0.9
3	F	1.9	0836 0.9	1.8	2107 1.2
4	SA	1.7	0938 1.1	1.7	2220 1.3
5	SU	1.6	1059 1.2	1.7	2344 1.3
6	M	1.6	1220 1.2	1.8	
7	TU	0057 1.2	1.6	1321 1.1	1.9
8	W	0150 1.0	1.8	1406 1.0	1.9
9	TH	0231 0.9	1.8	1446 0.8	2.0
10	F	0308 0.8	1.9	1523 0.8	2.0
11	SA	0344 0.7	1.9	1558 0.7	2.0
12	SU ●	0418 0.7	2.0	1632 0.7	2.1
13	M	0450 0.7	2.0	1704 0.7	
14	TU	2.1	0521 0.7	2.0	1735 0.7
15	W	2.1	0552 0.7	2.0	1809 0.8
16	TH	2.0	0628 0.7	2.0	1848 0.8
17	F	2.0	0709 0.8	2.0	1934 0.9
18	SA	1.9	0759 0.9	1.9	2031 1.0
19	SU	1.8	0902 1.0	1.9	2143 1.1
20	M	1.8	1020 1.0	1.8	2304 1.1
21	TU	1.8	1141 1.0	1.9	
22	W	0021 1.0	1.9	1252 0.9	2.0
23	TH	0125 0.9	2.0	1350 0.7	2.1
24	F	0220 0.7	2.1	1442 0.6	2.2
25	SA	0310 0.6	2.1	1530 0.6	2.3
26	SU ○	0358 0.5	2.2	1616 0.5	2.3
27	M	0443 0.5	2.2	1701 0.6	
28	TU	2.3	0527 0.5	2.2	1743 0.6
29	W	2.2	0608 0.6	2.1	1825 0.7
30	TH	2.1	0649 0.7	2.1	1906 0.8
31	F	2.0	0729 0.8	2.0	1950 0.9

JUNE

Date	Day	Time m	Time m	Time m	Time m
1	SA	1.9	0813 0.9	1.9	2039 1.1
2	SU	1.8	0904 1.0	1.8	2137 1.2
3	M	1.6	1006 1.2	1.8	2246 1.3
4	TU	1.6	1116 1.2	1.8	2357 1.3
5	W	1.6	1222 1.2	1.8	
6	TH	0057 1.2	1.6	1315 1.0	1.9
7	F	0145 1.0	1.8	1401 1.0	1.9
8	SA	0227 0.9	1.8	1442 0.9	2.0
9	SU	0307 0.8	1.9	1522 0.8	2.0
10	M ●	0345 0.8	2.0	1600 0.8	2.1
11	TU	0422 0.7	2.0	1638 0.8	2.1
12	W	0500 0.7	2.1	1718 0.7	
13	TH	2.1	0540 0.7	2.1	1759 0.7
14	F	2.1	0622 0.7	2.1	1843 0.8
15	SA	2.0	0708 0.7	2.1	1932 0.8
16	SU	2.0	0759 0.8	2.0	2027 0.9
17	M	1.9	0856 0.8	2.0	2128 0.9
18	TU	1.9	0958 0.9	2.0	2234 1.0
19	W	1.9	1105 0.9	2.0	2344 1.0
20	TH	1.9	1213 0.9	2.0	
21	F	0052 0.9	1.9	1318 0.8	2.1
22	SA	0154 0.8	2.0	1417 0.8	2.1
23	SU	0249 0.7	2.0	1509 0.7	2.1
24	M ○	0339 0.7	2.1	1558 0.7	2.2
25	TU	0427 0.6	2.1	1644 0.7	2.1
26	W	0511 0.6	2.1	1727 0.7	
27	TH	2.1	0553 0.7	2.1	1808 0.8
28	F	2.1	0632 0.7	2.1	1847 0.8
29	SA	2.0	0710 0.8	2.0	1927 0.9
30	SU	1.9	0747 0.9	2.0	2008 1.0

JULY

Date	Day	Time m	Time m	Time m	Time m
1	M	1.8	0827 0.9	1.9	2052 1.1
2	TU	1.8	0912 1.0	1.8	2143 1.2
3	W	1.7	1004 1.2	1.8	2243 1.2
4	TH	1.6	1106 1.2	1.8	2350 1.2
5	F	1.6	1213 1.2	1.8	
6	SA	0052 1.2	1.7	1312 1.1	1.9
7	SU	0145 1.0	1.8	1403 1.0	1.9
8	M	0232 0.9	1.9	1450 0.9	2.0
9	TU	0317 0.8	2.0	1535 0.8	2.1
10	W ●	0401 0.7	2.1	1620 0.8	2.1
11	TH	0445 0.6	2.1	1705 0.7	
12	F	2.1	0530 0.6	2.1	1750 0.7
13	SA	2.1	0616 0.6	2.2	1837 0.7
14	SU	2.1	0702 0.6	2.2	1925 0.7
15	M	2.1	0750 0.6	2.1	2014 0.7
16	TU	2.0	0840 0.7	2.1	2107 0.8
17	W	2.0	0933 0.8	2.0	2205 0.9
18	TH	1.9	1033 0.9	2.0	2311 1.0
19	F	1.8	1140 1.0	1.9	
20	SA	0023 1.0	1.8	1253 1.0	1.9
21	SU	0133 0.9	1.9	1359 1.0	2.0
22	M	0234 0.9	1.9	1457 0.9	2.0
23	TU	0327 0.8	2.0	1547 0.8	2.1
24	W ○	0414 0.7	2.1	1631 0.8	2.1
25	TH	0457 0.7	2.1	1713 0.8	
26	F	2.1	0535 0.7	2.1	1750 0.8
27	SA	2.0	0612 0.7	2.1	1826 0.8
28	SU	2.0	0646 0.7	2.0	1901 0.8
29	M	2.0	0718 0.8	2.0	1934 0.9
30	TU	1.9	0749 0.9	2.0	2008 1.0
31	W	1.8	0823 0.9	1.9	2046 1.1

AUGUST

Date	Day	Time m	Time m	Time m	Time m
1	TH	1.8	0902 1.1	1.8	2133 1.2
2	F	1.7	0954 1.2	1.8	2235 1.3
3	SA	1.6	1103 1.3	1.8	2355 1.3
4	SU	1.6	1225 1.3	1.8	
5	M	0110 1.2	1.8	1334 1.2	1.9
6	TU	0208 1.0	1.9	1430 1.0	2.0
7	W	0258 0.8	2.0	1519 0.9	2.1
8	TH ●	0345 0.7	2.1	1606 0.8	2.1
9	F	0431 0.6	2.2	1652 0.7	2.2
10	SA	0517 0.5	2.3	1738 0.6	
11	SU	2.2	0602 0.4	2.3	1823 0.6
12	M	2.2	0647 0.4	2.3	1908 0.6
13	TU	2.2	0732 0.5	2.3	1954 0.6
14	W	2.1	0817 0.6	2.1	2042 0.7
15	TH	2.0	0906 0.8	2.0	2136 0.9
16	F	1.9	1003 0.9	1.9	2241 1.0
17	SA	1.8	1114 1.1	1.8	
18	SU	0001 1.1	1.8	1236 1.2	1.8
19	M	0121 1.1	1.8	1351 1.1	1.9
20	TU	0226 1.0	1.9	1449 1.0	2.0
21	W	0317 0.8	2.0	1536 0.9	2.0
22	TH ○	0359 0.7	2.1	1617 0.8	2.1
23	F	0438 0.7	2.1	1654 0.7	2.1
24	SA	0514 0.6	2.1	1729 0.7	
25	SU	2.0	0547 0.6	2.1	1802 0.7
26	M	2.0	0618 0.7	2.1	1832 0.8
27	TU	2.0	0646 0.7	2.0	1859 0.8
28	W	2.0	0712 0.8	2.0	1927 0.9
29	TH	1.9	0740 0.9	1.9	2000 1.0
30	F	1.8	0815 1.0	1.9	2040 1.1
31	SA	1.8	0901 1.2	1.8	2136 1.3

Chart Datum: 1·40 metres below Ordnance Datum (Newlyn)

Note - HW times are not shown because they cannot be predicted with reasonable accuracy. Approximate times can be gained using LW times and the Tidal Curves at the start of this section.

TIME ZONE (UTC)
For Summer Time add ONE hour in **non-shaded areas**

ENGLAND – POOLE HARBOUR

LAT 50°42′N LONG 1°59′W

HIGH WATER HEIGHTS AND TIMES AND HEIGHTS OF LOW WATERS

SPRING & NEAP TIDES
Dates in red are SPRINGS
Dates in blue are NEAPS

YEAR **2002**

SEPTEMBER

Date	Day	Time	m	Time	m	Time	m	Time	m
1	SU		1.6	1009	1.3		1.7	2303	1.3
2	M		1.6	1151	1.4		1.7		
3	TU	0044	1.2		1.8	1317	1.3		1.8
4	W	0151	1.0		1.9	1415	1.0		2.0
5	TH	0243	0.8		2.0	1504	0.9		2.1
6	F	0329	0.7		2.2	1550	0.7		2.2
7	SA ●	0414	0.5		2.3	1635	0.6		2.3
8	SU	0459	0.4		2.3	1719	0.4		
9	M		2.3	0542	0.4		2.4	1803	0.4
10	TU		2.3	0625	0.4		2.4	1846	0.5
11	W		2.3	0708	0.5		2.3	1930	0.6
12	TH		2.1	0751	0.6		2.1	2015	0.7
13	F		2.0	0838	0.8		2.0	2107	0.9
14	SA		1.9	0936	1.0		1.9	2214	1.1
15	SU		1.8	1054	1.2		1.8	2342	1.2
16	M		1.7	1224	1.3		1.8		
17	TU	0110	1.2		1.8	1342	1.2		1.8
18	W	0214	1.0		2.0	1437	1.0		2.0
19	TH	0300	0.9		2.1	1519	0.9		2.0
20	F	0338	0.8		2.1	1555	0.8		2.1
21	SA ○	0414	0.7		2.1	1630	0.7		2.1
22	SU	0447	0.6		2.1	1703	0.7		2.1
23	M	0520	0.6		2.1	1734	0.7		
24	TU		2.1	0549	0.7		2.1	1801	0.7
25	W		2.1	0614	0.7		2.1	1826	0.8
26	TH		2.0	0638	0.8		2.0	1852	0.8
27	F		2.0	0705	0.9		2.0	1922	0.9
28	SA		1.9	0738	1.0		1.9	2001	1.1
29	SU		1.8	0822	1.2		1.8	2055	1.3
30	M		1.7	0932	1.4		1.7	2226	1.3

OCTOBER

Date	Day	Time	m	Time	m	Time	m	Time	m
1	TU		1.6	1126	1.4		1.7		
2	W	0020	1.3		1.8	1257	1.3		1.8
3	TH	0130	1.0		1.9	1356	1.0		2.0
4	F	0222	0.8		2.1	1444	0.8		2.1
5	SA	0307	0.6		2.3	1528	0.6		2.3
6	SU ●	0351	0.5		2.4	1612	0.5		2.3
7	M	0435	0.4		2.4	1656	0.4		2.4
8	TU	0518	0.4		2.4	1740	0.4		
9	W		2.4	0600	0.4		2.4	1822	0.5
10	TH		2.3	0642	0.6		2.3	1904	0.6
11	F		2.2	0725	0.7		2.1	1949	0.8
12	SA		2.0	0813	0.9		2.0	2039	1.0
13	SU		1.9	0912	1.2		1.8	2147	1.2
14	M		1.8	1032	1.3		1.7	2317	1.3
15	TU		1.8	1203	1.3		1.7		
16	W	0045	1.2		1.9	1320	1.2		1.8
17	TH	0149	1.1		2.0	1412	1.1		1.9
18	F	0232	0.9		2.1	1451	0.9		2.0
19	SA	0309	0.8		2.1	1526	0.8		2.0
20	SU	0343	0.7		2.1	1600	0.7		2.1
21	M ○	0416	0.7		2.1	1632	0.7		2.1
22	TU	0448	0.7		2.1	1703	0.7		
23	W		2.1	0517	0.7		2.1	1731	0.7
24	TH		2.1	0544	0.8		2.1	1756	0.8
25	F		2.1	0609	0.8		2.1	1824	0.8
26	SA		2.0	0638	0.9		2.0	1856	0.9
27	SU		2.0	0714	1.0		1.9	1937	1.0
28	M		1.9	0801	1.2		1.8	2033	1.2
29	TU		1.8	0913	1.4		1.8	2200	1.3
30	W		1.8	1057	1.4		1.7	2342	1.2
31	TH		1.8	1225	1.3		1.8		

NOVEMBER

Date	Day	Time	m	Time	m	Time	m	Time	m
1	F	0056	1.0		2.0	1327	1.0		2.0
2	SA	0152	0.8		2.1	1417	0.8		2.1
3	SU	0239	0.7		2.3	1503	0.7		2.3
4	M ●	0325	0.5		2.4	1548	0.5		2.3
5	TU	0409	0.4		2.4	1633	0.4		2.4
6	W	0453	0.4		2.4	1717	0.5		
7	TH		2.4	0536	0.5		2.4	1800	0.6
8	F		2.3	0619	0.7		2.3	1843	0.7
9	SA		2.2	0703	0.8		2.1	1928	0.8
10	SU		2.1	0751	1.0		2.0	2017	1.0
11	M		1.9	0848	1.2		1.8	2118	1.2
12	TU		1.8	1000	1.3		1.7	2235	1.3
13	W		1.8	1123	1.4		1.6	2357	1.3
14	TH		1.8	1238	1.3		1.7		
15	F	0103	1.2		1.9	1333	1.2		1.8
16	SA	0151	1.0		2.0	1415	1.0		1.9
17	SU	0230	0.9		2.0	1452	0.9		2.0
18	M	0306	0.8		2.1	1527	0.8		2.0
19	TU	0342	0.8		2.1	1601	0.8		2.0
20	W ○	0416	0.8		2.1	1634	0.8		2.1
21	TH	0447	0.8		2.1	1704	0.8		
22	F		2.1	0517	0.8		2.1	1734	0.8
23	SA		2.1	0548	0.9		2.1	1807	0.8
24	SU		2.1	0623	0.9		2.0	1844	0.9
25	M		2.0	0704	1.0		2.0	1929	0.9
26	TU		1.9	0756	1.2		1.9	2026	1.0
27	W		1.9	0902	1.2		1.8	2138	1.1
28	TH		1.9	1023	1.3		1.8	2258	1.1
29	F		1.9	1142	1.2		1.9		
30	SA	0011	1.0		2.0	1250	1.0		2.0

DECEMBER

Date	Day	Time	m	Time	m	Time	m	Time	m
1	SU	0114	0.9		2.1	1347	0.9		2.1
2	M	0209	0.7		2.3	1438	0.7		2.1
3	TU	0258	0.7		2.3	1527	0.6		2.3
4	W ●	0346	0.6		2.4	1614	0.6		2.3
5	TH	0433	0.6		2.4	1701	0.6		
6	F		2.3	0518	0.7		2.3	1745	0.6
7	SA		2.3	0602	0.7		2.2	1828	0.7
8	SU		2.2	0646	0.8		2.1	1911	0.8
9	M		2.1	0731	1.0		2.0	1956	0.9
10	TU		2.0	0821	1.1		1.9	2045	1.0
11	W		1.9	0918	1.3		1.8	2143	1.2
12	TH		1.8	1025	1.3		1.6	2249	1.2
13	F		1.8	1136	1.3		1.6	2356	1.2
14	SA		1.8	1239	1.3		1.7		
15	SU	0055	1.2		1.9	1330	1.2		1.8
16	M	0144	1.1		2.0	1413	1.0		1.9
17	TU	0228	1.0		2.0	1453	0.9		1.9
18	W	0308	0.9		2.1	1531	0.9		2.0
19	TH ○	0346	0.9		2.1	1608	0.8		2.1
20	F	0423	0.8		2.1	1645	0.8		2.1
21	SA	0459	0.8		2.1	1721	0.7		
22	SU		2.1	0536	0.8		2.1	1800	0.7
23	M		2.1	0617	0.9		2.1	1841	0.7
24	TU		2.1	0701	0.9		2.0	1927	0.8
25	W		2.0	0751	0.9		2.0	2019	0.8
26	TH		2.0	0848	1.0		1.9	2116	0.9
27	F		2.0	0951	1.0		1.9	2219	0.9
28	SA		2.0	1101	1.1		1.9	2328	1.0
29	SU		2.0	1212	1.0		1.9		
30	M	0037	0.9		2.0	1319	0.9		1.9
31	TU	0142	0.9		2.1	1419	0.8		2.0

Chart Datum: 1·40 metres below Ordnance Datum (Newlyn)

CHRISTCHURCH *9.2.14*

Dorset **50°43'·53N 01°44'·33W**

CHARTS AC *5601, 2172, 2035*; Imray C4; Stanfords 7, 12, 24; OS 195

TIDES HW Sp –0210, Np, –0140 Dover; ML 1·2; Zone 0 (UT)

Standard Port PORTSMOUTH (⟶)

Times				Height (metres)			
High Water		Low Water		MHWS	MHWN	MLWN	MLWS
0000	0600	0500	1100	4·7	3·8	1·9	0·8
1200	1800	1700	2300				
Differences BOURNEMOUTH							
–0240	+0055	–0050	–0030	–2·7	–2·2	–0·8	–0·3
CHRISTCHURCH (Entrance)							
–0230	+0030	–0035	–0035	–2·9	–2·4	–1·2	–0·2
CHRISTCHURCH (Quay)							
–0210	+0100	+0105	+0055	–2·9	–2·4	–1·0	0·0
CHRISTCHURCH (Tuckton bridge)							
–0205	+0110	+0110	+0105	–3·0	–2·5	–1·0	+0·1

NOTE: Double HWs occur, except near nps; predictions are for the higher HW. Near nps there is a stand; predictions are for mid-stand. Tidal levels are for inside the bar. Outside the bar the tide is about 0·6m lower at sp. Floods (or drought) in the Rivers Avon and Stour cause considerable variations from predicted hts. See 9.2.12.

SHELTER Good in lee of Hengistbury Hd, elsewhere exposed to SW winds. R Stour, navigable at HW up to Tuckton, and the R Avon up to the first bridge, give good shelter in all winds. Most ⚓s in the hbr dry. No ⚓ in chan. No berthing at ferry jetty by Mudeford sandbank. Hbr speed limit 4kn. Fishing licence obligatory.

NAVIGATION WPT 50°43'·53N 01°43'·58W, 090°/270° from/to NE end of Mudeford Quay 0·5M. The bar/chan is liable to shift. The ent is difficult on the ebb which reaches 4-5kn in 'The Run'. Recommended ent/dep at HW/stand. Chan inside hbr is narrow and mostly shallow (approx 0·3m) soft mud; mean ranges are 1·2m sp and 0·7m nps. Beware groynes S of Hengistbury Hd, Beerpan and Yarranton Rks.

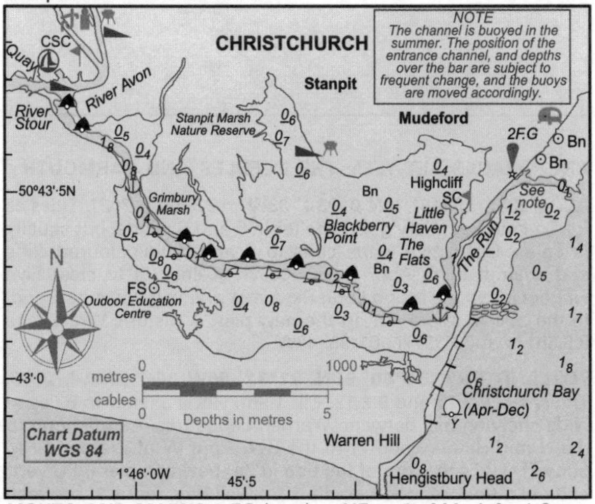

LIGHTS AND MARKS 2 FG (vert) at NE end of Mudeford Quay. Unlit chan buoys in hbr and apps are locally laid April-Oct inc; info from ☎ 483250.

RADIO TELEPHONE None.

TELEPHONE (Dial code 01202) MRSC (01305) 760439; ⊜ 0345 231110 (H24); Marinecall 09068 500457; Police 486333; 🄷 303626; Casualty 704167.

FACILITIES Elkins BY ☎ 483141, AB £15; **Rossiter Yachts** ☎ 483250, AB £14; **Christchurch SC (CSC)** ☎ 483150, limited AB £9.50, monohulls only, max LOA 9m.
Services: M*, L*, D, P (cans), FW, El, Sh, CH, ACA, Gas, C (10 ton), Slip. **Town** ✉, Ⓑ, ⇌, ✈ (Bournemouth).

KEYHAVEN *9.2.15*

Hampshire **50°42'·85N 01·33'·26W**

CHARTS AC *5600, 2021, 2035*; Imray C4, C3; Stanfords 7, 11, 12, 24, 25; OS 196

TIDES –0020, +0105 Dover; ML 2·0; Zone 0 (UT)

Standard Port PORTSMOUTH (⟶)

Times				Height (metres)			
High Water		Low Water		MHWS	MHWN	MLWN	MLWS
0000	0600	0500	1100	4·7	3·8	1·9	0·8
1200	1800	1700	2300				
Differences HURST POINT							
–0115	–0005	–0030	–0025	–2·0	–1·5	–0·5	–0·1
TOTLAND BAY							
–0130	–0045	–0035	–0045	–2·2	–1·7	–0·4	–0·1
FRESHWATER BAY							
–0210	+0025	–0040	–0020	–2·1	–1·5	–0·4	0·0

NOTE: Double HWs occur at or near sp; predictions are then for the 1st HW. Off springs there is a stand of about 2 hrs; predictions are then for mid-stand. See 9.2.12.

SHELTER Good, but the river gets extremely congested. Access HW ±4½. Ent difficult on ebb. All moorings and ⚓s are exposed to winds across the marshland. River is administered by New Forest DC aided by the Keyhaven Consultative Committee.

NAVIGATION WPT 50°42'·73N 01°32'·58W, 115°/295° from/to chan ent, 0·40M. Ent should not be attempted in strong E winds. Bar is constantly changing. Leave chan SHM buoys well to stbd. Beware lobster pots. Approaching from the W, beware The Shingles bank over which seas break and which partly dries. At Hurst Narrows give 'The Trap' a wide berth.

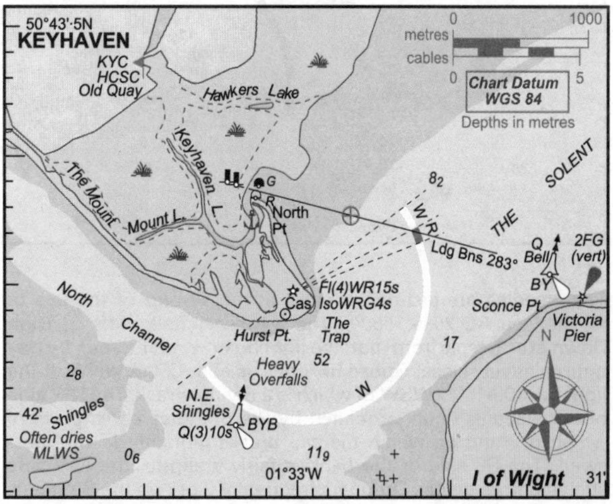

LIGHTS AND MARKS When E of Hurst Point lt, two ldg bns ('X' topmarks) lead 283° to ent of buoyed chan; the R & G ent buoys are the more visible. See 9.2.4 and chartlet above for sectors of light at Hurst Point. The sectors of Hurst Pt Iso WRG 4s have been deliberately omitted from the above chartlet for clarity.

RADIO TELEPHONE None.

TELEPHONE (Dial code 01590) R. Warden 645695; MRSC (01705) 552100; ⊜ 0345 231110 (H24); Marinecall 09068 500457; Police 615101; Dr 643022; 🄷 677011.

FACILITIES Quay Slip, L; **Keyhaven YC** ☎ 642165, C, M, L (on beach), FW, Bar; **New Forest District Council** ☎ (01703) 285000, Slip, M; **Milford-on-Sea** P, D, FW, CH, V, R, Bar; **Hurst Castle SC** M, L, FW;
Services: Slip, ME, El, Sh, C (9 ton), CH.
Village EC (Milford-on-Sea) Wed; R, Bar, CH, V, ✉ and Ⓑ (Milford-on-Sea), ⇌ (bus to New Milton), ✈ (Hurn).

NEEDLES CHANNEL *9.2.16*

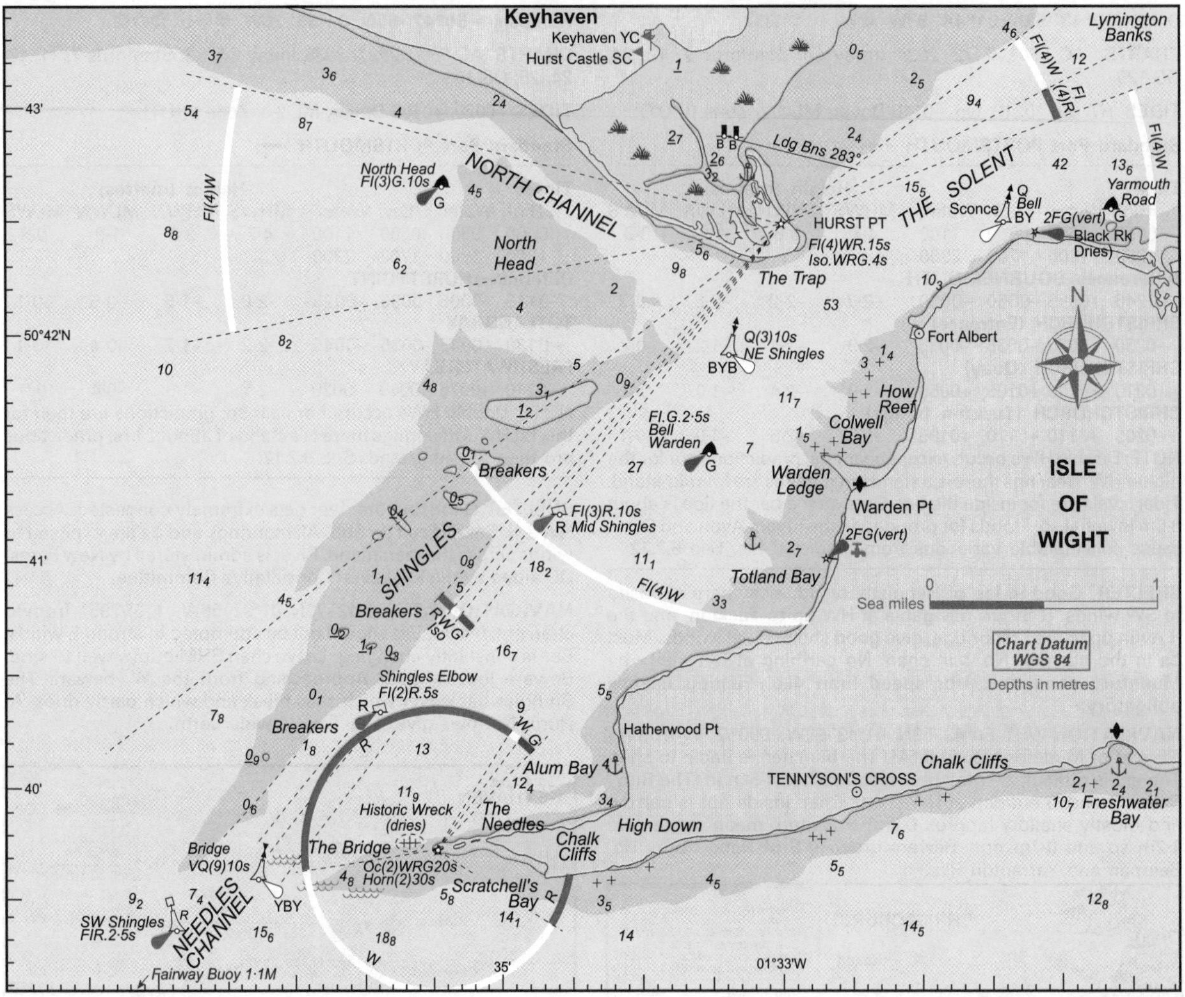

The Needles are distinctive rocks at the W end of the Isle of Wight (see AC 2035, *5600)*. The adjacent chalk cliffs of High Down are conspic from afar; the light ho may not be seen by day until relatively close. Goose Rk, dries, is about 50m WNW of the light ho, 100-150m WSW of which is a drying wreck. The NW side of the Needles Chan is defined by the Shingles bank, parts of which dry and on which the sea breaks violently in the least swell. The SE side of the bank is fairly steep-to, the NW side shelves more gently. Dredgers frequently work on the Shingles. On the ebb the stream sets very strongly (3-4kn) WSW across the Shingles. The Needles Chan is well lit/buoyed and in fair weather presents no significant problems. But even a SW Force 4 against the ebb will raise breaking seas near Bridge and SW Shingles buoys.

In bad weather broken water and overfalls extend along The Bridge, a reef which runs 8ca W of the lt ho with its W extremity marked by Bridge WCM lt buoy. S to W gales against the ebb raise very dangerous breaking seas in the Needles Chan, here only 250m wide. The sea state can be at its worst shortly after LW when the flood has just begun. There is then no wind-over-tide situation, but a substantial swell is raised as a result of the recently turned stream. In such conditions use the E route to the Solent, S of the IOW and via Nab Tower; or find shelter at Poole or Studland.

In strong winds the North Channel, N of the Shingles, is preferable to the Needles Channel. The two join S of Hurst Point where overfalls and tide rips may be met. Beware The Trap, a shoal spit extending 150m SE of Hurst Castle.

ANCHORAGES BETWEEN THE NEEDLES AND YARMOUTH

ALUM BAY, 50°40'·10N 01°34'·33W. *AC 5600.4, 2021.* Tides as for Totland Bay. Very good shelter in E and S winds, but squally in gales. Distinctive white cliffs to S and multi-coloured cliffs and chairlift to E. Appr from due W of chairlift to clear Five Fingers Rk, to the N and Long Rk, a reef drying 0·9m at its E end, to the S. ⚓ in about 4m off the new pier. A Historic Wreck (see 9.0.3h) is at 50°39'·7N 01°35'·45W.

TOTLAND BAY, 50°40'·98N 01°32'·86W. *AC 5600.4, 2219.* Tides, see 9.2.15 and 9.2.12; ML 1·9m. Good shelter in E'lies in wide shelving bay between Warden Ledge (rks 4ca offshore) to the N and Hatherwood Pt to the SW. Appr W of Warden SHM buoy Fl G 2·5s to ⚓ out of the tide in 2m between pier (2FG vert) and old LB house; good holding. Colwell Bay, to the N between Warden Pt and Fort Albert, is generally rky and shallow.

ANCHORAGE EAST OF THE NEEDLES, SOUTH IOW

FRESHWATER BAY, 50°40'·07N 01°30'·61W. AC *5600.4, 2021.* Tides see 9.2.15 and 9.2.12; ML 1·6m. Good shelter from the N, open to the S. The bay is 3·2M E of Needles lt ho and 1·2M E of Tennyson's Cross. Conspic marks:on W side Redoubt Fort; a hotel on N side; Stag, Arch and Mermaid Rks to the E. The bay is shallow, with rky drying ledges ¾ca either side and a rk (0·1m) almost in the centre. Best to ⚓ in about 2m just outside. V, R, Bar, ✉

THE SOLENT *9.2.17*

Charts In addition to normal ACs, the Solent and approaches are covered by AC 5600, intended for yachtsmen. This is a folio of 10 A2 size charts in a clear plastic wallet, price £35.00 (2000).

Vessel Traffic Service (VTS) A VTS, operated by Southampton on VHF Ch 12 14, controls shipping in the Solent between the Needles and Nab Tower including Southampton Water. Portsmouth Hbr and its appr's N of a line from Gilkicker Pt to Outer Spit buoy are controlled on Ch 11 by QHM Portsmouth.

The VTS is primarily intended to monitor and co-ordinate the safe passage of commercial ships which must report at designated points. It includes compulsory pilotage, a radar service on request, berthing instructions and tug assistance.

Pleasure craft, particularly at night or in poor visibility, can be forewarned of ship movements (and likely avoiding action), simply by listening on VHF Ch 12 Southampton, or Ch 11 for QHM Portsmouth. Traffic information is routinely broadcast by Southampton VTS on VHF Ch 12 every H, 0600 to 2200LT, Fri-Sun and Bank Hols from Easter to last weekend in Oct. From 1 Jun to 30 Sep broadcasts are daily at the same times.

Pleasure Craft and Commercial Shipping In the interests of safety it is important that good co-operation between pleasure craft and commercial shipping be maintained. Yachtsmen should always bear in mind the restricted field of vision from large ships at close quarters, their limited ability to manoeuvre at slow speeds, and the constraints imposed by narrow and shallow channels.

An **Area of Concern** (AOC) covers one of the busiest parts of the Solent to improve safety for large vessels. The AOC (see 9.2.18) covers the Western Approach and Thorn Channels. It is delineated by the following lt buoys, clockwise fom Prince Consort NCM: Gurnard NCM, NE Gurnard PHM, Bourne Gap PHM, Calshot lt Float, Castle Pt PHM, Black Jack PHM, Reach PHM, Calshot NCM, N Thorn SHM, Thorn Knoll SHM, W Bramble WCM and S Bramble SHM.

The AOC, which is criss-crossed by many pleasure craft, is also negotiated by large ships bound to/from Southampton normally via the E Solent. Inbound ships usually pass Prince Consort NCM and turn first to the southward toward Gurnard NCM, before starting their critical stbd turn into the Thorn Chan. They turn port around Calshot to clear the AOC.

To minimise the risk of collision with small craft, any large vessel >150m LOA, on entering the AOC, is enclosed by a **Moving Prohibited Zone** (MPZ) which extends 1000m ahead of the vessel and 100m on either beam.

Small craft <20m LOA must remain outside this MPZ, using seamanlike anticipation of likely turns.

The large vessel, displaying a B cylinder by day or 3 all-round ● lts (vert) by night, will normally be preceded by a Hbr patrol launch showing a Fl Bu lt and working Ch 12 (callsign *SP*).

The VTS will identify large ships and approx timings of MPZ as part of the hourly broadcasts (see above). All pleasure craft in the vicinity are strongly advised to monitor Ch 12 in order to create a mental picture. Be particularly alert when in, or approaching, the triangle defined by East Lepe, Hook and West Ryde Middle buoys.

VHF Radio Telephone The proliferation of VHF radios in yachts and, it must be said, often poor R/T procedures cause problems for legitimate users and can seriously hamper emergency situations. Yachtsmen are reminded that Ch 16 is a DISTRESS, SAFETY and CALLING Ch. If another calling Ch is available use it in preference to Ch 16; otherwise, use Ch 16 as briefly as possible to make contact before shifting to a working Ch. Note also that initial contact with Solent CG should be on Ch 67, NOT Ch 16 (see next column). For ship-to-ship messages the recognised VHF channels include 06, 08, 72 and 77.

Yachts in the Solent should listen on Ch 12 and on Ch 11 for Portsmouth. Other Ch's are listed under each port entry.

Local Signals Outward bound vessels normally hoist the following flag signals during daylight hours.

Signal	*Meaning*	
International 'E' Flag over Answering Pendant	I am bound East (Nab Tower)	
Answering Pendant Over International 'W' Flag	I am bound West (The Needles)	

Southampton patrol launches have HARBOUR MASTER painted on their after cabin in B lettering on Y background. At night a Fl Bu all-round lt is shown above the W masthead lt.

Reference Much useful information is given in the *Solent Year Book,* published by the Solent Cruising and Racing Association (SCRA); also in a free booklet *The Yachtsman's Guide to Southampton Water* and a leaflet *Enjoy the Solent.*

Solent Hazards by Peter Bruce, published by Boldre Marine, goes closer inshore than other Pilot books.

For Marinecall forecasts call ☎ 09068 500 457; for MetFax Marine 📠 09060 100 457. Southampton Weather Centre ☎ (02380) 228844.

Solent Coastguard The Maritime Rescue Sub Centre (MRSC) at Lee-on-Solent

☎ (02392) 552100 coordinates all SAR activities in Solent District, which is bounded by a line from Highcliffe south to mid-channel; E to the Greenwich Lt V; thence N to Beachy Head. It is the busiest CG District in the UK, because of the huge concentration of pleasure craft within its bounds.

It is manned H24, year round by at least 3 CG Officers who can call on the RNLI, Solent Safety rescue boats and the CG Rescue helicopter based at Lee. Sector and Auxiliary CGs are based on the IOW, Calshot, Eastney, Hayling, Littlehampton, Shoreham, Newhaven and elsewhere.

Solent CG keeps watch on VHF Ch 67 and 16. Uniquely, the initial call to *Solent Coastguard* should be made on Ch 67, the working channel; this is because Ch 16 is often very busy especially in the summer. Ch 67 is also heavily loaded and is only for essential traffic. Listen out before transmitting; be brief, to the point and use correct R/T procedures.

Weather message are broadcast by Solent CG on Ch 73 after an announcement on Ch 16. See Ch 5 for schedule.

Save valuable R/T time by telephoning Solent CG before sailing; they will be glad to advise you. In general terms, they will always stress: Up-to-date forecasts; awareness of tidal streams; sound knowledge of "Rule of the Road" and local Notices to Mariners; adequate fuel, plus reserves, for your passage, and a sharp lookout at all times. Bon voyage!

SOLENT AREA *continued*

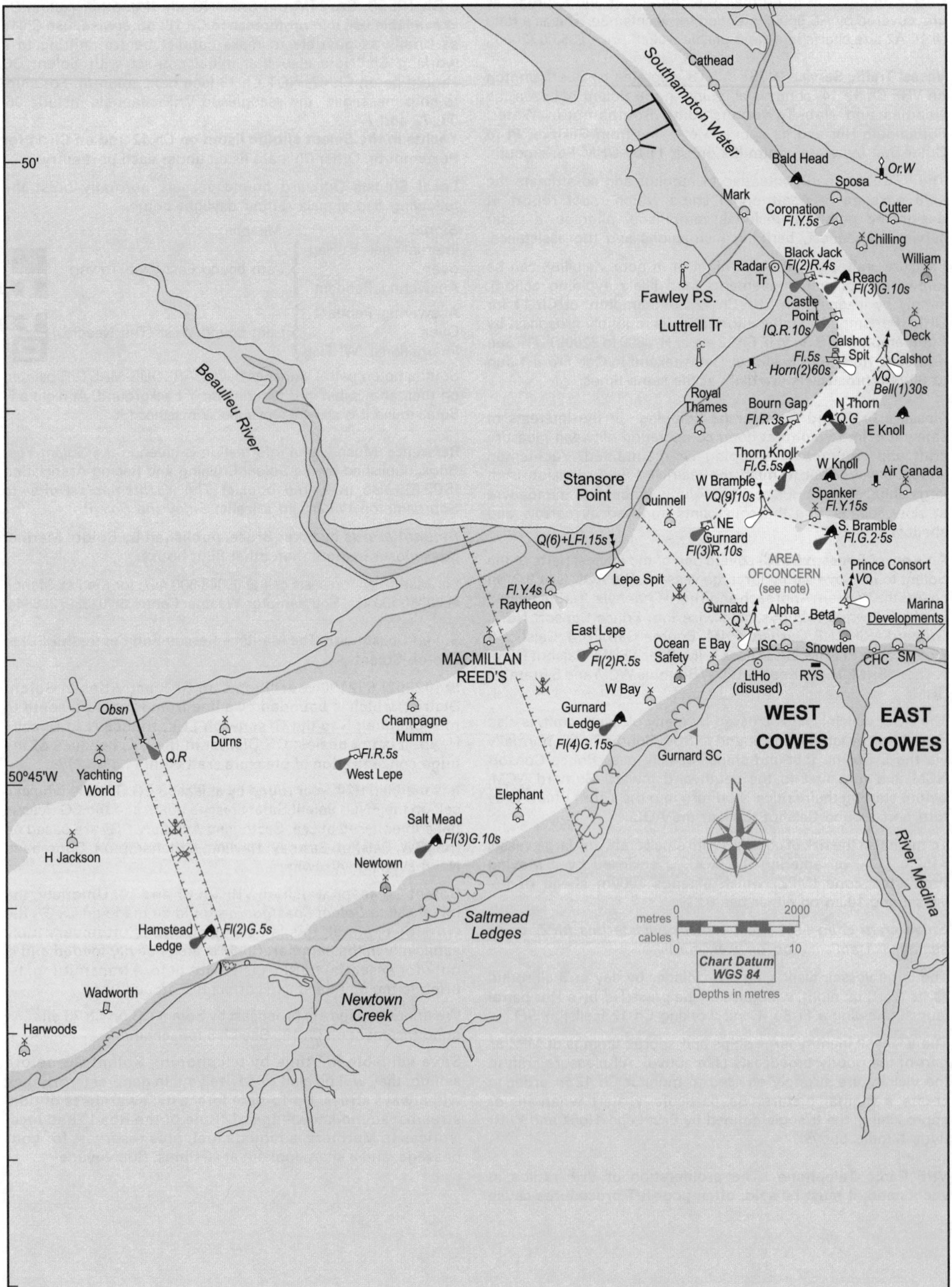

SOLENT AREA *continued*

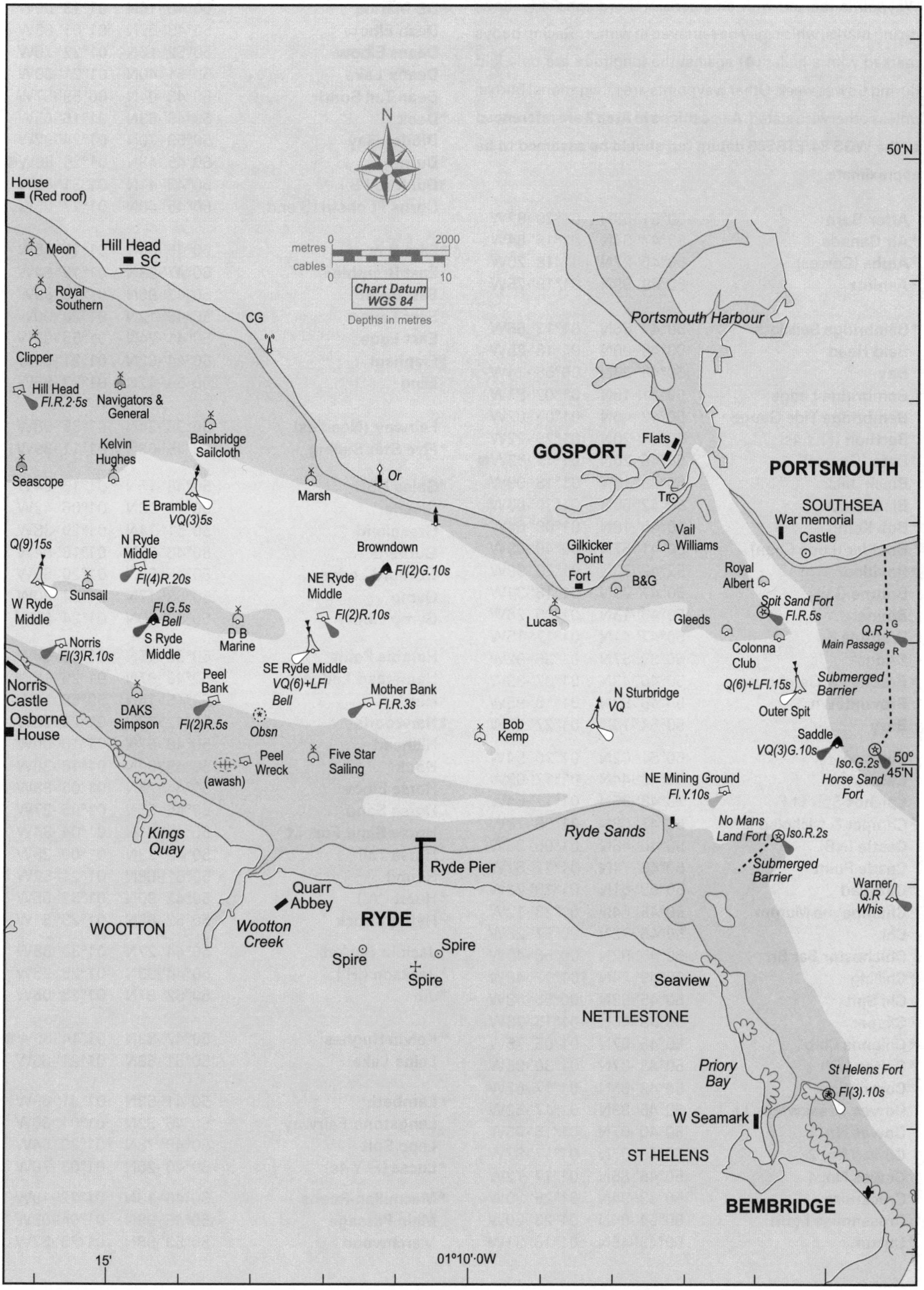
House (Red roof)
Meon
Hill Head SC
Royal Southern
Clipper
Hill Head Fl.R.2·5s
Navigators & General
CG
metres 0 2000
cables 0 10
Chart Datum WGS 84
Depths in metres
N
50'N
Bainbridge Sailcloth
Kelvin Hughes
Seascope
E Bramble VQ(3)5s
Marsh
Or
Portsmouth Harbour
Flats
GOSPORT
PORTSMOUTH
Tr
SOUTHSEA
War memorial
Castle
Vail Williams
Gilkicker Point
Fort
B&G
Royal Albert
Spit Sand Fort Fl.R.5s
Q(9)15s
W Ryde Middle
Sunsail
N Ryde Middle Fl(4)R.20s
Browndown
NE Ryde Middle Fl(2)G.10s
Fl(2)R.10s
Fl.G.5s Bell
S Ryde Middle
D B Marine
Norris Fl(3)R.10s
Norris Castle
Osborne House
Lucas
Gleeds
Colonna Club
Q.R G
Main Passage R
SE Ryde Middle VQ(6)+LFl Bell
Peel Bank Fl(2)R.5s
DAKS Simpson
Obsn
Mother Bank Fl.R.3s
N Sturbridge VQ
Q(6)+LFl.15s
Outer Spit
Submerged Barrier
Bob Kemp
Saddle VQ(3)G.10s
Iso.G.2s
Horse Sand Fort
50° 45'N
Peel Wreck
(awash)
Five Star Sailing
NE Mining Ground Fl.Y.10s
No Mans Land Fort Iso.R.2s
Submerged Barrier
Kings Quay
Ryde Sands
Ryde Pier
Quarr Abbey
RYDE
Warner Q.R Whis
WOOTTON
Wootton Creek
Spire
Spire
Spire
Seaview
NETTLESTONE
Priory Bay
St Helens Fort Fl(3).10s
W Seamark
ST HELENS
BEMBRIDGE
15'
01°10'·0W

SOLENT AREA WAYPOINTS *9.2.18*

Waypoints marked with an asterisk (*) are special (yellow) racing marks, which may be removed in winter. Racing buoys marked with a bullet (●) against the longitude are only laid during Cowes week. Other waypoints are navigational buoys, unless otherwise stated. **All positions in Area 2 are referenced to the WGS 84/ETRS89 datum but should be assumed to be approximate.**

After Barn	50°51'·53N	01°20'·82W
***Air Canada**	50°47'·34N	01°16'·84W
***Alpha** (Cowes)	50°46'·27N	01°18'·20W
***Ashlett**	50°49'·99N	01°19'·75W
***Bainbridge Sailcloth**	50°47'·66N	01°13'·65W
Bald Head	50°49'·90N	01°18'·25W
***Bay**	50°46'·23N	00°58'·14W
Bembridge Ledge	50°41'·15N	01°02'·81W
Bembridge Tide Gauge	50°42'·46N	01°05'·02W
***Berthon** (Fl Y 4s)	50°44'·20N	01°29'·22W
***Beta** (Cowes)	50°46'·20N	01°17'·62W●
Black Jack	50°49'·13N	01°18'·09W
Black Rock	50°42'·58N	01°30'·63W
***Bob Kemp**	50°45'·18N	01°09'·64W
Boulder (Looe Chan)	50°41'·57N	00°49'·09W
***Bouldnor**	52°42'·73N	01°28'·99W
Bourne Gap	50°47'·83N	01°18'·34W
Boyne	50°46'·15N	01°05'·26W
Bramble Bn	50°47'·41N	01°17'·15W
Bridge	50°39'·57N	01°36'·92W
***Brookes & Gatehouse**	50°46'·43N	01°07'·89W
Browndown	50°46'·57N	01°10'·95W
Bury	50°54'·14N	01°27'·12W
Cadland	50°51'·02N	01°20'·54W
Calshot	50°48'·44N	01°17'·03W
Calshot Spit Lt F	50°48'·35N	01°17'·64W
***Camper & Nicholsons**	50°47'·08N	01°06'·78W
Castle (NB)	50°46'·45N	01°05'·38W
Castle Point	50°48'·71N	01°17'·67W
***Cathead**	50°50'·61N	01°19'·23W
***Champagne Mumm**	50°45'·64N	01°23'·12W
Chi	50°45'·72N	00°57'·26W
Chichester Bar Bn	50°45'·92N	00°56'·46W
***Chilling**	50°49'·24N	01°17'·48W
Chi Spit	50°45'·68N	00°56'·48W
***Clipper**	50°48'·46N	01°15'·73W
***Colonna Club**	50°46'·07N	01°05'·75W
***Colten** ('C')	50°43'·87N	01°30'·95W
Coronation	50°49'·55N	01°17'·62W
Cowes Breakwater Lt	50°45'·88N	01°17'·52W
Cowes No. 1	50°46'·07N	01°18'·03W
Cowes No. 2	50°46'·07N	01°17'·87W
Cowes No. 4	50°45'·85N	01°17'·72W
Cracknore	50°53'·94N	01°25'·20W
Crosshouse Lt Bn	50°54'·04N	01°23'·20W
***Cutter**	50°49'·45N	01°16'·91W
***Daks-Simpson**	50°45'·53N	01°14'·39W
***DB Marine**	50°46'·16N	01°13'·09W
Dean Elbow	50°43'·69N	01°01'·88W
Deans Elbow	50°52'·16N	01°22'·76W
Deans Lake	50°51'·40N	01°21'·59W
Dean Tail South	50°43'·04N	00°59'·57W
***Deck**	50°48'·63N	01°16'·65W
Dibden Bay	50°53'·70N	01°24'·92W
***Durns**	50°45'·43N	01°25'·89W●
***Dunford** ('B')	50°43'·41N	01°31'·63W
Durns Pt obstn (S end)	50°45'·40N	01°27'·05W
***East Bay**	50°45'·95N	01°19'·45W
East Bramble	50°47'·23N	01°13'·64W
East Knoll	50°47'·96N	01°16'·83W
East Lepe	50°46'·12N	01°20'·90W
East Looe	50°41'·24N	01°55'·93W
***Elephant**	50°44'·63N	01°21'·88W
Eling	50°54'·47N	01°27'·85W
Fairway (Needles)	50°38'·24N	01°38'·98W
***Five Star Sailing**	50°45'·03N	01°11'·89W
***Gales HSB**	50°46'·15N	01°16'·64W
***Gleeds**	50°46'·08N	01°06'·42W
Greenland	50°51'·11N	01°20'·38W
Gurnard	50°46'·22N	01°18'·84W
Gurnard Ledge	50°45'·52N	01°20'·59W
Gymp	50°53'·17N	01°24'·30W
Gymp Elbow	50°53'·50N	01°24'·68W
Hamble Point	50°50'·15N	01°18'·66W
Hamstead Ledge	50°43'·87N	01°26'·18W
***Hard**	50°45'·15N	00°58'·14W
***Harwoods**	50°42'·83N	01°28'·79W
Hillhead	50°48'·07N	01°16'·00W
Hook	50°49'·52N	01°18'·30W
Horse Elbow	50°44'·26N	01°03'·88W
Horse Sand	50°45'·53N	01°05'·27W
Horse Sand Fort Lt	50°45'·01N	01°04'·34W
Horse Tail	50°43'·23N	01°00'·23W
Hound	50°51'·68N	01°21'·52W
***Hurst** ('A')	50°42'·90N	01°32'·55W
Hythe Knock	50°52'·83N	01°23'·81W
Jack in Basket	50°44'·27N	01°30'·58W
***Jackson** ('H')	50°44'·33N	01°28'·25W
***Jib**	50°52'·97N	01°23'·06W
***Kelvin Hughes**	50°47'·33N	01°14'·59W●
Lains Lake	50°51'·59N	01°21'·65W
***Lambeth**	50°41'·53N	01°41'·69W
Langstone Fairway	50°46'·32N	01°01'·36W
Lepe Spit	50°46'·78N	01°20'·64W
***Lucas** (Fl Y 4s)	50°46'·26N	01°08'·76W
***Macmillan-Reeds**	50°46'·13N	01°22'·19W
Main Passage	50°45'·99N	01°04'·09W
Marchwood	50°53'·98N	01°25'·57W

***Mark**	50°49'·57N	01°18'·95W
***Marsh**	50°47'·31N	01°12'·10W
		·70W
		·71W
		·82W
		·32W
		·90W
		·21W
		·52W
		·82W
		·12W
		·80W
		·49W
		·15W
		·64W
		·42W
		·39W
		·88W
		·41W
		·98W
		·81W
		·63W
		·79W●
		·91W
		·70W
		·51W
		·52W
		·44W
		·31W
		·23W
		·84W
		·73W
		·76W
		·19W
		·74W
		·50W
		·34W
		·41W
		·63W
		·66W
		·16W
		·24W
		·36W
		·55W
		·52
		·88W
		·46W
		·65W
		·65W
		·28W
		·96W
		·28W

***Royal Southern**	50°48'·86N	01°15'·59W
***Royal Southern ODM**	50°42'·53N	01°29'·74W
***Royal Thames**	50°47'·81N	01°19'·25W
***Ruthven**	50°42'·70N	01°03'·56W
Ryde Pier Hd (NW corner)	50°44'·34N	01°09'·72W
***RYS flagstaff**	50°45'·98N	01°18'·04W
Saddle	50°45'·20N	01°04'·98W
Salt Mead	50°44'·52N	01°23'·04W
Sconce	50°42'·53N	01°31'·43W
***Seascope**	50°47'·42N	01°15'·90W
SE Ryde Middle	50°45'·93N	01°12'·09W
Shingles Elbow	50°40'·32N	01°36'·06W
***Snowden** (ex Trap)	50°46'·25N	01°17'·59W
South Bramble	50°46'·98N	01°17'·72W
South Pullar	50°38'·84N	00°49'·29W
South Ryde Middle	50°46'·13N	01°14'·16W
***Southsea Marina**	50°46'·43N	01°03'·54W
***Spanker** (Fl Y 4s)	50°47'·11N	01°18'·08W
***Spinlock**	50°46'·09N	01°18'·43W
Spit Refuge	50°46'·15N	01°05'·46W
Spit Sand Fort Lt	50°46'·24N	01°05'·94W
***Sposa**	50°49'·67N	01°17'·60W
St Helens	50°40'·36N	01°02'·41W
Street	50°41'·69N	00°48'·88W
***Sunsail**	50°46'·43N	01°15'·09W
Swinging Ground No. 1	50°53'·00N	01°23'·44W
Swinging Ground No. 2	50°53'·82N	01°25'·12W
SW Mining Ground	50°44'·66N	01°08'·04W
SW Shingles	50°39'·35N	01°37'·39W
***Tanners** ('G')	50°44'·83N	01°28'·56W
Thorn Knoll	50°47'·50N	01°18'·44W
***Vail Williams** (ex Beta Portsmouth)	50°46'·83N	01°07'·34W
***Wadworth**	50°43'·15N	01°27'·49W
Warden	50°41'·46N	01°33'·61W
Warner	50°43'·87N	01°03'·99W
***West Bay**	50°45'·65N	01°20'·23W
West Bramble	50°47'·20N	01°18'·65W
***W – E**	50°45'·72N	00°59'·05W
West Knoll	50°47'·55N	01°17'·77W
West Lepe	50°45'·24N	01°24'·09W
West Pole Beacon	50°45'·71N	00°56'·50W
Weston Shelf	50°52'·71N	01°23'·26W
West Princessa	50°40'·16N	01°03'·65W
West Ryde Middle	50°46'·48N	01°15'·79W
***William**	50°49'·03N	01°16'·49W
Winner	50°45'·10N	01°00'·10W
***Woolwich**	50°43'·04N	01°38'·08W
Wootton Bn	50°44'·53N	01°12'·13W
***Yachting World**	50°45'·11N	01°27'·34W
***Yachthaven** ('D') **ODM**	50°44'·21N	01°30'·19W
***YMS 2** (Fl Y 10s)	50°42'·89N	01°29'·49W

YARMOUTH *9.2.19*

Isle of Wight **50°42'·42N 01°30'·05W** ❀❀❀◊◊◊✿✿✿

CHARTS AC *5600, 2021, 2037*; Imray C3, C15; Stanfords 11, 24, 25; OS 196

TIDES Sp –0050, +0150, Np +0020 Dover; ML 2·0; Zone 0 (UT)

Standard Port PORTSMOUTH (⟶)

Times				**Height (metres)**			
High Water		Low Water		MHWS	MHWN	MLWN	MLWS
0000	0600	0500	1100	4·7	3·8	1·9	0·8
1200	1800	1700	2300				
Differences YARMOUTH							
–0105	+0005	–0025	–0030	–1·7	–1·2	–0·3	0·0

NOTE: Double HWs occur at or near sp; at other times there is a stand lasting about two hrs. Predictions refer to the first HW when there are two; otherwise to the middle of the stand. See 9.2.12.

SHELTER Good from all directions of wind and sea, but swell enters if wind strong from N/NE. Hbr dredged 2m from ent to bridge; access H24. Moor fore-and-aft on piles, on the Town Quay, or on pontoon. Boats over 15m LOA, 4m beam or 2·4m draft should give notice of arrival. Berthing on S Quay is normally only for fuel, C, FW, or to load people/cargo. Hbr gets very full in season and may be closed to visitors signalled by R flag and notice. 36 Y ◈s outside hbr (see chartlet) and ⚓ further to the N or S.

NAVIGATION WPT 50°42'·58N 01°30'·01W, 008°/188° from/to abeam car ferry terminal, 2ca. Dangers on appr are Black Rock (SHM buoy Fl G 5s) and shoal water to the N of the E/W bkwtr. Beware ferries. Caution: strong ebb in the ent at sp. Speed limit 4kn in hbr and 6kn in approaches. ⚓ prohib in hbr and beyond R Yar road bridge. This swing bridge opens for 10 mins for access to the moorings and BYs up-river at Saltern Quay: (May-Sept) 0800, 0900, 1000, 1200, 1400, 1600, 1730, 1830, 2000LT; and on request (Oct-May). The river is navigable by dinghy at HW almost up to Freshwater.

A **Historic Wreck** (see 9.0.3h) is at 50°42'·55N 01°29'·67W, 2ca ExN from end of pier; marked by Y SPM buoy.

LIGHTS AND MARKS Ldg bns (2 W ◊ on B/W masts) and ldg lts (FG 5/9m 2M), on quay, 188°. When hbr is closed to visitors (eg when full in summer or at week-ends) a R flag is flown at the pier head and an illuminated board 'Harbour Full' is displayed at the ent, plus an extra ●. In fog a high intensity Ⓦ lt is shown from the pier hd and from the inner E pier, together with a ●.

RADIO TELEPHONE Hr Mr VHF Ch 68. Water Taxi Ch 15.

TELEPHONE (Dial code 01983 = code for whole of IOW) Hr Mr 760321, 📠 761192; MRSC (023 92) 552100; ⊜ 0345 231110 (H24); Marinecall 0898 500457; Police 52800; Dr 760434.

FACILITIES Hbr £9.00 (30ft) (£4 < 4hrs) on piles, Town Quay, pontoon or ◈; Slip, P, D, L, M, Gaz, FW, C (5 ton), Ice, Ⓢ, ♿;
Yarmouth SC ☎ 760512, Bar, L;
Royal Solent YC ☎ 760256, Bar, R, L, Slip;
Services Note: BY in SW corner but most marine services/BYs are located near Salterns Quay, 500m up-river above the bridge, or ½M by road. BY, Slip, M, ME, El, Sh, CH, Gas, Gaz, LPG, SM, C, Divers.
Town EC Wed; V, R, Bar, ✉, Ⓑ (May-Sept 1000-1445, Sept-May a.m. only), ⇌ (Lymington), ✈ (Bournemouth/Southampton).

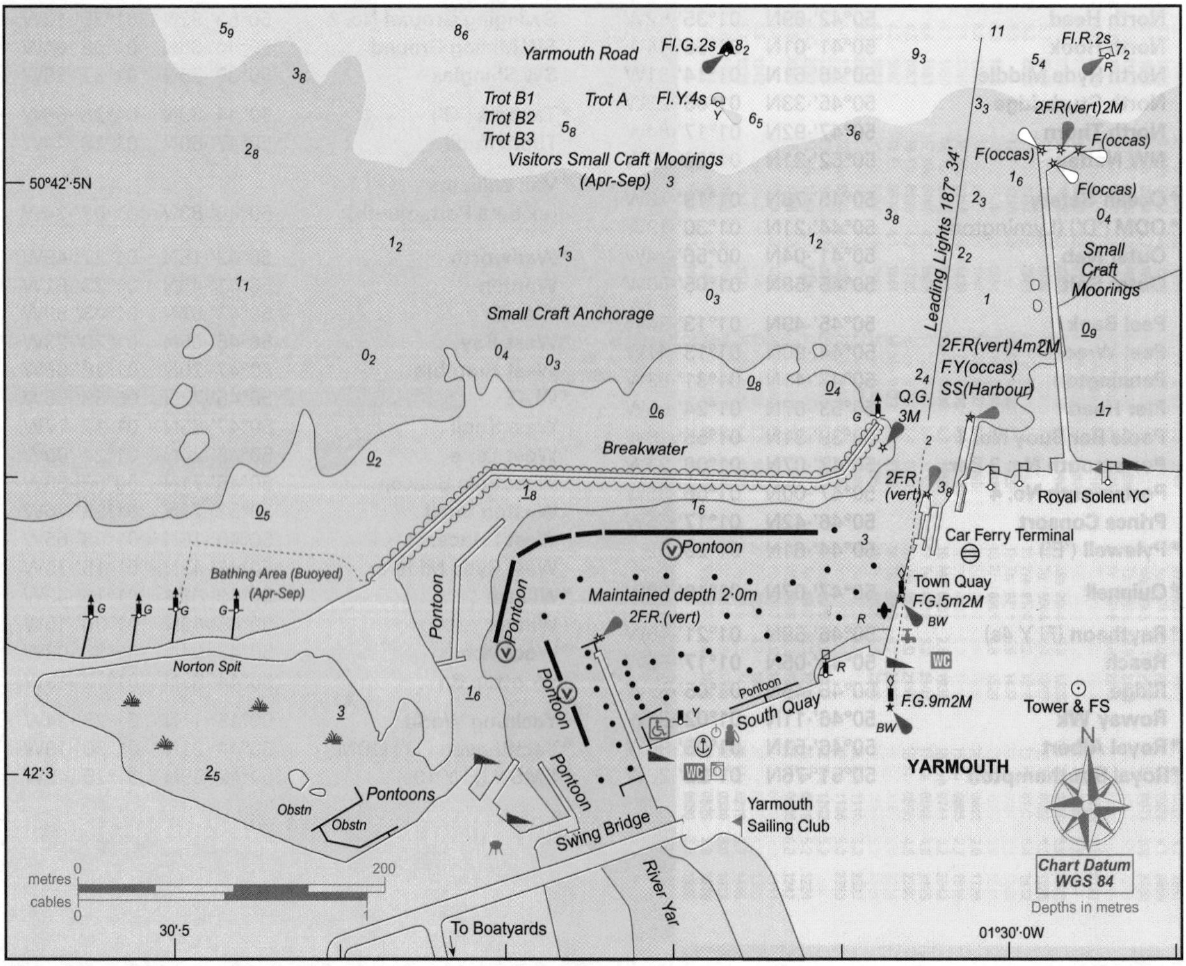

LYMINGTON *9.2.20*

Hampshire **50°45'·13N 01·31'·40W** ❁❁❁◊◊◊✿✿✿

CHARTS AC *5600, 2021, 2035*; Imray C3, C15; Stanfords 11, 25, 25; OS 196

TIDES Sp –0040, +0100, Np +0020 Dover; ML 2·0; Zone 0 (UT)

Standard Port PORTSMOUTH (⟶)

Times				Height (metres)			
High Water		Low Water		MHWS	MHWN	MLWN	MLWS
0000	0600	0500	1100	4·7	3·8	1·9	0·8
1200	1800	1700	2300				
Differences LYMINGTON							
–0110	+0005	–0020	–0020	–1·7	–1·2	–0·5	–0·1

NOTE: Double HWs occur at or near sp and on other occasions there is a stand lasting about 2hrs. Predictions refer to the first HW when there are two. At other times they refer to the middle of the stand. See 9.2.12.

RADIO TELEPHONE Marinas VHF Ch **80** M (office hrs).

TELEPHONE (Dial code 01590) Hr Mr 672014; MRSC (023 92) 552100; ⊜ 0345 231110 (H24); Marinecall 09068 500457; Police 675411; Dr 672953; Ⓗ 677011.

FACILITIES Marinas:
Lymington Yacht Haven (475+100 visitors), 2m depth, all tides access, ☎ 677071, 📠 678186, £1.87, P, D, AC, FW, BY, ME, El, Sh, C (10 ton), BH (40 ton), CH, Gas, Gaz, LPG, ▣, ♿ (mobile) ;
Lymington Marina (300+100 visitors), ☎ 673312, 📠 676353, £2.22, Slip, P, AC, D, FW, ME, El, Sh, CH, BH (100 ton), C, (37, 80 ton), Gas, Gaz, ▣, ♿;
Town Quay AB £1.05, M, FW, Slip (see Hr Mr); **Bath Road** public pontoon, FW, ♿.
Clubs: Royal Lymington YC ☎ 672677, R, Bar, ♿; **Lymington Town SC** ☎ 674514, AB, R, Bar.
Services: M, FW, ME, El, Sh, C (16 ton), CH, Ⓔ, SM, ACA.
Town every facility including ✉, Ⓑ, ⇌, ✈ (Bournemouth or Southampton).

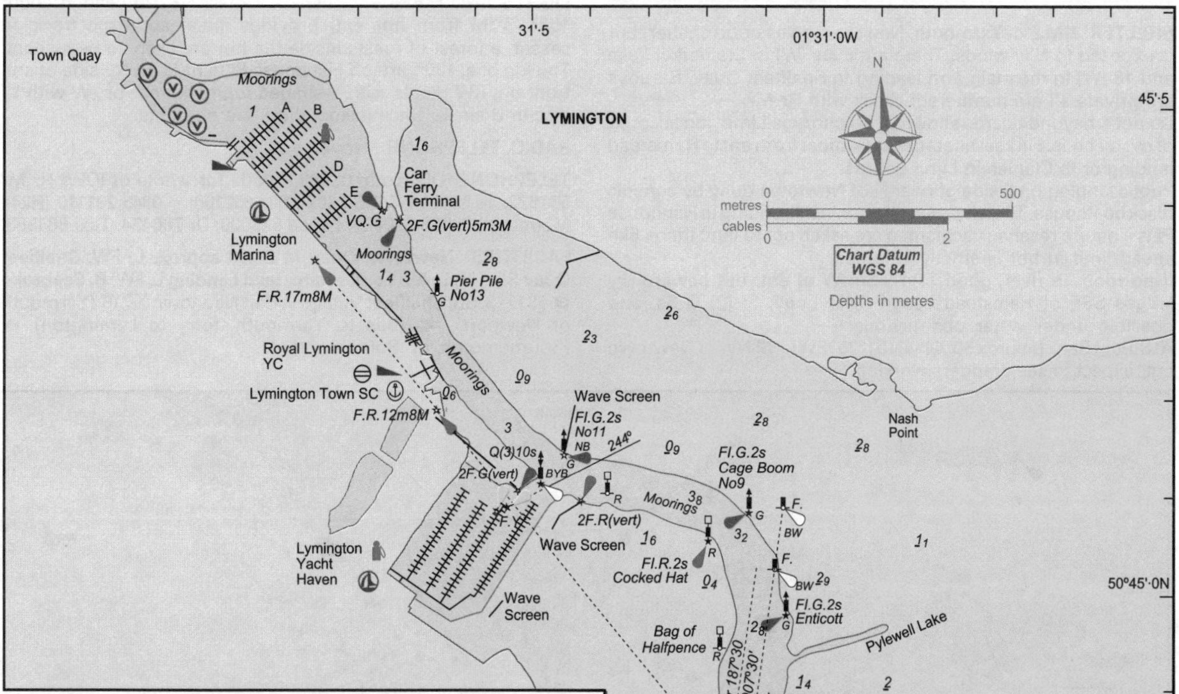

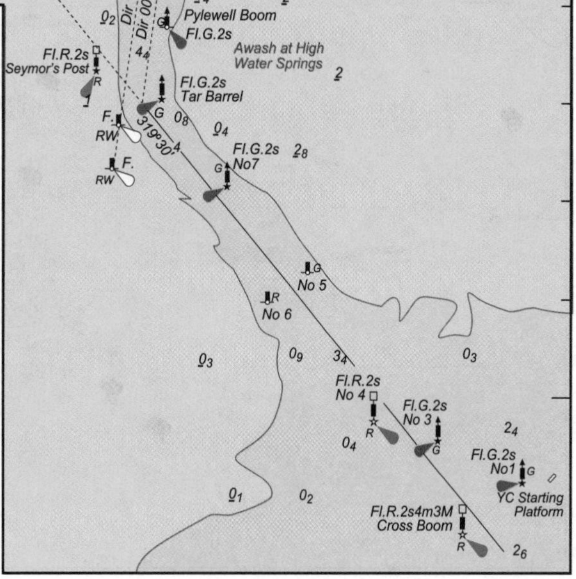

SHELTER Good in two large marinas and at Customs House Quay and Town Quay; the latter provide public AB (see Hr Mr) and up to 100 ⚓s (W). River is accessible at all states of the tide; speed limit 6kn. ⚓ in the river is prohib, but in off-shore winds yachts can ⚓ off the mud flats outside.

NAVIGATION WPT 50°44'·23N 01°30'·36W, 139·5°/319·5° from/to abeam Nos 1 and 2 piles, 1·9ca. There are extensive, but well marked mud banks around the ent. Entering, leave Jack- in-the-Basket about 45m to port to clear Cross Boom.
Min depth 1·8m in mid-chan from ent to Railway Pier; thence 1·1m to Town Quay. All craft must give way to and keep clear of ferries in very narrow chan; beware wave screens off Lymington Yacht Haven.

LIGHTS AND MARKS Ldg lts 319°, both FR 12/17m 8M. Ent marked by Jack-in-the-Basket, Fl R 2s, and by conspic YC starting platform, 60m E of No 1 bn, Fl G 2s. Narrow chan is marked by 8 PHM piles (four Fl R 2s) and 9 SHM piles (eight Fl G 2s). Two sets of ldg marks/lts on the central section ensure lateral clearance between opposite direction ferries: two BW posts, Dir FW, on flats to SE of Cage Boom in line at 007°30' for inbound ferries; two RW posts, Dir FW, on flats to SSE of Seymours Post in line at 187°30' for outbound ferries.
Harper's Post ECM bn, Q (3) 10s 5m 1M, and two FY ldg lts 244° mark the ent into Lymington Yacht Haven.

NEWTOWN RIVER 9.2.21

Isle of Wight **50°43'·45N 01°24'·66W** ❀❀◊◊✿✿✿

CHARTS AC *5600, 2021, 2035, 2036*; Imray C3, C15; Stanfords 11, 24, 25; OS 196

TIDES Sp –0108, Np +0058, Dover; ML 2·3; Zone 0 (UT)

Standard Port PORTSMOUTH (⟶)

Times				Height (metres)			
High Water		Low Water		MHWS	MHWN	MLWN	MLWS
0000	0600	0500	1100	4·7	3·8	1·9	0·8
1200	1800	1700	2300				
Differences SOLENT BANK (Data approximate)							
–0100	0000	–0015	–0020	–1·3	–1·0	–0·3	–0·1

NOTE: Double HWs occur at or near springs; at other times there is a stand which lasts about 2hrs. Predictions refer to the first HW when there are two. At other times they refer to the middle of the stand. See 9.2.12.

SHELTER 3½M E of Yarmouth, Newtown gives good shelter, but is exposed to N'ly winds. There are 6 ⚓s (W) in Clamerkin Lake and 18 (W) in the main arm leading to Shalfleet Quay, R buoys are private all are numbered; check with Hr Mr.

Do not ⚓ beyond boards showing "Anchorage Limit" on account of oyster beds. Fin keel boats can stay afloat from ent to Hamstead landing or to Clamerkin Limit Boards.

Public landing on E side of river N of Newtown quay by conspic black boathouse. The whole eastern peninsula ending in Fishhouse Pt is a nature reserve; yachtsmen are asked not to land there. 5kn speed limit in hbr is strictly enforced.

If no room in river, good ⚓ in 3-5m W of ent, but beware rky ledges SSE of Hamstead Ledge SHM buoy, Fl (2) G 5s, and possible under water obstructions.

At Solent Bank (approx 50°44'·5N 01°25'·5W), 1M NW of Newtown ent, expect to see dredgers working.

NAVIGATION WPT 50°43'·83N 01°25'·18W, 310°/130° from/to ldg bn, 0·46M. From W, make good Hamstead Ledge SHM buoy, thence E to pick up ldg marks. From E, keep N of Newtown gravel banks where W/SW winds over a sp ebb can raise steep breaking seas; leave PHM Fl.R4s bar buoy to port. Best ent is from about HW –4, on the flood but while the mud flats are still visible. Ent lies between two shingle spits and can be rough in N winds especially near HW. There is only about 0·9m over the bar.

Inside the ent so many perches mark the mud banks that confusion may result. Near junction to Causeway Lake depth is only 0·9m and beyond this water quickly shoals.

At ent to Clamerkin Lake (1·2 -1·8m) keep to SE to avoid gravel spit off W shore, marked by two PHM perches; the rest of chan is marked by occas perches. Beware many oyster beds in Western Haven and Clamerkin Lake.

There is a rifle range at top of Clamerkin Lake and in Spur Lake; R flags flown during firing. High voltage power line across Clamerkin at 50°42'·81N 01°22'·66W has clearance of only 9m and no shore markings.

LIGHTS AND MARKS Conspic TV mast (152m) bearing about 150° (3·3M from hbr ent) provides initial approach track. In season a forest of masts inside the hbr are likely to be evident. The ldg bns, 130°, are off Fishhouse Pt in mud on NE side of ent: front bn, RW bands with Y-shaped topmark; rear bn, W with W disc in B circle. Once inside, there are no lights.

RADIO TELEPHONE None.

TELEPHONE (Dial code 01983 = code for whole of IOW) Hr Mr 531622; 📠 531914; MRSC (023 92) 552100; ⊜ 0345 231110 (H24); Marinecall 09068 500457; Police 528000; Dr 760434; Taxi 884353.

FACILITIES **Newtown Quay** M £1.00 approx, L, FW; **Shalfleet Quay** Slip, M, L, AB; **Lower Hamstead Landing** L, FW; **R. Seabroke** ☎ 531213, Sh; **Shalfleet Village** V, Bar. **Newtown** ✉, Ⓑ (Yarmouth or Newport), ⇌ (bus to Yarmouth, ferry to Lymington), ✈ (Bournemouth or Southampton).

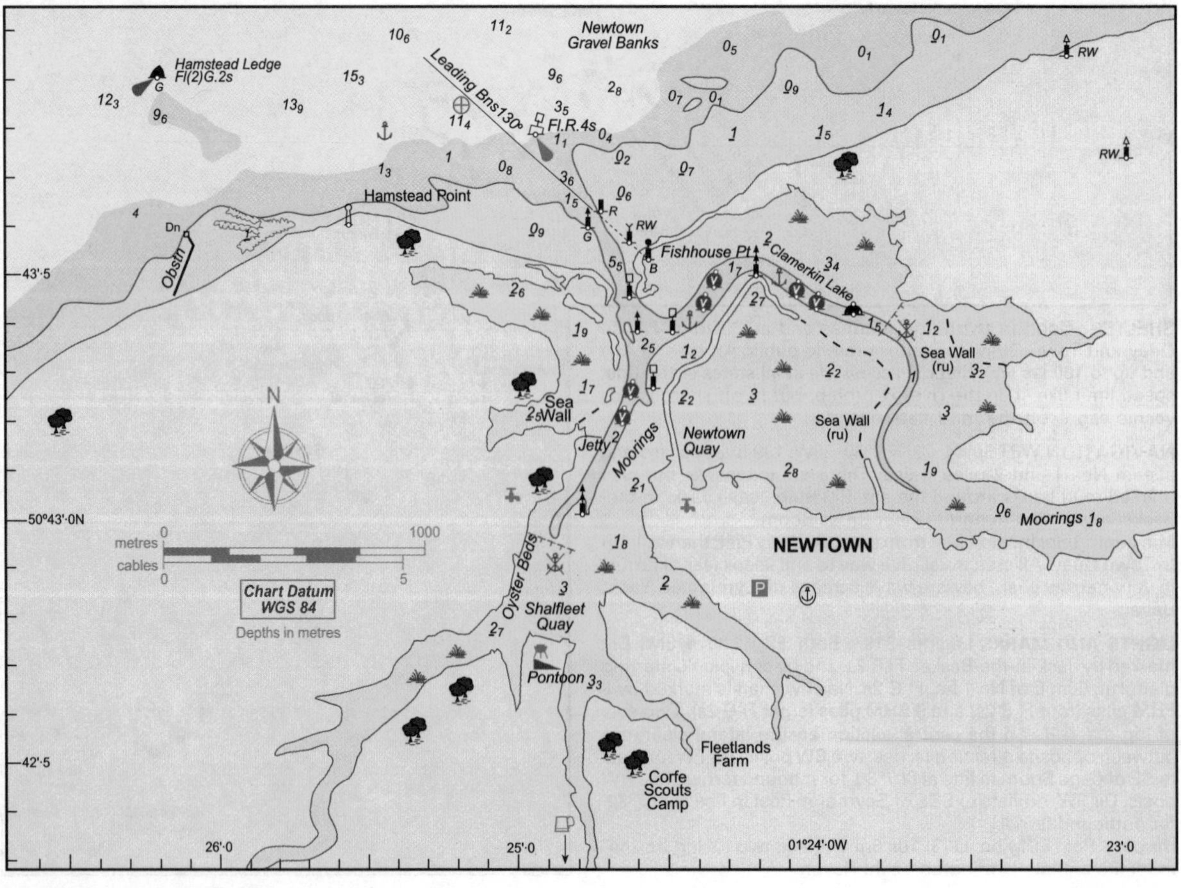

BEAULIEU RIVER *9.2.22*

Hampshire **50°46'·89N 01°21'·72W** (Ent)

CHARTS AC *5600, 2021, 2035, 2036*; Imray C3, C15; Stanfords 11, 24, 25; OS 196

TIDES –0100 and +0140 Dover; ML 2·4; Zone 0 (UT)

Standard Port PORTSMOUTH (⟶)

Times				Height (metres)			
High Water		Low Water		MHWS	MHWN	MLWN	MLWS
0000	0600	0500	1100	4·7	3·8	1·9	0·8
1200	1800	1700	2300				
BUCKLER'S HARD							
–0040	–0010	+0010	–0010	–1·0	–0·8	–0·2	–0·3
STANSORE POINT							
–0050	–0010	–0005	–0010	–0·8	–0·5	–0·3	–0·1

NOTE: Double HWs occur at or near springs; the 2nd HW is approx 1¾ hrs after the 1st. On other occasions there is a stand which lasts about two hrs. The predictions refer to the first HW when there are two, or to the middle of the stand. See 9.2.12.

SHELTER Very good in all winds. ⚓ possible in reach between Lepe Ho and Beaulieu River SC, but preferable to proceed to Buckler's Hard Yacht Hbr (AB and Ⓥ pile moorings).
Many of the landing stages/slips shown on the chartlet (and AC 2021) are privately owned and not to be used. The uppermost reaches of the river are best explored first by dinghy due to the lack of channel markers and the short duration of the HW stand.
Rabies: Craft with animals from abroad are prohibited in the river.

NAVIGATION WPT 50°46'·53N 01°21'·33W, 144°/324° from/to abeam Beaulieu Spit dolphin (Fl R 5s), 4ca. Ent dangerous LW±2. There are patches drying 0·3m approx 100m S of Beaulieu Spit. 1ca further SSE, close W of the ldg line, are shoal depths 0·1m. Lepe Spit SCM buoy, Q (6) + L Fl 15s, is 7ca E of Beaulieu Spit dolphin at 50°46'.78N 01°20'·63W.
The swatchway off Beaulieu River SC is closed. A speed limit of 5kn applies to the whole river.

LIGHTS AND MARKS Ldg marks at ent 324° must be aligned exactly due to shoal water either side of ldg line. The front is No 2 bn, R with Or dayglow topmark, △ shape above □; the rear is Lepe Ho. Beaulieu Spit, R dolphin with W band, Fl R 5s 3M vis 277°-037°; ra refl, should be left approx 40m to port. The old CG cottages and Boat House are conspic, approx 320m E of Lepe Ho.
The river is clearly marked by R and G bns and perches. SHM bns 5, 9, 19 and 21 are all Fl G 4s; PHM bns 12 & 20 are Fl R 4s. Marina pontoons A, C and E have 2FR (vert).

RADIO TELEPHONE None.

TELEPHONE (Dial code 01590) Hr Mr 616200/616234, 📠 616211; MRSC (023 92) 552100; ⊖ 0345 231110 (H24); Marinecall 09068 500457; Police (023 80) 335444; Dr 612451 or (023 80) 845955; Ⓗ 77011.

FACILITIES Buckler's Hard Yacht Hbr £2.20 (110+20 Ⓥ) ☎ 616200, 📠 616211, Slip, M (£1 on piles), P, D, AC, FW, ME, El, Sh, C (1 ton), BH (26 ton), SM, Gas, Gaz, CH, ▣, ♿, V, R, Bar.
Village V (Stores ☎ 616293), R, Bar, ✉ (Beaulieu), Ⓑ (Mon, Wed, Fri AM or Hythe), ⇄ (bus to Brockenhurst), ✈ (Bournemouth or Southampton).

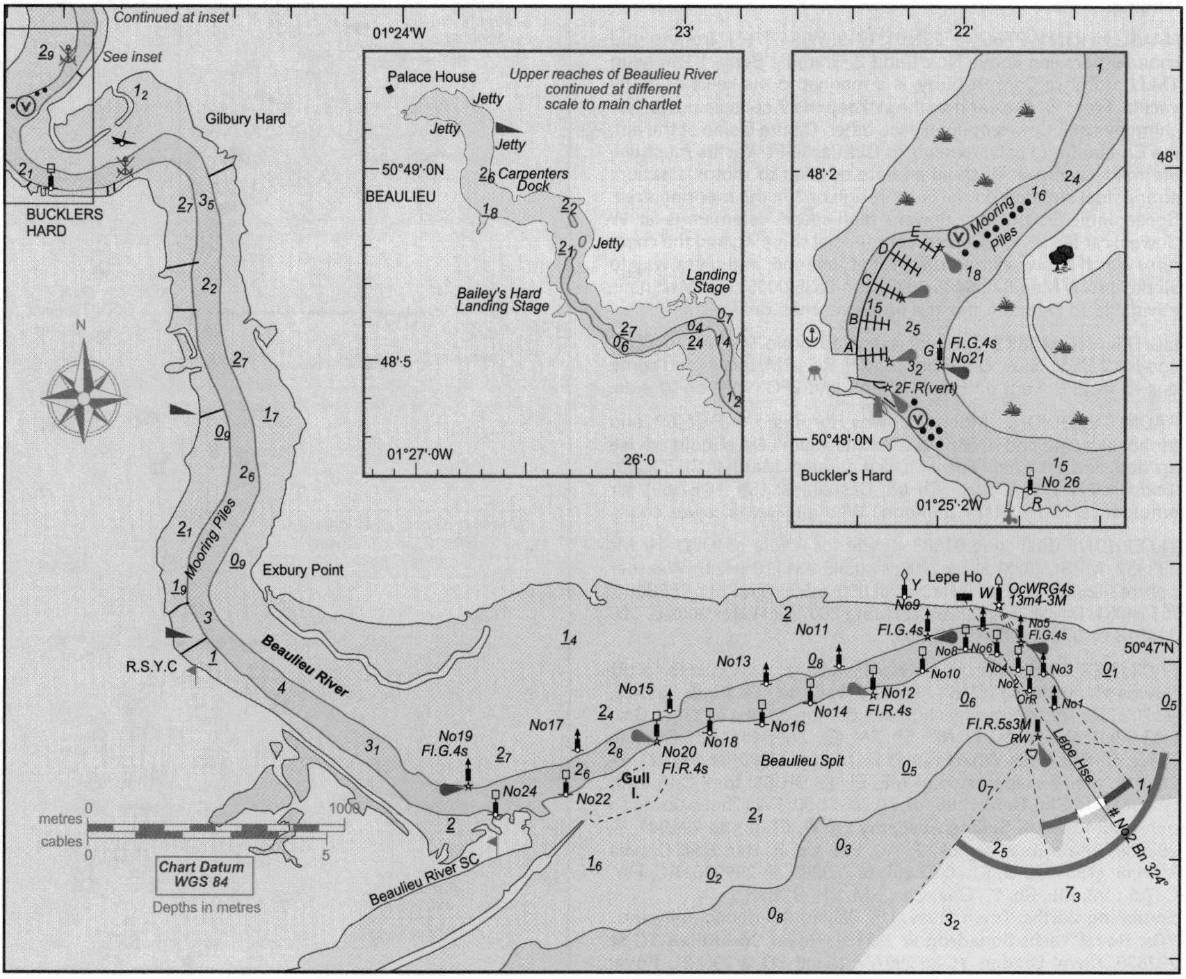

COWES/RIVER MEDINA *9.2.23*

Isle of Wight 50°45'·89N 01°17'·80W ❀❀❀◇◇◇✿✿✿

CHARTS AC *5600, 2793, 2035, 2036*; Imray C3, C15; Stanfords 11, 24, 25; OS 196

TIDES +0029 Dover; ML 2·7; Zone 0 (UT)

Standard Port PORTSMOUTH (⟶)

Times				Height (metres)			
High Water		Low Water		MHWS	MHWN	MLWN	MLWS
0000	0600	0500	1100	4·7	3·8	1·9	0·8
1200	1800	1700	2300				
Differences COWES							
–0015	+0015	0000	–0020	–0·5	–0·3	–0·1	0·0
FOLLY INN							
–0015	+0015	0000	–0020	–0·6	–0·4	–0·1	+0·2
NEWPORT							
No data		No data		–0·6	–0·4	+0·1	+0·8

NOTE: Double HWs occur at or near sp. On other occasions a stand occurs lasting up to 2hrs; times given represent the middle of the stand. See 9.2.12, especially for Newport.

SHELTER Good at Cowes Yacht Haven and above the chain ferry, but outer hbr exposed to N and NE winds. ⚓ prohib in hbr. Visitors may pick up/secure to any mooring/piles/pontoon so labelled, ie: 14 large Ⓥs off The Green and off The Parade; piles S of Cowes Yacht Haven; Thetis Pontoon (short stay/overnight only, dredged 2·5m); pontoons S of the chain ferry (W Cowes); 'E' Pontoon off E Cowes SC. See opposite for pontoons in Folly Reach; Island Harbour marina on E bank beyond Folly Inn and in Newport (dries). Good ⚓ in Osborne Bay, 2M E, sheltered from SE to W; no landing.

NAVIGATION WPT 50°46'·23N 01°17'·99W, 347°/167° from/to mid channel between Buoys Nos 1 and 2. Bramble Bank, 1·1m, lying 1M N of Prince Consort buoy, is a magnet to the keels of many yachts. From N, to clear it to the W keep the 2 conspic power stn chimneys at E Cowes open of each other. On the E side of the ent, the Shrape (mud flats) extends to Old Castle Pt. Yachts must use the main chan near W shore and are advised to motor. Caution: strong tidal streams; do not sail through or ⚓ in the mooring area. Speed limit 6kn in hbr. Beware high-speed catamarans at W Cowes; car ferries at E Cowes, commercial shipping and the chain ferry which shows all round Fl W lt at fore-end, and gives way to all tfc; it runs Mon-Sat: 0435-0005, Sun 0635-0005LT. R Medina is navigable to Newport, but the upper reaches dry.

LIGHTS AND MARKS Chan ent is marked by No 1 SHM buoy, QG, and No 2 PHM buoy, QR. E bkwtr hd Fl R 3s 3M. Jetties and some dns show 2FR (vert) on E side of hbr, and 2FG (vert) on W side.

RADIO TELEPHONE Monitor *Cowes Hbr Radio* VHF Ch **69**; and for hbr launches and Hr Mr's Ⓥs. Yachts >30m LOA should advise arr/dep, and call *Chain Ferry* Ch 69 if passing. Marinas Ch 80. *Hbr Taxi* Ch 77. *Water Taxi* Ch 06. Casualties: (Ch 16/67/69) for ambulance at Fountain pontoon. Web site www.cowes.co.uk.

TELEPHONE (Dial code 01983 = code for whole of IOW) Hr Mr 293952; MRSC (023) 9255 2100; ⊜ 0345 231110 (H24); Weather Centre (023) 8022 8844; Marinecall 09068 500457; Police 528000; Ⓗ 524081; Dr 295251; Cowes Yachting 280770; Water taxis 07050 344818 or 07831 331717/299033.

FACILITIES Marinas (from seaward) website www.cowes.co.uk: **Cowes Yacht Haven** (CYH), (35+ 200 Ⓥ, £1.80 - £2.35) ☎ 299975, 📠 200332, info@cowesyachthaven.demon.co.uk, ♿, Gas, Gaz, LPG (all H24), FW, AC, El, ME, Sh, SM, Ⓔ, C (2·5 ton), BH (35 ton), R, Ice, ▣. **Shepards Wharf** (up to 75 berths, £1.80) ☎ 297821, 📠 294814, mail@shepards.co.uk,ME, El, Ⓔ, BH (20 ton), C (6 ton), BY, SM, CH, Slip. **Hr Mr**: 100 AB, £0.70 -£1.00; FW (Thetis pontoon only), some ♿. **UK Sailing Academy** (10 Ⓥ, £1.32), ☎ 294941, 📠 295938, info@uksail.org.uk, ♿, AC, FW, Ice, R, Bar. **East Cowes Marina,** (180+120 Ⓥ, £1.20-£2.20), ☎ 293983, 📠 299276, AC, FW, C (7.5 ton), ME, Sh, V, Gas, Gaz, SM, CH, R, Bar.
Scrubbing berths: Town Quay, UK Sailing Academy, Folly Inn. **YCs: Royal Yacht Squadron** ☎ 292191; **Royal Corinthian YC** ☎ 292608; **Royal London YC** ☎ 299727; **Island SC** ☎ 296621; **Royal**

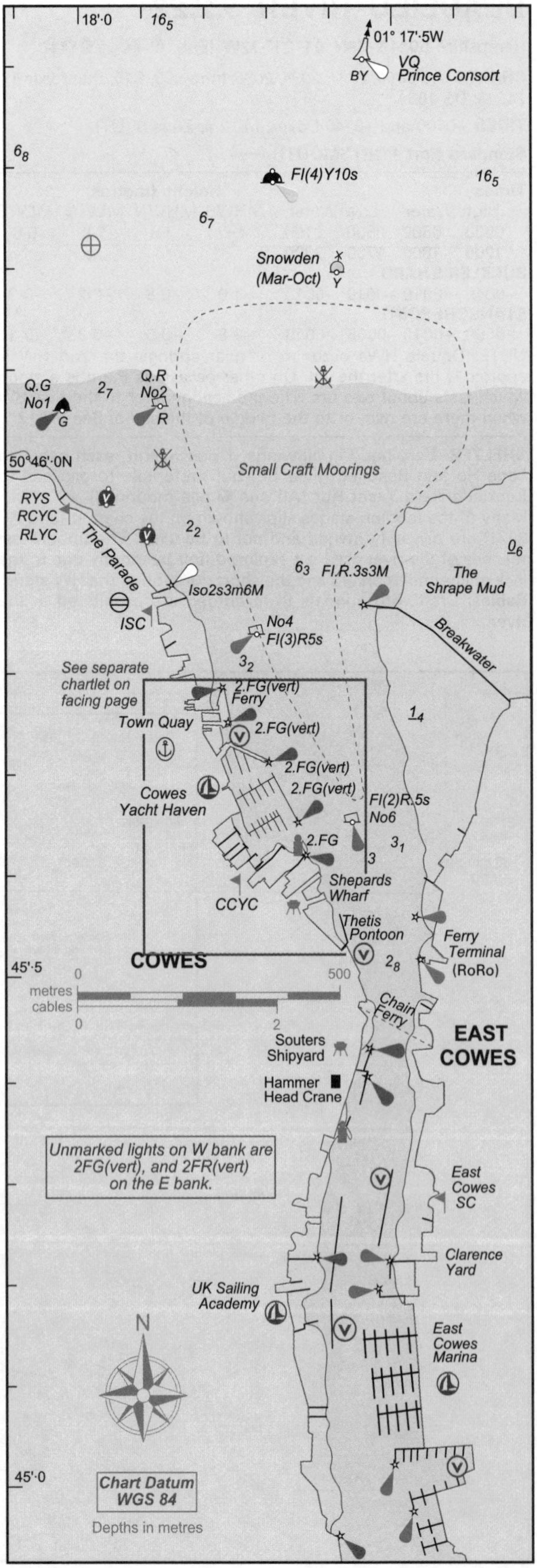

Ocean Racing Club ☎ 295144 (manned only in Cowes Week); **Cowes Corinthian YC** ☎ 296333; **East Cowes SC** ☎ 294394; **Cowes Combined Clubs** ☎ 295744, 📠 295329, ccc@cowesweek.co.uk. Cowes Week is normally 1st full week in Aug.
Ferries: Red Funnel ☎ (023 80) 334010, 📠 639438, post@redfunnel.co.uk, www.redfunnel.co.uk, all to Southampton: Car/pax from E Cowes; Catamaran (foot pax) from W Cowes; **Chain Ferry** ☎ 293041.
Services: All marine services are available. See *Port Handbook & Directory* for details (free from Hr Mr, hbr launches, marinas and Cowes Yachting). **FW** from marinas, Old Town Quay, Whitegates public pontoon, Thetis pontoon and Folly Inn pontoon. **Fuel:** CYH, D & LPG only, H24, ; Lallows BY (P & D); MST pontoon off Souters BY (P & D).
Town www.cowes.co.uk, Bar, ⊡, Slip, ✉, Ⓑ, Gas, Gaz Ⓔ, CH, R, V, El.

RIVER MEDINA, FOLLY REACH TO NEWPORT

FOLLY REACH, 50°44'·03N 01°16'·99W. Above Medham ECM bn, VQ (3) 5s, there are depths of 1m to S Folly bn, QG. There are Ⓥ pontoons along W bank, S of residents' ones. Hr Mr ☎ 295722 and Ch 69 *Folly Launch*. **Folly Inn** ♿, ☎ 297171, AB (pontoon) £1.10, M*, Slip, scrubbing berth.
Island Harbour Marina (5ca S of Folly Inn), (150 + 100 Ⓥ), £1.64; 2·1m), ☎ 822999, 📠 526020, ♿, AC, BH (25 ton), Gas, Gaz, ⊡, ME, CH, BY, Slip, Bar, R. VHF Ch 80 *Island Harbour Control*. Excellent shelter; appr via marked, dredged chan with waiting pontoon to stbd, withies to port. Access HW ±4 to lock with R/G tfc lts. *Ryde Queen* paddle steamer is conspic.

NEWPORT, 50°42'·21N 01°17'·43W. Tides see 9.2.12 and 9.2.23. Above Island Hbr marina the 1·2M long chan to Newport dries, but from HW Portsmouth –1½ to HW +2 it carries 2m or more. S from Folly Inn, the hbr authority is IoW Council. Speed limit 6kn up to Seaclose, S of Newport Rowing Club (NRC); thence 4kn to Newport. The chan, which is buoyed and partially lit, favours the W bank; night appr not recommended. Power lines have 33m clearance. Ldg marks/lts are 192°, W ◊ bns 7/11m, on the E bank, both lit 2FR (hor). Newport, Ⓥs' pontoons on the E/SE sides of the basin have 1·4m HW ±2. Bilge keelers lie alongside pontoons on soft mud; fin keelers against quay wall on firm, level bottom. Fender boards can be supplied.
Newport Yacht Hbr (40 Ⓥs, £1.10), ♿, Hr Mr ☎ 525994, 📠 823333, VHF Ch 69 (HO or as arranged), AC, FW, BY, C (10 ton), R; Classic Boat Centre.
Town P & D (cans), El, Sh, Slip, Gaz, Gas, Ⓑ, Bar, Dr, Ⓗ, ✉, ⊡, R, V.

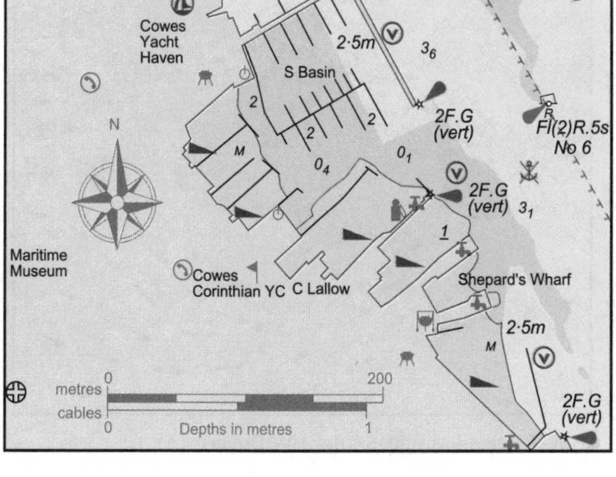

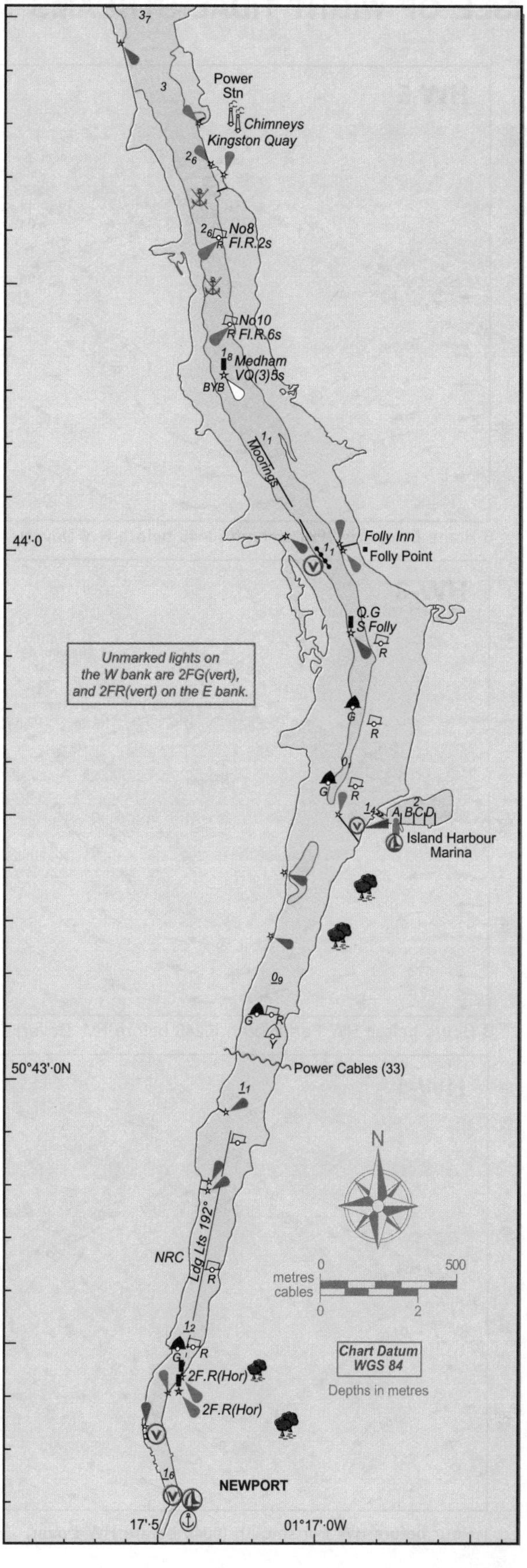

ISLE OF WIGHT TIDAL STREAMS *9.2.24*

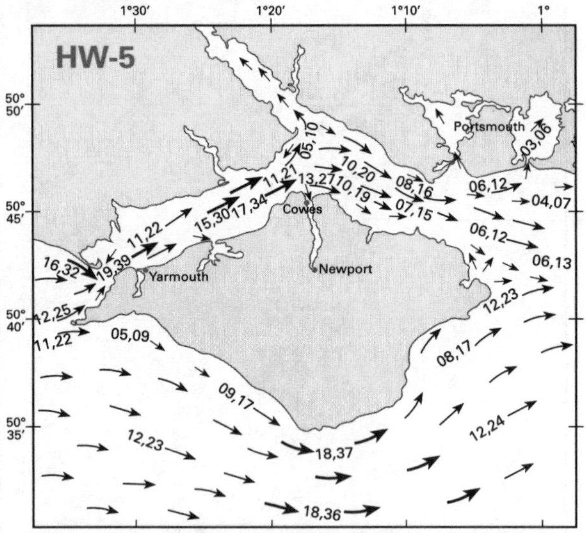

5 Hours before HW Portsmouth (0445 before HW Dover)

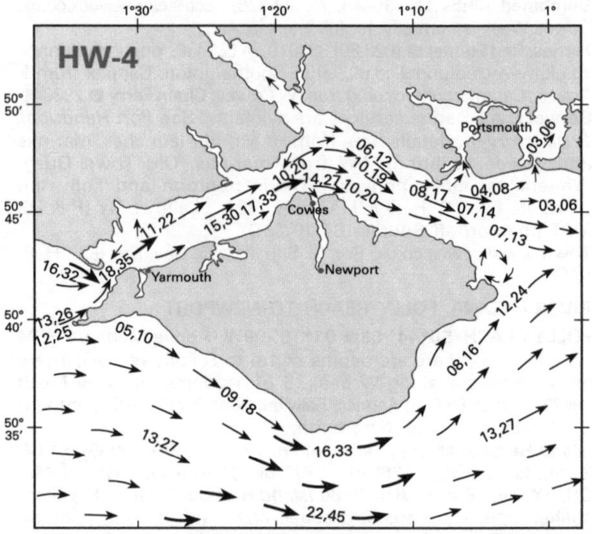

4 Hours before HW Portsmouth (0345 before HW Dover)

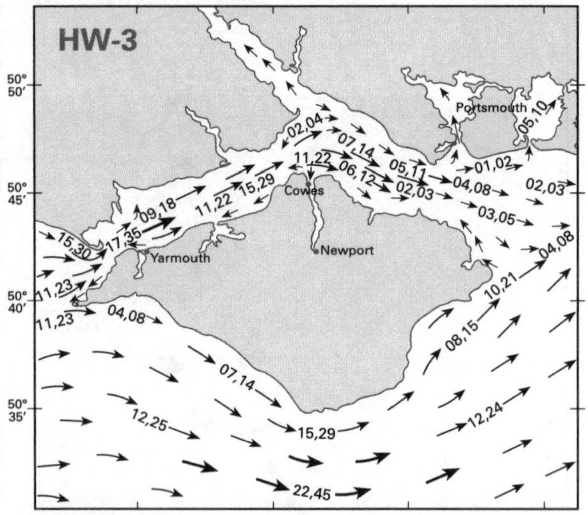

3 Hours before HW Portsmouth (0245 before HW Dover)

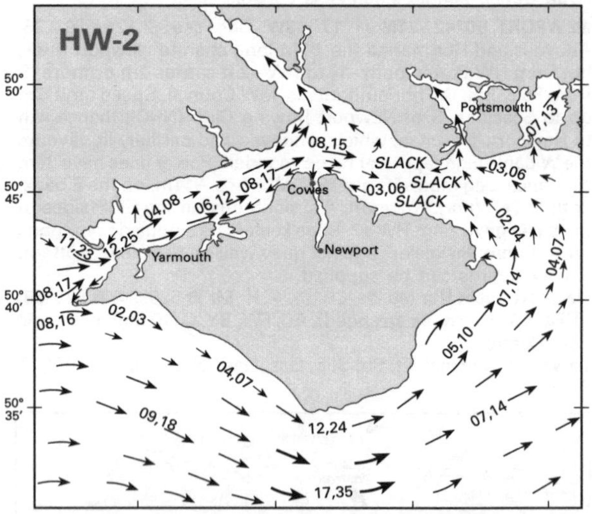

2 Hours before HW Portsmouth (0145 before HW Dover)

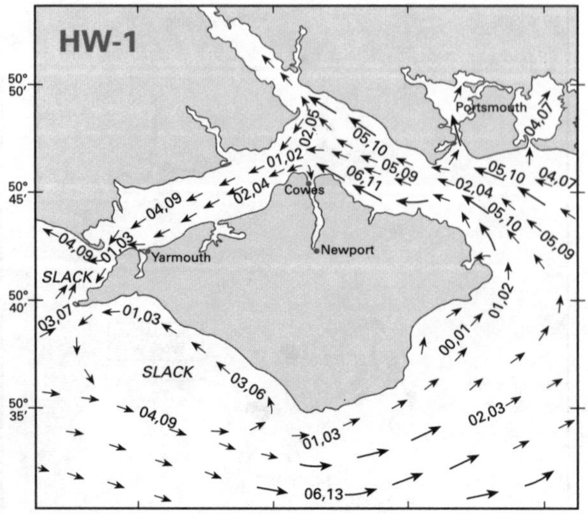

1 Hour before HW Portsmouth (0045 before HW Dover)

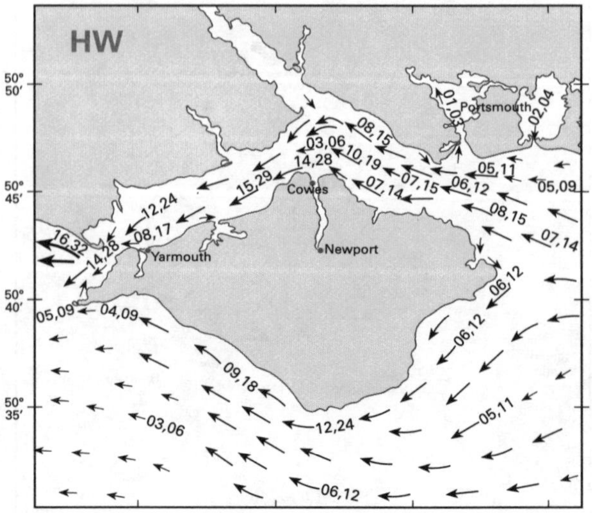

HW Portsmouth (0015 after HW Dover)

General Area 2: 9.2.3

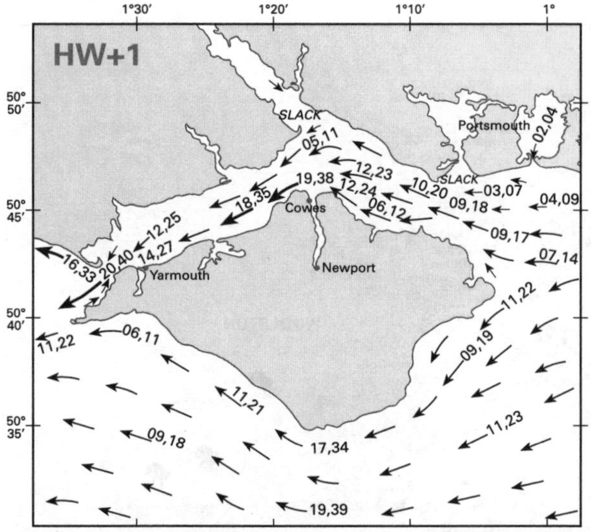

1 Hour after HW Portsmouth (0115 after HW Dover)

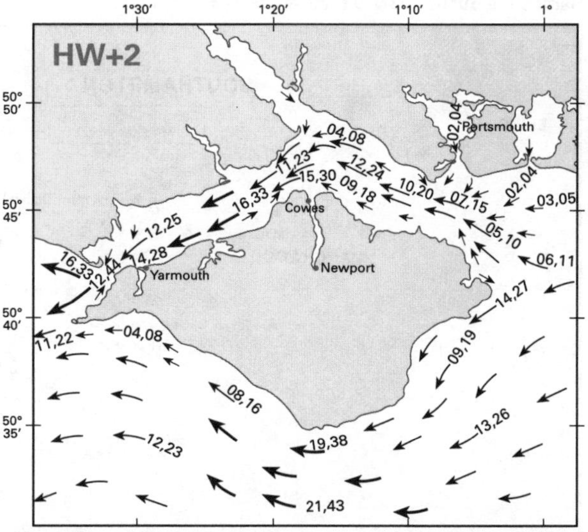

2 Hours after HW Portsmouth (0215 after HW Dover)

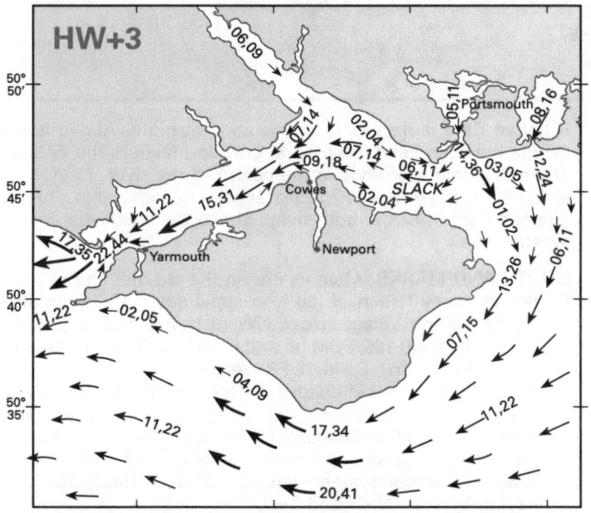

3 Hours after HW Portsmouth (0315 after HW Dover)

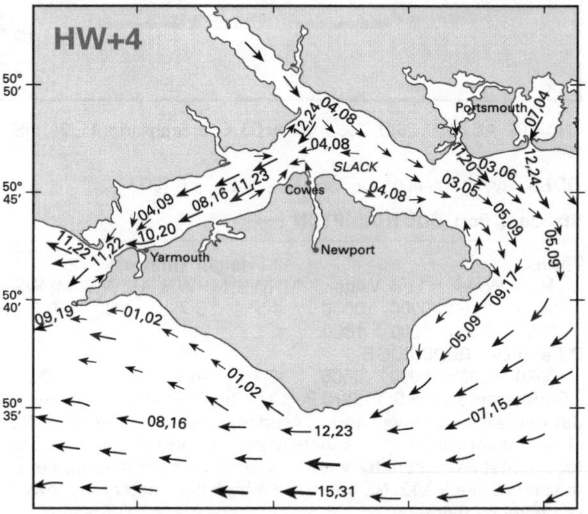

4 Hours after HW Portsmouth (0415 after HW Dover)

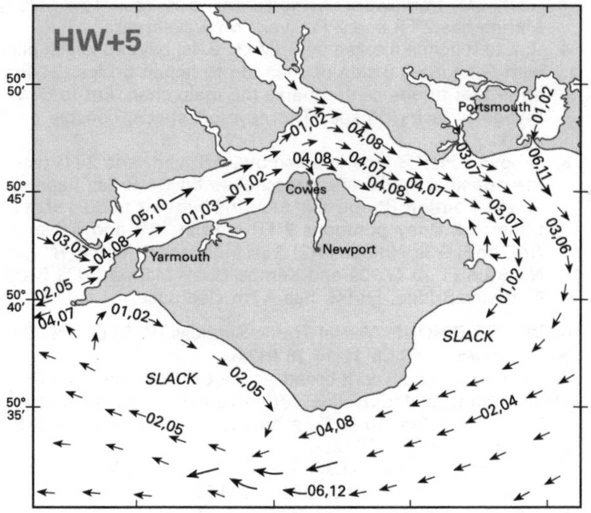

5 Hours after HW Portsmouth (0515 after HW Dover)

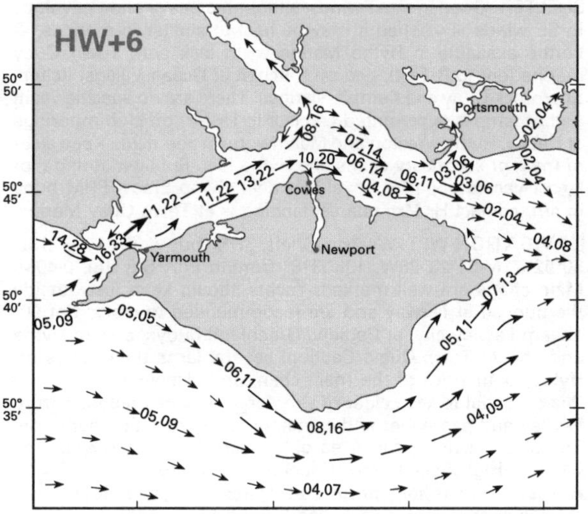

6 Hours after HW Portsmouth (0615 after HW Dover)

SOUTHAMPTON *9.2.25*

Hampshire **50°52′·93N 01°23′·49W**

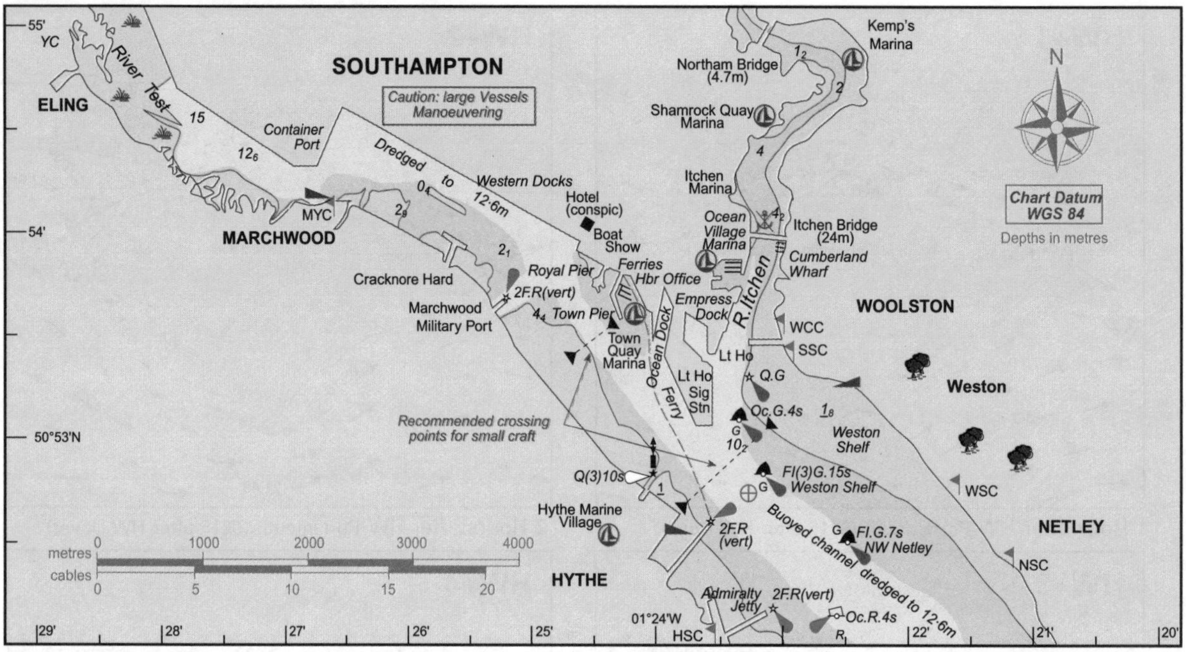

CHARTS AC *5600, 2041, 2036*; Imray C3, C15; Stanfords 11, 24; OS 196

TIDES HW (1st) –0001 Dover; ML 2·9; Zone 0 (UT)

Standard Port SOUTHAMPTON (⟶)

Times				Height (metres)			
High Water		Low Water		MHWS	MHWN	MLWN	MLWS
0400	1100	0000	0600	4·5	3·7	1·8	0·5
1600	2300	1200	1800				
Differences REDBRIDGE							
–0020	+0005	0000	–0005	–0·1	–0·1	–0·1	–0·1

Southampton is a Standard Port and tidal predictions for each day of the year are given above. At sp there are two separate HWs about two hrs apart; at nps there is a long stand. Predictions are for the first HW when there are two, otherwise for the middle of the stand. See 9.2.12. NE gales and a high barometer may lower sea level by 0·6m.

SHELTER Good in most winds, although a heavy chop develops in SE winds >F4, when it may be best to shelter in marinas. ⓥ berths available in Hythe Marina (with lock ent), Town Quay marina (ent to R Test), and on R Itchen at Ocean Village, Itchen, Shamrock Quay and Kemp's Marinas. There are no specific yacht ⚓s but temp ⚓ is permitted (subject to Hr Mr) off club moorings at Netley, Hythe, Weston and Marchwood in about 2m. Keep clear of main or secondary chans and Hythe Pier. Public moorings for larger yachts opposite Royal Pier near Gymp Elbow PHM buoy in 4m (contact Hr Mr); nearest landing is at Town Quay Marina.

NAVIGATION WPT Weston Shelf SHM buoy, Fl (3) G 15s, 50°52′·71N 01°23′·26W, 138°/318° from/to Port Sig Stn, 0·40M. Main chans are well marked. Yachts should keep just outside the buoyed lit fairway and are recommended to cross it at 90° abeam Fawley chy, at Cadland/Greenland buoys, abeam Hythe and abeam Town Quay. Caution: several large unlit buoys off Hythe, both sides of the main chan, and elsewhere.

It is essential to keep clear of very large tankers operating from Fawley and passenger and container ships from Southampton. See also 9.2.18 for the Area of Concern between Cowes and Calshot. High Speed Ferries operate in the area.

R Test There is foul ground at Marchwood and Royal Pier; extensive container port beyond. Eling Chan dries.

R Itchen Care is necessary, particularly at night. Above Itchen Bridge the chan bends sharply to port and favours the W bank. There are unlit moorings in the centre of the river. Navigation above Northam Bridge (4·7m clearance) is not advisable. There is a speed limit of 6kn in both rivers above the line Hythe Pier to Weston Shelf.

LIGHTS AND MARKS Main lts are on the chartlet and in 9.2.4. Fawley chimney (198m, R lts) is conspic day/night. Note also:

1. Hythe Marina Village, close NW of Hythe Pier: appr chan marked by Q (3) 10s, ECM bn and Fl (2) R 5s PHM bn. Lock ent, N side 2 FG (vert); S side 2 FR (vert).
2. Southampton Water divides at Dock Head which is easily identified by conspic silos and a high lattice mast showing traffic sigs which are mandatory for commercial vessels, but may be disregarded by yachts outside the main chans. Beware large ships manoeuvering off Dock Head, and craft leaving Rivers Itchen and Test.
3. Dock Hd, W side (Queen Elizabeth II Terminal, S end) 4 FG (vert) 3M; framework tr; marks ent to R Test. Town Quay Marina has 2 FR and 2 FG (vert) on wavebreaks.
4. Ent to R Itchen marked by SHM Oc G 4s, beyond which piles with G lts mark E side of chan ldg to Itchen bridge (24·4m); a FW lt at bridge centre marks the main chan. Ent to Ocean Village is facing Vosper Thorneycroft sheds, conspic on E bank.
5. Above Itchen Bridge, marked by 2 FR (vert) and 2 FG (vert), the principal marks are: Crosshouse bn Oc R 5s;Chapel bn Fl G 3s. **Caution:** 8 large unlit mooring buoys in middle of river. Shamrock Quay pontoons 2 FR (vert)at SW and NE ends; No 5 bn Fl G 3s; No 7 bn Fl (2) G 5s; Millstone Pt jetty 2 FR (vert); No 9 bn Fl (4) G 10s and Kemps Quay Marina 2 FG (vert). Northam Bridge, FR/FG, has 4·7m clearance.

RADIO TELEPHONE Vessel Traffic Services (VTS) Centre. Call: *Southampton VTS* Ch **12** 14 16 (H24).

Traffic info for small craft broadcast on Ch 12 on the hour 0600-2200 Fri-Sun and Bank Holiday Mons from Easter to last weekend in Oct. From 1 June to 30 Sept broadcasts are every day at the same times (see Fig 18 (28)).

Southampton Hbr Patrol Call: *Southampton Patrol* VHF Ch **12** 16, 01-28, 60-88 (H24). Marinas VHF Ch **80** M.

Fuel barges in R Itchen, call *Mr Diesel* or *Wyefuel* Ch 08.

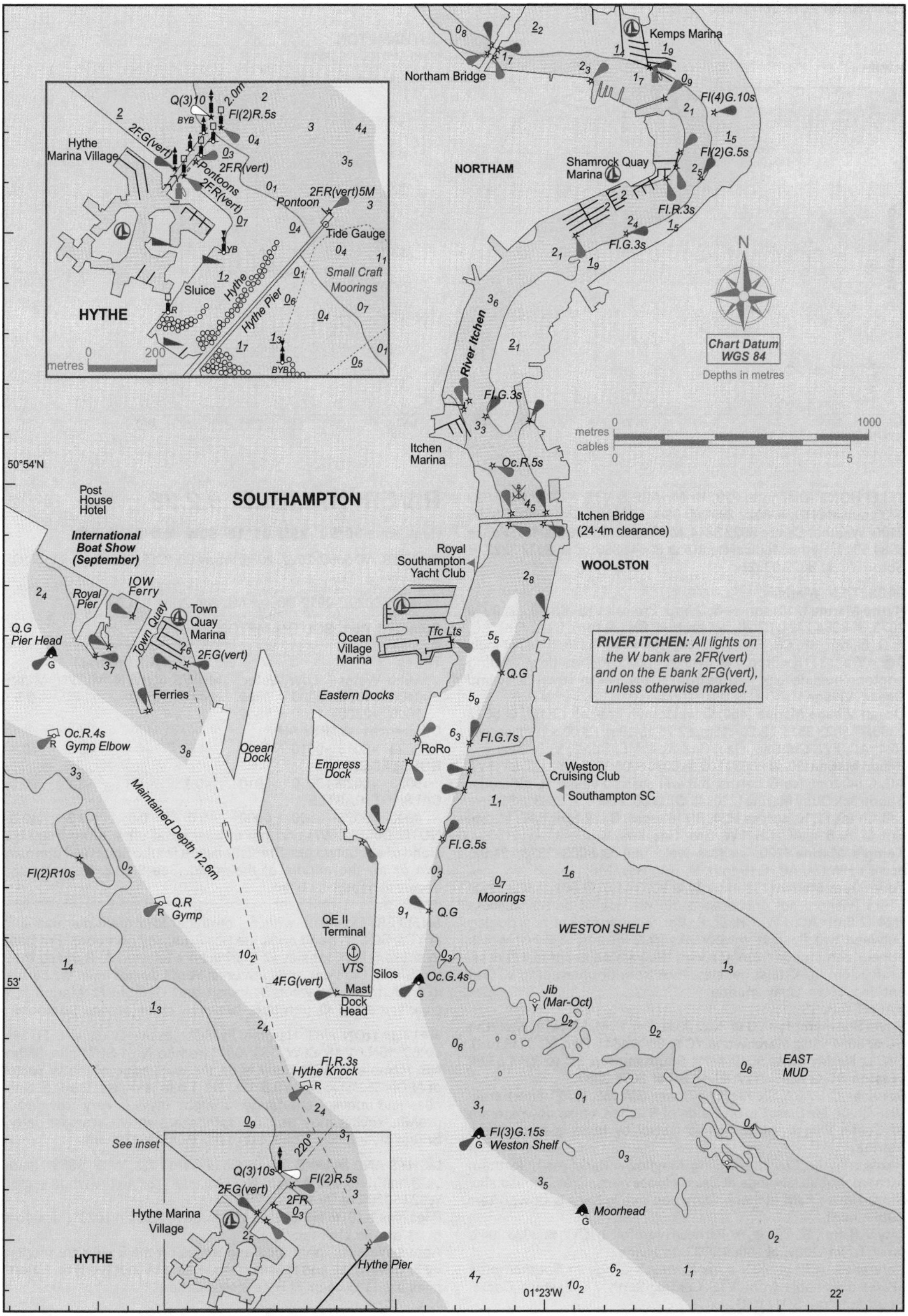
Kemps Marina
Northam Bridge
Fl(4)G.10s
NORTHAM
Fl(2)G.5s
Shamrock Quay Marina
Fl.R.3s
Fl.G.3s
N
Chart Datum WGS 84
Depths in metres
River Itchen
Fl.G.3s
metres
cables
0
1000
5
Itchen Marina
Oc.R.5s
50°54'N
Post House Hotel
SOUTHAMPTON
Itchen Bridge (24·4m clearance)
International Boat Show (September)
Royal Southampton Yacht Club
WOOLSTON
IOW Ferry
Royal Pier
Town Quay
Town Quay Marina
Q.G Pier Head
2F.G(vert)
Tfc Lts
Ocean Village Marina
RIVER ITCHEN: All lights on the W bank are 2FR(vert) and on the E bank 2FG(vert), unless otherwise marked.
Q.G
Ferries
Eastern Docks
Oc.R.4s Gymp Elbow
Ocean Dock
Empress Dock
Fl.G.7s
RoRo
Weston Cruising Club
Southampton SC
Maintained Depth 12.6m
Fl.G.5s
Fl(2)R10s
Moorings
Q.R Gymp
Q.G
QE II Terminal
WESTON SHELF
VTS
Silos
Oc.G.4s
53'
4F.G(vert)
Mast Dock Head
Jib (Mar-Oct)
EAST MUD
Fl.R.3s Hythe Knock
Fl(3)G.15s Weston Shelf
See inset
220°
Q(3)10s
Fl(2)R.5s
2F.G(vert)
2FR
Hythe Marina Village
Moorhead
HYTHE
Hythe Pier
01°23'W
22'
Q(3)10
2.0m
Fl(2)R.5s
BYB
Hythe Marina Village
2F.G(vert)
Pontoons
2F.R(vert)
2F.R(vert)5M
Pontoon
Tide Gauge
YB
Small Craft Moorings
Sluice
Hythe
Hythe Pier
HYTHE
metres
0
200

SOUTHAMPTON *continued*

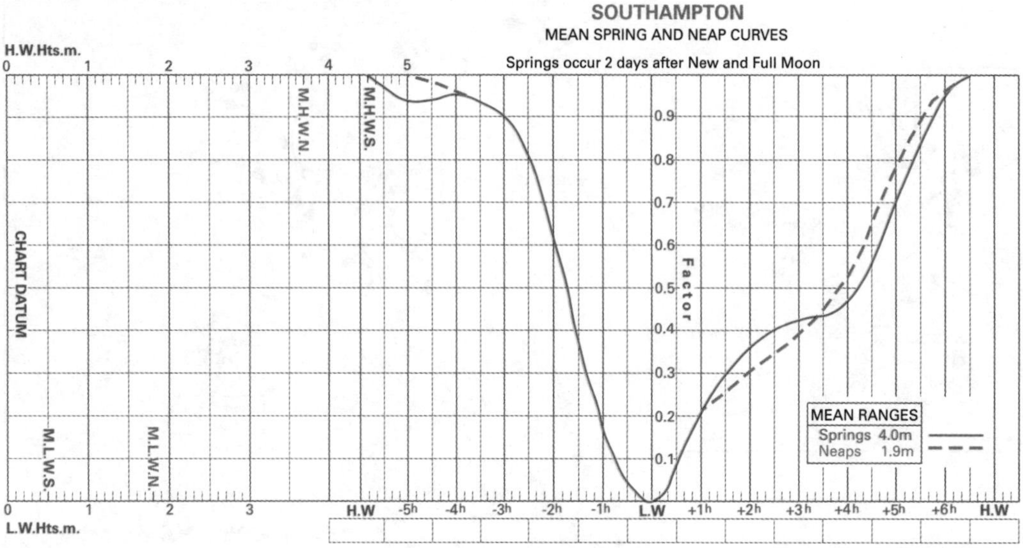
SOUTHAMPTON
MEAN SPRING AND NEAP CURVES
Springs occur 2 days after New and Full Moon
H.W.Hts.m.
L.W.Hts.m.
CHART DATUM
M.H.W.N.
M.H.W.S.
M.L.W.S.
M.L.W.N.
Factor
MEAN RANGES
Springs 4.0m
Neaps 1.9m
H.W -5h -4h -3h -2h -1h L.W +1h +2h +3h +4h +5h +6h H.W

TELEPHONE (Dial code 023) Hr Mr ABP & VTS 8033 0022, 8033 9733 outside HO; 📠 8023 2991; ⊖ 0345 231110 (H24); MRSC 9255 2100; Weather Centre 8022 8844; Marinecall 09068 500457; Police 8084 5511; Hythe Medical Centre ☎ 8084 5955; Ⓗ ☎ 8077 7222, R Soton YC ☎ 8022 3352.

FACILITIES Marinas:
Hythe Marina (210+some Ⓥ; 2·5m). Pre-call VHF Ch 80. ☎ 8020 7073, 📠 8084 2424, £2.20, access H24; BH (30 ton), C (12 ton), AC, P, D, El, ME, Sh, CH, FW, V, R, Bar, SM, ⚓, ♿. Tfc lts (vert) at lock: 3● = Wait; 3 Fl R = Stop; 2● over Ⓦ = proceed, free-flow. Waiting pontoon outside lock. Ferries from Hythe pier to Town Quay and Ocean Village.
Ocean Village Marina (450; Ⓥ welcome). Pre-call Ch 80, ☎ 8022 9385, 📠 8023 3515, £2.20 <15m, £2.75 15-18m, £3.00 > 18m, access H24, AC, FW, CH, Slip, Gas, Gaz, Kos, ME, Sh, ⊡, V, R, Bar, ♿;
Itchen Marina (50) ☎ 8063 1500, 📠 8033 5606; VHF Ch 12. D, BY, FW, AC, C (40 ton); No Ⓥ berths, but will assist a vessel in difficulty.
Shamrock Quay Marina (220+40 Ⓥ). ☎ 8022 9461, 📠 8033 3384. Pre-call Ch 80. £2.10, access H24, BH (63 ton), C (12 ton), ME, El, Sh, SM, ⊡, R, Bar, AC, CH, FW, Gas, Gaz, Kos, V;
Kemp's Marina (220; visitors welcome) ☎ 8063 2323, £1.93, access HW±3½, AC, C (5 ton), D, FW, Gas, ME;
Town Quay Marina (133 + few Ⓥ) ☎ 8023 4397, 📠 8023 5302, £2.35 <15m (visitors not encouraged due to lack of berths), access H24 (2·6m); AC, FW, CH, ⊡, R, Bar, ♿; marina ent is a dogleg between two floating wavebreaks (☆ 2 FR and ☆ 2 FG) which appear continuous from seaward. Beware adjacent fast ferries. Craft >20m LOA must get clearance from Southampton VTS to ent/dep Town Quay marina.
YACHT CLUBS
Royal Southampton YC ☎ 8022 3352, Bar, R, M, FW, L, ⊡, ♿; **Hythe SC** ☎ 8084 6563; **Marchwood YC** ☎ 8086 4641, Bar, M, C (10 ton), FW, L; **Netley SC** ☎ 8045 4272; **Southampton SC** ☎ 8044 6575; **Weston SC** ☎ 8045 2527; **Eling SC** ☎ 8086 3987.
Services CH, ACA, Sh, Rigging, Spars, SM, ME, El, Ⓔ. Fuel barge, VHF Ch 08 *Mr Diesel*, is on E side of R Itchen, close downstream of Ocean Village. Note: nearest petrol by hose is from Hythe marina.
Hards at Hythe, Cracknore, Eling, Mayflower Park (Test), Northam (Itchen). Public landings at Cross House hard, Cross House slip, Block House hard (Itchen), Carnation public hard & Cowporters public hard.
City V, R, Bar, Ⓑ, ✉, ⇌, ✈, Ferries/Hydrofoil to IOW, ☎ 8033 3042; ferry Town Quay, ☎ 8084 0722, to Hythe.
Reference ABP publish a *Yachtsman's Guide to Southampton Water* obtainable from VTS Centre, Berth 37, Eastern Docks, Southampton SO1 1GG.

RIVER HAMBLE *9.2.26*

Hampshire **50°50′·99N 01°18′·50W** ❀❀❀⚓⚓⚓✿✿

CHARTS AC *5600, 2022, 2036*; Imray C3, C15; Stanfords 11, 24; OS 196

TIDES +0020, –0010 Dover; ML 2·9; Zone 0 (UT)

Standard Port SOUTHAMPTON (⟶)

Times				**Height (metres)**			
High Water		Low Water		MHWS	MHWN	MLWN	MLWS
0400	1100	0000	0600	4·5	3·7	1·8	0·5
1600	2300	1200	1800				
Differences WARSASH							
+0020	+0010	+0010	0000	0·0	+0·1	+0·1	+0·3
BURSLEDON							
+0020	+0020	+0010	+0010	+0·1	+0·1	+0·2	+0·2
CALSHOT CASTLE							
0000	+0025	0000	0000	0·0	0·0	+0·2	+0·3

NOTE: Double HWs occur at or near sp; at other times there is a stand of about two hrs. Predictions are for the first HW if there are two or for the middle of the stand. See 9.2.12. NE gales can decrease depths by 0·6m.

SHELTER Excellent, with Ⓥs berths at four main marinas, and at YCs, SCs, BYs and on some Hbr Authority pontoons. Pre-book in season. Pontoons at all marinas are lettered A, B et seq from the S end. Crableck and Universal Yards do not have Ⓥs berths. In mid-stream between Warsash and Hamble Pt Marina is a clearly marked Ⓥ pontoon, between other private pontoons.

NAVIGATION WPT Hamble Pt SCM buoy, Q (6) + L Fl 15s, 50°50′·15N 01°18′·66W, 181°/001° from/to No 1 SHM pile, 350m. NB: Hamble Pt SCM buoy is on the west edge of the W sector of N Dir 352°, Oc (2) WRG 12s; No 1 pile is on the E edge. Unlit piles and buoys are a danger at night. River is very crowded; x prohib. Yachts may not use spinnakers above Warsash jetty. Bridge clearances: Road 4·0m; Rly 6·0m; M27 4·3m.

LIGHTS AND MARKS Dir ☆, Oc (2) WRG 12s, W351°-353°, leads 352° into river ent. Abeam No 7 bn alter 028° in the white sector, W027°-029°, of Dir ☆, Iso WRG 6s.
Piles Nos 1-10 (to either side of the above 352° and 028° tracks) are lit as on the chartlet.
Above Warsash, pontoons and jetties on the E side are marked by 2FG (vert) lts, and those on the W side by 2FR (vert) lts. Lateral piles are Fl G 4s or Fl R 4s (see chartlet).

RIVER HAMBLE *continued*

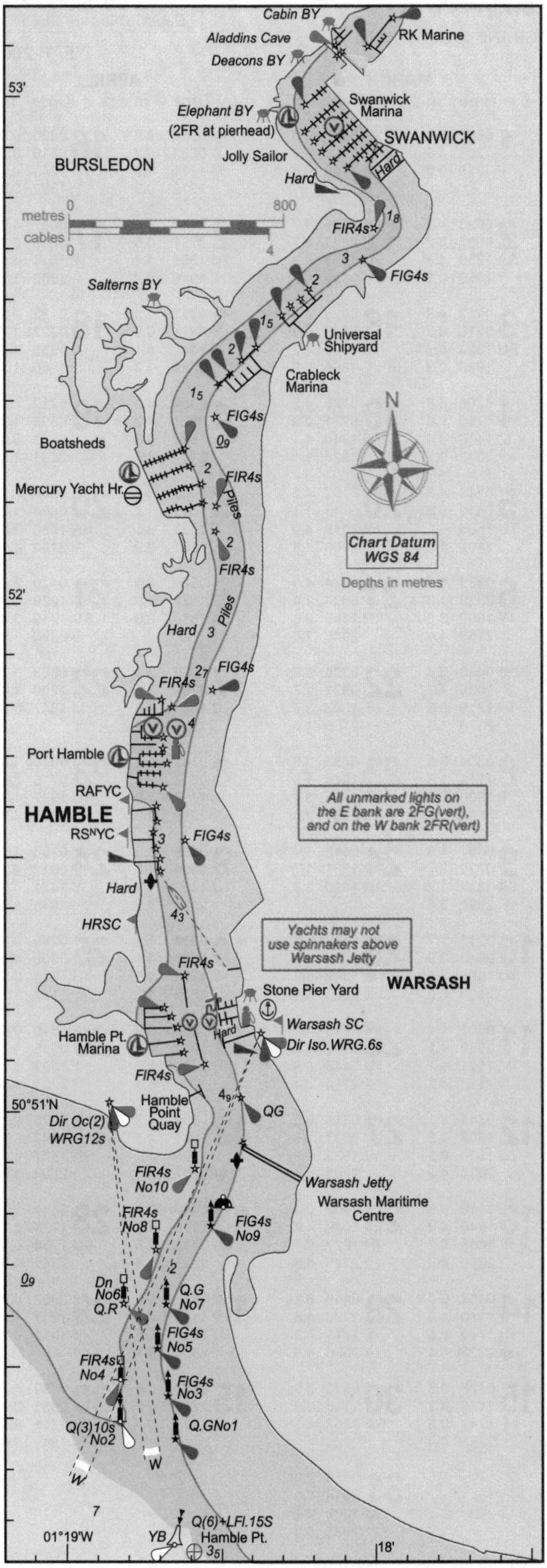

RADIO TELEPHONE Call: *Hamble Radio* Ch **68** (April-Sep: Daily 0600-2200. Oct-Mar: Dailly 0700-1830). Marinas Ch **80** M. Water Taxi Ch 77. See also 8.2.25 for VTS and info broadcasts.

TELEPHONE Dial codes are 023 on the W bank; and 01489 on E bank, where all ☎ numbers begin 57, 58 or 88.Hr Mr ☎/℻ 9255 576387; MRSC (023) 9255 2100; ⊖ 0345 231110 (H24); Marinecall 09068 500457; Police (West Bank) 8033 5444, (East Bank) 023 9283 9333; Dr 57318.

FACILITIES **Marinas** (from seaward):
Hamble Pt Marina (220+10 Ⓥ) ☎ 8045 2464, ℻ 8045 6440; pre-call Ch 80. Access H24; £2.10, AC, CH, D, BH (65 ton), C (7 ton), Ⓔ, El, FW, Gas, Gaz, LPG, ME, Sh, V, YC, Bar;
Port Hamble Marina (310+ Ⓥ) ☎ 8045 2741, ℻ 8045 5206; pre-call Ch 80. Access H24; £2, AC, ⊡, Bar, BH (60 ton), C (7 ton), CH, D, P, Ⓔ, FW, Gas, Gaz, ME, Sh, El, SM, Slip;
Mercury Yacht Hbr (346+ Ⓥ) ☎ 8045 5994, ℻ 8045 7369; pre-call Ch 80. Access H24; £2, AC, Bar, BH (20 ton), El, Slip, CH, D, Ⓔ, FW, Gas, Gaz, ME, P, Sh, SM, V, ⊡;
Universal Marina ☎ 574272, BY 570053; BH (30 ton), CH, ME
Swanwick Marina (380+ Ⓥ) ☎ 8088 5000 (after 1700, 8088 5262), ℻ 8088 5509, £12, AC, BH (60 ton), C (12 ton), CH, D, Ⓔ, FW, Gas, Gaz, ⊖, ⊡, ME, P, ✉, Sh, SM, V, (Access H24).
The Hbr Authority jetty in front of the conspic B/W Hr Mr's Office at Warsash has limited AB (£15 for 24hrs), ⚓, showers and toilets on shore; also Ⓥ pontoons in mid-stream. A public jetty is on the W bank near the Bugle carpark. Ⓥ pile moorings are opposite Port Hamble marina.
YACHT CLUBS
Hamble River SC ☎ 8045 2070; **RAFYC** ☎ 8045 2208, Bar, R, L; **Royal Southern YC** ☎ 8045 3271; **Warsash SC** ☎ 583575.
SERVICES
A very wide range of marine services is available; consult marina/Hr Mr for locations. CH, Ⓔ, BY, AB, C (12 ton), FW, Gas, Gaz, M, ME, R, Sh, Slip, SM; Riggers, BH (25 ton), ACA, Divers.
Piper Marine Services ☎ 8045 4563, (or call *Piper Fuel* Ch M), D, P.
Hards. At Warsash, Hamble and Swanwick.
Slips at Warsash, Hamble, Bursledon & Lower Swanwick.
Scrubbing piles at Warsash by Hr Mr's slipway; on W bank upriver of public jetty near Bugle; between Port Hamble and Mercury marinas; by slip opposite Swanwick marina.
✉ (Hamble, Bursledon, Warsash and Lower Swanwick); (Hamble, Bursledon, Sarisbury Green, Swanwick, Warsash); ≈ (Hamble and Bursledon); ✈ (Southampton).
Hamble River Guide available from Hr Mr.

ADJACENT HARBOURS

ASHLETT CREEK, Hants, **50°50'·01N 01°19'·49W**. AC *5600.8, 2022, 1905*. Tides approx as Calshot Castle (opposite). Small drying (2·1m) inlet across from R Hamble; best for shoal-draft vessels. Appr at HW close to Esso Marine Terminal. Unlit chan, marked by 3 PHM buoys, 1 SHM buoy and 2 PHM bns, has four 90° bends. Ldg bns are hard to find; local knowledge desirable. Berth at drying quay. Facilities: AB, M, FW, Slip, Hard, Pub. **Esso SC.**

HILL HEAD, Hants, **50°49'·08N 01°14'·54W**. AC *5600.8, 2022, 1905*. HW +0030 on Dover; see 9.2.30 LEE-ON-SOLENT diffs. Short term ⚓ for small craft at mouth of R Meon. Bar dries ¼M offshore. Ent dries 1·2m at MLWS. Appr on 030° towards Hill Head SC ho (W, conspic); Small hbr to W inside ent where yachts can lie in soft mud alongside wall. Facilities: **Hill Head SC** ☎ (01329) 664843. **Hill Head village** EC Thurs; ✉, CH, V, P & D (cans).

Note - Double HWs occur at Southampton. The predictions are for the first HW.

TIME ZONE (UTC)
For Summer Time add ONE hour in **non-shaded areas**

ENGLAND – SOUTHAMPTON

LAT 50°54′N LONG 1°24′W

TIMES AND HEIGHTS OF HIGH AND LOW WATERS

SPRING & NEAP TIDES
Dates in red are SPRINGS
Dates in blue are NEAPS

YEAR **2002**

JANUARY

Date	Day	Time	m	Time	m	Time	m	Time	m
1	TU	0528	0.8	1150	4.7	1755	0.6		
2	W	0018	4.6	0613	0.8	1236	4.7	1840	0.6
3	TH	0105	4.6	0700	0.9	1324	4.6	1927	0.7
4	F	0155	4.5	0750	1.0	1415	4.4	2017	0.9
5	SA	0249	4.4	0844	1.2	1510	4.3	2111	1.1
6	SU	0348	4.2	0944	1.4	1612	4.1	2212	1.3
7	M	0453	4.1	1050	1.5	1720	4.0	2320	1.4
8	TU	0602	4.1	1200	1.5	1831	3.9		
9	W	0029	1.5	0709	4.1	1308	1.5	1940	4.0
10	TH	0135	1.4	0810	4.2	1409	1.3	2041	4.1
11	F	0232	1.3	0904	4.3	1503	1.1	2133	4.2
12	SA	0323	1.2	0951	4.3	1550	1.0	2219	4.3
13	SU	0408	1.0	1033	4.4	1634	0.8	● 2259	4.3
14	M	0451	1.0	1112	4.4	1714	0.8	2337	4.4
15	TU	0530	0.9	1148	4.4	1751	0.7		
16	W	0013	4.4	0606	1.0	1224	4.4	1824	0.8
17	TH	0048	4.3	0641	1.0	1259	4.3	1855	0.9
18	F	0123	4.3	0713	1.2	1335	4.2	1925	1.1
19	SA	0159	4.2	0745	1.3	1411	4.1	1957	1.2
20	SU	0237	4.1	0820	1.5	1450	3.9	2034	1.5
21	M	0319	3.9	0903	1.7	1534	3.8	2120	1.7
22	TU	0409	3.8	0958	1.9	1630	3.6	2221	1.8
23	W	0511	3.8	1109	1.9	1740	3.6	2337	1.9
24	TH	0622	3.8	1225	1.8	1858	3.7		
25	F	0052	1.8	0731	3.9	1333	1.6	2006	3.9
26	SA	0157	1.5	0830	4.1	1431	1.3	2102	4.1
27	SU	0253	1.3	0921	4.3	1523	1.0	2151	4.3
28	M	0344	1.0	1008	4.5	1612	0.7	○ 2237	4.5
29	TU	0432	0.7	1054	4.7	1700	0.4	2322	4.7
30	W	0519	0.6	1138	4.8	1746	0.3		
31	TH	0007	4.7	0605	0.5	1224	4.8	1831	0.3

FEBRUARY

Date	Day	Time	m	Time	m	Time	m	Time	m
1	F	0053	4.7	0650	0.5	1310	4.7	1915	0.3
2	SA	0139	4.6	0735	0.6	1356	4.6	1959	0.5
3	SU	0226	4.5	0821	0.8	1445	4.4	2045	0.8
4	M	0317	4.3	0911	1.1	1537	4.1	2136	1.1
5	TU	0413	4.1	1008	1.4	1638	3.9	2237	1.5
6	W	0519	3.9	1119	1.6	1753	3.7	2353	1.7
7	TH	0637	3.8	1239	1.7	1918	3.7		
8	F	0113	1.7	0753	3.9	1352	1.5	2031	3.8
9	SA	0220	1.5	0854	4.0	1451	1.3	2127	4.0
10	SU	0313	1.3	0943	4.2	1538	1.1	2211	4.2
11	M	0357	1.1	1024	4.3	1619	0.9	2249	4.3
12	TU	0437	0.9	1059	4.3	1657	0.7	● 2322	4.3
13	W	0515	0.8	1132	4.4	1733	0.6	2353	4.4
14	TH	0549	0.7	1203	4.3	1805	0.6		
15	F	0024	4.3	0620	0.8	1235	4.3	1833	0.7
16	SA	0055	4.3	0648	0.9	1307	4.2	1859	0.8
17	SU	0127	4.2	0714	1.0	1339	4.1	1925	1.0
18	M	0159	4.1	0742	1.2	1412	4.0	1955	1.2
19	TU	0233	4.0	0816	1.4	1448	3.9	2032	1.4
20	W	0313	3.9	0900	1.6	1534	3.7	2121	1.7
21	TH	0407	3.7	1002	1.8	1640	3.6	2235	1.9
22	F	0522	3.7	1130	1.9	1809	3.6		
23	SA	0011	1.9	0649	3.7	1300	1.7	1935	3.7
24	SU	0133	1.7	0804	4.0	1410	1.3	2042	4.0
25	M	0236	1.3	0903	4.2	1507	0.9	2134	4.3
26	TU	0330	0.9	0952	4.5	1559	0.5	2221	4.6
27	W	0420	0.6	1038	4.7	1646	0.2	○ 2306	4.8
28	TH	0507	0.3	1123	4.8	1732	0.0	2350	4.8

MARCH

Date	Day	Time	m	Time	m	Time	m	Time	m
1	F	0552	0.2	1206	4.9	1815	0.0		
2	SA	0033	4.8	0634	0.2	1250	4.8	1856	0.1
3	SU	0117	4.8	0715	0.3	1334	4.7	1936	0.3
4	M	0200	4.6	0756	0.6	1418	4.4	2017	0.7
5	TU	0245	4.3	0839	0.9	1506	4.1	2101	1.1
6	W	0335	4.0	0929	1.3	1602	3.8	2158	1.6
7	TH	0438	3.7	1038	1.7	1719	3.6	2320	1.9
8	F	0604	3.6	1211	1.8	1900	3.6		
9	SA	0057	1.9	0736	3.7	1337	1.7	2021	3.8
10	SU	0211	1.7	0842	3.9	1436	1.4	2115	4.0
11	M	0301	1.4	0930	4.1	1521	1.1	2156	4.2
12	TU	0341	1.1	1008	4.2	1559	0.9	2230	4.3
13	W	0418	0.9	1040	4.3	1635	0.7	2300	4.3
14	TH	0453	0.7	1110	4.3	1709	0.5	● 2328	4.4
15	F	0525	0.6	1138	4.3	1740	0.5	2356	4.4
16	SA	0555	0.6	1208	4.3	1808	0.6		
17	SU	0025	4.3	0621	0.7	1238	4.3	1832	0.7
18	M	0055	4.3	0645	0.8	1309	4.2	1856	0.9
19	TU	0125	4.2	0711	0.9	1340	4.1	1924	1.1
20	W	0157	4.1	0743	1.1	1415	4.0	1959	1.3
21	TH	0234	4.0	0824	1.4	1458	3.8	2046	1.6
22	F	0324	3.8	0921	1.7	1603	3.7	2156	1.9
23	SA	0439	3.6	1048	1.8	1735	3.6	2341	2.0
24	SU	0615	3.7	1231	1.7	1910	3.8		
25	M	0113	1.7	0739	3.9	1349	1.3	2020	4.1
26	TU	0219	1.3	0842	4.2	1448	0.9	2114	4.4
27	W	0314	0.8	0933	4.5	1539	0.5	2201	4.7
28	TH	0403	0.4	1019	4.7	1627	0.1	○ 2245	4.8
29	F	0449	0.2	1103	4.8	1711	-0.1	2328	4.9
30	SA	0533	0.0	1146	4.9	1754	-0.1		
31	SU	0010	4.9	0614	0.0	1229	4.8	1833	0.0

APRIL

Date	Day	Time	m	Time	m	Time	m	Time	m
1	M	0052	4.8	0653	0.2	1311	4.7	1912	0.3
2	TU	0134	4.6	0731	0.5	1354	4.4	1950	0.7
3	W	0217	4.3	0811	0.9	1440	4.1	2033	1.2
4	TH	0304	4.0	0857	1.3	1536	3.8	2127	1.7
5	F	0403	3.7	1001	1.7	1653	3.6	2251	2.0
6	SA	0529	3.5	1137	1.9	1836	3.6		
7	SU	0035	2.1	0708	3.5	1308	1.8	1956	3.8
8	M	0148	1.8	0817	3.8	1407	1.5	2049	4.0
9	TU	0236	1.5	0904	4.0	1451	1.2	2128	4.2
10	W	0314	1.2	0940	4.1	1528	1.0	2200	4.3
11	TH	0350	0.9	1012	4.2	1604	0.7	2229	4.3
12	F	0424	0.7	1041	4.3	1638	0.6	● 2257	4.4
13	SA	0456	0.6	1109	4.3	1710	0.6	2325	4.4
14	SU	0526	0.6	1139	4.3	1739	0.6	2354	4.4
15	M	0553	0.6	1210	4.3	1805	0.7		
16	TU	0025	4.3	0619	0.7	1243	4.3	1832	0.9
17	W	0057	4.3	0648	0.9	1317	4.2	1902	1.1
18	TH	0132	4.2	0722	1.1	1355	4.1	1940	1.3
19	F	0212	4.0	0805	1.3	1443	3.9	2031	1.6
20	SA	0304	3.9	0904	1.6	1550	3.8	2144	1.9
21	SU	0420	3.7	1029	1.7	1719	3.8	2323	1.9
22	M	0553	3.7	1205	1.6	1847	3.9		
23	TU	0050	1.6	0715	3.9	1322	1.3	1955	4.2
24	W	0156	1.2	0817	4.2	1421	0.9	2049	4.5
25	TH	0250	0.8	0909	4.4	1513	0.5	2137	4.7
26	F	0340	0.5	0956	4.6	1601	0.2	2221	4.8
27	SA	0426	0.2	1041	4.7	1647	0.1	○ 2304	4.9
28	SU	0511	0.1	1124	4.7	1730	0.1	2347	4.8
29	M	0552	0.2	1207	4.7	1811	0.3		
30	TU	0029	4.7	0631	0.3	1251	4.5	1849	0.6

Chart Datum: 2·74 metres below Ordnance Datum (Newlyn)

Note - Double HWs occur at Southampton.
The predictions are for the first HW.

TIME ZONE (UTC)
For Summer Time add ONE hour in **non-shaded areas**

ENGLAND –SOUTHAMPTON

LAT 50°54′N LONG 1°24′W

TIMES AND HEIGHTS OF HIGH AND LOW WATERS

SPRING & NEAP TIDES
Dates in **red** are **SPRINGS**
Dates in **blue** are **NEAPS**

YEAR **2002**

MAY

Date	Day	Time	m	Time	m	Time	m	Time	m
1	W	0111	4.5	0710	0.6	1335	4.3	1928	1.0
2	TH	0153	4.3	0749	1.0	1422	4.1	2011	1.4
3	F	0240	4.0	0833	1.4	1516	3.9	2103	1.8
4	SA	0335	3.7	0930	1.7	1626	3.7	2219	2.1
5	SU	0449	3.5	1051	1.9	1753	3.6	2351	2.1
6	M	0618	3.5	1216	1.9	1911	3.8		
7	TU	0103	1.9	0730	3.7	1319	1.7	2005	4.0
8	W	0154	1.6	0822	3.8	1407	1.4	2047	4.1
9	TH	0235	1.4	0902	4.0	1448	1.2	2121	4.2
10	F	0313	1.1	0936	4.1	1526	1.0	2153	4.3
11	SA	0348	0.9	1008	4.2	1602	0.8	2223	4.3
12	SU	0423	0.7	1040	4.2	1637	0.8	● 2254	4.4
13	M	0456	0.7	1112	4.3	1710	0.8	2327	4.4
14	TU	0528	0.7	1147	4.3	1742	0.9		
15	W	0001	4.4	0559	0.7	1224	4.3	1814	1.0
16	TH	0038	4.3	0633	0.9	1303	4.3	1851	1.1
17	F	0118	4.2	0713	1.0	1347	4.2	1935	1.3
18	SA	0203	4.1	0800	1.2	1440	4.1	2030	1.6
19	SU	0300	4.0	0900	1.4	1547	4.0	2142	1.7
20	M	0412	3.8	1017	1.5	1705	4.0	2305	1.7
21	TU	0533	3.9	1138	1.4	1822	4.1		
22	W	0022	1.5	0648	4.0	1250	1.2	1927	4.3
23	TH	0127	1.2	0750	4.2	1351	1.0	2022	4.5
24	F	0223	0.9	0844	4.4	1445	0.7	2111	4.6
25	SA	0314	0.6	0934	4.5	1535	0.5	2158	4.7
26	SU	0403	0.5	1020	4.5	1622	0.5	○ 2242	4.7
27	M	0448	0.4	1106	4.5	1707	0.5	2326	4.6
28	TU	0532	0.4	1150	4.5	1750	0.6		
29	W	0009	4.5	0612	0.5	1235	4.4	1831	0.9
30	TH	0051	4.4	0651	0.8	1319	4.3	1911	1.1
31	F	0134	4.2	0730	1.0	1405	4.1	1953	1.4

JUNE

Date	Day	Time	m	Time	m	Time	m	Time	m
1	SA	0219	4.0	0812	1.3	1455	4.0	2041	1.7
2	SU	0308	3.8	0900	1.6	1551	3.8	2141	1.9
3	M	0406	3.7	1000	1.8	1657	3.8	2252	2.0
4	TU	0514	3.6	1110	1.8	1805	3.8		
5	W	0001	2.0	0624	3.6	1217	1.8	1905	3.9
6	TH	0059	1.8	0725	3.7	1312	1.6	1955	4.0
7	F	0147	1.6	0815	3.8	1400	1.4	2037	4.1
8	SA	0230	1.3	0857	4.0	1444	1.3	2115	4.2
9	SU	0311	1.1	0936	4.1	1526	1.1	2151	4.3
10	M	0350	0.9	1013	4.2	1606	1.0	● 2228	4.4
11	TU	0429	0.8	1051	4.3	1645	0.9	2305	4.4
12	W	0507	0.8	1130	4.3	1724	0.9	2345	4.4
13	TH	0546	0.8	1211	4.4	1804	1.0		
14	F	0026	4.4	0626	0.8	1255	4.3	1847	1.1
15	SA	0111	4.3	0710	0.9	1342	4.3	1935	1.2
16	SU	0200	4.2	0800	1.1	1436	4.2	2029	1.4
17	M	0256	4.1	0856	1.2	1537	4.1	2132	1.5
18	TU	0359	4.0	1000	1.3	1644	4.1	2241	1.5
19	W	0509	4.0	1109	1.3	1753	4.2	2350	1.4
20	TH	0618	4.0	1217	1.3	1857	4.2		
21	F	0055	1.3	0723	4.1	1320	1.2	1956	4.3
22	SA	0156	1.1	0822	4.2	1418	1.0	2049	4.4
23	SU	0251	0.9	0916	4.3	1512	0.9	2139	4.5
24	M	0342	0.8	1006	4.3	1603	0.9	○ 2226	4.5
25	TU	0431	0.7	1053	4.4	1650	0.8	2311	4.5
26	W	0515	0.7	1138	4.4	1735	0.9	2353	4.4
27	TH	0557	0.7	1221	4.3	1817	1.0		
28	F	0034	4.3	0636	0.8	1303	4.3	1856	1.1
29	SA	0115	4.2	0713	1.0	1345	4.2	1935	1.3
30	SU	0156	4.1	0749	1.2	1427	4.1	2014	1.5

JULY

Date	Day	Time	m	Time	m	Time	m	Time	m
1	M	0237	3.9	0827	1.4	1511	4.0	2058	1.7
2	TU	0322	3.8	0911	1.6	1600	3.9	2149	1.9
3	W	0414	3.7	1003	1.7	1655	3.8	2249	1.9
4	TH	0513	3.6	1105	1.8	1756	3.8	2353	1.9
5	F	0619	3.6	1211	1.8	1857	3.9		
6	SA	0053	1.8	0723	3.7	1312	1.7	1952	4.0
7	SU	0148	1.6	0819	3.8	1406	1.5	2041	4.1
8	M	0237	1.3	0907	4.0	1455	1.4	2125	4.2
9	TU	0323	1.1	0951	4.2	1542	1.2	2208	4.4
10	W	0408	0.9	1034	4.3	1627	1.0	● 2250	4.5
11	TH	0453	0.8	1117	4.4	1712	0.9	2332	4.5
12	F	0537	0.7	1200	4.5	1757	0.9		
13	SA	0016	4.5	0621	0.6	1246	4.5	1842	0.9
14	SU	0102	4.5	0706	0.7	1333	4.5	1929	0.9
15	M	0150	4.4	0753	0.8	1423	4.4	2018	1.0
16	TU	0241	4.3	0842	0.9	1517	4.3	2111	1.2
17	W	0337	4.2	0936	1.1	1616	4.2	2210	1.3
18	TH	0439	4.0	1037	1.3	1719	4.1	2316	1.5
19	F	0547	3.9	1144	1.4	1827	4.1		
20	SA	0026	1.5	0658	3.9	1255	1.5	1934	4.1
21	SU	0135	1.4	0807	4.0	1401	1.4	2036	4.2
22	M	0236	1.2	0907	4.1	1500	1.3	2130	4.3
23	TU	0330	1.1	1000	4.2	1552	1.1	2218	4.3
24	W	0419	0.9	1046	4.3	1639	1.0	○ 2301	4.3
25	TH	0502	0.8	1128	4.3	1722	1.0	2340	4.3
26	F	0543	0.7	1206	4.3	1802	1.0		
27	SA	0017	4.3	0619	0.8	1243	4.3	1838	1.0
28	SU	0053	4.2	0652	0.9	1318	4.3	1911	1.1
29	M	0128	4.2	0723	1.0	1353	4.2	1943	1.3
30	TU	0203	4.1	0753	1.2	1429	4.1	2015	1.5
31	W	0240	3.9	0825	1.4	1508	4.0	2052	1.6

AUGUST

Date	Day	Time	m	Time	m	Time	m	Time	m
1	TH	0321	3.8	0904	1.6	1552	3.9	2139	1.8
2	F	0410	3.7	0956	1.8	1646	3.8	2241	2.0
3	SA	0514	3.6	1105	2.0	1754	3.7	2357	2.0
4	SU	0631	3.6	1225	2.0	1907	3.8		
5	M	0110	1.8	0744	3.7	1335	1.8	2011	4.0
6	TU	0211	1.5	0844	4.0	1434	1.5	2104	4.2
7	W	0304	1.2	0933	4.2	1525	1.2	2150	4.4
8	TH	0353	0.9	1019	4.4	1614	1.0	● 2234	4.5
9	F	0440	0.6	1102	4.5	1701	0.8	2318	4.6
10	SA	0526	0.5	1146	4.6	1746	0.6		
11	SU	0002	4.7	0610	0.4	1231	4.7	1830	0.6
12	M	0047	4.7	0654	0.4	1316	4.7	1914	0.6
13	TU	0132	4.6	0737	0.5	1402	4.6	1959	0.8
14	W	0219	4.5	0821	0.7	1450	4.4	2045	1.0
15	TH	0309	4.3	0908	1.1	1543	4.2	2138	1.3
16	F	0407	4.0	1005	1.4	1645	4.0	2243	1.6
17	SA	0517	3.8	1116	1.7	1800	3.9		
18	SU	0002	1.7	0641	3.8	1240	1.8	1921	3.9
19	M	0124	1.7	0802	3.9	1356	1.7	2031	4.0
20	TU	0231	1.5	0906	4.0	1457	1.5	2126	4.2
21	W	0323	1.2	0956	4.2	1545	1.3	2210	4.3
22	TH	0407	1.0	1037	4.3	1627	1.1	○ 2248	4.4
23	F	0446	0.8	1112	4.4	1706	0.9	2322	4.4
24	SA	0523	0.7	1145	4.4	1742	0.8	2354	4.3
25	SU	0557	0.7	1215	4.4	1814	0.8		
26	M	0025	4.3	0627	0.7	1246	4.3	1843	0.9
27	TU	0056	4.2	0653	0.9	1316	4.3	1909	1.1
28	W	0128	4.2	0718	1.1	1348	4.2	1935	1.3
29	TH	0200	4.0	0744	1.3	1421	4.1	2004	1.5
30	F	0235	3.9	0816	1.6	1458	3.9	2043	1.7
31	SA	0317	3.8	0900	1.8	1546	3.8	2138	2.0

Chart Datum: 2·74 metres below Ordnance Datum (Newlyn)

Note - Double HWs occur at Southampton. The predictions are for the first HW.

TIME ZONE (UTC)
For Summer Time add ONE hour in **non-shaded areas**

ENGLAND –SOUTHAMPTON

LAT 50°54′N LONG 1°24′W

TIMES AND HEIGHTS OF HIGH AND LOW WATERS

SPRING & NEAP TIDES
Dates in red are SPRINGS
Dates in blue are NEAPS

YEAR **2002**

SEPTEMBER

Day	Time	m	Day	Time	m
1 SU	0417	3.6	16 M	0632	3.7
	1005	2.1		1232	2.0
	1655	3.7		1912	3.8
	2301	2.1			
2 M	0543	3.6	17 TU	0117	1.9
	1142	2.2		0758	3.9
	1824	3.7		1354	1.9
				2024	4.0
3 TU	0037	2.0	18 W	0222	1.6
	0714	3.7		0857	4.1
	1312	2.0		1448	1.6
	1943	3.9		2114	4.2
4 W	0150	1.6	19 TH	0308	1.3
	0822	4.0		0941	4.3
	1416	1.6		1529	1.3
	2042	4.2		2154	4.3
5 TH	0247	1.2	20 F	0346	1.0
	0914	4.3		1017	4.4
	1510	1.2		1606	1.1
	2131	4.4		2228	4.4
6 F	0337	0.8	21 SA	0422	0.8
	1000	4.5		1048	4.4
	1559	0.9		1641	0.9
	2216	4.6		○ 2257	4.4
7 SA	0424	0.5	22 SU	0456	0.7
	1043	4.7		1116	4.4
	1645	0.6		1714	0.8
	● 2259	4.8		2326	4.4
8 SU	0509	0.3	23 M	0528	0.7
	1126	4.8		1143	4.4
	1730	0.4		1745	0.8
	2342	4.9		2354	4.4
9 M	0552	0.1	24 TU	0557	0.7
	1209	4.9		1211	4.4
	1813	0.3		1812	0.8
10 TU	0025	4.9	25 W	0023	4.3
	0634	0.2		0621	0.9
	1253	4.8		1241	4.3
	1854	0.4		1836	1.0
11 W	0109	4.8	26 TH	0054	4.3
	0715	0.4		0644	1.1
	1336	4.7		1311	4.3
	1935	0.6		1900	1.2
12 TH	0154	4.6	27 F	0125	4.2
	0756	0.7		0710	1.3
	1422	4.5		1342	4.2
	2018	1.0		1928	1.4
13 F	0242	4.3	28 SA	0159	4.0
	0840	1.1		0741	1.6
	1512	4.2		1417	4.0
	2108	1.4		2005	1.6
14 SA	0338	4.0	29 SU	0240	3.9
	0934	1.6		0823	1.8
	1614	3.9		1503	3.9
	2212	1.7		2056	1.9
15 SU	0453	3.8	30 M	0339	3.7
	1052	1.9		0927	2.1
	1737	3.7		1613	3.7
	2344	1.9		2219	2.1

OCTOBER

Day	Time	m	Day	Time	m
1 TU	0510	3.7	16 W	0053	2.0
	1111	2.2		0737	3.9
	1749	3.7		1332	2.0
				1959	3.9
2 W	0007	2.0	17 TH	0155	1.7
	0646	3.8		0832	4.1
	1249	2.0		1422	1.7
	1915	3.9		2048	4.1
3 TH	0126	1.6	18 F	0238	1.4
	0757	4.1		0912	4.3
	1356	1.6		1501	1.4
	2018	4.2		2126	4.3
4 F	0224	1.2	19 SA	0314	1.1
	0850	4.4		0946	4.4
	1449	1.2		1535	1.1
	2108	4.5		2158	4.4
5 SA	0314	0.8	20 SU	0349	0.9
	0936	4.7		1016	4.5
	1538	0.8		1609	0.9
	2153	4.7		2227	4.4
6 SU	0401	0.4	21 M	0423	0.8
	1019	4.9		1043	4.5
	1624	0.5		1642	0.8
	● 2236	4.9		○ 2255	4.4
7 M	0446	0.2	22 TU	0455	0.8
	1102	5.0		1110	4.5
	1708	0.3		1713	0.8
	2319	5.0		2324	4.4
8 TU	0529	0.1	23 W	0525	0.8
	1145	5.0		1139	4.4
	1751	0.3		1741	0.9
				2354	4.4
9 W	0002	4.9	24 TH	0552	0.9
	0610	0.2		1209	4.4
	1228	4.9		1807	1.0
	1831	0.4			
10 TH	0046	4.8	25 F	0026	4.3
	0650	0.5		0617	1.1
	1311	4.7		1242	4.3
	1912	0.6		1833	1.1
11 F	0131	4.6	26 SA	0059	4.3
	0731	0.8		0645	1.3
	1356	4.5		1315	4.2
	1954	1.0		1904	1.3
12 SA	0219	4.3	27 SU	0136	4.2
	0815	1.3		0720	1.6
	1445	4.2		1353	4.1
	2041	1.4		1944	1.6
13 SU	0316	4.0	28 M	0221	4.0
	0909	1.8		0805	1.8
	1547	3.9		1441	4.0
	2145	1.8		2037	1.8
14 M	0434	3.7	29 TU	0323	3.9
	1031	2.1		0912	2.1
	1712	3.7		1551	3.8
	2320	2.0		2157	2.0
15 TU	0615	3.7	30 W	0449	3.8
	1215	2.2		1049	2.1
	1850	3.7		1722	3.8
				2336	1.9
			31 TH	0618	4.0
				1220	1.9
				1846	4.0

NOVEMBER

Day	Time	m	Day	Time	m
1 F	0054	1.6	16 SA	0154	1.6
	0727	4.2		0832	4.2
	1327	1.5		1420	1.5
	1950	4.3		2048	4.1
2 SA	0154	1.2	17 SU	0234	1.3
	0822	4.5		0908	4.3
	1422	1.1		1458	1.3
	2042	4.5		2123	4.2
3 SU	0246	0.8	18 M	0311	1.1
	0909	4.8		0939	4.4
	1512	0.8		1533	1.1
	2129	4.7		2155	4.3
4 M	0334	0.5	19 TU	0347	1.0
	0954	4.9		1010	4.5
	1559	0.5		1608	0.9
	● 2214	4.8		2226	4.4
5 TU	0419	0.3	20 W	0422	0.9
	1038	5.0		1040	4.5
	1644	0.4		1641	0.9
	2258	4.9		○ 2258	4.4
6 W	0504	0.3	21 TH	0455	0.9
	1121	5.0		1112	4.5
	1728	0.4		1713	0.9
	2342	4.8		2331	4.4
7 TH	0546	0.4	22 F	0526	1.0
	1205	4.9		1146	4.5
	1810	0.5		1744	1.0
8 F	0026	4.7	23 SA	0006	4.4
	0627	0.7		0557	1.1
	1249	4.7		1221	4.4
	1851	0.7		1816	1.1
9 SA	0112	4.5	24 SU	0044	4.3
	0709	1.0		0631	1.3
	1334	4.5		1259	4.3
	1933	1.1		1852	1.2
10 SU	0201	4.3	25 M	0125	4.3
	0754	1.4		0711	1.5
	1423	4.2		1341	4.2
	2019	1.4		1935	1.4
11 M	0257	4.0	26 TU	0213	4.1
	0848	1.8		0800	1.7
	1521	3.9		1432	4.1
	2118	1.8		2030	1.6
12 TU	0408	3.8	27 W	0313	4.0
	1001	2.1		0905	1.8
	1635	3.7		1537	3.9
	2237	2.0		2140	1.7
13 W	0534	3.8	28 TH	0427	4.0
	1132	2.2		1025	1.9
	1800	3.7		1655	3.9
				2301	1.7
14 TH	0002	2.0	29 F	0545	4.1
	0651	3.9		1145	1.7
	1246	2.0		1812	4.0
	1913	3.8			
15 F	0106	1.8	30 SA	0016	1.5
	0748	4.1		0653	4.3
	1339	1.8		1253	1.5
	2006	4.0		1918	4.2

DECEMBER

Day	Time	m	Day	Time	m
1 SU	0120	1.2	16 M	0148	1.6
	0751	4.5		0824	4.1
	1351	1.2		1417	1.5
	2014	4.4		2046	4.0
2 M	0215	0.9	17 TU	0232	1.4
	0843	4.7		0904	4.3
	1444	0.9		1458	1.3
	2105	4.6		2126	4.2
3 TU	0306	0.7	18 W	0313	1.2
	0931	4.8		0941	4.4
	1535	0.7		1538	1.1
	2154	4.7		2203	4.3
4 W	0355	0.6	19 TH	0353	1.1
	1017	4.8		1016	4.4
	1623	0.6		1616	1.0
	● 2241	4.7		○ 2239	4.3
5 TH	0442	0.6	20 F	0431	1.0
	1102	4.8		1052	4.5
	1708	0.5		1653	0.9
	2327	4.7		2315	4.4
6 F	0527	0.7	21 SA	0508	1.0
	1147	4.7		1129	4.5
	1752	0.6		1730	0.9
				2353	4.4
7 SA	0012	4.6	22 SU	0546	1.0
	0610	0.8		1208	4.5
	1231	4.6		1808	0.9
	1834	0.8			
8 SU	0059	4.5	23 M	0033	4.4
	0653	1.1		0624	1.1
	1316	4.4		1249	4.4
	1916	1.0		1847	1.0
9 M	0145	4.3	24 TU	0117	4.4
	0737	1.4		0707	1.2
	1402	4.2		1333	4.3
	1958	1.3		1931	1.1
10 TU	0235	4.1	25 W	0204	4.3
	0824	1.7		0755	1.3
	1451	4.0		1422	4.2
	2046	1.6		2021	1.2
11 W	0330	4.0	26 TH	0258	4.2
	0921	1.9		0851	1.5
	1547	3.8		1518	4.1
	2143	1.8		2119	1.4
12 TH	0433	3.9	27 F	0400	4.1
	1028	2.0		0955	1.6
	1652	3.7		1623	4.0
	2250	1.9		2225	1.4
13 F	0541	3.8	28 SA	0507	4.1
	1139	2.0		1105	1.6
	1802	3.7		1733	4.0
	2358	1.9		2336	1.4
14 SA	0646	3.9	29 SU	0616	4.2
	1240	1.9		1215	1.5
	1908	3.8		1844	4.0
15 SU	0057	1.8	30 M	0044	1.3
	0739	4.0		0720	4.3
	1332	1.7		1321	1.3
	2001	3.9		1949	4.2
			31 TU	0147	1.2
				0819	4.4
				1421	1.1
				2048	4.3

Chart Datum: 2·74 metres below Ordnance Datum (Newlyn)

WOOTTON CREEK *9.2.27*

Isle of Wight **50°44'·09N 01°12'·77W** ❁❁❁◊◊✿✿✿

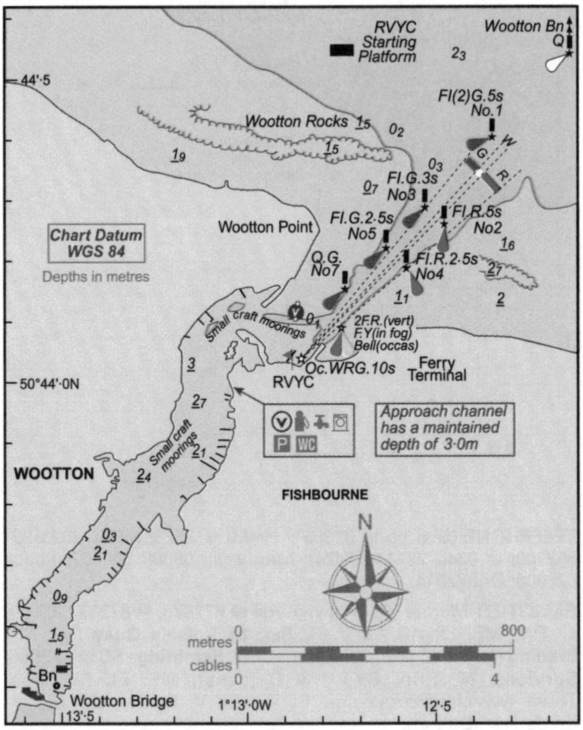

CHARTS AC *5600, 2022, 394*; Imray C3, C15; Stanfords 11, 24, 25; OS 196

TIDES +0023 Dover; ML 2·8; Zone 0 (UT). Use RYDE differences 9.2.28; see also 9.2.12.

SHELTER Good except in stormy N or E winds. Above the ferry, the creek dries. Moor to RVYC pontoons (dry); No ⚓ in the fairway. Speed limit 5kn.

NAVIGATION WPT Wootton NCM Bn, Q, 50°44'·53N 01°12'·13W, 044°/224° from/to ferry slip, 0·64M. Beware large ferries, leaving astern and turning at Wootton Bn. It is difficult to beat in on the ebb.

LIGHTS AND MARKS Ent to creek due S of SE Ryde Middle SCM and 1·75M W of Ryde Pier. Visitors from/to the W should round the starting platform and No 1 bn. The chan is marked by four SHM bns and two PHMs, all lit. Keep in W sector of Dir lt, Oc WRG 10s, G221°-224°, W224°-225½°, R225½°-230½°. By ferry terminal, turn onto ldg marks on W shore △ ▽, which form a ◊ when in transit 270°.

RADIO TELEPHONE None.

TELEPHONE (Dial code 01983) Royal Victoria YC 882325; MRSC (023 92) 552100; Fairway Association 883097; ⊖ 08457 231110 (H24); Marinecall 09068 500457; Police 528000; Dr 562955.

FACILITIES **Royal Victoria YC** ☎ 882325, Slip, AB £1.00/m (min £5.00), FW, R, Ⓛ, Bar; **Village** EC = Thurs, Wootton Bridge = Wed; ✉ (Wootton Bridge, Ryde), Ⓑ (Ryde), ⇌ (ferry to Portsmouth), ✈ (Southampton).

RYDE *9.2.28*

Isle of Wight **50°43'·98N 01°09'·31W** ❁❁◊◊✿✿

CHARTS AC *5600*,2037, *2045*; Imray C3, C15; Stanfords 11, 24; OS 196

TIDES +0022 Dover; ML 2·8m; Zone 0 (UT). See 9.2.12

Standard Port PORTSMOUTH (⟶)

Times				Height (metres)			
High Water		Low Water		MHWS	MHWN	MLWN	MLWS
0000	0600	0500	1100	4·7	3·8	1·9	0·8
1200	1800	1700	2300				
Differences RYDE							
–0010	+0010	–0005	–0010	–0·2	–0·1	0·0	+0·1

SHELTER Small hbr 300m E of Ryde Pier; dries approx 2·3m. Access for shoal draft approx HW–2½ to +2. Berth on E'ly of three pontoons; long and fin keel yachts should dry out against the bkwtr.

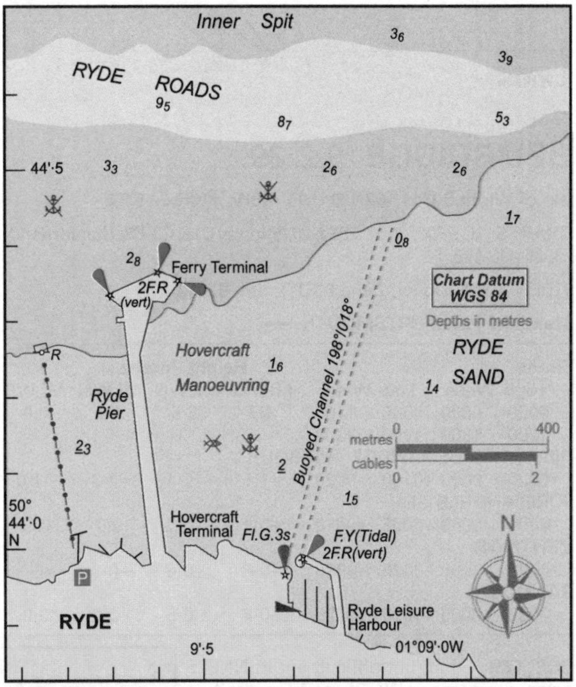

NAVIGATION WPT 50°44'·35N 01°09'·24W, No 1 SHM buoy, 018°/198° from/to hbr ent, 6ca. From the E, best to stay North of No Man's Land Fort and SW Mining Ground Y buoy to clear Ryde Sands. Drying channel 197° across Ryde Sands (1·5m - 1·7m) is marked by 3 SHM and 3 PHM unlit buoys. Beware hovercraft manoeuvering between Ryde pier and marina; and High Speed Ferries from/to pierhead.

LIGHTS AND MARKS Ryde Ch spire (Holy Trinity) brg 200° gives initial appr. Hbr ent lts are 2 FR and Fl G 3s 7m 1M. Ryde pier is lit by 3 sets of 2FR (vert) and a FY fog lt.

RADIO TELEPHONE *Ryde Harbour* VHF Ch 80.

TELEPHONE (Dial code 01983) Hr Mr 613879; MRSC (023 92) 552100; ⊖ 08457 231110 (H24); Marinecall 09068 500457; Police 0845 0454545; Ⓗ 524081.

FACILITIES **Marina** (100+70 Ⓥ) ☎/📠 613879, rydeharbour@amserve.net, £1.10, FW, Slip, Ⓞ, Ⓛ. **Services:** P & D (cans) from garage, Gas, V, R, Bar, contact Hr Mr before arrival. **Town** all domestic facilities nearby. Hovercraft from slip next to hbr to Southsea. Fast cat (passenger) from Ryde Pier to Portsmouth for mainland ⇌; ✈ Southampton.

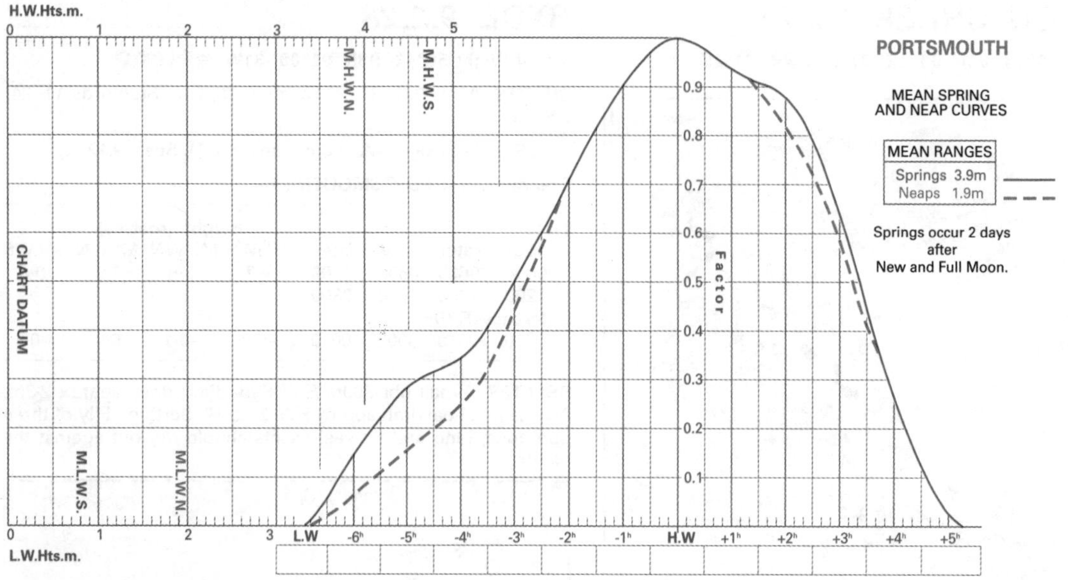

BEMBRIDGE *9.2.29*

Isle of Wight **50°41′·62N 01°06′·40W** ❁❁⛵⛵⛵✿✿

CHARTS AC *5600, 2022, 2037, 2045*; Imray C15, C3, C9; Stanfords 10, 24, 25; OS 196

TIDES +0020 Dover; Zone 0 (UT). See 9.2.12

Standard Port PORTSMOUTH (⟶)

Times				Height (metres)			
High Water		Low Water		MHWS	MHWN	MLWN	MLWS
0000	0600	0500	1100	4·7	3·8	1·9	0·8
1200	1800	1700	2300				
Differences BEMBRIDGE HARBOUR							
+0020	0000	+0100	+0020	−1·5	−1·4	−1·3	−1·0
FORELAND (LB Slip)							
−0005	0000	+0005	+0010	−0·1	−0·1	0·0	+0·1
VENTNOR							
−0025	−0030	−0025	−0030	−0·8	−0·6	−0·2	+0·2
SANDOWN							
0000	+0005	+0010	+0025	−0·6	−0·5	−0·2	0·0

SHELTER Good, but difficult ent in NNE gales. No access LW ±2½ for 1·5m draft; carefully check tide gauge which indicates depth over the bar. Speed limit 6kn. Visitors' berths at marina, Fisherman's Wharf and afloat on pontoon between Nos 15 & 17 SHM buoys. No ⚓ in chan and hbr, but Priory Bay is sheltered ⚓ in winds from S to WNW.

NAVIGATION WPT tide gauge, Fl Y 2s, 50°42′·33N 01°05′·09W, approx 2ca E of ent to well-buoyed, but unlit chan. The bar, between Nos 6 and 10 buoys, almost dries. Avoid the gravel banks between St Helen's Fort, Nodes Pt and N to Seaview, by keeping to ent times above.

LIGHTS AND MARKS St Helens Fort Fl (3) 10s 16m 8M; no ⚓ within 1ca radius of Fort. Conspic W seamark on shore where chan turns S. Caution: there are numerous unlit Y racing marks off Bembridge and Seaview (Mar-Oct).

RADIO TELEPHONE Call *Bembridge Marina* VHF Ch **80**; *Hbr Launch* Ch M.

TELEPHONE (Dial code 01983) Hr Mr 872828; MRSC (023 92) 552100; ⊖ 0345 231110 (H24); Marinecall 09068 500457; Police 528000; Dr 872614.

FACILITIES Marina (40+100 visitors) ☎ 872828, 📠 872922, £1.40, ♿, FW, ME, El, AC, ▣, V, R, Bar; **St Helen's Quay** FW, CH; **Brading Haven YC** ☎ 872289, Bar, R, FW; **Bembridge SC** ☎ 872686; **Services:** M, Slip, BY, P & D (cans), ME, El, Sh, Gas. **Town** www.harbours.co.uk, EC Thurs; V, R, Bar, ✉, Ⓑ, ⇌ (Ryde), ✈ (So'ton).

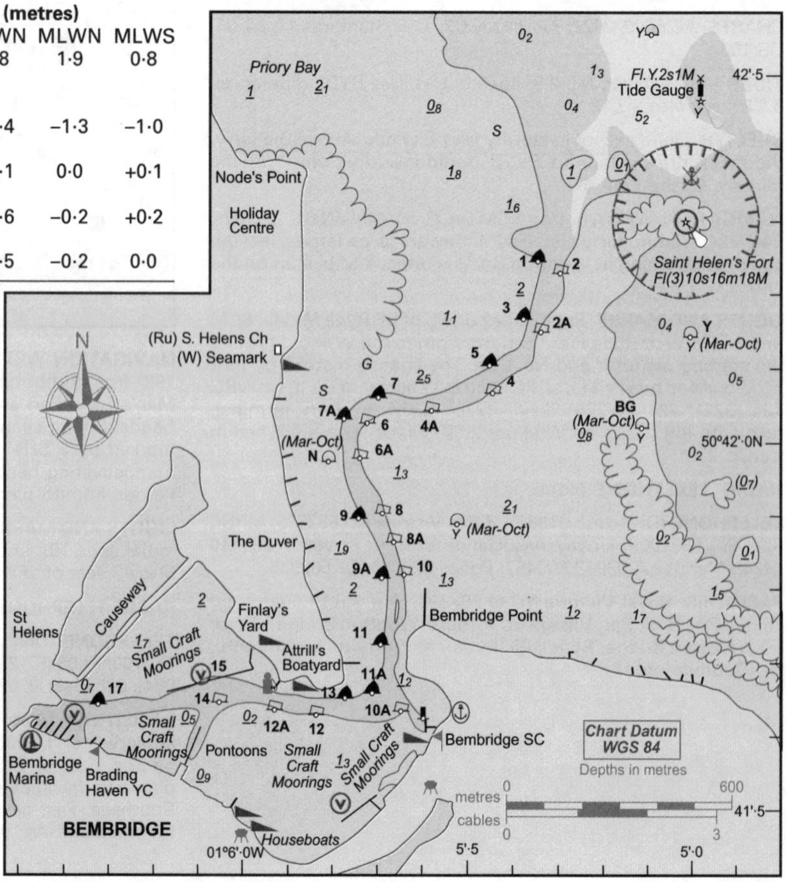

TIME ZONE (UTC)
For Summer Time add ONE hour in **non-shaded areas**

ENGLAND – PORTSMOUTH

LAT 50°48′N LONG 1°07′W

TIMES AND HEIGHTS OF HIGH AND LOW WATERS

SPRING & NEAP TIDES
Dates in red are SPRINGS
Dates in blue are NEAPS

YEAR **2002**

JANUARY

Day	Time	m	Day	Time	m
1	0010	4.7	16	0050	4.5
	0534	1.0		0613	1.2
TU	1224	4.7	W	1253	4.4
	1802	0.7		1834	1.0
2	0057	4.8	17	0124	4.5
	0622	1.0		0647	1.3
W	1310	4.7	TH	1328	4.4
	1849	0.7		1906	1.1
3	0145	4.7	18	0159	4.4
	0711	1.0		0720	1.4
TH	1358	4.6	F	1403	4.3
	1938	0.8		1937	1.2
4	0235	4.7	19	0235	4.3
	0802	1.1		0753	1.5
F	1448	4.5	SA	1440	4.1
	2029	0.9		2010	1.4
5	0329	4.6	20	0313	4.2
	0856	1.3		0828	1.7
SA	1542	4.3	SU	1518	4.0
	2123	1.1		2046	1.5
6	0425	4.5	21	0355	4.1
	0956	1.4		0911	1.8
SU	1640	4.2	M	1601	3.9
	2222	1.3		2131	1.7
7	0526	4.3	22	0443	4.0
	1101	1.6		1005	2.0
M	1745	4.1	TU	1654	3.8
	2328	1.5		2230	1.9
8	0632	4.3	23	0542	3.9
	1212	1.6		1115	2.0
TU	1857	4.0	W	1803	3.7
				2344	1.9
9	0038	1.5	24	0653	4.0
	0739	4.3		1236	1.9
W	1322	1.6	TH	1922	3.8
	2008	4.1			
10	0146	1.5	25	0102	1.8
	0841	4.4		0801	4.1
TH	1423	1.4	F	1345	1.7
	2113	4.2		2032	4.0
11	0244	1.4	26	0206	1.6
	0936	4.5		0900	4.3
F	1516	1.3	SA	1440	1.4
	2208	4.3		2131	4.2
12	0334	1.3	27	0300	1.4
	1025	4.5		0951	4.5
SA	1602	1.1	SU	1530	1.1
	2255	4.4		2223	4.5
13	0418	1.2	28	0350	1.1
	1107	4.6		1039	4.6
SU	1645	1.0	M	1619	0.8
●	2337	4.5	○	2311	4.7
14	0459	1.1	29	0439	0.9
	1145	4.6		1126	4.7
M	1724	1.0	TU	1707	0.6
				2359	4.8
15	0015	4.5	30	0527	0.8
	0537	1.1		1213	4.8
TU	1220	4.5	W	1754	0.5
	1800	0.9			
			31	0046	4.9
				0614	0.7
			TH	1301	4.8
				1840	0.5

FEBRUARY

Day	Time	m	Day	Time	m
1	0133	4.9	16	0132	4.5
	0700	0.7		0655	1.1
F	1348	4.7	SA	1341	4.3
	1926	0.5		1910	1.0
2	0221	4.8	17	0204	4.4
	0747	0.8		0721	1.2
SA	1436	4.6	SU	1413	4.3
	2011	0.7		1937	1.1
3	0308	4.7	18	0235	4.3
	0835	0.9		0751	1.3
SU	1524	4.5	M	1446	4.2
	2058	0.9		2008	1.3
4	0356	4.5	19	0309	4.2
	0925	1.2		0826	1.5
M	1614	4.2	TU	1522	4.0
	2150	1.2		2046	1.5
5	0449	4.3	20	0348	4.0
	1024	1.5		0911	1.7
TU	1711	4.0	W	1608	3.9
	2251	1.5		2137	1.8
6	0550	4.1	21	0441	3.9
	1135	1.7		1013	1.9
W	1822	3.8	TH	1713	3.7
				2251	2.0
7	0005	1.7	22	0556	3.8
	0704	4.0		1144	2.0
TH	1255	1.7	F	1840	3.7
	1947	3.8			
8	0125	1.8	23	0029	2.0
	0821	4.0		0722	3.9
F	1406	1.6	SA	1319	1.8
	2103	4.0		2007	3.9
9	0231	1.6	24	0150	1.7
	0924	4.2		0835	4.1
SA	1503	1.4	SU	1424	1.4
	2200	4.2		2113	4.2
10	0324	1.4	25	0249	1.4
	1014	4.3		0933	4.4
SU	1549	1.2	M	1517	1.0
	2246	4.4		2207	4.5
11	0407	1.2	26	0340	1.0
	1055	4.4		1024	4.6
M	1629	1.0	TU	1606	0.7
	2325	4.5		2256	4.7
12	0446	1.1	27	0428	0.7
	1131	4.4		1112	4.7
TU	1707	0.9	W	1653	0.5
●	2359	4.5	○	2343	4.9
13	0522	1.0	28	0515	0.5
	1204	4.4		1159	4.8
W	1742	0.9	TH	1739	0.3
14	0030	4.5			
	0555	1.0			
TH	1236	4.4			
	1814	0.9			
15	0101	4.5			
	0626	1.0			
F	1308	4.4			
	1843	0.9			

MARCH

Day	Time	m	Day	Time	m
1	0029	5.0	16	0035	4.5
	0600	0.4		0602	0.8
F	1246	4.9	SA	1246	4.4
	1824	0.3		1817	0.8
2	0115	5.0	17	0104	4.5
	0644	0.4		0628	0.9
SA	1332	4.8	SU	1317	4.4
	1907	0.4		1842	0.9
3	0159	4.9	18	0133	4.4
	0726	0.5		0653	1.0
SU	1418	4.7	M	1348	4.3
	1949	0.5		1908	1.0
4	0242	4.7	19	0202	4.4
	0809	0.7		0720	1.1
M	1502	4.5	TU	1419	4.3
	2031	0.8		1938	1.2
5	0325	4.5	20	0233	4.2
	0854	1.0		0754	1.2
TU	1549	4.3	W	1454	4.1
	2118	1.2		2014	1.4
6	0412	4.2	21	0309	4.1
	0947	1.4		0836	1.5
W	1642	4.0	TH	1540	3.9
	2218	1.6		2104	1.7
7	0508	3.9	22	0400	3.9
	1058	1.8		0935	1.8
TH	1752	3.8	F	1644	3.8
	2338	1.9		2219	2.0
8	0628	3.7	23	0515	3.7
	1228	1.9		1110	1.9
F	1931	3.7	SA	1814	3.7
9	0107	1.9	24	0009	2.0
	0804	3.7		0649	3.8
SA	1348	1.8	SU	1258	1.8
	2051	3.9		1946	3.9
10	0220	1.7	25	0136	1.7
	0912	3.9		0812	4.0
SU	1446	1.5	M	1407	1.4
	2146	4.2		2054	4.2
11	0310	1.5	26	0235	1.3
	1000	4.1		0913	4.3
M	1530	1.3	TU	1501	1.0
	2229	4.3		2148	4.6
12	0351	1.2	27	0325	0.9
	1040	4.3		1004	4.6
TU	1608	1.0	W	1548	0.6
	2305	4.4		2236	4.8
13	0427	1.0	28	0412	0.6
	1114	4.3		1053	4.7
W	1644	0.9	TH	1634	0.4
	2337	4.5	○	2322	4.9
14	0501	0.9	29	0457	0.4
	1145	4.4		1140	4.9
TH	1718	0.8	F	1719	0.3
●					
15	0006	4.5	30	0008	5.0
	0533	0.8		0540	0.3
F	1215	4.4	SA	1227	4.9
	1749	0.8		1802	0.3
			31	0052	5.0
				0623	0.3
			SU	1313	4.9
				1843	0.4

APRIL

Day	Time	m	Day	Time	m
1	0134	4.9	16	0105	4.5
	0704	0.4		0627	0.9
M	1357	4.8	TU	1326	4.4
	1924	0.6		1843	1.0
2	0215	4.7	17	0135	4.4
	0744	0.7		0657	1.0
TU	1441	4.6	W	1359	4.3
	2004	0.9		1915	1.2
3	0256	4.5	18	0208	4.3
	0826	1.0		0733	1.1
W	1526	4.3	TH	1438	4.2
	2050	1.3		1955	1.4
4	0339	4.1	19	0247	4.1
	0915	1.4		0817	1.4
TH	1618	4.0	F	1526	4.0
	2148	1.7		2048	1.7
5	0432	3.8	20	0340	3.9
	1024	1.8		0919	1.7
F	1728	3.8	SA	1632	3.9
	2310	2.0		2206	1.9
6	0550	3.6	21	0454	3.8
	1157	1.9		1052	1.8
SA	1908	3.7	SU	1757	3.8
				2347	1.9
7	0042	2.0	22	0623	3.8
	0739	3.6		1231	1.6
SU	1321	1.8	M	1923	4.0
	2026	3.9			
8	0155	1.8	23	0111	1.7
	0848	3.8		0745	4.0
M	1419	1.6	TU	1342	1.3
	2119	4.2		2030	4.3
9	0245	1.5	24	0212	1.3
	0935	4.0		0848	4.3
TU	1501	1.3	W	1436	0.9
	2200	4.3		2123	4.6
10	0324	1.2	25	0303	0.9
	1013	4.2		0941	4.5
W	1539	1.1	TH	1524	0.7
	2235	4.4		2212	4.8
11	0359	1.0	26	0350	0.6
	1046	4.2		1031	4.7
TH	1614	0.9	F	1610	0.5
	2306	4.5		2259	4.9
12	0433	0.9	27	0435	0.4
	1118	4.3		1119	4.8
F	1648	0.8	SA	1655	0.4
●	2335	4.5	○	2344	5.0
13	0506	0.8	28	0519	0.4
	1149	4.4		1206	4.8
SA	1720	0.8	SU	1738	0.4
14	0005	4.5	29	0028	4.9
	0535	0.8		0601	0.4
SU	1221	4.4	M	1252	4.8
	1748	0.8		1819	0.5
15	0035	4.5	30	0110	4.8
	0601	0.8		0642	0.5
M	1253	4.4	TU	1336	4.7
	1815	0.9		1900	0.8

Chart Datum: 2·73 metres below Ordnance Datum (Newlyn)

Register for your **FREE** weekly weather email service from Macmillan Reeds
›› at **www.nauticaldata.com – NOW!** ‹‹
weekend weather reports sent to your email address, every Thursday

TIME ZONE (UTC)
For Summer Time add ONE hour in **non-shaded areas**

ENGLAND – PORTSMOUTH

LAT 50°48′N LONG 1°07′W

TIMES AND HEIGHTS OF HIGH AND LOW WATERS

SPRING & NEAP TIDES
Dates in red are **SPRINGS**
Dates in blue are **NEAPS**

YEAR **2002**

MAY

Date	Day	Time	m	Time	m	Time	m	Time	m
1	W	0150	4.7	0722	0.8	1420	4.5	1941	1.1
2	TH	0230	4.4	0803	1.1	1506	4.3	2026	1.4
3	F	0313	4.1	0851	1.4	1557	4.0	2122	1.8
4	SA	0403	3.8	0953	1.7	1701	3.8	2235	2.0
5	SU	0510	3.6	1114	1.9	1825	3.8	2359	2.1
6	M	0645	3.6	1235	1.9	1942	3.9		
7	TU	0112	1.9	0802	3.7	1336	1.7	2036	4.1
8	W	0205	1.6	0853	3.9	1421	1.5	2118	4.2
9	TH	0246	1.4	0933	4.0	1501	1.2	2154	4.3
10	F	0323	1.2	1009	4.1	1538	1.1	2228	4.4
11	SA	0359	1.0	1044	4.2	1613	1.0	2301	4.4
12	SU	0433	0.9	1119	4.3	1647	0.9	● 2334	4.5
13	M	0505	0.9	1154	4.4	1719	0.9		
14	TU	0007	4.5	0536	0.9	1231	4.4	1750	1.0
15	W	0041	4.5	0607	0.9	1307	4.4	1824	1.1
16	TH	0116	4.4	0643	1.0	1346	4.4	1903	1.2
17	F	0153	4.3	0724	1.1	1429	4.3	1949	1.4
18	SA	0238	4.2	0814	1.3	1521	4.2	2046	1.6
19	SU	0333	4.0	0917	1.5	1625	4.1	2158	1.7
20	M	0441	3.9	1035	1.5	1740	4.0	2319	1.7
21	TU	0559	3.9	1156	1.5	1856	4.2		
22	W	0036	1.5	0715	4.1	1307	1.3	2000	4.4
23	TH	0140	1.3	0819	4.3	1405	1.0	2056	4.6
24	F	0235	1.0	0916	4.5	1457	0.8	2147	4.7
25	SA	0325	0.8	1009	4.6	1545	0.7	2235	4.8
26	SU	0413	0.6	1059	4.7	1631	0.6	○ 2322	4.9
27	M	0458	0.6	1147	4.7	1716	0.7		
28	TU	0006	4.8	0542	0.6	1234	4.7	1758	0.8
29	W	0048	4.7	0623	0.7	1318	4.6	1840	0.9
30	TH	0128	4.6	0704	0.9	1402	4.5	1921	1.2
31	F	0207	4.4	0744	1.1	1446	4.3	2005	1.4

JUNE

Date	Day	Time	m	Time	m	Time	m	Time	m
1	SA	0249	4.1	0828	1.4	1533	4.1	2054	1.7
2	SU	0335	3.9	0919	1.6	1625	4.0	2152	1.9
3	M	0429	3.7	1021	1.8	1726	3.9	2301	2.0
4	TU	0534	3.6	1131	1.9	1832	3.9		
5	W	0012	2.0	0645	3.6	1237	1.8	1932	4.0
6	TH	0112	1.8	0749	3.7	1330	1.6	2022	4.1
7	F	0200	1.6	0841	3.9	1416	1.5	2106	4.2
8	SA	0242	1.4	0926	4.0	1457	1.3	2147	4.3
9	SU	0322	1.2	1009	4.2	1537	1.2	2226	4.4
10	M	0400	1.1	1050	4.3	1615	1.1	● 2305	4.5
11	TU	0437	1.0	1131	4.4	1653	1.1	2343	4.5
12	W	0515	0.9	1211	4.5	1733	1.0		
13	TH	0022	4.5	0555	0.9	1253	4.5	1814	1.0
14	F	0102	4.5	0637	0.9	1337	4.5	1858	1.1
15	SA	0145	4.4	0723	1.0	1424	4.5	1947	1.2
16	SU	0233	4.3	0814	1.1	1516	4.4	2042	1.3
17	M	0326	4.2	0911	1.2	1614	4.3	2143	1.4
18	TU	0427	4.1	1013	1.3	1717	4.3	2249	1.5
19	W	0534	4.1	1120	1.3	1824	4.3	2359	1.5
20	TH	0644	4.1	1228	1.3	1929	4.4		
21	F	0107	1.3	0751	4.2	1333	1.2	2029	4.5
22	SA	0209	1.2	0854	4.3	1432	1.1	2124	4.6
23	SU	0304	1.0	0951	4.4	1524	1.0	2215	4.6
24	M	0354	0.9	1044	4.5	1613	1.0	○ 2303	4.7
25	TU	0442	0.8	1134	4.6	1659	1.0	2347	4.6
26	W	0526	0.8	1219	4.6	1742	1.0		
27	TH	0028	4.6	0608	0.9	1302	4.6	1823	1.1
28	F	0107	4.5	0647	1.0	1343	4.5	1902	1.2
29	SA	0145	4.3	0725	1.1	1423	4.4	1942	1.4
30	SU	0224	4.2	0802	1.3	1503	4.3	2023	1.5

JULY

Date	Day	Time	m	Time	m	Time	m	Time	m
1	M	0305	4.0	0842	1.4	1546	4.1	2107	1.7
2	TU	0349	3.9	0927	1.6	1632	4.0	2158	1.9
3	W	0439	3.8	1019	1.8	1723	3.9	2258	1.9
4	TH	0536	3.7	1121	1.9	1821	3.9		
5	F	0005	1.9	0641	3.7	1228	1.8	1921	4.0
6	SA	0107	1.8	0747	3.8	1327	1.7	2018	4.1
7	SU	0200	1.6	0846	4.0	1418	1.6	2109	4.2
8	M	0247	1.4	0938	4.1	1505	1.4	2156	4.3
9	TU	0332	1.2	1026	4.3	1550	1.2	2240	4.5
10	W	0416	1.0	1111	4.5	1635	1.1	● 2323	4.5
11	TH	0500	0.8	1156	4.6	1720	1.0		
12	F	0006	4.6	0545	0.8	1241	4.6	1805	0.9
13	SA	0051	4.6	0631	0.7	1327	4.7	1852	0.9
14	SU	0136	4.6	0717	0.7	1414	4.7	1940	0.9
15	M	0224	4.5	0805	0.8	1503	4.6	2029	1.0
16	TU	0315	4.4	0855	0.9	1554	4.5	2122	1.2
17	W	0408	4.3	0948	1.1	1649	4.4	2220	1.3
18	TH	0507	4.1	1048	1.3	1749	4.3	2326	1.5
19	F	0614	4.0	1155	1.5	1856	4.2		
20	SA	0038	1.5	0727	4.0	1308	1.5	2004	4.2
21	SU	0148	1.4	0839	4.1	1414	1.5	2107	4.3
22	M	0249	1.3	0942	4.2	1512	1.3	2202	4.4
23	TU	0342	1.1	1037	4.4	1602	1.2	2250	4.5
24	W	0429	1.0	1124	4.5	1646	1.1	○ 2332	4.5
25	TH	0512	0.9	1206	4.5	1728	1.1		
26	F	0011	4.5	0550	0.9	1245	4.5	1805	1.1
27	SA	0047	4.4	0627	0.9	1321	4.5	1841	1.1
28	SU	0121	4.3	0701	1.0	1355	4.4	1916	1.2
29	M	0156	4.3	0733	1.1	1429	4.4	1949	1.3
30	TU	0233	4.2	0804	1.3	1505	4.3	2023	1.5
31	W	0311	4.0	0838	1.4	1543	4.2	2101	1.7

AUGUST

Date	Day	Time	m	Time	m	Time	m	Time	m
1	TH	0351	3.9	0917	1.7	1624	4.0	2148	1.8
2	F	0440	3.8	1009	1.9	1716	3.9	2250	2.0
3	SA	0542	3.7	1118	2.0	1821	3.9		
4	SU	0010	2.0	0659	3.7	1240	2.0	1934	4.0
5	M	0125	1.8	0814	3.9	1349	1.8	2038	4.1
6	TU	0223	1.5	0915	4.1	1445	1.6	2132	4.3
7	W	0313	1.2	1007	4.4	1534	1.3	2219	4.5
8	TH	0400	0.9	1054	4.6	1621	1.1	● 2305	4.6
9	F	0446	0.7	1140	4.7	1707	0.9	2350	4.7
10	SA	0532	0.6	1225	4.8	1753	0.7		
11	SU	0036	4.7	0617	0.5	1311	4.8	1838	0.7
12	M	0122	4.7	0702	0.5	1357	4.8	1923	0.7
13	TU	0209	4.7	0747	0.6	1442	4.8	2009	0.8
14	W	0256	4.5	0832	0.8	1528	4.6	2057	1.0
15	TH	0345	4.4	0921	1.1	1617	4.4	2151	1.3
16	F	0440	4.1	1018	1.4	1714	4.2	2256	1.6
17	SA	0546	3.9	1129	1.7	1825	4.0		
18	SU	0016	1.7	0711	3.9	1251	1.8	1947	4.0
19	M	0136	1.7	0835	4.0	1406	1.7	2058	4.1
20	TU	0241	1.5	0939	4.2	1504	1.5	2154	4.3
21	W	0332	1.2	1029	4.4	1551	1.3	2239	4.4
22	TH	0414	1.0	1111	4.5	1632	1.2	○ 2318	4.5
23	F	0453	0.9	1149	4.6	1709	1.0	2352	4.5
24	SA	0529	0.8	1222	4.6	1744	1.0		
25	SU	0024	4.4	0602	0.8	1254	4.5	1817	1.0
26	M	0056	4.4	0633	0.9	1323	4.5	1847	1.1
27	TU	0128	4.4	0701	1.0	1354	4.4	1914	1.2
28	W	0200	4.3	0727	1.2	1425	4.4	1942	1.3
29	TH	0233	4.2	0755	1.3	1457	4.2	2015	1.5
30	F	0309	4.0	0830	1.6	1532	4.1	2055	1.7
31	SA	0351	3.9	0916	1.9	1618	3.9	2151	2.0

Chart Datum: 2·73 metres below Ordnance Datum (Newlyn)

Register for your FREE weekly weather email service from Macmillan Reeds
» at www.nauticaldata.com – NOW! «
weekend weather reports sent to your email address, every Thursday

TIME ZONE (UTC)
For Summer Time add ONE hour in **non-shaded areas**

ENGLAND – PORTSMOUTH

LAT 50°48'N LONG 1°07'W

TIMES AND HEIGHTS OF HIGH AND LOW WATERS

SPRING & NEAP TIDES
Dates in red are SPRINGS
Dates in blue are NEAPS

YEAR **2002**

SEPTEMBER

Date	Time	m	Time	m	Time	m	Time	m
1 SU	0452	3.7	1024	2.1	1725	3.8	2318	2.1
2 M	0618	3.7	1206	2.2	1853	3.8		
3 TU	0059	1.9	0748	3.9	1332	2.0	2012	4.0
4 W	0206	1.6	0856	4.2	1430	1.6	2111	4.3
5 TH	0258	1.2	0948	4.4	1519	1.3	2200	4.5
6 F	0344	0.9	1034	4.7	1605	0.9	2245	4.7
7 SA	0429	0.6	1119	4.8	1650	0.7	● 2331	4.8
8 SU	0514	0.4	1204	4.9	1734	0.5		
9 M	0017	4.9	0557	0.4	1249	5.0	1818	0.5
10 TU	0103	4.9	0640	0.4	1333	5.0	1901	0.6
11 W	0148	4.8	0723	0.6	1416	4.8	1945	0.7
12 TH	0234	4.6	0806	0.8	1500	4.6	2030	1.0
13 F	0321	4.4	0853	1.2	1546	4.4	2122	1.4
14 SA	0415	4.1	0951	1.6	1641	4.1	2229	1.7
15 SU	0524	3.9	1109	1.9	1757	3.9	2357	1.9
16 M	0702	3.8	1239	2.0	1938	3.9		
17 TU	0125	1.8	0829	4.0	1357	1.9	2051	4.0
18 W	0229	1.6	0927	4.3	1452	1.6	2142	4.3
19 TH	0315	1.3	1012	4.5	1534	1.3	2223	4.4
20 F	0353	1.1	1050	4.6	1610	1.1	2258	4.5
21 SA	0429	0.9	1124	4.6	1645	1.0	○ 2329	4.5
22 SU	0502	0.8	1154	4.6	1718	0.9	2358	4.5
23 M	0535	0.8	1222	4.6	1749	0.9		
24 TU	0028	4.5	0604	0.9	1250	4.5	1816	1.0
25 W	0059	4.5	0629	1.0	1319	4.5	1841	1.1
26 TH	0130	4.4	0653	1.1	1348	4.4	1907	1.2
27 F	0201	4.3	0720	1.3	1417	4.3	1937	1.4
28 SA	0234	4.2	0753	1.6	1451	4.1	2016	1.7
29 SU	0316	4.0	0837	1.9	1536	4.0	2110	2.0
30 M	0418	3.8	0947	2.2	1644	3.8	2241	2.1

OCTOBER

Date	Time	m	Time	m	Time	m	Time	m
1 TU	0546	3.7	1141	2.3	1816	3.8		
2 W	0035	2.0	0722	3.9	1312	2.0	1944	4.0
3 TH	0145	1.6	0832	4.2	1411	1.6	2047	4.3
4 F	0237	1.2	0924	4.5	1459	1.2	2136	4.6
5 SA	0322	0.8	1010	4.8	1543	0.8	2223	4.8
6 SU	0406	0.6	1055	5.0	1627	0.6	● 2309	4.9
7 M	0450	0.4	1139	5.0	1711	0.5	2355	5.0
8 TU	0533	0.4	1223	5.1	1755	0.5		
9 W	0040	5.0	0615	0.5	1307	5.0	1837	0.6
10 TH	0126	4.9	0657	0.7	1350	4.8	1919	0.8
11 F	0212	4.7	0740	1.0	1433	4.6	2004	1.1
12 SA	0259	4.4	0828	1.4	1519	4.3	2054	1.5
13 SU	0354	4.1	0927	1.8	1613	4.0	2202	1.8
14 M	0505	3.9	1047	2.1	1731	3.8	2332	2.0
15 TU	0646	3.9	1218	2.1	1919	3.8		
16 W	0100	1.9	0807	4.1	1335	1.9	2029	4.0
17 TH	0204	1.7	0901	4.3	1427	1.7	2118	4.2
18 F	0247	1.4	0944	4.5	1506	1.4	2157	4.3
19 SA	0324	1.2	1020	4.6	1541	1.2	2230	4.4
20 SU	0358	1.0	1051	4.6	1615	1.0	2300	4.5
21 M	0431	0.9	1120	4.6	1647	1.0	○ 2329	4.5
22 TU	0503	0.9	1149	4.6	1718	1.0		
23 W	0000	4.5	0532	1.0	1218	4.6	1746	1.0
24 TH	0032	4.5	0559	1.1	1248	4.5	1811	1.1
25 F	0104	4.5	0624	1.2	1317	4.5	1839	1.2
26 SA	0136	4.4	0653	1.4	1348	4.3	1911	1.4
27 SU	0212	4.3	0729	1.6	1423	4.2	1952	1.6
28 M	0257	4.1	0816	1.9	1511	4.0	2048	1.9
29 TU	0400	3.9	0928	2.2	1619	3.9	2215	2.0
30 W	0522	3.9	1112	2.2	1744	3.8	2357	1.9
31 TH	0651	4.0	1240	2.0	1911	4.0		

NOVEMBER

Date	Time	m	Time	m	Time	m	Time	m
1 F	0111	1.6	0801	4.3	1342	1.6	2016	4.3
2 SA	0207	1.2	0855	4.6	1432	1.2	2109	4.6
3 SU	0254	0.9	0942	4.9	1518	0.9	2158	4.8
4 M	0340	0.6	1029	5.0	1603	0.6	● 2246	4.9
5 TU	0424	0.5	1114	5.1	1648	0.5	2334	5.0
6 W	0508	0.5	1159	5.1	1732	0.6		
7 TH	0021	5.0	0551	0.6	1243	5.0	1815	0.7
8 F	0107	4.9	0634	0.9	1326	4.8	1858	0.9
9 SA	0153	4.7	0718	1.1	1409	4.6	1943	1.2
10 SU	0241	4.5	0806	1.5	1454	4.3	2032	1.5
11 M	0335	4.2	0903	1.8	1546	4.0	2133	1.8
12 TU	0441	4.0	1015	2.1	1654	3.8	2250	2.0
13 W	0605	3.9	1138	2.2	1829	3.7		
14 TH	0012	2.0	0723	4.0	1253	2.0	1946	3.8
15 F	0118	1.8	0819	4.2	1348	1.8	2038	4.0
16 SA	0206	1.6	0903	4.3	1430	1.6	2119	4.1
17 SU	0245	1.4	0940	4.4	1507	1.4	2154	4.3
18 M	0321	1.2	1013	4.5	1542	1.2	2227	4.4
19 TU	0357	1.1	1044	4.5	1616	1.1	2300	4.4
20 W	0431	1.1	1116	4.6	1649	1.1	○ 2334	4.5
21 TH	0502	1.1	1149	4.6	1719	1.1		
22 F	0009	4.5	0532	1.2	1222	4.6	1749	1.1
23 SA	0044	4.5	0603	1.3	1255	4.5	1822	1.2
24 SU	0121	4.5	0638	1.4	1330	4.4	1859	1.3
25 M	0201	4.4	0719	1.6	1410	4.3	1944	1.4
26 TU	0249	4.2	0811	1.8	1459	4.1	2041	1.6
27 W	0348	4.1	0917	1.9	1601	4.0	2153	1.7
28 TH	0500	4.1	1038	2.0	1715	4.0	2313	1.7
29 F	0616	4.2	1157	1.8	1833	4.1		
30 SA	0026	1.5	0725	4.4	1305	1.6	1942	4.3

DECEMBER

Date	Time	m	Time	m	Time	m	Time	m
1 SU	0129	1.3	0823	4.6	1402	1.3	2042	4.5
2 M	0224	1.0	0916	4.8	1453	1.0	2136	4.6
3 TU	0313	0.9	1005	4.9	1542	0.8	2228	4.8
4 W	0401	0.8	1052	5.0	1629	0.7	● 2318	4.8
5 TH	0448	0.8	1139	5.0	1716	0.7		
6 F	0006	4.8	0533	0.9	1223	4.9	1800	0.8
7 SA	0053	4.8	0617	1.0	1306	4.7	1843	0.9
8 SU	0139	4.7	0701	1.2	1349	4.5	1926	1.1
9 M	0225	4.5	0746	1.5	1432	4.3	2011	1.4
10 TU	0313	4.3	0836	1.7	1518	4.1	2100	1.6
11 W	0406	4.1	0933	2.0	1611	3.9	2158	1.8
12 TH	0506	4.0	1040	2.1	1712	3.7	2304	1.9
13 F	0610	4.0	1151	2.1	1822	3.7		
14 SA	0011	1.9	0712	4.0	1254	2.0	1930	3.8
15 SU	0110	1.8	0805	4.1	1345	1.8	2025	3.9
16 M	0159	1.7	0851	4.3	1428	1.6	2111	4.1
17 TU	0243	1.5	0932	4.4	1508	1.4	2154	4.2
18 W	0323	1.4	1011	4.5	1546	1.3	2234	4.3
19 TH	0401	1.3	1048	4.5	1623	1.1	○ 2312	4.5
20 F	0438	1.2	1125	4.6	1700	1.1	2351	4.5
21 SA	0514	1.2	1202	4.6	1736	1.0		
22 SU	0030	4.6	0551	1.2	1240	4.5	1815	1.0
23 M	0111	4.6	0632	1.3	1319	4.5	1856	1.0
24 TU	0154	4.5	0716	1.3	1402	4.4	1942	1.1
25 W	0241	4.4	0806	1.4	1451	4.3	2034	1.2
26 TH	0335	4.4	0903	1.5	1545	4.2	2131	1.3
27 F	0434	4.3	1006	1.6	1647	4.1	2234	1.4
28 SA	0539	4.3	1116	1.7	1755	4.1	2343	1.5
29 SU	0647	4.3	1227	1.6	1908	4.1		
30 M	0052	1.4	0752	4.4	1334	1.4	2017	4.2
31 TU	0157	1.3	0852	4.6	1434	1.2	2120	4.4

Chart Datum: 2·73 metres below Ordnance Datum (Newlyn)

PORTSMOUTH *9.2.30*

Hampshire **50°47'·38N 01°06'·67W** (Entrance) ❁❁❁◊◊◊✿✿

CHARTS AC *5600*, 2628, 2629, 2625, *2631*, *2037*, *2045*; Imray C3, C9, C15; Stanfords 10, 11; OS 197

TIDES +0029 Dover; ML 2·8; Zone 0 (UT)

Standard Port PORTSMOUTH (⟵)

Times				**Height (metres)**			
High Water		Low Water		MHWS	MHWN	MLWN	MLWS
0500	1000	0000	0600	4·7	3·8	1·9	0·8
1700	2200	1200	1800				
Differences LEE-ON-THE-SOLENT							
−0005	+0005	−0015	−0010	−0·2	−0·1	+0·1	+0·2

See also 9.2.12. Strong winds from NE to SE, coupled with a high barometer, may lower levels by 1m and delay times of HW and LW by 1hr; the opposite may occur in strong W'lies with low pressure.

SHELTER Excellent. This very large hbr affords shelter in some area for any wind. There are two marinas on the Gosport side, two at Fareham and one at the N end of Portchester Lake, plus several yacht pontoons/jetties and many moorings (see Facilities).
Good shelter in The Camber, but this is a busy little commercial dock and often full; beware the Isle of Wight car ferry docking near the ent.
Portsmouth is a major naval base and Dockyard Port; all vessels come under the QHM's authority. If > 20m LOA, ask QHM's permission (VHF Ch 11) to enter, leave or move in hbr, especially in fog. Fishing and ⚓ in chans are prohib.

NAVIGATION WPT No 4 Bar buoy, QR, 50°47'·01N 01°06'·36W, 150°/330° from/to hbr ent (W side), 4½ca. Beware very strong tides in hbr ent, commercial shipping and ferries, Gosport ferry and HM Ships. High Speed Ferries operate within the area.
Approaches: From the W, yachts can use the Swashway Chan (to NW of Spit Sand Fort) which carries about 2m; keep War Memorial and RH edge of block of flats on at 049°. The Inner Swashway Chan (Round Tr on 029°) carries only 0·1m; local knowledge required.
Approaching inshore from E, the submerged barrier, which extends from Southsea to Horse Sand Fort, should only be crossed via the unlit Inshore Boat passage (0·9m) 1ca off the beach, marked by R & G piles; or via the Main Passage (min depth 1·2m) 7ca further S, marked by G pile and dolphin, QR.
A Small Boat Channel for craft < 20m LOA lies at the hbr ent, parallel to and outboard of the W edge of the main dredged chan. It runs from abeam No 4 Bar buoy, QR (off Clarence Pier) to Ballast buoy, Fl R 2·5s, and extends about 50m off Fort Blockhouse. A depth gauge is on pile BC4.
Yachts should enter by the Small Boat Chan; they may also enter on the E side of the main chan, but clear of it and close inshore. All yachts must leave via the Small Boat Chan. Yachts may only cross the main chan N of Ballast buoy or S of No 4 Bar buoy. Yachts must motor (if so fitted) between No 4 Bar and Ballast buoys; winds at the ent may be fickle or gusty and tides run hard.
At night the Small Boat Chan is covered by the Oc R sector (324°-330°) of the Dir WRG lt on Fort Blockhouse (W side of hbr ent), until close to the hbr ent. Thereafter the Iso R 2s sector (337·5°-345°) of the Dir WRG lt 2m 1M (dolphin E of Gosport Marina) leads 341° through the ent and close abeam Ballast Bank PHM buoy, Fl R 2·5s.
Speed limit is 10kn within hbr and within 1000 yds of the shore in any part of the Dockyard Port; speed = speed through the water. Outside the hbr ent, the Dockyard Port limits embrace the Solent from Hillhead and Old Castle Pt (close NE of Cowes) eastward to Eastney and Shanklin (IOW), thence almost out to Nab Tr (see AC 394 & 2050).
Historic Wrecks (see 9.0.3h) are at: 50°45'·8N 01°06'·2W (site of *Mary Rose*), marked by SPM buoys; 5ca SSW of Spit Sand Ft. *Invincible* lies at 50°44'·34N 01°02'·23W, 117° Horse Sand Fort 1·45M, marked by SPM buoy.

LIGHTS AND MARKS From E of the IOW, Nab Tower, Fl 10s 27m 16M, is conspic about 10M SE of the hbr ent. In the inner appr's there are 3 conspic forts: Horse Sand Fort, Iso G 2s; No Man's Land Fort, Iso R 2s, and Spit Sand Fort, Fl R 5s.
Ldg marks/lts: St Jude's ✠ spire and Southsea Castle lt ho in transit 003° lead between Outer Spit SCM buoy, Q (6) + L Fl 15s, and Horse Sand SHM buoy, Fl G 2·5s. At night keep in the W sector (000°-003°) between the Al WG and Al WR sectors of the Dir lt (H24) on Southsea Castle, which also shows a lt Iso 2s 16m 11M, vis 337°-071° (94°).

FIRING RANGE **Tipner Rifle Range** as shown on chartlet. The danger area extends 2,500 metres from firing range. When firing is in progress, R flag or ● lt on Tipner Range FS indicates yachts should clear the range danger area or transit it as quickly as possible.

RADIO TELEPHONE Yachts should monitor Ch **11** (H24) for traffic/nav info. For the Camber call *Portsmouth Hbr Radio* (Commercial Port) Ch 11 14 (H24).
Haslar Marina and *Port Solent* Ch **80** M (H24). *Gosport Marina* call Ch **80** M (HO). Fareham Marina Ch M (summer 0900-1730). Wicor Marina Ch 80 (0900-1730, Mon-Sat). **Naval activities** to the S/SE of Portsmouth and IOW may be advised by Solent CG Ch 67 or ☎ 9255 2100; or Naval Ops ☎ 9272 2008. Naval vessels use Ch 13. The positions and times of naval firings and underwater explosions are broadcast daily at 0800 and 1400LT Ch 06; preceded by a Securité call on Ch 16. Warnings of underwater explosions will also be broadcast on Ch 16 at 1 hour, at 30 mins and just before the detonation.

TELEPHONE Dial codes: Portsmouth/Gosport 023; Fareham 01329. QHM 9272 3124; DQHM 9272 3794/📠 9272 2831; Hbr Control (H24) 9272 3694; Commercial Docks 9229 7395; Camber Berthing Offices ☎ 9229 7395 Ext 310; ⊜ 0345 231110 (H24); MRSC 9255 2100; Marinecall 09068 500457; Weather Centre 8022 8844; Police 9283 9333; Dr Fareham Health Centre (01329) 282911; Ⓗ 9282 2331.

FACILITIES **Marinas** (from seaward)
Haslar Marina, ☎ 9260 1201, 📠 9260 2201, £1.88, (550+ 50 Ⓥ); Access H24; Ⓥ at L pontoon, near conspic former lt ship, Bar & R (☎ 9221 9847); FW, AC, Gas, Gaz, CH, ME, Ⓔ, ◙, Slip (upstream of Haslar bridge). RNSA berths at S end.
Gosport Marina (350, some visitors) ☎ 9252 4811, 📠 9258 9541, www.cnmarinas.com, £0.36(low),£1.20(mid),£2.35(high), P, D, FW, ME, El, Sh, BH (150, 40 ton), CH, V, R, AC, Bar, Gas, Gaz, SM, ◙. Planned extension into Cold Hbr will create 270 new pontoon berths by 2001. Note: There are RNSA pontoons at the N end of Cold Hbr, inside the Fuel Jetty. Also 150 pile moorings (some dry); contact Haslar Marina.
Services: CH, P, D, ACA, El, Ⓔ, ME, Sh, BY, SM, Slip, C.
Gosport EC Wed; ✉, Ⓑ, ⇌ (Portsmouth), ✈ (Southampton).
Services SM, ACA; **Hbr** Moorings ☎ 9283 2484.
City of Portsmouth (3M) EC Wed (Southsea Sat); ✉, Ⓑ, ⇌, Ferries to Caen (Ouistreham), Cherbourg, Le Havre, St Malo, Bilbao, Santander (winter) and IoW (see 9.0.4); ✈ (Southampton).
Port Solent Marina, see over for chartlet and text.
FAREHAM (01329)
Fareham Lake is well marked, but only partially lit up to Bedenham Pier and unlit thereafter. Chan dries 0·9m in final 5ca to Town Quay.
Fareham Marina ☎ 822445, £5.00, M, Slip, D, FW, ME, El, Ⓔ, Sh, V, Bar, CH; (Access HW±3);
Wicor Marine (200) ☎ 237112, 📠 825660, Slip, M, D, ME, Sh, CH, AC, BH (10 ton), C (7 ton), FW, El, Ⓔ, Gas, Gaz.
Services: M, Sh, CH, ME, Slip, El, Ⓔ, D, FW, Gas, AC, SM.
Town EC Wed; ✉, Ⓑ, ⇌, ✈ (Southampton).
YACHT CLUBS
Royal Naval Sailing Association ☎ 9252 1100, 📠 9252 1122; **Royal Naval & Royal Albert YC** ☎ 9282 5924, M, Bar; **Portsmouth SC** ☎ 9282 0596; **Portchester SC** ☎ 9237 6375; **Hardway SC** ☎ 9258 1875, Slip, M, L, FW, C (mast stepping only), AB; **Gosport CC** ☎ (01329) 47014 or (0860) 966390; **Fareham Sailing & Motor Boat Club** ☎ (01329) 280738.

PORTSMOUTH *continued*

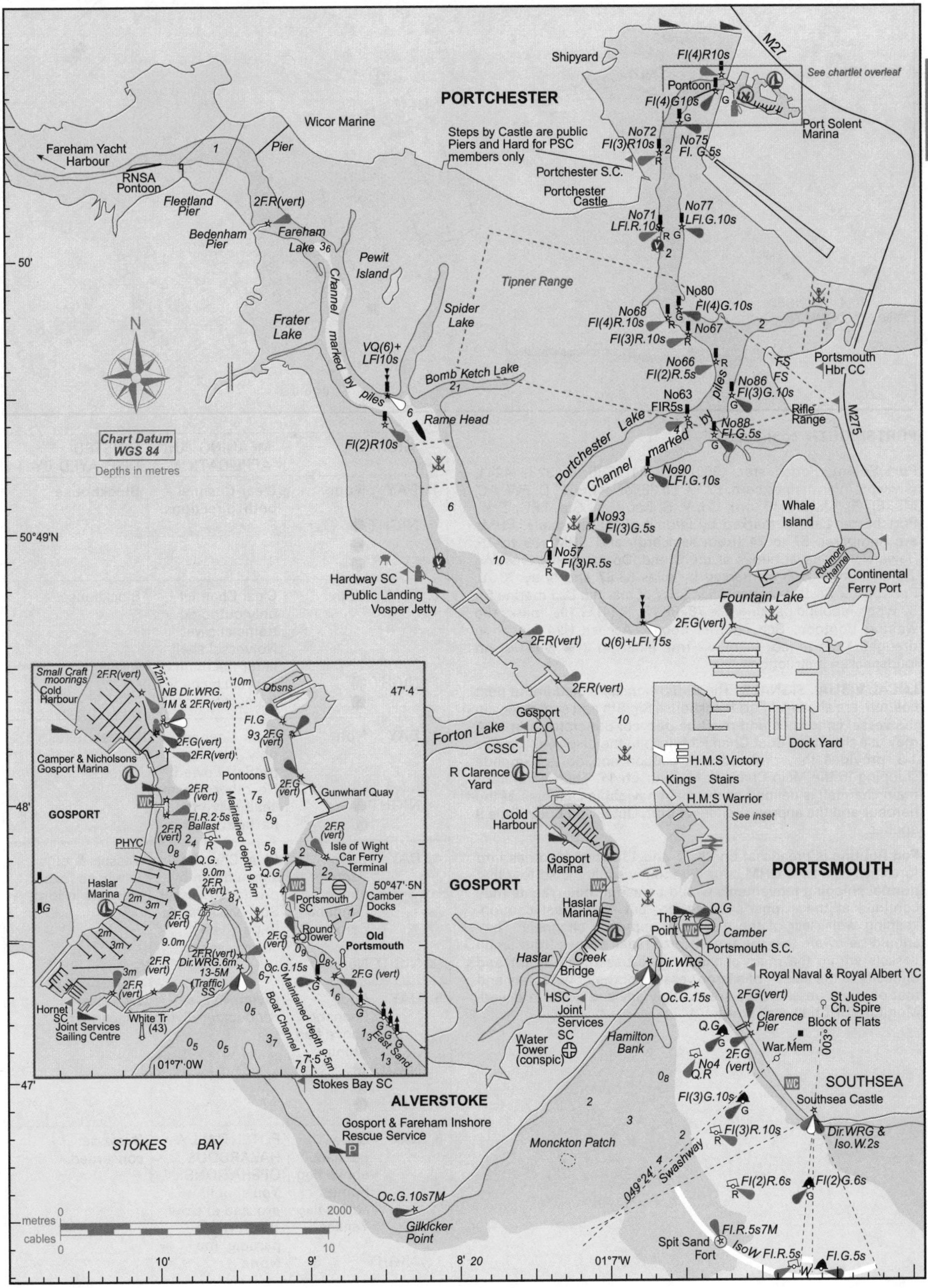

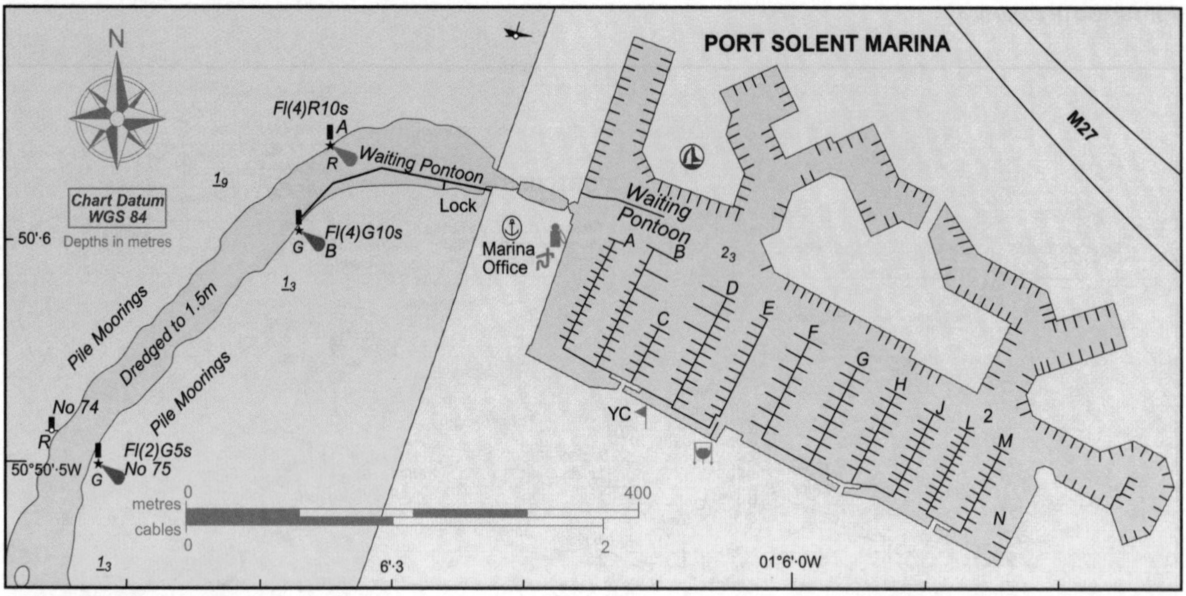

PORTSMOUTH *continued*

Port Solent, Portchester, (900) ☎ 9221 0765, 📠 9232 4241, www.premiermarinas.com, £2.17, £0.88 for <4hrs, P, D, FW, AC, ME, El, Ⓔ, Sh, BH (40 ton), CH, V, R, Bar, Gas, Gaz, LPG, 🅿, ♿. Portchester Lake is marked by lit/unlit piles; unusually, PHMs are numbered 57 to 74 (from seaward), and SHMs 95 to 75. Beware unlit naval buoys at the S end. Do not delay crossing Tipner Range, S limit marked by piles 63/87 and N by 70/78. Portchester Castle is conspic 5ca SSW of marina. Call marina Ch 80 when inbound passing pile 78. Pile B, Fl (4) G 10s, marks the waiting pontoon. See chartlet above. Access H24 via chan dredged 1·5m to lock (43m x 9·1m); enter on 3 ● (vert) or on loudspeaker instructions.

LOCAL VISUAL SIGNALS The traffic signals, tabled in the next column, are shown at Fort Blockhouse Sig Stn and sometimes in the vessel concerned and must be obeyed. But craft <20m LOA may use the Small Boat Chan H24 despite the displayed tfc sigs 1-3, provided they proceed with caution and do not impede shipping in the Main Channel. Monitor Ch 11. The Channel (or main channel) is defined as the main navigable channels of the harbour and the approach channel from Outer Spit buoy; Rule 9 applies.

Fog Routine is broadcast on Ch 11 and 13, when it comes into force, ie when the QHM considers that visibility is so low that normal shipping movements would be dangerous. Yachts may continue at the skipper's discretion, but with great caution, keeping well clear of the main and approach channels. They should be aware that the presence of radar echoes from small vessels within the main channel can cause much doubt and difficulty to the Master of a large vessel. For their own safety and that of major vessels they are strongly advised not to proceed. Monitor VHF Ch 11 at all times.

SIGNAL	MEANING AND APPLICATION	HOISTED/ DISPLAYED BY
1. DAY None. NIGHT ● ● ●	Clear Channel – both directions.	Blockhouse.
2. DAY None. NIGHT Ⓦ ●	Clear Channel – only outgoing traffic allowed. No vessel shall enter the main or approach channel from seaward.	Blockhouse.
3. DAY None. NIGHT ● Ⓦ	Clear Channel – only incoming traffic allowed. No other vessel shall leave the harbour.	Blockhouse.
4. DAY Code Pennant above Pennant Zero. NIGHT None	Clear Channel – signal flown by privileged vessel. Such vessels are to be given a clear passage.	Vessels & tugs in whose favour signal is in force
5. DAY Code Pennant above flag Alpha. NIGHT ● Ⓦ ●	Diving – vessel conducting diving.	By vessel concerned.
6. DAY Code Pennant above flag Romeo above flag Yankee. NIGHT	POTENTIALLY HAZARDOUS OPERATIONS. You should proceed at slow speed when passing me. None	By vessel concerned.

LANGSTONE HARBOUR *9.2.31*

Hampshire **50°47'·23N 01°01'·54W** (Ent) ❀❀◊◊◊✿✿

CHARTS AC *5600, 3418, 2045*; Imray C3, Y33; Stanfords 10, 11; OS 196, 197

TIDES +0022 Dover; Zone 0 (UT)

Standard Port PORTSMOUTH (⟵)

Times				Height (metres)			
High Water		Low Water		MHWS	MHWN	MLWN	MLWS
0500	1000	0000	0600	4·7	3·8	1·9	0·8
1700	2200	1200	1800				
Differences LANGSTONE							
0000	0000	+0010	+0010	+0·1	+0·1	0·0	0·0
NAB TOWER							
+0015	0000	+0015	+0015	–0·2	0·0	+0·2	0·0

SHELTER Very good in marina (2·4m) to W inside ent, access HW±3 over tidal flap 1·6m CD; waiting pontoon. Ent is 7m wide. 6 Y ⚓s at W side of hbr ent, 6 more on E side; max LOA 9m. Or ⚓ out of the fairway in Russell's Lake or Langstone Chan (water ski area); or see Hr Mr (E side of ent). Hbr speed limit 10kn, or 5kn in Southsea Marina channel.

NAVIGATION WPT 50°46'·31N 01°01'·36W, Langstone Fairway SWM beacon, L Fl 10s, 168°/348° from/to QR lt at ent, 0·94M. Bar has about 1·2m. Ent chan lies between East and West Winner drying banks, which afford some protection. Appr is easy in most weather, best from HW –3 to +1, but avoid entry against the ebb, esp at sp and in strong onshore winds. In strong S/SE winds do not attempt entry.

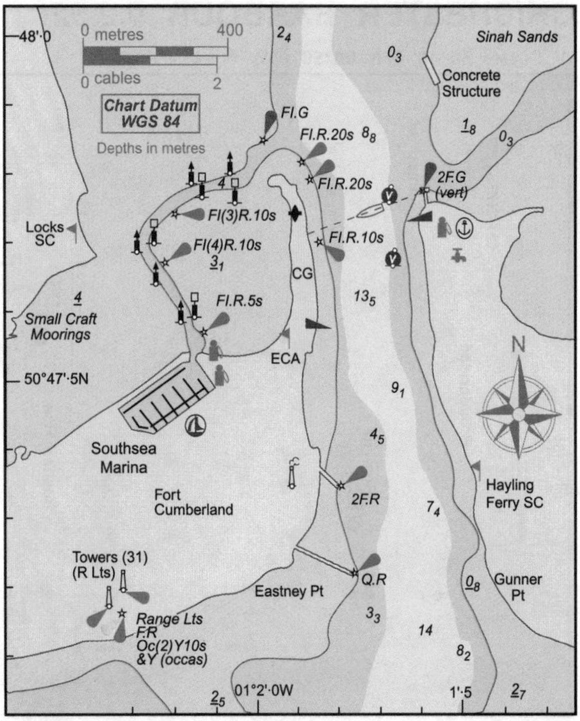

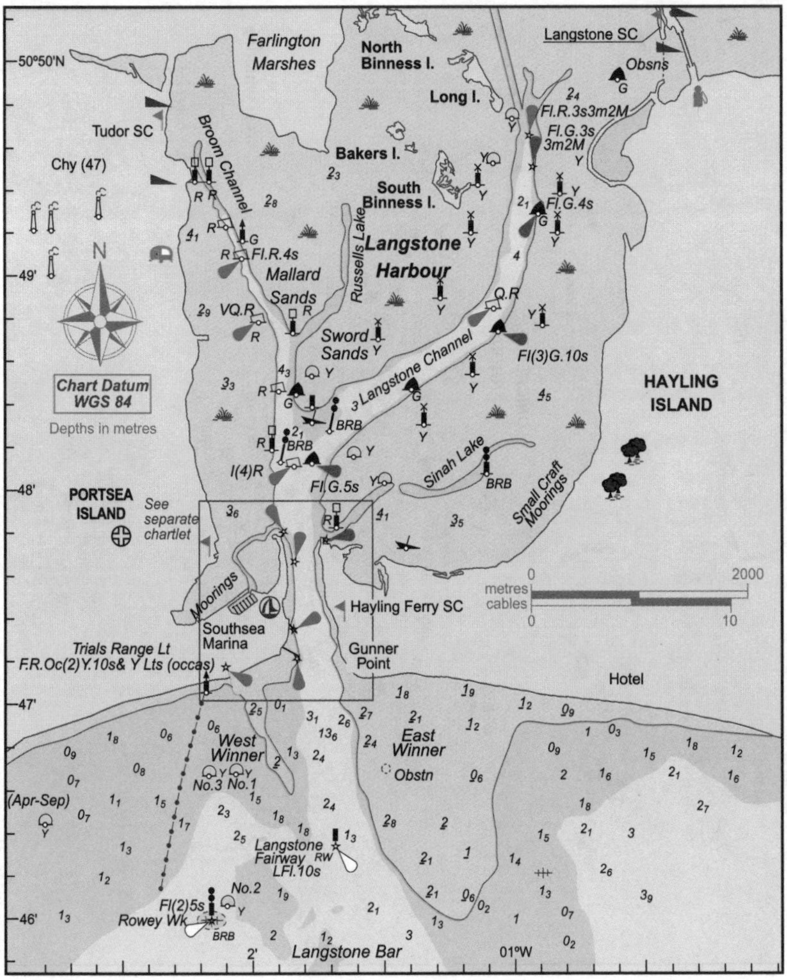

LIGHTS AND MARKS Ldg marks (concrete dolphins), or Fairway beacon on with conspic chy, lead 344° just clear of East Winner. The ent itself deepens and favours the W side. The narrow appr chan to Southsea Marina is marked by 7 SHM piles, only the first of which is lit, Fl G. There are 9 PHM piles; the 4th, 6th and 9th are Fl R. The lock has R/G ent sigs, as it is too narrow for 2 boats to pass; vessels going with the tide have priority.

RADIO TELEPHONE Harbour VHF Ch 12 16 (Summer 0830-1700 daily. Winter: Mon-Fri 0830-1700; Sat-Sun 0830-1300). Marina Ch **80** M (0800-1800 daily).

TELEPHONE Dial code 023 Hr Mr 9246 3419, 📠 9246 7144; MRSC 9255 2100; ⊖ 0345 231110 (H24); Marinecall 09068 500457; Police 9283 9333; Dr 9246 5721.

FACILITIES Southsea Marina (300) ☎ 9282 2719, 📠 9282 2220, www.southsea-marina.com, £1.47, £1 <4hrs on waiting pontoon, Access HW±3, AC, FW, D, CH, BH (20 ton), C (6 ton), Gaz, V, Bar, R; **Hayling Pontoon** (E side of ent), AB, P, D, FW, L, Slip; **Langstone SC** ☎ 9248 4577, Slip, M, L, FW, Bar; **Eastney Cruising Ass'n** (ECA) ☎ 9273 4103, 6 ⚓s; **Hayling Ferry SC; Locks SC** ☎ 9282 9833; **Tudor SC** (Hilsea) ☎ 9266 2002, Slip, M, FW, Bar.
Towns: EC Havant Wed; ✉ (Eastney, Hayling), Ⓑ (Havant, Hayling, Emsworth), ⇌ (bus to Havant), ✈ (Southampton).

CHICHESTER HARBOUR *9.2.32*

W. Sussex **50°46'·86N 00°56'·06W**

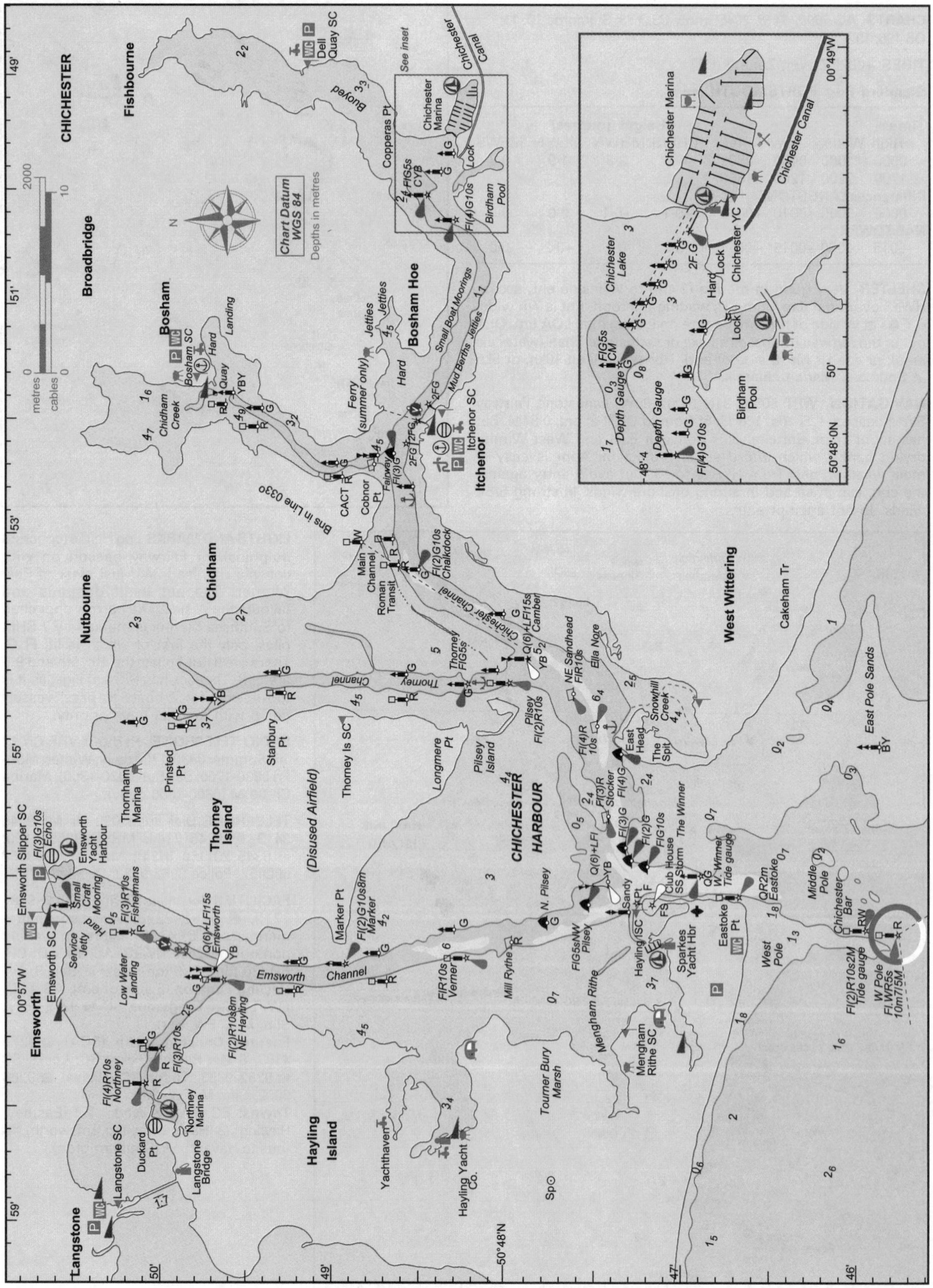

CHARTS AC *5600, 3418, 2045*; Imray C3, C9, Y33; Stanfords 10, 11; OS 197

TIDES +0027 Dover; ML 2·8; Zone 0 (UT); see curves on 8·2·13

Standard Port PORTSMOUTH (⟵)

Times				Height (metres)			
High Water		Low Water		MHWS	MHWN	MLWN	MLWS
0500	1000	0000	0600	4·7	3·8	1·9	0·8
1700	2200	1200	1800				
Differences CHICHESTER HARBOUR ENTRANCE							
–0010	+0005	+0015	+0020	+0·2	+0·2	0·0	+0·1
NORTHNEY							
+0010	+0015	+0015	+0025	+0·2	0·0	–0·2	–0·3
ITCHENOR							
–0005	+0005	+0005	+0025	+0·1	0·0	–0·2	–0·2
BOSHAM							
0000	+0010	No data		+0·2	+0·1	No data	
DELL QUAY							
+0005	+0015	No data		+0·2	+0·1	No data	
SELSEY BILL							
–0005	–0005	+0035	+0035	+0·6	+0·6	0·0	0·0

SHELTER Excellent in all five main chans, ie: Emsworth, Thorney, Chichester, Bosham, Itchenor Reach and Fishbourne. There are six yacht hbrs and marinas (see FACILITIES); also about 50 Ⓥs at Emsworth and Itchenor. Recognised ⚓s in Thorney Chan off Pilsey Is; off E Head (uncomfortable in NE winds); and in Chichester Chan off Chalkdock Point. Hbr speed limit of 8kn is rigidly enforced; max fine £2500.

NAVIGATION WPT 50°45′·53N 00°56′·59W, 193°/013° from/to West Pole Bn, 0·4M. Best entry is HW –3 to +1, to avoid confused seas on the ebb, esp in onshore winds >F 5. Do not attempt entry in S'ly gales. Bar is dredged 1·5m, but after gales depths may vary ±0·75m. Leave West Pole Bn (tide gauge) close to port; the chan N'ward is effectively only about 200m wide.

APPROACHES: **From the W**, the astern transit 255° of No Man's Land Fort and Ryde ✠ spire (hard to see) leads to the West Pole Bn. Closer in, transit 064° of Target NCM Bn with Cakeham Tr leads 4ca S of West Pole Bn; thence alter 013° as Eastoke Pt opens to E of West Pole Bn. West Pole PHM bn, Fl WR 5s, must be rounded to clear W Pole Spit, dries 0·2m.

From the E/SE, via Looe Chan, keep W for 2M, then alter NW to pick up an astern brg 184° of Nab Tr, toward the West Pole Bn, so as to clear the shoals of Bracklesham Bay. Note: An Historic Wreck (*Hazardous*) lies at 50°45′·13N 00°51′·56W, brg 105°/3·2M from Bar Bn; see 9.0.3h.

ENTRANCE: Pass between Eastoke bn QR and W Winner bn QG (tide gauge) leaving Eastoke bn 50m to port, to avoid a drying spit. Three SHM lt buoys mark the edge of The Winner shoal, dries, to stbd of the ent. Near Fishery SCM buoy, Q (6) + L Fl 15s, depths may change and buoys are moved accordingly. Here the chan divides: N toward Emsworth and ENE toward Chichester. Stocker's Sand, dries 2·4m, is marked by 3 PHM lt buoys. East Head SHM, Fl (4) G 10s, marks start of anchorage.

EMSWORTH CHANNEL: Chan is straight, broad, deep and well marked/lit in the 2·5M reach to Emsworth SCM bn, Q (6) + L Fl 15s, where Sweare Deep forks NW to Northney. An unlit ECM bn marks chan to Sparkes Yacht Hbr.

THORNEY CHANNEL: Strangers should go up at half-flood. Ent is at Camber SCM bn, Q (6) + L Fl 15s; pass between Pilsey and Thorney Lt bns, thereafter chan is marked by perches. Above Stanbury Pt chan splits, Prinsted Chan to port (full of moorings) and Nutbourne Chan to stbd; both dry at N ends. There is plenty of room to ⚓ in Thorney Chan, well protected from E and SE winds.

CHICHESTER CHANNEL runs up to Itchenor Reach and Bosham Chan. From NE Sandhead PHM by, Fl R 10s, transit 033° of Roman Transit bn on with Main Chan bn and distant clump of trees leads to Chalkdock Bn, Fl (2) G 10s. A measured half mile is marked by Y perches on the stbd side of Chichester ch running S of Chalkdock. Here alter 082° to Fairway buoy, Fl (3) G 10s; At Deep End SCM bn turn N into Bosham Chan, or ESE into Itchenor Reach, for Birdham Pool and Chichester Marina. ⚓ prohib in Itchenor Reach and Bosham Chan.

LIGHTS AND MARKS Bar Bn, R wooden bn, Fl (2) R 10s 14m 2M; tide gauge. 2ca S at 50°45′·71N 00°56′·48W is West Pole PHM bn, Fl WR 5s 10m 7/5M, vis W321°-081°, R081°-321°.

The E side of the ent chan is marked by W Winner SHM pile, QG, with tide gauge; and by 3 SHM buoys: NW Winner Fl G 10s; N Winner Fl (2) G10s; Mid Winner Fl (3) G 10s. All chans within the hbr are well marked by day. Emsworth & Thorney Chans are partly lit; Bosham Chan is unlit. Itchenor Reach is unlit except for Birdham Pool and CYB entrance bns.

RADIO TELEPHONE *Chichester Hbr Radio* VHF Ch **14** 16 (Apr-Sept: 0830-1700; Sat 0900-1300) or Chichester Hbr Patrol (weekends Apr-Sep). Tarquin Yacht Hbr and Northney Marina Ch **80** M. Chichester Marina Ch 80.

TELEPHONE (Dial code 01243, except Hayling Island 023) Chichester Hbr Office 512301, 📠513026,harbourmaster @conservancy.co.uk, www.conservancy.co.uk (incl current weather at bar); ⊜ 0345 231110 (H24); MRSC (023 92) 552100; Marinecall 09068 500457; Police 536733; Ⓗ 787970.

FACILITIES

EMSWORTH CHANNEL **Emsworth Yacht Hbr** (200+20 Ⓥ) ☎ 377727, 📠 373432, £1.50; access HW±2 over 2·4m sill which maintains 1·5m inside, Slip, Gas, ME, El, AC, Sh, P, D, FW, BH (60 ton), C (20 ton). **Service jetty** (E of Emsworth SC) 50m long, ☆ 2FR (vert); access HW±4. Free for <2 hrs stay, FW. **Slips** at South St, Kings St, and Slipper Mill; contact the Warden ☎ 376422. Ferry £1 to moorings Ch 14 *Emsworth Mobile*. **Services:** ME, Sh, CH, El, ACA; Emsworth EC Wed.

HAYLING ISLAND (023) **Sparkes Yacht Hbr** (150 + 30 Ⓥ) ☎ 9246 3572, mobile 07770 365610, 📠 9246 5741, £1.60, access all tides via chan dredged 2m; pontoons have 1·6m. ME, El, FW, P, D, AC, M, Gas, Gaz, LPG, ⊡, Sh, C (25 ton), CH. From close N of Sandy Pt, appr on transit 277° of two x bns; thence alter S, past 3 PHM bns to marina.

Northney Marina (228+27 Ⓥ) ☎ (023) 9246 6321, 📠 (023) 9246 1467; pre-call Ch 80. Access all tides via chan 1m; £2.10, D, FW, AC, LPG, El, Sh, CH, ME, BH (35 ton), Bar, R; **Services:** Slip, BH (8 ton), P. EC Wed.

THORNEY CHANNEL **Thornham Marina** (77+6 Ⓥ), ☎ 375335, 📠 371522, £0.60 all LOA, appr via drying chan, P & D (cans), FW, Sh, ME, C (10 ton), BH (12 ton), Slip, R, Bar. **Services:** CH, BY.

CHICHESTER CHANNEL/ITCHENOR REACH

Hard available at all stages of the tide. There are berths for approx 40 yachts at Itchenor on both buoys and pontoons. £5.00 per night. **Services:** Slip, P & D (cans), CH, Sh, FW, M, El, ⓔ, ME, showers in hbr office, ♿. Itchenor EC Thurs. Ferry Ch 08 to Bosham and Birdham.

BOSHAM CHANNEL For moorings (200+) contact the Quaymaster ☎ 573336. ⚓ prohib in chan which mostly dries, access HW±2.

Bosham Quay Hard, L, FW, AB; **Services:** SM. EC Wed.

CHICHESTER LAKE **Birdham Pool:** (230+10 Ⓥ) ☎ 512310, 📠 513163, £1.30, enter chan at Birdham SHM bn, Fl (4) G 10s, with depth gauge; access HW ±3 via lock. **Services:** Slip, P, D, FW, El, ⓔ, AC, Sh, CH, Gas, ME, SM, C (3 ton).

Chichester Marina: (1000+50 Ⓥ) ☎ 512731, 📠 513472, £1.90, £0.88 for <4hrs. Enter chan at CM SHM pile, Fl G 5s, with depth gauge; 6kn speed limit. The well marked chan dries 0·5m restricted access LW ±1½ springs; a waiting pontoon is outside the lock.

Traffic sigs:

Q ● (S of tr) = <1m water in chan.

Q ● (top of tr) = both gates open (free flow).

Lock sigs: ● = Wait; ● = Enter.

Yachts lock out in numerical sequence, as assigned by lock-keeper on Ch 80, except during free-flow. The lock is manned 24H 365 days a year: Contact ☎ 512731 or call VHF Ch 80. **Services:** Slip, P, D, FW, ME, El, Sh, AC, Gas, Gaz, LPG, CH, BY, BH (20 ton), V, R, Bar, ⊡, ACA, SM, ♿.

FISHBOURNE CHANNEL **Dell Quay:** Possible drying berth against the Quay, apply to Hbr Office, public slip. **Services:** Sh, Slip, BH, M, L.

YACHT CLUBS

Bosham SC ☎ 572341; **Chichester YC** ☎ 512918, R, Bar, ⊡; **Chichester Cruiser and Racing Club** ☎ 371731; **Dell Quay SC** ☎ 785080; **Emsworth SC** ☎ 373065; **Emsworth Slipper SC** ☎ 372523; **Hayling Island SC** ☎ (023) 9246 3768; **Itchenor SC** ☎ 512400; **Mengham Rithe SC** ☎ (023) 9246 3337; **Thorney Island SC; W Wittering SC.**

Cobnor Activities Centre Trust (at Cobnor Pt) gets many young people, inc disabled ♿, afloat. ☎ 01243 572791.

NAVAL EXERCISE AREAS (SUBFACTS & GUNFACTS) *9.2.33*

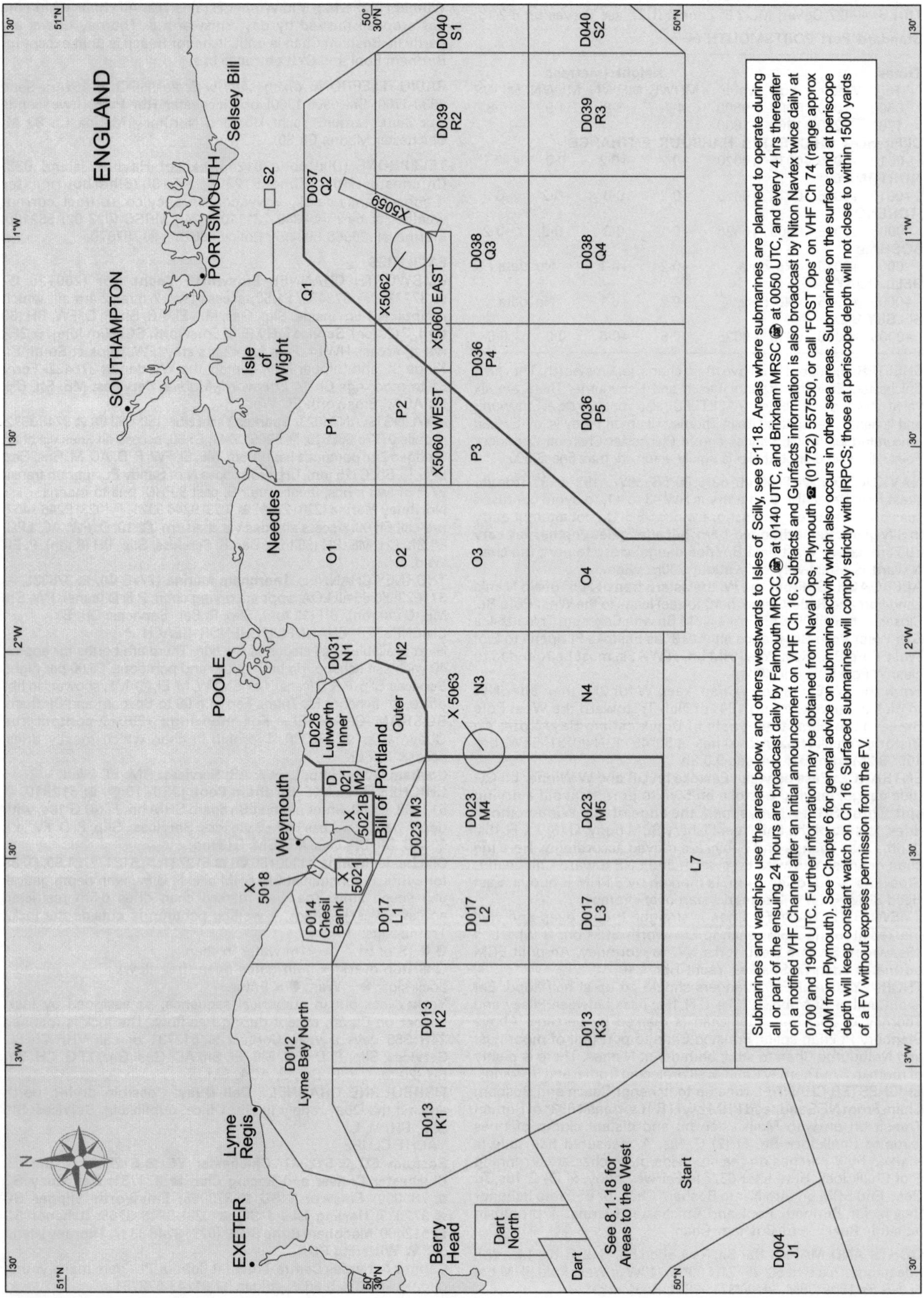

ENGLAND
EXETER
Lyme Regis
Berry Head
Weymouth
POOLE
SOUTHAMPTON
PORTSMOUTH
Selsey Bill
Isle of Wight
Needles
Bill of Portland
Dart
Dart North
See 8.1.18 for Areas to the West
Start
D004 J1
D013 K1
D013 K2
D013 K3
D012 Lyme Bay North
D014 Chesil Bank
X 5018
X 5021
X 5021B
D 021 M2
D017 L1
D017 L2
D017 L3
L7
D023 M3
D023 M4
D023 M5
D026 Lulworth Inner
Outer
X 5063
D031 N1
N2
N3
N4
O1
O2
O3
O4
P1
P2
P3
D036 P4
D036 P5
X5060 WEST
X5060 EAST
X5062
Q1
D037 Q2
D038 Q3
D038 Q4
X5059
S2
D039 R2
D039 R3
D040 S1
D040 S2
51°N
50° 30'N
50°N
3°W
2°W
1°W
30'
Submarines and warships use the areas below, and others westwards to Isles of Scilly, see 9·1·18. Areas where submarines are planned to operate during all or part of the ensuing 24 hours are broadcast daily by Falmouth MRCC at 0140 UTC, and Brixham MRCC at 0050 UTC, and every 4 hrs thereafter on a notified VHF Channel after an initial announcement on VHF Ch 16. Subfacts and Gunfacts information is also broadcast by Niton Navtex twice daily at 0700 and 1900 UTC. Further information may be obtained from Naval Ops, Plymouth ☎ (01752) 557550, or call 'FOST Ops' on VHF Ch 74 (range approx 40M from Plymouth). See Chapter 6 for general advice on submarine activity which also occurs in other sea areas. Submarines on the surface and at periscope depth will keep constant watch on Ch 16. Surfaced submarines will comply strictly with IRPCS; those at periscope depth will not close to within 1500 yards of a FV without express permission from the FV.

MAPTECH®

Leading the world in digital navigation

Maptech UK Ltd • +44 (0)1243 389352 • sales@maptech.co.uk

Sales and distribution centres in Area 3

West Sussex: ***Cruisemart Express***, 01243 773788, Donnington Park, Birdham Road, Chichester PO20 7DU.
East Sussex: ***Russell Simpson Marine (Brighton)***, 01273 681543, The Village Square, Brighton Marina, Brighton BN2 5UF.
Russell Simpson Marine (Newhaven), 01273 612612, Yacht Harbour, Newhaven BN9 9BY. ***Russell Simpson (Eastbourne)***, 01323 470213, The Chandlery, Sovereign Harbour, Eastbourne BN23 6JH.

www.maptech.co.uk

Area 3

South-East England

Selsey Bill to North Foreland

9.3.1	Index	Page 321
9.3.2	Area map	322
9.3.3	Tidal stream charts	324
9.3.4	Lights, buoys & waypoints	326
9.3.5	Passage information	328
9.3.6	Distance table	329
9.3.7	Littlehampton	330
9.3.8	Shoreham, Standard Port, tidal curves	331
9.3.9	Brighton	335
9.3.10	Newhaven	336
9.3.11	Eastbourne Hastings	336
9.3.12	Rye Hastings Lydd firing Ranges Hythe Firing Ranges	337
9.3.13	Folkestone	338
9.3.14	Dover, Standard Port, tidal curves Deal	338
9.3.15	Dover Strait diagram	343
9.3.16	Ramsgate Sandwich	344

Register for your FREE weekly weather email service from Macmillan Reeds
» at www.nauticaldata.com – NOW! «
weekend weather reports sent to your email address, every Thursday

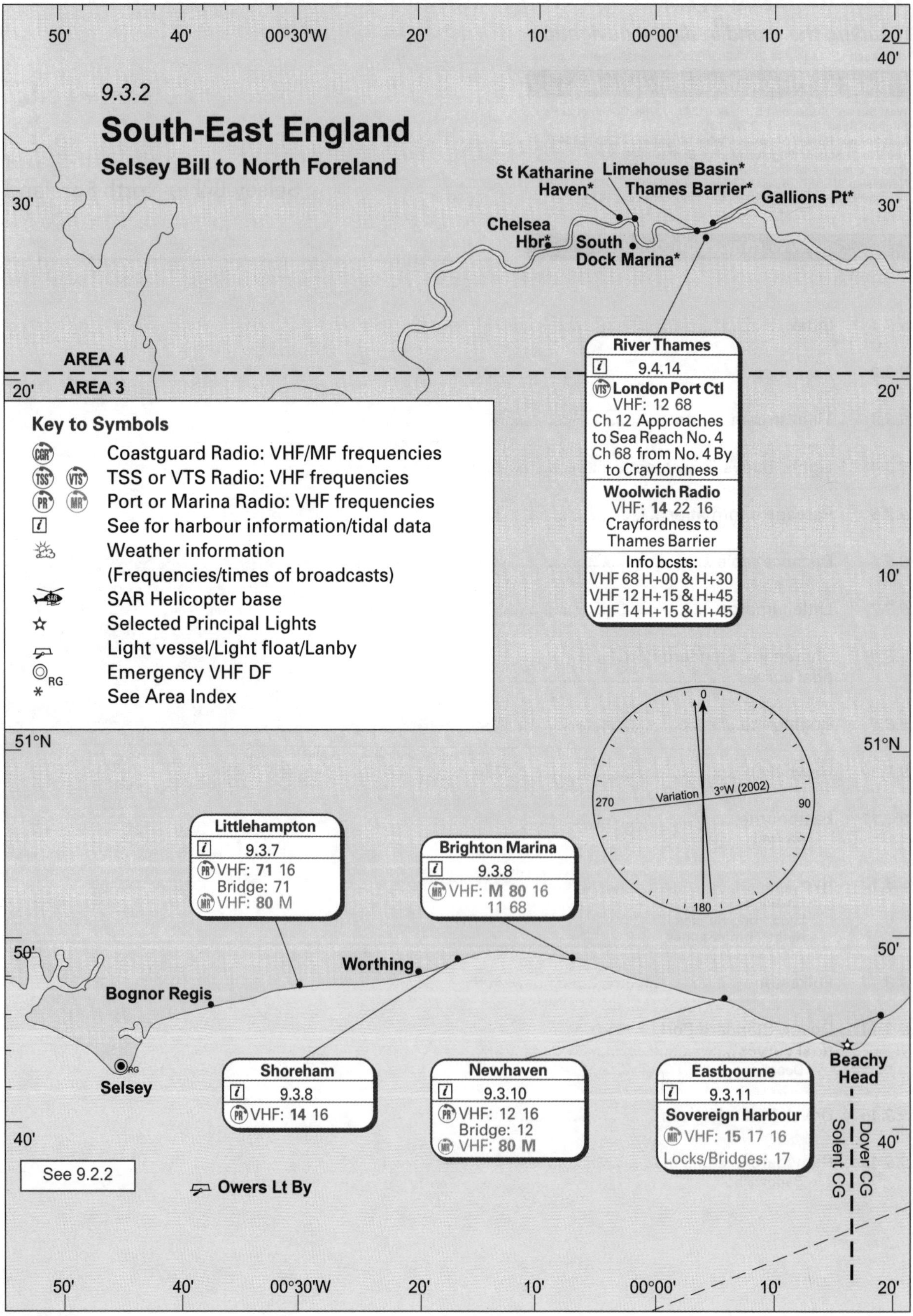

50'
40'
00°30'W
20'
10'
00°00'
10'
20'
40'
9.3.2
South-East England
Selsey Bill to North Foreland
St Katharine Haven*
Limehouse Basin*
Thames Barrier*
Gallions Pt*
Chelsea Hbr*
South Dock Marina*
30'
AREA 4
AREA 3
20'
River Thames
9.4.14
London Port Ctl
VHF: 12 68
Ch 12 Approaches to Sea Reach No. 4
Ch 68 from No. 4 By to Crayfordness
Woolwich Radio
VHF: 14 22 16
Crayfordness to Thames Barrier
Info bcsts:
VHF 68 H+00 & H+30
VHF 12 H+15 & H+45
VHF 14 H+15 & H+45
Key to Symbols
Coastguard Radio: VHF/MF frequencies
TSS or VTS Radio: VHF frequencies
Port or Marina Radio: VHF frequencies
See for harbour information/tidal data
Weather information
(Frequencies/times of broadcasts)
SAR Helicopter base
Selected Principal Lights
Light vessel/Light float/Lanby
Emergency VHF DF
See Area Index
10'
51°N
0
270
Variation
3°W (2002)
90
180
Littlehampton
9.3.7
VHF: 71 16
Bridge: 71
VHF: 80 M
Brighton Marina
9.3.8
VHF: M 80 16
11 68
Worthing
Bognor Regis
50'
Selsey
Shoreham
9.3.8
VHF: 14 16
Newhaven
9.3.10
VHF: 12 16
Bridge: 12
VHF: 80 M
Eastbourne
9.3.11
Sovereign Harbour
VHF: 15 17 16
Locks/Bridges: 17
Beachy Head
Solent CG
Dover CG
40'
See 9.2.2
Owers Lt By
50'
40'
00°30'W
20'
10'
00°00'
10'
20'

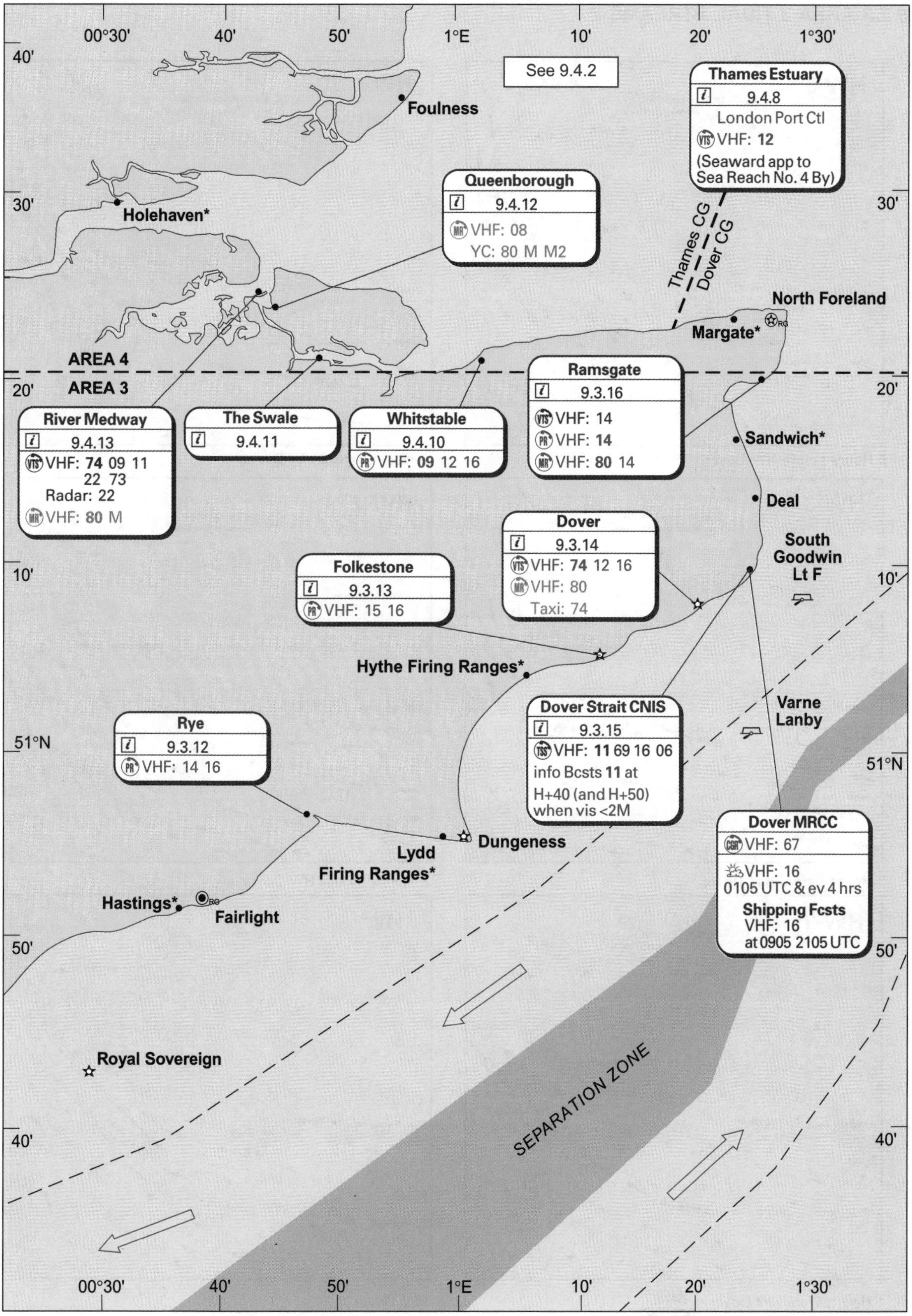
00°30'
40'
50'
1°E
10'
20'
1°30'
40'
30'
20'
10'
51°N
50'
40'
See 9.4.2
Foulness
Thames Estuary
9.4.8
London Port Ctl
VHF: 12
(Seaward app to Sea Reach No. 4 By)
Holehaven*
Queenborough
9.4.12
VHF: 08
YC: 80 M M2
Thames CG
Dover CG
North Foreland
Margate*
AREA 4
AREA 3
Ramsgate
9.3.16
VHF: 14
VHF: 14
VHF: 80 14
River Medway
9.4.13
VHF: 74 09 11 22 73
Radar: 22
VHF: 80 M
The Swale
9.4.11
Whitstable
9.4.10
VHF: 09 12 16
Sandwich*
Deal
Dover
9.3.14
VHF: 74 12 16
VHF: 80
Taxi: 74
South Goodwin Lt F
Folkestone
9.3.13
VHF: 15 16
Hythe Firing Ranges*
Dover Strait CNIS
9.3.15
VHF: 11 69 16 06
info Bcsts 11 at
H+40 (and H+50)
when vis <2M
Varne Lanby
Rye
9.3.12
VHF: 14 16
Dungeness
Lydd Firing Ranges*
Dover MRCC
VHF: 67
VHF: 16
0105 UTC & ev 4 hrs
Shipping Fcsts
VHF: 16
at 0905 2105 UTC
Hastings*
Fairlight
Royal Sovereign
SEPARATION ZONE

9.3.3 AREA 3 TIDAL STREAMS

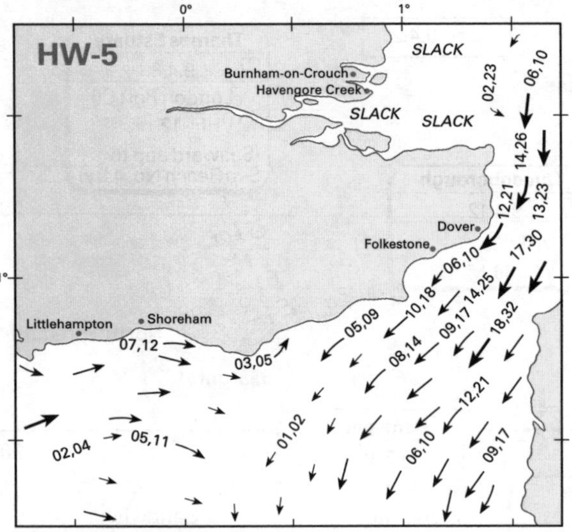

5 Hours before HW Dover

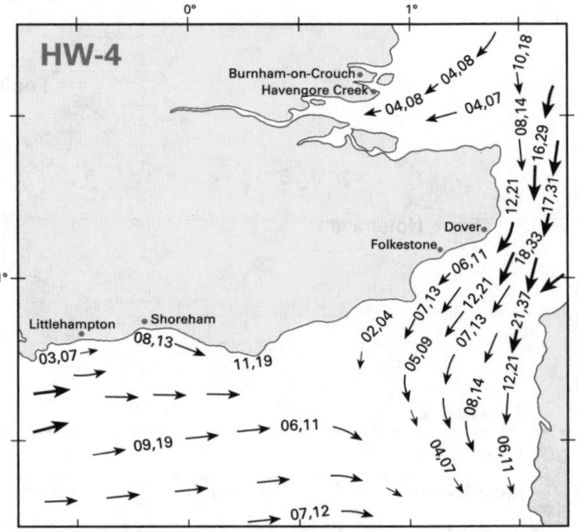

4 Hours before HW Dover

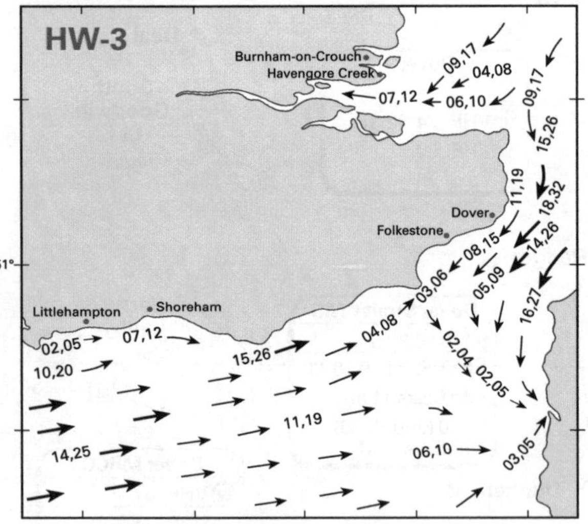

3 Hours before HW Dover

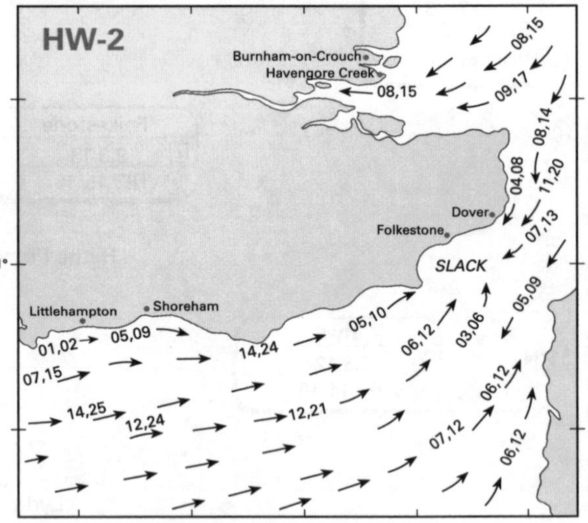

2 Hours before HW Dover

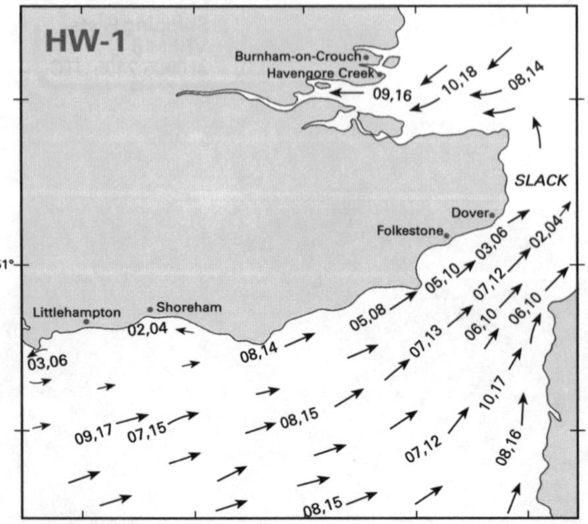

1 Hour before HW Dover

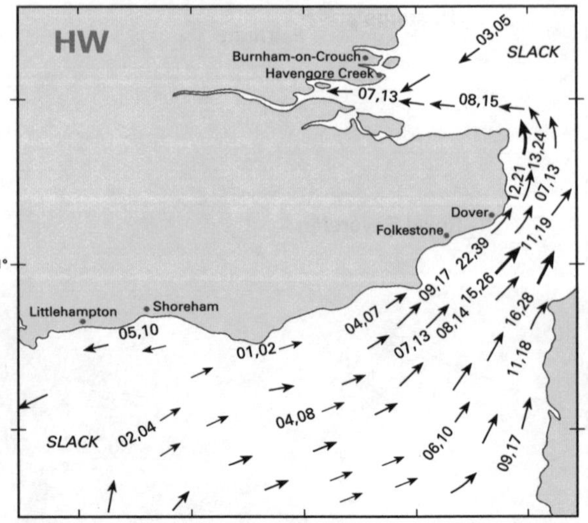

HW Dover

Westward 9.2.3 Southward 9.16.3 Northward 9.4.3 Thames Estuary 9.4.9 Eastward 9.20.3

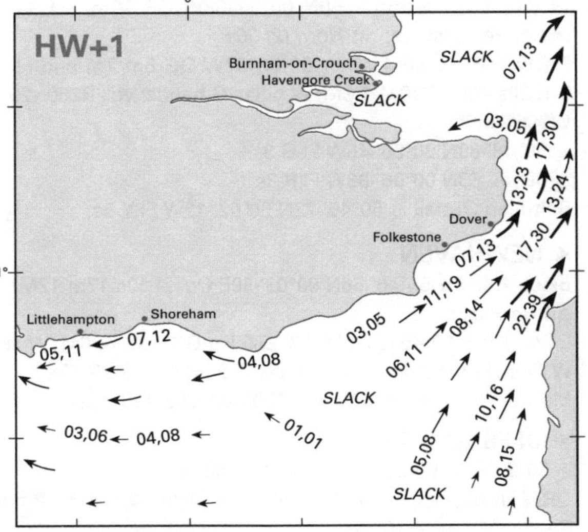

1 Hour after HW Dover

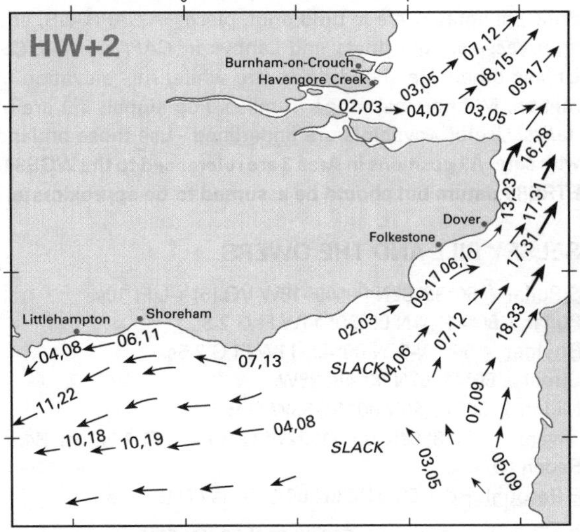

2 Hours after HW Dover

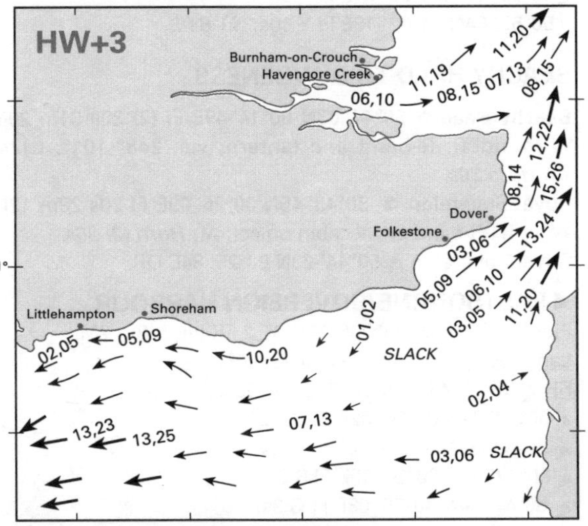

3 Hours after HW Dover

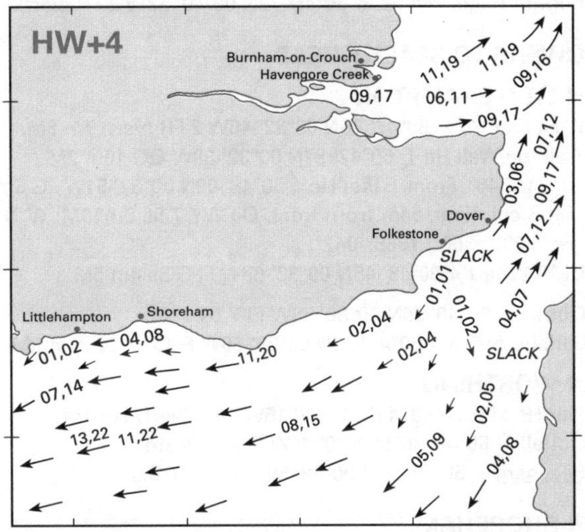

4 Hours after HW Dover

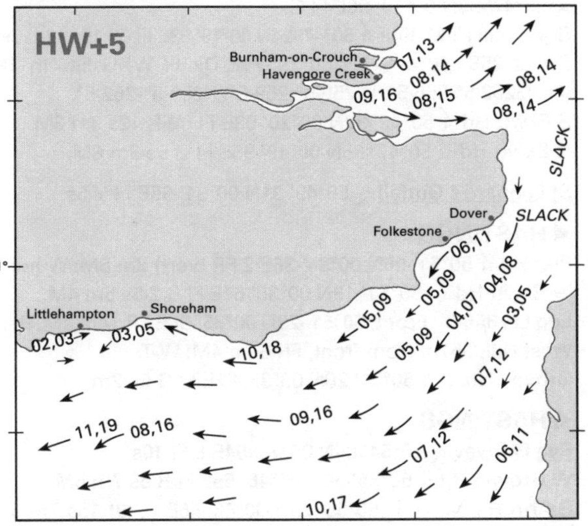

5 Hours after HW Dover

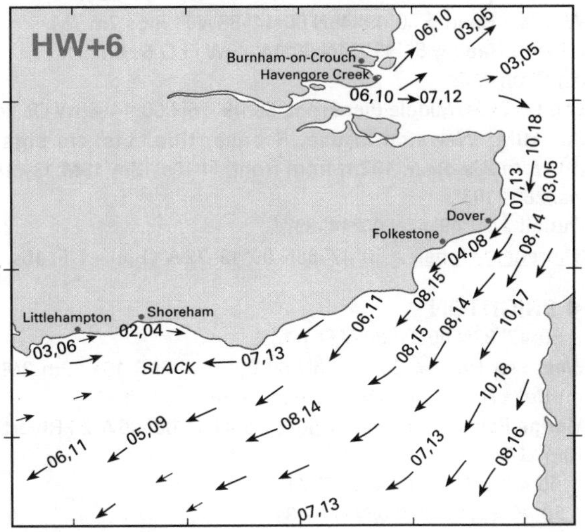

6 Hours after HW Dover

3

9.3.4 LIGHTS, BUOYS AND WAYPOINTS

Abbreviations used below are given in the Introduction. Principal lights ☆ are in **bold** print, places in CAPITALS, and light-vessels, light floats and Lanbys in *CAPITAL ITALICS*. Unless otherwise stated lights are white. m - elevation in metres; M - nominal range in miles. Fog signals are in *italics*. Useful waypoints are underlined - use those on land with care. **All positions in Area 3 are referenced to the WGS84/ ETRS89 datum but should be assumed to be approximate.**

SELSEY BILL AND THE OWERS

S Pullar 50°38'·82N 00°49'·18W VQ (6) + L Fl 10s.
Pullar 50°41'·47N 00°50'·11W Fl G 2·5s.
Boulder 50°41'·55N 00°49'·11W Fl G 2·5s.
Street 50°41'·67N 00°48'·88W.
Mixon 50°42'·36N 00°46'·33W Fl R 5s.
Owers 50°38'·63N 00°41'·22W Q (6) + L Fl 15s; *Whis*; Racon (O).
E Borough Hd 50°41'·52N 00°39'·11W Q (3) 10s.

Bognor Regis Outfall 50°45'·21N 00°41'·65W.
Bognor Regis Pier Hd ☆ 50°46'·72N 00°40'·53W 2 FR (vert).

OWERS TO BEACHY HEAD

◀ LITTLEHAMPTON

West Pier Hd 50°47'·88N 00°32'·46W 2 FR (vert) 7m 6M.
Training Wall Hd 50°47'·87N 00°32'·38W QG 10m 2M.
Ldg Lts 346°. Front, E Pier Hd ☆ 50°48'·09N 00°32'·51W FG 6m 7M; B col. Rear, 64m from front, Oc WY 7·5s 9m10M; W Tr; vis: W290°-356°, Y356°-042°.
UMA Wharf ☆ 50°48'·45N 00°32'·68W Fl G 3s 4m 5M.

Outfall 50°46'·26N 00°30'·55W Fl Y 5s.
Littlehampton ☆ 50°46'·26N 00°29'·55W Fl (5) Y 20s 9m 5M.

◀ WORTHING

Pier Head ☆ 50°48'·41N 00°22'·15W 2 FR (vert) 6m 1M.
Outfall 50°48'·36N 00°20'·31W Fl R 2·5s 3m.
Beecham 50°48'·45N 00°19'·50W Fl (2) R 10s.

◀ SHOREHAM

Express 50°47'·28N 00°17'·09W Fl Y 5s; (Apr-Oct).
W Bkwtr Head ☆ 50°49'·49N 00°14'·88W Fl R 5s 7m 7M.
E Bkwtr Head ☆ 50°49'·54N 00°14'·80W Fl G 5s 8M; *Siren 120s*.
Ldg Lts 355°. Middle Pier Front, 50°49'·75N 00°14'·88W Oc 5s 8m 10M; W watch-house, R base; tidal Lts, tfc sigs; *Horn 20s*. **Rear**, 192m from front, Fl 10s 13m **15M**; Gy Tr vis: 283°-103°.
Outfall 50°49'·47N 00°14'·39W.
Shoreham Outfall 50°47'·88N 00°13'·72W Q (6) + L Fl 15s.

◀ BRIGHTON

50°47'·83N 00°11'·30W Fl Y 10s.
West Pier Head ☆ 50°49'·15N 00°09'·15W Fl R 10s 13m 2M; *Bell (1) 13s* (when vessel expected).
Marine Palace Pier Head ☆ 50°48'·90N 00°08'·25W 2 FR(vert) 10m 2M.
50°47'·67N 00°08'·44W Fl Y 6s.
50°46'·62N 00°07'·08W Fl Y 3s.
50°46'·64N 00°04'·83W Fl Y 2s.

◀ BRIGHTON MARINA

Black Rk Ledge 50°47'·66N 00°08'·44W Fl Y 4s.
W Bkwtr Hd ☆ 50°48'·50N 00°06'·38W QR 10m 7M; W ○ structure, R bands; *Horn (2) 30s*.
E Bkwtr Hd ☆ 50°48'·47N 00°06'·37W QG 8m 7M and Fl (4) WR 20s 16m W10M, R8M; W pillar, G bands; vis: R260°-295°, W295°-100°.
50°48'·60N 00°06'·45W Fl G 3s.
50°48'·63N 00°06'·35W Fl R 3s.
Saltdean Outfall 50°46'·72N 00°02'·12W Fl Y 5s.

◀ NEWHAVEN

Bkwtr Head ☆ 50°46'·56N 00°03'·50E Oc (2) 10s 17m 12M; *Horn 30s*.
E Pier Hd ☆ 50°46'·81N 00°03'·58E Iso G 10s 12m 6M; W Tr.
W Pier Hd ☆ 50°46'·92N 00°03'·43E 2 FR (vert); SS Tfc.
Marina Ent S end ☆ 50°47'·20N 00°03'·25E 2 FR (vert).

◀ OFFSHORE MARKS

50°33'·69N 00°03'·92W Fl Y 2·5s; *Whis*.
GREENWICH 50°24'·54N 00°00'·10 Fl 5s 12m **21M**; R hull; Racon (M); *Horn 30s*.
50°39'·12N 00°32'·61E Fl Y 5s.
50°52'·04N 01°02'·18E Fl Y 10s; *Bell*.

BEACHY HEAD TO DUNGENESS

Beachy Head ☆ 50°44'·03N 00°14'·49E Fl (2) 20s 31m **20M**; W round Tr, R band and lantern; vis: 248°-101°; (H24); *Horn 30s*.
Royal Sovereign ☆ 50°43'·45N 00°26'·09E Fl 20s 28m 12M; W ○ Tr, R band on W cabin on col; *Horn (2) 30s*.
Royal Sovereign 50°44'·23N 00°25'·84E QR.

◀ EASTBOURNE/SOVEREIGN HARBOUR

Pier Hd ☆ 50°45'·95N 00°17'·73E 2 FR (vert) 8m 2M.
Langney Pt 50°46'·74N 00°19'·90E.
SH 50°47'·41N 00°20'·72E L Fl 10s.
50°47'·37N 00°20'·32E Fl G 5s.
50°47'·36N 00°20'·20E Fl G 3s.
50°47'·33N 00°20'·15E Fl R 5s.
50°47'·34N 00°20'·08E Fl G 3s.
50°47'·32N 00°20'·03E Fl R.
50°47'·33N 00°19'·96E Fl G.
Sovereign Hr Marina ☆ 50°47'·24N 00°19'·83E Fl (3) 15s 12m 7M.
Dir Lt 258° 50°47'·28N 00°19'·71E Dir Fl WRG 5s 4m 1M; vis: G252·5°-256·5°, W256·5°-259·5°, R259·5°-262·5°.
S Bkwtr Hd ☆ 50°47'·30N 00°20'·03E Fl (4) R 12s 3m 6M.
N Bkwtr Hd ☆ 50°47'·35N 00°19'·95E Fl G 5s 3m 6M.

St Leonard's Outfall 50°49'·31N 00°31'·95E Fl Y 5s.

◀ HASTINGS

Pier Hd ☆ 50°51'·06N 00°34'·36E 2 FR (vert) 8m 5M; W hut.
W Bkwtr Hd ☆ 50°51'·19N 00°35'·61E Fl R 2·5s 5m 4M.
Ldg Lts 356·3°. Front, 50°51'·29N 00°35'·38E FR 14m 4M. Rear, West Hill, 357m from front, FR 55m 4M; W Tr.
Groyne No. 3 ☆ 50°51'·28N 00°35'·82E Fl G 5s 2m.

◀ HASTINGS

Rye Fairway 50°54'·04N 00°48'·04E L Fl 10s.
W Groyne Hd ☆ 50°55'·58N 00°46'·55E Fl R 5s 7m 6M.
E Arm Hd No. 1 50°55'·73N 00°46'·46E Q (9) 15s 7m 5M; G △; *Horn 7s*.

E Bank No. 3 50°55'·92N 00°46'·29E QG 3m 2M.
E Bank No. 11 50°56'·27N 00°45'·94E Oc WG 4s 3m W7M, G6M; vis: W326°-331°, G331°-326°; Tfc sigs.

Dungeness Outfall 50°54'·45N 00°58'·21E Q (6) + L Fl 15s.
Dungeness ☆ 50°54'·81N 00°58'·56E Fl 10s 40m **21M**; B ○ Tr, W bands and lantern, floodlit; Part obsc 078°-shore; (H24). F RG 37m 10M (same Tr); vis: R057°-073°, G073°-078°, R196°-216°; *Horn (3) 60s.*
FR Lts shown between 2·4M and 5·2M WNW when firing taking place. QR on radio mast 1·2M NW.

DUNGENESS TO NORTH FORELAND

◀ OFFSHORE MARKS

Bullock Bank 50°46'·94N 01°07'·60E VQ; *Whis.*
Ridens SE 50°43'·47N 01°18'·87E VQ (3) 5s.
Colbart SW 50°48'·87N 01°16'·31E VQ (6) + L Fl 10s; *Whis.*
South Varne 50°55'·63N 01°17'·27E Q (6) + L Fl 15s; *Whis.*
Mid Varne 50°58'·94N 01°19'·88E QG.
East Varne 50°58'·22N 01°20'·87E Fl R 2·5s.
Colbart N 50°57'·47N 01°23'·30E VQ.
VARNE 51°01'·29N 01°23'·90E Fl R 20s12m **19M**; Racon (T); *Horn 30s.*
CS 4 51°08'·60N 01°33'·94E Fl (4) Y 15s; *Whis.*
CS 5 51°23'·02N 01°49'·90E Fl Y 2.5s.
MPC 51°06'·13N 01°38'·25E Fl Y 2·5s; Racon (O).

◀ FOLKESTONE

Hythe Flats Outfall 51°02'·52N 01°05'·32E Fl Y 5s.
Breakwater Head 51°04'·56N 01°11'·69E Fl (2) 10s 14m **22M**; *Dia (4) 60s.* In fog Fl 2s; vis: 246°-306°, intens 271·5°-280·5°.
Outer Hbr E Pier Hd 51°04'·76N 01°11'·38E QG 16m 1M.
Shakespeare Cliff W end 51°06'·08N 01°16'·01E Fl R 5s.
Shakespeare Cliff E end 51°06'·31N 01°16'·85E Fl R 5s.

◀ DOVER

Admiralty Pier Extension Head 51°06'·69N 01°19'·66E Fl 7·5s 21m **20M**; W Tr; vis: 096°-090°, obsc in The Downs by S Foreland inshore of 226°; *Horn 10s;* Int Port Tfc sigs.
S Bkwtr W Hd ☆ 51°06'·78N 01°19'·80E Oc R 30s 21m **18M**; W Tr.
Dunkirk Jetty Head 51°06'·88N 01°18'·98E QR 7m.
Dolphin Jetty Head 51°07'·05N 01°18'·71E QG 3m 2M.
Crosswall Quay (Ent to Dover Marina) 51°07'·08N 01°18'·65E F WR: vis: R283°-323°, W324°-333°; H24.
Knuckle ☆ 51°07'·04N 01°20'·49E Fl (4) WR 10s 15m **W15M**, R13M; W Tr; vis: R059°-239°, W239°-059°.
N Head 51°07'·20N 01°20'·61E Fl R 2·5s 11m 5M.
Eastern Arm Hd 51°07'·31N 01°20'·59E Fl G 5s 12m 5M; *Horn (2) 30s*; Int port tfc sigs.
S GOODWIN 51°07'·97N 01°28'·49E Fl (2) 20s 12m **15M**; R hull; *Horn (2) 60s.*
SW Goodwin 51°08'·58N 01°28'·68E Q (6) + L Fl 15s.
S Goodwin 51°10'·58N 01°32'·26E Fl (4) R 15s.
SE Goodwin 51°12'·97N 01°34'·44E Fl (3) R 10s.
E GOODWIN 51°13'·25N 01°36'·38E Fl 15s 12m **23M**; R hull with Lt Tr amidships; Racon (T); *Horn 30s.*
E Goodwin 51°15'·67N 01°35'·69E Q (3) 10s.
NE Goodwin 51°20'·30N 01°34'·18E Q (3) 10s; Racon (M).

◀ DEAL

Pier Hd 51°13'·42N 01°24'·54E 2 FR (vert) 7m 5M.
Sandown Outfall 51°14'·49N 01°24'·45E Fl R 2·5s; Ra refl.

◀ THE DOWNS

Deal Bank 51°12'·92N 01°25'·57E; QR.
Goodwin Fork 51°14'·33N 01°26'·84E Q (6) + L Fl 15s; *Bell.*
Downs 51°14'·50N 01°26'·22E Fl (2) R 5s; *Bell.*

◀ GULL STREAM

W Goodwin 51°15'·60N 01°27'·36E Fl G 5s.
S Brake 51°15'·77N 01°26'·82E Fl (3) R 10s.
NW Goodwin 51°16'·56N 01°28'·56E Q (9) 15s; *Bell.*
Brake 51°16'·98N 01°28'·19E Fl (4) R 15s; *Bell.*
N Goodwin 51°17'·90N 01°30'·20E Fl G 2·5s.
Gull Stream 51°18'·26N 01°29'·69E QR.
Gull 51°19'·57N 01°31'·30E VQ (3) 5s.
Goodwin Knoll 51°19'·57N 01°32'·20E Fl (2) G 5s.

◀ RAMSGATE CHANNEL

B2 51°18'·03N 01°24'·00E.
W Quern 51°18'·98N 01°25'·39E Q (9) 15s.

◀ RIVER STOUR/SANDWICH

Channel marked by small lateral buoys and beacons which are moved to meet changes in channel.

◀ RAMSGATE

RA 51°19'·60N 01°30'·13E Q(6) + L Fl 15s.
E Brake 51°19'·47N 01°29'·20E Fl R 5s.
No. 1 51°19'·56N 01°27'·29E QG.
No. 2 51°19'·46N 01°27'·28E Fl (4) R 10s.
No. 3 51°19'·56N 01°26'·61E Fl G 2·5s.
No. 4 51°19'·46N 01°26'·60E QR.
No. 5 51°19'·56N 01°25'·91E Q (6) + L Fl 15s.
No. 6 51°19'·46N 01°25'·91E Fl (2) R 5s.
N Quern 51°19'·41N 01°26'·11E Q.
South Bkwtr Hd 51°19'·46N 01°25'·41E VQ R 10m 5M; R pillar.
N Bkwtr Hd 51°19'·56N 01°25'·47E QG 10m 5M; G pillar.
Western Marine terminal Dir Lt 270°, 51°19'·51N 01°24'·85E Dir Oc WRG 10s 10m 5M; B △, Or stripe; vis: G259°-269°, W269°-271°, R271°-281°. Rear 493m from front Oc 5s 17m 5M; B ▽, Or stripe; vis: 263°-278°.

◀ BROADSTAIRS

Broadstairs Knoll 51°20'·88N 01°29'·48E Fl R 2·5s.
Pier SE End 51°21'·50N 01°26'·74E 2 FR (vert) 7m 4M.
Elbow 51°23'·23N 01°31'·59E Q.

North Foreland ☆ 51°22'·49N 01°26'·70E Fl (5) WR 20s 57m **W19M, R16M, R15M**; W 8-sided Tr; vis: Wshore-150°, R(**16M**)150°-181°, R(**15M**) 181°-200°, W200°-011°; H24.

◀ OFFSHORE MARKS

F1 51°11'·21N 01°44'·91E Fl (4) Y 15s.
South Falls 51°13'·84N 00°43'·93E Q (6) + L Fl 15s; *Bell.*
Mid Falls 51°18'·63N 01°47'·00E Fl (3) R 10s; *Bell.*
Inter Bank 51°16'·47N 01°52'·23E Fl Y 5s; *Bell;* Racon (M).
F2 51°20'·41N 01°56'·19E Fl (4) Y 15s; *Bell.*

9.3.5 PASSAGE INFORMATION

Reference books include: Admiralty *Channel Pilot*; *Shell Channel Pilot* (Imray/Cunliffe); and *South Coast Cruising* (YM/Fishwick). See 9.0.6 for cross-Channel distances. An Admiralty Small Craft Folio SC 5605, 11 A2 charts, price £35.00 covers Chichester to Ramsgate.

THE EASTERN CHANNEL This area embraces the greatest concentration of commercial shipping in the world. In such waters the greatest danger to a small yacht is being run down by a larger vessel, especially in poor visibility. In addition to the many ships plying up and down the traffic lanes, there are fast ferries, hovercraft and hydrofoils passing to and fro between English and Continental harbours; warships and submarines on exercises; fishing vessels operating both inshore and offshore; many other yachts; and static dangers such as lobster pots and fishing nets which are concentrated in certain places.

Even for coastal cruising it is essential to know about the TSS and ITZ; eg, note that the SW-bound TSS lane from the Dover Strait passes only 4M off Dungeness. Radar surveillance of the Dover Strait (9.3.15) is maintained at all times by the Channel Navigation Information Service (CNIS).

In this area the weather has a big effect on tidal streams, and on the range of tides. The rates of tidal streams vary with the locality, and are greatest in the narrower parts of the Channel and off major headlands. In the Dover Strait sp rates can reach 4kn, but elsewhere in open water they seldom exceed 2kn. Also N winds, which give smooth water and pleasant sailing off the shores of England, can cause rough seas on the French coast; and vice versa. With strong S'lies the English coast between Isle of Wight and Dover is very exposed, and shelter is hard to find. The Dover Strait has a funnelling effect and in strong winds can become very rough.

SELSEY BILL AND THE OWERS (chart *1652*) Selsey Bill is a low headland, off which lie the Owers, groups of rks and shoals extending 3M to the S, and 5M to the SE. Just W and SW of the Bill, The Streets (awash) extend 1·25M seaward. 1·25M SSW of the Bill are The Grounds (or Malt Owers) and The Dries (dry). 1M E of The Dries, and about 1·25M S of the lifeboat house on E side of Selsey Bill is The Mixon a group of rks marked by bn at E end.

Immediately S of the above dangers is the Looe Chan, which runs E/W about 7½ca S of Mixon bn. It is marked by buoys at W end, where it is narrowest between Brake (or Cross) Ledge on N side and Boulder Bank to the S. In daylight, good visibility and moderate weather, the Looe Chan is an easy and useful short cut. The E-going stream begins at HW Portsmouth + 0430, and the W-going at HW Portsmouth – 0135, sp rates 2·5 kn. Beware lobster pots in this area.

In poor visibility or in bad weather (and always in darkness) keep S of the Owers SCM lt buoy, 7M SE of Selsey Bill, marking SE end of Owers. Over much of the Owers there is less than 3m, and large parts virtually dry; so a combination of tidal stream and strong wind produces heavy breaking seas and overfalls over a large area.

OWERS TO BEACHY HEAD (chart *1652*) The coast from Selsey Bill to Brighton is low, faced by a shingle beach, and with few offlying dangers, Bognor Rks (dry in places) extend 1·75M E from a point 1M W of the pier, and Bognor Spit extends E and S from the end of them. Middleton ledge are rks running 8ca offshore, about 1·5M E of Bognor pier, with depths of less than 1m. Shelley Rks lie 5ca S of Middleton ledge, with depths of less than 1m.

Winter Knoll, about 2·5M SSW of Littlehampton (9.3.7) has depths of 2·1m. Kingston Rks, depth 2m, lie about 3·25M ESE of Littlehampton. An unlit outfall bn is 3ca off Goring-on-sea (2M W of Worthing pier). Grass Banks, an extensive shoal with 2m depth at W end, lie about 1M S of Worthing pier. Elbow shoal, with depth of 3·1m, lies E of Grass Banks.

Off Shoreham (9.3.8) Church Rks, with depth of 0·3m, lie 1·5M W of the hbr ent and 2½ca offshore. Jenny Rks, with depth 0·9m, are 1·25M E of the ent, 3ca offshore.

At Brighton (9.3.9) the S Downs form the coastline, and high chalk cliffs are conspic from here to Beachy Head. There are no dangers more than 3ca offshore, until Birling Gap, where a rky ledge begins, on which is built Beachy Head lt ho (fog sig). Head Ledge (dries) extends about 4ca S. 2M S of Beachy Hd the W-going stream begins at HW Dover + 0030, and the E-going at HW Dover – 0520, sp rates 2·25kn. In bad weather there are overfalls off the Head, which should then be given a berth of 2M.

BEACHY HEAD TO DUNGENESS (chart *536*) Royal Sovereign lt tr (fog sig) is 7·4M E of Beachy Head. The extensive Royal Sovereign shoals lie from 3M NW of the tr to 1·5M N of it, and have a minimum depth of 3·5m. There are strong eddies over the shoals at sp, and the sea breaks on them in bad weather.

On the direct course from Royal Sovereign lt tr to clear Dungeness there are no dangers. Along the coast in Pevensey B and Rye B there are drying rky ledges or shoals extending 5ca offshore in places. These include Boulder Bank near Wish tr, S of Eastbourne (9.3.11); Oyster Reef off Cooden; Bexhill Reef off Bexhill-on-Sea; Bopeep Rks off St Leonards; and the shoals at the mouth of R Rother, at entrance to Rye (9.3.12). There are also banks 2-3M offshore, on which the sea builds in bad weather. Avoid the firing range danger area between Rye and Dungeness (lt, fog sig, RC). The nuclear power station is conspic at SE extremity of the low-lying spit. The Pt is steep-to on SE side. Good anch close NE of Dungeness.

DUNGENESS TO NORTH FORELAND (charts *1892, 1828*) From Dungeness to Folkestone (9.3.13) the coast forms a bay. Beware Roar bank, depth 2·7m, E of New Romney: otherwise there are no offlying dangers, apart from Hythe firing range. Good anch off Sandgate in offshore winds. Off Folkestone the E-going stream starts at HW Dover – 0155, sp rate 2kn; the W-going at HW Dover + 0320, sp rate 1·5kn.

Passing Dover (9.3.14) and S Foreland keep 1M offshore. Do not pass too close to Dover, because ferries/jetfoils leave at speed, and there can be considerable backwash and lumpy seas off the breakwaters. 8M S of Dover in the TSS is the Varne, a shoal 7M long with least depth 3·3m and heavy seas in bad weather, marked by Lanby and 3 buoys. Between S and N Foreland the N-going stream begins at about HW Dover – 0150, and the S-going at about HW Dover + 0415.

The Goodwin Sands are drying, shifting shoals, extending about 10M from S to N, and 5M from W to E at their widest part. The E side is relatively steep-to; large areas dry up to 2·7m. The sands are well marked by lt Fs and buoys. Kellett Gut is an unmarked chan about 5ca wide, running SW/NE through the middle of the sands, but it is not regularly surveyed and is liable to change. The Gull Stream (buoyed) leads from The Downs, inside Goodwin Sands and outside Brake Sands to the S of Ramsgate (9.3.16). The Ramsgate chan leads inside the Brake Sands and Cross Ledge.

CROSS-CHANNEL PASSAGES This section applies broadly to any crossing, ranging from the short (4-5hrs) Dover Strait route, through the much used, medium length Solent-Cherbourg route (13hrs; see 9.15.5), to the longer passages (20+hrs) from

SW England to North Brittany. Distances are tabulated at 9.0.6. Whatever the length of passage, thorough planning is the key to a safe and efficient crossing. Maximum experience of crossing the Channel as crew/navigator is also invaluable, before the psychological hurdle of first skippering a boat across.

A **Planning check-list** must oblige a skipper/navigator to:

a. Study the meteorological situation several days before departure, so that windows of opportunity, eg high pressure, may be predicted and bad weather avoided.

b. Consider the forecast wind direction and likely shifts, so that the probability of obtaining a good slant can be improved. Prevailing winds are SW/W, except in the spring when NE/ E winds are equally likely. The advantages of getting well to windward cannot be over-emphasised. If heading for St Malo from Brighton, for example, it might pay to make westing along the coast (working the tides to advantage) so as to depart from St Catherine's Point, the Needles, Anvil Point or even Portland Bill when crossing towards Barfleur, Cherbourg, Cap de la Hague or Alderney.

c. Choose the route, departure points and landfalls so that time on passage and out of sight of identifiable marks is minimised. This can much reduce anxiety and fatigue (which may soon become apparent in a family crew). The risk of navigational errors, particularly those due to leeway and tidal streams, is also reduced. It is sound practice to take back bearings on the departure mark.

d. Take account of tidal constraints at the point of departure and destination; and en route tidal gates, eg Hurst Narrows.

e. Work out the hourly direction and rate of tidal streams expected during (and after) the crossing; so as to lay off the total drift angle required to make good the desired track. Only rarely do 6 hours of E-going tide cancel out 6 hours of W-going (or vice versa); streams off the French coast are usually stronger. Try to arrive up-tide of destination. Note the times and areas of races and overfalls and keep well clear.

f. Consider actions to be taken in poor visibility/fog when the range at which marks may be seen is much reduced (and risk of collision with other vessels equally increased). Fog is unlikely in summer (except in certain notorious areas, eg off Ushant) and visibility is often greater than 6M. A landfall at night or dawn/dusk is frequently easier due to the additional range provided by lights.

g. Observe the legal requirement to head at 90° across any TSS; consider motoring to expedite such crossing.

h. Make use of additional navigational info such as soundings, for example when crossing the distinctive contours of the Hurd Deep; the rising or dipping ranges of major lights; fixing on clearly identifiable radar targets, if so equipped; and the sighting of TSS buoys and light floats. Note: The charted 2M exclusion circle around EC2 buoy applies only to IMO-Convention vessels, ie not yachts.

j. Keep a harbour of refuge in mind if caught out by fog, gales or gear failure. For example, if unable to make Cherbourg in a strong SSW'ly and E-going tide, it may be better to bear away and run for St Vaast in the lee of the peninsular. Or heave to and stay at sea.

k. Finally, even if using electronic navigation, write up the ship's log and maintain a DR plot. This is both a safeguard, and a source of pride (when proven accurate); it also ensures the highest degree of navigational awareness.

Routes from ports within Area 3 Passages from Brighton, Newhaven or Eastbourne to Dieppe or adjacent French ports are relatively short and direct. The route crosses the Dover Strait TSS whose SW-bound lane lies only 7M S of Beachy Head. A departure from close W of CS2 buoy will satisfy the 90° crossing rule and minimise the time spent in the TSS. During the 19M crossing of the TSS, it is worth listening to the VHF broadcasts of navigational and traffic information made by CNIS. These include details of vessels which appear to be contravening Rule 10.

Dover to Calais or Boulogne is only about 25M (see 9.3.15) but the route crosses the congested Dover Strait TSS. Study the tidal streams. Keep a very sharp lookout for ships in the traffic lanes and ferries crossing them. Do not attempt to cross in fog or poor visibility.

9.3.6 DISTANCE TABLE

Approximate distances in nautical miles are by the most direct route, whilst avoiding dangers and allowing for Traffic Separation Schemes. Places in italics are in adjoining areas; places in **bold** are in 9.0.6, Cross-Channel Distances; places underlined are in 9.0.8, Distances across the North Sea.

1. *Portland Bill Lt*	**1**																	
2. *Nab Tower*	60	**2**																
3. Boulder Lt Buoy	65	5	**3**															
4. Owers Lt Buoy	69	11	8	**4**														
5. **Littlehampton**	78	19	13	12	**5**													
6. **Shoreham**	90	32	24	21	13	**6**												
7. **Brighton**	93	35	28	24	17	5	**7**											
8. **Newhaven**	97	40	34	29	24	12	7	**8**										
9. Beachy Head Lt	104	46	41	36	30	20	14	8	**9**									
10. Eastbourne	111	51	45	40	34	24	19	12	7	**10**								
11. **Rye**	129	72	67	62	56	46	41	34	25	23	**11**							
12. Dungeness Lt	134	76	71	66	60	50	44	38	30	26	9	**12**						
13. **Folkestone**	152	92	84	81	76	65	60	53	43	40	23	13	**13**					
14. Dover	157	97	89	86	81	70	65	58	48	45	28	18	5	**14**				
15. Ramsgate	172	112	104	101	96	85	80	73	63	60	43	33	20	15	**15**			
16. N Foreland Lt	175	115	107	104	99	88	83	76	66	63	46	36	23	18	3	**16**		
17. *Sheerness*	206	146	139	135	132	119	114	107	97	96	79	67	54	49	34	31	**17**	
18. *London Bridge*	248	188	184	177	177	161	156	149	139	141	124	109	96	91	76	73	45	**18**

LITTLEHAMPTON *9.3.7*

W. Sussex **50°47'·87N 00°32'·43W** ☸☸👍👍✿✿

CHARTS AC *5605, 1991, 1652*; Imray C9, C12; Stanfords 9; OS 197

TIDES +0015 Dover; ML 2·8; Zone 0 (UT)

Standard Port SHOREHAM (⟶)

Times				Height (metres)			
High Water		Low Water		MHWS	MHWN	MLWN	MLWS
0500	1000	0000	0600	6·3	4·8	1·9	0·6
1700	2200	1200	1800				
Differences LITTLEHAMPTON (ENT)							
+0010	0000	–0005	–0010	–0·4	–0·4	–0·2	–0·2
LITTLEHAMPTON (NORFOLK WHARF)							
+0015	+0005	0000	+0045	–0·7	–0·7	–0·3	+0·2
ARUNDEL							
No data	+0120	No data		–3·1	–2·8	No data	
PAGHAM							
+0015	0000	–0015	–0025	–0·7	–0·5	–0·1	–0·1
BOGNOR REGIS							
+0010	–0005	–0005	–0020	–0·6	–0·5	–0·2	–0·1

NOTE: Tidal hts in hbr are affected by flow down R Arun. Tide seldom falls lower than 0·9m above CD.

SHELTER Good. Ent dangerous in strong SE winds which cause swell up the hbr. The bar (0·7 to 1·0m) is rough in SW'lies. Visitors berth initially at Town Quay where marked and contact Hr Mr.

NAVIGATION WPT 50°47'·53N 00°32'·30W, 166°/346° from/to front ldg lt, 0·60M. Bar ½M offshore. Hbr accessible from HW–3 to HW+2½ for approx 1·5m draft. The ebb runs so fast (4 – 6 kn) at sp that yachts may have difficulty entering. From HW–1 to HW+4 a strong W-going tidal stream sets across the ent; keep to E side. Speed limit 6½kn.
On E side of ent chan a training wall which covers at half-tide is marked by 7 poles and lit bn at S end. The W pier is a long, prominent structure of wood piles; beware shoal ground within its arm. A tide gauge on end shows height of tide above CD. To obtain depth on the bar subtract 0·9m from indicated depth.
River Arun. A retractable footbridge (3·6m clearance MHWS; 9·4m above CD) 3ca above Town Quay gives access for masted craft to Littlehampton marina. It is opened by request to Hr Mr before 1630 previous day. The River Arun is navigable on the tide by small, unmasted craft for 24M via Ford, Arundel and beyond; consult Hr Mr.

LIGHTS AND MARKS High-rise bldg (38m) is conspic 0·4M NNE of hbr ent. A pile with small platform and ☆, Fl Y (5) 20s 5M, is 2·5M SE of hbr ent at 50°46'·1N 00°29'·5W.
Ldg lts 346°: Front FG on B column; Rear, lt ho Oc WY 7·5s at root of E bkwtr, W 290°-356°, Y 356°-042°. The Fl G 3s lt at Norfolk Wharf leads craft upstream, once inside hbr ent.
When Pilot boat with P1 at the bow displays the Pilot flag 'H' (WR vert halves) or Ⓦ over ● lts, all boats keep clear of ent; large ship moving.
Footbridge sigs, from high mast to port:
Fl G lt = open; Fl R = closed.
Bridge's retractable centre section (22m wide) has 2 FR (vert) to port and 2 FG (vert) to stbd at both upstream and downstream ends.

RADIO TELEPHONE Hr Mr VHF Ch 71 16 (0900-1700LT); Pilots Ch 71 16 when vessel due. Bridge Ch 71. Marinas Ch **80** M (office hrs).

TELEPHONE (Dial code 01903) Hr Mr 721215, 📠 739472, e-mail harbour@littlehampton.org.uk; MRSC (01705) 552100; ⊜ 0345 231110 (H24); Marinecall 09068 500456; Police 731733; Dr 714113.

FACILITIES **Town Quay** AB £10 <11m, £12.50 >11m, FW, C (5 ton), ME, Sh; **Services**: BY, M, Sh (Wood), ACA.
Littlehampton Sailing & Motor Club ☎ 715859, M, FW, Bar;
Arun YC (90+10 visitors), £7.50, ☎ 721215/6, (dries; access HW±3), M, AC, FW, Bar, Slip, R, Showers, ♿;
Littlehampton Marina (120 + 30 Ⓥ), £17.62, ☎ 713553, 📠 732264, Slip, BH (12 ton), CH, P, D, V, R, Bar, FW, AC, Sh, ME, ♿;
Ship and Anchor Marina, about 2M up-river at Ford, (50+, some visitors) ☎ (01243) 551262, (access HW±4), Slip, FW, ME, Sh, CH, V, R, Bar.
Town EC Wed; P, D, V, R, Bar, ✉, Ⓑ, ⇌, ✈ (Shoreham).

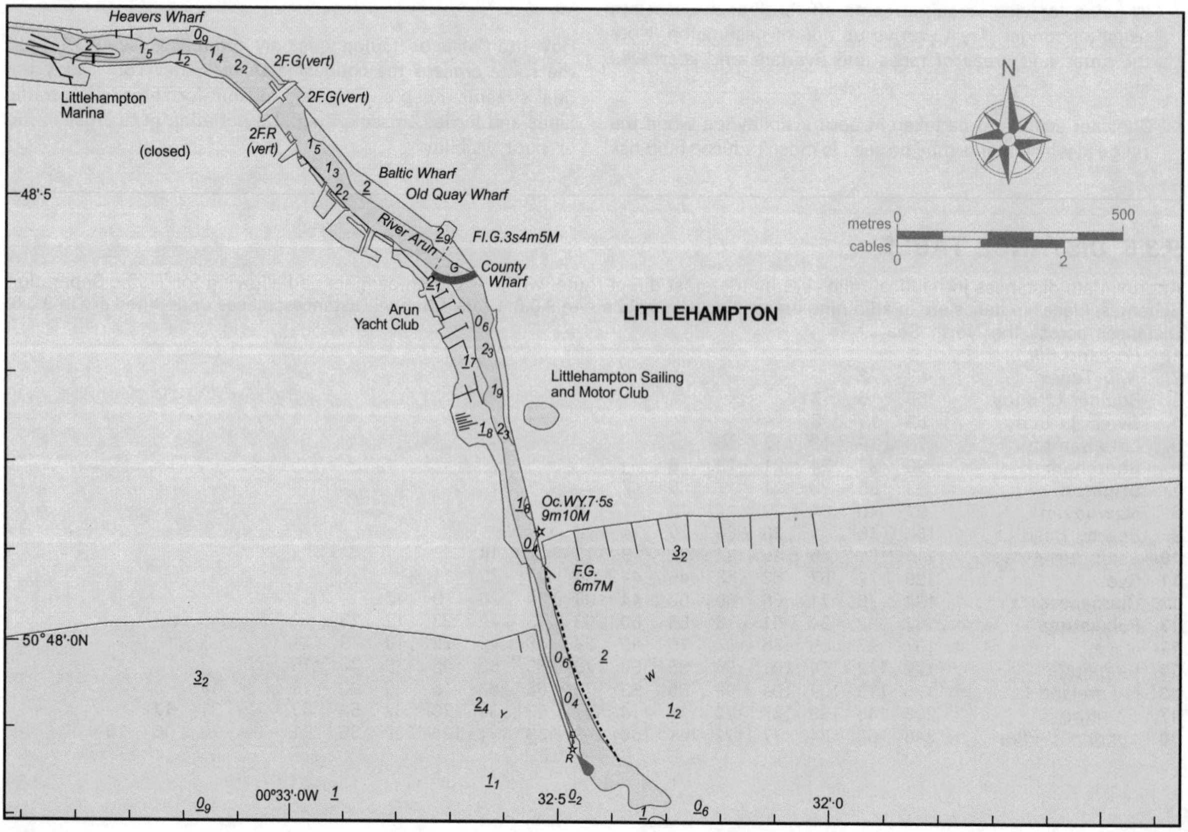

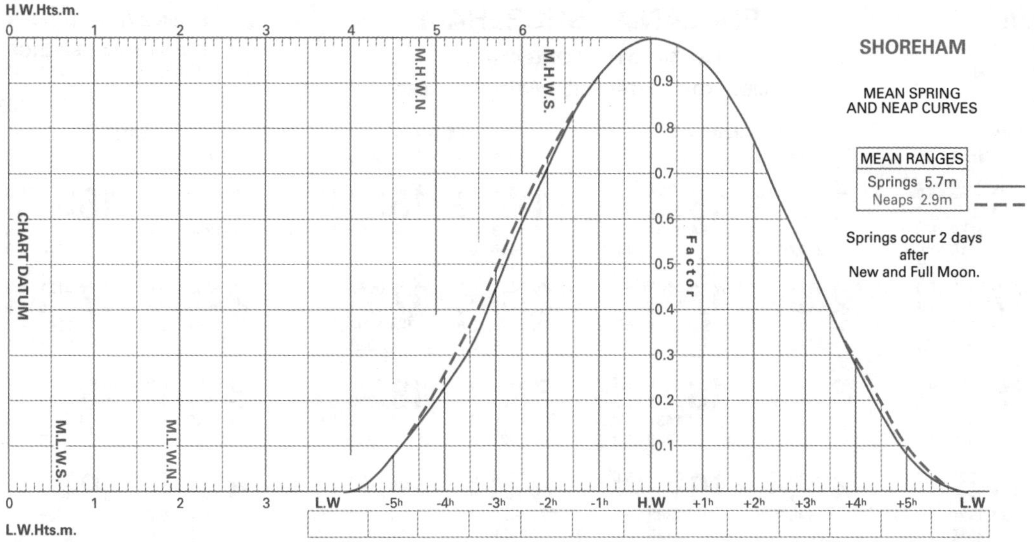

SHOREHAM *9.3.8*

W. Sussex **50°49'·53N 00°14'·85W** ❁❁☆☆✿✿

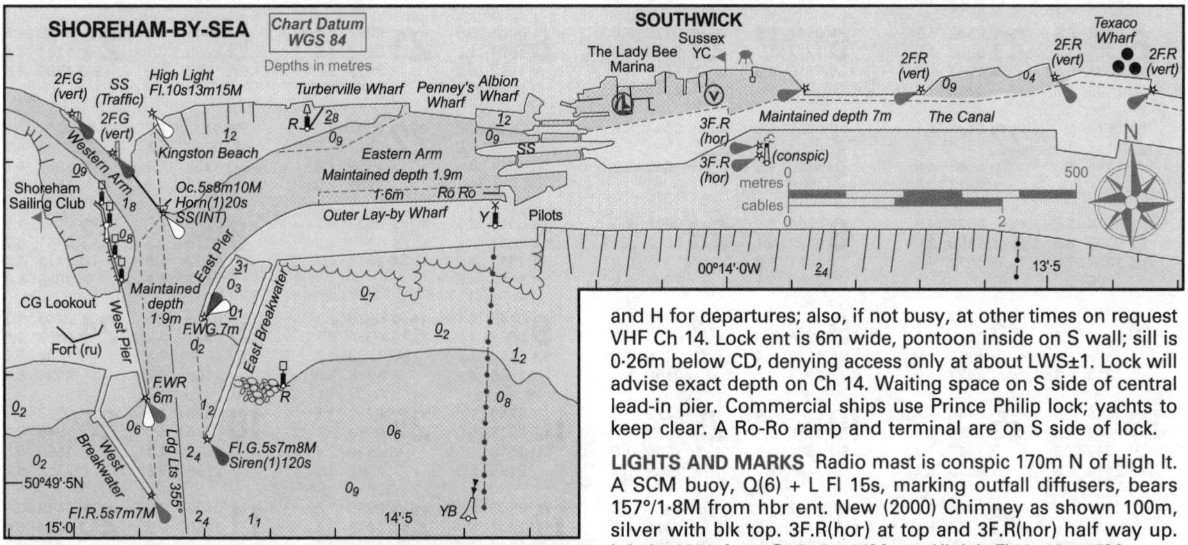

CHARTS AC *5605*, 2044, *1652*; Imray C9, C12; Stanfords 9; OS 197/8

TIDES +0009 Dover; ML 3·3; Duration 0605; Zone 0 (UT)

Standard Port SHOREHAM (⟶)

Times				Height (metres)			
High Water		Low Water		MHWS	MHWN	MLWN	MLWS
0500	1000	0000	0600	6·3	4·8	1·9	0·6
1700	2200	1200	1800				
Differences WORTHING							
+0010	0000	−0005	−0010	−0·1	−0·2	0·0	0·0

SHELTER Excellent, once through the lock and into The Canal. The shallow water (dredged 1·9m) at the ent can be very rough in strong on-shore winds and dangerous in onshore gales. Lady Bee and Aldrington (E end of The Canal) marinas, least depth 2m, both welcome visitors; they are managed by the Hbr Authority. Visitors are advised not to use the drying Western Arm if possible. Hbr speed limit = 4kn.

NAVIGATION WPT 50°49'·23N 00°14'·81W, 175°/355° from/to front ldg lt, 0·52M. From E, beware Jenny Rks (0·9m) and from the W, Church Rks (0·3m). The Eastern Arm leads to Prince George Lock, the N'ly of two locks, which opens H24 @ H+30 for arrivals and H for departures; also, if not busy, at other times on request VHF Ch 14. Lock ent is 6m wide, pontoon inside on S wall; sill is 0·26m below CD, denying access only at about LWS±1. Lock will advise exact depth on Ch 14. Waiting space on S side of central lead-in pier. Commercial ships use Prince Philip lock; yachts to keep clear. A Ro-Ro ramp and terminal are on S side of lock.

LIGHTS AND MARKS Radio mast is conspic 170m N of High lt. A SCM buoy, Q(6) + L Fl 15s, marking outfall diffusers, bears 157°/1·8M from hbr ent. New (2000) Chimney as shown 100m, silver with blk top. 3F.R(hor) at top and 3F.R(hor) half way up. Ldg lts 355°: front Oc 5s 8m 10M; rear High lt, Fl 10s 13m 15M.
Traffic Sigs IPTS (Sigs 2 and 5, Oc) are shown from Middle Pier.
Note : ● Fl lt exempts small craft.
Oc R 3s (from LB ho, directed at E or W Arms) = No exit.
Lock Sigs (Comply strictly to avoid turbulence):
3 ● (vert) = do not approach lock.
● Ⓦ ● (vert) = clear to approach lock.

RADIO TELEPHONE Call *Shoreham Hbr Radio* VHF Ch **14** 16 (H24) Hr Mr and lock. Lock will advise Lady Bee marina of arrivals, 0830-1800 M-Sat; 1000-1400 Sun.

TELEPHONE (Dial code 01273) Hr Mr 592613, 📠 592492; Locks 592366; MRSC (023 92) 552100; ⊜ 0345 231110 (H24); Marinecall 09068 500456; Police 454521; Ⓗ 455622; Dr 461101 (Health Centre).

FACILITIES **Lady Bee Marina** (110+10 Ⓥ) ☎ 593801 (0900-1700), 📠 870349, (best to pre-book), <7m £12.00 inc lock fee, £9.50 subsequent nights; <15m £16.50, £12 subsequent nights. Access as lock times, AB, P & D (cans), FW, AC, CH, ME, El, Sh, SM, R, V, Slip;
Sussex YC ☎/📠 464868, welcomes visitors, but has only one AB in The Canal, so prior notice advised; also a drying ½ tide pontoon in the Western Arm(limited Ⓥ), R, Bar, ♿.
Services: P & D also on N side of W Arm HW±3; ACA.
Town EC Wed; ⓟ, ✉, Ⓑ, ⇌, ✈.

TIME ZONE (UTC)
For Summer Time add ONE hour in **non-shaded areas**

ENGLAND – SHOREHAM

LAT 50°50′N LONG 0°15′W

TIMES AND HEIGHTS OF HIGH AND LOW WATERS

SPRING & NEAP TIDES
Dates in red are SPRINGS
Dates in blue are NEAPS

YEAR **2002**

JANUARY

Day		Time	m	Time	m	Time	m	Time	m
1	TU	0003	6.3	0612	0.9	1217	6.3	1839	0.7
2	W	0049	6.3	0658	0.8	1303	6.3	1926	0.7
3	TH	0136	6.3	0747	0.9	1351	6.2	2015	0.8
4	F	0225	6.2	0838	1.0	1441	6.0	2107	0.9
5	SA	0317	6.0	0933	1.2	1536	5.7	2204	1.1
6	SU	0414	5.8	1035	1.4	1637	5.5	2306	1.3
7	M	0517	5.6	1143	1.5	1745	5.3		
8	TU	0014	1.5	0627	5.5	1254	1.6	1900	5.2
9	W	0123	1.5	0739	5.5	1359	1.5	2014	5.3
10	TH	0226	1.5	0843	5.6	1457	1.3	2116	5.5
11	F	0321	1.3	0938	5.8	1549	1.1	2209	5.7
12	SA	0411	1.2	1026	5.9	1636	1.0	2255	5.9
13	SU	0455	1.1	1109	6.0	1719	0.9	● 2337	6.0
14	M	0537	1.0	1148	6.0	1759	0.9		
15	TU	0014	6.0	0615	1.1	1224	6.0	1835	0.9
16	W	0050	6.0	0651	1.1	1257	5.9	1910	1.0
17	TH	0123	5.9	0725	1.2	1328	5.8	1945	1.1
18	F	0154	5.8	0800	1.3	1358	5.6	2020	1.2
19	SA	0222	5.7	0836	1.4	1429	5.5	2056	1.4
20	SU	0253	5.5	0914	1.6	1506	5.3	2134	1.6
21	M	0332	5.3	0958	1.8	1551	5.0	2219	1.8
22	TU	0421	5.1	1053	2.0	1648	4.8	2316	2.0
23	W	0527	4.9	1159	2.0	1811	4.7		
24	TH	0027	2.0	0649	5.0	1310	1.9	1927	4.9
25	F	0140	1.9	0756	5.2	1417	1.7	2030	5.2
26	SA	0245	1.7	0853	5.5	1515	1.4	2126	5.6
27	SU	0339	1.4	0945	5.9	1606	1.0	2217	5.9
28	M	0428	1.1	1034	6.2	1654	0.8	○ 2306	6.2
29	TU	0515	0.8	1121	6.4	1741	0.5	2354	6.4
30	W	0602	0.6	1208	6.5	1828	0.4		
31	TH	0041	6.6	0648	0.6	1255	6.5	1915	0.4

FEBRUARY

Day		Time	m	Time	m	Time	m	Time	m
1	F	0127	6.6	0735	0.6	1341	6.5	2002	0.4
2	SA	0212	6.5	0823	0.6	1427	6.3	2049	0.6
3	SU	0258	6.3	0912	0.8	1515	6.0	2138	0.9
4	M	0346	6.0	1005	1.1	1606	5.7	2231	1.2
5	TU	0439	5.6	1104	1.5	1705	5.3	2334	1.6
6	W	0541	5.3	1217	1.7	1816	5.0		
7	TH	0051	1.8	0657	5.1	1335	1.8	1946	4.9
8	F	0206	1.8	0822	5.1	1441	1.6	2103	5.1
9	SA	0308	1.6	0926	5.3	1536	1.4	2159	5.4
10	SU	0359	1.4	1016	5.6	1622	1.1	2245	5.7
11	M	0442	1.2	1058	5.8	1703	1.0	2324	5.9
12	TU	0521	1.0	1136	5.9	1741	0.9	● 2359	6.0
13	W	0558	1.0	1209	6.0	1816	0.8		
14	TH	0031	6.0	0631	1.0	1239	5.9	1849	0.8
15	F	0100	6.0	0704	1.0	1305	5.9	1921	0.9
16	SA	0124	5.9	0734	1.0	1330	5.8	1952	1.0
17	SU	0148	5.9	0804	1.1	1358	5.7	2020	1.1
18	M	0216	5.7	0833	1.3	1431	5.6	2049	1.3
19	TU	0250	5.6	0907	1.5	1508	5.3	2125	1.6
20	W	0332	5.3	0951	1.7	1556	5.0	2216	1.8
21	TH	0425	5.0	1053	1.9	1701	4.8	2326	2.1
22	F	0544	4.8	1218	2.0	1846	4.7		
23	SA	0059	2.1	0722	4.9	1345	1.8	2005	5.0
24	SU	0221	1.8	0832	5.3	1455	1.4	2108	5.5
25	M	0323	1.4	0929	5.7	1550	1.0	2203	5.9
26	TU	0414	1.0	1021	6.1	1639	0.6	2253	6.3
27	W	0501	0.6	1110	6.4	1725	0.4	○ 2341	6.6
28	TH	0547	0.4	1157	6.6	1811	0.2		

MARCH

Day		Time	m	Time	m	Time	m	Time	m
1	F	0026	6.8	0632	0.3	1243	6.7	1856	0.1
2	SA	0111	6.8	0717	0.3	1327	6.6	1941	0.2
3	SU	0153	6.7	0802	0.4	1409	6.5	2024	0.4
4	M	0234	6.4	0846	0.6	1452	6.1	2108	0.8
5	TU	0317	6.0	0932	1.0	1538	5.7	2155	1.2
6	W	0405	5.5	1024	1.5	1633	5.2	2252	1.7
7	TH	0504	5.0	1135	1.9	1741	4.8		
8	F	0018	2.1	0618	4.7	1311	2.0	1916	4.6
9	SA	0148	2.1	0801	4.7	1422	1.8	2050	4.9
10	SU	0253	1.8	0913	5.0	1518	1.5	2145	5.3
11	M	0343	1.5	1002	5.4	1603	1.2	2228	5.7
12	TU	0424	1.2	1042	5.7	1642	1.0	2304	5.9
13	W	0501	1.0	1118	5.8	1718	0.8	2338	6.0
14	TH	0535	0.9	1149	5.9	1752	0.8	●	
15	F	0007	6.1	0607	0.8	1215	5.9	1824	0.7
16	SA	0031	6.0	0638	0.8	1239	5.9	1855	0.8
17	SU	0053	6.0	0707	0.9	1304	5.9	1922	0.9
18	M	0118	6.0	0733	0.9	1332	5.9	1947	1.0
19	TU	0146	5.9	0759	1.0	1402	5.7	2015	1.1
20	W	0218	5.7	0832	1.2	1438	5.5	2052	1.4
21	TH	0257	5.4	0916	1.5	1522	5.2	2142	1.7
22	F	0347	5.0	1016	1.8	1625	4.8	2253	2.0
23	SA	0502	4.7	1140	2.0	1815	4.7		
24	SU	0030	2.1	0656	4.7	1320	1.8	1945	5.0
25	M	0203	1.8	0813	5.1	1436	1.4	2052	5.5
26	TU	0306	1.3	0913	5.7	1531	0.9	2147	6.0
27	W	0356	0.8	1006	6.1	1619	0.5	2236	6.4
28	TH	0442	0.4	1054	6.4	1704	0.2	○ 2322	6.7
29	F	0527	0.2	1140	6.6	1749	0.1		
30	SA	0006	6.9	0611	0.1	1226	6.7	1833	0.1
31	SU	0049	6.8	0655	0.2	1309	6.6	1916	0.2

APRIL

Day		Time	m	Time	m	Time	m	Time	m
1	M	0130	6.7	0738	0.3	1350	6.4	1958	0.5
2	TU	0209	6.4	0820	0.6	1431	6.1	2040	0.8
3	W	0250	5.9	0903	1.0	1515	5.6	2125	1.3
4	TH	0336	5.4	0951	1.5	1609	5.2	2218	1.8
5	F	0434	4.9	1053	1.9	1714	4.7	2338	2.2
6	SA	0545	4.5	1238	2.1	1838	4.6		
7	SU	0123	2.2	0728	4.5	1356	1.9	2022	4.8
8	M	0229	1.9	0849	4.8	1452	1.6	2117	5.2
9	TU	0318	1.5	0937	5.2	1536	1.3	2159	5.6
10	W	0358	1.2	1016	5.5	1614	1.1	2235	5.8
11	TH	0433	1.0	1050	5.7	1648	0.9	2306	5.9
12	F	0507	0.9	1119	5.8	1722	0.8	● 2334	6.0
13	SA	0539	0.8	1145	5.9	1755	0.8	2358	6.0
14	SU	0611	0.8	1211	5.9	1826	0.8		
15	M	0023	6.0	0639	0.8	1240	5.9	1854	0.9
16	TU	0051	6.0	0706	0.9	1310	5.9	1920	1.0
17	W	0121	5.9	0735	0.9	1341	5.8	1953	1.1
18	TH	0155	5.7	0812	1.1	1419	5.6	2033	1.3
19	F	0235	5.4	0858	1.4	1506	5.3	2127	1.7
20	SA	0327	5.1	1000	1.7	1612	4.9	2239	1.9
21	SU	0446	4.8	1121	1.8	1755	4.8		
22	M	0012	1.9	0633	4.8	1257	1.7	1922	5.1
23	TU	0141	1.6	0751	5.2	1412	1.3	2029	5.6
24	W	0243	1.1	0853	5.6	1507	0.9	2124	6.1
25	TH	0333	0.7	0945	6.1	1555	0.5	2213	6.4
26	F	0419	0.4	1034	6.4	1641	0.3	2259	6.7
27	SA	0504	0.2	1121	6.5	1726	0.2	○ 2343	6.7
28	SU	0549	0.2	1206	6.6	1810	0.3		
29	M	0026	6.7	0632	0.3	1250	6.5	1853	0.4
30	TU	0107	6.5	0715	0.4	1331	6.3	1935	0.7

Chart Datum: 3·27 metres below Ordnance Datum (Newlyn)

TIME ZONE (UTC)
For Summer Time add ONE hour in **non-shaded areas**

ENGLAND – SHOREHAM

LAT 50°50′N LONG 0°15′W

TIMES AND HEIGHTS OF HIGH AND LOW WATERS

SPRING & NEAP TIDES
Dates in red are SPRINGS
Dates in blue are NEAPS

YEAR **2002**

MAY

Day		Time	m	Time	m	Time	m	Time	m
1	W	0147	6.2	0757	0.7	1413	6.0	2016	1.0
2	TH	0227	5.8	0839	1.0	1457	5.6	2101	1.4
3	F	0312	5.3	0925	1.4	1548	5.2	2152	1.8
4	SA	0408	4.9	1021	1.8	1647	4.9	2259	2.1
5	SU	0513	4.6	1140	2.0	1756	4.7		
6	M	0040	2.2	0628	4.5	1313	2.0	1922	4.8
7	TU	0151	1.9	0800	4.7	1412	1.7	2032	5.1
8	W	0241	1.6	0855	5.0	1458	1.5	2117	5.4
9	TH	0322	1.4	0936	5.3	1538	1.2	2153	5.6
10	F	0359	1.1	1009	5.5	1614	1.1	2224	5.8
11	SA	0434	1.0	1040	5.7	1650	1.0	2254	5.9
12	SU	0508	0.9	1112	5.8	1725	0.9	● 2325	6.0
13	M	0542	0.8	1145	5.9	1758	0.9	2356	6.0
14	TU	0614	0.8	1218	5.9	1830	0.9		
15	W	0029	6.0	0646	0.8	1253	5.9	1903	1.0
16	TH	0104	5.9	0721	0.9	1330	5.8	1940	1.1
17	F	0142	5.7	0803	1.1	1412	5.6	2026	1.3
18	SA	0227	5.5	0852	1.3	1504	5.4	2121	1.5
19	SU	0324	5.2	0953	1.5	1612	5.2	2231	1.7
20	M	0440	5.0	1108	1.6	1735	5.1	2353	1.7
21	TU	0607	5.0	1232	1.5	1854	5.3		
22	W	0112	1.5	0723	5.3	1343	1.2	2001	5.7
23	TH	0215	1.1	0827	5.6	1440	0.9	2058	6.0
24	F	0307	0.8	0922	5.9	1530	0.7	2148	6.3
25	SA	0356	0.6	1012	6.1	1618	0.5	2235	6.4
26	SU	0442	0.4	1101	6.3	1704	0.5	○ 2321	6.5
27	M	0528	0.4	1147	6.3	1749	0.6		
28	TU	0004	6.4	0612	0.5	1232	6.3	1833	0.7
29	W	0047	6.2	0655	0.6	1314	6.1	1915	0.9
30	TH	0127	6.0	0737	0.8	1356	5.9	1957	1.1
31	F	0208	5.7	0819	1.1	1439	5.7	2040	1.4

JUNE

Day		Time	m	Time	m	Time	m	Time	m
1	SA	0251	5.3	0902	1.4	1525	5.4	2127	1.7
2	SU	0340	5.0	0952	1.6	1617	5.1	2222	1.9
3	M	0437	4.7	1049	1.8	1714	4.9	2327	2.0
4	TU	0539	4.6	1156	1.9	1814	4.9		
5	W	0043	2.0	0642	4.6	1308	1.9	1915	5.0
6	TH	0148	1.8	0743	4.8	1407	1.7	2011	5.2
7	F	0237	1.6	0836	5.1	1454	1.5	2058	5.4
8	SA	0319	1.3	0921	5.3	1536	1.3	2139	5.6
9	SU	0358	1.2	1002	5.6	1616	1.2	2218	5.8
10	M	0437	1.0	1042	5.7	1655	1.1	● 2256	5.9
11	TU	0515	0.9	1121	5.9	1733	1.0	2334	6.0
12	W	0553	0.9	1201	5.9	1812	1.0		
13	TH	0013	6.0	0632	0.8	1243	6.0	1851	1.0
14	F	0054	6.0	0714	0.9	1325	5.9	1934	1.0
15	SA	0138	5.9	0759	0.9	1411	5.8	2022	1.1
16	SU	0226	5.7	0850	1.1	1503	5.7	2117	1.3
17	M	0321	5.5	0947	1.2	1602	5.6	2219	1.4
18	TU	0425	5.3	1052	1.3	1708	5.5	2329	1.4
19	W	0536	5.3	1203	1.3	1818	5.5		
20	TH	0041	1.4	0648	5.3	1312	1.3	1927	5.6
21	F	0146	1.2	0758	5.4	1413	1.1	2029	5.8
22	SA	0243	1.0	0859	5.6	1508	1.0	2125	6.0
23	SU	0336	0.9	0954	5.8	1559	0.9	2216	6.1
24	M	0425	0.7	1045	6.0	1648	0.8	○ 2303	6.1
25	TU	0512	0.7	1132	6.1	1734	0.9	2348	6.1
26	W	0557	0.7	1217	6.1	1817	0.9		
27	TH	0030	6.0	0639	0.8	1259	6.0	1859	1.0
28	F	0110	5.9	0720	0.9	1339	5.9	1938	1.1
29	SA	0149	5.7	0759	1.1	1418	5.8	2018	1.3
30	SU	0227	5.5	0838	1.2	1458	5.6	2059	1.5

JULY

Day		Time	m	Time	m	Time	m	Time	m
1	M	0307	5.2	0920	1.4	1539	5.4	2144	1.7
2	TU	0352	5.0	1006	1.6	1625	5.2	2235	1.8
3	W	0445	4.8	1058	1.8	1719	5.0	2331	1.9
4	TH	0545	4.7	1156	1.9	1817	4.9		
5	F	0033	1.9	0647	4.7	1259	1.9	1916	5.0
6	SA	0136	1.8	0746	4.9	1401	1.8	2011	5.2
7	SU	0234	1.6	0841	5.2	1457	1.6	2102	5.4
8	M	0324	1.4	0931	5.4	1546	1.4	2148	5.7
9	TU	0409	1.1	1018	5.7	1631	1.2	2232	5.9
10	W	0453	0.9	1103	5.9	1714	1.0	● 2316	6.0
11	TH	0536	0.8	1148	6.1	1757	0.9		
12	F	0000	6.1	0620	0.7	1233	6.2	1841	0.9
13	SA	0045	6.2	0705	0.7	1319	6.2	1927	0.8
14	SU	0131	6.1	0752	0.7	1404	6.2	2014	0.9
15	M	0218	6.0	0841	0.8	1452	6.1	2105	1.0
16	TU	0308	5.9	0932	0.9	1543	5.9	2200	1.1
17	W	0402	5.6	1028	1.1	1638	5.7	2301	1.3
18	TH	0503	5.4	1131	1.3	1740	5.5		
19	F	0009	1.4	0611	5.2	1241	1.5	1850	5.4
20	SA	0120	1.5	0728	5.2	1350	1.5	2003	5.4
21	SU	0225	1.4	0842	5.3	1452	1.4	2108	5.6
22	M	0322	1.2	0943	5.5	1547	1.2	2203	5.7
23	TU	0413	1.0	1036	5.8	1636	1.1	2252	5.9
24	W	0459	0.9	1122	5.9	1721	1.0	○ 2336	6.0
25	TH	0542	0.9	1204	6.0	1802	1.0		
26	F	0016	5.9	0622	0.9	1243	6.0	1841	1.0
27	SA	0053	5.9	0659	0.9	1319	6.0	1917	1.1
28	SU	0127	5.8	0734	1.0	1352	5.9	1952	1.2
29	M	0157	5.6	0809	1.1	1423	5.8	2027	1.3
30	TU	0227	5.5	0845	1.3	1451	5.6	2105	1.5
31	W	0258	5.3	0922	1.5	1523	5.4	2145	1.6

AUGUST

Day		Time	m	Time	m	Time	m	Time	m
1	TH	0337	5.1	1004	1.7	1604	5.2	2233	1.8
2	F	0428	4.8	1055	1.9	1701	4.9	2333	2.0
3	SA	0544	4.7	1200	2.1	1820	4.9		
4	SU	0041	2.0	0703	4.7	1313	2.0	1932	5.0
5	M	0153	1.8	0810	5.0	1424	1.8	2033	5.3
6	TU	0256	1.5	0907	5.3	1523	1.5	2126	5.6
7	W	0348	1.2	0959	5.7	1612	1.2	2215	5.9
8	TH	0435	0.9	1048	6.0	1657	1.0	● 2302	6.2
9	F	0520	0.7	1134	6.3	1742	0.8	2348	6.3
10	SA	0605	0.5	1220	6.4	1827	0.6		
11	SU	0033	6.4	0650	0.4	1305	6.5	1912	0.6
12	M	0118	6.4	0736	0.4	1349	6.5	1958	0.6
13	TU	0203	6.3	0822	0.5	1433	6.4	2045	0.7
14	W	0248	6.1	0909	0.8	1518	6.2	2135	1.0
15	TH	0337	5.8	0959	1.1	1608	5.8	2230	1.3
16	F	0432	5.4	1057	1.5	1707	5.4	2337	1.6
17	SA	0540	5.1	1212	1.8	1817	5.1		
18	SU	0058	1.8	0705	4.9	1334	1.9	1945	5.1
19	M	0212	1.7	0835	5.1	1442	1.7	2101	5.3
20	TU	0312	1.5	0938	5.4	1537	1.5	2157	5.6
21	W	0402	1.2	1027	5.7	1624	1.2	2243	5.8
22	TH	0445	1.0	1109	6.0	1705	1.1	○ 2323	5.9
23	F	0524	0.9	1148	6.1	1743	1.0	2359	6.0
24	SA	0601	0.8	1222	6.1	1819	1.0		
25	SU	0032	6.0	0634	0.9	1254	6.1	1851	1.0
26	M	0100	5.9	0707	0.9	1320	6.0	1923	1.1
27	TU	0124	5.8	0738	1.0	1342	5.9	1954	1.2
28	W	0149	5.7	0808	1.2	1406	5.8	2024	1.3
29	TH	0217	5.5	0837	1.4	1436	5.6	2056	1.5
30	F	0252	5.3	0911	1.6	1513	5.3	2136	1.8
31	SA	0335	5.0	0957	1.9	1602	5.0	2233	2.0

Chart Datum: 3·27 metres below Ordnance Datum (Newlyn)

TIME ZONE (UTC)
For Summer Time add ONE hour in **non-shaded areas**

ENGLAND – SHOREHAM

LAT 50°50′N LONG 0°15′W

TIMES AND HEIGHTS OF HIGH AND LOW WATERS

SPRING & NEAP TIDES
Dates in red are **SPRINGS**
Dates in blue are **NEAPS**

YEAR **2002**

SEPTEMBER

Date	Day	Time	m	Time	m	Time	m	Time	m
1	SU	0435	4.7	1104	2.2	1714	4.7	2352	2.1
2	M	0624	4.6	1233	2.2	1859	4.8		
3	TU	0119	2.0	0745	4.9	1400	2.0	2010	5.1
4	W	0235	1.6	0849	5.3	1505	1.6	2108	5.6
5	TH	0330	1.2	0942	5.8	1554	1.2	2159	6.0
6	F	0416	0.8	1031	6.2	1639	0.8	2246	6.3
7	SA	0501	0.5	1116	6.5	1723	0.6	● 2331	6.5
8	SU	0545	0.4	1201	6.7	1807	0.4		
9	M	0016	6.6	0628	0.3	1245	6.8	1851	0.4
10	TU	0100	6.6	0713	0.3	1327	6.7	1935	0.5
11	W	0143	6.5	0757	0.5	1408	6.5	2020	0.7
12	TH	0225	6.2	0841	0.8	1451	6.2	2106	1.0
13	F	0312	5.8	0929	1.2	1539	5.7	2158	1.4
14	SA	0406	5.3	1025	1.7	1638	5.2	2305	1.8
15	SU	0515	4.9	1145	2.1	1751	4.8		
16	M	0039	2.1	0648	4.7	1320	2.1	1933	4.8
17	TU	0159	1.9	0827	5.0	1431	1.9	2053	5.1
18	W	0259	1.6	0926	5.4	1524	1.6	2145	5.5
19	TH	0346	1.3	1010	5.8	1607	1.3	2226	5.8
20	F	0425	1.0	1049	6.0	1644	1.1	2304	6.0
21	SA	0501	0.9	1124	6.2	1719	0.9	○ 2337	6.0
22	SU	0534	0.8	1155	6.2	1752	0.9		
23	M	0005	6.0	0606	0.8	1223	6.1	1823	0.9
24	TU	0029	6.0	0637	0.9	1244	6.1	1853	1.0
25	W	0052	5.9	0706	1.0	1305	6.0	1920	1.1
26	TH	0117	5.8	0733	1.1	1331	5.9	1947	1.2
27	F	0145	5.7	0800	1.3	1400	5.7	2017	1.4
28	SA	0217	5.5	0834	1.6	1435	5.4	2056	1.7
29	SU	0258	5.2	0920	1.9	1522	5.0	2153	2.0
30	M	0355	4.8	1028	2.2	1630	4.7	2313	2.2

OCTOBER

Date	Day	Time	m	Time	m	Time	m	Time	m
1	TU	0549	4.6	1202	2.3	1832	4.7		
2	W	0051	2.1	0722	4.9	1338	2.0	1949	5.1
3	TH	0213	1.7	0828	5.4	1444	1.5	2049	5.6
4	F	0308	1.2	0922	6.0	1532	1.1	2139	6.1
5	SA	0354	0.8	1009	6.4	1617	0.7	2226	6.4
6	SU	0437	0.5	1054	6.7	1700	0.4	● 2311	6.7
7	M	0521	0.3	1137	6.9	1743	0.3	2356	6.8
8	TU	0604	0.3	1220	6.9	1827	0.3		
9	W	0039	6.7	0648	0.4	1302	6.8	1911	0.4
10	TH	0122	6.5	0731	0.6	1344	6.5	1955	0.7
11	F	0205	6.2	0815	0.9	1426	6.1	2040	1.1
12	SA	0251	5.8	0902	1.4	1514	5.6	2131	1.5
13	SU	0346	5.3	0958	1.8	1613	5.1	2234	2.0
14	M	0454	4.9	1117	2.2	1727	4.7		
15	TU	0013	2.2	0623	4.7	1300	2.2	1911	4.7
16	W	0135	2.1	0802	5.0	1409	2.0	2030	5.0
17	TH	0234	1.7	0859	5.4	1501	1.6	2120	5.4
18	F	0320	1.4	0942	5.7	1541	1.3	2201	5.7
19	SA	0358	1.2	1019	6.0	1617	1.1	2236	5.9
20	SU	0432	1.0	1052	6.1	1650	1.0	2307	6.0
21	M	0505	0.9	1121	6.1	1723	0.9	○ 2333	6.0
22	TU	0538	0.9	1145	6.1	1755	0.9	2357	6.0
23	W	0609	1.0	1209	6.1	1825	1.0		
24	TH	0023	6.0	0637	1.0	1235	6.0	1852	1.1
25	F	0052	5.9	0704	1.2	1303	5.9	1919	1.2
26	SA	0121	5.8	0734	1.3	1334	5.7	1952	1.4
27	SU	0155	5.6	0811	1.6	1411	5.5	2034	1.6
28	M	0237	5.3	0900	1.9	1458	5.1	2132	1.9
29	TU	0337	5.0	1008	2.1	1609	4.8	2248	2.1
30	W	0521	4.8	1137	2.2	1802	4.8		
31	TH	0022	2.0	0654	5.0	1309	1.9	1922	5.1

NOVEMBER

Date	Day	Time	m	Time	m	Time	m	Time	m
1	F	0142	1.6	0801	5.5	1415	1.5	2024	5.6
2	SA	0240	1.2	0855	6.0	1506	1.0	2116	6.1
3	SU	0328	0.8	0943	6.4	1551	0.6	2204	6.4
4	M	0412	0.5	1029	6.7	1636	0.4	● 2250	6.6
5	TU	0457	0.4	1113	6.8	1720	0.3	2335	6.7
6	W	0541	0.4	1156	6.8	1805	0.4		
7	TH	0020	6.6	0625	0.5	1239	6.6	1850	0.5
8	F	0104	6.4	0709	0.7	1322	6.4	1934	0.8
9	SA	0148	6.2	0754	1.1	1405	6.0	2020	1.1
10	SU	0235	5.8	0841	1.5	1453	5.5	2109	1.5
11	M	0328	5.4	0935	1.9	1550	5.1	2206	1.9
12	TU	0429	5.1	1044	2.2	1657	4.8	2325	2.1
13	W	0541	4.9	1219	2.2	1818	4.7		
14	TH	0053	2.1	0710	5.0	1332	2.1	1946	4.8
15	F	0155	1.9	0816	5.2	1425	1.8	2042	5.1
16	SA	0243	1.6	0903	5.5	1508	1.5	2124	5.4
17	SU	0324	1.4	0941	5.8	1545	1.3	2159	5.7
18	M	0400	1.2	1013	5.9	1620	1.1	2229	5.8
19	TU	0435	1.1	1042	6.0	1654	1.0	2259	5.9
20	W	0509	1.1	1110	6.0	1727	1.0	○ 2329	6.0
21	TH	0542	1.1	1140	6.0	1800	1.0		
22	F	0001	6.0	0613	1.1	1211	6.0	1831	1.1
23	SA	0034	5.9	0644	1.2	1244	5.9	1903	1.2
24	SU	0108	5.9	0719	1.3	1319	5.8	1941	1.3
25	M	0146	5.7	0800	1.5	1400	5.6	2025	1.5
26	TU	0232	5.5	0850	1.7	1451	5.3	2121	1.7
27	W	0332	5.2	0954	1.9	1558	5.1	2229	1.8
28	TH	0452	5.1	1111	1.9	1724	5.0	2349	1.8
29	F	0616	5.3	1232	1.8	1846	5.2		
30	SA	0105	1.6	0726	5.6	1341	1.4	1952	5.5

DECEMBER

Date	Day	Time	m	Time	m	Time	m	Time	m
1	SU	0207	1.3	0825	5.9	1437	1.1	2049	5.9
2	M	0301	1.0	0916	6.3	1527	0.8	2141	6.2
3	TU	0349	0.8	1005	6.5	1615	0.6	2230	6.4
4	W	0437	0.7	1051	6.6	1702	0.5	● 2318	6.4
5	TH	0523	0.7	1137	6.6	1748	0.6		
6	F	0005	6.4	0608	0.7	1221	6.4	1834	0.7
7	SA	0050	6.3	0653	0.9	1305	6.2	1918	0.9
8	SU	0135	6.1	0738	1.1	1349	5.9	2003	1.1
9	M	0220	5.9	0823	1.4	1434	5.6	2048	1.4
10	TU	0307	5.6	0911	1.7	1524	5.2	2137	1.7
11	W	0358	5.3	1006	2.0	1619	4.9	2232	1.9
12	TH	0455	5.1	1109	2.1	1720	4.8	2336	2.0
13	F	0556	5.0	1224	2.1	1824	4.7		
14	SA	0048	2.0	0659	5.0	1332	2.0	1929	4.8
15	SU	0151	1.9	0758	5.2	1424	1.8	2025	5.1
16	M	0242	1.7	0847	5.4	1508	1.5	2110	5.3
17	TU	0325	1.5	0928	5.6	1548	1.3	2150	5.6
18	W	0405	1.4	1005	5.8	1626	1.2	2228	5.7
19	TH	0443	1.3	1041	5.9	1704	1.1	○ 2306	5.9
20	F	0520	1.2	1117	6.0	1741	1.0	2344	6.0
21	SA	0556	1.1	1154	6.0	1817	1.0		
22	SU	0022	6.0	0632	1.1	1233	6.0	1855	1.0
23	M	0101	6.0	0711	1.2	1313	5.9	1935	1.1
24	TU	0143	5.9	0753	1.3	1356	5.8	2020	1.1
25	W	0229	5.8	0842	1.4	1445	5.7	2110	1.3
26	TH	0321	5.7	0938	1.5	1541	5.5	2208	1.4
27	F	0422	5.5	1043	1.6	1647	5.3	2315	1.5
28	SA	0531	5.5	1155	1.6	1800	5.3		
29	SU	0027	1.5	0643	5.5	1307	1.5	1914	5.4
30	M	0136	1.4	0752	5.7	1411	1.3	2022	5.5
31	TU	0237	1.3	0852	5.9	1508	1.1	2123	5.8

Chart Datum: 3·27 metres below Ordnance Datum (Newlyn)

BRIGHTON *9.3.9*

E. Sussex **50°48′·53N 00°06′·38W** ❁❁❁◊◊◊✿✿✿

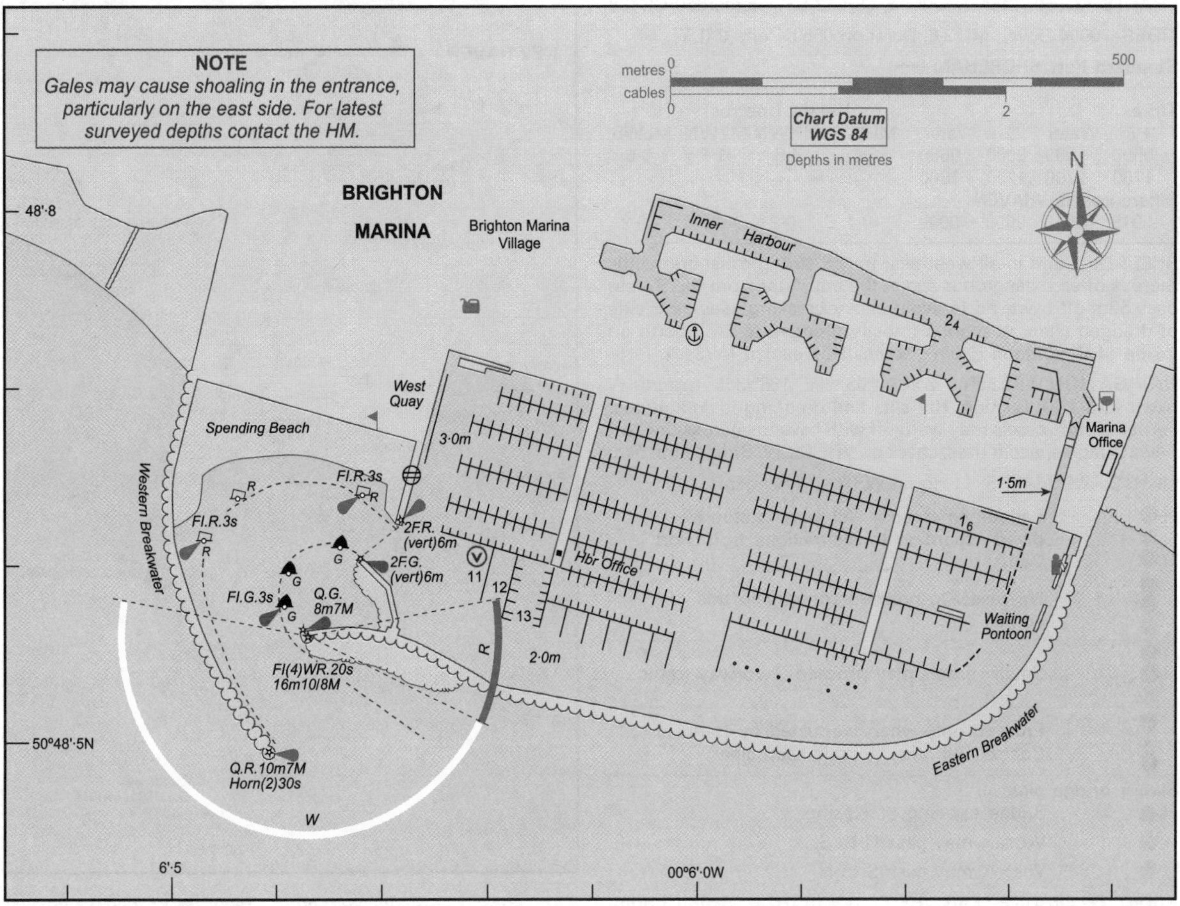

CHARTS AC *5605, 1991, 1652*; Imray C9, C12, C31; Stanfords 9; OS 198

TIDES +0004 Dover; ML 3·5; Duration 0605; Zone 0 (UT)

Standard Port SHOREHAM (⟵)

Times				Height (metres)			
High Water		Low Water		MHWS	MHWN	MLWN	MLWS
0500	1000	0000	0600	6·3	4·8	1·9	0·6
1700	2200	1200	1800				
Differences BRIGHTON							
–0010	–0005	–0005	–0005	+0·3	+0·1	0·0	–0·1

SHELTER Good in the marina under all conditions, but in strong S'ly winds confused seas can make the final appr very rough. Speed limit 5kn.

NAVIGATION WPT 50°48′·23N 00°06′·39W, 180°/000° from/to W bkwtr lt, 0·26M. Ent chan dredged 2·0m, but after gales shoaling occurs especially on E side; craft drawing >1·5m should keep to the W side of chan until past the first SHM buoy. In heavy weather, best appr is from SSE to avoid worst of the backlash from bkwtrs; beware shallow water E of ent in R sector of lt Fl (4) WR 20s. W-going stream starts at Brighton HW–1½ and E-going at HW+4½. Inshore the sp rate reaches approx 1·5kn. A Historic Wreck (see 9.0.3h) is at 50°48′·6N 00°06′·49W, immediately W of the marina's W bkwtr.

LIGHTS AND MARKS The marina is at the E end of the town, where white cliffs extend eastward. Daymark: conspic white hospital block, brg 334° leads to ent. six Y spar lt buoys used as racing buoys:

1. 50°48′·06N 00°06′·41W	2. 50°47′·61N 00°08′·43W
3. 50°46′·61N 00°07′·00W	4. 50°47′·00N 00°15′·33W
5. 50°48′·40N 00°19′·40W	6. 50°46′·63N 00°04′·76W

A sewer outfall can buoy, Fl Y 5s is 1·1M off the coast. Navigational lts may be hard to see against shore glare: E bkwtr Fl (4) WR 20s (intens) 16m 10/8M; vis R260°-295°, W295°-100°. E bkwtr hd QG 8m 7M. W bkwtr hd, tr R/W bands, QR 10m 7M; Horn (2) 30s. Inner Hbr lock controlled by normal R/G lts, 0800-1800LT.

RADIO TELEPHONE Call: *Brighton Control* VHF Ch **M** 80 16 (H24).

TELEPHONE (Dial code 01273) Hr Mr 819919, 📠 675082; BY 609235; MRSC (023 92) 552100; ⊜ 0345 231110 (H24); Marinecall 09068 500456; Police 606744; Ⓗ 696955; Dr 686863.

FACILITIES **Marina** (1300+200 visitors) ☎ 819919, 📠 675082, www.premiermarinas.com, £1.95, £5 for <6 hrs, ⊜, FW, AC, Gas, Gaz, ⊡, R, Bar, BY, BH (60 ton), C (35 ton), ⚓, ♿; Inner Hbr has least depth of 2·4m. Fuel pontoon (P, D, LPG, Gas): 0800-1730 summer; 0800-1100 winter; Diesel = self service H24.
Brighton Marina YC ☎ 818711, Bar, R.
Services El, Ⓔ, ME, Sh, SM, CH, ACA, Divers, Riggers, V, Superstore. Hbr Guides available from Hbr Office or by post. Bus service from marina; timetable info ☎ 674881. Electric railway runs from marina to Palace Pier, Mar-Oct. **Town** V, R, Bar, ✉, Ⓑ, ⇌, ✈ (Shoreham).

NEWHAVEN 9.3.10

E. Sussex **50°46′·84N 00°03′·53E** ❀❀❀⛵⛵⛵✿✿

CHARTS AC *5605*, 2154, *1652*; Imray C9, C12, C31; Stanfords 9; OS 198

TIDES +0004 Dover; ML 3·6; Duration 0550; Zone 0 (UT)

Standard Port SHOREHAM (⟵)

Times				**Height (metres)**			
High Water		Low Water		MHWS	MHWN	MLWN	MLWS
0500	1000	0000	0600	6·3	4·8	1·9	0·6
1700	2200	1200	1800				
Differences NEWHAVEN							
–0015	–0010	0000	0000	+0·4	+0·2	0·0	–0·2

SHELTER Good in all weathers, but in strong on-shore winds there is often a dangerous sea at the ent. Appr from the SW, to pass 50m off bkwtr hd to avoid heavy breaking seas on E side of dredged chan. At marina (mostly dredged to 2m), berth on inside of Ⓥ pontoon (0.0m), access H24 except LWS±2½.

NAVIGATION WPT 50°46′·24N 00°03′·60E, 168°/348° from/to W bkwtr lt, 0·32M. Caution: Hbr silts and dredging is continuous. Ferries/cargo vessels may warp off with hawsers across the hbr. Beware high speed ferries; check on VHF Ch 12. Speed limit 5kn.

LIGHTS AND MARKS Lt Ho on W bkwtr is conspic.

Fl ● Fl ● Fl ●	Serious emergency. All vessels stop or divert according to instructions from Port Control
● ● ●	No vessel to proceed contrary to this signal
● ● Ⓦ	Small vessels may proceed. Two way traffic
● Ⓦ ●	Proceed only when instructed by Port Control. All other vessels keep clear

Swing bridge sigs:

Fl ●	Bridge opening or closing.
●	Vessels may pass N to S.
●	Vessels may pass S to N.

RADIO TELEPHONE Port VHF Ch 12 16 (H24). Swing bridge opening Ch 12. Marina Ch **80** M (0800-1700).

TELEPHONE (Dial code 01273) Hr Mr 514131 (H24), 📠 517342; Hbr Sig Stn 517922; MRSC (023 92) 552100; ⊖ 0345 231110 (H24); Marinecall 09068 500456; Police 515801; Dr 515076; Ⓗ 609411 (Casualty 696955).

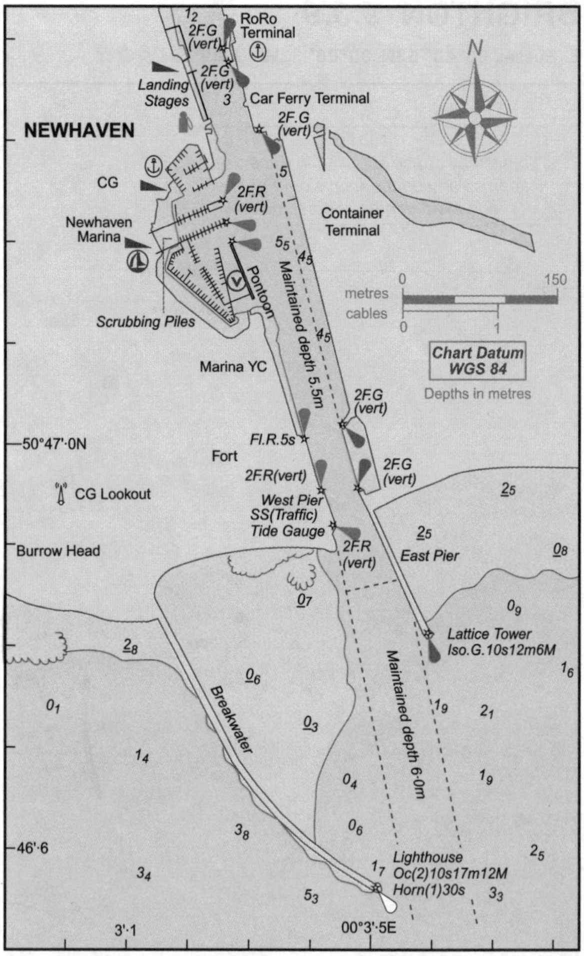

FACILITIES **Marina** (300+50 Ⓥ) ☎ 513881, 📠 517990, £1.60, FW, fuel pontoon D only 200 yds N of marina ent, ME, El, Sh, AC, BH (18 ton), C (10 ton), CH, Gas, Gaz, Slip, V, R, Bar, ⊡, ♿; **Newhaven & Seaford SC** ☎ (01323) 890077, M, FW. **Town** EC Wed; ACA, SM, P, Ⓔ, V, R, Bar, ✉, Ⓑ, ⇌, ✈ (Shoreham), Hoverspeed ferry to Dieppe.

EASTBOURNE 9.3.11

E. Sussex **50°47′·34N 00°19′·90E** ❀❀⛵⛵⛵✿✿

CHARTS AC *5605, 536*; Imray C8, C12, C31; Stanfords 9; OS 199

TIDES –0005 Dover; ML 3·8; Duration 0540; Zone 0 (UT)

Standard Port SHOREHAM (⟵)

Times				**Height (metres)**			
High Water		Low Water		MHWS	MHWN	MLWN	MLWS
0500	1000	0000	0600	6·3	4·8	1·9	0·6
1700	2200	1200	1800				
Differences EASTBOURNE							
–0010	–0005	+0015	+0020	+1·1	+0·6	+0·2	+0·1

SHELTER Good, but apprs exposed to NE/SE winds. Access H24 via buoyed chan and twin locks into inner basin (4m). The channel depth varies seasonally, even drying at LW. Call HM before entry.

NAVIGATION WPT 50°47′·37N 00°20′·81E, SWM buoy 'SH', L Fl 10s, 079°/259° from/to hbr ent, 0·45M. There are shoals to the NE in Pevensey Bay and from 2·5M SE toward Royal Sovereign lt (tide rips). From Beachy Hd, keep 0·75M offshore to clear Holywell Bank.

LIGHTS AND MARKS Beachy Hd lt, Fl (2) 20s, is 4·7M SW; Royal Sovereign lt, Fl 20s, is 5·5M to SE. Martello tr No 66 at root of S bkwtr has high intens Xenon lt, Fl (3) 15s 12m 7M, vis H24. From E, by day R roofs are conspic WSW of ent. Dir lt, Fl WRG 5s 4m 1M, W256·5°-259·5°, leads 258° through appr channel. A wreck on N side is marked by 2 SHM buoys, Fl G 5s and Fl G 3s. N and

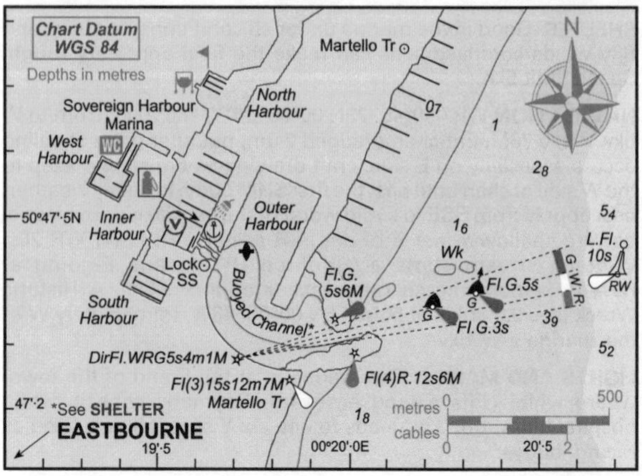

EASTBOURNE *continued*

S bkwtr hds, both painted white, are Fl G 5s 3m 6M and Fl (4) R 12s 3m 6M. Eastbourne pier, 2 FR, is 2M S of hbr ent; an unlit PHM buoy is approx 5ca S. 5kn speed limit in chan and hbr.

RADIO TELEPHONE Monitor *Sovereign Harbour* VHF Ch **17**, 15 (H24) for nav info and locks/berthing. IPTS (Sigs 2, 3 & 5) for each lock indicate lock availability; gates close every H and H+30. Waiting pontoon outside and pontoons inside the lock.

TELEPHONE (Dial code 01323) Hr Mr 470099; MRSC (01304) 210008; ⊖ 0345 231110 (H24); Marinecall 09068 500456; Police 722522; Dr 720555; Ⓗ 417400.

FACILITIES Sovereign Marina (496 berths, up to 800 planned and 300 in tidal hbr), ☎ 470099, 📠 470077, £1.95, FW, AC, D, P, LPG (H24), BH (50 tons), LPG, Gas, Gaz, ME, Sh, CH, ♂, ▣, ♿, YC, Bar, R, supermarket. **Town** (2½M) all needs, ⇌, ✈ (Gatwick).

ADJACENT ANCHORAGE

HASTINGS, E Sussex, **50°50′·88N 00°35′·50E.** AC *536.*

Tides, see 9.3.12; ML 3·8m; Duration 0530. Strictly a settled weather ⚓ or emergency shelter; landing places on pier. The stone bkwtr is in disrepair and serves only to protect FVs. Beware dangerous wreck 3ca SE of pier head. Ldg lts 356°, both FR 14/55m 4M: front on W metal column; rear 357m from front, on 5-sided W tr on West Hill. Pier hd 2 FR (vert) 8m 5M from white hut; W bkwtr hd Fl R 2·5s 5m 4M; Fl G 5s 2m, 30m from head of No3 Groyne (E bkwtr). A Historic Wreck (*Amsterdam*; see 9.0.3h) is about 2M W of pier, close inshore at 50°50′·7N 00°31′·65E. Facilities: EC Wed; ⊖ (01304) 224251. ACA (St Leonard's). Few marine services, but all shore needs at Hastings and St Leonard's. YC ☎ (01424) 420656.

3

RYE 9.3.12

E. Sussex **50°55′·60N 00°46′·58E** ❁❁◊◊✿✿✿

CHARTS AC *5605, 1991, 536*; Imray C8, C12, C31; Stanfords 9; OS 189

TIDES ML 2·0; Zone 0 (UT); Duration 3·25hrs sp, 5hrs nps

Standard Port DOVER (⟶)

Times				Height (metres)			
High Water		Low Water		MHWS	MHWN	MLWN	MLWS
0000	0600	0100	0700	6·8	5·3	2·1	0·8
1200	1800	1300	1900				
Differences RYE (approaches)							
+0005	−0010	No data		+1·0	+0·7	No data	
RYE HARBOUR							
+0005	−0010	Dries		−1·4	−1·7	Dries	
HASTINGS							
0000	−0010	−0030	−0030	+0·8	+0·5	+0·1	−0·1

SHELTER Very good in R Rother which dries completely to soft mud. Rye Bay is exposed to prevailing SW'lies with little shelter, when there is good ⚓ in lee of Dungeness (6M to E). In N'lies ⚓ 5ca N of the Rye Fairway buoy.
Rye Hbr is a small village, ¾M inside ent on W bank, used by commercial shipping. Berth initially on Admiralty Jetty (E bank) and see Hr Mr for AB or M. No ⚓. Max speed 6kn.
Rye Town (a Cinque Port) is 2M up river. Enter via Rock Channel for ⓥ AB along NE side of Strand Quay.

NAVIGATION WPT Rye Fairway SWM By, L Fl 10s, 50°54′·04N 00°48′·02E, 150°/330° from/to W Arm tripod lt, 1·81M. Bar dries 2·75m about 2ca offshore and needs care when wind >F6 from SE to SW. Enter HW −2 to HW +3. Beware: Bar and shoals E and W of ent with ground swell or surf; narrow ent (42m) and chan (30m); flood runs 4·5kn (max HW −3 to HW −1).
Depth of water over the bar can be judged by day from how many horizontal timbers can be seen on West Arm tripod structure (approx 2ca N of the bar): 3, 2 or 1 timbers indicate water depths over the bar of about 0·5m, 2·0m or 3·5m (1·6ft, 6·5ft or 11·5ft) respectively.

LIGHTS AND MARKS Dir Oc WG 4s lt on Hr Mr's office has W sector (326°-331°) covering ent/river. W Arm lt Fl R 5s 7m 6M, wooden tripod, radar reflector. E Arm hd, Q (9) 15s 7m 5M; Horn 7s, G △. On E Pier a floodlit "Welcome to Rye" sign is considered too bright by some, but helpful by others. Rock Chan ent marked by a QR and QG lt buoy in season.
IPTS (Sigs 2 & 5 only) are shown to seaward (3M) from Hr Mr's office and up-river (1M) from Admiralty Jetty.

RADIO TELEPHONE VHF Ch 14 16 (0900-1700LT, HW±2 or when vessel due). To avoid commercial ships monitor Ch 14 before arr/dep.

TELEPHONE (Dial code 01797) Hr Mr 225225, 📠 227429; MRCC (01304) 210008; ⊖ (01304) 224251; Marinecall 09068 500456; Police 222112; Dr 222031; Ⓗ 222109.

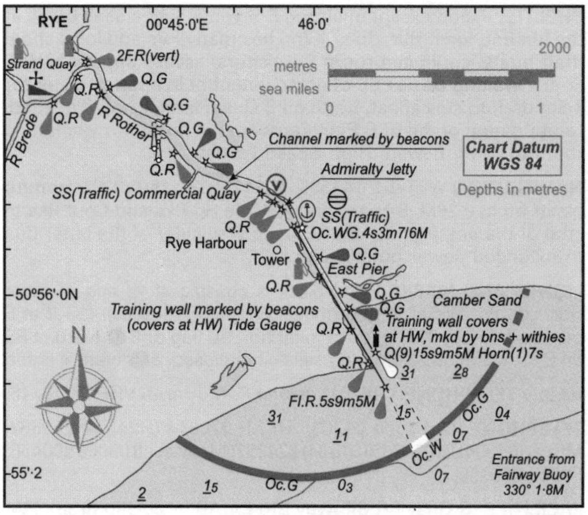

FACILITIES (from seaward) **Admiralty Jetty** £1.20, Slip, M, L, FW; **Rye Hbr** ME, El, BY, Sh, CH, C (15 ton), C (3 ton), Slip (26 ton), Ⓔ, ACA; **Rye Hbr SC** (Sec'y) ☎ 344645. **Rye Town, Strand Quay** AB £1.20, wood fendering posts against solid wall with numbered ladders. M, P & D (50m, cans), FW, Shwrs, ♿; **Town** EC Tues; ✉, Ⓑ, ⇌, ✈ (Lydd). Note: A Historic Wreck (*Anne*; see 9.0.3h) is about 4M WSW of Rye, close inshore at 50°53′·42N 00°41′·91E.

LYDD Firing Ranges off Lydd, centred on 50°54′N 00°53′E: a Sea Danger Area extends 3M offshore and stretches E from Rye Fairway buoy to a N/S line approx 1·5M W of Dungeness lt ho. When firing takes place, about 300 days p.a. 0830–1630LT (often to 2300), R flags/R lts are displayed ashore and a Range Safety Craft may be on station. Call *Lydd Ranges* Ch 73 13 or ☎ 01303 225518/225519. Radar fixes may also be obtained by VHF. Vessels may legally transit through the Sea Danger Area, but should not enter or remain in it for other purposes. If possible vessels should transit S of Stephenson Shoal.

HYTHE Firing Ranges (centred on 51°02′N 01°03′E) have a Sea Danger Area extending 2M offshore, from Hythe to Dymchurch (approx 5M and 8M WSW of Folkestone hbr). Vessels may legally transit through the Sea Danger Area, but should not enter or remain in it for other purposes. When firing takes place, about 300 days p.a. 0830–1630LT (often to 2300), R flags/R lts are displayed ashore and a Range Safety Craft may be on station. Radar fixes may also be obtained by VHF. Call *Hythe Ranges* Ch 73 13 or ☎ 01303 225836 Ext 8179/8133, 📠 Ext 8138.

FOLKESTONE *9.3.13*

Kent **51°04'·59N 01°11'·67E**

CHARTS AC *5605, 1991, 1892*; Imray C8, C12; Stanfords 9, 20; OS 179

TIDES –0010 Dover; ML 3·9; Duration 0500; Zone 0 (UT)

Standard Port DOVER (⟶)

Times				Height (metres)			
High Water		Low Water		MHWS	MHWN	MLWN	MLWS
0000	0600	0100	0700	6·8	5·3	2·1	0·8
1200	1800	1300	1900				
Differences FOLKESTONE							
–0020	–0005	–0010	–0010	+0·4	+0·4	0·0	–0·1
DUNGENESS							
–0010	–0015	–0020	–0010	+1·0	+0·6	+0·4	+0·1

SHELTER Good except in strong E-S winds when seas break at the hbr ent. Inner Hbr, dries 1·7m, has many FVs and local shoal draft boats, so limited room for visitors; access approx HW±2. Four Y waiting Ⓜs lie ESE of ent to inner hbr in enough water for 1·5m draft to stay afloat. Berth on S Quay; fender board needed. Depth gauge on hd of E Pier. Ferry area is prohib to yachts; no room to ⚓ off. Beware High Speed Ferries.

NAVIGATION WPT 51°04'·33N 01°11'·89E, 150°/330° from/to bkwtr hd lt, 0·26M. Beware drying Mole Hd Rks and Copt Rks to stbd of the ent; from/to the NE, keep well clear of the latter due to extended sewer outfall pipe.

LIGHTS AND MARKS Hotel block is conspic at W end of Inner Hbr. Ldg lts 295° at ferry terminal, FR and FG (occas). QG lt at E pierhead on brg 305° leads to inner hbr. Bu flag or 3 ● (vert) at FS on S arm, 5 mins before ferry sails = hbr closed. 3● (vert) = enter.

RADIO TELEPHONE Call *Folkestone Port Control* VHF Ch 15, 16.

TELEPHONE (Dial code 01303) Hr Mr 220544 (H24), 📠 221567; MRCC (01304) 210008; ⊖ (01304) 224251; Marinecall 09068 500456; Police 850055.

FACILITIES S Quay BR Slipway £10 for AB or ⚓, Slip (free), FW; **Folkestone Y & MB Club** ☎ 251574, D, FW, L, Slip, M, Bar, ♿. **Town** EC Wed (larger shops open all day); P & D (cans, 100 yds), V, R, Bar, ✉, Ⓑ, ⇌, ✈ (Lydd). Freight ferries and Hoverspeed (Seacat) to Boulogne.

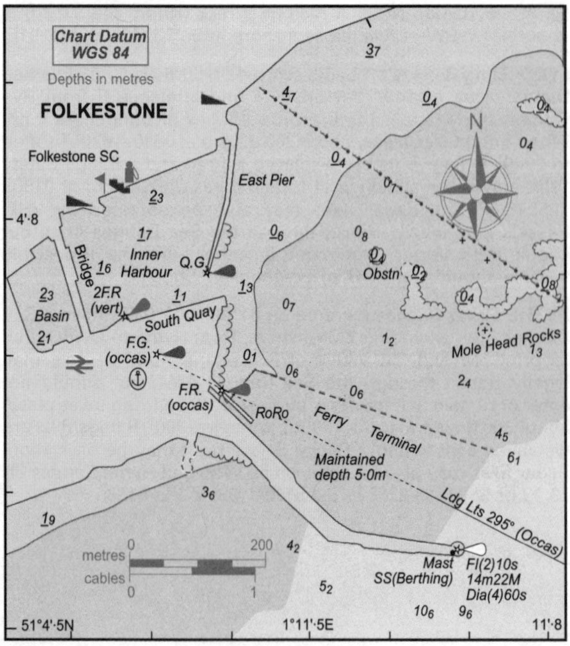

DOVER *9.3.14*

Kent **51°06'·74N 01°19'·73E** (W ent)
51°07'·25N 01°20'·61E (E ent)

CHARTS AC *5605, 1698, 1828, 1892*; Imray C8, C12, C30, 2100 series; Stanfords 9, 20; OS 179

TIDES 0000 Dover; ML 3·7; Duration 0505; Zone 0 (UT)

Standard Port DOVER (⟶)

Times				Height (metres)			
High Water		Low Water		MHWS	MHWN	MLWN	MLWS
0000	0600	0100	0700	6·8	5·3	2·1	0·8
1200	1800	1300	1900				
Differences DEAL							
+0010	+0020	+0010	+0005	–0·6	–0·3	0·0	0·0

SHELTER Very good in marina, 3 options: a. Tidal hbr, E of waiting pontoon (1·5m), access H24. 3 pontoons in about 2·5m. b. Granville Dock, access via gate approx HW±4, 120 AB. c. Wellington Dock. Dock gates, and swing bridge, open HW ±2 nps and approx HW–1½ to HW+2½ sp, depending on range; 147 AB. In the Outer Hbr the small craft moorings and ⚓ are tenable in offshore winds, but exposed to winds from NE through S to SW; in gales a heavy sea builds up. Small craft may not be left unattended at ⚓ in Outer Hbr. High Speed Ferries operate in the area.

NAVIGATION WPT from SW, 51°06'·18N 01°19'·67E, 180°/000° from/to Admiralty Pier lt ho, 0·5M. WPT from NE, 51°07'·30N 01°21'·41E, 090°/270° from/to S end Eastern Arm, 0·5M. Beware lumpy seas/overfalls outside the bkwtrs and the frequent ferries and catamarans using both ents. Strong tides across ents and high walls make ent under sail slow and difficult; use of engine very strongly recommended. Inside the W ent do not pass between NCM buoy, Q, (marking wreck) and the S bkwtr.
Specific permission to ent/leave the hbr via E or W ent must first be obtained from Port Control on VHF Ch 74. Comply with any VHF instructions from Port Control or hbr patrol launch. Clearance for small/slow craft is not normally given until within 200m of ent; advise if you have no engine. Visitors are welcomed and usually escorted by hbr launch to the marina.
If no VHF, Stay clear of entrance, attract attention of Port Control (E arm) with five short lamp flashes. Hbr launch will escort you in. Do not use W entrance.
Q Ⓦ lt from Port Control tr or patrol launch = keep clear of ent you are approaching. Beware catamarans on rounding Prince of Wales pier.
Marina sigs: In the final appr, especially near LW, stay in deep water as defined by the W sector (324°-333°) of the F WR lt, 3 unlit SHM poles. IPTS are shown, plus a small Fl ● lt 5 min before bridge is swung.
Note: A Historic Wreck (see 9.0.3h) is adjacent to the Eastern Arm bkwtr at 51°07'·6N 01°20'·7E (see chartlet). There are 4 more Historic Wrecks on the Goodwin Sands.

LIGHTS AND MARKS Lts as on chartlet & 9.3.4. Port Control tr (conspic) is at S end of E Arm and shows IPTS (for ferries only) for the E ent on panels; for W ent, IPTS are on panels near Admiralty Pier sig stn.

RADIO TELEPHONE Call: *Dover Port Control* VHF Ch **74** 12 16. Hbr launch and Water Taxi Ch 74. *Dover Marina* Ch 80, only within tidal hbr/marina. Chan Nav Info Service (CNIS) broadcasts tfc/nav/wx/tidal info Ch 11 at H+40; also, if vis < 2M, at H+55. *Dover Coastguard* Ch **69** 16 80, gives TSS surveillance.

TELEPHONE (Dial code 01304) Hr Mr 240400 xt 4540; Port Control 240400 ext 5530, Marina 241663, pr.doverport.co.uk; MRCC 210008; ⊖ 224251; Marinecall 09068 500456; Police 240055; Ⓗ 201624.

FACILITIES Marina (373 inc Ⓥ) ☎ 241663, 📠 242549, £1.80 tidal hbr, £1.60 Granville Dock, £1.50 Wellington Dock; all inc AC. **Services:** FW, C, Slip, D, LPG, ◙, BH (50 ton), ME, El, Sh, SM, CH, ACA, Ⓔ (H24). **Royal Cinque Ports YC** ☎ 206262, L, M, C, FW, Bar, R; **Town:** www.doverport.co.uk, P (cans), V, R, Bar, ✉, Ⓑ, ⇌, ✈ (Lydd).

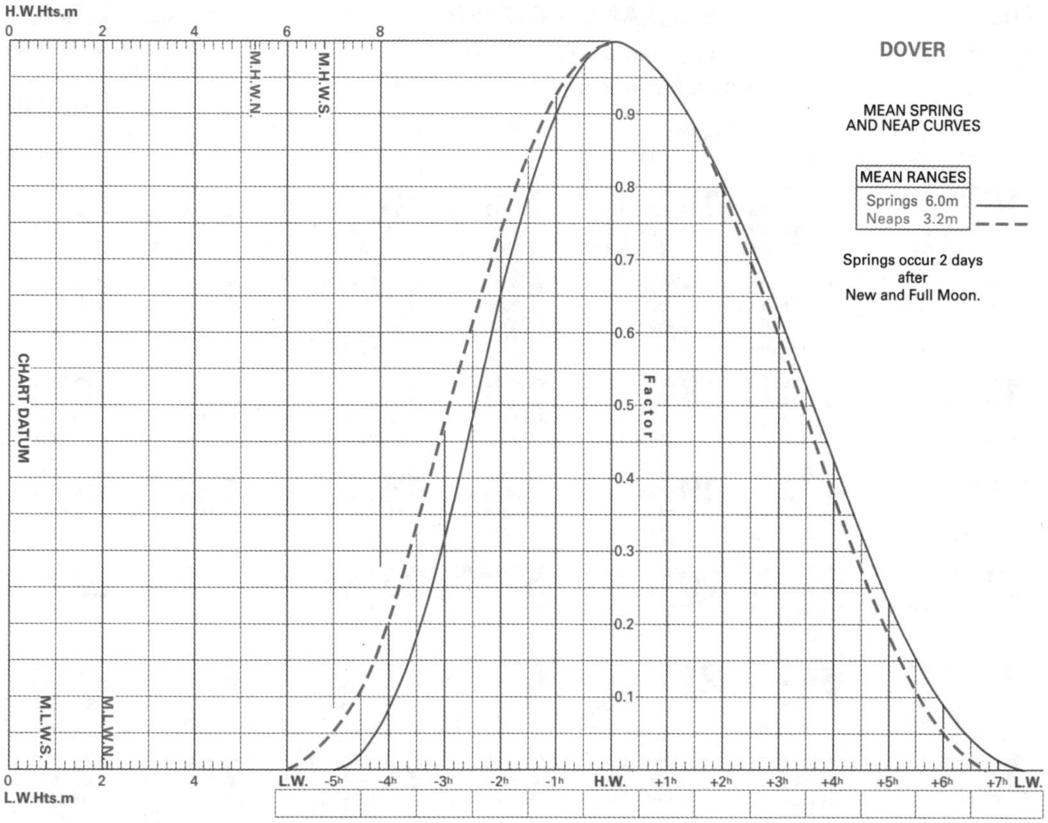
H.W.Hts.m
M.H.W.N.
M.H.W.S.
CHART DATUM
M.L.W.S.
M.L.W.N.
L.W.Hts.m
Factor
L.W.
H.W.
DOVER
MEAN SPRING
AND NEAP CURVES
MEAN RANGES
Springs 6.0m
Neaps 3.2m
Springs occur 2 days
after
New and Full Moon.

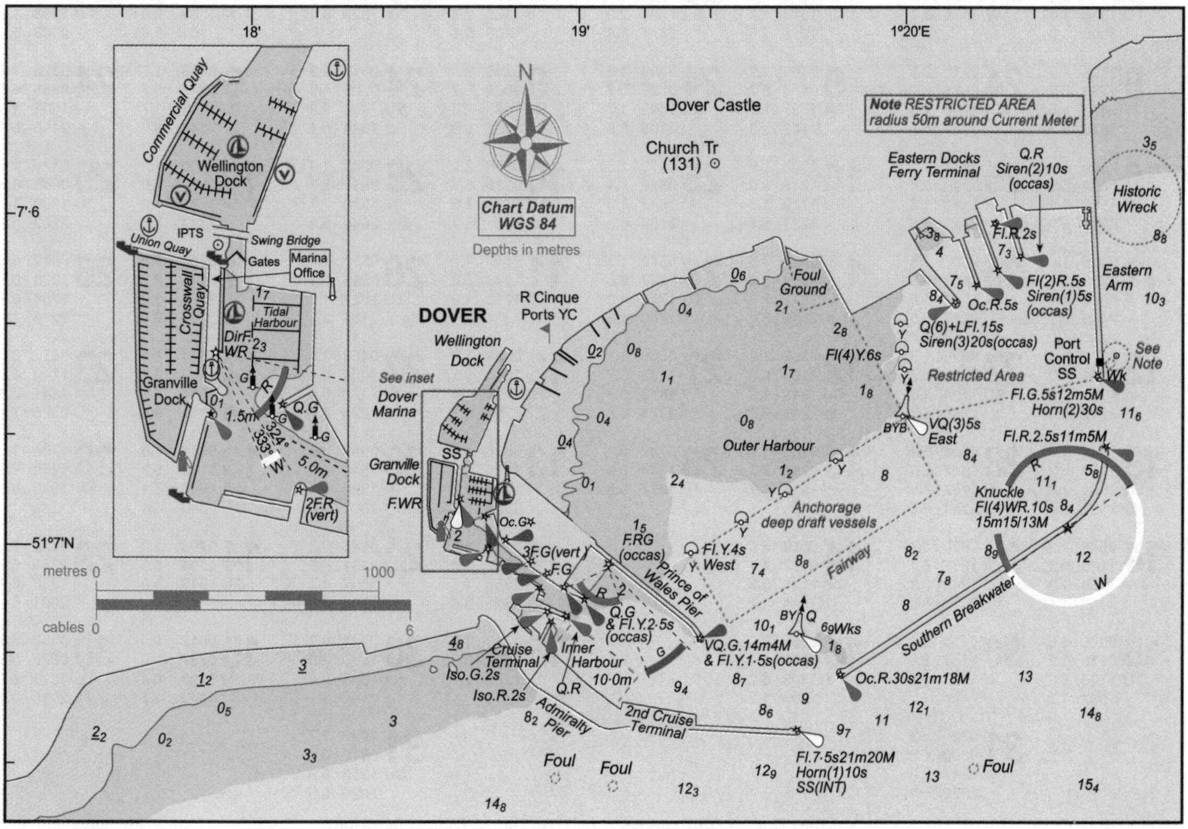
DOVER
Chart Datum
WGS 84
Depths in metres
Dover Castle
Church Tr
(131)
Note RESTRICTED AREA
radius 50m around Current Meter
Eastern Docks
Ferry Terminal
Q.R
Siren(2)10s
(occas)
Historic
Wreck
Eastern
Arm
Fl(2)R.5s
Siren(1)5s
(occas)
Oc.R.5s
Q(6)+LFl.15s
Siren(3)20s(occas)
Port
Control
SS
See
Note
Restricted Area
Fl.G.5s12m5M
Horn(2)30s
VQ(3)5s
East
Fl.R.2.5s11m5M
Knuckle
Fl(4)WR.10s
15m15/13M
Southern Breakwater
Oc.R.30s21m18M
Foul
Ground
Fl(4)Y.6s
Outer Harbour
Anchorage
deep draft vessels
Fairway
Fl.Y.4s
West
Prince of
Wales Pier
VQ.G.14m4M
& Fl.Y.1·5s(occas)
6 Wks
R Cinque
Ports YC
Wellington
Dock
See inset
Dover
Marina
Granville
Dock
F.WR
Oc.G
3F.G(vert)
F.RG
(occas)
Q.G
& Fl.Y.2·5s
(occas)
Cruise
Terminal
Inner
Harbour
Iso.G.2s
Iso.R.2s
Q.R
Admiralty
Pier
2nd Cruise
Terminal
Fl.7·5s21m20M
Horn(1)10s
SS(INT)
Foul
Commercial Quay
Wellington
Dock
IPTS
Swing Bridge
Union Quay
Gates
Marina
Office
Tidal
Harbour
Crosswell
Quay
Dir.F.
WR
Granville
Dock
Q.G
2F.R
(vert)
metres
cables
18'
19'
1°20'E
7'·6
51°7'N

TIME ZONE (UTC)
For Summer Time add ONE hour in **non-shaded areas**

ENGLAND – DOVER

LAT 51°07'N LONG 1°19'W

TIMES AND HEIGHTS OF HIGH AND LOW WATERS

SPRING & NEAP TIDES
Dates in red are SPRINGS
Dates in blue are NEAPS

YEAR **2002**

JANUARY

Date	Time	m	Date	Time	m
1 TU	0716 1203 1939	1.0 6.7 1.0	16 W	0038 0753 1255 2001	6.5 1.2 6.3 1.4
2 W	0029 0802 1250 2023	6.8 0.9 6.6 1.1	17 TH	0113 0823 1328 2029	6.5 1.3 6.1 1.4
3 TH	0117 0850 1340 2109	6.7 0.9 6.5 1.2	18 F	0144 0853 1400 2059	6.3 1.4 6.0 1.5
4 F	0207 0939 1434 2157	6.6 1.0 6.3 1.3	19 SA	0212 0925 1430 2134	6.2 1.5 5.8 1.6
5 SA	0301 1030 1534 2248	6.5 1.2 6.1 1.5	20 SU	0242 1001 1503 2212	6.0 1.6 5.6 1.8
6 SU	0359 1124 1640 2344	6.2 1.3 5.8 1.7	21 M	0320 1042 1546 2256	5.8 1.8 5.4 2.0
7 M	0504 1223 1753	6.0 1.5 5.7	22 TU	0409 1132 1649 2351	5.6 2.0 5.2 2.2
8 TU	0047 0615 1326 1905	1.9 5.9 1.6 5.6	23 W	0518 1238 1816	5.4 2.1 5.2
9 W	0155 0728 1432 2010	1.9 5.8 1.6 5.7	24 TH	0110 0638 1357 1927	2.3 5.4 2.1 5.3
10 TH	0305 0834 1542 2108	1.8 5.9 1.6 5.9	25 F	0231 0746 1507 2026	2.1 5.6 1.8 5.6
11 F	0415 0931 1649 2158	1.6 6.1 1.4 6.1	26 SA	0337 0844 1608 2117	1.8 5.9 1.5 6.0
12 SA	0514 1021 1741 2242	1.4 6.2 1.3 6.3	27 SU	0435 0935 1704 2205	1.5 6.2 1.3 6.3
13 SU	0602 1104 1823 ● 2322	1.3 6.3 1.3 6.4	28 M	0528 1024 1757 ○ 2251	1.2 6.5 1.0 6.6
14 M	0643 1143 1900	1.2 6.4 1.3	29 TU	0620 1111 1848 2336	0.9 6.7 0.9 6.8
15 TU	0000 0720 1220 1932	6.5 1.2 6.3 1.3	30 W	0711 1157 1937	0.7 6.8 0.8
			31 TH	0021 0800 1243 2022	6.9 0.6 6.8 0.7

FEBRUARY

Date	Time	m	Date	Time	m
1 F	0106 0847 1328 2104	7.0 0.5 6.7 0.8	16 SA	0116 0830 1328 2037	6.4 1.1 6.1 1.2
2 SA	0152 0931 1415 2145	6.9 0.6 6.5 0.9	17 SU	0137 0859 1350 2108	6.3 1.2 6.1 1.3
3 SU	0239 1014 1506 2227	6.8 0.8 6.3 1.1	18 M	0203 0930 1417 2141	6.3 1.3 6.0 1.5
4 M	0330 1058 1601 2313	6.5 1.1 6.0 1.5	19 TU	0236 1003 1454 2217	6.2 1.5 5.8 1.7
5 TU	0426 1148 1705	6.1 1.4 5.6	20 W	0318 1043 1541 2302	5.9 1.8 5.6 2.0
6 W	0008 0532 1248 1819	1.8 5.7 1.8 5.4	21 TH	0413 1136 1649	5.6 2.1 5.2
7 TH	0117 0651 1357 1939	2.1 5.5 2.0 5.3	22 F	0007 0540 1302 1848	2.3 5.3 2.2 5.1
8 F	0233 0816 1512 2051	2.1 5.5 1.9 5.5	23 SA	0147 0721 1435 2004	2.3 5.4 2.0 5.4
9 SA	0355 0926 1631 2147	1.9 5.7 1.7 5.8	24 SU	0308 0829 1545 2103	1.9 5.7 1.7 5.8
10 SU	0502 1018 1729 2231	1.6 6.0 1.5 6.1	25 M	0413 0926 1647 2154	1.5 6.1 1.3 6.3
11 M	0552 1058 1812 2309	1.3 6.2 1.3 6.4	26 TU	0512 1017 1745 2240	1.1 6.5 1.0 6.6
12 TU	0633 1133 1848 ● 2345	1.2 6.3 1.3 6.5	27 W	0609 1103 1839 ○ 2324	0.7 6.7 0.7 6.9
13 W	0708 1204 1918	1.1 6.3 1.2	28 TH	0702 1146 1927	0.4 6.9 0.6
14 TH	0019 0737 1235 1944	6.5 1.1 6.3 1.2			
15 F	0050 0803 1303 2009	6.5 1.1 6.2 1.2			

MARCH

Date	Time	m	Date	Time	m
1 F	0007 0750 1229 2009	7.1 0.3 6.9 0.5	16 SA	0022 0737 1235 1945	6.5 1.0 6.3 1.1
2 SA	0049 0833 1310 2048	7.2 0.2 6.9 0.5	17 SU	0045 0804 1257 2013	6.4 1.0 6.3 1.1
3 SU	0132 0913 1353 2124	7.1 0.3 6.7 0.7	18 M	0106 0832 1317 2042	6.4 1.1 6.3 1.2
4 M	0215 0950 1438 2201	6.9 0.6 6.4 1.0	19 TU	0131 0901 1345 2113	6.4 1.2 6.3 1.3
5 TU	0302 1030 1529 2243	6.5 1.0 6.1 1.4	20 W	0203 0932 1421 2147	6.3 1.4 6.1 1.6
6 W	0355 1115 1628 2334	6.1 1.5 5.6 1.9	21 TH	0243 1009 1506 2230	6.1 1.7 5.8 1.9
7 TH	0458 1213 1740	5.6 2.0 5.3	22 F	0335 1059 1609 2332	5.7 2.1 5.3 2.2
8 F	0044 0617 1327 1905	2.2 5.2 2.3 5.1	23 SA	0501 1217 1820	5.2 2.3 5.1
9 SA	0208 0804 1448 2032	2.3 5.2 2.2 5.3	24 SU	0113 0705 1408 1944	2.3 5.3 2.2 5.4
10 SU	0338 0920 1613 2131	2.0 5.5 1.9 5.7	25 M	0243 0817 1523 2046	1.9 5.7 1.7 5.9
11 M	0449 1008 1712 2214	1.6 5.8 1.6 6.1	26 TU	0351 0915 1627 2138	1.4 6.1 1.3 6.3
12 TU	0538 1044 1754 2251	1.3 6.1 1.4 6.3	27 W	0453 1004 1726 2224	1.0 6.5 0.9 6.7
13 W	0616 1115 1829 2324	1.1 6.2 1.2 6.5	28 TH	0552 1049 1820 ○ 2307	0.6 6.8 0.7 7.0
14 TH	0648 1142 1856 ● 2355	1.0 6.3 1.1 6.5	29 F	0645 1131 1907 2348	0.3 6.9 0.5 7.2
15 F	0713 1209 1920	1.0 6.3 1.1	30 SA	0732 1210 1948	0.2 7.0 0.4
			31 SU	0029 0812 1250 2025	7.2 0.2 6.9 0.5

APRIL

Date	Time	m	Date	Time	m
1 M	0110 0849 1331 2100	7.1 0.4 6.8 0.7	16 TU	0037 0807 1251 2019	6.5 1.1 6.4 1.1
2 TU	0152 0925 1414 2136	6.9 0.7 6.5 1.0	17 W	0105 0836 1322 2051	6.5 1.2 6.4 1.3
3 W	0237 1002 1503 2215	6.5 1.1 6.1 1.4	18 TH	0139 0909 1400 2127	6.3 1.4 6.2 1.5
4 TH	0329 1044 1600 2304	6.0 1.7 5.7 1.9	19 F	0221 0948 1449 2213	6.1 1.7 5.8 1.8
5 F	0432 1141 1708	5.5 2.2 5.3	20 SA	0317 1040 1558 2316	5.6 2.0 5.4 2.1
6 SA	0017 0547 1300 1828	2.3 5.1 2.4 5.1	21 SU	0459 1157 1756	5.3 2.2 5.3
7 SU	0145 0740 1422 2001	2.3 5.1 2.3 5.3	22 M	0053 0647 1344 1919	2.1 5.4 2.1 5.5
8 M	0310 0858 1538 2103	2.1 5.4 2.0 5.6	23 TU	0219 0758 1458 2023	1.8 5.7 1.7 5.9
9 TU	0418 0942 1636 2146	1.7 5.7 1.7 6.0	24 W	0326 0856 1601 2116	1.3 6.1 1.3 6.4
10 W	0506 1017 1721 2222	1.4 6.0 1.4 6.2	25 TH	0429 0945 1700 2202	0.9 6.5 1.0 6.7
11 TH	0544 1045 1756 2254	1.2 6.2 1.2 6.4	26 F	0529 1029 1754 2246	0.6 6.7 0.7 7.0
12 F	0614 1112 1824 ● 2323	1.1 6.3 1.2 6.4	27 SA	0622 1110 1841 ○ 2328	0.4 6.8 0.6 7.1
13 SA	0641 1139 1850 2350	1.0 6.3 1.1 6.4	28 SU	0708 1150 1923	0.3 6.9 0.5
14 SU	0708 1204 1919	1.0 6.3 1.0	29 M	0009 0748 1230 2001	7.1 0.4 6.8 0.6
15 M	0013 0737 1228 1949	6.4 1.0 6.4 1.1	30 TU	0050 0826 1311 2038	6.9 0.6 6.7 0.8

Chart Datum: 3·67 metres below Ordnance Datum (Newlyn)

TIME ZONE (UTC)
For Summer Time add ONE hour in **non-shaded areas**

ENGLAND – DOVER

LAT 51°07'N LONG 1°19'W

TIMES AND HEIGHTS OF HIGH AND LOW WATERS

SPRING & NEAP TIDES
Dates in red are SPRINGS
Dates in blue are NEAPS

YEAR **2002**

MAY

Day	Time	m	Time	m	Time	m	Time	m
1 W	0132	6.7	0901	0.9	1355	6.5	2114	1.1
2 TH	0217	6.3	0937	1.3	1443	6.1	2153	1.5
3 F	0309	5.9	1017	1.8	1537	5.8	2241	1.9
4 SA	0408	5.5	1110	2.2	1638	5.4	2350	2.2
5 SU	0516	5.1	1227	2.4	1748	5.2		
6 M	0111	2.3	0642	5.1	1344	2.4	1909	5.3
7 TU	0224	2.1	0810	5.3	1450	2.1	2018	5.6
8 W	0325	1.8	0859	5.6	1546	1.8	2106	5.8
9 TH	0414	1.5	0934	5.8	1633	1.6	2143	6.1
10 F	0455	1.3	1005	6.0	1712	1.4	2216	6.2
11 SA	0531	1.2	1035	6.2	1747	1.2	2246	6.3
12 SU	0605	1.1	1105	6.3	1820	1.1	● 2315	6.4
13 M	0640	1.1	1134	6.3	1854	1.1	2344	6.4
14 TU	0714	1.1	1203	6.4	1928	1.1		
15 W	0014	6.4	0746	1.1	1234	6.4	2002	1.1
16 TH	0048	6.4	0820	1.2	1310	6.4	2038	1.3
17 F	0127	6.3	0856	1.4	1354	6.2	2119	1.4
18 SA	0215	6.0	0939	1.6	1449	5.9	2208	1.7
19 SU	0320	5.7	1033	1.9	1603	5.7	2313	1.8
20 M	0454	5.5	1149	2.0	1728	5.6		
21 TU	0037	1.8	0621	5.6	1317	1.9	1846	5.7
22 W	0153	1.6	0732	5.8	1427	1.7	1953	6.0
23 TH	0257	1.3	0830	6.1	1529	1.4	2049	6.3
24 F	0400	1.0	0921	6.3	1630	1.1	2138	6.6
25 SA	0501	0.8	1007	6.5	1726	0.9	2225	6.7
26 SU	0557	0.7	1050	6.6	1816	0.8	○ 2309	6.8
27 M	0644	0.6	1132	6.7	1901	0.8	2352	6.8
28 TU	0726	0.7	1213	6.7	1941	0.8		
29 W	0034	6.7	0805	0.9	1256	6.6	2020	1.0
30 TH	0117	6.5	0841	1.2	1339	6.4	2058	1.2
31 F	0201	6.2	0917	1.5	1424	6.2	2137	1.5

JUNE

Day	Time	m	Time	m	Time	m	Time	m
1 SA	0249	5.9	0954	1.8	1513	5.9	2220	1.8
2 SU	0343	5.5	1037	2.0	1606	5.6	2314	2.0
3 M	0442	5.3	1138	2.3	1705	5.4		
4 TU	0021	2.1	0547	5.2	1249	2.3	1811	5.4
5 W	0126	2.1	0657	5.2	1353	2.2	1917	5.4
6 TH	0224	1.9	0756	5.4	1450	2.0	2011	5.6
7 F	0315	1.7	0842	5.6	1541	1.8	2055	5.8
8 SA	0404	1.5	0920	5.8	1628	1.5	2132	6.0
9 SU	0449	1.3	0957	6.0	1711	1.4	2208	6.2
10 M	0533	1.2	1033	6.2	1753	1.2	● 2245	6.3
11 TU	0614	1.1	1109	6.3	1833	1.1	2322	6.4
12 W	0654	1.1	1145	6.4	1912	1.1		
13 TH	0000	6.4	0733	1.1	1225	6.4	1952	1.1
14 F	0041	6.4	0812	1.2	1308	6.4	2034	1.1
15 SA	0126	6.3	0854	1.3	1355	6.3	2119	1.2
16 SU	0218	6.1	0940	1.5	1450	6.2	2211	1.4
17 M	0320	5.9	1033	1.6	1551	6.0	2310	1.5
18 TU	0431	5.8	1136	1.7	1657	5.9		
19 W	0015	1.5	0546	5.7	1245	1.7	1807	5.9
20 TH	0121	1.5	0658	5.8	1351	1.7	1917	6.0
21 F	0225	1.4	0801	5.9	1455	1.5	2021	6.1
22 SA	0329	1.3	0856	6.1	1600	1.4	2117	6.3
23 SU	0435	1.1	0947	6.2	1702	1.2	2209	6.4
24 M	0535	1.0	1035	6.4	1756	1.1	○ 2257	6.5
25 TU	0625	1.0	1119	6.5	1843	1.0	2341	6.5
26 W	0709	1.0	1200	6.5	1926	1.0		
27 TH	0023	6.4	0748	1.1	1242	6.5	2006	1.1
28 F	0104	6.3	0825	1.3	1323	6.4	2044	1.3
29 SA	0144	6.1	0859	1.5	1404	6.3	2120	1.4
30 SU	0226	5.9	0930	1.6	1445	6.1	2155	1.6

JULY

Day	Time	m	Time	m	Time	m	Time	m
1 M	0310	5.7	1003	1.8	1528	5.9	2233	1.8
2 TU	0359	5.5	1043	2.0	1614	5.6	2319	1.9
3 W	0454	5.3	1133	2.1	1708	5.5		
4 TH	0016	2.0	0554	5.2	1239	2.2	1809	5.4
5 F	0120	2.0	0656	5.3	1349	2.2	1911	5.4
6 SA	0223	1.9	0752	5.4	1452	2.0	2005	5.6
7 SU	0321	1.7	0841	5.6	1549	1.8	2054	5.8
8 M	0415	1.5	0926	5.9	1641	1.5	2139	6.1
9 TU	0506	1.3	1008	6.1	1729	1.3	2223	6.3
10 W	0554	1.2	1051	6.3	1815	1.1	● 2307	6.4
11 TH	0640	1.1	1133	6.5	1901	1.0	2351	6.5
12 F	0725	1.1	1216	6.6	1947	0.9		
13 SA	0035	6.5	0809	1.1	1301	6.6	2033	0.9
14 SU	0121	6.5	0854	1.1	1347	6.6	2119	0.9
15 M	0210	6.4	0938	1.1	1436	6.5	2206	1.0
16 TU	0303	6.2	1023	1.3	1529	6.4	2255	1.1
17 W	0401	6.0	1113	1.5	1626	6.2	2348	1.3
18 TH	0506	5.8	1210	1.7	1730	6.0		
19 F	0047	1.5	0618	5.7	1315	1.8	1841	5.8
20 SA	0152	1.6	0731	5.6	1424	1.8	1957	5.8
21 SU	0301	1.6	0837	5.7	1536	1.7	2105	5.9
22 M	0415	1.5	0935	6.0	1646	1.5	2204	6.1
23 TU	0520	1.4	1025	6.2	1744	1.3	2253	6.3
24 W	0612	1.3	1108	6.4	1833	1.2	○ 2335	6.3
25 TH	0656	1.2	1148	6.5	1915	1.1		
26 F	0013	6.3	0733	1.2	1227	6.5	1953	1.1
27 SA	0049	6.3	0807	1.3	1304	6.5	2026	1.2
28 SU	0124	6.2	0836	1.4	1340	6.4	2056	1.3
29 M	0158	6.0	0901	1.4	1412	6.3	2123	1.4
30 TU	0230	5.9	0929	1.5	1442	6.1	2153	1.5
31 W	0303	5.7	1002	1.7	1515	5.9	2229	1.7

AUGUST

Day	Time	m	Time	m	Time	m	Time	m
1 TH	0341	5.5	1041	1.9	1558	5.6	2312	1.9
2 F	0435	5.3	1130	2.1	1657	5.4		
3 SA	0011	2.1	0554	5.2	1240	2.3	1814	5.3
4 SU	0131	2.2	0709	5.2	1406	2.3	1927	5.4
5 M	0245	2.0	0810	5.5	1517	2.0	2028	5.7
6 TU	0348	1.7	0903	5.8	1616	1.6	2121	6.0
7 W	0444	1.4	0951	6.1	1709	1.3	2210	6.3
8 TH	0537	1.2	1036	6.4	1759	1.0	● 2256	6.5
9 F	0627	1.0	1119	6.7	1850	0.8	2340	6.6
10 SA	0716	0.9	1202	6.8	1939	0.7		
11 SU	0023	6.7	0801	0.8	1246	6.9	2025	0.6
12 M	0106	6.7	0843	0.8	1329	6.9	2108	0.6
13 TU	0150	6.6	0923	0.9	1415	6.8	2149	0.7
14 W	0237	6.4	1002	1.1	1503	6.6	2231	1.0
15 TH	0330	6.2	1045	1.3	1556	6.3	2317	1.3
16 F	0430	5.8	1136	1.7	1658	5.9		
17 SA	0014	1.7	0542	5.5	1242	2.0	1812	5.6
18 SU	0123	2.0	0703	5.4	1359	2.1	1941	5.5
19 M	0241	2.0	0823	5.5	1524	2.0	2105	5.7
20 TU	0407	1.8	0927	5.8	1642	1.7	2205	6.0
21 W	0514	1.6	1016	6.1	1738	1.4	2249	6.2
22 TH	0602	1.4	1055	6.4	1824	1.2	○ 2325	6.3
23 F	0642	1.3	1132	6.6	1902	1.1	2357	6.4
24 SA	0716	1.2	1207	6.6	1934	1.1		
25 SU	0027	6.4	0743	1.3	1241	6.6	2000	1.1
26 M	0057	6.3	0806	1.3	1311	6.5	2024	1.2
27 TU	0124	6.2	0828	1.3	1335	6.4	2048	1.3
28 W	0146	6.1	0855	1.4	1357	6.3	2116	1.4
29 TH	0208	6.0	0926	1.5	1424	6.1	2148	1.6
30 F	0239	5.8	1001	1.8	1501	5.9	2225	1.9
31 SA	0320	5.5	1042	2.1	1551	5.5	2312	2.2

Chart Datum: 3·67 metres below Ordnance Datum (Newlyn)

TIME ZONE (UTC)
For Summer Time add ONE hour in **non-shaded areas**

ENGLAND – DOVER

LAT 51°07′N LONG 1°19′W

TIMES AND HEIGHTS OF HIGH AND LOW WATERS

SPRING & NEAP TIDES
Dates in red are SPRINGS
Dates in blue are NEAPS

YEAR **2002**

SEPTEMBER

Date	Day	Time	m	Time	m	Time	m	Time	m
1	SU	0424	5.2	1139	2.4	1719	5.2		
2	M	0028	2.4	0633	5.1	1319	2.5	1901	5.3
3	TU	0214	2.3	0747	5.3	1448	2.2	2011	5.6
4	W	0325	1.9	0845	5.8	1552	1.7	2107	6.0
5	TH	0424	1.5	0934	6.2	1648	1.3	2156	6.4
6	F	0519	1.2	1019	6.6	1742	0.9	2241	6.7
7	SA	0610	1.0	1101	6.9	1834	0.7	● 2323	6.8
8	SU	0659	0.8	1143	7.1	1923	0.5		
9	M	0004	6.9	0742	0.7	1225	7.2	2006	0.4
10	TU	0044	6.9	0822	0.7	1307	7.2	2046	0.5
11	W	0126	6.8	0859	0.8	1350	7.0	2124	0.7
12	TH	0211	6.6	0936	1.0	1437	6.7	2203	1.0
13	F	0301	6.2	1017	1.4	1529	6.3	2247	1.5
14	SA	0401	5.8	1106	1.9	1632	5.8	2343	2.0
15	SU	0513	5.4	1214	2.3	1749	5.4		
16	M	0059	2.4	0637	5.3	1343	2.4	1935	5.3
17	TU	0229	2.3	0810	5.4	1522	2.1	2103	5.6
18	W	0401	2.0	0914	5.8	1634	1.7	2155	5.9
19	TH	0459	1.7	0959	6.2	1724	1.3	2233	6.2
20	F	0543	1.4	1035	6.4	1805	1.1	2305	6.3
21	SA	0619	1.3	1109	6.6	1839	1.1	○ 2333	6.4
22	SU	0649	1.2	1142	6.6	1906	1.1		
23	M	0000	6.4	0711	1.2	1212	6.6	1927	1.1
24	TU	0027	6.4	0732	1.2	1238	6.5	1949	1.2
25	W	0049	6.3	0757	1.3	1258	6.4	2015	1.3
26	TH	0107	6.3	0825	1.3	1318	6.4	2043	1.4
27	F	0129	6.2	0855	1.5	1345	6.3	2113	1.6
28	SA	0200	6.1	0928	1.8	1421	6.0	2148	1.9
29	SU	0241	5.8	1009	2.1	1508	5.6	2234	2.2
30	M	0337	5.3	1103	2.4	1628	5.2	2340	2.5

OCTOBER

Date	Day	Time	m	Time	m	Time	m	Time	m
1	TU	0601	5.1	1236	2.5	1842	5.2		
2	W	0143	2.5	0722	5.4	1420	2.2	1953	5.6
3	TH	0301	2.0	0823	5.8	1527	1.7	2050	6.1
4	F	0401	1.6	0913	6.3	1625	1.2	2138	6.5
5	SA	0456	1.2	0957	6.7	1719	0.8	2221	6.8
6	SU	0547	0.9	1039	7.0	1811	0.6	● 2302	7.0
7	M	0634	0.7	1120	7.2	1859	0.4	2341	7.0
8	TU	0717	0.7	1200	7.3	1942	0.4		
9	W	0020	7.0	0756	0.7	1242	7.2	2021	0.5
10	TH	0102	6.9	0833	0.8	1325	7.0	2058	0.8
11	F	0147	6.6	0911	1.1	1412	6.6	2136	1.2
12	SA	0237	6.3	0952	1.5	1506	6.2	2219	1.8
13	SU	0337	5.8	1042	2.0	1611	5.7	2316	2.3
14	M	0446	5.4	1153	2.4	1726	5.3		
15	TU	0037	2.6	0605	5.3	1326	2.5	1918	5.2
16	W	0209	2.5	0741	5.4	1501	2.1	2042	5.5
17	TH	0330	2.1	0846	5.8	1606	1.7	2129	5.9
18	F	0425	1.8	0930	6.1	1654	1.4	2205	6.1
19	SA	0508	1.5	1007	6.4	1732	1.2	2234	6.3
20	SU	0544	1.3	1040	6.5	1803	1.2	2301	6.4
21	M	0613	1.3	1110	6.6	1828	1.2	○ 2327	6.4
22	TU	0636	1.3	1138	6.6	1852	1.2	2353	6.4
23	W	0702	1.3	1202	6.5	1918	1.2		
24	TH	0016	6.4	0729	1.3	1224	6.5	1947	1.3
25	F	0036	6.4	0800	1.4	1247	6.4	2016	1.4
26	SA	0102	6.4	0831	1.5	1317	6.3	2047	1.6
27	SU	0135	6.2	0906	1.7	1355	6.1	2124	1.9
28	M	0219	5.9	0948	2.0	1445	5.7	2210	2.2
29	TU	0320	5.5	1043	2.3	1613	5.3	2315	2.5
30	W	0525	5.3	1209	2.4	1818	5.3		
31	TH	0107	2.5	0650	5.5	1349	2.1	1928	5.7

NOVEMBER

Date	Day	Time	m	Time	m	Time	m	Time	m
1	F	0230	2.1	0753	5.9	1457	1.6	2025	6.1
2	SA	0331	1.6	0845	6.4	1556	1.2	2114	6.5
3	SU	0426	1.2	0931	6.8	1652	0.9	2157	6.8
4	M	0518	1.0	1014	7.0	1745	0.6	● 2238	6.9
5	TU	0607	0.8	1056	7.2	1834	0.5	2319	7.0
6	W	0651	0.7	1138	7.2	1917	0.6		
7	TH	0000	7.0	0732	0.8	1221	7.1	1957	0.7
8	F	0043	6.9	0812	0.9	1305	6.8	2035	1.0
9	SA	0129	6.6	0852	1.2	1353	6.5	2114	1.4
10	SU	0219	6.3	0934	1.6	1447	6.1	2157	1.9
11	M	0315	5.9	1025	2.0	1549	5.6	2251	2.3
12	TU	0418	5.6	1132	2.3	1658	5.3		
13	W	0006	2.5	0527	5.4	1253	2.4	1825	5.2
14	TH	0127	2.5	0649	5.4	1411	2.2	1954	5.4
15	F	0237	2.3	0800	5.7	1514	1.9	2045	5.7
16	SA	0335	2.0	0850	5.9	1604	1.6	2123	5.9
17	SU	0422	1.7	0929	6.2	1644	1.4	2155	6.1
18	M	0500	1.5	1003	6.3	1718	1.3	2224	6.3
19	TU	0533	1.4	1034	6.4	1749	1.3	2253	6.3
20	W	0604	1.3	1103	6.4	1820	1.3	○ 2322	6.4
21	TH	0635	1.3	1131	6.4	1853	1.3	2349	6.4
22	F	0708	1.3	1159	6.4	1925	1.3		
23	SA	0016	6.4	0742	1.3	1229	6.4	1958	1.4
24	SU	0048	6.4	0816	1.5	1304	6.3	2032	1.6
25	M	0127	6.3	0854	1.6	1346	6.1	2111	1.8
26	TU	0215	6.0	0939	1.8	1441	5.8	2159	2.0
27	W	0319	5.8	1035	2.0	1603	5.5	2301	2.2
28	TH	0445	5.6	1150	2.0	1742	5.5		
29	F	0028	2.2	0608	5.7	1313	1.9	1855	5.7
30	SA	0148	2.0	0716	6.0	1421	1.6	1955	6.0

DECEMBER

Date	Day	Time	m	Time	m	Time	m	Time	m
1	SU	0253	1.7	0814	6.3	1522	1.3	2047	6.3
2	M	0352	1.4	0904	6.6	1622	1.0	2134	6.5
3	TU	0450	1.2	0951	6.8	1720	0.9	2219	6.7
4	W	0543	1.0	1037	6.9	1811	0.8	● 2303	6.8
5	TH	0631	0.9	1122	6.9	1857	0.8	2346	6.8
6	F	0716	0.9	1207	6.8	1940	1.0		
7	SA	0030	6.7	0758	1.1	1252	6.6	2019	1.2
8	SU	0115	6.6	0840	1.3	1339	6.4	2059	1.5
9	M	0202	6.4	0923	1.5	1428	6.0	2140	1.8
10	TU	0251	6.1	1009	1.8	1522	5.7	2224	2.1
11	W	0345	5.8	1101	2.0	1621	5.4	2318	2.3
12	TH	0444	5.6	1201	2.2	1727	5.2		
13	F	0023	2.4	0549	5.4	1305	2.2	1837	5.2
14	SA	0130	2.4	0657	5.5	1404	2.1	1941	5.4
15	SU	0231	2.2	0756	5.6	1459	1.9	2030	5.6
16	M	0326	2.0	0843	5.8	1548	1.7	2111	5.8
17	TU	0414	1.8	0922	6.0	1633	1.5	2147	6.0
18	W	0456	1.6	0958	6.2	1715	1.4	2222	6.2
19	TH	0536	1.4	1033	6.3	1755	1.3	○ 2257	6.3
20	F	0614	1.3	1108	6.4	1833	1.3	2331	6.4
21	SA	0652	1.2	1144	6.4	1911	1.3		
22	SU	0007	6.5	0731	1.2	1222	6.4	1948	1.3
23	M	0045	6.5	0810	1.3	1301	6.3	2027	1.4
24	TU	0127	6.4	0852	1.3	1346	6.2	2108	1.5
25	W	0214	6.3	0938	1.4	1437	6.0	2155	1.6
26	TH	0308	6.2	1030	1.5	1538	5.9	2248	1.8
27	F	0410	6.0	1129	1.6	1651	5.7	2352	1.9
28	SA	0520	5.9	1235	1.6	1809	5.7		
29	SU	0103	1.9	0633	5.9	1341	1.6	1919	5.8
30	M	0212	1.8	0741	6.0	1447	1.5	2020	5.9
31	TU	0319	1.6	0842	6.2	1553	1.3	2116	6.1

Chart Datum: 3·67 metres below Ordnance Datum (Newlyn)

DOVER STRAIT 9.3.15

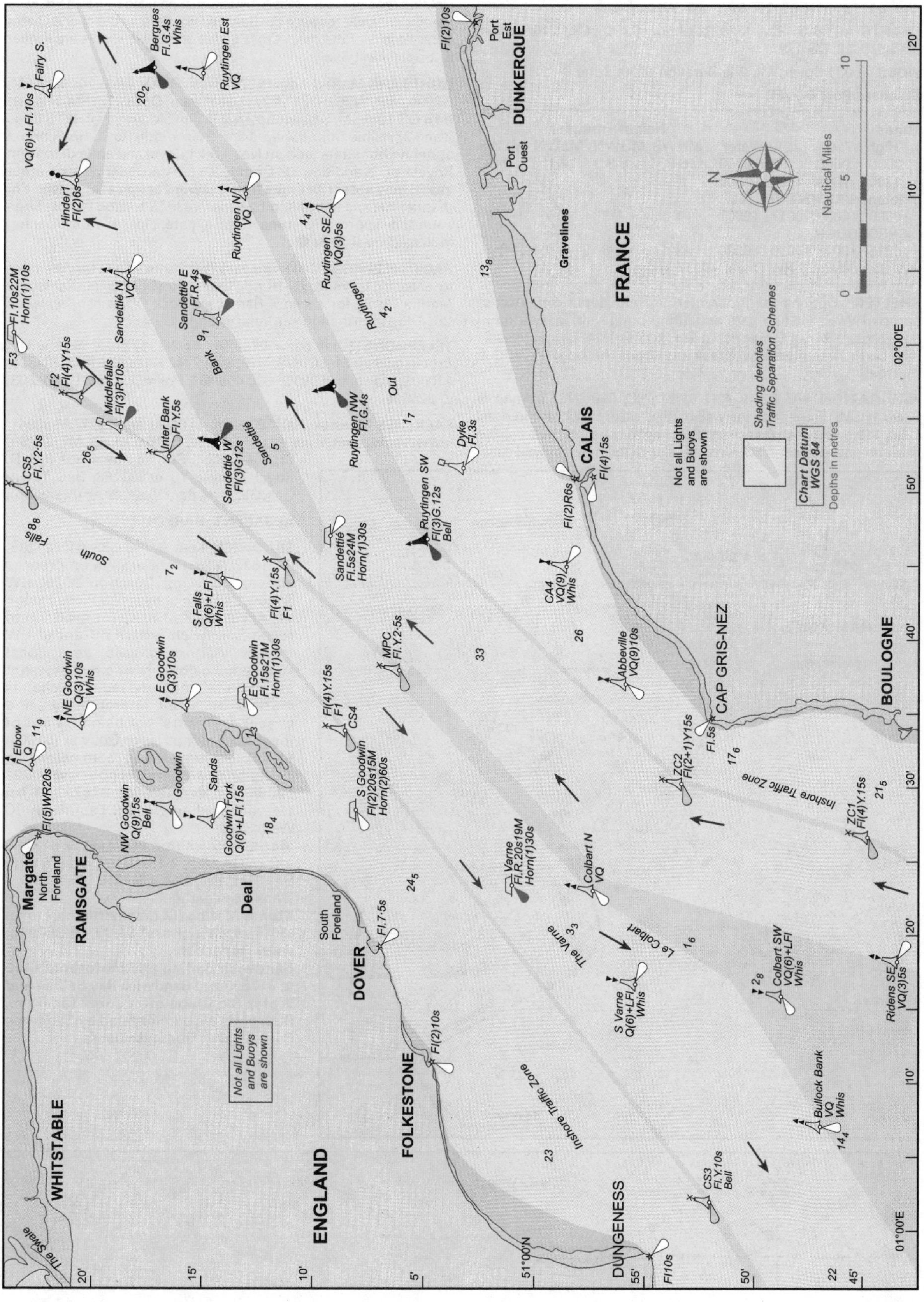

RAMSGATE 9.3.16

Kent **51°19′·51N 01°25′·50E** ❁❁❁⛵⛵⛵✿✿✿

CHARTS AC *5605*, 1827, *1828*, *323*; Imray C1, C8, C30, 2100 series; Stan 5, 9, 20; OS 179

TIDES +0030 Dover; ML 2·7; Duration 0530; Zone 0 (UT)

Standard Port DOVER (⟵)

Times				Height (metres)			
High Water		Low Water		MHWS	MHWN	MLWN	MLWS
0000	0600	0100	0700	6·8	5·3	2·1	0·8
1200	1800	1300	1900				
Differences RAMSGATE							
+0030	+0030	+0017	+0007	−1·6	−1·3	−0·7	−0·2
RICHBOROUGH							
+0015	+0015	+0030	+0030	−3·4	−2·6	−1·7	−0·7

HW Broadstairs = HW Dover +0037 approx.

SHELTER Options (a) inner marina, min depth 3m. Access approx HW ±2 via flap gate and lifting bridge, (b) W marina in 3m access H24, (c) E marina, in 2m, access H24. Larger vessels can berth on outer wavebreak pontoons of both W and E marinas.

NAVIGATION WPT 51°19′·43N 01°27′·70E, 090°/270° from/to S bkwtr, 1·45M. Ferries use the well-marked main E-W chan dredged 7·5m, 110m wide; as lower chartlet). For ent/dep yachts must use the Recommended Yacht Track on the S side of the main buoyed chan. Enter/dep under power, or advise Port Control if unable to motor. Ent/dep Royal Hbr directly; do not manoeuvre in the outer hbr. Holding area to the S of the S bkwtr must be used by yachts to keep the hbr ent clear for ferry tfc. Beware Dike Bank to the N and Quern Bank close S of the chan. Cross Ledge and Brake shoals are further S. Speed limit 5kn.

LIGHTS AND MARKS Ldg lts 270°: front Dir Oc WRG 10s 10m 5M, G259°-269°, W269°-271°, R271°-281°; rear, Oc 5s 17m 5M. N bkwtr hd = QG 10m 5M; S bkwtr hd = VQ R 10m 5M. At E Pier, **IPTS** (Sigs 2 and 3) visible from seaward and from within Royal Hbr, control appr into hbr limits (abeam Nos 1 & 2 buoys) and ent/exit to/from Royal Hbr. In addition a Fl Orange lt = ferry is under way; **no other vessel may enter Hbr limits from seaward or leave Royal Hbr.** Ent to inner marina controlled by separate IPTS to stbd of ent. Siren sounded approx 10 mins before gate closes; non-opening indicated by R ● or ●.

RADIO TELEPHONE Call Ramsgate Port Control Ch14 for clearance to enter or leave Royal Hbr. When in Royal Hbr call Ramsgate Marina Ch 80 for a berth. Ramsgate Dock Office can be called Ch14 for information on Inner Marina Lock.

TELEPHONE (Dial code 01843) Hr Mr 572100, 🖷 590941; Broadstairs Hr Mr 861879; ⊜ (01304) 224251 (H24); MRCC (01304) 210008; Marinecall 09068 500 455/456; Police 231055; Dr 852853; Ⓗ 225544.

FACILITIES Marinas (500+300 visitors) £1.60, ☎592277, 🖷590941, www. ramsgatemarina.co.uk, AC, FW, C (10 ton), Ⓔ, ME, El, Sh, CH, ACA, Gaz, SM, ⊡; **Royal Hbr** P & D. **Royal Temple YC** ☎ 591766, Bar. **Town**; Gas, Gaz, V, R, Bar, ✉, Ⓑ, ⇌, ✈ (Manston).

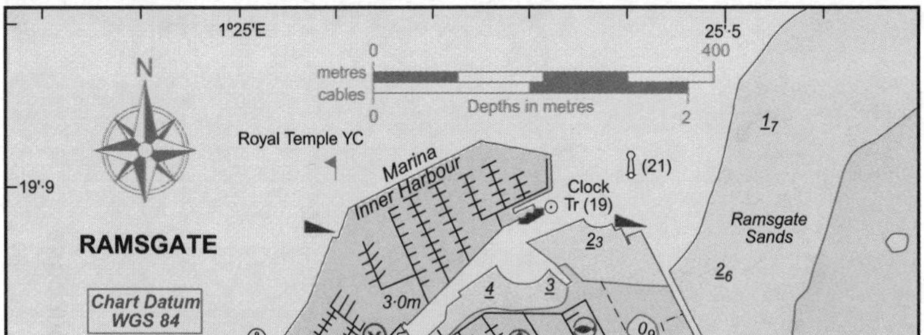

ADJACENT HARBOUR

SANDWICH, Kent, **51°16′·83N 01°21′·20E.** AC 1827 *1828*. Richborough differences above; ML 1·4m; Duration 0520. HW Sandwich Town quay is HW Richborough +1. Access HW ±1 at sp for draft 2m to reach Sandwich; arrive off ent at HW Dover. Visitors should seek local knowledge before arriving by day; night ent definitely not advised. The chan is marked by small lateral buoys and beacons. Visitors' berths on S bank of the River Stour at Town Quay ☎ (01304) 612162. Limited turning room before the swing bridge (opens 1H notice ☎ 01304 620644 or Mobile 0860 378792, 1·7m clearance when closed. Facilities: EC Wed; Slip;

Marina (50 + some visitors) ☎ 613783 (max LOA 18m, 2·1m draft), BH (15 ton), Sh, Slip, FW, SM, CH, ME, Gas; D & P (cans from garage);

Stonar Marina ½M downstream of town (50 + some visitors) £1.00, ☎ 867925, www.stonar.com.

Sandwich Sailing and Motorboat Club ☎ 617650 and **Sandwich Bay Sailing and Water Ski Clubs** offer some facilities. Both ports are administered by Sandwich Port & Haven Commissioners.

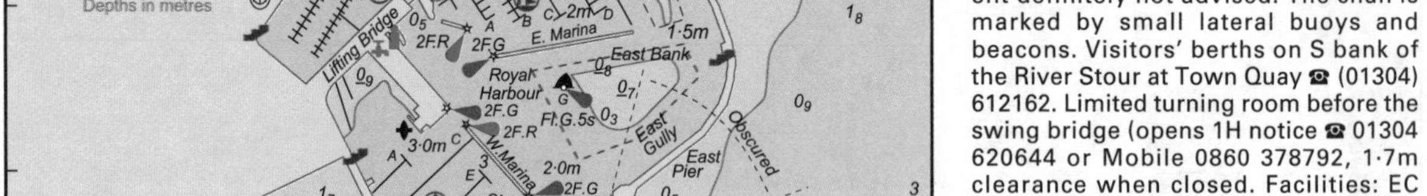

MAPTECH®
Leading the world in digital navigation
Maptech UK Ltd • +44 (0)1243 389352 • sales@maptech.co.uk

Sales and distribution centres in Area 4

Suffolk: *Fox's Electronics*, 01473 689111, Fox's Marina, The Strand, Wherstead, Ipswich IP28SA. *R&J Marine*, 01473 659737, Suffolk Yacht Harbour, Levington, Ipswich IP10 0LN. **London:** *Kelvin Hughes*, 0207 7099076, 142 Minories, London EC3N 1NH. *Cactus Navigation & Communication*, 020 7493 1115, Lower Ground Floor, 39A Curzon Street, London W1Y 7RF. *Captain O M Watts*, 020 7493 4633, 7 Dover Street, London W1S 4LD.

www.maptech.co.uk

Area 4

East England
North Foreland to Great Yarmouth

9.4.1 Index .... Page 345
9.4.2 Area map 346
9.4.3 Tidal stream charts 348
9.4.4 Lights, buoys & waypoints 350
9.4.5 Passage information 355
9.4.6 Distance table 356
9.4.7 East Anglian Waypoints 357
9.4.8 Thames Estuary 359
9.4.9 Thames Estuary tidal stream charts 360
9.4.10 Whitstable 362
Margate
Herne Bay
9.4.11 The Swale 363
9.4.12 Queenborough 364
9.4.13 River Medway (Sheerness, Standard Port, tidal curves) 365
9.4.14 River Thames (London Bridge, Standard Port, tidal curves) 370
Holehaven
Gravesend
Thames tidal barrier
Gallions Point marina
South Dock marina
Poplar Dock marina
Limehouse Basin marina
St Katharine Haven
Chelsea Harbour
Brentford Dock marina
9.4.15 Southend-on-Sea, Leigh-on-Sea 379
9.4.16 River Roach/Havengore 380
9.4.17 Burnham-on-Crouch (inc tidal predictions) 381
9.4.18 River Blackwater 385
9.4.19 River Colne 386
9.4.20 Walton Backwaters Standard Port, tidal curves 387
9.4.21 River Stour 391
9.4.22 River Orwell 392
9.4.23 River Deben 393
9.4.24 River Ore/Alde 393
9.4.25 Southwold 394
9.4.26 Lowestoft, Standard Port, tidal curves 395
9.4.27 Great Yarmouth 399
Norfolk Broads

Register for your FREE weekly weather email service from Macmillan Reeds
›› at www.nauticaldata.com – NOW!
weekend weather reports sent to your email address, every Thursday ‹‹

9.4.2
East England
North Foreland to Great Yarmouth

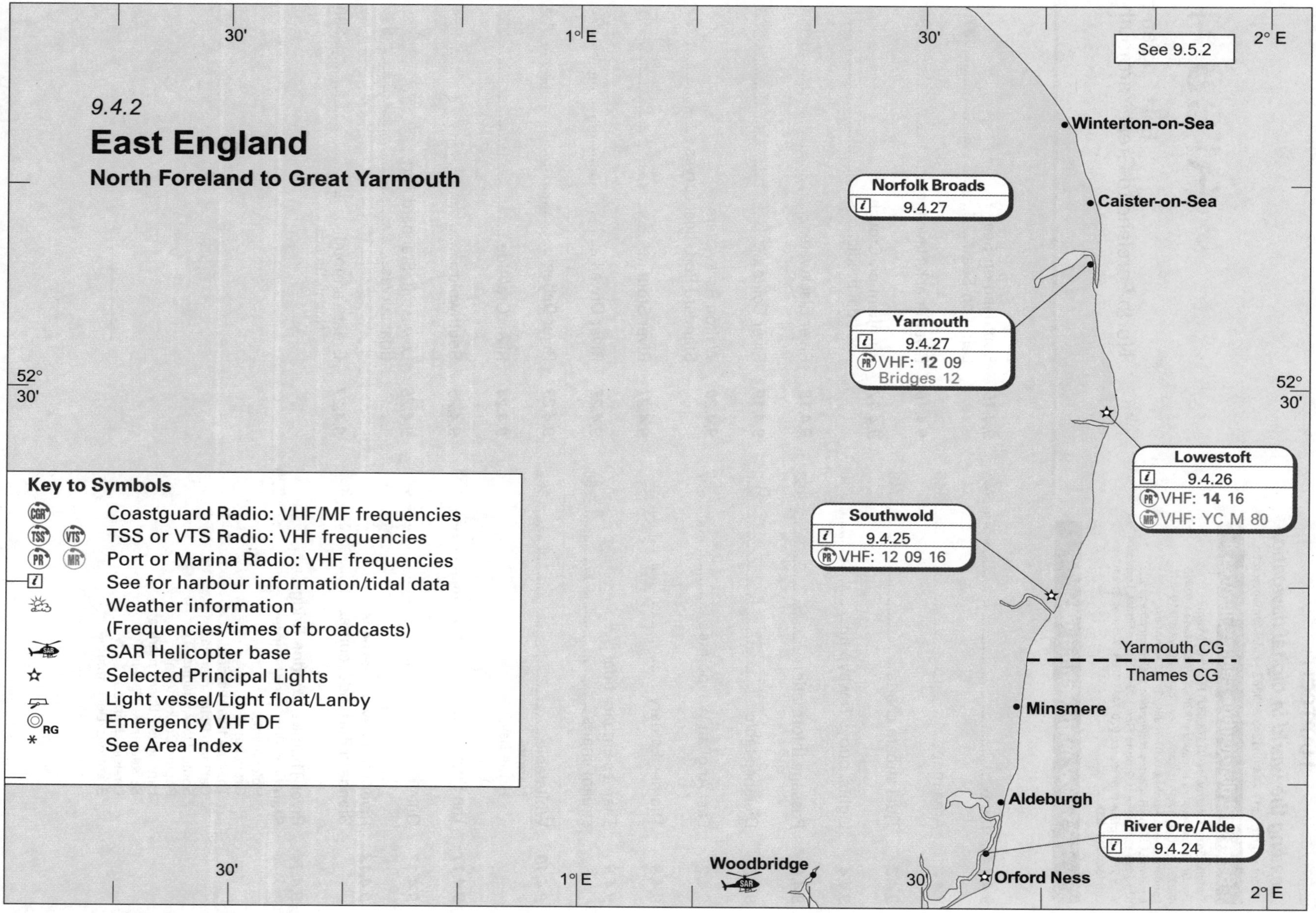
30'
1° E
30'
2° E
See 9.5.2
52° 30'
Winterton-on-Sea
Caister-on-Sea
Norfolk Broads 9.4.27
Yarmouth 9.4.27 VHF: 12 09 Bridges 12
Lowestoft 9.4.26 VHF: 14 16 VHF: YC M 80
Southwold 9.4.25 VHF: 12 09 16
Yarmouth CG
Thames CG
Minsmere
Aldeburgh
River Ore/Alde 9.4.24
Orford Ness
Woodbridge

Key to Symbols

- Coastguard Radio: VHF/MF frequencies
- TSS or VTS Radio: VHF frequencies
- Port or Marina Radio: VHF frequencies
- See for harbour information/tidal data
- Weather information (Frequencies/times of broadcasts)
- SAR Helicopter base
- Selected Principal Lights
- Light vessel/Light float/Lanby
- RG Emergency VHF DF
- * See Area Index

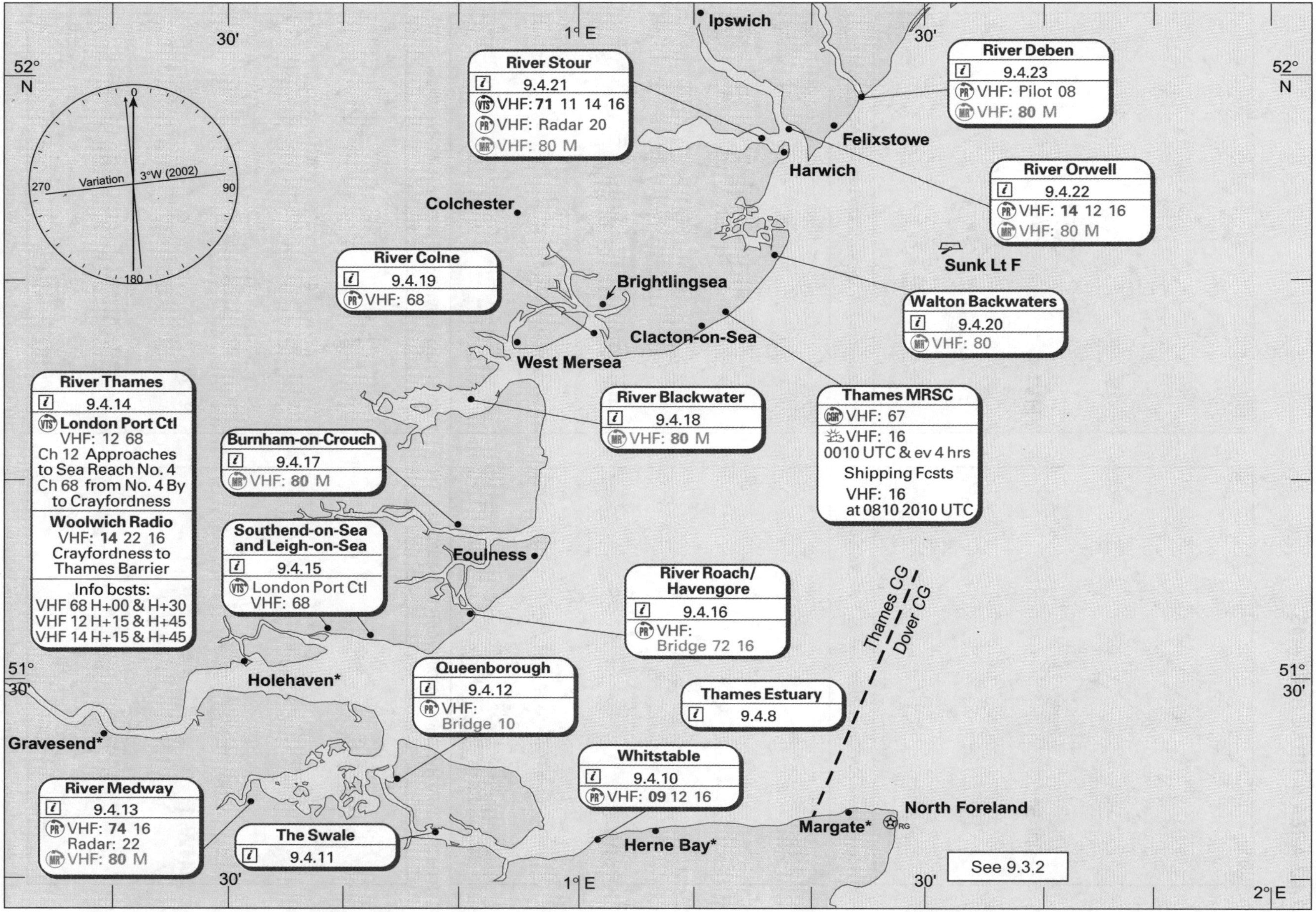
30'
1° E
30'
52° N
52° N
Variation 3°W (2002)
0
90
180
270
Ipswich
River Stour
9.4.21
VHF: 71 11 14 16
VHF: Radar 20
VHF: 80 M
River Deben
9.4.23
VHF: Pilot 08
VHF: 80 M
Felixstowe
Harwich
River Orwell
9.4.22
VHF: 14 12 16
VHF: 80 M
Colchester
Sunk Lt F
River Colne
9.4.19
VHF: 68
Brightlingsea
Walton Backwaters
9.4.20
VHF: 80
Clacton-on-Sea
West Mersea
River Thames
9.4.14
London Port Ctl
VHF: 12 68
Ch 12 Approaches to Sea Reach No. 4
Ch 68 from No. 4 By to Crayfordness
Woolwich Radio
VHF: 14 22 16
Crayfordness to Thames Barrier
Info bcsts:
VHF 68 H+00 & H+30
VHF 12 H+15 & H+45
VHF 14 H+15 & H+45
River Blackwater
9.4.18
VHF: 80 M
Thames MRSC
VHF: 67
VHF: 16
0010 UTC & ev 4 hrs
Shipping Fcsts
VHF: 16
at 0810 2010 UTC
Burnham-on-Crouch
9.4.17
VHF: 80 M
Southend-on-Sea and Leigh-on-Sea
9.4.15
London Port Ctl
VHF: 68
Foulness
River Roach/ Havengore
9.4.16
VHF:
Bridge 72 16
Thames CG
Dover CG
51° 30'
51° 30'
Holehaven*
Queenborough
9.4.12
VHF:
Bridge 10
Thames Estuary
9.4.8
Gravesend*
Whitstable
9.4.10
VHF: 09 12 16
River Medway
9.4.13
VHF: 74 16
Radar: 22
VHF: 80 M
The Swale
9.4.11
North Foreland
RG
Margate*
Herne Bay*
See 9.3.2
30'
1° E
30'
2° E

4

9.4.3 AREA 4 TIDAL STREAMS

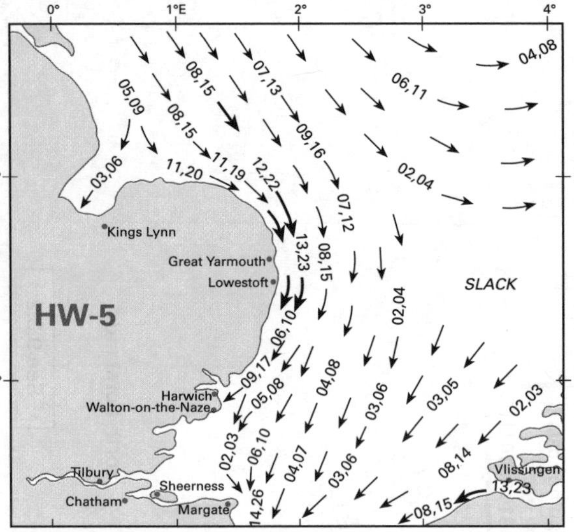

5 Hours before HW Dover (0530 before HW Walton)

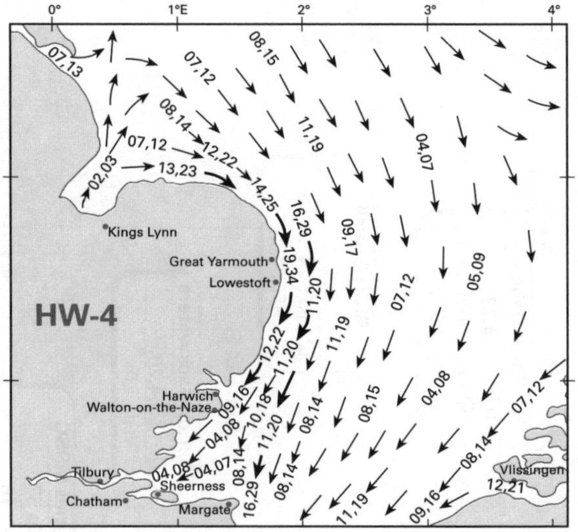

4 Hours before HW Dover (0430 before HW Walton)

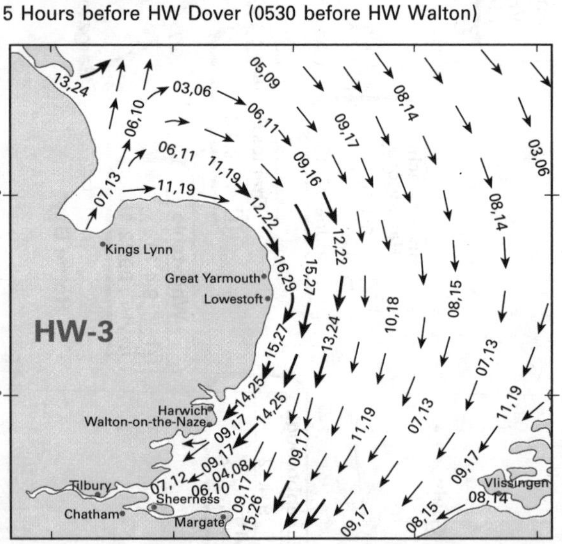

3 Hours before HW Dover (0330 before HW Walton)

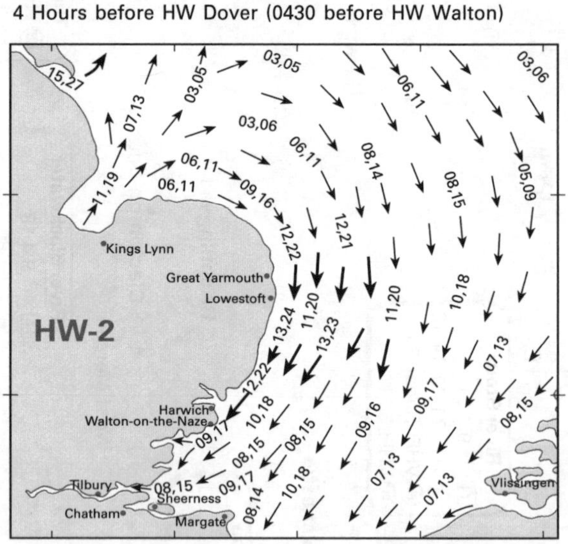

2 Hours before HW Dover (0230 before HW Walton)

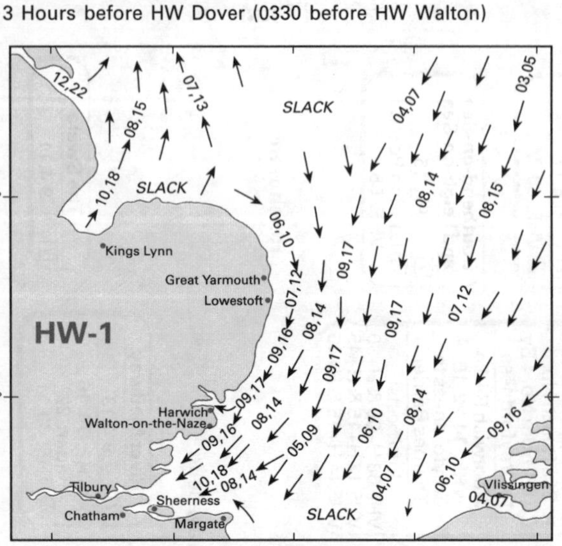

1 Hour before HW Dover (0130 before HW Walton)

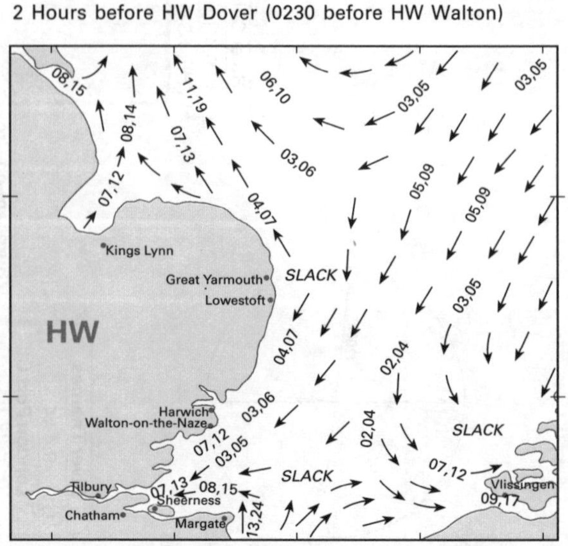

HW Dover (0030 before HW Walton)

Southward 9.3.3 Thames Estuary 9.4.9 Northward 9.5.3 Eastward 9.23.3

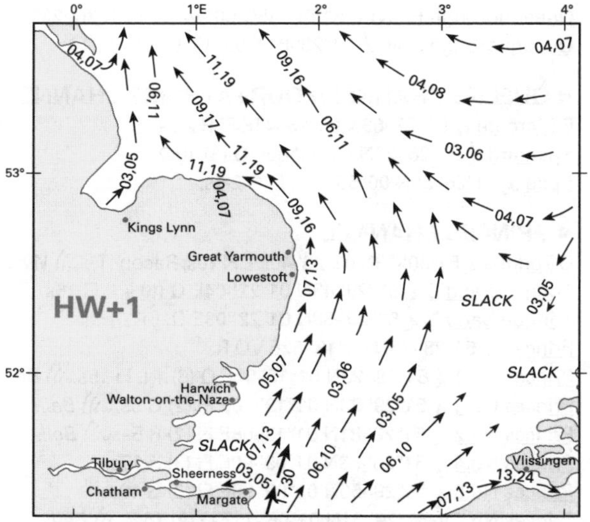

1 Hour after HW Dover (0030 after HW Walton)

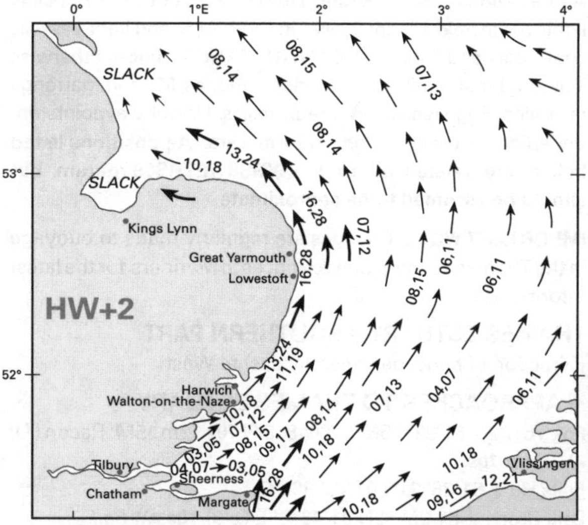

2 Hours after HW Dover (0130 after HW Walton)

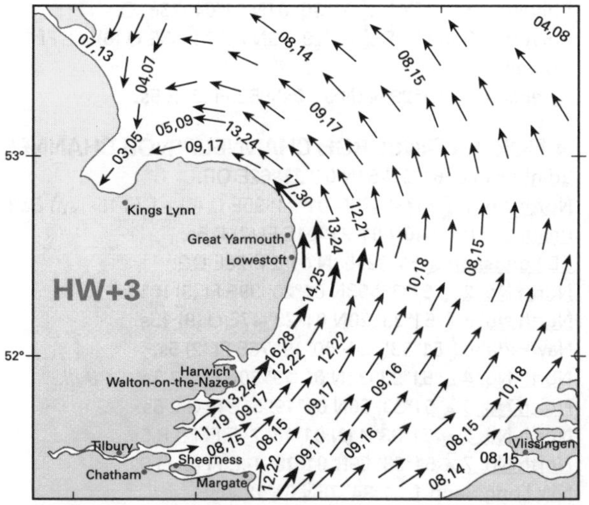

3 Hours after HW Dover (0230 after HW Walton)

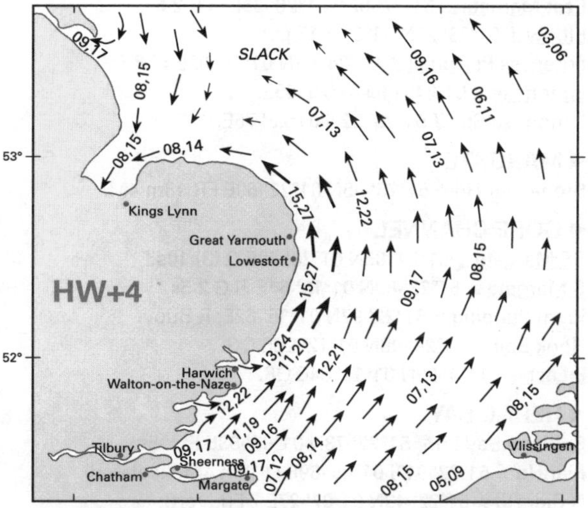

4 Hours after HW Dover (0330 after HW Walton)

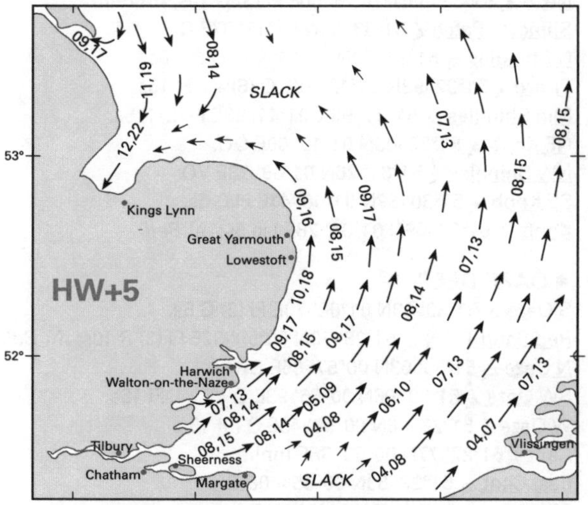

5 Hours after HW Dover (0430 after HW Walton)

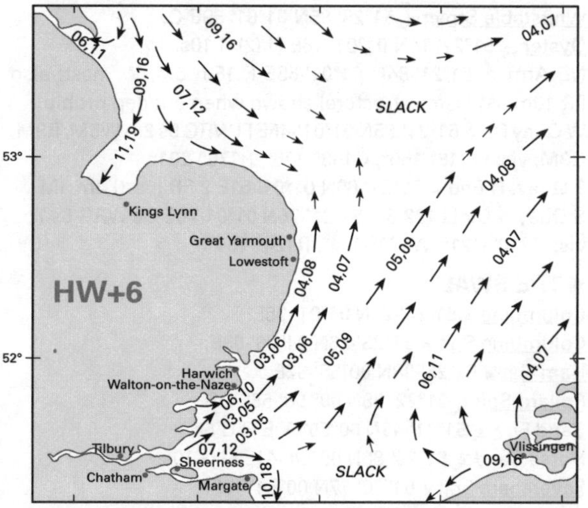

6 Hours after HW Dover (0530 after HW Walton)

9.4.4 LIGHTS, BUOYS AND WAYPOINTS

Abbreviations used below are given in the Introduction. Principal lights are in **bold** ☆ print, places in CAPITALS, and light-vessels, light floats and Lanbys in *CAPITAL ITALICS.* Unless otherwise stated lights are white. m – elevation in metres; M – nominal range in miles. Fog signals are in *italics.* Useful waypoints are underlined – use those on land with care. **All positions listed below are referenced to the WGS84/ETRS89 datum but should be assumed to be approximate.**

IMPORTANT NOTE. Changes are regularly made to buoyage in the Thames Estuary. Check Notices to Mariners for the latest information.

THAMES ESTUARY – SOUTHERN PART

(Direction of buoyage generally East to West)

◄ APPROACHES TO THAMES ESTUARY

Foxtrot 3 51°23'·85N 02°00'·51E Fl 10s 12m **15M**; Racon (T); *Horn 10s.*
Falls Hd 51°28'·21N 01°49'·86E Q.
Drill Stone 51°25'·82N 01°42'·85E Q (3) 10s *Bell.*
NE Spit 51°27'·92N 01°29'·85E VQ (3) 5s.
East Margate 51°27'·02N 01°26'·35E Fl R 2·5s.
Elbow 51°23'·23N 01°31'·61E Q.
Foreness Pt Outfall 51°24'·61N 01°26'·02E Fl R 5s.
Longnose 51°24'·14N 01°26'·09E.
Longnose Spit 51°23'·92N 01°25'·75E.

◄ MARGATE

Stone Pier Hd 51°23'·45N 01°22'·69E FR 18m 4M.

◄ GORE CHANNEL

SE Margate 51°24'·05N 01°20'·40E Q (3) 10s.
S Margate 51°23'·83N 01°16'·64E Fl G 2·5s.
Plum Pudding 51°22'·97N 01°15'·62E; R Buoy.
Hook Spit 51°24'·08N 01°12'·26E QG.
E Last 51°24'·06N 01°11'·84E QR.

◄ HERNE BAY

Beltinge Bay Bn 51°22'·73N 01°08'·63E Fl Y 5s.
Pier Hd 51°22'·91N 01°06'·89E Q 18m 4M, (isolated).
N Pier Hd 51°22'·43N 01°07'·27E 2 FR (vert).

◄ WHITSTABLE

Whitstable Street 51°23'·85N 01°01'·59E Q.
Oyster 51°22'·14N 01°01'·16E Fl (2) R 10s.
NE Arm 51°21'·84N 01°01'·58E F 15m 8M; W mast; also FR 10m 5M (same structure) shown when ent/dep prohib.
W Quay Dn 51°21'·85N 01°01'·46E Fl WRG 5s 2m W5M, R3M, G3M; vis: W118°-156°, G156°-178°, R178°-201°.
E Quay, N End 51°21'·86N 01°01'·51E 2 FR (vert) 4m 1M.
S Quay Dir Lt 122·5°. 51°21'·76N 01°01·70E Oc WRG 5s 7m: vis: G110°-121°, W121°-124°, R124°-134°.

◄ THE SWALE

Columbine 51°24'·26N 01°01'·35E.
Columbine Spit 51°23'·86N 01°00'·03E.
Ham Gat 51°23'·08N 00°58'·32E.
Pollard Spit 51°22'·98N 00° 58'·56E QR.
Sand End 51°21'·43N 00°55'·90E Fl G 5s.
Horse Sand 51°20'·86N 00°54'·41E Fl G 10s.
Faversham Spit 51°20'·77N 00°54'·19E.
Fowley Spit 51°21'·50N 00°51'·47E Q (3) 10s.
Queenborough Hard S1 51°24'·99N 00°44'·18E Fl R 3s.
Queenborough Pt (S) 51°25'·34N 00°44'·03E Fl R 4s.
Queenborough Pt (N) 51°25'·45N 00°44'·00E QR 3m 2M.
Queenborough Spit 51°25'·81N 00°43'·93E Q (3) 10s.

◄ QUEENS CHANNEL/FOUR FATHOMS CHANNEL

E Margate 51°27'·03N 01°26'·41E Fl R 2·5s.
Spaniard 51°26'·23N 01°04'·00E Q (3) 10s.
Spile 51°26'·38N 00°55'·70E Fl G 2·5s.

◄ PRINCES CHANNEL

O Tongue 51°30'·73N 01°26'·40E L Fl 10s; Racon (T); *Whis.*
Tongue Sand S 51°29'·43N 01°22'·04E Q (6) + L Fl 15s.
Tongue Sand N 51°29'·68N 01°22'·03E Q.
Princes 51°28'·75N 01°18'·62E VQ R.
Princes No.1 51°29'·23N 01°16'·02E Q (6) + L Fl 15s; *Bell.*
Princes No.3 51°29'·33N 01°13'·10E Fl (2) G 5s; *Bell.*
Princes No.2 51°28'·81N 01°13'·08E Fl (2) R 5s; *Bell.*
Princes No.4 51°28'·83N 01°09'·90E Fl (3) R 10s.
Princes No.5 51°29'·50N 01°09'·90E Fl (3) G 10s.
Princes No.7 51°29'·61N 01°06'·72E Q (9) 15s; *Bell.*
Princes No.6 51°29'·18N 01°06'·40E Fl (4) R 15s.
Shivering Sand Tr N 51°30'·01N 01°04'·76E. Q.
Shivering Sand Tr S 51°29'·79N 01°04'·83E Q (6) + L Fl 15s; Bell.
E Redsand 51°29'·41N 01°04'·05E Fl (2) R 5s.

◄ NORTH EDINBURGH CHANNEL/KNOB CHANNEL

Edinburgh 51°31'·51N 01°21'·62E QR.
North No. 1 51°31'·76N 01°21'·95E Q (6) + L Fl 15s; *Bell.*
Patch 51°32'·40N 01°21'·01E Fl (2) R 5s.
SE Longsand 51°32'·53N 01°21'·26E QG.
North No. 2 51°32'·93N 01°20'·39E Fl (3) R 10s.
North No. 3 51°33'·20N 01°20'·47E Q (9) 15s.
Hawksdale 51°33'·30N 00°19'·75E Fl (2) 5s.
North No. 4 51°33'·31N 01°19'·30E Fl R 2·5s; *Bell.*
North No. 5 51°33'·56N 01°19'·51E Fl G 2·5s.
North No. 6 51°33'·41N 01°18'·24E Fl (2) R 5s.
North No. 7 51°33'·69N 01°18'·14E Fl (2) G 5s.
NW Long Sand 51°34'·75N 01°18'·05E.
No. 8 51°33'·23N 01°16'·54E Fl (3) R 10s.
No. 9 51°33'·53N 01°16'·60E Fl (3) G 10s; *Bell.*
Shingles Patch 51°33'·01N 01°15'·37E Q.
N Shingles 51°32'·79N 01°14'·25E Fl R 2·5s.
Tizard 51°32'·93N 01°12'·90E Q (6) + L Fl 15s.
Mid Shingles 51°31'·96N 01°11'·98E Fl (2) R 5s.
NE Knob 51°32'·03N 01°10'·00E QG.
NW Shingles 51°31'·26N 01°09'·73E VQ.
SE Knob 51°30'·89N 01°06'·41E Fl G 5s.
Knob 51°30'·69N 01°04'·28E Iso 5s; *Bell.*

◄ OAZE DEEP

S Oaze 51°30'·03N 01°00'·70E Fl (2) G 5s.
Red Sand Trs N 51°28'·73N 00°59'·32E Fl (3) R 10s; *Bell.*
N Oaze 51°30'·03N 00°57'·65E QR.
SW Oaze 51°29'·06N 00°56'·93E Q (6) + L Fl 15s.
W Oaze 51°29'·06N 00°55'·43E Q (9) 15s.
Cant 51°27'·77N 00°53'·36E (unlit).
East Cant 51°28'·53N 00°55'·60E QR.
Mid Cant 51°26'·88N 00°49'·80E Q.

◀ **MEDWAY, SHEERNESS**
Medway 51°28'·83N 00°52'·81E Mo (A) 6s.
No. 1 51°28'·52N 00°50'·52E Fl G 2·5s.
No. 2 51°28'·29N 00°50'·52E Q.
No. 7 51°27'·91N 00°47'·52E Fl G 10s.
No. 9 51°27'·74N 00°46'·61E Fl G 5s.
No. 11 51°27'·51N 00°45'·80E Fl (3) G 10s.
Grain Edge 51°27'·61N 00°45'·46E.
W Cant 51°27'·22N 00°45'·50E QR.
Jacobs Bank Obstn 51°26'·97N 00°45'·18E VQ.
Grain Hard 51°26'·98N 00°44'·17E Fl G 5s.
Isle of Grain ☆ 51°26'·70N 00°43'·38E Q WRG 20m W13M, R7M, G8M; R & W ◊ on R Tr; vis R220°-234°, G234°-241°, W241°-013°.
N. Kent 51°26'·13N 00°43'·46E QG.
S. Kent 51°25'·98N 00°43'·66E QR.
Queenborough Spit 51°25'·81N 00°43'·93E Q (3) 10s.
Victoria 51°25'·96N 00°42'·96E Fl (3) G 10s.
Z1 51°25'·78N 00°41'·61E Fl (2) 10s.
Z2 51°25'·64N 00°41'·64E Q.
Stangate Spit 51°25'·41N 00°41'·55E VQ (3) 5s.
Stoke No. 13 51°25'·76N 00°39'·81E Fl G 5s.
East Bulwark 51°25'·36N 00°39'·24E Fl (3) G 15s.
No. 15 51°24'·75N 00°38'·43E Fl G 10s.
Bishop No. 16 51°24'·71N 00°38'·78E Fl (2) R 10s.
No. 22 51°24'·51N 00°36'·08E Fl R 5s.
Darnett No. 23 51°24'·59N 00°35'·62E IQ G.
Darnett Ness No. 6 51°24'·45N 01°35'·73E QR 12m 3M.
Folly No. 25 51°24'·09N 00°35'·24E Fl (3) G 10s.
Gillingham Reach No. 27 51°23'·91N 00°34'·71E Fl G 10s.

RIVER THAMES

◀ **SEA REACH, NORE AND YANTLET**
No. 1 51°29'·45N 00°52'·57E Fl Y 2·5s; Racon (T).
No. 2 51°29'·40N 00°49'·75E Iso 5s.
No. 3 51°29'·33N 00°46'·54E L Fl 10s.
No. 4 51°29'·61N 00°44'·18E Fl Y 2·5s.
No. 5 51°29'·95N 00°41'·44E Iso 5s.
No. 6 51°30'·03N 00°39'·83E Iso 2s.
No. 7 51°30'·10N 00°37'·04E Fl Y 2·5s; Racon (T).
Nore Swatch 51°28'·28N 00°45'·55E Fl (4) R 15s.
Mid Swatch 51°28'·68N 00°44'·16E Fl G 5s.
W Nore Sand 51°29'·41N 00°40'·85E Fl (3) R 10s.
East Blyth 51°29'·72N 00°37'·80E Fl (2) R 10s.
West Lee Middle 51°30'·48N 00°38'·82E QG.
Chapman 51°30'·43N 00°36'·93E Fl (3) G 10s; *Bell.*
Scars Elbow 51°30'·33N 00°34'·57E Fl G 2·5s.
Mid Blyth 51°30'·08N 00°32'·38E Q.
Mucking No. 1 51°29'·85N 00°28'·44E QG; *Bell.*
Mucking No. 3 51°29'·34N 00°27'·68E Fl G 2·5s.
Mucking No. 7 51°28'·03N 00°26'·77E Fl G 5s.
Higham 51°27'·40N 00°26'·84E Fl (2) R 5s.
Ovens 51°27'·49N 00°26'·35E QG; *Bell.*
Tilbury 51°27'·16N 00°25'·49E Q (6) + L Fl 15s.
Diver 51°27'·08N 00°24'·56E L Fl G 10s.

◀ **LEIGH-ON-SEA/SOUTHEND-ON-SEA**
Leigh 51°31'·07N 00°42'·56E.
Southend Pier E End ☆ 51°30'·87N 00°43'·40E 2 FG (vert) 7m; *Horn Mo (N) 30s, Bell (1) 5s (reserve).*
Pier W Head ☆ 51°30·89N 00°43'·28E 2 FG (vert) 13m 8M.
West Shoebury 51°30'·23N 00°45'·73E Fl G 2·5s.
SE Leigh 51°29'·42N 00°47'·07E Q (6) + L Fl 15s.
Shoebury 51°30'·29N 00°49'·26E Fl (3) G 10s 5m 5M.
Inner Shoebury 51°30'·99N 00°49'·16E Fl Y 2·5s.
S Shoebury 51°30'·43N 00°52'·39E Fl G 5s.

◀ **CANVEY ISLAND/HOLEHAVEN**
Jetty Hd E end ☆ 51°30'·39N 00°34'·13E 2 FG (vert); *Bell 10s.*
W end ☆ 51°30'·39N 00°34'·05E 2 FG (vert) 13m 8M.
Shornmead ☆ 51°26'·99N 00°26'·52E Fl (2) WRG 10s 12m W17M, R13M, G13M; vis G054°-081·5°, R081·5°-086·2°, W086·2°-088·7°, G088·7°-141°, W141°-205°, R205°-213°.

◀ **GRAVESEND**
Northfleet Lower ☆ 51°26'·88N 00°20'·26E Oc WR 5s 15m W17M, R14M; vis: W164°-271°, R271°-S shore.
Northfleet Upper ☆ 51°26'·93N 00°20'·06E Oc WRG 10s 30m W16M, R12M, G12M; vis: R126°-149°, W149°-159°, G159°-268°, W268°-279°.
Broadness ☆ 51°28'·02N 00°18'·60E Oc R 5s 12m 12M.
QEII Bridge Centre ☆ 51°27'·88N 00°15'·52E Iso 10s.
Crayford Ness ☆ 51°28'·94N 00°12'·71E Fl 5s 19m 14M and F17m 3M.
Cross Ness ☆ 51°30'·78N 00°07'·71E Fl 5s 11m 8M.

◀ **THAMES TIDAL BARRIER**
Span B (51°29'·73N 00°02'·23E) is used for small craft/yachts Eastbound and Span G (51°29'·91N 00°02'·21E) is used for small craft/yachts Westbound. Spans B, C, D, E, F & G are navigable. Spans C to F are for larger vessels. All spans display a F GR ☆. A **Green** ⟶ indicates span open for navigation. A **Red X** indicates span closed to navigation. In low visibility F lights are shown either side of those spans which are displaying a **Green** ⟶.

◀ **SOUTH DOCK MARINA**
Marina Ent 51°29'·65N 00°01'·97W.

◀ **LIMEHOUSE BASIN MARINA/REGENT'S CANAL**
Limehouse Basin Marina Lock ent 51°30'·56N 00°02'·26W.

◀ **ST KATHARINE YACHT HAVEN**
St Katherine Haven Ent 51°30'·36N 00°04'·35W.

◀ **CHELSEA HARBOUR MARINA**
Chelsea Harbour Ent 51°28'·48N 00°10'·81W.

THAMES ESTUARY – NORTHERN PART

◀ **KENTISH KNOCK**
Kentish Knock 51°38'·52N 01°40·41E Q (3) 10s; *Whis.*
S Knock 51°34'·13N 01°34'·29E Q (6) + L Fl 15s; *Bell.*

◀ **KNOCK JOHN CHANNEL**
No. 7 51°32'·03N 01°06'·40E Fl (4) G 15s.
No. 5 51°32'·78N 01°08'·58E Fl (3) G 10s.
No. 4 51°32'·63N 01°08'·72E L Fl R 10s.
No. 2 51°33'·11N 01°09'·85E Fl (3) R 10s.
No. 3 51°33'·23N 01°09'·70E Q (6) + L Fl 15s.
No. 1 51°33'·75N 01°10'·72E Fl G 5s.
Knock John 51°33'·53N 01°10'·98E Fl (2) R 5s.

◀ **BLACK DEEP**
No. 12 51°33'·83N 01°13'·49E Fl (4) R 15s.
No. 11 51°34'·33N 01°13'·40E Fl (3) G 10s.

4

No. 10 51°34'·73N 01°15'·60E QR.
No. 9 51°35'·13N 01°15'·09E Q (6) + L Fl 15s.
No. 8 51°36'·36N 01°20'·43E Q (9) 15s.
No. 7 51°37'·08N 01°17'·69E QG.
No. 6 51°38'·53N 01°24'·41E Fl R 2·5s.
No. 5 51°39'·53N 01°23'·00E VQ (3) 5s; *Bell.*
No. 4 51°41'·42N 01°28'·49E Fl (2) R 5s.
Long Sand Beacon 51°41'·47N 01°29'·46E.
No. 3 51°41'·98N 01°25'·97E Fl (3) G 15s.
No. 1 51°44'·03N 01°28'·10E Fl G 5s.
No. 2 51°45'·63N 01°32'·20E Fl (4) R 15s.
Sunk Head Tower 51°46'·63N 01°30'·51E Q; *Whis.*
Black Deep 51°46'·83N 01°34'·27E QR.
Trinity 51°49'·04N 01°36'·37E Q (6) + L Fl 15s; *Whis.*
Long Sand Head 51°47'·90N 01°39'·43E VQ; *Bell.*

◀ FISHERMANS GAT

Outer Fisherman 51°33'·89N 01°25'·01E Q (3) 10s.
Fisherman No. 1 51°34'·52N 01°23'·57E Fl G 2·5s.
Fisherman No. 2 51°34'·35N 01°23'·01E Fl R 2·5s.
Fisherman No. 3 51°34'·75N 01°22'·99E Fl G 5s.
Fisherman No. 4 51°35'·25N 01°21'·35E Fl (2) R 5s.
Fisherman No. 5 51°35'·52N 01°21'·75E Fl (2) G 5s.
Inner Fisherman 51°36'·06N 01°19'·86E Fl (3) R 10s.

◀ BARROW DEEP (selected Bys)

SW Barrow 51°32'·29N 01°00'·30E Q (6) + L Fl 15s; *Bell.*
Barrow No. 14 51°31'·83N 01°00'·42E Fl R 2·5s.
Barrow No. 13 51°32'·82N 01°03'·07E Fl (2) G 5s.
Barrow No. 12 51°32'·77N 01°04'·14E Fl (2) R 5s.
Barrow No.11 51°34'·07N 01°06'·70E Fl (3) G 10s.
Barrow No. 9 51°35'·34N 01°10'·30E VQ (3) 5s.
Barrow No. 8 51°35'·03N 01°11'·40E Fl (2) R 5s.
Barrow No. 6 51°37'·32N 01°14'·69E Fl (4) R 15s.
Barrow No. 5 51°40'·03N 01°16'·20E Fl G 10s.
Barrow No. 4 51°39'·88N 01°17'·48E VQ (9) 10s.
Barrow No. 3 51°42'·03N 01°20'·25E Q (3) 10s; Racon (M).
Barrow No. 2 51°41'·98N 01°22'·89E Fl (2) R 5s.

◀ WEST SWIN AND MIDDLE DEEP

Blacktail (W) 51°31'·46N 00°55'·19E Iso G 10s 10m 6M.
Blacktail Spit 51°31'·47N 00°56'·74E Fl (3) G 10s.
Blacktail (E) 51°31'·79N 00°56'·46E Iso G 5s 10m 6M.
Maplin 51°34'·03N 01°02'·29E Q (3) 10s; *Bell.*
W Swin 51°33'·38N 01°01'·98E.
Maplin Edge 51°35'·33N 01°03'·64E.
Maplin Bank 51°35'·50N 01°04'·70E Fl (3) R 10s.

◀ EAST SWIN (KING'S) CHANNEL

NE Maplin 51°37'·44N 01°04'·78E Fl G 5s; *Bell.*
W Hook Middle 51°39'·17N 01°07'·89E.
S Whitaker 51°40'·22N 01°09'·04E Fl (2) G 10s.
N Middle 51°41'·03N 01°11'·88E.
W Sunk 51°44'·33N 01°25'·80E Q (9) 15s.
Gunfleet Spit 51°45'·32N 01°21'·69E Q (6) + L Fl 15s; *Bell.*
Gunfleet Old Lt Ho 51°46'·12N 01°20'·43E.

WHITAKER CHANNEL AND RIVER CROUCH

Whitaker 51°40'·52N 01°03'·50E.
Whitaker 51°41'·44N 01°10'·50E Q (3) 10s; *Bell.*
Whitaker No. 6 51°40'·69N 01°08'·06E Q.
Swin Spitway 51°41'·96N 01°08'·32E Iso 10s; *Bell.*
Whitaker 51°39'·64N 01°06'·16E.
Swallow Tail 51°40'·47N 01°04'·70E.
Ridge 51°40'·12N 01°04'·88E Fl R 10s.
Foulness 51°39'·85N 01°03'·81E Fl (2) R 10s.
Sunken Buxey 51°39'·54N 01°00'·59E Q.
Buxey No. 1 51°39'·18N 01°01'·01E VQ (6) + L Fl 10s.
Buxey No. 2 51°38'·98N 01°00'·15E Q.
Outer Crouch 51°38'·38N 00°58'·48E Q (6) + L Fl 15s.
Crouch 51°37'·62N 00°56'·38E Fl R 10s.
Inner Crouch 51°37'·22N 00°55'·14E L Fl 10s.

◀ RIVER ROACH/HAVENGORE

Branklet By 51°36'·97N 00°52'·14E.

◀ BURNHAM-ON-CROUCH

Horse Shoal 51°37'·10N 00°51'·52E Q.
Fairway No. 1 51°37'·10N 00°51'·00E QG.
Fairway No. 3 51°37'·18N 00°49'·90E QG.
Fairway No. 5 51°37'·18N 00°49'·57E QG.
Fairway No. 9 51°37'·36N 00°48'·77E QG.
Fairway No. 2 51°37'·31N 00°48'·70E QR.
Fairway No. 11 51°37'·43N 00°48'·30E QG.
Burnham Yacht Hbr 51°37'·50N 00°48'·24E Fl Y 5s.

◀ RAY SAND CHANNEL

Buxey 51°41'·16N 01°01'·29E (unlit).

◀ GOLDMER GAT/WALLET

NE Gunfleet 51°49'·92N 01°27'·80E Q (3) 10s.
Wallet No. 2 51°48'·88N 01°22'·99E Fl R 5s.
Wallet No. 4 51°46'·53N 01°17'·23E Fl (4) R 10s.
Walton Pier Hd 51°50'·60N 01°16'·80E 2 FG (vert) 5m 2M.
Wallet Spitway 51°42'·86N 01°07'·32E L Fl 10s; *Bell.*
Knoll 51°43'·88N 01°05'·07E Q.
Eagle 51°44'·13N 01°03'·81E QG.
N Eagle 51°44'·71N 01°04'·32E Q.
NW Knoll 51°44'·35N 01°02'·15E Fl (2) R 5s.
Colne Bar 51°44'·60N 01°02'·58E Fl (2) G 5s.
Bench Head 51°44'·69N 01°01'·10E Fl (3) G 10s.

◀ RIVER BLACKWATER

The Nass 51°45'·83N 00°54'·83E VQ (3) 5s 6m 2M.
Thirslet 51°43'·73N 00°50'·39E Fl (3) G 10s.
No. 1 51°43'·44N 00°48'·02E.
Small 51°43'·22N 00°47'·47E Fl (2) R 3s.
No. 2 51°42'·81N 00°46'·47E Fl R 3s.
Osea Island Pier Hd 51°43'·10N 00°46'·48E 2 FG (vert).
No. 3 51°42'·91N 00°46'·05E Fl (2) G 6s.
Southey Creek No. 4 51°43'·06N 00°45'·20E.
N Double No. 7 51°43'·24N 00°44'·76E Fl G 3s.
S Double No. 6 51°43'·16N 00°44'·74E.
No. 8 51°43'·93N 00°43'·24E.

◀ RIVER COLNE/BRIGHTLINGSEA

Inner Bench Head No. 2 51°45'·96N 01°01'·74E Fl (2) R 5s.
Colne Pt No. 1 51°46'·01N 01°01'·92E Fl G 3s.
No. 8 51°46'·97N 01°00'·98E QR.
No. 9 51°47'·36N 01°01'·07E Fl G 3s.
No. 13 51°47'·74N 01°00'·76E Fl G.
Brightlingsea Spit 51°48'·08N 01°00'·70E Q (6) + L Fl 15s.
Brightlingsea 51°48'·22N 01°01'·08E Fl (3) G 5s.
Brightlingsea 51°48'·26N 01°01'·04E Fl R 5s.

Ldg Lts 041°. Front, 51°48'·39N 01°01'·20E FR 7m 4M; W □, R stripe on post; vis: 020°-080°. Rear, 50m from front, FR 10m 4M; W □, R stripe on post. FR Lts are shown on 7 masts between 1·5M and 3M NW when firing occurs.
Hardway Hd 51°48'·26N 01°01'·40E 2 FR (vert) 2m.
Batemans Tr 51°48'·34N 01°00'·65E FY 12m.
No. 24 51°50'·16N 00°58'·83E Fl R.
No. 23 51°50'·59N 00°58'·82E Fl G 5s 5m.
Rowhedge Wharf 51°51'·23N 00°57'·10E FY 11m.

◄ CLACTON-ON-SEA

Berthing arm 51°47'·04N 01°09'·42E 2 FG (vert) 5m 4M; *Reed (2) 120s* (occas).

◄ WALTON BACKWATERS

Naze Tower 51°51'·87N 01°17'·29E.
Pye End 51°55'·04N 01°17'·88E L Fl 10s.
Orwell YC No. 2 51°54'·62N 01°16'·80E.
Crab Knoll No. 3 51°54'·40N 01°16'·41E Fl (2) G 10s.
Heather J No. 5 51°54'·28N 01°16'·23E.
High Hill No. 4 51°54'·05N 01°15'·96E Fl R 10s.
No. 7 51°53'·83N 01°15'·62E Fl G 10s.
No. 6 51°53'·78N 01°15'·66E.
Picard No. 8 51°53'·63N 01°15'·55E.
Island Point 51°53'·36N 01°15'·36E Q.
Frank Bloom 51°53'·27N 01°15'·49E.
Colin Bloom 51°53'·33N 01°15'·42E.
Exchem No. 9 51°53'·18N 01°14'·91E.
Bains No. 10 51°53'·38N 01°15'·40E.
No. 12 51°53'·26N 01°15'·51E.
East Coast Sails 51°53'·21N 01°15'·54E Fl G 5s.
Stone Pt 51°53'·07N 01°15'·65E.

HARWICH APPROACHES

(Direction of buoyage North to South)

◄ MEDUSA CHANNEL

Medusa 51°51'·20N 01°20'·35E Fl G 5s.
Stone Banks 51°53'·19N 01°19'·21E.

◄ CORK SAND /ROUGH SHOALS

S Cork 51°51'·33N 01°24'·10E Q (6) + L Fl 15s.
Roughs Tower SE 51°53'·64N 01°28'·94E Q (3) 10s.
Roughs Tower NW 51°53'·80N 01°28'·76E Q (9) 15s.
Rough 51°55'·19N 01°31'·00E VQ.
Cork Sand Yacht Bn 51°55'·21N 01°25'·21E VQ 2M.
Cork Sand 51°55'·51N 01°25'·41E Q.

◄ HARWICH CHANNEL

SUNK 51°51'·02N 01°34'·89E Fl (2) 20s 12m **16M**; R hull with Lt Tr; Racon (T); *Horn (2) 60s*.
S Threshold 51°52'·21N 01°33'·14E Fl (4) Y 10s.
S Shipwash 51°52'·71N 01°33'·97E Q (6) + L Fl 15s.
Wave/Tide Gauge 51°52'·85N 01°32'·32E Mo (U) 15s 2m 3M.
E Fort Massac 51°53'·36N 01°32'·76E VQ (3) 5s.
W Fort Massac 51°53'·36N 01°32'·45E VQ (9) 10s.
Walker 51°53'·79N 01°33'·90E Fl R 5s.
N Threshold 51°54'·49N 01°33'·47E Fl Y 5s.
SW Shipwash 51°54'·75N 01°34'·21E Q (9)15s.
Haven 51°55'·76N 01°32'·56E Mo (A) 5s.
W Shipwash 51°57'·13N 01°35'·89E Fl (2) R 10s.
NW Shipwash 51°58'·98N 01°37'·01E Fl R 5s.
Harwich App (HA) 51°56'·76N 01°30'·66E Iso 5s.
Cross 51°56'·24N 01°30'·48E Fl (3) Y 10s.
Harwich Chan No. 1 51°56'·14N 01°27'·05E Fl Y 2·5s; Racon (T).
Harwich Chan No. 3 51°56'·04N 01°25'·53E Fl (3) Y 10s.
Harwich Chan No. 5 51°55'·96N 01°24'·01E Fl (5) Y 10s.
Harwich Chan No. 7 51°55'·88N 01°22'·48E Fl Y 10s.
S Bawdsey 51°57'·23N 01°30'·20E Q (6) + L Fl 15s; *Whis.*
Washington 51°56'·52N 01°26'·59E QG.
Felixstowe Ledge 51°56'·30N 01°23'·72E Fl (3) G 10s.
Wadgate Ledge 51°56'·16N 01°21'·98E Fl (4) G 15s.
Cobbolds Pt 51°57'·61N 01°22'·27E (Apr-Oct).
Platters 51°55'·64N 01°20'·96E; Q (6) + L Fl 15s.
Rolling Ground 51°55'·55N 01°19'·75E QG.
Beach End 51°55'·63N 01°19'·20E Fl (2) G 5s.
NW Beach 51°55'·88N 01°18'·88E Fl (3) G 10s; *Bell.*
Fort 51°56'·21N 01°18'·87E Fl (4) G 15s.

◄ EDGE OF RECOMMENDED YACHT TRACK

Rough 51°55'·19N 01°31'·00E VQ.
Cork Sand 51°55'·52N 01°25'·42E Q.
Cork Sand Yacht Beacon 51°55'·21N 01°25'·21E VQ 2M.
Cork Ledge 51°54'·50N 01°23'·40E (Racing Mark-seasonal).
Pitching Ground 51°55'·43N 01°21'·04E Fl (4) R 15s.
Inner Ridge 51°55'·38N 01°20'·20E QR.
Deane 51°55'·37N 01°19'·27E L Fl R 6s.
Landguard 51°55'·45N 01°18'·84E Q.
NW Beach 51°55'·88N 01°18'·88E Fl (3) G 10s; *Bell.*
Cliff Foot 51°55'·72N 01°18'·53E Fl R 5s.
S Shelf 51°56'·20N 01°18'·56E Fl (2) R 5s.
N Shelf 51°56'·68N 01°18'·59E QR.
Harwich Shelf 51°56'·84N 01°18'·07E Q (3) 10s (Apr-Oct).
Grisle 51°56'·89N 01°18'·32E Fl R 2·5s.

RIVERS STOUR AND ORWELL

◄ RIVER STOUR/HARWICH

Shotley Spit 51°57'·22N 01°17'·69E Q (6) + L Fl 15s.
Shotley Marina Lock E side Dir Lt 339·5° 51°57'·46N 01°16'·60E 3m 1M (uses Moiré pattern); Or structure.
Shotley Marina Ent E side 51°57'·26N 01°16'·74E Fl (4) G 15s.
Shotley Marina 51°57'·26N 01°16'·71E VQ (3) 5s.
Shotley Ganges Pier East Head 51°57'·21N 01°16'·23E 2 FG (vert) 4m 1M; G post.
Guard 51°57'·08N 01°17'·86E Fl R 5s; *Bell.*
Ganges 51°57'·10N 01°17'·03E Fl G 5s.
Bristol 51°57'·05N 01°16'·21E Fl (2) G 5s.
Parkeston 51°57'·09N 01°15'·33E Fl (3) G 10s.
Ramsey 51°57'·03N 01°14'·15E L Fl G 10s.
Erwarton Ness 51°57'·11N 01°13'·24E Q (6) + L Fl 15s 4M.
Holbrook 51°57'·22N 01°10'·36E VQ (6) + L Fl 10s 4M.

◄ RIVER ORWELL/IPSWICH

College 51°57'·55N 01°17'·33E Fl (2) R 10s.
Pepys 51°57'·74N 01°16'·89E Fl (4) R 15s.
Fagbury 51°57'·97N 01°16'·80E Fl G 2·5s.
Orwell 51°58'·17N 01°16'·54E Fl R 2·5s.
No. 1 51°58'·28N 01°16'·65E Fl G 5s.
Trimley 51°59'·06N 01°16'·66E Fl G 2·5s.
Stratton 51°59'·42N 01°16'·38E Fl G 5s.
Suffolk Yacht Harbour. Ldg Lts 51°59'·73N 01°16'·09E. Front Iso Y 1M, Rear Oc Y 4s 1M.

Woolverstone Marina 52°00'·48N 01°11'·58E 2 FR (vert).
Orwell Bridge 52°01'·63N 01°09'·83E FY 39m 3M at centre; 2 FR (vert) on Pier 9 and 2 FG (vert) on Pier 10.
No. 12 (off Fox's Marina) 52°02'·11N 01°09'·33E Fl R 5s.
Ipswich Lock SS (Tfc) 52°02'·81N 01°09'·65E.
Neptune Marina 52°03'·13N 01°09'·67E.

HARWICH TO ORFORDNESS

◄ FELIXSTOWE/R. DEBEN/WOODBRIDGE HAVEN

Felixstowe Town Pier Hd 51°57'·39N 01°20'·92E 2 FG (vert) 7m.
Woodbridge Haven 51°58'·18N 01°23'·78E.
Ldg Lts Fl or Fl Y moved as required (on request). Front W △ on R ▮. Rear; R line on ▮.
Martello Spit 51°58'·56N 01°23'·24E.
Deben 51°59'·30N 01°23'·53E.
Horse Sand 51°59'·85N 01°23'·27E.
Felixtowe Ferry, E side 51°59'·42N 01°23'·62E 2 FG (vert).
W side 51°59'·37N 01°23'·47E 2 FR (vert).

◄ RIVER ORE/RIVER ALDE

Orford Haven 52°01'·90N 01°28'·32E L Fl 10s; *Bell.*
Oxley 52°02'·08N 01°27'·87E (Apr-Oct).
Weir 52°02'·10N 01°27'·64W (Apr-Oct).
Dovey's Point 52°03'·81N 01°29'·85W.

◄ OFFSHORE MARKS

S Galloper 51°43'·98N 01°56'·40E Q (6) L Fl 15s; Racon (T); *Whis.*
N Galloper 51°50'·03N 01°59'·36E Q.
S Inner Gabbard 51°51'·23N 01°52'·28E Q (6) + L Fl 15s.
N Inner Gabbard 51°59'·13N 01°55'·98E Q.
Outer Gabbard 51°57'·83N 02°04'·19E Q (3) 10s; Racon (O); *Whis.*
NHR-SE 51°45'·39N 02°39'·89E Fl G 5s; Racon (N).
NHR-S 51°51'·35N 02°28'·71E Fl Y 10s; *Bell.*

◄ SHIPWASH/BAWDSEY BANK

E Shipwash 51°57'·08N 01°37'·89E VQ (3) 5s.
NW Shipwash 51°58'·98N 01°37'·01E Fl R 5s.
N Shipwash 52°01'·73N 01°38'·23E Q 7M; Racon (M); *Bell.*
S Bawdsey 51°57'·23N 01°30'·21E Q (6) + L Fl 15s; *Whis.*
Mid Bawdsey 51°58'·88N 01°33'·59E Fl (3) G 10s.
NE Bawdsey 52°01'·73N 01°36'·09E Fl G 10s.

◄ CUTLER/WHITING BANKS

Cutler 51°58'·51N 01°27'·48E QG.
SW Whiting 52°00'·96N 01°30'·69E Q (6) + L Fl 10s.
Whiting Hook 52°02'·98N 01°31'·82E.
NE Whiting 52°03'·61N 01°33'·32E Q (3) 10s.

ORFORDNESS TO WINTERTON (Direction of buoyage is South to North)

Orford Ness 52°05'·03N 01°34'·46E Fl 5s 28m **20M**; W ○ Tr, R bands. F WRG 14m **W17M**, R14M, **G15M** (same Tr). vis: R shore-210°, R038°-047°, G047°-shore; Racon (T).
Aldeburgh Ridge 52°06'·82N 01°37'·47E.
Sizewell Cooling Water intake and outfall 52°12'·91N 01°37'·97E each Fl R 5s 5m 3M.

◄ SOUTHWOLD

Southwold 52°19'·63N 01°40'·89E Fl (4) WR 20s 37m **W17M**, **R15M**, R14M; vis R (intens) 204°-220°, W220°-001°, R001°-032·3°.
S Pier Head 52°18'·79N 01°40'·49E QR 4m 2M.
N Pier Head 52°18'·80N 01°40'·53E Fl G 1·5s 4m 4M.

◄ LOWESTOFT AND APPROACHES VIA STANFORD CHANNEL

E Barnard 52°25'·14N 01°46'·38E Q (3) 10s.
Newcome Sand 52°26'·28N 01°46'·96E QR.
S Holm 52°27'·13N 01°47'·05E VQ (6) + L Fl 10s.
Stanford 52°27'·35N 01°46'·67E Fl R 2·5s.
SW Holm 52°27'·87N 01°46'·99E Fl (2) G 5s.
Claremont Pier 52°27'·89N 01°44'·87E 2 FR (vert) 5/4m 4M.
Outer Hbr S Pier Hd 52°28'·29N 01°45'·36E Oc R 5s 12m 6M; *Horn (4) 60s*; Tfc sigs.
N Pier Hd 52°28'·32N 01°45'·39E Oc G 5s 12m 8M.
N Newcome 52°28'·31N 01°46'·32E Fl (4) R 15s.
Lowestoft 52°29'·22N 01°45'·35E Fl 15s 37m **23M**; W Tr; part obscd 347°-shore.

◄ LOWESTOFT NORTH ROAD AND CORTON ROAD

Lowestoft Ness SE 52°28'·84N 01°46'·25E Q (6) + L Fl 15s.
Lowestoft Ness N 52°28'·89N 01°46'·23E VQ (3) 5s; *Bell.*
W Holm 52°29'·82N 01°47'·09E Fl (3) G 10s.
NW Holm 52°31'·94N 01°46'·69E Fl (4) G 15s.

◄ GREAT YARMOUTH APPROACHES VIA HOLM CHANNEL

E Newcome 52°28'·55N 01°49'·19E Fl (2) R 5s.
Corton 52°31'·13N 01°51'·36E Q (3) 10s; *Whis.*
E. Holm 52°30'·90N 01°49'·46E Fl (3) R 10s.
S Corton 52°32'·47N 01°49'·35E Q (6) + L Fl 15s; *Bell.*
NE Holm 52°32'·31N 01°48'·19E Fl R 2·5s.
Holm 52°33'·53N 01°47'·96E Fl G 2·5s.
White Swan 52°33'·40N 01°44'·29E.
Holm Sand 52°33'·70N 01°46'·89E Q.

◄ GREAT YARMOUTH/GORLESTON

W Corton 52°34'·57N 01°46'·61E Q (9) 15s.
Ldg Lts 264°. Front, 52°34'·33N 01°43'·97E Oc 3s 6m 10M. Rear, Brush Oc 6s 7m 10M, also FR 20m 6M; R ○ Tr.
Gorleston South Pier Hd 52°34'·33N 01°44'·28E Fl R 3s 11m 11M; vis: 235°-340°; *Horn (3) 60s.*
N Pier Hd 52°34'·38N 01°44'·38E QG 8m 6M; vis: 176°-078°.
Haven Bridge 52°36'·40N 01°43'·38E marked by pairs of 2 FR (vert) and 2 FG (vert) showing up and down stream.

◄ CAISTER ROADS/COCKLE GATEWAY

SW Scroby 52°35'·82N 01°46'·26E Fl G 2·5s.
Scroby Elbow 52°37'·34N 01°46'·38E Fl (2) G 5s.
52°37'·53N 01°45'·79E QR.
East Cross Sand 52°37'·85N 01°53'·30E Fl (4) R 15s.
Mid Caister 52°38'·97N 01°45'·64E Fl (2) R 5s; *Bell.*
N Scroby Platform 52°40'·21N 01°47'·15E Fl (5) Y 20s 10m 5M on N and S sides; same platform, mast Fl R 3s 50m 3M.
NW Scroby 52°40'·36N 01°46'·31E Fl (3) G 10s.
N Caister 52°40'·76N 01°45'·65E Fl (3) R 10s.
Hemsby 52°41'·82N 01°44'·71E Fl R 2·5s.
N Scroby 52°42'·53N 01°44'·66E VQ; *Whis.*
Winterton Lt Ho (disused) 52°42'·75N 01°41'·71E; Racon (T).
Cockle 52°44'·02N 01°43'·58E VQ (3) 5s; *Bell.*

9.4.5 PASSAGE INFORMATION

Reference books include: *East Coast Rivers* (Macmillan Reeds/Coote) from the Swale to Lowestoft. The Admiralty *Dover Strait Pilot* - (stops at Southwold). *North Sea Passage Pilot* (Imray/Navin). *The East Coast* (Imray/Bowskill). Admiralty Small Craft Folio 5606 covers The Thames Estuary and 5607 the R Roach to Orford Ness. The former contains 11 and the latter 12 A2 size charts in a clear plastic wallet and cost £35.00 (2000).

THE THAMES ESTUARY (chart *1183, 1975*) To appreciate the geography of the Thames Estuary there is a well-known analogy between its major sandbanks and the fingers and thumb of the left hand, outstretched palm-down: With the thumb lying E over Margate Sand, the index finger covers Long Sand; the middle finger represents Sunk Sand and the third finger delineates West and East Barrow; the little finger points NE along Buxey and Gunfleet Sands.

The intervening channels are often intricate, but the main ones, in sequence from south to north, are:

a. between the Kent coast and thumb – Four Fathoms, Horse, Gore and South Chans; sometimes known as the overland route due to relatively shallow water.
b. between thumb and index finger – Queens and Princes Chans leading seaward to Knock Deep.
c. between index and middle fingers – Knob Chan leading to Knock Deep via the Edinburgh Chans across Long Sand and the Shingles. Knock John Chan and Black Deep, the main shipping channels.
d. between middle and third fingers – Barrow Deep.
e. between third and little fingers – W and E Swin, Middle Deep and Whitaker Chan leading seaward to King's Chan.
f. between little finger and the Essex coast – The Wallet and Goldmer Gat.

The sandbanks shift constantly in the Thames Estuary. Up-to-date charts showing the latest buoyage changes are essential, but it is unwise to put too much faith in charted depths over the banks; a reliable echosounder is vital. The main chans carry much commercial shipping and are well buoyed and lit, but this is not so in lesser chans and swatchways which are convenient for yachtsmen, particularly when crossing the estuary from N to S, or vice versa. Unlit, unmarked minor chans (eg Fisherman's Gat or S Edinburgh Chan; in the latter there is a Historic Wreck (see 9.0.3h) at 51°31'·7N 01°14'·9E) should be used with great caution, which could indeed be the hallmark of all passage-making in the Thames Estuary. Good vis is needed to pick out buoys/marks, and to avoid shipping.

CROSSING THE THAMES ESTUARY (See 9.4.9) Study the tides carefully and understand them, so as to work the streams to best advantage and to ensure sufficient depth at the times and places where you expect to be, or might be later (see 9.4.3 and 9.4.7). In principle it is best to make most of the crossing on a rising tide, ie departing N Foreland or the vicinity of the Whitaker buoy at around LW. The stream runs 3kn at sp in places, mostly along the chans but sometimes across the intervening banks. With wind against tide a short, steep sea is raised, particularly in E or NE winds.

Making N from N Foreland to Orford Ness or beyond (or vice versa) it may be preferable to keep to seaward of the main banks, via Kentish Knock and Long Sand Head buoys, thence to N Shipwash lt buoy 14M further N.

Bound NW from N Foreland it is approximately 26M to the Rivers Crouch, Blackwater or Colne. A safe route is through either the Princes or the North Edinburgh Channels, thence S of the Tizard, Knob and West Barrow banks to the West Swin, before turning NE into Middle Deep and the East Swin. This is just one of many routes which could be followed, depending on wind direction, tidal conditions and confidence in electronic aids in the absence of marks.

A similar, well-used route in reverse, ie to the SE, lies via the Wallet Spitway, to the Whitaker lt buoy, through Barrow Swatchway to SW Sunk bn; thence via the N Edinburgh Chan, toward the E Margate lt buoy keeping E of Tongue Sand tr. Beware shoal waters off Barrow and Sunk Sands.

Port Control London can give navigational help to yachts on VHF Ch 12; Thames CG at Walton-on-the-Naze can also assist. The Thames Navigation Service has radar coverage between the Naze and Margate, eastward to near the Dutch coast.

NORTH FORELAND TO LONDON BRIDGE N Foreland has a conspic lt ho, (chart 1828), with buoys offshore. From HW Dover –0120 to +0045 the stream runs N from The Downs and W into Thames Estuary. From HWD + 0045 to + 0440 the N-going stream from The Downs meets the E-going stream from Thames Estuary, which in strong winds causes a bad sea. From HWD –0450 to –0120 the streams turn W into Thames Estuary and S towards The Downs. If bound for London, round N Foreland against the late ebb in order to carry a fair tide from Sheerness onward.

For vessels drawing less than 2m the most direct route from North Foreland to the Thames and Medway is via South Chan, Gore Chan, Horse Chan, Kentish Flats, Four Fathom Chan and Cant; but it is not well marked particularly over the Kentish Flats. An alternative, deeper route is East of Margate Sand and the Tongue, to set course through Princes Channel to Oaze Deep; larger vessels proceed via the North Edinburgh Channel. W-going streams begin at approx HW Sheerness –0600 and E-going at HW Sheerness +0030.

Margate or Whitstable (9.4.10) afford little shelter for yachts. The Swale (9.4.11) provides an interesting inside route S of the Isle of Sheppey with access to Sheerness and the R Medway (9.4.13). If sailing from N Foreland to the Thames, Queenborough (9.4.12) offers the first easily accessible, all-tide, deep-water shelter. The Medway Chan is the main appr to Sheerness from the Warp and the Medway Fairway buoy.

To clear tanker berths yachts should navigate as follows:

Inward from north - keep close to starboard hand buoys, at West Leigh Middle cross to the south side of the Yanlet Channel, making sure the fairway is clear, make for the E Blyth buoy before turning onto the inward track, remember outward vessels will pass close to the port hand buoys. The Mid Blyth, West Blyth and Lower Hope buoys can be safely passed to the south. Cross to the correct side in Lower Hope Reach as rapidly as possible, when it is safe to do so.

Outward to north - as above in reverse, but crossing to the north between Sea Reach Nos 4 & 5 buoys.

Inward from south - keep well clear of the Sea Reach Channel to the south, crossing to the north side in the Lower Hope as described above.

SHOEBURYNESS TO RIVER COLNE (charts *1185, 1975*) Maplin and Foulness Sands extend nearly 6M NE from Foulness Pt, the extremity being marked by Whitaker bn. On N side of Whitaker chan leading to R. Crouch (9.4.17) and R. Roach (9.4.16) lies Buxey Sand, inshore of which is the Ray Sand chan (dries), a convenient short cut between R. Crouch and R. Blackwater with sufficient rise of tide.

To seaward of Buxey Sand and the Spitway, Gunfleet Sand extends 10M NE, marked by buoys and drying in places. A conspic disused lt tr stands on SE side of Gunfleet Sand, about 6M SSE of the Naze tr, and here the SW-going (flood) stream begins about HW Sheerness + 0600, and the NE-going stream at about HW Sheerness – 0030, sp rates 2kn.

The Rivers Blackwater (9.4.18) and Colne (9.4.19) share a common estuary which is approached from the NE via NE Gunfleet lt buoy; thence along Goldmer Gat and the Wallet towards Knoll and Eagle lt buoys. For the Colne turn NNW via Colne Bar buoy towards Inner Bench Hd buoy keeping in mid-chan. For R. Blackwater, head WNW for NW Knoll and Bench Hd buoys. From the S or SE, make for the Whitaker ECM buoy, thence through the Spitway, via Swin Spitway and Wallet Spitway buoys to reach Knoll buoy and deeper water.

RIVER COLNE TO HARWICH (chart *1975*, 1593) 4M SW of the Naze tr at Hollands Haven a conspic radar tr (67m, unlit) is an excellent daymark. From the S, approach Walton and Harwich via the Medusa chan about 1M E of Naze tr. At N end of this chan, 1M off Dovercourt, Pye End buoy marks chan SSW to Walton Backwaters (9.4.20). Harwich and Landguard Point are close to the N. Making Harwich from the SE beware the drying Cork Sand, which lies N/S.

Sunk lt Float (Fog sig), 11M E of The Naze, marks the outer apprs to Harwich (9.4.21), an extensive and well sheltered hbr accessible at all times (chart *2693*). The Harwich DW channel begins 1·5M NNW of Sunk lt Float and runs N between Rough and Shipwash shoals, then W past the Cork Sand PHM lt buoy. It is in constant use by commercial shipping, so yachts should approach via the Recommended Track for yachts.

Approaching from NE and 2M off the ent to R. Deben (9.4.23), beware Cutler shoal, with least depth of 1·2m, marked by SHM buoy on E side; Wadgate Ledge and the Platters are about 1·5M ENE of Landguard Point. S of Landguard Point the W-going (flood) stream begins at HW Harwich + 0600, and the E-going stream at HW Harwich, sp rates about 1·5kn. Note: HW Harwich is never more than 7 mins after HW Walton; LW times are about 10 mins earlier.

HARWICH TO ORFORD NESS (chart *2052*) Shipwash shoal, buoyed and with a drying patch, runs NNE from 9M E of Felixstowe to 4M SSE of Orford Ness. Inshore of this is Shipway Chan, then Bawdsey Bank, buoyed with depths of 2m, on which the sea breaks in E'ly swell. The Sledway Chan lies between Bawdsey Bank and Whiting Bank (buoyed) which is close SW of Orford Ness, and has least depth of 1m. Hollesley Chan, about 1M wide, runs inshore W and N of this bank. In the SW part of Hollesley B is the ent to Orford Haven and the R Ore/Alde (9.4.24).

There are overfalls S of Orford Ness on both the ebb and flood streams. 2M E of Orford Ness the SW-going stream begins at HW Harwich +0605, sp rate 2·5kn; the NE-going stream begins at HW Harwich –0010, sp rate 3kn.

Note: The direction of local buoyage becomes S to N off Orford Ness (52°05'N).

ORFORD NESS TO GREAT YARMOUTH (chart 1543) N of Orford Ness seas break on Aldeburgh Ridge (1.3m), but the coast is clear of offlying dangers past Aldeburgh and Southwold (9.4.25), as far as Benacre Ness, 5M S of Lowestoft. Sizewell power stn is a conspic 3 bldg 1·5M N of Thorpe Ness. Keep 1·5M offshore to avoid fishing floats.

Lowestoft (9.4.26) is best approached from both S and E by the buoyed/lit Stanford chan, passing E of Newcome Sand and SW of Holm Sand; beware possible strong set across hbr ent. From the N, approach through Cockle Gatway, Caister Road, Yarmouth Road, passing Great Yarmouth; then proceed S through Gorleston, Corton and Lowestoft North Roads (buoyed). 1M E of hbr ent, the S-going stream begins at HW Dover –0600, and the N-going at HW Dover, sp rates 2·6kn.

In the approaches to Great Yarmouth (9.4.27) from seaward the banks are continually changing; use the buoyed chans which, from N and S, are those described in the preceding paragraph. But from the E the shortest approach is via Corton ECM lt buoy and the Holm Channel leading into Gorleston Road. The sea often breaks on North Scroby, Middle Scroby and Caister Shoal (all of which dry), and there are heavy tide rips over parts of Corton and South Scroby Sands, Middle and South Cross Sands, and Winterton Overfalls.

1M NE of ent to Gt Yarmouth the S-going stream begins at HW Dover –0600, and the N-going at HW Dover – 0015, sp rates 2·3kn. Breydon Water (tidal) affects streams in the Haven; after heavy rain the out-going stream at Brush Quay may exceed 5kn. For Norfolk Broads, see 9.4.27. About 12M NE of Great Yarmouth lie Newarp Banks, on which the sea breaks in bad weather.

CROSSING FROM THAMES ESTUARY TO BELGIUM OR THE NETHERLANDS (charts 1610, 1872, 3371, *1406*, 1408) Important factors in choosing a route include the need to head at 90° across the various TSSs; to avoid areas where traffic converges; to make full use of available ITZs and to keep well clear of offshore oil/gas activities (see 9.5.5). It is best to avoid the areas westward of W Hinder lt, around Nord Hinder lt buoy and the Maas routes W of the Hook of Holland. For Distances across N Sea, see 9.0.8 and for further notes on North Sea crossings, see 9.23.5.

From Rivers Crouch, Blackwater, Colne or from Harwich take departure from Long Sand Hd lt buoy to S Galloper lt buoy, thence to W Hinder lt (see 9.23.5), crossing the TSS at right angles near Garden City lt buoy. Care must be taken throughout with tidal streams, which may be setting across the yacht's track. The area is relatively shallow, and in bad weather seas are steep and short.

For ports between Hook of Holland and Texel it may be best to diverge to the NE so as to cross the several Deep Water (DW) routes, and their extensions, as quickly as possible, to the N of Nord Hinder lt buoy and the Maas TSS. If bound for ports NE of Texel keep well S of the TX1 lt buoy and then inshore of the Off Texel-Vlieland-Terschelling-German Bight TSS, which is well buoyed on its S side.

9.4.6 DISTANCE TABLE

Approximate distances in nautical miles are by the most direct route, whilst avoiding dangers and allowing for Traffic Separation Schemes. Places in *italics* are in adjoining areas; places in **bold** are in 9.0.8, Distances across the North Sea.

1. ***Ramsgate***	**1**																			
2. Whitstable	22	**2**																		
3. **Sheerness**	34	14	**3**																	
4. Gravesend	56	36	22	**4**																
5. **London Bridge**	76	55	45	23	**5**															
6. Southend-on-Sea	35	17	6	20	43	**6**														
7. Havengore	33	15	12	32	55	12	**7**													
8. **Burnham-on-Crouch**	44	36	34	53	76	33	30	**8**												
9. West Mersea	43	38	29	49	72	30	29	22	**9**											
10. **Brightlingsea**	**41**	**36**	**28**	**47**	**71**	**28**	**26**	**22**	**8**	**10**										
11. Walton-on-the-Naze	40	40	46	59	82	39	37	25	23	23	**11**									
12. **Harwich**	40	40	50	65	83	40	41	31	24	24	6	**12**								
13. Ipswich	49	49	59	74	92	49	50	40	33	33	15	9	**13**							
14. River Deben (ent)	45	45	55	71	89	46	46	35	38	38	10	6	15	**14**						
15. River Ore (ent)	47	47	60	75	93	50	51	38	43	43	14	10	19	4	**15**					
16. Southwold	62	67	80	95	113	70	71	58	63	63	33	30	39	23	20	**16**				
17. **Lowestoft**	72	77	90	105	123	80	81	68	73	73	43	40	49	33	30	10	**17**			
18. Great Yarmouth	79	84	97	112	130	87	88	76	81	80	51	52	61	41	38	18	7	**18**		
19. *Blakeney*	123	128	141	156	174	131	132	120	125	124	95	96	105	85	82	62	51	44	**19**	
20. Bridlington	207	198	224	226	244	201	215	204	205	204	181	175	184	169	165	145	135	114	79	**20**

9.4.7 EAST ANGLIAN WAYPOINTS

Selected waypoints for use between the Thames Estuary and the Wash are listed below. Further waypoints in adjacent waters are given in 9.3.4 and 9.4.4 for the English Coast, and 9.22.4, 9.23.4 and 9.24.4 for the coasts Central NE France, Belgium, the Netherlands and Germany. **All positions listed below are referenced to the WGS84/ETRS89 datum but should be assumed to be approximate.**

Aldeburgh Ridge By	52°06'·82N	01°37'·46E
Barnard E Lt By	52°25'·12N	01°46'·30E
Barrow No.3 Lt By	51°42'·03N	01°20'·25E
Barrow No.6 Lt By	51°37'·32N	01°14'·69E
Barrow No.9 Lt By	51°35'·34N	01°10'·30E
Barrow No.11 Lt By	51°33'·76N	01°05'·74E
Barrow SW Lt By	51°32'·29N	01°00'·30E
Bawdsey NE Lt By	52°01'·73N	01°36'·09E
Bawdsey S Lt By	51°57'·23N	01°30'·21E
Bawdsey Mid Lt By	51°58'·88N	01°33'·59E
Bench Head Lt By	51°44'·69N	01°01'·10E
Black Deep Lt By	51°46'·83N	01°34'·27E
Black Deep No. 1 Lt By	51°44'·03N	01°28'·10E
Black Deep No. 3 Lt By	51°41'·98N	01°25'·97E
Black Deep No. 5 Lt By	51°39'·53N	01°23'·00E
Black Deep No. 7 Lt By	51°37'·08N	01°17'·69E
Black Deep No. 11 Lt By	51°34'·33N	01°13'·40E
Blacktail E Lt Bn	51°31'·79N	00°56'·46E
Blakeney Overfalls Lt By	53°03'·01N	01°01'·37E
Blyth E Lt By	51°29'·73N	00°37'·81E
Blyth Mid Lt By	51°30'·08N	00°32'·38E
Boston No. 1 Lt By	52°57'·88N	00°15'·16E
Boston Roads Lt By	52°57'·66N	00°16'·04E
Burnham Flats Lt By	53°07'·53N	00°34'·89E
Buxey Bn	51°41'·15N	01°01'·28E
Buxey No. 1 Lt By	51°39'·18N	01°01'·01E
Buxey No. 2 Lt By	51°38'·98N	01°00'·15E
Buxey S Lt By	51°39'·84N	01°02'·49E
Caister Mid Lt By	52°38'·97N	01°45'·64E
Cant Bn	51°27'·77N	00°53'·36E
Cant E Lt By	51°28'·53N	00°55'·60E
Cant Mid Lt Bn	51°26'·88N	00°49'·80E
Chapman Lt By	51°30'·43N	00°36'·93E
Cliff Foot Lt By	51°55'·72N	01°18'·53E
Cockle Lt By	52°44'·02N	01°43'·58E
Colne Bar Lt By	51°44'·60N	01°02'·58E
Columbine By	51°24'·26N	01°01'·35E
Columbine Spit By	51°23'·86N	01°00'·03E
Cork S By	51°51'·33N	01°24'·10E
Cork Sand Lt Bn	51°55'·51N	01°25'·41E
Cork Sand Yacht Lt Bn	51°55'·21N	01°25'·21E
Corton Lt By	52°31'·13N	01°51'·36E
Corton S Lt By	52°32'·47N	01°49'·35E
Corton W Lt By	52°34'·57N	01°46'·61E
Cromer Lt	52°55'·48N	01°18'·99E
Cross Sand Lt By	52°37'·06N	01°59'·13E
Cross Sand NE Lt By	52°43'·03N	01°53'·63E
Cross Sand E Lt By	52°40'·85N	01°53'·30E
Crouch Lt By	51°37'·62N	00°56'·38E
Crouch Fairway No. 1 Lt By	51°37'·10N	00°51'·00E
Crouch Inner Lt By	51°37'·22N	00°55'·14E
CS 5 Lt By	51°23'·03N	01°49'·90E
Cutler Lt By	51°58'·51N	01°27'·48E
Docking N Lt By	53°14'·80N	00°41'·47E
Docking E Lt By	53°09'·83N	00°50'·40E
Drill Stone Lt By	51°25'·82N	01°42'·85E
Eagle Lt By	51°44'·13N	01°03'·81E
East Last Lt By	51°24'·06N	01°11'·84E
Edinburgh Lt By	51°31'·51N	01°21'·62E
Elbow Lt By	51°23'·23N	01°31'·61E
Falls Hd Lt By	51°28'·21N	01°49'·86E
Faversham Spit By	51°20'·77N	00°54'·19E
Felixstowe Ledge Lt By	51°56'·30N	01°23'·72E
Foulness Lt By	51°39'·85N	01°03'·81E
Foxtrot 3 Lt F	51°23'·85N	02°00'·51E
Gabbard N Inner Lt By	51°59'·13N	01°55'·98E
Gabbard S Inner Lt By	51°51'·23N	01°52'·28E
Galloper N Lt By	51°50'·03N	01°59'·36E
Galloper S Lt By	51°43'·98N	01°56'·40E
Grain Hard Lt By	51°26'·98N	00°44'·17E
Guard Lt By	51°57'·08N	01°17'·86E
Gunfleet NE Lt By	51°49'·91N	01°27'·84E
Gunfleet Old Lt Ho	51°46'·12N	01°20'·43E
Gunfleet Spit Lt By	51°45'·32N	01°21'·69E
Haisbro N Lt By	53°00'·22N	01°32'·28E
Haisbro Mid Lt By	52°54'·22N	01°41'·59E
Haisbro S Lt By	52°50'·82N	01°48'·24E
Hammond Knoll E Lt By	52°52'·28N	01°58'·60E
Harwich Chan No. 1 Lt By	51°56'·14N	01°27'·05E
Harwich Shelf Lt Bn	51°56'·84N	01°18'·07E
Haven Lt By	51°55'·76N	01°32'·56E
Hemsby Lt By	52°41'·82N	01°44'·71E
Holm Lt By	52°33'·53N	01°47'·96E
Holm E Lt By	52°30'·90N	01°49'·46E
Holm S Lt By	52°27'·13N	01°47'·05E
Holm SW Lt By	52°27'·87N	01°46'·99E
Holm W Lt By	52°29'·82N	01°47'·09E
Holm NW Lt By	52°31'·94N	01°46'·69E
Hook Middle W By	51°39'·17N	01°07'·89E
Hook Spit By	51°24'·09N	01°12'·27E
Horse Shoal Lt By	51°37'·10N	00°51'·52E
Kentish Knock Lt By	51°38'·52N	01°40'·41E
Knob Lt By	51°30'·70N	01°04'·27E
Knob NE Lt By	51°32'·04N	01°10'·00E
Knob SE Lt By	51°30'·89N	01°06'·40E
Knock S Lt By	51°34'·11N	01°34'·28E
Knock John Lt By	51°33'·53N	01°10'·98E
Knoll Lt By	51°43'·88N	01°05'·07E
Knoll NW Lt By	51°44'·35N	01°02'·15E
Landguard Lt By	51°55'·45N	01°18'·84E
Lee W Mid Lt By	51°30'·48N	00°38'·82E
Leigh By	51°31'·07N	00°42'·56E
Leigh SE Lt By	51°29'·42N	00°47'·07E
Little Sunk Bn	51°41'·93N	01°24'·75E
Long Sand Bn	51°41'·47N	01°29'·46E
Long Sand Hd Lt By	51°47'·90N	01°39'·43E
Long Sand SE Lt By	51°32'·53N	01°21'·26E
Long Sand NW Bn	51°34'·75N	01°18'·05E
Lowestoft Lt Ho	52°29'·22N	01°45'·35E

Lynn Knock Lt By	53°04'·37N	00°27'·19E
Maplin Lt By	51°34'·03N	01°02'·29E
Maplin NE Lt By	51°37'·44N	01°04'·78E
Maplin Bank Lt By	51°35'·50N	01°04'·70E
Margate E Lt By	51°27'·02N	01°26'·35E
Margate SE Lt By	51°24'·05N	01°20'·40E
Margate S Lt By	51°23'·83N	01°16'·64E
Margate Hook Bn	51°24'·18N	01°14'·28E
Margate Outfall Lt By	51°24'·61N	01°26'·01E
Medusa Lt By	51°51'·20N	01°20'·35E
Medway Lt By	51°28'·83N	00°52'·81E
Nass Lt Bn	51°45'·83N	00°54'·83E
Naze Tr	51°51'·87N	01°17'·27E
Newarp Lt F	52°48'·37N	01°55'·69 E
Newcome N Lt By	52°28'·31N	01°46'·32E
Newcome E Lt By	52°28'·55N	01°49'·19E
Newcome Sand Lt By	52°26'·28N	01°46'·96E
NHR-S Lt By	51°51'·35N	02°28'·71E
NHR-SE Lt By	51°45'·39N	02°39'·89E
Nore Sand W Lt By	51°29'·41N	00°40'·85E
Nore Swatch Lt By	51°28'·28N	00°45'·55E
North Foreland Lt	51°22'·49N	01°26'·71E
Oaze S Lt By	51°30'·03N	01°00'·70E
Oaze SW Lt By	51°29'·06N	00°56'·93E
Oaze W Lt By	51°29'·06N	00°55'·43E
Orford Haven Lt By	52°01'·90N	01°28'·32E
Orford Ness Lt Ho	52°05'·03N	01°34'·46E
Outer Crouch Lt By	51°38'·38N	00°58'·48E
Outer Gabbard Lt By	51°57'·83N	02°04'·19E
Outer Tongue Lt By	51°30'·73N	01°26'·40E
Oyster Lt By	51°22'·14N	01°01'·16E
Patch Lt By	51°32'·40N	01°21'·01E
Pitching Ground Lt By	51°55'·43N	01°21'·04E
Pollard Spit Lt By	51°22'·98N	00°58'·56E
Princes Lt By	51°28'·75N	01°18'·62E
Princes No. 1 Lt By	51°29'·23N	01°16'·02E
Princes No. 2 Lt By	51°28'·81N	01°13'·08E
Princes No. 4 Lt By	51°28'·83N	01°09'·90E
Princes No. 5 Lt By	51°29'·50N	01°09'·90E
Princes No. 7 Lt By	51°29'·61N	01°06'·72E
Princes No. 6 Lt By	51°29'·18N	01°06'·40E
Pye End Lt By	51°55'·04N	01°17'·88E
Race S Lt By	53°07'·80N	00°57'·31E
Redsand E Lt By	51°29'·41N	01°04'·05E
Red Sand Trs N Lt By	51°28'·73N	00°59'·32E
Ridge Lt By	51°40'·12N	01°04'·88E
Ridge Inner Lt By	51°55'·38N	01°20'·20E
Rough Lt By	51°55'·19N	01°31'·00E
Roughs Tr SE Lt By	51°53'·64N	01°28'·94E
Roughs Tr NW Lt By	51°53'·80N	01°28'·76E
Scott Patch Lt By	53°11'·13N	00°36'·36E
Scroby N Lt By	52°42'·53N	01°44'·66E
Scroby SW Lt By	52°35'·82N	01°46'·26E
Scroby NW Lt By	52°40'·36N	01°46'·31E
Scroby Elbow Lt By	52°37'·34N	01°46'·39E
Shelf N Lt By	51°56'·68N	01°18'·59E
Sheringham E Lt By	53°02'·21N	01°14'·84E
Sheringham W Lt By	53°02'·95N	01°06'·72E
Shingles N Lt By	51°32'·79N	01°14'·25E
Shingles Mid Lt By	51°31'·96N	01°11'·98E
Shingles NW Lt By	51°31'·26N	01°09'·73E
Shingles Patch Lt By	51°33'·01N	01°15'·37E
Shipwash N Lt By	52°01'·73N	01°38'·23E
Shipwash E Lt By	51°57'·08N	01°37'·89E
Shipwash S Lt By	51°52'·71N	01°33'·97E
Shipwash SW Lt By	51°54'·75N	01°34'·21E
Shipwash NW Lt By	51°58'·98N	01°37'·01E
Shivering Sand Trs N Lt By	51°30'·01N	01°04'·76E
Shivering Sand Trs S Lt By	51°29'·79N	01°04'·83E
Shoebury Lt Bn	51°30'·29N	00°49'·26E
Shoebury S Lt By	51°30'·43N	00°52'·39E
Shoebury W Lt By	51°30'·23N	00°45'·73E
Shoebury Inner Bn	51°30'·99N	00°49'·16E
Smiths Knoll Lt By	52°43'·52N	02°17'·89E
Southwold Lt Ho	52°19'·63N	01°40'·89E
Spaniard Lt By	51°26'·23N	01°04'·00E
Spile Lt By	51°26'·38N	00°55'·70E
Spit NE Lt By	51°27'·93N	01°29'·89E
Stanford Lt By	52°27'·35N	01°46'·67E
Stone Banks By	51°53'·19N	01°19'·21E
Sunk Lt F	51°51'·02N	01°34'·89E
Sunk Lt By (Wash – Cork Hole)	52°56'·29N	00°23'·40E
Sunk SW Bn	51°36'·55N	01°14'·74E
Sunk W Lt By	51°44'·34N	01°25'·78E
Sunk Head Tr Lt By	51°46'·63N	01°30'·51E
Sunken Buxey Lt By	51°39'·54N	01°00'·59E
Swallow Tail By	51°40'·47N	01°04'·70E
Swatch Mid Lt By	51°28'·68N	00°44'·16E
Swin Spitway Lt By	51°41'·96N	01°08'·32E
Swin W By	51°33'·38N	01°01'·98E
Tizard Lt By	51°32'·93N	01°12'·90E
Tongue Sand Tr N Lt By	51°29'·68N	01°22'·03E
Tongue Sand Tr S Lt By	51°29'·43N	01°22'·04E
Trinity Lt By	51°49'·04N	01°36'·37E
Walker Lt By	51°53'·79N	01°33'·90E
Wallet No.2 Lt By	51°48'·88N	01°22'·99E
Wallet No.4 Lt By	51°46'·53N	01°17'·23E
Wallet Spitway Lt By	51°42'·86N	01°07'·32E
Washington Lt By	51°56'·52N	01°26'·59E
Well N Lt By	53°02'·99N	00°27'·85E
Wells Fairway Lt By	52°59'·81N	00°49'·77E
Whitaker Bn	51°39'·64N	01°06'·16E
Whitaker Lt By	51°40'·52N	01°03'·50E
Whiting NE Lt By	52°03'·61N	01°33'·32E
Whiting SW Lt By	52°00'·96N	01°30'·69E
Whiting Hook By	52°02'·98N	01°31'·82E
Whitstable St Lt By	51°23'·85N	01°01'·59E
Winterton Ridge S Lt By	52°47'·21N	02°03'·44E
Woodbridge Haven By	51°58'·18N	01°23'·78E
Woolpack Lt By	53°02'·68N	00°31'·41E

THAMES ESTUARY *9.4.8*

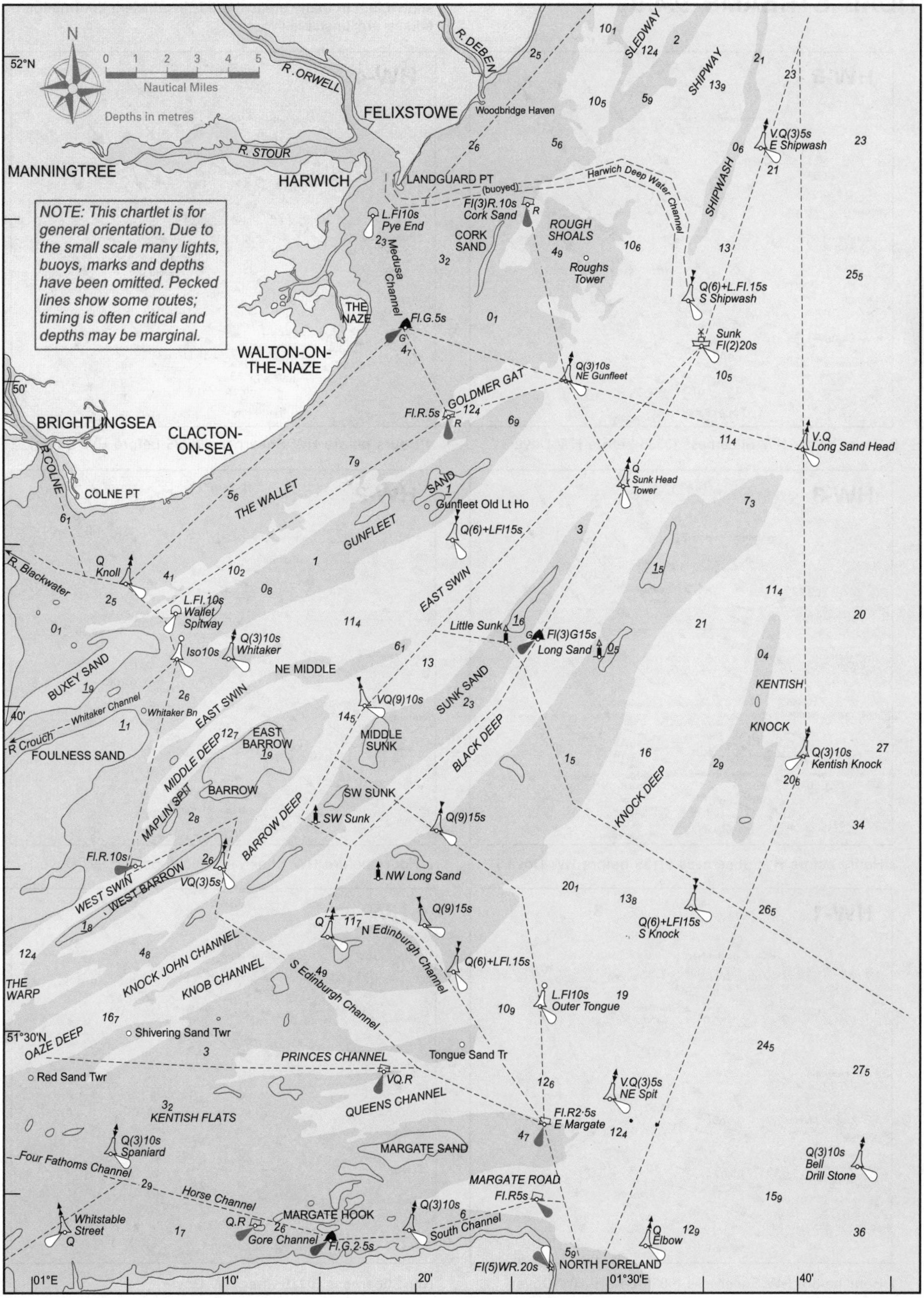
N
0 1 2 3 4 5
Nautical Miles
Depths in metres
52°N
NOTE: This chartlet is for general orientation. Due to the small scale many lights, buoys, marks and depths have been omitted. Pecked lines show some routes; timing is often critical and depths may be marginal.
R. DEBEN
R. ORWELL
FELIXSTOWE
Woodbridge Haven
R. STOUR
MANNINGTREE
HARWICH
LANDGUARD PT
(buoyed)
Harwich Deep Water Channel
SLEDWAY
SHIPWAY
SHIPWASH
V.Q(3)5s
E Shipwash
L.Fl10s
Pye End
Fl(3)R.10s
Cork Sand
CORK SAND
ROUGH SHOALS
Roughs Tower
Medusa Channel
THE NAZE
Fl.G.5s
Q(6)+L.Fl.15s
S Shipwash
Sunk
Fl(2)20s
WALTON-ON-THE-NAZE
Q(3)10s
NE Gunfleet
GOLDMER GAT
Fl.R.5s
50'
BRIGHTLINGSEA
CLACTON-ON-SEA
R COLNE
COLNE PT
V.Q
Long Sand Head
Q
Sunk Head Tower
SAND
Gunfleet Old Lt Ho
THE WALLET
GUNFLEET
Q(6)+LFl15s
R. Blackwater
Q
Knoll
EAST SWIN
L.Fl.10s
Wallet Spitway
Little Sunk
Fl(3)G15s
Long Sand
Iso10s
Q(3)10s
Whitaker
NE MIDDLE
KENTISH
BUXEY SAND
Whitaker Channel
Whitaker Bn
EAST SWIN
VQ(9)10s
SUNK SAND
40'
R Crouch
FOULNESS SAND
MIDDLE DEEP
EAST BARROW
MIDDLE SUNK
KNOCK
BLACK DEEP
Q(3)10s
Kentish Knock
MAPLIN SPIT
BARROW
SW SUNK
SW Sunk
Q(9)15s
KNOCK DEEP
BARROW DEEP
Fl.R.10s
WEST SWIN
WEST BARROW
VQ(3)5s
NW Long Sand
Q(6)+LFl15s
S Knock
Q(9)15s
Q
N Edinburgh Channel
KNOCK JOHN CHANNEL
Q(6)+LFl.15s
THE WARP
KNOB CHANNEL
S Edinburgh Channel
L.Fl10s
Outer Tongue
Shivering Sand Twr
51°30'N
OAZE DEEP
Tongue Sand Tr
PRINCES CHANNEL
Red Sand Twr
VQ.R
V.Q(3)5s
NE Spit
QUEENS CHANNEL
KENTISH FLATS
Fl.R2·5s
E Margate
Q(3)10s
Spaniard
MARGATE SAND
Q(3)10s
Bell
Drill Stone
Four Fathoms Channel
MARGATE ROAD
Horse Channel
Fl.R5s
Q(3)10s
Whitstable Street
Q
MARGATE HOOK
Q.R
Gore Channel
Fl.G.2·5s
South Channel
Q
Elbow
NORTH FORELAND
Fl(5)WR.20s
01°E
10'
20'
01°30'E
40'

THAMES ESTUARY TIDAL STREAMS *9.4.9*

Due to very strong rates of tidal streams in some areas, eddies may occur. Where possible, some indication of these is shown, but in many areas there is insufficient information or eddies are unstable.

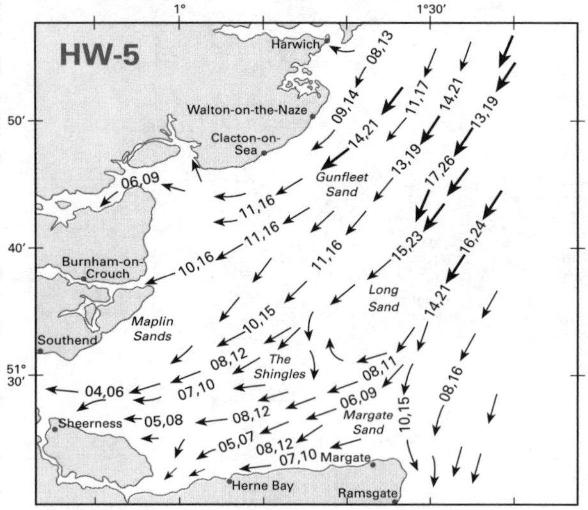
HW-5
Harwich
Walton-on-the-Naze
Clacton-on-Sea
Gunfleet Sand
Burnham-on-Crouch
Maplin Sands
Southend
The Shingles
Long Sand
Sheerness
Margate Sand
Margate
Herne Bay
Ramsgate

5 Hours before HW Sheerness (0335 before HW Dover)

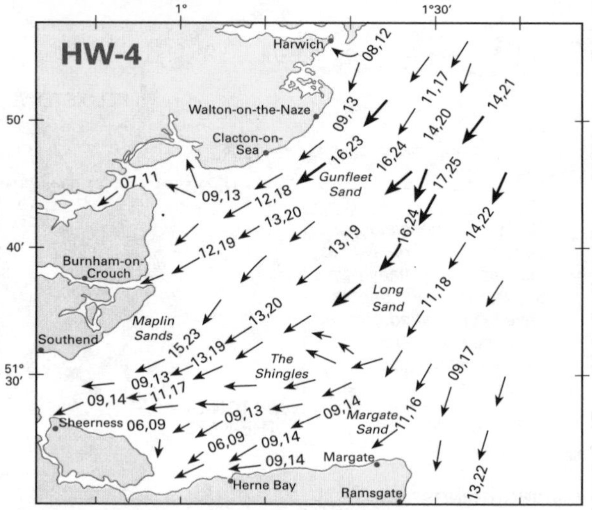
HW-4
Harwich
Walton-on-the-Naze
Clacton-on-Sea
Gunfleet Sand
Burnham-on-Crouch
Maplin Sands
Southend
The Shingles
Long Sand
Sheerness
Margate Sand
Margate
Herne Bay
Ramsgate

4 Hours before HW Sheerness (0235 before HW Dover)

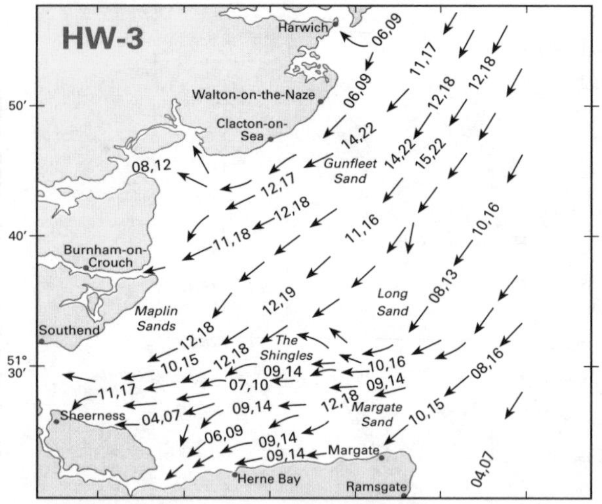
HW-3
Harwich
Walton-on-the-Naze
Clacton-on-Sea
Gunfleet Sand
Burnham-on-Crouch
Maplin Sands
Southend
The Shingles
Long Sand
Sheerness
Margate Sand
Margate
Herne Bay
Ramsgate

3 Hours before HW Sheerness (0135 before HW Dover)

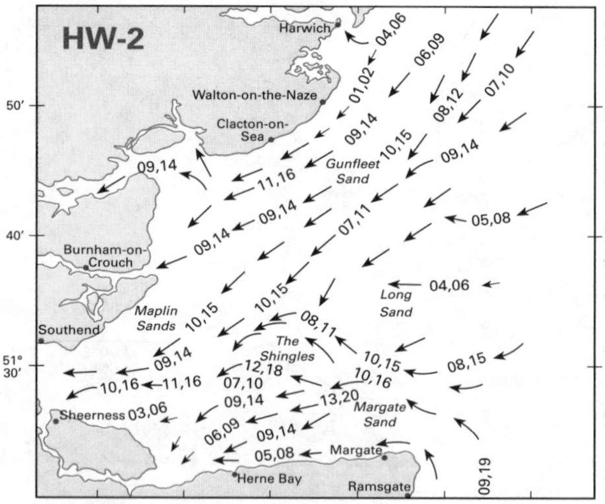
HW-2
Harwich
Walton-on-the-Naze
Clacton-on-Sea
Gunfleet Sand
Burnham-on-Crouch
Maplin Sands
Southend
The Shingles
Long Sand
Sheerness
Margate Sand
Margate
Herne Bay
Ramsgate

2 Hours before HW Sheerness (0035 before HW Dover)

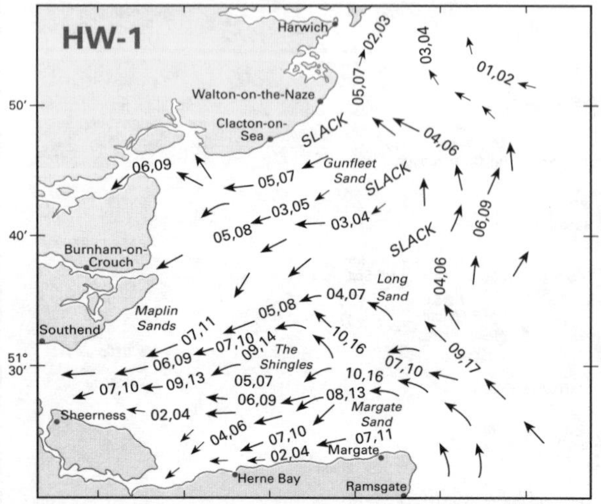
HW-1
Harwich
Walton-on-the-Naze
Clacton-on-Sea
SLACK
Gunfleet Sand
SLACK
SLACK
Burnham-on-Crouch
Maplin Sands
Southend
The Shingles
Long Sand
Sheerness
Margate Sand
Margate
Herne Bay
Ramsgate

1 Hour before HW Sheerness (0025 before HW Dover)

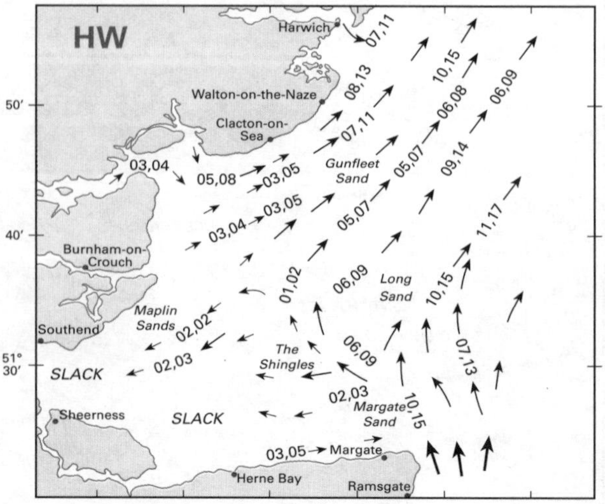
HW
Harwich
Walton-on-the-Naze
Clacton-on-Sea
Gunfleet Sand
Burnham-on-Crouch
Maplin Sands
Southend
SLACK
The Shingles
Long Sand
Sheerness
SLACK
Margate Sand
Margate
Herne Bay
Ramsgate

HW Sheerness (0125 after HW Dover)

Due to very strong rates of tidal streams in some areas, eddies may occur. Where possible, some indication of these is shown, but in many areas there is insufficient information or eddies are unstable.

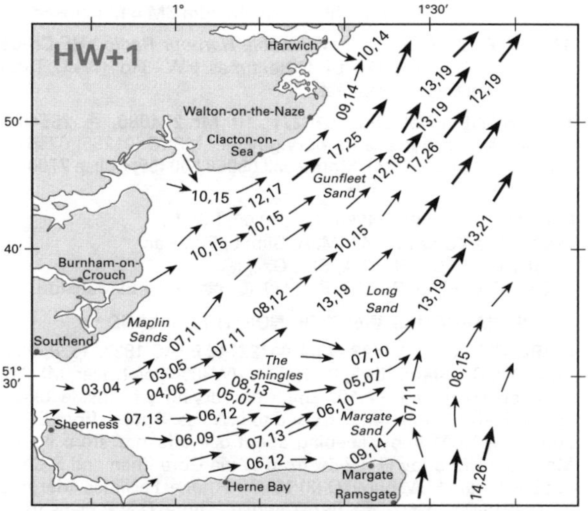

1 Hour after HW Sheerness (0225 after HW Dover)

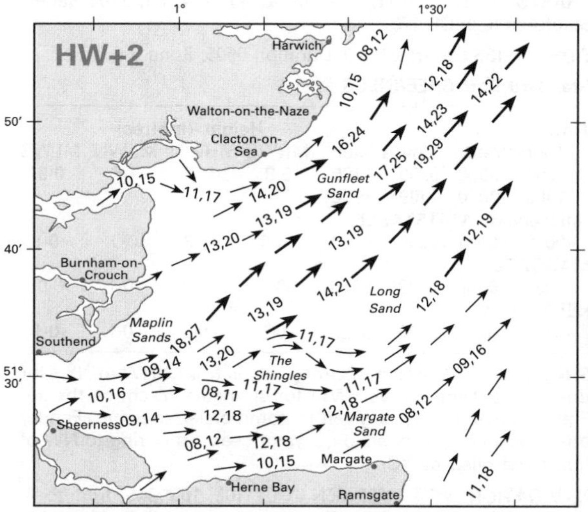

2 Hours after HW Sheerness (0325 after HW Dover)

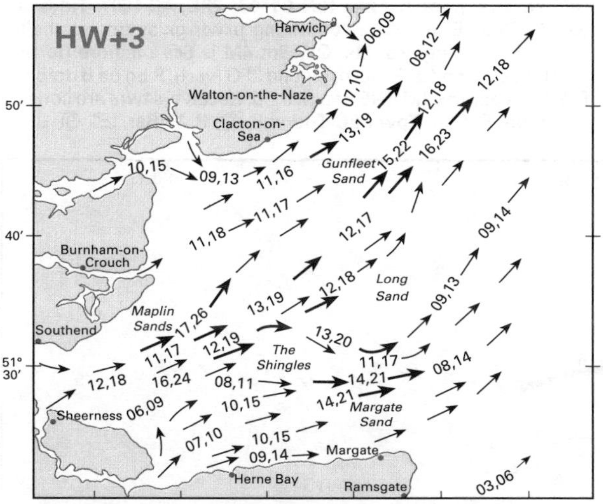

3 Hours after HW Sheerness (0425 after HW Dover)

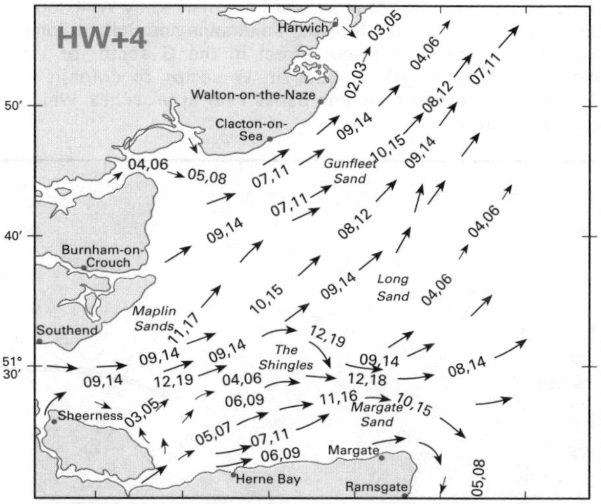

4 Hours after HW Sheerness (0525 after HW Dover)

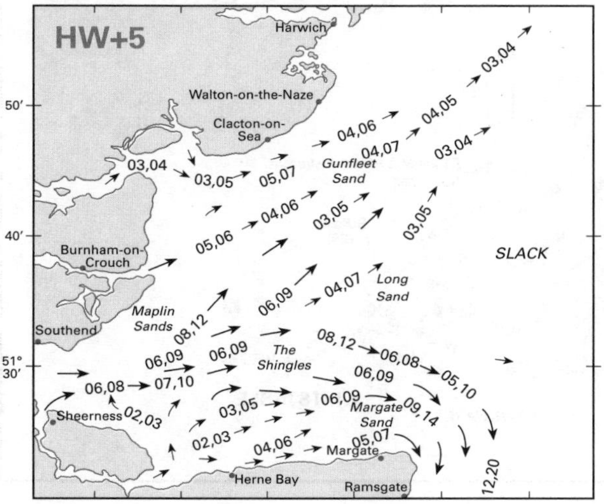

5 Hours after HW Sheerness (0600 before HW Dover)

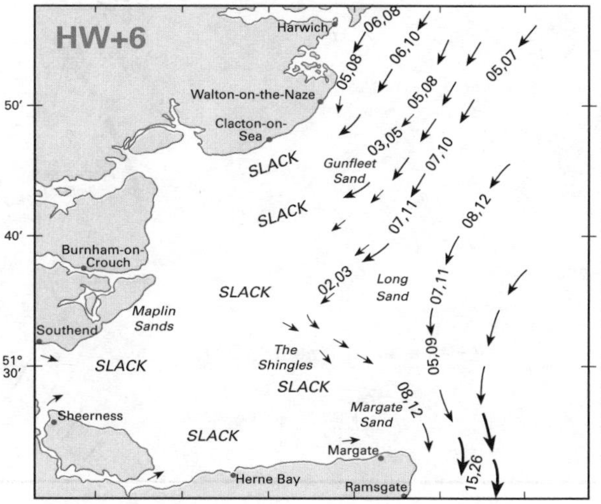

6 Hours after HW Sheerness (0500 before HW Dover)

WHITSTABLE 9.4.10

Kent **51°21'·86N 01°01'·46E** ❁❁◊◊✿✿

CHARTS AC *5606*, 2571, 1607; Imray Y7, Y14, C1, 2100 Series; Stanfords 5, 8; OS 179

TIDES +0135 Dover; ML 3·0; Duration 0605; Zone 0 (UT)

Standard Port SHEERNESS (⟶)

Times				Height (metres)			
High Water		Low Water		MHWS	MHWN	MLWN	MLWS
0200	0800	0200	0700	5·8	4·7	1·5	0·6
1400	2000	1400	1900				
Differences WHITSTABLE							
–0008	–0011	+0005	0000	–0·3	–0·3	0·0	–0·1
MARGATE							
–0050	–0040	–0020	–0050	–0·9	–0·9	–0·1	0·0
HERNE BAY							
–0025	–0015	0000	–0025	–0·5	–0·5	–0·1	–0·1

SHELTER Good, except in strong winds from NNW to NE. Hbr dries up to 0·4m; access HW±1 for strangers. Yacht berths are limited since priority is given to commercial shipping. Fender board needed against piled quays or seek a mooring to NW of hbr, (controlled by YC).

NAVIGATION WPT 51°22'·65N 01°01'·10E, 165°/345° from/to W Quay dolphin, 0·83M. From E keep well seaward of Whitstable Street, a hard drying sandspit, which extends 1M N from the coast; shoals a further 1M to seaward are marked by Whitstable Street NCM lt buoy. From W avoid Columbine and Pollard Spits. Appr (not before half flood) direct in the G sector or via Whitstable Oyster PHM lt buoy in W sector of dolphin lt. Beware many oyster beds and banks near approaches, which are very shallow.

LIGHTS AND MARKS Off head of W Quay on a dolphin, ☆ Fl WRG 5s 2m 5/3M, covers the approaches, vis W118°-156°, G156°-178°, R178°-201°. At the head of the hbr a Dir lt, Oc WRG 5s, leads 122½° into hbr ent, vis G110°-121°, W121°-124°(3°), R124°-134°. Tfc sigs at NE arm: FW 15m 8M = hbr open; FR 10m 5M = hbr closed.

RADIO TELEPHONE Call *Whitstable Harbour Radio* VHF Ch **09** 12 16 (Mon-Fri: 0830-1700LT. Other times: HW –3 to HW+1). Tidal info is available on request.

TELEPHONE (Dial code 01227) Hr Mr 274086, 📠 265441, whitstable.harbour@canterbury.gov.uk, MRSC (01255) 675518; ⊖ (01304) 224251 (H24); Marinecall 09068 500455; Police 770055; Dr 59440.

FACILITIES Hbr ☎ 274086, AB £10.00, FW, D.
Whitstable YC ☎ 272942, M, R, Slip, L, FW, Bar.
Services: ME, C, CH, ACA, SM, Gas, Ⓔ.
Town EC Wed; ⊡, P, V, R, Bar, ⊠, Ⓑ, ⇌, ✈ Lydd/Manston.

MINOR HARBOURS WEST OF NORTH FORELAND

MARGATE, Kent, **51°23'·43N 01°22'·65E**. AC 1827, 1828, 323; Imray Y7, C1; Stanfords 5, 8; OS 179. HW+0045 on Dover; ML 2·6; Duration 0610; see 9.4.10. Small hbr drying 3m, inside bkwtr (Stone Pier) FR 18m 4M; exposed to NW'lies. Appr's: from E, via Longnose NCM buoy, keeping about 5ca offshore; from N, via Margate PHM buoy Fl R 2·5s; from W via Gore Chan and S Chan to SE Margate ECM buoy, Q (3) 10s. VHF none. Facilities: Margate YC ☎ (01843) 292602, Ⓒ, Bar. Town EC Thurs; D & P (cans from garage), R, V, Bar, ⊠, Ⓑ, ⇌, ✈ Manston.

HERNE BAY, Kent, **51°22'·40N 01°07'·22E**. AC 1607. Tides see 9.4.10. Close E of pier, a 400m long bkwtr gives drying shelter for dayboats/dinghies. Lts: QW 8m 4M is 6ca offshore (former pier hd); bkwtr hd 2FR (vert); pier hd 2FG (vert); R bn on B dolphin, Fl Y 5s, is approx 1M ENE of bkwtr hd. Reculvers twrs are conspic 3M to the E. Slip. **Town** EC Thurs; P, Ⓔ, R, V, Bar, ⊠, Ⓑ, ⊡.

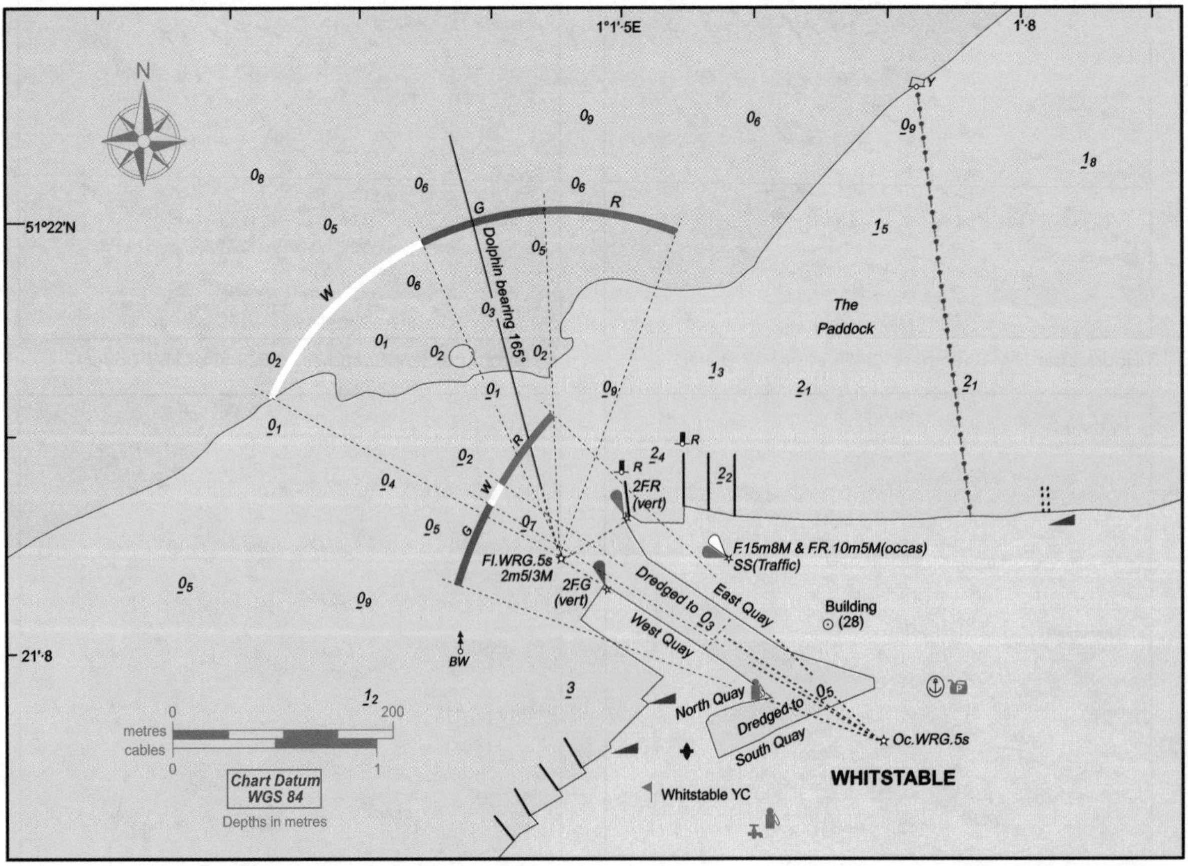

THE SWALE *9.4.11*

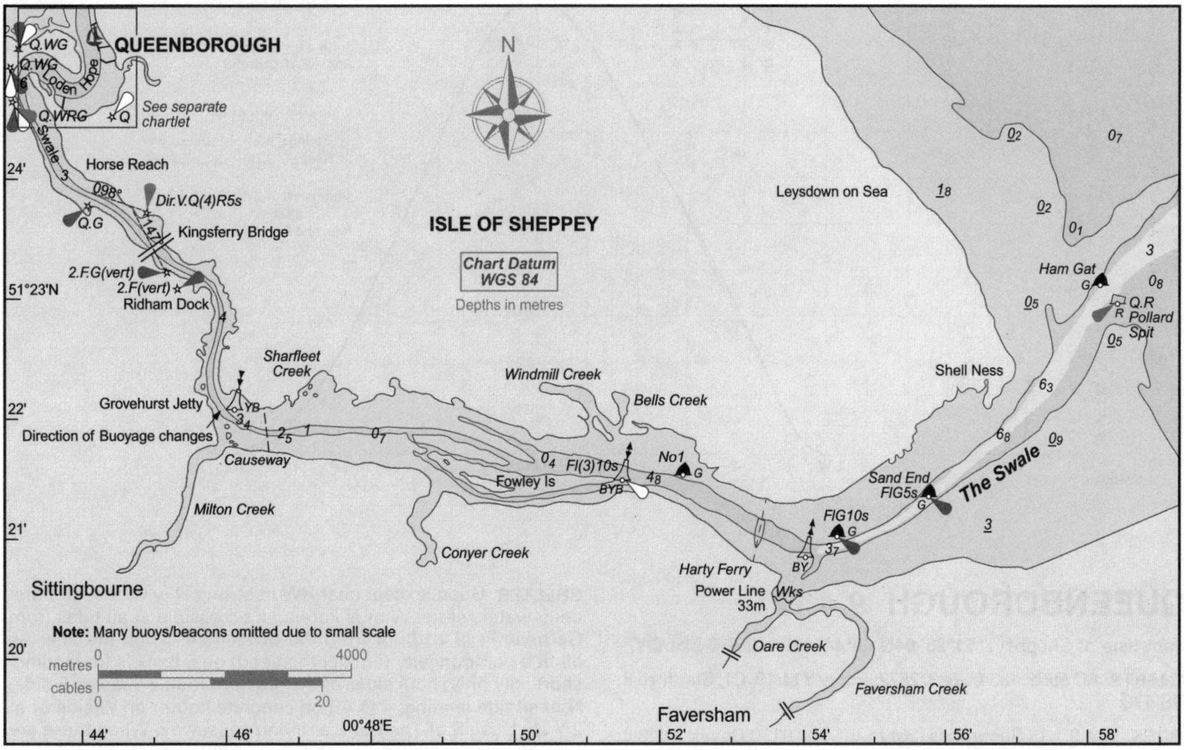

Kent

CHARTS AC *5606*, 2571, *2482*, 2572, *1834*, 3683; Imray Y18, Y14, C1 2100 Series; Stanfords 5, 8; OS 178

TIDES Queenborough +0130 Dover; Harty Ferry +0120 Dover; ML (Harty Ferry) 3·0; Duration 0610; Zone 0 (UT). Faversham HW differences are –0·2m on Sheerness; no other data.

Standard Port SHEERNESS (⟶)

Times				**Height (metres)**			
High Water		Low Water		MHWS	MHWN	MLWN	MLWS
0200	0800	0200	0700	5·8	4·7	1·5	0·6
1400	2000	1400	1900				
Differences R. SWALE (Grovehurst Jetty)							
–0007	0000	0000	+0016	0·0	0·0	0·0	–0·1

Grovehurst Jetty is close N of the ent to Milton Creek.

SHELTER Excellent in the Swale, the 14M chan between the Isle of Sheppey and the N Kent coast, from Shell Ness in the E to Queenborough in the W. Yachts can enter the drying creeks of Faversham, Oare, Conyer, and Milton. Beware wrecks at ent to Faversham Creek. Many moorings line the chan from Faversham to Conyer Creeks. See 9.4.12 for Queenborough, all-tide access.

NAVIGATION E ent WPT: Columbine Spit SHM, 51°23´·86N 01°00´·03E, 050°/230° from/to ent to buoyed chan 1·3M. The first chan buoys are Pollard Spit PHM QR and Ham Gat SHM unlit; buoys are moved to suit the shifting chan. Speed limit 8kn.
Chan is well marked from Faversham to Milton Creek. The middle section from 1·5M E of Conyer Creek to 0·5M E of Milton Creek is narrowed by drying mudbanks and carries least depths of 0·4m. At Milton Creek direction of buoyage changes. There are numerous oyster beds in the area. Kingsferry Bridge (see opposite) normally opens H and H+30 for masted craft on request, but subject to railway trains; temp anchs off SW bank. The power lines crossing SE of the br have a clearance of 31m.
The **W ent** is marked by Queenborough Spit ECM buoy, Q (3) 10s, 1M S of Garrison Pt, at 51°25´·81N 00°43´·93E.

LIGHTS AND MARKS No fixed lts at E ent. In W Swale the following lights are intended for large coasters using the narrow chan:
1. Dir ent lt Q 16m 5M; vis 163°-168°.
2. Round Loden Hope bend: two Q WG and one Q WRG on bns; keep in G sectors. See 9.4.12 chartlet.
3. Horse Reach ldg lts 113°: front QG 7m 5M; rear Fl G 3s 10m 6M. Dir lt 098°, VQ (4) R 5s 6m 5M.
4. Kingsferry Bridge ldg lts 147°: front 2FG(vert) 9m 7M; rear 2 FW (vert) 11m 10M. Lts on bridge: two x 2 FG (vert) on SW buttresses; two x 2 FR (vert) on NE.

Kingsferry Bridge traffic sigs:
No lts = Bridge down (3·35m MHWS).
Al Q ●/● = Centre span lifting.
F ● = Bridge open (29m MHWS).
Q ● = Centre span lowering. Keep clear.
Q ● = Bridge out of action.

Best to request bridge opening on VHF Ch 10; normally opens H and H+30.

RADIO TELEPHONE Call: *Medway Radio* VHF Ch **74** 16 22 (H24); Kingsferry Bridge Ch 10 (H24).

TELEPHONE (Dial code 01795) Hr Mr (Medway Ports Ltd) 561234; MRSC (01255) 675518; ⊖ (01474) 537115 (H24); Marinecall 09068 500455; Police 536639; Dr or Ⓗ via Medway Navigation Service 663025.

FACILITIES FAVERSHAM: **Services:** BY, AB £5, M, AC, FW, Ⓔ, ME, El, Sh, C (40 ton), SM, D, C (25 ton).
Town EC Thurs; V, R, Bar, Gas, ✉, Ⓑ, ⇌, ✈ Gatwick.
OARE CREEK: **Services:** AB £5, M, C (8 ton), ME, El, Sh, CH; **Hollow Shore Cruising Club** ☎ 533254, Bar.
CONYER CREEK: **Swale Marina** ☎ 521562, 📠 520788, £5, BH (15 ton), ME, Sh, C (3 ton), Slip, ♿, ▣; **Conyer CC**. **Conyer Marina** ☎ 521711 AB £5, CH, SM, Rigging, BY, ME, Sh, El, Ⓔ, Slip, D.
MILTON CREEK (Sittingbourne): **Crown Quay** M, FW.
Town EC Wed; V, R, Bar, ✉, Ⓑ, ⇌, ✈ (Gatwick); also the Dolphin Yard Sailing Barge Museum.
QUEENBOROUGH: See 9.4.12.

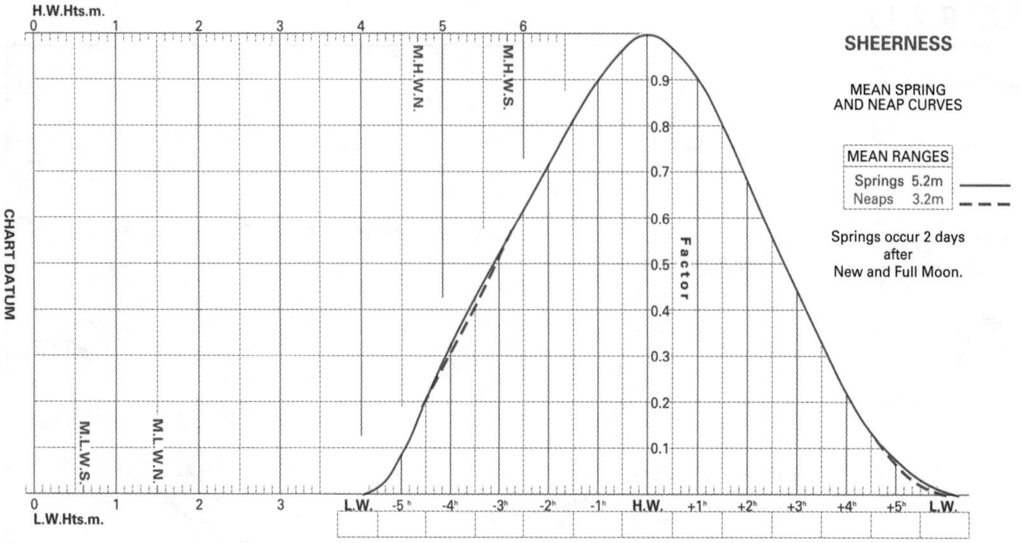

QUEENBOROUGH *9.4.12*

Kent (Isle of Sheppey) **51°25'·04N 00°44'·19E** ❁❁❁◊◊◊✿✿

CHARTS AC *5606, 1834,* 3683, 2572; Imray Y14/18, C1; Stanford 8; OS 178

TIDES Use 9.4.13 Sheerness, 2M to the N. +0130 Dover; ML 3·0; Duration 0610; Zone 0 (UT).

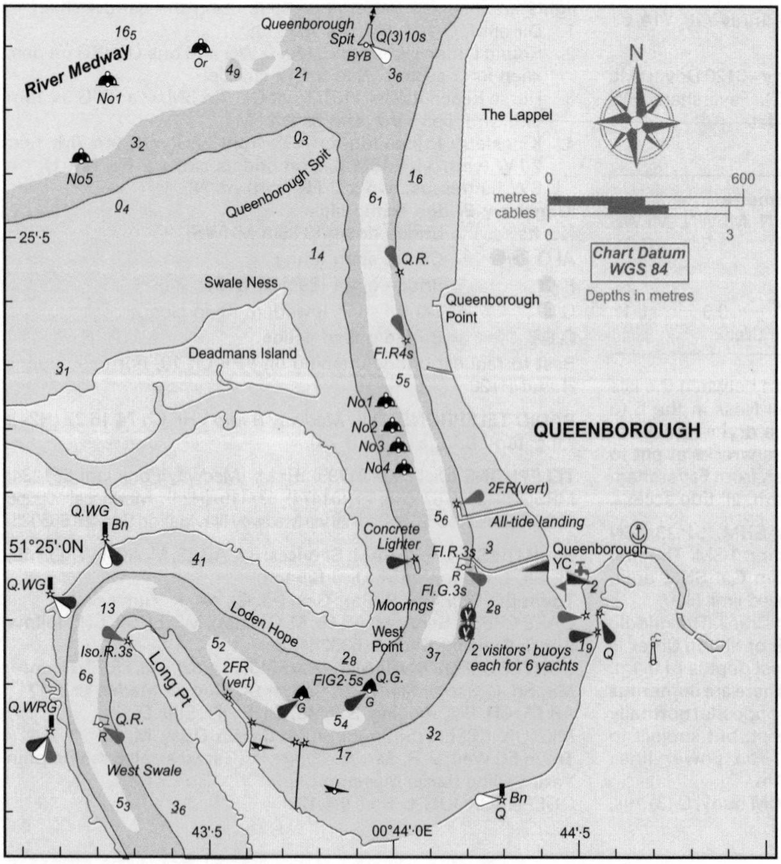

SHELTER Good, except near HW in strong N'ly winds. The first deep-water refuge W of N Foreland, accessible at all tides from Garrison Pt (9.4.13); or from the Swale (9.4.11) on the tide. An all-tide pontoon/jetty (5m depth at end) on E bank is for landing/short stay only; both sides of the jetty are foul. 2 Y 🅥s on E side, N of all-tide landing; 4 🅥 AB on concrete lighter on W side or at 2 Y 🅥s close S of The Hard, a drying causeway. When these are full the hbr controller will offer spare buoys. Smaller R buoys (numbered) are for locals. ⚓ is discouraged due to commercial traffic. Speed limit 8kn.

NAVIGATION WPT: see 9.4.13 for appr via Garrison Pt. Enter the river at Queenborough Spit ECM buoy, Q (3) 10s, 51°25'·75N 00°43'·93E. The chan narrows between drying banks and moorings. See 9.4.11 if approaching from the Swale.

LIGHTS AND MARKS Lights as chartlet. Note: Q 16m 5M lt, vis 163°-168°, on river bend covers the appr chan. All-tide landing 2 FR (vert). Concrete lighter Fl G 3s.

RADIO TELEPHONE Monitor *Medway Radio* VHF Ch **74** for tfc info. Call Ch 08 *Sheppey One* (Q'boro Hr Mr) for berths, also water taxi at weekends only.

TELEPHONE (Dial code 01795) Hr Mr 662051; MRSC (01255) 675518; ⊖ (01474) 537115 (H24); Marinecall 09068 500455; Police 580055; Dr 583828; ⊞ (01634) 830000 (Gillingham).

FACILITIES Hbr Controller (AB/🅥 £5.00 <11m, >11m AB on lighter £5) ☎/📠 662051, AC, FW on all-tide Landing jetty.
Queenborough YC Wed, Fri, Sat evenings, Sat, Sun lunchtimes, ☎ 663955, M, R, Bar, ♿, 🚿, ⛴; **The Creek** ☎ 07974 349018, (HW±1½) Slip, Scrubbing berth (FW, AC, D (cans)).
Services: BY, ME, El, Sh, CH, C (10 ton), Gas;
Town EC Wed; P & D (cans), V, R, Bar, ✉, ⇌, ✈ (Gatwick).

RIVER MEDWAY *9.4.13* (SHEERNESS to ROCHESTER)

Kent **51°27'·03N 00°44'·50E** (Off Garrison Pt) ❁❁❁◊◊◊✿✿✿

CHARTS AC *5606*, 3683, *2482*, 1835, *1834*, *1185*; Imray C1, Y18; Stanfords 5, 8; OS 178

TIDES +0130 Dover; ML 3·1; Duration 0610; Zone 0 (UT)

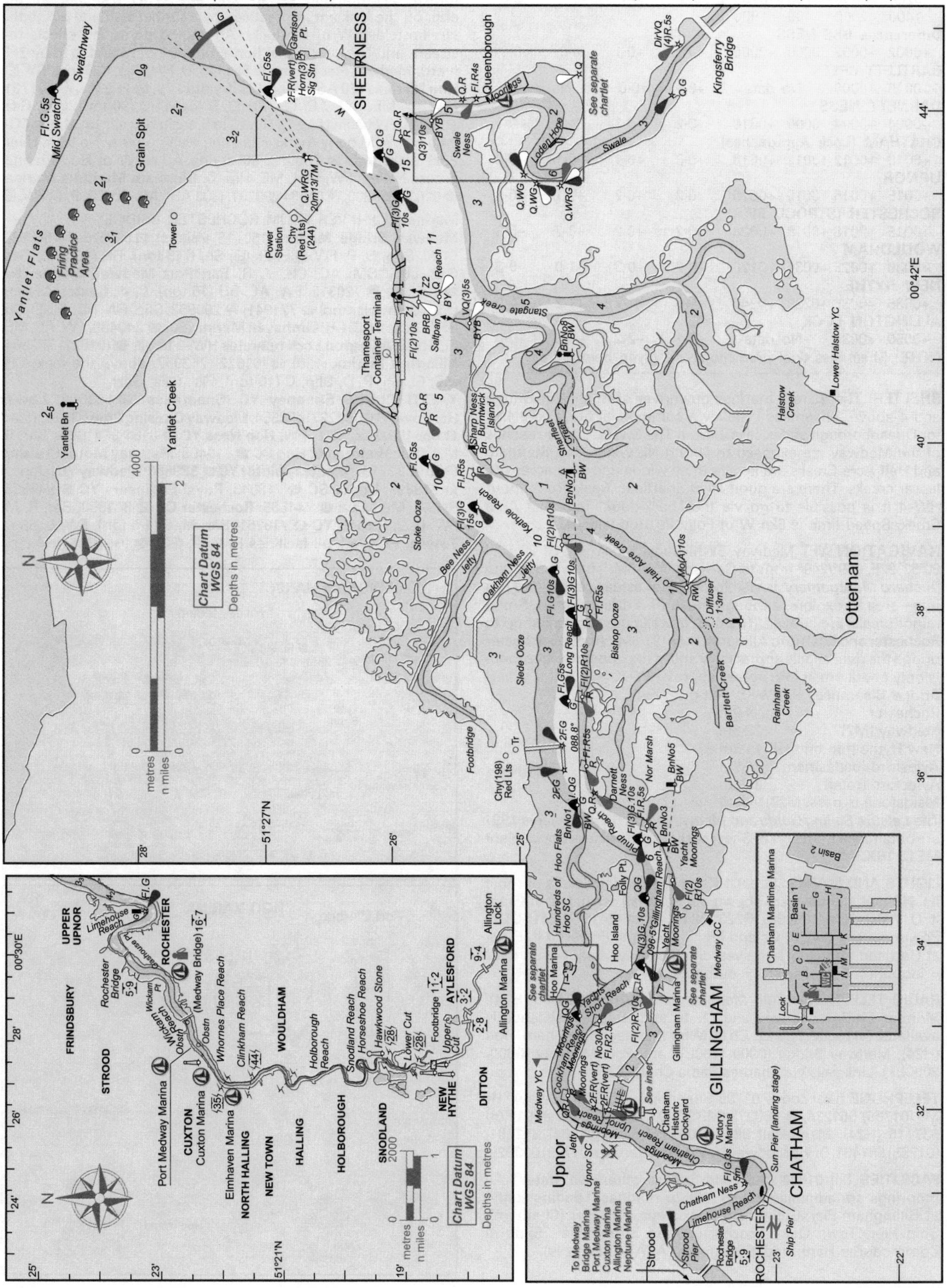

4

Standard Port SHEERNESS (⟶)

Times				Height (metres)			
High Water		Low Water		MHWS	MHWN	MLWN	MLWS
0200	0800	0200	0700	5·8	4·7	1·5	0·6
1400	2000	1400	1900				
Differences BEE NESS							
+0002	+0002	0000	+0005	+0·2	+0·1	0·0	0·0
BARTLETT CREEK							
+0016	+0008	No data		+0·1	0·0	No data	
DARNETT NESS							
+0004	+0004	0000	+0010	+0·2	+0·1	0·0	–0·1
CHATHAM (Lock Approaches)							
+0010	+0012	+0012	+0018	+0·3	+0·1	–0·1	–0·2
UPNOR							
+0015	+0015	+0015	+0025	+0·2	+0·2	–0·1	–0·1
ROCHESTER (STROOD PIER)							
+0018	+0018	+0018	+0028	+0·2	+0·2	–0·2	–0·3
WOULDHAM							
+0030	+0025	+0035	+0120	–0·2	–0·3	–1·0	–0·3
NEW HYTHE							
+0035	+0035	+0220	+0240	–1·6	–1·7	–1·2	–0·3
ALLINGTON LOCK							
+0050	+0035	No data		–2·1	–2·2	–1·3	–0·4

NOTE: Sheerness tidal predictions are given below.

SHELTER There are 3 marinas downriver of Rochester Bridge and 4 above. Sheerness is solely a commercial hbr. See 9.4.12 for Queenborough and access to/from The Swale. Lower reaches of the Medway are exposed to strong NE winds, but Stangate and Half Acre Creeks are secure in all winds and give access to lesser creeks. There are good ⚓s in Sharfleet Creek; from about HW–4 it is possible to go via the "back-door" into Half Acre Creek. Speed limit is 6kn W of Folly Pt (Hoo Island).

NAVIGATION WPT Medway SWM buoy, Mo(A) 6s, 51°28'·80N 00°52'·92E, 069°/249° from/to Garrison Pt, 5·5M. The wreck of the '*Richard Montgomery*' is visible 2M NE of estuary ent. There is a huge area to explore, although much of it dries to mud. Some minor creeks are buoyed. The river is well buoyed/marked up to Rochester and tidal up to Allington Lock (21·6M). Above Rochester bridge the river shoals appreciably and in the upper reaches there is only about 1m at LW; access approx HW±3.

Bridge Clearances (MHWS), going up-river:

Rochester	5·9m
Medway (M2)	29·6m
New Hythe (footbridge)	11·3m
Aylesford (pedestrian)	2·87m
Aylesford (road)	3·26m
Maidstone bypass (M20)	9·45m

The *Leisure Sailing Guide* and *Medway Ports River Byelaws 1991* are obtainable from Port of Sheerness Ltd, Sheerness Docks, Kent ME12 1RX.

LIGHTS AND MARKS See 9.4.4 and chartlet for details of most lts. NB: not all buoys are shown due to small scale. Isle of Grain lt Q WRG 20m 13/7/8M R220°-234°, G234°-241°, W241°-013°. Power stn chy (242m) Oc and FR lts. Tfc Sigs: Powerful lt, Fl 7s, at Garrison Pt means large vessel under way: if shown up river = inbound; if to seaward = outbound.

RADIO TELEPHONE Call: *Medway Radio* VHF Ch **74** 16 (H24). Monitor Ch 74 underway and Ch 16 at ⚓. Radar assistance is available on request Ch 22. Ch **80** M for marinas: Gillingham, Hoo (H24), Medway Bridge (0900-1700LT) and Port Medway (0800-2000LT). Link calls via Thames Radio Ch 02, 83.

TELEPHONE (Dial codes 01795 Sheerness; 01634 Medway) Hr Mr (01795) 561234, 📠 660072; MRSC (01255) 675518; ⊖ (01474) 537115 (H24); Marinecall 0891-500455; Police (01634) 811281, (01795) 661451; Dr via Medway Navigation Service (01795) 663025.

FACILITIES (all 01634 dial code, unless otherwise stated) All moorings are administered by YCs or marinas. Landing (only) at Gillingham Pier, Gillingham Dock steps, Sun Pier (Chatham), Ship Pier, Town Quay (Rochester) and Strood Pier. Slips at Commodores Hard, and Gillingham. ACA (Sheerness).

Marinas (FROM SEAWARD UP TO ROCHESTER BRIDGE) **Gillingham Marina** (250+12 Ⓥs) ☎ 280022, 📠 280164, pre-book. £1.60 locked basin (access via lock HW±4½), £1.10 tidal basin HW±2, P, D, AC foc, FW, ME, El, Ⓔ, Sh, Gas, Gaz, LPG, CH, BH (65 ton), ♆, C (1 ton), Slip, V, Bar. Note: effects of cross-tide, esp. the ebb, off the lock ent are reduced by a timber baffle at 90° to the stream (close W of the lock). An angled pontoon deflects the stream and is also the fuel berth; the outboard end is lit by 2FR (vert). **Medway Pier Marine** ☎ 851113, D, FW, Slip, C (6 ton), BY, Ⓔ; **Hoo Marina** (120 AB afloat; 125 drying) £10, ☎ 250311, 📠 251761, FW, Sh, ME, SM, AC, CH, El, Ⓔ, D (cans), C (20 ton), Gas, Gaz; access to W basin HW±1½; HW±3 to E basin (via sill 1m above CD); an unlit WCM buoy marks chan ent; waiting buoy No 53 in river. **Port Werburgh** ☎ 250593; 90 drying AB to W of Hoo marina; access HW±2; FW, fuel, ME, slip, C. **Chatham Maritime Marina.** ☎ 01634 899200, 📠 01634 899201, (300 AB), AC, C(15T), P, D, FW, Ⓑ.

Marinas (UP-RIVER FROM ROCHESTER BRIDGE) **Medway Bridge Marina** (160+15 visitors) ☎ 843576, 📠 843820, £1.20, Slip, D, P, FW, ME, El, Ⓔ, Sh, C (3 ton), BH (10 ton), Gas, Gaz, LPG, SM, AC, CH, V, R, Bar; **Port Medway Marina** (50) ☎ 720033, 📠 720315, FW, AC, BH (16 ton), C, ♆; **Cuxton Marina** (150+some visitors) ☎ 721941, 📠 290853, Slip, FW, ME, El, Ⓔ, Sh, BH (12 ton), AC, CH; **Elmhaven Marina** (60) ☎ 240489, FW, AC, ME, El, Sh, C; **Allington Lock** operates HW–3 to +2, ☎ (01622) 752864. **Allington Marina** (120) ☎ (01622) 752057, above the lock; CH, ME, El, Sh, P, D, Slip, C (10 ton), FW, Gas, Gaz;

YACHT CLUBS Sheppey YC (Sheerness) ☎ 663052; **Lower Halstow YC** ☎ (01227) 458554; **Medway Cruising Club** (Gillingham) ☎ 856489, Bar, M, L, FW; **Hoo Ness YC** ☎ 0181 304 1238, Bar, R, M, L, FW; **Hundred of Hoo SC** ☎ 710405; **Medway Motor Cruising Club** ☎ 827194; **Medway Motor YC** ☎ 389856; **Medway YC** (Upnor) ☎ 718399; **Upnor SC** ☎ 718043; **Royal Engineers YC** ☎ 844555; **RNSA** (Medway) ☎ 744565; **Rochester CC** ☎ 841350, Bar, R, M, FW, L, Ⓑ; **Strood YC** ☎ 718261, Bar, M, C (1·5 ton), FW, L, Slip.

Towns: EC Wed; all facilities R, V, Ⓑ, ⊠, ⇌, ✈ (Gatwick).

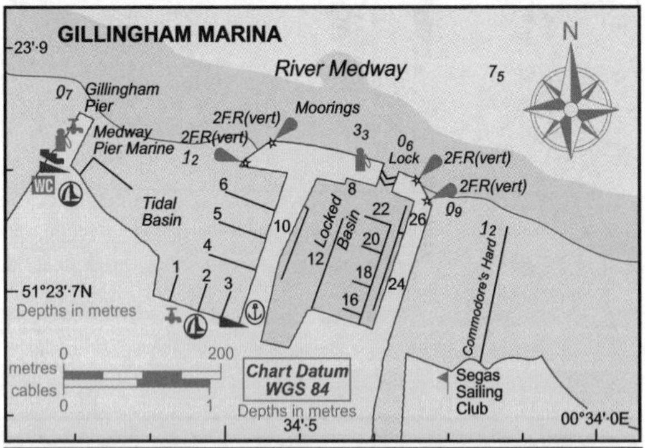

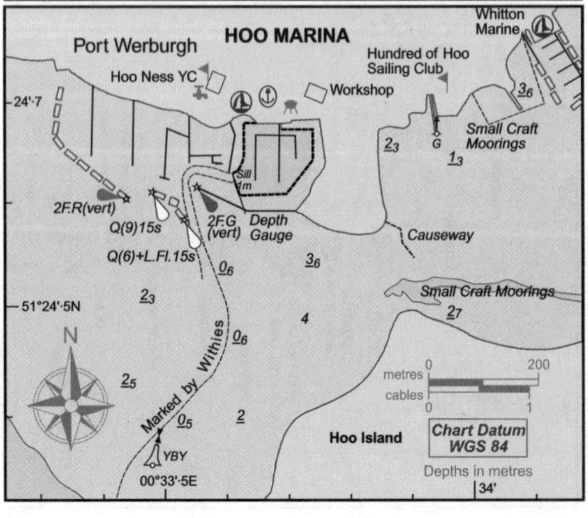

TIME ZONE (UTC)
For Summer Time add ONE hour in **non-shaded areas**

ENGLAND – SHEERNESS

LAT 51°27′N LONG 0°45′E

TIMES AND HEIGHTS OF HIGH AND LOW WATERS

SPRING & NEAP TIDES
Dates in red are **SPRINGS**
Dates in blue are **NEAPS**

YEAR **2002**

JANUARY

Date	Day	Time	m	Time	m	Time	m	Time	m
1	TU	0126	5.7	0739	0.6	1351	5.8	2000	0.7
2	W	0210	5.7	0827	0.5	1437	5.8	2045	0.7
3	TH	0254	5.7	0915	0.4	1525	5.7	2129	0.8
4	F	0341	5.6	1004	0.5	1614	5.6	2215	1.0
5	SA	0430	5.5	1055	0.5	1707	5.4	2305	1.1
6	SU	0524	5.3	1149	0.7	1805	5.2		
7	M	0001	1.3	0625	5.2	1250	0.8	1908	5.1
8	TU	0105	1.4	0733	5.1	1356	0.9	2016	5.0
9	W	0215	1.4	0843	5.1	1505	1.0	2123	5.1
10	TH	0327	1.3	0951	5.2	1610	1.0	2224	5.2
11	F	0434	1.2	1053	5.3	1705	0.9	2318	5.3
12	SA	0531	1.0	1146	5.4	1752	0.9		
13	SU	0005	5.4	0620	0.9	1233	5.5	● 1833	0.9
14	M	0047	5.5	0703	0.8	1315	5.5	1912	0.8
15	TU	0126	5.5	0742	0.7	1353	5.5	1948	0.9
16	W	0202	5.5	0817	0.7	1429	5.5	2021	0.9
17	TH	0236	5.5	0848	0.8	1502	5.4	2051	1.0
18	F	0309	5.4	0917	0.8	1535	5.2	2120	1.1
19	SA	0342	5.2	0947	0.8	1608	5.1	2150	1.2
20	SU	0416	5.1	1022	0.9	1644	5.0	2224	1.4
21	M	0454	4.9	1102	1.0	1726	4.8	2304	1.5
22	TU	0539	4.8	1150	1.2	1817	4.7	2356	1.7
23	W	0637	4.6	1253	1.3	1921	4.6		
24	TH	0107	1.7	0751	4.6	1415	1.4	2033	4.7
25	F	0237	1.7	0907	4.7	1532	1.2	2142	5.0
26	SA	0352	1.4	1014	5.0	1633	1.0	2244	5.2
27	SU	0454	1.1	1113	5.3	1728	0.9	2338	5.5
28	M	0550	0.8	1206	5.6	1818	0.7	○	
29	TU	0028	5.7	0643	0.6	1255	5.8	1906	0.6
30	W	0114	5.8	0735	0.4	1342	5.9	1952	0.6
31	TH	0159	5.9	0824	0.2	1428	6.0	2037	0.6

FEBRUARY

Date	Day	Time	m	Time	m	Time	m	Time	m
1	F	0243	5.9	0911	0.1	1513	5.9	2120	0.6
2	SA	0327	5.8	0955	0.1	1558	5.8	2200	0.8
3	SU	0411	5.7	1037	0.3	1644	5.6	2240	0.9
4	M	0459	5.5	1120	0.5	1734	5.3	2324	1.1
5	TU	0553	5.3	1210	0.8	1831	5.0		
6	W	0019	1.3	0657	5.0	1313	1.1	1936	4.8
7	TH	0132	1.4	0813	4.9	1428	1.2	2049	4.8
8	F	0259	1.4	0932	4.9	1544	1.2	2201	4.9
9	SA	0422	1.2	1042	5.1	1649	1.2	2302	5.1
10	SU	0526	1.0	1138	5.3	1740	1.1	2352	5.3
11	M	0614	0.9	1223	5.4	1822	1.0		
12	TU	0034	5.4	0653	0.8	1302	5.5	● 1858	0.9
13	W	0111	5.5	0728	0.7	1337	5.5	1932	0.8
14	TH	0145	5.6	0800	0.6	1408	5.5	2003	0.8
15	F	0216	5.6	0829	0.6	1438	5.5	2032	0.9
16	SA	0247	5.5	0858	0.6	1507	5.4	2058	0.9
17	SU	0316	5.4	0926	0.6	1537	5.3	2124	1.0
18	M	0346	5.3	0955	0.8	1609	5.2	2149	1.1
19	TU	0417	5.1	1025	0.9	1645	5.0	2218	1.3
20	W	0455	5.0	1100	1.1	1729	4.8	2300	1.4
21	TH	0544	4.7	1151	1.3	1827	4.7		
22	F	0003	1.6	0655	4.6	1314	1.5	1944	4.6
23	SA	0139	1.6	0824	4.6	1455	1.4	2106	4.8
24	SU	0319	1.4	0947	4.9	1609	1.2	2219	5.1
25	M	0433	1.0	1055	5.3	1710	0.9	2319	5.4
26	TU	0537	0.7	1151	5.6	1805	0.7		
27	W	0011	5.7	0634	0.4	1241	5.9	○ 1854	0.6
28	TH	0058	5.9	0725	0.2	1327	6.0	1939	0.5

MARCH

Date	Day	Time	m	Time	m	Time	m	Time	m
1	F	0142	6.0	0812	0.0	1411	6.1	2022	0.4
2	SA	0224	6.1	0855	-0.1	1453	6.1	2102	0.5
3	SU	0306	6.0	0935	0.0	1534	5.9	2138	0.6
4	M	0348	5.9	1012	0.3	1616	5.6	2213	0.8
5	TU	0432	5.6	1048	0.6	1701	5.3	2250	1.0
6	W	0523	5.3	1130	0.9	1752	5.0	2338	1.2
7	TH	0625	4.9	1229	1.3	1856	4.7		
8	F	0052	1.4	0745	4.7	1354	1.5	2015	4.6
9	SA	0237	1.5	0914	4.7	1522	1.5	2137	4.7
10	SU	0410	1.3	1027	5.0	1633	1.3	2243	5.0
11	M	0513	1.0	1122	5.3	1725	1.1	2333	5.2
12	TU	0558	0.8	1205	5.5	1805	1.0		
13	W	0013	5.4	0633	0.7	1241	5.5	1839	0.9
14	TH	0049	5.5	0704	0.6	1313	5.6	● 1910	0.8
15	F	0121	5.6	0734	0.5	1342	5.6	1940	0.8
16	SA	0152	5.6	0804	0.5	1410	5.6	2008	0.8
17	SU	0221	5.6	0833	0.5	1438	5.6	2035	0.8
18	M	0250	5.5	0902	0.6	1507	5.5	2100	0.9
19	TU	0319	5.4	0929	0.7	1538	5.4	2122	1.0
20	W	0349	5.2	0954	0.9	1612	5.2	2148	1.1
21	TH	0426	5.1	1023	1.1	1654	5.0	2228	1.2
22	F	0514	4.9	1111	1.3	1750	4.7	2330	1.4
23	SA	0622	4.6	1233	1.6	1907	4.6		
24	SU	0105	1.5	0754	4.6	1425	1.5	2036	4.7
25	M	0254	1.3	0925	4.9	1545	1.2	2155	5.0
26	TU	0414	0.9	1036	5.4	1650	0.9	2257	5.4
27	W	0521	0.5	1133	5.7	1746	0.7	2350	5.7
28	TH	0618	0.3	1221	6.0	1835	0.5	○	
29	F	0036	5.9	0706	0.1	1306	6.1	1919	0.4
30	SA	0119	6.1	0750	-0.1	1348	6.1	2000	0.4
31	SU	0201	6.1	0831	0.0	1428	6.1	2039	0.4

APRIL

Date	Day	Time	m	Time	m	Time	m	Time	m
1	M	0242	6.1	0909	0.1	1508	5.9	2115	0.5
2	TU	0324	5.9	0943	0.4	1548	5.6	2148	0.7
3	W	0408	5.6	1017	0.7	1629	5.3	2223	0.9
4	TH	0457	5.3	1057	1.1	1717	5.0	2308	1.2
5	F	0558	4.9	1152	1.5	1819	4.6		
6	SA	0019	1.4	0717	4.6	1319	1.7	1939	4.5
7	SU	0212	1.5	0846	4.7	1453	1.7	2105	4.6
8	M	0341	1.2	1001	4.9	1605	1.4	2213	4.9
9	TU	0442	1.0	1054	5.2	1657	1.2	2303	5.2
10	W	0526	0.8	1136	5.4	1737	1.0	2344	5.4
11	TH	0601	0.7	1211	5.5	1811	0.9		
12	F	0020	5.5	0632	0.6	1242	5.6	● 1842	0.8
13	SA	0052	5.6	0703	0.6	1311	5.6	1912	0.8
14	SU	0124	5.6	0734	0.5	1340	5.7	1942	0.7
15	M	0154	5.6	0806	0.5	1410	5.7	2012	0.8
16	TU	0225	5.5	0837	0.6	1440	5.6	2039	0.8
17	W	0255	5.4	0905	0.8	1513	5.4	2105	0.9
18	TH	0329	5.3	0933	1.0	1548	5.3	2136	1.0
19	F	0409	5.1	1006	1.2	1632	5.0	2219	1.1
20	SA	0500	4.9	1057	1.4	1728	4.8	2323	1.2
21	SU	0609	4.8	1219	1.6	1845	4.6		
22	M	0056	1.3	0736	4.8	1400	1.5	2012	4.8
23	TU	0234	1.0	0902	5.0	1518	1.2	2129	5.1
24	W	0352	0.7	1012	5.4	1623	1.0	2232	5.4
25	TH	0458	0.4	1109	5.7	1720	0.8	2324	5.7
26	F	0554	0.2	1158	5.9	1809	0.6		
27	SA	0011	5.9	0641	0.1	1242	6.0	○ 1854	0.5
28	SU	0056	6.0	0724	0.1	1323	6.0	1936	0.4
29	M	0138	6.1	0804	0.1	1403	6.0	2016	0.4
30	TU	0221	6.0	0842	0.3	1443	5.8	2054	0.5

Chart Datum: 2·90 metres below Ordnance Datum (Newlyn)

Register for your FREE weekly weather email service from Macmillan Reeds
at www.nauticaldata.com – NOW!
weekend weather reports sent to your email address, every Thursday

TIME ZONE (UTC)
For Summer Time add ONE hour in **non-shaded areas**

ENGLAND – SHEERNESS

LAT 51°27'N LONG 0°45'E

TIMES AND HEIGHTS OF HIGH AND LOW WATERS

SPRING & NEAP TIDES
Dates in red are SPRINGS
Dates in blue are NEAPS

YEAR **2002**

MAY

Day	Time	m	Day	Time	m
1	0304 0917 W 1522 2130	5.8 0.6 5.6 0.7	16	0239 0848 TH 1455 2059	5.5 0.8 5.5 0.8
2	0349 0952 TH 1603 2204	5.5 0.9 5.3 0.9	17	0318 0922 F 1535 2137	5.4 1.0 5.3 0.9
3	0437 1030 F 1649 2246	5.2 1.3 5.0 1.1	18	0403 1003 SA 1621 2226	5.2 1.2 5.1 0.9
4	0534 1121 SA 1746 2350	4.8 1.6 4.7 1.3	19	0457 1058 SU 1719 2330	5.1 1.3 4.9 1.0
5	0643 1238 SU 1900	4.6 1.8 4.5	20	0604 1211 M 1831	4.9 1.4 4.8
6	0129 0802 M 1408 2020	1.4 4.6 1.8 4.5	21	0052 0721 TU 1334 1949	1.0 5.0 1.4 4.9
7	0252 0916 TU 1519 2130	1.2 4.8 1.6 4.8	22	0214 0837 W 1446 2101	0.8 5.2 1.2 5.2
8	0352 1013 W 1614 2223	1.0 5.0 1.4 5.1	23	0325 0944 TH 1550 2204	0.6 5.4 1.0 5.4
9	0440 1056 TH 1658 2307	0.9 5.2 1.2 5.3	24	0430 1042 F 1649 2258	0.5 5.6 0.9 5.6
10	0520 1133 F 1735 2345	0.8 5.4 1.0 5.4	25	0526 1132 SA 1741 2348	0.4 5.8 0.7 5.8
11	0556 1206 SA 1810	0.7 5.5 0.9	26	0614 1217 SU 1830 ○	0.3 5.8 0.6
12	0020 0630 SU 1238 ● 1843	5.5 0.6 5.6 0.8	27	0034 0657 M 1301 1914	5.9 0.3 5.8 0.5
13	0055 0705 M 1311 1917	5.6 0.6 5.7 0.8	28	0120 0738 TU 1342 1958	5.9 0.4 5.8 0.5
14	0129 0740 TU 1345 1951	5.6 0.6 5.7 0.8	29	0205 0818 W 1422 2039	5.8 0.6 5.7 0.6
15	0203 0814 W 1419 2025	5.5 0.7 5.6 0.8	30	0249 0855 TH 1502 2117	5.7 0.8 5.5 0.7
			31	0333 0931 F 1543 2153	5.4 1.1 5.3 0.9

JUNE

Day	Time	m	Day	Time	m
1	0418 1007 SA 1626 2231	5.2 1.3 5.0 1.0	16	0400 1004 SU 1617 2236	5.4 1.0 5.3 0.7
2	0507 1050 SU 1716 2321	4.9 1.5 4.8 1.2	17	0454 1055 M 1711 2334	5.3 1.2 5.2 0.7
3	0602 1148 M 1816	4.7 1.7 4.6	18	0553 1156 TU 1814	5.2 1.3 5.1
4	0030 0704 TU 1304 1924	1.3 4.6 1.8 4.6	19	0039 0659 W 1303 1922	0.7 5.1 1.3 5.1
5	0147 0811 W 1418 2032	1.2 4.6 1.7 4.7	20	0148 0808 TH 1411 2031	0.7 5.2 1.2 5.2
6	0252 0913 TH 1519 2132	1.1 4.8 1.5 4.9	21	0256 0914 F 1517 2136	0.7 5.3 1.1 5.3
7	0347 1004 F 1610 2223	1.0 5.0 1.3 5.1	22	0400 1015 SA 1620 2236	0.6 5.4 1.0 5.4
8	0435 1048 SA 1654 2307	0.9 5.2 1.2 5.3	23	0459 1109 SU 1719 2331	0.6 5.5 0.9 5.6
9	0518 1129 SU 1735 2349	0.8 5.4 1.0 5.4	24	0550 1158 M 1812 ○	0.6 5.6 0.7
10	0559 1208 M 1815 ●	0.7 5.6 0.9	25	0022 0635 TU 1244 1900	5.6 0.6 5.6 0.6
11	0029 0639 TU 1247 1854	5.5 0.7 5.6 0.8	26	0109 0718 W 1326 1946	5.7 0.7 5.6 0.6
12	0109 0718 W 1326 1935	5.5 0.7 5.6 0.7	27	0154 0759 TH 1407 2028	5.6 0.8 5.6 0.6
13	0148 0757 TH 1405 2016	5.5 0.7 5.6 0.7	28	0237 0837 F 1447 2107	5.6 0.9 5.5 0.7
14	0229 0837 F 1445 2059	5.5 0.8 5.5 0.6	29	0317 0912 SA 1525 2141	5.4 1.1 5.3 0.8
15	0313 0919 SA 1529 2145	5.5 0.9 5.4 0.6	30	0357 0945 SU 1603 2213	5.2 1.3 5.1 0.9

JULY

Day	Time	m	Day	Time	m
1	0436 1019 M 1643 2250	5.0 1.4 5.0 1.0	16	0441 1042 TU 1656 2322	5.5 1.0 5.4 0.5
2	0518 1100 TU 1729 2336	4.9 1.5 4.8 1.1	17	0534 1131 W 1750	5.4 1.1 5.3
3	0606 1151 W 1823	4.7 1.7 4.7	18	0015 0631 TH 1227 1852	0.6 5.2 1.2 5.2
4	0035 0700 TH 1255 1925	1.2 4.6 1.8 4.6	19	0116 0735 F 1333 2002	0.8 5.1 1.3 5.1
5	0144 0802 F 1408 2032	1.2 4.7 1.7 4.7	20	0224 0843 SA 1446 2114	0.9 5.1 1.3 5.1
6	0252 0904 SA 1516 2134	1.2 4.8 1.6 4.8	21	0334 0950 SU 1600 2223	1.0 5.1 1.2 5.2
7	0352 1002 SU 1613 2230	1.1 5.1 1.4 5.1	22	0439 1052 M 1708 2324	0.9 5.3 1.0 5.4
8	0444 1054 M 1704 2321	1.0 5.3 1.1 5.3	23	0534 1145 TU 1805	0.9 5.4 0.9
9	0532 1142 TU 1752	0.9 5.5 1.0	24	0016 0621 W 1232 ○ 1854	5.5 0.9 5.5 0.7
10	0008 0617 W 1228 ● 1838	5.4 0.8 5.6 0.8	25	0102 0703 TH 1314 1937	5.6 0.9 5.6 0.7
11	0053 0701 TH 1312 1925	5.5 0.8 5.7 0.6	26	0143 0743 F 1353 2016	5.6 0.9 5.6 0.6
12	0137 0745 F 1355 2013	5.7 0.7 5.7 0.5	27	0221 0819 SA 1429 2050	5.5 0.9 5.5 0.7
13	0221 0830 SA 1437 2100	5.7 0.7 5.7 0.4	28	0256 0852 SU 1503 2120	5.5 1.0 5.4 0.7
14	0306 0914 SU 1521 2148	5.7 0.8 5.6 0.3	29	0329 0920 M 1536 2148	5.3 1.1 5.3 0.8
15	0353 0958 M 1607 2234	5.7 0.9 5.5 0.4	30	0402 0948 TU 1610 2218	5.2 1.3 5.2 0.9
			31	0436 1018 W 1645 2254	5.1 1.4 5.0 1.0

AUGUST

Day	Time	m	Day	Time	m
1	0514 1055 TH 1727 2337	4.9 1.5 4.8 1.2	16	0559 1149 F 1823	5.2 1.2 5.2
2	0600 1142 F 1819	4.8 1.7 4.7	17	0039 0701 SA 1257 1936	1.0 5.0 1.4 5.0
3	0034 0657 SA 1246 1927	1.3 4.7 1.8 4.5	18	0153 0813 SU 1424 2058	1.3 4.9 1.4 4.9
4	0152 0807 SU 1415 2044	1.4 4.7 1.7 4.6	19	0314 0929 M 1554 2215	1.3 4.9 1.3 5.1
5	0311 0919 M 1534 2156	1.4 4.9 1.5 4.9	20	0427 1038 TU 1707 2318	1.2 5.1 1.1 5.3
6	0415 1024 TU 1637 2257	1.2 5.1 1.2 5.2	21	0525 1133 W 1802	1.1 5.3 0.9
7	0510 1120 W 1733 2350	1.0 5.4 0.9 5.5	22	0008 0610 TH 1219 ○ 1844	5.5 1.0 5.5 0.7
8	0600 1210 TH 1826 ●	0.9 5.6 0.7	23	0050 0649 F 1258 1921	5.6 1.0 5.6 0.7
9	0038 0648 F 1257 1916	5.7 0.8 5.8 0.5	24	0126 0724 SA 1334 1953	5.6 0.9 5.6 0.6
10	0124 0734 SA 1340 2005	5.9 0.7 5.9 0.3	25	0159 0756 SU 1406 2024	5.6 0.9 5.6 0.6
11	0208 0818 SU 1423 2052	6.0 0.6 5.9 0.1	26	0229 0826 M 1437 2052	5.6 1.0 5.6 0.6
12	0252 0901 M 1505 2136	6.0 0.7 5.9 0.1	27	0258 0852 TU 1507 2119	5.5 1.0 5.5 0.7
13	0335 0941 TU 1548 2217	5.9 0.8 5.8 0.3	28	0327 0917 W 1536 2146	5.4 1.2 5.4 0.8
14	0420 1020 W 1632 2258	5.7 0.9 5.7 0.5	29	0357 0941 TH 1607 2216	5.3 1.3 5.2 1.0
15	0506 1100 TH 1722 2342	5.5 1.1 5.4 0.7	30	0431 1009 F 1642 2249	5.1 1.4 5.0 1.2
			31	0511 1047 SA 1726 2335	4.9 1.5 4.8 1.5

Chart Datum: 2·90 metres below Ordnance Datum (Newlyn)

Register for your FREE weekly weather email service from Macmillan Reeds
at www.nauticaldata.com – NOW!
weekend weather reports sent to your email address, every Thursday

TIME ZONE (UTC)
For Summer Time add ONE hour in **non-shaded areas**

ENGLAND – SHEERNESS

LAT 51°27′N LONG 0°45′E

TIMES AND HEIGHTS OF HIGH AND LOW WATERS

SPRING & NEAP TIDES
Dates in **red** are **SPRINGS**
Dates in **blue** are **NEAPS**

YEAR **2002**

SEPTEMBER

Date	Time	m
1 SU	0604	4.7
	1143	1.7
	1830	4.6
2 M	0049	1.7
	0715	4.6
	1313	1.8
	1957	4.5
3 TU	0232	1.6
	0839	4.7
	1458	1.6
	2124	4.8
4 W	0348	1.4
	0955	5.1
	1613	1.2
	2234	5.2
5 TH	0448	1.1
	1057	5.4
	1715	0.8
	2331	5.6
6 F	0542	0.9
	1149	5.7
	1811	0.5
7 SA	0020	5.9
	0631	0.7
	1236	5.9
●	1902	0.3
8 SU	0105	6.0
	0716	0.6
	1320	6.0
	1949	0.1
9 M	0148	6.1
	0759	0.6
	1401	6.1
	2032	0.1
10 TU	0230	6.1
	0840	0.6
	1442	6.1
	2113	0.1
11 W	0311	6.0
	0917	0.7
	1523	6.0
	2151	0.3
12 TH	0352	5.8
	0953	0.9
	1607	5.8
	2228	0.6
13 F	0436	5.5
	1030	1.0
	1656	5.5
	2308	1.0
14 SA	0526	5.1
	1116	1.3
	1756	5.1
15 SU	0003	1.3
	0627	4.8
	1225	1.5
	1913	4.8
16 M	0124	1.6
	0744	4.7
	1410	1.6
	2043	4.8
17 TU	0257	1.6
	0909	4.8
	1548	1.3
	2203	5.1
18 W	0413	1.5
	1020	5.1
	1657	1.0
	2303	5.4
19 TH	0510	1.3
	1114	5.3
	1745	0.9
	2349	5.6
20 F	0552	1.1
	1158	5.5
	1822	0.8
21 SA	0027	5.6
	0626	1.0
	1235	5.6
○	1853	0.7
22 SU	0100	5.7
	0657	1.0
	1308	5.7
	1922	0.7
23 M	0129	5.7
	0727	0.9
	1338	5.7
	1951	0.6
24 TU	0157	5.7
	0756	0.9
	1408	5.7
	2020	0.6
25 W	0224	5.6
	0822	1.0
	1436	5.6
	2048	0.7
26 TH	0253	5.6
	0847	1.1
	1505	5.5
	2115	0.9
27 F	0323	5.4
	0910	1.2
	1535	5.3
	2142	1.1
28 SA	0355	5.3
	0935	1.3
	1609	5.1
	2210	1.3
29 SU	0434	5.1
	1011	1.4
	1653	4.9
	2252	1.5
30 M	0525	4.8
	1107	1.6
	1755	4.7

OCTOBER

Date	Time	m
1 TU	0004	1.8
	0635	4.6
	1235	1.7
	1921	4.6
2 W	0154	1.8
	0805	4.7
	1427	1.5
	2055	4.8
3 TH	0319	1.5
	0927	5.0
	1547	1.1
	2209	5.3
4 F	0422	1.2
	1031	5.4
	1652	0.7
	2307	5.7
5 SA	0518	0.9
	1124	5.8
	1749	0.4
	2356	6.0
6 SU	0607	0.8
	1210	6.0
	1839	0.3
●		
7 M	0041	6.1
	0652	0.7
	1254	6.1
	1924	0.1
8 TU	0123	6.2
	0734	0.6
	1336	6.2
	2006	0.1
9 W	0204	6.1
	0814	0.6
	1417	6.2
	2046	0.3
10 TH	0244	6.0
	0852	0.7
	1500	6.0
	2122	0.5
11 F	0325	5.7
	0928	0.9
	1544	5.8
	2158	0.9
12 SA	0407	5.4
	1005	1.1
	1634	5.4
	2238	1.2
13 SU	0456	5.1
	1050	1.3
	1734	5.0
	2331	1.6
14 M	0556	4.8
	1159	1.5
	1851	4.8
15 TU	0053	1.9
	0714	4.6
	1351	1.6
	2018	4.8
16 W	0230	1.8
	0839	4.7
	1523	1.3
	2137	5.0
17 TH	0345	1.6
	0951	5.0
	1626	1.1
	2235	5.3
18 F	0440	1.4
	1045	5.3
	1712	0.9
	2320	5.5
19 SA	0521	1.2
	1128	5.5
	1747	0.8
	2356	5.6
20 SU	0555	1.1
	1204	5.6
	1818	0.8
21 M	0027	5.6
	0626	1.0
	1237	5.7
○	1847	0.7
22 TU	0056	5.7
	0655	0.9
	1308	5.7
	1917	0.7
23 W	0124	5.7
	0725	0.9
	1338	5.7
	1948	0.7
24 TH	0153	5.7
	0754	0.9
	1409	5.6
	2018	0.8
25 F	0223	5.6
	0822	1.0
	1439	5.5
	2048	0.9
26 SA	0255	5.5
	0849	1.1
	1512	5.3
	2116	1.1
27 SU	0329	5.3
	0918	1.2
	1549	5.2
	2146	1.3
28 M	0409	5.1
	0957	1.3
	1636	5.0
	2231	1.5
29 TU	0500	4.9
	1055	1.4
	1737	4.8
	2341	1.7
30 W	0609	4.7
	1218	1.5
	1859	4.7
31 TH	0119	1.8
	0735	4.8
	1359	1.3
	2025	5.0

NOVEMBER

Date	Time	m
1 F	0243	1.5
	0855	5.1
	1518	1.0
	2139	5.3
2 SA	0349	1.2
	1000	5.4
	1624	0.7
	2238	5.7
3 SU	0445	1.0
	1054	5.7
	1721	0.4
	2328	5.9
4 M	0537	0.8
	1142	6.0
	1811	0.3
●		
5 TU	0014	6.0
	0623	0.7
	1228	6.1
	1856	0.3
6 W	0057	6.0
	0708	0.6
	1312	6.1
	1938	0.3
7 TH	0139	6.0
	0750	0.6
	1356	6.1
	2018	0.5
8 F	0220	5.9
	0831	0.7
	1441	5.9
	2056	0.7
9 SA	0301	5.6
	0910	0.8
	1527	5.7
	2133	1.0
10 SU	0344	5.4
	0949	1.0
	1617	5.3
	2212	1.4
11 M	0431	5.1
	1033	1.2
	1714	5.0
	2301	1.7
12 TU	0528	4.8
	1135	1.4
	1821	4.7
13 W	0013	1.9
	0638	4.6
	1311	1.5
	1937	4.7
14 TH	0142	1.9
	0756	4.6
	1434	1.4
	2052	4.8
15 F	0256	1.8
	0908	4.8
	1535	1.2
	2153	5.0
16 SA	0354	1.5
	1005	5.1
	1624	1.0
	2240	5.2
17 SU	0439	1.3
	1050	5.3
	1703	0.9
	2317	5.4
18 M	0517	1.2
	1129	5.5
	1738	0.8
	2350	5.5
19 TU	0552	1.1
	1204	5.6
	1812	0.8
20 W	0022	5.6
	0624	1.0
	1239	5.6
○	1845	0.7
21 TH	0054	5.7
	0657	0.9
	1312	5.6
	1919	0.8
22 F	0127	5.7
	0730	0.9
	1346	5.6
	1953	0.8
23 SA	0201	5.6
	0804	0.9
	1421	5.5
	2027	0.9
24 SU	0235	5.5
	0838	1.0
	1458	5.4
	2100	1.1
25 M	0313	5.4
	0914	1.0
	1539	5.3
	2137	1.3
26 TU	0355	5.2
	0958	1.1
	1628	5.1
	2223	1.4
27 W	0447	5.0
	1055	1.2
	1727	5.0
	2327	1.6
28 TH	0551	4.9
	1208	1.2
	1838	4.9
29 F	0045	1.6
	0705	4.9
	1330	1.1
	1954	5.0
30 SA	0202	1.5
	0820	5.1
	1444	0.9
	2105	5.3

DECEMBER

Date	Time	m
1 SU	0309	1.3
	0926	5.3
	1550	0.7
	2206	5.5
2 M	0409	1.1
	1024	5.6
	1650	0.6
	2300	5.7
3 TU	0506	0.9
	1117	5.8
	1743	0.5
	2349	5.8
4 W	0558	0.8
	1206	5.9
	1830	0.5
●		
5 TH	0034	5.8
	0646	0.7
	1255	5.9
	1914	0.5
6 F	0118	5.8
	0733	0.6
	1341	5.9
	1956	0.6
7 SA	0201	5.7
	0818	0.7
	1428	5.8
	2036	0.8
8 SU	0244	5.6
	0901	0.8
	1514	5.6
	2114	1.1
9 M	0326	5.4
	0940	0.9
	1601	5.3
	2151	1.4
10 TU	0410	5.1
	1020	1.1
	1650	5.0
	2232	1.6
11 W	0459	4.9
	1107	1.2
	1742	4.8
	2323	1.8
12 TH	0555	4.7
	1209	1.3
	1841	4.6
13 F	0031	1.9
	0659	4.6
	1322	1.4
	1946	4.6
14 SA	0147	1.9
	0808	4.7
	1430	1.3
	2050	4.7
15 SU	0253	1.7
	0911	4.8
	1527	1.2
	2145	4.9
16 M	0349	1.6
	1005	5.0
	1617	1.1
	2231	5.1
17 TU	0436	1.4
	1052	5.2
	1701	0.9
	2312	5.3
18 W	0518	1.2
	1134	5.4
	1741	0.9
	2352	5.5
19 TH	0557	1.1
	1214	5.4
	1820	0.8
○		
20 F	0030	5.6
	0635	0.9
	1253	5.5
	1857	0.8
21 SA	0108	5.6
	0713	0.8
	1331	5.5
	1935	0.8
22 SU	0146	5.6
	0753	0.8
	1410	5.5
	2013	0.9
23 M	0225	5.5
	0835	0.7
	1450	5.5
	2052	0.9
24 TU	0305	5.4
	0918	0.7
	1534	5.4
	2132	1.1
25 W	0348	5.3
	1004	0.8
	1621	5.3
	2217	1.2
26 TH	0436	5.2
	1054	0.8
	1714	5.2
	2308	1.3
27 F	0531	5.1
	1151	0.9
	1814	5.1
28 SA	0008	1.4
	0633	5.0
	1257	0.9
	1921	5.0
29 SU	0117	1.4
	0743	5.1
	1407	0.9
	2030	5.1
30 M	0227	1.4
	0853	5.2
	1517	0.8
	2135	5.2
31 TU	0336	1.2
	0959	5.3
	1622	0.8
	2236	5.3

Chart Datum: 2·90 metres below Ordnance Datum (Newlyn)

Register for your **FREE** weekly weather email service from Macmillan Reeds
at www.nauticaldata.com – NOW!
weekend weather reports sent to your email address, every Thursday

RIVER THAMES *9.4.14*

London: from Canvey Island to Teddington lock

SEQUENCE Information is arranged as far as possible from seaward, starting abeam Canvey Island and continuing up-river to the head of the tidal Thames at Teddington. See 9.4.15 for Southend-on-Sea and Leigh-on-Sea.

CHARTS AC *5606*, 3319, *2484*, 3337, 2151, 1186, *1185*; Imray C2, C1, Y18, 2100 Series; Stanfords 5, 8; OS 176, 177, 178.

Books include: *Nicholsons Guide to the Thames*; *River Thames Book* (Imray). The Port of London Authority (PLA), Bakers Hall, 7 Harp Lane, London EC3R 6LB; ☎ 020 7743 7900, issues free: *General Directions, Permanent Notices: Yachtsman's Guide; Pleasure Users Guide; Leisure Guide. Port of London River Byelaws* & *Tide Tables* are available.

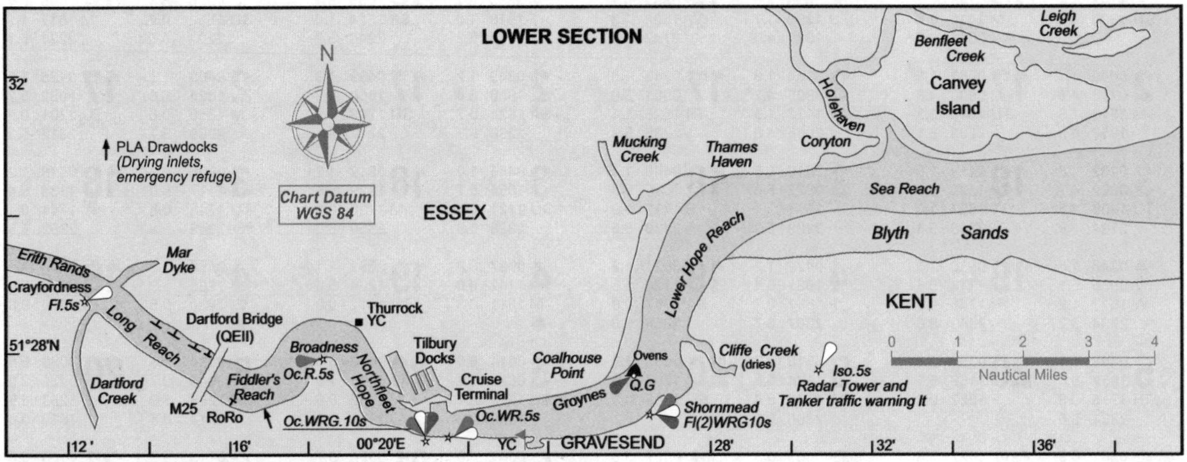

CANVEY ISLAND TO CRAYFORDNESS (AC 1185, 1186, 2484, 2151)

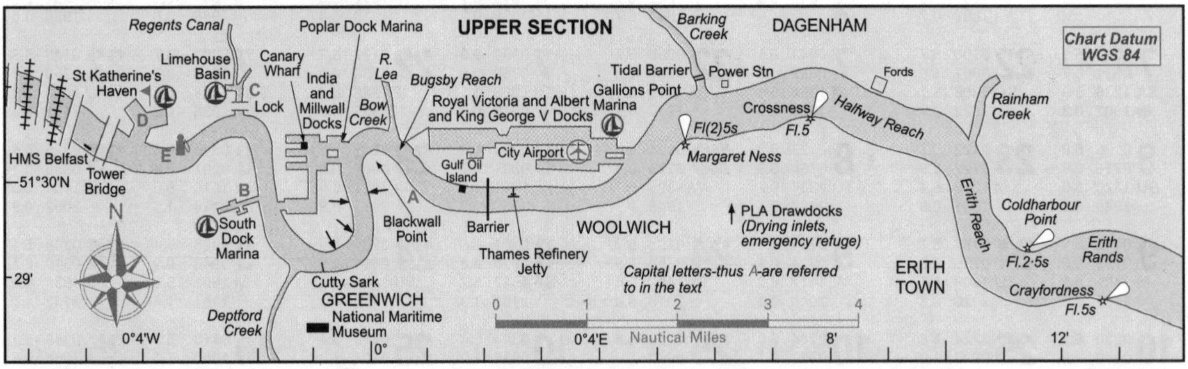

CRAYFORDNESS TO TOWER BRIDGE (AC 2484, 2151, 3337)

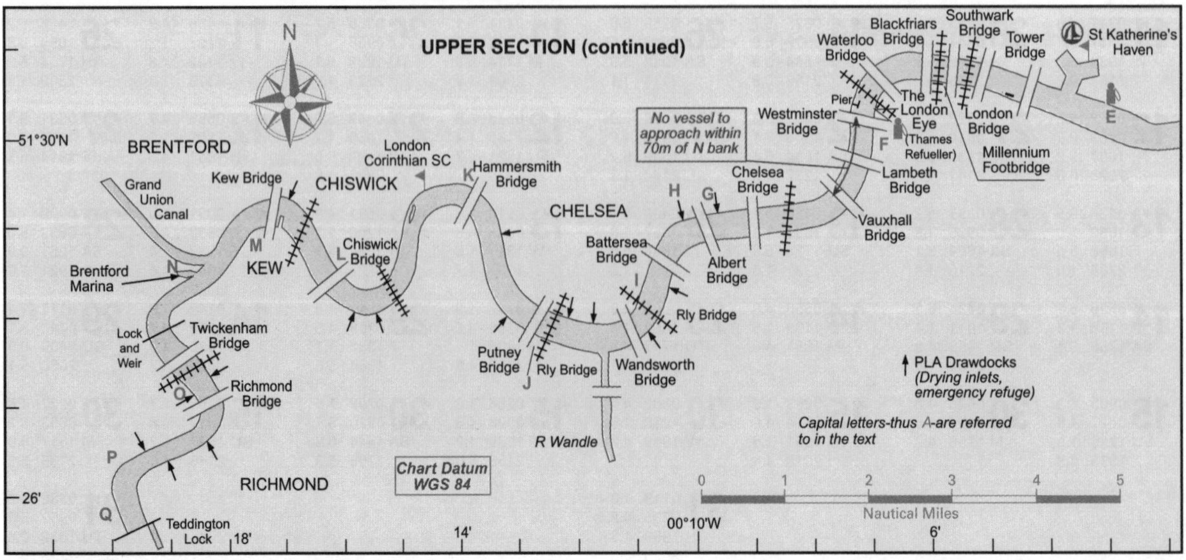

TOWER BRIDGE TO TEDDINGTON (AC 3319)

RIVER THAMES *continued*

HARBOURS IN LOWER REACHES OF RIVER THAMES

HOLEHAVEN, Essex, **51°30´·58N 00°33´·40E**. AC 2484, 1186. HW +0140 on Dover; use differences for CORYTON, see 9.4.15; ML 3·0m; Duration 068. Shelter is good, but beware swell from passing traffic. Note: There is an 8kn speed limit in the river off Coryton and Shellhaven; keep at least 60m clear of berthed tankers and refinery jetties. Keep to Canvey Is side on ent. ⚓ on W edge of chan as long stone groynes extend from E side. 0·5M N of ent an overhead oil pipe crosses chan with clearance of 11m, plus 2 FY lts (horiz). Lts Coryton Refinery Jetty No 4 2 FG (vert). FW from 'The Lobster Smack yard', P & D from Canvey Village (1M); EC Thurs; all other facilities on Canvey Is.

GRAVESEND, Kent, **51°26´·61N 00°22´·90E** (lock into Canal basin). AC 1186, 2151. HW +0150 on Dover; ML 3·3m; Duration 0610. Use Tilbury diffs overleaf. Caution: Off the N bank, from Coalhouse Pt to 7ca E of Gravesend, 6 groynes (tops dry 1·0m) project approx 400m almost into the fairway; their outer ends are marked by SHM bns, Fl G 2·5s. 5 Y buoys downstream of No 6 groyne (the most E'ly) indicate that **no passage exists inshore of the Y buoys and groyne bns**. A SHM buoy *Diver*, L Fl G 10s, between Nos 3 and 2 groynes, marks the N edge of the fairway. ⚓ E of the Sea School jetty, close to S shore, but remote from town. There are Øs off the Club. Lock opens HW −1½ to HW on request to lock-keeper, ☎ (01474) 352392 (24hrs notice required for night tides). Boats can be left unattended in canal basin but not at ⚓s. Royal Terrace Pier hd FR. Call *Port Control London* (located at Gravesend) VHF Ch 12 if E of Sea Reach No 4 buoy (1.4M SSE of Southend pier); and Ch 68 from No 4 buoy to Crayfordness. Broadcasts on Ch 68 every H & H+30 and on Ch 12 every H+15 and H+45. ⊖537115 (H24); **Gravesend SC** ☎ 533974, Bar, FW, M, P & D (cans); **Services:** C (at canal ent, ask at SC), CH, Ⓔ, ME, El, Sh. **Town** EC Wed, R, V.

Thurrock YC (51°28´·30N 00°19´·57E) at Grays, ☎ (01375) 373720 is 3M upriver on N bank opposite Broadness. 1 Ø, D, P (2M), Bar, R (occas). 1000-1500 M-F; 2000-2300 Thur.

THAMES TIDAL BARRIER

51°29´·91N 00°02´·21E (Span G)

Charts AC *5606*, 2484 and 3337.

Description Located at Woolwich Reach, it protects London from floods. There are 9 piers between which gates can be rotated upwards from the river bed to form a barrier. The piers are numbered 1-9 from N to S; the spans are lettered A-K from S to N (see diagram). A, H, J & K are not navigable. C-F, with depth 5·8m and 61m wide, are for larger ships. Spans B and G, with 1·25m, are for small craft/yachts which should lower sail and use engine: W-bound via G and E-bound via B (51°29´·70N 00°02´·33E).

Control & Communications The Thames Barrier Navigation Centre controls all traffic in a Zone from Margaret Ness (51°30´·5N 00°05´·6E) to Blackwall Point (51°30´·3N 00°00´·3E), using the callsign *Woolwich Radio* on VHF Ch **14**, 22, 16. **Inbound** vessels should pass their ETA at the Barrier to *Woolwich Radio* when abeam Crayford Ness (51°28´·9N 00°12´·8E). When passing Margaret Ness they should obtain clearance to proceed through the Barrier. **Outbound** vessels should use the same procedure abeam Tower Bridge (51°30´·3N 00°04´·3E) and Blackwall Point. **Non-VHF** craft should, if possible, pre-notify the Barrier Control ☎ 020 8855 0315; then observe all visual signals, proceed with caution keeping clear of larger vessels and use spans B or G as appropriate. Telephone Barrier Control when passage completed. Sailing vessels should transit the Barrier under power, not sail.

Lights and Signals At Thamesmead and Barking Power Station to the E, and Blackwall Stairs (N bank) and Blackwall Pt (S bank) to the W, noticeboards and lights indicate:
Fl ○ = proceed with extreme caution.
Fl ● = navigation within Zone is prohibited.
Loudhailers may pass instructions and Morse K (—·—) = Barrier closed.
On the Barrier piers:
St Andrew's Cross (R lts) = barrier or span closed.
Arrows (G lts) = span indicated is open to traffic.
Spans A, H, J and K are lit with 3 ● in ▽ = No passage.
In addition, in reduced visibility, spans open to navigation are marked by high intensity lts and racons.

Spans open for navigation Information will be included in routine broadcasts by *Woolwich Radio* on VHF Ch 14 at H + 15 and H + 45.

Testing The Barrier is completely closed for testing once a month, for about 3hrs, LW ±1½. An annual closure in Sept/Oct lasts about 10 hrs, LW to LW; this may affect passage plans.

Beware On N side of river (Spans E and F) a cross-tide component is reported; expect to lay-off a compensating drift angle. When all spans are closed, keep 200m clear to avoid turbulence. **It is dangerous to transit a closed span, as the gate may be semi-raised.** Small craft should not navigate between Thames Refinery Jetty and Gulf Oil Island, unless intending to transit the Barrier.

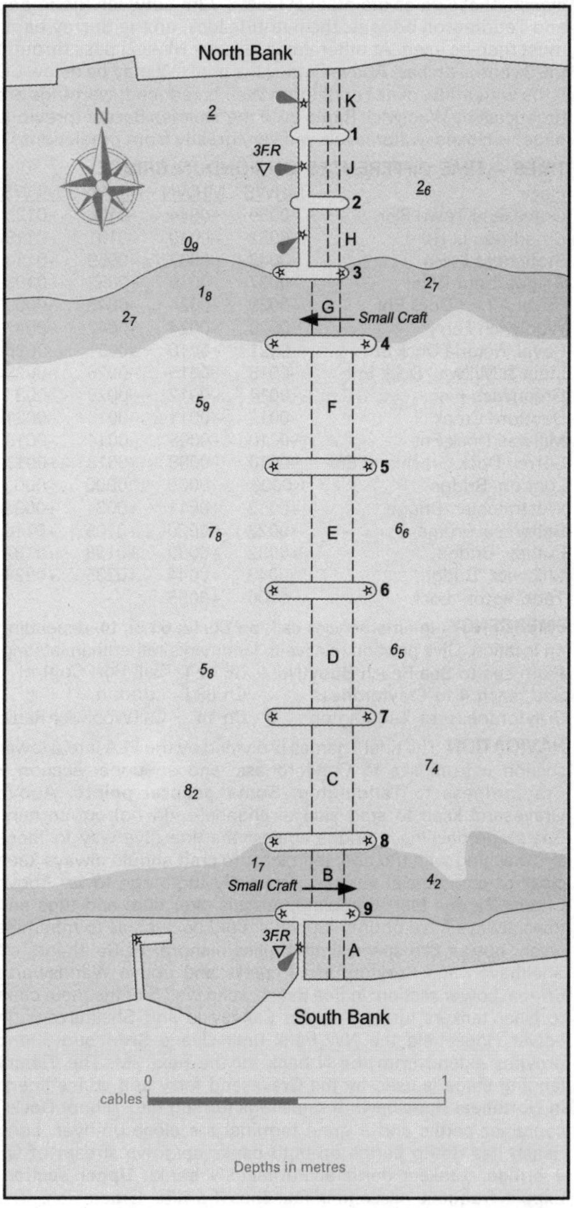

TIDES +0252 Dover; ML 3·6; Duration 0555; Zone 0 (UT)

Standard Port LONDON BRIDGE (⟶)

Times				Height (metres)			
High Water		Low Water		MHWS	MHWN	MLWN	MLWS
0300	0900	0400	1100	7·1	5·9	1·3	0·5
1500	2100	1600	2300				
Differences TILBURY							
−0055	−0040	−0050	−0115	−0·7	−0·5	+0·1	0·0
WOOLWICH (GALLIONS POINT)							
−0020	−0020	−0035	−0045	−0·1	0·0	+0·2	0·0
ALBERT BRIDGE							
+0025	+0020	+0105	+0110	−0·9	−0·8	−0·7	−0·4
HAMMERSMITH BRIDGE							
+0040	+0035	+0205	+0155	−1·4	−1·3	−1·0	−0·5
KEW BRIDGE							
+0055	+0050	+0255	+0235	−1·8	−1·8	−1·2	−0·5
RICHMOND LOCK							
+0105	+0055	+0325	+0305	−2·2	−2·2	−1·3	−0·5

The river is tidal up to Richmond Footbridge where there is a half-tide lock and a weir with overhead sluice gates. When down, ie closed, these gates maintain at least 1·72m between Richmond and Teddington bridges; the half-tide lock, on the Surrey bank, must then be used. At other times (approx HW ±2) pass through the 3 central arches. Above Putney the ht of LW may be below CD if the water flow over Teddington Weir is reduced; warnings are broadcast by Woolwich Radio qv. If the Thames Barrier (previous page) is closed, water levels will vary greatly from predictions.

TIDES – TIME DIFFERENCES ON LONDON BRIDGE

Place	MHWS	MHWN	MLWN	MLWS
Gravesend Town Pier	−0059	−0044	−0106	−0125
Broadness Lt Ho	−0052	−0040	−0101	−0119
Stoneness Lt Ho	−0048	−0037	−0059	−0114
Coldharbour Point	−0037	−0030	−0053	−0103
Royal Albert Dock Ent	−0029	−0024	−0043	−0050
Woolwich Ferry	−0028	−0024	−0042	−0047
Royal Victoria Dock Ent	−0021	−0018	−0031	−0025
India & Millwall Dock Ent	−0018	−0015	−0026	−0029
Greenwich Pier	−0014	−0012	−0020	−0023
Deptford Creek	−0012	−0011	−0018	−0021
Millwall Dock Ent	−0010	−0008	−0014	−0016
Surrey Dock Greenland Ent	−0010	−0008	−0013	−0015
London Bridge	0000	0000	0000	0000
Westminster Bridge	+0012	+0011	+0031	+0035
Battersea Bridge	+0023	+0020	+0109	+0110
Putney Bridge	+0032	+0030	+0138	+0137
Chiswick Bridge	+0049	+0044	+0235	+0224
Teddington Lock	+0106	+0056	–	–

EMERGENCY In emergencies call on Ch 12, 68 or 14, depending on location. Give position relative to landmarks rather than lat/long.

From sea to Sea Reach Buoy No 4	Ch 12	Call Port Control London
Sea reach 4 to Crayfordness	Ch 68	Call Port Control London
Crayfordness to Teddington	Ch 14	Call Woolwich Radio

NAVIGATION The tidal Thames is divided by the PLA into a lower section = from sea to Crayfordness; and an upper section = Crayfordness to Teddington. **Some general points**: Above Gravesend keep to stbd side of channel - do not cut corners. Boats approaching a bridge against the tide give way to those approaching with the tide; but pleasure craft should always keep clear of commercial vessels, especially tug/barge tows. Above Cherry Garden Pier (Wapping), vessels over 40m and tugs and tows always have priority. Speed should be such as to minimise wash, but an 8kn speed limit applies inshore off Southend, off Shellhaven and Coryton, in all creeks and above Wandsworth Bridge. **Lower section.** In Sea Reach, keep well S of the main chan to clear tankers turning abeam Canvey Is and Shellhaven. In Lower Hope hold the NW bank until Ovens SHM buoy; long groynes extend from the N bank for the next 2M. The Tilbury landing stage is used by the Gravesend ferry and cruise liners. In Northfleet Hope beware ships/tugs turning into Tilbury Docks; container berths and a grain terminal are close up-river. Long Reach has Ro-Ro berths on both banks up/down stream of QE II bridge. Tankers berth at Purfleet (N bank). **Upper section.** Expect frequent passenger launches from/to Greenwich, The Tower and Westminster. Thames Police and PLA launches are very helpful to yachts.

BRIDGES

Name of Bridge	Distance from London Bridge Nautical Miles	Clearance below centre span MHWS (m)
Dartford (QEII)	17·68 below	54.1
Tower	0·49 below	8·6 (42·5 open)
ALL BRIDGES UPSTREAM OF TOWER BRIDGE ARE FIXED		
London Bridge	0.00	8·9
Cannon St. Railway	0·16	7·1
Southwark	0·24	7·4
Millennium Bridge	0·41	9·4
Blackfriars Railway	0·62	7·0
Blackfriars	0·63	7·1
Waterloo	1·12	8·5
Charing Cross Railway	1·32	7·0
Westminster	1·64	5·4
Lambeth	2·02	6·5
Vauxhall	2·46	5·6
Victoria Railway	3·31	6·0
Chelsea	3·40	6·6
Albert	4·04	4·9
Battersea	4·27	5·5
Battersea Railway	4·83	6·1
Wandsworth	5·46	5·8
Fulham Railway	6·31	6·9
Putney	6·45	5·5
Hammersmith	7·97	3·7
Barnes Railway	9·55	5·4
Chiswick	10·22	6·9
Kew Railway	10·98	5·6
Kew	11·33	5·3
Richmond Footbridge	13·49	5·5
Twickenham	13·64	5·9
Richmond Railway	13·67	5·3
Richmond	13·97	5·3

Tower Bridge sounds horn for 10s, every 20s, in fog when bascules are open for shipping; standby is Bell 30s. A ▽ of R discs (● lts) below a bridge span = this arch closed.

PIERS WHERE LANDING CAN BE MADE BY ARRANGEMENT Piers with *, contact London River Services ☎ 020 7941 2400/20, 📠 020 7941 2410: Greenwich Pier*, Tower Pier*, Embankment*, Bankside, Blackfriars, Waterloo Millenium, Westminster Pier*, Festival Pier*, London Bridge City Pier 020 7403 5939; Cadogan Pier (G) 020 7349 8585; Putney Pier 020 7378 1211; Kew Pier, Richmond Landing Stage 020 7930 2062; Hampton Court Pier 020 8781 9758.

LIGHTS AND MARKS Glare from the many shore lts makes navigation by night difficult or even risky. Margaret Ness Fl (2) 5s 11m 8M. Special lts fitted on brs between Tower and Wandsworth: triggered by single large vessel Iso W 4s or by second large vessel VQFl. Other vessels keep clear.

RADIO TELEPHONE Sea Reach No 4 buoy is 1.35M SSE of Southend pierhead at 51°29′·61N 00°44′·18E. Craft >20m LOA must have VHF radio and call Woolwich Radio on Ch 14 if intending to navigate within the Thames Barrier control zone. Smaller craft with no VHF should call ☎ 020 8855 0315 before and after transiting the Thames Barrier. Routine traffic, weather, tidal and nav info is broadcast by *Port Control London* on Ch 12 at H +15 and H +45 and on Ch 68 at H and H +30; also by *Woolwich Radio* on Ch 14 at H +15 and H +45. The latter will warn if ht of LW upstream of Putney falls below CD. For marina VHF see next page. Yachts should avoid using the following tug Chs: 8, 10, 13, 15, 17, 36, 72, 77.

TELEPHONE (Dial code 020 7 Central London; 020 8 Outer London) PLA: Operational enquiries 01474 560311; General non-operational enquiries, below Crayfordness: (01474) 562200, 📠 562281; above Crayfordness: 020 7743 7912, 📠 020 7743 7996; Duty Port Controller Gravesend (01474) 560311; Duty Officer Woolwich 020 8855 0315; Port Health Authority (Tilbury 01375) 842663 (H24); Thames MRSC (01255) 675518; River Police HQ (Wapping) 020 7275 4421; London Weather Centre 020 7831 5968; Tower Bridge 020 7407 0922; ⊖ (01474) 537115 (H24); Richmond Lock 020 8940 0634; **Marinecall** 09068 500 455; 🄷 020 7987 7011.

SHELTER Very good in marinas. PLA Drawdocks (⟼) are drying inlets offering emergency refuge, subject to wash.

FACILITIES (Bold red letters in brackets appear on chartlets)
Greenwich YC (A) ☎ 020 88587339; VHF Ch M. FW, ⚓, ME.
Westminster Petroleum Ltd (F) (Fuel barge). Call *Thames Refueller* VHF Ch 14, ☎ 0831 110681, D, Gas, CH, L.
Chelsea Yacht & Boat Co (H) ☎ 020 7352 1427, M, Gas;
Hurlingham YC (J) ☎ 020 8788 5547, M, CH, ME, FW, El, Sh;
Dove Marina (K).

Chiswick Pier, 51°28'·90N 00°14'·95W. ☎ 020 8742 2713, 📠 0181 742 0057, £0.95m, long pontoon, 2FG (vert). All tide access, max draft 1·4m. FW, AC, ⛽. Visitors welcome.
Chiswick Quay Marina (L) (50) ☎ 020 8994 8743, Access HW±2 via lock, M, FW, BY, M, ME, El, Sh.
Kew Marina (M) ☎ 020 8940 8364, M, CH, D, P, Gas, SM;
(O), Richmond Slipway BY, CH, D, Gas, M, FW, ME, El, Sh.
(P) Eel Pie Island BY, CH, AC, ME, M, Gas, C (6 ton), Sh, El, FW;
(Q) Swan Island Hbr, D, M, ME, El, Sh, FW, Gas, Slip, AB, C (30 ton), CH.

MARINAS ON THE TIDAL THAMES (From seaward: Woolwich to Brentford)

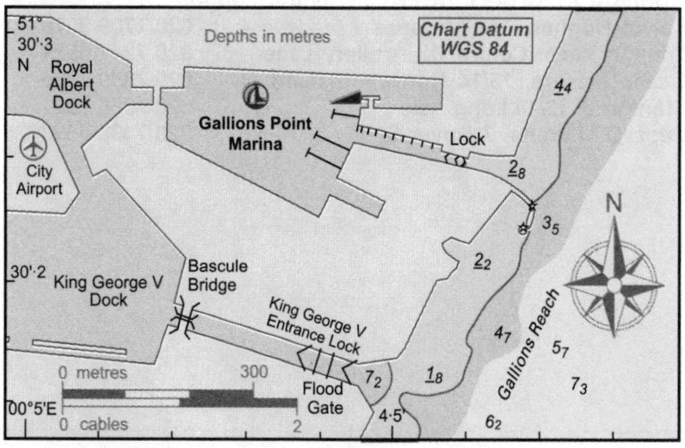

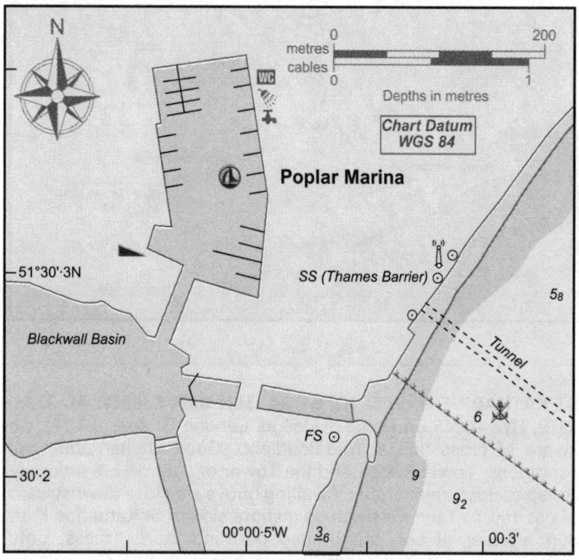

GALLIONS POINT MARINA, 51°30'·30N 00°04'·66E in entry basin for Royal Albert Dock. AC 2151, *2484*. Tides as for Gallions Pt (9.4.14). Marina ☎ 020 7476 7054 (H24). VHF Ch 37 & 80, when vessel expected. Access via lock HW±5; Locking from £5 each way; AB £1.10. Two ☆s 2FG (vert) on river pier. 8m depth in basin. Usual facilities, H24 security. The fuel barge LEONARD is conspic, berthed outside the lock; D, Gas 0900-1600 M-F; ☎ 020 7474 8714 VHF Ch 14. DLR from N Woolwich to central London, until 0030. Woolwich ferry & foot tunnel 15 mins walk. ✈ City airport is adjacent.

SOUTH DOCK MARINA (B), 51°29'·65N 00°01'·97W. AC 3337, *2484*. Tides as for Surrey Dock Greenland Ent (9.4.14). 1·1M above Greenwich, 2·5M below Tower Bridge. Baltic Quay building at SW end of marina is conspic with five arched rooftops. Waiting pontoon at Greenland Pier. Approx access via lock HW-2½ to HW+1½ for 2m draft; HW±3 for 1m draft. **Marina** ☎ 020 7252 2244, 📠 020 7237 3806, (250 + Ⓥ, £15 <15m, £20 >15.5m). VHF Ch **M** 80. **Facilities**: AC, ME, Sh, El, FW, CH, C (20 ton), Bar, R, V, ⊡, ♿, Dr ☎ 237 1078; Ⓗ ⛽ ☎ 020 7955 5000; Police ☎ 020 7252 2836. ⇌, Surrey Quays and Canada Water tube, ✈ City Airport.

POPLAR DOCK MARINA, 51°30'·07N 00°00'·50W (lock ent). AC 3337, *2484*. Tides: India & Millwall Docks ent (9.4.14). 4·5M below Tower Bridge. Canary Wharf twr (244m) is conspic 4ca W of marina and Millenium dome is 5ca E. Lock (200m x 24m) opens 0600-2200LT at HW for outbound and HW-1 to HW+1 for arrivals, foc, but OT £20. Bridge at lock and 2 other bridges open in unison. Least width 12·1m into marina. **Marina** ☎ 020 7515 1046, 📠 020 7538 5537, (90 + Ⓥ £25, all LOA). VHF Ch 13 (H24). **Facilities**: AC, FW, Slip, Bar, R, V, ⛽, ⊡, ♿; Dr ☎ 020 7237 1078; Ⓗ ☎ 020 7955 5000; Police ☎ 252 2836. ⇌, Blackwall DLR, Canary Wharf Tube (when Jubilee line open), ✈ City.

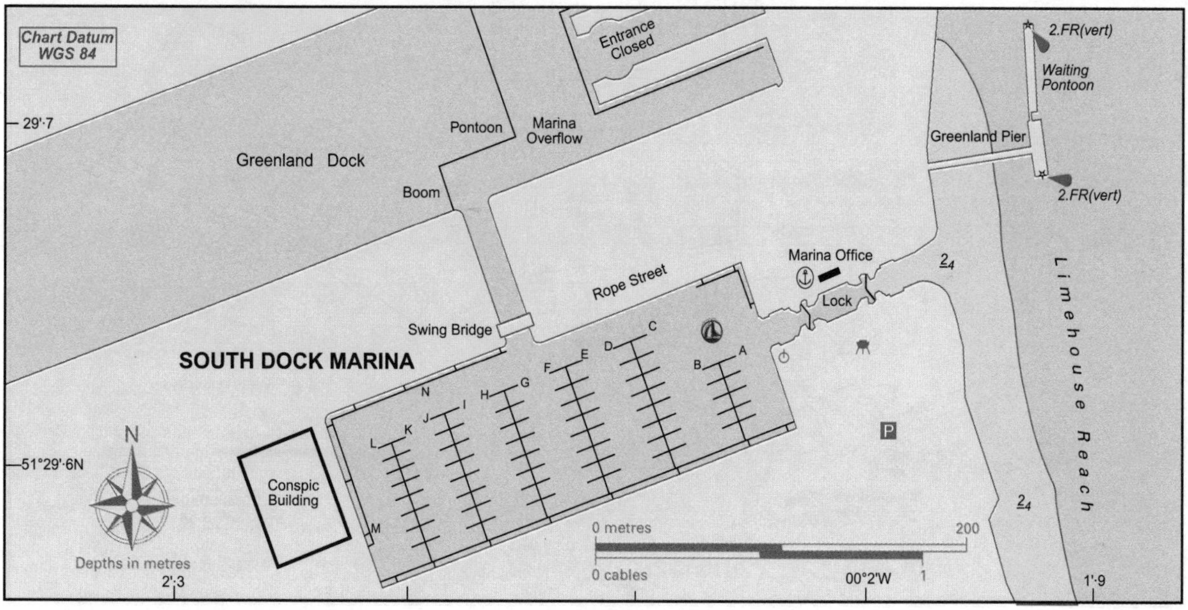

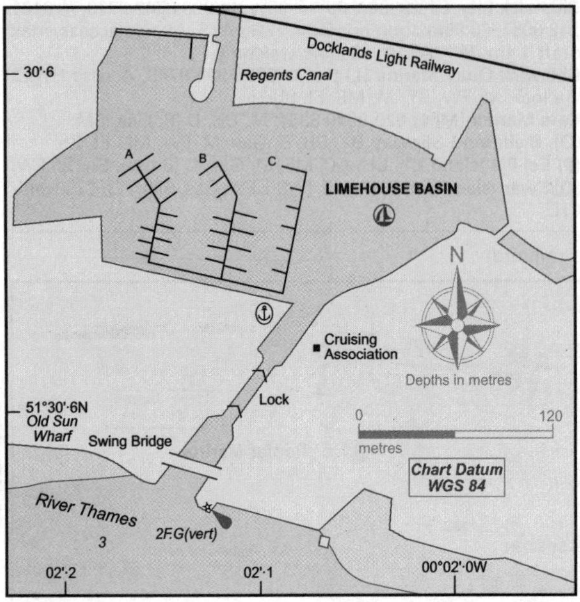

LIMEHOUSE BASIN (C), 51°30'·57N 00°02'·27W. Entry HW±3 via swing bridge/lock, 0800-1800LT daily Apr-Oct; 0800-1630 Nov-Mar; other times by prior arrangement to Hr Mr & BWB lock, ☎ 020 7308 9930. Waiting pontoon in lock entrance is accessible outside LW±1½. Call VHF Ch 80 *Limehouse Marina*. **Facilities:** (90 berths, £11.75 all LOA) H24 security, FW, AC, ⊡, ⇌, DLR; also entry to Regents Canal and R Lea. Marina is managed by Cruising Association at: 1 Northey St, Limehouse Basin, E14 8BT, ☎ 020 7537 2828, 🖷 020 7537 2266; temporary membership, open: 1130-1500 & 1700-2300 Mon-Fri, 1130-2300 Sat, 1200-1500 & 1900-2230 Sun; Bar, R, ♿, ⊡.

ADMIRALTY CHART AGENTS (Central London)

Kelvin Hughes, 142 Minories	020 7709 9076
London Yacht Centre, 13 Artillery Lane	020 7247 0521
Ocean Leisure, 13/14 Northumberland Av	020 7930 5050
Stanfords, 12/14 Long Acre	020 7836 1321
Capt. O.M.Watts, 7 Dover St	020 7493 4633

ST KATHARINE HAVEN, (D) 51°30´·36N 00°04´·35W. AC 3337, 3319. HW +0245 on Dover. Tides as London Bridge (9.4.14). Be aware of cross tide at mid-flood/ebb. Good shelter under all conditions. Tower Bridge and the Tower of London are uniquely conspic, close up-river. Six Y waiting buoys are close downstream of ent in 0.1 - 1.9m. Or berth on inshore side of St Katharine Pier, 30m upriver of ent, but limited berthing/shore access, only suitable for shoal draft. Pleasure launches berth on S side of pier. **St Katharine Haven** Call St Katharines VHF Ch **80** M. Lock (41m x 12·5m with 2 small lifting bridges), access HW –2 to HW +1½, season 0600-2030, winter 0800-1800LT; other times by prior arrangement. R/G tfc lts at ent. Lock is shut Tues and Wed, Nov to Feb. **Facilities** (100 + 50 ♥, usually in Centre Basin or East Dock; give 1 week's notice in season) ☎ 020 7481 8350, 🖷 020 7702 2252; £2.05, FW, AC, CH, ME, El, Sh, Gas, ⛽, YC, Bar, R, V, ⊖, ⊡. **Fuel Barge (E)** is 400m downstream of lock ent. ☎ 020 7481 1774; VHF Ch 14 *Burgan*. D & Gas, 0900-1600 Mon-Fri; 0900-1300 Sun.

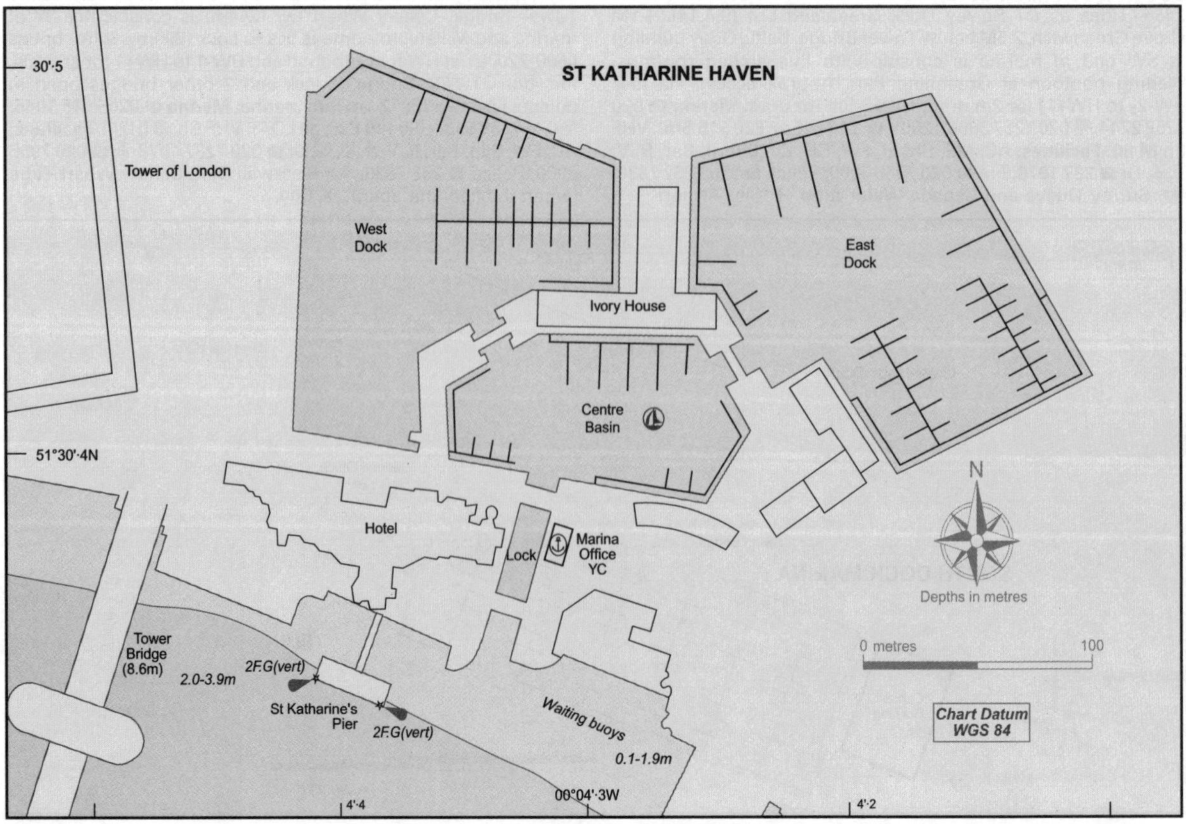

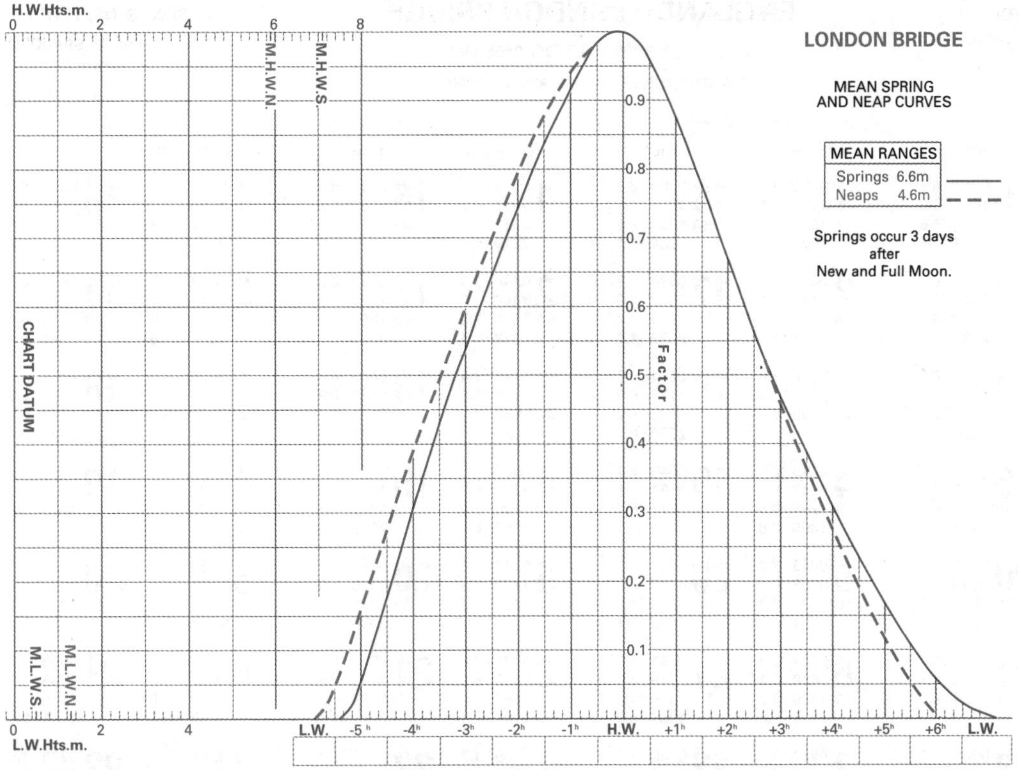
H.W.Hts.m.
0 2 4 6 8
M.H.W.N.
M.H.W.S.
LONDON BRIDGE
MEAN SPRING AND NEAP CURVES
MEAN RANGES
Springs 6.6m
Neaps 4.6m
Springs occur 3 days after New and Full Moon.
CHART DATUM
Factor
0.9
0.8
0.7
0.6
0.5
0.4
0.3
0.2
0.1
M.L.W.S.
M.L.W.N.
0 2 4
L.W.Hts.m.
L.W. -5h -4h -3h -2h -1h H.W. +1h +2h +3h +4h +5h +6h L.W.

CHELSEA HARBOUR, London, **51°28′·42N 00°10′·82W**. AC 3319. Tides: see 9.4.14. Good shelter in all conditions, 5M above Tower Bridge, reached via 14 fixed bridges. Battersea railway bridge is 120m upstream. Belvedere Tower (80m high with tide ball) is conspic, next to the lock. Basin ent is for max LOA 24m, beam 5·5m, draft 1·8m, with bascule bridge. Lock opens when 2·5m water above sill; tide gauge outside, access HW ±1½, R/G tfc lts. Limited waiting berths and shore access on Chelsea Hbr Pier (1·7m) close upriver. Call Chelsea Hbr VHF Ch 80. **Marina** (50+10 Ⓥ). ☎ 020 7225 9108, 📠 020 7352 7868, mobile ☎ 07770 542783, £12.50, AC, FW, Bar, Ⓑ, ♿, ⛽, V.

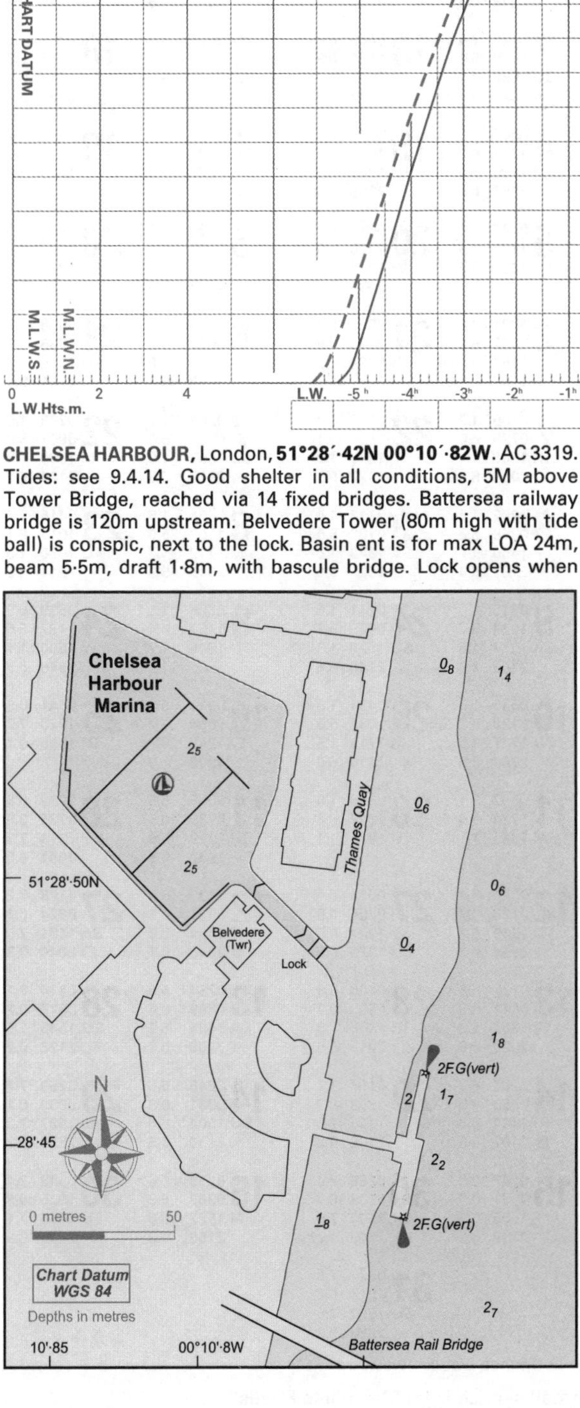
Chelsea Harbour Marina
Thames Quay
51°28'·50N
Belvedere (Twr)
Lock
2F.G(vert)
2F.G(vert)
28'·45
N
0 metres 50
Chart Datum WGS 84
Depths in metres
Battersea Rail Bridge
10'·85
00°10'·8W

BRENTFORD DOCK MARINA (N). 51°28′·88N 00°17′·95W, 1100m beyond Kew bridge. AC 3319. Tides, see Kew Bridge. 60 AB inc Ⓥ, £14.10 all LOA. ☎ 020 8232 8941, 📠 020 8560 5486, mobile 07970 143 987. No VHF. Access HW±2½ via lock 4·8m x 9·8m (longer LOA during freeflow); 18m waiting pontoon. **Facilities**: AC, El, FW, CH, ME, Bar, R, V, Sh; Gunnersbury & Ealing tubes. Ent to Grand Union Canal via lock is nearby: M, AB.

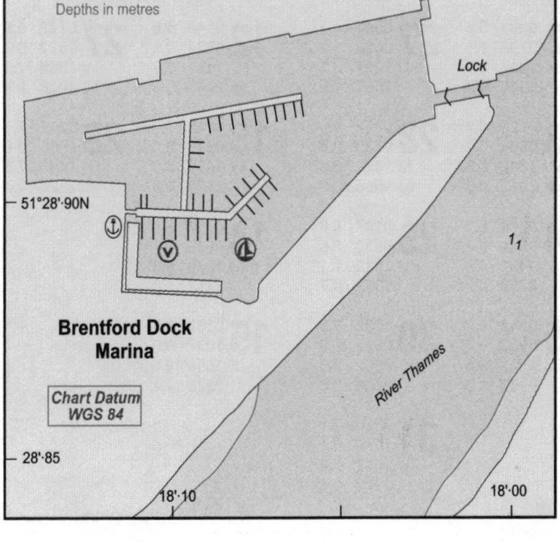
N
metres 0 100
cables 0 0.5
Depths in metres
Lock
51°28'·90N
Brentford Dock Marina
River Thames
Chart Datum WGS 84
28'·85
18'·10
18'·00

TIME ZONE (UTC)
For Summer Time add ONE hour in **non-shaded areas**

ENGLAND – LONDON BRIDGE

LAT 50°30′N LONG 0°05′W

TIMES AND HEIGHTS OF HIGH AND LOW WATERS

SPRING & NEAP TIDES
Dates in red are **SPRINGS**
Dates in blue are **NEAPS**

YEAR **2002**

JANUARY

Date	Day	Time	m	Time	m	Time	m	Time	m
1	TU	0248	6.9	0931	0.5	1514	7.1	2141	0.8
2	W	0332	6.9	1020	0.5	1601	7.2	2222	0.8
3	TH	0415	6.9	1105	0.4	1648	7.1	2302	0.9
4	F	0459	6.8	1150	0.5	1737	7.0	2343	1.0
5	SA	0546	6.6	1235	0.6	1828	6.7		
6	SU	0028	1.1	0637	6.4	1324	0.8	1925	6.4
7	M	0121	1.3	0738	6.2	1421	1.0	2029	6.2
8	TU	0223	1.5	0849	6.1	1527	1.1	2136	6.1
9	W	0337	1.6	0959	6.1	1638	1.1	2240	6.2
10	TH	0459	1.4	1104	6.3	1743	1.0	2338	6.4
11	F	0610	1.2	1202	6.5	1838	0.9		
12	SA	0031	6.6	0708	0.9	1256	6.7	1928	0.8
13	SU	0120	6.7	0801	0.7	1346	6.8	● 2015	0.8
14	M	0204	6.7	0849	0.7	1431	6.9	2058	0.8
15	TU	0243	6.7	0933	0.7	1512	6.8	2137	1.0
16	W	0317	6.6	1011	0.8	1548	6.6	2209	1.1
17	TH	0348	6.5	1042	1.0	1621	6.5	2231	1.2
18	F	0419	6.5	1102	1.1	1654	6.5	2250	1.2
19	SA	0453	6.4	1120	1.1	1730	6.4	2320	1.1
20	SU	0531	6.3	1150	1.0	1809	6.3	2357	1.1
21	M	0614	6.2	1228	1.1	1854	6.1		
22	TU	0041	1.3	0702	6.0	1315	1.2	1944	6.0
23	W	0135	1.4	0759	5.9	1414	1.3	2042	5.9
24	TH	0244	1.6	0903	5.8	1528	1.4	2148	5.9
25	F	0402	1.5	1013	5.9	1644	1.4	2258	6.0
26	SA	0514	1.3	1123	6.1	1754	1.2		
27	SU	0001	6.3	0623	1.1	1226	6.5	1857	1.0
28	M	0057	6.6	0730	0.8	1322	6.8	○ 1956	0.8
29	TU	0147	6.8	0832	0.5	1413	7.1	2049	0.7
30	W	0235	7.0	0927	0.3	1502	7.3	2138	0.6
31	TH	0320	7.1	1016	0.1	1549	7.4	2222	0.6

FEBRUARY

Date	Day	Time	m	Time	m	Time	m	Time	m
1	F	0403	7.1	1100	0.0	1635	7.4	2301	0.6
2	SA	0446	7.1	1140	0.1	1720	7.3	2337	0.7
3	SU	0529	7.0	1217	0.3	1806	7.0		
4	M	0013	0.8	0613	6.7	1254	0.6	1855	6.6
5	TU	0053	1.0	0703	6.4	1336	0.9	1951	6.1
6	W	0141	1.3	0808	6.1	1429	1.2	2058	5.8
7	TH	0242	1.6	0928	5.9	1539	1.5	2209	5.8
8	F	0400	1.7	1043	5.9	1705	1.5	2314	5.9
9	SA	0551	1.5	1147	6.2	1813	1.3		
10	SU	0011	6.2	0655	1.1	1243	6.5	1907	1.0
11	M	0103	6.5	0746	0.8	1333	6.7	1956	0.9
12	TU	0148	6.6	0834	0.6	1417	6.8	● 2041	0.8
13	W	0228	6.6	0917	0.6	1457	6.8	2122	0.9
14	TH	0302	6.6	0956	0.7	1530	6.6	2157	1.0
15	F	0332	6.5	1027	0.9	1559	6.6	2220	1.1
16	SA	0400	6.5	1047	1.0	1628	6.6	2234	1.1
17	SU	0430	6.5	1057	1.0	1700	6.6	2258	1.0
18	M	0504	6.5	1119	0.9	1736	6.5	2330	0.9
19	TU	0542	6.4	1151	0.8	1817	6.4		
20	W	0007	0.9	0626	6.3	1229	1.0	1903	6.1
21	TH	0051	1.2	0718	6.0	1316	1.2	1957	5.9
22	F	0148	1.4	0820	5.8	1423	1.5	2101	5.7
23	SA	0318	1.6	0931	5.8	1605	1.6	2218	5.7
24	SU	0447	1.5	1053	6.0	1731	1.4	2334	6.1
25	M	0609	1.1	1206	6.4	1843	1.1		
26	TU	0036	6.5	0722	0.7	1306	6.8	1944	0.8
27	W	0129	6.8	0822	0.3	1358	7.2	○ 2038	0.6
28	TH	0217	7.1	0915	0.0	1446	7.5	2126	0.4

MARCH

Date	Day	Time	m	Time	m	Time	m	Time	m
1	F	0302	7.3	1002	-0.2	1532	7.6	2210	0.4
2	SA	0344	7.4	1044	-0.2	1615	7.5	2248	0.4
3	SU	0425	7.4	1120	-0.1	1658	7.4	2321	0.4
4	M	0506	7.2	1151	0.2	1739	7.0	2352	0.6
5	TU	0547	7.0	1220	0.5	1821	6.6		
6	W	0024	0.8	0632	6.5	1257	0.9	1907	6.1
7	TH	0106	1.2	0729	6.0	1345	1.4	2008	5.6
8	F	0202	1.5	0858	5.6	1450	1.7	2137	5.4
9	SA	0315	1.8	1023	5.7	1617	1.8	2249	5.6
10	SU	0535	1.6	1128	6.0	1747	1.5	2348	6.0
11	M	0637	1.1	1224	6.4	1845	1.1		
12	TU	0041	6.4	0726	0.7	1313	6.7	1934	0.9
13	W	0127	6.6	0811	0.5	1357	6.8	2020	0.8
14	TH	0207	6.7	0853	0.5	1434	6.8	● 2102	0.8
15	F	0242	6.6	0931	0.6	1505	6.7	2138	0.9
16	SA	0311	6.5	1003	0.8	1533	6.6	2203	1.0
17	SU	0338	6.5	1023	0.9	1600	6.6	2216	1.0
18	M	0406	6.6	1031	0.9	1631	6.6	2237	0.9
19	TU	0438	6.6	1051	0.8	1705	6.6	2305	0.8
20	W	0515	6.6	1120	0.8	1744	6.5	2339	0.8
21	TH	0559	6.4	1155	0.9	1829	6.2		
22	F	0019	1.0	0650	6.1	1240	1.2	1922	5.9
23	SA	0112	1.4	0752	5.8	1342	1.6	2025	5.6
24	SU	0241	1.6	0905	5.7	1529	1.8	2146	5.6
25	M	0431	1.5	1032	5.9	1713	1.5	2310	6.0
26	TU	0559	1.0	1148	6.4	1826	1.1		
27	W	0013	6.4	0706	0.5	1247	6.9	1925	0.8
28	TH	0106	6.9	0803	0.1	1338	7.3	○ 2018	0.5
29	F	0154	7.2	0853	-0.2	1425	7.5	2106	0.3
30	SA	0238	7.4	0938	-0.3	1509	7.6	2149	0.2
31	SU	0321	7.5	1018	-0.2	1552	7.5	2228	0.2

APRIL

Date	Day	Time	m	Time	m	Time	m	Time	m
1	M	0403	7.4	1053	0.0	1632	7.3	2301	0.3
2	TU	0443	7.3	1122	0.2	1710	7.0	2331	0.5
3	W	0525	7.0	1151	0.6	1748	6.6		
4	TH	0000	0.7	0608	6.5	1225	1.0	1827	6.1
5	F	0039	1.1	0702	6.0	1310	1.4	1917	5.6
6	SA	0134	1.5	0832	5.6	1415	1.8	2059	5.3
7	SU	0247	1.7	0959	5.6	1537	1.9	2219	5.5
8	M	0455	1.6	1102	6.0	1712	1.7	2319	5.9
9	TU	0606	1.1	1157	6.4	1816	1.2		
10	W	0011	6.3	0654	0.7	1245	6.7	1906	0.9
11	TH	0058	6.5	0739	0.5	1328	6.8	1952	0.8
12	F	0139	6.6	0821	0.5	1404	6.8	● 2033	0.7
13	SA	0214	6.6	0859	0.6	1435	6.7	2109	0.8
14	SU	0245	6.5	0931	0.8	1504	6.6	2136	0.9
15	M	0313	6.5	0952	0.9	1532	6.6	2156	0.9
16	TU	0343	6.6	1006	0.9	1604	6.6	2219	0.8
17	W	0417	6.6	1028	0.8	1639	6.6	2247	0.7
18	TH	0456	6.6	1058	0.8	1718	6.4	2321	0.8
19	F	0541	6.4	1135	1.0	1803	6.2		
20	SA	0002	1.0	0633	6.2	1222	1.3	1856	5.8
21	SU	0058	1.3	0736	5.9	1325	1.6	2001	5.6
22	M	0233	1.5	0851	5.8	1509	1.8	2124	5.7
23	TU	0418	1.3	1017	6.1	1650	1.5	2244	6.0
24	W	0539	0.8	1127	6.6	1800	1.1	2346	6.5
25	TH	0641	0.3	1223	7.0	1859	0.7		
26	F	0039	6.9	0735	0.0	1314	7.3	1951	0.5
27	SA	0128	7.2	0824	-0.1	1401	7.5	○ 2040	0.3
28	SU	0214	7.4	0910	-0.2	1445	7.5	2126	0.2
29	M	0259	7.4	0950	-0.1	1527	7.3	2206	0.2
30	TU	0342	7.4	1025	0.1	1606	7.1	2242	0.3

Chart Datum: 2·90 metres below Ordnance Datum (Newlyn)

TIME ZONE (UTC)
For Summer Time add ONE hour in **non-shaded areas**

ENGLAND – LONDON BRIDGE

LAT 50°30′N LONG 0°05′W

TIMES AND HEIGHTS OF HIGH AND LOW WATERS

SPRING & NEAP TIDES
Dates in **red** are **SPRINGS**
Dates in **blue** are **NEAPS**

YEAR **2002**

MAY

Date	Time	m	Time	m	Time	m	Time	m
1 W	0424	7.2	1057	0.4	1644	6.9	2313	0.5
2 TH	0507	6.9	1126	0.7	1720	6.5	2343	0.8
3 F	0552	6.5	1159	1.1	1758	6.1		
4 SA	0020	1.0	0644	6.0	1243	1.5	1844	5.7
5 SU	0113	1.3	0802	5.6	1343	1.8	2005	5.4
6 M	0221	1.5	0924	5.6	1457	1.9	2138	5.5
7 TU	0338	1.5	1027	5.9	1616	1.8	2241	5.8
8 W	0510	1.2	1121	6.2	1730	1.4	2334	6.1
9 TH	0609	0.9	1208	6.5	1826	1.1		
10 F	0021	6.4	0656	0.7	1251	6.7	1912	0.9
11 SA	0103	6.5	0739	0.7	1328	6.7	1954	0.8
12 SU	0141	6.6	0818	0.7	1403	6.7	● 2032	0.8
13 M	0216	6.6	0852	0.8	1435	6.7	2105	0.8
14 TU	0250	6.6	0920	0.9	1509	6.7	2136	0.8
15 W	0325	6.6	0946	0.9	1543	6.6	2207	0.7
16 TH	0403	6.7	1014	0.9	1620	6.6	2240	0.7
17 F	0444	6.6	1048	0.9	1701	6.4	2318	0.8
18 SA	0532	6.5	1128	1.1	1747	6.2		
19 SU	0003	1.0	0625	6.3	1218	1.3	1840	6.0
20 M	0105	1.2	0728	6.1	1322	1.6	1946	5.8
21 TU	0232	1.2	0842	6.1	1452	1.6	2105	5.9
22 W	0357	1.0	0957	6.3	1619	1.4	2216	6.2
23 TH	0510	0.7	1102	6.7	1729	1.1	2318	6.6
24 F	0611	0.4	1158	7.0	1830	0.8		
25 SA	0013	6.9	0705	0.2	1250	7.2	1925	0.5
26 SU	0104	7.1	0755	0.1	1337	7.3	○ 2016	0.4
27 M	0153	7.2	0841	0.1	1422	7.3	2103	0.3
28 TU	0240	7.2	0923	0.2	1505	7.1	2147	0.3
29 W	0325	7.2	1001	0.4	1545	7.0	2226	0.4
30 TH	0409	7.0	1035	0.6	1622	6.7	2300	0.6
31 F	0452	6.8	1107	0.9	1658	6.5	2332	0.8

JUNE

Date	Time	m	Time	m	Time	m	Time	m
1 SA	0536	6.4	1139	1.2	1736	6.2		
2 SU	0007	1.0	0624	6.1	1218	1.4	1820	5.9
3 M	0052	1.2	0721	5.8	1308	1.7	1918	5.7
4 TU	0149	1.3	0829	5.7	1410	1.8	2035	5.6
5 W	0251	1.4	0935	5.8	1516	1.8	2146	5.7
6 TH	0354	1.3	1031	6.0	1619	1.6	2244	5.9
7 F	0457	1.1	1122	6.2	1720	1.4	2336	6.1
8 SA	0556	1.0	1208	6.4	1817	1.1		
9 SU	0023	6.3	0648	0.8	1251	6.6	1907	0.9
10 M	0107	6.5	0734	0.8	1331	6.7	● 1954	0.8
11 TU	0149	6.6	0816	0.8	1411	6.7	2039	0.7
12 W	0230	6.7	0855	0.8	1450	6.7	2121	0.6
13 TH	0311	6.8	0932	0.8	1529	6.7	2203	0.6
14 F	0354	6.8	1009	0.9	1610	6.6	2244	0.6
15 SA	0439	6.8	1047	0.9	1652	6.5	2327	0.6
16 SU	0527	6.7	1130	1.0	1738	6.4		
17 M	0014	0.7	0619	6.5	1219	1.2	1829	6.3
18 TU	0111	0.8	0718	6.4	1317	1.4	1931	6.1
19 W	0215	0.9	0824	6.3	1426	1.4	2040	6.1
20 TH	0326	0.9	0931	6.3	1541	1.4	2147	6.3
21 F	0436	0.7	1035	6.5	1655	1.2	2251	6.4
22 SA	0540	0.6	1133	6.7	1802	1.0	2350	6.7
23 SU	0636	0.5	1227	6.9	1902	0.7		
24 M	0045	6.9	0728	0.4	1317	7.0	○ 1956	0.6
25 TU	0137	7.0	0816	0.4	1404	7.0	2046	0.5
26 W	0226	7.0	0901	0.5	1447	6.9	2133	0.5
27 TH	0313	7.0	0942	0.6	1528	6.8	2214	0.5
28 F	0356	6.9	1019	0.8	1604	6.7	2251	0.7
29 SA	0437	6.7	1052	1.0	1639	6.5	2322	0.8
30 SU	0517	6.5	1121	1.2	1715	6.4	2351	0.9

JULY

Date	Time	m	Time	m	Time	m	Time	m
1 M	0556	6.3	1152	1.3	1755	6.2		
2 TU	0024	1.0	0639	6.1	1231	1.4	1841	6.0
3 W	0107	1.1	0728	5.9	1319	1.6	1935	5.8
4 TH	0159	1.2	0823	5.8	1418	1.6	2037	5.7
5 F	0258	1.3	0924	5.8	1522	1.6	2141	5.8
6 SA	0400	1.2	1025	6.0	1625	1.5	2244	5.9
7 SU	0502	1.1	1122	6.2	1727	1.3	2342	6.1
8 M	0603	1.0	1215	6.4	1827	1.0		
9 TU	0035	6.4	0658	0.8	1304	6.6	1925	0.8
10 W	0125	6.6	0750	0.8	1350	6.7	● 2020	0.6
11 TH	0213	6.8	0839	0.7	1435	6.8	2113	0.5
12 F	0259	7.0	0925	0.7	1518	6.8	2202	0.4
13 SA	0345	7.1	1009	0.8	1601	6.8	2248	0.3
14 SU	0431	7.1	1050	0.8	1643	6.8	2331	0.3
15 M	0517	7.0	1131	0.9	1727	6.8		
16 TU	0013	0.4	0606	6.8	1213	1.0	1813	6.6
17 W	0057	0.5	0658	6.6	1300	1.1	1906	6.4
18 TH	0146	0.7	0757	6.3	1354	1.3	2008	6.2
19 F	0244	0.9	0902	6.2	1458	1.5	2117	6.1
20 SA	0354	1.1	1008	6.2	1614	1.5	2227	6.2
21 SU	0508	1.0	1110	6.3	1738	1.3	2333	6.4
22 M	0611	0.9	1207	6.5	1845	1.0		
23 TU	0032	6.6	0705	0.7	1300	6.7	1942	0.7
24 W	0126	6.8	0756	0.7	1349	6.8	○ 2033	0.5
25 TH	0215	6.9	0843	0.7	1433	6.8	2120	0.5
26 F	0301	6.9	0927	0.7	1513	6.8	2203	0.5
27 SA	0342	6.8	1006	0.9	1547	6.7	2239	0.7
28 SU	0418	6.7	1039	1.0	1619	6.6	2309	0.8
29 M	0451	6.5	1104	1.2	1650	6.5	2330	0.9
30 TU	0524	6.4	1125	1.2	1726	6.4	2350	1.0
31 W	0600	6.3	1155	1.2	1805	6.3		

AUGUST

Date	Time	m	Time	m	Time	m	Time	m
1 TH	0020	1.0	0641	6.1	1234	1.3	1850	6.1
2 F	0101	1.1	0728	6.0	1323	1.4	1942	5.9
3 SA	0155	1.3	0823	5.8	1428	1.6	2042	5.7
4 SU	0306	1.4	0928	5.8	1541	1.6	2151	5.7
5 M	0420	1.4	1038	5.9	1651	1.4	2303	5.9
6 TU	0530	1.2	1143	6.2	1759	1.1		
7 W	0008	6.3	0633	1.0	1241	6.5	1907	0.8
8 TH	0105	6.7	0732	0.8	1332	6.7	● 2010	0.5
9 F	0156	7.0	0827	0.7	1419	6.9	2106	0.3
10 SA	0244	7.2	0918	0.6	1503	7.0	2155	0.1
11 SU	0330	7.3	1003	0.6	1545	7.1	2240	0.0
12 M	0415	7.3	1045	0.6	1626	7.1	2320	0.1
13 TU	0459	7.2	1122	0.6	1707	7.1	2356	0.2
14 W	0544	7.0	1158	0.8	1750	6.9		
15 TH	0031	0.5	0630	6.6	1236	1.0	1836	6.6
16 F	0109	0.8	0722	6.2	1320	1.2	1932	6.2
17 SA	0158	1.2	0827	5.9	1417	1.5	2047	5.9
18 SU	0305	1.5	0941	5.7	1531	1.7	2210	5.9
19 M	0433	1.5	1049	5.9	1722	1.5	2320	6.1
20 TU	0549	1.3	1150	6.2	1834	1.1		
21 W	0020	6.5	0647	1.0	1244	6.5	1928	0.7
22 TH	0114	6.8	0737	0.8	1332	6.8	○ 2017	0.5
23 F	0202	7.0	0825	0.7	1416	6.8	2103	0.4
24 SA	0244	7.0	0909	0.7	1454	6.8	2144	0.5
25 SU	0321	6.8	0949	0.8	1527	6.7	2219	0.6
26 M	0352	6.7	1022	1.0	1554	6.6	2247	0.8
27 TU	0420	6.6	1044	1.1	1623	6.5	2302	1.0
28 W	0448	6.5	1058	1.1	1654	6.5	2312	1.0
29 TH	0521	6.4	1122	1.1	1729	6.4	2335	0.9
30 F	0559	6.3	1155	1.1	1810	6.3		
31 SA	0009	1.0	0641	6.1	1236	1.3	1858	6.0

Chart Datum: 2·90 metres below Ordnance Datum (Newlyn)

TIME ZONE (UTC)
For Summer Time add ONE hour in **non-shaded areas**

ENGLAND – LONDON BRIDGE

LAT 50°30′N LONG 0°05′W

TIMES AND HEIGHTS OF HIGH AND LOW WATERS

SPRING & NEAP TIDES
Dates in red are **SPRINGS**
Dates in blue are **NEAPS**

YEAR **2002**

SEPTEMBER

Day	Time	m	Time	m	Time	m	Time	m
1 SU	0052	1.3	0733	5.8	1331	1.6	1956	5.8
2 M	0156	1.6	0835	5.6	1500	1.7	2105	5.7
3 TU	0340	1.7	0953	5.6	1624	1.6	2227	5.8
4 W	0504	1.5	1114	5.9	1741	1.2	2345	6.2
5 TH	0615	1.2	1217	6.4	1855	0.8		
6 F	0045	6.7	0716	0.9	1310	6.7	1956	0.4
7 SA	0137	7.1	0812	0.7	1357	7.0	● 2050	0.1
8 SU	0224	7.4	0902	0.5	1440	7.2	2138	-0.1
9 M	0309	7.5	0948	0.4	1522	7.3	2221	-0.1
10 TU	0352	7.5	1028	0.4	1603	7.3	2258	0.0
11 W	0434	7.3	1105	0.5	1643	7.3	2330	0.2
12 TH	0516	7.0	1137	0.7	1724	7.1	2359	0.6
13 F	0557	6.6	1209	0.9	1808	6.7		
14 SA	0032	0.9	0642	6.1	1249	1.2	1900	6.2
15 SU	0118	1.4	0742	5.6	1344	1.6	2021	5.7
16 M	0223	1.8	0913	5.4	1459	1.8	2155	5.7
17 TU	0356	1.9	1028	5.6	1712	1.6	2305	6.0
18 W	0527	1.6	1129	6.0	1817	1.1		
19 TH	0003	6.5	0625	1.1	1223	6.5	1907	0.6
20 F	0055	6.8	0715	0.8	1310	6.8	1953	0.4
21 SA	0140	7.0	0802	0.6	1353	6.9	○ 2036	0.3
22 SU	0220	7.0	0846	0.6	1430	6.8	2116	0.5
23 M	0254	6.8	0925	0.7	1501	6.7	2151	0.7
24 TU	0321	6.7	0958	0.9	1527	6.6	2217	0.9
25 W	0346	6.6	1018	1.1	1553	6.5	2226	1.1
26 TH	0413	6.6	1029	1.1	1623	6.6	2234	1.0
27 F	0444	6.6	1052	1.0	1657	6.5	2259	0.9
28 SA	0520	6.4	1122	1.0	1738	6.4	2331	1.0
29 SU	0602	6.2	1159	1.2	1826	6.1		
30 M	0012	1.3	0652	5.8	1249	1.5	1924	5.8

OCTOBER

Day	Time	m	Time	m	Time	m	Time	m
1 TU	0108	1.7	0754	5.6	1418	1.8	2033	5.7
2 W	0250	2.0	0912	5.5	1603	1.6	2158	5.8
3 TH	0440	1.7	1043	5.8	1726	1.1	2321	6.3
4 F	0553	1.3	1149	6.3	1835	0.7		
5 SA	0021	6.8	0654	0.9	1241	6.8	1933	0.3
6 SU	0113	7.2	0748	0.7	1328	7.1	● 2025	0.0
7 M	0159	7.5	0838	0.5	1413	7.3	2112	-0.1
8 TU	0244	7.5	0924	0.4	1456	7.4	2154	0.0
9 W	0326	7.5	1006	0.4	1538	7.5	2230	0.1
10 TH	0407	7.3	1043	0.5	1620	7.4	2302	0.4
11 F	0447	7.0	1116	0.6	1702	7.1	2330	0.7
12 SA	0526	6.6	1148	0.9	1747	6.7		
13 SU	0002	1.1	0605	6.1	1226	1.2	1839	6.1
14 M	0046	1.5	0654	5.6	1321	1.5	2003	5.6
15 TU	0150	2.0	0842	5.3	1437	1.8	2134	5.6
16 W	0319	2.1	1000	5.5	1642	1.6	2240	6.0
17 TH	0454	1.8	1100	5.9	1746	1.1	2337	6.4
18 F	0556	1.3	1153	6.4	1836	0.7		
19 SA	0026	6.8	0646	0.9	1241	6.7	1920	0.5
20 SU	0111	7.0	0733	0.7	1323	6.8	2002	0.5
21 M	0149	6.9	0816	0.7	1400	6.8	○ 2042	0.6
22 TU	0221	6.8	0854	0.8	1431	6.6	2116	0.8
23 W	0248	6.7	0926	0.9	1459	6.6	2140	1.0
24 TH	0314	6.6	0947	1.0	1527	6.6	2150	1.1
25 F	0342	6.6	1004	1.0	1558	6.6	2206	1.0
26 SA	0414	6.6	1029	1.0	1634	6.6	2233	1.0
27 SU	0450	6.5	1100	1.0	1716	6.4	2308	1.0
28 M	0533	6.2	1139	1.2	1805	6.2	2350	1.3
29 TU	0623	5.9	1230	1.4	1904	5.9		
30 W	0046	1.7	0724	5.6	1357	1.7	2013	5.8
31 TH	0212	2.0	0841	5.6	1543	1.5	2136	5.9

NOVEMBER

Day	Time	m	Time	m	Time	m	Time	m
1 F	0409	1.8	1008	5.9	1702	1.0	2253	6.4
2 SA	0523	1.3	1115	6.4	1807	0.6	2353	6.9
3 SU	0625	1.0	1209	6.8	1904	0.3		
4 M	0045	7.2	0720	0.7	1259	7.1	● 1955	0.1
5 TU	0133	7.4	0811	0.5	1346	7.3	2042	0.1
6 W	0218	7.5	0859	0.4	1432	7.4	2125	0.1
7 TH	0301	7.4	0943	0.4	1517	7.4	2203	0.3
8 F	0342	7.2	1023	0.5	1601	7.3	2236	0.5
9 SA	0422	6.9	1059	0.6	1646	7.0	2307	0.8
10 SU	0500	6.6	1133	0.9	1732	6.6	2340	1.2
11 M	0538	6.2	1211	1.2	1825	6.1		
12 TU	0021	1.6	0622	5.8	1304	1.4	1937	5.7
13 W	0120	1.9	0751	5.4	1411	1.6	2100	5.7
14 TH	0236	2.1	0921	5.5	1535	1.6	2205	5.9
15 F	0359	1.9	1023	5.8	1657	1.3	2300	6.2
16 SA	0511	1.6	1116	6.2	1752	1.0	2350	6.5
17 SU	0607	1.2	1204	6.4	1839	0.8		
18 M	0034	6.7	0654	1.0	1247	6.6	1921	0.7
19 TU	0112	6.7	0737	0.9	1326	6.6	2000	0.8
20 W	0146	6.7	0815	0.9	1400	6.6	○ 2034	0.9
21 TH	0217	6.7	0849	0.9	1433	6.6	2101	1.0
22 F	0248	6.7	0918	0.9	1506	6.6	2123	1.0
23 SA	0319	6.6	0947	0.9	1541	6.6	2149	1.0
24 SU	0353	6.6	1018	0.9	1620	6.6	2221	1.0
25 M	0431	6.5	1054	1.0	1704	6.5	2258	1.1
26 TU	0514	6.3	1136	1.1	1754	6.3	2343	1.3
27 W	0603	6.1	1230	1.3	1851	6.1		
28 TH	0038	1.6	0702	5.9	1348	1.4	1957	6.0
29 F	0152	1.8	0815	5.8	1514	1.2	2111	6.1
30 SA	0328	1.7	0934	6.0	1629	1.0	2222	6.4

DECEMBER

Day	Time	m	Time	m	Time	m	Time	m
1 SU	0447	1.4	1041	6.4	1735	0.7	2324	6.7
2 M	0553	1.1	1140	6.7	1833	0.5		
3 TU	0018	7.0	0652	0.8	1234	7.0	1925	0.3
4 W	0108	7.2	0746	0.6	1325	7.2	● 2014	0.3
5 TH	0155	7.2	0838	0.5	1414	7.3	2059	0.4
6 F	0240	7.1	0925	0.5	1501	7.3	2140	0.5
7 SA	0322	7.0	1009	0.5	1548	7.1	2218	0.7
8 SU	0402	6.8	1049	0.7	1633	6.9	2251	1.0
9 M	0440	6.6	1125	0.9	1718	6.6	2324	1.2
10 TU	0518	6.3	1201	1.1	1805	6.3		
11 W	0000	1.5	0559	6.0	1243	1.3	1858	5.9
12 TH	0046	1.7	0653	5.7	1335	1.4	2002	5.7
13 F	0144	1.9	0811	5.6	1433	1.5	2109	5.7
14 SA	0250	1.9	0926	5.6	1534	1.5	2208	5.8
15 SU	0355	1.8	1026	5.8	1637	1.4	2301	6.0
16 M	0457	1.6	1119	6.0	1737	1.2	2349	6.3
17 TU	0555	1.3	1207	6.3	1828	1.1		
18 W	0032	6.4	0645	1.1	1251	6.4	1913	1.0
19 TH	0112	6.6	0731	0.9	1332	6.5	○ 1954	1.0
20 F	0151	6.6	0815	0.9	1411	6.6	2032	1.0
21 SA	0228	6.7	0858	0.8	1451	6.7	2107	1.0
22 SU	0305	6.6	0939	0.8	1531	6.8	2142	1.0
23 M	0342	6.6	1019	0.8	1613	6.8	2219	1.0
24 TU	0421	6.6	1100	0.8	1658	6.7	2258	1.1
25 W	0503	6.5	1143	0.9	1745	6.6	2341	1.2
26 TH	0550	6.4	1232	1.0	1838	6.5		
27 F	0031	1.3	0643	6.2	1329	1.0	1936	6.3
28 SA	0130	1.5	0746	6.1	1434	1.1	2042	6.2
29 SU	0241	1.6	0858	6.1	1547	1.1	2151	6.2
30 M	0402	1.5	1009	6.2	1701	1.0	2256	6.4
31 TU	0521	1.3	1115	6.4	1805	0.8	2354	6.6

Chart Datum: 2·90 metres below Ordnance Datum (Newlyn)

SOUTHEND-ON-SEA/ LEIGH-ON-SEA *9.4.15*

Essex **51°31′·07N 00°42′·57E**

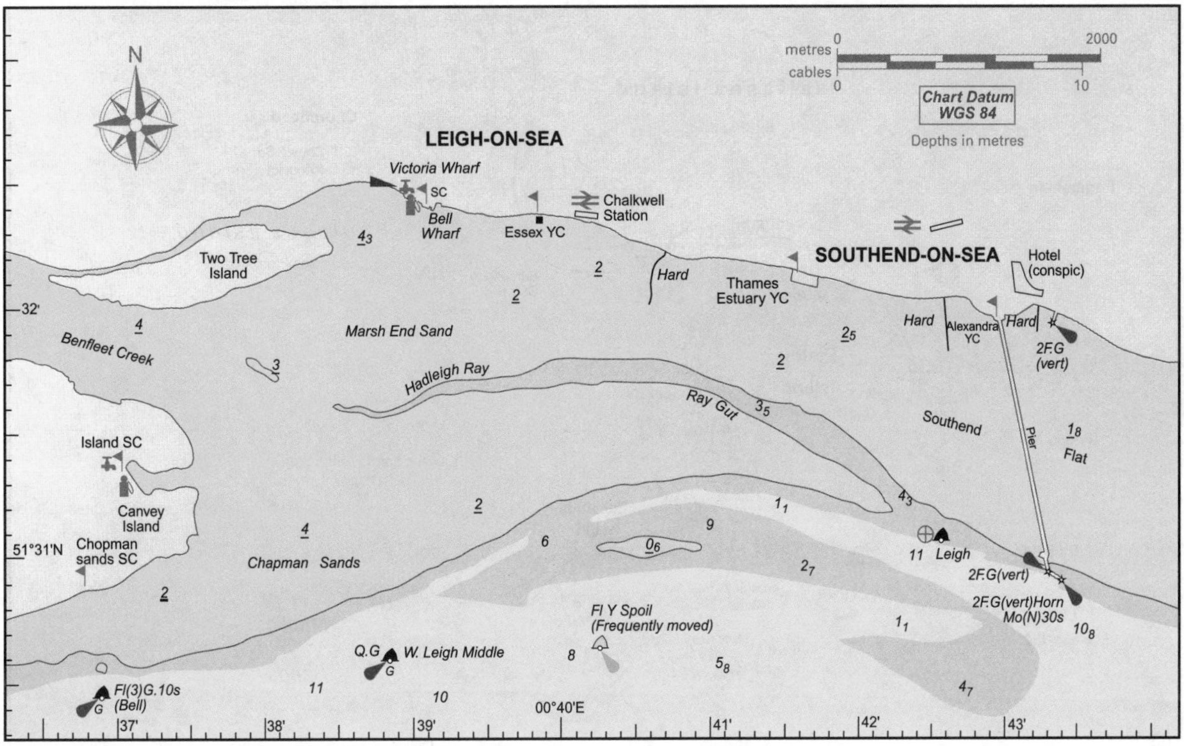

CHARTS AC *5606, 1185, 1183*; Imray C1, C2, Y18, 2100 Series; Stanfords 5, 8; OS 178

TIDES +0125 Dover; ML 3·0; Duration 0610; Zone 0 (UT)

Standard Port SHEERNESS (⟵)

Times				Height (metres)			
High Water		Low Water		MHWS	MHWN	MLWN	MLWS
0200	0800	0200	0700	5·8	4·7	1·5	0·6
1400	2000	1400	1900				
Differences SOUTHEND-ON-SEA							
−0005	0000	0000	+0005	0·0	0·0	−0·1	−0·1
CORYTON							
+0005	+0010	+0010	+0015	+0·4	+0·3	+0·1	−0·1

SHELTER The whole area dries soon after half ebb, except Ray Gut (0·4 - 4·8m) which leads to Leigh Creek and Hadleigh Ray, either side of Two Tree Island, thence to Benfleet Creek where the limit of W navigation is the Tidal Barrier just above Benfleet YC; all are buoyed, but echo-sounder is essential. At Leigh-on-Sea some drying moorings are available; or yachts can take the ground alongside Bell Wharf or Victoria Wharf. It is also possible to secure at the end of Southend Pier to collect stores, FW. NOTE: Southend-on-Sea and Leigh-on-Sea are both part of the lower PLA Area and an 8kn speed limit is enforced in inshore areas. Southend BC launches *Alec White II*, *Sidney Bates II* or *Low Way* patrol area (VHF Ch 68 16), Apr-Oct.

NAVIGATION WPT Leigh SHM buoy, 51°31′·07N 00°42′·57E, at ent to Ray Gut; this SHM buoy can be left close to port on entering Ray Gut, since there is now more water NE of it than to the SW. Appr from Shoeburyness, keep outside the W Shoebury SHM buoy, Fl G 2·5s. Beware some 3000 small boat moorings 1M either side of Southend Pier. Speed limit in Canvey Island/Hadleigh Ray areas is 8kn.

LIGHTS AND MARKS Pier lts as on chartlet.

RADIO TELEPHONE Thames Navigation Service: *Port Control London* VHF Ch 68.

TELEPHONE (Dial code 01702) Hr Mr 611889, 📠 355110; Hr Mr Leigh-on-Sea 710561; MRSC (01255) 675518; Essex Police Marine Section (01268) 775533; ⊖ (01473) 235704 (H24); Marinecall 09068 500455; Police 341212; Dr 225500; Ⓗ 348911.

FACILITIES

SOUTHEND-ON-SEA: **Southend Pier** ☎ 215620, AB first 24H free then £9.95 per day any size, M, L, FW, Bar; **Alexandra YC** ☎ 340363, Bar, FW; **Thorpe Bay YC** ☎ 587563, Bar, L, Slip, R, FW; **Thames Estuary YC** ☎ 345967; **Halfway YC** ☎ 582025, pre-book 1 ⚓, FW;**Town** EC Wed. CH, ACA, Ⓔ, V, R, Bar, ✉, Ⓑ, ⇌, ✈.

LEIGH-ON-SEA: **Essex YC** ☎ 478404, FW, Bar; **Leigh on Sea SC** ☎ 476788, FW, Bar; **Bell Wharf**, AB (1st 24hrs free, then £5.95 per subsequent 24 hrs); **Victoria Wharf** AB, SM, Slip; **Town:** EC Wed, P &D (cans), ME, El, Sh, C, CH, SM.

CANVEY ISLAND: (Dial code 01268) **Services:** Slip, M, D, FW, ME, El, Sh, C, Gas, CH, Access HW±2; **Island YC** ☎ 683729; **Benfleet YC** (on S side of Benfleet Creek on Canvey Island) ☎ 792278, Access HW±2½, M, Slip, FW, D (by day), CH, ME, El, Sh, C, Bar, V, ▣.

RIVER ROACH/HAVENGORE *9.4.16*

Essex **51°36′·98N 00°52′·14E** (Branklet SPM buoy), R Roach ❁❁❁⛵✿✿✿. **51°33′·62N 00°50′·52E**, Havengore Bridge ❁⛵✿

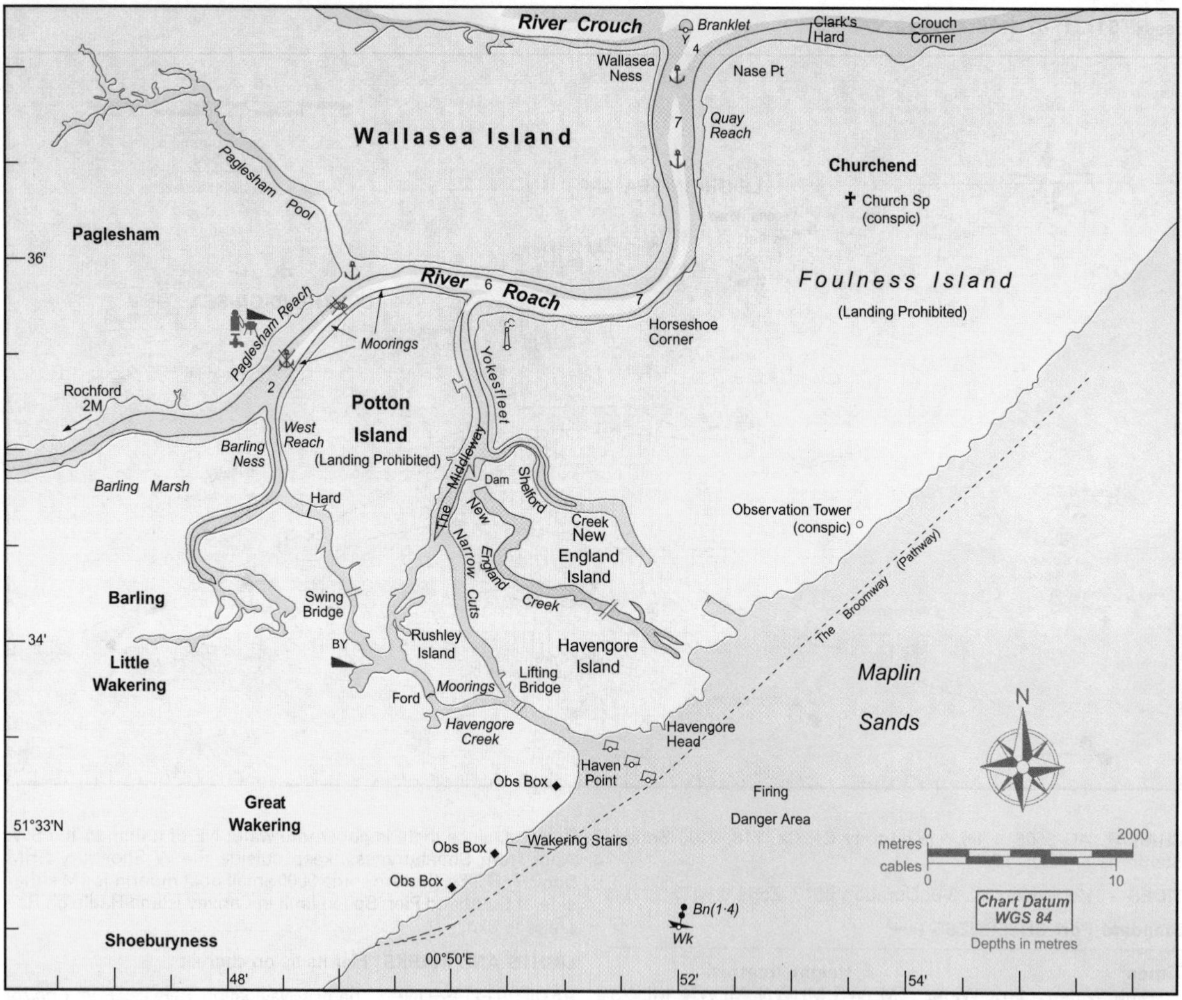

CHARTS AC *5607, 3750, 1185;* Imray C1, Y17, 2100 Series; Stanfords 4, 5; OS 178

TIDES +0110 Dover; ML 2·7; Duration 0615; Zone 0 (UT)

Standard Port WALTON-ON-THE-NAZE (⟶)

Times				Height (metres)			
High Water		Low Water		MHWS	MHWN	MLWN	MLWS
0000	0600	0500	1100	4·2	3·4	1·1	0·4
1200	1800	1700	2300				
Differences ROCHFORD							
+0050	+0040	Dries		–0·8	–1·1	Dries	

SHELTER Good. The Roach gives sheltered sailing and access to a network of secluded creeks, including Havengore (the "backdoor" from the Crouch to the Thames Estuary). No AB available in the area. ⚓s behind sea-walls can be found for all winds at: Quay Reach (often more protected than the Crouch), Paglesham Reach (possible moorings from BY at East End), West Reach, Barling Reach and Yokes Fleet. An ⚓ light is essential due to freighters H24. Speed limit 8kn. Crouch Hbr Authority controls R Roach and Crouch, out to Foulness Pt.

NAVIGATION Normal access H24 to the Roach is from R Crouch (see 9.4.17 for WPT from seaward); the ent between Branklet SPM buoy and Nase Pt is narrowed by mudbanks. Unlit buoys up-river to Barling Ness, above which few boats go. To exit at Havengore Creek, appr via Middleway and Narrow Cuts to reach the bridge before HW.

Entry via **Havengore Creek** is possible in good weather, with great care and adequate rise of tide (max draft 1·5m at HW sp). Shoeburyness Range is usually active Mon-Fri 0600-1700LT; give 24hrs notice to Range Officer by ☎. Subsequent clearance on VHF by Havengore lifting bridge (☎ HW±2, HJ); no passage unless bridge raised. Least water is over the shifting bar, just inside creek ent. From the S, cross Maplin Sands at HW –1 from S Shoebury SHM buoy, Fl G 5s (51°30′·40N 00°52′·50E), leaving Pisces wreck (conspic, 1M from ent) to port.

LIGHTS AND MARKS Unlit, but night entry to R Roach may be possible.

RADIO TELEPHONE VHF Ch 72 16 is worked by Range Officer (*Shoe Base*) (HO); Radar Control (*Shoe Radar*) (HO); & Bridge keeper (*Shoe Bridge*) (HW±2 by day). Radar guidance may be available.

TELEPHONE (Dial code 01702= Southend) Crouch Hbr Mr (01621) 783602; Range Officer 383211; Havengore Bridge 383436; Swing Br to Potton I. ☎ 219491; Marinecall 09068 500455; ⊖ (01473) 235704 (H24); MRSC (01255) 675518; Dr 218678.

FACILITIES Paglesham (East End) M £5, FW, D, slip, El, ME (from BY), Sh, Bar; **Gt Wakering:** Slip, P, D, FW, ME, El, Sh, C, CH (from BY); at Rochford **Wakering YC** ☎ 530926, M, L, Bar. **Towns** EC Wed Gt Wakering & Rochford; V, R, Bar, ✉ (Great Wakering and Barling); most facilities, Ⓑ and ⇌ in Rochford and Shoeburyness, ✈ (Southend).

BURNHAM-ON-CROUCH *9.4.17*

Essex **51°37'·50N 00°48'·23E** (Yacht Hbr)

CHARTS AC *5607, 3750, 1975, 1183*; Imray Y17, C1, 2000 Series; Stanfords 4, 5, 19, 1; OS168

TIDES +0115 Dover; ML 2·5; Duration 0610; Zone 0 (UT). Full daily predictions for Burnham are on following pages. Ranges: Sp = 5·0m; Np = 3·2m. Use Walton Tidal Curves (9.4.20)

Standard Port WALTON-ON-THE-NAZE (⟶)

Times				Height (metres)			
High Water		Low Water		MHWS	MHWN	MLWN	MLWS
0000	0600	0500	1100	4·2	3·4	1·1	0·4
1200	1800	1700	2300				
Differences WHITAKER BEACON							
+0022	+0024	+0033	+0027	+0·6	+0·5	+0·2	+0·1
HOLLIWELL POINT							
+0034	+0037	+0100	+0037	+1·1	+0·9	+0·3	+0·1
BURNHAM-ON-CROUCH (but see also full predictions)							
+0050	+0035	+0115	+0050	+1·0	+0·8	−0·1	−0·2
NORTH FAMBRIDGE							
+0115	+0050	+0130	+0100	+1·1	+0·8	0·0	−0·1
HULLBRIDGE							
+0115	+0050	+0135	+0105	+1·1	+0·8	0·0	−0·1
BATTLESBRIDGE							
+0120	+0110	Dries		−1·8	−2·0	Dries	

SHELTER River is exposed to most winds. Cliff Reach (off W edge of lower chartlet) is sheltered from SW'lies. There are six marinas or yacht hbrs. ⚓ prohib in fairway but possible just E or W of the moorings. Speed limit in moorings is 8kn. Ent to Bridge Marsh marina marked by PHM bn, Fl R 10s.

NAVIGATION WPT 51°39'·79N 01°02'·50E, S Buxey SHM buoy, Fl (3) G 15s. Appr from East Swin, or the Wallet via Spitway, into the Whitaker Chan. Near Sunken Buxey seas can be hazardous with strong wind over tide. Ray Sand Chan (dries 1·7m) is usable on the tide by shoal draft boats as a short cut from/to the Blackwater. Shoeburyness Artillery ranges lie E and S of Foulness Pt, clear of the fairway. Landing on Foulness and Bridgemarsh Is (up river) is prohibited. R. Crouch is navigable to Battlesbridge, 10M beyond Burnham.

LIGHTS AND MARKS There are few landmarks to assist entering, but Whitaker Chan and the river are lit/buoyed to 0·5M W of Essex Marina. From Sunken Buxey NCM buoy, Q, the spire of St Mary's ✠ leads 233° to Outer Crouch SCM buoy, Q (6) + L Fl 15s; thence steer 240° past Foulness Pt into the river. There is a 2·2M unlit gap between Inner Crouch SWM buoy, L Fl 10s, and Horse Shoal NCM buoy, Q.

RADIO TELEPHONE VHF Ch 80 for: Crouch Hr Mr Launch (0900-1700LT, w/e); Essex Marina; Burnham Yacht Harbour; W Wick Marina (1000-1700), also Ch M.

TELEPHONE (Dial code Maldon = 01621) Hr Mr 783602; MRSC (01255) 675518; ⊖ (01473) 235704; Marinecall 09068 500455; Police 782121; Dr 782054.

FACILITIES BURNHAM: **Burnham Yacht Hbr** ☎ 782150, 785848, Access H24, (350) £1.10 approx, D, AC, FW, ME, El, Sh, BH (30 ton), CH, Bar, Slip; **Royal Corinthian YC** ☎ 782105, AB, FW, M, L, R, Bar; **Royal Burnham YC** ☎ 782044, FW, L, R, Bar; **Crouch YC** ☎ 782252, L, FW, R, Bar; **Services:** AB, BY, C (15 ton), D, P, FW, ME, El, Sh, M, Slip, CH, ACA, Gas, SM, Gaz. **Town** EC Wed; V, R, Bar, ✉, Ⓑ, ≷, ✈ (Southend).
WALLASEA (01702): **Essex Marina** (400) ☎ (01702) 258531, 258227, BY, Gas, Bar, C (13 ton), BH (40 ton), CH, D, P, LPG, El, FW, M, ME, R, Sh, Slip, V; Ferry to Burnham Town Hard at w/ends in season, ☎ 258870; **Essex YC**; ACA.
FAMBRIDGE: **N Fambridge Yacht Stn** (150) ☎ 740370, Access HW±5, M, CH, Sh, ME, BY, C (5 ton), El, FW, Slip, Gas, Gaz; **W Wick Marina** (Stow Creek) (180) ☎ 741268, Access HW±5, Gas, Gaz, CH, El, Slip, FW, D, C (5 ton), YC, Bar; **Brandy Hole Yacht Stn** (120) ☎ (01702) 230248, L, M, ME, Sh, Slip, Gas, Gaz, Bar, BY, D, FW, Access HW±4.
ALTHORNE: **Bridge Marsh Marina** (125 + 6 Ⓥ) ☎ 740414, 742216, Access HW±4, FW, Sh, ME, El, C (8 ton), Slip.

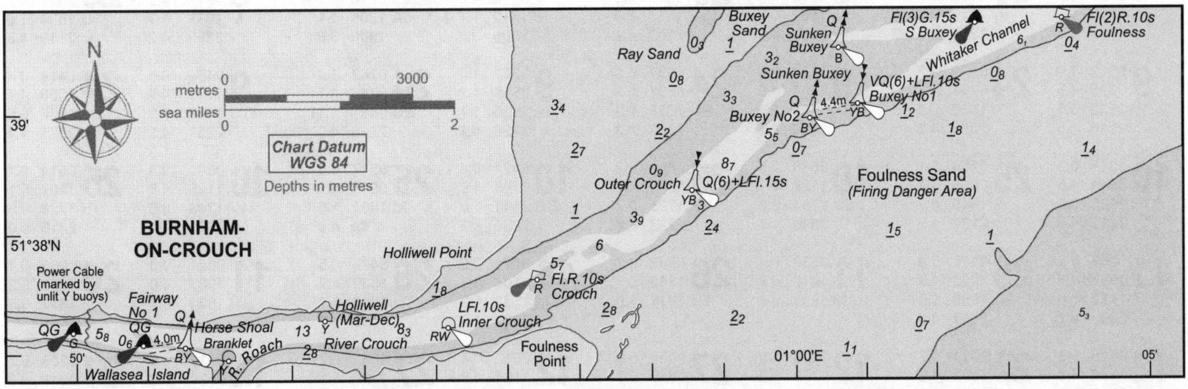

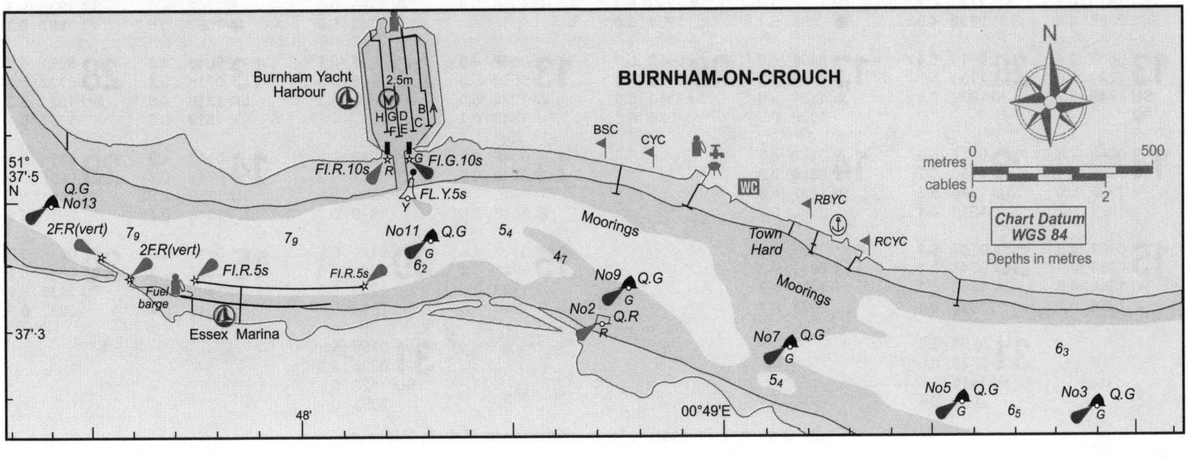

TIME ZONE (UTC)
For Summer Time add ONE hour in **non-shaded areas**

ENGLAND – BURNHAM-ON-CROUCH

LAT 51°37′N LONG 0°48′E

TIMES AND HEIGHTS OF HIGH AND LOW WATERS

SPRING & NEAP TIDES
Dates in red are SPRINGS
Dates in blue are NEAPS

YEAR **2002**

JANUARY

Date	Day	Time	m	Time	m	Time	m	Time	m
1	TU	0120	5.1	0750	0.3	1342	5.2	2003	0.5
2	W	0201	5.1	0835	0.2	1427	5.2	2042	0.7
3	TH	0243	5.0	0919	0.2	1513	5.2	2123	0.7
4	F	0328	5.0	1006	0.2	1601	5.1	2207	0.8
5	SA	0415	4.8	1056	0.2	1653	4.8	2256	0.9
6	SU	0507	4.7	1152	0.3	1749	4.6	2351	1.0
7	M	0606	4.6	1303	0.4	1852	4.5		
8	TU	0107	1.1	0715	4.5	1418	0.5	2002	4.5
9	W	0229	1.0	0826	4.5	1528	0.5	2110	4.5
10	TH	0345	0.9	0935	4.6	1628	0.5	2213	4.6
11	F	0450	0.8	1037	4.7	1723	0.5	2308	4.7
12	SA	0548	0.5	1132	4.8	1810	0.5	2358	4.8
13	SU ●	0638	0.4	1223	5.0	1849	0.7		
14	M	0043	4.8	0720	0.4	1306	5.0	1924	0.7
15	TU	0121	4.8	0759	0.3	1345	4.8	1956	0.7
16	W	0155	4.8	0833	0.4	1419	4.8	2026	0.8
17	TH	0224	4.8	0904	0.4	1451	4.7	2055	0.8
18	F	0254	4.7	0932	0.4	1523	4.7	2124	0.8
19	SA	0327	4.7	1002	0.5	1557	4.6	2158	0.8
20	SU	0404	4.6	1037	0.5	1635	4.5	2237	0.9
21	M	0446	4.5	1120	0.7	1720	4.3	2324	1.0
22	TU	0535	4.3	1215	0.8	1812	4.2		
23	W	0025	1.1	0633	4.2	1323	0.9	1917	4.1
24	TH	0139	1.2	0744	4.2	1435	0.9	2028	4.2
25	F	0254	1.1	0856	4.3	1545	0.9	2137	4.3
26	SA	0406	0.9	1002	4.5	1648	0.8	2237	4.6
27	SU	0511	0.7	1101	4.8	1743	0.7	2332	4.8
28	M ○	0610	0.4	1156	5.1	1832	0.5		
29	TU	0022	5.0	0658	0.2	1247	5.2	1913	0.4
30	W	0107	5.1	0743	0.1	1333	5.3	1952	0.4
31	TH	0151	5.2	0826	0.0	1416	5.5	2030	0.4

FEBRUARY

Date	Day	Time	m	Time	m	Time	m	Time	m
1	F	0233	5.2	0908	-0.1	1500	5.3	2110	0.4
2	SA	0314	5.2	0951	0.0	1545	5.2	2150	0.5
3	SU	0357	5.2	1034	0.1	1630	5.0	2233	0.7
4	M	0443	5.0	1121	0.2	1720	4.7	2321	0.8
5	TU	0535	4.7	1219	0.5	1814	4.5		
6	W	0023	1.0	0638	4.5	1331	0.8	1922	4.2
7	TH	0146	1.0	0757	4.3	1450	0.9	2038	4.1
8	F	0319	1.0	0916	4.3	1603	0.9	2150	4.2
9	SA	0437	0.8	1024	4.6	1704	0.9	2250	4.5
10	SU	0540	0.5	1122	4.7	1754	0.8	2343	4.7
11	M	0630	0.4	1212	4.8	1834	0.8		
12	TU	0028	4.8	0709	0.3	1255	5.0	● 1908	0.7
13	W	0106	4.8	0744	0.3	1331	4.8	1938	0.7
14	TH	0139	4.8	0814	0.3	1401	4.8	2006	0.7
15	F	0207	4.8	0840	0.3	1429	4.7	2032	0.7
16	SA	0233	4.8	0903	0.4	1456	4.7	2100	0.5
17	SU	0301	4.8	0930	0.4	1526	4.7	2131	0.5
18	M	0334	4.8	1001	0.4	1601	4.7	2205	0.7
19	TU	0411	4.7	1036	0.5	1641	4.6	2246	0.8
20	W	0453	4.5	1119	0.8	1728	4.3	2335	1.0
21	TH	0545	4.3	1221	0.9	1825	4.1		
22	F	0045	1.1	0653	4.1	1346	1.0	1939	4.0
23	SA	0211	1.1	0815	4.1	1510	1.0	2100	4.1
24	SU	0337	0.9	0937	4.3	1623	0.9	2213	4.3
25	M	0453	0.7	1045	4.7	1725	0.7	2313	4.7
26	TU	0557	0.3	1143	5.1	1817	0.5		
27	W	0006	5.0	0647	0.1	1233	5.3	○ 1857	0.4
28	TH	0053	5.2	0729	-0.1	1319	5.5	1936	0.3

MARCH

Date	Day	Time	m	Time	m	Time	m	Time	m
1	F	0135	5.3	0810	-0.3	1401	5.6	2014	0.2
2	SA	0216	5.5	0850	-0.3	1442	5.5	2053	0.2
3	SU	0256	5.5	0929	-0.1	1524	5.3	2131	0.3
4	M	0336	5.3	1008	0.0	1606	5.1	2211	0.4
5	TU	0419	5.1	1050	0.3	1649	4.7	2255	0.7
6	W	0507	4.8	1139	0.7	1738	4.3	2348	0.9
7	TH	0608	4.5	1247	0.9	1840	4.0		
8	F	0111	1.0	0732	4.2	1410	1.1	2006	3.8
9	SA	0257	1.0	0859	4.2	1535	1.1	2126	4.1
10	SU	0421	0.8	1009	4.5	1641	1.0	2230	4.3
11	M	0523	0.5	1106	4.7	1733	0.9	2323	4.6
12	TU	0613	0.4	1154	4.8	1816	0.8		
13	W	0008	4.8	0650	0.3	1236	5.0	1849	0.7
14	TH	0046	4.8	0720	0.3	1310	5.0	● 1918	0.5
15	F	0117	4.8	0746	0.3	1339	4.8	1944	0.5
16	SA	0144	4.8	0810	0.3	1403	4.8	2009	0.5
17	SU	0210	4.8	0834	0.3	1428	4.8	2037	0.4
18	M	0236	4.8	0900	0.3	1457	4.8	2108	0.4
19	TU	0308	4.8	0929	0.4	1531	4.8	2141	0.4
20	W	0343	4.8	1000	0.5	1610	4.6	2218	0.7
21	TH	0423	4.6	1039	0.8	1654	4.3	2303	0.8
22	F	0513	4.3	1132	1.0	1749	4.1		
23	SA	0009	1.0	0618	4.1	1305	1.1	1900	3.8
24	SU	0142	1.0	0746	4.1	1441	1.1	2029	4.0
25	M	0317	0.9	0918	4.3	1601	1.0	2149	4.3
26	TU	0437	0.5	1030	4.7	1702	0.7	2250	4.7
27	W	0539	0.2	1126	5.1	1755	0.5	2343	5.0
28	TH ○	0629	-0.1	1216	5.3	1838	0.3		
29	F	0030	5.2	0711	-0.3	1301	5.5	1918	0.2
30	SA	0114	5.5	0749	-0.4	1342	5.5	1955	0.1
31	SU	0156	5.5	0828	-0.3	1422	5.5	2034	0.1

APRIL

Date	Day	Time	m	Time	m	Time	m	Time	m
1	M	0235	5.5	0905	-0.1	1501	5.2	2113	0.2
2	TU	0316	5.3	0942	0.1	1541	5.0	2152	0.3
3	W	0358	5.1	1022	0.4	1621	4.7	2235	0.5
4	TH	0445	4.7	1108	0.8	1706	4.3	2328	0.8
5	F	0545	4.3	1208	1.1	1804	4.0		
6	SA	0047	0.9	0707	4.1	1331	1.3	1930	3.8
7	SU	0231	1.0	0832	4.1	1501	1.3	2052	4.0
8	M	0353	0.8	0943	4.3	1611	1.1	2159	4.2
9	TU	0454	0.5	1039	4.7	1705	0.9	2251	4.5
10	W	0541	0.4	1126	4.8	1748	0.8	2338	4.7
11	TH	0621	0.3	1207	5.0	1824	0.7		
12	F	0016	4.8	0650	0.3	1242	5.0	● 1853	0.5
13	SA	0049	4.8	0716	0.3	1310	4.8	1919	0.5
14	SU	0117	4.8	0740	0.3	1335	4.8	1946	0.4
15	M	0145	4.8	0807	0.4	1402	4.8	2016	0.4
16	TU	0215	4.8	0834	0.4	1433	4.8	2048	0.4
17	W	0247	4.8	0904	0.4	1506	4.7	2122	0.4
18	TH	0324	4.8	0935	0.5	1546	4.6	2200	0.5
19	F	0406	4.6	1015	0.8	1630	4.3	2248	0.7
20	SA	0457	4.3	1109	1.0	1725	4.1	2353	0.8
21	SU	0604	4.2	1237	1.2	1836	4.0		
22	M	0126	0.8	0730	4.1	1414	1.2	2003	4.0
23	TU	0259	0.7	0858	4.5	1534	1.0	2119	4.3
24	W	0414	0.3	1006	4.7	1636	0.8	2221	4.7
25	TH	0514	0.1	1102	5.1	1728	0.5	2315	5.0
26	F	0606	-0.1	1152	5.3	1817	0.3		
27	SA	0005	5.2	0649	-0.3	1239	5.3	○ 1857	0.2
28	SU	0051	5.3	0727	-0.3	1321	5.3	1937	0.1
29	M	0134	5.5	0805	-0.1	1401	5.2	2017	0.1
30	TU	0216	5.3	0842	0.1	1439	5.1	2057	0.2

Chart Datum: 2·35 metres below Ordnance Datum (Newlyn)

TIME ZONE (UTC)
For Summer Time add ONE hour in **non-shaded areas**

ENGLAND – BURNHAM-ON-CROUCH

LAT 51°37′N LONG 0°48′E

TIMES AND HEIGHTS OF HIGH AND LOW WATERS

SPRING & NEAP TIDES
Dates in red are SPRINGS
Dates in blue are NEAPS

YEAR **2002**

MAY

Date	Time	m	Time	m	Time	m	Time	m
1 W	0257	5.2	0919	0.3	1518	4.8	2139	0.3
2 TH	0341	5.0	0958	0.5	1557	4.6	2222	0.4
3 F	0428	4.7	1042	0.9	1640	4.3	2315	0.7
4 SA	0523	4.3	1136	1.2	1734	4.1		
5 SU	0024	0.8	0633	4.1	1251	1.3	1846	4.0
6 M	0153	0.9	0751	4.1	1416	1.3	2004	4.0
7 TU	0312	0.8	0901	4.3	1531	1.2	2112	4.2
8 W	0412	0.7	0959	4.5	1627	1.0	2208	4.5
9 TH	0500	0.5	1046	4.7	1713	0.8	2254	4.6
10 F	0540	0.4	1128	4.8	1752	0.7	2335	4.7
11 SA	0615	0.4	1205	4.8	1824	0.5		
12 SU	0013	4.7	0644	0.4	1238	4.8	● 1854	0.5
13 M	0048	4.8	0714	0.4	1308	4.8	1926	0.4
14 TU	0121	4.8	0744	0.4	1340	4.8	1959	0.4
15 W	0156	4.8	0814	0.5	1414	4.8	2034	0.4
16 TH	0232	4.8	0847	0.5	1450	4.7	2112	0.4
17 F	0312	4.8	0923	0.7	1530	4.6	2154	0.4
18 SA	0357	4.7	1005	0.9	1616	4.3	2246	0.5
19 SU	0452	4.5	1101	1.0	1713	4.2	2348	0.7
20 M	0557	4.3	1215	1.1	1821	4.1		
21 TU	0111	0.5	0713	4.3	1343	1.1	1937	4.2
22 W	0236	0.4	0830	4.5	1501	1.0	2046	4.5
23 TH	0348	0.2	0937	4.7	1606	0.8	2149	4.7
24 F	0448	0.1	1034	5.0	1701	0.5	2245	5.0
25 SA	0540	0.0	1126	5.1	1754	0.4	2339	5.1
26 SU ○	0626	0.0	1215	5.2	1840	0.3		
27 M	0029	5.2	0706	0.0	1300	5.1	1923	0.2
28 TU	0115	5.2	0745	0.1	1341	5.1	2005	0.2
29 W	0159	5.2	0822	0.3	1420	5.0	2047	0.2
30 TH	0241	5.1	0859	0.5	1459	4.8	2129	0.3
31 F	0325	4.8	0937	0.7	1537	4.6	2212	0.4

JUNE

Date	Time	m	Time	m	Time	m	Time	m
1 SA	0410	4.6	1018	0.9	1618	4.5	2259	0.5
2 SU	0458	4.5	1103	1.1	1705	4.2	2351	0.8
3 M	0554	4.2	1202	1.3	1802	4.1		
4 TU	0059	0.8	0657	4.1	1316	1.3	1907	4.1
5 W	0211	0.8	0804	4.2	1432	1.2	2013	4.2
6 TH	0314	0.8	0905	4.3	1535	1.1	2113	4.3
7 F	0407	0.7	0957	4.6	1626	1.0	2206	4.5
8 SA	0453	0.5	1044	4.7	1711	0.8	2252	4.6
9 SU	0534	0.5	1126	4.8	1752	0.7	2338	4.7
10 M ●	0616	0.5	1207	4.8	1831	0.5		
11 TU	0020	4.8	0651	0.5	1245	4.8	1908	0.4
12 W	0101	4.8	0726	0.5	1323	4.8	1946	0.4
13 TH	0140	5.0	0801	0.5	1400	4.8	2027	0.3
14 F	0221	5.0	0838	0.7	1439	4.7	2108	0.3
15 SA	0304	5.0	0917	0.8	1522	4.7	2152	0.3
16 SU	0352	4.8	1000	0.9	1609	4.6	2242	0.3
17 M	0445	4.7	1050	1.0	1702	4.5	2338	0.4
18 TU	0544	4.6	1149	1.1	1802	4.5		
19 W	0049	0.4	0649	4.6	1306	1.1	1907	4.5
20 TH	0205	0.4	0758	4.6	1424	1.0	2013	4.6
21 F	0317	0.3	0904	4.7	1535	0.9	2119	4.7
22 SA	0420	0.2	1006	4.8	1638	0.7	2220	4.8
23 SU	0515	0.2	1102	4.8	1736	0.5	2319	5.0
24 M ○	0606	0.2	1154	5.0	1828	0.4		
25 TU	0013	5.0	0649	0.3	1243	5.0	1914	0.3
26 W	0103	5.1	0727	0.4	1326	5.0	1957	0.3
27 TH	0147	5.0	0804	0.5	1405	4.8	2039	0.3
28 F	0229	5.0	0841	0.7	1442	4.8	2119	0.3
29 SA	0309	4.8	0916	0.8	1518	4.7	2155	0.4
30 SU	0349	4.7	0951	0.9	1553	4.6	2232	0.5

JULY

Date	Time	m	Time	m	Time	m	Time	m
1 M	0428	4.5	1028	1.0	1633	4.5	2311	0.7
2 TU	0511	4.3	1111	1.1	1719	4.3	2356	0.8
3 W	0559	4.2	1205	1.2	1811	4.2		
4 TH	0056	0.8	0655	4.2	1314	1.3	1912	4.2
5 F	0201	0.9	0800	4.2	1424	1.2	2016	4.2
6 SA	0305	0.8	0902	4.3	1530	1.1	2118	4.3
7 SU	0404	0.8	1000	4.6	1627	1.0	2215	4.5
8 M	0458	0.7	1051	4.7	1721	0.8	2307	4.7
9 TU	0547	0.7	1140	4.8	1812	0.7	2357	4.8
10 W ●	0632	0.5	1225	5.0	1855	0.4		
11 TH	0045	5.0	0711	0.5	1308	5.0	1937	0.3
12 F	0129	5.1	0749	0.7	1350	5.0	2019	0.2
13 SA	0213	5.1	0828	0.7	1431	5.0	2101	0.2
14 SU	0257	5.1	0908	0.7	1512	5.0	2144	0.1
15 M	0342	5.1	0949	0.8	1556	5.0	2229	0.2
16 TU	0430	5.0	1033	0.8	1643	4.8	2317	0.2
17 W	0523	4.8	1124	0.9	1736	4.7		
18 TH	0016	0.3	0619	4.6	1227	1.0	1834	4.6
19 F	0128	0.5	0724	4.5	1346	1.0	1944	4.6
20 SA	0244	0.5	0834	4.5	1507	1.0	2055	4.6
21 SU	0353	0.7	0942	4.6	1621	0.9	2205	4.7
22 M	0455	0.5	1044	4.7	1726	0.7	2308	4.8
23 TU	0548	0.5	1140	4.8	1823	0.4		
24 W	0005	5.0	0634	0.7	1229	5.0	○ 1908	0.4
25 TH	0054	5.0	0711	0.7	1313	5.0	1949	0.3
26 F	0136	5.0	0747	0.7	1351	5.0	2027	0.3
27 SA	0215	5.0	0821	0.8	1424	4.8	2100	0.3
28 SU	0249	4.8	0852	0.8	1455	4.8	2130	0.4
29 M	0321	4.7	0922	0.9	1526	4.8	2156	0.4
30 TU	0353	4.7	0953	0.9	1558	4.7	2227	0.5
31 W	0428	4.6	1030	1.0	1636	4.6	2304	0.7

AUGUST

Date	Time	m	Time	m	Time	m	Time	m
1 TH	0508	4.5	1114	1.1	1722	4.5	2351	0.8
2 F	0556	4.3	1209	1.2	1815	4.2		
3 SA	0056	0.9	0655	4.2	1322	1.2	1920	4.2
4 SU	0209	1.0	0806	4.2	1437	1.2	2032	4.2
5 M	0321	1.0	0918	4.3	1549	1.1	2142	4.3
6 TU	0426	0.9	1021	4.6	1655	0.9	2244	4.6
7 W	0524	0.8	1118	4.8	1755	0.7	2341	5.0
8 TH ●	0615	0.7	1208	5.0	1843	0.4		
9 F	0030	5.1	0656	0.7	1253	5.1	1926	0.2
10 SA	0116	5.3	0734	0.5	1335	5.2	2007	0.1
11 SU	0159	5.3	0813	0.5	1416	5.3	2047	0.0
12 M	0241	5.5	0851	0.5	1456	5.3	2127	0.0
13 TU	0325	5.3	0930	0.5	1536	5.2	2207	0.1
14 W	0409	5.2	1012	0.7	1620	5.1	2250	0.2
15 TH	0455	5.0	1059	0.8	1708	5.0	2340	0.4
16 F	0547	4.6	1153	1.0	1806	4.7		
17 SA	0047	0.8	0650	4.3	1312	1.1	1919	4.5
18 SU	0207	0.9	0807	4.2	1446	1.1	2041	4.3
19 M	0329	1.0	0923	4.3	1611	0.9	2157	4.6
20 TU	0437	1.0	1030	4.6	1721	0.7	2302	4.7
21 W	0532	0.9	1126	4.8	1816	0.4	2355	5.0
22 TH ○	0619	0.8	1214	5.0	1857	0.3		
23 F	0042	5.1	0655	0.8	1257	5.1	1933	0.3
24 SA	0121	5.1	0728	0.8	1333	5.0	2005	0.3
25 SU	0156	5.0	0759	0.8	1402	5.0	2033	0.4
26 M	0224	4.8	0827	0.8	1428	5.0	2056	0.4
27 TU	0249	4.8	0854	0.8	1454	4.8	2119	0.4
28 W	0316	4.8	0923	0.8	1524	4.8	2147	0.5
29 TH	0348	4.7	0956	0.8	1558	4.7	2219	0.7
30 F	0425	4.6	1035	0.9	1637	4.6	2259	0.8
31 SA	0508	4.5	1124	1.1	1725	4.3	2353	1.0

Chart Datum: 2·35 metres below Ordnance Datum (Newlyn)

TIME ZONE (UTC)
For Summer Time add ONE hour in **non-shaded areas**

ENGLAND – BURNHAM-ON-CROUCH

LAT 51°37′N LONG 0°48′E

TIMES AND HEIGHTS OF HIGH AND LOW WATERS

SPRING & NEAP TIDES
Dates in **red** are **SPRINGS**
Dates in **blue** are **NEAPS**

YEAR **2002**

SEPTEMBER

Date	Day	Time m	Time m	Time m	Time m
1	SU	0603 4.2	1232 1.2	1827 4.1	
2	M	0117 1.2	0714 4.1	1356 1.2	1949 4.1
3	TU	0244 1.2	0838 4.2	1519 1.1	2115 4.3
4	W	0358 1.1	0954 4.5	1634 0.9	2225 4.6
5	TH	0501 0.9	1054 4.8	1737 0.5	2323 5.0
6	F	0554 0.8	1146 5.1	1827 0.2	
7	SA	0013 5.3	0636 0.5	1231 5.3	● 1908 0.1
8	SU	0059 5.5	0715 0.5	1314 5.5	1947 -0.1
9	M	0141 5.6	0753 0.4	1355 5.5	2027 -0.1
10	TU	0221 5.6	0831 0.4	1434 5.6	2104 0.0
11	W	0301 5.5	0911 0.4	1514 5.5	2141 0.1
12	TH	0343 5.2	0952 0.5	1556 5.3	2222 0.3
13	F	0427 5.0	1036 0.7	1643 5.0	2308 0.7
14	SA	0515 4.6	1130 0.9	1741 4.6	
15	SU	0008 1.0	0616 4.2	1249 1.1	1859 4.3
16	M	0132 1.2	0740 4.1	1431 1.1	2030 4.3
17	TU	0304 1.3	0903 4.2	1558 0.9	2147 4.5
18	W	0417 1.2	1010 4.5	1704 0.7	2247 4.8
19	TH	0512 1.1	1105 4.8	1756 0.4	2338 5.0
20	F	0557 0.9	1152 5.0	1836 0.3	
21	SA	0021 5.1	0635 0.8	1233 5.1	○ 1908 0.3
22	SU	0059 5.1	0705 0.8	1307 5.1	1936 0.4
23	M	0130 5.0	0733 0.8	1334 5.0	2000 0.4
24	TU	0154 5.0	0800 0.7	1358 5.0	2022 0.5
25	W	0216 4.8	0827 0.7	1424 5.0	2046 0.5
26	TH	0242 4.8	0856 0.7	1453 4.8	2113 0.5
27	F	0313 4.8	0929 0.8	1527 4.8	2142 0.7
28	SA	0349 4.7	1005 0.9	1604 4.7	2217 0.9
29	SU	0430 4.6	1051 1.0	1650 4.5	2304 1.1
30	M	0523 4.2	1155 1.2	1751 4.2	

OCTOBER

Date	Day	Time m	Time m	Time m	Time m
1	TU	0027 1.3	0630 4.1	1325 1.2	1915 4.1
2	W	0209 1.3	0802 4.1	1454 1.0	2051 4.2
3	TH	0330 1.2	0924 4.3	1611 0.8	2204 4.7
4	F	0434 1.0	1025 4.7	1712 0.4	2300 5.1
5	SA	0527 0.8	1117 5.1	1804 0.1	2350 5.3
6	SU	0614 0.5	1205 5.3	1847 0.0	●
7	M	0036 5.6	0653 0.4	1249 5.5	1925 -0.1
8	TU	0117 5.6	0732 0.3	1331 5.6	2002 -0.1
9	W	0158 5.6	0812 0.3	1411 5.6	2040 0.0
10	TH	0237 5.3	0852 0.3	1452 5.5	2118 0.2
11	F	0318 5.2	0933 0.4	1535 5.2	2156 0.5
12	SA	0359 4.8	1019 0.7	1623 5.0	2241 0.9
13	SU	0445 4.5	1115 0.9	1722 4.5	2338 1.2
14	M	0545 4.2	1233 1.0	1839 4.2	
15	TU	0059 1.5	0709 4.0	1410 1.0	2007 4.2
16	W	0232 1.6	0832 4.1	1532 0.9	2121 4.5
17	TH	0347 1.3	0940 4.5	1634 0.7	2219 4.7
18	F	0442 1.1	1034 4.7	1724 0.5	2308 5.0
19	SA	0528 0.9	1120 5.0	1804 0.4	2350 5.1
20	SU	0608 0.8	1200 5.0	1836 0.4	
21	M	0026 5.1	0640 0.8	1235 5.0	○ 1904 0.5
22	TU	0057 5.0	0707 0.7	1304 5.0	1927 0.5
23	W	0122 5.0	0734 0.7	1330 4.8	1952 0.5
24	TH	0146 5.0	0803 0.7	1358 4.8	2017 0.7
25	F	0214 5.0	0834 0.7	1429 4.8	2045 0.7
26	SA	0245 4.8	0908 0.7	1503 4.8	2115 0.8
27	SU	0321 4.7	0946 0.8	1543 4.7	2150 0.9
28	M	0402 4.5	1033 0.9	1630 4.5	2237 1.1
29	TU	0453 4.2	1135 1.0	1731 4.2	2348 1.3
30	W	0601 4.1	1300 1.0	1850 4.2	
31	TH	0130 1.5	0729 4.1	1427 0.9	2021 4.3

NOVEMBER

Date	Day	Time m	Time m	Time m	Time m
1	F	0255 1.2	0847 4.3	1541 0.5	2134 4.7
2	SA	0401 1.0	0950 4.7	1643 0.3	2231 5.1
3	SU	0456 0.8	1044 5.1	1736 0.1	2321 5.3
4	M	0546 0.5	1134 5.3	1822 0.0	●
5	TU	0009 5.5	0632 0.4	1221 5.5	1903 0.0
6	W	0053 5.5	0713 0.3	1307 5.6	1940 0.1
7	TH	0134 5.3	0755 0.3	1350 5.5	2018 0.2
8	F	0215 5.2	0837 0.3	1433 5.3	2056 0.4
9	SA	0255 5.1	0921 0.4	1518 5.2	2136 0.7
10	SU	0335 4.8	1008 0.5	1607 4.8	2219 1.0
11	M	0419 4.5	1103 0.8	1702 4.5	2311 1.3
12	TU	0514 4.2	1212 0.9	1810 4.2	
13	W	0020 1.6	0626 4.1	1336 0.9	1928 4.2
14	TH	0146 1.6	0745 4.1	1451 0.9	2038 4.3
15	F	0303 1.5	0853 4.3	1552 0.8	2138 4.6
16	SA	0403 1.2	0949 4.6	1642 0.7	2226 4.7
17	SU	0452 1.0	1037 4.7	1724 0.5	2309 4.8
18	M	0533 0.8	1119 4.8	1800 0.5	2347 5.0
19	TU	0611 0.7	1156 4.8	1831 0.5	
20	W	0020 5.0	0641 0.7	1231 4.8	○ 1859 0.7
21	TH	0051 5.0	0711 0.5	1304 4.8	1927 0.7
22	F	0121 5.0	0744 0.5	1337 4.8	1957 0.7
23	SA	0152 4.8	0818 0.5	1412 4.8	2027 0.8
24	SU	0225 4.8	0856 0.5	1449 4.8	2100 0.9
25	M	0302 4.7	0936 0.7	1531 4.7	2138 1.0
26	TU	0344 4.6	1023 0.8	1620 4.6	2225 1.1
27	W	0434 4.3	1121 0.8	1718 4.5	2326 1.2
28	TH	0538 4.2	1234 0.8	1827 4.3	
29	F	0047 1.3	0653 4.2	1354 0.7	1946 4.5
30	SA	0210 1.2	0808 4.5	1508 0.5	2056 4.6

DECEMBER

Date	Day	Time m	Time m	Time m	Time m
1	SU	0323 1.0	0913 4.7	1611 0.3	2157 4.8
2	M	0424 0.8	1011 5.0	1707 0.2	2251 5.1
3	TU	0521 0.5	1106 5.2	1758 0.1	2343 5.2
4	W	0613 0.4	1158 5.3	1842 0.2	●
5	TH	0030 5.2	0659 0.3	1248 5.3	1922 0.2
6	F	0114 5.1	0743 0.3	1334 5.3	2000 0.4
7	SA	0156 5.1	0828 0.3	1419 5.2	2039 0.5
8	SU	0235 5.0	0913 0.3	1504 5.1	2118 0.8
9	M	0316 4.7	0959 0.4	1550 4.8	2157 1.0
10	TU	0357 4.6	1047 0.5	1638 4.6	2240 1.2
11	W	0443 4.5	1140 0.8	1731 4.3	2332 1.3
12	TH	0538 4.2	1243 0.9	1830 4.2	
13	F	0040 1.5	0642 4.1	1351 0.9	1938 4.1
14	SA	0157 1.5	0751 4.2	1453 0.9	2040 4.2
15	SU	0308 1.2	0854 4.3	1548 0.8	2136 4.5
16	M	0405 1.1	0948 4.5	1636 0.8	2223 4.6
17	TU	0453 0.9	1037 4.6	1718 0.7	2307 4.7
18	W	0536 0.8	1122 4.7	1759 0.7	2348 4.8
19	TH	0617 0.7	1204 4.8	1836 0.7	○
20	F	0025 4.8	0653 0.5	1244 4.8	1909 0.7
21	SA	0103 4.8	0730 0.5	1322 5.0	1943 0.7
22	SU	0138 4.8	0808 0.4	1359 5.0	2016 0.8
23	M	0214 4.8	0848 0.4	1439 5.0	2052 0.8
24	TU	0252 4.7	0930 0.4	1523 4.8	2130 0.9
25	W	0333 4.7	1015 0.4	1610 4.7	2215 0.9
26	TH	0420 4.6	1104 0.4	1702 4.6	2305 1.0
27	F	0515 4.5	1202 0.5	1802 4.5	
28	SA	0005 1.1	0618 4.5	1313 0.5	1909 4.5
29	SU	0122 1.1	0729 4.5	1429 0.5	2018 4.5
30	M	0242 1.0	0838 4.6	1539 0.4	2125 4.6
31	TU	0355 0.9	0945 4.7	1642 0.4	2226 4.7

Chart Datum: 2·35 metres below Ordnance Datum (Newlyn)

RIVER BLACKWATER *9.4.18*

Essex **51°45'·33N 00°54'·90E** (5ca S of Nass bn)
Rtgs: Maldon ; Heybridge Basin

CHARTS AC *5607, 3741, 1975, 1183*; Imray Y17, C1, 2000 Series; OS 168; Stanfords 5, 6.

TIDES Maldon +0130 Dover; ML 2·8; Duration 0620; Zone 0 (UT)

Standard Port WALTON-ON-THE-NAZE (⟶)

Times				Height (metres)			
High Water		Low Water		MHWS	MHWN	MLWN	MLWS
0000	0600	0500	1100	4·2	3·4	1·1	0·4
1200	1800	1700	2300				
Differences SUNK HEAD							
0000	+0002	–0002	+0002	–0·3	–0·3	–0·1	–0·1
WEST MERSEA							
+0035	+0015	+0055	+0010	+0·9	+0·4	+0·1	+0·1
BRADWELL							
+0035	+0023	+0047	+0004	+1·0	+0·8	+0·2	0·0
OSEA ISLAND							
+0057	+0045	+0050	+0007	+1·1	+0·9	+0·1	0·0
MALDON							
+0107	+0055	No data		–1·3	–1·1	No data	

SHELTER Good, as appropriate to wind. Marinas at Tollesbury, Bradwell and Maylandsea. ⚓ restricted by oyster beds and many moorings. At W Mersea there is a pontoon for landing (limited waiting); also pile moorings in Ray Chan or ⚓ in Mersea Quarters, access approx HW±1½. Berths at Heybridge Basin, access via lock approx HW –1 to HW; a SHM buoy opposite the lock marks the deep water ent. Access to Chelmer & Blackwater Canal (not navigable).

NAVIGATION WPT Knoll NCM, Q, 51°43'·88N 01°05'·07E, 107°/287° from/to Nass bn, ECM VQ (3) 5s, 6·7M. Speed limit 8kn W of Osea Is.
WEST MERSEA: Avoid oyster beds between Cobmarsh and Packing Marsh Is and in Salcott Chan. ⚓ in Mersea Quarters.
BRADWELL: No dangers, but only suitable for small craft and area gets very crowded; see below under Lts & Marks.
TOLLESBURY FLEET: Proceeding via S Chan up Woodrolfe Creek, a tide gauge shows depth over marina ent sill (approx 3m at MHWS and 2m at MHWN). Speed limits: Woodrolfe Creek 4kn upper reaches; Tollesbury Fleet S Chan 8kn.

LIGHTS AND MARKS Bradwell Creek ent has bn QR with tide gauge showing depth in ft in Creek; this bn must be left to **STBD** on entry. 4 PHM buoys, 3 SHM withies and 2 B/W △ ldg bns mark the chan which doglegs past a SHM buoy to marina ent. Power stn is conspic 7ca NNE.
MALDON: From S of Osea Is, 'The Doctor', No 3 SHM buoy on with Blackwater SC lt, Iso G 5s, lead 300° approx up the chan; or No 3 and No 8 buoys in line at 305°. Beyond No 8 buoy, the chan which shifts and carries 0·2m, is lighted and buoyed up to Maldon. Access near HW; pontoons dry to soft mud.

RADIO TELEPHONE Bradwell and Tollesbury Marinas VHF Ch **80** M (HO). Blackwater Marina VHF Ch M, 0900-2300.Heybridge Lock VHF Ch 80 HW -2+1. Clark and Carter launch - call CC1.

TELEPHONE (Dial code 01621 Maldon; 01206 Colchester/West Mersea) Hr Mr 856726; R. Bailiff (Maldon Quay) 856487, Office 875837, Mobile 0860 456802; Canal lockmaster 853506; MRSC (01255) 675518; ⊜ (01473) 235704 (H24); Marinecall 09068 500455; Police (Colchester) 762212, (W Mersea) 382930; Dr 854118, or W Mersea 382015.

FACILITIES
WEST MERSEA (01206): **W Mersea YC** 382947, 📠 386261, Bar, launch service call YC 1; **Town** EC Wed; P, D, FW, ME, El, CH, V, R, Bar, ✉, Ⓑ, ⇌ (bus to Colchester, Ⓗ ☎ 01206-853535), ✈ (Southend/Stansted).
TOLLESBURY (01621): **Tollesbury Marina** (220+20 Ⓥ) ☎ 869202, 📠 868489, £1.41, marina@woodrolfe.demon.co.uk Access HW±1½, Slip, D, AC, BH (20 ton), Gas, Gaz, LPG, FW, El, ME, Sh, C (5 ton), CH, R, Bar, ⊡; **Tollesbury Cruising Club** ☎ 869561, Bar, R, M. **Village** EC Wed; P, V, R, Bar, ✉, Ⓑ (Tues, Thurs 1000-1430), ⇌ (bus to Witham), ✈ (Southend or Cambridge).
BRADWELL (01621): **Bradwell Marina** (280, some Ⓥ) ☎ 776235, 📠 776393, £1.12 approx, Slip, AC, Gas, Gaz, LPG, D, P, FW, ME, El, Sh, BH (16 ton), CH, R, Bar, Access HW±4½, approx 2m; **Bradwell Quay YC** ☎ 776539, M, FW, Bar, L, Slip. **Town** ✉, ⇌ (bus/taxi to Southminster), ✈ (Southend).
MAYLANDSEA: **Blackwater Marina** (230) ☎ 740264, 📠 742122, £7, Slip, D, Sh, CH, R, Bar; Access HW±2. 150 moorings in chan. Taxi to Southminster ⇌.
MALDON (01621): **Maldon Quay** Hr Mr/River bailiff ☎ 856487, Mobile ☎ 0860 456802; M, P, D, FW, AB < 8m £8, > 8m £10, Slip; **Maldon Little Ship Club** ☎ 854139, Bar; **Services:** Slip, D, Sh, CH, M, ACA, SM, ME, El, Ⓔ. **Town** EC Wed; ✉, Ⓑ, ⇌ (bus to Chelmsford, Ⓗ ☎ (01245) 440761), ✈ (Southend, Cambridge or Stansted).
HEYBRIDGE BASIN (01621): **Lockmaster** ☎ 853506, VHF Ch80 opens HW±1 approx. **Blackwater SC** ☎ 853923, L, FW; **Services:** at CRS Marine ☎ 854684 (pontoon outside lock), Slip, D, L, M, FW, ME, El, SH, C. Bus to Heybridge/Maldon.

4

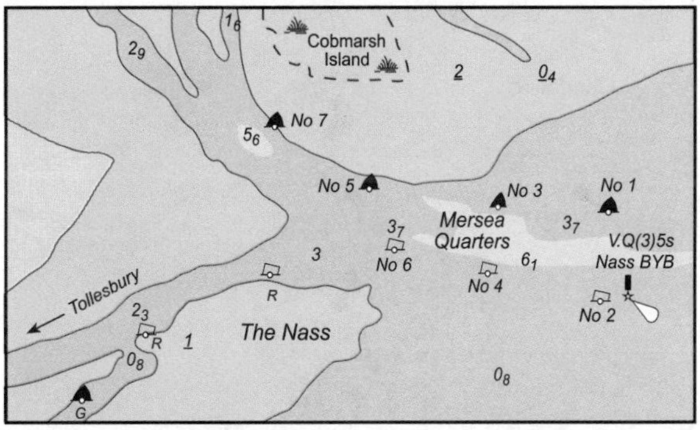

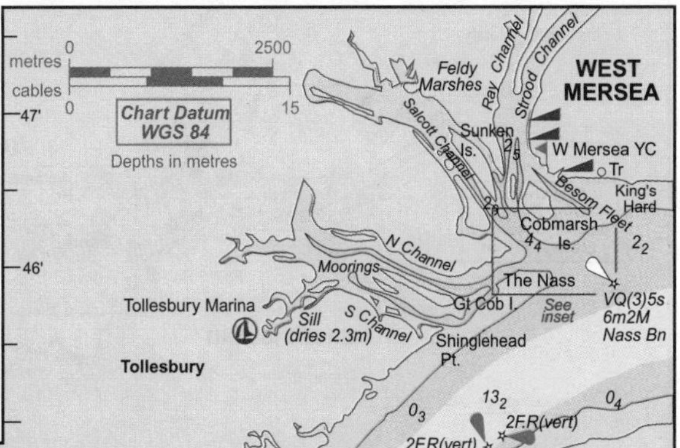
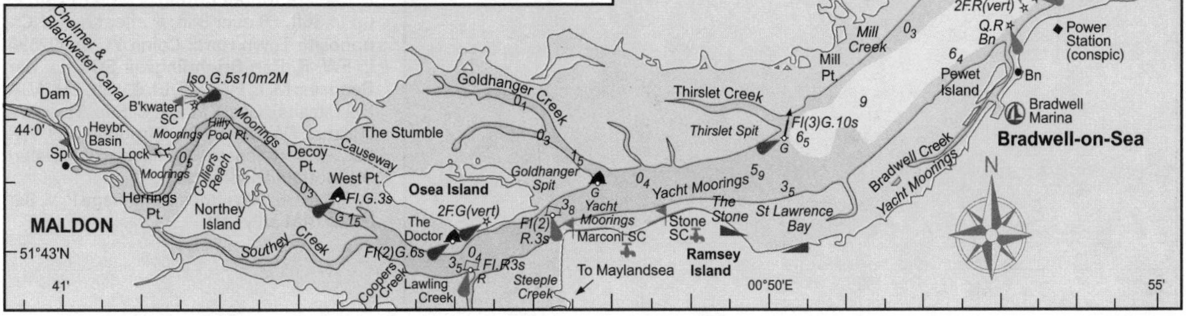

RIVER COLNE *9.4.19*

Essex **51°47′·98N 01°00′·60E** (Brightlingsea) ☸☸⚓⚓⚓✿✿

CHARTS AC *5607, 3741, 1975, 1183*; Imray Y17, C1, 2000 Series; Stan 5, 6; OS 168

TIDES +0050 Dover; ML 2·5; Duration 0615; Zone 0 (UT)

Standard Port WALTON-ON-THE-NAZE (⟶)

Times				Height (metres)			
High Water		Low Water		MHWS	MHWN	MLWN	MLWS
0000	0600	0500	1100	4·2	3·4	1·1	0·4
1200	1800	1700	2300				
Differences BRIGHTLINGSEA							
+0025	+0021	+0046	+0004	+0·8	+0·4	+0·1	0·0
COLCHESTER							
+0035	+0025	Dries		0·0	−0·3	Dries	
CLACTON-ON-SEA							
+0012	+0010	+0025	+0008	+0·3	+0·1	+0·1	+0·1

SHELTER Suitable shelter can be found from most winds, but outer hbr is exposed to W'lies. In the creek S of Cindery Island are moorings (as shown) and long pontoons in about 1·5m, with possible AB for ⓥs. ⚓ prohib in Brightlingsea Hbr, but there are ⚓s to the NW of Mersea Stone Pt and in Pyefleet Chan, E of Pewit Island. R Colne is navigable for 4·5m draft to Wivenhoe, where the river dries; and to The Hythe, Colchester (3m draft).

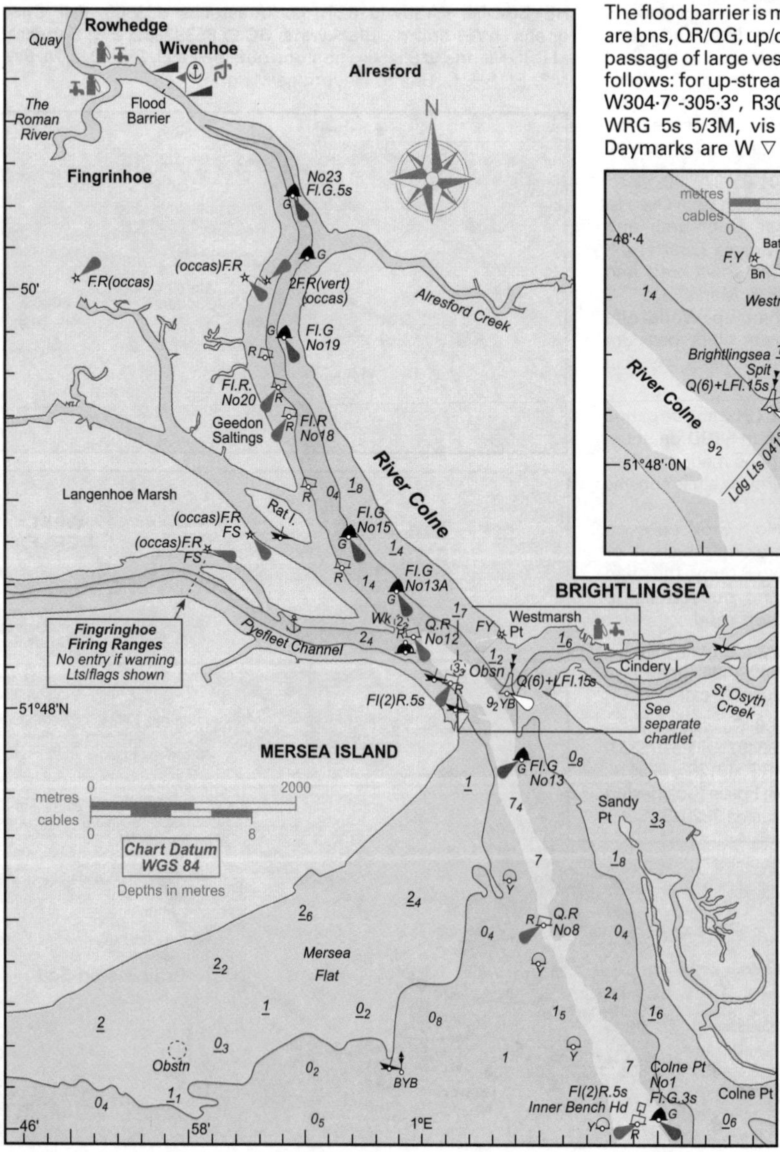

NAVIGATION WPT Colne Bar By, SHM Fl (2) G 5s, 51°44′·61N 01°02′·57E, 160°/340° from/to Mersea Stone, 3·6M. See also 9.4.18. Extensive mud and sand banks flank the ent chan. Large coasters use the Brightlingsea chans. The ent to Brightlingsea Creek is narrow at LW and carries about 1m.

A flood barrier 2ca below Wivenhoe church is normally open (30m wide) allowing unrestricted passage; keep to stbd, max speed 4kn. Tfc lts on N pier are 3FR (vert), vis up/downstream. When lit, they indicate either the barrier gates are shut or a large vessel is passing through; other traffic must keep clear and call on VHF Ch 13 for further info; see also LIGHTS AND MARKS.

Speed limits in the approaches and up-river: No 13 buoy to Fingringhoe (No 24 buoy) = 8kn; No 24 buoy to Colchester = 4kn; Brightlingsea Harbour = 4kn.

LIGHTS AND MARKS Well buoyed/lit up to Wivenhoe. Ldg lts/marks 041° for Brightlingsea: both FR 7/10m 4M; dayglo W □, orange stripe on posts; adjusted to suit the chan. Then Spit SCM buoy, Q (6) + L Fl 15s, and chan buoys Fl (3) G 5s and Fl R 5s, plus NCM bn Q where chan is divided by Cindery Is. Bateman's Tr (conspic) by Westmarsh Pt has a FY sodium lt 12m. Pyefleet Chan and other creeks are unlit.

The flood barrier is marked by 2FR/FG (vert) on both sides and there are bns, QR/QG, up/downstream on the river banks. To facilitate the passage of large vessels, Dir lts above and below the barrier are as follows: for up-stream tfc 305°, Oc WRG 5s 5/3M, vis G300°-304.7°, W304·7°-305·3°, R305·3°-310°; and for down-stream tfc 125°, Oc WRG 5s 5/3M, vis G120°-124.8, W°124.8°-125.2°, R125.2°-130°. Daymarks are W ▽ with Or vert stripe.

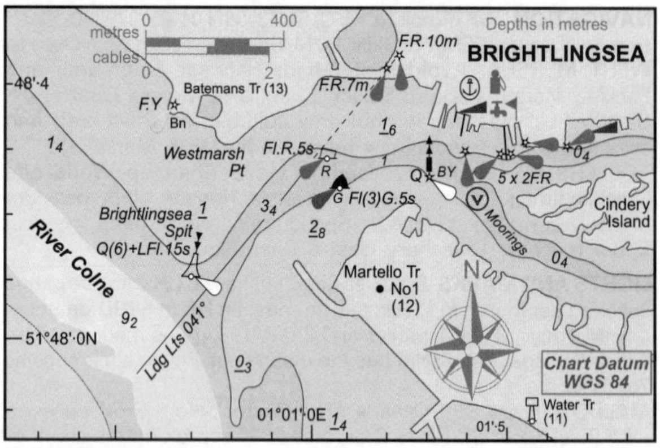

RADIO TELEPHONE *Brightlingsea Port Radio* VHF Ch 13. Colchester Ch 13 (Office hrs and HW–2 to HW+1).

TELEPHONE (Dial code 01206 Brightlingsea) Hr Mr (Brightlingsea) 302200; MRSC (01255) 675518; ⊜ (01473) 235704 (H24); Marinecall 09068 500455; Police (01255) 221312; Dr 302522.

FACILITIES

BRIGHTLINGSEA: **Town Hard** ☎ 303535, L, FW, Pontoon moorings £6 up to 26ft, £7 up to 36ft, £8 over 36ft, ⚓ afloat near NCM opposite Town Hard; **Colne YC** ☎ 302594, L, FW, R, Bar; **Brightlingsea SC** Slip, Bar; **Services:** M, L, FW, ME, El, Ⓔ, Sh, CH, ACA, P & D (cans), Gas, SM, BY, C, Slip. **Town** P & D (cans), FW, ME, El, Sh, C (mobile), CH, V, R, Bar, ✉, Ⓑ, ⇌ (bus to Wivenhoe or Colchester), ✈ (Southend or Stansted).

WIVENHOE: **Wivenhoe SC**. **Village** P, V, Bar, ✉, Ⓑ (AM only), ⇌.

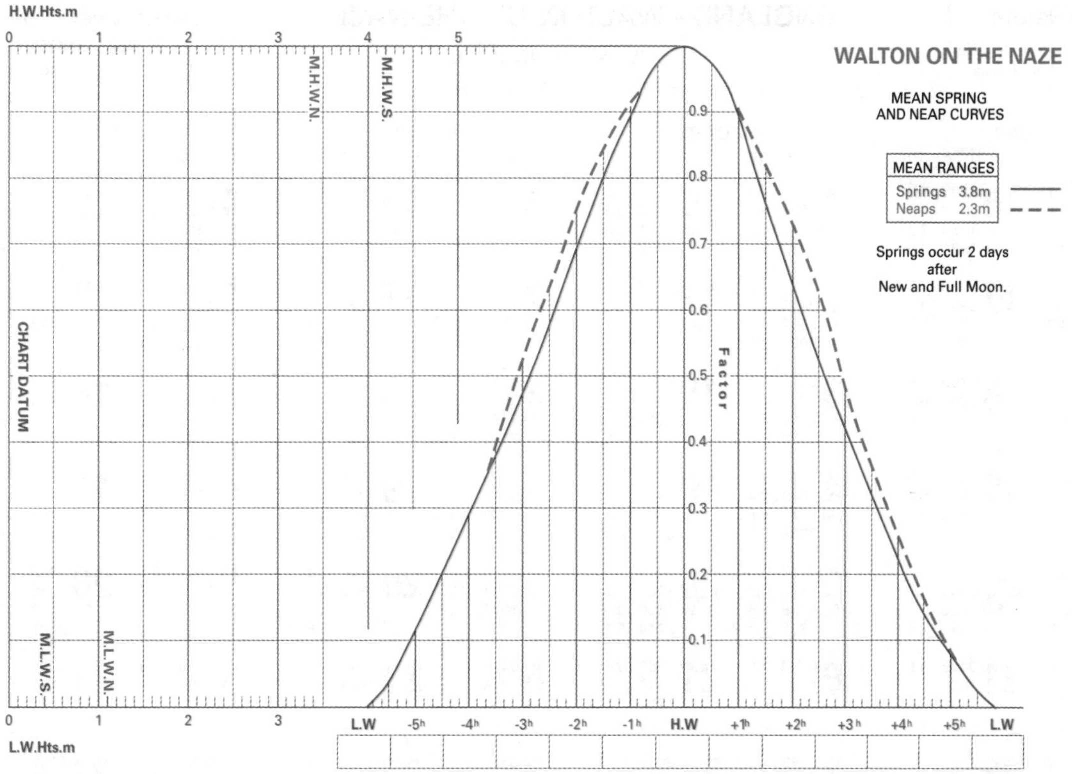

WALTON BACKWATERS *9.4.20*

Essex **51°54'·57N 01°16'·79E** (No 2 PHM buoy)

CHARTS AC *5607, 2695, 2052*; Imray Y16, C1, 2000 Series; Stanfords 5, 6; OS 169

TIDES +0030 Dover; ML 2·2; Duration 0615; Zone 0 (UT). Walton is a Standard Port. Predictions are for Walton Pier, ie to seaward. Time differences for Bramble Creek (N of Hamford Water) are +10, –7, –5, +10 mins; height differences are all +0·3m.

SHELTER Good in all weather, but ent not advised if a big sea is running from the NE. Berth HW±5 in Titchmarsh Marina (pontoons lettered A-H from ent), ent dredged 1·3m; or on adjacent pontoons in the Twizzle. Good ⚓s in Hamford Water (keep clear of Oakley Creek) and in N end of Walton Chan, 2ca S of Stone Pt on E side. Walton Yacht Basin more suited for long stay; appr dries.

NAVIGATION WPT Pye End SWM buoy, L Fl 10s, 51°55'·03N 01°17'·89E, 054°/234° from/to buoyed chan ent, 1·0M. NB this stretch carries only 0·9m. From S, appr via Medusa Chan; from N and E via the Harwich recomended yacht track. At narrow ent to Walton Chan leave NCM buoy to stbd, and 3 PHM buoys close to port; after a SHM Fl G 10s buoy abeam Stone Pt best water is on E side. Beware lobster pots off the Naze and Pye Sands and oyster beds in the Backwaters. Buoys may be moved to suit channel changes.

LIGHTS AND MARKS Naze Tr (49m) is conspic 3M S of Pye End buoy. 2M NNE at Felixstowe, cranes and Y flood lts are conspic D/N.

RADIO TELEPHONE Titchmarsh marina Ch 80, 0800-2000 in season.

TELEPHONE (Dial code 01255) Hr Mr 851899; MRSC 675518; ⊖ (01473) 235704 (H24); Marinecall 09068 500455; Police 241312; Ⓗ 421145.

FACILITIES **Titchmarsh Marina** (450+Ⓥ), ☎ 672185, 📠 851901, £1.32, Access HW±5 over sill 1·3m, D, FW, AC, Gas, Gaz, LPG, ME, CH, El, C (10 ton), BH (35 ton), Slip, R, Bar; **Walton & Frinton YC**, ☎ 675526/678161, R, Bar; **Yacht Basin** (60) run by YC; AB (long stay), FW, AC. **Services:** Slip, M, D, C (½ ton), El. **Town** EC Wed; P, SM, V, R, Bar, ✉, Ⓑ, ⇌, ✈ (Southend/Cambridge/Stansted).

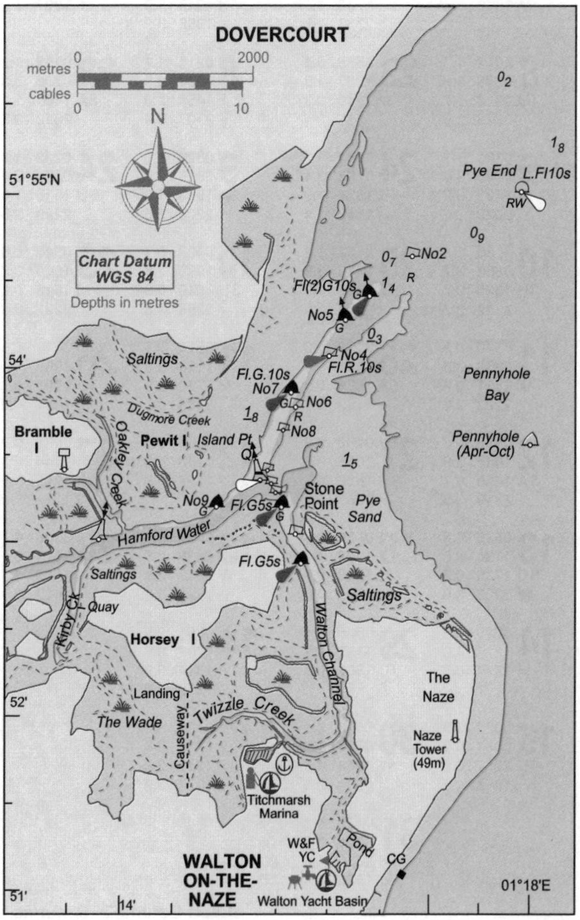

TIME ZONE (UTC)
For Summer Time add ONE hour in **non-shaded areas**

ENGLAND – WALTON-ON-THE-NAZE

LAT 51°51′N LONG 1°17′E

TIMES AND HEIGHTS OF HIGH AND LOW WATERS

SPRING & NEAP TIDES
Dates in **red** are **SPRINGS**
Dates in **blue** are **NEAPS**

YEAR **2002**

JANUARY

Date	Day	Time	m	Time	m	Time	m	Time	m
1	TU	0031	4.1	0642	0.5	1254	4.2	1856	0.7
2	W	0114	4.1	0730	0.4	1341	4.2	1938	0.8
3	TH	0158	4.0	0818	0.4	1429	4.2	2022	0.8
4	F	0244	4.0	0909	0.4	1519	4.1	2110	0.9
5	SA	0334	3.9	1002	0.4	1613	3.9	2202	1.0
6	SU	0428	3.8	1102	0.5	1712	3.7	2301	1.1
7	M	0530	3.7	1208	0.6	1816	3.6		
8	TU	0012	1.2	0638	3.6	1318	0.7	1923	3.6
9	W	0129	1.1	0746	3.6	1423	0.7	2029	3.6
10	TH	0239	1.0	0852	3.7	1520	0.7	2129	3.7
11	F	0340	0.9	0952	3.8	1611	0.7	2222	3.8
12	SA	0435	0.7	1045	3.9	1655	0.7	2310	3.9
13	SU	0525	0.6	1134	4.0	1736	0.8	● 2353	3.9
14	M	0610	0.6	1217	4.0	1814	0.8		
15	TU	0032	3.9	0651	0.5	1257	3.9	1848	0.8
16	W	0107	3.9	0728	0.6	1333	3.9	1920	0.9
17	TH	0138	3.9	0801	0.6	1406	3.8	1951	0.9
18	F	0209	3.8	0832	0.6	1439	3.8	2023	0.9
19	SA	0243	3.8	0904	0.7	1515	3.7	2100	0.9
20	SU	0322	3.7	0942	0.7	1555	3.6	2142	1.0
21	M	0406	3.6	1028	0.8	1641	3.5	2232	1.1
22	TU	0457	3.5	1123	0.9	1736	3.4	2333	1.2
23	W	0558	3.4	1227	1.0	1840	3.3		
24	TH	0042	1.3	0706	3.4	1334	1.0	1948	3.4
25	F	0152	1.2	0815	3.5	1439	1.0	2054	3.5
26	SA	0259	1.0	0918	3.6	1538	0.9	2152	3.7
27	SU	0400	0.8	1015	3.9	1630	0.8	2245	3.9
28	M	0455	0.6	1108	4.1	1718	0.7	○ 2333	4.0
29	TU	0546	0.4	1157	4.2	1802	0.6		
30	W	0018	4.1	0634	0.3	1244	4.3	1844	0.6
31	TH	0103	4.2	0720	0.2	1330	4.4	1925	0.6

FEBRUARY

Date	Day	Time	m	Time	m	Time	m	Time	m	
1	F	0147	4.2	0806	0.1	1416	4.3	2008	0.6	
2	SA	0230	4.2	0852	0.2	1502	4.2	2051	0.7	
3	SU	0315	4.2	0939	0.3	1550	4.0	2138	0.8	
4	M	0403	4.0	1029	0.4	1641	3.8	2229	0.9	
5	TU	0457	3.8	1127	0.7	1738	3.6	2331	1.1	
6	W	0603	3.6	1235	0.9	1845	3.4			
7	TH	0049	1.1	0718	3.5	1348	1.0	1958	3.3	
8	F	0215	1.1	0834	3.5	1456	1.0	2107	3.4	
9	SA	0328	0.9	0940	3.7	1553	1.0	2205	3.6	
10	SU	0427	0.7	1035	3.8	1640	0.9	2255	3.8	
11	M	0516	0.6	1123	3.9	1720	0.9	2339	3.9	
12	TU	0558	0.5	1205	4.0	1757	0.8			●
13	W	0017	3.9	0635	0.5	1242	3.9	1829	0.8	
14	TH	0051	3.9	0707	0.5	1314	3.9	1859	0.8	
15	F	0120	3.9	0735	0.5	1343	3.8	1927	0.8	
16	SA	0147	3.9	0800	0.6	1411	3.8	1957	0.7	
17	SU	0217	3.9	0829	0.6	1442	3.8	2031	0.7	
18	M	0251	3.9	0903	0.6	1519	3.8	2108	0.8	
19	TU	0329	3.8	0941	0.7	1601	3.7	2151	0.9	
20	W	0413	3.6	1027	0.9	1650	3.5	2244	1.1	
21	TH	0507	3.5	1129	1.0	1750	3.3	2352	1.2	
22	F	0617	3.3	1249	1.1	1901	3.2			
23	SA	0112	1.2	0736	3.3	1407	1.1	2019	3.3	
24	SU	0232	1.0	0854	3.5	1515	1.0	2129	3.5	
25	M	0343	0.8	1000	3.8	1613	0.8	2227	3.8	
26	TU	0443	0.5	1055	4.1	1702	0.7	2317	4.0	
27	W	0534	0.3	1144	4.3	1745	0.6			○
28	TH	0003	4.2	0619	0.1	1230	4.4	1827	0.5	

MARCH

Date	Day	Time	m	Time	m	Time	m	Time	m	
1	F	0047	4.3	0703	0.0	1314	4.5	1908	0.4	
2	SA	0129	4.4	0746	0.0	1357	4.4	1949	0.4	
3	SU	0211	4.4	0828	0.1	1440	4.3	2031	0.5	
4	M	0253	4.3	0911	0.2	1524	4.1	2114	0.6	
5	TU	0338	4.1	0956	0.5	1609	3.8	2201	0.8	
6	W	0428	3.9	1048	0.8	1700	3.5	2258	1.0	
7	TH	0532	3.6	1153	1.0	1805	3.2			
8	F	0016	1.1	0654	3.4	1311	1.2	1927	3.1	
9	SA	0154	1.1	0818	3.4	1430	1.2	2044	3.3	
10	SU	0313	0.9	0925	3.6	1532	1.1	2145	3.5	
11	M	0411	0.7	1020	3.8	1621	1.0	2236	3.7	
12	TU	0458	0.6	1106	3.9	1701	0.9	2319	3.9	
13	W	0537	0.5	1146	4.0	1736	0.8	2356	3.9	
14	TH	0610	0.5	1221	4.0	1808	0.7			●
15	F	0028	3.9	0638	0.5	1251	3.9	1835	0.7	
16	SA	0056	3.9	0703	0.5	1316	3.9	1902	0.7	
17	SU	0123	3.9	0729	0.5	1342	3.9	1932	0.6	
18	M	0151	3.9	0757	0.5	1412	3.9	2005	0.6	
19	TU	0224	3.9	0828	0.6	1448	3.9	2041	0.6	
20	W	0300	3.9	0902	0.7	1528	3.7	2121	0.8	
21	TH	0342	3.7	0944	0.9	1614	3.5	2210	0.9	
22	F	0434	3.5	1041	1.1	1712	3.3	2318	1.1	
23	SA	0542	3.3	1210	1.2	1824	3.1			
24	SU	0045	1.1	0708	3.3	1340	1.2	1949	3.2	
25	M	0213	1.0	0836	3.5	1454	1.1	2106	3.5	
26	TU	0328	0.7	0945	3.8	1552	0.8	2205	3.8	
27	W	0426	0.4	1039	4.1	1641	0.7	2255	4.0	
28	TH	0515	0.1	1127	4.3	1725	0.5	○ 2341	4.2	
29	F	0600	0.0	1211	4.4	1807	0.4			
30	SA	0025	4.4	0641	-0.1	1254	4.4	1847	0.3	
31	SU	0108	4.4	0722	0.0	1336	4.4	1929	0.3	

APRIL

Date	Day	Time	m	Time	m	Time	m	Time	m	
1	M	0149	4.4	0802	0.1	1417	4.2	2011	0.4	
2	TU	0232	4.3	0843	0.3	1458	4.0	2054	0.5	
3	W	0316	4.1	0926	0.6	1540	3.8	2140	0.7	
4	TH	0405	3.8	1015	0.9	1627	3.5	2236	0.9	
5	F	0507	3.5	1117	1.2	1727	3.2	2353	1.0	
6	SA	0630	3.3	1235	1.4	1852	3.1			
7	SU	0130	1.1	0752	3.3	1358	1.4	2011	3.2	
8	M	0247	0.9	0900	3.5	1504	1.2	2115	3.4	
9	TU	0344	0.7	0954	3.8	1554	1.0	2206	3.6	
10	W	0428	0.6	1039	3.9	1635	0.9	2250	3.8	
11	TH	0506	0.5	1118	4.0	1710	0.8	2327	3.9	
12	F	0538	0.5	1152	4.0	1741	0.7	● 2359	3.9	
13	SA	0605	0.5	1221	3.9	1809	0.7			
14	SU	0028	3.9	0631	0.5	1247	3.9	1838	0.6	
15	M	0057	3.9	0700	0.6	1315	3.9	1910	0.6	
16	TU	0128	3.9	0729	0.6	1347	3.9	1944	0.6	
17	W	0202	3.9	0801	0.6	1422	3.8	2021	0.6	
18	TH	0240	3.9	0835	0.7	1503	3.7	2102	0.7	
19	F	0324	3.7	0918	0.9	1550	3.5	2154	0.8	
20	SA	0418	3.5	1016	1.1	1647	3.3	2303	0.9	
21	SU	0527	3.4	1144	1.3	1801	3.2			
22	M	0030	0.9	0652	3.3	1315	1.3	1924	3.2	
23	TU	0156	0.8	0817	3.6	1429	1.1	2037	3.5	
24	W	0307	0.5	0922	3.8	1527	0.9	2137	3.8	
25	TH	0403	0.3	1016	4.1	1616	0.7	2229	4.0	
26	F	0452	0.1	1104	4.3	1702	0.5	2316	4.2	
27	SA	0536	0.0	1149	4.3	1745	0.4			○
28	SU	0001	4.3	0617	0.0	1232	4.3	1828	0.3	
29	M	0046	4.4	0658	0.1	1314	4.2	1911	0.3	
30	TU	0129	4.3	0738	0.3	1354	4.1	1954	0.4	

Chart Datum: 2·16 metres below Ordnance Datum (Newlyn)

TIME ZONE (UTC)
For Summer Time add ONE hour in **non-shaded areas**

ENGLAND – WALTON-ON-THE-NAZE

LAT 51°51′N LONG 1°17′E

TIMES AND HEIGHTS OF HIGH AND LOW WATERS

SPRING & NEAP TIDES
Dates in red are SPRINGS
Dates in blue are NEAPS

YEAR **2002**

MAY

Date	Day	Time	m	Time	m	Time	m	Time	m
1	W	0212	4.2	0818	0.5	1434	3.9	2039	0.5
2	TH	0258	4.0	0900	0.7	1515	3.7	2126	0.6
3	F	0347	3.8	0947	1.0	1600	3.5	2222	0.8
4	SA	0445	3.5	1045	1.3	1656	3.3	2332	0.9
5	SU	0558	3.3	1157	1.4	1810	3.2		
6	M	0055	1.0	0713	3.3	1317	1.4	1925	3.2
7	TU	0208	0.9	0820	3.5	1426	1.3	2030	3.4
8	W	0305	0.8	0915	3.6	1519	1.1	2124	3.6
9	TH	0350	0.7	1001	3.8	1602	0.9	2209	3.7
10	F	0427	0.6	1041	3.9	1638	0.8	2248	3.8
11	SA	0500	0.6	1116	3.9	1710	0.7	2324	3.8
12	SU	0531	0.6	1148	3.9	1742	0.7	● 2358	3.9
13	M	0603	0.6	1219	3.9	1816	0.6		
14	TU	0032	3.9	0635	0.6	1252	3.9	1851	0.6
15	W	0108	3.9	0708	0.7	1327	3.9	1929	0.6
16	TH	0146	3.9	0743	0.7	1405	3.8	2010	0.6
17	F	0228	3.9	0822	0.8	1447	3.7	2056	0.6
18	SA	0315	3.8	0908	1.0	1535	3.5	2151	0.7
19	SU	0412	3.6	1007	1.1	1634	3.4	2258	0.8
20	M	0520	3.5	1123	1.2	1745	3.3		
21	TU	0016	0.7	0636	3.5	1246	1.2	1859	3.4
22	W	0135	0.6	0750	3.6	1358	1.1	2006	3.6
23	TH	0242	0.4	0854	3.8	1459	0.9	2106	3.8
24	F	0338	0.3	0949	4.0	1551	0.7	2200	4.0
25	SA	0427	0.2	1039	4.1	1640	0.6	2251	4.1
26	SU	0512	0.2	1126	4.2	1727	0.5	○ 2340	4.2
27	M	0555	0.2	1210	4.1	1813	0.4		
28	TU	0026	4.2	0636	0.3	1253	4.1	1858	0.4
29	W	0112	4.2	0716	0.5	1334	4.0	1943	0.4
30	TH	0156	4.1	0756	0.7	1414	3.9	2028	0.5
31	F	0241	3.9	0837	0.8	1454	3.7	2115	0.6

JUNE

Date	Day	Time	m	Time	m	Time	m	Time	m
1	SA	0328	3.7	0921	1.0	1537	3.6	2205	0.7
2	SU	0419	3.6	1010	1.2	1626	3.4	2301	0.9
3	M	0517	3.4	1111	1.4	1725	3.3		
4	TU	0005	0.9	0621	3.3	1221	1.4	1830	3.3
5	W	0112	0.9	0725	3.4	1331	1.3	1934	3.4
6	TH	0210	0.9	0824	3.5	1430	1.2	2031	3.5
7	F	0300	0.8	0914	3.7	1518	1.1	2122	3.6
8	SA	0343	0.7	0959	3.8	1600	0.9	2207	3.7
9	SU	0422	0.7	1039	3.9	1638	0.8	2250	3.8
10	M	0501	0.7	1118	3.9	1717	0.7	● 2331	3.9
11	TU	0539	0.7	1155	3.9	1757	0.6		
12	W	0011	3.9	0616	0.7	1234	3.9	1838	0.6
13	TH	0052	4.0	0654	0.7	1313	3.9	1921	0.5
14	F	0135	4.0	0733	0.8	1354	3.8	2006	0.5
15	SA	0220	4.0	0815	0.9	1438	3.8	2054	0.5
16	SU	0310	3.9	0902	1.0	1527	3.7	2147	0.5
17	M	0405	3.8	0956	1.1	1623	3.6	2247	0.6
18	TU	0506	3.7	1059	1.2	1725	3.6	2355	0.6
19	W	0613	3.7	1211	1.2	1830	3.6		
20	TH	0106	0.6	0719	3.7	1324	1.1	1934	3.7
21	F	0213	0.5	0823	3.8	1430	1.0	2037	3.8
22	SA	0312	0.4	0922	3.9	1529	0.8	2136	3.9
23	SU	0404	0.4	1016	3.9	1623	0.7	2232	4.0
24	M	0452	0.4	1106	4.0	1714	0.6	○ 2324	4.0
25	TU	0536	0.5	1153	4.0	1803	0.5		
26	W	0013	4.1	0617	0.6	1237	4.0	1849	0.5
27	TH	0059	4.0	0657	0.7	1318	3.9	1934	0.5
28	F	0143	4.0	0736	0.8	1357	3.9	2017	0.5
29	SA	0225	3.9	0814	0.9	1434	3.8	2057	0.6
30	SU	0306	3.8	0852	1.0	1511	3.7	2136	0.7

JULY

Date	Day	Time	m	Time	m	Time	m	Time	m
1	M	0347	3.6	0932	1.1	1553	3.6	2218	0.8
2	TU	0432	3.5	1018	1.2	1640	3.5	2306	0.9
3	W	0522	3.4	1114	1.3	1735	3.4		
4	TH	0002	0.9	0619	3.4	1219	1.4	1835	3.4
5	F	0103	1.0	0721	3.4	1324	1.3	1937	3.4
6	SA	0202	0.9	0821	3.5	1425	1.2	2036	3.5
7	SU	0257	0.9	0916	3.7	1519	1.1	2131	3.6
8	M	0348	0.8	1006	3.8	1609	0.9	2221	3.8
9	TU	0434	0.8	1052	3.9	1657	0.8	2309	3.9
10	W	0518	0.7	1136	4.0	1743	0.6	● 2355	4.0
11	TH	0600	0.7	1219	4.0	1828	0.5		
12	F	0040	4.1	0641	0.8	1302	4.0	1913	0.4
13	SA	0126	4.1	0722	0.8	1345	4.0	1958	0.4
14	SU	0212	4.1	0805	0.8	1428	4.0	2045	0.3
15	M	0259	4.1	0850	0.9	1514	4.0	2133	0.4
16	TU	0350	4.0	0938	0.9	1603	3.9	2225	0.4
17	W	0444	3.9	1032	1.0	1658	3.8	2324	0.5
18	TH	0543	3.7	1135	1.1	1759	3.7		
19	F	0032	0.7	0647	3.6	1249	1.1	1906	3.7
20	SA	0142	0.7	0754	3.6	1404	1.1	2014	3.7
21	SU	0247	0.8	0859	3.7	1513	1.0	2121	3.8
22	M	0345	0.7	0959	3.8	1614	0.8	2222	3.9
23	TU	0435	0.7	1052	3.9	1709	0.6	2316	4.0
24	W	0520	0.8	1140	4.0	1757	0.6	○	
25	TH	0004	4.0	0600	0.8	1224	4.0	1841	0.5
26	F	0048	4.0	0639	0.8	1303	4.0	1921	0.5
27	SA	0128	4.0	0715	0.9	1338	3.9	1957	0.5
28	SU	0204	3.9	0748	0.9	1410	3.9	2029	0.6
29	M	0237	3.8	0821	1.0	1442	3.9	2058	0.6
30	TU	0311	3.8	0855	1.0	1516	3.8	2131	0.7
31	W	0347	3.7	0934	1.1	1556	3.7	2211	0.8

AUGUST

Date	Day	Time	m	Time	m	Time	m	Time	m
1	TH	0429	3.6	1021	1.2	1643	3.6	2301	0.9
2	F	0519	3.5	1118	1.3	1739	3.4		
3	SA	0002	1.0	0619	3.4	1226	1.3	1843	3.4
4	SU	0110	1.1	0727	3.4	1336	1.3	1952	3.4
5	M	0217	1.1	0836	3.5	1443	1.2	2059	3.5
6	TU	0318	1.0	0937	3.7	1545	1.0	2159	3.7
7	W	0412	0.9	1031	3.9	1641	0.8	2253	4.0
8	TH	0500	0.8	1119	4.0	1730	0.6	● 2341	4.1
9	F	0544	0.8	1203	4.1	1816	0.4		
10	SA	0027	4.3	0625	0.7	1247	4.2	1900	0.3
11	SU	0112	4.3	0706	0.7	1329	4.3	1943	0.2
12	M	0156	4.4	0747	0.7	1411	4.3	2026	0.2
13	TU	0241	4.3	0830	0.7	1453	4.2	2110	0.3
14	W	0327	4.2	0915	0.8	1539	4.1	2156	0.4
15	TH	0416	4.0	1005	0.9	1629	4.0	2249	0.6
16	F	0510	3.7	1103	1.1	1729	3.8	2353	0.9
17	SA	0614	3.5	1217	1.2	1842	3.6		
18	SU	0108	1.0	0728	3.4	1344	1.2	2001	3.5
19	M	0224	1.1	0841	3.5	1504	1.0	2114	3.7
20	TU	0328	1.1	0945	3.7	1609	0.8	2216	3.8
21	W	0420	1.0	1039	3.9	1701	0.6	2307	4.0
22	TH	0504	0.9	1125	4.0	1745	0.5	○ 2352	4.1
23	F	0543	0.9	1207	4.1	1824	0.5		
24	SA	0032	4.1	0618	0.9	1244	4.0	1858	0.5
25	SU	0108	4.0	0651	0.9	1315	4.0	1928	0.6
26	M	0138	3.9	0721	0.9	1342	4.0	1953	0.6
27	TU	0204	3.9	0750	0.9	1409	3.9	2018	0.6
28	W	0232	3.9	0822	0.9	1440	3.9	2048	0.7
29	TH	0305	3.8	0858	0.9	1516	3.8	2123	0.8
30	F	0344	3.7	0940	1.0	1557	3.7	2205	0.9
31	SA	0429	3.6	1032	1.2	1647	3.5	2303	1.1

Chart Datum: 2·16 metres below Ordnance Datum (Newlyn)

TIME ZONE (UTC)
For Summer Time add ONE hour in **non-shaded areas**

ENGLAND – WALTON-ON-THE-NAZE

LAT 51°51′N LONG 1°17′E

TIMES AND HEIGHTS OF HIGH AND LOW WATERS

SPRING & NEAP TIDES
Dates in red are **SPRINGS**
Dates in blue are **NEAPS**

YEAR **2002**

SEPTEMBER

Date	Day	Time	m	Time	m	Time	m	Time	m
1	SU	0526	3.4	1139	1.3	1752	3.3		
2	M	0022	1.3	0637	3.3	1258	1.3	1911	3.3
3	TU	0142	1.3	0758	3.4	1415	1.2	2033	3.5
4	W	0252	1.2	0911	3.6	1525	1.0	2141	3.7
5	TH	0351	1.0	1009	3.9	1624	0.7	2236	4.0
6	F	0440	0.9	1058	4.1	1713	0.4	2324	4.3
7	SA ●	0523	0.7	1142	4.3	1757	0.3		
8	SU	0009	4.4	0604	0.7	1225	4.4	1839	0.1
9	M	0053	4.5	0645	0.6	1307	4.4	1921	0.1
10	TU	0135	4.5	0726	0.6	1348	4.5	2001	0.2
11	W	0217	4.4	0809	0.6	1430	4.4	2042	0.3
12	TH	0300	4.2	0853	0.7	1514	4.3	2126	0.5
13	F	0346	4.0	0941	0.8	1603	4.0	2215	0.8
14	SA	0436	3.7	1039	1.0	1703	3.7	2317	1.1
15	SU	0540	3.4	1155	1.2	1823	3.5		
16	M	0036	1.3	0702	3.3	1330	1.2	1950	3.5
17	TU	0201	1.4	0822	3.4	1452	1.0	2104	3.6
18	W	0309	1.3	0926	3.6	1553	0.8	2202	3.9
19	TH	0401	1.2	1019	3.9	1642	0.6	2250	4.0
20	F	0443	1.0	1104	4.0	1722	0.5	2332	4.1
21	SA ○	0521	0.9	1144	4.1	1757	0.5		
22	SU	0009	4.1	0554	0.9	1218	4.1	1827	0.6
23	M	0041	4.0	0624	0.9	1246	4.0	1853	0.6
24	TU	0106	4.0	0652	0.8	1311	4.0	1916	0.7
25	W	0130	3.9	0721	0.8	1338	4.0	1942	0.7
26	TH	0157	3.9	0753	0.8	1408	3.9	2011	0.7
27	F	0229	3.9	0828	0.9	1443	3.9	2043	0.8
28	SA	0306	3.8	0908	1.0	1522	3.8	2120	1.0
29	SU	0350	3.7	0957	1.1	1610	3.6	2211	1.2
30	M	0444	3.4	1105	1.3	1714	3.4	2335	1.4

OCTOBER

Date	Day	Time	m	Time	m	Time	m	Time	m
1	TU	0555	3.3	1229	1.3	1838	3.3		
2	W	0110	1.4	0723	3.3	1352	1.1	2010	3.4
3	TH	0225	1.3	0842	3.5	1504	0.9	2120	3.8
4	F	0325	1.1	0941	3.8	1601	0.6	2214	4.1
5	SA	0415	0.9	1030	4.1	1650	0.3	2302	4.3
6	SU ●	0459	0.7	1116	4.3	1734	0.2	2346	4.5
7	M	0541	0.6	1159	4.4	1815	0.1		
8	TU	0028	4.5	0622	0.5	1242	4.5	1855	0.1
9	W	0111	4.5	0705	0.5	1324	4.5	1935	0.2
10	TH	0152	4.3	0748	0.5	1407	4.4	2016	0.4
11	F	0234	4.2	0833	0.6	1452	4.2	2058	0.7
12	SA	0317	3.9	0923	0.8	1542	4.0	2146	1.0
13	SU	0405	3.6	1022	1.0	1643	3.6	2247	1.3
14	M	0507	3.4	1140	1.1	1804	3.4		
15	TU	0005	1.5	0632	3.2	1311	1.1	1928	3.4
16	W	0131	1.6	0752	3.3	1427	1.0	2039	3.6
17	TH	0241	1.4	0857	3.6	1525	0.8	2135	3.8
18	F	0333	1.2	0949	3.8	1612	0.7	2222	4.0
19	SA	0416	1.0	1033	4.0	1650	0.6	2302	4.1
20	SU	0453	0.9	1112	4.0	1723	0.6	2337	4.1
21	M ○	0527	0.9	1145	4.0	1752	0.7		
22	TU	0007	4.0	0556	0.8	1214	4.0	1817	0.7
23	W	0033	4.0	0625	0.8	1241	3.9	1844	0.7
24	TH	0058	4.0	0656	0.8	1311	3.9	1911	0.8
25	F	0127	4.0	0729	0.8	1343	3.9	1941	0.8
26	SA	0200	3.9	0806	0.8	1419	3.9	2013	0.9
27	SU	0237	3.8	0847	0.9	1500	3.8	2051	1.0
28	M	0320	3.6	0937	1.0	1550	3.6	2142	1.2
29	TU	0413	3.4	1044	1.1	1653	3.4	2258	1.4
30	W	0524	3.3	1206	1.1	1814	3.4		
31	TH	0034	1.5	0651	3.3	1327	1.0	1942	3.5

NOVEMBER

Date	Day	Time	m	Time	m	Time	m	Time	m
1	F	0153	1.3	0807	3.5	1436	0.7	2051	3.8
2	SA	0254	1.1	0907	3.8	1534	0.5	2146	4.1
3	SU	0346	0.9	0959	4.1	1623	0.3	2234	4.3
4	M ●	0433	0.7	1047	4.3	1708	0.2	2320	4.4
5	TU	0518	0.6	1132	4.4	1751	0.2		
6	W	0003	4.4	0602	0.5	1218	4.5	1831	0.3
7	TH	0046	4.3	0647	0.5	1302	4.4	1912	0.4
8	F	0128	4.2	0732	0.5	1347	4.3	1953	0.6
9	SA	0210	4.1	0820	0.6	1434	4.2	2036	0.8
10	SU	0252	3.9	0911	0.7	1525	3.9	2122	1.1
11	M	0338	3.6	1010	0.9	1623	3.6	2218	1.4
12	TU	0435	3.4	1121	1.0	1734	3.4	2328	1.6
13	W	0551	3.3	1239	1.0	1850	3.4		
14	TH	0049	1.6	0707	3.3	1349	1.0	1958	3.5
15	F	0200	1.5	0812	3.5	1446	0.9	2055	3.7
16	SA	0256	1.3	0906	3.7	1533	0.8	2142	3.8
17	SU	0342	1.1	0952	3.8	1612	0.7	2223	3.9
18	M	0421	0.9	1032	3.9	1646	0.7	2259	4.0
19	TU	0456	0.8	1108	3.9	1717	0.7	2331	4.0
20	W ○	0528	0.8	1142	3.9	1747	0.8		
21	TH	0001	4.0	0600	0.7	1215	3.9	1817	0.8
22	F	0032	4.0	0635	0.7	1249	3.9	1849	0.8
23	SA	0104	3.9	0712	0.7	1325	3.9	1921	0.9
24	SU	0139	3.9	0752	0.7	1404	3.9	1957	1.0
25	M	0218	3.8	0836	0.8	1448	3.8	2038	1.1
26	TU	0301	3.7	0927	0.9	1539	3.7	2129	1.2
27	W	0354	3.5	1029	0.9	1639	3.6	2234	1.3
28	TH	0500	3.4	1141	0.9	1752	3.5	2353	1.4
29	F	0617	3.4	1256	0.8	1908	3.6		
30	SA	0111	1.3	0729	3.6	1405	0.7	2015	3.7

DECEMBER

Date	Day	Time	m	Time	m	Time	m	Time	m
1	SU	0219	1.1	0831	3.8	1504	0.5	2114	3.9
2	M	0316	0.9	0927	4.0	1556	0.4	2206	4.1
3	TU	0409	0.7	1020	4.2	1644	0.3	2255	4.2
4	W ●	0458	0.6	1110	4.3	1729	0.4	2341	4.2
5	TH	0547	0.5	1158	4.3	1812	0.4		
6	F	0025	4.1	0634	0.5	1246	4.3	1853	0.6
7	SA	0108	4.1	0722	0.5	1333	4.2	1934	0.7
8	SU	0150	4.0	0811	0.5	1420	4.1	2016	0.9
9	M	0232	3.8	0901	0.6	1507	3.9	2059	1.1
10	TU	0315	3.7	0953	0.7	1558	3.7	2145	1.3
11	W	0403	3.6	1049	0.9	1653	3.5	2241	1.4
12	TH	0500	3.4	1150	1.0	1755	3.4	2347	1.5
13	F	0607	3.3	1253	1.0	1900	3.3		
14	SA	0059	1.5	0713	3.4	1351	1.0	2000	3.4
15	SU	0205	1.3	0813	3.5	1442	0.9	2053	3.6
16	M	0258	1.2	0905	3.6	1527	0.9	2139	3.7
17	TU	0343	1.0	0952	3.7	1607	0.8	2221	3.8
18	W	0423	0.9	1035	3.8	1645	0.8	2300	3.9
19	TH ○	0502	0.8	1115	3.9	1722	0.8	2336	3.9
20	F	0541	0.7	1154	3.9	1758	0.8		
21	SA	0013	3.9	0620	0.7	1233	4.0	1834	0.8
22	SU	0050	3.9	0701	0.6	1312	4.0	1910	0.9
23	M	0127	3.9	0744	0.6	1354	4.0	1948	0.9
24	TU	0207	3.8	0829	0.6	1439	3.9	2030	1.0
25	W	0250	3.8	0918	0.6	1528	3.8	2118	1.0
26	TH	0339	3.7	1011	0.6	1623	3.7	2212	1.1
27	F	0436	3.6	1111	0.7	1725	3.6	2314	1.2
28	SA	0542	3.6	1218	0.7	1832	3.6		
29	SU	0026	1.2	0651	3.6	1329	0.7	1939	3.6
30	M	0141	1.1	0758	3.7	1434	0.6	2043	3.7
31	TU	0249	1.0	0902	3.8	1533	0.6	2142	3.8

Chart Datum: 2·16 metres below Ordnance Datum (Newlyn)

RIVERS STOUR, ORWELL AND DEBEN *9.4.21, 22 & 23*

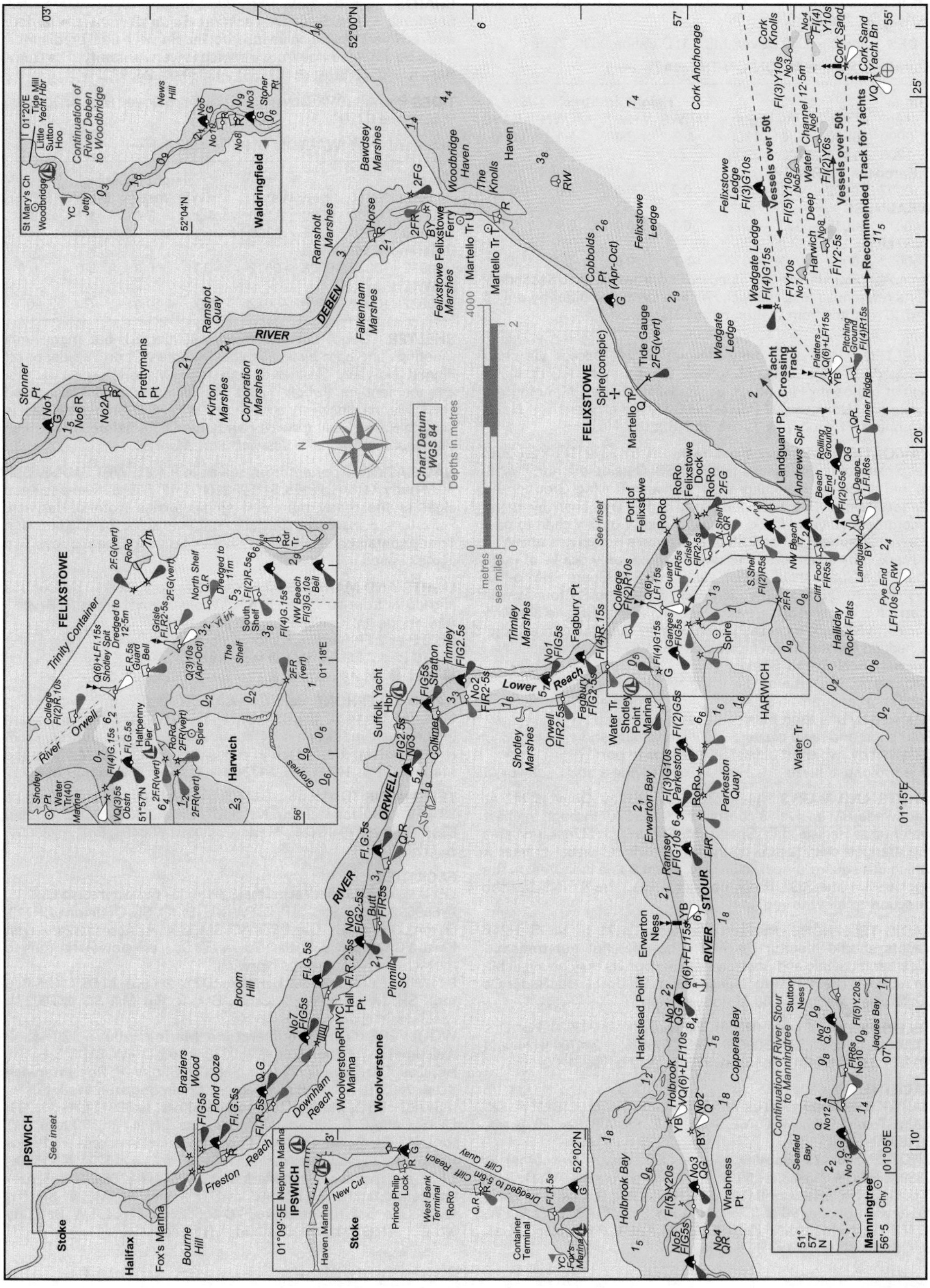

RIVER STOUR *9.4.21*

Essex/Suffolk **51°57'·06N 01°17'·77E** (Guard PHM buoy)

CHARTS AC *5607, 2693*, 1594, 1491, 1593, *2052*; Imray Y16, C1, 2000 Series; Stanfords 5, 6; OS 169

TIDES Harwich+0050 Dover; ML 2·1; Duration 0630; Zone 0 (UT)

Standard Port WALTON-ON-THE-NAZE (⟵)

Times				Height (metres)			
High Water		Low Water		MHWS	MHWN	MLWN	MLWS
0000	0600	0500	1100	4·2	3·4	1·1	0·4
1200	1800	1700	2300				
Differences HARWICH							
+0007	+0002	–0010	–0012	–0·2	0·0	0·0	0·0
WRABNESS							
+0017	+0015	–0010	–0012	–0·1	0·0	0·0	0·0
MISTLEY							
+0032	+0027	–0010	–0012	0·0	0·0	–0·1	–0·1

Note: Although Harwich is a Standard Port, it has only two Secondary Ports referenced to it. Harwich HW and LW times differ by only 5 and 10 minutes from Walton-on-the-Naze.

SHELTER Good at Shotley Marina; all tide access via chan dredged 2m, outer limits lit, to lock. Enter only on F.G tfc lt. AB also at Halfpenny Pier (dries; access H24), Mistley, Manningtree (both dry). No yachts at Parkeston Quay. ⚓s off Erwarton Ness, Wrabness Pt, Holbrook Creek and Stutton Ness.

NAVIGATION WPT Cork Sand Yacht Bn, 51°55'·21N 01°25'·20E. Keep clear of commercial shipping/HSS. Outside the hbr, yachts should cross the DW chan at 90° between Rolling Ground and Platters buoys. See 9.4.5. Stay out of the DW chan by using recommended yacht track, running S and W of DW chan to past Harwich. **Caution**: Bkwtr, ESE of Blackman's Hd, covers at HW; it is marked by small inconspic unlit PHM bn, only 5ca W of main chan. The Guard shoal (0·8m), about 2ca S of Guard PHM buoy, lies close to the recommended yacht track. The R Stour is well marked; speed limit 8kn. Beware 'The Horse' 4ca NE and a drying bank 1½ca NW of Wrabness Pt. From Mistley Quay local knowledge is needed for the narrow, tortuous chan to Manningtree.

Special Local Sound Signals

Commercial vessels may use these additional sigs:

Four short and rapid blasts followed by one short blast } = I am turning short around to stbd.

Four short and rapid blasts followed by two short blasts) } = I am turning short around to port.

One prolonged blast = I am leaving a dock, quay or ⚓.

LIGHTS AND MARKS The R Stour to Mistley Quay is lit. At Cattawade, 8M up river, a conspic chy leads 270° through the best water up to Harkstead Pt. Shotley Marina: a Dir lt at lock indicates the dredged chan (2·0m) by Inogen (or Moiré) visual marker lt which is a square, ambered display; a vert B line indicates on the appr centre line 339°. If off the centre line, arrows indicate the direction to steer to regain it.

RADIO TELEPHONE *Harwich Hbr Radio* Ch **71** 11 14 16 (H24). Yachts should monitor Ch 71 for tfc info, but not transmit. Weather, tidal info and possibly help in poor vis may be available on request. The Hbr Patrol launch listens on Ch 11. Hbr Radar Ch 20. Shotley Marina Ch **80** M (lock master).

TELEPHONE (Dial code 01255) Harwich Hr Mr 243030; Hbr Ops 243000; Marinecall 0891 500455; MRSC 675518; ⊖ 244700 (H24) and (01473) 235704 (H24); Police 241312; Dr 201299; Ⓗ 201200.

FACILITIES

HARWICH: **Halfpenny Pier** L, FW, AB £5 <5m, £10 <10m, £15 <15m, £20 <20m. **Town** EC Wed; P, D, ME, SM, Gas, El, Sh, V, R, Bar, ✉, Ⓑ, ⇌, ✈ (Cambridge).

SHOTLEY: (01473) **Shotley Marina** (350, visitors welcome) ☎ 788982 H24, 📠 788868, £1.59, access H24 via lock; FW, AC, D, ⊡, ♿, ME, El, Ⓔ, Sh, BH (40 ton), C, V, BY, CH, SM, Bar, R, Gas, Gaz, Ferry to Harwich; **Shotley SC** ☎ 787500, Slip, FW, Bar. WRABNESS: M, FW, V. MISTLEY and MANNINGTREE: AB, M, FW, V, P & D (cans), Gas, Bar. **Stour SC** ☎ (01206) 393924 M, Bar.

RIVER ORWELL *9.4.22*

Suffolk **51°57'·06N 01°17'·77E** (GuardPHM by) ❁❁❁◊◊◊✿✿✿

CHARTS AC *5607, 2693*, 1491, *2052*; Imray Y16, C1, 2000 Series; Stanfords 5, 6; OS 169. A *Yachting Guide to Harwich Harbour and its Rivers* has much useful info, inc Harwich tidal predictions; it can be obtained free from Harwich Haven Authority, The Quay, Harwich CO12 3HH; ☎ (01255) 243030, 📠 240933.

TIDES Pin Mill +0100 Dover; Ipswich +0115 Dover; ML 2·4; Duration 0555; Zone 0 (UT)

Standard Port WALTON-ON-THE-NAZE (⟵)

Times				Height (metres)			
High Water		Low Water		MHWS	MHWN	MLWN	MLWS
0000	0600	0500	1100	4·2	3·4	1·1	0·4
1200	1800	1700	2300				
Differences PIN MILL							
+0012	+0015	–0008	–0012	–0·1	0·0	0·0	0·0
IPSWICH							
+0022	+0027	0000	–0012	0·0	0·0	–0·1	–0·1

SHELTER Good. Ent and river well marked, but many unlit moorings line both banks. ⚓s above Shotley Pt on W side, or off Pinmill. No yacht facilities at Felixstowe. Visitors' berths (by pre-arrangement) at Suffolk Yacht Hbr, Woolverstone Marina and Fox's Marina (Ipswich) accessible 0800-2000 on request as is Ipswich Haven - call *Ipswich Port Radio* Ch 14 before arrival, then call *Neptune Marina* or *Ipswich Port Marina*.

NAVIGATION Appr/ent from sea as in 9.4.21. WPT Shotley Spit SCM buoy, Q (6)+L Fl 15s, 51°57'·21N 01°17'·68E, at river ent. Keep clear of the many merchant ships, ferries from/to Harwich, Felixstowe & Ipswich, especially container ships turning between Trinity container terminal and Shotley Spit and Guard buoys. 6kn is max speed in R Orwell.

LIGHTS AND MARKS Suffolk Yacht Hbr appr marked by four bns and ldg lts: front Iso Y; rear Oc Y 4s. Woolverstone Marina: 2 FR (vert). A14 bridge lts: Centre FY (clearance 38m)

No 9 Pier 2 FR (vert) } shown up and

No 10 Pier 2 FG (vert) } down stream.

● and ● tfc lts control ent to Ipswich Dock (H24).

RADIO TELEPHONE Call: *Ipswich Port Radio* and *Prince Philip Lock* VHF Ch **14** 16 12 (H24). Once above Shotley Pt or anywhere in the area, monitor Ch 14 continuously in fog. Suffolk Yacht Hbr, Woolverstone Marina, Fox'sMarina: Ch 80 M. Neptune Marina: Ch M 14 80 (0800-1730LT), Ipswich Marina Ch M 80.

TELEPHONE (Dial code 01473) Orwell Navigation Service 231010 (also Ipswich Hr Mr and Port Radio); MRSC (01255) 675518; ⊖ 235704 (H24); Marinecall 0891 500455; Police 233000; Ⓗ 712233.

FACILITIES

LEVINGTON: **Suffolk Yacht Hbr** (SYH) (500+ ⓥ welcome) ☎ 659240, 📠 659632, £1.23, Slip, ♿, P, D, FW, ME, El, Ⓔ, Sh, C (15 ton), BH (10/60 ton), CH, V, Gas, Gaz, LPG, AC, SM, ⊡, ♿, ✚, Access H24; **Haven Ports YC** ☎ 659658, R, Bar. **Town** ✉, Ⓑ (Felixstowe), ⇌ (bus to Ipswich), ✈ (Cambridge/Norwich).

PIN MILL: **Hr Mr** ☎ 780621, mobile 07714 260568, M £6, L, CH, C (6 ton), SH, ME, El, FW, D (cans), Bar, R; **Pin Mill SC** ☎ 780271; Facilities at Ipswich.

WOOLVERSTONE: **Woolverstone Marina** (200 + 120 ⓜ, ⓥ welcome) ☎ 780206 (H24), 📠 780273, £1.65, D, FW, BY, ME, El, Sh, AC, Gas, Gaz, ⊡, ♿, C (20 ton), SM, CH, Slip, V, R; **Royal Harwich YC** ☎ 780319, AB, R, Bar. **Town** EC Chelmondiston Wed; ✉, V.

IPSWICH: **Fox's Marina** (100+some visitors) ☎ 689111, 📠 601737, £1.15, FW, AC, D, P (cans), BY, Gas, Gaz, BH (44 and 70 ton), C (7 ton), ME, El, Ⓔ, Sh, CH, ACA, Rigging, Bar; H24 access via Prince Philip Lock to **Neptune Marina** (100+100 ⓥ), ☎ 215204 📠 215206, £1.32, and **Ipswich Haven Marina**, ☎ 236644 📠 236645, £1.55, near city centre, both with FW, AC, ⊡, D, P (cans), Sh, ME, C, BH, BY, El, Ⓔ, Gas, Gaz, R, Bar; **Orwell YC** ☎ 602288, Slip, L, FW, Bar. **City** No EC; ✉, Ⓑ, ⇌, ✈ (Cambridge/Norwich).

RIVER DEBEN *9.4.23*

Suffolk **51°59'·38N 01°23'·58E** (Felixstowe Ferry)

CHARTS AC *5607, 2693, 2052*; Imray Y16, C1, C28, 2000 Series; Stan 3, 5, 6; OS 169

TIDES Woodbridge Haven +0025 Dover; Woodbridge +0105 Dover; ML 1·9; Duration 0635; Zone 0 (UT)

Standard Port WALTON-ON-THE-NAZE (⟵)

Times				Height (metres)			
High Water		Low Water		MHWS	MHWN	MLWN	MLWS
0100	0700	0100	0700	4·2	3·4	1·1	0·4
1300	1900	1300	1900				
Differences FELIXSTOWE PIER							
–0005	–0007	–0018	–0020	–0·5	–0·4	0·0	0·0
BAWDSEY							
–0016	–0020	–0030	–0032	–0·8	–0·6	–0·1	–0·1
WOODBRIDGE HAVEN (Ent)							
0000	–0005	–0020	–0025	–0·5	–0·5	–0·1	+0·1
WOODBRIDGE (Town)							
+0045	+0025	+0025	–0020	–0·2	–0·3	–0·2	0·0

SHELTER Good in Tide Mill Yacht Harbour (TMYH) at Woodbridge. Ent by No 24 PHM buoy; depth over sill, dries 1·5m, is 1·6m @ MHWN and 2·5m MHWS, with very accurate tide gauge and 8 waiting buoys. ⚓s up-river N of Horse Sand, at: Ramsholt, Waldringfield, Methersgate, Kyson Point and Woodbridge (9M from ent), keeping clear of moorings.

NAVIGATION WPT Woodbridge Haven unlit SWM buoy, 51°58'·18N 01°23'·79E, thence leave G conical Bar buoy to Stbd and in 100m the Red PHM to port, clearing The Knolls, steer for entrance. If a pilot is required call VHF Ch 08 (call *Odd Times*). The shifting shingle bar may be crossed at HW–4 to HW depending on draft. Best to enter after half-flood, and leave on the flood. The ent is only 1ca wide and in strong on-shore winds gets dangerously choppy; chan is well buoyed/marked. Keep to the W shore until PHM opposite the SC, then move E of Horse Sand just up river of the ent. No commercial tfc. Speed limit is 8kn above Green Reach. For current sketch map of approach, send SAE (plus 2 1st-class stamps for RNLI) to: Tidemill Yacht Hbr, Woodbridge, Suffolk IP12 1BP.

LIGHTS AND MARKS Ldg marks (unlit) are now unreliable. No lights.

RADIO TELEPHONE Pilot Ch 08. Tide Mill Yacht Hbr VHF Ch **80** M (some VHF dead spots down-river).

TELEPHONE (Dial code 01394) Hr Mr 270106, mob 07803476621, Pilot 285005, mob 07778 401105; MRSC (01255) 675518; Marinecall 09068 500 455; ⊖ (01473) 235704 (H24); Police 383377; Ramsholt Hr Mr 07751 034959.

FACILITIES
FELIXSTOWE FERRY (01394) **Quay** Slip, M, L, FW, ME, El, Sh, CH, V, R, Bar; **Felixstowe Ferry SC** ☎ 283785; **Felixstowe Ferry BY** ☎ 282173, M (200), Gas, Slip. RAMSHOLT **Services:** M, FW, Bar. WALDRINGFIELD (01473) Hbr Mr 0410 598552) **Waldringfield SC** ☎ 736633, Bar; **Services:** BY, C, Slip, D, FW, CH, Gas, Gaz, V. WOODBRIDGE (01394) **Tide Mill Yacht Hbr** (150+50 Ⓥ) ☎ 385745, 📠 380735, £1.50, D, L, FW, ME, El, Sh, C (10 ton), AC, V; Tide Mill is conspic daymark. **Services:** CH, Slip, C, M, ACA; **Deben YC**. **Town** P, D, L, FW, CH, V, R, Bar, ✉, Ⓑ, ⇌, ✈ (Cambridge or Norwich).

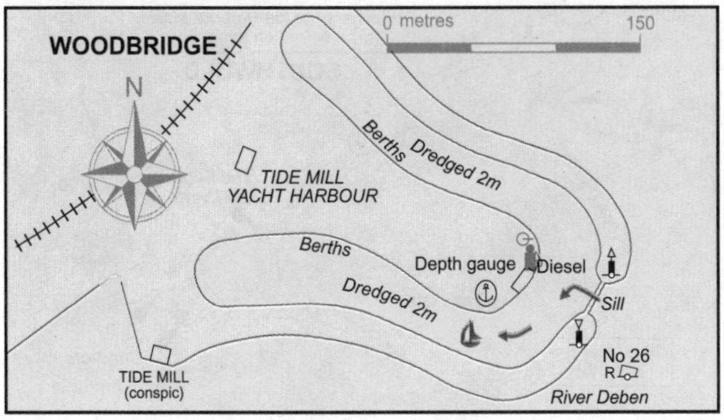

RIVER ORE/ALDE *9.4.24*

Suffolk **52°02'·13N 01°27'·49E** (Ent)

CHARTS AC *5607, 2695, 2693*, 1543, *2052*; Imray C28, 2000 Series; Stanfords 3, 5, 6; OS 169

TIDES Ent. +0015 Dover Slaughden Quay +0155 Dover; ML1·6; Duration 0620; Zone 0 (UT)

Standard Port WALTON-ON-THE-NAZE (⟵)

Times				Height (metres)			
High Water		Low Water		MHWS	MHWN	MLWN	MLWS
0100	0700	0100	0700	4·2	3·4	1·1	0·4
1300	1900	1300	1900				
Differences ORFORD HAVEN BAR							
–0026	–0030	–0036	–0038	–1·0	–0·8	–0·1	0·0
ORFORD QUAY							
+0040	+0040	+0055	+0055	–1·4	–1·1	0·0	+0·2
SLAUGHDEN QUAY							
+0105	+0105	+0125	+0125	–1·3	–0·8	–0·1	+0·2
IKEN CLIFF							
+0130	+0130	+0155	+0155	–1·3	–1·0	0·0	+0·2

SHELTER Good shelter within the river, but the entrance should not be attempted in strong E/ESE onshore winds and rough seas or at night. Good ⚓s as shown and at Iken; also as between Martello Tr and Slaughden Quay. Landing on Havergate Island, a bird sanctuary, is prohib. Visitors' moorings at Orford have small pick-up buoys marked V.

NAVIGATION WPT Orford Haven SWM buoy, 52°01'·91N 01°27'·32E *in Mar '01*; it may be moved. For latest position call Thames CG ☎ (01255) 675518. The chartlet below depicts a layout of the ent, to which current info can be referred. It is essential that the latest plan of ent and directions (£2, incl post) is obtained from: Small Craft Deliveries, 12 Quay St, Woodbridge, Suffolk IP12 1RJ, ☎ (01394) 383508; or local marinas or chandlers.

Navigation *continued overleaf*

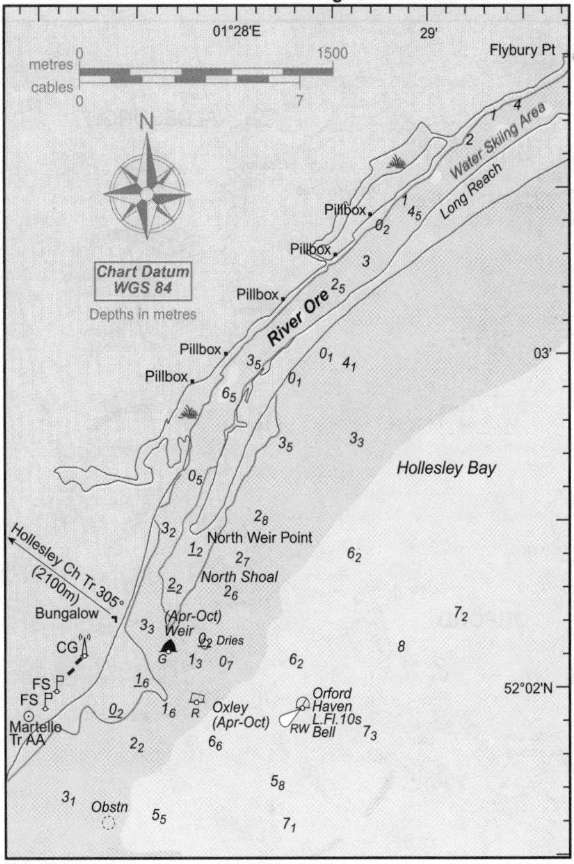

River Ore/Alde *continued*

The bar (approx 0·5m) shifts after onshore gales and is dangerous in rough or confused seas. These result from tidal streams offshore running against those within the shingle banks. Sp ebb reaches 6kn. Without local info do not enter before half flood or at night. For a first visit, appr at about LW+$2\frac{1}{2}$ in settled conditions and at nps. See previous warnings. Beware shoals S & SW of Dove Pt (SW tip of Havergate Island). R Ore (re-named R Alde between Orford and Slaughden Quay) is navigable up to Snape. The upper reaches are shallow and winding, and although marked by withies these may have been damaged. There are shelfish beds on the E bank centred on 52°08′·0N 01°35′·6E.

LIGHTS AND MARKS Orfordness lt ho, W tr/R bands, Fl 5s and F.G.RW, is 5·5M NE of Haven buoy. Ent and river are unlit. Shingle Street, about 2ca S of ent, is identified by Martello tr 'AA', CG Stn, terrace houses and DF aerial. Up-river, Orford Ch and Castle are conspic; also Martello Tr 'CC', 3ca S of Slaughden Quay.

RADIO TELEPHONE Call *Chantry* on Ch 08..

TELEPHONE (Dial codes 01394 Orford; 01728 Aldeburgh) Hr Mr Orford 450481; Hbr Office 459950; Hr Mr Aldeburgh 453047; Marinecall 09068 500455; MRSC (01255) 675518; Police (01473) 613500; Orford Dr 450315 (HO); Aldeburgh Dr 452027 (HO); for Dr outside HO and at weekends, call Ipswich (01474) 299622.

FACILITIES
ORFORD **Orford Quay** Slip, AB (1 hour free, then £10/hour), M £5 night, L, FW, D (cans), C (mobile 5 ton), CH, Sh (£5 deposit), Orford SC (OSC), R, Bar. **Village** ($\frac{1}{4}$M). EC Wed; P & D (cans), Gas, Gaz, ✉, V, R, Bar, ⇌ (twice daily bus to Woodbridge).
ALDEBURGH **Slaughden Quay** L, FW, Slip, BH (20 ton), CH; **Aldeburgh YC** (AYC) ☎ 452562, ♿, Sh. **Slaughden SC** (SSC). **Services:** M £4, Sh, Slip, D, ME, BY, Gas, Gaz, P. **Town** ($\frac{3}{4}$M), EC Wed; P, V, R, Bar, ✉, Ⓑ, ⇌ (bus to Wickham Market), ✈ (Norwich).

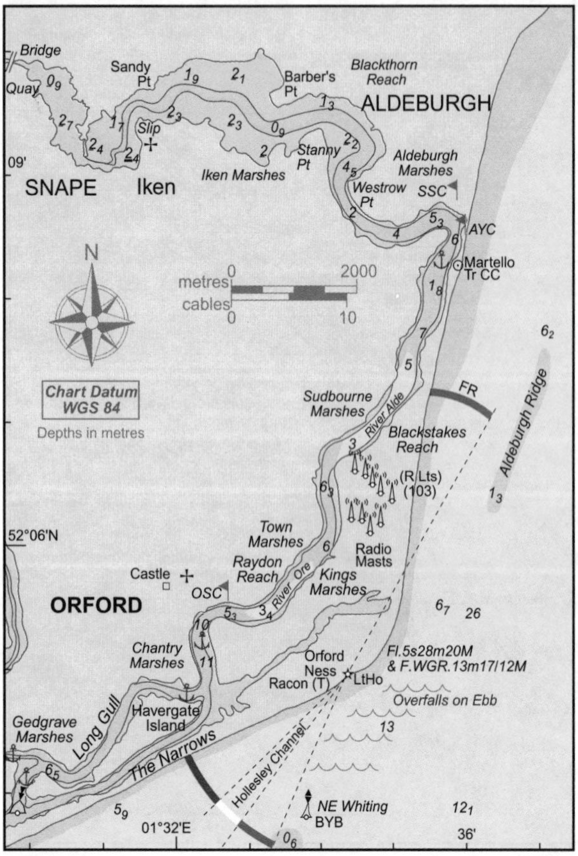

SOUTHWOLD *9.4.25*

Suffolk **52°18′·78N 01°40′·54E**

CHARTS AC *2695,* 1543; Imray C28, C29; Stanfords 3; OS 156

TIDES –0105 Dover; ML 1·5; Duration 0620; Zone 0 (UT)

Standard Port LOWESTOFT (⟶)

Times				Height (metres)			
High Water		Low Water		MHWS	MHWN	MLWN	MLWS
0300	0900	0200	0800	2·4	2·1	1·0	0·5
1500	2100	1400	2000				
Differences SOUTHWOLD							
+0105	+0105	+0055	+0055	0·0	0·0	–0·1	0·0
MINSMERE							
+0110	+0110	+0110	+0110	0·0	–0·1	–0·2	–0·2
ALDEBURGH (seaward)							
+0130	+0130	+0115	+0120	+0·3	+0·2	–0·1	–0·2
ORFORD NESS							
+0135	+0135	+0135	+0125	+0·4	+0·6	–0·1	0·0

Note: HW time differences (above) for Southwold apply up the hbr. At the ent mean HW is HW Lowestoft +0035.

SHELTER Good, but the ent is dangerous in strong winds from N through E to S. Visitors berth on a staging 6ca from the ent, on N bank near to the Harbour Inn. If rafted, shore lines are essential due to current.

NAVIGATION WPT 52°18′·09N 01°41′·69E, 135°/315° from/to N Pier lt, 1M. Enter on the flood since the ebb runs up to 6kn. Some shoals are unpredictable; a sand and shingle bar, extent/depth variable, lies off the hbr ent and a shoal builds inside N Pier. Obtain details of appr chans from Hr Mr before entering (Ch 12 or ☎ 724712). Enter between piers in midstream. When chan widens, at The Knuckle (2 FG vert), turn stbd towards LB House; keep within 30m of quay wall until it ends, when resume midstream. Unlit low footbridge $\frac{3}{4}$M upstream of ent.

LIGHTS AND MARKS Walberswick ⊕ on with N Pier lt = 268°. Hbr ent opens on 300°. 3 FR (vert) at N pier = port closed. Lt ho, W ○ tr, is in Southwold town, 0·86M NNE of hbr ent, Fl (4) WR 20s 37m 16/12M; vis R (intens) 204°-215°, W215°-001°, R001°-032°.

RADIO TELEPHONE *Southwold Port Radio* Ch 12 16 09 (as required).

TELEPHONE (Dial code 01502) Hr Mr 724712; MRCC (01493) 851338; ⊖ (01473) 235704 (H24); Marinecall 09068 500455; Weather (01603) 660779; Police 722666; Dr 722326; ⊞ 723333; Pilot 724712.

FACILITIES Hbr AB 20-30ft £11, FW, D (cans) also by bowser 100 litres min, BY, CH, ME, Sh, Slip, BH (20 ton), SM. **Southwold SC; Town** ($\frac{3}{4}$M), EC Wed (Southwold & Walberswick); Gas, Gaz, Kos, P (cans, 1M), R, V, ✉, Ⓑ, ⇌ (bus to Brampton/Darsham), ✈ (Norwich).

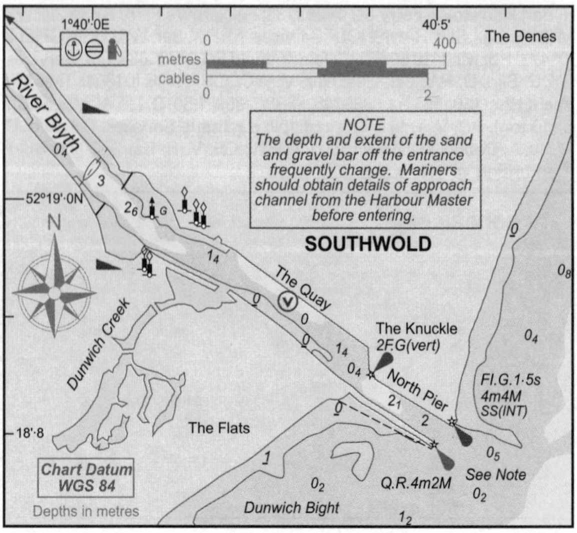

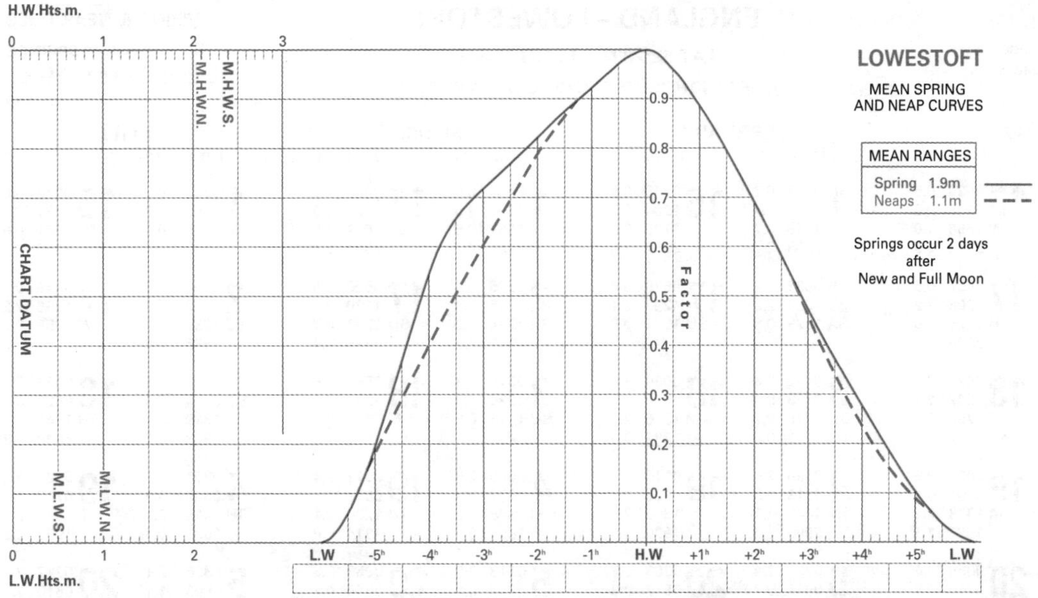

LOWESTOFT 9.4.26

Suffolk **52°28'·31N 01°45'·39E** ❀❀❀◊◊◊✿✿✿

CHARTS AC *1536, 1543*; Imray C28, C29; Stanfords 3; OS 156/134

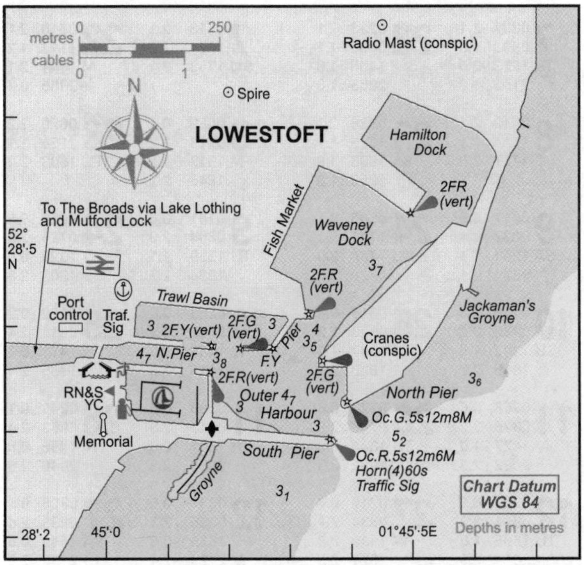

TIDES –0133 Dover; ML 1·6; Duration 0620; Zone 0 (UT).

SHELTER Good; hbr accessible H24. Wind over tide, esp ebb, can make the ent lively. Fairway is dredged 4·7m. Speed limit 4kn. Yacht Basin in SW corner of Outer Hbr is run by RN & S YC; on N side ent leads to pontoons B & A in 2·5m. No berthing on N side of S Pier.

Bridge to Inner Hbr (Lake Lothing and Lowestoft CC) lifts at the following local times (20 mins notice required):

Mon-Fri	0700, 0930, 1100, 1600, 1900, 2100
Sat/Sun, Bank Hols	0745, 0930, 1100, 1400, 1730, 1900, 2100

and also, by prior arrangement, when ships transit. Small craft may pass under the bridge (clearance 2·2m) at any time but VHF Ch 14 contact advisable.

NAVIGATION Listen on VHF Ch 14 when in vicinity of hbr. Sands continually shift and buoys are moved to suit. Beware shoals and drying areas; do not cross banks in bad weather nor at mid flood/ebb.

Speed limit in harbour 4 kn.

From S, WPT is E Barnard ECM buoy, Q (3) 10s, 52°25'·15N 01°46'·36E; thence via Stanford Chan E of Newcome Sand QR, Stanford Fl R 2.5s and N Newcome Fl (4) R 15s, all PHM buoys. S Holm SCM, VQ (6)+L Fl 10s, and SW Holm SHM, Fl (2) G 5s, buoys mark the seaward side of this chan.

From E, WPT is Corton ECM buoy, Q (3) 10s Whis, 52°31'·14N 01°51'·37E; then via Holm Chan (buoyed) into Corton Road. Or approach direct to S Holm SCM buoy for Stanford Chan.

From N, appr via Yarmouth, Gorleston and Corton Roads.

LIGHTS AND MARKS N Newcome PHM lt buoy bears 086°/5·5ca from hbr ent. Lowestoft lt ho, Fl 15s 37m 23M, is 1M N of hbr ent.

Tfc Sigs: Comply with IPTS (only Nos 2 and 5 are shown) on S pierhead; also get clearance on VHF Ch 14 when entering or leaving, due to restricted vis in appr and ent.

Bridge Sigs (on N side of bridge):

● = bridge operating, keep 150m clear.
= vessels may enter/leave Inner Hbr.

Yacht Basin tfc sigs on E arm (only visible from inside): 3 FR (vert) = no exit; GWG (vert) = proceed on instruction.

RADIO TELEPHONE *Lowestoft Hbr Control* (ABP) VHF Ch **14** 16 11 (H24). Pilot Ch 14. RN & SYC Ch 14, 80.

TELEPHONE (Dial code 01502) Hr Mr & Bridge Control 572286; Mutford Bridge and Lock 531778 (+Ansafone, checked daily at 0830, 1300 & 1730); Oulton Broad Yacht Stn 574946; MRCC (01493) 851338; Pilot 572286 ext 243; ⊖ (01473) 235704 (H24); Weather (01603) 660779; Marinecall 09068 500455; Police (01986) 835100; Ⓗ 600611.

FACILITIES **Royal Norfolk & Suffolk YC** ☎ 566726, 🖷 517981, £1.60 inc YC facilities, AC, D, FW, C (2 ton), ⛭, Slip, R, Bar; **Lowestoft Cruising Club** ☎ 574376 (occas), e-mail lowcruise@hotmail.com. AB £0.85, AC, FW, Slip (emergency only); **Services:** ME, El, Sh, CH, Gas, Gaz, Ⓔ, ACA. **Town** V, R, Bar, ✉, Ⓑ, ⇌, ✈ (Norwich).

Entry to the Broads: www.norfolkbroads.com. Passage to Oulton Broad, from Lake Lothing via two bridges and Mutford Lock (openings are coordinated; fee £6), is available 7 days/wk in working hrs HJ as pre-arranged with Mutford Br/Lock ☎ (01502) 531778/523003 or VHF Ch 09 14 (occas), who will also advise visitors drawing >1·7m. Mutford Control operates in response to bookings and daily 0800-1100 and 1300-1600LT. Oulton Broad Yacht Station ☎ (01502) 574946. From Oulton Broad, access into the R. Waveney is via Oulton Dyke. New Cut is a short cut from the R. Waveney to the R Yare for air draft <7·3m. See 9.4.27 for Broads.

TIME ZONE (UTC)
For Summer Time add ONE hour in **non-shaded areas**

ENGLAND – LOWESTOFT

LAT 52°28′N LONG 1°45′E

TIMES AND HEIGHTS OF HIGH AND LOW WATERS

SPRING & NEAP TIDES
Dates in **red** are **SPRINGS**
Dates in **blue** are **NEAPS**

YEAR **2002**

JANUARY

Date	Day	Time	m
1	TU	0428 1045 1639 2249	0.6 2.5 0.8 2.6
2	W	0515 1132 1721 2329	0.5 2.5 0.8 2.6
3	TH	0602 1221 1803	0.4 2.4 0.9
4	F	0012 0650 1315 1846	2.6 0.5 2.3 1.0
5	SA	0058 0744 1418 1934	2.5 0.5 2.2 1.1
6	SU	0149 0845 1529 2029	2.5 0.6 2.2 1.2
7	M	0246 0954 1636 2134	2.4 0.6 2.1 1.2
8	TU	0405 1107 1736 2320	2.3 0.7 2.2 1.2
9	W	0531 1215 1830	2.3 0.7 2.2
10	TH	0042 0639 1314 1917	1.0 2.3 0.7 2.2
11	F	0142 0739 1406 2002	0.9 2.3 0.8 2.3
12	SA	0233 0836 1452 2044	0.7 2.3 0.8 2.4
13	SU	0321 0929 1532 ● 2124	0.6 2.3 0.9 2.4
14	M	0404 1016 1607 2203	0.5 2.3 0.9 2.5
15	TU	0444 1058 1634 2239	0.5 2.3 1.0 2.5
16	W	0520 1135 1658 2312	0.5 2.2 1.0 2.5
17	TH	0552 1208 1725 2345	0.6 2.2 1.0 2.5
18	F	0625 1242 1754	0.6 2.1 1.0
19	SA	0020 0701 1323 1827	2.5 0.7 2.1 1.1
20	SU	0059 0744 1411 1908	2.4 0.8 2.0 1.1
21	M	0143 0839 1509 1958	2.3 0.9 2.0 1.2
22	TU	0233 0940 1612 2104	2.3 0.9 2.0 1.3
23	W	0329 1039 1713 2244	2.2 0.9 2.0 1.3
24	TH	0438 1135 1809 2354	2.2 0.9 2.1 1.2
25	F	0556 1229 1859	2.2 0.9 2.2
26	SA	0053 0700 1322 1944	1.0 2.2 0.8 2.3
27	SU	0150 0759 1412 2027	0.9 2.3 0.8 2.4
28	M	0244 0855 1501 ○ 2109	0.7 2.4 0.8 2.5
29	TU	0336 0948 1547 2152	0.5 2.4 0.7 2.6
30	W	0424 1037 1630 2234	0.4 2.5 0.7 2.7
31	TH	0509 1123 1710 2316	0.2 2.5 0.7 2.7

FEBRUARY

Date	Day	Time	m
1	F	0553 1208 1749 2358	0.2 2.4 0.7 2.7
2	SA	0637 1254 1829	0.2 2.3 0.8
3	SU	0042 0723 1346 1911	2.6 0.3 2.2 0.9
4	M	0130 0813 1448 2000	2.5 0.5 2.1 1.0
5	TU	0225 0911 1557 2100	2.4 0.7 2.0 1.1
6	W	0344 1021 1701 2222	2.2 0.8 2.0 1.1
7	TH	0518 1149 1759	2.2 0.9 2.1
8	F	0030 0632 1302 1851	1.0 2.2 0.9 2.1
9	SA	0134 0737 1357 1939	0.8 2.2 1.0 2.2
10	SU	0225 0835 1443 2024	0.7 2.2 1.0 2.3
11	M	0311 0925 1523 2106	0.6 2.3 1.0 2.4
12	TU	0353 1008 1556 ● 2144	0.5 2.3 1.0 2.4
13	W	0430 1042 1619 2220	0.5 2.2 1.0 2.5
14	TH	0500 1110 1638 2252	0.5 2.2 0.9 2.5
15	F	0527 1136 1701 2324	0.5 2.2 0.9 2.5
16	SA	0553 1204 1729 2357	0.6 2.2 0.9 2.5
17	SU	0620 1237 1801	0.6 2.1 0.9
18	M	0034 0650 1315 1837	2.4 0.7 2.1 0.9
19	TU	0116 0726 1358 1920	2.3 0.8 2.0 1.0
20	W	0203 0817 1449 2012	2.2 0.9 2.0 1.1
21	TH	0256 0949 1559 2127	2.1 1.0 1.9 1.2
22	F	0359 1101 1722 2322	2.1 1.0 2.0 1.1
23	SA	0520 1203 1823	2.1 1.0 2.1
24	SU	0033 0642 1303 1914	1.0 2.2 0.9 2.2
25	M	0137 0750 1359 2001	0.8 2.3 0.9 2.3
26	TU	0234 0847 1450 2046	0.5 2.4 0.8 2.5
27	W	0324 0937 1535 ○ 2132	0.3 2.4 0.7 2.6
28	TH	0411 1022 1617 2216	0.1 2.5 0.6 2.7

MARCH

Date	Day	Time	m
1	F	0454 1104 1657 2259	0.0 2.5 0.6 2.7
2	SA	0536 1145 1734 2342	0.0 2.4 0.6 2.7
3	SU	0616 1225 1811	0.1 2.3 0.6
4	M	0026 0657 1308 1851	2.6 0.3 2.2 0.7
5	TU	0113 0743 1358 1938	2.5 0.5 2.1 0.8
6	W	0209 0836 1508 2038	2.3 0.8 2.0 0.9
7	TH	0337 0938 1623 2156	2.1 1.0 2.0 1.0
8	F	0512 1114 1727	2.1 1.1 2.0
9	SA	0017 0627 1251 1824	0.9 2.1 1.1 2.1
10	SU	0119 0732 1343 1915	0.8 2.2 1.1 2.2
11	M	0208 0826 1427 2002	0.6 2.2 1.0 2.3
12	TU	0252 0911 1505 2044	0.5 2.3 1.0 2.3
13	W	0331 0947 1536 2122	0.5 2.3 0.9 2.4
14	TH	0405 1013 1559 ● 2157	0.5 2.3 0.9 2.4
15	F	0432 1036 1617 2229	0.5 2.2 0.8 2.4
16	SA	0455 1101 1639 2301	0.5 2.3 0.8 2.4
17	SU	0520 1130 1707 2335	0.5 2.2 0.7 2.4
18	M	0545 1201 1739	0.6 2.2 0.7
19	TU	0012 0613 1236 1814	2.4 0.7 2.1 0.8
20	W	0053 0648 1315 1854	2.3 0.8 2.1 0.8
21	TH	0140 0733 1401 1944	2.2 0.9 2.0 1.0
22	F	0233 0835 1456 2053	2.1 1.1 1.9 1.0
23	SA	0338 1025 1603 2255	2.1 1.1 1.9 1.0
24	SU	0506 1141 1734	2.1 1.1 2.0
25	M	0016 0638 1247 1839	0.8 2.2 1.0 2.1
26	TU	0121 0743 1344 1932	0.6 2.3 0.9 2.3
27	W	0216 0834 1433 2021	0.4 2.4 0.8 2.5
28	TH	0305 0919 1518 ○ 2109	0.2 2.4 0.6 2.6
29	F	0350 1000 1600 2155	0.0 2.5 0.5 2.7
30	SA	0433 1039 1639 2241	0.0 2.4 0.5 2.7
31	SU	0513 1117 1717 2325	0.0 2.4 0.4 2.7

APRIL

Date	Day	Time	m
1	M	0553 1155 1755	0.2 2.3 0.5
2	TU	0010 0632 1235 1835	2.6 0.4 2.2 0.6
3	W	0059 0714 1319 1923	2.4 0.6 2.1 0.7
4	TH	0201 0805 1418 2025	2.2 0.9 2.0 0.8
5	F	0336 0905 1542 2144	2.1 1.1 2.0 0.9
6	SA	0503 1018 1652 2349	2.1 1.3 2.0 0.9
7	SU	0613 1224 1753	2.1 1.2 2.1
8	M	0052 0713 1317 1846	0.7 2.2 1.2 2.2
9	TU	0141 0804 1359 1934	0.6 2.3 1.1 2.3
10	W	0223 0845 1436 2016	0.6 2.3 1.0 2.3
11	TH	0300 0913 1507 2054	0.6 2.3 0.9 2.3
12	F	0331 0935 1529 ● 2129	0.6 2.3 0.8 2.4
13	SA	0356 1001 1551 2204	0.6 2.3 0.8 2.4
14	SU	0421 1030 1617 2239	0.6 2.3 0.7 2.4
15	M	0448 1101 1647 2314	0.6 2.3 0.6 2.4
16	TU	0517 1131 1721 2352	0.6 2.3 0.6 2.4
17	W	0549 1205 1758	0.7 2.2 0.7
18	TH	0033 0625 1245 1840	2.3 0.8 2.1 0.8
19	F	0121 0710 1331 1933	2.2 1.0 2.1 0.8
20	SA	0217 0810 1424 2044	2.1 1.1 2.0 0.9
21	SU	0328 0934 1525 2233	2.1 1.2 2.0 0.9
22	M	0510 1113 1641 2355	2.1 1.2 2.1 0.7
23	TU	0629 1225 1803	2.2 1.1 2.2
24	W	0058 0725 1322 1903	0.5 2.3 0.9 2.3
25	TH	0152 0812 1411 1956	0.3 2.4 0.8 2.4
26	F	0241 0853 1456 2046	0.1 2.4 0.6 2.5
27	SA	0326 0933 1540 ○ 2135	0.1 2.4 0.5 2.6
28	SU	0409 1012 1621 2223	0.1 2.4 0.4 2.6
29	M	0450 1050 1702 2309	0.2 2.4 0.4 2.6
30	TU	0529 1129 1742 2357	0.3 2.3 0.4 2.4

Chart Datum: 1·50 metres below Ordnance Datum (Newlyn)

Register for your **FREE** weekly weather email service from Macmillan Reeds
» at **www.nauticaldata.com – NOW!** «
weekend weather reports sent to your email address, every Thursday

TIME ZONE (UTC)
For Summer Time add ONE hour in **non-shaded areas**

ENGLAND – LOWESTOFT

LAT 52°28′N LONG 1°45′E

TIMES AND HEIGHTS OF HIGH AND LOW WATERS

SPRING & NEAP TIDES
Dates in red are SPRINGS
Dates in blue are NEAPS

YEAR **2002**

MAY

Date	Day	Time	m	Time	m	Time	m	Time	m
1	W	0607	0.5	1208	2.3	1825	0.5		
2	TH	0049	2.3	0647	0.8	1251	2.2	1914	0.6
3	F	0158	2.1	0735	1.0	1344	2.1	2017	0.7
4	SA	0327	2.1	0833	1.2	1459	2.1	2130	0.8
5	SU	0441	2.1	0937	1.3	1610	2.1	2257	0.8
6	M	0545	2.1	1056	1.3	1713	2.1		
7	TU	0011	0.8	0642	2.2	1233	1.3	1808	2.2
8	W	0103	0.7	0730	2.2	1320	1.2	1857	2.2
9	TH	0144	0.7	0805	2.3	1357	1.0	1941	2.3
10	F	0218	0.6	0830	2.3	1426	0.9	2020	2.3
11	SA	0248	0.6	0857	2.3	1453	0.8	2059	2.3
12	SU	0317	0.6	0930	2.3	1523	0.8	● 2138	2.3
13	M	0347	0.6	1004	2.4	1556	0.7	2217	2.4
14	TU	0420	0.6	1036	2.4	1631	0.6	2255	2.4
15	W	0454	0.7	1109	2.3	1709	0.6	2335	2.3
16	TH	0530	0.8	1143	2.3	1750	0.6		
17	F	0019	2.3	0610	0.9	1223	2.3	1836	0.7
18	SA	0109	2.2	0657	1.0	1309	2.2	1932	0.7
19	SU	0208	2.2	0753	1.2	1401	2.2	2041	0.7
20	M	0332	2.1	0900	1.2	1500	2.1	2210	0.7
21	TU	0458	2.2	1026	1.2	1608	2.2	2327	0.6
22	W	0604	2.2	1151	1.1	1731	2.2		
23	TH	0031	0.4	0658	2.3	1254	1.0	1837	2.3
24	F	0126	0.3	0744	2.4	1346	0.8	1934	2.4
25	SA	0216	0.2	0826	2.4	1435	0.7	2028	2.5
26	SU	0302	0.2	0907	2.4	1521	0.5	○ 2119	2.5
27	M	0346	0.3	0947	2.4	1606	0.4	2210	2.5
28	TU	0428	0.4	1027	2.4	1650	0.4	2259	2.4
29	W	0506	0.5	1107	2.4	1733	0.4	2349	2.3
30	TH	0543	0.7	1147	2.4	1818	0.5		
31	F	0043	2.2	0621	0.9	1228	2.3	1906	0.6

JUNE

Date	Day	Time	m	Time	m	Time	m	Time	m
1	SA	0149	2.1	0703	1.1	1315	2.3	2002	0.7
2	SU	0300	2.1	0754	1.2	1414	2.2	2102	0.7
3	M	0404	2.1	0853	1.3	1521	2.2	2201	0.8
4	TU	0502	2.1	0955	1.4	1622	2.2	2300	0.8
5	W	0556	2.1	1059	1.3	1720	2.2	2354	0.8
6	TH	0640	2.2	1202	1.2	1812	2.2		
7	F	0041	0.8	0714	2.2	1255	1.1	1900	2.2
8	SA	0123	0.7	0748	2.3	1339	1.0	1946	2.3
9	SU	0201	0.7	0825	2.3	1419	0.9	2030	2.3
10	M	0240	0.7	0903	2.4	1459	0.8	● 2114	2.3
11	TU	0318	0.7	0941	2.4	1539	0.7	2158	2.3
12	W	0357	0.7	1016	2.4	1620	0.6	2241	2.4
13	TH	0436	0.7	1051	2.4	1703	0.6	2325	2.4
14	F	0516	0.8	1127	2.4	1748	0.6		
15	SA	0011	2.3	0558	0.9	1208	2.4	1835	0.6
16	SU	0102	2.3	0644	1.0	1253	2.4	1929	0.6
17	M	0204	2.2	0735	1.1	1343	2.3	2031	0.6
18	TU	0321	2.2	0832	1.2	1438	2.3	2142	0.6
19	W	0431	2.2	0937	1.2	1543	2.3	2255	0.5
20	TH	0533	2.2	1105	1.2	1705	2.3		
21	F	0001	0.5	0628	2.3	1224	1.0	1816	2.3
22	SA	0100	0.5	0716	2.3	1325	0.9	1918	2.3
23	SU	0154	0.5	0801	2.3	1418	0.7	2015	2.4
24	M	0243	0.5	0844	2.4	1509	0.6	○ 2111	2.4
25	TU	0328	0.6	0927	2.4	1556	0.5	2204	2.4
26	W	0410	0.6	1008	2.5	1642	0.4	2255	2.3
27	TH	0448	0.7	1048	2.5	1726	0.4	2344	2.3
28	F	0522	0.9	1127	2.5	1808	0.5		
29	SA	0032	2.2	0554	1.0	1206	2.5	1850	0.5
30	SU	0122	2.1	0629	1.1	1245	2.4	1935	0.6

JULY

Date	Day	Time	m	Time	m	Time	m	Time	m
1	M	0213	2.1	0710	1.2	1327	2.4	2023	0.7
2	TU	0306	2.0	0800	1.3	1418	2.3	2114	0.8
3	W	0358	2.0	0901	1.3	1518	2.2	2205	0.8
4	TH	0450	2.1	1006	1.3	1622	2.2	2257	0.8
5	F	0541	2.1	1109	1.3	1723	2.2	2348	0.8
6	SA	0629	2.2	1207	1.2	1820	2.2		
7	SU	0037	0.8	0714	2.3	1301	1.1	1913	2.2
8	M	0125	0.8	0757	2.3	1351	1.0	2004	2.3
9	TU	0210	0.8	0839	2.4	1440	0.8	2054	2.3
10	W	0255	0.8	0919	2.5	1527	0.7	● 2144	2.4
11	TH	0339	0.8	0958	2.5	1614	0.6	2232	2.4
12	F	0422	0.8	1035	2.6	1659	0.5	2318	2.4
13	SA	0504	0.8	1114	2.6	1744	0.4		
14	SU	0003	2.4	0545	0.8	1155	2.6	1829	0.4
15	M	0052	2.4	0628	0.9	1238	2.6	1918	0.4
16	TU	0146	2.3	0713	1.0	1325	2.5	2011	0.5
17	W	0251	2.2	0804	1.1	1418	2.4	2111	0.5
18	TH	0359	2.2	0903	1.1	1521	2.3	2219	0.6
19	F	0501	2.2	1019	1.1	1648	2.3	2331	0.7
20	SA	0559	2.2	1156	1.1	1805	2.3		
21	SU	0039	0.7	0650	2.2	1311	0.9	1911	2.3
22	M	0139	0.7	0738	2.3	1410	0.7	2012	2.3
23	TU	0231	0.8	0824	2.4	1502	0.6	2109	2.3
24	W	0318	0.8	0908	2.5	1549	0.5	○ 2201	2.3
25	TH	0358	0.9	0950	2.5	1633	0.4	2248	2.3
26	F	0433	0.9	1029	2.6	1713	0.4	2330	2.3
27	SA	0501	0.9	1106	2.6	1749	0.5		
28	SU	0006	2.2	0526	1.0	1140	2.6	1822	0.5
29	M	0039	2.2	0555	1.0	1214	2.5	1857	0.6
30	TU	0114	2.1	0627	1.1	1250	2.5	1936	0.7
31	W	0157	2.1	0704	1.1	1331	2.4	2024	0.8

AUGUST

Date	Day	Time	m	Time	m	Time	m	Time	m
1	TH	0252	2.0	0750	1.2	1418	2.3	2119	0.9
2	F	0353	2.0	0905	1.3	1514	2.2	2216	0.9
3	SA	0454	2.1	1028	1.3	1627	2.1	2311	0.9
4	SU	0551	2.1	1133	1.2	1741	2.1		
5	M	0005	0.9	0642	2.2	1234	1.1	1845	2.2
6	TU	0058	0.9	0729	2.3	1331	1.0	1945	2.3
7	W	0149	0.9	0813	2.4	1426	0.8	2041	2.3
8	TH	0239	0.9	0855	2.5	1518	0.6	● 2133	2.4
9	F	0326	0.8	0936	2.6	1605	0.5	2220	2.5
10	SA	0409	0.8	1016	2.7	1649	0.3	2304	2.5
11	SU	0450	0.7	1057	2.7	1732	0.2	2346	2.5
12	M	0530	0.7	1138	2.8	1814	0.2		
13	TU	0028	2.4	0609	0.8	1221	2.7	1857	0.3
14	W	0113	2.3	0651	0.8	1306	2.6	1944	0.5
15	TH	0207	2.2	0739	0.9	1358	2.5	2039	0.6
16	F	0318	2.1	0837	1.0	1505	2.3	2143	0.8
17	SA	0429	2.1	0952	1.1	1641	2.2	2301	0.9
18	SU	0531	2.1	1144	1.1	1801	2.2		
19	M	0028	1.0	0626	2.2	1305	0.9	1910	2.3
20	TU	0132	1.0	0716	2.3	1402	0.7	2011	2.3
21	W	0223	1.0	0803	2.4	1451	0.6	2105	2.4
22	TH	0306	1.0	0848	2.5	1535	0.5	○ 2151	2.4
23	F	0344	1.0	0929	2.5	1615	0.4	2231	2.4
24	SA	0415	1.0	1006	2.6	1650	0.5	2303	2.3
25	SU	0437	1.0	1040	2.6	1720	0.5	2328	2.3
26	M	0458	0.9	1112	2.6	1747	0.6	2351	2.3
27	TU	0524	0.9	1145	2.5	1814	0.7		
28	W	0020	2.2	0552	0.9	1220	2.5	1841	0.7
29	TH	0056	2.2	0625	1.0	1259	2.4	1912	0.9
30	F	0137	2.1	0704	1.1	1343	2.3	1959	1.0
31	SA	0229	2.1	0755	1.2	1435	2.2	2131	1.1

Chart Datum: 1·50 metres below Ordnance Datum (Newlyn)

Register for your FREE weekly weather email service from Macmillan Reeds
at **www.nauticaldata.com** – NOW!
weekend weather reports sent to your email address, every Thursday

TIME ZONE (UTC)
For Summer Time add ONE hour in **non-shaded areas**

ENGLAND – LOWESTOFT

LAT 52°28′N LONG 1°45′E

TIMES AND HEIGHTS OF HIGH AND LOW WATERS

SPRING & NEAP TIDES
Dates in red are SPRINGS
Dates in blue are NEAPS

YEAR **2002**

SEPTEMBER

Date	Day	Time	m	Time	m	Time	m	Time	m
1	SU	0351	2.1	0944	1.3	1540	2.1	2239	1.1
2	M	0510	2.1	1107	1.2	1709	2.1	2339	1.1
3	TU	0610	2.2	1213	1.1	1829	2.2		
4	W	0037	1.1	0659	2.3	1315	0.9	1935	2.3
5	TH	0133	1.0	0744	2.4	1411	0.7	2030	2.4
6	F	0224	0.9	0827	2.5	1502	0.5	2118	2.5
7	SA	0310	0.8	0910	2.7	1548	0.3	● 2201	2.6
8	SU	0353	0.7	0953	2.8	1631	0.2	2241	2.6
9	M	0433	0.7	1036	2.8	1712	0.1	2320	2.6
10	TU	0512	0.6	1119	2.8	1752	0.2	2358	2.5
11	W	0550	0.7	1202	2.8	1832	0.3		
12	TH	0038	2.4	0631	0.7	1248	2.6	1915	0.6
13	F	0123	2.3	0718	0.8	1341	2.4	2007	0.8
14	SA	0224	2.1	0818	1.0	1501	2.3	2110	1.0
15	SU	0353	2.1	0939	1.0	1640	2.2	2232	1.2
16	M	0502	2.1	1141	1.0	1759	2.2		
17	TU	0018	1.2	0600	2.2	1252	0.8	1906	2.3
18	W	0117	1.2	0653	2.3	1344	0.7	2002	2.4
19	TH	0204	1.1	0741	2.4	1430	0.6	2050	2.4
20	F	0245	1.1	0824	2.5	1512	0.5	2130	2.4
21	SA	0320	1.0	0904	2.5	1549	0.5	○ 2202	2.4
22	SU	0348	1.0	0939	2.6	1620	0.6	2225	2.4
23	M	0408	0.9	1012	2.6	1645	0.6	2245	2.4
24	TU	0429	0.9	1044	2.6	1707	0.6	2311	2.4
25	W	0455	0.8	1118	2.5	1730	0.7	2341	2.4
26	TH	0525	0.8	1154	2.5	1755	0.8		
27	F	0014	2.3	0557	0.9	1233	2.4	1824	0.9
28	SA	0052	2.2	0636	1.0	1317	2.3	1903	1.0
29	SU	0137	2.2	0724	1.1	1409	2.2	2000	1.2
30	M	0230	2.1	0842	1.2	1512	2.1	2159	1.3

OCTOBER

Date	Day	Time	m	Time	m	Time	m	Time	m
1	TU	0338	2.1	1043	1.2	1652	2.1	2313	1.3
2	W	0522	2.2	1154	1.0	1822	2.2		
3	TH	0017	1.2	0621	2.3	1256	0.8	1923	2.4
4	F	0114	1.1	0709	2.5	1350	0.6	2013	2.5
5	SA	0204	0.9	0756	2.6	1439	0.4	2056	2.5
6	SU	0249	0.8	0842	2.7	1524	0.2	● 2135	2.6
7	M	0332	0.7	0929	2.8	1607	0.1	2213	2.6
8	TU	0413	0.6	1014	2.8	1648	0.1	2251	2.6
9	W	0453	0.6	1100	2.8	1727	0.3	2329	2.5
10	TH	0533	0.6	1145	2.7	1806	0.5		
11	F	0008	2.4	0614	0.7	1233	2.5	1847	0.7
12	SA	0050	2.3	0704	0.8	1332	2.4	1936	1.0
13	SU	0142	2.2	0808	0.9	1504	2.2	2037	1.2
14	M	0310	2.2	0935	1.0	1635	2.2	2155	1.4
15	TU	0429	2.2	1120	0.9	1746	2.2	2351	1.4
16	W	0531	2.3	1226	0.8	1849	2.3		
17	TH	0049	1.3	0625	2.4	1318	0.7	1941	2.4
18	F	0136	1.2	0713	2.4	1402	0.6	2025	2.4
19	SA	0215	1.1	0756	2.5	1441	0.6	2059	2.4
20	SU	0249	1.0	0834	2.5	1515	0.6	2123	2.4
21	M	0314	1.0	0909	2.5	1542	0.7	○ 2144	2.4
22	TU	0335	0.9	0944	2.5	1605	0.7	2211	2.4
23	W	0401	0.8	1019	2.5	1629	0.7	2240	2.4
24	TH	0431	0.8	1055	2.5	1655	0.8	2311	2.4
25	F	0503	0.8	1131	2.4	1724	0.8	2344	2.4
26	SA	0539	0.9	1211	2.4	1757	0.9		
27	SU	0021	2.3	0619	0.9	1256	2.3	1837	1.1
28	M	0106	2.3	0710	1.0	1349	2.2	1931	1.3
29	TU	0157	2.2	0825	1.1	1455	2.1	2047	1.4
30	W	0255	2.2	1016	1.0	1647	2.2	2233	1.4
31	TH	0403	2.2	1129	0.9	1805	2.3	2348	1.3

NOVEMBER

Date	Day	Time	m	Time	m	Time	m	Time	m
1	F	0529	2.3	1230	0.7	1901	2.4		
2	SA	0047	1.1	0632	2.5	1324	0.5	1947	2.4
3	SU	0138	1.0	0726	2.6	1412	0.3	2028	2.5
4	M	0225	0.8	0817	2.7	1458	0.2	● 2107	2.5
5	TU	0310	0.7	0907	2.7	1542	0.2	2146	2.6
6	W	0354	0.6	0955	2.8	1624	0.3	2225	2.5
7	TH	0437	0.5	1044	2.7	1703	0.4	2304	2.5
8	F	0519	0.5	1132	2.6	1742	0.6	2344	2.5
9	SA	0604	0.6	1224	2.4	1822	0.9		
10	SU	0025	2.4	0655	0.7	1328	2.3	1906	1.1
11	M	0112	2.3	0800	0.8	1457	2.2	2001	1.3
12	TU	0223	2.3	0918	0.9	1615	2.2	2108	1.4
13	W	0345	2.3	1041	0.9	1720	2.2	2232	1.5
14	TH	0450	2.3	1149	0.8	1819	2.2		
15	F	0006	1.4	0548	2.4	1242	0.8	1909	2.3
16	SA	0058	1.3	0638	2.4	1326	0.7	1949	2.3
17	SU	0138	1.2	0722	2.4	1403	0.7	2017	2.4
18	M	0209	1.1	0802	2.4	1433	0.8	2041	2.4
19	TU	0235	1.0	0840	2.4	1459	0.8	2111	2.4
20	W	0304	0.9	0918	2.4	1527	0.8	○ 2144	2.5
21	TH	0337	0.8	0957	2.4	1558	0.8	2216	2.5
22	F	0413	0.8	1036	2.4	1630	0.8	2248	2.5
23	SA	0450	0.8	1115	2.4	1704	0.9	2321	2.5
24	SU	0529	0.8	1156	2.3	1741	1.0	2359	2.4
25	M	0613	0.9	1242	2.3	1823	1.1		
26	TU	0043	2.4	0705	0.9	1335	2.2	1913	1.2
27	W	0133	2.3	0811	0.9	1442	2.2	2015	1.3
28	TH	0228	2.3	0937	0.9	1623	2.2	2126	1.4
29	F	0327	2.3	1056	0.8	1733	2.2	2300	1.3
30	SA	0438	2.4	1159	0.6	1829	2.3		

DECEMBER

Date	Day	Time	m	Time	m	Time	m	Time	m
1	SU	0014	1.2	0558	2.4	1255	0.5	1916	2.4
2	M	0112	1.0	0701	2.5	1346	0.4	1959	2.4
3	TU	0203	0.8	0757	2.6	1434	0.4	2040	2.5
4	W	0252	0.7	0850	2.6	1520	0.4	● 2121	2.5
5	TH	0339	0.6	0943	2.6	1603	0.5	2203	2.5
6	F	0426	0.5	1034	2.5	1643	0.6	2243	2.5
7	SA	0512	0.5	1125	2.4	1721	0.8	2324	2.5
8	SU	0558	0.5	1219	2.3	1758	1.0		
9	M	0004	2.5	0647	0.6	1321	2.2	1836	1.1
10	TU	0047	2.4	0743	0.7	1432	2.1	1922	1.3
11	W	0138	2.4	0843	0.8	1538	2.1	2017	1.4
12	TH	0244	2.3	0945	0.8	1639	2.1	2120	1.5
13	F	0353	2.3	1045	0.9	1735	2.1	2227	1.4
14	SA	0455	2.3	1142	0.9	1823	2.2	2335	1.4
15	SU	0552	2.3	1228	0.9	1901	2.2		
16	M	0034	1.2	0642	2.3	1307	0.9	1933	2.3
17	TU	0119	1.1	0728	2.3	1344	0.9	2007	2.4
18	W	0200	1.0	0812	2.3	1420	0.8	2044	2.4
19	TH	0240	0.9	0856	2.4	1457	0.8	○ 2121	2.5
20	F	0320	0.8	0940	2.4	1534	0.8	2156	2.5
21	SA	0401	0.8	1024	2.4	1612	0.9	2230	2.5
22	SU	0442	0.7	1106	2.4	1650	0.9	2304	2.5
23	M	0525	0.7	1148	2.4	1729	1.0	2343	2.5
24	TU	0609	0.7	1233	2.3	1811	1.0		
25	W	0025	2.5	0658	0.7	1323	2.2	1857	1.1
26	TH	0113	2.4	0753	0.7	1422	2.2	1948	1.2
27	F	0204	2.4	0857	0.7	1542	2.1	2046	1.2
28	SA	0300	2.4	1012	0.7	1654	2.1	2154	1.2
29	SU	0404	2.3	1123	0.7	1754	2.2	2333	1.2
30	M	0532	2.3	1226	0.6	1846	2.2		
31	TU	0047	1.0	0644	2.4	1323	0.6	1932	2.3

Chart Datum: 1·50 metres below Ordnance Datum (Newlyn)

Register for your **FREE** weekly weather email service from Macmillan Reeds
» at **www.nauticaldata.com – NOW!** «
weekend weather reports sent to your email address, every Thursday

GREAT YARMOUTH 9.4.27

Norfolk **52°34'·36N 01°44'·39E** ❁❁◊✿✿

CHARTS AC *1536, 1543*; Imray C28, C29; Stanfords 3; OS 134

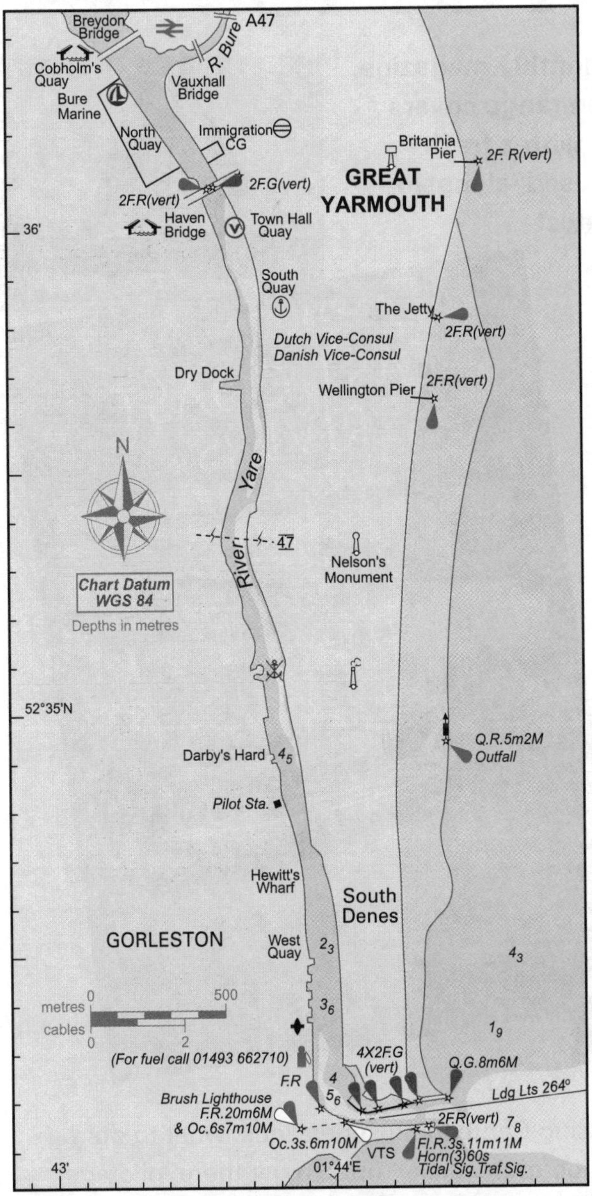

TIDES –0210 Dover; ML 1·5; Duration 0620; Zone 0 (UT)

Standard Port LOWESTOFT (⟵)

Times				Height (metres)			
High Water		Low Water		MHWS	MHWN	MLWN	MLWS
0300	0900	0200	0800	2·4	2·1	1·0	0·5
1500	2100	1400	2000				
Differences GORLESTON (To be used for Great Yarmouth)							
–0035	–0035	–0030	–0030	0·0	0·0	0·0	0·0
CAISTER-ON-SEA							
–0120	–0120	–0100	–0100	0·0	–0·1	0·0	0·0
WINTERTON-ON-SEA							
–0225	–0215	–0135	–0135	+0·8	+0·5	+0·2	+0·1

Rise of tide occurs mainly during 3½ hours after LW. From HW Lowestoft –3 until HW the level is usually within 0·3m of predicted HW. Flood tide runs until about HW +1½ and Ebb until about LW +2½. See also under NAVIGATION.

SHELTER Excellent on Town Hall Quay, close S of Haven Bridge; ⚓ prohib in hbr which is a busy commercial port.

NAVIGATION WPT 52°34'·43N 01°45'·56E, 084°/264° from/to front ldg lt, 1·0M. Access is H24, subject to clearance, but small craft must not attempt ent in strong SE winds which cause dangerous seas, especially on the ebb. Except at local slack water, which occurs at HW+1½ and LW+1¾, tidal streams at the ent are strong. On the flood, the stream eddies NW past S pier, thence up-river; beware being set onto N pier; a QY tidal lt on S pier warns of this D/N. Temp shoaling may occur in the ent during strong E'lies, with depths 1m less than those charted. Beware strong tidal streams that sweep through the Haven Bridge. Slow past Cobham's Quay.

LIGHTS AND MARKS Main lt Fl R 3s 11m 11M, vis 235°-340°, Horn (3) 60s. (Note: Tfc Sigs and the tidal QY are co-located with the Main lt on a R brick bldg, W lower half floodlit, at S pier). Ldg lts 264°: front Oc 3s 6m 10M; rear Oc 6s 7m 10M, (below the FR 20m 6M on Brush lt ho). N pier lt, QG 8m 6M, vis 176°-078° (262°). Ent and bend marked by five x 2 FG and seven x 2FR (all vert).

TRAFFIC SIGNALS VTS instructions (Ch 12) must always be obeyed. **Inbound**: now IALA sigs on S pier: 3 Fl ● = hbr closed; 3F ● = do not proceed; 3 F ● = vessels may proceed, one-way; ● Ⓦ ● = proceed only when told to; **Outbound**: 3 ● (vert) = no vessel to go down river south of LB shed. Haven and Breydon bridges: 3 ● (vert) = passage prohib.

RADIO TELEPHONE Call: *Yarmouth* or *Breydon Br* Ch **12** (both H24).

TELEPHONE (Dial code 01493) Hr Mr & Port Control 335511, 📠 653464; MRCC 851338; ⊖ (01473) 235704 (H24) or (01493) 843686 (Mon-Fri 0900-1600); Marinecall 09068 500455; Police 336200; Breydon Bridge 651275.

FACILITIES Town Hall Quay (50m stretch) AB £14, then £7 for successive days. **Bure Marine Cobham** H24 visitor pontoons planned for 2002. D, FW, El, ⛭, BH, C, Slip. **Burgh Castle Marina** (top of Breydon Water 5M) (90+10 visitors) ☎ 780331, £6, Slip, D, ⛭, FW, ME, El, Sh, ⊡, Gas, CH, V, R, Bar, Access HW ±4 (1m), diving ACA; **Burgh Castle Yacht Station** (top of Breydon Water 5M) (28+6 visitors) ☎ 782301, £10, D, ⛭, FW, ME, El, C (32 tons, including mast stepping) Gas, ⛭, Access 6ft at LW; **Services:** BY, P & D, ME, El, FW, Slip, Diving, AB, L, M, Sh, SM, ACA. **Town** EC Thurs; P, D, CH, V, R, Bar, ✉, Ⓑ, ⇌, ✈ (Norwich).

Entry to the Broads: Pass up R Yare at slack LW, under Haven Bridge (2·3m MHWS) thence to Breydon Water via Breydon Bridge (4·0m) or to R Bure. Both bridges lift in co-ordination to pass small craft in groups. All br lifts on request to Hbr Office (01493) 335503 during office hrs. Weekend and bank holiday lifts to be requested working afternoon before. Call the Bridge Officer on VHF Ch 12. R Bure has two fixed bridges (2·3m MHWS).

NORFOLK BROADS: The Broads comprise about 120 miles of navigable rivers and lakes in Norfolk and Suffolk. The main rivers (Bure, Yare and Waveney) are tidal, flowing into the sea at Great Yarmouth. The N Broads have a 2·3m headroom limit. Br clearances restrict cruising to R Yare (Great Yarmouth to Norwich, but note that 3M E of Norwich, Postwick viaduct on S bypass has 8.67m clearance) and River Waveney (Lowestoft to Beccles). The Broads may be entered also at Lowestoft (9.4.26). Broads Navigation Authority ☎ (01603) 610734.

Tidal data on the rivers and Broads is based on the time of LW at Yarmouth Yacht Stn (mouth of R Bure), which is LW Gorleston +0100 (see TIDES). Add the differences below to time of LW Yarmouth Yacht Stn to get local LW times:

R Bure		*R Waveney*	
Acle Bridge	+0230	Berney Arms	+0100
Horning	+0300	St Olaves	+0115
Potter Heigham	+0400	Oulton Broad	+0300
R Yare		Beccles	+0320
Reedham	+0115		
Cantley	+0200		
Norwich	+0430		

LW at Breydon (mouth of R Yare) is LW Yarmouth Yacht Stn +0100. Tide starts to flood on Breydon Water whilst still ebbing from R Bure. Max draft is 1·8m; 2m with care. Tidal range varies from 0·6m to 1·8m.

Licences are compulsory; get temp one from The Broads Authority, 18 Colegate, Norwich NR3 1BQ, ☎ 01603-610734; from Mutford Lock or from River Inspectors. *Hamilton's Guide to the Broads* is recommended.

MAPTECH
Leading the world in digital navigation
Maptech UK Ltd • +44 (0)1243 389352 • sales@maptech.co.uk

Maptech world class digital chart CDs
Worldwide coverage from over 4,500 charts

Maptech award winning software
Easy to use navigation software
• Chart Navigator • Cruising Navigator • Offshore Navigator

www.maptech.co.uk

Area 5

North East England
Winterton to Berwick-upon-Tweed

9.5.1	Index	Page 401
9.5.2	Area map	402
9.5.3	Tidal stream charts	404
9.5.4	Lights, buoys & waypoints	406
9.5.5	Passage information	409
9.5.6	Distance table	411
9.5.7	Blakeney	412
9.5.8	Wells-next-the-Sea	412
9.5.9	King's Lynn Burnham Overy Staithe Brancaster Staithe Wisbech	413
9.5.10	Boston River Welland Wainfleet	414
9.5.11	River Humber (Immingham, Standard Port, tidal curves) Grimsby Hull Goole South Ferriby Brough Haven Naburn	418
9.5.12	Bridlington Filey	421
9.5.13	Scarborough	421
9.5.14	Whitby Runswick Bay River Tees, Middlesbrough	422
9.5.15	Hartlepool	423
9.5.16	Seaham	424
9.5.17	Sunderland	424
9.5.18	River Tyne/North Shields, Standard Port, tidal curves Cullercoats	425
9.5.19	Blyth Newbiggin	429
9.5.20	Amble Boulmer Craster Newton Haven and Beadnell Bay North Sunderland (Seahouses) Farne Islands	430
9.5.21	Holy Island	431
9.5.22	Berwick-upon-Tweed	432

Register for your FREE weekly weather email service from Macmillan Reeds
›› at www.nauticaldata.com – NOW! ‹‹
weekend weather reports sent to your email address, every Thursday

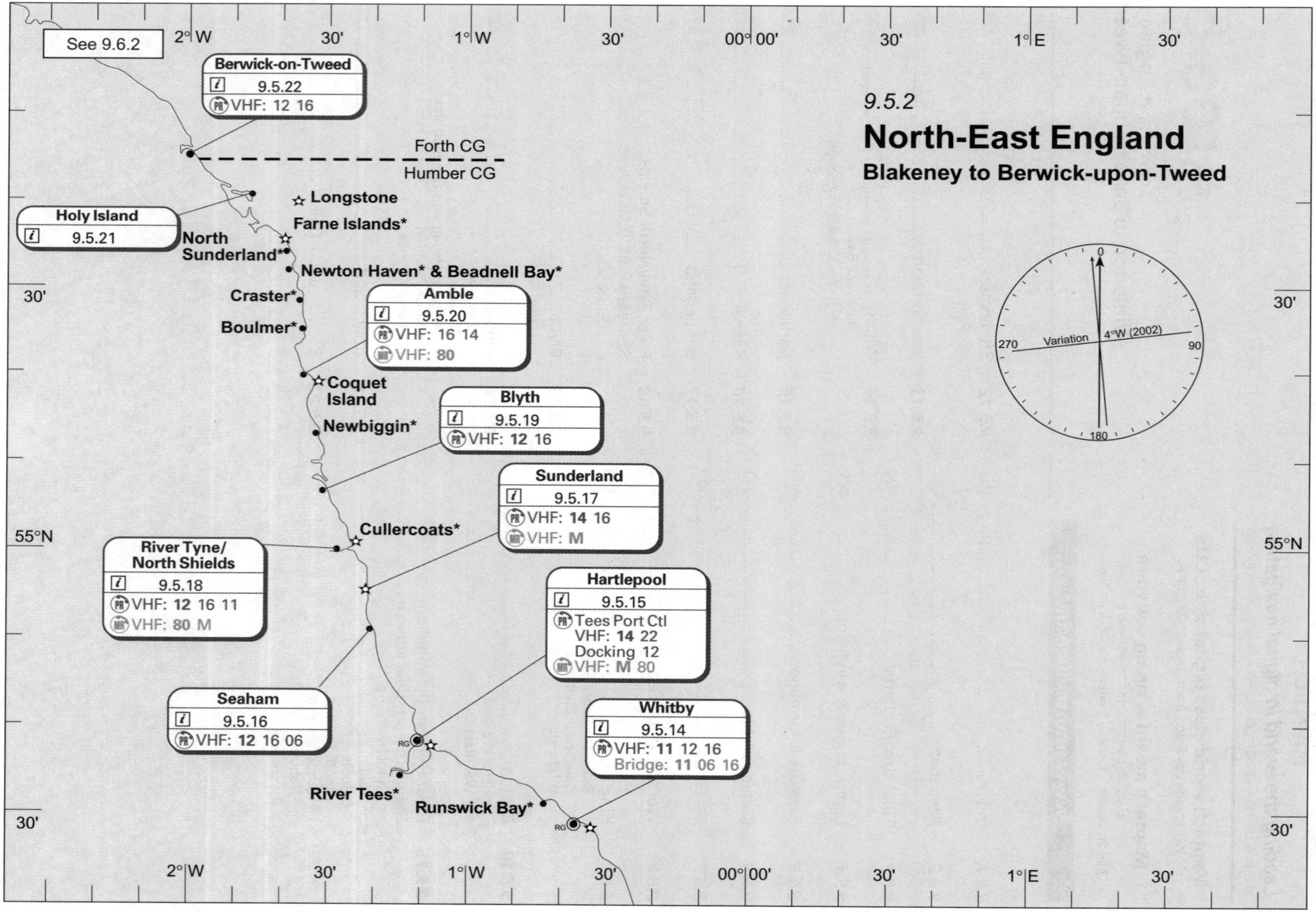
9.5.2
North-East England
Blakeney to Berwick-upon-Tweed
See 9.6.2
2°W
30'
1°W
30'
00°00'
30'
1°E
30'
55°N
Berwick-on-Tweed 9.5.22 VHF: 12 16
Forth CG
Humber CG
Holy Island 9.5.21
Longstone
Farne Islands*
North Sunderland**
Newton Haven* & Beadnell Bay*
Craster*
Boulmer*
Amble 9.5.20 VHF: 16 14 VHF: 80
Coquet Island
Newbiggin*
Blyth 9.5.19 VHF: 12 16
Sunderland 9.5.17 VHF: 14 16 VHF: M
Cullercoats*
River Tyne/ North Shields 9.5.18 VHF: 12 16 11 VHF: 80 M
Hartlepool 9.5.15 Tees Port Ctl VHF: 14 22 Docking 12 VHF: M 80
Seaham 9.5.16 VHF: 12 16 06
Whitby 9.5.14 VHF: 11 12 16 Bridge: 11 06 16
River Tees*
Runswick Bay*
RG
Variation 4°W (2002)
0
90
180
270

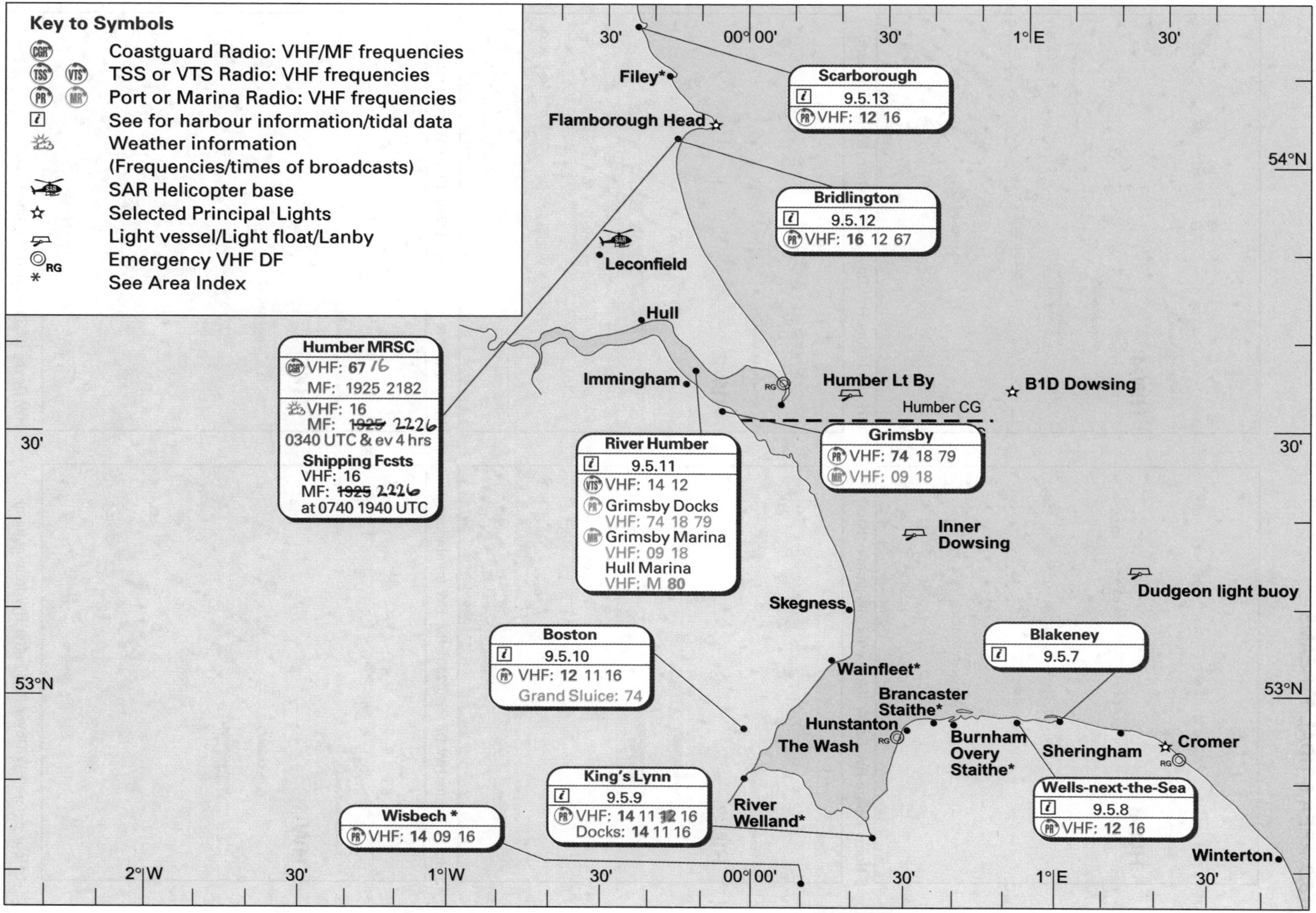
Key to Symbols
Coastguard Radio: VHF/MF frequencies
TSS or VTS Radio: VHF frequencies
Port or Marina Radio: VHF frequencies
See for harbour information/tidal data
Weather information
(Frequencies/times of broadcasts)
SAR Helicopter base
Selected Principal Lights
Light vessel/Light float/Lanby
Emergency VHF DF
RG
*
See Area Index
30'
00° 00'
30'
1° E
30'
54°N
30'
53°N
2° W
30'
1° W
30'
00° 00'
30'
1° E
30'
Filey*
Flamborough Head
Scarborough
9.5.13
VHF: 12 16
Bridlington
9.5.12
VHF: 16 12 67
SAR
Leconfield
Hull
Immingham
RG
Humber Lt By
B1D Dowsing
Humber CG
Humber MRSC
VHF: 67 16
MF: 1925 2182
VHF: 16
MF: 1925 2226
0340 UTC & ev 4 hrs
Shipping Fcsts
VHF: 16
MF: 1925 2226
at 0740 1940 UTC
River Humber
9.5.11
VHF: 14 12
Grimsby Docks
VHF: 74 18 79
Grimsby Marina
VHF: 09 18
Hull Marina
VHF: M 80
Grimsby
VHF: 74 18 79
VHF: 09 18
Inner
Dowsing
Dudgeon light buoy
Skegness
Boston
9.5.10
VHF: 12 11 16
Grand Sluice: 74
Wainfleet*
Blakeney
9.5.7
Brancaster
Staithe*
Hunstanton
RG
The Wash
Burnham
Overy
Staithe*
Sheringham
Cromer
RG
Wells-next-the-Sea
9.5.8
VHF: 12 16
King's Lynn
9.5.9
VHF: 14 11 12 16
Docks: 14 11 16
River
Welland*
Wisbech *
VHF: 14 09 16
Winterton

5

9.5.3 AREA 5 TIDAL STREAMS

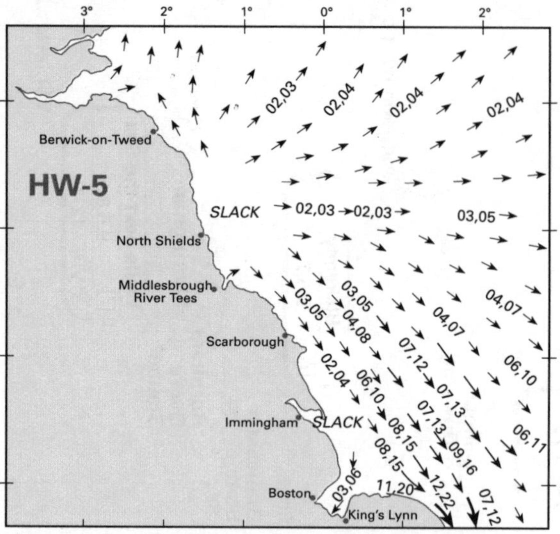

5 Hours before HW Dover (0030 after HW Immingham)

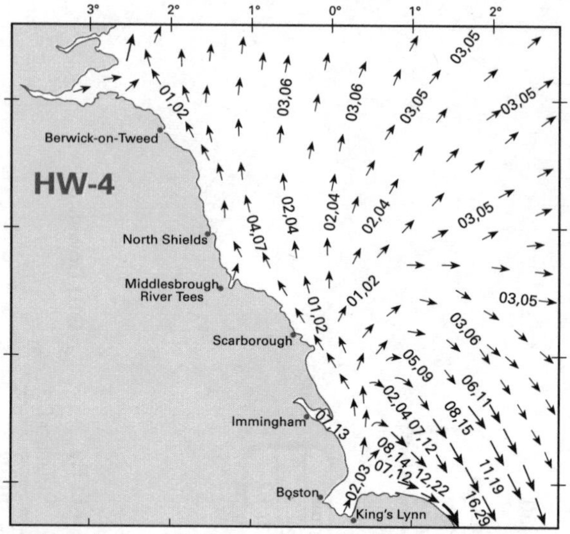

4 Hours before HW Dover (0130 after HW Immingham)

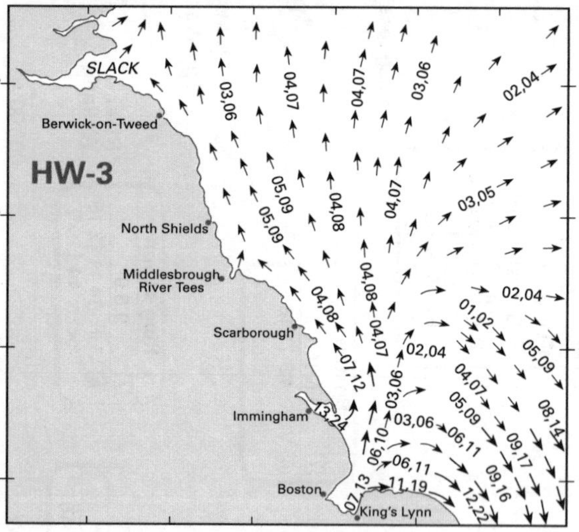

3 Hours before HW Dover (0230 after HW Immingham)

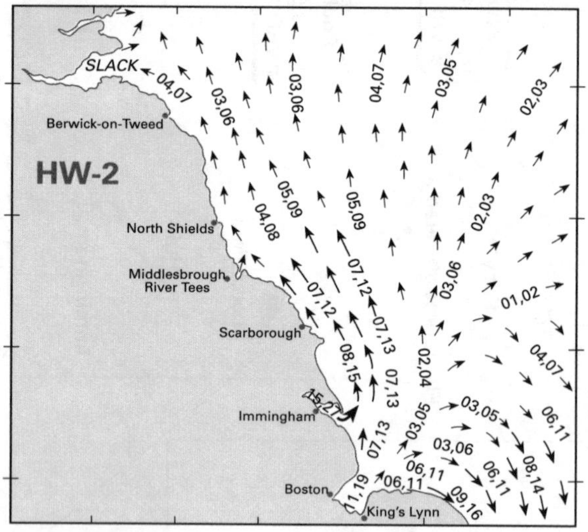

2 Hours before HW Dover (0330 after HW Immingham)

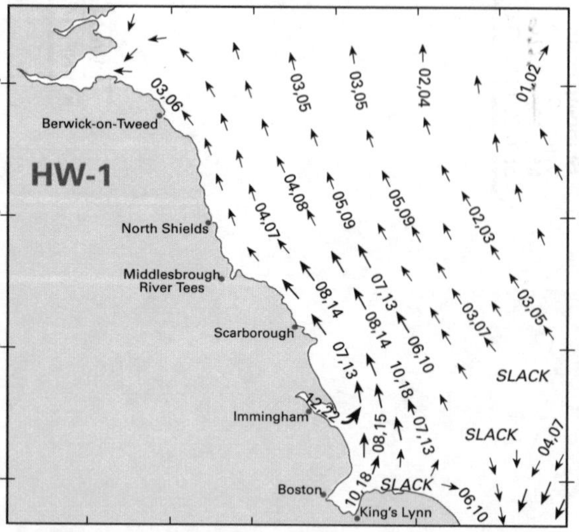

1 Hour before HW Dover (0430 after HW Immingham)

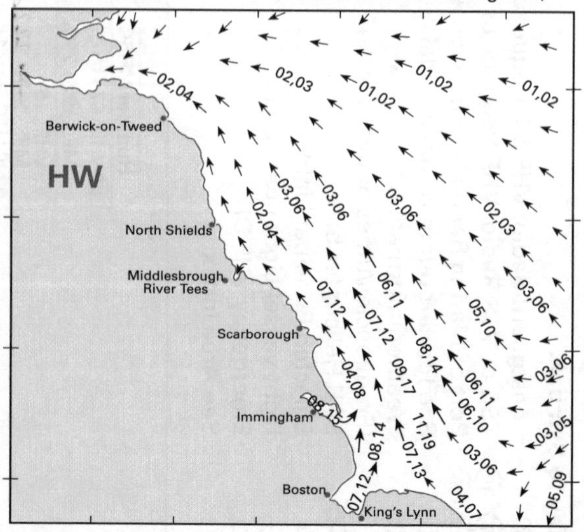

HW Dover (0530 after HW Immingham)

Northward 9.6.3 Southward 9.4.3

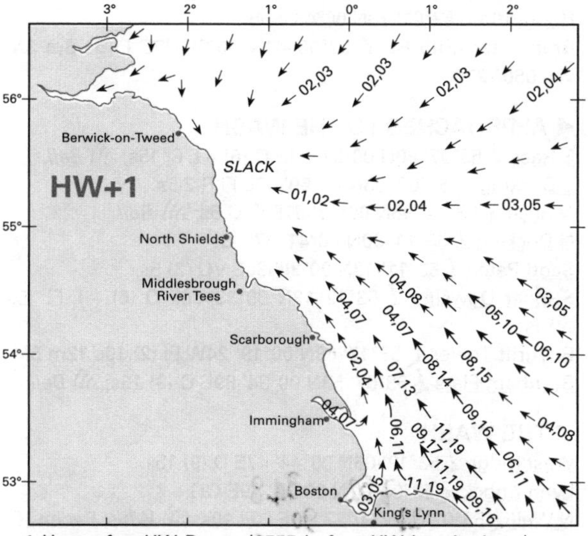

1 Hour after HW Dover (0555 before HW Immingham)

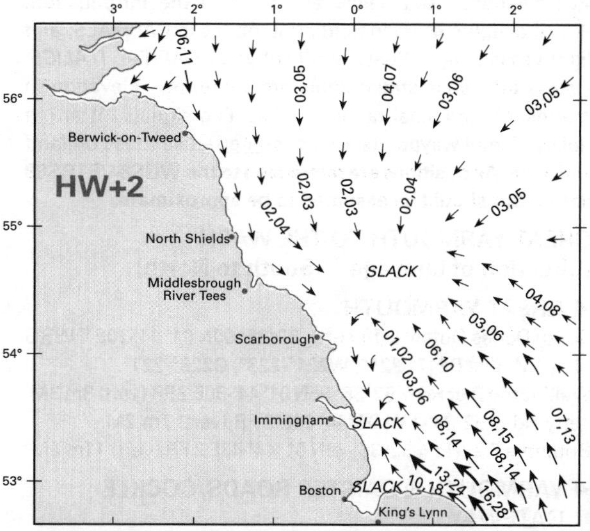

2 Hours after HW Dover (0455 before HW Immingham)

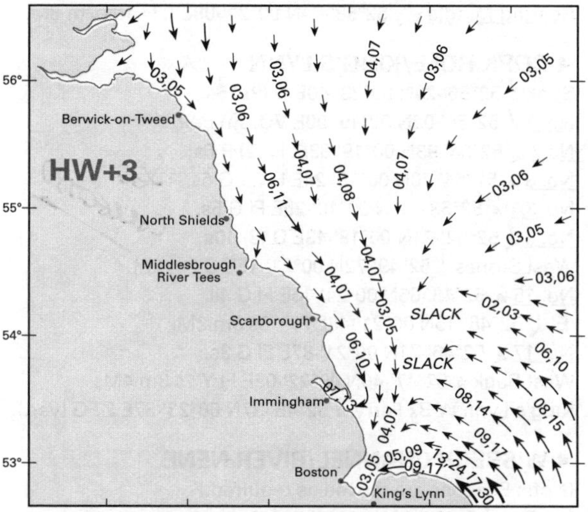

3 Hours after HW Dover (0355 before HW Immingham)

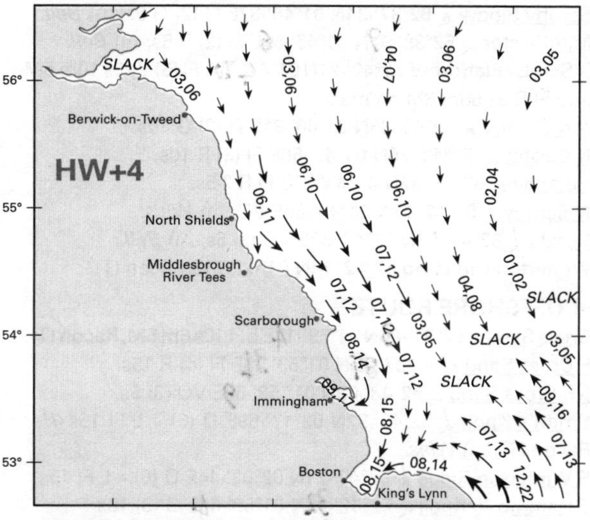

4 Hours after HW Dover (0255 before HW Immingham)

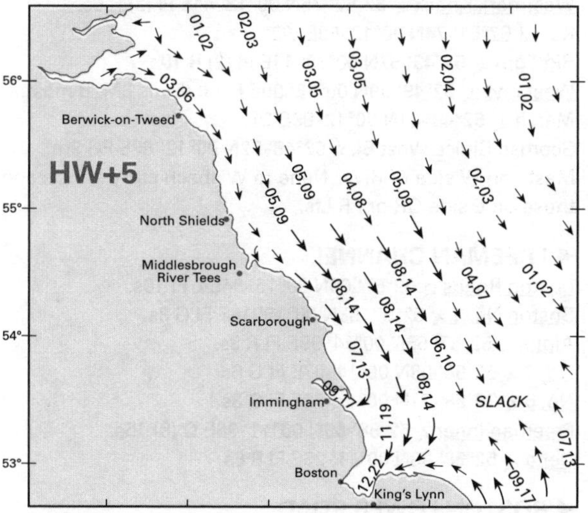

5 Hours after HW Dover (0155 before HW Immingham)

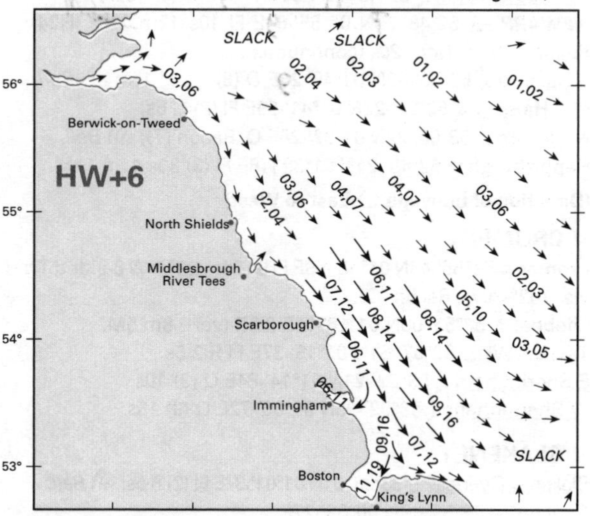

6 Hours after HW Dover (0055 before HW Immingham)

5

9.5.4 LIGHTS, BUOYS AND WAYPOINTS

Abbreviations used below are given in the Introduction. Principal lights ☆ are in **bold** print, places in CAPITALS, and light-vessels, light floats and Lanbys in *CAPITAL ITALICS*. Unless otherwise stated lights are white. m – elevation in metres; M – nominal range in miles. Fog signals ◦))) are in *italics*. Useful waypoints are underlined – use those on land with care. **All positions are referenced to the WGS84/ETRS89 datum but should be assumed to be approximate.**

GREAT YARMOUTH TO THE WASH (Direction of buoyage South to North)

◀ GREAT YARMOUTH

South Denes Outfall Diffuser 52°35'·00N 01°44'·20E F WRG 42m 1M; Vis: R217°-221°, W221°-223°, G223°-227°.
Wellington Pier Hd ☆ 52°35'·95N 01°44'·30E 2 FR (vert) 8m 3M.
Jetty Hd ☆ 52°36'·13N 01°44'·34E 2 FR (vert) 7m 2M.
Britannia Pier Hd ☆ 52°36'·49N 01°44'·43E 2 FR (vert) 11m 4M.

◀ YARMOUTH & CAISTER ROADS/COCKLE GATEWAY

SW Scroby 52°35'·82N 01°46'·26E Fl G 2·5s.
Scroby Elbow 52°37'·34N 01°46'·37E Fl (2) G 5s; ◦))) *Bell.*
Mid Caister 52°38'·97N 01°45'·66E Fl (2) R 5s; ◦))) *Bell.*
N Scroby Platform 52°40'·21N 01°47'·16E Fl (5) Y 20s 10m 5M and Fl R 3s 50m 3M on mast.
NW Scroby 52°40'·36N 01°46'·31E Fl (3) G 10s.
N Caister 52°40'·76N 01°45'·65E Fl (3) R 10s.
Hemsby 52°41'·82N 01°44'·71E Fl R 2·5s.
N Scroby 52°42'·53N 01°44'·66E VQ; ◦))) *Whis.*
Cockle 52°44'·02N 01°43'·58E VQ (3) 5s; ◦))) *Bell.*
Winterton Old Lt Ho 52°42'·75N 01°41'·71E Racon (T).

◀ OFFSHORE ROUTE

Cross Sand 52°37'·03N 01°59'·14E L Fl 10s 6m 5M; Racon (T).
E Cross Sand 52°37'·93N 01°53'·28E Fl (4) R 15s.
NE Cross Sand 52°43'·03N 01° 53'·69E VQ (3) 5s.
Smith's Knoll 52°43'·52N 02°17'·89E Q (6) + L Fl 15s 7M; Racon (T); ◦))) *Whis.*
S Winterton Ridge 52°47'·21N 02°03'·44E Q (6) + L Fl 15s.
E Hammond Knoll 52°52'·28N 01°58'·60E Q (3) 10s.
Hammond Knoll 52°49'·68N 01°57'·54E Q (9) 15s.
NEWARP 52°48'·35N 01°55'·63E Fl 10s 12m 21M (H24); Racon (O); ◦))) *Horn 20*s (continuous).
S Haisbro 52°50'·82N 01°48'·24E Q (6) + L Fl 15s; ◦))) *Bell.*
Mid Haisbro 52°54'·22N 01°41'·59E Fl (2) G 5s.
N Haisbro 53°00'·22N 01°32'·28E Q; Racon (T); ◦))) *Bell.*
Happisburgh ☆ 52°49'·21N 01°32'·18E Fl (3) 30s 41m 14M.

(Direction of buoyage East to West)

◀ CROMER

Cromer ☆ 52°55'·48N 01°18'·99E Fl 5s 84m **23M**; W 8-sided Tr; vis: 102°-307°; Racon (O).
Lifeboat ☆ 52°56'·03N 01°18'·08E 2 FR (vert) 8m 5M.
Tayjack Wk 52°57'·61N 01°15'·37E Fl R 2·5s.
E Sheringham 53°02'·21N 01°14'·84E Q (3) 10s.
W Sheringham 53°02'·95N 01°06'·72E Q (9) 15s.

◀ BLAKENEY

Blakeney Overfalls 53°03'·01N 01°01'·37E Fl (2) R 5s; ◦))) *Bell.*
Concord 52°59'·18N 00°58'·27E.
Hjordis Wk 52°59'·07N 00°58'·12E QR.

◀ WELLS-NEXT-THE-SEA/BRANCASTER STAITHE

Wells Fairway 52°59'·81N 00°49'·77E Q.
Bridgirdle 53°01'·73N 00°43'·95E.
Brancaster Club Ho ☆ 52°58'·41N 00°38'·17E Fl 5s 8m 3M; vis: 080°-270°.

◀ APPROACHES TO THE WASH

S Race 53°07'·80N 00°57'·31E Q (6) + L Fl 15s; ◦))) *Bell.*
E Docking 53°09'·83N 00°50'·40E Fl R 2·5s.
N Race 53°14'·98N 00°43'·87E Fl G 5s; ◦))) *Bell.*
N Docking 53°14'·80N 00°41'·47E Q.
Scott Patch 53°11'·13N 00°36'·36E VQ (3) 5s.
S Inner Dowsing 53°12'·12N 00°33'·66E Q (6) + L Fl 15s; ◦))) *Bell.*
Boygrift Tower 53°17'·63N 00°19'·24W Fl (2) 10s 12m 5M.
Burnham Flats 53°07'·53N 00°34'·89E Q (9) 15s; ◦))) *Bell.*

◀ THE WASH

West Ridge 53°19'·06N 00°44'·47E Q (9) 15s.
Lynn Knock 53°04'·32N 00°34'·89E QG.
N Well 53°02'·99N 00°27'·86E L Fl 10s; ◦))) *Whis*; Racon (T).
Woolpack 53°02'·68N 00°31'·41E Fl R 10s.
Roaring Middle 52°58'·64N 00°21'·08E L Fl 10s 7m 8M.

◀ CORK HOLE/KING'S LYNN

Sunk 52°56'·29N 00°23'·40E Q (9) 15s.
No. 1 52°56'·02N 00°19'·90E VQ; ◦))) *Bell.*
No 2 52°54'·93N 00°19'·83E. Fl (2) R 6s.
No. 3 52°54'·70N 00°19'·24E Fl (2) G 6s.
No. 3A 52°53'·22 N 00°18'·25E Fl G 5s.
No. 5 52°52'·21N 00°18'·43E Q (3) 10s.
West Stones 52°49'·72N 00°21'·15E Q 3m 2M.
No. 15 52°48'·66N 00°21'·16E Fl G 4s.
'E' 52°48'·15N 00°21'·48E Fl Y 3s 3m 2M.
No. 17 52°46'·71N 00°21'·87E Fl G 3s.
West Bank ☆ 52°47'·46N 00°22'·03E Fl Y 2s 3m 4M.
King's Lynn W Bk Ferry ☆ 52°45'·37N 00°23'·37E 2 FG (vert).

◀ WISBECH CHANNEL/RIVER NENE

(Note: Beacons are moved as required.)
Bar Flat 52°55'·25N 00°16'·72E Q (3) 10s.
Westmark Knock 52°52'·75N 00°13'·41E Fl (2) R 6s.
Kerr 52°51'·74N 00°13'·59E VQ.
Big Tom 52°49'·57N 00°13'·11E Fl (2) R 10s.
West End 52°49'·39N 00°12'·90E Fl (3) G 10s 3M; B mast.
Marsh 52°49'·01N 00°12'·89E QR.
Scottish Sluice West Bk ☆ 52°48'·52N 00°12'·62E FG 9m.
Masts on W side of River Nene to Wisbech carry FG Lts and those on E side QR or FR Lts.

◀ FREEMAN CHANNEL

Boston Roads 52°57'·66N 00°16'·04E L Fl 10s.
Boston No. 1 52°57'·88N 00°15'·16E Fl G 3s.
Alpha 52°57'·65N 00°14'·99E Fl R 3s.
No. 3 52°58'·08N 00°14'·07E Fl G 6s.
No. 5 52°58'·51N 00°12'·72E Fl G 3s.
Freeman Inner 52°58'·59N 00°11'·36E Q (9) 15s.
Delta 52°58'·38N 00°11'·25E Fl R 6s.

◀ BOSTON LOWER ROAD

Boston No. 7 52°58'·62N 00°10'·00E Fl G 3s.

Boston No. 9 52°57'·58N 00°08'·36E Fl G 3s.
Golf 52°56'·74N 00°07'·97E Fl (2) R 6s.
Black Boy 52°56'·72N 00°07'·54E Fl R 3s.
Boston No.11N 52°56'·66N 00°06'·55E Fl (2) G 6s.
Boston No.13N 52°56'·52N 00°06'·55E Fl G 3s.
Boston No.15 52°56'·34N 00°05'·95E Fl (2) G 6s.
Welland 52°56'·08N 00°05'·27E QR 5m.
Tabs Head 52°56'·00N 00°04'·91E Q WG 4m 1M; R □ on W mast; vis: W shore-251°, G251°-shore.

◀ BOSTON, NEW CUT AND RIVER WITHAM

Ent N side, Dollypeg 52°56'·13N 00°05'·03E QG 4m 1M; B △ on Bn.
New Cut 52°55'·98N 00°04'·67E Fl G 3s; △ on pile.
New Cut Ldg Lts 240°. Front, No. 1 52°55'·85N 00°04'·40E F 5m 5M. Rear, 90m from front, F 8m 5M.

◀ WELLAND CUT/RIVER WELLAND

SE side 52°55'·72E 00°04'·68E Iso R 2s; NW side Iso G 2s. Lts QR (to port) and QG (to stbd) mark the chan upstream.

(Direction of buoyage North to South)

◀ BOSTON DEEP/WAINFLEET ROADS

Wainfleet Range Control Tr 53°03'·66N 00°14'·11E UQ R (occas), with FR on Trs SW & NE.
Scullridge 52°59'·76N 00°13'·86E.
Friskney 53°00'·59N 00°16'·76E.
Long Sand 53°01'·27N 00°18'·30E.
Pompey 53°02'·19N 00°19'·26E.
Swatchway 53°03'·81N 00°19'·70E.
Off Ingoldmells Point 53°12'·49N 00°25'·85E Fl Y 5s 22m 5M; Mast; *Mo (U) 30s.*
Boygrift Tr 53°17'·63N 00°19'·24E Fl (2) 10s 12m 5M.

WASH TO THE RIVER HUMBER

(Direction of buoyage South to North)

Dudgeon 53°16'·62N 01°16'·90E Q (9) 15s 7M; Racon (O); *Whis.*

E Dudgeon 53°19'·70N 00°58'·69E Q (3) 10s; *Bell.*

Mid Outer Dowsing 53°24'·82N 01°07'·79E Fl (3) G 10s; *Bell.*

N Outer Dowsing 53°33'·52N 00°59'·59E Q.

B.1D Platform Dowsing 53°33'·68N 00°52'·63E Fl (2) 10s 28m **22M**; Morse (U) R 15s 28m 3M; *Horn (2) 60s*; Racon (T).

◀ RIVER HUMBER APPROACHES

W Ridge 53°19'·04N 00°44'·50E Q (9) 15s.
Inner Dowsing 53°19'·52N 00°33'·85E Fl 10s 12m **15M**; Racon (T); *Horn 60s.*
Protector 53°24'·84N 00°25'·12E Fl R 2·5s.
DZ No. 4 53°27'·15N 00°19'·06E Fl Y 5s.
DZ No. 3 53°29'·30N 00°19'·21E Fl Y 2·5s.
Rosse Spit 53°30'·41N 00°16'·91E Fl (2) R 5s.
Haile Sand No. 2 53°32'·42N 00°13'·18E Fl (3) R 10s.
Humber 53°39'·06N 00°19'·98E L Fl 10s 7M; *Horn (2) 30s*; Racon (T).
N Binks 53°36'·01N 00°18'·28E Fl G 4s.
S Binks 53°34'·74N 00°16'·55E Fl G 2s.
SPURN 53°33'·56N 00°14'·20E Q (3) 10s 10m 8M; *Horn 20s*; Racon (M).
SE CHEQUER 53°33'·38N 00°12'·55E VQ (6) + L Fl 10s 6m 6M; *Horn 30s.*
Chequer No. 3 53°33'·07N 00°10'·63E Q (6) + L Fl 15s.
No 2B 53°32'·33N 00°09'·10E Fl R 4s.
Tetney 53°32'·35N 00°06'·76E 2 VQ Y (vert); *Horn Mo (A) 60s*; QY on 290m floating hose.

◀ RIVER HUMBER/GRIMSBY/HULL

Binks No. 3A 53°33'·92N 00°07'·43E Fl G 4s.
Spurn Pt 53°34'·37N 00°06'·47E Fl G 3s 11m 5M.
BULL 53°33'·54N 00°05'·70E VQ 8m 6M; *Horn (2) 20s.*
North Fort 53°33'·80N 00°04'·19E Q.
South Fort 53°33'·65N 00°03'·96E Q (6) + L Fl 15s.
Haile Sand Fort 53°32'·07N 00°01'·99E Fl R 5s 21m 3M.
Haile Chan No. 4 53°33'·64N 00°02'·84E Fl R 4s.
Middle No. 7 53°35'·80N 00°01'·50E VQ (6) + L Fl 10s; *Horn 20s.*
Grimsby Royal Dock ent E side 53°35'·08N 00°04'·04W Fl (2) R 6s 10m 8M; Dn.
Killingholme Lts in line 292°. Front, 53°38'·78N 00°12'·96W Iso R 2s 10m 14M. Rear, 189m from front, Oc R 4s 21m 14M.
Immingham Oil Terminal SE end 53°37'·70N 00°09'·42W 2 QR (vert) 8m 5M; *Horn Mo (N) 30s.*
Clay Huts No.13 53°38'·54N 00°11'·34W Iso 2s 5m 9M.
Sand End No.16 53°42'·62N 00°14'·50W Fl R 4s 5m 3M.
Hebbles No. 21 53°44'·03N 00°15'·99W Fl G 1·3s.
Lower W Middle No. 24 53°44'·28N 00°18'·35W Fl R 4s.
Hull Marina 53°44'·24N 00°20'·16W 2 FG (vert).

RIVER HUMBER TO WHITBY

Canada & Giorgios Wreck 53°42'·37N 00°07'·16E VQ (3) 5s.
Hornsea Sewer Outfall 53°55'·01N 00°08'·41W Fl Y 20s.
Atwick Sewer Outfall 53°57'·14N 00°10'·34W Fl Y 10s.

◀ BRIDLINGTON

SW Smithic 54°02'·41N 00°09'·21W Q (9) 15s.
N Pier Hd 54°04'·77N 00°11'·19W Fl 2s 12m 9M; *Horn 60s*; (Tidal Lts) Fl R or Fl G.
N Smithic 54°06'·22N 00°03'·90W VQ; *Bell.*
Flamborough Hd 54°06'·98N 00°04'·96W Fl (4) 15s 65m **24M**; W ○ Tr; *Horn (2) 90s.*

◀ FILEY/SCARBOROUGH/WHITBY

Filey Brigg 54°12'·74N 00°14'·60W Q (3) 10s; *Bell.*
Scarborough E Pier Hd 54°16'·88N 00°23'·36W QG 8m 3M.
Scarborough Pier 54°16'·91N 00°23'·40W Iso 5s 17m 9M; W ○ Tr; vis: 219°-039°; vis: 233°-030°; (tide sigs); *Dia 60s.*
Scalby Ness Diffusers 54°18'·59N 00°23'·38W Fl R 5s.
Whitby 54°30'·33N 00°36'·58W Q; *Bell.*
Whitby High Ling Hill 54°28'·67N 00°34'·09W Iso WR 10s 73m **18M**, R16M; W 8-sided Tr and dwellings; vis: R128°-143°, W143°-319°.
Whitby E Pier Hd 54°29'·64N 00°36'·74W FR 14m 3M; R Tr.
Whitby W Pier Hd 54°29'·65N 00°36'·80W FG (occas) 14m 3M; G Tr; *Horn 30s.*

WHITBY TO RIVER TYNE

◀ RUNSWICK/REDCAR

Runswick Bay Pier 54°31'·99N 00°44'·95W 2 FY (occas).
Boulby Outfall 54°34'·52N 00°48'·29W Fl (4) Y 10s.
Redcar Outfall 54°36'·66N 01°00'·37W Fl Y 10s.
Salt Scar 54°38'·12N 01°00'·12W VQ; *Bell.*

Luff Way Ldg Lts 197°. Front, 54°37'·10N 01°03'·71W on Esplanade, FR 8m 7M; vis: 182°-212°. Rear, 115m from front, FR 12m 7M; vis: 182°-212°.
High Stone. Lade Way Ldg Lts 247°. Front, 54°37'·15N 01°03'·92W Oc R 2·5s 9m 7M. Rear, 43m from front, Oc R 2·5s 11m 7M; vis: 232°-262°.

◀ TEES APPROACHES/HARTLEPOOL

Tees Fairway 54°40'·94N 01°06'·48W Iso 4s 9m 8M; Racon (B); *Horn 5s.*
Tees N (Fairway) 54°40'·36N 01°07'·19W Fl G 5s.
Tees S (Fairway) 54°40'·29N 01°06'·98W Fl R 5s.
Bkwtr Hd S Gare ☆ 54°38'·85N 01°08'·27W Fl WR 12s 16m **W20M, R17M**; W ○ Tr; vis: W020°-274°, R274°-357°; Sig Stn; *Horn (2) 30s.*
Ldg Lts 210·1° Front, 54°37'·22N 01°10'·20W FR 18m 13M. **Rear**, 560m from front, FR 20m **16M**.
Longscar 54°40'·86N 01°09'·89W Q (3) 10s; *Bell.*
The Heugh ☆ 54°40'·09N 01°47'·98W Fl (2) 10s 19m **19M**; W Tr.
Hartlepool Old Pier Hd ☆ 54°41'·60N 01°11'·09W Q WG 13m 7M; vis: W317°-325°, G325°-317°.
W Hbr N Pier Hd ☆ 54°41'·31N 01°11'·57W Oc G 5s 12m 2M.
Harlepool Marina Lock Dir Lt 308° 54°41'·45N 01°11'·92W Dir Fl WRG 2s 6m 3M; vis: G305·5°-307°, W307°-309°, R309°-310·5°.
N Sands, Pipe Jetty Hd 54°42'·83N 01°12'·47W 2 FR (vert) 1M; *Bell 15s.*

◀ SEAHAM/SUNDERLAND

Seaham N Pier Hd ☆ 54°50'·26N 01°19'·26W Fl G 10s 12m 5M; W col, B bands; *Dia 30s.*
Sunderland Roker Pier Hd ☆ 54°55'·28N 01°21'·15W Fl 5s 25m **23M**; W □ Tr, 3 R bands and cupola: vis: 211°-357°; *Siren 20s.*
Old N Pier Hd ☆ 54°55'·13N 01°21'·61W QG 12m 8M; Y Tr; *Horn 10s.*
Whitburn Steel 54°56'·30N 01°20'·87W.
Whitburn Firing Range ☆ 54°57'·21N 01°21'·38W and 54°57'·76N 01°21'·35W both FR when firing is taking place.
DZ 54°57'·04N 01°18'·90W and 54°58'·61N 01°19'·90W, both Fl Y 2·5s.

◀ TYNE ENTRANCE/NORTH SHIELDS

Ent North Pier Hd ☆ 55°00'·88N 01°24'·18W Fl (3) 10s 26m 26M; Gy □ Tr, W lantern; *Horn 10s.*
South Pier Hd ☆ 55°00'·68N 01°24'·07W Oc WRG 10s 15m W13M, R9M, G8M; Gy □ Tr, R&W lantern; vis: W075°-161°, G161°-179° over Bellhues rock, W179°-255°, R255°-075°; *Bell (1) 10s.*
Herd Groyne Hd Ldg Lt 249°. 55°00'·49N 01°25'·44W Oc RG 10s 13m, R11M, G11M; R pile structure, R&W lantern; vis: G224°-246·5°, R251·5°-277°; FR (unintens) 080°-224°. Same structure Dir Oc 10s 14m **19M**; vis: W246·5°°-251·5°; *Bell (1) 5s.*
Royal Quay Marina ent (SS Tfc ⊙) 54°59'·78N 01°26'·98E.
Saint Peter's Marina ent (SS Tfc ⊙) 54°57'·93N 01°34'·35E.

RIVER TYNE TO BERWICK-ON-TWEED

◀ CULLERCOATS/BLYTH/NEWBIGGIN

Cullercoats Ldg Lts 256°. Front, 55°02'·06N 01°25'·91W FR 27m 3M. Rear, 38m from front, FR 35m 3M.
Blyth Ldg Lts 324°. Front, 55°07'·42N 01°29'·82W F Bu 11m 10M. Rear, 180m from front, F Bu 17m 10M. Both Or on Tr.
Blyth Fairway 55°06'·59N 01°28'·60W Fl G 3s; *Bell.*
Blyth E Pier Hd ☆ 55°06'·98N 01°29'·21W Fl (4) 10s 19m **21M**; W Tr; FR 13m 13M (same Tr); vis: 152°-249°; *Horn (3) 30s.*
Blyth W Pier Hd ☆ 55°06'·98N 01°29'·37W 2 FR (vert) 7m 8M.
Newbiggen Outfall 55°10'·13N 01°29'·60W Fl Y 5s.
Newbiggin Bkwtr Hd ☆ 55°10'·99N 01°30'·37W Fl G 10s 4M.

◀ COQUET ISLAND/WARKWORTH AND AMBLE

Coquet ☆ 55°20'·03N 01°32'·39W Fl (3) WR 30s 25m **W23M, R19M**; W □ Tr, turreted parapet, lower half Gy; vis: R330°-140°, W140°-163°, R163°-180°, W180°-330°; sector boundaries are indeterminate and may appear as Alt WR; *Horn 30s.*
Pan Rocks Outfall 55°20'·32N 01°33'·74W Fl R 10s; *Bell.*
Amble S Pier Head ☆ 55°20'·34N 01°34'·26W Fl R 5s 9m 5M.
N Pier Head ☆ 55°20'·39N 01°34'·25W Fl G 6s 12m 6M.

◀ BOULMER/CRASTER/NEWTON HAVEN/ BEADNELL BAY

Boulmer Haven 55°25'·00N 01°34'·93W.
Craster Harbour 55°28'·37N 01°35'·59W (unmarked).
Newton Rock 55°32'·15N 01°35'·85W.

◀ N SUNDERLAND (SEAHOUSES) BAMBURGH/ FARNE ISLANDS

The Falls 55°34'·61N 01°37'·12W Fl R 2·5s.
N Sunderland NW Pier Hd ☆ 55°35'·03N 01°38'·94W FG 11m 3M; W Tr; vis: 159°-294°; Tfc Sigs; *Siren 90s* (occas).
N. Sunderland Bkwtr Hd ☆ 55°35'·05N 01°38'·89W Fl R 2·5s 6m.
Shoreston Outcars 55°35'·88N 01°39'·34W QR.

Bamburgh Black Rocks Point ☆ 55°36'·99N 01°43'·45W Oc (2) WRG 15s 12m **W17M**, R13M, G13M; W bldg; vis: G122°-165°, W165°-175°, R175°-191°, W191°-238°, R238°-275°, W275°-289°, G289°-300°.

Inner Farne ☆ 55°36'·92N 01°39'·35W Fl (2) WR 15s 27m W10M, R7M; W ○ Tr; vis: R119°-280°, W280°-119°.
Longstone ☆ **W side** 55°38'·62N 01°36'·65W Fl 20s 23m **24M**; R Tr, W band; *Horn (2) 60s.*
Swedman 55°37'·65N 01°41'·63W Fl G 2·5s.

◀ HOLY ISLAND

Goldstone 55°40'·22N 01°43'·69W.
Ridge 55°39'·70N 01°45'·97W Q (3) 10s.
Triton Shoal 55°39'·61N 01°46'·59W QG.
Plough Rock 55°40'·24N 01°46'·00W.
Old Law E Bn ☆ (Guile Pt) 55°39'·49N 01°47'·60W Oc WRG 6s 9m 4M; vis: G182°-262°,W262°-264°, R264°-shore.
Heugh ☆ 55°40'·09N 01°47'·99W Oc WRG 6s 24m 5M; vis: G135°-308°, W308°-311°, R311°-shore.
Plough Seat 55°40'·37N 01°44'·97W QR.

◀ BERWICK-ON-TWEED

Bkwtr Hd ☆ 55°45'·88N 01°59'·06W Fl 5s 15m 10M; W ○ Tr, R cupola and base; vis: E of Seal Carr ledges-shore; FG (same Tr) 8m 1M; vis: 010°-154°.

9.5.5 PASSAGE INFORMATION

For directions and pilotage refer to: The East Coast (Imray/Bowskill) as far as The Wash; Tidal Havens of the Wash and Humber (Imray/Irving) carefully documents the hbrs of this little-frequented cruising ground. N from R Humber see the Royal Northumberland YC's Sailing Directions, Humber to Rattray Head. The Admiralty Pilot North Sea (West) covers the whole coast. North Sea Passage Pilot (Imray/Navin) goes as far N as Cromer and across to Den Helder.

NORTH NORFOLK COAST (charts 1503, 108) The coast of N Norfolk is unfriendly in bad weather, with no hbr accessible when there is any N in the wind. The hbrs all dry, and seas soon build up in the entrances or over the bars, some of which are dangerous even in a moderate breeze and an ebb tide. But in settled weather and moderate offshore winds it is a peaceful area to explore, particularly for boats which can take the ground. At Blakeney and Wells (see 9.5.7 and 9.5.8) chans shift almost every year, so local knowledge is essential and may best be acquired in advance from the Hr Mr; or in the event by following a friendly FV of suitable draft.

Haisborough Sand (buoyed) lies parallel to and 8M off the Norfolk coast at Happisburgh lt ho, with depths of less than 1m in many places, and drying 0·4m near the mid-point. The shoal is steep-to, on its NE side in particular, and there are tidal eddies. Even a moderate sea or swell breaks on the shallower parts. There are dangerous wks near the S end. Haisborough Tail and Hammond Knoll (with wk depth 1.6m) lie to the E of S end of Haisborough Sand. Newarp lt F is 5M SE. Similar banks lie parallel to and up to 60M off the coast.

The streams follow the generally NW/SE direction of the coast and offshore chans. But in the outer chans the stream is somewhat rotatory: when changing from SE-going to NW-going it sets SW, and when changing from NW-going to SE-going it sets NE, across the shoals. Close S of Haisborough Sand the SE-going stream begins at HW Immingham –0030; the NW-going at HW Immingham +0515, sp rates up to 2·5kn. It is possible to carry a fair tide from Gt Yarmouth to the Wash.

If proceeding direct from Cromer to the Humber, pass S of Sheringham Shoal (buoyed) where the ESE-going stream begins at HW Immingham –0225, and the WNW-going at +0430. Proceed to NE of Blakeney Overfalls and Docking Shoal, and to SW of Race Bank, so as to fetch Inner Dowsing lt tr (lt, fog sig). Thence pass E of Protector Overfalls, and steer for Rosse Spit buoy at SE ent to R Humber (9.5.11).

THE WASH (charts 108,1200) The Wash is formed by the estuaries of the rivers Great Ouse, Nene, Welland and Witham; it is an area of shifting sands, most of which dry. Important features are the strong tidal streams, the low-lying shore, and the often poor vis. Keep a careful watch on the echo sounder, because buoys may (or may not) have been moved to accommodate changes in the chan. Near North Well, the in-going stream begins at HW Immingham –0430, and the out-going at HW Immingham +0130, sp rates about 2kn. The in-going stream is usually stronger than the out-going, but its duration is less. Prolonged NE winds cause an in-going current, which can increase the rate and duration of the in-going stream and raise the water level at the head of the estuary. Do not attempt entry to the rivers too early on the flood, which runs hard in the rivers.

North Well SWM lt buoy and Roaring Middle lt F are the keys to entering the Wash from N or E. But from the E it is also possible to appr via a shallow route N of Stiffkey Overfalls and Bridgirdle PHM buoy; thence via Sledway and Woolpack PHM lt buoy to North Well and into Lynn Deeps. Near north end of Lynn Deeps there are overfalls over Lynn Knock at sp tides. For King's Lynn (9.5.9) and R Nene (Wisbech) follow the buoyed/lit Cork Hole and Wisbech Chans. Boston (9.5.10) and R Welland are reached via Freeman Chan, westward from Roaring Middle; or via Boston Deep, all lit.

The NW shore of The Wash is fronted by mudflats extending 2–3M offshore and drying more than 4m; a bombing range is marked by Y bns and buoys. Wainfleet Swatchway should only be used in good vis; the buoyed chan shifts constantly, and several shoals (charted depths unreliable) off Gibraltar Pt obstruct access to Boston Deep. For Wainfleet, see 9.5.10.

THE WASH TO THE RIVER HUMBER (charts 108, 107) Inner Dowsing is a narrow N/S sandbank with a least depth of 1·2m, 8M offshore between Skegness and Mablethorpe. There are overfalls off the W side of the bank at the N end. Inner Dowsing lt float (fog sig) is 1M NE of the bank.

In the outer approaches to The Wash and R. Humber there are many offlying banks, but few of them are of direct danger to yachts. The sea however breaks on some of them in bad weather, when they should be avoided. Fishing vessels may be encountered, and there are many oil/gas installations offshore (see over).

5

RIVER HUMBER (charts *109*, 1188, 3497) R. Humber is formed by R. Ouse and R. Trent, which meet 13M above Kingston-upon-Hull. It is commercially important and gives access to these rivers and inland waterways; it also drains most of Yorkshire and the Midlands. Where the Humber estuary reaches the sea between Northcoates Pt and Spurn Hd it is 4M wide. A VTS scheme is in operation to regulate commercial shipping in the Humber, Ouse and Trent and provide full radar surveillance. Yachts are advised to monitor the appropriate Humber VTS frequency.

Approaching from the S, a yacht should make good Rosse Spit and then Haile Sand No 2, both PHM lt buoys, before altering westward leading SW of Bull Ch.

If bound to/from the N, avoid The Binks, a shoal (dries 1·6m in places) extending 3M E from Spurn Hd, with a rough sea when wind is against tide. Depths offshore are irregular and subject to frequent change; it would be best to round the S Binks SPM buoy, unless in calm conditions and with local knowledge.

Haile Sand and Bull Sand Forts are both conspic to the SW of Spurn Head; beyond them it is advisable to keep just outside one of the buoyed chans, since shoals are liable to change. Hawke Chan (later Sunk) is the main dredged chan to the N. Haile Chan favours the S side and Grimsby. Bull Chan takes a middle course before merging with Haile Chan. There are good yachting facilities at Grimsby and Hull (9.5.11). ⚓ inside Spurn Head.

Streams are strong, even fierce at sp; local info suggests that they are stronger than shown in 9.5.3, which is based upon NP 251 (Admiralty Tidal Stream Atlas). 5ca S of Spurn Hd the flood sets NW from about HW Immingham –0520, sp rate 3·5kn; the ebb sets SE from about HW Immingham, sp rate 4kn. The worst seas are experienced in NW gales against a strong flood tide. 10M E of Spurn Hd the tidal streams are not affected by the river; relative to HW Immingham, the S-going stream begins at –0455, and the N-going at +0130. Nearer the entrance the direction of the S-going stream becomes more W'ly, and that of the N-going stream more E'ly.

R HUMBER TO HARTLEPOOL (charts 107, 121, 129, 134) Air gunnery and bombing practice is carried out 3M off Cowden, 17M S of Bridlington. The range is marked by 6 SPM buoys; 3 seaward ones Fl Y 10s, the 3 inner ones Fl Y 2s or 5s. Bridlington Bay (chart 1882) is clear of dangers apart from Smithic Shoals (marked by N and S cardinal lt buoys), about 3M off Bridlington (9.5.12); the seas break on these shoals in strong N or E winds even at HW.

Flamborough Head (lt, fog sig, RC) is a steep, W cliff with conspic lt ho on summit. The lt may be obsc by cliffs when close inshore. An old lt ho, also conspic, is 2½m WNW. Tides run hard around the Head which, in strong winds against a sp tide, is best avoided by 2M. From here the coast runs NW, with no offshore dangers until Filey Brigg where rky ledges extend 5ca ESE, marked by an ECM lt buoy. There is anch in Filey B (9.5.12) in N or offshore winds. NW of Filey Brigg beware Old Horse Rks and foul ground 5ca offshore; maintain this offing past Scarborough (9.5.13) to Whitby High lt. Off Whitby (9.5.14) beware Whitby Rk and The Scar (dry in places) to E of hbr, and Upgang Rks (dry in places) 1M to WNW; swell breaks heavily on all these rocks.

From Whitby to Hartlepool (9.5.15) there are no dangers more than 1M offshore. Runswick B (9.5.14 and AC 1612), 5M NW of Whitby, provides anch in winds from S and W but is dangerous in onshore winds. 2½M further NW the little hbr of Staithes is more suitable for yachts which can take the ground, but only in good weather and offshore winds.

Redcliff, dark red and 205m high is a conspic feature of this coast which, along to Hunt Cliff, is prone to landslides and is fringed with rky ledges which dry for about 3ca off. There is a conspic radio mast 4ca SSE of Redcliff. Off Redcar and Coatham beware Salt Scar and West Scar, drying rky ledges lying 1 – 8ca offshore. Other ledges lie close SE and S of Salt Scar which has NCM lt buoy. Between R. Tees (9.5.14) and Hartlepool beware Long Scar, detached rky ledge (dries 2m) with extremity marked by ECM lt buoy. Tees and Hartlepool Bays are exposed to strong E/SE winds. The R. Tees and Middlesbrough are highly industrialised at Hartlepool there is a centre specialising in the maintenance and restoration of Tall Ships.

HARTLEPOOL TO COQUET ISLAND (charts 134, 152, 156) From The Heugh an offing of 1M clears all dangers until past Seaham (9.5.16) and approaching Sunderland (9.5.17), where White Stones, rky shoals with depth 1·8m, lie 1·75M SSE of Roker Pier lt ho, and Hendon Rk, depth 0·9m, lies 1·25M SE of the lt ho. 1M N of Sunderland is Whitburn Steel, a rky ledge with less than 2m over it; a dangerous wreck (buoyed) lies 1ca SE of it. A firing range at Souter Pt is marked by R flags (R lts) when active. Along this stretch of coast industrial smoke haze may reduce vis and obscure lights.

The coast N of Tynemouth (9.5.18) is foul, and on passage to Blyth (9.5.19) it should be given an offing of 1M. 3·5M N of Tynemouth is St Mary's Island (with disused lt ho), joined to mainland by causeway. The small, drying hbr of Seaton Sluice, 1M NW of St Mary's Island, is accessible only in offshore winds via a narrow ent.

Proceeding N from Blyth, keep well seaward of The Sow and Pigs rks, and set course to clear Newbiggin Pt and Beacon Pt by about 1M. There are conspic measured mile bns here. Near Beacon Pt are conspic chys of aluminium smelter and power stn. 2M NNW of Beacon Pt is Snab Pt where rks extend 3ca seaward. Further offshore Cresswell Skeres, rky patches with depth 3m, lie about 1·5M NNE of Snab Pt.

COQUET ISLAND TO FARNE ISLANDS (chart 156) Coquet Is (lt, fog sig) lies about 5ca offshore at SE end of Alnmouth B, and nearly 1M NNE of Hauxley Pt, off which dangerous rks extend 6ca offshore, drying 1·9m. On passage, normally pass 1M E of Coquet Is in the W sector of the lt. Coquet chan may be used in good vis by day; but it is only 2ca wide, not buoyed, has least depth of 0·3m near the centre; and the stream runs strongly: S-going from HW Tyne – 0515 and N-going from HW Tyne + 0045. In S or W winds, there are good anchs in Coquet Road, W and NW of the Island.

Amble (Warkworth) hbr ent (9.5.20) is about 1M W of Coquet Is, and 1·5M SE of Warkworth Castle (conspic). 4ca NE and ENE of ent is Pan Bush, rky shoal with least depth of 0·3m on which dangerous seas can build in any swell. The bar has varying depths, down to less than 1m. The entrance is dangerous in strong winds from N/E when broken water may extend to Coquet Is. Once inside, the hbr is safe.

Between Coquet Is and the Farne Is, 19M to N, keep at least 1M offshore to avoid various dangers. To seaward, Craster Skeres lie 5M E of Castle Pt, and Dicky Shad and Newton Skere lie 1·75M and 4·5M E of Beadnell Pt; these are three rky banks on which the sea breaks heavily in bad weather. For Newton Haven and N Sunderland (Seahouses), see 9.5.20.

FARNE ISLANDS (charts 111, 160) The coast between N Sunderland Pt (Snook) and Holy Island, 8M NW, has fine hill (Cheviots) scenery fronted by dunes and sandy beaches. The Farne Is and offlying shoals extend 4·5M offshore, and are a mini-cruising ground well worth visiting in good weather. The islands are a bird sanctuary, owned and operated by the National Trust, with large colonies of sea birds and grey seals. AC 111 is essential.

Inner Sound separates the islands from the mainland. In good conditions it is a better N/S route than keeping outside the whole group; but the stream runs at 3kn at sp, and with strong wind against tide there is rough water. If course is set outside Farne Is, pass 1M E of Longstone (lt, fog sig) to clear Crumstone Rk 1M to S, and Knivestone (dries 3·6m) and Whirl Rks (depth 0·6m) respectively 5 and 6ca NE of Longstone lt ho. The sea breaks on these rks.

The islands, rks and shoals are divided by Staple Sound, running NW/SE, into an inner and outer group. The former comprises Inner Farne, W and E Wideopens and Knock's Reef. Inner Farne (lt) is the innermost Is; close NE there is anch called The Kettle, sheltered except from NW, but anch out of stream close to The Bridges connecting Knock's Reef and W Wideopen. 1M NW of Inner Farne Is and separated by Farne Sound, which runs NE/SW, lies the Megstone, a rk 5m high. Beware Swedman reef (dries 0·5m), marked by SHM buoy 4ca WSW of Megstone.

The outer group of Islands comprises Staple and Brownsman Islands, N and S Wamses, the Harcars and Longstone. There is occas anch between Staple and Brownsman Is. Piper Gut and Crafords Gut may be negotiated in calm weather and near HW, stemming the S-going stream.

HOLY ISLAND TO BERWICK (charts 1612, 111, 160) Near the Farne Is and Holy Is the SE-going stream begins at HW Tyne –0430, and the NW-going at HW Tyne +0130. Sp rates are about 2.5kn in Inner Sound, 4kn in Staple Sound and about 3·5kn 1M NE of Longstone, decreasing to seaward. There is an eddy S of Longstone on NW-going stream.

Holy Is (or Lindisfarne; 9.5.21) lies 6M WNW of Longstone, and is linked to mainland by a causeway covered at HW. There is a good anch on S side (chart 1612) with conspic daymarks and dir lts. The castle and a W obelisk at Emanuel Head are also conspic. The stream runs strongly in and out of hbr, W-going from HW Tyne + 0510, and E-going from HW Tyne –0045. E of Holy Is, Goldstone chan runs N/S between Goldstone Rk (dries) SHM buoy on E side and Plough Seat Reef and Plough Rk (both dry) on W side, with PHM buoy.

Berwick Bay has some offlying shoals. Berwick-upon-Tweed (9.5.22) is easily visible against the low shoreline, which rises again to high cliffs further north. The hbr entrance is restricted by a shallow bar, dangerous in onshore winds.

OIL AND GAS INSTALLATIONS Any yacht going offshore in the N Sea is likely to encounter oil or gas installations. These are shown on Admiralty charts, where scale permits; the position of mobile rigs is updated in weekly NMs. Safety zones of radius 500m are established round all permanent platforms, mobile exploration rigs, and tanker loading moorings, as described in the Annual Summary of Admiralty Notices to Mariners No 20. Some of these platforms are close together or inter-linked. Unauthorised vessels, including yachts, must not enter these zones except in emergency or due to stress of weather.

Platforms show a main lt, Fl Mo (U) 15s 15M. In addition secondary lts, Fl Mo (U) R 15s 2M, synchronised with the main lt, may mark projections at each corner of the platform if not marked by a W lt. The fog signal is Horn Mo (U) 30s. See the Admiralty List of Lights and Fog Signals, Vol A.

NORTH SEA PASSAGES See 9.0.8 for Distances across the North Sea. There are also further passage Notes in 9.4.5 for the Southern North Sea TSS; in 9.6.5 for crossing to Norway and the Baltic; in 9.23.5 for crossings from Belgium and the Netherlands; and in 9.24.5 for crossings from the Frisian Is and German Bight.

HARTLEPOOL TO SOUTHERN NETHERLANDS (charts 2182A, 1191, *1190*, 1503, 1408, 1610, 3371, 110) From abeam Whitby the passage can, theoretically, be made on one direct course, but this would conflict with oil/gas activities and platforms including Rough and Amethyst fields off Humber, Hewett off Cromer and very extensive fields further offshore. Commercial, oil-rig support and fishing vessels may be met S of Flamborough Hd and particularly off NE Norfolk where it is advisable to follow an inshore track.

After passing Flamborough Hd, Dowsing B1D, Dudgeon lt buoy and Newarp lt F, either:

Proceed SxE'ly to take departure from the Outer Gabbard; thence cross N Hinder South TSS at right angles before heading for Roompotsluis via Middelbank and subsequent buoyed chan.

Or set course ESE from the vicinity of Cross Sand lt buoy and Smith's Knoll, so as to cross the N/S deep-water traffic routes to the E (see 9.23.5). Thence alter SE toward Hoek van Holland, keeping N of Maas Approaches TSS.

HARTLEPOOL TO THE GERMAN BIGHT (charts 2182A, 1191, 266, 1405) Taking departure eastward from abeam Whitby High lt, skirt the SW Patch off Dogger Bank, keeping clear S of Gordon Gas Field and then N of German Bight W Approach TSS. Thence head for the Elbe or Helgoland; the latter may also serve as a convenient haven in order to adjust the passage for Elbe tides and streams (9.24.5), without greatly increasing passage distance. Tidal streams are less than 1kn away from the coast and run E/W along much of the route.

5

9.5.6 DISTANCE TABLE

Approximate distances in nautical miles are by the most direct route, whilst avoiding dangers and allowing for Traffic Separation Schemes. Places in *italics* are in adjoining areas; places in **bold** are in 9.0.8, Distances across the North Sea.

1.	*Great Yarmouth*	**1**																			
2.	Blakeney	44	**2**																		
3.	**King's Lynn**	85	42	**3**																	
4.	Boston	83	39	34	**4**																
5.	Humber Lt Buoy	82	45	55	54	**5**															
6.	**Grimsby**	99	54	61	58	17	**6**														
7.	Hull	113	68	75	72	31	14	**7**													
8.	Bridlington	114	79	87	83	35	44	58	**8**												
9.	Scarborough	130	96	105	98	50	59	81	20	**9**											
10.	Whitby	143	101	121	114	66	75	88	35	16	**10**										
11.	River Tees (ent)	166	122	138	135	87	96	118	56	37	21	**11**									
12.	**Hartlepool**	169	126	140	137	89	98	122	58	39	24	4	**12**								
13.	Seaham	175	137	151	145	100	106	133	66	47	33	15	11	**13**							
14.	Sunderland	180	142	156	149	105	110	138	70	51	36	20	16	5	**14**						
15.	Tynemouth	183	149	163	154	112	115	145	75	56	41	27	23	12	7	**15**					
16.	Blyth	190	156	171	162	120	123	153	83	64	49	35	31	20	15	8	**16**				
17.	Amble	203	170	185	176	126	143	157	102	81	65	46	42	32	27	21	14	**17**			
18.	Holy Island	225	191	196	198	148	166	180	126	104	88	68	65	54	50	44	37	22	**18**		
19.	**Berwick-on-Tweed**	232	200	205	205	157	166	189	126	107	91	82	78	67	61	55	47	31	9	**19**	
20.	Eyemouth	240	208	213	213	165	174	197	134	115	99	90	86	75	69	63	55	39	17	8	**20**

BLAKENEY *9.5.7*

Norfolk **52°59'·19N 00°57'·90E** (ent shifts)

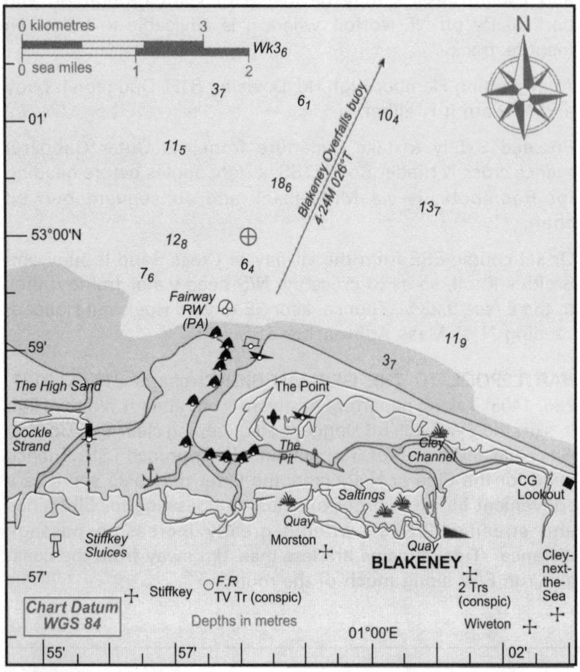

CHARTS AC 108, 1190; Imray C28; Stanfords 3, 19; OS 133

TIDES –0445 Dover; ML Cromer 2·8; Duration 0530; Zone 0 (UT)

Standard Port IMMINGHAM (⟶)

Times				Height (metres)			
High Water		Low Water		MHWS	MHWN	MLWN	MLWS
0100	0700	0100	0700	7·3	5·8	2·6	0·9
1300	1900	1300	1900				
Differences BLAKENEY BAR (approx 52°59'N 00°59'E)							
+0035	+0025	+0030	+0040	–1·6	–1·3	No data	
BLAKENEY (approx 52°57'N 01°01'E)							
+0115	+0055	No data		–3·9	–3·8	No data	
CROMER							
+0050	+0030	+0050	+0130	–2·1	–1·7	–0·5	–0·1

SHELTER Very good. Entry, sp HW ±2, nps HW ±1½. But no access in fresh on-shore winds when conditions at the entrance deteriorate very quickly, especially on the ebb. Moorings in The Pit area dry out. Speed limit 8kn.

NAVIGATION WPT 53°00'·00N 00°58'·20E, approx 045°/225° 1M from/to Fairway RW buoy which may not be on station or which may shift at ent to chan. Large dangerous wk, about close E of ent, marked by unlit PHM buoy. The bar is shallow and shifts often. The chan is marked by 15 unlit SHM buoys, relaid each spring. Beware mussel lays, drying, off Blakeney Spit.

LIGHTS AND MARKS Conspic marks: Blakeney and Langham churches; a chy on the house on Blakeney Pt neck; TV mast (R lts) approx 2M S of ent.

RADIO TELEPHONE None.

TELEPHONE (Dial code 01263) Hr Mr 740362; MRCC (01493) 851338; ⊖ (01473) 235704 (H24); Marinecall 09068 500455; Dr 740314.

FACILITIES Quay AB (Free), Slip, M, D, FW, C (15 ton); **Services:** CH (Stratton Long) ☎ 740362, AB, BY, M, P & D (cans), FW, ME, El, Sh, SM, Gaz, AC.
Village EC Wed; V, R, Bar, ✉, Ⓑ, ⇌ (Sheringham), ✈ (Norwich).

WELLS-NEXT-THE-SEA *9.5.8*

Norfolk **52°59'·30N 00°49'·75E** (ent shifts)

CHARTS AC 108, 1190; Imray C28, Y9; Stanfords 3, 19; OS 132

TIDES –0445 Dover; ML 1·2 Duration 0540; Zone 0 (UT)

Standard Port IMMINGHAM (⟶)

Times				Height (metres)			
High Water		Low Water		MHWS	MHWN	MLWN	MLWS
0100	0700	0100	0700	7·3	5·8	2·6	0·9
1300	1900	1300	1900				
Differences WELLS BAR (approx 52°59'N 00°49'E)							
+0020	+0020	+0020	+0020	–1·3	–1·0	No data	
WELLS-NEXT-THE-SEA (approx 52°57'N 00°51'E)							
+0035	+0045	+0340	+0310	–3·8	–3·8	Not below CD	

Note: LW time differences at Wells are for the end of a LW stand which lasts about 4 hrs at sp and about 5 hrs at nps.

SHELTER Good, but in strong N'lies swell renders entry impossible for small craft. Max draft 3m at sp. Access from HW –1½ to HW +1, but best on the flood. Quay berths mostly dry.

NAVIGATION WPT Fairway SWM buoy, Q, 52°59'·81N 00°49'·77E. The drying bar and ent vary in depth and position; buoys are altered to suit. Initially keep to W side of chan to counter E-going tide at HW–2; and to E side of chan from No 12 PHM lt buoy to quay. Best to seek Hr Mr's advice (send SAE for latest free plan) or follow FV of appropriate draft. Speed limits: W end of quay to LB house - 8kn, above this - 5kn.

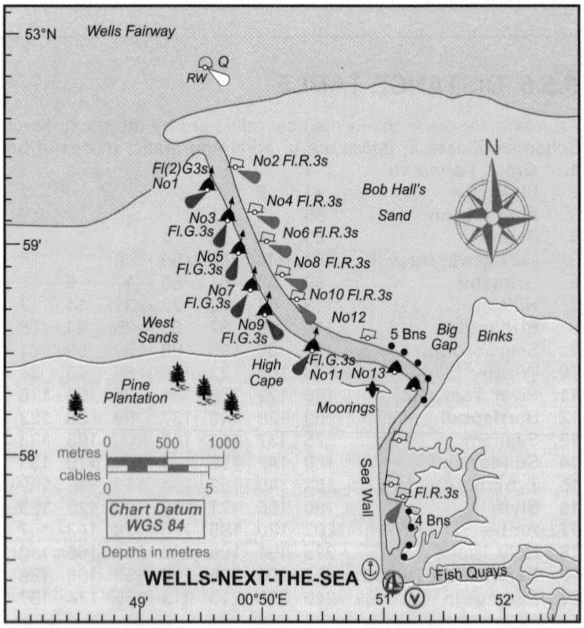

LIGHTS AND MARKS As plan. Temp buoys may be laid when chan changes. A pine plantation is conspic W of hbr ent; ditto white LB ho with R roof.

RADIO TELEPHONE *Wells Hbr Radio* Ch 12 16, HW–2 and when vessel due. Hbr launch may escort visitors into hbr and up to Quay.

TELEPHONE (Dial code 01328 Fakenham) Hr Mr 711646, 📠 710623; MRCC (01493) 851338; ⊖ (01473) 235704 (H24); Marinecall 09068 500 455; Police (01692) 402222; Dr 710741; Ⓗ 710097.

FACILITIES **Main Quay** AB (£1.30 approx), M (see Hr Mr), FW, ME, El, Sh, C (5 ton mobile), CH, V, R, Bar; **E Quay** Slip, M; **Wells SC** ☎ 710622, Slip, Bar; **Services:** Ⓔ, ACA. **Town** EC Thurs; P & D (bowser on quay; up to 500 galls), Gas, V, R, Bar, ✉, Ⓑ, ⇌ (bus to Norwich/King's Lynn), ✈ (Norwich).

KING'S LYNN *9.5.9*

Norfolk **52°49'·71N 00°21'·14E** (West Stones bn)
❁❁♿✿✿

CHARTS AC 1200, 108, 1190; Imray Y9; OS 132

TIDES –0443 Dover; ML 3·6; Duration 0340 Sp, 0515 Np; Zone 0 (UT)

Standard Port IMMINGHAM (⟶)

Times				Height (metres)			
High Water		Low Water		MHWS	MHWN	MLWN	MLWS
0100	0700	0100	0700	7·3	5·8	2·6	0·9
1300	1900	1300	1900				
Differences KING'S LYNN							
+0030	+0030	+0305	+0140	–0·5	–0·8	–0·8	+0·1
BURNHAM OVERY STAITHE							
+0045	+0055	No data		–5·0	–4·9	No data	
HUNSTANTON							
+0010	+0020	+0105	+0025	+0·1	–0·2	–0·1	0·0
WEST STONES							
+0025	+0025	+0115	+0040	–0·3	–0·4	–0·3	+0·2
WISBECH CUT							
+0020	+0025	+0200	+0030	–0·3	–0·7	–0·4	No data

SHELTER Port is well sheltered about 2M up river; entry is only recommended HW–3. A busy commercial and fishing port with very limited facilities for visiting leisure craft. Some mid-river moorings are available via local boating organisations, (contact Hr Mr for details), but due to strong tidal currents and distance from landing facilities are normally only used for boats overnight on passage to Denver (12M). The commercial docks are operated by ABP, and may offer limited facilities by prior arrangement with the Dock Master. North Sea Haven (Purfleet) is an enclosed dock operated by local council, notice required as a crane has to lift gate out. Drying moorings at S Quay, S side of Boal Quay or at Friars Fleet; keep clear of FV moorings.

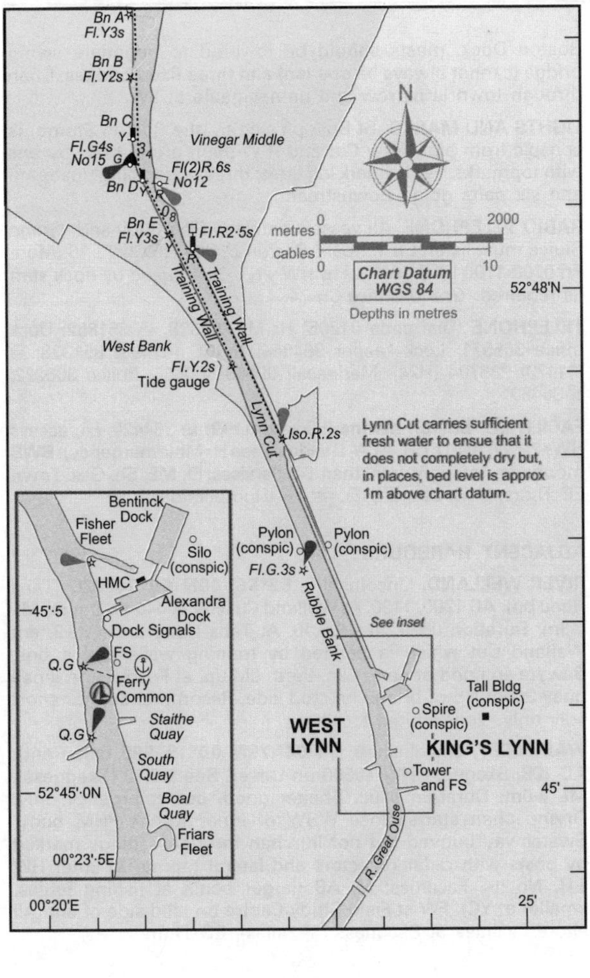

NAVIGATION WPT 52°58'·64N 00°21'·08E, Roaring Middle lt float SWM, L Fl 10s 7m 8M, 194°/014° to/from No 1 NCM lt byQ, 2·71M; continue 194° 1·35M to No 3 SHM by, Fl(2)G6s at 52°54'·67N 00°19'·24E marking ent to Teetotal ch, buoyed/lit appr to King's Lynn. From there to Denver Sluice (ent to inland routes) 6 bridges span river, min cl 9.15m less ht of tide at King's Lynn above Dock sill. Allow 1½H for passage. Extensive shifting sand banks extend several miles into the Wash. Chans are subject to frequent changes. Contact Hr Mr 1 wk prior for latest info.

LIGHTS AND MARKS Conspic white lt ho (disused, 18m) on Hunstanton cliffs. West Stones bn NCM, Q 3m 2M. Lynn Cut low lt Iso R 2s 11m 3M.

Entry sigs for Alexandra Dock:

Bu flag or ● = Vessels can enter;

R flag or ● = Vessels leaving dock.

RADIO TELEPHONE Call *King's Lynn Harbour Radio* VHF Ch **14** 16 11 (Mon-Fri: 0800-1730 LT. Other times: HW–4 to HW+1.) King's Lynn Docks (ABP) Ch **14** 16 11 (HW–2½ to HW).

TELEPHONE (Dial code 01553) Hr Mr 773411 🖷 763431; Dock 691555; MRCC (01493) 851338; Dr via Hr Mr; ⊖ (01473) 235704 (H24); Marinecall 09068 500455.

FACILITIES **Docks** ☎ 691555, AB £42 (9m LOA) for 48 hrs, FW, C (32 ton); **Services:** CH, Sh, ME, El, Ⓔ, D. **Town** EC Wed; P, D, V, R, Bar, ✉, Ⓑ, ⇌, ✈ (Humberside or Norwich). **Note:** 24M up the Great Ouse river, Ely Marina ☎ (01353) 664622, Slip, M, P, D, FW, ME, El, Sh, C (10 ton), CH. Lock half-way at Denver Sluice ☎ (01366) 382340/VHF Ch 73, and low bridges beyond.

ADJACENT HARBOURS

BURNHAM OVERY STAITHE, Norfolk, **52°58'·95N 00°46'·55E** ❁❁♿✿✿✿. AC 108, 1190. HW –0420 on Dover. See 9.5.9. Small drying hbr; ent chan has 0·3m MLWS. ⚓ off the Staithe only suitable in good weather. No lts. Scolt Hd is conspic to W and Gun Hill to E; Scolt Hd Island is conspic 3M long sandbank which affords some shelter. Chan varies constantly and buoys are moved to suit. Local knowledge advisable. Facilities: (01328) **Burnham Overy Staithe SC** ☎ 738348, M, L; **Services:** CH, M, ME, Sh, Slip, FW; **Burnham Market** EC Wed; Bar, P and D (cans), R, V.

BRANCASTER STAITHE, Norfolk, **52°59'·02N 00°37'·65E** ❁❁♿♿✿✿✿. AC 108, 1190. HW –0425 on Dover; See 9.5.9. Small drying hbr; dangerous to enter except by day in settled weather. Speed limit 6kn. Appr from due N. Conspic golf club house with lt, Fl 5s 8m 3M, is 0·5M S of chan ent and Fairway buoy. Beware wk shown on chart. Sandbanks vary constantly and buoys changed to suit. Scolt Hd conspic to E. Local knowledge or Pilot advised. Ⓥs available occas in The Hole. Hr Mr ☎ (01485) 210638. Facilities: **Brancaster Staithe SC** ☎ 210249, R, Bar; **Services:** BY, CH, El, FW, P & D (cans), ME, R, Sh, Bar, V.

WISBECH, Cambridgeshire, **52°40'·02N 00°09'·55E** ❁❁♿✿. AC 1200, 108. Imray Y9. HW –0450 on Dover; +0025 on Immingham. ML 3·5m; Duration 0520. See 9.5.9. Excellent shelter in river with Port of Wisbech Yacht Harbour pontoon berths (remain afloat) and shower/toilet facilities immediately below Freedom Bridge in Wisbech town. Vessels of 4·8m draft can reach Wisbech at sp (3·4m at nps), but depths vary. Ent to inland waterways above Wisbech to Peterborough, Oundle, Northampton. Mast lift out service available. Ent to R Nene from The Wash well marked with lit buoys/beacons from Wisbech No 1 Fl G 5s. Best ent HW–3. Ⓥs for waiting (Torbeau's) at RAF No 4 ECM. Cross Keys Swing Bridge in river opens by request given notice. Waiting pontoon 0.5M downstream from bridge thence 6M to Wisbech with FG lts to stbd. Call 'Wisbech Harbour' on VHF Ch 16 **09** or Hr Mr ☎ (01406) 350364 at Sutton Bridge HW –3 to HW. 24 hrs prior notice of intended visit recommended by calling Yacht Hr Mr (01945 588059 or Mobile 07860 576685. **Yt Hbr** (40AB + 20Ⓥ), VHF Ch 80, D barge. **Town** P (cans), Bar, R, V, Gas.

5

BOSTON *9.5.10*

Lincs **52°56′·00N 00°04′·92E** (Tabs Head bn)

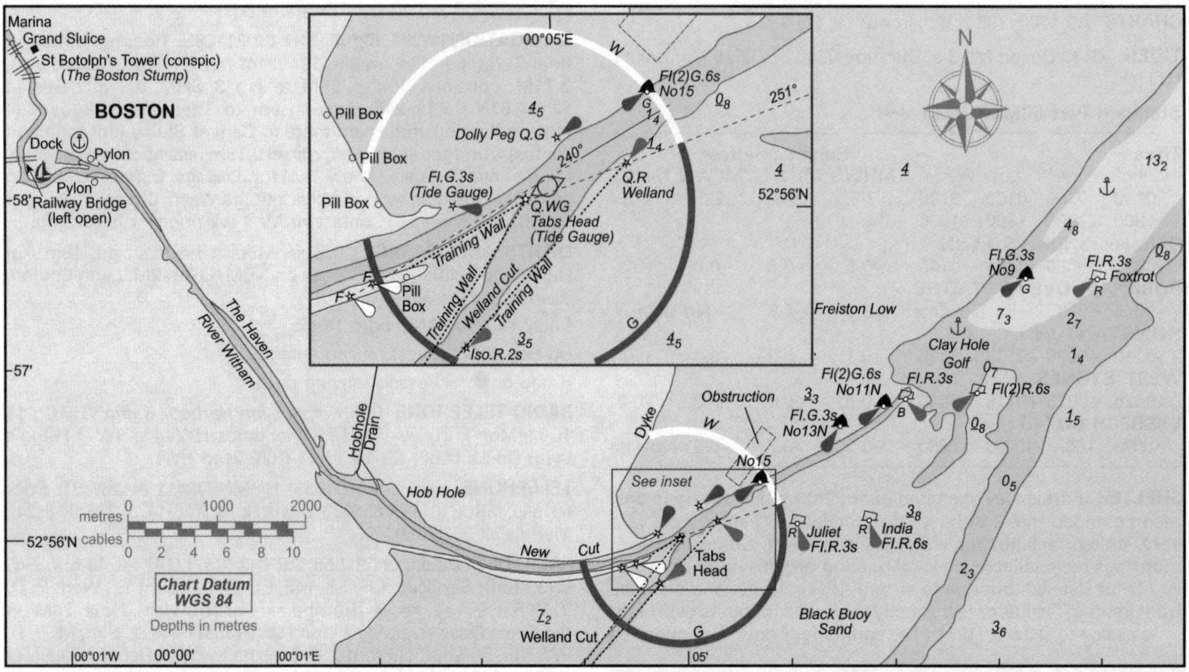

CHARTS AC 1200, 108; Imray Y9; OS 131

TIDES –0415 Dover; ML 3·3; Duration Flood 0500, Ebb 0700; Zone 0 (UT)

Standard Port IMMINGHAM (⟶)

Times				Height (metres)			
High Water		Low Water		MHWS	MHWN	MLWN	MLWS
0100	0700	0100	0700	7·3	5·8	2·6	0·9
1300	1900	1300	1900				
Differences BOSTON							
0000	+0010	+0140	+0050	–0·5	–1·0	–0·9	–0·5
TABS HEAD (WELLAND RIVER)							
0000	+0005	+0125	+0020	+0·2	–0·2	–0·2	–0·2
SKEGNESS							
+0010	+0015	+0030	+0020	–0·4	–0·5	–0·1	0·0
INNER DOWSING LIGHT TOWER							
0000	0000	+0010	+0010	–0·9	–0·7	–0·1	+0·3

SHELTER Very good. Except in emergency berthing in the Dock is prohib. Yachts secure just above Dock ent and see Hr Mr. The port is administered by Port of Boston Ltd. Moorings may be possible (on S side) below first fixed bridge.

Yachts which can lower masts should pass the Grand Sluice lock into fresh water (24 hrs notice required); the lock is 22·7m x 4·6m and opens approx HW±2. It leads into the R Witham Navigation which goes 31M to Lincoln. Marina is to stbd immediately beyond the sluice. British Waterways have 50 moorings, with FW and AC, beyond Grand Sluice, which can be manned at 6H notice. A telephone call (answerphone) will be diverted to a mobile.

NAVIGATION WPT Boston Rds SWM lt buoy, L Fl 10s, 52°57′·63N 00°16′·03E, 100°/280° from/to Freeman Chan ent, 0·70M. Thence Bar Chan is well marked, but liable to change. SW of Clay Hole a new chan has formed which dries 0.6m at entr; it is marked by SHM lt buoys Nos 11N, 13N, and 15. Note: former chan is still partially buoyed ufn. Tabs Head marks the ent to the river; it should be passed not earlier than HW–3 to enable the Grand Sluice to be reached before the start of the ebb. On reaching Boston Dock, masts should be lowered to negotiate swing bridge (cannot always be opened) and three fixed bridges. Chan through town is narrow and un-navigable at LW.

LIGHTS AND MARKS St Boltoph's ch tr, (the Boston Stump) is conspic from afar. New Cut and R Witham are marked by bns with topmarks. FW lts mark ldg lines: three pairs going upstream and six pairs going downstream.

RADIO TELEPHONE All vessels between Golf buoy and Grand Sluice must listen Ch 12. Call: *Boston Dock* VHF Ch 12 16 (Mon-Fri 0700-1700 LT & HW –2½ to HW +1½). Ch 11 used by dock staff as required. *Grand Sluice* Ch 74.

TELEPHONE (Dial code 01205) Hr Mr 362328, 🖷 351852; Dock office 365571; Lock keeper 364864; MRCC (01493) 851338; ⊖ (01473) 235704 (H24); Marinecall 09068 500455; Police 366222; ⊞ 364801.

FACILITIES Boston Marina (50 + some Ⓥ) ☎ 364420, £4, access HW±2; FW, AC, D, CH, ACA, C in dock, see Hr Mr (emergency); **BWB** moorings: 1st night free, then £4. **Services:** El, ME, Sh, Gas. **Town** EC Thurs; V, R, Bar, ✉, Ⓑ, ⇌, ✈ (Humberside).

ADJACENT HARBOURS

RIVER WELLAND, Lincolnshire, **52°56′·00N 00°04′·92E** (Tabs Head bn). AC 1200, 1190. At Welland Cut HW –0440 on Dover; ML 0·3m; Duration 0520. See 9.5.10. At Tabs Head bn HW ±3, ent Welland Cut which is defined by training walls and lt bns. Beware sp flood of up to 5kn. Berth 6M up, at Fosdyke on small quay 300m NE of bridge on stbd side. Recommended for short stay only. Very limited facilities.

WAINFLEET, Lincolnshire, **53°04′·79N 00°19′·89E** (chan ent). AC 108. Skegness HW +0500 on Dover. See 9.5.10 (Skegness). ML 4·0m; Duration 0600. Shelter good, but emergency only. Drying chan starts close WSW of Inner Knock PHM buoy. Swatchway buoyed but not lit; chan through saltings marked by posts with radar reflectors and lateral topmarks. Enter HW ±1½. No lts. Facilities: M, AB (larger boats at fishing jetties, smaller at YC), FW at Field Study Centre on stbd side of ent. All shore facilities at Skegness (3½ miles), EC Thurs.

TIME ZONE (UTC)
For Summer Time add ONE hour in **non-shaded areas**

ENGLAND – IMMINGHAM

LAT 53°38′N LONG 0°11′W

TIMES AND HEIGHTS OF HIGH AND LOW WATERS

SPRING & NEAP TIDES
Dates in red are **SPRINGS**
Dates in blue are **NEAPS**

YEAR **2002**

JANUARY

Date	Day	Time	m	Time	m	Time	m	Time	m	Moon
1	TU	0104	1.1	0701	7.2	1316	1.4	1913	7.3	
2	W	0151	1.0	0749	7.2	1400	1.4	1956	7.3	
3	TH	0239	1.0	0838	7.0	1445	1.6	2041	7.2	
4	F	0328	1.1	0929	6.8	1531	1.8	2129	7.1	
5	SA	0419	1.3	1025	6.6	1621	2.0	2224	6.8	
6	SU	0514	1.5	1128	6.3	1717	2.3	2327	6.6	
7	M	0615	1.7	1235	6.2	1823	2.5			
8	TU	0039	6.4	0721	1.9	1340	6.1	1939	2.5	
9	W	0152	6.3	0828	1.9	1442	6.2	2054	2.4	
10	TH	0300	6.4	0929	1.9	1539	6.3	2158	2.1	
11	F	0402	6.5	1022	1.8	1630	6.6	2253	1.8	
12	SA	0457	6.6	1111	1.7	1714	6.8	2343	1.6	
13	SU	0545	6.7	1155	1.6	1755	6.9			●
14	M	0028	1.4	0629	6.8	1236	1.6	1833	7.0	
15	TU	0109	1.4	0709	6.7	1313	1.6	1909	7.1	
16	W	0145	1.4	0745	6.7	1347	1.7	1943	7.0	
17	TH	0218	1.5	0817	6.5	1419	1.8	2016	6.9	
18	F	0249	1.6	0849	6.4	1449	1.9	2049	6.8	
19	SA	0320	1.7	0922	6.2	1519	2.1	2122	6.6	
20	SU	0353	1.9	0959	6.1	1554	2.3	2200	6.3	
21	M	0431	2.1	1041	5.8	1637	2.6	2245	6.1	
22	TU	0521	2.4	1136	5.7	1734	2.8	2343	5.9	
23	W	0624	2.5	1249	5.6	1846	2.9			
24	TH	0100	5.8	0734	2.5	1405	5.7	2001	2.8	
25	F	0220	5.9	0843	2.3	1509	6.0	2112	2.4	
26	SA	0326	6.2	0945	2.1	1604	6.3	2215	2.0	
27	SU	0424	6.6	1040	1.8	1652	6.7	2312	1.6	
28	M	0517	6.9	1131	1.5	1736	7.0			○
29	TU	0005	1.1	0606	7.1	1220	1.3	1819	7.3	
30	W	0056	0.8	0655	7.3	1307	1.2	1902	7.5	
31	TH	0144	0.6	0741	7.3	1352	1.1	1945	7.6	

FEBRUARY

Date	Day	Time	m	Time	m	Time	m	Time	m	Moon
1	F	0230	0.5	0827	7.3	1435	1.2	2029	7.6	
2	SA	0315	0.6	0912	7.1	1518	1.3	2114	7.4	
3	SU	0359	0.9	0959	6.8	1600	1.6	2202	7.1	
4	M	0445	1.3	1049	6.4	1646	2.0	2256	6.7	
5	TU	0536	1.8	1149	6.1	1739	2.4			
6	W	0003	6.3	0637	2.2	1257	5.8	1852	2.6	
7	TH	0124	6.0	0753	2.4	1407	5.8	2031	2.6	
8	F	0243	5.9	0905	2.4	1512	5.9	2146	2.3	
9	SA	0354	6.1	1005	2.3	1610	6.2	2243	2.0	
10	SU	0453	6.3	1055	2.0	1657	6.5	2332	1.6	
11	M	0540	6.5	1140	1.8	1739	6.8			
12	TU	0015	1.4	0619	6.6	1221	1.6	1816	7.0	●
13	W	0055	1.3	0653	6.7	1258	1.6	1851	7.1	
14	TH	0129	1.3	0724	6.7	1331	1.5	1924	7.1	
15	F	0200	1.3	0753	6.7	1400	1.6	1954	7.0	
16	SA	0228	1.4	0820	6.6	1426	1.7	2024	6.9	
17	SU	0253	1.5	0848	6.5	1452	1.8	2052	6.7	
18	M	0318	1.7	0918	6.3	1521	1.9	2123	6.5	
19	TU	0346	1.9	0952	6.1	1556	2.2	2200	6.3	
20	W	0424	2.2	1034	5.8	1643	2.5	2249	6.0	
21	TH	0519	2.5	1130	5.6	1751	2.7	2357	5.7	
22	F	0639	2.7	1301	5.5	1918	2.8			
23	SA	0139	5.7	0804	2.6	1436	5.7	2042	2.5	
24	SU	0309	6.0	0919	2.3	1541	6.1	2156	2.0	
25	M	0414	6.4	1022	1.9	1633	6.6	2259	1.4	
26	TU	0509	6.9	1117	1.5	1720	7.1	2353	0.9	
27	W	0558	7.2	1206	1.2	1804	7.4			○
28	TH	0043	0.5	0643	7.4	1253	1.0	1846	7.7	

MARCH

Date	Day	Time	m	Time	m	Time	m	Time	m	Moon
1	F	0129	0.2	0726	7.5	1337	0.8	1928	7.8	
2	SA	0213	0.2	0807	7.4	1419	0.8	2011	7.8	
3	SU	0254	0.4	0847	7.2	1458	1.0	2054	7.6	
4	M	0333	0.8	0927	6.9	1537	1.3	2138	7.2	
5	TU	0412	1.3	1010	6.5	1616	1.8	2229	6.6	
6	W	0455	1.9	1101	6.0	1702	2.3	2334	6.0	
7	TH	0551	2.5	1211	5.7	1809	2.7			
8	F	0103	5.7	0714	2.9	1332	5.5	2015	2.8	
9	SA	0231	5.6	0845	2.8	1446	5.7	2134	2.4	
10	SU	0348	5.9	0948	2.5	1548	6.1	2228	2.0	
11	M	0444	6.2	1038	2.2	1637	6.4	2314	1.6	
12	TU	0526	6.5	1121	1.8	1718	6.7	2354	1.3	
13	W	0600	6.6	1201	1.6	1754	6.9			
14	TH	0031	1.2	0629	6.7	1237	1.5	1827	7.0	●
15	F	0104	1.2	0657	6.8	1309	1.4	1859	7.0	
16	SA	0134	1.2	0724	6.8	1338	1.4	1929	7.0	
17	SU	0201	1.3	0750	6.7	1403	1.5	1956	6.9	
18	M	0225	1.4	0816	6.7	1428	1.6	2024	6.8	
19	TU	0247	1.6	0843	6.5	1455	1.7	2054	6.7	
20	W	0312	1.8	0915	6.3	1528	2.0	2131	6.4	
21	TH	0346	2.1	0955	6.0	1612	2.3	2219	6.1	
22	F	0437	2.4	1047	5.7	1718	2.6	2327	5.7	
23	SA	0556	2.8	1207	5.5	1850	2.7			
24	SU	0117	5.6	0735	2.8	1402	5.6	2022	2.4	
25	M	0258	6.0	0858	2.5	1516	6.1	2141	1.8	
26	TU	0403	6.5	1004	2.0	1611	6.7	2242	1.2	
27	W	0455	6.9	1059	1.5	1658	7.2	2334	0.6	
28	TH	0542	7.3	1148	1.1	1742	7.5			○
29	F	0022	0.3	0624	7.5	1234	0.8	1825	7.8	
30	SA	0107	0.1	0703	7.6	1318	0.6	1908	7.9	
31	SU	0149	0.2	0742	7.5	1359	0.7	1951	7.8	

APRIL

Date	Day	Time	m	Time	m	Time	m	Time	m	Moon
1	M	0228	0.4	0819	7.3	1438	0.9	2033	7.5	
2	TU	0305	0.9	0857	6.9	1514	1.2	2118	7.0	
3	W	0342	1.5	0936	6.5	1552	1.7	2207	6.4	
4	TH	0421	2.1	1022	6.0	1637	2.2	2314	5.8	
5	F	0513	2.7	1129	5.6	1742	2.6			
6	SA	0048	5.5	0631	3.1	1259	5.5	1954	2.7	
7	SU	0213	5.5	0815	3.0	1417	5.6	2110	2.4	
8	M	0325	5.8	0922	2.7	1520	6.0	2201	2.0	
9	TU	0418	6.1	1012	2.3	1609	6.3	2244	1.6	
10	W	0458	6.4	1054	1.9	1650	6.6	2323	1.4	
11	TH	0530	6.6	1133	1.6	1726	6.8	2358	1.2	
12	F	0559	6.7	1209	1.5	1758	6.9			●
13	SA	0032	1.2	0625	6.8	1242	1.4	1829	6.9	
14	SU	0103	1.2	0652	6.8	1311	1.4	1900	6.9	
15	M	0131	1.3	0720	6.8	1339	1.4	1930	6.9	
16	TU	0157	1.4	0747	6.8	1407	1.5	2001	6.8	
17	W	0222	1.6	0817	6.7	1438	1.6	2035	6.7	
18	TH	0251	1.8	0850	6.5	1513	1.8	2116	6.4	
19	F	0328	2.1	0931	6.2	1600	2.1	2208	6.0	
20	SA	0420	2.4	1026	5.9	1709	2.3	2321	5.7	
21	SU	0537	2.8	1145	5.7	1838	2.4			
22	M	0112	5.7	0713	2.8	1329	5.8	2005	2.1	
23	TU	0240	6.1	0835	2.4	1446	6.2	2119	1.5	
24	W	0342	6.5	0940	1.9	1543	6.7	2218	1.0	
25	TH	0433	7.0	1035	1.5	1633	7.2	2310	0.6	
26	F	0518	7.3	1125	1.1	1719	7.5	2357	0.3	
27	SA	0559	7.4	1212	0.8	1804	7.7			○
28	SU	0041	0.3	0638	7.5	1256	0.7	1848	7.7	
29	M	0123	0.4	0716	7.4	1339	0.7	1933	7.5	
30	TU	0203	0.7	0754	7.2	1419	0.9	2017	7.2	

Chart Datum: 3·90 metres below Ordnance Datum (Newlyn)

TIME ZONE (UTC)
For Summer Time add ONE hour in **non-shaded areas**

ENGLAND – IMMINGHAM

LAT 53°38′N LONG 0°11′W

TIMES AND HEIGHTS OF HIGH AND LOW WATERS

SPRING & NEAP TIDES
Dates in **red** are **SPRINGS**
Dates in **blue** are **NEAPS**

YEAR **2002**

MAY

Date	Day	Time	m	Time	m	Time	m	Time	m	Moon
1	W	0240	1.2	0831	6.9	1457	1.3	2102	6.8	
2	TH	0316	1.7	0909	6.5	1536	1.7	2152	6.2	
3	F	0356	2.2	0953	6.1	1621	2.1	2258	5.7	
4	SA	0445	2.7	1054	5.7	1723	2.5			
5	SU	0023	5.5	0552	3.1	1220	5.5	1855	2.6	
6	M	0139	5.5	0719	3.1	1338	5.6	2025	2.4	
7	TU	0245	5.7	0838	2.8	1441	5.9	2119	2.1	
8	W	0338	6.0	0933	2.4	1533	6.2	2203	1.8	
9	TH	0420	6.3	1018	2.1	1615	6.4	2242	1.6	
10	F	0454	6.5	1058	1.8	1651	6.6	2319	1.4	
11	SA	0523	6.7	1135	1.6	1725	6.7	2355	1.3	
12	SU	0552	6.8	1210	1.5	1800	6.8			●
13	M	0030	1.3	0622	6.8	1245	1.4	1834	6.9	
14	TU	0103	1.4	0654	6.9	1318	1.4	1910	6.9	
15	W	0133	1.4	0726	6.8	1352	1.4	1947	6.8	
16	TH	0205	1.6	0800	6.8	1429	1.5	2027	6.7	
17	F	0240	1.8	0837	6.6	1511	1.7	2113	6.4	
18	SA	0323	2.0	0922	6.4	1604	1.8	2210	6.1	
19	SU	0417	2.4	1019	6.1	1711	2.0	2324	5.9	
20	M	0528	2.6	1134	6.0	1828	2.0			
21	TU	0056	5.9	0650	2.6	1259	6.1	1943	1.7	
22	W	0212	6.2	0806	2.3	1413	6.4	2051	1.4	
23	TH	0313	6.5	0912	1.9	1514	6.7	2150	1.1	
24	F	0406	6.8	1010	1.5	1608	7.1	2243	0.8	
25	SA	0452	7.1	1102	1.2	1658	7.3	2331	0.7	
26	SU	0534	7.2	1150	1.0	1747	7.4			○
27	M	0016	0.7	0614	7.2	1237	0.9	1834	7.3	
28	TU	0100	0.8	0654	7.2	1322	0.9	1920	7.2	
29	W	0140	1.1	0733	7.1	1404	1.1	2006	6.9	
30	TH	0219	1.4	0811	6.9	1444	1.3	2051	6.6	
31	F	0256	1.8	0850	6.6	1525	1.6	2139	6.2	

JUNE

Date	Day	Time	m	Time	m	Time	m	Time	m	Moon
1	SA	0335	2.2	0932	6.3	1608	2.0	2233	5.8	
2	SU	0420	2.6	1023	6.0	1700	2.2	2338	5.6	
3	M	0515	2.8	1128	5.8	1801	2.4			
4	TU	0047	5.5	0619	2.9	1240	5.7	1906	2.4	
5	W	0150	5.6	0729	2.9	1345	5.8	2011	2.3	
6	TH	0246	5.8	0834	2.6	1442	6.0	2106	2.1	
7	F	0332	6.0	0929	2.3	1530	6.2	2155	1.8	
8	SA	0411	6.3	1016	2.0	1612	6.4	2239	1.7	
9	SU	0446	6.5	1059	1.8	1653	6.6	2320	1.5	
10	M	0521	6.7	1141	1.6	1734	6.7			●
11	TU	0000	1.5	0557	6.8	1221	1.4	1814	6.8	
12	W	0038	1.4	0634	6.9	1302	1.3	1857	6.9	
13	TH	0116	1.5	0712	6.9	1343	1.3	1940	6.9	
14	F	0155	1.5	0751	6.9	1427	1.3	2025	6.8	
15	SA	0236	1.7	0833	6.8	1515	1.3	2115	6.6	
16	SU	0322	1.9	0920	6.7	1607	1.4	2211	6.4	
17	M	0414	2.1	1014	6.5	1705	1.5	2317	6.2	
18	TU	0514	2.3	1119	6.4	1810	1.6			
19	W	0030	6.2	0622	2.3	1231	6.4	1916	1.6	
20	TH	0138	6.2	0734	2.3	1342	6.4	2022	1.5	
21	F	0240	6.4	0843	2.1	1448	6.6	2123	1.4	
22	SA	0337	6.6	0946	1.8	1548	6.8	2218	1.3	
23	SU	0427	6.7	1042	1.5	1644	6.9	2309	1.2	
24	M	0513	6.9	1135	1.3	1736	7.0	2356	1.2	○
25	TU	0556	7.0	1224	1.1	1826	7.0			
26	W	0041	1.3	0637	7.0	1311	1.1	1913	6.9	
27	TH	0123	1.4	0717	7.0	1354	1.2	1957	6.7	
28	F	0202	1.6	0755	6.9	1434	1.3	2038	6.5	
29	SA	0239	1.8	0833	6.7	1512	1.5	2118	6.3	
30	SU	0315	2.0	0911	6.5	1549	1.8	2157	6.0	

JULY

Date	Day	Time	m	Time	m	Time	m	Time	m	Moon
1	M	0352	2.3	0952	6.3	1629	2.0	2240	5.8	
2	TU	0434	2.5	1040	6.1	1715	2.2	2330	5.7	
3	W	0524	2.7	1136	5.9	1808	2.3			
4	TH	0030	5.6	0623	2.8	1239	5.8	1906	2.4	
5	F	0133	5.6	0728	2.8	1343	5.8	2008	2.3	
6	SA	0233	5.8	0833	2.6	1443	6.0	2108	2.2	
7	SU	0326	6.1	0933	2.3	1537	6.2	2201	2.0	
8	M	0412	6.3	1026	2.0	1627	6.4	2250	1.8	
9	TU	0456	6.6	1116	1.7	1715	6.7	2335	1.6	
10	W	0538	6.8	1203	1.4	1802	6.9			●
11	TH	0020	1.5	0619	7.0	1251	1.2	1848	7.0	
12	F	0104	1.4	0700	7.1	1338	1.0	1935	7.0	
13	SA	0147	1.4	0742	7.2	1425	0.9	2022	7.0	
14	SU	0231	1.4	0826	7.2	1511	0.9	2110	6.9	
15	M	0315	1.5	0911	7.1	1559	1.0	2200	6.7	
16	TU	0402	1.7	1001	7.0	1649	1.2	2255	6.5	
17	W	0452	2.0	1057	6.7	1743	1.5	2356	6.3	
18	TH	0551	2.2	1202	6.5	1845	1.7			
19	F	0102	6.1	0659	2.3	1314	6.3	1952	1.9	
20	SA	0207	6.1	0817	2.3	1427	6.3	2059	1.9	
21	SU	0309	6.2	0929	2.1	1535	6.4	2159	1.8	
22	M	0406	6.4	1031	1.8	1638	6.5	2253	1.7	
23	TU	0456	6.6	1126	1.5	1733	6.7	2341	1.6	
24	W	0540	6.8	1215	1.3	1821	6.7			○
25	TH	0026	1.5	0621	7.0	1301	1.2	1904	6.8	
26	F	0108	1.5	0700	7.0	1342	1.2	1943	6.7	
27	SA	0145	1.6	0737	7.0	1419	1.3	2017	6.6	
28	SU	0220	1.7	0812	6.9	1451	1.4	2048	6.5	
29	M	0251	1.8	0846	6.8	1522	1.6	2118	6.3	
30	TU	0321	2.0	0920	6.6	1552	1.8	2152	6.1	
31	W	0352	2.2	0957	6.3	1625	2.0	2230	5.9	

AUGUST

Date	Day	Time	m	Time	m	Time	m	Time	m	Moon
1	TH	0429	2.4	1039	6.1	1707	2.3	2320	5.7	
2	F	0519	2.7	1134	5.8	1804	2.5			
3	SA	0026	5.6	0624	2.8	1247	5.7	1912	2.6	
4	SU	0143	5.6	0739	2.8	1403	5.8	2024	2.5	
5	M	0250	5.9	0853	2.6	1511	6.0	2129	2.3	
6	TU	0347	6.2	1000	2.1	1610	6.3	2226	2.0	
7	W	0436	6.6	1058	1.7	1703	6.7	2317	1.7	
8	TH	0521	6.9	1151	1.3	1752	7.0			●
9	F	0005	1.5	0603	7.2	1241	0.9	1839	7.2	
10	SA	0052	1.3	0646	7.4	1328	0.7	1924	7.3	
11	SU	0136	1.2	0728	7.6	1413	0.5	2009	7.3	
12	M	0218	1.1	0811	7.6	1456	0.6	2052	7.2	
13	TU	0300	1.2	0854	7.5	1539	0.8	2136	7.0	
14	W	0342	1.4	0941	7.3	1623	1.1	2223	6.6	
15	TH	0426	1.8	1032	6.9	1711	1.6	2318	6.3	
16	F	0517	2.2	1134	6.4	1809	2.1			
17	SA	0023	6.0	0624	2.5	1252	6.1	1923	2.4	
18	SU	0136	5.8	0759	2.6	1414	5.9	2041	2.5	
19	M	0246	5.9	0923	2.4	1532	6.1	2146	2.3	
20	TU	0348	6.2	1025	2.0	1639	6.3	2240	2.1	
21	W	0440	6.5	1116	1.6	1729	6.6	2327	1.8	
22	TH	0523	6.8	1202	1.3	1810	6.7			○
23	F	0009	1.6	0602	7.0	1244	1.2	1846	6.8	
24	SA	0049	1.5	0639	7.1	1321	1.1	1918	6.8	
25	SU	0124	1.5	0713	7.1	1354	1.2	1947	6.7	
26	M	0156	1.5	0746	7.1	1423	1.3	2014	6.7	
27	TU	0223	1.6	0817	6.9	1449	1.5	2040	6.6	
28	W	0248	1.8	0846	6.8	1512	1.7	2108	6.4	
29	TH	0314	2.0	0916	6.5	1537	2.0	2139	6.2	
30	F	0346	2.2	0950	6.3	1609	2.2	2217	5.9	
31	SA	0428	2.5	1035	5.9	1658	2.6	2311	5.6	

Chart Datum: 3·90 metres below Ordnance Datum (Newlyn)

TIME ZONE (UTC)
For Summer Time add ONE hour in **non-shaded areas**

ENGLAND – IMMINGHAM

LAT 53°38′N LONG 0°11′W

TIMES AND HEIGHTS OF HIGH AND LOW WATERS

SPRING & NEAP TIDES
Dates in red are SPRINGS
Dates in blue are NEAPS

YEAR **2002**

SEPTEMBER

Date	Day	Time	m	Time	m	Time	m	Time	m	Moon
1	SU	0531	2.8	1143	5.7	1815	2.8			
2	M	0049	5.5	0656	2.9	1331	5.6	1944	2.8	
3	TU	0220	5.7	0823	2.7	1454	5.9	2103	2.6	
4	W	0323	6.1	0941	2.2	1557	6.3	2207	2.2	
5	TH	0415	6.6	1042	1.6	1651	6.8	2300	1.7	
6	F	0500	7.0	1135	1.1	1739	7.1	2348	1.4	
7	SA	0543	7.4	1223	0.7	1823	7.4			●
8	SU	0033	1.1	0624	7.7	1309	0.4	1905	7.5	
9	M	0117	0.9	0706	7.9	1352	0.3	1945	7.5	
10	TU	0158	0.9	0749	7.9	1433	0.4	2025	7.4	
11	W	0239	1.0	0832	7.7	1512	0.8	2105	7.1	
12	TH	0318	1.3	0917	7.3	1552	1.3	2147	6.7	
13	F	0358	1.7	1007	6.8	1634	1.9	2237	6.2	
14	SA	0444	2.2	1111	6.2	1728	2.5	2344	5.8	
15	SU	0552	2.7	1236	5.8	1853	2.9			
16	M	0106	5.7	0753	2.8	1406	5.7	2025	2.9	
17	TU	0223	5.8	0914	2.4	1527	6.0	2131	2.6	
18	W	0328	6.1	1010	1.9	1630	6.3	2222	2.2	
19	TH	0419	6.5	1057	1.6	1712	6.6	2306	1.9	
20	F	0501	6.9	1139	1.3	1747	6.8	2346	1.6	
21	SA	0538	7.1	1217	1.2	1818	6.9			○
22	SU	0024	1.5	0612	7.2	1252	1.2	1846	6.9	
23	M	0058	1.4	0645	7.2	1323	1.2	1913	6.9	
24	TU	0127	1.5	0716	7.1	1350	1.4	1938	6.8	
25	W	0153	1.6	0746	7.0	1413	1.5	2003	6.8	
26	TH	0218	1.7	0813	6.8	1435	1.7	2029	6.6	
27	F	0243	1.9	0842	6.6	1458	1.9	2058	6.4	
28	SA	0313	2.1	0916	6.4	1528	2.2	2134	6.1	
29	SU	0354	2.4	1000	6.0	1613	2.6	2223	5.8	
30	M	0455	2.7	1107	5.7	1725	3.0	2342	5.5	

OCTOBER

Date	Day	Time	m	Time	m	Time	m	Time	m	Moon
1	TU	0625	2.9	1307	5.6	1909	3.1			
2	W	0145	5.7	0759	2.6	1437	5.9	2036	2.7	
3	TH	0255	6.1	0920	2.0	1540	6.4	2143	2.2	
4	F	0349	6.7	1020	1.4	1632	6.9	2236	1.7	
5	SA	0434	7.2	1111	0.9	1718	7.3	2324	1.3	
6	SU	0517	7.6	1158	0.5	1759	7.5			●
7	M	0009	1.0	0559	7.9	1243	0.3	1838	7.6	
8	TU	0054	0.8	0642	8.0	1325	0.3	1917	7.6	
9	W	0136	0.8	0726	7.9	1405	0.5	1955	7.4	
10	TH	0216	1.0	0810	7.7	1443	1.0	2034	7.1	
11	F	0255	1.3	0856	7.2	1521	1.5	2114	6.7	
12	SA	0334	1.7	0947	6.6	1600	2.1	2200	6.3	
13	SU	0420	2.2	1053	6.0	1651	2.8	2306	5.8	
14	M	0529	2.7	1223	5.7	1813	3.2			
15	TU	0035	5.6	0736	2.7	1348	5.6	1957	3.2	
16	W	0154	5.8	0851	2.4	1503	5.9	2104	2.8	
17	TH	0259	6.1	0944	2.0	1600	6.3	2155	2.4	
18	F	0350	6.5	1028	1.6	1641	6.6	2238	2.0	
19	SA	0432	6.8	1107	1.4	1715	6.8	2317	1.7	
20	SU	0509	7.0	1143	1.3	1745	6.9	2353	1.5	
21	M	0543	7.1	1216	1.3	1813	7.0			○
22	TU	0026	1.5	0615	7.1	1247	1.3	1839	7.0	
23	W	0057	1.5	0646	7.1	1315	1.4	1905	7.0	
24	TH	0125	1.5	0717	7.0	1340	1.6	1932	6.9	
25	F	0152	1.7	0747	6.9	1404	1.7	1959	6.8	
26	SA	0220	1.8	0819	6.7	1431	1.9	2030	6.6	
27	SU	0253	2.0	0856	6.4	1504	2.2	2107	6.3	
28	M	0336	2.3	0944	6.1	1551	2.6	2156	6.0	
29	TU	0439	2.6	1054	5.7	1659	3.0	2309	5.7	
30	W	0605	2.6	1244	5.7	1834	3.1			
31	TH	0057	5.8	0734	2.4	1411	6.0	2003	2.8	

NOVEMBER

Date	Day	Time	m	Time	m	Time	m	Time	m	Moon
1	F	0217	6.2	0850	1.9	1514	6.5	2111	2.3	
2	SA	0315	6.7	0950	1.3	1605	6.9	2207	1.8	
3	SU	0404	7.2	1042	0.9	1651	7.3	2257	1.4	
4	M	0451	7.6	1129	0.6	1732	7.5	2344	1.0	●
5	TU	0536	7.8	1214	0.5	1812	7.6			
6	W	0030	0.9	0621	7.8	1257	0.6	1850	7.5	
7	TH	0114	0.9	0706	7.7	1338	0.8	1929	7.4	
8	F	0156	1.0	0753	7.4	1417	1.2	2008	7.1	
9	SA	0237	1.3	0840	7.0	1455	1.7	2048	6.8	
10	SU	0318	1.7	0933	6.5	1535	2.3	2133	6.4	
11	M	0405	2.1	1038	6.0	1623	2.8	2231	6.0	
12	TU	0509	2.5	1159	5.7	1729	3.2	2353	5.8	
13	W	0646	2.6	1314	5.6	1858	3.2			
14	TH	0113	5.8	0807	2.5	1420	5.8	2019	3.0	
15	F	0219	6.0	0903	2.2	1517	6.1	2115	2.6	
16	SA	0313	6.3	0947	1.9	1601	6.4	2201	2.2	
17	SU	0358	6.6	1026	1.7	1638	6.6	2242	1.9	
18	M	0436	6.8	1102	1.6	1710	6.8	2319	1.7	
19	TU	0511	6.9	1137	1.5	1739	6.9	2354	1.6	
20	W	0545	6.9	1210	1.5	1808	7.0			○
21	TH	0028	1.5	0619	7.0	1243	1.5	1838	7.0	
22	F	0100	1.6	0654	6.9	1312	1.6	1909	7.0	
23	SA	0132	1.6	0730	6.8	1342	1.7	1940	6.9	
24	SU	0207	1.7	0808	6.7	1415	1.9	2014	6.7	
25	M	0246	1.8	0850	6.5	1454	2.2	2054	6.5	
26	TU	0333	2.0	0941	6.2	1541	2.5	2144	6.3	
27	W	0433	2.2	1047	6.0	1643	2.7	2250	6.1	
28	TH	0546	2.2	1214	5.9	1801	2.8			
29	F	0012	6.1	0703	2.1	1334	6.1	1922	2.7	
30	SA	0133	6.3	0814	1.8	1438	6.4	2034	2.4	

DECEMBER

Date	Day	Time	m	Time	m	Time	m	Time	m	Moon
1	SU	0238	6.7	0916	1.4	1533	6.7	2136	1.9	
2	M	0335	7.0	1011	1.1	1622	7.0	2231	1.5	
3	TU	0428	7.3	1101	1.0	1706	7.2	2322	1.2	
4	W	0517	7.5	1148	0.9	1749	7.3			●
5	TH	0010	1.1	0606	7.5	1233	1.0	1829	7.4	
6	F	0057	1.0	0654	7.4	1316	1.2	1910	7.3	
7	SA	0142	1.1	0743	7.1	1356	1.5	1950	7.1	
8	SU	0226	1.3	0831	6.8	1436	1.8	2030	6.9	
9	M	0308	1.6	0920	6.4	1515	2.2	2112	6.6	
10	TU	0352	1.9	1014	6.1	1558	2.5	2200	6.3	
11	W	0441	2.2	1116	5.8	1648	2.9	2300	6.0	
12	TH	0538	2.4	1221	5.6	1749	3.0			
13	F	0011	5.9	0643	2.5	1324	5.6	1858	3.1	
14	SA	0120	5.9	0748	2.4	1422	5.8	2009	2.9	
15	SU	0221	6.0	0846	2.3	1514	6.0	2110	2.6	
16	M	0314	6.2	0935	2.1	1556	6.3	2159	2.3	
17	TU	0359	6.4	1019	1.9	1633	6.5	2243	2.0	
18	W	0440	6.6	1100	1.7	1708	6.7	2324	1.8	
19	TH	0520	6.7	1139	1.7	1743	6.9			○
20	F	0003	1.6	0559	6.8	1216	1.6	1818	7.0	
21	SA	0042	1.5	0639	6.9	1252	1.6	1854	7.0	
22	SU	0121	1.5	0721	6.9	1329	1.7	1929	7.0	
23	M	0202	1.5	0803	6.8	1407	1.8	2007	7.0	
24	TU	0245	1.5	0847	6.6	1449	1.9	2048	6.9	
25	W	0331	1.6	0936	6.5	1535	2.1	2135	6.7	
26	TH	0423	1.7	1032	6.3	1627	2.3	2231	6.6	
27	F	0522	1.8	1139	6.1	1728	2.5	2336	6.4	
28	SA	0627	1.8	1251	6.1	1839	2.5			
29	SU	0050	6.4	0735	1.8	1359	6.2	1955	2.4	
30	M	0204	6.5	0842	1.7	1500	6.4	2107	2.2	
31	TU	0311	6.7	0943	1.6	1556	6.6	2210	1.9	

Chart Datum: 3·90 metres below Ordnance Datum (Newlyn)

5

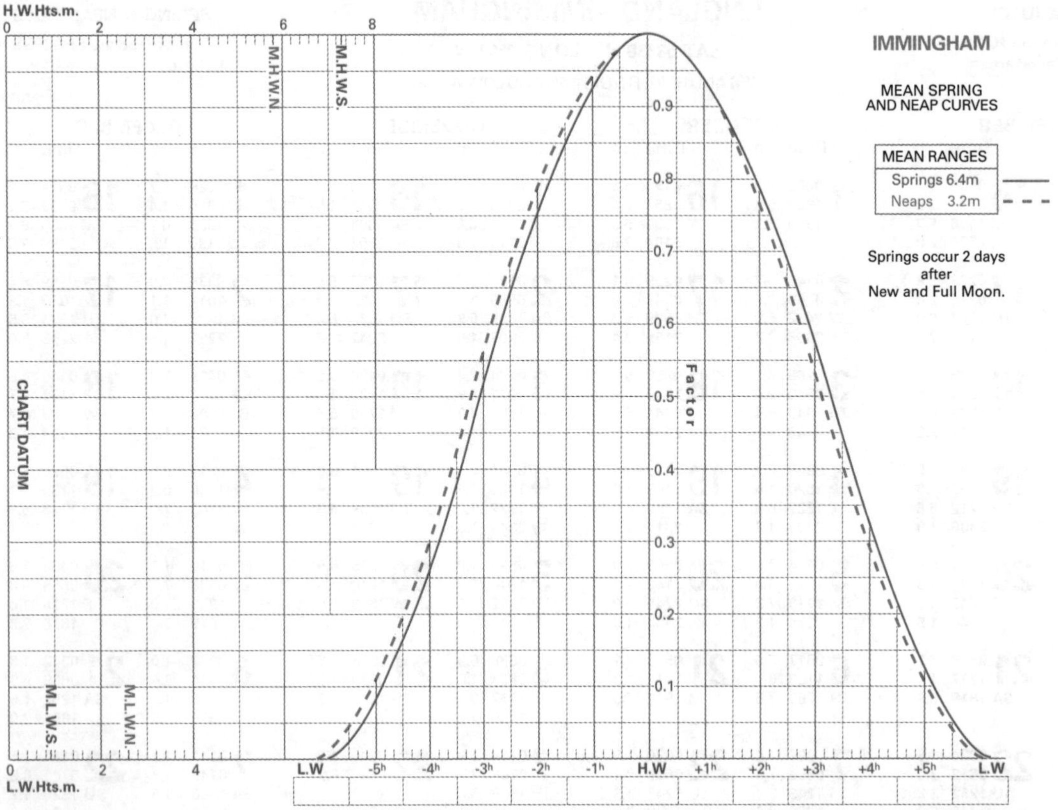
H.W.Hts.m.
0 2 4 6 8
M.H.W.N.
M.H.W.S.
CHART DATUM
M.L.W.S.
M.L.W.N.
0 2 4
L.W.Hts.m.
L.W -5h -4h -3h -2h -1h H.W +1h +2h +3h +4h +5h L.W
Factor
0.1 0.2 0.3 0.4 0.5 0.6 0.7 0.8 0.9
IMMINGHAM
MEAN SPRING AND NEAP CURVES
MEAN RANGES
Springs 6.4m
Neaps 3.2m
Springs occur 2 days after New and Full Moon.

RIVER HUMBER *9.5.11*

S bank: NE and N Lincolnshire
N bank: E Riding of Yorks and City of Kingston-upon-Hull
Hull marina: **53°44'·24N 00°20'·15W** Rtg

CHARTS AC 109, 3497, 1188, 1190; Imray C29; OS 107; ABP (local)

TIDES –0510 Immingham, –0452 Hull, Dover; ML 4·1; Duration 0555; Zone 0 (UT)

Standard Port IMMINGHAM (⟵)

Times				Height (metres)			
High Water		Low Water		MHWS	MHWN	MLWN	MLWS
0100	0700	0100	0700	7·3	5·8	2·6	0·9
1300	1900	1300	1900				
Differences BULL SAND FORT							
–0020	–0030	–0035	–0015	–0·4	–0·3	+0·1	+0·2
GRIMSBY							
–0010	–0010	–0012	–0012	–0·2	–0·1	0·0	+0·2
HULL (ALBERT DOCK)							
+0019	+0019	+0033	+0027	+0·3	+0·1	–0·1	–0·2
HUMBER BRIDGE							
+0027	+0022	+0049	+0039	–0·1	–0·4	–0·7	–0·6
BURTON STATHER (R. Trent)*							
+0105	+0045	+0335	+0305	–2·1	–2·3	–2·3	Dries
KEADBY (R. Trent)*							
+0135	+0120	+0425	+0410	–2·5	–2·8	Dries	
BLACKTOFT (R. Ouse)†							
+0100	+0055	+0325	+0255	–1·6	–1·8	–2·2	–1·1
GOOLE (R. Ouse)†							
+0130	+0115	+0355	+0350	–1·6	–2·1	–1·9	–0·6

NOTE: Daily predictions for Immingham are given above.

* Normal river level at Burton Stather is about 0·1m below CD, and at Keadby 0·1m to 0·2m below CD.
† Heights of LW can increase by up to 0·3m at Blacktoft and 0·6m at Goole when river in spate. HW heights are little affected.

SHELTER R Humber is the estuary of R Ouse and R Trent. ABP is the Authority for the Humber and owns the ports of Hull, Grimsby, Immingham and Goole.

Anchorages. Except in strong onshore winds, yachts can ⚓ inside Spurn Hd, or close off Haile Sand Fort. Immingham should be used by yachts only in emergency. If unable to reach Hull on the tide, in S to W winds there is a good ⚓ off the SW bank 8ca above N Killingholme Oil jetty, well out of main chan. In N'lies ⚓ off Hawkin's Pt, N of S9 buoy.

Marinas at Grimsby, Hull, S Ferriby and the docks at Goole are all entered by lock, access HW±3. S Ferriby should not be attempted without up-to-date ABP charts which cover the ever-changing buoyed chan above Hull.

Entry to Winteringham (HW±½) and Brough Havens (HW±1) should not be attempted without first contacting Humber Yawl Club for latest details of approach channel and mooring availability. Both havens dry to soft mud. Winteringham is prone to bad silting, but is dredged.

NAVIGATION Note new TSS (2001), see **Fig.8 (4)** and AC109. **From S**, WPT 53°30'·44N 00°16'·94E, Rosse Spit PHM buoy, Fl (2) R 5s. Thence make Haile Sand No 2, then via No 2B, Tetney monobuoy and No 2C into Haile Chan.

From N, WPT 53°34'·74N 00°16'·55E, S Binks SPM buoy, Fl G 2s. Thence passing N of Spurn Lt Float, SE Chequer and Chequer No 3 to make Binks 3A; then enter the estuary to the S of Spurn Hd outside Bull Chan. Best arrival at LW. Sp tides are fierce: 4·4kn ebb off Spurn Head and Immingham. There is a big ship ⚓ S of Spurn Hd. Keep clear of large commercial vessels using Hawke (8·4m) and Sunk (8·8m) Chans; these are marked by S1-S9 SHM buoys, all Fl G 1·5s (S8 is a SHM bn, Fl G 1·5s with tide gauge); and by P2-P9 PHM buoys, all Fl R 1·5s.

For **Grimsby** (lock into Fish Dock) make good 255°/1·35M from Lower Burcom No 6 Lt Float, Fl R 4s.

Off **Kingston-upon-Hull** there is a tidal eddy and streams can be rotatory, ie the flood makes W up Hull Roads for ¾hr whilst the ebb is already running down-river over Skitter Sand on the opposite bank (reaches 2½kn at sp). Humber bridge (conspic) has 30m clearance.

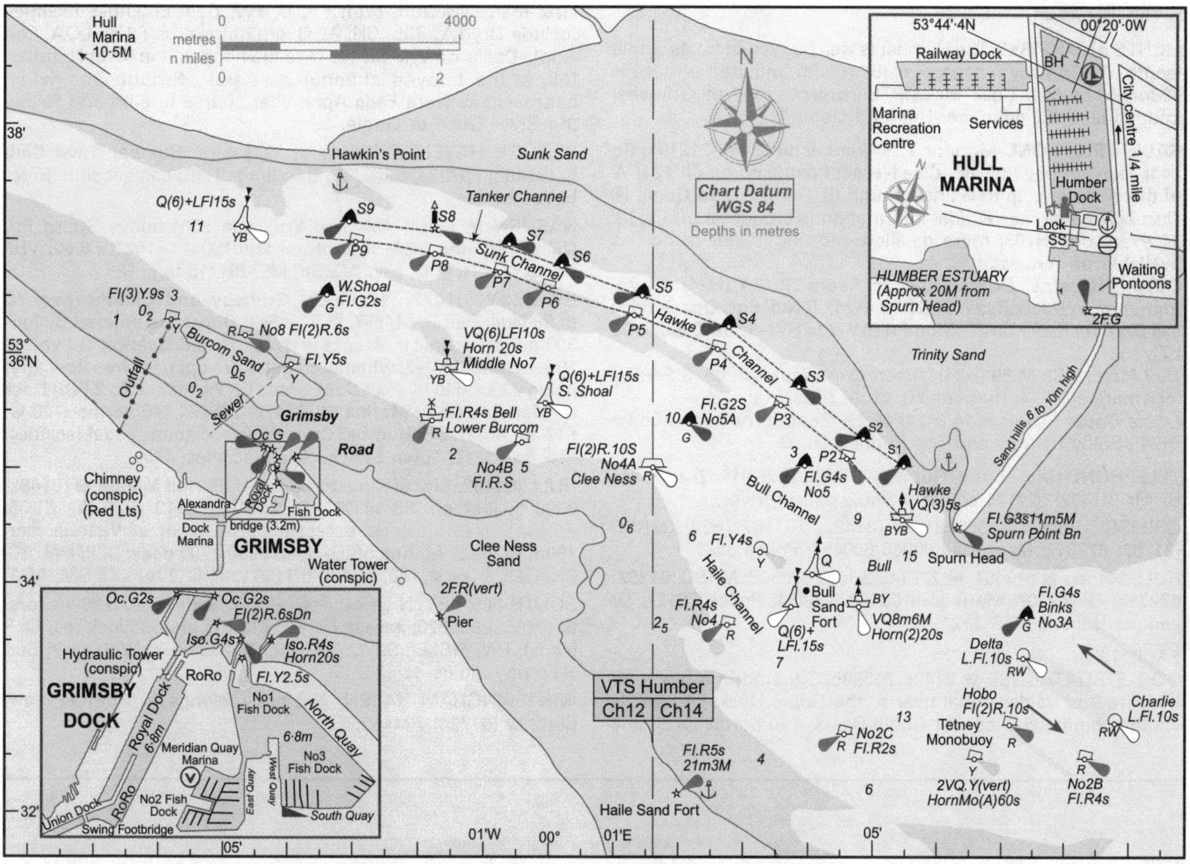
Hull Marina 10·5M
metres 0 4000
n miles 0 2
Hawkin's Point
Sunk Sand
Tanker Channel
Sunk Channel
Hawke Channel
Chart Datum WGS 84
Depths in metres
Q(6)+LFl15s
YB
S9
S8
S7
S6
S5
S4
S3
S2
S1
P9
P8
P7
P6
P5
P4
P3
P2
W.Shoal Fl.G2s
Fl(3)Y.9s
No8 Fl(2)R.6s
Burcom Sand
Fl.Y5s
Outfall
Sewer
VQ(6)LFl10s Horn 20s Middle No7
Q(6)+LFl15s S. Shoal
Fl.R4s Bell Lower Burcom
Grimsby Road
Oc G
No4B Fl.R.S
Fl.G2S No5A
Fl(2)R.10S No4A Clee Ness
Fl.G4s No5
Bull Channel
Hawke VQ(3)5s
BYB
Fl.G3s11m5M Spurn Point Bn
Spurn Head
Trinity Sand
Sand hills 6 to 10m high
Chimney (conspic) (Red Lts)
Alexandra
Royal Dock
Fish Dock
Dock Marina
bridge (3.2m)
GRIMSBY
Clee Ness Sand
Water Tower (conspic)
2F.R(vert)
Pier
Fl.Y4s
Haile Channel
Bull Sand Fort
Bull
Q(6)+ LFl.15s
BY
VQ8m6M Horn(2)20s
Fl.R4s No4
Fl.G4s Binks No3A
Delta L.Fl.10s
RW
Hobo Fl(2)R.10s
Charlie L.Fl.10s
Tetney Monobuoy
2VQ.Y(vert) HornMo(A)60s
No2C Fl.R2s
No2B Fl.R4s
Fl.R5s 21m3M
Haile Sand Fort
VTS Humber
Ch12
Ch14
Oc.G2s
Oc.G2s
Fl(2)R.6sDn
Iso.G4s
Iso.R4s Horn20s
Hydraulic Tower (conspic)
GRIMSBY DOCK
RoRo
Fl.Y2.5s
No1 Fish Dock
North Quay
Royal Dock 6·8m
6·8m
Meridian Quay Marina
No3 Fish Dock
West Quay
East Quay
No2 Fish Dock
Union Dock
Swing Footbridge
South Quay
53°44'·4N
00°20'·0W
Railway Dock
BH
City centre 1/4 mile
Marina Recreation Centre
Services
HULL MARINA
Humber Dock
Lock
SS
HUMBER ESTUARY (Approx 20M from Spurn Head)
Waiting Pontoons
2F.G
38'
53° 36'N
34'
32'
05'
01'W
00°
01'E
05'

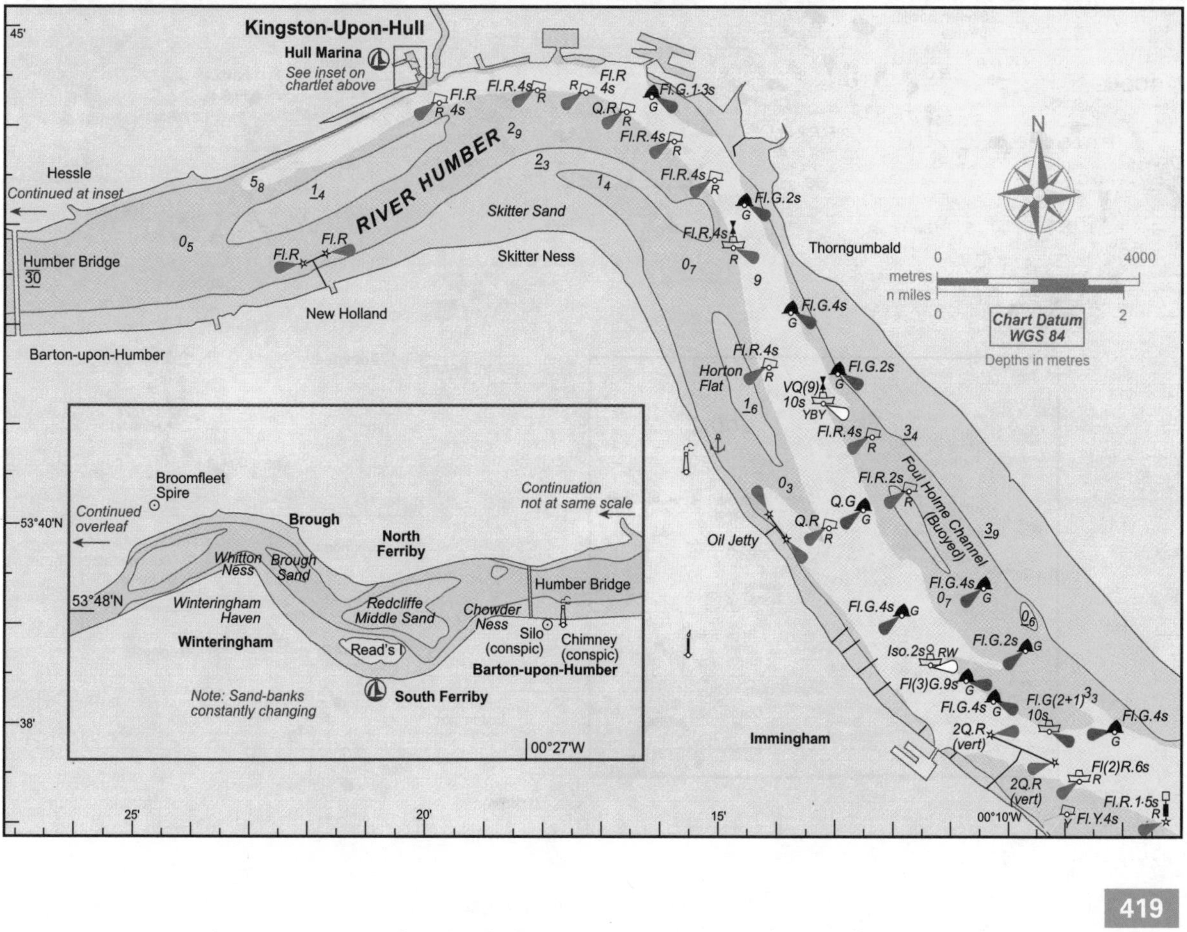
Kingston-Upon-Hull
Hull Marina
See inset on chartlet above
Hessle
Continued at inset
Humber Bridge 30
RIVER HUMBER
Skitter Sand
Skitter Ness
New Holland
Barton-upon-Humber
Fl.R
Fl.R 4s
Fl.R.4s
Fl.R 4s
Q.R
Fl.G.1·3s
Fl.R.4s
Fl.G.2s
Thorngumbald
Fl.G.4s
Fl.R.4s
Horton Flat
VQ(9) 10s
YBY
Fl.R.2s
Foul Holme Channel (Buoyed)
Q.G
Q.R
Oil Jetty
Fl.G.4s
Iso.2s RW
Fl(3)G.9s
Fl.G(2+1) 10s
2Q.R (vert)
Fl(2)R.6s
Fl.R.1·5s
Fl.Y.4s
Immingham
metres 0 4000
n miles 0 2
Chart Datum WGS 84
Depths in metres
Broomfleet Spire
Continued overleaf
Brough
North Ferriby
Whitton Ness
Brough Sand
Continuation not at same scale
Humber Bridge
Winteringham Haven
Redcliffe Middle Sand
Chowder Ness
Silo (conspic)
Chimney (conspic)
Winteringham
Read's I
Barton-upon-Humber
Note: Sand-banks constantly changing
South Ferriby
53°48'N
00°27'W
45'
53°40'N
38'
25'
20'
15'
00°10'W

5

RIVER HUMBER *continued*

LIGHTS AND MARKS The Humber is well buoyed/lit for its whole length. At Grimsby a conspic tr (94m with 'minaret' on top) is 300m W of Fish Dock lock. IPTS control entry to Grimsby, Immingham, Killingholme, Hull and Goole.

RADIO TELEPHONE Monitor *VTS Humber* (☎ 01482-212191) Ch 14 if seaward of 00°01´·8E (Clee Ness lt float); and on Ch 12 if W of this meridian, up to Gainsborough (R Trent) and to Goole (R Ouse). Weather, nav & tidal information is broadcast on Ch 12/ 14 every odd H+03; more detailed info, inc height of tide, is available on request.

Other VHF stns: *Grimsby Docks Radio* Ch 74 (H24) 18 79. *Immingham Docks Radio* Ch 19 68 (H24). R Hull Port Ops Service call *Drypool Radio* Ch 22 (Mon-Fri HW–2 to HW+1; Sat 0900-1100 LT).

Hull Marina, Ch M **80** (H24); *Albert Dock Radio* Ch 09. S Ferriby lock/marina Ch 74. Humber YC, Ch M (if racing).

Goole Docks Radio Ch 14 (H24) 09 19. Boothferry Bridge Ch 09 (H24). Selby Railway and Toll Bridges Ch 09.

TELEPHONE (Dial codes: Grimsby 01472; Hull 01482) Humber Hr Mr (01482) 327171 controls whole estuary/river.

GRIMSBY Port Mgr 359181; ⊖ (01482) 782107 (H24); MRSC (01262) 672317; Marinecall 09068 500454; Police 359171.

HULL Marina ☎ 613451, 🖷 222148 & lock 330508; MRSC (01262) 672317; ⊖ 782107; Marinecall 09068 500454; Police 26111; Dr contact Humber VTS 212191.

FACILITIES

GOOLE BOATHOUSE ☎ 01405 763985. Situated in a basin off the Aire and Calder Canal near to the Goole Docks. Access is via the commercial lock for Goole Docks. 140 berths £3.50 any size, max LOA 70ft, draft 6ft, D, FW, Gas, El. Other facilities include Dry Dk, Slip, CH, ♿. Overnight stay is £3 all LOA. Call Goole Docks on VHF Ch 14. Take the flood up the River Humber, follow the buoyed channel past Hull, Brough and when approaching Trent Falls Apex alter course to stbd and follow the River Ouse to Goole.

BROUGH HAVEN, E Riding of Yorkshire, **Humber Yawl Club** ☎ (01482) 667224, Slip, FW, Bar, limited AB; contact club. Enter HW±1½

NABURN (R Ouse, 4M S of York and 80M above Spurn Pt). **Naburn Marina** (300+50 visitors) ☎ (01904) 621021; £6.50; VHF Ch **80** M; CH, P, D, FW, AC, Sh, ME, BH (16 ton), R.

GRIMSBY (01472; NE Lincs) **Grimsby and Cleethorpes YC** ☎ 360404, Bar, R, M, FW, ▣. The **Fish Docks** are entered by lock 300m E of conspic tr. Access is HW±3, with R/G tfc lts, but yachts should enter HW±2, when both gates are open for free flow after being cleared in by *Fish Dock Island* Ch 74. Inside No 2 Fish Dock is: **Meridian Quay Marina** ☎ (01472) 268424,140 berths + 20 Ⓥ, £12 inc AC, D, BH. Humber Cruising Association ; usual facilities. ❁❁❁⚓⚓✿✿. **Town** EC Thurs; all facilities, ACA.

HULL (01482; City of Kingston-upon-Hull) **Hull Marina** ☎ (01482) 330505, lock ent 53°44'·28N 00°20'·10W, (310 + 20 Ⓥ), £1.35, access HW±3 via lock, accessible HW±4½; or at Victoria Pier, 150m to the E. Marina office open 0900-1700 daily; D, P, FW, AC, CH, Gas, ⊖, ♿, ⚓, ME, El, Sh, BH (50 ton), C (2 ton), ▣, SM, ACA.

SOUTH FERRIBY, N Lincs. ❁❁⚓⚓✿✿. **Marina** (100+20 visitors) ☎ (01652) 635620; access HW±3, £12 (60 hrs) inc lock fee, D, P (cans), FW, ME, El, Sh, C (30 ton), CH, Gas, Gaz. **Village** V, Bar. S Ferriby Sluice ☎ 635219.

WINTERINGHAM HAVEN, N Lincs (belongs to Humber Yawl Club) ☎ (01724) 734452, ✉.

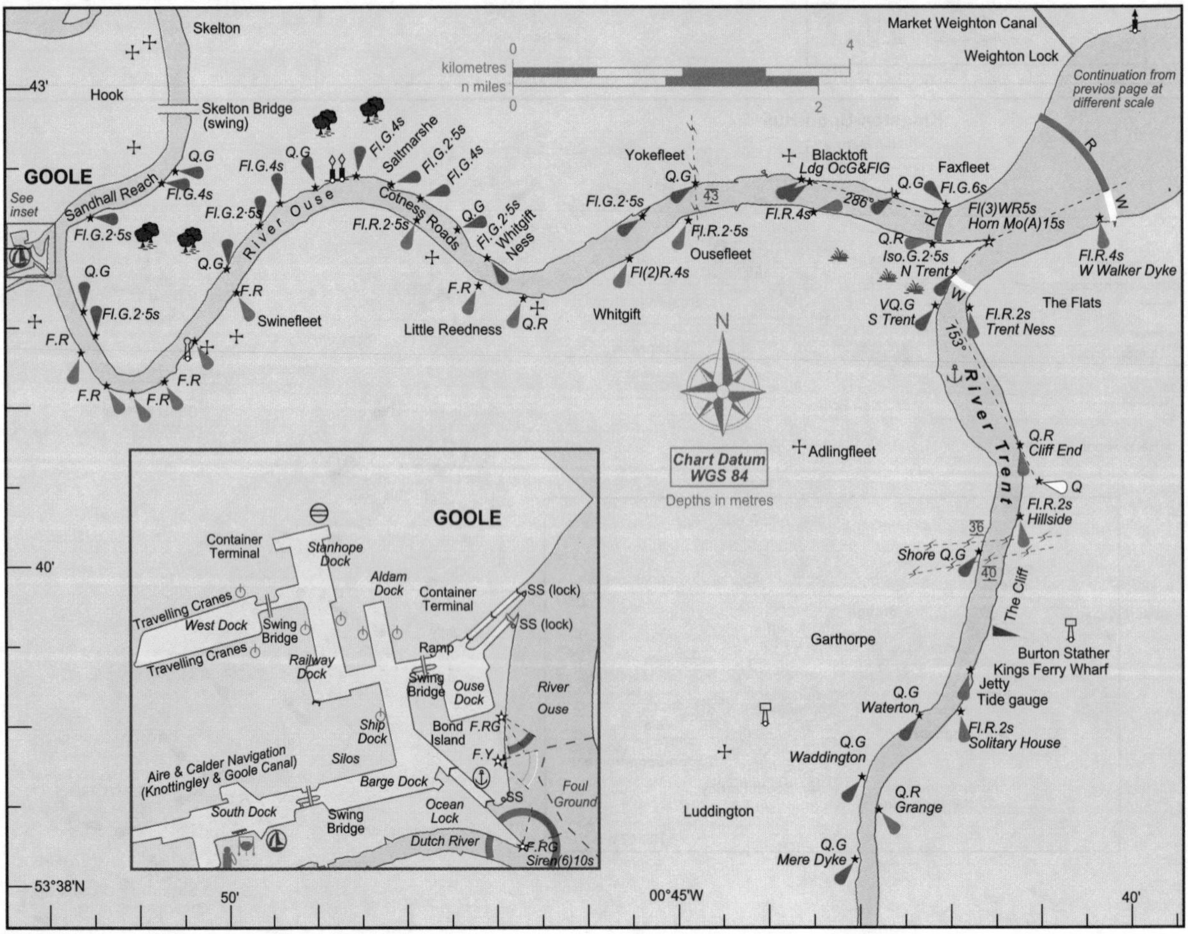

BRIDLINGTON *9.5.12*

E Riding of Yorkshire **54°04'·78N 00°11'·21W**

CHARTS AC 1882, 121, 129, 1191, 1190; Imray C29; OS 101

TIDES +0553 Dover; ML 3·6; Duration 0610; Zone 0 (UT)

Standard Port NORTH SHIELDS (→)

Times				Height (metres)			
High Water		Low Water		MHWS	MHWN	MLWN	MLWS
0200	0800	0100	0800	5·0	3·9	1·8	0·7
1400	2000	1300	2000				
Differences BRIDLINGTON							
+0119	+0109	+0109	+0104	+1·1	+0·8	+0·5	+0·4
FILEY BAY							
+0101	+0101	+0101	+0048	+0·8	+1·0	+0·6	+0·3

SHELTER Good, except in E, SE and S winds. Hbr dries completely to soft black mud; access HW±3 (for draft of 2·7m). Visitors normally berth on S pier or near Hr Mr's Office. A marina is planned but no starting date has been suggested.

NAVIGATION WPT SW Smithic WCM, Q (9) 15s, 54°02'·41N 00°09'·21W, 153°/333° from/to ent, 2·6M. Close-in appr is with N pier hd lt on brg 002° to keep W of drying patch (The Canch). Beware bar, 1m at MLWN, could dry out at MLWS.

LIGHTS AND MARKS Hbr is 4M WSW of Flamborough Hd lt, Fl (4) 15s 65m 24M. Y racing marks are laid in the Bay, Apr-Oct. Tidal sigs, by day from S pier: R flag = >2·7m in hbr; No flag = < 2·7m. At night from N pier: Fl ● = >2·7m in hbr; Fl ● = < 2·7m.

RADIO TELEPHONE Initial call on VHF Ch 16, then to Ch **12**, 67 for working.

TELEPHONE (Dial code 01262) Hr Mr 670148/9, 🖷 602041, mobile 0860 275150; MRSC 672317; Marinecall 09068 500454; ⊜ (01482) 782107 (H24); Police 672222; Ⓗ 673451.

FACILITIES **S Pier** FW, AB £2.19 m², D (tank/hose), C (5 ton), BH (70 ton), Slip; M, see Hr Mr; **Royal Yorks YC** ☎ 672041, L, FW, R, Bar. **Town** EC Thurs; P (cans), CH, ME, El, V, R, Bar, ✉, Ⓑ, ⇌, ✈ (Humberside).

ADJACENT ANCHORAGE (7M SE of Scarborough)

FILEY, N Yorkshire, 54°12'·80N 00°16'·20W, AC 1882, 129. HW +0532 on Dover; ML 3·5m; Duration 0605. See 9.5.12. Good ⚓ in winds from S to NNE in 4 – 5m on hard sand. Lt on cliff above CG Stn, G metal column, FR 31m 1M vis 272°-308°. Filey Brigg, a natural bkwtr, is marked by ECM buoy, Q(3)10s, Bell. Beware Old Horse Rks, 2M WNW of Filey Brigg, foul ground extending ½M offshore. Facilities: EC Wed; V, R, Bar, L, Ⓗ ☎ (01723) 68111, ✉, Ⓑ, ⇌.

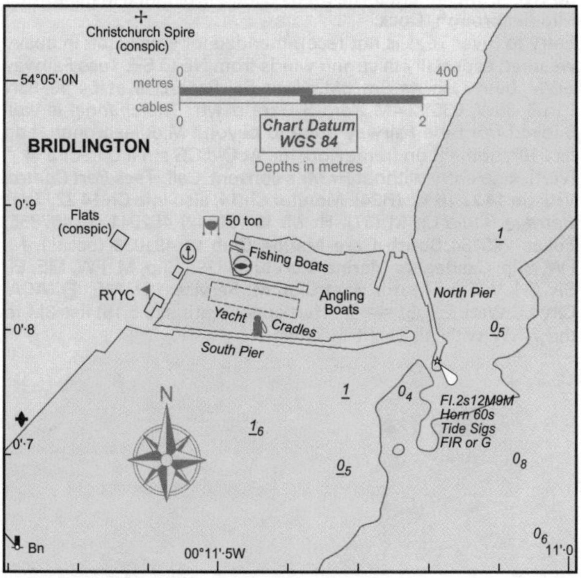

SCARBOROUGH *9.5.13*

N. Yorkshire **54°16'·88N 00°23'·36W**

CHARTS AC 1612, 129, 1191; Imray C29; OS 101

TIDES +0527 Dover; ML 3·5; Duration 0615; Zone 0 (UT)

Standard Port NORTH SHIELDS (→)

Times				Height (metres)			
High Water		Low Water		MHWS	MHWN	MLWN	MLWS
0200	0800	0100	0800	5·0	3·9	1·8	0·7
1400	2000	1300	2000				
Differences SCARBOROUGH							
+0059	+0059	+0044	+0044	+0·7	+0·7	+0·5	+0·2

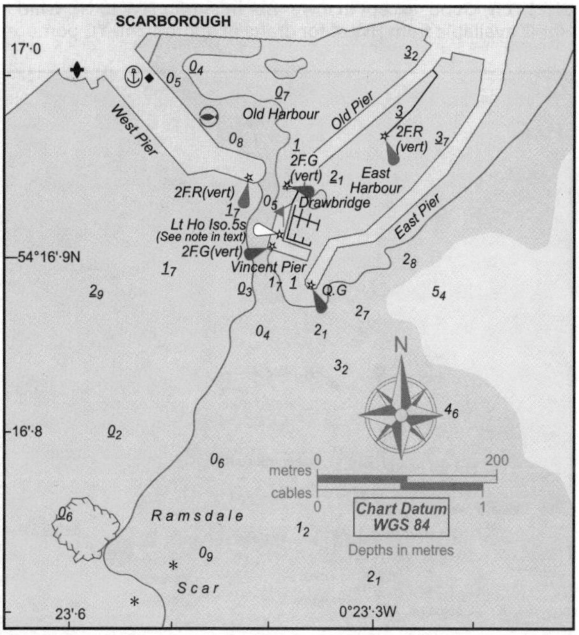

SHELTER Good in E Hbr, access HW±3 via narrow (10m) ent by E pier, but not in strong E/SE'lies. 7 Ⓥ pontoon berths, (max LOA 10.3m, draft 1.8m), in the SW corner of E Hbr, just below lt ho. 4 Ⓥ drying AB on Old Pier just N of the drawbridge. The Old Hbr is strictly for FVs. In winter months access to East Hbr is via the drawbridge only.

NAVIGATION WPT 54°16'·50N 00°22'·00W, 122°/302° from/to E pier lt, 0·83M. Appr from the E to avoid Ramsdale Scar, rky shoal 0·9m. Keep careful watch for salmon nets E & SE of ent. Beware rks extending approx 20m SW of E pier head.

LIGHTS AND MARKS Lt ho (conspic), Iso 5s, Dia 60s, on Vincent Pier is shown by night or B ● by day when there is =>3·7m over bar in entrance. Other lts as shown on plan.

RADIO TELEPHONE Call *Scarborough hbr* VHF Ch **12** 16 (H24). Watchkeeper will offer guidance to approaching visitors.

TELEPHONE (Dial code 01723) Hr Mr (HO) ☎ 373530, 360684 (OT), 🖷 350035; Lt Ho 360684; CG 372323; MRSC (01262) 672317; ⊜ (01482) 782107 (H24); Marinecall 09068 500454; Police 500300; Ⓗ 368111.

FACILITIES **East Hbr** AB £12.10 up to 10.3m LOA, M, FW, AC, D, C (3 ton), Slip; **Scarborough YC** ☎ 373821, AB, Slip, M*, FW, ME, El, Ⓢ; **Services:** ME, El, Sh, CH, P & D (cans), Ⓔ. **Town** EC Wed; P, D, V, R, Bar, ✉, Ⓑ, ⇌, ✈ (Humberside).

5

WHITBY *9.5.14*

N. Yorkshire **54°29'·65N 00°36'·78W** ❀❀⚓⚓⚓✿✿✿

CHARTS AC 1612, 134, 129; Imray C24, C29; OS 94

TIDES +0500 Dover; ML 3·3; Duration 0605; Zone 0 (UT)

Standard Port NORTH SHIELDS (⟶)

Times				Height (metres)			
High Water		Low Water		MHWS	MHWN	MLWN	MLWS
0200	0800	0100	0800	5·0	3·9	1·8	0·7
1400	2000	1300	2000				
Differences WHITBY							
+0034	+0049	+0034	+0019	+0·6	+0·4	+0·1	+0·1

SHELTER Good, except in lower hbr in strong NW to NE winds. Hbr is available from HW±4 for drafts of approx 2m. YC pontoon below br. Marina (dredged approx 2m) is 2ca beyond swing bridge; visitor berths at seaward end of long pontoon. Bridge opens on request HW±2 every H and H+30; extra openings at week-ends as arranged with WYC. FG lts = open; FR lts = shut.

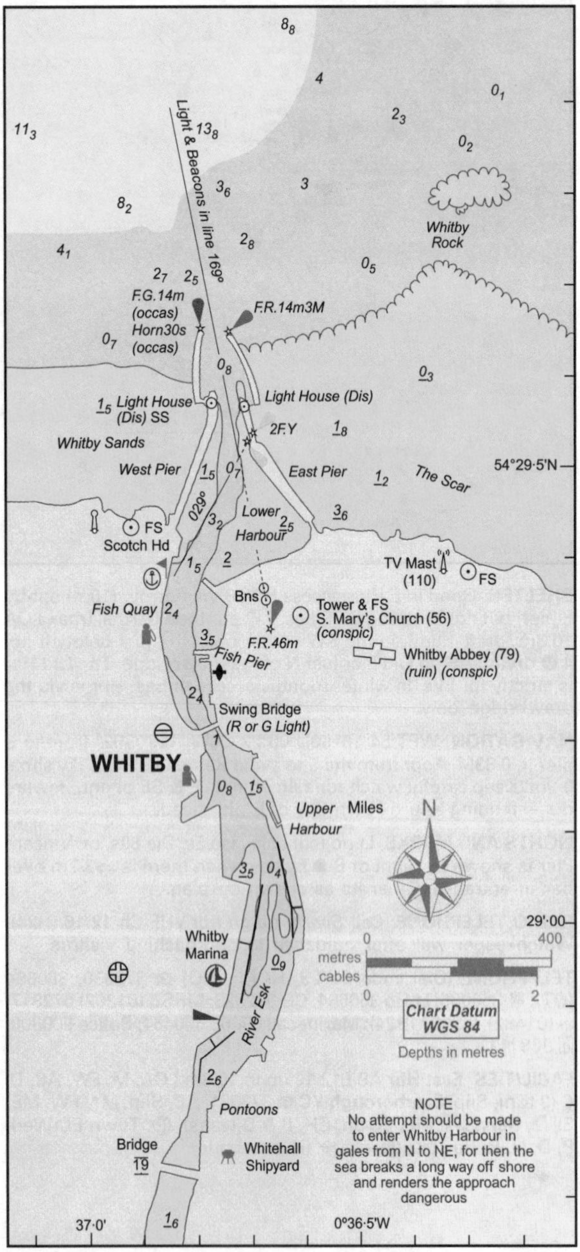

NAVIGATION WPT 54°30'·21N 00°36'96W, 349°/169° from/to ent, 0·57M. Hbr can be approached safely from any direction except when note on chartlet applies. From the SE beware Whitby Rk; leave Whitby NCM buoy, Q, to port. Beware strong set to E from HW –2 to HW, when nearing piers. Vessels >37m LOA must embark pilot; via Hr Mr.

LIGHTS AND MARKS TV mast to E of entr. Whitby High lt ho, Iso RW 10s 73m 18/16M, (R128°-143°, W143°-319°), is 2M ESE of hbr ent.

Ldg lines:

(1) Chapel spire in line 176° with E pier disused lt ho.

(2) FR lt or 2 bns, seen between disused lt houses, lead 169° into hbr. Hold this line until bns (W △ and W ○ with B stripe) on E pier (two FY lts) are abeam.

(3) On course 209° keep these same bns in line astern.

RADIO TELEPHONE Hbr and Marina VHF Ch **11** 16 12 (H24). Whitby Bridge Ch **11** 16 06 (listens on Ch 16 HW–2 to HW+2).

TELEPHONE (Dial code 01947) Hr Mr ☎ 602354, 📠 600380; MRSC (01262) 672317; ⊖ (01482) 782107 (H24); Marinecall 09068 500454/453; Police 603443; Dr 820888.

FACILITIES **Whitby Marina** (200+10 visitors) ☎ 600165, £1.56, AC, D, FW, P (cans), Slip, ME, El, Sh, C, CH; **Fish Quay** M, D (in commercial quantities only), L, FW, C (1 ton), CH, AB, R, Bar; **Whitby YC** ☎ 603623, M, L, Bar; **Services:** ME, El, Sh, CH, BH, ACA, SM, Gas, Gaz. **Town** EC Wed; usual amenities, ✉, Ⓑ, ⇌, ✈ (Teesside).

ADJACENT ANCHORAGE (5M WNW of Whitby)

RUNSWICK BAY, N. Yorkshire, **54°32'·11N 00°44'·20W**. AC 1612. HW +0505 on Dover: Differences on R Tyne are approx as Whitby; ML 3·1m; Duration 0605. Good shelter in all winds from SSE thru W to NW. Enter bay at 225° keeping clear of many rks at base of cliffs. Two W posts (2FY by night when required by lifeboat) 18m apart are ldg marks 270° to LB ho and can be used to lead into ⚓. Good holding in 6m to 9m in middle of bay. Facilities: **Runswick Bay Rescue Boat Station** ☎ (01947) 840965. **Village** Bar, R, V.

ADJACENT PORT (3M SSE of Hartlepool)

RIVER TEES/MIDDLESBROUGH, Middlesbrough/Stockton, **54°38'·94N 01°08'·48W.** ❀❀⚓✿. AC 2566, 2567, 152; Imray C29; OS 93. HW +0450 Dover; Differences see 9.5.15. ML 3·1; Duration 0605. R. Tees & Middlesbrough are a major industrial area. 5M up-river from hbr ent a Tall Ships Centre is planned in the former Middlesbrough Dock.

Entry to River Tees is not recommended for small craft in heavy weather, especially in strong winds from NE to SE. Tees Fairway SWM buoy, Iso 4s 9m 8M, Horn 5s, Racon, is at 54°40'·93N 01°06'·38W, 030°/2·4M from S Gare bkwtr. The channel is well buoyed from the Fairway buoy to beyond Middlesbrough. Ldg lts 210°, both FR on framework trs. At Old CG stn a Q lt, or 3 ● (vert), = no entry without Hr Mr's consent. Call: *Tees Port Control* VHF Ch **14** 22 16 12 (H24). Monitor Ch 14; also info Ch 14 22. *Tees Barrage Radio* Ch M (37). Hr Mr ☎ (01642) 452541, 📠 467855; Police 248184. **South Gare Marine Club** ☎ 491039 (occas), M, FW, Slip; **Castlegate Marine Club** ☎ 583299 Slip, M, FW, ME, El, Sh, CH, V; **Tees Motor Boat Club** M; **Services**: El, ME, Ⓔ, ACA. **City** EC Wed; ✉, Ⓑ, ⇌, ✈. Hartlepool marina (9.5.15) lies 3M to the NNW with all yacht facilities.

HARTLEPOOL *9.5.15*

Hartlepool **54°41′·26N 01°11′·90W** (West Hbr ent) ❁❁◊◊◊✿✿

CHARTS AC 2566, 2567, 152; Imray C24; OS 93

TIDES +0437 Dover; ML 3·0; Duration 0600; Zone 0 (UT)

Standard Port NORTH SHIELDS (⟶)

Times				Height (metres)			
High Water		Low Water		MHWS	MHWN	MLWN	MLWS
0200	0800	0100	0800	5·0	3·9	1·8	0·7
1400	2000	1300	2000				
Differences HARTLEPOOL							
+0015	+0015	+0008	+0008	+0·4	+0·3	0·0	+0·1
MIDDLESBROUGH							
+0019	+0021	+0014	+0011	+0·6	+0·6	+0·3	+0·1

SHELTER Excellent in marina (5m), access HW±5 via chan dredged 0·8m and lock H24 over tidal cill 0.8m below CD. Speed limit 4kn in W Hbr and marina. Strong E/SE winds raise broken water and swell in the bay, making ent channel hazardous, but possible. In such conditions, call VHF Ch M or 80 for advice. Or call *Tees Port Control* Ch 14 for short-stay in Victoria Hbr (commercial dock, not normally for yachts), access H24.

NAVIGATION WPT Longscar ECM buoy, Q (3) 10s, Bell, 54°40′·86N 01°09′·90W, 115°/295° from/to W Hbr ent 1·06M; (or, for Victoria Hbr, 128°/308° from/to Nos 1/2 buoys, 0·65M). From S, beware Longscar Rks, only 4ca WSW of WPT. Note: Tees Fairway SWM buoy, Iso 4s 8M, (54°40′·94N 01°06′·48W) is 2M E of Longscar ECM buoy and may assist the initial landfall.

LIGHTS AND MARKS The Heugh lt ho Fl (2) 10s 19m 19M, H24. Dir lt Fl WRG 2s 6m 3M leads 308° to W Hbr/marina lock; vis G305·5°-307°, W307°-309°, R309°-38·5°. W Hbr outer piers, Oc R/G 5s 12m 2M; bright street lts on S pier. Inner piers, FR/FG 7m 2M.
Lock sigs: ● = Proceed; ● = Wait; ●● = Lock closed.
Dir lt Iso WRG 3s 42m, W324·4°-325·4°, leads 325° via lit buoyed chan to Victoria Hbr. 2 FG (vert) on Kafiga pontoons.

RADIO TELEPHONE Marina Ch **M** 80. *Tees Port Control* info Ch 14 22 (H24). *Hartlepool Dock Radio* Ch 12, only for ship docking.

TELEPHONE (Dial code 01429) Marina 865744; ; MRSC (0191) 257 2691; Tees Port Authority (01642) 277205; Marinecall 09068 500453; ⊖ (0191) 257 9441; Police 221151; Dr 272679.

FACILITIES **Hartlepool Marina** H24 (500+100 Ⓥ) ☎ 865744, 📠 865947, £1.60, FW, AC, D (H24), P (cans), BY, El, Sh, ⊡, ♿, ⚓, BH (40 and 300 tons), C (13 tons), Gas, Gaz; **Tees & Hartlepool YC** ☎ 233423, Bar, Slip; **Services:** CH, ME, EL, Sh, C (mobiles). **Town:** P (cans), V (H24), R, Bar, ✉, Ⓑ, ⇌, ✈ (Teesside).

5

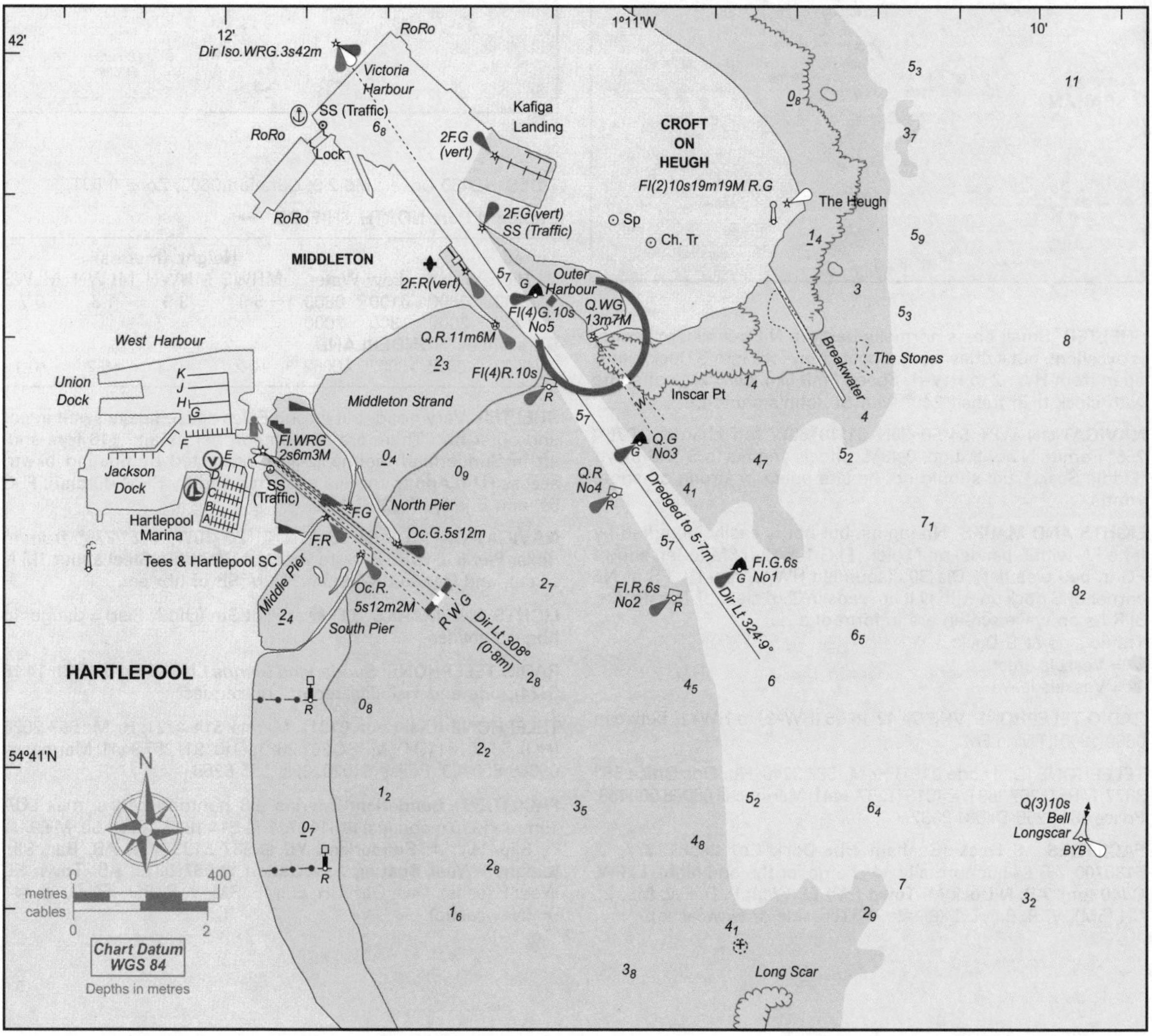

SEAHAM 9.5.16

Durham **54°50'·24N 01°19'·28W**

CHARTS AC 1627, 152; Imray C24; OS 88

TIDES +0435 Dover; ML 3·0; Duration 0600; Zone 0 (UT)

Standard Port NORTH SHIELDS (⟶)

Times				**Height (metres)**			
High Water		Low Water		MHWS	MHWN	MLWN	MLWS
0200	0800	0100	0800	5·0	3·9	1·8	0·7
1400	2000	1300	2000				
Differences SEAHAM							
+0004	+0004	–0001	–0001	+0·2	+0·2	+0·2	0·0

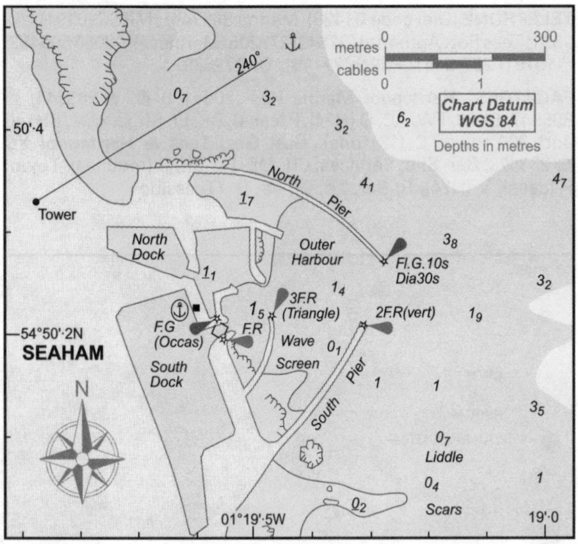

SHELTER Small boats normally berth in N Dock where shelter is excellent, but it dries. Larger boats may lock into S Dock; gates open from HW –2 to HW+1. Speed limit 5kn. Or ⚓ 2½ca offshore with clock tr in transit 240° with St John's church tr.

NAVIGATION WPT 54°50'·36N 01°18'·60W (off chartlet), 076°/256° from/to N bkwtr lt ho, 0·40M. Shoals and rks to S of S bkwtr (Liddle Scars). Ent should not be attempted in strong on-shore winds.

LIGHTS AND MARKS No ldg lts, but hbr is easily identified by lt ho (W with B bands) on N pier, Fl G 10s 12m 5M (often shows FG in bad weather), Dia 30s (sounded HW–2½ to +1½). FS at NE corner of S dock on with N lt ho leads in 256° clear of Tangle Rks. 3FR lts on wave screen are in form of a △.
Traffic sigs at S Dock:
● = Vessels enter
● = Vessels leave

RADIO TELEPHONE VHF Ch **12** 16 06 (HW–2½ to HW+1½ between 0800-1800 LT Mon-Fri).

TELEPHONE (Dial code 0191) Hr Mr 581 3246; Hbr Ops Office 581 3877; MRSC 257 2691; ⊖ (0191) 257 9441; Marinecall 09068 500453; Police 581 2255; Dr 581 2332.

FACILITIES **S Dock** (Seaham Hbr Dock Co) ☎ 5813877, 📠 5130700, AB £4 but normally no charge for the odd night, L, FW, C (40 ton), AB; **N Dock** M. **Town** (½M) EC Wed; P, D, FW, ME, El, CH (5M), V, R, Bar, ✉, Ⓑ, ⇌, ✈ (Teesside or Newcastle).

SUNDERLAND 9.5.17

Tyne and Wear **54°55'·23N 01°21'·15W**

CHARTS AC 1627, 152; Imray C24; OS 88

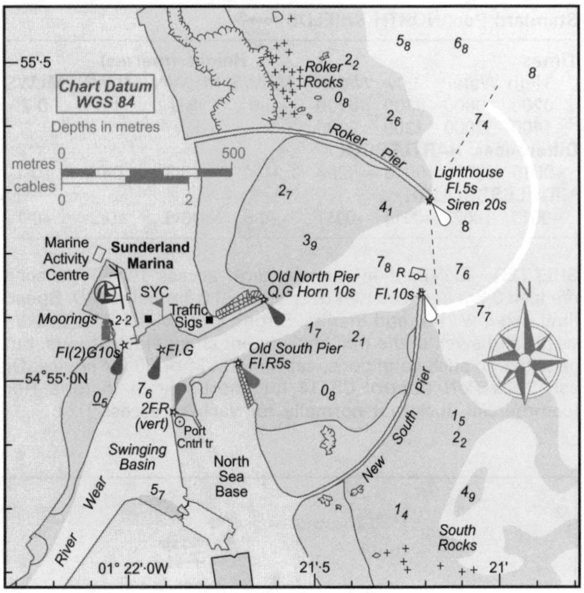

TIDES +0430 Dover; ML 2·9; Duration 0600; Zone 0 (UT)

Standard Port NORTH SHIELDS (⟶)

Times				**Height (metres)**			
High Water		Low Water		MHWS	MHWN	MLWN	MLWS
0200	0800	0100	0800	5·0	3·9	1·8	0·7
1400	2000	1300	2000				
Differences SUNDERLAND							
+0002	–0002	–0002	–0002	+0·2	+0·3	+0·2	+0·1

SHELTER Very good, but strong E'lies cause heavy swell in ent and outer hbr. There are 88 pontoon berths and 110 fore-and-aft in Sunderland Marina (2·3m), protected by floating bkwtr; access H24. App to marina ent is marked by SHM dolphin, Fl G 5s, and E jetty, Fl (2) G 10s.

NAVIGATION WPT 54°55'·21N 01°20'·10W, 098°/278° from/to Roker Pier lt, 0·61M. Beware wreck at Whitburn Steel about 1M N of ent, and Hendon Rk (0·9m), 1.2M SE of hbr ent.

LIGHTS AND MARKS 3 Fl ● at Pilot Stn (Old N Pier) = danger in hbr; no ent/dep.

RADIO TELEPHONE *Sunderland Marina* Ch M. Port VHF Ch 14 16 (H24); tide and visibility reports on request.

TELEPHONE (Dial code 0191) Marina 514 4721; Hr Mr 567 2626 (HO), 567 0161 (OT); MRSC 257 2691; ⊖ (0191) 257 9441; Marinecall 09068 500453; Police 5102020; Ⓗ 565 6256.

FACILITIES **Sunderland Marina** (88 pontoon berths, max LOA 15m; and 110 moorings) ☎ 514 4721, 📠 514 1847, AB £1.50, M £9, ♿, D, Slip, FW, ⚓; **Sunderland YC** ☎ 567 5133, FW, AB, Bar, Slip (dinghy); **Wear Boating Association** ☎ 567 5313, AB. **Town** EC Wed; P (cans), Gas, Gaz, CH, El, ME, SM, V, R, Bar, ✉, ⊡, Ⓑ, ⇌, ✈ (Newcastle).

R. TYNE/NORTH SHIELDS *9.5.18*

Tyne and Wear **55°00′·89N 01°24′·10W**

CHARTS AC 1934, 152; Imray C24; OS 88

TIDES +0430 Dover; ML 3·0; Duration 0604; Zone 0 (UT)

Standard Port NORTH SHIELDS (⟶)

Times				Height (metres)			
High Water		Low Water		MHWS	MHWN	MLWN	MLWS
0200	0800	0100	0800	5·0	3·9	1·8	0·7
1400	2000	1300	2000				
Differences NEWCASTLE-UPON-TYNE							
+0003	+0003	+0008	+0008	+0·3	+0·2	+0·1	+0·1

SHELTER Good in all weathers. Access H24, but in strong E and NE winds appr may be difficult for smaller craft due to much backwash off the piers; confused seas can build at the ent in severe weather. Royal Quays marina (in former Albert Edward Dock) is 2M upriver from pierheads. St Peter's Marina is 8M upriver, and 1M E of city. As a refuge or in emergency yachts may berth on Fish Quay; contact Hr Mr. A one-off £10 conservancy fee may be levied by the Port Authority on all visiting craft.

NAVIGATION WPT 55°01′·01N 01°22′·32W, 078°/258° from/to hbr ent, 1·1M. From S, no dangers. From N, beware Bellhues Rk (approx 1M N of hbr and $\frac{3}{4}$M off shore); give N pier a wide berth. Dredged chan in Lower Hbr is buoyed. The six bridges at Newcastle have least clearance 25m, or 4m when swing bridge closed.

LIGHTS AND MARKS Dir lt 249°, Oc GWR 10s,. Castle conspic on cliff, N of ent.

RADIO TELEPHONE Call: *Tyne Hbr Radio* VHF Ch **12** 16 11 (H24). Royal Quays marina Ch 80. St Peter's Marina Ch **80** M.

TELEPHONE (Dial code 0191) Hr Mr 257 2080, 📠 258 3238; Port Ops 257 0407; MRSC 257 2681; ⊖ 201 1700; Marinecall 09068 500453; Met 2326453; Police 232 3451; Dr via Tyne Hbr Radio 257 2080; 🄷 (Tynemouth) 259 6660; 🄷 (Newcastle) 232 5131.

FACILITIES (from seaward)
Royal Quays marina 54°59′·79N 01°26′·84W ☎ 272 8282, 📠 272 8288. 170 berths in 7·9m depth; £1.40. S lock (42.5m x 8·0m) operates locking-out H and H+30, locking-in H+15 and H+45 or on request at quiet times. H24. Waiting pontoon outside lock. Call *Royal Quays marina* VHF Ch 80. BY, BH (30 ton), D, P (H24), ⊡, CH, Bar, FW, El, Gas, Gaz, V.
St Peter's marina 54°57′·94N 01°34′·35W (140 + 20 Ⓥ) ☎ 265 4472, 📠 276 2618; £1.16. Access approx HW±3½ over sill 0·8m below CD; 2·5m retained within; tfc lts at ent; AC, FW, ⊡. D, P on pontoon outside ent in 2m.
Tynemouth SC ☎ 2529157; **South Shields SC ☎** 4565821; **Services:** Slip, M, L, FW, ME, El, Sh, C, CH, AB, ACA, Ⓔ. **City** EC Wed; All amenities, ⇌ (Newcastle/S Shields), ✈ (Newcastle). North Sea ferries as in 9.0.5.
www.aboard.co.uk/c.n.marinas

ADJACENT HARBOUR

CULLERCOATS, Tyne and Wear, **55°02′·08N 01°25′·81W.** AC 1191. +0430 Dover. Tides as 9.5.18. Small drying hbr 1·6M N of R Tyne ent. Appr on ldg line 256°, two bns (FR lts), between drying rks. An occas fair weather ⚓ or dry against S pier. Facilities at Tynemouth.

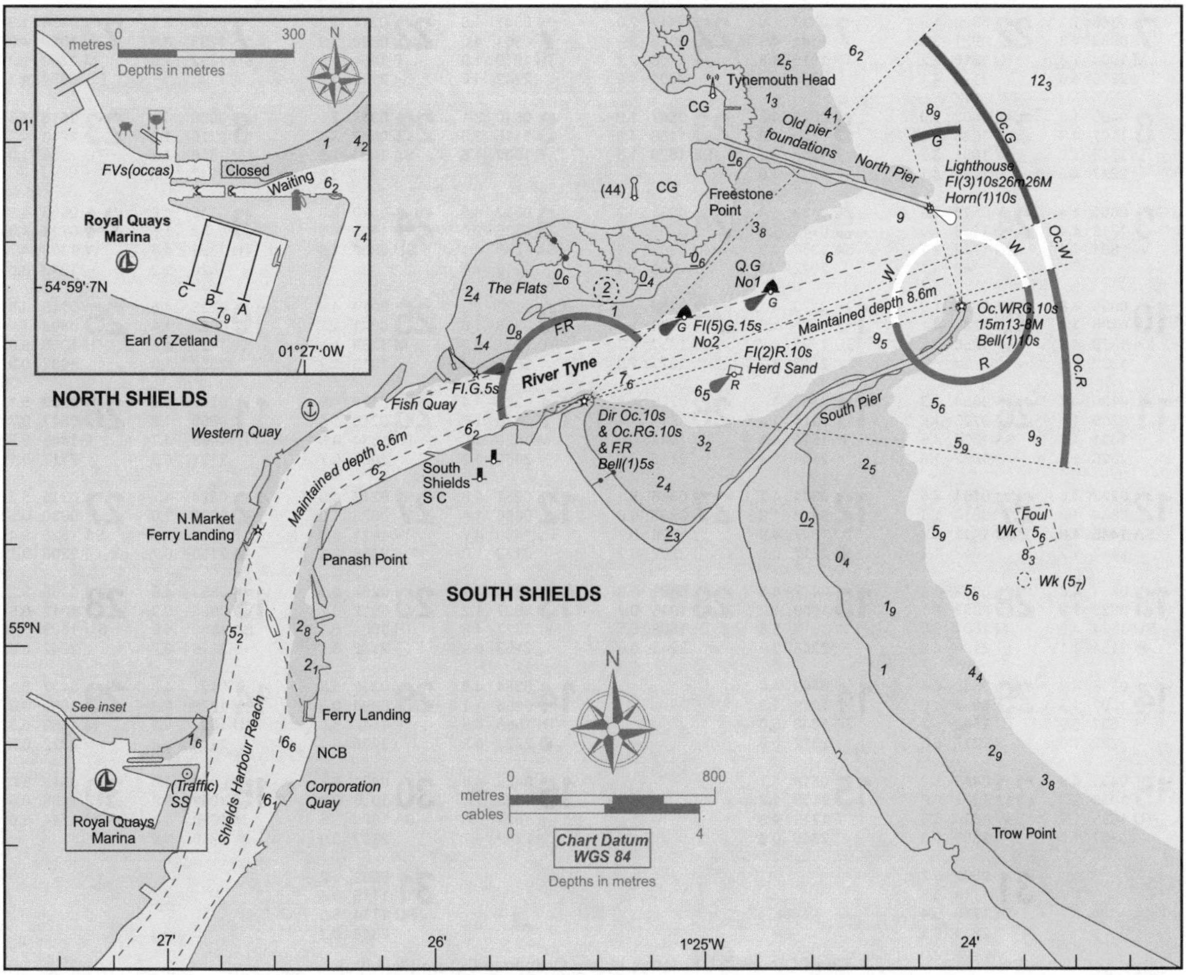

TIME ZONE (UTC)
For Summer Time add ONE hour in **non-shaded areas**

ENGLAND – NORTH SHIELDS

LAT 55°01′N LONG 1°26′W

TIMES AND HEIGHTS OF HIGH AND LOW WATERS

SPRING & NEAP TIDES
Dates in red are **SPRINGS**
Dates in blue are **NEAPS**

YEAR **2002**

JANUARY

Date	Day	Time	m	Date	Day	Time	m
1		0425	5.1	16		0510	4.8
		1041	1.0			1109	1.3
	TU	1639	5.2		W	1709	4.9
		2312	0.7			2341	1.0
2		0513	5.1	17		0545	4.7
		1125	1.1			1141	1.4
	W	1724	5.2		TH	1743	4.8
3		0000	0.6	18		0013	1.1
		0602	5.0			0621	4.5
	TH	1211	1.2		F	1213	1.5
		1811	5.1			1819	4.7
4		0051	0.7	19		0048	1.2
		0655	4.8			0658	4.4
	F	1300	1.4		SA	1248	1.7
		1903	5.0			1857	4.6
5		0144	0.8	20		0126	1.4
		0752	4.6			0740	4.2
	SA	1353	1.6		SU	1327	1.8
		2000	4.8			1940	4.4
6		0241	1.0	21		0209	1.6
		0853	4.4			0826	4.0
	SU	1453	1.7		M	1414	2.0
		2104	4.7			2030	4.3
7		0346	1.2	22		0300	1.8
		0959	4.3			0921	3.9
	M	1604	1.8		TU	1515	2.2
		2215	4.6			2128	4.1
8		0455	1.4	23		0403	1.9
		1107	4.3			1025	3.9
	TU	1719	1.8		W	1631	2.2
		2327	4.5			2236	4.1
9		0605	1.4	24		0515	1.9
		1212	4.4			1133	4.0
	W	1831	1.7		TH	1749	2.1
						2348	4.1
10		0035	4.6	25		0624	1.8
		0706	1.4			1236	4.2
	TH	1310	4.5		F	1856	1.8
		1932	1.5				
11		0136	4.7	26		0054	4.3
		0759	1.4			0723	1.6
	F	1401	4.7		SA	1330	4.5
		2026	1.3			1952	1.5
12		0228	4.8	27		0151	4.6
		0844	1.3			0814	1.4
	SA	1445	4.8		SU	1417	4.7
		2112	1.2			2042	1.2
13		0313	4.8	28		0242	4.8
		0925	1.3			0902	1.1
	SU	1524	4.9		M	1501	5.0
		● 2154	1.1			○ 2130	0.8
14		0355	4.8	29		0329	5.1
		1002	1.3			0947	1.0
	M	1601	5.0		TU	1543	5.2
		2232	1.0			2217	0.5
15		0433	4.8	30		0416	5.2
		1036	1.3			1031	0.9
	TU	1636	5.0		W	1626	5.3
		2307	1.0			2303	0.3
				31		0502	5.2
						1114	0.8
					TH	1710	5.4
						2349	0.3

FEBRUARY

Date	Day	Time	m	Date	Day	Time	m
1		0549	5.2	16		0550	4.6
		1157	0.9			1146	1.2
	F	1756	5.4		SA	1750	4.9
2		0035	0.4	17		0016	1.0
		0636	5.0			0621	4.5
	SA	1241	1.0		SU	1217	1.4
		1843	5.2			1823	4.7
3		0123	0.6	18		0048	1.2
		0726	4.7			0656	4.4
	SU	1326	1.3		M	1250	1.5
		1935	5.0			1900	4.6
4		0213	0.9	19		0123	1.4
		0820	4.5			0734	4.2
	M	1418	1.5		TU	1328	1.7
		2034	4.7			1943	4.4
5		0310	1.3	20		0205	1.6
		0920	4.2			0821	4.0
	TU	1523	1.8		W	1418	1.9
		2143	4.5			2036	4.2
6		0418	1.6	21		0300	1.9
		1030	4.1			0922	3.9
	W	1646	1.9		TH	1528	2.1
		2303	4.3			2145	4.0
7		0537	1.8	22		0417	2.0
		1144	4.1			1038	3.9
	TH	1815	1.8		F	1700	2.1
						2309	4.0
8		0023	4.3	23		0547	1.9
		0650	1.8			1158	4.0
	F	1254	4.3		SA	1828	1.8
		1927	1.6				
9		0132	4.4	24		0031	4.2
		0749	1.7			0701	1.7
	SA	1350	4.5		SU	1305	4.3
		2022	1.4			1933	1.4
10		0225	4.5	25		0136	4.5
		0835	1.5			0759	1.4
	SU	1436	4.7		M	1357	4.7
		2107	1.2			2027	1.0
11		0307	4.7	26		0229	4.8
		0914	1.4			0848	1.1
	M	1514	4.8		TU	1443	5.0
		2144	1.1			2116	0.6
12		0344	4.7	27		0316	5.1
		0948	1.3			0933	0.8
	TU	1547	4.9		W	1526	5.3
		● 2217	0.9			○ 2202	0.2
13		0417	4.8	28		0401	5.3
		1019	1.2			1015	0.7
	W	1618	5.0		TH	1608	5.5
		2248	0.9			2247	0.0
14		0449	4.8				
		1049	1.2				
	TH	1648	5.0				
		2317	0.9				
15		0519	4.7				
		1118	1.2				
	F	1719	4.9				
		2346	0.9				

MARCH

Date	Day	Time	m	Date	Day	Time	m
1		0444	5.3	16		0451	4.8
		1057	0.6			1053	1.0
	F	1651	5.6		SA	1653	4.9
		2331	0.0			2317	0.8
2		0528	5.2	17		0519	4.7
		1137	0.6			1121	1.0
	SA	1735	5.5		SU	1723	4.9
						2345	0.9
3		0013	0.2	18		0548	4.6
		0611	5.0			1150	1.1
	SU	1218	0.8		M	1754	4.8
		1821	5.3				
4		0056	0.5	19		0014	1.1
		0656	4.8			0619	4.5
	M	1300	1.0		TU	1222	1.3
		1911	5.0			1829	4.6
5		0141	1.0	20		0046	1.3
		0745	4.5			0654	4.3
	TU	1349	1.3		W	1258	1.5
		2008	4.6			1911	4.4
6		0233	1.4	21		0124	1.5
		0842	4.2			0739	4.1
	W	1451	1.7		TH	1345	1.7
		2117	4.3			2005	4.2
7		0341	1.8	22		0217	1.8
		0951	4.0			0838	3.9
	TH	1619	1.9		F	1454	1.9
		2242	4.0			2116	4.0
8		0510	2.1	23		0337	2.0
		1115	3.9			0957	3.8
	F	1802	1.8		SA	1630	1.9
						2247	3.9
9		0012	4.0	24		0520	2.0
		0635	2.0			1126	4.0
	SA	1235	4.1		SU	1804	1.6
		1918	1.6				
10		0123	4.2	25		0014	4.2
		0736	1.8			0641	1.7
	SU	1335	4.3		M	1239	4.3
		2010	1.4			1913	1.2
11		0213	4.4	26		0120	4.5
		0820	1.6			0740	1.4
	M	1420	4.5		TU	1334	4.6
		2050	1.2			2008	0.7
12		0251	4.6	27		0212	4.9
		0856	1.4			0828	1.0
	TU	1456	4.7		W	1421	5.0
		2123	1.0			2056	0.3
13		0324	4.7	28		0257	5.1
		0927	1.2			0912	0.7
	W	1527	4.8		TH	1504	5.3
		2153	0.9			○ 2142	0.1
14		0354	4.8	29		0340	5.3
		0956	1.1			0954	0.5
	TH	1555	4.9		F	1546	5.5
		● 2221	0.8			2225	-0.1
15		0423	4.8	30		0421	5.3
		1025	1.0			1035	0.4
	F	1624	5.0		SA	1630	5.6
		2249	0.7			2307	0.0
				31		0502	5.2
						1115	0.5
					SU	1714	5.5
						2348	0.3

APRIL

Date	Day	Time	m	Date	Day	Time	m
1		0544	5.0	16		0519	4.7
		1155	0.6			1129	1.0
	M	1801	5.2		TU	1731	4.7
						2346	1.0
2		0028	0.7	17		0551	4.6
		0626	4.8			1202	1.1
	TU	1239	0.9		W	1809	4.6
		1851	4.9				
3		0111	1.1	18		0019	1.3
		0713	4.5			0628	4.4
	W	1327	1.2		TH	1242	1.3
		1947	4.5			1854	4.4
4		0200	1.6	19		0100	1.5
		0807	4.2			0714	4.2
	TH	1428	1.6		F	1333	1.5
		2055	4.1			1952	4.1
5		0305	2.0	20		0156	1.8
		0914	3.9			0815	4.0
	F	1554	1.8		SA	1444	1.6
		2219	3.9			2106	4.0
6		0437	2.2	21		0319	2.0
		1039	3.8			0933	3.9
	SA	1737	1.8		SU	1614	1.6
		2349	3.9			2233	4.0
7		0609	2.1	22		0458	1.9
		1203	3.9			1058	4.0
	SU	1852	1.6		M	1740	1.3
						2354	4.2
8		0058	4.1	23		0616	1.7
		0710	1.9			1210	4.3
	M	1306	4.2		TU	1848	1.0
		1942	1.3				
9		0146	4.3	24		0057	4.5
		0753	1.6			0714	1.3
	TU	1351	4.4		W	1308	4.7
		2020	1.2			1943	0.6
10		0223	4.5	25		0149	4.8
		0827	1.4			0803	1.0
	W	1426	4.6		TH	1356	5.0
		2052	1.0			2032	0.3
11		0255	4.6	26		0233	5.1
		0859	1.2			0847	0.7
	TH	1458	4.7		F	1441	5.3
		2121	0.8			2117	0.1
12		0324	4.7	27		0315	5.2
		0929	1.0			0930	0.5
	F	1527	4.8		SA	1525	5.4
		● 2150	0.7			○ 2200	0.1
13		0353	4.8	28		0356	5.2
		0958	0.9			1013	0.5
	SA	1556	4.9		SU	1609	5.4
		2218	0.7			2242	0.2
14		0421	4.8	29		0437	5.1
		1028	0.9			1055	0.5
	SU	1627	4.9		M	1656	5.3
		2247	0.8			2322	0.5
15		0449	4.8	30		0518	5.0
		1058	0.9			1138	0.6
	M	1658	4.8		TU	1744	5.0
		2316	0.9				

Chart Datum: 2·60 metres below Ordnance Datum (Newlyn)

TIME ZONE (UTC)
For Summer Time add ONE hour in **non-shaded areas**

ENGLAND – NORTH SHIELDS

LAT 55°01'N LONG 1°26'W

TIMES AND HEIGHTS OF HIGH AND LOW WATERS

SPRING & NEAP TIDES
Dates in red are SPRINGS
Dates in blue are NEAPS

YEAR **2002**

MAY

Date	Time	m	Time	m	Time	m	Time	m
1 W	0002	0.9	0600	4.8	1222	0.9	1834	4.7
2 TH	0044	1.3	0645	4.5	1311	1.1	1929	4.3
3 F	0131	1.7	0736	4.2	1408	1.4	2032	4.0
4 SA	0230	2.0	0838	4.0	1522	1.6	2146	3.8
5 SU	0350	2.2	0953	3.9	1649	1.7	2305	3.8
6 M	0519	2.2	1113	3.9	1804	1.6		
7 TU	0014	3.9	0624	2.0	1220	4.0	1856	1.4
8 W	0105	4.1	0712	1.7	1309	4.2	1937	1.2
9 TH	0145	4.3	0750	1.5	1348	4.4	2012	1.1
10 F	0219	4.5	0825	1.3	1423	4.6	2045	0.9
11 SA	0251	4.6	0859	1.1	1456	4.7	2117	0.8
12 SU	0321	4.7	0931	1.0	1529	4.8	● 2148	0.8
13 M	0352	4.8	1004	0.9	1602	4.8	2220	0.8
14 TU	0423	4.8	1038	0.9	1638	4.8	2252	0.9
15 W	0456	4.7	1113	0.9	1716	4.7	2326	1.1
16 TH	0532	4.6	1153	1.0	1759	4.6		
17 F	0005	1.2	0613	4.5	1238	1.1	1848	4.4
18 SA	0051	1.5	0703	4.4	1333	1.2	1948	4.2
19 SU	0150	1.7	0803	4.2	1440	1.3	2058	4.1
20 M	0306	1.8	0914	4.1	1557	1.3	2215	4.1
21 TU	0430	1.8	1030	4.2	1713	1.1	2328	4.3
22 W	0543	1.6	1140	4.4	1819	0.9		
23 TH	0030	4.5	0643	1.3	1240	4.7	1916	0.6
24 F	0122	4.7	0735	1.1	1332	4.9	2006	0.5
25 SA	0209	4.9	0824	0.9	1420	5.1	2053	0.4
26 SU	0252	5.0	0910	0.7	1507	5.2	○ 2137	0.5
27 M	0333	5.1	0955	0.6	1554	5.1	2219	0.6
28 TU	0415	5.0	1040	0.6	1642	5.0	2300	0.8
29 W	0456	4.9	1125	0.7	1730	4.8	2341	1.1
30 TH	0539	4.8	1209	0.9	1819	4.6		
31 F	0021	1.4	0622	4.6	1255	1.1	1909	4.3

JUNE

Date	Time	m	Time	m	Time	m	Time	m
1 SA	0104	1.7	0709	4.4	1345	1.3	2003	4.1
2 SU	0154	1.9	0802	4.2	1441	1.5	2102	3.9
3 M	0256	2.1	0902	4.0	1546	1.6	2207	3.8
4 TU	0409	2.1	1010	3.9	1654	1.6	2313	3.9
5 W	0520	2.0	1117	4.0	1755	1.5		
6 TH	0010	4.0	0618	1.9	1215	4.1	1845	1.4
7 F	0058	4.2	0706	1.7	1304	4.3	1929	1.3
8 SA	0139	4.4	0749	1.5	1346	4.4	2008	1.1
9 SU	0216	4.5	0828	1.3	1426	4.6	2045	1.0
10 M	0251	4.7	0906	1.1	1504	4.7	● 2121	1.0
11 TU	0326	4.8	0944	1.0	1543	4.7	2158	1.0
12 W	0401	4.8	1023	0.9	1623	4.8	2236	1.0
13 TH	0438	4.8	1104	0.8	1706	4.7	2316	1.1
14 F	0519	4.8	1148	0.8	1753	4.7	2359	1.2
15 SA	0603	4.7	1236	0.8	1844	4.6		
16 SU	0047	1.3	0653	4.6	1330	0.9	1940	4.4
17 M	0143	1.5	0749	4.5	1429	1.0	2043	4.3
18 TU	0246	1.6	0853	4.4	1534	1.0	2150	4.3
19 W	0355	1.7	1001	4.4	1642	1.0	2257	4.3
20 TH	0506	1.6	1110	4.5	1749	1.0		
21 F	0000	4.4	0612	1.5	1214	4.6	1850	0.9
22 SA	0057	4.6	0712	1.3	1313	4.8	1944	0.9
23 SU	0147	4.7	0806	1.1	1407	4.9	2034	0.9
24 M	0233	4.8	0857	0.9	1458	4.9	○ 2119	0.9
25 TU	0317	4.9	0945	0.8	1546	4.9	2202	1.0
26 W	0358	4.9	1030	0.7	1632	4.8	2243	1.1
27 TH	0439	4.9	1113	0.8	1717	4.7	2321	1.2
28 F	0519	4.8	1154	0.9	1800	4.6	2358	1.4
29 SA	0559	4.7	1234	1.0	1843	4.4		
30 SU	0036	1.5	0640	4.6	1314	1.1	1927	4.2

JULY

Date	Time	m	Time	m	Time	m	Time	m
1 M	0116	1.7	0724	4.4	1357	1.3	2014	4.1
2 TU	0203	1.9	0813	4.2	1446	1.5	2107	3.9
3 W	0259	2.0	0909	4.1	1543	1.6	2205	3.9
4 TH	0405	2.1	1010	4.0	1646	1.7	2306	3.9
5 F	0515	2.0	1114	4.0	1748	1.6		
6 SA	0004	4.0	0618	1.9	1216	4.1	1844	1.6
7 SU	0057	4.2	0712	1.7	1310	4.3	1933	1.4
8 M	0143	4.4	0800	1.4	1359	4.4	2018	1.3
9 TU	0224	4.6	0844	1.2	1444	4.6	2100	1.2
10 W	0304	4.8	0927	1.0	1527	4.8	● 2142	1.0
11 TH	0343	4.9	1011	0.7	1611	4.9	2224	1.0
12 F	0423	5.0	1056	0.6	1656	4.9	2307	1.0
13 SA	0506	5.0	1141	0.5	1743	4.9	2351	1.0
14 SU	0550	5.0	1228	0.5	1832	4.8		
15 M	0036	1.1	0638	5.0	1317	0.6	1923	4.7
16 TU	0125	1.3	0730	4.9	1409	0.7	2018	4.5
17 W	0218	1.4	0827	4.7	1506	1.0	2119	4.3
18 TH	0320	1.6	0932	4.6	1610	1.2	2224	4.3
19 F	0431	1.7	1043	4.5	1720	1.3	2331	4.3
20 SA	0548	1.6	1156	4.5	1829	1.4		
21 SU	0035	4.4	0658	1.5	1304	4.5	1930	1.3
22 M	0133	4.5	0800	1.3	1404	4.6	2022	1.3
23 TU	0222	4.7	0853	1.1	1455	4.7	2108	1.2
24 W	0306	4.8	0939	0.9	1540	4.8	○ 2148	1.2
25 TH	0345	4.9	1020	0.8	1621	4.8	2226	1.2
26 F	0423	5.0	1058	0.8	1659	4.8	2300	1.2
27 SA	0458	4.9	1133	0.8	1736	4.7	2333	1.3
28 SU	0533	4.9	1206	0.9	1812	4.5		
29 M	0005	1.4	0608	4.8	1239	1.0	1848	4.4
30 TU	0039	1.5	0646	4.6	1314	1.2	1927	4.3
31 W	0116	1.7	0728	4.4	1354	1.4	2011	4.1

AUGUST

Date	Time	m	Time	m	Time	m	Time	m
1 TH	0200	1.8	0815	4.3	1441	1.6	2101	4.0
2 F	0256	2.0	0911	4.1	1539	1.8	2201	3.9
3 SA	0407	2.1	1016	4.0	1648	1.9	2308	3.9
4 SU	0527	2.1	1129	4.0	1801	1.9		
5 M	0015	4.1	0638	1.9	1239	4.2	1904	1.7
6 TU	0112	4.3	0736	1.6	1337	4.4	1956	1.5
7 W	0200	4.6	0826	1.2	1427	4.7	2043	1.3
8 TH	0244	4.8	0912	0.9	1513	4.9	● 2128	1.0
9 F	0325	5.1	0957	0.5	1557	5.1	2210	0.9
10 SA	0406	5.3	1042	0.3	1641	5.2	2253	0.8
11 SU	0447	5.4	1126	0.2	1726	5.2	2334	0.8
12 M	0531	5.4	1210	0.2	1811	5.0		
13 TU	0016	0.9	0616	5.3	1255	0.4	1858	4.9
14 W	0100	1.1	0706	5.1	1342	0.7	1948	4.6
15 TH	0148	1.3	0801	4.8	1435	1.1	2045	4.4
16 F	0247	1.6	0906	4.6	1538	1.5	2151	4.2
17 SA	0404	1.8	1023	4.3	1655	1.7	2305	4.1
18 SU	0535	1.8	1147	4.3	1816	1.8		
19 M	0019	4.3	0656	1.6	1304	4.4	1922	1.7
20 TU	0123	4.5	0758	1.3	1403	4.5	2014	1.6
21 W	0213	4.7	0847	1.1	1450	4.7	2056	1.4
22 TH	0255	4.8	0928	0.9	1528	4.8	○ 2133	1.3
23 F	0330	5.0	1003	0.8	1603	4.8	2205	1.2
24 SA	0402	5.0	1035	0.8	1635	4.8	2236	1.1
25 SU	0433	5.0	1105	0.8	1707	4.8	2306	1.2
26 M	0504	5.0	1134	0.8	1737	4.7	2335	1.2
27 TU	0536	4.9	1203	1.0	1809	4.6		
28 W	0005	1.3	0610	4.8	1234	1.1	1843	4.4
29 TH	0038	1.5	0647	4.6	1307	1.4	1920	4.3
30 F	0115	1.7	0729	4.4	1347	1.6	2005	4.1
31 SA	0204	1.9	0821	4.1	1439	1.9	2102	4.0

Chart Datum: 2·60 metres below Ordnance Datum (Newlyn)

TIME ZONE (UTC)
For Summer Time add ONE hour in **non-shaded areas**

ENGLAND – NORTH SHIELDS

LAT 55°01'N LONG 1°26'W

TIMES AND HEIGHTS OF HIGH AND LOW WATERS

SPRING & NEAP TIDES
Dates in red are **SPRINGS**
Dates in blue are **NEAPS**

YEAR **2002**

SEPTEMBER

Date	Time	m	Date	Time	m
1	0311	2.1	16	0528	1.8
	0928	4.0		1141	4.1
SU	1552	2.1	M	1805	2.1
	2215	3.9			
2	0440	2.1	17	0004	4.2
	1050	3.9		0651	1.6
M	1722	2.1	TU	1259	4.3
	2335	4.0		1912	1.9
3	0609	1.9	18	0110	4.4
	1213	4.1		0748	1.3
TU	1840	1.9	W	1353	4.5
				2000	1.7
4	0043	4.3	19	0158	4.6
	0714	1.5		0832	1.1
W	1319	4.4	TH	1434	4.7
	1937	1.6		2038	1.5
5	0137	4.6	20	0236	4.8
	0806	1.1		0907	1.0
TH	1410	4.8	F	1508	4.8
	2025	1.3		2110	1.3
6	0221	5.0	21	0308	5.0
	0853	0.7		0937	0.9
F	1455	5.1	SA	1538	4.9
	2109	1.0		○ 2140	1.2
7	0302	5.3	22	0338	5.0
	0938	0.3		1005	0.8
SA	1537	5.3	SU	1607	4.9
	● 2150	0.8		2209	1.1
8	0343	5.5	23	0406	5.1
	1021	0.1		1033	0.8
SU	1619	5.4	M	1635	4.9
	2231	0.7		2238	1.1
9	0424	5.6	24	0436	5.0
	1104	0.0		1100	0.8
M	1701	5.3	TU	1704	4.8
	2311	0.7		2306	1.1
10	0507	5.6	25	0506	5.0
	1146	0.2		1128	1.0
TU	1744	5.2	W	1733	4.7
	2352	0.8		2335	1.2
11	0553	5.5	26	0539	4.8
	1228	0.5		1157	1.2
W	1828	5.0	TH	1804	4.6
12	0034	1.0	27	0006	1.4
	0642	5.2		0613	4.6
TH	1313	0.9	F	1228	1.4
	1916	4.7		1838	4.4
13	0122	1.3	28	0043	1.6
	0738	4.8		0654	4.4
F	1403	1.4	SA	1304	1.7
	2011	4.4		1920	4.2
14	0222	1.6	29	0129	1.8
	0845	4.4		0746	4.2
SA	1508	1.8	SU	1352	2.0
	2118	4.2		2016	4.0
15	0345	1.8	30	0234	2.0
	1009	4.2		0855	4.0
SU	1634	2.1	M	1508	2.2
	2241	4.1		2132	3.9

OCTOBER

Date	Time	m	Date	Time	m
1	0407	2.1	16	0630	1.6
	1023	3.9		1236	4.2
TU	1651	2.2	W	1848	2.0
	2259	4.0			
2	0541	1.8	17	0043	4.4
	1151	4.1		0723	1.4
W	1816	2.0	TH	1328	4.4
				1934	1.8
3	0013	4.3	18	0131	4.6
	0649	1.4		0803	1.2
TH	1257	4.5	F	1406	4.6
	1914	1.6		2010	1.6
4	0109	4.7	19	0209	4.7
	0742	0.9		0836	1.1
F	1348	4.9	SA	1439	4.8
	2002	1.3		2042	1.4
5	0155	5.1	20	0240	4.9
	0829	0.5		0905	1.0
SA	1432	5.2	SU	1508	4.9
	2045	0.9		2112	1.2
6	0237	5.4	21	0310	5.0
	0913	0.2		0933	0.9
SU	1513	5.4	M	1537	4.9
	● 2126	0.7		○ 2142	1.1
7	0318	5.6	22	0340	5.0
	0956	0.1		1001	0.9
M	1554	5.4	TU	1605	5.0
	2207	0.6		2211	1.1
8	0400	5.7	23	0410	5.0
	1038	0.1		1029	0.9
TU	1634	5.4	W	1633	4.9
	2247	0.6		2241	1.1
9	0445	5.7	24	0441	4.9
	1120	0.3		1057	1.1
W	1716	5.2	TH	1702	4.8
	2329	0.7		2312	1.2
10	0532	5.4	25	0514	4.8
	1201	0.7		1126	1.2
TH	1759	5.0	F	1732	4.7
				2345	1.3
11	0013	0.9	26	0550	4.6
	0622	5.1		1158	1.5
F	1245	1.1	SA	1807	4.5
	1846	4.7			
12	0103	1.2	27	0022	1.5
	0720	4.7		0633	4.4
SA	1335	1.6	SU	1235	1.7
	1940	4.4		1850	4.4
13	0205	1.6	28	0111	1.7
	0829	4.3		0727	4.2
SU	1439	2.1	M	1325	2.0
	2048	4.2		1947	4.2
14	0329	1.8	29	0217	1.8
	0953	4.0		0837	4.0
M	1609	2.3	TU	1441	2.2
	2212	4.1		2100	4.0
15	0511	1.8	30	0342	1.8
	1123	4.0		1001	4.0
TU	1743	2.2	W	1620	2.2
	2337	4.2		2224	4.1
			31	0510	1.6
				1124	4.2
			TH	1744	2.0
				2339	4.4

NOVEMBER

Date	Time	m	Date	Time	m
1	0619	1.3	16	0053	4.4
	1228	4.5		0723	1.4
F	1844	1.6	SA	1330	4.5
				1935	1.7
2	0037	4.7	17	0134	4.6
	0713	0.9		0758	1.3
SA	1321	4.9	SU	1405	4.6
	1933	1.3		2010	1.5
3	0127	5.1	18	0209	4.7
	0802	0.5		0830	1.2
SU	1405	5.1	M	1437	4.8
	2018	1.0		2044	1.3
4	0211	5.4	19	0243	4.8
	0847	0.3		0901	1.1
M	1447	5.3	TU	1507	4.9
	● 2101	0.8		2116	1.2
5	0255	5.6	20	0315	4.9
	0931	0.3		0932	1.1
TU	1528	5.4	W	1537	4.9
	2144	0.6		○ 2149	1.2
6	0340	5.6	21	0348	4.9
	1014	0.4		1003	1.1
W	1609	5.4	TH	1607	4.9
	2228	0.6		2221	1.1
7	0427	5.5	22	0422	4.9
	1056	0.6		1033	1.2
TH	1651	5.2	F	1638	4.9
	2312	0.7		2256	1.2
8	0516	5.3	23	0458	4.8
	1138	1.0		1106	1.3
F	1735	5.0	SA	1711	4.8
	2359	0.9		2332	1.2
9	0609	4.9	24	0537	4.7
	1222	1.4		1141	1.5
SA	1821	4.8	SU	1749	4.7
10	0050	1.2	25	0014	1.3
	0706	4.6		0623	4.5
SU	1310	1.8	M	1222	1.7
	1913	4.5		1834	4.5
11	0150	1.5	26	0105	1.4
	0810	4.3		0717	4.3
M	1410	2.1	TU	1314	1.9
	2016	4.3		1929	4.4
12	0303	1.7	27	0206	1.5
	0924	4.0		0822	4.2
TU	1528	2.3	W	1422	2.0
	2131	4.1		2035	4.3
13	0428	1.8	28	0318	1.5
	1043	4.0		0936	4.2
W	1656	2.3	TH	1544	2.1
	2252	4.1		2149	4.3
14	0545	1.7	29	0434	1.4
	1154	4.1		1050	4.3
TH	1805	2.1	F	1702	1.9
				2301	4.5
15	0000	4.2	30	0543	1.2
	0641	1.5		1155	4.5
F	1248	4.3	SA	1807	1.7
	1855	1.9			

DECEMBER

Date	Time	m	Date	Time	m
1	0004	4.7	16	0051	4.3
	0642	1.0		0716	1.6
SU	1251	4.8	M	1327	4.4
	1902	1.4		1936	1.7
2	0100	5.0	17	0136	4.5
	0735	0.8		0756	1.5
M	1339	5.0	TU	1405	4.6
	1953	1.2		2016	1.5
3	0150	5.2	18	0216	4.6
	0824	0.7		0833	1.4
TU	1424	5.1	W	1440	4.7
	2041	0.9		2054	1.4
4	0239	5.4	19	0254	4.7
	0910	0.6		0908	1.3
W	1507	5.2	TH	1514	4.8
	● 2129	0.8		○ 2131	1.2
5	0328	5.4	20	0331	4.8
	0954	0.7		0942	1.3
TH	1550	5.2	F	1547	4.9
	2216	0.7		2208	1.1
6	0417	5.3	21	0408	4.8
	1038	0.9		1018	1.3
F	1632	5.2	SA	1621	4.9
	2303	0.8		2246	1.1
7	0507	5.1	22	0447	4.8
	1120	1.2		1054	1.3
SA	1716	5.0	SU	1657	4.9
	2350	0.9		2327	1.0
8	0557	4.8	23	0529	4.8
	1203	1.5		1133	1.4
SU	1801	4.9	M	1737	4.9
9	0038	1.1	24	0010	1.0
	0649	4.6		0615	4.7
M	1247	1.7	TU	1217	1.5
	1849	4.6		1822	4.8
10	0129	1.3	25	0059	1.1
	0743	4.3		0705	4.6
TU	1336	2.0	W	1304	1.6
	1941	4.4		1912	4.7
11	0224	1.6	26	0152	1.2
	0842	4.1		0802	4.4
W	1434	2.2	TH	1400	1.8
	2041	4.2		2010	4.6
12	0326	1.7	27	0251	1.2
	0946	4.0		0905	4.3
TH	1544	2.3	F	1504	1.9
	2149	4.1		2114	4.5
13	0434	1.8	28	0357	1.3
	1052	4.0		1013	4.3
F	1657	2.3	SA	1616	1.9
	2258	4.1		2224	4.6
14	0538	1.8	29	0506	1.3
	1153	4.1		1120	4.4
SA	1801	2.1	SU	1729	1.8
	2359	4.2		2333	4.6
15	0632	1.7	30	0613	1.2
	1244	4.2		1222	4.5
SU	1853	1.9	M	1836	1.6
			31	0038	4.8
				0713	1.2
			TU	1318	4.7
				1937	1.4

Chart Datum: 2·60 metres below Ordnance Datum (Newlyn)

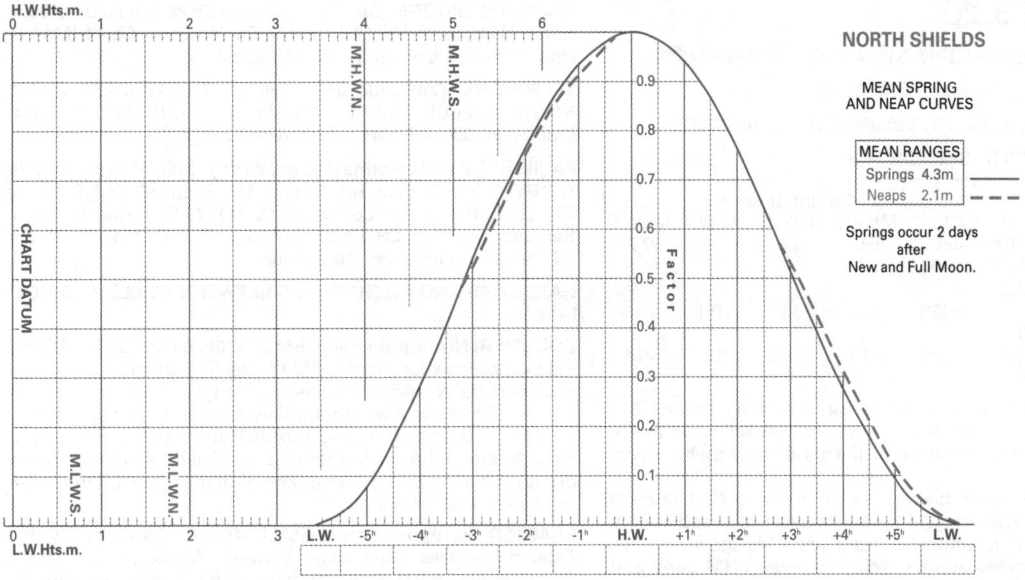

BLYTH *9.5.19*

Northumberland **55°06'·98N 01° 29'·27W**

CHARTS AC 1626, 152, 156; Imray C24; OS 81, 88

TIDES +0430 Dover; ML 2·8; Duration 0558; Zone 0 (UT)

Standard Port NORTH SHIELDS (⟵)

Times				Height (metres)			
High Water		Low Water		MHWS	MHWN	MLWN	MLWS
0200	0800	0100	0800	5·0	3·9	1·8	0·7
1400	2000	1300	2000				
Differences BLYTH							
+0005	–0007	–0001	+0009	0·0	0·0	–0·1	+0·1

SHELTER Very good; access H24. Yachts go to SE part of South Hbr; Ⓥ on N side of RNYC pontoons on E side of Middle Jetty (4·4m least depth).

NAVIGATION WPT Fairway SHM buoy, Fl G 3s, Bell, 55°06'·58N 01°28'·60W, 140°/320° from/to E pier lt, 0·53M. From N, beware The Pigs, The Sow and Seaton Sea Rks. No dangers from S. At LW in strong SE winds, seas break across ent. There are two wind turbines Fl. Y 2·5s on North Spit centred on 55°08'·2N 01°29'·3W.

LIGHTS AND MARKS 9 wind turbines are conspic on the E pier. Outer ldg lts 324°, F Bu 11/17m 10M, Or ◊ on framework trs. Inner ldg lts 338°, F Bu 5/11m 10M, front W 6-sided tr; rear W △ on mast.

RADIO TELEPHONE Call: *Blyth Hbr Control* VHF Ch **12** 11 16 (H24) for clearance to enter or depart.

TELEPHONE (Dial code 01670) Hr Mr 352678 📠 368540; MRSC (0191) 257 2691; ⊖ (0191) 257 9441; Marinecall 09068 500453; Police (01661) 872555; Dr 363334.

FACILITIES **R Northumberland YC** ☎ 353636, (50) AB £1.00 approx, FW, C (1½ ton), Bar; **South Hbr** ☎ 352678, FW, C (50 ton). **Town** EC Wed; P & D (cans), V, R, Bar, ✉, Ⓑ, Gas, Gaz, bus to Newcastle ⇌ ✈.

ADJACENT ANCHORAGE

NEWBIGGIN, Northumberland, **55°10'·75N 01°30'·10W**. AC 156. Tides approx as for Blyth, 3·5M to the S. Temp, fair weather ⚓ in about 4m in centre of Bay, sheltered from SW to N winds. Caution: offlying rky ledges to N and S. Conspic church on N side of bay; bkwtr lt Fl G 10s 4M. Facilities: **SC** (dinghies). **Town** V, R, Bar.

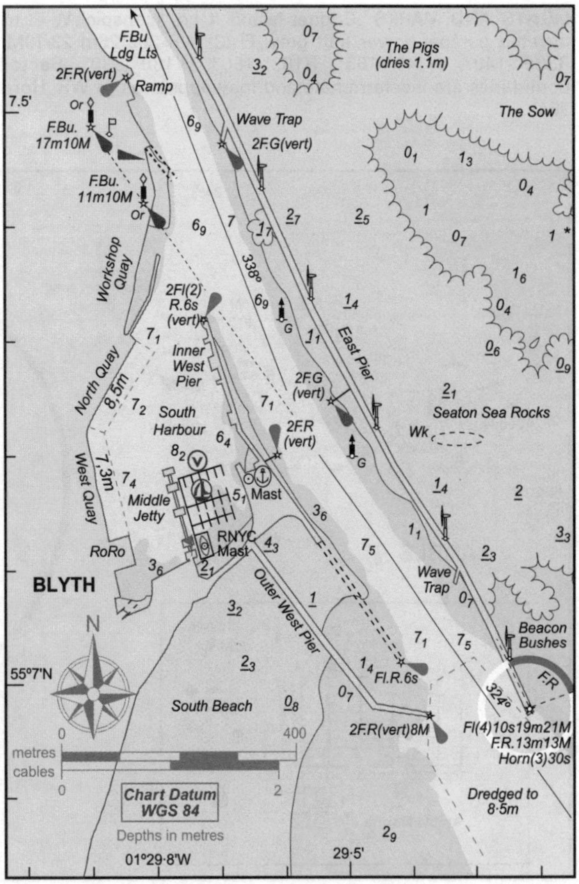

AMBLE *9.5.20*

Northumberland **55°20'·37N 01°34'·25W** ❁❁◊◊✿✿✿

CHARTS AC 1627, 156; Imray C24; OS 81

TIDES +0412 Dover; ML 3·1; Duration 0606; Zone 0 (UT)

Standard Port NORTH SHIELDS (⟵)

Times				Height (metres)			
High Water		Low Water		MHWS	MHWN	MLWN	MLWS
0200	0800	0100	0800	5·0	3·9	1·8	0·7
1400	2000	1300	2000				
Differences AMBLE							
–0013	–0013	–0016	–0020	0·0	0·0	+0·1	+0·1
COQUET ISLAND							
–0010	–0010	–0020	–0020	+0·1	+0·1	0·0	+0·1

SHELTER The hbr (alias Warkworth Hbr) is safe in all winds. But ent is dangerous in strong N to E winds or in swell, when heavy seas break on Pan Bush shoal and on the bar at hbr ent, where least depth is 0·8m.
Once inside the N bkwtr, beware drying banks to stbd, ie on N side of channel; keep close (15m) to S quays. 4kn speed limit in hbr. Amble marina is about 5ca from ent. Tidal gauge shows depth over sill; access approx HW±4 between PHM buoy and ECM bn, both unlit. Pontoons are 'A' to 'F' from sill; Ⓥ berth on 'B' initially.

NAVIGATION WPT 55°21'·00N 01°33'·10W, 045°/225° from/to hbr ent, 0·9M. Ent recommended from NE, passing N and W of Pan Bush. The S-going stream sets strongly across ent.
In NE'ly gales, when broken water can extend to Coquet Island, keep E of island and go to Blyth where app/ent may be safer.
Coquet Chan (min depth 0·3m) is not buoyed and is only advised with caution, by day, in good vis/ weather, slight sea state and with adequate rise of tide, ie HW–2.

LIGHTS AND MARKS Coquet Island lt ho, (conspic) W □ tr, turreted parapet, lower half grey; Fl (3) WR 30s 25m 23/19M, R330°-140°, W140°-163°, R163°-180°, W180°-330°. Sector boundaries are indeterminate and may appear as Al WR. Horn 30s.

RADIO TELEPHONE Call *Amble Marina* Ch **80** (seven days 0900-1700). *Warkworth Hbr* VHF, listens Ch 16, works Ch 14 (Mon-Fri 0900-1700 LT). Coquet YC Ch M (occas).

TELEPHONE (Dial code 01665) Hr Mr 710306; MRSC (01262) 672317; local CG 710575; ⊜ (N Shields) (0191) 257 9441 (H24); Marinecall 09068 500453; Ⓗ (01670) 521212.

FACILITIES Amble Marina (200+40 Ⓥ) ☎ 712168, 📠 713363, £1.70, AC, BY, C, FW, D , Slip, BH (20 ton), ME, El, Sh, Ⓔ, SM, R, Bar, V, CH, ⊡, ♿; **Hbr** D, AB; **Coquet YC** ☎ 711179 Slip, Bar, M, FW, L; **Services:** ME, Slip, CH, El, Sh, SM, Gas, Gaz, Ⓔ. **Town** V, R, Bar, ✉, ≠ (Alnmouth), ✈ (Newcastle).

HARBOURS AND ANCHORAGES BETWEEN AMBLE AND HOLY ISLAND

BOULMER, Northumberland, **55°25'·00N 01°33'·90W**. AC 156. Tides approx as for Amble, 4·5M to the S. A small haven almost enclosed by N and S Rheins, rky ledges either side of the narrow (30m) ent, Mar mouth; only advised in settled offshore weather. 2 unlit bns lead approx 262° through the ent, leaving close to stbd a bn on N Rheins. ⚓ just inside in about 1·5m or dry out on sand at the N end. Few facilities: Pub, ✉ in village. Alnwick is 4M inland.

CRASTER, Northumberland, **55°28'·40N 01°35'·30W**. AC 156. Tidal differences: interpolate between Amble (9.5.20) and N Sunderland (9.5.21). Strictly a fair weather ⚓ in offshore winds, 1M S of the conspic Dunstanburgh Castle (ru). The ent, 40m wide, is N of Muckle Carr and S of Little Carr which partly covers and has a bn on its S end. ⚓ in about 3·5m just inshore of these 2 rocky outcrops; or berth at the E pier on rk/sand inside the tiny drying hbr. Facilities: V, R, Bar.

NEWTON HAVEN and BEADNELL BAY, Northumberland, **55°30'·90N 01° 36'·70W**. AC 156. HW +0342 on Dover; Tidal differences: interpolate between Amble (9.5.20) and N Sunderland (9.5.21). ML 2·6m; Duration 0625. A safe ⚓ in winds from NNW to SE via S but susceptible to swell. Ent to S of Newton PHM buoy and Newton Pt. Beware Fills Rks. ⚓ between Fills Rks and Low Newton by the Sea in 4/5m. A very attractive ⚓ with no lts, marks or facilities except a pub. Further ⚓ S of Beadnell Pt (1M N of Newton Pt) in 4-6m; small, fishing hbr; Beadnell SC. Village 0·5M.

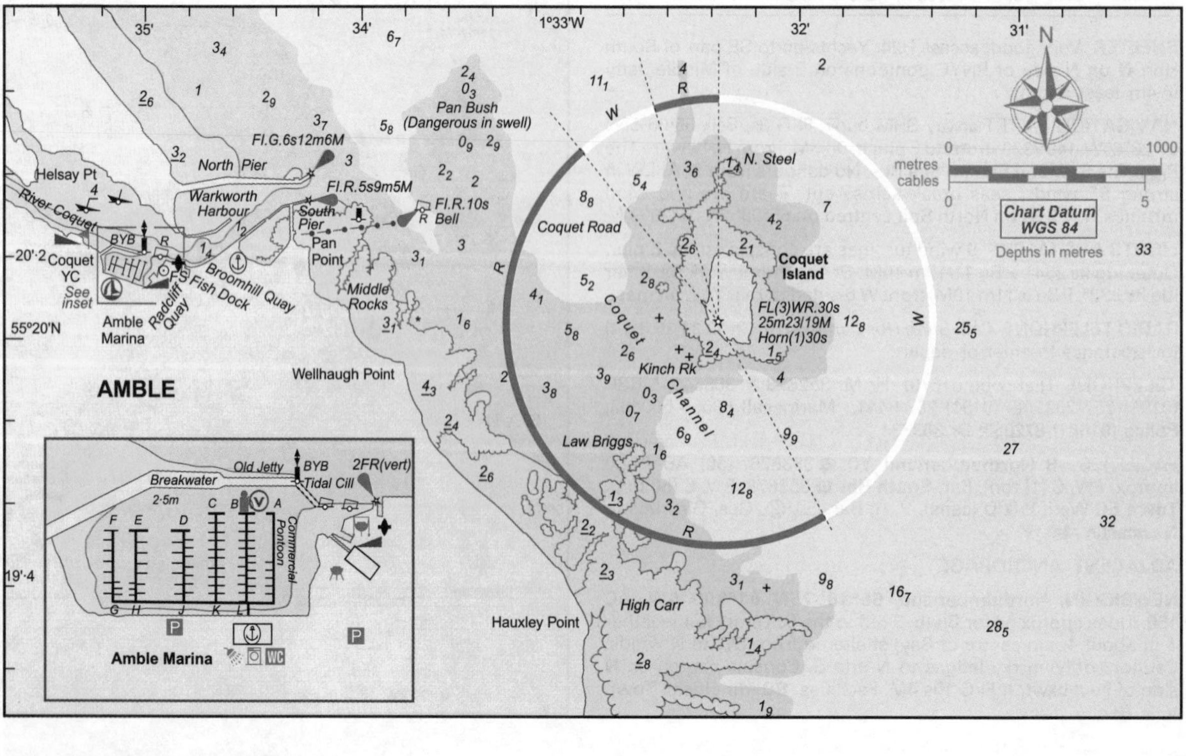

AMBLE *continued*

NORTH SUNDERLAND (Seahouses), Northumberland, **55°35′·04N 01°38′·91W**. AC 1612. HW +0340 on Dover; ML No data; Duration 0618. See 9.5.21. Good shelter except in on-shore winds when swell makes outer hbr berths (0·7m) very uncomfortable and dangerous. Access HW±3. Inner hbr has excellent berths but usually full of FVs. Beware The Tumblers (rks) to the W of ent and rks protruding NE from bkwtr hd Fl R 2·5s 6m; NW pier hd FG 11m 3M; vis 159°-294°, on W tr; traffic sigs; Siren 90s when vessels expected. When it is dangerous to enter a ● is shown over the FG lt (or R flag over a Bu flag) on NW pier hd. Facilities: EC Wed; Gas; all facilities.

FARNE ISLANDS, Northumberland, **55°37′·15N 01°39′·37W**. AC 111, 156, 160. HW +0345 on Dover; ML 2·6m; Duration 0630. See 9.5.21. The islands are a NT nature reserve in a beautiful area; they should only be attempted in good weather. Landing is only allowed on Farne Island, Staple Is and Longstone. In the inner group, ⚓ in The Kettle on the NE side of Inner Farne; near the Bridges (which connect Knocks Reef to West Wideopen); or to the S of West Wideopen. In the outer group, ⚓ in Pinnacle Haven (between Staple Is and Brownsman). Beware turbulence over Knivestone and Whirl Rks and eddy S of Longstone during NW tidal streams. Lts and marks: Black Rocks Pt, Oc (2) WRG 15s 12m 17/13M; G122°-165°, W165°-175°, R175°-191°, W191°-238°, R238°-275°, W275°-289°, G289°-300°. Bamburgh Castle is conspic 6ca to the SE. Farne Is lt ho at SW Pt, Fl (2) WR 15s 27m 8/6M; W ○ tr; R119°-280°, W280°-119°. Longstone Fl 20s 23m 24M, R tr with W band (conspic), RC, horn (2) 60s. Caution: reefs extend about 7ca seaward. No facilities.

NATIONAL NATURE RESERVE (Holy Island) A National Nature Reserve (NNR) extends from Budle Bay (**55°37′N 01°45′W**, close to Black Rocks Point lt ho) along the coast to Cheswick Black Rocks, 3M SE of Berwick-upon-Tweed. The NNR extends seaward from the HW shoreline to the drying line; it includes Holy Island and the adjacent islets.
Yachtsmen are asked to respect two constraints:

a. Landing is prohib on the small island of Black Law (55°39′·68N 01°47′·50W) from April to August inclusive.
b. Boats should not be landed or recovered any where in the NNR except at the designated and buoyed watersports zone on the SE side of Budle Bay.

HOLY ISLAND *9.5.21*

Northumberland **55°39′·57N 01°46′·81W**

CHARTS AC 1612, 111; Imray C24; OS 75

TIDES +0344 Dover; ML No data; Duration 0630; Zone 0 (UT)

Standard Port NORTH SHIELDS (⟵)

Times				**Height (metres)**			
High Water		Low Water		MHWS	MHWN	MLWN	MLWS
0200	0800	0100	0800	5·0	3·9	1·8	0·7
1400	2000	1300	2000				
Differences HOLY ISLAND							
−0043	−0039	−0105	−0110	−0·2	−0·2	−0·3	−0·1
NORTH SUNDERLAND (Seahouses)							
−0048	−0044	−0058	−0102	−0·2	−0·2	−0·2	0·0

SHELTER Good S of The Heugh in 3-6m, but ⚓ is uncomfortable in fresh W/SW winds esp at sp flood. Better shelter in The Ouse on sand/mud if able to dry out; but not in S/SE winds.

NAVIGATION WPT 55°39′·76N 01°44′·88W, 080°/260° from/to Old Law E bn 1·55M. From N identify Emanuel Hd, conspic W △ bn, then appr via Goldstone Chan leaving Plough Seat PHM buoy to stbd. From S, clear Farne Is thence to WPT. Outer ldg bns lead 260° close past Ridge ECM and Triton SHM buoys. Possible overfalls in chan across bar (2·1m) with sp ebb up to 4kn. Inner ldg marks lead 310° to ⚓. Inshore route, round Castle Pt via Hole Mouth and The Yares, may be more sheltered, but is not for strangers.

LIGHTS AND MARKS Outer ldg marks/lts are Old Law bns (conspic), 2 reddish obelisks 21/25m on 260°; E bn has dir lt, Oc WRG 6s 9m 4M, G182°-2620°, W262°-264°, R264°-shore. Inner ldg marks/lts are The Heugh tr, B △, on with St Mary's ch belfry 310°. The Heugh has dir lt, Oc WRG 6s 24m 5M, G135°-308°, W308°-311°, R311°-shore. Dir lts Oc WRG are aligned on 263° and 309·5° respectively.

RADIO TELEPHONE None.

TELEPHONE (Dial code 01289) Hr Mr 389217; CG 0191-257 2691; Marinecall 09068 500453.

FACILITIES Limited. FW on village green, R, Bar, limited V, P & D from Beal (5M); bus (occas) to Berwick. Note Lindisfarne is ancient name; Benedictine Abbey (ruins) and Castle (NT) are worth visiting. Causeway to mainland covers at HW. It is usable by vehicles HW+3½ to HW−2; less in adverse wx.

5

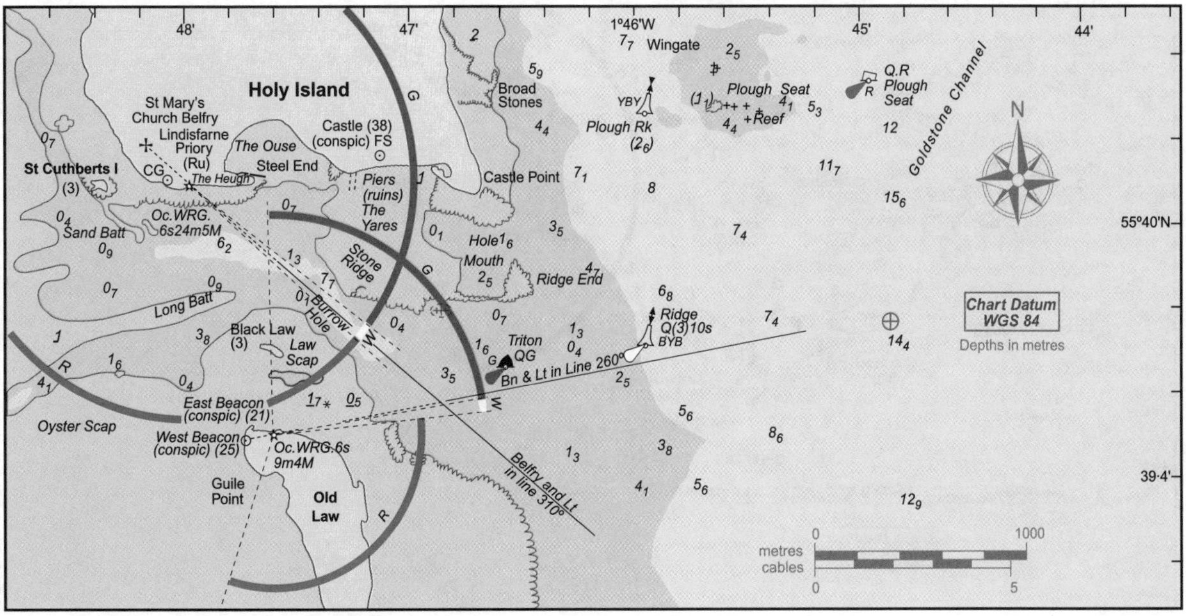

BERWICK-UPON-TWEED *9.5.22*

Northumberland **55°45'·87N 01°59'·05W**

CHARTS AC 1612, 111, 160; Imray C24; OS 75

TIDES +0348 Dover; ML 2·5; Duration 0620; Zone 0 (UT)

Standard Port NORTH SHIELDS (⟵)

Times				Height (metres)			
High Water		Low Water		MHWS	MHWN	MLWN	MLWS
0200	0800	0100	0800	5·0	3·9	1·8	0·7
1400	2000	1300	2000				
Differences BERWICK-UPON-TWEED							
–0053	–0053	–0109	–0109	–0·3	–0·1	–0·5	–0·1

SHELTER Good shelter or ⚓ except in strong E/SE winds. Yachts lie in Tweed Dock (the dock gates have been removed; 0·6m in ent, approx 1·2m inside at MLWS) or temporarily at W end of Fish Jetty (1·2m).

NAVIGATION WPT 55°45'·65N 01°58'·10W, 114°/294° from/to bkwtr lt ho, 0·58M. On-shore winds and ebb tides cause very confused state over the bar (0·6m). Access HW ±4 at sp. From HW–2 to HW+1 strong flood tide sets S across the ent; keep well up to bkwtr. The sands at the mouth of the Tweed shift so often that local knowledge is essential. The Berwick bridge (first and lowest) has about 3m clearance.

LIGHTS AND MARKS Town hall clock tr and lt ho in line at 294°. When past Crabwater Rk, keep bns at Spittal in line at 207°. Bns are B and Orange with △ top marks (both FR). Caution: The 207° ldg line may not clear the sands off Spittal Point which may encroach W'wards; best water is further W.

RADIO TELEPHONE Hr Mr VHF Ch 12 16 (HO).

TELEPHONE (Dial code 01289) Hr Mr 307404; MRSC 01333 450666; ⊜ 307547 or (01482) 782107 (H24); Marinecall 09068 500453/452; Police 307111; Dr 307484.

FACILITIES **Tweed Dock** ☎ 307404, AB £4.00, M, P, D, FW, ME, El, Sh, C (Mobile 3 ton), Slip, SM. **Town** EC Thurs; P, V, R, Bar, ✉, Ⓑ, ⇄ and ✈ (Newcastle or Edinburgh).

AGENTS WANTED If you are interested in becoming our agent for any of the following ports, please write to: The Editor, The Book Barn, Westbourne, Hampshire, PO10 8RS, England – and get your free copy of the Almanac annually. You do not have to live in a port to be the agent, but should at least be a fairly regular visitor.

Keyhaven	Lerwick
Rothesay	Malahide
Le Légué (St Brieuc)	Bénodet
River Loire/St Nazaire	L'Herbaudière
St Gilles-Croix-de-Vie	Les Sables d'Olonne
La Rochelle	La Seudre
La Gironde	Port Bloc
Anglet	St Jean-de-Luz
Dives-sur-Mer	River Seine
Le Touquet/Étaples	Nieupoort
Oostend	Stellendam & Hellevoetsluis
Nordeney	Spiekeroog

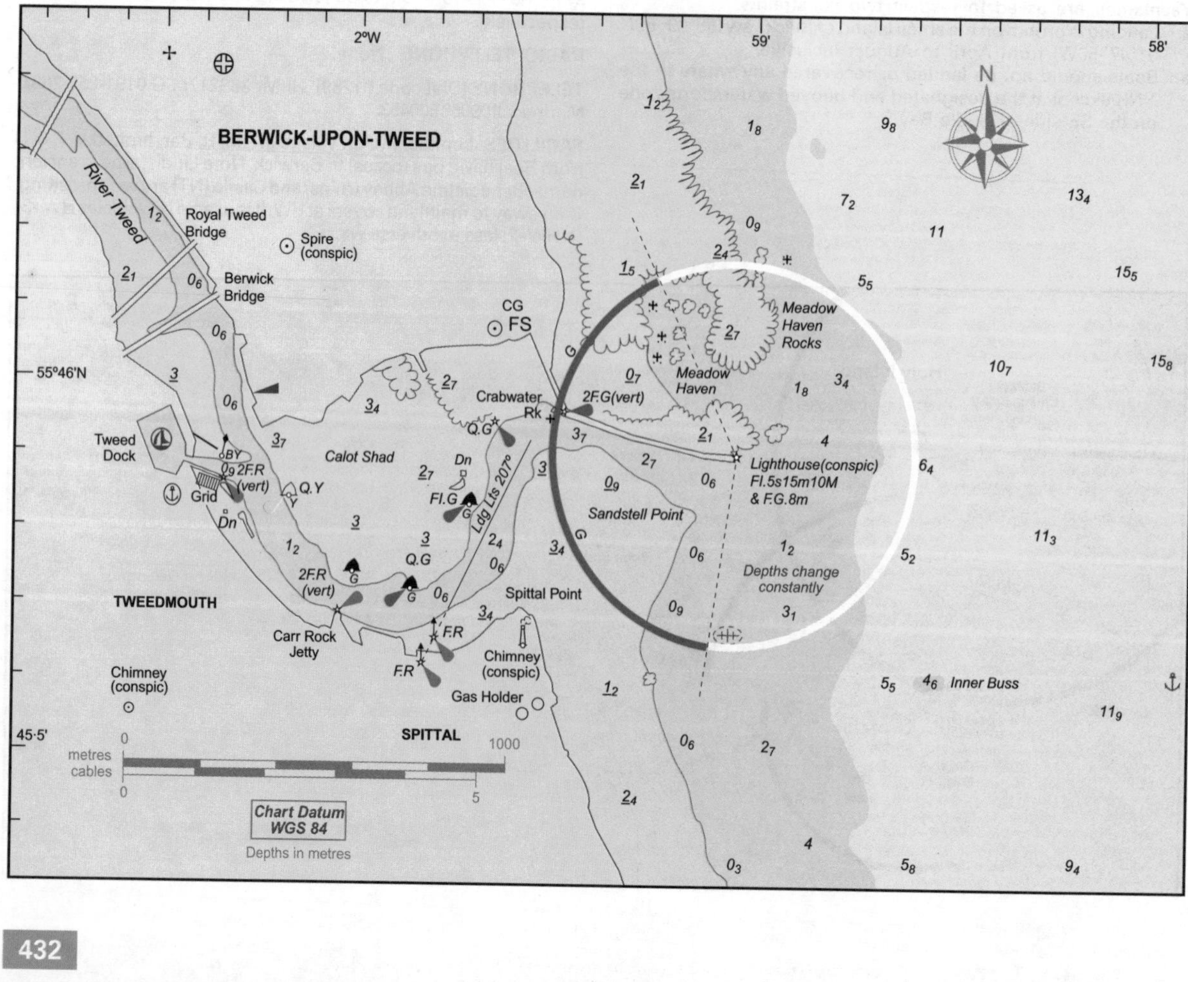

MAPTECH®
Leading the world in digital navigation
Maptech UK Ltd • +44 (0)1243 389352 • sales@maptech.co.uk

Sales and distribution centres in Area 6

Lothian: *Blue V Ltd*, Port Edgar Marina, Shore Road, South Queensferry, West Lothian EH30 9SQ.

www.maptech.co.uk

Area 6

South-East Scotland
Eyemouth to Rattray Head

9.6.1 Index .... **Page 433**
9.6.2 Area map 434
9.6.3 Tidal stream charts 436
9.6.4 Lights, buoys & waypoints 438
9.6.5 Passage information 441
9.6.6 Distance table 443
9.6.7 Eyemouth 443
Burnmouth
9.6.8 Dunbar 444
St Abbs
9.6.9 Firth of Forth, Leith, Standard Port, tidal curves 444
Inchcolm
Aberdour
Elie
St Monans
Pittenweem
Crail
Isle of May
North Berwick
Fisherrow
Cramond
9.6.10 Forth and Clyde Canal 446
9.6.11 Methil 451
Kirkcaldy
9.6.12 Anstruther 451
9.6.13 River Tay 452
Perth
St Andrews
9.6.14 Arbroath 453
9.6.15 Montrose 453
9.6.16 Stonehaven 454
Johnshaven
Gourdon
9.6.17 Aberdeen, Standard Port, tidal curves 455
9.6.18 Peterhead 459
Boddam

6

Register for your FREE weekly weather email service from Macmillan Reeds
» at www.nauticaldata.com – NOW! «
weekend weather reports sent to your email address, every Thursday

9.6.2

South-East Scotland

Eyemouth to Rattray Head

Key to Symbols

- (CGR) Coastguard Radio: VHF/MF frequencies
- (TSS) (VTS) TSS or VTS Radio: VHF frequencies
- (PR) (MR) Port or Marina Radio: VHF frequencies
- (i) See for harbour information/tidal data
- Weather information (Frequencies/times of broadcasts)
- SAR Helicopter base
- ☆ Selected Principal Lights
- Light vessel/Light float/Lanby
- ◎RG Emergency VHF DF
- * See Area Index

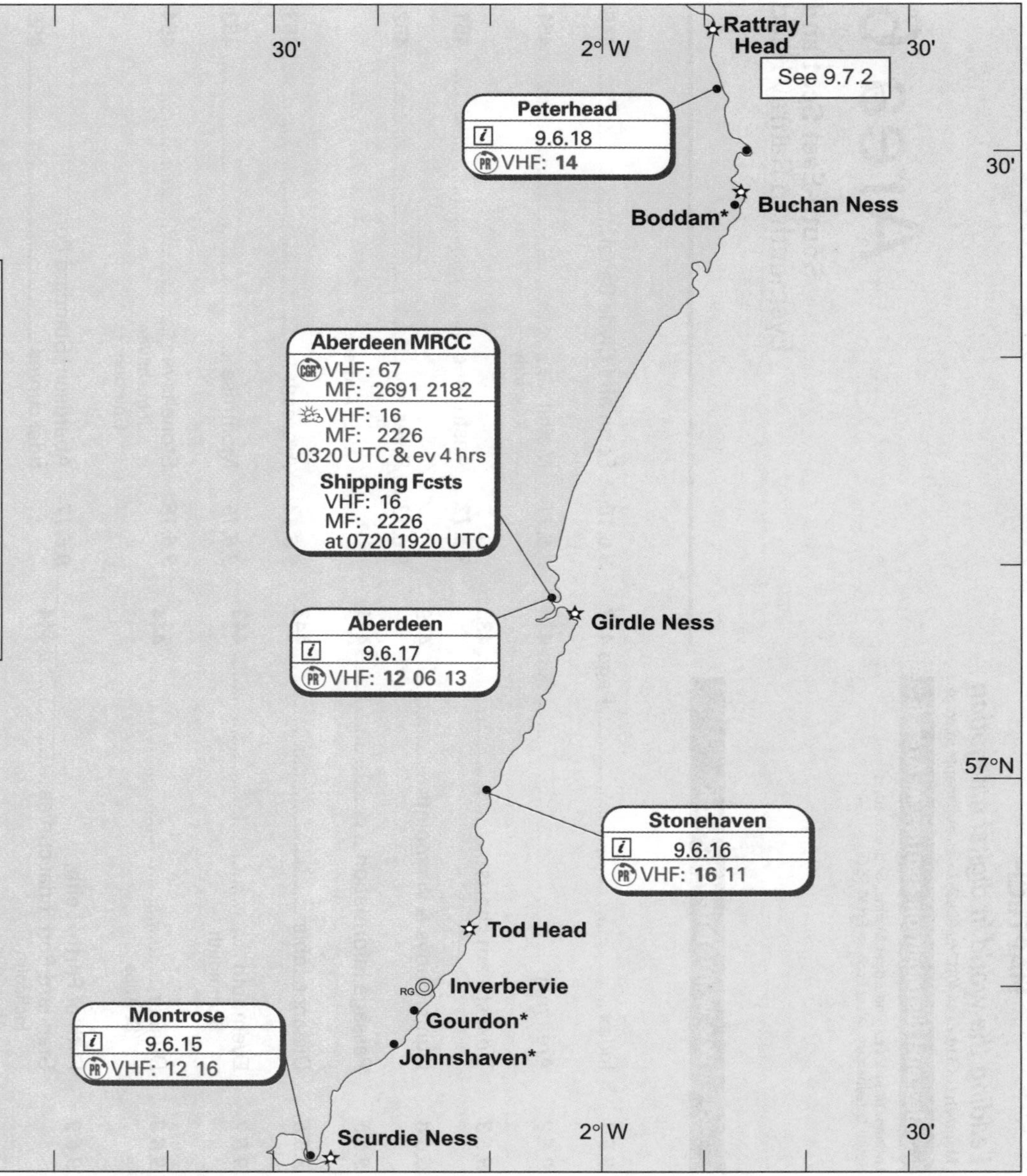
30'
3° W
30'
2° W
30'
57°N
Rattray Head
See 9.7.2
Peterhead
9.6.18
VHF: 14
Buchan Ness
Boddam*
Aberdeen MRCC
VHF: 67
MF: 2691 2182
VHF: 16
MF: 2226
0320 UTC & ev 4 hrs
Shipping Fcsts
VHF: 16
MF: 2226
at 0720 1920 UTC
Girdle Ness
Aberdeen
9.6.17
VHF: 12 06 13
Stonehaven
9.6.16
VHF: 16 11
Tod Head
Inverbervie
Gourdon*
Johnshaven*
Montrose
9.6.15
VHF: 12 16
Scurdie Ness

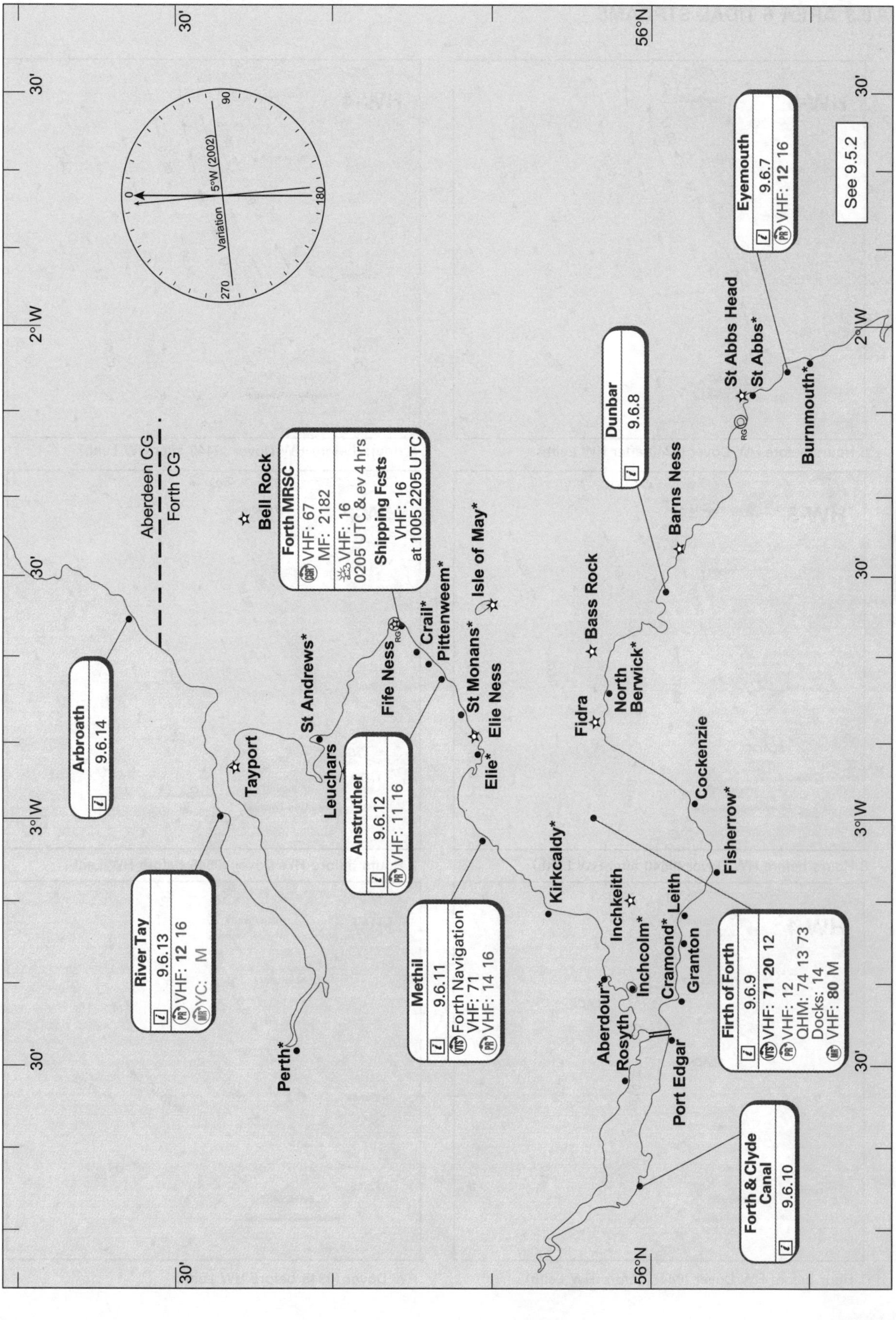
30'
2°W
3°W
56°N
Variation
5°W (2002)
0
90
180
270
Aberdeen CG
Forth CG
Bell Rock
Forth MRSC
VHF: 67
MF: 2182
VHF: 16
0205 UTC & ev 4 hrs
Shipping Fcsts
VHF: 16
at 1005 2205 UTC
Arbroath
9.6.14
River Tay
9.6.13
VHF: 12 16
YC: M
Perth*
Tayport
Leuchars
St Andrews*
Fife Ness
RG
Crail*
Pittenweem*
Isle of May*
St Monans*
Elie Ness
Elie*
Anstruther
9.6.12
VHF: 11 16
Methil
9.6.11
Forth Navigation
VHF: 71
VHF: 14 16
Kirkcaldy*
Inchkeith
Inchcolm*
Aberdour*
Rosyth
Port Edgar
Cramond*
Granton
Leith
Fisherrow*
Cockenzie
Fidra
North Berwick*
Bass Rock
Barns Ness
Dunbar
9.6.8
Firth of Forth
9.6.9
VHF: 71 20 12
VHF: 12
QHM: 74 13 73
Docks: 14
VHF: 80 M
Forth & Clyde Canal
9.6.10
St Abbs Head
St Abbs*
Burnmouth*
Eyemouth
9.6.7
VHF: 12 16
See 9.5.2

6

9.6.3 AREA 6 TIDAL STREAMS

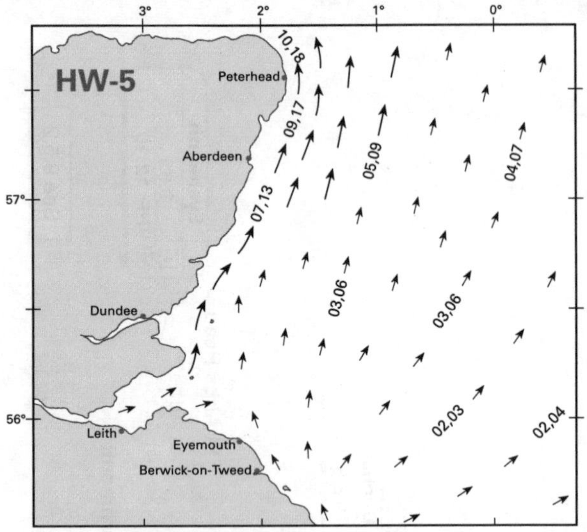

5 Hours before HW Dover (0340 after HW Leith)

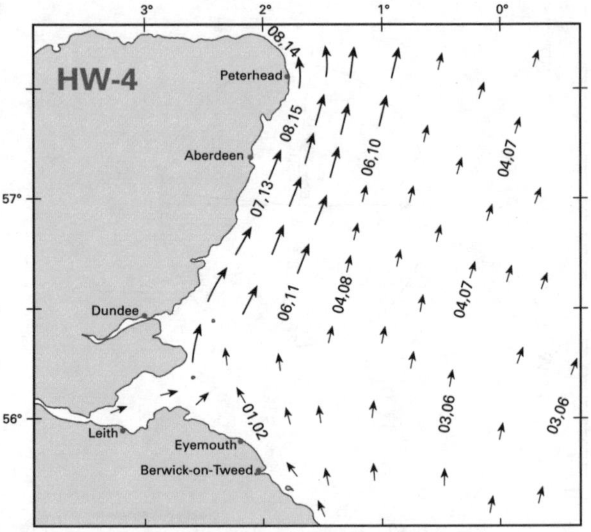

4 Hours before HW Dover (0440 after HW Leith)

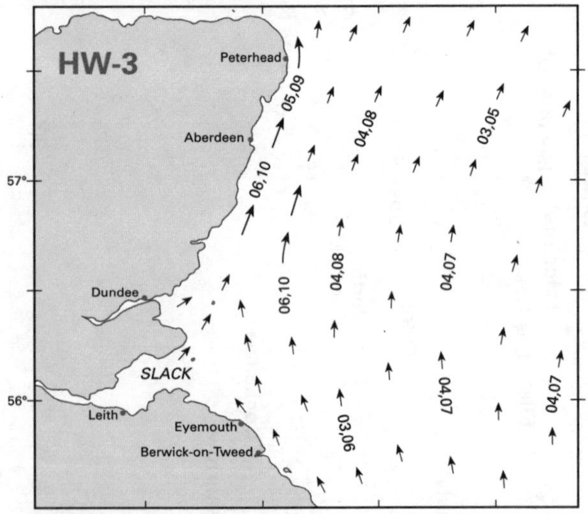

3 Hours before HW Dover (0540 after HW Leith)

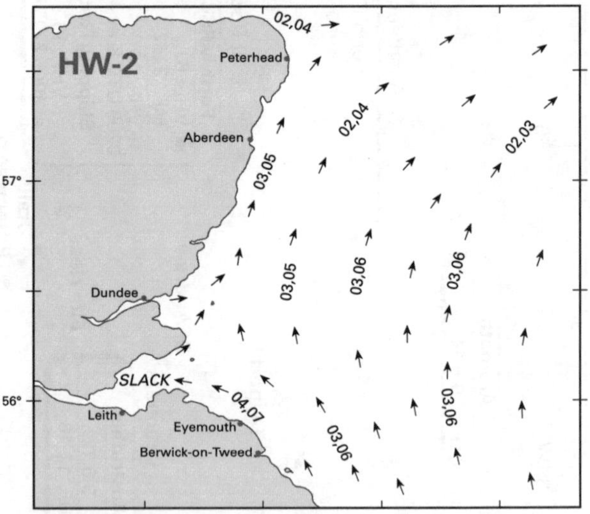

2 Hours before HW Dover (0545 before HW Leith)

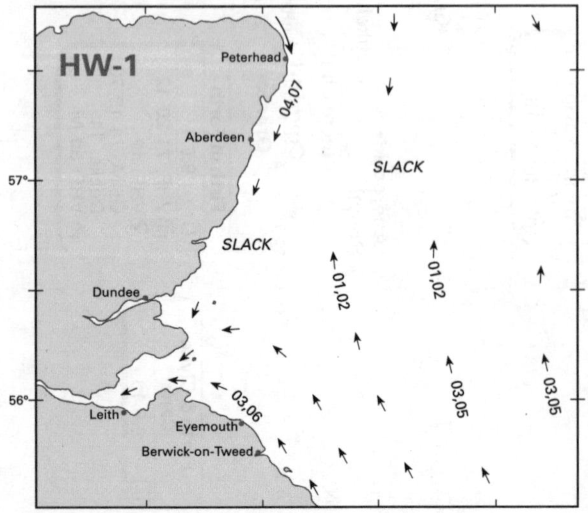

1 Hour before HW Dover (0445 before HW Leith)

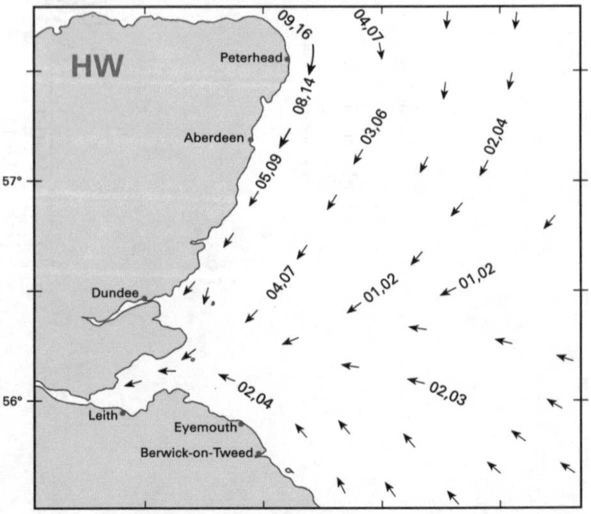

HW Dover (0345 before HW Leith)

Northward 9.7.3 Southward 9.5.3

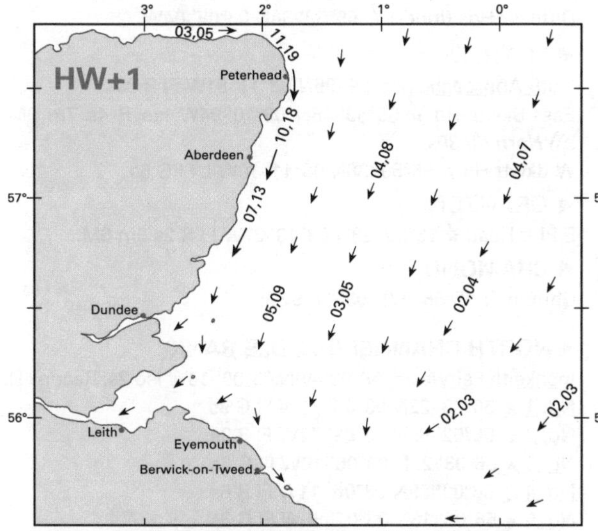

1 Hour after HW Dover (0245 before HW Leith)

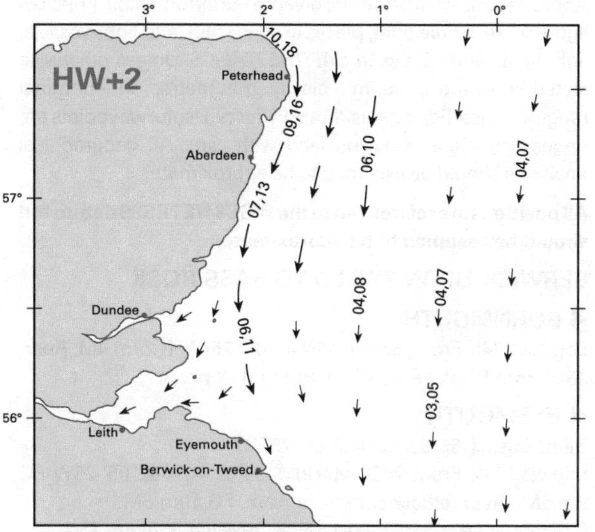

2 Hours after HW Dover (0145 before HW Leith)

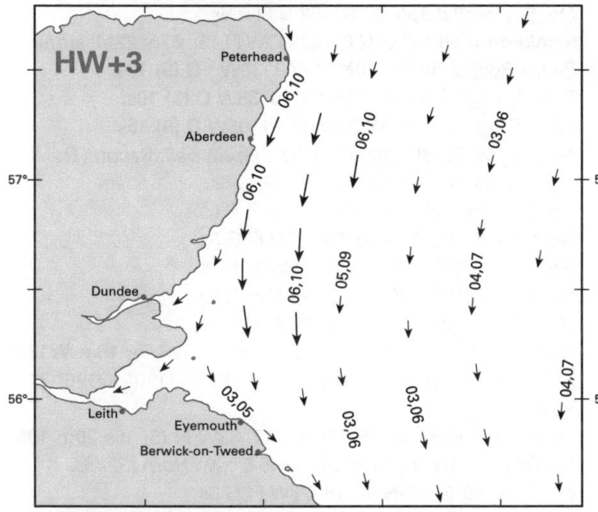

3 Hours after HW Dover (0045 before HW Leith)

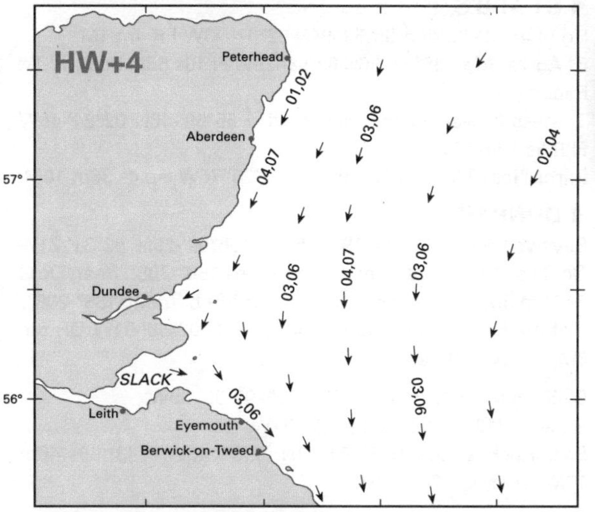

4 Hours after HW Dover (0015 after HW Leith)

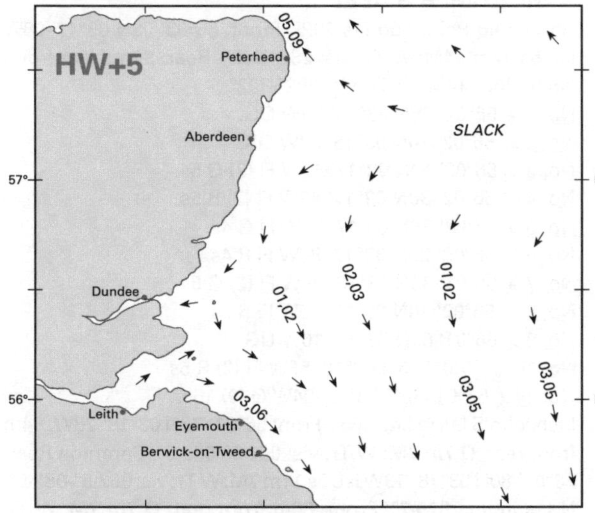

5 Hours after HW Dover (0115 after HW Leith)

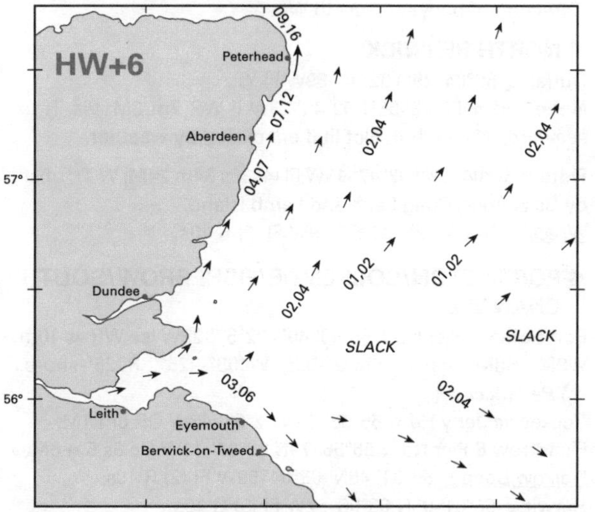

6 Hours after HW Dover (0215 after HW Leith)

9.6.4 LIGHTS, BUOYS AND WAYPOINTS

Abbreviations used below are given in the Introduction. Principal lights ☆ are in **bold** print, places in CAPITALS, and light-vessels, light floats and Lanbys in *CAPITAL ITALICS.* Unless otherwise stated lights are white. m – elevation in metres; M – nominal range in miles. Fog signals ◦))) are in *italics.* Useful waypoints are underlined – use those on land with care. All geographical positions should be assumed to be approximate.

All positions are referenced to the WGS84/ETRS89 datum but should be assumed to be approximate.

BERWICK-UPON-TWEED TO BASS ROCK

◀ BURNMOUTH

Ldg Lts 274°. Front, 55°50'·53N 02°04'·25W FR 29m 4M. Rear, 45m from front, FR 35m 4M. Both on W posts.

◀ EYEMOUTH

Blind Buss 55°52'·80N 02°05'·25E Q.
Ldg Lts 174°. Front, W Bkwtr Hd ☆, 55°52'·47N 02°05'·29W FG 9m 6M. Rear, elbow 55m from front, FG 10m 6M.
E Bkwtr Head ☆ 55°52'·50N 02°05'·29W Iso R 2s 8m 8M.

◀ ST ABB'S

Hd of inside Jetty ☆ 55°53'·94N 02°07'·73W FR 4m 1M.
St Abb's Hd ☆ 55°54'·96N 02°08'·29W Fl 10s 68m **26M**; W Tr; Racon (T).
Torness Power Station Pier Head ☆ 55°58'·40N 02°24'·45W Fl R 5s 10m 5M.
Barns Ness Tower ☆ 55°59'·22N 02°26'·76W Iso 4s 36m 10M.

◀ DUNBAR

Bayswell Hill Ldg Lts 198°. Front, 56°00'·25N 02°31'·21W Oc G 6s 15m 3M; W △ on Or col; intens 188°-208°. Rear, Oc G 6s 22m 3M; ▽ on Or col; synch with front, intens 188°-208°.
Victoria Hbr, Middle Quay ☆ 56°00'·31N 02°30'·91W QR 6m 3M; vis over hbr ent.

Bellhaven Bay Outfall 56°00'·99N 02°33'·09W.
S Carr (12) 56°03'·43N 02°37'·77W.
Bass Rock, S side, ☆ 56°04'·61N 02°38'·48W Fl (3) 20s 46m 10M; W Tr; vis: 241°-107°.

FIRTH OF FORTH AND SOUTH SHORE

(Direction of buoyage East to West)

◀ NORTH BERWICK

Outfall 56°04'·29N 02°40'·89W Fl Y.
N Pier Hd ☆ 56°03'·66N 02°43'·23W F WR 7m 3M; vis: R to seaward, W over hbr. Not lit if ent closed by weather.

Fidra ☆ 56°04'·39N 02°47'·13W Fl (4) 30s 34m **24M**; W Tr; obsc by Bass Rock, Craig Leith and Lamb Island.
Wreck 56°04'·39N 02°52'·39W Fl (2) R 10s.

◀ PORT SETON/COCKENZIE/FISHERROW/SOUTH CHANNEL

Port Seton, E Pier Hd ☆ 55°58'·40N 02°57'·23W Iso WR 4s 10m W9M, R6M; vis: R shore-105°, W105°-225°, R225°-shore; ◦))) *Bell (occas).*
Cockenzie Jetty Hd ☆ 55°58'·25N 02°58'·43W QR 6m 1M.
Fisherrow E Pier Hd ☆ 55°56'·79N 03°04'·11W Oc 6s 5m 6M.
Narrow Deep 56°01'·46N 03°04'·59W Fl (2) R 10s.
Herwit 56°01'·05N 03°06'·52W Fl (3) G 10s.
North Craig 56°01'·02N 03°03'·52W Q (3) 10s.
Craigh Waugh 56°00'·26N 03°04'·47W Q.
Diffuser Hds (Outer) 55°59'·81N 03°07'·84W.
Diffuser Hds (Inner) 55°59'·34N 03°08'·04W.

◀ LEITH

Leith Approach 55°59'·95N 03°11'·51W Fl R 3s.
East Bkwtr Hd ☆ 55°59'·48N 03°10'·94W Iso R 4s 7m 9M; ◦))) *Horn (3) 30s.*
W Bkwtr Hd ☆ 55°59'·36N 03°11'·10W L Fl G 6s.

◀ GRANTON

E Pier Head ☆ 55°59'·28N 03°13'·27W Fl R 2s 5m 6M.

◀ CRAMOND

Church Tr 55°58'·67N 03°17'·92W.

◀ NORTH CHANNEL/MIDDLE BANK

Inchkeith Fairway 56°03'·49N 03°00'·10W Iso 2s; Racon (T).
No. 1 56°03'·22N 03°03'·71W Fl G 9s.
No. 2 56°02'·89N 03°03'·72W Fl R 9s.
No. 3 56°03'·22N 03°06'·10W Fl G 6s.
No. 4 56°02'·89N 03°06'·11W Fl R 6s.
No. 5 56°03'·18N 03°07'·88W Fl G 3s.
No. 6 56°03'·05N 03°08'·44W Fl R 3s.
No. 8 56°02'·95N 03°09'·62W Fl R 9s.
Inchkeith ☆ 56°02'·01N 03°08'·17W Fl 15s 67m **22M**; stone Tr.
Pallas Rock 56°01'·50N 03°09'·30W VQ (9) 10s.
East Gunnet 56°01'·41N 03°10'·38W Q (3) 10s.
West Gunnet 56°01'·35N 03°11'·06W Q (9) 15s.
No. 7 56°02'·80N 03°10'·96W QG; ◦))) *Bell;* Racon (T).
No. 9 56°02'·32N 03°13'·48W Fl G 6s.
No. 10 56°02'·07N 03°13'·32W Fl R 6s.
No. 11 56°02'·08N 03°15'·26W Fl G 3s.
No. 12 56°01'·78N 03°15'·15W Fl R 3s.
No. 13 56°01'·77N 03°16'·94W Fl G 9s.
No. 14 56°01'·52N 03°16'·82W Fl R 9s.
Oxcars ☆ 56°01'·36N 03°16'·84W Fl (2) WR 7s 16m W13M, R12M; W Tr, R band; vis: W072°-087°, R087°-196°, W196°-313°, R313°-072°.
Inchcolm E Pt ☆ 56°01'·72N 03°17'·83W Fl (3) 15s 20m 10M; Gy Tr; part obsc by land 075°-145·5°; ◦))) *Horn (3) 45s.*
No. 15 56°01'·43N 03°18'·78W Fl G 6s.

◀ MORTIMER'S DEEP

Hawkcraig Point Ldg Lts 292°. Front, 56°03'·03N 03°17'·08W Iso 5s 12m 14M; W Tr; vis: 282°-302°. Rear, 96m from front, Iso 5s 16m 14M; W Tr; vis: 282°-302°.
No. 1 56°02'·66N 03°15'·26W QG.
No. 2 56°02'·70N 03°15'·83W QR.
No. 3 56°02'·50N 03°17'·52W Fl (2) G 5s.
No. 4 56°02'·38N 03°17'·43W Fl (2) R 5s.
No. 5 56°02'·36N 03°17'·93W Fl G 4s.
No. 6 56°02'·28N 03°17'·86W Fl R 4s.
No. 7 56°01'·93N 03°18'·99W Fl (2) G 5s.
No. 8 56°02'·10N 03°18'·25W Fl R 2s.
No. 9 56°01'·69N 03°19'·16W QG.
No. 10 56°01'·83N 03°18'·56W Fl (2) R 5s.
No. 14 56°01'·55N 03°19'·04W Q (9) 15s.
Inchcolm S Lts in line 066°. Front 56°01'·78N 03°18'·28W, 84m from rear, Q 7m 7M; W Tr; vis: 062·5°-082·5°. Common Rear, 56°01'·80N 03°18'·13W Iso 5s 11m 7M; W Tr; vis: 062·5°-082·5°. N Lts in line 076·7°. Front, 80m from rear, Q 7m 7M; W Tr; vis: 062·5°-082·5°.

◀ APPROACHES TO FORTH BRIDGES
No. 16 56°00'·87N 03°19'·60W Fl R 3s.
No. 17 56°01'·23N 03°19'·84W Fl G 3s.
No. 19 56°00'·71N 03°22'·47W Fl G 9s.
Hound Pt Terminal NE Dn ☆ 56°00'·46N 03°21'·34W 2 FR 7m 5M.
Centre Pier 56°00'·33N 03°21'·79W 2 Aero FR 47m 5M.
Hound Pt SW Dn ☆ 56°00'·28N 03°21'·92W FR 7m 5M.
Inch Garvie, NW end ☆ 56°00'·10N 03°23'·37W L Fl 5s 9m 11M.
N Queensferry ☆ Oc 5s and QR or QG tfc signals.
Forth Rail Bridge. Centres of spans have W Lts and ends of cantilevers R Lts, defining N and S chans.
Forth Road Bridge. N suspension Tr Iso G 4s 7m 6M on E and W sides; 2 Aero FR 155m 11M and 2 FR 109m 7M on same Tr. Main span, N part QG 50m 6M on E and W sides. Main span, centre Iso 4s 52m 8M on E and W sides. Main span, S part QR 50m 6M on E and W sides. S suspension Tr Iso R 4s 7m 6M on E and W sides; 2 Aero FR 155m and 2 Fr 109m 7M on same Tr.
Beamer Rk ☆ 56°00'·28N 03°24'·74W Fl 3s 6m 9M; W Tr, R top.

◀ PORT EDGAR
W Bkwtr Head ☆ 55°59'·86N 03°24'·78W Fl R 4s 4m 8M; W blockhouse; 3 QY mark floating bkwtr.
3 x 2 FR (vert) mark N ends of Marina pontoons inside hbr.

FIRTH OF FORTH – NORTH SHORE (INWARD)

◀ BURNTISLAND
W Pier Outer Hd ☆ 56°03'·22N 03°14'·26W Fl (2) R 6s 7m; W Tr.
E Pier Outer Hd ☆ 56°03'·24N 03°14'·17W Fl (2) G 6s 7m 5M.

◀ ABERDOUR/BRAEFOOT BAY/INCHCOLM
Hawkcraig Pt ☆ (see MORTIMER'S DEEP above)
Aberdour Bay Outfall Bn 56°02'·96N 03°17'·71W; Y Bn.
Braefoot Bay Terminal, W Jetty. Ldg Lts 247·25°. **Front,** 56°02'·16N 03°18'·71W Fl 3s 6m **15M;** W △ on E dolphin; vis: 237·2°-257·2°; four dolphins marked by 2 FG (vert). **Rear,** 88m from front, Fl 3s 12m **15M;** W ▽ on appr gangway; vis: 237·2°-257·2°; synch with front.
Inchcolm Abbey Tr 56°01'·81N 03°18'·11W.

◀ INVERKEITHING BAY
St David's Dir 56°01'·37N 03°22'·29W Dir 098° Fl G 5s 3m 7M; Or □, on pile.
Channel 56°01'·43N 03°23'·02W QG.
Channel 56°01'·41N 03°23'·15W QR.
Channel 56°01'·43N 03°23'·34W Fl R 3s.

◀ HM NAVAL BASE, ROSYTH
Main Chan Dir Lt 323·5°. Bn 'A' 56°01'·19N 03°25'·61W Dir Oc WRG 7m 4M; R □ on W post with R bands; vis: G318°-321°, W321°-326°, R326°-328° (H24).
Dir Lt 115°, Bn 'C' 56°00'·61N 03°24'·25W Dir Oc WRG 6s 7m 4M; W ▽ on W Bn; vis: R110°-113°, W113°-116·5°, G116·5°-120°.
Dir Lt 295°, Bn E 56°01'·30N 03°26'·91W Dir Oc 6s 11m 4M: vis: 293·5°-296·5°; (TE 1999).
No. 1 56°00'·54N 03°24'·56W Fl (2) G 10s.
Whale Bank No. 2 56°00'·70N 03°25'·19W Q (3) 10s.
No. 3 56°00'·87N 03°25'·05W Fl G 5s.
No. 4 56°00'·82N 03°25'·25W Fl R 3s.
No. 5 56°01'·08N 03°25'·89W QG.
No. 6 56°01'·01N 03°26'·00W QR.
S Arm Jetty Hd ☆ 56°01'·09N 03°26'·58W L Fl (2) WR 12s 5m W9M; R6M; vis: W010°-280°, R280°-010°.

RIVER FORTH

◀ ROSYTH TO GRANGEMOUTH
Dhu Craig 56°00'·74N 03°27'·23W Fl G 5s.
Blackness 56°01'·06N 03°30'·30W QR.
Charlestown. Lts in line. Front 56°02'·21N 03°30'·68W FG 4m 10M; Y △ on Y pile; vis: 017°-037°; marks line of HP gas main. Rear FG 6m 10M; Y ▽ on Y pile; vis: 017°-037°.
Crombie Jetty, downstream dolphin ☆ 56°01'·94N 03°31'·84W 2 FG (vert) 8m 4M.
Crombie Jetty, upstream dolphin ☆ 56°02'·00N 03°32'·12W 2 FG (vert) 8m 4M.
Tancred Bank 56°01'·58N 03°31'·91W Fl (2) R 10s.
Dods Bank 56°02'·03N 03°34'·07W Fl R 3s.
Bo'ness 56°02'·23N 03°35'·38W Fl R 10s.
Bo'ness. Carriden outfall 56°01'·33N 03°33'·71W Fl Y 5s 3M; Y □ on Y Bn.
Torry ☆ 56°02'·46N 03°35'·28W Fl G 10s 5m 7M; G ○ structure.
Bo'ness Platform 56°01'·85N 03°36'·22W 2 QR 3m 2M.

◀ GRANGEMOUTH
Grangemouth App No. 1 56°02'·12N 03°38'·10W Fl (3) R 20s 4m 6M.
Hen & Chickens 56°02'·35N 03°38'·08W Fl (3) G 20s.
No. 2 56°02'·35N 03°39'·21W Fl G 5s.
No. 3 56°02'·26N 03°39'·22W Fl R 5s 4m 6M.
No. 4 56°02'·37N 03°39'·91W Fl G 2s 4m 5M.
No. 5 56°02'·26N 03°39'·92W Fl R 2s 4m 5M.
Grangemouth W 56°02'·38N 03°40'·59W QG.
Dock entrance, E Jetty; *Horn 30s;* docking signals.
Longannet Power Station ☆ 56°02'·78N 03°40'·99W L Fl G 10s 5m 6M.
Inch Brake 56°03'·61N 03°43'·27W.

FIRTH OF FORTH – NORTH SHORE (OUTWARD)

◀ KIRKCALDY
East Pier Hd ☆ 56°06'·78N 03°08'·90W Fl WG 10s 12m 8M; vis: G156°-336°, W336°-156°.
Kirkcaldy Wreck 56°07'·27N 03°05'·32W Fl (3) G 20s.

◀ METHIL
Outer Pier Hd ☆ 56°10'·76N 03°00'·48W Oc G 6s 8m 5M; W Tr; vis: 280°-100°.

◀ ELIE
Thill Rock 56°10'·87N 02°49'·70W Fl (4) R 10s.
Elie Ness ☆ 56°11'·04N 02°48'·77W Fl 6s 15m **18M;** W Tr.

◀ ST MONANCE
Bkwtr Hd ☆ 56°12'·20N 02°45'·94W Oc WRG 6s 5m W7M, R4M, G4M; vis: G282°-355°, W355°-026°, R026°-038°.
E Pier Hd ☆ 2 FG (vert) 6m 4M; Or tripod; *Bell (occas).*
W Pier near Hd ☆ 2 FR (vert) 6m 4M.

◀ PITTENWEEM
Ldg Lts 037° Middle Pier Hd. Front, 56°12'·69N 02°43'·69W FR 4m 5M. Rear, FR 8m 5M. Both Gy Cols, Or stripes.
E Bkwtr Hd ☆ 56°12'·63N 02°43'·74W Fl (2) RG 5s 9m R9M, G6M; vis: R265°-345°, G345°-055°.
Beacon Rk ☆ 56°12'·62N 02°43'·82W QR 3m 2M.
W Pier Elbow *Horn 90s (occas).*

6

◄ ANSTRUTHER EASTER

Ldg Lts 019°. Front 56°13'·28N 02°41'·76W FG 7m 4M. Rear, 38m from front, FG 11m 4M, (both W masts).
W Pier Hd ☆ 56°13'·18N 02°41'·84W 2 FR (vert) 5m 4M; Gy mast; *Horn (3) 60s (occas).*
E Pier Hd ☆ 56°13'·14N 02°41'·83W Fl G 3s 6m 4M.

◄ MAY ISLAND

Isle of May ☆, Summit 56°11'·12N 02°33'·46W Fl (2) 15s 73m **22M**; □ Tr on stone dwelling.

◄ CRAIL

Ldg Lts 295°. Front, 56°15'·46N 02°37'·84W FR 24m 6M (not lit when hbr closed). Rear, 30m from front, FR 30m 6M.
Fife Ness ☆ 56°16'·74N 02°35'·19W Iso WR 10s 12m **W21M, R20M**; W bldg; vis: W143°-197°, R197°-217°, W217°-023°.

◄ FIFE NESS TO MONTROSE

N Carr 56°18'·05N 02°32'·94W Q (3) 10s.
Bell Rk ☆ 56°26'·05N 02°23'·07W Fl 5s 28m **18M**; Racon (M).

◄ RIVER TAY/TAYPORT/DUNDEE/PERTH

Tay Fairway 56°29'·24N 02°38'·27W L Fl 10s; *Bell.*
Middle Green (N) 56°28'·44N 02°39'·56W Fl (3) G 20s.
Middle Red (S) 56°28'·32N 02°38'·85W Fl (2) R 12s.
Abertay N 56°27'·39N 02°40'·36W Q (3) 10s; Racon (T).
Abertay S (Elbow) 56°27'·13N 02°39'·83W Fl R 6s.
Tayport High Lt Ho ☆ Dir Lt 269°, 56°27'·17N 02°53'·96W Dir Iso WRG 3s 24m **W22M, R17M, G16M**; W Tr; vis: G267°-268°, W268°-270°, R270°-271°.
Inner 56°27'·09N 02°44'·33W Fl (2) R 12s.
N Lady 56°27'·39N 02°46'·85W Fl (3) G 18s.
S Lady 56°27'·20N 02°46'·84W Fl (3) R 18s.
Pool 56°27'·14N 02°48'·54W Fl R 6s.
Tentsmuir Pt 56°26'·58N 02°49'·62W Fl Y 5s; Y ◇ on Y Bn; vis: 198°-208°; marks gas pipeline.
Monifieth 56°28'·83N 02°47'·90W Fl Y 5s; Y ◇ on Y Bn; vis: 018°-028°; marks gas pipeline.
Horse Shoe 56°27'·27N 02°50'·22W VQ (6) + L Fl 15s.
Larick Scalp 56°27'·17N 02°51'·60W Fl (2) R 12s; *Bell.*
Broughty Castle ☆ 56°27'·75N 02°52'·21W 2 FG (vert) 10m 4M; FR is shown at foot of old Lt Ho at Buddon Ness, 4M to E, and at other places on firing range when practice is taking place.
Craig 56°27'·47N 02°53'·00W QR.
Newcombe Shoal 56°27'·71N 02°53'·53W Fl R 6s.
Dundee Tidal Basin E Ent ☆ 56°27'·92N 02°56'·03W 2 FG (vert).
Middle Bank 56°27'·40N 02°56'·53W Q (3) 10s.
West Deep 56°27'·14W 02°56'·26W Fl R 3s.
Tay Road Bridge N navigation span, centre ☆ 56°27'·04N 02°56'·55W 2 x VQ 27m 4M.
Tay Road Bridge S navigation span, centre ☆ 56°27'·01N 02°56'·48W 2 x VQ 28m 4M.
Tay Railway Bridge navigation ☆ 56°26'·26N 02°59'·31W 2 x 2 F (vert) 23m.
Jock's Hole ☆ 56°21'·75N 03°12'·28W QR 8m 2M.
Cairnie Pier ☆ 56°21'·47N 03°17'·96W.
Pipeline S by Elcho Castle ☆ 56°22'·47N 03°20'·95W Iso R 4s 4m 4M.

◄ ARBROATH

Outfall 56°32'·64N 02°35'·07W Fl Y 3s.
Ldg Lts 299·2°. Front, 56°33'·29N 02°35'·16W FR 7m 5M; W col. Rear, 50m from front, FR 13m 5M; W col.
W Bkwtr E end, VQ (2) 6s 6m 4M; W post.
E Pier S Elbow ☆ 56°33'·24N 02°34'·96W Fl G 3s 8m 5M; W Tr; shows FR when hbr closed; *Siren (3) 60s* (occas).

◄ MONTROSE

Scurdie Ness ☆ 56°42'·10N 02°26'·24W Fl (3) 20s 38m **23M**; W Tr; Racon (T).
Ldg Lts 271·5°. Front 56°42'·21N 02°27'·41W, FR 11m 5M; W twin pillars, R bands. Rear, 272m from front, FR 18m 5M; W Tr, R cupola.
Scurdie Rks 56°42'·14N 02°25'·29W QR.
Annat 56°42'·23N 02°25'·95W Fl G 3s.
Annat Shoal 56°42'·37N 02°25'·19W QG.

MONTROSE TO RATTRAY HEAD

◄ JOHNSHAVEN

Ldg Lts 316°. Front, 56°47'·62N 02°20'·26W FR 5m. Rear, 85m from front, FG 20m; shows R when unsafe to enter hbr.

◄ GOURDON HARBOUR

Ldg Lts 358°. Front, 56°49'·69N 02°17'·24W FR 5m 5M; W Tr; shows G when unsafe to enter; *Siren (2) 60s* (occas). Rear, 120m from front, FR 30m 5M; W Tr.
W Pier Hd ☆ 56°49'·62N 02°17'·30W Fl WRG 3s 5m W9M, R7M, G7M; vis: G180°-344°, W344°-354°, R354°-180°.
E Bkwtr Hd ☆ 56°49'·58N 02°17'·18W Q 3m 7M.

Todhead ☆ 56°53'·00N 02°12'·97W Fl (4) 30s 41m **18M**; W Tr.

◄ STONEHAVEN

Outer Pier Hd ☆ 56°57'·59N 02°12'·00W Iso WRG 4s 7m W11M, R7M, G8M; vis: G214°-246°, W246°-268°, R268°-280°.
Girdle Ness ☆ 57°08'·34N 02°02'·91W Fl (2) 20s 56m **22M**; obsc by Greg Ness when brg more than about 020°; Racon (G).

◄ ABERDEEN

Fairway 57°09'·31N 02°01'·94W Mo (A); Racon (T).
Torry Ldg Lts 235·7°. Front, 57°08'·37N 02°04'·51W FR or G 14m 5M; R when ent safe, FG when dangerous to navigation; vis: 195°-279°. Rear, 205m from front, FR 19m 5M; W Tr; vis: 195°-279°.
S Bkwtr Hd ☆ 57°08'·69N 02°03'·34W Fl (3) R 8s 23m 7M.
N Pier Hd ☆ 57°08'·74N 02°03'·69W Oc WR 6s 11m 9M; W Tr; vis: W145°-055°, R055°-145°. In fog FY 10m (same Tr) vis: 136°-336°; *Bell (3) 12s.*
Buchan Ness ☆ 57°28'·23N 01°46'·51W Fl 5s 40m **28M**; W Tr, R bands; Racon (O).
Cruden Skares 57°23'·17N 01°50'·36W Fl R 10s; *Bell.*

◄ PETERHEAD

Kirktown Ldg Lts 314°. Front, 57°30'·22N 01°47'·21W FR 13m 8M; R mast, W △ on Or mast. Rear, 91m from front, FR 17m 8M.
S Bkwtr Hd ☆ 57°29'·79N 01°46'·54W Fl (2) R 12s 24m 7M.
N Bkwtr Hd ☆ 57°29'·84N 01°46'·32W Iso RG 6s 19m 11M; W tripod; vis: R171°-236°, G236°-171°; *Horn 30s.*
Marina N Bkwtr Hd ☆ 57°29'·81N 01°47'·49W QG 5m 2M; vis: 120°-005°.
Marina S Bkwtr Hd ☆ 57°29'·80N 01°47'·43W Fl R 4s 6m 2M.
Rattray Hd ☆ 57°36'·61N 01°49'·03W Fl (3) 30s 28m **24M**; W Tr; Racon (M); *Horn (2) 45s.*

9.6.5 PASSAGE INFORMATION

For these waters refer to the Admiralty *North Sea (West) Pilot*; R Northumberland YC's *Sailing Directions Humber to Rattray Head*, and the *Forth Yacht Clubs Association Pilot Handbook* (new edition 2000), which covers the Firth of Forth in detail.

A 'Rover Ticket', £16 from Aberdeenshire Council or Moray Council allows berthing for one week from the date of entry to the first harbour at Johnshaven, Gourdon, Stonehaven, Rosehearty, Banff, Portsoy, Portknockie, Findochty, Hopeman and Burghead.

BERWICK-UPON-TWEED TO BASS ROCK (charts 160,175) From Berwick-upon-Tweed to the Firth of Forth there is no good hbr which can be approached with safety in strong onshore winds. So, if on passage with strong winds from N or E, plan accordingly and keep well to seaward. In late spring and early summer fog (haar) is likely in onshore winds.

The coast N from Berwick is rky with cliffs rising in height to Burnmouth, then diminishing gradually to Eyemouth (9.6.7). Keep 5ca offshore to clear outlying rks. Burnmouth, although small, has more alongside space than Eyemouth, which is a crowded fishing hbr. 2M NW is St Abb's Hbr (9.6.8), with temp anch in offshore winds in Coldingham B close to the S.

St Abb's Hd (lt) is a bold, steep headland, 92m high, with no offlying dangers. The stream runs strongly round the Hd, causing turbulence with wind against tide; this can be largely avoided by keeping close inshore. The ESE-going stream begins at HW Leith –0345, and the WNW-going at HW Leith +0240. There is a good anch in Pettico Wick, on NW side of Hd, in S winds, but dangerous if the wind shifts onshore. There are no off-lying dangers between St Abb's Hd and Fast Castle Hd, 3M WNW. Between Fast Castle Hd and Barns Ness, about 8M NW, is the attractive little hbr of Cove; but it dries and should only be approached in ideal conditions.

Torness Power Station (conspic; lt on bkwtr) is 1·75M SE of Barns Ness (lt) which lies 2·5M ESE of Dunbar (9.6.8) and is fringed with rks; tidal streams as for St Abb's Hd. Conspic chys are 7½ca WSW inland of Barns Ness. Between here and Dunbar keep at least 2½ca offshore to clear rky patches. Sicar Rk (7·9m depth) lies about 1·25M ENE of Dunbar, and sea breaks on it in onshore gales.

The direct course from Dunbar to Bass Rk (lt) is clear of all dangers; inshore of this line beware Wildfire Rks (dry) on NW side of Bellhaven B. In offshore winds there is anch in Scoughall Road. Great Carr is ledge of rks, nearly covering at HW, 1M ESE of Gin Hd, with Carr bn (stone tr surmounted by cross) at its N end. Drying ledges of rks extend 1M SE of Great Carr, up to 3ca offshore. Keep at least 5ca off Carr bn in strong onshore winds. Tantallon Castle (ruins) is on cliff edge 1M W of Great Car. Bass Rk (lt) lies 1·25M NNE of Gin Hd, and is a sheer, conspic rk (115m) with no offlying dangers; landing difficult due to swell.

FIRTH OF FORTH, SOUTH SHORE (chart 734, 735) Westward of Bass Rk, Craigleith (51m), Lamb Is (24m) and Fidra (31m) lie 5ca or more offshore, while the coast is generally foul. Craigleith is steep-to, and temporary anchorage can be found on SE and SW sides; if passing inshore of it keep well to N side of chan. N Berwick hbr (dries) lies S of Craigleith, but is unsafe in onshore winds. Between Craigleith and Lamb Is, beware drying rks up to 3ca from land. Lamb Is is 1·5M WNW of N Berwick (9.6.9) and has a rky ledge extending 2½ca SW. Fidra Is (lt) is a bird reserve, nearly connected to the shore by rky ledges, and should be passed to the N; passage and anch on S side are tricky. Anchor on E or W sides, depending on wind, in good weather.

In the B between Fidra and Edinburgh some shelter can be found in SE winds in Aberlady B and Gosford B. The best anch is SW of Craigielaw Pt. Port Seton is a drying fishing hbr 7½ca E of the conspic chys of Cockenzie Power Station; the E side of the hbr can be entered HW ±3, but not advisable in strong onshore wind or sea. Cockenzie (dries) is close to power station; beware Corsik Rk 400m to E. Access HW ±2·5, but no attractions except boatyard. For Fisherrow, see 9.6.9.

There are no dangers on the direct course from Fidra to Inchkeith (lt), which stands between the buoyed deep water chans. Rks extend 7½ca SE from Inchkeith, and 5ca off the W side where there is a small hbr below the lt ho; landing is forbidden without permission. N Craig and Craig Waugh (least depth $\underline{0}$·2m) are buoyed shoals 2·5M SE from Inchkeith lt ho. For Cramond and Inchcolm, see 9.6.9.

In N Chan, close to Inchkeith the W-going (flood) stream begins about HW Leith –0530, and the E-going at HW Leith +0030, sp rates about 1kn. The streams gather strength towards the Forth bridges, where they reach 2·25kn and there may be turbulence.

Leith is wholly commercial; Granton has yacht moorings in the E hbr; Port Edgar (9.6.9) is a major yacht hbr close W of Forth road bridge. Hound Point oil terminal is an artificial 'island-jetty' almost in mid-stream, connected to the shore by underwater pipeline (no ⚓). Yachts may pass the terminal on either side at least 30m off and well clear of tankers berthing.

6

RIVER FORTH TO KINCARDINE (charts 736, 737, 738) The main shipping chan under the N span of the rail bridge is busy with commercial traffic for Grangemouth and warships to/from Rosyth dockyard. In the latter case a Protected Chan may be activated; see 9.6.9 for details. W of Beamer Rk the Firth widens as far as Bo'ness (small drying hbr) on the S shore where the chan narrows between drying mudbanks. Charlestown (N bank) dries, but is a secure hbr. Grangemouth is industrially conspic. Caution: gas carriers, tankers, cargo vessels; no yacht facilities. Few yachts go beyond Kincardine swing bridge, clearance 9m, which is no longer opened.

FIRTH OF FORTH, NORTH SHORE (charts 734, 190) From Burntisland the N shore of Firth of Forth leads E to Kinghorn Ness. 1M SSW of Kinghorn Ness Blae Rk (SHM lt buoy) has least depth of 4·1m, and seas break on it in E gales. Rost Bank lies halfway between Kinghorn Ness and Inchkeith, with tide rips at sp tides or in strong winds.

From Kinghorn Ness to Kirkcaldy, drying rks lie up to 3ca offshore. Kirkcaldy hbr (9.6.11) is effectively closed, but yachts can enter inner dock near HW by arrangement; ent is dangerous in strong E'lies, when seas break a long way out.

Between Kirkcaldy and Methil (9.6.11) the only dangers more than 2ca offshore are The Rockheads, extending 4ca SE of Dysart, and marked by 2 SHM buoys. Largo B is anch, well sheltered from N and E, but avoid gaspipes near E side. Close SW of Elie, beware W Vows (dries) and E Vows (dries, bn). There is anch close W of Elie Ness (9.6.9). Ox Rk (dries $\underline{2}$m) lies 5ca ENE of Elie Ness, and 2½ca offshore; otherwise there are no dangers more than 2ca offshore past St Monance, Pittenweem (9.6.9) and Anstruther (9.6.13), but in bad weather the sea breaks on Shield Rk 4ca off Pittenweem. From Anstruther to Crail (9.6.9) and on to Fife Ness keep 3ca offshore to clear Caiplie Rk and other dangers.

May Island (lt) (9.6.9) lies about 5M S of Fife Ness; its shores are bold except at NW end where rks extend 1ca off. Anch near N end at E or W Tarbert, on lee side according to winds; in good weather it is possible to land. It ho boats use Kirkhaven, close SE of lt ho

FIFE NESS TO MONTROSE (chart 190) Fife Ness is fringed by rky ledges, and a reef extends 1M NE to N Carr Rk (dries $\underline{1}$·4m, marked by bn). In strong onshore winds keep to seaward of N Carr ECM lt buoy. From here keep 5ca offshore to clear dangers entering St Andrews B, where there is anch; the little hbr (9.6.14) dries, and should not be approached in onshore winds.

Northward from Firth of Forth to Rattray Hd the coast is mostly rky and steep-to, and there are no out-lying dangers within 2M of the coast except those off R. Tay and Bell Rk. But in an onshore blow there are few safe havens; both yachts and crews need to be prepared for offshore cruising rather than coast-crawling.

R. Tay (9.6.13 and chart 1481) is approached from the NE via Fairway buoy; it is dangerous to cut corners from the S. The Bar, NE of Abertay lt buoy, is dangerous in heavy weather, particularly in strong onshore wind or swell. Abertay Sands extend nearly 4M E of Tentsmuir Pt on S side of chan (buoyed); Elbow is a shoal extension eastward. Gaa Sands running 1·75M E from Buddon Ness, are marked by Abertay lt buoy (Racon) on N side of chan. Passage across Abertay and Gaa Sands is very dangerous. The estuary is shallow, with many shifting sandbanks; Tayport is a good passage stop and best yacht hbr (dries) in the Tay. S of Buddon Ness the W-going (flood) stream begins about HW Aberdeen −0400, and the E-going at about HW Aberdeen +0230, sp rates 2kn.

Bell Rk (lt, Racon) lies about 11·5M E of Buddon Ness. 2M E of Bell Rk the S-going stream begins HW Aberdeen −0220, and the N-going at HW Aberdeen +0405, sp rates 1kn. W of Bell Rk the streams begin earlier.

N from Buddon Ness the coast is sandy. 1·25M SW of Arbroath (9.6.14) beware Elliot Horses, rky patches with depth 1·9m, which extend about 5ca offshore. Between Whiting Ness and Scurdie Ness, 9·5M NNE, the coast is clear of out-lying dangers, but is mostly fringed with drying rks up to 1ca off. In offshore winds there is temp anch in SW of Lunan B, off Ethie Haven.

Scurdie Ness (lt, Racon) is conspic on S side of ent to Montrose (9.6.15). Scurdie Rks (dry) extend 2ca E of the Ness. On N side of chan Annat Bank dries up to about 5ca E of the shore, opposite Scurdie Ness (chart 1438). The in-going stream begins at HW Aberdeen −0500, and the outgoing at HW Aberdeen +0115; both streams are very strong, up to 7kn at sp, and there is turbulence off the ent on the ebb. The ent is dangerous in strong onshore winds, with breaking seas extending to Scurdie Ness on the ebb. In marginal conditions the last quarter of the flood is best time to enter.

MONTROSE TO ABERDEEN (chart 210) N from Montrose the coast is sandy for 5M to Milton Ness, where there is anch on S side in N winds. Johnshaven (9.6.16), 2M NE, is a small hbr (dries) with tight entrance, which should not be approached with onshore wind or swell. 5ca NE, off Brotherton Cas, drying rks extend 4ca offshore. Gourdon (9.6.16) has a small hbr (mostly dries) approached on ldg line between rky ledges; inner hbr has storm gates. Outside the hbr rks extend both sides of entrance, and the sea breaks heavily in strong E winds. Keep a sharp lookout for lobster pot dan buoys between Montrose and Stonehaven.

North to Inverbervie the coast is fringed with rky ledges up to 2ca offshore. Just N of Todhead Pt (lt) is Catterline, a small B which forms a natural anch in W winds, but open to E. Downie Pt, SE of Stonehaven (9.6.16) should be rounded 1ca off. The Bay is encumbered by rky ledges up to 2ca from shore and exposed to the E; anch 6ca E of Bay Hotel or berth afloat in outer hbr.

From Garron Pt to Girdle Ness the coast is mostly steep-to. Fishing nets may be met off headlands during fishing season. Craigmaroinn and Seal Craig (dry) are parts of reef 3ca offshore SE of Portlethen, a fishing village with landing sheltered by rks. Cove B has a very small fishing hbr, off which there is anch in good weather; Mutton Rk (dries $\underline{2}$·1m) lie 1½ca offshore. From Cove to Girdle Ness keep 5ca offshore, avoiding Hasman Rks (dries $\underline{3}$·4m) 1ca off Altens .

Greg Ness and Girdle Ness (lt, RC, Racon), at SE corner of Aberdeen B (9.6.17), are fringed by rks. Girdlestone is a rky patch, depth less than 2m, 2ca ENE of lt ho. A drying patch lies 2ca SE of lt ho. Off Girdle Ness the S-going stream begins at HW Aberdeen −0430, and the N-going at HW Aberdeen +0130, sp rates 2·5kn. A race forms on S-going stream.

ABERDEEN TO RATTRAY HEAD (chart 213) From Aberdeen there are few offshore dangers to Buchan Ness. R. Ythan, 1·75M SSW of Hackley Hd, is navigable by small craft, but chan shifts constantly. 3M North is the very small hbr of Collieston (mostly dries), only accessible in fine weather. 4·75M NNE of Hackley Head lie The Skares, rks (marked by PHM lt buoy) extending 3½ca from S point of Cruden B, where there is anch in offshore winds. On N side of Cruden B is Port Erroll (dries $\underline{2}$·5m).

Buchan Ness (lt, fog sig, Racon) is a rky peninsula. 2ca N is Meikle Mackie islet, close W of which is the small hbr of Boddam (dries) (9.6.18). 3ca NE of Meikle Mackie is The Skerry, a rk 6m high on S side of Sandford B; rks on which the sea breaks extend 2ca NNE. The chan between The Skerry and the coast is foul with rks and not advised. Peterhead (9.6.18) is easy to enter in almost all conditions and is an excellent passage port with marina at SW corner of the Bay.

Rattray Hd (with lt, fog sig on The Ron, rk 2ca E of Hd) has rky foreshore, drying for 2ca off. Rattray Briggs is a detached reef, depth 0·2m, 2ca E of lt ho. Rattray Hard is a rky patch, depth 10·7m, 1·5M ENE of lt ho, which raises a dangerous sea during onshore gales. Off Rattray Hd the S-going stream begins at HW Aberdeen −0420, and the N-going at HW Aberdeen +0110, sp rates 3kn. In normal conditions keep about 1M E of Rattray Hd, but pass 5M off in bad weather, preferably at slack water. Conspic radio masts with R lts lie 2·5M WNW and 2·2M W of lt ho.

For notes on offshore oil/gas installations, see 9.5.5.

NORTH SEA PASSAGE For distances across the N Sea, see 9.0.8.

FORTH TO NORWAY AND BALTIC (charts 2182B, 2182C) Heading ENE'ly from the Firth of Forth the main hazards result from offshore industrial activities and their associated traffic. In summer particularly, oil/gas exploration, movement of drilling rigs, pipe laying etc create situations which could endanger other vessels. Rig movements and many of the more intense activities are published in Notices to Mariners, but even so it is wise to avoid the gas and oil fields where possible and never to approach within 500m of installations (see 9.5.5). There are TSS to be avoided off the S and SW coast of Norway. Strong currents and steep seas may be experienced in the approaches to the Skagerrak.

9.6.6 DISTANCE TABLE

Approximate distances in nautical miles are by the most direct route, whilst avoiding dangers and allowing for Traffic Separation Schemes. Places in italics are in adjoining areas; places in **bold** are in 9.0.8, Distances across the North Sea.

1.	*Great Yarmouth*	**1**																			
2.	***Berwick-on-Tweed***	232	**2**																		
3.	Eyemouth	240	10	**3**																	
4.	Dunbar	257	26	17	**4**																
5.	North Berwick	266	35	25	9	**5**															
6.	Granton	285	54	44	27	19	**6**														
7.	**Port Edgar**	290	58	50	34	26	7	**7**													
8.	Burntisland	283	53	43	26	18	5	8	**8**												
9.	Methil	276	45	36	20	13	14	20	12	**9**											
10.	Anstruther	269	38	29	14	10	23	29	22	11	**10**										
11.	Fife Ness	269	38	29	17	14	28	34	27	16	5	**11**									
12.	Bell Rock	276	43	36	27	25	40	47	39	28	17	12	**12**								
13.	**Dundee**	289	58	49	37	34	48	54	47	36	25	20	20	**13**							
14.	Arbroath	284	51	44	34	31	45	51	44	33	22	17	10	15	**14**						
15.	Montrose	291	59	51	43	41	55	61	54	43	32	27	17	27	12	**15**					
16.	Stonehaven	300	72	66	60	58	72	78	71	60	49	44	32	45	30	20	**16**				
17.	**Aberdeen**	308	82	78	73	70	84	90	83	72	61	56	44	57	42	32	13	**17**			
18.	Peterhead	318	105	98	93	95	106	108	105	94	83	78	68	80	64	54	35	25	**18**		
19.	***Fraserburgh***	334	121	114	109	108	122	128	121	110	99	94	83	96	79	68	51	39	16	**19**	
20.	***Wick***	391	178	171	166	165	179	185	178	167	156	151	140	153	136	125	108	96	72	57	**20**

EYEMOUTH *9.6.7*

Borders **55°52'·52N 02°05'·29W** ❀❀◊◊✿✿✿

CHARTS AC 1612, 160; Imray C24; OS 67

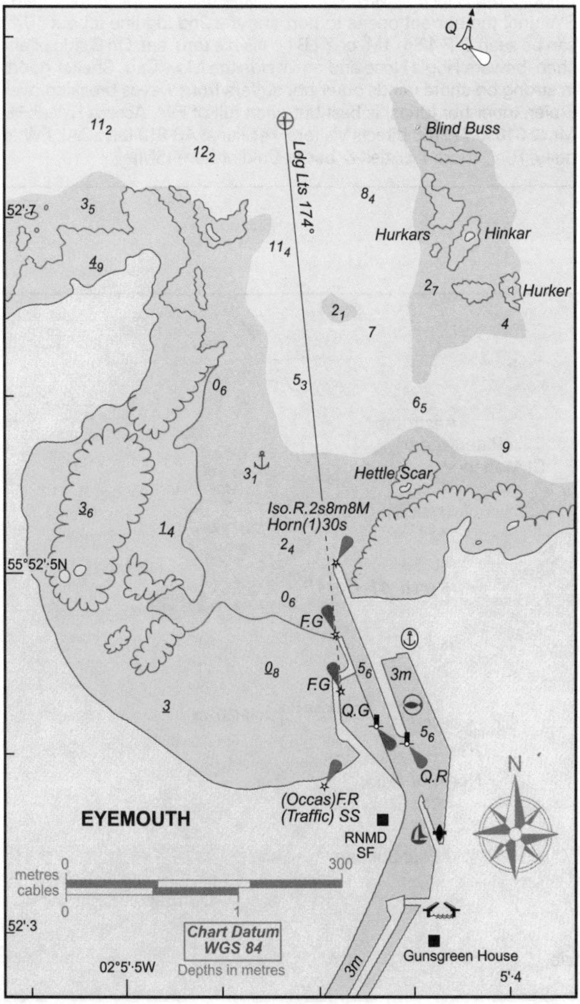

TIDES +0330 Dover; ML No data; Duration 0610; Zone 0 (UT)

Standard Port LEITH (⟶)

Times				**Height (metres)**			
High Water		Low Water		MHWS	MHWN	MLWN	MLWS
0300	0900	0300	0900	5·6	4·4	2·0	0·8
1500	2100	1500	2100				
Differences EYEMOUTH							
–0015	–0025	–0014	–0004	–0·9	–0·8	No data	

SHELTER Good in all weathers, though uncomfortable surge in N over F5, and entry should not be attempted in strong N to E winds. Caution, the entrance is 17m wide. Busy FV hbr which encourages yachtsman to visit. Berth as directed by HM, either (a) on the W wall of the N-pointing jetty by the LB; or (b) on the W wall of the centre jetty W of Gunsgreen House (conspic); or (c), for boats with draught >1·6m, at the NE corner of the FV basin. ⚓ in bay only in offshore winds. F.R (occas) lt indicates unsafe tp enter bay or hbr.

NAVIGATION WPT 55°52'·76N 02°05'·34W, 354°/174° from/to E bkwtr lt, 2½ca. Appr can be made N or S of Hurkars; from the N, beware Blind Buss 1·2m, marked by NCM buoy, Q 55°52'·79N 02°05'·14W, about 200m ENE of WPT. From the S, approach on 250° midway between Hurkars and Hettle Scar; there are no ldg marks, hbr ent is dredged to 3·0m.

LIGHTS AND MARKS St. Abbs Hd lt ho Fl 10s 68m 26M is 3M NW. Ldg lts 174° both FG 9/10m 6M, orange columns on W pier. ● or R flag = unsafe to enter.

RADIO TELEPHONE VHF Ch 16 12 (HO).

TELEPHONE (Dial code 01890) Hr Mr 750223, Mobile 07885 742505; MRSC (01333) 450666; ⊜ (0141) 887 9369 (H24); Marinecall 09068 500452; Police 750217; Dr 750599, Ⓗ (0131) 536 1000.

FACILITIES Hbr AB £9.00 (all LOA), FW, D (see Hr Mr for 25 ltr cans or larger quantities by delivery), P (cans), Slip, BY, ME, Sh, El, C (12 ton mobile), Ⓔ. Showers at Gunsgreen House and RNMDSF.

Town LB, P, CH, V, R, Bar, ✉, Ⓑ, Gas, Gaz, Ⓑ, ⇌ (bus to Berwick-on-Tweed and Edinburgh), ✈ (Edinburgh).

ADJACENT HARBOUR

BURNMOUTH, Borders, **55°50'·61N 02°04'·10W**. AC 160. HW +0315 on Dover, –0025 on Leith; Duration 0615. Use Eyemouth tides 9.6.7. From S beware Quarry Shoal Rks; and E & W Carrs from N. 2 W posts (FR 29/35m 4M) 45m apart, lead 253° to close N of the hbr; as hbr mouth opens, enter on about 185° with outer hbr ent in line with 2FG (vert). Min depth at ent at LWS is 0·6m. Shelter is good especially in inner hbr (dries). With on-shore winds, swell makes outer hbr uncomfortable. Hr Mr (018907) 81283 (home); also via Gull's Nest (bar at top of valley) 81306. Facilities: AB £5 (all LOA), FW, limited V.

6

DUNBAR *9.6.8*

East Lothian **56°00′·39N 02°31′·09W** ❁❁❁⛵⛵✿✿✿

CHARTS AC 734, 175; Imray C23, C27; OS 67

TIDES +0330 Dover; ML 3·0; Duration 0600; Zone 0 (UT)

Standard Port LEITH (⟶)

Times				Height (metres)			
High Water		Low Water		MHWS	MHWN	MLWN	MLWS
0300	0900	0300	0900	5·6	4·4	2·0	0·8
1500	2100	1500	2100				
Differences DUNBAR							
−0005	−0010	+0010	+0017	−0·4	−0·3	−0·1	−0·1
FIDRA							
−0001	0000	−0002	+0001	−0·2	−0·2	0·0	0·0

SHELTER Outer (Victoria) Hbr is subject to surge in strong NW to NE winds. N side dries; berth on S quay and contact Hr Mr. Keep steps clear. Inner (Old or Cromwell) Hbr dries, but is safe except in strong onshore winds near HWS when swell enters: entry is through a bridge, lifted on request to Hr Mr. New (2000) Hbr Trust plans improvements.

NAVIGATION WPT 56°00′·70N 02°30′·89W, 018°/198° from/to front ldg lt 198°, 0·50M. Beware Outer Bush Rk (0·6m), 4ca to E. Ent is unsafe in heavy on-shore swell. Min depth at ent 0·9m. Keep to port on entry to avoid rockfall off castle.

LIGHTS AND MARKS Church and Castle ruin both conspic. From NE, ldg lts, Oc G 6s 15/22m 3M, synch, intens 188°-208°, 2 W △ on Or cols, lead 198° through the outer rks to the Roads; thence narrow ent opens with QR brg 132°. From NW, appr on brg 132° between bns on Wallaces Head and Half Ebb Rk.

RADIO TELEPHONE None.

TELEPHONE (Dial code 01368) Hr Mr 863206; MRSC (01333) 450666; ⊖ (0141) 887 9369 (H24); Police 862718; Dr 863704; Ⓗ (0131) 536 1000.

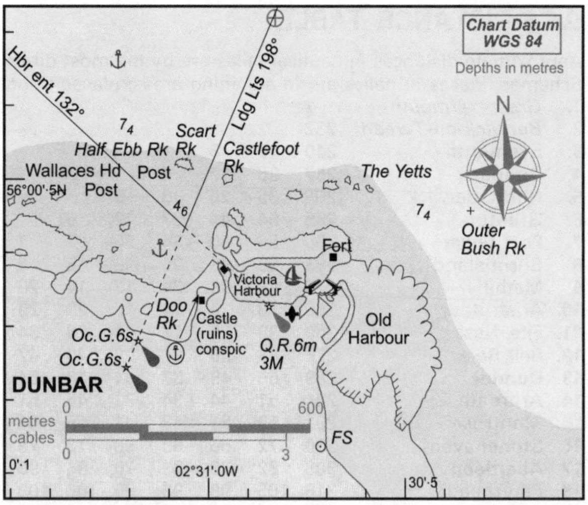

FACILITIES **Quay** AB £8 first night £5 thereafter (all LOA), Slip, FW, D (delivery), P (cans); **N Wall** M, AB; **Inner Hbr** Slip, AB; **Services** ME, Gas, Gaz. **Town** EC Wed; LB, P, ▣, V, R, Bar, ✉, Ⓑ, ⇌, ✈ Edinburgh.

ADJACENT HARBOUR

ST ABBS, Borders, **55°54′·10N 02°07′·74W**. AC 175. HW +0330 on Dover, −0017 on Leith; HW −0·6m on Leith; Duration 0605. Ldg line (about 228°) S face of Maw Carr on village hall (conspic R roof) leads SW until the hbr ent opens to port and the 2nd ldg line (about 167°) can be seen 2FR 4/8m 1M, or Y LB ho visible thru' ent. On E side of ent chan, beware Hog's Nose and on W side the Maw Carr. Shelter good. In strong on-shore winds outer hbr suffers from waves breaking over E pier. Inner hbr (dries) is best but often full of FVs. Access HW±3. Hr Mr ☎ 01890 771708 directs visitors. Facilities: AB £10 (all LOA), FW at quay, R, V, more facilities & bar at Coldingham (5M).

FIRTH OF FORTH *9.6.9*

E and W Lothian/City of Edinburgh/Fife

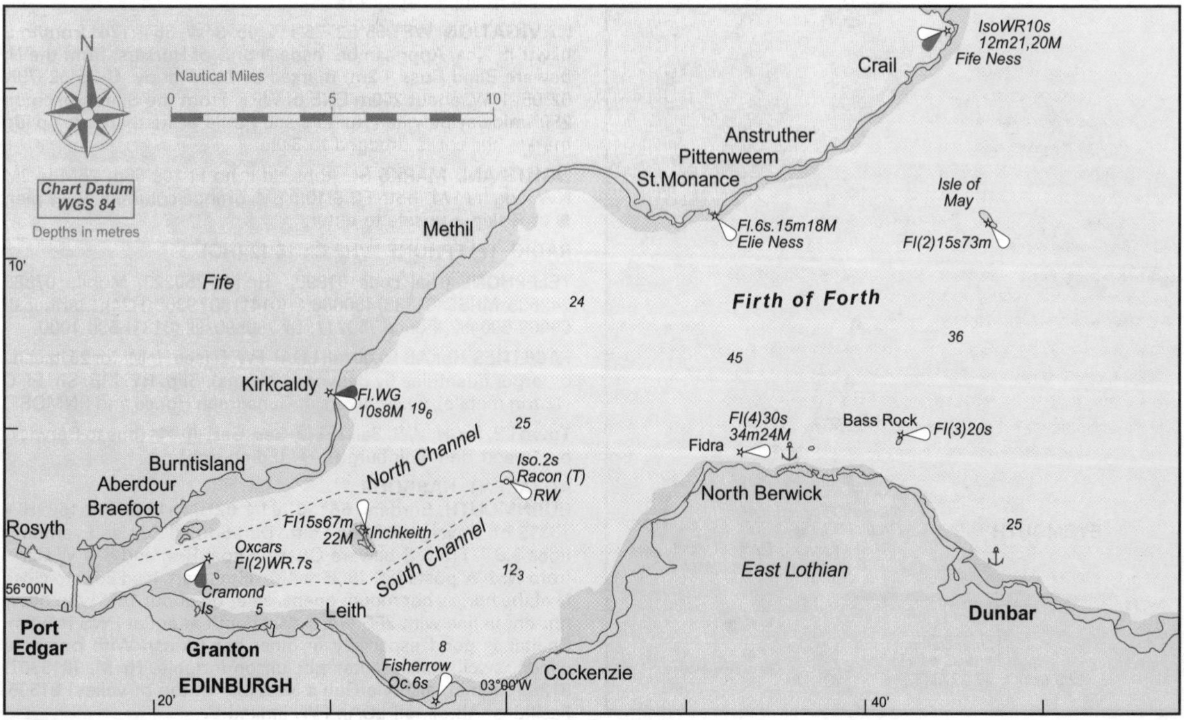

FIRTH OF FORTH *continued*

CHARTS AC 734, 735, 736; Imray C23, C27; OS 66, 59

TIDES +0350 (Granton) Dover; ML 3·3; Duration 0620; Zone 0 (UT)

Standard Port LEITH (⟶)

Times				Height (metres)			
High Water		Low Water		MHWS	MHWN	MLWN	MLWS
0300	0900	0300	0900	5·6	4·4	2·0	0·8
1500	2100	1500	2100				
Differences COCKENZIE							
–0007	–0015	–0013	–0005	–0·2	0·0	No data	
GRANTON: Same as LEITH							
GRANGEMOUTH							
+0025	+0010	–0052	–0015	–0·1	–0·2	–0·3	–0·3
KINCARDINE							
+0015	+0030	–0030	–0030	0·0	–0·2	–0·5	–0·3
ALLOA							
+0040	+0040	+0025	+0025	–0·2	–0·5	No data	–0·7
STIRLING							
+0100	+0100	No data		–2·9	–3·1	–2·3	–0·7

SHELTER Granton mostly dries but is open to violent swell in N'lies. There are pontoons on E side of Middle pier in about 2m. There are very few visitors' berths. Pilot boats berth at seaward end. W hbr is mainly commercial and for FVs. Port Edgar marina offers good shelter, except for a surge at LW esp in E winds, but prone to silting. Caution: strong tidal streams. Do not enter E of wavebreak; 3kn speed limit. Leith is wholly commercial. Rosyth Dockyard should only be used in emergency. Note: Forth Ports plc controls the Firth of Forth, Granton Hbr and all commercial impounded docks.

NAVIGATION WPT Granton 56°00'·00N 03°13'·31W, 000°/180° from/to ent, 0·72M. WPT Port Edgar 56°N 03°24'·3W, 064°/244° from/to Dir Lt, Fl R 4s, on W bkwtr, 3ca. Beware Hound Pt terminal; Forth railway and road bridges; vessels bound to/from Rosyth. On N shore, no vessel may enter Mortimer's Deep (Braefoot gas terminal) without prior approval from Forth Navigation Service. 12kn speed limit W of Forth Rly Bridge. A Protected Chan runs from Nos 13 & 14 buoys (NNW of Oxcars) under the bridges (N of Inch Garvie and Beamer Rk), to Rosyth. When activated (occas) via Forth Ports plc, other vessels must clear the chan for Rosyth traffic.

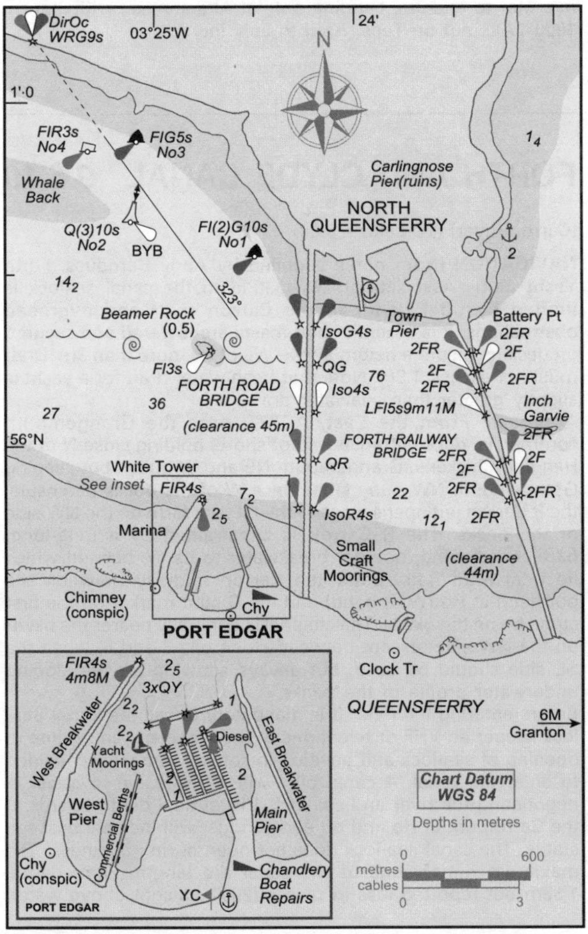

LIGHTS AND MARKS Granton: R flag with W diagonal cross (or ● lt) on signal mast at middle pier hd = Entry prohib. Port Edgar: On W pier Dir lt Fl R 4s 4m 8M 244°; 3 QY lts mark floating bkwtr; 3 x 2 FR (vert) mark N ends of marina pontoons.

RADIO TELEPHONE Call *Forth Navigation* (at Leith) Ch **71** (calling and short messages, H24) 16; **20** 12 will be requested if necessary. Traffic, nav and weather info available on request. Leith Hbr Radio Ch 12. Granton marina, call *Boswell* Ch M. Port Edgar Marina Ch M **80** (Apl-Sept 0900-1930; Oct-Mar 0900-1630 LT). Rosyth Dockyard, call *QHM* Ch 74 13 73 (Mon-Fri: 0730-1700). Grangemouth Docks Ch 14 (H24).

TELEPHONE (Dial code 0131) Forth Navigation Service 554 6473; QHM Rosyth (01383) 425050; MRSC (01333) 450666; ⊜ (0141) 887 9369 (H24); Weather (0141) 248 3451; Marinecall 09068 500452; Police (S. Queensferry) 331 1798; ⊞ Edinburgh Royal Infirmary 229-2477; Flag Officer Scotland/Northern Ireland (01436) 674321 ext 3206, for Naval activities off N and E Scotland; Forth Yacht Clubs Ass'n 552 3452.

FACILITIES

GRANTON Extensive development of the W hbr is proposed. Hr Mr via Leith, ☎ 555 8866, Access HW±3½, FW, Slip; **Royal Forth YC** ☎ 552 3006, 🖷 552 8560, Slip, M, L, FW, C (5 ton), D, El, Bar; **Forth Corinthian YC** ☎ 552 5939, Slip, M, L, Bar; **Services:** Gas, Gaz, Sh, CH, ME. **Town** D, P, V, R, Bar, ✉, Ⓑ, ⇌, ✈ (Buses to Edinburgh).

SOUTH QUEENSFERRY

Port Edgar Marina (300+8 visitors) ☎ 331 3330, 🖷 331 4878, £1.30, Access H24, M, Slip, AC, CH, D, C (5 ton) on N end of main pier, El, Ⓔ, ME, Sh, SM, Gas, Gaz, FW, R; Port Edgar YC, Bar. **Town** EC Wed; P, V, R, Bar, ✉, Ⓑ, ⇌ (Dalmeny), ✈ Edinburgh.

EDINBURGH: ACA.

GRANGEMOUTH: Hr Mr ☎ 01324 498566 (H24); Port Office ☎ 498597 (HO). VHF Ch 14 16. Commercial port.

Continued overleaf

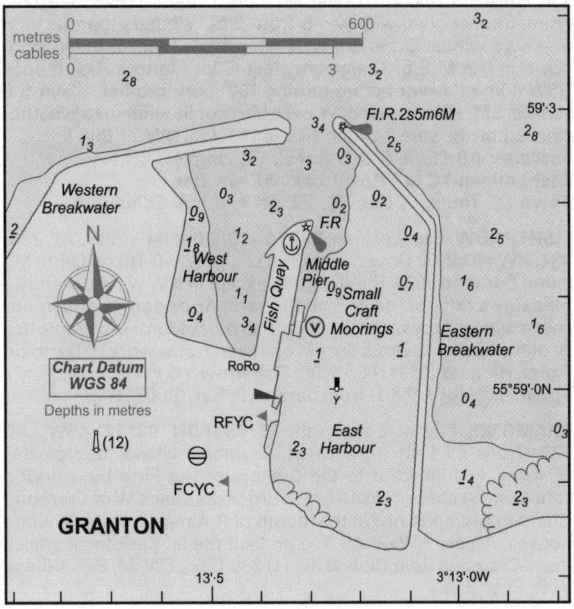

HARBOURS AND ANCHORAGES ON THE NORTH SHORE OF THE FIRTH OF FORTH

INCHCOLM, Fife, **56°01′·85N 03°17′·89W**. AC 736. Tides see 9.6.8. Best ⚓ in 4m, N of abbey (conspic); appr from NW or ESE, to land at pier close E (small fee). Meadulse Rks (dry) on N side. Ends of island foul. At SE end, lt Fl (3) 15s, obsc 075°-145°, horn (3) 45s. No facilities. ☎ 0131-244 3101. Keep clear of large ships under way in Mortimer's Deep.

ABERDOUR, Fife, **56°03′·00N 03°17′·49W**. AC 735, 736. HW +0345 on Dover; +0005 on Leith; HW 0·5m on Leith; ML 3·3m; Duration 0630. See 9.6.8. Good shelter except in SE winds when a swell occurs. The ⚓ between The Little Craigs and the disused pier is good but exposed to winds from E to SW. Temp berths £2 are available in hbr (dries) alongside the quay wall. Beware Little Craigs (dries 2·2m) and outfall 2ca N marked by bn. There are no lts/ marks. Hr Mr ☎ (01383) 860452. Facilities: FW (tap on pier), P, R, V, Bar in village, EC Wed; **Aberdour BC** ☎ (01592) 202827.

KIRKCALDY: See 9.6.11
METHIL: See 9.6.11

ELIE, Fife, **56°11′·20N 02°49′·29W**. AC 734. HW +0325 on Dover, –0015 on Leith; HW –0·1m on Leith; ML 3·0m; Duration 0620; Elie B provides good shelter from N winds for small craft but local knowledge is needed. Hbr dries; 3 short term waiting buoys available. Beware ledge off end of pier which dries. From E beware Ox Rk (dries 1m) 5M ENE of Elie Ness; from W beware rks off Chapel Ness, W Vows, E Vows (surmounted by cage bn) and Thill Rk, marked by PHM Fl(4)R.10s buoy. Lt: Elie Ness Fl 6s 15m 18M, W tr. Hr Mr (01333) 330502; AB (3) drying £5, M, AC, FW, CH, SC, Slip. Police 310333. Dr ☎ 330302; **Services:** P & D (tanker), Gas, Gaz. El. In Elie & Earlsferry: R, V, Bar, ✉, Ⓑ.

ST MONANS, Fife, **56°12′·25 N 02°45′·94W**. AC 734. HW +0335 on Dover, –0020 on Leith; HW –0·1m on Leith; ML 3·0m; Duration 0620. Shelter good except in strong SE to SW winds when scend occurs in the hbr (dries). Berth alongside E pier until contact with Hr Mr. From NE keep at least 2½ca from coast. Bkwtr hd Oc WRG 6s 5m 7/4M; E pier hd 2 FG (vert) 6m 4M. W pier hd 2 FR (vert) 6m 4M. Facilities: Hr Mr ☎ (01333) 730428; AB £5.10, FW, AC, El; **Services:** Gas, P & D (tanker), AC. **Village** R, Bar, V, ✉, Ⓑ.

PITTENWEEM, Fife, **56°12′·60N 02°43′·79W**. AC 734. HW +0325 Dover; –0015 and –0·1m on Leith; ML 3m. Duration 0620. Busy fishing hbr, dredged 1-2m, access all tides, but not in onshore winds. Yachts not encouraged; contact Hr Mr for berth at W end of inner hbr, but only for emergency use. Outer hbr dries to rock; is only suitable for temp stop in calm weather. Appr 037° on ldg marks/lts, Gy cols/Y stripe, both FR 3/8m 5M. Rks to port marked by bn, QR 3m 2M, and 3 unlit bns. E bkwtr lt Fl (2) RG 5s 9m 9/6M, R265°-345°, G345°-055°. No VHF. Hr Mr ☎ (01333) 312591. Facilities: FW, CH, D & P (tanker), Gas, V, Bar.

ANSTRUTHER: See 9.6.12

CRAIL, Fife, **56°15′·35N 02°37′·29W**. AC 175. HW +0320 on Dover, –0020 on Leith; HW –0·2m on Leith; ML 3·0m; Duration 0615. Good shelter but only for boats able to take the ground alongside. Appr between S pier and bn on rks to S following ldg line 295°, two W concrete pillars with FR lts, 24/30m 6M. Turn 150° to stbd for ent. Call Forth CG on VHF Ch 16 before entering. Hr Mr ☎ (01333) 450820. Facilities: AB £5.10, El, FW, AC, Slip, P. **Village** EC Wed; Bar, R, V, ✉, Ⓑ.

ISLE OF MAY, Fife, **56°11′·40N 02°33′·69W**. AC 734. HW +0325 on Dover, –0025 on Leith. In settled weather only, and depending on the wind, ⚓ at E or W Tarbert in 4m; landing at Altarstanes. Near the SE tip there is a tiny hbr at Kirkhaven, with narrow, rky ent; yachts can moor fore-and-aft to rings in rks, in about 1-1·5m. SDs are needed. Beware Norman Rk to N of Island, and Maiden Hair Rk to S. At the summit, a □ tr on stone ho, Fl (2) 15s 73m 22M. The island is a bird sanctuary, owned by Scottish Natural Heritage ☎ (01334) 654038. Avoid the breeding season, mid-Mar to end Jul. Landing only at Altarstanes or Kirkhaven, 1000-1700; not on Tues, April to July inc.

HARBOURS AND ANCHORAGES ON THE SOUTH SHORE OF THE FIRTH OF FORTH

NORTH BERWICK, East Lothian, **56°03′·74N 02°43′·04W**. AC 734. Fidra HW +0344 on Dover; ML 3·0m; Duration 0625. See 9.6.8 Fidra. Shelter good with winds from S to W but dangerous with on-shore winds. Ent is 8m wide. Hbr dries. From E or W, from position 0·25M S of Craigleith, steer S for Plattock Rks, thence SSW 40m off bkwtr before turning 180° port into hbr. Bkwtr lt F WR 7m 3M, R to seaward, W over hbr; not lit when bad weather closes hbr. Beware Maiden Rks (bn) 100m NW of this lt.
Facilities: AB £5.70, P & D (cans), FW on pier, CH;
East Lothian YC ☎ (01620) 2698, M, ⚓s, Bar.
Town EC Thurs; V, Gas, Ⓑ, ✉, ⇌ and bus Edinburgh.

FISHERROW, East Lothian, **55°56′·79N 03°04′·09W**. AC 735, 734. HW +0345 on Dover, –0005 on Leith; HW –0·1m on Leith; ML 3·0m; Duration 0620. Shelter good except in NW winds. Mainly a pleasure craft hbr, dries 5ca offshore. Appr dangerous in on-shore winds. Access HW±2. High-rise block (38m) is conspic 9ca W of hbr. E pier lt, Oc 6s 5m 6M on metal framework tr. Berth on E pier. Hr Mr ☎ (0131) 665 5900; **Fisherrow YC** FW.
Town EC Wed; V, P & D from garage, R, Bar, Ⓑ, ✉, SM.

CRAMOND, City of Edinburgh, **55°59′·80N 03°17′·49W**. AC 736. Tides as Leith (see 9.6.9). Cramond Island, approx 1M offshore, is connected to the S shore of the Firth by a drying causeway. A chan, marked by 7 SHM posts, leads W of Cramond Island to Cramond hbr at the mouth of R Almond, conspic white houses. Access HW±2; AB free or ⚓ off the Is. Seek local advice from: **Cramond Boat Club** ☎ (0131) 336 1356, FW, M, Bar. **Village** V, R, Pub, Bus.

FORTH AND CLYDE CANAL *9.6.10*

(Carron River) (TC Leith + 0.30).

NAVIGATION (from notes supplied by Andy Carnduss, Forth Yacht Clubs Association). Navigation to the canal sealock is limited by tidal depth in the Carron river and overhead obstructions. It is essential that masts are lowered and secured on deck to ensure a height above WL of no more than 3m. Draft must not exceed 1.8m. Note that fresh water draft for a yacht is slightly greater than seawater draft.
Approach: From the East, AC737, pass the Grangemouth commercial dock entrance well offshore, holding close N of the Hen and Chickens, Grangemouth NE and W buoys but keeping Grangemouth NW buoy stbd. Once W of the docks peninsula, the R Carron ent opens close to the oil tank farm on the NW side of the docks. The R Carron is constrained by a mile-long, partially covering, boulder breakwater to its W, beyond which lie tidal mud flats. Enter the Carron midway between the porthand Lt Ho (W, R band) and the G stbd marker on the first stone bn on the bkwtr. The channel is generally nearer the bkwtr on the NW side, except between stone bns 3 and 6, when the SE side should be used, but always allowing for the sloping underwater profile of the banks.
Before entering the river, it is mandatory to call the Canal Sea-lock keeper on VHF or telephone to request canal entry time of opening of sea-lock and position in convoy of boats scheduled to enter the canal. A canal pilot will be available to assist in negotiating the river and sea-lock. Visual tidal depth boards at the Carron ent Lt Ho and on each bridge, will indicate passage status. The canal sea-lock does not open during darkness. The maximum dimensions of the canal are length, 20m; depth, 1.83m but reported less in places (2001); height above water,

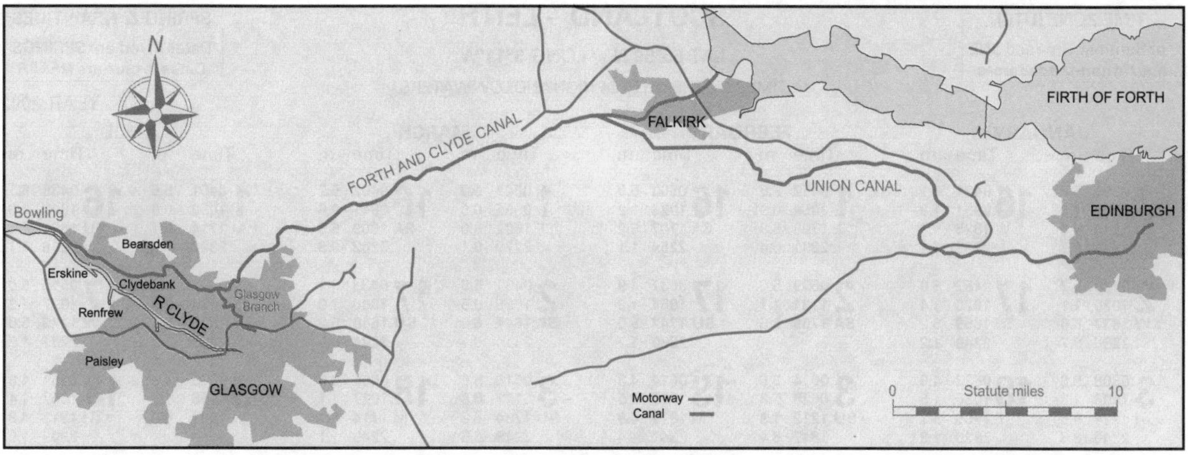

3.0m; width, 6.35m. The depth will be increased progressively by dredging out the silt to 2.3m; all structures have been built to these dimensions. Note that four fixed bridges cross the river Carron between the Firth of Forth and the canal sea-lock. The lowest is the concrete arched Glensburgh bridge on the A905, which has an underheight of 7.24m above CD. The first bridge is 2.3M and the sea-lock is 2.75M upstream from the MLWOST line at the Forth. The Carron can flow at over 6kn on the ebb, more if heavy rain has recently fallen. The Carron estuary dries at low water springs, the banks are soft mud, steep enough to cause a stranded vessel to founder. The flat bed is hard gravel reportedly safe to dry out a bilge keeler in emergency. This canal entry must only be commenced with the agreement of the canal Sealock Keeper, in a vessel well engined and with mast stowed on deck.

Return transit to the open Firth requires similar caution.

There are 38 locks on the 35 mile long canal. To make passage in two days it is necessary to attain the summit pound above lock 20 in the first day.

Rigging service with cranage is available at Port Edgar and Bowling but British Waterways hope to establish a pontoon in the Carron estuary where small yachts may moor while lowering their own mast. Fuel is available at Bowling dock, Port Edgar and from petrol stations along the route.

The Grangemouth Yacht Club have their pontoons at the original entrance basin to the canal, downstream of the bridges. The soft bottom is deeply gouged but temporary berthing may be available. Anchoring is not recommended but yachts must have an anchor prepared on deck available for immediate deployment in emergency. Mooring is available in the canal.

For information on the W entrance at Bowling, see 9.9.20.

Navigation should also be available in 2001 via the Falkirk Wheel and Union Canal to Edinburgh (draft max 1.06m; height, 2.74m; beam, 3.8m; length, 21m, limited by tight bends) where a basin is planned to open late 2002. Contact British Waterways, Lowland Canals Office at 1 Applecross St., Glasgow G4 9SP, or ☎ 0141 332 6936, or www.britishwaterways.com for Skippers' Guide, detailed maps, prices and information. See also www.scottishcanals.co.uk

6

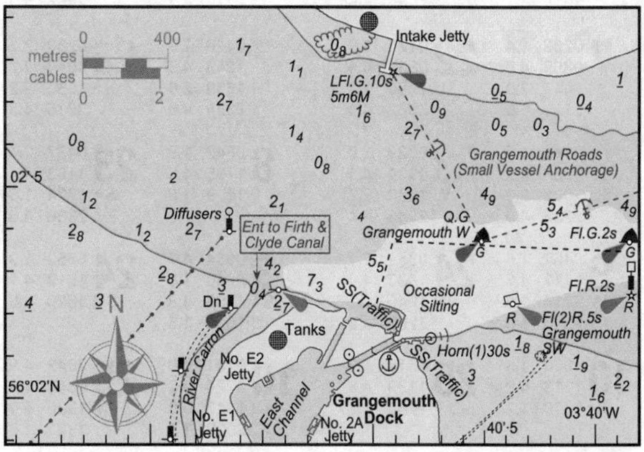

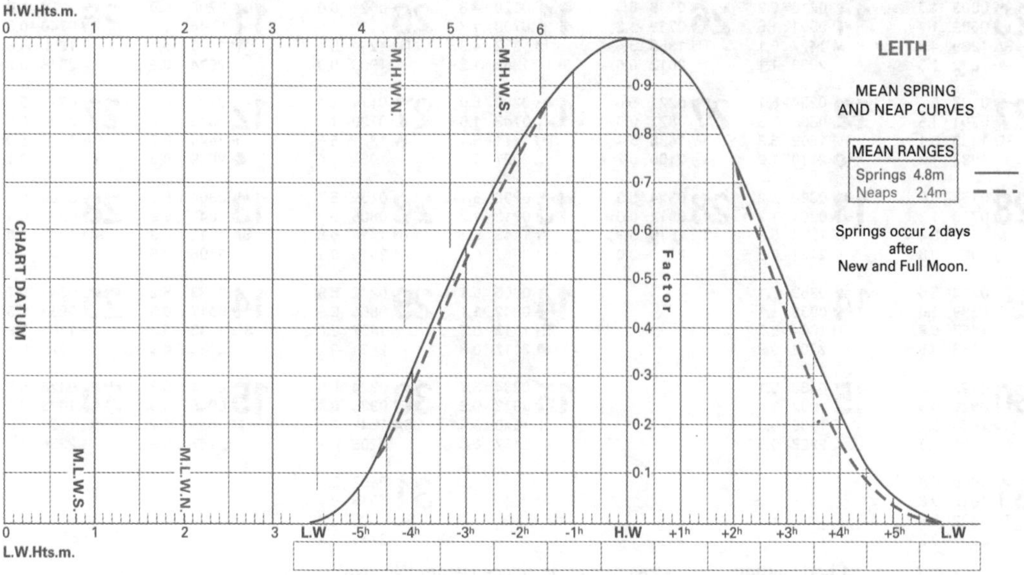

TIME ZONE (UTC)
For Summer Time add ONE hour in **non-shaded areas**

SCOTLAND – LEITH

LAT 55°59′N LONG 3°11′W

TIMES AND HEIGHTS OF HIGH AND LOW WATERS

SPRING & NEAP TIDES
Dates in red are **SPRINGS**
Dates in blue are **NEAPS**

YEAR **2002**

JANUARY

Date	Time	m	Time	m	Time	m	Time	m
1 TU	0335	5.6	0932	1.1	1554	5.6	2208	0.7
2 W	0420	5.7	1020	1.1	1637	5.6	2256	0.7
3 TH	0508	5.6	1106	1.3	1724	5.5	2345	0.8
4 F	0558	5.4	1152	1.5	1815	5.4		
5 SA	0035	0.9	0651	5.2	1241	1.7	1911	5.2
6 SU	0130	1.2	0752	4.9	1337	1.9	2018	5.1
7 M	0233	1.4	0859	4.8	1447	2.0	2128	5.0
8 TU	0346	1.5	1006	4.7	1603	2.0	2235	4.9
9 W	0457	1.6	1112	4.8	1714	1.9	2340	5.0
10 TH	0600	1.5	1213	4.9	1819	1.7		
11 F	0040	5.1	0651	1.5	1307	5.0	1915	1.4
12 SA	0134	5.2	0735	1.4	1354	5.2	2004	1.2
13 SU	0222	5.2	0814	1.4	1435	5.3	● 2046	1.1
14 M	0304	5.2	0849	1.3	1514	5.3	2124	1.0
15 TU	0344	5.2	0921	1.3	1550	5.3	2155	1.0
16 W	0421	5.1	0951	1.3	1625	5.3	2222	1.1
17 TH	0457	5.0	1020	1.4	1659	5.2	2249	1.2
18 F	0533	4.9	1050	1.5	1735	5.1	2320	1.3
19 SA	0611	4.8	1123	1.6	1815	4.9	2355	1.5
20 SU	0653	4.6	1200	1.8	1858	4.7		
21 M	0035	1.7	0739	4.5	1245	2.1	1946	4.6
22 TU	0125	1.9	0831	4.4	1350	2.3	2042	4.4
23 W	0229	2.0	0931	4.3	1520	2.3	2148	4.4
24 TH	0352	2.1	1035	4.4	1645	2.2	2257	4.5
25 F	0510	1.9	1139	4.6	1748	1.9		
26 SA	0003	4.7	0609	1.7	1239	4.8	1842	1.6
27 SU	0102	5.0	0701	1.5	1330	5.1	1933	1.2
28 M	0153	5.3	0750	1.2	1415	5.4	○ 2023	0.8
29 TU	0238	5.6	0839	1.0	1457	5.6	2113	0.5
30 W	0322	5.8	0926	0.9	1539	5.7	2201	0.3
31 TH	0406	5.8	1012	0.8	1622	5.8	2247	0.2

FEBRUARY

Date	Time	m	Time	m	Time	m	Time	m
1 F	0452	5.8	1054	0.9	1708	5.8	2331	0.4
2 SA	0539	5.6	1134	1.1	1755	5.6		
3 SU	0014	0.6	0628	5.3	1212	1.3	1847	5.4
4 M	0058	1.0	0722	5.0	1254	1.6	1948	5.1
5 TU	0148	1.4	0824	4.7	1354	1.9	2058	4.8
6 W	0259	1.8	0932	4.5	1526	2.1	2210	4.7
7 TH	0426	1.9	1043	4.5	1659	2.0	2324	4.6
8 F	0542	1.9	1155	4.6	1819	1.8		
9 SA	0034	4.7	0640	1.8	1258	4.8	1918	1.5
10 SU	0131	4.9	0724	1.7	1347	5.0	2003	1.3
11 M	0216	5.0	0801	1.5	1427	5.1	2039	1.1
12 TU	0254	5.1	0833	1.3	1502	5.3	● 2110	1.0
13 W	0328	5.2	0904	1.2	1534	5.3	2137	0.9
14 TH	0359	5.1	0933	1.1	1604	5.3	2202	0.9
15 F	0430	5.1	1002	1.1	1635	5.3	2228	0.9
16 SA	0503	5.0	1029	1.2	1707	5.2	2254	1.1
17 SU	0537	4.9	1054	1.3	1742	5.0	2320	1.2
18 M	0614	4.8	1118	1.5	1819	4.9	2347	1.4
19 TU	0655	4.6	1147	1.7	1901	4.7		
20 W	0022	1.7	0741	4.4	1232	2.0	1950	4.5
21 TH	0114	2.0	0838	4.3	1347	2.2	2056	4.3
22 F	0239	2.2	0948	4.2	1555	2.2	2216	4.3
23 SA	0437	2.1	1103	4.4	1724	1.9	2336	4.5
24 SU	0552	1.9	1212	4.7	1826	1.5		
25 M	0042	4.9	0648	1.5	1309	5.0	1921	1.0
26 TU	0136	5.3	0739	1.2	1355	5.4	2012	0.6
27 W	0221	5.6	0827	0.9	1438	5.7	○ 2100	0.2
28 TH	0304	5.9	0912	0.6	1519	5.9	2146	0.0

MARCH

Date	Time	m	Time	m	Time	m	Time	m
1 F	0347	5.9	0955	0.5	1602	6.0	2229	-0.1
2 SA	0431	5.8	1035	0.6	1647	6.0	2310	0.1
3 SU	0516	5.6	1111	0.8	1734	5.8	2348	0.5
4 M	0603	5.3	1144	1.1	1825	5.4		
5 TU	0024	1.0	0652	4.9	1220	1.4	1923	5.0
6 W	0105	1.5	0750	4.6	1315	1.8	2032	4.7
7 TH	0211	2.0	0859	4.4	1459	2.1	2147	4.4
8 F	0358	2.2	1014	4.3	1656	2.0	2308	4.4
9 SA	0525	2.2	1135	4.4	1819	1.7		
10 SU	0025	4.6	0627	2.0	1243	4.6	1912	1.5
11 M	0120	4.8	0709	1.7	1332	4.9	1951	1.2
12 TU	0202	5.0	0743	1.5	1411	5.1	2021	1.1
13 W	0236	5.1	0813	1.2	1443	5.2	2047	0.9
14 TH	0306	5.1	0842	1.1	1512	5.3	● 2112	0.8
15 F	0334	5.2	0912	0.9	1540	5.3	2137	0.8
16 SA	0402	5.2	0941	0.9	1609	5.3	2202	0.8
17 SU	0433	5.1	1006	1.0	1640	5.2	2226	0.9
18 M	0506	5.0	1027	1.1	1714	5.1	2245	1.1
19 TU	0541	4.9	1046	1.3	1750	4.9	2305	1.3
20 W	0619	4.7	1113	1.5	1831	4.7	2335	1.6
21 TH	0702	4.5	1154	1.7	1921	4.5		
22 F	0022	1.9	0756	4.3	1302	2.0	2025	4.3
23 SA	0151	2.2	0908	4.2	1519	2.1	2148	4.3
24 SU	0416	2.2	1032	4.3	1702	1.8	2312	4.6
25 M	0534	1.9	1146	4.6	1808	1.3		
26 TU	0021	5.0	0630	1.5	1244	5.1	1903	0.8
27 W	0114	5.4	0720	1.1	1331	5.5	1954	0.4
28 TH	0159	5.7	0806	0.7	1414	5.8	○ 2040	0.1
29 F	0242	5.9	0850	0.5	1457	6.0	2124	-0.1
30 SA	0324	5.9	0933	0.4	1541	6.1	2206	-0.1
31 SU	0407	5.8	1013	0.4	1626	6.0	2245	0.2

APRIL

Date	Time	m	Time	m	Time	m	Time	m
1 M	0451	5.6	1050	0.6	1714	5.7	2322	0.7
2 TU	0537	5.3	1123	0.9	1806	5.3	2353	1.2
3 W	0625	4.9	1158	1.3	1904	4.9		
4 TH	0028	1.7	0721	4.6	1251	1.7	2010	4.5
5 F	0132	2.2	0828	4.3	1439	2.0	2122	4.3
6 SA	0328	2.4	0943	4.2	1641	2.0	2242	4.3
7 SU	0456	2.3	1104	4.3	1757	1.7		
8 M	0000	4.5	0555	2.0	1214	4.5	1846	1.5
9 TU	0055	4.7	0638	1.8	1304	4.8	1921	1.3
10 W	0135	4.9	0712	1.5	1343	5.0	1949	1.1
11 TH	0208	5.0	0744	1.2	1415	5.1	2014	0.9
12 F	0237	5.1	0815	1.0	1444	5.2	● 2039	0.8
13 SA	0304	5.2	0846	0.9	1512	5.3	2106	0.8
14 SU	0333	5.2	0917	0.9	1543	5.3	2133	0.8
15 M	0404	5.2	0945	0.9	1615	5.2	2157	0.9
16 TU	0438	5.1	1007	1.0	1651	5.1	2216	1.1
17 W	0513	5.0	1027	1.2	1729	5.0	2237	1.3
18 TH	0551	4.8	1057	1.4	1813	4.8	2309	1.6
19 F	0635	4.6	1143	1.6	1905	4.6		
20 SA	0001	2.0	0729	4.4	1303	1.8	2008	4.5
21 SU	0154	2.2	0842	4.3	1506	1.8	2129	4.5
22 M	0355	2.2	1006	4.4	1638	1.5	2249	4.7
23 TU	0507	1.8	1118	4.7	1743	1.1	2355	5.0
24 W	0603	1.5	1216	5.1	1839	0.7		
25 TH	0048	5.4	0652	1.1	1305	5.5	1929	0.4
26 F	0134	5.6	0740	0.8	1350	5.8	2016	0.2
27 SA	0217	5.8	0826	0.5	1434	6.0	○ 2100	0.1
28 SU	0300	5.8	0910	0.4	1520	6.0	2142	0.2
29 M	0344	5.7	0953	0.5	1608	5.8	2221	0.5
30 TU	0428	5.5	1033	0.6	1657	5.6	2256	1.0

Chart Datum: 2·90 metres below Ordnance Datum (Newlyn)

Register for your **FREE** weekly weather email service from Macmillan Reeds
at **www.nauticaldata.com – NOW!**
weekend weather reports sent to your email address, every Thursday

TIME ZONE (UTC)
For Summer Time add ONE hour in **non-shaded areas**

SCOTLAND – LEITH

LAT 55°59′N LONG 3°11′W

TIMES AND HEIGHTS OF HIGH AND LOW WATERS

SPRING & NEAP TIDES
Dates in red are SPRINGS
Dates in blue are NEAPS

YEAR **2002**

MAY

Day	Time	m	Time	m	Time	m	Time	m
1 W	0513	5.3	1110	0.9	1749	5.2	2327	1.4
2 TH	0601	5.0	1146	1.3	1845	4.8		
3 F	0000	1.8	0655	4.7	1235	1.6	1945	4.5
4 SA	0058	2.2	0758	4.4	1400	1.9	2050	4.3
5 SU	0239	2.4	0907	4.3	1557	1.9	2200	4.2
6 M	0407	2.3	1018	4.3	1707	1.8	2313	4.3
7 TU	0506	2.1	1127	4.4	1757	1.6		
8 W	0012	4.6	0552	1.8	1222	4.7	1834	1.4
9 TH	0056	4.8	0632	1.6	1303	4.9	1904	1.2
10 F	0130	4.9	0709	1.3	1339	5.0	1932	1.1
11 SA	0202	5.1	0744	1.1	1411	5.1	2002	1.0
12 SU	0233	5.2	0819	1.0	1444	5.2	● 2033	0.9
13 M	0305	5.2	0853	0.9	1518	5.2	2104	0.9
14 TU	0338	5.2	0926	0.9	1554	5.2	2134	1.0
15 W	0413	5.2	0958	1.0	1632	5.2	2201	1.2
16 TH	0450	5.1	1031	1.1	1714	5.1	2230	1.4
17 F	0531	4.9	1110	1.2	1800	4.9	2311	1.7
18 SA	0618	4.8	1207	1.4	1853	4.8		
19 SU	0020	1.9	0713	4.6	1322	1.5	1956	4.7
20 M	0156	2.1	0823	4.6	1449	1.5	2109	4.7
21 TU	0324	2.0	0940	4.7	1609	1.3	2222	4.8
22 W	0434	1.8	1049	4.9	1713	1.1	2327	5.0
23 TH	0531	1.5	1147	5.2	1810	0.8		
24 F	0021	5.3	0623	1.2	1239	5.4	1902	0.6
25 SA	0110	5.4	0714	0.9	1328	5.6	1950	0.5
26 SU	0155	5.6	0804	0.7	1416	5.7	○ 2035	0.5
27 M	0239	5.6	0852	0.6	1504	5.7	2118	0.6
28 TU	0323	5.6	0937	0.6	1553	5.6	2157	0.9
29 W	0408	5.4	1020	0.7	1642	5.4	2233	1.2
30 TH	0453	5.2	1059	1.0	1732	5.1	2304	1.5
31 F	0539	5.0	1134	1.2	1822	4.8	2337	1.8

JUNE

Day	Time	m	Time	m	Time	m	Time	m
1 SA	0628	4.8	1213	1.5	1915	4.6		
2 SU	0023	2.1	0723	4.6	1306	1.7	2009	4.4
3 M	0130	2.2	0822	4.4	1423	1.9	2106	4.3
4 TU	0256	2.3	0923	4.4	1548	1.9	2206	4.3
5 W	0407	2.2	1024	4.4	1647	1.8	2305	4.4
6 TH	0503	2.0	1121	4.5	1734	1.6	2359	4.6
7 F	0551	1.7	1213	4.7	1814	1.5		
8 SA	0044	4.8	0633	1.5	1258	4.8	1851	1.3
9 SU	0124	5.0	0713	1.3	1339	5.0	1927	1.2
10 M	0202	5.1	0752	1.1	1418	5.1	● 2004	1.1
11 TU	0239	5.2	0831	1.0	1457	5.2	2042	1.1
12 W	0316	5.2	0912	0.9	1536	5.3	2121	1.1
13 TH	0354	5.3	0954	0.9	1617	5.3	2203	1.2
14 F	0434	5.2	1039	0.9	1701	5.3	2247	1.3
15 SA	0517	5.2	1127	0.9	1749	5.2	2336	1.5
16 SU	0604	5.1	1218	1.1	1841	5.0		
17 M	0031	1.7	0658	4.9	1317	1.2	1939	4.9
18 TU	0135	1.8	0801	4.9	1423	1.2	2045	4.8
19 W	0246	1.9	0912	4.9	1534	1.2	2153	4.8
20 TH	0355	1.8	1019	5.0	1641	1.2	2257	4.9
21 F	0459	1.6	1121	5.1	1742	1.1	2356	5.0
22 SA	0558	1.4	1219	5.2	1838	1.0		
23 SU	0048	5.2	0655	1.1	1314	5.4	1928	0.9
24 M	0137	5.3	0749	0.9	1405	5.4	○ 2014	0.9
25 TU	0223	5.4	0839	0.8	1454	5.4	2057	1.0
26 W	0308	5.4	0925	0.7	1541	5.4	2136	1.1
27 TH	0352	5.4	1007	0.8	1627	5.2	2211	1.3
28 F	0434	5.2	1044	0.9	1711	5.1	2242	1.4
29 SA	0516	5.1	1115	1.1	1754	4.9	2312	1.6
30 SU	0558	4.9	1145	1.3	1838	4.7	2349	1.8

JULY

Day	Time	m	Time	m	Time	m	Time	m
1 M	0643	4.8	1223	1.5	1923	4.5		
2 TU	0036	1.9	0732	4.6	1311	1.7	2012	4.4
3 W	0136	2.1	0825	4.5	1410	1.9	2105	4.3
4 TH	0251	2.2	0922	4.4	1522	1.9	2200	4.3
5 F	0407	2.1	1020	4.4	1633	1.8	2258	4.4
6 SA	0509	2.0	1120	4.5	1729	1.7	2356	4.6
7 SU	0600	1.7	1218	4.6	1817	1.6		
8 M	0049	4.8	0646	1.5	1310	4.8	1900	1.4
9 TU	0136	5.0	0730	1.2	1356	5.0	1943	1.3
10 W	0218	5.2	0815	1.0	1439	5.3	● 2028	1.1
11 TH	0258	5.3	0901	0.8	1521	5.4	2114	1.0
12 F	0338	5.4	0948	0.6	1603	5.5	2200	1.0
13 SA	0419	5.5	1035	0.5	1647	5.5	2246	1.1
14 SU	0502	5.5	1122	0.5	1734	5.4	2330	1.2
15 M	0549	5.4	1208	0.7	1823	5.3		
16 TU	0015	1.4	0639	5.3	1257	0.9	1917	5.1
17 W	0104	1.6	0736	5.1	1351	1.1	2017	4.9
18 TH	0203	1.7	0843	5.0	1456	1.3	2123	4.7
19 F	0317	1.8	0953	4.9	1610	1.5	2229	4.7
20 SA	0434	1.8	1101	4.9	1720	1.5	2334	4.8
21 SU	0545	1.6	1208	5.0	1822	1.4		
22 M	0035	4.9	0650	1.3	1308	5.1	1914	1.4
23 TU	0129	5.1	0746	1.1	1401	5.2	1959	1.3
24 W	0215	5.2	0834	0.9	1447	5.3	○ 2040	1.2
25 TH	0257	5.3	0916	0.8	1529	5.3	2116	1.2
26 F	0337	5.3	0952	0.8	1609	5.2	2148	1.2
27 SA	0414	5.3	1023	0.9	1646	5.1	2217	1.2
28 SU	0450	5.2	1049	1.0	1722	5.0	2245	1.3
29 M	0526	5.1	1114	1.1	1759	4.8	2316	1.5
30 TU	0604	5.0	1145	1.3	1839	4.7	2350	1.7
31 W	0645	4.8	1221	1.5	1923	4.5		

AUGUST

Day	Time	m	Time	m	Time	m	Time	m
1 TH	0032	1.9	0731	4.6	1306	1.8	2012	4.4
2 F	0129	2.1	0825	4.4	1405	2.0	2108	4.3
3 SA	0253	2.3	0927	4.3	1525	2.1	2209	4.3
4 SU	0425	2.2	1034	4.3	1649	2.0	2314	4.4
5 M	0532	1.9	1143	4.5	1751	1.8		
6 TU	0017	4.7	0625	1.6	1245	4.8	1842	1.6
7 W	0112	4.9	0714	1.2	1337	5.1	1929	1.3
8 TH	0158	5.2	0802	0.9	1421	5.4	● 2016	1.1
9 F	0239	5.5	0850	0.5	1504	5.6	2103	0.9
10 SA	0319	5.7	0937	0.3	1545	5.8	2148	0.8
11 SU	0400	5.8	1022	0.2	1629	5.8	2231	0.8
12 M	0443	5.8	1106	0.2	1713	5.7	2311	0.9
13 TU	0528	5.7	1148	0.4	1800	5.4	2350	1.1
14 W	0617	5.5	1230	0.8	1851	5.2		
15 TH	0030	1.4	0712	5.3	1317	1.2	1948	4.9
16 F	0123	1.7	0818	5.0	1418	1.6	2054	4.6
17 SA	0245	1.9	0933	4.7	1545	1.8	2205	4.5
18 SU	0424	1.9	1049	4.7	1708	1.9	2319	4.6
19 M	0549	1.7	1204	4.8	1815	1.8		
20 TU	0027	4.8	0655	1.4	1308	4.9	1906	1.6
21 W	0123	5.0	0746	1.1	1357	5.1	1947	1.5
22 TH	0207	5.2	0826	0.9	1437	5.2	○ 2022	1.3
23 F	0244	5.3	0900	0.8	1513	5.2	2053	1.2
24 SA	0319	5.4	0929	0.8	1546	5.2	2123	1.1
25 SU	0350	5.4	0955	0.8	1617	5.2	2151	1.1
26 M	0421	5.3	1018	0.9	1649	5.1	2217	1.1
27 TU	0453	5.2	1041	1.0	1723	5.0	2243	1.3
28 W	0528	5.1	1106	1.2	1759	4.8	2308	1.5
29 TH	0606	4.9	1133	1.4	1839	4.7	2336	1.7
30 F	0648	4.7	1205	1.7	1925	4.5		
31 SA	0017	2.0	0737	4.4	1253	2.0	2019	4.3

Chart Datum: 2·90 metres below Ordnance Datum (Newlyn)

Register for your FREE weekly weather email service from Macmillan Reeds
» at www.nauticaldata.com – NOW! «
weekend weather reports sent to your email address, every Thursday

TIME ZONE (UTC)
For Summer Time add ONE hour in **non-shaded areas**

SCOTLAND – LEITH

LAT 55°59′N LONG 3°11′W

TIMES AND HEIGHTS OF HIGH AND LOW WATERS

SPRING & NEAP TIDES
Dates in red are SPRINGS
Dates in blue are NEAPS

YEAR **2002**

SEPTEMBER

Date	Day	Time	m	Time	m	Time	m	Time	m
1	SU	0130	2.2	0840	4.3	1417	2.3	2125	4.3
2	M	0337	2.3	0955	4.3	1617	2.3	2238	4.4
3	TU	0508	2.0	1113	4.5	1732	2.0	2349	4.6
4	W	0607	1.6	1222	4.8	1827	1.7		
5	TH	0047	5.0	0658	1.1	1316	5.2	1914	1.3
6	F	0134	5.3	0747	0.7	1400	5.6	2000	1.0
7	SA	0216	5.7	0834	0.3	1442	5.9	● 2044	0.7
8	SU	0256	5.9	0919	0.0	1523	6.0	2128	0.6
9	M	0337	6.1	1002	-0.1	1605	6.0	2209	0.5
10	TU	0420	6.1	1044	0.1	1649	5.8	2248	0.7
11	W	0506	5.9	1123	0.4	1735	5.5	2324	1.0
12	TH	0555	5.6	1201	0.9	1824	5.2		
13	F	0001	1.3	0651	5.2	1243	1.4	1920	4.8
14	SA	0055	1.7	0759	4.8	1344	1.9	2028	4.6
15	SU	0229	2.0	0917	4.6	1526	2.2	2144	4.5
16	M	0427	2.0	1038	4.5	1659	2.2	2303	4.5
17	TU	0553	1.7	1158	4.7	1805	2.0		
18	W	0015	4.8	0651	1.4	1258	4.9	1851	1.8
19	TH	0108	5.0	0733	1.2	1343	5.1	1927	1.5
20	F	0150	5.2	0807	1.0	1419	5.2	1957	1.3
21	SA	0224	5.4	0834	0.9	1450	5.3	○ 2026	1.1
22	SU	0254	5.4	0858	0.8	1518	5.3	2055	1.0
23	M	0323	5.4	0921	0.8	1547	5.3	2124	1.0
24	TU	0352	5.4	0944	0.8	1617	5.2	2150	1.0
25	W	0423	5.3	1007	1.0	1649	5.1	2213	1.2
26	TH	0457	5.2	1028	1.2	1724	5.0	2233	1.4
27	F	0534	5.0	1049	1.4	1802	4.8	2259	1.6
28	SA	0616	4.7	1115	1.7	1845	4.6	2336	1.9
29	SU	0705	4.5	1155	2.1	1937	4.4		
30	M	0040	2.2	0806	4.3	1319	2.4	2046	4.3

OCTOBER

Date	Day	Time	m	Time	m	Time	m	Time	m
1	TU	0257	2.3	0925	4.3	1550	2.4	2206	4.4
2	W	0443	2.0	1046	4.5	1711	2.1	2320	4.7
3	TH	0546	1.5	1156	4.9	1805	1.7		
4	F	0019	5.1	0637	1.0	1250	5.4	1852	1.3
5	SA	0107	5.5	0725	0.6	1335	5.7	1936	1.0
6	SU	0149	5.8	0811	0.2	1417	6.0	● 2020	0.7
7	M	0230	6.1	0855	0.0	1458	6.1	2103	0.5
8	TU	0313	6.2	0938	0.0	1540	6.0	2146	0.5
9	W	0358	6.2	1019	0.2	1624	5.8	2226	0.7
10	TH	0446	5.9	1057	0.6	1710	5.5	2304	1.0
11	F	0537	5.6	1134	1.2	1759	5.2	2344	1.3
12	SA	0635	5.1	1212	1.7	1855	4.9		
13	SU	0039	1.7	0744	4.8	1314	2.2	2004	4.6
14	M	0221	2.0	0859	4.5	1504	2.5	2121	4.5
15	TU	0418	2.0	1018	4.5	1634	2.4	2238	4.5
16	W	0535	1.7	1136	4.6	1737	2.2	2348	4.8
17	TH	0628	1.5	1234	4.9	1821	1.9		
18	F	0041	5.0	0706	1.3	1317	5.1	1855	1.6
19	SA	0122	5.2	0735	1.2	1351	5.2	1926	1.4
20	SU	0156	5.3	0759	1.0	1421	5.3	1957	1.2
21	M	0226	5.4	0821	0.9	1448	5.3	○ 2028	1.1
22	TU	0254	5.4	0846	0.9	1516	5.3	2058	1.0
23	W	0324	5.4	0912	1.0	1547	5.3	2126	1.1
24	TH	0357	5.3	0936	1.1	1620	5.2	2151	1.2
25	F	0433	5.2	0957	1.3	1654	5.1	2213	1.4
26	SA	0511	5.0	1018	1.5	1732	4.9	2240	1.6
27	SU	0554	4.8	1046	1.8	1814	4.7	2321	1.8
28	M	0644	4.6	1129	2.1	1906	4.5		
29	TU	0035	2.0	0744	4.5	1302	2.4	2014	4.4
30	W	0232	2.1	0859	4.5	1519	2.4	2135	4.5
31	TH	0410	1.8	1018	4.7	1639	2.1	2248	4.8

NOVEMBER

Date	Day	Time	m	Time	m	Time	m	Time	m
1	F	0516	1.4	1126	5.0	1735	1.8	2347	5.2
2	SA	0609	1.0	1221	5.4	1823	1.4		
3	SU	0037	5.6	0658	0.6	1308	5.7	1908	1.0
4	M	0122	5.9	0744	0.4	1351	5.9	● 1954	0.8
5	TU	0206	6.1	0829	0.3	1433	6.0	2040	0.6
6	W	0252	6.1	0913	0.3	1517	5.9	2126	0.6
7	TH	0340	6.0	0955	0.6	1601	5.8	2210	0.7
8	F	0430	5.8	1034	1.0	1648	5.5	2252	1.0
9	SA	0523	5.5	1110	1.5	1737	5.2	2336	1.3
10	SU	0620	5.1	1147	1.9	1832	4.9		
11	M	0028	1.7	0724	4.7	1242	2.3	1938	4.7
12	TU	0153	2.0	0831	4.5	1416	2.5	2049	4.5
13	W	0338	2.0	0941	4.4	1545	2.5	2200	4.5
14	TH	0451	1.9	1052	4.5	1647	2.3	2306	4.7
15	F	0545	1.7	1153	4.7	1735	2.1		
16	SA	0001	4.8	0623	1.6	1239	4.9	1815	1.8
17	SU	0046	5.0	0651	1.4	1316	5.0	1852	1.5
18	M	0123	5.1	0717	1.3	1348	5.2	1927	1.3
19	TU	0156	5.2	0745	1.2	1418	5.3	2001	1.2
20	W	0228	5.3	0814	1.1	1449	5.3	○ 2035	1.1
21	TH	0302	5.3	0844	1.1	1522	5.3	2108	1.1
22	F	0337	5.3	0913	1.2	1556	5.3	2140	1.2
23	SA	0414	5.2	0941	1.4	1631	5.2	2212	1.3
24	SU	0454	5.1	1009	1.6	1710	5.0	2249	1.5
25	M	0538	5.0	1043	1.8	1753	4.9	2338	1.6
26	TU	0628	4.8	1134	2.1	1844	4.8		
27	W	0045	1.7	0725	4.7	1303	2.3	1946	4.7
28	TH	0206	1.8	0833	4.7	1438	2.3	2101	4.7
29	F	0329	1.6	0945	4.8	1556	2.1	2213	4.9
30	SA	0439	1.4	1052	5.0	1658	1.8	2314	5.2

DECEMBER

Date	Day	Time	m	Time	m	Time	m	Time	m
1	SU	0537	1.1	1150	5.2	1751	1.5		
2	M	0008	5.5	0630	0.9	1241	5.5	1842	1.2
3	TU	0059	5.7	0719	0.7	1328	5.6	1933	1.0
4	W	0148	5.8	0807	0.7	1412	5.7	● 2024	0.8
5	TH	0237	5.9	0852	0.8	1457	5.7	2113	0.7
6	F	0327	5.8	0935	0.9	1543	5.6	2200	0.8
7	SA	0417	5.6	1016	1.2	1630	5.5	2244	1.0
8	SU	0509	5.3	1052	1.5	1718	5.3	2326	1.2
9	M	0601	5.1	1125	1.9	1809	5.0		
10	TU	0007	1.5	0655	4.8	1205	2.1	1904	4.8
11	W	0055	1.8	0751	4.5	1303	2.3	2005	4.6
12	TH	0204	2.0	0849	4.4	1422	2.4	2106	4.5
13	F	0328	2.1	0948	4.4	1540	2.4	2206	4.5
14	SA	0431	2.0	1047	4.4	1641	2.2	2304	4.6
15	SU	0521	1.9	1143	4.6	1733	2.0	2357	4.7
16	M	0602	1.7	1231	4.8	1819	1.8		
17	TU	0044	4.9	0638	1.6	1313	5.0	1900	1.6
18	W	0127	5.0	0714	1.4	1350	5.1	1938	1.4
19	TH	0206	5.1	0749	1.4	1427	5.2	○ 2016	1.3
20	F	0244	5.2	0825	1.3	1502	5.3	2055	1.1
21	SA	0321	5.3	0902	1.3	1538	5.3	2135	1.1
22	SU	0400	5.3	0940	1.4	1615	5.3	2216	1.1
23	M	0441	5.3	1019	1.5	1654	5.2	2300	1.1
24	TU	0524	5.2	1101	1.6	1737	5.2	2347	1.2
25	W	0612	5.1	1146	1.8	1825	5.1		
26	TH	0037	1.3	0704	5.0	1242	1.9	1920	5.0
27	F	0136	1.4	0803	4.8	1349	2.0	2024	4.9
28	SA	0244	1.5	0910	4.8	1505	2.0	2135	4.9
29	SU	0357	1.5	1017	4.8	1618	1.9	2243	5.0
30	M	0505	1.4	1120	5.0	1723	1.7	2346	5.2
31	TU	0606	1.3	1218	5.1	1825	1.4		

Chart Datum: 2·90 metres below Ordnance Datum (Newlyn)

Register for your FREE weekly weather email service from Macmillan Reeds
at www.nauticaldata.com – NOW!
weekend weather reports sent to your email address, every Thursday

METHIL 9.6.11

Fife **56°10′·75N 03°00′·55W**

CHARTS AC 739, 734; Imray C23, C27; OS 59

TIDES +0330 Dover; ML 3·0; Duration 0615; Zone 0 (UT)

Standard Port LEITH (←)

Times				Height (metres)			
High Water		Low Water		MHWS	MHWN	MLWN	MLWS
0300	0900	0300	0900	5·6	4·4	2·0	0·8
1500	2100	1500	2100				
Differences METHIL							
–0005	–0001	–0001	–0001	–0·1	–0·1	–0·1	–0·1
KIRKCALDY							
+0005	0000	–0004	–0001	–0·3	–0·3	–0·2	–0·2

SHELTER Commercial port and only suitable as an emergency shelter in No 2 dock and dangerous to enter in bad weather.

NAVIGATION WPT 56°10′·49N 03°00′·10W, 140°/320° from/to pier hd lt, 0·34M. Beware silting. A sand bar forms rapidly to seaward of the lt ho and dredged depth is not always maintained.

LIGHTS AND MARKS
By day and night (vert lts):
● ● = Dangerous to enter; Bring up in roads.
● Ⓦ = Clear to enter No 2 dock.
● = Remain in roads until another signal is made.

RADIO TELEPHONE *Methil Docks Radio* VHF Ch 14 16 (HW–3 to +1). Forth Navigation Ch 71 (H24).

TELEPHONE (Dial code 01592) Hr Mr (Port Manager) (01333) 426725 📠 424873; MRSC (01333) 450666; ⊜ (0141) 887 9369 (H24); Marinecall 09068 500452; Police 418900; Dr (01333) 426913.

FACILITIES Hbr No 2 Dock £22.00 per week, FW, C (10 ton). **Town** EC Thurs; P, D, Gas, Gaz, V, R, Bar, ✉, Ⓑ, ≋ (bus to Markinch or Kirkcaldy), Ⓗ Kirkcaldy, ✈ Edinburgh.

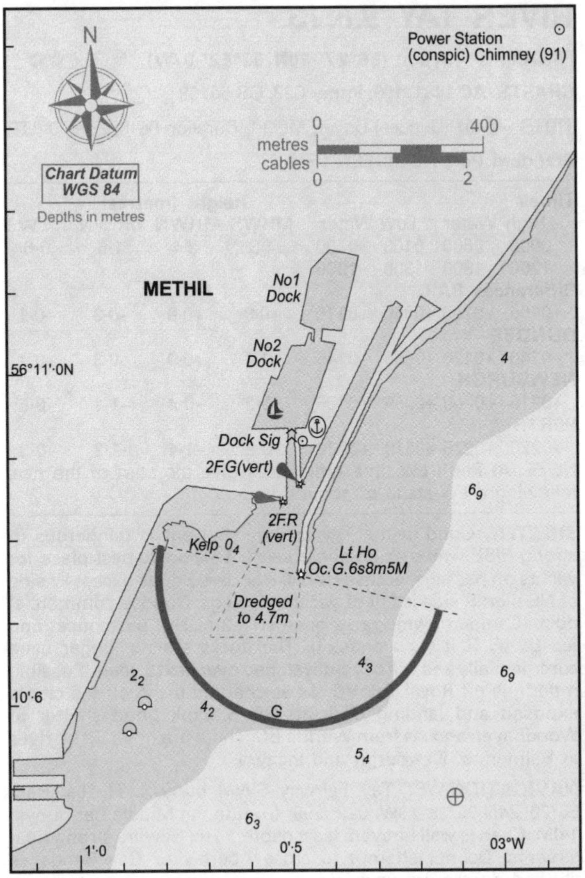

ADJACENT HARBOURS

KIRKCALDY, Fife, **56°06′·80N 03°08′·96W**. AC 739. HW +0345 on Dover, –0005 on Leith; HW –0·1m on Leith; ML 3·2m; Duration 0620. See 9.6.12. Shelter good except in strong E winds; an emergency refuge. Officially the hbr is closed (no commercial tfc, but some local FVs) and not manned; depths may be less than charted due to silting. The only hbr light is on E Pier head, Fl WG 10s 12m 8M. Small craft should contact Forth Ports Authority ☎ (01333) 426725, or call Forth Navigation Ch 71 (H24) or Methil Docks Radio Ch 16 14 for advice.

ANSTRUTHER 9.6.12

Fife **56°13′·15N 02°41′·82W**

CHARTS AC 734, 175; Imray C23, C27; OS 59

TIDES +0315 Dover; ML 3·1; Duration 0620; Zone 0 (UT)

Standard Port LEITH (←)

Times				Height (metres)			
High Water		Low Water		MHWS	MHWN	MLWN	MLWS
0300	0900	0300	0900	5·6	4·4	2·0	0·8
1500	2100	1500	2100				
Differences ANSTRUTHER EASTER							
–0018	–0012	–0006	–0008	–0·3	–0·2	0·0	0·0

SHELTER Good, but dangerous to enter in strong E & S winds. Hbr dries; access approx HW±2. Caution: ledge at base of W pier. No ⚓ to W of hbr; do not go N of W pier lt due to rks.

NAVIGATION WPT 56°12′·59N 02°42′·20W, 199°/019° from/to ent, 0·60M. Beware lobster pots and FVs.

LIGHTS AND MARKS Conspic tr on W pier. Ldg lts 019°, both FG 7/11m 4M. Pier lts as chartlet. Horn (3) 60s in conspic tr.

RADIO TELEPHONE Call *Anstruther Hbr* VHF Ch 11 16 (HO) or Forth CG 16 (OT).

TELEPHONE (Dial code 01333) Hr Mr ☎/📠 310836 (HO); MRSC (01333) 450666; ⊜ (0141) 887 9369 (H24); Marinecall 09068 500452; Police St Adrews 01334 418900, Cupar 01334 418700; Dr 310352, Ⓗ St Andrews 01334 472327, Kirkaldy 01592 643355.

FACILITIES Hbr AB (22 + 8Ⓥ) AB (wall) £11.40 + £5.70 per day; pontoons £13.50 + £7.80 per day all for 10m LOA, AB, Slip, FW, AC, ♿, Shwrs; **Services:** D (tanker), CH, ACA, ME, Gas, Gaz, El, Ⓔ, ⊡, LB. **Town** EC Wed; P, V, R, Bar, ✉, Ⓑ, ≋ (bus Cupar or Leuchars), ✈ Edinburgh/Dundee.

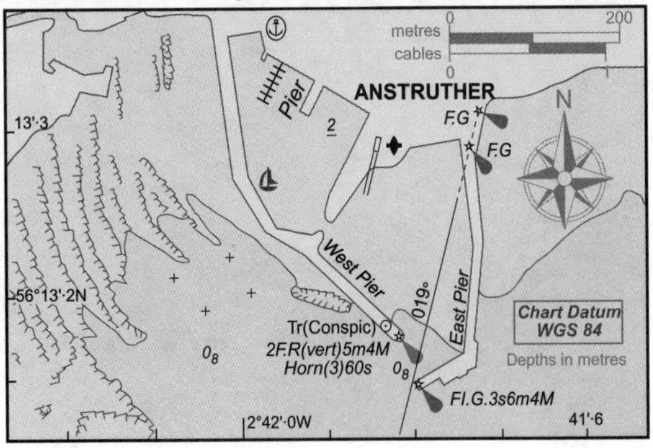

RIVER TAY *9.6.13*

Fife/Angus Tayport **(56°27'·10N 02°52'·87W)** ❁❁◊◊✿✿

CHARTS AC 1481, 190; Imray C23; OS 54, 59

TIDES +0401 (Dundee) Dover; ML 3·1; Duration 0610; Zone 0 (UT)

Standard Port ABERDEEN (⟶)

Times				Height (metres)			
High Water		Low Water		MHWS	MHWN	MLWN	MLWS
0000	0600	0100	0700	4·3	3·4	1·6	0·6
1200	1800	1300	1900				
Differences BAR							
+0100	+0100	+0050	+0110	+0·9	+0·8	+0·3	+0·1
DUNDEE							
+0140	+0120	+0055	+0145	+1·1	+0·9	+0·3	+0·1
NEWBURGH							
+0215	+0200	+0250	+0335	−0·2	−0·4	−1·1	−0·5
PERTH							
+0220	+0225	+0510	+0530	−0·9	−1·4	−1·2	−0·3

NOTE: At Perth LW time differences give the start of the rise, following a LW stand of about 4 hours.

SHELTER Good in the Tay Estuary, but ent is dangerous in strong E/SE winds or on-shore swell. **Tayport** is best place for yachts on passage, access HW±4. Hbr partly dries except W side of NE pier; S side is full of yacht moorings. **Dundee** commercial dock (Camperdown), gates open HW–2 to HW by request and fee £6 (Fl R lt = no ent/exit). The docks are no longer used commercially and will be re-developed over next 5 years. Possible moorings off Royal Tay YC. ⚓s as chartlet: the ⚓ off the city is exposed and landing difficult. Off S bank good shelter at Woodhaven and 🅐s from Wormit BC. There are other ⚓s up river at Balmerino, Newburgh and Inchyra.

NAVIGATION WPT Tay Fairway SWM buoy, L Fl 10s, Bell, 56°29'·24N 02°38'·29W, 029°/209° from/to the Middle Bar buoys, 1·0M. Chan is well buoyed, least depth 5·2m. Beware strong tidal streams. Do not attempt to cross Abertay or Gaa Sands as charted depths are unreliable.

LIGHTS AND MARKS Tayport High lt Dir 269° Iso WRG 3s, W sector 268°-270°. The HFP "Abertay" ECM buoy, Q (3) 10s (Racon), at E end of Gaa Sands is a clear visual mark. Keep N of Larick, a conspic disused lt bn. Bridge lts reported unreliable (2001).

RADIO TELEPHONE *Dundee Hbr Radio* VHF Ch **12** 16 (H24); local nav warnings, weather, vis and tides on request. Royal Tay YC, Ch M.

TELEPHONE (Dial code 01382) Port Control 878140 Hr Mr (Dundee) 224121/📠 200834 Port Control 459448; Hr Mr (Perth) (01738) 624056; MRSC (01333) 450666; ⊖ 200822; Marinecall 09068 500452; Tayport Boatowners' Ass'n 553679; Police (Tayport) 552222, (Dundee) 223200; Dr 221953; 🄷 223125.

FACILITIES N BANK: **Camperdown Dock**, AB £18 all LOA, £36 for week; FW, ME, El, C (8 ton); **Victoria Dock**, AB, FW, ME, C (8 ton); **Royal Tay YC** (Broughty Ferry) ☎ 477516, 🅐s free, R, Bar; **Services:** CH, M, L, ME, El, Sh, C (2 ton), ACA. **Dundee City** EC Wed; P, D, CH, V, R, Bar, ⊠, Ⓑ, ⇌, ✈. S BANK: **Tayport Hbr** ☎ 553679 AB £6.60, Slip, L, FW, AC; **Wormit Boating Club** ☎ 541400 🅐s free, Slip, L, FW, V.

ADJACENT HARBOURS

PERTH, Perth & Kinross, **56°22'·89N 03°25'·74W**. AC 1481; OS 53, 58. Tides, see 9.6.14. FYCA Pilot Handbook is needed. Leave Tay rly bridge at about HW Dundee –2 to carry a fair tide the 16·5M to Perth. The buoyed/lit chan favours the S bank for 9M to Newburgh. Here care is needed due to mudbanks in mid-stream; keep S of Mugdrum Is. Up-river, power cables have clearance of 33m and Friarton bridge 26m. Keep S of Willow Is, past the gasworks to hbr on the W bank. Hbr has approx 1·5m; keep clear of coasters. See Hr Mr, ☎ (01738) 624056, for berth. VHF Ch 09 16. FW, D & P (cans), usual city amenities, ⇌, ✈.

ST ANDREWS, Fife, **56°20'·32N 02°46'·79W**. AC 190. HW –0015 Leith. Small drying hbr 7M S of Tay Estuary and 8M NW of Fife Ness. In strong onshore winds breaking seas render appr/ent impossible. Appr at HW±2 on 270°, N bkwtr bn in transit with conspic cathedral tr; no lights. A recce by dinghy is useful. Keep about 10m S of the bkwtr for best water. 8m wide ent to inner hbr (drying 2·5m) has lock gates, usually open, and sliding footbridge; berth on W side. Facilities: FW, SC. EC Thurs; all amenities of university town, inc golf course.

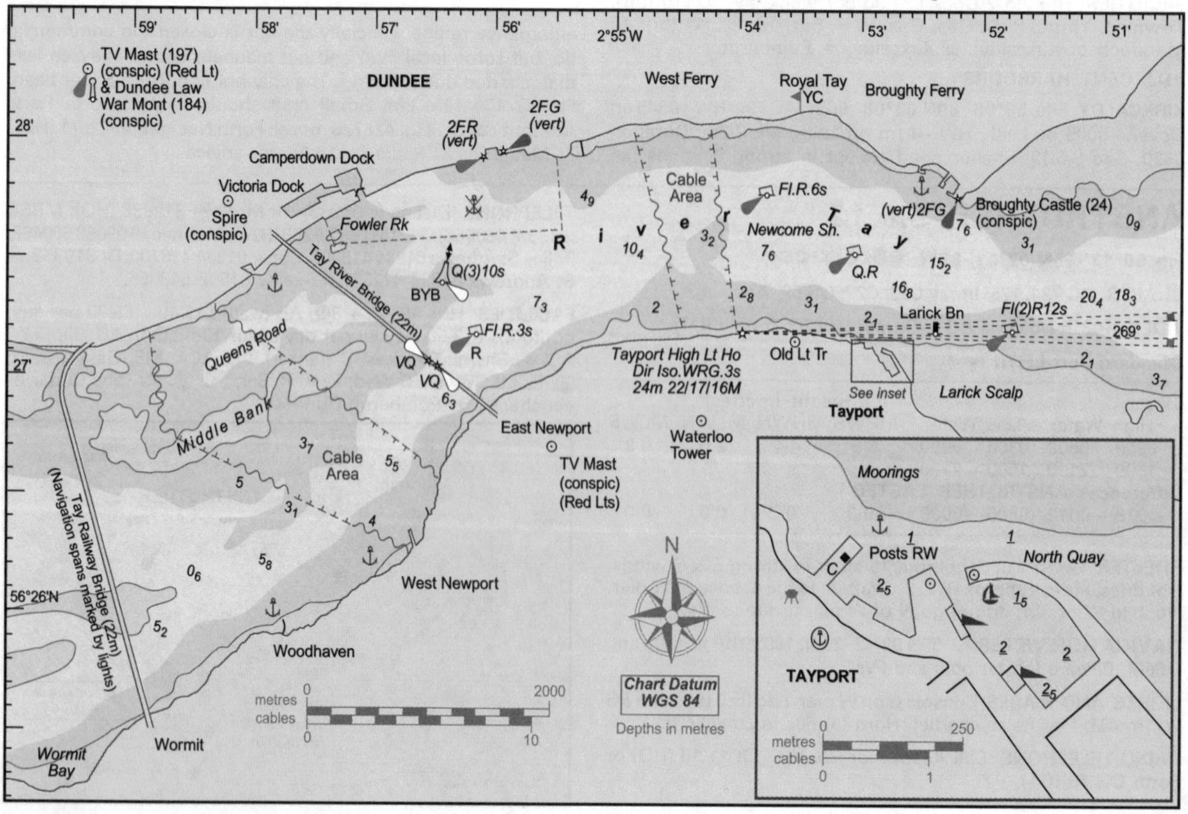

ARBROATH *9.6.14*

Angus **56°33'·22N 02°34'·99W**

CHARTS AC 1438, 190; Imray C23; OS 54

TIDES +0317 Dover; ML 2·9; Duration 0620; Zone 0 (UT)

Standard Port ABERDEEN (→)

Times				Height (metres)			
High Water		Low Water		MHWS	MHWN	MLWN	MLWS
0000	0600	0100	0700	4·3	3·4	1·6	0·6
1200	1800	1300	1900				
Differences ARBROATH							
+0056	+0037	+0034	+0055	+0·7	+0·7	+0·2	+0·1

SHELTER Good, especially in Wet Dock, but ent can be dangerous in moderate SE swell. Dock gates normally remain open, but will be closed on request. Or small craft can dry out in the SW corner of inner hbr; inside ent, turn stbd and stbd again.

NAVIGATION WPT 56°32'·98N 02°34'·21W, 119°/299° from/to ent, 0·5M. Entry should not be attempted LW±2½. Beware Knuckle rks to stbd and Cheek Bush rks to port on entering.

LIGHTS AND MARKS Ldg lts 299°, both FR 7/13m 5M; or twin trs of St Thomas' ✠ visible between N pier lt ho and W bkwtr bn. Hbr entry sigs: Fl G 3s on E pier = Entry safe. Same lt shows FR when hbr closed, entry dangerous. Siren (3) 60s at E pier lt is occas, for FVs.

RADIO TELEPHONE None.

TELEPHONE (Dial code 01241) Hr Mr 872166; MRSC (01224) 592334; ⊜ (0141) 887 9369 (H24); Marinecall 09068 500452; Police 722222; Dr 876836.

FACILITIES Pier AB £11, Slip, D, FW; **Services:** BY, Slip, L, ME, El, Sh, C (8 ton) Ⓔ, M, Gas, CH. **Town** EC Wed; P, D, V, R, Bar, ✉, Ⓑ, ⇄, ✈ (Dundee).

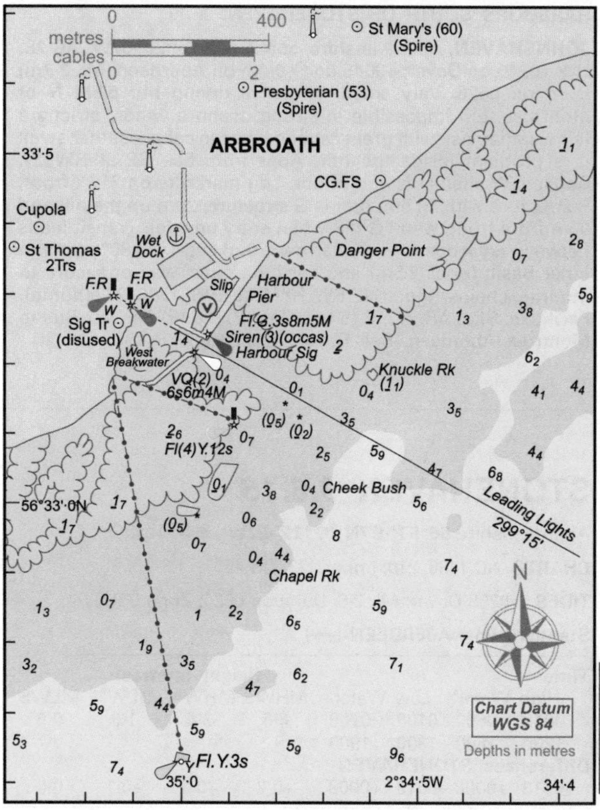

MONTROSE *9.6.15*

Angus **56°42'·19N 02°26'·60W**

CHARTS AC 1438, 190; Imray C23; OS 54

TIDES +0320 Dover; ML 2·9; Duration 0645; Zone 0 (UT)

Standard Port ABERDEEN (→)

Times				Height (metres)			
High Water		Low Water		MHWS	MHWN	MLWN	MLWS
0000	0600	0100	0700	4·3	3·4	1·6	0·6
1200	1800	1300	1900				
Differences MONTROSE							
+0055	+0055	+0030	+0040	+0·5	+0·4	+0·2	0·0

SHELTER Good; yachts are welcome in this busy commercial port. Contact Hr Mr for AB, usually available, but beware wash from other traffic. Double mooring lines advised due to strong tidal streams (up to 6kn).

NAVIGATION WPT 56°42'·18N 02°25'·11W, 091°/271° from/to front ldg lt, 1·25M. Beware Annat Bank to N and Scurdie Rks to S of ent chan. In quiet weather best access is LW to LW+1, but in strong onshore winds only safe access would be from HW –2 to HW. Ent is dangerous with strong onshore winds against ebb tide when heavy overfalls develop.

LIGHTS AND MARKS Scurdie Ness lt ho Fl (3) 20s 38m 23M (conspic). Two sets of ldg lts: Outer 271·5°, both FR 11/18m 5M, front W twin pillars, R bands; rear W tr, R cupola. Inner 265°, both FG 21/33m 5M, Orange △ front and ▽ rear. For position of outer SHM chan buoy (off chartlet), see 9.6.4.

RADIO TELEPHONE VHF Ch 12 16 (H24).

TELEPHONE (Dial code 01674) Hr Mr 672302; MRCC (01224) 592334; Marinecall 09068 500 452; ⊜ (01224) 844844; Police 672222; Dr 672554.

FACILITIES N Quay ☎ 672302, AB £6.00, D (by tanker via Hr Mr), FW, ME, El, C (1½ to 40 ton), CH, Gas. **Town** EC Wed; V, R, P, Bar, ✉, Ⓑ, ⇄, ✈ (Aberdeen).

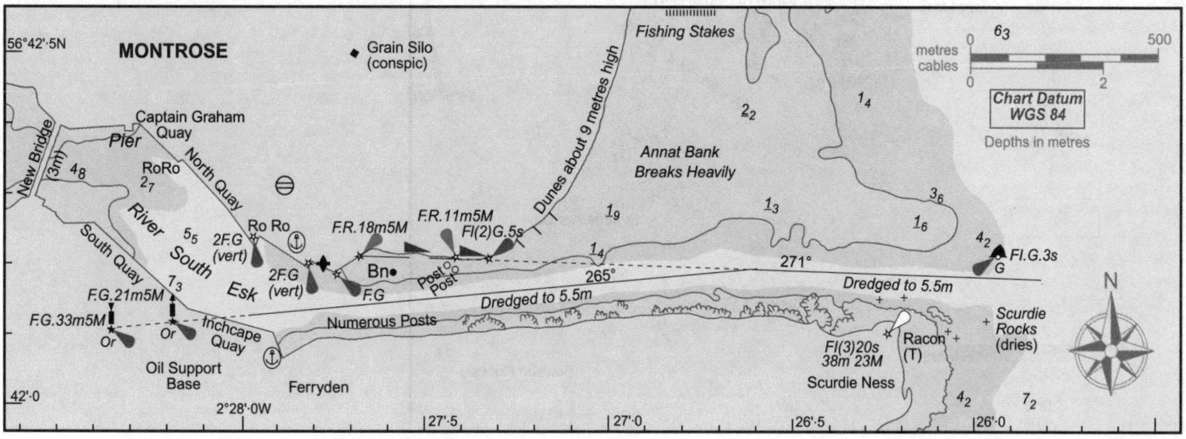

HARBOURS SOUTH OF STONEHAVEN

JOHNSHAVEN, Aberdeenshire, 56°47′·60N 02°20′·07W. AC 28. HW +0245 on Dover; +0045 and +0·4m on Aberdeen; ML 2·7m; Duration 0626. Very small, attractive drying hbr 6·5M N of Montrose. Ent impossible in strong onshore winds; strictly a fair weather visit with great caution. Even in calm weather swell is a problem inside the hbr. Appr from 5ca SE at HW±2½. Conspic W shed at N end of hbr. Ldg marks/lts on 316°: front, R structure with FR 5m; rear is G structure, 20m up the hill and 85m from front, with FG (FR when entry unsafe). Transit leads between rky ledges to very narrow (20m) ent. Turn 90° port into Inner Basin (dries 2·5m) and berth on outer wall or secure to mooring chains, rigged NE/SW. Hr Mr ☎ (01561) 362262 (home). Facilities: Slip, AB, AC, C (5 ton), FW, V, R, ME, Bar, ✉. Bus to Montrose/Aberdeen. See Rover Ticket 9.6.5.

GOURDON, Aberdeenshire, 56°49′·49N 02°17′·21W. AC 28. HW +0240 on Dover; +0035 on Aberdeen; HW +0·4m on Aberdeen; ML 2·7m; Duration 0620. Shelter good in inner W hbr (drys about 2m; protected by storm gates); access from about mid-flood. E (or Gutty) hbr is rky, with difficult access. Beware rky ledges marked by bn and extending 200m S from W pier end. A dangerous rk dries on the ldg line about 1½ca S of pier heads. Ldg marks/lts 358°, both FR 5/30m 5M, 2 W trs; front lt shows G when not safe to enter. W pier hd Fl WRG 3s 5m 9/7M, vis G180°-344°, W344°-354° (10°), R354°-180°. E bkwtr hd Q 3m 7M. Hr Mr ☎ (01569) 762741 (part-time, same as 9.6.16). Facilities: Slip, FW from standpipe, D, ME, AC, M, V, R, Bar. Fish market held Mon-Fri 1130 and 1530. See Rover Ticket, 9.6.5.

STONEHAVEN *9.6.16*

Aberdeenshire **56°57′·57N 02°12′·02W** ❁❁❁◊✿✿

CHARTS AC 1438, 210; Imray C23; OS 45

TIDES +0235 Dover; ML 2·6; Duration 0620; Zone 0 (UT)

Standard Port ABERDEEN (⟶)

Times				Height (metres)			
High Water		Low Water		MHWS	MHWN	MLWN	MLWS
0000	0600	0100	0700	4·3	3·4	1·6	0·6
1200	1800	1300	1900				
Differences STONEHAVEN							
+0013	+0008	+0013	+0009	+0·2	+0·2	+0·1	0·0

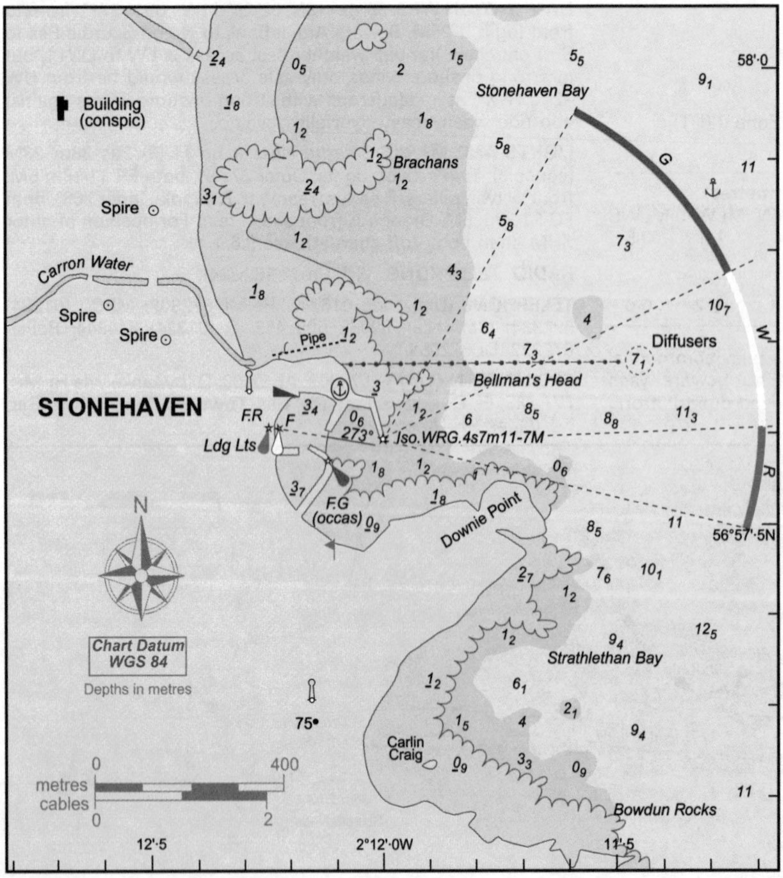

SHELTER Good, especially from offshore winds. Berth in outer hbr (1·2 to1·0m) on bkwtr or N wall; sandbank forms in middle to W side. Or ⚓ outside in fair weather. Hbr speed limit 3kn. Inner hbr dries 3·4m and in bad weather is closed, indicated by FG(occas) lt as shown. Do not go S of ldg line, to clear rks close E of inner hbr wall.

NAVIGATION WPT 56°57′·69N 02°11′·11W, 078°/258° from/to bkwtr lt, 0·50M. Give Downie Pt a wide berth. Do not enter in strong on-shore winds.

LIGHTS AND MARKS N pier Iso WRG 4s 7m 11/7M; appr in W sector, 246°-268°. Inner hbr ldg lts 273°, only apply to inner hbr: front FW 6m 5M; rear FR 8m 5M. FG on SE pier is shown when inner hbr is closed by a boom in bad weather. Conspic monument to S of hbr.

RADIO TELEPHONE Hr Mr VHF Ch 11.

TELEPHONE (Dial code 01569) Hr Mr (part-time) 762741, Mobile 07882 702831; MRCC (01224) 592334; ⊜ (0141) 887 9369 (H24); Marinecall 09068 500452; Police 762963; Dr 762945; Maritime Rescue International ☎ 764065.

FACILITIES Hbr AB £10.00 for 7 days, L, M, FW, AC, Slip, ♿, C (1·5 ton), LB, D by tanker, Fri early am; **Aberdeen & Stonehaven SC** Slip, Bar. **Town** EC Wed; P, Gas, V, R, Bar, Ⓗ, ✉, Ⓑ, ⇌, ✈ (Aberdeen).

BERTHING FEES; For details of a Rover Ticket see 9.6.5.

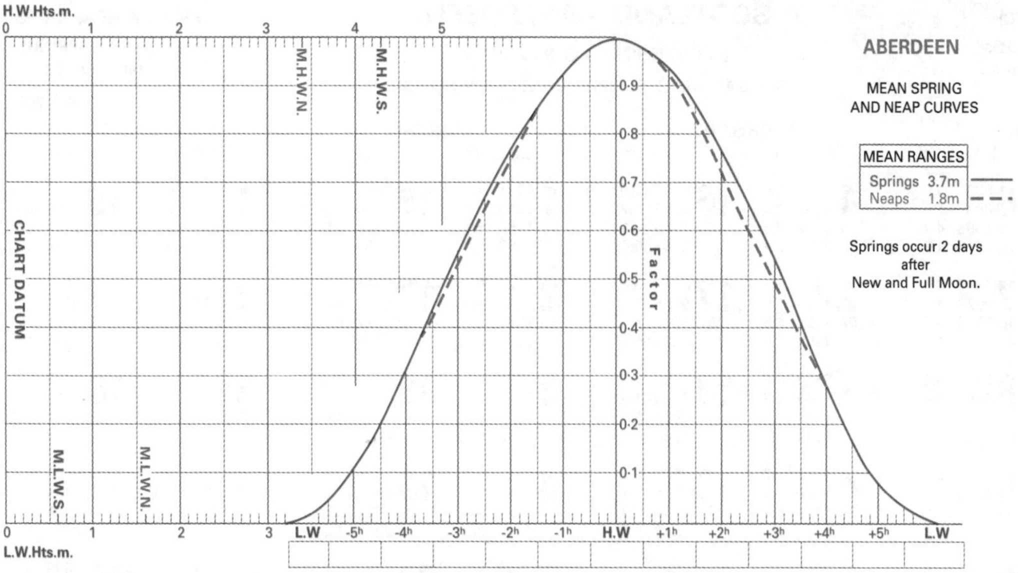

ABERDEEN *9.6.17*

Aberdeenshire **57°08'·70N 02°03'·59W** ❁❁❁◊✿✿

CHARTS AC 1446, 210; Imray C23; OS 38

TIDES +0231 Dover; ML 2·5; Duration 0620; Zone 0 (UT)

SHELTER Good in hbr; open at all tides, but do not enter in strong NE/ESE winds. Call Hr Mr VHF Ch 12 for berthing details. Yachts are not encouraged in this busy commercial port, but usually lie on N side of Albert Basin alongside floating linkspan. ⚓ in Aberdeen Bay gives some shelter from S and W winds. Peterhead is 25M to N; Stonehaven is 13M S.

NAVIGATION WPT Fairway SWM buoy, Mo (A) 5s, Racon, 57°09'·31N 02°01'·96W, 056°/236° from/to hbr ent 1·05M. Give Girdle Ness a berth of at least ¼M (more in bad weather) and do not pass close round pier hds. Strong tidal streams and, with river in spate, possible overfalls. Chan dredged to 6m on ldg line.

LIGHTS AND MARKS Ldg lts 236° (FR = port open; FG = port closed). Traffic sigs at root of N pier:

●	=	Entry prohib
●	=	Dep prohib
● & ●	=	Port closed

RADIO TELEPHONE VHF Ch 06 11 **12** 13 16 (H24).

TELEPHONE (Dial code 01224) Hr Mr 597000, 📠 584301; MRCC 592334, 📠 575920; ⊖ 844844; Weather 722334; Marinecall 09068 500 452/0839 406189; Police 386000.

FACILITIES **Services:** AB £16 for a period of up to 5 days , El, Ⓔ, CH, ME, ACA. **City** EC Wed/Sat; all amenities, ⇌, ✈.

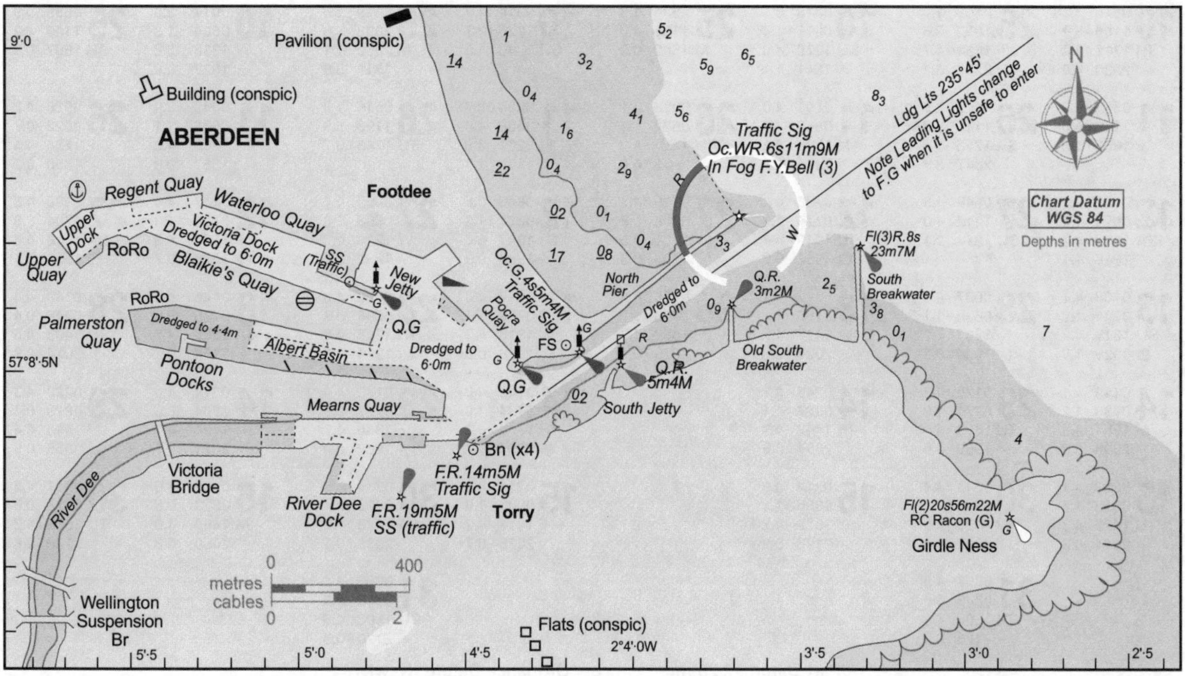

TIME ZONE (UTC)
For Summer Time add ONE hour in **non-shaded areas**

SCOTLAND – ABERDEEN

LAT 57°09′N LONG 2°05′W

TIMES AND HEIGHTS OF HIGH AND LOW WATERS

SPRING & NEAP TIDES
Dates in red are **SPRINGS**
Dates in blue are **NEAPS**

YEAR **2002**

JANUARY

Day	Time	m	Day	Time	m
1	0220	4.3	16	0305	4.0
	0815	1.0		0847	1.3
TU	1433	4.4	W	1503	4.2
	2046	0.6		2118	1.0
2	0308	4.3	17	0341	3.9
	0900	1.0		0920	1.3
W	1517	4.4	TH	1536	4.1
	2135	0.6		2151	1.1
3	0358	4.2	18	0417	3.8
	0947	1.1		0953	1.4
TH	1605	4.3	F	1611	4.0
	2226	0.7		2226	1.2
4	0451	4.1	19	0455	3.7
	1036	1.3		1028	1.6
F	1656	4.2	SA	1650	3.9
	2320	0.8		2304	1.3
5	0547	3.9	20	0536	3.6
	1131	1.5		1108	1.7
SA	1753	4.1	SU	1734	3.8
				2348	1.5
6	0019	1.0	21	0624	3.5
	0648	3.8		1156	1.8
SU	1233	1.6	M	1824	3.6
	1857	4.0			
7	0124	1.2	22	0040	1.6
	0754	3.7		0719	3.4
M	1343	1.7	TU	1258	2.0
	2008	3.9		1923	3.5
8	0233	1.3	23	0142	1.7
	0903	3.7		0822	3.4
TU	1458	1.7	W	1412	2.0
	2122	3.9		2031	3.5
9	0344	1.3	24	0252	1.7
	1009	3.8		0929	3.5
W	1610	1.6	TH	1528	1.9
	2231	3.9		2144	3.6
10	0445	1.3	25	0400	1.7
	1106	3.9		1032	3.6
TH	1711	1.4	F	1634	1.7
	2330	4.0		2251	3.7
11	0537	1.3	26	0459	1.5
	1155	4.0		1125	3.8
F	1803	1.3	SA	1728	1.4
				2347	3.9
12	0022	4.1	27	0549	1.3
	0621	1.3		1212	4.0
SA	1238	4.1	SU	1817	1.1
	1848	1.1			
13	0108	4.1	28	0037	4.1
	0701	1.2		0636	1.1
SU	1317	4.2	M	1255	4.2
	● 1929	1.0		○ 1904	0.8
14	0149	4.1	29	0125	4.3
	0738	1.2		0721	1.0
M	1354	4.3	TU	1338	4.4
	2008	0.9		1950	0.5
15	0228	4.1	30	0211	4.4
	0813	1.2		0805	0.9
TU	1429	4.3	W	1420	4.6
	2044	0.9		2037	0.4
			31	0257	4.5
				0849	0.8
			TH	1504	4.6
				2123	0.3

FEBRUARY

Day	Time	m	Day	Time	m
1	0343	4.4	16	0344	3.9
	0932	0.9		0925	1.2
F	1549	4.6	SA	1544	4.1
	2210	0.4		2153	1.0
2	0431	4.2	17	0417	3.8
	1016	1.0		0955	1.3
SA	1637	4.5	SU	1618	4.0
	2258	0.6		2225	1.1
3	0520	4.0	18	0452	3.7
	1104	1.2		1029	1.4
SU	1729	4.3	M	1656	3.9
	2349	0.9		2300	1.3
4	0614	3.8	19	0532	3.6
	1157	1.4		1108	1.6
M	1828	4.0	TU	1740	3.7
				2343	1.5
5	0047	1.2	20	0620	3.5
	0715	3.6		1158	1.7
TU	1304	1.6	W	1833	3.6
	1938	3.8			
6	0156	1.5	21	0039	1.7
	0825	3.5		0720	3.4
W	1426	1.7	TH	1311	1.9
	2059	3.7		1942	3.4
7	0316	1.7	22	0156	1.8
	0940	3.5		0835	3.3
TH	1554	1.7	F	1441	1.9
	2219	3.7		2106	3.4
8	0430	1.7	23	0324	1.8
	1048	3.7		0954	3.5
F	1705	1.5	SA	1606	1.7
	2326	3.8		2227	3.6
9	0527	1.6	24	0438	1.6
	1143	3.8		1100	3.7
SA	1758	1.3	SU	1710	1.3
				2331	3.8
10	0018	3.9	25	0534	1.3
	0611	1.4		1151	4.0
SU	1228	4.0	M	1802	0.9
	1841	1.1			
11	0101	4.0	26	0023	4.1
	0649	1.3		0622	1.1
M	1306	4.1	TU	1237	4.2
	1918	1.0		1849	0.6
12	0138	4.0	27	0110	4.3
	0724	1.2		0706	0.8
TU	1340	4.2	W	1320	4.5
	● 1952	0.9		○ 1935	0.3
13	0212	4.1	28	0155	4.5
	0756	1.1		0749	0.7
W	1412	4.2	TH	1402	4.7
	2024	0.8		2020	0.1
14	0243	4.1			
	0827	1.1			
TH	1442	4.2			
	2054	0.8			
15	0314	4.0			
	0856	1.1			
F	1512	4.2			
	2123	0.9			

MARCH

Day	Time	m	Day	Time	m
1	0238	4.5	16	0244	4.0
	0830	0.6		0830	0.9
F	1445	4.7	SA	1446	4.2
	2103	0.1		2052	0.8
2	0321	4.4	17	0312	4.0
	0911	0.6		0858	1.0
SA	1529	4.7	SU	1517	4.1
	2147	0.3		2120	0.9
3	0404	4.3	18	0342	3.9
	0952	0.8		0926	1.0
SU	1615	4.5	M	1550	4.0
	2230	0.6		2149	1.0
4	0450	4.0	19	0415	3.8
	1036	1.0		0958	1.2
M	1705	4.3	TU	1627	3.9
	2317	0.9		2221	1.2
5	0539	3.8	20	0452	3.7
	1127	1.2		1035	1.3
TU	1803	3.9	W	1709	3.7
				2301	1.4
6	0010	1.3	21	0536	3.5
	0636	3.6		1122	1.5
W	1232	1.5	TH	1803	3.5
	1913	3.6		2355	1.6
7	0119	1.7	22	0635	3.3
	0747	3.4		1233	1.7
TH	1359	1.7	F	1914	3.4
	2040	3.5			
8	0249	1.9	23	0117	1.8
	0910	3.4		0753	3.3
F	1543	1.7	SA	1410	1.7
	2209	3.5		2043	3.4
9	0416	1.8	24	0258	1.8
	1028	3.5		0921	3.3
SA	1656	1.5	SU	1542	1.5
	2317	3.6		2209	3.5
10	0514	1.7	25	0419	1.6
	1126	3.7		1033	3.6
SU	1746	1.3	M	1650	1.1
				2314	3.8
11	0006	3.7	26	0516	1.3
	0556	1.5		1128	3.9
M	1211	3.8	TU	1743	0.7
	1824	1.1			
12	0045	3.9	27	0005	4.1
	0631	1.3		0603	1.0
TU	1247	4.0	W	1214	4.2
	1858	0.9		1830	0.4
13	0117	4.0	28	0050	4.3
	0703	1.1		0646	0.7
W	1318	4.1	TH	1258	4.5
	1928	0.8		○ 1914	0.1
14	0148	4.0	29	0133	4.4
	0734	1.0		0727	0.5
TH	1348	4.2	F	1340	4.7
	● 1957	0.7		1957	0.0
15	0216	4.0	30	0214	4.5
	0803	1.0		0808	0.4
F	1417	4.2	SA	1423	4.7
	2025	0.7		2039	0.1
			31	0255	4.4
				0848	0.5
			SU	1508	4.6
				2120	0.3

APRIL

Day	Time	m	Day	Time	m
1	0336	4.2	16	0313	3.9
	0930	0.6		0903	0.9
M	1554	4.4	TU	1527	3.9
	2202	0.6		2120	1.0
2	0420	4.0	17	0346	3.8
	1014	0.8		0936	1.0
TU	1645	4.1	W	1606	3.8
	2246	1.0		2154	1.1
3	0506	3.8	18	0424	3.7
	1104	1.1		1016	1.1
W	1743	3.8	TH	1651	3.7
	2337	1.4		2235	1.3
4	0602	3.5	19	0509	3.5
	1208	1.4		1108	1.3
TH	1854	3.5	F	1748	3.5
				2333	1.6
5	0044	1.8	20	0609	3.4
	0710	3.3		1221	1.4
F	1334	1.6	SA	1902	3.3
	2018	3.3			
6	0216	2.0	21	0059	1.8
	0834	3.3		0727	3.3
SA	1521	1.6	SU	1353	1.4
	2147	3.3		2028	3.4
7	0350	1.9	22	0236	1.7
	0957	3.4		0851	3.4
SU	1632	1.4	M	1519	1.2
	2254	3.5		2149	3.5
8	0448	1.7	23	0354	1.5
	1057	3.5		1004	3.6
M	1719	1.2	TU	1626	0.9
	2340	3.6		2251	3.8
9	0530	1.5	24	0451	1.2
	1142	3.7		1100	3.9
TU	1756	1.0	W	1719	0.6
				2342	4.0
10	0017	3.8	25	0539	0.9
	0604	1.3		1149	4.2
W	1218	3.8	TH	1807	0.3
	1827	0.9			
11	0048	3.9	26	0026	4.2
	0636	1.1		0622	0.7
TH	1250	4.0	F	1234	4.4
	1857	0.8		1850	0.2
12	0117	4.0	27	0108	4.3
	0706	1.0		0704	0.5
F	1320	4.0	SA	1318	4.5
	● 1926	0.7		○ 1933	0.1
13	0146	4.0	28	0149	4.4
	0735	0.9		0746	0.4
SA	1350	4.1	SU	1403	4.5
	1954	0.7		2014	0.3
14	0214	4.0	29	0229	4.3
	0804	0.8		0828	0.4
SU	1421	4.1	M	1449	4.4
	2021	0.7		2055	0.5
15	0242	4.0	30	0311	4.2
	0833	0.8		0912	0.6
M	1453	4.0	TU	1538	4.2
	2050	0.8		2136	0.8

Chart Datum: 2·25 metres below Ordnance Datum (Newlyn)

TIME ZONE (UTC)
For Summer Time add ONE hour in **non-shaded areas**

SCOTLAND – ABERDEEN

LAT 57°09'N LONG 2°05'W

TIMES AND HEIGHTS OF HIGH AND LOW WATERS

SPRING & NEAP TIDES
Dates in red are **SPRINGS**
Dates in blue are **NEAPS**

YEAR **2002**

MAY

Date	Day	Time	m	Time	m	Time	m	Time	m
1	W	0353	4.0	0957	0.8	1629	3.9	2220	1.2
2	TH	0439	3.8	1048	1.0	1727	3.6	2309	1.5
3	F	0532	3.5	1148	1.3	1832	3.4		
4	SA	0010	1.8	0635	3.4	1303	1.4	1945	3.2
5	SU	0130	1.9	0750	3.3	1434	1.5	2104	3.2
6	M	0301	1.9	0907	3.3	1548	1.4	2212	3.3
7	TU	0406	1.7	1012	3.4	1638	1.2	2301	3.5
8	W	0452	1.5	1101	3.5	1717	1.1	2339	3.6
9	TH	0530	1.3	1140	3.7	1751	1.0		
10	F	0013	3.8	0604	1.2	1216	3.8	1822	0.9
11	SA	0044	3.9	0636	1.0	1250	3.9	1852	0.8
12	SU	0114	4.0	0707	0.9	1323	4.0	● 1923	0.8
13	M	0145	4.0	0739	0.8	1357	4.0	1954	0.8
14	TU	0216	4.0	0812	0.8	1433	4.0	2026	0.9
15	W	0249	4.0	0847	0.8	1511	3.9	2100	1.0
16	TH	0325	3.9	0926	0.9	1554	3.8	2139	1.1
17	F	0406	3.8	1011	1.0	1644	3.7	2227	1.3
18	SA	0455	3.6	1108	1.1	1743	3.5	2328	1.5
19	SU	0555	3.5	1218	1.2	1854	3.4		
20	M	0046	1.6	0707	3.5	1336	1.1	2010	3.5
21	TU	0208	1.6	0823	3.5	1452	1.0	2123	3.6
22	W	0321	1.4	0932	3.7	1558	0.8	2224	3.8
23	TH	0421	1.2	1032	3.9	1653	0.6	2316	3.9
24	F	0513	1.0	1125	4.1	1743	0.5		
25	SA	0002	4.1	0600	0.8	1214	4.3	1828	0.4
26	SU	0045	4.2	0645	0.6	1302	4.3	○ 1911	0.4
27	M	0127	4.2	0730	0.5	1349	4.3	1953	0.6
28	TU	0208	4.2	0814	0.5	1437	4.2	2035	0.8
29	W	0250	4.1	0859	0.6	1525	4.0	2116	1.0
30	TH	0332	4.0	0945	0.8	1615	3.8	2158	1.2
31	F	0416	3.8	1032	1.0	1707	3.6	2243	1.5

JUNE

Date	Day	Time	m	Time	m	Time	m	Time	m
1	SA	0504	3.7	1123	1.1	1802	3.4	2335	1.7
2	SU	0558	3.5	1221	1.3	1902	3.3		
3	M	0038	1.8	0659	3.4	1329	1.4	2006	3.2
4	TU	0151	1.9	0805	3.3	1440	1.4	2110	3.3
5	W	0304	1.8	0911	3.3	1541	1.4	2207	3.4
6	TH	0403	1.7	1009	3.4	1629	1.3	2253	3.5
7	F	0449	1.5	1057	3.6	1710	1.2	2333	3.7
8	SA	0529	1.3	1140	3.7	1746	1.1		
9	SU	0010	3.8	0605	1.1	1220	3.8	1821	1.0
10	M	0045	3.9	0641	1.0	1259	3.9	● 1856	0.9
11	TU	0120	4.0	0718	0.9	1338	4.0	1932	0.9
12	W	0155	4.0	0757	0.8	1418	4.0	2010	0.9
13	TH	0232	4.0	0838	0.7	1501	4.0	2050	1.0
14	F	0312	4.0	0922	0.7	1548	3.9	2135	1.1
15	SA	0356	3.9	1011	0.8	1638	3.8	2224	1.2
16	SU	0445	3.9	1106	0.8	1735	3.7	2321	1.4
17	M	0542	3.8	1207	0.9	1838	3.6		
18	TU	0025	1.5	0645	3.7	1313	0.9	1944	3.6
19	W	0136	1.5	0753	3.7	1421	0.9	2052	3.6
20	TH	0246	1.5	0902	3.8	1528	0.9	2155	3.7
21	F	0352	1.3	1008	3.9	1629	0.9	2252	3.8
22	SA	0451	1.2	1108	4.0	1723	0.8	2342	4.0
23	SU	0545	1.0	1202	4.1	1811	0.8		
24	M	0027	4.1	0634	0.8	1253	4.1	○ 1855	0.8
25	TU	0111	4.1	0721	0.7	1341	4.1	1938	0.9
26	W	0153	4.2	0806	0.7	1428	4.1	2019	1.0
27	TH	0233	4.1	0849	0.7	1513	4.0	2058	1.1
28	F	0314	4.1	0930	0.8	1557	3.8	2137	1.2
29	SA	0354	4.0	1011	0.9	1641	3.7	2216	1.4
30	SU	0435	3.8	1052	1.0	1726	3.5	2258	1.5

JULY

Date	Day	Time	m	Time	m	Time	m	Time	m
1	M	0519	3.7	1137	1.2	1813	3.4	2345	1.7
2	TU	0608	3.6	1227	1.3	1905	3.3		
3	W	0042	1.8	0703	3.4	1325	1.5	2001	3.3
4	TH	0148	1.9	0804	3.4	1428	1.5	2101	3.3
5	F	0258	1.8	0908	3.4	1531	1.5	2200	3.4
6	SA	0401	1.7	1011	3.5	1625	1.4	2252	3.6
7	SU	0453	1.5	1106	3.6	1712	1.3	2337	3.7
8	M	0538	1.3	1154	3.7	1754	1.2		
9	TU	0018	3.9	0620	1.1	1240	3.9	1835	1.1
10	W	0058	4.0	0702	0.9	1323	4.0	● 1917	1.0
11	TH	0138	4.1	0745	0.7	1407	4.1	1959	0.9
12	F	0218	4.2	0830	0.6	1452	4.1	2042	0.9
13	SA	0300	4.2	0916	0.5	1538	4.1	2127	1.0
14	SU	0344	4.2	1003	0.5	1627	4.0	2213	1.1
15	M	0431	4.2	1053	0.6	1718	3.9	2302	1.2
16	TU	0523	4.1	1146	0.7	1813	3.8	2358	1.3
17	W	0620	4.0	1244	0.9	1914	3.7		
18	TH	0101	1.5	0725	3.9	1349	1.1	2019	3.6
19	F	0212	1.5	0837	3.8	1459	1.2	2127	3.6
20	SA	0329	1.5	0952	3.8	1609	1.3	2231	3.7
21	SU	0439	1.3	1100	3.8	1710	1.2	2327	3.8
22	M	0539	1.2	1159	3.9	1801	1.2		
23	TU	0016	4.0	0629	1.0	1251	4.0	1845	1.2
24	W	0100	4.1	0715	0.8	1336	4.0	○ 1925	1.1
25	TH	0140	4.2	0756	0.7	1417	4.0	2003	1.1
26	F	0217	4.2	0834	0.7	1456	4.0	2039	1.1
27	SA	0253	4.2	0910	0.8	1533	3.9	2112	1.2
28	SU	0328	4.1	0943	0.8	1608	3.8	2146	1.3
29	M	0403	4.0	1017	1.0	1645	3.7	2220	1.4
30	TU	0440	3.9	1053	1.1	1724	3.6	2257	1.5
31	W	0521	3.8	1133	1.3	1808	3.5	2342	1.7

AUGUST

Date	Day	Time	m	Time	m	Time	m	Time	m
1	TH	0609	3.6	1220	1.5	1859	3.4		
2	F	0038	1.8	0705	3.5	1318	1.6	1957	3.3
3	SA	0149	1.9	0811	3.4	1427	1.7	2104	3.4
4	SU	0308	1.9	0924	3.4	1540	1.7	2210	3.5
5	M	0419	1.7	1035	3.5	1642	1.6	2307	3.7
6	TU	0515	1.4	1133	3.7	1734	1.4	2355	3.9
7	W	0603	1.1	1223	3.9	1819	1.2		
8	TH	0038	4.1	0647	0.8	1309	4.1	● 1903	1.0
9	F	0120	4.3	0732	0.5	1353	4.3	1945	0.9
10	SA	0201	4.4	0816	0.3	1437	4.4	2028	0.8
11	SU	0242	4.5	0900	0.2	1521	4.4	2110	0.8
12	M	0325	4.5	0945	0.3	1606	4.3	2152	0.9
13	TU	0411	4.5	1030	0.4	1652	4.1	2237	1.0
14	W	0500	4.3	1119	0.7	1743	3.9	2328	1.2
15	TH	0555	4.1	1213	1.0	1840	3.7		
16	F	0029	1.4	0701	3.9	1317	1.3	1946	3.6
17	SA	0146	1.6	0820	3.7	1435	1.6	2102	3.5
18	SU	0317	1.6	0945	3.6	1558	1.6	2216	3.6
19	M	0437	1.4	1100	3.7	1703	1.6	2317	3.8
20	TU	0537	1.2	1158	3.9	1753	1.5		
21	W	0007	4.0	0624	1.0	1245	4.0	1834	1.3
22	TH	0048	4.1	0704	0.9	1324	4.0	○ 1910	1.2
23	F	0124	4.2	0739	0.8	1359	4.1	1943	1.1
24	SA	0157	4.2	0812	0.7	1431	4.1	2015	1.1
25	SU	0228	4.2	0842	0.7	1502	4.0	2045	1.1
26	M	0259	4.2	0911	0.8	1532	4.0	2114	1.2
27	TU	0330	4.1	0940	0.9	1604	3.9	2144	1.3
28	W	0404	4.0	1010	1.1	1638	3.8	2216	1.4
29	TH	0442	3.9	1044	1.3	1717	3.6	2254	1.6
30	F	0525	3.7	1124	1.5	1803	3.5	2342	1.7
31	SA	0618	3.5	1216	1.7	1900	3.4		

Chart Datum: 2·25 metres below Ordnance Datum (Newlyn)

TIME ZONE (UTC)
For Summer Time add ONE hour in **non-shaded areas**

SCOTLAND – ABERDEEN

LAT 57°09'N LONG 2°05'W

TIMES AND HEIGHTS OF HIGH AND LOW WATERS

SPRING & NEAP TIDES
Dates in red are **SPRINGS**
Dates in blue are **NEAPS**

YEAR **2002**

SEPTEMBER

Date	Day	Time	m	Time	m	Time	m	Time	m
1	SU	0051	1.9	0724	3.4	1330	1.9	2011	3.3
2	M	0221	1.9	0847	3.4	1500	1.9	2131	3.4
3	TU	0349	1.7	1010	3.5	1619	1.7	2238	3.6
4	W	0454	1.4	1114	3.7	1715	1.5	2331	3.9
5	TH	0544	1.0	1205	4.0	1802	1.2		
6	F	0016	4.2	0628	0.7	1250	4.3	1844	1.0
7	SA	0057	4.4	0712	0.3	1333	4.5	● 1925	0.8
8	SU	0138	4.6	0755	0.1	1415	4.5	2006	0.7
9	M	0220	4.8	0838	0.1	1456	4.5	2046	0.6
10	TU	0302	4.7	0920	0.2	1539	4.4	2127	0.7
11	W	0348	4.6	1003	0.5	1623	4.2	2211	0.9
12	TH	0437	4.4	1049	0.8	1711	4.0	2301	1.2
13	F	0534	4.1	1141	1.3	1807	3.7		
14	SA	0003	1.4	0643	3.8	1247	1.6	1915	3.5
15	SU	0127	1.6	0809	3.6	1414	1.9	2038	3.5
16	M	0312	1.6	0941	3.5	1548	1.9	2159	3.6
17	TU	0433	1.5	1055	3.7	1652	1.7	2303	3.8
18	W	0528	1.2	1148	3.8	1738	1.6	2350	3.9
19	TH	0609	1.1	1228	4.0	1815	1.4		
20	F	0028	4.1	0642	0.9	1302	4.0	1847	1.2
21	SA	0101	4.2	0713	0.8	1333	4.1	○ 1918	1.1
22	SU	0131	4.3	0742	0.8	1401	4.1	1948	1.0
23	M	0200	4.3	0810	0.8	1429	4.1	2016	1.0
24	TU	0230	4.3	0837	0.8	1457	4.1	2043	1.1
25	W	0300	4.2	0904	0.9	1527	4.0	2112	1.2
26	TH	0334	4.1	0932	1.1	1559	3.9	2143	1.3
27	F	0410	3.9	1003	1.3	1635	3.8	2219	1.4
28	SA	0452	3.7	1040	1.5	1718	3.6	2305	1.6
29	SU	0544	3.5	1129	1.8	1813	3.5		
30	M	0012	1.8	0653	3.4	1247	2.0	1928	3.4

OCTOBER

Date	Day	Time	m	Time	m	Time	m	Time	m
1	TU	0147	1.8	0820	3.4	1429	2.0	2055	3.4
2	W	0321	1.6	0947	3.5	1555	1.8	2208	3.7
3	TH	0429	1.3	1052	3.8	1652	1.5	2303	4.0
4	F	0520	0.9	1142	4.1	1739	1.2	2349	4.3
5	SA	0605	0.5	1226	4.4	1821	0.9		
6	SU	0031	4.6	0648	0.3	1308	4.5	● 1901	0.7
7	M	0113	4.8	0730	0.1	1348	4.6	1941	0.6
8	TU	0156	4.8	0812	0.1	1429	4.6	2022	0.6
9	W	0240	4.8	0853	0.3	1511	4.4	2104	0.7
10	TH	0327	4.6	0936	0.7	1554	4.2	2149	0.9
11	F	0418	4.3	1021	1.1	1641	4.0	2241	1.1
12	SA	0517	4.0	1112	1.5	1737	3.7	2345	1.4
13	SU	0629	3.7	1218	1.9	1846	3.6		
14	M	0110	1.6	0754	3.5	1347	2.1	2009	3.5
15	TU	0256	1.6	0923	3.5	1525	2.0	2132	3.6
16	W	0413	1.5	1034	3.6	1628	1.8	2236	3.7
17	TH	0503	1.3	1124	3.8	1712	1.6	2323	3.9
18	F	0541	1.1	1201	3.9	1748	1.4		
19	SA	0000	4.0	0612	1.0	1233	4.0	1819	1.3
20	SU	0032	4.1	0642	0.9	1302	4.1	1850	1.1
21	M	0103	4.2	0710	0.9	1330	4.2	○ 1919	1.1
22	TU	0133	4.2	0738	0.9	1357	4.2	1948	1.0
23	W	0203	4.2	0805	0.9	1426	4.2	2017	1.0
24	TH	0235	4.2	0832	1.0	1455	4.1	2047	1.1
25	F	0310	4.1	0901	1.2	1527	4.0	2120	1.2
26	SA	0347	3.9	0934	1.3	1603	3.9	2158	1.3
27	SU	0431	3.8	1012	1.5	1647	3.7	2246	1.5
28	M	0525	3.6	1103	1.8	1742	3.5	2354	1.6
29	TU	0635	3.4	1222	2.0	1856	3.5		
30	W	0122	1.7	0758	3.4	1400	2.0	2019	3.5
31	TH	0249	1.5	0919	3.6	1522	1.8	2133	3.7

NOVEMBER

Date	Day	Time	m	Time	m	Time	m	Time	m
1	F	0358	1.2	1024	3.9	1622	1.5	2231	4.0
2	SA	0452	0.8	1115	4.1	1711	1.2	2321	4.3
3	SU	0539	0.5	1200	4.4	1755	1.0		
4	M	0006	4.6	0622	0.4	1242	4.5	● 1837	0.7
5	TU	0051	4.7	0705	0.3	1323	4.6	1919	0.6
6	W	0136	4.8	0747	0.4	1404	4.5	2002	0.6
7	TH	0223	4.7	0830	0.6	1446	4.4	2047	0.7
8	F	0312	4.5	0912	0.9	1529	4.3	2135	0.9
9	SA	0405	4.2	0957	1.3	1616	4.0	2227	1.1
10	SU	0504	3.9	1048	1.6	1710	3.8	2328	1.4
11	M	0611	3.6	1148	1.9	1814	3.6		
12	TU	0042	1.5	0725	3.5	1305	2.1	1928	3.5
13	W	0211	1.6	0843	3.4	1435	2.1	2046	3.5
14	TH	0330	1.5	0953	3.5	1545	2.0	2153	3.6
15	F	0423	1.4	1045	3.7	1635	1.8	2244	3.8
16	SA	0503	1.3	1124	3.8	1714	1.6	2325	3.9
17	SU	0537	1.2	1158	3.9	1749	1.4		
18	M	0001	4.0	0608	1.1	1229	4.1	1821	1.3
19	TU	0035	4.1	0638	1.0	1259	4.1	1853	1.2
20	W	0108	4.1	0708	1.0	1329	4.2	○ 1925	1.1
21	TH	0141	4.2	0738	1.1	1400	4.2	1957	1.1
22	F	0216	4.1	0808	1.1	1431	4.1	2031	1.1
23	SA	0253	4.1	0841	1.2	1505	4.1	2108	1.1
24	SU	0333	3.9	0917	1.4	1543	4.0	2150	1.2
25	M	0419	3.8	1000	1.5	1628	3.8	2241	1.3
26	TU	0514	3.7	1053	1.7	1722	3.7	2344	1.4
27	W	0619	3.6	1204	1.9	1829	3.6		
28	TH	0058	1.4	0732	3.6	1325	1.9	1943	3.7
29	F	0214	1.3	0846	3.7	1442	1.8	2054	3.8
30	SA	0322	1.1	0951	3.9	1547	1.6	2158	4.0

DECEMBER

Date	Day	Time	m	Time	m	Time	m	Time	m
1	SU	0421	0.9	1046	4.1	1642	1.3	2254	4.3
2	M	0513	0.8	1134	4.2	1731	1.1	2345	4.4
3	TU	0600	0.7	1219	4.4	1818	0.9		
4	W	0034	4.5	0645	0.7	1302	4.4	● 1904	0.8
5	TH	0123	4.6	0729	0.7	1344	4.5	1951	0.7
6	F	0212	4.5	0812	0.9	1427	4.4	2038	0.7
7	SA	0303	4.3	0855	1.1	1510	4.3	2126	0.9
8	SU	0354	4.1	0939	1.4	1556	4.1	2214	1.0
9	M	0447	3.9	1024	1.6	1644	4.0	2306	1.2
10	TU	0542	3.7	1114	1.8	1737	3.8		
11	W	0002	1.4	0641	3.5	1213	2.0	1837	3.6
12	TH	0106	1.6	0744	3.4	1323	2.1	1943	3.5
13	F	0216	1.6	0850	3.4	1438	2.1	2050	3.5
14	SA	0322	1.6	0949	3.5	1543	1.9	2152	3.6
15	SU	0414	1.5	1039	3.7	1634	1.8	2244	3.7
16	M	0457	1.5	1120	3.8	1716	1.6	2328	3.8
17	TU	0535	1.4	1157	3.9	1755	1.4		
18	W	0009	3.9	0609	1.3	1233	4.0	1830	1.3
19	TH	0047	4.0	0643	1.2	1306	4.1	○ 1906	1.2
20	F	0125	4.1	0717	1.2	1340	4.2	1943	1.1
21	SA	0203	4.1	0753	1.2	1414	4.2	2021	1.0
22	SU	0243	4.1	0830	1.2	1451	4.2	2102	1.0
23	M	0325	4.0	0910	1.3	1531	4.1	2146	1.0
24	TU	0411	4.0	0954	1.4	1615	4.1	2235	1.0
25	W	0502	3.9	1043	1.5	1705	4.0	2329	1.1
26	TH	0559	3.8	1140	1.6	1803	3.9		
27	F	0030	1.2	0701	3.7	1247	1.7	1907	3.9
28	SA	0136	1.2	0808	3.7	1358	1.7	2017	3.9
29	SU	0245	1.2	0915	3.8	1509	1.6	2127	4.0
30	M	0351	1.2	1018	3.9	1616	1.5	2234	4.1
31	TU	0452	1.1	1113	4.0	1716	1.3	2333	4.2

Chart Datum: 2·25 metres below Ordnance Datum (Newlyn)

PETERHEAD *9.6.18*

Aberdeenshire **57°29'·81N 01°46'·42W**

CHARTS AC 1438, 213; Imray C23; OS 30

TIDES +0140 Dover; ML 2·3; Duration 0620; Zone 0 (UT)

Standard Port ABERDEEN (⟵)

Times				**Height (metres)**			
High Water		Low Water		MHWS	MHWN	MLWN	MLWS
0000	0600	0100	0700	4·3	3·4	1·6	0·6
1200	1800	1300	1900				
Differences PETERHEAD							
−0035	−0045	−0035	−0040	−0·5	−0·3	−0·1	−0·1

SHELTER Good in marina (2·8m). A useful passage hbr, also a major fishing and oil/gas industry port. Access any weather/tide.

NAVIGATION WPT 57°29'·44N 01°45'·75W, 134°/314° from/to ent, 0·5M. No dangers. 5kn speed limit in Bay; 4kn in marina. Chan between marina bkwtr and SHM lt buoy is <30m wide.

LIGHTS AND MARKS Power stn chy (183m) is conspic 1·25M S of ent, with Fl W lts H24. Ldg marks 314°, front △, rear ▽ on W cols; lts as chartlet. Marina E bkwtr ☆ Fl R 4s 6m 2M; W bkwtr hd, QG 5m 2M, vis 185°-300°. Buchan Ness ☆ Fl 5s 40m 28M is 1·6M S of entr.

RADIO TELEPHONE All vessels, including yachts, **must** call *Peterhead Harbour Radio* VHF Ch **14** for clearance to enter/depart the Bay.

TELEPHONE (Dial code 01779) Marina Mr (Bay Authority: www.peterhead-bay.co.uk) 474020, 🖷 475712; Hr Control (H24) 4833630; MRCC (01224) 592334; ⊜ (01224) 212666; Marinecall 09068 500452; Police 472571; Dr 474841; ⊞ 472316.

FACILITIES Peterhead Bay Marina ☎ via 474020 (HO)/🖷 475712, ☎ 474281 (after hrs), 150 AB £10 for 7m LOA, £1 per m thereafter (7 days for price of 5), max LOA 20m; access all tides, 2·3m at ent. Pontoons are 'E' to 'A' from ent. AC, FW, Gas, CH; D from bowser at end of Princess Royal jetty (☆ Oc WRG 4s); R, V and ⊡ at caravan site. **Peterhead SC ☎** (01358) 751340 (Sec); **Services:** Slip, ME, El, Ⓔ, Sh, C, Gas. **Town** EC Wed; P, V, R, ✉, bus to Aberdeen for ⇌ & ✈Ⓨ.

ADJACENT HARBOUR

BODDAM, Aberdeenshire, **57°28'·47N 01°46'·56W.** AC 213. HW +0145 on Dover; Tides as 9.6.19. Good shelter in the lee of Meikle Mackie, the island just N of Buchan Ness, Fl 5s 40m 28M Horn (3) 60s. Inner hbr dries/unlit. Beware rks around Meikle Mackie and to the SW of it. Appr from 1½ca NW of The Skerry. Yachts on S side of outer hbr. All facilities at Peterhead, 2M N.

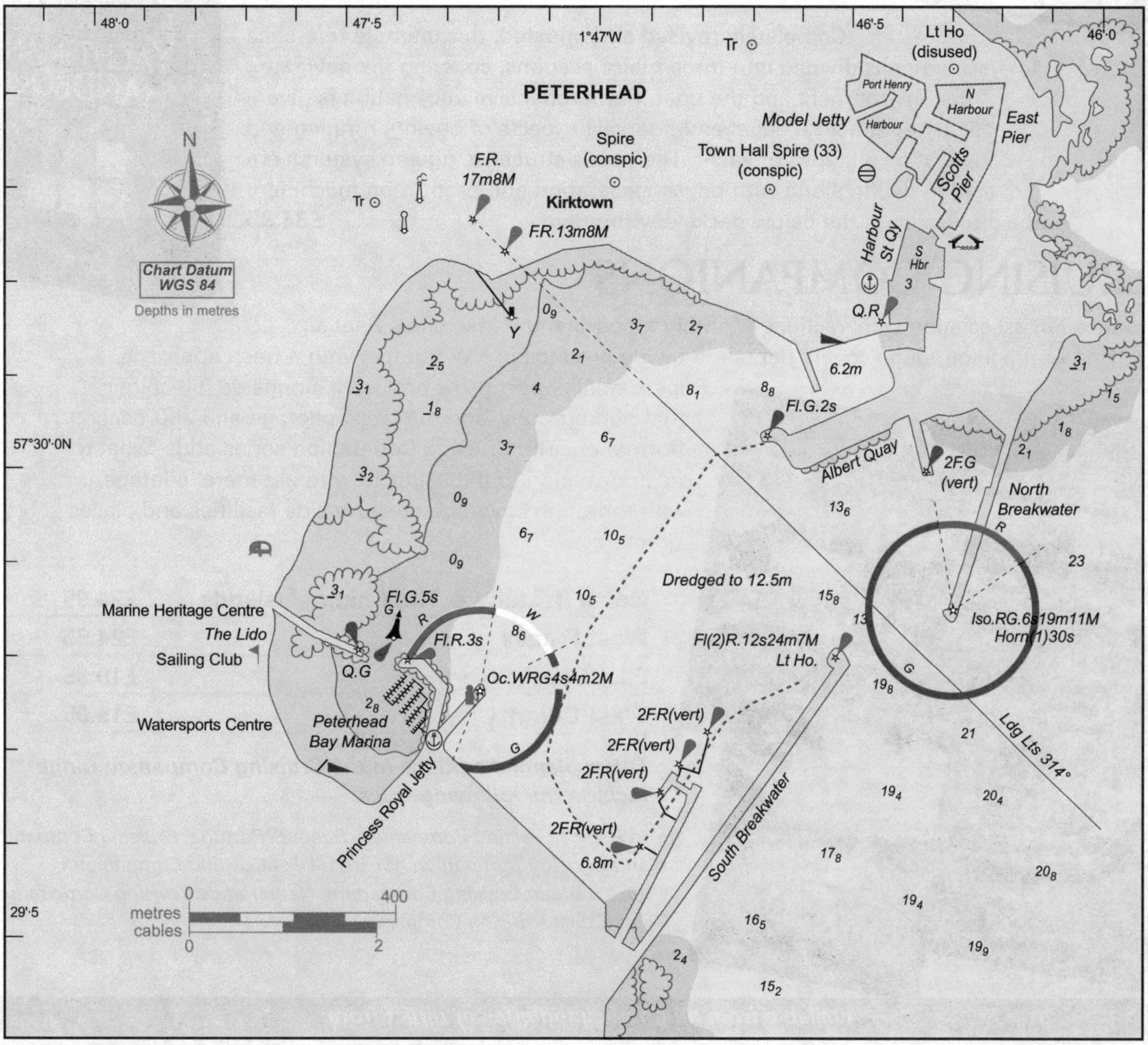

MAPTECH®
Leading the world in digital navigation
Maptech UK Ltd • +44 (0)1243 389352 • sales@maptech.co.uk

Maptech world class digital chart CDs
Worldwide coverage from over 4,500 charts

Maptech award winning software
Easy to use navigation software
• Chart Navigator • Cruising Navigator • Offshore Navigator

www.maptech.co.uk

Area 7

North-East Scotland
Rattray Head to Cape Wrath
including Orkney and Shetland Islands

9.7.1 Index .... Page 461

9.7.2 Area map 462

9.7.3 Tidal stream charts 464

9.7.4 Lights, buoys & waypoints 466

9.7.5 Passage information 470

9.7.6 Distance table 471

9.7.7 Fraserburgh 472
Rosehearty

9.7.8 Macduff and Banff 472
Portsoy

9.7.9 Whitehills 473
Cullen
Portknockie
Findochty

9.7.10 Buckie 473

9.7.11 Lossiemouth 474

9.7.12 Hopeman 474

9.7.13 Burghead 475

9.7.14 Findhorn 475

9.7.15 Nairn 476

9.7.16 Inverness 476
Fortrose
Avoch
Caledonian Canal

9.7.17 Portmahomack 478
Cromarty Firth
Dornoch Firth
Golspie

9.7.18 Helmsdale 479
Lybster

9.7.19 Wick, Standard Port, tidal curves 479

9.7.20 Scrabster 483
Kyle of Tongue
Loch Eriboll

9.7.21 Orkney Islands 484
Houton Bay
Shapinsay
Auskerry
Pierowall
Rapness

9.7.22 Stromness 485

9.7.23 Kirkwall 486

9.7.24 Stronsay 486

9.7.25 Shetland Islands 490

9.7.26 Lerwick, Standard Port, tidal curves 491
Foula
Balta Sound
Scalloway
Vaila Sound (Walls)
Fair Isle

Register for your FREE weekly weather email service from Macmillan Reeds
» at www.nauticaldata.com – NOW! «
weekend weather reports sent to your email address, every Thursday

9.7.2 North-East Scotland, Orkney and Shetland

Rattray Head to Cape Wrath

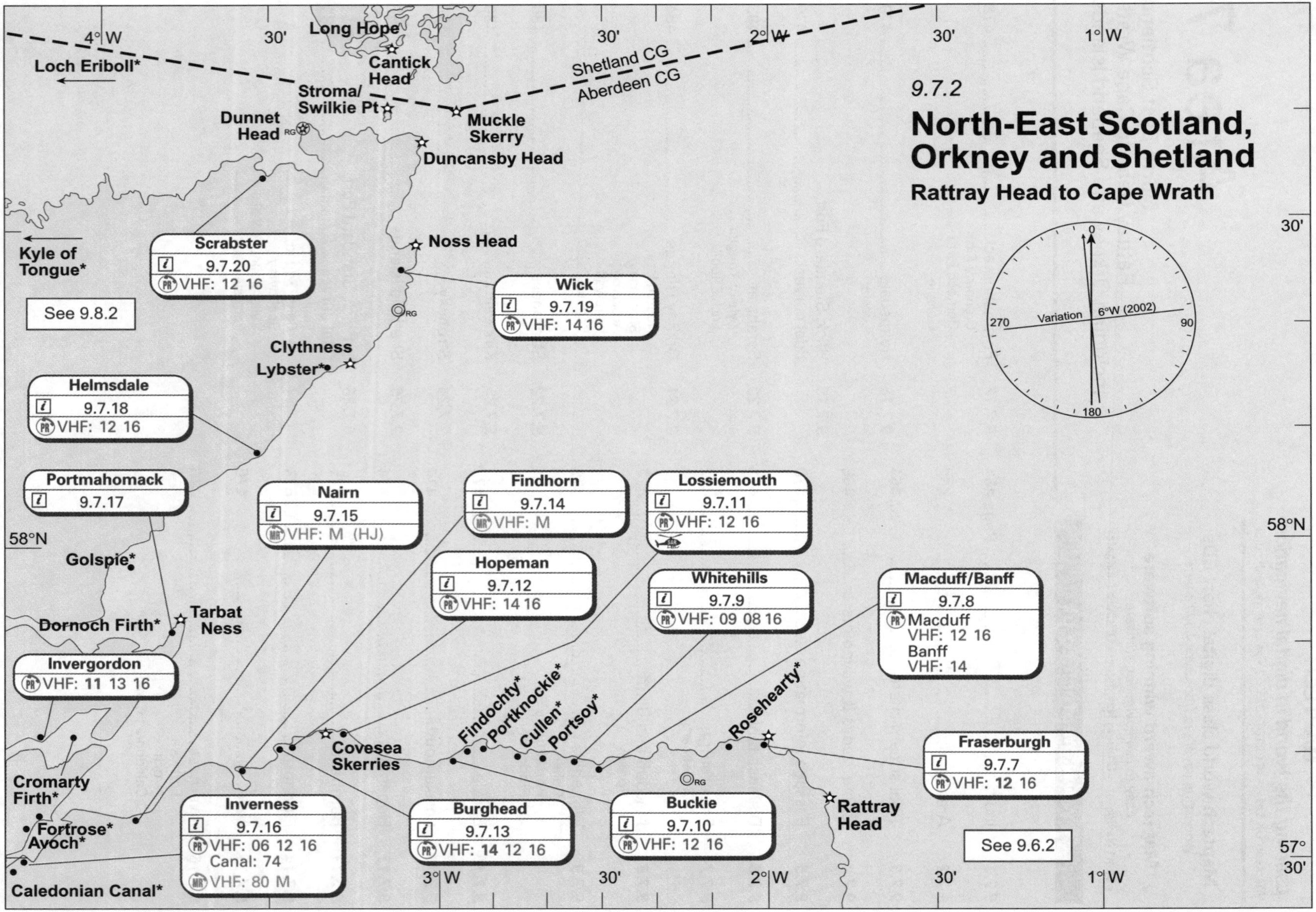

Key to Symbols

- (CGR) Coastguard Radio: VHF/MF frequencies
- (TSS) (VTS) TSS or VTS Radio: VHF frequencies
- (PR) (MR) Port or Marina Radio: VHF frequencies
- [i] See for harbour information/tidal data
- (weather symbol) Weather information (Frequencies/times of broadcasts)
- (SAR helicopter symbol) SAR Helicopter base
- ☆ Selected Principal Lights
- (light vessel symbol) Light vessel/Light float/Lanby
- ◎RG Emergency VHF DF
- * See Area Index

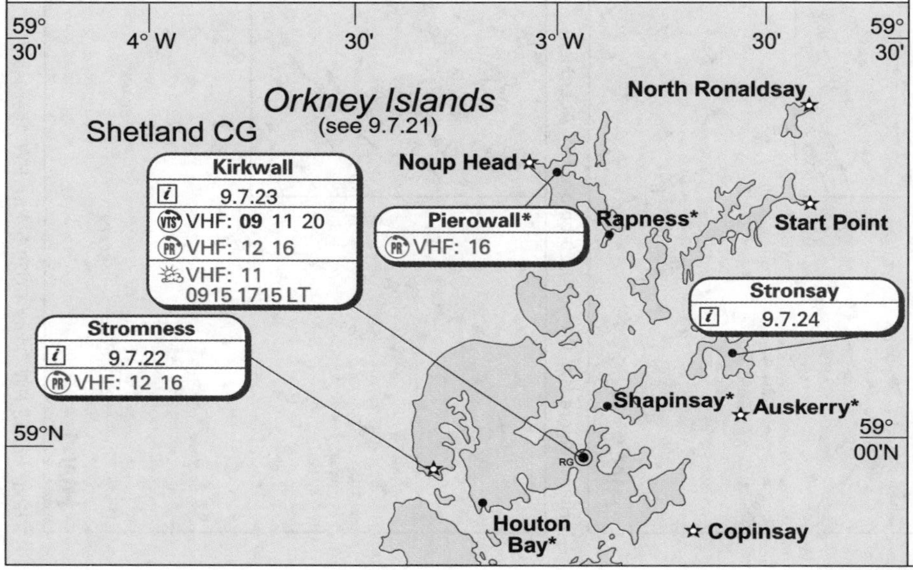
59° 30'
4° W
30'
3° W
30'
59° 30'
Orkney Islands
(see 9.7.21)
Shetland CG
North Ronaldsay
Noup Head
Kirkwall
9.7.23
VHF: 09 11 20
VHF: 12 16
VHF: 11
0915 1715 LT
Pierowall*
VHF: 16
Rapness*
Start Point
Stronsay
9.7.24
Stromness
9.7.22
VHF: 12 16
Shapinsay*
Auskerry*
59°N
59° 00'N
RG
Houton Bay*
Copinsay

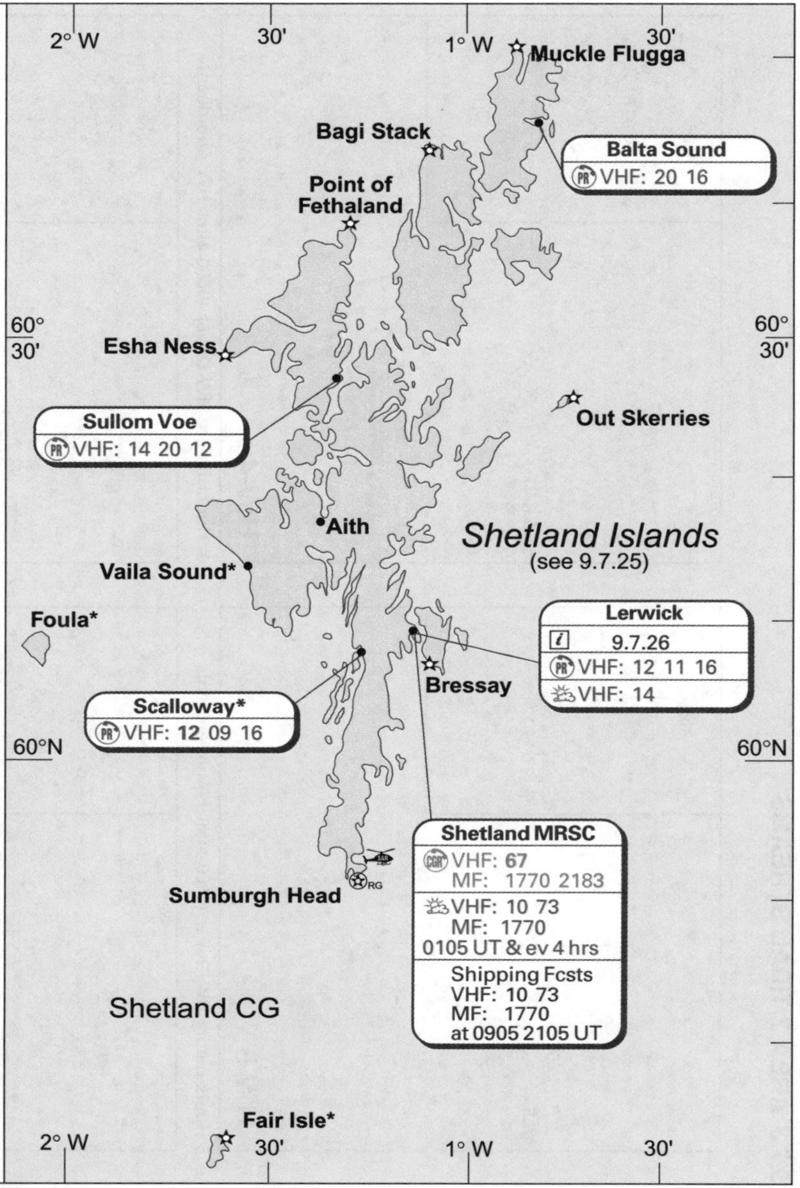
2° W
30'
1° W
Muckle Flugga
30'
Bagi Stack
Balta Sound
VHF: 20 16
Point of Fethaland
60° 30'
Esha Ness
60° 30'
Sullom Voe
VHF: 14 20 12
Out Skerries
Aith
Shetland Islands
(see 9.7.25)
Vaila Sound*
Foula*
Lerwick
9.7.26
VHF: 12 11 16
VHF: 14
Scalloway*
VHF: 12 09 16
Bressay
60°N
60°N
Shetland MRSC
VHF: 67
MF: 1770 2183
VHF: 10 73
MF: 1770
0105 UT & ev 4 hrs
Shipping Fcsts
VHF: 10 73
MF: 1770
at 0905 2105 UT
Sumburgh Head
RG
Shetland CG
Fair Isle*
2° W
30'
1° W
30'

7

9.7.3 AREA 7 TIDAL STREAMS

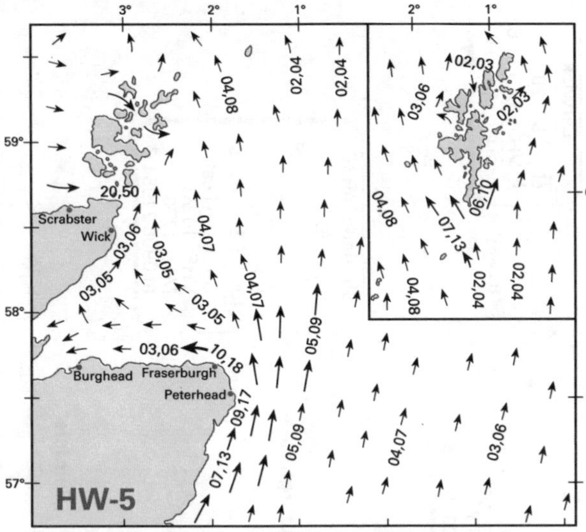

5 Hours before HW Dover (0500 after HW Aberdeen)

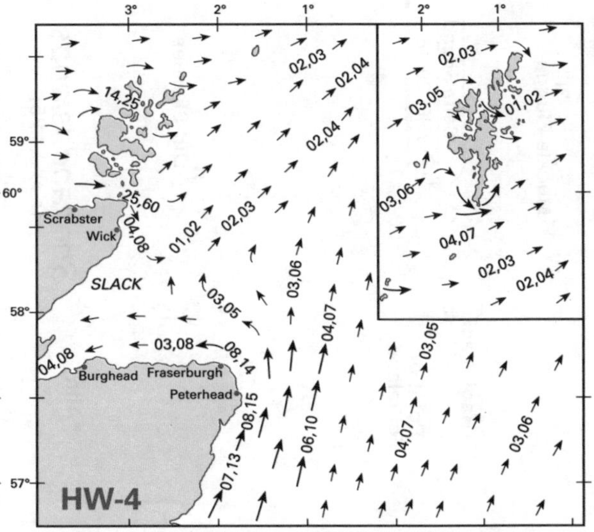

4 Hours before HW Dover (0600 after HW Aberdeen)

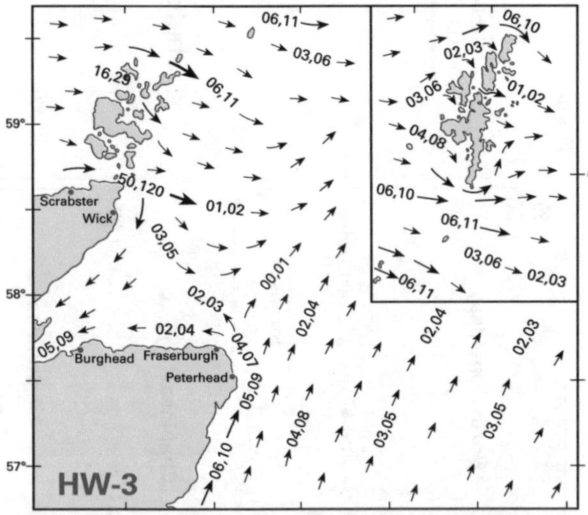

3 Hours before HW Dover (0520 before HW Aberdeen)

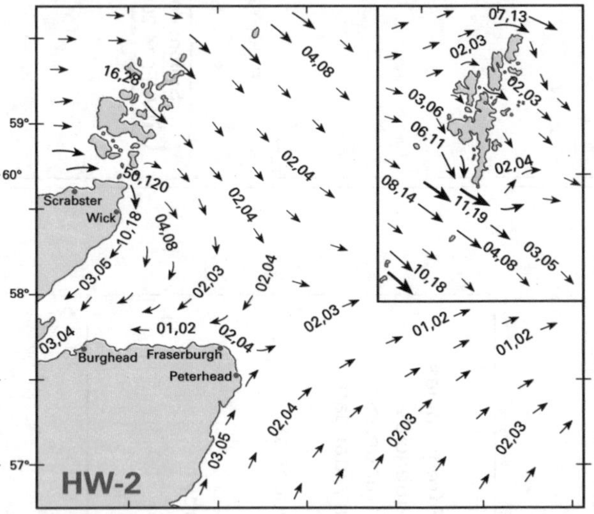

2 Hours before HW Dover (0420 before HW Aberdeen)

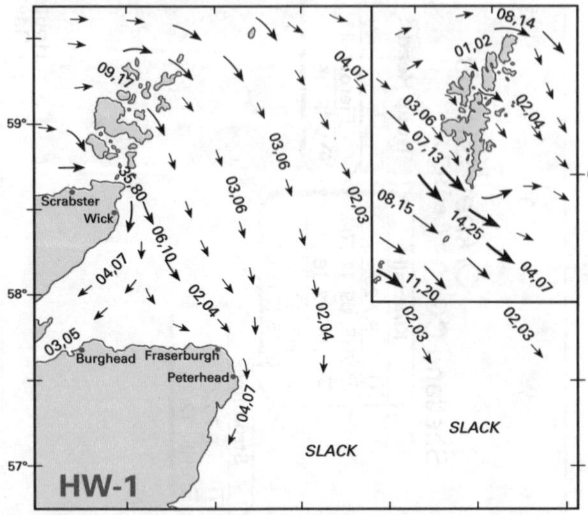

1 Hour before HW Dover (0320 before HW Aberdeen)

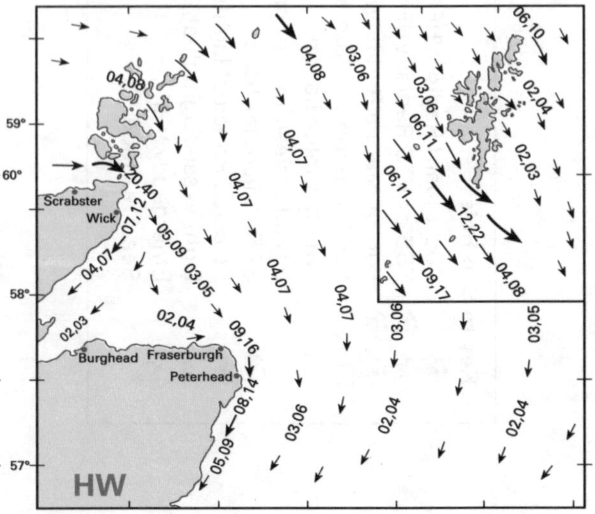

HW Dover (0220 before HW Aberdeen)

Southward 9.6.3 Westward 9.8.3

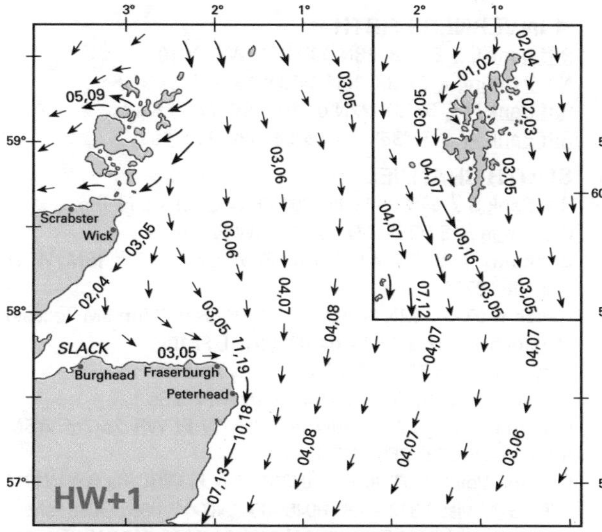

1 Hour after HW Dover (0120 before HW Aberdeen)

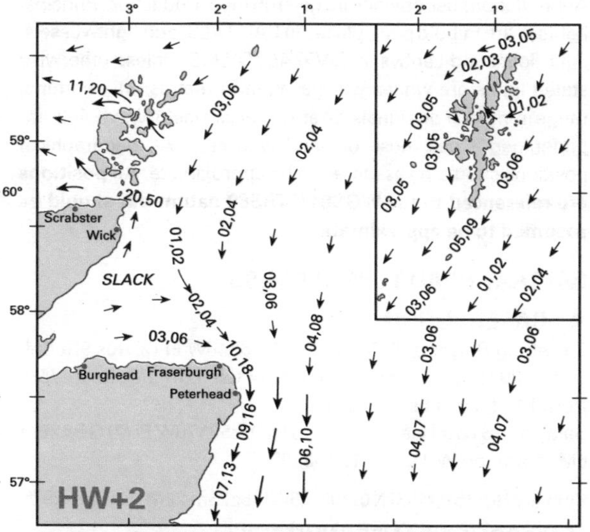

2 Hours after HW Dover (0020 before HW Aberdeen)

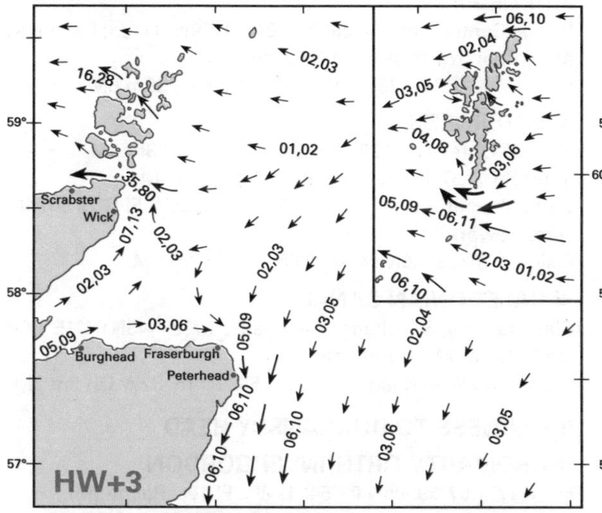

3 Hours after HW Dover (0040 after HW Aberdeen)

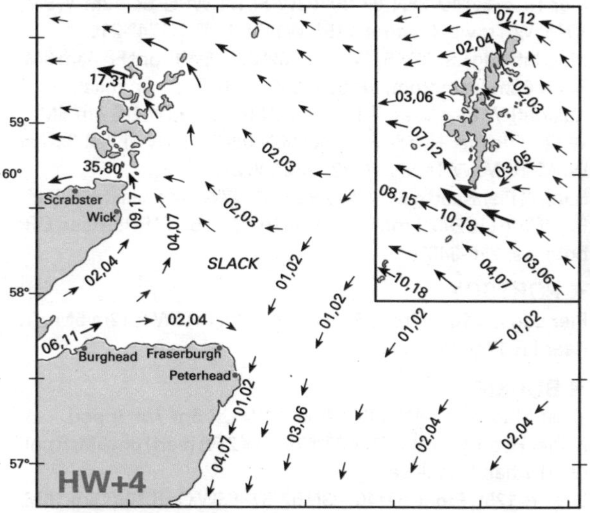

4 Hours after HW Dover (0140 after HW Aberdeen)

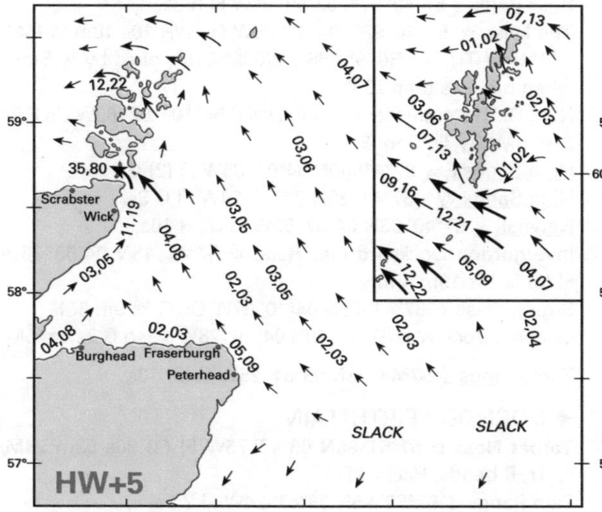

5 Hours after HW Dover (0240 after HW Aberdeen)

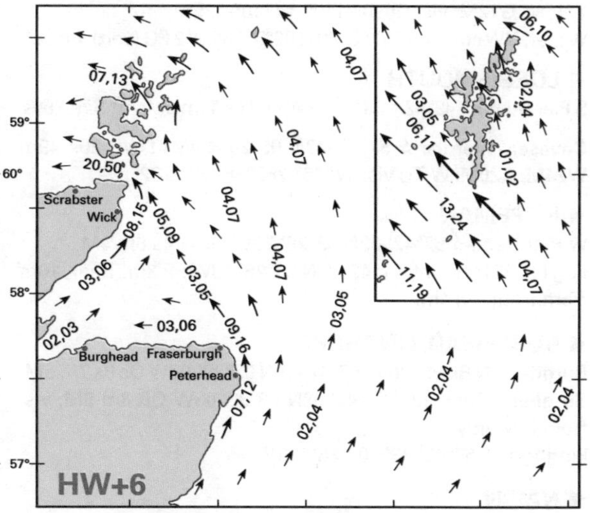

6 Hours after HW Dover (0340 after HW Aberdeen)

7

9.7.4 LIGHTS, BUOYS AND WAYPOINTS

Abbreviations used below are given in the Introduction. Principal lights ☆ are in **bold** print, places in CAPITALS, and light-vessels, light floats and Lanbys in *CAPITAL ITALICS*. Unless otherwise stated lights are white. m – elevation in metres; M – nominal range in miles. Fog signals))) are in *italics*. Useful waypoints are underlined – use those on land with care. All geographical positions should be assumed to be approximate. **All positions are referenced to the WGS84/ETRS89 datum but should be assumed to be approximate.**

RATTRAY HEAD TO INVERNESS

◄ FRASERBURGH

Cairnbulg Briggs 57°41'·10N 01°56'·46W Fl (2) 10s 9m 6M.
Ldg Lt 291°. 57°41'·57N 02°00'·13W QR 12m 5M. Rear, 75m from front, Oc R 6s 17m 5M.
Balaclava Bkwtr Head 57°41'·51N 01°59'·70W Fl (2) G 8s 26m 6M; dome on W Tr; vis: 178°-326°.

Kinnaird Hd ☆ 57°41'·87N 02°00'·26W Fl 5s 25m **22M**; vis: 092°-297°.

◄ MACDUFF/BANFF/WHITEHILLS

Pier Hd 57°40'·25N 02°30'·02W Fl (2) WRG 6s 12m W9M, R7M; W Tr; vis: G shore-115°, W115°-174°, R174°-210°.
Macduff Ldg Lts 127° 57°40'·12N 02°29'·75W Front FR 44m 3M. Rear, 60m from front, FR 55m 3M; both Or △ on mast.
Macduff W Pier Head 57°40'·22N 02°29'·98W QG 4m 5M.
Whitehills Pier Head 57°40'·80N 02°34'·88W Fl WR 3s 7m W9M, R6M; W Tr; vis: R132°-212°, W212°-245°.
Banff N Pier Head 57°40'·22N 02°31'·27W Fl 4s; vis: 105°-010°.
Banff Ldg Lts 295° Front 57°40·30N 02°31·36N Fl R 4s. Rear, QR: both vis: 210-345°.

◄ PORTSOY

Pier Ldg Lts 160°. Front 57°41'·17N 02°41'·49W F 12m 5M; Tr. Rear FR 17m 5M; mast.

◄ BUCKIE

West Muck 57°41'·06N 02°58'·01W QR 5m 7M; tripod.
N Pier Head 57°40'·83N 02°57'·71W 2 FR (vert) 6m 9M; R col. (3 FR when Hbr closed.)
Ldg Lts 125°. **Front,** 57°40'·83N 02°57'·65W Oc R 10s 15m **16M**; W Tr;))) *Siren (2) 60s.* **Rear,** 60m from head, Oc R 10s 15m **W15M**, G12M; vis: G090°-110°, W110°-225°.
W Pier, NW corner 57°40'·80 N 02°57'·65 W 2 FG (vert) 4m 9M.

◄ LOSSIEMOUTH

S Pier Hd 57°43'·42N 03°16'·69W Fl R 6s 11m 5M;))) *Siren 60s.*

Covesea Skerries ☆ 57°43'·47N 03°20'·45W Fl WR 20s 49m **W24M, R20M**; W Tr; vis: W076°-267°, R267°-282°.

◄ HOPEMAN

W Pier Head 57°42'·69N 03°26'·29W Oc G 4s 8m 4M.
Ldg Lts 081°. Front, 57°42'·71N 03°26'·18W FR 3m. Rear, 10m from front, FR 4m.

◄ BURGHEAD/FINDHORN

Burghead N Bkwtr Hd 57°42'·09N 03°30'·03W Oc 8s 7m 5M.
Burghead Spur Hd 57°42'·08N 03°30'·03W QR 3m 5M; vis: from SW only.
Findhorn 57°40'·33N 03°38'·76W.

◄ NAIRN

W Pier Head 57°35'·60N 03°51'·63W QG 5m 1M; Gy post.
E Pier Head 57°35'·62N 03°51'·65W Oc WRG 4s 6m 5M; 8-sided Tr; vis: Gshore-100°, W100°-207°, R207°-shore.

◄ INVERNESS FIRTH

Riff Bank E 57°38'·38N 03°58'·18W Fl Y 10s.
Navity Bank 57°38'·16N 04°01'·18W Fl (3) G 15s.
Riff Bank N 57°37'·22N 04°02'·75W Fl (2) R 12s.
Riff Bank W 57°35'·78N 04°04'·08W Fl Y 5s.

SOUTH CHANNEL

Riff Bank S 57°36'·73N 04°00'·97W Q (6) + L Fl 15s.
Craigmee 57°35'·30N 04°05'·04W Fl R 6s.
Chanonry ☆ 57°34'·44N 04°05'·57W Oc 6s 12m **15M**; W Tr; vis: 148°-073°.
Avoch 57°34'·02N 04°09'·93W 2 FR (vert) 7/5m 5M; (occas).
Munlochy 57°32'·91N 04°07'·65W L Fl 10s.
Petty Bank 57°31'·58N 04°08'·98W Fl R 5s.
Meikle Mee 57°30'·26N 04°12'·02W Fl G 3s.
Longman Pt 57°29'·99N 04°13'·31W Fl WR 2s 7m W5M, R4M; vis: W078°-258°, R258°-078°.
Craigton Point 57°30'·05N 04°14'·09W Fl WRG 4s 6m W11M, R7M, G7M; vis: W312°-048°, R048°-064°, W064°-085°, G085°-shore.
Kessock Bridge N Trs 57°30'·01N 04°13'·88W; QG 3m 3M; S Trs QR 3m 3M.
Bridge Centre mark 57°29'·97N 04°13'·79W; Or △; Racon (K).
Main Chan North side Oc G 6s 28m 5M.
South side 57°29'·93N 04°13'·74W Oc R 6s 28m 5M.

◄ INVERNESS

R. Ness Outer 57°29'·83N 04°13'·93W QR 3m 4M.
Inner Bn 57°29'·72N 04°14'·11W QR 3m 4M.
Embankment Head 57°29'·72N 04°14'·25W Fl G 2s 8m 4M; G framework Tr.
E side 57°29'·56N 04°14'·21W Fl R 3s 7m 6M.

◄ CALEDONIAN CANAL

Clachnaharry, S Training Wall Head 57°29'·43N 04°15'·86W Iso G 4s 5m 2M; tfc signals.
N Training Wall Head 57°29'·45N 04°15'·82W QR 5m 2M.

INVERNESS TO DUNCANSBY HEAD

◄ CROMARTY FIRTH/INVERGORDON

Fairway 57°39'·96N 03°54'·19W L Fl 10s; Racon (M).
Cromarty Bank 57°40'·66N 03°56'·78W Fl (2) G 10s.
Buss Bank 57°40'·97N 03°59'·54W Fl R 3s.
The Ness ☆ 57°40'·98N 04°02'·20W Oc WR 10s 18m **W15M**, R11M; W Tr; vis: R079°-088°, W088°-275°, obsc by N Sutor when brg less than 253°.
Nigg Oil Terminal Pier Head 57°41'·54N 04°02'·60W Oc G 5s 31m 5M; Gy Tr, floodlit.
Nigg Sands E 57°41'·60N 04°04'·35W Fl (2) G 10s.
Nigg Sands W 57°41'·28N 04°07'·24W Fl G 3s.
Newhall 57°40'·93N 04°07'·95W Fl (2) R 10s.
Invergordon Dockyard Pier Head 57°41'·15N 04°09'·75W Fl (3) G 10s 15m 4M.
Supply Base 57°41'·09N 04°10'·37W Oc G 8s 9m 6M.
Queen's Dock W 57°41'·10N 04°10'·78W Iso G 2s 9m 6M.

Three Kings 57°43'·73N 03°54'·25W Q (3) 10s.

◄ DORNOCH FIRTH/TAIN

Tarbat Ness ☆ 57°51'·88N 03°46'·76W Fl (4) 30s 53m **24M**; W Tr, R bands; Racon (T).
Tain Range 57°52'·96N 03°47'·24W Fl Y 5s.
Range 57°49'·46N 03°57'·54W Fl R 5s, when firing occurs.

◀ HELMSDALE/LYBSTER

Ben-a-Chielt ☆ 58°19'·69N 03°22'·36W Aero 5 FR (vert) (461).
Lybster, S Pier Hd ☆ 58°17'·79N 03°17'·41W Oc R 6s 10m 3M.
Clyth Ness ☆ 58°18'·64N 03°12'·74W Fl (2) 30s 45m **16M**.

◀ WICK

S Pier Head ☆ 58°26'·34N 03°04'·73W Fl WRG 3s 12m W12M, R9M, G9M; W 8-sided Tr; vis: G253°-270°, W270°-286°, R286°-329°; *Bell (2) 10s* (occas).

Dir Lt 288·5° 58°26'·54N 03°05'·34W Dir F WRG 9m W10M, R7M, G7M; col on N end of bridge; vis: G283·5°-287·2°, W287·2°-289·7°, R289·7°-293·5°.

Noss Head ☆ 58°28'·71N 03°03'·09W Fl WR 20s 53m **W25M, R 21M**; W Tr; vis: R shore-191°, W191°-shore.

DUNCANSBY HEAD TO CAPE WRATH

Duncansby Head ☆ 58°38'·65N 03°01'·58W Fl 12s 67m **22M**; W Tr; Racon (T).

Pentland Skerries ☆ 58°41'·41N 02°55'·49W Fl (3) 30s 52m **23M**; W Tr; *Horn 45s.*

Lother Rock ☆ 58°43'·80N 02°58'·68W Q 13m 6M; Racon (M).

S Ronaldsay, Burwick Bkwtr Head ☆ 58°44'·35N 02°58'·31W 2FR (vert) 8m 5M.

Swona ☆ 58°44'·25N 03°04'·24W Fl 8s 17m 9M; vis: 261°-210°.

Swona N Head ☆ 58°45'·11N 03°03'·10W Fl (3) 10s 16m 10M.

Stroma ☆, Swilkie Point 58°41'·75N 03°07'·01W Fl (2) 20s 32m **26M**; W Tr; *Horn (2) 60s.*

Inner sound, John O'Groats, Pier Head ☆ 58°38'·72N 03°04'·23W Fl R 3s 4m 2M; W post.

Dunnet Head ☆ 58°40'·28N 03°22'·60W Fl (4) 30s 105m **23M**.

◀ THURSO/SCRABSTER

Holburn (Little) Head ☆ 58°36'·88N 03°32'·37W Fl WR 10s 23m **W15M**, R11M; W Tr; vis: W198°-358°, R358°-shore.

Thurso Bkwtr Head ☆ 58°35'·97N 03°30'·48W QG 5m 4M; G post; shown 1/9-30/4.

Thurso Ldg Lts 195°. Front, 58°35'·96N 03°30'·76W FG 5m 4M; Gy post. Rear, FG 6m 4M; Gy mast.

Scrabster Outer Pier Hd ☆ 58°36'·61N 03°32'·58W QG 6m 4M.

Strathy Point ☆ 58°36'·04N 04°01'·12W Fl 20s 45m **26M**; W Tr on W dwelling.

Sule Skerry ☆ 59°05'·09N 04°24'·38W Fl (2) 15s 34m **21M**; W Tr; Racon (T).

North Rona ☆ 59°07'·27N 05°48'·91W Fl (3) 20s 114m **24M**.

Sula Sgeir ☆ 59°05'·61N 06°09'·57W Fl 15s 74m 11M; □ structure.

Loch Eriboll, White Head ☆ 58°31'·01N 04°38'·90W Fl WR 3s 18m W13M, R12M; W Tr and bldg; vis: W030°-172°, R172°-191°, W191°-212°.

Cape Wrath ☆ 58°37'·54N 04°59'·94W Fl (4) 30s 122m **22M**; W Tr; *Horn (3) 45s.*

ORKNEY ISLANDS

Tor Ness ☆ 58°46'·78N 03°17'·86W Fl 3s 21m 10M; W Tr.

Cantick Head (S Walls, SE end) ☆ 58°47'·23N 03°07'·88W Fl 20s 35m **18M**; W Tr.

SCAPA FLOW AND APPROACHES

Ruff Reef, off Cantick Hd ☆ 58°47'·43N 03°07'·80W Fl (2) 10s 10m 6M.

Long Hope, S Ness Pier Hd ☆ 58°48'·05N 03°12'·35W Fl WRG 3s 6m W7M, R5M, G5M; vis: G082°-242°, W242°-252°, R252°-082°.

Hoxa Head ☆ 58°49'·31N 03°02'·09W Fl WR 3s 15m W9M, R6M; W Tr; vis: W026°-163°, R163°-201°, W201°-215°.

Stanger Head ☆ 58°48'·96N 03°04'·74W Fl R 5s 25m 8M.

Roan Head ☆ 58°50'·72N 03°03'·94W Fl (2) R 6s 12m 7M.

Nevi Skerry ⍊ 58°50'·67N 03°02'·70W Fl (2) 6s 7m 6M.

Calf of Flotta ☆ 58°51'·27N 03°03'·92W QR 8m 4M.

Flotta Terminal, E Jetty ☆ 58°50'·75N 03°03'·91W 2 FR (vert) 10m 3M.

Mooring dolphins, E and W, both QR 8m 3M.

SPM Tr No. 1 58°52'·14N 03°07'·46W Fl Y 5s 12m 3M; *Horn Mo (A) 60s.*

SPM Tr No. 2 58°52'·23N 03°05'·96W Fl (4) Y 15s 12m 3M; *Horn Mo (N) 60s.*

Gibraltar Pier ☆ 58°50'·27N 03°07'·88W 2 FG (vert) 7m 3M.

Sutherland Pier ☆ 58°50'·19N 03°08'·07W QG 8m 3M.

Golden Wharf ☆ 58°50'·16N 03°11'·46W 2 FR (vert) 7m 3M.

Lyness Wharf ☆ 58°50'·02N 03°11'·42W 2 FR (vert) 7m 3M.

Needle Point ⍊ 58°50'·09N 02°57'·46W Fl G 3s 6m 3M.

St Margaret's Hope Pier Head ☆ 58°49'·93N 02°57'·67W 2 FG (vert) 6m 2M.

Ldg Lts 196°, 58°49'·57N 02°57'·64W both FR 7/11m.

Rose Ness ☆ 58°52'·33N 02°49'·97W Fl 6s 24m 8M; W Tr.

Scapa Pier ☆ 58°57'·39N 02°58'·42W Fl G 3s 6m 8M.

Scapa Skerry 58°56'·87N 02°59'·16W Fl (2) R 12s.

Barrel of Butter ☆ 58 53'·40N 03°07'·62W Fl (2) 10s 6m 7M.

Cava ☆ 58°53'·21N 03°10'·70W Fl WR 3s 11m W10M, R8M; W ○ Tr; vis: W351°-143°, R143°-196°, W196°-251°, R251°- 271°, W271°-298°.

Houton Bay Ldg Lts 316°. Front ⍊, 58°54'·97N 03°11'·56W Fl G 3s 8m. Rear ⍊, 200m from front, FG 16m; vis: 312°-320°.

Ro-Ro terminal S ☆ 58°55'·00N 03°11'·09W Iso R 4s 7m 5M.

◀ CLESTRAN SOUND

Peter Skerry 58°55'·25N 03°13'·51W Fl G 6s.

Riddock Shoal 58°55'·86N 03°15'·15W Fl (2) R 12s.

◀ HOY SOUND

Ebbing Eddy Rocks 58°56'·60N 03°17'·00W Q.

Graemsay Is Hoy Sound Low ☆ Ldg Lts 104°. **Front**, 58°56'·42N 03°18'·60W Iso 3s 17m **15M**; W Tr; vis: 070°-255°.

High Rear, 1·2M from front, Oc WR 8s 35m **W20M, R16M**; W Tr; vis: R097°-112°, W112°-163°, R163°-178°, W178°-332°; obsc on Ldg line within 0·5M.

Skerry of Ness ☆ 58°56'·95N 03°17'·83W Fl WG 4s 7m W7M, G4M; vis: W shore-090°, G090°-shore.

◀ STROMNESS

Stromness 58°57'·25N 03°17'·61W QR.

Stromness 58°57'·38N 03°17'·65W Fl G 3s.

Ldg Lts 317°. Front, 58°57'·61N 03°18'·15W FR 29m 11M; post on W Tr. Rear, 55m from front, FR 39m 11M; vis: 307°-327°.

N Pier Head ☆ 58°57'·75N 03°17'·71W Fl R 3s 8m 5M.

◀ AUSKERRY

Copinsay ☆ 58°53'·77N 02°40'·35W Fl (5) 30s 79m **21M**; W Tr; *Horn (4) 60s.* Fog Det Lt UQ, vis: 192°.

Auskerry ☆ 59°01'·51N 02°34'·34W Fl 20s 34m **20M**; W Tr.

Helliar Holm, S end ☆ 59°01'·13N 02°54'·09W Fl WRG 10s 18m W14M, R11M, G11M; W Tr; vis: G256°-276°, W276°-292°, R292°-098°, W098°-116°, G116°-154°.

Balfour Pier Shapinsay ☆ 59°01'·86N 02°54'·49W Q WRG 5m W3M, R2M, G2M; vis: G270°-010°, W010°-020°, R020°-090°.

◀ KIRKWALL

Scargun Shoal 59°00'·80N 02°58'·67W.
Pier N end ☆ 58°59'·29N 02°57'·72W Iso WRG 5s 8m **W15M**, R13M, G13M; W Tr; vis: G153°-183°, W183°-192°, R192°-210°.

◀ WIDE FIRTH

Linga Skerry 59°02'·39N 02°57'·56W Q (3) 10s.
Boray Skerries 59°03'·65N 02°57'·66W Q (6) + L Fl 15s.
Skertours 59°04'·11N 02°56'·72W Q.
Galt Skerry 59°05'·21N 02°54'·20W Q.
Brough of Birsay ☆ 59°08'·19N 03°20'·41W Fl (3) 25s 52m **18M**.
Papa Stronsay NE end, The Ness 59°09'·34N 02°34'·93W Fl(4)20s 8m 9M; W Tr.

◀ STRONSAY, PAPA SOUND

Quiabow 59°09'·82N 02°36'·30W Fl (2) G 12s.
No. 1 (off Jacks Reef) 59°09'·16N 02°36'·51W Fl G 5s.
No. 2 59°08'·92N 02°36'·61W Fl R 5s.
No. 4 59°08'·77N 02°36'·46W Fl (2) R 5s.
No. 3 59°08'·70N 02°36'·18W Fl (2) G 5s.
Whitehall Pier ☆ 50°08'·61N 02°35'·96W 2 FG (vert) 8m 4M.

◀ SANDAY ISLAND/NORTH RONALDSAY

Start Point ☆ 59°16'·69N 02°22'·71W Fl (2) 20s 24m **19M**.
Kettletoft Pier Head ☆ 59°13'·80N 02°35'·86W Fl WRG 3s 7m W7M, R5M, G5M; vis: W351°-011°, R011°-180°, G180°-351°.
N Ronaldsay ☆ NE end, 59°23'·37N 02°23'·03W Fl 10s 43m **24M**; R Tr, W bands; Racon (T); *Horn 60s*.
Nouster Pier Head ☆ 59°21'·30N 02°26'·48W QR 5m.

◀ EDAY/EGILSAY

Calf Sound ☆ 59°14'·26N 02°45'·86W Iso WRG 5s 8m W8M, R7M, G6M; W Tr; vis: R shore-216°, W216°-223°, G223°-302°, W302°-307°.
Backaland Pier ☆ 59°09'·43N 02°44'·88W Fl R 3s 5m 4M; vis: 192°-250°.
Egilsay Graand 59°06'·86N 02°54'·42W Q (6) + L Fl 15s.
Egilsay Pier, S end ☆ 59°09'·29N 02°56'·81W Fl G 3s 4m 4M.

◀ WESTRAY/PIEROWALL

Noup Head ☆ 59°19'·86N 03°04'·23W Fl 30s 79m **22M**; W Tr; vis: 335°-242°, 248°-282°; obsc on E bearings within 0·8M, part obsc 240°-275°.
Pierowall E Pier Head ☆ 59°19'·35N 02°58'·53W Fl WRG 3s 7m W11M, R7M, G7M; vis: G254°-276°, W276°-291°, R291°-308°, G308°-215°.
Papa Westray, Moclett Bay Pier Head ☆ 59°19'·60N 02°53'·52W Fl WRG 5s 7m W5M, R3M, G3M; vis: G306°-341°, W341°-040°, R040°-074°.

SHETLAND ISLES

◀ FAIR ISLE

Skadan South ☆, 59°30'·84N 01°39'·16W Fl (4) 30s 32m **22M**; W Tr; vis: 260°-146°, obsc inshore 260°-282°; *Horn (2) 60s*.
Skroo ☆ N end 59°33'·13N 01°36'·58W Fl (2) 30s 80m **22M**; W Tr; vis: 086·7°-358°; *Horn (3) 45s*.

◀ MAINLAND, SOUTH

Sumburgh Head ☆ 59°51'·21N 01°16'·58W Fl (3) 30s 91m **23M**.
Pool of Virkie, Marina E Bkwtr Head ☆ 59°53'·01N 01°17'·16W 2 FG (vert) 6m 5M.
Mousa, Perie Bard ☆ 59°59'·84N 01°09'·51W Fl 3s 20m 10M.
Aithsvoe ☆ 60°02'·26N 01°12'·97W Fl R 3s 3m 2M.

◀ BRESSAY/LERWICK

Bressay, Kirkabister Ness ☆ 60°07'·20N 01°07'·29W Fl (2) 20s 32m **23M**.
Cro of Ham ☆ 60°08'·26N 01°07'·57W Fl 3s 12m 3M.
Twageos Point ☆ 60°08'·91N 01°07'·95W L Fl 6s 8m 6M.
Maryfield Ferry Terminal ☆ 60°09'·43N 01°07'·45W Oc WRG 6s 5m 5M; vis: W008°-013°, R013°-111°, G111°-008°.
Bkwtr N Head ☆ 60°09'·24N 01°08'·41W 2 FR (vert) 5m 4M.
North Ness ☆ 60°09'·57N 01°08'·77W Iso WG 4s 4m 5M; vis: G158°-216°, W216°-158°.
Loofa Baa 60°09'·72N 01°08'·79W Q (6) + L Fl 15s 4m 5M.
Soldian Rock 60°12'·51N 01°04'·73W Q (6) + L Fl 15s.
N ent Dir Lt 215° 60°10'·47N 01°09'·53W Dir Oc WRG 6s 27m 8M; Y △, Or stripe; vis: R211°-214°, W214°-216°, G216°-221°.
Gremista Marina S Hd ☆ 60°10'·20N 01°09'·61W Iso R 4s 3m 2M.
Green Head ☆ 60°10'·84N 01°09'·10W Q (4) R 10s 4m 3M.
Rova Hd ☆ 60°11'·46N 01°08'·60W Fl (3) WRG 18s 10m W8M, R7M, G7M; W Tr; vis: R shore-182°, W182°-191°, G191°-213°, R213°-241°, W241°-261·5°, G261·5°-009°, W009°-shore.
The Brethren Rock 60°12'·35N 01°08'·24W Q (9) 15s.
The Unicorn Rock 60°13'·51N 01°08'·48W VQ (3) 5s.
Dales Voe ☆ 60°11'·79N 01°11'·23W Fl (2) WRG 8s 5m W4M, R3M, G3M; vis: G220°-227°, W227°-233°, R233°-240°.
Dales Voe Quay ☆ 60°11'·60N 01°10'·48W 2 FR (vert) 9m 3M.
Laxfirth Pier Hd ☆ 60°12'·74N 01°12'·14W 2 FG (vert) 4m 2M.
Hoo Stack ☆ 60°14'·96N 01°05'·38W Fl (4) WRG 12s 40m W7M, R5M, G5M; W pylon; vis: R169°-180°, W180°-184°, G184°-193°, W193°-169°. Same structure, Dir Lt 182°. Dir Fl (4) WRG 12s 33m W9M, R6M, G6M; vis: R177°-180°, W180°-184°, G184°-187°; synch with upper Lt.
Mull (Moul) of Eswick ☆ 60°15'·74N 01°05'·90W Fl WRG 3s 50m W9M, R6M, G6M; W Tr; vis: R028°-200°, W200°-207°, G207°-018°, W018°-028°.

◀ WHALSAY/SKERRIES

Symbister Ness ☆ 60°20'·43N 01°02'·29W Fl (2) WG 12s 11m W8M, G6M; W Tr; vis: W shore-203°, G203°-shore.
Symbister Bay N Bkwtr Head ☆ 60°20'·63N 01°01'·72W Oc G 7s 3m 3M.
E Bkwtr Head ☆ 60°20'·67N 01°01'·66W Oc R 7s 3m 3M..
S Bkwtr Hd ☆ 60°20'·58N 01°01'·63W QG 4m 2M.
Marina N pontoon ☆ 60°20'·50N 01°01'·59W 2 FG (vert) 2m 3M.
Skate of Marrister ☆ 60°21'·35N 01°01'·39W Fl G 6s 4m 4M.
Suther Ness ☆ 60°22'·12N 01°00'·20W Fl WRG 3s 8m W10M, R8M, G7M; vis: W shore-038°, R038°-173°, W173°-206°, G206°-shore.
Mainland, Laxo Voe ferry terminal ☆ 60°21'·13N 01°10'·27W 2 FG (vert) 4m 2M.
Bound Skerry ☆ 60°25'·47N 00°43'·72W Fl 20s 44m **20M**; W Tr.
South Mouth. Ldg Lts 014°. Front, 60°25'·33N 00°45'·01W FY3m 2M. Rear, FY 12m 2M.
Bruray Bn 'D' ☆ Fl (3) G 6s 3m 3M.
Bruray Bn 'B' ☆ VQ G 3m 3M.
Housay Bn 'A' ☆ VQ R 3m 3M.
Bruray ferry berth ☆ 60°25'·36N 00°45'·12W 2 FG (vert) 6m 4M.
Muckle Skerry ☆ 60°26'·41N 00°51'·84W Fl (2) WRG 10s 13m W7M, R5M, G5M; W Tr; vis: W046°-192°, R192°-272°, G272°-348°, W348°-353°, R353°-046°.

◀ YELL SOUND

S ent, Lunna Holm ☆ 60°27'·34N 01°02'·52W Fl (3) WRG 15s 19m W10M,R7M,G7M; W ◯Tr; vis: R shore-090°, W090°-094°, G094°-209°, W209°-275°, R275°-shore.

Firths Voe ☆, N shore 60°27'·21N 01°10'·63W Oc WRG 8s 9m **W15M**, R10M, G10M; W Tr; vis: W189°-194°, G194°-257°, W257°-261°, R261°-339°, W339°-066°.

Linga Is. Dir Lt ☆ 60°26'·80N 01°09'·13W Dir Q (4) WRG 8s 10m W9M, R9M, G9M; vis: R145°-148°, W148°-152°, G152°-155°. Q (4) WRG 8s 10m W7M, R4M, G4M; same structure; vis: R052°-146°, G154°-196°, W196°-312°; synch with Dir Lt.

The Rumble Bn ☆ 60°28'·16N 01°07'·26W; R Bn; Racon (O).

Yell, Ulsta Ferry Terminal Breakwater Head ☆ 60°29'·74N 01°09'·52W Oc RG 4s 7m R5M, G5M; vis: G shore-354°, R044°-shore. Same structure; Oc WRG 4s 5m W8M, R5M, G5M; vis: G shore-008°, W008°-036°, R036°-shore.

Toft ferry terminal ☆ 60°28'·02N 01°12'·40W 2 FR (vert) 5m 2M.

Ness of Sound, W side ☆ 60°31'·34N 01°11'·28W Fl (3) WRG 12s 18m W9M, R6M, G6M; vis: G shore-345°, W345°-350°, R350°-160°, W160°-165°, G165°-shore.

Brother Is. Dir Lt 329° 60°30'·95N 01°14'·11W Dir Fl (4) WRG 8s 16m W10M, R7M, G7M; vis: G323·5°-328°, W328°-330°, R330°-333·5°.

Mio Ness ☆ 60°29'·66N 01°13'·68W Q (2) WR 10s 12m W7M, R4M; W ○ Tr; vis: W282°-238°, R238°-282°.

Tinga Skerry ☆ 60°30'·48N 01°14'·86W Q (2) G 10s 9m 5M. W ○ Tr.

◀ YELL SOUND, NORTH ENTRANCE

Bagi Stack ☆ 60°43'·53N 01°07'·54W Fl (4) 20s 45m 10M.

Gruney Is ☆ 60°39'·15N 01°18'·17W Fl WR 5s 53m W8M, R6M; W Tr; vis: R064°-180°, W180°-012°; Racon (T).

Pt of Fethaland ☆ 60°38'·05N 01°18'·70W Fl (3) WR 15s 65m **W24M, R20M**; vis R080°-103°, W103°-160°, R160°-206°, W206°-340°.

Muckle Holm ☆ 60°34'·83N 01°16'·01W Fl (4) 10s 32m 10M.

Little Holm ☆ 60°33'·42N 01°15'·88W Iso 4s 12m 6M; W Tr.

Outer Skerry ☆ 60°33'·03N 01°18'·32W Fl 6s 12m 8M.

Quey Firth ☆ 60°31'·43N 01°19'·58W Oc WRG 6s 22m W12M, R8M, G8M; W Tr; vis: W shore (through S and W-290°, G290°-327°, W327°-334°, R334°-shore.

Lamba, S side ☆ 60°30'·73N 01°17'·84W Fl WRG 3s 30m W8M, R5M, G5M; W Tr; vis: G shore-288°, W288°-293°, R293°-327°, W327°-044°, R044°-140°, W140°-shore. Dir Lt 290·5° Dir Fl WRG 3s 24m W10M, R7M, G7M; vis: 285·5°-288°, W288°-293°, R293°-295·5°.

◀ SULLOM VOE

Gluss Is ☆ Ldg Lts 194·7° (H24). **Front**, 60°29'·77N 01°19'·44W F 39m **19M**; □ on Gy Tr; H24. **Rear**, 0·75M from front, F 69m **19M**; □ on Gy Tr. Both Lts 9M by day.

Little Roe ☆ 60°29'·99N 01°16'·46W Fl (3) WR 10s 16m W5M, R4M; W structure, Or band; vis: R036°-095·5°, W095·5°-036°.

Skaw Taing ☆ Ldg Lts 150·5°. Front, 60°29'·10N 01°16'·86W Fl (2) WRG 5s 21m W8M, R5M, G5M; Or and W structure; vis: W049°-078°, G078°-147°, W147°-154°, R154°-169°, W169°-288°. Rear, 195m from front, Fl (2) 5s 35m 8M; vis: W145°-156°.

Ness of Bardister ☆ 60°28'·19N 01°19'·63W Oc WRG 8s 20m W9M, R6M, G6M; Or and W structure; vis: W180·5°-240°, R240°-310·5°, W310·5°-314·5°, G314·5°-030·5°.

Fugla Ness. Lts in line 212·3°. Rear, 60°27'·25N 01°19'·74W Iso 4s 45m 14M. Common front 60°27'·45N 01°19'·57W Iso 4s 27m 14M; synch with rear Lts. Lts in line 203°. Rear, 60°27'·26N 01°19'·81W Iso 4s 45m 14M.

Sella Ness ☆ Dir Lt 135·5° 60°26'·76N 01°16'·66W Dir Oc WRG 10s 19m **W16M**, R3M, G3M; vis: G123·5°-130·5°, Al WG 130·5°-132·5°, white phase increasing with brg, W132·5°-134·5°. Al WR134·5°-136·5°, R phase inc with brg. R136·5°-143·5°; H24. By day Dir Oc WRG 10s 19m W2M, R1M,G1M as above.

Tug Jetty Pier Head ☆ 60°26'·81N 01°16'·30W Iso G 4s 4m 3M.

Garth Pier N arm Head ☆ 60°26'·69N 01°16'·35W Fl (2) G 5s 4m 3M.

Scatsa Ness Upper ☆ 60°26'·48N 01°18'·25W Oc WRG 5s 14m 7M; Gy Tr; vis: G161·5°-187·2°, W187·2°-188·2°, W207·2°-208·2°, R208·2°-251·5°; by day F WRG 2M (occas). Lower Lt Oc WRG 5s 10m 7M; vis: G161·5°-197·2°, W197·2°-202·2°, R202·2°-251·5°; by day F WRG 2M (occas).

Ungam Is ☆ 60°27'·23N 01°18'·61W VQ (2) 5s 2m 2M.

◀ EAST YELL/UNST/BALTA SOUND

Whitehill ☆ 60°34'·80N 01°00'·25W Fl WR 3s 24m W9M, R6M; vis: W shore-163°, R163°-211°, W211°-349°, R349°-shore.

Uyea Sound ☆ 60°41'·15N 00°55'·48W Fl (2) 8s 8m 7M.

Balta Sound ☆ 60°44'·43N 00°47'·68W Fl WR 10s 17m 10M, R7M; vis: W249°-010°, R010°-060°, W060°-154°.

Balta Marina Bkwtr Hd ☆ 60°45'·57N 00°50'·38W Fl R 6s 2m 2M.

Holme of Skaw ☆ 60°49'·87N 00°46'·33W Fl 5s 8m 8M.

Muckle Flugga ☆ 60°51'·32N 00°53'·14W Fl (2) 20s 66m **22M**.

Yell. Cullivoe Bkwtr Hd ☆ 60°41'·91N 00°59'·66W Fl (2) WRG 10s 3m 4M; vis: G080°-294°, W294°-355°, R355°-080°.

◀ MAINLAND, WEST

Esha Ness ☆ 60°29'·34N 01°37'·65W Fl 12s 61m **25M**.

Ness of Hillswick ☆ 60°27'·21N 01°29'·80W Fl (4) WR 15s 34m W9M, R6M; vis: W217°-093°, R093°-114°.

Muckle Roe, Swarbacks Minn ☆ 60°20'·98N 01°27'·07W Fl WR 3s 30m W9M, R6M; vis: W314°-041°, R041°-075°, W075°-137°.

W Burra Firth Outer ☆ 60°17'·79N 01°33'·56W Oc WRG 8s 27m W9M, R7M, G7M; vis: G136°-142°, W142°-150°, R150°-156°.

W Burra Firth Inner ☆ 60°17'·78N 01°32'·17W F WRG 9m **W15M**, R9M, G9M; vis: G095°-098°, W098°-102°, W098°-102°, R102°-105°.

Aith Breakwater ☆ 60°17'·22N 01°22'·43W QG 5m 3M.

W Burra Firth Transport Pier Head ☆ 60°17'·71N 01°32'·41W Iso G 4s 4m 4M.

Ve Skerries ☆ 60°22'·36N 01°48'·78W Fl (2) 20s 17m 11M; W Tr; Racon (T).

Papa Stour Housa Voe Dir Lt 228° ☆ 60°19'·58N 01°40'·47W Dir F WRG 2m W9M, R7M, G7M; vis: G219°-226°, W226°-230°, R230°-239°.

Rams Head ☆ 60°11'·96N 01°33'·47W Fl WRG 8s 16m W9M, R6M; G6M; W house; vis: G265°-355°, W355°-012°, R012°-090°, W090°-136°, obsc by Vaila I when brg more than 030°.

North Havra ☆ 60°09'·85N 01°20'·31W Fl WRG 12s 24m W7M, R5M, G5M; W Tr; vis: G001°-053·5°, W053·5°-060·5°, R060°-182°, G274°-334°, W334°-337·5°, R337·5°-001°.

◀ SCALLOWAY

Point of the Pund ☆ 60°07'·99N 01°18'·31W Fl WRG 5s 20m W7M, R5M, G5M; W Tr; vis: R350°-090°,G090°-111°, R111°-135°, W135°-140°, G140°-177°, W267°-350°.

Whaleback Skerry ⚓ 60°07'·95N 01°18'·90W Q.

Pier SW corner ☆ 60°08'·02N 01°16'·59W Oc WRG 10s 10m W11M, G8M, R8M; vis: G052°-063·5°, W063·5°-065·5°, R065·5°-077°. Fugla Ness ☆ 60°06'·38N 01°20'·85W Fl (2) WRG 10s 20m W10M, R7M, G7M; W Tr; vis: G014°-032°, W032°-082°, R082°-134°, W134°-shore.

◀ FOULA

South Ness ☆ 60°06'·75N 02°03'·87W Fl (3) 15s 36m **18M**; W Tr; vis: obscured 123°-221°.

9.7.5 PASSAGE INFORMATION

Refer to the *N Coast of Scotland Pilot*; the CCC's SDs (3 vols) for *N and NE coasts of Scotland; Orkney;* and *Shetland.*

A 'Rover Ticket', £16 from Aberdeenshire Council or the Moray Council allows berthing for one week from the date of entry to the first harbour at Johnshaven, Gourdon, Stonehaven, Rosehearty, Banff, Portsoy, Portknockie, Findochty, Hopeman and Burghead.

MORAY FIRTH: SOUTH COAST (charts 115, 222, 223) Crossing the Moray Firth from Rattray Hd (lt, fog sig) to Duncansby Hd (lt, Racon) heavy seas may be met in strong W winds. Most hbrs in the Firth are exposed to NE-E winds. For oil installations, see 9.5.5; the Beatrice Field is 20M S of Wick. Tidal streams attain 3kn at sp close off Rattray Hd, but 5M NE of the Head the NE-going stream begins at HW Aberdeen + 0140, and the SE-going stream at HW Aberdeen – 0440, sp rates 2kn. Streams are weak elsewhere in the Moray Firth, except in the inner part. In late spring/early summer fog (haar) is likely in onshore winds.

In strong winds the sea breaks over Steratan Rk and Colonel Rk, respectively 3M E and 1M ENE of Fraserburgh (9.7.7). Rosehearty firing range is N & W of Kinnairds Hd (lt); tgt buoys often partially submerged. Banff B is shallow; N of Macduff (9.7.8) beware Collie Rks. Banff hbr dries, and should not be approached in fresh NE-E winds, when seas break well offshore; Macduff would then be a feasible alternative.

From Meavie Pt to Scar Nose dangers extend up to 3ca from shore in places. Beware Caple Rk (depth 0·2m) 7½ca W of Logie Hd. Spey B is clear of dangers more than 7½ca from shore; anch here, but only in offshore winds. Beware E Muck (dries) 5ca SW of Craigenroan, an above-water rky patch 5ca SW of Craig Hd, and Middle Muck and W Muck in approach to Buckie (9.7.10); Findochty & Portknockie are 2 and 3.5M ENE. Halliman Skerries (dry; bn) lie 1·5M WNW of Lossiemouth (9.7.11). Covesea Skerries (dry) lie 5ca NW of their lt ho.

Inverness Firth is approached between Nairn (9.7.15) and S Sutor. In heavy weather there is a confused sea with overfalls on Guillam Bank, 9M S of Tarbat Ness. The sea also breaks on Riff Bank (S of S Sutor) which dries in places. Chans run both N and S of Riff Bank. Off Fort George, on E side of ent to Inverness Firth (chart 1078), the SW-going stream begins HW Aberdeen + 0605, sp rate 2·5kn; the NE-going stream begins at HW Aberdeen – 0105, sp rate 3·5kn. There are eddies and turbulence between Fort George and Chanonry Pt when stream is running hard. There is a firing range between Nairn and Inverness marked, when in operation, by flags at Fort George. Much of Inverness Firth is shallow, but a direct course from Chanonry Pt to Kessock Bridge, via Munlochy SWM and Meikle Mee SHM lt buoys, carries a least depth of 2·1m. Meikle Mee bank dries 0·2m. For Fortrose and Avoch, see 9.7.16.

MORAY FIRTH: NORTH WEST COAST (chart 115) Cromarty Firth (charts 1889, 1890) is entered between N Sutor and S Sutor, both fringed by rks, some of which dry. Off the entrance the in-going stream begins at HW Aberdeen + 0605, and the out-going at HW Aberdeen – 0105, sp rates 1·5 kn. Good sheltered anchs within the firth, see 9.7.17.

The coast NE to Tarbat Ness (lt) is fringed with rks. Beware Three Kings (dries) about 3M NE of N Sutor. Culloden Rk, a shoal with depth of 1·8m, extends 2½ca NE of Tarbat Ness, where stream is weak. Beware salmon nets between Tarbat Ness and Portmahomack (9.7.17). Dornoch Firth (9.7.17) is shallow, with shifting banks, and in strong E winds the sea breaks heavily on the bar E of Dornoch Pt.

At Lothbeg Pt, 5M SW of Helmsdale (9.7.18), a rky ledge extends 5ca offshore. Near Berriedale, 7M NE of Helmsdale, The Pinnacle, a detached rk 61m high, stands close offshore. The Beatrice oil field lies on Smith Bank, 28M NE of Tarbat Ness, and 11M off Caithness coast. Between Dunbeath and Lybster (9.7.18) there are no dangers more than 2ca offshore. Clyth Ness (lt) is fringed by detached and drying rks. From here to Wick (9.7.19) the only dangers are close inshore. There is anch in Sinclair's B in good weather, but Freswick B further N is better to await the tide in Pentland Firth (beware wreck in centre of bay). Stacks of Duncansby and Baxter Rk (depth 2·7m) lie 1M and 4ca S of Duncansby Hd.

PENTLAND FIRTH (charts 2162, 2581) This potentially dangerous chan should only be attempted with moderate winds (less than F4), good vis, no swell and a fair np tide; when it presents few problems. A safe passage depends on a clear understanding of tidal streams and correct timing. The Admiralty Tidal Stream Atlas for Orkney and Shetland (NP 209) gives large scale vectors and is essential. Even in ideal conditions the races off Duncansby Hd, Swilkie Pt (N end of Stroma), and Rks of Mey (Merry Men of Mey) must be avoided as they are always dangerous to small craft. Also avoid the Pentland Skerries, Muckle Skerry, Old Head, Lother Rock (S Ronaldsay), and Dunnet Hd on E-going flood. For passages across the Firth see CCC *SDs for Orkney*.

At E end the Firth is entered between Duncansby Hd and Old Hd (S Ronaldsay), between which lie Muckle Skerry and the Pentland Skerries. Near the centre of Firth are the Islands of Swona (N side) and Stroma (S side). Outer Sound (main chan, 2·5M wide) runs between Swona and Stroma; Inner Sound (1·5M wide) between Stroma and the mainland. Rks of Mey extend about 2ca N of St John's Pt. The W end of the Firth is between Dunnet Hd and Tor Ness (Hoy).

Tidal streams reach 8-9kn at sp in the Outer Sound, and 9-12kn between Pentland Skerries and Duncansby Hd. The resultant dangerous seas, very strong eddies and violent races should be avoided by yachts at all costs. Broadly the E-going stream begins at HW Aberdeen + 0500, and the W-going at HW Aberdeen – 0105. **Duncansby Race** extends ENE towards Muckle Skerry on the SE-going stream, but by HW Aberdeen – 0440 it extends NW from Duncansby Hd. Note: HW at Muckle Skerry is the same time as HW Dover. A persistent race off **Swilkie Pt** at N end of Stroma, is very dangerous with a strong W'ly wind over a W-going stream. The most dangerous and extensive race in the Firth is **Merry Men of Mey**, which forms off St John's Pt on W-going stream at HW Aberdeen – 0150 and for a while extends right across to Tor Ness with heavy breaking seas even in fine weather.

Passage Westward: This is the more difficult direction due to prevailing W winds. Freswick B, 3·5M S of Duncansby Hd, is a good waiting anch; here an eddy runs N for 9 hrs. Round Duncansby Hd close in at HW Aberdeen –0220, as the ebb starts to run W. Take a mid-course through the Inner Sound to appr the Rks of Mey from close inshore. Gills Bay is a temp anch if early; do not pass Rks of Mey until ebb has run for at least 2 hrs. Pass 100m N of the Rks (awash).

Passage Eastward: With a fair wind and tide, no race forms and the passage is easier. Leave Scrabster at local LW+1 so as to be close off Dunnet Hd not before HW Aberdeen +0340 when the E-going flood starts to make. If late, give the Hd a wide berth. Having rounded the Rks of Mey, steer S initially to avoid being set onto the rky S tip of Stroma, marked by unlit SCM bn. Then keep mid-chan through the Inner Sound and maintain this offing to give Duncansby Hd a wide berth.

PENTLAND FIRTH TO CAPE WRATH (chart 1954) Dunnet B, S of Dunnet Hd (lt) gives temp anch in E or S winds, but dangerous seas enter in NW'lies. On W side of Thurso B is Scrabster (9.7.20) sheltered from S and W. Between Holborn Hd and Strathy Pt the E-going stream begins at HW Ullapool – 0150, and the W-going at HW Ullapool + 0420, sp rates 1·8kn. Close to Brims Ness off Ushat Hd the sp rate is 3kn, and there is often turbulence.

SW of Ushat Hd the Dounreay power stn is conspic, near shore. Dangers extend 2½ca seaward off this coast.

Along E side of Strathy Pt (lt) an eddy gives almost continuous N-going stream, but there is usually turbulence off the Pt where this eddy meets the main E or W stream. Several small B's along this coast give temp anch in offshore winds, but must not be used or approached with wind in a N quarter.

Kyle of Tongue (9.7.20) is entered from E through Caol Raineach, S of Eilean nan Ron, or from N between Eilean Iosal and Cnoc Glass. There is no chan into the kyle W of Rabbit Is,to which a drying spit extends 0·5M NNE from the mainland shore. Further S there is a bar across entrance to inner part of kyle. There are anchs on SE side of Eilean nan Ron, SE side of Rabbit Is, off Skullomie, or S of Eilean Creagach off Talmine. Approach to the latter runs close W of Rabbit Islands, but beware rks to N and NW of them.

Loch Eriboll, (chart 2076 and 9.7.20), provides secure anchs, but in strong winds violent squalls blow down from mountains. Eilean Cluimhrig lies on W side of entrance; the E shore is fringed with rks up to 2ca offshore. At White Hd (lt) the loch narrows to 6ca. There are chans W and E of Eilean Choraidh. Best anchs in Camas an Duin (S of Ard Neackie) or in Rispond B close to entrance (but not in E winds, and beware Rispond Rk which dries).

The coast to C. Wrath (9.8.5) is indented, with dangers extending 3ca off the shore and offlying rks and Is. Once a yacht has left Loch Eriboll she is committed to a long and exposed passage until reaching Loch Inchard. The Kyle of Durness is dangerous if the wind or sea is onshore. Give Cape Wrath a wide berth when wind-against-tide which raises a severe sea. A firing exercise area extends 8M E of C. Wrath, and 4M offshore. When in use, R flags or pairs of R lts (vert) are shown from E and W limits, and yachts should keep clear.

ORKNEY ISLANDS (9.7.21 and charts 2249, 2250) The Islands are mostly indented and rky, but with sandy beaches especially on NE sides. Pilotage is easy in good vis, but in other conditions great care is needed since tides run strongly. For details refer to Clyde Cruising Club's *Orkney Sailing Directions* and the Admiralty Tidal Atlas NP 209.

When cruising in Orkney it is essential to understand and use the tidal streams to the best advantage, avoiding the various tide races and overfalls, particularly near sp. A good engine is needed since, for example, there are many places where it is dangerous to get becalmed. Swell from the Atlantic or North Sea can contribute to dangerous sea conditions, or penetrate to some of the anchorages. During summer months winds are not normally unduly strong, and can be expected to be Force 7 or more on about two days a month. But in winter the wind reaches this strength for 10-15 days per month, and gales can be very severe in late winter and early spring. Cruising conditions are best near midsummer, when of course the hours of daylight are much extended.

Stronsay Firth and Westray Firth run SE/NW through the group. The many good anchs, include: Deer Sound (W of Deer Ness); B of Firth, B of Isbister, and off Balfour in Elwick B (all leading from Wide Firth); Rysa Sound, B of Houton, Hunda Sound (in Scapa Flow); Rousay Sound; and Pierowall Road (Westray). Plans for some of these are on chart 2622. For Houton Bay, Shapinsay, Auskerry and Pierowall see 9.7.21. There is a major oil terminal and prohibited area at Flotta, on the S side of Scapa Flow.

Tide races or dangerous seas occur at the entrances to most of the firths or sounds when the stream is against strong winds. This applies particularly to Hoy Sound, Eynhallow Sound, Papa Sound (Westray), Lashy Sound, and North Ronaldsay Firth. Also off Mull Head, over Dowie Sand, between Muckle Green Holm and War Ness (where violent turbulence may extend right across the firth), between Faraclett Head and Wart Holm, and off Sacquoy Hd. Off War Ness the SE-going stream begins at HW Aberdeen + 0435, and the NW-going at HW Aberdeen – 0200, sp rates 7kn.

SHETLAND ISLANDS (9.7.25 and charts 3281, 3282, 3283) These Islands mostly have bold cliffs and are relatively high, separated by narrow sounds through which the tide runs strongly, so that in poor vis great care is needed. Avoid sp tides, swell and wind against tide conditions. Although there are many secluded and attractive anchs, remember that the weather can change very quickly, with sudden shifts of wind. Also beware salmon fisheries and mussel rafts (unlit) in many Voes, Sounds and hbrs. Lerwick (9.7.26) is the busy main port and capital; for Scalloway, Vaila Sound and Balta Sound see 9.7.26. Refer to the CCC's *Shetland Sailing Directions*.

Coming from the S, beware a most violent and dangerous race (roost) off Sumburgh Hd (at S end of Mainland) on both streams. Other dangerous areas include between Ve Skerries and Papa Stour; the mouth of Yell Sound with strong wind against N-going stream; and off Holm of Skaw (N end of Unst). Tidal streams run mainly NW/SE and are not strong except off headlands and in the major sounds; the Admiralty Tidal Atlas NP 209 gives detail. The sp range is about 2m.

The 50M passage from Orkney can conveniently be broken by a stop at Fair Isle (North Haven). Note that races form off both ends of the Is, especially S (Roost of Keels); see 9.7.26.

Recommended Traffic Routes: NW-bound ships pass to the NE (no closer than 10M to Sumburgh Hd) or SW of Fair Isle; SE-bound ships pass no closer than 5M off N Ronaldsay (Orkney). Lerwick to Bergen, Norway is about 210M.

9.7.6 DISTANCE TABLE

Approximate distances in nautical miles are by the most direct route, whilst avoiding dangers and allowing for Traffic Separation Schemes. Places in *italics* are in adjoining areas; places in **bold** are in 9.0.8, Distances across the North Sea.

1.	*Peterhead*	**1**																			
2.	Fraserburgh	16	**2**																		
3.	Banff/Macduff	33	18	**3**																	
4.	Buckie	46	31	15	**4**																
5.	Lossiemouth	56	41	25	11	**5**															
6.	Findhorn	69	54	38	24	13	**6**														
7.	Nairn	79	64	48	34	23	10	**7**													
8.	Inverness	90	75	59	45	34	23	13	**8**												
9.	Tarbat Ness	72	57	41	27	18	14	17	27	**9**											
10.	Helmsdale	74	59	44	33	26	28	32	43	16	**10**										
11.	Wick	72	57	50	46	44	51	58	69	42	29	**11**									
12.	Duncansby Head	82	67	62	58	57	64	71	81	54	41	13	**12**								
13.	Scrabster	100	85	80	76	75	82	89	99	72	59	31	18	**13**							
14.	Kirkwall	115	100	95	91	90	97	104	114	87	74	46	34	50	**14**						
15.	Stromness	104	89	84	80	79	85	92	103	76	63	35	22	25	32	**15**					
16.	Fair Isle	122	111	116	118	120	130	137	148	121	108	79	68	85	55	77	**16**				
17.	Lerwick	160	150	156	160	162	172	170	190	162	148	120	109	124	95	110	42	**17**			
18.	Loch Eriboll (ent)	137	122	117	113	112	119	126	136	109	96	68	55	37	80	50	110	150	**18**		
19.	Cape Wrath	145	130	125	121	120	127	126	144	117	104	76	63	47	79	58	120	155	13	**19**	
20.	*Ullapool*	198	183	178	174	173	180	179	197	170	157	129	116	100	132	111	173	208	66	53	**20**

FRASERBURGH 9.7.7

Aberdeenshire 57°41'·50N 01°59'·79W ❀❀◊◊✿✿

CHARTS AC 1462, 222,115; Imray C22, C23; OS 30

TIDES +0120 Dover; ML 2·3; Duration 0615; Zone 0 (UT)

Standard Port ABERDEEN (⟵)

Times				Height (metres)			
High Water		Low Water		MHWS	MHWN	MLWN	MLWS
0000	0600	0100	0700	4·3	3·4	1·6	0·6
1200	1800	1300	1900				
Differences FRASERBURGH							
–0105	–0115	–0120	–0110	–0·6	–0·5	–0·2	0·0

SHELTER A safe refuge, but ent is dangerous in NE/SE gales. A very busy FV hbr; yachts are not encouraged but may find a berth in S Hbr (3.2m). FVs come and go H24.

NAVIGATION WPT 57°41'·30N 01°58'·80W, 111°/291° from/to ent, 0·57M. The ent chan is dredged 5·9m. Good lookout on entering/ leaving. Yachts can enter under radar control in poor vis.

LIGHTS AND MARKS Kinnairds Hd lt ho, Fl 5s 25m 22M, is 0·45M NNW of ent. Cairnbulg Briggs bn, Fl (2) 10s 9m 6M, is 1·8M ESE of ent. Ldg lts 291°: front QR 12m 5M; rear Oc R 6s 17m 5M.

RADIO TELEPHONE Call on approach VHF Ch **12** 16 (H24) for directions/berth.

TELEPHONE (Dial code 01346) Port Office 515858; Watch Tr 515926; MRCC (01224) 592334; ⊖ (0141) 887 9369 (H24); Marinecall 09068 500 451; Police 513151; Dr 518088.

FACILITIES **Port** ☎ 515858, AB £10 (in S Hbr) any LOA, Slip, P (cans), D, FW, CH, ME, El, Sh, C (30 ton & 70 ton mobile), SM, V, R, Bar; **Town** EC Wed; ✉, Ⓑ, ⇌, ✈ (bus to Aberdeen).

ADJACENT HARBOURS

ROSEHEARTY, Aberdeen, **57°42'·08N 02°06'·87W**. ❀❀✿✿. AC 222, 213. HW Aberdeen –1. E pier and inner hbr dry, but end of W pier is accessible at all tides. Ent exposed in N/E winds; in E/SE winds hbr can be uncomfortable. Ldg marks B/W now (2001) lit on approx 220°; rks E of ldg line. When 30m from pier, steer midway between ldg line and W pier. Port Rae, close to E, has unmarked rks; local knowledge. Hr Mr ☎ (01261) 813412, AB £10 any LOA. **Town** V, R, Bar, ✉. Firing range: for info ☎ (01346) 571634; see also 9.7.5. **Pennan Bay**, 5M W: ⚓ on sand between Howdman (2·9m) and Tamhead (2·1m) rks, 300m N of hbr (small craft only). **Gardenstown** (Gamrie Bay). Appr from E of Craig Dagerty rk (4m, conspic). Access HW±3 to drying hbr or ⚓ off. For details of Rover berthing ticket see 9.7.5.

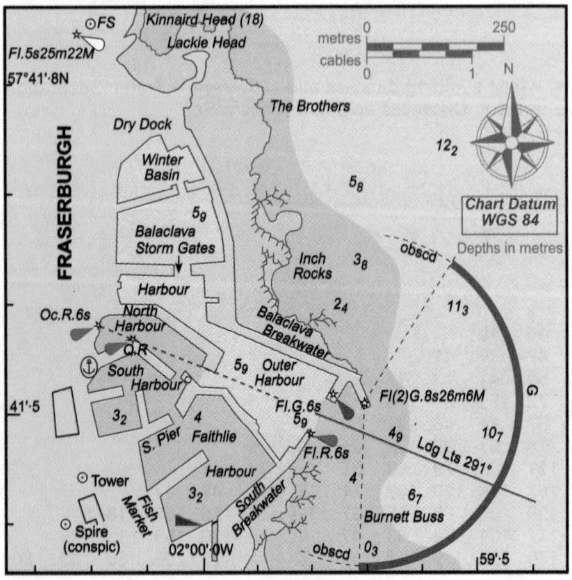

MACDUFF/BANFF 9.7.8

Aberdeenshire Macduff **57°40'·25N 02°30'·03W** ❀❀◊◊✿✿
Banff **57°40'·22N 02°31'·27W** ❀❀◊◊✿✿

CHARTS AC 1462, 222, 115; Imray C22, C23; OS 29

TIDES + 0055 Dover; ML 2·0; Duration 0615; Zone 0 (UT)

Standard Port ABERDEEN (⟵)

Times				Height (metres)			
High Water		Low Water		MHWS	MHWN	MLWN	MLWS
0200	0900	0400	0900	4·3	3·4	1·6	0 · 6
1400	2100	1600	2100				
Differences BANFF							
–0100	–0150	–0150	–0050	–0·4	–0·2	–0·1	+0·2

SHELTER **Macduff**: Reasonably good, but ent not advised in strong NW winds. Slight/moderate surge in outer hbr with N/ NE gales. Hbr ent is 17m wide with 3 basins; approx 2·6m in outer hbr and 2m inner hbr. A busy cargo/fishing port with limited space for yachts. **Banff**: Popular hbr (dries); access HW±4. When Macduff ent is very rough in strong NW/N winds, Banff can be a safe refuge; berth in outer basin and contact Hr Mr. In strong E/ENE winds Banff is unusable.

NAVIGATION WPT 57°40'·48N 02°30'·59W, 307°/127° from/to **Macduff** ent, 0·4M. WPT 57°40'·11N 02°30'·85W, 295°/115° from/ to **Banff** ent, 0·25M. Beware Feachie Craig, Collie Rks and rky coast N and S of hbr ent.

LIGHTS AND MARKS **Macduff**: Ldg lts/marks 127° both FR 44/ 55m 3M, orange △s. Pier hd lt, Fl (2) WRG 6s 12m 9/7M, W tr; W115°-174°, Horn (2) 20s. **Banff**: Fl 4s end of New Quay and ldg lts 295° rear Fl R 2s, front Fl R 4s.

RADIO TELEPHONE **Macduff** VHF Ch 12 16 (H24); **Banff** Ch 14 (part time).

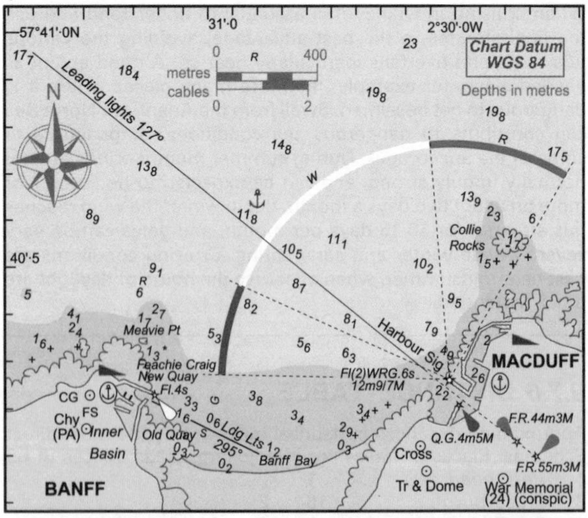

TELEPHONE (Dial code 01261) Hr Mr (**Macduff**) 832236, 📠 833612, Watch tr 833962; Hr Mr (**Banff**) 815544 (part time); MRCC (01224) 592334; ⊖ (0141) 887 9369 (H24); Marinecall 09068 500 451; Police 812555; Dr (**Banff**) 812027.

FACILITIES Macduff: **Hbr** £10 any LOA, Slip, P (cans), D, FW, ME, El, Sh, CH. **Town** EC Wed; V, R, Bar, ✉, ⇌ (bus to Keith). Banff: **Hbr** £10 any LOA, FW, AC, Slip, new toilet block; **Banff SC**: showers. **Town**, P, D, V, R, Bar, ⇌, Ⓑ, ✈ (Aberdeen). For details of Rover berthing ticket see 9.7.5.

ADJACENT HARBOURS

PORTSOY, Aberdeenshire, **57°41'·34N 02°41'·59W**. ❀❀◊✿✿✿. AC 222. HW +0047 on Dover; –0132 and Ht –0·3m on Aberdeen. Small drying hbr; ent exposed to NW/NE'lies. New Hbr to port of ent partially dries; inner hbr dries to clean sand. Ldg lts 160°, front FW 12m 5M on twr; rear FR 17m 5M. Hr Mr ☎ (01261) 815544. Facilities: few. AB £10, FW, Slip, V, R, Bar, ✉. For details of Rover berthing ticket see 9.7.5. **Sandend Bay**, 1·7M W (57°41'N 02°44'·5W). ⚓ on sand E of hbr.

WHITEHILLS *9.7.9*

Aberdeenshire **57°40'·80N 02°34'·87W**

CHARTS AC 222, 115; Imray C22, C23; OS 29

TIDES +0050 Dover; ML 2·4; Duration 0610; Zone 0 (UT)

Standard Port ABERDEEN (⟵)

Times				Height (metres)			
High Water		Low Water		MHWS	MHWN	MLWN	MLWS
0200	0900	0400	0900	4·3	3·4	1·6	0·6
1400	2100	1600	2100				
Differences WHITEHILLS							
–0122	–0137	–0117	–0127	–0·4	–0·3	+0·1	+0·1

SHELTER Safe. In strong NW/N winds beware surge in the narrow ent and outer hbr (2·4m), when ent is best not attempted. See Hr Mr for vacant pontoon berth (1·2m). Entr. reported 0.8m (2001).

NAVIGATION WPT 57°41'·98N 02°34'·89W, 000°/180° from/to bkwtr lt, 1·2M. Reefs on S side of chan marked by 2 rusty/white SHM bns. Beware fishing floats.

LIGHTS AND MARKS Fl WR 3s on pier hd, vis R132°–212°, W212°–245°; appr in R sector.

RADIO TELEPHONE Whitehills Hbr Radio VHF Ch 14 16.

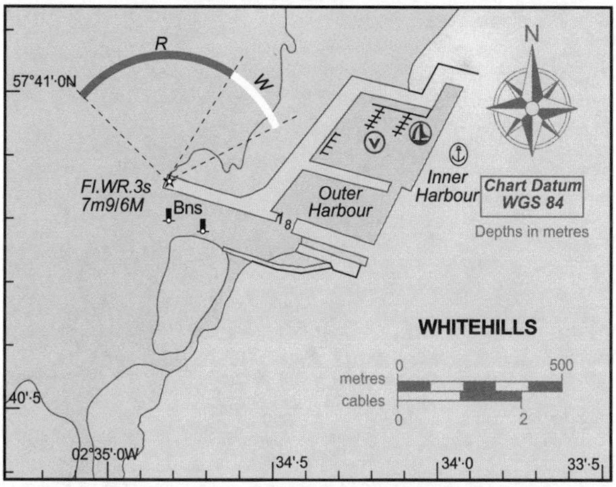

TELEPHONE (Dial code 01261) Hr Mr 861291; MRCC (01224) 592334; ⊖ (0141) 887 9369 (H24); Marinecall 09068 500451; Police Banff 812515; Dr 812027.

FACILITIES Marina £15 incl AC, AB £12, D, FW, ME, El, CH. **Town** V, R, Bar, ✉, ⇌ (bus to Keith), ✈ (Aberdeen).

ADJACENT HARBOURS

CULLEN, Moray, **57°41'·63N 02°49'·29W.** AC 222. HW +0045 on Dover, HW –0135 & –0·3m on Aberdeen; Duration 0555; ML 2·4m. Shelter good, but ent hazardous in strong W/N winds. Appr on 180° toward conspic viaduct and W bn on N pier. Caple Rk, 0·2m, is 5ca NE of hbr. Access HW ±2 approx to small drying unlit hbr, best for shoal draft. Moor S of Inner jetty if < 1m draft. Beware moorings across inner basin ent. Pontoons in inner hbr. Hr Mr ☎ (01261) 842477 (home, part-time). **Town** V, R, Bar, ✉. For details of Rover Ticket see 9.7.5.

PORTKNOCKIE, Moray, **57°42'·28N 02°51'·79W.** AC 222. HW +0045 on Dover; –0135 and ht –0·3m Aberdeen; ML 2·3m; Duration 0555; access H24. Good shelter in one of the safest hbrs on S side of Moray Firth, but scend is often experienced; care needed in strong NW/N winds. FW ldg lts, on white-topped poles, lead approx 143°, to ent. Orange street lts surround the hbr. Berth N quay of outer hbr on firm sand; most of inner hbr dries. Hr Mr ☎ (01542) 840833 (home, part-time); Facilities: Slip, AB, for details of Rover Ticket see 9.7.5., FW, Sh; Dr ☎ 840272. **Town** EC Wed; Ⓑ, P & D, ✉, V, Bar.

ADJACENT HARBOUR (2M ENE of BUCKIE)

FINDOCHTY, Moray, **57°41'·94N 02°54'·29W.** AC 222. HW +0045 on Dover, HW –0140 & ht –0·2m on Aberdeen; ML 2·3m; Duration 0550. Ent is about 2ca W of conspic church belfry. 1ca N of ent, leave Beacon Rock (3m high) to stbd. Ldg lts, FW, lead approx 166° into Outer Basin which dries 0·2m and has many rky outcrops; access HW ±2 for 1·5m draft. Ent faces N and is 20m wide; unlit white bn at hd of W pier. Good shelter in inner basin for 100 yachts on 3 pontoons (the 2 W'ly pontoons dry); AB, for details of Rover Ticket see 9.7.5. Hr Mr ☎ (01542) 831466 (home, part-time). **Town** V, R, Bar, ✉, Ⓑ.

BUCKIE *9.7.10*

Moray **57°40'·84N 02°57'·63W**

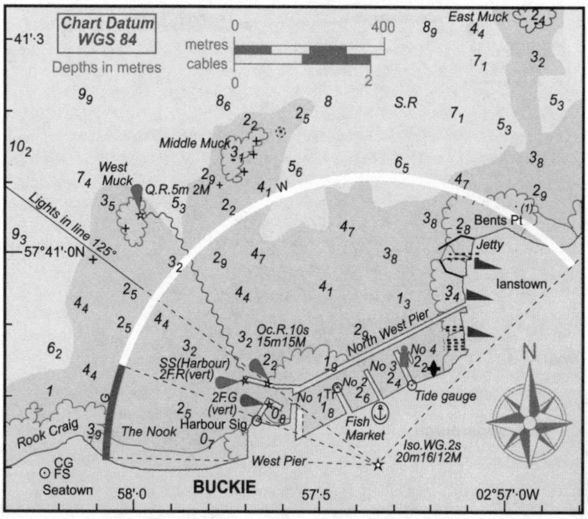

CHARTS AC 1462, 222, 115; Imray C22, C23; OS 28

TIDES +0040 Dover; ML 2·4; Duration 0550; Zone 0 (UT)

Standard Port ABERDEEN (⟵)

Times				Height (metres)			
High Water		Low Water		MHWS	MHWN	MLWN	MLWS
0200	0900	0400	0900	4·3	3·4	1·6	0·6
1400	2100	1600	2100				
Differences BUCKIE							
–0130	–0145	–0125	–0140	–0·2	–0·2	0·0	+0·1

SHELTER Good in all weathers, but in strong NNW to NE winds there is a dangerous swell over the bar at hbr ent; Entrance dredged to 4m but subject to silting. Access H24. Berth in No 4 basin as directed by Hr Mr.

NAVIGATION WPT 57°41'·30N 02°58'·89W, 306°/126° from/to ent, 0·80M. Beware W Muck (QR 5m tripod, 2M), Middle Muck and E Muck Rks, 3ca off shore.

LIGHTS AND MARKS The Oc R 10s 15m 15M, W tr on N bkwtr, in line 125° with Iso WG 2s 20m 16/12M, W tr, R top, leads clear of W Muck. NB: this line does not lead into hbr ent; but the transit of 2FG (vert) on W pier with same Iso WG 2s **does** lead 119° to ent (24m wide). White tr of ice plant on pier No. 2 is conspic. Entry sigs on N pier: 3 ● lts = hbr closed. Traffic is controlled by VHF.

RADIO TELEPHONE VHF Ch 12 16 (H24).

TELEPHONE (Dial code 01542) Hr Mr 831700 📠 834742; MRCC (01224) 592334; ⊖ (0141) 887 9369 (H24); Marinecall 09068 500 451; Police 832222; Dr 831555.

FACILITIES No 4 Basin AB £10, FW; **Services:** D & P (delivery), BY, ME, El, Sh, CH, Slip, C (15 ton), Gas. **Town** EC Wed; V, Bar, Ⓑ, ✉, ⊡ at Strathlene caravan site 1·5M E, ⇌ (bus to Elgin), ✈ (Aberdeen or Inverness).

LOSSIEMOUTH *9.7.11*

Moray **57°43'·41N 03°16'·63W** ❀❀◊◊✿✿

CHARTS AC 1462, 223; Imray C22, C23; OS 28

TIDES +0040 Dover; ML 2·3; Duration 0605; Zone 0 (UT)

Standard Port ABERDEEN (⟵)

Times				Height (metres)			
High Water		Low Water		MHWS	MHWN	MLWN	MLWS
0200	0900	0400	0900	4·3	3·4	1·6	0 · 6
1400	2100	1600	2100				
Differences LOSSIEMOUTH							
–0125	–0200	–0130	–0130	–0·2	–0·2	0·0	0·0

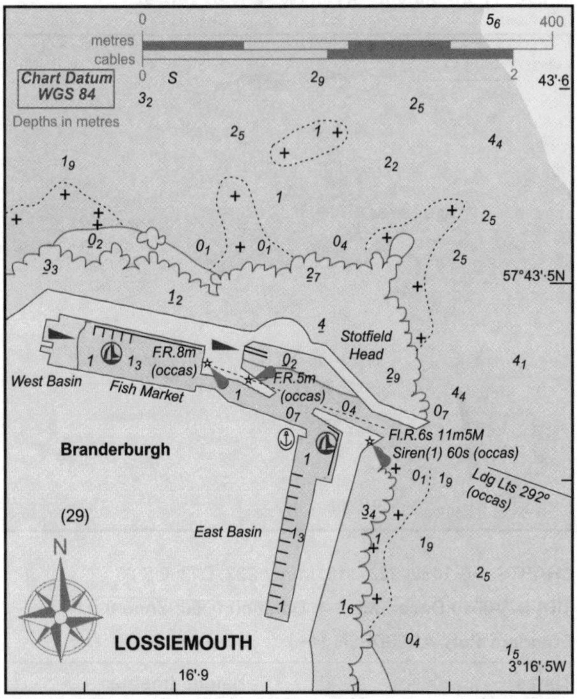

SHELTER Very good in winds from SSE to NW. In N to SE winds >F6 appr to ent can be dangerous, with swell in outer hbr. Turn hard port for marina in S Basin, dredged 2m; access HW±4. But chan and Basins are prone to silting; a vessel drawing 2m would have little clearance at LWS ±1. West basin also used by FV's.

NAVIGATION WPT 57°43'·38N 03°16'·09W, 097°/277° from/to ent, 0·30M. Rks to N and S of hbr ent; appr from E. Near ent, beware current from R Lossie setting in N'ly direction, causing confused water in N to SE winds at sp.

LIGHTS AND MARKS Covesea Skerries, W lt ho, Fl WR 20s 49m 24M, is 2M W of the hbr ent. Ldg lts 292°, both FR 5/8m; S pier hd Fl R 6s 11m 5M. Traffic sigs: B ● at S pier (● over Fl R 6s) = hbr shut.

RADIO TELEPHONE VHF Ch 12 16 HO.

TELEPHONE (Dial code 01343) Hr Mr ☎/📠 813066; MRCC (01224) 592334; ⊖ (0141) 887 9369 (H24); Marinecall 09068 500451; Police 812022; Dr 812277.

FACILITIES **Marina** (43), ☎ 543855, £16.50 inc AC, FW, ⊡, ♿; **Hbr** ME, El, Sh, C, SM; **Lossiemouth CC** ☎ 813767; **Hbr Service Stn** ☎ 813001, Mon-Fri 0800-2030, Sat 0800-1930, Sun 0930-1900, P & D cans, Gas. **Town** EC Thurs; V, R, Bar, ✉, Ⓑ, ⇌ (bus to Elgin), ✈ (Inverness).

HOPEMAN *9.7.12*

Moray **57°42'·70N 03°26'·31W** ❀❀◊◊✿✿

CHARTS AC 1462, 223; Imray C22, C23; OS 28

TIDES +0050 Dover; ML 2·4; Duration 0610; Zone 0 (UT)

Standard Port ABERDEEN (⟵)

Times				Height (metres)			
High Water		Low Water		MHWS	MHWN	MLWN	MLWS
0200	0900	0400	0900	4·3	3·4	1·6	0 · 6
1400	2100	1600	2100				
Differences HOPEMAN							
–0120	–0150	–0135	–0120	–0·2	–0·2	0·0	0·0

SHELTER Once in Inner basin, shelter good from all winds; but hbr dries, access HW ± 2 (for 1·5m draft). Ent is difficult in winds from NE to SE. A popular yachting hbr with AB. For details of Rover berthing see 9.7.17.

NAVIGATION WPT 57°42'·66N, 03°26'·59W, 263°/083° from/to ent, 0·17M. Dangerous rks lie off hbr ent. Do not attempt entry in heavy weather. Beware lobster pot floats E and W of hbr (Mar-Aug).

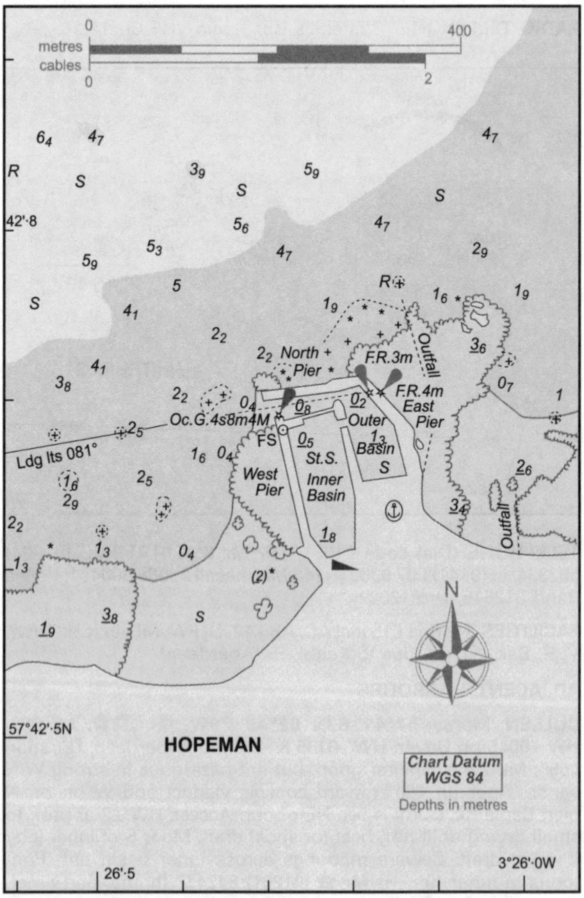

LIGHTS AND MARKS Ldg lts 081°, FR 3/4m; S pier hd FG 4s 8m 4M.

RADIO TELEPHONE Call *Burghead Radio* Ch 14 (HX).

TELEPHONE (Dial code 01343) Hr Mr ☎/📠 835337 (part-time); MRCC (01224) 592334; ⊖ (0141) 887 9369 (H24); Marinecall 09068 500 451; Police 830222; Dr 543141.

FACILITIES **Hbr** AB, for details of Rover Ticket see 9.7.5., FW, Slip. **Services:** CH, ME, Gas, Sh, El, P (cans). **Town** EC Wed; V, R, Bar, ✉, Ⓑ, ⇌ (bus to Elgin), ✈ (Inverness).

BURGHEAD 9.7.13

Moray **57°42'·06N 03°30'·02W**

CHARTS AC 1462, 223; Imray C22, C23; OS 28

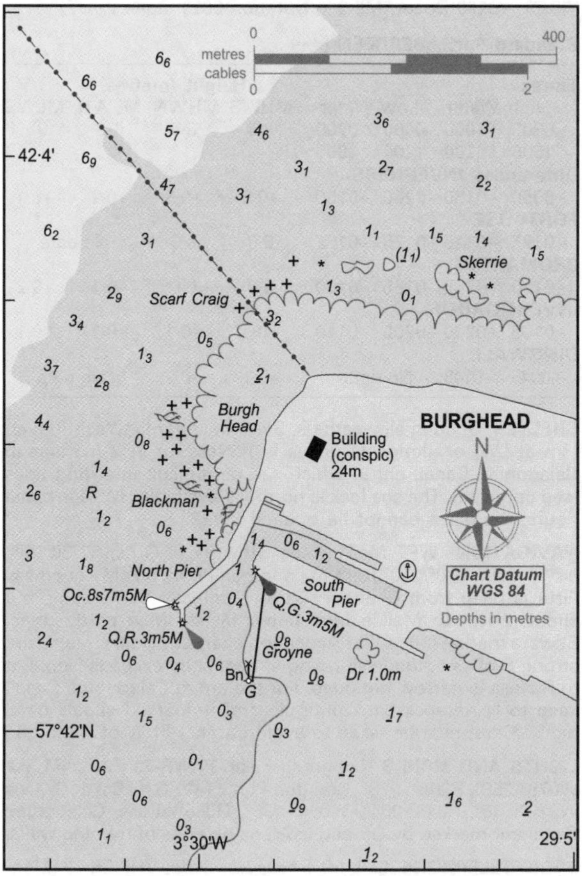

TIDES +0035 Dover; ML 2·4; Duration 0610; Zone 0 (UT)

Standard Port ABERDEEN (⟵)

Times				Height (metres)			
High Water		Low Water		MHWS	MHWN	MLWN	MLWS
0200	0900	0400	0900	4·3	3·4	1·6	0·6
1400	2100	1600	2100				
Differences BURGHEAD							
–0120	–0150	–0135	–0120	–0·2	–0·2	0·0	0·0

SHELTER One of the few Moray Firth hbrs accessible in strong E winds. 0·6m depth in ent chan and 1·4m in hbr. Go alongside where available and contact Hr Mr. Can be very busy with FVs.

NAVIGATION WPT 57°42'·28N 03°30'·39W, 317°/137° from/to N pier lt QR, 0·28M. Access HW ±4. Chan is variable due to sand movement. Advisable to contact Hr Mr if entering at LW.

LIGHTS AND MARKS No ldg lts but night ent is safe after identifying the N pier lts: QR 3m 5M and Oc 8s 7m 5M. S pier hd QG 3m 5M.

RADIO TELEPHONE Call *Burghead Radio* VHF Ch **14** 12 (HO and when vessel due).

TELEPHONE (Dial code 01343) Hr Mr 835337; MRCC (01224) 592334; ⊖ (0141) 887 9369 (H24); Marinecall 09068 500 451; Dr 812277.

FACILITIES Hbr For details of Rover Ticket see 9.7.5., FW, AB, C (50 ton mobile), L, Slip, BY, Sh. **Town** EC Thurs; Bar, ✉, V, Ⓑ, ⇌ (bus to Elgin), ✈ (Inverness).

FINDHORN 9.7.14

Moray **57°39'·64N 03°37'·47W**

CHARTS AC 223; Imray C22, C23; OS 27

TIDES +0110 Dover; ML 2·5; Duration 0615; Zone 0 (UT)

Standard Port ABERDEEN (⟵)

Times				Height (metres)			
High Water		Low Water		MHWS	MHWN	MLWN	MLWS
0200	0900	0400	0900	4·3	3·4	1·6	0·6
1400	2100	1600	2100				
Differences FINDHORN							
–0120	–0150	–0135	–0130	0·0	–0·1	0·0	+0·1

SHELTER ⚓ in pool off boatyard or off N pier or dry out alongside, inside piers and ask at YC; or pick up Y 🅐 off N pier. Do not attempt entry in strong NW/NE winds or with big swell running; expect breakers/surf either side of ent.

NAVIGATION WPT 57°40'·33N 03°37'·77W, SWM spar buoy, 313°/133° from/to Ee Point, 0·85M. Access HW±2. 100m SE of the spar buoy there are 2 Y waiting 🅐s in 4m. From WPT, the bar is marked (R marker) and thence by Fl R or G buoys all of which are moved to suit the channel into the bay, and may be lifted Nov to early Apr. Once past The Ee, turn port inside G buoys. The S part of Findhorn Bay dries extensively.

LIGHTS AND MARKS Unlit. There is a windsock on FS by The Ee. Boatyard building is conspic.

RADIO TELEPHONE VHF Ch M *Chadwick Base* (when racing in progress). Findhorn BY: Ch 16, 80.

TELEPHONE (Dial code 01309) Fairways Committee (via BY) 690099; MRCC (01224) 592334; ⊖ (0141) 887 9369 (H24); Findhorn Pilot (Robin Miller) 690213; Marinecall 09068 500 451; Police 672224; Dr 672221.

FACILITIES Royal Findhorn YC ☎ 690247, M, FW, Bar; **Services:** BY, L, M, AC, FW, Slip, C (16 ton), P & D (cans), El, ME, CH, ACA, Gas, Sh. **Town** V, R, Bar, ✉, Ⓑ, ⇌ (Forres), ✈ (Inverness).

7

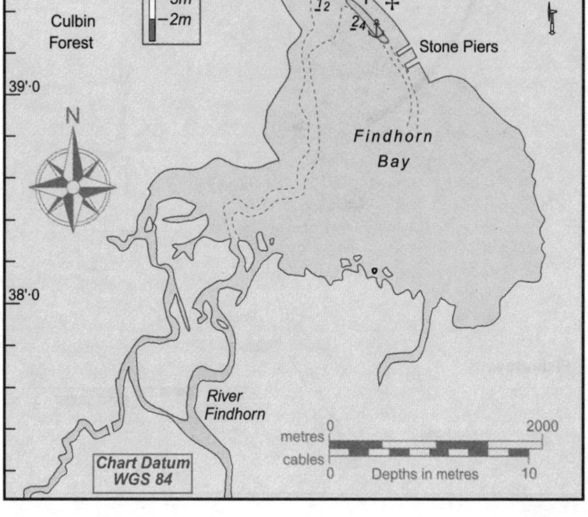

NAIRN *9.7.15*

Highland **57°35'·61N 03°51'·65W**

CHARTS AC 1462, 223; Imray C22, C23; OS 27

TIDES +0110 Dover; ML 2·2; Duration 0615; Zone 0 (UT)

Standard Port ABERDEEN (⟵)

Times				Height (metres)			
High Water		Low Water		MHWS	MHWN	MLWN	MLWS
0200	0900	0400	0900	4·3	3·4	1·6	0 · 6
1400	2100	1600	2100				
Differences NAIRN							
–0120	–0150	–0135	–0130	0·0	–0·1	0·0	+0·1
McDERMOTT BASE							
–0110	–0140	–0120	–0115	–0·1	–0·1	+0·1	+0·3

SHELTER Good, but entry difficult in fresh NNE'ly. Pontoons in hbr with Ⓥ berths. Best entry HW ± 1½. A Y buoy is close to the WPT, approx 400m NNW of the pierheads; the W'ly buoy in 2·5m, the E'ly in 1·5m. No commercial shipping.

NAVIGATION WPT 57°35'·88N 03°51'·89W, 335°/155° from/to ent, 0·3M. The approach dries to 100m off the pierheads. Inside, the best water is to the E side of the river chan.

LIGHTS AND MARKS Lt ho on E pier hd, Oc WRG 4s 6m 5M, vis G shore-100°, W100°-207°, R207°-shore. Keep in W sector. McDermott Base, 4·5M to the W, has a large conspic cream-coloured building; also useful if making for Inverness Firth.

RADIO TELEPHONE None. Ch M (weekends only).

TELEPHONE (Dial code 01667) Hr Mr 454704; MRCC (01224) 592334; ⊖ (0141) 887 9369 (H24); Clinic 455092; Marinecall 09068 500 451; Police 452222; Dr 453421.

FACILITIES Nairn Basin AB £2, Slip, AC (110 volts), P, D; **Nairn SC** ☎ 453897, Bar. **Town** EC Wed; V, R, Bar, ✉, Ⓑ, ⇌, ✈ (Inverness).

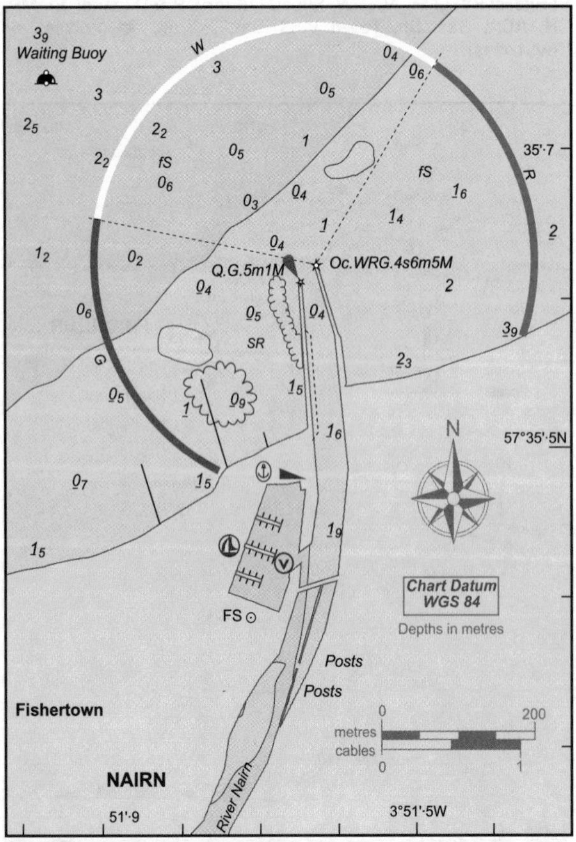

INVERNESS *9.7.16*

Highland **57°29'·73N 04°14'·17W**

CHARTS AC 1078, 1077, 223; Imray C22, C23; OS 26/27

TIDES +0100 Dover; ML 2·7; Duration 0620; Zone 0 (UT)

Standard Port ABERDEEN (⟵)

Times				Height (metres)			
High Water		Low Water		MHWS	MHWN	MLWN	MLWS
0300	1000	0000	0700	4·3	3·4	1·6	0 · 6
1500	2200	1200	1900				
Differences INVERNESS							
–0050	–0150	–0200	–0150	+0·5	+0·3	+0·2	+0·1
FORTROSE							
–0125	–0125	–0125	–0125	0·0	0·0	No data	
CROMARTY							
–0120	–0155	–0155	–0120	0·0	0·0	+0·1	+0·2
INVERGORDON							
–0105	–0200	–0200	–0110	+0·1	+0·1	+0·1	+0·1
DINGWALL							
–0045	–0145	No data		+0·1	+0·2	No data	

SHELTER Good in all weathers. Berth at Longman Yacht Haven (3m at LW) or alongside quays in R Ness; or at 2 marinas in Caledonian Canal, ent to which can be difficult in strong tides (see opposite). The sea lock is normally available HW±4 in canal hours; the gates cannot be opened LW±2.

NAVIGATION WPT Meikle Mee SHM By Fl G 3s, 57°30'·25N 04°12'·03W, 070°/250° from/to Longman Pt bn, 0·74M. Inverness Firth is deep from Chanonry Pt to Munlochy SWM buoy, but shoal (2·1m) to Meikle Mee buoy. Meikle Mee partly dries. Beware marine farms S of Avoch (off chartlet). Tidal streams are strong S of Craigton Pt (E-going stream at sp exceeds 5kn). Ent to R Ness is narrow but deep. For the ent to Caledonian Canal, keep to N Kessock bank until clear of unmarked shoals on S bank. Care must be taken to avoid Carnare Pt W of R mouth.

LIGHTS AND MARKS Longman Pt bn Fl WR 2s 7m 5/4M, vis W078°-258°, R258° -078°. Craigton Pt lt, Fl WRG 4s 6m 11/7M vis W312°-048°, R048°-064°, W064°-085°, G085°-shore. Caledonian Canal ent marked by QR and Iso G 4s on ends of training walls.

RADIO TELEPHONE Call: *Inverness Hbr Office* VHF Ch 12 (Mon-Fri: 0900 -1700 LT). Inverness Boat Centre Ch 80 M (0900-1800 LT). Caledonian Canal: Ch 74 is used by all stations. Call: *Clachnaharry Sea Lock*; or for office: *Caledonian Canal.*

TELEPHONE (Dial code 01463) Hr Mr 715715; Clachnaharry Sea Lock 713896; Canal Office 233140; MRCC (01224) 592334; ⊖ 222787; Marinecall 09068 500 451; Police 239191; Dr 234151.

FACILITIES Longman Yacht Haven (18+4 visitors), £10, ☎ 715715, FW, access H24 (3m at LW); **Citadel and Shore Street Quays** (R Ness) ☎ 715715, AB £10, P, D, FW, ME, El; (For commercial ships unless directed by Hr Mr). **Services:** Slip, M, ME, El, C (100 ton), CH, FW, P, SM, Gas. **Town** EC Wed; V, R, Bar, ✉, Ⓑ, ⇌, ✈.

MINOR HARBOURS IN INVERNESS FIRTH

FORTROSE, Highland, **57°34'·71N 04°08'·04W**. AC 1078. Tides 9.7.16. HW +0055 on Dover; ML 2·5m; Duration 0620. Small drying unlit hbr, well protected by Chanonry Ness to E; access HW±2, limited space. Follow ldg line 296°, Broomhill Ho (conspic on hill to NW) in line with school spire until abeam SPM buoy; then turn W to avoid Craig an Roan rks (1·8m) ESE of ent. Chanonry Pt lt, Oc 6s 12m 15M, obscd 073°-shore. Hr Mr ☎ (01381) 620861; Dr ☎ 620909. Facilities: EC Thurs; AB £3, L, M, P, D, Slip, Gas, R, V, ✉, Ⓑ; **Chanonry SC** (near pier) ☎ 01381 621973.

AVOCH, Highland, **57°34'·03N 04°09'·94W**. AC 1078. Tides as Fortrose (1·25M to the ENE). Hbr dries, mostly on the N side, but is bigger than Fortrose; access HW±2. Small craft may stay afloat at nps against the S pier, which has 2FR (vert) at E-facing ent. Facilities: AB, FW. **Village:** ✉, V, R, Bar, P & D (cans), ME.

INVERNESS *continued*

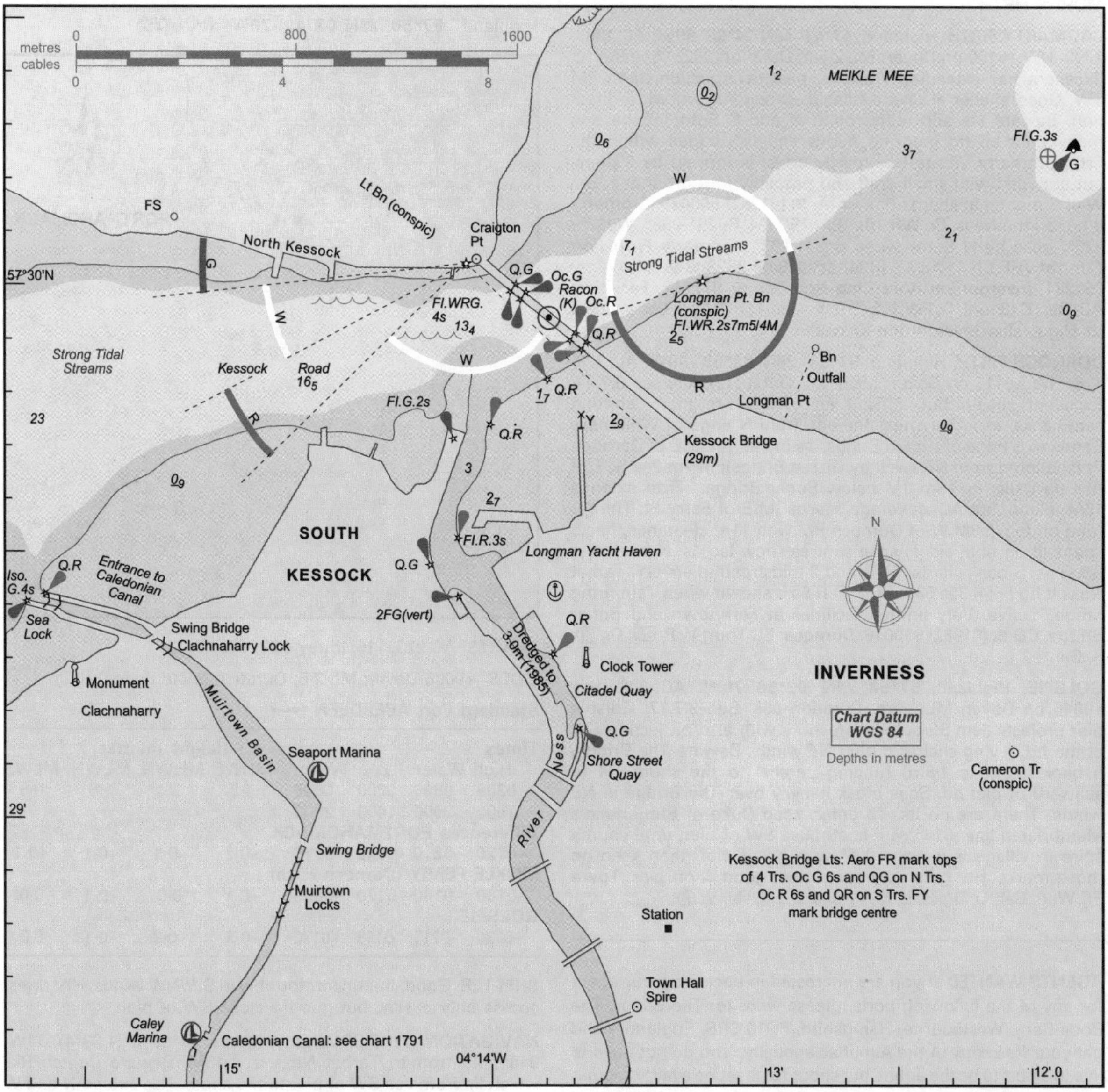

CALEDONIAN CANAL (Sea lock 57°29'·44N 04°15'·84W). These notes are for the convenience of those entering the Canal at Inverness, qv. They supplement and partly duplicate the main information and chartlet in 9.8.18.

CHARTS AC 1078, 1791; OS 26, 27, 34, 41. *Skipper's Guide* advised.

TIDES Differences: Clachnaharry +0116 on Dover; see 9.7.16.

SHELTER Clachnaharry sea lock operates HW±4 (sp) within canal hours. The road and rail swing bridges may cause delays up to 25 mins. Seaport and Caley marinas: see Facilities.

NAVIGATION The 60M Caledonian Canal consists of 38M through three lochs, (Lochs Ness, Oich and Lochy), connected by 22M through canals. It can take vessels 45m LOA, 10m beam, 4m draft and max mast ht 27·4m. The passage normally takes two full days, possibly longer in the summer; 14 hrs is absolute minimum. Speed limit is 5kn in canal sections. There are 10 swing bridges; road tfc has priority at peak hrs. Do not pass bridges without the keeper's instructions. From Clachnaharry sea lock to Loch Ness (Bona Ferry lt ho) is approx 7M, via Muirtown and Dochgarroch locks.

LOCKS All 29 locks are manned and operate early May to early Oct, 0800-1800LT daily. Dues: see 9.8.18. For regulations and *Skipper's Guide* apply: Canal Manager, Muirtown Wharf, Inverness IV3 5LS, ☎ (01463) 233140; 📠 710942.

LIGHTS & MARKS Chans are marked by posts, cairns and unlit buoys, PHM on the NW side of the chan and SHM on the SE side.

BOAT SAFETY SCHEME Transient/visiting vessels will be checked for apparent dangerous defects eg leaking gas or fuel, damaged electrical cables, taking in water, risk of capsize. £1M 3rd party insurance is required. For details see 9.8.18.

RADIO TELEPHONE Sea locks and main lock flights operate VHF Ch **74** (HO).

TELEPHONE Clachnaharry sea lock (01463) 713896; Canal Office, Inverness (01463) 233140.

FACILITIES **Seaport marina** (20+ 20 Ⓥ), £6 all LOA, ☎ (01463) 239475, AC, FW, D, El, ME, Sh, Gas, Gaz, ⊡, C (40 ton), ♂, ♿. **Caley marina** (25+25 Ⓥ) ☎ (01463) 236539, £6.50, FW, CH, D, ME, El, Sh, AC, C (20 ton), ACA.

OTHER HARBOURS ON THE NORTH WEST SIDE OF THE MORAY FIRTH

CROMARTY FIRTH, Highland, **57°41'·18N 04°02'·09W**. AC 1889, 1890. HW +0100 on Dover; ML 2·5m; Duration 0625. See 9.7.16. Excellent hbr extending 7·5M W, past Invergordon, then 9M SW. Good shelter always available, depending on wind direction. Beware rks and reefs round N and S Sutor at the ent; many unlit oil rig mooring buoys and fish cages within the firth. Cromarty Village Hbr (partly dries) is formed by 2 piers, but crowded with small craft and probably foul ground; ⚓ 2ca W of S pier hd in approx 6m. Hr Mr ☎ (01381) 600479. Cromarty lt ho, on the Ness, Oc WR 10s 18m 15/11M, R079°–088°, W088°–275°, obsc by N Sutor when brg < 253°. *Cromarty Firth Port Control* VHF Ch 11 16 13 (H24) ☎ (01349) 852308 📠 854172; ⊜ 852221. **Invergordon Boat Club** Hon Sec ☎ 877612. Facilities: AB, Bar, C (3 ton), D, FW, ⊠, P, R, V, Gas, L; EC Wed. Ferry: Local to Nigg; also Invergordon-Kirkwall.

DORNOCH FIRTH, Highland. **57°51'·28N 03°59'·39W**. AC 223, 115. HW +0115 on Dover; ML 2·5m; Duration 0605; see 9.7.17. Excellent shelter but difficult ent. There are many shifting sandbanks, especially near the ent, from N edge of Whiteness Sands to S edge of Gizzen Briggs. ⚓s in 7m ¾M ESE of Dornoch Pt (sheltered from NE swell by Gizzen Briggs); in 7m 2ca SSE of Ard na Cailc; in 3·3m 1M below Bonar Bridge. Firth extends 15M inland, but AC coverage ceases ¼M E of Ferry Pt. The A9 road bridge, 3·3M W of Dornoch Pt, with 11m clearance, has 3 spans lit on both sides; span centres show Iso 4s, N bank pier Iso G 4s, S bank pier Iso R 4s and 2 midstream piers QY. Tarbat Ness lt ho Fl (4) 30s 53m 24M. Fl R 5s lt shown when Tain firing range active. Very limited facilities at Ferrytown and Bonar Bridge. CG ☎ (01862) 810016. **Dornoch**: EC Thur; V, P, ⊠, Dr, Ⓑ, R, Bar.

GOLSPIE, Highland, **57°58'·71N 03°56'·79W**. AC 223. HW +0045 on Dover; ML 2·3m; Duration 068. See 9.7.17. Golspie pier projects 60m SE across foreshore with arm projecting SW at the hd, giving shelter during NE winds. Beware The Bridge, a bank (0·3m to 1·8m) running parallel to the shore ¼M to seaward of pier hd. Seas break heavily over The Bridge in NE winds. There are no lts. To enter, keep Duke of Sutherland's Memorial in line 316° with boathouse SW of pier, until church spire in village is in line 006° with hd of pier, then keep on those marks. Hbr gets very congested; good ⚓ off pier. **Town** EC Wed; Bar, D, Dr, ⊞, L, M, P, Gas, ⊠, R, ⇌, V, Ⓑ.

AGENTS WANTED If you are interested in becoming our agent for any of the following ports, please write to: The Editor, The Book Barn, Westbourne, Hampshire, PO10 8RS, England – and get your free copy of the Almanac annually. You do not have to live in a port to be the agent, but should at least be a fairly regular visitor.

Keyhaven	Lerwick
Rothesay	Malahide
Le Légué (St Brieuc)	Bénodet
River Loire/St Nazaire	L'Herbaudière
St Gilles-Croix-de-Vie	Les Sables d'Olonne
La Rochelle	La Seudre
La Gironde	Port Bloc
Anglet	St Jean-de-Luz
Dives-sur-Mer	River Seine
Le Touquet/Étaples	Nieuwpoort
Oostend	Stellendam & Hellevoetsluis
Nordeney	Spiekeroog

PORTMAHOMACK 9.7.17

Highland **57°50'.28N 03°49'·79W** ❁❁⛵✿✿

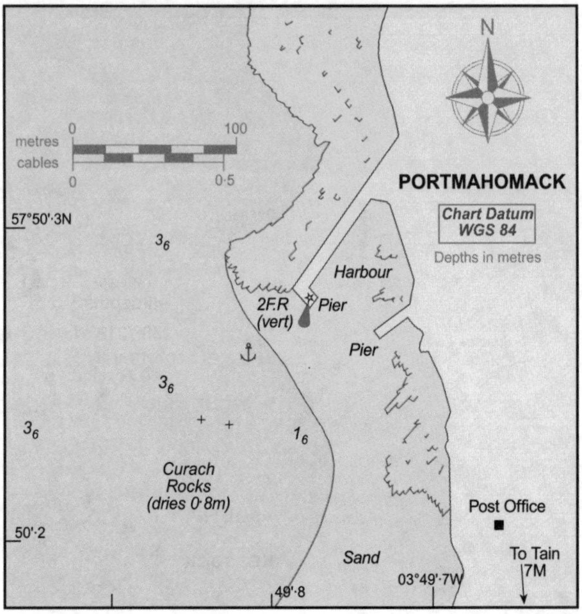

CHARTS AC 223, 115; Imray C22, C23; OS 21

TIDES +0035 Dover; ML 2·5; Duration 0600; Zone 0 (UT)

Standard Port ABERDEEN (⟵)

Times				Height (metres)			
High Water		Low Water		MHWS	MHWN	MLWN	MLWS
0300	0800	0200	0800	4·3	3·4	1·6	0·6
1500	2000	1400	2000				
Differences PORTMAHOMACK							
–0120	–0210	–0140	–0110	–0·2	–0·1	+0·1	+0·1
MEIKLE FERRY (Dornoch Firth)							
–0100	–0140	–0120	–0055	+0·1	0·0	–0·1	0·0
GOLSPIE							
–0130	–0215	–0155	–0130	–0·3	–0·3	–0·1	0·0

SHELTER Good, but uncomfortable in SW/NW winds. Hbr dries, access only at HW, but good ⚓ close SW of pier.

NAVIGATION WPT SPM buoy, FlY 5s, 57°53'·01N 03°47'·11W, 346°/166° from/to Tarbat Ness lt, 1·13M. Beware Curach Rks which lie from 2ca SW of pier to the shore. Rks extend N and W of the pier. Beware lobster pot floats and salmon nets N of hbr. Tain firing & bombing range is about 3M to the W, S of mouth of Dornoch Firth; R flags, R lts, shown when active.

LIGHTS AND MARKS Tarbert Ness lt ho Fl (4) 30s 53m 24M, W twr R bands, is 2·6M to NE of hbr. Pier hd 2 FR (vert) 7m 5M.

RADIO TELEPHONE None.

TELEPHONE (Dial code 01862) Hr Mr 671705; MRCC (01224) 592334; ⊜ (0141) 887 9369 (H24); **Marinecall** 09068 500 451; Dr 892759.

FACILITIES **Hbr**, AB £13, M, L, FW. **Town** EC Wed; R, V, Bar, ⊠, ⇌ (bus to Tain), ✈ (Inverness).

HELMSDALE *9.7.18*

Highland **58°06'·83N 03°38'·89W**

CHARTS AC 1462, 115; Imray C22; OS 17

TIDES +0035 Dover; ML 2·2; Duration 0615; Zone 0 (UT)

Standard Port WICK (⟶)

Times				Height (metres)			
High Water		Low Water		MHWS	MHWN	MLWN	MLWS
0000	0700	0200	0700	3·5	2·8	1·4	0·7
1200	1900	1400	1900				
Differences HELMSDALE							
+0025	+0015	+0035	+0030	+0·4	+0·3	+0·1	0·0

SHELTER Good, except in strong E/SE'lies. AB on NW pier, approx 1m. 30m of Pontoon berths through Hr Mr. Limited depths at LWS.

NAVIGATION WPT 58°06'·59N 03°38'·39W, 133°/313° from/to ent, 0·35M, ldg marks are dark poles with Or topmarks. Beware spate coming down river after heavy rain. Shoal both sides of chan and bar builds up when river in spate.

LIGHTS AND MARKS Ldg lts 313° (occas).

RADIO TELEPHONE VHF Ch 13 16.

TELEPHONE (Dial code 01431) Hr Mr 821692 (Office), 821386 (Home); MRCC (01224) 592334; ⊜ (01955) 603650; Marinecall 09068 500 451; Dr 821221, or 821225 (Home).

FACILITIES **Hbr** AB £5 first 5m + £1.25 per m over 24H; 1-7 days £7.50 up to 5m + £2.50 per m, M (See Hr Mr), FW, Slip. **Town** EC Wed; P, D, Gas, V, R, Bar, ✉, Ⓑ (Brora), ⇌ (Wick).

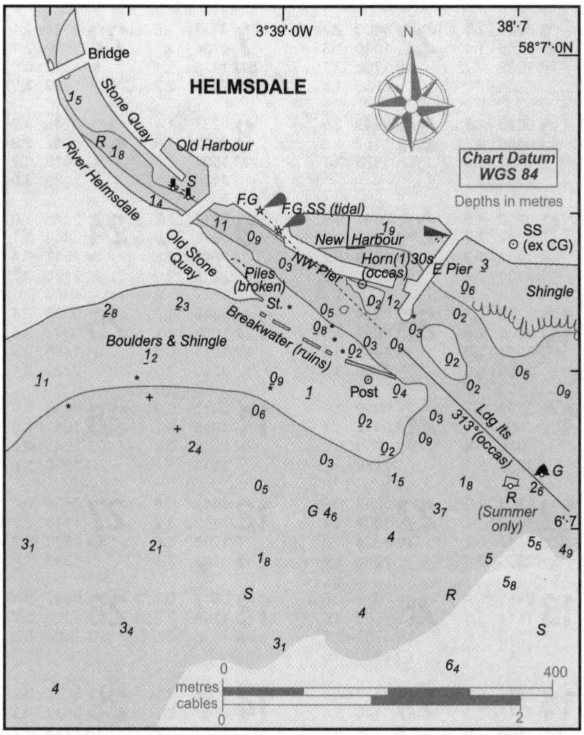

ADJACENT HARBOUR

LYBSTER, Highland, **58°17'·72N 03°17'·39W**. AC 115. HW +0020 on Dover; HW –0150 sp, –0215 np; HW ht –0·6m on Aberdeen; ML 2·1m; Duration 0620. Excellent shelter in basin (SW corner of inner hbr); AB on W side of pier in about 1·2m. Most of hbr dries to sand/mud and is much used by FVs; no bollards on N wall. Appr on about 350°. Beware rks close on E side of ent; narrow (10m) ent is difficult in strong E to S winds. Min depth 2·5m in ent. S pier hd, Oc R 6s 10m 3M, occas in fishing season. AB £7.00 per week, FW on W quay. **Town** EC Thurs; Bar, D, P, R, V.

WICK *9.7.19*

Highland **58°26'·38N 03°04'·72W**

CHARTS AC 1462, 115; Imray C22, C68; OS 12

TIDES +0010 Dover; ML 2·0; Duration 0625; Zone 0 (UT). Wick is a Standard Port. Daily tidal predictions are given below.

Standard Port WICK (⟶)

Times				Height (metres)			
High Water		Low Water		MHWS	MHWN	MLWN	MLWS
0000	0700	0200	0700	3·5	2·8	1·4	0·7
1200	1900	1400	1900				
Differences DUNCANSBY HEAD							
–0115	–0115	–0110	–0110	–0·4	–0·4	No data	

SHELTER Good, except in strong NNE to SSE winds. A good hbr to await right conditions for W-bound passage through the Pentland Firth (see 9.7.5). Berth where directed in the Inner Hbr, 2·4m. NB: The River Hbr (commercial) is leased and must **not** be entered without prior approval.

NAVIGATION WPT 58°26'·18N 03°03'·39W, 104°/284° from/to S pier, 0·72M. From the N, open up hbr ent before rounding North Head so as to clear drying Proudfoot Rks. Hbr ent is dangerous in strong E'lies as boats have to turn port 90° at the end of S pier. On S side of bay, an unlit bn, 300m ENE of LB slip, marks end of ruined bkwtr.

LIGHTS AND MARKS S pier lt, Fl WRG 3s 12m 12/9M, G253°-270°, W270°-286°, R286°-329°, Bell (2) 10s (fishing). Ldg lts , both FR 5/8m, lead 234° into outer hbr. Traffic signals:

B ● (●) at CG stn on S Head = hbr closed by weather.
B ● (●) at S pier head = caution; hbr temp obstructed.

RADIO TELEPHONE VHF Ch 14 16 (when vessel expected).

TELEPHONE (Dial code 01955) Hr Mr 602030; MRSC (01224) 592334; ⊜ 603650; Police 603551; ⊞ 602434, 602261.

FACILITIES **Inner Hbr** AB (£8.00 for 48H, £25 per week), Slip, ME; **Fish Jetty** D, FW, CH; **Services:** ME, El, Sh, Slip, Gas, C (15/ 100 ton). **Town** EC Wed; P, V, R, Bar, ✉, Ⓑ, ⇌, ✈.

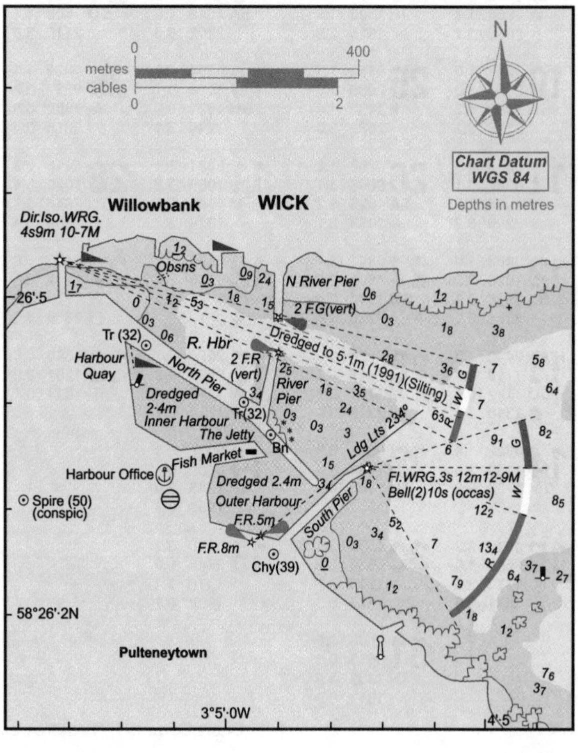

TIME ZONE (UTC)
For Summer Time add ONE hour in **non-shaded areas**

SCOTLAND – WICK

LAT 58°26′N LONG 3°05′W

TIMES AND HEIGHTS OF HIGH AND LOW WATERS

SPRING & NEAP TIDES
Dates in red are SPRINGS
Dates in blue are NEAPS

YEAR **2002**

JANUARY

Date	Day	Time	m	Time	m	Time	m	Time	m
1	TU	0014	3.5	0602	0.9	1232	3.6	1834	0.6
2	W	0101	3.5	0644	1.0	1315	3.6	1921	0.6
3	TH	0149	3.4	0729	1.1	1401	3.5	2011	0.6
4	F	0241	3.3	0817	1.2	1452	3.4	2106	0.7
5	SA	0336	3.1	0914	1.3	1548	3.3	2209	0.8
6	SU	0437	3.0	1021	1.4	1651	3.2	2317	0.9
7	M	0542	2.9	1135	1.4	1757	3.1		
8	TU	0025	1.0	0648	2.9	1249	1.4	1906	3.0
9	W	0130	1.0	0752	2.9	1358	1.3	2013	3.1
10	TH	0229	1.0	0851	3.0	1459	1.2	2115	3.1
11	F	0319	1.0	0942	3.1	1551	1.0	2209	3.2
12	SA	0403	1.0	1028	3.3	1636	0.9	2256	3.2
13	SU	0443	1.0	1110	3.4	1717	0.8	● 2340	3.2
14	M	0520	1.0	1150	3.5	1755	0.8		
15	TU	0020	3.2	0555	1.0	1228	3.5	1831	0.8
16	W	0059	3.2	0630	1.1	1304	3.5	1905	0.9
17	TH	0135	3.1	0703	1.1	1339	3.4	1938	0.9
18	F	0210	3.0	0738	1.2	1413	3.3	2013	1.0
19	SA	0246	2.9	0814	1.3	1449	3.2	2051	1.1
20	SU	0326	2.9	0856	1.4	1531	3.1	2135	1.3
21	M	0413	2.8	0945	1.6	1621	2.9	2228	1.4
22	TU	0507	2.7	1048	1.6	1717	2.9	2333	1.4
23	W	0606	2.7	1205	1.6	1820	2.8		
24	TH	0044	1.4	0707	2.8	1323	1.6	1925	2.9
25	F	0152	1.3	0809	2.9	1430	1.4	2032	3.0
26	SA	0250	1.2	0908	3.1	1525	1.2	2133	3.1
27	SU	0341	1.1	1000	3.3	1614	0.9	2228	3.3
28	M	0428	1.0	1049	3.4	1700	0.7	○ 2318	3.4
29	TU	0512	0.9	1134	3.6	1744	0.5		
30	W	0004	3.5	0554	0.8	1219	3.7	1827	0.3
31	TH	0050	3.6	0635	0.8	1302	3.8	1911	0.3

FEBRUARY

Date	Day	Time	m	Time	m	Time	m	Time	m
1	F	0135	3.5	0717	0.8	1347	3.8	1955	0.4
2	SA	0221	3.4	0800	0.9	1433	3.6	2043	0.5
3	SU	0309	3.2	0847	1.0	1523	3.4	2136	0.8
4	M	0401	3.0	0943	1.2	1621	3.2	2238	1.0
5	TU	0500	2.8	1054	1.4	1726	3.0	2349	1.2
6	W	0606	2.8	1217	1.4	1841	2.9		
7	TH	0105	1.3	0719	2.8	1343	1.3	2000	2.9
8	F	0216	1.3	0830	2.8	1455	1.2	2108	2.9
9	SA	0311	1.2	0927	3.0	1549	1.0	2202	3.0
10	SU	0354	1.1	1014	3.1	1631	0.9	2248	3.1
11	M	0431	1.1	1056	3.3	1708	0.8	2328	3.1
12	TU ●	0505	1.0	1135	3.4	1740	0.7		
13	W	0004	3.1	0537	0.9	1212	3.4	1810	0.7
14	TH	0039	3.1	0609	0.9	1245	3.4	1839	0.7
15	F	0110	3.1	0640	0.9	1316	3.4	1909	0.7
16	SA	0139	3.1	0712	0.9	1345	3.3	1939	0.8
17	SU	0209	3.0	0745	1.0	1417	3.2	2012	1.0
18	M	0243	2.9	0820	1.2	1453	3.1	2047	1.1
19	TU	0325	2.8	0858	1.3	1537	2.9	2129	1.2
20	W	0415	2.7	0948	1.4	1632	2.8	2225	1.4
21	TH	0513	2.7	1059	1.5	1737	2.8	2341	1.5
22	F	0617	2.7	1230	1.5	1848	2.8		
23	SA	0115	1.4	0726	2.8	1402	1.3	2005	2.9
24	SU	0233	1.3	0836	2.9	1508	1.1	2116	3.0
25	M	0329	1.1	0937	3.2	1600	0.8	2215	3.2
26	TU	0416	0.9	1029	3.4	1646	0.5	2305	3.4
27	W	0459	0.8	1117	3.6	1729	0.2	○ 2350	3.6
28	TH	0540	0.6	1201	3.8	1811	0.1		

MARCH

Date	Day	Time	m	Time	m	Time	m	Time	m
1	F	0033	3.6	0619	0.6	1245	3.9	1852	0.1
2	SA	0115	3.6	0659	0.6	1328	3.9	1933	0.2
3	SU	0156	3.5	0739	0.7	1412	3.7	2016	0.5
4	M	0238	3.3	0822	0.9	1500	3.5	2103	0.8
5	TU	0325	3.1	0912	1.1	1554	3.2	2200	1.1
6	W	0419	2.9	1022	1.3	1700	2.9	2315	1.4
7	TH	0524	2.7	1156	1.4	1822	2.7		
8	F	0043	1.5	0646	2.7	1331	1.3	1951	2.7
9	SA	0203	1.5	0807	2.7	1447	1.2	2100	2.8
10	SU	0259	1.3	0908	2.9	1537	1.0	2150	2.9
11	M	0339	1.2	0955	3.1	1615	0.8	2232	3.0
12	TU	0413	1.0	1037	3.2	1647	0.7	2308	3.0
13	W	0445	0.9	1114	3.3	1715	0.6	2342	3.1
14	TH ●	0515	0.8	1148	3.3	1743	0.6		
15	F	0013	3.1	0544	0.7	1220	3.3	1809	0.6
16	SA	0041	3.1	0614	0.7	1248	3.3	1837	0.6
17	SU	0107	3.1	0645	0.8	1316	3.2	1907	0.7
18	M	0134	3.0	0717	0.9	1347	3.2	1938	0.8
19	TU	0206	3.0	0749	1.0	1422	3.1	2010	1.0
20	W	0243	2.9	0825	1.1	1505	2.9	2047	1.2
21	TH	0330	2.8	0911	1.2	1601	2.8	2139	1.3
22	F	0430	2.7	1020	1.3	1708	2.7	2256	1.5
23	SA	0540	2.6	1157	1.3	1825	2.7		
24	SU	0047	1.5	0653	2.7	1338	1.2	1947	2.8
25	M	0214	1.3	0807	2.9	1445	0.9	2100	3.0
26	TU	0310	1.1	0912	3.1	1538	0.6	2158	3.2
27	W	0357	0.9	1007	3.4	1624	0.3	2246	3.4
28	TH	0439	0.6	1055	3.6	1707	0.1	○ 2330	3.6
29	F	0519	0.5	1140	3.8	1748	0.1		
30	SA	0011	3.6	0558	0.4	1224	3.9	1828	0.1
31	SU	0051	3.6	0638	0.5	1308	3.8	1908	0.3

APRIL

Date	Day	Time	m	Time	m	Time	m	Time	m
1	M	0130	3.5	0718	0.6	1352	3.7	1949	0.6
2	TU	0210	3.4	0801	0.8	1439	3.4	2032	1.0
3	W	0253	3.1	0850	1.0	1533	3.1	2124	1.3
4	TH	0344	2.9	1002	1.2	1639	2.8	2241	1.6
5	F	0447	2.7	1138	1.4	1802	2.7		
6	SA	0012	1.7	0609	2.7	1306	1.3	1931	2.6
7	SU	0133	1.6	0734	2.7	1418	1.1	2038	2.7
8	M	0231	1.4	0837	2.8	1507	1.0	2125	2.8
9	TU	0312	1.2	0926	3.0	1543	0.8	2204	2.9
10	W	0346	1.1	1008	3.1	1614	0.7	2240	3.0
11	TH	0417	0.9	1045	3.1	1642	0.7	2313	3.1
12	F	0447	0.8	1119	3.2	1709	0.6	● 2342	3.1
13	SA	0517	0.7	1149	3.2	1738	0.6		
14	SU	0009	3.1	0547	0.7	1218	3.2	1807	0.6
15	M	0035	3.1	0619	0.7	1249	3.2	1837	0.7
16	TU	0104	3.1	0652	0.8	1322	3.2	1908	0.8
17	W	0136	3.0	0726	0.8	1400	3.1	1941	1.0
18	TH	0214	2.9	0805	1.0	1446	2.9	2021	1.1
19	F	0301	2.8	0855	1.1	1544	2.8	2114	1.3
20	SA	0403	2.7	1007	1.2	1654	2.7	2234	1.5
21	SU	0515	2.7	1144	1.1	1811	2.7		
22	M	0024	1.4	0630	2.7	1312	0.9	1930	2.8
23	TU	0146	1.3	0742	2.9	1418	0.7	2039	3.0
24	W	0243	1.0	0846	3.1	1511	0.4	2135	3.2
25	TH	0330	0.8	0942	3.4	1558	0.3	2222	3.4
26	F	0414	0.6	1031	3.6	1641	0.2	2306	3.5
27	SA	0456	0.5	1118	3.7	1723	0.2	○ 2347	3.6
28	SU	0537	0.4	1203	3.7	1804	0.3		
29	M	0026	3.6	0617	0.5	1249	3.7	1843	0.5
30	TU	0105	3.5	0659	0.6	1334	3.5	1923	0.8

Chart Datum: 1·71 metres below Ordnance Datum (Newlyn)

TIME ZONE (UTC)
For Summer Time add ONE hour in **non-shaded areas**

SCOTLAND – WICK

LAT 58°26′N LONG 3°05′W

TIMES AND HEIGHTS OF HIGH AND LOW WATERS

SPRING & NEAP TIDES
Dates in red are **SPRINGS**
Dates in blue are **NEAPS**

YEAR **2002**

MAY

Date	Day	Time	m	Date	Day	Time	m
1		0145	3.4	16		0117	3.1
		0744	0.8			0711	0.8
	W	1422	3.3		TH	1348	3.1
		2005	1.1			1924	1.0
2		0228	3.2	17		0158	3.0
		0836	1.0			0756	0.8
	TH	1515	3.0		F	1438	2.9
		2053	1.4			2008	1.1
3		0316	3.0	18		0247	2.9
		0946	1.2			0852	0.9
	F	1617	2.8		SA	1537	2.8
		2201	1.6			2104	1.3
4		0415	2.8	19		0348	2.8
		1110	1.3			1006	0.9
	SA	1731	2.6		SU	1645	2.7
		2328	1.7			2223	1.4
5		0528	2.7	20		0459	2.8
		1226	1.3			1129	0.9
	SU	1849	2.6		M	1757	2.7
						2355	1.3
6		0044	1.7	21		0610	2.8
		0645	2.7			1243	0.7
	M	1331	1.2		TU	1908	2.8
		1955	2.6				
7		0145	1.5	22		0109	1.2
		0752	2.8			0717	2.9
	TU	1421	1.0		W	1346	0.6
		2046	2.8			2012	2.9
8		0232	1.3	23		0210	1.0
		0845	2.9			0819	3.1
	W	1501	0.9		TH	1441	0.4
		2127	2.9			2107	3.1
9		0311	1.1	24		0302	0.8
		0929	3.0			0916	3.3
	TH	1534	0.8		F	1530	0.4
		2204	3.0			2156	3.2
10		0345	1.0	25		0349	0.7
		1008	3.0			1009	3.4
	F	1605	0.7		SA	1616	0.4
		2238	3.0			2241	3.3
11		0417	0.8	26		0434	0.6
		1044	3.1			1058	3.5
	SA	1635	0.7		SU	1659	0.4
		2309	3.1		○	2324	3.4
12		0450	0.7	27		0518	0.5
		1117	3.2			1146	3.5
	SU	1707	0.7		M	1741	0.5
	●	2338	3.2				
13		0523	0.7	28		0004	3.4
		1150	3.2			0602	0.5
	M	1739	0.7		TU	1233	3.4
						1821	0.7
14		0008	3.2	29		0045	3.4
		0557	0.7			0646	0.6
	TU	1226	3.2		W	1320	3.3
		1812	0.7			1902	0.9
15		0041	3.2	30		0125	3.4
		0633	0.7			0732	0.8
	W	1305	3.1		TH	1407	3.2
		1847	0.8			1942	1.2
				31		0207	3.3
						0822	0.9
					F	1456	3.0
						2025	1.4

JUNE

Date	Day	Time	m	Date	Day	Time	m
1		0253	3.1	16		0238	3.1
		0920	1.1			0850	0.7
	SA	1550	2.8		SU	1528	2.9
		2115	1.5			2057	1.2
2		0344	3.0	17		0335	3.0
		1027	1.2			0956	0.7
	SU	1649	2.7		M	1629	2.8
		2224	1.6			2205	1.2
3		0443	2.8	18		0439	2.9
		1134	1.2			1105	0.7
	M	1752	2.6		TU	1734	2.8
		2342	1.6			2321	1.2
4		0548	2.8	19		0546	2.9
		1235	1.2			1212	0.7
	TU	1856	2.6		W	1839	2.8
5		0048	1.5	20		0032	1.2
		0653	2.8			0651	3.0
	W	1328	1.1		TH	1315	0.6
		1953	2.7			1941	2.8
6		0144	1.4	21		0138	1.0
		0752	2.8			0755	3.1
	TH	1412	1.0		F	1413	0.6
		2041	2.8			2039	3.0
7		0231	1.2	22		0237	0.9
		0843	2.9			0855	3.1
	F	1452	1.0		SA	1507	0.6
		2123	2.9			2132	3.1
8		0311	1.1	23		0331	0.8
		0927	3.0			0952	3.2
	SA	1528	0.9		SU	1555	0.6
		2201	3.0			2220	3.2
9		0349	0.9	24		0421	0.7
		1008	3.0			1045	3.3
	SU	1604	0.8		M	1640	0.7
		2236	3.1		○	2305	3.3
10		0426	0.8	25		0508	0.6
		1048	3.1			1134	3.3
	M	1641	0.8		TU	1723	0.8
	●	2311	3.2			2348	3.4
11		0504	0.7	26		0553	0.6
		1129	3.2			1221	3.3
	TU	1718	0.8		W	1803	0.9
		2347	3.2				
12		0542	0.7	27		0028	3.4
		1210	3.2			0636	0.6
	W	1756	0.8		TH	1306	3.2
						1841	1.0
13		0025	3.3	28		0109	3.4
		0622	0.6			0718	0.7
	TH	1254	3.2		F	1349	3.1
		1834	0.8			1919	1.1
14		0105	3.2	29		0148	3.3
		0706	0.6			0800	0.8
	F	1340	3.1		SA	1432	3.0
		1916	0.9			1956	1.2
15		0148	3.2	30		0229	3.2
		0754	0.6			0843	1.0
	SA	1431	3.0		SU	1516	2.8
		2002	1.0			2035	1.3

JULY

Date	Day	Time	m	Date	Day	Time	m
1		0311	3.1	16		0316	3.2
		0929	1.1			0934	0.6
	M	1603	2.7		TU	1604	2.9
		2122	1.5			2139	1.1
2		0359	2.9	17		0414	3.1
		1022	1.2			1035	0.7
	TU	1653	2.6		W	1703	2.8
		2220	1.5			2247	1.2
3		0452	2.8	18		0518	3.0
		1122	1.2			1140	0.8
	W	1748	2.6		TH	1806	2.8
		2332	1.6				
4		0550	2.8	19		0000	1.2
		1222	1.2			0625	3.0
	TH	1846	2.6		F	1247	0.9
						1910	2.8
5		0044	1.5	20		0114	1.2
		0649	2.8			0735	2.9
	F	1318	1.2		SA	1353	0.9
		1943	2.7			2015	2.9
6		0146	1.4	21		0225	1.0
		0749	2.8			0844	3.0
	SA	1409	1.1		SU	1452	0.9
		2035	2.8			2114	3.0
7		0238	1.2	22		0326	0.9
		0846	2.9			0945	3.0
	SU	1455	1.1		M	1543	0.9
		2122	3.0			2205	3.1
8		0325	1.1	23		0418	0.8
		0938	3.0			1039	3.1
	M	1539	1.0		TU	1628	0.9
		2206	3.1			2251	3.2
9		0409	0.9	24		0503	0.7
		1026	3.1			1126	3.1
	TU	1622	0.9		W	1708	0.9
		2248	3.2		○	2333	3.3
10		0451	0.7	25		0544	0.6
		1113	3.2			1209	3.2
	W	1704	0.8		TH	1745	0.9
	●	2329	3.3				
11		0534	0.6	26		0013	3.4
		1159	3.3			0621	0.6
	TH	1745	0.8		F	1249	3.1
						1819	0.9
12		0011	3.4	27		0051	3.4
		0617	0.5			0656	0.7
	F	1244	3.3		SA	1327	3.1
		1826	0.8			1853	1.0
13		0053	3.4	28		0126	3.4
		0701	0.4			0729	0.7
	SA	1331	3.3		SU	1403	3.0
		1908	0.8			1926	1.1
14		0137	3.4	29		0200	3.3
		0747	0.4			0802	0.8
	SU	1418	3.2		M	1439	2.9
		1953	0.9			2001	1.2
15		0224	3.4	30		0235	3.2
		0838	0.5			0838	1.0
	M	1509	3.1		TU	1516	2.8
		2042	1.0			2040	1.3
				31		0315	3.0
						0918	1.1
					W	1558	2.8
						2125	1.4

AUGUST

Date	Day	Time	m	Date	Day	Time	m
1		0401	2.9	16		0451	3.0
		1006	1.3			1110	1.1
	TH	1647	2.7		F	1731	2.8
		2222	1.5			2335	1.3
2		0456	2.8	17		0605	2.9
		1105	1.4			1225	1.2
	F	1742	2.7		SA	1843	2.7
		2335	1.6				
3		0556	2.7	18		0103	1.3
		1215	1.4			0727	2.8
	SA	1841	2.7		SU	1343	1.3
						1958	2.8
4		0057	1.5	19		0227	1.2
		0701	2.7			0843	2.9
	SU	1327	1.4		M	1448	1.2
		1943	2.8			2101	3.0
5		0209	1.4	20		0329	1.0
		0809	2.8			0943	3.0
	M	1429	1.3		TU	1536	1.2
		2044	2.9			2153	3.1
6		0306	1.1	21		0415	0.8
		0914	3.0			1031	3.0
	TU	1522	1.1		W	1615	1.1
		2138	3.1			2237	3.3
7		0355	0.9	22		0453	0.7
		1010	3.1			1113	3.1
	W	1609	1.0		TH	1650	1.0
		2226	3.3		○	2317	3.4
8		0440	0.7	23		0527	0.6
		1059	3.3			1151	3.1
	TH	1652	0.9		F	1723	0.9
	●	2311	3.5			2353	3.4
9		0523	0.5	24		0558	0.6
		1146	3.4			1226	3.2
	F	1734	0.8		SA	1754	0.9
		2354	3.6				
10		0606	0.3	25		0027	3.4
		1230	3.5			0626	0.6
	SA	1814	0.7		SU	1259	3.1
						1825	0.9
11		0037	3.7	26		0059	3.4
		0647	0.2			0654	0.7
	SU	1314	3.5		M	1329	3.1
		1854	0.7			1856	0.9
12		0120	3.7	27		0128	3.3
		0731	0.2			0724	0.8
	M	1358	3.4		TU	1359	3.0
		1936	0.8			1929	1.0
13		0204	3.6	28		0158	3.2
		0816	0.4			0756	0.9
	TU	1443	3.3		W	1431	3.0
		2020	0.9			2004	1.2
14		0252	3.5	29		0233	3.1
		0905	0.6			0831	1.1
	W	1533	3.1		TH	1509	2.9
		2111	1.1			2042	1.3
15		0347	3.3	30		0316	3.0
		1003	0.8			0912	1.3
	TH	1628	2.9		F	1555	2.8
		2215	1.2			2131	1.5
				31		0410	2.8
						1005	1.4
					SA	1651	2.7
						2239	1.6

Chart Datum: 1·71 metres below Ordnance Datum (Newlyn)

TIME ZONE (UTC)
For Summer Time add ONE hour in **non-shaded areas**

SCOTLAND – WICK

LAT 58°26′N LONG 3°05′W

TIMES AND HEIGHTS OF HIGH AND LOW WATERS

SPRING & NEAP TIDES
Dates in red are **SPRINGS**
Dates in blue are **NEAPS**

YEAR **2002**

SEPTEMBER

Day	Time	m	Time	m	Time	m	Time	m
1 SU	0514	2.7	1119	1.6	1754	2.7		
2 M	0012	1.6	0625	2.7	1252	1.5	1901	2.8
3 TU	0144	1.4	0742	2.8	1411	1.4	2010	2.9
4 W	0247	1.1	0855	3.0	1507	1.3	2112	3.1
5 TH	0337	0.8	0954	3.2	1553	1.1	2204	3.4
6 F	0422	0.6	1043	3.4	1636	0.9	2250	3.6
7 SA	0505	0.3	1128	3.6	1716	0.7	● 2334	3.8
8 SU	0546	0.2	1210	3.7	1755	0.6		
9 M	0016	3.9	0626	0.1	1251	3.7	1834	0.6
10 TU	0059	3.9	0707	0.2	1332	3.6	1914	0.7
11 W	0142	3.8	0750	0.5	1414	3.4	1956	0.9
12 TH	0229	3.6	0836	0.8	1459	3.2	2045	1.1
13 F	0323	3.3	0930	1.1	1552	3.0	2150	1.3
14 SA	0429	3.0	1042	1.4	1657	2.8	2322	1.4
15 SU	0553	2.8	1209	1.6	1819	2.8		
16 M	0100	1.4	0726	2.8	1335	1.6	1942	2.8
17 TU	0225	1.2	0841	2.9	1439	1.5	2046	3.0
18 W	0320	1.0	0933	3.0	1522	1.3	2135	3.2
19 TH	0359	0.9	1015	3.1	1556	1.2	2216	3.3
20 F	0431	0.8	1052	3.1	1627	1.0	2254	3.4
21 SA	0459	0.7	1126	3.2	1657	0.9	○ 2328	3.4
22 SU	0526	0.7	1157	3.2	1726	0.9		
23 M	0000	3.4	0552	0.7	1227	3.2	1756	0.9
24 TU	0028	3.4	0620	0.7	1254	3.2	1827	0.9
25 W	0056	3.4	0649	0.8	1321	3.2	1859	1.0
26 TH	0125	3.3	0720	1.0	1351	3.1	1932	1.1
27 F	0159	3.2	0752	1.2	1426	3.0	2008	1.3
28 SA	0240	3.0	0829	1.3	1511	2.9	2052	1.4
29 SU	0335	2.9	0918	1.5	1609	2.8	2200	1.6
30 M	0444	2.8	1035	1.7	1717	2.7	2341	1.5

OCTOBER

Day	Time	m	Time	m	Time	m	Time	m
1 TU	0600	2.8	1227	1.7	1829	2.8		
2 W	0118	1.3	0721	2.8	1350	1.5	1941	2.9
3 TH	0222	1.1	0836	3.0	1445	1.3	2045	3.2
4 F	0312	0.8	0933	3.3	1531	1.1	2139	3.5
5 SA	0358	0.5	1021	3.5	1613	0.9	2227	3.7
6 SU	0440	0.3	1105	3.7	1653	0.7	● 2311	3.9
7 M	0521	0.2	1146	3.8	1732	0.6	2354	4.0
8 TU	0602	0.2	1226	3.8	1812	0.6		
9 W	0037	4.0	0642	0.4	1305	3.7	1852	0.7
10 TH	0122	3.8	0723	0.7	1346	3.6	1935	0.9
11 F	0210	3.6	0808	1.0	1430	3.3	2025	1.1
12 SA	0304	3.3	0901	1.4	1520	3.1	2134	1.4
13 SU	0412	3.0	1015	1.7	1626	2.9	2311	1.5
14 M	0539	2.8	1146	1.8	1750	2.8		
15 TU	0042	1.4	0712	2.8	1309	1.8	1913	2.9
16 W	0200	1.3	0822	2.9	1411	1.6	2017	3.0
17 TH	0251	1.1	0909	3.0	1453	1.4	2106	3.2
18 F	0327	1.0	0948	3.1	1527	1.3	2148	3.3
19 SA	0357	0.9	1022	3.2	1559	1.1	2225	3.3
20 SU	0425	0.8	1055	3.2	1629	1.0	2259	3.4
21 M	0451	0.8	1126	3.3	1659	0.9	○ 2329	3.4
22 TU	0519	0.8	1154	3.3	1730	0.9	2358	3.4
23 W	0548	0.8	1220	3.3	1802	0.9		
24 TH	0027	3.4	0618	0.9	1249	3.3	1834	1.0
25 F	0059	3.3	0650	1.0	1320	3.2	1908	1.1
26 SA	0136	3.2	0722	1.2	1356	3.1	1945	1.2
27 SU	0219	3.1	0759	1.4	1439	3.0	2031	1.3
28 M	0315	2.9	0848	1.6	1537	2.9	2140	1.4
29 TU	0425	2.8	1006	1.7	1648	2.8	2320	1.4
30 W	0543	2.8	1157	1.7	1803	2.9		
31 TH	0047	1.2	0701	2.9	1318	1.5	1914	3.0

NOVEMBER

Day	Time	m	Time	m	Time	m	Time	m
1 F	0150	1.0	0811	3.1	1415	1.3	2017	3.2
2 SA	0242	0.7	0907	3.3	1502	1.1	2112	3.5
3 SU	0329	0.5	0955	3.5	1546	0.9	2202	3.7
4 M	0413	0.4	1039	3.6	1628	0.7	● 2249	3.9
5 TU	0455	0.4	1121	3.7	1710	0.7	2334	3.9
6 W	0537	0.5	1201	3.8	1752	0.7		
7 TH	0019	3.9	0618	0.7	1242	3.7	1835	0.8
8 F	0106	3.7	0700	0.9	1323	3.6	1921	0.9
9 SA	0155	3.5	0744	1.2	1406	3.5	2013	1.1
10 SU	0250	3.3	0834	1.5	1455	3.3	2121	1.3
11 M	0354	3.0	0941	1.8	1555	3.1	2246	1.4
12 TU	0510	2.8	1105	1.9	1709	3.0		
13 W	0004	1.4	0630	2.8	1221	1.9	1826	3.0
14 TH	0112	1.3	0738	2.9	1324	1.7	1933	3.0
15 F	0204	1.2	0829	3.0	1413	1.5	2027	3.1
16 SA	0245	1.1	0910	3.1	1454	1.4	2112	3.2
17 SU	0319	1.0	0947	3.2	1529	1.2	2152	3.3
18 M	0349	1.0	1022	3.3	1603	1.1	2227	3.3
19 TU	0419	0.9	1054	3.3	1635	1.0	2300	3.3
20 W	0449	0.9	1124	3.4	1709	0.9	○ 2333	3.4
21 TH	0521	0.9	1154	3.4	1743	0.9		
22 F	0006	3.3	0554	1.0	1227	3.4	1817	1.0
23 SA	0043	3.3	0628	1.1	1301	3.3	1854	1.0
24 SU	0123	3.2	0703	1.2	1339	3.2	1934	1.1
25 M	0209	3.1	0743	1.4	1422	3.1	2024	1.2
26 TU	0304	3.0	0834	1.5	1517	3.0	2130	1.2
27 W	0410	2.9	0945	1.6	1624	2.9	2254	1.2
28 TH	0522	2.8	1117	1.6	1735	3.0		
29 F	0010	1.1	0633	2.9	1235	1.5	1843	3.1
30 SA	0114	0.9	0739	3.0	1338	1.3	1947	3.2

DECEMBER

Day	Time	m	Time	m	Time	m	Time	m
1 SU	0210	0.7	0836	3.2	1432	1.1	2045	3.4
2 M	0300	0.6	0927	3.4	1521	1.0	2139	3.6
3 TU	0347	0.6	1014	3.5	1608	0.8	2230	3.7
4 W	0432	0.6	1059	3.6	1655	0.8	● 2319	3.7
5 TH	0516	0.7	1142	3.7	1740	0.7		
6 F	0007	3.7	0559	0.9	1224	3.7	1826	0.8
7 SA	0055	3.6	0641	1.1	1306	3.6	1913	0.9
8 SU	0144	3.4	0724	1.3	1349	3.5	2003	1.0
9 M	0234	3.2	0808	1.5	1435	3.4	2059	1.2
10 TU	0328	3.0	0858	1.7	1525	3.2	2204	1.3
11 W	0427	2.9	1003	1.8	1623	3.1	2311	1.4
12 TH	0530	2.8	1119	1.8	1728	3.0		
13 F	0015	1.4	0635	2.8	1228	1.8	1834	3.0
14 SA	0111	1.4	0734	2.8	1327	1.6	1936	3.0
15 SU	0159	1.3	0825	3.0	1418	1.5	2029	3.0
16 M	0240	1.2	0909	3.1	1501	1.3	2116	3.1
17 TU	0317	1.1	0949	3.2	1541	1.2	2157	3.2
18 W	0352	1.1	1025	3.3	1618	1.1	2236	3.2
19 TH	0427	1.0	1100	3.4	1655	1.0	○ 2314	3.3
20 F	0503	1.0	1135	3.4	1732	0.9	2353	3.3
21 SA	0539	1.0	1211	3.4	1809	0.9		
22 SU	0033	3.3	0616	1.1	1249	3.4	1848	0.9
23 M	0115	3.2	0654	1.1	1328	3.4	1931	0.9
24 TU	0201	3.2	0735	1.2	1411	3.3	2019	0.9
25 W	0252	3.0	0823	1.3	1501	3.2	2116	0.9
26 TH	0350	2.9	0921	1.4	1559	3.1	2222	0.9
27 F	0453	2.9	1034	1.5	1704	3.1	2330	0.9
28 SA	0558	2.9	1149	1.4	1811	3.1		
29 SU	0036	0.9	0702	2.9	1300	1.3	1917	3.1
30 M	0139	0.9	0804	3.0	1405	1.2	2022	3.2
31 TU	0237	0.9	0902	3.2	1504	1.1	2123	3.3

Chart Datum: 1·71 metres below Ordnance Datum (Newlyn)

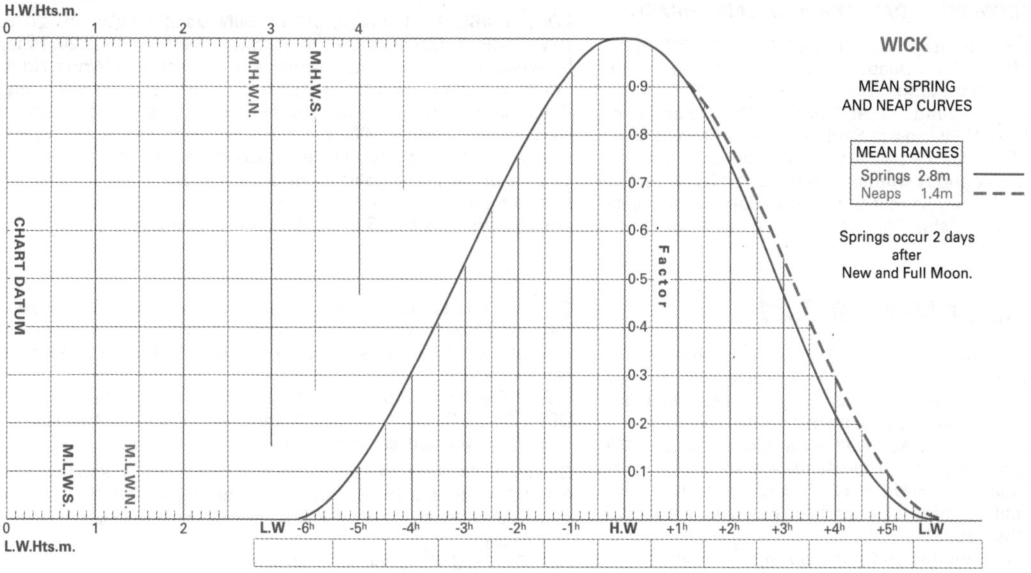

SCRABSTER *9.7.20*

Highland **58°36'·61N 03°32'·61W**

CHARTS AC 1462, 2162, 1954; Imray C68; OS 12

TIDES -0240 Dover; ML 3·2; Duration 0615; Zone 0 (UT)

Standard Port WICK (⟵)

Times				Height (metres)			
High Water		Low Water		MHWS	MHWN	MLWN	MLWS
0200	0700	0100	0700	3·5	2·8	1·4	0·7
1400	1900	1300	1900				
Differences SCRABSTER							
−0255	−0225	−0240	−0230	+1·5	+1·2	+0·8	+0·3
GILLS BAY							
−0150	−0150	−0202	−0202	+0·7	+0·7	+0·6	+0·3
STROMA							
−0115	−0115	−0110	−0110	−0·4	−0·5	−0·1	−0·2
LOCH ERIBOLL (Portnancon) (overleaf)							
−0340	−0255	−0315	−0255	+1·6	+1·3	+0·8	+0·4
KYLE OF DURNESS							
−0350	−0350	−0315	−0315	+1·1	+0·7	+0·4	−0·1
SULE SKERRY (59°05'N 04°24'W)							
−0320	−0255	−0315	−0250	+0·4	+0·3	+0·2	+0·1
RONA (59°08'N 05°49'W)							
−0410	−0345	−0330	−0340	−0·1	−0·2	−0·2	−0·1

SHELTER Very good except for swell in NW and N winds. Yachts usually lie in the Inner (0·9 - 1·2m) or Centre Basins (0·9 - 2·7m). ⚓ is not advised. A good hbr to await the right conditions for E-bound passage through Pentland Firth (see 9.7.5). Beware floating creel lines E and W of hbr ent.

NAVIGATION WPT 58°36'·58N 03°32'·09W, 098°/278° from/to E pier lt, 0·25M. Can be entered at all tides in all weathers. Beware FVs and the Orkney ferries.

LIGHTS AND MARKS No ldg marks/lts. Entry is simple once the conspic ice plant tr and/or the pier lt, QG 6m 4M, have been located. Do not confuse hbr lts with the shore lts of Thurso.

RADIO TELEPHONE Call Hr Mr VHF Ch 12 16 (H24) for berthing directions, before entering hbr. From the W reception is very poor due to masking by Holborn Head.

TELEPHONE (Dial code 01847) Hr Mr 892779, 📠 892353, Mobile 07803 290366, harbour@scrabster.co.uk, www.scrabster.co.uk; MRSC (01224) 592334; ⊜ (01955) 603650; Marinecall 09068 500 451; Police 893222; Dr 893154.

FACILITIES **Hbr** AB £5.40 (£6.58 for 4th and subsequent days), FW, D, P (cans), ME, El, C (15, 30 & 100 ton mobiles), Slip, CH, ♿; **Pentland Firth YC** M, R, Bar, Showers (keys held by Duty Hr Mr). **Thurso** EC Thurs; V, R, Bar, ✉, Ⓑ, ⇌, ✈ (Wick). Ferry to Stromness.

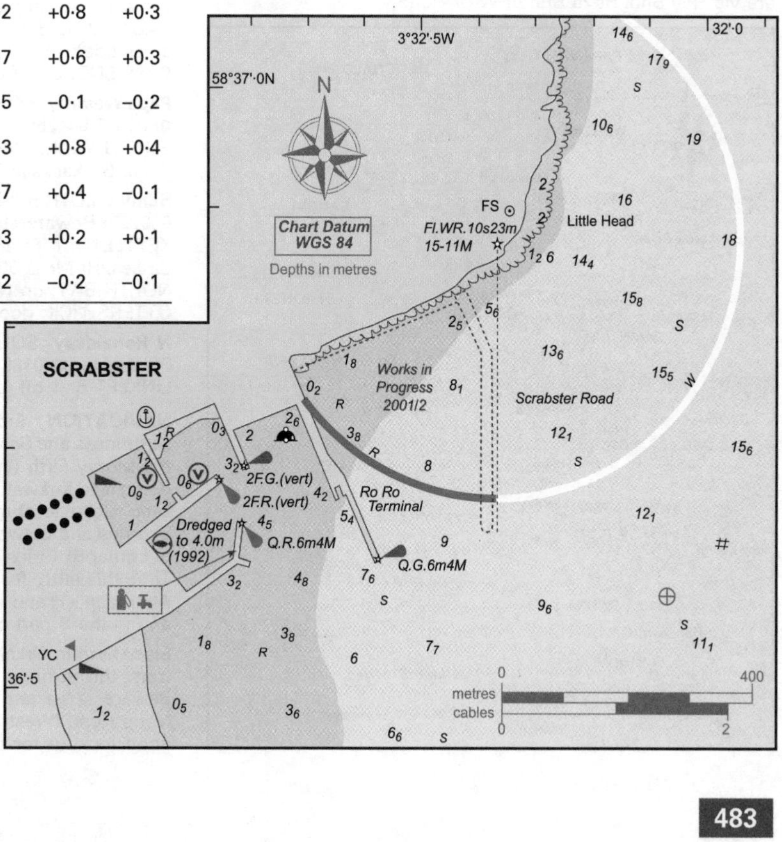

ANCHORAGES BETWEEN SCRABSTER AND CAPE WRATH

KYLE OF TONGUE, Highland, **58°31'·97N 04°22'·67W** (ent). AC 1954, 2720. HW +0050 on Ullapool; HW ht –0·4m; see 9.7.20. The Kyle runs about 7M inland. Entry (see 9.7.5) should not be attempted in strong N winds. ⚓ at Talmine (W of Rabbit Is) protected from all but NE winds; at Skullomie Hr, protected from E'lies; off Mol na Coinnle, a small bay on SE side of Eilean nan Ron, protected from W and N winds; off S of Rabbit Is, protected from W to N winds. No ldg lts/marks. Facilities: Limited supplies at Talmine (½M from slip) or at Coldbachie (1½M from Skullomie).

LOCH ERIBOLL, Highland, **58°32'·58N 04°37'·48W**. AC 2076. HW –0345 on Dover; ML 2·7m; Duration 0608. See 9.7.20. Enter between Whiten Hd and Klourig Is in W sector of White Hd lt, Fl WR 3s, vis W030°-172°, R172°-191°, W191°-212°. In SW winds fierce squalls funnel down the loch. Yachts can enter Rispond Hbr, access approx HW ± 3, and dry out alongside; no lts/marks and very limited facilities. Good ⚓s: at Rispond Bay on W side of loch, ent good in all but E winds, in approx 5m; off Portnancon in 5·5m; at the head of the loch; at Camus an Duin and in bays to N and S of peninsula at Heilam on E side of loch.

ORKNEY ISLANDS *9.7.21*

The Orkney Islands number about 70, of which some 24 are inhabited. They extend from Duncansby Hd 5 to 50M NNE, and are mostly low-lying, but Hoy in the SW of the group reaches 475m (1560ft). Coasts are generally rky and much indented, but there are many sandy beaches. A passage with least width of about 3M runs NW/SE through the group. The islands are separated from Scotland by the Pentland Firth, a very dangerous stretch of water. The principal island is Mainland (or Pomona) on which stands Kirkwall, the capital.
Severe gales blow in winter and early spring. The climate is mild but windy, and very few trees grow. There are LBs at Longhope, Stromness and Kirkwall. Enquire for 4 or 14 day berthing fees, good value.

CHARTS AC 2249, 2250 and 2162 at medium scale. For larger scale charts, see under individual hbrs. Imray C68; OS sheets 5 and 6.

TIDES Wick (9.7.19) is the Standard Port. Tidal streams are strong, particularly in Pentland Firth and in the firths and sounds among the islands.

SHELTER There are piers (fender board advised) at all main islands. Yachts can pay 4 or 14 day hbr dues (£10.40 or £23.00) to berth on all Council-operated piers, except St Margaret's Hope. Some of the many ⚓s are listed below:

Mainland SCAPA BAY: good except in S winds. No yacht berths alongside pier due to heavy hbr traffic. Only ents to Scapa Flow are via Hoy Snd, Hoxa Snd or W of Flotta.

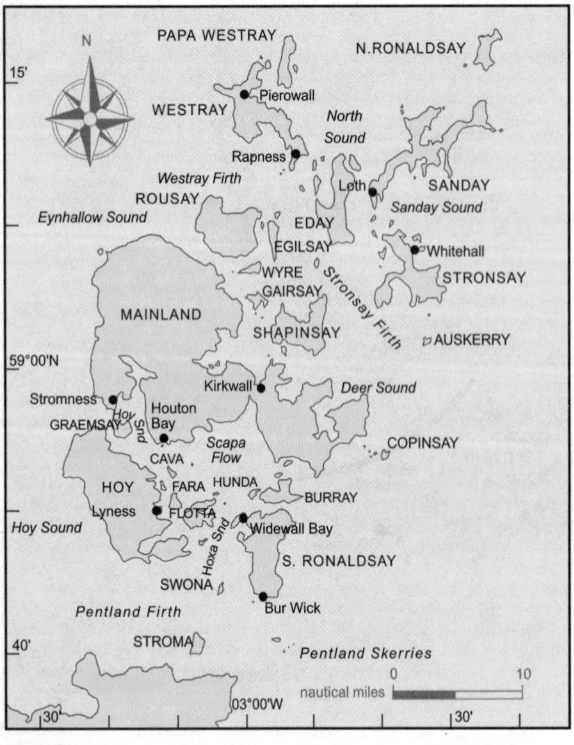

ST MARYS (known as Holm, pronounced Ham): Piermaster ☎01856 731365; N side of Kirk Sound; ⚓ in B of Ayre or berth E side of pier HW±4. P & D (cans), ✉, Bar, R, Bus to Kirkwall & Burwick Ferry.
KIRK SOUND (E ent): ⚓ N of Lamb Holm; beware fish cages.
DEER SOUND: ⚓ in Pool of Mirkady or off pier on NW side of sound; very good shelter, no facilities.

Burray E WEDDEL SOUND: ⚓ to E of pier in E'lies, sheltered by No 4 Churchill Barrier; Piermaster ☎ 01856 731365; pier is exposed in strong W'lies. P & D (cans), BY, Slip, V, ✉, Bar, R, Bus to Kirkwall.
HUNDA SOUND: good ⚓ in all winds.

S Ronaldsay ST MARGARET'S HOPE: ☸☸👍👍✿✿. ⚓ in centre of bay; or AB £6.50 at pier, (keep clear of ferry berth on S side of pier), beware salmon farm. Hr Mr ☎ 831454; Dr 831206. FW, P & D (cans), V, R, Bar, ✉, Bus Kirkwall, Vehicle ferry to Gill's Bay/ Caithness. WIDEWALL BAY: ⚓ sheltered from all but SW winds.

Flotta Berth on Sutherland Pier, SW of oil terminal. Hr Mr ☎ 701411. P & D (cans), V, ✉.

Hoy LONG HOPE: ⚓ E of S Ness pier, used by steamers, or berth on pier (safest at slack water) ☎ 701273; Dr 701209. Facilities: FW, P & D (cans), ✉, V, Bar.
LYNESS: berth on pier; avoid disused piles; ⚓ in Ore Bay. Hr Mr ☎ 791228. FW, P & D (cans), Bar, ✉. Beware fish cages.
PEGAL B: good ⚓ except in strong W winds.

Rousay WYRE SOUND: ⚓ E of Rousay pier, or berth on it ✉, V, R.

Eday FERSNESS Bay: good holding, sheltered from S winds.Piermaster ☎ 01857 622265;
BACKALAND Bay: berth on pier clear of ferry or ⚓ to NW. Beware cross tides. FW, P & D, V, ✉.
CALF SND: ⚓ in Carrick B; good shelter from SW-NW'lies.

Papa Westray B OF MOCLETT: Good ⚓ but open to S. Piermaster ☎ 01857 644259;
SOUTH WICK: ⚓ off the old pier or ESE of pier off Holm of Papa. Backaskaill: P & D (cans), V, ✉.

Sanday LOTH B: berth on pier, clear of ferry. Piermaster ☎ 01857 600227; Beware strong tides.
KETTLETOFT B: ⚓ in bay or berth on pier; very exposed to SE'lies. Hr Mr ☎ 600227. P & D (cans), FW, Gas, ✉, Ⓑ, V, hotel.
NORTH BAY: on NW side of island, exposed to NW.
OTTERSWICK: good ⚓ except in N or E winds.

N Ronaldsay SOUTH B: ⚓ in middle of bay or berth on pier; Piermaster ☎ 01857 633239; open to S & W and swell. V, ✉.
LINKLET B: ⚓ off jetty at N of bay, open to E.

NAVIGATION From the mainland, appr from Scrabster to Stromness and Scapa Flow via Hoy Mouth and Hoy Sound. From the Moray Firth (Wick) keep well E of the Pentland Skerries if going N to Kirkwall. Or, if bound for Scapa Flow via Hoxa Sound, keep close to Duncansby Head, passing W of the Pentland Skerries and between Swona and S Ronaldsay. Keep well clear of Lother Rk (dries 1·8m; lt, Q, Racon) off SW tip of S Ronaldsay. Time this entry for slack water in the Pentland Firth (about HW Aberdeen –1¾ and +4). Be aware of tankers off Flotta oil terminal and in the S part of Scapa Flow.

Elsewhere in Orkney navigation is easy in clear weather, apart from the strong tidal streams in all the firths and sounds. Beware races and overfalls off Brough of Birsay (Mainland), Noup Head (Westray) and Dennis Head (N Ronaldsay). Keep a good lookout for the many lobster pots (creels).

LIGHTS AND MARKS The main hbrs and sounds are well lit; for details see 9.7.4. Powerful lts are shown offshore from Cantick Hd, Graemsay Island, Copinsay, Auskerry, Kirkwall, Brough of Birsay, Sanday Island, N Ronaldsay and Noup Hd.

RADIO TELEPHONE Orkney Hbrs Navigation Service (call: *Orkney Hbr Radio*, Ch 09 11 20 16 (H24)) covers Scapa Flow and appr's, Wide Firth, Shapinsay Sound and Kirkwall Bay.

TELEPHONE Area Code for islands SW of Stronsay and Westray Firths is 01856; islands to the NE are 01857.

MEDICAL SERVICES Doctors are available at Kirkwall, Stromness, Rousay, Hoy, Shapinsay, Eday, S and N Ronaldsay, Stronsay, Sanday and Westray (Pierowall); Papa Westray is looked after by Westray. The only hospital (and dentist) are at Kirkwall. Serious cases are flown to Aberdeen (1 hour).

FISH FARMS Fish cages/farms approx 30m x 50m may be found anywhere in sheltered waters within anchoring depths. Some are well buoyed, others are marked only by poles. Too many to list but the following will show the scale of the operations:

Beware **salmon cages** (may be marked by Y buoys/lts) at:

Rysa Sound	St Margaret's Hope
Bring Deeps	Backaland Bay (Eday)
Pegal Bay (Hoy)	Hunda Sound
Lyrawa Bay	Kirk Sound
Ore Bay (Hoy)	Carness Bay
Widewall Bay (S Ronaldsay)	Bay of Ham
	Bay of London (Eday)

Beware **oysters and longlines** at:

Widewall Bay	Bay of Firth
Swandister Bay	Damsay Sound
Water Sound	Millburn Bay (Gairsay)
Hunda Sound	Pierowall
Deer Sound	Bay of Skaill (Westray)
Inganess Bay	Longhope

MINOR HARBOURS IN THE ORKNEY ISLANDS

HOUTON BAY, Mainland, **58°54'·85N 03°11'·33W**. AC 2568, 35. HW –0140 on Dover, –0400 on Aberdeen; HW ht +0·3m on Kirkwall; ML 1·8m; Duration 0615. ⚓ in the bay in approx 5·5m at centre, sheltered from all winds. The ent is to the E of the island Holm of Houton; ent chan dredged 3·5m for 15m each side of ldg line. Keep clear of merchant vessels/ferries plying to Flotta. Ldg lts 316°: front Fl G 3s 8m, rear FG 16m; both R △ on W pole, B bands. Ro Ro terminal in NE corner marked by Iso R 4s. Bus to Kirkwall; Slip close E of piers. Yachtsmen may contact **M. Grainger** ☎ 811356 for help.

SHAPINSAY, Orkney Islands, **59°01'·97N 02°54'·10W**. AC 2584, 2249. HW –0015 on Dover, –0330 on Aberdeen; HW ht –1·0m on Aberdeen. Good shelter in Elwick Bay off Balfour on SW end of island in 2·5-3m. Enter bay passing W of Helliar Holm which has lt Fl WRG 10s on S end. Keep mid-chan. Balfour Pier lt Q WRG 5m 3/2M; vis G270°–010°, W010°–020°, R020°–090°. Piermaster ☎ 01856 711358; Tides in The String reach 5kn at sp. Facilities: FW, P & D (cans), ⊠, shop, Bar.

AUSKERRY, Orkney Islands, **59°02'·02N 02°34'·65W**. AC 2250. HW –0010 on Dover, –0315 on Aberdeen, HW ht –1m on Aberdeen. Small island at ent to Stronsay Firth with small hbr on W side. Safe ent and good shelter except in SW winds. Ent has 3·5m; 1·2m alongside pier. Yachts can lie secured between ringbolts at ent and the pier. Auskerry Sound and Stronsay Firth are dangerous with wind over tide. Auskerry lt at S end, Fl 20s 34m 18M, W tr. No facilities.

PIEROWALL, Westray, **59°19'·32N 02°58'·51W**. AC 2622, 2250. HW –0135 on Dover; ML 2·2m; Duration 0620. See 9.7.24. The bay is a good ⚓ in 2-7m and well protected. Deep water AB at Gill Pt piers may be available; see Hr Mr. From S, beware Skelwick Skerry rks, and from the N the rks extending approx 1ca off Vest Ness. The N ent via Papa Sound needs local knowledge; tide race on the ebb. A dangerous tide race runs off Mull Hd at the N of Papa Westray. Lights: E pier hd Fl WRG 3s 7m 11/7M, G254°–276°, W276°–291°, R291°–308°, G308°–215°. W pier hd 2 FR (vert) 4/6m 3M. VHF Ch 16. Hr Mr ☎ (01857) 677273. Facilities: FW (Gill Pier), P & D (cans), Gas, Bar, ⊠, Ⓑ, R, V.

RAPNESS: Berth on pier, clear of Ro-Ro. Piermaster ☎ 01857 677212; Open to SSW.

STROMNESS *9.7.22*

Orkney Islands, Mainland **58°57'·78N 03°17'·72W** ❁❁◊◊◊✿✿✿

CHARTS AC 2568, 2249; Imray C68; OS 6

TIDES -0145 Dover; ML 2·0; Duration 0620; Zone 0 (UT)

Standard Port WICK (⟵)

Times				Height (metres)			
High Water		Low Water		MHWS	MHWN	MLWN	MLWS
0000	0700	0200	0700	3·5	2·8	1·4	0·7
1200	1900	1400	1900				
Differences STROMNESS							
–0225	–0135	–0205	–0205	+0·1	–0·1	0·0	0·0
ST MARY'S (Scapa Flow)							
–0140	–0140	–0140	–0140	–0·2	–0·2	0·0	–0·1
BURRAY NESS (Burray)							
+0005	+0005	+0015	+0015	–0·2	–0·3	–0·1	–0·1
WIDEWALL BAY (S Ronaldsay)							
–0155	–0155	–0150	–0150	+0·1	–0·1	–0·1	–0·3
BUR WICK (S Ronaldsay)							
–0100	–0100	–0150	–0150	–0·1	–0·1	+0·2	+0·1
MUCKLE SKERRY (Pentland Firth)							
–0025	–0025	–0020	–0020	–0·9	–0·8	–0·4	–0·3

SHELTER Very good. Northern Lights Board have sole use of pier near to ldg lts. ⚓ in hbr or berth at ferry piers further N.

NAVIGATION WPT 58°56'·93N 03°17'·00W, 137°/317° from/to front ldg lt, 0·88M. Entry from the W should not be attempted with strong wind against tide due to heavy overfalls; if entering against the ebb, stand on to avoid being swept onto Skerry of Ness. Tides in Hoy Sound are very strong (>7kn sp). No tidal stream in hbr.

LIGHTS AND MARKS For Hoy Sound, ldg lts 104° on Graemsay Is: front Iso 3s 17m 15M, W tr; rear Oc WR 8s 35m 20/16M, ldg sector is R097°-112°. Skerry of Ness, Fl WG 4s 7m 7/4M; W shore-090°, G090°-shore. Hbr ldg lts 317°, both FR 29/39m 11M (H24), W trs, vis 307°-327°.

RADIO TELEPHONE VHF Ch 12 16 (0900-1700 LT). (See also 9.7.23).

TELEPHONE (Dial code 01856) Hr Mr 850744; Fuel 851286; MRSC 01595 692976; ⊜ 0845 744 2266; Marinecall 09068 500 451; Police 850222; Dr 850205; Dentist 850658.

FACILITIES Services: FW, Sh, El, Ⓔ, ME, C (mobile, 30 ton), Slip. **Town** EC Thurs; FW, D, V, R, Bar, Gas, ⊠, ▣, Ⓑ, ⇌ (ferry to Scrabster, bus to Thurso), ✈ (Kirkwall). Yachtsmen may contact for help/advice: **Mr J. Stout** ☎ 850100, **Mr S. Mowat** ☎ 850624 or **Capt A. Johnston** ☎ 850366.

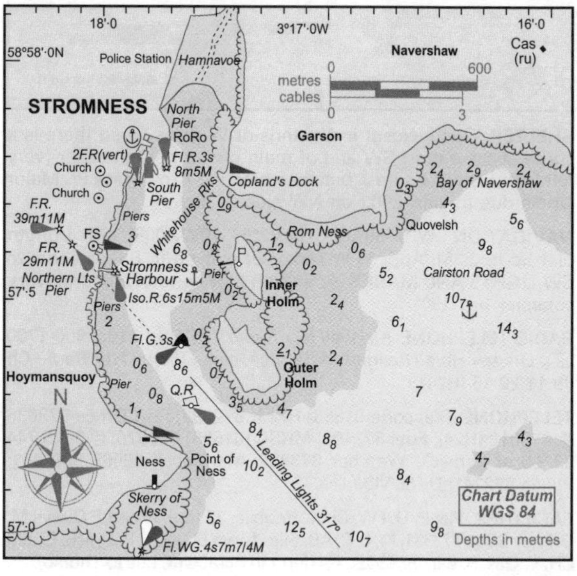

KIRKWALL *9.7.23*

Orkney Islands, Mainland **58°59'·30N 02°57'·70W**

CHARTS AC 1553, 2584, 2249, 2250; Imray C68; OS 6

TIDES –0045 Dover; ML 1·8; Duration 0620; Zone 0 (UT)

Standard Port WICK (⟵)

Times				**Height (metres)**			
High Water		Low Water		MHWS	MHWN	MLWN	MLWS
0000	0700	0200	0700	3·5	2·8	1·4	0·7
1200	1900	1400	1900				
Differences KIRKWALL							
–0042	–0042	–0041	–0041	–0·5	–0·4	–0·1	–0·1
DEER SOUND							
–0040	–0040	–0035	–0035	–0·3	–0·3	–0·1	–0·1
TINGWALL							
–0200	–0125	–0145	–0125	–0·4	–0·4	–0·1	–0·1

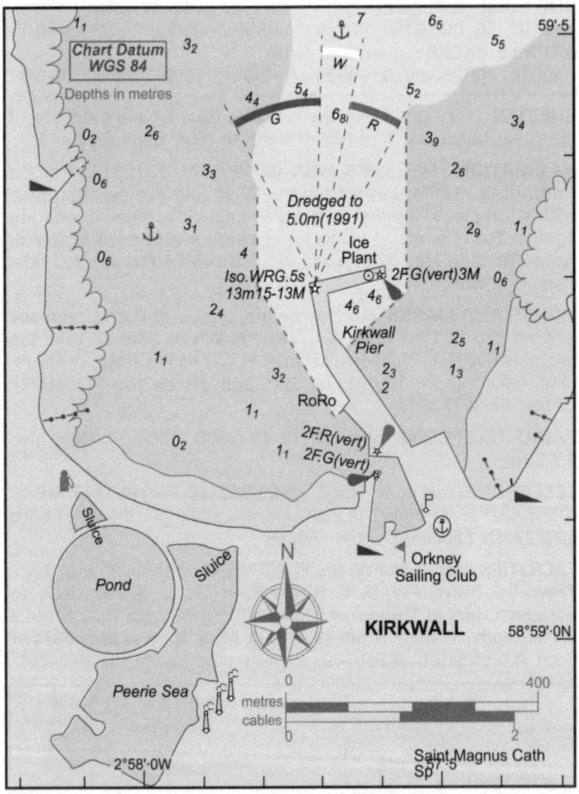

SHELTER Good except in N winds or W gales when there is a surge at the ent. At SW end of main pier, enter inner hbr (very full in Jun/Jul); or safe ⚓ between pier and Crow Ness Pt. Major works due to start 2002 on NW side of bay.

NAVIGATION WPT 59°01'·37N 02°57'·10W, 008°/188° from/to pier hd lt, 2·2M. Appr in W sector of pier hd lt. Bay is shoal to SW. **LIGHTS AND MARKS** Appr with St Magnus Cathedral (very conspic) brg 190°.

RADIO TELEPHONE *Kirkwall Hbr Radio* VHF Ch 12 16 (0800-1700 LT). Orkney Hbrs Navigation Service, call: *Orkney Hbr Radio* Ch 09 11 20 16 (H24).

TELEPHONE (Dial code 01856) Hr Mr 872292; Port Office 873636 Fax 873012 (H24); Fuel 873105; MRSC (01595) 692976; ⊖ 0845 744 22266 at Lerwick; Weather 873802; Marinecall 09068 500 451; Police 872241; Dr 885400 (H).

FACILITIES **Pier** P, D, FW, CH, C (mobile, 25 ton); **N and E Quays** M; **Orkney SC** ☎ 872331, M, L, C, AB, Slip. **Town** EC Wed; P, D, ME, El, Sh, CH, V, Gas, R, Bar, Ⓑ, ✉, ⇌ (ferry to Scrabster, bus to Thurso), ✈.

STRONSAY *9.7.24*

Orkney Islands, Stronsay **59°08'·57N 02°36'·01W**

CHARTS AC 2622, 2250; Imray C68; OS 6

TIDES As Dover; ML 1·7; Duration 0620; Zone 0 (UT)

Standard Port WICK (⟵)

Times				**Height (metres)**			
High Water		Low Water		MHWS	MHWN	MLWN	MLWS
0000	0700	0200	0700	3·5	2·8	1·4	0·7
1200	1900	1400	1900				
Differences LOTH (Sanday)							
–0052	–0052	–0058	–0058	–0·1	0·0	+0·3	+0·4
KETTLETOFT PIER (Sanday)							
–0025	–0025	–0015	–0015	0·0	0·0	+0·2	+0·2
RAPNESS (Westray)							
–0205	–0205	–0205	–0205	+0·1	0·0	+0·2	0·0
PIEROWALL (Westray)							
–0150	–0150	–0145	–0145	+0·2	0·0	0·0	–0·1

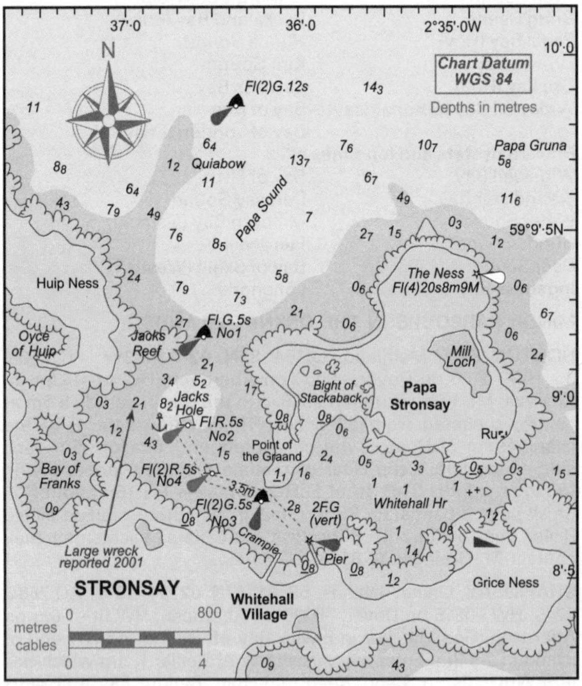

SHELTER Good from all winds. Good ⚓ between seaward end of piers, or berth on outer end of W pier and contact Hr Mr. The extended E pier head is berth for Ro-Ro ferry. There are many other sheltered ⚓s around the bay.

NAVIGATION WPT 59°09'·82N 02°36'·31W, Quiabow SHM By, Fl (2) G 12s, 009°/189° from/to No 1 lt buoy, 6·5ca. 800m NE of Huip Ness is Quiabow, a submerged rk. Jack's Reef extends 400m E from Huip Ness, and is marked by No 1 SHM buoy Fl G 5. A bank extends 350m SW from Papa Stronsay. Crampie Shoal is in mid-chan, marked by No 3 buoy. The buoyed chan to Whitehall pier is dredged 3·5m. Spit to E of Whitehall pier extends 400m N. The E ent is narrow and shallow and should not be attempted.

LIGHTS AND MARKS As chartlet. Pier hd lts, 2FG (vert).

RADIO TELEPHONE See Kirkwall.

TELEPHONE (Dial code 01857) Piermaster 616317; MRSC (01595) 692976; ⊖ (0845) 744 2266; Marinecall 09068 500451; Police (01856) 872241; Dr 616321.

FACILITIES **W Pier** M, L, AB; **Main (E) Pier** M, L, FW, AB clear of ferry. **Village (Whitehall)** EC Thurs; P, D, V, Bar, ✉, Ⓑ, ⇌ (ferry to Scrabster, bus to Thurso), ✈.

TIME ZONE (UTC)
For Summer Time add ONE hour in **non-shaded areas**

SCOTLAND – LERWICK

LAT 60°09′N LONG 1°08′W

TIMES AND HEIGHTS OF HIGH AND LOW WATERS

SPRING & NEAP TIDES
Dates in red are **SPRINGS**
Dates in blue are **NEAPS**

YEAR **2002**

JANUARY

Day	Time	m	Time	m	Time	m	Time	m
1 TU	0547	0.7	1203	2.3	1819	0.4		
2 W	0042	2.2	0632	0.7	1249	2.3	1906	0.4
3 TH	0132	2.1	0718	0.8	1336	2.2	1956	0.4
4 F	0225	2.0	0808	0.8	1428	2.2	2050	0.5
5 SA	0319	1.9	0901	0.9	1525	2.1	2148	0.6
6 SU	0417	1.8	1001	1.0	1628	2.0	2257	0.7
7 M	0520	1.8	1118	1.0	1737	1.9		
8 TU	0014	0.7	0626	1.8	1244	1.0	1849	1.9
9 W	0120	0.8	0732	1.8	1351	0.9	2000	1.9
10 TH	0217	0.8	0831	1.9	1447	0.8	2102	2.0
11 F	0306	0.8	0922	2.0	1537	0.7	2155	2.0
12 SA	0351	0.8	1007	2.1	1621	0.7	2241	2.0
13 SU	0432	0.8	1047	2.2	1703	0.6	● 2323	2.1
14 M	0510	0.8	1125	2.2	1742	0.6		
15 TU	0001	2.0	0546	0.8	1202	2.2	1818	0.6
16 W	0038	2.0	0621	0.8	1235	2.2	1853	0.6
17 TH	0112	2.0	0653	0.8	1308	2.1	1928	0.6
18 F	0146	1.9	0725	0.9	1342	2.1	2003	0.7
19 SA	0222	1.8	0800	0.9	1418	2.0	2042	0.8
20 SU	0301	1.7	0840	1.0	1500	1.9	2126	0.8
21 M	0347	1.7	0930	1.0	1548	1.8	2218	0.9
22 TU	0440	1.7	1035	1.1	1645	1.7	2325	1.0
23 W	0544	1.7	1205	1.1	1755	1.7		
24 TH	0041	1.0	0654	1.7	1319	1.0	1911	1.7
25 F	0141	0.9	0756	1.8	1414	0.9	2018	1.8
26 SA	0233	0.9	0848	1.9	1503	0.8	2114	1.9
27 SU	0321	0.8	0936	2.1	1550	0.6	2206	2.1
28 M	0407	0.7	1022	2.2	1636	0.5	○ 2256	2.2
29 TU	0452	0.6	1108	2.3	1722	0.3	2344	2.2
30 W	0536	0.6	1153	2.3	1807	0.2		
31 TH	0031	2.2	0619	0.5	1238	2.3	1852	0.2

FEBRUARY

Day	Time	m	Time	m	Time	m	Time	m
1 F	0118	2.1	0703	0.6	1323	2.3	1938	0.2
2 SA	0205	2.1	0747	0.6	1411	2.2	2026	0.4
3 SU	0253	1.9	0835	0.7	1502	2.1	2118	0.5
4 M	0343	1.8	0928	0.8	1559	2.0	2217	0.7
5 TU	0440	1.7	1036	0.9	1706	1.8	2336	0.8
6 W	0545	1.7	1218	1.0	1825	1.8		
7 TH	0057	0.9	0701	1.7	1338	0.9	1950	1.8
8 F	0203	0.9	0813	1.8	1443	0.8	2058	1.8
9 SA	0258	0.9	0910	1.9	1534	0.7	2149	1.9
10 SU	0342	0.9	0956	2.0	1615	0.6	2231	1.9
11 M	0421	0.8	1035	2.1	1652	0.6	2308	2.0
12 TU	0456	0.7	1111	2.1	1725	0.5	● 2343	2.0
13 W	0528	0.7	1144	2.2	1757	0.5		
14 TH	0015	2.0	0558	0.7	1215	2.1	1827	0.5
15 F	0046	1.9	0627	0.7	1244	2.1	1856	0.5
16 SA	0115	1.9	0656	0.7	1313	2.1	1927	0.6
17 SU	0145	1.8	0728	0.7	1346	2.0	2000	0.6
18 M	0219	1.8	0803	0.8	1423	1.9	2037	0.7
19 TU	0258	1.7	0844	0.9	1505	1.8	2119	0.8
20 W	0345	1.7	0937	1.0	1558	1.7	2214	0.9
21 TH	0443	1.6	1052	1.0	1706	1.6	2335	1.0
22 F	0556	1.6	1238	1.0	1831	1.6		
23 SA	0110	1.0	0716	1.7	1349	0.9	1955	1.7
24 SU	0214	0.9	0823	1.8	1445	0.7	2100	1.9
25 M	0307	0.8	0917	2.0	1535	0.5	2153	2.0
26 TU	0354	0.6	1006	2.1	1621	0.3	2242	2.1
27 W	0438	0.5	1052	2.3	1705	0.1	○ 2329	2.2
28 TH	0519	0.4	1136	2.3	1748	0.0		

MARCH

Day	Time	m	Time	m	Time	m	Time	m
1 F	0013	2.2	0600	0.4	1220	2.4	1831	0.0
2 SA	0056	2.1	0642	0.4	1304	2.3	1914	0.1
3 SU	0138	2.1	0724	0.4	1350	2.2	1959	0.3
4 M	0221	1.9	0810	0.6	1439	2.1	2047	0.5
5 TU	0307	1.8	0901	0.7	1533	1.9	2141	0.8
6 W	0359	1.7	1007	0.8	1638	1.7	2256	0.9
7 TH	0503	1.6	1158	0.9	1804	1.6		
8 F	0035	1.0	0627	1.6	1326	0.9	1944	1.6
9 SA	0148	1.0	0754	1.7	1433	0.8	2049	1.7
10 SU	0245	0.9	0852	1.8	1521	0.7	2134	1.8
11 M	0327	0.8	0936	1.9	1558	0.6	2211	1.8
12 TU	0403	0.7	1015	2.0	1631	0.5	2245	1.9
13 W	0435	0.6	1049	2.0	1701	0.4	2317	1.9
14 TH	0505	0.6	1121	2.1	1729	0.4	● 2347	2.0
15 F	0532	0.5	1150	2.1	1756	0.4		
16 SA	0015	1.9	0600	0.5	1217	2.1	1823	0.4
17 SU	0042	1.9	0629	0.5	1246	2.0	1853	0.5
18 M	0110	1.9	0701	0.6	1317	2.0	1925	0.6
19 TU	0141	1.8	0736	0.7	1353	1.9	1959	0.7
20 W	0217	1.8	0816	0.7	1434	1.8	2039	0.8
21 TH	0300	1.7	0906	0.8	1527	1.7	2131	0.9
22 F	0356	1.6	1016	0.9	1637	1.6	2249	1.0
23 SA	0512	1.6	1201	0.9	1807	1.6		
24 SU	0047	1.0	0641	1.6	1326	0.8	1939	1.7
25 M	0157	0.9	0759	1.7	1425	0.6	2044	1.8
26 TU	0250	0.7	0856	1.9	1515	0.3	2136	2.0
27 W	0335	0.6	0946	2.1	1600	0.2	2223	2.1
28 TH	0417	0.4	1031	2.2	1643	0.0	○ 2306	2.1
29 F	0458	0.3	1115	2.3	1725	0.0	2348	2.2
30 SA	0539	0.3	1159	2.3	1807	0.0		
31 SU	0028	2.1	0619	0.3	1243	2.3	1849	0.2

APRIL

Day	Time	m	Time	m	Time	m	Time	m
1 M	0108	2.0	0702	0.3	1329	2.1	1932	0.4
2 TU	0149	1.9	0749	0.5	1418	2.0	2018	0.6
3 W	0232	1.8	0841	0.6	1512	1.8	2110	0.8
4 TH	0322	1.7	0948	0.7	1616	1.6	2219	1.0
5 F	0423	1.6	1134	0.8	1742	1.5		
6 SA	0004	1.1	0547	1.6	1301	0.8	1925	1.5
7 SU	0122	1.0	0720	1.6	1406	0.7	2024	1.6
8 M	0219	0.9	0821	1.7	1453	0.6	2105	1.7
9 TU	0301	0.8	0907	1.8	1529	0.5	2141	1.8
10 W	0336	0.7	0945	1.9	1600	0.5	2215	1.8
11 TH	0408	0.6	1020	1.9	1629	0.4	2246	1.9
12 F	0436	0.5	1052	2.0	1656	0.4	● 2316	1.9
13 SA	0504	0.5	1121	2.0	1723	0.4	2343	1.9
14 SU	0534	0.5	1150	2.0	1752	0.4		
15 M	0010	1.9	0605	0.5	1221	2.0	1823	0.5
16 TU	0040	1.9	0639	0.5	1254	1.9	1856	0.6
17 W	0111	1.9	0716	0.6	1332	1.9	1931	0.7
18 TH	0147	1.8	0759	0.6	1416	1.8	2013	0.8
19 F	0230	1.7	0851	0.7	1512	1.6	2108	0.9
20 SA	0327	1.6	1001	0.8	1626	1.6	2229	1.0
21 SU	0444	1.6	1136	0.7	1754	1.5		
22 M	0023	0.9	0613	1.6	1300	0.6	1919	1.6
23 TU	0134	0.8	0731	1.7	1400	0.4	2022	1.8
24 W	0226	0.7	0831	1.9	1451	0.3	2112	1.9
25 TH	0312	0.5	0922	2.0	1536	0.1	2158	2.0
26 F	0354	0.4	1008	2.1	1619	0.1	2240	2.1
27 SA	0435	0.3	1054	2.2	1701	0.1	○ 2320	2.1
28 SU	0517	0.2	1138	2.2	1743	0.2		
29 M	0000	2.1	0600	0.2	1224	2.2	1824	0.3
30 TU	0040	2.0	0644	0.3	1311	2.0	1908	0.5

Chart Datum: 1·22 metres below Ordnance Datum (Local)

TIME ZONE (UTC)
For Summer Time add ONE hour in **non-shaded areas**

SCOTLAND – LERWICK

LAT 60°09′N LONG 1°08′W

TIMES AND HEIGHTS OF HIGH AND LOW WATERS

SPRING & NEAP TIDES
Dates in red are **SPRINGS**
Dates in blue are **NEAPS**

YEAR **2002**

MAY

Day	Time	m	Time	m	Time	m	Time	m
1 W	0121	2.0	0733	0.4	1401	1.9	1953	0.7
2 TH	0204	1.9	0826	0.6	1453	1.7	2044	0.9
3 F	0252	1.7	0930	0.7	1552	1.6	2146	1.0
4 SA	0348	1.6	1053	0.7	1705	1.5	2310	1.1
5 SU	0459	1.6	1217	0.7	1835	1.5		
6 M	0035	1.0	0628	1.6	1322	0.7	1939	1.5
7 TU	0137	0.9	0737	1.6	1411	0.6	2024	1.6
8 W	0223	0.8	0827	1.7	1450	0.6	2103	1.7
9 TH	0301	0.7	0909	1.8	1523	0.5	2139	1.8
10 F	0335	0.6	0946	1.8	1553	0.5	2212	1.9
11 SA	0406	0.6	1020	1.9	1622	0.5	2242	1.9
12 SU	0437	0.5	1052	1.9	1652	0.5	● 2312	2.0
13 M	0510	0.5	1125	2.0	1724	0.5	2342	2.0
14 TU	0545	0.5	1200	1.9	1759	0.5		
15 W	0015	2.0	0622	0.5	1239	1.9	1835	0.6
16 TH	0050	1.9	0703	0.5	1321	1.8	1915	0.7
17 F	0129	1.9	0750	0.5	1410	1.7	2001	0.8
18 SA	0216	1.8	0845	0.6	1509	1.7	2100	0.9
19 SU	0314	1.7	0952	0.6	1619	1.6	2214	0.9
20 M	0428	1.6	1111	0.6	1736	1.6	2347	0.9
21 TU	0548	1.7	1230	0.5	1851	1.6		
22 W	0102	0.8	0701	1.7	1332	0.4	1953	1.7
23 TH	0159	0.7	0803	1.9	1425	0.3	2045	1.9
24 F	0247	0.5	0857	2.0	1512	0.3	2131	2.0
25 SA	0332	0.4	0948	2.1	1556	0.2	2215	2.0
26 SU	0416	0.3	1036	2.1	1639	0.3	○ 2256	2.1
27 M	0500	0.3	1124	2.1	1722	0.4	2337	2.1
28 TU	0545	0.3	1211	2.0	1805	0.5		
29 W	0017	2.0	0631	0.3	1258	1.9	1848	0.6
30 TH	0100	2.0	0720	0.4	1345	1.8	1932	0.8
31 F	0143	1.9	0810	0.5	1433	1.7	2019	0.9

JUNE

Day	Time	m	Time	m	Time	m	Time	m
1 SA	0227	1.8	0904	0.6	1524	1.6	2110	1.0
2 SU	0316	1.7	1003	0.7	1620	1.5	2210	1.0
3 M	0412	1.6	1109	0.7	1727	1.5	2322	1.0
4 TU	0521	1.6	1217	0.7	1837	1.5		
5 W	0036	0.9	0638	1.6	1315	0.7	1934	1.6
6 TH	0134	0.9	0740	1.6	1401	0.7	2020	1.7
7 F	0220	0.8	0828	1.7	1440	0.6	2100	1.8
8 SA	0259	0.7	0910	1.8	1515	0.6	2136	1.8
9 SU	0335	0.6	0948	1.8	1549	0.6	2210	1.9
10 M	0412	0.6	1026	1.9	1625	0.6	● 2244	2.0
11 TU	0449	0.5	1105	1.9	1702	0.6	2320	2.0
12 W	0529	0.5	1146	1.9	1741	0.6	2358	2.0
13 TH	0611	0.4	1230	1.9	1822	0.6		
14 F	0038	2.0	0655	0.4	1317	1.9	1906	0.7
15 SA	0122	2.0	0744	0.4	1408	1.8	1955	0.7
16 SU	0210	1.9	0837	0.4	1504	1.7	2049	0.8
17 M	0307	1.8	0936	0.5	1605	1.7	2151	0.8
18 TU	0412	1.8	1043	0.5	1711	1.6	2304	0.8
19 W	0522	1.8	1157	0.5	1817	1.7		
20 TH	0026	0.8	0632	1.8	1304	0.5	1920	1.7
21 F	0131	0.7	0738	1.8	1401	0.5	2017	1.8
22 SA	0226	0.6	0839	1.9	1452	0.5	2108	1.9
23 SU	0317	0.5	0935	2.0	1538	0.5	2155	2.0
24 M	0404	0.5	1027	2.0	1623	0.5	○ 2239	2.0
25 TU	0451	0.4	1116	2.0	1707	0.6	2321	2.1
26 W	0536	0.4	1201	2.0	1749	0.6		
27 TH	0003	2.1	0620	0.4	1245	1.9	1830	0.7
28 F	0043	2.0	0704	0.4	1327	1.8	1910	0.7
29 SA	0123	2.0	0747	0.5	1408	1.7	1950	0.8
30 SU	0202	1.9	0830	0.6	1449	1.7	2030	0.9

JULY

Day	Time	m	Time	m	Time	m	Time	m
1 M	0243	1.8	0915	0.7	1533	1.6	2116	0.9
2 TU	0329	1.7	1004	0.7	1623	1.5	2212	1.0
3 W	0420	1.7	1103	0.8	1722	1.5	2324	1.0
4 TH	0522	1.6	1209	0.8	1830	1.6		
5 F	0038	1.0	0635	1.6	1309	0.8	1930	1.6
6 SA	0137	0.9	0741	1.7	1358	0.8	2018	1.7
7 SU	0225	0.8	0833	1.7	1441	0.8	2101	1.8
8 M	0309	0.7	0920	1.8	1523	0.7	2141	1.9
9 TU	0351	0.6	1005	1.9	1604	0.7	2222	2.0
10 W	0433	0.5	1050	2.0	1647	0.6	● 2303	2.1
11 TH	0516	0.4	1136	2.0	1729	0.6	2346	2.1
12 F	0601	0.3	1223	2.0	1813	0.6		
13 SA	0029	2.1	0645	0.3	1310	2.0	1856	0.6
14 SU	0114	2.1	0732	0.3	1358	1.9	1942	0.6
15 M	0201	2.1	0821	0.3	1449	1.8	2031	0.7
16 TU	0253	2.0	0914	0.4	1542	1.8	2124	0.8
17 W	0351	1.9	1012	0.5	1640	1.7	2227	0.8
18 TH	0455	1.8	1123	0.6	1742	1.7	2351	0.8
19 F	0606	1.8	1238	0.7	1849	1.7		
20 SA	0111	0.8	0720	1.8	1343	0.7	1954	1.8
21 SU	0215	0.7	0831	1.8	1439	0.7	2053	1.9
22 M	0311	0.6	0932	1.9	1529	0.7	2144	2.0
23 TU	0401	0.6	1023	1.9	1614	0.7	2229	2.1
24 W	0445	0.5	1108	2.0	1655	0.7	○ 2310	2.1
25 TH	0526	0.4	1149	2.0	1734	0.7	2349	2.1
26 F	0605	0.4	1227	1.9	1811	0.7		
27 SA	0025	2.1	0642	0.4	1303	1.9	1844	0.7
28 SU	0100	2.1	0717	0.5	1337	1.8	1917	0.7
29 M	0133	2.0	0752	0.6	1411	1.8	1950	0.8
30 TU	0208	1.9	0828	0.6	1447	1.7	2028	0.8
31 W	0247	1.8	0908	0.7	1529	1.7	2113	0.9

AUGUST

Day	Time	m	Time	m	Time	m	Time	m
1 TH	0332	1.8	0956	0.8	1617	1.6	2213	1.0
2 F	0425	1.7	1057	0.9	1715	1.6	2337	1.0
3 SA	0529	1.6	1214	1.0	1825	1.6		
4 SU	0057	1.0	0647	1.6	1321	0.9	1934	1.7
5 M	0156	0.9	0801	1.7	1415	0.9	2029	1.8
6 TU	0247	0.8	0858	1.8	1503	0.8	2117	1.9
7 W	0333	0.6	0948	1.9	1549	0.7	2203	2.1
8 TH	0418	0.5	1036	2.0	1633	0.6	● 2247	2.2
9 F	0502	0.3	1123	2.1	1716	0.6	2331	2.2
10 SA	0545	0.2	1209	2.1	1758	0.5		
11 SU	0014	2.3	0628	0.2	1254	2.1	1839	0.5
12 M	0059	2.3	0712	0.2	1338	2.1	1922	0.5
13 TU	0144	2.2	0758	0.3	1424	2.0	2007	0.6
14 W	0233	2.1	0847	0.4	1512	1.9	2057	0.7
15 TH	0327	2.0	0941	0.6	1606	1.8	2158	0.8
16 F	0430	1.9	1049	0.8	1707	1.7	2328	0.9
17 SA	0546	1.8	1219	0.9	1820	1.7		
18 SU	0103	0.9	0714	1.7	1332	0.9	1938	1.8
19 M	0213	0.8	0832	1.8	1432	0.9	2043	1.9
20 TU	0310	0.7	0929	1.9	1522	0.9	2134	2.0
21 W	0356	0.6	1014	1.9	1603	0.8	2217	2.1
22 TH	0434	0.5	1053	2.0	1640	0.7	○ 2255	2.1
23 F	0509	0.5	1129	2.0	1714	0.7	2330	2.2
24 SA	0542	0.4	1202	2.0	1745	0.7		
25 SU	0002	2.2	0613	0.5	1233	2.0	1815	0.7
26 M	0032	2.1	0643	0.5	1302	1.9	1844	0.7
27 TU	0101	2.1	0712	0.6	1332	1.9	1915	0.7
28 W	0133	2.0	0744	0.7	1404	1.8	1949	0.8
29 TH	0208	1.9	0820	0.8	1441	1.8	2030	0.9
30 F	0250	1.8	0900	0.9	1525	1.7	2121	1.0
31 SA	0341	1.7	0951	1.0	1619	1.7	2234	1.1

Chart Datum: 1·22 metres below Ordnance Datum (Local)

TIME ZONE (UTC)
For Summer Time add ONE hour in **non-shaded areas**

SCOTLAND – LERWICK

LAT 60°09'N LONG 1°08'W

TIMES AND HEIGHTS OF HIGH AND LOW WATERS

SPRING & NEAP TIDES
Dates in red are **SPRINGS**
Dates in blue are **NEAPS**

YEAR **2002**

SEPTEMBER

Date	Day	Time	m	Time	m	Time	m	Time	m
1	SU	0444	1.7	1109	1.1	1727	1.7		
2	M	0021	1.1	0605	1.6	1250	1.1	1848	1.7
3	TU	0132	1.0	0735	1.7	1355	1.0	2001	1.8
4	W	0226	0.8	0841	1.8	1447	0.9	2055	2.0
5	TH	0314	0.6	0932	2.0	1533	0.8	2143	2.1
6	F	0359	0.4	1019	2.1	1615	0.6	2228	2.3
7	SA	0442	0.2	1104	2.2	1656	0.5	● 2311	2.4
8	SU	0524	0.1	1147	2.2	1736	0.4	2354	2.4
9	M	0606	0.1	1229	2.2	1817	0.4		
10	TU	0037	2.4	0648	0.2	1311	2.2	1859	0.5
11	W	0122	2.3	0732	0.3	1353	2.1	1944	0.6
12	TH	0211	2.2	0819	0.5	1439	2.0	2034	0.7
13	F	0306	2.0	0911	0.8	1531	1.9	2137	0.9
14	SA	0411	1.8	1020	1.0	1633	1.8	2320	0.9
15	SU	0532	1.7	1203	1.1	1752	1.7		
16	M	0056	0.9	0716	1.7	1321	1.1	1922	1.8
17	TU	0207	0.8	0828	1.8	1421	1.0	2028	1.9
18	W	0300	0.7	0916	1.9	1507	0.9	2116	2.0
19	TH	0339	0.6	0954	2.0	1544	0.8	2156	2.1
20	F	0413	0.6	1029	2.0	1618	0.8	2232	2.2
21	SA	0444	0.5	1101	2.1	1648	0.7	○ 2304	2.2
22	SU	0513	0.5	1132	2.1	1717	0.7	2334	2.2
23	M	0540	0.5	1200	2.1	1745	0.6		
24	TU	0002	2.2	0607	0.5	1227	2.0	1814	0.7
25	W	0030	2.1	0636	0.6	1254	2.0	1845	0.7
26	TH	0101	2.1	0707	0.7	1324	2.0	1920	0.8
27	F	0136	2.0	0740	0.8	1359	1.9	1959	0.9
28	SA	0217	1.9	0817	1.0	1440	1.8	2048	1.0
29	SU	0308	1.8	0905	1.1	1533	1.8	2157	1.1
30	M	0415	1.7	1021	1.2	1644	1.7	2344	1.1

OCTOBER

Date	Day	Time	m	Time	m	Time	m	Time	m
1	TU	0540	1.7	1224	1.2	1810	1.7		
2	W	0106	0.9	0714	1.7	1335	1.1	1932	1.8
3	TH	0203	0.8	0821	1.9	1427	0.9	2030	2.0
4	F	0251	0.6	0911	2.0	1511	0.8	2119	2.2
5	SA	0336	0.4	0956	2.2	1553	0.6	2204	2.3
6	SU	0418	0.2	1039	2.3	1633	0.5	● 2248	2.4
7	M	0500	0.2	1120	2.3	1713	0.4	2331	2.5
8	TU	0541	0.2	1200	2.3	1754	0.4		
9	W	0015	2.5	0623	0.3	1241	2.3	1837	0.5
10	TH	0102	2.3	0706	0.5	1323	2.2	1924	0.6
11	F	0152	2.2	0753	0.7	1408	2.1	2017	0.7
12	SA	0249	2.0	0845	1.0	1459	1.9	2124	0.9
13	SU	0354	1.8	0954	1.1	1601	1.8	2306	0.9
14	M	0516	1.7	1137	1.2	1721	1.8		
15	TU	0037	0.9	0701	1.7	1257	1.2	1853	1.8
16	W	0145	0.8	0805	1.8	1357	1.1	1959	1.9
17	TH	0234	0.8	0848	1.9	1442	1.0	2047	2.0
18	F	0312	0.7	0924	1.9	1518	0.9	2127	2.1
19	SA	0344	0.6	0957	2.0	1550	0.8	2202	2.1
20	SU	0413	0.6	1029	2.1	1620	0.7	2235	2.2
21	M	0440	0.6	1059	2.1	1649	0.7	○ 2305	2.2
22	TU	0507	0.6	1127	2.1	1718	0.7	2334	2.2
23	W	0535	0.6	1154	2.1	1749	0.7		
24	TH	0004	2.2	0604	0.7	1222	2.1	1822	0.7
25	F	0037	2.1	0636	0.8	1253	2.1	1858	0.8
26	SA	0114	2.0	0710	0.9	1328	2.0	1939	0.9
27	SU	0156	1.9	0748	1.0	1409	1.9	2030	0.9
28	M	0249	1.8	0839	1.1	1502	1.8	2136	1.0
29	TU	0358	1.7	0954	1.2	1613	1.8	2307	1.0
30	W	0521	1.7	1147	1.2	1739	1.8		
31	TH	0034	0.9	0647	1.8	1307	1.1	1859	1.9

NOVEMBER

Date	Day	Time	m	Time	m	Time	m	Time	m
1	F	0134	0.7	0753	1.9	1400	0.9	2001	2.0
2	SA	0224	0.5	0844	2.1	1446	0.8	2052	2.2
3	SU	0310	0.4	0929	2.2	1528	0.6	2139	2.3
4	M	0353	0.3	1012	2.3	1610	0.5	● 2225	2.4
5	TU	0435	0.3	1053	2.3	1652	0.5	2311	2.4
6	W	0518	0.4	1133	2.3	1735	0.4	2357	2.4
7	TH	0600	0.5	1214	2.3	1821	0.5		
8	F	0046	2.3	0644	0.7	1257	2.2	1910	0.6
9	SA	0139	2.1	0731	0.9	1343	2.1	2005	0.7
10	SU	0234	2.0	0823	1.1	1434	2.0	2109	0.8
11	M	0335	1.8	0925	1.2	1532	1.9	2230	0.9
12	TU	0445	1.7	1045	1.3	1641	1.8	2356	0.9
13	W	0610	1.7	1212	1.2	1804	1.8		
14	TH	0104	0.9	0718	1.7	1317	1.1	1915	1.9
15	F	0155	0.8	0806	1.8	1406	1.0	2008	1.9
16	SA	0235	0.8	0846	1.9	1446	0.9	2052	2.0
17	SU	0309	0.7	0922	2.0	1520	0.9	2130	2.1
18	M	0339	0.7	0956	2.1	1552	0.8	2206	2.1
19	TU	0408	0.7	1027	2.1	1623	0.7	2238	2.1
20	W	0437	0.7	1057	2.2	1655	0.7	○ 2310	2.1
21	TH	0507	0.7	1126	2.2	1729	0.7	2344	2.1
22	F	0540	0.8	1158	2.2	1805	0.7		
23	SA	0021	2.1	0614	0.9	1232	2.2	1845	0.7
24	SU	0101	2.0	0652	0.9	1309	2.1	1929	0.8
25	M	0147	2.0	0735	1.0	1352	2.0	2020	0.8
26	TU	0241	1.9	0827	1.1	1445	1.9	2121	0.8
27	W	0346	1.8	0934	1.1	1551	1.9	2233	0.8
28	TH	0459	1.8	1057	1.1	1708	1.9	2354	0.8
29	F	0614	1.8	1226	1.1	1824	1.9		
30	SA	0101	0.7	0719	1.9	1328	1.0	1930	2.0

DECEMBER

Date	Day	Time	m	Time	m	Time	m	Time	m
1	SU	0156	0.6	0814	2.0	1419	0.8	2026	2.1
2	M	0245	0.5	0902	2.1	1506	0.7	2119	2.2
3	TU	0331	0.5	0947	2.2	1551	0.6	2209	2.3
4	W	0415	0.5	1031	2.3	1637	0.5	● 2258	2.3
5	TH	0459	0.6	1113	2.3	1723	0.5	2348	2.3
6	F	0543	0.7	1156	2.3	1811	0.5		
7	SA	0038	2.2	0628	0.8	1240	2.3	1900	0.6
8	SU	0128	2.1	0714	0.9	1325	2.2	1951	0.6
9	M	0217	2.0	0801	1.0	1412	2.1	2045	0.7
10	TU	0308	1.8	0851	1.1	1501	2.0	2143	0.8
11	W	0402	1.7	0947	1.2	1556	1.9	2247	0.9
12	TH	0504	1.7	1054	1.2	1700	1.8	2359	0.9
13	F	0612	1.7	1213	1.2	1815	1.8		
14	SA	0100	0.9	0713	1.7	1318	1.1	1920	1.8
15	SU	0149	0.9	0803	1.8	1407	1.0	2013	1.9
16	M	0229	0.9	0846	1.9	1449	0.9	2058	1.9
17	TU	0305	0.8	0924	2.0	1526	0.9	2138	2.0
18	W	0338	0.8	0958	2.1	1601	0.8	2215	2.1
19	TH	0412	0.8	1032	2.2	1637	0.7	○ 2252	2.1
20	F	0447	0.8	1106	2.2	1715	0.7	2331	2.1
21	SA	0524	0.8	1142	2.2	1754	0.6		
22	SU	0012	2.1	0602	0.8	1220	2.2	1836	0.6
23	M	0056	2.1	0643	0.9	1300	2.2	1921	0.6
24	TU	0142	2.0	0727	0.9	1343	2.1	2009	0.6
25	W	0232	1.9	0816	0.9	1433	2.0	2102	0.6
26	TH	0329	1.9	0911	1.0	1531	2.0	2201	0.7
27	F	0430	1.8	1015	1.0	1638	1.9	2310	0.7
28	SA	0536	1.8	1133	1.0	1749	1.9		
29	SU	0025	0.7	0642	1.8	1255	1.0	1900	2.0
30	M	0130	0.7	0744	1.9	1357	0.9	2006	2.0
31	TU	0225	0.7	0840	2.0	1451	0.8	2107	2.1

Chart Datum: 1·22 metres below Ordnance Datum (Local)

SHETLAND ISLANDS *9.7.25*

The Shetland Islands consist of approx 100 islands, holms and rks of which fewer than 20 are inhabited. They lie 90 to 150M NNE of the Scottish mainland. By far the biggest island is Mainland with Lerwick (9.7.26), the capital, on the E side and Scalloway (overleaf), the only other town and old capital, on the W side. At the very S is Sumburgh airport and there are airstrips at Baltasound, Scalsta and Tingwall. Two islands of the Shetland group not shown on the chartlet are Fair Isle (see overleaf), 20M SSW of Sumburgh Hd and owned by the NT for Scotland, and Foula (see below) 12M WSW of Mainland. There are LBs at Lerwick and Aith. The CG MRSC is at Lerwick ☎ (01595) 692976, with an Auxiliary Station (Watch & Rescue) at Fair Isle.

CHARTS AC: Med scale 3281, 3282, 3283; larger scale 3271, 3272, 3292, 3293, 3294, 3295, 3297, 3298; OS sheets 1-4.

TIDES Lerwick is the Standard Port. Tidal streams run mostly N/S or NW/SE and in open waters to the E and W are mostly weak. But rates >6kn can cause dangerous disturbances at the N and S extremities of the islands and in the two main sounds (Yell Sound and BlueMull/Colgrave Sounds). Keep 3M off Sumburgh Head to clear a dangerous race (roost) or pass close inshore.

SHELTER Weather conditions are bad in winter; yachts should only visit Apr – Sept. Around mid-summer it is day light H24. Some 12 small, non-commercial "marinas" are asterisked below; they are mostly full of local boats but supposedly each reserves 1 berth for visitors. Often only 1 boat lies between 2 fingers so that she can be held off by warps all round. Of the many ⚓s, the following are safe to enter in most weathers:

Mainland (anti-clockwise from Sumburgh Head)
GRUTNESS VOE*: 1·5M N of Sumburgh Hd, a convenient passage ⚓, open to NE. Beware 2 rks awash in mid-ent.
CAT FIRTH: excellent shelter, ⚓ in approx 6m. Facilities: ✉ (Skellister), FW, V (both at Lax Firth).
GRUNNA VOE: off S side of Dury Voe, good shelter and holding, ⚓ in 5-10m; beware prohib ⚓ areas. Facilities: V, FW, ✉ (Lax Firth).
WHALSAY*: FV hbr at Symbister. FW, D, V, ✉.
OUT SKERRIES*: Quay and ⚓ at Bruray. FW, D, V, ✉.
S OF YELL SOUND*: Tides –0025 on Lerwick. W of Lunna Ness, well-protected ⚓s with good holding include: Boatsroom Voe, W Lunna Voe (small hotel, FW), Colla Firth* (excellent pier) and Dales Voe. Facilities: none.
SULLOM VOE: tides –0130 on Lerwick. 6·5M long deep water voe, partly taken over by the oil industry. ⚓ S of the narrows. Facilities at Brae: FW, V, ✉, D, ME, El, Sh, Bar.
HAMNA VOE: Tides –0200 on Lerwick; very good shelter. Ldg line 153° old house on S shore with prominent rk on pt of W shore 3ca within ent. Almost land-locked; ⚓ in 6m approx, but bottom foul with old moorings. Facilities: ✉ (0·5M), Vs, D (1·5M), L (at pier).
URA FIRTH: NE of St Magnus Bay, ⚓ off Hills Wick on W side or in Hamar Voe on E side, which has excellent shelter in all weathers and good holding, but no facilities. Facilities: Hills Wick FW, ✉, D, ME, El, Sh, V, R, Bar.
OLNA FIRTH: NE of Swarbacks Minn, beware rk 1ca off S shore which dries. ⚓ in firth, 4-8m or in Gon Firth or go alongside pier at Voe. Facilities: (Voe) FW, V, D, ✉, Bar.
SWARBACKS MINN*: a large complex of voes and isles SE of St Magnus Bay. Best ⚓ Uyea Sound or Aith Voe*, both well sheltered and good holding. Facilities: former none; Aith FW, ✉, V, Bar, LB.
VAILA SOUND: on SW of Mainland, ent via Easter Sound (do not attempt Wester Sound); very good shelter, ⚓ N of Salt Ness in 4-5m in mud. See WALLS* overleaf: FW, V, ✉.
GRUTING VOE*: HW –0150 on Lerwick, ⚓ in main voe or in Seli, Scutta or Browland* voes. Facilities: V and ✉ at Bridge of Walls (hd of Browland Voe).

Yell. MID YELL VOE: tides –0040 on Lerwick, enter through S Sd or Hascosay Sd, good ⚓ in wide part of voe 2·5-10m. Facilities: ✉, FW at pier on S side, D, V, ME, Sh, El.
BASTA VOE: good ⚓ above shingle bank in 5-15m; good holding in places. Facilities: FW, V, Hotel, ✉.

BLUE MULL SND*: ⚓ at Cullivoe, pier and slip. D, FW, V.

Foula: Ham Voe on E side has tiny hbr/pier, unsafe in E'ly; berth clear of mailboat. Avoid Hoevdi Grund, 2M ESE.

NAVIGATION A careful lookout must be kept for salmon farming cages, over 100 in 1999 mostly marked by Y buoys and combinations of Y lts. The Clyde Cruising Club's *Shetland Sailing Directions and Anchorages* are essential for visitors. For general passage information see 9.7.5. Weather forecasting and the avoidance of wind-over-tide conditions assume yet more significance than elsewhere in the UK. Local magnetic anomalies may be experienced.
Note: There are two Historic Wrecks (*Kennemerland* and *Wrangels Palais*) on Out Skerries at 60°25'·2N 00°45'·0W and 60°25'·5N 00°43'·3W (see 9.0.3h).

LIGHTS AND MARKS See 9.7.4. Powerful lights show offshore from Fair Isle, Sumburgh Head, Kirkabister Ness, Bound Skerry, Muckle Flugga, Pt of Fethaland, Esha Ness and Foula.

RADIO TELEPHONE For Port Radio services see 9.7.26. There is no Coast Radio Station.

TELEPHONE (Dial code 01595; 01806 for Sullom Voe) MRSC 692976; Sullom Voe Port Control (01806) 242551; Weather 692239; Forecaster (01806) 242069; Sumburgh Airport (01950) 460654.

FACILITIES See SHELTER. All stores can be obtained in Lerwick and to a lesser extent in Scalloway. Elsewhere in Shetland there is little available and yachts should be well provisioned for extended offshore cruising.

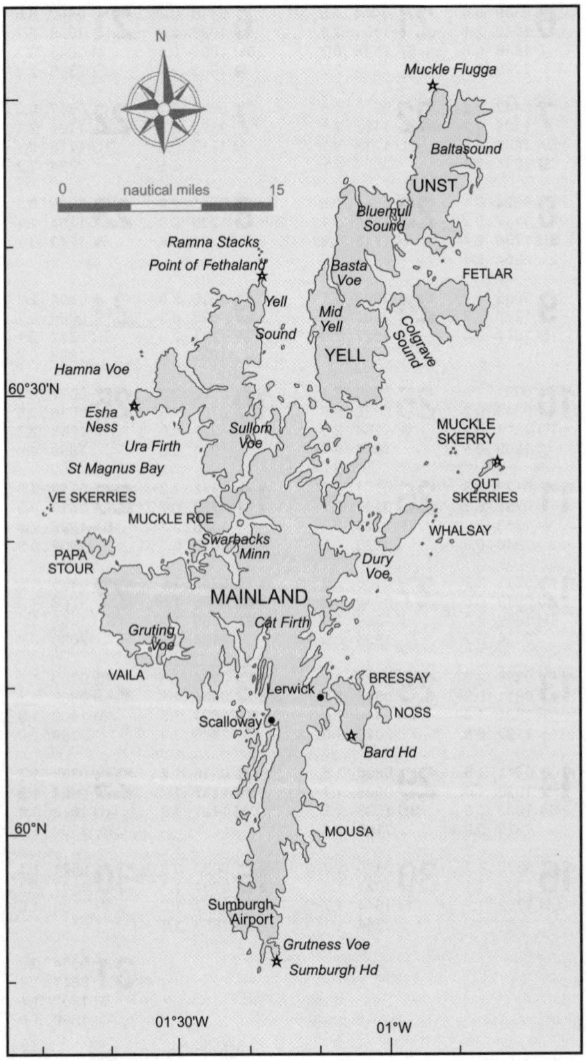

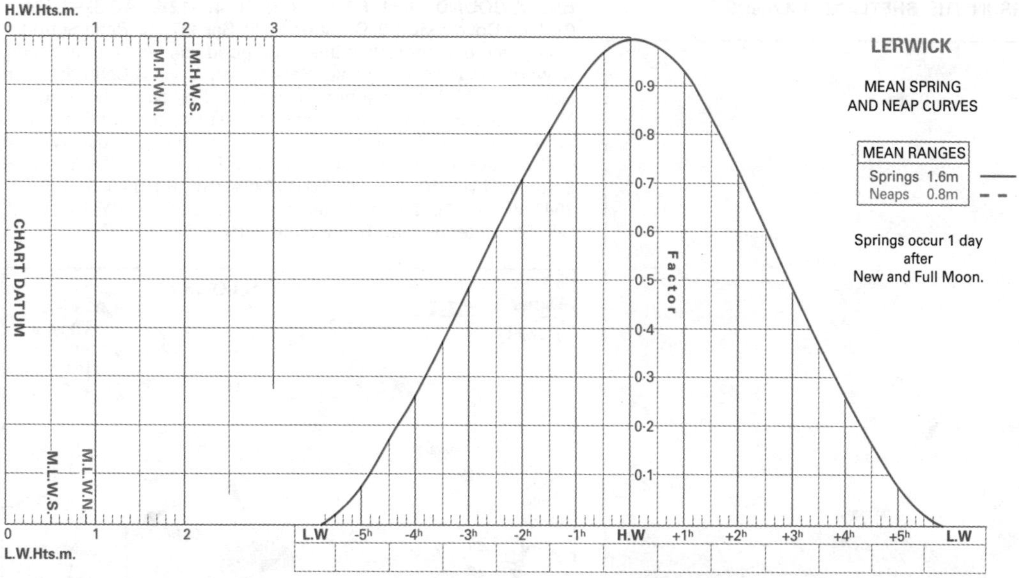

LERWICK *9.7.26*

Shetland Is, Mainland 60°09'·26N 01°08'·42W

CHARTS AC 3271, 3272, 3283; OS 4

TIDES –0001 Dover; ML 1·4; Duration 0620; Zone 0 (UT)

Standard Port LERWICK (←)

Times				Height (metres)			
High Water		Low Water		MHWS	MHWN	MLWN	MLWS
0000	0600	0100	0800	2·1	1·7	0·9	0·5
1200	1800	1300	2000				
Differences FAIR ISLE							
–0006	–0015	–0031	–0037	+0·1	0·0	+0·1	+0·1
SUMBURGH (Grutness Voe)							
+0006	+0008	+0004	–0002	–0·3	–0·3	–0·2	–0·1
DURY VOE							
–0015	–0015	–0010	–0010	0·0	–0·1	0·0	–0·2
BURRA VOE (YELL SOUND)							
–0025	–0025	–0025	–0025	+0·2	+0·1	0·0	–0·1
BALTA SOUND							
–0055	–0055	–0045	–0045	+0·2	+0·1	0·0	–0·1
BLUE MULL SOUND							
–0135	–0135	–0155	–0155	+0·5	+0·2	+0·1	0·0
SULLOM VOE							
–0135	–0125	–0135	–0120	0·0	0·0	–0·2	–0·2
HILLSWICK (URA FIRTH)							
–0220	–0220	–0200	–0200	–0·1	–0·1	–0·1	–0·1
SCALLOWAY							
–0150	–0150	–0150	–0150	–0·5	–0·4	–0·3	0·0
FOULA (23M West of Scalloway)							
–0140	–0130	–0140	–0120	–0·1	–0·1	0·0	0·0

SHELTER Good. Hr Mr allocates berths in Small Dock or Albert Dock. FVs occupy most alongside space. ⚓ prohib for about 2ca off the waterfront. Gremista marina in N hbr, is mainly for local boats, and is about 1M from the town.

NAVIGATION WPT 60°05'·97N 01°08'·62W, 190°/010° from/to Maryfield lt, 3·5M, in W sector. From S, Bressay Sound is clear of dangers. From N, WPT 60°11'·60N 01°07'·88W, 035°/215° from/to N ent Dir lt, 1·34M; lt Oc WRG 6s, W sector 214°-216°. Beware Soldian Rk (dries), Nive Baa (0·6m), Green Holm (10m) and The Brethren (two rks 2m and 1·5m).

LIGHTS AND MARKS Kirkabister Ness, Fl (2) 20s 32m 23M; Cro of Ham, Fl 3s 3M; Maryfield, Oc WRG 6s, W 008°-013°; all on Bressay. Twageos Pt, L Fl 6s 8m 6M. Loofa Baa SCM lt bn, as on chartlet. 2 SHM lt buoys mark Middle Ground in N Hbr.

RADIO TELEPHONE *Lerwick Harbour* VHF Ch **12** 11 16 (H24) for VTS, radar and information. Other stns: *Sullom Voe Hbr Radio* broadcasts traffic info and local forecasts on request Ch **14** 12 20 16 (H24).

TELEPHONE (Dial code 01595) Hr Mr 692991 Fax 695911; MRSC 692976; ⊖ 696166; Weather 692239; Police 692110; Dr 693201.

FACILITIES **Hbr** Slip, M, P, D, L, FW, ME, Sh, Gas; **Lerwick Hbr Trust** ☎ 692991, AB £0.50, M, FW, D, P, ♿ ramps/toilet; **Lerwick Boating Club** ☎ 692407, L, C, Bar, ⓘ; **Services:** ME, El, Ⓔ, Sh, Slip, BY, CH, SM, Gas, ACA. **Town** EC Wed (all day); V, R, Bar, ✉, Ⓑ, ⇌, (ferry to Aberdeen), ✈. www.shetland.news.co.uk.

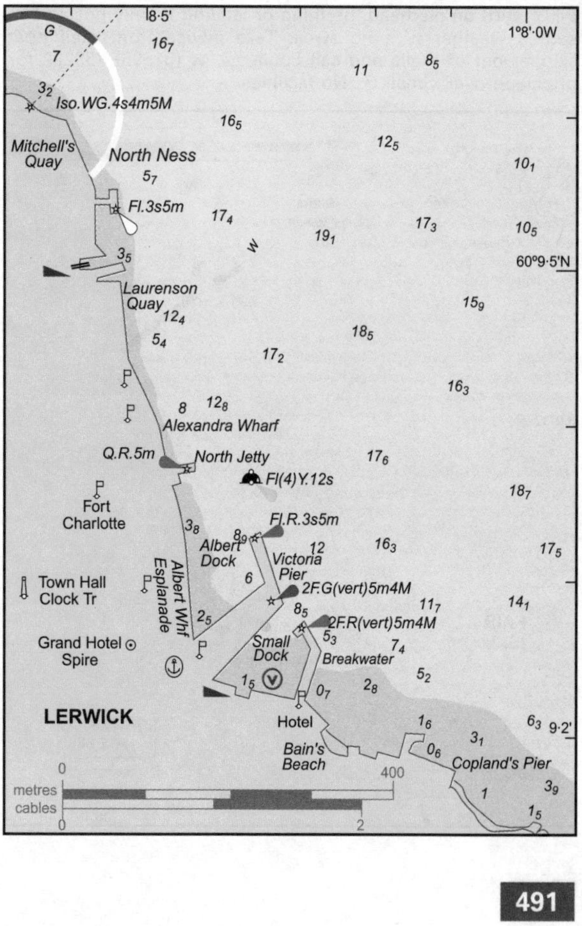

7

OTHER HARBOURS IN THE SHETLAND ISLANDS

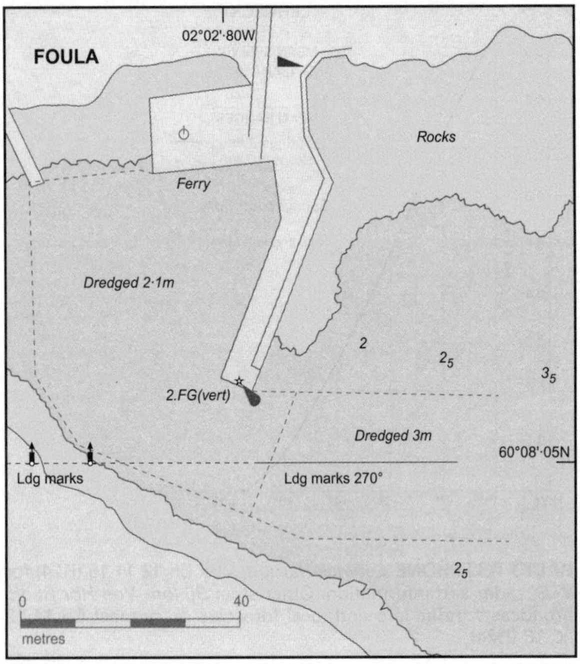

FOULA, Shetland Islands, **60°08'·02N 02°02'·92W** (Ham Voe). AC 3283. HW –0150 on Dover; ML 1·3m. See 9.7.26. Foula is 12M WSW of Mainland. Highest ground is 416m. S Ness lt ho, Fl (3) 15s, is at the S tip. Beware Foula Shoal (7·6m) and Hœvdi Grund (1·4m), respectively 4·3M E and 2M SE of Ham Voe.

Ham Voe is a narrow inlet on the E coast with a quay; rks on both sides. Two R ▲ ldg marks, approx 270°, are hard to see. ☆ 2 FG (vert) on pierhead. Berthing or landing is only possible in settled weather with no swell. Take advice from mail boat skipper out of Walls and call Foula ✉, ☎ (01595) 753222 for prior approval. Small ✈. No facilities.

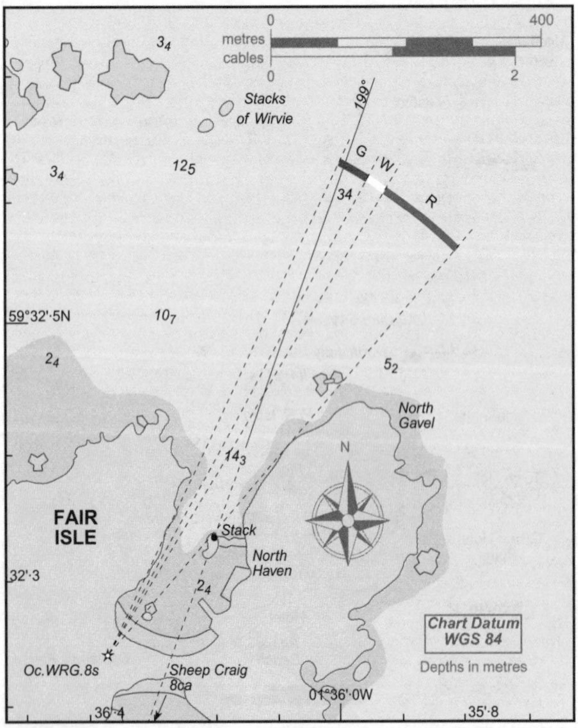

BALTA SOUND, Unst, **60°44'·32N 00°48'·12W**. AC 3293. HW –0105 on Dover; ML 1·3; Duration 0640. See 9.7.26. Balta Sound is a large almost landlocked inlet with good shelter from all winds. Beware bad holding on kelp. Safest entry is via S Chan between Huney Is and Balta Is; inner chan marked by two PHM lt buoys. N Chan is deep but narrow; keep to Unst shore. ⚓ off Sandisons Wharf (2FG vert) in approx 6m or enter marina close W (one visitor's berth, very shallow); jetty has Fl R 6s 2m 2M. S end of Balta Is, Fl WR 10s 17m 10/7M, W249°–010°, R010°–060°, W060°–154°. VHF Ch 16; 20 (HO or as required). Facilities: BY, FW, D, El, ME, Sh; Hotel by pier. **Baltasound village**, Bar, R, V, ✉.

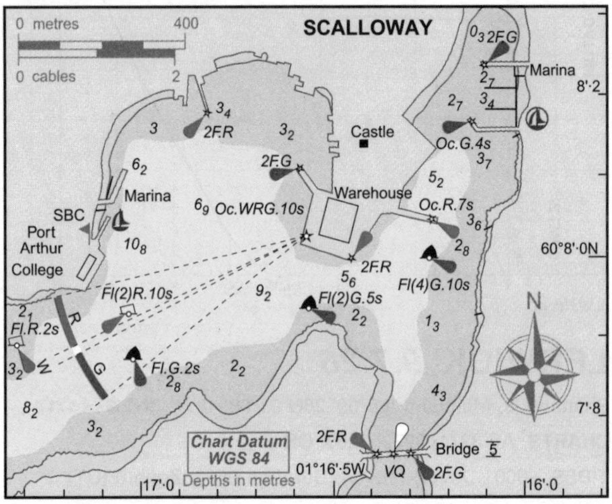

SCALLOWAY, Mainland, **60°08'·02N 01°16'·59W**. AC 3294. HW –0200 on Dover; ML 0·9m; Duration 0620. See 9.7.26. A busy fishing port; good shelter and ⚓ in all weathers. Care is needed negotiating the islands in strong SW'lies. The N Chan is easier and safer than the S Chan, both are well lit and marked. Castle and warehouse (both conspic) lead 054° through S Chan. Dir Oc WRG 10s on hbr quay leads 064·5° into hbr. Hbr lts as chartlet. ❶ pontoon in 3m off SBC is best option; marina close N or new marina in E Voe (though mostly full of local boats. ⚓s in hbr 6 -10m or in Hamna Voe (W Burra). Call *Scalloway Hbr Radio* VHF Ch **12** 09 16 (Mon-Fri 0600-1800; Sat 0600-1230LT). Piermaster ☎ (01595) 880574 (H24). **Facilities: Scalloway Boat Club** (SBC) ☎ 880409 welcomes visitors; AB (free), Bar. **Town** EC Thurs; Slip, P, D, FW, SM, BY, CH, C, El, ME, Sh, ✉, R, V, Bar.

VAILA SOUND (WALLS), Mainland, **60°13'·65N 01°33'·87W**. AC 3295. Tides approx as Scalloway (above); see 9.7.26. Appr to E of Vaila island (do not attempt Wester Sound) in the W sector (355°-012°) of Rams Head lt, Fl WRG 8s 16m 9/6M. Gruting Voe lies to the NE. Enter Easter Sound and go N for 1·5M, passing E of Linga islet, to Walls at the head of Vaila Voe. Navigate by echo sounder. Beware fish farms. Temp'y AB on Bayhaa pier (covers). Close E of this, AB £1 on pontoon of Peter Georgeson **marina**; Sec ☎ (01595) 809273, FW. **Walls Regatta Club** welcomes visitors; showers, Bar, Slip. **Village**: P & D (cans), V, ✉.

FAIR ISLE, Shetland Islands, **59°32'·37N 01°36'·21W** (North Haven). AC 2622. HW –0030 on Dover; ML 1·4m; Duration 0620. See 9.7.26 Good shelter in North Haven, except in NE winds. AB on pier or ⚓ in approx 2m. Beware strong cross-tides in the apprs; beware also rocks all round Fair Isle, particularly in S Haven and South Hbr which are not recommended. Ldg marks 199° into North Haven: front, Stack of N Haven (only visible as a dark "tooth" sticking up from the jumble of blocks which form the bkwtr) in transit with conspic summit of Sheep Craig (rear). Dir lt, 209·5° into N Haven, Oc WRG 8s 10m 6M, vis G204°-208°, W208°- 211°, R211°-221°. Other lts: At N tip, Skroo Fl (2) 30s 80m **22**M, vis 086·7°–358°, Horn (3) 45s. At S tip, Skadan Fl (4) 30s 32m **22**M, vis 260°–146°, but obscd close inshore from 260°–282°, Horn (2) 60s. **Facilities**: V, ✉ at N Shriva, ✈ and a bi-weekly mail boat ("Good Shepherd") to Shetland.

MAPTECH®
Leading the world in digital navigation
Maptech UK Ltd • +44 (0)1243 389352 • sales@maptech.co.uk

Maptech world class digital chart CDs
Worldwide coverage from over 4,500 charts

Maptech award winning software
Easy to use navigation software
• Chart Navigator • Cruising Navigator • Offshore Navigator

www.maptech.co.uk

Area 8

North-West Scotland
Cape Wrath to Crinan Canal

9.8.1 Index .... Page 493

9.8.2 Area map 494

9.8.3 Tidal stream charts 496

9.8.4 Lights, buoys & waypoints 498

9.8.5 Passage information 502

9.8.6 Distance table 503

9.8.7 Stornoway, Standard Port 504
- Loch Shell (Lewis)
- Shiant Islands
- E Loch Tarbert (Harris)
- Sound of Harris
- N Uist: Loch Maddy, Loch Eport
- S Uist: Loch Carnan,
- Loch Skipport, Loch Eynort,
- Loch Boisdale
- Acairseid Mhór (Eriskay)
- North Bay, Castlebay (Barra)
- Loch Rodall
- Kallin
- Flannan, St Kilda, Rockall and Monach Islands

9.8.8 Kinlochbervie 510
- Loch Laxford, Loch Inver

9.8.9 Ullapool, StMandard Port 511
- Summer Isles
- Loch Ewe
- Loch Gairloch

9.8.10 Portree 515
- Loch Torridon
- Loch A'Bhraige (Rona)
- Acairseid Mhór
- Around Skye:
  - Loch Dunvegan
  - Loch Harport
  - Soay, Armadale Bay, Crowlin Islands

9.8.11 Plockton 516
- Loch Carron

9.8.12 Loch Alsh 516
- Kyle of Lochalsh
- Kyleakin
- Sound of Sleat
- Loch Hourn
- Loch Nevis

9.8.13 Mallaig 517
- Small Islands:
  - Canna
  - Rhum
  - Eigg
  - Muck
  - Arisaig

9.8.14 Loch Sunart 518
- Arinagour (Coll)
- Gott Bay (Tiree)

9.8.15 Tobermory 519
- Sound of Mull
- Craignure

9.8.16 Loch Aline 519
- Around Mull:
  - Treshnish Isles
  - Staffa, Gometra
  - Loch na Keal
  - Loch Lathaich
  - Sound of Iona
  - Tinker's Hole
  - Carsaig Bay
  - Loch Spelve

9.8.17 Fort William/Corpach 520
- Lynn of Lorn
- Loch Creran
- Loch Leven
- Corran Narrows

9.8.18 Caledonian Canal 521

9.8.19 Oban, Standard Port 525
- Dunstaffnage Bay
- Loch Etive
- Loch Feochan
- Puilladobhrain
- Cuan Sound

9.8.20 Loch Melfort 527
- Ardinamar

9.8.21 Craobh Marina (Loch Shuna) 528

9.8.22 Loch Craignish 528

9.8.23 Submarine exercise areas 529

9.8.24 Ferries on the West coast 529

Register for your FREE weekly weather email service from Macmillan Reeds
at www.nauticaldata.com – NOW!
weekend weather reports sent to your email address, every Thursday

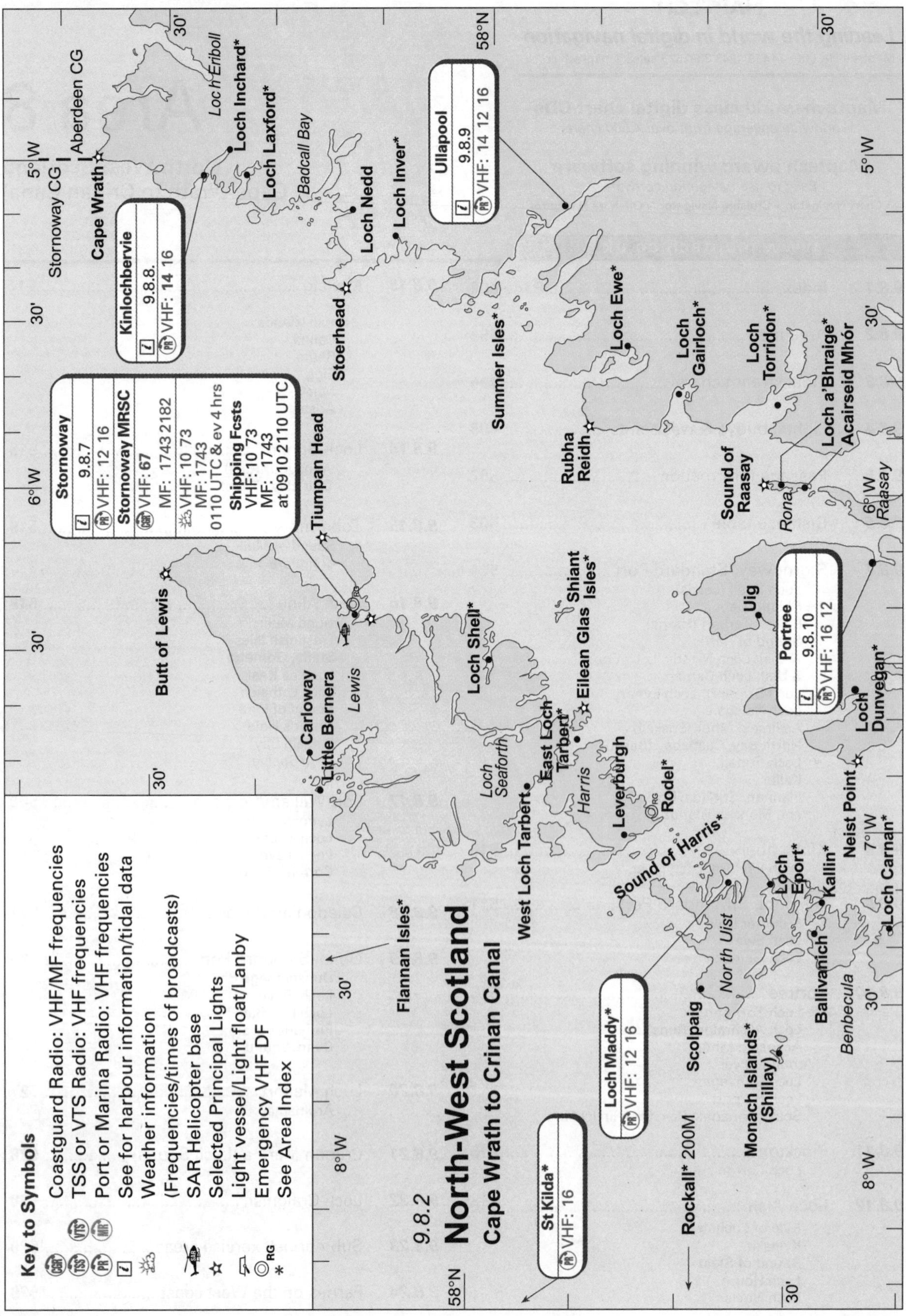
Key to Symbols
CGR Coastguard Radio: VHF/MF frequencies
TSS VTS TSS or VTS Radio: VHF frequencies
PR MR Port or Marina Radio: VHF frequencies
See for harbour information/tidal data
Weather information
(Frequencies/times of broadcasts)
SAR Helicopter base
Selected Principal Lights
Light vessel/Light float/Lanby
RG Emergency VHF DF
* See Area Index
9.8.2
North-West Scotland
Cape Wrath to Crinan Canal
St Kilda*
VHF: 16
Loch Maddy*
VHF: 12 16
Rockall* 200M
Flannan Isles*
Stornoway CG
Aberdeen CG
Cape Wrath
Kinlochbervie
9.8.8.
VHF: 14 16
Loch Eriboll
Loch Inchard*
Loch Laxford*
Badcall Bay
Loch Nedd
Loch Inver*
Ullapool
9.8.9
VHF: 14 12 16
Stornoway
9.8.7
VHF: 12 16
Stornoway MRSC
VHF: 67
MF: 1743 2182
VHF: 10 73
MF: 1743
0110 UTC & ev 4 hrs
Shipping Fcsts
VHF: 10 73
MF: 1743
at 0910 2110 UTC
Butt of Lewis
Tiumpan Head
Stoerhead
Summer Isles*
Loch Ewe*
Rubha Reidh
Loch Gairloch*
Loch Torridon*
Sound of Raasay
Rona
Raasay
Loch a'Bhraige*
Acairseid Mhór
Carloway
Little Bernera
Lewis
Loch Shell*
Shiant Isles*
Eilean Glas
East Loch Tarbert*
Loch Seaforth
Harris
Leverburgh
Rodel*
West Loch Tarbert
Sound of Harris*
Uig
Portree
9.8.10
VHF: 16 12
Loch Dunvegan*
Neist Point
Loch Eport*
Kallin*
Ballivanich
Loch Carnan*
North Uist
Scolpaig
Monach Islands* (Shillay)
Benbecula
58°N
5° W
6° W
7° W
8° W
30'

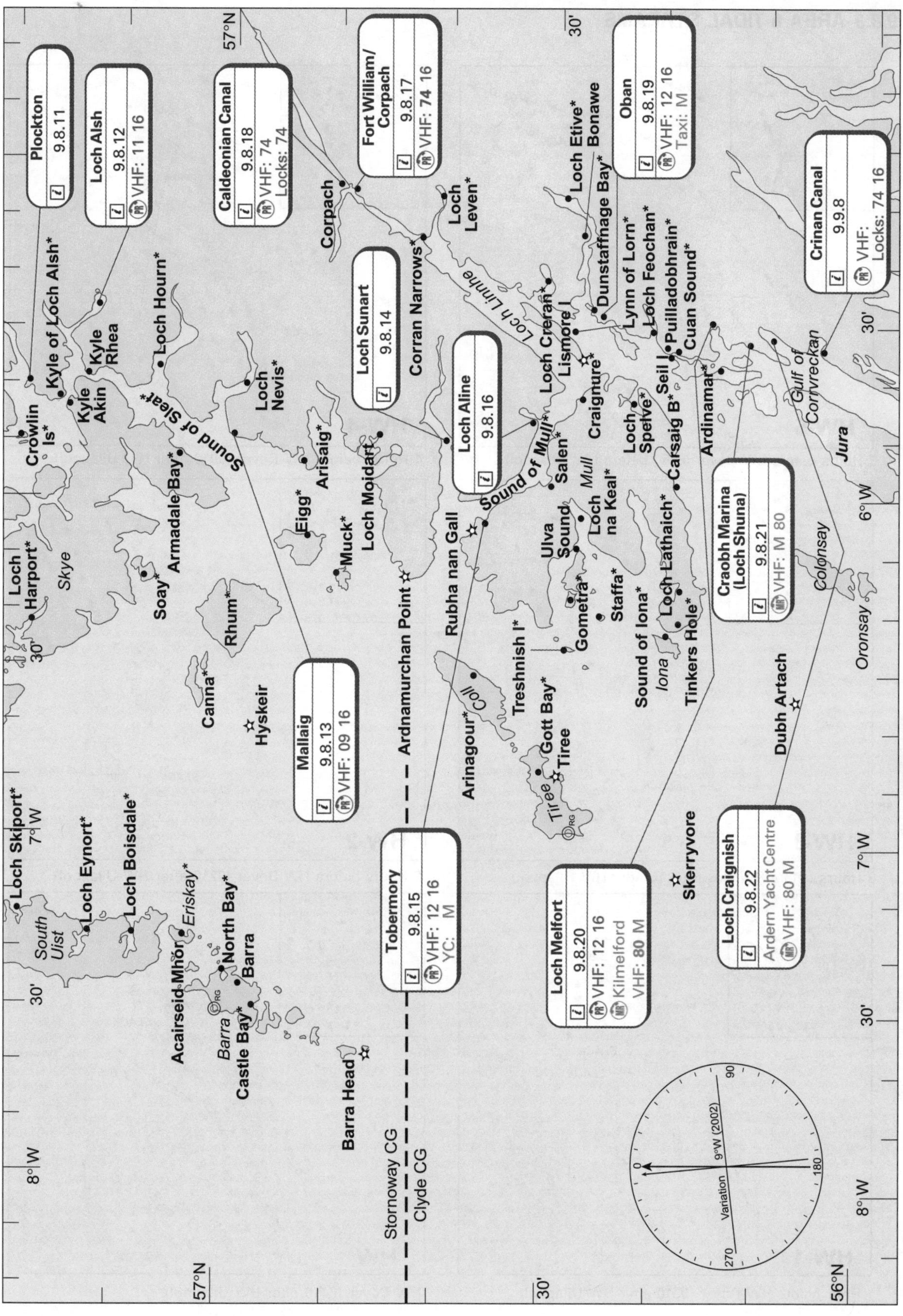

Plockton
9.8.11
Loch Alsh
9.8.12
VHF: 11 16
Caldeonian Canal
9.8.18
VHF: 74
Locks: 74
Fort William/ Corpach
9.8.17
VHF: 74 16
Oban
9.8.19
VHF: 12 16
Taxi: M
Crinan Canal
9.9.8
VHF:
Locks: 74 16
Loch Sunart
9.8.14
Loch Aline
9.8.16
Mallaig
9.8.13
VHF: 09 16
Tobermory
9.8.15
VHF: 12 16
YC: M
Loch Melfort
9.8.20
VHF: 12 16
Kilmelford
VHF: 80 M
Craobh Marina (Loch Shuna)
9.8.21
VHF: M 80
Loch Craignish
9.8.22
Ardern Yacht Centre
VHF: 80 M
Crowlin Is*
Kyle of Loch Alsh*
Kyle Akin
Kyle Rhea
Loch Hourn*
Sound of Sleat*
Loch Nevis*
Corpach
Loch Leven*
Corran Narrows*
Loch Linnhe
Loch Etive*
Bonawe
Dunstaffnage Bay*
Lynn of Lorn*
Loch Feochan*
Puilladobhrain*
Cuan Sound*
Loch Creran*
Lismore I
Craignure*
Seil I
Loch Spelve*
Carsaig B*
Ardinamar*
Gulf of Corryvreckan
Jura
Loch Harport*
Skye
Armadale Bay*
Soay*
Rhum*
Canna*
Hyskeir
Eigg*
Arisaig*
Muck*
Loch Moidart
Ardnamurchan Point
Rubha nan Gall
Sound of Mull*
Salen*
Mull
Loch na Keal*
Ulva Sound
Gometra*
Staffa*
Treshnish I*
Coll
Arinagour*
Gott Bay*
Tiree
Sound of Iona*
Iona
Loch Lathaich*
Tinkers Hole*
Colonsay
Oronsay
Dubh Artach
Skerryvore
Loch Skiport*
Loch Eynort*
Loch Boisdale*
South Uist
Eriskay*
North Bay*
Barra
Acairseid Mhòr
Castle Bay*
Barra Head
Stornoway CG
Clyde CG
Variation
9°W (2002)
0
90
180
270
57°N
56°N
30'
8°W
7°W
6°W

9.8.3 AREA 8 TIDAL STREAMS

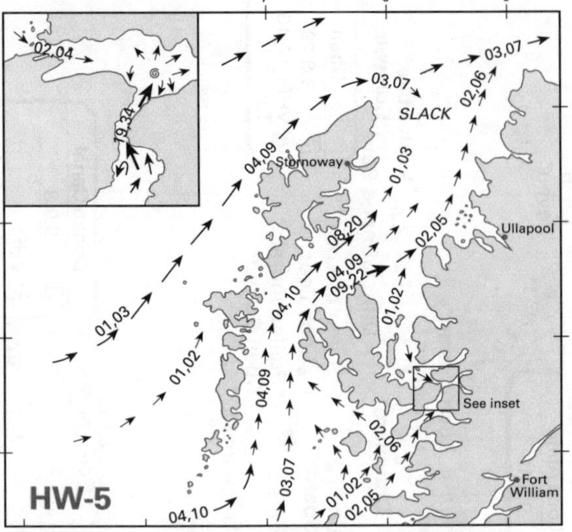

5 Hours before HW Dover (0050 before HW Ullapool)

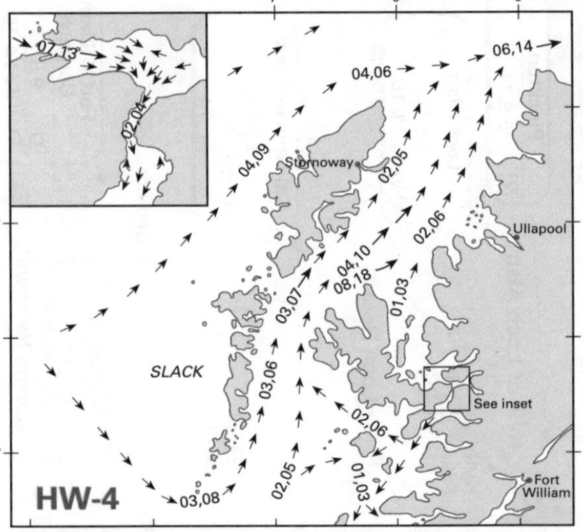

4 Hours before HW Dover (0010 after HW Ullapool)

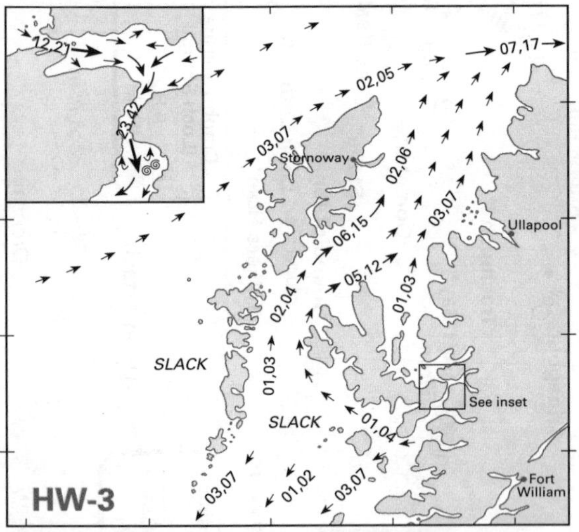

3 Hours before HW Dover (0110 after HW Ullapool)

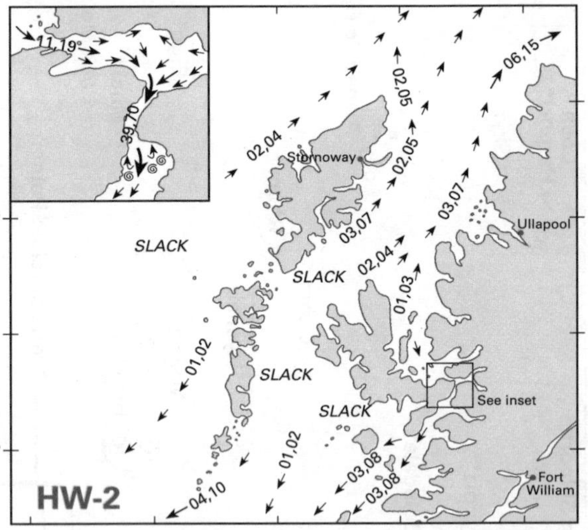

2 Hours before HW Dover (0210 after HW Ullapool)

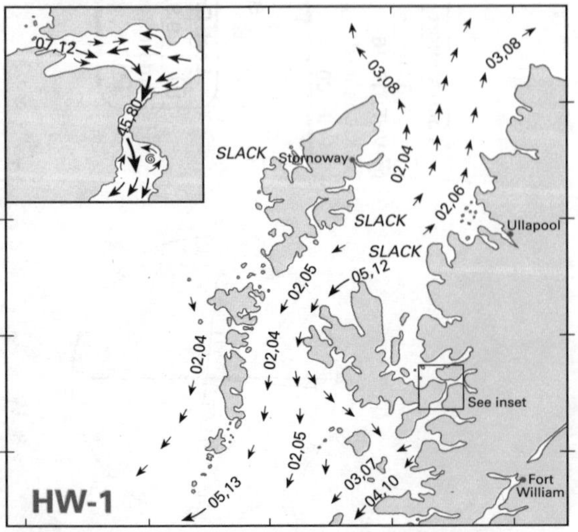

1 Hour before HW Dover (0310 after HW Ullapool)

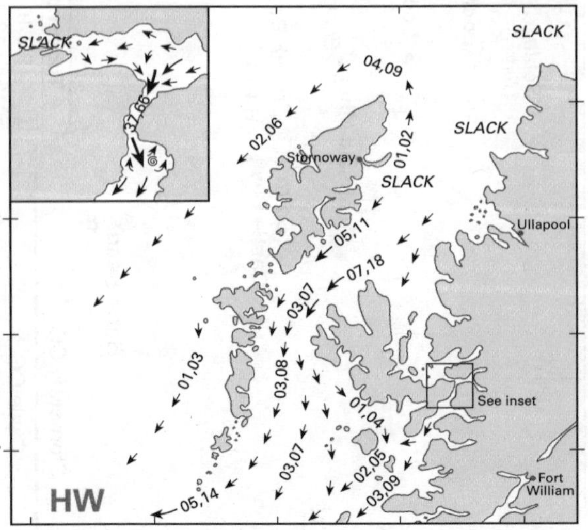

HW Dover (0410 after HW Ullapool)

Eastward 9.7.3   Southward 9.9.3   Mull of Kintyre 9.9.12

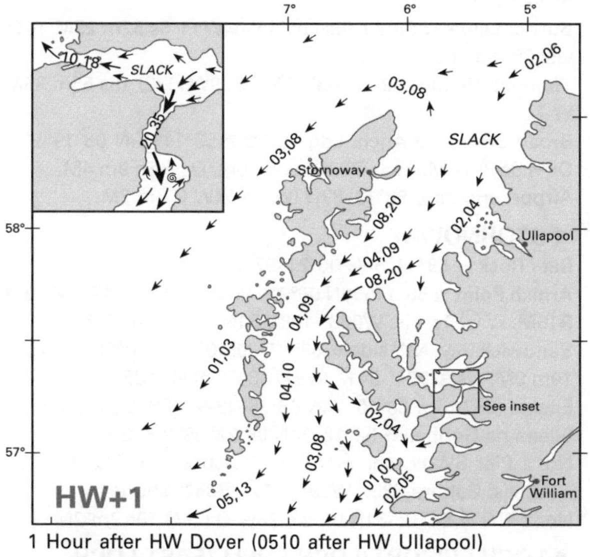

1 Hour after HW Dover (0510 after HW Ullapool)

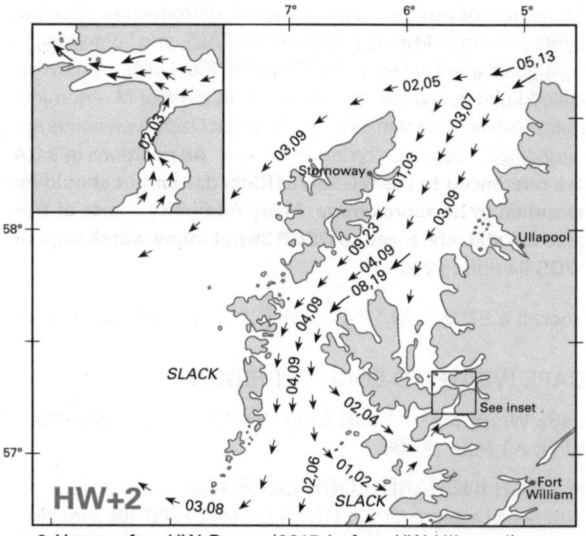

2 Hours after HW Dover (0615 before HW Ullapool)

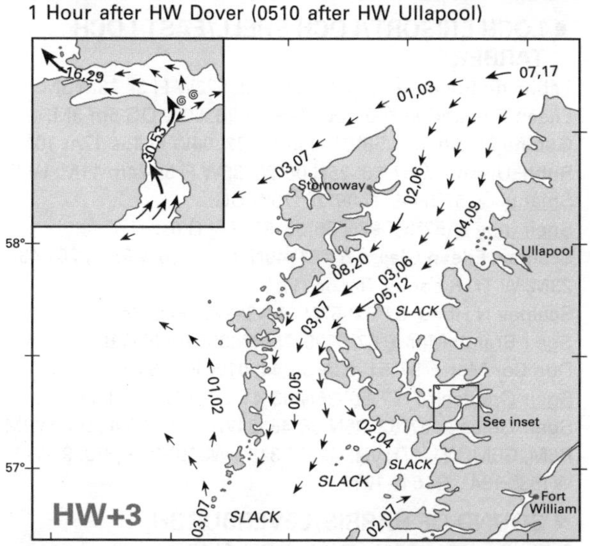

3 Hours after HW Dover (0515 before HW Ullapool)

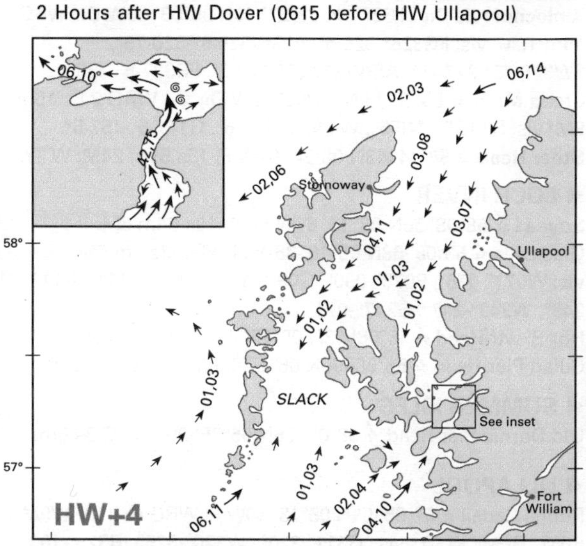

4 Hours after HW Dover (0415 before HW Ullapool)

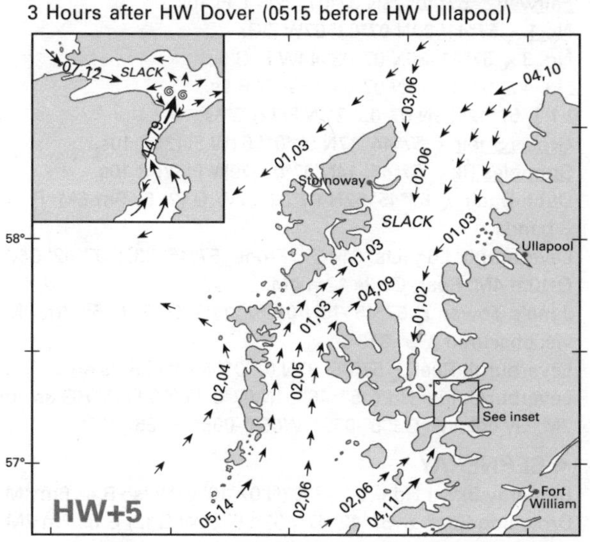

5 Hours after HW Dover (0315 before HW Ullapool)

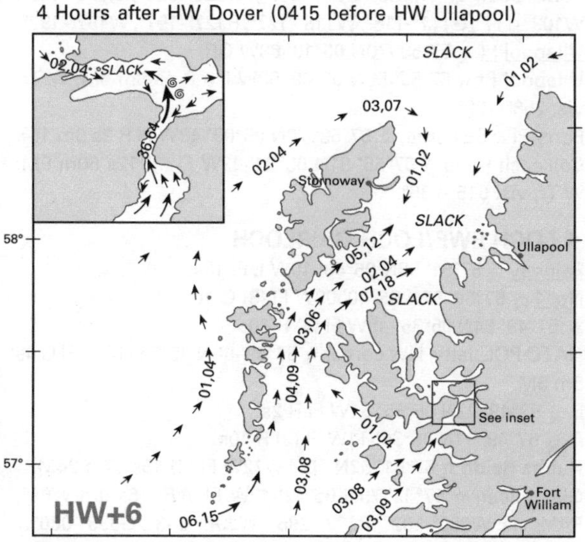

6 Hours after HW Dover (0215 before HW Ullapool)

9.8.4 LIGHTS, BUOYS AND WAYPOINTS

Abbreviations used below are given in the Introduction. Principal lights ☆ are in **bold** print, places in CAPITALS, and light-vessels, light floats and Lanbys in *CAPITAL ITALICS*. Unless otherwise stated lights are white. m – elevation in metres; M – nominal range in miles. Fog signals are in *italics*. Useful waypoints are underlined – use those on land with care. **All positions in 9.8.4 are referenced to the WGS84/ETRS89 datum but should be assumed to be approximate. Many Admiralty charts of this area are still referenced to OSGB 36 but many will change to WGS 84 during 2001.**

Rockall 57°35'·76N 13°41'·27W Fl 15s 19m 8M (unreliable).

CAPE WRATH TO LOCH TORRIDON

Cape Wrath ☆ 58°37'·54N 04°59'·99W Fl (4) 30s 122m **22M**; W Tr; *Horn (3) 45s*.

◀ LOCH INCHARD/LOCH LAXFORD

Rubha na Lecaig 58°27'·41N 05°04'·58W Fl (2) 10s 30m 8M.
Kinlochbervie Dir Lt 327° ☆. 58°27'·49N 05°03'·08W Dir WRG 15m **16M**; vis: FG326°-326·5°, AlGW326·5°-326·75°, FW326·75°-327·25°, AlRW327·25°-327·5°, FR327·5°-328°.
Creag Mhòr 58°26'·99N 05°02'·45W Dir Oc WRG 2·8s 16m 9M; vis: R136·5°-146·5°, W146·5°-147·5°, G147·5°-157·5°.
Stoer Head ☆ 58°14'·43N 05°24'·07W Fl 15s 59m **24M**; W Tr.

◀ LOCH INVER

Soyea I 58°08'·56N 05°19'·67W Fl (2) 10s 34m 6M.
Glas Leac 58°08'·68N 05°16'·36W Fl WRG 3s 7m 5M; vis: W071°-078°, R078°-090°, G090°-103°, W103°-111°, R111°-243°, W243°-247°, G247°-071°.
Hbr Bkwtr Head 58°08'·93N 05°15'·08W QG 3m 1M.
Culag Pier Head 58°08'·90N 05°14'·89W 2 FG (vert) 6m.

◀ SUMMER ISLES

Old Dornie Pier Head 58°02'·56N 05°25'·39W Fl G 3s 5m.

◀ ULLAPOOL

Rubha Cadail 57°55'·51N 05°13'·40W Fl WRG 6s 11m W9M, R6M, G6M; W Tr; vis: G311°-320°, W320°-325°, R325°-103°, W103°-111°, G111°-118°, W118°-127°, R127°-157°, W157°-199°.
Ullapool Pt 57°53'·70N 05°10'·68W QR.
Ullapool Pt 57°53'·59N 05°09'·93W Iso R 4s 8m 6M; W Tr; vis: 258°-108°.
Ferry Pier SE corner 57°53'·70N 05°09'·43W Fl R 3s 6m 1M.
Cailleach Head 57°55'·81N 05°24'·23W Fl (2) 12s 60m 9M; W Tr; vis: 015°-236°.

◀ LOCH EWE/LOCH GAIRLOCH

Fairway 57°51'·98N 05°40'·10W L Fl 10s.
No. 1 57°50'·97N 05°40'·09W Fl (3) G 10s.
57°49'·84N 05°35'·49W Fl (4) R 10s.
NATO POL Jetty, NW corner 57°49'·66N 05°35'·12W Fl G 4s 5m 3M.
E 57°49'·42N 05°35'·51W Fl R 2s.
D 57°49'·11N 05°36'·11W Fl (2) R 10s.
Rubha Reidh ☆ 57°51'·52N 05°48'·72W Fl (4) 15s 37m 24M.
Glas Eilean 57°42'·79N 05°42'·42W Fl WRG 6s 9m W6M, R4M; vis: W080°-102°, R102°-296°, W296°-333°, G333°-080°.
Gairloch Pier 57°42'·59N 05°41'·03W QR 6m 2M; occas.

OUTER HEBRIDES – EAST SIDE

◀ LEWIS

Butt of Lewis ☆ 58°30'·89N 06°15'·84W Fl 5s 52m **25M**; R Tr; vis: 056°-320°.
Tiumpan Head ☆ 58°15'·66N 06°08'·29W Fl (2) 15s 55m **25M**; W Tr.
Broad Bay Tong Anch. Ldg Lts 320° 58°14'·48N 06°19'·98W Oc R 8s 8m 4M. Rear, 70m from front, Oc R 8s 9m 4M.
Airport app lts 58°13'·87N 06°20'·04W Q 3m 2M.

◀ STORNOWAY

Reef Rock 58°11'·58N 06°21'·97W QR.
Arnish Point ☆ 58°11'·50N 06°22'·16W Fl WR 10s 17m **W19M, R15M**; W ○ Tr; vis: W088°-198°, R198°-302°, W302°-013°.
Sandwick Bay, NW side 58°12'·20N 06°22'·11W Oc WRG 6s 10m 9M; vis: G334°-341°, W341°-347°, R347°-354°.
Eitshal (367m) 58°10'·74N 06°35'·13W 4 FR (vert) on mast.
Eilean na Gobhail 58°12'·14N 06°22'·99W Fl G 6s 8m.
No. 1 Pier SW corner 58°12'·36N 06°23'·43W Q WRG 5m 11M; vis: Gshore-335°, W335°-352°, R352°-shore.
No. 3 Pier 58°12'·31N 06°23'·28W Q (2) G 10s 7m 2M.

◀ LOCH ERISORT/LOCH SHELL/EAST LOCH TARBERT

Tabhaidh Bheag 58°07'·19N 06°23'·22W Fl 3s 13m 3M.
Eilean Chalabrigh 58°06'·79N 06°26'·69W QG 5m 3M.
Gob na Milaid Pt 58°01'·08N 06°22'·04W Fl 15s 17m 10M.
Rubh' Uisenis 57°56'·25N 06°28'·36W Fl 5s 24m 11M; W Tr.
Shiants 57°54'·57N 06°25'·70W QG.
Sgeir Inoe 57°50'·92N 06°33'·95W Fl G 6s.
Scalpay, **Eilean Glas** ☆ 57°51'·40N 06°38'·55W Fl (3) 20s 43m **23M**; W Tr, R bands; Racon (T).
Scalpay N Hbr 57°52'·57N 06°42'·22W Fl G 2s.
Sgeir Bràigh Mor 57°51'·51N 06°43'·84W Fl G 6s.
Dun Cor Mòr 57°51'·03N 06°44'·01W Fl R 5s 10m 5M.
Sgeir Graidach 57°50'·36N 06°41'·37W Q (6) + L Fl 15s.
Sgeir Ghlas 57°52'·36N 06°45'·24W Iso WRG 4s 9m W9M, R6M, G6M; W ○ Tr; vis: G282°-319°, W319°-329°, R329°-153°, W153°-164°, G164°-171°.

◀ SOUND OF HARRIS/LEVERBURGH

Fairway 57°40'·23N 07°01'·39W L Fl 10s.
No.1 57°41'·20N 07°02'·67W QG.
No. 3 57°41'·86N 07°03'·44W Fl G 5s.
No. 4 57°41'·76N 07°03'·63W Fl R 5s.
L1 57°42'·59N 07°03'·21W Fl (2) G 5s.
Grocis Sgeir 57°44'·17N 07°01'·51W Fl (3) R 10s.
Stumbles Rk 57°45'·14N 07°01'·79W Fl (2) R 10s.
Dubh Sgeir 57°45'·52N 07°02'·62W Q (2) 5s 9m 6M; R Tr, B bands.
Leverburgh Ldg Lts 014·7°. Front, 57°46'·23N 07°02'·04W Q 10m 4M. Rear, Oc 3s 12m 4M.
Jane's Tower 57°45'·76N 07°02'·12W Q (2) G 5s 6m 4M; vis: obscured 273°-318°.
Leverburgh Reef 57°45'·97N 07°01'·86W Fl R 2s 4m.
Leverburgh Pier Hd 57°46'·01N 07°01'·62W Oc WRG 8s 5m 2M; Gy col; vis: G305°-059°, W059°-066°, R066°-125°.

◀ BERNERAY

Berneray Bkwtr Hd 57°42'·87N 07°10'·07W Iso R 4s 6m 4M.
Drowning Rock 57°42'·47N 07°09'·34W Q (2) G 8s 2m 2M.
BA3 57°41'·74N 07°08'·14W Fl (2) R.

BA4 57°42'·33N 07°09'·59W Q (3) 10s.
Reef Chan No. 1 57°42'·93N 07°09'·11W QG 2m 4M.
Reef Chan No. 2 57°42'·96N 07°09'·09W Iso G 4s 2m 4M.

◀ NORTH UIST

Fairway 57°40'·23N 07°01'·39W L Fl 10s.
No.1 57°41'·20N 07°02'·67W QG.
No. 3 57°41'·86N 07°03'·44W Fl G 5s.
No. 4 57°41'·76N 07°03'·63W Fl R 5s.
NF 3 57°41'·47N 07°06'·68W Fl G 10s.
NF 6 57°41'·57N 07°08'·03W Fl R.
Eilean Fuam 57°41'·93N 07°10'·69W Q 6m 2M; W col.
Newton Jetty Root 57°41'·54N 07°11'·63W 2 FG (vert) 9m 4M.
Vallay Island 57°39'·69N 07°26'·42W Fl WRG 3s 4m 8M; vis: W206°-085°, G085°-140°, W140°-145°, R145°-206°.
Griminish Hbr Ldg Lts 183°. Front, 57°39'·38N 07°26'·75W QG 6m 4M. Rear, 110m from front, QG 7m 4M.
Pier Hd 57°39'·26N 07°26'·36W 2 FG (vert) 6m 4M; Gy col.

◀ LOCH MADDY

Weaver's Pt 57°36'·49N 07°06'·00W Fl 3s 21m 7M; W hut.
Glas Eilean Mòr 57°35'·95N 07°06'·70W Fl G 4s 8m 5M.
Rubna Nam Pleàc 57°35'·76N 07°06'·76W Fl R 4s 7m 5M.
Ruigh Liath E Islet 57°35'·72N 07°08'·42W QG 6m 5M.
Vallaquie I 57°35'·50N 07°09'·40W Fl (3) WRG 8s 11m W7M, R5M, G5M; W pillar; vis: G shore-205°, W205°-210°, R210°-240°, G240°-254°, W254°-257°, R257°-shore (P).
Lochmaddy Ldg Lts 298°. Front, Ro-Ro Pier 57°35'·76N 07°09'·36W 2 FG (vert) 8m 4M. Rear, 110m from front, Oc G 8s 10m 4M; vis: 284°-304°.
57°35'·92N 07°08'·68W Fl R 3s 4M.

◀ GRIMSAY

No. 1 57°28'·26N 07°11'·82W Fl (2) R 8°s.
No. 2 57°28'·62N 07°11'·80W Fl R 5s.
No. 3 57°28'·71N 07°11'·84W Fl G 2s.
Kallin Harbour Bkwtr NE corner, 57°28'·88N 07°12'·31W 2 FR (vert) 6m 5M; Gy col.

◀ SOUTH UIST, LOCH CARNAN

Landfall 57°22'·30N 07°11'·45W L Fl 10s.
No. 1 57°22'·42N 07°14'·93W Fl G 2·5s.
No. 2 57°22'·39N 07°14'·93W Fl R 2s.
No. 3 57°22'·31N 07°15'·60W Fl R 5s.
No. 4 57°22'·25N 07°15'·88W QR.
No. 2 57°22'·11N 07°16'·19W QG.
Ldg Lts 222°. Front 57°22'·00N 07°16'·34W Fl R 2s 7m 5M; W ◊ on post. Rear, 58m from front, Iso R 10s 11m 5M; W ◊ on post.
Ushenish ☆ (S Uist) 57°17'·89N 07°11'·58W Fl WR 20s 54m **W19M, R15M**; W Tr; vis: W193°-356°, R356°-018°.

◀ LOCH BOISDALE

McKenzie Rk 57°08'·24N 07°13'·71W Fl (3) R 15s.
Calvay E End 57°08'·53N 07°15'·38W Fl (2) WRG 10s 16m W7M, R4M, G4M; W Tr; vis: W111°-190°, G190°-202°, W202°-286°, R286°-111°.
N side 57°08'·99N 07°16'·98W Fl G 6s 3m 3M.
Eilean Dubh 57°09'·07N 07°18'·18W Fl (2) R 5s 2m 3M.
Gasay I 57°08'·93N 07°17'·39W Fl WR 5s 10m W7M, R4M; W Tr; vis: W120°-284°, R284°-120°.
Gasay Spar 57°09'·02N 07°17'·45W QG 4m 5M.
Sgeir Rock 57°09'·09N 07°17'·76W Fl G 3s.
Eilean Dubh 57°09'·07N 07°18'·18W Fl (2) R 5s 2m 3M.

Ro-Ro Jetty Head 57°09'·12N 07°18'·22W Iso RG 4s 8m 2M; vis: Gshore-283°, R283°-shore; 2 FG (vert) 8m 3M on dn.

◀ LUDAIG

The Witches 57°05'·72N 07°20'·84W Fl R 5s.
Off Ludaig 57°05'·94N 07°19'·56W.
Ludaig Pier 57°06'·18N 07°19'·42W 2 FG (vert) 5m 3M.

◀ ERISKAY

Bank Rk 57°05'·56N 07°17'·60W Q (2) 4s 5m 4M.
Pier 2 FG (vert) 5m 5M.
Acairseid Mhor Ldg Lts 285°. Front, 57°03'·88N 07°17'·24W Oc R 6s 9m 4M. Rear, 24m from front, Oc R 6s 10m 4M.
57°03'·89N 07°17'·10W.
Acairseid Pier 57°04'·03N 07°17'·61W 2 FG (vert) 8m 4M.

◀ BARRA/CASTLEBAY, VATERSAY SOUND

Drover Rocks 57°04'·15N 07°23'·66W Fl (2) 10s.
Binch Rock 57°01'·70N 07°17'·14W Q (6) + L Fl 15s.
Curachan 56°58'·58N 07°20'·51W Q (3) 10s.
Ardveenish 57°00'·21N 07°24'·43W Oc WRG 6m 9/6M; vis: G300°-304°, W304°-306°, R306°-310°.
Bo Vich Chuan 56°56'·15N 07°23'·31W Q (6) + L Fl 15s; Racon (M).
Channel Rk 56°56'·24N 07°28'·94W Fl WR 6s 4m W6M, R4M; vis: W121·5°-277°, R277°-121·5°.
Castle Bay S 56°56'·09N 07°27'·21W Fl (2) R 8s; Racon (T).
Sgeir Dubh 56°56'·40N 07°28'·92W Q (3) WG 6s 6m W6M, G4M; vis: W280°-117°, G117°-280°. In line 283° with Sgeir Leadh (Liath) below.
Sgeir Leadh (Liath) 56°56'·64N 07°30'·77W Fl 3s 7m 8M.
Castlebay 56°57'·16N 07°29'·62W Fl R 5s 2m 3M.
Rubha Glas. Ldg Lts 295°. Front á, 56°56'·77N 07°30'·64W FG 9m 11M; Or △ on W Tr. Rear, 457m from front, FG 15m 11M; Or ▽ on W Tr.
Barra Hd ☆ 56°47'·11N 07°39'·26W Fl 15s 208m **18M**; W Tr; obsc by islands to NE.

OUTER HEBRIDES – WEST SIDE

Flannan I ☆, Eilean Mór 58°17'·32N 07°35'·23W Fl (2) 30s 101m **20M**; W Tr; obsc in places by Is to W of Eilean Mór.
Whale Rock 57°54'·40N 07°59·91W Q (3) 10s.
Haskeir I ☆ 57°41'·98N 07°41·36W Fl 20s 44m **23M**; W Tr.

◀ EAST LOCH ROAG

Aird Laimishader Carloway 58°17'·06N 06°49'·50W Fl 6s 63m 8M; W hut; obsc on some brgs.
Ardvanich Pt 58°13'·48N 06°47'·68W Fl G 3s 4m 2M.
Tidal Rk 58°13'·45N 06°47'·57W Fl R 3s 2m 2M (synch with Ardvanich Pt above).
Gt Bernera Kirkibost Jetty 2 FG (vert) 7m 2M.
Grèinam 58°13'·30N 06°46'·16W Fl WR 6s 8m W8M, R7M; W Bn; vis: R143°-169°, W169°-143°.
Rubha Arspaig Jetty Hd 2 FR (vert) 10m 4M.

◀ NORTH UIST/SOUTH UIST

Vallay I 57°39'·70N 07°26'·34W Fl WRG 3s 8M; vis: W206°-085°, G085°-140°, W140°-145°, R145°-206°.
Falconet Tr 57°22'·04N 07°23'·58W FR 25m 8M (3M by day); shown 1h before firing, changes to Iso R 2s 15 min before firing until completion.

8

◀ ST KILDA
Ldg Lts 270°. Front, 57°48'·32N 08°34'·31W Oc 5s 26m 3M. Rear, 100m from front, Oc 5s 38m 3M; synch.

◀ SKYE
Eilean Trodday ☆ 57°43'·64N 06°17'·89W Fl (2) WRG 10s 49m W12M, R9M, G9M; W Bn; vis: W062°-088°, R088°-130°, W130°-322°, G322°-062°.
Comet Rock ⛵ 57°44'·60N 06°20'·50W Fl R 6s.

◀ RONA/LOCH A'BHRAIGE
Rona NE Point ☆ 57°34'·68N 05°57'·56W Fl 12s 69m **19M**; W Tr; vis: 050°-358°.
Loch A'Bhraige, Sgeir Shuas ☆ 57°35'·02N 05°58'·61W Fl R 2s 6m 3M; vis: 070°-199°.
Jetty, NE end ☆ 57°34'·66N 05°57'·93W 2 FR (vert).
Rock 57°34'·59N 05°58'·01W QR 4m 3M.
Ldg Lts 136·5°. Front, No. 9 57°34'·41N 05°58'·09W Q WRG 3m W4M, R3M; vis: W135°-138°, R138°-318°, G318°-135°. Rear, No. 10 Iso 6s 28m 5M.
No. 1 57°34'·30N 05°58'·27W Fl G 3s 91m 3M; Or bn.
Rubha Chùiltairbh 57°34'·11N 05°57'·18W Fl 3s 6m 5M.
No. 11 57°33'·12N 05°57'·60W QY 6m 4M.
No. 3 57°32'·59N 05°57'·87W Fl (2) 10s 9m 4M.
No. 12 57°32'·04N 05°58'·15W QR 5m 3M.
Garbh Eilean SE Pt No. 8 57°30'·67N 05°58'·61W Fl 3s 8m 5M; W Bn.

◀ INNER SOUND
Ru Na Lachan ☆ 57°29'·02N 05°52'·14W Oc WR 8s 21m 10M; Tr; vis: W337°-022°, R022°-117°, W117°-162°.

◀ SOUND OF RAASAY, PORTREE
<u>Sgeir Mhór</u> 57°24'·57N 06°10'·53W Fl G 5s.
Portree Pier Head ☆ 57°24'·64N 06°11'·42W 2 FR (vert) 6m 4M; (occas).

◀ CROWLIN ISLANDS
Eilean Beag ☆ 57°21'·21N 05°51'·42W Fl 6s 32m 6M; W Bn.

◀ RAASAY/LOCH SLIGACHAN
Suisnish ☆ 57°19'·87N 06°03'·91W 2 FG (vert) 8m 2M.
Eyre Point ☆ 57°20'·01N 06°01'·29W Fl WR 3s 6m W9M, R6M; W Tr; vis: W215°-266°, R266°-288°, W288°-063°.
Sconser Ferry Terminal ☆ 57°18'·88N 06°06'·67W QR 8m 3M.
<u>McMillan's Rock</u> 57°21'·11N 06°06'·31W Fl (2) G 12s.
<u>Penfold Rock</u> 57°20'·62N 06°05'·54W Fl R 5s.
<u>Jackal Rock</u> 57°20'·34N 06°04'·76W Fl G 5s.

◀ LOCH CARRON
Sgeir Golach 57°21'·20N 05°39'·01W.
Bogha Dubh Sgeir 57°20'·92N 05°37'·85W.
Old Lt Ho (13) 57°20'·95N 05°38'·88W (unlit).

◀ KYLE AKIN AND KYLE OF LOCH ALSH
Kyle Akin Lt Ho 57°16'·65N 05°44'·55W (unlit).
<u>Carragh Rk</u> 57°17'·20N 05°45'·30W Fl (2) G 12s; Racon (T).
<u>Bow Rk</u> 57°16'·78N 05°45'·85W Fl (2) R 12s.
<u>Fork Rks</u> 57°16'·86N 05°44'·87W Fl G 6s.
<u>Black Eye Rk</u> 57°16'·73N 05°45'·24W Fl R 6s.
Kyle Akin Bridge Centre ☆ 57°16'·58N 05°44'·51W Oc 6s.
Eileanan Dubha East ☆ 57°16'·58N 05°42'·25W Fl (2) 10s 9m 8M; vis: obscured 104°-146°.
Eileanan Dubha West ☆ 57°16'·62N 05°42'·61W Fl G 6s 5m 4M.
<u>String Rock</u> 57°16'·51N 05°42'·82W Fl R 6s.
Allt-an-Avaig Jetty ☆ 2 FR (vert) 10m; vis: 075°-270°.
S shore, ferry slipway ☆ 57°16'·44N 05°43'·33W QR 6m (vis in Kyle of Loch Alsh).
Mooring dolphin ☆ 57°16'·38N 05°43'·36W Q 5m 3M.
Ferry Pier, W and E sides ☆ 2 FG (vert) 6/5m 5/4M.
Butec Jetty W end, N corner ☆ 57°16'·77N 05°42'·37W Oc G 6s 5m 3M each end, synch.
<u>Sgeir-na-Caillich</u> ☆ 57°15'·59N 05°38'·90W Fl (2) R 6s 3m 4M.

◀ SOUND OF SLEAT
Kyle Rhea ☆ 57°14'·22N 05°39'·93W Fl WRG 3s 7m W11M, R9M, G8M; W Bn; vis: R shore-219°, W219-228°, G228°-338°, W338°-346°, R346°-shore.
Sandaig I, NW point ☆ 57°10'·05N 05°42'·29W Fl 6s 12m 8M; W 8-sided Tr.
Ornsay, N end ☆ 57°09'·08N 05°46'·95W Fl R 6s 8m 4M; W Tr.
Ornsay, SE end ☆ 57°08'·59N 05°46'·88W Oc 8s 18m **15M**; W Tr; vis: 157°-030°.
Eilean Iarmain, off Pier Hd ☆ 57°08'·78N 05°47'·89W 2 FR (vert) 3m 2M.
Armadale Bay Pier Centre ☆ 57°03'·86N 05°53'·58W Oc R 6s 6m 6M.
Point of Sleat ☆ 57°01'·08N 06° 01'·08W Fl 3s 20m 9M; W Tr.
Elgol ☆ 57°08'·78N 06°06'·53W Fl G 3s 4m 4M.

◀ MALLAIG, ENTRANCE TO LOCH NEVIS
<u>Sgeir Dhearg</u> 57°00'·74N 05°49'·50W QG.
Northern Pier E end ☆ 57°00'·47N 05°49'·50W Iso WRG 4s 6m W9M, R6M, G6M; Gy Tr; vis: G181°-185°, W185°-197°, R197°-201°. Fl G 3s 14m 6M; same structure.
Sgeir Dhearg ☆ 57°00'·63N 05°49'·61W Fl (2) WG 8s 6m 5M; Gy Bn; vis: G190°-055°, W055°-190°.

◀ NW SKYE, UIG/LOCH DUNVEGAN/LOCH HARPORT
Uig, Edward Pier Hd ☆ 57°35'·09N 06°22'·29W Iso WRG 4s 9m W7M, R4M, G4M; vis: W180°-008°, G008°-052°, W052°-075°, R075°-180°.
Bo Na Farmachd 57°26'·79N 06°35'·86W Fl G 5s.
Waternish Pt ☆ 57°36'·48N 06°37'·99W Fl 20s 21m 8M; W Tr.
Loch Dunvegan, Uiginish Pt ☆ 57°26'·84N 06°36'·53W Fl WG 3s 14m W7M, G5M; W hut; vis: G040°-128°, W128°-306°, obsc by Fiadhairt Pt when brg more than 148°.
Neist Point ☆ 57°25'·41N 06°47'·30W Fl 5s 43m **16M**; W Tr.
Loch Harport, Ardtreck Pt ☆ 57°20'·38N 06°25'·80W Iso 4s 17m 9M; small W Tr.

SMALL ISLES AND WEST OF MULL

◀ CANNA, RHUM
E end, Sanday Is ☆ 57°02'·82N 06°28'·02W Fl 6s 32m 9M; W Tr; vis: 152°-061°.

◀ ÒIGH SGEIR/EIGG/ARISAIG
<u>Humla</u> 57°00'·46N 06°37'·39W Fl G 6s.
Hyskeir ☆ 56°58'·14N 06°40'·87W Fl (3) 30s 41m **24M**; W Tr. N end *Horn 30s;* Racon (T).
SE point of Eigg (Eilean Chathastail) ☆ 56°52'·25N 06°07'·28W Fl 6s 24m 8M; W Tr; vis: 181°-shore.
<u>Bo Faskadale</u> 56°48'·18N 06°06'·31W Fl (3) G 18s.
Ardnamurchan ☆ 56°43'·63N 06°13'·52W Fl (2) 20s 55m **24M**; Gy Tr; vis: 002°-217°; *Horn (2) 20s.*
Cairns of Coll, Suil Ghorm ☆ 56°42'·26N 06°26'·75W Fl 12s 23m 10M; W Tr.

◄ COLL/ARINAGOUR

Loch Eatharna, Bogha Mór 56°36'·63N 06°30'·95W Fl G 6s.
Arinagour Pier ☆ 56°36'·85N 06°31'·31W 2 FR (vert) 12m.

◄ TIREE

Roan Bogha 56°32'·23N 06°40'·17W Q (6) + L Fl 15s.
Placaid Bogha 56°33'·22N 06°44'·06W Fl G 4s.
Scarinish ☆, S side of ent 56°30'·01N 06°48'·27W Fl 3s 11m **16M**; W □ Tr; vis: 210°-030°.
Gott Bay Ldg Lts 286·5°. Front 56°30'·61N 06°47'·82W FR 8m. Rear 30m from front FR 11m.
Skerryvore ☆ 56°19'·36N 07°06'·88W Fl 10s 46m **23M**; Gy Tr; Racon (M); *Horn 60s*.

◄ LOCH NA LÀTHAICH (LOCH LATHAICH)

Eileanan na Liathanaich, SE end ☆ 56°20'·56N 06°16'·38W Fl WR 6s 12m W8M, R6M; vis: R088°-108°, W108°-088°.
Dubh Artach ☆ 56°07'·94N 06°38'·08W Fl (2) 30s 44m **20M**; Gy Tr, R band.

SOUND OF MULL

◄ LOCH SUNART/TOBERMORY/LOCH ALINE

Ardmore Pt ☆ 56°39'·37N 06°07'·70W Fl (2) 10s 17m 8M.
New Rks 56°39'·05N 06°03'·30W Fl G 6s.
Rubha nan Gall ☆ 56°38'·33N 06°04'·00W Fl 3s 17m **15M**, W Tr.
Bogha Bhuilg 56°36'·13N 05°59'·13W Fl G 5s.
Hispania Wreck 56°34'·95N 05°59'·12W Fl (2) R 10s.
Bo Rocks 56°31'·53N 05°55'·53W Fl (2) G 6s.
Eileanan Glasa (Dearg Sgeir) ☆ 56°32'·25N 05°54'·80W Fl 6s 7m 8M; W ○ Tr.
Fiunary Spit 56°32'·65N 05°53'·16W Fl G 6s.
Avon Rock 56°30'·78N 05°46'·75W Fl (4) R 12s.
Lochaline 56°32'·09N 05°46'·48W QR.
Lochaline Ldg Lts 356°. Front, 56°32'·40N 05°46'·46W F 2M. Rear, 88m from front, F 4M; both H24.
Ardtornish Pt ☆ 56°31'·10N 05°45'·23W Fl (2) WRG 10s 7m W8M, R5M, G5M; W Tr; vis: G shore-302°, W302°-310°, R310°-342°, W342°-057°, R057°-095°, W095°-108°, G108°-shore.
Yule Rock 56°30'·01N 05°43'·96W Fl R 15s.
Glas Eileanan Gy Rks ☆ 56°29'·76N 05°42'·82W Fl 3s 11m 6M; W ○ Tr on W base.
Craignure Ldg Lts 240·9°. Front, 56°28'·26N 05°42'·27W FR 10m. Rear, 150m from front, FR 12m; vis: 225·8°-255·8°.

MULL TO CALEDONIAN CANAL AND OBAN

Lismore ☆, SW end 56°27'·33N 05°36'·45W Fl 10s 31m **19M**; W Tr; vis: 237°-208°.
Lady's Rk 56°26'·91N 05°37'·05W Fl 6s 12m 5M.
Duart Pt ☆ 56°26'·84N 05°38'·77W Fl (3) WR 18s 14m W5M, R3M; vis: W162°-261°, R261°-275°, W275°-353°, R353°-shore.

◄ LOCH LINNHE

Corran Shoal 56°43'·69N 05°14'·39W QR.
Ent W side, Corran Pt ☆ 56°43'·25N 05°14'·54W Iso WRG 4s 12m W10M, R7M; W Tr; vis: R shore-195°, W195°-215°, G215°-305°, W305°-030°, R030°-shore.
Corran Narrows NE ☆ 56°43'·59N 05°13'·89W Fl 5s 4m 4M; W Tr; vis: S shore-214°.
Jetty ☆ 56°43'·40N 05°14'·64W Fl R 5s 7m 3M; Gy mast.
Clovullin Spit 56°42'·29N 05°15'·56W Fl (2) R 15s.

◄ FORT WILLIAM/CALEDONIAN CANAL

Corpach, Caledonian Canal Lock ent ☆ 56°50'·52N 05°07'·44W Iso WRG 3s 6m 5M; W Tr; vis: G287°-310°, W310°-335°, R335°-030°.
Eilean na Creiche 56°50'·40N 05°07'·38W Fl R 3s.
Lochy Flat S 56°49'·53N 05°07'·02W QG.
McLean Rock 56°49'·81N 05°07'·04W Fl (2) R 12s.

◄ LYNN OF LORN

Sgeir Bhuidhe Appin 56°33'·63N 05°24'·65W Fl (2) WR 7s 7m 9M; W Bn; vis: R184°-220°, W220°-184°.
Appin Point 56°32'·69N 05°25'·97W Fl G 6s.
Dearg Sgeir, off Aird's Point 56°32'·20N 05°25'·22W Fl WRG 2s 2m W3M, R1M, G1M; vis: R196°-246°, W246°-258°, G258°-041°, W041°058°, R058°-093°, W093°-139°.
Rubha nam Faoileann (Eriska) ☆, QG 2m 2M; G col; vis 128°-329°.

◄ DUNSTAFFNAGE BAY

Pier Hd ☆, NE end 56°27'·21N 05°26'·18W 2 FG (vert) 4m 2M.

◄ OBAN

N spit of Kerrera ☆ 56°25'·49N 05°29'·56W Fl R 3s 9m 5M; W col, R bands.
Dunollie ☆ 56°25'·37N 05°29'·05W Fl (2) WRG 6s 7m W5M, G4M, R4M; vis: G351°-009°, W009°-047°, R047°-120°, W120°-138°, G138°-143°.
Rubbh'a' Chruidh ☆ 56°25'·32N 05°29'·29W QR 3m 2M.
Corran Ledge 56°25'·19N 05°29'·11W VQ (9) 10s.
Oban N Pier ☆ 56°24'·87N 05°28'·49W

OBAN TO LOCH CRAIGNISH

Sgeir Rathaid North 56°24'·92N 05°29'·24W Q.
Sgeir Rathaid South 56°24'·74N 05°29'·37W Q (6) + L Fl 15s.
Ardbhan 56°24'·18N 05°30'·39W Fl G 5s.
Ferry Rocks NW 56°24'·11N 05°30'·70W QG.
Ferry Rocks SE 56°23'·99N 05°30'·53W Fl R 5s.
Little Horse Shoe 56°23'·25N 05°31'·83W Fl (4) R 12s.
Kerrera Sound, Dubh Sgeir ☆ 56°22'·81N 05°32'·27W Fl (2) 12s 7m 5M; W ○ Tr.
Port Lathaich ☆ 56°22'·84N 05°31'·42W Oc G 6s 6M; vis: 037°-072°.
Bono Rock 56°16'·23N 05°40'·98W Fl (4) R 12s.
Fladda ☆ 56°14'·89N 05°40'·83W Fl (2) WRG 9s 13m W11M, R9M, G9M; W Tr; vis: R169°-186°, W186°-337°, G337°-344°. W344°-356°, R356°-026°.
Dubh Sgeir (Luing) ☆ 56°14'·76N 05°40'·20W Fl WRG 6s 9m W6M, R4M. G4M; W Tr; vis: W000°-010°, R010°-025°, W025°-199°, G199°-000°; Racon (M).
The Garvellachs, Eileach an Naoimh, SW end ☆ 56°13'·04N 05°49'·06W Fl 6s 21m 9M; W Bn; vis: 240°-215°.

◄ LOCH MELFORT/CRAOBH HAVEN

Melfort Pier ☆ 56°16'·14N 05°30'·19W Dir FR 6m 3M; (Private shown 1/4 to 31/10).
56°12'·88N 05°33'·59W.
Craobh Marina Bkwtr Hd ☆ 56°12'·78N 05°33'·52W Iso WRG 5s 10m W5M, R3M, G3M; vis: G114°-162°, W162°-183°, R183°-200°.

For Colonsay, and Sounds of Jura and Islay see 9.9.4.

9.8.5 PASSAGE INFORMATION

It is essential to carry large scale charts, and current Pilots, ie Admiralty *W Coast of Scotland Pilot*; Clyde Cruising Club's *Sailing Directions* (awaiting reprint), *Pt 2 Kintyre to Ardnamurchan* and *Pt 3 Ardnamurchan to Cape Wrath*; and the *Yachtsman's Pilot to W Coast of Scotland (Vol 2 Crinan to Canna), (Vol 3 The Western Isles), (Vol 4 Skye & NW Scotland)*, Lawrence/Imray.

The West coast of Scotland provides splendid, if sometimes boisterous, sailing and matchless scenery. In summer the long daylight hours and warmth of the Gulf Stream compensate for the lower air temperatures and higher wind speeds experienced when depressions run typically north of Scotland. Inshore winds are often unpredictable, due to geographical effects of lochs, mountains and islands offshore; calms and squalls can alternate rapidly.

Good anchors, especially on kelp/weed, are essential. ⚓s are listed, but it should not be assumed that these will always be available. Particularly in N of area, facilities are very dispersed. VHF communications with shore stations may be limited by high ground. Beware ever more fish farms in many inlets. Local magnetic anomalies occur in Kilbrannan Sound, Passage of Tiree, Sound of Mull, Canna, and East Loch Roag. Submarines exercise throughout these waters; see 9.8.23.

CAPE WRATH TO ULLAPOOL (charts 1785, 1794) C Wrath (lt, fog sig) is a steep headland (110m). To N of it the E-going stream begins at HW Ullapool −0350, and W- going at HW Ullapool +0235, sp rates 3kn. Eddies close inshore cause almost continuous W-going stream E of Cape, and N-going stream SW of it. Where they meet is turbulence, with dangerous seas in bad weather. Duslic Rk, 7ca NE of lt ho, dries 3·4m. 6M SW of C Wrath, islet of Am Balg (45m)is foul for 2ca around.

There are anchs in Loch Inchard (chart 2503), the best shelter being in Kinlochbervie (9.8.8) on N shore; also good anchs among Is along S shore of Loch Laxford, entered between Ardmore Pt and Rubha Ruadh. Handa Is to WSW is a bird sanctuary. Handa Sound is navigable with care, but beware Bogha Morair in mid-chan and associated overfalls. Tide turns 2hrs earlier in the Sound than offshore.

Strong winds against tide raise a bad sea off Pt of Stoer. The best shelter is 8M S at Loch Inver (chart 2504), with good anch off hotel near head of loch. S lies Enard Bay.

ULLAPOOL TO LOCH TORRIDON (charts 1794, 2210) The Summer Isles (chart 2501), 12M NW of the major fishing port of Ullapool (9.8.9), offer some sheltered anchs and tight approaches. The best include the Bay on E side of Tanera Mor; off NE of Tanera Beg (W of Eilean Fada Mor); and in Caolas Eilean Ristol, between the Is and mainland.

Loch Ewe (9.8.9 and chart 3146) provides good shelter and easy access. Best anchs are in Poolewe Bay (beware Boor Rks off W shore) and in SW corner of Loch Thuirnaig (entering, keep close to S shore to avoid rks extending from N side). Off Rubha Reidh (lt) seas can be dangerous. The NE-going stream begins at HW Ullapool −0335; the SW-going at HW Ullapool +0305. Sp rates 3kn, but slacker to SW of point.

Longa Is lies N of ent to Loch Gairloch (9.8.9 and chart 2528). The chan N of it is navigable but narrow at E end. Outer loch is free of dangers, but exposed to swell. Best anch is on S side of loch in Caolas Bad a' Chrotha, W of Eilean Horrisdale.

Entering L Torridon (chart 2210) from S or W beware Murchadh Breac (dries 1·5m) 3ca NNW of Rubha na Fearna. Best anchs are SW of Eilean Mor (to W of Ardheslaig); in Loch a 'Chracaich, 7ca further SE; E of Shieldaig Is; and near head of Upper L Torridon. Streams are weak except where they run 2-3 kn in narrows between L Shieldaig and Upper L Torridon.

OUTER HEBRIDES (charts 1785, 1794, 1795) The E sides of these Is have many good, sheltered anchs, but W coasts give little shelter. The CCC's *Outer Hebrides SDs* or *The Western Isles* (Imray) are advised. The Minches and Sea of the Hebrides can be very rough, particularly in the Little Minch between Skye and Harris, and around Shiant Is where tide runs locally 4kn at sp, and heavy overfalls can be met.

The NE-going stream begins at HW Ullapool −0335; the SW-going stream at HW Ullapool +0250, sp rates 2·5kn.

From N to S, the better hbrs in Outer Hebrides include:

Lewis. Stornoway (9.8.7); Loch Grimshader (beware Sgeir a'Chaolais, dries in entrance); Loch Erisort; Loch Odhairn; Loch Shell (9.8.7). Proceeding S from here, or to E Loch Tarbert beware Sgeir Inoe (dries 2·3m) 3M ESE of Eilean Glas lt ho at SE end of Scalpay.

Harris. E Loch Tarbert; Loch Scadaby; Loch Stockinish; Loch Finsby; W Loch Tarbert; Loch Rodel (⚓). A well buoyed/lit ferry chan connects Leverburgh (South Harris) to Berneray.

N Uist. Loch Maddy (⚓); Loch Eport, Kallin Hbr (⚓).

S Uist. Loch Carnan (⚓); Loch Skiport; Loch Eynort; Loch Boisdale (⚓).

Barra. Castlebay (⚓), see 9.8.7, and Berneray, on N side, E of Shelter Rk.

Activity at the Hebrides Range, S. Uist ☎ (01870) 604441, is broadcast daily at 0950LT and Mon-Fri 1100-1700LT on VHF Ch **12** (Ch 73 in emergency) and on MF 2660 kHz.

SKYE TO ARDNAMURCHAN PT (charts 1795, 2210, 2209, 2208, 2207) Skye and the islands around it provide many good and attractive anchs, of which the most secure are: Acairseid Mhor on the W side of Rona; Portree (9.8.10); Isleornsay; Portnalong, near the ent to Loch Harport, and Carbost at the head; Loch Dunvegan; and Uig Bay in Loch Snizort. ⚓s at Stein (Loch Dunvegan), Portree, Acairseid Mhor (Rona), Churchton Bay (Raasay) and Armadale Bay (S tip).

Tides are strong off Rubha Hunish at N end of Skye, and heavy overfalls occur with tide against fresh or strong winds. Anch behind Fladday Is near the N end of Raasay can be squally and uncomfortable; and Loch Scavaig (S. Skye, beneath the Cuillins) more so, though the latter is so spectacular as to warrant a visit in fair weather. Soay Is has a small, safe hbr on its N side, but the bar at ent almost dries at LW sp.

Between N Skye and the mainland there is the choice of Sound of Raasay or Inner Sound. **The direction of buoyage in both Sounds is Northward.** In the former, coming S from Portree, beware Sgeir Chnapach (3m) and Ebbing Rk (dries 2·9m), both NNW of Oskaig Pt. At the Narrows (chart 2534) the SE- going stream begins at HW Ullapool −0605, and the NW-going at HW Ullapool +0040; sp rate 1·4kn in mid-chan, but more near shoals each side. Beware McMillan's Rk (0·4m depth) in mid-chan, marked by SHM lt buoy.

The chan between Scalpay and Skye narrows to 2½ca with drying reefs each side and least depth 0·1m. Here the E-going stream begins at HW Ullapool +0550, and W-going at HW Ullapool −0010, sp rate 1kn.

Inner Sound, which is a Submarine exercise area, is wider and easier than Sound of Raasay; the two are connected by Caol Rona and Caol Mor, respectively N and S of Raasay. Dangers extend about 1M N of Rona, and Cow Is lies off the mainland 8M to S; otherwise approach from N is clear to Crowlin Is, which should be passed to W. There is a good anch between Eilean Mor and Eilean Meadhonach.

A torpedo range in the Inner Sound does not normally restrict passage, but vessels may be requested to keep to the E side of the Sound if the range is active. Range activity is broadcast at 0800 and 1600LT on VHF Ch 08, 16 and is indicated by R Flags and International Code NE4 flown at the range building at

Applecross, by all range vessels and at the naval pier at Kyle of Lochalsh (9.8.12), ☎ (01599) 534262.

Approaching Kyle Akin (chart 2540) from W, beware dangerous rks to N, off Bleat Is (at S side of entrance to Loch Carron); on S side of chan, Bogha Beag (dries 0·6m) and Black Eye Rk (depth 3·8m), respectively 6ca and 4ca W of bridge. For Plockton (Loch Carron), see 9.8.11. Pass at least 100m N or S of Eileanan Dubha in Kyle Akin. On S side of chan String Rk (dries) is marked by PHM lt buoy. For Loch Alsh, see 9.8.12.

Kyle Rhea connects Loch Alsh with NE end of Sound of Sleat. The tidal streams are very strong: N-going stream begins HW Ullapool +0600, sp rate 6-7kn; S-going stream begins at HW Ullapool, sp rate 8kn. Eddies form both sides of the Kyle and there are dangerous overfalls off S end in fresh S'ly winds on S-going stream. Temp anch in Sandaig Bay, 3M to SW.

The Sound of Sleat widens to 4M off Point of Sleat and is exposed to SW winds unless Eigg and Muck give a lee. Mallaig (9.8.13) is a busy fishing and ferry hbr, convenient for supplies. Further S the lochs require intricate pilotage. 6M NE of Ardnamurchan Pt (lt, fog sig) are Bo Faskadale rks, drying 0·5m and marked by SHM lt buoy, and Elizabeth Rk with depth of 0·7m. Ardnamurchan Pt is an exposed headland onto which the ebb sets. With onshore winds, very heavy seas extend 2M offshore and it should be given a wide berth. Here the N-going stream begins at HW Oban −0525, and the S-going at HW Oban +0100, sp rates 1·5kn.

THE SMALL ISLES (charts 2207, 2208) These consist of Canna, Rhum, Eigg (9.8.13) and Muck. Dangers extend SSW from Canna: at 1M Jemina Rk (depth 1·5m) and Belle Rk (depth 3·6m); at 2M Humla Rk (5m high), marked by buoy and with offlying shoals close W of it; at 5M Oigh Sgeir (lt, fog sig), the largest of a group of small islands; and at 7M Mill Rks (with depths of 1·8m).

The tide runs hard here, and in bad weather the sea breaks heavily up to 15M SW of Canna. Between Skerryvore and Neist Pt the stream runs generally N and S, starting N-going at HW Ullapool +0550, and S-going at HW Ullapool −008. It rarely exceeds 1kn, except near Skerryvore, around headlands of The Small Isles, and over rks and shoals.

1M off the N side of Muck are Godag Rks, some above water but with submerged dangers extending 2ca further N. Most other dangers around the Small Isles are closer inshore, but there are banks on which the sea breaks heavily in bad weather. A local magnetic anomaly exists about 2M E of Muck. The hbrs at Eigg (SE end), Rhum (Loch Scresort) and Canna (between Canna and Sanday) are all exposed to E'lies; Canna has best shelter and is useful for the Outer Hebrides.

ARDNAMURCHAN TO CRINAN (charts 2171, 2169) S of Ardnamurchan the route lies either W of Mull via Passage of Tiree (where headlands need to be treated with respect in bad weather); or via the more sheltered Sound of Mull and Firth of Lorne. The former permits a visit to Coll and Tiree, where best anchs are at Arinagour (⚓s) and Gott Bay respectively. Beware Cairns of Coll, off the N tip.

The W coast of Mull is rewarding in settled weather, but careful pilotage is needed. Beware tide rip off Caliach Pt (NW corner) and Torran Rks off SW end of Mull (large scale chart 2617 required). Apart from the attractions of Iona and of Staffa (Fingal's Cave), the remote Treshnish Is are worth visiting. The best anchs in this area are at Ulva, Gometra, Bull Hole and Tinker's Hole in Iona Sound. The usual passage through Iona Sound avoids overfalls W of Iona, but heed shoal patches. Loch Lathaich on the N side of Ross of Mull is 5M to the E; a good base with anch at Bunessan.

The Sound of Mull gives access to Tobermory (9.8.15, ⚓), Dunstaffnage Bay, Oban (9.8.19), and up Loch Linnhe through Corran Narrows (where tide runs strongly) to Fort William (9.8.17) and to Corpach for the Caledonian Canal (9.8.18). But, apart from these places, there are dozens of lovely anchs in the sheltered lochs inside Mull, as for example in Loch Sunart (9.8.14)with ⚓s at Kilchoan; also at Craignure and Salen Bays on Sound of Mull. For Loch Aline see 9.8.16.

On the mainland shore Puilladobhrain is a sheltered anch. Cuan Sound (see 9.8.19 for details) is a useful short cut to Loch Melfort, (9.8.20) and Craobh Marina (9.8.21). Good shelter, draft permitting, in Ardinamar B, SW of Torsa.

Sound of Luing (chart *2326*) between Fladda (lt), Lunga and Scarba on the W side, and Luing and Dubh Sgeir (lt) on the E side, is the normal chan to or from Sound of Jura, despite dangers at the N end and strong tidal streams. The N and W-going flood begins at HW Oban +0430; the S and E-going ebb at HW Oban −0155. Sp rates are 2·5kn at S end of Sound, increasing to 6kn or more in Islands off N entrance, where there are eddies, races and overfalls.

From the N, beware very strong streams, eddies and whirlpools in Dorus Mór, off Craignish Pt. Streams begin to set W and N away from Dorus Mór at HW Oban +0345, and E and S towards Dorus Mór at HW Oban −0215, sp rates 7kn. At N end of Sound of Jura (chart *2326*) is Loch Craignish (9.8.22).

For Gulf of Corryvreckan, Colonsay, Islay, Loch Crinan and passage south through the Sound of Jura, see 9.9.5.

9.8.6 DISTANCE TABLE

Approximate distances in nautical miles are by the most direct route, keeping East of Skye and Mull where appropriate, and avoiding dangers. Places in *italics* are in adjoining areas.

1. *Cape Wrath*	**1**																			
2. Ullapool	54	**2**																		
3. Stornoway	53	45	**3**																	
4. East Loch Tarbert	75	56	33	**4**																
5. Portree	83	57	53	42	**5**															
6. Loch Harport	110	82	65	45	66	**6**														
7. Kyle of Lochalsh	91	63	62	63	21	53	**7**													
8. Mallaig	112	82	83	84	42	33	21	**8**												
9. Eigg	123	98	97	75	54	34	35	14	**9**											
10. Castlebay (Barra)	133	105	92	69	97	43	76	59	46	**10**										
11. Tobermory	144	114	115	87	74	52	53	32	20	53	**11**									
12. Loch Aline	157	127	128	100	87	65	66	45	33	66	13	**12**								
13. Fort William	198	161	162	134	121	99	98	75	63	96	43	34	**13**							
14. Oban	169	138	139	111	100	76	77	56	44	77	24	13	29	**14**						
15. Loch Lathaich	160	130	124	98	91	62	67	49	35	56	31	53	77	48	**15**					
16. Loch Melfort	184	154	155	117	114	92	93	69	61	92	40	27	45	18	45	**16**				
17. Craobh Haven	184	155	155	117	114	93	92	70	60	93	40	27	50	21	43	5	**17**			
18. Loch Craignish	188	158	159	131	118	95	96	76	64	98	44	31	55	26	46	17	14	**18**		
19. Crinan	187	157	158	129	112	95	95	74	63	97	42	30	54	25	45	14	9	6	**19**	
20. Mull of Kintyre	232	203	189	175	159	133	143	121	105	120	89	87	98	72	78	62	57	54	51	**20**

STORNOWAY 9.8.7

Lewis (Western Isles) **58°11′·58N 06°21′·82W** ❀❀❀◊◊✿✿

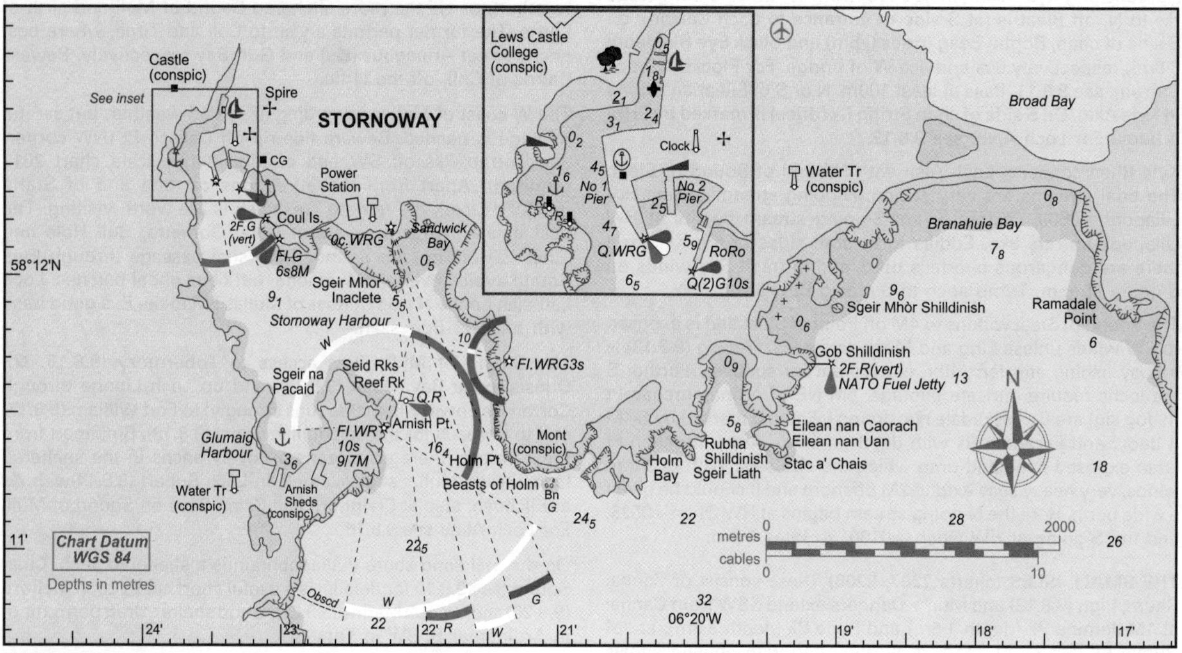

CHARTS AC 2529, 1794, 1785; Imray C67; OS 8

TIDES –0428 Dover; ML 2·8; Duration 0610; Zone 0 (UT)

Standard Port STORNOWAY (⟶)

Times				Height (metres)			
High Water		Low Water		MHWS	MHWN	MLWN	MLWS
0100	0700	0300	0900	4·8	3·7	2·0	0·7
1300	1900	1500	2100				
East side of Outer Hebrides, N to S							
Differences LOCH SHELL (Harris)							
–0013	0000	0000	–0017	0·0	–0·1	–0·1	0·0
EAST LOCH TARBERT (Harris)							
–0025	–0010	–0010	–0020	+0·2	0·0	+0·1	+0·1
LOCH MADDY (N Uist)							
–0044	–0014	–0016	–0030	0·0	–0·1	–0·1	0·0
LOCH CARNAN (S Uist)							
–0050	–0010	–0020	–0040	–0·3	–0·5	–0·1	–0·1
LOCH SKIPORT (S Uist)							
–0100	–0025	–0024	–0024	–0·2	–0·4	–0·3	–0·2
LOCH BOISDALE (S Uist)							
–0055	–0030	–0020	–0040	–0·7	–0·7	–0·3	–0·2
BARRA (North Bay)							
–0103	–0031	–0034	–0048	–0·6	–0·5	–0·2	–0·1
CASTLE BAY (Barra)							
–0115	–0040	–0045	–0100	–0·5	–0·6	–0·3	–0·1
BARRA HEAD (Berneray)							
–0115	–0040	–0045	–0055	–0·8	–0·7	–0·2	+0·1
West side of Outer Hebrides, N to S							
CARLOWAY (W Lewis)							
–0040	+0020	–0035	–0015	–0·6	–0·5	–0·4	–0·1
LITTLE BERNERA (W Lewis)							
–0021	–0011	–0017	–0027	–0·5	–0·6	–0·4	–0·2
WEST LOCH TARBERT (W Harris)							
–0015	–0015	–0046	–0046	–1·1	–0·9	–0·5	0·0
SCOLPAIG (W North Uist)							
–0033	–0033	–0040	–0040	–1·0	–0·9	–0·5	0·0
SHILLAY (Monach Islands)							
–0103	–0043	–0047	–0107	–0·6	–0·7	–0·7	–0·3
BALIVANICH (W Benbecula)							
–0103	–0017	–0031	–0045	–0·7	–0·6	–0·5	–0·2

SHELTER Good. A small marina, max LOA 12m, at the N end of the Inner Hbr, beyond the LB berth, has depths 1·4 - 3·3m. Or AB for larger boats on adjacent Cromwell St Quay, close S; or lie alongside FVs in the inner hbr. Visitors should report to Hr Mr. Ullapool ferries use the new No 3 pier and commercial vessels on Nos 1 and 2 Piers. S'ly swells can make anchoring uncomfortable. Much of the hbr is foul with old wire hawsers. ⚓s as on chartlet at: Poll nam Portan on the W side of inner chan, opposite No 1 Pier; Glumaig Hbr is best ⚓, but oil works may preclude this; in bay NW of Coul Island (Eilean na Gobhail).

NAVIGATION WPT 58°09′·98N 06°20′·87W, 163°/343° from/to Oc WRG lt, 2·3M. Reef Rk, N of Arnish Pt on W side of ent, is marked by PHM buoy, QR. At the E side of ent an unlit G bn marks the Beasts of Holm, a rky patch off Holm Pt, on which is a conspic memorial. A local magnetic anomaly exists over a small area in mid-hbr, 1·75ca N of Seid Rks PHM bn.

LIGHTS AND MARKS Arnish sheds are conspic 3ca SW of Arnish Pt lt, Fl WR 10s 17m 19/15M, W tr; W sector 302°-013° covers ent. Then in turn follow W sectors of: Sandwick Bay lt, (close E of water tr, 3 power stn chys and fuel tanks; all conspic) Oc WRG 6s 10m 9M, W341°-347°; then Stoney Field Fl WRG 3s 8m 11M, vis W102°-109° across hbr; and finally No 1 Pier, Q WRG 5m 11M, W335°-352°.

RADIO TELEPHONE VHF Ch 12 16 (H24).

TELEPHONE (Dial code 01851) Hr Mr 702688, 📠 705714; MRSC 702013; ⊜ 703626; Marinecall 09068 500464; Police 702222; Dr 703145.

FACILITIES Marina 27 berths, inc 8 ❶, £8 via Hr Mr Ch 12; FW, AC. **Nos 1 & 2 Piers** FW, C (10 ton), CH, AB, Slip, P. **Services**: ACA, ME, El, Sh. **Town** EC Wed; P (cans), D, El, V, R, Bar, Gas, ✉, Ⓑ, ⇌ (ferry to Ullapool, bus to Garve), ✈.

HARBOURS AND ANCHORAGES ON THE EAST SIDE OF THE OUTER HEBRIDES (Western Isles), from N to S:

LOCH SHELL, Harris, **57°59'·98N 06°25'·07W**. AC 1794. HW –0437 on Dover; ML 2·7m. See 9.8.7. Pass S of Eilean Iuvard; beware rks to W of Is. ⚓ in Tob Eishken, 2½M up loch on N shore (beware rk awash on E side of ent), or at head of loch (exposed to E winds; dries some distance). Facilities: ✉/Stores at Lemreway.

SHIANT ISLANDS, Lewis, **57°53'·68N 06°21'·37W**. AC 1794, 1795. Tides as Loch Shell 9.8.7. Beware strong tidal streams and overfalls in Sound of Shiant. Strictly a fair weather ⚓; in W winds ⚓ E of Mol Mor, isthmus between Garbh Eileen (160m) and Eileen an Tighe. In E winds ⚓ W of Mol Mor. No lights or facilities.

EAST LOCH TARBERT, Harris, **57°49'·98N 06°41'·07W**. AC 2905. HW –0446 on Dover; ML 3·0m; Duration 0605. See 9.8.7. Appr via Sound of Scalpay; beware Elliot Rk (2m) 2½ca SSW of Rubha Crago. A bridge (20m cl'nce) at 57°52'·80N 06°41'·73W joins Scalpay to Harris. Bridge lts: Centre Oc 6s; N side Iso G 4s 35m; S side Iso R 4s 35m. Eilean Glas lt ho at E end of Scalpay, Fl (3) 20s 43m 23M; W tr, R bands. In Sound of Scalpay, stream sets W from HW +3, and E from HW –3. ⚓ off Tarbert WSW of steamer pier in about 2·5m. Facilities: EC Thurs; Bar, D, Dr, FW, P, ✉, R, V, ferry to Uig. Alternatively Scalpay N Hbr gives good shelter. Beware rk 5ca off Aird an Aiseig, E side of ent. SHM buoy marks wk off Coddem; 5ca E of the buoy is a rk, depth 1·1m. Fish pier at SE end of hbr has 2FG (vert) lts; ⚓ 7ca N, in about 3m. Facilities: FW at pier, ✉, V, ferry to Harris.

SOUND OF HARRIS, 57°43'N 06°58'W. Passages through this difficult Sound are detailed in the *W Coast of Scotland Pilot*. The Stanton and Outer Stromay Chans off the Harris shore are the most feasible for yachts. AC 2642 shows the newly marked ferry routes from Leverburgh to Berneray.

LOCH MADDY, North Uist, **57°35'·98N 07°06'·07W**. AC 2825 HW –0500 on Dover. See 9.8.7. With strong wind against tide there can be bad seas off ent. Appr clear, but from S beware submerged rk ½ca N of Leacnam Madadh. Lts: Weaver's Pt Fl 3s 21m 7M; Glas Eilean Mor Fl (2) G 4s 8m 5M; Rubna Nam Pleac Fl R 4s 7m 5M. Inside loch: Ruigh Liath QG 6m 5M; Vallaquie Is dir Fl (3) WRG 8s. Ferry pier ldg lts 298°: front 2FG(vert) 4M; rear Oc G 8s 10m 4M, vis 284°-304°. 2 🛟s Bagh Aird nam Madadh; 2 🛟s W of and 4 🛟s SW of ferry pier ☎ (01870) 602425; 2 🛟s E of Oronsay. ⚓s: clear S of ferry pier; NE of Vallaquie Is; Charles Hbr; Oronsay (⚓ not advised due to moorings), tidal berth on private pier; Sponish Hbr; Loch Portain. VHF Ch 12 16. Port Manager ☎ (01876) 5003337 (day), 5003226 (night). Facilities: Lochmaddy, EC Wed; Shop, Ⓑ, Gas, ✉, P, D, FW; Loch Portain ✉, Shop.

LOCH EPORT, North Uist, **57°33'·45N 07°08'·12W**. AC 2825, but not the head of loch. Tides, approx as L Maddy; 3kn sp stream. On the S side of ent are rks, some drying. The ent proper is clean but very narrow (about 100m) for 5ca, then widens. Follow the charted clearing line 082°. Best ⚓s are: Bàgh a' Bhiorain (S of chan); and Acairseid Lee (N bank) E or W of Deer Is. V, R, Bar, ✉ at Clachan, hd of loch.

LOCH CARNAN, South Uist, **57°22'·03N 07°16'·39W**. AC 2825. Tides, see 9.8.7. SWM buoy, L Fl 10s, at 57°22'·30N 07°11'·57W is almost 2M E of app chan proper, marked by Nos 1 and 2 buoys, Fl G 2·5s and Fl R 2s, at 57°22'·45N 07°14'·90W. Round No 3 PHM buoy, Fl R 5s, between Gasay and Taigh lamain, then pick up ldg lts 222° to Sandwick quay; front Fl R 2s, rear Iso R 10s, both 5M, W ◊s on posts. Power stn and 2 chys are conspic close to SE of quay. Call ☎ (01870) 602425 for permission to berth on the quay (MoD property). There is ⚓ or 2 🛟s about 2ca WNW of the quay in deep water. The passage S of Gasay is unmarked and needs careful pilotage. FW, D available.

LOCH SKIPPORT, South Uist, **57°19'·98N 07°13'·67W**. AC 2825, 2904. HW –0602 on Dover; see 9.8.7. Easy ent 3M NNE of Hecla (604m). No lights, but 2¼M SSE is Usinish lt ho Fl WR 20s 54m 19/15M. ⚓s at: Wizard Pool in 7m; beware Float Rk, dries 2·3m; on N side of Caolas Mor in 7m; Bagh Charmaig in 5m. Linne Arm has narrow ent, many fish farms and poor holding. No facilities.

LOCH EYNORT, South Uist, **57°13'·13N 07°16'·87W**. AC 2825. Tides: interpolate between Lochs Skipport and Boisdale, see 9.8.7. ⚓s in the outer loch at Cearcdal Bay and on the N side just before the narrows are exposed to the E. The passage to Upper L Eynort is very narrow and streams reach 5-7kn; best not attempted unless local fishermen offer guidance. Good ⚓ inside at Bàgh Lathach.

LOCH BOISDALE, South Uist, **57°08'·78N 07°16'·07W**. AC 2770. HW –0455 on Dover; ML 2·4m; Duration 0600. See 9.8.7. Good shelter except in SE gales when swell runs right up the 2M loch. From N, appr between Rubha na Cruibe and Calvay Is; ldg line 245°: Hollisgeir (0·3m) on with pier (ru). From S beware Clan Ewan Rk, dries 1·2m, and McKenzie Rk (2·4m), marked by PHM lt buoy Fl (3) R 15s. Chan to Boisdale Hbr lies N of Gasay Is; beware rks off E end. ⚓ off pier in approx 4m, or SW of Gasay Is in approx 9m. 4 🛟s NE of pier ☎ (01870) 602425. There are fish cages W of Rubha Bhuailt. Lts: E end of Calvay Is Fl (2) WRG 10s 16m 7/4M. Gasay Is Fl WR 5s 10m 7/4M. N side of loch, opp Gasay Is, Fl G 6s. Ro-Ro terminal Iso RG 4s 8m 2M; and close SE, Fl (2) R 5s. See 9.8.4. Facilities: EC Tues; Bar, FW (on pier), P, ✉, R, V, ferry to mainland. Plans for extensive development (2001).

ACAIRSEID MHÓR, Eriskay, ⊕ **57°03'·78N 07°16'·35W**. AC 2770. Tides approx as for North Bay (Barra), see 9.8.7. Ben Scrien (183m) is conspic, pointed peak N of hbr. Ldg lts 285°, both Oc R 6s 9/10m 4M, W △ ▽ on orange posts, lead for 0·5M from the above lat/long between two drying rks into the outer loch. A SHM buoy, Fl G 6s, marks a rk drying 3m. 3 🛟s are at 57°03'·95N 07°17'·40W on S side of inner loch, opp pier, 2 FG (vert). ☎ (01870) 602425. V, R, Bar, ✉ at Haun, 1·5M at N end of island.

NORTH BAY, Barra, **57°00'·11N 07°24'·67W**. AC 2770. Tides see 9.8.7. Well marked approach to inlet sheltered from S and W winds. WPT 56°58'·68N 07°20'·31W is about 200m NE of Curachan ECM buoy, Q (3) 10s, and in the white sector (304°-306°) of Ardveenish dir ☆ 305°, Oc WRG 3s, 2·5M to the WNW. ⚓ 1ca WNW of Black Island or in N part of Bay Hirivagh where there are 🛟s; or tempy AB on the quay in 4·5m. FW, Bar, V, bus to Castlebay.

CASTLEBAY, Barra, **56°56'·78N 07°29'·67W**. AC 2769. HW –0525 on Dover; ML 2·3m; Duration 0600. See 9.8.7. Very good shelter & holding. Best ⚓ in approx 8m NW of Kiessimul Castle (on an island); NE of castle are rks. 8 🛟s lie to W of pier ☎ (01870) 602425. Or ⚓ in Vatersay Bay in approx 9m. W end of Vatersay Sound is closed by a causeway. Beware rks NNW of Sgeir Dubh a conspic W/G tr, Fl (2) WG 6s 6m 7/5M, vis W280°-117°, G117°-280°; which leads 283° in transit with Sgeir Liath, Fl 3s 7m 8M. Chan Rk, 2ca to the S, is marked by Fl WR 6s 4m 6/4M. Close-in ldg lts 295°, both FG 11M on W framework trs: front 9m Or △ on Rubha Glas; rear, 457m from front, 15m Or ▽. Facilities: Bar, D, FW, P, ✉, R, V, Ferry to mainland.

HIE as are also located in the Outer Hebrides at:
Loch Rodel, Harris. AC 2642. 3 🛟s at 57°44'·2N 06°57'·4W in Poll an Tigh-mhàil; enter from SW past jetties. No lts. ☎ (01851) 703773.
Kallin, Grimsay. AC 2904. 1 🛟 at 57°28'·9N 07°12'·2W, NE of hbr. 3 chan lt buoys and 2 FR (vert) on hbr bkwtr. ☎ (01870) 602425.

TIME ZONE (UTC)
For Summer Time add ONE hour in **non-shaded areas**

SCOTLAND – STORNOWAY

LAT 58°12′N LONG 6°23′W

TIMES AND HEIGHTS OF HIGH AND LOW WATERS

SPRING & NEAP TIDES
Dates in red are SPRINGS
Dates in blue are NEAPS

YEAR 2002

JANUARY

Day	Time	m	Day	Time	m
1 TU	0152	0.8	16 W	0232	1.0
	0752	4.9		0824	4.6
	1429	0.7		1459	1.0
	2024	4.6		2045	4.1
2 W	0235	0.8	17 TH	0306	1.1
	0837	4.9		0900	4.5
	1515	0.7		1533	1.1
	2112	4.5		2120	4.0
3 TH	0319	1.0	18 F	0341	1.3
	0925	4.8		0937	4.4
	1603	0.8		1609	1.2
	2205	4.3		2158	3.8
4 F	0405	1.1	19 SA	0418	1.5
	1021	4.6		1019	4.2
	1655	0.9		1648	1.4
	2306	4.1		2242	3.7
5 SA	0457	1.4	20 SU	0459	1.7
	1125	4.4		1106	3.9
	1752	1.1		1731	1.6
				2336	3.5
6 SU	0013	3.9	21 M	0546	1.9
	0557	1.6		1201	3.8
	1235	4.2		1819	1.7
	1855	1.3			
7 M	0123	3.8	22 TU	0039	3.4
	0707	1.8		0641	2.1
	1347	4.1		1301	3.7
	2005	1.4		1915	1.9
8 TU	0234	3.8	23 W	0148	3.5
	0824	1.8		0747	2.1
	1458	4.0		1406	3.7
	2117	1.5		2021	1.9
9 W	0338	3.9	24 TH	0257	3.6
	0940	1.7		0902	2.1
	1602	4.0		1514	3.7
	2221	1.4		2131	1.8
10 TH	0433	4.0	25 F	0357	3.8
	1044	1.6		1012	1.9
	1658	4.1		1618	3.9
	2313	1.3		2234	1.6
11 F	0520	4.2	26 SA	0448	4.1
	1139	1.4		1111	1.6
	1745	4.1		1713	4.1
	2359	1.2		2327	1.4
12 SA	0601	4.4	27 SU	0534	4.4
	1226	1.2		1202	1.2
	1826	4.2		1801	4.4
13 SU	0040	1.1	28 M	0015	1.1
	0638	4.5		0617	4.7
	1309	1.1		1250	0.9
	● 1903	4.2		○ 1846	4.6
14 M	0120	1.0	29 TU	0100	0.8
	0715	4.6		0700	4.9
	1347	1.0		1335	0.6
	1938	4.2		1929	4.8
15 TU	0156	1.0	30 W	0143	0.6
	0750	4.7		0741	5.1
	1424	1.0		1419	0.4
	2012	4.2		2012	4.8
			31 TH	0225	0.5
				0823	5.1
				1502	0.3
				2054	4.7

FEBRUARY

Day	Time	m	Day	Time	m
1 F	0307	0.6	16 SA	0316	1.0
	0907	5.0		0901	4.4
	1546	0.4		1537	0.9
	2140	4.5		2117	4.0
2 SA	0349	0.7	17 SU	0348	1.1
	0954	4.8		0935	4.2
	1631	0.6		1611	1.1
	2230	4.3		2151	3.9
3 SU	0435	1.0	18 M	0422	1.4
	1049	4.5		1012	4.0
	1720	0.9		1648	1.3
	2331	4.0		2230	3.7
4 M	0526	1.3	19 TU	0500	1.6
	1157	4.2		1059	3.8
	1815	1.3		1730	1.6
				2326	3.5
5 TU	0043	3.7	20 W	0546	1.9
	0625	1.6		1203	3.6
	1316	3.9		1821	1.8
	1920	1.6			
6 W	0201	3.6	21 TH	0042	3.4
	0744	1.9		0646	2.0
	1437	3.7		1319	3.5
	2042	1.7		1925	1.9
7 TH	0315	3.6	22 F	0203	3.4
	0921	1.9		0808	2.1
	1552	3.7		1441	3.6
	2204	1.7		2048	2.0
8 F	0419	3.8	23 SA	0321	3.6
	1040	1.7		0945	1.9
	1654	3.8		1559	3.8
	2304	1.6		2210	1.8
9 SA	0510	4.0	24 SU	0426	4.0
	1136	1.5		1055	1.6
	1742	3.9		1659	4.1
	2350	1.4		2311	1.4
10 SU	0551	4.2	25 M	0518	4.3
	1221	1.2		1148	1.1
	1819	4.0		1748	4.4
11 M	0030	1.2	26 TU	0001	1.1
	0626	4.4		0602	4.7
	1300	1.0		1236	0.7
	1851	4.1		1832	4.7
12 TU	0107	1.0	27 W	0046	0.7
	0659	4.6		0644	5.1
	1334	0.9		1319	0.3
	● 1921	4.2		○ 1912	4.9
13 W	0142	0.9	28 TH	0128	0.5
	0730	4.7		0724	5.3
	1406	0.8		1401	0.1
	1950	4.2		1952	5.0
14 TH	0214	0.8			
	0800	4.7			
	1436	0.8			
	2018	4.2			
15 F	0245	0.8			
	0830	4.6			
	1506	0.8			
	2046	4.2			

MARCH

Day	Time	m	Day	Time	m
1 F	0208	0.3	16 SA	0220	0.7
	0804	5.4		0800	4.6
	1441	0.0		1435	0.7
	2031	5.0		2014	4.3
2 SA	0248	0.3	17 SU	0248	0.8
	0844	5.2		0829	4.5
	1522	0.2		1504	0.8
	2112	4.7		2042	4.2
3 SU	0329	0.5	18 M	0318	1.0
	0927	5.0		0858	4.3
	1603	0.5		1535	1.0
	2156	4.4		2110	4.1
4 M	0411	0.8	19 TU	0350	1.2
	1017	4.6		0930	4.1
	1648	0.9		1610	1.2
	2250	4.1		2142	3.9
5 TU	0457	1.2	20 W	0425	1.4
	1122	4.1		1011	3.8
	1737	1.4		1648	1.5
				2225	3.7
6 W	0005	3.8	21 TH	0507	1.7
	0552	1.6		1118	3.6
	1253	3.7		1735	1.8
	1839	1.8		2349	3.5
7 TH	0131	3.6	22 F	0605	1.9
	0710	2.0		1252	3.5
	1422	3.5		1840	2.0
	2010	2.1			
8 F	0252	3.6	23 SA	0127	3.5
	0909	2.0		0736	2.0
	1545	3.5		1424	3.5
	2149	2.0		2015	2.1
9 SA	0402	3.7	24 SU	0254	3.6
	1036	1.8		0926	1.8
	1650	3.6		1544	3.8
	2251	1.8		2150	1.9
10 SU	0454	4.0	25 M	0404	4.0
	1128	1.5		1038	1.4
	1734	3.8		1643	4.1
	2335	1.5		2252	1.5
11 M	0534	4.2	26 TU	0458	4.4
	1207	1.3		1130	1.0
	1806	4.0		1730	4.5
				2341	1.1
12 TU	0013	1.2	27 W	0543	4.8
	0608	4.4		1215	0.5
	1241	1.0		1812	4.8
	1833	4.1			
13 W	0048	1.0	28 TH	0025	0.7
	0638	4.6		0624	5.2
	1312	0.8		1258	0.2
	1859	4.3		○ 1851	5.0
14 TH	0121	0.8	29 F	0107	0.4
	0707	4.7		0703	5.4
	1340	0.7		1338	0.0
	● 1924	4.3		1929	5.1
15 F	0151	0.7	30 SA	0148	0.3
	0733	4.7		0742	5.4
	1407	0.7		1417	0.0
	1948	4.4		2006	5.1
			31 SU	0227	0.3
				0822	5.2
				1456	0.2
				2045	4.9

APRIL

Day	Time	m	Day	Time	m
1 M	0307	0.5	16 TU	0252	0.9
	0904	4.9		0832	4.3
	1536	0.6		1505	0.9
	2128	4.6		2043	4.2
2 TU	0349	0.8	17 W	0325	1.1
	0952	4.5		0908	4.1
	1618	1.1		1539	1.2
	2219	4.2		2117	4.0
3 W	0435	1.3	18 TH	0401	1.3
	1057	4.0		0954	3.8
	1704	1.6		1618	1.5
	2333	3.9		2204	3.8
4 TH	0529	1.7	19 F	0447	1.6
	1233	3.6		1108	3.6
	1803	2.0		1705	1.8
				2330	3.6
5 F	0102	3.7	20 SA	0550	1.8
	0647	2.0		1242	3.5
	1402	3.4		1813	2.0
	1936	2.3			
6 SA	0222	3.6	21 SU	0107	3.6
	0847	2.1		0727	1.9
	1527	3.5		1409	3.6
	2120	2.2		1953	2.1
7 SU	0332	3.8	22 M	0229	3.8
	1014	1.8		0905	1.6
	1633	3.6		1523	3.8
	2224	2.0		2124	1.8
8 M	0427	3.9	23 TU	0338	4.1
	1103	1.6		1013	1.2
	1713	3.8		1621	4.1
	2309	1.7		2226	1.5
9 TU	0508	4.1	24 W	0433	4.5
	1139	1.3		1105	0.9
	1742	4.0		1708	4.5
	2347	1.4		2316	1.1
10 W	0542	4.3	25 TH	0520	4.8
	1212	1.1		1150	0.5
	1808	4.1		1749	4.8
11 TH	0021	1.1	26 F	0001	0.8
	0612	4.5		0602	5.1
	1242	0.9		1233	0.3
	1832	4.3		1827	5.0
12 F	0054	0.9	27 SA	0044	0.6
	0639	4.6		0642	5.2
	1309	0.8		1313	0.2
	● 1856	4.4		○ 1905	5.1
13 SA	0124	0.8	28 SU	0126	0.5
	0705	4.6		0722	5.2
	1336	0.7		1352	0.3
	1920	4.5		1943	5.0
14 SU	0152	0.8	29 M	0207	0.5
	0732	4.6		0802	5.0
	1404	0.7		1432	0.5
	1946	4.5		2023	4.8
15 M	0221	0.8	30 TU	0249	0.7
	0801	4.5		0846	4.7
	1433	0.8		1511	0.8
	2014	4.4		2106	4.6

Chart Datum: 2·71 metres below Ordnance Datum (Newlyn)

TIME ZONE (UTC)
For Summer Time add ONE hour in **non-shaded areas**

SCOTLAND – STORNOWAY

LAT 58°12′N LONG 6°23′W

TIMES AND HEIGHTS OF HIGH AND LOW WATERS

SPRING & NEAP TIDES
Dates in red are **SPRINGS**
Dates in blue are **NEAPS**

YEAR **2002**

MAY

Day	Time	m
1 W	0332	1.0
	0936	4.3
	1553	1.2
	2157	4.3
2 TH	0418	1.3
	1040	3.9
	1638	1.7
	2305	4.0
3 F	0513	1.7
	1205	3.6
	1734	2.1
4 SA	0025	3.8
	0625	2.0
	1328	3.4
	1855	2.3
5 SU	0140	3.8
	0801	2.0
	1448	3.4
	2032	2.3
6 M	0248	3.8
	0924	1.9
	1554	3.5
	2141	2.1
7 TU	0346	3.9
	1019	1.7
	1638	3.7
	2231	1.8
8 W	0432	4.0
	1100	1.5
	1711	3.9
	2312	1.6
9 TH	0509	4.2
	1135	1.3
	1738	4.1
	2349	1.4
10 F	0541	4.3
	1206	1.1
	1804	4.3
11 SA	0022	1.2
	0610	4.4
	1236	0.9
	1828	4.4
12 SU	0054	1.0
	0639	4.5
	1305	0.8
	● 1854	4.5
13 M	0125	1.0
	0709	4.5
	1336	0.8
	1923	4.5
14 TU	0158	0.9
	0743	4.4
	1408	0.9
	1955	4.5
15 W	0232	1.0
	0819	4.3
	1442	1.0
	2030	4.4
16 TH	0309	1.1
	0902	4.1
	1519	1.2
	2111	4.2
17 F	0352	1.2
	0956	3.9
	1600	1.4
	2207	4.0
18 SA	0443	1.4
	1109	3.7
	1651	1.7
	2326	3.8
19 SU	0552	1.6
	1229	3.6
	1801	1.9
20 M	0047	3.8
	0714	1.6
	1345	3.6
	1929	1.9
21 TU	0202	3.9
	0834	1.4
	1455	3.8
	2050	1.8
22 W	0309	4.1
	0941	1.1
	1553	4.1
	2154	1.5
23 TH	0406	4.4
	1036	0.9
	1642	4.4
	2248	1.2
24 F	0456	4.6
	1124	0.7
	1726	4.6
	2336	1.0
25 SA	0541	4.8
	1208	0.6
	1806	4.8
26 SU	0022	0.8
	0623	4.8
	1251	0.5
	○ 1845	4.8
27 M	0108	0.7
	0706	4.8
	1332	0.6
	1925	4.8
28 TU	0152	0.8
	0749	4.6
	1412	0.8
	2006	4.7
29 W	0235	0.9
	0835	4.4
	1452	1.0
	2050	4.6
30 TH	0320	1.1
	0923	4.1
	1533	1.3
	2139	4.4
31 F	0406	1.3
	1018	3.9
	1617	1.6
	2235	4.2

JUNE

Day	Time	m
1 SA	0456	1.5
	1122	3.6
	1708	1.9
	2338	4.0
2 SU	0554	1.8
	1232	3.4
	1810	2.1
3 M	0045	3.8
	0701	1.9
	1347	3.4
	1928	2.2
4 TU	0151	3.8
	0815	1.9
	1457	3.4
	2044	2.2
5 W	0253	3.8
	0920	1.8
	1552	3.6
	2143	2.0
6 TH	0346	3.9
	1010	1.7
	1632	3.8
	2231	1.8
7 F	0430	4.0
	1052	1.5
	1704	4.0
	2312	1.6
8 SA	0507	4.1
	1128	1.3
	1733	4.2
	2349	1.4
9 SU	0542	4.2
	1202	1.2
	1802	4.3
10 M	0025	1.2
	0617	4.3
	1238	1.0
	● 1832	4.5
11 TU	0103	1.1
	0654	4.4
	1313	0.9
	1907	4.5
12 W	0141	1.0
	0733	4.4
	1350	0.9
	1943	4.5
13 TH	0221	0.9
	0815	4.3
	1428	1.0
	2024	4.5
14 F	0303	0.9
	0902	4.2
	1509	1.1
	2109	4.4
15 SA	0350	1.0
	0956	4.0
	1553	1.3
	2204	4.2
16 SU	0443	1.1
	1058	3.9
	1644	1.5
	2311	4.1
17 M	0543	1.2
	1205	3.7
	1746	1.6
18 TU	0022	4.0
	0649	1.3
	1313	3.7
	1858	1.7
19 W	0132	4.0
	0758	1.2
	1421	3.8
	2013	1.7
20 TH	0239	4.1
	0905	1.2
	1524	3.9
	2122	1.5
21 F	0341	4.2
	1007	1.1
	1618	4.1
	2223	1.4
22 SA	0436	4.3
	1100	1.0
	1706	4.3
	2318	1.2
23 SU	0526	4.4
	1149	0.9
	1749	4.5
24 M	0009	1.1
	0613	4.4
	1235	0.9
	○ 1831	4.6
25 TU	0058	1.0
	0658	4.4
	1318	0.9
	1911	4.7
26 W	0143	0.9
	0741	4.3
	1358	1.0
	1952	4.7
27 TH	0226	0.9
	0823	4.2
	1438	1.1
	2033	4.6
28 F	0308	1.0
	0905	4.1
	1517	1.2
	2115	4.5
29 SA	0349	1.1
	0948	3.9
	1557	1.4
	2200	4.3
30 SU	0431	1.3
	1035	3.7
	1639	1.6
	2249	4.1

JULY

Day	Time	m
1 M	0515	1.5
	1126	3.5
	1726	1.9
	2343	3.9
2 TU	0603	1.7
	1226	3.4
	1821	2.0
3 W	0041	3.8
	0656	1.8
	1335	3.4
	1925	2.1
4 TH	0143	3.7
	0756	1.8
	1446	3.5
	2036	2.1
5 F	0245	3.7
	0901	1.8
	1542	3.6
	2140	2.0
6 SA	0343	3.7
	1000	1.7
	1624	3.8
	2232	1.8
7 SU	0432	3.9
	1049	1.6
	1702	4.0
	2318	1.6
8 M	0518	4.0
	1133	1.4
	1738	4.2
9 TU	0002	1.4
	0601	4.2
	1216	1.2
	1815	4.4
10 W	0046	1.1
	0644	4.3
	1257	1.0
	● 1854	4.6
11 TH	0129	0.9
	0726	4.4
	1338	0.9
	1934	4.7
12 F	0212	0.7
	0809	4.5
	1419	0.9
	2015	4.7
13 SA	0256	0.6
	0854	4.4
	1500	0.9
	2059	4.7
14 SU	0341	0.6
	0941	4.3
	1543	1.0
	2148	4.6
15 M	0428	0.7
	1034	4.1
	1630	1.2
	2245	4.4
16 TU	0520	0.9
	1133	3.9
	1723	1.4
	2351	4.2
17 W	0617	1.1
	1239	3.8
	1825	1.6
18 TH	0101	4.0
	0719	1.3
	1348	3.7
	1936	1.7
19 F	0213	4.0
	0830	1.4
	1457	3.8
	2055	1.7
20 SA	0324	3.9
	0943	1.4
	1559	3.9
	2211	1.6
21 SU	0428	4.0
	1047	1.3
	1653	4.1
	2313	1.4
22 M	0523	4.0
	1139	1.2
	1739	4.3
23 TU	0006	1.2
	0610	4.1
	1226	1.1
	1820	4.5
24 W	0054	1.1
	0652	4.2
	1307	1.1
	○ 1859	4.6
25 TH	0135	0.9
	0729	4.2
	1346	1.0
	1936	4.7
26 F	0213	0.9
	0805	4.2
	1422	1.0
	2011	4.7
27 SA	0249	0.9
	0839	4.1
	1457	1.1
	2046	4.6
28 SU	0323	1.0
	0914	4.0
	1532	1.2
	2123	4.4
29 M	0358	1.1
	0950	3.9
	1607	1.4
	2202	4.2
30 TU	0434	1.3
	1030	3.7
	1645	1.6
	2247	4.0
31 W	0513	1.5
	1118	3.6
	1729	1.9
	2339	3.8

AUGUST

Day	Time	m
1 TH	0558	1.7
	1215	3.5
	1819	2.1
2 F	0038	3.6
	0649	1.9
	1320	3.4
	1920	2.2
3 SA	0144	3.6
	0749	2.0
	1432	3.5
	2036	2.2
4 SU	0255	3.6
	0903	2.0
	1539	3.7
	2154	2.0
5 M	0403	3.7
	1014	1.8
	1632	3.9
	2255	1.8
6 TU	0500	3.9
	1111	1.6
	1718	4.2
	2345	1.4
7 W	0548	4.2
	1159	1.3
	1800	4.5
8 TH	0031	1.1
	0631	4.4
	1243	1.1
	● 1840	4.8
9 F	0115	0.7
	0713	4.6
	1325	0.8
	1919	5.0
10 SA	0157	0.5
	0754	4.7
	1405	0.7
	1959	5.1
11 SU	0239	0.3
	0834	4.8
	1445	0.6
	2040	5.1
12 M	0321	0.3
	0917	4.6
	1526	0.7
	2124	4.9
13 TU	0404	0.5
	1004	4.4
	1609	0.9
	2215	4.6
14 W	0451	0.8
	1059	4.1
	1657	1.2
	2319	4.3
15 TH	0542	1.1
	1206	3.9
	1752	1.5
16 F	0037	4.0
	0642	1.5
	1321	3.7
	1903	1.8
17 SA	0159	3.8
	0759	1.7
	1437	3.7
	2042	1.9
18 SU	0319	3.7
	0931	1.8
	1548	3.8
	2214	1.8
19 M	0429	3.8
	1041	1.7
	1646	4.1
	2316	1.5
20 TU	0524	3.9
	1132	1.5
	1731	4.3
21 W	0004	1.3
	0605	4.0
	1216	1.3
	1809	4.5
22 TH	0044	1.1
	0640	4.1
	1253	1.1
	○ 1843	4.7
23 F	0119	0.9
	0711	4.2
	1328	1.0
	1915	4.8
24 SA	0152	0.8
	0740	4.3
	1401	0.9
	1945	4.8
25 SU	0222	0.8
	0808	4.3
	1432	0.9
	2015	4.7
26 M	0251	0.9
	0837	4.2
	1503	1.1
	2045	4.5
27 TU	0321	1.0
	0906	4.1
	1534	1.2
	2117	4.3
28 W	0353	1.2
	0940	4.0
	1607	1.5
	2153	4.1
29 TH	0429	1.4
	1019	3.8
	1644	1.7
	2239	3.8
30 F	0509	1.7
	1112	3.6
	1728	2.0
	2344	3.6
31 SA	0557	1.9
	1223	3.5
	1825	2.2

Chart Datum: 2·71 metres below Ordnance Datum (Newlyn)

TIME ZONE (UTC)
For Summer Time add ONE hour in **non-shaded areas**

SCOTLAND – STORNOWAY

LAT 58°12′N LONG 6°23′W

TIMES AND HEIGHTS OF HIGH AND LOW WATERS

SPRING & NEAP TIDES
Dates in red are SPRINGS
Dates in blue are NEAPS

YEAR **2002**

SEPTEMBER

Date	Day	Time	m	Time	m	Time	m	Time	m
1	SU	0101	3.5	0656	2.1	1340	3.5	1944	2.3
2	M	0224	3.5	0817	2.2	1500	3.6	2127	2.1
3	TU	0343	3.7	0948	2.0	1606	3.9	2237	1.8
4	W	0443	4.0	1052	1.7	1658	4.3	2328	1.4
5	TH	0531	4.3	1140	1.4	1741	4.7		
6	F	0013	0.9	0613	4.7	1224	1.0	1821	5.1
7	SA	0055	0.5	0653	4.9	1305	0.7	● 1900	5.3
8	SU	0136	0.3	0731	5.1	1345	0.5	1938	5.4
9	M	0216	0.1	0810	5.1	1424	0.5	2017	5.4
10	TU	0255	0.2	0850	4.9	1504	0.6	2059	5.1
11	W	0337	0.5	0934	4.7	1546	0.9	2147	4.8
12	TH	0420	0.9	1027	4.3	1631	1.2	2251	4.3
13	F	0508	1.3	1138	4.0	1725	1.7		
14	SA	0022	3.9	0607	1.8	1300	3.8	1839	2.0
15	SU	0152	3.7	0734	2.1	1421	3.8	2043	2.1
16	M	0317	3.7	0924	2.1	1536	3.9	2216	1.9
17	TU	0430	3.8	1031	1.9	1634	4.1	2309	1.6
18	W	0520	3.9	1118	1.7	1717	4.4	2349	1.3
19	TH	0553	4.1	1156	1.4	1751	4.6		
20	F	0023	1.1	0620	4.2	1232	1.2	1821	4.7
21	SA	0054	1.0	0646	4.4	1304	1.0	○ 1850	4.8
22	SU	0123	0.9	0712	4.5	1335	0.9	1917	4.8
23	M	0150	0.8	0736	4.5	1404	0.9	1943	4.8
24	TU	0217	0.9	0801	4.5	1433	1.0	2010	4.6
25	W	0245	1.0	0828	4.4	1502	1.2	2039	4.4
26	TH	0316	1.1	0856	4.2	1533	1.4	2110	4.2
27	F	0350	1.4	0928	4.0	1608	1.7	2148	3.9
28	SA	0427	1.7	1010	3.8	1648	2.0	2255	3.7
29	SU	0512	2.0	1136	3.6	1744	2.2		
30	M	0036	3.5	0614	2.2	1307	3.6	1912	2.3

OCTOBER

Date	Day	Time	m	Time	m	Time	m	Time	m
1	TU	0206	3.6	0745	2.3	1430	3.7	2105	2.1
2	W	0324	3.8	0925	2.2	1540	4.1	2216	1.7
3	TH	0422	4.2	1028	1.8	1634	4.5	2305	1.2
4	F	0509	4.5	1117	1.4	1719	4.9	2349	0.8
5	SA	0550	4.9	1200	1.0	1759	5.2		
6	SU	0030	0.5	0629	5.1	1242	0.7	● 1838	5.5
7	M	0110	0.2	0707	5.3	1322	0.6	1916	5.6
8	TU	0150	0.2	0744	5.3	1402	0.5	1956	5.4
9	W	0229	0.4	0824	5.1	1442	0.7	2038	5.2
10	TH	0309	0.7	0907	4.8	1525	1.0	2127	4.7
11	F	0352	1.1	1000	4.5	1611	1.4	2233	4.3
12	SA	0439	1.6	1115	4.2	1705	1.8		
13	SU	0009	3.9	0536	2.1	1238	4.0	1824	2.1
14	M	0136	3.7	0708	2.4	1356	3.9	2027	2.2
15	TU	0303	3.7	0859	2.4	1509	4.0	2157	2.0
16	W	0416	3.8	1006	2.1	1609	4.2	2245	1.7
17	TH	0500	4.0	1051	1.8	1651	4.4	2322	1.5
18	F	0529	4.1	1129	1.6	1726	4.5	2353	1.3
19	SA	0555	4.3	1203	1.4	1756	4.7		
20	SU	0023	1.1	0619	4.5	1236	1.2	1823	4.7
21	M	0051	1.0	0643	4.6	1307	1.1	○ 1849	4.8
22	TU	0117	0.9	0706	4.6	1336	1.0	1915	4.7
23	W	0144	0.9	0731	4.6	1405	1.1	1943	4.6
24	TH	0214	1.0	0758	4.5	1435	1.2	2013	4.5
25	F	0245	1.2	0827	4.4	1508	1.4	2047	4.2
26	SA	0319	1.4	0900	4.2	1543	1.6	2129	4.0
27	SU	0356	1.7	0944	4.0	1626	1.9	2242	3.7
28	M	0441	2.0	1109	3.8	1725	2.1		
29	TU	0020	3.6	0545	2.2	1243	3.7	1857	2.1
30	W	0144	3.7	0719	2.3	1400	3.9	2035	1.9
31	TH	0257	3.9	0853	2.1	1509	4.2	2145	1.6

NOVEMBER

Date	Day	Time	m	Time	m	Time	m	Time	m
1	F	0355	4.2	0958	1.8	1606	4.5	2236	1.2
2	SA	0443	4.6	1048	1.4	1653	4.9	2321	0.8
3	SU	0525	4.9	1133	1.1	1736	5.2		
4	M	0003	0.6	0604	5.1	1217	0.8	● 1816	5.3
5	TU	0045	0.4	0643	5.2	1259	0.7	1857	5.4
6	W	0125	0.5	0722	5.2	1342	0.7	1938	5.2
7	TH	0205	0.6	0803	5.1	1425	0.8	2023	4.9
8	F	0246	0.9	0848	4.9	1509	1.1	2114	4.6
9	SA	0329	1.3	0941	4.6	1557	1.4	2220	4.2
10	SU	0416	1.7	1049	4.3	1653	1.8	2343	3.8
11	M	0512	2.1	1204	4.1	1805	2.1		
12	TU	0102	3.7	0630	2.4	1316	4.0	1938	2.1
13	W	0222	3.6	0806	2.4	1425	4.0	2104	2.0
14	TH	0334	3.7	0920	2.3	1526	4.1	2200	1.8
15	F	0423	3.9	1012	2.0	1615	4.2	2241	1.7
16	SA	0457	4.1	1054	1.8	1654	4.3	2316	1.5
17	SU	0526	4.2	1132	1.6	1727	4.5	2348	1.3
18	M	0552	4.4	1206	1.4	1757	4.5		
19	TU	0018	1.2	0616	4.5	1239	1.3	1825	4.6
20	W	0047	1.1	0641	4.6	1311	1.2	○ 1854	4.6
21	TH	0117	1.1	0709	4.7	1343	1.2	1926	4.5
22	F	0149	1.1	0740	4.6	1417	1.2	2001	4.4
23	SA	0223	1.2	0813	4.5	1453	1.3	2041	4.2
24	SU	0259	1.4	0852	4.3	1533	1.5	2130	4.0
25	M	0339	1.6	0942	4.1	1620	1.6	2238	3.8
26	TU	0426	1.8	1054	4.0	1721	1.8	2358	3.7
27	W	0528	2.0	1214	3.9	1838	1.8		
28	TH	0112	3.7	0649	2.1	1326	4.0	1956	1.7
29	F	0221	3.9	0811	2.0	1433	4.2	2106	1.4
30	SA	0322	4.1	0920	1.8	1534	4.4	2203	1.2

DECEMBER

Date	Day	Time	m	Time	m	Time	m	Time	m
1	SU	0414	4.4	1017	1.5	1626	4.7	2253	0.9
2	M	0500	4.7	1107	1.2	1714	4.8	2339	0.8
3	TU	0542	4.9	1156	1.0	1759	5.0		
4	W	0023	0.7	0624	5.0	1243	0.9	● 1843	5.0
5	TH	0106	0.7	0705	5.0	1329	0.9	1928	4.9
6	F	0148	0.9	0748	5.0	1415	0.9	2015	4.7
7	SA	0230	1.1	0834	4.9	1501	1.1	2104	4.4
8	SU	0313	1.3	0923	4.7	1548	1.3	2158	4.1
9	M	0358	1.6	1017	4.5	1637	1.5	2259	3.9
10	TU	0447	1.9	1117	4.2	1733	1.8		
11	W	0007	3.6	0545	2.2	1221	4.1	1836	1.9
12	TH	0120	3.5	0658	2.3	1326	4.0	1947	2.0
13	F	0232	3.6	0815	2.3	1431	3.9	2055	2.0
14	SA	0332	3.7	0921	2.1	1528	4.0	2150	1.8
15	SU	0418	3.8	1013	2.0	1616	4.0	2235	1.7
16	M	0455	4.0	1058	1.8	1657	4.1	2313	1.5
17	TU	0526	4.2	1137	1.6	1733	4.2	2348	1.4
18	W	0554	4.4	1215	1.4	1807	4.3		
19	TH	0022	1.2	0623	4.5	1252	1.3	○ 1842	4.4
20	F	0058	1.1	0655	4.6	1329	1.2	1918	4.4
21	SA	0134	1.1	0730	4.6	1407	1.1	1957	4.4
22	SU	0211	1.1	0807	4.6	1447	1.1	2039	4.3
23	M	0249	1.2	0848	4.5	1529	1.1	2126	4.1
24	TU	0330	1.3	0934	4.4	1616	1.2	2220	4.0
25	W	0416	1.5	1031	4.2	1709	1.3	2324	3.8
26	TH	0510	1.6	1138	4.1	1809	1.4		
27	F	0032	3.8	0614	1.8	1248	4.1	1914	1.4
28	SA	0141	3.8	0726	1.8	1356	4.1	2023	1.4
29	SU	0246	3.9	0839	1.7	1503	4.2	2129	1.3
30	M	0346	4.1	0948	1.6	1604	4.3	2229	1.2
31	TU	0439	4.3	1049	1.4	1700	4.4	2322	1.1

Chart Datum: 2·71 metres below Ordnance Datum (Newlyn)

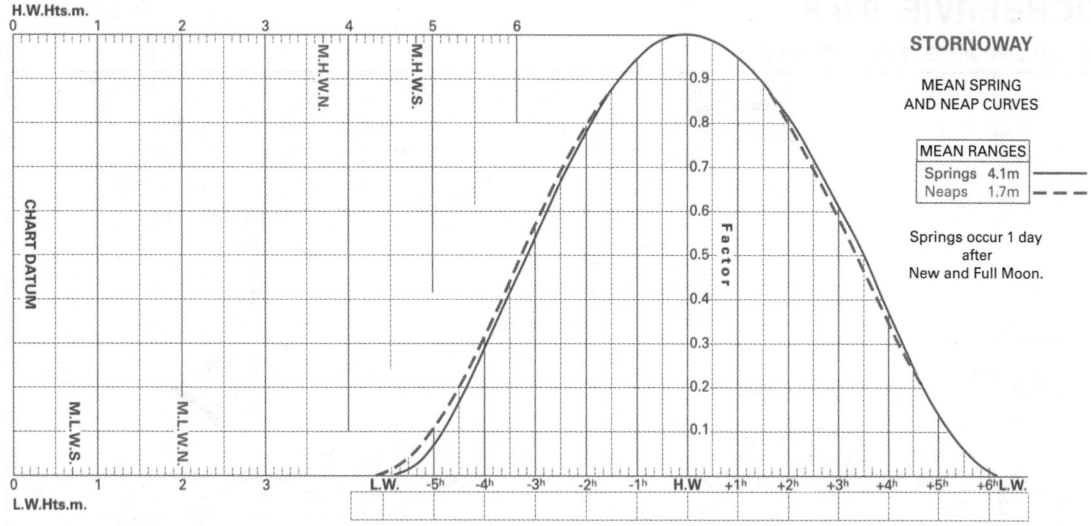
H.W.Hts.m.
0 1 2 3 4 5 6
M.H.W.N.
M.H.W.S.
CHART DATUM
M.L.W.S.
M.L.W.N.
0 1 2 3
L.W.Hts.m.
0.9
0.8
0.7
0.6
0.5
0.4
0.3
0.2
0.1
Factor
L.W. -5h -4h -3h -2h -1h H.W +1h +2h +3h +4h +5h +6h L.W.
STORNOWAY
MEAN SPRING AND NEAP CURVES
MEAN RANGES
Springs 4.1m
Neaps 1.7m
Springs occur 1 day after New and Full Moon.

ISLANDS WEST OF THE OUTER HEBRIDES (N to S)

TIDES

Standard Port STORNOWAY (⟵)

Times				**Height (metres)**			
High Water		Low Water		MHWS	MHWN	MLWN	MLWS
0100	0700	0300	0900	4·8	3·7	2·0	0·7
1300	1900	1500	2100				
Differences FLANNAN ISLES							
–0026	–0016	–0016	–0026	–0·9	–0·7	–0·6	–0·2
VILLAGE BAY (St Kilda)							
–0040	–0040	–0045	–0045	–1·4	–1·2	–0·8	–0·3
ROCKALL							
–0055	–0055	–0105	–0105	–1·8	–1·5	–0·9	–0·2

FLANNAN ISLES, Western Isles, centred on **58°17´·28N 07°35´·27W** (Eilean Mór). AC 2524, 2721. Tides, as above. Uninhabited group of several rky islets, 18M WNW of Gallan Head (Lewis). The main islet is Eilean Mór where landing can be made on SW side in suitable conditions. Lt ho, Fl (2) 30s 101m 20M, is a 23m high W tr on NE tip of Eilean Mór; the lt is obscured by islets to the W which are up to 57m high. No recommended ⚓s and the few charted depths are by lead-line surveys.

ST KILDA, Western Isles, **57°48´·28N 08°33´·07W.** AC 2524, 2721. Tides at Village Bay, Hirta: HW –0510 on Dover; ML 1·9m; Duration 0615; see above. A group of four isles and three stacks, the main island is Hirta from which the Army withdrew in April 1998 after 30 years. The facility is now manned by a civilian company, Serco ☎ (01870) 604443, based at South Uist. Hirta is owned by National Trust for Scotland and leased to Scottish National Heritage whose Warden lives at Village Bay. ⚓ in Village Bay, SE-facing, in approx 5m about 1·5ca off the pier. Ldg lts 270°, both Oc 5s 26/38m 3M. If wind is between NE and SSW big swells enter the bay; good holding, but untenable if winds strong. Levenish Is (55m) is 1·5M E of Hirta with offlying rks. Call *Kilda Radio* VHF Ch 16 12 73 (HJ) for permission to land; ☎ (01870) 604406 (HO), 604612 (OT); 📠 604601. Alternative ⚓ at Glen Bay on N side is only safe in S & E winds. Facilities: FW from wells near landings.

ROCKALL, 57°35´·7N 13°41´·2W. AC 2524, 1128. Tides, as above. A 19m high granite rock, 200M W of N Uist. Best access by helicopter. Lt, Fl 15s 13M, is often extinguished for long periods due to weather damage. Helen's Reef, 1·4m, on which the sea breaks is 2M ENE.

MONACH ISLANDS (or Heisker Is), centred on 57°31´·28N 07°38´·07W. AC 2721, 2721. Tides, see 9.8.7 Shillay. The group lies 5M SW of N Uist and 8M WNW of Benbecula. The 5 main islands (W-E) are Shillay, Ceann Iar, Shivinish, Ceann Ear and Stockay; all uninhabited. There are many rky offliers from NW through N to SE of the group. On Shillay there is a conspic, disused, red brick lt ho. ⚓s at: E of disused lt ho; Croic Hbr, bay N of Shivinish; and S Hbr on W side of Shivinish.

KINLOCHBERVIE *9.8.8*

Highland **58°27'·26N 05°02'·78W** ❁❁❁◊◊✿✿

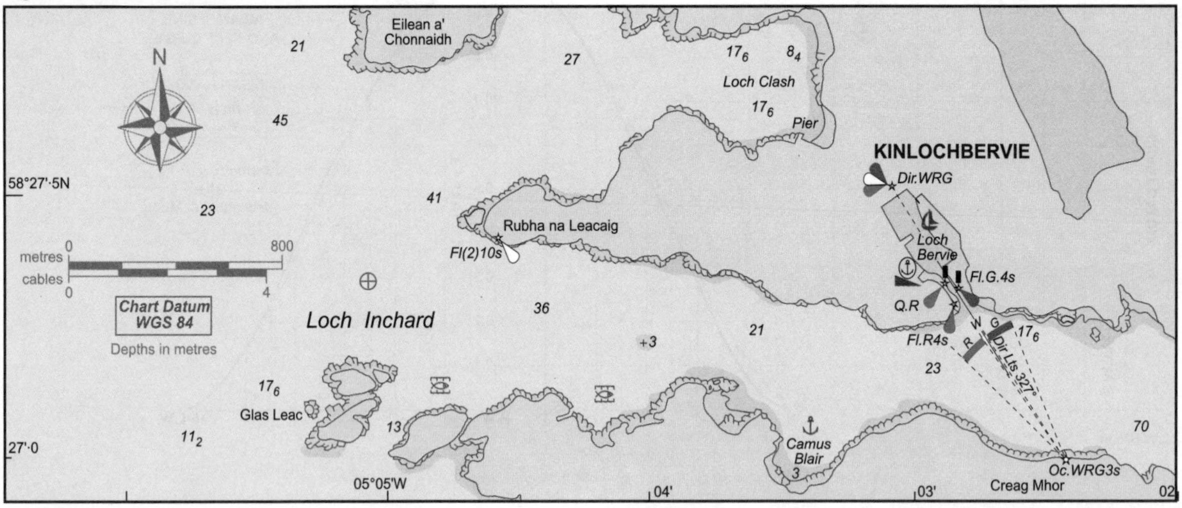

CHARTS AC 2503, 1785, 1954; Imray C67; OS 9

TIDES –0400 Dover; ML 2·7; Duration 0610; Zone 0 (UT)

Standard Port ULLAPOOL (⟶)

Times				Height (metres)			
High Water		Low Water		MHWS	MHWN	MLWN	MLWS
0000	0600	0300	0900	5·2	3·9	2·1	0·7
1200	1800	1500	2100				
Differences LOCH BERVIE							
+0030	+0010	+0010	+0020	–0·3	–0·3	–0·2	0·0
LOCH LAXFORD							
+0015	+0015	+0005	+0005	–0·3	–0·4	–0·2	0·0
BADCALL BAY							
+0005	+0005	+0005	+0005	–0·7	–0·5	–0·5	+0·2
LOCH NEDD							
0000	0000	0000	0000	–0·3	–0·2	–0·2	0·0
LOCH INVER							
–0005	–0005	–0005	–0005	–0·2	0·0	0·0	+0·1

SHELTER Very good in Kinlochbervie Hbr off the N shore of Loch Inchard. A useful passage port, only 14.5 track miles S of Cape Wrath. It is also a busy FV port, but in NNE corner yachts AB on 18m long pontoon in 4m on SW side only; NE side is shoal/foul. If full, ⚓ at Loch Clash, open to W; landing jetty in 2·7m. Other ⚓s at: Camus Blair on S shore, 5ca SW of hbr ent, and up the loch at L Sheigra, Achriesgill Bay and 5ca short of the head of the loch.

NAVIGATION WPT 58°27'·34N 05°05'·08W (at mouth of Loch Inchard), 280°/100° from/to hbr ent, 1·3M. The sides of the loch are clean, but keep to N side of Loch Inchard to clear a rk (3m depth) almost in mid-chan.

LIGHTS AND MARKS From offshore in good vis Ceann Garbh, a conspic mountain 899m (6M inland), leads 110° toward ent of Loch Inchard. Rubha na Leacaig, Fl (2) 10s 30m 8M, marks N side of loch ent. Dir ☆ WRG (H24) 15m 16M, Y framework tr (floodlit) leads 327° into hbr; see 9.8.4 for vis sectors. The 25m wide ent chan (and hbr) is dredged 4m and marked by 2 PHM poles, Fl R 4s and QR, and by a SHM pole, Fl G 4s. On S shore of loch Creag Mhòr, Dir Oc lt WRG 2.8s 16m 9M, is aligned 147°/327° with hbr ent chan; see 9.8.4.

RADIO TELEPHONE VHF Ch **14** 16 HX. Ch 06 is used by FVs in the Minches.

TELEPHONE (Dial code 01971) Hr Mr ☎ 521235, 📠 521718; MRSC (01851) 702013; ⊖ (0141) 887 9369 (H24); Marinecall 09068 500 464; Police 521222; Dr 502002.

FACILITIES FW, D at FV quay, P (cans), Gas, CH, ME, ✉, Bar, V, R. Showers (Mission), ♿. In summer, bus to Inverness.

ANCHORAGE/HARBOUR BETWEEN KINLOCHBERVIE AND ULLAPOOL

LOCH LAXFORD Highland, **58°24'·78N 05°07'·18W**. AC 2503. HW –0410 on Dover. ML 2·7m. See 9.8.8. Ent between Rubha Ruadh and Ardmore Pt, 1M ENE, clearly identified by 3 isolated mountains (N-S) Ceann Garbh, Ben Arkle and Ben Stack. The many ⚓s in the loch include: Loch a'Chadh-fi, on N/NE sides of islet (John Ridgeway's Adventure School on Pt on W side of narrows has moorings); Bagh nah-Airde Beag, next bay to E, (beware rk 5ca off SE shore which covers at MHWS); Weaver's Bay on SW shore, 3M from ent (beware drying rk off NW Pt of ent); Bagh na Fionndalach Mor on SW shore (4-6m); Fanagmore Bay on SW shore (beware head of bay foul with old moorings). Beware many fish farming cages. Facilities: none, nearest stores at Scourie (5M).

LOCH INVER Highland, **58°08'·98N 05°15'·08W**. AC 2504. HW –0433 on Dover; ML 3·0m. See 9.8.8. Good shelter in all weathers at head of loch in busy fishing hbr on S side. Appr N or S of Soyea Is, Fl (2) 10s 34m 6M; beware rk drying 1·7m about 50m off Kirkaig Point (S side of ent). Glas Leac, a small islet 7ca WSW of hbr, may be passed on either side. Its ☆, Fl WRG 3s, has 3 WRG sectors (see 9.8.4) covering the chans N and S of Soyea Is and into the hbr. The church, hotel (S side) and white ho (N side) are all conspic. A pontoon for yachts, <12m LOA, is in 5m between the bkwtr (QG) and the first FV pier. Or, in W'ly gales, ⚓ in the lee of bkwtr in about 8m; or where Hr Mr directs. Other ⚓s on S shore of Loch Inver. VHF Ch 09 16. Hr Mr ☎ (01571) 844247. **Facilities**: FW, P, D, V, ✉, Gas.

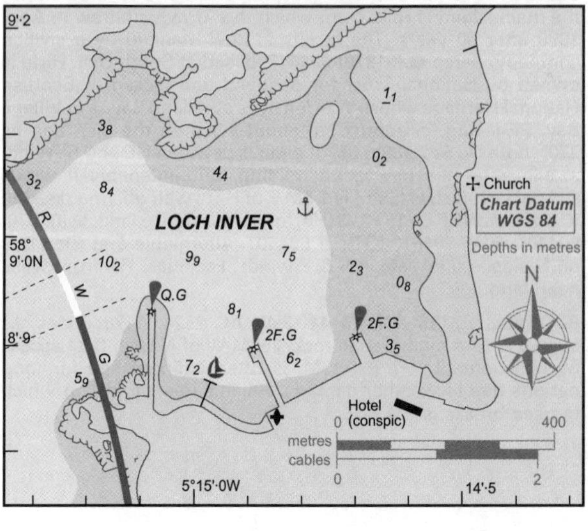

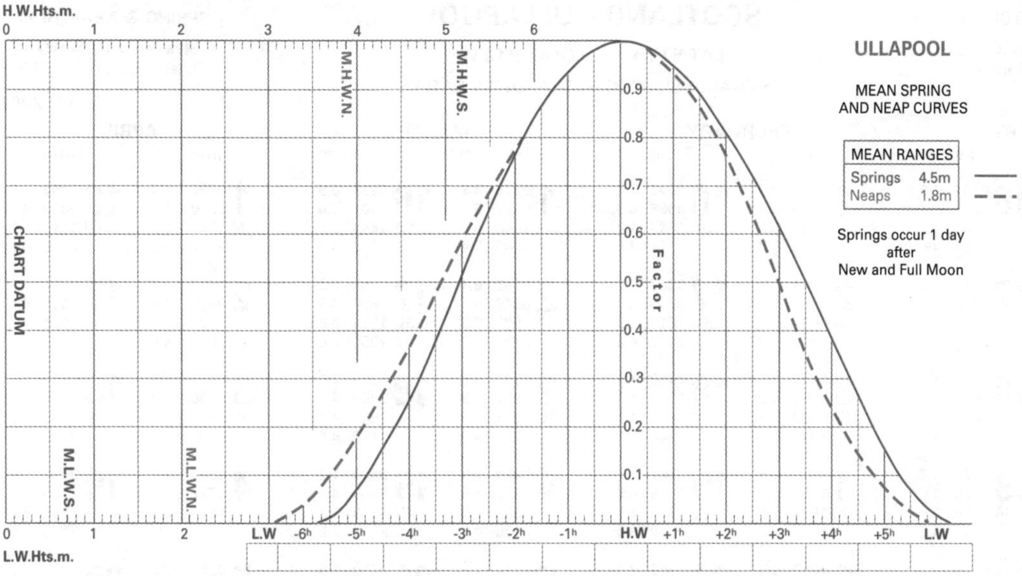

ULLAPOOL *9.8.9*

Highland **57°53´·70N 05°09´·38W**

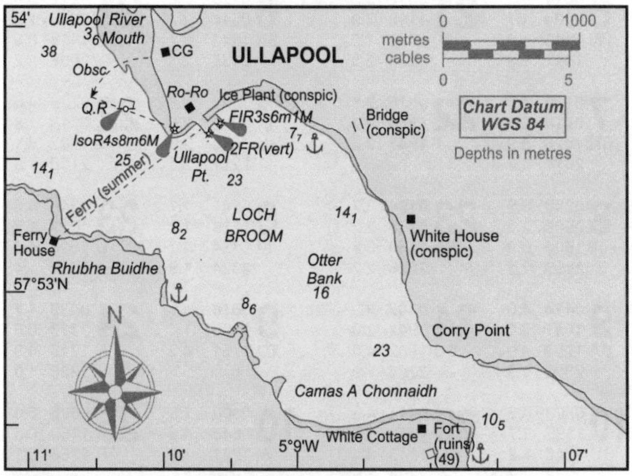

CHARTS AC 2500, 2501, 2509, 1794; Imray C67; OS 19

TIDES –0415 Dover; ML 3·0; Duration 0610; Zone 0 (UT)

Standard Port ULLAPOOL (⟶)

Times				Height (metres)			
High Water		Low Water		MHWS	MHWN	MLWN	MLWS
0000	0600	0300	0900	5·2	3·9	2·1	0·7
1200	1800	1500	2100				
Differences SUMMER ISLES (Tanera Mor)							
–0005	–0005	–0010	–0010	–0·1	+0·1	0·0	+0·1
LOCH EWE (Mellon Charles, 57°51'N 05°38'W)							
–0010	–0010	–0010	–0010	–0·1	–0·1	–0·1	0·0
LOCH GAIRLOCH							
–0020	–0020	–0010	–0010	0·0	+0·1	–0·3	–0·1

Ullapool is a Standard Port and detailed tidal predictions for each day of the year are given below.

SHELTER Good in ⚓ E of pier; access at all tides. See Hr Mr for temp moorings. From Aug to Mar Ullapool is mainly a FV port and the pier may be congested. Loch Kanaird (N of ent to Loch Broom) has good ⚓ E of Isle Martin. Possible ⚓s 6ca S of Ullapool Pt, and beyond the narrows 3ca ESE of W cottage. The upper loch is squally in strong winds.

NAVIGATION WPT L Broom ent 57°55´·78N 05°15´·08W, 309°/129° from/to Ullapool Pt lt, 3.5M. N of Ullapool Pt extensive drying flats off the mouth of Ullapool R are marked by QR buoy. Beware fish pens and unlit buoys SE of narrows off W shore.

LIGHTS AND MARKS Rhubha Cadail, N of L. Broom ent, Fl WRG 6s 11m 9/6M. Cailleach Hd, W of ent, Fl (2) 12s 60m 9M. Ullapool Pt Iso R 4s 8m 6M; grey mast, vis 258°-108°.

RADIO TELEPHONE VHF Ch 14 16 12 (July-Nov: H24. Dec-June: HO).

TELEPHONE (Dial code 01854) Hr Mr 612091/612165; MRSC (01851) 702013; ⊖ (0141) 887 9369; Marinecall 09068 500464; Police 612017; Dr 612015.

FACILITIES **Pier** AB £5 for 1 or more nights, D, FW, CH; **Ullapool YC** Gas; **Services:** ME, El, Ⓔ, Sh. **Town** EC Tues (winter); P, ⊡, V, R, Bar, ⊠, Ⓑ, ⇌ (bus to Garve). Daily buses to Inverness (✈), ferries twice daily (summer) to Stornoway. No Sunday bus, train or ferry services.

ADJACENT ANCHORAGES

SUMMER ISLES, High. **58°01'N 05°25'W**. AC 2501, 2509. HW –0425 Dover; See 9.8.9; streams are weak and irregular. In the N apps to Loch Broom some 30 islands and rks, the main ones being Eilean Mullagrach, Isle Ristol, Glas-leac Mor, Tanera Beg, Eilean a' Char, Eilean Fada Mor. ⚓s: Isle Ristol, ⚓ to the S of drying causeway; close to slip is lt Fl G 3s. Tanera Beg, ⚓ in the chan to the E inside Eilean Fada Mor (beware bys, nets and drying rks). Tanera Mor on E side, ⚓ in bay (the "Cabbage Patch"); new pier but many moorings; or in NW, ⚓ close E of Eilean na Saille, but N of drying rk. Temp ⚓ at Badentarbat B for Achiltibuie on mainland. Facilities: V, R, Gas, FW, D (emerg) ☎ (01854) 622261.

LOCH EWE, Highland, **57°52´·0N 05°40´·0W** (SWM buoy, L Fl 10s). AC 3146, 2509. Tides: See 9.8.9; HW –0415 on Dover; ML 2·9m; Duration 0610. Shelter in all winds. Easy ent with no dangers in loch. Rhubha Reidh lt, Fl (4) 15s 37m 24M, W tr, is 4·5M W of ent. No 1 buoy Fl (3) G 10s. Loch approx 7M long with Isle Ewe and 2 small islets about 2M from ent in centre; can be passed on either side. Beware unlit buoys E side Isle Ewe. Aultbea Pier, 2 FG (vert), to NE. NATO fuelling jetty and dolphins, all Fl G 4s. Sheltered ⚓ in Loch Thurnaig to S. **Aultbea**: Dr, P, ⊠, R, V, Bar. Poolewe Bay (3·5m, at head of loch): Boor Rks off W shore about 7ca from loch hd. **Inverewe Gdns** on NE side. Poolewe: FW, D, L on pier, P (at garage), ⊠, R, Bar, V, Gas.

LOCH GAIRLOCH, Highland, **57°43´N 05°45´W**. AC 2528, 228. HW –0440 on Dover. See 9.8.9. A wide loch facing W. Ent clear of dangers. Quite heavy seas enter in bad weather. Good shelter in Badachro, SW of Eilean Horrisdale on S side of loch or in Loch Shieldaig at SE end of the loch. Or ⚓ in Flowerdale Bay in approx 6m near Gairloch pier. Lts: Glas Eilean Fl WRG 6s 9m 6/4M, W080°-102°, R102°-296°, W296°-333°, G333°-080°. Pier hd, QR 9m. Hr Mr ☎ (01445) 712140, 📠 710184. VHF Ch 16 (occas). Gairloch Pier: AB fees charged. P (cans), D, FW, Hotel, Gas, V, CH, Bar, ⊠.

TIME ZONE (UTC)
For Summer Time add ONE hour in **non-shaded areas**

SCOTLAND – ULLAPOOL

LAT 57°54′N LONG 5°10′W

TIMES AND HEIGHTS OF HIGH AND LOW WATERS

SPRING & NEAP TIDES
Dates in **red** are **SPRINGS**
Dates in **blue** are **NEAPS**

YEAR **2002**

JANUARY

Date	Day	Time	m	Time	m	Time	m	Time	m
1	TU	0201	1.0	0757	5.3	1434	0.9	2033	5.1
2	W	0245	1.0	0841	5.3	1520	0.9	2123	5.0
3	TH	0330	1.1	0929	5.2	1609	1.0	2218	4.8
4	F	0418	1.3	1022	5.0	1701	1.1	2317	4.6
5	SA	0511	1.5	1124	4.8	1758	1.4		
6	SU	0022	4.4	0609	1.8	1234	4.6	1902	1.6
7	M	0132	4.3	0716	2.0	1350	4.4	2014	1.7
8	TU	0242	4.3	0832	2.0	1506	4.4	2128	1.7
9	W	0347	4.4	0949	1.9	1614	4.5	2232	1.6
10	TH	0444	4.6	1054	1.8	1711	4.6	2325	1.5
11	F	0531	4.8	1148	1.6	1757	4.7		
12	SA	0011	1.4	0611	4.9	1235	1.4	1837	4.7
13	SU	0053	1.4	0646	5.0	1317	1.3	● 1913	4.8
14	M	0131	1.3	0721	5.1	1356	1.2	1949	4.8
15	TU	0207	1.3	0756	5.1	1432	1.2	2024	4.7
16	W	0241	1.3	0830	5.1	1508	1.2	2058	4.6
17	TH	0316	1.4	0905	4.9	1543	1.3	2133	4.5
18	F	0351	1.5	0941	4.8	1619	1.4	2208	4.3
19	SA	0427	1.7	1020	4.6	1656	1.6	2249	4.1
20	SU	0506	1.9	1105	4.4	1736	1.8	2339	4.0
21	M	0549	2.1	1159	4.2	1822	2.0		
22	TU	0040	3.8	0642	2.3	1305	4.0	1919	2.1
23	W	0154	3.8	0750	2.4	1417	4.0	2030	2.1
24	TH	0308	3.9	0914	2.3	1528	4.1	2147	2.0
25	F	0410	4.2	1028	2.1	1629	4.3	2249	1.8
26	SA	0459	4.5	1123	1.7	1721	4.6	2339	1.5
27	SU	0543	4.8	1211	1.4	1807	4.9		
28	M	0024	1.2	0624	5.1	1256	1.0	○ 1851	5.1
29	TU	0107	1.0	0704	5.4	1339	0.7	1935	5.3
30	W	0150	0.8	0745	5.5	1423	0.5	2019	5.3
31	TH	0233	0.7	0826	5.5	1507	0.4	2104	5.2

FEBRUARY

Date	Day	Time	m	Time	m	Time	m	Time	m
1	F	0317	0.7	0910	5.4	1552	0.5	2153	5.0
2	SA	0401	0.9	0957	5.2	1639	0.7	2245	4.8
3	SU	0448	1.1	1051	4.9	1728	1.1	2344	4.5
4	M	0539	1.5	1155	4.6	1823	1.5		
5	TU	0050	4.3	0637	1.8	1313	4.3	1928	1.8
6	W	0204	4.1	0749	2.1	1442	4.1	2052	2.0
7	TH	0322	4.1	0926	2.1	1606	4.1	2214	2.0
8	F	0430	4.3	1046	1.9	1708	4.2	2314	1.8
9	SA	0522	4.5	1143	1.7	1755	4.4		
10	SU	0001	1.6	0602	4.7	1228	1.5	1830	4.5
11	M	0042	1.4	0634	4.8	1307	1.2	1901	4.6
12	TU	0117	1.3	0705	5.0	1341	1.1	● 1930	4.7
13	W	0150	1.1	0736	5.1	1413	1.0	1959	4.7
14	TH	0222	1.0	0806	5.1	1444	0.9	2027	4.7
15	F	0254	1.0	0835	5.0	1515	1.0	2054	4.6
16	SA	0325	1.1	0906	4.9	1546	1.1	2125	4.5
17	SU	0357	1.3	0939	4.7	1619	1.2	2159	4.3
18	M	0430	1.5	1015	4.5	1653	1.4	2240	4.1
19	TU	0507	1.7	1058	4.2	1733	1.7	2330	3.9
20	W	0552	2.0	1156	4.0	1821	2.0		
21	TH	0041	3.8	0650	2.3	1318	3.9	1926	2.2
22	F	0212	3.7	0812	2.3	1451	3.9	2059	2.2
23	SA	0336	4.0	1002	2.1	1608	4.1	2228	1.9
24	SU	0438	4.3	1107	1.7	1706	4.5	2323	1.5
25	M	0525	4.7	1157	1.2	1753	4.8		
26	TU	0009	1.1	0607	5.1	1242	0.8	1835	5.2
27	W	0053	0.8	0647	5.4	1324	0.4	○ 1917	5.4
28	TH	0135	0.5	0726	5.6	1406	0.2	1958	5.5

MARCH

Date	Day	Time	m	Time	m	Time	m	Time	m
1	F	0216	0.3	0806	5.7	1448	0.1	2040	5.4
2	SA	0258	0.4	0848	5.6	1530	0.2	2124	5.2
3	SU	0341	0.5	0932	5.3	1613	0.5	2212	4.9
4	M	0425	0.8	1022	4.9	1657	1.0	2306	4.5
5	TU	0511	1.2	1122	4.4	1747	1.5		
6	W	0011	4.2	0604	1.7	1243	4.0	1847	1.9
7	TH	0129	4.0	0714	2.1	1426	3.8	2017	2.2
8	F	0258	3.9	0909	2.2	1600	3.9	2159	2.2
9	SA	0414	4.0	1041	2.0	1702	4.0	2303	2.0
10	SU	0508	4.3	1135	1.7	1746	4.2	2348	1.7
11	M	0546	4.5	1215	1.4	1816	4.4		
12	TU	0025	1.4	0616	4.7	1249	1.2	1841	4.5
13	W	0058	1.2	0644	4.9	1319	1.0	1906	4.6
14	TH	0129	1.0	0712	5.0	1347	0.8	● 1931	4.7
15	F	0158	0.9	0739	5.0	1415	0.8	1954	4.8
16	SA	0228	0.8	0805	5.0	1444	0.8	2020	4.7
17	SU	0258	0.9	0834	4.9	1514	0.8	2050	4.6
18	M	0328	1.0	0906	4.7	1545	1.0	2122	4.4
19	TU	0400	1.2	0940	4.5	1618	1.3	2159	4.2
20	W	0436	1.5	1021	4.2	1656	1.6	2244	4.0
21	TH	0519	1.8	1118	3.9	1742	1.9	2353	3.8
22	F	0616	2.1	1246	3.7	1847	2.2		
23	SA	0134	3.7	0739	2.2	1430	3.8	2026	2.2
24	SU	0307	3.9	0942	2.0	1552	4.0	2206	1.9
25	M	0414	4.2	1049	1.5	1649	4.4	2303	1.5
26	TU	0504	4.7	1138	1.0	1735	4.8	2350	1.0
27	W	0547	5.1	1222	0.6	1817	5.2		
28	TH	0033	0.6	0626	5.4	1304	0.2	○ 1856	5.4
29	F	0115	0.4	0706	5.6	1345	0.0	1936	5.5
30	SA	0157	0.2	0745	5.6	1426	0.0	2016	5.4
31	SU	0239	0.2	0826	5.5	1506	0.2	2057	5.2

APRIL

Date	Day	Time	m	Time	m	Time	m	Time	m
1	M	0320	0.4	0910	5.2	1547	0.6	2142	4.9
2	TU	0403	0.8	0959	4.8	1630	1.0	2233	4.5
3	W	0448	1.2	1100	4.3	1716	1.6	2337	4.2
4	TH	0540	1.7	1222	3.9	1814	2.1		
5	F	0057	3.9	0650	2.1	1410	3.7	1945	2.4
6	SA	0228	3.8	0844	2.2	1543	3.7	2135	2.3
7	SU	0347	3.9	1022	2.0	1644	3.9	2241	2.0
8	M	0441	4.1	1113	1.7	1724	4.1	2324	1.8
9	TU	0518	4.3	1150	1.4	1751	4.3		
10	W	0000	1.5	0548	4.6	1221	1.2	1815	4.5
11	TH	0032	1.2	0617	4.7	1249	1.0	1839	4.6
12	F	0102	1.0	0644	4.9	1316	0.8	● 1902	4.7
13	SA	0131	0.9	0711	4.9	1345	0.8	1925	4.8
14	SU	0201	0.8	0738	4.9	1414	0.7	1952	4.8
15	M	0232	0.9	0809	4.9	1444	0.8	2022	4.7
16	TU	0303	1.0	0842	4.7	1516	1.0	2056	4.5
17	W	0338	1.2	0919	4.5	1551	1.2	2134	4.3
18	TH	0416	1.4	1006	4.2	1630	1.5	2222	4.1
19	F	0502	1.7	1110	3.9	1719	1.9	2335	3.9
20	SA	0602	1.9	1241	3.7	1827	2.1		
21	SU	0112	3.8	0728	2.0	1414	3.8	2006	2.2
22	M	0239	4.0	0916	1.8	1532	4.1	2138	1.9
23	TU	0346	4.3	1023	1.3	1629	4.4	2237	1.4
24	W	0439	4.7	1113	0.9	1715	4.8	2326	1.0
25	TH	0525	5.0	1159	0.5	1756	5.1		
26	F	0011	0.7	0606	5.3	1242	0.3	1835	5.4
27	SA	0055	0.4	0647	5.4	1323	0.2	○ 1914	5.4
28	SU	0138	0.3	0728	5.4	1404	0.2	1954	5.4
29	M	0220	0.4	0810	5.3	1444	0.5	2034	5.2
30	TU	0303	0.6	0856	5.0	1525	0.8	2118	4.9

Chart Datum: 2·75 metres below Ordnance Datum (Newlyn)

TIME ZONE (UTC)
For Summer Time add ONE hour in **non-shaded areas**

SCOTLAND – ULLAPOOL

LAT 57°54′N LONG 5°10′W

TIMES AND HEIGHTS OF HIGH AND LOW WATERS

SPRING & NEAP TIDES
Dates in red are SPRINGS
Dates in blue are NEAPS

YEAR **2002**

MAY

Date	Day	Time	m	Date	Day	Time	m
1		0346	0.9	16		0323	1.1
		0946	4.6			0914	4.4
	W	1606	1.2		TH	1533	1.3
		2208	4.5			2124	4.4
2		0432	1.3	17		0406	1.3
		1047	4.2			1008	4.2
	TH	1652	1.7		F	1617	1.5
		2311	4.2			2218	4.2
3		0524	1.6	18		0456	1.5
		1203	3.8			1115	4.0
	F	1749	2.1		SA	1709	1.8
						2329	4.1
4		0026	4.0	19		0558	1.7
		0631	2.0			1232	3.9
	SA	1335	3.6		SU	1818	2.0
		1909	2.4				
5		0146	3.8	20		0050	4.0
		0759	2.1			0717	1.7
	SU	1503	3.6		M	1351	3.9
		2043	2.3			1942	2.0
6		0259	3.9	21		0207	4.1
		0928	2.0			0841	1.5
	M	1605	3.8		TU	1504	4.1
		2156	2.1			2103	1.8
7		0355	4.0	22		0315	4.3
		1027	1.8			0949	1.3
	TU	1646	4.0		W	1603	4.4
		2244	1.9			2206	1.5
8		0437	4.2	23		0413	4.6
		1107	1.5			1045	1.0
	W	1716	4.2		TH	1653	4.7
		2323	1.6			2300	1.2
9		0513	4.4	24		0503	4.8
		1141	1.3			1134	0.7
	TH	1744	4.4		F	1736	5.0
		2357	1.4			2349	0.9
10		0546	4.6	25		0549	5.0
		1212	1.1			1220	0.6
	F	1811	4.5		SA	1817	5.2
11		0030	1.2	26		0036	0.7
		0616	4.7			0632	5.1
	SA	1243	1.0		SU	1304	0.5
		1835	4.7		○	1857	5.2
12		0103	1.1	27		0121	0.6
		0645	4.8			0716	5.1
	SU	1314	0.9		M	1345	0.6
	●	1900	4.8			1936	5.2
13		0135	1.0	28		0206	0.7
		0717	4.8			0800	5.0
	M	1346	0.9		TU	1426	0.8
		1930	4.8			2017	5.1
14		0209	1.0	29		0249	0.8
		0751	4.7			0846	4.7
	TU	1419	0.9		W	1507	1.0
		2004	4.7			2101	4.8
15		0244	1.0	30		0333	1.0
		0830	4.6			0936	4.5
	W	1455	1.1		TH	1548	1.4
		2041	4.6			2149	4.6
				31		0419	1.3
						1030	4.2
					F	1633	1.7
						2244	4.3

JUNE

Date	Day	Time	m	Date	Day	Time	m
1		0508	1.5	16		0451	1.2
		1131	3.9			1106	4.2
	SA	1724	2.0		SU	1702	1.5
		2348	4.1			2314	4.4
2		0604	1.8	17		0548	1.3
		1240	3.7			1211	4.1
	SU	1826	2.2		M	1803	1.7
3		0055	4.0	18		0023	4.3
		0706	1.9			0653	1.4
	M	1354	3.6		TU	1321	4.1
		1938	2.3			1912	1.8
4		0201	3.9	19		0134	4.2
		0812	1.9			0803	1.4
	TU	1500	3.7		W	1430	4.2
		2048	2.2			2024	1.7
5		0259	3.9	20		0244	4.3
		0915	1.9			0913	1.3
	W	1552	3.8		TH	1535	4.3
		2148	2.0			2134	1.6
6		0350	4.1	21		0349	4.4
		1008	1.7			1016	1.2
	TH	1634	4.0		F	1630	4.5
		2237	1.8			2236	1.4
7		0434	4.2	22		0446	4.5
		1053	1.6			1112	1.1
	F	1710	4.2		SA	1719	4.7
		2319	1.6			2332	1.2
8		0513	4.4	23		0538	4.7
		1133	1.4			1202	1.0
	SA	1742	4.4		SU	1803	4.9
		2358	1.4				
9		0549	4.5	24		0022	1.0
		1210	1.2			0624	4.8
	SU	1811	4.6		M	1248	1.0
					○	1844	5.0
10		0035	1.3	25		0111	0.9
		0624	4.6			0709	4.8
	M	1247	1.1		TU	1331	1.0
	●	1842	4.7			1923	5.0
11		0113	1.1	26		0156	0.9
		0701	4.7			0751	4.7
	TU	1323	1.0		W	1412	1.0
		1916	4.8			2003	5.0
12		0151	1.0	27		0238	0.9
		0742	4.7			0834	4.6
	W	1401	1.0		TH	1451	1.2
		1953	4.8			2043	4.9
13		0231	1.0	28		0320	1.0
		0825	4.6			0917	4.4
	TH	1440	1.1		F	1530	1.3
		2034	4.7			2125	4.7
14		0313	1.0	29		0401	1.2
		0913	4.5			1002	4.3
	F	1523	1.2		SA	1611	1.5
		2120	4.6			2211	4.5
15		0400	1.1	30		0442	1.3
		1007	4.4			1049	4.1
	SA	1609	1.3		SU	1653	1.7
		2213	4.5			2301	4.3

JULY

Date	Day	Time	m	Date	Day	Time	m
1		0526	1.5	16		0527	1.0
		1141	3.9			1142	4.4
	M	1740	1.9		TU	1739	1.4
		2357	4.1			2351	4.5
2		0613	1.7	17		0622	1.2
		1239	3.7			1246	4.2
	TU	1834	2.1		W	1839	1.6
3		0057	4.0	18		0101	4.3
		0704	1.8			0724	1.4
	W	1344	3.7		TH	1356	4.1
		1935	2.2			1947	1.7
4		0158	3.9	19		0217	4.2
		0802	1.9			0836	1.5
	TH	1449	3.7		F	1507	4.2
		2042	2.2			2104	1.8
5		0257	3.9	20		0332	4.2
		0904	1.9			0952	1.6
	F	1546	3.8		SA	1612	4.3
		2146	2.1			2221	1.6
6		0351	4.0	21		0440	4.3
		1004	1.8			1057	1.5
	SA	1634	4.0		SU	1707	4.5
		2241	1.9			2324	1.4
7		0440	4.1	22		0536	4.4
		1057	1.7			1150	1.4
	SU	1714	4.3		M	1754	4.7
		2329	1.7				
8		0525	4.3	23		0016	1.3
		1143	1.5			0622	4.5
	M	1751	4.5		TU	1237	1.3
						1833	4.8
9		0013	1.4	24		0103	1.1
		0607	4.5			0702	4.6
	TU	1226	1.3		W	1319	1.2
		1826	4.7		○	1910	4.9
10		0055	1.2	25		0145	1.0
		0649	4.7			0738	4.6
	W	1306	1.1		TH	1357	1.1
	●	1904	4.9			1945	5.0
11		0136	1.0	26		0223	0.9
		0731	4.8			0814	4.6
	TH	1347	1.0		F	1433	1.1
		1942	5.0			2020	4.9
12		0219	0.8	27		0259	0.9
		0815	4.8			0849	4.5
	F	1428	0.9		SA	1508	1.2
		2023	5.0			2056	4.8
13		0302	0.7	28		0334	1.0
		0901	4.8			0924	4.4
	SA	1512	0.9		SU	1543	1.3
		2107	5.0			2131	4.7
14		0348	0.7	29		0409	1.1
		0950	4.7			0959	4.2
	SU	1557	1.0		M	1619	1.4
		2155	4.8			2208	4.5
15		0436	0.8	30		0444	1.3
		1043	4.5			1035	4.1
	M	1646	1.2		TU	1656	1.6
		2249	4.6			2250	4.2
				31		0522	1.5
						1118	3.9
					W	1737	1.9
						2341	4.0

AUGUST

Date	Day	Time	m	Date	Day	Time	m
1		0604	1.7	16		0034	4.2
		1214	3.7			0648	1.6
	TH	1825	2.1		F	1325	4.1
						1914	1.9
2		0043	3.9	17		0200	4.0
		0652	1.9			0803	1.9
	F	1327	3.7		SA	1445	4.1
		1926	2.3			2045	2.0
3		0155	3.8	18		0330	4.0
		0755	2.1			0937	1.9
	SA	1449	3.7		SU	1600	4.2
		2048	2.3			2220	1.8
4		0307	3.8	19		0443	4.1
		0914	2.1			1049	1.8
	SU	1557	3.9		M	1659	4.4
		2210	2.1			2322	1.6
5		0411	4.0	20		0536	4.3
		1028	1.9			1142	1.6
	M	1649	4.2		TU	1745	4.6
		2308	1.8				
6		0505	4.2	21		0011	1.3
		1122	1.7			0617	4.4
	TU	1731	4.5		W	1226	1.4
		2356	1.4			1821	4.8
7		0551	4.5	22		0052	1.1
		1208	1.4			0649	4.5
	W	1809	4.8		TH	1303	1.2
					○	1852	4.9
8		0039	1.1	23		0128	1.0
		0633	4.8			0718	4.6
	TH	1250	1.1		F	1337	1.1
	●	1847	5.1			1923	5.0
9		0121	0.8	24		0200	0.9
		0714	5.0			0746	4.7
	F	1331	0.8		SA	1409	1.0
		1925	5.3			1953	5.0
10		0202	0.5	25		0230	0.8
		0756	5.1			0814	4.7
	SA	1413	0.7		SU	1441	1.0
		2004	5.4			2022	5.0
11		0245	0.4	26		0301	0.9
		0839	5.1			0841	4.6
	SU	1455	0.6		M	1512	1.1
		2045	5.3			2051	4.8
12		0328	0.4	27		0332	1.0
		0925	5.0			0910	4.5
	M	1538	0.7		TU	1544	1.2
		2129	5.1			2122	4.6
13		0412	0.5	28		0403	1.1
		1014	4.8			0943	4.3
	TU	1623	0.9		W	1616	1.5
		2220	4.9			2158	4.4
14		0459	0.8	29		0437	1.4
		1109	4.6			1021	4.1
	W	1712	1.2		TH	1652	1.7
		2320	4.5			2240	4.1
15		0550	1.2	30		0514	1.7
		1212	4.3			1108	3.9
	TH	1807	1.5		F	1733	2.0
						2337	3.9
				31		0558	2.0
						1216	3.7
					SA	1829	2.3

Chart Datum: 2·75 metres below Ordnance Datum (Newlyn)

TIME ZONE (UTC)
For Summer Time add ONE hour in **non-shaded areas**

SCOTLAND – ULLAPOOL

LAT 57°54'N LONG 5°10'W

TIMES AND HEIGHTS OF HIGH AND LOW WATERS

SPRING & NEAP TIDES
Dates in red are SPRINGS
Dates in blue are NEAPS

YEAR **2002**

SEPTEMBER

Day		Time	m	Time	m	Time	m	Time	m
1	SU	0100	3.7	0657	2.2	1355	3.7	1950	2.4
2	M	0233	3.7	0825	2.3	1524	3.8	2150	2.2
3	TU	0350	3.9	1006	2.1	1624	4.2	2252	1.8
4	W	0447	4.3	1104	1.7	1709	4.6	2338	1.3
5	TH	0532	4.6	1149	1.3	1748	5.0		
6	F	0020	0.9	0613	5.0	1231	1.0	1825	5.3
7	SA	0100	0.5	0653	5.3	1311	0.6	● 1903	5.6
8	SU	0141	0.2	0732	5.4	1352	0.4	1941	5.6
9	M	0222	0.1	0813	5.4	1433	0.4	2021	5.6
10	TU	0303	0.2	0856	5.3	1516	0.5	2104	5.3
11	W	0346	0.5	0943	5.0	1559	0.8	2153	5.0
12	TH	0430	0.9	1036	4.7	1646	1.2	2253	4.5
13	F	0518	1.4	1141	4.4	1739	1.6		
14	SA	0016	4.1	0615	1.9	1300	4.1	1848	2.0
15	SU	0156	3.9	0738	2.2	1428	4.0	2043	2.2
16	M	0330	3.9	0930	2.2	1548	4.1	2221	1.9
17	TU	0439	4.1	1042	2.0	1647	4.4	2317	1.6
18	W	0528	4.3	1130	1.8	1729	4.6	2358	1.4
19	TH	0603	4.4	1208	1.5	1801	4.8		
20	F	0032	1.2	0628	4.6	1242	1.3	1829	5.0
21	SA	0103	1.0	0652	4.7	1312	1.1	○ 1857	5.1
22	SU	0130	0.9	0716	4.8	1342	1.0	1924	5.1
23	M	0158	0.8	0739	4.8	1411	1.0	1950	5.1
24	TU	0226	0.9	0803	4.8	1441	1.0	2017	4.9
25	W	0256	1.0	0831	4.7	1512	1.2	2047	4.8
26	TH	0326	1.1	0904	4.5	1543	1.4	2120	4.5
27	F	0358	1.4	0939	4.3	1617	1.7	2200	4.2
28	SA	0434	1.7	1023	4.1	1658	2.0	2258	3.9
29	SU	0517	2.0	1131	3.8	1752	2.3		
30	M	0032	3.7	0616	2.3	1319	3.7	1917	2.5

OCTOBER

Day		Time	m	Time	m	Time	m	Time	m
1	TU	0212	3.7	0752	2.5	1451	3.9	2130	2.2
2	W	0331	4.0	0943	2.2	1555	4.3	2230	1.7
3	TH	0427	4.4	1040	1.8	1643	4.7	2315	1.2
4	F	0511	4.8	1125	1.3	1724	5.1	2356	0.8
5	SA	0551	5.2	1207	0.9	1803	5.5		
6	SU	0036	0.4	0630	5.5	1249	0.6	● 1840	5.7
7	M	0117	0.2	0709	5.6	1330	0.4	1919	5.8
8	TU	0157	0.2	0748	5.6	1412	0.4	2000	5.7
9	W	0238	0.3	0830	5.5	1454	0.6	2043	5.4
10	TH	0320	0.6	0914	5.2	1538	0.9	2133	5.0
11	F	0403	1.1	1006	4.8	1624	1.3	2237	4.5
12	SA	0450	1.6	1113	4.4	1718	1.8		
13	SU	0005	4.1	0548	2.1	1237	4.2	1832	2.2
14	M	0148	3.9	0715	2.5	1406	4.1	2030	2.3
15	TU	0317	3.9	0910	2.5	1525	4.2	2206	2.0
16	W	0421	4.1	1021	2.2	1622	4.4	2255	1.7
17	TH	0507	4.3	1105	1.9	1703	4.6	2332	1.5
18	F	0538	4.5	1141	1.7	1734	4.8		
19	SA	0003	1.3	0600	4.6	1213	1.4	1801	5.0
20	SU	0031	1.1	0623	4.8	1243	1.2	1829	5.1
21	M	0057	1.0	0646	4.9	1313	1.1	○ 1856	5.1
22	TU	0125	1.0	0708	5.0	1343	1.1	1922	5.1
23	W	0154	1.0	0733	5.0	1414	1.1	1951	5.0
24	TH	0224	1.1	0803	4.9	1445	1.3	2022	4.8
25	F	0255	1.2	0836	4.7	1518	1.5	2058	4.5
26	SA	0329	1.5	0913	4.5	1554	1.7	2143	4.3
27	SU	0406	1.8	0959	4.2	1637	2.0	2248	4.0
28	M	0451	2.1	1110	4.0	1735	2.2		
29	TU	0021	3.8	0553	2.4	1250	4.0	1901	2.3
30	W	0150	3.9	0728	2.5	1415	4.1	2055	2.1
31	TH	0304	4.1	0908	2.2	1521	4.4	2159	1.7

NOVEMBER

Day		Time	m	Time	m	Time	m	Time	m
1	F	0401	4.5	1009	1.8	1614	4.8	2247	1.2
2	SA	0447	4.9	1058	1.4	1659	5.2	2330	0.8
3	SU	0529	5.2	1142	1.0	1740	5.5		
4	M	0012	0.5	0608	5.5	1226	0.7	● 1821	5.7
5	TU	0054	0.4	0648	5.7	1309	0.6	1902	5.7
6	W	0135	0.4	0727	5.6	1353	0.6	1945	5.5
7	TH	0217	0.6	0809	5.5	1436	0.7	2031	5.3
8	F	0258	0.9	0853	5.2	1521	1.0	2124	4.9
9	SA	0342	1.3	0944	4.9	1609	1.4	2228	4.5
10	SU	0429	1.8	1048	4.6	1704	1.8	2347	4.1
11	M	0525	2.2	1205	4.3	1814	2.1		
12	TU	0117	3.9	0642	2.5	1327	4.2	1943	2.2
13	W	0240	3.9	0816	2.6	1441	4.2	2115	2.1
14	TH	0344	4.0	0935	2.4	1539	4.3	2211	1.9
15	F	0430	4.2	1025	2.1	1623	4.5	2251	1.7
16	SA	0502	4.4	1104	1.9	1659	4.7	2324	1.5
17	SU	0529	4.6	1139	1.7	1732	4.8	2354	1.4
18	M	0555	4.7	1212	1.5	1804	4.9		
19	TU	0024	1.3	0620	4.9	1245	1.4	1833	5.0
20	W	0056	1.2	0645	5.0	1318	1.3	○ 1903	5.0
21	TH	0127	1.2	0713	5.0	1351	1.3	1935	4.9
22	F	0200	1.2	0746	5.0	1426	1.4	2011	4.8
23	SA	0234	1.3	0822	4.8	1502	1.5	2053	4.6
24	SU	0310	1.5	0902	4.7	1543	1.6	2144	4.4
25	M	0351	1.7	0951	4.5	1629	1.8	2248	4.2
26	TU	0439	2.0	1057	4.3	1727	2.0		
27	W	0002	4.1	0539	2.2	1216	4.2	1841	2.0
28	TH	0118	4.1	0659	2.3	1333	4.3	2008	1.9
29	F	0228	4.2	0823	2.2	1442	4.5	2119	1.6
30	SA	0329	4.5	0932	1.9	1542	4.7	2215	1.3

DECEMBER

Day		Time	m	Time	m	Time	m	Time	m
1	SU	0421	4.8	1028	1.5	1634	5.0	2304	1.1
2	M	0507	5.1	1119	1.2	1722	5.2	2350	0.9
3	TU	0550	5.4	1207	1.0	1808	5.4		
4	W	0035	0.8	0631	5.5	1254	0.9	● 1852	5.4
5	TH	0118	0.8	0713	5.5	1340	0.9	1938	5.3
6	F	0201	0.9	0755	5.4	1425	0.9	2025	5.1
7	SA	0243	1.2	0838	5.3	1511	1.1	2115	4.8
8	SU	0326	1.4	0926	5.0	1558	1.4	2211	4.5
9	M	0411	1.8	1020	4.7	1648	1.6	2312	4.2
10	TU	0500	2.1	1122	4.5	1743	1.9		
11	W	0020	4.0	0558	2.3	1230	4.3	1845	2.1
12	TH	0132	3.9	0706	2.5	1338	4.2	1952	2.2
13	F	0238	3.9	0819	2.5	1440	4.2	2058	2.1
14	SA	0333	4.0	0925	2.3	1534	4.3	2153	2.0
15	SU	0417	4.2	1019	2.2	1620	4.4	2238	1.9
16	M	0455	4.4	1103	2.0	1702	4.5	2318	1.7
17	TU	0529	4.6	1144	1.8	1740	4.7	2355	1.6
18	W	0600	4.7	1222	1.6	1816	4.8		
19	TH	0031	1.4	0629	4.9	1259	1.5	○ 1850	4.9
20	F	0107	1.3	0701	5.0	1336	1.4	1927	4.9
21	SA	0143	1.3	0737	5.0	1414	1.3	2007	4.8
22	SU	0220	1.3	0815	5.0	1453	1.3	2050	4.7
23	M	0300	1.4	0856	4.9	1535	1.3	2138	4.6
24	TU	0342	1.5	0942	4.8	1622	1.4	2233	4.4
25	W	0429	1.6	1035	4.7	1714	1.5	2333	4.3
26	TH	0523	1.8	1138	4.5	1814	1.6		
27	F	0039	4.3	0626	2.0	1247	4.5	1921	1.7
28	SA	0147	4.3	0737	2.0	1400	4.5	2033	1.7
29	SU	0254	4.4	0851	1.9	1511	4.5	2142	1.5
30	M	0356	4.6	1000	1.8	1615	4.7	2242	1.4
31	TU	0450	4.8	1101	1.5	1712	4.9	2334	1.3

Chart Datum: 2·75 metres below Ordnance Datum (Newlyn)

PORTREE *9.8.10*

Skye (Highland) **57°24'·73N 06°11'·07W** ✪✪✪◊◊✿✿✿

CHARTS AC 2534, 2209; Imray C66; OS 23

TIDES –0445 Dover; ML no data; Duration 0610; Zone 0 (UT)

Standard Port ULLAPOOL (⟵)

Times				Height (metres)			
High Water		Low Water		MHWS	MHWN	MLWN	MLWS
0000	0600	0300	0900	5·2	3·9	2·1	0·7
1200	1800	1500	2100				
Differences PORTREE (Skye)							
–0025	–0025	–0025	–0025	+0·1	–0·2	–0·2	0·0
SHIELDAIG (Loch Torridon)							
–0020	–0020	–0015	–0015	+0·4	+0·3	+0·1	0·0
LOCH A'BHRAIGE (Rona)							
–0020	0000	–0010	0000	–0·1	–0·1	–0·1	–0·2
PLOCKTON							
+0005	–0025	–0005	–0010	+0·5	+0·5	+0·5	+0·2
LOCH SNIZORT (Uig Bay, Skye)							
–0045	–0020	–0005	–0025	+0·1	–0·4	–0·2	0·0
LOCH DUNVEGAN (Skye)							
–0105	–0030	–0020	–0040	0·0	–0·1	0·0	0·0
LOCH HARPORT (Skye)							
–0115	–0035	–0020	–0100	–0·1	–0·1	0·0	+0·1
SOAY (Camus nan Gall)							
–0055	–0025	–0025	–0045	–0·4	–0·2	No data	
KYLE OF LOCHALSH							
–0040	–0020	–0005	–0025	0·0	–0·1	–0·2	–0·2
DORNIE BRIDGE (Loch Alsh)							
–0040	–0010	–0005	–0020	+0·1	–0·1	0·0	0·0
GLENELG BAY (Kyle Rhea)							
–0105	–0035	–0035	–0055	–0·4	–0·4	–0·9	–0·1
LOCH HOURN							
–0125	–0050	–0040	–0110	–0·2	–0·1	–0·1	+0·1

SHELTER Secure in all but strong SW'lies, when Camas Bàn is more sheltered. In the N of the bay there are 8 HIE Ⓐs for <15 tons. Short stay pontoon on pier.

NAVIGATION WPT 57°24'·58N 06°10'·07W, 095°/275° from/to pier, 0·72M. From the S, avoid rks off An Tom Pt (1·5M to E, off chartlet).

LIGHTS AND MARKS Only lts are a SHM buoy Fl G 5s marking Sgeir Mhór, 2 FR (vert) 6m 4M (occas) on the pier and a SPM buoy Fl Y 5s.

RADIO TELEPHONE VHF Ch 16 12 (occas).

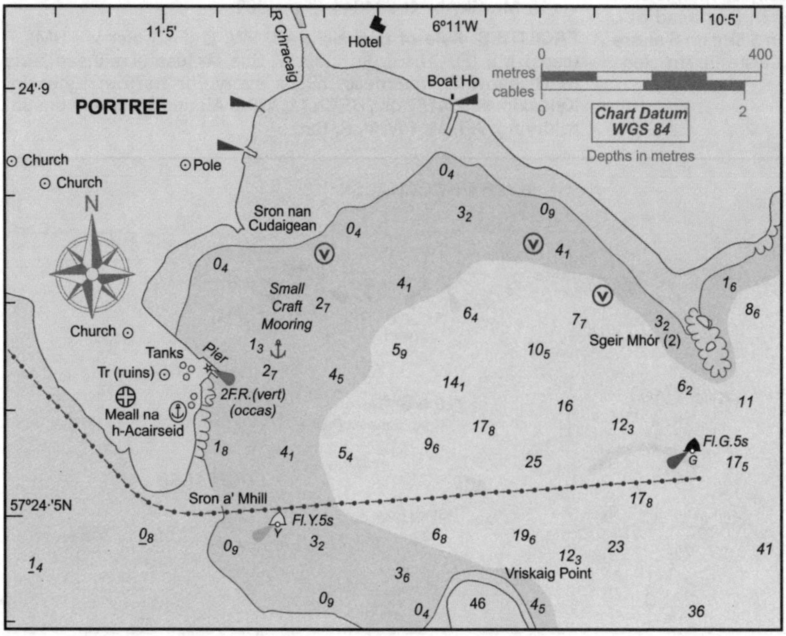

TELEPHONE (Dial code 01478) Hr Mr ☎ 612926; Moorings 612341; MRSC (01851) 702013; ⊖ (0141) 887 9369; Marinecall 09068 500464; Police 612888; Dr 612013; Ⓗ 612704.

FACILITIES Pier D (cans), L, FW. **Town** EC Wed; P, V, Gas, Gaz, ▣, R, Bar, ✉, Ⓑ, bus to Kyle of Lochalsh, ≷.

ANCHORAGES AROUND OR NEAR SKYE

LOCH TORRIDON, Highland, **57°36'N 05°49'W**. AC 228. Tides, see 9.8.8. Three large lochs: ent to outer loch (Torridon) is 3M wide, with isolated Sgeir na Trian (2m) almost in mid-chan; ⚓s on SW side behind Eilean Mór and in L Beag. L Sheildaig is middle loch with good ⚓ between the Is and village. 1M to the N, a 2ca wide chan leads into Upper L Torridon; many fish cages and prone to squalls. Few facilities, except Shieldaig: FW, V, R, Bar, ✉, Garage.

LOCH A'BHRAIGE, Rona (Highland), **57°34'·6N 05°57'·9W**. AC 2534, 2479. HW –0438 on Dover; ML 2·8m; Duration 0605. See 9.8.8. A good ⚓ in NW of the island, safe except in NNW winds. Beware rks on NE side up to 1ca off shore. Hbr in NE corner of loch head. Ldg lts 137°, see 9.8.4. Facilities: jetty, FW and a helipad, all owned by MOD (DRA). Before ent, call *Rona* Range Control VHF Ch 16.

Acarseid Mhor is ⚓ on W of Rona. App S of Eilean Garbh marked by W arrow. SD sketch of rks at ent is necessary. FW (cans), showers. At **Churchton Bay**, SW tip of Raasay, there are 4 HIE Ⓐs; ☎ (01478) 612341; Slip, showers, R, ▣.

LOCH DUNVEGAN, 4 Ⓐs off Stein, **57°30'·9N 06°34'·5W**. 3 Ⓐs off Dunvegan, 57°26'·3N 06°35'·2W. Fuel, FW, R. ☎ (01478) 612341.

LOCH HARPORT, Skye (Highland), **57°20'·6N 06°25'·8W**. AC 1795. HW –0447 (sp), –0527 (np) on Dover. See 9.8.8. On E side of Loch Bracadale, entered between Oronsay Is and Ardtreck Pt (W lt ho, Iso 4s 17m 9M). SW end of Oronsay has conspic rk pillar, called The Castle; keep ¼M off-shore here and off E coast of Oronsay which is joined to Ullinish Pt by drying reef. ⚓ Oronsay Is, N side of drying reef (4m), or on E side, but beware rk (dries) 0·5ca off N shore of Oronsay. Fiskavaig Bay 1M S of Ardtreck (7m); Loch Beag on N side of loch, exposed to W winds; Port na Long E of Ardtreck, sheltered except from E winds (beware fish farm); Ⓐ off distillery at Carbost on SW shore. Facilities: EC Wed (Carbost); V (local shop), Bar, R, P (garage), ✉, FW. (Port na Long) Bar, FW, V (shop).

SOAY HARBOUR, Skye (Highland), **57°09'·5N 06°13'·4W**. AC 2208. Tides see 9.8.8. Narrow inlet on NW side of Soay; enter from Soay Sound above half flood to clear bar, dries 0·6m. Appr on 135° from 5ca out to avoid reefs close each side of ent. Cross bar slightly E of mid-chan, altering 20° stbd for best water; ent is 15m wide between boulder spits marked by W poles with Or tops. ⚓ in 3m mid-pool or shoal draft boats can enter inner pool. Good shelter and holding. Camas nan Gall (poor holding) has public ☎; no other facilities.

ARMADALE BAY, Skye (Highland), 4M NW of Mallaig. AC 2208. 6 Ⓐs at **57°04'·0N 05°53'·6W**, ☎ (01478) 612341. Bay is sheltered from SE to N winds but subject to swell in winds from N to SE. From S, beware the Eilean Maol and Sgorach rocks. Ferry pier, Oc R 6s 6m 6M, with conspic W shed. Facilities, Sleat Marine ☎ 01471 844216, 📠 844387: M (£3.52 <10m, £5.87 >10m), FW at ferry pier or by hose to charter moorings, D, V, ▣, showers, Gas, ferry to Mallaig for ≷. Ardvasar ¾ mile: P (cans), Gaz at ¼ mile; R, Bar.

CROWLIN ISLANDS, Highland, **57°21'·1N 05°50'·6W**. AC 2498, 2209. HW –0435 on Dover, –0020 on Ullapool; HW +0·3m on Ullapool. See 9.8.8. ⚓ between Eilean Meadhonach and Eilean Mor, appr from N, keep E of Eilean Beg. Excellent shelter except in strong N winds. There is an inner ⚓ with 3½m but ent chan dries. Eilean Beg lt ho Fl 6s 32m 6M, W tr. There are no facilities.

8

PLOCKTON *9.8.11*

Highland **57°20´·52N 05°38´·47W** ❀❀⛵⛵✿✿✿

CHARTS AC 2528, 2209; Imray C66; OS 24, 33

TIDES –0435 Dover; ML 3·5m; Duration 0600; See 9.8.10

SHELTER Good, exposed only to N/NE'lies. 5 Y ◍s or ⚓ in centre of bay in approx 3·5m. Inner part of bay shoals and dries to the SW.

NAVIGATION WPT 57°21´·16N 05°39´·44W; thence track towards Bogha Dubh Sgeir PHM bn, between Cat Is disused ltho and Sgeir Golach PHM bn and High Stone (1m) to the N. Hawk (0.1m) will be cleared when Duncraig Castle bears 158°. Alter S to the ⚓. Beware Plockton Rks (3·1m) on E side of bay.

LIGHTS AND MARKS No lts or buoys. Old lt ho (13m) on Cat Is is conspic, as is Duncraig Castle.

RADIO TELEPHONE None.

TELEPHONE Hr Mr ☎/📠 (01599) 534167 at Kyle of Lochalsh, mobile 0802 367253; MRSC (01851) 702013; ⊖ (0141) 887 9369; Marinecall 09068 500 464; Police/Dr via Hr Mr.

FACILITIES **Village** FW, M £5, L at 24m long pontoon, D (cans), CH, V, R, Bar, ✉, ⇋, airstrip, (bus to Kyle of Lochalsh).

LOCH CARRON. Strome Narrows are no longer buoyed or lit. At head of loch are 3 Y ◍s (max LOA 14m) in 3m off drying jetty at 57°23´·95N 05°29´·0W; call ☎ 01520 722321. Appr on 328° between Sgeir Chreagach and Sgeir Fhada.

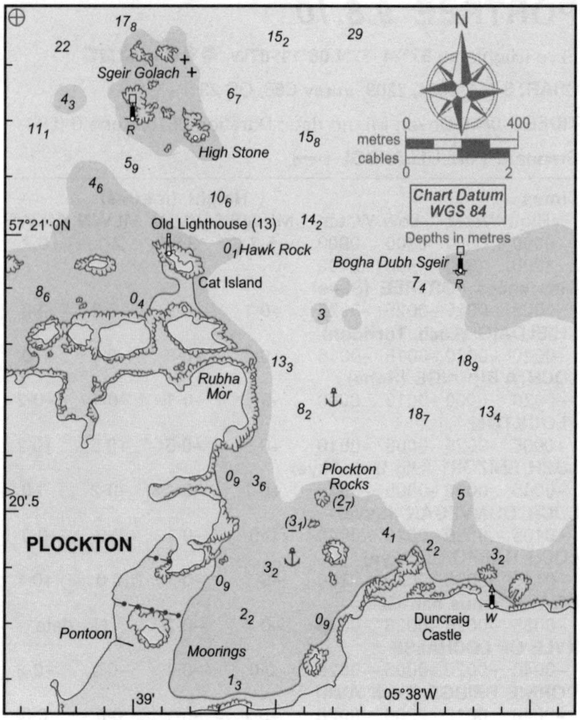

LOCH ALSH *9.8.12*

Highland **57°16´·68N 05°42´·87W** ❀❀❀⛵⛵✿✿✿

CHARTS AC 2540, 2541; Imray C66; OS 33

TIDES –0450 Dover; ML 3·0m; Duration 0555; See 9.8.10

SHELTER **Kyle (of Lochalsh)**: AB on Railway Pier, with FVs, or on 40m pontoon (seasonal), close W of Railway Pier; or ⚓ off the hotel there in 11m. **Kyleakin:** 4 free ◍s are subject to tidal stream. Lit pontoon on NW side of hbr.

⚓s, safe depending on winds, are (clockwise from Kyle): Avernish B, (2ca N of Racoon Rk) in 3m clear of power cables, open to SW; NW of Eilean Donnan Cas (conspic); in Ratagan B at head of L Duich in 7m; in Totaig B facing Loch Long ent in 3·5m; on S shore in Ardintoul B in 5·5m; at head of Loch na Béiste in 7m close inshore and W of fish cages.

NAVIGATION WPT (from Inner Sound) 57°16´·98N 05°45´·77W, 303°/123° from/to bridge, 7½ca. Chan to bridge is marked by 2 PHM and 2 SHM lt buoys. Bridge to Skye, 30m clearance, is lit Oc 6s in centre of main span, Iso R 4s on S pier and Iso G4s on N pier. The secondary NE span is lit, but has only 4.5m clearance.

LIGHTS AND MARKS Lts/marks as chartlet. Direction of buoyage is N in Kyle Rhea, thence E up Loch Alsh; but W through Kyle Akin and the bridge, ie SHMs are on N side of chan.

RADIO TELEPHONE VHF Ch 11 16. Sky br VHF Ch 12.

TELEPHONE (Dial code 01599) Hr Mr ☎/📠 534167; MRSC (01851) 702013; ⊖ (0141) 887 9369; Marinecall 09068 500 464; Police, Dr, Ⓗ: via Hr Mr. Sky br ☎ 534844, 📠 534969.

FACILITIES **Kyle of Lochalsh**: AB, FW, D (Fish pier via HM), P (cans), ME, Ⓔ, CH, ✉, Ⓑ, R, Bar, V, Gas, ⇋ (useful railhead), Bus to Glasgow & Inverness; buses every ½hr to/from Kyleakin. **Kyleakin:** ☎ 534167 or VHF Ch 11, 120m AB depth varies from 3m to drying: AB, M, FW, V, R, Bar.

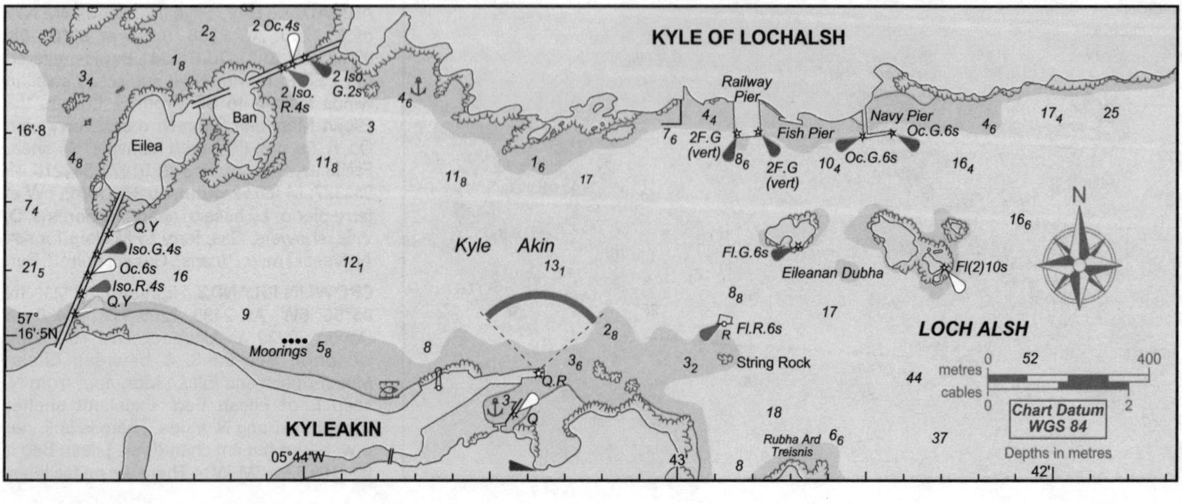

ANCHORAGES IN THE SOUND OF SLEAT

SOUND OF SLEAT: There are ⚓s at: **Glenelg Bay (57°12'·57N 05°37'·95W)** SW of pier out of the tide, but only moderate holding. Usual facilities in village. At **Sandaig Bay** (57°10'·0N 05°41'·4W), exposed to SW. Sandaig Is are to NW of the bay; beware rks off Sgeir nan Eun. Eilean Mór has lt Fl 6s. At **Isleornsay Hbr** (57°09'N 05°48'W) 2ca N of pier, 2FR (vert) and floodlit. Give drying N end of Ornsay Is a wide berth. Lts: SE tip of Ornsay, Oc 8s 18m 15M, W tr; N end, Fl R 6s 8m 4M. Facilities: FW, P, V, ✉, Hotel.

LOCH HOURN, Highland, **57°08'N 05°42'W**. AC 2541, 2208. Tides see 9.8.10. Ent is S of Sandaig Is and opposite Isle Ornsay, Skye. Loch extends 11M inland via 4 narrows to Loch Beag; it is scenically magnificent, but violent squalls occur in strong winds. Sgeir Ulibhe, drying 2·1m, bn, lies almost in mid-ent; best to pass S of it to clear Clansman Rk, 2·1m, to the N. ⚓s on N shore at Eilean Ràrsaidh and Camas Bàn, within first 4M. For pilotage further E, consult SDs. Facilities at Arnisdale (Camas Bàn): FW, V, R, Bar, ✉. Doune Marine (01687 462667) FW, V, D.

LOCH NEVIS, Highland, **57°02'·2N 05°43'·3W**. AC 2541, 2208. HW –0515 on Dover. See 9.8.10. Beware rks Bogha cas Sruth (dries 1·8m), Bogha Don and Sgeirean Glasa both marked by bns. ⚓ NE of Eilean na Glaschoille, good except in S winds; or 6 Or 🅐s off Inverie, £5 (free if dining), 10m max LOA. Call *Old Forge* VHF Ch 16, 12; FW, Bar, R, showers, ▣. In strong winds expect violent unpredictable squalls. Enter the inner loch with caution, and ⚓ N or SE of Eilean Maol.

ANCHORAGES IN THE SMALL ISLANDS RoRo ferry berths are to be constructed on all four islands.

CANNA, The Small Islands, **57°03'·3N 06°29'·4W**. AC 2208, 1796. HW –0457 (Sp), –0550 (Np) on Dover; HW –0035 and –0·4m on Ullapool; Duration 0605. Good holding and shelter, except in strong E'lies, in hbr between Canna and Sanday Is. Appr along Sanday shore, keeping N of Sgeir a' Phuirt, dries 4·6m. Ldg marks as in SDs. ⚓ in 3 - 4m W of Canna pier, off which beware drying rky patch. ⚓ Lt is advised due to FVs. Conspic W lt bn, Fl 6s 32m 9M, vis 152°-061°, at E end of Sanday Is. Magnetic anomaly off NE Canna. Facilities: FW only. Note: National Trust for Scotland runs island; please do not ditch rubbish.

RUM, The Small Islands, **57°00'·1N 06°15'·7W**. AC 2207, 2208. HW –0500 on Dover; –0035 and –0·3m on Ullapool; ML 2·4m; Duration 0600. Nature Conservancy Council owns Is. The mountains (809m) are unmistakeable. Landing is only allowed at L Scresort on E side; no dogs. Beware drying rks 1ca off N point of ent and almost 3ca off S point. The head of the loch dries 2ca out; ⚓ off slip on S side or further in, to NE of jetty. Hbr is open to E winds/swell. Facilities: Hotel, ✉, FW, V, R, Bar, ferry to Mallaig.

EIGG HARBOUR, The Small Islands, **56°52'·6N 06°07'·6W**. AC 2207. HW –0523 on Dover. See 9.8.13. Coming from N or E enter between Garbh Sgeir and Flod Sgeir (bn, ○ top-mark), drying rks. An Sgùrr is a conspic 391m high peak/ridge brg 290°/1·3M from pier. Most of hbr dries, but good ⚓ 1ca NE of Galmisdale Pt pier, except in NE winds when yachts should go through the narrows and ⚓ in South Bay in 6-8m; tide runs hard in the narrows. Also ⚓ in 2·5m at Poll nam Partan, about 2ca N of Flod Sgeir. SE point of Eilean Chathastail Fl 6s 24m 8M, vis 181°-shore, W tr. VHF Ch 08 *Eigg Hbr*. Hr Mr ☎ via (01687) 482428. FW, repairs. **Cleadale village** (2M to N) Bar, ✉, R, V, Gas.

MUCK, The Small Islands, **56°49'·8N 06°13'·3W**. AC 2207. Tides approx as Eigg, 9.8.13. Port Mór at SE end is the main hbr, with a deep pool inside offlying rks, but open to S'lies. Approach: tree plantation brg exactly 329° leads between Dubh Sgeir and Bogha Ruadh rks. ⚓ towards the NW side of inlet; NE side has drying rks. On N side of Is, Bagh a' Ghallanaich is ⚓ protected from S; ent needs SDs and careful identification of marks. Few facilities.

MALLAIG *9.8.13*

Highland **57°00'·47N 05°49'·47W**

CHARTS AC 2541, 2208; Imray C65, C66; OS 40

TIDES –0515 Dover; ML 2·9; Duration 0605; Zone 0 (UT)

Standard Port OBAN (⟶)

Times				Height (metres)			
High Water		Low Water		MHWS	MHWN	MLWN	MLWS
0000	0600	0100	0700	4·0	2·9	1·8	0·7
1200	1800	1300	1900				
Differences MALLAIG							
+0017	+0017	+0017	+0017	+1·0	+0·7	+0·3	+0·1
INVERIE BAY (Loch Nevis)							
+0030	+0020	+0035	+0020	+1·0	+0·9	+0·2	0·0
BAY OF LAIG (Eigg)							
+0015	+0030	+0040	+0005	+0·7	+0·6	–0·2	–0·2
LOCH MOIDART							
+0015	+0015	+0040	+0020	+0·8	+0·6	–0·2	–0·2
LOCH EATHARNA (Coll)							
+0025	+0010	+0015	+0025	+0·4	+0·3	No data	
GOTT BAY (Tiree)							
0000	+0010	+0005	+0010	0·0	+0·1	0·0	0·0

SHELTER Good in SW'lies but open to N. Access H24. ⚓ in SE part of hbr or find a berth on Fish Pier. No 🅐s. Hbr is often full of FVs; also Skye ferry.

NAVIGATION WPT 57°00'·75N 05°49'·49W, 011°/191° from/to Steamer Pier lt, 540m, passing E of Sgeir Dhearg lt bn. The former W chan is now permanently closed to navigation.

LIGHTS AND MARKS As chartlet & 9.8.4. Town lts may obscure Sgeir Dhearg lt. IPTS (3 FR vert at pier hd) indicate ferries operating Easter-Oct, no other traffic allowed except by Hr Mr's permission.

RADIO TELEPHONE Call: *Mallaig Hbr Radio* VHF Ch 09 16 (HO).

TELEPHONE (Dial code 01687) Hr Mr 462154, outside office hrs 462249; MRSC (01851) 702013; ⊖ (0141) 887 9369; Marinecall 09068 500464; Police 462177.

FACILITIES Hbr AB £5.88 whenever alongside for FW/fuel/stores (⚓ is free), M, P (cans), D (tanker), FW, ME, El, Sh, C (mobile 10 ton), CH, Ⓔ, ACA, Slip; a busy FV hbr, yacht berths may be provided at a later date near root of the Fish Pier. **Town** EC Wed; Dr 462202. V, R, Gas, Gaz, Bar, ✉, Ⓑ, ⇌.

ADJACENT ANCHORAGE

ARISAIG, (Loch nan Ceall), Highland, **56°53'·64N 05°55'·77W** (ent). AC 2207. HW –0515 on Dover; +0030 and +0·9m on Oban. S side of ent is identifiable by W mark on Rubh' Arisaig. SDs essential. S Chan is winding, but marked by 8 perches; each must be identified. Appr HW±4 to avoid strongest streams LW±1½. Caution: many unmarked rks; no lts. Sheltered ⚓ at head of loch, clear of moorings. Call **Arisaig Marine** ☎ (01687) 450224, 📠 450678, VHF Ch 16, M; few 🅐s, C (10 ton), CH, D & FW at ferry pier (HW), P (cans), El, ME, Sh, Slip. **Village** EC Thurs; FW at hotel, Bar, ✉, R, Gas, V, ⇌.

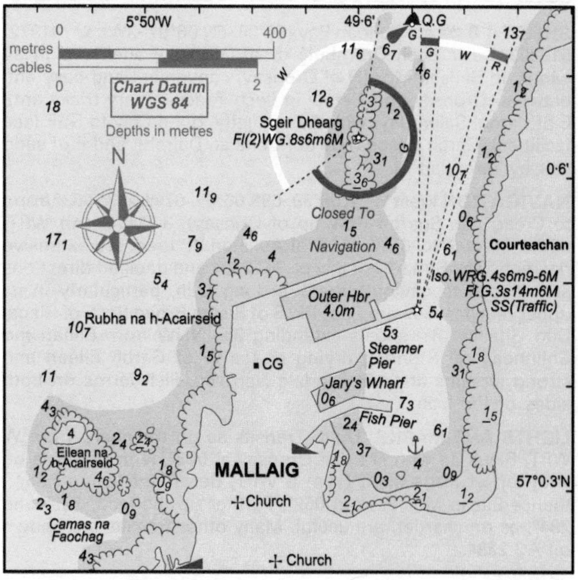

LOCH SUNART *9.8.14*

Highland **56°39′·49N 06°00′·07W** ❁❁◇◇✿✿

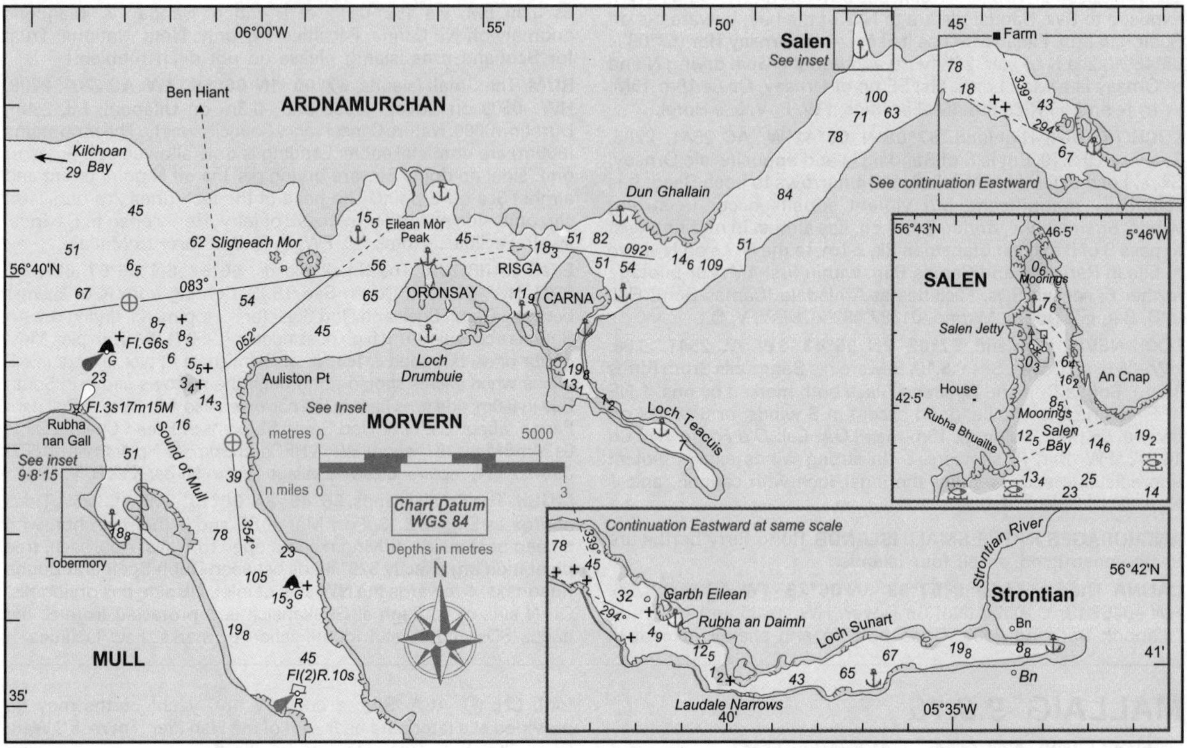

CHARTS AC 2394, 2392, *2171*; Imray C65; OS 45, 47, 49

TIDES Salen –0500 Dover; ML 2·0; Zone 0 (UT)

Standard Port OBAN (⟶)

Times				Height (metres)			
High Water		Low Water		MHWS	MHWN	MLWN	MLWS
0100	0700	0100	0800	4·0	2·9	1·8	0·7
1300	1900	1300	2000				
Differences SALEN (Loch Sunart)							
–0015	+0015	+0010	+0005	+0·6	+0·5	–0·1	–0·1

SHELTER 8 Ⓐs at Kilchoan Bay (56°24′·5N 06°07′·3W); ☎ (01972) 510209. ⚓s in Loch Drumbuie (S of Oronsay) sheltered in all winds; in Sailean Mór (N of Oronsay) convenient and easy ent; between Oronsay and Carna; in Loch Teacuis (very tricky ent); E of Carna; Salen Bay, with Ⓐs and jetty, open only to SSE (see facilities); Garbh Eilean (NW of Rubha an Daimh), and E of sand spit by Strontian R.

NAVIGATION West WPT, 56°39′·69N 06°03′·07W, 263°/083° from/ to Creag nan Sgarbh (NW tip of Orinsay), 3·7M. **South WPT**, 56°38′·00N 06°00′·65W, 1M S of Auliston Pt; there are extensive rky reefs, The Stirks W of this pt. AC 2394 and detailed directions are needed to navigate the 17M long loch, particularly in its upper reaches. Beware Ross Rk, S of Risga; Broad Rk, E of Risga; Dun Ghallain Rk; shoals extending 3ca NNW from Eilean mo Shlinneag off S shore; drying rk 1ca W of Garbh Eilean and strong streams at sp in Laudale Narrows. Fish farms on both sides of the loch.

LIGHTS AND MARKS Unlit. Transits as on the chart: from W WPT, Risga on with N tip of Oronsay at 083°; N pt of Carna on with top of Risga 092°. From S WPT, Ben Hiant bearing 354°, thence Eilean Mor Peak at 052°. Further up the loch, 339° and 294°, as on chartlet, are useful. Many other transits are shown on AC 2394.

RADIO TELEPHONE None, except under Salen Bay below.

TELEPHONE (Dial code 01967) MRSC (01475) 729014; ⊖ (0141) 887 9369; Marinecall 09068 500463; Dr 431231.

FACILITIES SALEN BAY jetty (56°42′·39N 05°46′·17W). ☎ 01967 431333. VHF Ch 16 (occas). Access HW±2 to jetty, keeping on E side of ent to avoid a drying reef on W side; two R Ⓐs (15 ton) £10 (other moorings are private); ⚓ buoy advised as bottom is generally foul. L, FW, D by hose, AC, Slip, SM, ME, El, CH, Gas, Gaz, Diver, limited V, R, Bar. **Acharacle** (2½M), P, V, ✉, Ⓑ (Tues/ Wed, mobile), ⇌ (bus to Loch Ailort/Fort William), ✈ (Oban). STRONTIAN FW, P, V, hotel, ✉, Gas, Gaz, Bar. Bus to Fort William.

ANCHORAGES IN COLL AND TIREE (Argyll and Bute)

ARINAGOUR, Loch Eatharna, Coll, **56°37′·0N 06°31′·2W**. AC 2474, 2171. HW –0530 on Dover; ML 1·4m; Duration 0600; see 9.8.14. Good shelter except with SE swell or strong winds from ENE to SSW. Enter at SHM buoy, Fl G 6s, marking Bogha Mòr. Thence NW to Arinagour ferry pier, 2 FR(vert) 10m. Beware McQuarrie's Rk (dries 2·9m) 1ca E of pier hd and unmarked drying rks further N on E side of fairway. Ch and hotel are conspic ahead. Continue N towards old stone pier; ⚓ S of it or pick up a buoy. Six Ⓐs on W side of hbr, between the two piers. Also ⚓ E of Eilean Eatharna. Piermaster ☎ (01879) 230347; VHF Ch 31. **Facilities**: HIE Trading Post ☎ 230349, M, D, FW, Gas, V, CH, R. **Village** ⊡, FW, P, ✉, ferry to Oban (⇌).

GOTT BAY, Tiree, **56°30′·74N 06°48′·07W**. AC 2474. Tides as 9.8.13; HW –0540 on Dover. Hr Mr ☎ (01879) 230337, VHF Ch 31. Adequate shelter in calm weather, but exposed in winds ENE to S. The bay, at NE end of island, can be identified by conspic latticed tr at Scarinish about 8ca SW of ent, with lt Fl 3s 11m 16M close by (obscd over hbr). Appr on NW track, keeping to SW side of bay which is obstructed on NE side by Soa Is and drying rks. The ferry pier at S side of ent has FR ldg lts 286½°. ⚓ about 1ca NW of pier head in 3m on sand; dinghy landing at pier. Facilities: P & D (cans), Gas, V, R, Bar, ✉ at Scarinish (¼M), ferry to Oban (⇌).

TOBERMORY *9.8.15*

Mull (Argyll and Bute) **56°37'·19N 06°03'·87W** ❀❀❀◊◊✿✿✿

CHARTS AC 2474, *2390, 2171*; Imray C65; OS 47

TIDES –0519 Dover; ML 2·4; Duration 0610; Zone 0 (UT)

Standard Port OBAN (⟶)

Times				Height (metres)			
High Water		Low Water		MHWS	MHWN	MLWN	MLWS
0100	0700	0100	0800	4·0	2·9	1·8	0·7
1300	1900	1300	2000				
Differences TOBERMORY (Mull)							
+0025	+0010	+0015	+0025	+0·4	+0·4	0·0	0·0
CARSAIG BAY (S Mull)							
–0015	–0005	–0030	+0020	+0·1	+0·2	0·0	–0·1
IONA (SW Mull)							
–0010	–0005	–0020	+0015	0·0	+0·1	–0·3	–0·2
BUNESSAN (Loch Lathaich, SW Mull)							
–0015	–0015	–0010	–0015	+0·3	+0·1	0·0	–0·1
ULVA SOUND (W Mull)							
–0010	–0015	0000	–0005	+0·4	+0·3	0·0	–0·1

SHELTER Good, but some swell in strong N/NE winds. 22 🅥s are marked by a blue ◌ with a Y pick-up. ⚓ clear of fairway, where marked; at SE end of The Doirlinn.

NAVIGATION WPT 56°37'·59N 06°03'·17W, 044°/224° from/to moorings 0·5M. N ent is wide and clear of dangers. S ent via The Doirlinn is only 80m wide at HW, and dries at LW; at HW±2 least depth is 2m. Enter between 2 bns on 300°.

LIGHTS AND MARKS Rhubha nan Gall, Fl 3s 17m 15M, W tr is 1M N of ent. Ch spire and hotel turret are both conspic.

RADIO TELEPHONE VHF Ch 16 12 (HO), M.

TELEPHONE (Dial code 01688) Piermaster 302017; MRSC (01475) 729014; Local CG 302200; Marinecall 09068 500463; Police 302016; Dr 302013.

FACILITIES Ferry Pier, only short stay AB for P, D, FW £2; **Western Isles YC** ☎ 302371; **Services:** 🅥 £7 < 8m £10 > 8m. ME, CH, ACA, Gaz, Gas, Divers. **Town** EC Wed (winter); FW, P, Dr, V, R, Bar, ✉, Ⓑ, 🅛, ⇄ (ferry to Oban), ✈ (grass strip; helipad on golf course).

SOUND OF MULL (Mull, **56°31'·44N 05°56'·82W**). Beware drying rks 6ca E of the bay; ent on SE side. **Salen Jetty,** 🅥 £10. Landing from yacht at ⚓ £1 per person/H24. FW, D. **Village**, V, ME, Ⓔ, CH, R, Dr, ✉. Land at jetty in SW corner.

CRAIGNURE, (Mull, **56°28'·37N 05°42'·25W**) ldg lts 241°, both FR 10/12m. Facilities: V, Bar, ✉, Gas, ferry to Oban. Tides, see 9.8.13.

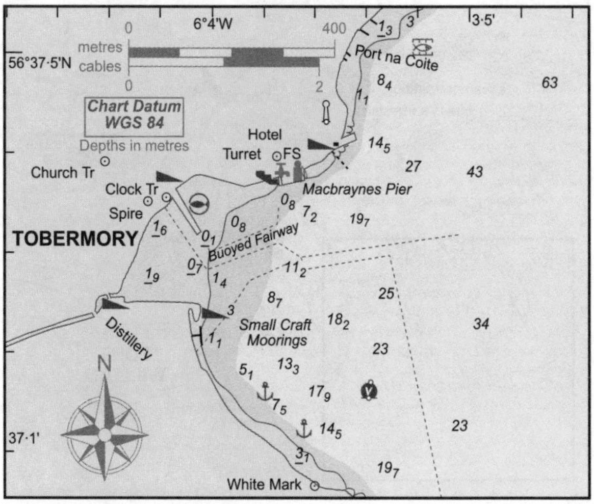

LOCH ALINE *9.8.16*

Highland **56°32'·09N 05°46'·47W** ❀❀❀◊✿✿✿

CHARTS AC *2390*; Imray C65; OS 49

TIDES –0523 Dover; Duration 0610; Zone 0 (UT)

Standard Port OBAN (⟶)

Times				Height (metres)			
High Water		Low Water		MHWS	MHWN	MLWN	MLWS
0100	0700	0100	0800	4·0	2·9	1·8	0·7
1300	1900	1300	2000				
Differences LOCH ALINE							
+0012	+0012	No data		+0·5	+0·3	No data	
SALEN (Sound of Mull)							
+0045	+0015	+0020	+0030	+0·2	+0·2	–0·1	0·0
CRAIGNURE (Sound of Mull)							
+0030	+0005	+0010	+0015	0·0	+0·1	–0·1	–0·1

SHELTER Very good. ⚓s in SE end of loch and in N and E part of loch. Temp berth on the old stone slip in the ent on W side, depth and ferries permitting.

NAVIGATION WPT 56°31'·49N 05°46'·37W, 356°/176° from/to front ldg bn, 0·9M. Bns (not easily seen) lead 356°, 100m W of Bogha Lurcain, drying rk off Bolorkle Pt on E side of ent. The buoyed ent is easy, but narrow with a bar (min depth 2·1m); stream runs 2½kn at sp. Beware coasters from the sand mine going to/from the jetty (which completely fill the entr) and ferries to/from Mull. Last 5ca of loch dries.

LIGHTS AND MARKS Ardtornish Pt lt ho, 1M SSE of ent, Fl (2) WRG 10s 7m 8/5M. Lts and buoys as chartlet. War memorial (conspic, 9m high) stands on W side of ent. Ldg lts are FW 2/4m (H24). 1M up the loch on E side a Y bn with Y ○ topmark marks a reef, and ½M further up similar bn marks a larger reef on W side. Both top marks need new coat of paint. Clock tr is very conspic at head of loch.

RADIO TELEPHONE None.

TELEPHONE (Dial code 01967) MRSC (01475) 729014; ⊖ (0141) 887 9369; Marinecall 09068 500463; 🅗 (01631) 563727; Dr 421252.

FACILITIES Village FW at pier, Gas, V, R, Bar, P, ✉, (Ⓑ, ⇄, ✈ at Oban), Ferry to Fishnish Bay (Mull).

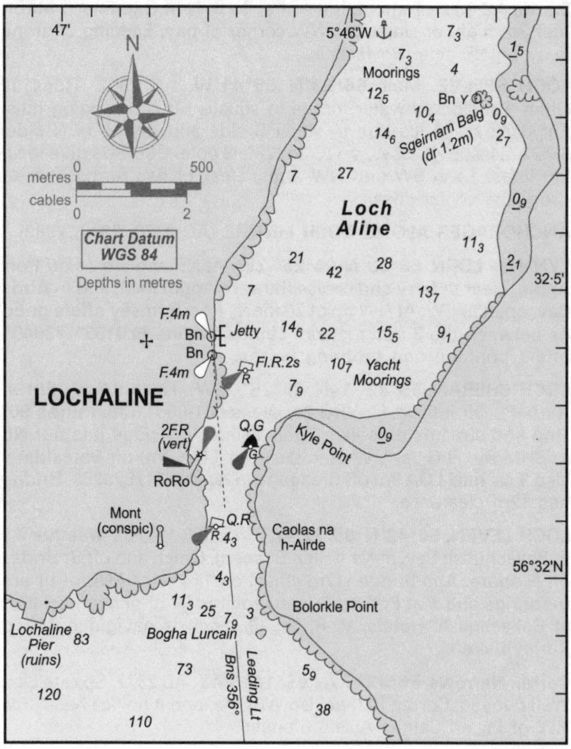

ANCHORAGES on WEST and SOUTH COASTS OF MULL (Anti-clockwise from the North. SDs essential)

TRESHNISH ISLES, 56°29'N 06°31'W. AC 2652. The main Is (N to S) are: Cairn na Burgh, Fladda, Lunga, Bac Mòr and Bac Beag. Tides run hard and isles are exposed to swell, but merit a visit in calm weather. Appr with caution on ldg lines as in CCC SDs; temp ⚓ off Lunga's N tip in 4m.

STAFFA, 56°25'·96N 06°20'·34W. AC 2652. Spectacular isle with Fingal's Cave, but same caveats as above. Very temp ⚓ off SE tip where there is landing; beware unmarked rks.

GOMETRA, 56°28'·85N 06°23'W. AC 2652. Tides as 9.8.15. The narrow inlet between Gometra and Ulva Is offers sheltered ⚓, except in S'lies. Appr on 020° between Staffa and Little Colonsay, or N of the former. Beware rks drying 3·2m, to stbd and 5ca S of ent. Inside, E side is cleaner.

LOCH NA KEAL, 56°26'N 06°18'W (ent). AC 2652. Tides in 9.8.15. Appr S of Geasgill Is and N of drying rks off **Inch Kenneth**; E of this Is and in **Sound of Ulva** are sheltered ⚓s, except in S'lies. Beware MacQuarrie's Rk, dries 0·8m.

LOCH LATHAICH, Mull, **56°19'·29N 06°15'·47W**. AC 2617. HW –0545 on Dover; ML 2·4. See 9.8.15. Excellent shelter with easy access; good base for cruising W Mull. Eilean na Liathanaich (a group of islets) lie off the ent, marked by a W bn at the E end, Fl WR 6s 12m 8/6M, R088°-108°, W108°-088°. Keep to W side of loch and ⚓ off Bendoran BY in SW, or SE of Eilean Ban off the pier in approx 5m. **Facilities:** (Bunessan) Shop, ✉, Bar, R, FW.

SOUND OF IONA, 56°19'·45N 06°23'·12W. AC 2617. Tides see 9.8.15. From N, enter in mid-chan; from S keep clear of Torran Rks. Cathedral brg 012° closes the Iona shore past 2 SHM buoys and SCM buoy. Beware a bank 0·1m in mid-sound, between cathedral and Fionnphort; also tel cables and ferries. ⚓ S of ferry close in to Iona, or in Bull Hole. Consult SDs. Crowded in season; limited facilities.

TINKER'S HOLE, Ross of Mull, **56°17'·49N 06°23'·07W**. AC 2617. Beware Torran Rks, reefs extending 5M S and SW of Erraid. Usual app from S, avoiding Rankin's Rks, drying 0·8m, and rk, dries 2·3m, between Eilean nam Muc and Erraid. Popular ⚓ in mid-pool between Eilean Dubh and Erraid.

CARSAIG BAY, Ross of Mull, **56°19'·19N 05°59'·07W**. Tides see 9.8.15. AC 2386. Temp, fair weather ⚓s to N of Gamhnach Mhòr, reef 2m high, or close into NW corner of bay. Landing at stone quay on NE side. No facilities.

LOCH SPELVE, Mull, **56°23'N 05°41'W**. AC 2387. Tides as Oban. Landlocked water, prone to squalls off surrounding hills. Ent narrows to ½ca due to shoal S side and drying rk N side, 56°23'·24N 05°41'·95W, ☆ QG 3m 2M, G pole. CCC SDs give local ldg lines. ⚓s in SW and NW arms, clear of fish farms. Pier at Croggan; no facilities.

ANCHORAGES ALONG LOCH LINNHE (AC 2378, 2379, 2380)

LYNN OF LORN, 56°33'N 05°25'·2W: At NE end are ⚓s off **Port Appin**, clear of ferry and cables (beware Appin Rks); and in **Airds Bay**, open to SW. At NW tip of Lismore, **Port Ramsey** offers good ⚓s between the 3 main islets. **Linnhe Marina** ☎ 01631 730401 offers pontoon and mooring berths.

LOCH CRERAN, 56°32'·14N 05°25'·22W. Tides 9.8.17. Ent at Airds Pt, Dir lt 050°, Fl WRG 2s, W vis 041-058°. Chan turns 90° stbd and streams runs 4kn. Sgeir Callich, rky ridge juts out NE to SHM By, Fl G 3s; ⚓ W of it. 🅥s (max LOA 7m) off Barcaldine; also 3 🅥s max LOA 9m off Creagan Inn, ☎ (01631) 573250. Bridge has 12m clearance.

LOCH LEVEN, 56°42'N 05°12'W. Tides 9.8.17. Fair weather ⚓s in Ballachulish Bay, at Kentallen B (deep), Onich and off St Brides on N shore. App bridge (17m clnce) on 114°; 4ca ENE of br are moorings and ⚓ at Poll an Dùnan, entered W of perch. Facilities at Ballachulish: Hotels, V, R, ✉, Ⓑ. Loch is navigable 7M to Kinlochleven.

Corran Narrows, 56°43'·27N 05°14'·34W. AC 2372. Sp rate 6kn. Well buoyed; Corran Pt lt ho, Iso WRG 4s, and lt bn 5ca NE. ⚓ 5ca NW of Pt, off Camas Aiseig pier/slip.

FORT WILLIAM/CORPACH *9.8.17*

Highland 56°48'·99N 05°07'·07W (off Fort William)

CHARTS AC 2372, 2380; Imray C65, C23; OS 41

TIDES –0535 Dover; ML 2·3; Duration 0610; Zone 0 (UT)

Standard Port OBAN (⟶)

Times				**Height (metres)**			
High Water		Low Water		MHWS	MHWN	MLWN	MLWS
0100	0700	0100	0800	4·0	2·9	1·8	0·7
1300	1900	1300	2000				
Differences CORPACH							
0000	+0020	+0040	0000	0·0	0·0	–0·2	–0·2
LOCH EIL (Head)							
+0025	+0045	+0105	+0025		No data		No data
CORRAN NARROWS							
+0007	+0007	+0004	+0004	+0·4	+0·4	–0·1	0·0
LOCH LEVEN (Head)							
+0045	+0045	+0045	+0045		No data		No data
LOCH LINNHE (Port Appin)							
–0005	–0005	–0030	0000	+0·2	+0·2	+0·1	+0·1
LOCH CRERAN (Barcaldine Pier)							
+0010	+0020	+0040	+0015	+0·1	+0·1	0·0	+0·1
LOCH CRERAN (Head)							
+0015	+0025	+0120	+0020	–0·3	–0·3	–0·4	–0·3

SHELTER Exposed to winds SW thro' N to NE. ⚓s off Fort William pier; in Camus na Gall; SSW of Eilean A Bhealaidh; and off Corpach Basin, where there is also a waiting pontoon; or inside the canal. The sea lock is normally available HW±4 during canal hrs. For Caledonian Canal see 9.8.18.

NAVIGATION Corpach WPT 56°50'·29N 05°07'·07W, 135°/315° from/to lock ent, 0·30M. Beware McLean Rk, dries 0·3m, buoyed, 8ca N of Fort William. Lochy Flats dry 3ca off the E bank. In Annat Narrows at ent to Loch Eil streams reach 5kn.

LIGHTS AND MARKS Iso WRG 4s lt is at N jetty of sea-lock ent, W310°-335°. A long pier/viaduct off Ft William is unlit.

RADIO TELEPHONE Call: *Corpach Lock* VHF Ch **74** 16 (during canal hours).

TELEPHONE (Dial code 01397) Hr Mr 772249 (Corpach); MRSC (01475) 729014; ⊖ 702948; Marinecall 09068 500463; Police 702361; Dr 703136.

FACILITIES Fort William. Pier ☎ 703881, AB; **Services:** Slip, L, CH, ACA. **Town** EC Wed; P, ME, El, Sh, YC, V, R, Bar, Ⓗ, ✉, Ⓑ, ⇌. CORPACH. **Corpach Basin** ☎ 772249, AB, L, FW; **Lochaber YC** ☎ 703576, M, FW, L, Slip; **Services:** ME, El, Sh, D (cans), M, CH, Slip, Divers. **Village** P, V, R, Bar, ✉, Ⓑ, ⇌.

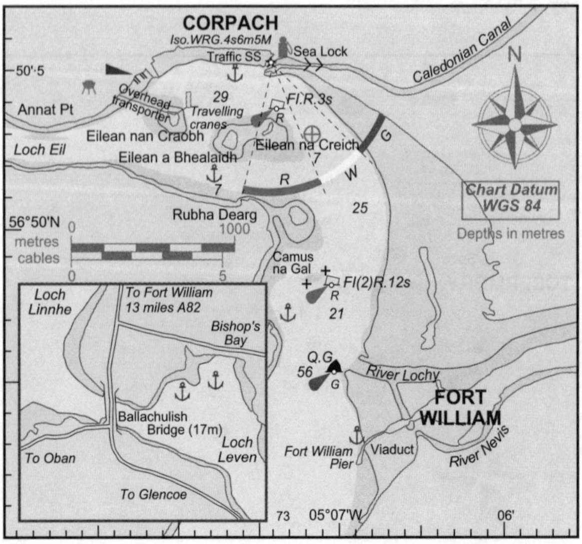

CALEDONIAN CANAL *9.8.18*

Highland ❁❁◊◊◊✿✿✿

CHARTS AC 1791; Imray C23; OS 41, 34, 26; Skippers Brief

TIDES Tidal differences: Corpach –0455 on Dover; See 9.8.17. Clachnaharry: +0116 on Dover; See 9.7.16.

SHELTER Corpach is at the SW ent of the Caledonian Canal, and is not suitable of yachts; the sea locks at both ends do not open LW±2 at springs. For best shelter transit the sea lock and lie above the double lock. Numerous pontoons along the canal; cost is included in the canal dues. For Inverness see 9.7.16.

NAVIGATION The 60M canal consists of 38M through 3 lochs, (Lochs Lochy, Oich and Ness), connected by 22M through canals. Loch Oich is part of a hydro-electric scheme which may vary the water level. The passage normally takes two full days, possibly longer in the summer; absolute minimum is 14 hrs. Speed limit is 5kn in the canal sections. There are 10 swing bridges; road tfc has priority at peak hrs. Do not pass bridges without the keeper's instructions.

LOCKS There are 29 locks: 14 between Loch Linnhe (Corpach), via Lochs Lochy and Oich up to the summit (106′ above sea level); and 15 locks from the summit down via Loch Ness to Inverness.
Hours: All locations: 3rd Jan to 11 Mar, 0900-1530, Mon-Fri; 12 Mar to 6 May, 0830-1650, Mon-Sat; 7 May to 30 Sep, 0800-1730, Mon-Sun; 1 Oct to 27 Oct, 0830-1650, Mon-Sat; 29 Oct to 10 Mar, 0900-1530, Mon-Fri. Additional hours 3 Jun to 31 Aug: Sealocks 0700-2200; Dochgarroch 0800-1900; Gairlochy 0800-1900; Fort Augustus 0800-1930.
Dues, payable at Corpach, at 2001 rates inc VAT: £9.50 per metre for 1 day; £15.65 for 3 days, plus special offers. For regulations and useful booklet *Skipper's Brief* apply: Canal Manager, Canal Office, Seaport Marina, Muirtown Wharf, Inverness IV3 5LE, ☎ (01463) 233140/📠 710942.

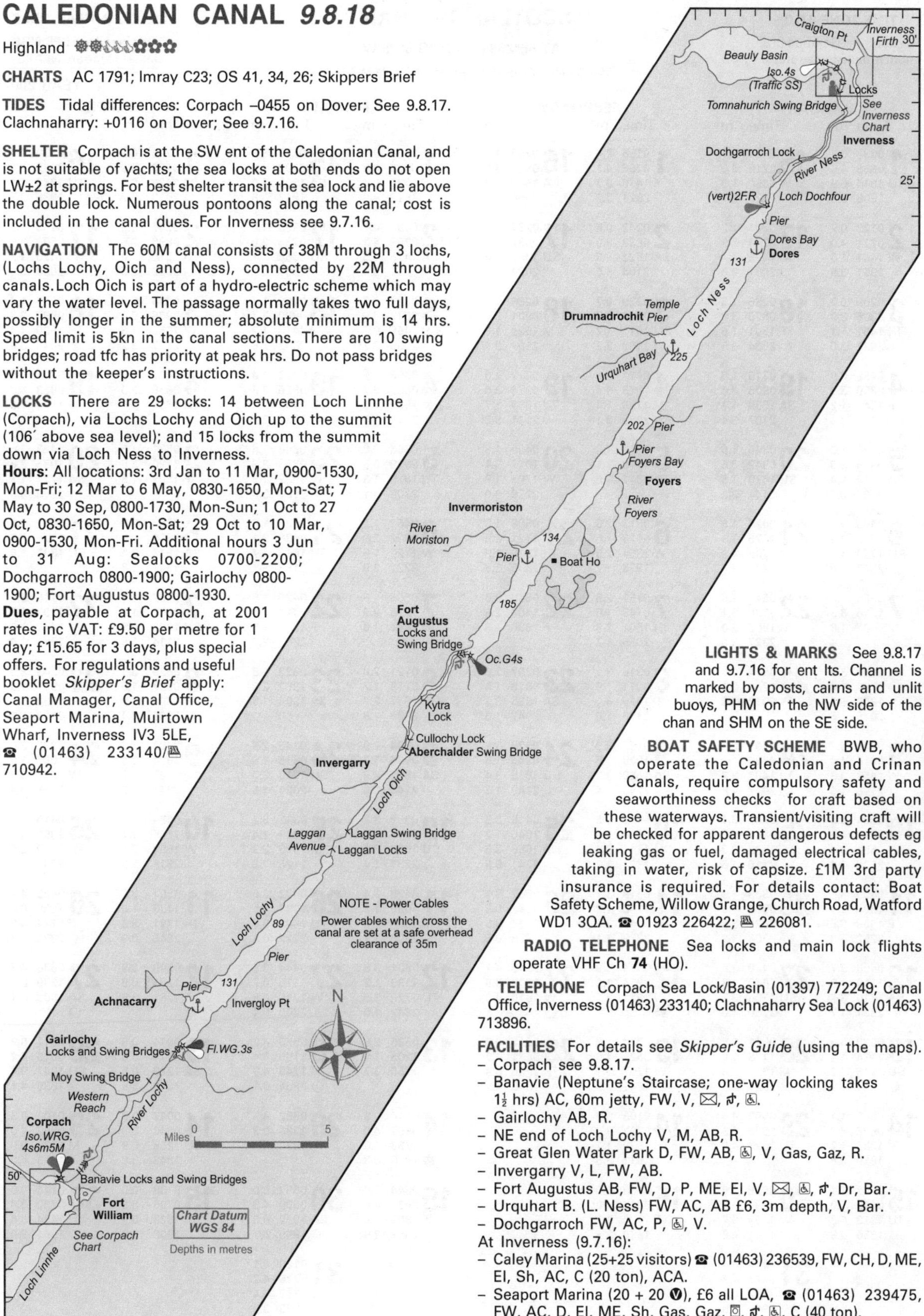

LIGHTS & MARKS See 9.8.17 and 9.7.16 for ent lts. Channel is marked by posts, cairns and unlit buoys, PHM on the NW side of the chan and SHM on the SE side.

BOAT SAFETY SCHEME BWB, who operate the Caledonian and Crinan Canals, require compulsory safety and seaworthiness checks for craft based on these waterways. Transient/visiting craft will be checked for apparent dangerous defects eg leaking gas or fuel, damaged electrical cables, taking in water, risk of capsize. £1M 3rd party insurance is required. For details contact: Boat Safety Scheme, Willow Grange, Church Road, Watford WD1 3QA. ☎ 01923 226422; 📠 226081.

RADIO TELEPHONE Sea locks and main lock flights operate VHF Ch **74** (HO).

TELEPHONE Corpach Sea Lock/Basin (01397) 772249; Canal Office, Inverness (01463) 233140; Clachnaharry Sea Lock (01463) 713896.

FACILITIES For details see *Skipper's Guide* (using the maps).
- Corpach see 9.8.17.
- Banavie (Neptune's Staircase; one-way locking takes 1½ hrs) AC, 60m jetty, FW, V, ✉, ⛪, ♿.
- Gairlochy AB, R.
- NE end of Loch Lochy V, M, AB, R.
- Great Glen Water Park D, FW, AB, ♿, V, Gas, Gaz, R.
- Invergarry V, L, FW, AB.
- Fort Augustus AB, FW, D, P, ME, El, V, ✉, ♿, ⛪, Dr, Bar.
- Urquhart B. (L. Ness) FW, AC, AB £6, 3m depth, V, Bar.
- Dochgarroch FW, AC, P, ♿, V.

At Inverness (9.7.16):
- Caley Marina (25+25 visitors) ☎ (01463) 236539, FW, CH, D, ME, El, Sh, AC, C (20 ton), ACA.
- Seaport Marina (20 + 20 Ⓥ), £6 all LOA, ☎ (01463) 239475, FW, AC, D, El, ME, Sh, Gas, Gaz, ⊡, ⛪, ♿, C (40 ton).

www.scottishcanals.co.uk.

TIME ZONE (UTC)
For Summer Time add ONE hour in **non-shaded areas**

SCOTLAND – OBAN

LAT 56°25′N LONG 5°29′W

TIMES AND HEIGHTS OF HIGH AND LOW WATERS

SPRING & NEAP TIDES
Dates in red are **SPRINGS**
Dates in blue are **NEAPS**

YEAR **2002**

JANUARY

Date	Day	Time	m	Time	m	Time	m	Time	m
1	TU	0038	0.7	0638	4.0	1314	0.9	1908	3.9
2	W	0123	0.7	0721	4.0	1401	1.0	1951	3.8
3	TH	0209	0.7	0806	3.9	1451	1.1	2037	3.6
4	F	0258	0.8	0855	3.8	1545	1.2	2127	3.4
5	SA	0350	1.0	0949	3.6	1644	1.4	2226	3.2
6	SU	0448	1.1	1052	3.4	1750	1.5	2342	3.0
7	M	0553	1.3	1216	3.3	1902	1.6		
8	TU	0113	3.0	0702	1.4	1347	3.3	2015	1.6
9	W	0228	3.1	0814	1.4	1457	3.3	2118	1.5
10	TH	0324	3.3	0922	1.4	1551	3.4	2209	1.4
11	F	0409	3.5	1020	1.3	1633	3.5	2252	1.3
12	SA	0450	3.7	1110	1.3	1710	3.6	2331	1.2
13	SU ●	0528	3.9	1154	1.2	1745	3.7		
14	M	0009	1.1	0606	4.0	1235	1.2	1819	3.8
15	TU	0047	1.1	0642	4.0	1313	1.3	1854	3.8
16	W	0124	1.1	0718	4.0	1350	1.3	1928	3.7
17	TH	0201	1.2	0754	3.9	1425	1.4	2001	3.6
18	F	0236	1.3	0829	3.8	1501	1.6	2034	3.5
19	SA	0310	1.5	0905	3.6	1539	1.7	2107	3.4
20	SU	0345	1.6	0942	3.5	1620	1.8	2144	3.2
21	M	0424	1.8	1025	3.3	1709	1.9	2229	3.1
22	TU	0513	1.9	1120	3.1	1808	2.0	2327	3.0
23	W	0614	2.0	1253	3.1	1913	1.9		
24	TH	0101	2.9	0725	1.9	1432	3.2	2017	1.8
25	F	0239	3.1	0840	1.8	1533	3.3	2116	1.6
26	SA	0339	3.3	0951	1.6	1621	3.5	2208	1.3
27	SU	0428	3.6	1049	1.3	1704	3.7	2256	1.0
28	M	0511	3.8	1138	1.0	1744	3.9	○ 2341	0.7
29	TU	0553	4.0	1224	0.8	1823	4.0		
30	W	0026	0.5	0634	4.1	1309	0.7	1901	4.0
31	TH	0111	0.4	0715	4.2	1352	0.7	1940	3.9

FEBRUARY

Date	Day	Time	m	Time	m	Time	m	Time	m
1	F	0156	0.4	0756	4.1	1436	0.7	2021	3.7
2	SA	0242	0.5	0839	3.9	1522	0.9	2104	3.5
3	SU	0329	0.7	0924	3.7	1611	1.2	2152	3.3
4	M	0421	0.9	1015	3.4	1706	1.4	2249	3.1
5	TU	0519	1.2	1119	3.1	1811	1.6		
6	W	0013	2.9	0625	1.5	1304	2.9	1928	1.7
7	TH	0151	2.9	0743	1.6	1501	2.9	2055	1.7
8	F	0310	3.1	0911	1.6	1623	3.1	2159	1.6
9	SA	0403	3.3	1020	1.5	1650	3.2	2245	1.4
10	SU	0442	3.5	1108	1.4	1711	3.4	2324	1.2
11	M	0519	3.7	1148	1.2	1740	3.6	2359	1.1
12	TU ●	0554	3.9	1224	1.2	1811	3.7		
13	W	0034	1.0	0629	4.0	1257	1.1	1841	3.8
14	TH	0108	0.9	0702	4.0	1329	1.1	1911	3.8
15	F	0139	1.0	0733	4.0	1400	1.2	1939	3.8
16	SA	0209	1.1	0803	3.9	1430	1.3	2006	3.7
17	SU	0234	1.2	0832	3.7	1457	1.4	2034	3.5
18	M	0258	1.4	0901	3.5	1526	1.6	2104	3.4
19	TU	0327	1.6	0934	3.3	1605	1.7	2141	3.2
20	W	0406	1.8	1017	3.1	1703	1.9	2229	3.0
21	TH	0508	1.9	1121	2.9	1819	1.9	2338	2.9
22	F	0642	2.0	1404	2.9	1936	1.8		
23	SA	0207	2.9	0818	1.8	1525	3.1	2047	1.6
24	SU	0328	3.2	0948	1.5	1615	3.4	2149	1.2
25	M	0419	3.5	1046	1.2	1656	3.6	2241	0.9
26	TU	0502	3.9	1132	0.8	1734	3.8	2328	0.5
27	W ○	0543	4.1	1215	0.6	1810	4.0		
28	TH	0012	0.3	0621	4.3	1256	0.4	1845	4.1

MARCH

Date	Day	Time	m	Time	m	Time	m	Time	m
1	F	0056	0.1	0700	4.3	1335	0.4	1922	4.0
2	SA	0139	0.1	0739	4.2	1415	0.5	1959	3.9
3	SU	0223	0.2	0817	4.0	1455	0.7	2038	3.7
4	M	0308	0.5	0857	3.7	1539	1.0	2119	3.4
5	TU	0356	0.8	0939	3.3	1628	1.3	2208	3.1
6	W	0450	1.2	1032	2.9	1728	1.6	2321	2.9
7	TH	0555	1.5	1215	2.7	1844	1.8		
8	F	0121	2.8	0719	1.7	1537	2.7	2030	1.8
9	SA	0304	2.9	0914	1.7	1632	2.9	2144	1.6
10	SU	0358	3.2	1018	1.5	1658	3.1	2231	1.4
11	M	0428	3.4	1059	1.3	1659	3.3	2308	1.1
12	TU	0501	3.6	1133	1.2	1722	3.5	2342	1.0
13	W	0535	3.8	1203	1.0	1750	3.7		
14	TH	0014	0.8	0607	4.0	1233	1.0	● 1819	3.8
15	F	0044	0.8	0639	4.0	1302	0.9	1847	3.9
16	SA	0113	0.9	0708	4.0	1330	1.0	1912	3.8
17	SU	0139	1.0	0735	3.9	1356	1.1	1937	3.7
18	M	0159	1.1	0800	3.7	1418	1.2	2002	3.6
19	TU	0220	1.3	0826	3.6	1445	1.3	2032	3.5
20	W	0248	1.4	0858	3.3	1522	1.5	2107	3.3
21	TH	0326	1.6	0938	3.1	1616	1.7	2152	3.1
22	F	0425	1.8	1042	2.8	1737	1.8	2302	2.9
23	SA	0622	1.9	1352	2.8	1904	1.8		
24	SU	0145	2.9	0815	1.8	1510	3.0	2022	1.5
25	M	0312	3.2	0939	1.4	1559	3.3	2128	1.2
26	TU	0402	3.6	1031	1.0	1640	3.6	2222	0.8
27	W	0444	3.9	1115	0.7	1715	3.8	2309	0.4
28	TH	0523	4.2	1155	0.4	1749	4.0	○ 2354	0.1
29	F	0602	4.3	1234	0.3	1824	4.1		
30	SA	0037	0.0	0639	4.3	1312	0.3	1859	4.1
31	SU	0120	0.1	0716	4.2	1350	0.4	1935	3.9

APRIL

Date	Day	Time	m	Time	m	Time	m	Time	m
1	M	0203	0.3	0753	3.9	1429	0.7	2013	3.7
2	TU	0247	0.6	0830	3.6	1510	1.0	2052	3.5
3	W	0334	0.9	0909	3.2	1558	1.3	2137	3.2
4	TH	0427	1.3	0955	2.8	1655	1.6	2242	2.9
5	F	0531	1.6	1120	2.5	1808	1.8		
6	SA	0053	2.8	0659	1.8	1513	2.6	1951	1.8
7	SU	0237	2.9	0901	1.7	1606	2.8	2114	1.6
8	M	0329	3.1	0957	1.6	1624	3.0	2203	1.4
9	TU	0402	3.3	1034	1.4	1627	3.2	2241	1.2
10	W	0434	3.6	1105	1.2	1652	3.4	2315	1.0
11	TH	0507	3.8	1133	1.0	1721	3.6	2345	0.9
12	F ●	0540	3.9	1201	0.9	1751	3.8		
13	SA	0014	0.8	0611	3.9	1229	0.8	1818	3.8
14	SU	0042	0.9	0640	3.9	1258	0.9	1843	3.8
15	M	0108	0.9	0706	3.8	1323	0.9	1908	3.8
16	TU	0130	1.1	0733	3.7	1349	1.1	1936	3.7
17	W	0155	1.2	0802	3.5	1420	1.2	2008	3.5
18	TH	0227	1.4	0837	3.3	1500	1.4	2046	3.4
19	F	0311	1.6	0923	3.0	1555	1.5	2136	3.1
20	SA	0423	1.8	1035	2.8	1711	1.7	2253	3.0
21	SU	0621	1.8	1326	2.7	1837	1.6		
22	M	0115	3.0	0803	1.6	1443	3.0	1955	1.4
23	TU	0243	3.3	0915	1.3	1533	3.3	2102	1.1
24	W	0335	3.6	1007	1.0	1614	3.5	2158	0.7
25	TH	0419	3.9	1050	0.7	1650	3.8	2247	0.4
26	F	0459	4.1	1130	0.5	1724	4.0	2333	0.2
27	SA ○	0538	4.2	1209	0.4	1800	4.1		
28	SU	0017	0.2	0616	4.2	1247	0.4	1836	4.1
29	M	0101	0.3	0653	4.0	1325	0.6	1913	4.0
30	TU	0144	0.5	0730	3.8	1404	0.8	1951	3.8

Chart Datum: 2·10 metres below Ordnance Datum (Newlyn)

TIME ZONE (UTC)
For Summer Time add ONE hour in **non-shaded areas**

SCOTLAND – OBAN

LAT 56°25′N LONG 5°29′W

TIMES AND HEIGHTS OF HIGH AND LOW WATERS

SPRING & NEAP TIDES
Dates in red are SPRINGS Dates in blue are NEAPS

YEAR **2002**

MAY

Date	Day	Time	m	Time	m	Time	m	Time	m
1	W	0228	0.8	0807	3.5	1446	1.0	2032	3.5
2	TH	0315	1.1	0846	3.1	1533	1.3	2117	3.3
3	F	0407	1.4	0932	2.8	1628	1.5	2216	3.0
4	SA	0508	1.7	1042	2.6	1733	1.7		
5	SU	0000	2.9	0628	1.9	1350	2.6	1855	1.8
6	M	0150	2.9	0813	1.8	1454	2.7	2025	1.7
7	TU	0246	3.1	0914	1.6	1522	2.9	2122	1.5
8	W	0325	3.3	0954	1.5	1546	3.1	2204	1.3
9	TH	0400	3.5	1025	1.3	1616	3.3	2238	1.2
10	F	0434	3.6	1055	1.1	1647	3.5	2309	1.1
11	SA	0509	3.8	1124	1.0	1719	3.7	2339	1.0
12	SU ●	0542	3.8	1155	0.9	1748	3.8		
13	M	0010	1.0	0613	3.8	1226	0.9	1816	3.8
14	TU	0041	1.0	0643	3.8	1257	0.9	1846	3.8
15	W	0112	1.1	0714	3.7	1330	1.0	1919	3.7
16	TH	0146	1.2	0749	3.5	1407	1.1	1956	3.6
17	F	0227	1.3	0832	3.3	1452	1.2	2041	3.4
18	SA	0322	1.5	0925	3.1	1547	1.3	2137	3.3
19	SU	0439	1.6	1036	2.9	1655	1.4	2252	3.1
20	M	0610	1.6	1235	2.8	1810	1.4		
21	TU	0035	3.2	0735	1.5	1405	3.0	1924	1.3
22	W	0206	3.3	0844	1.3	1500	3.2	2031	1.1
23	TH	0304	3.6	0938	1.0	1545	3.5	2131	0.8
24	F	0352	3.8	1023	0.8	1623	3.7	2223	0.7
25	SA	0435	3.9	1105	0.7	1701	3.9	2312	0.5
26	SU ○	0516	4.0	1145	0.7	1739	4.0	2358	0.5
27	M	0556	3.9	1224	0.7	1817	4.0		
28	TU	0043	0.6	0634	3.8	1304	0.8	1856	3.9
29	W	0128	0.8	0713	3.6	1344	0.9	1936	3.8
30	TH	0212	1.0	0751	3.4	1426	1.1	2017	3.6
31	F	0258	1.3	0831	3.2	1511	1.3	2101	3.4

JUNE

Date	Day	Time	m	Time	m	Time	m	Time	m
1	SA	0346	1.5	0915	3.0	1600	1.5	2152	3.2
2	SU	0441	1.7	1010	2.8	1655	1.6	2256	3.1
3	M	0543	1.8	1131	2.7	1756	1.7		
4	TU	0025	3.0	0654	1.9	1322	2.7	1904	1.8
5	W	0146	3.0	0803	1.8	1417	2.9	2013	1.7
6	TH	0238	3.2	0856	1.6	1458	3.0	2107	1.6
7	F	0321	3.3	0937	1.5	1536	3.2	2150	1.4
8	SA	0400	3.5	1013	1.3	1612	3.4	2228	1.3
9	SU	0439	3.6	1048	1.1	1648	3.5	2305	1.2
10	M ●	0517	3.7	1123	1.0	1723	3.7	2343	1.1
11	TU	0553	3.7	1159	0.9	1758	3.7		
12	W	0022	1.0	0628	3.7	1237	0.9	1833	3.8
13	TH	0103	1.0	0705	3.6	1317	0.8	1911	3.7
14	F	0147	1.1	0745	3.5	1359	0.9	1954	3.7
15	SA	0235	1.2	0830	3.4	1446	1.0	2041	3.6
16	SU	0330	1.3	0922	3.2	1538	1.1	2135	3.4
17	M	0433	1.4	1023	3.0	1636	1.2	2239	3.3
18	TU	0545	1.4	1142	3.0	1742	1.2	2357	3.3
19	W	0700	1.4	1315	3.0	1851	1.2		
20	TH	0124	3.3	0808	1.3	1423	3.1	2000	1.2
21	F	0234	3.4	0908	1.2	1517	3.3	2104	1.1
22	SA	0331	3.5	0959	1.1	1603	3.5	2203	1.0
23	SU	0419	3.6	1045	1.0	1644	3.7	2256	0.9
24	M ○	0503	3.7	1127	0.9	1725	3.8	2344	0.9
25	TU	0545	3.7	1208	0.9	1805	3.9		
26	W	0031	0.9	0623	3.7	1249	0.9	1844	3.9
27	TH	0115	1.0	0701	3.6	1329	1.0	1923	3.9
28	F	0158	1.1	0739	3.5	1409	1.1	2003	3.7
29	SA	0240	1.3	0816	3.3	1449	1.2	2043	3.6
30	SU	0322	1.5	0854	3.2	1531	1.4	2124	3.4

JULY

Date	Day	Time	m	Time	m	Time	m	Time	m
1	M	0406	1.6	0936	3.1	1615	1.5	2210	3.3
2	TU	0454	1.7	1023	2.9	1702	1.7	2303	3.1
3	W	0548	1.8	1123	2.9	1754	1.8		
4	TH	0011	3.1	0647	1.8	1243	2.8	1850	1.8
5	F	0130	3.1	0747	1.8	1358	2.9	1951	1.8
6	SA	0237	3.2	0843	1.6	1455	3.1	2052	1.7
7	SU	0330	3.3	0933	1.5	1543	3.2	2149	1.5
8	M	0417	3.4	1017	1.3	1627	3.4	2240	1.3
9	TU	0501	3.6	1059	1.1	1708	3.6	2327	1.2
10	W ●	0542	3.7	1140	0.9	1748	3.7		
11	TH	0013	1.0	0621	3.7	1222	0.7	1827	3.8
12	F	0058	0.9	0659	3.7	1304	0.6	1908	3.9
13	SA	0144	0.9	0739	3.7	1348	0.6	1949	3.9
14	SU	0230	0.9	0821	3.5	1434	0.6	2034	3.8
15	M	0319	1.0	0907	3.4	1522	0.8	2122	3.6
16	TU	0412	1.1	0959	3.2	1615	0.9	2216	3.4
17	W	0512	1.3	1101	3.1	1714	1.1	2321	3.3
18	TH	0619	1.4	1223	3.0	1820	1.2		
19	F	0045	3.1	0731	1.5	1349	3.0	1930	1.3
20	SA	0213	3.1	0842	1.4	1459	3.2	2043	1.3
21	SU	0325	3.2	0944	1.4	1555	3.4	2151	1.3
22	M	0421	3.3	1034	1.2	1639	3.6	2249	1.2
23	TU	0505	3.4	1118	1.1	1718	3.7	2338	1.1
24	W ○	0543	3.5	1158	1.0	1757	3.9		
25	TH	0021	1.1	0617	3.6	1237	0.9	1833	3.9
26	F	0102	1.1	0651	3.6	1314	0.9	1909	4.0
27	SA	0140	1.1	0723	3.6	1350	1.0	1944	3.9
28	SU	0216	1.2	0755	3.5	1425	1.1	2018	3.8
29	M	0252	1.3	0827	3.5	1459	1.3	2053	3.6
30	TU	0328	1.5	0859	3.3	1533	1.4	2128	3.5
31	W	0407	1.6	0934	3.2	1611	1.6	2206	3.3

AUGUST

Date	Day	Time	m	Time	m	Time	m	Time	m
1	TH	0452	1.8	1016	3.0	1655	1.8	2253	3.1
2	F	0547	1.9	1109	2.9	1751	1.9		
3	SA	0004	3.0	0650	1.9	1237	2.8	1858	2.0
4	SU	0158	3.0	0757	1.8	1424	2.9	2012	1.9
5	M	0314	3.1	0900	1.6	1528	3.1	2130	1.7
6	TU	0408	3.3	0954	1.4	1617	3.4	2233	1.4
7	W	0452	3.5	1042	1.1	1700	3.6	2323	1.1
8	TH ●	0533	3.7	1125	0.8	1740	3.9		
9	F	0007	0.9	0611	3.8	1208	0.5	1819	4.0
10	SA	0050	0.7	0648	3.9	1250	0.4	1858	4.1
11	SU	0132	0.6	0724	3.8	1333	0.3	1937	4.1
12	M	0214	0.6	0802	3.7	1417	0.4	2017	4.0
13	TU	0258	0.8	0843	3.6	1503	0.5	2100	3.8
14	W	0344	1.0	0928	3.4	1553	0.8	2146	3.5
15	TH	0437	1.2	1022	3.1	1648	1.1	2243	3.2
16	F	0539	1.5	1140	3.0	1752	1.4		
17	SA	0009	2.9	0654	1.6	1327	2.9	1907	1.6
18	SU	0211	2.9	0822	1.6	1457	3.1	2035	1.6
19	M	0400	3.0	0936	1.5	1559	3.3	2157	1.5
20	TU	0447	3.1	1028	1.3	1636	3.5	2251	1.3
21	W	0510	3.3	1109	1.1	1709	3.7	2332	1.2
22	TH ○	0534	3.5	1146	1.0	1742	3.9		
23	F	0009	1.1	0602	3.6	1221	0.9	1815	4.0
24	SA	0043	1.0	0632	3.7	1255	0.8	1848	4.1
25	SU	0115	1.0	0700	3.8	1327	0.9	1919	4.0
26	M	0147	1.1	0728	3.8	1357	1.0	1949	3.9
27	TU	0218	1.2	0755	3.7	1425	1.2	2019	3.8
28	W	0248	1.3	0822	3.5	1451	1.4	2047	3.6
29	TH	0319	1.5	0852	3.4	1519	1.6	2117	3.4
30	F	0356	1.7	0928	3.2	1555	1.8	2154	3.2
31	SA	0450	1.9	1013	3.0	1652	2.0	2249	2.9

Chart Datum: 2·10 metres below Ordnance Datum (Newlyn)

TIME ZONE (UTC)
For Summer Time add ONE hour in **non-shaded areas**

SCOTLAND – OBAN

LAT 56°25′N LONG 5°29′W

TIMES AND HEIGHTS OF HIGH AND LOW WATERS

SPRING & NEAP TIDES
Dates in red are SPRINGS
Dates in blue are NEAPS

YEAR **2002**

SEPTEMBER

Day	Time	m	Day	Time	m
1 SU	0603 1120 1822	1.9 2.8 2.1	16 M	0300 0804 1501 2048	2.7 1.7 3.1 1.8
2 M	0143 0720 1412 1957	2.8 1.9 2.9 2.0	17 TU	0410 0922 1556 2201	2.9 1.6 3.3 1.6
3 TU	0310 0833 1522 2132	3.0 1.7 3.2 1.7	18 W	0447 1012 1621 2242	3.1 1.3 3.5 1.4
4 W	0400 0935 1607 2229	3.3 1.4 3.5 1.3	19 TH	0454 1051 1648 2315	3.3 1.1 3.7 1.2
5 TH	0441 1024 1646 2313	3.5 1.0 3.8 1.0	20 F	0509 1125 1718 2345	3.5 1.0 3.9 1.1
6 F	0518 1108 1725 2353	3.8 0.7 4.1 0.7	21 SA ○	0536 1158 1750	3.7 0.9 4.1
7 SA ●	0553 1150 1802	3.9 0.4 4.3	22 SU	0015 0604 1229 1820	1.0 3.9 0.8 4.1
8 SU	0032 0627 1232 1838	0.5 4.0 0.2 4.3	23 M	0045 0632 1259 1850	1.0 3.9 0.9 4.1
9 M	0111 0701 1314 1915	0.4 4.0 0.1 4.3	24 TU	0114 0658 1326 1918	1.0 3.9 1.0 4.0
10 TU	0150 0737 1358 1953	0.5 3.9 0.2 4.1	25 W	0143 0723 1350 1944	1.1 3.8 1.2 3.9
11 W	0230 0816 1442 2032	0.6 3.8 0.5 3.8	26 TH	0209 0748 1411 2010	1.2 3.7 1.4 3.7
12 TH	0314 0857 1531 2114	0.9 3.5 0.8 3.4	27 F	0235 0817 1435 2038	1.4 3.5 1.6 3.4
13 F	0404 0947 1625 2205	1.2 3.2 1.2 3.1	28 SA	0308 0851 1508 2113	1.6 3.3 1.9 3.2
14 SA	0504 1102 1730 2334	1.5 3.0 1.5 2.7	29 SU	0358 0934 1603 2207	1.8 3.1 2.1 2.9
15 SU	0621 1317 1852	1.7 2.9 1.8	30 M	0519 1041 1805	2.0 2.9 2.2

OCTOBER

Day	Time	m	Day	Time	m
1 TU	0140 0646 1401 1958	2.8 1.9 3.0 2.0	16 W	0346 0852 1526 2140	2.9 1.6 3.3 1.7
2 W	0253 0805 1503 2121	3.0 1.7 3.3 1.7	17 TH	0417 0943 1552 2216	3.1 1.4 3.5 1.5
3 TH	0341 0910 1546 2210	3.3 1.4 3.6 1.3	18 F	0417 1023 1619 2246	3.3 1.2 3.7 1.3
4 F	0420 1001 1624 2252	3.6 1.0 4.0 0.9	19 SA	0437 1058 1649 2314	3.5 1.1 3.9 1.1
5 SA	0455 1046 1701 2330	3.8 0.6 4.3 0.6	20 SU	0504 1130 1720 2342	3.7 1.0 4.1 1.0
6 SU ●	0528 1129 1737	4.0 0.3 4.4	21 M ○	0533 1159 1751	3.9 1.0 4.1
7 M	0008 0600 1212 1814	0.4 4.1 0.2 4.5	22 TU	0011 0601 1228 1820	1.0 4.0 1.0 4.1
8 TU	0046 0635 1254 1850	0.4 4.2 0.2 4.3	23 W	0041 0627 1255 1849	1.0 4.0 1.1 4.0
9 W	0123 0711 1337 1927	0.5 4.1 0.3 4.1	24 TH	0110 0654 1320 1915	1.1 3.9 1.3 3.9
10 TH	0203 0750 1422 2005	0.7 3.9 0.6 3.8	25 F	0137 0721 1343 1943	1.2 3.8 1.5 3.7
11 F	0246 0831 1511 2045	1.0 3.6 1.0 3.4	26 SA	0206 0751 1410 2014	1.4 3.6 1.7 3.4
12 SA	0335 0919 1606 2132	1.3 3.3 1.4 3.0	27 SU	0242 0827 1450 2054	1.6 3.5 1.9 3.2
13 SU	0434 1030 1712 2252	1.6 3.1 1.7 2.7	28 M	0331 0914 1555 2155	1.7 3.3 2.1 2.9
14 M	0548 1302 1839	1.8 3.0 1.9	29 TU	0444 1025 1756	1.9 3.1 2.1
15 TU	0244 0730 1437 2042	2.7 1.8 3.1 1.9	30 W	0105 0609 1311 1939	2.8 1.9 3.1 1.9
			31 TH	0222 0729 1428 2051	3.0 1.7 3.4 1.6

NOVEMBER

Day	Time	m	Day	Time	m
1 F	0312 0836 1515 2141	3.3 1.4 3.7 1.3	16 SA	0333 0949 1546 2208	3.2 1.4 3.6 1.5
2 SA	0352 0932 1555 2224	3.6 1.0 4.0 1.0	17 SU	0400 1026 1618 2237	3.5 1.3 3.8 1.3
3 SU	0427 1021 1634 2303	3.8 0.7 4.3 0.7	18 M	0431 1058 1650 2307	3.7 1.2 3.9 1.2
4 M ●	0500 1106 1712 2341	4.0 0.5 4.4 0.6	19 TU	0502 1128 1723 2338	3.8 1.2 4.0 1.1
5 TU	0535 1151 1750	4.2 0.4 4.4	20 W ○	0533 1158 1755	3.9 1.2 4.0
6 W	0020 0611 1235 1827	0.6 4.2 0.4 4.3	21 TH	0011 0602 1229 1826	1.1 3.9 1.3 4.0
7 TH	0059 0650 1320 1905	0.6 4.2 0.6 4.0	22 F	0043 0632 1300 1857	1.1 3.9 1.4 3.8
8 F	0140 0730 1405 1944	0.8 4.0 0.9 3.7	23 SA	0115 0703 1331 1929	1.2 3.8 1.5 3.7
9 SA	0223 0813 1454 2024	1.0 3.8 1.2 3.4	24 SU	0150 0738 1407 2007	1.3 3.7 1.6 3.5
10 SU	0312 0901 1548 2110	1.3 3.5 1.6 3.0	25 M	0230 0819 1454 2053	1.4 3.6 1.8 3.3
11 M	0407 1003 1650 2215	1.6 3.2 1.8 2.8	26 TU	0319 0909 1602 2153	1.5 3.4 1.9 3.1
12 TU	0513 1210 1810	1.8 3.1 2.0	27 W	0420 1016 1732 2318	1.6 3.3 1.9 2.9
13 W	0131 0636 1346 1950	2.7 1.8 3.2 2.0	28 TH	0532 1150 1859	1.7 3.3 1.8
14 TH	0245 0804 1440 2056	2.9 1.8 3.3 1.8	29 F	0130 0647 1336 2011	3.0 1.6 3.4 1.6
15 F	0314 0904 1515 2136	3.0 1.6 3.5 1.6	30 SA	0232 0758 1438 2107	3.2 1.4 3.7 1.4

DECEMBER

Day	Time	m	Day	Time	m
1 SU	0318 0900 1526 2154	3.5 1.1 3.9 1.2	16 M	0321 0946 1547 2158	3.3 1.6 3.6 1.5
2 M	0358 0955 1609 2237	3.7 0.9 4.1 1.0	17 TU	0358 1024 1625 2234	3.5 1.5 3.7 1.4
3 TU	0436 1046 1651 2318	3.9 0.8 4.2 0.8	18 W	0435 1059 1702 2310	3.6 1.5 3.8 1.2
4 W ●	0515 1134 1731 2359	4.1 0.7 4.2 0.8	19 TH ○	0511 1135 1739 2346	3.7 1.4 3.9 1.1
5 TH	0555 1220 1811	4.2 0.7 4.1	20 F	0546 1212 1814	3.8 1.3 3.9
6 F	0040 0635 1306 1851	0.8 4.1 0.9 3.9	21 SA	0022 0620 1250 1848	1.1 3.9 1.3 3.8
7 SA	0122 0717 1352 1930	0.9 4.0 1.1 3.7	22 SU	0100 0656 1329 1924	1.1 3.9 1.3 3.7
8 SU	0206 0800 1439 2011	1.1 3.9 1.3 3.4	23 M	0138 0734 1410 2003	1.1 3.8 1.4 3.6
9 M	0252 0845 1528 2053	1.3 3.7 1.6 3.2	24 TU	0220 0816 1457 2047	1.1 3.7 1.5 3.4
10 TU	0341 0936 1621 2142	1.5 3.5 1.8 3.0	25 W	0306 0904 1551 2138	1.2 3.6 1.6 3.3
11 W	0435 1039 1721 2248	1.7 3.3 2.0 2.9	26 TH	0359 0959 1656 2239	1.3 3.5 1.7 3.1
12 TH	0535 1213 1829	1.8 3.2 2.0	27 F	0459 1107 1809 2358	1.4 3.4 1.7 3.1
13 F	0041 0644 1338 1938	2.8 1.9 3.2 2.0	28 SA	0608 1232 1922	1.4 3.4 1.7
14 SA	0156 0758 1430 2036	2.9 1.8 3.3 1.9	29 SU	0132 0720 1358 2029	3.1 1.4 3.5 1.5
15 SU	0242 0900 1510 2120	3.1 1.7 3.4 1.7	30 M	0243 0830 1503 2126	3.3 1.3 3.6 1.4
			31 TU	0336 0934 1556 2217	3.5 1.2 3.7 1.2

Chart Datum: 2·10 metres below Ordnance Datum (Newlyn)

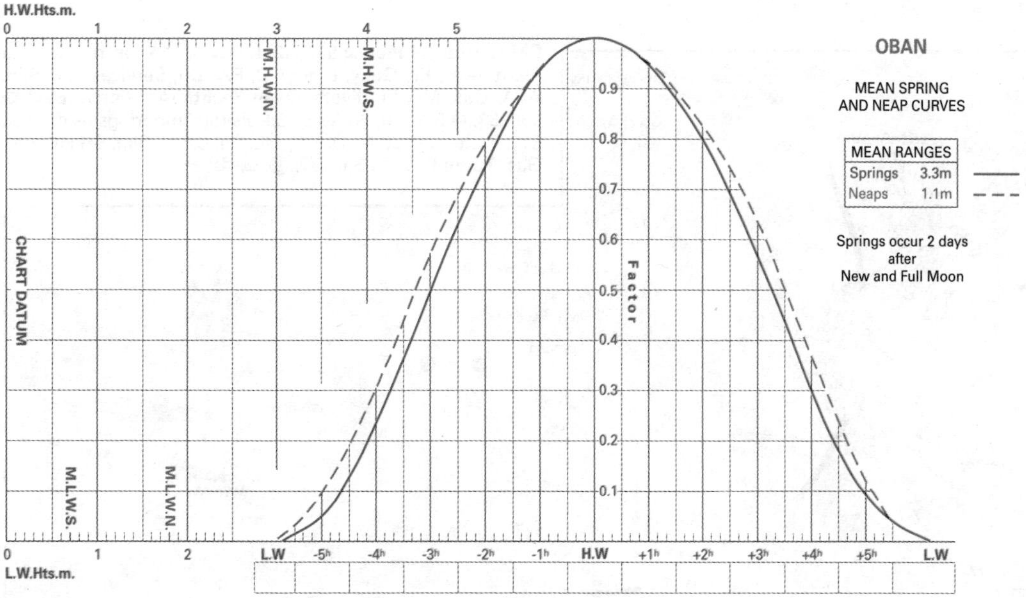
H.W.Hts.m.
0 1 2 3 4 5
M.H.W.N.
M.H.W.S.
OBAN
MEAN SPRING
AND NEAP CURVES
MEAN RANGES
Springs 3.3m
Neaps 1.1m
Springs occur 2 days after New and Full Moon
0.9
0.8
0.7
0.6
0.5
0.4
0.3
0.2
0.1
Factor
CHART DATUM
M.L.W.S.
M.L.W.N.
0 1 2
L.W.Hts.m.
L.W -5h -4h -3h -2h -1h H.W +1h +2h +3h +4h +5h L.W

ADJACENT ANCHORAGES/HAVEN

DUNSTAFFNAGE BAY, Argyll & Bute, **56°27′·04N 05°25′·97W**. ❁❁❁◊◊◊✿✿✿. AC 2378, 2387. HW –0530 on Dover; see 9.8.19. Good shelter at marina pontoons, SE side of bay entered 'twixt Rubha Garbh and Eilean Mór; little room to ⚓, within the bay the tidal stream is rotary but sets E through the marina most of the time. No navigational hazards; W and SW sides of bay dry. Private pier on NW side has 2 FG (vert) 4m 2M. **Dunstaffnage Marina** ☎ (01631) 566555, 📠 567422, VHF Ch M, 80+ approx AB £1.46, FW, D, Slip, BH (8 ton), AC, CH, C (masting), ⊡, SM, R, Bar; Facilities: P (cans, ¾M), V (½M), Bus, ⇌ Oban (2M) & Connel (airstrip).

LOCH ETIVE, AC 2378 to Bonawe, thence AC 5076. Connel Bridge, 15m clrnce, and Falls of Lora can be physical and tidal barriers. HT cables at Bonawe have 13m clrnce. See CCC SDs.

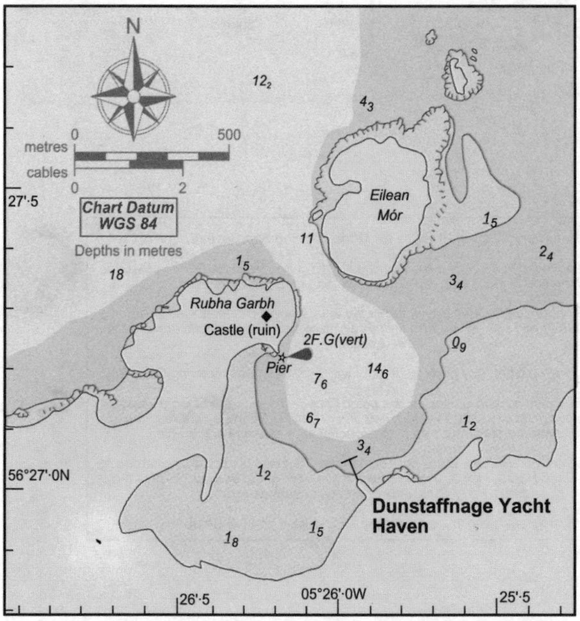
N
metres 0 500
cables 0 2
Chart Datum WGS 84
Depths in metres
27′·5
12₂
4₃
Eilean Mór
1₅
11
2₄
18
1₅
3₄
Rubha Garbh
Castle (ruin)
2F.G(vert)
Pier
0₉
7₆
14₆
6₇
1₂
3₄
56°27′·0N
1₂
Dunstaffnage Yacht Haven
1₈
1₅
26′·5
05°26′·0W
25′·5

OBAN *9.8.19*

Argyll and Bute **56°24′·99N 05°29′·07W** ❁❁❁◊◊◊✿✿

CHARTS AC 1790, 2387, *2171*; Imray C65; OS 49

TIDES –0530 Dover; ML 2·4; Duration 0610; Zone 0 (UT)

Standard Port OBAN (⟶)

Times				Height (metres)			
High Water		Low Water		MHWS	MHWN	MLWN	MLWS
0100	0700	0100	0800	4·0	2·9	1·8	0·7
1300	1900	1300	2000				
Differences DUNSTAFFNAGE BAY							
+0005	0000	0000	+0005	+0·1	+0·1	+0·1	+0·1
CONNEL							
+0020	+0005	+0010	+0015	–0·3	–0·2	–0·1	+0·1
BONAWE							
+0150	+0205	+0240	+0210	–2·0	–1·7	–1·3	–0·5

SHELTER Good except in strong SW/NW winds, but Ardantrive Bay (20 🅐s, some pontoon berths and water taxi 0800-2300) is sheltered from these winds. See chartlet for 🅐s. ⚓s off town, but in deep water. ⚓ or M off Brandystone and in Kerrera Sound at: Horseshoe Bay, Gallanachbeg (rk dries 0·3m) and Little Horseshoe Bay. Dunstaffnage Bay, 3M NE: see facing column.

NAVIGATION WPT (N) 56°25′·84N 05°30′·07W, 309°/129° from/to Dunollie lt, 0·73M and WPT (S) 56°21′·99N 05°32′·95W, 210°/030° from/to 140m ESE of Sgeirean Dubha 9 cables. Beware Sgeir Rathaid, buoyed, in middle of the bay; also CalMac ferries running to/from Railway Quay. Ferry Rks in mid-channel at 56°24′·0N can be passed on either side but note the direction of the buoyage is NE, thus pass to the E'ward of the port-hand unlit buoy or to the W'ward of the stbd-conical QG buoy. The N'ly stbd-hand buoy must always be passed to the W'ward.

LIGHTS AND MARKS N Spit of Kerrera Fl R 3s 9m 5M, W col, R bands. Dunollie Fl (2) WRG 6s 7m 5/4M; G351°-009°, W009°-047°, R047°-120°, W120°-138°, G138°-143°. N Pier 2FG (vert). S Quay 2FG (vert). Northern Lights Wharf Oc G 6s.

RADIO TELEPHONE Call *North Pier* Ch 12 16 (0900-1700). For Railway Quay, call *CalMac* Ch 06 12 16. For Ardantrive Bay, call *Oban Yachts* and Water taxi Ch 80.

TELEPHONE (Dial code 01631) Pier 562892; Marinecall 09068 500 463; ⊖ 563079; MRSC (01475) 729014; Police 562213; Dr 563175.

8

OBAN *continued*

FACILITIES N Pier ☎ 562892, L, FW, C (15 ton mobile) via Piermaster; **Rly Quay,** L, Slip, D, FW, CH; **Services:** BY, Slip, ACA, Gas, ME, El, divers; **Oban Yachts** (Ardantrive Bay) ☎ 565333, 📠 565888, 20 AB £1.38, visitors' moorings as marked £10; Water taxi Ch M; D, FW, ME, Sh, C, CH, Slip, BH (16 ton), Gas. **Town** P, V, R, Bar, ✉, Ⓑ, ▣, ⇌, ✈.

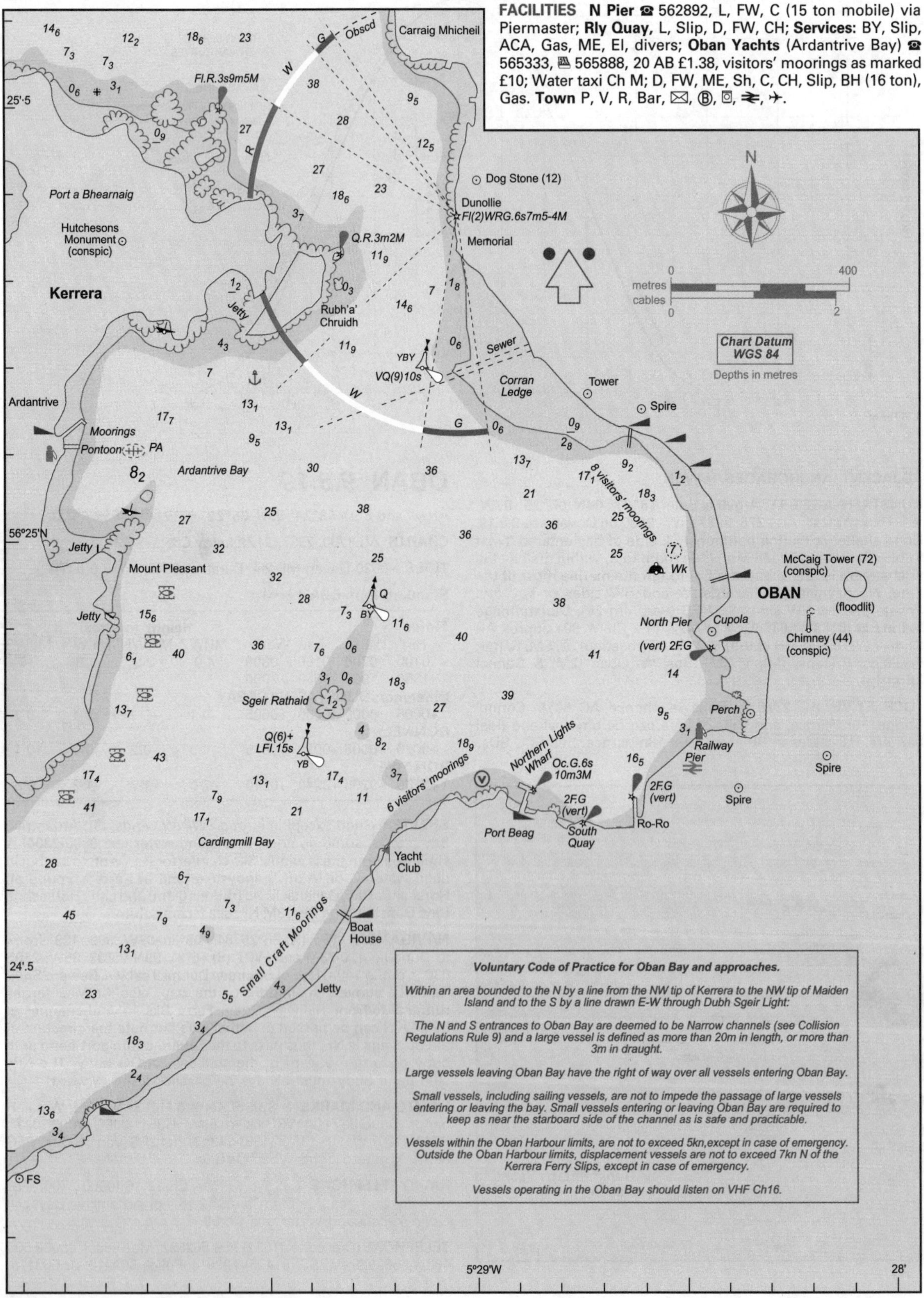

Voluntary Code of Practice for Oban Bay and approaches.

Within an area bounded to the N by a line from the NW tip of Kerrera to the NW tip of Maiden Island and to the S by a line drawn E-W through Dubh Sgeir Light:

The N and S entrances to Oban Bay are deemed to be Narrow channels (see Collision Regulations Rule 9) and a large vessel is defined as more than 20m in length, or more than 3m in draught.

Large vessels leaving Oban Bay have the right of way over all vessels entering Oban Bay.

Small vessels, including sailing vessels, are not to impede the passage of large vessels entering or leaving the bay. Small vessels entering or leaving Oban Bay are required to keep as near the starboard side of the channel as is safe and practicable.

Vessels within the Oban Harbour limits, are not to exceed 5kn,except in case of emergency. Outside the Oban Harbour limits, displacement vessels are not to exceed 7kn N of the Kerrera Ferry Slips, except in case of emergency.

Vessels operating in the Oban Bay should listen on VHF Ch16.

ANCHORAGES ON MAINLAND SHORE OF FIRTH OF LORN

LOCH FEOCHAN, Argyll and Bute, **56°21′.39N 05°29′·77W**. AC 2387. HW = HW Oban; flood runs 4 hrs, ebb for 8 hrs. Caution: strong streams off Ardentallan Pt. Good shelter, 5M S of Oban and 1·5M SE of Kerrera. Best appr at local slack LW = LW Oban +0200. Narrow chan marked by 3 PHM buoys, 2 PHM perches on shore and 5 SHM buoys. ⚓ off pier, or moor off **Ardoran Marine** ☎ (01631) 566123, 📠 566611; 4 ♦s £10 <11m, D, FW, ME, CH, Slip, Showers.

PUILLADOBHRAIN, Argyll & Bute, **56°19′·47N 05°35′·22W**. AC 2386/2387. Tides as Oban. Popular ⚓ on the SE shore of the Firth of Lorne, approx 7M S of Oban, sheltered by the islets to the W of it. At N end of Ardencaple Bay identify Eilean Dùin (18m) and steer SE keeping 1½ca off to clear a rk awash at its NE tip. Continue for 4ca between Eilean nam Beathach, with Orange drum on N tip, and Dun Horses rks drying 2·7m. Two W cairns on E side of Eilean nam Freumha lead approx 215° into the inner ⚓ in about 4m. Landing at head of inlet. Nearest facilities: Bar, P at Clachan Br (½M); ☎, ✉ at Clachan Seil.

CUAN SOUND, Argyll & Bute, **56°15′·84N 05°37′·47W**. AC 2326, 2386. Tides see 9.8.20 Seil Sound. Streams reach 6kn at sp; N-going makes at HW Oban +0420, S-going at HW Oban –2. The Sound is a useful doglegged short cut from Firth of Lorne to Lochs Melfort and Shuna, but needs care due to rks and tides. There are ⚓s at either end to await the tide. At the 90° dogleg, pass close N of Cleit Rk onto which the tide sets; it is marked by a Y △ perch. The chan is only ¾ca wide here due to rks off Seil. Overhead cables (35m) cross from Seil to Luing. There are ⚓s out of the tide to the S of Cleit Rk. No lts/facilities. See CCC SDs.

ARDINAMAR, Luing/Torsa, **56°14′·92N 05°37′·04W**. AC *2326*. HW –0555 on Dover; ML 1·7m; see 9.8.20 SEIL SOUND. A small cove and popular ⚓ between Luing and Torsa, close W of ent to L. Melfort. Appr with W paint mark inside cove on brg 290°. Narrow, shallow (about 1m CD) ent has drying rks either side, those to N marked by 2 SHM perches. Keep about 15m S of perches to ⚓ in 2m in centre of cove; S part dries. Few facilities: V, ✉, ☎, at Cullipool 1·5M WNW. Gas at Cuan Sound ferry 2M NNW.

LOCH MELFORT *9.8.20*

Argyll and Bute **56°14′·59N 05°34′·07W** ❁❁❁⚓⚓⚓✿✿✿

CHARTS AC *2326, 2169*; Imray C65; OS 55

TIDES Loch Shuna –0615 Dover; ML Loch Melfort 1·7; Duration Seil Sound 0615; Zone 0 (UT)

Standard Port OBAN (⟵)

Times				Height (metres)			
High Water		Low Water		MHWS	MHWN	MLWN	MLWS
0100	0700	0100	0800	4·0	2·9	1·8	0·7
1300	1900	1300	2000				
Differences LOCH MELFORT							
–0055	–0025	–0040	–0035	–1·2	–0·8	–0·5	–0·1
SEIL SOUND							
–0035	–0015	–0040	–0015	–1·3	–0·9	–0·7	–0·3

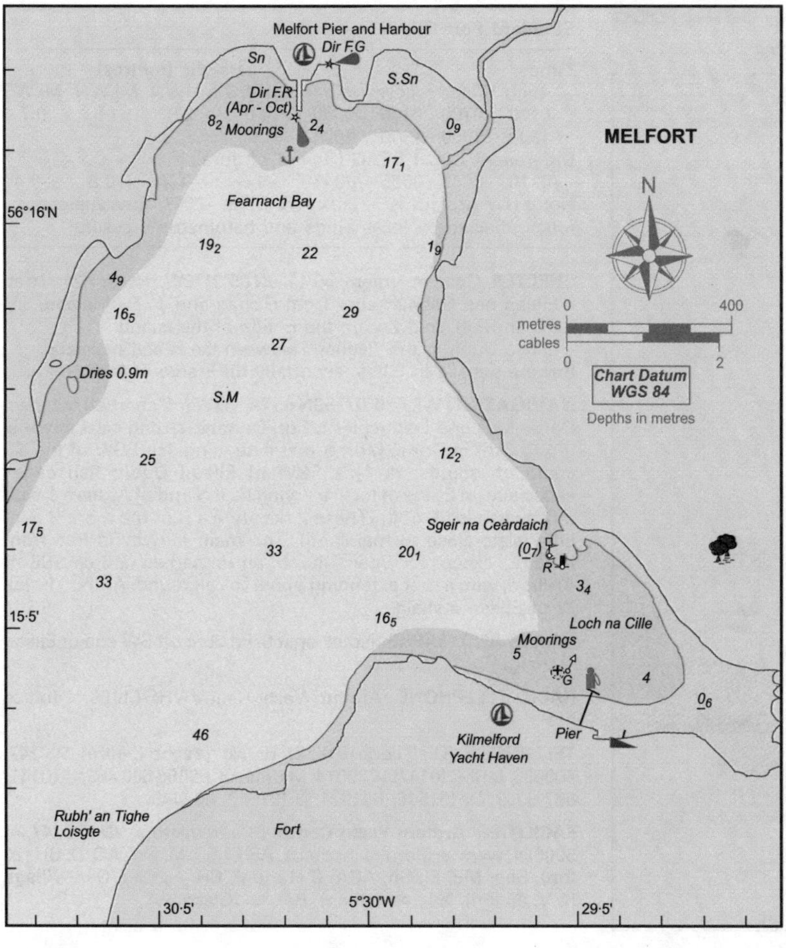

SHELTER Good at Kilmelford Yacht Haven in Loch na Cille; access at all tides for 3m draft, but no lights. Or at Melfort Pier (Fearnach Bay at N end of loch): pier/ pontoon in 2m, but chan to inner hbr dries; good ⚓ in N winds. ⚓s sheltered from S–W at: a bay with one or two private moorings ½M inside the ent on S shore, but beware rk drying 1·5m; in Kames Bay (1·5M further E) clear of moorings, rks and fish farm.

NAVIGATION WPT 56°13′·99N 05°35′·07W, 210°/030° from/to summit Eilean Gamhna, 4ca. Pass either side of Eilean Gamhna. 8ca NE lies Campbell Rk (1·8m). A rk drying 1m lies 1½ca ESE of the FS on Eilean Coltair. The S side of L Melfort is mostly steep-to, except in Kames Bay. At Loch na Cille, beware drying reef ¾ca off NE shore (PHM perch), and rk near S shore (SHM perch); boats may obscure perches.

LIGHTS AND MARKS A Dir FR ☆ 6m 3M on Melfort pier (also depth gauge) and a Dir FG ☆ close NE on the shore are not ldg lts, nor do they form a safe transit. Approach on a N'ly track keeping them an equal angle off each bow.

RADIO TELEPHONE Kilmelford VHF Ch **80** M (HO).

TELEPHONE (Dial code 01852) MRSC (01475) 729014; ⊜ (0141) 887 9369; Police (01631) 562213; Marinecall 09068 500463; Ⓗ (01546) 602323.

FACILITIES Kilmelford Yacht Haven ☎ 200248, 📠 200343, £11.75, D, FW, BH (12 ton), Slip, ME, El, Sh, Gas, ♿; **Melfort Pier** ☎ 200333, 📠 200329, AB £10, M, D, FW, ME, Slip, R, Bar, 🅾. **Village** (¾M) V, Bar, ✉.

CRAOBH MARINA (L Shuna) *9.8.21*

Argyll & Bute **56°12′·80N 05°33′·54W**

CHARTS AC *2326, 2169*; Imray C65; OS 55

TIDES HW Loch Shuna –0100 Oban; –0615 Dover; Seil Sound Duration 0615, ML 1·4; Zone 0 (UT). For tidal figures see 9.8.20.

SHELTER Very good. Craobh (pronounced Croove) Marina (access H24) on SE shore of Loch Shuna is enclosed by N and S causeways between islets. The ent is between 2 bkwtrs on the N side. In the marina, a shoal area S of the E bkwtr is marked by nine PHM and two SHM buoys. A Y perch in W corner of hbr marks a spit; elsewhere ample depth. There are ⚓s in Asknish Bay 1M to the N, and in the bays E of Eilean Arsa and at Bàgh an Tigh-Stòir, S of Craobh.

NAVIGATION WPT 56°13′·01N 05°33′·57W, 353°/173° from/to ent, 2ca. Tidal streams in Loch Shuna are weak. Beware lobster pots in appr's and unmarked rks (dr 1·5m) 4ca NNE of ent. An unlit SHM buoy marks a rk (1m) 150m NNW of the W bkwtr. 1M N of marina, Eich Donna, an unmarked reef (dr 1·5m), lies between Eilean Creagach and Arduaine Pt.

LIGHTS AND MARKS The W sector, 162°-183°, of Dir Lt, Iso WRG 5s 10m 5/3M, on E bkwtr hd leads 172° between the close-in rks above. Multi coloured marina buildings are conspic.

RADIO TELEPHONE VHF Ch M, 80 (summer 0830-2000LT; winter 0830-1800).

TELEPHONE (Dial code 01852) Hr Mr 500222; MRSC (01475) 729014; ⊖ (0141) 887 9369; Marinecall 09068 500463; Police (01546) 602222; Ⓗ (01546) 602323.

FACILITIES **Craobh Marina** (200+50 Ⓥ) ☎ 500222, 📠 500252, £1.94, AC, D, FW, SM, BY, CH, Slip, BH (15 ton), C (12 ton), Gas, Gaz, ME, El, Sh, R, SC, Ⓔ, ⊡, Divers. **Village** V, Bar, Ⓑ (Fri), ✉ (Kilmelford), ⇌ (Oban by bus), ✈ (Glasgow).

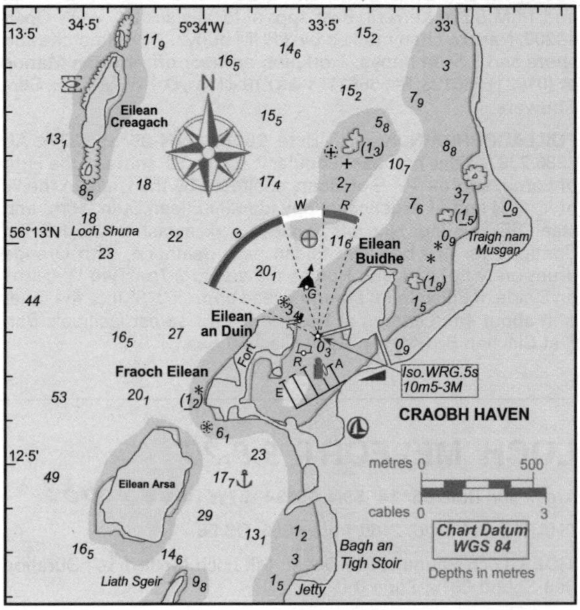

LOCH CRAIGNISH *9.8.22*

Argyll and Bute **56°07′·99N 05°35′·07W** (Ardfern)

CHARTS AC *2326, 2169*; Imray C63, C65; OS 55

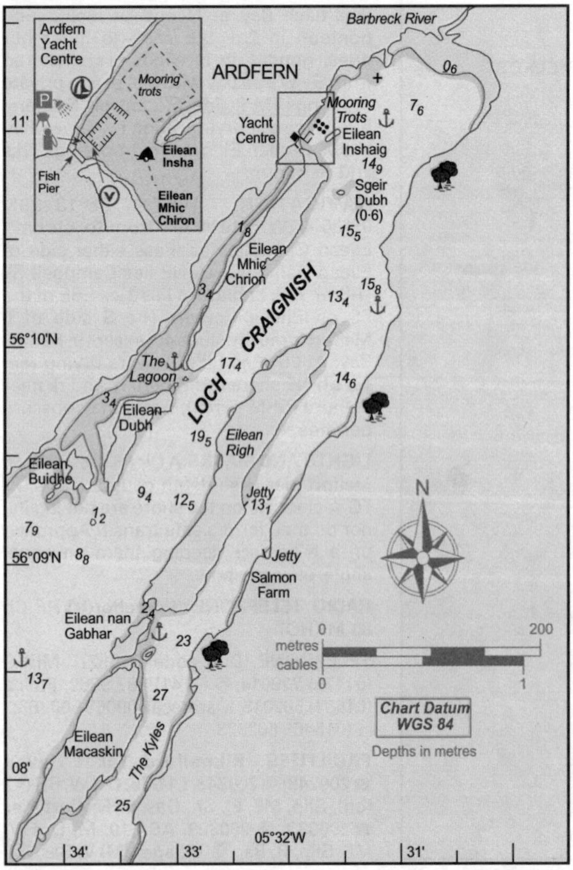

TIDES +0600 Dover; ML (Loch Beag)1·2; Duration (Seil Sound) 0615; Zone 0 (UT)

Standard Port OBAN (⟵)

Times				Height (metres)			
High Water		Low Water		MHWS	MHWN	MLWN	MLWS
0100	0700	0100	0800	4·0	2·9	1·8	0·7
1300	1900	1300	2000				
Differences LOCH BEAG (Sound of Jura)							
–0110	–0045	–0035	–0045	–1·6	–1·2	–0·8	–0·4

Note: HW Ardfern is approx HW Oban –0045; times/heights much affected by local winds and barometric pressure

SHELTER Good at Ardfern, 56°11′·0N 05°31′·8W, access H24; ⚓s at:
- Eilean nan Gabhar; appr from E chan and ⚓ E of island.
- Eilean Righ; midway up the E side of the island.
- Eilean Dubh in the "lagoon" between the Is and mainland.

Beware squalls in E'lies, especially on E side of loch.

NAVIGATION WPT 56°07′·59N 05°35′·37W (off chartlet) between Dorus Mór and Liath-sgier Mhòr. Beware: strong tidal streams (up to 8kn) in Dorus Mór; a reef extending 1ca SSW of the SE chain of islands; rk 1½ca SSW of Eilean Dubh; fish cages especially on E side of loch; a drying rk at N end of Ardfern ⚓ with a rk awash ¼ca E of it. (These 2 rks are ½ca S of the more S'ly of little islets close to mainland). The main fairway is free from hazards, except for Sgeir Dhubh, an unmarked rk 3½ca SSE of Ardfern, with a reef extending about ½ca all round. Ardfern is 1ca W of Eilean Inshaig.

LIGHTS AND MARKS Note: unlit SHM 25m off SW end of Eilean Inshaig.

RADIO TELEPHONE Ardfern Yacht Centre VHF Ch 80 M (office hrs).

TELEPHONE (Dial code 01852) Hr Mr (Yacht Centre) 500247/500636; MRSC (01475) 729014; Marinecall 09068 500 463; ⊖ (0141) 887 9369; Dr (01546) 602921; Ⓗ (01546) 602449.

FACILITIES **Ardfern Yacht Centre** (87+20 visitors); ☎ 500247, 📠 500624, www.ardfernyacht.co.uk, AB £1.50, M, FW, AC, D, BH (20 ton), Slip, ME, El, Sh, ACA, C (12 ton), CH, ⊡, Gas, Gaz. **Village** R, V, Ⓑ (Fri), ✉, ⇌ (Oban), Bar, ✈ (Glasgow).

SUBMARINE EXERCISE AREAS (SUBFACTS) *9.8.23*

Areas North of Mull in which submarine activity is planned for the next 16 hrs are broadcast by CG Coordination Centres on a notified VHF Ch after an initial announcement on VHF Ch 16 at the times below. The areas are referred to by names given below, rather than by numbers indicated. For Areas 22 – 81 (South of Mull), see 9.9.24.

Stornoway 0110 0510 0910 1310 1710 and 2110 UTC
Clyde 0020 0420 0820 1220 1620 and 2020 UTC

During notified NATO exercises, Subfacts are also broadcast on MF by **Stornoway** 1743 kHz and **Clyde** 1883 kHz, at the same times as above.

General information on Subfacts is also broadcast twice daily at 0930 & 2130 UTC by **Portpatrick Navtex (O). Stornoway** and **Clyde** CG will also supply Subfacts on request Ch 16.

A Fisherman's hotline ☎ 01436 677201 deals with queries. FOSNNI Ops ☎ (01436) 674321 ext 3206, may help. Submarines on the suface and at periscope depth always listen on Ch 16. See also 9.9.24.

1	Tiumpan	**14**	Raasay
2	Minch North	**15**	Neist
3	Stoer	**16**	Bracadale
4	Shiant	**17**	Ushenish
5	Minch South	**18**	Hebrides North
6	Ewe	**19**	Canna
7	Trodday	**20**	Rhum
8	Rona West	**21**	Sleat
9	Rona North	**22**	Barra
10	Lochmaddy	**23**	Hebrides Central
11	Dunvegan	**24**	Hawes
12	Portree	**25**	Eigg
13	Rona South	**26**	Hebrides South

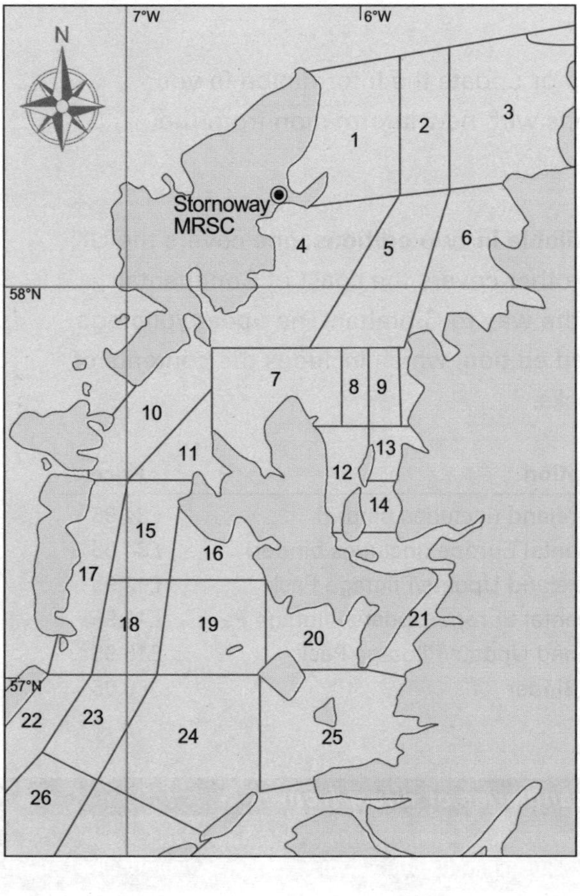

FERRIES ON THE WEST COAST OF SCOTLAND *9.8.24*

The following is a brief summary of the many ferries plying between mainland and island harbours. It supplements the UK and Continental ferry services listed in 9.0.5, and may prove useful when cruise plans or crews change, often in remote places. It covers Area 8 (Stornoway to Oban) and Area 9 (Jura to the Clyde).

The major operator is Caledonian MacBrayne: Head Office, The Ferry Terminal, Gourock PA19 1QP; ☎ 08705-650000 for reservations, 📠 (08705) 650000. Many routes are very short and not be pre-bookable; seasonal routes are *asterisked.

From	To	Time	Remarks
Area 8			
Otternish	Leverburgh	1¼	Not Sun
Ullapool	Stornoway	2¾ hrs	See 9.
Uig (Skye)	Tarbert (Harris)	1¾ hrs	Not Sun
Uig	Lochmaddy (N Uist)	1¾ hrs	
Oban	Castlebay/Lochboisdale	5-7 hrs	
Sconser (Skye)	Raasay	15 mins	Not Sun
Mallaig*	Armadale (Skye)	30 mins	
Mallaig	Eigg-Muck-Rhum-Canna	Varies	Not Sun
Oban	Coll-Tiree	Varies	Not Sun/ Thurs
Tobermory	Kilchoan	35 mins	
Fionnphort	Iona	5 mins	
Lochaline	Fishnish (Mull)	15 mins	
Oban	Craignure (Mull)	45 mins	
Oban	Lismore	50 mins	Not Sun
Areas 8/9			
Oban	Colonsay	2¼ hrs	Sun/W/Fri
Area 9			
Kennacraig	Port Askaig/Colonsay	Varies	Wed
Kennacraig	Port Ellen	2h 10m	
Kennacraig	Port Askaig	2 hrs	Not Sun
Tayinloan	Gigha	20 mins	
Ardrossan	Brodick	55 mins	
Claonaig	Lochranza (Arran)	30 mins	
Largs	Cumbrae Slip	10 mins	
Tarbert (L Fyne)	Portavadie*	25 mins	
Colintraive	Rhubodach (Bute)	5 mins	
Wemyss Bay	Rothesay (Bute)	35 mins	
Gourock	Dunoon	20 mins	

Other Operators/services

Serco Denholm ☎ 01496 840681:			
Port Askaig	Feolin (Jura)	Short	
Argyll & Bute Council ☎ 01631 562125:			
Seil	Luing	15 mins	
D.J.Rodgers, ☎ 01878 720261:			
South Uist	Eriskay		
Caledonian McBrayne, ☎ 08705 650000:			
South Uist	Barra		

8

Is this almanac too BIG?

Have you tried the Looseleaf version?

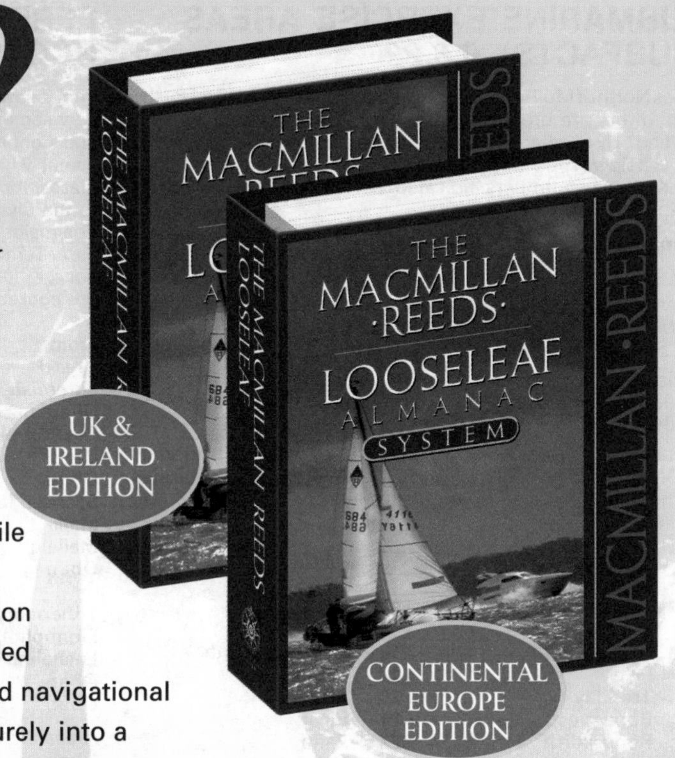

The Macmillan Reeds Looseleaf Almanac is an innovative and versatile system that lets you completely customise the navigational information you carry on board. Remove unneeded sections and add your own notes and navigational data from other sources. Bound securely into a sturdy binder, your almanac will always include just as much, or as little, information as you need for your cruising area – or even for a single voyage.

The ongoing cost is low, too. It is easy to extend or update the information in your Looseleaf Almanac – replace the relevant sections with new information from the Update/Pilotage packs as and when needed.

The Macmillan Reeds Looseleaf Almanac is available in two editions: one covers the UK and Ireland (including the Channel Islands), the other covers the coast of Continental Europe, from Skagen at the tip of Denmark, all the way to Gibraltar. The update/pilotage packs follow the same areas, adding a Combined edition, which includes the contents of both the Continental and the UK and Ireland packs.

- **Versatile**
- **Value for money**
- **Convenient**
- **Flexible**
- **Updateable**

Code	Description	Price
ND50	UK & Ireland (includes binder)	£34.95
ND51	Continental Europe (includes binder)	£34.95
ND52	UK & Ireland Update/Pilotage Pack	£12.95
ND53	Continental Europe Update/Pilotage Pack	£12.95
ND54	Combined Update/Pilotage Pack	£15.95
ND2	Spare Binder	£6.95

Available from all good chandleries or direct from:

Nautical Data Limited • The Book Barn • Westbourne • Hampshire PO10 8RS • UK
tel: +44 (0)1243 389352 • fax: +44 (0)1243 379136 • email: sales@nauticaldata.com • web: www.nauticaldata.com

Prices include UK VAT at 17.5% where applicable, but exclude delivery

e&oe

MAPTECH
Leading the world in digital navigation
Maptech UK Ltd • +44 (0)1243 389352 • sales@maptech.co.uk

Sales and distribution centres in Area 9

Strathclyde: *Marinac*, Unit41/43, 24-26 Boswell Sq., Hillington Ind.Est., Hillington, Glasgow G52 4BQ.
Kelvin Hughes, 0141 221 5452, 26 Holland Street, Glasgow G2 4LR.

www.maptech.co.uk

Area 9

South-West Scotland
Crinan Canal to Mull of Galloway

9.9.1 Index .... Page 531

9.9.2 Area map 532

9.9.3 Tidal stream charts 534

9.9.4 Lights, buoys & waypoints 536

9.9.5 Passage information 539

9.9.6 Distance table 540

9.9.7 Port Ellen 541
Scalasaig (Colonsay)
Loch Tarbert (Jura)
Port Askaig (Islay)
Craighouse (Jura)
Loch Sween
West Loch Tarbert (Kintyre)
Gigha Island

9.9.8 Crinan Canal 542

9.9.9 Ardrishaig 543

9.9.10 Tarbert, Loch Fyne 543
Inverary

9.9.11 Campbeltown 544
Carradale Bay

9.9.12 Tidal stream charts for Mull of Kintyre 545

9.9.13 Lamlash 546
Brodick (Arran)
Loch Ranza (Arran)
St Ninian's Bay (Bute)
West Kyle
Caladh Harbour
Loch Riddon
Burnt Islands
Kames Bay (Bute)
Kilchattan Bay (Bute)

9.9.14 Rothesay 547
Millport (Cumbraes)

9.9.15 Largs 547

9.9.16 Inverkip (Kip marina) 548
Dunoon
Gourock

9.9.17 Holy Loch 548

9.9.18 Firth of Clyde area 549

9.9.19 Gareloch/Rhu 550
Loch Long/Loch Goil

9.9.20 Dumbarton and Bowling
Greenock Standard Port/tidal curves 551

9.9.21 Ardrossan 555
Irvine

9.9.22 Troon 556
Ayr
Girvan
Loch Ryan

9.9.23 Portpatrick 557

9.9.24 Submarine exercise areas 558

9.9.25 Clyde waypoints 559

9

Register for your **FREE** weekly weather email service from Macmillan Reeds
at **www.nauticaldata.com – NOW!**
weekend weather reports sent to your email address, every Thursday

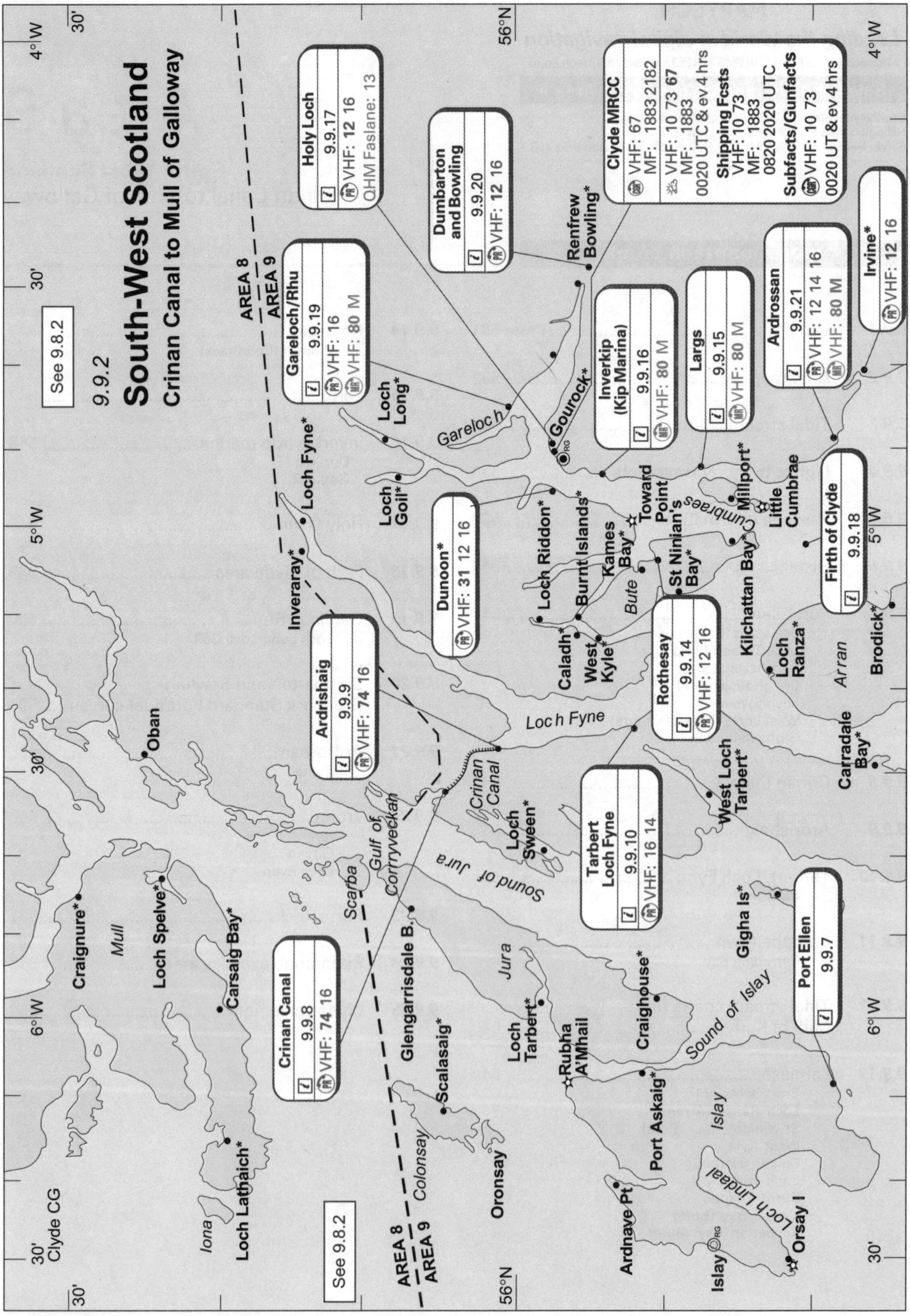
9.9.2
South-West Scotland
Crinan Canal to Mull of Galloway
See 9.8.2
See 9.8.2
AREA 8
AREA 9
AREA 8
AREA 9
Holy Loch
9.9.17
VHF: 12 16
QHM Faslane: 13
Dumbarton and Bowling
9.9.20
VHF: 12 16
Clyde MRCC
VHF: 67
MF: 1883 2182
VHF: 10 73 67
MF: 1883
0020 UTC & ev 4 hrs
Shipping Fcsts
VHF: 10 73
MF: 1883
0820 2020 UTC
Subfacts/Gunfacts
VHF: 10 73
0020 UT & ev 4 hrs
Gareloch/Rhu
9.9.19
VHF: 16
VHF: 80 M
Inverkip (Kip Marina)
9.9.16
VHF: 80 M
Largs
9.9.15
VHF: 80 M
Ardrossan
9.9.21
VHF: 12 14 16
VHF: 80 M
Irvine*
VHF: 12 16
Ardrishaig
9.9.9
VHF: 74 16
Dunoon*
VHF: 31 12 16
Rothesay
9.9.14
VHF: 12 16
Firth of Clyde
9.9.18
Tarbert Loch Fyne
9.9.10
VHF: 16 14
Port Ellen
9.9.7
Crinan Canal
9.9.8
VHF: 74 16
Renfrew
Bowling*
Gourock*
Gareloch
Loch Long*
Loch Fyne*
Loch Goil*
Inveraray*
Loch Riddon*
Burnt Islands*
Kames Bay*
Toward Point
Cumbraes
Millport*
Little Cumbrae
St Ninian's Bay*
Kilchattan Bay*
Bute
Caladh*
West Kyle*
Loch Ranza*
Arran
Brodick*
Carradale Bay*
West Loch Tarbert*
Loch Fyne
Crinan Canal
Loch Sween*
Sound of Jura
Gulf of Corryvreckan
Scarba
Oban
Craignure*
Mull
Loch Spelve*
Carsaig Bay*
Glengarrisdale B.
Jura
Gigha Is*
Craighouse*
Loch Tarbert*
Rubha A'Mhail
Sound of Islay
Scalasaig*
Port Askaig*
Islay
Colonsay
Oronsay
Loch Lathaich*
Iona
Clyde CG
Ardnave Pt
Loch Lindeal
Orsay I
Islay
4°W
5°W
6°W
30'
56°N

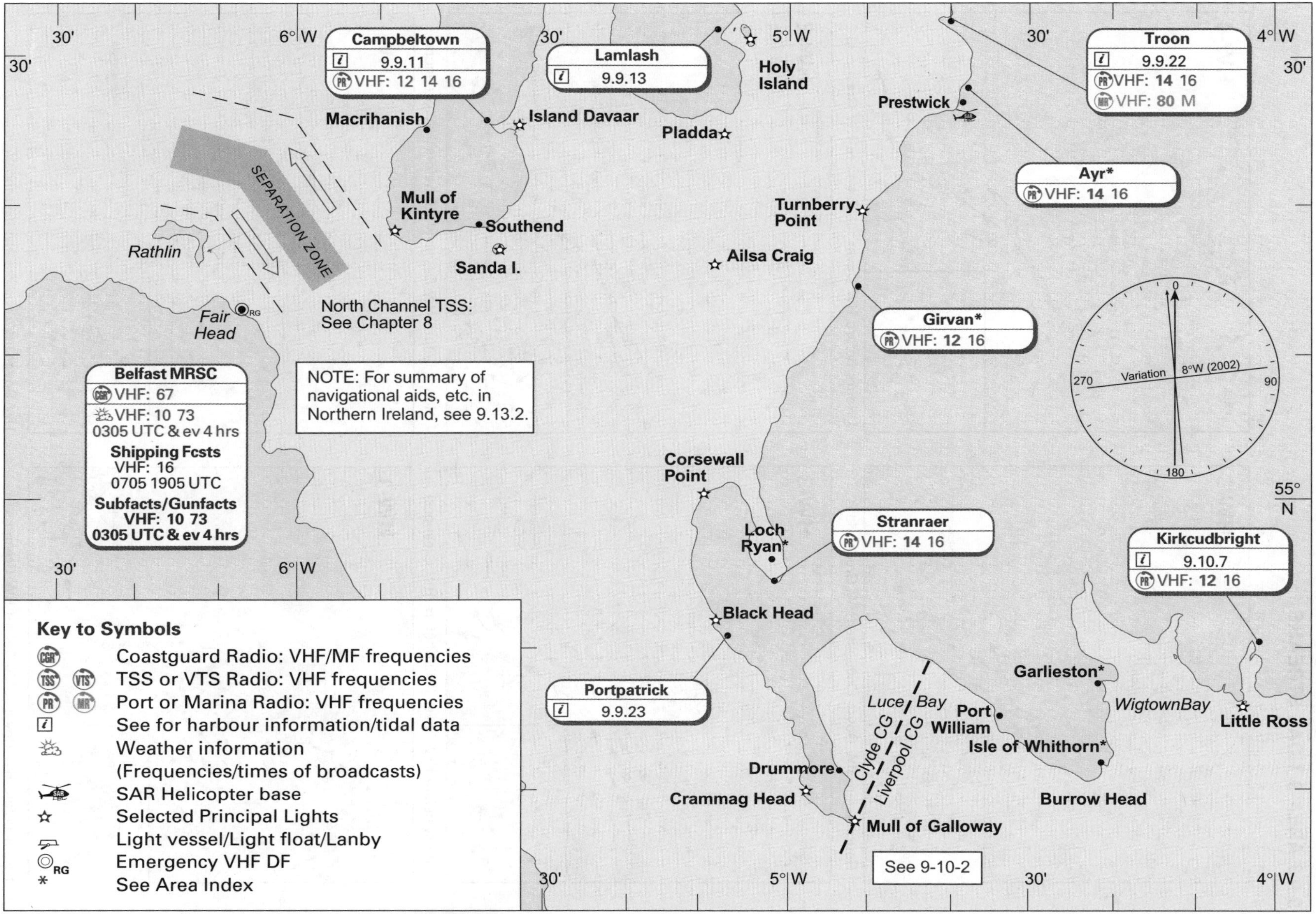
Campbeltown
9.9.11
VHF: 12 14 16
Lamlash
9.9.13
Holy Island
Troon
9.9.22
VHF: 14 16
VHF: 80 M
Macrihanish
Island Davaar
Pladda
Prestwick
Ayr*
VHF: 14 16
SEPARATION ZONE
Mull of Kintyre
Southend
Sanda I.
Turnberry Point
Ailsa Craig
Rathlin
Fair Head
North Channel TSS:
See Chapter 8
Girvan*
VHF: 12 16
Belfast MRSC
VHF: 67
VHF: 10 73
0305 UTC & ev 4 hrs
Shipping Fcsts
VHF: 16
0705 1905 UTC
Subfacts/Gunfacts
VHF: 10 73
0305 UTC & ev 4 hrs
NOTE: For summary of navigational aids, etc. in Northern Ireland, see 9.13.2.
Variation 8°W (2002)
Corsewall Point
Loch Ryan*
Stranraer
VHF: 14 16
Kirkcudbright
9.10.7
VHF: 12 16
Black Head
Portpatrick
9.9.23
Garlieston*
Luce Bay
Port William
WigtownBay
Little Ross
Clyde CG
Liverpool CG
Isle of Whithorn*
Drummore
Crammag Head
Mull of Galloway
Burrow Head
See 9-10-2
Key to Symbols
Coastguard Radio: VHF/MF frequencies
TSS or VTS Radio: VHF frequencies
Port or Marina Radio: VHF frequencies
See for harbour information/tidal data
Weather information
(Frequencies/times of broadcasts)
SAR Helicopter base
Selected Principal Lights
Light vessel/Light float/Lanby
Emergency VHF DF
See Area Index

9.9.3 AREA 9 TIDAL STREAMS

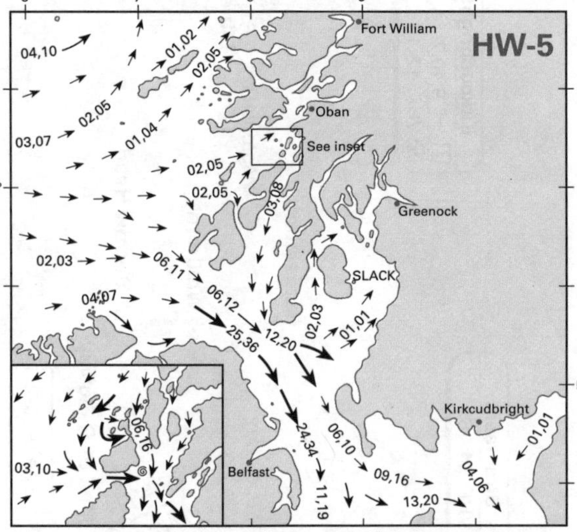

5 Hours before HW Dover (0605 after HW Greenock)

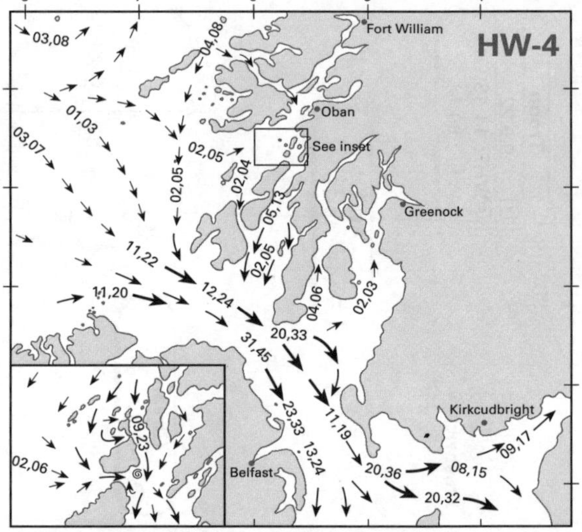

4 Hours before HW Dover (0520 before HW Greenock)

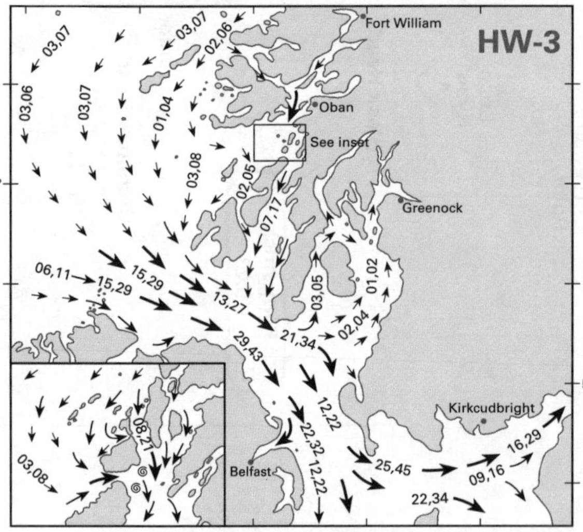

3 Hours before HW Dover (0420 before HW Greenock)

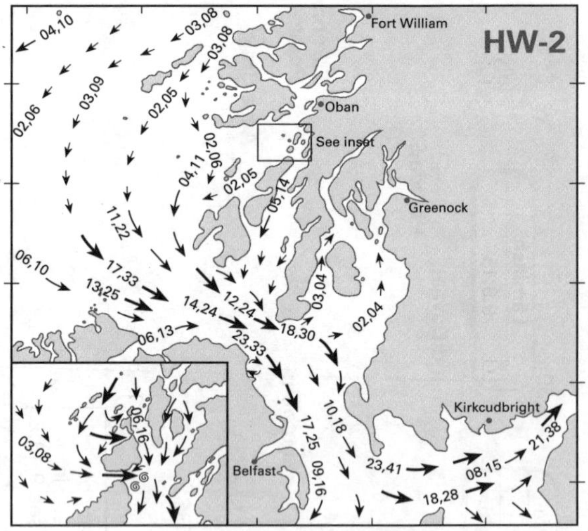

2 Hours before HW Dover (0320 before HW Greenock)

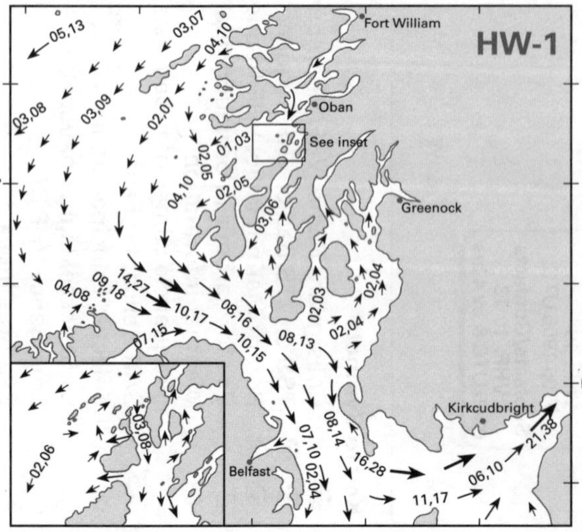

1 Hour before HW Dover (0220 before HW Greenock)

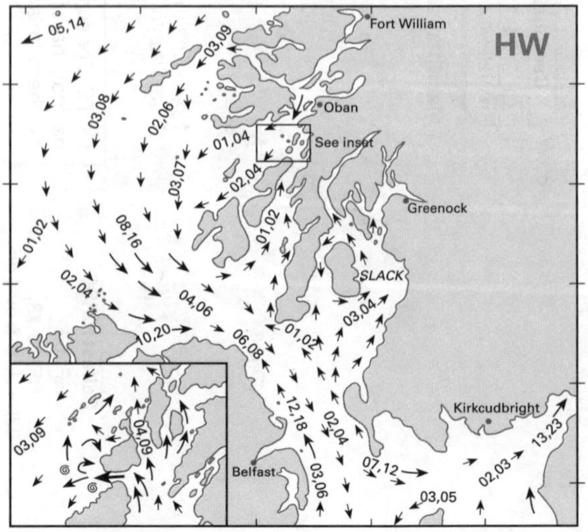

HW Dover (0120 before HW Greenock)

Northward 9.8.3   Mull of Kintyre 9.9.12   Irish Sea 9.10.3   Northern Ireland 9.13.3

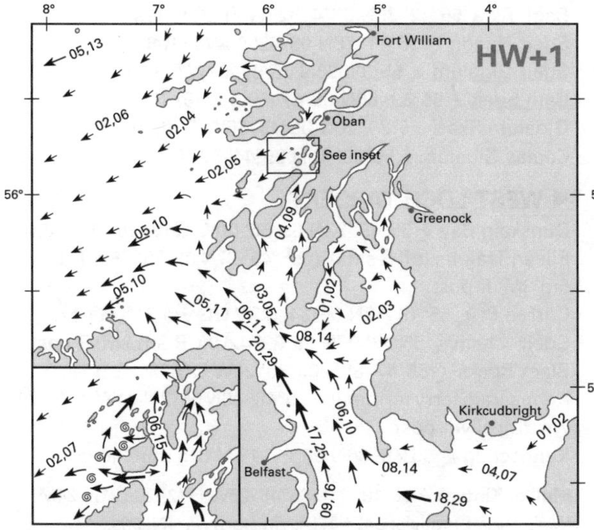

1 Hour after HW Dover (0020 before HW Greenock)

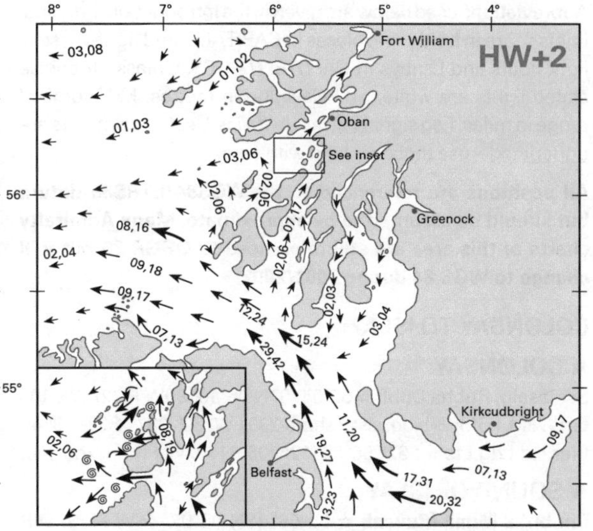

2 Hours after HW Dover (0040 after HW Greenock)

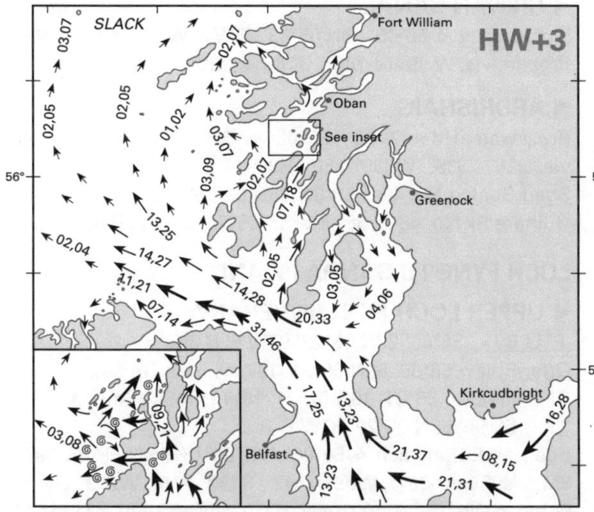

3 Hours after HW Dover (0140 after HW Greenock)

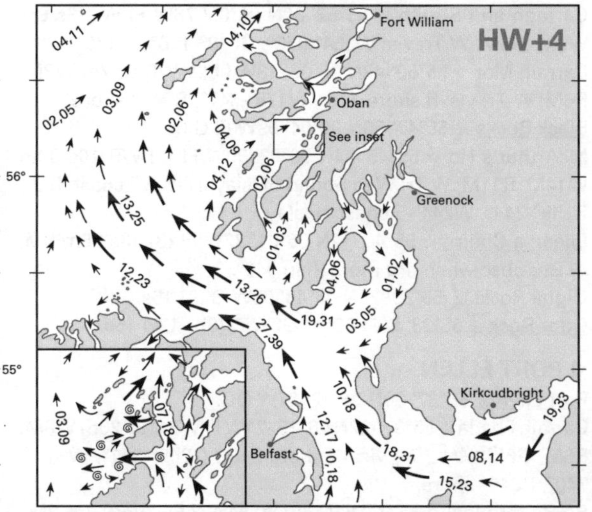

4 Hours after HW Dover (0240 after HW Greenock)

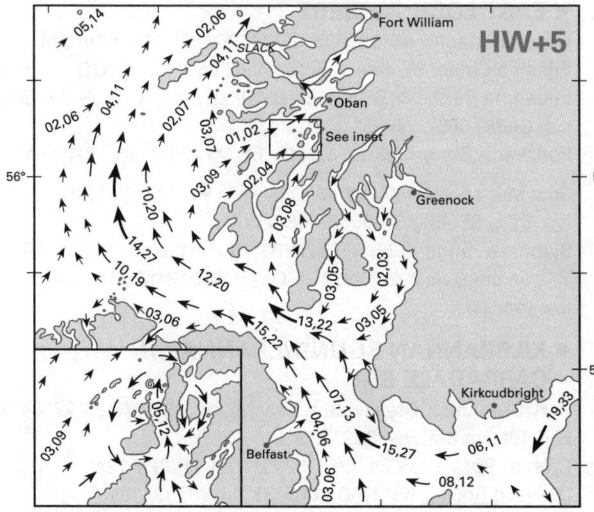

5 Hours after HW Dover (0340 after HW Greenock)

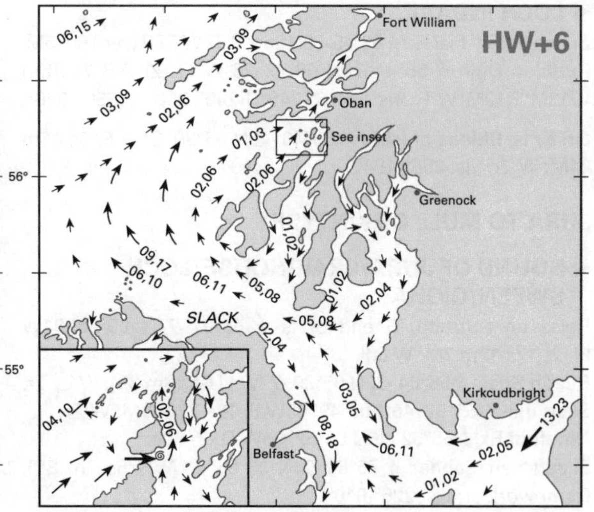

6 Hours after HW Dover (0440 after HW Greenock)

9

9.9.4 LIGHTS, BUOYS AND WAYPOINTS

Abbreviations used below are given in the Introduction. Principal lights ☆ are in **bold** print, places in CAPITALS, and light-vessels, light floats and Lanbys in *CAPITAL ITALICS*. Unless otherwise stated lights are white. m – elevation in metres; M – nominal range in miles. Fog signals are in *italics*. Useful waypoints are underlined – use those on land with care.

All positions are referenced to the WGS84/ETRS89 datum but should be assumed to be approximate. Many Admiralty charts of this area are still referenced to OSGB 36 but will change to WGS 84 during 2001/2002.

COLONSAY TO ISLAY

◀ COLONSAY

Scalasaig, Rubha Dubh ☆ 56°04'·01N 06°10'·90W Fl (2) WR 10s 6m W8M, R5M; W bldg; vis: R shore-230°, W230°-337°, R337°-354°.
Pier Hd Ldg Lts ☆ 262° 56°04'·12N 06°11'·02W FR 8m (occas).

◀ SOUND OF ISLAY

Rhubh' a Mháil (Ruvaal) ☆ 56°56'·18N 06°07'·46W Fl (3) WR 15s 45m **W24M, R21M**; W Tr; vis: R075°-180°, W180°-075°.
Carragh an t'Struith ☆ 55°52'·30N 06°05'·78W Fl WG 3s 8m W9M, G6M, W Tr; vis: W354°-078°, G078°-170°, W170°-185°.
Carraig Mòr ☆ 55°50'·42N 06°06'·13W Fl (2) WR 6s 7m W8M, R6M; W Tr; vis: R shore-175°, W175°-347°, R347°-shore.
Black Rocks 55°47'·50N 06°04'·09W Fl G 6s.
McArthur's Hd ☆ 55°45'·84N 06°02'·90W Fl (2) WR 10s 39m W14M, R11M; W Tr; W in Sound of Islay from NE coast-159°, R159°-244°, W244°-E coast of Islay.
Eilean a Chùirn ☆ 55°40'·12N 06°01'·22W Fl (3) 18s 26m 8M; W Bn; obsc when brg more than 040°.
Gigha Rocks 55°39'·20N 05°43'·65W Q (9) 15s.
Otter Rock 55°33'·86N 06°07'·92W Q (6) + L Fl 15s.

◀ PORT ELLEN

Port Ellen 55°37'·00N 06°12'·27W QG.
Carraig Fhada ☆ 55°37'·22N 06°12'·71W Fl WRG 3s 20m W8M, R6M, G6M; W □ Tr; vis: W shore-248°, G248°-311°, W311°-340°, R340°-shore.
Ro-Ro terminal ☆ 55°37'·61N 06°11'·44W 2 FG (vert) 7m 3M.

◀ LOCH INDAAL

Bruichladdich Pier Hd ☆ 55°45'·83N 06°21'·67 W 2 FR (vert) 6m 5M.
Rubh'an Dùin ☆ 55°44'·70N 06°22'·28 W Fl (2) WR 7s 15m W13M, R12M; W Tr; vis: W218°-249°, R249°-350°, W350°-036°.

Orsay Is, **Rhinns of Islay** ☆ 55°40'·40N 06°30'·84W Fl 5s 46m **24M**; W Tr; vis: 256°-184°.

JURA TO MULL OF KINTYRE

◀ SOUND OF JURA/CRAIGHOUSE/LOCH SWEEN/GIGHA

Reisa an t-Struith, S end of Is ☆ 56°07'·77N 05°38'·91W Fl (2) 12s 12m 7M; W col.
Ruadh Sgeir ☆ 56°04'·32N 05°39'·77W Fl 6s 13m 8M; W ○ Tr.
Skervuile ☆ 55°52'·46N 05°49'·85W Fl 15s 22m 9M; W Tr.
Ninefoot Rk 55°52'·46N 05°52'·95W Q (3) 10s.
Eilean nan Gabhar ☆ 55°50'·04N 05°56'·25W Fl 5s 7m 8M; framework Tr; vis: 225°-010°.
Na Cùiltean ☆ 55°48'·64N 05°54'·90W Fl 10s 9m 9M.
Gamhna Gigha ☆ 55°43'·78N 05°41'·11W Fl (2) 6s 7m 5M.
Badh Rk 55°42'·30N 05°41'·24W Fl (2) G 12s.
Sgeir Nuadh 55°41'·78N 05°42'·08W Fl R 6s.
Sgeir Gigalum 55°39'·96N 05°42'·67W Fl G 6s.
Cath Sgeir 55°39'·66N 05°47'·50W Q (9) 15s.
Gigalum Rks 55°39'·20N 05°43'·65W Q (9) 15s.
Caolas Gigalum 55°39'·15N 05°44'·57W.

◀ WEST LOCH TARBERT

Dunskeig Bay ☆ 55°45'·22N 05°35'·00W Q (2) 10s 11m 8M.
Eileen Tráighe (off S side) 55°45'·37N 05°35'·75W Fl (2) R 5s 5m 3M; R post.
Corran Pt 55°46'·12N 05°34'·35W QG 3m 3M; G post.
Sgeir Mhein 55°47'·06N 05°32'·42W QR 3m 3M; R post.
Black Rocks 55°47'·89N 05°30'·20W QG 3M; G post.
Kennacraig ferry terminal ☆ 55°48'·40N 05°29'·01W 2 FG (vert) 7m 3M; silver post.
Kennacraig 55°48'·66N 05°29'·18W QR; unreliable.

Mull of Kintyre ☆ 55°18'·64N 05°48'·25W Fl (2) 20s 91m **24M**; W Tr on W bldg; vis: 347°-178°; *Horn Mo (N) 90s.*

◀ CRINAN CANAL

E of lock ent ☆ 56°05'·48N 05°33'·37W Fl WG 3s 8m 4M; W Tr, R band; vis: W shore-146°, G146°-shore.

◀ ARDRISHAIG

Breakwater Hd ☆ 56°00'·76N 05°26'·59W L Fl WRG 6s 9m 4M; vis: G287°-339°, W339°-350°, R350°-035°.
Sgeir Sgalag No. 49 56°00'·36N 05°26'·30W.
Gulnare Rk No. 48 56°00'·18N 05°26'·31W Fl R 4s.

LOCH FYNE TO SANDA ISLAND

◀ UPPER LOCH FYNE/INVERARY

'P' Lt By 56°00'·23N 05°22'·07W Fl R 3s.
Otter Spit ☆ 56°00'·63N 05°21'·10W Fl G 3s 7m 8M.
Glas Eilean ☆ 56°01'·10N 05°21'·16W Fl R 5s 12m 7M.
'Q' 56°00'·95N 05°20'·67W Fl R 3s.
Sgeir an Eirionnaich ☆ 56°06'·47N 05°13'·55W Fl WR 3s 7m 8M; vis: R044°-087°, W087°-192°, R192°-210°, W210°-044°.
Furnace Wharf ☆ 56°09'·05N 05°10'·45W 2 FR (vert) 9m 5M.

◀ EAST LOCH TARBERT

Madadh Maol ☆ 55°52'·02N 05°24'·25W Fl R 2·5s 4m 3M.
Eilean a'Choic, SE side ☆ 55°51'·99N 05°24'·37W QG 3m 2M.
Eilean na Beithe ☆ 55°52'·68N 05°19'·62W Fl WRG 3s 7m 5M; vis: G036°-065°, W065°-078°, R078°-106°.
Portavadie Bkwtr ☆ 55°52'·52N 05°19'·24W 2 FG (vert) 6/4m 4M.

Sgat Mór ☆ 55°50'·85N 05°18'·50W Fl 3s 9m 12M; W ○ Tr.
No. 51 55°45'·56N 05°19'·68W Fl R 4s.
Skipness range ☆ 55°46'·72N 05°19'·06W Iso R 8s 7m 10M; Y ◇ on bldg; vis 292·2°-312·2°. Oc (2) Y 10s **24M** when range in use (occas).

◀ KILBRANNAN SOUND/CRANNAICH/CARRADALE BAY

Port Crannaich Breakwater Head ☆ 55°35'·60N 05°27'·84W Fl R 10s 5m 6M; vis: 099°-279°.
Crubon Rock 55°34'·48N 05°27'·07W Fl (2) R 12s.
Otterard Rock 55°27'·07N 05°31'·11W Q (3) 10s.

◄ CAMPBELTOWN LOCH

Davaar N Pt ☆ 55°25'·69N 05°32'·42W Fl (2) 10s 37m **23M**; W Tr; vis: 073°-330°; *Horn (2) 20s.*
Methe Bank 'C' 55°25'·30N 05°34'·42W Fl (2) 6s.
Arranman's Barrels 55°19'·40N 05°32'·87W Fl (2) R 12s.
Macosh Rock 55°17'·95N 05°37'·00W Fl R 6s.
Sanda Island ☆ 55°16'·50N 05°35'·01W Fl 10s 50m **15M**; W Tr.
Patersons Rock 55°16'·90N 05°32'·48W Fl (3) R 18s.

KYLES OF BUTE TO RIVER CLYDE

◄ KYLES OF BUTE/CALADH

Ardlamont Point No. 47 55°49'·59N 05°11'·76W Fl R 4s.
Carry Point No. 46 55°51'·39N 05°12'·24W Fl R 4s.
Rubha Ban 55°54'·95N 05°12'·40W Fl R 4s.
Burnt Is (NE of Eilean Fraoich) 55°55'·78N 05°10'·49W Fl G 3s.
Burnt I No. 42 (S of Eilean Buidhe) 55°55'·76N 05°10'·39W Fl R 2s.
Creyke Rock No. 45 55°55'·67N 05°10'·89W.
Beere Rock No. 44 55°55'·55N 05°10'·63W.
Wood Farm Rock No. 43 55°55'·41N 05°10'·34W.
Rubha á Bhodaich 55°55'·38N 05°09'·59W Fl G.
Ardmaleish Point No. 41 55°53'·02N 05°04'·70W Q.

◄ ROTHESAY

Front Pier, E end ☆ 55°50'·32N 05°03'·10W 2 FG (vert) 7m 5M.
Pier W end ☆ 55°50'·35N 05°03'·32W 2 FR (vert) 7m 5M.
Albert Pier near N end ☆ 2 FR (vert) 8m 5M.

◄ FIRTH OF CLYDE

Ascog Patches No. 13 55°49'·71N 05°00'·25W Fl (2) 10s 5m 5M.
Toward Pt ☆ 55°51'·73N 04°58'·79W Fl 10s 21m **22M**; W Tr.
No. 34 55°51'·44N 04°59'·11W.
Toward Bank No. 35 55°51'·04N 04°00'·01W Fl G 3s.
Skelmorlie 55°51'·65N 04°56'·34W Iso 5s.

◄ WEMYSS/INVERKIP

Wemyss Bay Pier ☆ 55°52'·56N 04°53'·47W 2 FG (vert) 7m 5M.
No. 12 55°52'·97N 04°53'·78W Oc (2) Y 10s 5m 3M.
'M' 55°53'·52N 04°54'·41W Fl G 5s.
'O' 55°54'·55N 04°54'·55W Fl G 2·5s.
Kip 55°54'·49N 04°52'·98W QG.
Warden Bank 55°54'·77N 04°54'·54W Fl G 2s.
Cowal 55°56'·00N 04°54'·83W L Fl 10s.
Lunderston Bay No. 8 55°55'·50N 04°52'·96W Fl (4) Y 10s 5m 3M.
The Gantocks 55°56'·45N 04°55'·08W Fl R 6s 12m 6M; ○ Tr.

◄ DUNOON

Dunoon Pier, S end 55°56'·76N 04°55'·31W and N end ☆ both 2 FR (vert) 5m 6M.
Cloch Point ☆ 55°56'·55N 04°52'·74W Fl 3s 24m 8M; W ○ Tr, B band, W dwellings.
No. 5 55°56'·95N 04°51'·70W Oc (2) Y 10s 5m 3M.
McInroy's Point, Ro-Ro Ferry terminal Head ☆ 55°57'·08N 04°51'·26W 2 FG (vert) 5/3m 6M.

◄ HOLY LOCH

Hunter's Quay, Ro-Ro terminal ☆ 55°58'·26N 04°54'·50W 2 FR (vert) 6/4m 6M.

◄ LOCH LONG/LOCH GOIL

Loch Long 55°59'·15N 04°52'·42W Oc 6s.
Baron's Pt No. 3 ☆ 55°59'·18N 04°51'·12W Oc (2) Y 10s 5m 3M.
Ravenrock Pt ☆ 56°02'·14N 04°54'·39W Fl 4s 12m 10M; W Tr on W col. Dir Lt 204°, Dir WRG 9m (same Tr); vis: F R201·5°-203°, Al WR203°-203·5° (W phase incr with brg), F 203·5°-204·5°, Al WG204·5°-205° (G phase incr with brg), FG205°-206·5°.
Port Dornaige ☆ 56°03·75N 04°53'·65W Fl 6s 8m 11M; W col; vis: 026°-206°.
Carraig nan Ron (Dog Rock) ☆ 56°06'·00N 04°51'·71W Fl 2s 7m 11M; W col.
Rubha Ardnahein ☆ 56°06'·15N 04°53'·60W Fl R 5s 3m 3M; vis: 132°-312°.
The Perch, Ldg Lts 318° Front, 56°06'·90N 04°54'·31W Dir F WRG 3m 5M; vis: G311°-317°, W317°-320°, R320°-322°. Same structure, Fl R 3s 3m 3M; vis: 187°-322°. Rear, 700m from front, F 7m 5M; vis: 312°-322·5°.
Cnap Pt ☆ 56°07'·40N 04°49'·97W Ldg Lts 031°. Front, Q 8m 10M; W col. Rear, 87m from front F 13m; R line on W Tr.
Ashton 55°58'·10N 04°50'·65W Iso 5s.

◄ GOUROCK

Railway Pier Hd ☆ 55°57'·77N 04°49'·06W 2 FG (vert) 10m 3M.
Kempock Pt No. 4 ☆ 55°57'·71N 04°49'·37W Oc (2) Y 10s 6m 3M.
Whiteforeland 55°58'·11N 04°47'·28W L Fl 10s.
Rosneath Patch 55°58'·52N 04°47'·45W Fl (2) 10s 5m 10M.

◄ ROSNEATH/RHU NARROWS/GARELOCH

Ldg Lts 356°. **Front, No. 7N** 56°00'·05N 04°45'·36W Dir Lt 356°. Dir WRG 5m **W16M**, R13M, G13M; vis: Al WG 353°-355°, FW 355°-357°, Al WR 357°-000°, FR000°-002°.
Dir Lt 115° WRG 5m **W16M**, R13M, G13M; vis: Al WG 111°-114°; F 114°-116°, Al WR 116°-119°; F R119°-121°. Passing Lt Oc G 6s 6m 3M; G △ on G pile. Rear, Ardencaple Castle Centre ☆ 56°00'·54N 04°45'·43W 2 FG (vert) 26m 12M; Tr on Castle NW corner; vis: 335°-020°.
No. 8N Lt Bn 56°59'·09N 04°44'·21W Dir Lt 080° Dir WRG 4m; **W16M**, R13M, G13M; vis: F G 075°-077·5°, Al WG077·5°-079·5°, F079·5°-080·5°, Alt WR080·5°-082·5°, FR082·5°-085°.
Dir Lt 138° WRG 4m **W16M**, R13M, G13M; vis: FG132°-134°, Al WG134°-137°, F 137°-139°, Al WR139°-142°. Passing lt Fl Y 3s 6m 3M.
Gareloch No. 1 Lt Bn ☆ 55°59'·12N 04°43'·89W VQ (4) Y 5s 9m; Y 'X' on Y structure.
Row 55°59'·84N 04°45'·13W Fl G 5s.
Cairndhu 56°00'·35N 04°46'·00W Fl G 2·5s.
Castle Pt ☆ 56°00'·19N 04°46'·50W Fl (2) R 10s 8m 6M; R mast.
56°00'·61N 04°46'·53W Fl G 4s.
No. 3 N Lt Bn 56°00'·07N 04°46'·72W Dir Lt 149° WRG 9m **W16M**, R13M, G13M F & Al; vis: FG144°-145°, Al WG145°-148°, F148°-150°, Al WR150°-153°, FR153°-154°. Passing Lt Oc R 8s 9m 3M.
Rosneath DG Jetty ☆ 56°00'·39N 04°47'·51W 2 FR (vert) 5M; W col; vis: 150°-330°.
Rhu SE 56°00'·64N 04°47'·17W Fl G 3s.
Rhu Pt 56°00'·95N 04°47'·19W Q (3) WRG 6s 9m W10M, R7M, G7M; vis: G270°-000°, W000°-114°, R114°-188°.
Dir Lt 318° Dir WRG **W16M**, R13M, G13M; vis: Al WG 315°-317°, F317°-319°, Al WR319°-321°, FR321°-325°.
Limekiln No. 2N Lt Bn 56°00'·67N 04°47'·64W Dir Lt 295° WRG 5m **W16M**, R13M, G13M F & Al; R □ on R Bn; vis: Al WG291°-294°, F294°-296°, Al WR 296°-299°, FR299°-301°.
Rhu NE 56°01'·02N 04°47'·58W QG.

9

Rhu Spit 56°00'·84N 04°47'·34W Fl 3s 6m 6M.
Mambeg Dir Lt 331° 56°03'·74N 04°50'·47W Dir Q (4) WRG 8s 10m 14M; vis: G328·5°-330°, W330°-332°, R332°-333°; H24.

◀ GREENOCK

Anchorage Lts in line 196°. Front, 55°57'·62N 04°46'·58W FG 7m 12M; Y col. Rear, 32m from front, FG 9m 12M. Y col.
Lts in line 194·5°. Front, 55°57'·45N 04°45'·91W FG 18m. Rear, 360m from front, FG 33m.
Clydeport Container Terminal NW corner QG 8m 8M.
Victoria Hbr W side 55°56'·77N 04°44'·70W 2 FG 5m (vert).
Garvel W end 55°56'·81N 04°43'·55W Oc G 10s 9m 4M.
E end, Maurice Clark Pt 55°56'·60N 04°42'·85W QG 7m 2M.

◀ PORT GLASGOW

Beacon off ent 55°56'·25N 04°41'·26W FG 7m 9M.
Steamboat Quay, W end 55°56'·25N 04°41'·44W FG 12m 12M; B&W chequered col; vis 210°-290°. From here to Glasgow Lts on S bank are Fl G and Lts on N bank are Fl R.

CLYDE TO MULL OF GALLOWAY

◀ LARGS

Approach 55°46'·40N 04°51'·85W L Fl 10s.
Marina S Bkwtr Hd 55°46'·36N 04°51'·73W Oc G 10s 4m 4M.
W Bkwtr Hd 55°46'·37N 04°51'·67W Oc R 10s 4m 4M.
Largs Pier Hd N end 2 FG (vert) 7/5m 5M (H24).

◀ FAIRLIE

Fairlie Patch 55°45'·38N 04°52'·36W Fl G 1·5s.
Hunterston Jetty S 55°45'·10N 04°52'·88W 2 FG (vert) 11m 5M.
Pier N 55°45'·30N 04°52'·65W 2 FG (vert) 11m 5M.
NATO Pier Hd N 55°46'·06N 04°51'·78W 2 FG (vert).

◀ MILLPORT, GREAT CUMBRAE

The Eileans, W end 55°44'·89N 04°55'·59W QG 5m 2M.
Ldg Lts 333°. Pier Head front, 55°45'·04N 04°55'·85W FR 7m 5M. Rear, 137m from front, FR 9m 5M.
Mountstuart 55°48'·00N 04°57'·57W L Fl 10s.
Portachur 55°44'·35N 04°58'·52W Fl G 3s.
Runnaneun Pt (Rubha'n Eun) 55°43'·79N 05°00'·23W Fl R 6s 8m 12M; W Tr.
Sheanawally Point 55°44'·12N 04°56'·37W Fl 10s 6m 5M; vis: 061°300°.
Little Cumbrae I Cumbrae Elbow 55°43'·22N 04°58'·06W Fl 6s 28m 14M; W Tr; vis: 334°-193°.

◀ ARDROSSAN

Approach Dir Lt 055° 55°38'·66N 04°49'·21W Dir F WRG 15m W14M, R11M, G11M; vis: F G050°-051·2°, Alt WG 051·2°-053·8°, W phase increasing with Brg; F W053·8°-056·2°; Alt WR 056·2°-058·8°. R phase increasing with brg; F R058·8°-060°. Same structure FR 13m 6M; vis: 325°-145°.
N Bkwtr Hd 55°38'·53N 04°49'·64W Fl R 5s 7m 5M; R gantry.
Lighthouse Pier Head 55°38'·47N 04°49'·57W Iso WG 4s 11m 9M; W Tr; vis: W035°-317°, G317°-035°.
Eagle Rock 55°38'·21N 04°49'·69W Fl G 5s.

◀ IRVINE

Ent N side 55°36'·21N 04°42'·08W Fl R 3s 6m 5M; R col.
S side 55°36'·17N 04°42'·04W Fl G 3s 6m 5M; G col.
Ldg Lts 051°. Front, 55°36'·40N 04°41'·57W FG 10m 5M. Rear, 101m from front, FR 15m 5M; G masts, vis: 019°-120°.

◀ TROON

Troon 55°33'·07N 04°41'·35W Fl G 4s.
West Pier Head 55°33'·07N 04°41'·02W Fl (2) WG 5s 11m 9M; W Tr; vis: G036°-090°, W090°-036°.
East Pier Head 55°33'·02N 04°40'·96W Fl R 10s 6m 3M.
Lady I 55°31'·63N 04°44'·04W Fl (4) 30s 19m 8M; W Bn.

◀ ARRAN/RANZA/LAMLASH/BRODICK

Hamilton Rk 55°32'·63N 05°04'·92W Fl R 6s.
Brodick Pier Hd 55°32'·64N 05°08'·28W 2 FR (vert) 9m 4M.
Pillar Rk Pt ☆ (Holy Island), 55°31'·04N 05°03'·67W Fl (2) 20s 38m **25M**; W □ Tr.
South Channel 55°30'·64N 05°04'·57W Fl (2) R 12s.
Holy I SW end 55°30'·73N 05°04'·21W Fl G 3s 14m 10M; W Tr; vis: 282°-147°.
Pladda ☆ 55°25'·50N 05°07'·12W Fl (3) 30s 40m **17M**; W Tr.

◀ AYR

S. Nicholas 55°28'·12N 04°39'·44W Fl G 2s.
North Breakwater Head 55°28'·22N 04°38'·78W QR 9m 5M.
South Pier Head 55°28'·17N 04°38'·74W Q 7m 7M; R Tr; vis: 012°-161°. Also FG 5m 5M; vis: 012°-082°.
Ldg Lts 098°. Front, 55°28'·15N 04°38'·38W FR 10m 5M; R Tr. Rear, 130m from front Oc R 10s 18m 9M.
Turnberry Point ☆, near castle ruins 55°19'·56N 04°50'·71W Fl 15s 29m **24M**; W Tr.
Ailsa Craig ☆ 55°15'·12N 05°06'·52W Fl 4s 18m **17M**; W Tr; vis: 145°-028°.

◀ GIRVAN

S Pier Hd 55°14'·72N 04°51'·90W 2 FG (vert) 8m 4M; W Tr.
N Bkwtr Hd 55°14'·74N 04°51'·85W Fl (2) R 6s 7m 4M.
N Groyne Hd 55°14'·71N 04°51'·71W Iso 4s 3m 4M.

◀ LOCH RYAN

Cairn Pt 54°58'·46N 05°01'·85W Fl (2) R 10s 14m 12M; W Tr.
Cairnryan 54°57'·77N 05°00'·99W Fl R 5s 5m 5M.
Forbes Shoal 54°59'·47N 05°02'·96W QR.
Loch Ryan W 54°59'·23N 05°03'·24W QG.
Stranraer No.1 54°56'·67N 05°01'·32W Oc G 6s.
No. 3 54°55'·87N 05°01'·59W QG.
No. 5 54°55'·08N 05°01'·86W Fl G 3s.

◀ STRANRAER

Ross Pier Head 54°54'·54N 05°01'·64W 2 F Bu (vert).
E Pier Head 54°54'·61N 05°01'·59W 2 FR (vert) 9m.
W Pier Head 54°54'·51N 05°01'·75W 2 FG (vert) 8m 4M; Gy col.
Milleur Point 54°01'·28N 05°05'·66W Q.
Corsewall Point ☆ 55°00'·41N 05°09'·58W Fl (5) 30s 34m **22M**; W Tr; vis: 027°-257°.
Killantringan Black Head ☆ 54°51'·70N 05°08'·85W Fl (2) 15s 49m **25M**; W Tr.

◀ PORTPATRICK

Ldg Lts 050·5°. Front, 54°50'·50N 05°07'·02W FG (occas). Rear, 68m from front, FG 8m (occas).
Crammag Hd ☆ 54°39'·90N 04°57'·92W Fl 10s 35m **18M**; W Tr.
Mull of Galloway ☆, SE end 54°38'·08N 04°51'·45W Fl 20s 99m **28M**; W Tr; vis: 182°-105°.

9.9.5 PASSAGE INFORMATION

Although conditions in the South-West of Scotland are in general less rugged than from Mull northwards, some of the remarks at the start of 9.8.5 are equally applicable to this area. Refer to the Admiralty *West Coast of Scotland Pilot*; to *Yachtsman's Pilot to the W Coast of Scotland, Clyde to Colonsay* (Imray/Lawrence) and to the Clyde Cruising Club's SDs. Submarines exercise throughout these waters; see 9.8.23 for information on active areas (Subfacts).

Some of the following more common Gaelic terms may help with navigation: *Acairseid*: anchorage. *Ailean*: meadow. *Aird, ard*: promontory. *Aisir, aisridh*: passage between rocks. *Beag*: little. *Beinn*: mountain. *Bo, boghar, bodha*: rock. *Cala*: harbour. *Camas*: channel, bay. *Caol*: strait. *Cladach*: shore, beach. *Creag*: cliff. *Cumhamn*: narrows. *Dubh, dhubh*: black. *Dun*: castle. *Eilean, eileanan*: island. *Garbh*: rough. *Geal, gheal*: white. *Glas, ghlas*: grey, green. *Inis*: island. *Kyle*: narrow strait. *Linn, Linne*: pool. *Mor, mhor:* large. *Mull*: promontory. *Rinn, roinn*: point. *Ruadh*: red, brown. *Rubha, rhu*: cape. *Sgeir*: rock. *Sruth*: current. *Strath*: river valley. *Tarbert*: isthmus. *Traigh*: beach. *Uig*: bay.

CORRYVRECKAN TO CRINAN (charts *2326*, 2343) Between Scarba and Jura is the Gulf of Corryvreckan (chart 2343) which is best avoided, and should never be attempted by yachts except at slack water and in calm conditions. (In any event the Sound of Luing is always a safer and not much longer alternative). The Gulf has a least width of 6ca and is free of dangers, other than its very strong tides which, in conjunction with a very uneven bottom, cause extreme turbulence. This is particularly dangerous with strong W winds over a W-going (flood) tide which spews out several miles to seaward of the gulf, with overfalls extending 5M from the W of ent (The Great Race). Keep to the S side of the gulf to avoid the worst turbulence and the whirlpool known as The Hag, caused by depths of only 29m, as opposed to more than 100m in the fairway. The W-going stream in the gulf begins at HW Oban + 0410, and the E-going at HW Oban – 0210. Sp rate W-going is 8·5kn, and E-going about 6kn.

The range of tide at sp can vary nearly 2m between the E end of the gulf (1·5m) and the W end (3·4m), with HW ½ hr earlier at the E end. Slack water occurs at HW Oban +4 and –2½ and lasts almost 1 hr at nps, but only 15 mins at sps. On the W-going (flood) stream eddies form both sides of the gulf, but the one on the N (Scarba) shore is more important. Where this eddy meets the main stream off Camas nam Bairneach there is violent turbulence, with heavy overfalls extending W at the division of the eddy and the main stream. There are temp anchs with the wind in the right quarter in Bàgh Gleann a' Mhaoil in the SE corner of Scarba, and in Bàgh Gleann nam Muc at N end of Jura but the latter has rks in approaches E and SW of Eilean Beag.

SE of Corryvreckan is Loch Crinan, which leads to the Crinan Canal (9.9.8). Beware Black Rk, 2m high and 2ca N of the canal sea lock, and dangers extending 100m from the rk.

WEST OF JURA TO ISLAY (charts 2481, 2168) The W coasts of Colonsay and Oronsay (chart *2169*) are fringed with dangers up to 2M offshore. The two islands are separated by a narrow chan which dries and has an overhead cable (10m). There are HIE 🅥s at Scalasaig; see 9.9.7.

The Sound of Islay presents no difficulty; hold to the Islay shore, where all dangers are close in. The N-going stream begins at HW Oban + 0440, and the S-going at HW Oban – 0140. The sp rates are 2·5kn at N entrance and 1·5kn at S entrance, but reaching 5kn in the narrows off Port Askaig. There are anchs in the Sound, but mostly holding ground is poor. The best places are alongside at Port Askaig (9.9.7), or at anch off the distillery in Bunnahabhain B, 2·5M to N. There are overfalls off McArthur's Hd (Islay side of S entrance) during the S-going stream.

The N coast of Islay and Rhinns of Islay are very exposed. In the N there is anch SE of Nave Island at entrance to Loch Gruinart; beware Balach Rks which dry, just to N. To the SW off Orsay (lt), Frenchman's Rks and W Bank there is a race and overfalls which should be cleared by 3M. Here the NW-going stream begins at HW Oban + 0530, and the SE-going at HW Oban – 0040; sp rates are 6-8kn inshore, but decrease to 3kn 5M offshore. Loch Indaal gives some shelter; beware rks extending from Laggan Pt on E side of ent. Off the Mull of Oa there are further overfalls. Port Ellen, the main hbr on Islay, has HIE 🅥s; there are some dangers in approach, and it is exposed to S; see 9.9.7 and chart 2474.

SOUND OF JURA TO GIGHA (charts 2397, 2396, 2168) From Crinan to Gigha the Sound of Jura is safe if a mid-chan course is held. Ruadh Sgeir (lt) are rky ledges in mid-fairway, about 3M W of Crinan. Loch Sween (chart 2397) can be approached N or SE of MacCormaig Islands, where there is an attractive anch on NE side of Eilean Mor, but exposed to NE. Coming from N beware Keills Rk and Danna Rk. Sgeirean a Mhain is a rk in fairway 1·5M NE of Castle Sween (conspic on SE shore). Anch at Tayvallich, near head of loch on W side.

W Loch Tarbert (chart 2477) is long and narrow, with good anchs and lts near ent, but unmarked shoals. On entry give a berth of at least 2½ca to Eilean Traighe off N shore, E of Ardpatrick Pt. Dun Skeig, an isolated hill, is conspic on S shore. Good anch near head of loch, 1M by road from E Loch Tarbert, Loch Fyne; see 9.9.7.

On W side of Sound, near S end of Jura, are The Small Is (chart 2396) across the mouth of Loch na Mile. Beware Goat Rk (dries 0·3m) 1½ca off southernmost Is, Eilean nan Gabhar, behind which is good anch. Also possible to go alongside Craighouse Pier (HIE 🅥) (9.9.7). Another anch is in Lowlandman's B, about 3M to N, but exposed to S winds; Ninefoot Rks with depth of 2·4m and ECM lt buoy lie off ent. Skervuile (lt) is a reef to the E, in middle of the Sound.

S of W Loch Tarbert, and about 2M off the Kintyre shore, is Gigha Is (chart 2475 and 9.9.7). Good anchs on E side in Druimyeon B and Ardminish B (HIE 🅥s), respectively N and S of Ardminish Pt. Outer and Inner Red Rks (least depth 2m) lie 2M SW of N end of Gigha Is. Dangers extend 1M W off S end of Gigha Is. Gigalum Is and Cara Is are off the S end. Gigha Sound needs very careful pilotage, since there are several dangerous rks, some buoyed/lit, others not. The N-going stream begins at HW Oban + 0430, and S-going at HW Oban – 0155, sp rates 1·3kn.

MULL OF KINTYRE (charts 2126, 2199, 2798) From Crinan to Mull of Kintyre is about 50M. This long peninsula much affects the tidal streams in North Chan. Off Mull of Kintyre (lt, fog sig) the N-going stream begins at HW Oban + 0400, and the S-going at HW Oban – 0225, sp rate 5kn. A strong race and overfalls exist S and SW of Mull of Kintyre, dangerous in strong S winds against S-going tide. Careful timing is needed, especially W-bound (9.9.12). The Traffic Separation Scheme in the North Channel, is only 2M W of the Mull and may limit sea-room in the ITZ.

Sanda Sound separates Sanda Is (lt) and its rks and islets, from Kintyre. On the mainland shore beware Macosh Rks (dry, PHM lt buoy) forming part of Barley Ridges, 2ca offshore; Arranman Barrels, drying and submerged, marked by PHM lt buoy; and Blindman Rk (depth 2m) 1·3M N of Ru Stafnish, where 3 radio masts are 5ca inland. Sanda Is has Sheep Is 3ca to the N; Paterson's Rk (dries) is 1M E. There is anch in Sanda hbr on N side. In Sanda Sound the E-going stream begins at HW Greenock + 0340, and the W-going at HW Greenock – 0230, sp rates 5kn. Tide races extend W, N and NE from Sanda, and in strong S or SW winds the Sound is dangerous. In these conditions pass 2M S of Mull of Kintyre and Sanda and E of Paterson's Rk.

MULL OF KINTYRE TO UPPER LOCH FYNE (charts *2126*, 2383, 2381, 2382). Once E of Mull of Kintyre, tidal conditions and pilotage much improve. Campbeltown (9.9.11) is entered N of Island Davaar (lt, fog sig). 1·5M N of lt ho is Otterard Rk (depth 3·8m), with Long Rk (dries 1·1m) 5ca W of it; both are buoyed. E of Island Davaar tide runs 3kn at sp, and there are overfalls.

Kilbrannan Sound runs 21M from Island Davaar to Skipness Pt, where it joins Inchmarnock Water, Lower Loch Fyne and Bute Sound. There are few dangers apart from overfalls on Erins Bank, 10M S of Skipness, on S-going stream. Good anch in Carradale B (9.9.11), off Torrisdale Castle. There are overfalls off Carradale Pt on S-going stream.

Lower L. Fyne (chart 2381) is mainly clear of dangers to East L. Tarbert (9.9.10). On E shore beware rks off Ardlamont Pt; 4M to NW is Skate Is which is best passed to W. 3M S of Ardrishaig (9.9.9) beware Big Rk (depth 2·1m). Further N, at entrance to Loch Gilp (mostly dries) note shoals (least depth 1·5m) round Gulnare Rk, PHM lt buoy; also Duncuan Is with dangers extending SW to Sgeir Sgalag (depth 0·6m), buoyed.

Where Upper L. Fyne turns NE (The Narrows) it is partly obstructed by Otter Spit (dries 0·9m), extending 8ca WNW from E shore and marked by lt bn. The stream runs up to 2kn here. A buoyed/lit rk, depth less than 2m, lies about 7ca SW of Otter Spit bn. In Upper L. Fyne (chart 2382) off Minard Pt, the chan between rks and islands in the fairway is buoyed/lit. For Inveraray, see 9.9.10.

ARRAN, BUTE AND FIRTH OF CLYDE (charts 1906, 1907) Bute Sound leads into Firth of Clyde, and is clear in fairway. Arran's mountains tend to cause squalls or calms, but it has good anchs at Lamlash (9.9.13), Brodick and Loch Ranza. Sannox Rock (depth 1·5m) is 2½ca off Arran coast 8M N of Lamlash (9.9.13). 1ca off W side of Inchmarnock is Tra na-h-uil, a rk drying 1·5m. In Inchmarnock Sound, Shearwater Rk (depth 0·9m) lies in centre of S entrance.

Kyles of Bute are attractive chan N of Bute from Inchmarnock Water to Firth of Clyde, and straightforward apart from Burnt Islands. Here it is best to take the north channel, narrow but well buoyed, passing S of Eilean Buidhe, and N of Eilean Fraoich and Eilean Mor. Care is needed, since sp stream may reach 5kn. Caladh Hbr is a beautiful anch 7ca NW of Burnt Is.

In contrast, the N lochs in Firth of Clyde are less attractive. Loch Goil is worth a visit but Loch Long is squally and has few anchs, while Gareloch (9.9.19) has little to attract cruising yachts other than Rhu marina. Navigation in Firth of Clyde is easy since tidal streams are weak, seldom exceeding 1kn and chans are well marked; but beware commercial and naval shipping and also unlit moorings, see 9.9.19. There are marinas on the mainland at Largs (9.9.15) and Inverkip (9.9.16). Rothesay hbr (9.9.14) on E Bute, and Kilchattan B (anch 6M to S) are both sheltered from SSE to WNW.

FIRTH OF CLYDE TO MULL OF GALLOWAY (charts *2131*, *2126*, 2199, 2198) Further S the coast is less inviting, with mostly commercial hbrs until reaching Ardrossan (9.9.21) and Troon (9.9.22), NW of which there are various dangers: beware Troon Rk (depth 5·6m, but sea can break), Lappock Rk (dries 0·6m, marked by bn), and Mill Rk (dries 0·4m, buoyed). Lady Isle (lt), shoal to NE, is 2M WSW of Troon.

There is a severe race off Bennane Hd (8M SSE of Ailsa Craig, conspic) when tide is running strongly. Loch Ryan offers little for yachtsmen but there is anch S of Kirkcolm Pt, inside the drying spit which runs in SE direction 1·5M from the point. There is also useful anch in Lady Bay, sheltered except from NE. Between Corsewall Pt and Mull of Galloway the S-going stream begins HW Greenock + 0310, and the N-going at HW Greenock – 0250. Sp rate off Corsewall Pt is 2-3 kn, increasing to 5kn off and S of Black Hd. Portpatrick (9.9.23) is a useful passage hbr, but not in onshore winds. Races occur off Morroch B, Money Hd and Mull of Logan. A race SSE of Crammag Hd is bad if wind against tide. Mull of Galloway (lt) is a high (82m), steep-to headland. Beware dangerous race extending nearly 3M to S. On E-going stream the race extends NNE into Luce B; on W-going stream it extends SW and W. Best to give the race a wide berth, or pass close inshore at slack water nps and calm weather. SW wind >F4 against W-going stream, do not attempt inshore route.

See 9.10.5 for continuation E into Solway Firth and S into the Irish Sea. For notes on crossing the Irish Sea, see 9.13.5.

9.9.6 DISTANCE TABLE

Approximate distances in nautical miles are by the most direct route, whilst avoiding dangers and allowing for Traffic Separation Schemes. Places in *italics* are in adjoining areas; places in **bold** are in 9.0.7, Distances across the Irish Sea.

1. *Loch Craignish*	1																			
2. **Port Ellen (Islay)**	42	2																		
3. Crinan	5	39	3																	
4. Ardrishaig	14	48	9	4																
5. East Loch Tarbert	24	58	19	10	5															
6. **Campbeltown**	55	47	50	39	31	6														
7. Mull of Kintyre	56	27	51	54	45	20	7													
8. Lamlash	48	61	43	34	25	24	34	8												
9. Largs	48	94	43	34	24	39	47	17	9											
10. Rothesay	49	95	44	35	25	43	48	23	9	10										
11. Kip Marina	53	85	48	39	28	50	58	25	10	8	11									
12. Greenock	59	90	54	45	36	53	63	31	16	14	6	12								
13. Rhu (Helensburgh)	62	94	57	48	37	59	67	33	19	17	9	4	13							
14. **Troon**	54	71	49	40	33	33	44	16	20	25	29	34	38	14						
15. Girvan	67	58	62	53	43	29	31	20	33	40	46	49	51	21	15					
16. Stranraer	89	62	84	75	65	34	35	39	56	63	69	65	74	44	23	16				
17. **Portpatrick**	88	63	83	74	66	39	36	44	61	67	68	77	77	49	28	23	17			
18. **Mull of Galloway**	104	78	99	90	82	56	52	60	78	82	84	93	93	65	62	39	16	18		
19. ***Kirkcudbright***	136	111	131	122	114	88	84	92	110	114	116	124	125	97	94	71	48	32	19	
20. *Douglas (IoM)*	146	120	141	132	124	106	94	102	141	130	126	141	135	107	104	84	60	42	45	20

HARBOURS AND ANCHORAGES IN COLONSAY, JURA, ISLAY AND THE SOUND OF JURA

SCALASAIG, Colonsay, **56°04´·14N 06°10´·86W**. AC 2474, *2169*. HW +0542 on Dover; ML 2·2m. See 9.9.7. Conspic monument ½M SW of hbr. Beware group of rks N of pier hd marked by bn. 2 HIE Ⓥ berths on N side of pier, inner end approx 2·5m. Inner hbr to SW of pier is safe, but dries. Ldg lts 262°, both FR 8/10m on pier. Also ⚓ clear of cable in **Loch Staosnaig**; SW of Rubha Dubh lt, Fl (2) WR 10s 6m 8/5M; R shore-230°, W230°-337°, R337°-354°. Facilities: D, P, V (all at ✉), FW, Hotel ☎ (01951) 200316.

LOCH TARBERT, W Jura, **55°57´·69N 06°00´·06W**. AC 2481, *2169*. Tides as Rubha A'Mhàil (N tip of Islay). See 9.9.7. HW –0540 on Dover; ML 2·1m; Duration 0600. Excellent shelter inside the loch, but subject to squalls in strong winds; ⚓ outside in Glenbatrick Bay in approx 6m in S winds, or at Bagh Gleann Righ Mor in approx 2m in N winds. To enter inner loch via Cumhann Beag, there are four pairs of ldg marks (W stones) at approx 120°, 150°, 077°, and 188°, the latter astern, to be used in sequence; pilot book required. There are no facilities.

PORT ASKAIG, Islay, **55°50´·87N 06°06´·26W**. AC 2481, 2168. HW +0610 on Dover; ML 1·2m. See 9.9.7. Hbr on W side of Sound of Islay. ⚓ close inshore in 4m or secure to ferry pier. Beware strong tide/eddies. ☆ FR at LB. Facilities: FW (hose on pier), Gas, P, R, Hotel, V, ✉, ferries to Jura and Kintyre. Other ⚓s in the Sound at: Bunnahabhain (2M N); Whitefarland Bay, Jura, opp Caol Ila distillery; NW of Am Fraoch Eilean (S tip of Jura); Aros Bay, N of Ardmore Pt.

CRAIGHOUSE, SE Jura, **55°49´·99N 05°56´·31W**. AC 2396, 2481, 2168. HW +0600 on Dover; ML 0·5m; Duration 0640 np, 0530 sp. See 9.9.7. Good shelter, but squalls occur in W winds. Enter between lt bn on SW end of Eilean nan Gabhar, Fl 5s 7m 8M vis 225°-010°, and unlit bn close SW. There are 8 HIE Ⓜs N of pier (☎ (01496) 810332), where yachts may berth alongside; or ⚓ in 5m in poor holding at the N end of Loch na Mile. Facilities: very limited, Bar, FW, ✉, R, V, Gas, P & D (cans). **Lowlandman's Bay** is 1M further N, with ECM buoy, Q (3) 10s, marking Nine Foot Rk (2·4m) off the ent. ⚓ to SW of conspic houses, off stone jetty.

LOCH SWEEN, Argyll and Bute, **55°55´·69N 05°41´·26W**. AC 2397. HW +0550 on Dover; ML 1·5m; Duration = 0610. See 9.9.8 Carsaig Bay. Off the ent to loch, **Eilean Mòr** (most SW'ly of MacCormaig Isles) has tiny ⚓ on N side in 3m; local transit marks keep clear of two rks, 0·6m and 0·9m. Inside the loch, beware Sgeirean a'Mhain, a rk in mid-chan to S of Taynish Is, 3M from ent. Good shelter in Loch a Bhealaich (⚓ outside **Tayvallich** in approx 7m on boulders) or enter inner hbr to ⚓ W of central reef. There are no lts. Facilities: Gas, Bar, ✉, FW (🚰 by ✉), R, V. Close to NE are ⚓s at **Caol Scotnish** and **Fairy Is**, the former obstructed by rks 3ca from ent.

WEST LOCH TARBERT, Argyll and Bute, (Kintyre), **55°45'N 05°36'W**. AC 2477. Tides as Gigha Sound, 9.9.7. Good shelter. Ent is S of Eilean Traighe, Fl (2) R 5s, and NW of Dun Skeig, Q (2) 10s, where there is also conspic conical hill (142m). Loch is lit for 5M by 3 bns, QG, QR and QG in sequence, up to Kennacraig ferry pier, 2FG (vert). PHM buoy, QR, is 2½ca NW of pier. Caution: many drying rks and fish farms outside the fairway and near head of loch. ⚓s are NE of Eilean Traighe (beware weed & ferry wash); near Rhu Pt, possible Ⓜs; NE of Eilean dà Gallagain, and at loch hd by pier (ru). Tarbert (9.9.10) is 1·5M walk/bus.

GIGHA ISLAND, Argyll and Bute, **55°40´·6N 05°44´·0W**. AC 2475, 2168. HW +0600 on Dover; ML 0·9m; Duration 0530. See 9.9.7. Main ⚓ is **Ardminish Bay**: 12 HIE Ⓜs in the centre. Reefs extend off both points, the S'ly reef marked by an unlit PHM buoy. Kiln Rk (dries 1·5m) is close NE of the old ferry jetty. **Druimyeon Bay** is more sheltered in E'lies, but care needed entering from S. ⚓s sheltered from winds in ( ): Port Mór (S-W), Bàgh na Dòirlinne (SE-S), W Tarbert Bay (NE). Caolas Gigalum (⚓ 50m SE of pier) is safe in all but NE-E winds. Beware many rks in Gigha Sound. Lts: Fl (2) 6s, on Gamhna Gigha (off NE tip); WCM buoy Fl (9) 15s marks Gigalum Rks, at S end of Gigha. **Ardminish** ☎/📠 (01583) 505254: FW, Gas, P & D (cans), 🅾, ✉, Bar, R, V.

PORT ELLEN *9.9.7*

Islay (Argyll and Bute) **55°37´·29N 06°12´·26W** ❁❁❁✿✿

CHARTS AC 2474, 2168; Imray C64

TIDES HW +0620 np, +0130 sp on Dover; ML 0·6. Sea level is much affected by the weather, rising by 1m in S/E gales; at nps the tide is sometimes diurnal and range negligible.

Standard Port OBAN (⟵)

Times				**Height (metres)**			
High Water		Low Water		MHWS	MHWN	MLWN	MLWS
0100	0700	0100	0800	4·0	2·9	1·8	0·7
1300	1900	1300	2000				
Differences PORT ELLEN (S Islay)							
–0530	–0050	–0045	–0530	–3·1	–2·1	–1·3	–0·4
SCALASAIG (E Colonsay)							
–0020	–0005	–0015	+0005	–0·1	–0·2	–0·2	–0·2
GLENGARRISDALE BAY (N Jura)							
–0020	0000	–0010	0000	–0·4	–0·2	0·0	–0·2
CRAIGHOUSE (SE Jura)							
–0230	–0250	–0150	–0230	–3·0	–2·4	–1·3	–0·6
RUBHA A'MHÀIL (N Islay)							
–0020	0000	+0005	–0015	–0·3	–0·1	–0·3	–0·1
ARDNAVE POINT (NW Islay)							
–0035	+0010	0000	–0025	–0·4	–0·2	–0·3	–0·1
ORSAY ISLAND (SW Islay)							
–0110	–0110	–0040	–0040	–1·4	–0·6	–0·5	–0·2
BRUICHLADDICH (Islay, Loch Indaal)							
–0105	–0035	–0110	–0110	–1·8	–1·3	–0·4	+0·1
PORT ASKAIG (Sound of Islay)							
–0110	–0030	–0020	–0020	–1·9	–1·4	–0·8	–0·3
GIGHA SOUND (Sound of Jura)							
–0450	–0210	–0130	–0410	–2·5	–1·6	–1·0	–0·1
MACHRIHANISH							
–0520	–0350	–0340	–0540	Mean range 0·5 metres.			

SHELTER Good shelter close S of pier and clear of ferries/FVs, but in S winds swell sets into the bay. 10 HIE Ⓜs to W of Rubha Glas; adjacent rks are marked by 3 perches with reflective topmarks. Inner hbr dries. In W'lies ⚓ in Kilnaughton Bay, N of Carraig Fhada lt ho; or 4M ENE at Loch-an-t-Sàilein.

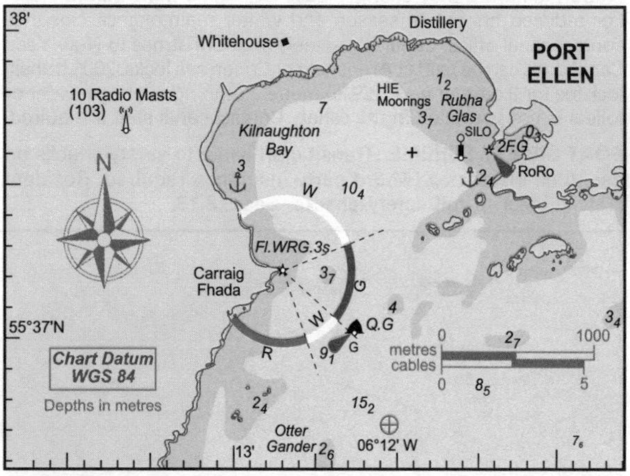

NAVIGATION WPT 55°36´·69N 06°12´·06W, 146°/326° from/to Carraig Fhada lt ho, 0·63M. Beware Otter Rk 4M SE of hbr, and rks closer in on both sides of ent and in NE corner of bay.

LIGHTS AND MARKS On W side 10 Radio masts (103m) and Carraig Fhada lt ho (conspic), Fl WRG 3s 20m 8/6M; W shore-248°, G248°-311°, W311°-340°, R340°-shore; keep in W sector until past the SHM buoy, QG. Ro-Ro pier shows 2 FG (vert).

RADIO TELEPHONE. None.

TELEPHONE (Dial code 01496) Moorings 810332; ⊖ 810337; MRCC (01475) 729988.

FACILITIES Village Bar, FW, ✉, R, V, Gas. 4 malt whisky distilleries in or near Port Ellen and 4 more on the island.

9

CRINAN CANAL *9.9.8*

Argyll and Bute **56°05·50N 05°33'·38W** Crinan ❀❀♁♁✿✿✿

CHARTS AC 2320, *2326*; Imray C65; OS 55

TIDES –0608 Dover; ML 2·1; Duration 0605; Zone 0 (UT) HW Crinan is at HW Oban –0045

Standard Port OBAN (⟵)

Times				Height (metres)			
High Water		Low Water		MHWS	MHWN	MLWN	MLWS
0100	0700	0100	0800	4·0	2·9	1·8	0·7
1300	1900	1300	2000				
Differences CARSAIG BAY (4·5M SSW of Loch Crinan)							
–0105	–0040	–0050	–0050	–2·1	–1·6	–1·0	–0·4

Note: In the Sound of Jura, S of Loch Crinan, the rise of tide occurs mainly during the 3½hrs after LW; the fall during the 3½hrs after HW. At other times the changes in level are usually small and irregular.

SHELTER Complete shelter in canal basin; yachts are welcome, but often full of FVs. Good shelter in Crinan Hbr (E of Eilean da Mheinn) but full of moorings. Except in strong W/N winds, ⚓ E of the canal ent, clear of fairway. Gallanach Bay on N side of L Crinan has good holding in about 3m. Berths may be reserved at Bellanoch Bay.

NAVIGATION WPT 56°05'·70N 05°33'·64W, 326°/146° from/to Fl WG 3s lt, 0·27M. Beware Black Rock (2m high) in appr NE of ldg line 146° to dir Fl WG 3s lt. Off NW corner of chartlet, no ⚓ in a nearly rectangular shellfish bed, 6ca by 6ca. SPM lt buoys mark each corner: Fl (4) Y 12s at the NE and NW corners, Fl Y 6s at the SW and SE corners; the latter being about 100m NE of Black Rock.

CANAL Canal is 9M long with 15 locks and 7 opening bridges. Least transit time is 5 to 6 hrs, observing 4kn speed limit. If short-handed, helpers may be available via canal staff or 01546 602458. Entry at all tides. Max LOA: 26·82m, 6·09m beam, 2·89m FW draft, mast 28.95m. Vessels NW-bound have right of way. **Lock hrs**: In season sea locks open 0830-1630 (later at peak season) daily. Sea lock outer gates are left open after hours for yachts to shelter. Inland locks and bridges operate 0830-1730 daily; lock 14 and Crinan Bridge open 0830-2100 Fri-Sun (all times may change). **Last locking 30 mins before close.** For reduced hrs out of season and winter maintenance closures, contact canal office. Canal is routinely shut Christmas to New Year. **Canal dues** can be paid at Ardrishaig or Crinan sea locks. 2001 transit/lock fee for 3 days or part = £9.30/metre. Pumping out bilge water or toilets is not permitted in the canal. Contact canal staff if required.

BOAT SAFETY SCHEME Transit craft liable to safety checks on gas, fuel, electrics; £1M 3rd party insurance required. Resident craft subject to full safety checks. See 9.8.18.

LIGHTS AND MARKS Crinan Hotel is conspic W bldg. A conspic chy, 3ca SW of hotel, leads 187° into Crinan Hbr. E of sea-lock: Dir Fl WG 3s 8m 4M, vis W 114°-146°, G146°-280°. Ent: 2 FG (vert) and 2FR (vert).

RADIO TELEPHONE VHF Ch **74** 16 only at sea locks.

TELEPHONE (Dial code 01546) Sea lock 830285; Canal HQ 603210; MRCC (01475) 729988; ⊖ (0141) 887 9369 (H24); Marinecall 09068 500463; Police 602222; Dr 602921.

FACILITIES **Canal HQ** ☎ 603210, www.scottishcanals.co.uk, M, L, FW, *Skippers Brief* is essential reading; **Sea Basin** AB £2.25/m, D. **Services:** BY, Slip, ME, El, Sh, Gas, ACA, C (5 ton), ▣, CH, P (cans), V, R, Bar. Use shore toilets, not yacht heads, whilst in canal. **Village** ✉, Ⓑ (Ardrishaig), ⇌ (Oban), ✈ (Glasgow or Macrihanish). There is a wintering park, plus BY and CH, at Cairnbaan for yachts <10m LOA.

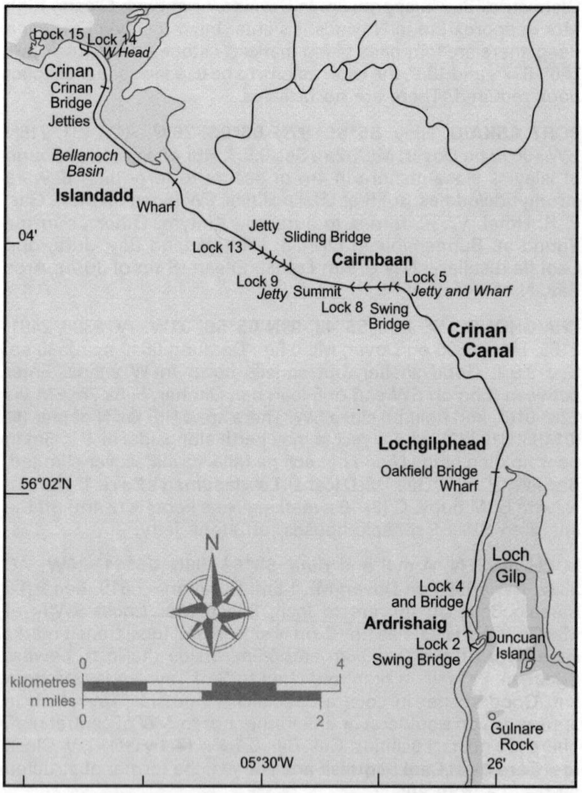

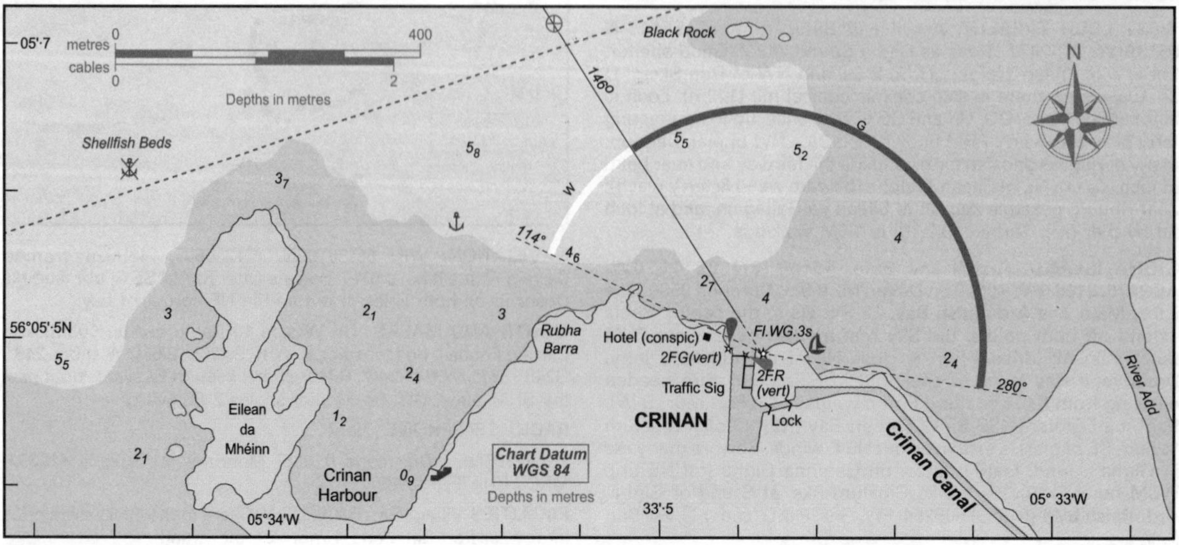

ARDRISHAIG *9.9.9*

Argyll and Bute **56°00′·78N 05°26′·62W** ❀❀◊◊✿✿

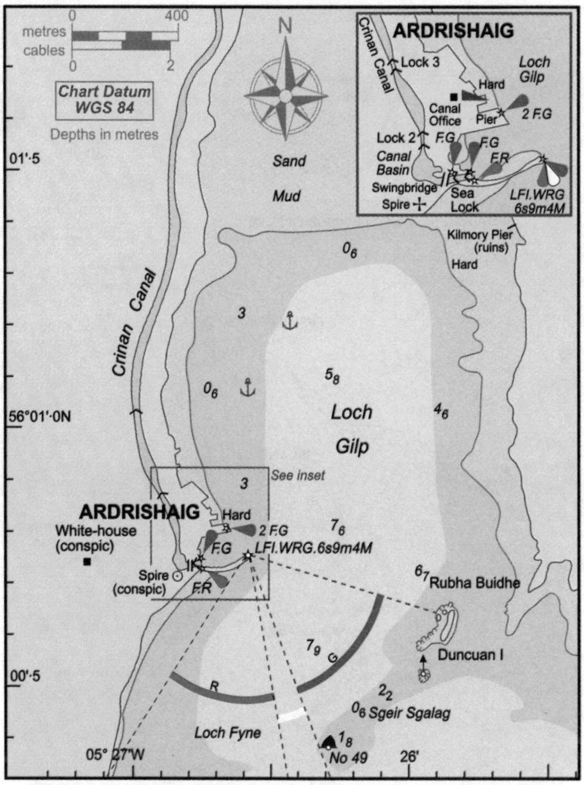

CHARTS AC 2381, *2131*; Imray C63; OS 55

TIDES +0120 Dover; ML 1·9; Duration 0640; Zone 0 (UT)

Standard Port GREENOCK (⟶)

Times				Height (metres)			
High Water		Low Water		MHWS	MHWN	MLWN	MLWS
0000	0600	0000	0600	3·4	2·8	1·0	0·3
1200	1800	1200	1800				
Differences ARDRISHAIG							
+0006	+0006	-0015	+0020	0·0	0·0	+0·1	–0·1
INVERARAY							
+0011	+0011	+0034	+0034	–0·1	+0·1	–0·5	–0·2

SHELTER Hbr is sheltered except from strong E'lies; do not berth on pier or ⚓ due to commercial vessels H24. Sea lock into the Crinan Canal is usually left open; access at all tides. Complete shelter in the canal basin, or beyond lock No 2; see 9.9.8. Also ⚓ 2ca N of hbr, off the W shore of L Gilp.

NAVIGATION WPT No 48 PHM buoy, Fl R 4s, 56°00′·18N 05°26′·31W, 165°/345° from/to bkwtr lt, 0·61M. Dangerous drying rks to E of appr chan are marked by No 49 unlit SHM buoy.

LIGHTS AND MARKS Conspic W Ho on with block of flats leads 315°between Nos 48 and 49 buoys. Bkwtr lt, L Fl WRG 6s, W339°-350°. Pier is floodlit. Other lights as plan.

RADIO TELEPHONE VHF Ch **74** 16.

TELEPHONE (Dial code 01546) Hr Mr 603210, 📠 603941; Sea lock 620458; MRCC (01475) 729988; ⊜ (0141) 887 9369; Marinecall 09068 500462; Police 603233; Dr 602921.

FACILITIES Pier/Hbr ☎ 603210, AB, Slip, FW; **Sea Lock ☎** 602458, AB £2.25; **Crinan Canal** www.scottishcanals.co.uk, AB, M, L, FW, R, Bar; dues, see 9.9.8. **Services:** BY, ME, El, Sh, CH, D (cans), Gas; C (20 ton) at Lochgilphead (2M). **Village** EC Wed; P & D (cans), V, R, Bar, ✉, Ⓑ, ⇌ (bus to Oban), ✈ (Glasgow or Campbeltown).

TARBERT, LOCH FYNE *9.9.10*

Also known as East Loch Tarbert

Argyll and Bute **55°52′·05N 05°24′·22W** ❀❀❀◊◊◊✿✿

CHARTS AC 2381, *2131*; Imray C63; OS 62

TIDES +0120 Dover; ML 1·9; Duration 0640; Zone 0 (UT)

Standard Port GREENOCK (⟶)

Times				Height (metres)			
High Water		Low Water		MHWS	MHWN	MLWN	MLWS
0000	0600	0000	0600	3·4	2·8	1·0	0·3
1200	1800	1200	1800				
Differences EAST LOCH TARBERT							
–0005	–0005	0000	–0005	+0·2	+0·1	0·0	0·0

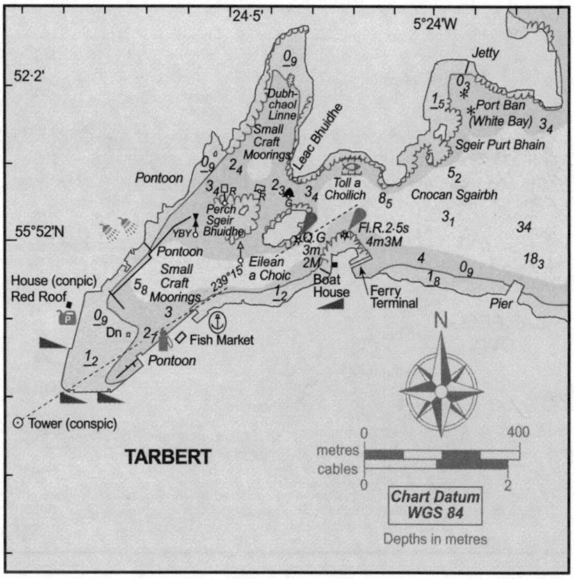

SHELTER Very good in all weathers but gets crowded. Access H24. Visitors berth only on SE side of yacht pontoons in 5m.

NAVIGATION WPT 55°52′·02N 05°23′·03W, 090°/270° from/to Fl R 2·5s lt, 0·70M. Ent is very narrow. Cock Isle divides the ent in half: Main hbr to the S, Buteman's Hole to the N, where ⚓s are fouled by heavy moorings and lost chains. Speed limit 3kn.

LIGHTS AND MARKS Outer ldg lts 252° to S ent: Fl R 2·5s on with Cock Is lt QG. Inner ldg line 239°: same QG, G column, on with conspic ⊕ tr. Note: The W sector, 065°-078°, of Eilean na Beithe ☆, Fl WRG 3s 7m 5M (on E shore of Lower Loch Fyne), could be used to position for the initial appr to Tarbert.

RADIO TELEPHONE Call VHF Ch 16; work Ch 14 (0900-1700LT).

TELEPHONE (Dial code 01880) Hr Mr 820344, 📠 820719; MRCC (01475) 729988; ⊜ (0141) 887 9369 (H24); Marinecall 09068 500462; Police 820200; Ⓗ (01546) 602323.

FACILITIES Yacht Berthing Facility 100 visitors, AB £1.35, FW, AC; **Old Quay** D, FW; **Tarbert YC** Slip, L; **Services:** SM, ◙, ACA, Sh, CH. **Town** EC Wed; P & D (cans), Gas, Gaz, L, V, R, Bar, ✉, Ⓑ, ⇌ (bus to Glasgow), ✈ (Glasgow/Campbeltown).

ANCHORAGES IN LOCH FYNE

INVERARAY, Argyll and Bute, **56°13′·95N 05°04′·07W.** AC 2382, *2131*. HW +0126 on Dover. See 9.9.9. For Upper Loch Fyne see 9.9.5. Beyond Otter Spit, are ⚓s on NW bank at Port Ann, Loch Gair and Minard Bay; and on SE bank at Otter Ferry, Strachur Bay (5 ⚓s off Creggans Inn, ☎ (01369) 860279) and St Catherine's.
Inveraray: beware An Oitir drying spit 2ca offshore, ½M S of pier. Some ⚓s or ⚓ SSW of pier in 4m or dry out NW of the pier. FW (on pier), ✉, V, R, Bar, Gas, bus to Glasgow. In Lower L Fyne, 6M NNE of East Loch Tarbert there is a ⚓ at Kilfinan Bay, ☎ (01700) 821201.

9

CAMPBELTOWN *9.9.11*

Argyll & Bute **55°25'·90N 05°32'·56W** Hbr ent ❀❀❀◊◊◊✿✿✿

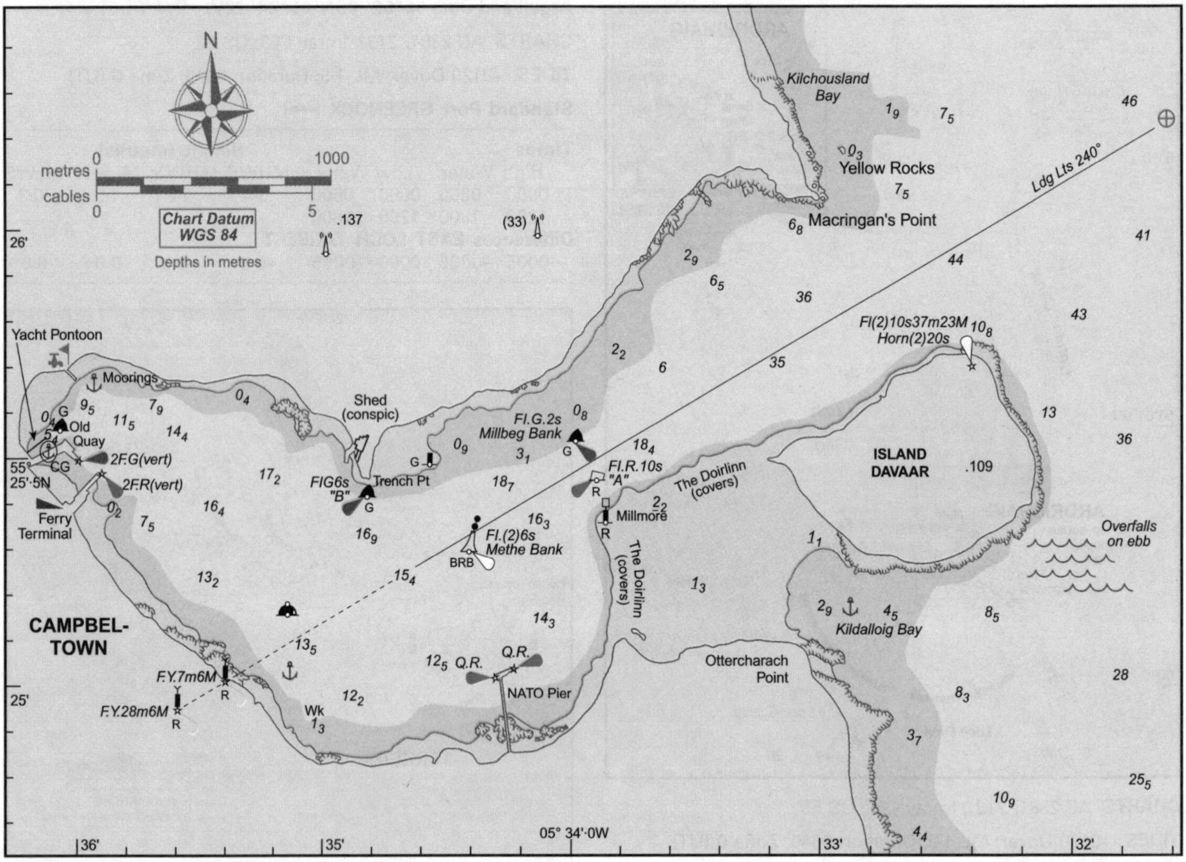

CHARTS AC 1864, *2126*; Imray C63; OS 68

TIDES +0125 Dover; ML 1·8; Duration 0630; Zone 0 (UT)

Standard Port GREENOCK (⟶)

Times				Height (metres)			
High Water		Low Water		MHWS	MHWN	MLWN	MLWS
0000	0600	0000	0600	3·4	2·8	1·0	0·3
1200	1800	1200	1800				
Differences CAMPBELTOWN							
−0025	−0005	−0015	+0005	−0·5	−0·3	+0·1	+0·2
CARRADALE BAY							
−0015	−0005	−0005	+0005	−0·3	−0·2	+0·1	+0·1
SOUTHEND, (Mull of Kintyre)							
−0030	−0010	+0005	+0035	−1·3	−1·2	−0·5	−0·2

SHELTER Good, but gusts off the hills in strong SW'lies. Yacht pontoon (6+34 visitors) dredged 3·0m is close NW of Old Quay and gives excellent sheltered berthing. Yachts >12m LOA should notify ETA to Berthing Master by ☎ (below). Excellent ⚓ close E of front ldg lt (240°), also near moorings NNE of the hbr. S of Island Davaar there is a temp ⚓ in Kildalloig Bay, but no access to the loch.

NAVIGATION WPT 55°26'·24N 05°31'·61W, 060°/240° from/to first chan buoys, 1·4M. The ent is easily identified by radio masts N and NE of Trench Pt (conspic W bldg) and conspic lt ho on N tip of Island Davaar off which streams are strong (4kn sp). Caution: The Dhorlin, a bank drying 2·5m which covers at HW, is close S of the ldg line.

LIGHTS AND MARKS Davaar Fl (2) 10s 37m 23M. Otterard Rk (3·8m depth, off chartlet, 1·5M NNE of Island Davaar), is marked by ECM buoy Q (3) 10s. Ldg lts 240°, both FY 7/28m 6M, are sodium vapour lts, H24. The ☆ 2FR (vert) at the NE end of the ferry terminal pier is on a dolphin, standing clear of the pier head.

RADIO TELEPHONE VHF Ch 12 14 16 (Mon-Fri 0900-1700).

TELEPHONE (Dial code 01586) Hr Mr 552552, 📠 554739; Yacht pontoon Berthing Master ☎ & 📠 552199, mobile 07798 524821, night 554266; MRCC (01475) 729988; ⊜ 552261; Marinecall 09068 500462; Police 552253; Dr 552105.

FACILITIES Yacht pontoon £10.00, FW, AC; Bath/shower in hotel opposite. **Old Quay** ☎ 552552, D, FW, AB, LB; **New Quay** Slip; **Campbeltown SC** Slip (dinghies), Bar, regular racing. **Town** EC Wed; BY, ME, ACA, C (25 ton), CH, P, D, El, Ⓔ, Gas, Gaz, V (2 supermarkets), R, Bar, ✉, Ⓑ, ⓓ, Ⓗ, ♿ toilet about 100m from yacht pontoon, key at Tourist office or police station (H24). Bus thrice daily to Glasgow, ✈ twice daily to Glasgow, ⇌ (nearest is Arrochar, 90 miles N by road). Car hire/taxi.

ADJACENT ANCHORAGE IN KILBRANNAN SOUND

CARRADALE BAY, Argyll and Bute, **55°34'·40N 05°28'·66W.** AC *2131*, HW+0115 on Dover. ML 1·8m. See 9.9.11. Good ⚓ in 7m off Torrisdale Castle in SW corner of Carradale Bay. In N & E winds ⚓ in NE corner of bay, W of Carradale Pt. 3ca E of this Pt, a PHM buoy Fl (2) R 12s marks Cruban Rk. With S & SE winds a swell sets into bay, when good shelter can be found 1M N in **Carradale Harbour** (Port Crannaich); if full of FVs, ⚓ 100m N of Hbr. Bkwtr lt, Fl R 10s 5m 6M. Piermaster ☎ (01586) 431228. Facilities: FW on pier, D & P (cans), Gas, V, R, Bar, ✉.

TIDAL STREAMS AROUND THE MULL OF KINTYRE *9.9.12*

HW –6

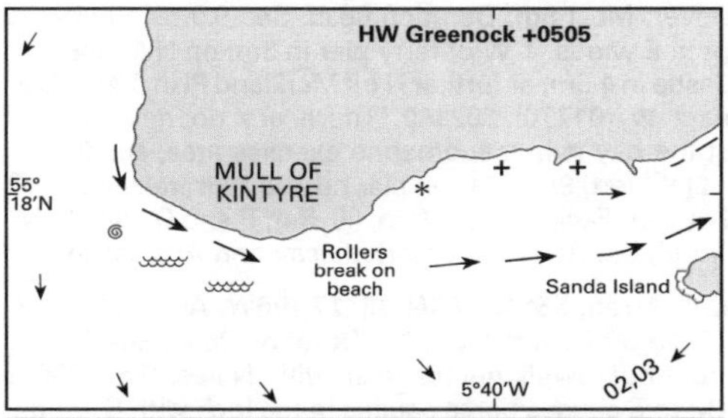

HW –5

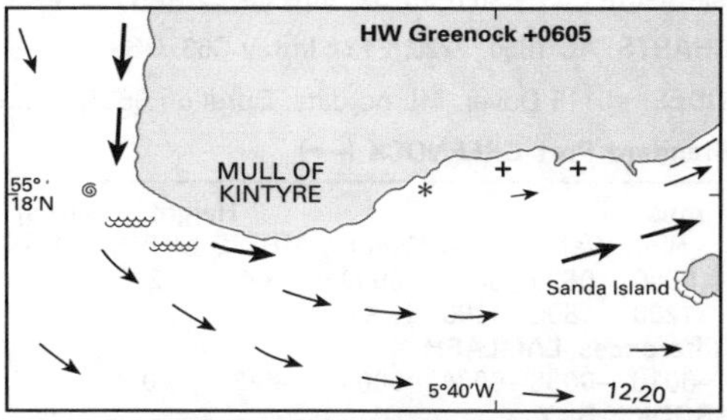

HW –4

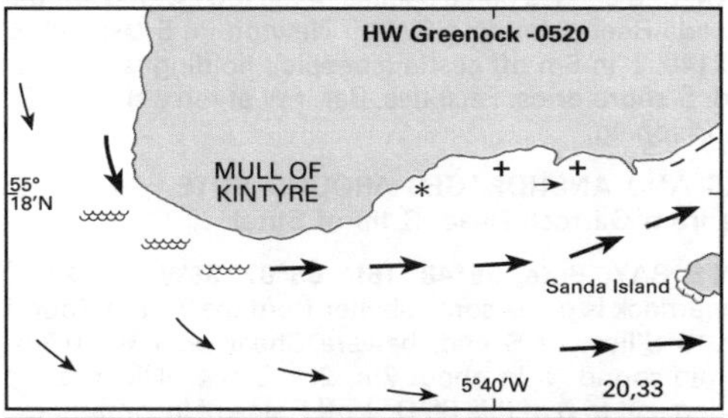

HW –3

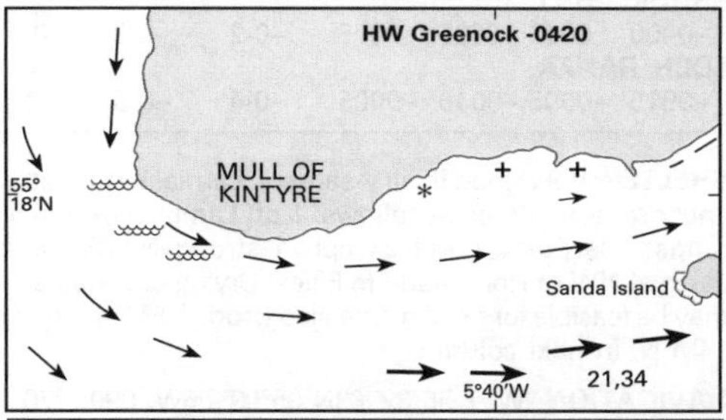

HW –2

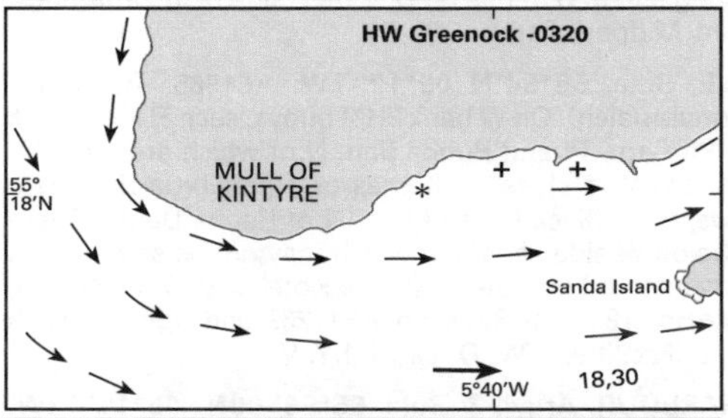

HW –1

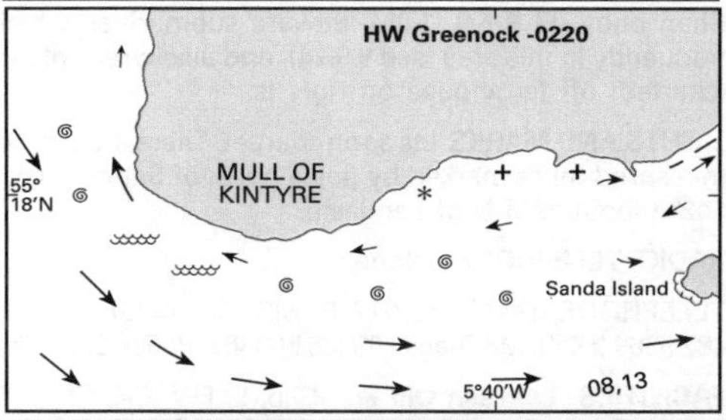

HW Dover

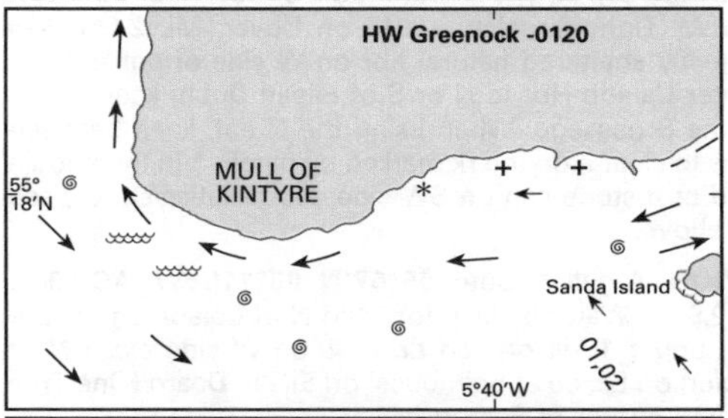

HW +1

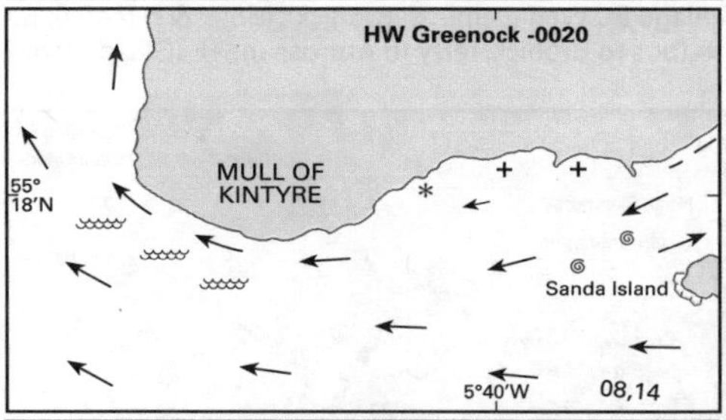

HW +2

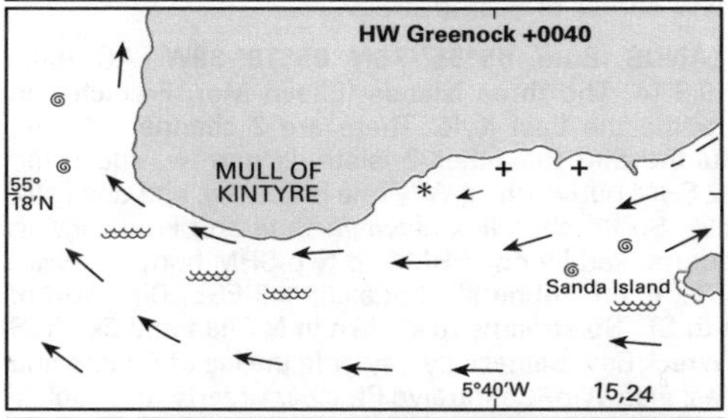

HW +3

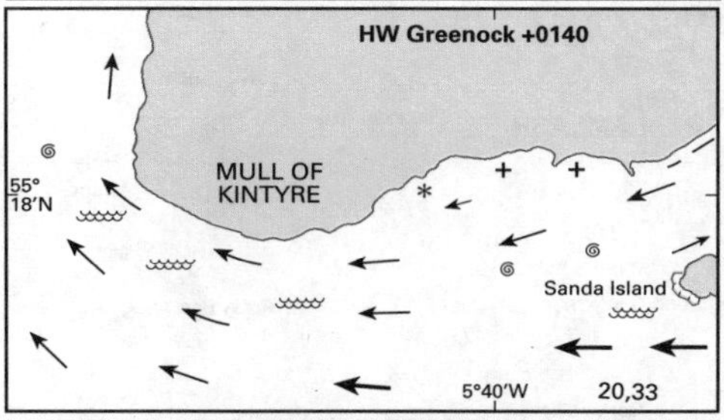

HW +4

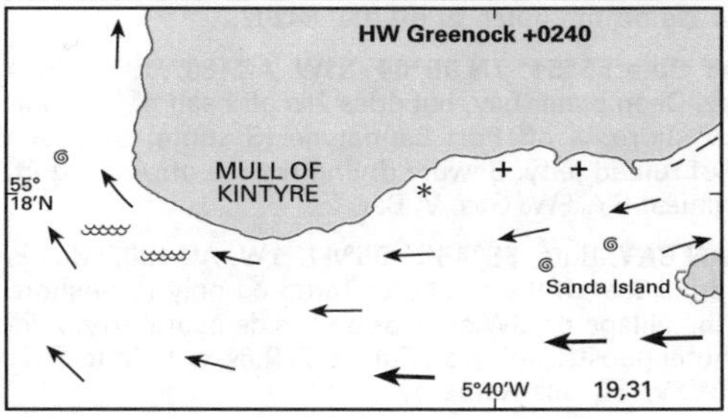

HW +5

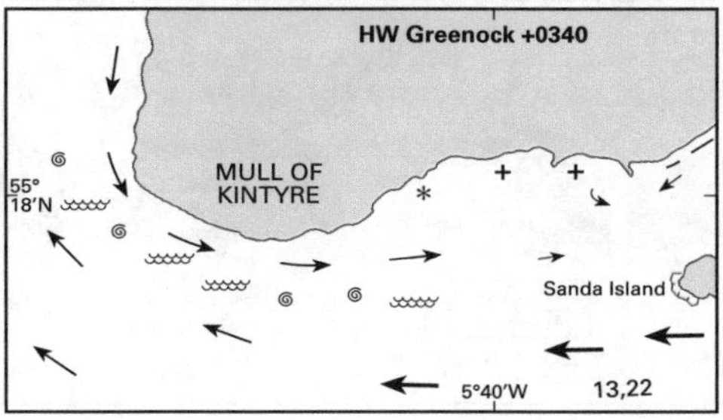

LAMLASH *9.9.13*

Isle of Arran, N Ayrshire **55°32'·00N 05°07'·06W** ❀❀❀⚓⚓⚓✿✿✿

CHARTS AC 1864, *2220*, *2131*; Imray C63; OS 69

TIDES +0115 Dover; ML no data; Duration 0635; Zone 0 (UT)

Standard Port GREENOCK (⟶)

Times				Height (metres)			
High Water		Low Water		MHWS	MHWN	MLWN	MLWS
0000	0600	0000	0600	3·4	2·8	1·0	0·3
1200	1800	1200	1800				
Differences LAMLASH							
–0016	–0036	–0024	–0004	–0·2	–0·2	No data	
BRODICK BAY							
0000	0000	+0005	+0005	–0·2	–0·2	0·0	0·0
LOCH RANZA							
–0015	–0005	–0010	–0005	–0·4	–0·3	–0·1	0·0

SHELTER Very good in all weathers. Lamlash is a natural hbr and anchorage sheltered as follows: ⚓ off Lamlash except in E'lies; off Kingscross Point, good except in strong N/NW winds; off the Farm at NW of Holy Island in E'lies. Drying out against the Old Pier may be feasible for repairs. See also Brodick 5M N, and Loch Ranza 14M N, in next column.

NAVIGATION WPT 55°32'·63N 05°03'·06W, 090°/270° from/to N Chan buoy (Fl R 6s), 1·0M. Beware submarines which exercise frequently in this area (see 9.9.24), and also wreck of landing craft (charted) off farmhouse on Holy Is.

LIGHTS AND MARKS Lts as on chartlet. There are two consecutive measured miles marked by poles north of Sannox, courses 322°/142° (about 12M N of Lamlash).

RADIO TELEPHONE None.

TELEPHONE (Dial code 01770) MRCC (01475) 729988; ⊖ (0141) 887 9369 (H24); Marinecall 09068 500462; Police 302573; Ⓗ 600777.

FACILITIES **Lamlash Old Pier** Slip, L, FW, CH, Sh (hull repairs); **Village** EC Wed (Lamlash/Brodick); ME, P & D (cans), Bar, R, V, ✉, ⇌ (bus to Brodick, ferry to Ardrossan), ✈ (Glasgow or Prestwick).

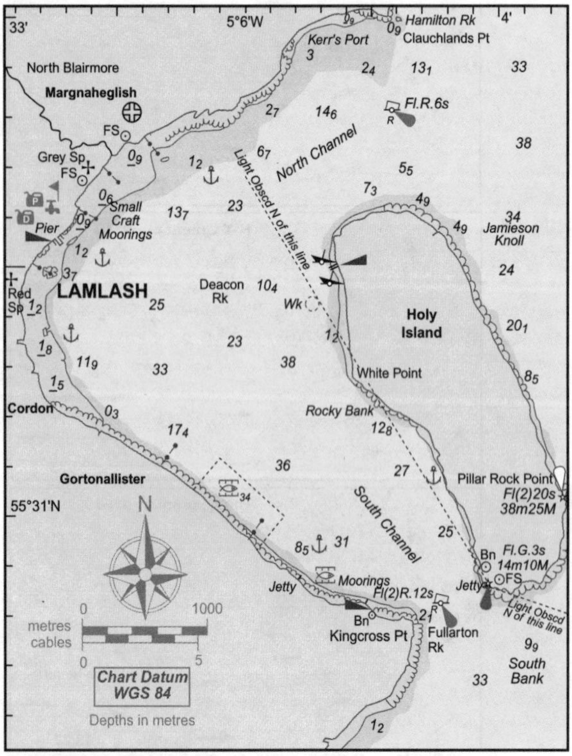

OTHER HARBOURS ON ARRAN

BRODICK, Arran, **55°35'·50N 05°08'·66W**. AC 1864, 2220, *2131*. HW +0115 on Dover; ML 1·8m; Duration 0635. See 9.9.13. Shelter is good except in E winds. ⚓ W of ferry pier in 3m; on NW side just below the Castle in 4·5m, or further N off Merkland Pt in 3-4m. Also 5 🅜s: contact ☎ (01770) 302140. There are no navigational dangers but the bay is in a submarine exercise area; see 9.9.24. Only lts are 2FR (vert) 9/7m 4M on pier hd and Admiralty buoy, Fl Y 2s, 5ca N of pier. Facilities: EC Wed; Ⓑ, Bar, P and D (cans), FW (at pier hd), ME, ✉, R, V. Ferry to Rothesay and Ardrossan.

LOCH RANZA, Arran, **55°42'·60N 05°17'·96W**. AC 2221, 2383, *2131*. HW +0120 on Dover; ML 1·7m; Duration 0635. See 9.9.13. Good shelter, but swell enters loch with N'lies. The 850m mountain 4M to S causes fierce squalls in the loch with S winds. Beware Screda Reef extending SW off Newton Pt. 5 🅜s; call ☎ (01770) 302140. ⚓ in 5m off castle (conspic); holding is suspect in soft mud. S shore dries. Facilities: Bar, FW at ferry slip, ✉, R, V. Ferry to Claonaig.

HARBOURS AND ANCHORAGES AROUND BUTE
(Clockwise from Garroch Head, S tip of Bute)

ST NINIAN'S BAY, Bute, **55°48'·15N 05°07'·86W**. AC 2383, 2221. Inchmarnock Is gives some shelter from the W, but Sound is exposed to S'lies. At S end, beware Shearwater Rk, 0·9m, almost in mid-sound. ⚓ in about 7m, 2ca E of St Ninian's Pt; beware drying spit to S of this Pt. Or ⚓ off E side of Inchmarnock, close abeam Midpark Farm.

WEST KYLE, Bute, **55°54'N 05°12'·7W**. AC1906. Tides, see 9.9.14 (Tighnabruaich). On W bank PHM buoys, each Fl R 4s, mark Ardlamont Pt, Carry Pt and Rubha Ban; N of which are two Fl Y buoys (fish farms). ⚓ close off Kames or Tighnabruaich, where space allows; or in Black Farland Bay (N of Rubha Dubh). There are some 🅜s on W side, some of which may not be safe though some are maintained by hotels: Karnes Hotel ☎ (01700) 811489; Kyles of Bute Hotel 811350; Royal Hotel 811239; and Tighnabruaich Hotel 811615. Facilities: FW, D (cans), BY, V.

CALADH HARBOUR, Argyll & Bute, **55°56'·00N, 05°11'·73W**. AC 1906. HW (Tighnabruaich) +0015 on Dover; ML 2·1m. See 9.9.14. Perfectly sheltered natural hbr on W side of ent to Loch Riddon. Enter Caladh Hbr to N or S of Eilean Dubh; keep to the middle of the S passage. When using the N ent, keep between R and G bns to clear a drying rk marked by perch. ⚓ in the middle of hbr; land at a stone slip on SW side. No facilities/stores; see West Kyle above.

LOCH RIDDON, Argyll & Bute, **55°57'N 05°11'·6W**. AC 1906. Tides, see 9.9.14. Water is deep for 1·3M N of Caladh and shore is steep-to; upper 1·5M of loch dries. ⚓ on W side close N of Ormidale pier; on E side at Salthouse; off Eilean Dearg (One Tree Is); and at NW corner of Fearnoch Bay.

BURNT ISLANDS, Bute, **55°55'·76N 05°10'·39W**. AC 1906. Tides, see 9.9.14. The three islands (Eilean Mor, Fraoich and Buidhe) straddle the East Kyle. There are 2 channels: North, between Buidhe and the other 2 islets, is narrow, short and marked by 2 SHM buoys (the NW'ly one is Fl G 3s), and one PHM buoy, Fl R 2s. South chan lies between Bute and Fraoich/Mor; it is unlit, but marked by one PHM and two SHM buoys. A SHM buoy, Fl G 3s, is off Rubha a' Bhodaich, 4ca ESE. Direction of buoyage is to SE. Sp streams reach 5kn in N Chan and 3kn in S Chan. ⚓ in Wreck Bay, Balnakailly Bay or in the lee of Buidhe and Mor in W'lies; also W of Colintraive Pt, clear of ferry and cables. There are 4 🅜s off the hotel, ☎ (01700) 84207.

KAMES BAY, Bute, **55°51'·7N 05°04'·81W**. AC 1867, 1906. Tides as Rothesay. Deep water bay, but dries 2ca off head of loch and 1ca off NW shore. ⚓ off Port Bannatyne (S shore) as space permits W of ruined jetty. Beware drying rks 1ca off Ardbeg Pt. No lts. Facilities: BY, FW, Gas, V, Bar, ✉.

KILCHATTAN BAY, Bute, **55°45'N 05°01'·1W**. AC 1907. Bay is deep, but dries 3ca off the W shore. Temp ⚓s only in offshore winds: off the village on SW side, or on N side near Kerrytonlia Pt. 🅜s for hotel guests. Rubh' an Eun Lt, Fl R 6s, is 1·1M to SSE. Facilities: FW, V, ✉, bus Rothesay.

ROTHESAY *9.9.14*

Isle of Bute, Argyll & Bute **55°50'·32N 05°03'·08W** ❀❀❀◊◊◊✿✿✿

CHARTS AC *1867, 1906, 1907, 2131;* Imray C63, 2900 Series; OS 63

TIDES +0100 Dover; ML 1·9; Duration 0640; Zone 0 (UT)

Standard Port GREENOCK (⟶)

Times				Height (metres)			
High Water		Low Water		MHWS	MHWN	MLWN	MLWS
0000	0600	0000	0600	3·4	2·8	1·0	0·3
1200	1800	1200	1800				
Differences ROTHESAY BAY							
−0020	−0015	−0010	−0002	+0·2	+0·2	+0·2	+0·2
RUBHA BHODACH (Burnt Is)							
−0020	−0010	−0007	−0007	−0·2	−0·1	+0·2	+0·2
TIGHNABRUAICH							
+0007	−0010	−0002	−0015	0·0	+0·2	+0·4	+0·5

SHELTER Good on yacht pontoons in Outer Hbr (2m) and at W end inside the Front pier (2m) (Mar-Oct). 40 ♦s WNW of pier or good ⚓ in bay ¼M W, off Isle of Bute SC; except in strong N/NE'lies when Kyles of Bute or Kames Bay offer better shelter.

NAVIGATION WPT 55°51'·00N 05°02'·76W, 014°/194° from/to Outer hbr ent, 0·69M. From E keep 1ca off Bogany Pt, and off Ardbeg Pt from N.

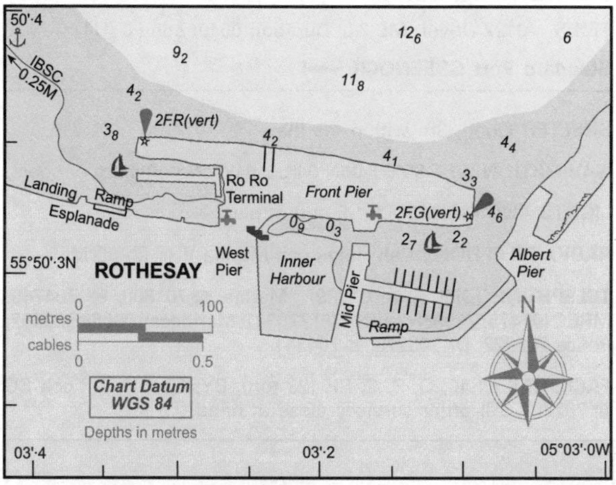

LIGHTS AND MARKS Lts as chartlet, hard to see against shore lts. Conspic Ch spire leads 190° to outer hbr; at night beware large, unlit Admiralty buoy "MK" on this brg 5½ca from hbr. 3½ca N of hbr is Rothesay 'A' mooring buoy, Fl Y 2s.

RADIO TELEPHONE VHF Ch 12 16 (1 May-30 Sept: 0600-2100; 1 Oct-30 Apl: 0600-1900 LT).

TELEPHONE (Dial code 01700) Hr Mr 503842; Berthing 500630; Moorings 504750; MRCC (01475) 729988; ⊖ (0141) 887 9369 (H24); Marinecall 09068 500462; Police 502121; Dr 503985; Ⓗ 503938.

FACILITIES **Outer Hbr** AB £1.49, AC, FW, Slip, D*, L, FW, ME, El, CH, ♿; **Inner Hbr** L, FW, AB,; **Front Pier (W)** FW, AC, R, ☐; **Albert Pier** D*, L, FW, C (4 ton mobile). **Town** EC Wed; P, D, CH, V, R, Bar, ✉, Ⓑ, ⇌ (ferry to Wemyss Bay), ✈ (Glasgow). *By arrangement (min 200 galls).

GREAT CUMBRAE ISLAND

MILLPORT, Great Cumbrae, N Ayrshire, 55°45'·00N 04°55'·82W. AC 1867, 1907. HW +0100 on Dover; ML 1·9m; Duration 0640. See 9.9.15. Good shelter, except in S'lies. ⚓ in approx 3m S of pier or E of the Eileans. 12 HIE ♦s 1½ca SSE of pier; call ☎ (01475) 530741. Ldg marks: pier hd on with ✠ twr 333°; or ldg lts 333°, both FR 7/9m 5M, between the Spoig and the Eileans, QG. Unmarked, drying rk is close E of ldg line. Hr Mr ☎ (01475) 530826. **Town** EC Wed; CH, Bar, Gas, D, P, FW, ✉, R, Slip, V.

LARGS *9.9.15*

N Ayrshire **55°46'·40N 04°51'·84W** ❀❀❀◊◊◊✿✿

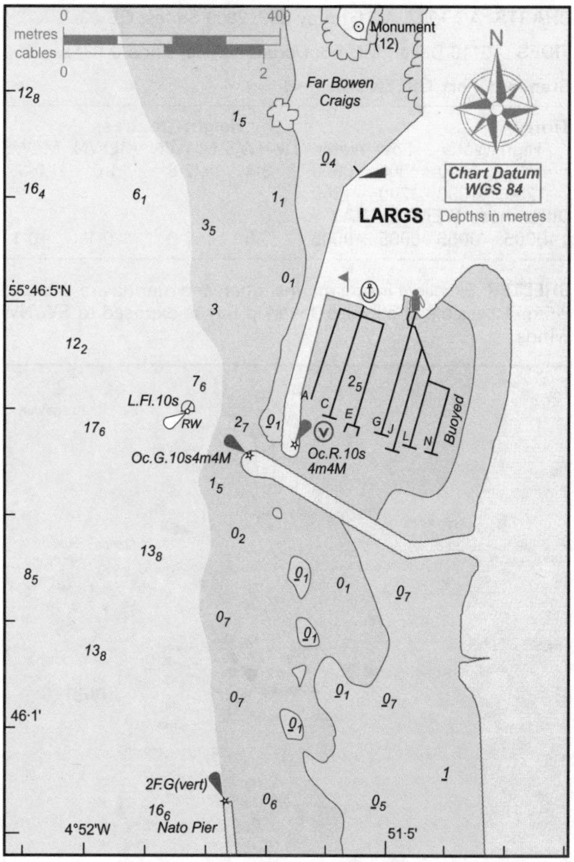

CHARTS AC 1867, 1907, *2131*; Imray C63, 2900 Series; OS 63

TIDES +0105 Dover; ML 1·9; Duration 0640; Zone 0 (UT)

Standard Port GREENOCK (⟶)

Times				Heights (metres)			
High Water		Low Water		MHWS	MHWN	MLWN	MLWS
0000	0600	0000	0600	3·4	2·8	1·0	0·3
1200	1800	1200	1800				
Differences MILLPORT							
−0005	−0025	−0025	−0005	0·0	−0·1	0·0	+0·1

SHELTER Excellent in Yacht Haven, access all tides (2·5m in ent; 3m deep berths). 6 pontoons; Ⓥ on 'C/D'. Cumbrae Is gives shelter from W'lies; Largs Chan is open to S or N winds.

NAVIGATION WPT 55°46'·40N 04°51'·84W, SWM buoy, L Fl 10s, off ent. From S beware Hunterston and Southannan sands and outfalls from Hunterston Power Stn (conspic). From the S bkwtr to the NATO pier is a restricted, no ⚓ area.

LIGHTS AND MARKS "Pencil" monument (12m) is conspic 4ca N of ent. Lts as on chartlet. Largs Pier, 2 FG (vert) when vessel expected.

RADIO TELEPHONE *Largs Yacht Haven* Ch **80** M (H24).

TELEPHONE (Dial code 01475) Yacht Haven 675333; MRCC 729988; ⊖ (0141) 308 3600 (H24); Dr 673380; Ⓗ 733777; Marinecall 09068 500 462; Police 674651.

FACILITIES **Yacht Haven** (630, some Ⓥ) ☎ 675333, 📠 672245, £1.88, FW, Fuel H24: D, P, LPG; AC, ♿, SM, BY, C (17 ton), ME, El, Sh, BH (45 ton), Divers, Ⓔ,CH, ☐, Gas, Gaz, Slip (access H24), Bar, R; **Largs SC** ☎ 670000; **Fairlie YC**; **Town** V, R, Bar, ✉, Ⓑ, ⇌ (dep Largs every H −10; 50 mins to Glasgow), ✈.

9

INVERKIP (KIP MARINA) *9.9.16*

Inverclyde **55°54′·50N 04°53′·00W** ❁❁❁◊◊◊✿✿

CHARTS AC *1907, 2131;* Imray C63, 2900 Series; OS 63

TIDES +0110 Dover; ML 1·8; Duration 0640; Zone 0 (UT)

Standard Port GREENOCK (⟶)

Times				**Height (metres)**			
High Water		Low Water		MHWS	MHWN	MLWN	MLWS
0000	0600	0000	0600	3·4	2·8	1·0	0·3
1200	1800	1200	1800				
Differences WEMYSS BAY							
−0005	−0005	−0005	−0005	0·0	0·0	+0·1	+0·1

SHELTER Excellent inside marina. Chan and marina are dredged 3·5m; accessible at all tides. Inverkip Bay is exposed to SW/NW winds.

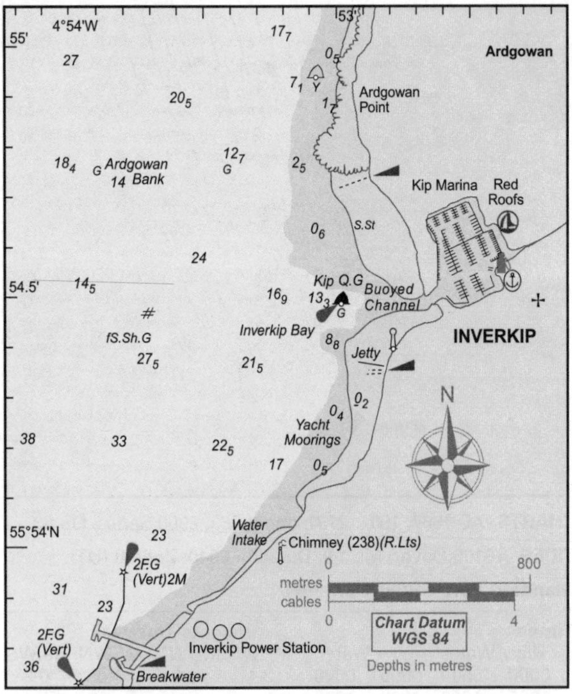

NAVIGATION WPT 55°54′·49N 04°52′·95W, Kip SHM buoy, QG, at ent to buoyed chan; beware shifting bank to the N.

LIGHTS AND MARKS SHM 55°54′·55N 04°54′·47W Fl G 1·06M 093° to entr which is ½M N of conspic chmy (238m). SPM buoy marks sewer outfall off Ardgowan Pt. From Kip SHM buoy, 3 SHM and 3 PHM buoys mark 365m long appr chan.

RADIO TELEPHONE VHF Ch **80** M (H24).

TELEPHONE (Dial code 01475) Hr Mr 521485; MRCC 729988; ⊖ (0141) 887 9369 (H24); Marinecall 09068 500462; Police 521222; Dr 520248; Ⓗ 33777.

FACILITIES Kip Marina (540+40 Ⓥ), ☎ 521485, 📠 521298, £1.59, AC, FW, D, P (cans), Sh, C, ME, El, Ⓔ, SM, CH, Diver, BH (50 ton), V, R, Bar, 🅻, Gas, Gaz, YC. **Town** ✉, Ⓑ (Gourock), ⇌, ✈ (Glasgow).

ADJACENT ANCHORAGES

DUNOON, Argyll and Bute, **55°56′·70N 04°55′·20W**. AC 1994, 1907, *2131.* Use Greenock tides. Temp ⚓ in West or East Bays (S and N of Dunoon Pt). The former is open to the S; the latter more shoal. Six HIE Ⓥs (free) in each bay; call ☎ (01369) 703785. The Gantocks, drying rks 3ca SE of Dunoon Pt, have W○ bn tr, Fl R 6s 12m 6M. 2FR (vert) on ferry pier. Facilities: P & D (cans), V, R, Bar, ✉, Gas, ferry to Gourock. 3 Ⓥs off Inellan, 3·7M S of Dunoon, ☎ (01369) 830445.

GOUROCK, Inverclyde **55°58′·00N 04°49′·00W** (As WPT) ❁❁❁◊✿. AC 1*994, 2131;* Imray C63, 2900 Series; OS 63. Use Greenock tides. Gourock: good ⚓ in West Bay, but open to N/NE winds. Greenock is a large port with a major container terminal (Clydeport) and other commercial facilities. Hbrs are controlled by Clyde Port Authority. Gourock WPT 55°57′·90N 04°49′·00W, 000°/180° from/to Kempock Pt, 1ca. No navigational dangers, but much shipping and ferries in the Clyde. The S edge of the Firth of Clyde recommended channel lies 2ca N of Kempock Pt. Beware foul ground in Gourock Bay. The pier at the S end of Gourock Bay is disused and unsafe. Call: *Clydeport Estuary Radio* VHF Ch 12 16 (H24). Info on weather and traffic available on request. (Dial codes: Gourock/Greenock 01475; Glasgow 0141) General Mgr Marine 725775; Estuary Control 726221; MRCC 729988; ⊖ (0141) 308 3618; Police 724444; Marinecall 09068 500462; Dr 634617. **Royal Gourock YC** ☎ 632983 M, L, FW, ME, V, R, Bar; **Services:** SM. **Town** EC Wed; P, D, V, R, Bar, ✉, Ⓑ, ⇌, ✈ (Glasgow).

HOLY LOCH *9.9.17*

Argyll **55°59′·06N 04°56′·84W** ❁❁❁◊◊◊✿✿✿

CHARTS AC 1*994, 2131;* Imray C63, 2900 Series; OS 63

TIDES +0122 Dover; ML 2·0; Duration 0640; Zone 0 (UT)

Standard Port GREENOCK (⟶)

SHELTER Good, 3m within marina

NAVIGATION WPT 55°59′·06N 04°56′·84W. No offshore dangers.

LIGHTS AND MARKS F.R SE end of pier.

RADIO TELEPHONE Call Holy Loch Marina VHF Ch 80 M.

TELEPHONE (Dial code 01369) Marina ☎ 701800, 📠 704749; MRCC (01475) 729988; ⊖ (01475) 726331; Marinecall 09068 500462; Police 702222; Dr 703279; Ⓗ 704341.

FACILITIES £1.40, D, P, C, BH (23 ton), BY, Gas, Holy Loch SC ☎ 702707. All other services close at hand.

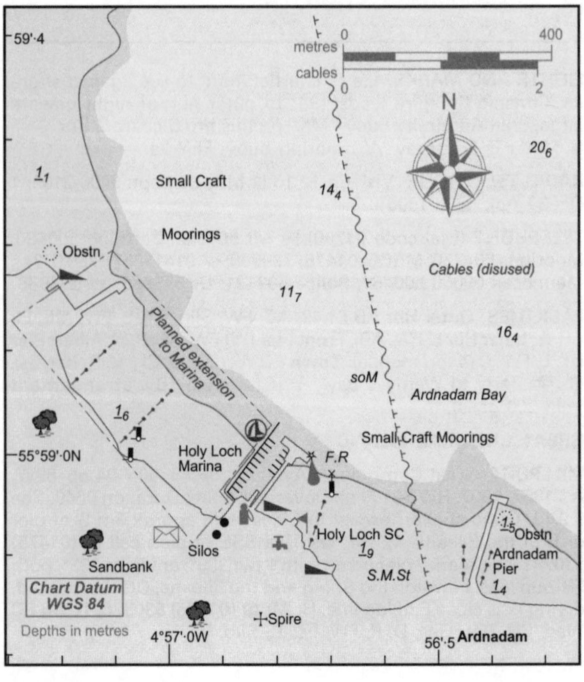

FIRTH OF CLYDE AREA *9.9.18*

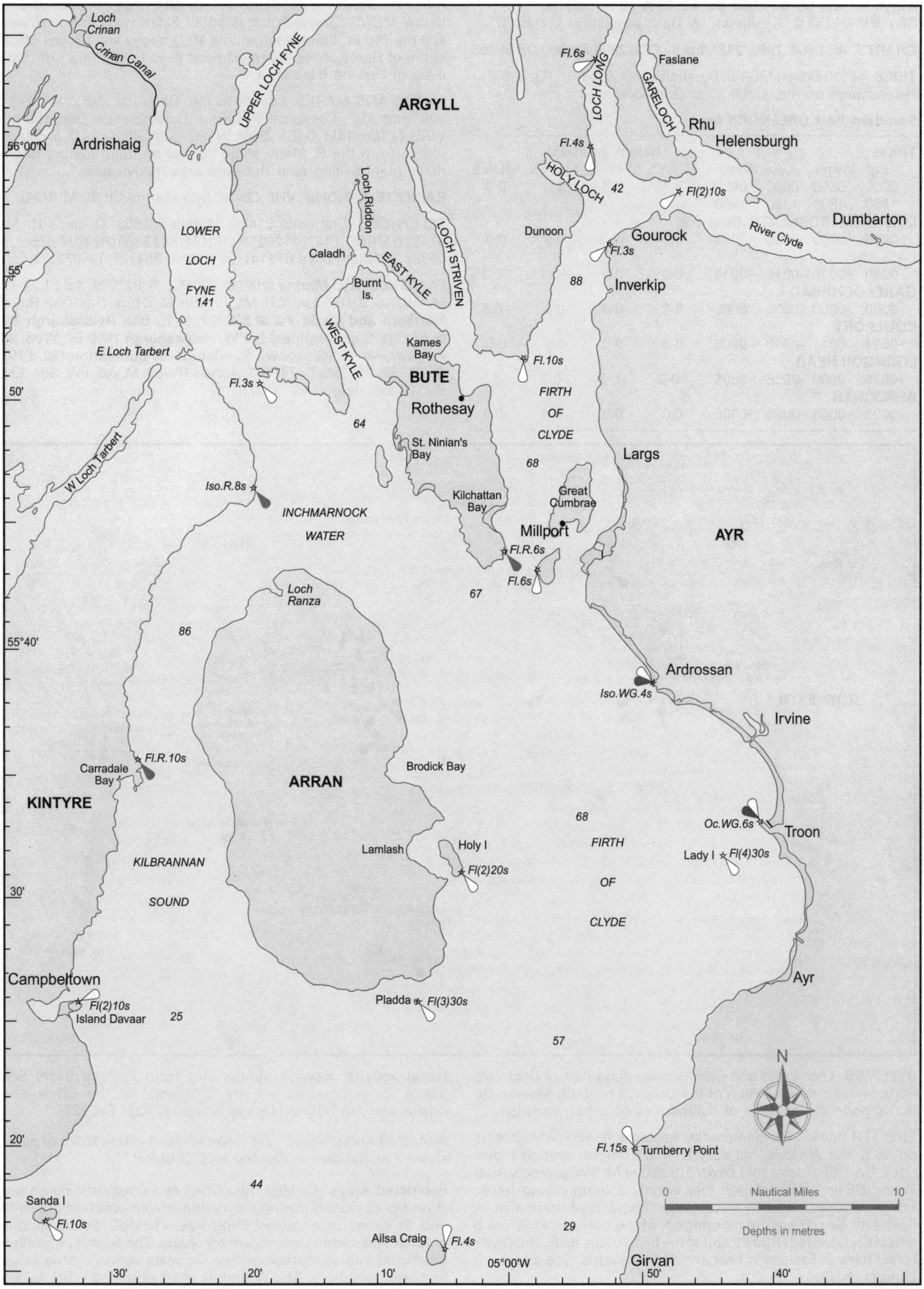

GARELOCH/RHU *9.9.19*

Argyll & Bute **56°00'·70N 04°46'·57W** (Rhu marina)
Rhu ❁❁❁◊◊✿✿; Sandpoint (W Dunbartonshire) ❁❁❁◊✿

CHARTS AC *2000, 1994, 2131;* Imray C63, 2900 Series; OS 56, 63

TIDES +0110 Dover; ML 1·9; Duration 0640; Zone 0 (UT). Tides at Helensburgh are the same as at Greenock

Standard Port GREENOCK (⟶)

Times				Height (metres)			
High Water		Low Water		MHWS	MHWN	MLWN	MLWS
0000	0600	0000	0600	3·4	2·8	1·0	0·3
1200	1800	1200	1800				
Differences ROSNEATH (Rhu pier)							
–0005	–0005	–0005	–0005	0·0	–0·1	0·0	0·0
FASLANE							
–0010	–0010	–0010	–0010	0·0	0·0	–0·1	–0·2
GARELOCHHEAD							
0000	0000	0000	0000	0·0	0·0	0·0	–0·1
COULPORT							
–0011	–0011	–0008	–0008	0·0	0·0	0·0	0·0
LOCHGOILHEAD							
+0015	0000	–0005	–0005	–0·2	–0·3	–0·3	–0·3
ARROCHAR							
–0005	–0005	–0005	–0005	0·0	0·0	–0·1	–0·1

NAVIGATION WPT 55°59'·29N 04°45'·26W, 176°/356° from/to bn No 7, 1·3M. Beaches between Cairndhu Pt and Helensburgh Pier (dries almost to the head) are strewn with large boulders above/ below MLWS. Gareloch ent is about 225m wide due to drying spit off Rhu Pt. Beware large unlit MoD buoys and barges off W shore of Gareloch; for Garelochhead keep to W shore until well clear of Faslane Base area.

LIGHTS AND MARKS Ldg/dir lts into Gareloch 356°, 318°, 295°, 329° and 331°. Conspic ✠ tr at Rhu. Gareloch Fuel Depot lt, Iso WRG 4s 10m 14M, G351°-356°, W356°-006°, R006°-011°, is clearly visible from the S. Many shore lts and an unlit floating boom make night sailing near the Base area inadvisable.

RADIO TELEPHONE VHF Ch 16. Rhu Marina Ch **80** M (H24).

TELEPHONE (Dial code 01436) Marina 820652; Queen's Hr Mr 674321; MRCC (01475) 729014; ⊖ (0141) 887 9369 (H24); Marinecall 09068 500462; Police 672141; Ⓗ (01389) 754121; Dr 672277.

FACILITIES **Rhu Marina** (200) ☎ 820652, 🖷 821039, AB £1.74, D, M, FW, AC, BH (35 ton), CH, ME, El, Slip, M, C hire, Gas, Gaz; **Royal Northern and Clyde YC** ☎ 820322, L, R, Bar; **Helensburgh SC** ☎ 672778 Slip (dinghies) L, FW; **Helensburgh** (1M) EC Wed; all services, ⇌, ✈ (Glasgow). **Sandpoint**, at Dumbarton (20, £10), ☎ (01389) 762396, 🖷 732605, Access HW±3, M, AC, FW, Slip, CH, BH (20 ton, vessels 80' x 20').

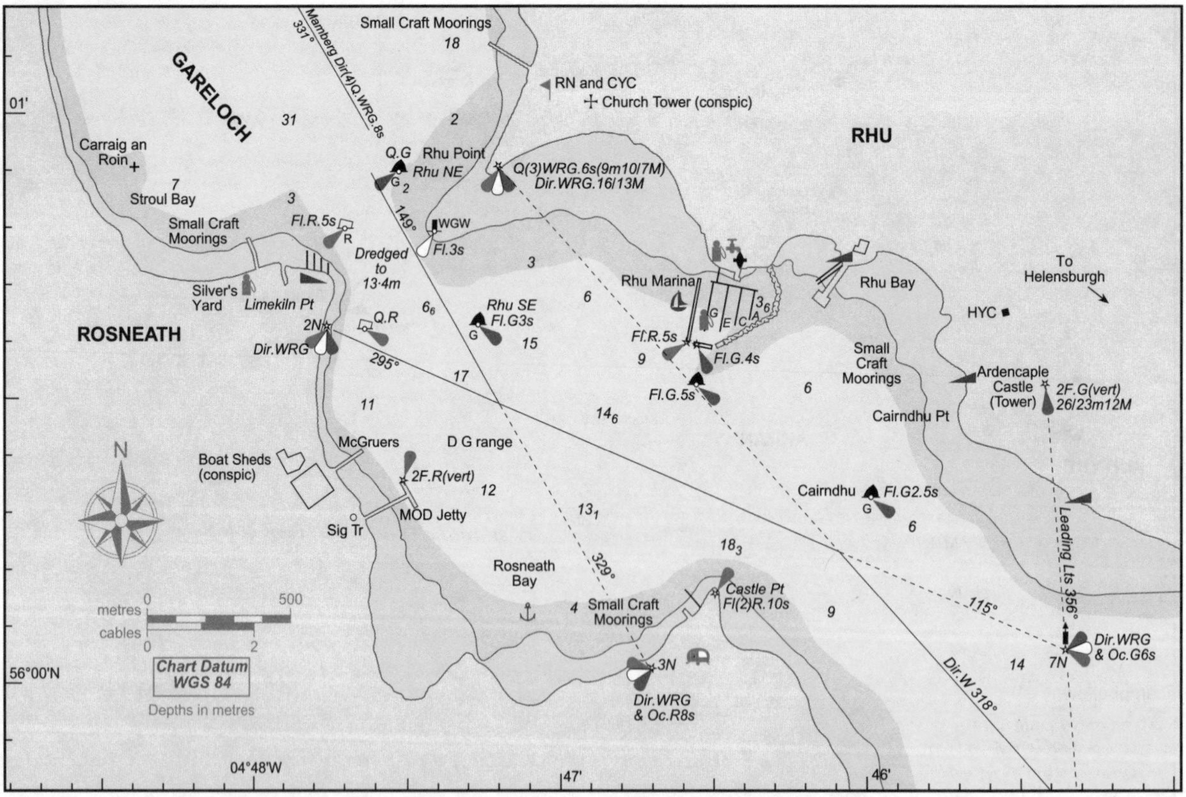

BYELAWS Loch Long and Gareloch are classified as Dockyard Ports under the jurisdiction of the Queen's Harbour Master. Do not impede the passage of submarines or other warships.

SHELTER Rhu Marina is entered between low, floating wavebreaks on its S and W sides, not easy to find at night; caution cross-tides. On E/SE sides a rock bkwtr 1m above MHWS protects from strong SE'lies. Helensburgh Pier is only a temp drying berth, rather exposed, used by occas steamers. ⚓ E of marina or in Rosneath Bay. There are moorings N of the narrows at Stroul B and at Clynder; N of Rhu Pt; and at the head of the loch. The Clyde Naval Base at Faslane is best avoided by yachts. See also Loch Long/Loch Goil.

Naval activity: Beware submarines from Faslane Base. See 9.9.24 for submarine activity (Subfacts) in the Clyde and offshore or call FOSNNI Ops ☎ (01436) 674321 Ext 3206.

Protected Areas: Vessels are never allowed within 150m of naval shore installations at Faslane and Coulport.

Restricted Areas (Faslane, Rhu Chan and Coulport): These are closed to all vessels during submarine movements (see opposite and *W Coast of Scotland Pilot*, App 2). MoD Police patrols enforce areas which are shown on charts. The S limit of Faslane Restricted area is marked by two Or posts with X topmarks on Shandon foreshore. The W limit is marked by Iso WRG 4s, vis

W356°-006°, at Gareloch Oil fuel depot N jetty. The following signals are shown when restrictions are in force:

1. Entrance to Gareloch
   by day : ● ● ● (vert), supplemented by R flag with W diagonal bar.
   by night : ● ● ● (vert).
2. Faslane and Coulport
   by day : 3 ● (vert), supplemented by International Code pendant over pendant Nine.
   by night : 3 ● (vert) in conspic position.

Holy Loch, Argyll & Bute, 55°58'·5N 04°54'·0W is no longer a restricted or protected area, but nominally is still under the control of QHM Clyde. A new marina is expected to open in 2000 at 55°59·00N 04°56·60W with 46 berths and most facilities increasing to 300 berths in future. £1.65 ☎ (01369) 701800, 📠 704749. VHF Ch M, 80. ⚓ not advised as the bottom is reported to be foul.

LOCH LONG/LOCH GOIL, Argyll and Bute, approx 56°00'N 04°52'·5W to 56°12'·00N 04°45'·00W. AC 3746. Tides: See 9.9.19 for differences. ML 1·7m; Duration 0645.

Shelter: Loch Long is about 15M long. Temp ⚓s (S→N) at Cove, Blairmore (not in S'lies), Ardentinny, Portincaple, Coilessan (about 1M S of Ardgartan Pt), and near head of loch (Arrochar) on either shore. In Loch Goil ⚓ at Swines Hole and off Carrick Castle (S of the pier, in N'lies a swell builds). Avoid ⚓ near Douglas Pier. The head of the loch is crowded with private/dinghy moorings, and is either too steep-to or too shallow to ⚓.

Lights: Coulport Jetty, 2FG (vert) each end and two Fl G 12s on N jetty; Port Dornaige Fl 6s 8m 11M, vis 026°-206°; Dog Rock (Carraig nan Ron) Fl 2s 11M; Finnart Oil Terminal has FG lts and ldg lts 031° QW/FW on Cnap Pt. Upper Loch Long is unlit. Loch Goil ent is marked by 2 PHM buoys (Fl R 3s and QR), a SHM buoy (QG) and ldg lts 318°: front (The Perch) Dir FWRG and Fl R 3s; rear FW. Rubha Ardnahein Fl R5s.

Facilities: Loch Long (Cove), Cove SC, FW, Bar; V, FW (pier); (Portincaple) shops, hotel, ✉, FW; (Ardentinny) shop, V, R, hotel, M; (Blairmore) shops, ✉, Slip, FW; (Arrochar) shops, hotel, FW, Gas, ✉. Loch Goil (Carrick Castle) has ✉, shop, hotel; (Lochgoilhead) has a store, ✉, hotel, FW, Gas.

DUMBARTON (SANDPOINT) AND BOWLING *9.9.20*

Inverclyde **55°60'·00N 04°34'·27W** ❀❀❀◊✿

CHARTS AC *1994, 2007, 2131:* BW Skipper's Guide for Forth and Clyde Canal, BW Skipper's Brief for Lowland Canals; Imray 63, 2900 Series.

TIDES +0122 Dover; ML 2·0; Duration 0640; Zone 0 (UT)

Standard Port GREENOCK (⟶)

Times				Height (metres)			
High Water		Low Water		MHWS	MHWN	MLWN	MLWS
0000	0600	0000	0600	3·4	2·8	1·0	0·3
1200	1800	1200	1800				
Differences PORT GLASGOW (55°56'·10N 04°40'·50W)							
+0010	+0005	+0010	+0020	+0·2	+0·1	0·0	0·0
DUMBARTON							
+0015	+0010	+0020	+0040	+0·4	+0·3	+0·1	0·0
BOWLING							
+0020	+0010	+0030	+0055	+0·6	+0·5	+0·3	+0·1
RENFREW							
+0025	+0015	+0035	+0100	+0·9	+0·8	+0·5	+0·2
GLASGOW							
+0025	+0015	+0035	+0105	+1·3	+1·2	+0·6	+0·4

SHELTER Good. From seaward, AB at: Dumbarton (Sandpoint marina), Bowling Hbr (within HO, lock access HW±2 to Basin and Forth & Clyde Canal); and at Renfrew Hbr for laying-up/repairs. Hbrs are controlled by Clyde Port Authority.

NAVIGATION WPT No 1 SHM buoy, FL G 5s, 55°57'·61N 04°45'·96W, 2ca NNW of Clydeport container terminal (conspic blue cranes). No navigational dangers, but much shipping and

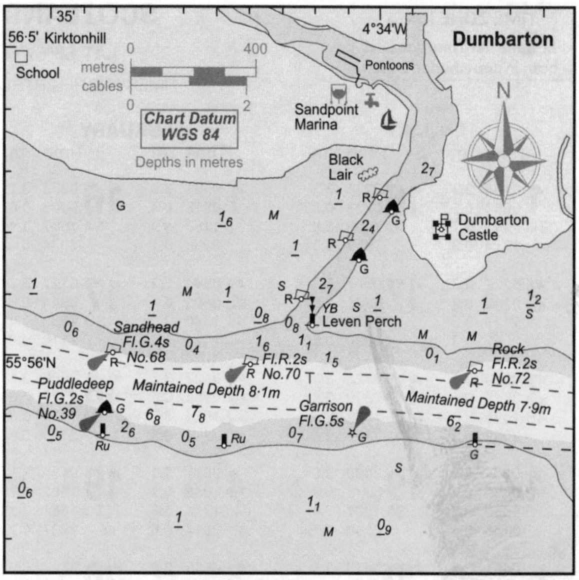

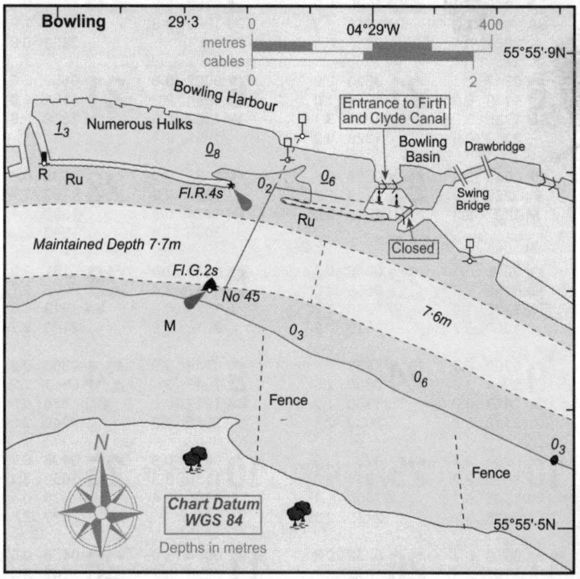

ferries in the Clyde. Keep just inboard of chan lateral marks as depths shoal rapidly outboard. For Dumbarton see plan follow buoyed ch closely. For Bowling Hbr (N bank) cross the river at 90° abeam No 45 SHM buoy, Fl G 2s; follow ldg marks as plan.

LIGHTS AND MARKS The R Clyde is well buoyed/lit, but yachts may not transit at night.

RADIO TELEPHONE Call *Clydeport Estuary Control* VHF Ch **12** 16 (H24) when appr No 1 buoy on way up river. Weather and traffic info on request. Marina Ch M. Lock Keeper Ch 16 74, HW±2.

TELEPHONE (Dial codes: Greenock 01475; Glasgow 0141, followed by 7 digit Tel No). General Mgr Marine 725775; Estuary Control 726221; British Waterways Board 332 6936, in emergency dial 100 and ask for Freephone Canals; MRCC 729988; ⊖ 308 3618; Dr 634617; Marinecall 09068 500462; 🅗 (01389) 754121.

FACILITIES **Sandpoint Marina** ☎ (01389) 762396, 731500, 📠 732605. £5 any LOA. Limited visitors berths. Call marina on Ch M and report to office on arrival. BH (40T), AC, FW, BY, D (can). **Town** V, R, Bar, Ⓑ, ✉, ≹ 30 mins to Glasgow. www.scottishcanals.co.uk. **Bowling Basin** 55°55'·8N 04°29'·0W ☎ (01389) 877969. W end of Forth and Clyde Canal. See 9.6.10 Lock hrs, call ahead for current position; call on VHF Ch 16 74 HW±2 as far ahead as possible. *Skipper's Brief* is essential. **Facilities:** AB £2.25m, FW, D by prior notice; lift out for max 7 ton craft. **Town** P&D (cans), V, R, Bar, ✉, Ⓑ, ≹ 40 mins to Glasgow.

TIME ZONE (UTC)
For Summer Time add ONE hour in **non-shaded areas**

SCOTLAND – GREENOCK

LAT 55°57′N LONG 4°46′W

TIMES AND HEIGHTS OF HIGH AND LOW WATERS

SPRING & NEAP TIDES
Dates in **red** are **SPRINGS**
Dates in **blue** are **NEAPS**

YEAR **2002**

JANUARY

Day	Time	m	Time	m	Time	m	Time	m
1 TU	0134	3.3	0654	0.5	1341	3.7	1914	0.3
2 W	0222	3.3	0742	0.5	1423	3.8	2002	0.3
3 TH	0310	3.3	0832	0.6	1506	3.8	2052	0.3
4 F	0359	3.2	0924	0.7	1552	3.7	2146	0.4
5 SA	0451	3.2	1019	0.8	1641	3.6	2244	0.5
6 SU	0547	3.1	1119	0.9	1735	3.5	2348	0.6
7 M	0648	3.0	1225	1.0	1837	3.3		
8 TU	0055	0.7	0759	3.0	1335	1.0	1950	3.2
9 W	0202	0.7	0914	3.0	1443	0.9	2115	3.2
10 TH	0304	0.7	1015	3.2	1543	0.7	2223	3.2
11 F	0359	0.7	1106	3.3	1634	0.6	2319	3.2
12 SA	0447	0.7	1151	3.4	1719	0.5		
13 SU	0008	3.2	0531	0.7	1233	3.5	● 1801	0.4
14 M	0053	3.2	0611	0.7	1311	3.6	1839	0.4
15 TU	0134	3.2	0650	0.8	1348	3.6	1917	0.4
16 W	0211	3.2	0726	0.8	1423	3.6	1953	0.5
17 TH	0247	3.2	0803	0.8	1457	3.6	2030	0.5
18 F	0323	3.2	0840	0.8	1532	3.5	2109	0.6
19 SA	0400	3.2	0919	0.9	1607	3.4	2150	0.7
20 SU	0438	3.1	1000	0.9	1646	3.3	2236	0.8
21 M	0520	3.0	1046	1.0	1728	3.1	2329	0.9
22 TU	0606	2.9	1140	1.2	1818	3.0		
23 W	0029	0.9	0658	2.9	1243	1.2	1916	2.9
24 TH	0133	0.9	0800	2.8	1350	1.2	2030	2.8
25 F	0236	0.9	0915	2.9	1458	1.1	2149	2.9
26 SA	0333	0.8	1022	3.1	1557	0.8	2254	3.0
27 SU	0424	0.6	1114	3.3	1647	0.6	2347	3.1
28 M	0510	0.5	1200	3.4	1732	0.4	○	
29 TU	0038	3.2	0555	0.4	1245	3.6	1816	0.2
30 W	0128	3.3	0641	0.4	1330	3.7	1902	0.1
31 TH	0216	3.3	0728	0.3	1413	3.8	1948	0.0

FEBRUARY

Day	Time	m	Time	m	Time	m	Time	m
1 F	0301	3.3	0815	0.4	1457	3.9	2035	0.1
2 SA	0344	3.3	0903	0.4	1540	3.9	2124	0.2
3 SU	0427	3.3	0953	0.5	1624	3.7	2216	0.3
4 M	0511	3.2	1048	0.7	1710	3.6	2314	0.6
5 TU	0558	3.0	1152	0.8	1800	3.3		
6 W	0022	0.8	0654	2.9	1307	0.9	1859	3.1
7 TH	0138	0.9	0823	2.9	1424	0.9	2035	2.9
8 F	0249	1.0	0952	3.0	1529	0.8	2216	2.9
9 SA	0349	0.9	1049	3.1	1622	0.6	2316	3.0
10 SU	0439	0.8	1136	3.3	1708	0.4		
11 M	0004	3.0	0522	0.7	1219	3.4	1747	0.3
12 TU	0047	3.1	0559	0.7	1258	3.5	● 1824	0.3
13 W	0124	3.1	0633	0.6	1334	3.5	1857	0.3
14 TH	0157	3.1	0704	0.6	1407	3.5	1929	0.4
15 F	0227	3.1	0736	0.6	1437	3.4	2001	0.4
16 SA	0256	3.1	0809	0.6	1507	3.4	2034	0.4
17 SU	0327	3.2	0844	0.6	1539	3.4	2110	0.5
18 M	0400	3.1	0921	0.6	1613	3.3	2150	0.6
19 TU	0436	3.1	1002	0.7	1651	3.1	2237	0.7
20 W	0517	3.0	1051	0.9	1734	2.9	2333	0.8
21 TH	0604	2.8	1151	1.0	1829	2.8		
22 F	0038	0.9	0703	2.7	1300	1.1	1943	2.7
23 SA	0151	1.0	0825	2.7	1418	1.0	2121	2.7
24 SU	0306	0.8	0951	2.9	1534	0.8	2240	2.9
25 M	0406	0.7	1052	3.1	1630	0.4	2337	3.1
26 TU	0455	0.5	1142	3.4	1716	0.2		
27 W	0027	3.2	0539	0.3	1229	3.6	○ 1759	0.0
28 TH	0116	3.3	0623	0.2	1314	3.7	1843	-0.1

MARCH

Day	Time	m	Time	m	Time	m	Time	m
1 F	0200	3.3	0707	0.1	1358	3.8	1926	-0.1
2 SA	0241	3.4	0751	0.1	1441	3.9	2011	-0.1
3 SU	0319	3.4	0837	0.2	1522	3.9	2057	0.1
4 M	0355	3.4	0924	0.3	1603	3.8	2144	0.3
5 TU	0433	3.3	1016	0.5	1645	3.5	2238	0.6
6 W	0515	3.1	1118	0.7	1730	3.2	2345	0.9
7 TH	0605	2.9	1241	0.9	1824	2.9		
8 F	0114	1.1	0711	2.8	1405	0.9	1938	2.7
9 SA	0233	1.1	0928	2.8	1510	0.7	2212	2.7
10 SU	0335	1.0	1030	3.0	1604	0.5	2306	2.9
11 M	0424	0.8	1118	3.2	1648	0.4	2350	3.0
12 TU	0505	0.7	1200	3.3	1726	0.3		
13 W	0028	3.0	0539	0.6	1239	3.4	1800	0.2
14 TH	0103	3.0	0609	0.5	1314	3.3	● 1831	0.3
15 F	0133	3.0	0637	0.5	1344	3.3	1900	0.3
16 SA	0159	3.1	0705	0.4	1411	3.3	1929	0.3
17 SU	0225	3.1	0736	0.4	1439	3.3	2000	0.3
18 M	0253	3.2	0810	0.4	1511	3.3	2035	0.3
19 TU	0325	3.2	0846	0.4	1545	3.2	2115	0.4
20 W	0358	3.1	0927	0.5	1621	3.0	2200	0.6
21 TH	0434	3.0	1016	0.7	1702	2.9	2255	0.8
22 F	0517	2.8	1116	0.8	1755	2.7		
23 SA	0001	0.9	0615	2.7	1227	0.9	1914	2.6
24 SU	0117	1.0	0742	2.7	1348	0.8	2104	2.6
25 M	0241	0.9	0922	2.8	1511	0.6	2227	2.8
26 TU	0346	0.6	1029	3.1	1608	0.3	2322	3.0
27 W	0435	0.4	1120	3.4	1655	0.0		
28 TH	0010	3.2	0519	0.2	1208	3.6	○ 1737	-0.1
29 F	0055	3.3	0601	0.1	1254	3.7	1819	-0.2
30 SA	0137	3.4	0644	0.0	1339	3.8	1902	-0.1
31 SU	0215	3.4	0726	0.0	1421	3.8	1945	0.0

APRIL

Day	Time	m	Time	m	Time	m	Time	m
1 M	0250	3.5	0810	0.1	1502	3.8	2030	0.2
2 TU	0325	3.4	0856	0.2	1541	3.7	2115	0.4
3 W	0402	3.3	0946	0.4	1623	3.4	2205	0.7
4 TH	0443	3.2	1047	0.7	1708	3.1	2309	1.1
5 F	0532	3.0	1216	0.8	1802	2.8		
6 SA	0044	1.3	0635	2.8	1339	0.8	1915	2.6
7 SU	0205	1.3	0848	2.7	1442	0.7	2150	2.6
8 M	0308	1.1	1002	2.9	1535	0.5	2241	2.8
9 TU	0358	0.9	1050	3.1	1619	0.4	2322	2.9
10 W	0438	0.7	1132	3.2	1657	0.3	2359	3.0
11 TH	0512	0.6	1210	3.2	1731	0.2		
12 F	0032	3.0	0541	0.5	1245	3.2	● 1801	0.3
13 SA	0102	3.0	0607	0.4	1314	3.2	1829	0.3
14 SU	0127	3.1	0635	0.4	1341	3.2	1858	0.3
15 M	0153	3.2	0706	0.3	1412	3.2	1931	0.3
16 TU	0222	3.2	0741	0.3	1445	3.2	2008	0.3
17 W	0254	3.3	0819	0.3	1521	3.1	2050	0.4
18 TH	0328	3.2	0903	0.4	1559	3.0	2137	0.6
19 F	0403	3.1	0954	0.5	1643	2.8	2233	0.7
20 SA	0446	2.9	1056	0.7	1742	2.6	2339	0.9
21 SU	0546	2.8	1209	0.7	1908	2.6		
22 M	0055	1.0	0714	2.7	1329	0.7	2050	2.6
23 TU	0215	0.9	0854	2.9	1445	0.4	2206	2.8
24 W	0321	0.6	1002	3.1	1542	0.2	2300	3.0
25 TH	0412	0.4	1056	3.4	1630	0.0	2346	3.2
26 F	0457	0.2	1144	3.5	1713	-0.1		
27 SA	0030	3.3	0539	0.0	1231	3.6	○ 1755	-0.1
28 SU	0111	3.4	0621	0.0	1317	3.7	1838	0.0
29 M	0148	3.4	0704	0.0	1400	3.7	1922	0.2
30 TU	0224	3.5	0748	0.1	1442	3.6	2007	0.3

Chart Datum: 1·62 metres below Ordnance Datum (Newlyn)

Register for your **FREE** weekly weather email service from Macmillan Reeds
at **www.nauticaldata.com – NOW!**
weekend weather reports sent to your email address, every Thursday

TIME ZONE (UTC)
For Summer Time add ONE hour in **non-shaded areas**

SCOTLAND – GREENOCK

LAT 55°57′N LONG 4°46′W

TIMES AND HEIGHTS OF HIGH AND LOW WATERS

SPRING & NEAP TIDES
Dates in red are SPRINGS
Dates in blue are NEAPS

YEAR **2002**

MAY

Day	Time	m	Day	Time	m
1 W	0300	3.5	**16** TH	0232	3.3
	0833	0.2		0801	0.2
	1523	3.5		1505	3.0
	2053	0.6		2035	0.4
2 TH	0338	3.4	**17** F	0307	3.3
	0923	0.4		0849	0.3
	1606	3.3		1548	2.9
	2142	0.8		2125	0.6
3 F	0419	3.2	**18** SA	0346	3.2
	1023	0.6		0943	0.4
	1653	3.0		1639	2.8
	2241	1.1		2221	0.7
4 SA	0508	3.0	**19** SU	0432	3.1
	1144	0.8		1046	0.5
	1749	2.8		1745	2.7
				2325	0.8
5 SU	0000	1.3	**20** M	0534	2.9
	0608	2.8		1156	0.5
	1302	0.8		1904	2.6
	1857	2.6			
6 M	0120	1.3	**21** TU	0035	0.9
	0734	2.7		0656	2.9
	1404	0.7		1310	0.5
	2049	2.6		2025	2.7
7 TU	0226	1.2	**22** W	0146	0.8
	0916	2.8		0824	3.0
	1457	0.6		1417	0.3
	2156	2.7		2136	2.9
8 W	0320	1.0	**23** TH	0252	0.6
	1012	3.0		0934	3.2
	1543	0.4		1515	0.2
	2242	2.9		2232	3.0
9 TH	0404	0.8	**24** F	0348	0.4
	1056	3.1		1030	3.3
	1623	0.3		1605	0.1
	2321	2.9		2320	3.1
10 F	0440	0.6	**25** SA	0436	0.2
	1134	3.1		1120	3.4
	1658	0.3		1651	0.1
	2356	3.0			
11 SA	0511	0.5	**26** SU	0004	3.3
	1208	3.1		0520	0.1
	1729	0.3		1209	3.5
				○ 1735	0.1
12 SU	0026	3.1	**27** M	0046	3.3
	0539	0.4		0604	0.1
	1240	3.1		1256	3.5
	● 1759	0.3		1819	0.2
13 M	0055	3.1	**28** TU	0125	3.4
	0609	0.3		0647	0.1
	1311	3.1		1341	3.4
	1831	0.3		1904	0.4
14 TU	0124	3.2	**29** W	0203	3.5
	0642	0.3		0731	0.1
	1347	3.1		1425	3.4
	1908	0.3		1950	0.5
15 W	0157	3.3	**30** TH	0241	3.5
	0720	0.2		0817	0.2
	1425	3.1		1508	3.3
	1949	0.4		2036	0.7
			31 F	0320	3.4
				0906	0.4
				1553	3.1
				2124	0.8

JUNE

Day	Time	m	Day	Time	m
1 SA	0401	3.3	**16** SU	0338	3.4
	1000	0.5		0935	0.3
	1640	3.0		1640	2.9
	2215	1.0		2211	0.6
2 SU	0447	3.1	**17** M	0426	3.3
	1104	0.7		1035	0.3
	1733	2.8		1741	2.8
	2313	1.1		2309	0.7
3 M	0541	3.0	**18** TU	0524	3.1
	1215	0.7		1140	0.4
	1829	2.7		1845	2.8
4 TU	0019	1.2	**19** W	0011	0.7
	0644	2.8		0632	3.1
	1318	0.7		1246	0.4
	1929	2.7		1952	2.8
5 W	0127	1.2	**20** TH	0117	0.7
	0758	2.8		0749	3.1
	1413	0.6		1350	0.3
	2036	2.7		2101	2.9
6 TH	0229	1.1	**21** F	0224	0.6
	0913	2.8		0904	3.1
	1502	0.6		1449	0.3
	2142	2.8		2203	3.0
7 F	0321	0.9	**22** SA	0326	0.5
	1009	2.9		1007	3.2
	1545	0.5		1544	0.3
	2234	2.9		2256	3.1
8 SA	0403	0.8	**23** SU	0420	0.4
	1052	2.9		1102	3.2
	1624	0.4		1634	0.3
	2315	3.0		2344	3.2
9 SU	0440	0.6	**24** M	0508	0.2
	1130	3.0		1153	3.3
	1659	0.4		1721	0.4
	2352	3.1		○	
10 M	0514	0.5	**25** TU	0027	3.3
	1207	3.0		0552	0.2
	1734	0.4		1242	3.2
	●			1806	0.5
11 TU	0026	3.2	**26** W	0109	3.4
	0548	0.4		0636	0.2
	1246	3.0		1329	3.2
	1811	0.4		1851	0.5
12 W	0101	3.3	**27** TH	0148	3.4
	0625	0.3		0719	0.2
	1328	3.0		1414	3.1
	1852	0.4		1936	0.6
13 TH	0138	3.3	**28** F	0226	3.5
	0706	0.2		0802	0.3
	1412	3.0		1457	3.1
	1937	0.4		2019	0.7
14 F	0216	3.4	**29** SA	0304	3.4
	0751	0.2		0845	0.4
	1457	3.0		1539	3.0
	2026	0.4		2102	0.7
15 SA	0256	3.4	**30** SU	0343	3.3
	0841	0.2		0931	0.5
	1546	2.9		1622	3.0
	2117	0.5		2145	0.8

JULY

Day	Time	m	Day	Time	m
1 M	0424	3.2	**16** TU	0416	3.5
	1021	0.6		1015	0.2
	1706	2.9		1720	3.0
	2230	0.9		2246	0.5
2 TU	0508	3.1	**17** W	0506	3.4
	1118	0.7		1114	0.3
	1752	2.9		1812	2.9
	2319	1.0		2345	0.6
3 W	0557	2.9	**18** TH	0603	3.2
	1220	0.8		1219	0.4
	1840	2.8		1909	2.9
4 TH	0016	1.1	**19** F	0049	0.7
	0651	2.8		0708	3.1
	1320	0.8		1325	0.5
	1930	2.8		2020	2.8
5 F	0119	1.1	**20** SA	0201	0.7
	0753	2.7		0831	3.0
	1415	0.7		1430	0.6
	2028	2.8		2137	2.9
6 SA	0224	1.1	**21** SU	0311	0.6
	0903	2.8		0951	3.0
	1505	0.7		1531	0.6
	2135	2.8		2238	3.0
7 SU	0323	0.9	**22** M	0410	0.5
	1006	2.8		1054	3.0
	1551	0.6		1625	0.6
	2234	2.9		2329	3.2
8 M	0411	0.7	**23** TU	0501	0.3
	1057	2.9		1148	3.1
	1633	0.5		1714	0.6
	2320	3.0			
9 TU	0453	0.6	**24** W	0014	3.3
	1143	3.0		0544	0.2
	1714	0.5		1238	3.1
				○ 1758	0.6
10 W	0002	3.2	**25** TH	0056	3.4
	0533	0.4		0625	0.2
	1229	3.0		1323	3.1
	● 1756	0.4		1839	0.6
11 TH	0043	3.3	**26** F	0135	3.4
	0613	0.3		0704	0.2
	1316	3.0		1404	3.0
	1840	0.4		1918	0.6
12 F	0123	3.4	**27** SA	0212	3.4
	0656	0.2		0741	0.3
	1405	3.0		1441	3.0
	1926	0.4		1955	0.6
13 SA	0205	3.5	**28** SU	0247	3.4
	0742	0.1		0819	0.4
	1453	3.0		1517	3.0
	2013	0.4		2032	0.7
14 SU	0247	3.5	**29** M	0321	3.4
	0829	0.1		0857	0.4
	1541	3.0		1553	3.0
	2102	0.4		2109	0.7
15 M	0330	3.5	**30** TU	0355	3.3
	0920	0.1		0937	0.6
	1630	3.0		1630	3.0
	2152	0.4		2148	0.7
			31 W	0432	3.2
				1021	0.7
				1709	3.0
				2230	0.8

AUGUST

Day	Time	m	Day	Time	m
1 TH	0512	3.0	**16** F	0531	3.3
	1112	0.8		1148	0.7
	1751	2.9		1820	2.9
	2318	1.0			
2 F	0559	2.9	**17** SA	0024	0.8
	1212	0.9		0628	3.0
	1838	2.8		1304	0.9
				1925	2.8
3 SA	0014	1.1	**18** SU	0146	0.9
	0656	2.7		0752	2.8
	1317	0.9		1419	0.9
	1932	2.8		2115	2.8
4 SU	0120	1.1	**19** M	0302	0.8
	0807	2.7		0952	2.8
	1422	0.9		1525	0.9
	2040	2.8		2224	3.0
5 M	0237	1.0	**20** TU	0401	0.6
	0927	2.7		1056	3.0
	1521	0.8		1619	0.8
	2154	2.9		2316	3.2
6 TU	0344	0.8	**21** W	0450	0.4
	1036	2.9		1147	3.0
	1611	0.7		1705	0.7
	2253	3.0			
7 W	0435	0.6	**22** TH	0001	3.3
	1130	3.0		0531	0.3
	1657	0.5		1232	3.1
	2341	3.2		○ 1745	0.7
8 TH	0518	0.4	**23** F	0042	3.4
	1219	3.1		0609	0.2
	1740	0.4		1311	3.1
	●			1820	0.7
9 F	0025	3.4	**24** SA	0120	3.4
	0559	0.2		0643	0.3
	1308	3.1		1347	3.1
	1823	0.4		1853	0.7
10 SA	0108	3.5	**25** SU	0154	3.4
	0641	0.0		0715	0.3
	1356	3.2		1418	3.1
	1908	0.3		1924	0.6
11 SU	0151	3.6	**26** M	0225	3.4
	0725	0.0		0746	0.4
	1441	3.2		1447	3.1
	1953	0.3		1956	0.6
12 M	0234	3.7	**27** TU	0254	3.4
	0810	0.0		0819	0.5
	1524	3.2		1517	3.2
	2039	0.3		2030	0.6
13 TU	0316	3.7	**28** W	0325	3.3
	0857	0.1		0853	0.5
	1605	3.2		1549	3.2
	2127	0.4		2106	0.6
14 W	0358	3.7	**29** TH	0357	3.2
	0947	0.2		0931	0.7
	1646	3.2		1624	3.1
	2218	0.5		2146	0.7
15 TH	0443	3.5	**30** F	0434	3.1
	1043	0.5		1016	0.8
	1730	3.1		1703	3.0
	2316	0.6		2231	0.9
			31 SA	0516	2.9
				1111	1.0
				1748	2.9
				2326	1.1

Chart Datum: 1·62 metres below Ordnance Datum (Newlyn)

Register for your **FREE** weekly weather email service from Macmillan Reeds
at **www.nauticaldata.com – NOW!**
weekend weather reports sent to your email address, every Thursday

9

TIME ZONE (UTC)
For Summer Time add ONE hour in **non-shaded areas**

SCOTLAND – GREENOCK

LAT 55°57′N LONG 4°46′W

TIMES AND HEIGHTS OF HIGH AND LOW WATERS

SPRING & NEAP TIDES
Dates in red are SPRINGS
Dates in blue are NEAPS

YEAR **2002**

SEPTEMBER

Date	Day	Time	m	Time	m	Time	m	Time	m
1	SU	0612	2.7	1218	1.1	1844	2.8		
2	M	0032	1.2	0726	2.6	1337	1.1	1955	2.8
3	TU	0152	1.1	0901	2.7	1454	1.0	2120	2.9
4	W	0319	0.9	1024	2.9	1551	0.8	2228	3.1
5	TH	0414	0.6	1119	3.1	1637	0.6	2319	3.3
6	F	0458	0.3	1207	3.2	1720	0.5		
7	SA	0005	3.5	0539	0.1	1253	3.3	● 1801	0.3
8	SU	0050	3.7	0619	0.0	1337	3.3	1844	0.3
9	M	0133	3.8	0701	-0.1	1418	3.4	1927	0.2
10	TU	0216	3.9	0744	0.0	1456	3.4	2012	0.3
11	W	0257	3.9	0829	0.2	1533	3.4	2058	0.4
12	TH	0337	3.8	0916	0.4	1610	3.4	2148	0.5
13	F	0418	3.6	1008	0.7	1651	3.2	2246	0.7
14	SA	0504	3.3	1115	1.0	1739	3.1		
15	SU	0003	0.9	0557	3.0	1247	1.2	1839	2.9
16	M	0135	1.0	0719	2.7	1408	1.3	2053	2.9
17	TU	0247	0.8	0955	2.8	1512	1.2	2207	3.1
18	W	0344	0.6	1050	3.0	1604	1.0	2257	3.3
19	TH	0430	0.5	1134	3.1	1647	0.9	2340	3.4
20	F	0510	0.3	1213	3.2	1724	0.8		
21	SA	0020	3.5	0544	0.3	1248	3.2	○ 1755	0.7
22	SU	0057	3.5	0616	0.3	1319	3.2	1824	0.7
23	M	0129	3.4	0644	0.4	1347	3.2	1851	0.6
24	TU	0158	3.4	0712	0.5	1413	3.3	1921	0.6
25	W	0225	3.4	0742	0.5	1441	3.3	1954	0.6
26	TH	0255	3.3	0815	0.6	1511	3.3	2029	0.6
27	F	0327	3.3	0852	0.7	1545	3.3	2108	0.7
28	SA	0402	3.1	0935	0.9	1621	3.2	2154	0.9
29	SU	0442	2.9	1029	1.1	1703	3.0	2251	1.0
30	M	0536	2.7	1137	1.2	1758	2.9	2359	1.1

OCTOBER

Date	Day	Time	m	Time	m	Time	m	Time	m
1	TU	0659	2.6	1258	1.3	1916	2.8		
2	W	0120	1.1	0844	2.7	1424	1.2	2048	2.9
3	TH	0249	0.9	1010	2.9	1525	0.9	2201	3.2
4	F	0347	0.5	1102	3.2	1613	0.7	2254	3.4
5	SA	0432	0.3	1147	3.3	1656	0.5	2341	3.6
6	SU ●	0514	0.1	1230	3.4	1737	0.3		
7	M	0027	3.8	0554	0.0	1311	3.5	1818	0.3
8	TU	0112	3.9	0635	0.0	1350	3.6	1901	0.2
9	W	0155	3.9	0718	0.1	1427	3.6	1945	0.3
10	TH	0236	3.9	0802	0.3	1502	3.6	2031	0.4
11	F	0316	3.8	0848	0.6	1540	3.6	2121	0.6
12	SA	0357	3.6	0939	0.9	1621	3.4	2220	0.8
13	SU	0443	3.3	1044	1.3	1709	3.2	2344	1.0
14	M	0539	2.9	1222	1.5	1810	3.0		
15	TU	0112	1.0	0708	2.7	1342	1.5	2008	3.0
16	W	0219	0.9	0937	2.9	1446	1.4	2137	3.1
17	TH	0315	0.7	1027	3.0	1538	1.2	2229	3.3
18	F	0401	0.6	1107	3.2	1620	1.0	2313	3.4
19	SA	0441	0.5	1143	3.3	1657	0.8	2352	3.5
20	SU	0515	0.4	1216	3.3	1727	0.8		
21	M	0028	3.4	0545	0.5	1247	3.3	○ 1754	0.7
22	TU	0100	3.4	0613	0.5	1314	3.4	1821	0.7
23	W	0128	3.3	0641	0.6	1340	3.4	1850	0.6
24	TH	0156	3.3	0711	0.6	1408	3.5	1923	0.6
25	F	0228	3.3	0745	0.6	1440	3.5	2000	0.6
26	SA	0303	3.3	0825	0.8	1514	3.5	2042	0.7
27	SU	0340	3.1	0910	0.9	1549	3.4	2130	0.8
28	M	0421	3.0	1004	1.1	1630	3.2	2228	1.0
29	TU	0517	2.8	1112	1.3	1724	3.1	2338	1.0
30	W	0643	2.7	1230	1.3	1842	3.0		
31	TH	0057	1.0	0822	2.8	1349	1.2	2014	3.1

NOVEMBER

Date	Day	Time	m	Time	m	Time	m	Time	m
1	F	0214	0.8	0942	3.0	1454	1.0	2130	3.3
2	SA	0314	0.5	1035	3.2	1546	0.8	2227	3.5
3	SU	0403	0.3	1121	3.4	1631	0.5	2316	3.7
4	M ●	0447	0.2	1203	3.5	1714	0.4		
5	TU	0003	3.8	0529	0.1	1244	3.6	1756	0.3
6	W	0050	3.9	0611	0.2	1323	3.7	1839	0.3
7	TH	0134	3.9	0655	0.4	1401	3.7	1924	0.3
8	F	0217	3.8	0740	0.6	1439	3.8	2011	0.5
9	SA	0259	3.7	0828	0.8	1517	3.7	2101	0.6
10	SU	0343	3.5	0919	1.1	1600	3.6	2200	0.8
11	M	0431	3.2	1021	1.4	1648	3.4	2315	1.0
12	TU	0529	3.0	1141	1.5	1747	3.2		
13	W	0035	1.0	0644	2.8	1300	1.6	1907	3.1
14	TH	0141	1.0	0842	2.9	1405	1.5	2048	3.1
15	F	0237	0.8	0943	3.0	1501	1.3	2150	3.3
16	SA	0325	0.7	1027	3.2	1547	1.1	2238	3.3
17	SU	0406	0.6	1105	3.3	1626	0.9	2319	3.4
18	M	0443	0.6	1141	3.3	1658	0.8	2356	3.3
19	TU	0516	0.6	1213	3.4	1728	0.8		
20	W	0029	3.3	0545	0.6	1243	3.5	○ 1756	0.7
21	TH	0100	3.3	0615	0.6	1311	3.5	1827	0.7
22	F	0132	3.3	0648	0.7	1343	3.6	1902	0.6
23	SA	0208	3.3	0726	0.7	1417	3.6	1941	0.6
24	SU	0246	3.2	0809	0.8	1452	3.6	2026	0.6
25	M	0327	3.1	0857	0.9	1530	3.5	2116	0.7
26	TU	0413	3.0	0951	1.1	1613	3.4	2214	0.8
27	W	0512	2.9	1054	1.2	1706	3.2	2321	0.8
28	TH	0627	2.8	1204	1.2	1816	3.2		
29	F	0031	0.8	0748	2.9	1314	1.2	1936	3.2
30	SA	0140	0.7	0904	3.0	1420	1.0	2054	3.3

DECEMBER

Date	Day	Time	m	Time	m	Time	m	Time	m
1	SU	0241	0.5	1003	3.2	1517	0.8	2158	3.5
2	M	0335	0.4	1053	3.4	1608	0.6	2252	3.6
3	TU	0423	0.3	1138	3.5	1655	0.4	2342	3.7
4	W ●	0509	0.4	1221	3.6	1739	0.4		
5	TH	0031	3.7	0553	0.4	1302	3.7	1824	0.3
6	F	0118	3.7	0639	0.6	1342	3.8	1909	0.4
7	SA	0204	3.6	0726	0.7	1422	3.8	1956	0.4
8	SU	0248	3.5	0814	0.9	1502	3.8	2046	0.6
9	M	0333	3.4	0903	1.1	1545	3.7	2139	0.7
10	TU	0421	3.2	0955	1.2	1630	3.5	2238	0.9
11	W	0513	3.1	1054	1.4	1722	3.3	2346	1.0
12	TH	0610	3.0	1201	1.5	1821	3.2		
13	F	0052	1.0	0710	2.9	1310	1.5	1928	3.1
14	SA	0152	0.9	0818	2.9	1413	1.4	2046	3.1
15	SU	0244	0.9	0927	3.0	1507	1.2	2152	3.1
16	M	0330	0.8	1020	3.1	1552	1.1	2242	3.1
17	TU	0411	0.7	1104	3.3	1630	0.9	2324	3.2
18	W	0448	0.7	1141	3.4	1705	0.8		
19	TH	0001	3.2	0522	0.7	1215	3.4	○ 1737	0.7
20	F	0037	3.2	0557	0.7	1248	3.5	1812	0.6
21	SA	0115	3.2	0634	0.7	1323	3.6	1849	0.6
22	SU	0155	3.2	0714	0.7	1400	3.6	1931	0.5
23	M	0237	3.2	0759	0.7	1439	3.6	2016	0.5
24	TU	0321	3.1	0847	0.8	1519	3.6	2105	0.5
25	W	0408	3.1	0938	0.8	1603	3.5	2159	0.5
26	TH	0500	3.0	1034	0.9	1652	3.4	2259	0.6
27	F	0559	2.9	1135	1.0	1749	3.3		
28	SA	0002	0.6	0703	2.9	1240	1.0	1854	3.3
29	SU	0108	0.6	0816	3.0	1347	1.0	2011	3.2
30	M	0211	0.6	0928	3.1	1452	0.8	2128	3.3
31	TU	0311	0.6	1028	3.2	1550	0.7	2233	3.4

Chart Datum: 1·62 metres below Ordnance Datum (Newlyn)

Register for your FREE weekly weather email service from Macmillan Reeds
at www.nauticaldata.com – NOW!
weekend weather reports sent to your email address, every Thursday

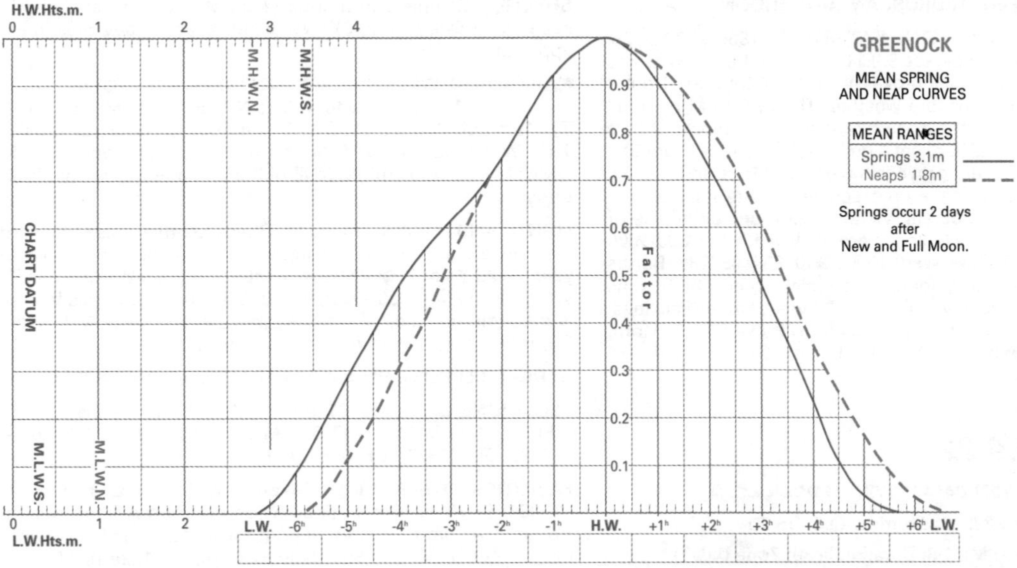

ARDROSSAN *9.9.21*

N Ayrshire **55°38'·50N 04°49'·61W**

CHARTS AC *1866*, *2491*, 2221, *2126*; Imray C63; OS 63/70

TIDES +0055 Dover; ML 1·9; Duration 0630; Zone 0 (UT)

Standard Port GREENOCK (⟵)

Times				**Height (metres)**			
High Water		Low Water		MHWS	MHWN	MLWN	MLWS
0000	0600	0000	0600	3·4	2·8	1·0	0·3
1200	1800	1200	1800				
Differences ARDROSSAN							
−0020	−0010	−0010	−0010	−0·2	−0·2	+0·1	+0·1
IRVINE							
−0020	−0020	−0030	−0010	−0·3	−0·3	−0·1	0·0

SHELTER Good in marina (formerly Eglinton Dock), access at all tides over sill, 5·2m least depth. A storm gate is fitted; max acceptable beam is 8·6m (28ft). Strong SW/NW winds cause heavy seas in the apprs and the hbr may be closed in SW gales. Ferries berth on both sides of Winton Pier.

NAVIGATION WPT 55°38'·13N 04°50'·55W, 235°/055° from/to hbr ent, 0·65M. From the W/NW keep clear of low-lying Horse Isle (conspic W tower on its S end) ringed by drying ledges. The passage between Horse Isle and the mainland is obstructed by unmarked drying rks and should not be attempted. Be aware of following dangers: From the S/SE, Eagle Rk 3ca S of hbr ent, marked by SHM buoy, Fl G 5s. 3ca SE of Eagle Rk lies unmarked Campbell Rk (0·2m). W Crinan Rk (1·1m) is 300m W of hbr ent, marked by PHM buoy, Fl R 4s.

LIGHTS AND MARKS Dir lt WRG 15m W14M, R/G11M (see 9.9.4); W sector leads 055° to hbr ent between lt ho and detached bkwtr. Lt ho Iso WG 4s 11m 9M, G317°-035°, W elsewhere. On S end of detached bkwtr, Fl WR 2s 7m 5M, R041°-126°, W elsewhere.

Tfc signals, shown H24 from control twr at ent to marina:

3 F ● lts (vert) = hbr and marina closed; no entry/exit for commercial and pleasure vessels.

3 F ● lts (vert) = marina open, hbr closed; pleasure craft may enter/exit the marina, no commercial movements.

2 F ● lts over 1 F ● = hbr open, marina closed; in severe weather marina storm gate is closed. Commercial vessels may enter/exit hbr, subject to approval by Hbr Control on VHF. Pleasure craft must clear the approach channel, ferry turning area (between the detached bkwtr and Winton Pier) and the outer basin. Yachts may not manoeuvre under sail alone until to seaward of the outer breakwater.

RADIO TELEPHONE *Clyde Marina* VHF Ch **80** M. *Hbr Control* Ch 12 14 16 (H24).

TELEPHONE (Dial code 01294) Marina 607077, Fax 607076; Control Twr 463972, Fax 605305; MRCC (01475) 729988; ⊖ (0141) 887 9369 (H24); Marinecall 09068 500462; Police 468236; Dr 463011; Ⓗ (01563) 521133.

FACILITIES **Clyde Marina** (250+50 Ⓥ) ☎ 607077, Fax 607076, £1.41, access all tides. D, AC, FW, ME, El, Ⓔ, CH, BH (20 ton). **Town** EC Wed; V, R, Bar, ⓞ, Gas, Gaz, ✉, Ⓑ, ⇌, ✈ (Prestwick/Glasgow). Ferry to Brodick (Arran).

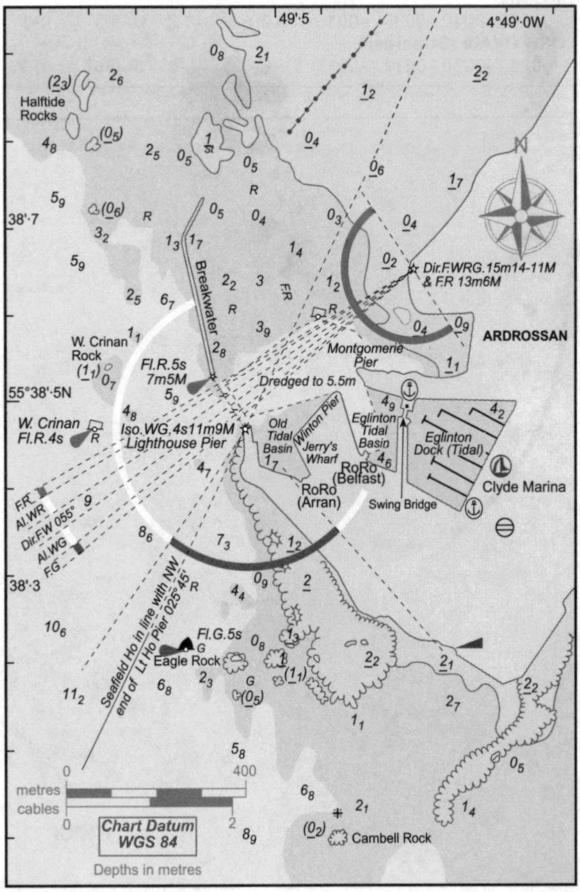

HARBOUR BETWEEN ARDROSSAN AND TROON

IRVINE, N Ayrshire, 55°36'·17N 04°42'·07W. AC 1866, 2220, *2126*. HW +0055 on Dover. Tides: see 9.9.21. Good shelter once across the bar (0·5m CD); access approx HW ±3½ for 1·4m draft. Do not attempt ent in heavy onshore weather. The IB-B SPM buoy, Fl Y 3s, is 1·15M from hbr ent, close NW of ldg line. 5 blocks of flats and chys are conspic ENE of ent. Ldg lts 051°: front, FG 10m 5M; rear, FR 15m 5M. The ent groynes have bns, Fl R 3s and Fl G 3s; groynes inside the ent have unlit perches. White Pilot tr with mast is conspic 3ca inside ent. Visitors' pontoons on N side or on S side at visitors' quay (2·2m). ⚓ prohib. VHF Ch 12 (0800-1600 Tues and Thurs; 0800-1300 Wed). Hr Mr ☎ (01294) 487286. Berths available above opening footbridge which opens at 5 mins notice ☎ 08708 403123 or VHF Ch 12 (call *Irvine Bridge*). Facilities: **Quay** AB <5m £4, >5m <10m £6, >10m <15m £9, FW, Slip, C (3 ton), Showers, SM. **Town** P & D (cans, 1·5km), Gas, V, R, ≈, ✈ (Prestwick).

TROON *9.9.22*

S Ayrshire **55°33'·10N 04°40'·97W** ✽✽✽◊◊◊✿✿

CHARTS AC *1866, 2220, 2126*; Imray C63; OS 70

TIDES +0050 Dover; ML 1·9; Duration 0630; Zone 0 (UT)

Standard Port GREENOCK (⟵)

Times				**Height (metres)**			
High Water		Low Water		MHWS	MHWN	MLWN	MLWS
0000	0600	0000	0600	3·4	2·8	1·0	0·3
1200	1800	1200	1800				
Differences TROON							
–0025	–0025	–0020	–0020	–0·2	–0·2	0·0	0·0
AYR							
–0025	–0025	–0030	–0015	–0·4	–0·3	+0·1	+0·1
GIRVAN							
–0025	–0040	–0035	–0010	–0·3	–0·3	–0·1	0·0
LOCH RYAN (Stranraer)							
–0020	–0020	–0017	–0017	–0·4	–0·4	–0·4	–0·2

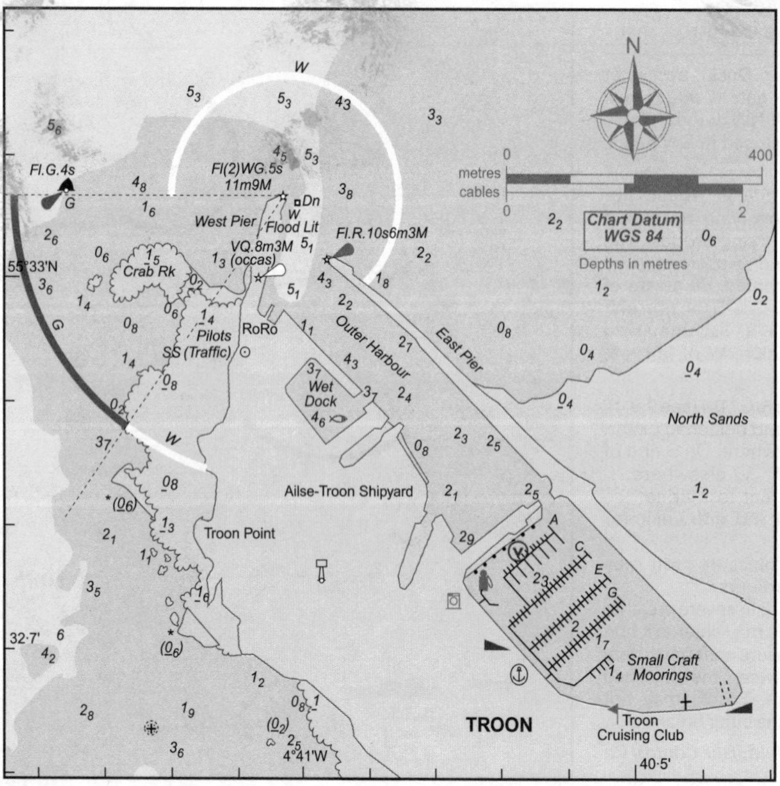

SHELTER Complete in marina (2·4m at ent, 1·6m at SE end); speed limit 5kn. Strong SW/NW winds cause heavy seas in the apprs. Inside hbr.

NAVIGATION WPT 55°33'·20N 04°42'·00W, 283°/103° from/to W pier lt, 0·61M. Appr in sector SW to NW. Beware Lady Isle, Fl (4) 30s 19m 8M, W bn, 2·2M SW; Troon Rock (5·6m, occas breaks) 1·1M W; Lappock Rock (0̲·6m, bn with G barrel topmark) 1·6M NNW; Mill Rock (0̲·4m) ½M NNE of hbr ent, marked by unlit PHM buoy.

LIGHTS AND MARKS No ldg lts. Sheds (35m) at Ailsa Shipyard are conspic and floodlit at night. Ent sigs (not applicable to yachts): 2B ●s or 2F● lts (vert) = ent/exit prohib. W pier hd Fl (2) WG 5s 11m 9M, G036°-090°, W090°-036°. 14m SE of this lt there is a floodlit dolphin, W with dayglow patches. A SHM lt buoy, FG, marks the chan in the ent to marina.

RADIO TELEPHONE Hr Mr VHF Ch 16 14. Marina VHF Ch **80** M (H24).

TELEPHONE (Dial code 01292) Hr Mr 281687; Marina 315553; MRCC (01475) 729988; ⊜ 478548; Marinecall 09068 500 462; Police 313100; Dr 313593; Ⓗ 610555 (Ayr).

FACILITIES **Troon Yacht Haven** (250+50 Ⓥ) ☎ 315553, 📠 312836, £1.73, access all tides. Ⓥ on pontoon A, first to stbd. AB for LOA 36m x 3m draft at pontoon ends. D (H24), LPG, FW, ME, El, Ⓔ, CH, AC, Sh , SM (daily pick-up), BH (12 ton), C (2 ton), Slip, V, R ☎ 311523, Bar, 🅾, Gas, Gaz; **Troon CC** ☎ 311865; **Troon YC** ☎ 316770. **Town** EC Wed; ✉, Ⓑ, ≈, ✈ (Prestwick/Glasgow). Fast RoRo ferry to Belfast.

HARBOURS ON THE FIRTH OF CLYDE SOUTH OF TROON

AYR, S Ayrshire, **55°28'·22N 04°38'·78W**. AC 1866, 2220, *2126*. HW +0050 on Dover; ML 1·8m. Duration 0630. See 9.9.22. After heavy rains large amounts of debris may be washed down the R Ayr. From the W, hbr ent lies between conspic gasholder to the N and townhall spire to the S. Outer St Nicholas SHM buoy, Fl G 2s, warns of shoals and eponymous Rock (0̲·8m) 150m S of ent. Ldg lts 098°: front, by Pilot Stn, FR 10m 5M R tr, also tfc sigs; rear (130m from front), Oc R 10s 18m 9M. N bkwtr hd, QR 9m 5M. S pier hd, Q 7m 7M, vis 012°-161°, and FG 5m 5M, same structure, vis 012°-082°, over St Nicholas Rk. Tfc sigs (near front ldg lt): 2 ● (vert) = hbr closed to incoming traffic. Hr Mr ☎ (01292) 281687; VHF Ch 14 16; ⊜ 478548; **Ayr Y & CC** at S dock, M. **Services**: Sh, ME, El, CH. **Town** EC Wed; Ⓑ, Bar, Gas, P & D, FW, ✉, R, ≈, V.

GIRVAN, S Ayrshire, **55°14'·77N 04°51'·87W**. AC 1866, 2199. HW +0043 on Dover; ML 1·8m; Duration 0630. See 9.9.22. Good shelter at inner hbr for 16 yachts on 60m pontoon (1·7m) beyond LB. Coasters and FVs berth on adjacent quay. No access LW±2 over bar 1·5m. Beware Girvan Patch, 1·7m, 4ca SW of ent, and Brest Rks, 3·5M N of hbr extending 6ca offshore. Ch spire (conspic) brg 104° leads between N bkwtr, Fl (2) R 6s 7m 4M, and S pier, 2 FG (vert) 8m 4M. Inner N groyne, Iso 4s 3m 4M. Tfc sigs at root of S pier: 2 B discs (hor), at night 2 ● (hor) = hbr shut. VHF Ch 12 16 (HO). Hr Mr ☎ (01465) 713648, 📠 714454; FW, Slip. **Town** EC Wed; Ⓑ, ✉, V, R, ≈, P & D (cans).

ANCHORAGES WITHIN LOCH RYAN

LOCH RYAN, Dumfries and Galloway, **55°01´N 05°05´W**. AC 1403, 2198. HW (Stranraer) +0055 on Dover; ML 1·6m; Duration 0640. See 9.9.22. Very good shelter except in strong NW winds. Ent between Milleur Pt and Finnarts Pt. ⚓s in Lady Bay, 1·3M SSE of Milleur Pt, but exposed to heavy wash from fast catamaran ferries; in The Wig in 3m (avoid weed patches); or off Stranraer 3ca NW of W pier hd. Larger yachts berth on NE side of E pier, by arrangement with Hr Mr, VHF Ch 14 (H24) or ☎ (01776) 702460. Beware The Beef Barrel, rk 1m high 6ca SSE of Milleur Pt; the sand spit running 1·5M to SE from W shore opposite Cairn Pt lt ho Fl (2) R 10s 14m 12M. Lt at Cairnryan ferry terminal Fl R 5s 5m 5M. Lts at Stranraer: centre pier hd 2FBu (vert), E pier hd 2FR (vert), W pier hd 2 FG (vert) 8m 4M. Facilities (Stranraer): EC Wed; Ⓑ, Bar, D, FW, P, ✉, R, ≷, V.

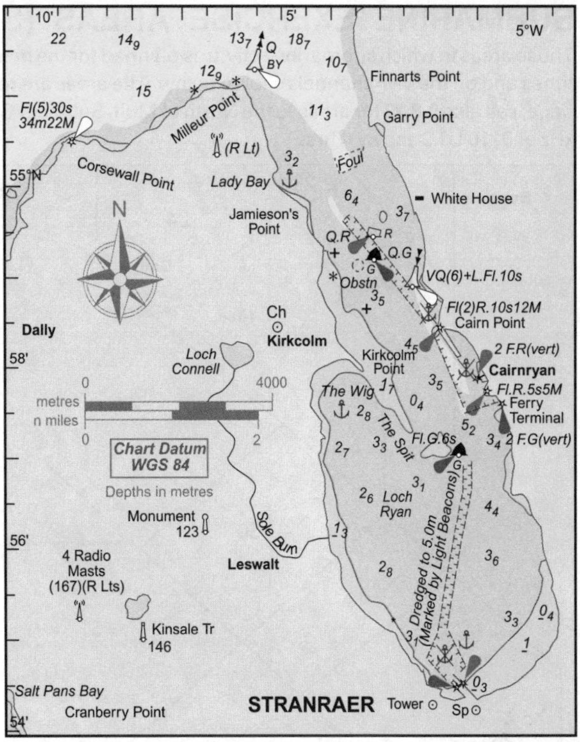

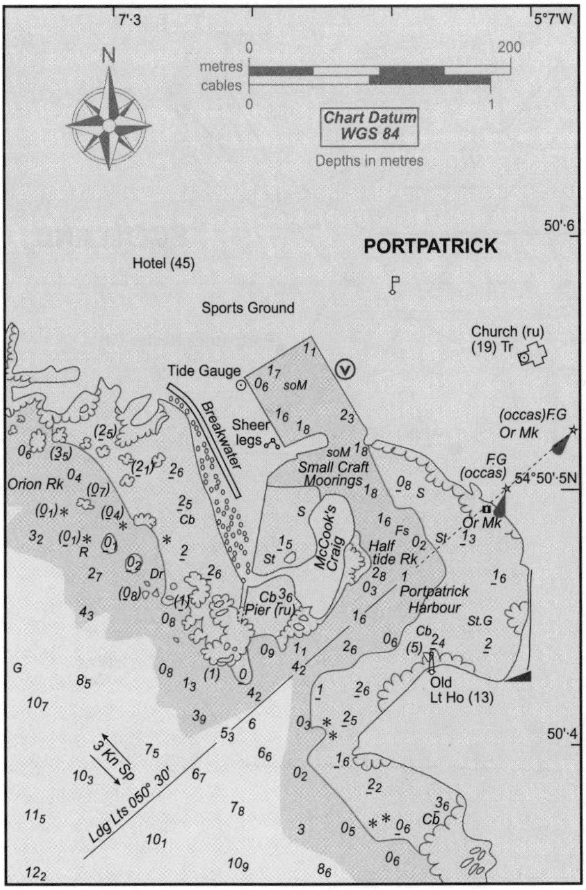

PORTPATRICK *9.9.23*

Dumfries and Galloway **54°50´·42N 05°07´·18W**

CHARTS AC 2198, *2724*; Imray C62; OS 82

TIDES +0032 Dover; ML 2·1; Duration 0615; Zone 0 (UT)

Standard Port LIVERPOOL (⟶)

Times				**Heights (metres)**			
High Water		Low Water		MHWS	MHWN	MLWN	MLWS
0000	0600	0200	0800	9·3	7·4	2·9	0·9
1200	1800	1400	2000				
Differences PORTPATRICK							
+0018	+0026	0000	−0035	−5·5	−4·4	−2·0	−0·6

SHELTER Good in tiny Inner hbr, but ent is difficult in strong SW/NW winds. Beware cross tides off ent, up to 3kn springs.

NAVIGATION WPT 54°50´·00N 05°08´·07W, 235°/055° from/to ent, 0·70M. Ent to outer hbr by short narrow chan with hazards either side, including rky shelf covered at HW. Barrel buoy (a mooring buoy) marks end of Half Tide Rk; do not cut inside.

LIGHTS AND MARKS Killantringan lt ho, Fl (2) 15s 49m 25M, is 1.6M NW of ent. Ldg lts 050°, FG (H24) 6/8m: Front on sea wall; rear on bldg; 2 vert orange stripes by day. Conspic features include: TV mast 1M NE, almost on ldg line; large hotel on cliffs about 1½ca NNW of hbr ent; Dunskey Castle (ru) 4ca SE of hbr.

RADIO TELEPHONE None.

TELEPHONE (Dial code 01776) Hr Mr 810355; MRSC (01475) 729988; ⊖ (0141) 887 9369 (H24); Marinecall 09068 500462; Police 810222; Ⓗ 702323.

FACILITIES **Hbr** Slip (small craft), AB £6, M, FW, L. Note: Pontoons are planned in inner hbr, to be dredged approx 2·5m. **Village** EC Thurs; P (cans), D (bulk tanker), Gas, V, R, Bar, ✉, Ⓑ (Stranraer), ≷ (bus to Stranraer), ✈ (Carlisle).

9

SUBMARINE EXERCISE AREAS (SUBFACTS) *9.9.24*

Those areas in which submarine activity is planned for the next 16 hrs are broadcast by Coastguard Coordination Centres at the times and on the VHF channels shown below. The areas are referred to not by numbers, but by names as listed on the previous page; see also 9.8.23 for areas to the North of Mull. Subfacts/Gunfacts are also broadcast by Stornoway on Ch 10 or 73 and 1743 kHz at 0110 UTC and ev 4 hrs.

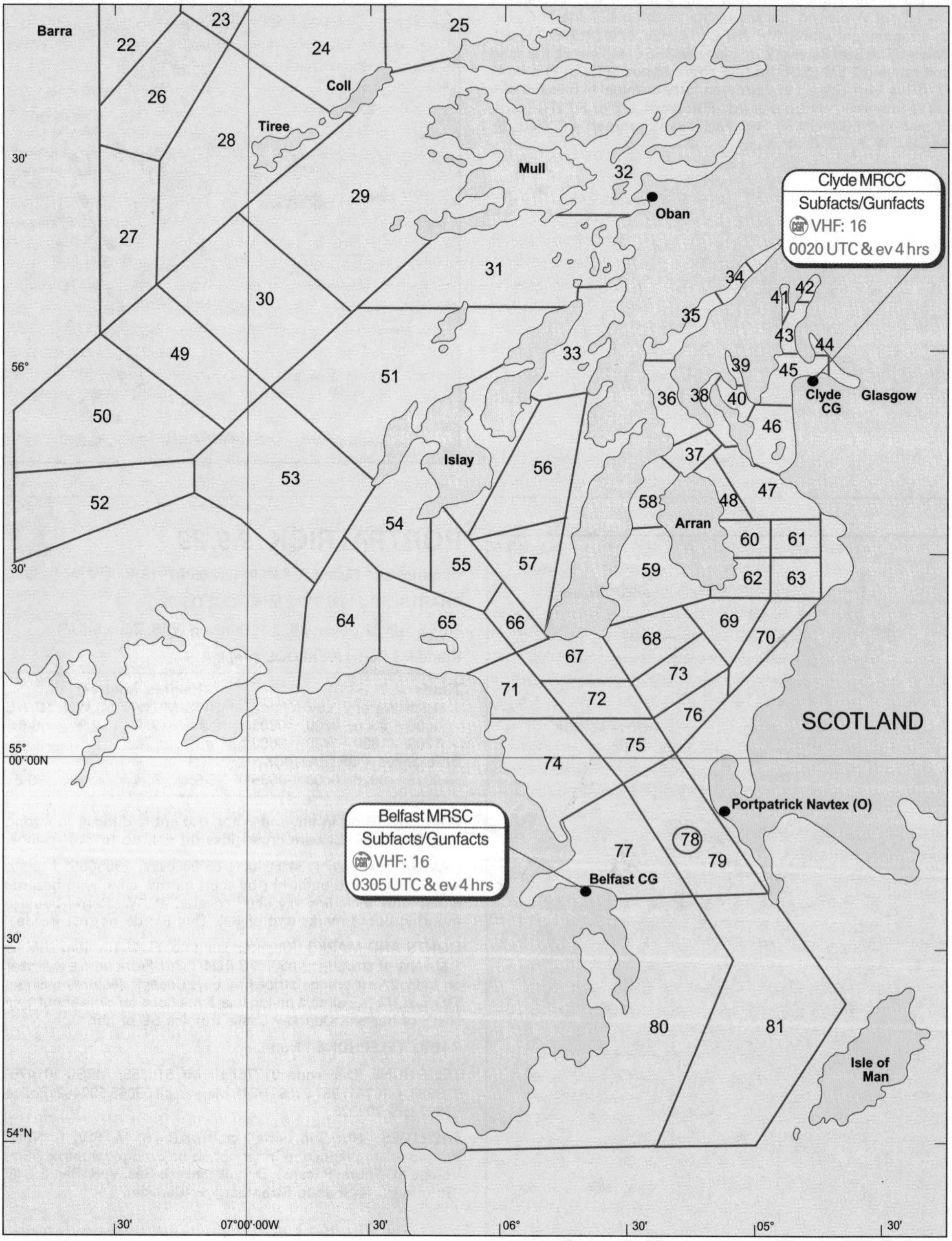

SUBMARINE EXERCISE AREAS *9.9.24*

Obtaining Subfacts and Gunfacts

Subfacts for areas between Barra and the Isle of Man are broadcast by the Coastguard Radio Stations below on a notified VHF Ch, after an initial announcement on Ch 16, at the following times:

Stornoway	0110 0510 0910 1310 1710 and 2110 UTC
Clyde	0020 0420 0820 1220 1620 and 2020 UTC
Belfast	0305 0705 1105 1505 1905 and 2305 UTC

During notified NATO exercises, Subfacts are also broadcast on MF SSB by Stornoway 1743 kHz, and Clyde 1883 kHz, at the same times as above.

General information on Subfacts is also broadcast twice daily at 0930 and 2130 UTC by Portpatrick (O) Navtex. Clyde, Portpatrick and Belfast Coastguards will also supply Subfacts on request Ch 16.

A Fisherman's Hotline, ☎ 01436 677201, answers queries. FOSNNI Ops, ☎ 01436 674321 ext 3206/6778 may help.

Submarines on the surface and at periscope depth always listen on Ch 16. Submarines on the surface will comply strictly with IRPCS; Submarines at periscope depth will not close to within 1500 yds of a FV without its express permission. See Chapter 6 for general advice on submarine activity which also occurs in other sea areas.

Subfacts areas (see 9.9.25 overleaf).
The numbered areas, as shown on the chartlet overleaf, are referred to in broadcasts by their names; these are listed below. For areas 1-26, North of Mull, see 9.8.23.

22	Barra	**52**	Boyle
23	Hebrides Central	**53**	Orsay
24	Hawes	**54**	Islay
25	Eigg	**55**	Otter
26	Hebrides South	**56**	Gigha
27	Ford	**57**	Earadale
28	Tiree	**58**	Lochranza
29	Staffa	**59**	Davaar
30	Mackenzie	**60**	Brodick
31	Mull	**61**	Irvine
32	Linnhe	**62**	Lamlash
33	Jura Sound	**63**	Ayr
34	Fyne	**64**	Skerries
35	Minard	**65**	Rathlin
36	Tarbert	**66**	Kintyre
37	Skipness	**67**	Sanda
38	West Kyle	**68**	Stafnish
39	Striven	**69**	Pladda
40	East Kyle	**70**	Turnberry
41	Goil	**71**	Torr
42	Long	**72**	Mermaid
43	Cove	**73**	Ailsa
44	Gareloch	**74**	Maiden
45	Rosneath	**75**	Corsewall
46	Cumbrae	**76**	Ballantrae
47	Garroch	**77**	Magee
48	Laggan	**78**	Londonderry
49	Blackstone	**79**	Beaufort
50	Place	**80**	Ardglass
51	Colonsay	**81**	Peel

CLYDE AREA WAYPOINTS *9.9.25*

The following selected waypoints in the Firth of Clyde area supplement those given in 9.9.4. **All positions are referenced to WGS 84.**

Ardgowan Outfall By	55°54'·93N	04°53'·07W
Ardmore No. 4 Lt By	55°58'·74N	04°48'·39W
Ardmore No. 5 Lt By	55°58'·66N	04°47'·51W
Ardmore No. 8 Lt By	55°58'·94N	04°46'·73W
Ardmore No.10 Lt By	55°59'·02N	04°45'·70W
Ardyne Lt By	55°52'·10N	05°03'·21W
Arranman's Barrels Lt By	55°19'·40N	05°32'·87W
Ashton Lt By	55°58'·10N	04°50'·65W
Ayr Bar Lt By	55°28'·12N	04°39'·44W
Beere Rk No. 44 Lt By	55°55'·55N	05°10'·63W
Burnt Islands No. 43 Lt By	55°55'·41N	05°10'·34W
Cairndhu Lt By	56°00'·35N	04°46'·00W
Carry Pt No. 46 Lt By	55°51'·39N	05°12'·24W
Cowal Lt By	55°56'·00N	04°54'·83W
Creyke Rk (No. 45) By	55°55'·67N	05°10'·89W
Crubon Rk Lt By	55°34'·48N	05°27'·07W
Dunoon Bank SE Lt By	55°56'·64N	04°54'·16W
Eilean Buidhe Lt By	55°55'·78N	05°10'·39W
Eilean Fraoich Lt By	55°55'·79N	05°10'·49W
Fairlie Patch Lt By	55°45'·38N	04°52'·36W
Fullerton Rk Lt By	55°30'·65N	05°04'·57W
Gantock By	55°56'·57N	04°55'·11W
Green Isle No. 24 Lt By	55°59'·39N	04°45'·53W
Hun 1 Lt By	55°48'·11N	04°54'·22W
Hun 3 Lt By	55°47'·60N	04°53'·51W
Hun 5 Lt By	55°45'·87N	04°52'·52W
Hun 7 Lt By	55°44'·97N	04°53'·94W
Hun 8 Lt By	55°44'·79N	04°53'·72W
Hun 9 Lt By	55°44'·66N	04°54'·45W
Hun 10 Lt By	55°44'·15N	04°54'·86W
Hun 11 Lt By	55°43'·45N	04°55'·17W
Hun 12 Lt By	55°43'·45N	04°55'·62W
Hun 13 Lt By	55°42'·53N	04°55'·17W
Hun 14 Lt By	55°42'·53N	04°55'·62W
Ironotter Outfall Lt By	55°58'·36N	04°48'·39W
Iron Rk Ledges Lt By	55°26'·83N	05°18'·88W
Kilcreggan No. 1 Lt By	55°58'·67N	04°50'·28W
Kilcreggan No. 2 Lt By	55°58'·81N	04°50'·20W
Kilcreggan No. 3 Lt By	55°59'·19N	04°51'·46W
Kip Marina Lt By	55°54'·49N	04°52'·98W
Lamlash N Chan Lt By	55°32'·69N	05°04'·83W
Lamlash S Chan Lt By	55°30'·68N	05°04'·53W
Loch Long Lt By	55°59'·15N	04°52'·42W
Macosh Rk Lt By	55°17'·95N	05°37'·00W
Methe Bank Lt By	55°25'·30N	05°34'·42W
Millbeg Bank Lt By	55°25'·53N	05°33'·99W
Mountstuart Lt By	55°48'·00N	05°57'·57W
Otterard Rk Lt By	55°27'·07N	05°31'·11W
Outer St Nicholas Lt By	55°28'·11N	04°39'·45W
Outfall Lt By (off Hunterston)	55°43'·57N	04°54'·77W
Patersons Rk Lt By	55°16'·90N	05°32'·48W
Pillar Rk Lt Ho	55°31'·04N	05°03'·67W
Perch Rk By	55°59'·44N	04°45'·66W
Portachur Lt By	55°44'·35N	04°58'·52W
Rosneath Patch Lt Bn	55°58'·52N	04°47'·45W
Rosneath Patch No. 27 Lt By	55°58'·30N	04°47'·27W
Row Lt By	55°59'·84N	04°45'·13W
Rubha Ban Lt By	55°54'·95N	05°12'·41W
Skelmorlie Bank Lt By	55°51'·65N	04°56'·35W
Skelmorlie 'A' Lt By	55°46'·50N	04°57'·77W
Skelmorlie 'B' Lt By	55°47'·13N	04°57'·55W
Skelmorlie 'C' Lt By	55°48'·10N	04°55'·31W
Skelmorlie 'D' Lt By	55°47'·85N	04°56'·28W
Skelmorlie 'F' Lt By	55°48'·63N	04°54'·96W
Skelmorlie 'G' Lt By	55°49'·00N	04°54'·32W
Tann Spit (No. 38) By	55°44'·42N	04°57'·14W
Warden Bank Lt By	55°54'·77N	04°54'·54W
West Crinan Lt By	55°38'·47N	04°49'·89W

MAPTECH®
Leading the world in digital navigation
Maptech UK Ltd • +44 (0)1243 389352 • sales@maptech.co.uk

Sales and distribution centres in Area 10

Cumbria: ***Sharlo Marine***, 07775 770973, Kingstown Truck Park, Millbrook Road, Carlisle, CA3 0EU.
Lancs: ***Electro-Com Systems***, 07253 875241, Exchange Buildings, 8 Station Road, Fleetwood FY7 6NW.

www.maptech.co.uk

Area 10

North-West England, Isle of Man and North Wales

Mull of Galloway to Bardsey Island

9.10.1 Index .... **Page 561**

9.10.2 Area map **562**

9.10.3 Tidal stream charts **564**

9.10.4 Lights, buoys & waypoints **566**

9.10.5 Passage information **569**

9.10.6 Distance table **570**

9.10.7 Kirkcudbright **571**
Isle of Whithorn
Garlieston
Kippford

9.10.8 Maryport **572**
Silloth

9.10.9 Workington **572**
Harrington

9.10.10 Whitehaven **573**
Ravenglass

9.10.11 Glasson Dock **574**
Barrow-in-Furness
Heysham

9.10.12 Fleetwood **575**

9.10.13 River Ribble/Preston **576**

9.10.14 Liverpool, Standard Port, tidal curves **580**
River Alt

9.10.15 Isle of Man **582**
Port Erin
Castletown
Laxey

9.10.16 Peel **582**

9.10.17 Port St Mary **583**
Derby Haven

9.10.18 Douglas **583**

9.10.19 Ramsey **584**

9.10.20 Conwy **584**

9.10.21 Menai Strait **585**
Caernarfon
Port Dinorwic
Beaumaris
Bangor
The Swellies

9.10.22 Holyhead, Standard Port, tidal curves **587**
Porth Dinllaen

Register for your **FREE** weekly weather email service from Macmillan Reeds
›› at **www.nauticaldata.com – NOW!** ‹‹
weekend weather reports sent to your email address, every Thursday

9.10.2 North-West England, Isle of Man and North Wales

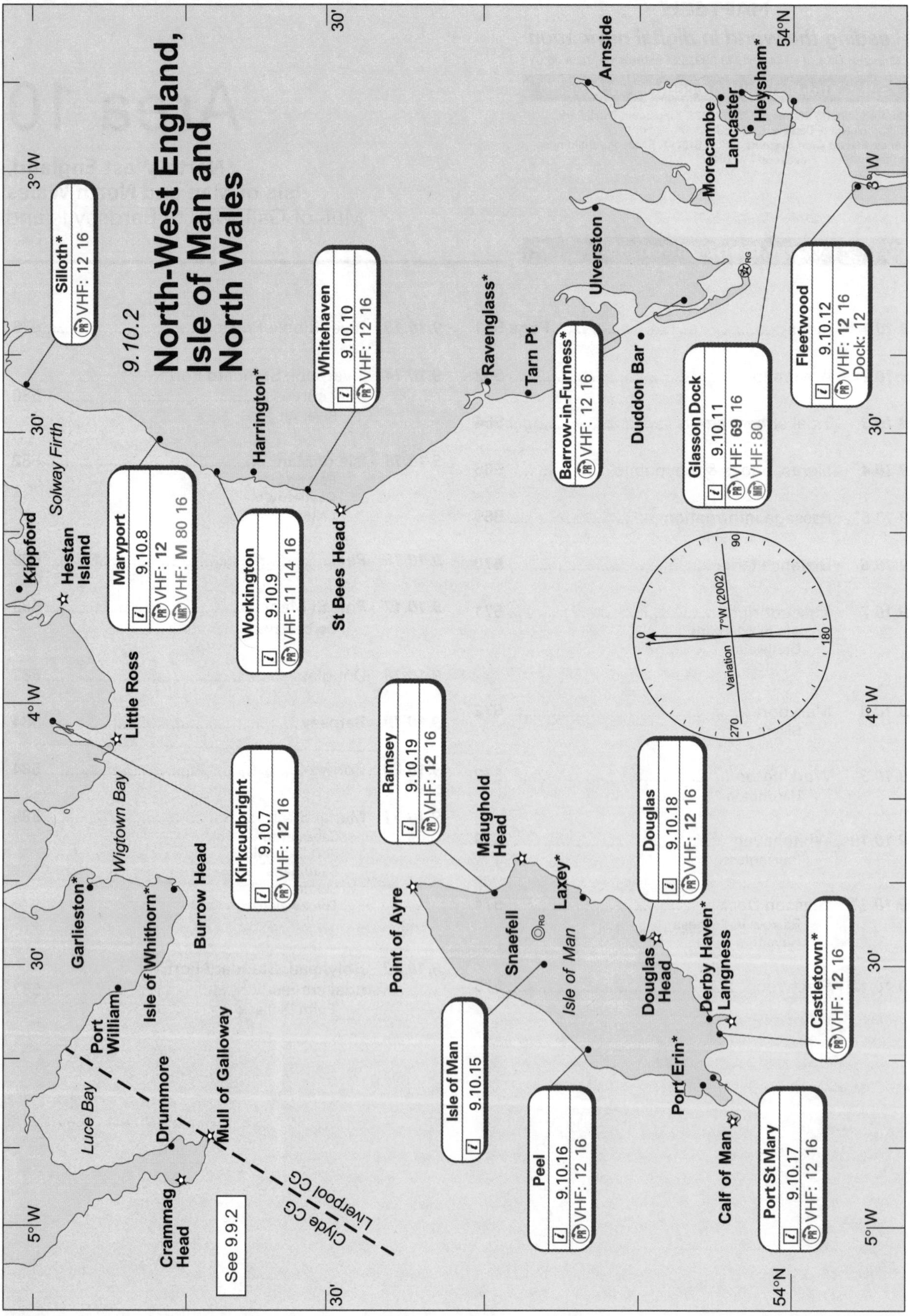

Silloth* VHF: 12 16
Kippford
Hestan Island
Solway Firth
Maryport 9.10.8 VHF: 12 VHF: M 80 16
Workington 9.10.9 VHF: 11 14 16
Harrington*
Whitehaven 9.10.10 VHF: 12 16
St Bees Head
Ravenglass*
Tarn Pt
Barrow-in-Furness* VHF: 12 16
Duddon Bar
Ulverston
Glasson Dock 9.10.11 VHF: 69 16 VHF: 80
Fleetwood 9.10.12 VHF: 12 16 Dock: 12
Morecambe
Lancaster
Heysham*
Arnside
Little Ross
Kirkcudbright 9.10.7 VHF: 12 16
Wigtown Bay
Garlieston*
Isle of Whithorn*
Burrow Head
Port William
Luce Bay
Drummore
Mull of Galloway
Crammag Head
See 9.9.2
Clyde CG
Liverpool CG
Ramsey 9.10.19 VHF: 12 16
Maughold Head
Point of Ayre
Snaefell
Laxey*
Isle of Man
Isle of Man 9.10.15
Douglas 9.10.18 VHF: 12 16
Douglas Head
Derby Haven*
Langness
Castletown* VHF: 12 16
Port Erin*
Calf of Man
Peel 9.10.16 VHF: 12 16
Port St Mary 9.10.17 VHF: 12 16
Variation 7°W (2002)
0
90
180
270
5°W
4°W
3°W
30'
54°N

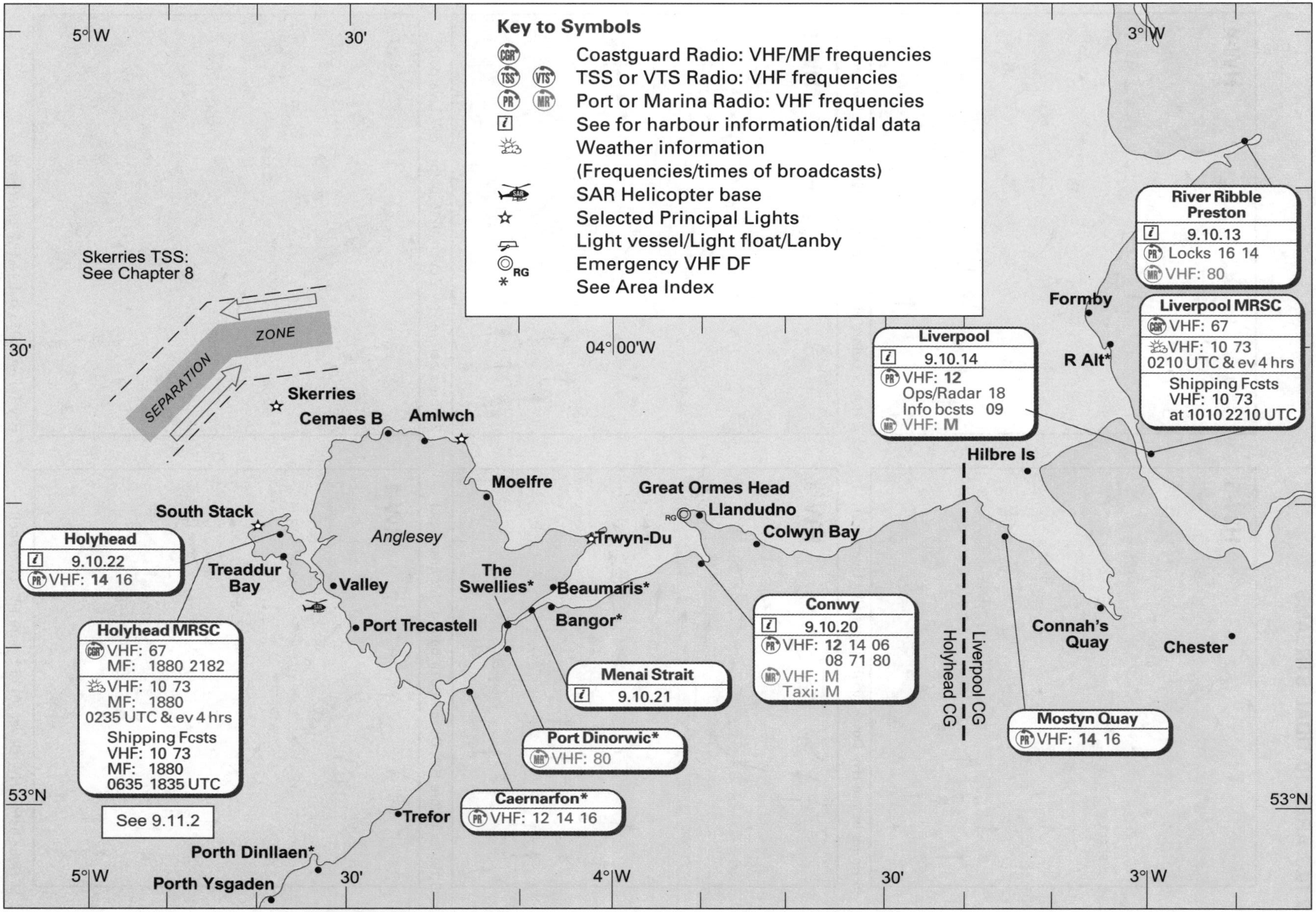
Key to Symbols
Coastguard Radio: VHF/MF frequencies
TSS or VTS Radio: VHF frequencies
Port or Marina Radio: VHF frequencies
See for harbour information/tidal data
Weather information
(Frequencies/times of broadcasts)
SAR Helicopter base
Selected Principal Lights
Light vessel/Light float/Lanby
Emergency VHF DF
See Area Index
RG
5° W
30'
04° 00'W
3° W
53°N
4° W
Skerries TSS:
See Chapter 8
SEPARATION
ZONE
Skerries
Cemaes B
Amlwch
Moelfre
Anglesey
South Stack
Treaddur Bay
Valley
Port Trecastell
The Swellies*
Beaumaris*
Bangor*
Trwyn-Du
Great Ormes Head
Llandudno
Colwyn Bay
Hilbre Is
Formby
R Alt*
Connah's Quay
Chester
Trefor
Porth Dinllaen*
Porth Ysgaden
Liverpool CG
Holyhead CG
River Ribble Preston
9.10.13
Locks 16 14
VHF: 80
Liverpool MRSC
VHF: 67
VHF: 10 73
0210 UTC & ev 4 hrs
Shipping Fcsts
VHF: 10 73
at 1010 2210 UTC
Liverpool
9.10.14
VHF: 12
Ops/Radar 18
Info bcsts 09
VHF: M
Holyhead
9.10.22
VHF: 14 16
Holyhead MRSC
VHF: 67
MF: 1880 2182
VHF: 10 73
MF: 1880
0235 UTC & ev 4 hrs
Shipping Fcsts
VHF: 10 73
MF: 1880
0635 1835 UTC
See 9.11.2
Menai Strait
9.10.21
Port Dinorwic*
VHF: 80
Caernarfon*
VHF: 12 14 16
Conwy
9.10.20
VHF: 12 14 06
08 71 80
VHF: M
Taxi: M
Mostyn Quay
VHF: 14 16

10

9.10.3 AREA 10 TIDAL STREAMS

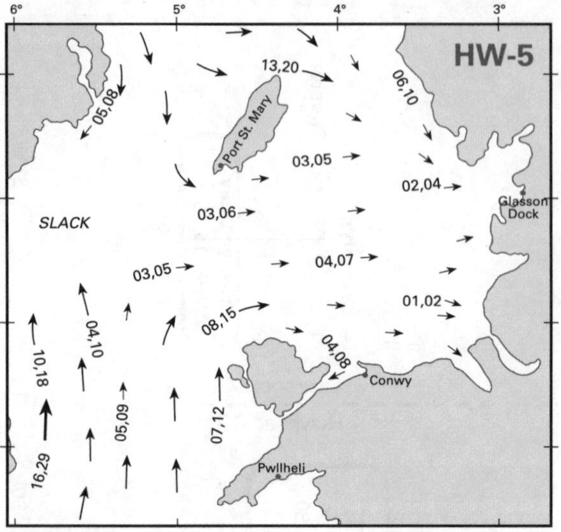

5 Hours before HW Dover (0515 before HW Liverpool)

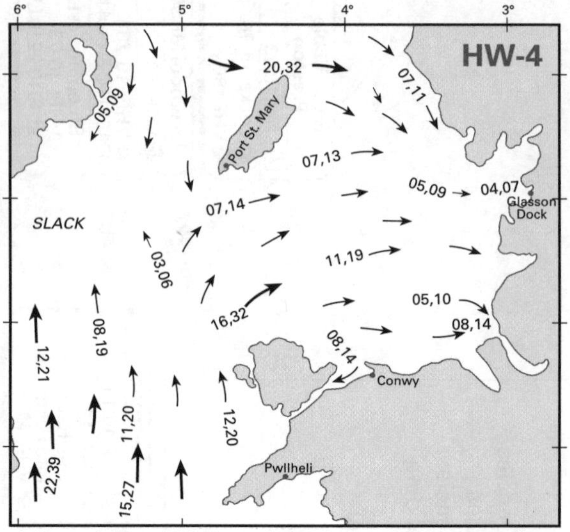

4 Hours before HW Dover (0415 before HW Liverpool)

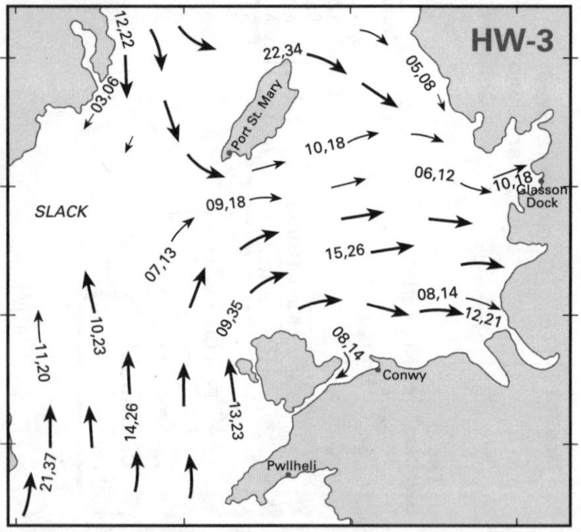

3 Hours before HW Dover (0315 before HW Liverpool)

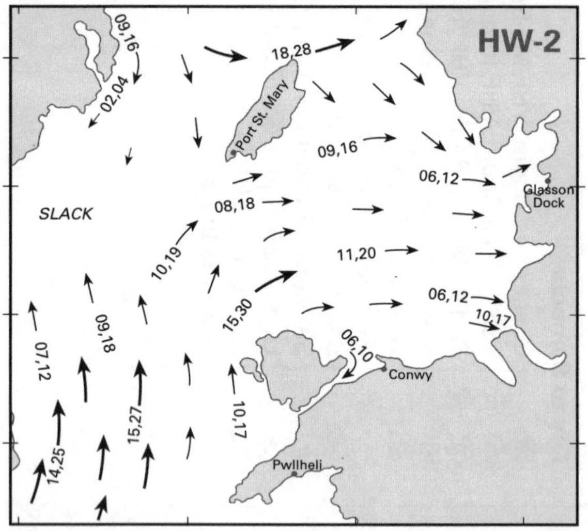

2 Hours before HW Dover (0215 before HW Liverpool)

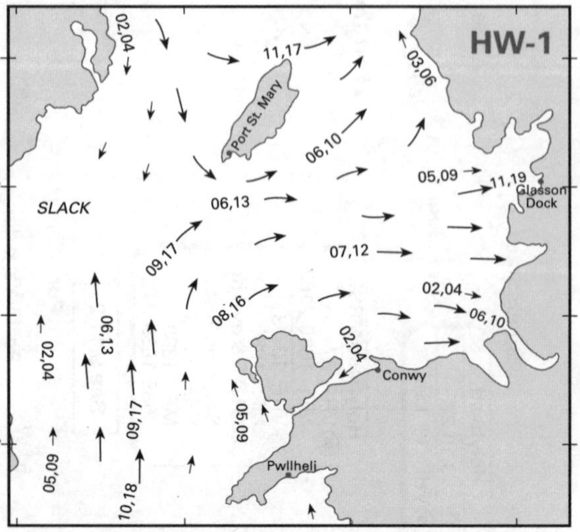

1 Hour before HW Dover (0115 before HW Liverpool)

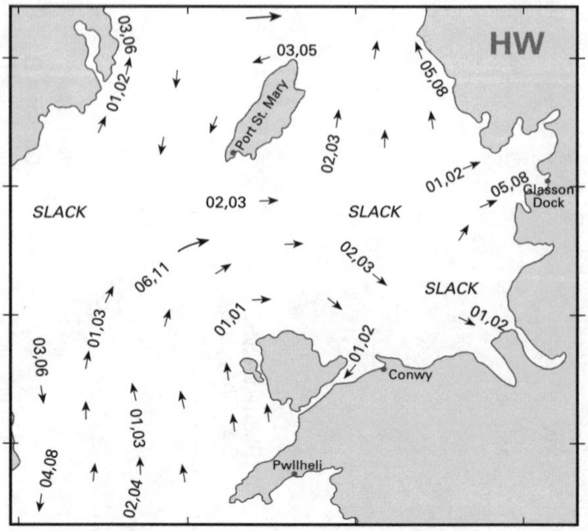

HW Dover (0015 before HW Liverpool)

Northward 9.9.3 Southward 9.11.3 Northern Ireland 9.13.3 Mull of Kintyre 9.9.12 South Ireland 9.12.3

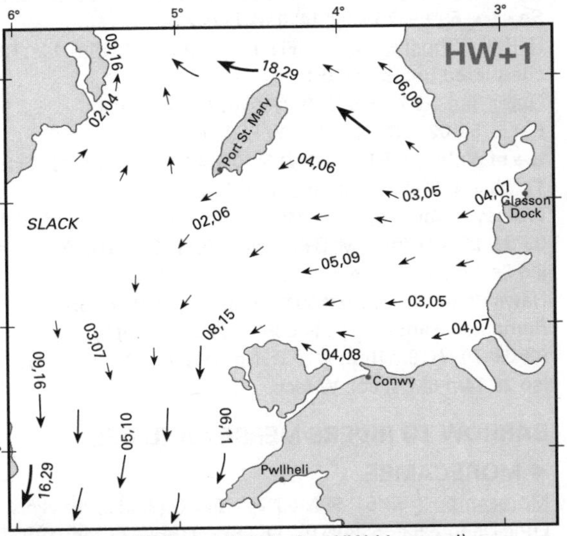

1 Hour after HW Dover (0045 after HW Liverpool)

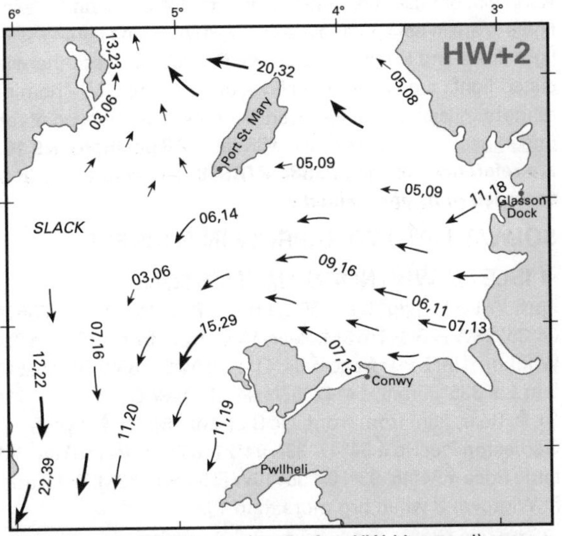

2 Hours after HW Dover (0145 after HW Liverpool)

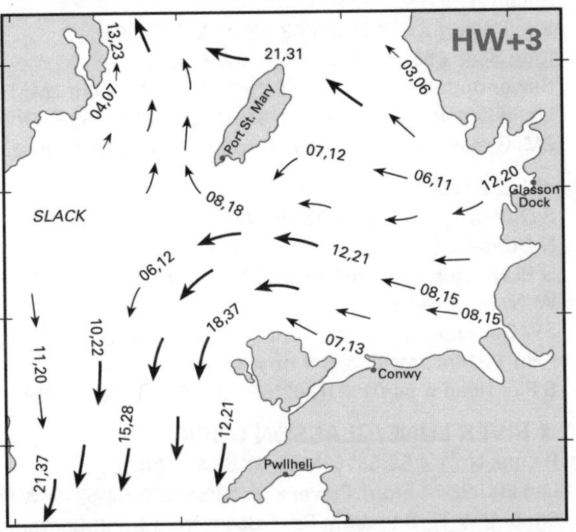

3 Hours after HW Dover (0245 after HW Liverpool)

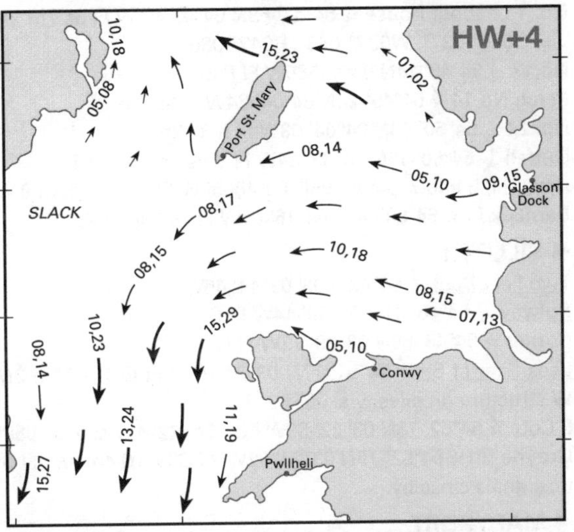

4 Hours after HW Dover (0345 after HW Liverpool)

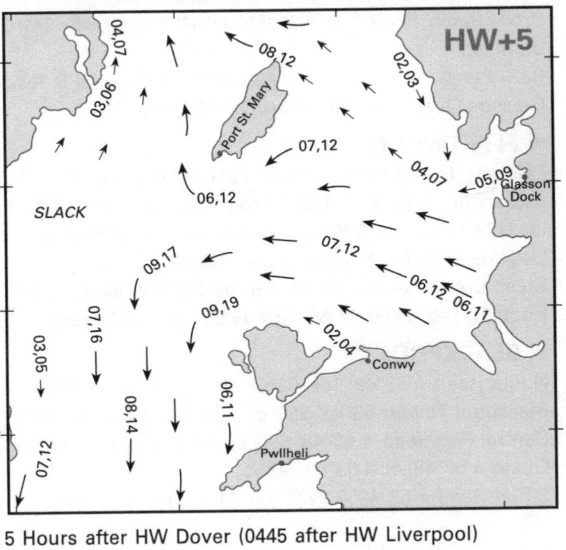

5 Hours after HW Dover (0445 after HW Liverpool)

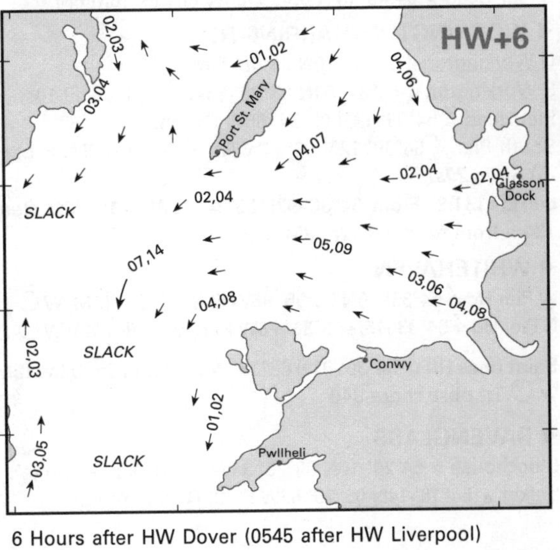

6 Hours after HW Dover (0545 after HW Liverpool)

10

9.10.4 LIGHTS, BUOYS AND WAYPOINTS

Abbreviations used below are given in the Introduction. Principal lights ☆ are in **bold** print, places in CAPITALS, and light-vessels, light floats and Lanbys in *CAPITAL ITALICS*. Unless otherwise stated lights are white. m – elevation in metres; M – nominal range in miles. Fog signals are in *italics*. Useful waypoints are underlined – use those on land with care. **All positions in 9.10.4 are referenced to the WGS84/ETRS89 datum but should be assumed to be approximate.**

SOLWAY FIRTH TO BARROW-IN-FURNESS

◄ ISLE OF WHITHORN/GARLIESTON

Port William Ldg Lts 105°. Front, Pier Head 54°45'·66N 04°35'·28W Fl G 3s 7m 3M. Rear, 130m from front, FG 10m 2M.
Whithorn Hbr E Pier Head ☆ 54°41'·88N 04°21'·86W QG 4m 5M. Ldg Lts 335°. Front, 54°42'·01N 04°22'·05W Oc R 8s 7m 7M; Or ♦. Rear, 35m from front, Oc R 8s 9m 7M; Or ♦, synch.
Garlieston Pier Hd ☆ 54°47'·33N 04°21'·80W 2 FR (vert) 8m 3M.
Little Ross ☆ 54°45'·93N 04°05'·10W Fl 5s 50m 12M; W Tr; obsc in Wigtown B when brg more than 103°.

◄ KIRKCUDBRIGHT BAY/KIPPFORD

No. 1 Lifeboat House ☆ 54°47'·68N 04°03'·75W Fl 3s 7m 3M; vis: G080°-037°, W037°-043°, R043°-080°.
No.12 54°49'·14N 04°04'·85W Fl R 3s.
Perch No.14 ☆ 54°49'·24N 04°04'·84W Fl 3s 5m.
No. 22 54°50'·08N 04°04'·03W Fl R 3s 2m.
Outfall 54°50'·18N 04°03'·84W Fl Y 5s 3m 2M; Y Tr.
Hestan I, E end ☆ 54°49'·96N 03°48'·55W Fl (2) 10s 42m 9M.
Barnkirk Pt ☆ 54°58'·00N 03°16'·01W Fl 2s 18m 2M.

◄ SILLOTH

Two Feet Bank 54°42'·40N 03°44'·46W.
Solway 54°46'·81N 03°30'·14W Fl G.
Corner ☆ 54°48'·88N 03°29'·72W Fl G.
Lees Scar Lt Bn ☆ 54°51'·77N 03°24'·82W Fl G 10s 11m 2M; W structure on piles; vis: 005°-317°.
E Cote ☆ 54°52'·78N 03°22'·89W FG 15m 12M; vis: 046°-058°.
Groyne Hd ☆ 54°52'·16N 03°23'·92W 2 FG (vert) 4m 4M; Fl Bu tfc signals close by.

◄ MARYPORT

S Pier Head ☆ 54°43'·07N 03°30'·64W Fl 1·5s 10m 6M.

◄ WORKINGTON/HARRINGTON

N Workington 54°40'·10N 03°38'·50W.
S Workington 54°37'·01N 03°38'·58W VQ (6) + L Fl 10s.
Pier Head ☆ 54°39'·14N 03°34'·80W QG 5m.
South Pier ☆ 54°39'·12N 03°34'·67W Fl 5s 11m 8M; R bldg; *Siren 20s.*
Ldg Lts 131·8°. Front, 54°38'·92N 03°34'·12W FR 10m 3M. Rear, 134m from front, FR 12m 3M.

◄ WHITEHAVEN

W Pier Hd ☆ 54°33'·16N 03°35'·96W Fl G 5s 16m 13M; W ○ Tr.
N Pier Hd ☆ 54°33'·15N 03°35'·78W 2 FR (vert) 8m 9M; W ○ Tr.
Saint Bees Hd ☆ 54°30'·81N 03°38'·24W Fl (2) 20s 102m **18M**; W ○ Tr; obsc shore-340°.

◄ RAVENGLASS

Blockhouse ☆ 54°20'·16N 03°25'·34W FG; (Eskdale Range).
Selker 54°16'·14N 03°29'·63W Fl (3) G 10s; *Bell.*

◄ BARROW-IN-FURNESS

Lightning Knoll 53°59'·84N 03°14'·28W L Fl 10s; *Bell.*
Sea 1 53°59'·75N 03°14'·09W Fl G 2·5s.
Halfway Shoal 54°01'·46N 03°11'·88W QR 19m 10s; R&W chequered Bn; Racon (B).
Outer Bar 54°02'·00N 03°11'·10W Fl (4) R 10s.
Bar 54°02'·54N 03°10'·31W Fl (2) R 5s.
Isle of Walney ☆ 54°02'·92N 03°10'·64W Fl 15s 21m **23M**; stone Tr; obsc 122°-127° within 3M of shore.
Walney Chan Ldg Lts 040·7°. No.1 Front, 54°03'·19N 03°09'·22W Q 7m 10M; B Pile. No. 2 Rear, 0·61M from front, Iso 2s 13m 10M; Pile.
Haws Point W 54°02'·99N 03°10'·11W QR 8m 6M.
Rampside Sands Ldg Lts 005·1°. No. 3 Front, 54°04'·41N 03°09'·79W Q 9m 10M; W ○ Tr. No. 4 Rear, 0·77M from front, Iso 2s 14m 6M; R col, W face.

BARROW TO RIVERS MERSEY AND DEE

◄ MORECAMBE

Morecambe 53°51'·99N 03°24'·10W Q (9) 15s; *Whis.*
Lune Deep 53°55'·80N 03°11'·08W Q (6) + L Fl 15s; *Whis*; Racon (T).
Shell Wharf 53°55'·45N 03°08'·97W Fl G 2·5s.
King Scar 53°56'·96N 03°04'·40W Fl G 5s.
Sewer outfall ☆ 54°04'·33N 02°53'·84W Fl G 2s 4m 2M; Tr.
Lts in line about 090°. Front, 54°04'·41N 02°52'·63W FR 10m 2M; G mast. Rear, 140m from front, FR 14m 2M; G mast.

◄ HEYSHAM

S Outfall 54°01'·73N 02°55'·80W Fl (2) G 10s 5m 2M.
N Outfall ☆ 54°01'·85N 02°55'·77W Fl G 5s 5m 2M.
S Bkwtr Head ☆ 54°01'·90N 02°55'·72W 2 FG (vert) 9m 5M; W Tr; *Siren 30s.*
SW Quay Ldg Lts 102·2°. Front, 54°01'·91N 02°55'·22W both F Bu 11/14m 2M; Or & B ♦ on masts.
S Pier Head ☆ 54°01'·91N 02°55'·43W Oc G 7·5s 9m 6M.

◄ RIVER LUNE/GLASSON DOCK

R Lune No.1 53°58'·63N 03°00'·06W Q (9) 15s.
Ldg Lts 083·7°. Front, Plover Scar 53°58'·89N 02°52'·96W Fl 2s 6m 6M; W Tr, B lantern. Rear, 854m from front, Cockersand Abbey F 18m 8M; R Tr (chan liable to change).
Crook Perch, No. 7 53°59'·46N 02°52'·35W Fl G 5s 3M; G △ on mast.
Bazil Perch, No.16 54°00'·20N 02°51'·65W Fl (3) R 10s 3M.
Glasson Quay ☆ 54°00'·03N 02°51·03W FG 1M.

◄ FLEETWOOD

Fairway No. 1 53°57'·67N 03°02'·03W Q; *Bell.*
Esplanade Ldg Lts 156°. Front, 53°55'·71N 03°00'·56W Iso G 2s 14m. Rear, 320m from front, Iso G 4s 28m. Both vis on Ldg line only. (H24) (chan liable to change).
Steep Breast Perch ☆ 53°55'·75N 03°00'·56W Iso G 2s 3m 2M.
Knott End slip Hd ☆ 53°55'·73N 03°00'·10W 2 FR (vert) 3m 2M.

◄ BLACKPOOL

N Pier Head ☆ 53°49'·16N 03°03'·92W 2 FG (vert) 3M.
Blackpool Towerr 53°48'·95N 03°03'·30W Aero FR 158m.
Central Pier Head ☆ 53°48'·65N 03°03'·67W 2 FG (vert) 4M.
Obstn 53°48'·45N 03°04'·30W.
S Pier Head ☆ 53°47'·74N 03°03'·71W 2 FG (vert) 4M.

◀ RIVER RIBBLE

Gut 53°41'·74N 03°08'·98W L Fl 10s.
Perches show Fl R on N side, and Fl G on S side of chan.
S side, 14·3M Perch ☆ 53°42'·75N 03°04'·90W Fl G 5s 6m 3M.

Southport Pier Head ☆ 53°39'·33N 03°01'·31W 2 FG (vert) 6m 5M; W post; vis: 033°-213°.
Jordan's Spit 53°35'·76N 03°19'·28W Q (9) 15s.
FT 53°34'·52N 03°13'·20W Q.
Spoil Ground 53°34'·27N 03°17'·41W Fl Y 3s.

◀ RIVER MERSEY/LIVERPOOL

BAR 53°32'·01N 03°20'·98W Fl 5s 10m 12M; R structure on By; Racon (T); *Horn (2) 20s.*
Q1 53°31'·00N 03°16'·76W VQ.
Q2 53°31'·47N 03°14'·95W VQ R.
Q3 53°30'·95N 03°15'·10W Fl G.
BT 53°30'·41N 03°17'·61W Fl (3) G 9s.
Formby 53°31'·13N 03°13'·50W Iso 4s 11m 6M; R hull, W stripes.
C4 53°31'·82N 03°08'·51W Fl R 3s R hull.
Crosby 53°30'·72N 03°06'·29W Oc 5s 11m 8M; R hull, W stripes.
C14 53°29'·91N 03°05'·34W Fl R 3s; R hull.
Brazil 53°26'·84N 03°02'·24W QG; G hull.
Seacombe Ferry N and S corners ☆ 53°24'·63N 03°00'·91W 3 FG 5m 5M; near N corner FY 8m 6M; *Bell (3) 20s.*
Birkenhead, Woodside Ferry N end ☆ 53°23'·76N 03°00'·49W 3 FG 5m 4M and S end 2 FG (vert) with *Bell (4) 15s.*
Cammell Laird slip, SE corner ☆ 53°22'·98N 03°00'·31W Fl (2) G 6s 5m 5M.
Pluckington Bank 53°23'·00N 02°59'·56W VQ (9)10s.
Brombro 53°21'·83N 02°58'·68W Q (3) 10s.
Eastham Locks E Dn ☆ 53°19'·58N 02°57'·00W Fl (2) R 6s 5m 8M.
Garston NW Dn ☆ 53°20'·89N 02°54'·63W 2 FG (vert) 12m 9M; *Horn 11s.*

◀ RIVER DEE

HE1 53°26'·31N 03°18'·10W Q (9) 15s.
HE2 53°25'·13N 03°13'·17W Q (3) 10s.
HE3 53°24'·76N 03°12'·99W.
Hilbre I ☆ 53°22'·99N 03°13'·72W Fl R 3s 14m 5M; W Tr.
HE4 53°22'·32N 03°14'·29W.

◀ MOSTYN/CONNAH'S QUAY

MostynTraining Wall Hd ☆ 53°19'·56N 03°15'·70W 2 FR (vert) 10m 3M; B mast.
Mostyn Ldg Lts 215·7°. Front, 53°19'·20N 03°16'·24W FR 12m; W ◇ on B mast. Rear, 135m from front, FR 22m; W ◇ on B mast.
Flint Sands, N Training wall Head ☆ 53°15'·07N 03°06'·52W Fl R 3s 4m 6M; Tr.
Connah's Quay, South Training Wall Head ☆ 53°13'·97N 03°04'·48W Fl G 5s 3m 6M.

◀ WELSH CHANNEL

M2 53°20'·17N 03°15'·89W Fl R 5s.
Mostyn 53°21'·02N 03°16'·49W Fl (4) G 15s.
NE Mostyn 53°21'·50N 03°17'·81W Fl (3) G 10s.
Dee 53°21'·99N 03°18'·87W Q (6) + L Fl 15s.
Air 53°21'·85N 03°19'·29W.
E Hoyle Spit 53°22'·52N 03°19'·07W Fl G 5s.
Mid Hoyle 53°22'·91N 03°19'·72W.
Hoyle 53°23'·15N 03°21'·39W QR.
NW Hoyle 53°23'·32N 03°23'·89W Fl R 2·5s.
Earwig 53°21'·34N 03°23'·58W Fl (2) G 5s; *Bell*
S Hoyle 53°21'·34N 03°24'·86W Fl (3) R 10s.
N Hoyle 53°26'·67N 03°30'·50W VQ.

ISLE OF MAN

Point of Ayre ☆ 54°24'·94N 04°22'·13W Fl (4) 20s 32m **19M**; W Tr, two R bands; Racon (M); *Horn (3) 60s.*
Low Lt ☆ 54°25'·03N 04°21'·86W Fl 3s 10m 8M; R Tr, lower part W, on B Base; part obsc 335°-341°.

◀ JURBY/PEEL

Cronk y Cliwe ☆ 54°22'·28N 04°31'·48W 2 Fl R 5s (vert); synch.
Orrisdale ☆ 54°19'·30N 04°34'·21W 2 Fl R 5s (vert).
Peel Bkwtr Head ☆ 54°13'·67N 04°41'·69W Oc 7s 11m 6M; W Tr; *Bell (4) 12s* (occas).
Peel Groyne Head ☆ 54°13'·54N 04°41'·84W Oc R 2s 4m.

◀ PORT ERIN

Ldg Lts 099·1°. Front, 54°05'·23N 04°45'·57W FR 10m 5M; W Tr, R band. Rear, 39m from front, FR 19m 5M; W col, R band.
Raglan Pier Head ☆ 54°05'·12N 04°45'·86W Oc G 5s 8m 5M.
Thousla Rock ☆ 54°03'·73N 04°48'·05W Fl R 3s 9m 4M.
Calf of Man ☆ W Pt 54°03'·18N 04°49'·78W Fl 15s 93m **26M**; W 8-sided Tr; vis 274°-190°; *Horn 45s.*
Chicken Rock ☆ 54°02'·26N 04°50'·32W Fl 5s 38m 13M;Tr; *Horn 60s.*

◀ PORT ST MARY

The Carrick 54°04'·30N 04°42'·68W Q (2) 5s 6m 3M.
Alfred Pier Head ☆ 54°04'·33N 04°43'·82W Oc R 10s 8m 6M; W Tr, R band.
Inner Pier Head ☆ 54°04'·42N 04°44'·15W Oc R 3s 8m 5M.

◀ CASTLETOWN/DERBY HAVEN

54°03'·73N 04°38'·62W Fl R 3s: *Bell.*
New Pier Head ☆ 54°04'·33N 04°38'·97W Oc R 15s 8m 5M.
Dreswick Pt ☆ 54°03'·29N 04°37'·45W Fl (2) 30s 23m 12M; W Tr.
Derby Haven, Bkwtr SW end ☆ 54°04'·58N 04°37'·06W Iso G 2s 5m 5M; W Tr, G band.

◀ DOUGLAS

Douglas Head ☆ 54°08'·60N 04°27'·95W Fl 10s 32m **24M**; W Tr; obsc brg more than 037°. FR Lts on radio masts 1 and 3M West.
No. 1 54°09'·04N 04°27'·68W Q (3) G 5s.
Princess Alexandra Pier Head ☆ 54°08'·84N 04°27'·85W Fl R 5s 16m 8M; R mast; *Whis (2) 40s.*
Ldg Lts 229·3°, Front, 54°08'·72N 04°28'·25W Oc 10s 9m 5M; W △ R border on mast. Rear, 62m from front, Oc 10s 12m 5M; W ▽ on R border; synch with front.
Victoria Pier Head ☆ 54°08'·84N 04°28'·08W Iso G 10s 10m 3M; W col; vis: 225°-327°; Intnl Port Tfc Signals.
Conister Rock Refuse Tr 54°09'·03N 04°28'·12W Q 3M; vis: 234°-312°.

◀ LAXEY

Pier Head ☆ 54°13'·50N 04°23'·43W Oc R 3s 7m 5M; W Tr, R band; obsc when brg less than 318°.
Bkwtr Hd ☆ 54°13'·45N 04°23'·32W Oc G 3s 7m; W Tr, G band.
Maughold Head ☆ 54°17'·72N 04°18'·58W Fl (3) 30s 65m **21M.**
Bahama 54°20'·02N 04°08'·56W VQ (6) + L Fl 10s; *Bell.*

◀ RAMSEY

Queens Pier Dn 54°19'·28N 04°21'·94W Fl R 5s.

S Pier Head 54°19'·43N 04°22'·50W QR 8m 10M; W Tr, R band, B base.

N Pier Hd 54°19'·46N 04°22'·50W QG 9m 10M; W Tr, B base.

Whitestone Bank 54°24'·58N 04°20'·41W Q (9) 15s.

King William Bank 54°25'·95N 04°00'·06W Q (3) 10s.

WALES – NORTH COAST

Chester Flat 53°21'·67N 03°27'·47W Fl (2) R 5s.

Mid Patch Spit 53°21'·83N 03°31'·57W Fl R 5s.

N Rhyl 53°22'·76N 03°34'·58W Q.

W Constable 53°23'·14N 03°49'·26W Q (9) 15s.

◀ RHYL/LLANDUDNO/CONWY

River Clwyd Outfall 53°19'·60N 03°30'·65W

River Clwyd Bkwtr Head 53°19'·46N 03°30'·35W QR 7m 2M.

Llanddulas, Llysfaen Jetty 53°17'·59N 03°39'·49W Fl G 10s.

Raynes Quarry Jetty Hd 53°17'·62N 03°40'·37W 2 FG (vert).

Llandudno Pier Hd 53°19'·90N 03°49'·51W 2 FG (vert) 8m 4M.

Great Ormes Hd Lt Ho 53°20'·56N 03°52'·17W (unlit).

Conwy Fairway 53°17'·95N 03°55'·58W L Fl 10s.

Conway R ent S side 53°18'·04N 03°50'·90W Fl WR 5s 5m 2M; vis: W076°-088°, R088°-171°, W171°-319°, R319°-076°.

◀ ANGLESEY

Pilot Station Pier 53°24'·90N 04°17'·20W 2 FR (vert).

Point Lynas ☆ 53°24'·98N 04°17'·35W Oc 10s 39m **20M**; W castellated Tr; vis: 109°-315°; (H24). Fog Det Lt F 25m 16M vis: 211·8°-214·3°; *Horn 45s;* H24.

◀ AMLWCH

Main Bkwtr 53°25'·02N 04°19'·91W Fl G 15s 11m 3M; W mast; vis: 141°-271°.

Inner Bkwtr 53°24'·99N 04°19'·95W 2 FR (vert) 12m 5M; W mast; vis: 164°-239°.

Inner Harbour 53°24'·95N 04°20'·02W F 9m 8M; W post; vis: 233°-257°.

Wylfa power station 53°25'·09N 04°29'·29W 2 FG (vert) 13m 6M.

Furlong 53°25'·41N 04°30'·49W.

Archdeacon Rock 53°26'·71N 04°30'·89W.

Victoria Bank 53°25'·61N 04°31'·37W.

Coal Rk 53°25'·90N 04°32'·83W.

Ethel Rk 53°26'·63N 04°33'·71W.

W Mouse 53°25'·03N 04°33'·29W.

The Skerries ☆ 53°25'·27N 04°36'·50W Fl (2) 10s 36m **22M**; W ○ Tr, R band; Racon (T). FR 26m **16M**; same Tr; vis: 231°-254°; *Horn (2) 20s*; H24.

Langdon 53°22'·74N 04°38'·74W Q (9) 15s.

Bolivar 53°21'·51N 04°35'·32W.

Wk 53°20'·43N 04°36'·60W Fl (2) R 10s.

Clipera 53°20'·10N 04°36'·20W Fl (4) R 15s; *Bell.*

◀ HOLYHEAD

Bkwtr Head 53°19'·86N 04°37'·16W Fl (3) G 15s 21m 14M; W □ Tr, B band; *Siren 20s.*

Old Hbr, Admiralty Pier Dn 53°18'·87N 04°37'·07W 2 FG (vert) 8m 5M; *Horn* 15s (occas).

South Stack ☆ 53°18'·40N 04°41'·98W Fl 10s 60m **24M**; (H24); W ○ Tr; obsc to N by N Stack and part obsc in Penrhos bay: *Horn 30s.* Fog Det Lt vis: 145°-325°.

Llanddwyn I 53°08'·07N 04°24'·82W Fl WR 2·5s 12m W7M, R4M; W Tr; vis: R280°-013°, W015°-120°.

MENAI STRAIT TO BARDSEY ISLAND

Trwyn-Du 53°18'·77N 04°02'·44W Fl 5s 19m 12M; W ○ castellated Tr, B bands; vis: 101°-023°; *Bell (1) 30s,* sounded continuously. FR on radio mast 2M SW.

Ten Feet Bank 53°19'·47N 04°02'·82W QR.

Dinmor 53°19'·35N 04°03'·27W QG.

◀ BEAUMARIS/BANGOR

(Direction of buoyage NE to SW)

Perch Rock 53°18'·73N 04°02'·09W.

B2 53°18'·32N 04°02'·07W Fl (2) R 5s.

B1 53°18'·12N 04°02'·37W Fl (2) G 10s.

B3 53°17'·72N 04°02'·77W QG.

B8 53°16'·47N 04°04'·47W Fl (3) R 10s.

B5 53°15'·77N 04°04'·87W Fl G 5s.

Beaumaris Pier 53°15'·67N 04°05'·37W F WG 5m 6M; vis: G212°-286°, W286°-014°, G014°-071°.

B10 53°15'·62N 04°05'·22W Fl (2) R 10s.

B12 53°15'·47N 04°05'·57W QR.

B7 53°15'·12N 04°06'·17W Fl (2) G 5s.

Bangor 53°14'·49N 04°07'·57W.

St George's Pier 53°13'·53N 04°09'·54W Fl G 10s.

Price's Point 53°13'·11N 04°10'·53W Fl WR 2s 5m 3M; W Bn; vis: R059°-239°, W239°-259°.

Britannia Tubular Bridge, S chan Ldg Lts 231° E side. Front, 53°12'·92N 04°11'·05W FW. Rear, 45m from front, FW. Centre span of bridge Iso 5s 27m 3M, one either side. SE end of bridge, FR 21m 3M either side, NW end of bridge section FG 21m 3M either side.

◀ PORT DINORWIC

Pier Head 53°11'·18N 04°12'·64W F WR 5m 2M; vis: R225°-357°, W357°-225°.

C9 53°08'·52N 04°16'·87W.

Channel 53°10'·34N 04°15'·19W.

C14 53°10'·19N 04°15'·37W.

C11 53°09'·92N 04°15'·67W.

C13 53°09'·52N 04°15'·92W.

(Direction of buoyage SW to NE)

Change 53°08'·82N 04°16'·72W.

◀ CAERNARFON

Caernarfon N Pier Hd 53°08'·72N 04°16'·57W 2 FG (vert) 5m 2M.

C10 53°07'·96N 04°18'·27W QR.

Abermenai Point 53°07'·62N 04°19'·72W Fl WR 3·5s 6m 3M; W mast; vis: R065°-245°, W245°-065°.

Mussel Bank 53°07'·27N 04°20'·79W Fl (2) R 5s.

C6 53°07'·20N 04°21'·93W Fl R 5s.

C5 53°07'·29N 04°22'·94W.°

C4 53°07'·32N 04°22'·90W QR.

C3 53°07'·18N 04°23'·70W QG.

C1 53°06'·58N 04°24'·24W Fl G 5s.

C2 53°06'·69N 04°24'·33W Fl R 10s.

Poole 53°00'·02N 04°34'·10W Fl Y 6s; (Apr-Oct).

◀ PORTH DINLLÄEN

CG Stn 52°56'·82N 04°33'·89W FR when firing taking place 10M North.

Careg y Chwislen 52°56'·99N 04°33'·51W.

Bardsey I ☆ 52°44'·99N 04°47'·98W Fl (5) 15s 39m **28M**; W □ Tr, R bands; obsc by Bardsey I 198°-250° and in Tremadoc B when brg less than 260°; *Horn Mo (N) 45s.*

9.10.5 PASSAGE INFORMATION

For detailed directions covering these waters and harbours refer to the Admiralty Pilot *W Coast of England and Wales*; *A Cruising Guide to NW England & Wales* (Griffiths/Imray) and *Lundy and Irish Sea Pilot* (Taylor/Imray). *Solway SDs* cover from Loch Ryan to Ravenglass; by post £5.60 from: Matheson, Decca Stn, Kidsdale, Whithorn, Newton Stewart DG8 8HZ.

SCOTLAND – SW COAST

The Scares, two groups of rocks, lie at the mouth of Luce Bay which elsewhere is clear more than 3ca offshore; but the whole bay is occupied by a practice bombing range, marked by 12 DZ SPM lt buoys. Good anch at E Tarbert B to await the tide around the Mull of Galloway, or dry out alongside in shelter of Drummore. Off Burrow Hd there is a bad race in strong W winds with W-going tide. In Wigtown B the best anch is in Isle of Whithorn B, but exposed to S. It is also possible to dry out in Garlieston, see 9.10.7.

A tank firing range, between the E side of ent to Kirkcudbright Bay (9.10.7) and Abbey Hd, 4M to E, extends 14M offshore. If unable to avoid the area, cross it at N end close inshore. For information contact the Range safety boat "Gallovidian" on VHF Ch 16, 73. The range operates 0900-1600LT Mon-Fri, but weekend and night firing may also occur.

SOLWAY FIRTH (chart 1346) Between Abbey Head and St Bees Head lies the Solway Firth, most of which is encumbered by shifting sandbanks.The *Solway SDs* (see above) are virtually essential. Off the entrances to the Firth, and in the approaches to Workington (9.10.9) beware shoals over which strong W winds raise a heavy sea. There are navigable, buoyed chans as far as Annan on the N shore, but buoys are laid primarily for the aid of Pilots.

Local knowledge is required, particularly in the upper Firth, where streams run very strongly in the chans when the banks are dry, and less strongly over the banks when covered. In Powfoot chan for example the in-going stream begins at HW Liverpool – 0300, and the outgoing at HW Liverpool + 0100, sp rates up to 6kn. For Silloth and Maryport see 9.10.8; Workington and Harrington 9.10.9, Whitehaven and Ravenglass 9.10.10. South along the Cumbrian coast past St Bees Hd to Walney Is there are no dangers more than 2M offshore, but no shelter either.

BARROW TO CONWY (AC 2010, 1981, *1978*) Ent to Barrow-in-Furness (9.10.11 and chart 3164) is about 1M S of Hilpsford Pt at S end of Walney Island where the lt ho is prominent. The stream sets across the narrow chan, which is well marked but shallow in patches. W winds cause rough sea in the ent. Moorings and anch off Piel and Roa Islands, but space is limited and stream runs hard on ebb. Coming from the S it is possible with sufficient rise of tide to cross the sands between Fleetwood and Barrow.

Lune Deep, 2M NW of Rossall Pt, is ent to Morecambe B (chart 2010), and gives access to the ferry/commercial port of Heysham, Glasson Dock (9.10.11), and Fleetwood (9.10.12); it is well buoyed. Streams run 3·5kn at sp. Most of Bay is encumbered with drying sands, intersected by chans which are subject to change. S of Morecambe B, beware shoals extending 3M W of Rossall Pt. Further S, R. Ribble (9.10.13) gives access via a long drying chan to the marina at Preston.

Queen's Chan and Crosby Chan (charts 1951 and *1978*) are entered E of the Bar Lanby. They are well buoyed, dredged and preserved by training banks, and give main access to R. Mersey and Liverpool (9.10.14). Keep clear of commercial shipping. From the N the old Formby chan is abandoned, but possible near HW. Towards HW and in moderate winds a yacht can cross the training bank (level of which varies between 2m and 3m above CD) E of Great Burbo Bank, if coming from the W. Rock Chan, parts of which dry and which is unmarked, may also be used but beware wrecks.

In good weather and at nps, the Dee Estuary (charts 1953, *1978*) is accessible for boats able to take the ground. But most of estuary dries and banks extend 6M seaward. Chans shift, and buoys are moved as required. Stream runs hard in chans when banks are dry. Main ent is Welsh Chan, but if coming from N, Hilbre Swash runs W of Hilbre Is (lit). This area is being extensively dredged and developed.

Sailing W from the Dee on the ebb, it is feasible to take the Inner Passage (buoyed) S of West Hoyle Spit, and this enjoys some protection from onshore winds at half tide or below. Rhyl is a tidal hbr, not accessible in strong onshore winds, but gives shelter for yachts able to take the ground. Abergele Road, Colwyn B and Llandudno B are possible anchs in settled weather and S winds. Conwy (9.10.20) offer good shelter in both marina and harbour. Between Point of Ayr and Great Ormes Head the E-going stream begins at HW Liverpool + 0600, and the W-going at HW Liverpool – 0015, sp rates 3kn.

ISLE OF MAN (IOM) (charts 2094, 2696) For general pilotage information, tidal streams and hbr details of IOM, see *IOM Sailing Directions, Tidal Streams and Anchorages*, published by Hunter Publications (9.10.15). For notes on crossing the Irish Sea, see 9.13.5.

There are four choices when rounding South of Isle of Man: **a**, In bad weather, or at night, keep S of Chicken Rk (lt, fog sig). **b**, In good conditions, pass between Chicken Rk and Calf of Man (lt, fog sig). **c**, With winds of Force 3 or less and a reliable engine giving at least 5kn, and only by day use Calf Sound between Calf of Man and IOM, passing W of Kitterland Island but E of Thousla Rock, which is marked by lt bn and is close to Calf of Man shore. **d**, Little Sound, a minor chan, runs E of Kitterland Is.

The stream runs strongly through Calf Sound, starting N-going at HW Liverpool – 0145, and S-going at HW Liverpool + 0345, sp rates 3·5kn. W of Calf of Man the stream runs N and S, but changes direction off Chicken Rk and runs W and E between Calf of Man and Langness Pt 6M to E. Overfalls extend E from Chicken Rk on E-going stream, which begins at HW Liverpool + 0610, and N from the rk on W-going stream, which begins at HW Liverpool.

Off Langness Pt (lt) the Skerranes (dry) extend 1ca SW, and tidal stream runs strongly, with eddies and a race. E side of Langness peninsula is foul ground, over which a dangerous sea can build in strong winds. Here the NE-going stream begins at HW Liverpool + 0545, and the SW-going at HW Liverpool – 0415, sp rates 2·25kn.

There is anch in Derby Haven, N of St Michael's Is, but exposed to E. From here to Douglas (9.10.18) and on to Maughold Hd (lt), there are no dangers more than 4ca offshore. Near the coast the SW-going stream runs for 9 hours and the NE-going for 3 hours, since an eddy forms during the second half of the main NE-going stream. Off Maughold Hd the NE-going stream begins at HW Liverpool + 0500, and the SW-going at HW Liverpool – 0415.

SE, E and NW of Pt of Ayre are dangerous banks, on which seas break in bad weather. These are Whitestone Bk (least depth 2·0m), Bahama Bk (1·5m, buoy), Ballacash Bk (2·7 m), King William Bks (3·3m, buoy), and Strunakill Bk (6·7m).

The W coast of IOM has few pilotage hazards. A spit with depth of 1·4m runs 2ca offshore from Rue Pt. Jurby Rk (depth 2·7m) lies 3ca off Jurby Hd. Craig Rk (depth 4 m) and shoals lie 2·5M NNE of Peel (9.10.16).

MENAI STRAIT (9.10.21 and chart *1464*) The main features of this narrow chan include: Puffin Is, seaward of NE end; Beaumaris; Garth Pt at Bangor, where NE end of Strait begins; Menai Suspension Bridge (30·5m); The Swellies, a narrow 1M stretch with strong tide and dangers mid-stream; Britannia Rail Bridge (27·4m), with cables close W at elevation of 22m; Port Dinorwic and Caernarfon (9.10.21); Abermenai Pt and Fort Belan, where narrows mark SW end of Strait; and Caernarfon Bar.

The following brief notes only cover very basic pilotage. For detailed directions see *W Coasts of England and Wales Pilot*, or *Cruising Anglesey and N Wales* (NW Venturers Yacht Club). For tidal streams 'Arrowsmiths' is recommended, from Arrowsmiths, Winterstoke Rd., Bristol, BS3 2NT, cost £3.00. The Swellies should be taken near local HW slack, and an understanding of tidal streams is essential. The tide is about 1 hour later, and sp range about 2·7m more, at NE end of Strait than at SW end. Levels differ most at about HW+1 (when level at NE end is more than 1·8m above level at SW end); and at about HW – 0445 (when level at NE end is more than 1·8m below level at SW end). Normally the stream runs as follows (times referred to HW Holyhead). HW – 0040 to HW + 0420: SW between Garth Pt and Abermenai Pt. HW + 0420 to HW + 0545: outwards from about The Swellies, ie NE towards Garth Pt and SW towards Abermenai Pt. HW + 0545 to HW – 0040: NE between Abermenai Pt and Garth Pt. Sp rates are generally about 3kn, but more in narrows, eg 5kn off Abermenai Pt, 6kn between the bridges, and 8kn at The Swellies. The timings and rates of streams may be affected by strong winds in either direction.

From NE, enter chan W of Puffin Island, taking first of ebb to reach the Swellies at slack HW (HW Holyhead – 0100). Slack HW only lasts about 20 mins at sps, a little more at nps. Pass under centre of suspension bridge span, and steer to leave Platters (dry) on mainland shore to port and Swellies lt bn close to stbd. From Swellies lt bn to Britannia Bridge hold mainland shore, leaving bn on Price Pt to port, and Gored Goch and Gribbin Rk to stbd. Leave Britannia Rk (centre pier of bridge) to stbd. Thence to SW hold to buoyed chan near mainland shore. (A Historic Wreck (see 9.0.3h) is 4ca SW of Britannia Bridge at 53°12'·77N 04°11'·72W). Port Dinorwic is useful to await right tidal conditions for onward passage in either direction. **Note: Direction of buoyage becomes NE off Caernarfon.**

Caernarfon Bar is impassable even in moderately strong winds against ebb, and narrows at Abermenai Pt demand a fair tide, or slackish water, since tide runs strongly here. Going seaward on first of ebb, when there is water over the banks, it may not be practicable to return to the Strait if conditions on the bar are bad. Then it is best to anch near Mussel Bank buoy and await slack water, before returning to Caernarfon (say). Leaving Abermenai Pt on last of ebb means banks to seaward are exposed and there is little water in chan or over bar.

Going NE'ward it is safe to reach the Swellies with last of flood, leaving Caernarfon about HW Holyhead – 0230. Do not leave too late, or full force of ebb will be met before reaching Bangor.

ANGLESEY TO BARDSEY ISLAND (AC *1977*, 1970, 1971) On N coast of Anglesey, a race extends 5ca off Pt Lynas (lt, fog sig, RC) on E-going stream. Amlwch is a small hbr (partly dries) 1·5M W of Pt Lynas. A drying rk lies 100m offshore on W side of appr, which should not be attempted in strong onshore winds. From here to Carmel Hd beware E Mouse (and shoals to SE), Middle Mouse, Harry Furlong's Rks (dry), Victoria Bank (least depth 1·8m), Coal Rk (awash), and W Mouse (with dangers to W and SW). The outermost of these dangers is 2M offshore. There are overfalls and races at headlands and over many rks and shoals along this coast.

Between Carmel Hd and The Skerries (lt, fog sig, Racon) the NE-going stream begins at HW Holyhead + 0550, and the SW-going at HW Holyhead – 0010, sp rates 5kn. 1M NW of Skerries the stream turns $1\frac{1}{2}$ hours later, and runs less strongly. Simplest passage, or at night or in bad weather, is to pass 1M off Skerries, in the TSS ITZ. In good conditions by day and at slack water, Carmel Hd can be rounded close inshore; but beware short, steep, breaking seas here in even moderate winds against tide.

Holyhead (9.10.22) is a port of refuge, access H24 in all weathers, within New Hbr; beware fast ferries. Races occur off N Stack and (more severe) off S Stack (lt, fog sig), up to 1·5M offshore on NNE-going stream which begins at HW Holyhead – 0605, sp rate 5kn. Races do not extend so far on SSW-going stream which begins at HW Holyhead + 0020, sp rate 5kn. The W coast of Anglesey is rugged with rks, some drying, up to 1·5M offshore. There are races off Penrhyn Mawr and Rhoscolyn Hd. Pilot's Cove, E of Llanddwyn Is, is good anch to await the right conditions for Menai Strait.

On the Lleyn Peninsula Porth Dinllaen (9.10.22) is good anch, but exposed to N and NE. Braich y Pwll is the steep, rky point at end of Lleyn Peninsula (chart 1971). About 1M N of it and up to 1M offshore lie The Tripods, a bank on which there are overfalls and a bad sea with wind against tide.

Bardsey Sound, 1·5M wide, can be used by day in moderate winds. Stream reaches 6kn at sp, and passage should be made at slack water, – 0015 HW or + 0035 LW Holyhead. Avoid Carreg Ddu on N side and Maen Bugail Rk (dries 4·1m) on S side of Sound, where there are dangerous races. If passing outside Bardsey Is (lt, fog sig) make a good offing to avoid overfalls which extend 1·5M W and 2·5M S of Island. Turbulence occurs over Bastram Shoal, Devil's Tail and Devil's Ridge, which lie SSE and E of Bardsey Is.

9.10.6 DISTANCE TABLE

Approximate distances in nautical miles are by the most direct route, whilst avoiding dangers and allowing for Traffic Separation Schemes. Places in *italics* are in adjoining areas; places in **bold** are in 9.0.7, Distances across the Irish Sea.

1.	***Portpatrick***	1																		
2.	***Mull of Galloway***	16	2																	
3.	**Kirkcudbright**	48	32	3																
4.	**Maryport**	65	49	26	4															
5.	Workington	63	47	25	6	5														
6.	Ravenglass	70	54	40	30	23	6													
7.	**Point of Ayre**	38	22	28	37	31	34	7												
8.	Peel	41	26	46	55	49	52	18	8											
9.	**Port St Mary**	56	41	61	63	57	50	35	18	9										
10.	Douglas	60	42	46	50	44	39	19	30	13	10									
11.	Ramsey	44	28	34	41	35	34	6	24	27	15	11								
12.	Glasson Dock	101	85	74	66	60	37	64	85	69	63	61	12							
13.	**Fleetwood**	95	79	68	59	53	30	58	80	63	57	55	10	13						
14.	**Liverpool**	118	102	97	89	83	60	80	86	76	70	77	52	46	14					
15.	Conwy	111	95	95	92	86	58	72	72	57	59	68	62	56	46	15				
16.	Beaumaris	109	93	94	95	89	72	71	73	58	58	70	66	60	49	12	16			
17.	Caernarfon	117	103	104	105	99	82	81	73	68	68	80	76	70	59	22	10	17		
18.	**Holyhead**	93	81	94	96	90	69	68	62	46	50	65	79	73	68	36	32	26	18	
19.	Bardsey Island	127	113	129	129	123	114	107	94	80	88	98	107	101	90	53	41	31	43	19	
20.	***Fishguard***	171	158	175	175	169	160	153	140	126	134	144	153	147	136	100	88	78	89	45	20

KIRKCUDBRIGHT *9.10.7*

Dumfries and Galloway **54°50'·31N 04°03'·48W**

CHARTS AC1344, 1346, 2094, *1826*; Imray C62; OS 84

TIDES +0030 Dover; ML 4·1; Duration 0545; Zone 0 (UT)

Standard Port LIVERPOOL (⟶)

Times				Height (metres)			
High Water		Low Water		MHWS	MHWN	MLWN	MLWS
0000	0600	0200	0800	9·3	7·4	2·9	0·9
1200	1800	1400	2000				
Differences KIRKCUDBRIGHT BAY							
+0015	+0015	+0010	0000	–1·8	–1·5	–0·5	–0·1
DRUMMORE							
+0030	+0040	+0015	+0020	–3·4	–2·5	–0·9	–0·3
PORT WILLIAM							
+0030	+0030	+0025	0000	–2·9	–2·2	–0.8	No data
GARLIESTON							
+0025	+0035	+0030	+0005	–2·3	–1·7	–0·5	No data
ISLE OF WHITHORN							
+0020	+0025	+0025	+0005	–2·4	–2·0	–0.8	–0.2
HESTAN ISLET (Kippford)							
+0025	+0025	+0020	+0025	–1·0	–1·1	–0.5	0.0
SOUTHERNESS POINT							
+0030	+0030	+0030	+0010	–0·7	–0·7	No data	
ANNAN WATERFOOT							
+0050	+0105	+0220	+0310	–2·2	–2·6	–2·7	*
TORDUFF POINT							
+0105	+0140	+0520	+0410	–4·1	–4·9	*Not below CD	
REDKIRK							
+0110	+0215	+0715	+0445	–5·5	–6·2	*Not below CD	

Notes: At Annan Waterfoot, Torduff Pt and Redkirk the LW time differences are for the start of the rise, which at sp is very sudden. *At LW the tide does not usually fall below CD.

SHELTER Very good. Depths at LW: 1-1·5m at the floating pontoon/jetty. Alternatively dry out on 40 Ⓐs or against town quay. Down-river there are good ⚓s behind Ross Is and ½ca N of Torrs Pt, except in S'lies which raise heavy swell.

NAVIGATION WPT 54°45'·51N 04°04'·08W, 185°/005° from/to Torrs Pt, 1·4M. The Bar is 1ca N of Torrs Pt; access HW±3. R Dee has many shoal patches of 0·3m or less. Spring tides run up to 3-4kn. A firing range crosses the ent; call Range Safety Officer ☎ (01557) 500271 (out of hours), 830236 office hours) or VHF 73 Range Safety Boat Gallavidian on Ch 16.

LIGHTS AND MARKS Little Ross lt ho, W of ent, Fl 5s 50m 12M, (obscured in Wigtown bay when brg more than 103°). No 1 lt bn, Fl WRG 3s, is atop the LB shed (54°47'·70N); vis G080°-037°, W037°-043°, R043°-080°. The river is well lit/buoyed. There are Fl G lts on the mooring piles off the town.

RADIO TELEPHONE VHF Ch 12 16 (0730-1700). *Range Control* Ch 16 73.

TELEPHONE (Dial code 01557) Hr Mr ☎/📠 331135; ⊖ (0141) 887 9369; MRCC 0151-931 3341; Marinecall 09068 500 461; Police 330600; Dr 330755.

FACILITIES **Pontoon/jetty** £7.80, AC, FW; **Town Quay** P (hose), D (road tanker), FW, El, C (15 ton) CH, ME. **KYC** ☎ 330963; **SC** ☎ 330032, Slip, M, FW; **Town** EC Thur; V, R, Bar, ✉, Ⓑ, ≋ (Dumfries 30M), ✈ (Glasgow 100M).

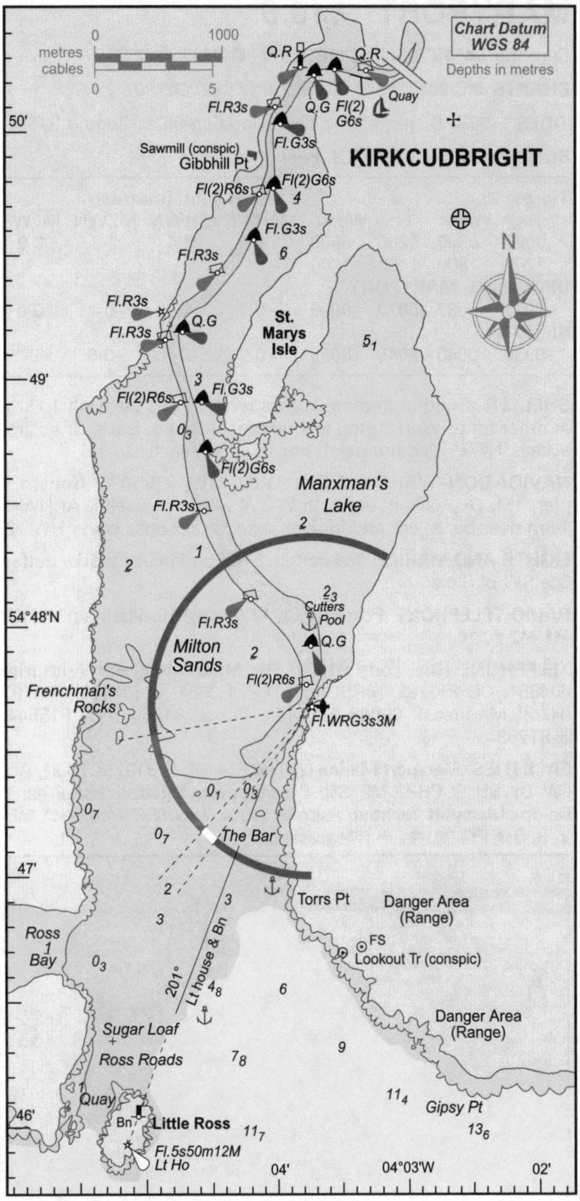

Luce Bay Firing Range (D402/403) lies to the NW. For info on activity ☎ (01776) 888792.

OTHER HARBOURS ON THE COASTS OF DUMFRIES AND GALLOWAY

ISLE OF WHITHORN, Dumfries and Galloway, **54°41'·91N 04°21'·88W.** AC2094, *1826*. HW +0035 on Dover; ML 3·7m; Duration 0545. See 9.10.7. Shelter good but hbr dries, having approx 2·5m at HW±3. On W side of ent beware the Skerries, a ledge with PHM pole/radar reflector. St Ninian's Tr (W □ tr) is conspic at E side of ent. E pier hd has QG 4m 5M; ldg lts 335°, both Oc R 8s 7/9m 7M, synch, Or masts and ◇. Hr Mr ☎ (01988) 500246; Facilities: AB on quay £3, Slip, P, D, FW, ME, Sh, CH, V, Bar, ✉, VHF Ch 80 (occas).

GARLIESTON, Dumfries and Galloway, **54°47'·36N 04°21'·83W.** AC 2094, *1826*. HW +0035 on Dover; ML no data; Duration 0545. See 9.10.7. Hbr affords complete shelter but dries. Access (2m) HW±3. Pier hd lt 2FR (vert) 5m 3M. Beware rky outcrops in W side of bay marked by a perch. Hr Mr ☎ (01988) 600274. Facilities: M £3, FW, AC on quay, Slip. **Town**: V, ME, P, D.

KIPPFORD, Dumfries & Galloway, **54°52'·36N 03°48'·93W.** AC 1346, *1826*. HW +0040 on Dover; ML 4·2m (Hestan Is). See 9.10.7. Good shelter on drying moorings/pontoons off Kippford, 2·75M up drying Urr Estuary from Hestan Is lt ho Fl (2) 10s 42m 9M. Access HW±2 via marked, unlit chan. CCC or Solway SDs (from Solway YC) are strongly advised. Beware Craig Roan on E side of ent. Temp ⚓s NE or W of Hestan Is to await tide. VHF: Ch M call *Kippford Startline* (YC) HW±2 in season. Ch 16 *Kippford Slipway* (Pilotage). Facilities: **Solway YC** (01556) 620249, AB, AC, FW, M; **Services:** AB £6, M, Slip, D (cans), CH, Gaz, BY, ME. **Town** P, SM, V, ✉, Bar, Slip

MARYPORT 9.10.8

Cumbria **54°43'·03N 03°30'·38W** ❁❁◊◊◊✿✿✿

CHARTS AC 2013, 1346, *1826*; Imray C62; OS 89

TIDES +0038 Dover; ML no data; Duration 0550; Zone 0 (UT)

Standard Port LIVERPOOL (⟶)

Times				Height (metres)			
High Water		Low Water		MHWS	MHWN	MLWN	MLWS
0000	0600	0200	0800	9·3	7·4	2·9	0·9
1200	1800	1400	2000				
Differences MARYPORT							
+0017	+0032	+0020	+0005	−0·7	−0·8	−0·4	0·0
SILLOTH							
+0030	+0040	+0045	+0055	−0·1	−0·3	−0·6	−0·1

SHELTER Good in marina, access HW ±2½ nps over sill 1·75m; at other times Workington is a refuge. Elizabeth Basin dries 2m, access HW±1½; commercial, not used by yachts.

NAVIGATION WPT 54°43'·09N 03°32'·47W, 270°/090° from/to S pier, 1M. Overfalls at ent with W/SW winds over ebb. At HW−3 1·8m over bar at ent and in river chan; mud banks cover HW −2.

LIGHTS AND MARKS As chartlet. SHM bn Fl G 5s marks outfall 6ca SW of S pier.

RADIO TELEPHONE Port VHF Ch 12 (occas) 16. Marina (H24) Ch M1 M2 80 16.

TELEPHONE (Dial code 01900) Hr Mr 817440; Hbr Authority 604351; CG 812782; MRSC (0151) 931 3341; ⊖ (01482) 782107 (H24); Marinecall 09068 500 461; Police 812601; Dr 815544; Ⓗ 812634.

FACILITIES **Maryport Marina** (200) ☎ 814431, 📠 810212, £0.31, AC, FW, BY, BH, El, CH, ⓔ, ME, Slip, P (cans), (fresh fish from Fisherman's Co-op); **Maryport Yachting Ass'n** ☎ 64964. **Town** EC Wed; P, D, ME, V, R, Bar, ✉, Ⓑ, ⇌, ✈ (Newcastle).

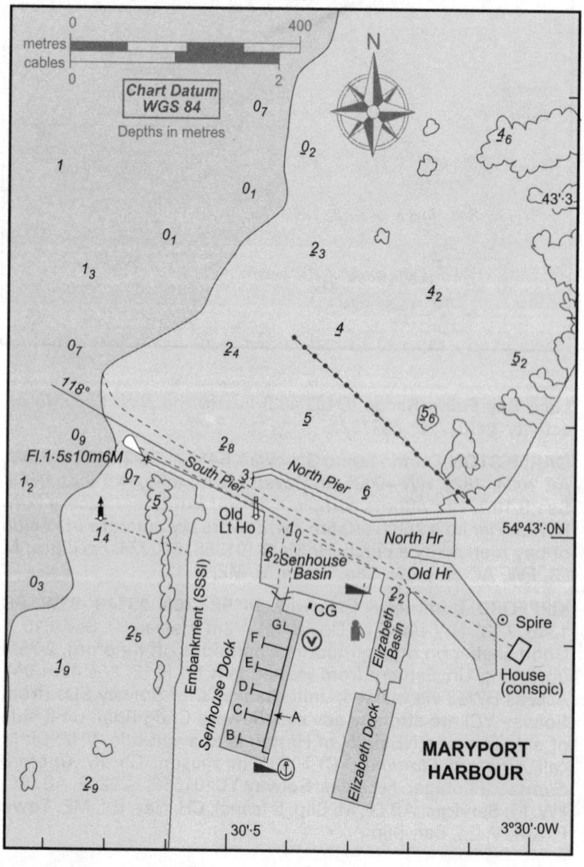

WORKINGTON 9.10.9

Cumbria 54°39'·03N 03°34'·38W ❁❁◊◊✿

CHARTS AC 2013, 1346, *1826*; Imray C62; OS 89

TIDES +0025 Dover; ML 4·5; Duration 0545; Zone 0 (UT)

Standard Port LIVERPOOL (⟶)

Times				Height (metres)			
High Water		Low Water		MHWS	MHWN	MLWN	MLWS
0000	0600	0200	0800	9·3	7·4	2·9	0·9
1200	1800	1400	2000				
Differences WORKINGTON							
+0020	+0020	+0020	+0010	−1·2	−1·1	−0·3	0·0

SHELTER Good; ent and chan to Prince of Wales Dock are dredged 1·8m. Berth where you can (free) or ⚓ in Turning Basin. Lock (HW±1½) into PoW Dock 1·8m (for coasters). Low (1·8m) fixed railway bridge across ent to inner tidal hbr.

NAVIGATION WPT 54°39'·59N 03°35'·38W, 311°/131° from/to front ldg lt, 1·0M. Tide sets strongly across ent. In periods of heavy rain a strong freshet from R Derwent may be encountered in the hbr ent.

LIGHTS AND MARKS Workington Bank, least depth 5·5m, is 2M W of hbr ent; it is marked by a NCM buoy Q.Fl and a SCM buoy, VQ (6) + L Fl 10s, (see 9.10.4). A SHM buoy, Fl G 5s, 1·3M NW of hbr ent is a mark for English Chan. Ldg lts 132°, both FR 10/12m 3M, on W pyramidal trs with Y bands. Two sets of F Bu lts in line mark NE and SW edges of chan. There are 16 wind-turbines between ¾M and 2M NE of hbr ent.

RADIO TELEPHONE VHF Ch 14 16 (HW−2½ to HW+2 approx).

TELEPHONE (Dial code 01900) Hr Mr 602301 📠 604696 ; CG 2238; ⊖ (01482) 782107 (H24); MRSC (0151) 931 3341; Marinecall 09068 500 461; Police 812601; Dr 64866; Ⓗ 602244.

FACILITIES **Dock** D, FW, ME, El; **Vanguard SC** ☎ 826886, M, FW. **Town** EC Thurs; P, V, R, Bar, ✉, Ⓑ, ⇌, ✈ (Carlisle).

MINOR HARBOUR 10M NNE OF MARYPORT

SILLOTH, Cumbria, **54°52'·16N 03°23'·86W**. AC 2013, 1346, *1826*. HW −0050 on Dover; ML no data; Duration 0520. See 9.10.8. Appr via English or Middle Chans, approx 8M long, requires local knowledge. Beware constantly shifting chans and banks. Yachts are not encouraged. ⚓ SW of ent in about 4m off Lees Scar, Fl G 10s 11m 2M; exposed to SW winds. Outer hbr dries; lock into New Dock, which is mainly commercial. East Cote Dir lt 052° FG 15m 12M; vis 046°-058°, intens 052°. Ldg lts, both F, 115°. Groyne 2 FG (vert). Tfc sigs on mast at New Dock: no entry unless Y signal arm raised by day or Q Bu lt by night. VHF Ch 16 12 (HW−2½ to HW+1½). Hr Mr ☎ (016973) 31358; ⊖ (01900) 604611. Facilities: EC Tues; FW, Ⓑ, Bar, ✉, R, V.

MINOR HARBOUR 2M SOUTH OF WORKINGTON

HARRINGTON, Cumbria, **54°36'·77N 03°34'·29W**. AC 2013, 1346, *1826*. HW +0025 on Dover; Duration 0540; Use Diff's Workington 9.10.9. Good shelter in small hbr only used by local FVs and yachts; dries 3ca offshore. Ent difficult in strong W winds. Berth on N wall of inner hbr (free). Call ☎ (01946) 823741 Ext 148 for moorings. Limited facilities. **SC**.

WORKINGTON *continued*

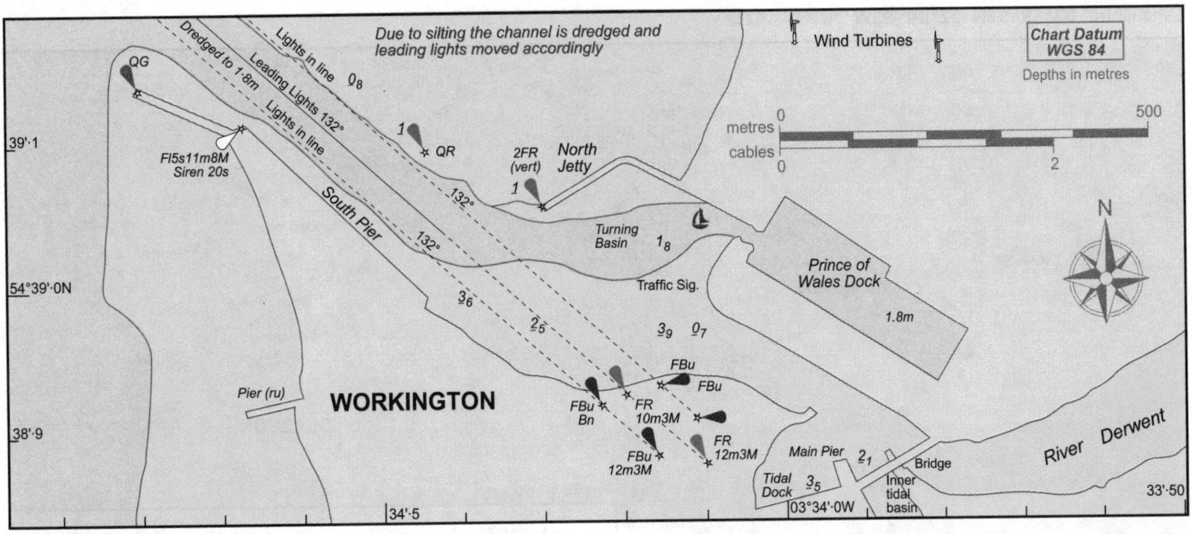
Due to silting the channel is dredged and leading lights moved accordingly
Wind Turbines
Chart Datum WGS 84
Depths in metres
metres 0 500
cables 0 2
Dredged to 1·8m
Leading Lights 132°
Lights in line
QG
Fl5s11m8M
Siren 20s
QR
2FR (vert)
North Jetty
South Pier
132°
Turning Basin
Traffic Sig.
Prince of Wales Dock
1.8m
FBu
FBu Bn
FR 10m3M
FBu 12m3M
FR 12m3M
Pier (ru)
WORKINGTON
Main Pier
Tidal Dock
Inner tidal basin
Bridge
River Derwent
39'·1
54°39'·0N
38'·9
34'·5
03°34'·0W
33'·50
N

WHITEHAVEN *9.10.10*

Cumbria **54°33'·18N 03°35'·82W**

CHARTS AC 2013, 1346, *1826*; Imray C62; OS 89

TIDES +0015 Dover; ML 4·5; Duration 0550; Zone 0 (UT)

Standard Port LIVERPOOL (⟶)

Times				**Height (metres)**			
High Water		Low Water		MHWS	MHWN	MLWN	MLWS
0000	0600	0200	0800	9·3	7·4	2·9	0·9
1200	1800	1400	2000				
Differences WHITEHAVEN							
+0005	+0015	+0010	+0005	−1·3	−1·1	−0·5	+0·1
TARN POINT (3M S of Ravenglass)							
+0005	+0005	+0010	0000	−1·0	−1·0	−0·4	0·0
DUDDON BAR (54°09'N 03°20'W)							
+0003	+0003	+0008	+0002	−0·8	−0·8	−0·3	0·0

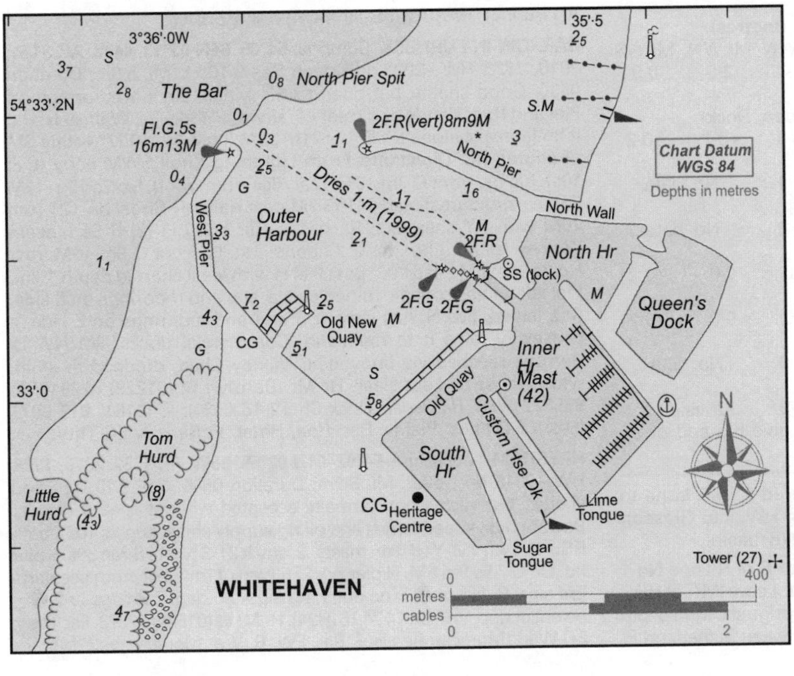
3°36'·0W
35'·5
54°33'·2N
33'·0
The Bar
North Pier Spit
S.M
Fl.G.5s 16m13M
2F.R(vert)8m9M
North Pier
Dries 1m (1999)
Chart Datum WGS 84
Depths in metres
North Wall
West Pier
Outer Harbour
M 2F.R
SS (lock)
North Hr
Queen's Dock
2F.G
2F.G
Old New Quay
CG
Inner Hr
Mast (42)
Old Quay
Custom Hse Dk
South Hr
Lime Tongue
Tom Hurd
Little Hurd
CG Heritage Centre
Sugar Tongue
Tower (27)
WHITEHAVEN
metres 0 400
cables 0 2
N

SHELTER Very good, entry safe in most weathers. One of the more accessible ports of refuge in NW England, with a new marina in the inner hbr. Appr chan across the outer hbr is dredged to $\underline{1}$·0m above CD giving access approx HW±4. Sea lock (30m x 13.7m), with sill at CD, maintains 5·5m within inner hbr. Yacht pontoons are in Inner Hbr. Queen's Dock (from which the lock gates have been removed) and N Hbr remain for commercial and FV use.

NAVIGATION WPT 54°33'·34N 03°36'·21W, 313°/133° from/to W pier hd, 4½ca. There are no hazards in the offing. Hold closer to the North Pier.

LIGHTS AND MARKS Several tall chimneys are charted within 1·5M S of hbr. St Bees Head, Fl (2) 20s 102m 21M, is 2·7M SSW of hbr ent. SHM bn, Fl G 2·5s, 4½ca S of W pierhead marks sewer outfall. IPTS sigs 1-3 shown from N side of lock ent to seaward only at present: priority to inward bound vessels.

RADIO TELEPHONE Hr Mr VHF Ch 12 16 (as for access times).

TELEPHONE (Dial code 01946) Hr Mr 692435, 📠 691135; ⊖ (01482) 782107 (H24); MRSC (0151) 931 3341; Marinecall 09068 500 461.

FACILITIES **Marina** (155) ☎ 692435, AC, FW, D, Slip, showers and toilets in portacabins, BH, **SC**. **Town** EC Wed, Market days Thurs, Sat; P (cans), Bar, Ⓑ, ✉, R, V, ⇌.

MINOR HARBOUR BETWEEN ST BEES HEAD AND MORECAMBE BAY

RAVENGLASS, Cumbria, **54°20'·00N 03°26'·80W** (drying line). AC 1346, *1826*. HW +0020 on Dover; ML no data; Duration 0545. See 9.10.10 (Tarn Point). Large drying hbr, into which R's Mite, Irt and Esk flow; has approx 2·5m in ent at HW–2. Sellafield power stn with WCM lt buoy and outfall buoys are 5M NNW. FG ☆ (occas) is on blockhouse at S side of ent. *Solway Sailing Directions* with pilotage notes by Ravenglass Boating Ass'n or local knowledge are advised. From N beware Drigg Rk and from S Selker Rks, marked by SHM buoy Fl (3) G 10s, 5M SSW of ent. Firing range D406 is close S at Eskmeals; Mon-Thur 0800-1600LT (1500 Fri). When in use R flags flown, R lts at night; call *Eskmeals Gun Range* VHF Ch 16 13, ☎ (01229) 717631 Ext 245/6. **Village**: EC Wed; FW, Slip, Bar, V, ✉.

GLASSON DOCK *9.10.11*

Lancashire **53°59'·98N 02°50'·93W** ❁❁◊◊◊✿✿

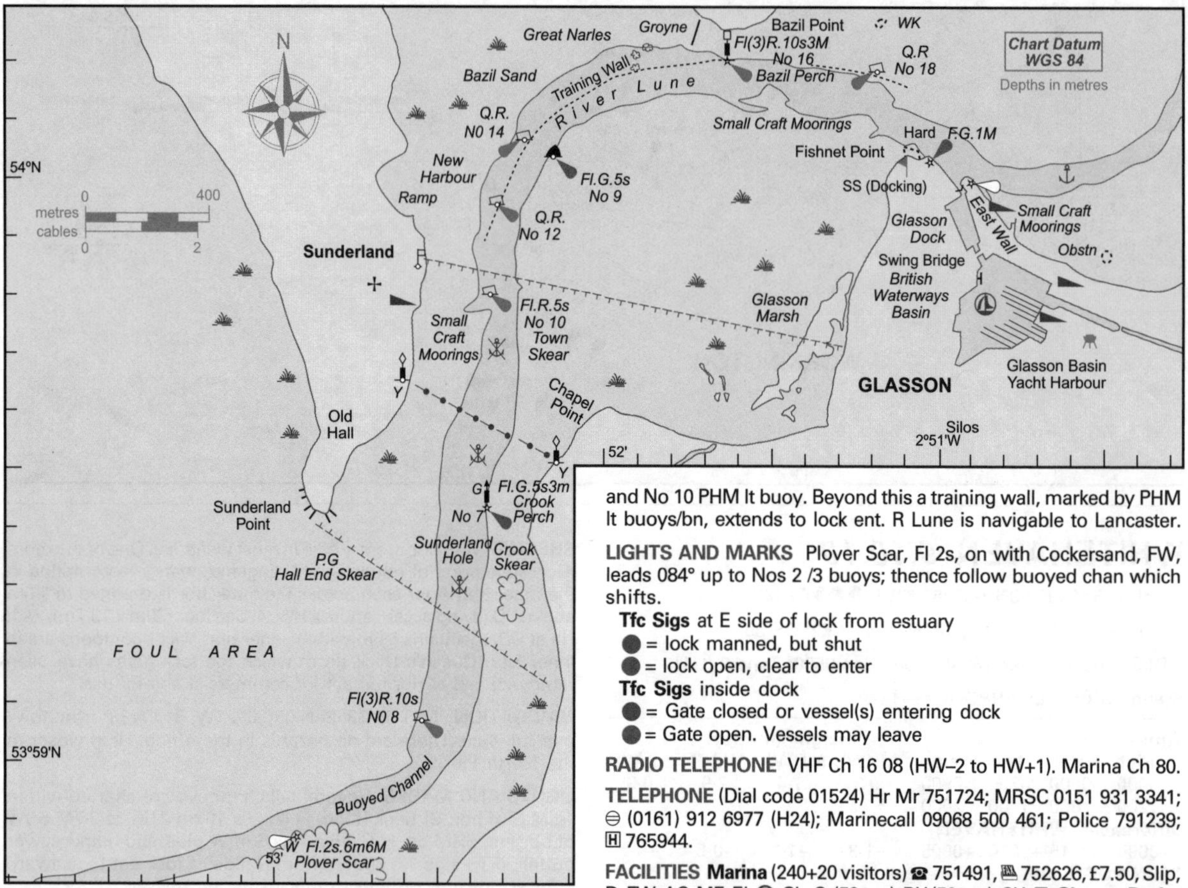

CHARTS AC 1552, 2010, *1826*; Imray C62; OS 102, 97

TIDES +0020 Dover; ML No data; Duration 0535; Zone 0 (UT)

Standard Port LIVERPOOL (⟶)

Times				Height (metres)			
High Water		Low Water		MHWS	MHWN	MLWN	MLWS
0000	0600	0200	0700	9·3	7·4	2·9	0·9
1200	1800	1400	1900				
Differences BARROW-IN-FURNESS (Ramsden Dock)							
+0015	+0015	+0015	+0015	0·0	–0·3	+0·1	+0·2
ULVERSTON							
+0020	+0040	No data		0·0	–0·1	No data	
ARNSIDE							
+0100	+0135	No data		+0·5	+0·2	No data	
MORECAMBE							
+0005	+0010	+0030	+0015	+0·2	0·0	0·0	+0·2
HEYSHAM							
+0005	+0005	+0015	0000	+0·1	0·0	0·0	+0·2
GLASSON DOCK							
+0020	+0030	+0220	+0240	–2·7	–3·0	No data	
LANCASTER							
+0110	+0030	Dries out		–5·0	–4·9	Dries out	

Note: At Glasson Dock LW time differences give the end of a LW stand which lasts up to 2 hours at sp.

SHELTER Very good in marina; also sheltered ⚓ in R Lune to await sea lock, opens HW Liverpool –0045 to HW, into Glasson Dock. Inner lock/swing bridge lead into BWB basin.

NAVIGATION WPT 53°58'·41N 03°00'·09W (2ca S of R Lune No 1 WCM By), 264°/084° from/to front ldg lt 084°, 4·2M. Leave WPT at HW–2 via buoyed/lit chan. Plover Scar lt bn has a tide gauge showing depth over the lock sill at Glasson Dock. ⚓ is prohib between Sutherland Pt and No 10 PHM lt buoy. Beyond this a training wall, marked by PHM lt buoys/bn, extends to lock ent. R Lune is navigable to Lancaster.

LIGHTS AND MARKS Plover Scar, Fl 2s, on with Cockersand, FW, leads 084° up to Nos 2 /3 buoys; thence follow buoyed chan which shifts.

Tfc Sigs at E side of lock from estuary
● = lock manned, but shut
● = lock open, clear to enter

Tfc Sigs inside dock
● = Gate closed or vessel(s) entering dock
● = Gate open. Vessels may leave

RADIO TELEPHONE VHF Ch 16 08 (HW–2 to HW+1). Marina Ch 80.

TELEPHONE (Dial code 01524) Hr Mr 751724; MRSC 0151 931 3341; ⊜ (0161) 912 6977 (H24); Marinecall 09068 500 461; Police 791239; Ⓗ 765944.

FACILITIES Marina (240+20 visitors) ☎ 751491, ℻ 752626, £7.50, Slip, D, FW, AC, ME, El, Ⓔ, Sh, C, (50 ton), BH (50 ton), CH, ♿; **Glasson Basin**, M, AB; **Glasson SC** ☎ 751089 Slip, M, C; **Lune CC** Access HW±2. **Town** EC Lancaster Wed; P (cans), V, R, Bar, ✉, Ⓑ (Lancaster), ⇌ (bus to Lancaster 4M), ✈ (Blackpool).

ADJACENT HARBOURS IN MORECAMBE BAY

BARROW-IN-FURNESS, Cumbria, **54°05'·64N 03°13'·44W**. AC 3164, 2010, *1826*. HW +0030 on Dover; See 9.10.11. ML 5·0m; Duration 0530. Good shelter but open to SE winds. Drying moorings off Piel and Roa Islands or ⚓ clear of fairway. Marks/lts: Walney Island lt ho (conspic stone tr), Fl 15s 21m 23M (obsc 122°-127° within 3M of shore), RC. Directions: From Lightning Knoll SWM buoy (L Fl 10s), ldg lts, front Q 7m 10M; rear (6ca from front), Iso 2s 13m 10M (lattice structures) lead 041°/3·7M past Halfway Shoal bn, QR 16m 10M with RY chequers, Racon, to Bar buoy Fl (2) R 5s (abeam Walney Island lt ho). Inner Channel ldg lts, front Q 9m 10M, rear Iso 2s 14m 6M, lead 006° past Piel Is with least charted depth 1·7m. Piel Island has conspic ruined castle, slip and moorings on E side. Roa Island, 5ca N, has jetty at S end and moorings on E side; a causeway joins it to mainland. Commercial docks, 3M NW at Barrow, reached via buoyed/lit Walney Chan, dredged to 2·5m, which must be kept clear. Hr Mr (Barrow) ☎ (01229) 822911, ℻ 835822; VHF *Ramsden Dock* Ch 12 16 (H24). ⊜ (0161) 912 6977 (H24). Facilities: Piel Is, Bar; Roa, Hotel, V. **Barrow** EC Thurs.

HEYSHAM, Lancashire, **54°02'·01N 02°55'·96W**. AC 1552, 2010, *1826*. HW +0015 on Dover; ML 5·1m; Duration 0545. See 9.10.11. Good shelter, but yachts not normally accepted without special reason. Beware high speed ferries and oil rig supply ships. Ldg lts 102°, both F Bu 11/14m 2M, Y+B ◊ on masts. S jetty lt 2 FG (vert), Siren 30s. S pier hd ,Oc G 7·5s 9m 6M. N pier hd, 2FR (vert) 11m, obsc from seaward. Ent sigs: R flag or ● = no entry; no sig = no dep; 2 R flags or 2 ● = no ent or dep. VHF Ch 14 74 16 (H24). Hr Mr ☎ (01524) 52373. Facilities: EC Wed (Morecambe also); Bar, FW, R, V at Morecambe (2M).

FLEETWOOD *9.10.12*

Lancashire **53°55'·49N 03°00'·15W** ❀❀❀◊◊◊✿✿

CHARTS AC 1552, 2010, *1826*; Imray C62; OS 102

TIDES +0015 Dover; ML 5.2; Duration 0530; Zone 0 (UT)

Standard Port LIVERPOOL (⟶)

Times				**Height (metres)**			
High Water		Low Water		MHWS	MHWN	MLWN	MLWS
0000	0600	0200	0700	9·3	7·4	2·9	0·9
1200	1800	1400	1900				
Differences WYRE LIGHTHOUSE							
−0010	−0010	+0005	0000	−0·1	−0·1	No data	
FLEETWOOD							
−0008	−0008	−0003	−0003	−0·1	−0·1	+0·1	+0·3
BLACKPOOL							
−0015	−0005	−0005	−0015	−0·4	−0·4	−0·1	+0·1

SHELTER Very good in Wyre Dock Marina 5·5m. Sheltered ⚓ off Knott End pier on E bank to await tide. Passage up-river to Skippool (5M) needs local knowledge and shoal draft; access HW±1 (if ht of tide is >8·0m).

NAVIGATION WPT 53°57´·57N 03°02´·33W, Fairway NCM buoy, VQ, 323°/143° from/to No 3 SHM lt buoy, 3ca; here the appr chan turns S. Caution: avoid ferries and dredgers turning in lower hbr, dredged 4·5m. Further up the hbr, Nos 23 SHM and 24 PHM buoys mark start of marina ent chan dredged to drying height of $\underline{3}$m, giving access HW±2 to lock. For best water keep 15m NW of the 300m long training wall (5 Y perches, △ topmarks).

LIGHTS AND MARKS Chan is well buoyed/lit, but AC 1552 no longer depicts individual buoys which are subject to frequent change due to silting. Ldg lts, front Fl G 2s; rear Fl G 4s, 156° (only to be used between Nos 8 and 13 buoys). Lock sigs (only enter on instructions): 1 ● (1 ●) = Gates open for entry; 2 ● (2 ●) = open for departures.

RADIO TELEPHONE Call *RoRo Ships* directly on Ch 11 for info on movements. Call *Fleetwood Dock* Ch **12**, HW±2 for marina/Fish Dock.

TELEPHONE (Dial code 01253) Hr Mr (ABP) ☎ 872323, 📠 777549; MRSC (0151) 931 3341/3; ⊖ (0161) 912 6977 (H24); Marinecall 09068 500 461; Police (01524) 63333; Dr 873312.

FACILITIES Marina (210) ☎ 872323, 📠 777549, £1.56, D, FW, AC, ⊡, C (25 ton), CH, SM, ACA, ME, El, Sh, Ⓔ, C (mobile 50 ton by arrangement). **Wardley's YC** ☎ 700429, 1 Ⓥ. **Blackpool & Fleetwood YC** (Skippool) ☎ 884205, AB, Slip, FW, Bar; **Town** EC Wed; P & D (cans), ME, El, Sh, CH, V, R, Bar, ✉, Ⓑ, ⇌ (Poulton-le-Fylde or Blackpool), ✈ (Blackpool).

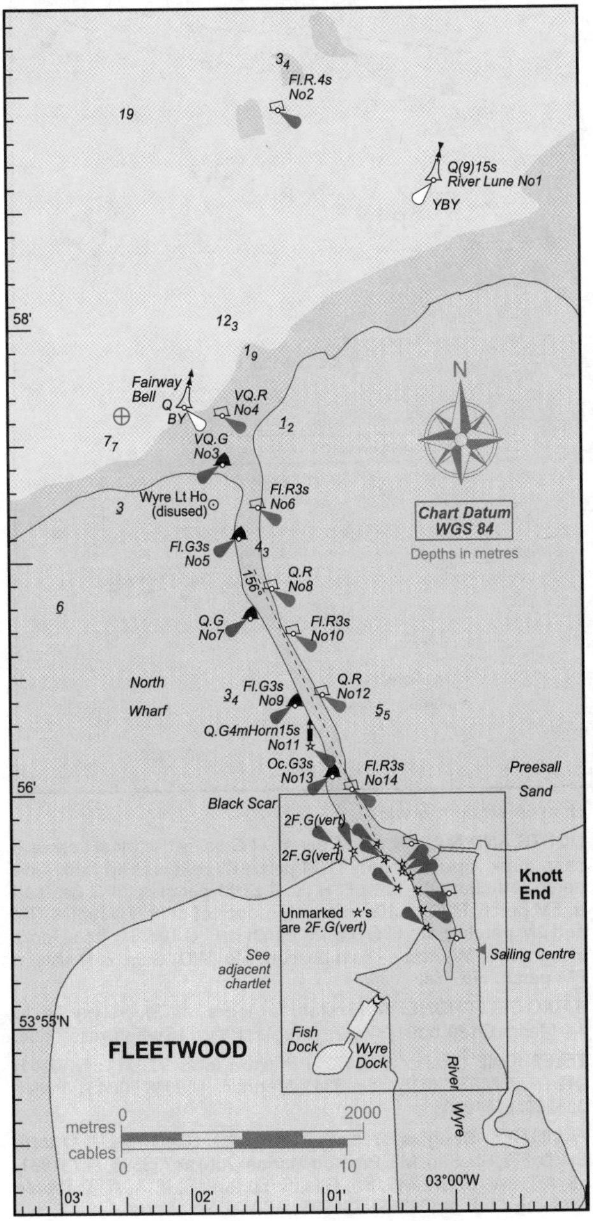

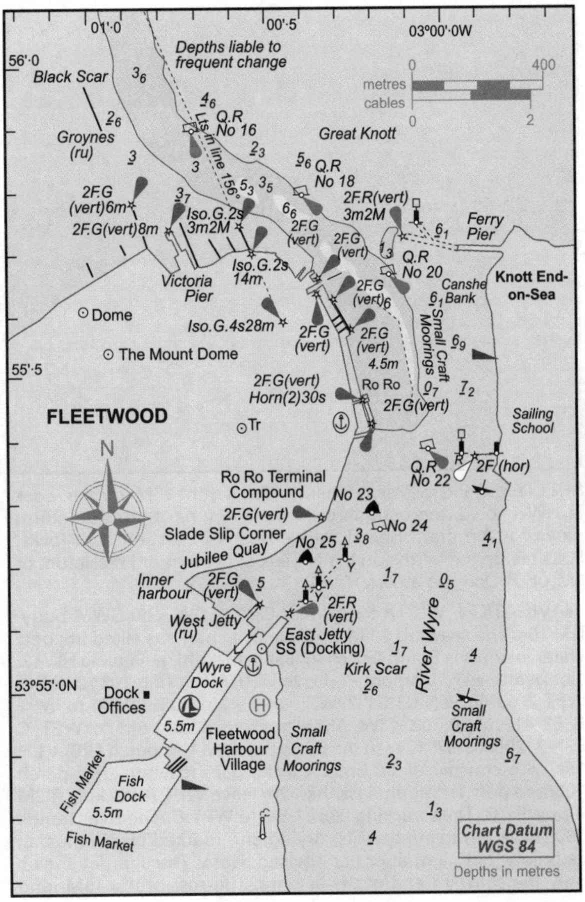

RIVER RIBBLE/PRESTON *9.10.13*

Lancashire **53°43′·51N 03°00′·08W**

CHARTS AC 1981, *1826*; Imray C62; OS 102

TIDES +0013 Dover; ML No data; Duration 0520; Zone 0 (UT)

Standard Port LIVERPOOL (⟶)

Times				Height (metres)			
High Water		Low Water		MHWS	MHWN	MLWN	MLWS
0000	0600	0200	0700	9·3	7·4	2·9	0·9
1200	1800	1400	1900				
Differences PRESTON							
+0010	+0010	+0335	+0310	−4·0	−4·1	−2·8	−0·8

LW time differences give the end of a LW stand lasting 3½ hrs.

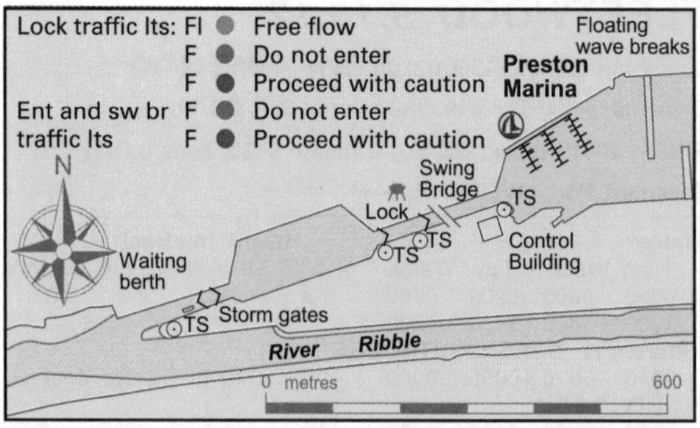

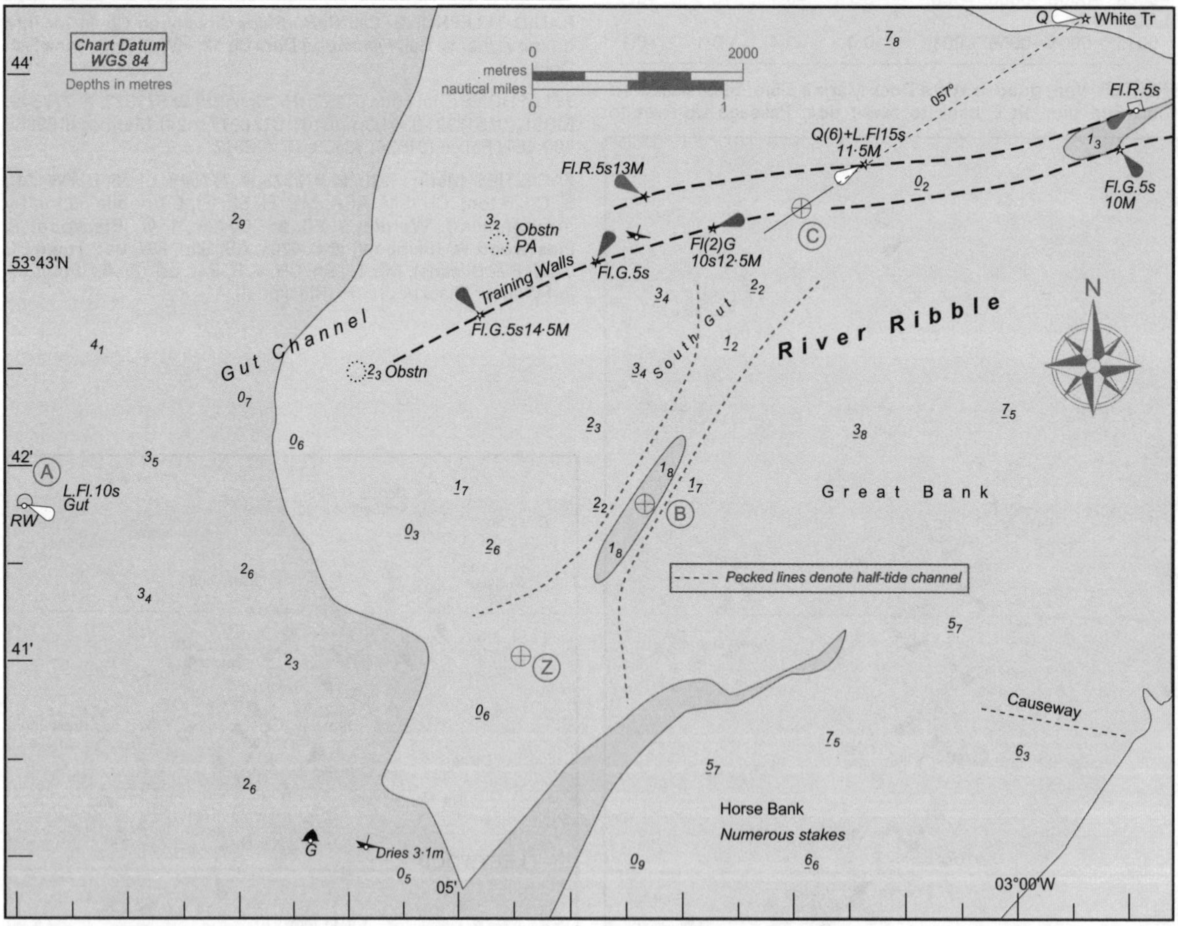

SHELTER Good in Preston marina (5m depth) 15M upriver. Lock in HW-1 to +2, (no commercial tfc); lay-by berth outside storm gates for 2m draft. Swing bridge opens in unison with locks. Possible drying berths on the N bank at Lytham or Freckleton, or 2M up R Douglas access HW±1.

NAVIGATION WPT **A** 53°41′·75N 03°08′·90W, Gut SWM buoy, L Fl 10s. The seaward 2·5M of original lit chan has silted up; best water is now via South Gut chan (liable to shift), navigable HW±2. Not before HW Liverpool −2, leave WPT **A** tracking 105° 2·9M to WPT **Z** 53°40′·96N 03°04′·22W, then tracking 032° 0·9M to WPT **B** 53°41′·70N 03°03′·43W. Then tracking 026° 1·8M to WPT **C** 53°43′·29N 03°02′·10W to the transit of the 11½M perch Q(6) + LFl 15s with conspic W Tr. Enter via the gap, leaving 11½M perch 100m to port. If draught less than 2m leave WPT **A** tracking 3·2M E to WPT **B**. Then tracking 026° 1·8M to WPT **C**. The river trends 080° between training walls, drying 3m, marked by perches; lit as below, but night appr not advised. Note: The chartlet shows only the seaward end of the estuary. The rest of the 15M long chan is straightforward.

LIGHTS AND MARKS 14½M perch, Fl G 5s, is the most seaward chan mark. Up-river from 11½M perch there is a PHM buoy and perch (off chartlet), both Fl R 5s. 4 SHM perches, Fl G 5s, lead to 5M perch, Fl (2) G 10s, marking mouth of unlit R Douglas. 3M and 2M perches are Fl G 5s; 1M perch is Fl G 10s. Tfc lts at locks into marina. Warton airfield beacon, Mo (WQ) G 9s, is N abeam 6M perch, Fl G 5s.

RADIO TELEPHONE At Preston, for locks call *Riversway* Ch 16 14; Marina Ch **80**, both (HW±2). Douglas BY Ch 16 when vessel due.

TELEPHONE (Dial code 01772) Preston locks 726711; ⊖ (0161) 912 6977; MRSC (0151) 9313341; Marinecall 09068 500461; Police 203203; H 710408.

FACILITIES **Douglas BY**, ☎/📠 812462, AB, £0.40/ft/wk, C (7 ton), CH, D, FW, Sh, Slip, ME. **Preston Marina** (250) ☎ 733595, 📠 731881, £5, AC, FW, D, CH, ME, Sh, Gas, C (50 ton), R, V, ACA, ♿. **Ribble Cruising Club** ☎ (01253) 739983. ACA at Southport.

TIME ZONE (UTC)
For Summer Time add ONE hour in **non-shaded areas**

ENGLAND – LIVERPOOL (ALFRED DOCK)

LAT 53°24′N LONG 3°01′W

TIMES AND HEIGHTS OF HIGH AND LOW WATERS

SPRING & NEAP TIDES
Dates in red are SPRINGS
Dates in blue are NEAPS

YEAR **2002**

JANUARY

Day	Time	m	Day	Time	m
1 TU	0005	9.4	16 W	0041	8.8
	0642	1.2		0717	1.8
	1226	9.5		1256	9.1
	1917	1.1		1944	1.7
2 W	0053	9.4	17 TH	0115	8.7
	0726	1.3		0750	1.9
	1313	9.6		1331	9.0
	2004	1.1		2016	1.8
3 TH	0141	9.3	18 F	0150	8.5
	0812	1.4		0819	2.1
	1401	9.5		1408	8.8
	2052	1.2		2046	2.0
4 F	0230	9.1	19 SA	0226	8.3
	0858	1.7		0849	2.4
	1451	9.3		1445	8.6
	2141	1.4		2119	2.3
5 SA	0322	8.8	20 SU	0304	8.0
	0948	1.9		0927	2.6
	1544	9.0		1525	8.3
	2234	1.7		2158	2.5
6 SU	0418	8.4	21 M	0347	7.7
	1043	2.3		1013	2.9
	1642	8.6		1611	7.9
	2332	2.1		2247	2.8
7 M	0522	8.1	22 TU	0439	7.4
	1145	2.6		1110	3.2
	1747	8.3		1707	7.6
				2349	3.0
8 TU	0038	2.3	23 W	0542	7.2
	0631	7.9		1220	3.3
	1256	2.7		1812	7.5
	1858	8.2			
9 W	0151	2.3	24 TH	0100	3.0
	0741	8.0		0654	7.3
	1413	2.6		1334	3.2
	2008	8.2		1921	7.7
10 TH	0300	2.2	25 F	0209	2.8
	0843	8.3		0802	7.7
	1524	2.3		1443	2.8
	2109	8.4		2027	8.0
11 F	0356	1.9	26 SA	0312	2.4
	0936	8.6		0901	8.2
	1621	2.0		1544	2.2
	2202	8.7		2125	8.5
12 SA	0444	1.7	27 SU	0408	1.9
	1023	8.9		0952	8.8
	1709	1.7		1640	1.7
	2247	8.8		2217	8.9
13 SU	0526	1.6	28 M	0459	1.5
	1104	9.1		1040	9.2
	1752	1.6		1732	1.2
	● 2328	8.9		○ 2307	9.3
14 M	0605	1.6	29 TU	0548	1.2
	1143	9.2		1127	9.6
	1832	1.5		1823	0.8
				2354	9.6
15 TU	0005	8.9	30 W	0635	0.9
	0642	1.7		1214	9.9
	1220	9.2		1910	0.5
	1909	1.6			
			31 TH	0042	9.7
				0720	0.8
				1301	10.0
				1956	0.4

FEBRUARY

Day	Time	m	Day	Time	m
1 F	0129	9.7	16 SA	0126	8.7
	0804	0.8		0755	1.7
	1348	10.0		1343	9.0
	2040	0.5		2016	1.7
2 SA	0214	9.5	17 SU	0158	8.6
	0846	1.0		0822	1.9
	1434	9.7		1415	8.8
	2123	0.9		2043	1.9
3 SU	0300	9.2	18 M	0230	8.4
	0929	1.4		0854	2.1
	1521	9.3		1450	8.5
	2208	1.4		2116	2.2
4 M	0349	8.7	19 TU	0305	8.1
	1016	1.9		0932	2.5
	1612	8.7		1529	8.2
	2258	2.0		2156	2.6
5 TU	0444	8.1	20 W	0349	7.7
	1111	2.4		1020	2.9
	1711	8.1		1619	7.7
	2357	2.5		2249	3.0
6 W	0551	7.7	21 TH	0447	7.3
	1218	2.8		1125	3.3
	1825	7.7		1724	7.4
7 TH	0110	2.8	22 F	0004	3.3
	0710	7.5		0601	7.2
	1341	3.0		1251	3.3
	1948	7.6		1841	7.3
8 F	0233	2.8	23 SA	0130	3.2
	0824	7.8		0723	7.4
	1511	2.7		1414	2.9
	2058	7.9		2000	7.7
9 SA	0342	2.5	24 SU	0246	2.7
	0922	8.2		0835	7.9
	1614	2.3		1526	2.3
	2152	8.2		2107	8.2
10 SU	0433	2.2	25 M	0351	2.1
	1010	8.6		0934	8.6
	1702	1.9		1626	1.5
	2237	8.5		2203	8.9
11 M	0515	1.9	26 TU	0446	1.5
	1052	9.0		1024	9.3
	1743	1.6		1720	0.9
	2317	8.7		2252	9.4
12 TU	0553	1.7	27 W	0536	0.9
	1129	9.1		1112	9.8
	1819	1.5		1809	0.3
	● 2351	8.8		○ 2339	9.8
13 W	0629	1.6	28 TH	0623	0.6
	1204	9.2		1158	10.1
	1853	1.4		1855	0.0
14 TH	0023	8.8			
	0702	1.5			
	1238	9.2			
	1924	1.4			
15 F	0055	8.8			
	0731	1.6			
	1310	9.1			
	1951	1.5			

MARCH

Day	Time	m	Day	Time	m
1 F	0024	10.0	16 SA	0030	8.9
	0706	0.3		0706	1.3
	1243	10.3		1245	9.1
	1938	0.0		1921	1.3
2 SA	0109	9.9	17 SU	0059	8.8
	0748	0.3		0730	1.4
	1328	10.2		1315	9.0
	2019	0.1		1944	1.4
3 SU	0152	9.7	18 M	0128	8.8
	0827	0.6		0756	1.5
	1411	9.9		1346	8.8
	2058	0.6		2012	1.6
4 M	0235	9.3	19 TU	0158	8.6
	0907	1.0		0827	1.8
	1455	9.3		1419	8.6
	2139	1.3		2043	1.9
5 TU	0318	8.8	20 W	0231	8.3
	0950	1.6		0902	2.2
	1542	8.6		1456	8.2
	2224	2.0		2118	2.4
6 W	0408	8.1	21 TH	0311	7.9
	1041	2.3		0944	2.6
	1638	7.8		1545	7.8
	2320	2.7		2205	2.9
7 TH	0512	7.5	22 F	0407	7.5
	1148	2.9		1046	3.1
	1755	7.2		1650	7.3
				2318	3.3
8 F	0033	3.2	23 SA	0524	7.1
	0639	7.2		1217	3.2
	1314	3.1		1813	7.2
	1929	7.1			
9 SA	0206	3.2	24 SU	0054	3.3
	0802	7.4		0653	7.3
	1459	2.9		1351	2.8
	2042	7.5		1939	7.5
10 SU	0326	2.8	25 M	0222	2.8
	0903	7.9		0812	7.9
	1602	2.3		1507	2.1
	2135	8.0		2049	8.2
11 M	0418	2.4	26 TU	0332	2.1
	0951	8.4		0913	8.6
	1647	1.9		1609	1.3
	2219	8.4		2144	8.9
12 TU	0459	1.9	27 W	0428	1.4
	1032	8.8		1004	9.3
	1724	1.5		1701	0.6
	2256	8.7		2233	9.5
13 W	0535	1.6	28 TH	0517	0.7
	1109	9.1		1051	9.9
	1758	1.3		1748	0.1
	2329	8.8		○ 2318	9.9
14 TH	0609	1.4	29 F	0603	0.3
	1142	9.1		1137	10.2
	1829	1.2		1833	-0.2
	●				
15 F	0000	8.9	30 SA	0002	10.0
	0640	1.3		0646	0.1
	1214	9.1		1221	10.2
	1856	1.2		1914	-0.2
			31 SU	0045	10.0
				0726	0.2
				1305	10.1
				1953	0.1

APRIL

Day	Time	m	Day	Time	m
1 M	0127	9.7	16 TU	0059	8.8
	0806	0.4		0733	1.4
	1347	9.7		1319	8.8
	2031	0.7		1944	1.5
2 TU	0208	9.3	17 W	0131	8.7
	0844	0.9		0805	1.6
	1430	9.1		1355	8.6
	2109	1.4		2017	1.8
3 W	0250	8.7	18 TH	0206	8.4
	0926	1.6		0841	2.0
	1515	8.4		1435	8.2
	2152	2.2		2054	2.3
4 TH	0336	8.1	19 F	0249	8.1
	1016	2.3		0926	2.4
	1610	7.6		1525	7.8
	2247	2.9		2143	2.8
5 F	0438	7.4	20 SA	0346	7.6
	1122	2.9		1029	2.8
	1728	7.0		1631	7.4
				2254	3.2
6 SA	0000	3.4	21 SU	0502	7.3
	0607	7.1		1157	2.9
	1247	3.1		1754	7.3
	1901	6.9			
7 SU	0131	3.4	22 M	0026	3.2
	0730	7.3		0629	7.5
	1427	2.9		1327	2.6
	2013	7.2		1918	7.6
8 M	0253	3.0	23 TU	0154	2.7
	0832	7.7		0747	8.0
	1532	2.4		1443	1.9
	2106	7.8		2026	8.3
9 TU	0348	2.5	24 W	0305	2.0
	0922	8.2		0848	8.7
	1617	1.9		1544	1.1
	2149	8.2		2120	8.9
10 W	0430	2.0	25 TH	0403	1.3
	1003	8.6		0940	9.3
	1653	1.6		1636	0.5
	2226	8.5		2209	9.4
11 TH	0507	1.6	26 F	0453	0.8
	1041	8.9		1028	9.8
	1726	1.4		1723	0.1
	2259	8.7		2254	9.8
12 F	0540	1.4	27 SA	0539	0.4
	1115	9.0		1114	10.0
	1755	1.2		1807	0.0
	● 2330	8.8		○ 2337	9.9
13 SA	0610	1.3	28 SU	0623	0.2
	1146	9.0		1158	10.0
	1822	1.2		1848	0.1
14 SU	0000	8.9	29 M	0019	9.8
	0636	1.3		0704	0.3
	1217	9.0		1242	9.7
	1847	1.2		1926	0.5
15 M	0029	8.8	30 TU	0101	9.5
	0703	1.3		0744	0.6
	1247	8.9		1325	9.3
	1915	1.3		2004	1.0

Chart Datum: 4·93 metres below Ordnance Datum (Newlyn)

TIME ZONE (UTC)
For Summer Time add ONE hour in **non-shaded areas**

ENGLAND – LIVERPOOL (ALFRED DOCK)

LAT 53°24′N LONG 3°01′W

TIMES AND HEIGHTS OF HIGH AND LOW WATERS

SPRING & NEAP TIDES
Dates in red are SPRINGS
Dates in blue are NEAPS

YEAR **2002**

MAY

Date	Day	Time	m	Time	m	Time	m	Time	m
1	W	0142	9.1	0824	1.1	1407	8.8	2041	1.6
2	TH	0224	8.7	0907	1.7	1452	8.2	2124	2.3
3	F	0310	8.1	0956	2.3	1544	7.5	2216	3.0
4	SA	0408	7.6	1057	2.8	1655	7.0	2324	3.4
5	SU	0529	7.2	1208	3.0	1819	6.9		
6	M	0043	3.5	0647	7.3	1329	2.9	1929	7.1
7	TU	0201	3.2	0751	7.6	1440	2.6	2025	7.5
8	W	0303	2.7	0843	8.0	1530	2.2	2110	8.0
9	TH	0349	2.3	0927	8.4	1610	1.8	2149	8.3
10	F	0428	1.9	1006	8.6	1644	1.6	2225	8.6
11	SA	0502	1.6	1042	8.8	1715	1.4	2257	8.7
12	SU	0534	1.4	1115	8.8	1745	1.3	● 2329	8.8
13	M	0606	1.3	1148	8.8	1817	1.3		
14	TU	0001	8.8	0639	1.3	1222	8.8	1849	1.4
15	W	0035	8.8	0714	1.4	1259	8.8	1924	1.5
16	TH	0112	8.7	0752	1.6	1339	8.6	2000	1.8
17	F	0153	8.6	0833	1.8	1424	8.4	2042	2.2
18	SA	0240	8.3	0922	2.2	1516	8.0	2134	2.6
19	SU	0338	8.0	1025	2.4	1620	7.7	2242	2.8
20	M	0448	7.8	1140	2.5	1736	7.6		
21	TU	0001	2.8	0605	7.9	1259	2.2	1851	7.8
22	W	0120	2.5	0717	8.2	1412	1.8	1957	8.3
23	TH	0232	2.0	0820	8.7	1515	1.3	2054	8.8
24	F	0333	1.5	0915	9.1	1609	0.8	2144	9.2
25	SA	0426	1.1	1005	9.4	1657	0.6	2230	9.5
26	SU	0515	0.8	1053	9.6	1741	0.5	○ 2314	9.6
27	M	0600	0.7	1138	9.5	1822	0.7	2357	9.5
28	TU	0644	0.8	1222	9.3	1902	1.0		
29	W	0039	9.3	0726	1.0	1306	9.0	1940	1.4
30	TH	0121	9.0	0808	1.3	1348	8.6	2018	1.9
31	F	0203	8.7	0850	1.8	1431	8.2	2059	2.4

JUNE

Date	Day	Time	m	Time	m	Time	m	Time	m
1	SA	0247	8.3	0936	2.2	1518	7.7	2146	2.8
2	SU	0337	7.9	1027	2.6	1613	7.3	2243	3.2
3	M	0439	7.5	1123	2.8	1722	7.0	2346	3.3
4	TU	0552	7.4	1223	2.9	1833	7.1		
5	W	0052	3.3	0657	7.5	1324	2.8	1933	7.3
6	TH	0156	3.0	0755	7.7	1422	2.5	2025	7.7
7	F	0252	2.6	0844	8.0	1512	2.2	2109	8.1
8	SA	0338	2.2	0927	8.3	1555	1.9	2148	8.4
9	SU	0420	1.9	1007	8.5	1635	1.6	2224	8.6
10	M	0500	1.6	1045	8.7	1714	1.5	● 2300	8.8
11	TU	0540	1.5	1123	8.8	1752	1.4	2337	8.9
12	W	0621	1.4	1203	8.8	1831	1.4		
13	TH	0017	9.0	0703	1.4	1245	8.8	1911	1.5
14	F	0100	8.9	0747	1.4	1330	8.8	1953	1.7
15	SA	0146	8.9	0833	1.5	1418	8.6	2038	1.9
16	SU	0235	8.7	0923	1.7	1509	8.4	2129	2.2
17	M	0330	8.5	1019	1.9	1607	8.2	2228	2.4
18	TU	0431	8.4	1120	2.0	1712	8.0	2334	2.5
19	W	0538	8.3	1226	2.0	1821	8.0		
20	TH	0044	2.4	0646	8.3	1336	1.9	1927	8.2
21	F	0156	2.2	0752	8.5	1444	1.7	2028	8.5
22	SA	0304	1.9	0852	8.7	1543	1.5	2122	8.8
23	SU	0403	1.6	0947	8.9	1634	1.3	2211	9.1
24	M	0456	1.3	1037	9.0	1719	1.2	○ 2256	9.2
25	TU	0544	1.2	1124	9.0	1802	1.3	2340	9.2
26	W	0629	1.2	1208	8.9	1843	1.4		
27	TH	0022	9.2	0713	1.3	1250	8.8	1921	1.7
28	F	0103	9.0	0754	1.5	1330	8.5	1959	1.9
29	SA	0143	8.8	0833	1.7	1409	8.3	2036	2.3
30	SU	0223	8.5	0912	2.0	1449	8.0	2114	2.6

JULY

Date	Day	Time	m	Time	m	Time	m	Time	m
1	M	0305	8.2	0951	2.3	1531	7.7	2156	2.9
2	TU	0351	7.9	1035	2.6	1620	7.4	2248	3.1
3	W	0444	7.6	1125	2.8	1718	7.2	2348	3.2
4	TH	0545	7.5	1222	2.9	1825	7.2		
5	F	0052	3.2	0650	7.5	1322	2.8	1928	7.4
6	SA	0155	2.9	0751	7.7	1421	2.6	2023	7.8
7	SU	0252	2.6	0845	7.9	1515	2.3	2111	8.2
8	M	0345	2.2	0933	8.3	1604	2.0	2155	8.5
9	TU	0434	1.8	1019	8.5	1650	1.7	2237	8.8
10	W	0522	1.5	1103	8.8	1735	1.5	● 2320	9.1
11	TH	0609	1.3	1149	8.9	1819	1.4		
12	F	0004	9.2	0656	1.1	1235	9.1	1903	1.4
13	SA	0050	9.3	0743	1.0	1321	9.1	1947	1.4
14	SU	0137	9.3	0829	1.0	1408	9.1	2032	1.5
15	M	0225	9.3	0915	1.2	1456	8.9	2118	1.7
16	TU	0315	9.1	1003	1.4	1547	8.6	2209	2.0
17	W	0408	8.8	1054	1.7	1643	8.3	2306	2.3
18	TH	0508	8.4	1153	2.1	1747	8.0		
19	F	0011	2.5	0615	8.1	1301	2.3	1857	7.9
20	SA	0125	2.6	0728	8.1	1415	2.3	2006	8.1
21	SU	0243	2.4	0837	8.2	1523	2.1	2106	8.4
22	M	0351	2.1	0937	8.4	1619	1.9	2159	8.7
23	TU	0447	1.7	1028	8.6	1706	1.7	2245	9.0
24	W	0536	1.5	1114	8.7	1749	1.6	○ 2327	9.1
25	TH	0620	1.4	1156	8.8	1829	1.6		
26	F	0007	9.1	0700	1.4	1235	8.7	1906	1.7
27	SA	0044	9.1	0737	1.5	1310	8.6	1940	1.8
28	SU	0120	9.0	0811	1.6	1344	8.5	2011	2.0
29	M	0156	8.8	0842	1.8	1418	8.3	2040	2.2
30	TU	0232	8.5	0912	2.1	1453	8.1	2112	2.5
31	W	0310	8.2	0945	2.3	1532	7.8	2152	2.8

AUGUST

Date	Day	Time	m	Time	m	Time	m	Time	m
1	TH	0353	7.9	1027	2.7	1617	7.5	2246	3.1
2	F	0444	7.6	1122	2.9	1714	7.3	2354	3.3
3	SA	0546	7.3	1229	3.1	1824	7.2		
4	SU	0108	3.3	0656	7.3	1339	3.0	1936	7.5
5	M	0218	2.9	0806	7.6	1443	2.7	2039	7.9
6	TU	0320	2.4	0906	8.0	1541	2.2	2131	8.4
7	W	0416	1.9	0959	8.5	1633	1.8	2219	8.9
8	TH	0508	1.4	1048	8.9	1722	1.5	● 2304	9.3
9	F	0558	1.0	1135	9.2	1809	1.2	2350	9.6
10	SA	0646	0.7	1221	9.4	1854	1.0		
11	SU	0035	9.8	0731	0.5	1306	9.5	1937	0.9
12	M	0121	9.8	0815	0.5	1351	9.4	2019	1.0
13	TU	0207	9.7	0857	0.7	1435	9.2	2101	1.2
14	W	0253	9.4	0939	1.1	1521	8.9	2145	1.7
15	TH	0342	8.9	1026	1.7	1612	8.4	2238	2.2
16	F	0438	8.3	1121	2.3	1713	7.9	2343	2.7
17	SA	0548	7.7	1230	2.7	1831	7.6		
18	SU	0103	2.9	0712	7.5	1353	2.9	1951	7.7
19	M	0238	2.7	0830	7.7	1513	2.6	2056	8.1
20	TU	0350	2.3	0930	8.1	1611	2.3	2148	8.6
21	W	0443	1.9	1019	8.4	1657	2.0	2233	8.9
22	TH	0527	1.5	1102	8.6	1737	1.7	○ 2313	9.1
23	F	0606	1.4	1139	8.7	1814	1.6	2349	9.2
24	SA	0641	1.3	1213	8.8	1848	1.6		
25	SU	0022	9.1	0713	1.4	1244	8.7	1918	1.6
26	M	0055	9.0	0742	1.5	1315	8.6	1944	1.8
27	TU	0126	8.9	0807	1.6	1345	8.5	2007	1.9
28	W	0158	8.7	0831	1.9	1416	8.3	2036	2.2
29	TH	0232	8.4	0901	2.2	1450	8.1	2111	2.5
30	F	0310	8.1	0937	2.6	1530	7.7	2155	3.0
31	SA	0357	7.6	1026	3.0	1622	7.3	2259	3.4

Chart Datum: 4·93 metres below Ordnance Datum (Newlyn)

TIME ZONE (UTC)
For Summer Time add ONE hour in **non-shaded areas**

ENGLAND – LIVERPOOL (ALFRED DOCK)

LAT 53°24'N LONG 3°01'W

TIMES AND HEIGHTS OF HIGH AND LOW WATERS

SPRING & NEAP TIDES
Dates in red are SPRINGS
Dates in blue are NEAPS

YEAR **2002**

SEPTEMBER

Day	Time	m	Time	m	Time	m	Time	m
1 SU	0458	7.2	1137	3.3	1731	7.1		
2 M	0028	3.5	0613	7.1	1302	3.3	1854	7.2
3 TU	0151	3.1	0736	7.4	1418	3.0	2012	7.7
4 W	0301	2.5	0846	7.9	1522	2.4	2111	8.4
5 TH	0400	1.8	0942	8.5	1618	1.8	2200	9.1
6 F	0453	1.1	1030	9.1	1708	1.2	2246	9.6
7 SA	0542	0.6	1116	9.5	1754	0.8	● 2331	9.9
8 SU	0628	0.2	1200	9.7	1838	0.6		
9 M	0015	10.1	0711	0.1	1244	9.8	1919	0.5
10 TU	0059	10.1	0752	0.2	1327	9.7	1959	0.6
11 W	0143	9.8	0832	0.6	1410	9.4	2039	1.0
12 TH	0228	9.4	0912	1.2	1453	8.9	2122	1.6
13 F	0315	8.7	0957	1.9	1541	8.3	2212	2.2
14 SA	0410	8.0	1052	2.6	1642	7.7	2319	2.9
15 SU	0526	7.3	1204	3.2	1808	7.3		
16 M	0050	3.1	0703	7.2	1339	3.3	1935	7.5
17 TU	0236	2.8	0819	7.5	1503	2.9	2040	8.0
18 W	0342	2.3	0915	8.0	1558	2.4	2131	8.5
19 TH	0429	1.8	1001	8.4	1641	2.0	2213	8.9
20 F	0507	1.5	1040	8.7	1718	1.7	2251	9.1
21 SA	0542	1.3	1115	8.8	1752	1.5	○ 2325	9.2
22 SU	0613	1.2	1146	8.8	1823	1.4	2356	9.1
23 M	0642	1.3	1214	8.8	1851	1.5		
24 TU	0026	9.0	0707	1.4	1243	8.8	1914	1.6
25 W	0056	8.9	0730	1.5	1312	8.7	1938	1.7
26 TH	0126	8.7	0755	1.8	1342	8.5	2007	2.0
27 F	0158	8.5	0825	2.1	1414	8.3	2040	2.3
28 SA	0235	8.1	0859	2.5	1452	7.9	2120	2.8
29 SU	0321	7.7	0943	3.0	1543	7.5	2218	3.3
30 M	0423	7.2	1051	3.5	1653	7.1	2354	3.5

OCTOBER

Day	Time	m	Time	m	Time	m	Time	m
1 TU	0543	7.0	1228	3.5	1821	7.2		
2 W	0126	3.1	0713	7.3	1353	3.1	1945	7.7
3 TH	0240	2.4	0825	8.0	1501	2.4	2047	8.5
4 F	0341	1.6	0920	8.7	1558	1.7	2137	9.2
5 SA	0432	0.8	1007	9.3	1648	1.1	2223	9.8
6 SU	0519	0.3	1052	9.7	1733	0.6	● 2308	10.1
7 M	0604	0.0	1135	9.9	1817	0.4	2351	10.2
8 TU	0646	0.0	1218	9.9	1858	0.3		
9 W	0035	10.1	0726	0.2	1301	9.8	1938	0.6
10 TH	0119	9.7	0805	0.7	1343	9.4	2018	1.0
11 F	0204	9.2	0845	1.4	1426	8.9	2101	1.6
12 SA	0251	8.5	0929	2.2	1514	8.3	2152	2.3
13 SU	0346	7.7	1025	2.9	1615	7.6	2301	2.9
14 M	0507	7.1	1139	3.4	1743	7.3		
15 TU	0033	3.2	0642	7.0	1313	3.5	1908	7.4
16 W	0212	2.9	0754	7.4	1435	3.1	2012	7.9
17 TH	0315	2.4	0848	7.9	1530	2.6	2102	8.4
18 F	0400	1.9	0932	8.3	1613	2.1	2145	8.8
19 SA	0437	1.6	1010	8.6	1649	1.7	2223	9.0
20 SU	0509	1.4	1044	8.8	1723	1.5	2257	9.1
21 M	0539	1.3	1115	8.9	1753	1.4	○ 2327	9.1
22 TU	0606	1.3	1143	8.9	1820	1.4	2356	9.0
23 W	0631	1.4	1212	8.9	1846	1.5		
24 TH	0026	8.9	0657	1.5	1242	8.8	1914	1.7
25 F	0058	8.7	0727	1.8	1313	8.6	1945	1.9
26 SA	0132	8.5	0758	2.1	1347	8.4	2019	2.2
27 SU	0211	8.2	0834	2.5	1428	8.1	2101	2.7
28 M	0259	7.8	0918	3.0	1520	7.7	2159	3.1
29 TU	0401	7.3	1025	3.4	1629	7.4	2328	3.2
30 W	0520	7.2	1156	3.5	1752	7.4		
31 TH	0057	2.9	0646	7.4	1321	3.1	1913	7.9

NOVEMBER

Day	Time	m	Time	m	Time	m	Time	m
1 F	0212	2.2	0757	8.1	1432	2.4	2017	8.6
2 SA	0314	1.5	0853	8.8	1531	1.7	2110	9.3
3 SU	0406	0.8	0941	9.4	1622	1.1	2158	9.8
4 M	0454	0.4	1026	9.8	1709	0.7	● 2244	10.1
5 TU	0538	0.2	1110	9.9	1754	0.5	2329	10.1
6 W	0620	0.2	1153	9.9	1837	0.5		
7 TH	0013	9.9	0701	0.5	1237	9.7	1919	0.7
8 F	0058	9.5	0741	1.0	1320	9.4	2001	1.1
9 SA	0143	9.0	0822	1.6	1404	8.9	2046	1.7
10 SU	0230	8.4	0907	2.3	1451	8.4	2137	2.3
11 M	0324	7.7	1000	3.0	1549	7.8	2240	2.8
12 TU	0436	7.2	1107	3.4	1705	7.5	2355	3.1
13 W	0601	7.0	1225	3.5	1825	7.4		
14 TH	0117	3.0	0713	7.2	1344	3.3	1931	7.7
15 F	0227	2.6	0809	7.6	1446	2.9	2025	8.1
16 SA	0317	2.3	0856	8.1	1534	2.4	2110	8.5
17 SU	0356	1.9	0935	8.4	1613	2.1	2150	8.7
18 M	0429	1.7	1011	8.7	1648	1.8	2225	8.9
19 TU	0500	1.5	1043	8.8	1720	1.6	2258	8.9
20 W	0530	1.5	1114	8.9	1751	1.6	○ 2329	8.9
21 TH	0601	1.5	1145	8.9	1823	1.6		
22 F	0002	8.9	0633	1.6	1218	8.9	1856	1.7
23 SA	0038	8.8	0706	1.8	1254	8.8	1932	1.9
24 SU	0116	8.6	0742	2.0	1333	8.6	2011	2.1
25 M	0159	8.4	0822	2.4	1417	8.4	2057	2.4
26 TU	0248	8.1	0909	2.7	1509	8.1	2154	2.7
27 W	0346	7.7	1010	3.0	1612	7.9	2306	2.8
28 TH	0456	7.6	1125	3.1	1724	7.9		
29 F	0023	2.6	0612	7.7	1241	2.9	1837	8.1
30 SA	0136	2.2	0723	8.1	1354	2.5	1943	8.6

DECEMBER

Day	Time	m	Time	m	Time	m	Time	m
1 SU	0241	1.7	0823	8.7	1459	1.9	2042	9.1
2 M	0338	1.2	0915	9.1	1556	1.4	2135	9.5
3 TU	0428	0.8	1003	9.5	1647	1.1	2224	9.7
4 W	0515	0.7	1049	9.7	1735	0.9	● 2311	9.7
5 TH	0558	0.7	1134	9.7	1821	0.9	2357	9.6
6 F	0641	0.9	1218	9.6	1906	1.0		
7 SA	0042	9.3	0722	1.3	1302	9.4	1950	1.3
8 SU	0127	8.9	0804	1.8	1346	9.0	2035	1.7
9 M	0213	8.4	0848	2.3	1431	8.7	2122	2.1
10 TU	0300	7.9	0935	2.8	1520	8.2	2212	2.5
11 W	0353	7.5	1028	3.1	1617	7.8	2307	2.8
12 TH	0458	7.2	1128	3.4	1724	7.6		
13 F	0006	3.0	0610	7.1	1232	3.4	1832	7.6
14 SA	0109	3.0	0715	7.3	1337	3.2	1934	7.7
15 SU	0209	2.8	0810	7.7	1437	2.9	2027	8.0
16 M	0301	2.5	0856	8.0	1527	2.5	2113	8.3
17 TU	0344	2.1	0936	8.4	1609	2.2	2153	8.5
18 W	0423	1.9	1013	8.7	1648	1.9	2230	8.7
19 TH	0501	1.7	1049	8.8	1727	1.8	○ 2307	8.8
20 F	0538	1.6	1124	9.0	1806	1.7	2344	8.9
21 SA	0616	1.6	1202	9.0	1847	1.6		
22 SU	0024	8.9	0655	1.7	1242	9.0	1928	1.7
23 M	0107	8.8	0735	1.8	1325	9.0	2011	1.7
24 TU	0151	8.7	0817	2.0	1410	8.9	2057	1.9
25 W	0238	8.5	0903	2.2	1459	8.7	2146	2.0
26 TH	0331	8.3	0955	2.4	1553	8.6	2242	2.2
27 F	0429	8.1	1054	2.6	1654	8.4	2345	2.3
28 SA	0536	7.9	1200	2.7	1801	8.3		
29 SU	0054	2.3	0645	8.0	1312	2.6	1910	8.4
30 M	0206	2.1	0753	8.3	1426	2.3	2017	8.6
31 TU	0311	1.8	0853	8.7	1533	1.9	2117	8.9

Chart Datum: 4·93 metres below Ordnance Datum (Newlyn)

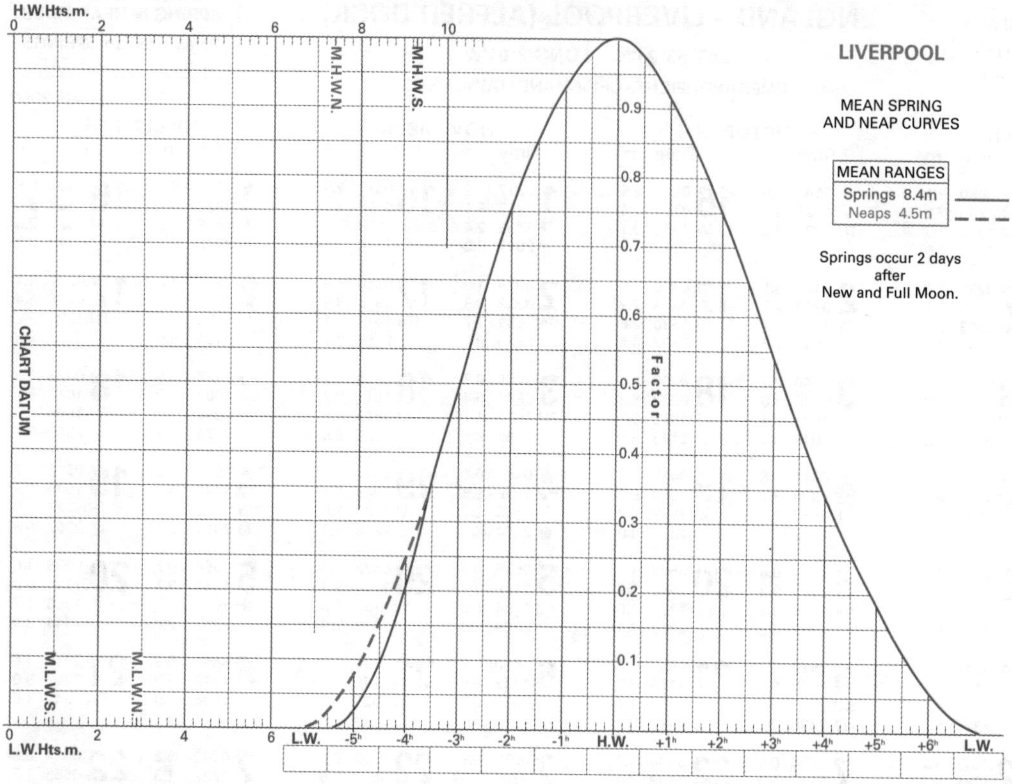
H.W.Hts.m.
M.H.W.N.
M.H.W.S.
CHART DATUM
M.L.W.S.
M.L.W.N.
L.W.Hts.m.
Factor
L.W. -5h -4h -3h -2h -1h H.W. +1h +2h +3h +4h +5h +6h L.W.
LIVERPOOL
MEAN SPRING AND NEAP CURVES
MEAN RANGES
Springs 8.4m
Neaps 4.5m
Springs occur 2 days after New and Full Moon.

LIVERPOOL *9.10.14*

Merseyside **53°24'·22N 03°00'·28W** (Liver Bldg) ❁❁❁◊◊◊✿✿

CHARTS AC 3490, 1951, *1978, 1826*; Imray C62; OS 108

TIDES +0015 Dover; ML 5·2; Duration 0535; Zone 0 (UT)

Standard Port LIVERPOOL (ALFRED DOCK) (⟵)

Times				Height (metres)			
High Water		Low Water		MHWS	MHWN	MLWN	MLWS
0000	0600	0200	0700	9·3	7·4	2·9	0·9
1200	1800	1400	1900				
Differences SOUTHPORT							
−0020	−0010	No data		−0·3	−0·3	No data	
FORMBY							
−0015	−0010	−0020	−0020	−0·3	−0·1	0·0	+0·1
GLADSTONE DOCK							
−0003	−0003	−0003	−0003	−0·1	−0·1	0·0	−0·1
EASTHAM (River Mersey)							
+0010	+0010	+0009	+0009	+0·3	+0·1	−0·1	−0·3
HALE HEAD (River Mersey)							
+0030	+0025	No data		−2·4	−2·5	No data	
WIDNES (River Mersey)							
+0040	+0045	+0400	+0345	−4·2	−4·4	−2·5	−0·3
FIDDLER'S FERRY (River Mersey)							
+0100	+0115	+0540	+0450	−5·9	−6·3	−2·4	−0·4
HILBRE ISLAND (River Dee)							
−0015	−0012	−0010	−0015	−0·3	−0·2	+0·2	+0·4
MOSTYN QUAY (River Dee)							
−0020	−0015	−0020	−0020	−0·8	−0·7	No data	
CONNAH'S QUAY (River Dee)							
0000	+0015	+0355	+0340	−4·6	−4·4	Dries	
CHESTER (River Dee)							
+0105	+0105	+0500	+0500	−5·3	−5·4	Dries	
COLWYN BAY							
−0020	−0020	No data		−1·5	−1·3	No data	
LLANDUDNO							
−0015	−0020	−0030	−0035	−1·7	−1·4	−0·7	−0·3

NOTE: LW time differences at Connah's Quay give the end of a LW stand lasting about 3¾hrs at sp and 5hrs at nps. A bore occurs in the R Dee at Chester.

SHELTER Good at marina in Brunswick and Coburg docks. Ent is 1M S of Liver Bldg, abeam Pluckington Bank (PB) WCM buoy; access approx HW ±2¼ sp, ±1¾ nps, 0600-2200 Mar-Oct. Good shelter also in Canning and Albert Docks but access HW−2 to HW, and not on every tide. ⚓ on the SW side of river but only in fair weather.

NAVIGATION WPT Bar PHM lt F 53°32'·02N 03°20'·98W, 291°/111° from/to Q1 NCM lt F, 2·8M. From Q1 to marina is 15·5M via Queen's and Crosby Chans. Both chans have training banks which cover and it is unwise to navigate between the floats/buoys and the trng banks. In strong NW'lies there is swell on the bar. Wind against tide causes steep, breaking seas in outer reaches of River Mersey. Inside the buoyed chan is safe; elsewhere local knowledge and great caution needed as the whole area (R Dee, R Mersey to R Alt and N to Morecambe Bay) is littered with sandbanks. Sp tidal streams exceed 5kn within the river. For **R Dee**: WPT 53°25'·13N 03°13'·17W, Hilbre Swash HE2 ECM buoy, Q(3) 10s, (chan shifts). From the W use Welsh Chan. The Dee estuary mostly dries.

Leeds & Liverpool Canal (BWB) gives access to E Coast, ent at Stanley Dock. Max draft 1·0m, air draft 2·2m, beam 4·3m, LOA 18·3m. Liverpool to Goole 161M, 103 locks.

Manchester Ship Canal, ent at Eastham Locks, leads 31M to Salford Quays (marina) or R Weaver for boatyards at Northwich. Obtain licence from MSC Co ☎ 0151 327 1461.

LIGHTS AND MARKS Bar PHM lt F, Fl 5s 12m 21M, Horn (2) 20s, Racon. Formby SWM lt F, Iso 4s, is at the ent to Queen's Chan which is marked by PHM lt Flts and SHM buoys, and 3 NCM buoys, numbered Q1-Q12. Crosby Chan is similarly marked, C1-C23. From Crosby SWM lt F, Oc 5s, the track up-river is approx 145°. See also 9.10.4. The Liver Bldg (twin spires) and Port of Liverpool Bldg (dome) are conspic on the E bank opposite Birkenhead Docks.

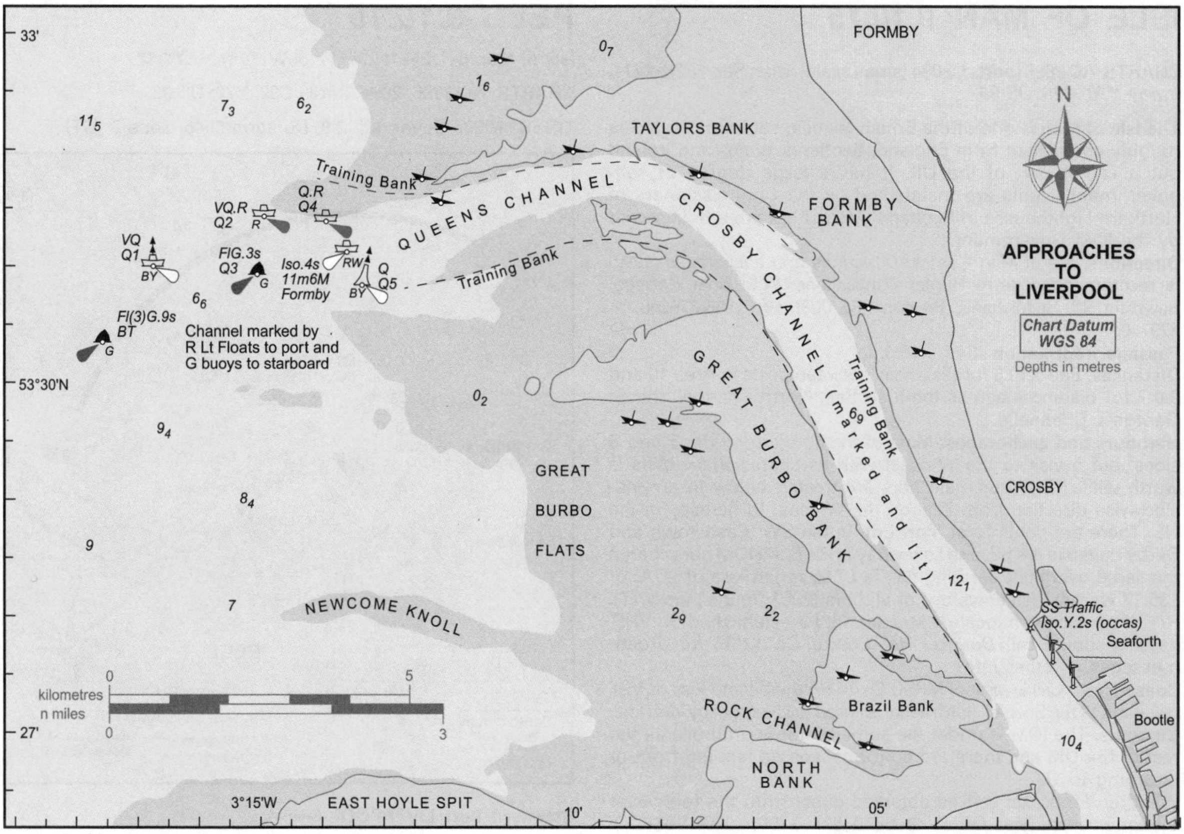

RADIO TELEPHONE Monitor *Mersey Radio* VHF Ch **12** 16 (H24). Local nav and gale warnings are broadcast on receipt on Ch 12. Traffic movements, nav warnings and weather reports are broadcast on Ch 09 at HW–3 and –2. Radar Ch 18 covers a radius of 20M and in poor vis can offer continuous fixing. *Liverpool Marina* Ch M. Eastham Locks Ch 07 (H24). Manchester Ship Canal Ch 14.

TELEPHONE (Dial code 0151) Port Ops 949 6134/5; MRSC 931 3341; ⊜ (0161) 912 6977; Marinecall 09068 500 461; Police 709 6010; 🄷 709 0141.

FACILITIES **Liverpool Marina** (300 + 50) ☎ 708 5228, (0600-2200 Mar–Oct), 📠 709 8731; liverpoolmarina@btinternet.com. Ent via Brunswick Dock lock, pontoons inside, min depth 3·5m; night locking as pre-arranged. Conspic black control bldg at lock ent has IPTS (sigs 2, 3 & 5). £1.35, D, P (½M), AC, FW, BH (60 ton), Slip, CH, SM, ⌼, ♿, Bar, R (☎ 709 2683); **Albert Dock** ☎ 709 6558; access through Canning Dock, VHF Ch M when ent manned, AB, FW, AC; **Royal Mersey YC** ☎ 645 3204, Slip, M, P, D, L, FW, R, Bar. **W Kirby SC** ☎ 625 5579, AB (at HW), Slip, M (in Dee Est), L, FW, C (30ton), Bar; **Hoylake SC** ☎ 632 2616, Slip, M, FW, Bar; **Services:** CH, SM, ME, El, Sh, ACA, Ⓔ. **City** EC Wed; all facilities, ✉, Ⓑ, ⇌, ✈.

ADJACENT ANCHORAGE

RIVER ALT, Merseyside, **53°31´·42N 03°03´·80W**. AC 1951, *1978*. HW –0008 on Dover; see 9.10.14. Good shelter but only for LOA <8·5m x 1·2m draft on a HW of at least 8m. Mersey E training wall can be crossed HW±2. Ent to chan (shifts frequently) is E of C14 PHM lt float, thence marked by locally-laid Y Fairway buoy and perches on the training wall. Unsafe to ⚓ in R Alt; pick up a free mooring off the SC and contact club. Local knowledge advised. Facilities very limited. **Blundellsands SC** ☎ (0151) 929 2101 (occas), Slip, L (at HW), FW, Bar.

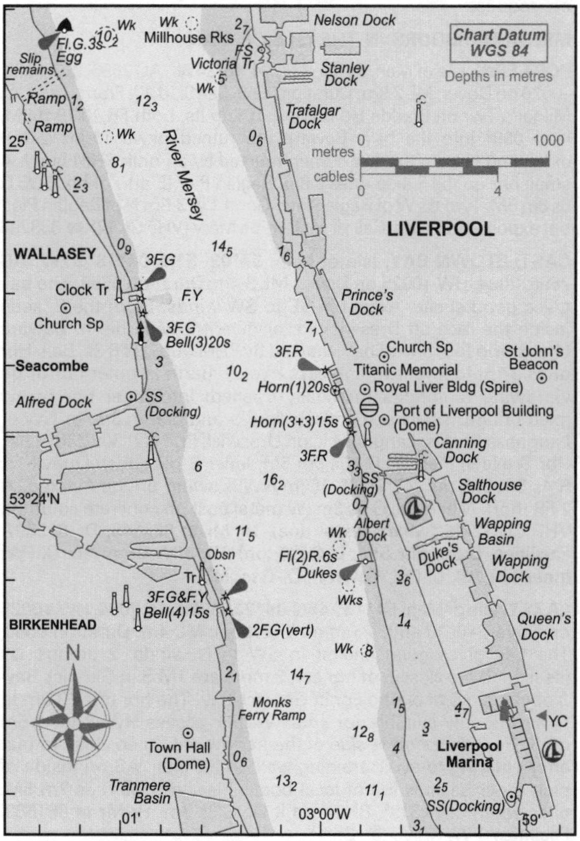

10

ISLE OF MAN *9.10.15*

CHARTS AC 2696 (ports), 2094 (small scale). Irish Sea *1826, 1411. Imray Y70, C26. OS 95.*

The Isle of Man is one of the British Islands, set in the Irish Sea roughly equidistant from England, Scotland, Wales and Ireland but it is not part of the UK. It has a large degree of self-government. Lights are maintained by the Commissioners of Northern Lighthouses in Scotland. Manx hbrs are administered by the IOM Government.

Directions. *Isle of Man - Tides, Directions and anchorages (1997)* is recommended; from Hunter Publications, Wild Boar Cottage, Rawcliffe Rd, St Michaels, Preston PR3 0UH, ☎ 01995-679240, 📠 679740.

Passage information. See 9.10.5.

Distances. See 9.10.6 for distances between ports in Area 10 and 9.0.7 for distances across the Irish Sea, North Channel and St George's Channel.

Harbours and anchorages. Most of the hbrs are on the E and S sides, but a visit to the W coast with its characteristic cliffs is worth while. The four main hbrs are treated below in an anti-clockwise direction from Peel on the W coast to Ramsey in the NE. There are good ⚓s at: Port Erin in the SW, Castletown and Derby Haven in the SE, and Laxey Bay in the E. All IOM hbrs charge the same overnight berthing fee, ie £7.05 regardless of LOA; or £35.17 weekly fee allows use of all hbrs (2001 figures, inc VAT).

R/T. If contact with local Hr Mrs cannot be established on VHF, vessels should call *Douglas Hbr Control* Ch 12 16 for urgent messages or other info.

Coastguard. Call Liverpool MRSC Ch 16 67; there is no loss of VHF coverage as the Snaefell (IoM) aerial is linked to Liverpool by land line.

Customs. The IOM is under the same customs umbrella as the rest of the UK, and there are no formalities on landing from or returning to UK.

Weather. Forecasts can be obtained direct from the forecaster at Ronaldsway Met Office ☎ 0900 624 3200, (0700-2030LT). **Douglas Hbr** Control (9.10.18) can supply visibility and wind info on request.

MINOR HARBOURS IN THE ISLE OF MAN

PORT ERIN, Isle of Man, **54°05'·31N 04°46'·34W.** AC 2696, 2094. HW –0020 on Dover; ML 2·9m; Duration 0555. See 9.10.17. From S and W, Milner's Twr on Bradda Hd is conspic. Ldg lts, both FR 10/19m 5M, lead 099° into the bay. Beware the ruined bkwtr (dries $\underline{2}$·9m) extending N from the SW corner, marked by an unlit SHM buoy. A small hbr on the S side dries $\underline{0}$·8m. Raglan Pier (E arm of hbr), Oc G 5s 8m 5M. Two Ⓥs W of Raglan Pier. Good ⚓ in 3-8m N of Raglan Pier, but exposed to W'lies. Call Hr Mr Port St. Mary (VHF Ch 12) ☎ 833206

CASTLETOWN BAY, Isle of Man, **54°03'·51N 04°38'·57W.** AC 2696, 2094. HW +0025 on Dover; ML 3·4m; Duration 0555. The bay gives good shelter except in SE to SW winds. From the E, keep inside the race off Dreswick Pt, or give it a wide berth. Beware Lheeah-rio Rks in W of bay, marked by PHM buoy, Fl R 3s, Bell. Hbr dries $\underline{3}$·1m to level sand. Access HW±2½. Berth in outer hbr or go via swing footbridge (manually opened) into inner hbr below fixed bridge. ⚓ between Lheeah-rio Rks and pier in 3m; or NW of Langness Pt. Lts: Langness lt, on Dreswick Pt, Fl (2) 30s 23m 12M. Hbr S (New) Pier, Oc R 15s 8m 5M; Inner S pier (Irish Quay), Oc R 4s 5m 5M, vis 142°-322°. 150m NW is swing bridge marked by 2 FR (hor). N pier, Oc G 4s 3m (W metal post on concrete column). VHF Ch 12 16 (when vessel due). Hr Mr ☎ 823549; Dr 823597. Facilities: **Outer hbr** Slip, L, C (20 ton) AB; **Irish Quay** AB, C, FW; **Inner hbr** AB, C, FW; **Town** P, D, Gas, ME.

LAXEY, Isle of Man, **54°13'·46N 04°23'·32W.** AC 2094. HW +0025 on Dover; +0010 and –2·0m on Liverpool; ML 4m; Duration 0550. The bay gives good shelter in SW to N winds. 2 orange Ⓥs (seasonal) are close E of hbr ent; 2 more are 1M S in Garwick Bay. ⚓ about 2ca S of pierhds or in Garwick Bay. The hbr dries $\underline{3}$·0m to rk and is only suitable for small yachts; access HW±3 for 1·5m draft. Beware rks on N side of the narrow ent. Keep close to pier after entering to avoid training wall on NE side. AB on inside of pier; inner basin is full of local boats. Pier hd lt Oc R 3s 7m 5M, obsc when brg <318°. Bkwtr hd lt Oc G 3s 7m. Hr Mr ☎ 861663. Facilities: FW, R, ✉, Ⓑ, Bar.

PEEL *9.10.16*

Isle of Man 54°13'·61N 04°41'·68W ❁❁◈◈✿✿✿

CHARTS AC 2696, 2094; Imray C62; Y70; OS 95

TIDES +0005 Dover; ML 2·9; Duration 0545; Zone 0 (UT)

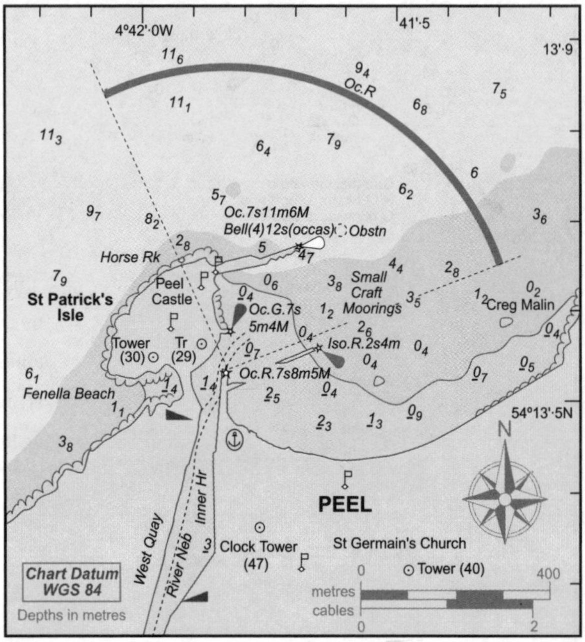

Standard Port LIVERPOOL (⟵)

Times				Height (metres)			
High Water		Low Water		MHWS	MHWN	MLWN	MLWS
0000	0600	0200	0700	9·3	7·4	2·9	0·9
1200	1800	1400	1900				
Differences PEEL							
+0005	+0005	-0015	–0025	–4·1	–3·1	–1·4	–0·5

SHELTER Good, except in strong NW to NE winds when ent should not be attempted. 3 Or Ⓥs (lifted mid Sep) off S groyne in about 2m. Hbr dries. Fin keelers may be able to berth on N bkwtr in 5m. Inner hbr dries approx $\underline{2}$·8m to flat sand; access HW±3, possible AB on W quay.

NAVIGATION WPT 54°13'·97N 04°41'·43W, 020°/200° from/to groyne lt, 0·42M. When close in, beware groyne on S side of hbr ent, submerged at half tide.

LIGHTS AND MARKS Power stn chy (80m, grey with B top) at S end of inner hbr is conspic from W and N, R Lts are unreliable; chy brg 203° leads to hbr ent. Groyne lt and Clock Tr (conspic) in transit 200° are almost on same line. Peel Castle and 2 twrs are conspic on St Patrick's Isle to NW of hbr. No ldg lts. N bkwtr Oc 7s 11m 6M. Groyne Iso R 2s 4m. S pier hd Oc R 7s 8m 5M; vis 156°-249°. Castle jetty Oc G 7s 5m 4M.

RADIO TELEPHONE VHF Ch 12 16 (when vessel expected; at other times call *Douglas Hbr Control* Ch 12).

TELEPHONE (Dial code 01624) Hr Mr ☎/📠 842338, Mobile 07624 495036; MRSC 0151-931 3341; ⊖ 674321; Weather 0696 888322; Marinecall 09068 500 461; Police 842208; Dr 843636.

FACILITIES **Outer & Inner Hbrs**, AB see 9.10.15, M, Slip, FW, ME, El, Sh, C (30 ton mobile); **Peel Sailing and Cruising Club** ☎ 842390, Showers (key via Hr Mr), R, ⊡, Bar; **Services:** Gas, BY, CH, ACA. **Town** EC Thurs; P & D (cans), V, R, Bar, ✉, Ⓑ, ⇌ (bus to Douglas, qv for ferries), ✈ Ronaldsway. Facilities: EC Thurs; Bar, D, P, FW, R, Slip, V.

PORT ST MARY *9.10.17*

Isle of Man **54°04'·43N 04°43'·73W**

CHARTS AC 2696, 2094; Imray C62; Y70; OS 95

TIDES +0020 Dover; ML 3·2; Duration 0605; Zone 0 (UT)

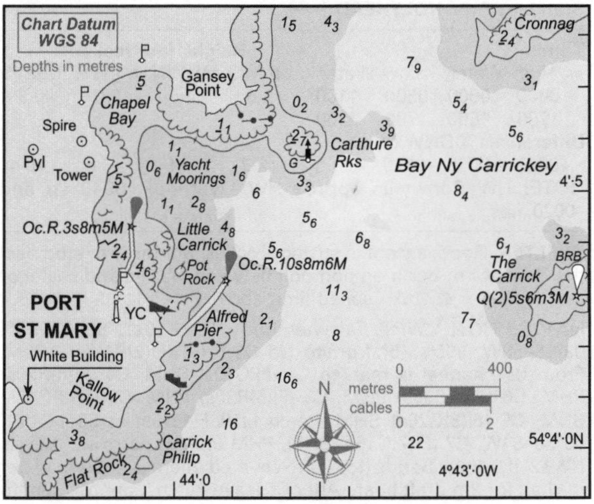

Standard Port LIVERPOOL (⟵)

Times				Height (metres)			
High Water		Low Water		MHWS	MHWN	MLWN	MLWS
0000	0600	0200	0700	9·3	7·4	2·9	0·9
1200	1800	1400	1900				
Differences PORT ST MARY							
+0005	+0015	−0010	−0030	−3·4	−2·6	−1·3	−0·4
CALF SOUND							
+0005	+0005	−0015	−0025	−3·2	−2·6	−0·9	−0·3
PORT ERIN							
−0005	+0015	−0010	−0050	−4·1	−3·2	−1·3	−0·5

SHELTER Very good except in E or SE winds. ⚓ S of Gansey Pt, but poor holding. 6 Or ⚓s between Alfred Pier and Little Carrick.

NAVIGATION WPT 54°04′·21N 04°43′·37W, 115°/295° from/to Alfred Pier lt, 0·30M. Rky outcrops to SE of pier to 2ca offshore. Beware lobster/crab pots, especially between Calf Island and Langness Pt.

LIGHTS AND MARKS Alfred Pier, Oc R 10s 8m 6M. Inner pier, Oc R 3s 8m 5M; both lts on W trs + R band, in transit 295° lead clear S of The Carrick Rk, in centre of bay, which is marked by IDM bn, Q (2) 5s 6m 3M. A conspic TV mast (133m), 5ca WNW of hbr, in transit with Alfred Pier lt leads 290° towards the hbr and also clears The Carrick rock.

RADIO TELEPHONE Call *Port St Mary Hbr* VHF Ch 12 16 (when vessel due or through Douglas Hbr Control Ch 12).

TELEPHONE (Dial code 01624) Hr Mr 833205; MRSC 0151-931 3341; ⊖ 674321; Marinecall 09068 500 461; Police 822222; Dr 832281.

FACILITIES **Alfred Pier** AB see 9.10.15, Slip, D (road tanker), L, FW, C (20 ton mobile); **Inner Hbr** dries 2·4m on sand; AB, Slip, D, L, FW; **Isle of Man YC** ☎ 832088, FW, Showers, Bar; **Services:** ME, CH, D, El, SM. **Town** EC Thurs; CH, V, R, Bar, ✉, Ⓑ, ≹ (bus to Douglas, qv for ferries), ✈ Ronaldsway.

MINOR HARBOUR EAST OF CASTLETOWN

DERBY HAVEN, Isle of Man, **54°04′·65N 04°36′·45W**. Tides & charts as above. Rather remote bay exposed only to NE/E winds. ⚓ in centre of bay, NW of St Michael's Island, in 3-5m. A detached bkwtr on NW side of the bay gives shelter to craft able to dry out behind it. Lts: Iso G 2s on S end of bkwtr. Aero FR (occas) at Ronaldsway airport, NW of bay. Facilities: at Castletown (1½M) or Port St Mary.

DOUGLAS *9.10.18*

Isle of Man **54°08'·87N 04°27'·96W**

CHARTS AC 2696, 2094; Imray C62; Y70; OS 95

TIDES +0009 Dover; ML 3·8; Duration 0600; Zone 0 (UT)

Standard Port LIVERPOOL (⟵)

Times				Height (metres)			
High Water		Low Water		MHWS	MHWN	MLWN	MLWS
0000	0600	0200	0700	9·3	7·4	2·9	0·9
1200	0800	1400	1900				
Differences DOUGLAS							
+0005	+0015	−0015	−0025	−2·4	−2·0	−0·5	−0·1

SHELTER Good except in NE winds. Very heavy seas run in during NE gales. Outer hbr: Victoria and King Edward VIII piers are for commercial vessels/ferries. At inner end of Battery Pier about 18 boats can raft up on pontoon; untenable in NE/E winds. Complete shelter in inner hbr, with possible pontoon berths, flapgate lowers on the flood and rises on the ebb at 4·4m above CD, lifting bridge opens every ½H subject to tide and road traffic conditions.

NAVIGATION WPT 54°09′·01N 04°27′·67W (abeam No 1 SHM buoy, Q (3) G 5s), 049°/229° from/to front ldg lt, 0·47M. Appr from NE of No 1 buoy (to avoid overfalls E of Princess Alexandra Pier) and await port entry sig, or call on VHF Ch 12. There is no bar. Keep clear of large vessels and ferries. Beware concrete step at end of dredged area (◊ mark on King Edward VIII Pier) and cill at ent to inner hbr.

LIGHTS AND MARKS Douglas Head Fl 10s 32m 24M. Ldg lts 229°, both Oc 10s 9/12m 5M, synch; front W △; rear W ▽, both on R border. IPTS Nos 2, 3 & 5 shown from mast on Victoria Pier. Dolphin at N end of Alexandra Pier 2FR (vert).

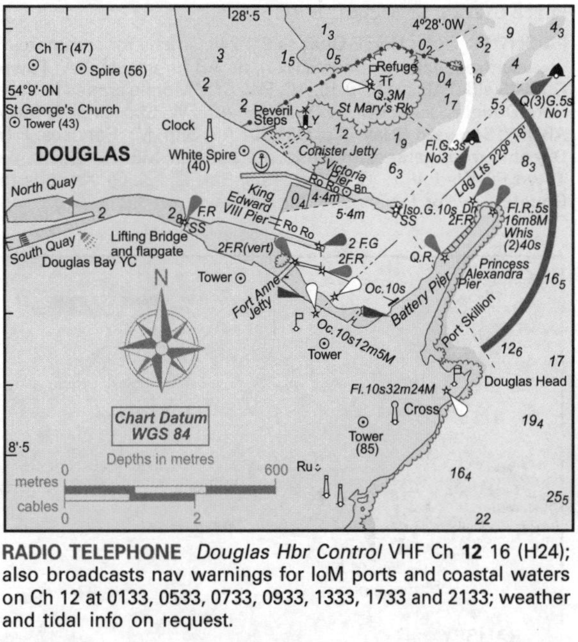

RADIO TELEPHONE *Douglas Hbr Control* VHF Ch **12** 16 (H24); also broadcasts nav warnings for IoM ports and coastal waters on Ch 12 at 0133, 0533, 0733, 0933, 1333, 1733 and 2133; weather and tidal info on request.

TELEPHONE (Dial code 01624) Hr Control 686628 626403 (H24); MRSC 0151-931 3341; ⊖ 674321; Marinecall 09068 500 461; Police 631212; Ⓗ 642642.

FACILITIES **Outer Hbr** AB see 9.10.15, M, FW at pontoon, P & D (cans) across the road from pontoon, ME, El, Sh, C (10, 5 ton), Slip; **Inner Hbr (N and S Quays)** AB, M, AC, FW, ME, C, El, Sh, CH, Slip; **Douglas Bay YC** ☎ 673965, Bar, Slip, L, showers 0930-2300. **Services:** P & D (cans), CH, ACA, El, Divers, Gas, Gaz, Kos. **Town** www.gov.im, EC Thurs; V, R, Bar, ✉, Ⓑ, ⊡, Ferry to Heysham and Liverpool; also in summer to Dublin and Belfast; ✈ Ronaldsway.

10

RAMSEY *9.10.19*

Isle of Man **54°19'·44N 04°22'·49W** ❁❁◊◊✿✿

CHARTS AC 2696, 2094; Imray C62; Y70; OS 95

TIDES +0020 Dover; ML 4·2; Duration 0545; Zone 0 (UT)

Standard Port LIVERPOOL (⟵)

Times				Height (metres)			
High Water		Low Water		MHWS	MHWN	MLWN	MLWS
0000	0600	0200	0700	9·3	7·4	2·9	0·9
1200	1800	1400	1900				
Differences RAMSEY							
+0005	+0015	–0005	–0015	–1·9	–1·5	–0·6	0·0

SHELTER Very good except in strong NE winds. Hbr dries 1·8m-6m. Access and ent only permitted HW –2½ to HW +2. Berth on Town quay (S side) or as directed by Hr Mr on entry. 2 orange ⚓s are close NW of Queen's Pier hd (only in summer). Note: Landing on Queen's Pier is prohibited. Possible water retention scheme as Douglas.

NAVIGATION WPT 54°19´·44N 04°21´·89W, 090°/270° from/to ent, 0·37M. The foreshore dries out 1ca to seaward of the pier hds.

LIGHTS AND MARKS No ldg lts/marks. Relative to hbr ent, Pt of Ayre, Fl (4) 20s 32m 19M, is 5·5M N; Maughold Hd, Fl (3) 30s 65m 21M, is 3M SE; Albert Tr (□ stone tr 14m, on hill 130m) is conspic 7ca S; and Snaefell (617m) bears 220°/5M. Inside the hbr an Iso G 4s, G SHM post, marks the S tip of Mooragh Bank; it is not visible from seaward. 2FR (hor) on each side mark the centre of swing bridge.

RADIO TELEPHONE *Ramsey Hbr* VHF Ch **12** 16 (0730-1600LT and when a vessel is due); OT call *Douglas Hbr Control* Ch **12**.

TELEPHONE (Dial code 01624) Hr Mr (non-resident) 812245; MRSC 0151-931 3341; ⊜ 674321; Marinecall 09068 500 461; Police 812234; Dr 813881; ⊞ 811811.

FACILITIES Outer Hbr: E Quay ☎ 812245, strictly for commercial vessels (frequent movements H24), no AB for yachts, FW; **Town Quay** (S side) AB see 9.10.15, AC, FW, C*; *Mobile cranes for hire from Douglas. **Inner Hbr, W Quay** AB, AC, FW, Slip (Grid); **N Quay** AB, FW; **Shipyard Quay** Slip; **Old Hbr** AB, Slip, M; **Services:** P & D (cans) from garages; none located at hbr. ME, El, Ⓔ, Sh, ♿. **Town** EC Wed; V, R, Gas, Gaz, Kos, Bar, ▣, ✉, Ⓑ, ⇌ (bus to Douglas, qv for ferries), ✈ Ronaldsway.

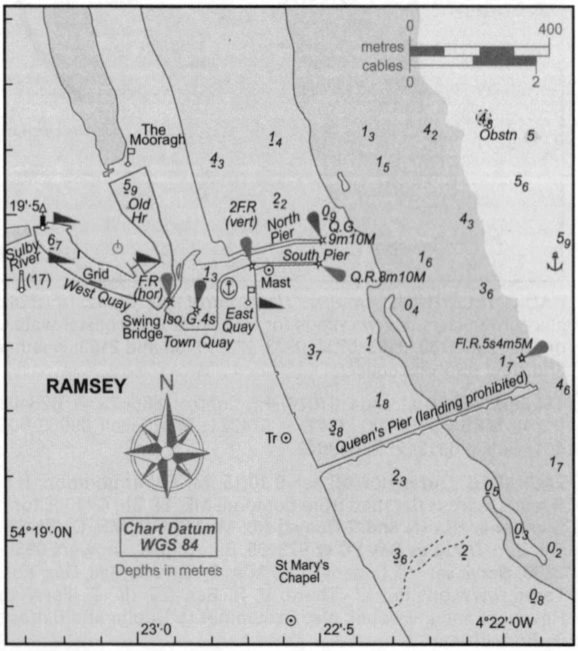

CONWY *9.10.20*

Conwy **53°17'·25N 03°50'·00W** (marina) ❁❁◊◊◊✿✿✿

CHARTS AC *1978, 1977, 1826*; Imray C52; OS 115; Stanfords 27

TIDES –0015 Dover; ML 4·3; Duration 0545; Zone 0 (UT)

Standard Port HOLYHEAD (⟶)

Times				Height (metres)			
High Water		Low Water		MHWS	MHWN	MLWN	MLWS
0000	0600	0500	1100	5·6	4·4	2·0	0·7
1200	1800	1700	2300				
Differences CONWY							
+0025	+0035	+0120	+0105	+2·3	+1·8	+0·6	+0·4

NOTE: HW Conwy is approx HW Liverpool –0040 sp and –0020 nps.

SHELTER Good, except in strong NW'lies. Marina is to stbd past the Narrows or berth on pontoon between marina and castle or ask Hr Mr for ⚓. 10kn speed limit above Perch lt.

NAVIGATION WPT Fairway buoy (L.Fl.10s), 53°17´·95N 03°55´·58W, 295°/115° from/to No C2 PHM (Fl(2)R10s), 0·80M. From C2 channel is marked C1 (Fl.G10s) SHM, C4 (Fl(4)R20s) PHM, C6 (Fl(6)R30s) PHM, C8 (Fl(8)R30s) PHM, C3 (Fl(3)G15s) SHM, C5 (Fl(5)G20s) SHM, Perch Lt (L.Fl.G15s) at 53°18´·06N 03°50´·84W, C7 (Fl(7)G15s) SHM, PHM unlit at narrows. Access HW±2; if Conwy Sands (to N) are covered, there is enough water in chan for 2m draft boat. After C5 leave Perch lt approx 30m to stbd. Pass unlit PHM. Marina ent to stbd has R/G entry lts. Beware unlit moorings. Sp ebb reaches 5kn. "Inshore Passage" (close SW of Gt Orme's Hd) is only advised with local knowledge.

LIGHTS AND MARKS Penmaenmawr Sewer Outfall (Fl.Y.5s) 53°17´·46N 03°54´·95W is not a ch mark. Ent ch buoyage is lit as above up to C7. The PHMs are unlit bns. Jetty unlit to stbd. Marina breakwater lt Fl.G. Two floating pontoons in hbr unlit.

RADIO TELEPHONE Hr Mr Ch **14** 16 (Summer 09-1700LT every day; winter, same times Mon-Fri). Conwy Marina Ch 80 (H24). N Wales CC Ch M, water taxi. Conwy YC Ch M.

TELEPHONE (Dial code 01492) Hr Mr 596253; MRSC (01407) 762051; ⊜ (01407) 760626; Marinecall 09068 500 460; Police 592222; Dr 592424.

FACILITIES Marina (500) access LW ±3½ ☎ 593000, 📠 572111, £1.90, AC, FW, D & P (0700-2359), BH (30 ton), ⛴, CH, Gas, ▣, SM, R, Bar, BY, Sh; **Harbour** ☎ 596253, Pontoon AB £8.00, Quay AB dries (12·3m max LOA; short stay for loading), M, D, P, FW, ♿; **Deganwy Dock** (dries), but marina development planned for 2002, AB, Slip, FW, C (mobile); **Conwy YC** ☎ 583690, Slip, M, L, FW, R, Bar; **N Wales Cruising Club** ☎ 593481, AB, M, FW, Bar. **Services:** ME, Gas, Gaz, Sh, El, Ⓔ. **Town** EC Wed; P & D (cans), V, R, Bar, ✉, Ⓑ, ⇌, ✈ (Liverpool).

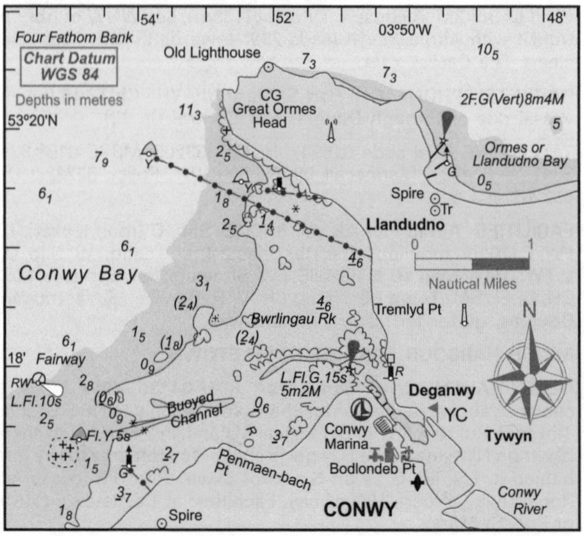

MENAI STRAIT *9.10.21*

Gwynedd/Isle of Anglesey

CHARTS AC *1464*, Imray C52; Stanfords 27; OS 114, 115. NOTE: The definitive Pilot book is *Cruising Anglesey and the North Wales Coast* by R Morris, 5th edition 1995: North West Venturers YC

TIDES Beaumaris –0025 Dover; ML Beaumaris 4·2; Duration 0540
Standard Port HOLYHEAD (⟶)

Times				Height (metres)			
High Water		Low Water		MHWS	MHWN	MLWN	MLWS
0000	0600	0500	1100	5·6	4·4	2·0	0·7
1200	1800	1700	2300				
Differences BEAUMARIS							
+0025	+0010	+0055	+0035	+2·0	+1·6	+0·5	+0·1
MENAI BRIDGE							
+0030	+0010	+0100	+0035	+1·7	+1·4	+0·3	0·0
PORT DINORWIC							
–0015	–0025	+0030	0000	0·0	0·0	0·0	+0·1
CAERNARFON							
–0030	–0030	+0015	–0005	–0·4	–0·4	–0·1	–0·1
FORT BELAN							
–0040	–0015	–0025	–0005	–1·0	–0·9	–0·2	–0·1
LLANDDWYN ISLAND							
–0115	–0055	–0030	–0020	–0·7	–0·5	–0·1	0·0

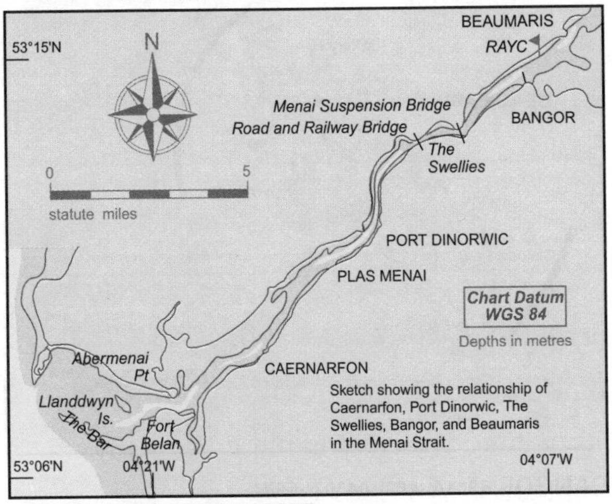

Sketch showing the relationship of Caernarfon, Port Dinorwic, The Swellies, Bangor, and Beaumaris in the Menai Strait.

SOUTH WEST ENTRANCE

NAVIGATION WPT 53°07'·61N 04°26'·08W, 270°/090° from/to Abermenai Pt, 3·8M. A dangerous sea can build in even a moderate breeze against tide, especially if a swell is running in the Irish Sea. Caernarfon Bar shifts often and unpredictably. See 9.10.5.

LIGHTS AND MARKS Llanddwyn Is lt, Fl WR 2·5s 12m 7/4M, R280°-015°, W015°-120°. Abermenai Pt lt, Fl WR 3·5s; R065°-245°, W245°-065°. **Direction of buoyage changes at Caernarfon.**

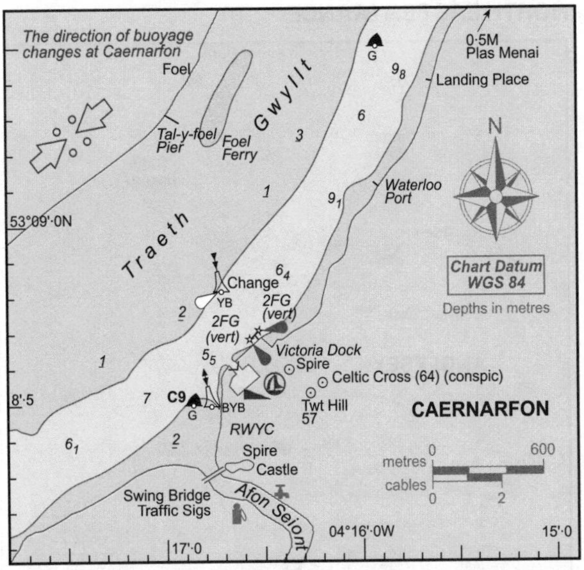

CAERNARFON 53°08'·51N 04°16'·83W

Direction of buoyage changes at Caernarfon.

SHELTER Good in Victoria Dock marina, access HW±2 via gates, trfc lts; pontoons at SW end in 2m. Or in river hbr (S of conspic castle), dries to mud/gravel, access HW±3 via swing bridge; for opening sound B (–···). ⚓ off Foel Ferry, with local knowledge; or temp ⚓ in fair holding off Abermenai Pt, sheltered from W'lies, but strong streams. Ø waiting 1½ca SW of C9.

RADIO TELEPHONE Victoria Dk mna VHF Ch 80. Port Ch 14 16 (HJ).

TELEPHONE (Dial code 01286) Hr Mr 672118, 📠 678729, Mobile 0410 541364; Police 673333; Ⓗ 01248 384384 Emergency 01248 384001.

FACILITIES Dock £1.35 **River Hbr** £8.15, 0700-2300 (Summer), FW, Slip, C (2 ton), V, ME, El, Ⓔ, Sh, CH, ⛴; **Caernarfon SC ☎** 672861, L, Bar; **Royal Welsh YC ☎** 672599, Bar; **Town** P (cans), ⊠, Ⓑ.

PORT DINORWIC 53°11'·23N 04°13'·70W

TELEPHONE (Dial code 01248) Marina 671500; MRSC (01407) 762051; Dr 670423.

FACILITIES Port Dinorwic Marina (230 berths in fresh water) £15 upto 9m, £18 up to 15m. Call *Dinorwic Marina* VHF Ch **80** M (HO)3 Ø 1ca NE of lock. **Tidal basin** dries at sp; lock opens HW±2. ☎ 671500 📠 671252, mobile 07768 794361, D, P (cans), AC, CH, SM; Pier hd F WR 5m 2M, vis R225°-357°, W357°-225°. **Services:** SM, ME, El, Sh, Slip, C, CH. Dinas Boatyard ☎ 671642 all BY facilities. **Town** Ⓔ, ⊠ (Bangor or Caernarfon), Ⓑ, ⇌ (Bangor), ✈ (Liverpool). **Note:** Between Port Dinorwic and Caernarfon is **Plas Menai ☎** 670964, the Sport Council for Wales Sailing and Sports Centre. *Menai Base* Ch **80** M. Day moorings only. All facilities for the disabled.

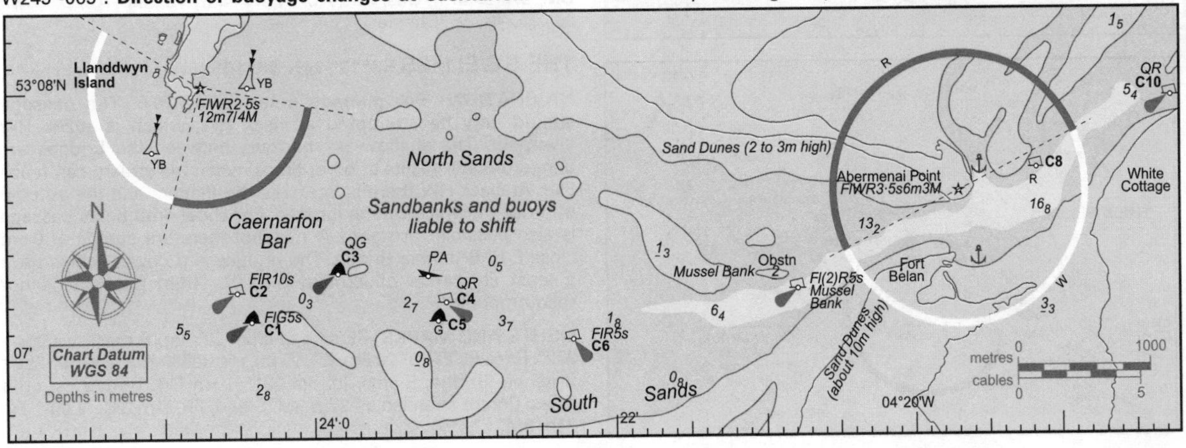

NORTH EAST ENTRANCE

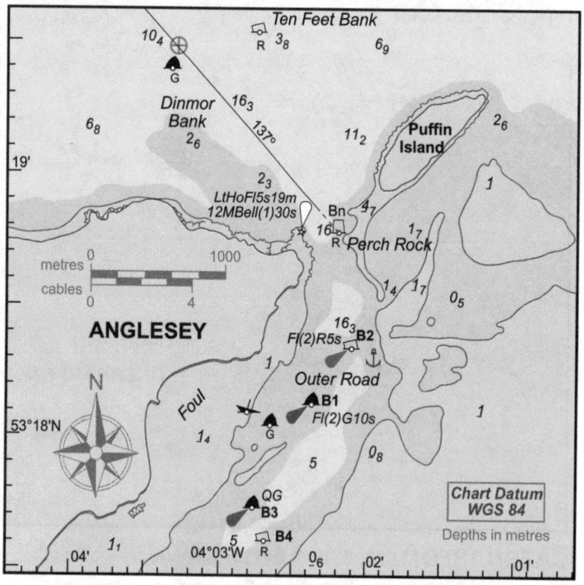

NAVIGATION WPT 53°19'·48N 04°03'·28W, 317°/137° from/to Perch Rk PHM bn, 1·0M. In N'ly gales seas break on Ten Foot Bank. In N Strait keep to buoyed chan, nearer Anglesey. Night pilotage not advised due to many unlit buoys/moorings.

LIGHTS AND MARKS At NE end of Strait, Trwyn-Du lt, W tr/B bands, Fl 5s 19m 12M, vis 101°-023° (282°), Bell 30s. Conspic tr on Puffin Is. Chan is laterally buoyed, some lit. Beaumaris pier has FWG sectored lt (see 9.10.4).

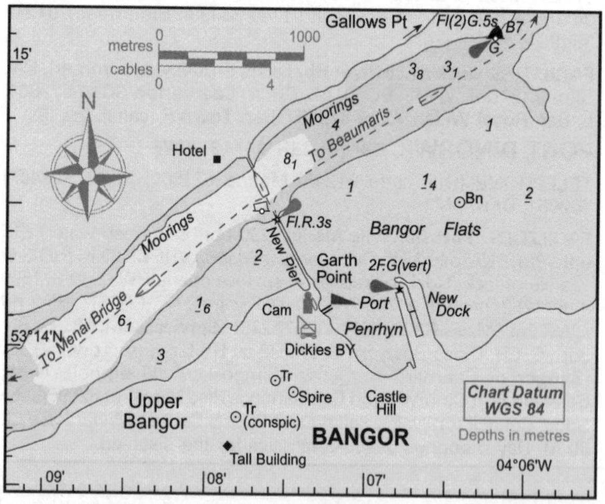

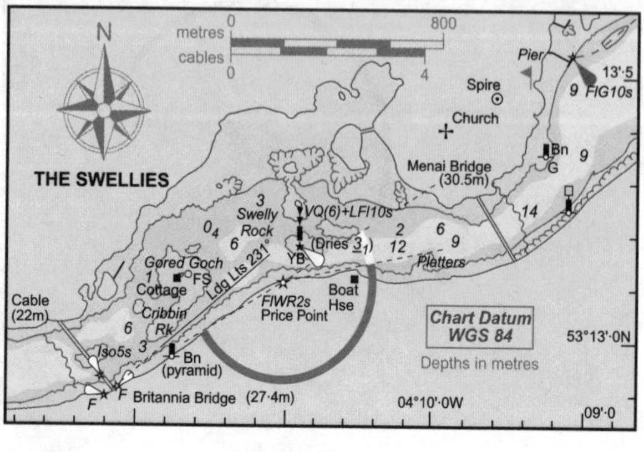

MENAI BRIDGE/BEAUMARIS 53°15'·66N 04°05'·38W

SHELTER Reasonable off Beaumaris except from NE winds. ⚓ S of B10 PHM buoy or call YCs for mooring. At Menai Bridge, call Hr Mr VHF Ch 69 16 for mooring or temp'y berth on St George's Pier (S of which a marina is planned).

TELEPHONE (Dial code 01248) Hr Mr Menai 712312, mobile 0378 253178; MRSC (01407) 762051; Marinecall 09068 500 460; ⊜ (01407) 762714; Police (01407) 762323; Dr 810501.

FACILITIES **St George's Pier** (Fl G 10s) L at all tides; **Royal Anglesey YC** ☎ 810295, Slip, M, L, R, Bar, P; **North West Venturers YC** ☎ 810023, M, L, FW, water taxi at w/ends only; **Menai Bridge SC. Services:** Slip, P & D (cans), FW, ME, BH (20 ton), Sh, C (2 ton), CH, El, Ⓔ, Gas. **Both towns** EC Wed; ✉, Ⓑ, ⇌ (bus to Bangor), ✈ (Liverpool).

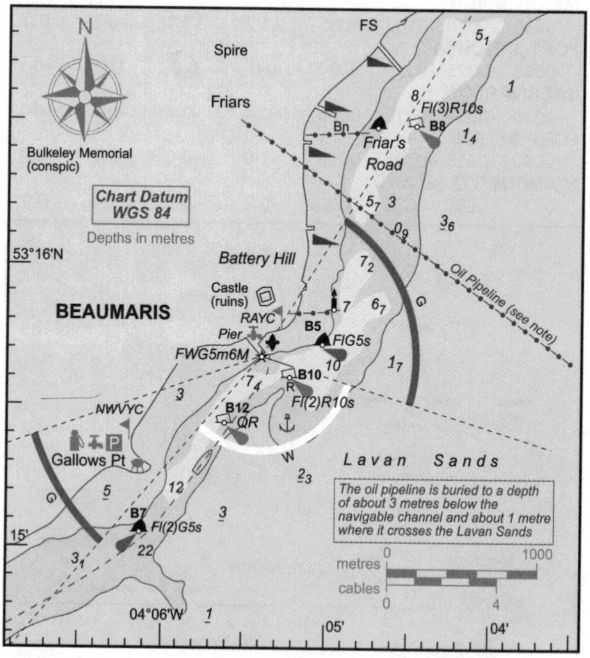

BANGOR 53°14'·46N 04°07'·58W

SHELTER Good, except in E'lies, at Dickies BY or Port Penrhyn dock (both dry; access HW±2).

RADIO TELEPHONE *Dickies* VHF Ch 09 M 16, all year.

TELEPHONE (Dial code 01248) Penrhyn Hr Mr 352525; MRSC (01407) 762051; ⊜ (01407) 762714; Dr 362055.

FACILITIES **Services:** Slip, D, P (cans), FW, ME, El, Sh, C, CH, Ⓔ, SM, BH (30 ton), Gas, Gaz, ACA; **Port Penrhyn**, Slip, AB, D. **Town** ✉, Ⓑ, ⇌, ✈ (Chester).

THE SWELLIES 53°13'·14N 04°10'·46W

NAVIGATION For pilotage notes, see 9.10.5. The passage should only be attempted at slack HW, which is –0200 HW Liverpool. The shallow rky narrows between the bridges are dangerous for yachts at other times, when the stream can reach 8kn. At slack HW there is 3m over The Platters and the outcrop off Price Pt, which can be ignored. For shoal-draft boats passage is also possible at slack LW nps, but there are depths of 0·5m close E of Britannia Bridge. The bridges and power cables have a least clearance of 22m at MHWS. Night passage is not recommended.

LIGHTS AND MARKS SE side of chan QR 4m, R mast, vis 064°-222°. Price Pt, Fl WR 2s 5m 3M, W Bn, vis R059°-239°, W239°-259°. Britannia Bridge, E side, ldg lts 231°, both FW. Bridge lts, both sides: Centre span Iso 5s 27m 3M; S end, FR 21m 3M; N end, FG 21m 3M.

HOLYHEAD *9.10.22*

Isle of Anglesey **53°19'·72N 04°37'·07W**

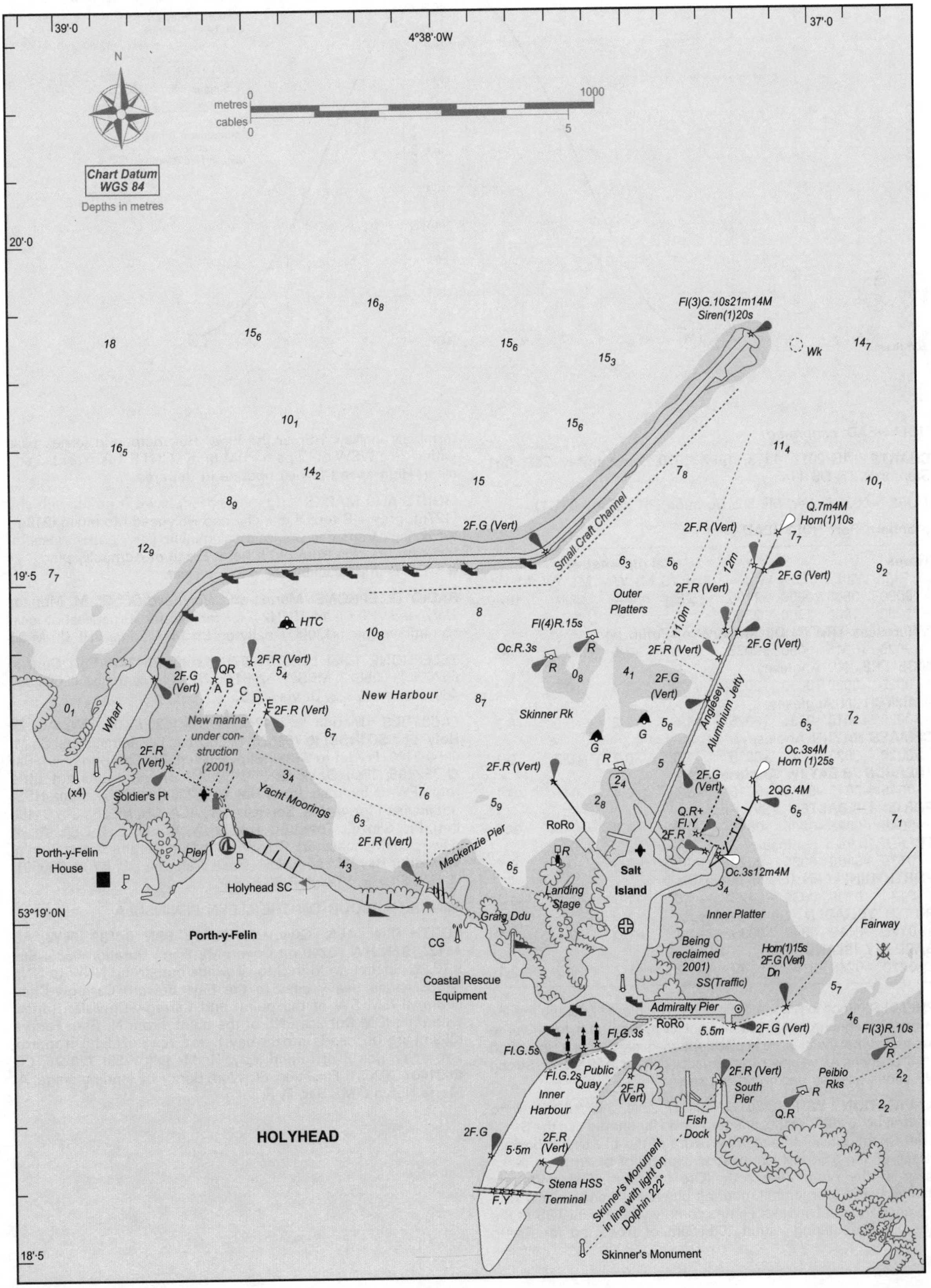

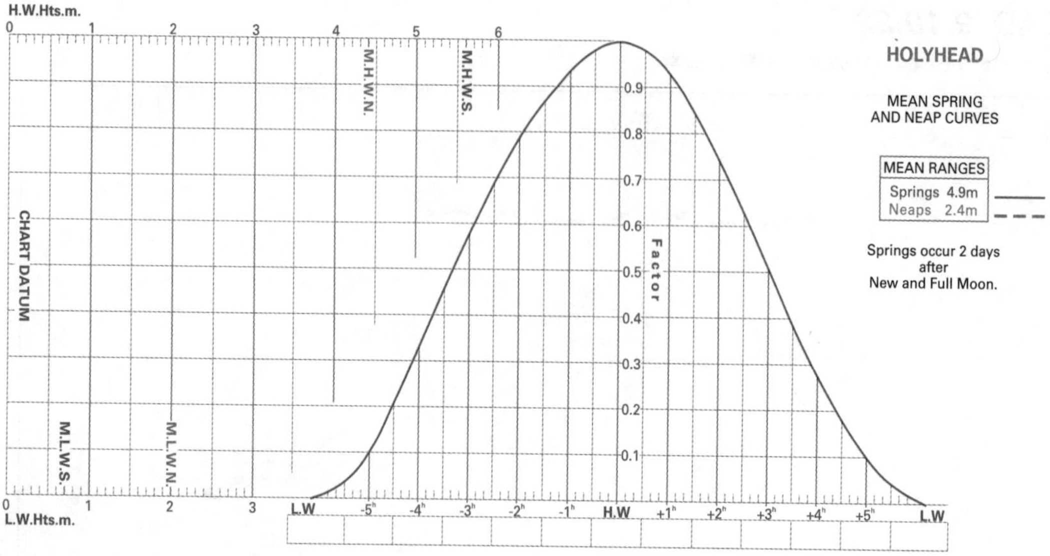
H.W.Hts.m.
CHART DATUM
M.H.W.N.
M.H.W.S.
M.L.W.S.
M.L.W.N.
Factor
L.W.Hts.m.
L.W -5h -4h -3h -2h -1h H.W +1h +2h +3h +4h +5h L.W
HOLYHEAD
MEAN SPRING AND NEAP CURVES
MEAN RANGES
Springs 4.9m
Neaps 2.4m
Springs occur 2 days after New and Full Moon.

HOLYHEAD *continued*

CHARTS AC 2011, 1413, *1977*, 1970, *1826*; Imray C52, C61; Stanfords 27; OS 114

TIDES –0035 Dover; ML 3·2; Duration 0615; Zone 0 (UT)

Standard Port HOLYHEAD (⟶)

Times				Height (metres)			
High Water		Low Water		MHWS	MHWN	MLWN	MLWS
0000	0600	0500	1100	5·6	4·4	2·0	0·7
1200	1800	1700	2300				
Differences TRWYN DINMOR (W of Puffin Is)							
+0025	+0015	+0050	+0035	+1·9	+1·5	+0·5	+0·2
MOELFRE (NE Anglesey)							
+0025	+0020	+0050	+0035	+1·9	+1·4	+0·5	+0·2
AMLWCH (N Anglesey)							
+0020	+0010	+0035	+0025	+1·6	+1·3	+0·5	+0·2
CEMAES BAY (N Anglesey)							
+0020	+0025	+0040	+0035	+1·0	+0·7	+0·3	+0·1
TREARDDUR BAY (W Anglesey)							
–0045	–0025	–0015	–0015	–0·4	–0·4	0·0	+0·1
PORTH TRECASTELL (SW Anglesey)							
–0045	–0025	–0005	–0015	–0·6	–0·6	0·0	0·0
TREFOR (Lleyn peninsula)							
–0115	–0100	–0030	–0020	–0·8	–0·9	–0·2	–0·1
PORTH DINLLAEN (Lleyn peninsula)							
–0120	–0105	–0035	–0025	–1·0	–1·0	–0·2	–0·2
PORTH YSGADEN (Lleyn peninsula)							
–0125	–0110	–0040	–0035	–1·1	–1·0	–0·1	–0·1
BARDSEY ISLAND							
–0220	–0240	–0145	–0140	–1·2	–1·2	–0·5	–0·1

SHELTER Good in marina, least depth 2m; please note the marina is under long-term construction. Contact marina prior to arrival to ascertain what facilities are in place. Alternatively ⚓ or pick up Y 🛟 off HSC; or drying AB on bkwtr in emergency only; or in Fish Dock. Strong NE winds raise an uncomfortable sea.

NAVIGATION WPT 53°20′·12N 04°37′·27W, 345°/165° from/to bkwtr lt ho, 0·28M. Yachts entering New Hbr should use the Small Craft Chan, parallel to and within 70m of the bkwtr; but beware shoal, drying 0·5m, which extends 35m SE of bkwtr head. Keep clear of the Aluminium Jetty (Ore terminal), Outer Platters (buoyed) and 3 large unlit mooring buoys at W end of New Hbr. No anchoring in fairways. Ferries comply with a mini-TSS at the hbr ent by entering within 100-500m of bkwtr hd for Ro-Ro terminals in New Hbr or the Inner Hbr; outbound ferries pass within 2½ca WSW of Clipera PHM buoy, Fl(4) R 15s. Yachts keep clear. High speed ferries operate in the area.

LIGHTS AND MARKS Ldg marks 165°: bkwtr lt ho on with chy (127m, grey + B top; R lts); chy and Holyhead Mountain (218m) are conspic from afar. Cranes on aluminium jetty conspic closer to. Inner hbr tfc sigs from old lt ho at E end of Admiralty pier: ● = Ent is impracticable. Ⓦ = Ent is clear.

RADIO TELEPHONE Marina and *Holyhead SC*: Ch M. Monitor *Holyhead* VHF Ch 14 16 (H24) for ferry traffic. Broadcast of local nav info/warnings1200UT daily on Ch 14. Marina: VHF Ch M 80

TELEPHONE (Dial code 01407) Marina 764242; Port Control 667006 📠 606622; MRSC 762051; ⊖ 762714; Marinecall 09068 500 460; Police 762323; Dr via MRSC.

FACILITIES Marina ☎ 764242, 📠 769152, £2.00, FW, AC, D. **Holyhead SC (HSC)** ☎ 762526, M £6.25, L, FW, launch (call Ch M: 0900-2100, Fri/Sat to 2330), Slip, R (Wed, Fri, Sat, Sun only), Bar ☎ 762496; **Fish Dock** ☎ 760139 AB on pontoons,but little room,FW, D by hose. **Inner Hbr** ☎ 762304, used by Stena HSS; not advised for yachts. **Services:** BY, ACA, CH, ME, El, Sh, C (100 ton), BH, Slip, Ⓔ. **Town** EC Tues; P, V, R, Bar, ⊡, ✉, Ⓑ, ⇌, ✈ (Liverpool/Manchester). Ferry/HSS to Dun Laoghaire and Dublin. **Trearddur Bay** (3M south) M (small craft only), L; **BY** ☎ 860501, D, FW, Sh, CH. **Village** P, V, R, Bar.

MINOR HARBOUR ON THE LLEYN PENINSULA

PORTH DINLLAEN, Gwynedd, **52°56′·68N 04°33′·66W**. AC 1512, 1971. HW –0240 on Dover; ML 2·5m; Duration 0535. See 9.10.22. Shelter good in S to W winds but strong NNW to NNE winds cause heavy seas in the bay. Beware Carreg-y-Chad (1·8m) 0·75M SW of the point, and Carreg-y-Chwislen (dries, with unlit IDM Bn) 2ca ENE of the point. From N, Garn Fadryn (369m) brg 182° leads into the bay. Best ⚓ 1ca S of LB ho in approx 2m, or 🛟 1½ca E of ruined jetty. Hr Mr ☎ (01758) 720276; CG ☎ 01407 762051. Facilities: EC Wed; Bar, V by landing stage. At Morfa Nefyn (1M), Bar, P, R, V.

TIME ZONE (UTC)
For Summer Time add ONE hour in **non-shaded areas**

WALES – HOLYHEAD

LAT 53°19′N LONG 4°37′W

TIMES AND HEIGHTS OF HIGH AND LOW WATERS

SPRING & NEAP TIDES
Dates in red are SPRINGS
Dates in blue are NEAPS

YEAR **2002**

JANUARY

Date	Day	Time	m	Time	m	Time	m	Time	m
1	TU	0510	0.9	1126	5.8	1742	0.7	2354	5.6
2	W	0556	0.9	1212	5.8	1830	0.7		
3	TH	0043	5.5	0643	1.0	1301	5.7	1920	0.8
4	F	0135	5.3	0733	1.2	1353	5.6	2015	0.9
5	SA	0230	5.1	0828	1.4	1449	5.4	2115	1.1
6	SU	0332	4.9	0930	1.6	1552	5.2	2220	1.3
7	M	0440	4.8	1039	1.8	1702	5.0	2329	1.4
8	TU	0551	4.7	1151	1.8	1813	5.0		
9	W	0035	1.5	0657	4.8	1301	1.7	1921	5.0
10	TH	0137	1.4	0756	5.0	1403	1.5	2021	5.1
11	F	0232	1.4	0847	5.2	1457	1.4	2113	5.2
12	SA	0319	1.3	0931	5.4	1543	1.2	2157	5.2
13	SU	0400	1.2	1012	5.5	1625	1.1	● 2238	5.2
14	M	0439	1.2	1050	5.6	1703	1.1	2315	5.2
15	TU	0515	1.2	1126	5.6	1740	1.1	2350	5.2
16	W	0549	1.2	1201	5.5	1814	1.1		
17	TH	0024	5.1	0623	1.3	1235	5.4	1849	1.2
18	F	0058	5.0	0658	1.5	1311	5.3	1925	1.4
19	SA	0134	4.8	0734	1.6	1348	5.1	2003	1.5
20	SU	0213	4.7	0815	1.9	1429	4.9	2046	1.7
21	M	0258	4.5	0902	2.1	1517	4.7	2137	1.9
22	TU	0354	4.4	1000	2.2	1616	4.6	2239	2.0
23	W	0505	4.3	1112	2.3	1728	4.5	2349	2.0
24	TH	0620	4.4	1225	2.2	1842	4.6		
25	F	0056	1.9	0724	4.6	1330	1.9	1945	4.8
26	SA	0154	1.7	0818	4.9	1426	1.6	2039	5.0
27	SU	0245	1.4	0904	5.2	1515	1.2	2127	5.3
28	M	0331	1.1	0947	5.5	1601	0.8	○ 2212	5.5
29	TU	0415	0.8	1030	5.7	1645	0.5	2257	5.7
30	W	0459	0.6	1114	5.9	1730	0.4	2342	5.7
31	TH	0543	0.6	1159	6.0	1816	0.3		

FEBRUARY

Date	Day	Time	m	Time	m	Time	m	Time	m
1	F	0028	5.7	0627	0.6	1245	6.0	1903	0.4
2	SA	0115	5.5	0714	0.8	1333	5.8	1952	0.6
3	SU	0204	5.3	0803	1.0	1423	5.5	2045	1.0
4	M	0257	5.0	0858	1.4	1520	5.2	2144	1.3
5	TU	0358	4.7	1003	1.7	1627	4.9	2253	1.6
6	W	0512	4.6	1120	1.9	1748	4.7		
7	TH	0008	1.8	0631	4.6	1242	1.9	1911	4.6
8	F	0122	1.8	0742	4.7	1355	1.7	2020	4.8
9	SA	0223	1.7	0839	5.0	1453	1.5	2113	4.9
10	SU	0311	1.5	0924	5.2	1538	1.3	2154	5.0
11	M	0351	1.3	1001	5.4	1615	1.1	2228	5.1
12	TU	0426	1.2	1035	5.5	1649	1.0	● 2259	5.2
13	W	0458	1.1	1107	5.6	1720	1.0	2329	5.2
14	TH	0528	1.0	1138	5.6	1750	1.0	2358	5.2
15	F	0559	1.1	1210	5.5	1820	1.0		
16	SA	0028	5.1	0629	1.2	1242	5.4	1851	1.1
17	SU	0100	5.0	0702	1.3	1315	5.3	1924	1.3
18	M	0133	4.9	0736	1.5	1350	5.1	2000	1.5
19	TU	0209	4.7	0816	1.7	1430	4.8	2043	1.7
20	W	0254	4.5	0905	2.0	1521	4.6	2138	2.0
21	TH	0355	4.3	1013	2.2	1632	4.4	2253	2.1
22	F	0521	4.3	1140	2.2	1804	4.4		
23	SA	0018	2.1	0648	4.4	1302	1.9	1923	4.6
24	SU	0130	1.8	0754	4.8	1406	1.5	2024	4.9
25	M	0228	1.4	0845	5.1	1458	1.0	2113	5.3
26	TU	0316	1.0	0930	5.5	1545	0.6	2158	5.6
27	W	0400	0.7	1013	5.8	1628	0.3	○ 2241	5.8
28	TH	0442	0.4	1056	6.1	1712	0.1	2323	5.9

MARCH

Date	Day	Time	m	Time	m	Time	m	Time	m
1	F	0524	0.3	1139	6.2	1755	0.0		
2	SA	0006	5.8	0606	0.3	1224	6.1	1839	0.2
3	SU	0050	5.6	0651	0.5	1310	5.9	1925	0.5
4	M	0135	5.4	0737	0.8	1357	5.5	2013	0.9
5	TU	0223	5.1	0829	1.2	1450	5.1	2109	1.4
6	W	0319	4.7	0932	1.6	1557	4.7	2217	1.9
7	TH	0432	4.5	1053	1.9	1727	4.4	2341	2.1
8	F	0603	4.4	1225	2.0	1905	4.4		
9	SA	0105	2.1	0725	4.6	1345	1.8	2016	4.6
10	SU	0210	1.9	0825	4.8	1441	1.5	2104	4.8
11	M	0257	1.6	0908	5.1	1522	1.3	2139	5.0
12	TU	0334	1.4	0942	5.3	1556	1.1	2209	5.1
13	W	0406	1.2	1013	5.4	1625	1.0	2236	5.2
14	TH	0435	1.0	1042	5.5	1653	0.9	● 2303	5.3
15	F	0503	0.9	1112	5.5	1721	0.9	2330	5.3
16	SA	0532	0.9	1142	5.5	1750	0.9	2359	5.2
17	SU	0601	1.0	1213	5.4	1819	1.0		
18	M	0028	5.2	0632	1.1	1245	5.3	1850	1.1
19	TU	0059	5.0	0705	1.3	1318	5.1	1924	1.3
20	W	0133	4.9	0743	1.5	1356	4.9	2004	1.6
21	TH	0214	4.7	0831	1.8	1445	4.6	2057	1.9
22	F	0311	4.4	0936	2.0	1556	4.4	2212	2.1
23	SA	0436	4.3	1108	2.1	1736	4.3	2347	2.1
24	SU	0616	4.4	1237	1.8	1904	4.5		
25	M	0107	1.8	0728	4.7	1345	1.4	2006	4.9
26	TU	0207	1.4	0822	5.2	1438	0.9	2055	5.3
27	W	0256	1.0	0908	5.6	1523	0.4	2138	5.6
28	TH	0339	0.6	0951	5.9	1606	0.1	○ 2219	5.8
29	F	0420	0.3	1034	6.1	1649	0.0	2300	5.9
30	SA	0502	0.2	1117	6.2	1731	0.0	2342	5.8
31	SU	0544	0.2	1201	6.1	1814	0.2		

APRIL

Date	Day	Time	m	Time	m	Time	m	Time	m
1	M	0024	5.7	0628	0.4	1247	5.8	1858	0.6
2	TU	0108	5.4	0714	0.7	1334	5.4	1944	1.1
3	W	0155	5.1	0806	1.2	1427	4.9	2037	1.6
4	TH	0248	4.8	0907	1.6	1532	4.5	2144	2.0
5	F	0357	4.5	1028	1.9	1704	4.2	2310	2.3
6	SA	0527	4.4	1200	2.0	1844	4.2		
7	SU	0037	2.3	0653	4.5	1318	1.8	1953	4.5
8	M	0144	2.0	0755	4.7	1413	1.6	2038	4.7
9	TU	0231	1.7	0838	4.9	1453	1.3	2112	4.9
10	W	0307	1.5	0912	5.1	1526	1.1	2140	5.1
11	TH	0338	1.2	0943	5.3	1555	1.0	2207	5.2
12	F	0407	1.0	1013	5.4	1623	0.9	● 2234	5.3
13	SA	0435	0.9	1043	5.4	1650	0.8	2301	5.3
14	SU	0504	0.9	1114	5.4	1719	0.9	2330	5.3
15	M	0535	0.9	1145	5.4	1750	1.0		
16	TU	0000	5.3	0607	1.0	1219	5.2	1821	1.1
17	W	0033	5.2	0642	1.2	1255	5.1	1858	1.3
18	TH	0109	5.0	0723	1.4	1336	4.9	1941	1.6
19	F	0153	4.8	0813	1.6	1429	4.6	2036	1.8
20	SA	0252	4.6	0921	1.8	1542	4.4	2151	2.1
21	SU	0414	4.4	1049	1.8	1718	4.4	2322	2.1
22	M	0546	4.5	1212	1.6	1841	4.6		
23	TU	0040	1.8	0658	4.8	1318	1.2	1941	5.0
24	W	0141	1.4	0754	5.2	1412	0.7	2030	5.3
25	TH	0230	1.0	0842	5.6	1459	0.4	2114	5.5
26	F	0314	0.6	0927	5.8	1542	0.2	2155	5.7
27	SA	0357	0.4	1011	6.0	1625	0.1	○ 2236	5.8
28	SU	0440	0.3	1056	6.0	1707	0.2	2319	5.8
29	M	0524	0.3	1141	5.8	1751	0.5		
30	TU	0002	5.6	0609	0.5	1228	5.6	1834	0.8

Chart Datum: 3·05 metres below Ordnance Datum (Newlyn)

TIME ZONE (UTC)
For Summer Time add ONE hour in **non-shaded areas**

WALES – HOLYHEAD

LAT 53°19′N LONG 4°37′W

TIMES AND HEIGHTS OF HIGH AND LOW WATERS

SPRING & NEAP TIDES
Dates in red are SPRINGS
Dates in blue are NEAPS

YEAR **2002**

MAY

Date	Day	Time	m	Time	m	Time	m	Time	m
1	W	0046	5.4	0656	0.8	1315	5.2	1920	1.2
2	TH	0132	5.2	0747	1.2	1407	4.8	2011	1.7
3	F	0223	4.9	0846	1.6	1509	4.4	2111	2.1
4	SA	0325	4.6	0958	1.9	1630	4.2	2229	2.3
5	SU	0442	4.4	1119	2.0	1758	4.2	2351	2.3
6	M	0602	4.4	1232	1.9	1908	4.3		
7	TU	0059	2.1	0706	4.6	1329	1.7	1957	4.6
8	W	0150	1.9	0754	4.8	1413	1.5	2034	4.8
9	TH	0230	1.6	0833	5.0	1448	1.3	2105	5.0
10	F	0304	1.4	0908	5.1	1519	1.1	2134	5.1
11	SA	0335	1.2	0941	5.2	1550	1.0	2203	5.2
12	SU	0406	1.1	1014	5.3	1620	0.9	● 2233	5.3
13	M	0438	1.0	1047	5.3	1652	0.9	2304	5.3
14	TU	0512	1.0	1122	5.3	1725	1.0	2338	5.3
15	W	0548	1.0	1159	5.2	1802	1.1		
16	TH	0015	5.2	0628	1.1	1241	5.1	1842	1.3
17	F	0056	5.1	0713	1.2	1327	4.9	1929	1.5
18	SA	0145	5.0	0808	1.4	1424	4.7	2026	1.7
19	SU	0245	4.8	0914	1.5	1535	4.5	2137	1.9
20	M	0359	4.7	1031	1.5	1656	4.5	2256	1.9
21	TU	0517	4.8	1145	1.3	1811	4.7		
22	W	0009	1.7	0626	5.0	1249	1.1	1912	4.9
23	TH	0111	1.4	0725	5.2	1344	0.8	2003	5.2
24	F	0203	1.1	0816	5.5	1434	0.6	2049	5.4
25	SA	0251	0.8	0905	5.6	1520	0.5	2133	5.6
26	SU	0337	0.6	0952	5.7	1604	0.5	○ 2216	5.6
27	M	0423	0.5	1038	5.7	1648	0.6	2259	5.7
28	TU	0509	0.6	1125	5.5	1731	0.8	2343	5.6
29	W	0555	0.7	1212	5.3	1815	1.0		
30	TH	0027	5.4	0641	0.9	1259	5.0	1859	1.3
31	F	0113	5.2	0730	1.2	1347	4.7	1946	1.6

JUNE

Date	Day	Time	m	Time	m	Time	m	Time	m
1	SA	0159	5.0	0822	1.5	1440	4.5	2038	1.9
2	SU	0251	4.8	0920	1.7	1542	4.3	2139	2.2
3	M	0351	4.6	1024	1.9	1653	4.2	2249	2.3
4	TU	0458	4.5	1130	1.9	1802	4.3	2357	2.2
5	W	0603	4.5	1230	1.8	1900	4.4		
6	TH	0055	2.1	0700	4.6	1321	1.6	1946	4.6
7	F	0144	1.8	0748	4.8	1404	1.5	2025	4.8
8	SA	0225	1.6	0831	4.9	1442	1.3	2100	5.0
9	SU	0303	1.4	0910	5.1	1517	1.2	2134	5.1
10	M	0339	1.2	0947	5.2	1553	1.1	● 2208	5.3
11	TU	0416	1.1	1025	5.2	1629	1.0	2243	5.3
12	W	0455	1.0	1105	5.2	1707	1.0	2322	5.4
13	TH	0536	0.9	1146	5.2	1748	1.1		
14	F	0003	5.4	0619	0.9	1232	5.1	1832	1.2
15	SA	0049	5.3	0708	1.0	1322	5.0	1921	1.3
16	SU	0139	5.2	0801	1.1	1417	4.9	2016	1.5
17	M	0236	5.1	0901	1.2	1520	4.8	2118	1.6
18	TU	0339	5.0	1007	1.2	1628	4.7	2227	1.7
19	W	0447	5.0	1115	1.2	1738	4.7	2336	1.6
20	TH	0555	5.0	1219	1.1	1842	4.9		
21	F	0041	1.5	0658	5.1	1319	1.0	1938	5.0
22	SA	0140	1.3	0756	5.2	1413	1.0	2029	5.2
23	SU	0234	1.1	0850	5.3	1503	0.9	2116	5.4
24	M	0325	0.9	0940	5.4	1549	0.9	○ 2201	5.5
25	TU	0413	0.8	1028	5.4	1633	0.9	2245	5.5
26	W	0458	0.8	1114	5.3	1716	1.0	2328	5.5
27	TH	0543	0.9	1158	5.2	1757	1.1		
28	F	0010	5.5	0625	1.0	1240	5.0	1837	1.3
29	SA	0051	5.3	0707	1.2	1322	4.8	1918	1.5
30	SU	0132	5.1	0750	1.4	1404	4.6	2001	1.7

JULY

Date	Day	Time	m	Time	m	Time	m	Time	m
1	M	0214	5.0	0835	1.6	1449	4.5	2048	1.9
2	TU	0301	4.8	0925	1.7	1542	4.3	2143	2.1
3	W	0354	4.6	1021	1.9	1644	4.3	2245	2.2
4	TH	0456	4.5	1122	1.9	1751	4.3	2351	2.2
5	F	0601	4.5	1222	1.9	1852	4.4		
6	SA	0052	2.1	0702	4.6	1317	1.7	1943	4.6
7	SU	0146	1.8	0756	4.7	1405	1.6	2028	4.8
8	M	0233	1.6	0843	4.9	1449	1.4	2108	5.0
9	TU	0317	1.3	0927	5.1	1531	1.2	2147	5.2
10	W	0359	1.1	1009	5.2	1612	1.1	● 2227	5.4
11	TH	0441	0.9	1051	5.3	1653	1.0	2308	5.5
12	F	0525	0.7	1135	5.4	1737	0.9	2352	5.6
13	SA	0610	0.7	1221	5.4	1821	0.9		
14	SU	0037	5.6	0656	0.7	1310	5.3	1908	1.0
15	M	0126	5.5	0746	0.8	1400	5.1	1958	1.2
16	TU	0217	5.4	0840	0.9	1455	5.0	2053	1.3
17	W	0314	5.2	0939	1.1	1556	4.8	2156	1.5
18	TH	0417	5.1	1044	1.3	1703	4.7	2306	1.6
19	F	0527	4.9	1152	1.4	1813	4.7		
20	SA	0018	1.6	0639	4.9	1259	1.4	1919	4.9
21	SU	0127	1.5	0747	4.9	1400	1.4	2017	5.0
22	M	0228	1.4	0847	5.0	1454	1.3	2108	5.2
23	TU	0321	1.2	0938	5.1	1541	1.2	2153	5.4
24	W	0408	1.0	1023	5.2	1622	1.1	○ 2234	5.5
25	TH	0449	0.9	1103	5.2	1701	1.1	2312	5.5
26	F	0528	0.9	1140	5.1	1738	1.1	2349	5.5
27	SA	0604	1.0	1215	5.1	1813	1.2		
28	SU	0025	5.4	0639	1.1	1250	5.0	1848	1.3
29	M	0100	5.3	0714	1.2	1324	4.8	1924	1.5
30	TU	0136	5.1	0751	1.4	1401	4.7	2002	1.7
31	W	0215	4.9	0831	1.6	1443	4.5	2046	1.9

AUGUST

Date	Day	Time	m	Time	m	Time	m	Time	m
1	TH	0259	4.7	0917	1.8	1533	4.4	2139	2.1
2	F	0353	4.5	1014	2.0	1637	4.3	2247	2.3
3	SA	0501	4.4	1122	2.1	1753	4.3		
4	SU	0002	2.2	0617	4.4	1232	2.0	1902	4.5
5	M	0111	2.0	0726	4.6	1334	1.8	1959	4.7
6	TU	0209	1.7	0823	4.8	1427	1.6	2046	5.0
7	W	0259	1.4	0911	5.0	1513	1.3	2129	5.3
8	TH	0343	1.0	0954	5.3	1556	1.0	● 2210	5.6
9	F	0426	0.7	1037	5.5	1638	0.8	2252	5.8
10	SA	0509	0.5	1120	5.6	1720	0.6	2335	5.9
11	SU	0552	0.3	1203	5.6	1803	0.6		
12	M	0019	5.9	0636	0.4	1249	5.5	1847	0.7
13	TU	0105	5.8	0723	0.5	1335	5.4	1934	0.9
14	W	0153	5.6	0812	0.8	1425	5.1	2026	1.2
15	TH	0246	5.3	0908	1.1	1522	4.9	2126	1.5
16	F	0349	5.0	1013	1.5	1630	4.7	2240	1.8
17	SA	0506	4.7	1128	1.8	1750	4.6		
18	SU	0003	1.8	0633	4.6	1246	1.8	1907	4.7
19	M	0123	1.7	0751	4.7	1354	1.7	2012	5.0
20	TU	0228	1.5	0851	4.9	1449	1.6	2102	5.2
21	W	0318	1.3	0936	5.0	1532	1.4	2143	5.4
22	TH	0358	1.1	1013	5.1	1609	1.2	○ 2218	5.5
23	F	0433	1.0	1045	5.2	1642	1.1	2251	5.6
24	SA	0506	0.9	1116	5.2	1714	1.1	2323	5.6
25	SU	0536	0.9	1145	5.2	1745	1.1	2355	5.5
26	M	0607	1.0	1215	5.1	1816	1.2		
27	TU	0027	5.4	0637	1.1	1247	5.0	1847	1.3
28	W	0100	5.2	0709	1.3	1319	4.9	1922	1.6
29	TH	0134	5.1	0744	1.5	1354	4.7	2000	1.8
30	F	0212	4.8	0824	1.8	1437	4.6	2047	2.1
31	SA	0301	4.6	0915	2.0	1533	4.4	2151	2.3

Chart Datum: 3·05 metres below Ordnance Datum (Newlyn)

TIME ZONE (UTC)
For Summer Time add ONE hour in **non-shaded areas**

WALES – HOLYHEAD

LAT 53°19'N LONG 4°37'W

TIMES AND HEIGHTS OF HIGH AND LOW WATERS

SPRING & NEAP TIDES
Dates in red are SPRINGS
Dates in blue are NEAPS

YEAR **2002**

SEPTEMBER

Date	Day	Time	m	Time	m	Time	m	Time	m
1	SU	0408	4.3	1025	2.3	1655	4.3	2317	2.3
2	M	0540	4.3	1152	2.3	1825	4.4		
3	TU	0042	2.1	0704	4.5	1308	2.0	1933	4.7
4	W	0147	1.7	0806	4.8	1407	1.7	2025	5.1
5	TH	0239	1.3	0854	5.1	1454	1.3	2108	5.4
6	F	0323	0.8	0936	5.4	1537	0.9	2149	5.8
7	SA	0405	0.4	1017	5.7	1617	0.6	● 2230	6.0
8	SU	0447	0.2	1058	5.8	1658	0.4	2312	6.2
9	M	0528	0.1	1140	5.8	1740	0.4	2356	6.1
10	TU	0612	0.2	1222	5.7	1823	0.5		
11	W	0041	6.0	0656	0.5	1308	5.5	1909	0.8
12	TH	0128	5.7	0744	0.9	1355	5.2	2000	1.1
13	F	0221	5.3	0838	1.4	1450	4.9	2101	1.6
14	SA	0326	4.8	0944	1.8	1601	4.6	2221	1.9
15	SU	0453	4.5	1108	2.1	1730	4.6	2354	2.0
16	M	0634	4.5	1234	2.2	1856	4.7		
17	TU	0117	1.8	0752	4.6	1345	2.0	2001	5.0
18	W	0219	1.5	0844	4.9	1436	1.7	2047	5.2
19	TH	0303	1.3	0922	5.0	1516	1.5	2124	5.4
20	F	0339	1.1	0953	5.2	1548	1.3	2155	5.5
21	SA	0409	1.0	1020	5.3	1618	1.1	○ 2225	5.6
22	SU	0438	1.0	1047	5.3	1647	1.1	2254	5.6
23	M	0505	0.9	1114	5.3	1715	1.1	2324	5.6
24	TU	0533	1.0	1142	5.3	1745	1.1	2355	5.5
25	W	0602	1.1	1212	5.2	1815	1.3		
26	TH	0026	5.3	0632	1.3	1243	5.1	1848	1.5
27	F	0059	5.1	0705	1.5	1316	4.9	1925	1.7
28	SA	0136	4.9	0744	1.8	1355	4.7	2011	2.0
29	SU	0223	4.6	0833	2.1	1449	4.5	2114	2.2
30	M	0331	4.3	0943	2.3	1610	4.4	2243	2.3

OCTOBER

Date	Day	Time	m	Time	m	Time	m	Time	m
1	TU	0511	4.3	1118	2.4	1750	4.4		
2	W	0014	2.0	0641	4.5	1242	2.1	1904	4.8
3	TH	0122	1.6	0744	4.9	1342	1.7	1958	5.2
4	F	0214	1.1	0831	5.3	1430	1.2	2043	5.6
5	SA	0259	0.7	0913	5.6	1512	0.8	2124	5.9
6	SU	0340	0.3	0953	5.8	1553	0.5	● 2206	6.2
7	M	0421	0.1	1033	6.0	1634	0.3	2248	6.3
8	TU	0503	0.1	1114	6.0	1716	0.3	2332	6.2
9	W	0546	0.3	1157	5.8	1801	0.5		
10	TH	0018	6.0	0630	0.6	1242	5.6	1848	0.8
11	F	0107	5.6	0718	1.1	1330	5.3	1940	1.2
12	SA	0201	5.1	0811	1.6	1425	5.0	2043	1.6
13	SU	0308	4.7	0918	2.1	1535	4.7	2204	1.9
14	M	0440	4.4	1043	2.4	1704	4.6	2336	2.0
15	TU	0620	4.4	1211	2.3	1830	4.7		
16	W	0055	1.9	0732	4.6	1321	2.1	1934	4.9
17	TH	0154	1.6	0821	4.8	1411	1.8	2019	5.1
18	F	0236	1.4	0856	5.0	1449	1.6	2055	5.3
19	SA	0310	1.2	0925	5.2	1521	1.4	2126	5.4
20	SU	0339	1.1	0951	5.3	1550	1.2	2155	5.5
21	M	0407	1.0	1017	5.4	1618	1.1	○ 2225	5.6
22	TU	0434	1.0	1044	5.4	1647	1.1	2255	5.5
23	W	0502	1.1	1113	5.4	1717	1.2	2327	5.4
24	TH	0531	1.2	1142	5.3	1749	1.3	2359	5.3
25	F	0603	1.3	1214	5.2	1824	1.4		
26	SA	0034	5.1	0637	1.5	1249	5.1	1902	1.6
27	SU	0114	4.9	0718	1.8	1331	4.9	1951	1.8
28	M	0204	4.7	0809	2.1	1426	4.7	2054	2.0
29	TU	0313	4.4	0919	2.3	1544	4.5	2219	2.1
30	W	0446	4.4	1048	2.3	1716	4.6	2344	1.9
31	TH	0613	4.6	1210	2.1	1831	4.9		

NOVEMBER

Date	Day	Time	m	Time	m	Time	m	Time	m
1	F	0051	1.5	0715	5.0	1312	1.7	1927	5.3
2	SA	0145	1.0	0804	5.3	1402	1.2	2015	5.6
3	SU	0231	0.6	0847	5.6	1446	0.9	2059	5.9
4	M	0315	0.4	0928	5.8	1529	0.6	● 2142	6.1
5	TU	0357	0.3	1009	5.9	1612	0.4	2227	6.2
6	W	0440	0.3	1052	5.9	1657	0.4	2313	6.0
7	TH	0524	0.5	1136	5.8	1743	0.6		
8	F	0001	5.8	0609	0.9	1222	5.7	1832	0.9
9	SA	0051	5.4	0657	1.3	1310	5.4	1925	1.2
10	SU	0146	5.0	0749	1.7	1403	5.1	2026	1.6
11	M	0250	4.6	0850	2.1	1507	4.8	2138	1.9
12	TU	0410	4.4	1007	2.4	1624	4.7	2259	2.0
13	W	0538	4.3	1128	2.4	1742	4.7		
14	TH	0012	2.0	0649	4.5	1238	2.3	1848	4.8
15	F	0112	1.8	0741	4.7	1332	2.0	1938	5.0
16	SA	0157	1.6	0819	4.9	1414	1.8	2018	5.1
17	SU	0234	1.4	0851	5.1	1449	1.6	2053	5.3
18	M	0306	1.3	0920	5.2	1521	1.4	2126	5.4
19	TU	0335	1.2	0949	5.3	1552	1.3	2158	5.4
20	W	0405	1.2	1018	5.4	1624	1.2	○ 2231	5.4
21	TH	0436	1.2	1048	5.4	1656	1.2	2305	5.4
22	F	0508	1.2	1121	5.4	1731	1.3	2340	5.3
23	SA	0543	1.3	1156	5.3	1809	1.3		
24	SU	0019	5.1	0620	1.5	1235	5.2	1852	1.5
25	M	0104	5.0	0704	1.7	1320	5.1	1942	1.6
26	TU	0156	4.8	0756	1.9	1415	4.9	2042	1.7
27	W	0300	4.6	0901	2.1	1523	4.8	2154	1.8
28	TH	0418	4.6	1017	2.1	1640	4.8	2309	1.6
29	F	0535	4.7	1132	2.0	1752	5.0		
30	SA	0016	1.4	0640	4.9	1237	1.7	1853	5.3

DECEMBER

Date	Day	Time	m	Time	m	Time	m	Time	m
1	SU	0114	1.1	0734	5.2	1333	1.4	1947	5.5
2	M	0205	0.8	0822	5.5	1423	1.0	2037	5.7
3	TU	0252	0.7	0907	5.7	1510	0.8	2125	5.9
4	W	0338	0.6	0951	5.8	1557	0.7	● 2213	5.9
5	TH	0423	0.6	1035	5.8	1645	0.7	2301	5.8
6	F	0508	0.8	1120	5.8	1732	0.7	2349	5.6
7	SA	0553	1.0	1206	5.7	1821	0.9		
8	SU	0038	5.3	0639	1.3	1253	5.5	1911	1.2
9	M	0129	5.0	0727	1.6	1342	5.3	2003	1.5
10	TU	0222	4.7	0818	2.0	1434	5.0	2101	1.7
11	W	0322	4.5	0917	2.2	1532	4.8	2204	1.9
12	TH	0431	4.3	1025	2.4	1637	4.7	2310	2.0
13	F	0542	4.3	1135	2.4	1744	4.6		
14	SA	0012	2.0	0643	4.5	1238	2.3	1843	4.7
15	SU	0106	1.9	0733	4.7	1330	2.1	1935	4.8
16	M	0152	1.7	0814	4.9	1414	1.8	2019	5.0
17	TU	0231	1.6	0850	5.0	1453	1.6	2059	5.1
18	W	0307	1.4	0924	5.2	1529	1.5	2136	5.2
19	TH	0341	1.3	0957	5.3	1605	1.3	○ 2213	5.3
20	F	0416	1.3	1030	5.4	1642	1.2	2250	5.3
21	SA	0452	1.2	1106	5.5	1720	1.1	2329	5.3
22	SU	0530	1.2	1144	5.5	1801	1.1		
23	M	0010	5.2	0610	1.3	1226	5.4	1844	1.2
24	TU	0056	5.1	0655	1.4	1312	5.4	1932	1.2
25	W	0145	5.0	0744	1.5	1403	5.2	2026	1.3
26	TH	0241	4.9	0839	1.7	1500	5.1	2126	1.4
27	F	0344	4.8	0943	1.8	1604	5.1	2233	1.4
28	SA	0454	4.7	1053	1.8	1713	5.0	2340	1.4
29	SU	0603	4.8	1202	1.7	1822	5.1		
30	M	0044	1.3	0705	5.0	1307	1.5	1925	5.2
31	TU	0143	1.2	0801	5.2	1406	1.3	2023	5.4

Chart Datum: 3·05 metres below Ordnance Datum (Newlyn)

MAPTECH®
Leading the world in digital navigation
Maptech UK Ltd • +44 (0)1243 389352 • sales@maptech.co.uk

Sales and distribution centres in Area 11

Avon: ***Marine Electronic Services (MES)***, 0117 982 1522, Innovation House, 130 - 132 Nibley Road, Bristol BS11 9XN.
Wales: ***Rowlands Marine***, 01758 613193, Pwllheli Marine Centre, Glandon, Pwllheli, Gwynedd, LL53 5YT.

www.maptech.co.uk

Area 11

South Wales and Bristol Channel
Bardsey Island to Lands End

9.11.1 Index .... Page 593

9.11.2 Area map 594

9.11.3 Tidal stream charts 596

9.11.4 Lights, buoys & waypoints 598

9.11.5 Passage information 602

9.11.6 Distance table 603

9.11.7 Abersoch 604

9.11.8 Pwllheli 604
Mochras

9.11.9 Porthmadog 605

9.11.10 Barmouth 605

9.11.11 Aberdovey 606

9.11.12 Aberystwyth 606
Aberaeron
New Quay
Port Cardigan

9.11.13 Fishguard 607
Solva
St Brides Bay
Skomer Island

9.11.14 Milford Haven, Standard Port, tidal curves 608

9.11.15 Tenby 613
Saundersfoot
Carmarthen

9.11.16 Burry Inlet 614
Firing ranges

9.11.17 Swansea 615
Mumbles
River Neath
Porthcawl

9.11.18 Barry 616

9.11.19 Cardiff 616
Newport

9.11.20 Sharpness 618
The Severn Bridges

9.11.21 Bristol (City Docks). (Avonmouth, Standard Port, tidal curves) 622

9.11.22 Portishead 624
Weston-super-Mare

9.11.23 Burnham-on-Sea 624

9.11.24 Watchet 625
Minehead
Porlock Weir
Lynmouth
Watermouth

9.11.25 Ilfracombe 626

9.11.26 Rivers Taw and Torridge 626
Clovelly
Lundy Island
Bude
Boscastle

9.11.27 Padstow 628
Port Isaac
Newquay
Portreath
Hayle
St Ives

Register for your **FREE** weekly weather email service from Macmillan Reeds
at **www.nauticaldata.com – NOW!**
weekend weather reports sent to your email address, every Thursday

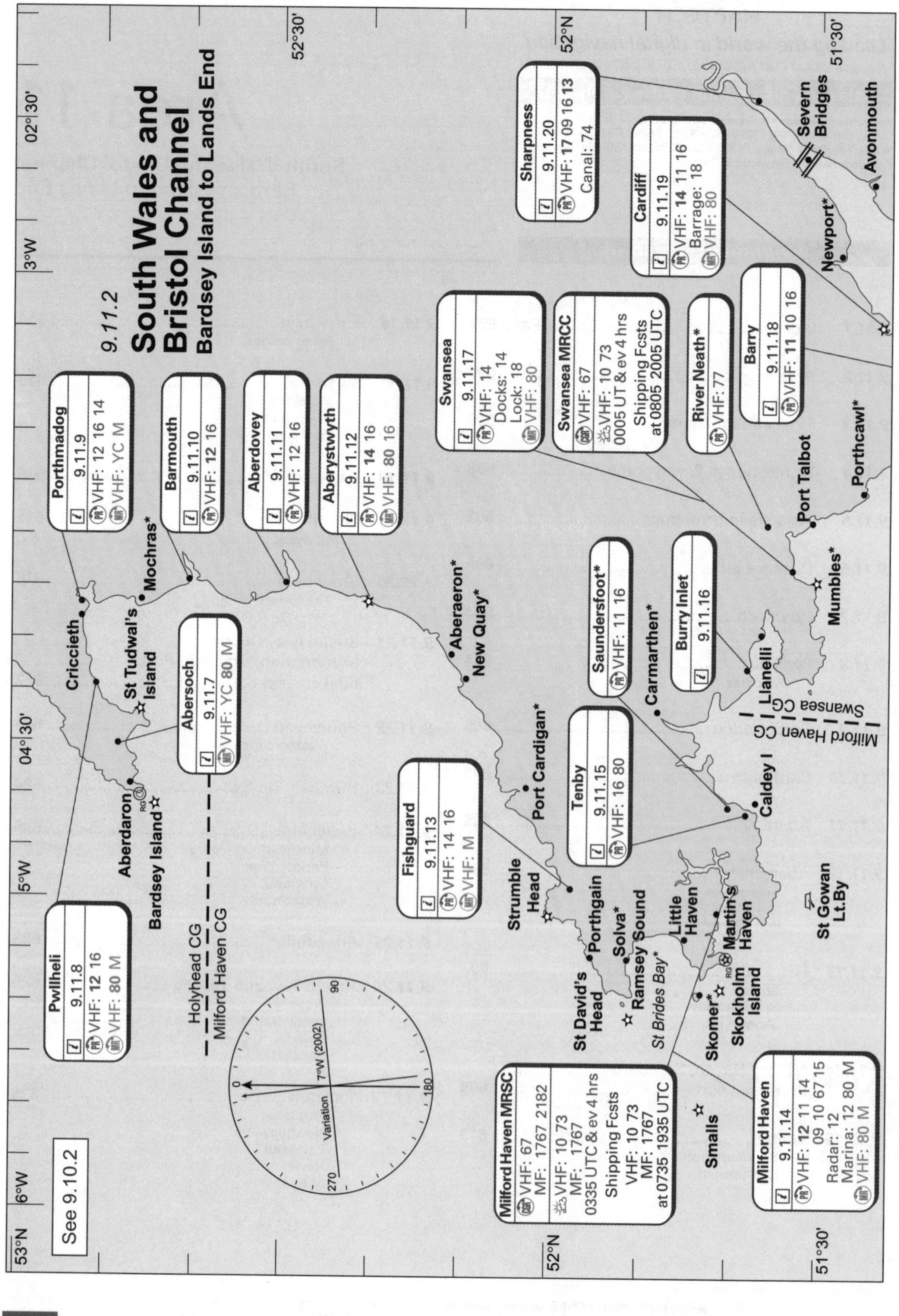
9.11.2
South Wales and Bristol Channel
Bardsey Island to Lands End
See 9.10.2
53°N
6°W
5°W
04°30'
3°W
02°30'
52°30'
52°N
51°30'
Variation 7°W (2002)
0
90
180
270
Holyhead CG
Milford Haven CG
Swansea CG
Milford Haven CG
Pwllheli 9.11.8 VHF: 12 16 VHF: 80 M
Porthmadog 9.11.9 VHF: 12 16 14 VHF: YC M
Barmouth 9.11.10 VHF: 12 16
Aberdovey 9.11.11 VHF: 12 16
Aberystwyth 9.11.12 VHF: 14 16 VHF: 80 16
Abersoch 9.11.7 VHF: YC 80 M
Fishguard 9.11.13 VHF: 14 16 VHF: M
Tenby 9.11.15 VHF: 16 80
Saundersfoot* VHF: 11 16
Burry Inlet 9.11.16
Swansea 9.11.17 VHF: 14 Docks: 14 Lock: 18 VHF: 80
Swansea MRCC VHF: 67 VHF: 10 73 0005 UT & ev 4 hrs Shipping Fcsts at 0805 2005 UTC
River Neath* VHF: 77
Barry 9.11.18 VHF: 11 10 16
Cardiff 9.11.19 VHF: 14 11 16 Barrage: 18 VHF: 80
Sharpness 9.11.20 VHF: 17 09 16 13 Canal: 74
Milford Haven MRSC VHF: 67 MF: 1767 2182 VHF: 10 73 MF: 1767 0335 UTC & ev 4 hrs Shipping Fcsts VHF: 10 73 MF: 1767 at 0735 1935 UTC
Milford Haven 9.11.14 VHF: 12 11 14 09 10 67 15 Radar: 12 Marina: 12 80 M VHF: 80 M
Aberdaron
Bardsey Island
St Tudwal's Island
Criccieth
Mochras*
Aberaeron*
New Quay*
Port Cardigan*
Strumble Head
Porthgain
St David's Head
Solva*
Ramsey Sound
St Brides Bay*
Little Haven
Martin's Haven
Skomer*
Skokholm Island
Smalls
St Gowan Lt.By
Caldey I
Carmarthen*
Llanelli
Mumbles*
Port Talbot
Porthcawl*
Newport*
Severn Bridges
Avonmouth

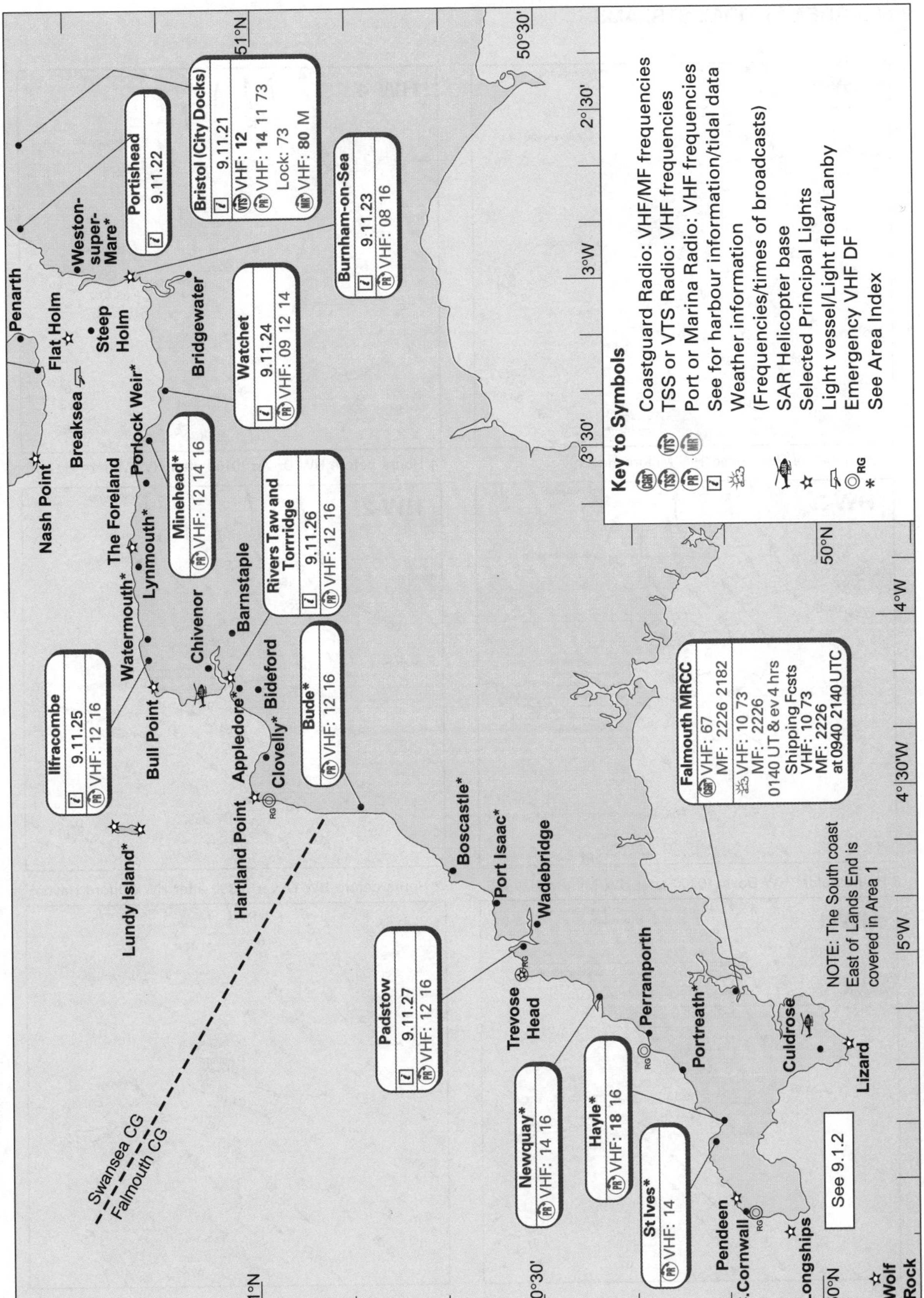
Key to Symbols
Coastguard Radio: VHF/MF frequencies
TSS or VTS Radio: VHF frequencies
Port or Marina Radio: VHF frequencies
See for harbour information/tidal data
Weather information
(Frequencies/times of broadcasts)
SAR Helicopter base
Selected Principal Lights
Light vessel/Light float/Lanby
Emergency VHF DF
See Area Index
Bristol (City Docks)
9.11.21
VHF: 12
VHF: 14 11 73
Lock: 73
VHF: 80 M
Portishead
9.11.22
Burnham-on-Sea
9.11.23
VHF: 08 16
Watchet
9.11.24
VHF: 09 12 14
Minehead*
VHF: 12 14 16
Rivers Taw and Torridge
9.11.26
VHF: 12 16
Ilfracombe
9.11.25
VHF: 12 16
Bude*
VHF: 12 16
Padstow
9.11.27
VHF: 12 16
Newquay*
VHF: 14 16
Hayle*
VHF: 18 16
St Ives*
VHF: 14
Falmouth MRCC
VHF: 67
MF: 2226 2182
VHF: 10 73
MF: 2226
0140 UT & ev 4 hrs
Shipping Fcsts
VHF: 10 73
MF: 2226
at 0940 2140 UTC
NOTE: The South coast East of Lands End is covered in Area 1
See 9.1.2
Swansea CG
Falmouth CG
Penarth
Flat Holm
Steep Holm
Weston-super-Mare*
Breaksea
Nash Point
Bridgewater
Porlock Weir*
The Foreland
Lynmouth*
Watermouth*
Bull Point
Chivenor
Barnstaple
Appledore*
Bideford
Clovelly*
Hartland Point
Lundy Island*
Boscastle*
Port Isaac*
Wadebridge
Trevose Head
Perranporth
Portreath*
Culdrose
Lizard
Pendeen
C.Cornwall
Longships
Wolf Rock
RG
51°N
50°30'
50°N
2°30'
3°W
3°30'
4°W
4°30'W
5°W

9.11.3 AREA 11 TIDAL STREAMS

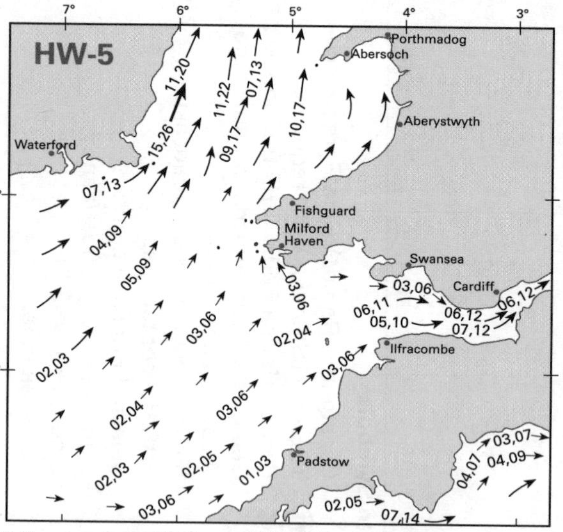

5 Hours before HW Dover (HW Milford Haven)

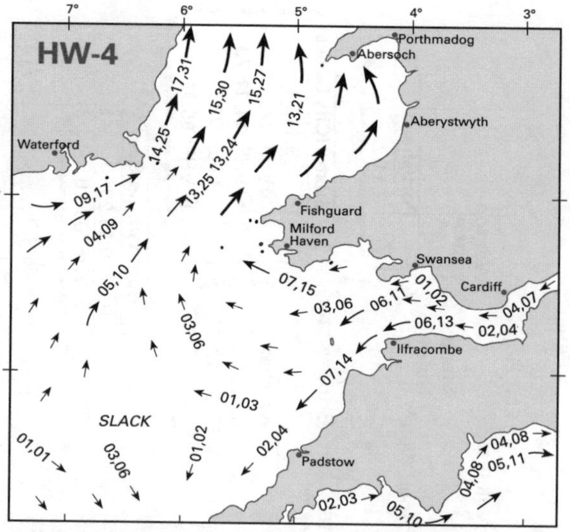

4 Hours before HW Dover (0100 after HW Milford Haven)

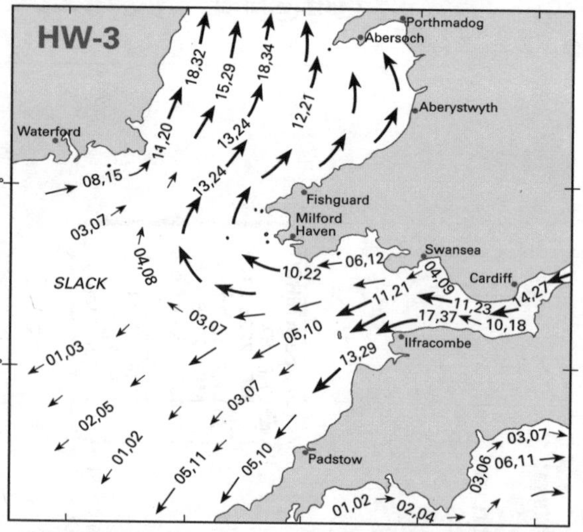

3 Hours before HW Dover (0200 after HW Milford Haven)

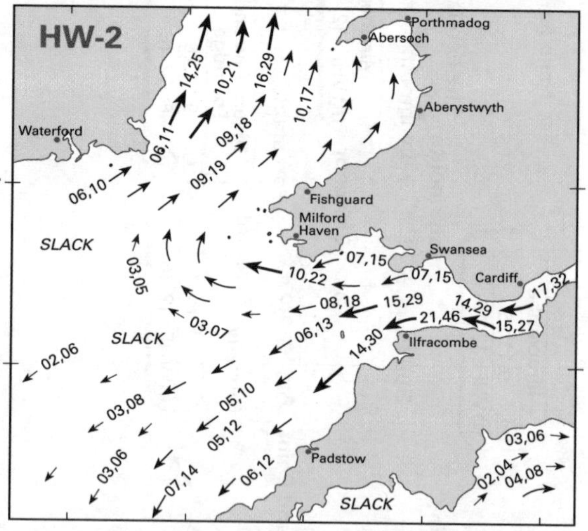

2 Hours before HW Dover (0300 after HW Milford Haven)

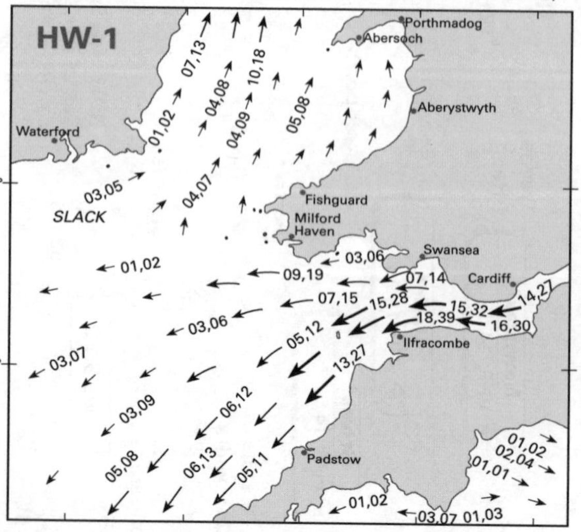

1 Hour before HW Dover (0400 after HW Milford Haven)

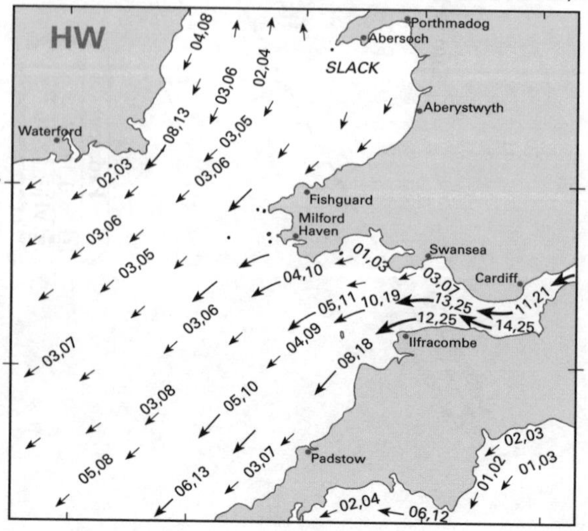

HW Dover (0500 after HW Milford Haven)

Southward 9.1.3   Northward 9.10.3   South Ireland 9.12.3

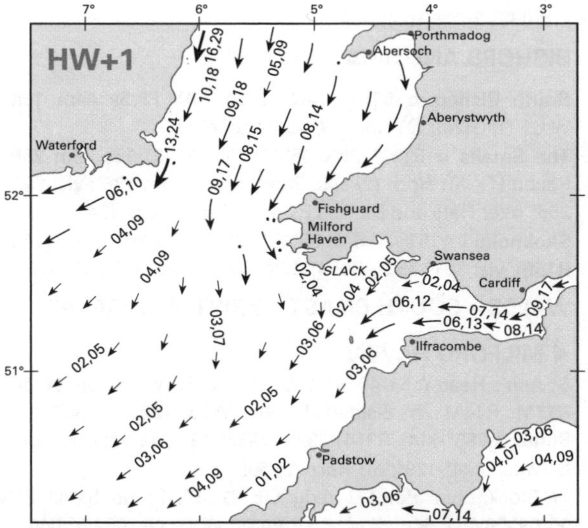

1 Hour after HW Dover (0600 after HW Milford Haven)

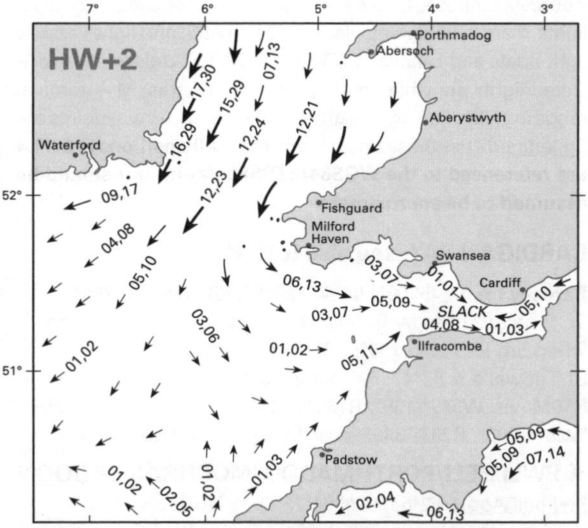

2 Hours after HW Dover (0525 before HW Milford Haven)

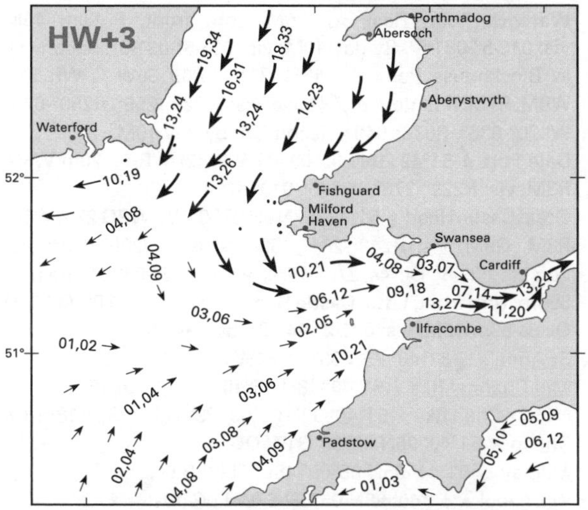

3 Hours after HW Dover (0425 before HW Milford Haven)

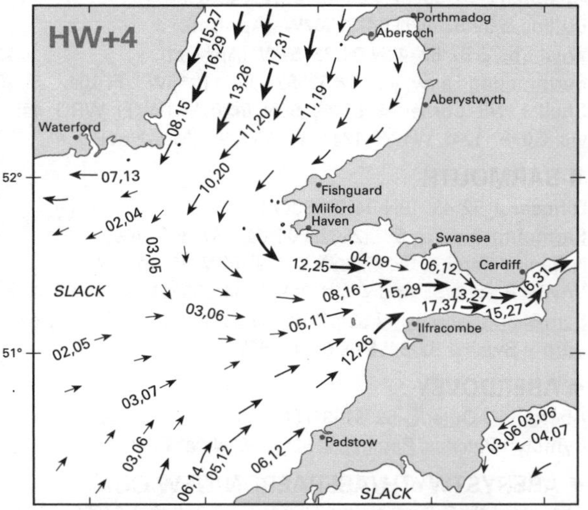

4 Hours after HW Dover (0325 before HW Milford Haven)

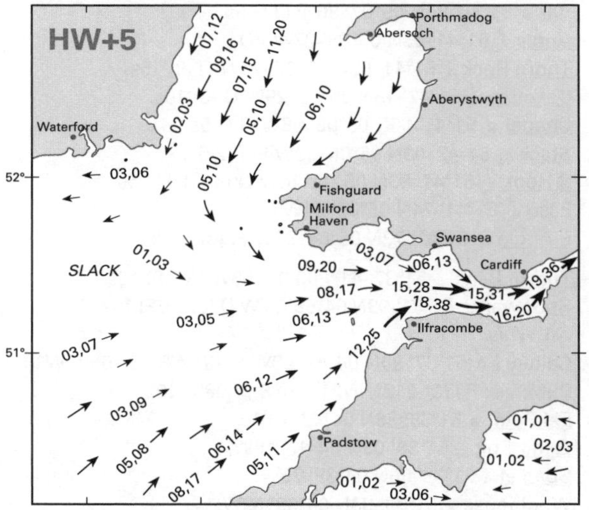

5 Hours after HW Dover (0225 before HW Milford Haven)

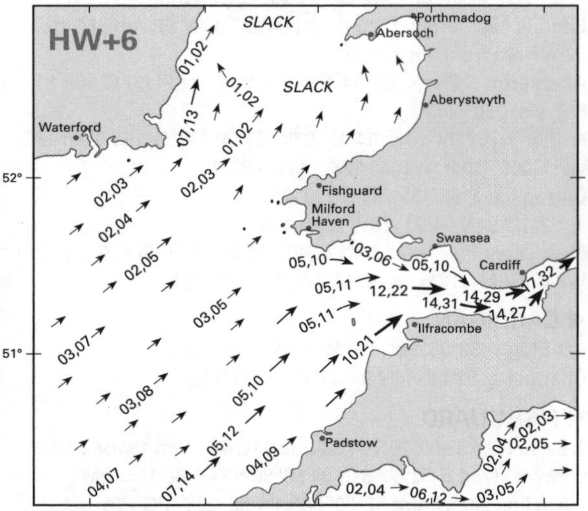

6 Hours after HW Dover (0125 before HW Milford Haven)

9.11.4 LIGHTS, BUOYS AND WAYPOINTS

Abbreviations used below are given in the Introduction. Principal lights ☆ are in **bold** print, places in CAPITALS, and light-vessels, light floats and Lanbys in *CAPITAL ITALICS.* Unless otherwise stated lights are white. m – elevation in metres; M – nominal range in miles. Fog signals are in *italics.* Useful waypoints are underlined – use those on land with care. **All positions in 9.11.4 are referenced to the WGS84/ETRS89 datum but should be assumed to be approximate.**

CARDIGAN BAY (see also 9.10.4)

Bardsey I ☆ 52°45'·00N 04°47'·98W Fl (5) 15s 39m **26M;** W □ Tr, R bands; obsc by Bardsey I 198°-250° and in Tremadoc B when brg less than 260°; *Horn Mo(N) 45s.*
St Tudwal's 52°47'·92N 04°28'·30W Fl WR 15s 46m W14, R10M; vis: W349°-169°, R169°-221°, W221°-243°, R243°-259°, W259°-293°, R293°-349°; obsc by East I 211°-231°.

◄ PWLLHELI/PORTHMADOG/MOCHRAS LAGOON

Pwllheli App 52°53'·02N 04°23'·07W Iso 2s.
Training Arm Head 52°53'·25N 04°23'·74W QG 3m 3M.
Abererch 52°53'·52N 04°23'·07W; (Apr-Oct).
Butlins 52°53'·02N 04°22'·07W; (Apr-Oct).
West End 52°52'·42N 04°25'·57W; (Apr-Oct).
Porthmadog Fairway 52°52'·97N 04°11'·18W L Fl 10s.
Shell I, NE Corner 52°49'·56N 04°07'·71W Fl WRG 4s; vis: G079°-124°, W124°-134°, R134°-179°; (Mar-Nov).

◄ BARMOUTH

Diffuser 52°43'·19N 04°05'·38W Fl Y 5s.
Barmouth Outer 52°42'·62N 04°04'·83W L Fl 10s.
N Bank Y Perch 52°42'·83N 04°03'·74W QR 4m 5M.
Ynys y Brawd, SE end 52°42'·99N 04°03'·12W Fl R 5s 5M.
Sarn Badrig Causeway 52°41'·19N 04°25'·36W Q (9) 15s; *Bell.*
Sarn-y-Bwch 52°34'·81N 04°13'·58W.

◄ ABERDOVEY

Aberdovey Outer 52°31'·31N 04°05'·12W; L Fl 10s.
Cynfelyn Patches, Patches 52°25'·83N 04°16'·41W.

◄ ABERYSTWYTH/ABERAERON/NEW QUAY

Aberystwyth S Breakwater Head 52°24'·40N 04°05'·52W Fl (2) WG 10s 12m 10M; vis: G030°-053°, W053°-210°.
Ldg Lts 133°. Front, 52°24'·37N 04°05'·39W FR 4m 5M. Rear, 52m from front, FR 7m 6M.
Aberaeron S Pier 52°14'·61N 04°15'·94W Fl (3) G 10s 11m 6M; vis: 050°-243°.
N Pier 52°14'·61N 04°15'·87W Fl (4) WRG 15s 10m 6M; vis: G050°-104°, W104°-178°, R178°-232°.
Carreg Ina 52°13'·25N 04°20'·75W Q.
52°12'·94N 04°21'·29W Q (3) 10s.
New Quay Pier Hd 52°12'·95N 04°21'·35W Fl WG 3s 12m W8M, G5M; G △; vis: W135°-252°, G252°-295.

◄ CARDIGAN

CG Bldg 52°06'·98N 04°41'·21W 2 FR (vert).
Channel 52°06'·44N 04°41'·43W Fl (2) 5s.

◄ FISHGUARD

N Bkwtr Hd 52°00'·76N 04°58'·23W Fl G 4·5s 18m 13M; *Bell (1) 8s.*
E Bkwtr Head 52°00'·31N 04°58'·86W Fl R 3s 10m 5M.
Lts in line 282°. Front 52°00'·68N 04°59'·27W FG 77m 5M W ◇ on mast. Rear, 46m from front, FG 89m 5M.
Penanglas, 152m S of Pt, *Dia (2) 60s;* W obelisk.
Strumble Head ☆ 52°01'·79N 05°04'·43W Fl (4) 15s 45m **26M;** vis: 038°-257°; (H24).

BISHOPS AND SMALLS

South Bishop ☆ 51°51'·14N 05°24'·74W Fl 5s 44m **16M;** W ○ Tr; (H24); *Horn (3) 45s;* Racon (O).
The Smalls ☆ 51°43'·28N 05°40'·19W Fl (3) 15s 36m **25M;** Racon (T); *Horn (2) 60s.* Same Tr, FR 33m 13M; vis: 253°-285° over Hats and Barrels Rk; both Lts shown H24.
Skokholm I ☆, 51°41'·64N 05°17'·22W Fl WR 10s 54m **W18M, R15M;** vis: 301°-154°, R154°-129°; part obsc 226°-258°; (H24).

WALES – SOUTH COAST – BRISTOL CHANNEL

◄ MILFORD HAVEN

St Ann's Head ☆ 51°40'·87N 05°10'·42W Fl WR 5s 48m **W18M, R17M,** R14M; W 8-sided Tr; vis: W233°-247°, R247°-285°, R(intens)285°-314°, R314°-332°, W332°-131°, partially obscured between 124°-129°; *Horn (2) 60s.*
W Blockhouse Point Ldg Lts 022·5°. Front, 51°41'·31N 05°09'·56W F 54m 13M; B stripe on W Tr; vis: 004·5°-040·5°. By day 10M; vis: 004·5°-040·5°.
Watwick Point Rear ☆, 0·5M from front, F 80m **15M;** vis: 013·5°-031·5°. By day 10M; vis: 013·5°-031·5°; Racon (Y).
W Blockhouse Point 51°41'·31N 05°09'·56W Q WR 21m W9M, R7M; R lantern on W base: vis: W220°-250°, R250°-020°, W020°-036°, R036°-049°; Racon (Q); by day 10M.
Dale Fort 51°42'·16N 05°09'·01W Fl (2) WR 5s 20m W5M, R3M; vis: R222°-276°, W276°-019°.
Great Castle Head 51°42'·67N 05°07'·07W F WRG 27m W5M, R3M, G3M; vis: R243°-281°, G281°-299°, W299°-029°; also Ldg Lts 039·8° Oc 4s 27m **15M;** vis: 031·2°-048·2°. **Rear** ☆, 890m from front, **Little Castle Head** 51°43'·04N 05°06'·60W Oc 8s 53m **15M;** vis: 031·2°-048·2°; by day 10M.
St Anne's 51°40'·25N 05°10'·51W Fl R 2·5s.
Mid Channel Rks 51°40'·18N 05°10'·14W Q (9) 15s.
Middle Chan Rks 51°40'·32N 05°09'·83W Fl (3) G 7s 18m 8M.
Sheep 51°40'·06N 05°08'·31W QG.
Millbay 51°41'·05N 05°09'·45W Fl (2) R 5s.
W Chapel 51°40'·98N 05°08'·67W Fl G 10s.
E Chapel 51°40'·87N 05°08'·15W Fl R 5s.
Rat 51°40'·80N 05°07'·86W Fl G 5s.
Angle 51°41'·63N 05°08'·27W VQ.
Thorn Rock 51°41'·53N 05°07'·76W Q (9) 15s.
Dakotian 51°42'·15N 05°08'·29W Q (3) 10s.
Chapel 51°41'·66N 05°06'·86W Fl G 5s.
Stack 51°42'·03N 05°06'·52W Fl R 2·5s.
S Hook 51°41'·83N 05°06'·10W Q (6) +L Fl 15s.
Esso 51°41'·74N 05°05'·24W Q.
E Angle 51°41'·72N 05°04'·26W Fl (3) G 10s.

Turbot Bank 51°37'·41N 05°10'·08W VQ (9) 10s.
St Gowan 51°31'·93N 04°59'·77W Q (6) + L Fl 15s; Racon (T); *Whis.*
Caldey I 51°37'·90N 04°41'·08W Fl (3) WR 20s 65m W13M, R9M; vis: R173°-212°, W212°-088°, R088°-102°.
Eel Point 51°38'·86N 04°42'·24W.
Giltar Spit 51°39'·03N 04°42'·10W.
Spaniel 51°38'·06N 04°39'·75W.
Woolhouse 51°39'·33N 04°39'·69W.
North Highcliff 51°39'·38N 04°40'·77W.

◀ TENBY/SAUNDERSFOOT/CARMARTHEN BAY/ BURRY INLET

Tenby Pier Head 51°40'·40N 04°41'·89W FR 7m 7M.
Saundersfoot Pier Hd 51°42'·59N 04°41'·73W Fl R 5s 6m 7M.
DZ1 51°42'·05N 04°36'·00W.
DZ2 51°39'·98N 04°37'·73W Fl Y 2·5s.
DZ3 51°37'·37N 04°37'·84W.
DZ7 51°38'·09N 04°30'·12W Fl Y 10s.
DZ4 51°35'·73N 04°30'·05W Fl Y 5s.
DZ8 51°41'·51N 04°24'·42W.
DZ6 51°38'·02N 04°24'·37W.
DZ5 51°36'·37N 04°24'·39W Fl Y 2·5s.
Burry Port Barrel Post 51°40'·49N 04°15'·01W Fl R 3s 5M.
Burry Port Inlet 51°40'·62N 04°15'·06W Fl 5s 7m **15M**.
Llanelli Ent N side Fl R 5s 2M
West Helwick (W HWK) 51°31'·40N 04°23'·65W Q (9) 15s; Racon (T); *Whis.*
East Helwick 51°31'·80N 04°12'·68W VQ (3) 5s; *Bell.*

◀ SWANSEA BAY/SWANSEA

Ledge 51°29'·93N 03°58'·77W VQ (6) + L Fl 10s.
Mixon 51°33'·12N 03°58'·78W Fl (2) R 5s; *Bell.*
Outer Spoil Gnd 51°32'·11N 03°55'·73W Fl Y 2·5s.
Grounds 51°32'·81N 03°53'·47W VQ (3) 5s.

Mumbles ☆ 51°34'·01N 03°58'·27W Fl (4) 20s 35m **15M**; W Tr; *Horn (3) 60s.*
Railway Pier Hd 51°34'·21N 03°58'·44W 2 FR (vert) 11m 9M.
SW Inner Green Grounds 51°34'·06N 03°57'·03W Q (6) + L Fl 15s; *Bell.*
Outer Fairway 51°35'·52N 03°56'·09W QG; *Bell.*
Swansea West Fairway 51°35'·56N 03°56'·24W QR.
Swansea Inner Fairway 51°36'·23N 03°55'·67W Fl G 2·5s; *Bell.*
E Bkwtr Head 51°36'·38N 03°55'·62W 2 FG (vert) 10m 6M; *Siren 30s.*
W Pier Head 51°36'·50N 03°55'·73W Fl (2) R 10s 11m 9M.
Lts in line 020°. Jetty Head Front, 51°36'·55N 03°55'·52W Oc G 4s 5m 2M. Rear, 260m from front, FG 6M.

◀ SWANSEA BAY/RIVER NEATH/PORT TALBOT

Neath App Chan 51°35'·71N 03°52'·83W Fl G 5s.
Monkstone 51°36'·32N 03°51'·97W Fl (2) G 6s 6m 5M.
Neath SE Trg Wall N End 51°37'·09N 03°50'·85W 3 FG (vert) 6m 5M.
Neath SE Trg Wall Middle 51°36'·70N 03°51'·41W FG 6m 5M.
Cabenda 51°33'·36N 03°52'·23W VQ (6) + L Fl 10s; Racon (Q).
P Talbot S Outer 51°33'·71N 03°51'·30W Fl G 5s.
P Talbot N Outer 51°33'·78N 03°51'·38W Fl R 5s.
North Inner 51°34'·22N 03°50'·25W Fl R 3s.
Ldg Lts 059·8° (occas). Front 51°34'·92N 03°48'·10W Oc R 3s 12m 6M. Rear, 400m from front, Oc R 6s 32m 6M.
N Bkwtr Head 51°34'·77N 03°49'·00W Fl (4) R 10s 11m 3M.
S Bkwtr Head 51°34'·46N 03°49'·04W Fl G 3s 11m 3M.

BRISTOL CHANNEL – EASTERN PART (NORTH SHORE)

Kenfig 51°29'·44N 03°46'·06W VQ (3) 5s.
W Scar 51°28'·31N 03°55'·57W Q (9) 15s; Racon (T); *Bell.*
South Scar (S SCAR) 51°27'·61N 03°51'·58W Q (6) + L Fl 15s.
Hugo 51°28'·63N 03°48'·07W QR.
East Scarweather 51°27'·98N 03°46'·95W Q (3) 10s; *Bell.*

◀ PORTHCAWL

Fairy 51°27'·86N 03°42'·07W Q (9) 15s.
Tusker 51°26'·85N 03°40'·74W Fl (2) R 5s.
Porthcawl Bkwtr Head 51°28'·39N 03°41'·98W F WRG 10m W6M, R4M, G4M; vis: G302°-036°, W036°-082°, R082°-122°.
W Nash 51°25'·98N 03°45'·96W VQ (9) 10s ; *Bell.*
Middle Nash 51°24'·83N 03°39'·41W Q (6) + L Fl 15s.
East Nash 51°24'·06N 03°34'·10W Q (3) 10s.

Nash ☆ 51°24'·05N 03°33'·14W Fl (2) WR 15s 56m **W21M**, **R16M**; vis: R280°-290°, W290°-100°, R100°-120°, W120°-128°; *Siren (2) 45s.*
Saint Hilary 51° 27'·43N 03°24'·18W Aero QR 346m 11M; radio mast; 4 FR (vert) on same mast 6M.
Breaksea Point intake 51°22'·51N 03°24'·53W Fl R 11m.

Breaksea 51°19'·88N 03°19'·08W Fl 15s 11m 12M; Racon (T); *Horn (2) 30s.*
Wenvoe 51°27'·55N 03°16'·93W Aero Q 365m 12M; radio mast (H24).
Merkur 51°21'·88N 03°15'·95W QR.
Welsh Water Barry W 51°22'·27N 03°16'·94W Fl R 5s.

◀ BARRY

W Breakwater Head 51°23'·46N 03°15'·52W Fl 2·5s 12m 10M.
E Breakwater Head 51°23'·50N 03°15'·43W QG 7m 8M.
Lavernock Spit 51°23'·00N 03°10'·82W VQ (6) + L Fl 10s.
North One Fathom 51°20'·94N 03°12'·17W Q.
Mackenzie 51°21'·75N 03°08'·24W QR.
Holm Middle 51°21'·71N 03°06'·72W Fl G 2·5s.
Wolves 51°23'·12N 03°08'·89W VQ.

Flat Holm ☆, SE Pt 51°22'·54N 03°07'·14W Fl (3) WR 10s 50m **W15M**, R12M; W ○ Tr; vis: R106°-140°, W140°-151°, R151°-203°, W203°-106°; (H24).
Weston 51°22'·60N 03°05'·75W Fl (2) R 5s.
Monkstone Rock 51°24'·89N 03°06'·02W Fl 5s 13m 12M.

◀ CARDIFF and PENARTH ROADS

Lavernock Outfall 51°23'·95N 03°09'·50W Fl Y 5s.
Ranie 51°24'·23N 03°09'·39W Fl (2) R 5s.
S Cardiff 51°24'·18N 03°08'·57W Q (6) + L Fl 15s; *Bell.*
Mid Cardiff 51°25'·60N 03°08'·09W Fl (3) G 10s.
Cardiff Spit 51°24'·57N 03°07'·12W QR.
N Cardiff 51°26'·52N 03°07'·19W QG.

◀ PENARTH/CARDIFF

Penarth Pier near Head 51°26'·08N 03°09'·90W 2 FR (vert) 8/6m 3M; *Reed Mo (BA) 60s.* when vessel expected.
Dir Lt 350·4°. 51°27'·16N 03°09'·75W Dir Oc WRG 10s 5m; vis: G346·25N 348·75°, W348·5°-351·75°, R351·75-354·25°; H24.
Outer Wrach 51°26'·20N 03°09'·46W Q (9) 15s.
Inner Wrach 51°26'·74N 03°09'·65W Fl G 2·5s.
Queen Alexandra Dock ent South Jetty Head 51°27'·09N 03°09'·58W 2 FG (vert); Tfc sigs; *Dia 60s.*
Tail Patch 51°23'·53N 03°03'·65W QG.
Hope 51°24'·84N 03°02'·68W Q (3) 10s.
NW Elbow 51°26'·28N 02°59'·93W VQ (9) 10s; *Bell.*
EW Grounds 51°27'·12N 02°59'·95W L Fl 10s 7M; Racon (T); *Whis.*

◀ NEWPORT DEEP

Newport Deep 51°29'·36N 02°59'·12W Fl (3) G 10s; *Bell.*

◀ RIVER USK/NEWPORT

East Usk ☆ 51°32'·40N 02°58'·01W Fl (2) WRG 10s 11m **W15M**, R11M, G11M; vis: W284°-290°, R290°-017°, W017°-037°, G037°-115°, W115°-120°. Also Oc WRG 10s 10m W11M, R9M, G9M; vis: G018°-022°, W022°-024°, R024°-028°.

Alexandra Dock, S Lock W Pier Hd ☆ 51°32'·87N 02°59'·26W 2 FR (vert) 9m 6M; *Horn 60s*.

E Pier Head ☆ 51°32'·96N 02°59'·11W 2 FG (vert) 9m 6M.

Julians Pill Ldg Lts about 057°. Common Front, 51°33'·30N 02°57'·94W FG 8m 4M. Rear, 61m from front, FG 8m 4M.

Ldg Lts 149°. Rear, 137m from common front, FG 9m 4M.

Birdport Jetty ☆ 51°33'·66N 02°58'·10W 2 FG (vert) 6m.

Dallimores Wharf ☆ 51°33'·88N 02°58'·60W 2 FG (vert).

Transporter Bridge, W side ☆ 51°34'·25N 02°59'·23W 2 FR (vert); 2 FY (vert) shown on transporter car.

E side ☆ 2 FG (vert). Centres of George Street and Newport Bridges marked by FY Lts.

BRISTOL CHANNEL – EASTERN PART (SOUTH SHORE)

◀ BRISTOL DEEP

N Elbow 51°26'·97N 02°58'·65W QG; *Bell*.

S Mid Grounds 51°27'·62N 02°58'·68W VQ (6) + L Fl 10s.

E Mid Grounds 51°27'·97N 02°53'·57W Fl R 5s.

Clevedon 51°27'·39N 02°54'·93W VQ.

Welsh Hook 51°28'·53N 02°51'·86W Q (6) + L Fl 15s; *Bell*.

Avon 51°27'·92N 02°51'·73W Fl G 2·5s.

Clevedon Pier ☆ 51°26'·63N 02°51'·94W 2 FG (vert) 7m 3M.

Black Nore Point ☆ 51°29'·09N 02°48'·05W Fl (2) 10s 11m **17M**; obsc by Sand Pt when brg less than 049°; vis: 044°-243°.

Newcome 51°30'·01N 02°46'·71W Fl (3) R 10s.

Denny Shoal 51°30'·15N 02°45'·45W VQ (6) + L Fl 10s.

Firefly 51°29'·96N 02°45'·35W Fl (2) G 5s.

Outer 51°29'·99N 02°44'·79W Fl G 5s.

Middle 51°29'·93N 02°44'·22W QG.

Inner 51°29'·86N 02°43'·87W Fl (3) G 15s.

Cockburn 51°30'·46N 02°44'·07W Fl R 2·5s.

Portishead Point ☆ 51°29'·68N 02°46'·42W Q (3) 10s 9m **16M**; B Tr, W base; vis: 060°-262°; *Horn 20s*.

◀ PORTISHEAD

Pier Head ☆ 51°29'·69N 02°45'·27W Iso G 2s 5m 3M.

Seabank. Lts in line 086·8°. Front, 51°30'·07N 02°43'·81W IQ 13m 5M; vis: 070·3°-103·3°; by day 1M vis: 076·8°-096·8°. Rear, 500m from front, IQ 16m 5M; vis: 070·3°-103·3°; by day 1M, vis: 076·8°-096·8°.

Royal Portbury Dock ☆ 51°30'·15N 02°43'·75W L Fl G 15s 5m 6M.

Pier corner ☆ 51°30'·12N 02°43'·84W Fl G 2s 7m 7M; Gy pillar; *Dia 30s*, sounded HW–4 to HW+3.

Knuckle Lts in line 099·6° 51°29'·94N 02°43'·67W Oc G 5s 6m 6M. Rear, 165m from front, FG 13m 6M; vis: 044°-134°.

◀ AVONMOUTH

Royal Edward Dock N Pier Head ☆ 51°30'·49N 02°43'·09W Fl 4s 15m 10M; vis: 060°-228·5°.

King Road Ldg Lts 072·4°. N Pier Head ☆ Front, 51°30'·49N 02°43'·09W Oc R 5s 5m 9M; W obelisk, R bands; vis: 062°-082°. Rear ☆, 546m from front, QR 15m 10M; vis: 066°-078°.

◀ RIVER AVON

S Pier Head ☆ 51°30'·37N 02°43'·10W Oc RG 30s 9m 10M; vis: R294°-036°, G036°-194°.

Ldg Lts 127·2°. Front, 51°30'·08N 02°42'·55W FR 7m 3M; W □, R stripes; vis: 010°-160°. Rear, 142m from front, FR 17m 3M; W ○, vis: 048°-138°.

Monoliths 51°30'·25N 02°42'·76W Fl R 5s 5m 3M; vis: 317°-137°.

Saint George Ldg Lts 173·3°, 51°29'·76N 02°42'·67W both Oc G 5s 6/9m 1M, vis: 158°-305°; synch with front.

Nelson Point ☆ 51°29'·86N 02°42'·50W Fl R 3s 9m 3M.

Broad Pill ☆ 51°29'·68N 02°41'·97W QR 9m 1M.

Avonmouth Bridge, NE end ☆ 51°29'·39N 02°41'·55W L Fl R 10s 5m 3M, SW end L Fl G 10s 5m 3M, show up and downstream. From here to City Docks, Oc G Lts are shown on S bank, and R or Y Lts on N bank.

◀ CUMBERLAND BASIN

Ent N side ☆ 51°26'·98N 02°37'·44W 2 FR (vert) 6m 1M; S side W end 2 FG (vert) 7m 1M.

◀ AVON BRIDGE

N side ☆ 51°26'·83N 02°37'·43W FR 6m 1M on Bridge pier.

Centre of span ☆ 51°26'·82N 02°37'·44W Iso 5s 6m 1M.

S side ☆ 51°26'·81N 02°37'·44W FG 6m 1M on Bridge pier.

SEVERN ESTUARY

◀ THE SHOOTS

Redcliffe Ldg Lts 012·9° Front 51°36'·20N 02°41'·37W F Bu 16m; vis: 358°-028°. Rear, 320m from front, F Bu 33m 10M.

Lower Shoots 51°33'·85N 02°42'·05W Q (9) 15s 6m 7M.

North Mixoms 51°34'·04N 02°42'·61W Fl (3) R 10s 6M.

Second Severn Crossing, Centre span ☆ 51°34'·45N 02°42'·03W Q Bu 5M; Racon (O).

Old Man's Hd 51°34'·74N 02°41'·69W VQ (9) W 10s.

Lady Bench 51°34'·85N 02°42'·20W QR 6m 6M.

Charston Rock ☆ 51°35'·35N 02°41'·68W Fl 3s 5m 8M.

Chapel Rock ☆ 51°36'·44N 02°39'·21W Fl WRG 2·6s 6m 8M, vis: W213°-284°, R284°-049°, W049°-051·5°, G051·5°-160°.

◀ RIVER WYE

Wye Bridge ☆ 51°37'·05N 02°39'·65W 2 F Bu (hor); centre span.

◀ SEVERN BRIDGE

Aust ☆ 51°36'·16N 02°38'·00W 2 QG (vert) 11/5m 6M.

West Tower ☆ 51°36'·73N 02°38'·80W 3 QR (hor) on upstream/ downstream sides; *Horn (3) 45s*; obscured 040°-065°.

Centre of span ☆ 51°36'·59N 02°38'·43W Q Bu, each side.

East Tower ☆ 51°36'·46N 02°38'·07W 3 QG (hor) on upstream/ downstream sides.

Lyde Rock ☆ 51°36'·89N 02°38'·67W Q WR 5m 5M; vis: R148°-237°, W237°-336°, R336°-067°.

Sedbury ☆ 51°37'·81N 02°39'·04W 2 FR (vert) 10m 3M.

Slimeroad Ldg Lts 210·4°. Front, 51°37'·24N 02°39'·08W F Bu 9m 5M. Rear, 91 m from front, F Bu 16m 5M; B Tr,

Inward Rocks Ldg Lts 252·5°. Front, 51°39'·26N 02°37'·47W F 6m 6M; B Tr. Rear, 183m from front, F 23m 2M.

Counts 51°39'·48N 02°35'·84W .

Sheperdine Ldg Lts 070·4°. Front, 51°40'·06N 02°33'·31W F 8m 5M. Rear, 168m from front, F 13m 5M.

Ledges 51°39'·77N 02°34'·15W Fl (3) G 10s.

Narlwood Rocks Ldg Lts 224·9°. Front, 51°39'·57N 02°34'·77W Fl 2s 5m 8M. Rear, 198m from front Fl 2s 9m 8M.

Hills Flats 51°40'·68N 02°32'·67W Fl G 4s.

Hayward Rock 51°41'·24N 02°31'·18W Q 6m 4M.

Conigre Ldg Lts 077·5°. Front, 51°41'·46N 02°30'·03W F Bu 21m 8M. Rear, 213m from front, F Bu 29m 8M.

Fishing House Ldg Lts 217·7°. Front, 51°40'·98N 02°31'·00W F 5m 2M. Rear, F 11m 2M.

◀ BERKELEY

Power Station Centre ☆ 51°41'·65N 02°29'·94W 3x2 FG (vert); *Siren (2) 30s.*
Bull Rock ☆ 51°41'·80N 02°29'·89W Iso (2) 6m 8M.
Berkeley Pill Ldg Lts 187·8°. Front, 51°41'·99N 02°29'·41W FG 5m 2M. Rear, 152m from front, FG 11m 2M.
Panthurst Pill ☆ 51°42'·59N 02°29'·02W F Bu 6m 1M; Y pillar.
Lydney Pier Hd ☆ 51°42'·63N 02°30'·35W 2 FR (vert).

◀ SHARPNESS DOCKS

S Pier Hd ☆ 51°42'·97N 02°29'·12W 2 FG (vert) 6m 3M; *Siren 20s.*
N Pier ☆ 51°43'·07N 02°29'·10W 2 FR (vert) 6m 3M.
Old ent, S side 51°43'·52N 02°28'·93W; *Siren 5s* (tidal).

BRISTOL CHANNEL (SOUTH SHORE)

◀ WESTON-SUPER-MARE

Pier Head ☆ 51°20'·88N 02°59'·26W 2 FG (vert) 6m.
E Culver 51°18'·00N 03°15'·44W Q (3) 10s.
W Culver 51°17'·37N 03°18'·68W VQ (9) 10s.
Gore 51°13'·94N 03°09'·79W Iso 5s; *Bell.*

◀ BURNHAM-ON-SEA/RIVER PARRETT

Ent ☆ 51°14'·89N 03°00'·36W Fl 7·5s 7m 12M; vis: 074°-164°.
Bridgewater Bar No. 1 51°14'·53N 03°03'·75W QR.
Dir Lt 076°. 51°14'·89N 03°00'·36W Dir F WRG 4m W12M, R10M, G10M; same Tr; vis: G071°-075°, W075°-077°, R077°-081°.
Seafront Lts in line 112°, moved for changing chan, Front, 51°14'·39N 02°59'·95W FR 6m 3M W □, Or stripe on sea wall. Rear, FR 12m 3M; on church Tr.
Stert Reach ☆ 51°13'·53N 03°00'·29W Fl 3s 4m 7M; vis: 187°-217°.
Brue Bn ☆ 51°13'·53N 03°00'·29W Fl R 3s 4m 3M.

DZ No. 1 51°15'·28N 03°09'·49W Fl Y 2·5s.
Hinkley Point ☆ 51°12'·93N 03°08'·05W 2 FG (vert) 7m 3M.
DZ No. 2 51°13'·77N 03°17'·19W Fl Y 10s.
DZ No. 3 51°15'·52N 03°14'·98W Fl Y 5s.

◀ WATCHET

W Bkwtr Head ☆ 51°11'·03N 03°19'·74W FG 9m 9M.
E Pier ☆ 51°11'·01N 03°19'·72W 2 FR (vert) 3M.

◀ MINEHEAD/PORLOCK WEIR

Bkwtr Hd ☆ 51°12'·81N 03°28'·36W Fl (2) G 5s 4M; vis: 127°-262°.
Sewer Outfall 51°12'·97N 03°28'·31W QG 6m 7M.

Lynmouth Foreland ☆ 51°14'·73N 03°47'·21W Fl (4) 15s 67m **18M**; W ○ Tr; vis: 083°-275°; (H24).

◀ LYNMOUTH/WATERMOUTH

River training arm ☆ 51°13'·90N 03°49'·83W 2 FR (vert) 6m 5M.
Harbour arm ☆ 51°13'·92N 03°49'·84W 2 FG (vert) 6m 5M.
Sand Ridge 51°15'·01N 03°49'·78W.
Copperas Rock 51°13'·78N 04°00'·60W.
Watermouth ☆ 51°12'·93N 04°04'·60W Oc WRG 5s 1m; W △; vis: G149·5°-151·5°, W151·5°-154·5°, R154·5°-156·5°.

◀ ILFRACOMBE

Lantern Hill ☆ 51°12'·66N 04°06'·78W Fl G 2·5s 39m 6M.
Promenade Pier N end ☆ 51°12'·69N 04°06'·68W 2 FG (vert).
Horseshoe 51°15'·02N 04°12'·96W Q.
Bull Point ☆ 51°11'·94N 04°12'·09W Fl (3) 10s 54m **24M**; W ○ Tr, obscd shore-056°. Same Tr; FR 48m 12M; vis: 058°-096°.
Morte Stone 51°11'·30N 04°14'·95W.
Baggy Leap 51°08'·92N 04°16'·97W.

◀ BIDEFORD, RIVERS TAW AND TORRIDGE

Bideford Fairway 51°05'·25N 04°16'·25W L Fl 10s; *Bell.*
Bideford Bar 51°04'·95N 04°14'·83W.
Instow ☆ Ldg Lts 118°. **Front**, 51°03'·62N 04°10'·67W Oc 6s 22m **15M**; vis: 104·5°-131·5°. **Rear**, 427m from front, Oc 10s 38m **15M**; vis: 104°-132°; (H24).
Crow Pt ☆ 51°03'·96N 04°11'·40W Fl WR 5s 8m W6M R5M; vis: R225°-232°, W232°-237°, R237°-358°, W358°,015°,R 015°-045°.

Clovelly Hbr Quay Hd ☆ 50°59'·92N 04°23'·83W Fl G 5s 5m 5M.

◀ LUNDY

Near North Point ☆ 51°12'·10N 04°40'·65W Fl 15s 48m **17M**; vis: 009°-285°.
South East Point 51°09'·72N 04°39'·37W Fl 5s 53m **15M**; vis: 170°-073°; *Horn 25s.*
Jetty Head ☆ 51°09'·80N 04°39'·20W Fl R 3s 8m 3M.
Hartland Point ☆ 51°01'·29N 04°31'·59W Fl (6) 15s 37m **25M**; (H24); *Horn 60s.*

NORTH CORNWALL

◀ BUDE

Compass Point Tr 50°49'·71N 04°33'·42W.

◀ PADSTOW

Stepper Point ☆ 50°34'·12N 04°56'·72W L Fl 10s 12m 4M.
Greenaway 50°33'·78N 04°56'·06W Fl (2) R 10s.
Bar 50°33'·46N 04°56'·12W Fl G 5s.
St Saviour's Pt ☆ 50°32'·76N 04°56'·06W L Fl G 10s 1M.
N Quay Head ☆ 50°32'·50N 04°56'·16W 2 FG (vert) 6m 2M.
Trevose Head ☆ 50°32'·94N 05°02'·13W Fl 7·5s 62m **21M**; *Horn (2) 30s.*

◀ NEWQUAY

North Pier Head ☆ 50°25'·07N 05°05'·19W 2 FG (vert) 5m 2M.
South Pier Head ☆ 50°25'·05N 05°05'·20W 2 FR (vert) 4m 2M.
The Stones 50°15'·64N 05°25'·51W Q.
Godrevy I ☆ 50°14'·54N 05°24'·04W Fl WR 10s 37m W12M, R9M; vis: W022°-101°, R101°-145°, W145°-272°.

◀ HAYLE

App 50°12'·26N 05°26'·30W QR.
Lts in line 180°. Front, 50°11'·50N 05°26'·18W F 17m 4M. Rear, 110m from front, F 23m 4M.

◀ ST IVES

App 50°12'·85N 05°28'·42W
East Pier Head ☆ 50°12'·80N 05°28'·61W 2 FG (vert) 8m 5M.
West Pier Head ☆ 50°12'·77N 05°28'·73W 2 FR (vert) 5m 3M.
Pendeen ☆ 50°09'·90N 05°40'·32W Fl (4) 15s 59m **16M**; vis: 042°-240°; in bay between Gurnard Hd and Pendeen it shows to coast; *Horn 20s.* For Lts further SW see 9.1.4.

9.11.5 PASSAGE INFORMATION

For directions on this coast refer to the Admiralty *W Coasts of England and Wales Pilot. A Cruising Guide to NW England & Wales* (Imray/Griffiths) covers as far S as Tenby; *Lundy and Irish Sea Pilot* (Imray/Taylor) continues to Land's End.

It is useful to know some Welsh words with navigational significance. *Aber:* estuary. *Afon:* river. *Bach, bychan, fach:* little. *Borth:* cove. *Bryn:* hill. *Careg, craig:* rock. *Coch, goch:* red. *Dinas:* fort. *Ddu:* black. *Fawr, Mawr:* big. *Ffrydiau:* tiderip. *Llwyd:* grey. *Moel:* bare conical hill. *Mor:* sea. *Morfa:* sandy shore. *Mynydd:* mountain. *Penrhyn:* headland. *Porth:* cove. *Ynys, Ynysoedd:* island(s).

CARDIGAN BAY (charts 1971, 1972, 1973) Hbrs are mostly on a lee shore, and/or have bars which make them dangerous to approach in bad weather. Abersoch (9.11.7) and Pwllheli (9.11.8) offer best shelter from prevailing W'lies. There may be overfalls off Trwyn Cilan, SW of St Tudwal's Is (lit). In N part of bay there are three major dangers to coasting yachts, as described briefly below: St Patrick's Causeway (Sarn Badrig) runs 12M SW from Mochras Pt. It is mostly large loose stones, and dries (up to 1·5m) for much of its length. In strong winds the sea breaks heavily at all states of tide. The outer end is marked by a WCM lt buoy. At the inner end there is a chan about 5ca offshore, which can be taken with care at half tide.

Sarn-y-Bwch runs 4M WSW from Pen Bwch Pt. It is composed of rky boulders, drying in places close inshore and with least depth 0·3m over 1M offshore. There is a WCM buoy off W end. NW of Aberystwyth (9.11.12), Sarn Cynfelyn and Cynfelyn Patches extend a total of 6·5M offshore, with depths of 1·5m in places. A WCM buoy is at the outer end. Almost halfway along the bank is Main Channel, 3ca wide, running roughly N/S, but not marked.

A military firing area occupies much of Cardigan B. Beware targets and buoys, some unlit. Range activity is broadcast on VHF Ch 16, 0800-1600LT Mon-Fri or ☎ (01239) 813462.

If on passage N/S through St George's Chan (ie not bound for Cardigan B or Milford Haven) the easiest route, and always by night, is W of the Bishops and the Smalls, noting the TSS. If bound to/from Milford Haven or Cardigan Bay, passage inside both the Smalls and Grassholm is possible.

RAMSEY SOUND AND THE BISHOPS (chart 1482) The Bishops and the Clerks are islets and rks 2·5M W and NW of Ramsey Is, a bird sanctuary SSW of St David's Hd. N Bishop is the N'ly of the group, 3ca ENE of which is Bell Rk (depth 1·9m). S Bishop (Lt, fog sig, RC) is 3M to the SSW.

Between S Bishop and Ramsey Is the dangers include Daufraich with offliers to the E and heavy overfalls; Llech Isaf and Llech Uchaf drying rks are further ENE. Carreg Rhoson and offliers are between Daufraich and N Bishop. The navigable routes between most of these islets and rks trend NE/SW, but use only by day, in good visibility and with local knowledge. The N/S route close W of Ramsey Island is said to be easier than Ramsey Sound (see below).

2M W of The Bishops the S-going stream begins at HW Milford Haven +4, and the N-going at HW –2½, sp rates 2kn. Between The Bishops and Ramsey Is the SW-going stream begins at HW Milford Haven +3½, and the NE-going at HW –3, sp rates 5kn.

Ramsey Sound should be taken at slack water. The S-going stream begins at HW Milford Haven +3, and the N-going at HW –3½, sp rates 6kn at The Bitches, where chan is narrowest (2ca), decreasing N and S. The Bitches are rks up to 4m high and extending 2ca from E side of Ramsey Is. Other dangers are: Gwahan and Carreg-gafeiliog, both 3m high at N end of Sound, to W and E; Horse Rk (dries 0·9m) almost in mid-chan about 5ca NNE of The Bitches, with associated overfalls; Shoe Rk (dries 3m) at SE end of chan; and rks extending 5ca SSE from S end of Ramsey Is.

THE SMALLS TO MILFORD HAVEN (chart *1478*) St Brides Bay (9.11.13) provides anch in settled weather or offshore winds, but is a trap in westerlies. Solva is a little hbr with shelter for boats able to take the ground, or anch behind Black Rk (dries 3·6m) in the middle of the entrance.

The Smalls Lt, where there is a Historic Wreck (see 9.0.3h) is 13M W of the Welsh mainland (Wooltack Pt). 2M and 4M E of The Smalls are the Hats and Barrels, rky patches on which the sea breaks. 7M E of The Smalls is Grassholm Island with a race either end and strong tidal eddies so that it is advisable to pass about 1M off. The chan between Barrels and Grassholm is 2·5M wide, and here the S-going stream begins at HW Milford Haven + 0440, and the N-going at HW Milford Haven – 0135, sp rates 5kn. 5M of clear water lie between Grassholm and Skomer Is/Skokholm Is to the E. But Wildgoose Race, which forms W of Skomer and Skokholm is very dangerous, so keep 2M W of these two Islands.

To E of Skomer is Midland Is, and between here and Wooltack Pt is Jack Sound, least width about 1ca. Do not attempt it without AC 1482, detailed pilotage directions, and only at slack water nps. Correct timing is important. The S-going stream begins at HW Milford Haven +2, and the N-going at HW –4½, sp rates 6-7kn. Rocks which must be identified include, from N to S: On E side of chan off Wooltack Pt, Tusker Rk (2m), steep-to on its W side; and off Anvil Pt, The Cable (dries 2·4m), The Anvil and Limpet Rks (3·7m). On the W side lie the Crabstones (3·7m) and the Blackstones (1·5m).

MILFORD HAVEN TO MUMBLES HD (charts *1179*, 1076) Milford Haven (9.11.14) is a long natural, all-weather hbr with marinas beyond the oil terminals. 3M S of the ent, beware Turbot Bank (WCM lt buoy). Crow Rk (dries 5·5m) is 5ca SSE of Linney Hd, and The Toes are dangerous submerged rks close W and SE of Crow Rk. There is a passage inshore of these dangers. There are overfalls on St Gowan Shoals which extend 4M SW of St Govan's Hd, and the sea breaks on the shallow patches in bad weather. For firing areas from Linney Hd to Carmarthen Bay, see 9.11.16.

Caldey Is (Lt) lies S of Tenby (9.11.15). Off its NW pt is St Margaret's Is connected by a rky reef. Caldey Sound, between St Margaret's Is and Giltar Pt (chart 1482), is buoyed, but beware Eel Spit near W end of Caldey Is where there can be a nasty sea with wind against tide, and Woolhouse Rks (dry 3·6m) 1ca NE of Caldey Is. Saundersfoot hbr (dries) is 2M N of Tenby, with anch well sheltered from N and W but subject to swell. Streams are weak here. Carmarthen Bay has no offshore dangers for yachts, other than the extensive drying sands at head of B and on its E side off Burry Inlet (9.11.16).

S of Worms Head, Helwick Sands (buoyed at each end) extend 7M W from Port Eynon Pt; least depth of 1·3m is near their W end. Stream sets NE/SW across the sands. There is a narrow chan inshore, close to Port Eynon Pt. Between here and Mumbles Hd the stream runs roughly along coast, sp rates 3kn off Pts, but there are eddies in Port Eynon B and Oxwich B (both yacht anchs), and overfalls SSE of Oxwich Pt.

MUMBLES HEAD TO CARDIFF (charts 1165, 1182) Off Mumbles Hd (Lt, fog sig) beware Mixon Shoal (dries 0·3m), marked by PHM buoy. In good conditions pass N of shoal, 1ca off Mumbles Hd. Anch N of Mumbles Hd, good holding but exposed to swell. At W side of Swansea Bay, Green Grounds, rky shoals, lie in appr's to Swansea (9.11.17).

Scarweather Sands, much of which dry (up to 3·3m) and where sea breaks heavily, extend 7M W from Porthcawl (9.11.17) and are well buoyed (chart 1161). There is a chan between the sands and coast to E, but beware Hugo Bank (dries 2·6m) and Kenfig Patches (0·5m) with overfalls up to 7ca offshore between Sker Pt and Porthcawl.

Nash Sands extend 7·5M WNW from Nash Pt. Depths vary and are least at inshore end (dries 3m), but Nash Passage, 1ca wide, runs close inshore between E Nash ECM buoy and ledge off Nash Pt. On E-going stream there are heavy overfalls off Nash Pt and at W end of Nash Sands. Between Nash Pt and Breaksea Pt the E-going stream begins at HW Avonmouth + 0535, and the W-going at HW Avonmouth – 0035, sp rates 3kn. Off Breaksea Pt there may be overfalls.

From Rhoose Pt to Lavernock Pt the coast is fringed with foul ground. Lavernock Spit extends 1·75M S of Lavernock Pt, and E of the spit is main chan to Cardiff (9.11.19); the other side of the chan being Cardiff Grounds, a bank drying 5·4m which lies parallel with the shore and about 1·5M from it.

SEVERN ESTUARY (charts 1176, 1166) Near the centre of Bristol Chan, either side of the buoyed fairway are the islands of Flat Holm (Lt, fog sig) and Steep Holm. 7M SW of Flat Holm lies Culver Sand (0·9m), 3M in length, with W & ECM bys. Monkstone Rk (Lt, dries) is 2M NW of the buoyed chan to Avonmouth and Bristol (9.11.21). Extensive drying banks cover the N shore of the estuary, beyond Newport and the Severn bridges (chart 1176).

The range of tide in the Bristol Chan is exceptionally large, 12·2m sp and 6·0m np, and tidal streams are very powerful, particularly above Avonmouth. Between Flat Holm and Steep Holm the E-going stream begins at HW Avonmouth – 0610, sp 3kn, and the W-going at HW Avonmouth + 0015, sp 4kn.

The ent to the R. Avon is just to the S of Avonmouth S Pier Hd. Bristol City Docks lie some 6M up river. Approach the ent via King Road and the Newcombe and Cockburn lt buoys and thence via the Swash chan into the Avon. The ent dries at LW but the river is navigable at about half tide. Tidal streams are strong in the approaches to Avonmouth, up to 5kn at sp. The tide is also strong in the R. Avon which is best entered no earlier than HW Avonmouth – 0200.

From Avonmouth it is 16M to Sharpness which yachts should aim to reach at about HW Avonmouth. Spring streams can run 8kn at the Shoots, and 6kn at the Severn bridges (9.11.20). At the Shoots the flood begins at HW Avonmouth –0430 and the ebb at HW Avonmouth + 0045. The Severn Bore can usually be seen if Avonmouth range is 13·5m or more.

AVONMOUTH TO HARTLAND POINT (AC 1152, 1165) From Avonmouth to Sand Pt, the part-drying English Grounds extend 3M off the S shore. Portishead Dock (9.11.22) is being developed as a marina. Extensive mud flats fill the bays S to Burnham-on-Sea (9.11.23). Westward, the S shore of Bristol Chan is cleaner than N shore. But there is less shelter since the approaches to hbrs such as Watchet (9.11.24), Minehead, Porlock Weir and Watermouth dry out, see 9.11.24. In bad weather dangerous overfalls occur NW and NE of Foreland Pt. 5M to W there is a race off Highveer Pt. Between Ilfracombe (9.11.25) and Bull Pt the E-going stream begins at HW Milford Haven + 0540, and the W-going at HW Milford Haven – 0025, sp rates 3kn. Overfalls occur up to 1·5M N of Bull Pt and over Horseshoe Rks, which lie 3M N. There is a dangerous race off Morte Pt, 1·5M to W of Bull Pt.

Shelter is available under lee of Lundy Is (9.11.26); but avoid bad races to NE (White Horses), the NW (Hen and Chickens), and to SE; also overfalls over NW Bank. W of Lundy streams are moderate, but strong around the Is and much stronger towards Bristol Chan proper.

Proceeding WSW from Rivers Taw/Torridge (9.11.26), keep 3M off to avoid the race N of Hartland Pt (Lt, fog sig, conspic radome). There is shelter off Clovelly in S/SW winds.

HARTLAND POINT TO LAND'S END (charts 1156, 1149) The N coast of Cornwall and SW approaches to Bristol Chan are very exposed. Yachts need to be sturdy and well equipped, since if bad weather develops no shelter may be at hand. Bude (9.11.26) dries, and is not approachable in W winds; only accessible in calm weather or offshore winds. Boscastle is a tiny hbr (dries) 3M NE of Tintagel Hd. Only approach in good weather or offshore winds; anch off or dry out alongside.

Padstow is a refuge, but in strong NW winds the sea breaks on bar and prevents entry. Off Trevose Hd (Lt) beware Quies Rks which extend 1M to W. From here S the coast is relatively clear to Godrevy Is, apart from Bawden Rks 1M N of St Agnes Hd. Newquay B (9.11.27) is good anch in offshore winds, and the hbr (dries) is sheltered but uncomfortable in N winds. Off Godrevy Is (Lt) are The Stones, drying rky shoals extending 1·5M offshore and marked by NCM lt buoy.

In St Ives Bay (chart 1168), Hayle (9.11.27) is a commercial port (dries); seas break heavily on bar at times, especially with a ground swell. Stream is strong, so enter just before HW. The bottom is mostly sand. St Ives (dries) (9.11.27) gives shelter from winds E to SW, but is very exposed to N; there is sometimes a heavy breaking sea if there is ground swell.

From St Ives to Land's End coast is rugged and exposed. There are overfalls SW of Pendeen Pt (lt, fog sig). Vyneck Rks lie awash about 3ca NW of C Cornwall. The Brisons are two high rky islets 5ca SW of C Cornwall, with rky ledges inshore and to the S. The Longships (lt, fog sig) group of rks is about 1M W of Land's End. The inshore passage (001° on Brisons) is about 4ca wide with unmarked drying rks on the W side; only to be considered in calm weather. See 9.1.5 for tides.

For Isles of Scilly and South Cornwall, see 9.1.5.

9.11.6 DISTANCE TABLE

Approximate distances in nautical miles are by the most direct route, whilst avoiding dangers and allowing for Traffic Separation Schemes. Places in *italics* are in adjoining areas; places in **bold** are in 9.0.7, Distances across the Irish Sea.

1. *Bardsey Island*	**1**																			
2. Abersoch	14	**2**																		
3. **Pwllheli**	18	5	**3**																	
4. Barmouth	27	18	18	**4**																
5. Aberdovey	31	26	25	14	**5**															
6. Aberystwyth	33	30	30	20	10	**6**														
7. **Fishguard**	45	54	58	56	47	40	**7**													
8. South Bishop	60	70	74	74	67	61	25	**8**												
9. **Milford Haven**	83	93	97	97	90	84	48	23	**9**											
10. Tenby	106	116	120	120	113	107	71	46	28	**10**										
11. **Swansea**	129	139	143	143	136	130	94	69	55	36	**11**									
12. Barry	151	161	165	165	158	152	116	91	77	57	37	**12**								
13. Cardiff	160	170	174	174	167	161	125	100	86	66	46	9	**13**							
14. Sharpness	191	201	205	205	198	192	156	131	117	106	75	39	33	**14**						
15. **Avonmouth**	174	184	188	188	181	175	139	114	100	89	58	22	20	18	**15**					
16. Burnham-on-Sea	168	178	182	182	175	169	133	108	94	70	48	18	53	50	33	**16**				
17. **Ilfracombe**	127	137	141	141	134	128	92	67	53	35	25	35	44	74	57	45	**17**			
18. Lundy Island	110	120	124	124	117	111	75	50	38	30	37	54	63	95	78	66	22	**18**		
19. **Padstow**	141	151	155	155	148	142	106	81	70	70	76	88	97	127	110	98	55	39	**19**	
20. ***Longships***	168	178	182	182	175	169	133	108	105	110	120	130	139	169	152	140	95	82	50	**20**

11

ABERSOCH *9.11.7*

Gwynedd **52°49'·29N 04°29'·20W** (⚓) ❀❀❀◊◊✿✿

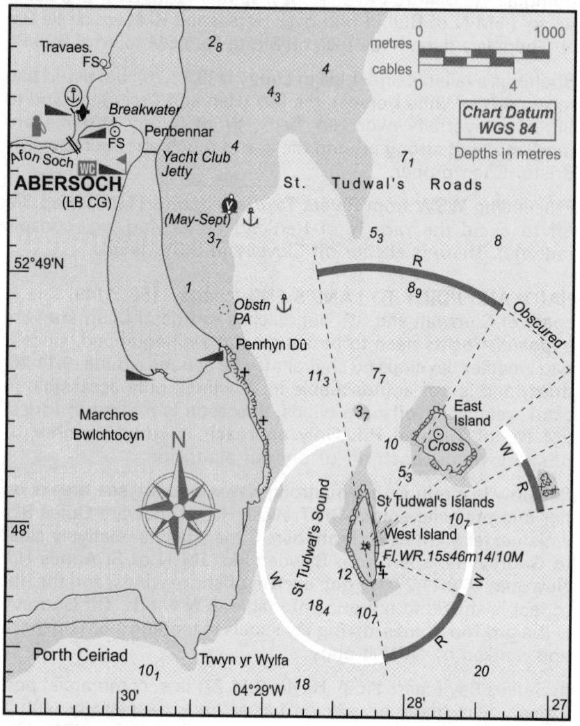

CHARTS AC 1512, 1971, *1410*; Imray C52, C61; Stanfords 27; OS 123

TIDES –0315 Dover; ML 2·5; Duration 0520; Zone 0 (UT)

Standard Port MILFORD HAVEN (⟶)

Times				Height (metres)			
High Water		Low Water		MHWS	MHWN	MLWN	MLWS
0100	0800	0100	0700	7·0	5·2	2·5	0·7
1300	2000	1300	1900				
Differences ST TUDWAL'S ROADS							
+0155	+0145	+0240	+0310	–2·2	–1·9	–0·7	–0·2
ABERDARON							
+0210	+0200	+0240	+0310	–2·4	–1·9	–0·6	–0·2

SHELTER There are few moorings for visitors. Apply to Hr Mr or SC. ⚓ in St Tudwal's Roads clear of moored yachts; sheltered from SSE through S to NE.

NAVIGATION WPT 52°48'·52N 04°26'·13W, 113°/293° from/to YC jetty, 2·4M. There are no navigational dangers, but steer well clear of the drying rks to the E of East Island; an unlit PHM buoy is 2ca E of these rks (just off chartlet). St Tudwal's islands themselves are fairly steep-to, except at N ends. St Tudwal's Sound is clear of dangers.

LIGHTS AND MARKS The only lt is on St Tudwal's West Island, Fl WR 15s 46m 14/10M (see chartlet and 9.11.4).

RADIO TELEPHONE S Caernarfon YC Ch **80** M.

TELEPHONE (Dial code 01758) Hr Mr 812684; MRSC (01407) 762051; ⊖ (01407) 762714; Marinecall 09068 500 460; Police 2022; Dr 612535.

FACILITIES S. Caernarvonshire YC ☎ 712338, Slip, M, L, FW, R, Bar (May-Sept), D; **Abersoch Power Boat Club** ☎ 812027. **Services:** BY, Slip, ME, El, Sh, ACA, CH, P, C (12 ton), LPG. **Town** EC Wed; CH, V, R, Bar, ✉, Ⓑ, ⥂ (Pwllheli), ✈ (Chester).

PWLLHELI *9.11.8*

Gwynedd **52°53'·23N 04°23'·75W** ❀❀❀◊◊◊✿✿✿

CHARTS AC 1512, 1971, *1410*; Imray C52, C61; OS 123; Stanfords 27

TIDES –0315 Dover; ML 2·6; Duration 0510; Zone 0 (UT)

Standard Port MILFORD HAVEN (⟶)

Times				Height (metres)			
High Water		Low Water		MHWS	MHWN	MLWN	MLWS
0100	0800	0100	0700	7·0	5·2	2·5	0·7
1300	2000	1300	1900				
Differences PWLLHELI							
+0210	+0150	+0245	+0320	–2·0	–1·8	–0·6	–0·2
CRICCIETH							
+0210	+0155	+0255	+0320	–2·0	–1·8	–0·7	–0·3

SHELTER Good in hbr & marina, pontoons are numbered 4–12 from S–N. Pile berths on S side of appr chan. Drying moorings in inner hbr (SW and NW bights).

NAVIGATION WPT 52°53'·02N 04°23'·07W, SWM lt buoy, Iso 2s, 119°/299° from/to QG lt at head of Training Arm, 0·47M. Ent is safe in most winds, but in strong E to SW winds sea breaks on offshore shoals. Bar and hbr chan are dredged to at least 0·6m; 3 tide gauges. No ⚓ in hbr; 4kn speed limit. Max tidal stream 2kn.

LIGHTS AND MARKS No ldg lts/marks, but ent chan well marked (see chartlet). Gimblet Rock (30m) is conspic conical rock 3ca SW of ent.

RADIO TELEPHONE Marina: Ch **80** M H24. Hr Mr: VHF Ch **12** 16 (0900-1715).

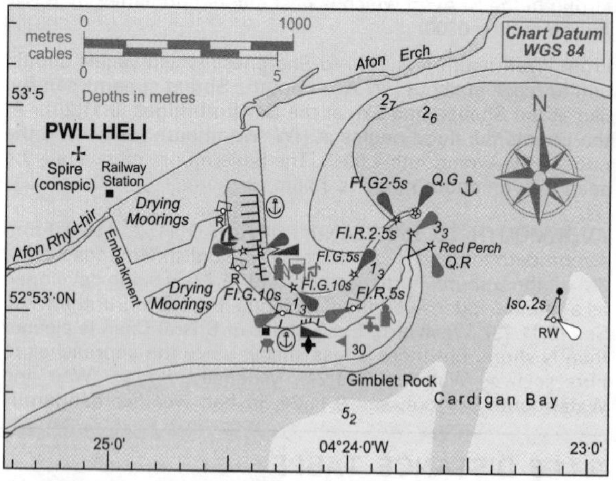

TELEPHONE (Dial code 01758) Hr Mr 704081 or weekends 0402 719022; MRSC (01407) 762051; ⊖ (01407) 386400; Ⓗ Bangor (A&E) 01248 384384; Marinecall 09068 500 460; Police 701177; Dr 701457.

FACILITIES Marina (400) ☎ 701219 (H24), 📠 701443, £1.58, FW, P, D, LPG, AC, BH (40 ton), C, Slip, ⓘ, Ⓓ, ⚲; **Marina Boat Club** ☎ 612271, Slip, FW; **Hbr Authority** Slip, M, L, FW, AB; **Pwllheli SC** ☎ 614442, 📠 612134; pwllhelisailingclub@bt internet.com; **Services:** BY, Slip, L, FW, ME, Gas, Gaz, LPG, Sh, CH, ACA, D, C (14 ton), El, Ⓔ, SM. **Town** EC Thurs; V, R, Bar, ✉, Ⓑ, ⥂, ✈ (Chester).

ADJACENT HARBOUR

MOCHRAS, Gwynedd, **52°49'·57N 04°07'·77W.** AC 1512, 1971. HW –0245 on Dover. Small yacht hbr on SE side of Shell Is. Mochras lagoon dries. Bar, about 2ca seaward. Entry advised HW±2. Tide runs strongly in the narrows on the ebb; at sp beware severe eddies inside ent. Ent between Shell Is (lt Fl WRG 4s; G079°-124°, W124°-134°, R134°-179°; shown mid Mar-Nov) and sea wall. 3 grey posts, R topmarks, mark N side of chan. Shifting chan, marked by posts & buoys, runs NE to Pensarn, where permanent moorings limit space. To S, buoyed chan runs to Shell Is Yacht Hbr ☎ (0134123) 453 with facilities: M, FW, Slip, R, Bar, shwrs. Pensarn: drying AB, ⥂.

PORTHMADOG 9.11.9

Gwynedd **52°55'·32N 04°07'·77W**

CHARTS AC 1512, 1971, *1410*; Imray C51, C61; Stanfords 27; OS 124

TIDES –0247 Dover; ML no data; Duration 0455; Zone 0 (UT)

Standard Port MILFORD HAVEN (⟶)

Times				**Height (metres)**			
High Water		Low Water		MHWS	MHWN	MLWN	MLWS
0100	0800	0100	0700	7·0	5·2	2·5	0·7
1300	2000	1300	1900				
Differences PORTHMADOG							
+0235	+0210	No data		–1·9	–1·8	No data	

SHELTER Inner hbr (N of Cei Ballast): Good all year round; visitors' drying AB adjacent Madoc YC or afloat rafted on moored yachts off YC. (Greaves Wharf is obstructed by dinghies and salmon nets). Outer hbr: Summer only, exposed to S winds. Speed limit 6kn in hbr upstream of No 8 buoy.

NAVIGATION WPT Fairway SWM buoy, 52°52'·97N 04°11'·09W, 221°/041° from/to conspic white Ho at W side of ent,-1·91M; chan shifts and may divide. Bar changes frequently, but is near to No 3 and 4 buoys; dries approx 0·3m. Latest info from Hr Mr on request. Advise entering HW±1½. In SW'lies, waves are steep-sided and close, especially on the ebb.

LIGHTS AND MARKS Fairway buoy RW, L Fl 10s. Chan marker buoys (14) have R/G reflective top marks and numbers in W reflective tape. Moel-y-Gest is conspic hill (259m) approx 1M WNW of hbr. Harlech Castle (ru) is about 3M SE of appr chan.

RADIO TELEPHONE Hr Mr Ch 12 16 (0900-1715 and when vessel due). Madoc YC: Ch M.

TELEPHONE (Dial code 01766) Hr Mr 512927, mobile (07879) 433147; MRSC (01407) 762051; Pilot 530684, Home 75684; Hbr Authority Gwynedd Council (01758) 613131; ⊜ (01407) 762714; Marinecall 09068 500 460; Police 512226; Dr 512239.

FACILITIES **Hbr** (265 berths) ☎ 512927, £6.00 < 12m, £6.50 >12m; D, FW, C, Slip; **Madoc YC** ☎ 512976, AB, M, FW, Bar; **Porthmadog SC** ☎ 513546, AB, M, FW, Slip; **Services:** CH, ACA, Sh, D, P (cans), C (3½ ton), M, BY, El, Pilot. **Town** EC Wed; ✉, Ⓑ, ≷, ✈ (Chester).

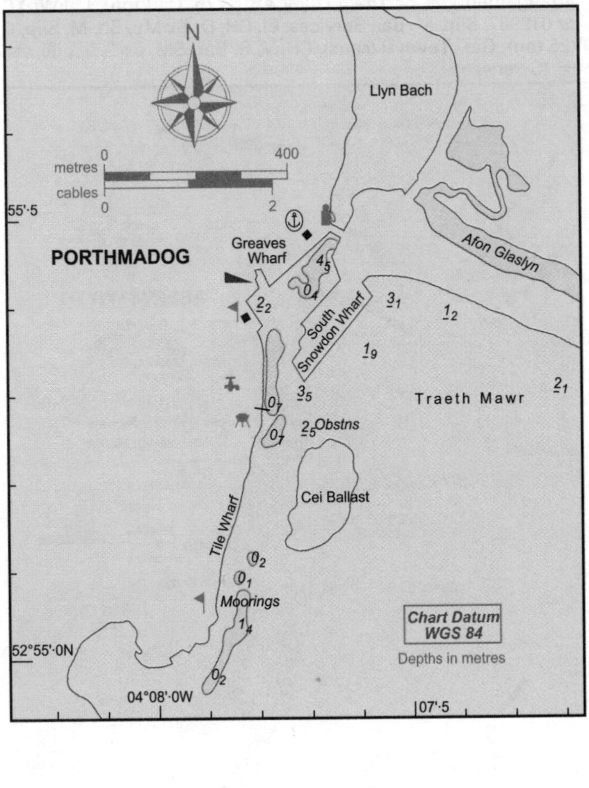

BARMOUTH 9.11.10

Gwynedd **52°42'·97N 04°03'·07W**

CHARTS AC 1484, 1971, *1410*; Imray C51, C61; Stanfords 27; OS 124

TIDES –0305 Dover; ML 2·6; Duration 0515; Zone 0 (UT)

Standard Port MILFORD HAVEN (⟶)

Times				**Height (metres)**			
High Water		Low Water		MHWS	MHWN	MLWN	MLWS
0100	0800	0100	0700	7·0	5·2	2·5	0·7
1300	2000	1300	1900				
Differences BARMOUTH							
+0215	+0205	+0310	+0320	–2·0	–1·7	–0·7	0·0

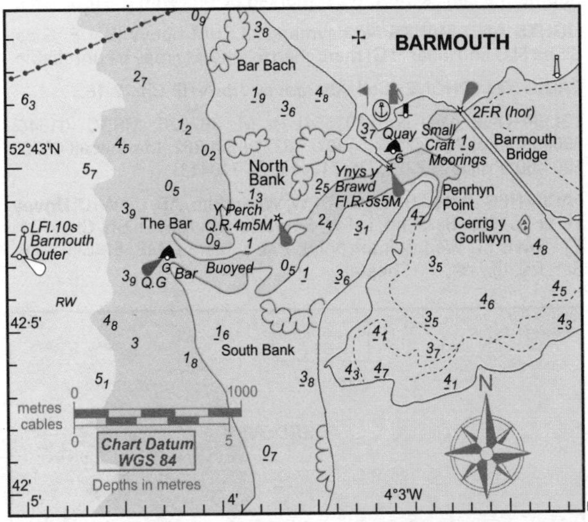

SHELTER Good. Entry HW±2½ safe, but impossible with strong SW'lies. Exposed ⚓ W of Barmouth Outer buoy in 6 to 10m. Serious silting up has recently been reported. In hbr there are 5 🅥s; secure as directed by Hr Mr, because of submarine cables and strong tidal streams. A 🅥 berth is marked at W end of quay, dries at half-tide. The estuary and river (Afon Mawddach) are tidal and can be navigated for about 7M above railway bridge (clearance approx 5·5m); but chan is not buoyed, and sandbanks move constantly - local knowledge essential.

NAVIGATION WPT, Barmouth Outer SWM buoy, L Fl 10s, 52°42'·72N 04°05'·02W, 262°/082° from/to Y perch lt, QR, 0·78M. Appr from SW between St Patrick's Causeway (Sarn Badrig) and Sarn-y-Bwch (see 9.11.5). Barmouth can be identified by Cader Idris, a mountain 890m high, 5M ESE. Fegla Fawr, a rounded hill, lies on S side of hbr. The Bar, 0·75M W of Penrhyn Pt, with min depth 0·3m is subject to considerable change. Chan is marked by buoys, all unlit, fitted with radar reflectors and reflective tape and moved as required; . Spring ebb runs 3 - 5kn. Note: A Historic Wreck (see 9.0.3h) is at 52°46'·73N 04°07'·53W, 4·5M NNW of Barmouth Outer SWM buoy.

LIGHTS AND MARKS Y perch, QR 4m 5M, R framework tr, marks S end of stony ledge extending 3ca SW from Ynys y Brawd across N Bank. Ynys y Brawd groyne, SE end, marked by bn with lt, Fl R 5s 5M. NW end of rly bridge 2 FR (hor).

RADIO TELEPHONE Call *Barmouth Hbr* VHF Ch **12** 16 (Apl-Sept 0900-2200LT; Oct-Mar 0900-1600LT); wind and sea state are available.

TELEPHONE (Dial code 01341) Hr Mr 280671; MRSC (01407) 762051; ⊜ (01407) 762714; Marinecall 09068 500460; Police 280222; Dr 280521.

FACILITIES Quay £6.50 < 9m £9.50 > 9m, M (contact Hr Mr in advance if deep water a required), D, FW, El, AC, Slip; Merioneth YC ☎ 280000; Services: CH, ACA. **Town** EC Wed; P, D, V, R, Bar, ✉, Ⓑ, ≷, ✈ (Chester), Ferry across to Penrhyn Pt.

ABERDOVEY *9.11.11*

Gwynedd **52°32'·57N 04°02'·72W** (Jetty) ❁❁◊◊✿✿✿

CHARTS AC 1484, 1972, *1410*; Imray C51, C61; Stanfords 27; OS 135

TIDES –0320 Dover; ML 2·6; Duration 0535; Zone 0 (UT). For differences see 9.11.12.

SHELTER Good except in strong W/SW winds. Berth on jetty in 3m; to the E there is heavy silting.

NAVIGATION WPT Aberdovey Outer SWM buoy, L Fl 10s, 52°31′·32N 04°05′·12W, 201°/021° from/to Bar buoy, 0.73M. Bar (0·7m though more water rep'd 1999) and chan constantly shift and are hazardous below half-tide; buoys moved accordingly. Visitors should call Hr Mr on VHF before entering or ☎ the Pilot. Submarine cables (prohib ⚓s) marked by bns with R ◊ topmarks.

LIGHTS AND MARKS No daymarks. 3 SHM buoys (Bar Fl G 5s, S Spit Fl G and Inner Fl G) mark chan to jetty. Lts may be unreliable.

RADIO TELEPHONE Call *Aberdovey Hbr* VHF Ch 12 16.

TELEPHONE (Dial code 01654) Hr Mr 767626; MRSC (01646) 690909; Pilot 767247; ⊖ (01407) 762714 Ext 262; Marinecall 09068 500 460; Police 767222; Dr 710414; 🄷 710411.

FACILITIES **Jetty** AB £6.00, M, FW; **Wharf** Slip, AB, L, FW, C; **Dovey YC** ☎ 767607, Bar, Slip, L, FW; **Services:** BY, ME, El, Sh, CH, ACA, Ⓔ. **Town** EC Wed (winter only); P & D (cans), ME, El, CH, V, R, Bar, ✉, Ⓑ, ⇌, ✈ (Chester).

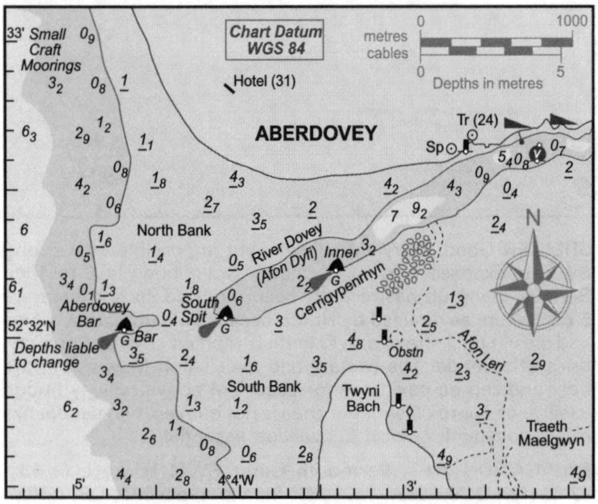

OTHER HARBOURS IN SOUTH PART OF CARDIGAN BAY

ABERAERON, Ceredigion, **52°14′·62N 04°15′·94W**. AC 1484, 1972, *1410*. HW –0325 on Dover; +0140 and –1·9m on Milford Haven; ML 2·7m; Duration 0540. A small, popular drying hbr at the mouth of the R Aeron; access HW±1½. Short drying piers extend each side of river ent. In strong NW'lies there is little shelter. AB £4 on NW wall. Foul ground with depths of 1·5m extend 3ca offshore to SW of Aberaeron. Beware Carreg Gloyn (0·3m) 4ca WSW of hbr, and Sarn Cadwgan (1·8m) shoals 5ca N of the hbr ent. Lts (see 9.11.4 for sectors): N pier Fl (4) WRG 15s 10m 6M. S pier Fl (3) G 10s 11m 6M. VHF **14** 16. Hr Mr ☎ (01545) 571645; FW, D (hose) via aquarium. **YC** ☎ 570077.

NEW QUAY, Ceredigion, **52°12′·92N 04°21′·22W**. AC 1484, 1972, *1410*. HW –0335 on Dover; Duration 0540; see 9.11.12. Good shelter in offshore winds, but untenable in NW'lies. On E side of bay Carreg Ina, rks drying 1·3m, are marked by NCM buoy, Q. Two Y bns mark a sewer outfall running 7ca NNW from Ina Pt. The hbr (dries 1·6m) is protected by a pier with lt, Fl WG 3s 12m 8/5M; W135°-252°, G252°-295°. Groyne extends 80m SSE of pierhd to a SHM bn; close ENE of which is a ECM bn, Q (3) 10s. ⚓s are 1ca E of pier; £4. VHF Ch **14** 16. Hr Mr ☎ (01545) 560368. MRSC (01646) 690909; Dr ☎ 560203; YC ☎ 560516. Facilities: FW, D (from fishermen). **Town** P (3M), ✉, R, Bar.

ABERYSTWYTH *9.11.12*

Ceredigion **52°24'·42N 04°05'·47W** ❁❁◊◊✿✿✿

CHARTS AC 1484, 1972, *1410*; Imray C51, C61; Stanfords 27; OS 135

TIDES –0330 Dover; ML 2·7; Duration 0540; Zone 0 (UT)

Standard Port MILFORD HAVEN (⟶)

Times				Height (metres)			
High Water		Low Water		MHWS	MHWN	MLWN	MLWS
0100	0800	0100	0700	7·0	5·2	2·5	0·7
1300	2000	1300	1900				
Differences ABERDOVEY							
+0215	+0200	+0230	+0305	–2·0	–1·7	–0·5	0·0
ABERYSTWYTH							
+0145	+0130	+0210	+0245	–2·0	–1·7	–0·7	0·0
NEW QUAY							
+0150	+0125	+0155	+0230	–2·1	–1·8	–0·6	–0·1
ABERPORTH							
+0135	+0120	+0150	+0220	–2·1	–1·8	–0·6	–0·1

SHELTER Good, in marina (1·7m) on E side of chan; or dry against Town Quay. Access approx HW±3 (HW±2 for strangers). The Bar, close off S pier hd, has 0·7m least depth. E edge of inner hbr chan 0·3m is defined by WCM beacon which in line with Y day mark gives a daytime lead into the Hbr.

NAVIGATION WPT 52°24′·83N 04°06′·22W, 313°/133° from/to ent, 0·6M. Approach dangerous in strong on-shore winds. From N, beware Castle Rks, within R sector 141°-175° of N bkwtr lt, QWR 9m 2M; also rks drying 0·5m W of N bkwtr and boulders below S pier hd. Turn 90° port inside narrow ent.

LIGHTS AND MARKS N bkwtr hd ≠ 140° Wellington Mon't (on top Pendinas, conspic hill 120m high) clears to S of Castle Rks. Ldg lts 133°, both FR on Ystwyth Bridge, white daymarks. WCM bn on with Y daymark leads 100° across bar into hbr ent.

RADIO TELEPHONE Hr Mr VHF Ch 14 16. Marina Ch 80.

TELEPHONE (Dial code 01970) Hr Mr 611433 623465 Mobile 07768 566457; Marina 611422; MRSC (01646) 690909; ⊖ (02920) 763880 (H24); Marinecall 09068 500460; Police 612791; Dr 624855.

FACILITIES **Marina (Y Lanfa)**, ☎ 611422, 📠 624122, (88 + 15 Ⓥ), £1.35, access HW±2, AC, FW, D, Slip, BH (10 ton), C (max 15 ton by arrangement), ♿, 🄴; **Town Quay** AB £3.75, C (3 ton), L, FW; **YC** ☎ 612907, Slip, M, Bar; **Services:** El, CH, D, Ⓔ, ME, Sh, M, Slip, C (25 ton), Gas. **Town** P (cans), CH, V, R, Bar, SM, 🄴, 🄾, ✉, Ⓑ, ⇌, ✈ (Swansea).

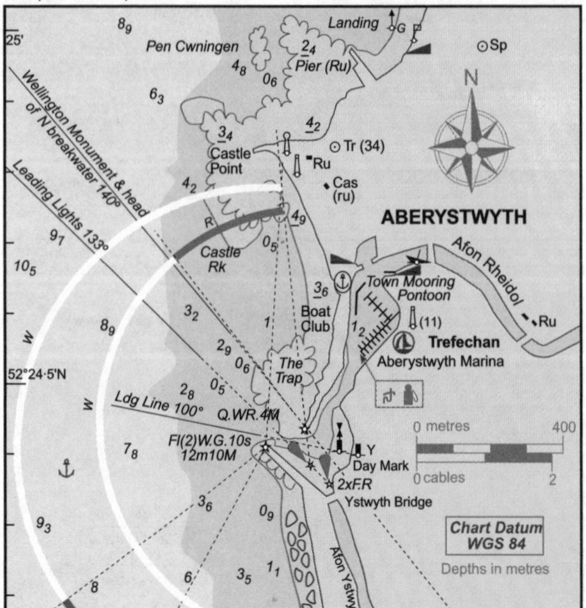

MINOR HARBOUR, 12M NE of Fishguard

PORT CARDIGAN, Ceredigion, **52°07′·02N 04°42′·07W**. AC 1484, 1973. HW –0405 on Dover; ML 2·4m; Duration 0550. Shelter is good, but ent dangerous in strong N/NW winds. **Large scale chart (1484) and local advice essential**. Bar has 0·3m or less; breakers form esp on sp ebb. ⚓ near Hotel (conspic) on E side of ent by 2 FR (vert). Chan is close to E side; IDM bn, Fl (2) 5s, should be left to stbd when clear of the bar. From Pen-yr-Ergyd to Bryn-Du chan is marked with mid channel markers but shifts constantly. ⚓ in pools off Pen-yr-Ergyd or near St Dogmaels. Possible Ⓜs off Teifi Boating Club. **Moorings**: administered by Afon Teifi Fairway Committee, Mooring Master ☎ (01239) 613890, Sec ☎ 613704;
Teifi Boating Club ☎ 613846, FW, Bar; **Services**: ME, Sh. **Town** EC Wed; Ⓑ, V, CH, P&D (cans), FW, ME, Bar, R.

FISHGUARD *9.11.13*

Pembrokeshire **52°00′·12N 04°58′·40W**
Commercial Hbr ❀❀❀◊◊✿; Lower Hbr ❀❀◊✿✿✿

CHARTS AC 1484, 1973, *1410, 1178*; Imray C51, C61/60; Stanfords 27; OS 157

TIDES –0400 Dover; ML 2·6; Duration 0550; Zone 0 (UT)

Standard Port MILFORD HAVEN (⟶)

Times				Height (metres)			
High Water		Low Water		MHWS	MHWN	MLWN	MLWS
0100	0800	0100	0700	7·0	5·2	2·5	0·7
1300	2000	1300	1900				
Differences FISHGUARD							
+0115	+0100	+0110	+0135	–2·2	–1·8	–0·5	+0·1
PORT CARDIGAN							
+0140	+0120	+0220	+0130	–2·3	–1·8	–0·5	0·0
CARDIGAN (Town)							
+0220	+0150	No data		–2·2	–1·6	No data	
PORTHGAIN							
+0055	+0045	+0045	+0100	–2·5	–1·8	–0·6	0·0
RAMSEY SOUND							
+0030	+0030	+0030	+0030	–1·9	–1·3	–0·3	0·0
SOLVA							
+0015	+0010	+0035	+0015	–1·5	–1·0	–0·2	0·0
LITTLE HAVEN							
+0010	+0010	+0025	+0015	–1·1	–0·8	–0·2	0·0
MARTIN'S HAVEN							
+0010	+0010	+0015	+0015	–0·8	–0·5	+0·1	+0·1
SKOMER IS							
–0005	–0005	+0005	+0005	–0·4	–0·1	0·0	0·0

SHELTER Good, except in strong NW/NE winds. Access H24 to Goodwick (upper, commercial) hbr with only 2 Ⓥ berths; no ⚓, except SW of ferry quay. Lower Town (Fishguard) dries 3·2m; access HW±1, limited AB. Good holding in most of the bay; ⚓ off Saddle Pt in 2m or as shown. Strong S'lies funnel down the hbr.

NAVIGATION WPT 52°01′·02N 04°57′·57W, 057°/237° from/to N bkwtr lt, 0·48m. Beware large swell, especially in N winds. Keep clear of ferries and high-speed SeaCat manoeuvring.

LIGHTS AND MARKS Strumble Hd lt, Fl (4) 15s 45m 26M, is approx 4M WNW of hbr. N bkwtr Fl G 4·5s 18m 13M, Bell 8s. E bkwtr Fl R 3s 10m 5M. Ldg lts 282° (to ferry berths), both FG; W ◊ on masts. The SHM (bn) at Aber gwavn is very small.

RADIO TELEPHONE Hr Mr Ch 14 16. Goodwick Marine Ch M (occas).

TELEPHONE (Dial code 01348) Commercial Hbr Supervisor 404453; Hr Mr (Lower hbr) 874726; MRSC (01646) 690909; ⊜ (01222) 763880 (H24); Marinecall 09068 500 460; Police 873073; Dr 872802.

FACILITIES Goodwick Hbr AB £10 all LOA, D from bowser; **Lower Town, Fishguard,** M (£5 AB) via Hr Mr; **Fishguard Bay YC** ☎ (home) 872866 (office) 873369, FW, Bar, ♿; **Services:** BY, Sh, ME, ACA, Slip, CH, El. **Town** EC Wed; P & D (cans), V, R, Gas, Bar, ✉, Ⓟ, Ⓑ, ⇌, ✈ (Cardiff), Ferry–Rosslare.

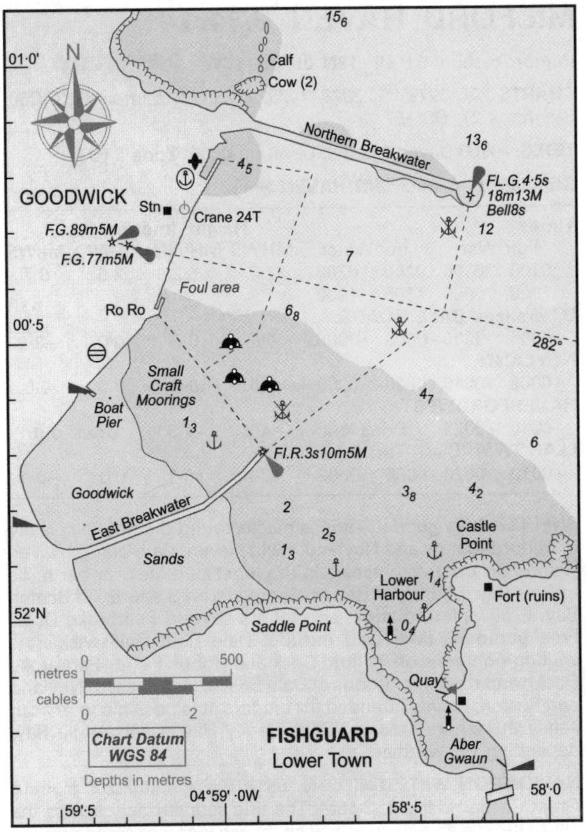

HARBOURS IN ST BRIDES BAY

SOLVA, Pembrokeshire, **51°52′02N 05°11′·67W.** AC *1478*. HW –0450 on Dover; ML 3·2m; Duration 0555. See 9.11.13. Good shelter for small boats that can take the ground; access HW±3. Avoid in strong S winds. Black Scar, Green Scar and The Mare are rks 5ca S. Ent via SSE side; best water near Black Rk in centre of ent. Beware stone spit at Trwyn Caws on W just inside ent. There are 9 R Ⓜs and some drying moorings available; or ⚓ behind the rk in approx 3m. Small craft can go up to the quay. Facilities limited; stores in village. FW on quay. Hr Mr (01437) 720153, M, CH. **Solva Boat Owners Assn** ☎ 721489.

ST BRIDES BAY, Pembrokeshire, **51°49′02N 05°10′·07W.** AC *1478*. HW (Little Haven) –0450 on Dover; ML 3·2m; Duration 0555. See 9.11.13. A SPM buoy, Fl (5) Y 20s, is midway between Ramsey and Skomer islands at 51°48′·2N 05°20′·0W. Keep at least 100m offshore 1/9-28/2 to avoid disturbing seals, and ditto nesting sea birds 1/3-31/7. Many good ⚓s, especially between Little Haven and Borough Head in S or E winds or between Solva and Dinas Fawr in N or E winds. In W'lies boats should shelter in Solva (above), Skomer (below) or Pendinas Bach. For apprs from the N or S see 9.11.5. Facilities: (Little Haven) CH, V, R, Bar, FW (cans).

SKOMER, Pembrokeshire, **51°44′·42N 05°16′·77W.** AC 2878, *1478*. HW –0455 Dover. See 9.11.13. The island is a National Nature Reserve (fee payable to Warden on landing) and also a Marine Nature Reserve, extending to Marloes Peninsula. Keep at least 100m offshore 1/9-28/2 to avoid disturbing seals and ditto nesting sea birds 1/3-31/7. There is a 5kn speed limit within 100m of the island. ⚓ in N or S Haven. Enter N Haven close to W shore, and land on W side of bay on beach or at steps. In N Haven pick up Ⓜs provided or ⚓ to seaward of them. No access to the island from S Haven. For Jack Sound see 9.11.5. There are no lts, marks or facilities. For info, Marine Conservation Officer ☎ (01646) 636736.

MILFORD HAVEN *9.11.14*

Pembrokeshire **51°40'·13N 05°08'·16W** ☸☸☸👍👍👍✿✿

CHARTS AC 3273/4/5, *2878, 1478, 1178, 1410*; Imray C13, C60; Stanfords 27; OS 157

TIDES –0500 Dover; ML 3·8; Duration 0605; Zone 0 (UT)

Standard Port MILFORD HAVEN (⟶)

Times				Height (metres)			
High Water		Low Water		MHWS	MHWN	MLWN	MLWS
0100	0800	0100	0700	7·0	5·2	2·5	0·7
1300	2000	1300	1900				
Differences DALE ROADS							
–0005	–0005	–0008	–0008	0·0	0·0	0·0	–0·1
NEYLAND							
+0002	+0010	0000	0000	0·0	0·0	0·0	0·0
HAVERFORDWEST							
+0010	+0025	Dries out		–4·8	–4·9	Dries out	
LLANGWM (Black Tar)							
+0010	+0020	+0005	0000	+0·1	+0·1	0·0	–0·1

SHELTER Very good in various places round the hbr, especially in Milford Marina and Neyland Yacht Haven. Call *Milford Haven Radio Port Control* to ascertain the most suitable ⚓ or berth. ⚓s in Dale Bay; off Chapel Bay and Angle Pt on S shore; off Scotch Bay, E of Milford marina; and others beyond Pembroke Dock. Free pontoons (May-Oct) include: Dale Bay, Gelliswick Bay; waiting pontoons off Milford Dock and Hobbs Pt (for Pembroke Dock); and drying pontoons at Dale Beach, Hazelbeach, Neyland and Burton; mainly intended for tenders. It is possible to dry out safely at inshore areas of Dale, Sandy Haven and Angle Bay, depending on weather.

NAVIGATION WPT 51°40'·21N, 05°10'·28W, 040°/220° from/to Great Castle Hd ldg lt, 3·18M. The tide sets strongly across the ent to the Haven particularly at sp. In bad weather avoid passing over Mid Chan Rks and St Ann's Hd shoal, where a confused sea and swell will be found (see AC 3273). Give St Ann's Head a wide berth especially on the ebb, when East Chan by Sheep Island is better. Beware large tankers entering and leaving the Haven and ferries moving at high speed in the lower Haven. Caution: Only 15m clearance below cables between Thorn Island and Thorn Pt. NB: Milford Haven Port Authority has a jetty, Port Control and offices near Hubberston Pt. Their launches have G hulls and W upperworks with 'PILOT' in black letters and fly a Pilot flag (HOTEL) while on patrol; Fl Bu lt at night. Their instructions must be obeyed. No vessel may pass within 100m of any terminal or any tanker, whether at ⚓ or under way.
River Cleddau is navigable 6M to Picton Pt, at junction of West and East arms, at all tides for boats of moderate draught. Clearance under Cleddau Bridge above Neyland is 37m; and 25m under power cable 1M upstream. Chan to Haverfordwest has 2m at HW and clearances of only 6m below cables and bridge; only feasible for shoal draft/lifting keel and unmasted craft.
Firing Ranges to the S and SE, see 9.11.16 and AC 1076.
Call Port Control VHF Ch 12 or tel/fax as below for navigational advice or port operational information.

LIGHTS AND MARKS See 9.11.4 for details. Many ldg lts have deliberately been omitted from the chartlet for clarity, since virtually all are "Big Ship" orientated. The Haven is very well buoyed and lit as far as the Cleddau bridge. Milford Dock ldg lts 348°, both FG, with W○ daymarks. Dock entry sigs on E side of lock: 2 FG (vert) = gates open, vessels may enter. Exit sigs are given via VHF Ch 14. VHF is normally used for ent/exit by day and night.

RADIO TELEPHONE Within the Haven keep a listening watch on Ch 12. Port Authority: *Milford Haven Port Control*, Ch **12** 11 14 16 (H24); 09 10 67. *Milford Haven Patrol* launches, Ch 11 12 (H24). To lock into Milford Marina first call *Milford Pier Head* Ch **14** for instructions (for lock hrs see Facilities); then call *Milford Marina* Ch M for a berth. Neyland Yacht Haven Ch **80,** M.
Broadcasts: Local forecasts on Ch 12 14 at 0300, 0900, 1500 and 2100 (all UT). Nav warnings follow on Ch14. Gale warnings issued on receipt Ch 12 14. Expected shipping movements for next 24 hours on Ch 12, 0800–0830, 2000–2030LT and on request. Tide hts and winds on request. Bcsts on Ch 16 67 at 0335 then every 4 hrs to 2335

TELEPHONE (Dial code 01646) Lock 696310; Port Ctrl 696100, 📠 696125; MRSC 690909; ⊜ 622777 (H24); Marinecall 09068 500 459; Police (01437) 763355; Ⓗ Haverfordwest (01437) 764545; Dr 690674.

FACILITIES Marinas/ Berthing (from seaward):
Dale Bay V, FW, R, Slip, Pontoon, YC.
Milford Haven Port Authority jetty ☎ 696133 (occas use by visitors with approval from Hr Mr), AB, FW.
Milford Marina (258) ☎ 696312, 📠 696314, Pierhead☎ 696310; £1.05 for 10m LOA. VHF Ch M. Lock hrs: ent HW–4, exit –3½, free flow HW –2¼ to HW–¼, ent +1½, exit +1¾, ent +2¾, exit +3¼; waiting pontoon or shelter in lock, 3·5m water at MLWS. FW, D, AC, C, BH (10 ton), CH, El, ME, Sh, Ⓔ, Gas, Gaz, V, R, Bar, Ice, ▣, ♿, ✉, Ⓑ.
Neyland Yacht Haven (360 inc Ⓥ) ☎ 601601, 📠 600713, £1.34, FW, D, AC, CH, Ⓔ, Gas, Gaz, ▣, C (20 ton), SM, SC, ME, El, Sh, R, V; Access lower basin H24, upper basin HW±3½ (sill + depth gauges and R/G lit perches);
Lawrenny Yacht Station (100) ☎ 651212/651065, ⚓ £5, L, FW, BY, CH, D, P, Sh, C (15 ton), ME, Slip, ▣, Bar, R, V, ♿, ✉, Gas.
Services: All marine services available; check with Hr Mr, marinas or YC/SC. **Dale Sailing Co** (@ Neyland), BY, CH, ME, Sh, D, LPG, BH (35T). **East Llannion Marine**: access HW±3, Slip, scrubbing piles, BH (30 ton), fuel. **Rudder's BY**, small but useful, is just upstream of Burton Pt.
Yacht Clubs: Dale YC ☎ 636362; Pembrokeshire YC ☎ 692799; Neyland YC ☎ 600267; Pembroke Haven YC ☎ 684403; Lawrenny YC ☎ 651212.
Towns: Milford Haven, EC Thurs; ✉, Ⓑ, ⇌. Pembroke Dock, EC Wed; ✉, Ⓑ, ⇌, Ⓗ. Neyland, EC Wed; ✉, Ⓑ. Haverfordwest, EC Thurs; ✉, Ⓗ, Ⓑ, ⇌, ✈ (Swansea or Cardiff). Ferry: Pembroke Dock–Rosslare.

SMALL BOAT PASSAGES The following small boat passages, suitable for dinghies, canoes etc, are in operation in the port of Milford Haven in the following positions:

Herbrandston Jetty	51°42'·32N	05°04'·70W approx
Elf Jetty	51°42'·29N	05°03'·72W approx
Texaco West end	51°41'·76N	05°03'·06W approx
Texaco Jetty centre	51°41'·83N	05°02'·25W approx
Texaco East end	51°41'·82N	05°01'·69W approx

All the above small boat passages exhibit all round fixed yellow lights at night and are marked by day with high visibility orange on the jetty legs. The maximum headroom above MHWS for the small boat passages are:

Herbrandston	3.40m	Texaco Centre	3.35m
Elf	2.78m	Texaco East	4.60m
Texaco West	4.36m		

WGS SHIFT Since so many yachts use GPS receivers for navigation, it is important to realise that care should be taken in plotting the instrument reading directly on the chart. Some British Admiralty and foreign charts now have a WGS84 base but most still have Ordnance Survey or appropriate foreign bases. It is important therefore to read the title of the chart in use to check the base and to plot any GPS readings in conformity. A number of sections in editions of the Macmillan Reeds range of almanacs have been converted to WGS84 - generally in line with the British Hydrographic Office's chart conversion programme - these are clearly marked at the head of each page. For example:

GPS reading	50°20'·00N	04°08'·00W
WGS shift	00'·03S	00'·07E
Position applied to chart	50°19'·97N	04°07'·93W

The usual rule applies, viz **add** similar headings, **subtract** dissimilar ones. At first sight this may seem academic but failure to apply the shift may easily give a plotted position on the wrong side of a narrow passage.

MILFORD HAVEN *continued*

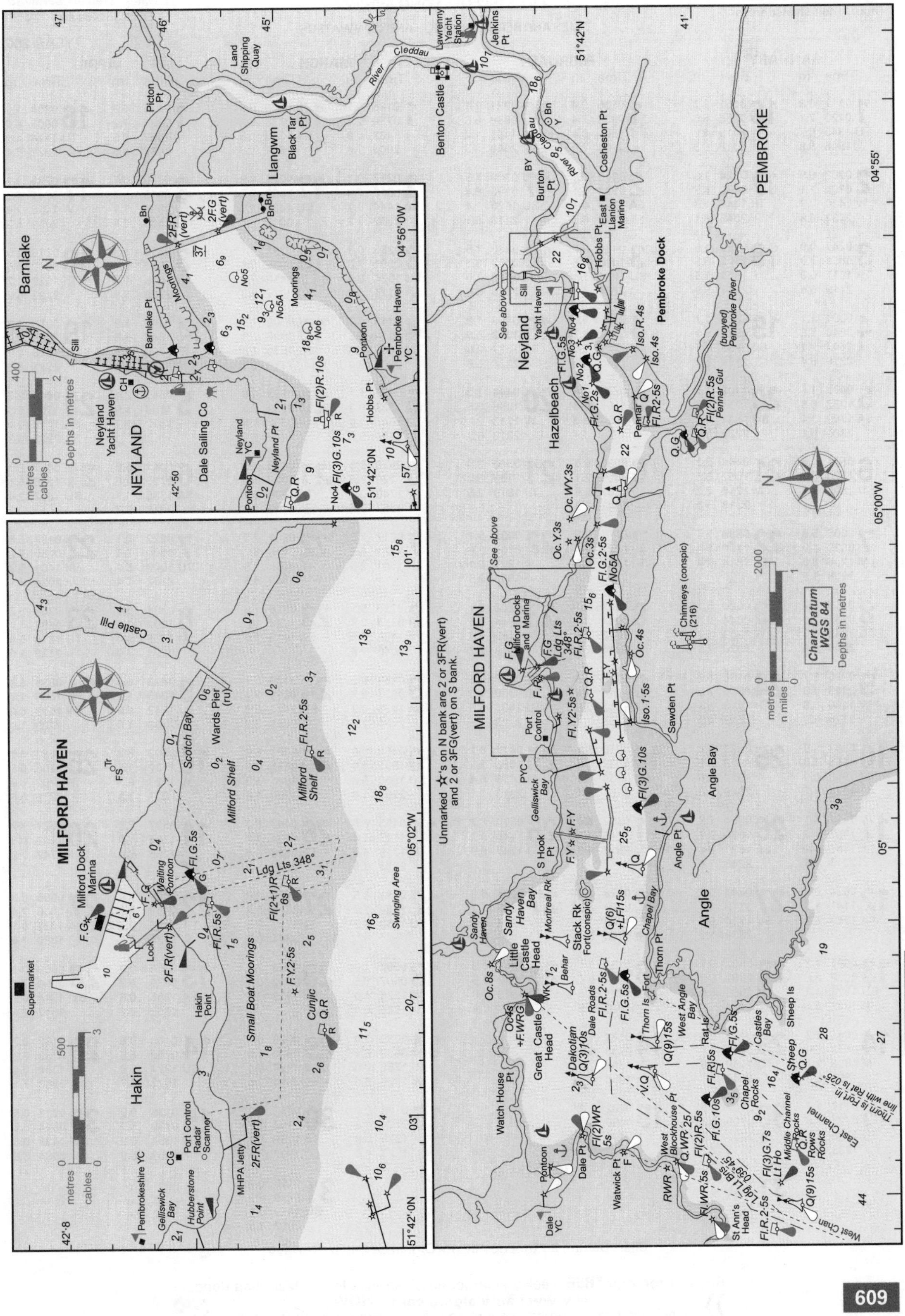

TIME ZONE (UTC)
For Summer Time add ONE hour in **non-shaded areas**

WALES – MILFORD HAVEN

LAT 51°42′N LONG 5°03′W

TIMES AND HEIGHTS OF HIGH AND LOW WATERS

SPRING & NEAP TIDES
Dates in red are SPRINGS
Dates in blue are NEAPS

YEAR **2002**

JANUARY

Date	Day	Time	m	Time	m	Time	m	Time	m
1	TU	0117	0.8	0720	7.1	1345	0.7	1946	6.9
2	W	0202	0.8	0804	7.1	1430	0.7	2032	6.8
3	TH	0247	0.9	0851	7.0	1517	0.9	2119	6.6
4	F	0334	1.1	0940	6.8	1607	1.1	2210	6.4
5	SA	0425	1.4	1032	6.5	1700	1.4	2305	6.1
6	SU	0521	1.6	1130	6.2	1800	1.7		
7	M	0006	5.8	0625	1.9	1235	6.0	1908	1.9
8	TU	0115	5.7	0737	2.0	1345	5.8	2020	1.9
9	W	0226	5.7	0849	1.9	1456	5.8	2128	1.8
10	TH	0332	5.9	0955	1.8	1600	6.0	2227	1.7
11	F	0430	6.1	1052	1.5	1655	6.1	2317	1.5
12	SA	0520	6.3	1141	1.3	1743	6.3		
13	SU	0001	1.3	0603	6.5	1224	1.2	● 1825	6.4
14	M	0041	1.2	0643	6.6	1303	1.1	1903	6.4
15	TU	0117	1.2	0721	6.6	1339	1.1	1939	6.4
16	W	0151	1.2	0756	6.6	1413	1.2	2013	6.3
17	TH	0224	1.3	0829	6.5	1446	1.3	2045	6.1
18	F	0255	1.5	0902	6.3	1519	1.5	2117	5.9
19	SA	0327	1.7	0937	6.1	1553	1.7	2152	5.7
20	SU	0402	1.9	1014	5.9	1631	2.0	2230	5.5
21	M	0444	2.2	1057	5.6	1716	2.2	2318	5.3
22	TU	0536	2.4	1150	5.4	1814	2.4		
23	W	0020	5.1	0644	2.6	1259	5.2	1926	2.5
24	TH	0136	5.1	0806	2.5	1413	5.3	2043	2.3
25	F	0251	5.4	0920	2.2	1522	5.6	2148	2.0
26	SA	0354	5.8	1020	1.8	1621	6.0	2243	1.6
27	SU	0447	6.3	1113	1.3	1714	6.4	2333	1.1
28	M	0537	6.7	1202	0.9	1803	6.8	○	
29	TU	0021	0.8	0623	7.1	1250	0.6	1849	7.1
30	W	0107	0.5	0709	7.3	1335	0.3	1935	7.2
31	TH	0152	0.4	0754	7.4	1420	0.3	2020	7.2

FEBRUARY

Date	Day	Time	m	Time	m	Time	m	Time	m
1	F	0236	0.4	0838	7.4	1504	0.4	2104	7.0
2	SA	0320	0.6	0924	7.1	1548	0.7	2149	6.7
3	SU	0404	0.9	1010	6.8	1634	1.1	2237	6.3
4	M	0452	1.3	1100	6.3	1723	1.6	2330	5.9
5	TU	0547	1.8	1157	5.8	1824	2.0		
6	W	0033	5.5	0656	2.1	1307	5.5	1941	2.3
7	TH	0151	5.3	0821	2.3	1429	5.3	2104	2.3
8	F	0312	5.4	0941	2.1	1547	5.5	2214	2.0
9	SA	0418	5.8	1044	1.8	1647	5.8	2308	1.7
10	SU	0510	6.1	1133	1.5	1734	6.0	2351	1.4
11	M	0552	6.4	1213	1.3	1813	6.3		
12	TU	0028	1.2	0629	6.5	1249	1.1	● 1848	6.4
13	W	0101	1.1	0704	6.6	1321	1.0	1920	6.5
14	TH	0132	1.0	0735	6.7	1352	1.0	1950	6.4
15	F	0202	1.0	0806	6.6	1421	1.0	2019	6.4
16	SA	0231	1.1	0836	6.6	1451	1.2	2048	6.3
17	SU	0300	1.3	0906	6.4	1520	1.4	2118	6.1
18	M	0330	1.5	0937	6.1	1552	1.6	2150	5.8
19	TU	0403	1.8	1012	5.9	1627	2.0	2228	5.6
20	W	0444	2.2	1056	5.5	1713	2.3	2318	5.3
21	TH	0540	2.5	1156	5.2	1819	2.5		
22	F	0032	5.1	0706	2.6	1321	5.1	1953	2.5
23	SA	0206	5.1	0844	2.4	1450	5.3	2119	2.2
24	SU	0327	5.6	0958	1.9	1601	5.8	2223	1.7
25	M	0428	6.1	1056	1.3	1658	6.4	2316	1.1
26	TU	0520	6.7	1146	0.7	1747	6.9		
27	W	0005	0.6	0607	7.2	1234	0.3	○ 1833	7.2
28	TH	0051	0.3	0652	7.5	1319	0.0	1917	7.4

MARCH

Date	Day	Time	m	Time	m	Time	m	Time	m
1	F	0135	0.1	0736	7.7	1402	0.0	2000	7.4
2	SA	0217	0.1	0819	7.6	1444	0.1	2042	7.3
3	SU	0259	0.3	0901	7.3	1524	0.5	2124	6.9
4	M	0340	0.7	0944	6.8	1604	1.0	2207	6.4
5	TU	0422	1.2	1028	6.3	1647	1.6	2254	5.9
6	W	0510	1.8	1120	5.6	1740	2.2	2353	5.4
7	TH	0617	2.3	1229	5.1	1901	2.5		
8	F	0115	5.1	0754	2.5	1405	4.9	2043	2.6
9	SA	0253	5.2	0927	2.3	1535	5.2	2200	2.2
10	SU	0403	5.6	1031	1.9	1633	5.6	2253	1.8
11	M	0453	6.0	1117	1.5	1716	5.9	2333	1.5
12	TU	0533	6.3	1154	1.2	1753	6.2		
13	W	0007	1.2	0607	6.5	1226	1.0	1825	6.4
14	TH	0039	1.0	0639	6.7	1256	0.9	● 1855	6.5
15	F	0108	0.9	0709	6.8	1325	0.8	1923	6.6
16	SA	0136	0.9	0738	6.8	1353	0.8	1951	6.6
17	SU	0204	0.9	0807	6.7	1422	1.0	2019	6.5
18	M	0233	1.1	0836	6.5	1450	1.2	2047	6.3
19	TU	0302	1.3	0906	6.3	1519	1.5	2118	6.1
20	W	0333	1.6	0939	6.0	1552	1.8	2153	5.8
21	TH	0410	2.0	1020	5.6	1633	2.2	2240	5.4
22	F	0502	2.3	1116	5.2	1735	2.5	2349	5.1
23	SA	0626	2.6	1244	5.0	1915	2.6		
24	SU	0130	5.1	0815	2.4	1424	5.2	2052	2.2
25	M	0301	5.6	0935	1.8	1541	5.8	2200	1.6
26	TU	0406	6.2	1034	1.2	1638	6.4	2255	1.0
27	W	0459	6.8	1126	0.6	1727	6.9	2344	0.5
28	TH	0546	7.3	1212	0.2	1812	7.3	○	
29	F	0029	0.1	0630	7.6	1257	-0.1	1855	7.5
30	SA	0113	0.0	0714	7.7	1339	-0.1	1937	7.5
31	SU	0155	0.0	0756	7.5	1419	0.1	2017	7.3

APRIL

Date	Day	Time	m	Time	m	Time	m	Time	m
1	M	0235	0.3	0837	7.2	1457	0.5	2057	6.9
2	TU	0315	0.7	0918	6.7	1535	1.1	2138	6.4
3	W	0355	1.3	1000	6.1	1615	1.7	2223	5.9
4	TH	0442	1.9	1049	5.5	1704	2.3	2319	5.3
5	F	0545	2.4	1156	4.9	1822	2.7		
6	SA	0041	5.0	0725	2.6	1335	4.7	2012	2.7
7	SU	0222	5.1	0900	2.4	1509	5.0	2132	2.4
8	M	0334	5.4	1002	2.0	1606	5.4	2224	1.9
9	TU	0423	5.9	1046	1.6	1647	5.9	2303	1.6
10	W	0503	6.2	1122	1.3	1723	6.2	2337	1.3
11	TH	0537	6.5	1154	1.0	1755	6.4		
12	F	0008	1.0	0609	6.6	1225	0.9	● 1824	6.6
13	SA	0038	0.9	0639	6.7	1255	0.8	1853	6.7
14	SU	0108	0.8	0709	6.8	1324	0.8	1922	6.7
15	M	0138	0.9	0739	6.7	1354	0.9	1951	6.6
16	TU	0208	1.0	0809	6.6	1424	1.1	2021	6.4
17	W	0239	1.2	0841	6.3	1455	1.4	2054	6.2
18	TH	0313	1.5	0917	6.0	1529	1.7	2132	5.9
19	F	0353	1.9	1001	5.7	1613	2.1	2221	5.6
20	SA	0448	2.2	1100	5.3	1718	2.4	2332	5.3
21	SU	0611	2.3	1226	5.1	1852	2.4		
22	M	0107	5.3	0750	2.2	1401	5.3	2024	2.1
23	TU	0233	5.7	0907	1.7	1515	5.8	2133	1.6
24	W	0339	6.3	1008	1.1	1612	6.4	2229	1.0
25	TH	0433	6.8	1100	0.6	1702	6.9	2319	0.6
26	F	0521	7.2	1147	0.3	1747	7.2		
27	SA	0005	0.3	0606	7.4	1232	0.1	○ 1830	7.4
28	SU	0050	0.1	0650	7.4	1314	0.2	1912	7.4
29	M	0132	0.2	0733	7.3	1354	0.4	1953	7.1
30	TU	0213	0.5	0814	6.9	1433	0.8	2034	6.8

Chart Datum: 3·71 metres below Ordnance Datum (Newlyn)

TIME ZONE (UTC)
For Summer Time add ONE hour in **non-shaded areas**

WALES – MILFORD HAVEN

LAT 51°42'N LONG 5°03'W

TIMES AND HEIGHTS OF HIGH AND LOW WATERS

SPRING & NEAP TIDES
Dates in **red** are **SPRINGS**
Dates in **blue** are **NEAPS**

YEAR **2002**

MAY

Date	Day	Time	m	Time	m	Time	m	Time	m
1	W	0254	0.9	0855	6.4	1511	1.3	2115	6.3
2	TH	0335	1.4	0937	5.9	1550	1.8	2159	5.9
3	F	0420	1.9	1025	5.4	1637	2.3	2252	5.4
4	SA	0520	2.3	1126	5.0	1745	2.6		
5	SU	0004	5.1	0644	2.5	1250	4.8	1921	2.7
6	M	0132	5.1	0810	2.4	1420	4.9	2041	2.5
7	TU	0247	5.3	0914	2.1	1522	5.3	2138	2.1
8	W	0341	5.7	1002	1.8	1607	5.7	2222	1.8
9	TH	0423	6.0	1041	1.5	1645	6.0	2259	1.5
10	F	0500	6.3	1117	1.2	1719	6.3	2334	1.2
11	SA	0535	6.5	1150	1.1	1751	6.5		
12	SU ●	0007	1.1	0607	6.6	1224	1.0	1823	6.6
13	M	0041	1.0	0640	6.7	1257	0.9	1855	6.7
14	TU	0114	1.0	0714	6.6	1330	1.0	1928	6.6
15	W	0149	1.0	0749	6.5	1404	1.1	2003	6.5
16	TH	0225	1.2	0826	6.3	1440	1.3	2041	6.3
17	F	0304	1.4	0907	6.1	1520	1.6	2124	6.1
18	SA	0349	1.7	0955	5.8	1609	1.9	2218	5.8
19	SU	0447	1.9	1057	5.5	1714	2.1	2326	5.6
20	M	0601	2.0	1213	5.4	1834	2.1		
21	TU	0046	5.7	0723	1.9	1333	5.6	1953	1.9
22	W	0203	5.9	0836	1.6	1444	5.9	2101	1.5
23	TH	0308	6.3	0938	1.2	1543	6.3	2200	1.2
24	F	0405	6.6	1032	0.9	1635	6.7	2253	0.8
25	SA	0456	6.9	1121	0.6	1723	6.9	2341	0.6
26	SU ○	0544	7.0	1207	0.5	1808	7.1		
27	M	0027	0.5	0629	7.0	1251	0.6	1851	7.0
28	TU	0112	0.6	0713	6.9	1332	0.7	1933	6.9
29	W	0155	0.8	0755	6.6	1412	1.0	2015	6.6
30	TH	0237	1.1	0837	6.2	1452	1.4	2056	6.3
31	F	0318	1.4	0919	5.9	1531	1.8	2139	5.9

JUNE

Date	Day	Time	m	Time	m	Time	m	Time	m
1	SA	0402	1.8	1003	5.5	1614	2.1	2227	5.6
2	SU	0451	2.1	1054	5.1	1707	2.4	2324	5.3
3	M	0553	2.4	1157	4.9	1817	2.6		
4	TU	0032	5.2	0704	2.4	1311	4.9	1933	2.5
5	W	0143	5.3	0811	2.3	1420	5.1	2038	2.3
6	TH	0245	5.5	0907	2.0	1515	5.4	2131	2.0
7	F	0335	5.8	0954	1.8	1601	5.8	2217	1.8
8	SA	0419	6.0	1037	1.5	1641	6.1	2258	1.5
9	SU	0459	6.2	1116	1.3	1719	6.3	2338	1.3
10	M ●	0538	6.4	1154	1.2	1756	6.5		
11	TU	0016	1.1	0616	6.5	1233	1.1	1833	6.6
12	W	0056	1.1	0655	6.6	1312	1.0	1912	6.7
13	TH	0135	1.0	0735	6.5	1351	1.1	1952	6.6
14	F	0217	1.1	0818	6.4	1432	1.2	2035	6.5
15	SA	0300	1.2	0903	6.3	1517	1.4	2122	6.4
16	SU	0348	1.3	0953	6.1	1607	1.6	2215	6.2
17	M	0443	1.5	1050	5.9	1705	1.7	2315	6.1
18	TU	0545	1.6	1153	5.8	1810	1.8		
19	W	0021	6.0	0653	1.7	1303	5.7	1921	1.8
20	TH	0131	6.0	0802	1.6	1411	5.9	2029	1.7
21	F	0238	6.1	0907	1.5	1514	6.1	2133	1.5
22	SA	0339	6.3	1006	1.3	1611	6.3	2231	1.2
23	SU	0436	6.4	1100	1.1	1703	6.5	2323	1.1
24	M ○	0527	6.5	1148	1.0	1752	6.7		
25	TU	0012	1.0	0615	6.6	1234	1.0	1836	6.7
26	W	0058	0.9	0659	6.5	1316	1.0	1919	6.7
27	TH	0141	1.0	0741	6.4	1356	1.2	2000	6.5
28	F	0221	1.2	0821	6.2	1434	1.4	2039	6.4
29	SA	0300	1.4	0859	6.0	1511	1.6	2118	6.1
30	SU	0338	1.6	0937	5.7	1548	1.9	2158	5.9

JULY

Date	Day	Time	m	Time	m	Time	m	Time	m
1	M	0418	1.9	1018	5.5	1628	2.1	2242	5.7
2	TU	0502	2.1	1104	5.2	1716	2.3	2333	5.5
3	W	0555	2.3	1200	5.1	1817	2.5		
4	TH	0033	5.3	0657	2.4	1306	5.1	1926	2.5
5	F	0138	5.3	0803	2.3	1413	5.2	2035	2.4
6	SA	0241	5.4	0904	2.1	1513	5.5	2134	2.1
7	SU	0337	5.7	0958	1.9	1604	5.8	2225	1.8
8	M	0427	5.9	1046	1.6	1650	6.1	2312	1.5
9	TU	0513	6.2	1131	1.4	1734	6.4	2357	1.3
10	W ●	0557	6.4	1214	1.1	1817	6.6		
11	TH	0041	1.0	0641	6.6	1258	1.0	1900	6.8
12	F	0125	0.9	0725	6.7	1341	0.9	1943	6.9
13	SA	0209	0.8	0809	6.7	1425	0.9	2028	6.9
14	SU	0254	0.8	0855	6.7	1509	1.0	2114	6.8
15	M	0340	0.9	0942	6.5	1556	1.1	2202	6.7
16	TU	0428	1.2	1032	6.3	1646	1.4	2255	6.4
17	W	0521	1.4	1127	6.0	1743	1.6	2353	6.1
18	TH	0620	1.7	1230	5.8	1848	1.8		
19	F	0058	5.9	0728	1.9	1339	5.7	2000	1.9
20	SA	0210	5.8	0841	1.9	1450	5.8	2113	1.9
21	SU	0321	5.8	0949	1.8	1556	6.0	2218	1.7
22	M	0425	6.0	1047	1.6	1653	6.2	2315	1.4
23	TU	0519	6.1	1138	1.4	1742	6.4		
24	W ○	0004	1.3	0606	6.3	1222	1.2	1825	6.6
25	TH	0047	1.1	0648	6.4	1302	1.2	1905	6.6
26	F	0126	1.1	0726	6.4	1339	1.2	1943	6.6
27	SA	0202	1.1	0801	6.3	1413	1.3	2018	6.5
28	SU	0236	1.2	0834	6.2	1445	1.4	2051	6.4
29	M	0309	1.4	0907	6.0	1517	1.6	2125	6.2
30	TU	0341	1.6	0940	5.8	1550	1.8	2200	6.0
31	W	0416	1.9	1016	5.6	1627	2.1	2240	5.7

AUGUST

Date	Day	Time	m	Time	m	Time	m	Time	m
1	TH	0457	2.1	1058	5.3	1713	2.3	2328	5.4
2	F	0548	2.4	1153	5.1	1815	2.6		
3	SA	0029	5.2	0654	2.5	1305	5.1	1934	2.6
4	SU	0144	5.2	0813	2.5	1424	5.2	2055	2.4
5	M	0258	5.3	0924	2.2	1532	5.5	2159	2.1
6	TU	0401	5.7	1021	1.9	1627	6.0	2252	1.6
7	W	0454	6.1	1111	1.4	1716	6.4	2340	1.2
8	TH ●	0541	6.5	1158	1.1	1801	6.8		
9	F	0026	0.8	0627	6.8	1243	0.8	1845	7.1
10	SA	0111	0.6	0711	7.1	1327	0.6	1929	7.3
11	SU	0155	0.4	0755	7.1	1411	0.5	2013	7.4
12	M	0239	0.4	0838	7.1	1454	0.6	2057	7.2
13	TU	0321	0.6	0922	6.9	1537	0.8	2142	7.0
14	W	0405	1.0	1008	6.5	1622	1.2	2229	6.5
15	TH	0451	1.4	1058	6.1	1713	1.6	2323	6.1
16	F	0546	1.9	1156	5.7	1816	2.1		
17	SA	0027	5.6	0656	2.2	1309	5.4	1938	2.3
18	SU	0148	5.4	0823	2.3	1434	5.4	2105	2.2
19	M	0313	5.4	0942	2.2	1549	5.7	2216	1.9
20	TU	0421	5.7	1042	1.8	1646	6.1	2311	1.6
21	W	0512	6.0	1130	1.5	1732	6.4	2355	1.3
22	TH ○	0555	6.3	1210	1.3	1812	6.6		
23	F	0032	1.1	0631	6.4	1245	1.2	1847	6.7
24	SA	0106	1.0	0705	6.5	1317	1.1	1920	6.7
25	SU	0137	1.0	0736	6.5	1347	1.1	1951	6.7
26	M	0207	1.1	0805	6.4	1416	1.2	2021	6.6
27	TU	0236	1.2	0834	6.3	1445	1.4	2051	6.4
28	W	0305	1.4	0903	6.1	1514	1.6	2121	6.2
29	TH	0336	1.7	0934	5.9	1546	1.9	2155	5.9
30	F	0409	2.0	1009	5.6	1624	2.3	2234	5.5
31	SA	0451	2.4	1054	5.3	1717	2.6	2329	5.2

Chart Datum: 3·71 metres below Ordnance Datum (Newlyn)

TIME ZONE (UTC)
For Summer Time add ONE hour in **non-shaded areas**

WALES – MILFORD HAVEN

LAT 51°42′N LONG 5°03′W

TIMES AND HEIGHTS OF HIGH AND LOW WATERS

SPRING & NEAP TIDES
Dates in red are **SPRINGS**
Dates in blue are **NEAPS**

YEAR **2002**

SEPTEMBER

Date	Day	Time	m	Time	m	Time	m	Time	m	Phase
1	SU	0551	2.7	1201	5.0	1838	2.8			
2	M	0050	5.0	0724	2.8	1339	5.0	2022	2.7	
3	TU	0226	5.1	0855	2.5	1505	5.4	2137	2.2	
4	W	0340	5.6	1000	2.0	1607	6.0	2233	1.6	
5	TH	0435	6.2	1052	1.4	1657	6.6	2322	1.0	
6	F	0523	6.7	1139	0.9	1742	7.1			
7	SA	0008	0.6	0608	7.1	1224	0.5	1826	7.5	●
8	SU	0052	0.2	0651	7.4	1308	0.3	1909	7.7	
9	M	0135	0.1	0734	7.5	1350	0.2	1952	7.7	
10	TU	0217	0.2	0816	7.4	1432	0.4	2034	7.4	
11	W	0258	0.5	0858	7.1	1514	0.7	2117	7.0	
12	TH	0338	1.0	0941	6.6	1557	1.2	2202	6.5	
13	F	0421	1.5	1028	6.1	1645	1.8	2253	5.9	
14	SA	0512	2.1	1125	5.6	1749	2.3	2359	5.3	
15	SU	0628	2.6	1244	5.2	1925	2.6			
16	M	0131	5.0	0812	2.7	1423	5.3	2102	2.4	
17	TU	0309	5.2	0936	2.4	1540	5.6	2211	2.0	
18	W	0412	5.6	1033	1.9	1632	6.1	2259	1.6	
19	TH	0457	6.0	1115	1.6	1714	6.4	2337	1.3	
20	F	0535	6.3	1150	1.3	1750	6.7			
21	SA	0009	1.1	0607	6.5	1221	1.1	1822	6.8	○
22	SU	0039	1.0	0638	6.6	1250	1.0	1852	6.9	
23	M	0108	1.0	0707	6.7	1318	1.0	1921	6.8	
24	TU	0136	1.0	0734	6.6	1346	1.1	1950	6.8	
25	W	0204	1.1	0802	6.5	1415	1.2	2018	6.6	
26	TH	0232	1.3	0830	6.3	1444	1.5	2048	6.3	
27	F	0301	1.6	0859	6.1	1514	1.8	2119	6.0	
28	SA	0332	2.0	0933	5.8	1549	2.2	2157	5.6	
29	SU	0409	2.4	1015	5.4	1638	2.6	2248	5.2	
30	M	0507	2.7	1119	5.1	1759	2.8			

OCTOBER

Date	Day	Time	m	Time	m	Time	m	Time	m	Phase
1	TU	0012	4.9	0645	2.9	1302	5.1	1954	2.7	
2	W	0159	5.1	0828	2.5	1438	5.5	2113	2.2	
3	TH	0317	5.6	0936	2.0	1542	6.1	2210	1.5	
4	F	0413	6.3	1029	1.3	1633	6.8	2259	0.9	
5	SA	0501	6.9	1116	0.8	1719	7.3	2345	0.4	
6	SU	0545	7.3	1201	0.4	1804	7.6			●
7	M	0029	0.1	0628	7.6	1245	0.2	1846	7.8	
8	TU	0112	0.1	0710	7.6	1328	0.2	1929	7.7	
9	W	0153	0.2	0752	7.5	1410	0.4	2011	7.4	
10	TH	0233	0.6	0833	7.1	1451	0.8	2054	6.9	
11	F	0313	1.1	0915	6.6	1534	1.3	2138	6.3	
12	SA	0355	1.7	1002	6.1	1622	1.9	2228	5.7	
13	SU	0445	2.3	1059	5.5	1728	2.5	2334	5.1	
14	M	0602	2.8	1218	5.2	1908	2.7			
15	TU	0111	4.9	0752	2.8	1400	5.2	2044	2.5	
16	W	0249	5.1	0914	2.5	1515	5.6	2147	2.1	
17	TH	0348	5.5	1007	2.1	1605	6.0	2231	1.7	
18	F	0431	6.0	1047	1.7	1645	6.4	2307	1.4	
19	SA	0506	6.3	1121	1.4	1720	6.6	2338	1.2	
20	SU	0538	6.5	1151	1.2	1753	6.8			
21	M	0008	1.0	0608	6.7	1221	1.1	1823	6.8	○
22	TU	0038	1.0	0637	6.7	1250	1.0	1852	6.8	
23	W	0106	1.0	0705	6.7	1320	1.1	1922	6.8	
24	TH	0136	1.1	0734	6.6	1350	1.2	1951	6.6	
25	F	0205	1.3	0803	6.5	1421	1.5	2022	6.3	
26	SA	0235	1.6	0835	6.2	1453	1.8	2056	6.0	
27	SU	0308	1.9	0911	5.9	1531	2.1	2136	5.7	
28	M	0349	2.3	0956	5.6	1623	2.5	2231	5.3	
29	TU	0448	2.6	1101	5.3	1741	2.6	2352	5.1	
30	W	0620	2.7	1234	5.3	1923	2.5			
31	TH	0129	5.2	0756	2.4	1404	5.6	2041	2.0	

NOVEMBER

Date	Day	Time	m	Time	m	Time	m	Time	m	Phase
1	F	0247	5.7	0906	1.9	1511	6.2	2141	1.4	
2	SA	0345	6.3	1001	1.3	1605	6.8	2232	0.9	
3	SU	0435	6.9	1051	0.8	1654	7.2	2319	0.5	
4	M	0520	7.3	1137	0.5	1740	7.5			●
5	TU	0004	0.3	0604	7.5	1223	0.3	1824	7.6	
6	W	0048	0.3	0647	7.5	1307	0.3	1908	7.5	
7	TH	0130	0.4	0730	7.4	1350	0.5	1951	7.2	
8	F	0211	0.8	0812	7.0	1433	0.9	2035	6.7	
9	SA	0252	1.3	0856	6.6	1518	1.4	2119	6.1	
10	SU	0335	1.8	0942	6.1	1606	1.9	2209	5.6	
11	M	0424	2.3	1036	5.6	1707	2.4	2309	5.1	
12	TU	0531	2.7	1146	5.3	1830	2.6			
13	W	0030	4.9	0705	2.8	1312	5.2	1956	2.5	
14	TH	0200	5.0	0826	2.6	1429	5.5	2101	2.3	
15	F	0305	5.4	0924	2.3	1524	5.8	2149	1.9	
16	SA	0352	5.7	1008	1.9	1608	6.1	2228	1.6	
17	SU	0431	6.1	1046	1.6	1646	6.4	2303	1.4	
18	M	0506	6.3	1120	1.4	1721	6.6	2336	1.2	
19	TU	0538	6.5	1153	1.2	1754	6.7			
20	W	0009	1.1	0609	6.6	1226	1.2	1826	6.7	○
21	TH	0041	1.1	0641	6.7	1259	1.2	1859	6.6	
22	F	0114	1.2	0713	6.6	1332	1.3	1932	6.5	
23	SA	0147	1.3	0746	6.5	1407	1.4	2007	6.3	
24	SU	0221	1.5	0822	6.4	1444	1.6	2046	6.1	
25	M	0259	1.8	0902	6.1	1527	1.9	2130	5.8	
26	TU	0344	2.0	0951	5.9	1619	2.1	2226	5.6	
27	W	0442	2.3	1053	5.7	1728	2.2	2337	5.4	
28	TH	0557	2.4	1209	5.7	1848	2.2			
29	F	0056	5.5	0718	2.2	1328	5.9	2003	1.9	
30	SA	0211	5.8	0830	1.9	1436	6.2	2108	1.5	

DECEMBER

Date	Day	Time	m	Time	m	Time	m	Time	m	Phase
1	SU	0313	6.2	0931	1.4	1536	6.6	2204	1.1	
2	M	0407	6.6	1025	1.1	1629	6.9	2255	0.8	
3	TU	0457	7.0	1116	0.8	1719	7.1	2343	0.7	
4	W	0544	7.2	1204	0.6	1807	7.2			●
5	TH	0028	0.6	0630	7.2	1251	0.6	1852	7.1	
6	F	0113	0.7	0714	7.1	1337	0.7	1937	6.8	
7	SA	0155	1.0	0758	6.9	1421	1.0	2021	6.5	
8	SU	0237	1.3	0841	6.6	1505	1.4	2104	6.1	
9	M	0319	1.7	0925	6.2	1550	1.8	2149	5.7	
10	TU	0403	2.1	1013	5.8	1639	2.1	2239	5.3	
11	W	0453	2.4	1106	5.5	1736	2.4	2337	5.1	
12	TH	0558	2.6	1210	5.3	1844	2.5			
13	F	0047	5.0	0712	2.7	1321	5.3	1953	2.4	
14	SA	0159	5.1	0822	2.5	1426	5.5	2052	2.2	
15	SU	0300	5.4	0919	2.3	1522	5.7	2143	2.0	
16	M	0349	5.7	1006	2.0	1608	6.0	2226	1.7	
17	TU	0432	6.0	1049	1.7	1650	6.2	2306	1.5	
18	W	0510	6.2	1128	1.5	1729	6.3	2344	1.4	
19	TH	0547	6.4	1206	1.3	1806	6.5			○
20	F	0021	1.3	0622	6.6	1244	1.2	1843	6.5	
21	SA	0058	1.2	0659	6.6	1321	1.2	1921	6.5	
22	SU	0135	1.2	0736	6.6	1400	1.2	2000	6.5	
23	M	0214	1.3	0816	6.6	1440	1.3	2041	6.4	
24	TU	0255	1.4	0859	6.5	1524	1.4	2127	6.2	
25	W	0340	1.6	0946	6.3	1612	1.6	2217	6.0	
26	TH	0431	1.7	1040	6.2	1708	1.7	2315	5.8	
27	F	0531	1.9	1142	6.0	1812	1.8			
28	SA	0021	5.7	0639	2.0	1251	6.0	1922	1.8	
29	SU	0132	5.8	0751	1.9	1401	6.0	2033	1.7	
30	M	0240	6.0	0901	1.7	1508	6.2	2138	1.5	
31	TU	0343	6.2	1005	1.4	1610	6.4	2236	1.3	

Chart Datum: 3·71 metres below Ordnance Datum (Newlyn)

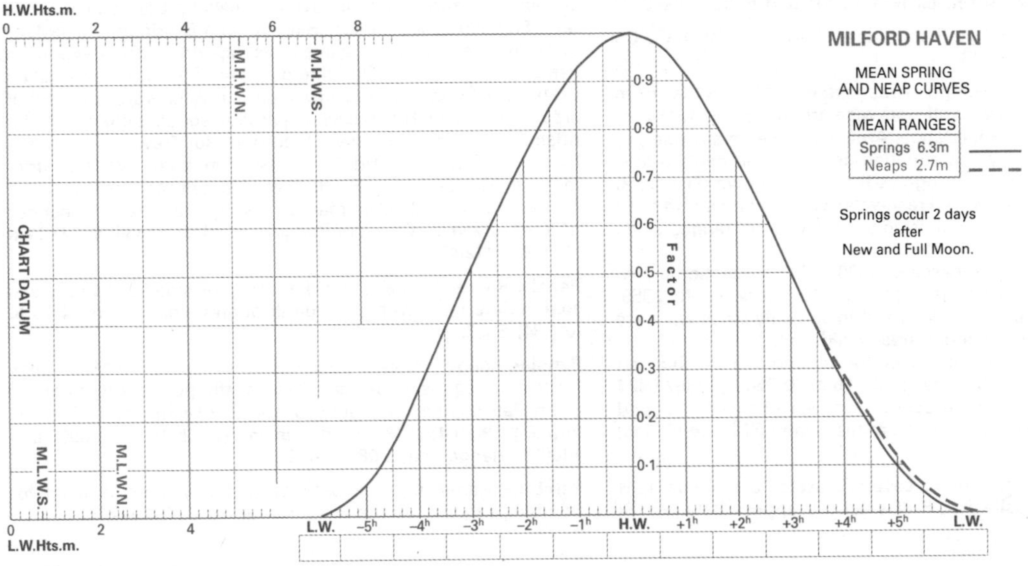

TENBY *9.11.15*

Pembrokeshire **51·40'·42N 04°41'·93W** ❁❁◊◊✿✿✿

CHARTS AC 1482, *1076, 1179;* Imray C60; Stanfords 14; OS 158

TIDES –0510 Dover; ML 4·5; Duration 0610; Zone 0 (UT)

Standard Port MILFORD HAVEN (⟵)

Times				**Height (metres)**			
High Water		Low Water		MHWS	MHWN	MLWN	MLWS
0100	0800	0100	0700	7·0	5·2	2·5	0·7
1300	2000	1300	1900				
Differences TENBY							
–0015	–0010	–0015	–0020	+1·4	+1·1	+0·5	+0·2
STACKPOLE QUAY (7M W of Caldey Island)							
–0005	+0025	–0010	–0010	+0·9	+0·7	+0·2	+0·3

SHELTER Good, but hbr dries up to 5m; access HW±2½. Sheltered ⚓s, depending on wind direction, to NE in Tenby Roads, in Lydstep Haven (2·5M SW), and around Caldey Island as follows:

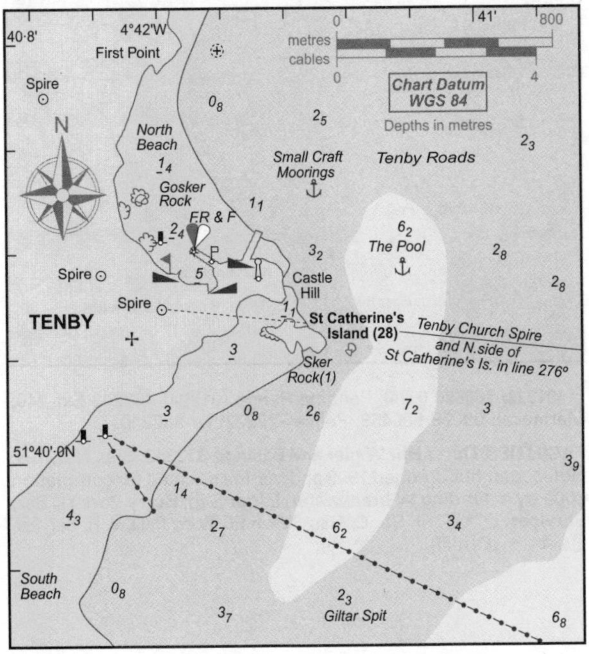

Priory Bay (shallow, to the N), Jone's Bay (NE), Drinkim Bay (E) or Sandtop Bay (W). Also at Saundersfoot about 2M to the N; see below.

NAVIGATION WPT 51°40´·02N 04°38´·08W, 099°/279° from/to monument on Castle Hill, 2·2M. The ⊕ WPT (off chartlet) is 2ca W of DZ2 SPM buoy, Fl Y 2·5s. Beware Woolhouse Rks (3·6m) 1·5M SExE of the hbr, marked by unlit SCM buoy; and Sker Rk (1m high) closer in off St Catherine's Island (28m). From the W, Caldey Sound is navigable with care by day between Eel Pt SHM and Giltar Spit PHM unlit buoys. Approaching Tenby Roads, keep outside the line of mooring buoys. For adjacent Firing ranges, see overleaf.

LIGHTS AND MARKS Church spire and N side of St Catherine's Is in line at 276°. FR 7m 7M on pier hd. Inside hbr, FW 6m 1M marks landing. PHM beacon (unlit) marks outcrop from Gosker Rk on beach close N of hbr ent. Hbr is floodlit.

RADIO TELEPHONE VHF Ch 16 80 (listening during HO).

TELEPHONE (Dial code 01834) Hr Mr 842717 (end May-end Sept), Mobile 07977 609947; MRSC (01646) 690909; ⊖ (01222) 763880 (H24); Marinecall 09068 500459; Police 842303; Dr 844161; Ⓗ 842040.

FACILITIES **Hbr** ☎/📠 842717, Slip (up to 4·2m), L, AB, Sh, FW; **Tenby YC** ☎ 842762; **Town** EC Wed; P & D (cans), ▣, CH, V, R, Bar, Gas, ✉, Ⓑ, ⇌, ✈ (Swansea; and a small airfield at Haverfordwest).

OTHER ADJACENT HARBOURS

SAUNDERSFOOT, Pembrokeshire, **51°42´·60N 04°41´·76W.** AC 1482, 1076, *1179.* HW –0510 on Dover; ML 4·4m; Duration 0605. See 9.11.15. A half-tide hbr with good shelter, but there may be a surge in prolonged E winds. On appr, beware buoys marking restricted area (power boats, etc) between Coppett Hall Pt and Perry's Pt. AB may be available (see Hr Mr), or moorings in the middle. Pier hd lt Fl R 5s 6m 7M on stone cupola. VHF: Hr Mr 11 16. Hr Mr ☎/📠 (01834) 812094/(Home 813782). Facilities: CH, FW (on SW wall), Slip, P & D (cans), ME, BH. **Town** EC Wed; V, R, Bar, ✉, Ⓑ, ⇌ (Tenby/Saundersfoot).

CARMARTHEN, Carmarthenshire, **51°46´·27N 04°22´·53W.** AC 1076, *1179.* HW –0455 on Dover. See 9.11.16. R Towy & Taf dry; access HW±2. Beware Carmarthen Bar and very strong sp streams. Appr on N'ly hdg toward Wharley Pt, leaving DZ8 & 9 buoys 5ca to stbd. Local knowledge or a pilot are advised; chan shifts frequently and is unmarked. ⚓ in mid-stream or Ⓜs at R Towy BC off Ferryside (7M below Carmarthen), access HW±3 (liable to dry). 4 power lines, min clearance 7·4m, cross in last 2·5M before Carmarthen. **R Towy BC** ☎ (01267) 267366, M, FW, Bar. **Town** Usual facilities, Ⓑ, Bar, Gas, ✉, V, ⇌, ✈ (Cardiff).

FIRING RANGES between LINNEY HEAD and BURRY INLET

For daily info on all range firing times call *Milford Haven CG* Ch 16/67 or ☎ 01646 690909.

Castlemartin Range Danger Area extends 12M WNW from Linney Hd, thence in an anti-clockwise arc to a point 12M S of St Govan's Hd. The exact Danger Area operative on any one day depends on the ranges/ammunition used; it is primarily a tank range. When firing is in progress R flags are flown (Fl R lts at night) along the coast from Freshwater West to Linney Hd to St Govan's Hd. Yachts are requested to keep clear of ranges when active.
Firing takes place on weekdays 0900 -1630, exceptionally to 1700. Night firing takes place on Mon to Thurs, up to 2359, depending on the hours of darkness. In Jan only small arms are usually fired and the danger area is reduced.
Days/times of firing are published locally and can be obtained by VHF from *Castlemartin Range* Ch 16 or ☎ 0646 662367 (H24 answering service); Range safety launches Ch 16 or 12; and Milford Haven CG Ch 16. Also from the Range Office ☎ (01646) 661321 ext 4336 .

Manorbier Range (further E) covers a sector arc radius 12M centred on Old Castle Hd; E/W extent is approx between St Govan's Hd and Caldey Is (see AC Q6402). It is usually active Mon-Fri 0900-1700LT, occas Sat/Sun, and is primarily a surface to air missile range, but active parts depend on the weapons in use on any given day. On firing days warnings are broadcast on Ch 16, 73 at 0830, 1430 and on completion; R flags are flown either side of Old Castle Hd. Yachts on passage should either stay 12M offshore or close inshore via Stackpole Hd, Trewent Pt, Priest's Nose and Old Castle Hd. Firing days/times are available from local Hr Mrs and YCs. For further info call: *Manorbier Range Control* Ch 16, 73 (also manned by Range safety launches); *Milford Haven CG* Ch 16; or Range Control ☎ (01834) 871282 ext 209, 📠 871283.

Penally Range (further E at Giltar Pt) is for small arms only and seldom interferes with passage through Caldey Sound. Info ☎ (01834) 843522.

Pendine Range (between Tenby and Burry Inlet) is a MOD range for testing explosive devices. It is usually possible to steer the rhumb line course from Tenby to Worms Hd without interference. Info ☎ (01994) 453243. Broadcasts on VHF Ch 16, 73 at 0900 and 1400LT. Range active 0800-1615.

Pembrey Range (approx 5M NW of Burry Inlet) is used for bombing practice by the RAF. Info ☎ (01554) 891224.

BURRY INLET *9.11.16*

Carmarthenshire **51°40'·52N 04°14'·93W** (Burry Port)

CHARTS AC 1167, 1076, *1179*; Imray C59, C60; Stanfords 14; OS 159

TIDES –0500 Dover; ML 4·7; Duration 0555; Zone 0 (UT)

Standard Port MILFORD HAVEN (⟵)

Times				**Height (metres)**			
High Water		Low Water		MHWS	MHWN	MLWN	MLWS
0100	0800	0100	0700	7·0	5·2	2·5	0·7
1300	2000	1300	1900				
Differences BURRY PORT							
+0003	+0003	+0007	+0007	+1·6	+1·4	+0·5	+0·4
LLANELLI							
–0003	–0003	+0150	+0020	+0·8	+0·6	No data	
FERRYSIDE							
0000	–0010	+0220	0000	–0·3	–0·7	–1·7	–0·6
CARMARTHEN							
+0010	0000	Dries		–4·4	–4·8	Dries	

SHELTER Good in Burry Port hbr (dries); access HW±2. Inspect before entry as it is entirely filled with moorings, none for visitors. ⚓ 1 to 2ca E of barrel post. Sp tides run hard. Note: If bad weather precludes access to Burry Inlet, see 9.11.15 for ⚓s around Caldey Island, especially in W'lies.

NAVIGATION WPT 51°36'·37N 04°24'·38W, 267°/087° from/to Burry Holms 3·3M; thence 4·5M to Burry Port. Carmarthen Bar, extending from the R Towy ent SE to Burry Holms, should not be attempted in W winds >F5 nor at night. Best entry is close NW of Burry Holms at HW–2; thence track 018° with Worms Hd on a stern transit (198°) between Burry Holms and Limekiln Pt. When Whiteford lt ho (disused) bears about 082°, alter to approx 050° into deeper water and steer to leave the barrel post about 1½ ca to port. Continue on this line to ⚓ in deep water beyond hbr ent, as shown. Chan is not buoyed/lit and is liable to shift. Before appr, check Firing Range activity (above).

LIGHTS AND MARKS Whiteford lt ho is conspic, but no longer lit. On head of W bkwtr is Barrel post, Fl R 3s 5M; 1½ca N is conspic old lt ho (W tr, R top) Fl 5s 7m 15M, and flagstaff.

RADIO TELEPHONE Superintendent: hand-held VHF Ch 16 (occas).

TELEPHONE (Dial code 01554) Superintendent 834315 (office) 834303 (home) or 0385 593748 (mobile); MRCC (01792) 366534;

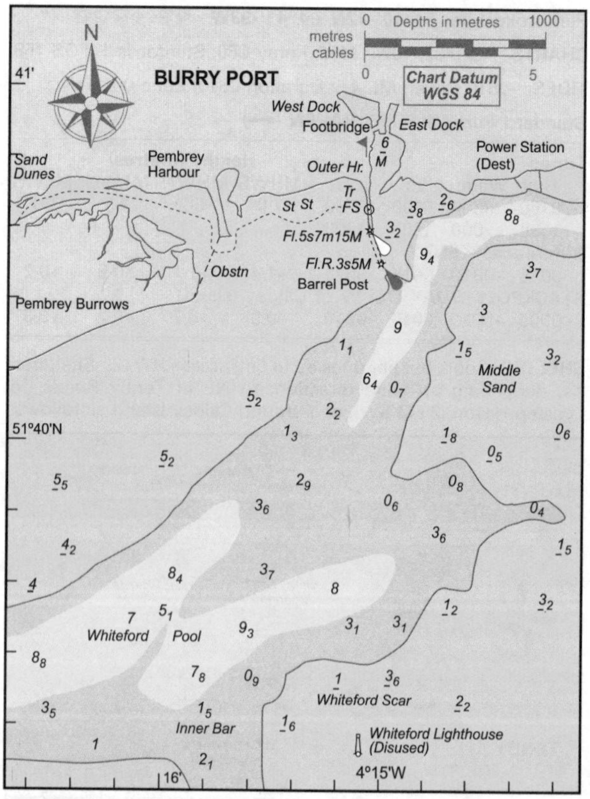

⊖ (01222) 763880 (H24); Pendine Range (01994) 453243 Ext 240; Marinecall 09068 500459; Police 772222; Dr 832240.

FACILITIES **Outer Hbr W pier and Basin** ☎ 833342, Slip, M, L, CH; Note: outer hbr dredged 1999 and marina planned for completion 2000 by extending W breakwater. **E Pier** Slip; **Burry Port YC** Bar; **Services:** D, ME, El, Sh, C, Gas. **Town** EC Tues; P, D, V, R, Bar, ✉, Ⓑ, ⇌, ✈ (Cardiff).

SWANSEA *9.11.17*

Swansea 51°36'·43N 03°55'·67W

CHARTS AC 1161, *1165, 1179*; Imray C59; Stanfords 14; OS 159

TIDES –0500 Dover; ML 5·2; Duration 0620; Zone 0 (UT)

Standard Port MILFORD HAVEN (⟵)

Times				Height (metres)			
High Water		Low Water		MHWS	MHWN	MLWN	MLWS
0100	0800	0100	0700	7·0	5·2	2·5	0·7
1300	2000	1300	1900				
Differences SWANSEA							
+0004	+0006	–0006	–0003	+2·6	+2·1	+0·7	+0·3
MUMBLES							
+0005	+0010	–0020	–0015	+2·3	+1·7	+0·6	+0·2
PORT TALBOT							
+0003	+0005	–0010	–0003	+2·6	+2·2	+1·0	+0·5
PORTHCAWL							
+0005	+0010	–0010	–0005	+2·9	+2·3	+0·8	+0·3

SHELTER Very good in marina; enter via R Tawe barrage lock, which operates on request HW±4½ (co-ordinated with the marina lock), 0700-2200BST; out of season, 0700-1900UT, but to 2200 at w/ends. Lock fee £2.24 per week. There are pontoons in both locks. Yachts usually exit Tawe barrage lock at H+00, and enter at H+30. Locks are closed when ht of tide falls to 1·5m above CD, usually at MLWS. At sp, do not enter river until LW+1½. Two large Or holding buoys below barrage in mid-stream; also, at W side of barrage lock, a landing pontoon (dries, foul ground). No Ⓥ berths at SY & SAC pontoons close N of marina ent.

NAVIGATION WPT SHM By, QG, Bell, 51°35'·53N 03°56'·08W, 200°/020° from/to E bkwtr lt, 0·92M. In Swansea Bay tidal streams flow anti-clockwise for 9½ hrs (Swansea HW –3½ to +6), with at times a race off Mumbles Hd. From HW–6 to –3 the stream reverses, setting N past Mumbles Hd towards Swansea. Keep seaward of Mixon Shoal. When N of SW Inner Green Grounds (SWIGG) SCM lt buoy, Q (6)+L Fl 15s, keep to W of dredged chan and clear of commercial ships. Yachts must motor in hbr and appr, max speed 4kn.

LIGHTS AND MARKS Mumbles Hd, Fl (4) 20s35m16M, is 3M SSW of hbr ent. A conspic TV mast (R lts) NNE of hbr is almost aligned with the fairway. Ldg lts 020°: front Oc G 4s 5m 2M; rear FG 6M; these mark E side of chan dredged 3m. When N of QR and QG chan buoys stay inside dredged chan. **Port Traffic sigs** are conspic at W side of ent to King's Dock; there are 9 lts, ● or ●, arranged in a 3 x 3 frame. Yachts arriving must obey the middle lt in left column:

●= Do not enter the river; hold SW of W Pier.
●= Yachts may enter the river, keeping to mid-chan, then to W of holding buoys.

Lock Master will advise on tfc movements Ch 18.
Lock sigs for barrage and marina locks alike are:

●● } = Lock closed. Do not proceed
● = Wait
● = Enter with caution
●● } = Free flow operating; proceed with caution

Barrage lock lit by 2FR/FG (vert) to seaward.

RADIO TELEPHONE For barrage, call *Tawe Lock* Ch 18. For marina call *Swansea Marina* Ch **80**. For commercial docks call *Swansea Docks Radio* VHF Ch14 (H24).

TELEPHONE (Dial code 01792) Hr Mr 650855 Ext 260 Fax 650729; Barrage 456014; MRCC 366534; Police 456999; ⊖ 652373/4 and (01222) 763880 (H24); Marinecall 09068 500 459; Ⓗ 205666; Dr 653452; DVLA (for SSR) 783355.

FACILITIES **Swansea Marina** (350+50 visitors) ☎ 470310, Fax 463948, £1.29, D (no P), LPG, AC, FW, C (1 ton), BH (25 ton), ⚓, Gas, Gaz, Ice, CH, ME, El, Ⓔ, Sh, ⊡, ♿, Bar, R; **Swansea Yacht & Sub Aqua Club (SY & SAC)** ☎ 654863, M, L, (no visitors' berths), FW, C (5 ton static), R, Bar; **Services:** ME, SM, ACA, CH, El, Ⓔ, Sh. **City** Sh, V, R, Bar, ✉, Ⓑ, ⇌, ✈.

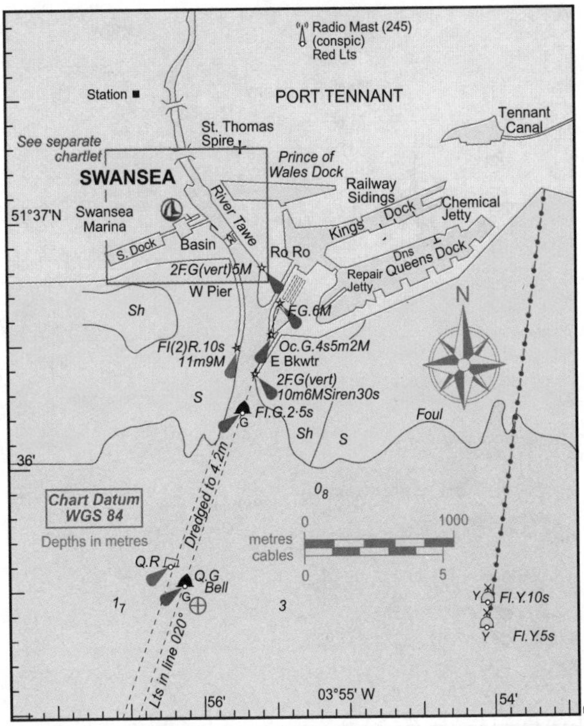

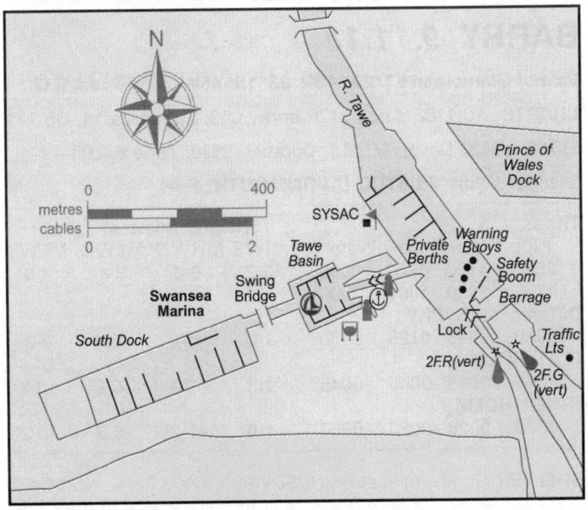

ADJACENT HARBOURS AND ANCHORAGES

MUMBLES, 51°34'·2N 03°58'·2W. Good ⚓ in W'lies 5ca N of Mumbles Hd lt ho. **Bristol Chan YC** ☎ (01792) 366000, Slip, M; **Mumbles YC** ☎ 369321, Slip, M, L, FW, C (hire).

R NEATH, 51°37'·88N 03°49'·97W. Ent over bar HW±2½ via 1·5M chan, marked/lit training wall to stbd. Tfc info from *Neath Pilot* VHF Ch 77, if on stn. **Monkstone Marina**, W bank just S of bridge, dries 4m: AB, 2 Y Ⓥs, D, FW, Slip, BH (15 ton), R, Bar, Visitors welcome. **Monkstone C & SC**, ☎ (01792) 812229; VHF Ch M (occas).

PORTHCAWL, Bridgend, **51°28'·48N 03°42'·02W.** AC 1169, *1165.* HW –0500 on Dover; ML 5·3m. See 9.11.17. A tiny drying hbr (access HW±2) protected by bkwtr running SE from Porthcawl Pt. Beware rk ledge (dries) W of bkwtr. Porthcawl lt ho, F WRG (see 9.11.4) in line 094° with St Hilary radio mast (QR & FR) leads through Shord chan. Tidal streams can reach 6kn at sp off end of bkwtr. 3 Ⓥs or ⚓ approx 3ca SSE of lt ho. Hr Mr ☎ (01656) 782756. Facilities: **Porthcawl Hbr B C** ☎ 782342. **Town** EC Wed; P & D (cans), CH, V, R, Bar, ✉, Ⓑ, ⇌ (Bridgend), ✈ (Cardiff).

11

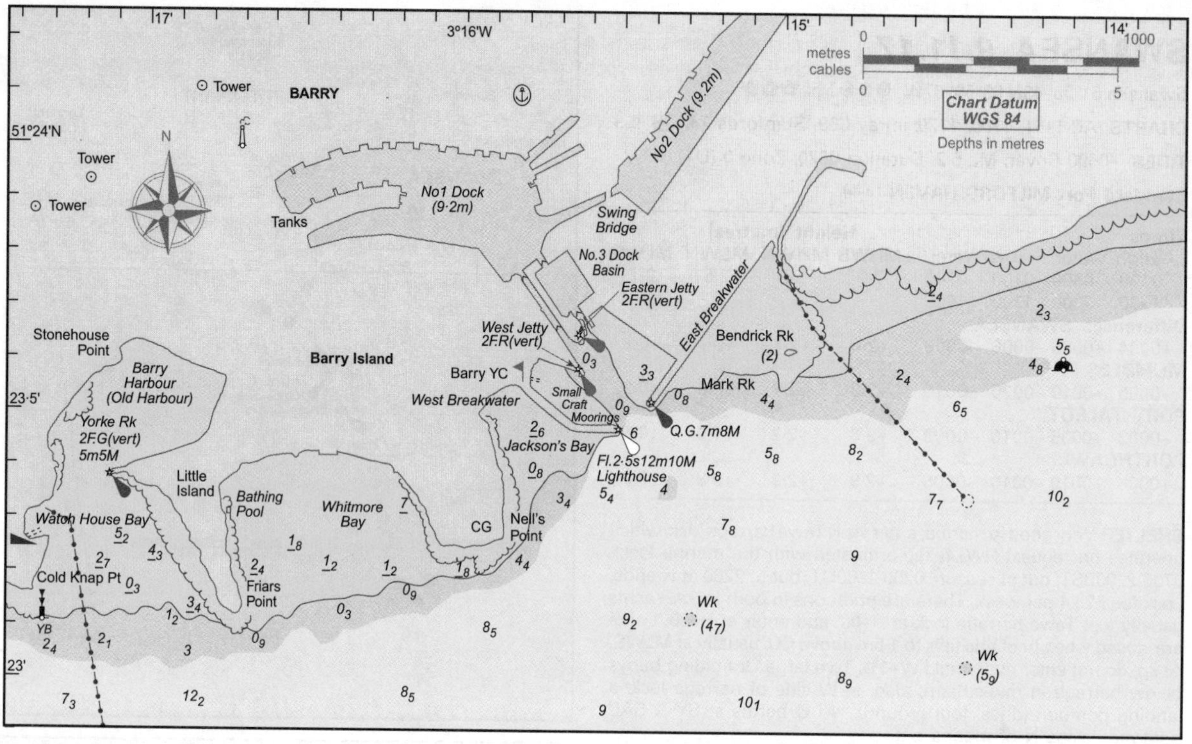

BARRY *9.11.18*

Vale of Glamorgan **51°23'·48N 03°15'·45W**

CHARTS AC *1182, 1152, 1179*; Imray C59; Stanfords 14; OS 171

TIDES –0423 Dover; ML 6·1; Duration 0630; Zone 0 (UT)

Standard Port BRISTOL (AVONMOUTH) (⟶)

Times				Height (metres)			
High Water		Low Water		MHWS	MHWN	MLWN	MLWS
0600	1100	0300	0800	13·2	9·8	3·8	1·0
1800	2300	1500	2000				
Differences BARRY							
–0030	–0015	–0125	–0030	–1·8	–1·3	+0·2	0·0
FLAT HOLM							
–0015	–0015	–0045	–0045	–1·3	–1·1	–0·2	+0·2
STEEP HOLM							
–0020	–0020	–0050	–0050	–1·6	–1·2	–0·2	–0·2

SHELTER Good, but in strong E/SE winds avoid Barry; No 1 Dock is no longer available to pleasure craft. Access H24 to the Outer hbr. No AB; pick up a mooring (free) and see YC. The Old Hbr to W of Barry Island dries and is not used.

NAVIGATION WPT 51°23'·03N 03°15'·08W, 152°/332° from/to ent, 0·53M. Beware heavy merchant traffic. Approaching from E keep well out from the shore. Strong tidal stream across ent.

LIGHTS AND MARKS Welsh Water Barry West PHM buoy, Fl R 5s, and Merkur PHM buoy, Fl R 2·5s, lie respectively 217°/1·5M and 191°/1·65M from hbr ent. W bkwtr Fl 2·5s 10M. E bkwtr QG 8M.

RADIO TELEPHONE *Barry Radio* VHF Ch **11** 10 16 (HW–4 to HW+3); tidal info on request. *Bristol Pilot* Ch 12 may advise on vacant moorings.

TELEPHONE (Dial code 01446) Hr Mr 700754 ℻ 700100; MRCC (01792) 366534; ⊜ (029) 2076 3880 (H24); Marinecall 09068 500 459; Police 734451; Dr 739543.

FACILITIES Barry YC (130) ☎ 735511, access HW±3½, Slip, M, Bar, FW; **Services:** Slip, D, FW, Gas, ME, El, Sh, CH, SM. **Town** EC Wed; P (cans, 1M away), D, CH, V, R, Bar, ✉, Ⓑ, ⇌, ✈ (Cardiff).

CARDIFF (Penarth) *9.11.19*

Vale of Glamorgan **51°26'·74N 03°09'·92W** (marina)

CHARTS AC *1182, 1176, 1179*; Imray C59; Stanfords 14; OS 171

TIDES –0425 Dover; ML 6·4; Duration 0610; Zone 0 (UT)

Standard Port BRISTOL (AVONMOUTH) (⟶)

Times				Height (metres)			
High Water		Low Water		MHWS	MHWN	MLWN	MLWS
0600	1100	0300	0800	13·2	9·8	3·8	1·0
1800	2300	1500	2000				
Differences CARDIFF							
–0015	–0015	–0100	–0030	–1·0	–0·6	+0·1	0·0
NEWPORT							
–0020	–0010	0000	–0020	–1·1	–1·0	–0·6	–0·7
CHEPSTOW (River Wye)							
+0020	+0020	No data		No data		No data	

Note: At Newport the ht of LW does not normally fall below MLWS. Tidal hts are based on a minimum river flow; max flow may raise ht of LW by as much as 0·3m.

SHELTER Very good in marina. Access via barrage not LW ± 1 and marina lock usually H24 but see below. Depth gauge shows ht of water above sill. See opposite for barrage locks. Waiting trot berths in outer hbr; or ⚓ off Penarth seafront in W'lies; in E'lies cramped ⚓ off Alexandra Dock ent in 2m.

NAVIGATION WPT 51°24'·03N 03°08'·81W (2½ca SW of S Cardiff SCM lt buoy), 169°/349° from/to barrage locks, 2·9M. The outer appr's from W or SW are via Breaksea lt float and N of One Fathom Bank. Keep S of Lavernock Spit (SCM lt buoy) and NW of Flat Holm and Wolves drying rk (NCM lt buoy). From NE, drying ledges and shoals extend >1M offshore. From E, appr via Monkstone lt ho and S Cardiff SCM buoy. Ranny Spit (dries 0·4m) is 3½ca to the W, and Cardiff Grounds (dries 5·4m) 3½ca to the E. The Wrach Chan is buoyed/lit and dredged 1·2m; it passes 1½ca E of Penarth Head. Do not impede merchant ships, especially those entering/leaving Alexandra Dock. The appr chan to the locks is dredged 0·7m below CD.

CARDIFF *continued*

Cardiff Bay Barrage

a. Call *Barrage Control* VHF Ch 18 or ☎ 029 2070 0234 to request lock-in or lock-out. Waiting berth on a barge in outer hbr.
b. Subject to VHF instructions, enter the outer hbr (Wpt 51°26'·71N 03°09'·84W) and lock in.
c. IPTS (sigs 1, 2, 3, 5 in 9.0.4) are shown at lock ent.
d. Outbound locks run on the hour and half hour. Inbound locks run on quarter past and quarter to the hour.

LIGHTS AND MARKS Ldg lts 349°, both FW 4/24m 17M, hard to identify due to other adjacent lts; front ldg lt is obscured by the Barrage at certain states of the tide.

RADIO TELEPHONE Port VHF Ch **14** 16 (HW–4 to HW+3). *Barrage Control* Ch 18. Penarth marina Ch 80 H24.

TELEPHONE (Dial code 029) Hr Mr 2040 0500; 📠 2040 0501 Barrage control 2070 0234; Marina 2070 5021; MRCC (01792) 366534; ⊖ For clearance 2038 6100 (H24); Marinecall 09068 500 459; Weather Centre 2039 7020; Police (01446) 734451; Dr 2041 5258.

FACILITIES **Penarth Marina** (350+50 Ⓥ; max draft 3m), ☎ 2070 5021 H24, 📠 2071 2170, www.aboard.co.uk/c.n.marinas £1.60, < 5 hrs £5.25, FW, AC, P (0930-1730, F pontoon), D (Daily 0900-1730, E pontoon), EI, ME, Sh, C, CH, BY, BH (20T) Gas, LPG, ⊡, R; **Penarth YC** ☎ 2070 8196, Slip, FW, Bar; **Cardiff YC** ☎ 2046 3697, Slip, M, FW, L (floating pontoon), Bar; **Penarth MB & SC** ☎ 2022 6575, M, L, C, FW, Bar, Slip; **Services:** D, SM, Sh, C (20 ton), CH, ACA, ME, EI, Ⓔ, BY, Slip, BH (20 ton), Gas. **City** P, D, ME, EI, V, R, Bar, ✉, Ⓑ, ≥, ✈ (15 mins).

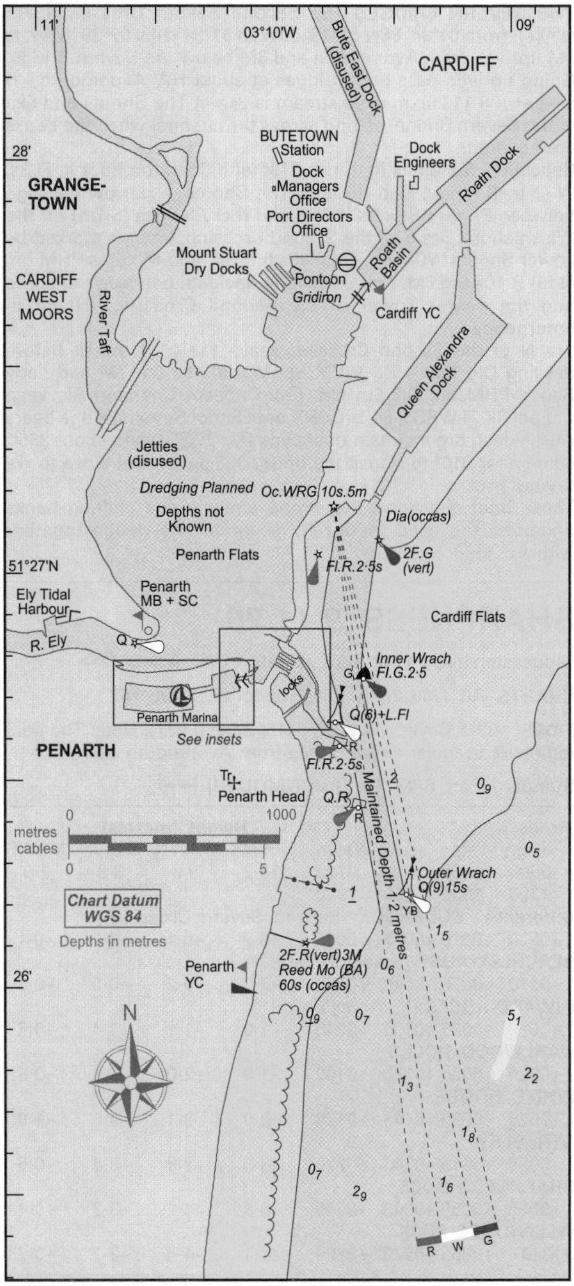

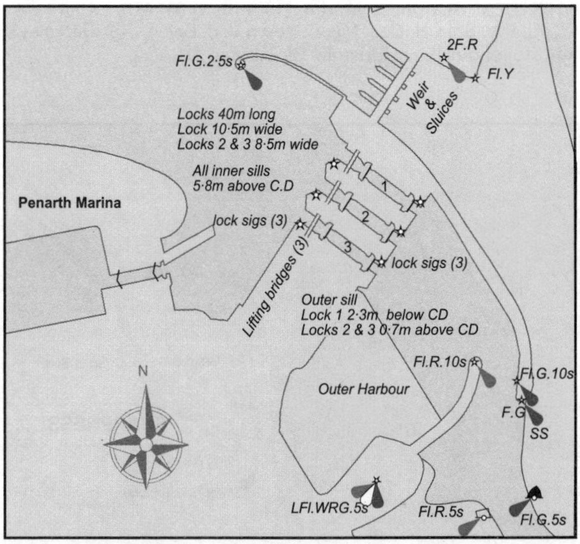

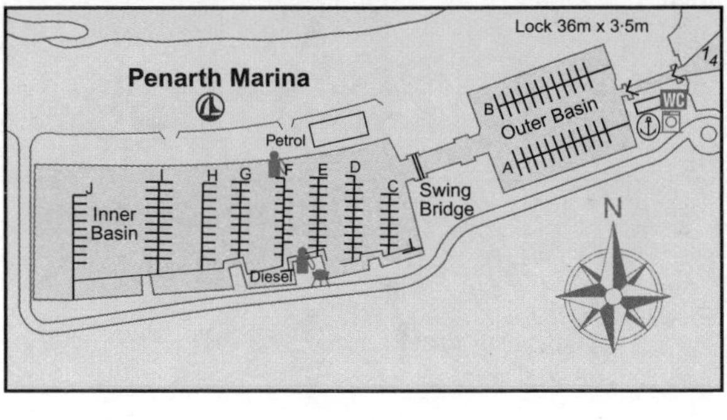

ADJACENT HARBOUR

NEWPORT, Newport, **51°32'·95N 02°59'·13W**. AC *1176, 1152, 1179*. HW –0425 on Dover; ML 6·0m; Duration 0620. See 9.11.19. A commercial port controlled by ABP, but a safe shelter for yachts. Enter R Usk over bar (approx 0·5m) E of West Usk buoy, QR Bell) and follow buoyed and lit chan to S Lock ent; turn NE (ldg lts 057°) for yacht moorings on S side between power stn pier and YC. Beware overhead cables in Julian's Pill, clearance 3 8m. East Usk lt ho Fl (2) WRG 10s 11m 15/11M, W284°-290°, R290°-017°, W017°-037°, G037°-115°, W115°-120°. Ldg lts 057°, both FG. Alexandra Dock, S lock W pier head 2 FR (vert) 9/7m 6M. E pier head 2 FG (vert) 9/7m 6M. Port VHF Ch 16 09 69 **71** (HW ±4). VTS, not compulsory for yachts, is on same chans/times, call *Newport Radio*. Hr Mr (ABP) ☎ (01633) 244411, 📠 221285. ⊖ ☎ 273709; Facilities: **Newport and Uskmouth SC** Bar, M; **Services:** CH, EI, ME, Sh, Ⓔ. **Town** EC Thurs; all facilities.

THE SEVERN BRIDGES The Second Severn Crossing (37m cl'nce), from 51°34'·88N 02°43'·80W to 51°34'·14N 02°39'·82W, is 4M upriver from Avonmouth and 3M below the Severn Bridge. Going upriver, pass both bridges at about HW Avonmouth −1¾ (see also 9.11.20); max sp stream is 8kn at The Shoots and 6kn at the Severn Bridge, setting across the channel when the banks are covered.

Redcliffe F Bu ldg lts in transit 013° with Charston Rock lt, Fl 3s, W ○ tr, B stripe, lead through The Shoots, a narrow passage between English Stones (6·2m) and rocky ledges (5·1m) off the Welsh shore. 5ca S of the Second Crossing, chan is marked by Lower Shoots WCM bn, Q (9) 15s 6m 7M, and Mixoms PHM bn, Fl (3) R 10s 6m 6M. No vessel may navigate between the shore and the nearer Tower of the Second Crossing, except in emergency.

4ca N of the Second Crossing, leave the 013° transit before passing Old Man's Hd WCM bn, VQ (9) 10s 6m 7M and Lady Bench PHM bn, QR 6m 6M. From abeam Charston Rk, keep Chapel Rk, Fl WRG 2·6s, brg 050° until E tr of Severn Bridge bears 068°; which brg maintain until Lyde Rk, QWR, bears about 355°, when alter 010° to transit the bridge (36·6m cl'nce) close to rks drying 1m.

These brief directions, the strong streams and shifting banks underline the need for locally acquired knowledge together with AC 1166.

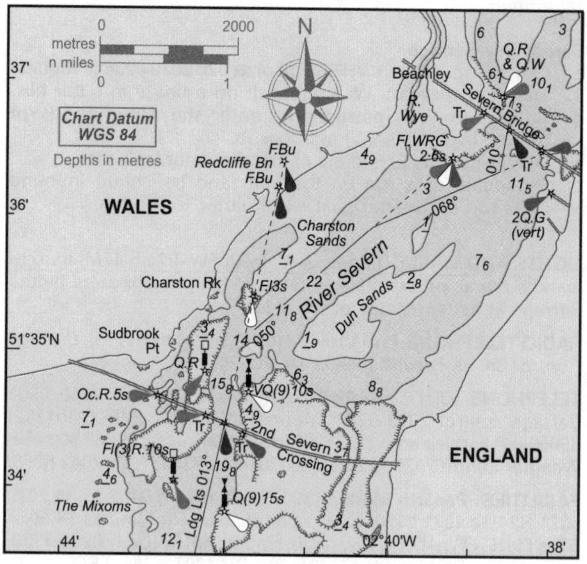

SHARPNESS *9.11.20*

Gloucestershire **51°43'·03N 02°29'·08W**

CHARTS AC *1166*, Imray C59; Stanfords 14; OS 162

TIDES −0315 Dover; Duration 0415; Zone 0 (UT). Note: The tidal regime is irregular and deviates from Avonmouth curve.

Standard Port BRISTOL (AVONMOUTH) (⟶)

Times				Height (metres)			
High Water		Low Water		MHWS	MHWN	MLWN	MLWS
0000	0600	0000	0700	13·2	9·8	3·8	1·0
1200	1800	1200	1900				
Differences SUDBROOK (Second Severn Crossing)							
+0010	+0010	+0025	+0015	+0·2	+0·1	−0·1	+0·1
BEACHLEY/AUST (Severn Bridge)							
+0010	+0015	+0040	+0025	−0·2	−0·2	−0·5	−0·3
INWARD ROCKS (River Severn)							
+0020	+0020	+0105	+0045	−1·0	−1·1	−1·4	−0·6
NARLWOOD ROCKS							
+0025	+0025	+0120	+0100	−1·9	−2·0	−2·3	−0·8
WHITE HOUSE							
+0025	+0025	+0145	+0120	−3·0	−3·1	−3·6	−1·0
BERKELEY							
+0030	+0045	+0245	+0220	−3·8	−3·9	−3·4	−0·5
SHARPNESS DOCK							
+0035	+0050	+0305	+0245	−3·9	−4·2	−3·3	−0·4
WELLHOUSE ROCK							
+0040	+0055	+0320	+0305	−4·1	−4·4	−3·1	−0·2

SHELTER Very good. The sea lock into the commercial dock is generally open HW-2 to HW but this is dependant on commercial shipping movements. The advice is plan your passage to arrive no sooner than HW-1 and no later than HW. For more detailed information on lock fees, canal licences and the passage from Avonmouth contact the HM at Sharpness on 01453 811862. The fog signal on Sharpness Point is available on request to Sharpness Radio on VHF channel 13 or 01453 511968.

NAVIGATION WPT 51°42'·83N 02°29'·28W, 208°/028° from/to ent, 2ca. Leave King Road, Avonmouth (17M downriver) not before HW Sharpness −3, to be off hbr ent about HW −½. Stem strong flood S of F Bu lt; beware Tidal eddy. Do not proceed above the Severn Bridge except HW±2. There is a 5H flood and a 7H ebb. Use the transits shown on AC 1166. Request pilot notes from Sharpness HM in good time.

LIGHTS AND MARKS Lts as chartlet, but night passage not advised without local knowledge/pilot (0777 4226143) .

RADIO TELEPHONE Call *Sharpness Radio* VHF Ch 17 (HW −6 to +1) for lock. Gloucester & Sharpness Canal Ch 74 for bridges (no locks).

TELEPHONE (Dial code 01453) Pierhead 511968 (HW−5 to HW+1); Hr Mr 811862/64 (HO), 811863; ⊖ (01222) 763880 (H24); Marinecall 09068 500 459; MRCC (01792) 366534; Police 810477; Ⓗ 810777.

FACILITIES **Sharpness Marine** (100+15) ☎ 811476, £4 all LOA, AC, El, FW, Sh, CH, Gas, ME, C. **Town** V, R, Bar, ✉, Ⓑ (Berkeley), ⇌ (Stonehouse), ✈ (Bristol). Gloucester: D, ACA.

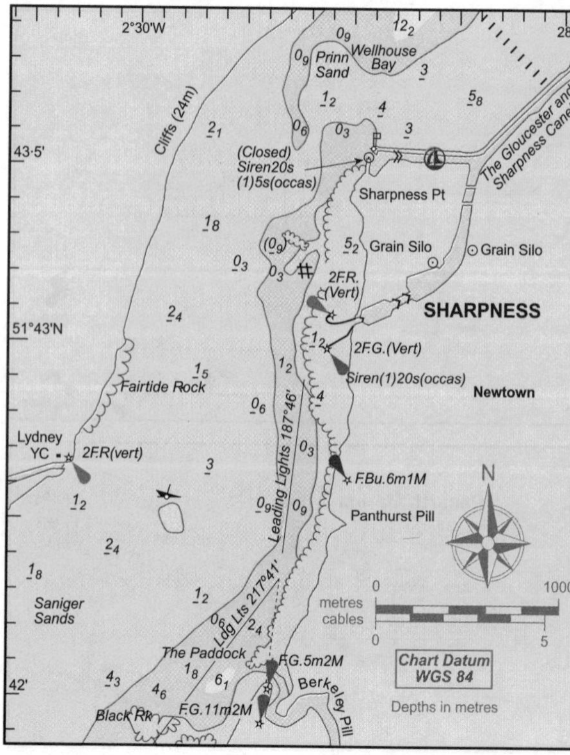

TIME ZONE (UTC)
For Summer Time add ONE hour in **non-shaded areas**

ENGLAND – PORT OF BRISTOL (AVONMOUTH)

LAT 51°30′N LONG 2°44′W

TIMES AND HEIGHTS OF HIGH AND LOW WATERS

SPRING & NEAP TIDES
Dates in red are **SPRINGS**
Dates in blue are **NEAPS**

YEAR **2002**

JANUARY

Day		Time	m	Time	m	Time	m	Time	m
1	TU	0246	1.3	0820	13.4	1513	1.4	2049	13.1
2	W	0330	1.3	0906	13.4	1556	1.4	2134	13.0
3	TH	0411	1.4	0951	13.2	1637	1.6	2219	12.7
4	F	0451	1.7	1037	12.8	1718	1.8	2305	12.3
5	SA	0532	2.0	1125	12.3	1801	2.2	2354	11.7
6	SU	0618	2.4	1220	11.7	1850	2.6		
7	M	0052	11.1	0712	2.9	1327	11.2	1949	3.0
8	TU	0205	10.7	0822	3.2	1441	11.0	2109	3.3
9	W	0318	10.8	0945	3.2	1549	11.1	2226	3.1
10	TH	0422	11.1	1055	2.9	1650	11.5	2329	2.6
11	F	0519	11.6	1154	2.4	1745	11.9		
12	SA	0023	2.2	0609	12.2	1247	1.9	1834	12.3
13	SU	0114	1.8	0655	12.6	1336	1.7	● 1919	12.5
14	M	0201	1.6	0738	12.7	1422	1.6	2001	12.5
15	TU	0243	1.6	0818	12.7	1504	1.7	2040	12.4
16	W	0320	1.8	0855	12.5	1538	2.0	2114	12.1
17	TH	0348	2.1	0928	12.2	1605	2.2	2144	11.8
18	F	0409	2.3	0958	11.8	1628	2.4	2213	11.5
19	SA	0431	2.4	1027	11.5	1653	2.5	2242	11.2
20	SU	0459	2.6	1058	11.1	1726	2.6	2316	10.9
21	M	0535	2.8	1136	10.7	1806	3.0	2358	10.5
22	TU	0620	3.2	1226	10.3	1856	3.4		
23	W	0054	10.1	0718	3.7	1333	10.0	2004	3.7
24	TH	0207	10.0	0838	3.9	1453	10.1	2129	3.6
25	F	0331	10.3	1005	3.5	1611	10.6	2247	3.1
26	SA	0443	11.1	1119	2.9	1716	11.4	2352	2.4
27	SU	0542	12.0	1222	2.2	1812	12.2		
28	M	0051	1.8	0633	12.8	1322	1.7	○ 1903	12.9
29	TU	0147	1.4	0723	13.4	1417	1.3	1952	13.4
30	W	0239	1.0	0810	13.8	1509	0.9	2039	13.7
31	TH	0327	0.8	0857	14.0	1554	0.8	2124	13.7

FEBRUARY

Day		Time	m	Time	m	Time	m	Time	m
1	F	0409	0.8	0941	14.0	1634	0.8	2207	13.5
2	SA	0445	0.9	1024	13.6	1709	1.1	2248	13.1
3	SU	0519	1.3	1106	13.0	1741	1.6	2329	12.4
4	M	0553	1.8	1150	12.2	1815	2.2		
5	TU	0014	11.5	0632	2.6	1243	11.3	1856	3.0
6	W	0112	10.6	0723	3.3	1354	10.5	1954	3.7
7	TH	0235	10.1	0840	3.9	1517	10.2	2138	4.0
8	F	0353	10.2	1024	3.7	1627	10.5	2302	3.5
9	SA	0458	10.8	1132	3.0	1728	11.1		
10	SU	0002	2.8	0553	11.6	1228	2.3	1819	11.7
11	M	0054	2.1	0641	12.2	1318	1.8	1905	12.2
12	TU	0142	1.7	0723	12.6	1405	1.5	● 1946	12.5
13	W	0227	1.5	0802	12.8	1448	1.5	2022	12.5
14	TH	0306	1.5	0837	12.7	1525	1.6	2054	12.4
15	F	0338	1.8	0908	12.5	1553	1.9	2122	12.2
16	SA	0359	2.0	0936	12.2	1612	2.1	2149	12.0
17	SU	0413	2.1	1001	11.9	1629	2.1	2214	11.8
18	M	0434	2.1	1028	11.6	1654	2.2	2243	11.5
19	TU	0504	2.3	1101	11.2	1727	2.5	2320	11.1
20	W	0541	2.7	1143	10.7	1807	3.0		
21	TH	0008	10.5	0627	3.3	1241	10.1	1903	3.6
22	F	0113	10.0	0735	3.9	1358	9.8	2031	3.9
23	SA	0240	9.9	0920	3.9	1536	10.1	2215	3.5
24	SU	0414	10.6	1055	3.2	1656	11.0	2331	2.7
25	M	0523	11.7	1208	2.3	1758	12.1		
26	TU	0036	1.9	0619	12.8	1311	1.5	1849	13.1
27	W	0135	1.2	0709	13.7	1407	0.9	○ 1938	13.8
28	TH	0228	0.7	0756	14.2	1458	0.4	2023	14.2

MARCH

Day		Time	m	Time	m	Time	m	Time	m
1	F	0315	0.3	0841	14.5	1542	0.2	2106	14.3
2	SA	0356	0.2	0923	14.5	1619	0.4	2147	14.1
3	SU	0430	0.5	1003	14.1	1649	0.8	2224	13.5
4	M	0458	1.0	1041	13.3	1713	1.5	2300	12.6
5	TU	0525	1.7	1119	12.3	1739	2.2	2338	11.6
6	W	0557	2.5	1202	11.1	1813	3.1		
7	TH	0025	10.5	0640	3.4	1304	10.0	1903	4.0
8	F	0149	9.6	0747	4.2	1448	9.5	2029	4.6
9	SA	0327	9.6	0953	4.2	1606	9.8	2239	4.0
10	SU	0437	10.3	1112	3.3	1709	10.6	2340	3.0
11	M	0534	11.3	1206	2.4	1800	11.5		
12	TU	0031	2.1	0620	12.1	1255	1.7	1843	12.2
13	W	0119	1.6	0701	12.6	1341	1.3	1922	12.5
14	TH	0204	1.3	0738	12.8	1425	1.2	● 1956	12.6
15	F	0244	1.3	0812	12.8	1503	1.4	2027	12.6
16	SA	0318	1.5	0842	12.6	1533	1.7	2056	12.4
17	SU	0341	1.8	0909	12.3	1551	1.9	2121	12.2
18	M	0352	2.0	0934	12.1	1603	2.0	2145	12.1
19	TU	0409	1.9	1000	11.9	1625	2.0	2215	11.8
20	W	0436	2.0	1033	11.5	1655	2.2	2251	11.4
21	TH	0510	2.3	1115	10.9	1732	2.7	2336	10.8
22	F	0552	3.0	1209	10.2	1822	3.5		
23	SA	0038	10.1	0654	3.7	1325	9.7	1942	4.1
24	SU	0205	9.8	0845	4.0	1511	9.9	2152	3.7
25	M	0351	10.4	1040	3.2	1639	10.9	2315	2.7
26	TU	0505	11.7	1154	2.1	1740	12.2		
27	W	0019	1.7	0601	12.9	1254	1.2	1831	13.2
28	TH	0116	0.9	0650	13.8	1348	0.6	○ 1917	14.0
29	F	0208	0.4	0736	14.4	1436	0.1	2001	14.4
30	SA	0254	0.1	0820	14.6	1519	0.1	2043	14.4
31	SU	0334	0.1	0901	14.5	1555	0.3	2122	14.1

APRIL

Day		Time	m	Time	m	Time	m	Time	m
1	M	0407	0.4	0940	14.0	1623	0.9	2158	13.5
2	TU	0434	1.0	1016	13.1	1643	1.6	2232	12.5
3	W	0457	1.7	1051	12.0	1706	2.3	2307	11.4
4	TH	0526	2.6	1129	10.8	1738	3.2	2349	10.3
5	F	0608	3.5	1224	9.6	1826	4.1		
6	SA	0108	9.3	0714	4.3	1418	9.1	1950	4.7
7	SU	0300	9.3	0904	4.4	1539	9.5	2210	4.2
8	M	0408	10.1	1042	3.5	1639	10.4	2312	3.2
9	TU	0503	11.0	1136	2.5	1730	11.3		
10	W	0001	2.2	0549	11.9	1225	1.7	1812	12.0
11	TH	0048	1.6	0629	12.4	1310	1.4	1849	12.5
12	F	0132	1.3	0706	12.6	1353	1.2	● 1924	12.6
13	SA	0214	1.3	0741	12.6	1432	1.4	1956	12.6
14	SU	0249	1.5	0813	12.5	1504	1.6	2026	12.5
15	M	0315	1.8	0842	12.3	1525	1.9	2053	12.4
16	TU	0330	1.9	0909	12.2	1540	1.9	2120	12.2
17	W	0348	1.9	0939	12.0	1602	1.9	2152	12.0
18	TH	0416	1.9	1015	11.6	1633	2.1	2231	11.5
19	F	0451	2.2	1057	11.0	1711	2.6	2317	10.9
20	SA	0534	2.9	1152	10.3	1801	3.4		
21	SU	0019	10.2	0636	3.6	1308	9.8	1921	4.0
22	M	0147	10.0	0831	3.8	1452	10.0	2131	3.6
23	TU	0330	10.6	1020	3.0	1616	11.0	2251	2.6
24	W	0441	11.7	1129	2.0	1716	12.2	2353	1.6
25	TH	0537	12.8	1227	1.1	1807	13.2		
26	F	0048	0.9	0626	13.7	1320	0.6	1852	13.9
27	SA	0140	0.4	0712	14.2	1408	0.3	○ 1936	14.2
28	SU	0226	0.2	0756	14.3	1451	0.3	2017	14.1
29	M	0308	0.3	0837	14.1	1528	0.6	2057	13.8
30	TU	0343	0.7	0917	13.5	1557	1.2	2134	13.1

Chart Datum: 6·50 metres below Ordnance Datum (Newlyn)

TIME ZONE (UTC)
For Summer Time add ONE hour in **non-shaded areas**

ENGLAND – PORT OF BRISTOL (AVONMOUTH)

LAT 51°30′N LONG 2°44′W

TIMES AND HEIGHTS OF HIGH AND LOW WATERS

SPRING & NEAP TIDES
Dates in red are SPRINGS
Dates in blue are NEAPS

YEAR **2002**

MAY

Date	Day	Time	m	Time	m	Time	m	Time	m
1	W	0411	1.3	0954	12.7	1619	1.9	2208	12.2
2	TH	0436	2.0	1029	11.7	1642	2.5	2243	11.3
3	F	0505	2.7	1107	10.6	1714	3.2	2325	10.3
4	SA	0547	3.4	1157	9.7	1801	4.0		
5	SU	0035	9.4	0649	4.1	1331	9.1	1917	4.5
6	M	0221	9.4	0812	4.1	1458	9.4	2056	4.3
7	TU	0328	9.9	0942	3.6	1557	10.1	2224	3.5
8	W	0422	10.7	1050	2.8	1648	10.9	2320	2.6
9	TH	0509	11.4	1143	2.1	1732	11.7		
10	F	0008	2.0	0551	12.0	1230	1.7	1811	12.2
11	SA	0054	1.7	0630	12.3	1315	1.5	1848	12.4
12	SU	0136	1.6	0707	12.4	1356	1.5	● 1924	12.6
13	M	0214	1.6	0743	12.4	1431	1.6	1957	12.5
14	TU	0246	1.7	0817	12.3	1500	1.7	2030	12.5
15	W	0312	1.8	0851	12.2	1525	1.8	2103	12.3
16	TH	0337	1.8	0926	12.0	1552	1.9	2140	12.1
17	F	0408	2.0	1006	11.7	1625	2.1	2221	11.7
18	SA	0446	2.3	1052	11.2	1706	2.6	2310	11.1
19	SU	0534	2.7	1147	10.6	1800	3.1		
20	M	0012	10.6	0640	3.2	1258	10.3	1920	3.5
21	TU	0134	10.4	0816	3.2	1427	10.4	2102	3.2
22	W	0303	10.9	0947	2.7	1545	11.1	2218	2.5
23	TH	0411	11.7	1056	2.0	1646	12.0	2322	1.7
24	F	0509	12.5	1155	1.4	1739	12.8		
25	SA	0018	1.1	0600	13.2	1249	1.0	1826	13.3
26	SU	0110	0.8	0647	13.5	1338	0.7	○ 1911	13.6
27	M	0158	0.6	0732	13.6	1423	0.8	1954	13.5
28	TU	0242	0.8	0816	13.3	1503	1.1	2035	13.2
29	W	0322	1.1	0858	12.9	1537	1.6	2114	12.7
30	TH	0355	1.6	0937	12.2	1603	2.1	2151	12.0
31	F	0423	2.1	1014	11.5	1628	2.6	2227	11.3

JUNE

Date	Day	Time	m	Time	m	Time	m	Time	m
1	SA	0453	2.6	1051	10.8	1700	3.0	2308	10.5
2	SU	0532	3.1	1134	10.1	1742	3.5		
3	M	0000	9.9	0622	3.5	1232	9.6	1840	3.9
4	TU	0117	9.6	0725	3.7	1349	9.5	1952	4.0
5	W	0231	9.8	0832	3.5	1458	9.9	2105	3.7
6	TH	0329	10.3	0939	3.1	1555	10.5	2215	3.2
7	F	0421	10.9	1045	2.6	1645	11.1	2316	2.6
8	SA	0509	11.4	1142	2.2	1731	11.7		
9	SU	0008	2.1	0553	11.8	1233	1.8	1814	12.2
10	M	0056	1.8	0635	12.1	1319	1.6	● 1854	12.5
11	TU	0140	1.7	0717	12.3	1402	1.6	1934	12.6
12	W	0222	1.7	0758	12.4	1441	1.6	2013	12.7
13	TH	0301	1.7	0839	12.4	1517	1.7	2053	12.6
14	F	0337	1.7	0921	12.3	1553	1.8	2135	12.4
15	SA	0415	1.8	1005	12.0	1630	2.0	2219	12.1
16	SU	0456	2.0	1051	11.7	1713	2.2	2308	11.7
17	M	0544	2.3	1142	11.3	1804	2.6		
18	TU	0004	11.3	0640	2.6	1243	11.0	1907	2.8
19	W	0114	11.1	0749	2.7	1355	10.8	2024	2.9
20	TH	0230	11.1	0906	2.7	1509	11.1	2141	2.6
21	F	0339	11.5	1019	2.4	1614	11.5	2249	2.2
22	SA	0440	11.9	1123	2.0	1711	12.1	2349	1.8
23	SU	0536	12.3	1220	1.7	1803	12.5		
24	M	0043	1.4	0626	12.6	1312	1.4	○ 1850	12.8
25	TU	0134	1.2	0714	12.8	1401	1.3	1935	12.9
26	W	0222	1.3	0800	12.7	1445	1.5	2018	12.8
27	TH	0306	1.4	0843	12.4	1524	1.7	2059	12.5
28	F	0344	1.8	0923	12.1	1556	2.1	2137	12.1
29	SA	0415	2.1	0959	11.6	1621	2.4	2213	11.6
30	SU	0443	2.4	1032	11.2	1648	2.7	2247	11.1

JULY

Date	Day	Time	m	Time	m	Time	m	Time	m
1	M	0514	2.7	1107	10.7	1721	2.9	2326	10.6
2	TU	0552	2.9	1147	10.3	1803	3.2		
3	W	0012	10.2	0639	3.1	1238	10.0	1855	3.5
4	TH	0113	9.9	0735	3.3	1341	9.9	2001	3.7
5	F	0221	10.0	0839	3.3	1450	10.1	2111	3.6
6	SA	0325	10.3	0948	3.1	1555	10.5	2222	3.1
7	SU	0425	10.8	1055	2.7	1652	11.2	2326	2.6
8	M	0519	11.4	1154	2.2	1744	11.8		
9	TU	0022	2.1	0609	11.9	1248	1.8	1831	12.4
10	W	0114	1.8	0656	12.3	1339	1.6	● 1916	12.8
11	TH	0205	1.6	0743	12.6	1428	1.5	2001	13.0
12	F	0255	1.5	0830	12.7	1514	1.4	2046	13.1
13	SA	0341	1.4	0915	12.8	1556	1.4	2131	13.0
14	SU	0422	1.4	1000	12.7	1636	1.5	2215	12.9
15	M	0502	1.5	1043	12.5	1714	1.6	2300	12.5
16	TU	0541	1.7	1128	12.1	1756	2.0	2348	12.0
17	W	0624	2.1	1218	11.6	1843	2.4		
18	TH	0045	11.5	0713	2.5	1319	11.0	1941	2.9
19	F	0154	11.0	0817	3.0	1431	10.7	2057	3.1
20	SA	0308	10.9	0941	3.2	1543	10.8	2219	3.0
21	SU	0416	11.1	1055	2.9	1648	11.2	2326	2.6
22	M	0517	11.4	1157	2.4	1745	11.8		
23	TU	0023	2.1	0611	11.9	1252	2.0	1835	12.3
24	W	0117	1.7	0700	12.2	1343	1.7	○ 1922	12.6
25	TH	0207	1.5	0746	12.4	1431	1.5	2005	12.7
26	F	0253	1.5	0829	12.4	1513	1.6	2045	12.6
27	SA	0333	1.6	0906	12.2	1548	1.9	2120	12.4
28	SU	0405	1.9	0939	11.9	1613	2.1	2152	12.0
29	M	0430	2.2	1009	11.6	1633	2.4	2222	11.6
30	TU	0452	2.3	1037	11.3	1656	2.5	2251	11.2
31	W	0519	2.5	1108	11.0	1726	2.7	2323	10.7

AUGUST

Date	Day	Time	m	Time	m	Time	m	Time	m
1	TH	0553	2.8	1145	10.5	1805	3.1		
2	F	0006	10.2	0637	3.2	1234	10.1	1856	3.6
3	SA	0106	9.9	0738	3.6	1341	9.9	2010	3.9
4	SU	0225	9.8	0857	3.6	1504	10.0	2136	3.7
5	M	0345	10.2	1016	3.3	1618	10.7	2253	3.1
6	TU	0452	10.9	1125	2.6	1719	11.5	2358	2.4
7	W	0550	11.7	1226	2.0	1813	12.4		
8	TH	0058	1.8	0641	12.4	1324	1.6	● 1901	13.0
9	F	0155	1.4	0730	12.9	1418	1.3	1949	13.5
10	SA	0249	1.1	0818	13.3	1508	1.0	2035	13.7
11	SU	0336	0.9	0903	13.5	1552	0.9	2119	13.8
12	M	0418	0.8	0945	13.4	1629	0.9	2201	13.6
13	TU	0453	1.0	1026	13.2	1703	1.2	2242	13.2
14	W	0525	1.4	1107	12.6	1735	1.7	2325	12.4
15	TH	0556	2.0	1149	11.8	1811	2.3		
16	F	0012	11.5	0633	2.7	1241	10.9	1857	3.1
17	SA	0116	10.6	0724	3.5	1356	10.2	2007	3.8
18	SU	0242	10.1	0858	4.0	1520	10.1	2156	3.8
19	M	0359	10.2	1036	3.7	1632	10.6	2311	3.2
20	TU	0504	10.8	1141	2.9	1732	11.4		
21	W	0008	2.4	0558	11.5	1236	2.2	1823	12.1
22	TH	0101	1.7	0647	12.1	1326	1.6	○ 1907	12.7
23	F	0149	1.3	0730	12.5	1413	1.3	1948	12.9
24	SA	0235	1.2	0809	12.6	1455	1.3	2025	12.9
25	SU	0315	1.3	0843	12.5	1531	1.6	2057	12.6
26	M	0348	1.7	0913	12.2	1558	1.9	2126	12.3
27	TU	0411	2.0	0939	12.0	1613	2.2	2152	11.9
28	W	0425	2.2	1004	11.7	1627	2.3	2216	11.5
29	TH	0443	2.4	1030	11.3	1651	2.5	2243	11.1
30	F	0511	2.6	1102	10.9	1722	2.8	2320	10.5
31	SA	0547	3.0	1145	10.4	1803	3.4		

Chart Datum: 6·50 metres below Ordnance Datum (Newlyn)

TIME ZONE (UTC)
For Summer Time add ONE hour in **non-shaded areas**

ENGLAND – PORT OF BRISTOL (AVONMOUTH)

LAT 51°30′N LONG 2°44′W

TIMES AND HEIGHTS OF HIGH AND LOW WATERS

SPRING & NEAP TIDES
Dates in **red** are **SPRINGS**
Dates in **blue** are **NEAPS**

YEAR **2002**

SEPTEMBER

Day	Time	m	Time	m	Time	m	Time	m
1 SU	0011	9.9	0636	3.7	1245	9.8	1905	4.1
2 M	0128	9.5	0759	4.1	1413	9.6	2054	4.2
3 TU	0311	9.7	0946	3.8	1551	10.3	2232	3.5
4 W	0433	10.6	1105	3.0	1700	11.4	2345	2.5
5 TH	0534	11.7	1211	2.2	1756	12.5		
6 F	0046	1.7	0625	12.7	1310	1.5	1845	13.4
7 SA	0143	1.1	0713	13.4	1404	1.0	● 1932	14.0
8 SU	0235	0.7	0759	13.9	1453	0.6	2017	14.3
9 M	0321	0.4	0842	14.0	1536	0.5	2059	14.3
10 TU	0400	0.5	0923	13.9	1612	0.6	2140	14.1
11 W	0433	0.9	1002	13.5	1643	1.1	2219	13.4
12 TH	0459	1.5	1040	12.8	1710	1.7	2258	12.5
13 F	0523	2.2	1119	11.8	1739	2.5	2340	11.3
14 SA	0554	3.1	1205	10.6	1819	3.5		
15 SU	0038	10.1	0639	4.0	1326	9.7	1924	4.4
16 M	0224	9.4	0809	4.7	1505	9.6	2144	4.4
17 TU	0344	9.8	1024	4.1	1616	10.3	2256	3.4
18 W	0448	10.6	1124	3.1	1714	11.3	2350	2.4
19 TH	0541	11.5	1214	2.1	1803	12.2		
20 F	0038	1.6	0625	12.3	1302	1.5	1845	12.8
21 SA	0125	1.1	0705	12.7	1347	1.1	○ 1923	13.1
22 SU	0209	1.0	0741	12.8	1430	1.2	1957	13.0
23 M	0249	1.2	0813	12.7	1506	1.4	2028	12.7
24 TU	0322	1.6	0842	12.4	1534	1.9	2056	12.4
25 W	0345	2.0	0908	12.1	1547	2.2	2120	12.0
26 TH	0355	2.3	0931	11.9	1557	2.3	2143	11.7
27 F	0410	2.3	0957	11.6	1619	2.4	2211	11.3
28 SA	0436	2.5	1029	11.2	1649	2.7	2248	10.7
29 SU	0509	2.9	1111	10.5	1727	3.3	2338	10.0
30 M	0553	3.6	1208	9.8	1821	4.0		

OCTOBER

Day	Time	m	Time	m	Time	m	Time	m
1 TU	0050	9.4	0704	4.3	1335	9.5	2009	4.5
2 W	0244	9.5	0921	4.2	1528	10.1	2217	3.7
3 TH	0414	10.5	1048	3.1	1640	11.4	2330	2.5
4 F	0514	11.8	1153	2.1	1736	12.6		
5 SA	0028	1.5	0605	12.9	1249	1.3	1824	13.6
6 SU	0122	0.8	0651	13.7	1341	0.8	● 1910	14.3
7 M	0211	0.4	0735	14.2	1429	0.4	1954	14.6
8 TU	0256	0.3	0817	14.3	1512	0.4	2036	14.5
9 W	0335	0.5	0858	14.1	1548	0.6	2117	14.1
10 TH	0406	1.0	0937	13.5	1618	1.2	2155	13.3
11 F	0430	1.7	1014	12.7	1644	1.9	2233	12.2
12 SA	0452	2.5	1051	11.6	1712	2.8	2313	11.0
13 SU	0522	3.3	1136	10.4	1751	3.7		
14 M	0008	9.7	0606	4.3	1303	9.5	1856	4.6
15 TU	0205	9.1	0732	5.0	1444	9.5	2122	4.6
16 W	0321	9.6	1001	4.3	1550	10.3	2231	3.5
17 TH	0421	10.4	1058	3.2	1646	11.2	2322	2.5
18 F	0512	11.4	1146	2.2	1733	12.1		
19 SA	0009	1.7	0555	12.2	1232	1.6	1814	12.7
20 SU	0053	1.2	0633	12.6	1315	1.3	1851	12.9
21 M	0136	1.1	0708	12.8	1357	1.3	○ 1925	12.9
22 TU	0216	1.2	0740	12.7	1434	1.5	1957	12.7
23 W	0250	1.6	0810	12.5	1503	1.9	2027	12.4
24 TH	0314	2.0	0837	12.3	1520	2.2	2053	12.1
25 F	0328	2.2	0903	12.0	1534	2.3	2119	11.8
26 SA	0345	2.3	0932	11.8	1557	2.4	2151	11.4
27 SU	0413	2.4	1007	11.4	1629	2.6	2230	10.9
28 M	0447	2.9	1051	10.8	1708	3.2	2320	10.2
29 TU	0532	3.5	1148	10.1	1802	3.9		
30 W	0030	9.6	0639	4.2	1310	9.8	1939	4.3
31 TH	0214	9.6	0850	4.1	1459	10.3	2148	3.6

NOVEMBER

Day	Time	m	Time	m	Time	m	Time	m
1 F	0347	10.6	1020	3.2	1613	11.4	2302	2.5
2 SA	0448	11.8	1124	2.1	1709	12.6		
3 SU	0000	1.6	0539	12.9	1221	1.3	1759	13.5
4 M	0053	0.9	0625	13.7	1312	0.8	● 1845	14.1
5 TU	0141	0.5	0709	14.1	1400	0.5	1930	14.4
6 W	0227	0.5	0752	14.2	1444	0.6	2013	14.2
7 TH	0307	0.7	0834	13.9	1523	0.9	2055	13.7
8 F	0341	1.2	0914	13.4	1557	1.4	2135	13.0
9 SA	0408	1.9	0953	12.5	1626	2.1	2214	12.0
10 SU	0432	2.6	1032	11.5	1656	2.9	2255	10.9
11 M	0502	3.4	1117	10.5	1735	3.7	2346	9.8
12 TU	0546	4.1	1230	9.7	1834	4.3		
13 W	0122	9.2	0657	4.7	1408	9.6	1959	4.5
14 TH	0243	9.5	0855	4.6	1513	10.1	2141	3.9
15 F	0342	10.1	1015	3.7	1607	10.9	2240	3.0
16 SA	0433	10.9	1107	2.8	1654	11.6	2329	2.3
17 SU	0517	11.7	1153	2.2	1737	12.1		
18 M	0014	1.8	0556	12.2	1237	1.8	1816	12.4
19 TU	0058	1.5	0633	12.5	1319	1.7	1852	12.6
20 W	0138	1.5	0708	12.6	1358	1.7	○ 1928	12.5
21 TH	0215	1.6	0742	12.6	1431	1.9	2001	12.3
22 F	0246	1.8	0813	12.4	1458	2.1	2033	12.1
23 SA	0310	2.0	0845	12.2	1521	2.2	2106	11.9
24 SU	0334	2.2	0919	12.0	1549	2.4	2142	11.6
25 M	0405	2.4	0958	11.7	1624	2.6	2224	11.2
26 TU	0442	2.7	1043	11.2	1707	3.0	2314	10.7
27 W	0529	3.2	1139	10.7	1803	3.4		
28 TH	0017	10.2	0633	3.6	1251	10.4	1922	3.7
29 F	0139	10.2	0807	3.7	1420	10.7	2103	3.4
30 SA	0307	10.7	0939	3.2	1537	11.4	2223	2.7

DECEMBER

Day	Time	m	Time	m	Time	m	Time	m
1 SU	0414	11.6	1049	2.4	1639	12.2	2326	2.0
2 M	0510	12.4	1149	1.7	1733	13.0		
3 TU	0021	1.4	0600	13.1	1243	1.2	1822	13.5
4 W	0112	1.0	0646	13.6	1333	1.0	● 1909	13.7
5 TH	0200	0.9	0731	13.7	1420	0.9	1954	13.6
6 F	0244	1.1	0814	13.5	1504	1.2	2039	13.2
7 SA	0322	1.5	0857	13.1	1542	1.6	2121	12.7
8 SU	0355	2.0	0938	12.5	1616	2.1	2202	11.9
9 M	0422	2.6	1018	11.8	1647	2.7	2241	11.2
10 TU	0452	3.1	1100	11.0	1722	3.2	2322	10.4
11 W	0530	3.5	1150	10.3	1807	3.6		
12 TH	0015	9.8	0620	4.0	1300	9.9	1903	3.9
13 F	0129	9.6	0725	4.2	1414	9.9	2007	3.9
14 SA	0241	9.8	0837	4.1	1513	10.3	2117	3.6
15 SU	0339	10.3	0951	3.7	1606	10.7	2226	3.1
16 M	0431	10.9	1058	3.1	1655	11.3	2325	2.6
17 TU	0517	11.5	1151	2.5	1740	11.7		
18 W	0015	2.1	0559	12.0	1239	2.1	1822	12.1
19 TH	0101	1.8	0640	12.4	1323	1.9	○ 1903	12.3
20 F	0144	1.7	0719	12.6	1404	1.9	1942	12.3
21 SA	0223	1.7	0757	12.6	1443	2.0	2022	12.3
22 SU	0300	1.8	0835	12.5	1519	2.0	2101	12.2
23 M	0334	2.0	0914	12.4	1555	2.1	2141	12.1
24 TU	0408	2.1	0955	12.2	1632	2.2	2223	11.8
25 W	0447	2.3	1040	12.0	1714	2.4	2309	11.5
26 TH	0531	2.5	1130	11.6	1801	2.7		
27 F	0001	11.1	0622	2.9	1228	11.2	1858	3.0
28 SA	0104	10.8	0727	3.1	1339	11.0	2009	3.2
29 SU	0220	10.7	0847	3.2	1457	11.1	2136	3.1
30 M	0336	11.0	1010	2.9	1607	11.5	2252	2.7
31 TU	0441	11.6	1119	2.4	1709	12.0	2353	2.2

Chart Datum: 6·50 metres below Ordnance Datum (Newlyn)

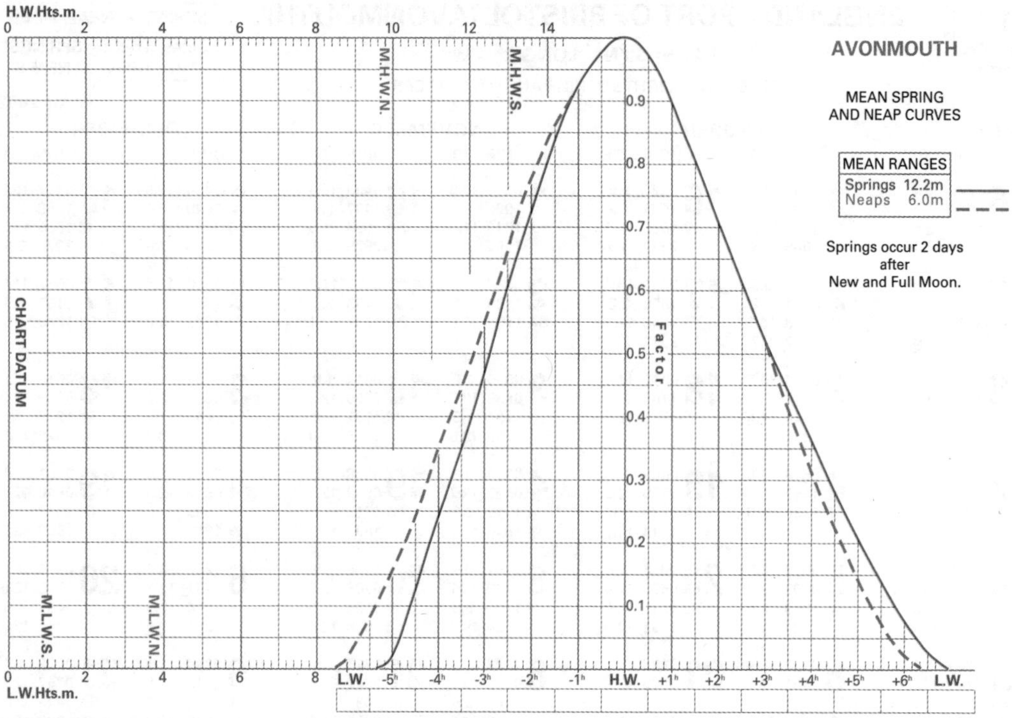
H.W.Hts.m.
0 2 4 6 8 10 12 14
M.H.W.N.
M.H.W.S.
CHART DATUM
M.L.W.S.
M.L.W.N.
Factor
0.9
0.8
0.7
0.6
0.5
0.4
0.3
0.2
0.1
L.W.Hts.m.
L.W. -5h -4h -3h -2h -1h H.W. +1h +2h +3h +4h +5h +6h L.W.
AVONMOUTH
MEAN SPRING AND NEAP CURVES
MEAN RANGES
Springs 12.2m
Neaps 6.0m
Springs occur 2 days after New and Full Moon.

BRISTOL (CITY DOCKS) *9.11.21*

City of Bristol **51°26'·95N 02°37'·44W** ❀❀❀◊◊◊✿✿✿

CHARTS AC 1859, *1176, 1179*; Imray C59; Stanfords 14; OS 172

TIDES –0410 on Dover; ML 7·0; Duration 0620; Zone 0 (UT)

Standard Port BRISTOL (AVONMOUTH) (⟵)

Times				**Height (metres)**			
High Water		Low Water		MHWS	MHWN	MLWN	MLWS
0200	0800	0300	0800	13·2	9·8	3·8	1·0
1400	2000	1500	2000				
Differences SHIREHAMPTON (R Avon, 51°29'N 02°41'W)							
0000	0000	+0035	+0010	–0·7	–0·7	–0·8	0·0
SEA MILLS (R Avon, 51°29'N 02°39'W)							
+0005	+0005	+0105	+0030	–1·4	–1·5	–1·7	–0·1
CUMBERLAND BASIN (Ent)							
+0010	+0010	Dries		–2·9	–3·0	Dries	

SHELTER Excellent in Bristol Floating Harbour and in Bristol marina. Avonmouth and Royal Portbury Docks are prohib to yachts, except in emergency. Crockerne Pill has drying moorings and a grid for emergency repairs. Speed limit in R Avon = 6kn. Drying moorings (soft mud) may be found at Lamplighters Quay just up stream of the M5 motorway br. and convenient when carrying the ebb from Sharpness. ☎ 0117 9381757 📠 0117 9382085. For R Avon, Cumberland Basin and Bristol Hbr refer to *Bristol Harbour: Info for Boat Owners*, from Hr Mr, Underfall Yard, Cumberland Rd, Bristol BS1 6XG.

NAVIGATION Avonmouth WPT 51°30´·45N 02°43´·33W, 307°/127° from/to front ldg lt, 0·61M. The chan from Flatholm is buoyed. See R/T below for compliance with VTS and reporting.Sp tidal stream across ent reaches 5kn.

Locking in: Best to reach Cumberland Basin by HW (approx 7M upriver from WPT); waiting pontoon (dries). Ent lock opens approx HW–2½, –1½ and –¼hr for arrivals; departing craft lockout approx 15 mins after these times. Swing bridge opens in unison with lock, but not Mon-Fri during road tfc rush hrs 0800-0900 and 1700-1800. Inner (Junction) lock is always open,unless ht of HW >9·6m ('stopgate' tide) when it closes; read special instructions. If you miss the last lock-in, call VHF Ch 12 for advice. Options: dry out in soft mud at pontoons, or on N Wall (bow abreast ladder No 4 Survey Mark; no nearer the lock gate). Other areas are foul.

Bridges: Prince St bridge is manned 0915-2215 summer, by appointment only in winter; openings are normally at H+15. Pre-notify Bridgemaster ☎ 9299338, call VHF Ch 73 or sound ·–·(R). Redcliffe bridge opening: pre-arrange with Hr Mr. Clearances above hbr datum: Prince St 2·2m; Redcliffe 3·6m; St Augustine 3·1m. Water level can be 0·5m above hbr datum.

LIGHTS AND MARKS R Avon ent is abeam S pier lt Oc RG 30s, vis R294°-036°, G036°-194°. Ldg lts 127° both FR. St George ldg lts 173°, both Oc G 5s synch; front R/Or post; rear W/Or chequers on Or post. Upriver, G or R ☆s mark the outside of bends.

Ent sigs to Bristol Hbr may be shown from E bank, 1½ and 2¼ca beyond Clifton Suspension Bridge: ● = continue with caution; ● = stop and await orders.

RADIO TELEPHONE Yachts bound for Bristol should call *Avonmouth Radio* VHF Ch **12** 09 at English and Welsh Grounds SWM buoy and at Welsh Hook PHM buoy; comply with any VTS orders. On entering R Avon call again, low power, stating that you are bound for City Docks. If no radio fitted, signal Avonmouth Sig Stn with Flag R or flash morse R (·–·). The sig stn will reply by light or loud hailer. Keep well clear of large vessels. At Black Rks (0·8M to run) call *City Docks Radio*, low power, Ch **14** 11 (HW–3 to HW+1) for locking instructions. For berths, call *Bristol Hbr* Ch 73 16 (HO), and/or Bristol Marina Ch **80** M. Prince St br and Netham lock Ch 73.

TELEPHONE (Dial code 0117) Hr Mr 9264797; Dock Master, Cumberland Basin 9273633; Prince St and Redcliffe Bridges 9299338; Netham Lock 9776590; ⊜ 9826451 (H24); MRCC (01792) 366534; Bristol weather centre 9279298; Marinecall 09068 500 459; Police 9277777; Ⓗ 9230000.

FACILITIES **Portishead CC** (Crockerne Pill), drying M; **Lamplighters Quay** ½M above M5 br on E Bank; drying AB, VHF Ch 80, C (20 ton), BH (9 ton) ☎ 938 1757 📠 938 2085; **Bristol Hbr** ☎ 9264797, 📠 9294454, approx 40 Ⓥ AB £0.75 inc locking fee, FW, D, AC, 🚲, Slip, CH, Gas, V, R, Bar; ferries ply around the hbr. **Bristol Marina** (80, inc Ⓥ; 20m max LOA) ☎ 921 3198, 📠 929 7672, £9.04, AC,D,FW, access HW–3 to +1, El, Ⓔ, ME, Sh, SM, Slip, CH, C (6&12 ton), BH (30 ton), ♿, 🗊; **Baltic Wharf Leisure Centre** ☎ 9297608, Slip, L, Bar; **Cabot Cruising Club** ☎ 9268318, M, L, FW, AB, Bar; **Portavon Marina** ☎ 9861626, 📠 986 6455, Bitton Road, Keynsham BS18 2DD; Slip, M, FW, ME, Sh, CH, R; **Bathurst Basin** Toilets and showers; **City** EC Wed/Sat; all facilities, ACA, P, D, ✉, Ⓑ, ⇌, ✈.

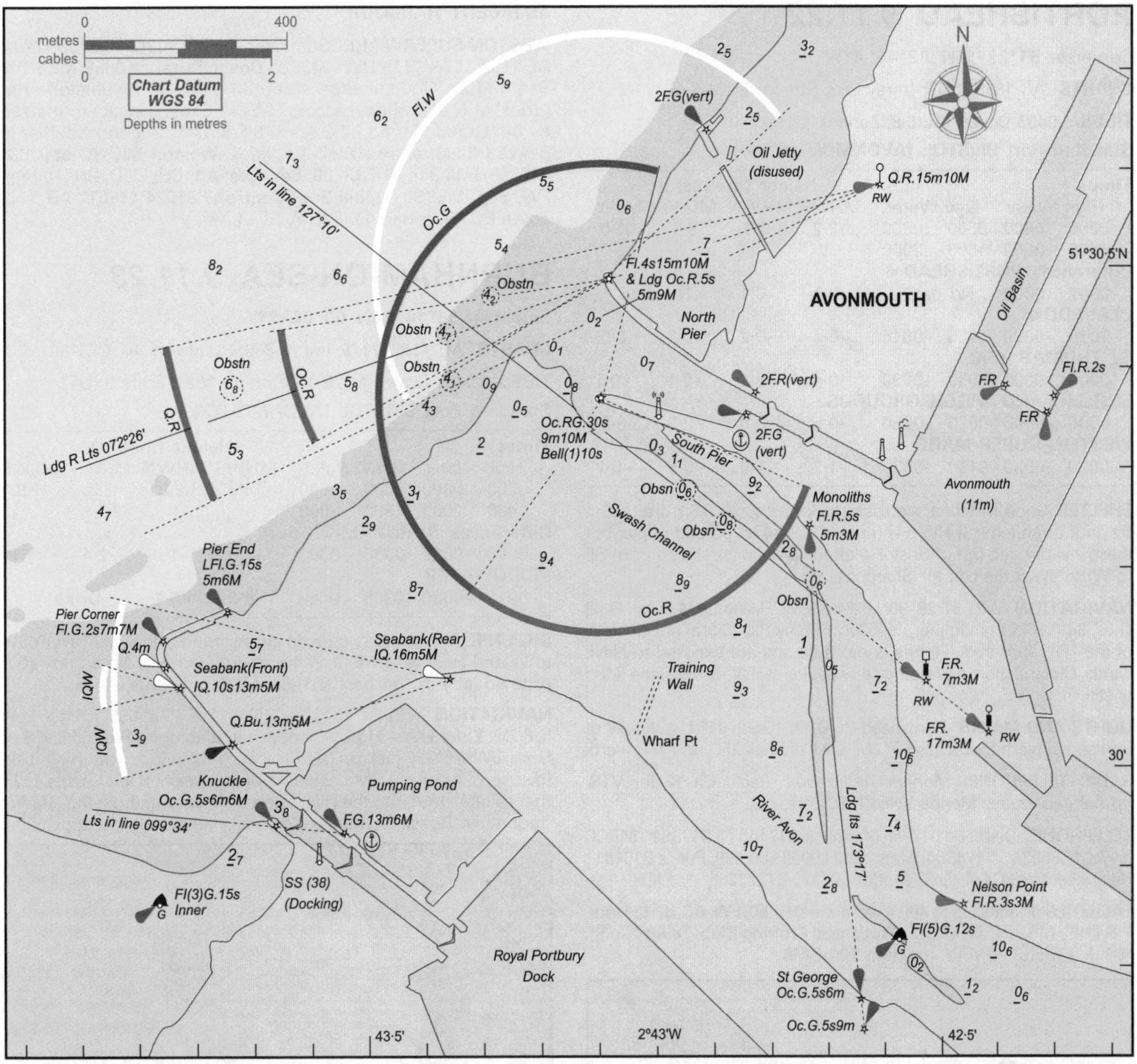
metres
cables
0
400
2
Chart Datum
WGS 84
Depths in metres
N
Fl.W
Oc.G
Lts in line 127°10'
2F.G(vert)
Oil Jetty
(disused)
Q.R.15m10M
RW
Fl.4s15m10M
& Ldg Oc.R.5s
5m9M
Obstn
AVONMOUTH
51°30·5'N
Oil Basin
North
Pier
Obstn
Oc.R
Q.R
Ldg R Lts 072°26'
2F.R(vert)
Fl.R.2s
F.R
F.R
2F.G
(vert)
South Pier
Oc.RG.30s
9m10M
Bell(1)10s
Avonmouth
(11m)
Obsn
Obsn
Monoliths
Fl.R.5s
5m3M
Swash Channel
Obsn
Oc.R
Pier End
LFl.G.15s
5m6M
Pier Corner
Fl.G.2s7m7M
Q.4m
Seabank(Rear)
IQ.16m5M
Seabank(Front)
IQ.10s13m5M
IQW
IQW
Training
Wall
F.R.
7m3M
RW
F.R.
17m3M
RW
30'
Q.Bu.13m5M
Wharf Pt
Pumping Pond
Knuckle
Oc.G.5s6m6M
Lts in line 099°34'
F.G.13m6M
River Avon
Ldg lts 173°17'
Fl(3)G.15s
Inner
G
SS (38)
(Docking)
Nelson Point
Fl.R.3s3M
Fl(5)G.12s
G
Royal Portbury
Dock
St George
Oc.G.5s6m
Oc.G.5s9m
43·5'
2°43'W
42·5'

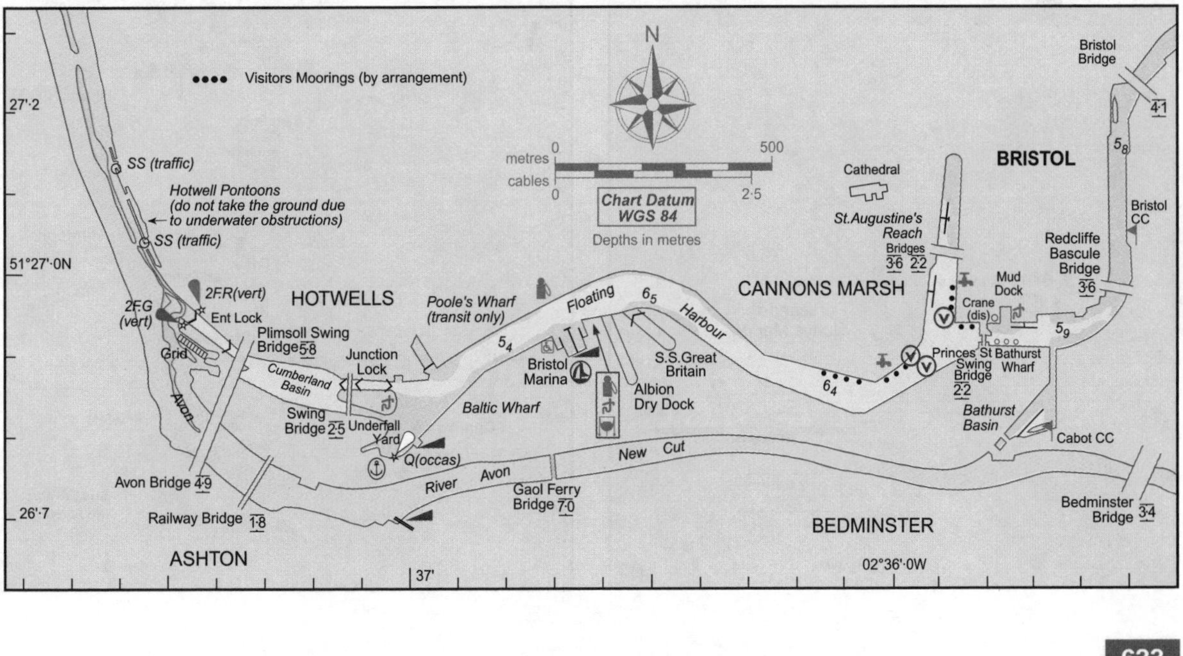
N
Visitors Moorings (by arrangement)
27'·2
SS (traffic)
Hotwell Pontoons
(do not take the ground due
to underwater obstructions)
SS (traffic)
51°27'·0N
metres
cables
0
500
2·5
Chart Datum
WGS 84
Depths in metres
Cathedral
BRISTOL
Bristol
Bridge
St.Augustine's
Reach
Bridges
3·6
2·2
Bristol
CC
Redcliffe
Bascule
Bridge
3·6
2F.R(vert)
2F.G
(vert)
Ent Lock
HOTWELLS
Poole's Wharf
(transit only)
Floating
Harbour
CANNONS MARSH
Mud
Dock
Crane
(dis)
Plimsoll Swing
Bridge 5·8
Grid
Junction
Lock
Cumberland
Basin
Bristol
Marina
S.S.Great
Britain
Princes St
Swing
Bridge
2·2
Bathurst
Wharf
Avon
Swing
Bridge 2·5
Underfall
Yard
Baltic Wharf
Albion
Dry Dock
Bathurst
Basin
Cabot CC
Q(occas)
New Cut
River Avon
Avon Bridge 4·9
Gaol Ferry
Bridge 7·0
26'·7
Railway Bridge 1·8
BEDMINSTER
Bedminster
Bridge 3·4
ASHTON
37'
02°36'·0W

11

PORTISHEAD *9.11.22*

Somerset **51°29'·56N 02°45'·41W**

CHARTS AC 1859, *1176*; Imray C59; Stanfords 14; OS 171/2

TIDES –0405 Dover; ML 6·8; Zone 0 (UT)

Standard Port BRISTOL (AVONMOUTH) (⟵)

Times				Height (metres)			
High Water		Low Water		MHWS	MHWN	MLWN	MLWS
0200	0800	0300	0800	13·2	9·8	3·8	1·0
1400	2000	1500	2000				
Differences PORTISHEAD							
–0002	0000	No data		–0·1	–0·1	No data	
CLEVEDON							
–0010	–0020	–0025	–0015	–0·4	–0·2	+0·2	0·0
ST THOMAS HEAD							
0000	0000	–0030	–0030	–0·4	–0·2	+0·1	+0·1
ENGLISH AND WELSH GROUNDS							
–0008	–0008	–0030	–0030	–0·5	–0·8	–0·3	0·0
WESTON-SUPER-MARE							
–0020	–0030	–0130	–0030	–1·2	–1·0	–0·8	–0·2

SHELTER Good in marina. Access by lock 9m x 40m x 3·5m draft (5·5m by prior arrangement) HW ±4½ (nps) ±3¾ (sp). ⚓ off end of pier but these will dry out. Out of Bristol, ⚓ off the pier hd (sheltered from SE to W) to await the tide for Sharpness.

NAVIGATION WPT 51°29'·96N 02°45'·35W, Firefly SHM buoy, Fl (2) G 5s, 348°/168° from/to pier hd, 500m. Firefly Rks (0·9m) are close W of the 168° appr track. Appr's dry to mud and are exposed to N/NE winds. Close inshore a W-going eddy begins at HW –3 whilst the flood is still making E.

LIGHTS AND MARKS Portishead Pt, Q (3) 10s9m 16M, is 7ca W of Portishead pierhd, Iso G 2s 5m 3M. Lock ent has 2FG and 2FR (vert).

RADIO TELEPHONE Monitor *Avonmouth Radio* Ch 12 for VTS. Portishead Quays Marina VHF Ch 80 24H.

TELEPHONE (Dial code 01275) Marina ☎ 817440 📠 817882 ; MRCC (01792) 366534; ⊜ 474864; Marinecall 09068 500 459; Police 818181 ; Health centre 847474; Ⓗ (Clevedon) 01179 872212

FACILITIES Marina (up to 400/450 planned) £1.50, FW, AC, BH (35 ton), P & D, El, ME, CH, BY, Gas, ⊡. **Portishead Cruising Club; Town** ✉, Ⓑ, ⇌, ✈ (Bristol). 3M to Junction 19 of M5.

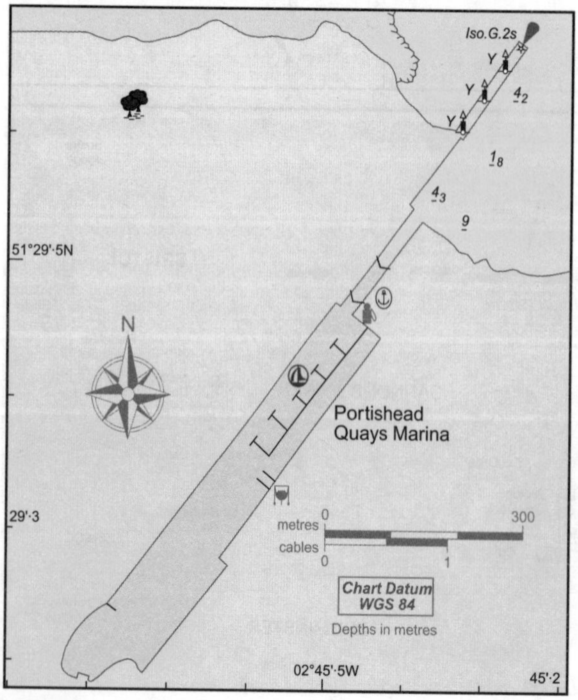

ADJACENT HARBOUR

WESTON-SUPER-MARE, Somerset, **51°21'·03N 02°59'·28W.** AC 1152, 1176, *1179*. HW –0435 on Dover; Duration 0655; ML 6·1m. See 9.11.22. Good shelter, except in S'lies, in Knightstone Hbr (dries) at N end of bay; access HW±1½. Causeway at ent marked by bn. Grand Pier hd 2 FG (vert) 6/5m. Or ⚓ in good weather in R Axe (dries), entry HW±2. Facilities: **Weston Bay YC** ☎ 01934 413366, FW, Bar, VHF Ch **80; Services**: AB, CH, El, D, BH (10 ton), FW, Slip, ME, Sh; **Uphill Boat Centre** ☎ 01934 418617 AB, slip; **Town** EC Mon; Bar, Ⓑ, FW, P, ✉, R, ⇌, V.

BURNHAM-ON-SEA *9.11.23*

Somerset **51°14'·23N 03°00'·33W**

CHARTS AC *1152, 1179*; Imray C59; Stanfords 14; OS 182

TIDES –0435 Dover; ML 5·4; Duration 0620; Zone 0 (UT)

Standard Port BRISTOL (AVONMOUTH) (⟵)

Times				Height (metres)			
High Water		Low Water		MHWS	MHWN	MLWN	MLWS
0200	0800	0300	0800	13·2	9·8	3·8	1·0
1400	2000	1500	2000				
Differences BURNHAM-ON-SEA							
–0020	–0025	–0030	0000	–2·3	–1·9	–1·4	–1·1
BRIDGWATER							
–0015	–0030	+0305	+0455	–8·6	–8·1	Dries	

SHELTER Ent is very choppy in strong winds, especially from SW to W and from N to NE. ⚓ in 4m about 40m E of No 1 buoy or S of town jetty or, for best shelter, AB/⚓ in R Brue (dries).

NAVIGATION WPT 51°15'·32N 03°08'·22W, 275°/095° from/to Low lt, 6·2M. Enter HW –3 to HW; not advised at night. From 5·0M S of Gore SWM buoy pick up 076° transit of Low lt ho with High lt ho (disused). Approx 1·3M past No 1 buoy, steer on ldg line/lts 112°; thence alter 180° into the river chan but banks and depths change frequently. Beware unmarked fishing stakes outside appr chan.

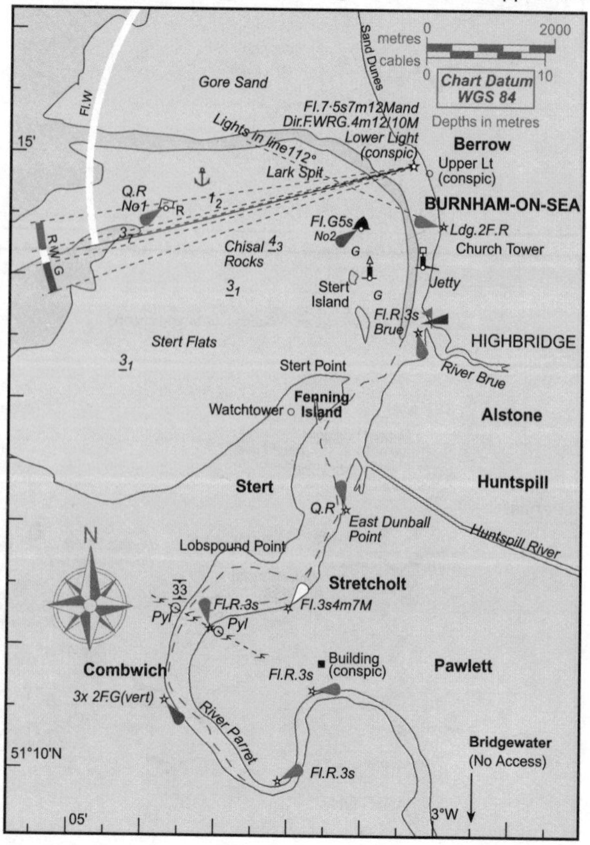

BURNHAM *continued*

LIGHTS AND MARKS Low lt ho Dir 076° as chartlet and 9.11.4. Ldg lts/marks 112° (moved as chan shifts): front FR 6m 3M, Or stripe on □ W background on sea wall; rear FR 12m 3M, church tr.

RADIO TELEPHONE Hr Mr and Pilot VHF Ch 08 16 (when vessel expected).

TELEPHONE (Dial code 01278) Hr Mr and Pilot 782180; MRCC (01792) 366534; ⊖ (01446) 420241; Marinecall 09068 500 459; Police 782288; 🅗 782262.

FACILITIES **Burnham-on-Sea YC** ☎ 792911, M, few drying ⚓s in River Brue, L, Slip, Bar; **Brue Yachts** ☎ 783275, drying pontoon £7, FW, D, V. **Services:** ME, El, Sh, ACA (Bridgwater). **Town** EC Wed; Gas, ✉, Ⓑ, ≹ (Highbridge), ✈ (Bristol). Note: No access to Bridgwater marina from sea/R Parrett.

WATCHET *9.11.24*

Somerset **51°11′·03N 03°19′·72W**

CHARTS AC *1160, 1152, 1179*; Imray C59; Stanfords 14; OS 181

TIDES –0450 Dover; ML 5·9; Duration 0655; Zone 0 (UT)

Standard Port BRISTOL (AVONMOUTH) (⟵)

Times				Height (metres)			
High Water		Low Water		MHWS	MHWN	MLWN	MLWS
0200	0800	0300	0800	13·2	9·8	3·8	1·0
1400	2000	1500	2000				
Differences HINKLEY POINT							
–0020	–0025	–0100	–0040	–1·7	–1·4	–0·2	–0·2
WATCHET							
–0035	–0050	–0145	–0040	–1·9	–1·5	+0·1	+0·1
MINEHEAD							
–0037	–0052	–0155	–0045	–2·6	–1·9	–0·2	0·0
PORLOCK BAY							
–0045	–0055	–0205	–0050	–3·0	–2·2	–0·1	–0·1
LYNMOUTH							
–0055	–0115	No data		–3·6	–2·7	No data	

SHELTER Good, but open to N and E winds. The outer hbr ent dries 6·5m, but has about 6m depth at MHWS; access approx HW±2½.
When the tide is higher than the retaining wall level in the marina the gate will drop with a minimum water depth at the entrance of 2·5m. The entrance width is 8m and the minimum depths in the marina will be up to 3.0m

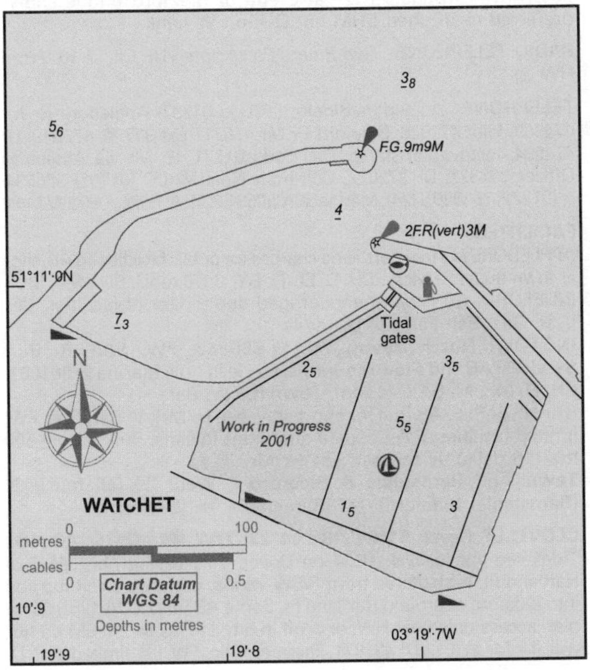

NAVIGATION WPT 51°12′·03N 03°18′·88W, 028°/208° from/to hbr ent, 1·1M. Rks/mud dry 5ca to seaward. Beware tidal streams 4-5kn at sp offshore and around W pier hd. Culver Sand (0·9m) is approx 6M NNE, marked by ECM and WCM lt buoys. 5M E of hbr are Lilstock range target buoys. DZ No 2 SPM buoy, Fl Y 10s, bears 030°/3·2M from Watchet.

LIGHTS AND MARKS Two unlit radio masts (206m) bearing 208°/1·6M from hbr ent are conspic approach marks. Hinkley Pt nuclear power stn is conspic 7·5M to the E. W pier hd FG 9m 9M on Red (R) tr. E pier hd 2 FR (vert) 3M.

RADIO TELEPHONE VHF Ch 09 12 14 16 (from HW–2, but occas).

TELEPHONE (Dial code 01984) Hr Mr 631264; Watchet Boat Owners Association 634242; ⊖ (01446) 420241; MRCC (01792) 366534; Marinecall 09068 500 459; Police (01643) 703361 (Minehead).

FACILITIES Work on marina due to be completed in 2001. **Planned Services:** FW, Slip, ACA (Bridgwater). **Town** EC Wed; ✉, Ⓑ, V, R, Bar. At Williton (2M): Gas, D & P (cans); 🅗 (Minehead 8M), ≹ (Taunton 18M), ✈ (Bristol).

OTHER HARBOURS ON S SHORE OF BRISTOL CHANNEL

MINEHEAD, Somerset, **51°12′·79N 03°28′·37W.** AC 1160, 1165, *1179.* HW –0450 on Dover. ML 5·7m. See 9.11.24. Small hbr, dries 7·5m; access HW±2. Good shelter within pier curving E and then SE, over which seas may break in gales at MHWS; exposed to E'lies. Best appr from N or NW; beware The Gables, shingle bank (dries 3·7m) about 5ca ENE of pier. Keep E of a sewer outfall which passes ½ca E of pierhd and extends 1¾ca NNE of it; outfall is protected by rk covering, drying 2·8m and N end marked by SHM bn QG 6m 7M. There are 8 R ⚓s at hbr ent just seaward of 3 posts or dry out against pier. Hbr gets very crowded. Holiday camp is conspic 6ca SE. Pierhd lt Fl (2) G 5s 4M, vis 127°-262°. VHF Ch 16 12 14 (occas). Hr Mr ☎ (01643) 702566; Facilities: **Hbr** FW, Slip. **Town** EC Wed; D, P, El, Gas, ME, Sh, R, Bar, V, ✉, Ⓑ, ≹ (Taunton).

PORLOCK WEIR, Somerset, **51°13′·17N 03°37′·64W.** AC 1160, 1165, *1179.* HW –0500 on Dover; ML 5·6m. See 9.11.24. Access HW±1½. Ent chan (250°), about 15m wide marked by withies (3 PHM and 1 SHM), between shingle bank/wood pilings to stbd and sunken wooden wall to port is difficult in any seas. A small pool (1m) just inside ent is for shoal draft boats; others dry out on pebble banks. Or turn 90° stbd, via gates (usually open), into inner drying dock with good shelter. No lts. Hr Mr ☎ (01643) 863277. **Porlock Weir SC** ☎ 862028. Facilities: FW and limited V.

LYNMOUTH, Devon, **51°14'·16N 03°49'·79W.** AC 1160,1165. HW–0515 on Dover. See 9.11.24. Tiny hbr, dries approx 5m; access HW±1, but only in settled offshore weather. Appr from Sand Ridge SHM buoy, 1·6M W of Foreland Pt and 9ca N of hbr ent. The narrow appr chan between drying boulder ledges is marked by 7 unlit posts. Hbr ent is between piers, 2FR/FG lts, on W side of river course. Berth on E pier, which covers at MHWS. Resort facilities.

WATERMOUTH, Devon, **51°13′·03N 04°04′·6W.** AC 1165, *1179.* HW –0525 on Dover; ML 4·9m; Duration 0625. Use 9.11.25. Good shelter in drying hbr, but heavy surge runs in strong NW winds. Access HW±3 at sp; only as far as inner bkwtr at np. Dir lt 153° Oc WRG 5s 1m, vis W151·5°-154·5°, W △ on structure, 1½ca inside ent on S shore. Bkwtr, covered at half tide, has Fl G 5s 2M. Eight Y ⚓s with B handles. Hr Mr ☎ (01271) 865422. Facilities: **Hbr** D (cans), FW (cans), CH, C (12 ton), Slip; **YC** ☎ 865048, Bar.

ILFRACOMBE *9.11.25*

Devon **51°12'·65N 04°06'·65W**

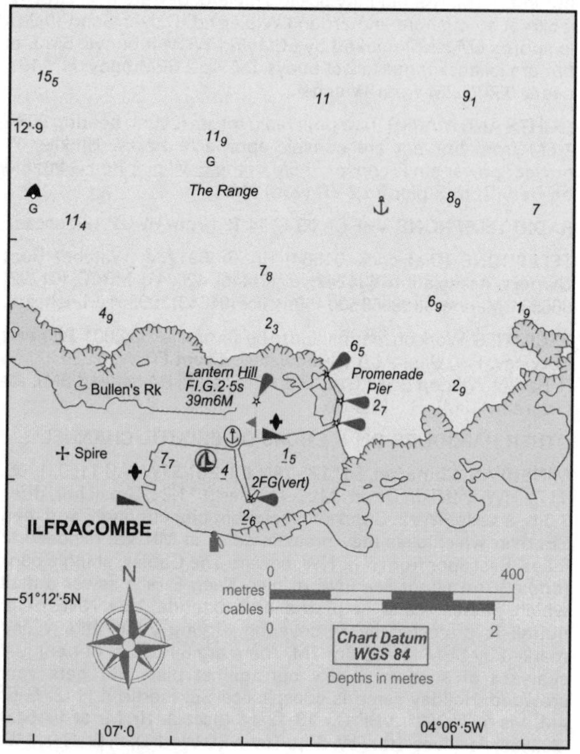

CHARTS AC 1160, *1165, 1179*; Imray C59; Stanfords 14; OS 180

TIDES –0525 Dover; ML 5·0; Duration 0625; Zone 0 (UT)

Standard Port MILFORD HAVEN (⟵)

Times				Height (metres)			
High Water		Low Water		MHWS	MHWN	MLWN	MLWS
0100	0700	0100	0700	7·0	5·2	2·5	0·7
1300	1900	1300	1900				
Differences ILFRACOMBE							
–0016	–0016	–0041	–0031	+2·3	+1·8	+0·6	+0·3
LUNDY ISLAND							
–0025	–0025	–0020	–0035	+1·0	+0·7	+0·2	0·0

SHELTER Good except in NE/E winds. SW gales can cause surge in hbrs, which dry. 6 Ⓜs in outer hbr, access HW±3. Or ⚓ clear of pier and LB Slip. Visitors AB on N wall of inner hbr, access HW±2.

NAVIGATION WPT 51°13'·23N 04°06'·67W, 000°/180° from/to pier hd, 0·55M. From E, beware Copperas Rks (4M to E), (SHM buoy) and tiderips on Buggy Pit, 7ca NE of ent. On entry keep toward Promenade Pier to clear drying ledges and lobster keep-pots obstructing hbr ent on SE side.

LIGHTS AND MARKS No ldg marks/lts. Lantern Hill lt, Fl G 2·5s 39m 6M, on small conspic chapel. Promenade Pier has three 2FG (vert). Inner bkwtr 2 FG (vert).

RADIO TELEPHONE Call: *Ilfracombe Hbr* VHF Ch 12 16 (Apl-Oct 0800-2000 when manned; Nov-Mar occas). Ch **80** M (occas).

TELEPHONE (Dial code 01271) Hr Mr 862108; MRCC (01792) 366534; ⊖ (01222) 763880 ; Marinecall 09068 500 459; Police 863633; Dr 863119.

FACILITIES **Hbr** AB £0·60, M, D, FW, CH, Slip, ME, El, Sh; **Ilfracombe YC** ☎ 863969, M, ⓘ, Bar, C (35 ton, as arranged) **Town** EC Thurs, V, R, Bar, ✉, Ⓑ, bus to Barnstaple (⇌), ✈ (Exeter).

RIVERS TAW & TORRIDGE *9.11.26*

Devon **51°04'·37N 04°12'·88W**

CHARTS AC *1160, 1164, 1179*; Imray C58; Stanfords 14; OS 180

TIDES –0525 (Appledore) Dover; ML 3·6; Duration 0600; Zone 0 (UT)

Standard Port MILFORD HAVEN (⟵)

Times				Height (metres)			
High Water		Low Water		MHWS	MHWN	MLWN	MLWS
0100	0700	0100	0700	7·0	5·2	2·5	0·7
1300	1900	1300	1900				
Differences APPLEDORE							
–0020	–0025	+0015	–0045	+0·5	0·0	–0·9	–0·5
YELLAND MARSH (R Taw)							
–0010	–0015	+0100	–0015	+0·1	–0·4	–1·2	–0·6
FREMINGTON (R Taw)							
–0010	–0015	+0030	–0030	–1·1	–1·8	–2·2	–0·5
BARNSTAPLE (R Taw)							
0000	–0015	–0155	–0245	–2·9	–3·8	–2·2	–0·4
BIDEFORD (R Torridge)							
–0020	–0025	0000	0000	–1·1	–1·6	–2·5	–0·7
CLOVELLY							
–0030	–0030	–0020	–0040	+1·3	+1·1	+0·2	+0·2

SHELTER Very well protected, but ent is dangerous in strong on-shore winds. Yachts can ⚓ or pick up RNLI buoy (please donate to RNLI, Boathouse ☎ 473969) or Appledore Shipbuilders buoy (☎ 473281 📠 462500) in Appledore Pool, N of Skern Pt where sp stream can reach 5kn. Bideford quay dries to soft mud; used by coasters.

NAVIGATION WPT 51°05'·43N 04°16'·11W (abeam Fairway buoy), 298°/118° from/to Bar buoy, 0·9M. Bar and sands constantly shift; buoys are moved occasionally to comply. Advice on bar, least depths of 0·1 and 0·4m, from Pilot Ch 12 or Swansea CG. Estuary dries; access is only feasible from HW–2 to HW. Once tide is ebbing, breakers quickly form between Bar SHM buoy and Middle Ridge SHM buoy. Hold the ldg line 118° only up to Outer Pulley where chan deviates stbd toward Pulley buoy and Grey Sand Hill, thence to Appledore Pool. 2M passage to Bideford is not difficult. Barnstaple (7M): seek local advice or take pilot.

LIGHTS AND MARKS Entry at night is NOT advised. Only lts, apart from jetties, are Bideford SWM buoy, Outer Pulley SHM buoy, Crow Pt and the ldg lts as on chartlet; ldg marks are W trs, lit H24. R Torridge: Lt QY at E end of Bideford bridge shows preferred chan; then SHM bn, QG, on W bank.

RADIO TELEPHONE *Two Rivers Port/Pilots* VHF Ch 12 16 (From HW–2).

TELEPHONE Appledore/Bideford: Code 01237. Appledore Hr Mr 474569; Pilot 477928; Bideford Hr Mr 476711 Ext 317 📠 478849; Dr 474994. Instow/Barnstaple: Dial code 01271. Hr Mr via Amenities Officer 388327; Dr 372672. Common Nos: MRCC (01792) 366534; ⊖ (01222) 763880 (H24); Marinecall 09068 500 459; Police 0990 777444.

FACILITIES

APPLEDORE is a free port, ie no charges for public facilities eg AB, slips at town quay. **Services:** CH, D, El, Ⓔ, BY, C (70 tons), Slip, ME, Sh.

BIDEFORD: AB few/not encouraged due to lack of facilities; CH, V, R, Gas, Bar. Ferry to Lundy Is.

INSTOW: **North Devon YC**, ☎ 860367, FW, Slip, R, Bar; **Services:** AB and a few moorings, £5 via Instow Marine ☎ 861081, CH, D, ME, M, Ⓔ, C (4 ton). **Town** R, FW, Bar.

BARNSTAPLE: AB (foc for short stay, see Hr Mr), V, Bar, Gas. FW: limited facilities; P & D: small quantities in cans. Bulk D (min 500 ltrs/110 galls) by bowser, see Hr Mr.

Towns: EC Barnstaple & Bideford = Wed; ✉ (all four), Ⓑ (Barnstaple, Bideford), ⇌ (Barnstaple, ✈ (Exeter).

CLOVELLY, Devon, **51°00'·18N 04°23'·77W**. AC *1164*. Tides see above. HW –0524 on Dover. Tiny drying hbr, 5M E of Hartland Pt, is sheltered from S/SW winds; useful to await the tide into Bideford or around Hartland Pt. Some AB (max LOA 12m) £5 on pier, access only near HW; or ⚓ off in 5m. Lt Fl G 5s 5m 5M on hbr wall. Hr Mr ☎ (01237) 431871. Facilities: Slip, FW, ✉, limited V, P, D.

RIVERS TAW & TORRIDGE *continued*

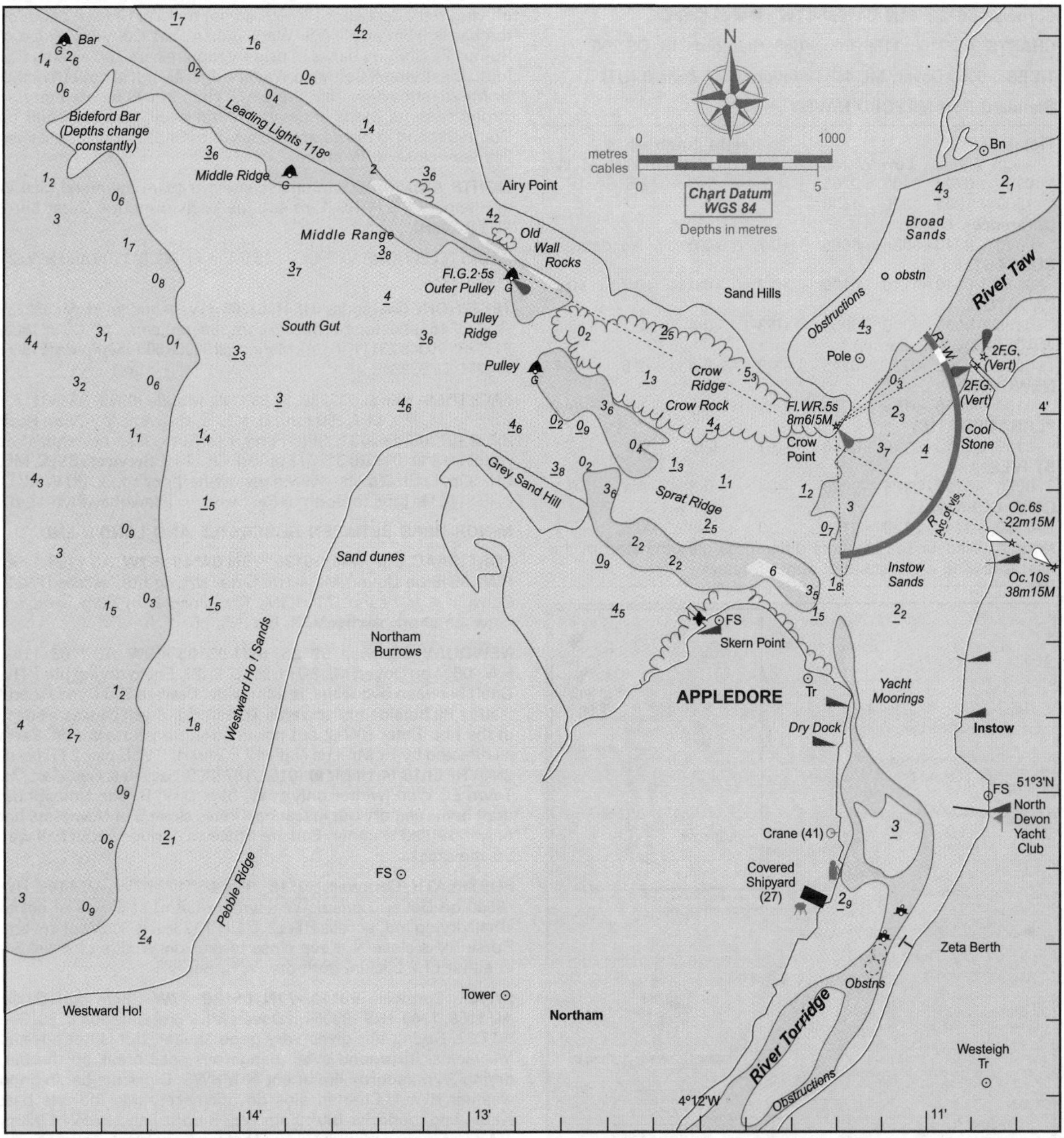

ISLAND IN BRISTOL CHANNEL, 10M NNW of Hartland Pt

LUNDY ISLAND, Devon, **51°09´·83N 04°39´·27W**. AC *1164, 1179.* HW–0530 on Dover; ML 4·3m; Duration 0605. See 9.11.25 ☎ 01237 470074. Beware bad tide races, esp on E-going flood, off the N and SE tips of the Is; and to the SW on the W-going ebb. A violent race forms over Stanley Bank 3M NE of the N tip. Shelter good in lee of island's high ground (145m). In SSW to NW winds, usual ⚓ is close inshore to NW of SE Pt and Rat Is, clear of ferry. In N'lies ⚓ in The Rattles, small bay on S side. In E'lies Jenny's Cove is safe if no W'ly swell. Lts: NW Pt, Fl 15s 48m 17M, vis 009°-285°, W ○ tr. On SE Pt, Fl 5s 53m 15M, vis 170°-073°, W ○ tr, horn 25s. Two Historic Wrecks (see 9.0.3h) lie on the E side of the island, at 51°11'N 04°39'·4W, and 4ca further E. Facilities: Landing by the ⚓ off SE end of Island or using N side of jetty to disembark passengers only, vessels not permitted to remain alongside; £3.50, £10 season per head landing fee. The waters around Lundy are a Marine Nature Reserve. **Lundy Co** CH, Gas, bar and hotel.

MINOR HARBOURS ON THE NW COAST OF CORNWALL

BUDE, Cornwall, **50°49´·93N 04°33´·37W**. AC 1156. HW–0540 on Dover. Duration 0605. See 9.11.27. Limited shelter in drying hbr, access for average yacht HW±2. Conspic W radar dish aerials 3·3M N of hbr. Outer ldg marks 075°, front W spar with Y ◊ topmark, rear W flagstaff; hold this line until inner ldg marks in line at 131°, front W pile, rear W spar, both with Y △ topmarks. There are no lts. VHF Ch 16 12 (when vessel expected). Hr Mr ☎ (01288) 353111; very limited facilities; **Town** EC Thurs; Ⓑ, Bar, ✉, R, V, Gas.

BOSCASTLE, Cornwall, **50°41'·48N 04°42·17W**. AC 1156. HW –0543 on Dover; see 9.11.27. A tiny, picturesque hbr, almost a land-locked cleft in the cliffs. Access HW±2, but not in onshore winds when swell causes surge inside. An E'ly appr, S of Meachard Rk (37m high, 2ca NW of hbr), is best. 2 short bkwtrs at ent; moor bows-on to drying S quay.

PADSTOW *9.11.27*

Cornwall **50°32'·51N 04°56'·17W**

CHARTS AC 1168, 1156; Imray C58; Stanfords 13; OS 200

TIDES –0550 Dover; ML 4·0; Duration 0600; Zone 0 (UT)

Standard Port MILFORD HAVEN (⟵)

Times				Height (metres)			
High Water		Low Water		MHWS	MHWN	MLWN	MLWS
0100	0700	0100	0700	7·0	5·2	2·5	0·7
1300	1900	1300	1900				
Differences BUDE							
–0040	–0040	–0035	–0045	+0·7	+0·6	No data	
BOSCASTLE							
–0045	–0010	–0110	–0100	+0·3	+0·4	+0·2	+0·2
PADSTOW							
–0055	–0050	–0040	–0050	+0·3	+0·4	+0·1	+0·1
WADEBRIDGE (R Camel)							
–0052	–0052	+0235	+0245	–3·8	–3·8	–2·5	–0·4
NEWQUAY							
–0100	–0110	–0105	–0050	0·0	+0·1	0·0	–0·1
PERRANPORTH							
–0100	–0110	–0110	–0050	–0·1	0·0	0·0	+0·1
ST IVES							
–0050	–0115	–0105	–0040	–0·4	–0·3	–0·1	+0·1
CAPE CORNWALL							
–0130	–0145	–0120	–0120	–1·0	–0·9	–0·5	–0·1

Note: At Wadebridge LW time differences give the start of the rise, following a LW stand of about 5 hours.

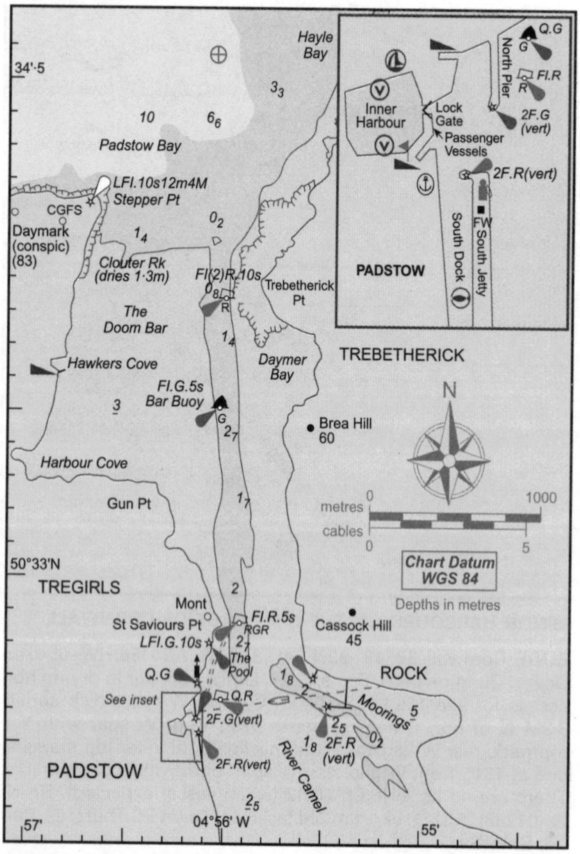

SHELTER Good in inner hbr 3m+, access via tidal gate HW±2 sp, ±1½ nps via tidal gate. If too late for gate, moor in the Pool or ⚓ close N in 1·5m LWS. Drying moorings available for smaller craft.

NAVIGATION WPT 50°34'·56N 04°56'·07W, 305°/125° from/to Stepper Pt, 1·5M. From SW, beware Quies Rks, Gulland Rk, The Hen, Gurley Rk, Chimney Rks and a wreck 5ca W of Stepper Pt (all off the chartlet). From N, keep well off Newland Island and its offlying reef. Best appr HW–2½, do not try LW±1½; least depth on the bar is 0·5m at MLWS. Waiting ⚓ in Port Quin Bay in lee of Rumps Pt. Shifting banks in estuary require care and a rising tide (ditto the drying R Camel to Wadebridge, 4M). If in doubt, consult Hr Mr. Identify/align 180° the first 2 chan buoys before entry. In strong onshore winds or heavy ground swell, seas can break on Doom Bar and in the adjacent chan. S of St Saviour's Pt the chan lies very close to W shore.

LIGHTS AND MARKS Conspic stone tr (83m daymark), 3ca W of Stepper Pt, L Fl 10s 12m 4M, marks river mouth. Outer hbr 2 FG/FR (vert).

RADIO TELEPHONE VHF Ch 12 16 (Mon-Fri 0800–1700 and HW±2). Water taxi.

TELEPHONE (Dial codes 01841; 01208 = Wadebridge) Hr Mr 532239 📠 533346 padstowharbour@compuserve.com; MRCC (01326) 317575; ⊖ 0345 231110 (H24); Marinecall 09068 500 458; Police (01566) 774211; Dr 532346.

FACILITIES Hbr ☎ 532239, 📠 533346, Mobile (0379) 338531, AB £1, Slip, M, FW, El, C (60 ton), D, ME, ⓔ, showers, V, R, Bar; **Rock SC** ☎ (01208) 862431, Slip; **Ferry 1** to Rock, also on request as water taxi, ☎ (01326) 317575 or VHF Ch 12 16. **Services:** BY, C, ME, CH, Slip, L, Sh. **Town** www.padstow-harbour.co.uk, EC Wed; ⓔ, P, ✉, Ⓑ, ⇌ (bus to Bodmin Parkway), ✈ (Newquay/Plymouth).

MINOR HBRS BETWEEN BOSCASTLE AND LAND'S END

PORT ISAAC, Cornwall, **50°35'·75N 04°49'·57W**. AC 1168, 1156. HW –0548 on Dover; ML 4·1m. Small drying hbr, access HW±2. Conspic ✠ tr bears 171°/1·3M. Rks close E of 50m wide ent between short bkwtrs. V, R, Bar, ✉, LB.

NEWQUAY, Cornwall, **50°25'·06N 05°05'·19W**. AC 1168, 1149. HW –0604 on Dover; ML 3·7m; see 9.11.27. Ent to drying hbr ('The Gap') between two walls, is 23m wide. Beware Old Dane Rk and Listrey Rk outside hbr towards Towan Hd. Swell causes a surge in the hbr. Enter HW±2 but not in strong onshore winds. Berth as directed by Hr Mr. Lts: N pier 2 FG (vert) 2M; S pier 2 FR (vert) 2M. VHF Ch16 14. Hr Mr ☎ (01637) 872809. Facilities: Gas, Gaz, CH. **Town** EC Wed (winter only); FW, Slip, D, V, R, Bar. Note: Shoal draft boats can dry out in Gannel Creek, close S of Newquay, but only in settled weather. Beware causeway bridge about half way up the creek.

PORTREATH, Cornwall, **50°15'·88N 05°17'·57W**. AC 1149. HW –0600 on Dover. Conspic W daymark (38m) at E side of ent to small drying hbr, access HW±2. Gull Rk (23m) is 3ca W of ent and Horse Rk is close N. Keep close to pier on W side of chan. AB in either of 2 basins, both dry. V, R, Bar, ✉.

HAYLE, Cornwall, **50°11'·77N 05°26'·17W** (Chan ent). AC 1168, 1149. HW –0605 on Dover; ML 3·6m; Duration 0555. See 9.11.27. Drying hbr gives very good shelter, but is not advised for yachts. In ground swell dangerous seas break on the bar, drying 2·7m; approx 4m at ent @ MHWS. Cross the bar in good weather HW±1. Charted aids do not necessarily indicate best water. Ldg marks/lts 180°: both W □ R horiz band, ☆ FW 17/23m 4M. PHM buoy, QR is about 8ca N of the front ldg lt. Training wall on W side of ent chan is marked by 4 perches (FG lts). The hbr is divided by long central island (about 700m long, with lt bn Q at NW end) which should be left to stbd. Follow the SE arm of hbr to Hayle; the S arm leads to Lelant Quay. VHF Ch **18** 16 (0900-1700). Hr Mr ☎ (01736) 754043, AB £6. Facilities: EC Thurs; Ⓑ, Bar, FW (can), ⇌, R, V, Gas, P & D (cans). A marina is proposed.

ST IVES, Cornwall, **50°12'·79N 05°28'·67W**. AC 1168, 1149. HW –0610 on Dover; ML 3·6m; Duration 0555. See 9.11.27. Drying hbr with about 4·5m @ MHWS. Good shelter except in on-shore winds when heavy swell works in. Ⓞs and ⚓ in 3m between the hbr and Porthminster Pt to S. From the NW beware Hoe Rk off St Ives Hd, and from SE The Carracks. Keep E of SHM buoy about 1½ ca ENE of E pier. Lts: E pier hd 2 FG (vert) 8m 5M. W pier hd 2 FR (vert) 5m 3M. VHF Ch 12 16 (occas). Hr Mr ☎ (01736) 795018. Facilities: Ⓞs £8; **E Pier** FW. **Town** EC Thurs; Gas, Gaz, Ⓑ, ⓔ, Bar, ✉, R, V, ⇌.

MAPTECH®
Leading the world in digital navigation
Maptech UK Ltd • +44 (0)1243 389352 • sales@maptech.co.uk

Maptech world class digital chart CDs
Worldwide coverage from over 4,500 charts

Maptech award winning software
Easy to use navigation software
• **Chart Navigator** • **Cruising Navigator** • **Offshore Navigator**

www.maptech.co.uk

Area 12

South Ireland
Malahide clockwise to Liscannor Bay

9.12.1 Index .... **Page 629**

9.12.2 Area map **630**

9.12.3 Tidal stream charts **632**

9.12.4 Lights, buoys & waypoints **634**

9.12.5 Passage information **638**

9.12.6 Distance table **640**

9.12.7 Special notes for Ireland **640**

9.12.8 Malahide **641**

9.12.9 Howth **642**

9.12.10 Dublin, Standard Port, tidal curves. Dun Laoghaire **643**

9.12.11 Wicklow **648**

9.12.12 Arklow **648**

9.12.13 Wexford **649**

9.12.14 Rosslare Harbour **650**

9.12.15 Kilmore Quay **651**

9.12.16 Waterford **652**

9.12.17 Dunmore East **653**

9.12.18 Youghal **653**

9.12.19 Cork Harbour, (Cobh, Standard Port, tidal curves) **657**
Dungarvan Bay
Ballycotton

9.12.20 Kinsale **659**
Oysterhaven

9.12.21 Courtmacsherry **659**

9.12.22 Glandore **660**

9.12.23 Castle Haven **660**
Barloge Creek

9.12.24 Baltimore **661**
Horseshoe Harbour
Clear Island, North Harbour
Roaring Water Bay

9.12.25 Schull **662**

9.12.26 Crookhaven **662**
Goleen
Dunmanus Bay

9.12.27 Bantry Bay **663**
Castletown
Lawrence Cove
Lonehort Harbour
Adrigole
Glengariff
Bantry

9.12.28 Kenmare River **664**
Garnish Bay
Cleanderry
Ardgroom
Kilmakilloge
Kenmare
Dunkerron Harbour
Sneem
Darrynane

9.12.29 Dingle **665**
Portmagee
Valentia
Ventry
Smerwick Harbour
Brandon Bay
Tralee Bay (Fenit)

9.12.30 Shannon Estuary **666**

9.12.31 Kilrush **667**

Register for your **FREE** weekly weather email service from Macmillan Reeds
» at **www.nauticaldata.com – NOW!** «
weekend weather reports sent to your email address, every Thursday

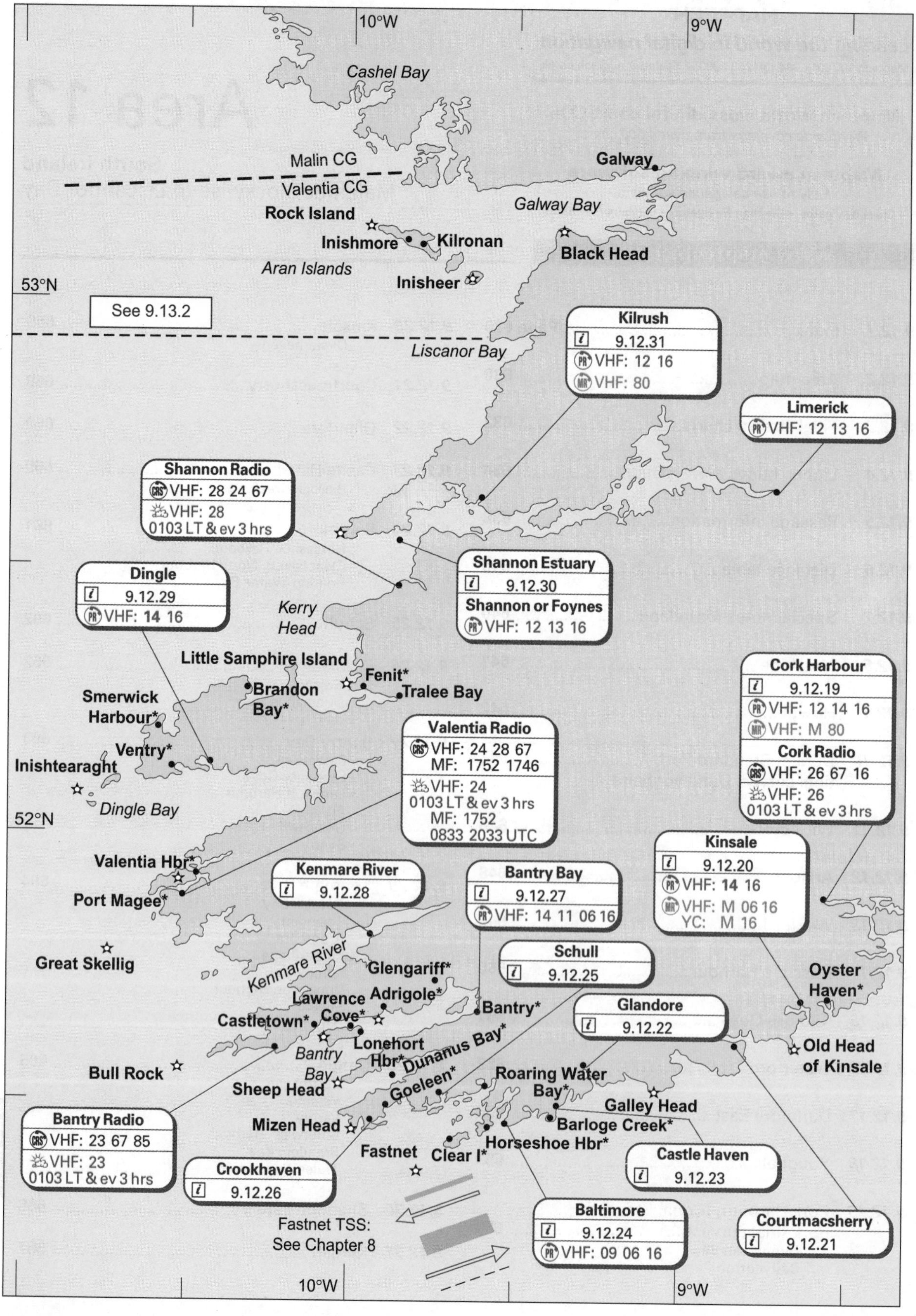
10°W
9°W
Cashel Bay
Malin CG
Valentia CG
Galway
Galway Bay
Rock Island
Inishmore
Kilronan
Aran Islands
Inisheer
Black Head
53°N
See 9.13.2
Liscanor Bay
Kilrush
9.12.31
VHF: 12 16
VHF: 80
Limerick
VHF: 12 13 16
Shannon Radio
VHF: 28 24 67
VHF: 28
0103 LT & ev 3 hrs
Shannon Estuary
9.12.30
Shannon or Foynes
VHF: 12 13 16
Dingle
9.12.29
VHF: 14 16
Kerry Head
Little Samphire Island
Fenit*
Brandon Bay*
Tralee Bay
Smerwick Harbour*
Ventry*
Inishtearaght
Dingle Bay
52°N
Valentia Radio
VHF: 24 28 67
MF: 1752 1746
VHF: 24
0103 LT & ev 3 hrs
MF: 1752
0833 2033 UTC
Cork Harbour
9.12.19
VHF: 12 14 16
VHF: M 80
Cork Radio
VHF: 26 67 16
VHF: 26
0103 LT & ev 3 hrs
Kinsale
9.12.20
VHF: 14 16
VHF: M 06 16
YC: M 16
Valentia Hbr*
Port Magee*
Kenmare River
9.12.28
Bantry Bay
9.12.27
VHF: 14 11 06 16
Schull
9.12.25
Great Skellig
Kenmare River
Glengariff*
Adrigole*
Lawrence Cove*
Castletown*
Bantry*
Lonehort Hbr*
Dunanus Bay*
Bantry Bay
Bull Rock
Sheep Head
Goeleen*
Glandore
9.12.22
Oyster Haven*
Old Head of Kinsale
Roaring Water Bay*
Galley Head
Barloge Creek*
Horseshoe Hbr*
Mizen Head
Fastnet
Clear I*
Bantry Radio
VHF: 23 67 85
VHF: 23
0103 LT & ev 3 hrs
Crookhaven
9.12.26
Castle Haven
9.12.23
Fastnet TSS:
See Chapter 8
Baltimore
9.12.24
VHF: 09 06 16
Courtmacsherry
9.12.21
10°W
9°W

9.12.2 South Ireland

Malahide clockwise to Liscanor Bay

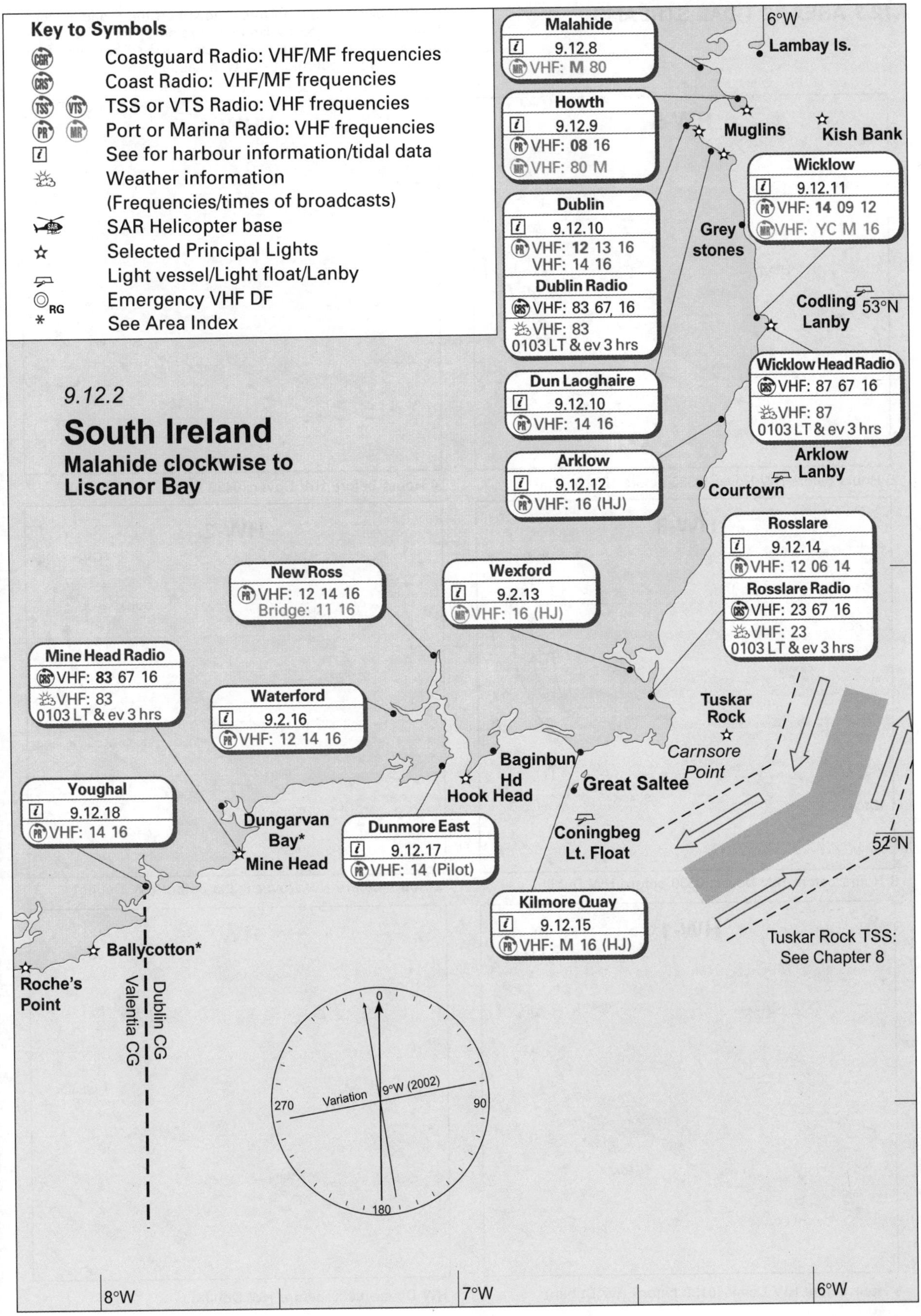
Key to Symbols
Coastguard Radio: VHF/MF frequencies
Coast Radio: VHF/MF frequencies
TSS or VTS Radio: VHF frequencies
Port or Marina Radio: VHF frequencies
See for harbour information/tidal data
Weather information
(Frequencies/times of broadcasts)
SAR Helicopter base
Selected Principal Lights
Light vessel/Light float/Lanby
Emergency VHF DF
See Area Index
9.12.2
South Ireland
Malahide clockwise to Liscanor Bay
6°W
Lambay Is.
Malahide 9.12.8 VHF: M 80
Howth 9.12.9 VHF: 08 16 VHF: 80 M
Muglins
Kish Bank
Dublin 9.12.10 VHF: 12 13 16 VHF: 14 16
Dublin Radio VHF: 83 67, 16 VHF: 83 0103 LT & ev 3 hrs
Wicklow 9.12.11 VHF: 14 09 12 VHF: YC M 16
Grey stones
Codling Lanby
53°N
Wicklow Head Radio VHF: 87 67 16 VHF: 87 0103 LT & ev 3 hrs
Dun Laoghaire 9.12.10 VHF: 14 16
Arklow 9.12.12 VHF: 16 (HJ)
Arklow Lanby
Courtown
Rosslare 9.12.14 VHF: 12 06 14
Rosslare Radio VHF: 23 67 16 VHF: 23 0103 LT & ev 3 hrs
New Ross VHF: 12 14 16 Bridge: 11 16
Wexford 9.2.13 VHF: 16 (HJ)
Mine Head Radio VHF: 83 67 16 VHF: 83 0103 LT & ev 3 hrs
Waterford 9.2.16 VHF: 12 14 16
Tuskar Rock
Carnsore Point
Baginbun Hd
Hook Head
Great Saltee
Youghal 9.12.18 VHF: 14 16
Dungarvan Bay*
Mine Head
Dunmore East 9.12.17 VHF: 14 (Pilot)
Coningbeg Lt. Float
52°N
Kilmore Quay 9.12.15 VHF: M 16 (HJ)
Tuskar Rock TSS: See Chapter 8
Ballycotton*
Roche's Point
Dublin CG
Valentia CG
0
270
Variation 9°W (2002)
90
180
8°W
7°W
6°W

9.12.3 AREA 12 TIDAL STREAMS

The tidal arrows (with no rates shown) off the S and W coasts of Ireland are printed by kind permission of the Irish Cruising Club, to whom the Editor is indebted. They have been found accurate, but should be used with caution.

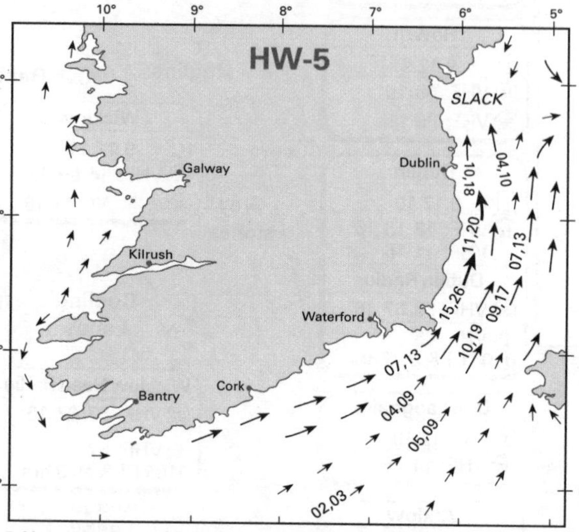

5 Hours before HW Dover (0530 before HW Dublin)

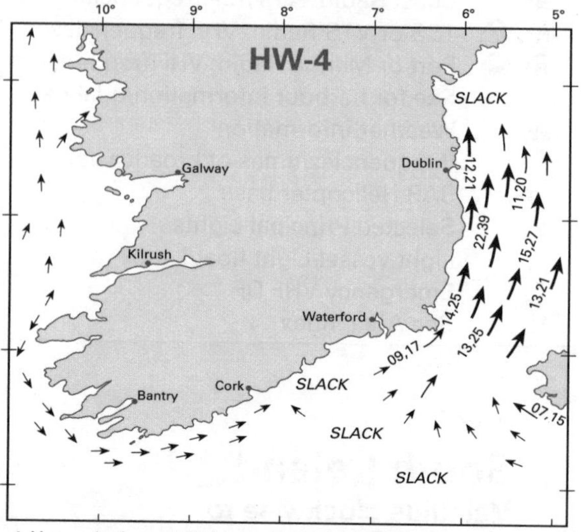

4 Hours before HW Dover (0430 before HW Dublin)

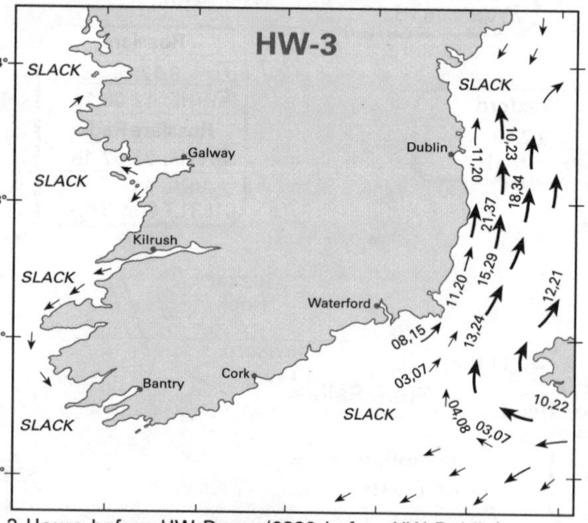

3 Hours before HW Dover (0330 before HW Dublin)

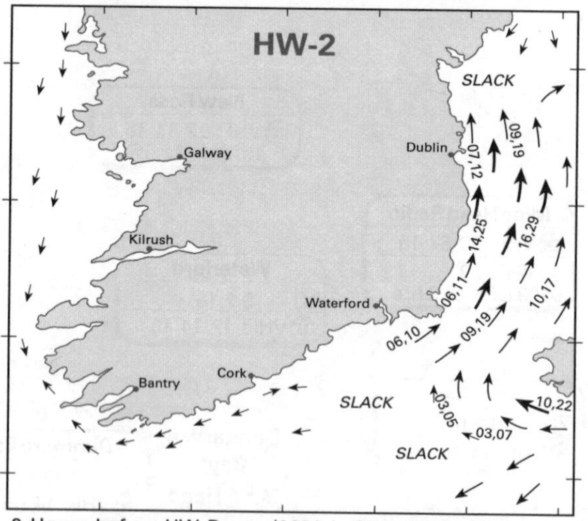

2 Hours before HW Dover (0230 before HW Dublin)

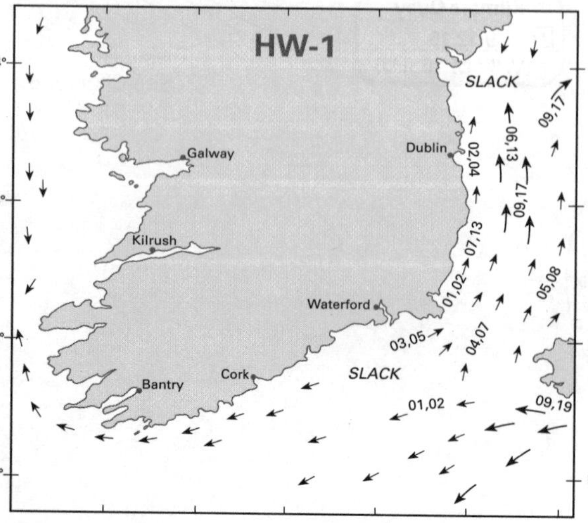

1 Hour before HW Dover (0130 before HW Dublin)

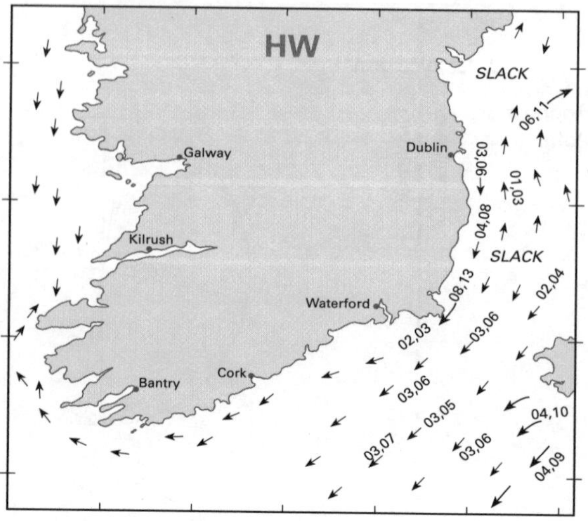

HW Dover (0030 before HW Dublin)

Northward 9.13.3 South Irish Sea 9.11.3

The tidal arrows (with no rates shown) off the S and W coasts of Ireland are printed by kind permission of the Irish Cruising Club, to whom the Editor is indebted. They have been found accurate, but should be used with caution.

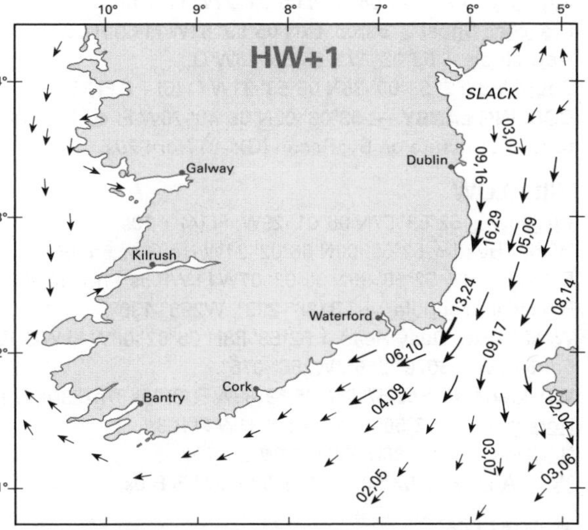

1 Hour after HW Dover (0030 after HW Dublin)

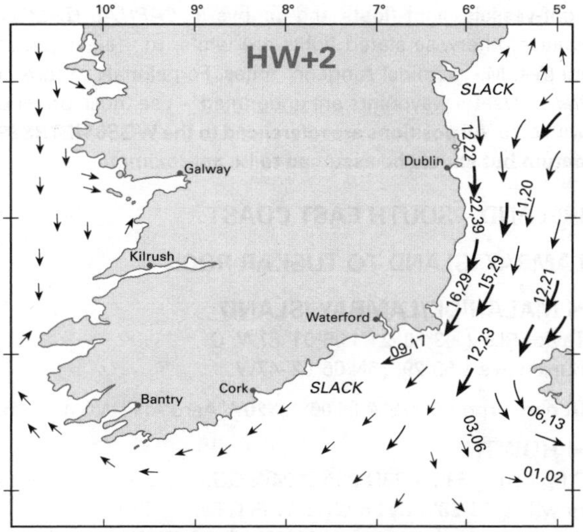

2 Hours after HW Dover (0130 after HW Dublin)

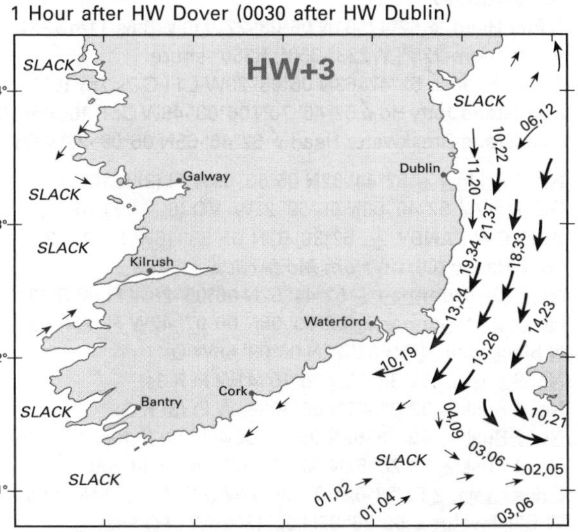

3 Hours after HW Dover (0230 after HW Dublin)

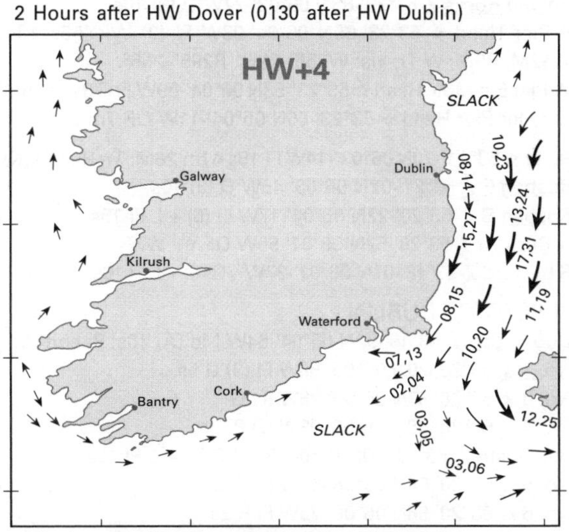

4 Hours after HW Dover (0330 after HW Dublin)

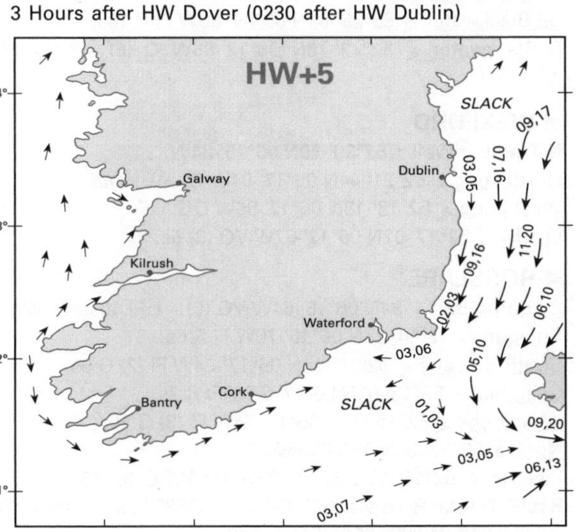

5 Hours after HW Dover (0430 after HW Dublin)

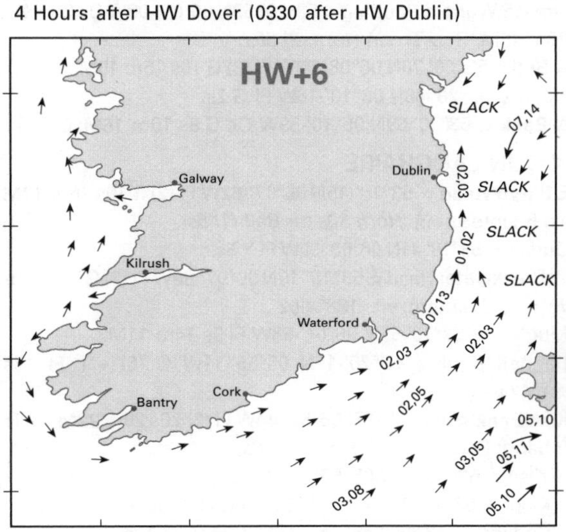

6 Hours after HW Dover (0530 after HW Dublin)

12

9.12.4 LIGHTS, BUOYS AND WAYPOINTS

Abbreviations used below are given in the Introduction. Principal lights ☆ are in **bold** print, places in CAPITALS, and light-vessels, light floats and Lanbys in *CAPITAL ITALICS*. Unless otherwise stated lights are white. m – elevation in metres; M – nominal range in miles. Fog signals are in *italics*. Useful waypoints are underlined – use those on land with care. **All positions are referenced to the WGS84/ETRS89 datum but should be assumed to be approximate.**

IRELAND – SOUTH EAST COAST

LAMBAY ISLAND TO TUSKAR ROCK

◀ MALAHIDE/LAMBAY ISLAND

Taylor Rks 53°30'·21N 06°01'·87W; Q.
Burren Rks 53°29'·35N 06°02'·47W.

Dublin Airport 53°25'·28N 06°16'·20W Aero Al Fl WG 4s 95m.

◀ HOWTH

S Rowan 53°23'·78N 06°03'·94W QG.
Howth 53°23'·74N 06°03'·59W Fl G 5s.
Rowan Rocks 53°23'·88N 06°03'·27W Q (3) 10s.
E Pier Head 53°23'·66N 06°04'·03W Fl (2) WR 7·5s 13m W12M, R9M; W Tr; vis: W256°-295°, R295°-256°.
W Pier Ext Mole Head 53°23'·53N 06°04'·09W Fl G 3s 7m 6M.
Trawler Pier Head 53°23'·50N 06°04'·11W QR 7m 6M.

Baily ☆ 53°21'·70N 06°03'·14W Fl 15s 41m **26M**; Tr; Racon (K).
Rosbeg E 53°21'·02N 06°03'·45W Q (3) 10s.
Rosbeg S 53°20'·22N 06°04'·17W Q (6) + L Fl 15s.
N Burford 53°20'·52N 06°01'·50W Q; *Whis.*
S Burford 53°18'·07N 06°01'·27W VQ (6) + L Fl 10s; *Whis*

◀ PORT OF DUBLIN

Dublin Bay 53°19'·92N 06°04'·64W Mo (A) 10s; Racon (M).
No. 1 53°20'·30N 06°05'·56W Fl (3) G 5s.
No. 3 53°20'·57N 06°06'·76W IQ G.
No. 4 53°20'·48N 06°06'·93W IQ R.
Bar Obstn 53°20'·70N 06°06'·96W Q (6) + L Fl 15s.
No. 5 53°20'·64N 06°08'·60W Fl G 2s.
No. 6 53°20'·56N 06°08'·75W Fl R 2s.
Great S Wall Hd **Poolbeg** ☆ 53°20'·53N 06°09'·08W Oc (2) R 20s 20m **15M**; R ○ Tr; *Horn (2) 60s.*
N Bull ☆ 53°20'·70N 06°08'·98W Fl (3) G 10s 15m **15M**; G ○ Tr.
No. 9 53°20'·68N 06°10'·16W Fl G 2s.
N Bank ☆ 53°20'·69N 06°10'·59W Oc G 8s 10m **16M**; G □ Tr.

◀ DUN LAOGHAIRE

E Bkwtr Head 53°18'·15N 06°07'·62W Fl (2) R 10s 16m **17M**; Tr, R lantern; *Horn 30s* (or *Bell (1) 6s*).
Outfall 53°18'·41N 06°08'·35W Fl Y 5s.
W Breakwater Head 53°18'·19N 06°07'·88W Fl (3) G 7·5s 11m 7M; Tr, G lantern; vis: 188°-062°.
Muglins 53°16'·55N 06°04'·58W Fl 5s 14m 11M.
Bennett Bank 53°20'·17N 05°55'·11W Q (6) + L Fl 15s; *Whis.*
Kish Bank ☆ 53°18'·70N 05°55'·44W Fl (2) 20s 29m **22M**; W Tr, R band; Racon (T); *Horn (2) 30s.*
N Kish 53°18'·56N 05°56'·44W VQ.
E Kish 53°14'·35N 05°53'·56W Fl (2) R 10s.
E Codling 53°08'·54N 05°47'·11W Fl (4) R 10s.
W Codling 53°06'·97N 05°54'·51W Fl G 10s.
S Codling 53°04'·74N 05°49'·76W VQ (6) + L Fl 10s.
Greystones 53°08'·37N 06°02'·43W Fl Y 5s.
Moulditch Bk 53°08'·42N 06°01'·22W Fl R 10s.
Breaches Shoal 53°05'·67N 05°59'·81W Fl (2) R 6s.
North India 53°03'·17N 05°53'·46W Q.
South India 53°00'·36N 05°53'·31W Q (6) + L Fl 15s.
CODLING LANBY 53°03'·02N 05°40'·76W Fl 4s 12m **15M**; tubular structure on By; Racon (G); *Horn 20s.*

WICKLOW

Wicklow 52°59'·57N 06°01'·29W; Fl (4) Y 10s.
W Pier Head 52°59'·00N 06°02'·21W Iso G 4s 5m 6M.
E Pier Head 52°58'·99N 06°02'·07W Fl WR 5s 11m 6M; W Tr, R base and cupola; vis: R136°-293°, W293°-136°.
West Packet Quay Head 52°58'·88N 06°02'·08W Fl WG 10s 5m 6M; vis: G076°-256°, W256°-076°.
Wicklow Head ☆ 52°57'·95N 05°59'·89W Fl (3) 15s 37m **23M**; W Tr.
Horseshoe 52°56'·62N 05°59'·31W Fl R 3s.
N Arklow 52°53'·86N 05°55'·21W Q; *Whis.*
No. 2 Arklow 52°50'·22N 05°54'·56W Fl R 6s.

◀ ARKLOW

S Pier Head 52°47'·61N 06°08'·22W Fl WR 6s 11m 13M; Tr; vis: R shore-223°, W223°-350°; R350°-shore.
N Pier Head 52°47'·63N 06°08'·29W L Fl G 7s 7m 10M.
Roadstone Jetty Hd 52°46'·70N 06°08'·46W Oc R 10s 9m 9M.
Roadstone Breakwater Head 52°46'·65N 06°08'·23W QY.

No. 1 Arklow 52°44'·32N 05°56'·05W Fl (3) R 10s.
S Arklow 52°40'·82N 05°59'·21W VQ (6) + L Fl 10s.
ARKLOW LANBY 52°39'·52N 05°58'·16W Fl (2) 12s 12m **15M**; Racon (O); *Horn Mo (A) 30s.*
No. 2 Glassgorman 52°44'·52N 06°05'·28W Fl (4) R 10s.
No. 1 Glassgorman 52°39'·08N 06°07'·42W Fl (2) R 6s.
N Blackwater 52°32'·22N 06°09'·56W Q.
No. 6 Rusk 52°32'·65N 06°10'·41W Fl R 3s.
No. 4 Rusk 52°31'·07N 06°10'·84W Fl (3) R 6s.
No. 2 Rusk 52°28'·62N 06°12'·66W Fl (3) R 10s.
No. 1 Rusk 52°28'·52N 06°11'·76W (to be lit 2002).
E Blackwater 52°28'·02N 06°08'·06W Q (3) 10s; *Horn (3) 20s.*
W Blackwater 52°25'·87N 06°13'·56W Fl G 6s.
SE Blackwater 52°25'·64N 06°09'·66W Fl R 10s.
S Blackwater 52°22'·76N 06°12'·86W Q (6) + L Fl 15s; *Whis.*

◀ WEXFORD

N Training Wall 52°20'·20N 06°26'·84W.
North Long 52°21'·44N 06°17'·04W Q; *Whis.*
West Long 52°18'·18N 06°17'·96W QG.
Lucifer 52°17'·02N 06°12'·67W VQ (3) 5s.

◀ ROSSLARE

S Long 52°14'·84N 06°15'·64W VQ (6) + L Fl 10s; *Whis.*
Splaugh 52°14'·37N 06°16'·76W Fl R 6s.
South Holdens 52°15'·14N 06°17'·24W Fl (2) G 6s.
Calmines 52°15'·01N 06°17'·77W Fl R 2s.
W Holdens 52°15'·77N 06°18'·74W Fl (3) G 10s.
No. 3 52°15'·38N 06°20'·68W QG.
Pier Hd 52°15'·43N 06°20'·29W Oc WRG 5s 15m W13M, R10M, G10M; R Tr; vis: G098°-188°, W188°-208°, R208°-246°, G246°-283°, W283°-286°, R286°-320°.

Ballygeary ☆ 52°15'·25N 06°20'·48W Oc WR 1·7s 7m 4M vis: Rshore-152°, W152°-200°, W(unintens)200°-205°, R205°-shore.
Tuskar ☆ 52°12'·19N 06°12'·46W Q (2) 7·5s 33m **24M**; W Tr; Racon (T); *Horn (4) 45s.*

IRELAND – SOUTH COAST

TUSKAR ROCK TO OLD HEAD OF KINSALE

S Rock 52°10'·82N 06°12'·86W Q (6) + L Fl 15s.
Fundale 52°10'·68N 06°20'·26W Fl (2) R 10s.
Barrels 52°08'·32N 06°22'·05W Q (3) 10s; *Whis.*

◀ CARNA

Pier Head ☆ 52°11'·92N 06°20'·89W Fl R 3s 6m 4M.

◀ KILMORE

St Patrick's Bridge 52°09'·30N 06°34'·71W Fl R 6s; (Apr-Sep).
St Patrick's Bridge 52°09'·13N 06°34'·71W Fl G 6s; (Apr-Sep)
Kilmore Breakwater Head ☆ 52°10'·20N 06°35'·15W Q RG 6m 5M; vis: R269°-354°, G354°-003°, R003°-077°.
Ldg Lts 007·9°, Front 52°10'·37N 06°35'·08W Oc 4s 3m 6M. Rear, 100m from front, Oc 4s 6m 6M; sync with front.

CONINGBEG 52°02'·40N 06°39'·49W Fl (3) 30s 12m **24M**; R hull, and Tr, Racon (M); *Horn (3) 60s.*

◀ WATERFORD

Hook Head ☆ 52°07'·32N 06°55'·85W Fl 3s 46m **23M**; W Tr, two B bands; Racon (K); *Horn (2) 45s.*
Waterford 52°08'·95N 06°57'·00W Fl R 3s. Fl (3) R 10s.
Duncannon No. 1 52°11'·02N 06°56'·28W Fl G 2s.
Duncannon No. 2 52°11'·02N 06°56'·47W QR.
Duncannon No. 3 52°12'·02N 06°56'·21W Fl G 4s.
Duncannon No. 4 52°12'·02N 06°56'·42W Fl R 3s.
Duncannon No. 5 52°12'·42N 06°56'·20W Fl (2) G 4s.
Duncannon Dir Lt 002°. 52°13'·23N 06°56'·25W Oc WRG 4s 13m W11M, R8M, G8M; W Tr on fort; vis: G358°-001·7°, W001·7°-002·2°, R002·2°-006°. Same Tr, Oc WR 4s 13m W9M, R7M; vis: R119°-149°, W149°-172°.
Drumroe Bank 52°13'·56N 06°56'·70W QR.
Passage Point ☆ 52°14'·26N 06°57'·77W Fl WR 5s 7m W6M, R5M; R pile structure; vis: W shore-127°, R127°-302°.
Seedes Bank 52°15'·27N 06°59'·63W Fl G 2s.
Cheek Point ☆ 52°16'·12N 06°59'·38W Q WR 6m 5M; W mast; vis: W007°-289°, R289°-007°.
Sheagh ☆ 52°16'·29N 06°59'·34W Fl R 3s 29m 3M; Gy Tr; vis: 090°-318°.
Kilmokea ☆ 52°16'·50N 06°58'·93W Fl 5s.
River Barrow Railway Bridge ☆ 2 FR (Hor); tfc sigs.
Garraunbaun Rock No. 2 ☆ 52°17'·38N 07°00'·94W.
Snowhill Point Ldg Lts 255°. Front, 52°16'·39N 07°00'·91W Fl WR 2·5s 5m 3M; vis: W222°-020°, R020°-057°, W057°-107°. Rear, Flour Mill, 750m from front, Q 12m 5M.
Queen's Chan Ldg Lts 098°. Front, 52°15'·32N 07°02'·38W QR 8m 5M; B Tr, W band; vis: 030°-210°. Rear, 550m from front, Q 15m 5M; W mast.
Giles Quay ☆ 52°15'·50N 07°04'·21W Fl 3s 9m; vis: 255°-086°.
Cove ☆ 52°15'·05N 07°05'·16W Fl WRG 6s 6m 2M; W Tr; vis: R111°-161°, G161°-234°, W234°-111°.
Smelting Ho Pt ☆ 52°15'·15N 07°05'·27W Q 8m 3M; W mast.
Ballycar ☆ 52°15'·06N 07°05'·51W Fl RG 3s 5m; vis: G127°-212°, R212°-284°.

◀ DUNMORE EAST

East Pier Head ☆ 52°08'·93N 06°59'·37W Fl WR 8s 13m **W17M**, R13M; Gy Tr, vis: W225°-310°, R310°-004°.
East Breakwater extn ☆ 52°08'·98N 06°59'·37W Fl R 2s 6m 4M; vis: 000°-310°.
West Wharf ☆ 52°08'·97N 07°59'·45W Fl G 2s 6m 4M; vis: 165°-246°.

◀ DUNGARVAN

Ballinacourty Point ☆ 52°04'·69N 07°33'·18W Fl (2) WRG 10s 16m W10M, R8M, G8M; W Tr; vis: G245°-274°, W274°-302°, R302°-325°, W325°-117°.
Helvick 52°03'·61N 07°32'·25W Q (3) 10s.
Mine Head ☆ 51°59'·52N 07°35'·25W Fl (4) 20s 87m **28M**; W Tr, B band; vis: 228°-052°.

◀ YOUGHAL

Bar Rocks 51°54'·85N 07°50'·05W Q (6) + L Fl 15s.
Blackball Ledge 51°55'·33N 07°48'·53W Q (3) 10s.
W side of ent ☆ 51°56'·57N 07°50'·53W Fl WR 2·5s 24m **W17M**, R13M; W Tr; vis: W183°-273°, R273°-295°, W295°-307°, R307°-351°, W351°-003°.

◀ BALLYCOTTON

Ballycotton ☆ 51°49'·52N 07° 59'·05W Fl WR 10s 59m **W21M**, **R17M**; B Tr, within W walls, B lantern; vis: W238°-048°, R048°-238°; *Horn (4) 90s.*
The Smiths 51°48'·62N 08°00'·71W Fl (3) R 10s.
Power 51°45'·59N 08°06'·67W Q (6) + L Fl 15s.
Pollock Rock 51°46'·22N 08°07'·85W Fl R 6s.

◀ CORK

Cork 51°42'·92N 08°15'·60W L Fl 10s; *Whis;* Racon (T).
Daunt Rock 51°43'·52N 08°17'·65W Fl (2) R 6s.
Fort Davis Ldg Lts 354·1°. **Front**, 51°48'·82N 08°15'·80W Dir Lt Dir WRG 29m **17M**; vis: FG351·5°-352·25°, AlWG352·25°-353°, FW353°-355°, AlWR355°-355·75°, FR355·75°-356·5°. Rear, Dognose Quay, 203m from front, Oc 5s 37m 10M; Or 3, synch with front.
Roche's Point ☆ 51°47'·59N 08°15'·29W Fl WR 3s 30m **W20M**, **R16M**; vis: Rshore-292°, W292°-016°, R016°-033°, W(unintens) 033°-159°, R159°-shore.
Outer Hbr Rk E2 51°47'·52N 08°15'·67W Fl R 2·5s.
Chicago Knoll E1 51°47'·66N 08°15'·54W Fl G 5s.
W1 51°47'·69N 08°16'·05W Fl G 10s.
W2 51°47'·69N 08°16'·34W Fl R 10s.
The Sound E4 51°47'·92N 08°15'·77W Q.
W4 51°48'·02N 08°15'·94W Fl R 5s.
W3 51°48'·12N 08°15'·61W Fl G 2·5s.
White Bay Ldg Lts 034·6°. Front, 51°48'·53N 08°15'·22W Oc R 5s 11m 5M; W hut. Rear, 113m from front, Oc R 5s 21m 5M; W hut; synch with front.
W6 51°48'·28N 08°15'·94W Fl R 2·5s.
Curraghbinney Ldg Lts 252°. Front, 51°48'·66N 08°17'·60W F 10m 3M; W 2 on col. Rear, 61m from front, F 15m 3M; W ♦ on col; vis: 229·5°-274·5°.
Dognose Bk 51°49'·02N 08°16'·20W Fl G 5s.
Spit Bank Pile ☆ 51°50'·72N 08°16'·45W Iso WR 4s 10m W10M, R7M; W house on R piles; vis: R087°-196°, W196°-221°, R221°358°.

C1 51°48'·82N 08°16'·97W Fl G 10s.
C2 51°48'·70N 08°17'·34W Fl R 5s.
East Ferry Marina, E Passage ☆ 51°51'·91N 08°12'·82W 2 FR (vert) at N and S ends.

KINSALE/OYSTER HAVEN

Bulman 51°40'·13N 08°29'·75W Q (6) + L Fl 15s; *Bell.*
Charle's Fort ☆ 51°41'·74N 08°29'·99W Fl WRG 5s 18m W8M, R5M, G6M; vis: G348°-358°, W358°-004°, R004°-168°; H24.
Spur 51°41'·80N 08°30'·31W Fl (2) R 6s.
Split 51°42'·17N 08°30'·48W QR.
Crohague 51°42'·21N 08°30'·81W QR.

IRELAND – SOUTH COAST

OLD HEAD OF KINSALE TO MIZEN HEAD

Old Head of Kinsale ☆, S point 51°36'·28N 08°32'·03W Fl (2) 10s 72m **25M**; B Tr, two W bands; *Horn (3) 45s.*

COURTMACSHERRY

Barrel Rock 51°37'·00N 08°37'·31W.
Black Tom 51°36'·41N 08°38'·05W, Fl G 5s.
Courtmacsherry 51°38'·27N 08°40'·91W Fl G 3s.
Wood Point (Land Pt) ☆ 51°38'·16N 08°41'·00W Fl (2) WR 5s 15m 5M; vis: W315°-332°, R332°-315°.

Galley Head ☆ summit 51°31'·80N 08°57'·19W Fl (5) 20s 53m **23M**; W Tr; vis: 256°-065°.

Wind Rock 51°35'·66N 08°50'·97W.

◀ GLANDORE

Glandore Harbour SW 51°33'·14N 09°06'·65W. Fl (2+1) G 10s 4M; G △ on G mast, R band.
Sunk Rock 51°33'·52N 09°06'·84W Q.

◀ CASTLE HAVEN

Reen Point ☆ 51°30'·98N 09°10'·50W Fl WRG 10s 9m W5M, R3M, G3M; W Tr; vis: Gshore-338°, W338°-001°, R001°-shore.
Kowloon Bridge 51°27'·57N 09°13'·76W Q (6) + L Fl 15s.

◀ BALTIMORE

Barrack Point ☆ 51°28'·33N 09°23'·65W Fl (2) WR 6s 40m W6M, R3M; vis: R168°-294°, W294°-038°.
Loo Rock 51°28'·44N 09°23'·47W Fl G 3s.
Lousy Rocks 51°28'·95N 09°23'·03W
Wallis Rock 51°28'·95N 09°23'·03W QR.

Fastnet ☆, W end 51°23'·35N 09°36'·19W Fl 5s 49m **27M**; Gy Tr; Racon (G); *Horn (4) 60s.*

Copper Point Long Island, E end ☆ 51°30'·24N 09°32'·08W Q(3)10s 16m 8M; W □ Tr.
Amelia Rk 51°29'·98N 09°31'·48W Fl G 3s.

◀ SCHULL/LONG ISLAND CHANNEL

Bull Rock 51°30'·75N 09°32'·22W Fl (2) R 6s 4m 4M.
Ldg Lts 346° Front, 51°31'·68N 09°32'·43W Oc 5s 5m 11M, W mast. Rear, 91m from front, Oc 5s 8m11M; W mast.
Cush Spit 51°30'·30N 09°33'·04W Q.

◀ CROOKHAVEN

Black Horse Rocks 51°28'·45N 09°41'·70W.
Rock Island Point ☆ 51°28'·60N 09°42'·29W L Fl WR 8s 20m W13M, R11M; W Tr; vis: W over Long Island B to 281°, R281°-340°; inside harbour R281°-348°, W348° towards N shore.

Mizen Head ☆ 51°27'·00N 09°49'·24W Iso 4s 55m **15M**; vis: 313°-133°; Racon (T).

IRELAND – SOUTH WEST COAST

◀ MIZEN HEAD TO DINGLE BAY

Sheep's Head ☆ 51°32'·60N 09°50'·95W Fl (3) WR 15s 83m **W18M, R15M**; W bldg; vis: R007°-017°, W017°-212°.

◀ BANTRY BAY/CASTLETOWN BEARHAVEN/ WHIDDY ISLE/BANTRY/GLENGARIFF

Roancarrigmore ☆ 51°39'·20N 09°44'·85W Fl WR 3s 18m **W18M**, R14M; W □ Tr, B band; vis: W312°-050°, R050°-122°, R(unintens) 122°-242°, R242°-312°. Reserve Lt W8M, R6M obsc 140°-220°.
Whiddy Island W clearing Light ☆ 51°41'·01N 09°31'·81W Oc 2s 22m 3M; vis: 073°-106°.
Ardnakinna Pt ☆ 51°37'·11N 09°55'·12W Fl (2) WR 10s 62m **W17M**, R14M; W ○ Tr; vis: R319°-348°, W348°-066°, R066°-shore.
Walter Scott Rock 51°38'·55N 09°54'·27W Q (6) + L Fl 15s.
Castletown Dir Lt 024° ☆ 51°38'·81N 09°54'·34W Dir Oc WRG 5s 4m W14M, R11M, G11M; W hut, R stripe; vis: G020·5°-024°, W024°-024·5°, R024·5°-027·5°.
Oilean na gCadrach (Sheep Islands) ☆ 51°38'·38N 09°53'·90W Q 3m 3M.
Castletown Ldg Lts 010°. Front, 51°39'·16N 09°54'·40W Oc 3s 4m 1M; W col, R stripe; vis: 005°-015°. Rear, 80m from front, Oc 3s 7m 1M; W with R stripe; vis: 005°-015°.
Perch Rock ☆ 51°38'·84N 09°54'·47W QG 4m 1M; G col.
Cametringane Spit 51°38'·94N 09°54'·48W QR.

Bull Rock ☆ 51°35'·53N 10°18'·08W Fl 15s 83m **21M**; W Tr; vis: 220°-186°.

◀ KENMARE RIVER/DARRYNANE/ BALLYCROVANE

Ballycrovane Hbr ☆ 51°42'·63N 09° 57'·53W Fl R 3s.
Darrynane Ldg Lts 034°. Front, 51°45'·90N 10°09'·20W Oc 3s 10m 4M. Rear, Oc 3s 16m 4M.
Skelligs Rock ☆ 51°46'·12N 10°32'·51W Fl (3) 10s 53m **27M**; W Tr; vis: 262°-115°; part obsc within 6M 110°-115°.

◀ VALENTIA/PORTMAGEE

Fort (Cromwell) Point ☆ 51°56'·03N 10°19'·31W Fl WR 2s 16m **W17M, R15M**; W Tr; vis: R304°-351°, W102°-304°; obsc from seaward by Doulus Head when brg more than 180°.
FR Lts on radio masts on Geokaun hill 1·20M WSW.
Harbour Rock 51°55'·82N 10°18'·93W Q (3) 10s 4m 5M; vis: 080°-040°.
Ldg Lts 141°. Front, 51°55'·52N 10°18'·45W Oc WRG 4s 25m W11M, R8M, G8M; W Tr, R stripe; vis: G134°-140°, W140°-142°, R142°-148°. Rear, 122m from front, Oc 4s 43m 5M; vis:128°-157·5° synch with front.
The Foot 51°55'·73N 10°17'·10W VQ (3) 5s.

DINGLE BAY TO LOOP HEAD

◀ DINGLE BAY/VENTRY/DINGLE

Dingle, NE side of entrance ☆ 52°07'·30N 10°15'·51W Fl G 3s 20m 6M.
Black Point 52°07'·40N 10°15'·84W Fl (3) G 5s.
Flaherty Point 52°07'·51N 10°16'·05W QR.

Pier Head ☆ 52°08'·22N 10°16'·52W 2 FG (vert) 5m 2M.
Ldg Lts 182°. Front 52°07'·41N 10°16'·59W, rear 100m from front, both Oc 3s.
Inishtearaght ☆, W end Blasket Islands 52°04'·54N 10°39'·72W Fl (2) 20s 84m **27M**; W Tr; vis: 318°-221°; Racon (O).

◀ BRANDON BAY

Brandon Pier Head ☆ 52°16'·00N 10°09'·61W 2 FG (vert) 5m 4M.

◀ TRALEE BAY

Little Samphire I ☆ 52°16'·26N 09°52'·94W Fl WRG 5s 27m **W16M**, R13M; G13M; Bu I Tr; vis: R262°-275°, R280°-090°, G090°-140°, W140°-152°, R152°-172°.
Great Samphire I ☆ 52°16'·15N 09°51'·82W QR 15m 3M; vis: 242°-097°.
Fenit Hbr Pier Head ☆ 52°16'·24N 09°51'·55W 2 FR (vert) 12m 3M; vis: 148°-058°.
Fenit Marina Ent Hd ☆ 52°16'·25N 09°51'·66W Iso G 6s 6m.

SHANNON ESTUARY

Ballybunnion 52°32'·53N 09°46'·96W VQ; Racon (M).
Kilstiffin 52°33'·81N 09°43'·86W Fl R 3s.
Kilcredaune Head ☆ 52°34'·82N 09°42'·64W Fl 6s 41m 13M; W Tr; obsc 224°-247° by hill within 1M.
Kilcredaune 52°34'·45N 09°41'·73W Fl (2+1) R 10s.
Tail of Beal 52°34'·40N 09°40'·77W Q (9) 15s.
Carrigaholt 52°34'·93N 09°40'·53W Fl (2) R 6s.
Beal Spit 52°34'·83N 09°40'·00W VQ (9) 10s.
Beal Bar 52°35'·18N 09°39'·23W Q.
Doonaha 52°35'·49N 09°38'·50W Fl (3) R 10s.
Letter Point 52°35'·44N 09°35'·89W Fl R 7s.
Asdee 52°35'·09N 09°34'·55W Fl R 5s.
Rineanna 52°35'·59N 09°31'·24W QR.
North Carraig 52°35'·60N 09°29'·76W Q.
Scattery I, Rineana Point ☆ 52°36'·35N 09°31'·07W Fl (2) 7·5s 15m 10M; W Tr; vis: 208°-092° (H24).

◀ KILRUSH

Off Cappagh Pier 52°37'·64N 09°30'·21WL Fl 10s.
Marina Ent Chan Ldg Lts 355°. Front, 52°37'·99N 09°30'·27W Oc 3s. Rear, 75m from front, Oc 3s.
Tarbert I North Point ☆ 52°35'·52N 09°21'·83W Q WR 4s 18m W14M, R10M; W ○ Tr; vis: W069°-277°, R277°-287°, W287°-339°.
Tarbert (Ballyhoolahan Pt) Ldg Lts 128·2°. Front, 52°34'·35N 09°18'·80W Iso 3s 13m 3M; △ on W Tr; vis: 123·2°-133·2°. Rear, 400m from front, Iso 5s 18m 3M; G stripe on W Bn.
Kilkerin 52°35'·53N 09°21'·02W Fl (2) R 6s.
Gorgon 52°35'·18N 09°20'·84W Fl (2) G 6s.
Bolands 52°34'·96N 09°19'·63W Fl (2) R 6s.
Carraig Fada 52°35'·26N 09°16'·03W Fl G 5s.
Garraunbaun Point ☆ 51°35'·62N 09°13'·94W Fl (3) WR 10s 16m W8M, R5M; W □ col, vis: R shore-072°, W072°-242°, R242°-shore.
Loghill 52°36'·32N 09°12'·85W Fl G 3s.
Rinealon Point ☆ 52°37'·12N 09°09'·82W Fl 2·5s 4m 7M; B col, W bands; vis: 234°-088°.

◀ FOYNES

W Chan Ldg Lts 108·8° (may be moved for changes in chan). Front, 52°36'·91N 09°06'·59W Oc 4s 34m 12M. Rear, Oc 4s 39m 12M.
Hunts (Weir) Pt No. 4 ☆ 52°37'·02N 09°07'·00W VQ (4) R 10s 2m 2M; W col, B bands.

◀ RIVER SHANNON

Beeves Rock ☆ 52°39'·01N 09°01'·35W Fl WR 5s 12m W12M, R9M; vis: W064·5°-091°, R091°-238°, W238°-265°, W(unintens) 265°-064·5°.
Shannon Airport ☆ 52°42'·12N 08°55'·48W Aero Al Fl WG 7·5s 40m.
Dernish I Pier Head ☆ 52°40'·73N 08°55'·09W 2 FR (vert) 4m 2M each end.
Conor Rock ☆ 52°40'·93N 08°54'·24W Fl R 4s 6m 6M; W Tr; vis: 228°-093°.
North Channel Ldg Lts 093°. Front, Tradree Rock 52°41'·00N 08°49'·87W Fl R 2s 6m 5M; W Trs; vis: 246°-110°. Rear 0·65M from front, Iso 6s 14m 5M; W Tr, R bands; vis: 327°-190°.
Bird Rock ☆ 52°40'·95N 08°50'·26W QG 6m 5M; W Tr.
Grass I ☆ 52°40'·43N 08°48'·45W Fl G 2s 6m 4M.
Logheen Rock ☆ 52°40'·33N 08°48'·15W QR 4m 5M.
S side Spilling Rock ☆ 52°40'·04N 08°47'·07W Fl G 5s 5m 5M.
N side, Ldg Lts 061°. Front, 52°40'·72N 08°45'·27W, Crawford Rock 490m from rear, Fl R 3s 6m 5M. Crawford No. 2, Common Rear, 52°40'·85N 08°44'·88W Iso 6s 10m 5M.
Ldg Lts 302·1°. 52°40'·66N 08°44'·40W Flagstaff Rock, 670m from rear, Fl R 7s 7m 5M.
The Whelps ☆ 52°40'·68N 08°45'·09W Fl G 3s 5m 5M; W pile.
Ldg Lts 106·5°. Meelick Rock, Front 52°40'·25N 08°42'·36W Iso 4s 6m 3M. Meelick No. 2, rear 275m from front Iso 6s 9m 5M; both W pile structures.
Ldg Lts 146°, Braemar Point, Front 52°39'·17N 08°41'·94W Iso 4s 5m 5M. Rear, Braemar No. 2, 122m from front, Iso 6s 6m 4M; both W pile structures.
N side Clonmacken Point ☆ 52°39'·52N 08°40'·69W Fl R 3s 7m 4M.
E side Spillane's Tower ☆ 52°39'·34N 08°39'·70W Fl 3s 11m 6M; turret on Tr.

◀ LIMERICK DOCK

Lts in line 098·5°. Front, 52°39'·49N 08°38'·80W. Rear, 100m from front; both FR ◊ on cols; occas.
Loop Head ☆ 52°33'·68N 09°55'·96W Fl (4) 20s 84m **28M**.

9.12.5 PASSAGE INFORMATION

For all Irish waters the Sailing Directions published by the Irish Cruising Club are strongly recommended, and particularly on the W coast, where other information is scarce. They are published in two volumes: *E and N coasts of Ireland* which runs anti-clockwise from Carnsore Pt to Bloody Foreland, and *S and W coasts of Ireland* which goes clockwise. For notes on crossing the Irish Sea, see 9.13.5; and for Distances across it see 9.0.7.

MALAHIDE TO TUSKAR ROCK (charts 1468, 1787) Malahide (9.12.8), 4M from both Lambay Is and Howth, can be entered in most weather via a channel which constantly shifts through drying sandbanks. Ireland's Eye, a rky island which rises steeply to a height of 99m, lies about 7½ca N of Howth (9.12.9) with reefs running SE and SW from Thulla Rk at its SE end. Ben of Howth, on N side of Dublin Bay, is steep-to, with no dangers more than 1ca offshore.

Rosbeg Bank lies on the N side of Dublin Bay. Burford Bank, on which the sea breaks in E gales, and Kish Bank lie offshore in the approaches. The N-going stream begins at HW Dublin – 0600, and the S-going at HW Dublin, sp rates 3kn.

From Dublin (9.12.10) to Carnsore Pt the shallow offshore banks cause dangerous overfalls and dictate the route which is sheltered from the W winds. Tidal streams run mainly N and S, but the N-going flood sets across the banks on the inside, and the S-going ebb sets across them on the outside. As a cruising area, hbr facilities are starting to improve (1999).

Leaving Dublin Bay, yachts normally use Dalkey Sound, but with a foul tide or light wind it is better to use Muglins Sound. Muglins (lt) is steep-to except for a rk about 1ca WSW of the lt. Beware Leac Buidhe (dries) 1ca E of Clare Rk. The inshore passage is best as far as Wicklow (9.12.11).

Thereafter yachts may either route offshore, passing east of Arklow Bank and its Lanby to fetch Tuskar Rock or Greenore Pt. Or keep inshore of Arklow Bank, avoiding Glassgorman Banks; through the Rusk Channel, inside Blackwater and Lucifer Banks, to round Carnsore Pt NW of Tuskar Rock. Arklow (9.12.12) is safe in offshore winds; Wexford (9.12.13) has a difficult entrance. Rosslare (9.12.14) lacks yacht facilities, but provides good shelter to wait out a SW'ly blow.

TUSKAR ROCK TO OLD HEAD OF KINSALE (chart 2049) Dangerous rks lie up to 2ca NW and 6½ca SSW of Tuskar Rk and there can be a dangerous race off Carnsore Pt. In bad weather or poor visibility, use the Inshore Traffic Zone of the Tuskar Rock TSS, passing to seaward of Tuskar Rk (lt), the Barrels ECM lt buoy and Coningbeg lt float.

If taking the inshore passage from Greenore Pt, stay inside The Bailies to pass 2ca off Carnsore Pt. Watch for lobster pots in this area. Steer WSW to pass N of Black Rk and the Bohurs, S of which are extensive overfalls. The little hbr of Kilmore Quay (9.12.15) has been rebuilt with a new marina, but beware rks and shoals in the approaches.

Saltee Sound (chart 2740) is a safe passage, least width 3ca, between Great and Little Saltee, conspic islands to S and N. Sebber Bridge extends 7½ca N from the NE point of Great Saltee and Jackeen Rk is 1M NW of the S end of Little Saltee, so care is needed through the sound, where the stream runs 3·5 kn at sp. There are several rks S of the Saltees, but yachts may pass between Coningbeg Rk and the lt float. There are no obstructions on a direct course for a point 1M S of Hook Head, to avoid the overfalls and Tower Race, which at times extend about 1M S of the Head.

Dunmore East (9.12.17 and chart 2046) is a useful passage port at the mouth of Waterford Hbr (9.12.16). To the W, beware salmon nets and Falskirt, a dangerous rk off Swines Pt. There are few offlying rks from Tramore Bay to Ballinacourty Pt on the N side of Dungarvan Bay (9.12.19 and chart 2017). Helvick is a small sheltered hbr approached along the S shore of the bay, keeping S of Helvick Rk (ECM lt buoy) and other dangers to the N.

Mine Hd (lt) has two dangerous rks, The Rogue about 2½ca E and The Longship 1M SW. To the W, there is a submerged rk 100m SE of Ram Hd. Here the W-going stream starts at HW Cobh + 0230, and the E-going at HW Cobh –0215, sp rates 1·5 kn. For Youghal, see 9.12.18. Pass 1ca S of Capel Island. The sound is not recommended.

The N side of Ballycotton B is foul up to 5ca offshore. Ballycotton Hbr (9.12.19) is small and crowded, but usually there is sheltered anch outside. Sound Rk and Small Is lie between the mainland and Ballycotton Is (lt, fog sig). From Ballycotton to Cork keep at least 5ca off for dangers including The Smiths (PHM lt buoy) 1·5M WSW of Ballycotton Island. Pass between Hawk Rk, close off Power Hd, and Pollock Rk (PHM lt buoy) 1.25M SE.

Near the easy entrance and excellent shelter of Cork Harbour (9.12.19 and chart 1777), Ringabella Bay offers temp anch in good weather. 7ca SE of Robert's Hd is Daunt Rk (3·5m) on which seas break in bad weather; marked by PHM lt buoy. Little Sovereign on with Reanies Hd 241° leads inshore of it. The Sovereigns are large rks off Oyster Haven, a good hbr but prone to swell in S'lies. The ent is clear except for Harbour Rk which must be passed on its W side, see 9.12.20. Bulman Rk (SCM lt buoy) is 4ca S of Preghane Pt at the ent to Kinsale's fine harbour (9.12.20).

Old Head of Kinsale (lt, fog sig) is quite steep-to, but a race extends 1M to SW on W-going stream, and to SE on E-going stream. There is an inshore passage in light weather, but in strong winds keep 2M off.

OLD HEAD OF KINSALE TO MIZEN HEAD (chart 2424) From Cork to Mizen Hd there are many natural hbrs. Only the best are mentioned here. Offshore the stream seldom exceeds 1·5kn, but it is stronger off headlands causing races and overfalls with wind against tide. Prolonged W winds increase the rate/duration of the E-going stream, and strong E winds have a similar effect on the W-going stream.

In the middle of Courtmacsherry Bay are several dangers, from E to W: Blueboy Rk, Barrel Rk (with Inner Barrels closer inshore), and Black Tom; Horse Rk is off Barry's Pt at the W side of the bay. These must be avoided going to or from Courtmacsherry, where the bar breaks in strong S/SE winds, but the river carries 2·3m; see 9.12.21. Beware Cotton Rk and Shoonta Rk close E of Seven Heads, off which rks extend 50m. Clonakilty B has little to offer. Keep at least 5ca off Galley Hd to clear Dhulic Rk, and further off in fresh winds. Offshore the W-going stream makes at HW Cobh + 0200, and the E-going at HW Cobh – 0420, sp rates 1·5 kn.

Across Glandore Bay there are good anchs off Glandore (9.12.22), or off Union Hall. Sailing W from Glandore, pass outside or inside High Is and Low Is, but if inside beware Belly Rk (awash) about 3ca S of Rabbit Is. On passage Toe Head has foul ground 100m S, and 7½ca S is a group of rks called the Stags. Castle Haven (9.12.23), a sheltered and attractive hbr, is entered between Reen Pt (lt) and Battery Pt. Baltimore (9.12.24) is 10M further W.

Fastnet Rk (lt, fog sig) is nearly 4M WSW of C Clear; 2½ca NE of it is an outlying rk. An E/W TSS lies between 2 and 8M SSE of the Fastnet. Long Island Bay can be entered from C Clear or through Gascanane Sound, between Clear Is and Sherkin Is. Carrigmore Rks lie in the middle of this chan, with Gascanane Rk 1ca W of them. The chan between Carrigmore Rks and Badger Island is best. If bound for Crookhaven, beware Bullig Reef, N of Clear Is.

Schull (9.12.25) is N of Long Island, inside which passage can be made W'ward to Crookhaven (9.12.26). This is a well sheltered hbr, accessible at all states of tide, entered between Rock Is lt Ho and Alderman Rks, ENE of Streek Hd. Anch off the village.

Off Mizen Hd (lt ho) the W-going stream starts at HW Cobh + 0120, and the E-going at HW Cobh – 0500. The sp rate is 4 kn, which with wind against tide forms a dangerous race, sometimes reaching to Brow Hd or Three Castle Hd , with broken water right to the shore.

THE WEST COAST

This coast offers wonderful cruising, although exposed to the Atlantic and any swell offshore; but this diminishes mid-summer. In bad weather however the sea breaks dangerously on shoals with quite substantial depths. There is usually a refuge close by, but if caught out in deteriorating weather and poor vis, a stranger may need to make an offing until conditions improve, so a stout yacht and good crew are required. Even in mid-summer at least one gale may be meet in a two-week cruise. Fog is less frequent than in the Irish Sea.

Tidal streams are weak, except round headlands. There are few lights, so inshore navigation is unwise after dark. Coastal navigation is feasible at night in good visibility. Keep a good watch for drift nets off the coast, and for lobster pots in inshore waters. Stores, fuel and water are not readily available.

MIZEN HEAD TO DINGLE BAY (chart 2423) At S end of Dunmanus Bay Three Castle Hd has rks 1ca W, and sea can break on S Bullig 4ca off Hd. Dunmanus B (chart 2552) has three hbrs: Dunmanus, Kitchen Cove and Dunbeacon. Carbery, Cold and Furze Is lie in middle of B, and it is best to keep N of them. Sheep's Hd (lt) is at the S end of Bantry Bay (9.12.27; charts 1838, 1840) which has excellent hbrs, notably Glengariff and Castletown. There are few dangers offshore, except around Bear and Whiddy Islands. Off Blackball Hd at W entrance to Bantry B there can be a nasty race, particularly on W-going stream against the wind. Keep 3ca off Crow Is to clear dangers.

Dursey Island is steep-to except for rk 7½ca NE of Dursey Hd and Lea Rk (1·4m)1½ca SW . The Bull (lt, fog sig, Racon) and two rks W of it lie 2·5M WNW of Dursey Hd. The Cow is midway between The Bull and Dursey Hd, with clear water each side. Calf and Heifer Rks are 7½ca SW of Dursey Hd, where there is often broken water. 2M W of The Bull the stream turns NW at HW Cobh + 0150, and SE at HW Cobh – 0420. Dursey Sound (chart 2495) is a good short cut, but the stream runs 4kn at sp; W-going starts at HW Cobh + 0135, and E-going at HW Cobh – 0450. Flag Rk lies almost awash in mid-chan at the narrows, which are crossed by cables 25m above MHWS. Hold very close to the Island shore. Beware wind changes in the sound, and broken water at N entrance.

Kenmare R. (chart 2495 and 9.12.28) has attractive hbrs and anchs, but its shores are rky, with no lights. The best places are Sneem, Kilmakilloge and Ardgroom. Off Lamb's Head, Two Headed Island is steep-to; further W is Moylaun Is with a rk 300m SW of it. Little Hog (or Deenish) Island is rky 1·5M to W, followed by Great Hog (or Scariff) Is which has a rk close N, and a reef extending 2ca W.

Darrynane is an attractive, sheltered hbr NNW of Lamb Hd. The entrance has ldg lts and marks, but is narrow and dangerous in bad weather. Ballinskelligs Bay has an anch N of Horse Is, which has two rks close off E end. Centre of bay is a prohib anch (cables reported).

Rough water is met between Bolus Hd and Bray Hd with fresh onshore winds or swell. The SW end of Puffin Island is steep-to, but the sound to the E is rky and not advised. Great Skellig (lit) is 6M, and Little Skellig 5M WSW of Puffin Is. Lemon Rk lies between Puffin Is and Little Skellig. Here the stream turns N at HW Cobh + 0500, and S at HW Cobh – 018. There is a rk 3ca SW of Great Skellig. When very calm it is possible to go alongside at Blind Man's Cove on NE side of Great Skellig, where there are interesting ruins.

DINGLE BAY TO LISCANOR BAY (chart 2254) Dingle Bay (charts 2789, 2790) is wide and deep, with few dangers around its shores. Dingle (9.12.29) has a small marina. The best anchs are at Portmagee and Ventry. At the NW ent to the bay, 2·5M SSW of Slea Hd, is Wild Bank (or Three Fathom Pinnacle), a shallow patch with overfalls. 3M SW of Wild Bank is Barrack Rk, which breaks in strong winds.

The Blasket Islands are very exposed, with strong tides and overfalls, but worth a visit in settled weather (chart 2790). Great Blasket and Inishvickillane each have anch and landing on their NE side. Inishtearaght is the most W'ly Is (lt), but further W lie Tearaght Rks, and 3M S are Little Foze and Gt Foze Rks. Blasket Sound is the most convenient N-S route, 1M wide, and easy in daylight and reasonable weather with fair wind or tide; extensive rks and shoals form its W side. The N-going stream starts at HW Galway + 0430, and the S-going at HW Galway – 0155, with sp rate 3 kn.

Between Blasket Sound and Sybil Pt there is a race in W or NW winds with N-going tide, and often a nasty sea. Sybil Pt has steep cliffs, and offlying rks extend 3½ca.

Smerwick hbr, entered between Duncapple Is and the E Sister is sheltered, except from NW or N winds. From here the scenery is spectacular to Brandon Bay on the W side of which there is an anch, but exposed to N winds and to swell.

There is no lt from Inishtearaght to Loop Hd, apart from Little Samphire Is in Tralee B, where Fenit hbr provides the only secure refuge until entering the Shannon Estuary. The coast from Loop Hd to Liscanor Bay has no safe anchs, and no lts. Take care not to be set inshore, although there are few offlying dangers except near Mutton Is and in Liscanor Bay.

THE SHANNON ESTUARY (charts 1819, 1547, 1548, 1549) The estuary and lower reaches of the Shannon (9.12.30), are tidal for 50M, from its mouth between Loop Hd and Kerry Hd up to Limerick Dock, some 15M beyond the junction with R. Fergus. The tides and streams are those of a deep-water inlet, with roughly equal durations of rise and fall, and equal rates of flood and ebb streams. In the entrance the flood stream begins at HW Galway – 0555, and the ebb at HW Galway + 0015.

There are several anchs available for yachts on passage up or down the coast. Kilbaha Bay (chart 1819) is about 3M E of Loop Hd, and is convenient in good weather or in N winds, but exposed to SE and any swell. Carrigaholt B (chart 1547), entered about 1M N of Kilcredaun Pt, is well sheltered from W winds and has little tidal stream. In N winds there is anch SE of Querrin Pt (chart 1547), 4·5M further up river on N shore. At Kilrush (9.12.31) there is a marina and anchs E of Scattery Is and N of Hog Is. Note that there are overfalls 0·75M S of Scattery Is with W winds and ebb tide.

Off Kilcredaun Pt the ebb reaches 4kn at sp, and in strong winds between S and NW a bad race forms. This can be mostly avoided by keeping near the N shore, which is free from offlying dangers, thereby cheating the worst of the tide. When leaving the Shannon in strong W winds, aim to pass Kilcredaun Pt at slack water, and again keep near the N shore. Loop Hd (lt) marks the N side of Shannon est, and should be passed 3ca off. Here the stream runs SW from HW Galway + 0300, and NE from HW Galway – 0300.

Above the junction with R. Fergus (chart 1540) the tidal characteristics become more like those of most rivers, ie the flood stream is stronger than the ebb, but it runs for a shorter time. In the Shannon the stream is much affected by the wind. S and W winds increase the rate and duration of the flood stream, and reduce the ebb. Strong N or E winds have the opposite effect. Prolonged or heavy rain increases the rate and duration of the ebb. The Shannon is the longest river in Ireland, rising at Lough Allen 100M above Limerick, thence 50M to the sea.

9.12.6 DISTANCE TABLE

Approximate distances in nautical miles are by the most direct route, whilst avoiding dangers and allowing for Traffic Separation Schemes. Places in *italics* are in adjoining areas; places in **bold** are in 9.0.7, Distances across the Irish Sea.

1.	***Carlingford Lough***	**1**																			
2.	Howth	39	**2**																		
3.	**Dun Laoghaire**	48	8	**3**																	
4.	**Wicklow**	63	25	21	**4**																
5.	**Arklow**	75	37	36	15	**5**															
6.	**Tuskar Rock**	113	73	70	52	37	**6**														
7.	**Rosslare**	108	70	66	47	34	8	**7**													
8.	**Dunmore East**	139	101	102	84	69	32	32	**8**												
9.	**Youghal**	172	134	133	115	100	63	65	34	**9**											
10.	**Crosshaven**	192	154	155	137	122	85	85	59	25	**10**										
11.	Kinsale	202	164	168	150	135	98	95	69	35	17	**11**									
12.	**Baltimore**	239	201	196	177	164	128	132	102	70	54	42	**12**								
13.	**Fastnet Rock**	250	212	207	189	174	137	144	112	78	60	49	10	**13**							
14.	Bantry	281	243	241	223	208	171	174	146	112	94	83	42	34	**14**						
15.	Darrynane	283	245	240	221	208	172	176	146	114	98	86	44	39	38	**15**					
16.	Valentia	295	257	252	242	227	184	188	165	131	113	102	56	48	55	16	**16**				
17.	Dingle	308	270	265	246	233	197	201	171	139	123	111	69	61	63	29	13	**17**			
18.	Kilrush	361	323	318	299	286	250	254	224	192	176	164	122	114	116	82	66	64	**18**		
19.	*Galway*	366	362	357	339	324	287	291	262	228	210	199	159	150	155	119	103	101	76	**19**	
20.	*Slyne Head*	317	351	346	328	313	276	283	251	217	199	188	153	139	144	113	97	95	75	49	**20**

9.12.7 SPECIAL NOTES FOR IRELAND

Céad Míle Fáilte! One hundred thousand Welcomes!

Ordnance Survey map numbers refer to the Irish OS maps, scale 1:50,000 or 1¼ inch to 1 mile, which cover the whole island, including Ulster, in 89 sheets.

Irish Customs: First port of call should preferably be at Customs posts in one of the following hbrs: Dublin, Dun Laoghaire, Waterford, New Ross, Cork, Ringaskiddy, Bantry, Foynes, Limerick, Galway, Sligo and Killybegs. Yachts may, in fact, make their first call anywhere and if no Customs officer arrives within a reasonable time, the skipper should inform the nearest Garda (Police) station of the yacht's arrival. Only non-EC members should fly flag Q or show ● over Ⓦ lts on arrival. Passports are not required by UK citizens. All current Northern Ireland 5 and 6 digit telephone numbers have become 8 digits **028 90**12 3456

Telephone: To call the Irish Republic from the UK, dial 00 -353, then the area code (given in UK ☎ directories and below) minus the initial 0, followed by the ☎ number. To call UK from the Irish Republic: dial 00-44, followed by the area code minus the initial 0, then the number.

Salmon drift nets are everywhere along the S and W coasts, off headlands and islands during the summer and especially May-Jul. They may be 1½ to 3M long and are hard to see. FVs may give warnings on VHF Ch 16, 06, 08.

Liquified petroleum gas: In Eire LPG is supplied by Kosan, a sister company of Calor Gas Ltd, but the bottles have different connections, and the smallest bottle is taller than the normal Calor one fitted in most yachts. Calor Gas bottles can be filled in most larger towns. Camping Gaz is widely available. The abbreviation Kos indicates where Kosan gas is available.

Information: The Irish Cruising Club publishes 2 highly recommended books of Sailing Directions, one for the S and W coasts of Ireland, the other for the N and E coasts. They are distributed by Imray and are available in good UK bookshops and chandleries. Further info is available from: Irish Sailing Association, 3 Park Road, Dun Laoghaire, Co Dublin, ☎ (01) 2800239, 📠 2807558; or the Irish Tourist Board, 150 New Bond St, London W1Y 0AQ, ☎ (020 7) 518 0800.

Currency is the Euro (€). Cash is most readily obtained via Euro or Travellers' cheques.

ACCESS BY AIR: There are airports in Eire at Dublin, Waterford, Cork, Kerry, Shannon, Galway, Connaught, Sligo and Donegal/Carrickfin. See also Ferries in 9.0.5.

Northern Ireland: Belfast CG (MRSC) is at Bangor, Co Down, ☎ (028 91) 463933, 📠 465886. HM Customs (⊜) should be contacted H24 on ☎ (028 90) 358250 at the following ports, if a local Customs Officer is not available: Belfast, Warrenpoint, Kilkeel, Ardglass, Portavogie, Larne, Londonderry, Coleraine. Northern Ireland's main airport is Belfast (Aldergrove).

Gaelic: It helps to understand some of the commoner words for navigational features (courtesy of the Irish Cruising Club):

Ail, alt	cliff, height	*Inish, illaun*	island
Aird, ard	height, high	*Inver*	river mouth
Anna, annagh	marsh		
Ath	ford	*Keal, keel*	narrow place, sound
Bal, Bally	town	*Kill*	church, cell
Barra	sandbank	*Kin, ken*	promontory, head
Bel, beal	mouth, strait		
Beg	little	*Knock*	hill
Ben, binna	hill		
Bo	sunken rock	*Lag*	hollow
Boy, bwee	yellow	*Lahan*	broad
Bullig	shoal, round rock, breaker	*Lea*	grey
		Lenan	weed-covered rock
Bun	end, river mouth	*Lis*	ancient fort
		Long, luing	ship
Caher	fort		
Camus	bay, river bend	*Maan*	middle
		Maol, mwee	bare
Carrick	rock	*Mara*	of the sea
Cladach	shore	*More, mor*	big
Cuan, coon	harbour		
		Rannagh	point
Derg, dearg	red	*Ron, roan*	seal
Drum	hill, ridge	*Roe, ruadh*	red
Duff, dubh	black	*Scolt*	split, rky gut
Dun, doon	fort	*Scrow*	boggy, grassy sward
Ennis	island		
Fad, fadda	long	*Slieve*	mountain
Fan	slope	*Slig*	shells
Fin	white	*Stag, stac*	high rock
Freagh, free	heather		
		Tawney	low hill
Gall	stranger	*Tigh, ti*	house
Glas, glass	green	*Togher*	causeway
Glinsk	clear water	*Tra, traw*	strand
Gorm	blue	*Turlin*	boulder beach
Gub	point of land		
Hassans	swift current	*Vad, bad*	boat

MALAHIDE 9.12.8

Dublin **53°27'·20N 06°08'·90W** ❀❀◊◊◊✿✿

CHARTS AC 633, 1468; Imray C61, C62; Irish OS 50

TIDES +0030 Dover; ML 2·4; Duration 0615; Zone 0 (UT)

Standard Port DUBLIN (NORTH WALL) (⟶)

Times				Height (metres)			
High Water		Low Water		MHWS	MHWN	MLWN	MLWS
0000	0700	0000	0500	4·1	3·4	1·5	0·7
1200	1900	1200	1700				
Differences MALAHIDE							
+0002	+0003	+0009	+0009	+0·1	−0·2	−0·4	−0·2

SHELTER Good in the marina, dredged approx 2·3m. Access HW±4. Visitors berth on end of pontoon D. ⚓ between marina and Grand Hotel on S edge of fairway, clear of moorings.

NAVIGATION WPT: SWM LFl 10s 53°27'·10N 06°06'·81W. The approach channel lies between drying sandbanks with constantly changing depths. It is marked by 5 PHM buoys and 5 SHM buoys all lit. Entry not advised in strong onshore winds against the ebb. The flood reaches 3kn sp, and the ebb 3½kn. Speed limit 4kn in fairway and marina.

LIGHTS AND MARKS The marina and apartment blocks close S of it are visible from the WPT. The Grand Hotel is no longer conspic from seaward, due to trees and bldgs.

RADIO TELEPHONE Marina Ch **M** 80 (H24) . MYC, call *Yacht Base* Ch M (occas).

TELEPHONE (Dial code 01) Marina 8454129, 📠 8454255; MRCC 6620922/3; ⊖ 8746571; Police 845 0216; Dr 845 5994; Ⓗ 837 7755.

FACILITIES Marina (350) ☎ 8454129, 📠 8454255, €2·22, FW, AC, D, P, Gas, BH (30 ton), BY, R, Bar, Ice, ⊡; **Malahide YC** ☎ 8453372, Slip, Scrubbing posts for <10m LOA; **Services:** Ⓔ, Sh, Kos. **Town** ⊡, ✉, Ⓑ, ⇌, ✈ (Dublin).

Visiting yachtsmen are advised to obtain up-to-date information by ☎ or VHF from the marina as to the latest depths and buoyage.

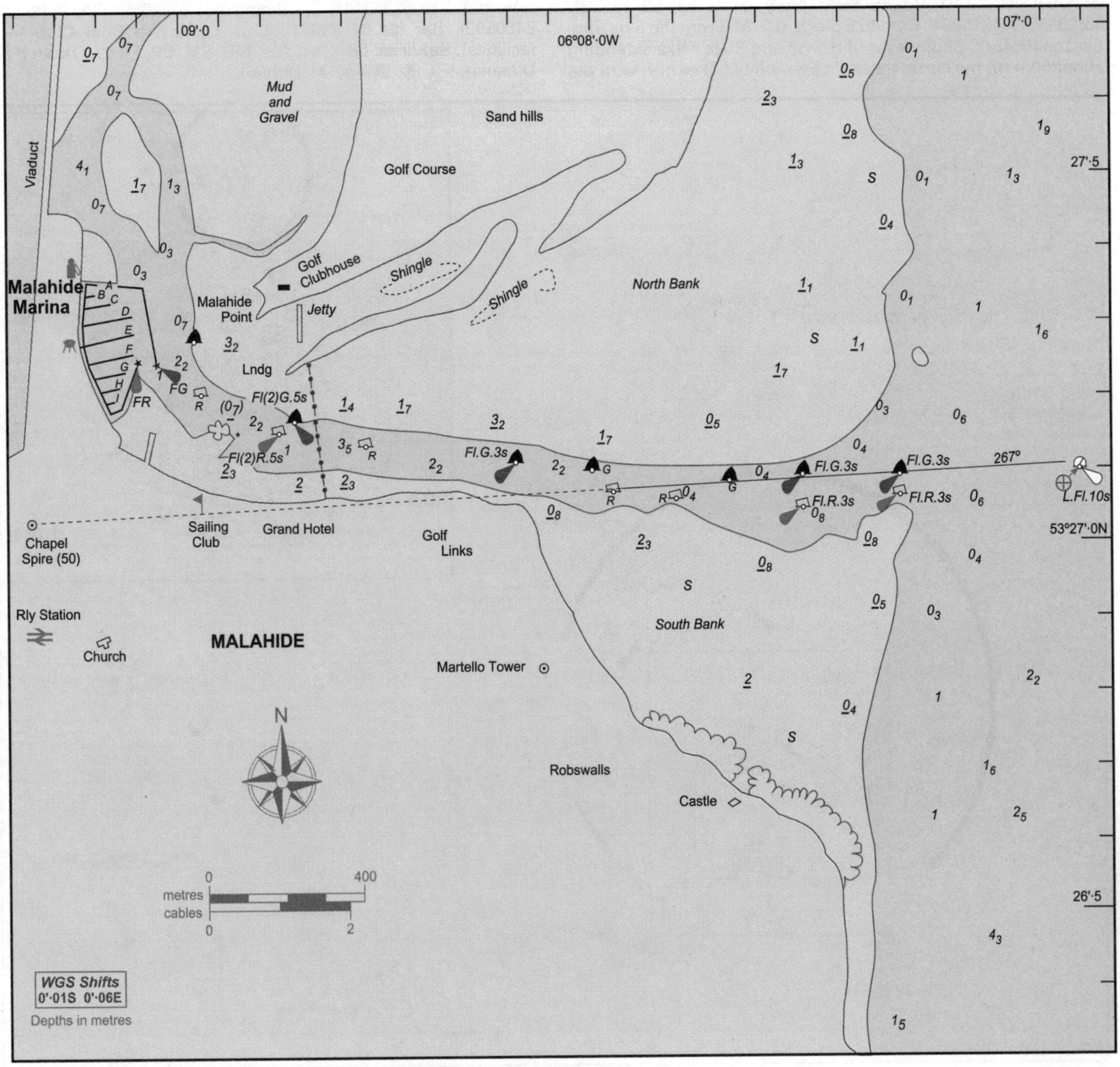

HOWTH *9.12.9*

Dublin **53°23'·60N 06°04'·00W** ❀❀❀◇◇✿✿✿

CHARTS AC 1415, 1468; Imray C61, C62; Irish OS 50

TIDES +0025 Dover; ML 2·4; Duration 0625; Zone 0 (UT)

Standard Port DUBLIN (NORTH WALL) (⟶)

Times				**Height (metres)**			
High Water		Low Water		MHWS	MHWN	MLWN	MLWS
0000	0700	0000	0500	4·1	3·4	1·5	0·7
1200	1900	1200	1700				
Differences HOWTH							
–0007	–0005	+0001	+0005	0·0	–0·1	–0·2	–0·2

SHELTER Good, available at all tides and in almost any conditions. After a severe ENE'ly storm, expect a dangerous scend in the app chan. Caution: many moorings in E part of outer hbr. No ent to FV basin for yachts. Inside the inner hbr keep strictly to chan to avoid drying shoals either side and a substantial wavebreak (gabion). Marina dredged to 2·5m; R PHM posts mark the outer limit of dredging around the marina. 4kn speed limit. There is a fair weather ⚓ in 2-3m at Carrigeen Bay, SW side of Ireland's Eye.

NAVIGATION WPT Howth SHM buoy, Fl G 5s, 53°23'·72N 06°03'·53W, 071°/251° from/to E pier lt, 0·27M. From the S beware Casana Rk 4ca S of the Nose of Howth and Puck's Rks extending about 50m off the Nose. Ireland's Eye is 0·6M N of hbr, with the Rowan Rks SE and SW from Thulla, marked by Rowan Rks ECM, and S Rowan SHM lt buoys. The usual appr passes S of Ireland's Eye. Between the Nose and the hbr, watch out for lobster pots. Beware rks off both pier hds. Howth Sound has 2·4m min depth. Give way to FVs (constrained by draft) in the Sound and hbr entrance.

LIGHTS AND MARKS Baily lt ho, Fl 15s 41m 26M, is 1·5M S of Nose of Howth. Disused lt ho on E pier is conspic. E pier lt, Fl (2) WR 7·5s 13m 12/9M; W 256°–295°, R elsewhere. W sector leads safely to NE pierhead which should be rounded 50m off. Ent to FV Basin has QR and Fl G 3s. The chan to marina is marked by 8 unlit R & G floating perches with W reflective tape (2 bands = port, 1 = stbd); these are reported to be difficult to see at night.

RADIO TELEPHONE Marina Ch M 80 (H24). Hr Mr VHF Ch 16 11 (Mon-Fri 0700–2300LT; Sat/Sun occas).

TELEPHONE (Dial code 01) Hr Mr 832 2252; MRCC 6620922/3; ⊖ 8746571; Police 832 2806; Dr 832 3191; ⊞ 837 7755.

FACILITIES Howth YC Marina (350 inc Ⓥ) ☎ 839 2777, 📠 839 2430; €1·59, M, D (H24), , FW, Slip, C (7 ton), AC, ⊡, ♿. The marina is run by the YC for its members. Visitors are normally very welcome, but visitor berthing ma be limited mid Sept to mid Oct. **Howth YC** ☎ 832 2141, Scrubbing posts <20m LOA, R (☎ 01 8450599), Bar (☎ 01 8392100), ⊡, ♿. **Howth Boat Club** (no facilities). **Services:** LB, Gas, Kos, ME, SM, CH, El, Ⓔ. **Town** P & D (cans), ✉, Ⓑ, ⊡, ⥲, ✈ (Dublin).

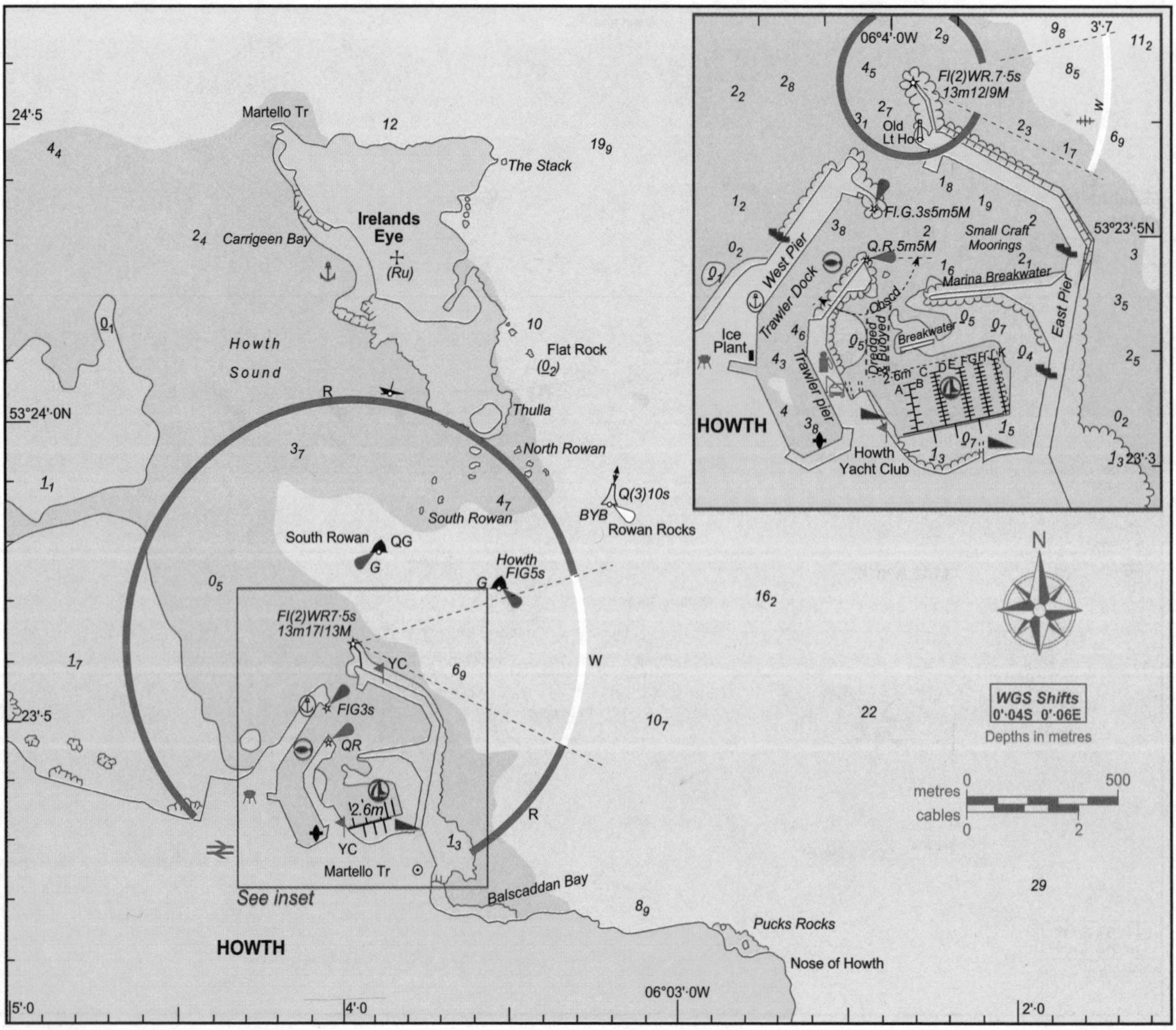

DUBLIN/DUN LAOGHAIRE *9.12.10*

Dun Laoghaire (Port ent) **53°18'·16N 06°07'·68W**

Dun Laoghaire ❀❀❀◊◊◊✿✿; Dublin ❀❀❀◊◊✿✿✿

CHARTS AC 1447, 1415, 1468; Imray C61, C62; Irish OS 50

TIDES +0042 Dover; ML 2·4; Duration 0640; Zone 0 (UT)

Standard Port DUBLIN (NORTH WALL) (⟶)

Times				Height (metres)			
High Water		Low Water		MHWS	MHWN	MLWN	MLWS
0000	0700	0000	0500	4·1	3·4	1·5	0·7
1200	1900	1200	1700				
Differences DUBLIN BAR and DUN LAOGHAIRE							
−0006	−0001	−0002	−0003	0·0	0·0	0·0	+0·1
GREYSTONES (53°09'N 06°04'W)							
−0008	−0008	−0008	−0008	−0·5	−0·4	No data	

Dublin is a Standard Port; daily predictions (⟶)

SHELTER Dublin Port For clearance to enter call *Dublin Port Radio* Ch 12. East Link Lifting Br (2·2m closed) opens 1100, 1500 and 2100, or on request normal H and BH. Call 00 353 1 855 5779. **Dun Laoghaire**, one of the main Dublin yachting centres, is accessible H24, and has a new 680 berth marina. In addition, all YCs advertise Ⓥs and have pontoons, but maybe for Ⓥ/fuel/stores/FW only. Possible AB inshore of Traders Wharf (priority to FVs).

NAVIGATION WPT 53°18'·40N 06°07'·00W, 060°/240° from/to ent to Dun Laoghaire, 0·47M. Keep clear of coasters, ferries and the HSS catamarans (41kn), which turn off St Michael's Pier. Beware drying rks approx 10m off the E Pierhead. **TSS**: Dublin Bay SWM buoy, Mo (A) 10s, (53°19'·90N 06°04'·58W, 2·5M NE of Dun Laoghaire and 2·75M ESE of Dublin Port) is the centre of a circular TSS, radius 2·3ca. Ships bound to/from Dublin Port follow this TSS in an anti-clockwise direction. Yachts must not impede large vessels and should keep clear of the TSS and fairway.

LIGHTS AND MARKS No ldg lts/marks. Poolbeg power stn 2 R/W chimneys (VQ R) are conspic from afar. **Dun Laoghaire**: On W Pier 2 △ bns in transit define the E edge of the triangular ⚓age. Off St Michael's Pierhd is a pile, ☆ 2 FG (vert). On the pierhd 2 ☆ QY = "HSS under way; small craft keep clear of No 1 Fairway" (which extends 600m seaward of the pierhds).

RADIO TELEPHONE Call *Dun Laoghaire Hbr* VHF Ch **14** 16 (H24). YCs Ch M. At Dublin: call *Dublin Port Radio* Ch **12** 13 16 (H24). Lifting bridge (call *Eastlink*) Ch 12. Poolbeg YC Ch 12 16. Dublin Coast Radio Stn 16 67 83.

TELEPHONE (Dial code 00 353 1) Hr Mr Dun Laoghaire 2801130 📠 2808062; Berthing Mr Dublin 8555779; MRCC 6620922/3; Coast/Cliff Rescue Service 2803900; ⊖ 2803992; Weather 1550 123855; Police (Dun Laoghaire) 2801285, (Dublin) 6778141; Dr 2859244; Ⓗ 2806901.

FACILITIES Dublin City Moorings ☎ 818 3300, mobile 086856 8113, 25 Ⓥ's in 3·3m, €2·28, FW, AC, Showers; **Dun Laoghaire Hbr Marina** 325 AB + 50 Ⓥ €2·22 AC, FW, ⊡, ♿; **Yacht Clubs** (E to W): **National YC** ☎ 2805725, 📠 2807837, Slip, M, L, C (12 ton), FW, D, R, Bar; **Royal St George YC** ☎ 2801811, 📠 2843002, Boatman ☎ 2801208; AB by prior agreement, €1·80, Slip, M, D, L, FW, C (5 ton), R, Bar; **Royal Irish YC** ☎ 2809452, 📠 2809723, Slip, M, D, L, FW, C (5 ton), R, Bar; **Dun Laoghaire Motor YC** ☎ 2801371, 📠 2800870, Slip, FW, AB, Bar, R. **Services** SM, CH, ACA, Sh, Ⓔ, El, Gas. HSS to Holyhead. At Dublin Port: **Poolbeg YC** ☎ 6604681, M, AB only for 20ft max LOA, Slip, Bar, FW. Ferry to Holyhead. City of Dublin, all needs, ⇌, ✈.

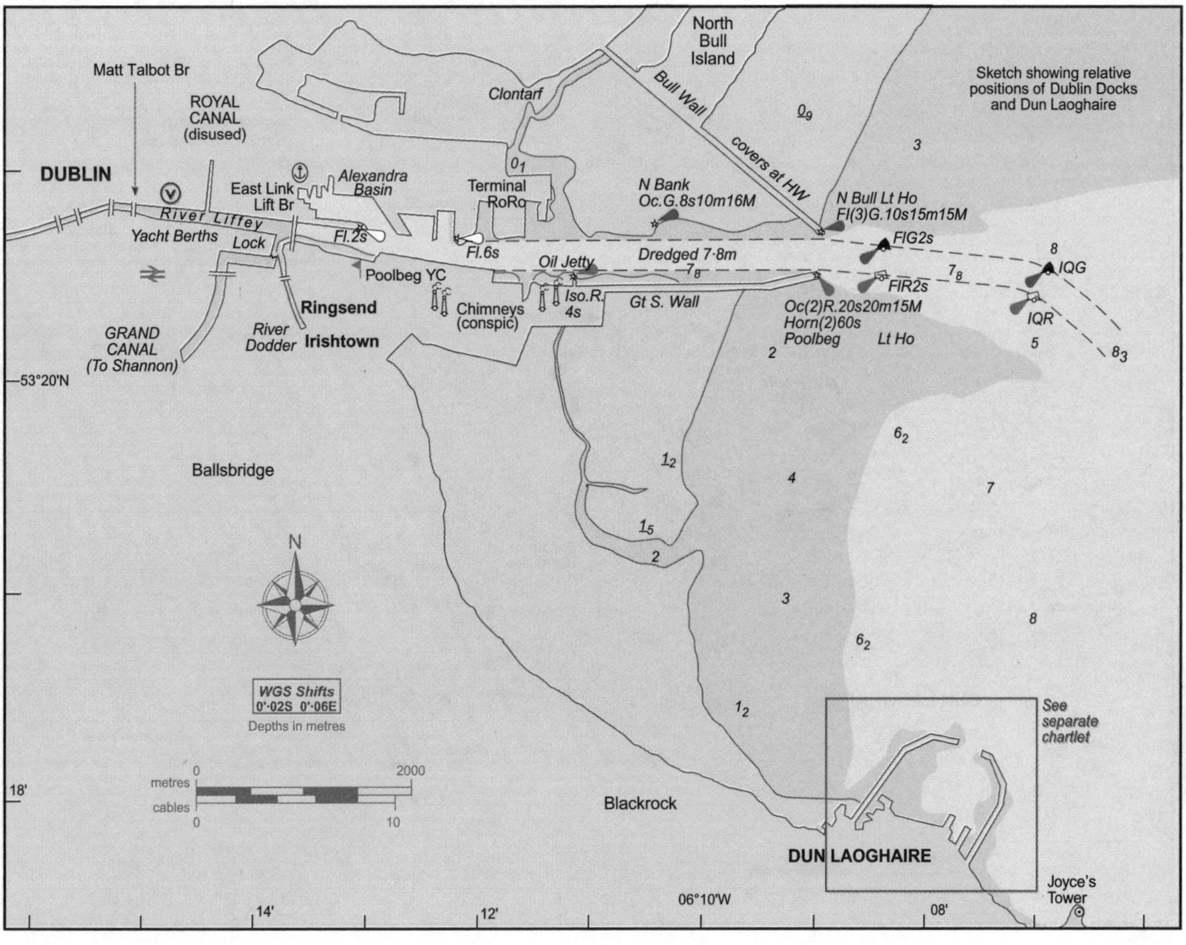

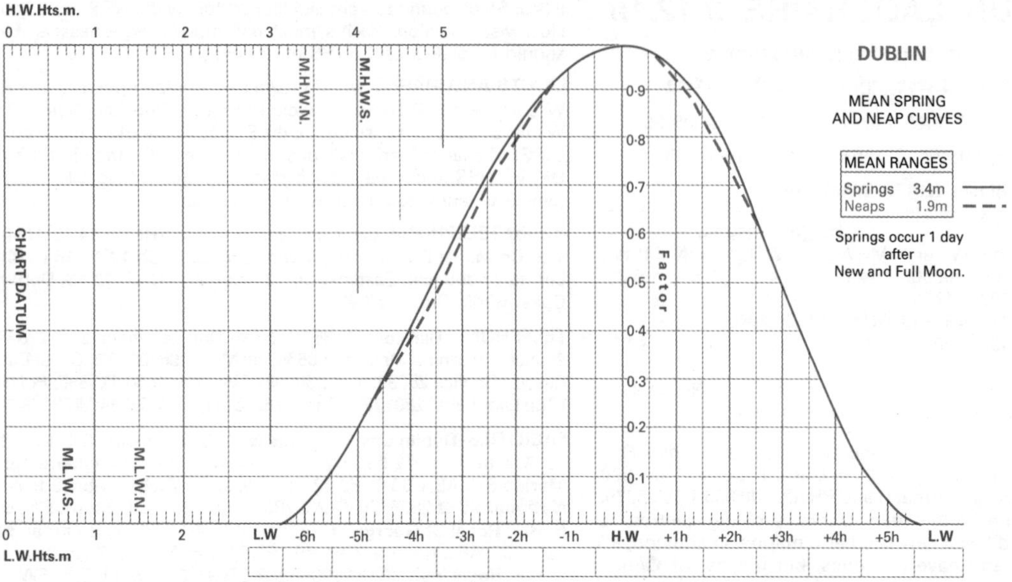
H.W.Hts.m.
DUBLIN
MEAN SPRING AND NEAP CURVES
MEAN RANGES
Springs 3.4m
Neaps 1.9m
Springs occur 1 day after New and Full Moon.
CHART DATUM
M.H.W.N.
M.H.W.S.
M.L.W.S.
M.L.W.N.
Factor
L.W -6h -5h -4h -3h -2h -1h H.W +1h +2h +3h +4h +5h L.W
L.W.Hts.m

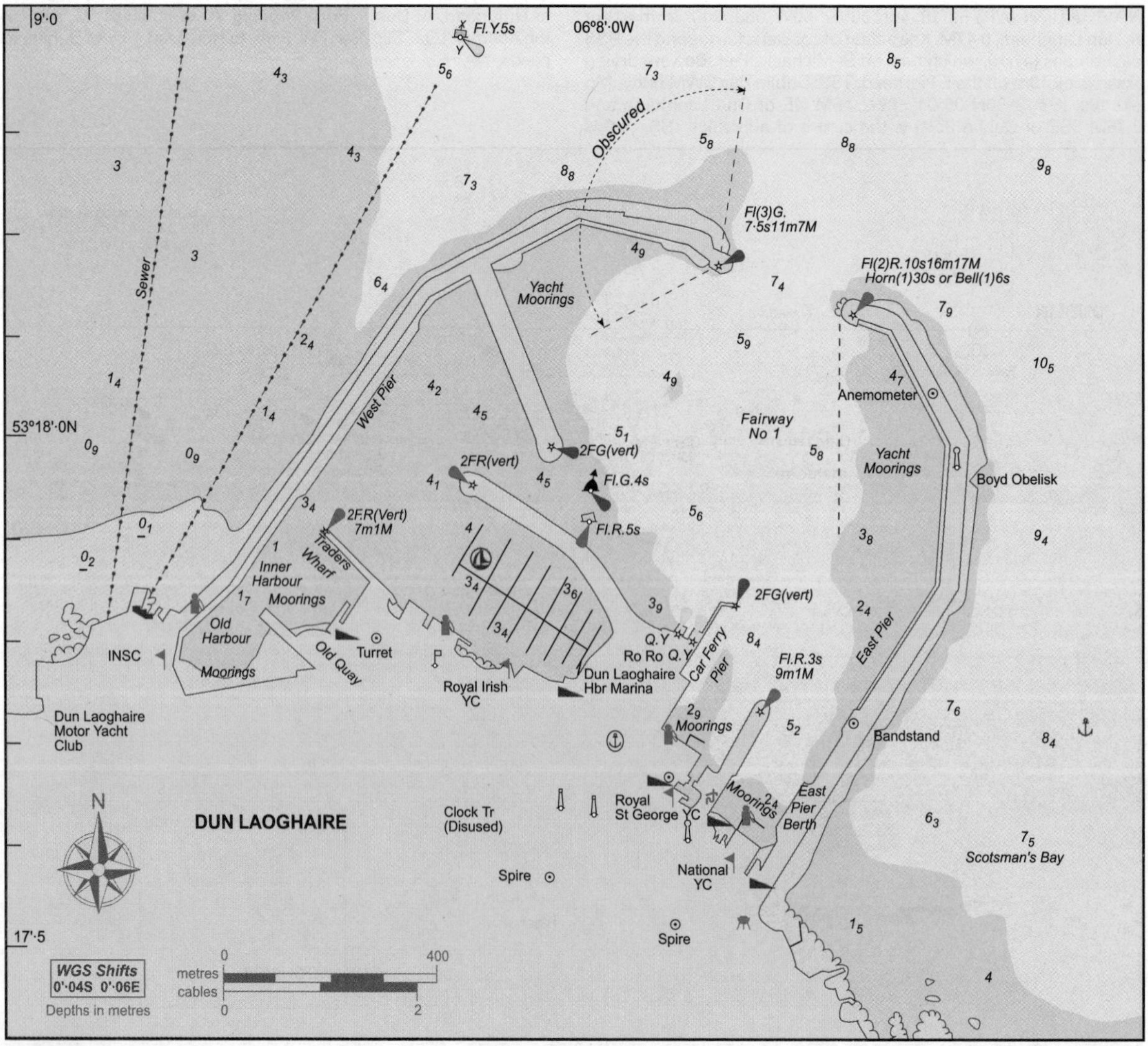
06°8'·0W
53°18'·0N
Fl.Y.5s
Obscured
Fl(3)G. 7·5s11m7M
Fl(2)R.10s16m17M Horn(1)30s or Bell(1)6s
Yacht Moorings
Sewer
West Pier
Anemometer
Fairway No 1
Boyd Obelisk
2FG(vert)
2FR(vert)
Fl.G.4s
Fl.R.5s
2F.R(Vert) 7m1M
Traders Wharf
Inner Harbour Moorings
Old Harbour
Moorings
Old Quay
Turret
INSC
Royal Irish YC
Dun Laoghaire Hbr Marina
Q.Y
Ro Ro Q.Y
Car Ferry Pier
Fl.R.3s 9m1M
East Pier
Bandstand
Dun Laoghaire Motor Yacht Club
DUN LAOGHAIRE
Clock Tr (Disused)
Royal St George YC
National YC
East Pier Berth
Spire
Scotsman's Bay
WGS Shifts 0'·04S 0'·06E
metres 0 400
cables 0 2
Depths in metres

TIME ZONE (UTC)
For Summer Time add ONE hour in **non-shaded areas**

IRELAND – DUBLIN (NORTH WALL)

LAT 53°21'N LONG 6°13'W

TIMES AND HEIGHTS OF HIGH AND LOW WATERS

SPRING & NEAP TIDES
Dates in red are **SPRINGS**
Dates in blue are **NEAPS**

YEAR **2002**

JANUARY

Day	Time	m	Time	m	Time	m	Time	m
1 TU	0022	4.0	0554	0.8	1239	4.2	1827	0.5
2 W	0109	4.0	0639	0.8	1327	4.2	1917	0.5
3 TH	0200	4.0	0729	0.9	1418	4.2	2012	0.6
4 F	0255	3.9	0824	1.0	1513	4.1	2109	0.7
5 SA	0353	3.8	0924	1.2	1611	4.1	2210	0.8
6 SU	0456	3.7	1029	1.3	1714	3.9	2314	0.9
7 M	0604	3.6	1137	1.4	1822	3.8		
8 TU	0022	1.0	0711	3.6	1249	1.4	1932	3.8
9 W	0130	1.1	0816	3.7	1358	1.4	2040	3.8
10 TH	0234	1.1	0916	3.8	1501	1.2	2143	3.8
11 F	0330	1.0	1009	3.9	1555	1.1	2237	3.8
12 SA	0417	1.0	1055	4.0	1642	1.0	2323	3.8
13 SU ●	0458	1.0	1134	4.0	1723	0.9		
14 M	0001	3.8	0534	0.9	1207	4.0	1801	0.8
15 TU	0035	3.8	0609	0.9	1240	4.0	1838	0.8
16 W	0108	3.7	0643	1.0	1314	4.0	1915	0.8
17 TH	0143	3.7	0719	1.0	1351	4.0	1951	0.9
18 F	0221	3.6	0757	1.1	1430	3.9	2029	1.0
19 SA	0302	3.5	0837	1.2	1511	3.8	2109	1.1
20 SU	0346	3.4	0922	1.4	1556	3.6	2152	1.2
21 M	0435	3.3	1014	1.5	1645	3.5	2241	1.3
22 TU	0534	3.3	1114	1.6	1742	3.4	2342	1.4
23 W	0641	3.2	1219	1.6	1849	3.3		
24 TH	0047	1.5	0745	3.3	1323	1.6	1958	3.4
25 F	0150	1.4	0842	3.5	1421	1.4	2059	3.5
26 SA	0246	1.2	0931	3.7	1513	1.1	2152	3.7
27 SU	0334	1.0	1015	3.9	1600	0.8	2239	3.9
28 M	0417	0.8	1058	4.1	1644	0.6	○ 2324	4.0
29 TU	0459	0.7	1140	4.2	1729	0.4		
30 W	0008	4.1	0541	0.6	1224	4.3	1813	0.2
31 TH	0054	4.1	0624	0.6	1310	4.4	1901	0.2

FEBRUARY

Day	Time	m	Time	m	Time	m	Time	m
1 F	0141	4.1	0711	0.6	1358	4.3	1951	0.3
2 SA	0231	4.0	0801	0.7	1450	4.2	2044	0.5
3 SU	0323	3.8	0856	0.9	1545	4.1	2140	0.7
4 M	0421	3.7	0956	1.1	1645	3.9	2239	0.9
5 TU	0526	3.6	1102	1.3	1755	3.7	2345	1.2
6 W	0637	3.5	1216	1.4	1910	3.6		
7 TH	0100	1.3	0747	3.5	1338	1.4	2023	3.5
8 F	0216	1.3	0853	3.6	1451	1.3	2132	3.6
9 SA	0318	1.3	0953	3.7	1548	1.1	2230	3.6
10 SU	0406	1.2	1042	3.8	1633	1.0	2315	3.7
11 M	0445	1.0	1121	3.9	1711	0.9	2350	3.7
12 TU ●	0519	0.9	1151	4.0	1745	0.8		
13 W	0017	3.7	0551	0.9	1220	4.0	1817	0.7
14 TH	0043	3.7	0621	0.8	1250	4.0	1847	0.8
15 F	0112	3.7	0651	0.8	1322	3.9	1916	0.8
16 SA	0144	3.6	0721	0.9	1357	3.9	1945	0.8
17 SU	0219	3.6	0755	0.9	1436	3.8	2019	0.9
18 M	0259	3.5	0834	1.1	1517	3.7	2057	1.0
19 TU	0343	3.4	0917	1.2	1603	3.5	2142	1.2
20 W	0433	3.3	1008	1.4	1655	3.4	2235	1.4
21 TH	0534	3.2	1115	1.5	1800	3.2	2347	1.5
22 F	0650	3.2	1238	1.5	1921	3.2		
23 SA	0112	1.5	0805	3.3	1352	1.3	2035	3.4
24 SU	0223	1.3	0905	3.5	1453	1.0	2134	3.6
25 M	0318	1.1	0955	3.8	1544	0.7	2224	3.8
26 TU	0404	0.8	1040	4.1	1630	0.3	2308	4.0
27 W	0445	0.5	1123	4.3	1713	0.1	○ 2350	4.1
28 TH	0526	0.4	1205	4.4	1756	0.0		

MARCH

Day	Time	m	Time	m	Time	m	Time	m
1 F	0032	4.1	0606	0.3	1250	4.4	1840	0.0
2 SA	0116	4.1	0650	0.4	1336	4.3	1926	0.2
3 SU	0201	4.0	0737	0.5	1425	4.2	2016	0.4
4 M	0250	3.8	0829	0.7	1518	4.0	2108	0.7
5 TU	0343	3.7	0927	0.9	1617	3.8	2205	1.0
6 W	0445	3.5	1032	1.2	1729	3.5	2308	1.3
7 TH	0600	3.4	1146	1.3	1848	3.4		
8 F	0025	1.5	0716	3.4	1318	1.4	2007	3.3
9 SA	0157	1.5	0829	3.4	1437	1.3	2121	3.4
10 SU	0302	1.4	0932	3.6	1533	1.1	2217	3.5
11 M	0349	1.2	1022	3.7	1615	0.9	2259	3.6
12 TU	0426	1.0	1100	3.8	1650	0.8	2330	3.6
13 W	0458	0.9	1130	3.9	1721	0.7	2353	3.6
14 TH ●	0528	0.8	1157	3.9	1750	0.7		
15 F	0016	3.7	0555	0.7	1224	3.9	1815	0.7
16 SA	0041	3.7	0621	0.7	1253	3.9	1839	0.7
17 SU	0110	3.7	0649	0.7	1327	3.9	1907	0.7
18 M	0144	3.7	0722	0.8	1406	3.8	1941	0.8
19 TU	0223	3.6	0759	0.9	1447	3.7	2021	0.9
20 W	0306	3.5	0843	1.0	1532	3.5	2105	1.1
21 TH	0354	3.4	0934	1.2	1624	3.4	2159	1.3
22 F	0452	3.2	1041	1.3	1729	3.2	2310	1.5
23 SA	0607	3.2	1207	1.4	1855	3.2		
24 SU	0043	1.5	0732	3.3	1329	1.2	2014	3.4
25 M	0202	1.3	0839	3.5	1434	0.9	2116	3.6
26 TU	0300	1.0	0933	3.8	1527	0.5	2206	3.8
27 W	0347	0.7	1020	4.1	1612	0.2	2249	4.0
28 TH	0428	0.4	1104	4.3	1655	0.0	○ 2330	4.1
29 F	0507	0.3	1146	4.4	1736	-0.1		
30 SA	0010	4.1	0547	0.2	1230	4.4	1818	0.0
31 SU	0051	4.1	0630	0.2	1315	4.3	1902	0.2

APRIL

Day	Time	m	Time	m	Time	m	Time	m
1 M	0134	4.0	0716	0.4	1404	4.1	1949	0.5
2 TU	0220	3.9	0808	0.6	1456	3.9	2039	0.8
3 W	0311	3.7	0905	0.8	1555	3.6	2134	1.1
4 TH	0410	3.5	1008	1.1	1706	3.4	2235	1.4
5 F	0524	3.4	1120	1.3	1824	3.2	2348	1.6
6 SA	0643	3.3	1249	1.3	1944	3.2		
7 SU	0121	1.6	0757	3.4	1410	1.2	2057	3.3
8 M	0233	1.5	0902	3.5	1505	1.0	2151	3.5
9 TU	0321	1.3	0952	3.7	1546	0.9	2230	3.6
10 W	0358	1.1	1031	3.8	1621	0.8	2259	3.6
11 TH	0431	0.9	1102	3.8	1651	0.7	2324	3.7
12 F	0501	0.8	1130	3.8	1718	0.7	● 2347	3.7
13 SA	0527	0.7	1156	3.8	1741	0.7		
14 SU	0010	3.7	0552	0.7	1226	3.8	1805	0.7
15 M	0039	3.8	0620	0.7	1301	3.8	1835	0.7
16 TU	0115	3.8	0654	0.7	1341	3.8	1912	0.8
17 W	0155	3.7	0735	0.8	1424	3.7	1953	0.9
18 TH	0240	3.6	0822	0.9	1512	3.6	2042	1.1
19 F	0329	3.5	0918	1.1	1606	3.4	2140	1.3
20 SA	0428	3.4	1028	1.2	1713	3.3	2253	1.5
21 SU	0541	3.3	1150	1.2	1835	3.3		
22 M	0019	1.5	0702	3.4	1307	1.0	1951	3.4
23 TU	0136	1.3	0811	3.6	1412	0.7	2053	3.6
24 W	0235	1.0	0909	3.8	1505	0.4	2144	3.8
25 TH	0324	0.7	0959	4.1	1552	0.2	2228	4.0
26 F	0408	0.5	1045	4.2	1635	0.1	2309	4.1
27 SA	0449	0.4	1129	4.3	1717	0.1	○ 2349	4.1
28 SU	0531	0.3	1213	4.3	1758	0.2		
29 M	0029	4.1	0613	0.3	1259	4.2	1841	0.4
30 TU	0111	4.0	0700	0.4	1347	4.0	1926	0.6

Chart Datum: 0·20 metres above Ordnance Datum (Dublin)

TIME ZONE (UTC)
For Summer Time add ONE hour in **non-shaded areas**

IRELAND – DUBLIN (NORTH WALL)

LAT 53°21′N LONG 6°13′W

TIMES AND HEIGHTS OF HIGH AND LOW WATERS

SPRING & NEAP TIDES
Dates in red are **SPRINGS**
Dates in blue are **NEAPS**

YEAR **2002**

MAY

Date	Day	Time	m	Time	m	Time	m	Time	m
1	W	0157	3.9	0752	0.6	1439	3.8	2015	0.9
2	TH	0246	3.8	0848	0.8	1537	3.6	2108	1.2
3	F	0343	3.6	0948	1.0	1642	3.3	2207	1.4
4	SA	0452	3.4	1054	1.2	1754	3.2	2312	1.6
5	SU	0607	3.4	1208	1.2	1907	3.2		
6	M	0028	1.6	0717	3.4	1325	1.2	2014	3.3
7	TU	0144	1.5	0819	3.5	1424	1.1	2108	3.4
8	W	0240	1.3	0911	3.6	1509	1.0	2148	3.5
9	TH	0322	1.2	0953	3.7	1545	0.9	2222	3.6
10	F	0357	1.0	1029	3.7	1616	0.8	2251	3.7
11	SA	0428	0.9	1100	3.8	1643	0.8	2316	3.7
12	SU	0456	0.8	1129	3.8	1708	0.8	● 2342	3.8
13	M	0524	0.8	1201	3.8	1736	0.8		
14	TU	0013	3.8	0556	0.7	1239	3.8	1810	0.8
15	W	0052	3.8	0634	0.8	1321	3.8	1849	0.9
16	TH	0135	3.8	0719	0.8	1408	3.7	1935	1.0
17	F	0222	3.8	0812	0.9	1459	3.6	2028	1.1
18	SA	0315	3.7	0912	0.9	1556	3.5	2129	1.3
19	SU	0414	3.6	1020	1.0	1701	3.4	2239	1.4
20	M	0522	3.6	1132	1.0	1813	3.4	2353	1.4
21	TU	0635	3.6	1242	0.9	1924	3.5		
22	W	0104	1.3	0742	3.7	1345	0.7	2025	3.7
23	TH	0205	1.1	0843	3.9	1441	0.5	2120	3.8
24	F	0259	0.9	0938	4.0	1531	0.4	2208	3.9
25	SA	0348	0.7	1028	4.1	1617	0.3	2251	4.0
26	SU	0433	0.6	1116	4.1	1700	0.4	○ 2332	4.0
27	M	0518	0.5	1201	4.1	1742	0.5		
28	TU	0012	4.0	0602	0.5	1247	4.0	1823	0.6
29	W	0054	4.0	0649	0.6	1334	3.9	1907	0.8
30	TH	0138	3.9	0739	0.7	1422	3.7	1953	1.0
31	F	0225	3.8	0831	0.8	1515	3.5	2043	1.2

JUNE

Date	Day	Time	m	Time	m	Time	m	Time	m
1	SA	0317	3.7	0927	1.0	1612	3.4	2138	1.4
2	SU	0416	3.6	1024	1.1	1714	3.3	2237	1.5
3	M	0523	3.5	1125	1.2	1819	3.2	2339	1.6
4	TU	0630	3.4	1228	1.2	1920	3.2		
5	W	0044	1.6	0730	3.5	1329	1.2	2014	3.3
6	TH	0145	1.5	0824	3.5	1420	1.1	2101	3.5
7	F	0235	1.3	0911	3.6	1502	1.1	2141	3.6
8	SA	0317	1.2	0952	3.6	1537	1.0	2216	3.7
9	SU	0353	1.1	1029	3.7	1609	0.9	2246	3.8
10	M	0426	1.0	1104	3.8	1640	0.9	● 2317	3.8
11	TU	0500	0.9	1141	3.8	1714	0.8	2353	3.9
12	W	0538	0.8	1221	3.8	1752	0.8		
13	TH	0033	4.0	0620	0.7	1306	3.8	1834	0.9
14	F	0118	4.0	0708	0.7	1355	3.8	1921	1.0
15	SA	0208	3.9	0803	0.8	1447	3.7	2015	1.1
16	SU	0301	3.9	0902	0.8	1543	3.7	2114	1.2
17	M	0359	3.9	1005	0.8	1643	3.6	2217	1.2
18	TU	0501	3.8	1110	0.8	1748	3.6	2324	1.3
19	W	0608	3.8	1214	0.8	1854	3.6		
20	TH	0031	1.2	0715	3.8	1317	0.8	1957	3.7
21	F	0136	1.2	0820	3.9	1417	0.8	2056	3.7
22	SA	0237	1.1	0921	3.9	1512	0.7	2149	3.8
23	SU	0332	0.9	1017	4.0	1601	0.7	2237	3.9
24	M	0423	0.8	1107	4.0	1647	0.7	○ 2319	4.0
25	TU	0510	0.8	1153	3.9	1729	0.8	2359	4.0
26	W	0555	0.7	1236	3.9	1809	0.8		
27	TH	0037	4.0	0638	0.7	1318	3.8	1848	0.9
28	F	0118	4.0	0723	0.8	1400	3.7	1930	1.0
29	SA	0201	3.9	0810	0.8	1445	3.5	2015	1.1
30	SU	0246	3.8	0858	0.9	1533	3.4	2103	1.3

JULY

Date	Day	Time	m	Time	m	Time	m	Time	m
1	M	0335	3.7	0947	1.1	1624	3.3	2156	1.4
2	TU	0428	3.6	1039	1.2	1721	3.3	2252	1.5
3	W	0528	3.5	1133	1.3	1822	3.2	2350	1.5
4	TH	0632	3.4	1228	1.3	1920	3.3		
5	F	0049	1.5	0733	3.4	1324	1.3	2013	3.4
6	SA	0145	1.5	0828	3.4	1414	1.3	2100	3.5
7	SU	0235	1.4	0917	3.5	1459	1.2	2142	3.6
8	M	0320	1.2	1001	3.6	1539	1.1	2220	3.8
9	TU	0401	1.0	1043	3.7	1617	1.0	2257	3.9
10	W	0441	0.9	1124	3.8	1656	0.9	● 2335	4.0
11	TH	0523	0.7	1207	3.9	1736	0.8		
12	F	0017	4.1	0607	0.6	1251	3.9	1819	0.8
13	SA	0102	4.1	0654	0.5	1339	3.9	1905	0.8
14	SU	0150	4.2	0747	0.5	1429	3.9	1956	0.9
15	M	0242	4.1	0843	0.6	1521	3.8	2051	1.0
16	TU	0337	4.1	0941	0.7	1617	3.7	2150	1.1
17	W	0436	4.0	1042	0.8	1718	3.6	2253	1.2
18	TH	0541	3.9	1144	0.9	1824	3.6		
19	F	0000	1.3	0652	3.8	1250	1.0	1931	3.6
20	SA	0112	1.3	0803	3.7	1355	1.1	2036	3.7
21	SU	0222	1.2	0910	3.8	1457	1.1	2135	3.8
22	M	0325	1.1	1010	3.8	1550	1.0	2226	3.9
23	TU	0418	1.0	1103	3.8	1636	1.0	2309	3.9
24	W	0504	0.9	1147	3.8	1716	0.9	○ 2346	4.0
25	TH	0545	0.8	1224	3.8	1752	0.9		
26	F	0019	4.0	0623	0.8	1257	3.7	1827	0.9
27	SA	0054	4.0	0701	0.8	1332	3.6	1903	1.0
28	SU	0131	4.0	0740	0.8	1408	3.6	1941	1.0
29	M	0210	3.9	0819	0.9	1448	3.5	2022	1.1
30	TU	0252	3.8	0901	1.0	1530	3.4	2106	1.2
31	W	0336	3.7	0944	1.1	1616	3.3	2155	1.4

AUGUST

Date	Day	Time	m	Time	m	Time	m	Time	m
1	TH	0425	3.5	1033	1.3	1709	3.3	2251	1.5
2	F	0523	3.4	1128	1.4	1814	3.2	2354	1.6
3	SA	0634	3.3	1229	1.5	1922	3.3		
4	SU	0059	1.6	0746	3.3	1331	1.5	2021	3.4
5	M	0200	1.5	0847	3.4	1428	1.4	2112	3.6
6	TU	0254	1.2	0940	3.6	1517	1.2	2157	3.8
7	W	0342	1.0	1026	3.7	1600	1.0	2238	4.0
8	TH	0425	0.7	1108	3.9	1640	0.8	● 2317	4.1
9	F	0507	0.5	1150	4.0	1720	0.7	2358	4.3
10	SA	0550	0.3	1232	4.1	1801	0.6		
11	SU	0040	4.3	0635	0.3	1317	4.0	1844	0.6
12	M	0127	4.3	0723	0.3	1403	4.0	1931	0.7
13	TU	0216	4.3	0815	0.4	1453	3.9	2023	0.8
14	W	0309	4.1	0911	0.6	1546	3.8	2120	1.0
15	TH	0407	4.0	1010	0.8	1645	3.6	2223	1.2
16	F	0515	3.8	1113	1.1	1754	3.5	2334	1.3
17	SA	0635	3.6	1223	1.3	1908	3.5		
18	SU	0054	1.4	0752	3.6	1338	1.4	2018	3.6
19	M	0216	1.3	0904	3.6	1446	1.3	2122	3.7
20	TU	0322	1.2	1007	3.7	1540	1.2	2215	3.8
21	W	0412	1.0	1057	3.7	1623	1.1	2258	3.9
22	TH	0453	0.8	1137	3.7	1700	1.0	○ 2331	4.0
23	F	0529	0.8	1207	3.7	1733	0.9	2358	4.0
24	SA	0602	0.7	1232	3.7	1804	0.9		
25	SU	0028	4.0	0633	0.7	1300	3.7	1835	0.9
26	M	0100	4.0	0703	0.8	1332	3.7	1906	0.9
27	TU	0136	3.9	0734	0.9	1406	3.6	1940	1.0
28	W	0214	3.8	0807	1.0	1444	3.6	2018	1.1
29	TH	0256	3.7	0845	1.1	1526	3.5	2100	1.3
30	F	0342	3.5	0929	1.3	1614	3.4	2150	1.4
31	SA	0435	3.4	1022	1.5	1711	3.2	2256	1.6

Chart Datum: 0·20 metres above Ordnance Datum (Dublin)

TIME ZONE (UTC)
For Summer Time add ONE hour in **non-shaded areas**

IRELAND – DUBLIN (NORTH WALL)

LAT 53°21′N LONG 6°13′W

TIMES AND HEIGHTS OF HIGH AND LOW WATERS

SPRING & NEAP TIDES
Dates in red are SPRINGS
Dates in blue are NEAPS

YEAR **2002**

SEPTEMBER

Date	Time	m	Time	m	Time	m	Time	m
1 SU	0542	3.2	1135	1.6	1827	3.2		
2 M	0018	1.6	0710	3.2	1256	1.6	1945	3.3
3 TU	0133	1.5	0824	3.3	1404	1.5	2046	3.5
4 W	0235	1.2	0921	3.6	1459	1.2	2134	3.8
5 TH	0325	0.8	1008	3.8	1543	1.0	2217	4.1
6 F	0408	0.5	1050	4.0	1623	0.7	2257	4.3
7 SA	0449	0.2	1130	4.1	1701	0.5	● 2337	4.4
8 SU	0530	0.1	1209	4.2	1741	0.4		
9 M	0018	4.5	0612	0.1	1251	4.2	1822	0.4
10 TU	0102	4.4	0657	0.2	1335	4.1	1907	0.5
11 W	0150	4.3	0746	0.4	1422	4.0	1957	0.7
12 TH	0242	4.1	0840	0.7	1514	3.8	2054	0.9
13 F	0341	3.9	0938	1.0	1612	3.7	2158	1.2
14 SA	0454	3.6	1042	1.3	1724	3.5	2312	1.4
15 SU	0619	3.5	1156	1.5	1844	3.5		
16 M	0041	1.4	0742	3.4	1321	1.6	1959	3.6
17 TU	0210	1.3	0858	3.5	1432	1.5	2106	3.7
18 W	0311	1.1	0957	3.6	1523	1.3	2159	3.9
19 TH	0356	0.9	1043	3.7	1604	1.1	2240	4.0
20 F	0433	0.8	1118	3.7	1639	1.0	2311	4.0
21 SA	0505	0.7	1144	3.7	1710	0.9	○ 2337	4.0
22 SU	0535	0.7	1206	3.7	1740	0.8		
23 M	0003	4.0	0601	0.7	1231	3.8	1807	0.8
24 TU	0032	4.0	0626	0.8	1258	3.8	1835	0.8
25 W	0106	3.9	0652	0.9	1331	3.7	1906	0.9
26 TH	0143	3.8	0724	0.9	1409	3.7	1942	1.0
27 F	0224	3.7	0802	1.1	1450	3.6	2024	1.2
28 SA	0310	3.6	0846	1.3	1537	3.5	2114	1.4
29 SU	0403	3.4	0940	1.5	1632	3.3	2219	1.5
30 M	0509	3.2	1054	1.7	1744	3.2	2347	1.6

OCTOBER

Date	Time	m	Time	m	Time	m	Time	m
1 TU	0640	3.2	1226	1.7	1909	3.3		
2 W	0108	1.4	0800	3.4	1341	1.5	2016	3.6
3 TH	0214	1.1	0900	3.6	1438	1.2	2109	3.8
4 F	0305	0.7	0947	3.9	1523	0.9	2154	4.1
5 SA	0349	0.4	1028	4.1	1602	0.6	2235	4.3
6 SU	0429	0.1	1107	4.2	1641	0.4	● 2316	4.5
7 M	0509	0.0	1146	4.3	1720	0.3	2357	4.5
8 TU	0550	0.1	1226	4.2	1802	0.3		
9 W	0041	4.4	0633	0.2	1309	4.2	1847	0.5
10 TH	0129	4.3	0720	0.5	1356	4.0	1937	0.7
11 F	0222	4.0	0812	0.8	1447	3.9	2034	0.9
12 SA	0323	3.8	0909	1.2	1545	3.7	2139	1.2
13 SU	0438	3.5	1013	1.5	1657	3.6	2252	1.3
14 M	0601	3.4	1126	1.7	1816	3.5		
15 TU	0021	1.4	0724	3.4	1253	1.7	1931	3.6
16 W	0147	1.3	0839	3.5	1406	1.6	2038	3.7
17 TH	0246	1.1	0935	3.6	1457	1.4	2132	3.8
18 F	0330	1.0	1017	3.7	1538	1.2	2213	3.9
19 SA	0406	0.8	1050	3.8	1613	1.0	2245	4.0
20 SU	0437	0.8	1116	3.8	1645	0.9	2313	4.0
21 M	0506	0.8	1139	3.8	1715	0.9	○ 2339	4.0
22 TU	0531	0.8	1203	3.8	1742	0.9		
23 W	0007	3.9	0553	0.8	1230	3.9	1809	0.9
24 TH	0041	3.9	0619	0.9	1303	3.8	1840	0.9
25 F	0118	3.8	0653	1.0	1341	3.8	1918	1.0
26 SA	0201	3.7	0732	1.2	1424	3.7	2002	1.2
27 SU	0248	3.6	0818	1.3	1512	3.6	2055	1.3
28 M	0343	3.4	0915	1.5	1607	3.5	2201	1.4
29 TU	0450	3.3	1029	1.7	1714	3.4	2322	1.4
30 W	0612	3.3	1156	1.7	1831	3.5		
31 TH	0040	1.2	0729	3.4	1311	1.5	1940	3.7

NOVEMBER

Date	Time	m	Time	m	Time	m	Time	m
1 F	0146	1.0	0831	3.7	1409	1.3	2038	3.9
2 SA	0240	0.6	0920	3.9	1457	1.0	2128	4.1
3 SU	0326	0.4	1004	4.1	1541	0.7	2213	4.3
4 M	0409	0.2	1045	4.2	1622	0.5	● 2257	4.4
5 TU	0450	0.2	1125	4.3	1704	0.4	2341	4.4
6 W	0531	0.2	1206	4.3	1747	0.4		
7 TH	0027	4.3	0614	0.4	1250	4.2	1833	0.5
8 F	0117	4.2	0659	0.7	1336	4.1	1924	0.7
9 SA	0210	4.0	0749	1.0	1427	4.0	2020	0.9
10 SU	0310	3.7	0845	1.3	1523	3.8	2121	1.1
11 M	0419	3.5	0946	1.5	1629	3.7	2228	1.3
12 TU	0533	3.4	1053	1.7	1742	3.6	2344	1.4
13 W	0649	3.4	1208	1.7	1852	3.6		
14 TH	0104	1.3	0759	3.4	1323	1.7	1956	3.7
15 F	0207	1.2	0855	3.6	1421	1.5	2051	3.7
16 SA	0255	1.1	0938	3.7	1506	1.3	2136	3.8
17 SU	0334	1.0	1013	3.8	1545	1.2	2214	3.9
18 M	0406	0.9	1043	3.8	1619	1.1	2247	3.9
19 TU	0435	0.9	1112	3.9	1650	1.0	2317	3.9
20 W	0501	0.9	1138	3.9	1719	1.0	○ 2347	3.9
21 TH	0526	1.0	1206	3.9	1748	1.0		
22 F	0021	3.9	0555	1.0	1240	3.9	1821	1.0
23 SA	0100	3.8	0630	1.1	1320	3.9	1902	1.0
24 SU	0144	3.7	0712	1.2	1405	3.8	1948	1.1
25 M	0234	3.7	0801	1.3	1454	3.8	2043	1.1
26 TU	0329	3.6	0859	1.5	1548	3.7	2146	1.2
27 W	0432	3.5	1006	1.6	1650	3.7	2256	1.2
28 TH	0542	3.5	1121	1.6	1757	3.7		
29 F	0007	1.1	0652	3.6	1233	1.5	1903	3.8
30 SA	0113	0.9	0755	3.7	1335	1.3	2005	3.9

DECEMBER

Date	Time	m	Time	m	Time	m	Time	m
1 SU	0211	0.7	0850	3.9	1430	1.1	2102	4.1
2 M	0303	0.6	0940	4.0	1520	0.9	2155	4.2
3 TU	0350	0.5	1026	4.1	1608	0.7	2245	4.2
4 W	0435	0.5	1110	4.2	1653	0.6	● 2333	4.2
5 TH	0517	0.5	1152	4.2	1739	0.6		
6 F	0020	4.2	0600	0.7	1236	4.2	1825	0.6
7 SA	0108	4.0	0643	0.8	1321	4.2	1914	0.7
8 SU	0159	3.9	0730	1.0	1409	4.1	2006	0.8
9 M	0252	3.7	0820	1.2	1500	3.9	2100	1.0
10 TU	0351	3.5	0916	1.4	1557	3.8	2157	1.1
11 W	0454	3.4	1015	1.6	1659	3.7	2258	1.3
12 TH	0559	3.3	1119	1.7	1804	3.6		
13 F	0004	1.4	0702	3.4	1227	1.7	1906	3.6
14 SA	0111	1.4	0759	3.4	1331	1.6	2003	3.6
15 SU	0209	1.3	0848	3.6	1426	1.5	2054	3.6
16 M	0255	1.2	0931	3.7	1512	1.4	2139	3.7
17 TU	0333	1.2	1009	3.8	1550	1.2	2219	3.7
18 W	0405	1.1	1044	3.9	1625	1.1	2255	3.8
19 TH	0435	1.1	1115	3.9	1658	1.1	○ 2329	3.8
20 F	0505	1.1	1146	4.0	1731	1.0		
21 SA	0006	3.8	0537	1.0	1222	4.0	1807	0.9
22 SU	0046	3.8	0615	1.0	1303	4.0	1849	0.9
23 M	0130	3.8	0657	1.1	1348	4.0	1936	0.9
24 TU	0219	3.8	0745	1.2	1436	4.0	2028	0.9
25 W	0311	3.7	0839	1.2	1528	3.9	2125	0.9
26 TH	0408	3.7	0939	1.3	1624	3.9	2226	0.9
27 F	0509	3.6	1044	1.4	1724	3.9	2330	1.0
28 SA	0614	3.6	1152	1.4	1829	3.8		
29 SU	0037	1.0	0720	3.7	1301	1.3	1936	3.8
30 M	0142	0.9	0822	3.8	1406	1.2	2042	3.9
31 TU	0242	0.9	0920	3.9	1506	1.1	2144	4.0

Chart Datum: 0·20 metres above Ordnance Datum (Dublin)

WICKLOW *9.12.11*

Wicklow **52°58'·98N 06°02'·70W** ❀❀❀◊◊✿✿

CHARTS AC 633, 1468; Imray C61; Irish OS 56

TIDES –0010 Dover; ML 1·7; Duration 0640; Zone 0 (UT)

Standard Port DUBLIN (NORTH WALL) (⟵)

Times				Height (metres)			
High Water		Low Water		MHWS	MHWN	MLWN	MLWS
0000	0700	0000	0500	4·1	3·4	1·5	0·7
1200	1900	1200	1700				
Differences WICKLOW							
–0019	–0019	–0024	–0026	–1·4	–1·1	–0·4	0·0

SHELTER Very safe, and access H24. Outer hbr is open to NE winds which cause a swell. Moorings in NW of hbr belong to SC and may not be used without permission. 4 berths on E Pier (2·5m) are convenient with fender boards/ladders provided. W pier is not recommended. ⚓ in hbr is restricted by ships' turning circle. Inner hbr (river) gives excellent shelter in 2·5m on N and S Quays, which are used by FVs. Packet Quay is for ships (2·5m), but may be used if none due; fender board needed. Yachts should berth on N or S quays as directed and/or space available.

NAVIGATION WPT 52°59'·20N 06°01'·80W, 040°/220° from/to ent, 0·27M. Appr presents no difficulty; keep in the R sector of the E pier lt to avoid Planet Rk and Pogeen Rk.

LIGHTS AND MARKS No ldg marks/lts; lts are as on the chartlet. W pier head lt, Iso G 4s, is shown H24. ☆ Fl WG 10s on Packet Quay hd is vis G076°-256°, W256°-076°.

RADIO TELEPHONE VHF Ch 12, **14**, 16. Wicklow SC Ch M 16 (occas).

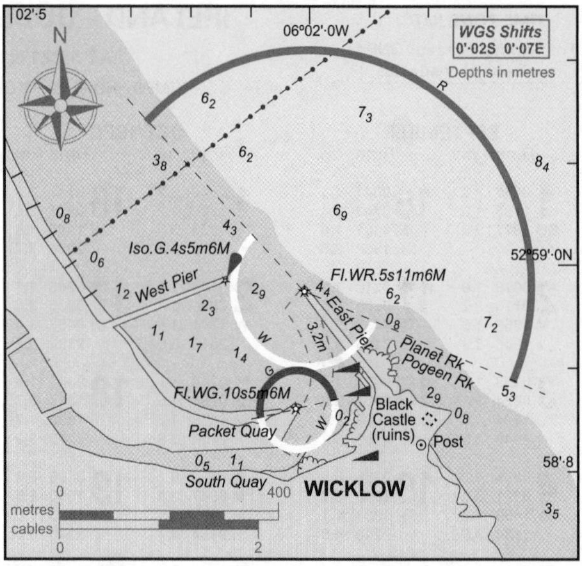

TELEPHONE (Dial code 0404) Hr Mr ☎/📠 67455; MRCC (01) 6620922; Coast/Cliff Rescue Service 69962; ⊖ 67222; Police 67107; Dr 67381.

FACILITIES **East Pier, S and N Quays**, L, FW, AB €4.44, reductions for longer stay, P & D (cans; bulk: see Hr Mr); **Wicklow SC** ☎ 67526, Slip (HW), M, L, FW, Bar; **Services**: ME, El, C, Kos, Gaz. **Town** CH, V, R, Bar, ✉, Ⓑ, ≷, ✈ (Dublin).

ARKLOW *9.12.12*

Wicklow **52°47'·60N 06°08'·20W** ❀❀❀◊◊✿✿

CHARTS AC 633, 1468; Imray C61; Irish OS 62

TIDES –0150 Dover; ML 1·0; Duration 0640; Zone 0 (UT)

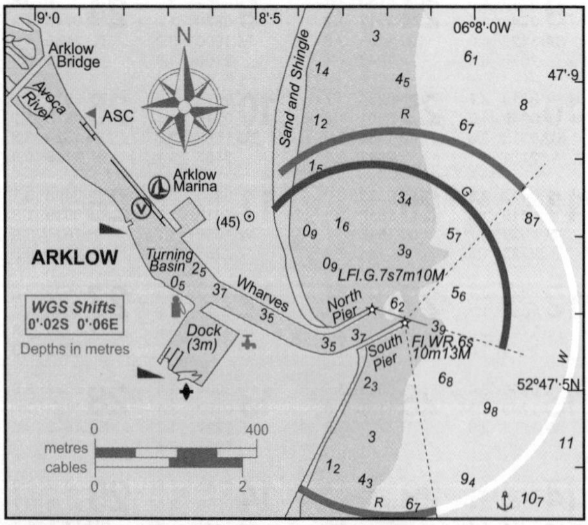

Standard Port DUBLIN (NORTH WALL) (⟵)

Times				Height (metres)			
High Water		Low Water		MHWS	MHWN	MLWN	MLWS
0000	0700	0000	0500	4·1	3·4	1·5	0·7
1200	1900	1200	1700				
Differences ARKLOW (Note small Range)							
–0315	–0201	–0140	–0134	–2·7	–2·2	–0·6	–0·1
COURTOWN							
–0328	–0242	–0158	–0138	–2·8	–2·4	–0·5	0·0

SHELTER Good, access H24; but ent unsafe in strong or prolonged NE to SE winds, when seas break across the bar. AB on SE wall of Dock (ent is 13·5m wide; 3m depth) in perfect shelter, but amidst FVs. A 60 berth marina lies on NE side of river. One ASC 🅐 up-river off slipway and one AB for Ⓥ (1.4m) at ASC quay. Good ⚓ in bay; avoid whelk pots. **Arklow Roadstone Hbr**, 1M S of Arklow, is not for yachts. **Courtown**, 10M S of Arklow at 52°38'·55N 06°13'·50W, is feasible in settled weather and offshore winds. Caution: 10m wide ent; only 1m at MLWS due to silting. AB on E wall or pick up vacant mooring.

NAVIGATION WPT 52°47'·60N 06°07'·50W, 090°/270° from/to ent, 0·40M. No navigational dangers, but beware ebb setting SE across hbr ent; give S pierhd a wide berth. Ent is difficult without power, due to blanking by piers. 3kn speed limit. Night entry, see below. Caution: Up-river of Dock ent keep to NE side of river.

LIGHTS AND MARKS No ldg lts/marks. Conspic factory chy 2·5ca NW of piers. N pier L Fl G 7s 7m 10M, vis shore-287°. S pier Fl WR 6s 11m 13M; vis R shore–223°, W223°–350°, R350°–shore. **Caution**: The pier head lts are very difficult to see due to powerful orange flood lts near the root of both piers shining E/ENE onto the piers (to assist pilotage of departing commercial vessels). Best advice to visitors is to approach from the NE with R sector just showing, or enter by day.

RADIO TELEPHONE VHF Ch 16 (HJ).

TELEPHONE (Dial code 0402) Hr Mr 32466; MRCC (01) 6620922/3; Coast/Cliff Rescue Service 32430; RNLI 32901; ⊖ 32553; Police 32304/5; Dr 32421.

FACILITIES (from seaward) **Dock** €10·16, use showers and toilets in LB Hse; **Marina** (60) ☎ 39901/32610, AC, FW. **Arklow SC** (NE bank, 500m up-river from Dock), showers, pontoon €13·97, 1 🅐. **Services**: FW, ME, El, Sh, C (5 ton mobile), Kos. **Town** EC Wed; limited CH for yachts, V, R, P & D (cans), Bar, ✉, Ⓑ, ≷, ✈ (Dublin).

WEXFORD *9.12.13*

Wexford **52°20'·10N 06°27'·00W** ❁◊◊✿✿

CHARTS AC 1772, 1787; Imray C61; Irish OS 77

TIDES –0450 Dover; ML 1·3; Duration 0630; Zone 0 (UT)

Standard Port COBH (⟶)

Times				Height (metres)			
High Water		Low Water		MHWS	MHWN	MLWN	MLWS
0500	1100	0500	1100	4·1	3·2	1·3	0·4
1700	2300	1700	2300				
Differences WEXFORD							
+0126	+0126	+0118	+0108	–2·1	–1·7	–0·3	+0·1

SHELTER 250m of AB available just below bridge. Sheltered ⚓ off town quays in 2·3m, but streams are strong. Some 🅰s are provided by WHBC, close N of Ballast Bank. There are no commercial users, other than FVs. On W side of river work continues on new waterfront. A decision is still pending on a small marina.

NAVIGATION WPT 52°21'·51N 06°20'·09W, Bar buoy (tall Y conical), 061°/241° from/to first channel mark, 5ca. The Bar partly dries and shifts, access approx HW±2. The ent, between drying sandbanks on which the sea breaks, requires careful pilotage. Do not enter in strong E/S winds, when seas break on the bar.

The chan from the Bar buoy to Ballast Bank is about 6·5M long, shallow (only 1m in places) and follows a winding track. It is at times difficult for a visitor to locate the next mark; good visibility essential. The Hbr Board has ceased to function. In summer 22 orange oil drums on end are locally laid to mark the chan. Other buoys may be seen, but they have no navigational significance. Within the training walls, Ballast Bank (small islet) can be passed either side. There are no pilots, but WHBC may, by prior arrangement, provide a launch to escort vistors from the Bar buoy. The club house is beyond the 5·8m clearance bridge.

LIGHTS AND MARKS The marks and tracks on chartlet should be treated with great caution. Channel buoys are re-laid annually using a depth sounder to find best water. The white marks on the embankment along the N side of hbr have only limited relevance to the shifting chan. There are no ldg lts. The 2 church spires at Wexford give useful general orientation.

RADIO TELEPHONE Wexford Hbr BC VHF Ch 16 occas.

TELEPHONE (Dial code 053) MRSC (01) 6620922/3; ⊜ 33116; Police 22333; Dr 31154; ⊞ 42233.

FACILITIES Wexford Quays AB (free), Slip, P, D, FW, ME, El, V, CH; **Wexford Hbr Boat Club** ☎ 22039, Slip, C (5 ton), Bar; **Town** ✉, Ⓑ, ⇌, ✈ (Waterford).

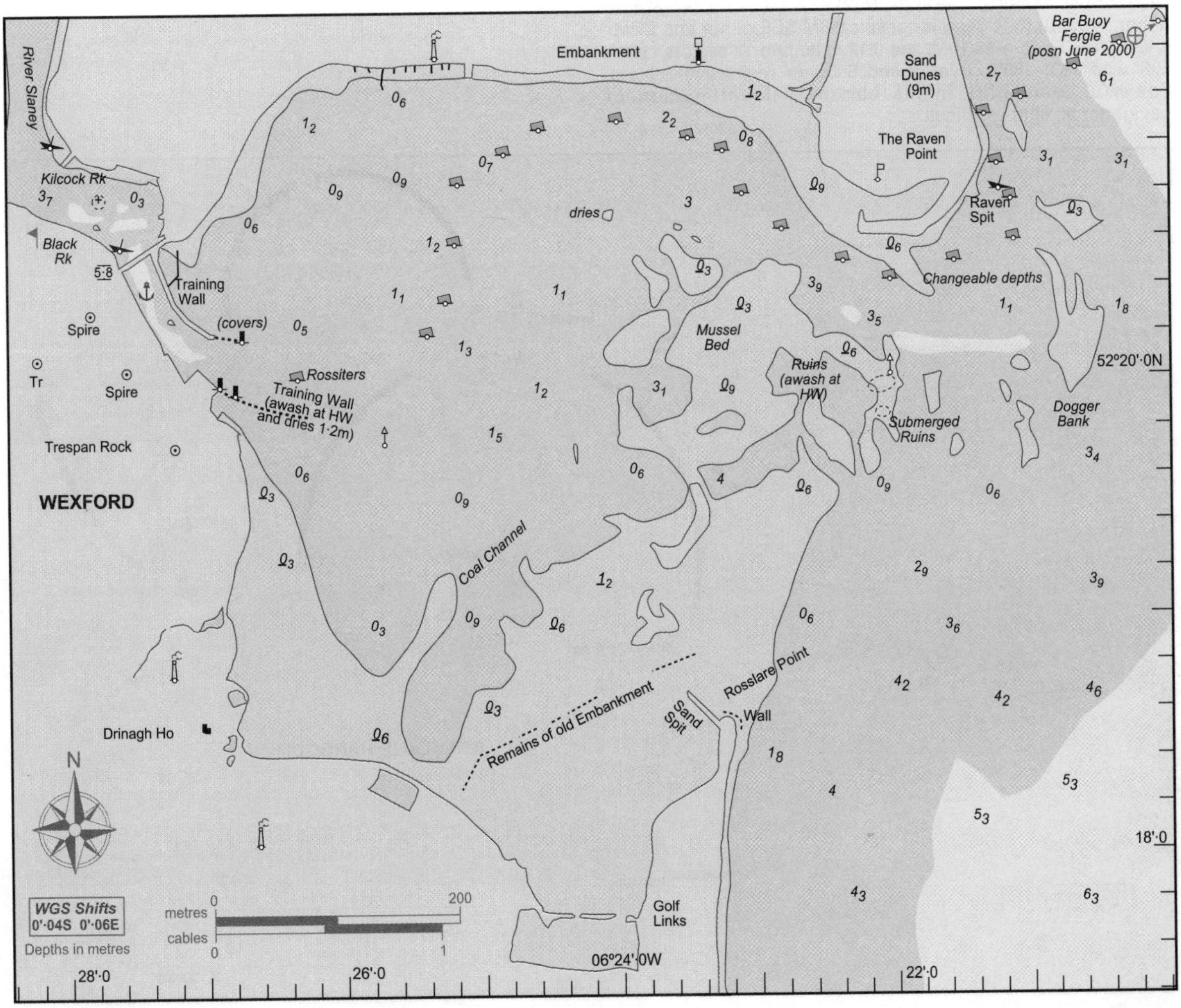

ROSSLARE HARBOUR *9.12.14*

Dublin **52°15'·30N 06°20'·90W** ❀❀❀◊◊✿

CHARTS AC 1772, 1787; Imray C57, C61; Irish OS 77

TIDES –0510 Dover; ML 1·1; Duration 0640; Zone 0 (UT)

Standard Port COBH (⟶)

Times				Height (metres)			
High Water		Low Water		MHWS	MHWN	MLWN	MLWS
0500	1100	0500	1100	4·1	3·2	1·3	0·4
1700	2300	1700	2300				
Differences ROSSLARE HARBOUR							
+0045	+0035	+0015	–0005	–2·2	–1·8	–0·5	–0·1

SHELTER Useful passage shelter from SW'lies, but few facilities for yachts which may berth on E wall of marshalling area (⛵ on the chartlet, 3·7m), or ⚓ about 0·5M W of hbr. Small craft hbr not advised. In winds from WNW-NNE it is often uncomfortable and, if these winds freshen, dangerous; leave at once, via S Shear. Rosslare has 160 ferry/high-speed catamaran (41kn) movements per week.

NAVIGATION WPT 52°14'·82N 06°15·60W, (abeam S Long SCM buoy, VQ (6)+L Fl 10s), 105°/285° from/to bkwtr lt, 2·92M. Main appr from E, S and W is via S Shear, buoyed/lit chan to S of Holden's Bed, a shoal of varying depth; the tide sets across the chan. From S, beware rks off Greenore Pt, and overfalls here and over The Baillies. From the N, appr via N Shear. Tuskar TSS (next col) is approx 8M ESE of hbr.

LIGHTS AND MARKS Tuskar Rk, Q (2) 7·5s 33m 28M, is 5·8M SE of hbr. Water tr (R lt, 35m) is conspic 0·8M SSE of hbr ent. Bkwtr lt, Oc WRG 5s 15m 13/10M, see 9.12.4. Its two W sectors (188°-208° and 283°–286°) cover N and S Shear respectively. Note: Powerful floodlights in the hbr make identification of navigational lights difficult.

RADIO TELEPHONE Call: *Rosslare Hbr* VHF Ch **12** (H24) before entering hbr.

TELEPHONE (Dial code 053) Hr Mr 33162, mobile 087 598535, 📠 33206; MRCC (01) 6620922/3; LB Lookout Stn 33205; ⊜ 33116; Police 22333; Dr 31154; Ⓗ 42233.

FACILITIES Hbr Ops ☎ 33162, No dues, P&D (cans), L, FW (by hose on Berths 2 & 3), ME, C, Divers, Kos, El. **Village**; V, R, Bar, ✉, Ⓑ, ⇌, ✈ (Dublin). Ferries to Fishguard, Pembroke Dock, Cherbourg and Roscoff.

OFF TUSKAR ROCK TRAFFIC SEPARATION SCHEME Centred on **52°08'·5N 06°03'·8W**. The 3M wide lanes are orientated 199°/019° and 232°/052° and the separation zone is 2M wide. Monitor Ch 16 whilst crossing. The ITZ lies between Tuskar Rk and the NW boundary of the TSS. Yachts, bound N/S, will usually navigate to the W of Tuskar Rk where the 3·5M wide chan lies to seaward of The Bailies. A passage inshore of The Bailies requires local knowledge and should not be attempted at night. In heavy weather or poor vis, passage E of Tuskar Rk is advised.

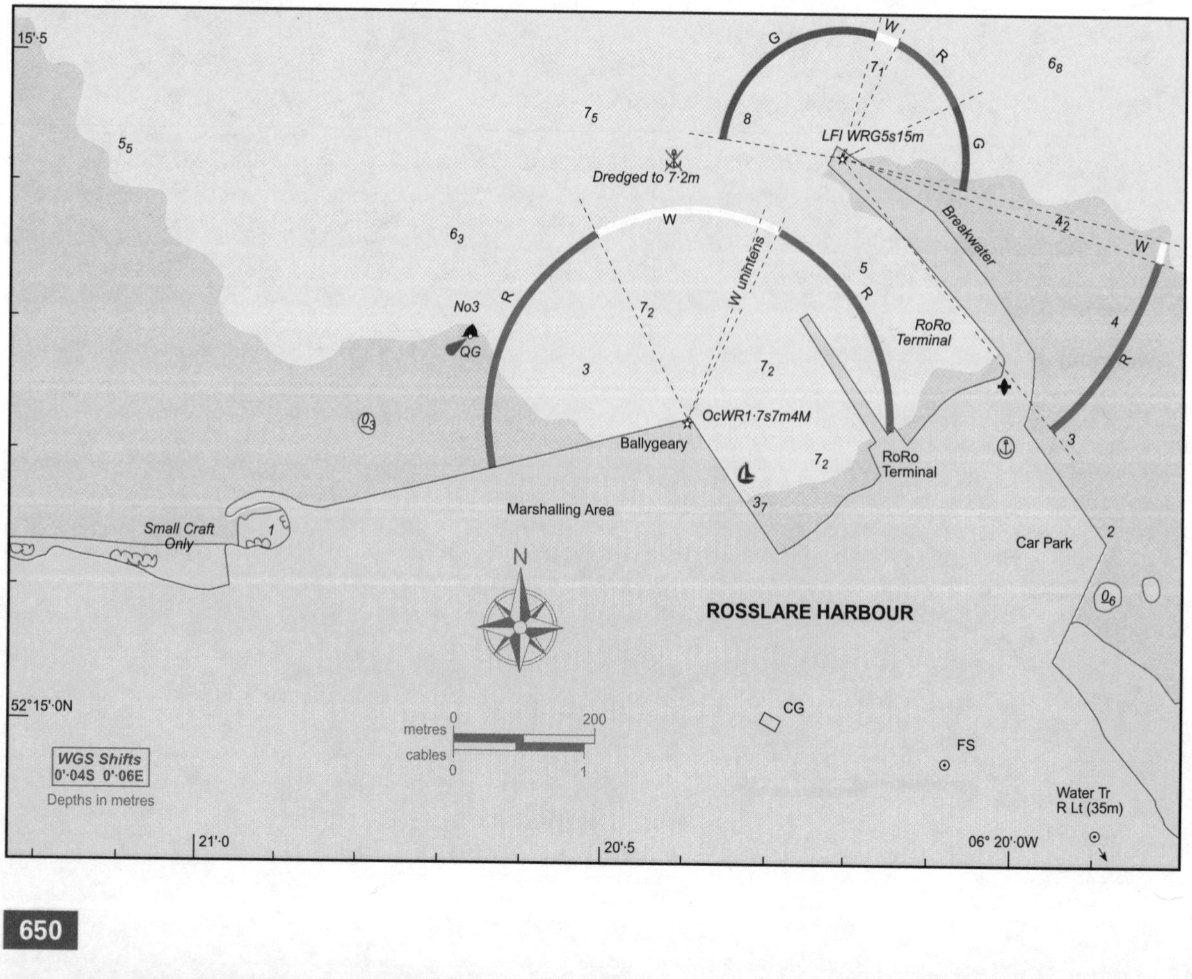

KILMORE QUAY *9.12.15*

Wexford **52°10'·25N 06°35'·15W**

CHARTS AC 2740, *2049*; Imray C61, C57; Irish OS 77

TIDES –0535 Dover; ML No data; Duration 0605; Zone 0 (UT)

Standard Port COBH (⟶)

Times				**Height (metres)**			
High Water		Low Water		MHWS	MHWN	MLWN	MLWS
0500	1100	0500	1100	4·1	3·2	1·3	0·4
1700	2300	1700	2300				
Differences BAGINBUN HEAD (5M NE of Hook Hd)							
+0003	+0003	–0008	–0008	–0·2	–0·1	+0·2	+0·2
GREAT SALTEE							
+0019	+0009	–0004	+0006	–0·3	–0·4	No data	
CARNSORE POINT							
+0029	+0019	–0002	+0008	–1·1	–1·0	No data	

SHELTER Excellent in marina (3·0m depth), but hbr ent is exposed to SE'lies. FVs berth on W and E piers, close S of marina.

NAVIGATION WPT 52°09'·20N 06°35'·28W, 187°/007° from/to pierhd lt, 1·0M, on ldg line. Great (57m) and Little (35m) Saltee Islands lie 3M and 1·7M to SSW and S, respectively, of hbr, separated by Saltee Sound. From the E, safest appr initially is via Saltee Sound, then N to WPT. Caution: In bad weather seas break on the Bohurs and The Bore, rks 2M E of Saltee Islands. Beware Goose Rk (2·6m) close W of Little Saltee and Murroch's Rk (2·1m) 6ca NW of Little Saltee. St Patrick's Bridge, 650m E of the WPT, is a 300m wide E/W chan used by FVs and yachts, but carrying only 2·4m; care needed in strong onshore winds. It is marked by a PHM buoy, Fl R 6s, and a SHM buoy, Fl G 6s, (laid Apr to mid-Sep); general direction of buoyage is E. From the W, appr is clear but keep at least 5ca off Forlorn Pt to avoid Forlorn Rk (1·5m).

LIGHTS AND MARKS Ldg lts/marks, both Oc 4s 3/6m 6M, W pylons with R stripe, lead 008° to the hbr. From W, ldg lts are obsc'd by piers until S of hbr ent. Turn 90° port into hbr ent, just past ☆ QRG at head of W Quay; do not overshoot into shoal water ahead. The R sectors of this ☆, QRG 7m 5M, R269°-354°, G354°-003°(9°), R003°-077°, warn of Forlorn Rock and The Lings to W of the ldg line and shingle banks drying 0·6m close E of the ldg line. A white-gabled church is conspic from afar, as are two 20m high flood lt pylons on the E quay. A disused lt ship at the inner end of W quay is a museum; its lt housing is of no navigational significance. Ballyteige Castle (AC 2740) is hard to see and of no navigational use.

RADIO TELEPHONE VHF Ch 09 M (occas).

TELEPHONE (Dial code 053) Hr Mr ☎/℻ 29955; ⊖ 33741; MRCC (01) 6620922/3; Emergency/Dr/Police 999.

FACILITIES Marina (35+20 Ⓥ) ☎/℻ 29955, €1·59, AC, FW, Slip, LB; **Village** Showers at Stella Maris (10 mins walk), Gaz, CH, ME, El, D & P (cans) is 3M away, R, Bar, V, ✉, Ⓗ (Wexford 15M).

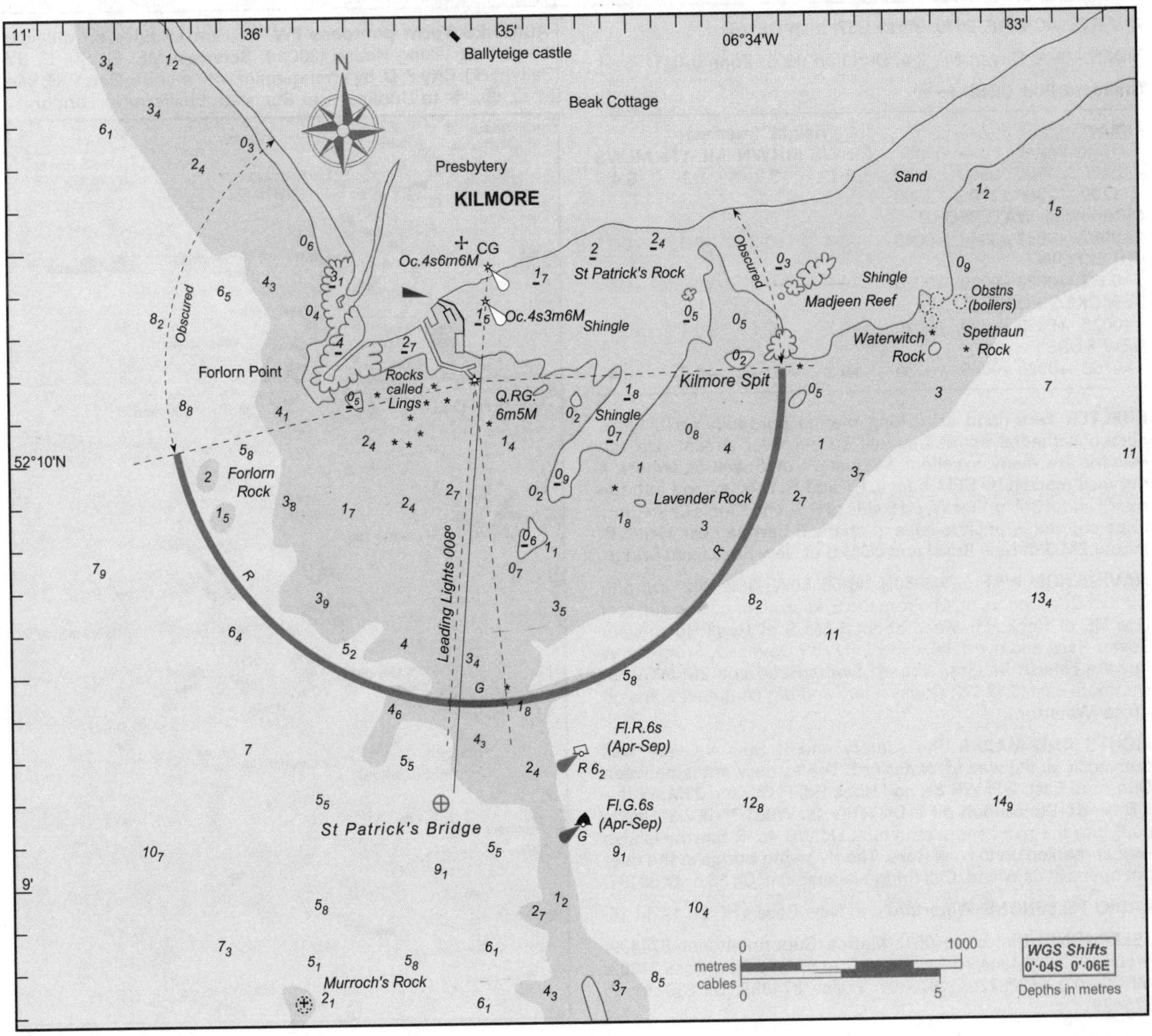

WATERFORD *9.12.16*

Waterford **52°15'·50N 07°06'·00W**

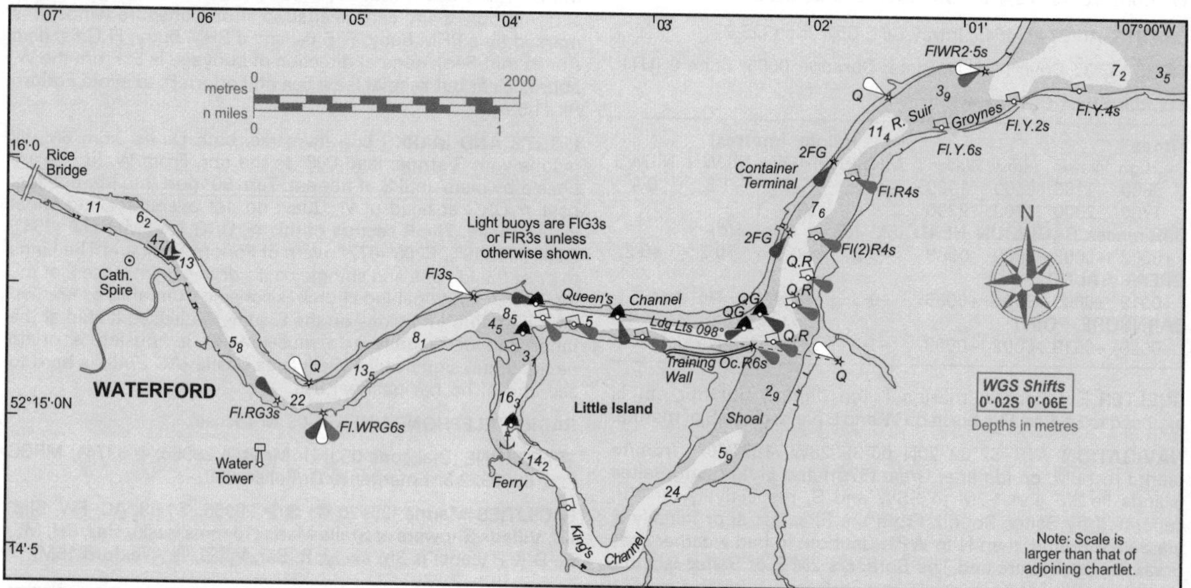

CHARTS AC *2046, 2049;* Imray C57; Irish OS 76

TIDES –0520 Dover; ML 2·4; Duration 0605; Zone 0 (UT)

Standard Port COBH (⟶)

Times				Height (metres)			
High Water		Low Water		MHWS	MHWN	MLWN	MLWS
0500	1100	0500	1100	4·1	3·2	1·3	0·4
1700	2300	1700	2300				
Differences WATERFORD							
+0057	+0057	+0046	+0046	+0·4	+0·3	–0·1	+0·1
CHEEKPOINT							
+0022	+0020	+0020	+0020	+0·3	+0·2	+0·2	+0·1
KILMOKEA POINT							
+0026	+0022	+0020	+0020	+0·2	+0·1	+0·1	+0·1
NEW ROSS							
+0100	+0030	+0055	+0130	+0·3	+0·4	+0·3	+0·4

SHELTER Very good on 2 long marina pontoons on S bank, abeam cathedral spire. Caution: strong tidal stream. Up the estuary are many excellent ⚓s: just W of Cheek Pt (where 4 groynes marked by SPM buoys, FY and Fl Y 2s, extend into the river); about 3M further W, off S side of R Suir in King's Chan (only to be entered W of Little Is); and up the R Barrow near Marsh Pt (about 2M S of New Ross) and 0·5M S of New Ross fixed bridge.

NAVIGATION WPT 52°06'·50N 06°56'·50W, 182°/002° from/to Dir lt at Duncannon, 6·7M. From the E, keep clear of Brecaun reef (2M NE of Hook Hd). Keep about 1·5M S of Hook Hd to clear Tower Race and overfalls, especially HW Dover ±2. From the W beware Falskirt Rk (3m), 2ca off Swine Head and 2M WSW of Dunmore East (9.12.17). Cruise liners and big container ships go up to Waterford.

LIGHTS AND MARKS The estuary and R Suir are very well buoyed/lit all the way to Waterford. The estuary ent is between Dunmore East, L Fl WR 8s, and Hook Hd, Fl 3s 46m 23M, W tr + 2 B bands. Duncannon dir lt Oc WRG 4s, W001·7°–002·2°, leads 002° into the river; same structure, Oc WR 4s. R Barrow is also well lit/marked up to New Ross. The rly swing bridge at the river ent opens at its W end. Call bridge-keeper VHF Ch 16 or ☎ 88137.

RADIO TELEPHONE Waterford and New Ross VHF Ch 12 14 16.

TELEPHONE (Dial code 051) Marina Superintendent 874499, mobile 087 238 4944; Hr Mrs Waterford 874907/New Ross 21303; MRCC (01) 6620922; ⊖ 875391; Police 874888; Dr 883194; Ⓗ 875429.

FACILITIES Yacht pontoons FW, AC, 2m all tides on outside; showers at Viking House (300m). **Services:** ME, El, Sh, C, BY (Ballyhack). **City** P, D, by arrangement with marina, Gaz, V, R, Bar, ✉, Ⓓ, Ⓑ, ⇌ to Dublin, ✈ to Stansted, bus/ferry to London.

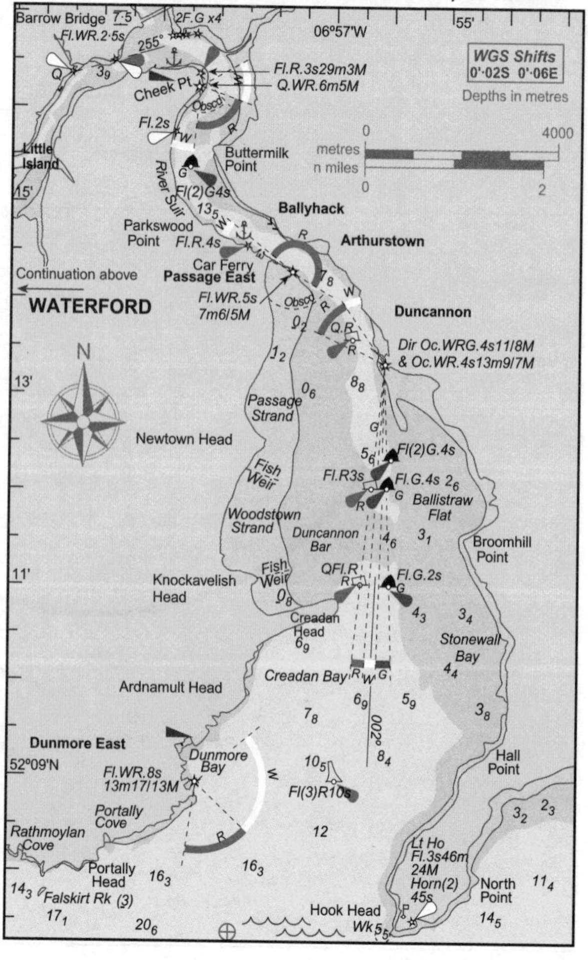

DUNMORE EAST *9.12.17*

Waterford **52°08'·95N 06°59'·37W**

CHARTS AC *2046, 2049*; Imray C61, C57; Irish OS 76

TIDES –0535 Dover; ML 2·4; Duration 0605; Zone 0 (UT)

Standard Port COBH (⟶)

Times				Height (metres)			
High Water		Low Water		MHWS	MHWN	MLWN	MLWS
0500	1100	0500	1100	4·1	3·2	1·3	0·4
1700	2300	1700	2300				
Differences DUNMORE EAST							
+0008	+0003	0000	0000	+0·1	0·0	+0·1	+0·2
DUNGARVAN HARBOUR							
+0004	+0012	+0007	–0001	0·0	+0·1	–0·2	0·0

SHELTER Very good in hbr, but yacht moorings are exposed to E'lies. ⚓ N of the hbr, no ⚓s. A useful passage port and refuge, but primarily a busy FV hbr. In bad weather berth on FVs at W Wharf, clear of ice plant, in at least 2m. Or go up R Suir to Waterford (9.12.16).

NAVIGATION WPT (see also 9.12.16) 52°08'·00N, 06°58'·00W, 137°/317° from/to bkwtr lt, 1·2M. Enter under power. From E, stay 1·5M off Hook Hd to clear Tower Race; then alter course for hbr in R sector of E pier lt ho. In calm weather Hook Hd can be rounded 1ca off. From W, beware Falskirt Rk (off Swines Hd, 2M WSW) dries 3·0m. By night track E for Hook Hd until in R sector of E pier lt, then alter to N.

LIGHTS AND MARKS Lts as chartlet and see 9.12.4.

RADIO TELEPHONE VHF Ch 14 16 (Pilot Station).

TELEPHONE (Dial code 051) Hr Mr 383166; Pilot 383119; ⊖ 875391; MRCC (01) 6620922/3; Coast Life Saving Service 383115; Dr 383194.

FACILITIES Hbr ☎ 83166, D, FW (E pier), Slip, Kos, CH, BH (230 ton); **Waterford Hbr SC** ☎ 83389, R, Bar; **Village** P (cans), Bar, R, V, Ⓑ, ⊠, ⇌ (Waterford), ✈ (Dublin).

DUNGARVAN BAY (22M W of Dunmore East): See 9.12.19.

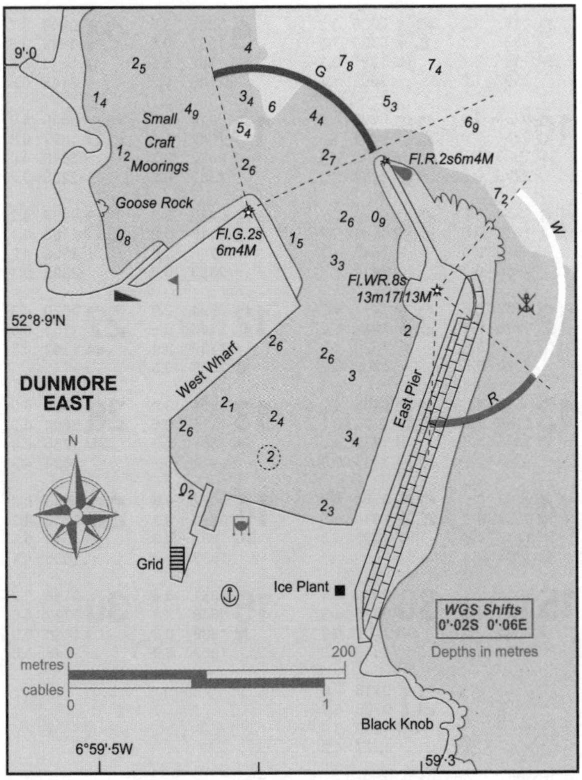

YOUGHAL *9.12.18*

Cork **51°56'·54N 07°50'·20W**

CHARTS AC 2071, *2049*; Imray C57; Irish OS 81, 82

TIDES –0556 Dover; ML 2·1; Duration 0555; Zone 0 (UT)

Standard Port COBH (⟶)

Times				Height (metres)			
High Water		Low Water		MHWS	MHWN	MLWN	MLWS
0500	1100	0500	1100	4·1	3·2	1·3	0·4
1700	2300	1700	2300				
Differences YOUGHAL							
0000	+0010	+0010	0000	–0·2	–0·1	–0·1	–0·1

SHELTER Good, but strong S'lies cause swell inside the hbr. No feasible AB. ⚓s as chartlet; no dues. 2½kn ebb stream.

NAVIGATION WPT, East Bar, 51°55'·62N 07°48'·00W, 122°/302° from/to Fl WR 2·5s lt, 1·8M. Beware Blackball Ledge (ECM buoy Q(3)10s) and Bar Rks (SCM buoy Q(6)+L.Fl.15s), both outside hbr ent in R sector of lt ho. From W, appr via West Bar (1·7m) is shorter; E Bar has 2·0m. In winds E to SSW >F6 both Bars are likely to have dangerous seas. Beware salmon nets May-July.

LIGHTS AND MARKS W of ent, Fl WR 2·5s 24m 17/14M, W tr (15m), has two W sectors ldg over the bars (see 9.12.4). Water tr is conspic from seaward; clock tr and ✠ tr within hbr. Up-river, 175° transit of convent belfry tr/town hall clears W of Red Bank.

RADIO TELEPHONE VHF Ch 14 16 HW±3 (Youghal Shipping)

TELEPHONE (Dial code 024) Hr Mr 92577; MRCC (066) 9476109; Coast/Cliff Rescue Service 93252; ⊖ (021) 968783; Police 92200; Dr 92702.

FACILITIES Services: ME, El, Sh, CH, L, FW (see Hr Mr), Slip. **Town** P & D (cans), V, R, Bar, ⊠, Ⓑ, Bus (Cork/Waterford), ✈(Cork).

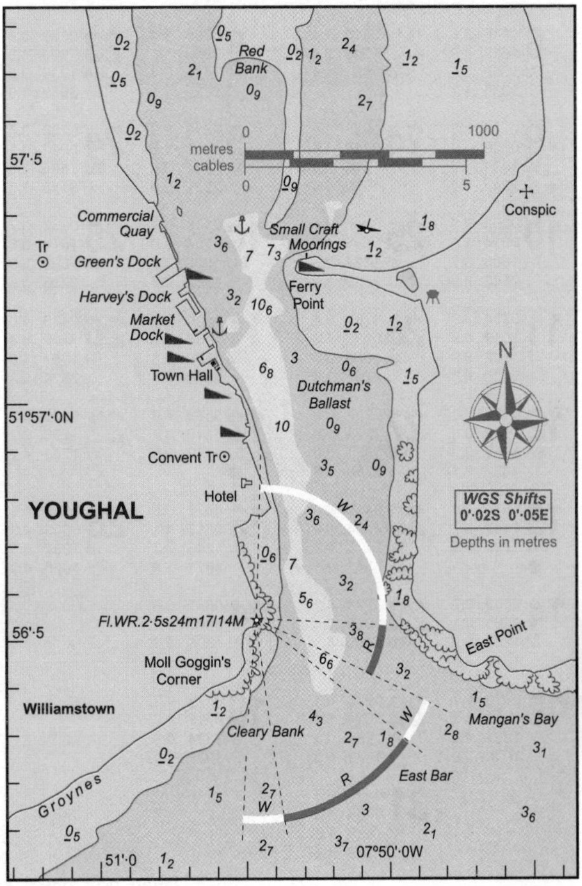

TIME ZONE (UTC)
For Summer Time add ONE hour in **non-shaded areas**

IRELAND – COBH

LAT 51°51′N LONG 8°18′W

TIMES AND HEIGHTS OF HIGH AND LOW WATERS

SPRING & NEAP TIDES
Dates in red are SPRINGS
Dates in blue are NEAPS

YEAR **2002**

JANUARY

Date	Day	Time	m	Time	m	Time	m	Time	m
1	TU	0037	0.5	0635	4.2	1305	0.6	1854	4.1
2	W	0121	0.5	0720	4.2	1350	0.6	1940	4.1
3	TH	0208	0.6	0808	4.1	1438	0.7	2028	4.0
4	F	0257	0.6	0858	4.0	1528	0.8	2119	3.8
5	SA	0349	0.8	0950	3.9	1621	0.9	2212	3.7
6	SU	0446	0.9	1047	3.8	1720	1.0	2311	3.6
7	M	0548	1.0	1148	3.6	1826	1.1		
8	TU	0015	3.5	0657	1.0	1256	3.6	1935	1.1
9	W	0125	3.5	0808	1.0	1404	3.6	2042	1.0
10	TH	0233	3.6	0914	1.0	1506	3.7	2142	0.9
11	F	0334	3.8	1013	0.9	1602	3.8	2236	0.8
12	SA	0428	3.9	1104	0.8	1651	3.9	2322	0.7
13	SU	0514	4.0	1147	0.7	1733	3.9	●	
14	M	0002	0.7	0555	4.1	1224	0.7	1810	4.0
15	TU	0038	0.7	0632	4.1	1257	0.8	1844	3.9
16	W	0112	0.7	0707	4.0	1329	0.8	1916	3.9
17	TH	0145	0.8	0741	4.0	1401	0.9	1949	3.8
18	F	0218	0.9	0816	3.9	1436	1.0	2024	3.7
19	SA	0254	1.0	0853	3.8	1514	1.1	2102	3.7
20	SU	0333	1.1	0933	3.7	1556	1.2	2145	3.6
21	M	0419	1.2	1016	3.6	1645	1.3	2233	3.5
22	TU	0514	1.4	1107	3.5	1743	1.4	2331	3.4
23	W	0619	1.4	1208	3.4	1851	1.4		
24	TH	0038	3.4	0728	1.4	1316	3.4	1959	1.4
25	F	0149	3.4	0835	1.3	1424	3.5	2103	1.2
26	SA	0257	3.6	0937	1.0	1528	3.7	2201	1.0
27	SU	0357	3.8	1034	0.8	1624	3.9	2253	0.7
28	M	0450	4.0	1124	0.6	1713	4.0	○ 2341	0.5
29	TU	0538	4.2	1210	0.4	1759	4.1		
30	W	0025	0.3	0624	4.3	1254	0.3	1843	4.2
31	TH	0109	0.3	0709	4.3	1338	0.3	1928	4.2

FEBRUARY

Date	Day	Time	m	Time	m	Time	m	Time	m
1	F	0154	0.3	0754	4.2	1423	0.4	2013	4.1
2	SA	0240	0.4	0840	4.1	1508	0.5	2058	4.0
3	SU	0327	0.5	0926	4.0	1555	0.7	2145	3.8
4	M	0417	0.7	1015	3.8	1646	0.9	2236	3.6
5	TU	0512	0.9	1110	3.6	1744	1.1	2335	3.5
6	W	0616	1.1	1215	3.4	1854	1.2		
7	TH	0047	3.3	0732	1.2	1331	3.3	2011	1.2
8	F	0206	3.4	0853	1.1	1445	3.4	2125	1.1
9	SA	0316	3.5	1001	1.0	1547	3.5	2225	0.9
10	SU	0413	3.7	1054	0.8	1638	3.7	2312	0.7
11	M	0500	3.9	1136	0.7	1720	3.8	2350	0.6
12	TU	0539	4.0	1210	0.7	1756	3.9	●	
13	W	0022	0.6	0615	4.1	1240	0.7	1827	3.9
14	TH	0052	0.6	0647	4.1	1306	0.7	1857	3.9
15	F	0119	0.7	0718	4.0	1334	0.8	1926	3.9
16	SA	0148	0.7	0748	3.9	1405	0.8	1957	3.8
17	SU	0220	0.8	0820	3.9	1439	0.9	2030	3.8
18	M	0255	0.9	0854	3.8	1515	1.1	2106	3.7
19	TU	0334	1.1	0932	3.7	1555	1.2	2148	3.6
20	W	0421	1.2	1018	3.5	1644	1.3	2240	3.4
21	TH	0522	1.4	1116	3.4	1754	1.5	2348	3.3
22	F	0640	1.4	1228	3.3	1916	1.4		
23	SA	0107	3.3	0800	1.3	1349	3.3	2032	1.3
24	SU	0228	3.4	0912	1.1	1505	3.5	2138	1.0
25	M	0337	3.7	1014	0.8	1606	3.8	2235	0.6
26	TU	0433	4.0	1107	0.4	1657	4.0	2324	0.3
27	W	0521	4.2	1153	0.2	1743	4.2	○	
28	TH	0008	0.1	0606	4.3	1237	0.1	1826	4.3

MARCH

Date	Day	Time	m	Time	m	Time	m	Time	m
1	F	0052	0.0	0649	4.4	1319	0.1	1908	4.3
2	SA	0134	0.0	0732	4.3	1401	0.1	1951	4.2
3	SU	0218	0.1	0815	4.2	1444	0.3	2033	4.1
4	M	0302	0.3	0858	4.0	1527	0.5	2116	3.9
5	TU	0348	0.6	0943	3.7	1614	0.8	2202	3.6
6	W	0438	0.8	1033	3.4	1708	1.0	2257	3.4
7	TH	0539	1.1	1136	3.2	1816	1.2		
8	F	0012	3.2	0656	1.3	1302	3.0	1940	1.3
9	SA	0143	3.2	0831	1.2	1426	3.1	2107	1.2
10	SU	0258	3.4	0946	1.0	1530	3.4	2210	0.9
11	M	0354	3.6	1038	0.8	1619	3.6	2256	0.7
12	TU	0439	3.8	1118	0.7	1700	3.8	2332	0.6
13	W	0518	4.0	1150	0.6	1736	3.9		
14	TH	0002	0.5	0552	4.0	1217	0.6	● 1806	3.9
15	F	0028	0.5	0623	4.0	1240	0.6	1834	3.9
16	SA	0052	0.6	0651	4.0	1306	0.6	1900	3.9
17	SU	0119	0.6	0718	3.9	1335	0.7	1928	3.9
18	M	0149	0.7	0746	3.9	1407	0.8	1959	3.8
19	TU	0223	0.8	0819	3.8	1441	0.9	2033	3.8
20	W	0301	1.0	0856	3.7	1518	1.1	2113	3.6
21	TH	0346	1.1	0941	3.5	1605	1.2	2203	3.5
22	F	0445	1.3	1039	3.3	1712	1.4	2311	3.3
23	SA	0604	1.4	1154	3.2	1840	1.4		
24	SU	0035	3.2	0729	1.3	1321	3.2	2002	1.2
25	M	0203	3.4	0846	1.0	1442	3.4	2113	0.9
26	TU	0314	3.7	0951	0.7	1545	3.7	2212	0.5
27	W	0411	4.0	1044	0.3	1636	4.0	2302	0.2
28	TH	0459	4.2	1131	0.1	1722	4.2	○ 2347	0.0
29	F	0544	4.3	1214	0.0	1805	4.3		
30	SA	0030	-0.1	0626	4.3	1257	0.0	1846	4.3
31	SU	0113	0.0	0708	4.3	1338	0.0	1927	4.2

APRIL

Date	Day	Time	m	Time	m	Time	m	Time	m
1	M	0156	0.1	0749	4.1	1420	0.2	2008	4.1
2	TU	0239	0.3	0831	3.9	1503	0.4	2049	3.9
3	W	0324	0.5	0914	3.6	1549	0.7	2134	3.6
4	TH	0413	0.8	1001	3.3	1641	1.0	2228	3.3
5	F	0511	1.1	1102	3.1	1747	1.2	2343	3.1
6	SA	0626	1.3	1231	2.9	1911	1.3		
7	SU	0118	3.1	0759	1.3	1400	3.0	2037	1.2
8	M	0231	3.3	0915	1.1	1503	3.3	2140	0.9
9	TU	0326	3.5	1007	0.8	1552	3.5	2226	0.7
10	W	0410	3.7	1047	0.7	1632	3.7	2303	0.6
11	TH	0449	3.9	1119	0.6	1708	3.8	2333	0.5
12	F	0524	3.9	1146	0.5	1739	3.9	● 2358	0.5
13	SA	0554	3.9	1210	0.6	1807	3.9		
14	SU	0022	0.6	0621	3.9	1237	0.6	1833	3.9
15	M	0051	0.6	0648	3.9	1308	0.6	1902	3.9
16	TU	0123	0.7	0718	3.9	1341	0.7	1934	3.9
17	W	0159	0.8	0752	3.8	1417	0.8	2010	3.8
18	TH	0239	0.9	0832	3.7	1458	1.0	2052	3.7
19	F	0327	1.0	0920	3.5	1548	1.1	2145	3.5
20	SA	0427	1.2	1020	3.3	1654	1.3	2252	3.3
21	SU	0542	1.3	1134	3.2	1816	1.3		
22	M	0014	3.3	0704	1.2	1258	3.2	1936	1.1
23	TU	0139	3.4	0819	0.9	1415	3.5	2046	0.8
24	W	0248	3.7	0923	0.6	1518	3.8	2145	0.5
25	TH	0345	4.0	1017	0.3	1610	4.0	2238	0.2
26	F	0434	4.2	1106	0.1	1658	4.2	2325	0.1
27	SA	0520	4.3	1151	0.0	1742	4.3	○	
28	SU	0009	0.0	0604	4.3	1235	0.0	1824	4.3
29	M	0053	0.0	0646	4.2	1318	0.1	1905	4.2
30	TU	0136	0.2	0727	4.0	1400	0.3	1946	4.0

Chart Datum: 0·13 metres above Ordnance Datum (Dublin)

TIME ZONE (UTC)
For Summer Time add ONE hour in **non-shaded areas**

IRELAND – COBH

LAT 51°51′N LONG 8°18′W

TIMES AND HEIGHTS OF HIGH AND LOW WATERS

SPRING & NEAP TIDES
Dates in red are SPRINGS
Dates in blue are NEAPS

YEAR **2002**

MAY

Date	Day	Time	m	Time	m	Time	m	Time	m
1	W	0219	0.4	0808	3.8	1444	0.5	2028	3.8
2	TH	0304	0.6	0850	3.6	1530	0.7	2113	3.6
3	F	0352	0.9	0937	3.3	1621	1.0	2205	3.3
4	SA	0448	1.1	1033	3.1	1723	1.2	2314	3.1
5	SU	0556	1.3	1151	3.0	1837	1.2		
6	M	0039	3.1	0713	1.3	1318	3.0	1951	1.2
7	TU	0151	3.2	0823	1.1	1422	3.2	2052	1.0
8	W	0246	3.4	0917	0.9	1512	3.4	2141	0.8
9	TH	0332	3.6	1001	0.8	1554	3.6	2221	0.7
10	F	0412	3.7	1037	0.7	1631	3.7	2254	0.6
11	SA	0449	3.8	1109	0.6	1705	3.8	2325	0.6
12	SU	0522	3.9	1139	0.6	1737	3.9	● 2355	0.6
13	M	0552	3.9	1212	0.6	1808	3.9		
14	TU	0028	0.6	0623	3.9	1247	0.7	1841	3.9
15	W	0105	0.7	0658	3.8	1324	0.7	1917	3.9
16	TH	0144	0.7	0737	3.8	1405	0.8	1957	3.8
17	F	0229	0.8	0821	3.7	1451	0.9	2044	3.7
18	SA	0320	0.9	0912	3.5	1544	1.0	2138	3.6
19	SU	0419	1.0	1012	3.4	1646	1.1	2243	3.5
20	M	0527	1.1	1120	3.3	1758	1.1	2357	3.5
21	TU	0641	1.0	1234	3.4	1911	0.9		
22	W	0113	3.6	0751	0.8	1346	3.6	2018	0.7
23	TH	0219	3.7	0854	0.6	1447	3.8	2119	0.5
24	F	0317	3.9	0951	0.4	1543	3.9	2214	0.3
25	SA	0410	4.0	1042	0.3	1634	4.1	2304	0.2
26	SU	0459	4.1	1130	0.2	1721	4.2	○ 2351	0.2
27	M	0544	4.1	1216	0.2	1805	4.2		
28	TU	0035	0.3	0627	4.0	1300	0.3	1847	4.1
29	W	0119	0.4	0708	3.9	1343	0.4	1928	4.0
30	TH	0201	0.5	0749	3.8	1426	0.6	2010	3.8
31	F	0245	0.7	0830	3.6	1511	0.8	2054	3.6

JUNE

Date	Day	Time	m	Time	m	Time	m	Time	m
1	SA	0331	0.9	0914	3.4	1559	1.0	2143	3.4
2	SU	0422	1.1	1003	3.2	1653	1.1	2239	3.3
3	M	0519	1.2	1102	3.1	1754	1.2	2345	3.2
4	TU	0622	1.2	1212	3.1	1857	1.2		
5	W	0054	3.2	0723	1.2	1321	3.2	1954	1.1
6	TH	0153	3.4	0817	1.1	1417	3.3	2045	1.0
7	F	0244	3.5	0906	1.0	1505	3.5	2131	0.9
8	SA	0329	3.6	0951	0.9	1549	3.6	2214	0.8
9	SU	0411	3.7	1033	0.8	1630	3.8	2254	0.7
10	M	0450	3.8	1113	0.7	1710	3.8	● 2333	0.7
11	TU	0528	3.9	1152	0.7	1748	3.9		
12	W	0012	0.6	0606	3.9	1232	0.6	1827	3.9
13	TH	0053	0.6	0646	3.9	1314	0.6	1907	3.9
14	F	0136	0.6	0729	3.8	1358	0.7	1952	3.9
15	SA	0223	0.7	0816	3.8	1446	0.7	2040	3.8
16	SU	0314	0.8	0907	3.7	1537	0.8	2133	3.7
17	M	0409	0.8	1003	3.6	1634	0.8	2232	3.7
18	TU	0509	0.9	1103	3.5	1736	0.9	2336	3.6
19	W	0615	0.9	1207	3.5	1843	0.9		
20	TH	0043	3.6	0722	0.9	1314	3.6	1949	0.8
21	F	0149	3.7	0826	0.8	1417	3.7	2053	0.7
22	SA	0250	3.8	0926	0.7	1517	3.8	2152	0.6
23	SU	0347	3.8	1022	0.6	1613	3.9	2247	0.5
24	M	0440	3.9	1113	0.5	1704	4.0	○ 2336	0.5
25	TU	0528	3.9	1200	0.5	1750	4.0		
26	W	0020	0.5	0611	3.9	1244	0.5	1832	4.0
27	TH	0102	0.5	0652	3.8	1325	0.5	1912	3.9
28	F	0142	0.7	0730	3.7	1406	0.6	1952	3.8
29	SA	0222	0.8	0809	3.6	1447	0.8	2032	3.7
30	SU	0303	0.9	0848	3.5	1529	0.9	2114	3.6

JULY

Date	Day	Time	m	Time	m	Time	m	Time	m
1	M	0346	1.0	0931	3.4	1613	1.0	2159	3.5
2	TU	0433	1.1	1017	3.3	1702	1.1	2249	3.4
3	W	0525	1.2	1109	3.3	1757	1.2	2344	3.3
4	TH	0622	1.2	1209	3.3	1855	1.2		
5	F	0046	3.3	0720	1.2	1312	3.3	1951	1.2
6	SA	0146	3.4	0816	1.1	1412	3.4	2046	1.1
7	SU	0242	3.5	0910	1.0	1507	3.5	2138	0.9
8	M	0334	3.6	1002	0.9	1559	3.7	2228	0.8
9	TU	0423	3.7	1051	0.8	1647	3.8	2315	0.7
10	W	0509	3.8	1136	0.6	1732	3.9	● 2359	0.6
11	TH	0553	3.9	1219	0.5	1815	4.0		
12	F	0042	0.5	0636	3.9	1303	0.5	1859	4.0
13	SA	0126	0.5	0721	3.9	1347	0.5	1944	4.0
14	SU	0212	0.5	0807	3.9	1434	0.5	2031	4.0
15	M	0300	0.6	0855	3.8	1522	0.6	2120	3.9
16	TU	0350	0.6	0945	3.8	1613	0.6	2212	3.8
17	W	0444	0.8	1038	3.7	1708	0.8	2308	3.7
18	TH	0543	0.9	1136	3.6	1810	0.9		
19	F	0010	3.6	0648	0.9	1241	3.5	1918	0.9
20	SA	0118	3.5	0757	1.0	1350	3.5	2029	0.9
21	SU	0226	3.5	0905	0.9	1457	3.6	2137	0.8
22	M	0330	3.6	1007	0.8	1558	3.7	2236	0.7
23	TU	0426	3.7	1101	0.7	1651	3.9	2325	0.6
24	W	0515	3.8	1148	0.6	1737	4.0	○	
25	TH	0008	0.6	0557	3.8	1229	0.5	1817	4.0
26	F	0045	0.6	0634	3.8	1306	0.6	1854	4.0
27	SA	0120	0.7	0710	3.8	1341	0.6	1930	3.9
28	SU	0153	0.8	0743	3.7	1415	0.7	2005	3.8
29	M	0227	0.9	0818	3.7	1449	0.8	2041	3.7
30	TU	0303	1.0	0855	3.6	1525	1.0	2118	3.6
31	W	0342	1.1	0934	3.5	1604	1.1	2158	3.5

AUGUST

Date	Day	Time	m	Time	m	Time	m	Time	m
1	TH	0426	1.2	1018	3.4	1651	1.2	2245	3.4
2	F	0518	1.3	1110	3.3	1750	1.3	2340	3.3
3	SA	0622	1.3	1212	3.3	1858	1.3		
4	SU	0046	3.3	0730	1.3	1323	3.3	2005	1.3
5	M	0157	3.4	0836	1.2	1432	3.4	2109	1.1
6	TU	0303	3.5	0936	1.0	1534	3.6	2206	0.9
7	W	0401	3.7	1030	0.8	1628	3.8	2257	0.6
8	TH	0451	3.8	1118	0.6	1715	4.0	● 2343	0.4
9	F	0537	4.0	1202	0.4	1800	4.1		
10	SA	0027	0.3	0621	4.1	1246	0.3	1843	4.2
11	SU	0110	0.3	0704	4.1	1329	0.2	1926	4.2
12	M	0154	0.3	0749	4.0	1413	0.3	2011	4.1
13	TU	0239	0.4	0834	4.0	1459	0.4	2056	4.0
14	W	0325	0.5	0920	3.9	1546	0.5	2144	3.8
15	TH	0414	0.7	1009	3.7	1637	0.7	2235	3.6
16	F	0509	0.9	1104	3.5	1736	0.9	2336	3.4
17	SA	0615	1.1	1210	3.4	1847	1.1		
18	SU	0050	3.3	0731	1.1	1330	3.3	2010	1.1
19	M	0210	3.3	0851	1.1	1446	3.4	2129	1.0
20	TU	0318	3.4	0959	0.9	1548	3.6	2229	0.8
21	W	0414	3.6	1052	0.7	1639	3.8	2316	0.7
22	TH	0500	3.8	1135	0.6	1721	4.0	○ 2353	0.6
23	F	0540	3.9	1211	0.5	1759	4.0		
24	SA	0025	0.6	0614	3.9	1242	0.5	1832	4.0
25	SU	0053	0.6	0645	3.9	1311	0.6	1903	4.0
26	M	0120	0.7	0715	3.8	1338	0.7	1933	3.9
27	TU	0149	0.8	0745	3.8	1407	0.8	2004	3.8
28	W	0221	0.9	0817	3.7	1440	0.9	2036	3.7
29	TH	0257	1.0	0853	3.6	1516	1.0	2113	3.6
30	F	0336	1.1	0933	3.5	1558	1.2	2155	3.5
31	SA	0423	1.3	1022	3.4	1653	1.4	2249	3.4

Chart Datum: 0·13 metres above Ordnance Datum (Dublin)

TIME ZONE (UTC)
For Summer Time add ONE hour in **non-shaded areas**

IRELAND – COBH

LAT 51°51'N LONG 8°18'W

TIMES AND HEIGHTS OF HIGH AND LOW WATERS

SPRING & NEAP TIDES
Dates in red are **SPRINGS**
Dates in blue are **NEAPS**

YEAR **2002**

SEPTEMBER

Date	Day	Time	m	Time	m	Time	m	Time	m
1	SU	0526	1.4	1124	3.2	1808	1.5	2357	3.2
2	M	0647	1.5	1241	3.2	1929	1.4		
3	TU	0118	3.2	0804	1.3	1403	3.3	2042	1.2
4	W	0238	3.4	0911	1.0	1513	3.6	2144	0.9
5	TH	0340	3.7	1008	0.7	1608	3.9	2237	0.6
6	F	0431	3.9	1057	0.4	1655	4.1	2323	0.3
7	SA ●	0517	4.1	1141	0.2	1739	4.3		
8	SU	0006	0.2	0559	4.2	1224	0.1	1821	4.3
9	M	0048	0.1	0642	4.2	1306	0.1	1903	4.3
10	TU	0130	0.2	0725	4.2	1349	0.2	1946	4.2
11	W	0214	0.3	0808	4.1	1434	0.3	2029	4.0
12	TH	0258	0.5	0852	3.9	1520	0.5	2114	3.8
13	F	0346	0.7	0940	3.7	1609	0.8	2204	3.5
14	SA	0440	1.0	1034	3.4	1707	1.1	2304	3.3
15	SU	0546	1.2	1146	3.2	1822	1.3		
16	M	0028	3.1	0712	1.3	1317	3.2	1959	1.3
17	TU	0158	3.2	0842	1.1	1435	3.4	2121	1.1
18	W	0306	3.4	0948	0.9	1534	3.6	2216	0.9
19	TH	0358	3.6	1037	0.7	1620	3.8	2258	0.7
20	F	0441	3.8	1116	0.6	1700	4.0	2332	0.6
21	SA	0518	3.9	1148	0.5	1735	4.1	○ 2359	0.6
22	SU	0550	3.9	1215	0.5	1806	4.1		
23	M	0022	0.6	0618	3.9	1239	0.6	1834	4.0
24	TU	0046	0.7	0645	3.9	1303	0.7	1900	3.9
25	W	0114	0.8	0712	3.8	1331	0.8	1927	3.9
26	TH	0145	0.9	0742	3.8	1403	0.9	1958	3.8
27	F	0219	1.0	0816	3.7	1439	1.1	2033	3.7
28	SA	0257	1.1	0855	3.6	1521	1.2	2116	3.6
29	SU	0343	1.3	0944	3.4	1616	1.4	2210	3.4
30	M	0447	1.5	1048	3.3	1731	1.5	2322	3.2

OCTOBER

Date	Day	Time	m	Time	m	Time	m	Time	m
1	TU	0612	1.5	1209	3.2	1858	1.5		
2	W	0048	3.2	0735	1.3	1337	3.4	2015	1.2
3	TH	0212	3.4	0844	1.0	1448	3.7	2119	0.9
4	F	0315	3.7	0942	0.7	1543	4.0	2212	0.5
5	SA	0407	4.0	1033	0.4	1631	4.2	2259	0.3
6	SU	0453	4.2	1118	0.2	1715	4.4	● 2343	0.1
7	M	0536	4.3	1201	0.1	1758	4.4		
8	TU	0025	0.1	0618	4.3	1245	0.1	1839	4.4
9	W	0107	0.2	0700	4.3	1328	0.2	1921	4.2
10	TH	0151	0.3	0743	4.1	1412	0.4	2004	4.0
11	F	0236	0.5	0828	3.9	1458	0.6	2048	3.8
12	SA	0324	0.8	0915	3.7	1548	0.9	2137	3.5
13	SU	0418	1.0	1011	3.4	1646	1.2	2237	3.2
14	M	0526	1.3	1126	3.2	1802	1.4		
15	TU	0005	3.0	0652	1.3	1259	3.2	1940	1.4
16	W	0138	3.1	0821	1.2	1414	3.4	2056	1.2
17	TH	0244	3.3	0922	1.0	1509	3.6	2148	1.0
18	F	0333	3.6	1009	0.8	1553	3.8	2229	0.8
19	SA	0414	3.8	1047	0.6	1631	4.0	2302	0.7
20	SU	0450	3.9	1118	0.6	1706	4.0	2328	0.7
21	M	0521	4.0	1144	0.6	1737	4.1	○ 2351	0.7
22	TU	0550	4.0	1207	0.7	1804	4.0		
23	W	0015	0.7	0616	4.0	1234	0.8	1829	4.0
24	TH	0045	0.8	0644	3.9	1303	0.8	1857	3.9
25	F	0117	0.9	0715	3.9	1337	1.0	1929	3.9
26	SA	0153	1.0	0750	3.8	1415	1.1	2007	3.8
27	SU	0233	1.1	0831	3.7	1501	1.2	2052	3.6
28	M	0323	1.3	0923	3.5	1557	1.4	2148	3.4
29	TU	0427	1.4	1027	3.4	1709	1.5	2259	3.3
30	W	0546	1.4	1145	3.4	1831	1.4		
31	TH	0022	3.3	0706	1.3	1309	3.5	1947	1.2

NOVEMBER

Date	Day	Time	m	Time	m	Time	m	Time	m
1	F	0142	3.5	0816	1.0	1419	3.8	2051	0.9
2	SA	0246	3.8	0915	0.7	1515	4.0	2146	0.6
3	SU	0339	4.1	1008	0.4	1605	4.2	2235	0.4
4	M	0428	4.3	1056	0.3	1652	4.4	● 2321	0.2
5	TU	0513	4.4	1142	0.2	1736	4.4		
6	W	0005	0.2	0557	4.4	1227	0.2	1819	4.3
7	TH	0049	0.3	0641	4.3	1311	0.3	1901	4.2
8	F	0133	0.4	0724	4.2	1356	0.5	1944	4.0
9	SA	0218	0.6	0809	4.0	1442	0.8	2028	3.7
10	SU	0307	0.9	0857	3.7	1532	1.0	2115	3.5
11	M	0401	1.1	0952	3.5	1628	1.3	2212	3.2
12	TU	0504	1.3	1100	3.3	1737	1.4	2328	3.1
13	W	0621	1.4	1222	3.2	1858	1.4		
14	TH	0056	3.1	0737	1.3	1334	3.4	2009	1.3
15	F	0204	3.3	0838	1.1	1430	3.5	2103	1.1
16	SA	0255	3.5	0927	1.0	1516	3.7	2146	1.0
17	SU	0337	3.7	1007	0.9	1556	3.9	2222	0.9
18	M	0415	3.9	1042	0.8	1633	4.0	2253	0.8
19	TU	0450	3.9	1113	0.8	1706	4.0	2322	0.8
20	W	0522	4.0	1142	0.8	1737	4.0	○ 2352	0.8
21	TH	0553	4.0	1213	0.8	1806	4.0		
22	F	0024	0.8	0624	4.0	1247	0.9	1837	4.0
23	SA	0100	0.9	0659	4.0	1324	1.0	1913	3.9
24	SU	0140	1.0	0737	3.9	1405	1.1	1954	3.8
25	M	0224	1.1	0822	3.8	1453	1.2	2041	3.7
26	TU	0315	1.2	0914	3.7	1548	1.3	2137	3.6
27	W	0415	1.3	1014	3.6	1652	1.3	2243	3.5
28	TH	0524	1.3	1124	3.6	1805	1.3	2355	3.5
29	F	0636	1.2	1237	3.6	1917	1.2		
30	SA	0108	3.6	0745	1.0	1346	3.8	2021	0.9

DECEMBER

Date	Day	Time	m	Time	m	Time	m	Time	m
1	SU	0213	3.8	0847	0.8	1445	4.0	2119	0.7
2	M	0311	4.0	0944	0.6	1540	4.1	2212	0.6
3	TU	0404	4.2	1037	0.5	1631	4.2	2302	0.4
4	W	0455	4.3	1127	0.4	1719	4.2	● 2349	0.4
5	TH	0542	4.3	1213	0.4	1804	4.2		
6	F	0034	0.4	0627	4.3	1259	0.5	1846	4.1
7	SA	0119	0.5	0711	4.2	1343	0.6	1928	4.0
8	SU	0203	0.7	0755	4.0	1428	0.8	2010	3.8
9	M	0250	0.9	0841	3.8	1514	1.0	2055	3.6
10	TU	0339	1.0	0930	3.6	1604	1.2	2143	3.4
11	W	0434	1.2	1024	3.5	1700	1.4	2239	3.3
12	TH	0534	1.3	1127	3.4	1802	1.4	2346	3.2
13	F	0639	1.3	1234	3.4	1906	1.4		
14	SA	0057	3.3	0739	1.3	1335	3.4	2003	1.3
15	SU	0159	3.4	0832	1.2	1428	3.6	2053	1.2
16	M	0250	3.6	0920	1.1	1515	3.7	2138	1.1
17	TU	0336	3.7	1004	1.0	1558	3.8	2220	1.0
18	W	0418	3.9	1044	0.9	1638	3.9	2258	0.9
19	TH	0458	4.0	1123	0.9	1716	4.0	○ 2335	0.8
20	F	0536	4.0	1200	0.8	1751	4.0		
21	SA	0012	0.8	0613	4.1	1238	0.8	1827	4.0
22	SU	0051	0.8	0651	4.0	1318	0.8	1906	4.0
23	M	0132	0.8	0732	4.0	1400	0.9	1948	3.9
24	TU	0217	0.9	0817	4.0	1446	1.0	2035	3.8
25	W	0306	0.9	0906	3.9	1536	1.0	2126	3.7
26	TH	0359	1.0	1000	3.8	1631	1.1	2223	3.6
27	F	0457	1.1	1058	3.7	1733	1.2	2324	3.6
28	SA	0602	1.1	1203	3.7	1841	1.2		
29	SU	0031	3.6	0710	1.1	1310	3.7	1949	1.1
30	M	0139	3.7	0819	1.0	1415	3.8	2053	1.0
31	TU	0244	3.8	0924	0.9	1518	3.9	2154	0.8

Chart Datum: 0·13 metres above Ordnance Datum (Dublin)

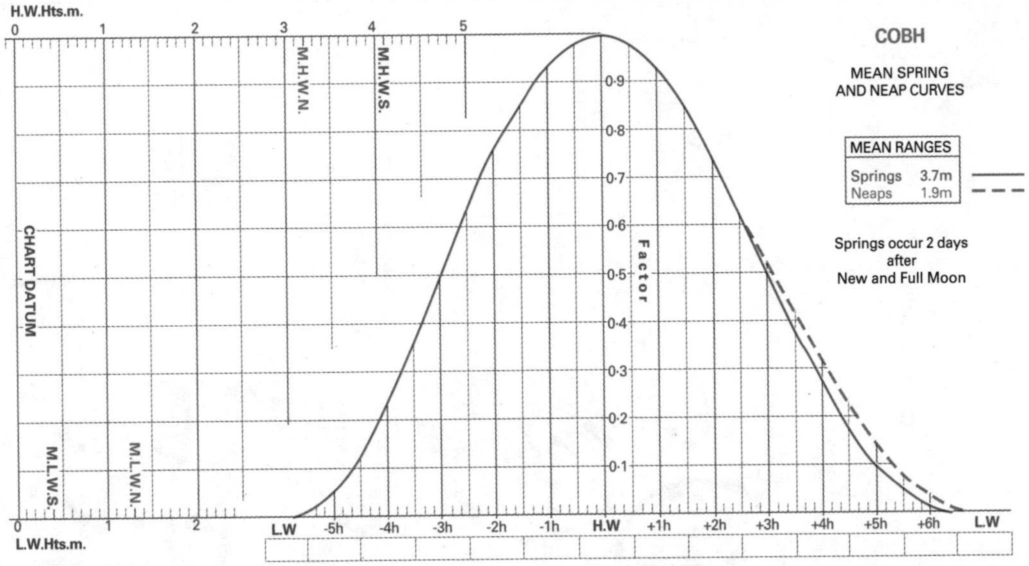
H.W.Hts.m.
0 1 2 3 4 5
M.H.W.N.
M.H.W.S.
CHART DATUM
M.L.W.S.
M.L.W.N.
0 1 2
L.W.Hts.m.
Factor
0·9 0·8 0·7 0·6 0·5 0·4 0·3 0·2 0·1
L.W -5h -4h -3h -2h -1h H.W +1h +2h +3h +4h +5h +6h L.W
COBH
MEAN SPRING AND NEAP CURVES
MEAN RANGES
Springs 3.7m
Neaps 1.9m
Springs occur 2 days after New and Full Moon

CORK HARBOUR *9.12.19*

Cork **51°47'·50N 08°15'·54W**

CHARTS AC 1773, *1777*, 1765; Imray C56, C57; Irish OS 81, 87

TIDES –0523 Dover; ML 2·3; Duration 0555; Zone 0 (UT)

Standard Port COBH (⟵)

Times				Height (metres)			
High Water		Low Water		MHWS	MHWN	MLWN	MLWS
0500	1100	0500	1100	4·1	3·2	1·3	0·4
1700	2300	1700	2300				
Differences BALLYCOTTON (15M ENE of Roche's Point)							
–0011	+0001	+0003	–0009	0·0	0·0	–0·1	0·0
RINGASKIDDY							
+0005	+0020	+0007	+0013	+0·1	+0·1	+0·1	+0·1
MARINO POINT							
0000	+0010	0000	+0010	+0·1	+0·1	0·0	0·0
CORK CITY							
+0005	+0010	+0020	+0010	+0·4	+0·4	+0·3	+0·2
ROBERTS COVE (approx 4M SW of Roche's Point)							
–0005	–0005	–0005	–0005	–0·1	0·0	0·0	+0·1

SHELTER Very good in all conditions, esp in Crosshaven and East Passage. There are 3 main marinas at Crosshaven (see Facilities), plus a small private marina and several ⚓s up the Owenboy River, in particular at Drake's Pool. There is a marina at E Ferry in E Passage at the E end of Great Island. Cobh, Ringaskiddy and Cork City are commercial and ferry ports; contact Port Ops for advice on yacht berths.

NAVIGATION WPT 51°46'·57N, 08°15'·39W, 185°/005° from/to Roche's Pt lt, 1M; also on 354°ldg line. Safe hbr with no dangers for yachts; ent is deep and well marked. Sp rate is about 1½kn in ent. Main chan up to Cork and the chan to E Ferry are marked, but shoal outside navigable chan. Ent to Owenboy River carries at least 3m at LWS, and the chan is buoyed. Head for Cage buoy (C1), Fl G 10s, to pick up the ldg marks/lts 252°, close S of pink ho, R roof.

LIGHTS AND MARKS The 24·5m high hammerhead water tr S of Crosshaven and the R/W power stn chy NE of Corkbeg Is are conspic from seaward. Two sets of ldg lts/marks (see 9.12.4) lead through The Sound, either side of Hbr Rk (5·2m), not a hazard for yachts; but do not impede merchant ships. Ldg lts, FW 10/15m 3M, with W◊ day marks, lead 252° to Crosshaven. The chan is marked by C1 SHM buoy Fl G 10s; C2 PHM buoy Fl (2) R 5s, and C4 PHM buoy Fl R 10s.

RADIO TELEPHONE Call: *Cork Hbr Radio* (Port Ops) VHF Ch 12 14 16 (H24); *Crosshaven BY* Ch M (Mon– Fri: 0830– 1700LT). *Royal Cork* YC Marina Ch M (0900– 2359LT); also Ch M for RC water taxi. *East Ferry Marina* Ch 80 (0800– 2200LT).

TELEPHONE (Dial code 021) Hr Mr 4273125, info@portofcork.ie; Port Ops 4811380; MRCC (066) 9476109; IMES 4831448; ⊜ 4311024; Police 4831222; Dr 4831716; ⊞ and Emergency 4546400.

FACILITIES Crosshaven BY Marina (100 + 20 Ⓥ) ☎ 4831161, 📠 4831603, cby@eircom.net, €1·56, FW, AC, BH (40 ton), C (1.5 tons), M, Ⓔ, CH, D, P (cans), El, Gas, Gaz, Kos, SM, ME, Sh, Slip (100 tons); **Salve Marine** (45 + 12 Ⓥ) ☎ 4831145, 📠 4831747, AB €1·71, M, FW, AC, BY, El, ME, C, CH, D, P (cans), Slip; **Royal Cork YC Marina** (170 + 30 Ⓥ) ☎ 4831023, 📠 4831586, office@royalcork.com, €2·34, AC, FW, P (cans), Bar, R, Slip, ♿; **Crosshaven Pier/Pontoon** AB €19·05 any size. **East Ferry Marina** (85 + 15 Ⓥ) ☎ 4811342, €1·56, D, AC, FW, Bar, R, Slip; access all tides, max draft 5·5m. **Crosshaven Village** FV pier in 3·5m at Town quay, L, Slip, Grid, SM, ACA, Bar, Dr, ✉, R, V, ▣. **Cork City** All facilities. Ferries (to UK and France), ⇌, ✈.

MINOR HARBOUR 16M ENE of YOUGHAL

DUNGARVAN BAY, Waterford, **52°05'·15N 07°36'·70W**. AC 2017. HW –0540 on Dover; Duration 0600. See 9.12.17. A large bay, drying to the W, entered between Helvick Hd to the S and to the N Ballynacourty Pt, Fl (2) WRG 10s; see 9.12.4. Appr in W sector (274°–302°) of this lt, to clear Carricknamoan islet to the N, and Carrickapane Rk and Helvick Rk (ECM buoy Q (3) 10s) to the S. 5ca W of this buoy are The Gainers, a large unmarked rky patch (dries 0·8m). Beware salmon nets. Off Helvick hbr are 8 Y ⚓s or ⚓ in approx 4m. Dungarvan town hbr is accessible HW+3, via buoyed (FlG/FlR) chan which shifts, the buoys being moved to suit; there are now no ldg lts. Appr is difficult in SE'lies >F6. ⚓ in the pool below the town or AB on pontoon (dries to soft mud), S bank below bridge; craft can stay upright beyond double Y lines. Facilities: D & P (cans), Bar, Ⓑ, ✉, ▣, R, V, Kos.

MINOR HARBOUR 15M ENE of ROCHE'S POINT

BALLYCOTTON, Cork, **51°49'·70N 08°00·19W**. AC 2424. HW –0555 on Dover; Duration 0550. See above. Small, NE-facing hbr at W end of bay suffers from scend in strong SE winds; 3m in ent and about 1·5m against piers. Many FVs alongside piers, on which yachts should berth, rather than ⚓ in hbr, which is foul with old ground tackle. 6 Y ⚓s are outside hbr, or good ⚓ in offshore winds in 6m NE of pier, protected by Ballycotton Is. Lt ho Fl WR 10s 59m 21/17M, B tr in W walls; W238°–048°, R048°–238°; Horn (4) 90s. Facilities: FW on pier. **Village** Hotel, R, ✉, V, LB, Kos.

12

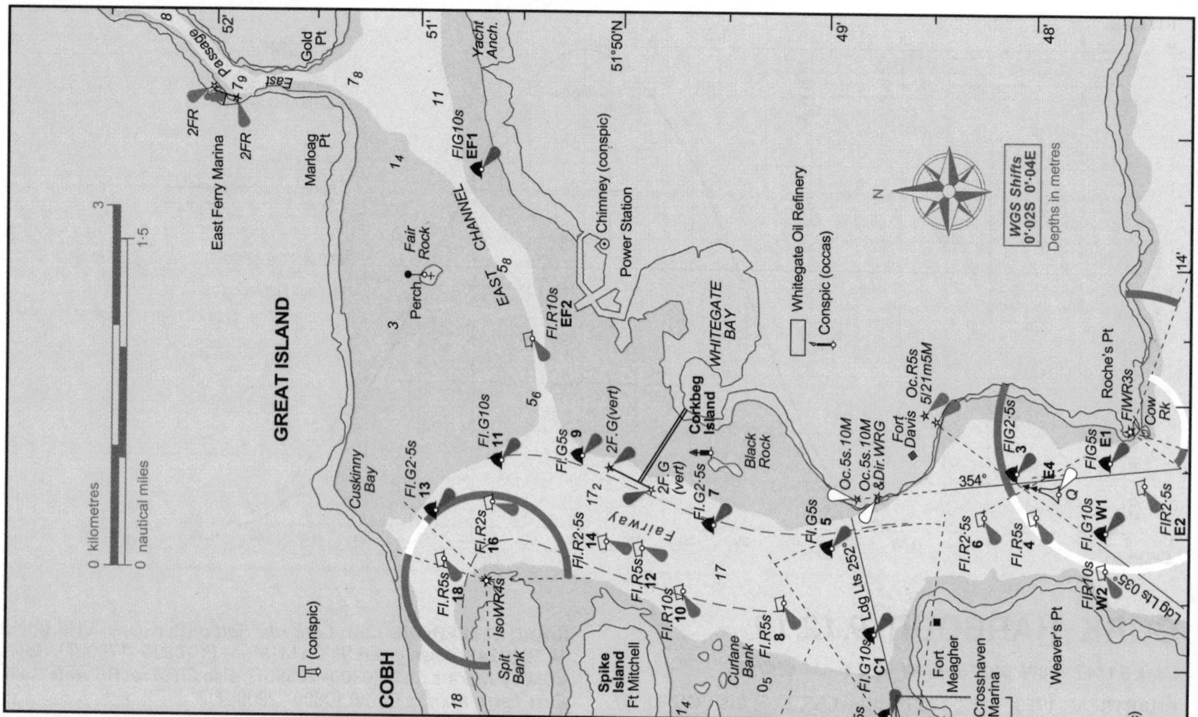
GREAT ISLAND
COBH
East Ferry Marina
2FR
East Passage
Marloag Pt
Gold Pt
Yacht Anch.
Fair Rock
Perch
EAST CHANNEL
Fl.G10s EF1
Fl.R10s EF2
Chimney (conspic)
Power Station
WHITEGATE BAY
Whitegate Oil Refinery
Conspic (occas)
Corkbeg Island
Black Rock
Cuskinny Bay
Fl.G2·5s 13
Fl.G10s 11
Fl.G5s 9
2F.G(vert)
Fl.R2s 16
Fl.R5s 18
IsoWR4s
Spit Bank
Fl.R2·5s 14
Fl.R5s 12
Fl.R10s 10
Fairway
Fl.G2·5s 7
Fl.G5s 5
Fl.R5s 8
Spike Island
Ft Mitchell
Curlane Bank
Ldg Lts 252°
Fl.G10s C1
Fl.G5s C1A
Oc.5s.10M
Oc.5s.10M &Dir.WRG
Fort Davis
Oc.R5s 5/21m5M
354°
FlG2·5s 3
Fl.R2·5s 6
Fl.R5s 4
Fl.G10s W1
Fl.G5s E1
FlWR3s
Cow Rk
Roche's Pt
FlR2·5s E2
FlR10s W2
Ldg Lts 035°
Weaver's Pt
Fort Meagher
Crosshaven Marina
Pier
See inset
RCYC
CROSSHAVEN
LOUGH BEG
CURRAGHBINNY
Owenboy River
Quay
Moorings
Drakes Pool
(conspic)
WGS Shifts 0'·02S 0'·04E
Depths in metres
kilometres
nautical miles
51°50'N
08°18'W

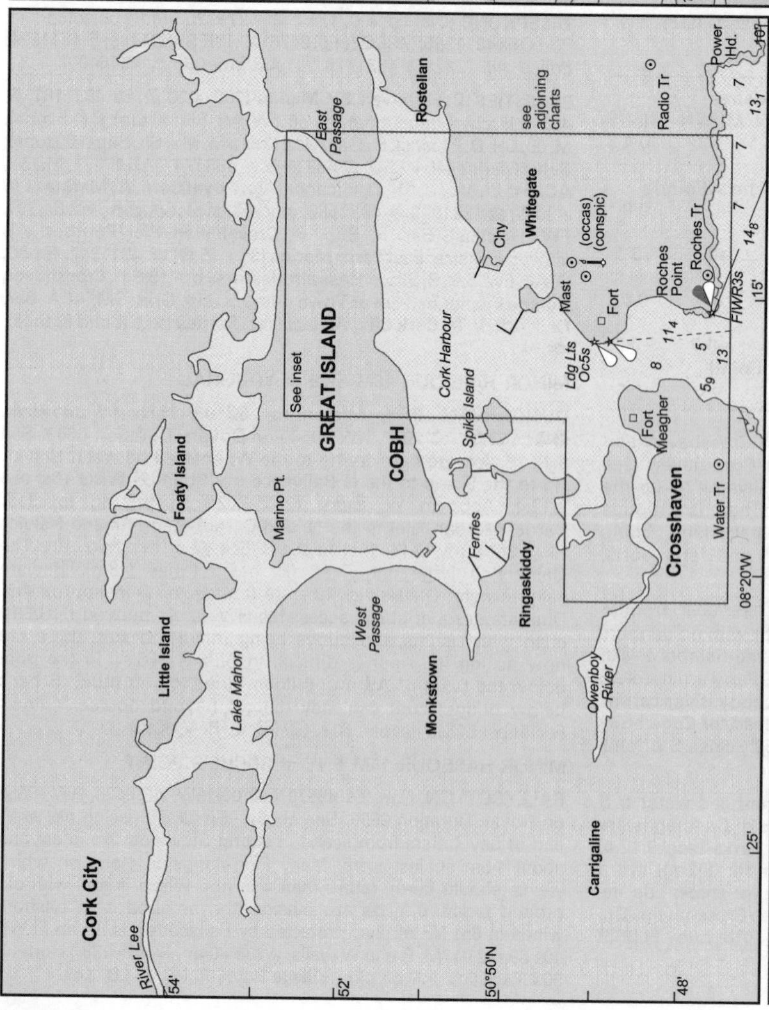
Cork City
River Lee
Little Island
Lake Mahon
Foaty Island
Marino Pt.
Monkstown
West Passage
Ringaskiddy
Ferries
Carrigaline
Owenboy River
GREAT ISLAND
COBH
See inset
Spike Island
Cork Harbour
East Passage
Rostellan
see adjoining charts
Whitegate
Chy
Mast
Fort
(occas) (conspic)
Ldg Lts Oc5s
Roches Point
Roches Tr
FlWR3s
Radio Tr
Power Hd.
Fort Meagher
Crosshaven
Water Tr
50°50'N
08°20'W

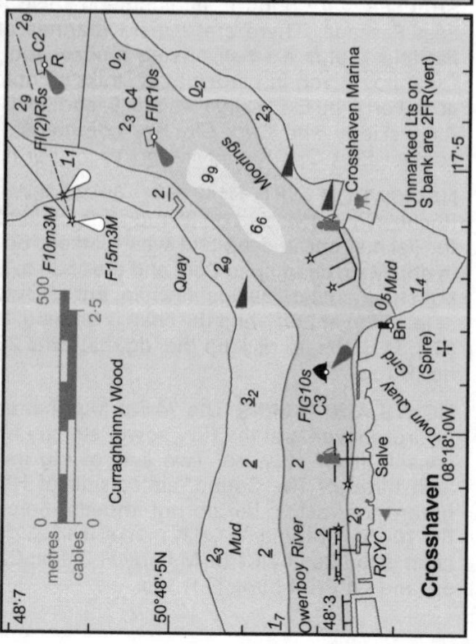
metres
cables
Curraghbinny Wood
F10m3M
F15m3M
Fl(2)R5s
C2
R
FlR10s
C4
Quay
Moorings
Crosshaven Marina
Unmarked Lts on S bank are 2FR(vert)
Mud
Bn
(Spire)
Grid
Town Quay
FlG10s C3
Salve
RCYC
Owenboy River
Crosshaven
50°48'·5N
08°18'·0W

KINSALE *9.12.20*

Cork **51°40'·80N 08°30'·00W**

CHARTS AC 2053, 1765; Imray C56; Irish OS 87

TIDES –0600 Dover; ML 2·2; Duration 0600; Zone 0 (UT)

Standard Port COBH (⟵)

Times				Height (metres)			
High Water		Low Water		MHWS	MHWN	MLWN	MLWS
0500	1100	0500	1100	4·1	3·2	1·3	0·4
1700	2300	1700	2300				
Differences KINSALE							
–0019	–0005	–0009	–0023	–0·2	0·0	+0·1	+0·2

SHELTER Excellent, except in very strong SE winds. Access H24 in all weathers/tides. Marinas at Kinsale YC and Castlepark; NNW of latter is FV pontoon and no ⚓ area. Hbr speed limit 6kn. Possible AB (Sun-Thurs) at Trident Hotel. No ⚓ permitted in main channel or within 700m of Town Pier. Contact HM prior to ⚓ or as soon as possible afterwards.

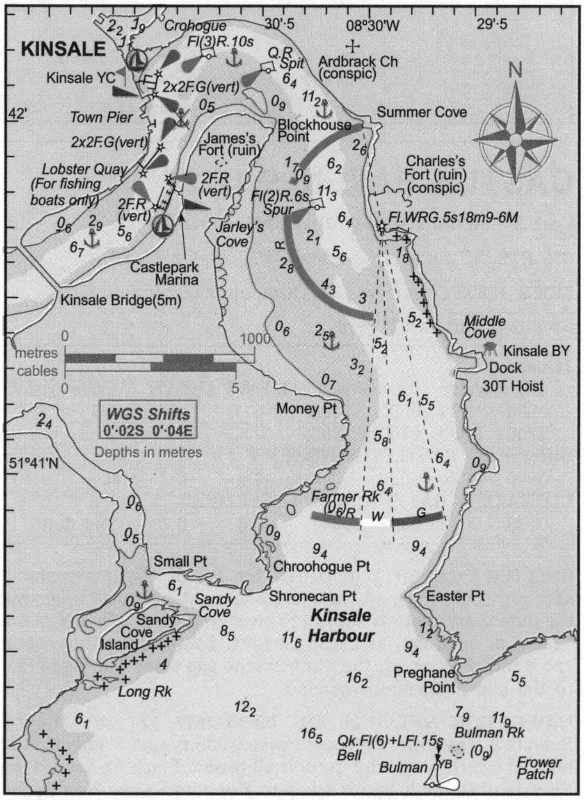

NAVIGATION WPT 51°40'·00N 08°30'·00W, 181°/001° from/to Charles's Fort lt, 1·7M. Beware: Bulman Rk (0·9m; SCM lt buoy) 4ca S of Preghane Pt; and Farmer Rk (0·6m) $\frac{3}{4}$ca off W bank.

LIGHTmS AND MARKS Charles's Fort Dir 001°, Fl WRG 5s 18m 9/6M, vis W358°-004° (H24). Chan is marked by PHM lt buoys. Marina lts are 2 FG or FR as appropriate.

RADIO TELEPHONE KYC VHF Ch M 16. Castlepark marina 06 16 M. Hr Mr **14** 16.

TELEPHONE (Dial code 021) Hr Mr 4772503 (HO), 4773047 (OT), ℻ 4774695; MRCC (066) 9476109; Coast/Cliff Rescue Service 4772346; ⊖ 4311044/4315422; Police 4772302; Dr 4772253, 4772717; Ⓗ 546400.

FACILITIES (from seaward) **Kinsale BY,** ☎ 4774774, ℻ 4775405. D, Ⓥ, FW, ME, Sh, El, BH (30 ton). **Kinsale YC Marina** (170+50 Ⓥ; 10m depth), ☎ 4772196, ℻ 4774455, €1·65, FW, AC, Slip, D, R, Bar, Ⓢ; **Trident Hotel,** D, FW, AB, Sun-Thur try Sail Ireland ☎ 4772927, ℻ 4774170. **Castlepark Marina** (70+20 Ⓥ) ☎ 4774959, ℻ 4774958 €1·65, D, Slip, FW, AC, R, Bar, El, Ⓢ; ferry (3 mins) to town. **Services:** ME, El, Ⓔ, Divers, C (30 ton), D, SM, Gas, Gaz. **Town** P (cans), V, R, Bar, ✉, Ⓑ, (bus to Cork), ⇌, ✈.

MINOR HARBOUR 2M EAST OF KINSALE

OYSTER HAVEN, Cork, **51°41'·20N 08°26'·90W.** AC 2053, 1765. HW –0600 on Dover; ML 2·2m; Duration 0600. Use 9.12.20. Good shelter but subject to swell in S winds. Enter 0·5M N of Big Sovereign, a steep islet divided into two. Keep to S of Little Sovereign on E side of ent. There is foul ground off Ballymacus Pt on W side, and off Kinure Pt on E side. Pass W of Hbr Rk (0·9m) off Ferry Pt, the only danger within hbr. ⚓ NNW of Ferry Pt in 4–6m on soft mud/weed. NW arm shoals suddenly about 5ca NW of Ferry Pt. Also ⚓ up N arm of hbr in 3m off the W shore. Weed in higher reaches may foul ⚓. No lts, marks or VHF radio. Coast/Cliff Rescue Service ☎ (021) 4770711. Facilities at Kinsale. See 9.12.20.

COURTMACSHERRY *9.12.21*

Cork **51°38'·22N 08°40'·90W**

CHARTS AC 2081, *2092*; Imray C56; Irish OS 87

TIDES HW –0610 on Dover; Duration 0545; Zone 0 (UT)

Standard Port COBH (⟵)

Times				Height (metres)			
High Water		Low Water		MHWS	MHWN	MLWN	MLWS
0500	1100	0500	1100	4·1	3·2	1·3	0·4
1700	2300	1700	2300				
Differences COURTMACSHERRY							
–0029	–0007	+0005	–0017	–0·4	–0·3	–0·2	–0·1

SHELTER Good shelter up-river, but in strong S/SE winds seas break on the bar (2·3m), when ent must not be attempted. Dry out in small inner hbr or AB afloat on jetty (FVs) or on yacht pontoon (18·5m). ⚓ NE of Ferry Pt in about 2·5m or N of pontoon. Weed may foul ⚓; best to moor using two ⚓s.

NAVIGATION WPT, 51°37'·50N 08°40'·17W, 144°/324° from/to Wood Pt, 0·8M. Appr in the W sector of Wood Pt lt, between Black Tom and Horse Rk (dries 3·6m); the latter is 3-4$\frac{1}{2}$ca E of Barry Pt on the W shore. Black Tom (2·3m), with SHM buoy Fl.G.5s 5ca SSE, is close NE of the appr. Further to NE, in centre of bay, Barrel Rk (dries 2·6m), has unlit SCM perch (no topmark). To NNW and E of it are Inner Barrels (0·5m) and Blueboy Rk. Hbr ent is between Wood Pt and SHM buoy 2ca NE, Fl G 3s. Chan (2m) is marked by 4 unlit SHM spar buoys after these; keep close N of moorings.

LIGHTS AND MARKS Wood Pt, Fl (2) WR 5s 15m 5M, W315°–332°, R332°–315°.

RADIO TELEPHONE None.

TELEPHONE (023) Hr Mr/RNLI 46311/40394; Dr 46186; Police 46122; Coast Rescue Service ☎ 40110.

FACILITIES Quay AB €1·27, min €12·70. AC, FW, Ⓢ, D, Slip, LB, R, Sh. **Village,** Bar, R, V, (bus to Cork), ⇌, ✈.

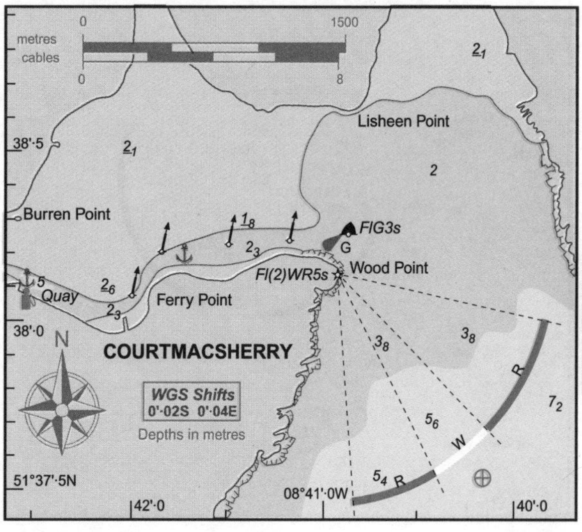

12

GLANDORE *9.12.22*

Cork, **51°33'·70N 09°07'·20W** ❅❅◊◊✿✿✿

CHARTS AC *2092*; Imray C56; Irish OS 89

TIDES Approx as for 9.12.23 Castletownshend. Zone 0 (UT)

SHELTER Excellent. 12 Y ⓜs or ⚓ 1½ca SW of Glandore Pier in 2m or 1ca NE of the New pier at Unionhall in 3m.

NAVIGATION WPT 51°32'·35N 09°05'·10W, 309°/129° from/to Outer Dangers 1·2M. Approach between Adam Is and Goat's Hd, thence keep E of Eve Is and W of the chain of rks: Outer, Middle and Inner Dangers and Sunk Rk. Before altering W for Unionhall, stand on to clear mudbank 1ca off S shore.

LIGHTS AND MARKS Galley Hd, Fl (5) 20s, is 5M E of the ent. Outer Dangers are marked by a preferred-chan-to-port bn (GRG), Fl (2+1) G 10s, and a PHM bn (not on chartlet); Middle and Inner Dangers by 2 SHM bns; and Sunk Rk by a NCM lt buoy, Q.

RADIO TELEPHONE None. No Hr Mr.

TELEPHONE (Dial code 028) Hbr Mr 339419; Police (023) 48162; Dr 23456; Coast Rescue ☎ 33115.

FACILITIES FW at both piers; **Glandore** CH, GHYC, ✉, R, Bar, Kos. **Unionhall** D, P, ME, Gas, ✉, R, Bar, V.

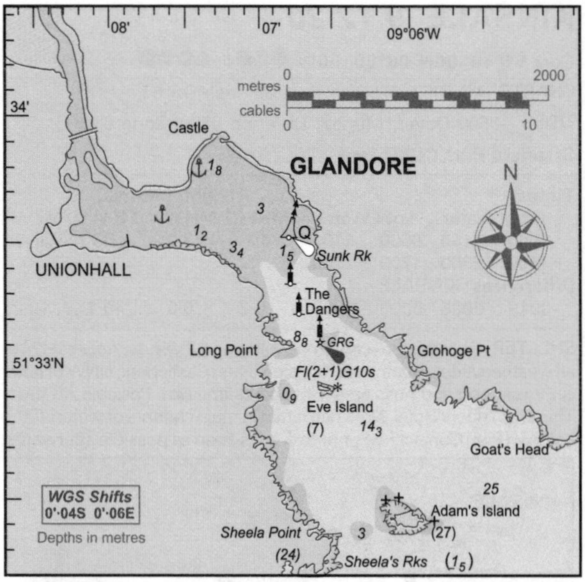

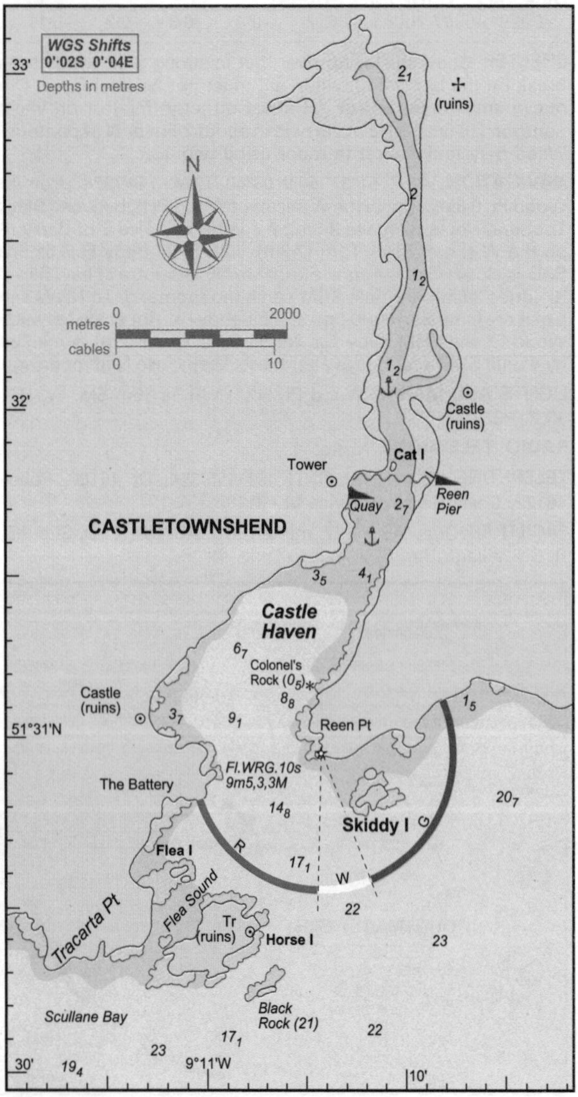

CASTLE HAVEN *9.12.23*

Cork **51°30'·90N 09°10'·70W** ❅❅◊◊✿✿✿

CHARTS AC *2129, 2092*; Imray C56; Irish OS 88, 89

TIDES +0605 Dover; ML 2·2; Duration 0605; Zone 0 (UT)

Standard Port COBH (⟵)

Times				Height (metres)			
High Water		Low Water		MHWS	MHWN	MLWN	MLWS
0500	1100	0500	1100	4·1	3·2	1·3	0·4
1700	2300	1700	2300				
Differences CASTLETOWNSHEND							
−0020	−0030	−0020	−0050	−0·4	−0·2	+0·1	+0·3
CLONAKILTY BAY (5M NE of Galley Head)							
−0033	−0011	−0019	−0041	−0·3	−0·2	No data	

SHELTER Excellent ⚓ in midstream SE of Castletownshend slip, protected from all weathers and available at all tides; but the outer part of hbr is subject to swell in S winds. Or ⚓ N of Cat Island, or upstream as depth permits. Caution: An underwater cable runs E/W across the hbr from the slip close N of Reen Pier to the slip at Castletownshend.

NAVIGATION WPT 51°30'·28N, 09°10'·26W, 171°/351° from/to Reen Pt lt, 7ca. Enter between Horse Is (35m) and Skiddy Is (9m) both of which have foul ground all round. Black Rk lies off the SE side of Horse Is and is steep-to along its S side. Flea Sound is a narrow boat chan, obstructed by rks. Colonel's Rk (0·5m) lies close to the E shore, 2ca N of Reen Pt. Beware salmon nets.

LIGHTS AND MARKS Reen Pt, Fl WRG 10s; a small slender W bn; vis G shore-338°, W338°-001°, R001°-shore. A ruined tr is on Horse Is.

RADIO TELEPHONE None.

TELEPHONE (Dial code 028) MRCC (066) 9746109; Coast/Cliff Rescue Service 21039; ⊖ Bantry (027) 50061; Police 36144; Dr 23456; Ⓗ 21677.

FACILITIES **Reen Pier** L, FW; **Sailing Club** ☎ 36100; **Castletownsend Village** Slip, Bar, R, V, FW, ✉, Ⓑ (Skibbereen), ⇌, ✈ (Cork).

BARLOGE CREEK, Cork, **51°29'·57N 09°17'·58W**. AC 2129. Tides approx as Castletownsend. A narrow creek, well sheltered except from S/SE winds. Appr with Gokane Pt brg 120°. Enter W of Bullock Is, keeping to the W side to clear rks S of the island. ⚓ W of the Is in 3m but weedy. No facilities.

BALTIMORE *9.12.24*

Cork **51°28'·30N 09°23'·40W** ❀❀❀⛵⛵✪✪✪

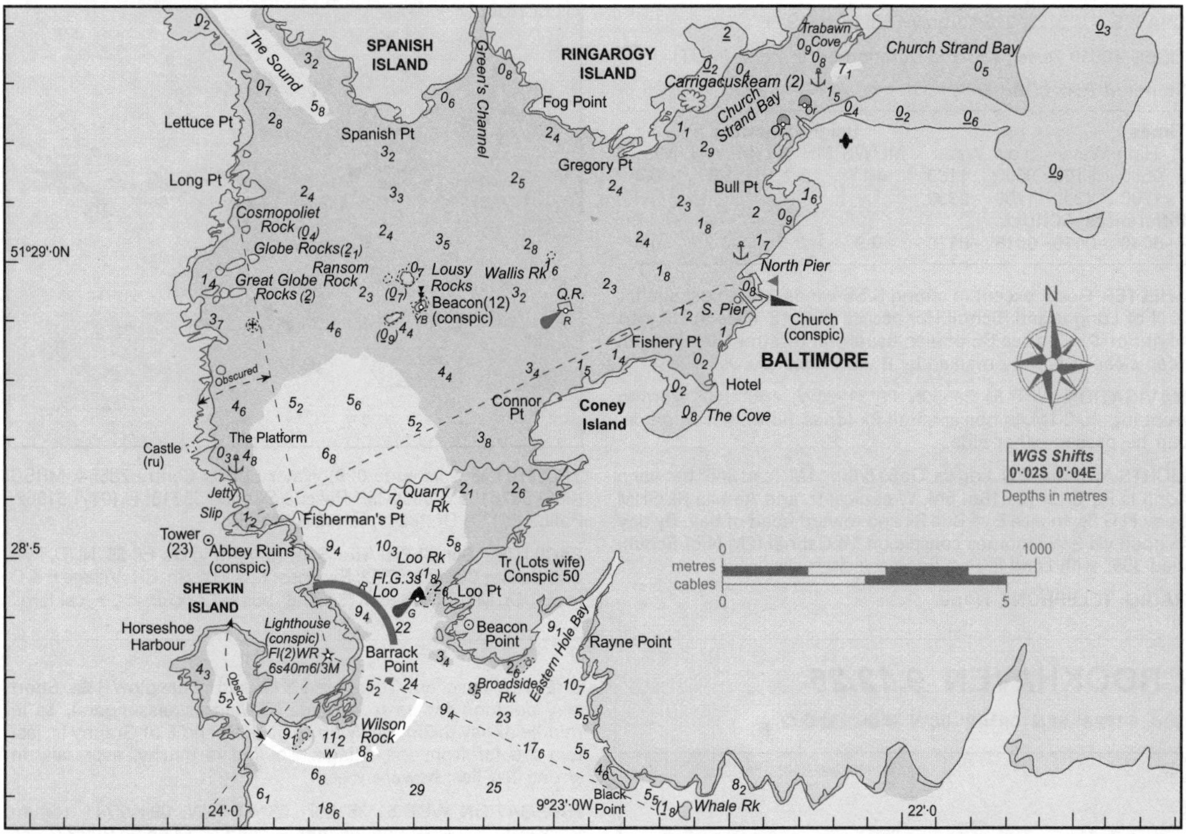

CHARTS AC 3725, 2129; Imray C56; Irish OS 88

TIDES –0605 Dover; ML 2·1; Duration 0610; Zone 0 (UT)

Standard Port COBH (⟵)

Times				Height (metres)			
High Water		Low Water		MHWS	MHWN	MLWN	MLWS
0500	1100	0500	1100	4·1	3·2	1·3	0·4
1700	2300	1700	2300				
Differences BALTIMORE							
–0025	–0005	–0010	–0050	–0·6	–0·3	+0·1	+0·2

SHELTER Excellent; access H24 from the S. At Baltimore a large water barge secured to outer end of the S pier provides AB for up to 20 yachts in 1·5m depth. Inner Hbr, partly drying between N and S piers, is mostly used by local boats and FVs; the latter also berth on N pier. ⚓ SW of S pier, or N of N pier; or in strong NW'lies in Church Strand Bay as shown. ⚓ lts are required. Do not ⚓ in the dredged chan between Wallis Rk buoy and N pier. In strong W winds ⚓ in lee of Sherkin Is off Castle ruins. A similar water barge with AB is secured to the jetty.

NAVIGATION WPT 51°27'·80N 09°23'·42W, 180°/000° from/to Loo Rk SHM buoy, Fl G 3s, 0·62M. Do not cut between this buoy and mainland. Beware Lousy Rks (SCM bn) and Wallis Rk (PHM buoy, QR) in the middle of the bay. From/to the N The Sound needs careful pilotage; AC 3725 and ICC SDs essential. R Ilen is navigable on the flood for at least 4M above The Sound.

LIGHTS AND MARKS Ent easily identified by conspic W tr (Lot's Wife) to stbd on Beacon Pt and Barrack Pt lt ho, Fl (2) WR 6s, to port.

RADIO TELEPHONE VHF Ch 06 09 16.

TELEPHONE (Dial code 028) Hr Board sec ☎/📠 22145; MRSC (066) 9476109; Coast/Cliff Rescue Service 20125; ⊜ (027) 50061; Police 20102; Dr 21488; 🄷 21677.

FACILITIES Berthing barges (up to 20 ⓥ) ☎ (021) 774959, 📠 (021) 774958, (May-Sept), €12·70, Slip, AB, FW, AC; **Baltimore SC** ☎/📠 20426, visitors welcome, bar, showers; **Glenans Irish Sailing School** ☎ (01) 6611481. **Services:** D (hose), P (cans), BY, ME, El, CH, V, Gas, Gaz, Kos, Sh, ACA; **Village** Bar, ✉, bus to Cork for ⥄, ✈.

ADJACENT ANCHORAGES

HORSESHOE HARBOUR, 51°28'·20N 09°23'·86W. Small unlit hbr on Sherkin Is, 3ca WSW of ent to Baltimore. Keep to the W at narrow ent. ⚓ in about 5m in centre of cove.

CLEAR ISLAND, NORTH HARBOUR, 51°26'·60N 09°30'·20W. AC 2129. Tides approx as Schull, 9.12.25. A tiny, partly drying inlet on N coast of Clear Is, exposed to N'ly swell. There are rks either side of the outer appr 196°. Inside the narrow (30m), rky ent keep to the E. Lie to 2⚓s on E side in about 1·5m or berth at inner end of pier. Few facilities.

ROARING WATER BAY Long Island Bay, entered between Cape Clear and Mizen Hd, extends NE into Roaring Water Bay (AC 2129). The Fastnet Rk, Fl 5s 49m 28M, Horn (4) 60s, is 4M to seaward. Safest appr, S of Schull, is via Carthy's Sound (51°30'N 09°30'W). From the SE appr via Gascanane Sound, but beware Toorane Rks, Anima Rk and outlying rks off many of the islands. Shelter in various winds at ⚓s clockwise from Horse Island: 3ca E and 7ca NE of E tip of Horse Is; in Ballydehob B 2m; Poulgorm B 2m; 5ca ENE of Mannin Is in 4m; 2ca SE of Carrigvalish Rks in 6m. Rincolisky Cas (ru) is conspic on S side of bay. The narrow chan E of Hare Is and N of Sherkin Is has two ⚓s; it also leads via The Sound into Baltimore hbr. Local advice is useful. There are temp fair weather ⚓s in the Carthy's Islands. Rossbrin Cove, 2·5M E of Schull, is a safe ⚓, but many local moorings; no access from E of Horse Is due to drying Horse Ridge. No facilities at most of the above ⚓s.

SCHULL 9.12.25

Cork **51°30'·80N 09°32'·00W** ❀❀❀◊◊◊✿✿

CHARTS AC 2129, 2184; Imray C56; Irish OS 88

TIDES +0610 Dover; ML 1·8; Duration 0610; Zone 0 (UT)

Standard Port COBH (⟵)

Times				Height (metres)			
High Water		Low Water		MHWS	MHWN	MLWN	MLWS
0500	1100	0500	1100	4·1	3·2	1·3	0·4
1700	2300	1700	2300				
Differences SCHULL							
−0040	−0015	−0015	−0110	−0·9	−0·6	−0·2	0·0

SHELTER Good, except in strong S/SE winds when best shelter is N of Long Island. Schull Hbr access H24. 12 Y Ⓐs in NE part of hbr or ⚓ in 3m 1ca SE of pier, usually lit by street lts all night; keep clear of fairway marked by 8 unlit lateral buoys.

NAVIGATION WPT 51°29'·60N 09°31'·60W, 166°/346° from/to front ldg lt, 2·1M. In hbr ent, Bull Rk (dries 1·8m), R iron perch, can be passed either side.

LIGHTS AND MARKS Ldg lts, Oc 5s 5/8m 11M, lead 346° between Long Is Pt, Q (3) 10s 16m 8M, W conical tr, and Amelia Rk SHM buoy Fl G 3s; thence E of Bull Rk and toward head of bay. By day in good vis 2 W radomes conspic on Mt Gabriel (2M N of Schull) lead 355° with Long Is Pt lt ho in transit.

RADIO TELEPHONE None.

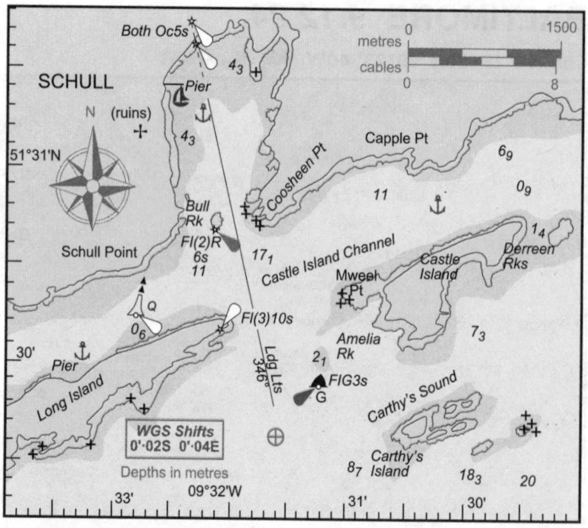

TELEPHONE (Dial code 028) Water Sports Centre 28554; MRSC (066) 9476109; Coast/Cliff Rescue Service 35318; ⊖ (027) 51562; Police 28111; Dr 28311; Ⓗ (027) 50133.

FACILITIES Schull Pier/Hbr Slip, AB tempy, Ⓐs €6·35, M, D, FW, SM; **Sailing Club** ☎ 37352; **Services:** Kos, BY, Sh, CH. **Village** P & D (cans), Dr, ME, El, V, R, Bar, ⊡, ✉, Ⓑ, bus to Cork for: ⇌, ✈, car ferry.

CROOKHAVEN 9.12.26

Cork **51°28'·50N 09°42'·00W** ❀❀◊◊✿✿✿

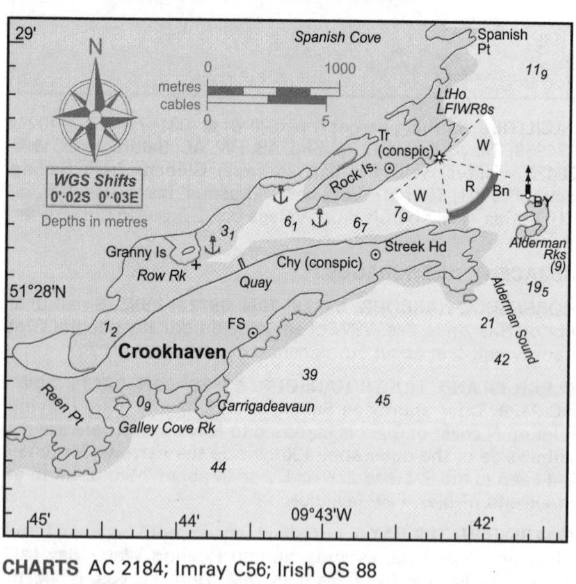

CHARTS AC 2184; Imray C56; Irish OS 88

TIDES +0550 Dover; ML 1·8; Duration 0610; Zone 0 (UT)

Standard Port COBH (⟵)

Times				Height (metres)			
High Water		Low Water		MHWS	MHWN	MLWN	MLWS
0500	1100	0500	1100	4·1	3·2	1·3	0·4
1700	2300	1700	2300				
Differences CROOKHAVEN							
−0057	−0033	−0048	−0112	−0·8	−0·6	−0·4	−0·1
DUNMANUS HARBOUR							
−0107	−0031	−0044	−0120	−0·7	−0·6	−0·2	0·0
DUNBEACON HARBOUR							
−0057	−0025	−0032	−0104	−0·8	−0·7	−0·3	−0·1

SHELTER Excellent. There are 8 Y Ⓐs and 10 dayglow R Ⓐs. Short stay pontoon for up to 4 boats (FW/stores/passengers). ⚓s in middle of bay in 3m; off W tip of Rock Is; and E of Granny Is; last two are far from the village. Holding is patchy, especially in strong SW'lies; beware weed.

NAVIGATION WPT 51°28'·50N 09°40'·50W, 094°/274° from/to Rock Is lt ho, 1M. Ent between this lt and NCM bn on Black Horse Rks (3½ca ESE). From S, keep 1ca E of Alderman Rks and ½ca off Black Horse Rks bn. Passage between Streek Hd and Alderman Rks is not advised for strangers. Inside the bay the shores are steep to.

LIGHTS AND MARKS Lt ho on Rock Is (conspic W tr) L Fl WR 8s 20m 13/11M; vis outside hbr: W over Long Is Bay–281°, R281°–340°; vis inside hbr: R 281°–348°, W348°–N shore.

RADIO TELEPHONE None.

TELEPHONE (Dial code 028) Hr Mr (O'Sullivan's Bar) 35319; MRSC (066) 9476109; Coast/Cliff Rescue at Goleen 35318; ⊖ (027) 50061; Dr 35148; ✉ 35200.

FACILITIES Village Ⓐs €6·35, Bar, R, FW, V, Kos, ✉, D (cans), ME, Gas, Ⓑ (Schull), taxi to Goleen then bus to Cork, ✈, ⇌.

ADJACENT HARBOURS

GOLEEN (Kireal-coegea), Cork, **51°29'·65N 09°42'·21W**. AC 2184. Tides as Crookhaven. A narrow inlet 6ca N of Spanish Pt; good shelter in fair weather, except from SE. 2 churches are easily seen, but ent not visible until close. Keep to S side of ent and ⚓ fore-and-aft just below quay, where AB also possible. Facilities: P, V, Bar.

DUNMANUS BAY, Cork. AC 2552. Tides see 9.12.26. Appr between Three Castle Hd and Sheep's Hd, Fl (3) WR 15s 83m 18/15M; no other lts. Ent to **Dunmanus Hbr**, 51°32'·70N 09°39'·86W, is 1ca wide; breakers both sides. ⚓ in 4m centre of B. **Kitchen Cove,** 51°35'·50N 09°38'·05W, is the best of the 3 hbrs; enter W of Owens Is and ⚓ 1ca NNW of it or 2ca further N in 3m. Exposed to S, but good holding. Quay at Ahakista village: V, R, Bar. **Dunbeacon Hbr**, 51°36'·35N 09°33'·60W, is shallow and rock-girt. ⚓ E or SE of Mannion Is. At Durrus (1¼M): Fuel (cans), R, Bar.

BANTRY BAY *9.12.27*

Cork **51°34'N 09°57'W** ❀❀❀⛵⛵✿✿✿

CHARTS AC 1838, 1840, *2552*; Imray C56; Irish OS 84, 85, 88

TIDES +0600 Dover; ML 1·8; Duration 0610; Zone 0 (UT)

Standard Port COBH (⟵)

Times				**Height (metres)**			
High Water		Low Water		MHWS	MHWN	MLWN	MLWS
0500	1100	0500	1100	4·1	3·2	1·3	0·4
1700	2300	1700	2300				
Differences BANTRY							
−0045	−0025	−0040	−0105	−0·9	−0·8	−0·2	0·0
CASTLETOWN (Bearhaven)							
−0048	−0012	−0025	−0101	−0·9	−0·6	−0·1	0·0
BLACK BALL HARBOUR (51°36N 10°02W)							
−0115	−0035	−0047	−0127	−0·7	−0·6	−0·1	+0·1

SHELTER/NAVIGATION Bantry Bay extends 20M ENE from Sheep's Hd, Fl (3) WR 15s 83m 18/15M. Access is easy, but the Bay is exposed to W'lies. The shore is clean everywhere except off Bear Is and Whiddy Is. Some of the many well sheltered ⚓s on the N shore are detailed on this page. The S shore has few ⚓s.

CASTLETOWN, 51°38'·80N 09°54'·45W. AC 1840. Sheltered ⚓ in 2·4m NW of Dinish Is, to E of 010° ldg line, but never far from FVs; also ⚓ at **Dunboy Bay,** W of Piper Sound (open to E). 4 Y 🛟s are laid Apr-Sep 3ca E of Dinish Is. Lts: At W ent, Ardnakinna Pt, Fl (2) WR 10s 62m 17/14M, H24. At E ent to Bearhaven: Roancarrigmore, Fl WR 3s 18m 18/14M. Appr W of Bear Is on 024° Dir lt, Oc WRG 5s 4m 14/11M (W024°–024·5°); then inner ldg lts 010°, both Oc 3s 4/7m 1M, vis 005°-015°, via ent chan which narrows to 50m abeam Perch Rk lt bn, QG. Beware Walter Scott Rk (2·7m), SCM buoy, Q (6) + L Fl 15s, and Carrigaglos (0·6m high) S of Dinish Is. VHF Ch 14 16. Hr Mr ☎ (027) 70220, 📠 70329. Facilities: FW & D on quay; BH on Dinish Is. **Town** El, ME, Sh, P (cans), Bar, Ⓑ, ✉, V, R, Kos.

LAWRENCE COVE, 51°38'·28N 09°49'·28W; AC 1840. Good shelter on N side of Bear Island. Marina on S side of cove has NE/SW pontoon 90m long (40 AB in 3-3·5m). From E keep clear of Palmer Rk and a shoal patch, both 1·8m. ☎/📠 027 75044; VHF Ch 16 M. AB (€1·52), FW, AC, D, BH, ▣. Friendly welcome at the only marina between Kinsale and Dingle. There are 4 Y 🛟s in 3m close S of Ardagh Pt, or ⚓ in 4m to W of Turk Is. At Rerrin village: BY, Slip, V, R, Bar, ✉, storage facilities. Bus to Cork and all storage facilities.

LONEHORT HARBOUR, 51°38'·12N 09°47'·80W. AC 1840. At E tip of Bear Is, good shelter but keep S at ent to clear unmarked rks; then turn ENE to ⚓ in 2·7m at E end of cove.

ADRIGOLE, 51°40'·51N 09°43'·22W. AC 1840. Good shelter, but squally in W/N gales. Beware Doucallia Rk, dries 1·2m, 1M SSW of ent. Beyond the 2ca wide ent, keep E of Orthons Is (rks on W side). 7 Y 🛟s NE of Orthons Is. ⚓s to suit wind direction: off pier on E shore 4m; N or NW of Orthons Is. Drumlave (½M E): V.

Trafrask Bay, 2M to the E, has 1 Y 🛟 at **51°40'·8N 09°40'·1W.**

GLENGARIFF, 51°44'·20N 09°31'·90W. AC 1838. Tides as Bantry. Beautiful ⚓ S of Bark Is in 7-10m; or to NE in 3m, where there are 6 Y 🛟s. Better for yachts than Bantry hbr. Ent between Big Pt and Gun Pt. No lts/marks. Keep 1ca E of rks off Garinish Island (Illnacullen) and Ship Is; beware marine farms. Rky chan W of Garinish, with HT cable 15m clearance, should not be attempted. Facilities: Eccles hotel, showers. **Village** FW, Bar, D & P (cans), ✉, R, V, Kos.

BANTRY, 51°40'·85N 09°27'·85W. AC 1838. Beware Gerane Rks 1M W of Whiddy Is lt, Oc 2s 22m 3M, vis 073°-106°. Appr via the buoyed/lit N chan (10m) to E of Horse and Chapel Is; keep 2ca off all islands to clear unlit mussel rafts. The S chan, fair weather only, has a bar 2m; ldg marks 091°, front RW post, FW lt; rear W post, FR lt. 🛟 call Bantry Hbr Ch 14 or ☎ 027 51253; VHF Ch 14 11 16 (H24). Hr Mr (027) 505205; ⊖ 50061; Police 50045; Dr 50405; Ⓗ 50133. MRCC (066) 9476109. Facilities: **Pier** L, FW; **Bantry Bay SC** ☎ 50081 Slip, L; **Town** EC Wed; P & D (cans), Kos, ME, CH, V, R, Bar, ✉, Ⓑ, bus to Cork.

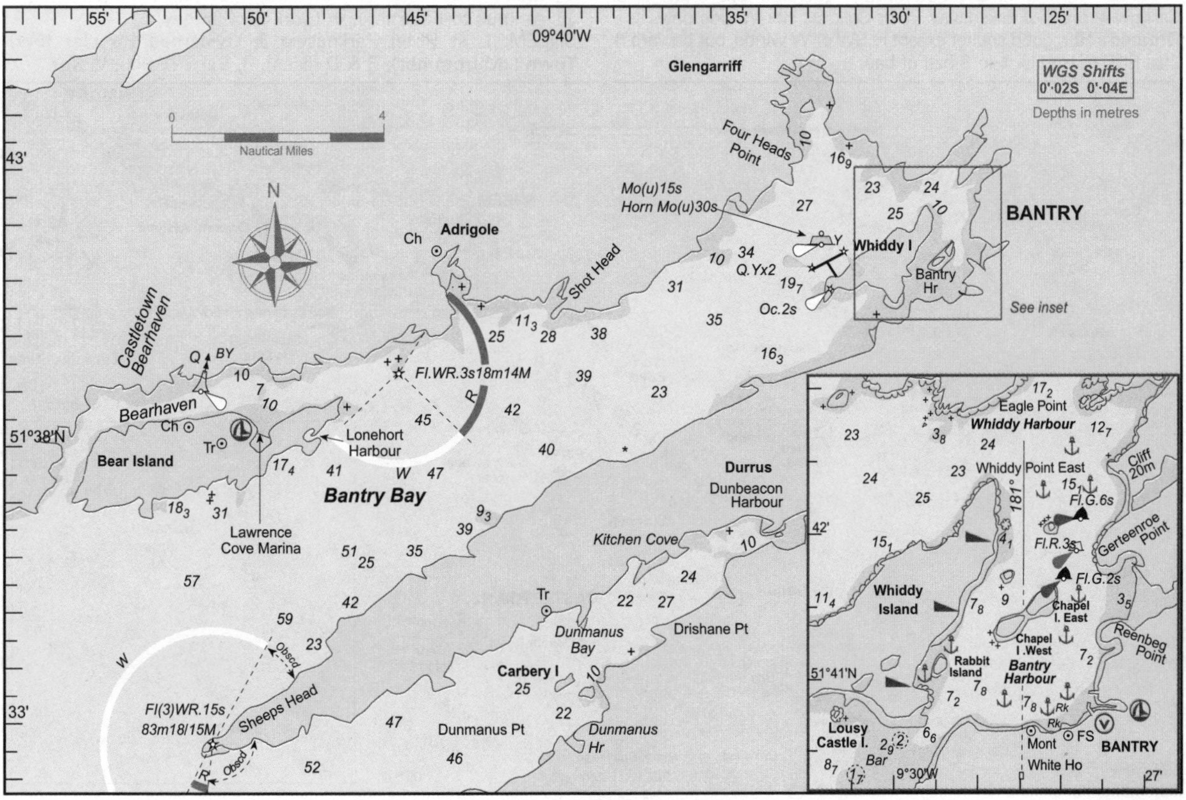

KENMARE RIVER *9.12.28*

Kerry **51°45'·00N 10°00'·00W** ❀❀❀◊✿✿

CHARTS AC *2495*; Imray C56; Irish OS 84

TIDES +0515 Dover; Duration Dunkerron 0620; West Cove 068. Zone 0 (UT)

Standard Port COBH (⟵)

Times				Height (metres)			
High Water		Low Water		MHWS	MHWN	MLWN	MLWS
0500	1100	0500	1100	4·1	3·2	1·3	0·4
1700	2300	1700	2300				
Differences BALLYCROVANE HARBOUR (Coulagh Bay)							
−0116	−0036	−0053	−0133	−0·6	−0·5	−0·1	0·0
DUNKERRON HARBOUR							
−0117	−0027	−0050	−0140	−0·2	−0·3	+0·1	0·0
WEST COVE (51°46'N 10°03'W)							
−0113	−0033	−0049	−0129	−0·6	−0·5	−0·1	0·0
BALLINSKELLIGS BAY							
−0119	−0039	−0054	−0134	−0·5	−0·5	−0·1	0·0
VALENTIA HARBOUR (Knights Town)							
−0118	−0038	−0056	−0136	−0·6	−0·4	−0·1	0·0

SHELTER **Garnish Bay (S of Long I)**: is only good in settled weather and W'ly winds. ⚓ either W or 1ca S of the Carrigduff concrete bn.
Ballycrovane: in NE of Coulagh B is a good ⚓, but open to W'ly swell which breaks on submerged rks in SE. N and E shores are foul. ⚓ ½ca NE of Bird Is.
Cleanderry: Ent NE of Illaunbweeheen (Yellow Is) is only 7m wide and rky. ⚓ ENE of inner hbr. Beware mussel farms
Ardgroom: excellent shelter, but intricate ent over rky bar. Appr with B bn brg 135°; then 2 W bns (front on Black Rk, rear ashore) lead 099° through bar. Alter 206° as two bns astern come in transit. When clear, steer WNW to ⚓ ½ca E of Reenavade pier; power needed. Beware fish farms.
Kilmakilloge: is a safe ⚓ in all winds. Beware mussel beds and rky shoals. On appr keep S side of ent, steer W of Spanish Is, but pass N of it. Bunaw Hbr ldg lts 041°, front Oc R 3s, rear Iso R 2s, (access only near HW; AB for shoal draft). Keep S side of ent; ⚓ 2ca W of Carrigwee bn; S of Eskadawer Pt; or Collorus Hbr W side only.
Ormond's Hbr: good shelter except in SW or W winds, but beware rk 2½ca ENE of Hog Is. ⚓ in S half of bay.
Kenmare: Good shelter. Access only near HW via narrow ch marked by withies. AB at pier at N side of river, just below town.
Dunkerron Hbr: Ent between Cod Rks and The Boar to ⚓ 1ca NW of Fox Is in 3·2m; land at Templenoe pier. 4ca E of Reen Pt behind pier, AB (€8.89) at floating jetty in 1·8m but appr may be less at LW.
Sneem: enter between Sherky Is and Rossdohan Is. Hotel conspic NE of hbr. 3 Y ♠s and ⚓ NE of Garinish Is, but uncomfortable if swell enters either side of Sherky Is.
Darrynane: 1½M NW of Lamb's Hd, is appr'd from the S between Deenish and Moylaun Islands, but not with high SW swell. Enter with care on the ldg marks/lts 034°, 2 W bns, both Oc 3s 10/16m 4M. 3 Y ♠s and safe ⚓ (3m) NE of Lamb's Is. Also ⚓s in Lehid Hbr, R Blackwater, Coongar Hbr & W Cove.

NAVIGATION WPT 51°40'·00N 10°17'·20W, 245°/065° from/to 0.5M S of Sherky Island, 15·6M. From SW, keep NW of The Bull and Dursey Is. From SE, Dursey Sound is possible in fair wx but narrow (beware Flag Rk 0·3m) and with cable car, 21m clearance. To clear dangerous rks off Coulagh Bay, keep twr on Dursey Is well open of Cod's Head 220°. From NW, there are 3 deep chans off Lamb's Head: between Scarriff Is and Deenish Is which is clear; between Deenish and Moylaun Is which has rky shoals; and between Moylaun and Two Headed Is which is clear and 4½ca wide. A night appr into the river is possible, but close appr to hbrs or ⚓s is not advised. Up-river from Sneem Hbr, keep N of Maiden Rk, dries 0·5m, and Church Rks; also Lackeen Rks and Carrignarona beg. Beware salmon nets Jun -Sep. See 9.12.5.

LIGHTS AND MARKS On Dursey Is: Old Watch Twr (conspic) 250m. Eagle Hill (Cod's Hd) 216m. The few lights are as on chartlet.

RADIO TELEPHONE None.

TELEPHONE (Dial code 064) MRCC (066) 9476109; Coast/Cliff Rescue Service (Waterville) (066) 74320; ⊖ Bantry (027) 50061; Ⓗ 41088; Police 91177.

FACILITIES
ARDGROOM (Pallas Hbr): D & P (cans), V, R, Bar, Kos, ✉ at Ardgroom village (2M SSW of Reenavade pier).
KILMAKILLOGE: **Bunaw Pier**, AB, V, Bar; 2M to D, Kos, ✉.
KENMARE: AB. **Town** D & P (cans), Kos, Gaz, R, V, Bar, Ⓗ, ✉, Ⓑ, ⇌ (bus to Killarney), ✈ (Cork or Killarney).
SNEEM: L at Hotel Parknasilla & Oysterbed Ho pier (FW). **Town** (2M from hbr), P & D (cans), R, Bar, ✉, Slip, V, Kos.

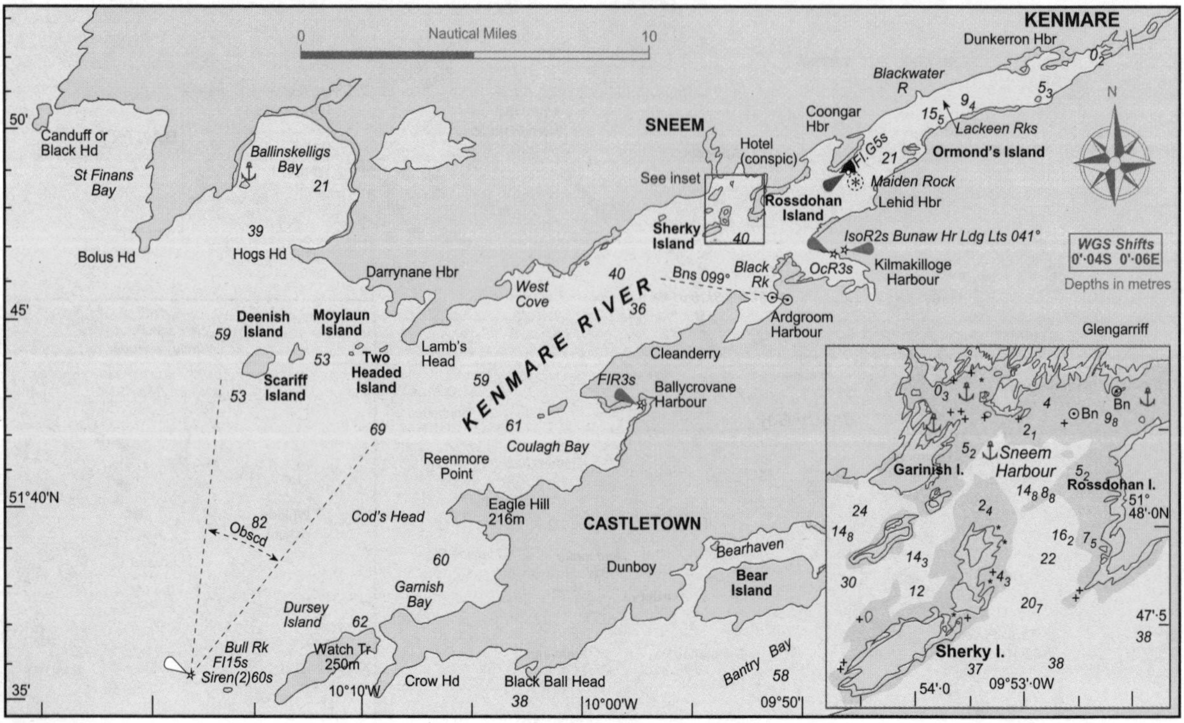

ANCHORAGES OFF VALENTIA ISLAND

PORTMAGEE, Kerry, **51°53'·20N 10°22'·29W**. AC 2125. HW +0550 on Dover; ML 2·0m; Duration 0610; See 9.12.28 under VALENTIA HBR. A safe ⚓ 2·5M E of Bray Head in Portmagee Sound between the mainland and Valentia Is. The ent to the Sound often has bad seas, but dangers are visible. Care required E of Reencaheragh Pt (S side) due rks either side. Deepest water is N of mid-chan. 6 Y ◆s at 51°53'·3N 10°22'·5W (N side), or ⚓ off the pier (S side) in 5m, opposite Skelling Heritage Centre (well worth a visit). AB on pier is not recommended due to strong tides. Facilities: FW, V, R, Bar, Kos. 1ca E of pier, road bridge centre span opens, if pre-arranged with ☎ (066) 77174 or call *Valentia Radio* VHF Ch 24, 28; giving access to Valentia Hbr (Knight's Town) via intricate chan with 1·5m.

VALENTIA HARBOUR, Kerry, **51°56'·20N 10°19'·31W**. AC 2125. Tides at 9.12.31. The only ent is at NE end of Valentia Is, between Fort Pt and Beginish Is as the swing br on the SW end is out of action to yachts. Easy access except in strong NW'lies. Fort Pt lt, Fl WR 2s 16m 17/15M, W102°-304°, R304°-351°, obsc'd from seaward when E of Doulus Head. Ldg lts 141°: Front Dir Oc WRG 4s 25m 11/8M, W sector 140°-142°; rear, Oc 4s 43m 5M, synch. Beware Hbr Rk, 2·6m, 3ca SE of Fort Pt and 100m SW of ldg line; marked by ECM bn Q (3) 10s. Good ⚓s at: Glanleam B, 6ca S of Fort Pt in 4m; 1ca NW of LB slip in 2·5m, with 6 Y ◆s (beware The Foot, spit drying 1·2m, marked by ECM buoy, Q (3) 5s); SEof the ferry pier at Knight's Town (E end of the island) in 4m, with 6 Y ◆s; in bay on the S side of Beginish Is in 3m. Hr Mr ☎ (066) 76124. Facilities (Knightstown): BY, Sh, ME, Gas, P & D (cans), Kos, some V, R, Bar, ⊡. Ferry/bus to Cahersiveen (2½M) for usual shops; EC Thurs. Marina (80 AB) planned in river at Cahersiveen.

DINGLE *9.12.29*

Kerry **52°07'·14N 10°15'·48W** ✿✿✿◊◊◊✿✿✿

CHARTS AC 2790, 2789; Imray C55, C56; Irish OS 70

TIDES +0540 Dover; ML 2·1m; Duration 0605; Zone 0 (UT)

Standard Port COBH (⟵)

Times				**Height (metres)**			
High Water		Low Water		MHWS	MHWN	MLWN	MLWS
0500	1100	0500	1100	4·1	3·2	1·3	0·4
1700	2300	1700	2300				
Differences DINGLE							
−0111	−0041	−0049	−0119	−0·1	0·0	+0·3	+0·4
SMERWICK HARBOUR							
−0107	−0027	−0041	−0121	−0·3	−0·4	No data	
FENIT PIER (Tralee Bay)							
−0057	−0017	−0029	−0109	+0·5	+0·2	+0·3	+0·1

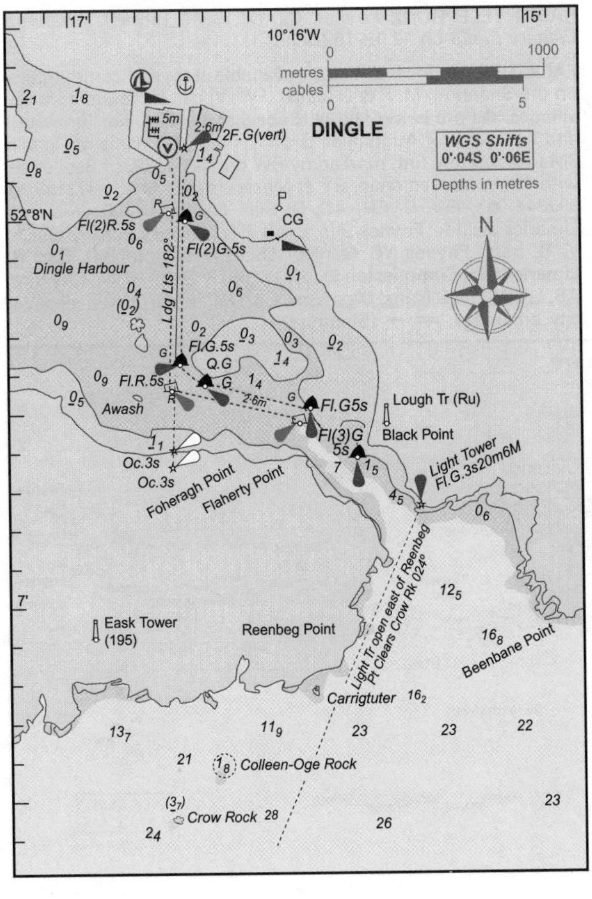

SHELTER Excellent at marina (5m depth) in landlocked hbr. A busy fishing port. There are 4 Y ◆s at **Kells Bay** (52°01'·6N 10°06'·3W), 8M SE of Dingle ent.

NAVIGATION WPT 52°06'·20N 10° 15'·48W, 180°/360° from/to lt Fl G 3s, 1·06M. Easy ent H24. Beware Crow Rk (dries 3·7m), 0·8M SW of Reenbeg Pt; and rky ledge SW of Black Pt.
Note: **Castlemaine Hbr**, approx 15M E at the head of Dingle Bay, largely dries and should not be attempted without local knowledge or inspection at LW.

LIGHTS AND MARKS Eask Twr (195m, with fingerpost pointing E) is conspic 0·85M WSW of ent. Lt tr, Fl G 3s 20m 6M, on NE side of ent. Ent chan, dredged 2·6m, is marked by 5 SHM lt buoys and 3 PHM lt buoys, as chartlet. Ldg lts, both Oc 3s, (W ◊s on B poles) lead from astern 182° to hbr bkwtrs.

RADIO TELEPHONE Ch **14** 16, but no calls required. Valentia Radio (Ch 24 28) will relay urgent messages to Dingle Hr Mr.

TELEPHONE (Dial code 066) Hr Mr 51629; Coastguard (066) 9476109; ⊜ 7121480; Dr 9152225; ⊞ 9151455; Police 9151522. All emergencies: 999 or 112.

FACILITIES Marina (60 + 20 Ⓥ) ☎ 9151629, 📠 9152629, €1·40, AC, FW, D, Slip, ⊡, ♿, C (hire). **Town** P (cans), Kos, ME, Ⓔ, Gas, Gaz, SM, ✉, R, Bar, V, Ⓑ, ⇌ Tralee (by bus), ✈ (Kerry 30M).

ANCHORAGE CLOSE WEST OF DINGLE BAY

VENTRY Kerry, **52°06·70N 10°20'·30W**. AC 2790, 2789. HW +0540 on Dover; ML 2·1m; Duration 0605; Use 9.12.29. Ent is 2M W of conspic Eask Tr. A pleasant hbr with easy ent 1M wide and good holding on hard sand; sheltered from SW to N winds, but open to swell from the SE, and in fresh W'lies prone to sharp squalls. Beware Reenvare Rks 1ca SE of Parkmore Pt; also a rky ridge 2·9m, on which seas break, extends 2·5ca SSE of Ballymore Pt. No lts. ⚓s in about 4m off Ventry Strand (✠ brg W, the village NE); or in 3m SW side of bay, 1ca N of pier; also 3 Y ◆s. On N side 3 Y ◆s off pier at Ventry village. Both piers access HW±3 for landing. Facilities: P, Slip, V, Kos, Bar, R, ✉.

ANCHORAGES BETWEEN THE BLASKETS AND KERRY HD

SMERWICK HARBOUR, Kerry, **52°13'·00N 10°24'·00W**. AC 2789. Tides 9.12.29. Adequate shelter in 1M wide bay, except from NW'ly when considerable swell runs in. Ent between East Sister (150m hill) and Dunacapple Is to the NE. ⚓s at: the W side close N or S of the Boat Hr in 3-10m; to the S, off Carrigveen Pt in 2·5m; or in N'lies at the bay in NE corner inside 10m line. Facilities at Ballynagall village on SE side: 4 Y ◆s, pier (0·5m), limited V, Bar, Bus.

BRANDON BAY, Kerry, **52°16'·10N 10°09'·92W**. AC 2739. Tides as Fenit 9.12.29. A 4M wide bay, very exposed to the N, but in moderate SW-W winds there is safe ⚓ in 6m close E of drying Brandon Pier, 2FG (vert). Cloghane Inlet in SW of Bay is not advised. Facilities at Brandon: limited V, P (1M), ✉, R, Bar, bus.

TRALEE BAY, Kerry, **52°18'·00N 09°56'·00W**. AC 2739. HW −0612 on Dover; ML 2·6m; Duration 0605. See 9.12.29. Enter the bay passing 3M N of Magharee Islands. Pick up the W sector (W140°–152°) of Little Samphire Is lt, Fl WRG 5s 17m 16/13M; see 9.12.4 for sectors. Approach between Magharee Is and Mucklaghmore (30m high).

12

FENIT HARBOUR, 52°16'·20N 09°51'·61W, is in SE corner of Tralee Bay. Appr on 146° to Little Samphire Is, conspic lt ho, Fl WRG 5s 17m 16/13M, thence 7ca E to Samphire Is; 3 conspic fuel tanks and lt QR 15m 3M vis 242°–097°. Good shelter in marina, but a few berths exposed to SE winds. Fenit Pier head 2 FR (vert) 12m 3M, vis 148°–058°. For 🅜s call *Neptune* (Tralee SC) VHF Ch 14 16, or ⚓ N of breakwater in 4m on good holding. Port Manager: VHF Ch 16 14 M (0900-2100UT), ☎ (066) 7136231, 📠 (066) 7136231; ⊖ ☎ (066) 7121480. **Marina** (110 inc 20 Ⓥ; max LOA 15m), €1·27 (min charge €12·70), FW, AC, D, 🅾, ♿; **Village** Slip, C, P (cans), ME, V, Bar, R, ✉.

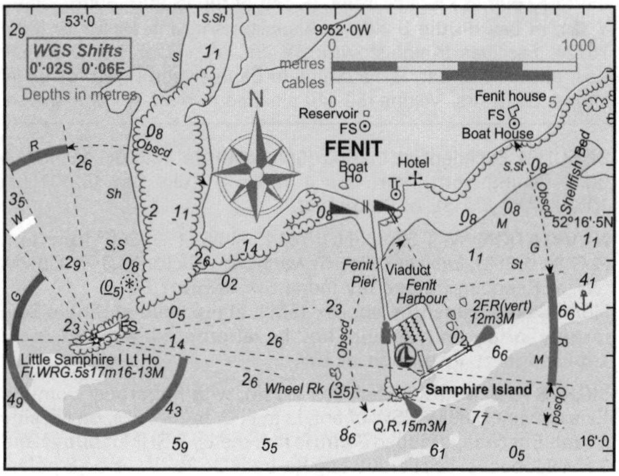

SHANNON ESTUARY *9.12.30*

Clare (N); Kerry and Limerick (S) **52°35'·00N 09°40'·00W**

CHARTS AC 1819, 1547, 1548, 1549, 1540; L. Derg 5080; L. Ree 5078. Imray C55. OS 63, 64. The ICC's *Sailing Directions for S & W Ireland* and/or Admiralty *Irish Coast Pilot* are essential.

TIDES

HW at	**HW Galway**	**HW Dover**
Kilbaha & Carrigaholt	–0015	+0605
Tarbert Island	+0035	–0530
Foynes	+0050	–0515
Limerick	+0130	–0435

At Limerick strong S-W winds increase the height and delay the times of HW; strong N-E winds do the opposite.

SHELTER The Shannon Estuary is 50M long, (Loop Hd to Limerick). For boats on passage N/S the nearest ⚓ is Kilbaha Bay, 3M inside Loop Hd; it has 🅜s sheltered in winds from W to NE, but is exposed to swell and holding is poor. 6M further E, Carrigaholt Bay has 🅜s and good shelter from W'lies; ⚓ just N of the new quay, out of the tide. Kilrush marina (9.12.31) with all facilities is 7M further E. From Kilcredaun Head in the W to the R Fergus ent (about 25M) there are ⚓s or 🅜s, protected from all but E winds, at Tarbert Is, Glin, Labasheeda, Killadysert (pontoon) and among the islands in the Fergus mouth. The best ⚓ in the estuary is at Foynes on the S bank, with also a pontoon off the YC. There are drying quays at Ballylongford Creek (Saleen), Knock and Clarecastle (S of Ennis, off chartlet). Yachts may enter Limerick Dock, but this is a commercial port with usual problems; major improvements planned.

NAVIGATION WPT 52°32'·50N 09°46'·90W, Ballybunnion NCM By VQ, 244°/064° from/to Tail of Beal Bar buoy WCM, Q (9) 15s, 4·2M. For notes on ent and tidal streams see 9.12.5. The ebb can reach 4kn. Thes are new ldg lts, Oc. 5s, 046°25' on Corlis Pt. The lower estuary between Kerry and Loop Heads is 9M wide, narrowing to 2M off Kilcredaun Pt. Here the chan is well buoyed in mid-stream and then follows the Kerry shore, S of Scattery Is. From Tarbert Is to Foynes Is the river narrows to less than 1M in places, before widening where the R Fergus joins from the N, abeam Shannon airport. Above this point the buoyed chan narrows and becomes shallower although there is a minimum of 2m at LWS. AC 1540 is essential for the final 15M stretch to Limerick.

RIVER SHANNON The Shannon, the longest navigable river in the UK or Ireland, is managed by Limerick Hbr Commissioners up to Limerick. Up-stream it effectively becomes an inland waterway; progress is restricted by locks and bridges. Info on navigation and facilities can be obtained from the Waterways Service, Dept of Art, Culture & the Gaeltacht, 51 St Stephen's Green, Dublin 2, ☎ 01-6613111; or from the Inland Waterways Association of Ireland, Kingston House, Ballinteer, Dublin 4, ☎ 01-983392; also from Tourist Offices and inland marinas.

LIGHTS AND MARKS Principal lts are listed in 9.12.4. There are QW (vert) aero hazard lts on tall chimneys at Money Pt power station 3M ESE of Kilrush. 2 chys at Tarbert Is are conspic (R lts).

RADIO TELEPHONE Foynes Ch 12 13 16 (occas). *Shannon Estuary Radio* Ch 12 13 16 (HO).

FACILITIES Marine facilities are available at several communities on the Shannon; M, P & D (cans), FW, V, can be found at many villages. 🅜s are being laid at Labasheeda, Glin Pier (pontoon) and Foynes. E of Aughanish Is on S shore, R Deal is navigable 3M to Askeaton. Ent, marked by RW bn, is 8ca SE of Beeves Rk with 1m in buoyed chan. BY at Massey's Pier ☎ 061-392198, 📠 392344, 🅜s, FW, C, CH, AC, D, Slip. Facilities at Foynes and Limerick include: **Foynes** Slip, L, AB, P & D (cans), FW, ✉, Ⓑ, Dr, V, R, Bar; **Foynes YC** ☎ (069) 65261, AB (pontoon), Bar, R. **Limerick**: **Hbr Commission** ☎ (061) 315377; ⊖ ☎ 415366. **City** Slip, AB, L, FW, P & D (cans), Kos, Gas, Gaz, ME, El, Dr, Ⓗ, ✉, all usual city amenities, ⇌, ✈ (Shannon).

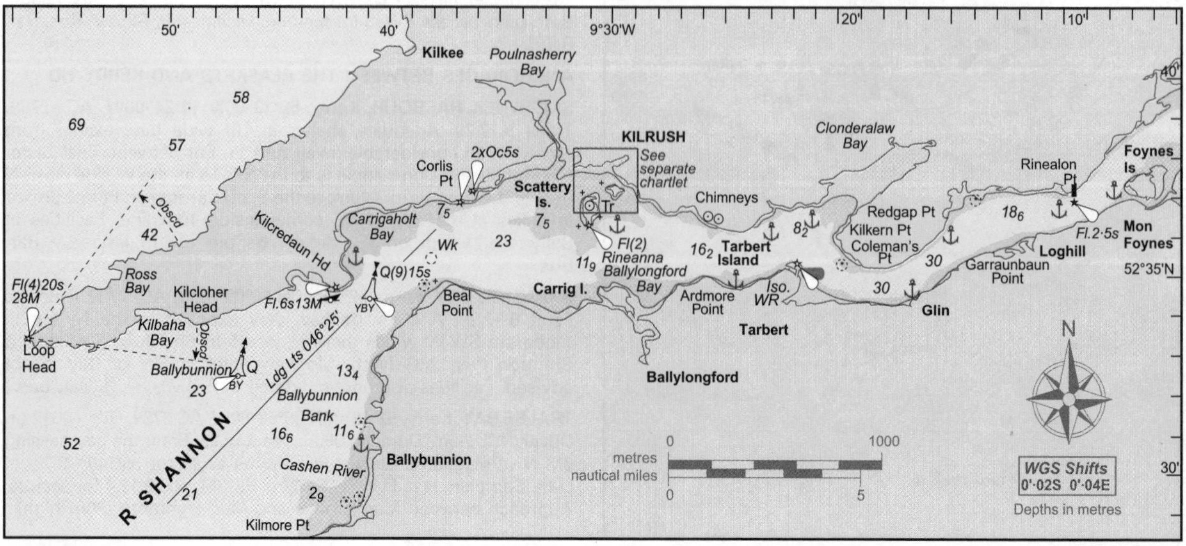

KILRUSH *9.12.31*

Clare **52°37'·90N 09°29'·70W** ❁❁❁◊◊◊✿✿✿

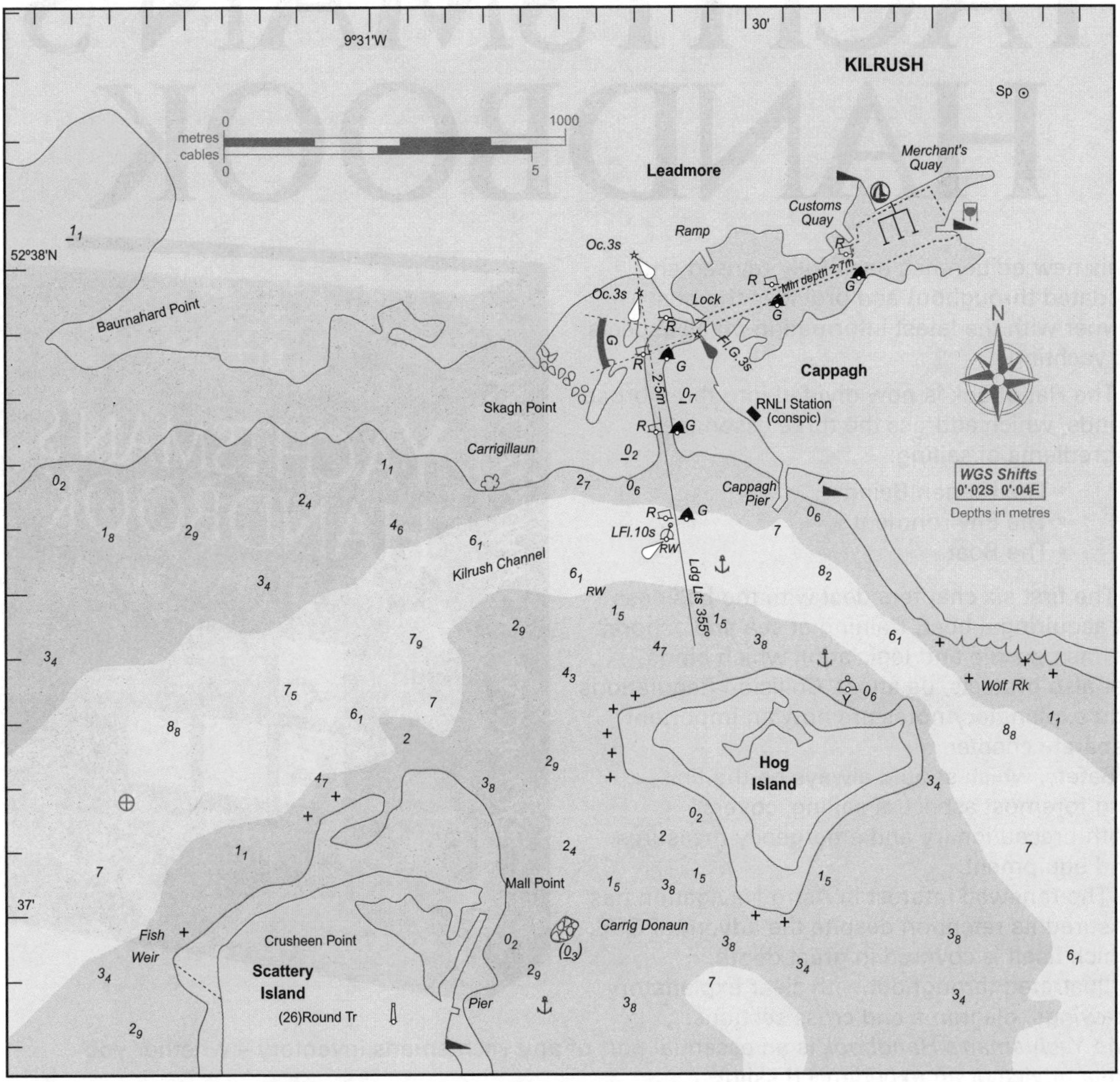

CHARTS AC 1547, 1819; Imray C55; Irish OS 63

TIDES –0555 Dover; ML 2·6; Duration 0610; Zone 0 (UT)

Standard Port GALWAY (⟶)

Times				Height (metres)			
High Water		Low Water		MHWS	MHWN	MLWN	MLWS
1000	0500	0000	0600	5·1	3·9	2·0	0·6
2200	1700	1200	1800				
Differences KILRUSH							
–0006	+0027	+0057	–0016	–0·1	–0·2	–0·3	–0·1

SHELTER Excellent in Kilrush Creek Marina (2·7m), access via lock H24. Day ⚓ in lee of Scattery Is.

NAVIGATION WPT 52°37'·18N 09°31'·64W, 243°/063° from/to SWM buoy, 1·00M. From seaward usual appr is N of Scattery Is (conspic Round Twr, 26m); beware Baurnahard Spit and Carrigillaun to the N. Coming down-river between Hog Is and mainland, beware Wolf Rk.

LIGHTS AND MARKS SWM By L Fl 10s marks ent to buoyed chan (dredged 2·5m), with ldg lts 355°, both Oc 3s, to lock. Fl G 3s 2M, S side of lock.

RADIO TELEPHONE Marina Ch 80.

TELEPHONE (Dial code 06590) Marina 52072 Mobile 087 2313870; Lock 52155; MRCC (066) 9476109; Coast/Cliff Rescue Service 51004; ⊜ (061) 415366; Weather (061) 62677; Police 51017; Dr (065) 51581 also 51470.

FACILITIES Marina (120+50) ☎ 52072, 📠 51692, Lock 52155, €1·52, AC, FW, D, P (cans), Slip, BY, CH, Gas, Gaz, Kos, BH (45 ton), C (26 ton), ME, El, Ⓔ, V; **Town** EC Thurs; El, CH, V, R, Bar, Dr, ✉, Ⓑ, ⇌ (bus to Limerick), ✈ (Shannon).

12

MAPTECH®
Leading the world in digital navigation
Maptech UK Ltd • +44 (0)1243 389352 • sales@maptech.co.uk

Maptech world class digital chart CDs
Worldwide coverage from over 4,500 charts

Maptech award winning software
Easy to use navigation software
• Chart Navigator • Cruising Navigator • Offshore Navigator

www.maptech.co.uk

Area 13

North Ireland
Lambay Island anti-clockwise
to Liscannor Bay

9.13.1 Index .... Page 669

9.13.2 Area map 670

9.13.3 Tidal stream charts 672

9.13.4 Lights, buoys & waypoints 674

9.13.5 Passage information 678

9.13.6 Distance table 680

9.13.7 Special notes for Ireland See *9.12.7*

9.13.8 Carlingford Lough 680
Skerries
Balbriggan
Kilkeel
Annalong
Dundrum Bay

9.13.9 Ardglass 682

9.13.10 Strangford Lough 682
Strangford
Portaferry

9.13.11 Belfast Lough, Standard Port, tidal curves 684
Bangor
Carrickfergus
Portavogie
Donaghadee

9.13.12 Larne 689
Carnlough
Red Bay
Ballycastle
Rathlin Island

9.13.13 Tidal streams off Rathlin Island 691

9.13.14 Portrush 692
Portstewart

9.13.15 River Bann and Coleraine 692

9.13.16 Lough Foyle 693

9.13.17 Lough Swilly 694
Mulroy Bay
Sheep Haven
Gweedore/Bunbeg
Burtonport
Inishkeel
Teelin Harbour

9.13.18 Killybegs 695

9.13.19 Sligo 696
Mullaghmore
Killala Bay

9.13.20 Westport and Clew Bay 697
Broadhaven
Portnafrankagh
Blacksod Bay
Clare Island
Inishturk
Killary Harbour
Ballynakill
Inishboffin
Clifden Bay

9.13.21 Galway Bay, Standard Port, tidal curves 698
Galway Harbour
Aran Islands

Register for your **FREE** weekly weather email service from Macmillan Reeds
» at **www.nauticaldata.com – NOW!** «
weekend weather reports sent to your email address, every Thursday

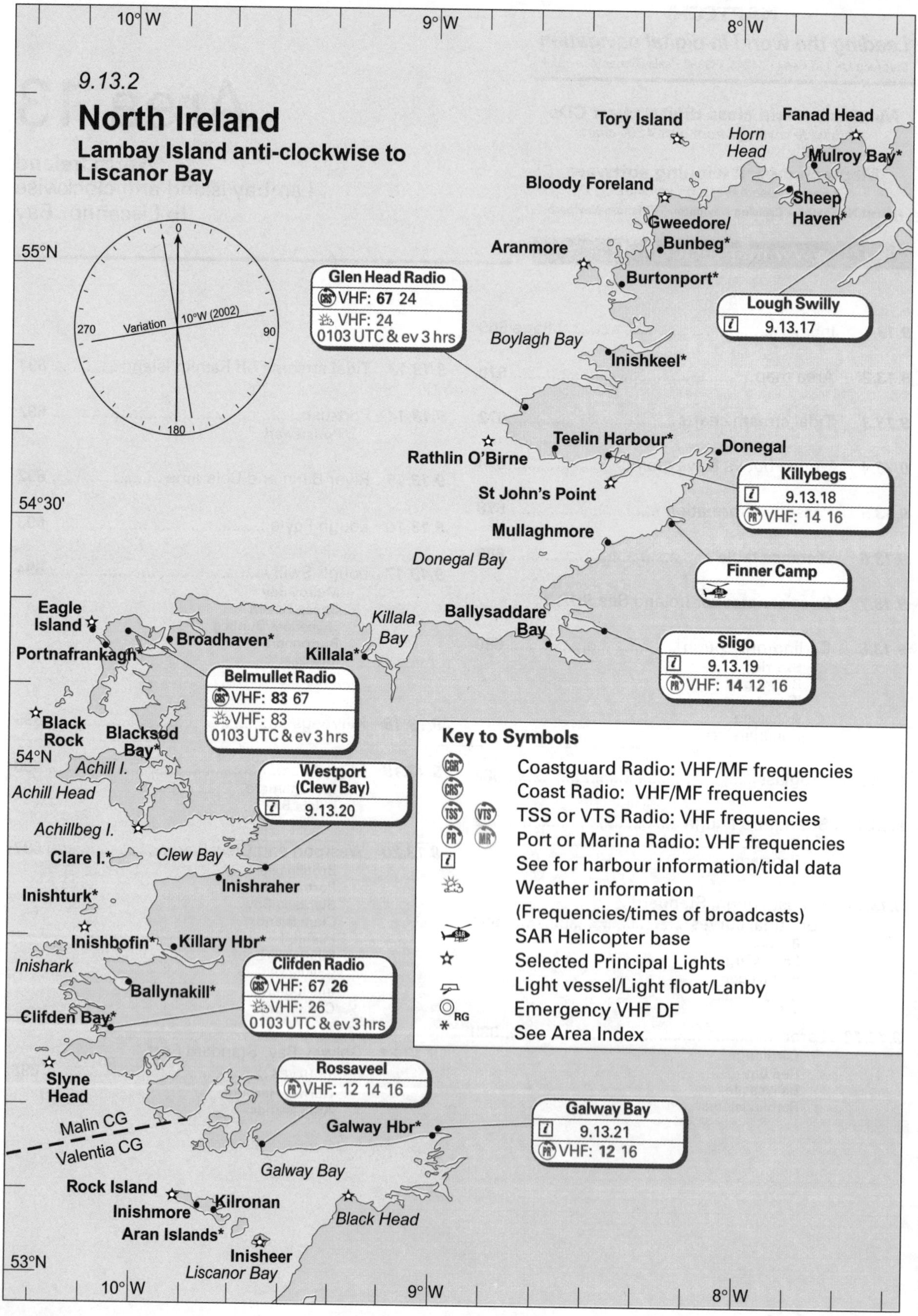
9.13.2
North Ireland
Lambay Island anti-clockwise to Liscanor Bay
10° W
9° W
8° W
55°N
54°30'
54°N
53°N
0
90
180
270
Variation
10°W (2002)
Tory Island
Fanad Head
Horn Head
Mulroy Bay*
Bloody Foreland
Sheep Haven*
Gweedore/ Bunbeg*
Aranmore
Burtonport*
Glen Head Radio
VHF: 67 24
VHF: 24
0103 UTC & ev 3 hrs
Lough Swilly
9.13.17
Boylagh Bay
Inishkeel*
Rathlin O'Birne
Teelin Harbour*
Donegal
Killybegs
9.13.18
VHF: 14 16
St John's Point
Mullaghmore
Donegal Bay
Finner Camp
Eagle Island
Portnafrankagh
Broadhaven*
Killala Bay
Killala*
Ballysaddare Bay
Sligo
9.13.19
VHF: 14 12 16
Belmullet Radio
VHF: 83 67
VHF: 83
0103 UTC & ev 3 hrs
Black Rock
Blacksod Bay*
Achill I.
Achill Head
Westport (Clew Bay)
9.13.20
Achillbeg I.
Clare I.*
Clew Bay
Inishraher
Inishturk*
Inishbofin*
Killary Hbr*
Inishark
Ballynakill*
Clifden Radio
VHF: 67 26
VHF: 26
0103 UTC & ev 3 hrs
Clifden Bay*
Slyne Head
Rossaveel
VHF: 12 14 16
Galway Hbr*
Galway Bay
9.13.21
VHF: 12 16
Malin CG
Valentia CG
Galway Bay
Rock Island
Kilronan
Inishmore
Aran Islands*
Black Head
Inisheer
Liscanor Bay
Key to Symbols
Coastguard Radio: VHF/MF frequencies
Coast Radio: VHF/MF frequencies
TSS or VTS Radio: VHF frequencies
Port or Marina Radio: VHF frequencies
See for harbour information/tidal data
Weather information (Frequencies/times of broadcasts)
SAR Helicopter base
Selected Principal Lights
Light vessel/Light float/Lanby
Emergency VHF DF
See Area Index

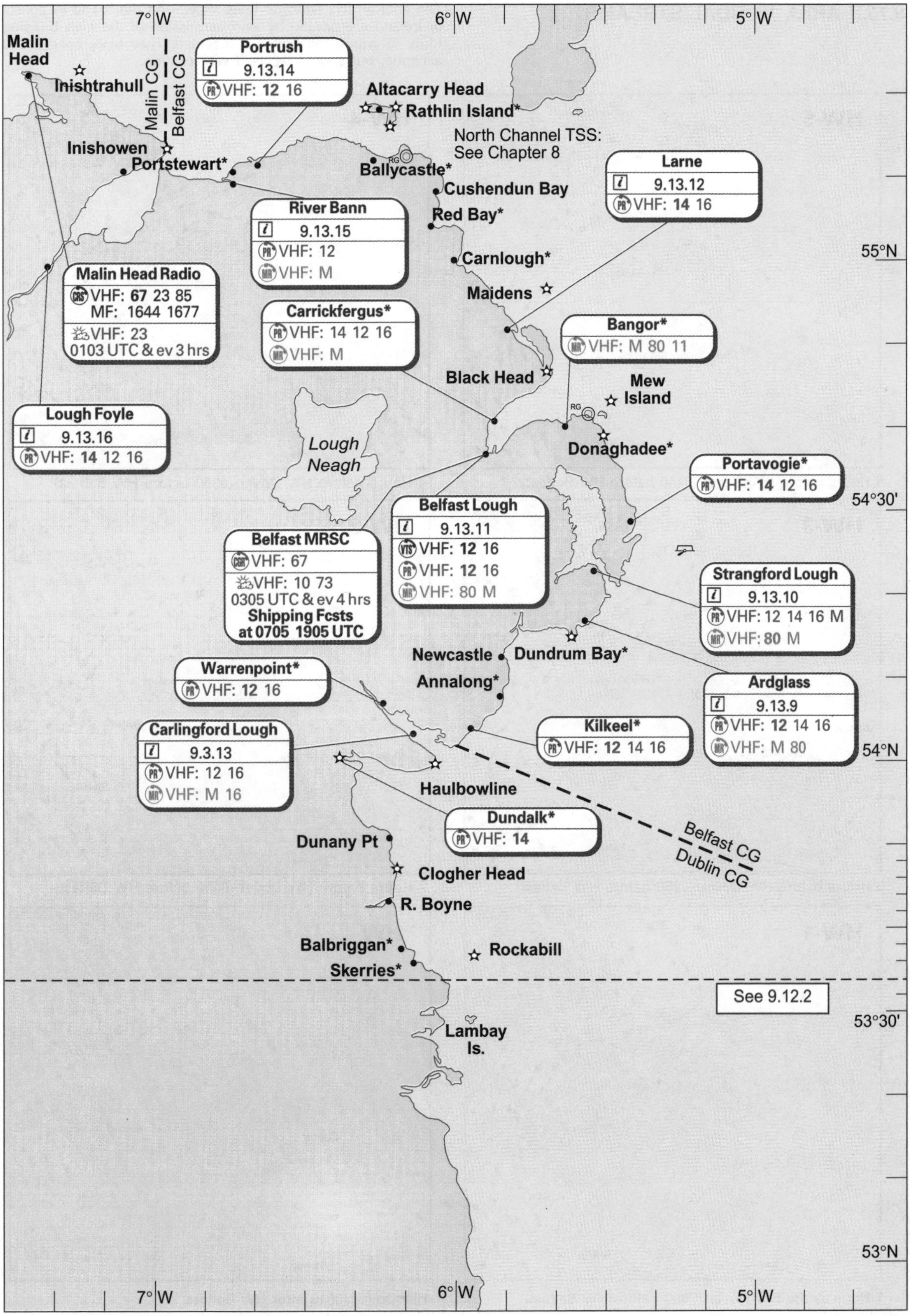
7° W
6° W
5° W
Malin Head
Inishtrahull
Malin CG
Belfast CG
Portrush
9.13.14
VHF: 12 16
Altacarry Head
Rathlin Island*
North Channel TSS: See Chapter 8
Inishowen
Portstewart*
Ballycastle*
Cushendun Bay
Larne
9.13.12
VHF: 14 16
River Bann
9.13.15
VHF: 12
VHF: M
Red Bay*
55°N
Carnlough*
Malin Head Radio
VHF: 67 23 85
MF: 1644 1677
VHF: 23
0103 UTC & ev 3 hrs
Maidens
Carrickfergus*
VHF: 14 12 16
VHF: M
Bangor*
VHF: M 80 11
Black Head
Mew Island
Lough Foyle
9.13.16
VHF: 14 12 16
Lough Neagh
Donaghadee*
Portavogie*
VHF: 14 12 16
54°30'
Belfast Lough
9.13.11
VHF: 12 16
VHF: 12 16
VHF: 80 M
Belfast MRSC
VHF: 67
VHF: 10 73
0305 UTC & ev 4 hrs
Shipping Fcsts at 0705 1905 UTC
Strangford Lough
9.13.10
VHF: 12 14 16 M
VHF: 80 M
Newcastle
Dundrum Bay*
Warrenpoint*
VHF: 12 16
Annalong*
Ardglass
9.13.9
VHF: 12 14 16
VHF: M 80
Carlingford Lough
9.3.13
VHF: 12 16
VHF: M 16
Kilkeel*
VHF: 12 14 16
54°N
Haulbowline
Dundalk*
VHF: 14
Belfast CG
Dublin CG
Dunany Pt
Clogher Head
R. Boyne
Balbriggan*
Rockabill
Skerries*
See 9.12.2
53°30'
Lambay Is.
53°N

13

9.13.3 AREA 13 TIDAL STREAMS

The tidal arrows (with no rates shown) off the S and W coasts of Ireland are printed by kind permission of the Irish Cruising Club, to whom the Editor is indebted. They have been found accurate, but should be used with caution.

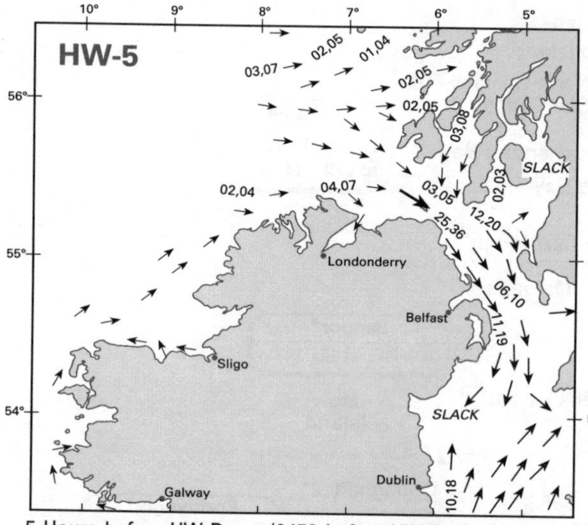

5 Hours before HW Dover (0450 before HW Belfast)

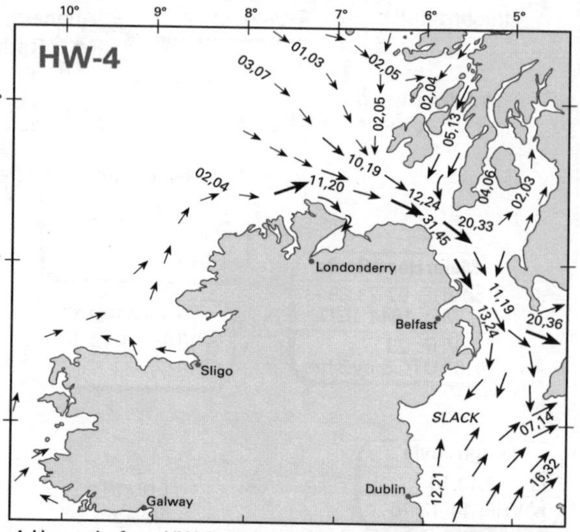

4 Hours before HW Dover (0350 before HW Belfast)

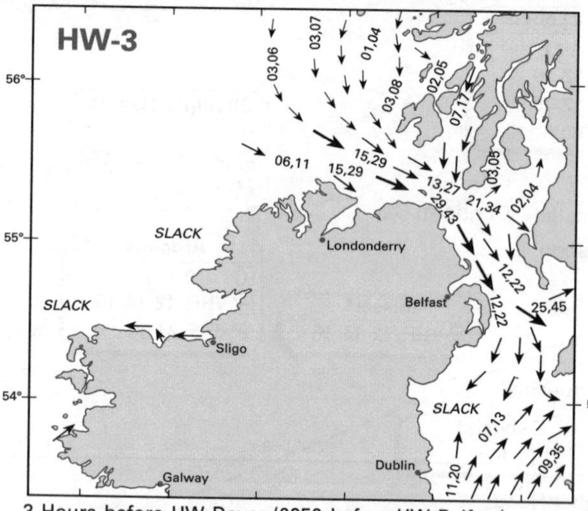

3 Hours before HW Dover (0250 before HW Belfast)

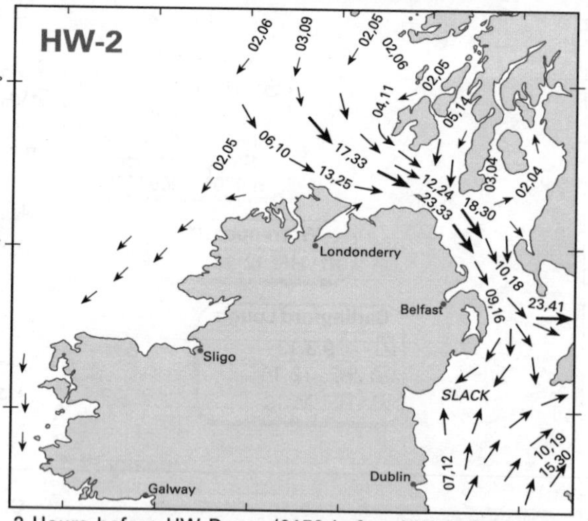

2 Hours before HW Dover (0150 before HW Belfast)

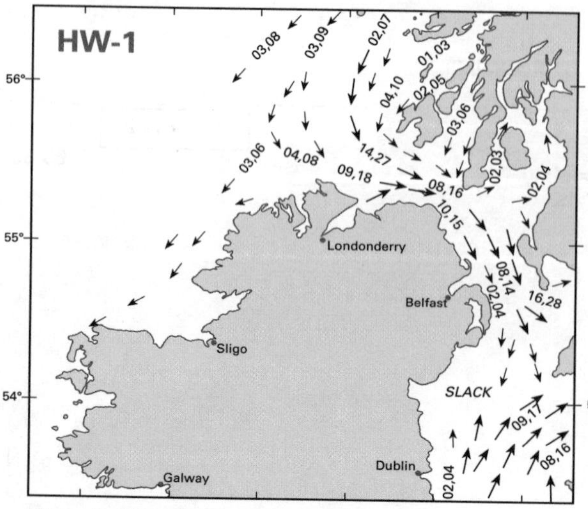

1 Hour before HW Dover (0050 before HW Belfast)

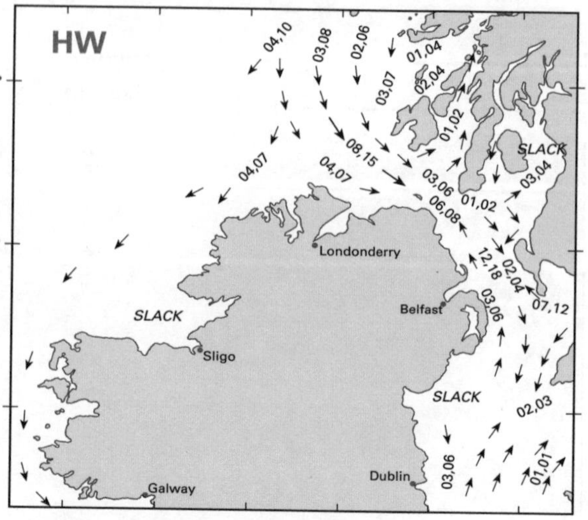

HW Dover (0010 after HW Belfast)

Rathlin Island 9.13.13
Mull of Kintyre 9.9.12
North Irish Sea 9.10.3
SW Scotland 9.9.3
South Ireland 9.12.3

The tidal arrows (with no rates shown) off the S and W coasts of Ireland are printed by kind permission of the Irish Cruising Club, to whom the Editor is indebted. They have been found accurate, but should be used with caution.

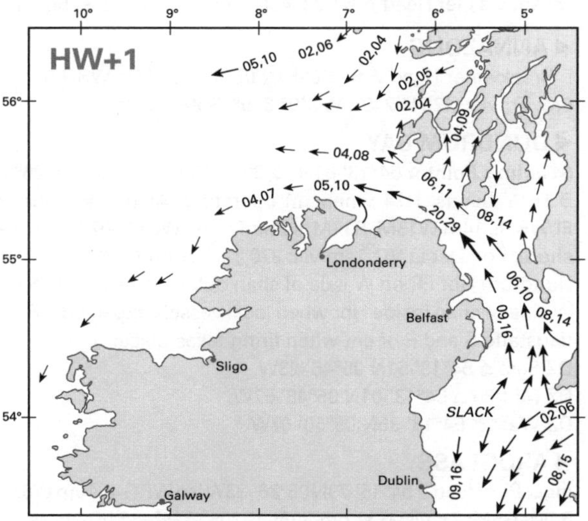

1 Hour after HW Dover (0110 after HW Belfast)

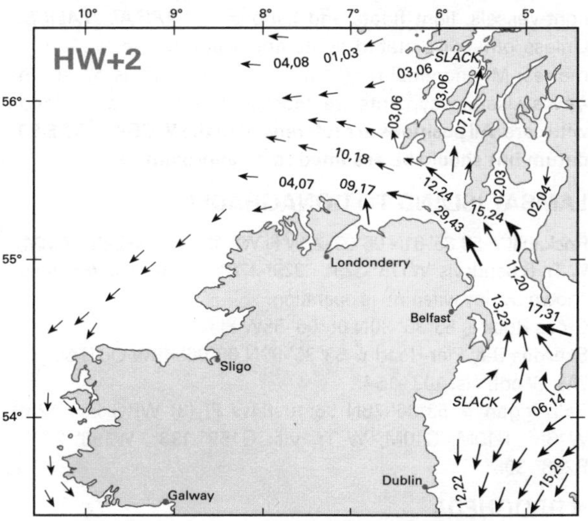

2 Hours after HW Dover (0210 after HW Belfast)

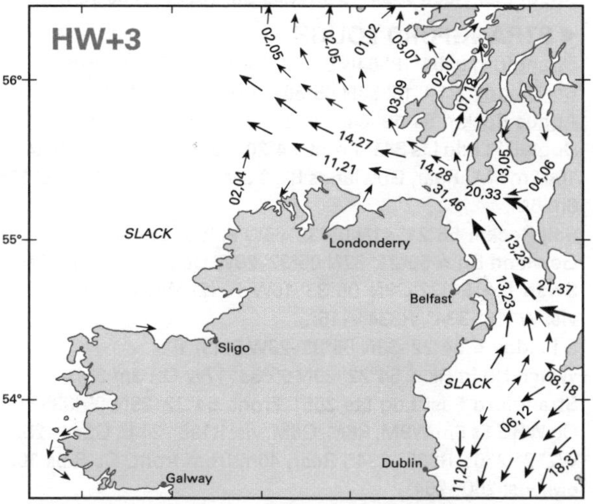

3 Hours after HW Dover (0310 after HW Belfast)

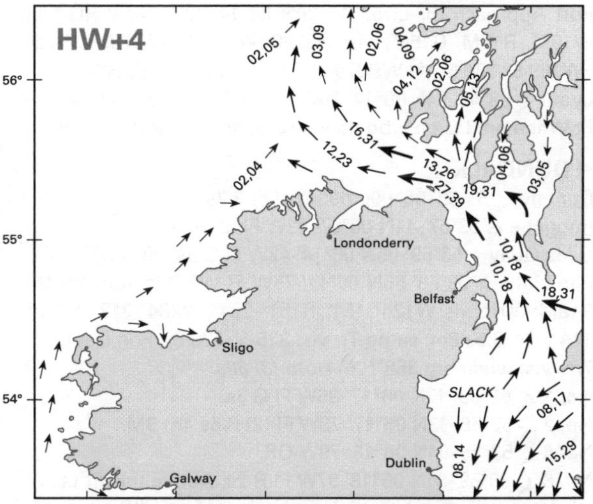

4 Hours after HW Dover (0410 after HW Belfast)

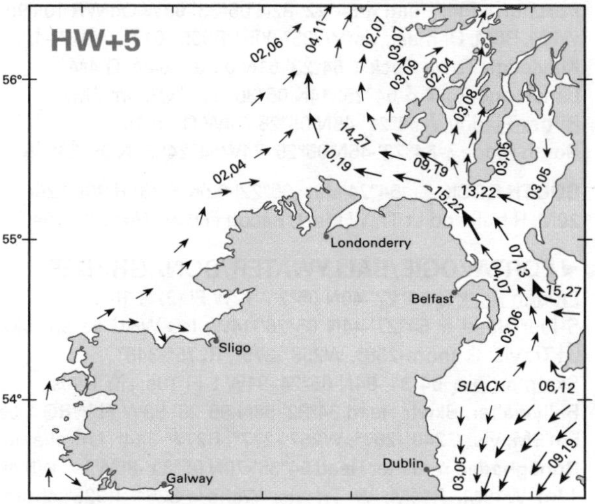

5 Hours after HW Dover (0510 after HW Belfast)

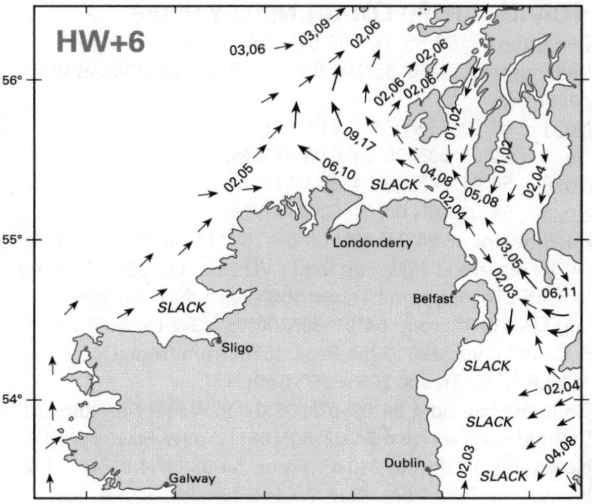

6 Hours after HW Dover (0610 after HW Belfast)

9.13.4 LIGHTS, BUOYS AND WAYPOINTS

Abbreviations used below are given in the Introduction. Principal lights ☆ are in **bold** print, places in CAPITALS, and light-vessels, light floats and Lanbys in *CAPITAL ITALICS*. Unless otherwise stated lights are white. m – elevation in metres; M – nominal range in miles. Fog signals are in *italics*. Useful waypoints are underlined – use those on land with care. **All positions are referenced to the WGS84/ETRS 89 datum but should be assumed to be approximate.**

LAMBAY ISLAND TO DONAGHADEE

Rockabill ☆ 53°35'·81N 06°00'·27W Fl WR 12s 45m **W22M, R18M**; W Tr, B band; vis: W178°-329°, R329°-178°; *Horn (4) 60s.* Also shown by day when it is operating.

Cross Rock 53°35'·30N 06°06'·55W Fl R 10s.

Skerries Bay Pier Head ☆ 53°35'·09N 06°06'·49W Oc R 6s 7m 7M; W col; vis: 103°-154°.

Balbriggan ☆ 53°36'·76N 06°10'·84W Fl (3) WRG 20s 12m W13M, R10M, G10M; W Tr; vis: G159°-193°, W193°-288°, R288°-305°.

◄ DROGHEDA

Aleria 53°43'·35N 06°14'·33W QG 18m 3M.

Port Approach Dir Lt 53°43'·30N 06°14'·73W Dir WRG 10m W19M, R15M, G15M; vis: FG268°-269°, Al WG269°-269·5°, FW269·5°-270·5°, Al WR270·5°-271°, FR271°-272°; H24.

Lyons 53°43'·24N 06°14'·26W Fl (3) R 5s 10m 3M. Above this Pt When ent Lts on stbd hand are G, and on port hand R.

◄ DUNDALK

Dunany 53°53'·56N 06°09'·47W Fl R 3s.

Imogene 53°57'·41N 06°07'·02W Fl (2) R 10s.

Giles Quay ☆ 53°59'·05N 06°14'·42W Fl G 3s; vis: 030°-210°.

Pile Light ☆ 53°58'·55N 06°17'·75W Fl WR 15s 10m **W21M, R18M**; W Ho; vis: W124°-151°, R151°-284°, W284°-313°, R313°-124°. Oc G 5s 8m; same Tr; vis: 325·5°-328·5°; Fog Det Lt VQ 7m, vis: when brg 358°; *Horn (3) 60s.*

No. 1 53°58'·17N 06°17'·36W Fl G 3s.

No. 2 53°58'·33N 06°17'·73W Fl (2) R 5s 4m 3M.

No. 6 53°58'·04N 06°18'·70W QR.

No. 8 53°59'·31N 06°18'·97W Fl R 2s. Above this Pt Lts on stbd hand when ent are QG, and on port hand QR.

◄ CARLINGFORD LOUGH/NEWRY RIVER

Carlingford 53°58'·76N 06°01'·13W L Fl 10s; *Whis.*

Hellyhunter 54°00'·35N 06°02'·06W Q (6) + L Fl 15s; *Whis;* Racon (K).

No. 1 54°00'·73N 06°03'·41W Fl (3) G 6s.

No. 4 54°01'·08N 06°04'·07W Fl R 4s.

No. 6 54°01'·24N 06°04'·39W Fl R 2s.

No. 5 54°01'·38N 06°04'·50W Fl R 2s.

Haulbowline ☆ 54°01'·19N 06°04'·75W Fl (3) 10s 32m **17M**; Gy Tr; reserve Lt 15M; Fog Det Lt VQ 26m; vis: 330°. Turning Lt ☆ FR 21m 9M; same Tr; vis: 196°-208°; *Horn 30s.*

Ldg Lts 310·4° Front, 54°01'·80N 06°05'·43W Oc 3s 7m 11M; R △ on Tr; vis: 295°-325°. Rear, 457m from front, Oc 3s 12m 11M; R ▽ on Tr; vis: 295°-325°; both H24.

Greenore Pier Hd ☆ 54°02'·07N 06°07'·97W Fl R 7·5s 10m 5M.

Carlingford Quay Hd ☆ 54°02'·60N 06°11'·09W Fl G 3s 5m 3M.

Newry River Ldg Lts 310·4°. Front, 54°06'·37N 06°16'·51W. Rear, 274m from front. Both Iso 4s 5/15m 2M; stone cols.

Warren Pt Bkwtr Hd ☆ 54°05'·79N 06°15'·26W Fl G 3s 6m 3M.

◄ KILKEEL

Pier Head ☆ 54°03'·46N 05°59'·30W Fl WR 2s 8m 8M; vis: R296°-313°, W313°-017°.

Meeney's Pier Head ☆ 54°03'·48N 05°59'·31W Fl G 3s 6m 2M.

◄ ANNALONG

E Breakwater Head ☆ 54°06'·51N 05°53'·73W Oc WRG 5s 8m 9M; Tr; vis: G204°-249°, W249°-309°, R309°-024°.

◄ DUNDRUM BAY

St John's Point ☆ 54°13'·61N 05°39'·30W Q (2) 7·5s 37m **25M**; B Tr, Y bands; H24 when it is operating. **Auxiliary Light** ☆ Fl WR 3s 14m **W15M**, R11M; same Tr, vis: W064°-078°, R078°-shore; Fog Det Lt VQ 14m vis: 270°; *Horn (2) 60s.*

Dundrum Hbr FR on W side of chan outside Hbr and 3 FR on W side of chan inside Hbr when local vessels expected. FR on flagstaffs S and E of ent when firing takes place.

DZ East 54°13'·51N 05°46'·23W.

DZ Middle 54°13'·01N 05°48'·57W.

DZ West 54°13'·35N 05°50'·07W.

◄ ARDGLASS

Inner Pier Head ☆ 54°15'·79N 05°36'·33W Iso WRG 4s 10m W8M, R7M, G5M; Tr; vis: G shore-308°, W308°-314°, R314°-shore.

South Pier Head ☆ 54°15'·67N 05°36'·16W Fl R 3s 10m 5M.

◄ STRANGFORD LOUGH

Strangford 54°18'·64N 05°28'·70W L Fl 10s; *Whis.*

Bar Pladdy 54°19'·33N 05°30'·51W Q (6) + L Fl 15s.

Angus Rock ☆ 54°19'·84N 05°31'·56W Fl R 5s 15m 6M.

Dogtail Pt Ldg Lts 341° Front, 54°20'·79N 05°31'·83W Oc (4) G 10s 2m 5M. Rear, Gowlands Rk, 0·8M from front, Oc (4) G 10s 6m 5M.

Salt Rock ☆ 56°21'·41N 05°32'·66W Fl R 3s 8m 3M.

Gowland Bn ☆ 56°21'·57N 05°32'·29W Oc (2) G 10s 6m 5M.

Swan I ☆ 54°22'·38N 05°33'·16W Fl (2) WR 6s 5m; W col; vis: W115°-334°, R334°-115°.

S Pladdy ☆ 54°22'·33N 05°33'·23W Fl (3) 10s.

Watch Ho Pt Rk ☆ 54°22'·29N 05°33'·17W QR 3m 3M.

Strangford East Ldg Lts 256°. Front, 54°22'·29N 05°33'·27W Oc WRG 5s 6m W9M, R6M, G6M: vis: R190°-244°, G244°-252°, W252°-260°, R260°-294°. Rear, 46m from front, Oc R 5s 10m 6M; vis: 250°-264°.

Church Point Bn 54°22'·59N 05°33'·40W Fl (4) R 10s.

Portaferry Pier Head ☆ 54°22'·82N 05°33'·03W Oc WR 10s 9m W9M, R6M; Or mast; vis: W335°-005°, R005°-017°, W017°-128°.

Killyleagh Town Rock 54°23'·61N 05°38'·54W Q 4M.

Limestone Rock ☆ 54°25'·14N 05°36'·11W QR 3m 3M.

Butter Pladdy 54°22'·45N 05°25'·74W Q (3) 10s.

South Ridge 54°22'·45N 05°25'·74W54°24'·37N 05°23'·15W.

SOUTH ROCK 54°24'·49N 05°22'·02W Fl (3) R 30s 12m **20M**; R hull and Lt Tr, W Mast; Racon (T); *Horn (3) 45s.*

◄ PORTAVOGIE/BALLYWATER/DONAGHADEE

Plough Rock 54°27'·40N 05°25'·12W Fl (2) R 10s.

S Pier Head ☆ 54°27'·44N 05°26'·14W, Iso WRG 5s 9m 9M; □ Tr; vis: G shore-258°, W258°-275°, R275°-348°.

Skulmartin 54°31'·84N 05°24'·91W L Fl 10s; *Whis.*

Ballywalter, Bkwtr Head 54°32'·68N 05°28'·83W Fl WRG 1·5s 5m 9M; vis: G240°-267°, W267°-277°, R277°-314°. Unreliable.

Donaghadee ☆, S Pier Head 54°38'·70N 05°31'·86W Iso WR 4s 17m **W18M**, R14M; W Tr; vis: Wshore-326°, R326°-shore; *Siren 12s.*

DONAGHADEE TO RATHLIN ISLAND

Governor Rocks 54°39'·36N 05°31'·99W Fl R 3s.
Deputy Reefs 54°39'·51N 05°31'·94W Fl G 2s.
Foreland Spit 54°39'·64N 05°32'·31W Fl R 6s.
Ninion Bushes 54°41'·08N 05°30'·48W.

◀ BELFAST LOUGH

Mew I ☆ NE end 54°41'·91N 05°30'·81W Fl (4) 30s 37m; B Tr, W band; Racon (O).
S Briggs 54°41'·19N 05°35'·74W Fl (2) R 10s.

◀ BANGOR

N Pier Head ☆ 54°40'·03N 05°40'·33W Iso R 12s 9m14M.
Dir Lt 105°. 54°39'·98N 05°40'·15W Dir Oc 10s WRG 1M; vis: G093°-104·8°, W104·8°-105·2°, R105·2°-117°.
Marina ent ☆ 54°39'·97N 05°40'·29W Fl G 3s 5m 1M.
Belfast Fairway 54°41'·70N 05°46'·23W L Fl 10s; *Horn (1) 16s*; Racon (G).
Cloghan Jetty 54°44'·10N 05°41'·60W QG.
Kilroot power station intake ☆ 54°43'·20N 05°45'·88W Oc G 4s; 2 QR on chy 500m N.

◀ CARRICKFERGUS

E Pier Head ☆ 54°42'·63N 05°48'·37W Fl G 7·5s 5m 4M; G col.
Marina E Bkwtr Head ☆ 54°42'·58N 05°48'·69W QG 8m 3M.
W Breakwater ☆ 54°42'·58N 05°48'·78W QR 7m 3M; R □ pillar.
Pier Head ☆ 54°42'·58N 05°48'·78W F WRG 5m 3M; vis: G308°-317·5°, W317·5°-322·5°, R322·5°-332°.
Black Hd ☆ 54°45'·99N 05°41'·35W Fl 3s 45m 27M; W 8-sided Tr.
N Hunter Rock 54°53'·04N 05°45'·13W Q.
S Hunter Rock 54°52'·69N 05°45'·30W Q (6) + L Fl 15s.

◀ LARNE

Barr Point ☆ 54°51'·50N 05°46'·81W; Horn 30s. Fog Det Lt VQ.
Larne No. 1 54°51'·62N 05°47'·69W Q (3) 10s.
Larne No. 3 54°51'·27N 05°47'·64W Fl (2) G 6s.
Larne No. 5 54°50'·48N 05°47'·74W QG.
Larne No. 7 54°50'·46N 05°47'·46W QG.
Chaine Tr ☆ 54°51'·27N 05°47'·90W Iso WR 5s 23m 16M; Gy Tr; vis: W230°-240°, R240°-shore.
Larne No. 2 54°51'·07N 05°47'·55W Fl R 3s.
Ent Ldg Lts 184°, No. 11 Front, 54°49'·60N 05°47'·81W Oc 4s 6m 12M; W 2 with R stripe on R pile structure; vis: 179°-189°. No. 12 Rear, 610m from front, Oc 4s 14m 12M; W 2 with R stripe on R □ Tr; synch with front, vis: 179°-189°.
Maidens ☆ 54°55'·73N 05°43'·67W Fl (3) 20s 29m 24M; W Tr, B band; Racon (M). Auxiliary Lt Fl R 5s 15m 8M; same Tr; vis:142°-182° over Russel and Highland Rks.

◀ CARNLOUGH/RED BAY

Carnlough Hbr N Pier ☆ 54°59'·59N 05°59'·29W Fl G 3s 4m 5M.
Red Bay Pier ☆ 55°03'·93N 06°03'·21W Fl 3s 10m 5M.

RATHLIN ISLAND TO INISHTRAHULL

◀ RATHLIN ISLAND

Rue Point ☆ 55°15'·53N 06°11'·47W Fl (2) 5s 16m 14M; W 8-sided Tr, B bands.
Drake Wreck 55°17'·00N 06°12'·48W Q (6) + L Fl 15s.
Altacarry Head Rathlin East ☆ 55°18'·06N 06°10'·30W Fl (4) 20s 74m **26M**; W Tr, B band; vis: 110°-006° and 036°-058°; Racon (G).
Rathlin W 0·5M NE of Bull Pt ☆ 55°18'·05N 06°16'·82W Fl R 5s 62m **22M**; W Tr, lantern at base; vis: 015°-225°; H24.
Manor House ☆ 55°17'·52N 06°11'·73W Oc WRG 4s 5M; vis: G020°-023°, W023°-026°, R026°-029°.
Rathlin Hbr Bkwtr ☆ 55°17'·5N 06°11'·8W Fl (3) G 6s 6m 6M.
Rathlin Hbr S Breakwater ☆ 55°17'·5N 06°11'·72W Fl (2) R 4s 5m 1M: vis: 130°-062°

◀ PORTRUSH

N Pier Hd ☆ 55°12'·34N 06°39'·58W Fl R 3s 6m 3M; vis: 220°-160°.
Portstewart Point ☆ 55°11'·33N 06°43'·26W Oc R 10s 21m 5M; R □ hut; vis: 040°-220°.

◀ RIVER BANN/COLERAINE

Ldg Lts 165°. Front, 55°09'·96N 06°46'·23W Oc 5s 6m 2M; W Tr. Rear, 245m from front, Oc 5s 14m 2M; W □ Tr. River Bann marked by Fl G on stbd hand, and Fl R on port.
W Mole ☆ 56°10'·25N 06°46'·45W Fl G 5s 4m 2M; Gy mast; vis: 170°-000°.
Foyle 55°15'·32N 06°52'·60W L Fl 10s; *Whis.*
Tuns 55°14'·00N 06°53'·52W Fl R 3s.
Inishowen ☆ 55°13'·56N 06°55'·75W Fl (2) WRG 10s 28m **W18M**, R14M, G14M; W Tr, 2 B bands; vis: G197°-211°, W211°-249°, R249°-000°; *Horn (2) 30s.* Fog Det Lt VQ 16m vis: 270°.

◀ LOUGH FOYLE

Greencastle Ldg Lts 032°. Front, 55°12'·17N 06°59'·13W Fl 3s 11m 2M; Or ◇ on mast. Rear, 50m from front, Fl 3s 13m 2M; Or ◇ on mast. F WR 10m; vis: R072°-082°, W082°-072°. FWR 5m; vis: R037°-052°, W052°-037°.
Warren Point Lt Bn Tr ☆ 55°12'·58N 06°57'·14W Fl 1·5s 9m 10M; Tr, G abutment; vis: 232°-061°.
Magilligan Point ☆ 55°11'·73N 06°58'·06W QR 7m 10M; R structure. FR, 700m SE, when firing taking place.
McKinney's Bank 55°10'·92N 07°00'·58W Fl R 5s 6m 4M; R pile structure.
Moville 55°10'·98N 07°02'·13W Fl WR 2·5s 11m 4M; W house on G piles vis: W240°-064°, R064°-240°.
Above this point the channel to R.Foyle is marked by Lts Fl G, when entering, on stbd hand, and Fl R on port hand. G Lts are shown from W structures on G or B piles; R Lts from W structures on R piles.
Kilderry 55°04'·10N 07°14'·03W Fl G 2s 4m 3M; 3 G △.
Muff 55°03'·62N 07°14'·28W Fl G 2s 4m 3M; G structure.
Coneyburrow 55°03'·32N 07°14'·49W QG 4m 3M.
Faughan 55°03'·12N 07°14'·50W Fl R 4s 5m 3M.
Culmore Pt ☆ 55°02'·77N 07°15'·22W Q 6m 3M; G ○ Tr.
Culmore Bay 55°02'·71N 07°15'·70W QG.
Ballynagard 55°02'·27N 07°16'·43W Fl 3s 6m 3M; W lantern on G □ house.
Otter Bank 55°01'·94N 07°16'·71W Fl R 4s 6m 3M; W structure on R □ Tr.
Brook Hall ☆ 55°01'·69N 07°17'·11W QG 6m 3M.
Mountjoy ☆ 55°01'·25N 07°17'·54W QR 5m 3M.
Inishtrahull ☆ 55°25'·85N 07°14'·64W Fl (3) 15s 59m **19M**; W Tr; Racon (T).

INISHTRAHULL TO BLOODY FORELAND

◀ LOUGH SWILLY/BUNCRANA/RATHMULLAN

Fanad Head ☆ 55°16'·57N 07°37'·91W Fl (5) WR 20s 39m **W18M**, R14M; W Tr; vis R100°-110°, W110°-313°, R313°-345°, W345°-100°. FR on radio mast 3·08M 200°.
Swilly More 55°15'·11N 07°35'·79W Fl G 3s.
Dunree ☆ 55°11'·88N 07°33'·25W Fl (2) WR 5s 46m W12M, R9M; vis: R320°-328°, W328°-183°, R183°-196°.

Colpagh 55°10'·42N 07°31'·55W Fl R 6s.
White Strand Rocks 55°09'·06N 07°29'·95W Fl R 10s.
Buncrana Pier near Head ☆ 55°07'·61N 07°27'·87W Iso WR 4s 8m W14M, R11M; vis: R shore-052° over Inch spit, W052°-139°, R139°-shore over White Strand Rock.
Rathmullan Pier Head ☆ 55°05'·70N 07°31'·66W Fl G 3s 5M; vis: 206°-345°.

◀ MULROY BAY

Limeburner 55°18'·54N 07°48'·40W Q Fl; *Whis.*
Ravedy Island ☆ 55°15'·14N 07°46'·90W Fl 3s 9m 3M; Tr; vis: 177°-357°.
Dundooan Rocks ☆ 55°13'·13N 07°47'·98W QG 4m 1M; G Tr.
Crannoge Point 55°12'·28N 07°48'·43W Fl G 5s 5m 2M; G Tr.

◀ SHEEPHAVEN

Downies Bay Pier Head ☆ 55°11'·35N 07°50'·51W Fl R 3s 5m 2M; vis: 283° through N till obsc by Downies Pt.
Portnablahy Ldg Lts 125·3°. Front 55°10'·79N 07°55'·65W Oc 6s 7m 2M; B col, W bands. Rear, 81m from front, Oc 6s 12m 2M; B col, W bands.
Tory Island ☆ 55°16'·36N 08°14'·97W Fl (4) 30s 40m **27M**; B Tr, W band; vis: 302°-277°; Racon (M); H24.
Inishbofin Pier ☆ 55°10'·08N 08°10·57W Fl 8s 3m 3M; part obsc.
Ballyness Hbr. Ldg Lts 119·5°. Front, 55°09'·06N 08°06'·98W Iso 4s 25m 1M. Rear, 61m from front, Iso 4s 26m 1M.
Bloody Foreland ☆ 55°09'·51N 08°17'·03W Fl WG 7·5s 14m W6M, G4M; vis: W062°-232°, G232°-062°.

BLOODY FORELAND TO RATHLIN O'BIRNE

Glassagh. Ldg Lts 137·4°. Front, 55°06'·83N 08°18'·97W Oc 8s 12m 3M. Rear, 46m from front, Oc 8s 17m 3M; synch.
Inishsirrer, NW end ☆ 55°07'·40N 08°20'·93W Fl 3·7s 20m 4M; W □ Tr vis: 083°-263°.

◀ BUNBEG/MULLAGHDOO/OWEY SOUND

Gola I Ldg Lts 171·2°. Front, 55°05'·11N 08°21'·07W Oc 3s 9m 2M; W Bn, B band. Rear, 86m from front, Oc 3s 13m 2M; B Bn, W band; synch with front.
Middle Rock 55°04'·50N 08°21'·02W Fl R 3s.
Gola Spit 55°04'·92N 08°20'·39W Fl (2) R 6s.
Bo I East Point 55°04'·78N 08°20'·15W Fl G 3s 3m; G Bn.
Inishinny No. 1 ☆ 55°04'·47N 08°19'·84W QG 3m 1M; G □ col.
Carrickbullog No. 2 ☆ 55°04'·38N 08°19'·60W QR.
Inishcoole No. 4 ☆ 55°03'·91N 08°18'·91W QR 4m 2M; R □ col.
Yellow Rks No. 6 ☆ 55°03'·66N 08°18'·95W QR 3m 1M; □ col with steps; Neon.
Cruit I. Owey Sound Ldg Lts 068·3°. Front, 55°03'·06N 08°25'·85W Oc 10s. Rear, 107m from front, Oc 10s.
Rinnalea Point ☆ 55°02'·59N 08°23'·72W Fl 7·5s 19m 9M; □ Tr; vis: 132°-167°.

Aranmore, Rinrawros Pt ☆ 55°00'·00N 08°33'·66W Fl (2) 20s 71m **29M**; W Tr; obsc by land about 234°-007° and about 013°. Auxiliary Lt Fl R 3s 61m 13M, same Tr; vis: 203°-234°.

◀ NORTH SOUND OF ARAN/RUTLAND NORTH CHANNEL

Ldg Lts 186°. Front, 54°58'·94N 08°29'·27W Oc 8s 8m 3M; B Bn, W band. Rear, 395m from front, Oc 8s 17m 3M; B Bn.
Ballagh Rocks ☆ 54°59'·96N 08°28'·86W Fl 2·5s 13m 5M.
Black Rocks ☆ 54°59'·43N 08°29'·63W Fl R 3s 3m 1M; R col.
Inishcoo Ldg Lts 119·3°. Front, 54°59'·12N 08°27'·74W Iso 6s 6m 1M; W Bn, B band. Rear, 248m from front, Iso 6s 11m 1M.
Carrickatine No. 2 Bn ☆ 54°59'·26N 08°28'·06W QR 6m 1M.
Rutland I Ldg Lts 137·6°. Front, 54°58'·97N 08°27'·68W Oc 6s 8m 1M; W Bn, B band. Rear, 330m from front, Oc 6s 14m 1M.

◀ BURTONPORT

Ldg Lts 068·1°. Front 54°58'·95N 08°26'·40W FG 17m 1M; Gy Bn, W band. Rear, 355m from front, FG 23m 1M; Gy Bn, Y band.

◀ SOUTH SOUND OF ARAN/RUTLAND SOUTH CHANNEL

Illancrone I ☆ 54°56'·27N 08°28'·57W Fl 5s 7m 6M; W □ Tr.
Wyon Point ☆ 54°56'·51N 08°27'·54W Fl (2) WRG 10s 8m W6M, R3M; W □ Tr; vis: G shore-021°, W021°-042°, R042°-121°, W121°-150°, R 150°-shore.
Turk Rocks ☆ 54°57'·30N 08°28'·18W Fl G 5s 6m 2M; G □ Tr.
Aileen Reef ☆ 54°58'·18N 08°28'·82W QR 6m 1M. R □ Bn.
Leac na bhFear ☆ 54°58'·19N 08°29'·22W Q (2) 5s 4m 2M.
Carrickbealatroha, Upper ☆ 54°58'·64N 08°28'·63W Fl 5s 3m 2M; W □ brickwork Tr.
Corren's Rock ☆ 54°58'·11N 08°26'·68W Fl R 3s 4m 2M; R □ Tr.
Teige's Rock ☆ 54°58'·60N 08°26'·81W Fl 3s 4m 2M.
Dawros Hd ☆ 54°49'·62N 08°33'·69W L Fl 10s 39m 4M; W □ col.
Dawros Bay ☆ 54°49'·3N 08°32'W Fl (2) 10s 5m 3M.
Rathlin O'Birne, W side ☆ 54°39'·80N 08°49'·94W Fl WR 15s 35m **W18M**, R14M; W Tr; vis: R195°-307°, W307°-195°; Racon (O).

RATHLIN O'BIRNE TO EAGLE ISLAND

◀ DONEGAL BAY, TEELIN/KILLYBEGS

Teelin Hbr ☆ 54°37'·33N 08°37'·76W Fl R 10s; R structure.
St John's Pt ☆ 54°34'·16N 08°27'·64W Fl 6s 30m 14M; W Tr.
Bullockmore 54°33'·98N 08°30'·14W Qk Fl (9) 15s.
Rotten I ☆ 54°36'·87N 08°26'·43W Fl WR 4s 20m **W15M**, R11M; W Tr; vis: W255°-008°, R008°-039°, W039°-208°.
New Landing Dir Lt 338°. 54°38'·14N 08°26'·38W Dir WRG; vis: G328°°-334°, Al WG334°-336°,W336°-340°, Al WR340°-342°, R342°-348°.
Killybegs Outer 54°37'·92N 08°29'·15W VQ (6) + L Fl 10s.
Killybegs Inner 54°38'·02N 08°26'·09W VQ.
Black Rock Pier ☆ 54°38'·03N 08°26'·59W 2 FR (vert) 7m.
Finner Camp ☆ 54°29'·70N 08°13'·90W Aero Q WRG 67m.

◀ SLIGO

Wheat Rock 54°18'·84N 08°39'·10W Q (6) + LFl 15s.
Black Rock ☆ 54°18'·45N 08°37'·07W Fl 5s 24m 13M; W Tr, B band. Auxiliary Lt Fl R 3s 12m 5M; same Tr; vis: 107°-130° over Wheat and Seal rks.
Lower Rosses, N of Point (Cullaun Bwee) ☆ 54°19'·72N 08°34'·41W Fl (2) WRG 10s 8m W10M, R8M, G8M; W hut on piles; vis: G over Bungar bank-066°, W066°-070°, R070° over Drumcliff bar; shown H24.
Bungar Bank Fl (2) G 5s.
Ldg Lts 125°. Front, Metal Man 54°18'·24N 08°34'·56W Fl 4s 3m 7M. Rear, Oyster I, 365m from front, Oc 4s 13m 10M; H24.

◀ KILLALA

Inishcrone Pier Root ☆ 54°13'·21N 09°05'·79W Fl WRG 1·5s 8m 2M; vis: W098°-116°, G116°-136°, R136°-187°.

Ldg Lts 230°. Rinnaun Point, Front No. 1, 54°13'·53N 09°12'·27W Oc 10s 7m 5M; □ Tr. Rear, 150m from front, No. 2 Oc 10s 12m 5M; □ Tr.

Dir Lt 215°, Inch I, 54°13'·29N 09°12'·30W Fl WRG 2s 6m 3M; □ Tr; vis: G205°-213°, W213°-217°, R217°-225°.

Ldg Lts 196°. Kilroe, Front, 54°12'·63N 09°12'·33W Oc 4s 5m 2M; □ Tr. Rear,120m from front, Oc 4s 10m 2M; □ Tr.

Ldg Lts 236°. Pier, Front, 54°13'·02N 09°12'·84W Iso 2s 5m 2M; W ◇ on Tr. Rear, 200m from front, Iso 2s 7m 2M; W ◇ on pole.

Killala Bay. Bone Rock, NE end ⫯ 54°15'·80N 09°11'·24W Q 7m.

◀ BROAD HAVEN BAY

Gubacashel Point ✩ 54°16'·06N 09°53'·33W Iso WR 4s 27m W12M, R9M; W Tr; vis: W shore (S side of bay)-355°, R355°-shore.

Ballyglass ✩ 54°15'·27N 09°53'·41W Fl G 3s.

EAGLE ISLAND TO SLYNE HEAD

Eagle I, W end ☆ 54°17'·03N 10°05'·54W Fl (3) 10s 67m **23M**; W Tr. Shown H24.

Black Rock ☆ 54°04'·03N 10°19'·25W Fl WR 12s 86m **W22M, R16M**; W Tr; vis: W276°-212°, R212°-276°.

◀ BLACKSOD BAY

Blacksod ⫯ 54°05'·89N 10°03'·01W Q (3) 10s.

Blacksod Pier Root ✩ 54°05'·92N 10°03'·65W Fl (2) WR 7·5s 13m W12M, R9M; W Tr on dwelling; vis: R189°-210°, W210°-018°.

Achill I Ridge Point ✩ 54°01'·78N 09°58'·50W Fl 5s 21m 5M.

◀ ACHILL SOUND

Achill Sound ✩ 53°56'·05N 09°55'·30W QR; R Bn.

Ldg Lts 330° 53°52'·50N 09°56'·91W Whitestone Point, Front and rear both Oc 4s 5/6m; W ◇, B stripe.

Saulia Pier ✩ 53°57'·03N 09°55'·56W Fl G 3s 12m.

Achillbeg E Lt Bn ▭ 53°52'·11N 09°56'·60W Fl R 2s 5m; R □ Tr.

Carrigin-a-tShrutha ✩ 53°52'·28N 09°56'·78W Q (2) R 5s; R Bn.

Achill I Ldg Lts 310° Purteen 53°57'·83N 10°05'·93W (PA) Oc 8s 5m. Rear, 46m from front Oc 8s 6m.

◀ CLEW BAY/WESTPORT

Achillbeg I S Point ☆ 53°51'·51N 09°56'·85W Fl WR 5s 56m **W18M, R18M, R15M**; W □ Tr on □ building; vis: R262°-281°, W281°-342°, R342°-060°, W060°-092°, R(intens) 092°-099°, W099° -118°.

Clare I, E Pier ✩ 53°48'·04N 09°57'·06W Fl R 3s 5m 3M.

Cloughcormick ⫯ 53°50'·56N 09°43'·20W.

Dorinish ▲ 53°49'·48N 09°40'·50W Fl G 3s.

Inishgort S Point ✩ 53°49'·61N 09°40'·25W L Fl 10s 11m 10M; W Tr. Shown H24.

Westport Appr ✩ 53°47'·98N 09°34'·33W Fl 3s.

Roonagh Quay Ldg Lts 144°. Front 53°45'·75N 09°54'·23W. Rear, 54m from front, both Iso 10s 9/15m.

◀ INISHBOFIN/CLIFDEN BAY

Inishlyon Lyon Head ✩ 53°36'·74N 10°09'·56W Fl WR 7·5s 13m W7M, R4M; W post; vis: W036°-058°, R058°-184°, W184°-325°, R325°-036°.

Gun Rock ✩ 53°36'·59N 10°13'·23W Fl (2) 6s 8m 4M; W col; vis: 296°-253°.

Cleggan Point ✩ 53°34'·49N 10°07'·73W Fl (3) WRG 15s 20m W6M, R3M, G3M; W col on W hut; vis: W shore-091°, R091°-124°, G124°-221°.

Carrickrana Rocks Bn 53°29'·24N 10°09'·48W; large W Bn.

Slyne Head, North Tr, Illaunamid ☆ 53°23'·99N 10°14'·07W Fl (2) 15s 35m **24M**; B Tr.

SLYNE HEAD TO BLACK HEAD

Inishnee ✩ 53°22'·75N 09°54'·53W Fl (2) WRG 10s 9m W5M, R3M, G3M; W col on W □ base; vis: G314°-017°, W017°-030°, R030°-080°, W080°-194°.

Croaghnakeela Is ✩ 53°19'·40N 09°58'·21W Fl 3·7s 7m 5M; W col; vis: 034°-045°, 218°-286°, 311°-325°.

◀ GALWAY BAY/INISHMORE

Eeragh, Rock Is ☆ 53°08'·10N 09°51'·39W Fl 15s 35m **23M**; W Tr, two B bands; vis: 297°-262°.

Killeany ▲ 53°07'·26N 09°38'·24W Fl G 3s.

Straw Is ☆ 53°07'·06N 09°37'·85W Fl (2) 5s 11m **15M**; W Tr.

Killeany Ldg Lts 192°. Front, 53°06'·25N 09°39'·74W Oc 5s 6m 3M; W col on W □ base; vis: 142°-197°. Rear, 43m from front, Oc 5s 8m 2M; W col on W □ base; vis: 142°-197°.

Kilronan Pier Head ✩ 53°07'·10N 09°39'·98W Fl WG 1·5s 5m 3M; W col; vis: G240°-326°, W326°-000°.

◀ KIGGAUL BAY

Kiggaul Bay ✩ 53°14'·02N 09°43'·04W Fl WR 3s 5m W5M, R3M; vis: W329°-359°, R359°-059°, part obsc by W shore of bay.

◀ CASHLA BAY/SPIDDLE

Ship Rock ▭ 53°15'·73N 09°34'·28W Fl R 3s.

Lion Rock ▲ 53°15'·79N 09°34'·16W Fl G 3s.

Ent W side ✩ 53°14'·23N 09°35'·20W Fl (3) WR 10s 8m W6M, R3M; W col on concrete structure; vis: W216°-000°, R000°-069°.

Cannon Rock ▲ 53°14'·06N 09°34'·34W Fl G 5s.

Lion Pt Dir Lt 53°15'·83N 09°33'·95W Dir Iso WRG 4s 6m W8M, R6M, G6M; vis: G357·5°-008·5°, W008·5°-011·5°, R011·5°-017·5°.

Rossaveel Pier Ldg Lts 116° Front, 53°16'·02N 09°33'·38W Oc 3s 7m 3M; W mast. Rear, 90m from front, Oc 3s 8m 3M.

Spiddle Pier Head ✩ 53°14'·42N 09°18'·55W Fl WRG 3·5s 11m W6M, R4M, G4M; Y col; vis: G102°-282°, W282°-024°, R024°-066°.

◀ GALWAY

Margaretta Shoal ▲ 53°13'·68N 09°05'·99W Fl G 3s;))) *Whis.*

Black Rock ▭ 53°14'·00N 09°06'·55W Fl R 3s.

Tawin Shoals ▲ 53°14'·30N 09°04'·26W Fl (3) G 10s.

Mutton Is ▭ 53°15'·07N 09°02'·93W Fl (2)R 6s.

Peter Rock ⫯ 53°15'·17N 09°01'·09W.

Leverets ✩ 53°15'·33N 09°01'·90W Q WRG 9m 10M; B □ Tr, W bands; vis: G015°-058°, W058°-065°, R065°-103°, G103°-143·5°, W143·5°-146·5°, R146·5°-015°.

Rinmore ✩ 53°16'·12N 09°01'·97W Iso WRG 4s 7m 5M; W □ Tr; vis: G359°-008°, W008°-018°, R018°-027°.

Nimmo's Pier Head ✩ 53°16'·00N 09°02'·81W Iso Y 6s 7m 6M.

Approach chan Dir Lt. 53°16'·12N 09°02'·83W Dir WRG 7m 3M; vis: FG322·25°-323·75°, AlGW323·75°-324·75°, F324·75°-325·25°, AlRW325·25°-326·25°, FR326·25°-331·25° FlR 331·25°-332·25°.

Black Head ✩ 53°09'·26N 09°15'·83W Fl WR 5s 20m W11M, R8M, W □ Tr; vis: 045°-268°, R268°-276°.

Finnis Rock ⫯ 53°02'·82N 09°29'·14W Q (3) 10s.

Inisheer ☆ 53°02'·79N 09°31'·64W Iso WR 12s 34m **W20M, R16M**; vis: 225°-231°, W231°-245°, R245°-269°, W280°-218°; Racon (K).

13

9.13.5 PASSAGE INFORMATION

For all Irish waters the Sailing Directions published by the Irish Cruising Club are strongly recommended, and particularly on the N and W coasts, where other information is scarce. They are published in 2 volumes: *E and N coasts of Ireland* which runs anti-clockwise from Carnsore Pt to Bloody Foreland, and *S and W coasts of Ireland* which goes clockwise.

CROSSING THE IRISH SEA (charts 1123, 1121, 1411) Passages across the Irish Sea can range from the fairly long haul from Land's End to Cork (140M), to the relatively short hop from Mull of Kintyre to Torr Pt (11M). But such distances are deceptive, because the average cruising yacht needs to depart from and arrive at a reasonably secure hbr; also in the North Chan strong tidal streams can cause heavy overfalls. So each passage needs to be treated on its merits. See 9.0.7 for distances across the Irish Sea.

Many yachts use the Land's End/Cork route on their way to (and from) the delightful cruising ground along the S coast of Ireland, see 9.12.5. Penzance Bay, or one of the Scilly Is anchs, make a convenient place from which to leave, with good lights to assist departure.

Although the Celtic Sea is exposed to the Atlantic, there are no dangers on passage and the tidal streams are weak. A landfall between Ballycotton and Old Hd of Kinsale (both have good lights) presents no offlying dangers, and in poor vis decreasing soundings indicate approach to land. There is a likelihood, outward bound under sail, that the boat will be on the wind – a possible benefit on the return passage. If however the wind serves, and if it is intended to cruise along the southern coast, a landfall at the Fastnet with arrival at (say) Baltimore will place the yacht more to windward, for little extra distance.

From Land's End the other likely destination is Dun Laoghaire. A stop at (say) Milford Haven enables the skipper to select the best time for passing the Smalls or Bishops (see 9.11.5) and roughly divides the total passage into two equal parts. From S Bishop onwards there are the options of making the short crossing to Tuskar Rk and going N inside the banks (theoretically a good idea in strong W winds), or of keeping to seaward. But in bad weather the area off Tuskar is best avoided; apart from the Traffic Separation Scheme, the tide is strong at sp and the sea can be very rough.

The ferry route Holyhead/Dun Laoghaire is another typical crossing, and is relatively straightforward with easy landfalls either end. The tide runs hard round Anglesey at sp, so departure just before slack water minimises the set N or S. Beware also the TSS off The Skerries.

The Isle of Man (9.10.5) is a good centre for cruising in the Irish Sea, and its hbrs provide convenient staging points whether bound N/S or E/W.

CROSSING TO SCOTLAND (charts 2198, 2199, 2724) Between Scotland and Northern Ireland there are several possible routes, but much depends on weather and tide. Time of departure must take full advantage of the stream, and avoid tide races and overfalls (see 9.9.5). Conditions can change quickly, so a flexible plan is needed.

From Belfast Lough ent, the passage distance to Mull of Kintyre is about 35M and, with a departure at HW Dover (also local HW) providing at least 6hrs of N-going tides, fair winds make it possible to get past the Mull or Sanda Is on one tide. But to be more confident of reaching Port Ellen or Gigha Is a departure from Carnlough or Red Bay at HW makes a shorter passage with better stream advantage. The inshore side of the TSS coincides with the outer limit of the race S and SW off the Mull of Kintyre; this occurs between HW Dover +0430 and +0610 when a local S-going stream opposes the main N-going stream (9.9.12).

For information on submarine hazards see 6.13.1

LAMBAY ISLAND TO FAIR HEAD (AC 44, 2093, 2198/9) The coast is fairly steep-to except in larger bays, particularly Dundalk. Streams offshore run up to 2·5kn as far as Rockabill, but are weaker further N until approaching Belfast Lough. Lambay Island is private, and steep-to except on W side, where there can be overfalls. Skerries Islands (Colt, Shenick's and St Patrick's) are 1M E and SE of Red Island, to E of Skerries hbr. Shenick's Island is connected to shore at LW. Pass between Colt and St Patrick's Islands, but the latter has offliers 3ca to S. Rockabill, two steep-to rks with lt ho, is 2·5M E of St Patrick's Island.

Going NE from Carlingford Lough (9.13.8), after rounding Hellyhunter By, there are no offshore dangers until Strangford Lough (9.13.10). For Ardglass, see 9.13.9. N of Strangford keep 5ca off Ballyquintin Pt. 3M to NE are Butter Pladdy Rks; keep to E of these. 2M further N is South Rk, with disused lt ho, part of group of rks to be avoided in poor vis or bad weather by closing South Rk lt float. In good vis pass inshore of South Rk, between it and North Rks (chart 2156), rounding South Ridge PHM buoy.

Three routes lead into Belfast Lough (9.13.11): **a.** E of Mew Is, but beware Ram Race (to the N on the ebb, and the S on the flood); **b.** Copeland Sound, between Mew Is and Copeland Is, is passable but not recommended; **c.** Donaghadee Sound is buoyed and a good short cut for yachts. Here the stream runs SSE from HW Belfast +0530 and NW from HW Belfast −0030, 4·5kn max. An eddy extends S to Ballyferris Pt, and about 1M offshore. For Donaghadee, see chart 3709.

N from Belfast Lough, Black Hd is clean. Pass E of Muck Is, which is steep-to. Hunter Rk (0·8m), 2·5M NE of Larne, is marked by N & S cardinals. 2M further N are the Maidens, two dangerous groups of rks extending 2·5M N/S; E Maiden is lit.

The very small hbr of Carnlough (9.13.12) provides shelter for small yachts, but should not be approached in strong onshore winds. Other anchs in offshore winds are at Red Bay (9.13.12) 5M further N, and in Cushendun B, 5M NNW of Garron Pt. All provide useful anch on passage to/from the Clyde or Western Is. Fair Hd is a bold 190m headland, steep-to all round, but with extensive overfalls in Rathlin Sound.

FAIR HEAD TO BLOODY FORELAND (chart 2723) This is a good cruising area, under the lee of land in SW'lies, but very exposed to NW or N. Beware fishing boats and nets in many places and the North Channel TSS.

A fair tide is essential through Rathlin Sound (9.13.13), as sp rates reach 6kn, with dangerous overfalls. The main stream sets W from HW Dover $+\frac{1}{2}$ for 5 hrs, and E from HW Dover $-5\frac{1}{2}$ for 5 hrs. The worst overfalls are S of Rue Pt (Slough-na-more) from HW Dover $+1\frac{1}{2}$ to $+2\frac{1}{2}$, and it is best to enter W-bound at the end of this period, on the last of fair tide. E-bound enter the Sound at HW Dover −5. Close inshore between Fair Hd and Carrickmannanon Rk a counter eddy runs W from HW Dover −3, and an E-going eddy runs from HW Dover +2 to +3. Pass outside Carrickmannanon Rk (0·3m) and Sheep Is. There are small hbrs in Church Bay (Rathlin Is) and at Ballycastle.

Proceeding to Portrush (9.13.14), use Skerries Sound in good weather. Enter Lough Foyle by either the North Chan W of The Tuns, or S chan passing 2ca N of Magilligan Pt and allowing for set towards The Tuns on the ebb (up to 3·5kn).

Tor Rks, Inishtrahull and Garvan Isles lie NE and E of Malin Hd. In bad weather it is best to pass at least 3M N of Tor Rks. Inishtrahull is lit and about 1M long; rks extend N about 3ca into Tor Sound. Inishtrahull Sound, between Inishtrahull and Garvan Isles, is exposed; tidal streams up to 4kn sp can raise a dangerous sea with no warning. Stream also sets hard through Garvan Isles, S of which Garvan Sound can be passed safely in daylight avoiding two sunken rks, one $1\frac{1}{2}$ca NE of Rossnabarton, and the other 5ca NW. The main stream runs W for only 3hrs, from HW Galway −0500 to −0200. W of Malin Hd a W-going eddy starts at HW Galway +0400, and an E-going one at HW Galway −0300.

W of Malin Head the direction of buoyage changes to E. From Malin Head SW to Dunaff Head, at ent to Lough Swilly (9.13.17), keep 5ca offshore. Trawbreaga Lough (AC 2697) gives shelter, but is shallow, and sea can break on bar; only approach when no swell, and at half flood. Ent to L Swilly is clear except for Swilly Rks off the W shore, SSE of Fanad Hd.

W from Lough Swilly the coast is very foul. Beware Limeburner Rk (2m), 6·8M WNW of Fanad Hd. Mulroy Bay (9.13.17) has good anchs but needs accurate pilotage, as in *ICC SDs*.

Between Mulroy B and Sheephaven there is inshore passage S of Frenchman's Rk, and between Guill Rks and Carnabollion, safe in good weather; otherwise keep 1M offshore. Sheep Haven B (9.13.17) is easy to enter between Rinnafaghla Pt and Horn Hd, and has good anchs except in strong NW or N winds. Beware Wherryman Rks, dry 1·5m, 1ca off E shore.

Between Horn Hd and Bloody Foreland (chart 2752) are three low-lying islands: Inishbeg, Inishdooey and Inishbofin. The latter is almost part of the mainland; it has a temp anch on S side and a more sheltered anch on NE side in Toberglassan B. 6M offshore is Tory Is (lt, fog sig, RC) with rks for 5ca off SW side. Temp anch in good weather in Camusmore B. In Tory Sound the stream runs W from HW Galway + 0230, and E from HW Galway – 0530, sp rates 2kn.

BLOODY FORELAND TO EAGLE ISLAND (chart 2725) Off low-lying Bloody Foreland (lt) there is often heavy swell. The coast and islands 15M SW to Aran Is give good cruising (chart 1883). An inshore passage avoids offlying dangers: Buniver and Brinlack shoals, which can break; Bullogconnell 1M NW of Gola Is; and Stag Rks 2M NNW of Owey Is. Anchs include Bunbeg and Gweedore hbr, and Cruit B which has easier access. Behind Aran Is are several good anchs. Use N ent, since S one is shallow (chart 2792). Rutland N Chan is main appr to Burtonport (9.13.17).

Boylagh B has shoals and rks N of Roaninish Is. Connell Rk (0·3m) is 1M N of Church Pool, a good anch, best approached from Dawros Hd 4·5M to W. On S side of Glen B a temp anch (but not in W or NW winds) is just E of Rinmeasa Pt. Rathlin O'Birne Is has steps E side; anch SE of them 100m offshore. Sound is 5ca wide; hold Is side to clear rks off Malin Beg Hd.

In Donegal B (chart 2702) beware uncharted rks W of Teelin, a good natural hbr but exposed to S/SW swell. Killybegs (9.13.18) has better shelter and is always accessible. Good shelter with fair access in Donegal Hbr (chart 2715). Good anch or ♁ via YC at Mullaghmore in fair weather; sea state is calm with winds from SE through S to NW. Inishmurray is worth a visit in good weather, anch off S side. There are shoals close E and NE of the Is, and Bomore Rks 1·5M to N. Keep well clear of coast S to Sligo (9.13.19) in onshore winds, and watch for lobster pots.

Killala B has temp anch 1M S of Kilcummin Hd, on W side. Proceeding to Killala beware St Patrick's Rks. Ent has ldg lts and marks, but bar is dangerous in strong NE winds.

The coast W to Broadhaven is inhospitable. Only Belderg and Portacloy give a little shelter. Stag Rks are steep-to and high. Broadhaven (chart 2703) is good anch and refuge, but in N/NW gales sea can break in ent. In approaches beware Slugga Rk on E side with offlier, and Monastery Rk (0·3m) on S side.

EAGLE ISLAND TO SLYNE HEAD (chart 2420) This coast has many inlets, some sheltered. Streams are weak offshore. There are few lights. Keep 5ca off Erris Hd, and further in bad weather. Unless calm, keep seaward of Eagle Is (lt) where there is race to N. Frenchport (chart 2703) is good temp anch except in strong W winds. Inishkea Is (chart 2704) can be visited in good weather; anch N or S of Rusheen Is. On passage keep 5ca W of Inishkea to avoid bad seas if wind over tide. The sound off Mullett Peninsula is clear, but for Pluddany Rk 6ca E of Inishkea N.

Blacksod B (chart 2704 and 9.13.20) has easy ent (possible at night) and good shelter. In the approaches Black Rk (lt) has rks up to 1·25M SW. From N, in good weather, there is chan between Duvillaun Beg and Gaghta Is, but in W gales beware breakers 1M SE of Duvillaun More.

Rough water is likely off impressive Achill Hd. Achill Sound (chart 2667) is restricted by cables 11m high at swing bridge. Anchs each end of Sound, but the stream runs strongly.

Clare Is has Two Fathom Rk (3·4m) 5ca off NW coast, and Calliaghcrom Rk 5ca to the N; anch on NE side. In Clew Bay Newport and Westport (AC 2667, 2057 and 9.13.20) need detailed pilotage directions. S of Clare Is beware Meemore Shoal 1·5M W of Roonagh Hd. 2M further W is the isolated rk Mweelaun. The islands of Caher, Ballybeg, Inishturk (with anch on E side) and Inishdalla have few hidden dangers, but the coast to the E must be given a berth of 1·5M even in calm weather; in strong winds seas break much further offshore.

Killary B (chart 2706) and Little Killary both have good anchs in magnificent scenery. Consult sailing directions, and only approach in reasonable weather and good vis.

Ballynakill Hbr (chart 2706), easily entered either side of Freaghillaun South, has excellent shelter; Tully mountain is conspic to N. Beware Mullaghadrina and Ship Rk in N chan. Anch in Fahy, Derryinver or Barnaderg B. There is anch on S side of Inishbofin (lt), but difficult access/exit in strong SW wind or swell (9.13.20). Rks and breakers exist E of Inishbofin and S of Inishshark; see chart 2707 for clearing lines. Lecky Rks lie 1M SSE of Davillaun. Carrickmahoy is a very dangerous rk (1·9m) between Inishbofin and Cleggan Pt.

Cleggan B is moderate anch, open to NW but easy access. High Is Sound is usual coasting route, not Friar Is Sound or Aughrus Passage. Clifden B (chart 2708) has offlying dangers with breakers; enter 3ca S of Carrickrana Bn and anch off Drinagh Pt, in Clifden Hbr or Ardbear B; see 9.13.20.

Slyne Hd (lt, Racon) marks SW end of the rocks and islets stretching 2M WSW from coast. Here the stream turns N at HW Galway – 0320, and S at HW Galway + 0300. It runs 3kn at sp,and in bad weather causes a dangerous race; keep 2M offshore. Seas break on Barret Shoals, 3M NW of Slyne Hd.

SLYNE HEAD TO LISCANNOR BAY (chart 2173) In good visibility the Connemara coast (charts 2709, 2096) and Aran Islands (chart 3339) give excellent cruising. But there are many rks, and few navigational marks. Between Slyne Head and Roundstone B are many offlying dangers. If coasting, keep well seaward of Skerd Rks. A conspic twr (24m) on Golan Head is a key feature. Going E the better hbrs are Roundstone B, Cashel B, Killeany B, Greatman B and Cashla B. Kilronan (Killeany B) on Inishmore is only reasonable hbr in Aran Islands, but is exposed in E winds. Disused lt ho on centre of island is conspic.

Normal approach to Galway B is through N Sound or S Sound. N Sound is 4M wide from Eagle Rk and other dangers off Lettermullan shore, to banks on S side which break in strong winds. S Sound is 3M wide, with no dangers except Finnis Rk (0·4m) 5ca SE of Inisheer. The other channels are Gregory Sound, 1M wide between Inishmore and Inishmaan, and Foul Sound between Inishmaan and Inisheer. The latter has one danger, Pipe Rk and the reef inshore of it, extending 3ca NW of Inisheer.

The N side of Galway Bay is exposed, with no shelter. Galway (9.13.21) is a commercial port, with possible marina plans. 3M SE, New Hbr (chart 1984) is a more pleasant anch with moorings off Galway Bay SC. Westward to Black Hd there are many bays and inlets, often poorly marked, but providing shelter and exploration. The coast SW to Liscannor Bay is devoid of shelter. O'Brien's Twr is conspic just N of the 199m high Cliffs of Moher.

9.13.6 DISTANCE TABLE

Approximate distances in nautical miles are by the most direct route, whilst avoiding dangers and allowing for Traffic Separation Schemes. Places in *italics* are in adjoining areas; places in **bold** are in 9.0.7, Distances across the Irish Sea.

Place	1	2	3	4	5	6	7	8	9	10	11	12	13	14	15	16	17	18	19	20
1. ***Dun Laoghaire***																				
2. **Carlingford Lough**	50																			
3. **Strangford Lough**	71	36																		
4. **Bangor**	96	61	34																	
5. **Carrickfergus**	101	66	39	6																
6. **Larne**	108	73	45	16	16															
7. **Carnlough**	118	78	50	25	26	11														
8. Altacarry Head	135	102	74	45	45	31	21													
9. **Portrush**	150	115	87	58	60	48	35	19												
10. **Lough Foyle**	157	121	92	72	73	55	47	30	11											
11. L Swilly (Fahan)	200	166	138	109	104	96	81	65	48	42										
12. **Tory Island**	209	174	146	117	113	105	90	74	57	51	35									
13. Burtonport	218	182	153	130	130	116	108	90	74	68	49	18								
14. Killybegs	267	232	204	175	171	163	148	132	115	109	93	58	43							
15. Sligo	281	246	218	189	179	177	156	146	123	117	107	72	51	30						
16. Eagle Island	297	262	234	205	198	193	175	162	147	136	123	88	72	62	59					
17. Westport	337	323	295	266	249	240	226	207	193	187	168	137	120	108	100	57				
18. Slyne Head	352	317	289	260	257	248	234	217	201	195	178	143	128	117	114	55	44			
19. Galway	348	366	338	309	307	297	284	266	253	245	227	192	178	166	163	104	94	49		
20. *Kilrush*	318	361	364	335	332	323	309	291	276	270	251	220	203	191	183	142	119	75	76	

9.13.7 Special notes for Ireland: See 9.12.7.

MINOR HARBOURS AND ANCHORAGES TO THE NORTH WEST OF LAMBAY ISLAND

SKERRIES, Dublin, **53°35'·1N 06°06'·66W**. AC 633. Tides as Balbriggan, 9.13.8. E & SE of Red Island (a peninsula) lie Colt, Shenick's and St Patrick's Islands, the latter foul to S and SW. Inshore passage between Colt and St Patrick's Is uses transit/brg as on chart to clear dangers. Good shelter and holding in 3m at Skerries Bay, W of Red Is. Appr from E or NE outside PHM buoy, Fl R 10s, off Red Is. ⚓ WNW of pier, Oc R 6s 7m 7M, vis 103°-154°; clear of moorings. Most facilities; Skerries SC ☎ 1-849 1233. Rockabill Lt, Fl WR 12s 45m 23/19M, is conspic 2·4M ExN of St Patrick's Is.

BALBRIGGAN, Dublin, **53°36'·8N 06°10'·7W**. AC 1468, 44. Tides see 9.13.8. Good shelter in small hbr, dries about 0·9m, access approx HW ±2. Appr on SW, to open the outer hbr which is entered on SE; thence to inner hbr and AB on SE quay. Beware shoaling on both sides of outer hbr. Lt, Fl (3) WRG 20s 12m 13/10M, conspic W tr on E bkwtr head, vis G159°-193°, W193°-288°, R288°-305°. Facilities: FW, D, Gas, Slip, BH (9 ton), R, Bar, V. EC Thurs.

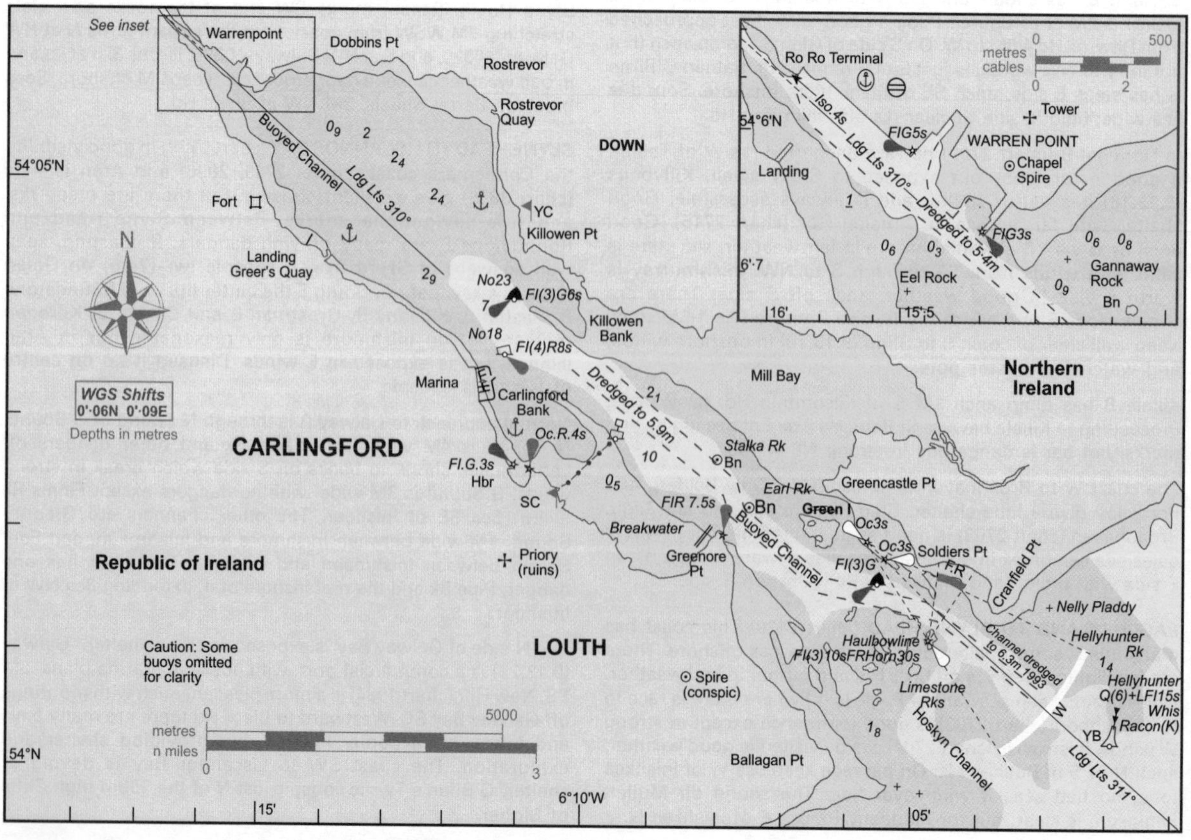

CARLINGFORD LOUGH *9.13.8*

Louth/Down **54°01'·25N 06°04'·30W**

CHARTS AC 2800, 44; Imray C62; Irish OS 29, 36

TIDES Cranfield Pt +0025 and Warrenpoint +0035 Dover; ML 2·9; Duration Cranfield Pt 0615, Warrenpoint 0540; Zone 0 (UT)

Standard Port DUBLIN (NORTH WALL) (←)

Times				Height (metres)			
High Water		Low Water		MHWS	MHWN	MLWN	MLWS
0000	0700	0000	0500	4·1	3·4	1·5	0·7
1200	1900	1200	1700				
Differences CRANFIELD POINT							
−0027	−0011	+0005	−0010	+0·7	+0·9	+0·3	+0·2
WARRENPOINT							
−0020	−0010	+0025	+0035	+1·0	+0·7	+0·2	0·0
NEWRY (VICTORIA LOCK)							
−0010	−0010	+0025	Dries	+1·1	+1·0	+0·1	Dries
DUNDALK (SOLDIERS POINT)							
−0010	−0010	0000	+0045	+1·0	+0·8	+0·1	−0·1
DUNANY POINT							
−0028	−0018	−0008	−0006	+0·7	+0·9	No data	
RIVER BOYNE BAR							
−0005	0000	+0020	+0030	+0·4	+0·3	−0·1	−0·2
BALBRIGGAN							
−0021	−0015	+0010	+0002	+0·3	+0·2	No data	

SHELTER Good. **Carlingford Marina** protected on S side by sunken barge; depths 1·4m – 3·5m. Appr from N with Nos 18 and 23 buoys in transit astern 012°, to clear the tail of Carlingford Bank (dries).
There are harbours at: **Carlingford Hbr** (dries 2·2m), AB at piers. **Warrenpoint** has pontoons on NW side of bkwtr (Fl G 3s); access dredged 1·1m. ⚓s clockwise from ent include: at Greenore Pt, between SW end of quay and bkwtr, in 3m clear of commercial tfc; off Greer's Quay in 2m; off Rostrevor Quay, Killowen Pt (YC) and off derelict pier at Greencastle Pt (beware rks).

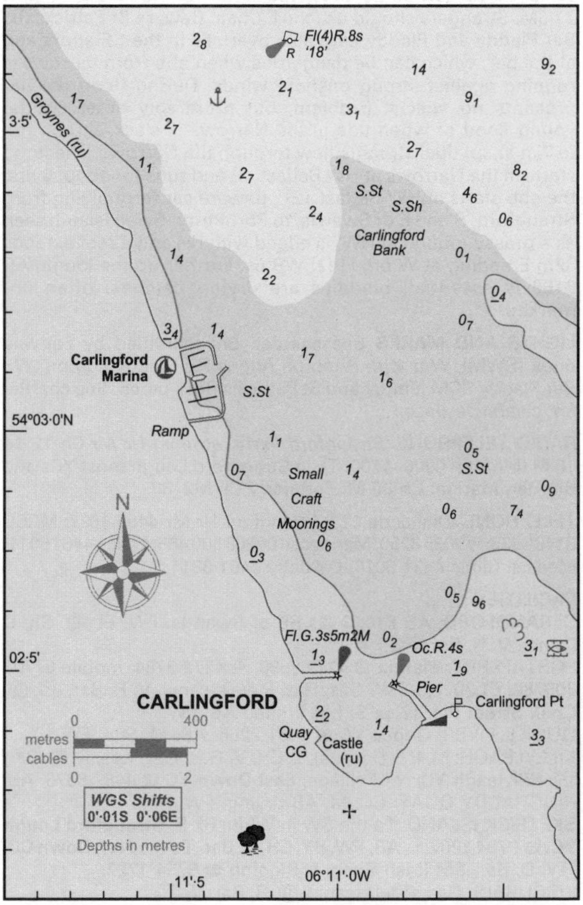
Fl(4)R.8s
R '18'
Groynes (ru)
3·5'
S.St
S.Sh
Carlingford Bank
Carlingford Marina
54°03·0'N
Ramp
Small Craft Moorings
N
Fl.G.3s5m2M
Oc.R.4s
Pier
Carlingford Pt
02·5'
CARLINGFORD
metres
cables
400
WGS Shifts
0'·01S 0'·06E
Quay
CG
Castle (ru)
Depths in metres
11'·5
06°11'·0W

NAVIGATION WPT 54°00'·09N 06°02'·00W, (2½ ca S of Hellyhunter SCM lt buoy) 131°/311° from/to first chan buoys, 1M. The main chan is Carlingford Cut (6·3m), about 3ca SW of Cranfield Pt, and passing 2ca NE of Haulbowline lt ho. Drying rks and shoals obstruct most of the ent. The lough becomes choppy in S winds: due to the funnelling effect of the mountains NW winds cause a worse sea state within the lough than outside it. The ent is impassable in strong on-shore winds. Tides run up to 5kn off Greenore Pt and entry is impracticable against the ebb. Beware sudden squalls and waterspouts. Caution: much shipping in narrow chan dredged 5·4m, but the head of the lough is shallow. Note: The NE bank is Ulster, SW bank is the Republic of Ireland. Yachts may be stopped by Naval vessels.

LIGHTS AND MARKS Haulbowline Fl (3) 10s 32m 17M; granite tr; also turning lt FR 21m 9M, vis 196°-208°, horn 30s. Ldg lts 310°26': both Oc 3s 7/12m 11M, vis 295°-325°; R △ front, ▽ rear, on framework trs. Greenore Pier Fl R 7·5s 10m 5M. Newry R: Ldg lts 310°, both Iso 4s 5/15m 2M, stone columns.

RADIO TELEPHONE Greenore (*Ferry Greenore*) Ch 12 16 (HJ). Carlingford marina Ch M 16. Warrenpoint Ch 12 16 (H24); call Ch 12 at By No. 23 to enter dredged chan. Dundalk Ch 14 16 (HW±3).

TELEPHONE (Dial code Greenore/Carlingford 042; Warrenpoint 028). MRCC (01) 6620922/3 or (02891) 463933; ⊖ (028) 9035 8250; Irish ⊖, Dundalk (042) 34114; Marinecall 09068 500 465; Dr (042) 73110; [hosp] Newry (028) 3026 5511, Dundalk (042) 34701; Police (042) 73102, (028) 4172 2222.

FACILITIES **Carlingford Marina** (80 with planned additional 50 by 2001), [tel] (042)937 3073 [fax] (042)937 3075, £1.30, AC, D, FW, C, CH, BH (50T), Divers, Slip, [launderette], Bar, R. **Carlingford YC** [tel] (041) 685 1951, Slip, Bar, M, FW; **Village** P (cans), V, R, Bar, Ⓑ, [post]. **Hbr** AB, Slip; **Dundalk SC** FW, Slip; **Services:** ME, El, Sh, Kos, Gas. **Warrenpoint** Hr Mr [tel] (02841) 752878, [fax] (02841) 773962; EC Wed; AB, M (but no access at LW), FW, P, D, [post] (also at Rostrevor, Carlingford), Ⓑ (also Dundalk), [rail] (Dundalk, Newry), ✈ (Dublin).

MINOR HARBOURS BETWEEN CARLINGFORD LOUGH AND ST. JOHN'S POINT

KILKEEL, Down, **54°03'·47N 05°59'·26W**. AC 2800, 44. HW +0015 on Dover; ML 2·9m; Duration 0620. See 9.13.9. Inner basin is completely sheltered, but gets crowded by FVs; depth off quays approx 1m. Secure in inner basin and see Hr Mr. There are drying banks both sides of ent chan and SW gales cause a sandbank right across ent. This is dredged or slowly eroded in E winds. S bkwtr lt Fl WR 2s 8m 8M, R296°-313°, W313°-017°, storm sigs. Meeney's pier (N bkwtr) Fl G 3s 6m 2M. VHF Ch **12** 14 16 (Mon-Fri: 0900-2000). Hr Mr [tel] (028 417) 62287; ⊖ (028 90) 358250 or (028 417) 62158; Facilities: FW on quay, BY (between fish market and dock), El, ME, Sh, Slip. **Town** (¾M) EC Thurs; Bar, [post], R, V, Gas, [launderette].

ANNALONG HBR, Down, **54°06'·50N 05°53'·65W**. AC 44. Tides as Kilkeel, see 9.13.9. Excellent shelter in small drying hbr, approx 2m from HW±3. Appr in W sector of S bkwtr lt, Oc WRG 5s 8m 9M, vis G204°-249°, W249°-309°, R309°-024°. Hug N side of the bkwtr to avoid rky shore to stbd. 40m beyond a spur on N side, turn hard port into the basin; berth as available. Caution: many warps are rigged across hbr. Surge gate at hbr ent may be closed in SE winds. Facilities: V, Bar, [post].

DUNDRUM BAY, Down. AC 44. Tides see 9.13.9. This 8M wide bay to the W of St John's Pt is shoal to 5ca offshore and unsafe in onshore winds. The small drying hbr at **Newcastle** (54°11'·8N 05°53'·0W) is for occas use in fair weather. Hr Mr [tel] (013967) 22106. **Dundrum Hbr** (**54°14'·2N 05°49'·4W**) provides ⚓ in 2m for shoal draft; the bar carries about 0·3m. A steep sea can run at the bar in onshore winds. HW Dundrum is approx that of HW Liverpool; see also 9.13.9 Newcastle. ICC SDs are essential for the 1M long, buoyed appr chan. 3 unlit DZ buoys offshore are part of the Ballykinler firing range, 2M E of hbr; R flag/lts indicate range active.

ARDGLASS *9.13.9*

Down 54°15'·63N 05°35'·96W ❀❀❀◊◊✿✿

CHARTS AC 633, 2093; Imray C62; Irish OS 21

TIDES HW +0025 Dover; ML 3·0; Duration 0620; Zone 0 (UT)

Standard Port BELFAST (⟶)

Times				Height (metres)			
High Water		Low Water		MHWS	MHWN	MLWN	MLWS
0100	0700	0000	0600	3·5	3·0	1·1	0·4
1300	1900	1200	1800				
Differences KILKEEL							
+0040	+0030	+0010	+0010	+1·2	+1·1	+0·4	+0·4
NEWCASTLE							
+0025	+0035	+0020	+0040	+1·6	+1·1	+0·4	+0·1
KILLOUGH HARBOUR							
0000	+0020	No data		+1·8	+1·6	No data	
ARDGLASS							
+0010	+0015	+0005	+0010	+1·7	+1·2	+0·6	+0·3

SHELTER Good, except in strong winds from E to S. It is the only all-weather, all-tide shelter between Howth and Bangor. Phennick Cove marina is on W side of hbr, with depths 1·0m to 2·8m. The busy fishing port is in South Hbr, with quays (2·1m) on inside of extended S pier. At NW end of hbr, old drying N Dock is also used by FVs.

NAVIGATION WPT 54°15'·30N 05°35'·32W, 311°/131° from/to hbr ent, 5ca. Appr 311° in W sector of WRG Dir lt. Depth in chan 2·4m. The inner bkwtr is marked by an ECM buoy, VQ (3) 4s. Thence chan 232° into the marina is marked by Nos 2 and 4 PHM buoys, QR and Fl R 4s; and by Nos 3 and 5 SHM buoys, QG and Fl G 4s. (These buoys are not shown on chartlet due to small scale). Do not cross the drying SW portion of inner bkwtr, marked by two unlit SCM perches.

LIGHTS AND MARKS Dir lt, 311°, conspic W tr at inner hbr, Iso WRG 4s 10m 8/7/5M, W308°-314°; reported hard to see against shore lts. S bkwtr Fl R 3s 10m 5M. W roof of shed on S bkwtr is conspic. If entering S Hbr, avoid Churn Rk, unlit SCM bn. Entrance to marina is buoyed. Castle, spire and water tr (off plan) are conspic to W.

RADIO TELEPHONE Hbr VHF Ch 12 14 16. Marina Ch M, 80.

TELEPHONE (Dial code 028) Hr Mr 4484 1291; MRSC 9046 3933; ⊖ 9035 8250; Marinecall 09068 500 465; Police 9084 1202; Dr 9084 1242.

FACILITIES Marina (55, inc 20 Ⓥ), ☎/℻ 4484 2332, £1·60, AC, D (in 20 & 25 ltr cans), FW, ⊡, ⓑ. **Town** P (cans), Bar, ✉, R, V, Gas.

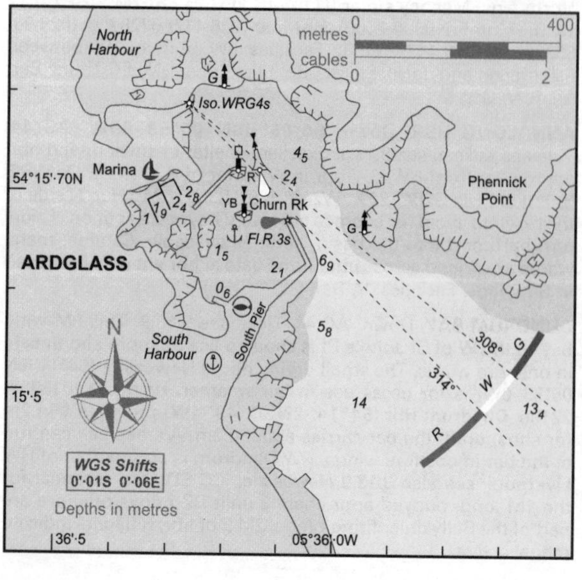

STRANGFORD LOUGH *9.13.10*

Down **54°19'·33N 05°30'·85W** (Narrows) ❀❀◊◊✿✿✿

CHARTS AC 2159, 2156; Imray C62; Irish OS 21

TIDES Killard Pt 0000, Strangford Quay +0200 Dover; ML 2·0; Duration 0610; Zone 0 (UT)

Standard Port BELFAST (⟶)

Times				Height (metres)			
High Water		Low Water		MHWS	MHWN	MLWN	MLWS
0100	0700	0000	0600	3·5	3·0	1·1	0·4
1300	1900	1200	1800				
Differences STRANGFORD (The Narrows)							
+0147	+0157	+0148	+0208	+0·1	+0·1	−0·2	0·0
KILLARD POINT (Entr)							
+0011	+0021	+0005	+0025	+1·0	+0·8	+0·1	+0·1
QUOILE BARRIER							
+0150	+0200	+0150	+0300	+0·2	+0·2	−0·3	−0·1
KILLYLEAGH							
+0157	+0207	+0211	+0231	+0·3	+0·3	No data	
SOUTH ROCK							
+0023	+0023	+0025	+0025	+1·0	+0·8	+0·1	+0·1
PORTAVOGIE							
+0010	+0020	+0010	+0020	+1·2	+0·9	+0·3	+0·2

SHELTER Excellent, largest inlet on E coast. Good ⚓s in the Narrows at Cross Roads seldom used; in Strangford Creek (NW of Swan Island, which is marked by 3 lt bns to S, E and N); in Audley Rds and Ballyhenry Bay. 3 Ⓥs at Strangford; AB on piers depends on state of tide. Portaferry has a small marina with visitors' berths. Many good ⚓s and some Ⓥs up the lough, by villages and YCs; dues, if applicable, are seldom collected.

NAVIGATION WPT Strangford Fairway SWM buoy, L Fl 10s, Whis, 54°18'·63N 05°28'·62W, 126°/306° from/to Angus Rk lt tr, 2·05M. Strangers should use the E Chan. Beware St Patricks Rk, Bar Pladdy and Pladdy Lug; also overfalls in the SE apprs and at the bar, which can be dangerous when ebb from narrows is running against strong onshore winds. During flood the bar presents no special problem, but preferably enter on the young flood or when tide in the Narrows is slack. Strong (up to 7kn at sp) tidal streams flow through the Narrows. The flood starts in the Narrows at HW Belfast -3½ and runs for about 6 hrs; the ebb starts at HW Belfast +2½. Beware car ferry plying from Strangford, S and E of Swan Is, to Portaferry. Swan Island, seen as a grassy mound at HW, is edged with rks and a reef extends 32m E ending at W bn, Fl (2) WR 6s. Further up the lough, AC 2156 is essential; pladdies are drying patches, often unmarked.

LIGHTS AND MARKS See chartlet. Ent identified by Fairway buoy (SWM), W tr with R top on Angus Rk, Pladdy Lug bn (W), Bar Pladdy SCM lt buoy and St Patrick's Rock perch. See chartlet for clearance lines.

RADIO TELEPHONE *Strangford FerryTerminal Hr Mr* Ch 12 14 16 M (Mon-Fri 0900- 1700LT). In Strangford Lough most YCs and Riordan Marine: Ch **80** M. Portaferry Ch M2, 80.

TELEPHONE (Dial code 028) Strangford Hr Mr 4488 1637; MRSC 9146 3933; ⊖ 9035 8250; Marinecall 09068 500 465; Police 4461 5011; Medical Clinic 4431 3016; Casualty 4461 3311.

FACILITIES
STRANGFORD: AB £10, 3 Ⓥs SE of Swan Is, FW, El, Ⓔ, Sh, D (cans), V, R, Bar, ✉.
PORTAFERRY: **Marina** ☎ 4272 9598, ℻ 4272 9784, mobile 07703 209780. £1.20, AC, FW, Gas, Gaz, P & D (cans), V, R, Bar, ✉, Ⓑ. **Cook Street Pier** (2¼ca S) has limited AB, FW.
QUOILE RIVER: **Quoile YC** ☎ 4461 2266. AB, M, Slip, FW.
KILLYLEAGH: M, P & D (cans), L, CH, V, Gas, Gaz, Kos, R, Ⓑ, Bar, ✉; **Killyleagh YC**; N of village, **East Down YC** ☎ 4482 8375, AB.
RINGHADDY QUAY: CC, M, AB drying, FW, Slip.
SKETRICK ISLAND: To the SW in White Rk B, **Strangford Lough YC**, ☎ 9754 1202, L, AB, FW, BY, CH, R, Bar. To the NW, **Down CC**, FW, D, Bar, SM (Irish Spars & Rigging ☎ 9754 1727.
KIRCUBBIN: Gas, P & D (cans), Ⓑ, R, Bar, V, ✉.

STRANGFORD LOUGH *continued*

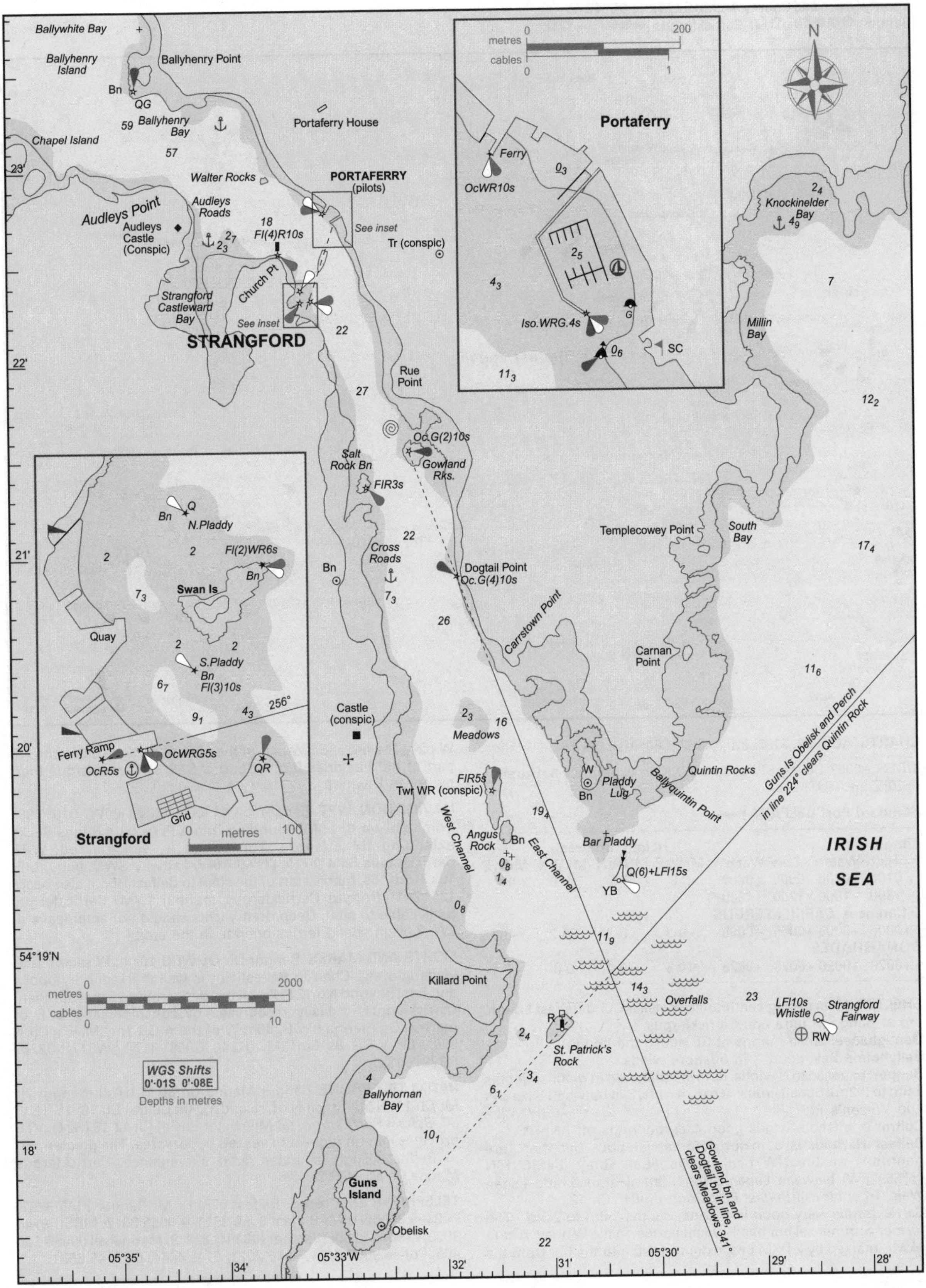
Ballywhite Bay
Ballyhenry Island
Ballyhenry Point
Bn
QG
Ballyhenry Bay
Portaferry House
Chapel Island
Walter Rocks
PORTAFERRY (pilots)
Audleys Point
Audleys Roads
Audleys Castle (Conspic)
Fl(4)R10s
See inset
Tr (conspic)
Strangford Castleward Bay
Church Pt
STRANGFORD
Rue Point
Oc.G(2)10s
Salt Rock Bn
Fl R3s
Gowland Rks.
Cross Roads
Dogtail Point
Oc.G(4)10s
Carrstown Point
Castle (conspic)
Meadows
Twr WR (conspic)
West Channel
East Channel
Angus Rock
Killard Point
St. Patrick's Rock
Ballyhornan Bay
Guns Island
Obelisk
Gowland bn and Dogtail bn in line, clears Meadows 341°
Guns Is Obelisk and Perch in line 224° clears Quintin Rock
Portaferry
metres
cables
Ferry
OcWR10s
Iso.WRG.4s
SC
Knockinelder Bay
Millin Bay
Templecowey Point
South Bay
Carnan Point
Quintin Rocks
Ballyquintin Point
Pladdy Lug
Bar Pladdy
Q(6)+LFl15s
YB
IRISH SEA
Overfalls
LFl10s Whistle
Strangford Fairway
RW
N.Pladdy
Fl(2)WR6s
Swan Is
Quay
S.Pladdy Bn Fl(3)10s
Ferry Ramp
OcR5s
OcWRG5s
QR
Grid
Strangford
WGS Shifts
0'·01S 0'·08E
Depths in metres
54°19'N
05°35'
05°33'W
05°30'

BELFAST LOUGH *9.13.11*

County Down and County Antrim **54°42'N 05°45'W**
Bangor ; Carrickfergus

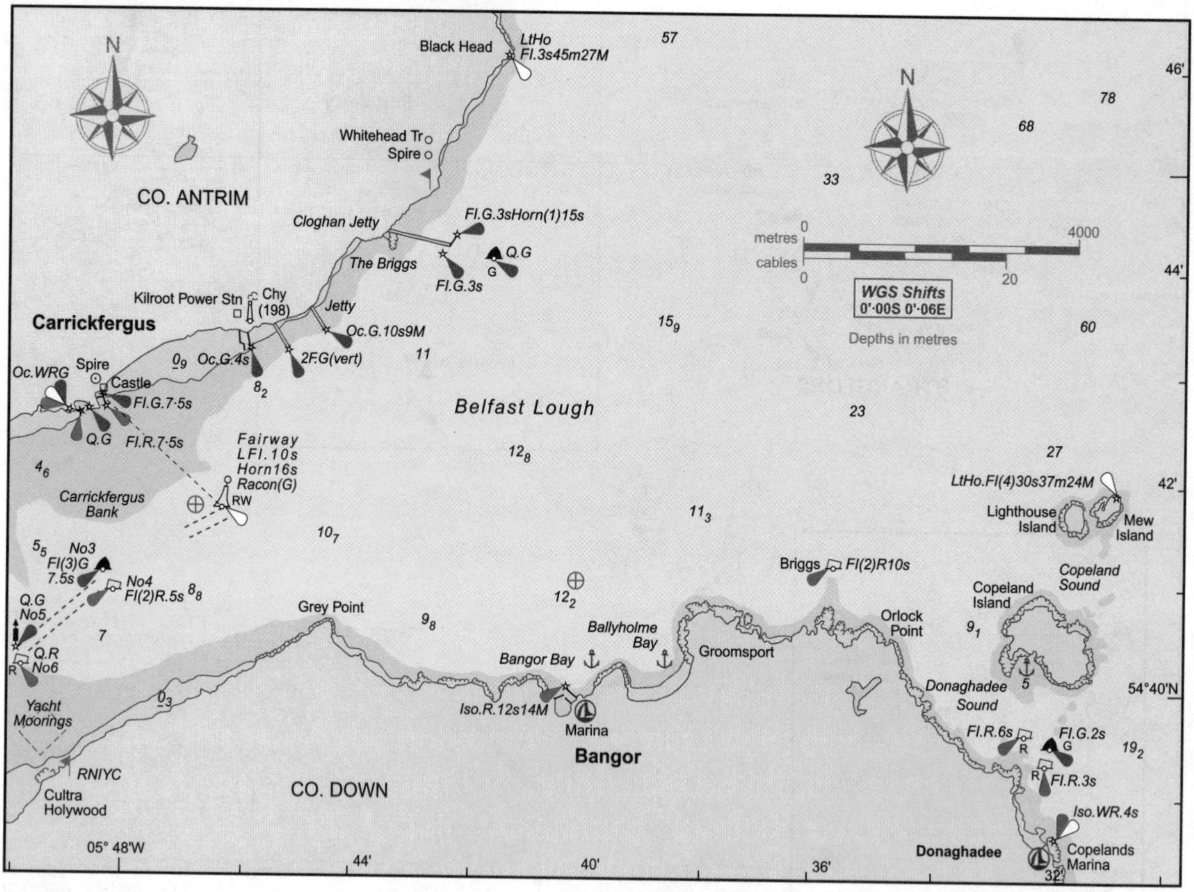

CHARTS AC 1753, 2198; Imray C62, C64; Irish OS 15

TIDES +0007 Dover; ML Belfast 2·0, Carrickfergus 1·8; Duration 0620; Zone 0 (UT)

Standard Port BELFAST (⟶)

Times				Height (metres)			
High Water		Low Water		MHWS	MHWN	MLWN	MLWS
0100	0700	0000	0600	3·5	3·0	1·1	0·4
1300	1900	1200	1800				
Differences CARRICKFERGUS							
+0005	+0005	+0005	+0005	−0·3	−0·3	−0·2	−0·1
DONAGHADEE							
+0020	+0020	+0023	+0023	+0·5	+0·4	0·0	+0·1

SHELTER Main sailing centres, clockwise around Belfast Lough, are at Bangor, Cultra and Carrickfergus.
Donaghadee: small marina at SE ent to the Lough.
Ballyholme Bay: good ⚓ in offshore winds.
Bangor: exposed to N winds, but well sheltered in marina (depths 2·9m to 2·2m). Speed limits: 4kn in marina, 8kn between Luke's Pt and Wilson's Pt.
Cultra: in offshore winds good ⚓ & moorings off RNoIYC.
Belfast Harbour is a major commercial port, but there are pontoons on the NW bank at Donegall Quay (54°36'·16N 05°55'·20W) between Lagan Bridge, 8m clearance, and Lagan Weir. To enter call *Belfast Port Control* VHF Ch **12**.
Carrickfergus: very good in marina, depths 1·8m to 2·3m. The former commercial hbr has 10 yacht berths on the W quay. A stub bkwtr, marked by 2 PHM bns, extends NNE into the hbr from the W pier. The ent and SW part of the hbr are dredged 2·3m; the NE part of the hbr dries 0·7m. Good ⚓ SSE of Carrickfergus Pier, except in E winds.

NAVIGATION WPT Bangor 54°41'·00N 05°40'·00W, 010°/190° from/to bkwtr lt, 1·0M. Rounding Orlock Pt beware Briggs Rocks extending ¾M offshore. The Lough is well marked. **WPT** Carrickfergus 54°41'·71N 05°46'·16W, Fairway SWM buoy, L Fl 10s, Horn 16s, marks start of the chan to Belfast Hbr. It also bears 121°/301° from/to Carrickfergus marina, 1.7M. Carrickfergus Bank liable to shift. Deep draft yachts should not enter/leave at LW±2. High speed ferries operate in the area.

LIGHTS AND MARKS Bangor Dir Oc WRG 10s lt; W sector 105° leads into ent. Chan to Belfast Hbr is well marked/lit by buoys and bns. Beyond No 12 PHM bn it is dangerous to leave the chan. Carrickfergus is easily recognised by conspic castle to E of marina. On marina bkwtr, 30m W of the ☆ QR 7m 3M, is a Dir lt 320°, Oc WRG 3s 5m 3M, (H24), G308°-317½°, W317½°-322½°, R322½°-332°.

RADIO TELEPHONE Bangor Marina Ch **80** M (H24); Bangor Hr Mr Ch 11 (H24). Royal N of Ireland YC (at Cultra) Ch **16**; 11 (H24) 80. *Belfast Port Control* (at Milewater Basin) Ch **12** 16 (H24); VTS provides info on request to vessels in port area. The greater part of Belfast Lough is under radar surveillance. Carrickfergus Marina Ch M, 80, M2.

TELEPHONE (Dial codes: Belfast 028) Hr Mr Bangor 9145 3297, 📠 9145 3450; Hr Mr Belfast 9055 3011/📠 9055 3017; MRSC 9146 3933; ⊖ 9035 8250; Weather (08494) 22339; Marinecall 09068 500 465; Police 9055 8411, 9336 2021, 9145 4444; Dr 9146 8521.

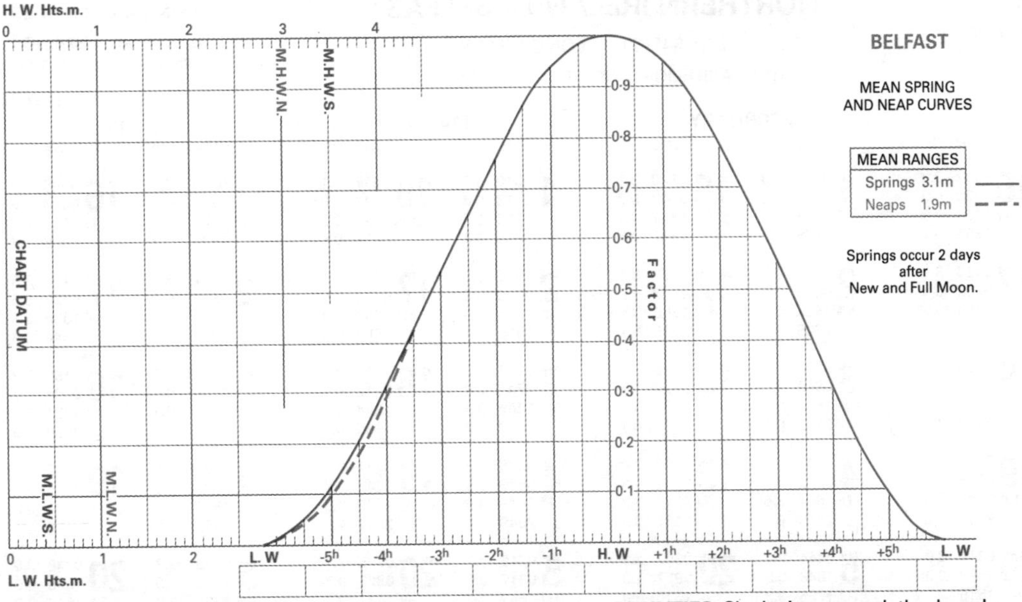

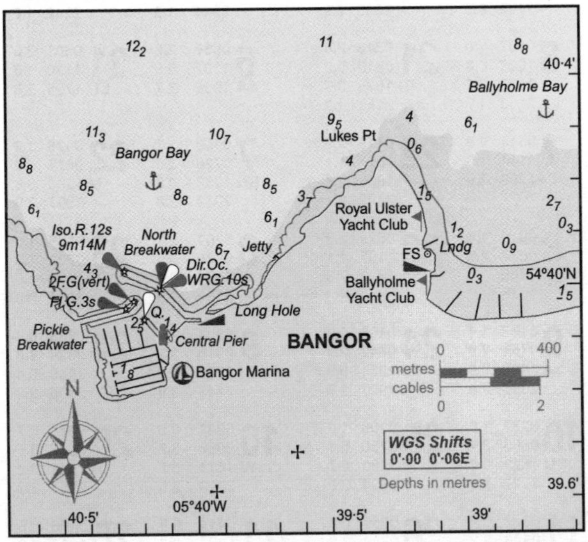

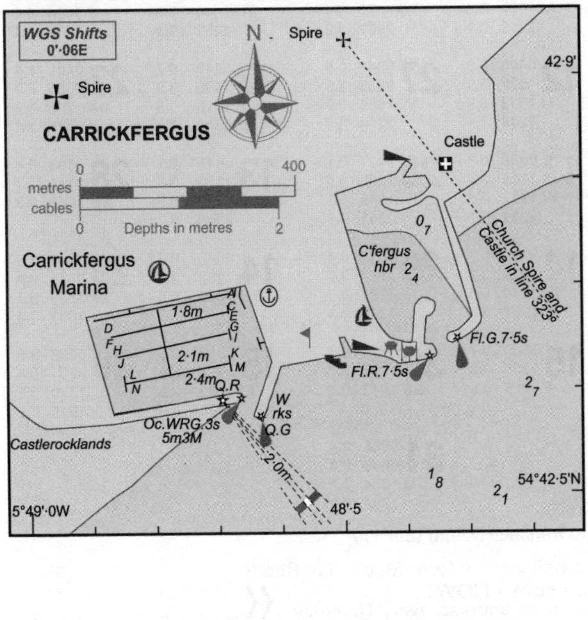

FACILITIES Clockwise around the Lough:
GROOMSPORT BAY: Hr Mr ☎ 9146 4733, M, Slip, FW; **Cockle Island Boat Club**, Slip, M, FW, L, R.
BALLYHOLME BAY: **Ballyholme YC** ☎ 9127 1467, two ⚓s, R, Bar; **Royal Ulster YC** ☎ 9127 0568, M, R, Bar.
BANGOR: **Bangor Marina** (560 + 40 Ⓥ), (£1.50) ☎ 9145 3297, 📠 9145 3450, FW, AC, P, D, C, CH, BH (40 ton), ME, El, Ⓔ, Sh, Gas, Gaz, Slip, SM, V, 🗊; **Todd Chart Agency** ☎ 9146 6640, 📠 9147 1070 ACA, CH. **Services:** BY, Diving, Gas, ME, El, Sh. **Town** EC Thurs; V, R, Bar, ✉, Ⓑ, ⇌, ✈ (Belfast).
CULTRA: **Royal North of Ireland YC,** ☎ 9042 8041, M, L, AB, FW, Slip, P (½M), D, R, Bar. **Services:** ME, El, Sh; **Town** P, CH, V, R, Bar, ✉, Ⓑ, ⇌, ✈.
BELFAST: River manager ☎ 9031 5304, AB, P, D, FW, ME, El, Sh, CH, C (200 ton), SM, Gas. **City** EC Wed; all facilities, ⇌, ✈.
CARRICKFERGUS: **Marina** (280 inc Ⓥ) ☎ 9336 6666, 📠 9335 0505, carrick.marina@virgin.net; £1.50, AC, FW, El, Sh, Gas, Rigging, ME, El, Sh, Ⓔ. **Carrick SC** ☎ 351402, M, L, FW, C, AB; **Hbr:** 10 AB, D, BH (45 ton).**Town** EC Wed; V, R, Ⓑ, ✉, ⇌, ✈ (Belfast).

MINOR HARBOURS BETWEEN STRANGFORD AND BELFAST LOUGHS

PORTAVOGIE, Down, **54°27´·45N 05°26´·08W.** ❀❀◊◊✿. AC 2156. HW +0016 on Dover; ML 2·6m; Duration 0620. See 9.13.10. Good shelter, but hbr so full of FVs as to risk damage; best only for overnight or emergency. Entrance dangerous in strong onshore winds. Beware Plough Rks to SE marked by PHM buoy, Fl (2) R 10s, and McCammon Rks to NE of ent. Keep in W sector of outer bkwtr lt, Iso WRG 5s 9m 9M, G shore-258°, W258°-275°, R275°-348°. Inner bkwtr 2 FG (vert) 6m 4M. VHF Ch 12 14 16 (Mon-Fri: 0900-1700LT). Hr Mr ☎ (028) 4277 1470. Facilities: Slip, FW (on central quay) Sh, ME, El. **Town** EC Thurs; CH, D & P (cans), ✉, R, Gas, V. No licenced premises.

DONAGHADEE, Down, **54°38´·71N 05°31´·85W.** ❀❀◊◊✿✿✿. AC 3709, 1753. HW +0025 on Dover; see 9.13.11; ML no data; Duration 0615. Excellent shelter and basic facilities in tiny marina, access HW±4 over sill; covers approx 1.1m at half tide. Appr on about 275° on ldg marks, orange △s to tricky ent with sharp 90° port turn into marina (pilots available). Appr in strong winds or at night not advised. 3ca to the N, the Old Hbr is small and very full; scend often sets in. Beware rky reef with less than 2m extends 1·5ca ENE from S pier hd. Max depth in hbr is approx 2·5m, dries at SW end; best berth alongside SE quay. S pier lt, Iso WR 4s 17m 18/14M, W shore–326°, R326°–shore. Hr Mr ☎ (028) 9188 2377. Police 9188 2526. Facilities: **Copelands Marina** ☎ 9188 2184, mobile 07802 363382; VHF Ch **16** 11 80; AB for 6 Ⓥ, FW, D, AC, C (20 ton). **Old Hbr** AB £4. **Town** Bar, D, P, Gas, ✉, R, V, Ⓑ, ⇌ (Bangor), ✈ (Belfast).

13

TIME ZONE (UTC)
For Summer Time add ONE hour in **non-shaded areas**

NORTHERN IRELAND – BELFAST

LAT 54°36′N LONG 5°55′W

TIMES AND HEIGHTS OF HIGH AND LOW WATERS

SPRING & NEAP TIDES
Dates in red are **SPRINGS**
Dates in blue are **NEAPS**

YEAR **2002**

JANUARY

Date	Time	m	Date	Time	m
1 TU	0554 1213 1819	0.7 3.7 0.5	16 W	0037 0626 1257 1904	3.2 0.9 3.5 0.7
2 W	0035 0641 1258 1905	3.4 0.7 3.7 0.5	17 TH	0116 0702 1333 1937	3.1 0.9 3.5 0.7
3 TH	0125 0729 1345 1953	3.3 0.8 3.7 0.4	18 F	0155 0739 1408 2012	3.1 0.9 3.4 0.7
4 F	0219 0819 1435 2045	3.2 0.8 3.6 0.5	19 SA	0235 0818 1442 2050	3.0 0.9 3.4 0.8
5 SA	0316 0912 1529 2142	3.1 0.9 3.6 0.6	20 SU	0317 0859 1519 2134	3.0 0.9 3.2 0.9
6 SU	0418 1010 1629 2246	3.0 1.0 3.5 0.7	21 M	0404 0944 1603 2225	2.9 1.0 3.1 0.9
7 M	0522 1118 1735 2357	3.0 1.0 3.3 0.8	22 TU	0455 1038 1658 2328	2.9 1.1 3.0 1.0
8 TU	0629 1233 1846	3.0 1.0 3.3	23 W	0552 1144 1803	2.9 1.2 2.9
9 W	0108 0735 1344 1954	0.8 3.0 1.0 3.3	24 TH	0041 0653 1303 1911	1.0 2.9 1.2 2.9
10 TH	0212 0836 1447 2055	0.8 3.1 0.9 3.3	25 F	0147 0755 1410 2017	1.0 3.0 1.1 3.0
11 F	0304 0929 1541 2148	0.8 3.3 0.8 3.4	26 SA	0241 0851 1504 2113	0.9 3.2 0.9 3.2
12 SA	0350 1016 1629 2235	0.8 3.4 0.7 3.4	27 SU	0328 0940 1552 2202	0.8 3.3 0.7 3.3
13 SU	0432 1100 1713 ● 2318	0.8 3.5 0.7 3.3	28 M	0413 1026 1638 ○ 2249	0.7 3.5 0.5 3.3
14 M	0512 1141 1755 2358	0.9 3.5 0.7 3.2	29 TU	0458 1112 1723 2337	0.6 3.6 0.4 3.3
15 TU	0550 1220 1831	0.9 3.6 0.7	30 W	0543 1158 1809	0.6 3.7 0.3
			31 TH	0026 0629 1246 1854	3.3 0.6 3.7 0.2

FEBRUARY

Date	Time	m	Date	Time	m
1 F	0116 0715 1333 1939	3.3 0.6 3.8 0.2	16 SA	0120 0709 1331 1937	3.1 0.7 3.4 0.6
2 SA	0205 0801 1420 2026	3.3 0.6 3.8 0.3	17 SU	0151 0743 1359 2010	3.1 0.7 3.4 0.7
3 SU	0254 0849 1510 2117	3.2 0.6 3.7 0.4	18 M	0226 0820 1433 2047	3.1 0.7 3.3 0.7
4 M	0347 0943 1604 2215	3.1 0.7 3.5 0.6	19 TU	0307 0902 1515 2132	3.0 0.9 3.2 0.9
5 TU	0444 1048 1706 2325	3.0 0.9 3.3 0.8	20 W	0357 0952 1610 2231	2.9 1.0 3.0 1.1
6 W	0552 1207 1818	2.9 1.0 3.1	21 TH	0458 1056 1721 2354	2.9 1.2 2.9 1.1
7 TH	0043 0708 1325 1938	1.0 2.9 1.0 3.1	22 F	0606 1228 1837	2.8 1.2 2.8
8 F	0154 0819 1435 2046	1.0 3.0 0.9 3.1	23 SA	0123 0715 1350 1949	1.1 2.9 1.0 2.9
9 SA	0252 0916 1533 2140	0.9 3.2 0.8 3.2	24 SU	0223 0819 1448 2052	0.9 3.1 0.8 3.1
10 SU	0340 1004 1621 2226	0.9 3.3 0.7 3.2	25 M	0313 0914 1538 2145	0.8 3.3 0.6 3.2
11 M	0421 1047 1703 2306	0.9 3.4 0.6 3.2	26 TU	0359 1003 1624 2233	0.7 3.5 0.4 3.3
12 TU	0458 1126 1738 ● 2344	0.8 3.5 0.6 3.1	27 W	0444 1050 1709 ○ 2322	0.6 3.6 0.2 3.3
13 W	0532 1203 1808	0.8 3.5 0.6	28 TH	0529 1139 1753	0.5 3.7 0.1
14 TH	0017 0603 1236 1837	3.1 0.8 3.4 0.7			
15 F	0049 0636 1304 1906	3.1 0.8 3.4 0.6			

MARCH

Date	Time	m	Date	Time	m
1 F	0010 0613 1228 1836	3.3 0.4 3.8 0.1	16 SA	0017 0610 1228 1836	3.1 0.6 3.3 0.6
2 SA	0058 0656 1315 1919	3.3 0.4 3.8 0.1	17 SU	0043 0640 1253 1904	3.1 0.6 3.4 0.6
3 SU	0144 0740 1402 2002	3.3 0.4 3.8 0.2	18 M	0113 0712 1324 1935	3.2 0.6 3.3 0.6
4 M	0228 0826 1449 2049	3.3 0.5 3.6 0.4	19 TU	0147 0748 1359 2011	3.2 0.6 3.3 0.7
5 TU	0315 0917 1541 2142	3.2 0.6 3.4 0.7	20 W	0225 0829 1442 2055	3.1 0.7 3.1 0.9
6 W	0407 1022 1639 2252	3.0 0.8 3.2 1.0	21 TH	0313 0918 1538 2152	3.0 0.9 3.0 1.1
7 TH	0511 1144 1753	2.9 1.0 2.9	22 F	0416 1021 1655 2309	2.9 1.1 2.8 1.2
8 F	0016 0637 1306 1925	1.1 2.8 1.0 2.9	23 SA	0529 1157 1813	2.9 1.1 2.8
9 SA	0133 0759 1422 2035	1.1 2.9 0.8 2.9	24 SU	0100 0642 1331 1927	1.2 2.9 0.9 2.9
10 SU	0237 0858 1522 2127	1.0 3.1 0.7 3.0	25 M	0205 0750 1430 2034	1.0 3.1 0.7 3.0
11 M	0327 0946 1607 2210	0.9 3.2 0.6 3.1	26 TU	0257 0848 1520 2127	0.8 3.3 0.4 3.2
12 TU	0406 1027 1643 2248	0.8 3.3 0.5 3.1	27 W	0343 0939 1605 2214	0.6 3.5 0.2 3.3
13 W	0439 1105 1712 2322	0.8 3.4 0.6 3.1	28 TH	0427 1028 1649 ○ 2301	0.5 3.6 0.1 3.3
14 TH	0510 1138 1740 ● 2352	0.7 3.3 0.6 3.1	29 F	0510 1117 1731 2349	0.4 3.7 0.1 3.4
15 F	0540 1205 1808	0.7 3.3 0.6	30 SA	0554 1206 1813	0.4 3.7 0.1
			31 SU	0035 0636 1254 1854	3.4 0.3 3.7 0.2

APRIL

Date	Time	m	Date	Time	m
1 M	0119 0719 1341 1937	3.4 0.3 3.7 0.3	16 TU	0045 0646 1256 1906	3.3 0.6 3.3 0.7
2 TU	0202 0804 1428 2022	3.4 0.4 3.5 0.6	17 W	0119 0722 1335 1944	3.3 0.6 3.3 0.8
3 W	0247 0855 1519 2115	3.3 0.6 3.3 0.8	18 TH	0159 0804 1421 2030	3.3 0.7 3.1 0.9
4 TH	0336 1002 1617 2222	3.1 0.8 3.0 1.1	19 F	0247 0855 1521 2128	3.1 0.9 2.9 1.1
5 F	0435 1121 1729 2344	2.9 0.9 2.8 1.2	20 SA	0348 1000 1640 2242	3.0 1.0 2.8 1.2
6 SA	0556 1237 1906	2.8 0.9 2.7	21 SU	0501 1130 1755	3.0 1.0 2.8
7 SU	0059 0728 1353 2012	1.2 2.9 0.8 2.8	22 M	0026 0614 1304 1907	1.2 3.0 0.8 2.9
8 M	0207 0830 1454 2102	1.1 3.0 0.7 2.9	23 TU	0138 0723 1406 2012	1.0 3.1 0.6 3.0
9 TU	0301 0918 1537 2143	1.0 3.1 0.6 3.0	24 W	0233 0824 1456 2105	0.8 3.3 0.4 3.2
10 W	0341 0958 1611 2219	0.9 3.2 0.5 3.0	25 TH	0321 0917 1541 2152	0.7 3.5 0.2 3.3
11 TH	0414 1034 1640 2252	0.8 3.2 0.5 3.1	26 F	0406 1007 1624 2239	0.5 3.6 0.2 3.4
12 F	0445 1105 1710 ● 2320	0.7 3.2 0.5 3.1	27 SA	0450 1056 1706 ○ 2325	0.4 3.7 0.2 3.4
13 SA	0515 1130 1739 2346	0.7 3.3 0.6 3.2	28 SU	0533 1144 1748	0.4 3.7 0.3
14 SU	0545 1153 1807	0.6 3.3 0.6	29 M	0011 0617 1233 1831	3.5 0.4 3.7 0.4
15 M	0013 0614 1222 1835	3.2 0.6 3.3 0.6	30 TU	0056 0701 1320 1915	3.5 0.4 3.5 0.5

Chart Datum: 2·01 metres below Ordnance Datum (Belfast)

Register for your **FREE** weekly weather email service from Macmillan Reeds
at **www.nauticaldata.com – NOW!**
weekend weather reports sent to your email address, every Thursday

TIME ZONE (UTC)
For Summer Time add ONE hour in **non-shaded areas**

NORTHERN IRELAND – BELFAST

LAT 54°36′N LONG 5°55′W

TIMES AND HEIGHTS OF HIGH AND LOW WATERS

SPRING & NEAP TIDES
Dates in red are SPRINGS
Dates in blue are NEAPS

YEAR **2002**

MAY

Date	Day	Time	m	Time	m	Time	m	Time	m
1	W	0139	3.4	0748	0.5	1408	3.4	2001	0.7
2	TH	0223	3.4	0841	0.6	1458	3.2	2054	0.9
3	F	0312	3.2	0946	0.7	1555	2.9	2157	1.1
4	SA	0407	3.1	1055	0.8	1701	2.8	2308	1.2
5	SU	0512	2.9	1201	0.9	1824	2.7		
6	M	0015	1.2	0631	2.9	1307	0.8	1932	2.7
7	TU	0119	1.2	0744	2.9	1406	0.7	2023	2.8
8	W	0217	1.1	0837	3.0	1454	0.7	2104	2.9
9	TH	0303	1.0	0919	3.1	1531	0.6	2141	3.0
10	F	0341	0.9	0956	3.1	1605	0.6	2214	3.1
11	SA	0415	0.8	1028	3.2	1637	0.6	2246	3.2
12	SU	0448	0.7	1058	3.2	1708	0.6	● 2318	3.3
13	M	0519	0.7	1127	3.3	1739	0.6	2350	3.3
14	TU	0552	0.6	1200	3.3	1811	0.7		
15	W	0024	3.4	0626	0.6	1238	3.3	1847	0.7
16	TH	0102	3.4	0705	0.6	1320	3.2	1929	0.8
17	F	0144	3.4	0750	0.7	1410	3.1	2018	1.0
18	SA	0233	3.3	0842	0.8	1513	3.0	2115	1.1
19	SU	0331	3.2	0946	0.8	1625	2.9	2223	1.2
20	M	0438	3.1	1105	0.8	1737	2.9	2341	1.1
21	TU	0549	3.1	1227	0.7	1845	2.9		
22	W	0058	1.0	0658	3.2	1333	0.6	1947	3.1
23	TH	0202	0.9	0800	3.4	1428	0.4	2040	3.2
24	F	0255	0.7	0856	3.5	1515	0.3	2129	3.3
25	SA	0344	0.6	0947	3.6	1559	0.3	2216	3.4
26	SU	0430	0.5	1036	3.6	1642	0.4	○ 2303	3.5
27	M	0516	0.5	1125	3.6	1726	0.5	2349	3.5
28	TU	0603	0.5	1212	3.5	1811	0.6		
29	W	0034	3.5	0650	0.5	1300	3.4	1857	0.8
30	TH	0119	3.5	0738	0.6	1348	3.3	1944	0.9
31	F	0204	3.4	0829	0.6	1438	3.1	2034	1.0

JUNE

Date	Day	Time	m	Time	m	Time	m	Time	m
1	SA	0250	3.3	0924	0.7	1531	2.9	2128	1.1
2	SU	0340	3.2	1021	0.8	1627	2.8	2224	1.1
3	M	0435	3.1	1118	0.8	1725	2.8	2321	1.2
4	TU	0532	3.0	1215	0.9	1824	2.8		
5	W	0021	1.2	0633	2.9	1312	0.8	1920	2.8
6	TH	0121	1.2	0734	2.9	1404	0.8	2010	2.9
7	F	0215	1.1	0828	3.0	1448	0.7	2055	3.0
8	SA	0301	1.0	0914	3.1	1527	0.7	2136	3.1
9	SU	0342	0.9	0954	3.2	1603	0.7	2215	3.2
10	M	0419	0.8	1031	3.2	1639	0.7	● 2253	3.3
11	TU	0457	0.7	1107	3.3	1716	0.7	2329	3.4
12	W	0535	0.7	1144	3.3	1754	0.8		
13	TH	0007	3.5	0614	0.6	1226	3.3	1835	0.8
14	F	0049	3.5	0657	0.6	1312	3.2	1921	0.8
15	SA	0133	3.5	0743	0.6	1403	3.1	2010	0.9
16	SU	0221	3.5	0834	0.6	1502	3.0	2104	0.9
17	M	0315	3.4	0933	0.6	1607	3.0	2203	1.0
18	TU	0417	3.3	1039	0.7	1713	2.9	2308	1.0
19	W	0523	3.3	1150	0.7	1818	3.0		
20	TH	0020	1.0	0631	3.3	1259	0.6	1919	3.0
21	F	0130	0.9	0737	3.4	1400	0.6	2017	3.2
22	SA	0231	0.8	0837	3.4	1453	0.5	2109	3.3
23	SU	0326	0.7	0931	3.5	1540	0.6	2158	3.4
24	M	0416	0.6	1021	3.5	1625	0.6	○ 2245	3.5
25	TU	0505	0.6	1109	3.5	1710	0.7	2331	3.5
26	W	0554	0.6	1156	3.4	1755	0.8		
27	TH	0016	3.5	0641	0.6	1242	3.3	1840	0.9
28	F	0100	3.5	0726	0.6	1328	3.1	1924	0.9
29	SA	0143	3.5	0809	0.7	1414	3.0	2006	1.0
30	SU	0226	3.4	0850	0.7	1501	3.0	2048	1.0

JULY

Date	Day	Time	m	Time	m	Time	m	Time	m
1	M	0310	3.3	0932	0.8	1550	2.9	2132	1.0
2	TU	0355	3.2	1019	0.8	1639	2.9	2219	1.1
3	W	0444	3.1	1112	0.9	1730	2.8	2313	1.1
4	TH	0538	2.9	1210	0.9	1823	2.9		
5	F	0015	1.2	0636	2.9	1310	0.9	1918	2.9
6	SA	0122	1.2	0738	2.9	1404	0.9	2012	3.0
7	SU	0221	1.1	0836	3.0	1452	0.8	2101	3.2
8	M	0311	1.0	0925	3.1	1534	0.8	2146	3.3
9	TU	0356	0.8	1009	3.2	1616	0.7	2227	3.4
10	W	0439	0.7	1049	3.3	1657	0.7	● 2307	3.5
11	TH	0521	0.6	1131	3.3	1740	0.8	2349	3.5
12	F	0605	0.5	1215	3.3	1825	0.8		
13	SA	0033	3.6	0648	0.4	1302	3.2	1910	0.8
14	SU	0119	3.6	0733	0.4	1352	3.2	1957	0.8
15	M	0207	3.6	0821	0.4	1445	3.1	2046	0.8
16	TU	0257	3.6	0912	0.5	1543	3.1	2139	0.8
17	W	0353	3.5	1010	0.6	1643	3.0	2239	0.9
18	TH	0455	3.4	1117	0.7	1746	3.0	2351	1.0
19	F	0604	3.3	1230	0.8	1853	3.0		
20	SA	0106	1.0	0716	3.2	1340	0.8	1957	3.1
21	SU	0216	0.9	0825	3.3	1438	0.8	2055	3.2
22	M	0316	0.8	0923	3.3	1528	0.8	2146	3.4
23	TU	0409	0.7	1013	3.3	1614	0.8	2233	3.4
24	W	0458	0.6	1059	3.3	1658	0.9	○ 2317	3.5
25	TH	0545	0.6	1143	3.2	1740	0.9	2359	3.5
26	F	0627	0.6	1224	3.1	1819	0.9		
27	SA	0040	3.5	0704	0.7	1305	3.1	1855	0.9
28	SU	0118	3.4	0735	0.7	1344	3.0	1931	0.9
29	M	0155	3.4	0805	0.7	1424	3.0	2007	0.9
30	TU	0230	3.3	0839	0.7	1505	3.0	2046	0.9
31	W	0306	3.2	0918	0.8	1550	2.9	2129	1.0

AUGUST

Date	Day	Time	m	Time	m	Time	m	Time	m
1	TH	0346	3.1	1005	0.9	1639	2.9	2218	1.1
2	F	0438	3.0	1103	1.0	1732	2.9	2318	1.2
3	SA	0542	2.9	1217	1.1	1831	2.9		
4	SU	0036	1.2	0651	2.8	1328	1.1	1931	3.0
5	M	0150	1.1	0800	2.9	1425	1.0	2027	3.1
6	TU	0248	1.0	0900	3.1	1513	0.9	2116	3.3
7	W	0337	0.8	0948	3.2	1557	0.8	2200	3.4
8	TH	0422	0.6	1032	3.3	1641	0.7	● 2243	3.5
9	F	0507	0.5	1116	3.3	1724	0.7	2328	3.6
10	SA	0550	0.4	1201	3.3	1809	0.7		
11	SU	0014	3.7	0633	0.3	1248	3.3	1853	0.6
12	M	0101	3.7	0716	0.3	1335	3.3	1937	0.6
13	TU	0148	3.7	0800	0.3	1423	3.2	2023	0.6
14	W	0237	3.7	0846	0.4	1513	3.2	2112	0.7
15	TH	0329	3.5	0939	0.6	1608	3.1	2211	0.9
16	F	0429	3.3	1044	0.8	1711	3.0	2328	1.0
17	SA	0539	3.1	1206	1.0	1826	3.0		
18	SU	0051	1.0	0701	3.0	1324	1.0	1942	3.0
19	M	0207	0.9	0819	3.1	1428	1.0	2045	3.2
20	TU	0311	0.8	0918	3.2	1520	1.0	2136	3.3
21	W	0404	0.7	1006	3.2	1605	0.9	2221	3.4
22	TH	0450	0.6	1049	3.2	1645	0.9	○ 2302	3.5
23	F	0530	0.6	1128	3.1	1721	0.9	2340	3.5
24	SA	0604	0.7	1204	3.1	1753	0.9		
25	SU	0015	3.4	0631	0.7	1237	3.1	1824	0.9
26	M	0047	3.4	0657	0.7	1308	3.1	1855	0.8
27	TU	0115	3.4	0724	0.7	1340	3.1	1928	0.8
28	W	0144	3.3	0755	0.7	1414	3.1	2004	0.8
29	TH	0216	3.3	0829	0.8	1453	3.1	2044	0.9
30	F	0254	3.2	0910	1.0	1541	3.0	2132	1.1
31	SA	0345	3.0	1004	1.1	1640	2.9	2231	1.2

Chart Datum: 2·01 metres below Ordnance Datum (Belfast)

Register for your **FREE** weekly weather email service from Macmillan Reeds
at **www.nauticaldata.com** – **NOW!**
weekend weather reports sent to your email address, every Thursday

TIME ZONE (UTC)
For Summer Time add ONE hour in **non-shaded areas**

NORTHERN IRELAND – BELFAST

LAT 54°36′N LONG 5°55′W

TIMES AND HEIGHTS OF HIGH AND LOW WATERS

SPRING & NEAP TIDES
Dates in red are SPRINGS
Dates in blue are NEAPS

YEAR **2002**

SEPTEMBER

Date	Day	Time	m	Time	m	Time	m	Time	m
1	SU	0457	2.8	1121	1.3	1745	2.9	2355	1.3
2	M	0615	2.8	1300	1.2	1852	3.0		
3	TU	0126	1.1	0730	2.9	1404	1.1	1954	3.1
4	W	0228	0.9	0837	3.0	1455	0.9	2047	3.3
5	TH	0319	0.7	0929	3.2	1540	0.8	2134	3.5
6	F	0404	0.5	1013	3.3	1623	0.7	2219	3.6
7	SA	0447	0.4	1057	3.3	1706	0.6	● 2305	3.7
8	SU	0529	0.3	1142	3.4	1748	0.6	2353	3.7
9	M	0611	0.2	1228	3.4	1831	0.5		
10	TU	0041	3.8	0652	0.2	1313	3.4	1913	0.5
11	W	0129	3.8	0734	0.3	1357	3.4	1957	0.6
12	TH	0216	3.7	0818	0.5	1443	3.3	2046	0.7
13	F	0307	3.5	0909	0.7	1535	3.2	2146	0.9
14	SA	0406	3.2	1012	1.0	1637	3.0	2309	1.0
15	SU	0518	3.0	1141	1.2	1757	2.9		
16	M	0035	1.0	0653	2.9	1305	1.3	1925	3.0
17	TU	0156	0.9	0811	3.0	1415	1.2	2030	3.2
18	W	0303	0.8	0906	3.1	1510	1.1	2120	3.3
19	TH	0352	0.6	0951	3.1	1553	1.0	2203	3.4
20	F	0432	0.6	1030	3.2	1628	0.9	2241	3.4
21	SA	0505	0.6	1106	3.1	1658	0.9	○ 2316	3.4
22	SU	0532	0.7	1137	3.1	1726	0.9	2345	3.4
23	M	0556	0.7	1205	3.2	1754	0.8		
24	TU	0010	3.4	0621	0.7	1232	3.2	1822	0.8
25	W	0035	3.4	0647	0.7	1301	3.3	1854	0.8
26	TH	0105	3.4	0716	0.8	1333	3.3	1929	0.8
27	F	0138	3.3	0750	0.9	1409	3.2	2009	0.9
28	SA	0218	3.2	0831	1.0	1454	3.1	2056	1.0
29	SU	0309	3.0	0924	1.2	1553	3.0	2156	1.2
30	M	0426	2.8	1036	1.4	1706	2.9	2317	1.3

OCTOBER

Date	Day	Time	m	Time	m	Time	m	Time	m
1	TU	0548	2.8	1231	1.4	1817	3.0		
2	W	0101	1.1	0703	2.9	1341	1.2	1922	3.1
3	TH	0205	0.9	0812	3.0	1434	1.0	2020	3.3
4	F	0256	0.6	0905	3.2	1520	0.8	2110	3.5
5	SA	0340	0.4	0950	3.3	1602	0.7	2157	3.6
6	SU	0422	0.3	1035	3.4	1643	0.6	● 2244	3.7
7	M	0502	0.3	1120	3.5	1724	0.5	2332	3.8
8	TU	0543	0.3	1205	3.5	1806	0.5		
9	W	0021	3.8	0625	0.3	1250	3.5	1849	0.5
10	TH	0110	3.7	0707	0.5	1334	3.5	1934	0.6
11	F	0158	3.6	0753	0.7	1418	3.4	2025	0.7
12	SA	0249	3.4	0844	0.9	1508	3.3	2127	0.9
13	SU	0348	3.1	0948	1.2	1607	3.1	2250	1.0
14	M	0500	2.9	1112	1.4	1724	3.0		
15	TU	0009	1.0	0635	2.8	1234	1.4	1855	3.0
16	W	0128	0.9	0749	2.9	1346	1.3	2002	3.1
17	TH	0236	0.8	0842	3.0	1445	1.2	2054	3.2
18	F	0325	0.7	0925	3.1	1529	1.0	2136	3.3
19	SA	0402	0.7	1003	3.2	1603	0.9	2214	3.3
20	SU	0431	0.7	1037	3.2	1631	0.9	2247	3.3
21	M	0457	0.7	1107	3.2	1658	0.9	○ 2314	3.3
22	TU	0523	0.8	1135	3.3	1726	0.8	2339	3.4
23	W	0549	0.8	1202	3.4	1755	0.8		
24	TH	0005	3.4	0615	0.8	1233	3.4	1826	0.8
25	F	0037	3.4	0645	0.9	1305	3.4	1902	0.8
26	SA	0113	3.3	0722	1.0	1342	3.4	1943	0.9
27	SU	0155	3.2	0805	1.1	1425	3.3	2031	1.0
28	M	0249	3.0	0900	1.3	1521	3.1	2131	1.1
29	TU	0406	2.9	1008	1.4	1632	3.1	2246	1.1
30	W	0525	2.8	1135	1.4	1745	3.1		
31	TH	0019	1.0	0636	2.9	1305	1.3	1852	3.2

NOVEMBER

Date	Day	Time	m	Time	m	Time	m	Time	m
1	F	0130	0.8	0743	3.1	1403	1.1	1952	3.3
2	SA	0224	0.6	0838	3.2	1452	0.9	2046	3.5
3	SU	0310	0.5	0926	3.4	1536	0.7	2136	3.7
4	M	0352	0.4	1011	3.5	1618	0.6	● 2224	3.7
5	TU	0433	0.4	1057	3.5	1701	0.5	2313	3.8
6	W	0516	0.4	1143	3.6	1745	0.5		
7	TH	0003	3.7	0559	0.5	1229	3.6	1830	0.5
8	F	0052	3.7	0645	0.7	1314	3.6	1918	0.6
9	SA	0142	3.5	0733	0.8	1400	3.5	2011	0.7
10	SU	0233	3.3	0826	1.0	1448	3.4	2114	0.8
11	M	0331	3.1	0928	1.2	1544	3.3	2226	0.9
12	TU	0437	2.9	1039	1.3	1649	3.1	2334	1.0
13	W	0557	2.8	1149	1.4	1805	3.0		
14	TH	0040	0.9	0708	2.8	1256	1.3	1917	3.0
15	F	0146	0.9	0803	2.9	1358	1.2	2014	3.1
16	SA	0239	0.8	0849	3.0	1449	1.1	2101	3.2
17	SU	0319	0.8	0928	3.1	1528	1.0	2141	3.2
18	M	0351	0.8	1003	3.2	1601	1.0	2216	3.3
19	TU	0421	0.8	1037	3.3	1631	0.9	2247	3.3
20	W	0451	0.8	1109	3.4	1701	0.8	○ 2316	3.3
21	TH	0521	0.8	1141	3.5	1733	0.8	2346	3.4
22	F	0552	0.9	1213	3.5	1808	0.8		
23	SA	0019	3.4	0626	0.9	1248	3.5	1845	0.8
24	SU	0059	3.3	0706	1.0	1326	3.5	1927	0.8
25	M	0144	3.2	0751	1.1	1410	3.4	2016	0.9
26	TU	0238	3.1	0844	1.2	1502	3.3	2113	0.9
27	W	0346	3.0	0945	1.3	1604	3.2	2220	1.0
28	TH	0458	2.9	1054	1.3	1712	3.2	2334	0.9
29	F	0606	2.9	1209	1.2	1820	3.3		
30	SA	0045	0.8	0711	3.0	1321	1.1	1924	3.4

DECEMBER

Date	Day	Time	m	Time	m	Time	m	Time	m
1	SU	0147	0.7	0809	3.2	1420	0.9	2023	3.5
2	M	0239	0.6	0901	3.3	1510	0.8	2116	3.6
3	TU	0325	0.5	0950	3.5	1558	0.7	2207	3.7
4	W	0410	0.5	1038	3.6	1644	0.6	● 2257	3.7
5	TH	0455	0.6	1125	3.6	1731	0.6	2347	3.6
6	F	0541	0.7	1212	3.7	1820	0.6		
7	SA	0036	3.5	0629	0.8	1259	3.7	1909	0.6
8	SU	0126	3.4	0718	0.9	1345	3.6	2002	0.7
9	M	0217	3.2	0809	1.0	1432	3.5	2057	0.7
10	TU	0310	3.1	0902	1.1	1521	3.4	2154	0.8
11	W	0406	2.9	0957	1.2	1615	3.2	2251	0.9
12	TH	0504	2.9	1055	1.3	1712	3.1	2348	0.9
13	F	0603	2.8	1155	1.3	1812	3.0		
14	SA	0046	1.0	0702	2.8	1258	1.3	1915	3.0
15	SU	0142	1.0	0757	2.9	1357	1.2	2014	3.0
16	M	0231	0.9	0846	3.0	1446	1.1	2103	3.1
17	TU	0311	0.9	0929	3.2	1528	1.0	2146	3.2
18	W	0348	0.9	1010	3.3	1605	0.9	2224	3.2
19	TH	0423	0.8	1048	3.4	1641	0.9	○ 2259	3.3
20	F	0459	0.9	1123	3.5	1718	0.8	2332	3.3
21	SA	0537	0.9	1158	3.5	1757	0.7		
22	SU	0008	3.3	0615	0.9	1234	3.6	1836	0.7
23	M	0048	3.3	0657	0.9	1313	3.6	1919	0.7
24	TU	0134	3.2	0742	0.9	1356	3.6	2005	0.6
25	W	0224	3.1	0830	1.0	1445	3.5	2056	0.7
26	TH	0322	3.0	0923	1.0	1539	3.4	2154	0.7
27	F	0425	3.0	1021	1.1	1640	3.4	2259	0.8
28	SA	0529	3.0	1128	1.1	1746	3.3		
29	SU	0008	0.8	0636	3.0	1244	1.1	1855	3.3
30	M	0117	0.7	0741	3.1	1354	1.0	2002	3.4
31	TU	0217	0.7	0841	3.2	1453	0.8	2101	3.5

Chart Datum: 2·01 metres below Ordnance Datum (Belfast)

Register for your FREE weekly weather email service from Macmillan Reeds
at www.nauticaldata.com – NOW!
weekend weather reports sent to your email address, every Thursday

LARNE 9.13.12

Antrim **54°51'·20N 05°47'·50W**

CHARTS AC 1237, 2198; Imray C62, C64; Irish OS 9

TIDES +0005 Dover; ML 1·6; Duration 0620; Zone 0 (UT)

Standard Port BELFAST (⟵)

Times				**Height (metres)**			
High Water		Low Water		MHWS	MHWN	MLWN	MLWS
0100	0700	0000	0600	3·5	3·0	1·1	0·4
1300	1900	1200	1800				
Differences LARNE							
+0005	0000	+0010	–0005	–0·7	–0·5	–0·3	0·0
RED BAY							
+0022	–0010	+0007	–0017	–1·9	–1·5	–0·8	–0·2
CUSHENDUN BAY							
+0010	–0030	0000	–0025	–1·7	–1·5	–0·6	–0·2

SHELTER Secure shelter in Larne Lough or ⚓ overnight outside hbr in Brown's Bay (E of Barr Pt) in 2–4m. Hbr can be entered H24 in any conditions. Larne is a busy commercial and ferry port; W side is commercial until Curran Pt where there are two YCs with congested moorings. ⚓ S of Ballylumford Power Stn. No AB available for visitors. Yachts should not berth on any commercial quays, inc Castle Quay, without Hr Mr's express permission. Boat Hbr (0·6m) 2ca S of Ferris Pt only for shoal draft craft. Note: Work continues (started 1993) to extend the harbour southward and will eventually result in E Antrim BC moving to Curran Point, with fewer moorings.

NAVIGATION WPT 54°51'·70N 05°47'·47W, 004°/184° from/to front ldg lt, 2·1M. Beware Hunter Rk 2M NE of hbr ent. Magnetic anomalies exist near Hunter Rk and between it and the mainland. Inside the narrow ent, the recommended chan is close to the E shore. Tide in the ent runs at up to 3½kn.

LIGHTS AND MARKS Ldg lts 184°, Oc 4s 6/14m 12M, synch and vis 179°-189°; W ◊ with R stripes. Chaine Tr and fairway lts as chartlet. Note: Many shore lts on W side of ent may be mistaken for nav lts.

RADIO TELEPHONE VHF Ch 14 16 *Larne Harbour.* Traffic, weather and tidal info available on Ch 14.

TELEPHONE (Dial code 02828) Hr Mr 872100 📠 872209; MRSC 9146 3933; Pilot 2827 3785; ⊖ 9035 8250; Marinecall 09068 500 465; Dr 275331; Police 2827 2266.

FACILITIES **Pier** ☎ 2827 9221, M, L, FW, C (32 ton); **E Antrim Boat Club** ☎ 2827 7204, Visitors should pre-contact Sec'y for advice on moorings; Slip, L, V, FW, Bar; **Services:** D, Gas, Sh, El. **Town** EC Tues; P & D (delivered, tidal), CH, V, R, Bar, ✉, Ⓑ, ⇌, Ferry to Cairnryan and Stranraer, ✈ (Belfast City and Belfast/Aldergrove).

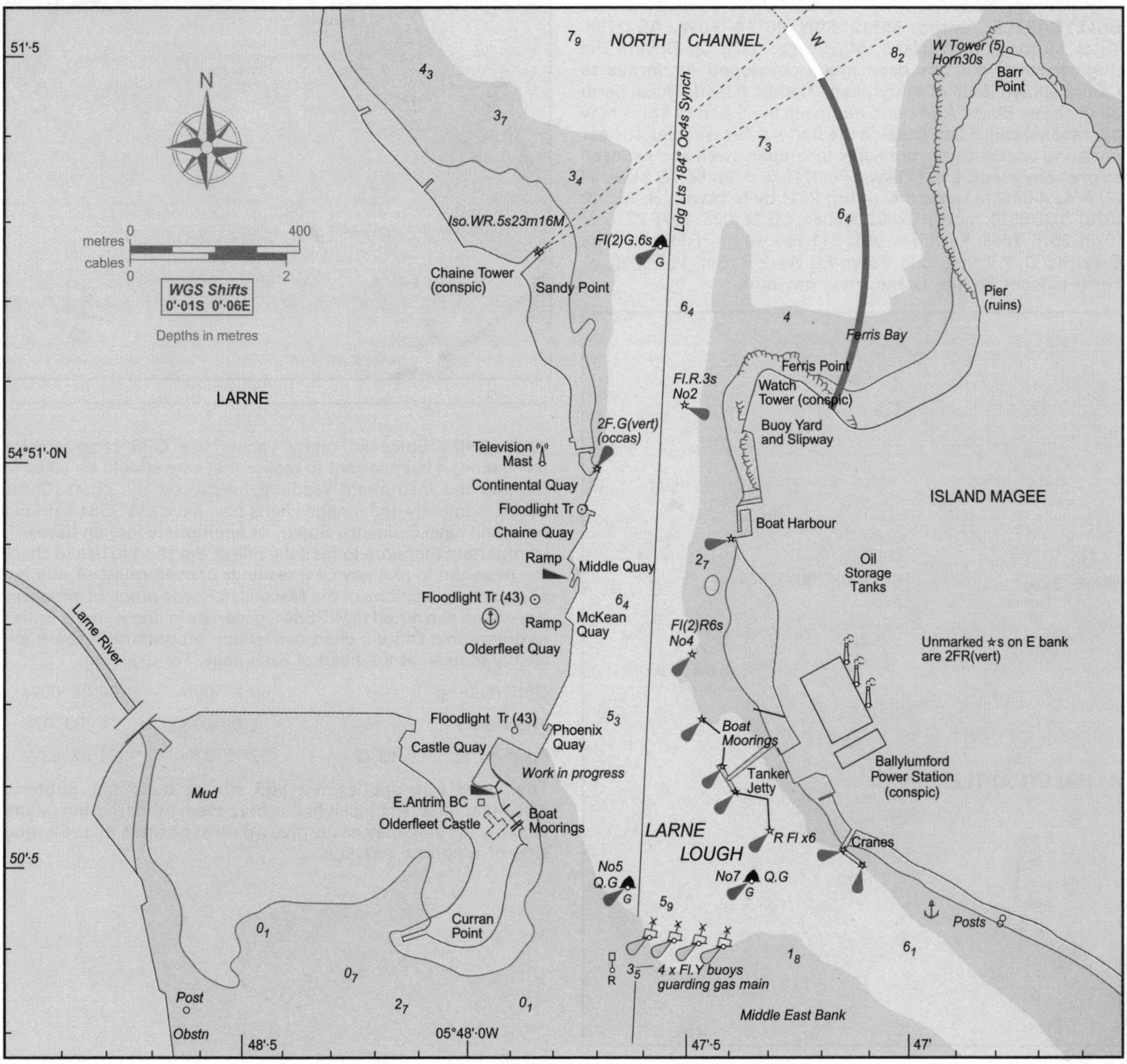

MINOR HARBOURS AND ANCHORAGES BETWEEN LARNE AND PORTRUSH

GLENARM, Antrim, **54°58′N 05°57′W**. Hr Mr and Marina ☎ 07703 606763. 60+30Ⓥ in 5m, FW, D, AC, ⊡. **Village** V, P (cans).

CARNLOUGH HARBOUR, Antrim, **54°59′·87N 05°59′·20W**. AC 2198. HW +0006 on Dover, +0005 on Belfast; HW –1·6m on Belfast; ML no data; Duration 0625. Good shelter, but often full, except in SE gales; do not ent in onshore winds >F6. Ldg marks 310°, Y ▽s on B/W posts. N pier lt, Fl G 3s 4m 5M; S pier Fl R 3s 6m 5M, both lts on B/W columns. Beware: fish farms in the bay marked by lt buoys (unreliable); and rks which cover at HW on either side of ent. Small hbr used by yachts and small FVs; visitors welcome. Ent and hbr dredged 2m every May. Hr Mr ☎ (028) 2827 2373. Facilities: **Quay** AB £9, AC (see Hr Mr), FW, Slip. **Town** P & D (cans), Gas, Gaz, ⊠, R, V, Bar, ♿.

RED BAY, Antrim, **55°03′·91N 06°03′·13W**. AC 2199. HW +0010 on Dover; ML 1·1m; Duration 0625. See 9.13.12. Good holding, but open to E winds. Beware rks, 2 ruined piers W of Garron Pt and fish farms, marked by lt buoys, on S side of bay, approx ½M from shore. Glenariff pier has lt Fl 3s 10m 5M. In S and E winds ⚓ 2ca off W stone arch near hd of bay in approx 3·5m; in N or W winds ⚓ S of small pier in 2 – 5m, ½M NE of Waterfoot village. Facilities: **Cushendall** (1M N of pier) Bar, D & P (cans), ⊠, R, V, Gas; **Services:** CH, El, Slip. **Waterfoot** Bar, R, ⊠.

BALLYCASTLE, Antrim, **55°12'·50N 06°14'·30W**. AC 2798. Tides as for Rathlin Island; ML 0·8m; –0320 on Dover. The original small hbr has been much developed for ferries to Campbeltown (Mull of Kintyre) and Rathlin Island. These berth on the outer bkwtr. A 74 berth marina in the S part of hbr is now operational with 3·2m. Outside the hbr is a fair weather ⚓, clear of strong tidal streams, but liable to sudden swell and exposed to onshore winds. Lts: N bkwtr Fl (3) G 6s 6·5m 6M; S bkwtr Fl (2) R 4s 4·6m 1M, obsc'd N of brg 261° by N bkwtr. Hr Mr ☎ (028) 2076 8525, mobile 07803 505084; CG ☎ (028) 2076 2226; Ⓗ (028) 2076 2666. **Facilities**: AB, £11.75 <9·14m, E,FW, L, Slip. **Services:** D, P (cans), Gas. **Town** EC Wed; R, Bar, V, ⊠, Ⓑ, ♿. Ferry to/from Rathlin Island (next column).

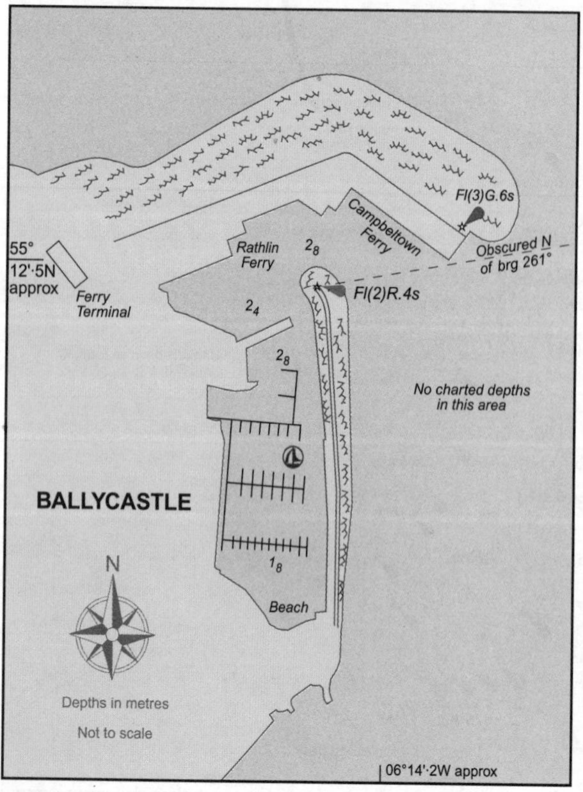

RATHLIN ISLAND, Antrim, **55°17'·52N 06°11'·60W**. AC 2798. HW sp –0445, nps –0200 on Dover. Small hbr in NE corner of Church Bay, sheltered from winds NW through E to SSE. New outer piers and ramp have equipped it for ferry service to Ballycastle. Beware sp streams up to 6kn in Rathlin Sound and the North Channel TSS (above), 2M to the N and E of the island. Pass N or E of a wreck 6ca SW of hbr, marked on its SE side by a SCM buoy, Q(6)+L Fl 15s. When clear, appr on NNE to the new W and S piers which form an outer hbr. White sector of Manor House pier dir lt, Oc WRG 4s 5M, G020°-023°, W023°-026°, R026°-029°, leads 024·5° to inner hbr (2m) ent via chan dredged 3·5m. W pier Fl R 2s 5·3m 3M; S pier Fl (2) G 6s 3·5m 3M, obsc'd 062°-130° (68°) by W pier. Possible AB in inner hbr. ⚓ in outer hbr on NW side in about 1.2m clear of ferry ramp; or outside hbr, close to W pier in about 5m. Other lts on Rathlin Is: Rue Point (S tip), Fl (2) 5s 16m 14M, W 8-sided tr, B bands. Rathlin East (Altacarry Head), Fl (4) 20s 74m 26M, H24, vis 110°–006°, 036°–058°, W tr, B band, Racon. Rathlin West, Fl R 5s 62m 22M, vis 015°–225°, shown by day in low vis, W tr, lamp at base; fog det lt VQ, 69m, vis 119°. **Facilities**: Church Bay R, Bar, V, ⊠. Ferry to Ballycastle.

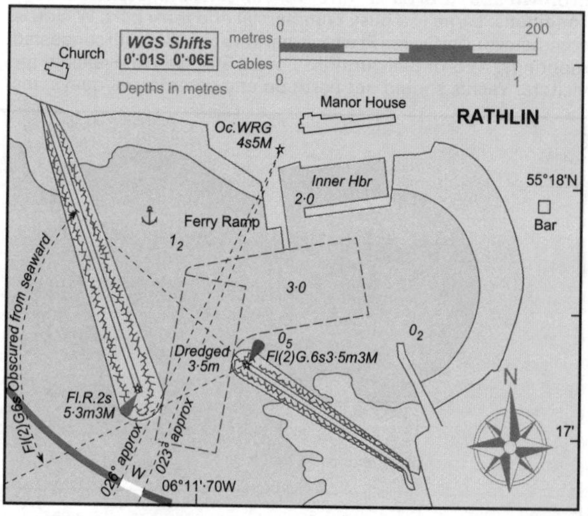

WGS SHIFT Since so many yachts use GPS receivers for navigation, it is important to realise that care should be taken in plotting the instrument reading directly on the chart. Some British Admiralty and foreign charts now have a WGS84 base but most still have Ordnance Survey or appropriate foreign bases. It is important therefore to read the title of the chart in use to check the base and to plot any GPS readings in conformity. A number of sections in editions of the Macmillan Reeds range of almanacs have been converted to WGS84 - generally in line with the British Hydrographic Office's chart conversion programme - these are clearly marked at the head of each page. For example:

GPS reading	50°20′·00N	04°08′·00W
WGS shift	00′·03S	00′·07E
Position applied to chart	50°19′·97N	04°07′·93W

The usual rule applies, viz **add** similar headings, **subtract** dissimilar ones. At first sight this may seem academic but failure to apply the shift may easily give a plotted position on the wrong side of a narrow passage.

TIDAL STREAMS AROUND RATHLIN ISLAND *9.13.13*

North Ireland 9.13.3 | Off Mull of Kintyre 9.9.12 | South Ireland 9.12.3
North Irish Sea 9.10.3 | SW Scotland 9.9.3

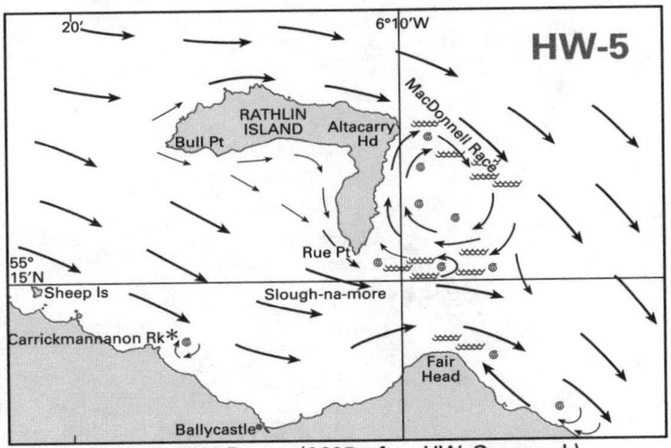

5 Hours before HW Dover (0605 after HW Greenock)

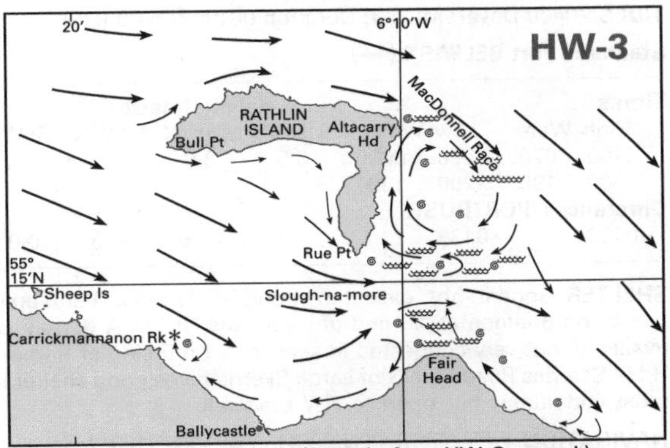

3 Hours before HW Dover (0420 before HW Greenock)

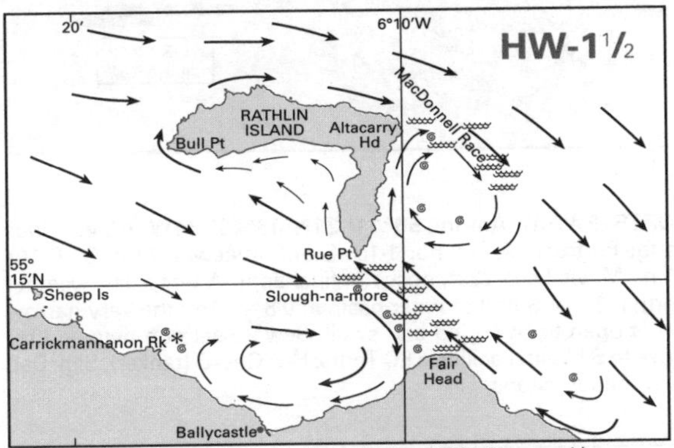

1½ Hours before HW Dover (0250 before HW Greenock)

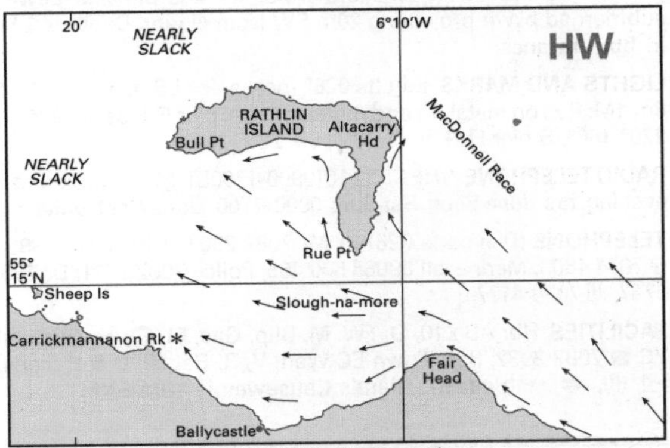

HW Dover (0120 before HW Greenock)

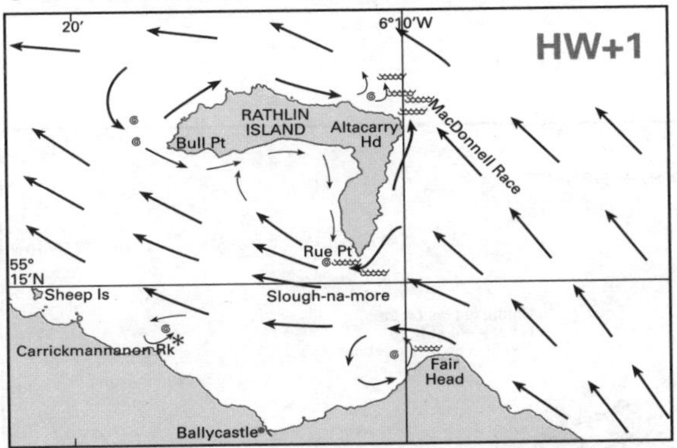

1 Hour after HW Dover (0020 before HW Greenock)

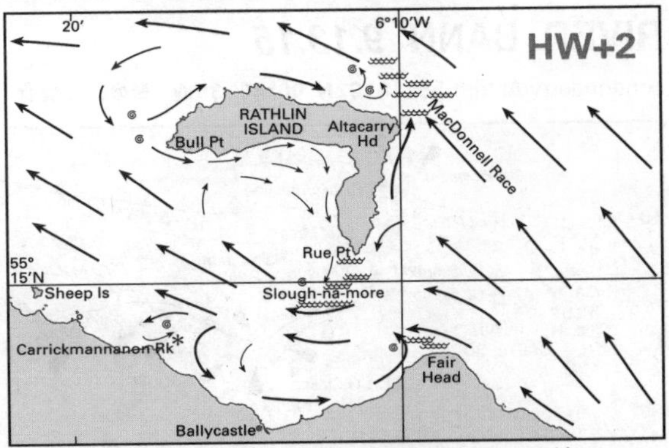

2 Hours after HW Dover (0040 after HW Greenock)

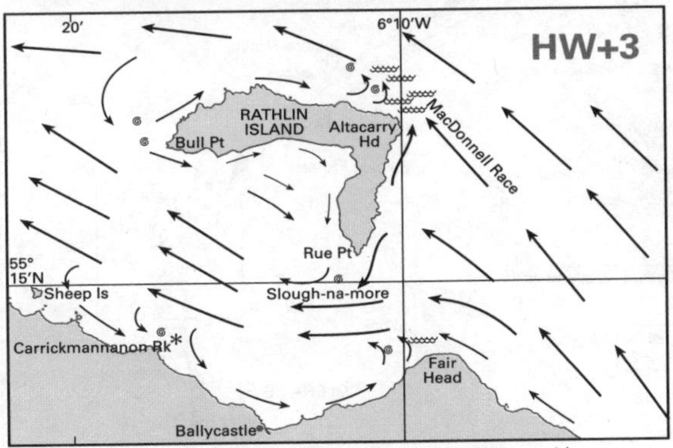

3 Hours after HW Dover (0140 after HW Greenock)

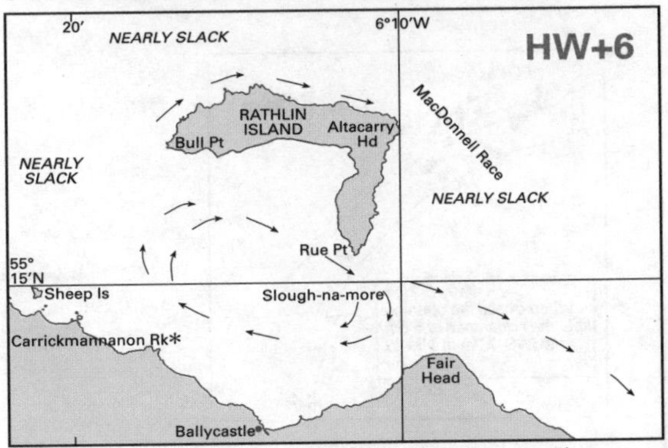

6 Hours after HW Dover (0440 after HW Greenock)

PORTRUSH *9.13.14*

Antrim **55°12'·34N 06°39'·49W**

CHARTS AC 49, 2499, 2798; Imray C53, C64; Irish OS 4

TIDES –0400 Dover; ML 1·1; Duration 0610; Zone 0 (UT)

Standard Port BELFAST (⟵)

Times				**Height (metres)**			
High Water		Low Water		MHWS	MHWN	MLWN	MLWS
0100	0700	0000	0600	3·5	3·0	1·1	0·4
1300	1900	1200	1800				
Differences PORTRUSH							
–0433		–0433		–1·6	–1·6	–0·3	0·0

SHELTER Good in hbr, except in strong NW/N winds. Berth on N pier or on pontoon at NE end of it and see Hr Mr. A ⚓ may be available, but very congested in season. ⚓ on E side of Ramore Hd in Skerries Roads 1ca S of Large Skerrie gives good shelter in most conditions, but open to NW sea/swell.

NAVIGATION WPT 55°13'·00N 06°41'·00W, 308°/128° from/to N pier lt, 1·1M. Ent with on-shore winds >F 4 is difficult. Beware submerged bkwtr projecting 20m SW from N pier. Depth is 2·8m in hbr entrance.

LIGHTS AND MARKS Ldg lts 028° (occas, for LB use) both FR 6/8m 1M; R △ on metal bn and metal mast. N pier Fl R 3s 6m 3M; vis 220°-160°. S pier Fl G 3s 6m 3M; vis 220°-100°.

RADIOTELEPHONE VHF Ch 12 16 (0900-1700LT, Mon-Fri; extended evening hrs June-Sept; Sat-Sun: 0900–1700, June-Sept only).

TELEPHONE (Dial code 028) Hr Mr 7082 2307; MRSC 9146 3933; ⊖ 7034 4803; Marinecall 09068 500 465; Police 7082 2721; Dr 7082 3767; Ⓗ 7034 4177.

FACILITIES Hbr AB £10, D, FW, M, Slip, Gas, El, Ⓔ, ♿; Portrush YC ☎ 7082 3932, Bar; Town EC Wed; V, R, Bar, ▣, D & P (cans), ✉, Ⓑ, ⇌, ✈ (Belfast). Giant's Causeway is 10M ENE.

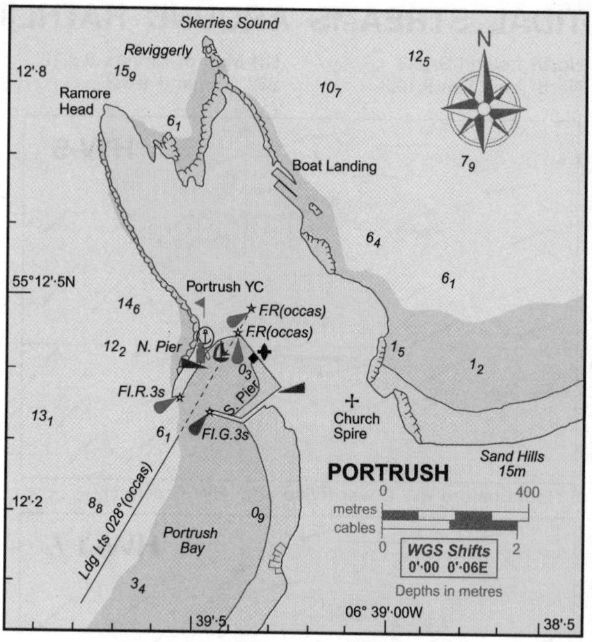

PORTSTEWART, Antrim, **55°11'·21N 06°43'·21W**. AC 49. Tides as for Portrush. A tiny hbr 1·1ca S of Portstewart Pt lt, Oc R 10s 21m 5M, vis 040°–220°, obscd in final appr. A temp, fair weather berth (£10) at S end of inner basin in 0·8 – 1·7m; the very narrow ent is open to SW wind and swell. Beware salmon nets and rks close to S bkwtr. Facilities: EC Thurs; FW, Gas, D (tanker), Slip, Bar, V, R, handy shops.

RIVER BANN *9.13.15*

Londonderry/Antrim **55°10'·32N 06°46'·35W**

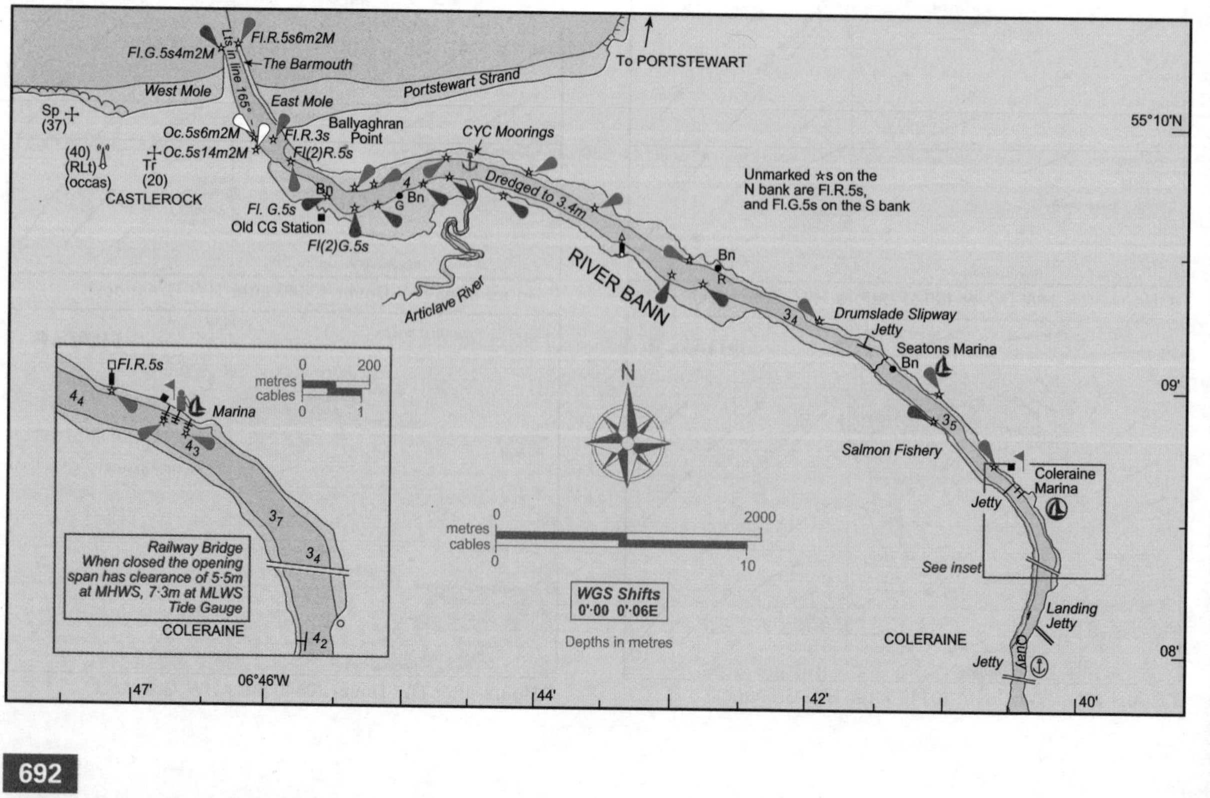

RIVER BANN *continued*

CHARTS AC 2499, 2798, 2723; Imray C64; Irish OS 4

TIDES –0345 Dover (Coleraine); ML 1·1; Duration 0540; Zone 0 (UT)

Standard Port BELFAST (⟵)

Times				Height (metres)			
High Water		Low Water		MHWS	MHWN	MLWN	MLWS
0100	0700	0000	0600	3·5	3·0	1·1	0·4
1300	1900	1200	1800				
Differences COLERAINE							
–0403		–0403		–1·3	–1·2	–0·2	0·0

SHELTER Good, once inside the river ent (The Barmouth) between 2 training walls, extending 2ca N from the beaches. Do not try to enter in strong on-shore winds or when swell breaks on the pierheads. If in doubt call Coleraine Hbr Radio or ring Hr Mr. ⚓ upstream of old CG stn, or berth at Seaton's or Coleraine marinas, 3½M & 4½M from ent, on NE bank.

NAVIGATION WPT 55°11′·00N, 06°46′·65W, 345°/165° from/to ent, 0·72M. Appr from E of N to bring ldg lts into line at bkwtr ends. The sand bar is constantly moving but ent is dredged to approx 3·5m. Beware salmon nets across the width of the river at 2M or 4M above ent, May to July. Also beware commercial traffic.

LIGHTS AND MARKS Ldg lts 165°, both Oc 5s 6/14m 2M, front on W pyramidal metal tr; rear W □ tr. Portstewart Pt, Oc R 10s, is 2M ENE.

RADIO TELEPHONE Coleraine Hbr Radio Ch 12 (Mon-Fri: HO and when vessel due). Coleraine Marina Ch M.

TELEPHONE (Dial code 028) Hr Mr 7034 2012, 🖷 7035 2000; ⊖ 9035 8250 or 7034 4803; MRSC 9146 3933; Marinecall 09068 500 465; Rly Bridge 7034 2403; Police 7034 4122; Ⓗ 7034 4177; Dr 7034 4831.

FACILITIES **Seatons Marina** ☎ 7083 2086 mobile 07733 100915, £8.00, FW, BH (10 ton), CH, Slip. **Coleraine Hbr** ☎ 7034 2012, BH (35 ton); **Coleraine (Borough Council) Marina** (45+15 visitors), ☎ 7034 4768, £10, Slip, D, FW, R, BH (15 ton), AC; **Coleraine YC** ☎ 7034 4503, Bar, M; **Services**: Gas, Kos, El, Ⓔ. **Town** EC Thurs; P & D (cans), V, R, ✉, Ⓑ, ⇌, ✈ (Belfast).

LOUGH FOYLE *9.13.16*

Londonderry (to SE)/Donegal (to NW) **55°14'N 06°54W**

CHARTS AC 2499, 2798, 2723; Imray C53, C64; Irish OS 3, 4, 7

TIDES
Warren Point: –0430 Dover
Moville: –0350 Dover; –0055 Londonderry; –0400 Belfast
Culmore Point: –0025 Londonderry
Londonderry: –0255 Dover
ML 1·6; Duration 0615; Zone 0 (UT)

Standard Port GALWAY (⟵)

Times				Height (metres)			
High Water		Low Water		MHWS	MHWN	MLWN	MLWS
0200	0900	0200	0800	5·1	3·9	2·0	0·6
1400	2100	1400	2000				
Differences LONDONDERRY							
+0254	+0319	+0322	+0321	–2·4	–1·8	–0·8	–0·1
INISHTRAHULL							
+0100	+0100	+0115	+0200	–1·8	–1·4	–0·4	–0·2
PORTMORE							
+0120	+0120	+0135	+0135	–1·3	–1·1	–0·4	–0·1
TRAWBREAGA BAY							
+0115	+0059	+0109	+0125	–1·1	–0·8	No data	

SHELTER The SE side of the Lough is low lying and shallow. The NW rises steeply and has several village hbrs between the ent and Londonderry (often referred to as Derry).
Greencastle: a busy fishing hbr, open to swell in winds SW to E. Only advised for yachts in emergency.
Moville: the pier, with 1·5m at the end, is near the village (shops closed all day Wed), but is much damaged. ⚓ outside hbr is exposed; inside hbr for shoal draft only. 8 Y 🅐s are about 600m up-stream.
Carrickarory: pier/quay is condemned as unsafe. ⚓ in bay is sheltered in winds from SW to NNW.
Culmore Bay: Complete shelter. ⚓ 1½ca W of Culmore Pt in pleasant cove, 4M from Londonderry.
Londonderry: Little used by yachts, although commercial operations have been transferred to new facilities at Lisahally (55°02'·6N 07°15'·6W). AB on non-commercial quay below Guildhall or ⚓ close below Craigavon Bridge clearance 1·7m.

NAVIGATION WPT Tuns PHM buoy, Fl R 3s, 55°14′·00N 06°53′·49W, 055°/235° from/to Warren Pt lt, 2·5M. The Tuns bank lies 3M NE of Magilligan Pt. The main or N Chan, ¾M wide, runs NW of The Tuns; a lesser chan, min depth 4m, runs 3ca off shore around NE side of Magilligan Pt. Beware commercial traffic. Foyle Bridge at Rosses Pt has 32m clearance. In June and July the chan is at times obstructed by salmon nets at night. N Chan tides reach 3½kn, and up-river the ebb runs up to 6kn.

LIGHTS AND MARKS Inishowen Fl (2) WRG 10s 28m 18/14M; W tr, 2 B bands; vis G197°–211°, W211°–249°, R249°–000°; Horn (2) 30s. Warren Pt Fl 1·5s 9m 10M; W tr, G abutment; vis 232°–061°. Magilligan Pt QR 7m 4M; R structure. The main chan up to Londonderry is very well lit. Foyle Bridge centre FW each side; VQ G on W pier; VQ R on E.

RADIO TELEPHONE VHF Ch 14 12 16 (H24). Traffic and nav info Ch 14.

TELEPHONE (Dial code 028) Hr Mr (at Lisahally) 7186 0555, 🖷 7186 1168; MRSC 9146 3933; ⊖ 7126 1937 or 9035 8250; Marinecall 09068 500 465; Police 7126 1893; Dr 7126 4868; Ⓗ 7034 5171.

FACILITIES (Londonderry) **Hbr Mr** ☎ 7186 0555, M, FW; **Prehen Boat Club** ☎ 7034 3405. **City** P & D (cans), ME, El, V, R, Bar, ✉, Ⓑ, ⇌, ✈. CULDAFF BAY (10M W of Foyle SWM buoy) 6 Y 🅐s are at 55°18'N 07°09'·1W, off Bunnagee Port.

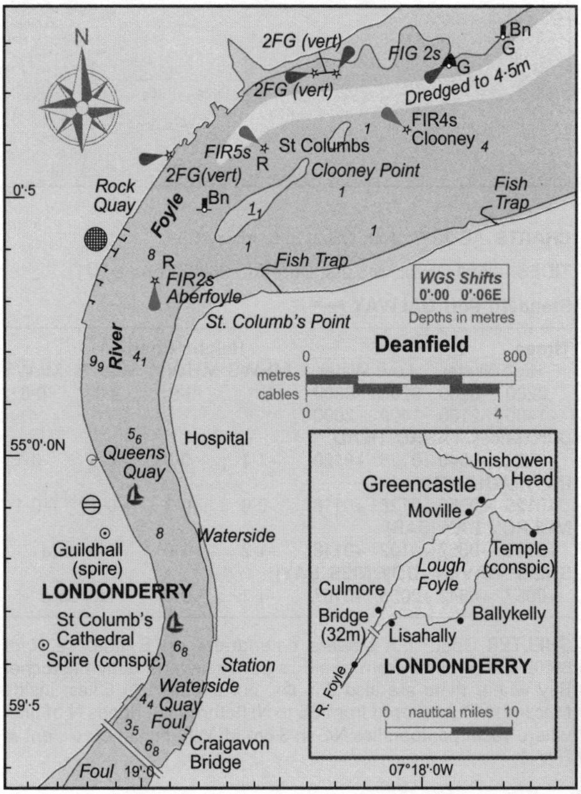

13

LOUGH SWILLY *9.13.17*

Donegal **55°17'N 07°34'W**

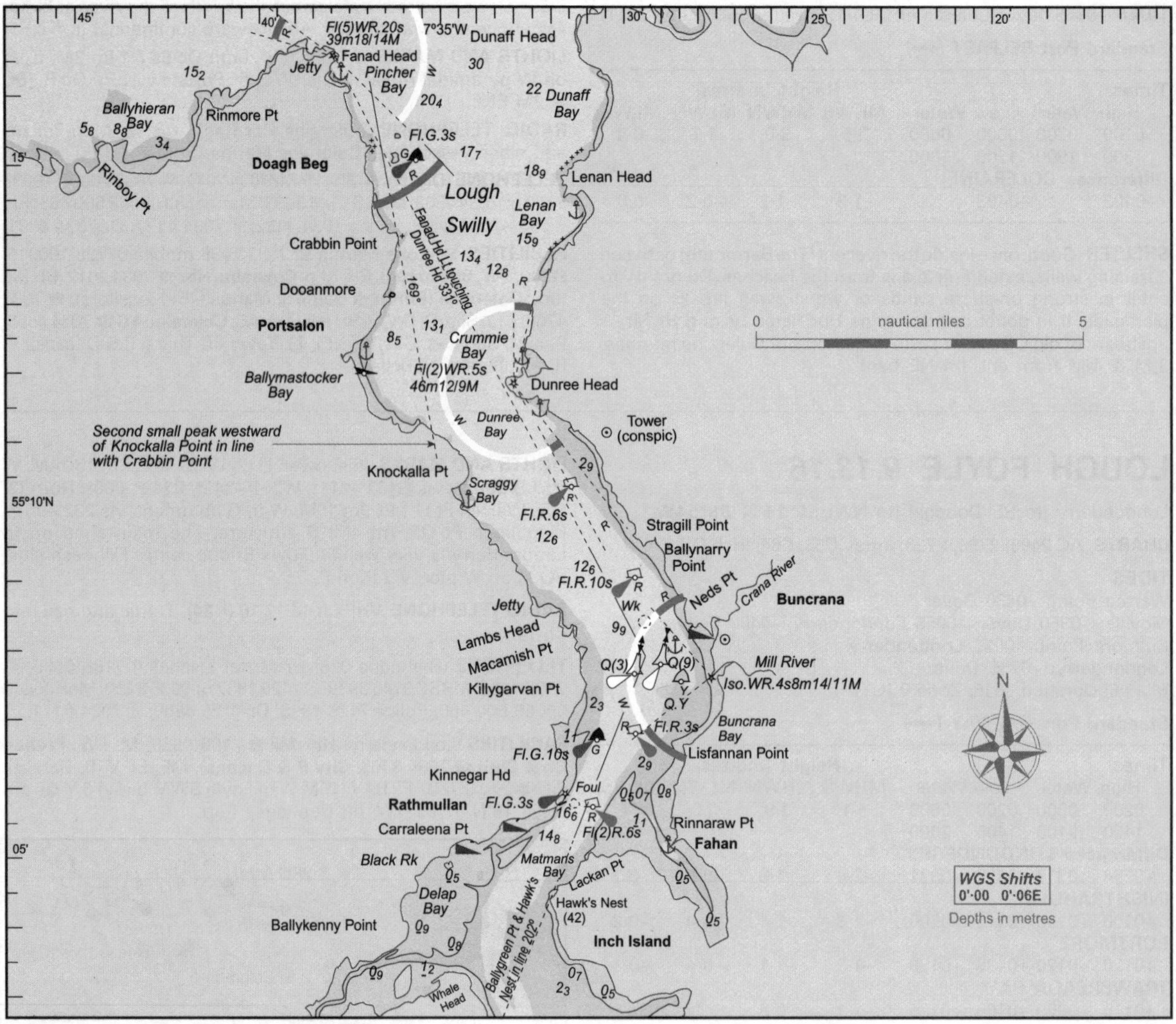

CHARTS AC 2697; Irish OS 2, 3, 6; Imray C53

TIDES –0500 Dover; ML 2·3; Duration 0605; Zone 0 (UT)

Standard Port GALWAY (⟶)

Times				Height (metres)			
High Water		Low Water		MHWS	MHWN	MLWN	MLWS
0200	0900	0200	0800	5·1	3·9	2·0	0·6
1400	2100	1400	2000				
Differences FANAD HEAD							
+0115	+0040	+0125	+0120	–1·1	–0·9	–0·5	–0·1
RATHMULLAN							
+0125	+0050	+0126	+0118	–0·8	–0·7	–0·1	–0·1
MULROY BAY (BAR)							
+0108	+0052	+0102	+0118	–1·2	–1·0	No data	
SHEEP HAVEN (DOWNIES BAY)							
+0057	+0043	+0053	+0107	–1·1	–0·9	No data	

SHELTER Good, but beware downdrafts on E side. ⚓s N of 55°05'N may suffer from swell. ⚓s from seaward: Ballymastocher Bay where there are also 8 Y 🅜s, but exposed to E'lies; inside Macamish Pt, sheltered from SE to N; Rathmullan Roads N of pier, where yacht pontoon lies N/S in 3·6m MLWS; Fahan Creek, ent at HW–1.

NAVIGATION WPT 55°17'·50N 07°34'·50W, 352°/172° from/to Dunree Hd lt, 5·7M. Ent is easy and main chan is well lit/buoyed. Beware: off W shore Swilly More Rks, Kinnegar Spit and Strand; off E shore Colpagh Rks and Inch Flats. These dangers are buoyed, as is Fahan Creek. There are mussel lines off Knockalla Pt, Killygarvan Pt and Macamish Pt and a salmon farm S of Scraggy Bay (☎ 074 51072/59071 for permission to use their pier).

LIGHTS AND MARKS Fanad Hd lt, Fl (5) WR 20s 39m 18/14M, touching Dunree Hd lt, Fl (2) WR 5s 46m 12/9M, leads 151° into the Lough. Thence Ballygreen Pt and Hawk's Nest in line at 202°.

RADIO TELEPHONE None.

TELEPHONE (Dial codes: W side of lough 074; E side 077) Rathmullan Pontoon 58131, 58315 (eves); MRCC 077 70243; ⊖ 074 26324; Police (074) 51002 and (077) 61555; Dr (074) 58416 (Rathmullan) and (077) 63611 (Buncrana).

FACILITIES **Rathmullan** Pontoon berth €6·35/day, €12·70 overnight, FW, slip. Services: ▣, R, Hotel, Bar, D & P (cans), Kos, V, ✉, EC Wed. **Ramelton** AB (drying), BY ☎ 074 51082, Bar, R, D & P (cans), FW, Kos, V, ✉. **Fahan** Slip, FW, Bar, R, ✉, **Lough Swilly YC** ☎ 077 60189. Services (1M SE): V, D & P (cans), ⇌, ✈ (Londonderry 10M bus/taxi). **Buncrana** AB(drying), Hotel, R, Bar, Ⓑ, ✉, V, ▣, D & P (cans), Kos.

OTHER HARBOURS AND ANCHORAGES IN DONEGAL

MULROY BAY, Donegal, **55°15´·30N 07°46´·30W**. AC 2699; HW (bar) –0455 on Dover. See 9.13.17. Beware Limeburner Rk, (marked by NCM buoy, Q, whis) 3M N of ent and the bar which is dangerous in swell or onshore winds. Ent at half flood (not HW); chan lies between Bar Rks and Sessiagh Rks, thence through First, Second and Third Narrows (with strong tides) to Broad Water. HW at the head of the lough is 2¼ hrs later than at the bar. ⚓s: Close SW of Ravedy Is (Fl 3s 9m 3M); Fanny's Bay (2m), excellent; Rosnakill Bay (3·5m) in SE side; Cranford Bay; Milford Port (3 to 4m). Beware power cable 6m, over Moross chan, barring North Water to masted boats. Facilities: **Milford Port** AB, FW, V; **Fanny's Bay** ✉, Shop at Downings village (1M), hotel at Rosepenna (¾M).

SHEEP HAVEN, Donegal, **55°11´·00N 07°51´·00W**. AC 2699. HW –0515 on Dover. See 9.13.17. Bay is 2M wide with many ⚓s, easily accessible in daylight, but exposed to N winds. Beware rks off Rinnafaghla Pt, and further S: Black Rk (6m) and Wherryman Rks, which dry, 1ca off E shore. ⚓ or 8 Y ⚲s in Downies Bay to SE of pier; in Pollcormick inlet close W in 3m; in Ards Bay for excellent shelter, but beware the bar in strong winds. Lts: Portnablahy ldg lts 125°, both Oc 6s 7/12m 2M, B col, W bands; Downies pier hd, Fl R 3s 5m 2M, R post. Facilities: (Downies) EC Wed; V, FW, P (cans 300m), R, Bar; (Portnablahy Bay) V, P (cans), R, Bar.

GWEEDORE HBR/BUNBEG, Donegal, **55°03'·75N 08°18'·87W**. AC 1883. Tides see 9.13.18. Gweedore hbr, the estuary of the R Gweedore, has sheltered ⚓s or temp AB at Bunbeg Quay, usually full of FVs. Apprs via Gola N or S Sounds are not simple especially in poor visibility. N Sound is easier with ldg lts 171°, both Oc 3s 9/13m 2M, B/W bns, on the SE tip of Gola Is. (There are also ⚓s on the S and E sides of Gola Is). E of Bo Is the bar 0·4m has a Fl G 3s and the chan, lying E of Inishinny Is and W of Inishcoole, is marked by a QG and 3 QR. A QG marks ent to Bunbeg. Night ent not advised. Facilities: FW, D at quay; V, ✉, Ⓑ, Bar at village ½M.

BURTONPORT, Donegal, **54°58´·93N 08°26´·60W**. AC 2792, 1879. HW –0525 on Dover; ML 2·0m; Duration 0605. See 9.13.18. Usual appr via N Chan. Ent safe in all weathers except NW gales. Hbr very full, no space to ⚓; berth on local boat at pier or go to Rutland Hbr or Aran Roads: 6 Y ⚲s 250m NE of Black Rks, Fl R 3s. Ldg marks/lts: N Chan ldg lts on Inishcoo 119·3°, both Iso 6s 6/11m 1M; front W bn, B band; rear B bn, Y band. Rutland Is ldg lts 138°, both Oc 6s 8/14m 1M; front W bn, B band; rear B bn, Y band. Burtonport ldg lts 068°, both FG 17/23m 1M; front Gy bn, W band; rear Gy bn, Y band. Hr Mr ☎ (075) 42258 (43170 home), 📠 (074) 41205; VHF Ch 06, 12, **14**, 16. Facilities: D (just inside pier), FW (root of pier), P (½M inland). **Village** Bar, ✉, R, V, Kos.

INISHKEEL, Donegal, **54°50´·82N 08°26´·50W**. AC 2792. 6 Y ⚲s in Church Pool, 3ca E of Inishkeel. Open to N/NE'lies.

TEELIN HARBOUR, Donegal, **54°37´·50N 08°37´·87W**. AC 2792. Tides as 9.13.18. A possible passage ⚓, mid-way between Rathlin O'Birne and Killybegs. But Hbr is open to S'ly swell and prone to squalls in NW winds. Ent, 1ca wide, is close E of Teelin Pt lt, Fl R 10s, which is hard to see by day. 4 Y ⚲s and ⚓ on E side in 3m to N of pier, or ⚓ on E side near pier. Many moorings and, in the NE, mussel rafts. Facilities: possible FW, D, V at Carrick, 3M inland.

KILLYBEGS *9.13.18*

Donegal **54°36'·90N 08°26'·80W** ❁❁❁◊◊✿

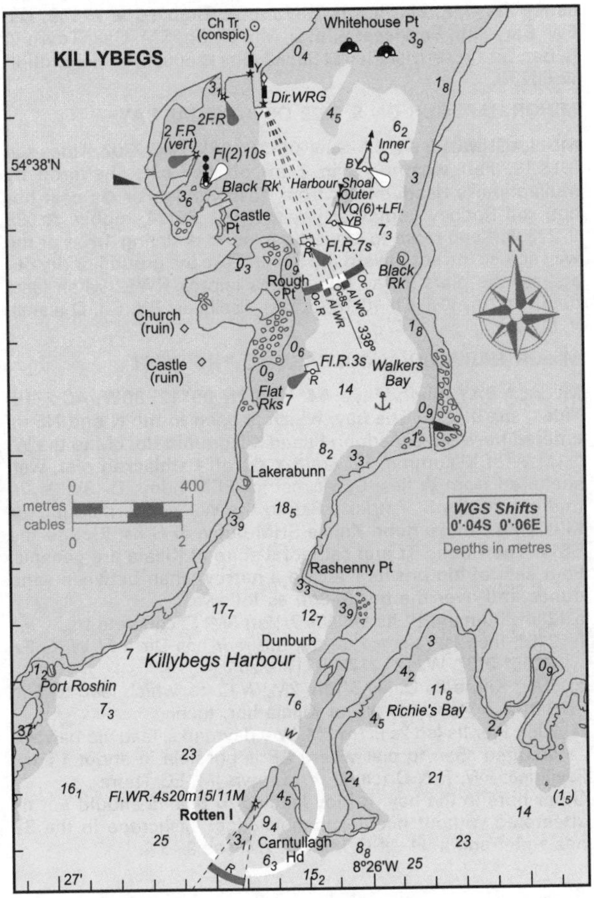

CHARTS AC 2792, 2702; Irish OS 10; Imray C53

TIDES –0520 Dover; ML 2·2; Duration 0620; Zone 0 (UT)

Standard Port GALWAY (⟶)

Times				Height (metres)			
High Water		Low Water		MHWS	MHWN	MLWN	MLWS
0600	1100	0000	0700	5·1	3·9	2·0	0·6
1800	2300	1200	1900				
Differences KILLYBEGS							
+0040	+0050	+0055	+0035	–1·0	–0·9	–0·5	0·0
GWEEDORE HARBOUR							
+0048	+0100	+0055	+0107	–1·3	–1·0	–0·5	–0·1
BURTONPORT							
+0042	+0055	+0115	+0055	–1·2	–1·0	–0·6	–0·1
DONEGAL HARBOUR (SALTHILL QUAY)							
+0038	+0050	+0052	+0104	–1·2	–0·9	No data	

SHELTER Secure natural hbr, but some swell in SSW winds. A busy major FV port, H24 access. ⚓ about 2½ca NE of the Pier, off blue shed (Gallagher Bros) in 3m, clear of FV wash. Or **Bruckless Hbr**, about 2M E at the head of McSwyne's Bay, is a pleasant ⚓ in 1 8m, sheltered from all except SW winds. Ent on 038° between rks; ICC SDs are essential.

NAVIGATION WPT 54°36´·00N 08°27´·00W, 202°/022° from/to Rotten Is lt, 0·94M. From W, beware Manister Rk (covers at HW; dries at LW) off Fintragh B. Keep mid chan until off Rough Pt, then follow the Dir lt or Y ◊ ldg marks 338° into hbr.

LIGHTS AND MARKS Rotten Is lt, Fl WR 4s 20m 15/11M, W tr, vis W255°–008°, R008°–039°, W039°–208°. Dir lt 338°, Oc WRG 6s 17m; W sector 336°-340° (see 9.13.4). Harbour Shoal (2·3m) is marked by a SCM and NCM lt buoy.

RADIO TELEPHONE Hr Mr VHF Ch 16 14; essential to request a berth.

TELEPHONE (Dial code 073) Hr Mr 31032; MRCC (01) 6620922/3; Bundoran Inshore Rescue ☎ (072) 41713; ⊜ 31070; Police 31002; Dr 31148 (Surgery).

FACILITIES **Town Pier** ☎ 31032, AB (free), M, D & P (cans), FW, ME, El, CH, Slip, V, R, Bar; **Black Rock Pier** AB, M, Slip, D; **Services:** Sh, C (12 ton), ME, El, Sh, Kos, Ⓔ. **Town** EC Wed; ✉, Ⓑ, ⇌ (bus to Sligo), ✈ (Strandhill).

13

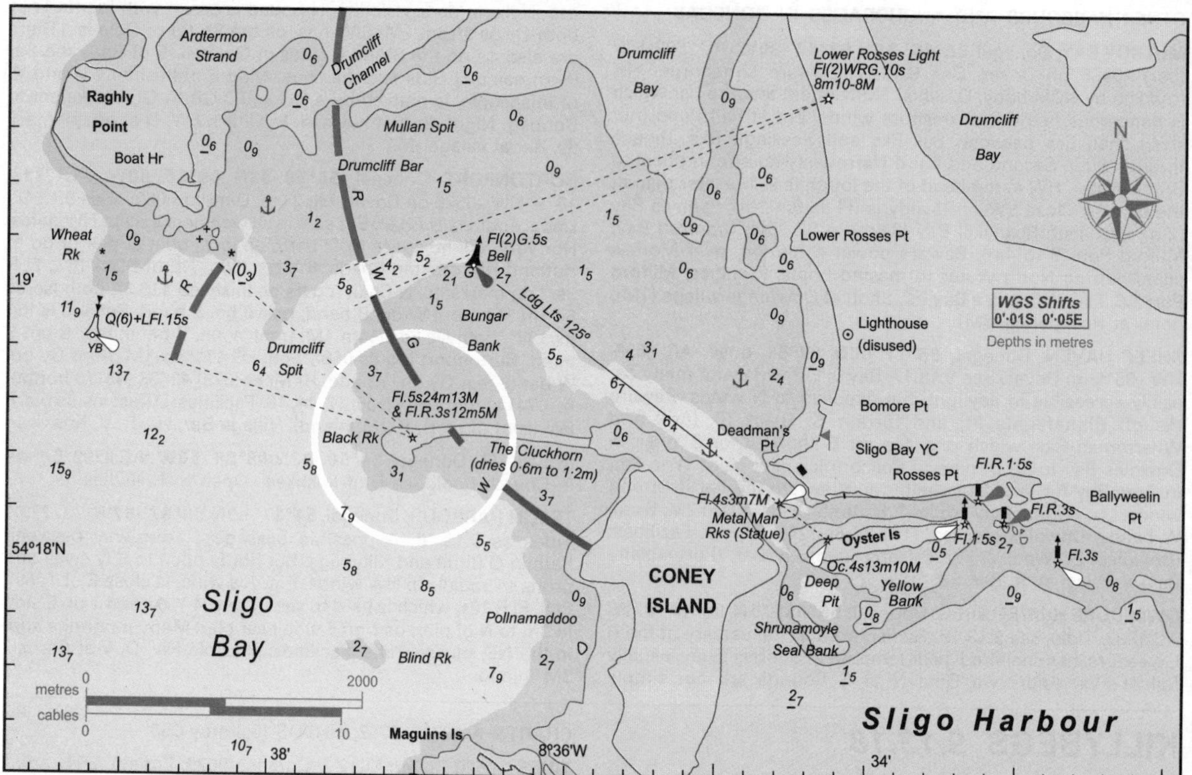

SLIGO *9.13.19*

Sligo **54°18'·30N 08°34'·70W** ❀❀👍👍✿✿✿

CHARTS AC 2852, 2767; Imray C54; Irish OS 16, 25

TIDES –0511 Dover; ML 2·3; Duration 0620; Zone 0 (UT)

Standard Port GALWAY (⟶)

Times				Height (metres)			
High Water		Low Water		MHWS	MHWN	MLWN	MLWS
0600	1100	0000	0700	5·1	3·9	2·0	0·6
1800	2300	1200	1900				
Differences SLIGO HARBOUR (Oyster Is)							
+0043	+0055	+0042	+0054	–1·0	–0·9	–0·5	–0·1
MULLAGHMORE							
+0036	+0048	+0047	+0059	–1·4	–1·0	–0·4	–0·2
BALLYSADARE BAY (Culleenamore)							
+0059	+0111	+0111	+0123	–1·2	–0·9	No data	
KILLALA BAY (Inishcrone)							
+0035	+0055	+0030	+0050	–1·3	–1·2	–0·7	–0·2

SHELTER The lower hbr is fairly exposed; ⚓ along N side of Oyster Island, or proceed 4M (not at night) up to the shelter of Sligo town; 2nd berth below bridge for yachts.

NAVIGATION WPT 54°19'·15N 08°36'·77W, 305°/125° from/to front ldg lt, 1·6M. The passage between Oyster Island and Coney Island is marked 'Dangerous'. Pass N of Oyster Is leaving Blennick Rks to port. Passage up to Sligo town between training walls. Some perches are in bad repair. Pilots at Raghly Pt and Rosses Pt. Approach quays at half tide or higher.

LIGHTS AND MARKS Cullaun Bwee Dir lt (1·5M ENE off chartlet), Fl (2) WRG 10s 8m10/8M (H24), W sector 066°-070°. Ldg lts (H24) lead 125° into ent: front, Fl 4s 3m 7M, Metal Man Rks (statue of a man on a twr); rear, Oyster Is lt ho, Oc 4s 13m 10M. Lts up-channel are unreliable.

RADIO TELEPHONE Pilots VHF Ch 12 16. Hr Mr Ch 16.

TELEPHONE (Dial code 071) Hbr Office ☎/📠 61197; MRCC (01) 6620922/3; ⊖ 61064; Police 42031; Dr 42886; Ⓗ 71111.

FACILITIES No 3 berth (next to bridge) AB €12·70, P & D (in cans), FW, ME, El, Sh, CH, C (15 ton); **Sligo YC** ☎ 77168, ⚓s, FW, Bar, Slip. **Services:** Slip, D, ME, El, Sh, SM, Gas; **Town** V, R, Bar, ✉, Ⓑ, ⇌ Irish Rail ☎ 69888, Bus ☎ 60066, ✈ (Strandhill) ☎ 68280.

MINOR HARBOUR ON S SIDE OF DONEGAL BAY

MULLAGHMORE 54°27'·90N 08°26'·80W. AC 2702. Tides see 9.13.19. Fair weather ⚓ in 2-3m off hbr ent, sheltered by Mullaghmore Head, except from N/NE winds. For ⚓s near hbr ent, call Rodney Lomax at BY, ☎/📠 071 66124, mobile ☎ 088 2727358. Keep close to N pier to avoid a rk drying 1m, ⅔ of the way across the ent toward the S pier. Take the ground or dry out against the piers inside hbr, access approx HW±2 when least depth is 2m. VHF Ch 16 18 (occas). Facilities: BY, Sh, D (cans), V, R, Bar.

MINOR HARBOUR/ANCHORAGE TO THE WEST

KILLALA BAY, Sligo/Mayo, **54°13'·02N 09°12'·80W.** AC 2715. Tides, see 9.13.19 The bay, which is open to the N and NE, is entered between Lenadoon Pt and Kilcummin Hd, 6M to the W. 1·1M W of Kilcummin Hd are 8 Y ⚓s off Rathlackan pier, well sheltered from W'lies. Carrickpatrick ECM buoy, Q (3) 10s, in mid-bay marks St Patrick's Rks to the W. Thence, if bound for Killala hbr, make good Killala SHM buoy, Fl G 6s, 7½ca to the SSW. The Round Tr and cathedral spire at Killala are conspic. Four sets of ldg bns/lts lead via a narrow chan between sand dunes and over the bar (0·3m) as follows:

a. 230°, Rinnaun Pt lts Oc 10s 7/12m 5M, □ concrete trs.
b. 215°, Inch Is, □ concrete trs; the rear has Dir lt Fl WRG 2s, G205°-213°, W213°-217°, R217°-225°.
c. 196°, Kilroe lts Oc 4s 5/10m 2M, W □ trs, which lead to ⚓ in Bartragh Pool, 6ca NE of Killala hbr; thence
d. 236°, Pier lts Iso 2s 5/7m 2M, W ◇ daymarks, lead via narrow, dredged chan to pier where AB is possible in about 1·5m.

Facilities: FW, P & D (cans), V in town ½M, EC Thurs.
Other hbrs in the bay: R Moy leading to Ballina should not be attempted without pilot/local knowledge. Inishcrone in the SE has a pier and lt, Fl WRG 1·5s 8m 2M; see 9.13.4.

WESTPORT (CLEW BAY) *9.13.20*

Mayo **53°47'·85N 09°35'·40W**

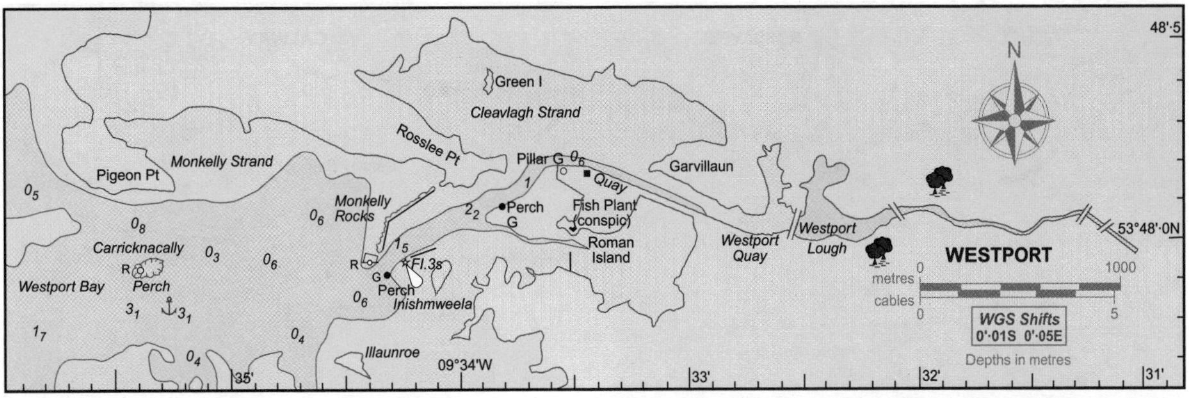

CHARTS AC 2057, 2667; Imray C54; Irish OS 30, 31

TIDES –0545 Dover; ML 2·5; Duration 0610; Zone 0 (UT)

Standard Port GALWAY (⟶)

Times				Height (metres)			
High Water		Low Water		MHWS	MHWN	MLWN	MLWS
0600	1100	0000	0700	5·1	3·9	2·0	0·6
1800	2300	1200	1900				
Differences INISHRAHER							
+0030	+0012	+0058	+0026	–0·6	–0·5	–0·3	–0·1
BROADHAVEN							
+0040	+0050	+0040	+0050	–1·4	–1·1	–0·4	–0·1
BLACKSOD QUAY							
+0025	+0035	+0040	+0040	–1·2	–1·0	–0·6	–0·2
BULL'S MOUTH (BLACKSOD BAY)							
+0101	+0057	+0109	+0105	–1·5	–1·0	–0·6	–0·1
CLARE ISLAND							
+0019	+0013	+0029	+0023	–1·0	–0·7	–0·4	–0·1
KILLARY HARBOUR							
+0021	+0015	+0035	+0029	–1·0	–0·8	–0·4	–0·1
INISHBOFIN HARBOUR							
+0013	+0009	+0021	+0017	–1·0	–0·8	–0·4	–0·1
CLIFDEN BAY							
+0005	+0005	+0016	+0016	–0·7	–0·5	No data	
SLYNE HEAD							
+0002	+0002	+0010	+0010	–0·7	–0·5	No data	

SHELTER Secure ⚓s amongst the islands at all times, as follows: E of Inishlyre in 2m; 2ca NE of Dorinish More, good holding in lee of Dorinish Bar (dries); 6 🟡s in Rosmoney Hbr 53°49'·75N 09°37'·34W; Westport Quay HW±1½, to dry out on S side; Newport Hbr (dries) can be reached above mid-flood with careful pilotage (AC 2667); dry out against N quay or ⚓ at E end of Rabbit Is.

NAVIGATION WPT 53°49'·20N 09°42'·10W, 251°/071° from/to Inishgort lt ho, 1·2M. Contact Tom Gibbons (Inishlyre Is) ☎ (098) 26381 for pilotage advice. Beware of Monkellys Rks (PHM buoy) and the Spit (G perch). Beware fish farms E of Clare I. and in Newport Bay.

LIGHTS AND MARKS Westport B entered via Inishgort lt, L Fl 10s 11m 10M (H24), and a series of ldg lines, but not advised at night. Final appr line 080° towards lt bn, Fl 3s. Chan from Westport Bay to Westport Quay, 1½M approx, is marked by bns.

RADIO TELEPHONE None.

TELEPHONE (Dial code 098) MRCC (01) 6620922/3; ⊖ (094) 21131; Police 25555; Ⓗ (094) 21733.

FACILITIES **Westport Quays** M, AB free, Slip, V, R, Bar; **Services:** Kos, El, Ⓔ; **Town** EC Wed; P & D (cans), ✉, Ⓑ, ⇌, ✈ (Galway/ Knock).**Mayo SC Rosmoney** ☎ 26160, Slip, Bar; **Glénans Irish SC** ☎ 26046 on Collanmore Is;

OTHER ANCHORAGES FROM EAGLE IS TO SLYNE HEAD

BROAD HAVEN, Mayo, **54°16'·00N 09°53'·20W.** AC 2703. See 9.13.20 for tides; ML 1·9m. A safe refuge except in N'lies. Easy appr across Broad Haven Bay to the ent between Brandy Pt and Gubacashel Pt, Iso WR 4s27m 12/9M, W tr. 7ca S of this lt is Ballyglas Fl G 3s on W side. ⚓ close N or S of Ballyglas which has pier (2m) and 8 Y 🟡s. In E'lies ⚓ 3ca S of Inver Pt out of the tide. Further S off Barrett Pt, the inlet narrows and turns W to Belmullet. Facilities: V, ✉.

PORTNAFRANKAGH Mayo, **54°14'·95N 10°06'·00W.** AC 2703. Tides approx as Broad Haven. A safe passage ⚓, close to the coastal route, but swell enters in all winds. Appr toward Port Pt, thence keep to the N side for better water; middle and S side break in onshore winds. ⚓ in 4–5m on S side, close inshore. L and slip at new pier. Unlit, but Eagle Is lt, Fl (3) 10s 67m 26M H24, W tr, is 2M N. No facilities; Belmullet 4M, V.

BLACKSOD BAY, Mayo, **54°05'·00N 10°02'·00W.** AC 2704. HW –0525 on Dover; ML 2·2m; Duration 0610. See 9.13.20. Easy appr, accessible by night. Safe ⚓s depending on wind: NW of Blacksod Pt (3m) 6 Y 🟡s; at Elly B (1·8m); Elly Hbr 6 Y 🟡s; Saleen B; N of Claggan Pt. Beware drying rk 3·5ca SSE of Ardmore Pt. Lts: Blacksod Pt, Fl (2) WR 7·5s 13m 9M, see 8.13.4. ECM buoy Q (3) 10s. Blacksod pier hd, 2 FR (vert). Few facilities; nearest town is Belmullet.

CLARE ISLAND, Mayo, **53°48'·1N 09°56'·7W.** 6 🟡s on SE side untenable in E winds. Hotel, Bar, some V.

INISHTURK, Mayo, **53°42'·3N 10°05'·2W.** 8 Y 🟡s Garranty Hbr. sheltered SW to NNW winds. Slip, quay, Bar, R, ✉, 6 🟡s on E side.

KILLARY HARBOUR, Mayo/Galway, **53°37'·83N 09°54'·00W,** 4ca W of Doonee Is. AC 2706. Tides 9.13.20. A spectacular 7M long inlet, narrow and deep. Caution fish farms, some with Fl Y lts. Appr in good vis to identify Doonee Is and Inishbarna bns ldg 099° to ent. ⚓s off Dernasliggaun, Bundorragha and, at head of inlet, Leenaun with 8 Y 🟡s. (Village: L, V, Bar, hotel). Enter **Little Killary Bay** 4ca S of Doonee Is; drying rks at ent. Good ⚓ in 3m at head of bay.

BALLYNAKILL, Galway, **53°34'·95N 10°03'·00W.** AC 2706. Tides as Inishbofin/Killary. Easy appr between Cleggan Pt, Fl (3) WRG 15s and Rinvyle Pt. Then pass N of Freaghillaun South Is, E of which is good passage ⚓ in 7m. Further E, Carrigeen and Ardagh Rks lie in mid-chan. Keep N for ⚓ in Derryinver B. S chan leads to ⚓s: off Ross Pt; S of Roeillaun; in Fahy Bay with 8 Y 🟡s sheltered by bar dries 0 2m. No facilities.

INISHBOFIN, Mayo, **53°36'·60N 10°13'·20W.** AC 2707, 1820. HW – 0555 on Dover; ML 1·9m. See 9.13.20. Very safe hbr once inside narrow ent. 2 conspic W trs lead 032°. ⚓ between new pier and Port Is. Old pier to the E dries. Gun Rock, Fl (2) 6s 8m 4M, vis 296°-253°. Facilities: FW, R, Bar, V, Hotel ☎ (095) 45803.

CLIFDEN BAY, Galway, **53°29'·40N 10°05'·90W.** AC 2708, 1820. HW –0600 on Dover; Duration 0610. Tides at 9.13.20. Before entering identify the conspic W bn on Carrickrana Rks. To the E keep clear of Coghan's Rks and Doolick Rks. Ldg marks: W bn at Fishing Pt on 080° with Clifden Castle (ruin); caution bar 2·4m off Fishing Pt. 8 Y 🟡s are 3ca S of Castle ruins, or ⚓ NE of Drinagh Pt. In the drying creek to Clifden beware ruined trng wall; dry out against the quay. Or enter Ardbear Bay to ⚓ SE of Yellow Slate Rks in 3·4m. Keep clear of fish farms. Facilities: **Town** EC Thurs; Bar, Ⓑ, CH, D, P, ✉, R, V, Kos, FW, V, R, Dr, Ⓗ. Bus to Galway.

GALWAY BAY *9.13.21*

Galway **53°12'N 09°08'W**

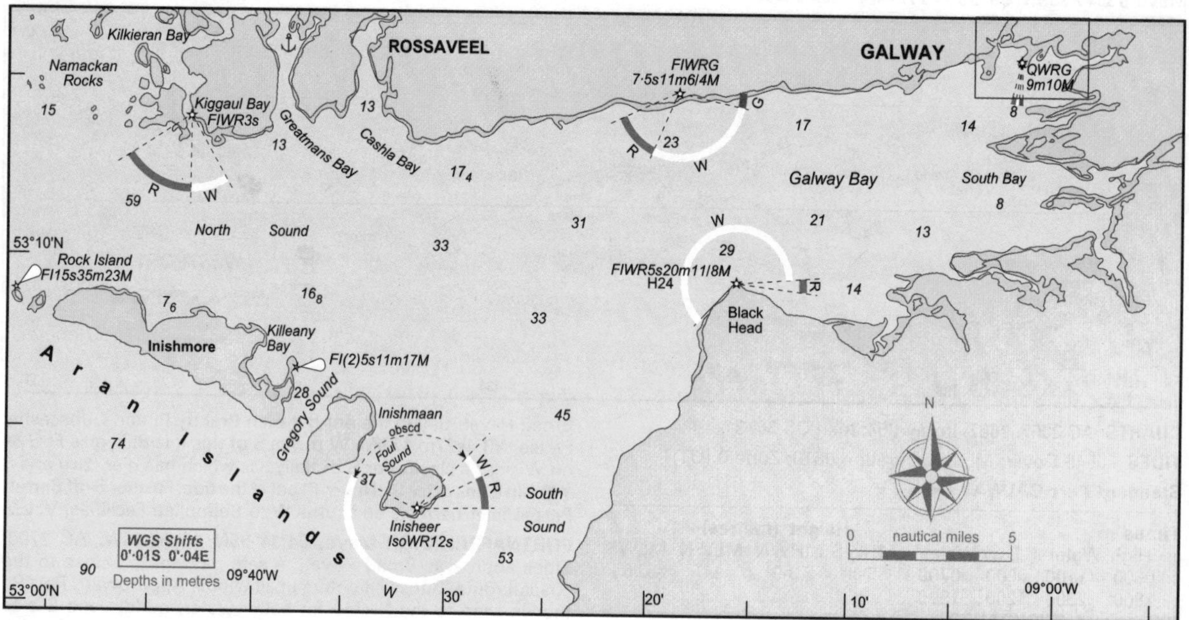

CHARTS AC 1903, 1984, 3339, 2173; Imray C55; Irish OS 45, 46, 51

TIDES –0555 Dover; ML 2·9; Duration 0620; Zone 0 (UT)

Standard Port GALWAY (⟶)

Times				Height (metres)			
High Water		Low Water		MHWS	MHWN	MLWN	MLWS
0600	1100	0000	0700	5·1	3·9	2·0	0·6
1800	2300	1200	1900				
Differences KILKIERAN COVE							
+0005	+0005	+0016	+0016	–0·3	–0·2	–0·1	0·0
ROUNDSTONE BAY							
+0003	+0003	+0008	+0008	–0·7	–0·5	–0·3	–0·1
KILLEANY BAY (Aran Islands)							
–0008	–0008	+0003	+0003	–0·4	–0·3	–0·2	–0·1
LISCANNOR							
–0003	–0007	+0006	+0002	–0·4	–0·3	No data	

SHELTER Galway Bay is sheltered from large swells by Aran Is, but seas get up in the 20M from Aran Is to Galway. Beware salmon drift nets in the apps to many bays. The better ⚓s from Slyne Head and clock-wise around Galway Bay are:

Bunowen Bay: (53°24'·6N 10°06'·9W). Sheltered in W-NE winds; unsafe in S'ly. Easy appr with Bunowen House brg 000°, leaving Mullauncarrickscoltia Rk (1·1m) to port. ⚓ in 3-4m below conspic Doon Hill.

Roundstone Bay: (Off chartlet at 53°23'N 09°54'·5W). Safe shelter/access, except in SE'ly. 4 Y 🅐s are 5ca SSE of Roundstone, or ⚓ in 2m off N quay. There are other ⚓s E'ward in Bertraghboy and Cashel Bays.

Kilkieran Bay: Easy ent abm Golam Tr (conspic). 12 Y 🅐s off Kilkieran. Many ⚓s in 14M long, sheltered bay.

Kiggaul Bay: Easy ent, H24; ⚓ close W/NW of lt Fl WR 3s 5/3M. Depth 3 to 4m; exposed to S/SE winds.

Greatman Bay: Beware English Rk (dries 1·2m), Keeraun Shoal (breaks in heavy weather), Arkeena Rk, Trabaan Rk, Rin Rks and Chapel Rks. ⚓ off Natawny Quay (E side), or on 4 Y 🅐s off Maumeen Quay (dries), AB possible.

Cashla Bay: Easiest hbr on this coast; ent in all weather. ⚓ and 8 Y 🅐s (planned) off Sruthan Quay. Rossaveel, on E side, is a busy fishing and ferry hbr.

Note: There is no safe hbr from Cashla to Galway (20M).

Bays between Black Hd and Galway have rks and shoals, but give excellent shelter. Kinvarra B, Aughinish B, South B and Ballyvaghan B are the main ones. Enter Kinvarra B with caution on the flood; beware rks. Berth in small drying hbr. Ballvaghan B, entered either side of Illaunloo Rk, leads to two piers (both dry) or ⚓ close NE in pool (3m). Best access HW±2.

NAVIGATION Enter the Bay by one of four Sounds:

1. North Sound between Inishmore and Golam Tr (conspic), 4½M wide, is easiest but beware Brocklinmore Bank in heavy weather.
2. Gregory Sound between Inishmore and Inishmaan, is free of dangers, but give Straw Island a berth of 2-3ca.
3. Foul Sound between Inishmaan and Inisheer; only danger is Pipe Rock (dries) at end of reef extending 3ca NW of Inisheer.
4. South Sound between Inisheer and mainland. Only danger Finnis Rock (dries 0·4m) 4½ca SE of E point of Inisheer (marked by ECM buoy Q (3) 10s). From S, beware Kilstiffin Rocks off Liscanor Bay.

LIGHTS AND MARKS Roundstone Bay: Croaghnakeela Is Fl 3·7s 7m 5M. Inishnee lt Fl (2) WRG 10s 9m 5/3M, W sector 017°-030°. Kiggaul Bay: Fl WR 3s 5m 5/3M, W329°-359°, R359°-059°. Cashla Bay: Killeen Pt Fl (3) WR 10s 6/3M; Lion Pt Dir lt 010°, Iso WRG 4s 8/6M, W008·5°-011·5°. Rossaveel ldg lts 116°, Oc 3s. Black Head lt Fl WR 5s 20m 11/8M H24, vis W045°-268°, R268°-276° covers Illanloo Rk.

FACILITIES

BUNOWEN Bay: No facilities.
ROUNDSTONE Bay: V, FW, Bar, ✉, Bus to Galway.
KILKIERAN Bay: Bar, ☎, P, V, Bus to Galway.
KIGGAUL Bay: Bar (no ☎), shop at Lettermullen (1M).
GREATMAN Bay: Maumeen V, P (1M), Bar.
CASHLA Bay: **Carraroe** (1M SW) V, Hotel, ☎; **Rossaveel** Hr Mr ☎ 091-72109, FW, D, ME; **Costelloe** (1½M E), Hotel, ✉, Gge.

Aran Islands The only reasonable shelter is on Inishmore in Killeany Bay, but exposed to E/NE winds and crowded with FVs. 8 Y 🅐s available; or ⚓ S of Kilronan pier; or ⚓ E of Killeany Pt; or in good weather ⚓ at Portmurvy. Kilronan, facilities: V, D, FW, ✉; Ferry to Galway, ✈ to Galway from airstrip on beach. **Lights and marks**: Inishmore: Eeragh Island (Rk Is) Fl 15s 35m 23M, W tr, B bands. Killeany Bay: Straw Is, Fl (2) 5s 11m 17M. Kilronan pier Fl WG 1·5s. Ldg lts 192° both Oc 5s for Killeany hbr. Inishmaan is not lit. Inisheer: Iso WR 12s 34m 20/16M, Racon, vis W225°-245° (partially obscd 225°-231° beyond 7M), R245°-269° covers Finnis Rk, W269°-115°; obscd 115°-225°.

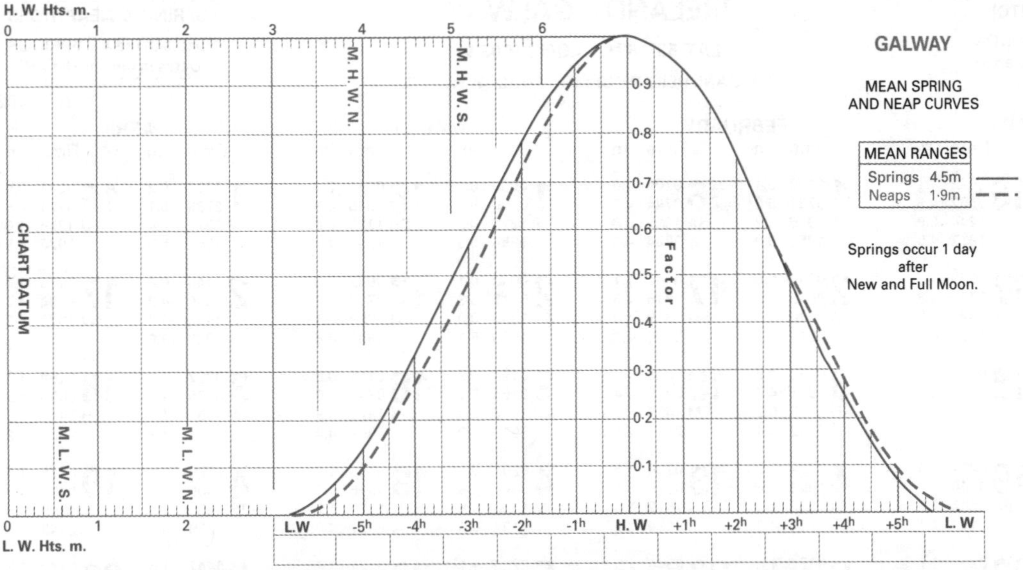

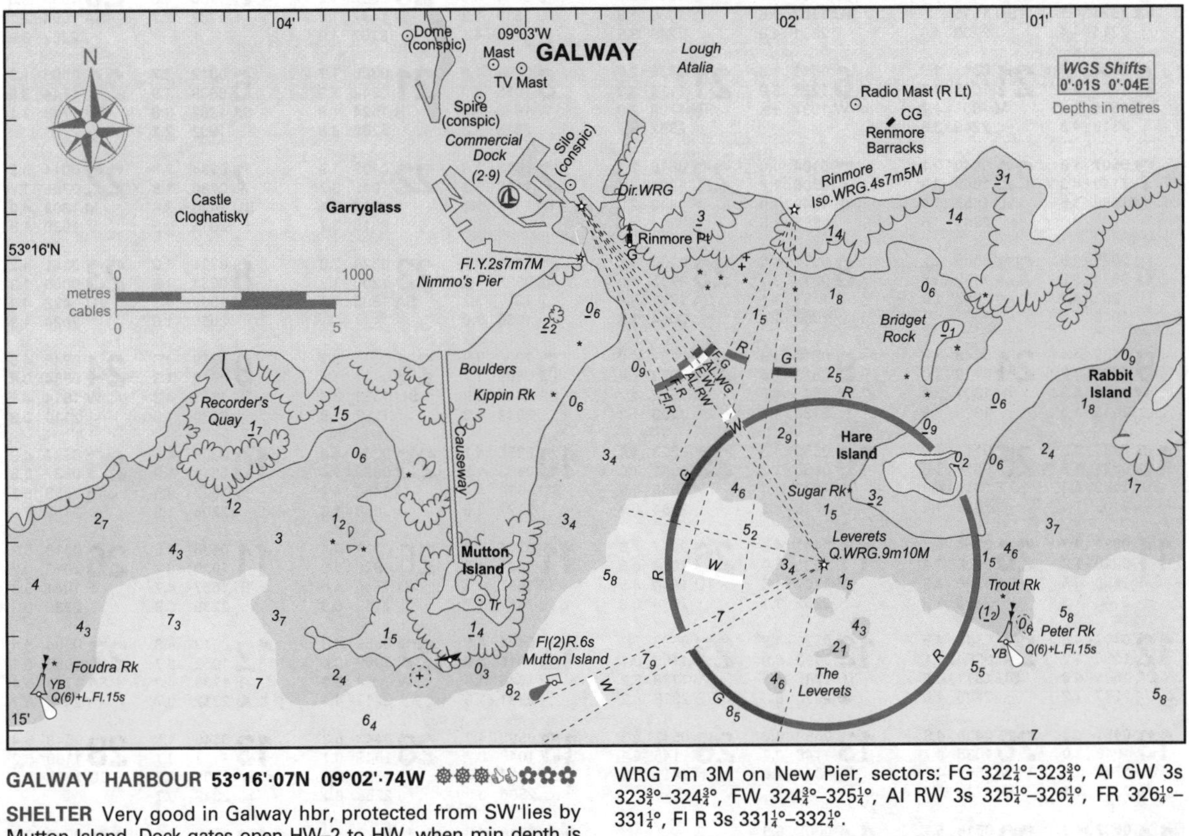

GALWAY HARBOUR 53°16'·07N 09°02'·74W

SHELTER Very good in Galway hbr, protected from SW'lies by Mutton Island. Dock gates open HW–2 to HW, when min depth is 6m. Enter Galway Dock and secure in SW corner of basin, or ask Hr Mr for waiting berth on lead-in pier. It is dangerous to lie in the 'Layby' (a dredged cut NE of New pier) when wind is SE or S; if strong from these points, seas sweep round the pierhead. New Harbour (2·5M ESE and home of Galway Bay SC) is nearest safe ⚓ to Galway.

NAVIGATION Galway WPT 53°14'·80N 09°03'·40W, 241°/061° from/to Leverets lt, 1·1M.

LIGHTS AND MARKS Leverets Q WRG 9m 10M; B tr, W bands; G015°-058°, W058°-065°, R065°-103°, G103°-143°, W143°-146°, R146°-015°. Rinmore Iso WRG 4s 7m 5M; W □ tr ; G359°-008°, W008°-018°, R018°-027°. Appr chan 325° is defined by a Dir lt WRG 7m 3M on New Pier, sectors: FG 322¼°–323¾°, Al GW 3s 323¾°–324¾°, FW 324¾°–325¼°, Al RW 3s 325¼°–326¼°, FR 326¼°–331¼°, Fl R 3s 331¼°–332¼°.

RADIO TELEPHONE Call *Hr Mr Galway* VHF Ch 12 16 (HW–2½ to HW+1).

TELEPHONE (Dial code 091) Hr Mr 561874, 📠 563738; MRCC (066) 9476109; Coast/Cliff Rescue Service (099) 61107; Police 563161; Dr 562453.

FACILITIES **Dock** AB €12.70 if space available, FW, El, ME, Sh, C (35 ton), CH, LB, PV, SM, V, R, Bar; **Galway YC** M, Slip, FW, C, CH, Bar; **Galway Bay SC** ☎ 794527, M, CH, Bar; **Town** EC Mon; P, D, ACA, Gas, Gaz, Kos, V, R, Bar, ✉, Ⓑ, ⇌, ✈ Carnmore (6M to the E of Galway City).

13

TIME ZONE (UTC)
For Summer Time add ONE hour in **non-shaded areas**

IRELAND – GALWAY

LAT 53°16′N LONG 9°03′W

TIMES AND HEIGHTS OF HIGH AND LOW WATERS

SPRING & NEAP TIDES
Dates in red are SPRINGS
Dates in blue are NEAPS

YEAR **2002**

JANUARY

Date	Time	m	Date	Time	m
1	0612	5.1	16	0022	1.1
	1212	0.5		0652	4.9
	TU 1842	5.0		W 1244	0.9
				1917	4.5
2	0026	0.8	17	0059	1.2
	0657	5.1		0730	4.8
	W 1256	0.5		TH 1320	1.0
	1928	4.9		1955	4.4
3	0112	0.9	18	0136	1.3
	0743	5.0		0808	4.6
	TH 1341	0.6		F 1357	1.1
	2018	4.8		2035	4.3
4	0200	1.1	19	0214	1.5
	0832	4.9		0846	4.5
	F 1430	0.9		SA 1434	1.3
	2112	4.6		2116	4.1
5	0252	1.4	20	0255	1.7
	0929	4.6		0925	4.3
	SA 1524	1.1		SU 1515	1.5
	2214	4.4		2200	4.0
6	0354	1.6	21	0342	1.9
	1033	4.4		1008	4.1
	SU 1629	1.4		M 1601	1.7
	2319	4.3		2249	3.9
7	0507	1.8	22	0440	2.1
	1140	4.3		1057	3.9
	M 1752	1.6		TU 1655	1.9
				2341	3.8
8	0025	4.3	23	0555	2.2
	0624	1.8		1152	3.8
	TU 1251	4.3		W 1807	1.9
	1912	1.6			
9	0132	4.4	24	0043	3.8
	0733	1.7		0713	2.0
	W 1400	4.3		TH 1301	3.8
	2013	1.5		1929	1.9
10	0231	4.5	25	0154	4.0
	0831	1.5		0816	1.8
	TH 1459	4.4		F 1419	4.0
	2102	1.4		2031	1.6
11	0322	4.7	26	0254	4.2
	0920	1.3		0908	1.4
	F 1550	4.5		SA 1520	4.3
	2146	1.3		2120	1.3
12	0407	4.8	27	0343	4.5
	1006	1.2		0954	1.1
	SA 1635	4.6		SU 1611	4.6
	2227	1.2		2205	1.0
13	0451	4.8	28	0430	4.8
	1048	1.0		1038	0.7
	SU 1718	4.6		M 1658	4.8
	● 2306	1.1		○ 2249	0.7
14	0532	4.9	29	0516	5.1
	1129	0.9		1120	0.4
	M 1759	4.6		TU 1744	5.0
	2345	1.1		2333	0.5
15	0613	4.9	30	0602	5.2
	1208	0.9		1202	0.2
	TU 1839	4.6		W 1830	5.1
			31	0016	0.4
				0646	5.3
				TH 1244	0.1
				1914	5.1

FEBRUARY

Date	Time	m	Date	Time	m
1	0100	0.4	16	0109	1.0
	0731	5.2		0744	4.7
	F 1326	0.2		SA 1326	0.8
	1959	5.0		2004	4.4
2	0144	0.6	17	0142	1.1
	0816	5.0		0816	4.6
	SA 1410	0.5		SU 1359	1.0
	2047	4.7		2036	4.3
3	0231	0.9	18	0216	1.4
	0906	4.7		0848	4.4
	SU 1458	0.9		M 1433	1.2
	2142	4.4		2111	4.1
4	0324	1.3	19	0254	1.6
	1003	4.4		0925	4.1
	M 1553	1.3		TU 1512	1.5
	2244	4.2		2154	3.9
5	0427	1.6	20	0340	1.9
	1108	4.1		1014	3.9
	TU 1703	1.6		W 1600	1.8
	2351	4.0		2249	3.8
6	0545	1.8	21	0438	2.0
	1221	3.9		1114	3.8
	W 1837	1.8		TH 1700	2.0
				2352	3.7
7	0104	4.0	22	0616	2.1
	0706	1.8		1222	3.7
	TH 1342	3.9		F 1842	2.0
	1957	1.8			
8	0216	4.1	23	0106	3.8
	0818	1.7		0755	1.8
	F 1451	4.1		SA 1351	3.8
	2053	1.6		2014	1.8
9	0312	4.3	24	0231	4.0
	0912	1.4		0853	1.4
	SA 1543	4.2		SU 1506	4.1
	2136	1.4		2108	1.3
10	0359	4.5	25	0329	4.4
	0956	1.2		0941	1.0
	SU 1627	4.4		M 1558	4.5
	2215	1.2		2154	0.9
11	0441	4.6	26	0417	4.8
	1036	1.0		1024	0.5
	M 1707	4.5		TU 1644	4.9
	2252	1.1		2236	0.5
12	0521	4.8	27	0503	5.1
	1113	0.8		1105	0.1
	TU 1745	4.6		W 1728	5.2
	● 2328	0.9		○ 2318	0.2
13	0559	4.8	28	0547	5.3
	1148	0.7		1145	-0.1
	W 1821	4.6		TH 1812	5.3
14	0003	0.9			
	0635	4.9			
	TH 1222	0.7			
	1856	4.6			
15	0037	0.9			
	0710	4.8			
	F 1254	0.7			
	1931	4.6			

MARCH

Date	Time	m	Date	Time	m
1	0000	0.1	16	0011	0.7
	0630	5.4		0646	4.8
	F 1226	-0.2		SA 1225	0.6
	1854	5.3		1902	4.7
2	0042	0.1	17	0042	0.8
	0713	5.3		0717	4.7
	SA 1306	0.0		SU 1254	0.7
	1936	5.1		1932	4.6
3	0124	0.3	18	0112	0.9
	0755	5.1		0747	4.6
	SU 1346	0.3		M 1325	0.9
	2019	4.9		1959	4.4
4	0208	0.6	19	0145	1.2
	0840	4.8		0816	4.4
	M 1430	0.8		TU 1358	1.2
	2107	4.5		2027	4.2
5	0256	1.1	20	0222	1.4
	0931	4.4		0852	4.2
	TU 1519	1.3		W 1437	1.5
	2204	4.1		2107	4.0
6	0355	1.5	21	0306	1.7
	1035	4.0		0942	3.9
	W 1625	1.8		TH 1524	1.8
	2315	3.8		2208	3.8
7	0512	1.8	22	0402	1.9
	1155	3.7		1048	3.7
	TH 1802	2.0		F 1624	2.1
				2318	3.7
8	0039	3.7	23	0524	2.0
	0638	1.9		1200	3.7
	F 1327	3.7		SA 1803	2.1
	1938	2.0			
9	0200	3.9	24	0035	3.7
	0805	1.7		0734	1.8
	SA 1441	3.9		SU 1331	3.8
	2042	1.8		1957	1.8
10	0258	4.1	25	0210	4.0
	0903	1.5		0833	1.4
	SU 1530	4.1		M 1450	4.2
	2122	1.5		2050	1.3
11	0344	4.3	26	0311	4.4
	0941	1.2		0920	0.9
	M 1611	4.3		TU 1540	4.6
	2157	1.2		2135	0.9
12	0424	4.5	27	0359	4.8
	1015	0.9		1002	0.4
	TU 1648	4.5		W 1624	5.0
	2231	1.0		2217	0.4
13	0502	4.7	28	0443	5.2
	1049	0.7		1043	0.1
	W 1724	4.7		TH 1707	5.3
	2306	0.8		○ 2258	0.1
14	0538	4.8	29	0527	5.4
	1122	0.6		1123	-0.1
	TH 1758	4.7		F 1749	5.4
	● 2339	0.7		2339	0.0
15	0613	4.9	30	0610	5.5
	1154	0.6		1202	-0.1
	F 1831	4.7		SA 1830	5.4
			31	0021	0.0
				0652	5.4
				SU 1242	0.1
				1910	5.2

APRIL

Date	Time	m	Date	Time	m
1	0102	0.2	16	0045	0.9
	0733	5.1		0721	4.6
	M 1322	0.4		TU 1255	1.0
	1952	5.0		1928	4.5
2	0145	0.6	17	0119	1.1
	0816	4.8		0754	4.4
	TU 1403	0.9		W 1330	1.2
	2036	4.6		1958	4.4
3	0232	1.0	18	0158	1.3
	0905	4.3		0833	4.2
	W 1450	1.5		TH 1411	1.5
	2128	4.2		2039	4.2
4	0330	1.5	19	0245	1.6
	1006	3.9		0926	4.0
	TH 1555	1.9		F 1500	1.8
	2239	3.8		2143	3.9
5	0447	1.8	20	0342	1.8
	1130	3.6		1032	3.8
	F 1732	2.2		SA 1604	2.1
				2257	3.8
6	0012	3.7	21	0506	1.9
	0609	1.9		1144	3.8
	SA 1307	3.6		SU 1748	2.1
	1902	2.1			
7	0134	3.8	22	0014	3.9
	0730	1.8		0705	1.7
	SU 1420	3.8		M 1309	4.0
	2015	1.9		1930	1.8
8	0234	4.0	23	0141	4.2
	0834	1.5		0805	1.3
	M 1508	4.1		TU 1423	4.4
	2055	1.6		2024	1.3
9	0319	4.3	24	0245	4.6
	0912	1.3		0854	0.8
	TU 1547	4.3		W 1514	4.8
	2130	1.3		2110	0.9
10	0359	4.5	25	0334	4.9
	0946	1.0		0937	0.5
	W 1622	4.5		TH 1559	5.1
	2205	1.0		2153	0.5
11	0436	4.6	26	0419	5.2
	1020	0.8		1019	0.2
	TH 1657	4.7		F 1641	5.3
	2239	0.8		2235	0.3
12	0512	4.8	27	0504	5.4
	1052	0.7		1059	0.1
	F 1730	4.8		SA 1723	5.4
	● 2312	0.7		○ 2317	0.2
13	0546	4.8	28	0548	5.4
	1123	0.7		1139	0.2
	SA 1801	4.8		SU 1805	5.4
	2343	0.7			
14	0619	4.8	29	0000	0.2
	1153	0.7		0631	5.3
	SU 1832	4.8		M 1219	0.4
				1846	5.2
15	0013	0.8	30	0043	0.4
	0650	4.7		0713	5.0
	M 1223	0.8		TU 1259	0.7
	1900	4.7		1928	5.0

Chart Datum: 0·20 metres above Ordnance Datum (Dublin)

TIME ZONE (UTC)
For Summer Time add ONE hour in **non-shaded areas**

IRELAND – GALWAY

LAT 53°16′N LONG 9°03′W

TIMES AND HEIGHTS OF HIGH AND LOW WATERS

SPRING & NEAP TIDES
Dates in red are SPRINGS
Dates in blue are NEAPS

YEAR **2002**

MAY

Day	Time	m	Time	m	Time	m	Time	m
1 W	0126	0.7	0757	4.7	1341	1.1	2012	4.6
2 TH	0214	1.1	0844	4.3	1428	1.6	2102	4.3
3 F	0310	1.4	0942	3.9	1531	2.0	2207	4.0
4 SA	0421	1.7	1059	3.7	1659	2.2	2334	3.8
5 SU	0535	1.8	1227	3.6	1818	2.2		
6 M	0054	3.8	0642	1.8	1342	3.8	1924	2.0
7 TU	0156	4.0	0743	1.6	1434	4.0	2016	1.7
8 W	0245	4.1	0831	1.4	1514	4.3	2056	1.4
9 TH	0326	4.3	0910	1.2	1550	4.5	2133	1.2
10 F	0404	4.5	0946	1.0	1624	4.6	2209	1.0
11 SA	0440	4.6	1020	0.9	1656	4.7	2243	0.9
12 SU	0515	4.7	1052	0.9	1727	4.8	● 2316	0.8
13 M	0549	4.7	1123	0.9	1759	4.8	2348	0.9
14 TU	0624	4.7	1155	0.9	1832	4.7		
15 W	0022	0.9	0700	4.6	1231	1.0	1905	4.6
16 TH	0101	1.0	0739	4.5	1311	1.2	1943	4.5
17 F	0144	1.2	0822	4.3	1355	1.5	2029	4.3
18 SA	0233	1.4	0916	4.2	1447	1.7	2131	4.2
19 SU	0332	1.6	1019	4.0	1552	1.9	2242	4.1
20 M	0451	1.6	1127	4.0	1724	1.9	2354	4.1
21 TU	0629	1.5	1240	4.2	1856	1.7		
22 W	0109	4.3	0733	1.2	1351	4.5	1955	1.4
23 TH	0215	4.6	0826	1.0	1446	4.8	2044	1.0
24 F	0308	4.9	0912	0.7	1532	5.0	2130	0.7
25 SA	0356	5.0	0955	0.6	1616	5.2	2213	0.5
26 SU	0442	5.1	1037	0.5	1659	5.3	○ 2257	0.4
27 M	0528	5.1	1118	0.6	1742	5.2	2341	0.5
28 TU	0613	5.0	1159	0.7	1825	5.1		
29 W	0025	0.6	0656	4.8	1241	1.0	1908	4.9
30 TH	0110	0.8	0740	4.6	1323	1.3	1953	4.7
31 F	0157	1.1	0827	4.3	1408	1.6	2041	4.4

JUNE

Day	Time	m	Time	m	Time	m	Time	m
1 SA	0247	1.3	0919	4.0	1502	1.9	2137	4.1
2 SU	0346	1.6	1019	3.8	1614	2.1	2243	3.9
3 M	0451	1.7	1128	3.7	1728	2.1	2352	3.8
4 TU	0552	1.7	1237	3.7	1832	2.0		
5 W	0058	3.8	0650	1.7	1341	3.9	1929	1.8
6 TH	0157	3.9	0743	1.6	1431	4.1	2018	1.6
7 F	0245	4.1	0830	1.4	1511	4.2	2100	1.4
8 SA	0326	4.2	0911	1.3	1546	4.4	2139	1.2
9 SU	0405	4.4	0948	1.2	1620	4.6	2216	1.0
10 M	0443	4.5	1023	1.1	1654	4.7	● 2252	0.9
11 TU	0522	4.6	1059	1.0	1731	4.8	2329	0.8
12 W	0602	4.7	1136	1.0	1809	4.8		
13 TH	0008	0.8	0643	4.7	1217	1.0	1850	4.8
14 F	0051	0.8	0726	4.6	1300	1.1	1933	4.7
15 SA	0135	0.9	0812	4.5	1346	1.2	2021	4.5
16 SU	0224	1.0	0903	4.4	1437	1.5	2119	4.4
17 M	0320	1.2	1002	4.3	1538	1.6	2225	4.3
18 TU	0426	1.3	1105	4.2	1653	1.7	2332	4.3
19 W	0545	1.4	1211	4.3	1817	1.6		
20 TH	0040	4.3	0658	1.3	1318	4.4	1925	1.4
21 F	0147	4.5	0758	1.2	1418	4.6	2021	1.2
22 SA	0245	4.6	0849	1.1	1509	4.8	2110	1.0
23 SU	0337	4.7	0935	1.0	1556	4.9	2156	0.8
24 M	0425	4.8	1019	0.9	1640	5.0	○ 2242	0.7
25 TU	0512	4.8	1102	0.9	1725	5.0	2327	0.7
26 W	0558	4.7	1143	1.0	1809	4.9		
27 TH	0011	0.7	0642	4.7	1225	1.1	1852	4.8
28 F	0054	0.8	0724	4.5	1305	1.2	1935	4.7
29 SA	0136	0.9	0807	4.3	1345	1.4	2019	4.5
30 SU	0219	1.1	0851	4.2	1430	1.6	2106	4.3

JULY

Day	Time	m	Time	m	Time	m	Time	m
1 M	0305	1.3	0939	4.0	1520	1.8	2156	4.1
2 TU	0356	1.5	1030	3.9	1623	2.0	2249	3.9
3 W	0452	1.7	1123	3.8	1732	2.0	2343	3.8
4 TH	0550	1.8	1221	3.8	1838	2.0		
5 F	0044	3.8	0649	1.8	1325	3.8	1936	1.8
6 SA	0149	3.8	0746	1.7	1422	4.0	2028	1.6
7 SU	0245	3.9	0837	1.6	1507	4.2	2113	1.4
8 M	0332	4.1	0921	1.4	1548	4.4	2155	1.1
9 TU	0417	4.3	1003	1.2	1628	4.6	2236	0.9
10 W	0501	4.5	1044	1.0	1709	4.8	● 2317	0.7
11 TH	0545	4.7	1125	0.8	1753	4.9	2358	0.5
12 F	0629	4.8	1207	0.8	1837	4.9		
13 SA	0040	0.5	0712	4.8	1250	0.8	1921	4.9
14 SU	0124	0.5	0757	4.7	1335	0.9	2008	4.8
15 M	0209	0.6	0844	4.6	1422	1.1	2100	4.6
16 TU	0259	0.9	0938	4.4	1516	1.3	2201	4.4
17 W	0356	1.1	1037	4.3	1620	1.5	2306	4.3
18 TH	0503	1.4	1140	4.2	1736	1.6		
19 F	0013	4.2	0621	1.5	1247	4.2	1856	1.6
20 SA	0124	4.2	0733	1.5	1355	4.3	2003	1.4
21 SU	0230	4.3	0832	1.4	1454	4.5	2058	1.2
22 M	0326	4.4	0921	1.3	1544	4.6	2145	1.0
23 TU	0416	4.5	1006	1.2	1629	4.7	2230	0.9
24 W	0502	4.5	1048	1.1	1713	4.8	○ 2313	0.8
25 TH	0546	4.6	1128	1.0	1755	4.8	2354	0.7
26 F	0627	4.6	1206	1.0	1836	4.8		
27 SA	0032	0.7	0705	4.5	1243	1.0	1915	4.7
28 SU	0109	0.8	0744	4.5	1319	1.1	1954	4.6
29 M	0146	0.9	0822	4.3	1356	1.3	2033	4.4
30 TU	0224	1.1	0900	4.2	1435	1.5	2114	4.2
31 W	0304	1.4	0940	4.0	1518	1.8	2158	4.0

AUGUST

Day	Time	m	Time	m	Time	m	Time	m
1 TH	0348	1.6	1023	3.9	1612	2.0	2246	3.8
2 F	0439	1.8	1111	3.8	1729	2.1	2340	3.7
3 SA	0543	1.9	1207	3.7	1856	2.0		
4 SU	0044	3.6	0703	1.9	1318	3.8	2002	1.8
5 M	0204	3.7	0810	1.8	1432	4.0	2054	1.5
6 TU	0308	4.0	0903	1.5	1525	4.3	2139	1.1
7 W	0358	4.3	0948	1.2	1610	4.6	2221	0.8
8 TH	0444	4.6	1031	0.9	1654	4.8	● 2303	0.4
9 F	0528	4.8	1113	0.6	1738	5.0	2343	0.2
10 SA	0612	5.0	1154	0.4	1822	5.2		
11 SU	0024	0.1	0654	5.1	1236	0.4	1904	5.1
12 M	0105	0.1	0736	5.0	1317	0.5	1948	5.0
13 TU	0148	0.4	0820	4.8	1401	0.7	2035	4.8
14 W	0233	0.7	0908	4.6	1449	1.1	2131	4.5
15 TH	0324	1.1	1003	4.3	1547	1.4	2236	4.2
16 F	0427	1.5	1107	4.1	1701	1.7	2348	4.0
17 SA	0550	1.8	1220	4.0	1833	1.8		
18 SU	0107	3.9	0714	1.8	1340	4.0	1955	1.6
19 M	0222	4.0	0820	1.7	1446	4.3	2054	1.4
20 TU	0320	4.2	0909	1.5	1536	4.5	2137	1.1
21 W	0406	4.4	0951	1.3	1619	4.7	2216	0.9
22 TH	0449	4.5	1030	1.1	1700	4.8	○ 2254	0.7
23 F	0528	4.6	1108	1.0	1739	4.9	2330	0.6
24 SA	0606	4.7	1143	0.9	1816	4.9		
25 SU	0005	0.6	0642	4.7	1217	0.9	1851	4.8
26 M	0039	0.7	0717	4.6	1250	0.9	1926	4.7
27 TU	0112	0.8	0750	4.5	1322	1.1	2000	4.5
28 W	0144	1.0	0822	4.4	1355	1.3	2033	4.3
29 TH	0218	1.3	0854	4.2	1431	1.6	2112	4.1
30 F	0256	1.6	0932	4.0	1513	1.9	2202	3.8
31 SA	0340	1.9	1021	3.8	1608	2.1	2300	3.7

Chart Datum: 0·20 metres above Ordnance Datum (Dublin)

TIME ZONE (UTC)
For Summer Time add ONE hour in **non-shaded areas**

IRELAND – GALWAY

LAT 53°16′N LONG 9°03′W

TIMES AND HEIGHTS OF HIGH AND LOW WATERS

SPRING & NEAP TIDES
Dates in red are SPRINGS
Dates in blue are NEAPS

YEAR **2002**

SEPTEMBER

Date	Time	m	Date	Time	m
1 SU	0438	2.1	16 M	0057	3.8
	1120	3.7		0658	2.1
	1813	2.2		1327	3.9
				1957	1.8
2 M	0006	3.6	17 TU	0215	4.0
	0622	2.2		0806	1.9
	1227	3.7		1433	4.2
	1943	1.9		2051	1.5
3 TU	0131	3.7	18 W	0308	4.2
	0752	2.0		0853	1.6
	1400	3.9		1521	4.5
	2037	1.5		2124	1.2
4 W	0250	4.0	19 TH	0349	4.4
	0846	1.6		0932	1.3
	1508	4.3		1602	4.7
	2121	1.1		2156	1.0
5 TH	0341	4.4	20 F	0428	4.6
	0931	1.2		1008	1.1
	1554	4.7		1640	4.9
	2202	0.6		2229	0.8
6 F	0424	4.7	21 SA	0504	4.7
	1013	0.8		1043	0.9
	1636	5.0		1716	5.0
	2242	0.3		○ 2302	0.7
7 SA	0507	5.0	22 SU	0540	4.8
	1054	0.4		1117	0.8
	1719	5.3		1751	5.0
	● 2322	0.0		2335	0.7
8 SU	0549	5.2	23 M	0614	4.8
	1134	0.2		1149	0.8
	1802	5.4		1825	4.9
9 M	0001	-0.1	24 TU	0006	0.7
	0630	5.3		0646	4.8
	1215	0.2		1220	0.9
	1843	5.4		1857	4.8
10 TU	0042	0.0	25 W	0037	0.9
	0711	5.2		0717	4.7
	1256	0.3		1250	1.1
	1925	5.2		1928	4.6
11 W	0122	0.3	26 TH	0107	1.1
	0752	5.0		0746	4.5
	1338	0.6		1322	1.3
	2009	4.9		1958	4.4
12 TH	0205	0.8	27 F	0140	1.4
	0836	4.7		0814	4.3
	1423	1.0		1356	1.5
	2100	4.5		2035	4.2
13 F	0254	1.3	28 SA	0217	1.7
	0927	4.4		0848	4.1
	1518	1.5		1437	1.8
	2206	4.1		2126	3.9
14 SA	0357	1.8	29 SU	0301	2.0
	1032	4.0		0940	3.9
	1633	1.8		1529	2.1
	2327	3.8		2231	3.7
15 SU	0528	2.1	30 M	0400	2.3
	1157	3.9		1046	3.8
	1813	1.9		1647	2.3
				2341	3.7

OCTOBER

Date	Time	m	Date	Time	m
1 TU	0543	2.4	16 W	0156	4.0
	1156	3.8		0740	2.0
	1918	2.0		1409	4.2
				2030	1.6
2 W	0105	3.8	17 TH	0245	4.3
	0731	2.1		0828	1.7
	1325	4.0		1457	4.5
	2012	1.6		2058	1.3
3 TH	0227	4.2	18 F	0325	4.5
	0824	1.6		0906	1.5
	1444	4.4		1537	4.7
	2057	1.1		2128	1.1
4 F	0317	4.6	19 SA	0401	4.7
	0909	1.2		0942	1.2
	1531	4.9		1614	4.8
	2138	0.6		2200	0.9
5 SA	0359	5.0	20 SU	0436	4.8
	0950	0.7		1017	1.0
	1614	5.2		1649	4.9
	2217	0.3		2232	0.9
6 SU	0441	5.3	21 M	0510	4.9
	1031	0.4		1050	0.9
	1656	5.5		1723	5.0
	● 2256	0.1		○ 2303	0.9
7 M	0522	5.5	22 TU	0542	4.9
	1111	0.2		1121	0.9
	1739	5.6		1756	4.9
	2336	0.0		2333	0.9
8 TU	0604	5.5	23 W	0614	4.9
	1152	0.2		1151	1.0
	1821	5.5		1828	4.8
9 W	0016	0.2	24 TH	0003	1.1
	0644	5.4		0644	4.8
	1234	0.3		1222	1.1
	1903	5.3		1859	4.7
10 TH	0057	0.5	25 F	0035	1.3
	0725	5.2		0714	4.6
	1316	0.6		1255	1.3
	1947	5.0		1933	4.5
11 F	0140	1.0	26 SA	0110	1.5
	0808	4.8		0744	4.5
	1401	1.0		1332	1.5
	2037	4.5		2012	4.3
12 SA	0228	1.5	27 SU	0149	1.8
	0857	4.5		0820	4.3
	1455	1.5		1415	1.8
	2141	4.1		2105	4.1
13 SU	0332	2.0	28 M	0236	2.1
	1001	4.1		0913	4.1
	1609	1.9		1508	2.0
	2308	3.8		2211	3.9
14 M	0507	2.3	29 TU	0337	2.3
	1133	3.9		1021	4.0
	1747	2.0		1622	2.1
				2321	3.9
15 TU	0040	3.8	30 W	0512	2.4
	0632	2.2		1131	4.0
	1303	4.0		1842	1.9
	1938	1.9			
			31 TH	0037	4.1
				0659	2.1
				1250	4.2
				1940	1.6

NOVEMBER

Date	Time	m	Date	Time	m
1 F	0152	4.4	16 SA	0253	4.4
	0755	1.7		0835	1.7
	1409	4.6		1506	4.5
	2028	1.1		2055	1.4
2 SA	0246	4.8	17 SU	0330	4.6
	0842	1.2		0913	1.4
	1503	5.0		1544	4.6
	2111	0.7		2129	1.2
3 SU	0331	5.1	18 M	0404	4.7
	0925	0.8		0949	1.3
	1548	5.3		1619	4.7
	2151	0.5		2201	1.1
4 M	0413	5.4	19 TU	0437	4.8
	1007	0.5		1024	1.2
	1632	5.5		1653	4.8
	● 2231	0.3		2233	1.1
5 TU	0455	5.6	20 W	0510	4.9
	1049	0.4		1056	1.1
	1716	5.6		1727	4.8
	2312	0.3		○ 2304	1.1
6 W	0538	5.6	21 TH	0543	4.9
	1131	0.3		1128	1.1
	1801	5.5		1802	4.8
	2353	0.5		2336	1.2
7 TH	0621	5.5	22 F	0616	4.8
	1214	0.5		1201	1.2
	1845	5.3		1838	4.7
8 F	0036	0.8	23 SA	0011	1.3
	0704	5.2		0650	4.8
	1259	0.7		1238	1.2
	1930	4.9		1916	4.6
9 SA	0120	1.2	24 SU	0050	1.5
	0748	4.9		0727	4.6
	1345	1.1		1318	1.4
	2020	4.5		1959	4.4
10 SU	0209	1.7	25 M	0134	1.7
	0837	4.6		0807	4.5
	1437	1.5		1404	1.5
	2120	4.2		2050	4.2
11 M	0310	2.1	26 TU	0223	1.9
	0937	4.2		0858	4.4
	1544	1.8		1457	1.7
	2240	3.9		2152	4.1
12 TU	0435	2.3	27 W	0323	2.1
	1057	4.0		1001	4.3
	1708	2.0		1603	1.8
				2259	4.1
13 W	0004	3.9	28 TH	0441	2.2
	0553	2.3		1109	4.3
	1221	4.0		1740	1.8
	1827	1.9			
14 TH	0117	4.0	29 F	0007	4.2
	0657	2.1		0615	2.0
	1329	4.1		1219	4.4
	1934	1.8		1901	1.5
15 F	0211	4.2	30 SA	0115	4.5
	0751	1.9		0721	1.7
	1422	4.3		1332	4.6
	2019	1.6		1957	1.2

DECEMBER

Date	Time	m	Date	Time	m
1 SU	0214	4.8	16 M	0253	4.3
	0814	1.4		0843	1.7
	1434	4.9		1508	4.3
	2044	1.0		2056	1.5
2 M	0303	5.1	17 TU	0331	4.5
	0901	1.0		0923	1.5
	1524	5.1		1548	4.4
	2128	0.8		2133	1.4
3 TU	0348	5.3	18 W	0406	4.6
	0946	0.8		1001	1.3
	1612	5.3		1625	4.5
	2210	0.7		2209	1.3
4 W	0433	5.4	19 TH	0441	4.7
	1031	0.6		1038	1.2
	1658	5.3		1703	4.6
	● 2253	0.7		○ 2244	1.2
5 TH	0518	5.4	20 F	0518	4.8
	1115	0.6		1115	1.1
	1745	5.2		1742	4.7
	2336	0.8		2321	1.2
6 F	0603	5.4	21 SA	0556	4.8
	1200	0.7		1152	1.0
	1831	5.1		1823	4.7
7 SA	0020	1.0	22 SU	0000	1.2
	0648	5.2		0635	4.9
	1246	0.8		1230	1.0
	1917	4.8		1904	4.7
8 SU	0105	1.3	23 M	0041	1.3
	0733	5.0		0715	4.8
	1331	1.0		1311	1.0
	2005	4.5		1947	4.6
9 M	0152	1.6	24 TU	0125	1.4
	0820	4.7		0757	4.7
	1419	1.3		1355	1.1
	2058	4.2		2035	4.5
10 TU	0244	1.9	25 W	0213	1.5
	0912	4.4		0844	4.6
	1512	1.6		1444	1.2
	2201	4.0		2131	4.4
11 W	0349	2.1	26 TH	0307	1.7
	1013	4.2		0940	4.5
	1615	1.8		1540	1.4
	2309	3.9		2232	4.3
12 TH	0501	2.2	27 F	0411	1.8
	1118	4.0		1043	4.4
	1724	1.9		1647	1.5
				2335	4.3
13 F	0015	3.9	28 SA	0525	1.8
	0606	2.2		1149	4.4
	1226	4.0		1808	1.5
	1828	1.9			
14 SA	0117	4.0	29 SU	0040	4.4
	0705	2.1		0641	1.7
	1329	4.0		1301	4.4
	1927	1.8		1924	1.4
15 SU	0210	4.2	30 M	0144	4.6
	0757	1.9		0747	1.5
	1424	4.1		1409	4.6
	2015	1.7		2022	1.3
			31 TU	0241	4.8
				0842	1.3
				1507	4.7
				2112	1.1

Chart Datum: 0·20 metres above Ordnance Datum (Dublin)

Register for your FREE weekly weather email service from Macmillan Reeds
» at www.nauticaldata.com – NOW! «
weekend weather reports sent to your email address, every Thursday

MAPTECH®
Leading the world in digital navigation
Maptech UK Ltd • +44 (0)1243 389352 • sales@maptech.co.uk
Sales and distribution centres in Area 14
Channel Isles: *JE Marine*, 01534 626930, La Route du Port Elizabeth, St Helier, Jersey.
www.maptech.co.uk

14

Area 14

Channel Islands
Alderney to Jersey

9.14.1 Index .... Page 703

9.14.2 Area map 704

9.14.3 Tidal stream charts 706

9.14.4 Lights, buoys & waypoints 708

9.14.5 Passage information 710

9.14.6 Distance table 711

9.14.7 English Channel waypoints see *9.1.7*

9.14.8 Special notes for The Channel Islands 712

9.14.9 Braye (Alderney) 712
Saye Bay
Corblet Bay
Longy Bay
La Tchue
Telegraph Bay
Hannaine Bay
Platte Saline Bay
Burhou

9.14.10 Beaucette (Guernsey) 714

9.14.11 The Little Russel Channel 714
Minor harbours and anchorages around Guernsey:
Bordeaux Harbour
St Sampson
Havelet Bay
Soldier's Bay
Fermain Bay
Petit Port
Moulin Huet
Saints Bay
Icart Bay
Jaonnet
Petit Bôt Bay
Portelet
Portelet Harbour
Lihou Island
Perelle Bay
Vazon Bay
Cobo Bay
Grande Havre
L'Ancresse Bay
Fontenelle Bay

9.14.12 St Peter Port (Guernsey), Standard Port, tidal curves 716
Herm Island

9.14.13 Sark 721
Saignie Bay
Port à la Jument
Havre Gosselin
Port és Saies
La Grande Grève
Port Gorey
Rouge Terrier
Dixcart Bay
Derrible Bay
Grève de la Ville
Les Fontaines

8.14.14 St Helier (Jersey), Standard Port, tidal curves 722
Minor harbours and anchorages around Jersey:
St Aubin
Belcroute Bay
Portelet Bay
St Brelade
Grève au Lancon
Grève de Lecq
Bonne Nuit Bay
Bouley Bay
Rozel Bay
St Catherine
La Rocque
Les Ecrehou
Plateau des Minquiers

9.14.15 Gorey (Jersey) 724

Register for your **FREE** weekly weather email service from Macmillan Reeds
at **www.nauticaldata.com – NOW!**
weekend weather reports sent to your email address, every Thursday

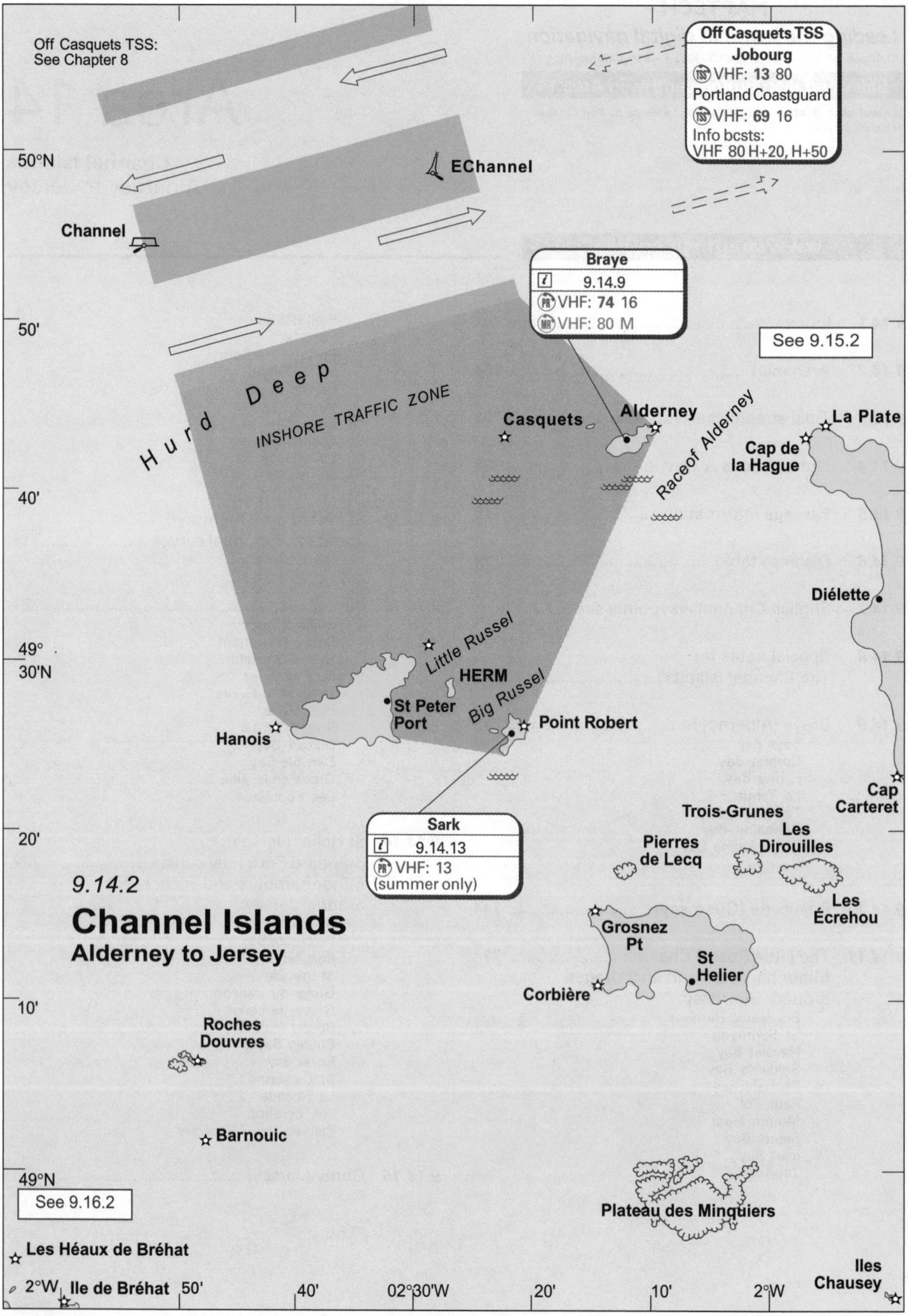
Off Casquets TSS:
See Chapter 8
Off Casquets TSS
Jobourg
VHF: 13 80
Portland Coastguard
VHF: 69 16
Info bcsts:
VHF 80 H+20, H+50
50°N
EChannel
Channel
Braye
9.14.9
VHF: 74 16
VHF: 80 M
See 9.15.2
50'
Hurd Deep
INSHORE TRAFFIC ZONE
Casquets
Alderney
Race of Alderney
La Plate
Cap de la Hague
40'
Diélette
49° 30'N
Little Russel
HERM
Big Russel
St Peter Port
Point Robert
Hanois
Sark
9.14.13
VHF: 13
(summer only)
Cap Carteret
Trois-Grunes
20'
Pierres de Lecq
Les Dirouilles
Les Écrehou
Grosnez Pt
St Helier
Corbière
10'
Roches Douvres
Barnouic
49°N
See 9.16.2
Plateau des Minquiers
Les Héaux de Bréhat
2°W
Ile de Bréhat
50'
40'
02°30'W
20'
10'
2°W
Iles Chausey

9.14.2

Channel Islands

Alderney to Jersey

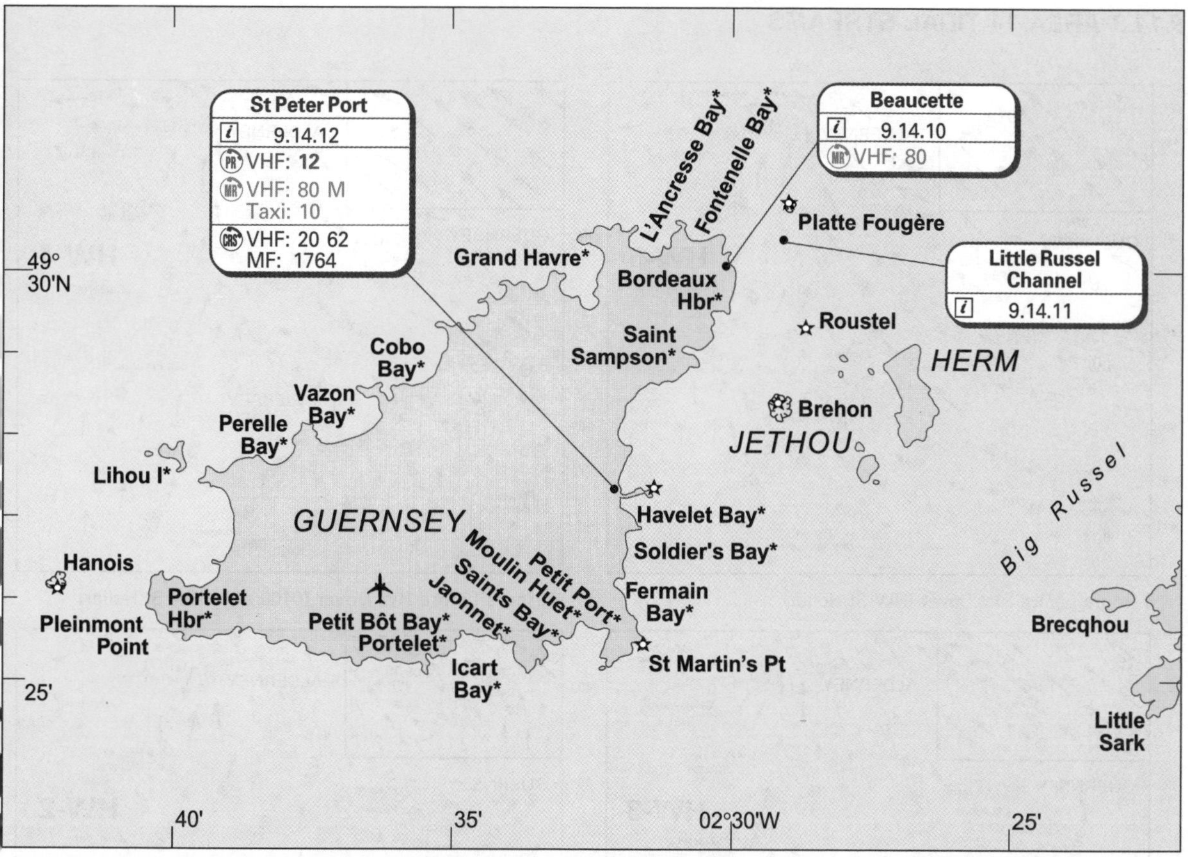
St Peter Port
9.14.12
VHF: 12
VHF: 80 M
Taxi: 10
VHF: 20 62
MF: 1764
Beaucette
9.14.10
VHF: 80
L'Ancresse Bay*
Fontenelle Bay*
Platte Fougère
Little Russel Channel
9.14.11
Grand Havre*
Bordeaux Hbr*
Saint Sampson*
Roustel
HERM
Brehon
JETHOU
Cobo Bay*
Vazon Bay*
Perelle Bay*
Lihou I*
GUERNSEY
Havelet Bay*
Soldier's Bay*
Fermain Bay*
Big Russel
Hanois
Moulin Huet*
Petit Port*
Saints Bay*
Jaonnet*
Portelet Hbr*
Pleinmont Point
Petit Bôt Bay*
Portelet*
Icart Bay*
St Martin's Pt
Brecqhou
Little Sark
49° 30'N
25'
40'
35'
02°30'W
25'

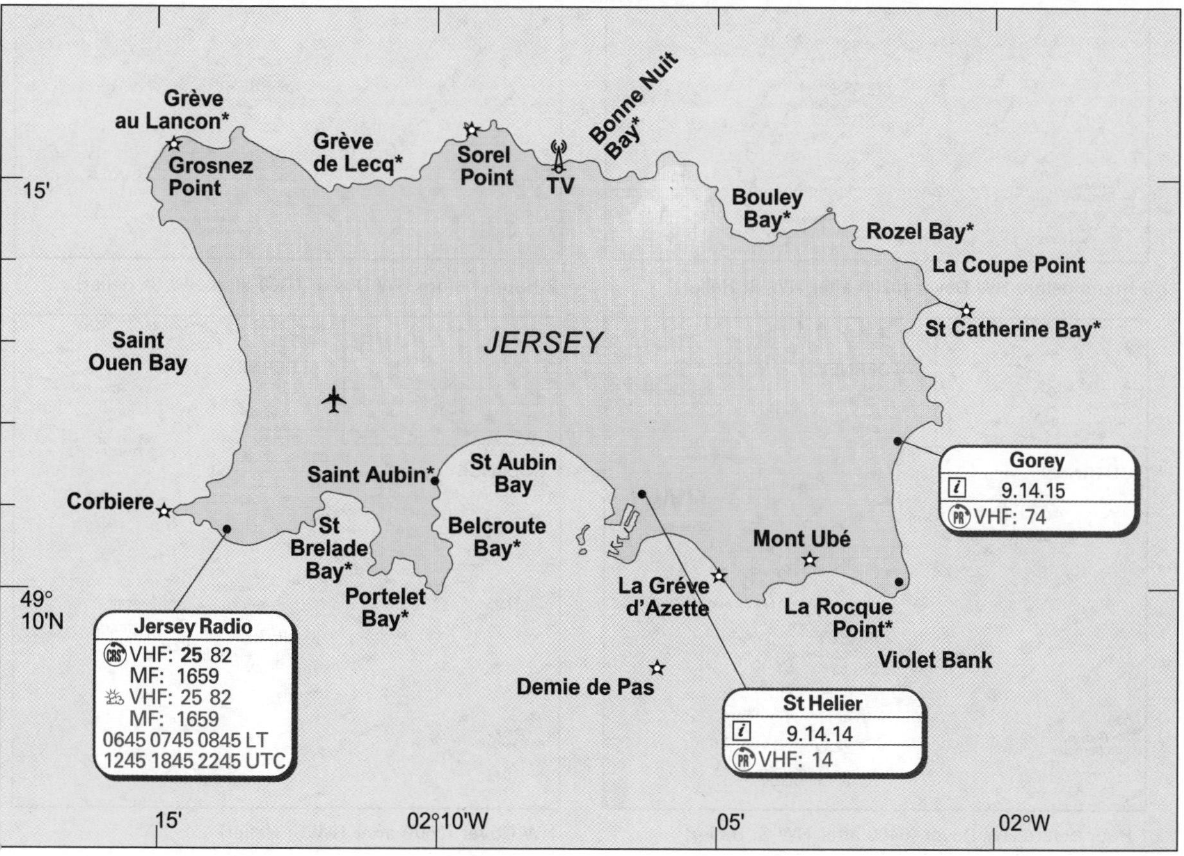
Grève au Lancon*
Grosnez Point
Grève de Lecq*
Sorel Point
TV
Bonne Nuit Bay*
Bouley Bay*
Rozel Bay*
La Coupe Point
St Catherine Bay*
Saint Ouen Bay
JERSEY
Gorey
9.14.15
VHF: 74
Saint Aubin*
St Aubin Bay
Corbiere
St Brelade Bay*
Belcroute Bay*
Mont Ubé
La Gréve d'Azette
La Rocque Point*
Portelet Bay*
Violet Bank
Jersey Radio
VHF: 25 82
MF: 1659
VHF: 25 82
MF: 1659
0645 0745 0845 LT
1245 1845 2245 UTC
Demie de Pas
St Helier
9.14.14
VHF: 14
15'
49° 10'N
15'
02°10'W
05'
02°W

9.14.3 AREA 14 TIDAL STREAMS

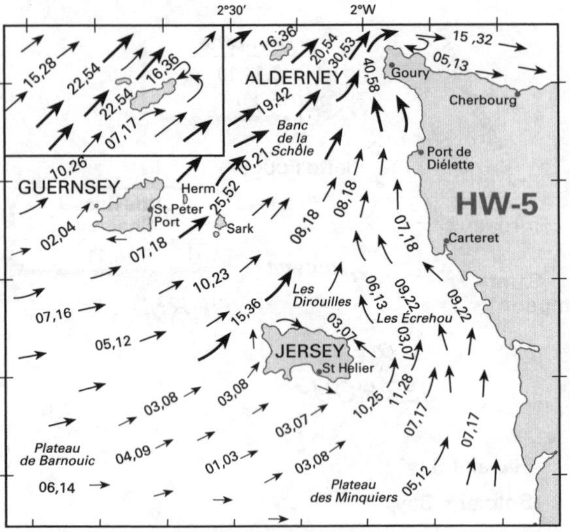

5 Hours before HW Dover (HW St Helier)

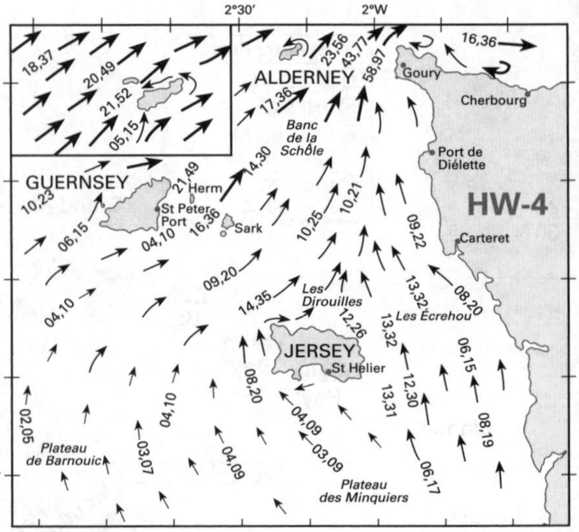

4 Hours before HW Dover (0100 after HW St Helier)

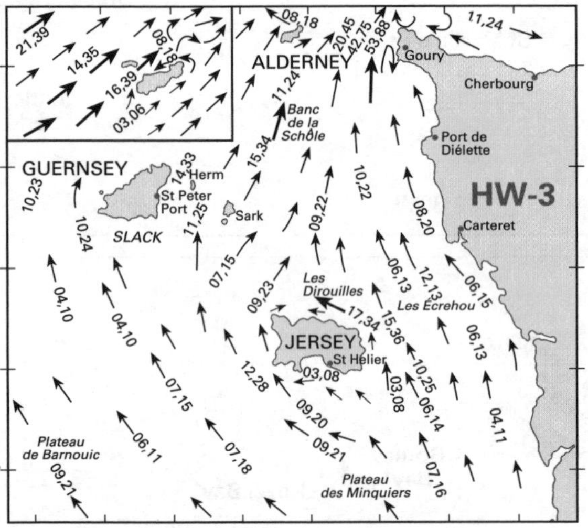

3 Hours before HW Dover (0200 after HW St Helier)

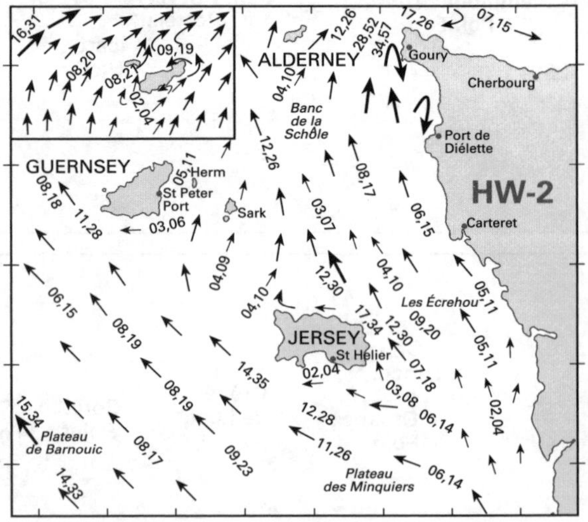

2 Hours before HW Dover (0300 after HW St Helier)

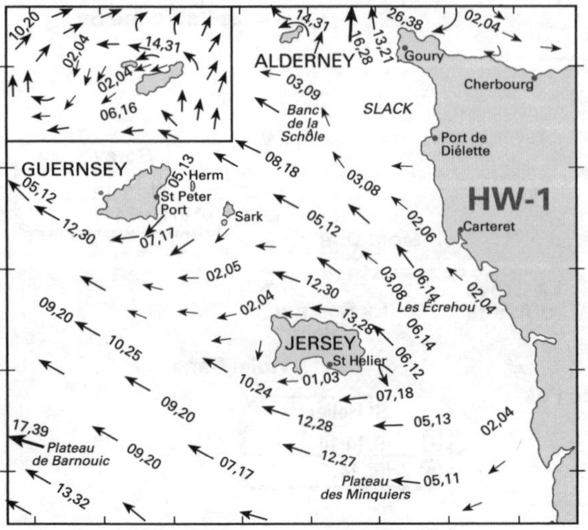

1 Hour before HW Dover (0400 after HW St Helier)

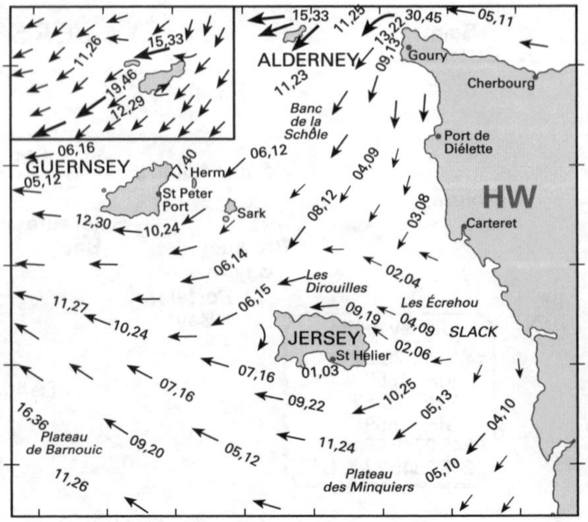

HW Dover (0500 after HW St Helier)

Westward 9.16.3   Southward 9.15.3   Northward 9.2.3   Eastward 9.22.3

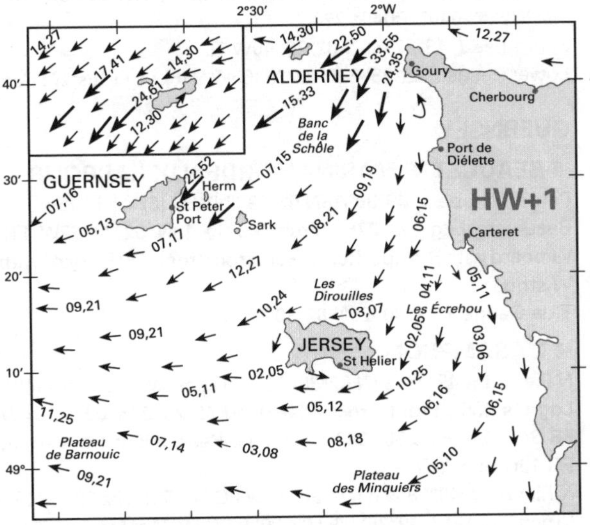

1 Hour after HW Dover (0600 after HW St Helier)

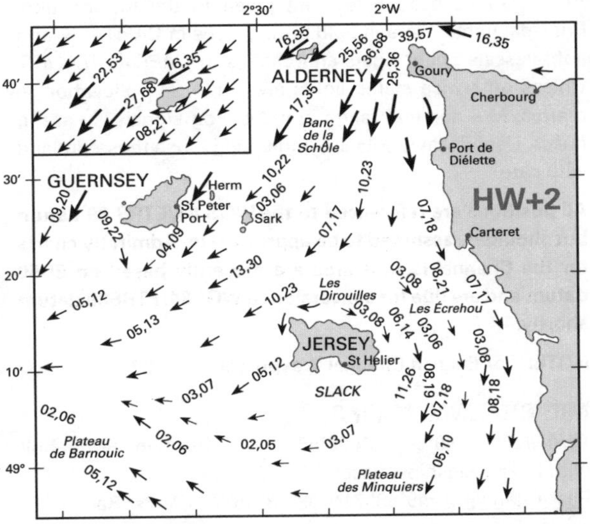

2 Hours after HW Dover (0530 before HW St Helier)

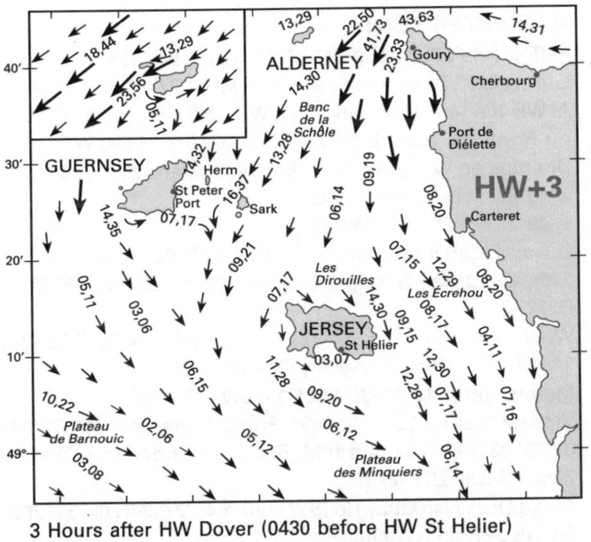

3 Hours after HW Dover (0430 before HW St Helier)

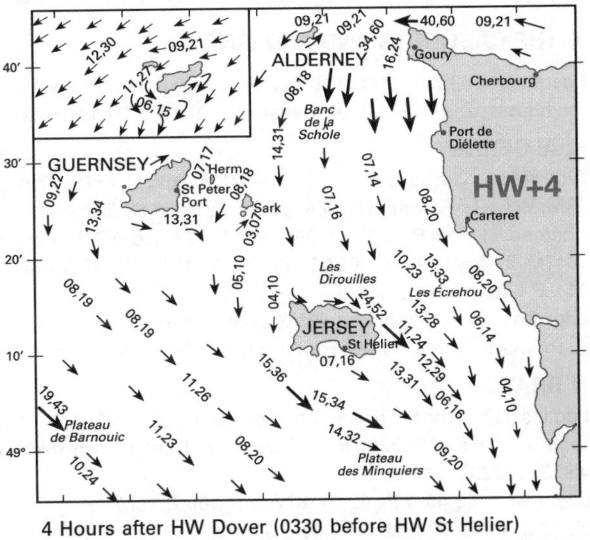

4 Hours after HW Dover (0330 before HW St Helier)

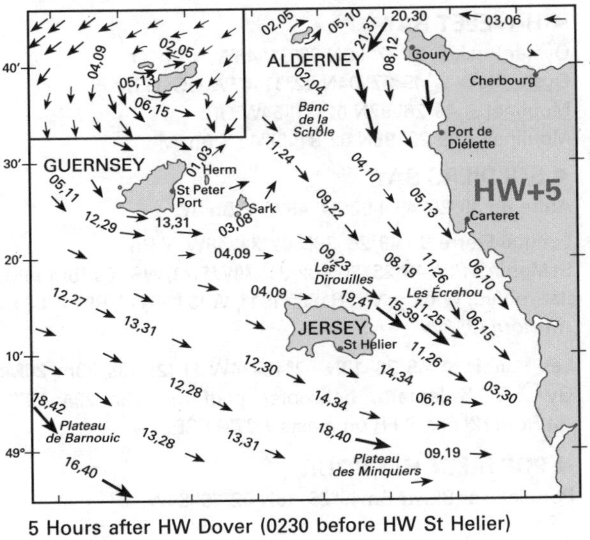

5 Hours after HW Dover (0230 before HW St Helier)

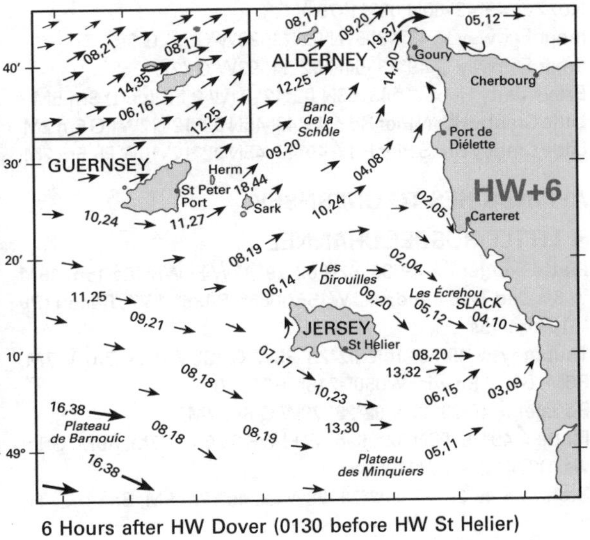

6 Hours after HW Dover (0130 before HW St Helier)

9.14.4 LIGHTS, BUOYS AND WAYPOINTS

Abbreviations used below are given in the Introduction. Principal lights ☆ are in **bold** print, places in CAPITALS, and light-vessels , light floats and Lanbys in *CAPITAL ITALICS*. Unless otherwise stated lights are white. m – elevation in metres; M – nominal range in miles. Fog signals are in *italics*. Useful waypoints are underlined – use those on land with care.

All positions are referenced to the WGS 84/ETRS 89 datum but should be assumed to be approximate. Admiralty charts for the Channel Islands area are presently based on ED50 datum and are due for conversion to WGS84/ETRS89 datum shortly.

NOTE: For English Channel Waypoints see 9.1.7.

MID-CHANNEL MARKS

CHANNEL 49°54'·46N 02°53'·94W Fl 15s 12m **25M**; R hull with Lt Tr amidships; Racon (O); *Horn (1) 20s.*

East Channel 49°58'·71N 02°28'·95W Fl Y 5s; Racon (T); *Whis.*

EC 2 50°12'·16N 01°12'·57W Fl (4) Y 15s; Racon (T); *Whis.*

◀ THE CASQUETS AND ALDERNEY

Casquets ☆ 49°43'·32N 02°22'·62W Fl (5) 30s 37m **25M**; W Tr, the highest and NW of three; Racon (T); *Horn (2) 60s*; H24.

◀ ALDERNEY

Alderney ☆ (Quenard Pt) 49°43'·75N 02°09'·86W Fl (4) 15s 37m **23M**; W ○ Tr, B band; vis: 085°-027°; *Horn (1) 30s*; H24.

Château à L'Étoc Pt 49°43'·94N 02°10'·63W Iso WR 4s 20m W10M, R7M; W col; vis: R071·1°-111·1°, W111·1°-151·1°; in line 111·1° with main Lt.

Ldg Bns 142°. Front, 49°43'·90N 02°10'·97W; W Bn, □ topmark. Rear, 720m from front, BW Bn, △ topmark.

◀ BRAYE

Ldg Lts 215°. **Front**, elbow of old pier, 49°43'·39N 02°11'·91W Q 8m **17M**; vis: 210°-220°. **Rear**, 335m from front, Q 17m **18M**; vis: 210°-220°.

Bkwtr Hd 49°43'·81N 02°11'·67W L Fl 10s 7m 5M.

No. 1 49°43'·72N 02°11'·71W QG.

No. 2 49°43'·60N 02°11'·75W QR.

Inner Fairway 49°43'·57N 02°11'·98W Q (2) G 5s.

Inner Fairway 49°43'·54N 02°11'·93W Q (2) R 5s.

Braye Jetty Hd 49°43'·53N 02°12'·01W 2 FR (vert) 8m 5M.

Little Crabby Hbr N Pier Hd 49°43'·45N 02°12'·12W FG 5m 2M.

Little Crabby Hbr S Pier Hd 49°43'·45N 02°12'·10W FR 5m 2M.

APPROACHES TO GUERNSEY

◀ LITTLE RUSSEL CHANNEL

Platte Fougère ☆ 49°30'·82N 02°29'·17W Fl WR 10s 15m **16M** W 8-sided Tr, B band; vis: W155°-085°, R085°-155°; Racon (P); *Horn 45s.*

Tautenay 49°30'·10N 02°26'·83W Q (3) WR 6s 7m W7M, R6M; B&W Bn; vis: W050°-215°, R215°-050°.

Roustel 49°29'·22N 02°28'·79W Q 8m 7M.

Platte 49°29'·08N 02°29'·57W Fl WR 3s 6m W7M, R5M; G Tr; vis: R024°-219°, W219°-024°.

Brehon 49°28'·27N 02°29'·28W Iso 4s 19m 9M; Bn on ○ Tr.

◀ BIG RUSSEL

Noire Pute 49°28'·27N 02°24'·93W Fl (2) WR 15s 8m 6M; vis: W220°-040°, R040°-220°.

Fourquies 49°27'·40N 02°26'·40W Q.

Lower Heads 49°25'·84N 02°28'·55W Q (6) + L Fl 15s; *Bell.*

GUERNSEY

◀ BEAUCETTE MARINA/BORDEAUX HARBOUR

Petite Canupe 49°30'·18N 02°29'·14W Q (6) + L Fl 15s.

Beaucette Ldg Lts 276°. Front 49°30'·18N 02°30'·22W FR; W board with R stripe. Rear, 185m from front, FR; R board with W stripe.

Tide Gauge 49°30'·20N 02°30'·17W.

◀ ST SAMPSON

N Pier Hd 49°28'·91N 02°30'·71W FG 3m 5M; vis: 230°-340°.

Ldg Lts 286°. Front Crocq Pier Head 49°28'·90N 02°30'·74W FR 3m 5M; vis: 230°-340°; Tfc sigs. Rear, 390m from front, FG 13m; clock Tr.

N Pier Hd 49°28'·91N 02°30'·71W FG 3m 5M; vis: 230°-340°.

Crocq Pier Hd 49°28'·99N 02°30'·99W FR 11m 5M; vis: 250°-340°.

◀ ST PETER PORT

Reffée 49°27'·74N 02°31'·27W VQ (6) + L Fl 15s.

Ldg Lts 220°. **Front**, Castle Bkwtr Head 49°27'·31N 02°31'·44W Al WR 10s 14m **16M**; dark ○ Tr, W on NE side; vis: 187°-007°; *Horn 15s.* Rear, Belvedere, Oc 10s 61m 14M; W □ with Or stripe on W Tr; vis: 179°-269°; both intens 217°-223°.

49°27'·76N 02°31'·74W QG.

49°27'·72N 02°31'·74W QR.

Queen Elizabeth II Marina 49°27'·72N 02°31'·86W. Dir Lt 270°. Dir Oc WRG 3s 5m 6M; vis: G258°-268°, W268°-272°, R272°-282°.

White Rock Pier Head 49°27'·38N 02°31'·59W Oc G 5s 11m 14M; ○ Tr; intens 174°-354°; Tfc sigs.

Marina app 49°27'·30N 02°31'·76W QG.

Victoria Marina Ldg Lts 265°. Front, S Pier Hd, 49°27'·32N 02°32'·03W Oc R 5s 10m 14M. Rear, 160m from front, Iso R 2s 22m 3M; vis: 260°-270°.

Albert Dock Fish Quay Hd (SW end) 49°27'·24N 02°31'·96W FR. Also FR on NW end.

◀ HAVELET BAY

Oyster Rock 49°27'·09N 02°31'·46W; Y Bn 'O'.

Oyster Rock 49°27'·04N 02°31'·47W QG; G By.

Moulinet 49°26'·97N 02°31'·54W QR.

Moulinet 49°26'·95N 02°31'·58W; Y Bn 'M'.

◀ SOLDIERS BAY

Anfré Bn 49°26'·45N 02°31'·48W; Y Bn 'A'.

Longue Pierre Bn 49°25'·36N 02°31'·48W; Y Bn.

St Martin's Pt ☆ 49°25'·30N 02°31'·70W Fl (3) WR 10s 15m 14M; flat-roofed, W bldg; vis: R185°-191°, W191°-011°, R011°-081°. *Horn (3) 30s.*

Les Hanois ☆ 49°26'·10N 02°42'·14W Fl (2) 13s 33m **20M**; Gy ○ Tr, B lantern, helicopter platform; vis: 294°-237°; *Horn (2) 60s.* 4 FR on masts 1·27M ESE.

◀ PORTELET HARBOUR

Portelet Hbr Bkwtr Bn 49°26'·15N 02°39'·84W.

◀ COBO BAY/GRAND HAVRE

Grosse Rock Bn 49°29'·01N 02°36'·19W 11m; B Bn.

Rousse Point Breakwater Beacon 49°29'·91N 02°33'·06W; B Bn.

◀ HERM

Petit Creux 49°28'·08N 02°28'·72W QR.

Alligande 49°27'·85N 02°28'·78W Fl (3) G 5s; Orange 'A' on B mast.

Épec 49°27'·98N 02°27'·89W Fl G 3s; Black 'E' on G mast.

Vermerette 49°28'·11N 02°27'·75W Fl (2) Y 5s; Orange 'V' on Bn.

Percée Pass, Gate Rock 49°27'·88N 02°27'·54W Q (9) 15s.

◀ SARK

Courbée du Nez 49°27'·08N 02°22'·17W Fl (4) WR 15s 14m 8M; W structure; vis: W057°-230°, R230°-057°.

Founiais 49°26'·02N 02°20'·36W; Topmark 'F'.

◀ GRÈVE LA VILLE/MASELINE

Point Robert ☆ 49°26'·19N 02°20'·74W Fl 15s 65m **20M**; W 8-sided Tr; vis: 138°-353°; *Horn (2) 30s.*

Blanchard 49°25'·35N 02°17'·42W Q (3) 10s; *Bell.*

JERSEY

Desormes 49°18'·94N 02°18'·02W Q (9) 15s.

Grosnez Point ☆ 49°15'·48N 02°14'·81W Fl (2) WR 15s 50m **W19M, R17M**; W hut; vis: W081°-188°, R188°-241°.

La Frouquie 49°11'·25N 02°15'·27.

La Corbière ☆ 49°10'·79N 02°15'·01W Iso WR 10s 36m **W18M, R16M**; W ○ stone Tr; vis: W shore-294°, R294°-328°, W328°-148°, R148°-shore; *Horn Mo (C) 60s.*

◀ WESTERN PASSAGE/ST BRELADE

Ldg Lts 082°. Front, La Gréve d'Azette 49°10'·12N 02°05'·12W Oc 5s 23m 14M; vis: 034°-129°. Rear, Mont Ubé 1M from front, Oc R 5s 46m 12M; vis: 250°-095°.

Noirmont Point 49°09'·91N 02°10'·08W Fl (4) 12s 18m 13M.

Passage Rock 49°09'·53N 02°12'·27W VQ.

Les Fours 49°09'·58N 02°10'·16W Q.

Pignonet 49°09'·87N 02°09'·68W.

Les Grunes du Port 49°10'·02N 02°09'·14W.

Ruaudière Rock 49°09'·74N 02°08'·60W Fl G 3s; *Bell.*

Diamond Rock 49°10'·11N 02°08'·64W Fl (2) R 6s.

◀ SAINT AUBIN

Baleine 49°10'·41N 02°08'·23W.

La Vrachére 49°10'·90N 02°07'·60W.

Beach Rock 49°11'·29N 02°08'·42W (Apr-Oct).

North Pier Hd 49°11'·21N 02°10'·04W Iso R 4s 12m 10M; and Dir Lt 254°. Dir F WRG 5m, vis: G248°-253°, W253°-255°, R255°-260°.

Fort Pier Head 49°11'·12N 02°09'·64W Fl R 4s 8m 1M.

◀ ST HELIER

Red and Green Passage (Small Roads) Ldg Lts 022·7°. Front, Elizabeth East Berth Dn 49°10'·63N 02°06'·94W Oc G 5s 10m 11M; R stripe on Tr. Rear, Albert Pier elbow, 230m from front, Oc R 5s 18m 12M; R stripe on Tr; synch with front.

East Rock 49°09'·95N 02°07'·28W QG.

Oyster Rocks 49°10'·09N 02°07'·49W.

Platte Rock 49°10'·16N 02°07'·34W Fl R 1·5s 6m 5M; R col.

No. 2 49°10'·38N 02°07'·24W QR.

Ldg Lts 078°. Front, 49°10'·62N 02°06'·66W FG. Rear, 80m from front, FG; both on W cols.

La Collette Yacht Basin 49°10'·54N 02°06'·95W QG.

La Collette Yacht Basin 49°10'·55N 02°06'·91W QR.

Victoria Pier Head 49°10'·57N 02°06'·88W; *Bell*; Tfc sigs.

◀ EASTERN PASSAGE/VIOLET CHANNEL/LA ROCQUE

Hinguette 49°09'·32N 02°07'·32W Fl (4) R 15s.

Demie de Pas Lt Bn Tr 49°09'·00N 02°06'·15W Mo (D) WR 12s 11m W14M, R10M; B Tr, Y top; vis: R130°-303°, W303°-130°; Racon (T); *Horn (3) 60s.*

Icho Tower 49°08'·88N 02°02'·90W (conspic).

Canger Rock 49°07'·34N 02°00'·38W Q (9) 15s.

La Conchere 49°08'·21N 02°00'·17W.

Frouquier Aubert 49°06'·09N 01°58'·84W Q (6) + L Fl 15s.

Violet 49°07'·81N 01°57'·14W L Fl 10s.

Petite Anquette 49°08'·46N 01°56'·30W; W Bn.

Grand Anquette 49°08'·32N 01°55'·21W; W Bn.

Le Cochon 49°09'·77N 01°58'·80W.

La Noire 49°10'·13N 01°59'·23W.

Le Giffard 49°10'·59N 01°59'·00W.

◀ GOREY

Ldg Lts 298°. Front, Pier Head 49°11'·80N 02°01'·34W Oc RG 5s 8m 12M; W Tr; vis: R304°-353°, G353°-304°. Rear, 490m from front, Oc R 5s 24m 8M; W □, Or sides on wall.

Horn Rock 49°10'·96N 01°59'·86W.

Inner Road 49°11'·49N 02°00'·34W QG.

Écureuil Rock 49°11'·66N 02°00'·78W.

Les Arch 49°12'·03N 02°00'·59W.

◀ ST CATHERINE BAY/ROZEL BAY

St Catherine Bay, Le Fara 49°12'·85N 02°00'·48W.

Verclut Bkwtr Hd 49°13'·33N 02°00'·65W Fl 1·5s 18m 13M.

La Coupe Pt Turret 49°13'·95N 02°01'·57W.

Rozel Bay Dir Lt 245° 49°14'·20N 02°02'·76W Dir F WRG 11m 5M; vis: G240°-244°, W244°-246°, R246°-250°.

◀ BONNE NUIT BAY TO GRÈVE AU LANCON

Demi Rock 49°15'·55N 02°07'·36W.

Bonne Nuit Bay Ldg Lts 223°. Front, Pier Hd 49°15'·09N 02°07'·17W FG 7m 6M. Rear, 170m from front, FG 34m 6M.

Sorel Point ☆ 49°15'·60N 02°09'·54W L Fl WR 7·5s 50m **15M**; B&W chequered ○ Tr; vis: W095°-112°, R112°-173°, W173°-230°, R230°-269°, W269°-273°.

OFFLYING ISLANDS

◀ LES ÉCREHOU

Écrevière 49°15'·26N 01°52'·17W Q (6) + L Fl 15s.

Maître I 49°17'·08N 01°55'·61W.

◀ PLATEAU DES MINQUIERS

NW Minquiers 48°59'·64N 02°20'·60W Q; *Bell.*

Refuge 49°00'·12N 02°10'·18W.

Demi de Vascelin 49°00'·80N 02°05'·18W.

Grand Vascelin Bn 48°59'·97N 02°07'·27W.

SW Minquiers 48°54'·34N 02°19'·41W Q (9) 15s; *Whis.*

S Minquiers 48°53'·07N 02°10'·11W Q (6) + L Fl 15s.

Maîtresse Île Bn Tr 48°58'·23N 02°03'·80W; B&W.

Récif Le Coq Bn 48°57'·88N 02°01'·31W

SE Minquiers 48°53'·43N 02°00'·10W Q (3) 10s; *Bell.*

NE Minquiers 49°00'·84N 01°55'·31W VQ (3) 5s; *Bell.*

N Minquiers 49°01'·63N 02°00'·60W Q.

9.14.5 PASSAGE INFORMATION

Current Pilots for this popular area include: *The Channel Islands* (Imray/RCC Pilotage Foundation, Heath); *Shell Channel Pilot* (Imray/Cunliffe); *Normandy and CI Pilot* (Adlard Coles/ Brackenbury); *Brittany and CI Cruising Guide* (Adlard Coles/ Jefferson - currently out of print); *N Brittany and CI Cruising* (YM/ Cumberlidge - awaiting reprint).

CHANNEL ISLANDS – GENERAL (chart *2669*) In an otherwise delightful cruising area, the main problems around the Channel Islands include fog and thick weather, the very big tidal range, strong tidal streams, overfalls and steep seas which get up very quickly. The shoreline is generally rugged with sandy bays and many offlying rks. It is important to use large scale charts, and recognised leading marks (of which there are plenty) when entering or leaving many of the hbrs and anchs. Several passages are marked by bns/perches identified by an alphabetical letter(s) in lieu of topmark. High speed ferries operate in the area.

From the N, note the Casquets TSS and ITZ. Soundings of Hurd Deep can help navigation. The powerful lights at the Casquets, Alderney (Quenard Pt), Cap de la Hague, Cap Levi and Barfleur greatly assist a night or dawn landfall. By day Alderney is relatively high and conspic. Sark is often seen before Guernsey which slopes down from S to N. Jersey is low-lying in the SE. The islands are fringed by many rky dangers. In bad visibility it is prudent to stay in hbr.

It is important to appreciate that over a 12 hour period tidal streams broadly rotate anti-clockwise around the Islands, particularly in open water and in wider chans (see 9.14.3). The E-going (flood) stream is of less duration than the W-going, but is stronger. The islands lie across the main direction of the streams, so eddies are common along the shores. The range of tide is greatest in Jersey (9·6m sp, 4·1m np), and least in Alderney (5·3m sp, 2·2m np). Streams run hard through the chans and around headlands and need to be worked carefully; neaps are easier, particularly for a first visit. Strong W'lies cause a heavy sea, usually worst from local HW – 3 to + 3.

Apart from the main hbrs described in Area 14, there are also many attractive minor hbrs and anchs. In the very nature of islands a lee can usually be found somewhere. Boats which can take the ground are better able to explore the quieter hbrs. Avoid lobster pots and oyster beds.

THE CASQUETS AND ORTAC ROCK (chart *60*) Casquets lt ho (fog sig) is conspic on the largest island of this group of rks 5·5M W of Braye, Alderney (9.14.9). Off-lying dangers extend 4ca W and WSW (The Ledge and Noire Roque) and 4ca E (Pte Colotte). The tide runs very hard round and between these various obstructions. A shallow bank, on which are situated Fourquie and l'Equêt rks (dry), lies from 5ca to 1M E of Casquets, and should not be approached. Ortac rk (24m) is 3·5M E of Casquets. Ortac Chan runs N/S 5ca W of Ortac; here the stream begins to run NE at HW St Helier – 0230, and SW at HW St Helier + 0355, with sp rates up to 5½kn (7kn reported). Ortac Chan should not be used in bad weather due to tremendous overfalls; these also occur over Eight-fathom Ledge (8½ca W of Casquets), and over the Banks SW, SSW and SSE of the Casquets. An Historic Wreck lies about 300m E of Casquets lt ho (see 9.0.3h).

ALDERNEY AND THE SWINGE (chart *60*) See 9.14.9 for Braye Harbour (chart *2845*) and approaches, together with pleasant bays and anchs around the island, offering shelter from different wind/sea directions. The sunken NE extremity of Admiralty Breakwater should not be crossed except in calm conditions, outside LW±2 and keeping about 50m off the hd of the Breakwater where there is 2·3m.

The Swinge lies between Burhou with its bordering rks, and the NW coast of Alderney. It can be a dangerous chan, and should only be used in reasonable vis and fair weather. On N side of the Swinge the main dangers are Boues des Kaines, almost awash at LW about 7½ca ESE of Ortac, and North Rk 2½ca SE of Burhou. On S side of the Swinge beware Barsier Rk (dries) 3½ca NNW of Fort Clonque, and Corbet Rk (0·5m high), with drying outliers, 5ca N of Fort Clonque.

The SW-going stream begins at HW St Helier + 0340, and the NE stream at HW St Helier – 0245, sp rates 7-8kn. On the NE-going stream, beware the very strong northerly set in vicinity of Ortac. The tide runs very hard, and in strong or gale force winds from S or W there are very heavy overfalls on the SW-going stream between Ortac and Les Etacs (off W end of Alderney). In strong E winds, on the NE-going stream, overfalls occur between Burhou and Braye breakwater. These overfalls can mostly be avoided by choosing the best time and route (see below), but due to the uneven bottom and strong tides broken water may be met even in calm conditions.

The best time to pass SW through the Swinge is at about HW St Helier +0400, when the SW-going stream starts; hold to the SE side of the chan since the strongest stream runs on the Burhou side. But after HW St Helier +0500, to clear the worst of the overfalls keep close to Burhou and Ortac, avoiding North Rk and Boues des Kaines.

Heading NE at about HW St Helier –0200, Great Nannel in transit with E end of Burhou clears Pierre au Vraic to the E, but passes close W of Les Etacs. On this transit, when Roque Tourgis fort is abeam, alter slightly to stbd to pass 1ca NW of Corbet Rk; keep near SE side of chan.

Pierre au Vraic (dries 1·2m) is an isolated, unmarked rock 1·8M S of Ortac and 1·8M WSW of Les Étacs, almost in the fairway to/ from the Swinge. On a fair tide from Guernsey it will be well covered, but it is a serious hazard if leaving the Swinge on a SW-going Spring tide close to LW (HW Dover to HW Dover +4). See AC 60 for clearing bearings.

THE ALDERNEY RACE (chart *3653*) (see 9.15.5)

APPROACHES TO GUERNSEY (charts *808, 3654*) From the N/ NE, The Little Russel Channel (chartlet at 9.14.11) between Guernsey and Herm gives the most convenient access to Beaucette marina (9.14.10) and St Peter Port (9.14.12 and chart *3140*). With lts on Platte Fougère, Tautenay, Platte and Bréhon, plus the ldg lts (220°) for St Peter Port, the Little Russel can be navigated day or night in reasonable vis, even at LW. But it needs care, due to rks which fringe the chan and appr, and the strong tide which also sets across the ent. In mid chan, S of Platte and NW of Bréhon, the NE-going stream begins at HW St Peter Port – 0245, and the SW stream at HW St Peter Port +0330, sp rates both 5·25kn which can raise a very steep sea with wind against tide.

The Big Russel is wider and easier; in bad weather or poor vis it may be a better approach to St Peter Port, via Lower Heads SCM lt buoy. From the NW, Doyle Passage, which is aligned 146°/326° off Beaucette, can be used but only by day with local knowledge. From S or W, the natural route is around St Martin's Pt rounding Longue Pierre bn (LP) 1·5ca ENE.

Minor hbrs and anchs around Guernsey are briefly described in 9.14.11. In onshore winds keep well clear of Guernsey's W coast, where in bad weather the sea breaks on dangers up to 4M offshore.

HERM AND JETHOU (charts *807, 808*). Herm (9.14.12) and Jethou (private) are reached from Little Russel via any of 7 passages all of which require reasonable vis and care with tidal streams; Alligande pass is most direct from St Peter Port. The appr from the Big Russel is more open and leads easily to pleasant ⚓s at Belvoir Bay and Shell Bay.

SARK (9.14.13 and chart *808*) La Maseline and Creux on the E coast are the only proper hbrs, the former much used by ferries. Elsewhere around the island, whatever the wind direction, a sheltered anch can usually be found in a lee, although swell may intrude. On the NW coast, Port à La Jument and Port du Moulin in Banquette Bay offer some shelter from S and E winds. Fontaines Bay and La Grève de la Ville offer different degrees of protection on the NE coast. Derrible B, Dixcart B and Rouge Terrier are good anchs on the SE coast. Port Gorey, Les Fontaines B, La Grande Grève and Havre Gosselin are all on the W coast; the last named is crowded in season due to easy access from Guernsey. Tidal streams around Sark need careful study, especially returning from the E coast towards Guernsey when the choice between going N or S-about Sark can make a significant difference. A more detailed study is under 9.14.13.

JERSEY (charts *3655*, 1136, *1137*, 1138) The rotatory pattern of tidal streams affecting the Channel Islands as a whole dictates that when streams are slack on the N and S coasts of Jersey, they are running strongly on the E and W coasts; and vice versa. If reaching Jersey from Guernsey/Alderney at HW St Helier +4, a fair tide can be carried for at least 6 hrs down the W coast and along the S coast to St Helier. From the S, leave St Malo at about HW, keeping E of the Minquiers, in order to carry a fair tide for 6 hrs to St Helier. Follow similar tidal tactics when coasting around the island.

To N and NE of Jersey, Les Pierres de Lecq (Paternosters), Les Dirouilles and Les Ecrehou are groups of islets and drying rks, 2-4M offshore. On the N coast several bays (9.14.14) offer anchs sheltered in offshore winds. Coming from N, a convenient landfall is Desormes WCM buoy, 4M NNW of Grosnez Pt (conspic lookout tr). In St Ouen B on the W coast, which has drying rks almost 1M offshore, there are no good anchorages except NW of La Rocco tr which is sheltered in offshore winds. Rounding the SW tip, to clear offlying dangers by 1M, keep the top of La Corbière lt ho (conspic) level with or below the clifftops behind (FR lt).

Along the S coast the NW and W Passages (buoyed) lead E past Noirmont Pt toward St Helier (9.14.14). St Brelade and St Aubin Bays (9.14.14) provide some shelter from W'lies. From the SW and S St Helier can be approached via Danger Rk Passage, Red & Green Passage or South Passage. All require good visibility to identify the transit marks and care to maintain the transits exactly. Only the R & G Passage is lit, but it needs sufficent water to pass over Fairway Rk (1·2m). The new Elizabeth marina at St Helier can be entered either from the R & G Passage or, with sufficient rise of tide, from St Aubin Bay. The latter appr on 106° passes N of Elizabeth Castle, crossing the causeway which dries approx 5·3m. It is well marked and lit.

SE of St Helier the drying, rky Violet Bank extends 1M S to Demie de Pas lt beacon, thence E past Icho Twr (conpic). It extends 1·7M S and 2M SE of La Rocque Pt. Further rky plateaux extend 1M to seaward. The Violet Channel (chart 1138), although buoyed is best avoided in bad weather, wind-over-tide or poor vis. From St Helier make good Canger Rk WCM lt buoy, thence track 078° for 2·2M to Violet SWM lt buoy. Turn N to pick up the charted ldg lines toward Gorey (9.14.15; dries) or to St Catherine Bay, both popular hbrs. The safe width of Violet Chan is only 5ca in places. Beware Decca problems due to being in the baseline extension area. The E coast of Jersey is sheltered from W'lies, but requires careful pilotage.

If bound for the adjacent French coast, proceed NE from Violet buoy via the Anquette Channel, between Petite and Grande Anquette beacons.

Les Minquiers (9.14.14), 10-18M S of St Helier, should only be entered by visitors in settled weather, with extreme caution and a good Pilot book.

9.14.6 DISTANCE TABLE

Approximate distances in nautical miles are by the most direct route, whilst avoiding dangers and allowing for Traffic Separation Schemes. Places in *italics* are in adjoining areas; places in **bold** are in 9.0.6, Cross-Channel Distances.

1.	***Cherbourg***	**1**																			
2.	*Cap de la Hague*	14	**2**																		
3.	*Carteret*	41	23	**3**																	
4.	*Granville*	75	61	38	**4**																
5.	***St Malo***	87	73	49	23	**5**															
6.	Casquets	31	17	32	63	70	**6**														
7.	**Braye (Alderney)**	23	9	26	66	73	8	**7**													
8.	Beaucette	39	25	34	59	58	15	19	**8**												
9.	**St Peter Port**	42	28	31	55	54	18	23	4	**9**											
10.	Les Hanois	49	35	37	58	56	23	29	14	10	**10**										
11.	Creux (Sark)	37	23	23	50	52	18	22	11	10	16	**11**									
12.	**St Helier**	59	45	28	30	38	43	46	33	29	32	24	**12**								
13.	Gorey (Jersey)	47	33	16	29	38	36	35	32	29	35	20	13	**13**							
14.	*Dahouet*	88	74	62	44	28	70	72	62	58	57	53	41	47	**14**						
15.	***St Quay-Portrieux***	88	74	64	54	35	71	73	55	56	48	51	46	52	12	**15**					
16.	*Paimpol*	91	77	65	56	42	67	70	54	50	45	50	45	53	24	24	**16**				
17.	***Lézardrieux***	88	74	68	54	49	65	68	52	48	42	38	47	55	33	21	14	**17**			
18.	***Tréguier***	94	80	72	72	60	66	72	56	52	42	58	53	63	58	46	29	22	**18**		
19.	***Roscoff***	117	103	95	96	84	87	94	77	73	63	79	80	93	71	59	58	54	41	**19**	
20.	***L'Aberwrac'h***	145	131	126	128	116	115	122	107	103	93	109	110	123	103	91	88	84	72	32	**20**

9.14.7 ENGLISH CHANNEL WAYPOINTS see 9.1.7

9.14.8 SPECIAL NOTES FOR THE CHANNEL ISLANDS

The Channel Islands (Jersey, Guernsey, Alderney, Sark and other smaller islands) lie, not in the Channel, but in the Bay of St. Malo. Alderney is part of the Bailiwick of Guernsey and the States of Alderney have seats in the States of Guernsey. Sark, Brecqhou, Herm and Jethou are all part of Guernsey.

History The Islands were originally part of Normandy and therefore French; the eastern ends of Jersey & Alderney are only 15 and 8·5 miles respectively from France. They could not be thought of as British until the 13th century, after King John lost mainland Normandy. The French call them Les Iles Anglo-Normandes (Jersey, Guernesey, Aurigny et Sercq).

Customs The Islands are British but are not part of the UK nor of the EU. They are self-governing, with their own laws and customs regulations. British yachts entering Channel Island ports will be required to complete the local Customs declaration form and may have to produce the vessel's registration documents; they will also be subject to customs formalities on return to UK. Yachts going to France need the normal documents (passports etc) and British yachts returning to the Channel Islands from France, must, like all French yachts, wear the Q flag. (It is advisable to do so when arriving from UK, but not mandatory, except in Alderney). Channel Islands do not have reciprocal medical arrangements with UK and medical insurance may be desirable as costs are high though hospital in-patient treatment is free.

Charts A folio of 10 small craft Admiralty charts of the Channel Islands 5604 costs £35.00.

Ports of Entry are Braye, Beaucette, St Sampson, St Peter Port, St Helier and Gorey.

SAR operations are directed by the Hr Mrs of St Peter Port (for the N area) and St Helier (for the S area), via St Peter Port and Jersey Radio respectively. Major incidents are co-ordinated with CROSSMA Joburg and Falmouth MRCC. Unlike the UK there are no CGs, but there are LBs at Braye, St Peter Port, St Helier and St Catherines (Jersey).

Telephones All CI telephones are part of the UK BT system.

Courtesy Flags Many yachts fly a courtesy flag in Channel Island ports as a mark of politeness but it is not essential. The local flags are:

Jersey W flag with R diagonal cross, with the Jersey Royal Arms (three lions passant with gold crown above) in the canton.

Guernsey R ensign with Duke William's cross in the fly. Vessels owned by Guernsey residents may wear this ensign.

Sark The English (St George's) flag with the Normandy arms in the canton.

Alderney The English (St George's) flag and in the centre a G disc charged with a gold lion.

Herm The English (St George's) flag, and in the canton the Arms of Herm (three cowled monks on a gold diagonal stripe between blue triangles containing a silver dolphin).

Cars can be hired in Jersey, Guernsey and Alderney. All cars are forbidden in Sark.

Animals The rules regarding animals are as strict as they are in UK. Landing of animals from boats is permitted only from UK, Ireland, Isle of Man or other Chan Islands, but not if the boat has visited France. Unless expressly permitted by a Revenue Officer, no vessel may lie alongside a pontoon or quay with an animal on board.

UK Currency is freely usable in the Islands but CI currency may not be in the UK. Postage stamps, issued by Jersey, Guernsey and Alderney must be used in the appropriate island. There is only one class of post.

BRAYE (Alderney) *9.14.9*

Alderney **49°43'·77N 02°11'·51W** ❁❁❁◊◊◊✿✿✿

CHARTS AC *5604*, 2845, *60*, *3653*, *2669*; SHOM 6934, 7158; ECM 1014; Imray C33A; Stanfords 7, 16, 26

TIDES –0400 Dover; ML 3·5; Duration 0545; Zone 0 (UT)

Standard Port ST HELIER (⟶)

Times				Height (metres)			
High Water		Low Water		MHWS	MHWN	MLWN	MLWS
0300	0900	0200	0900	11·0	8·1	4·0	1·4
1500	2100	1400	2100				
Differences BRAYE							
+0050	+0040	+0025	+0105	–4·8	–3·4	–1·5	–0·5

SHELTER Good in Braye Hbr, except in strong N/NE winds. A total of 64 Y ⚓s are laid parallel to the Admiralty bkwtr, E of Braye jetty and near Toulouse Rk, bn. Secure with chain if possible to avoid chafe due to persistent swell. Orange buoys are for locals. No landing on Admiralty bkwtr; at its NE end beware submerged extension. ⚓ in hbr is good on sand, but only fair on rock or weed patches; keep clear of the fairway and jetty due to steamer traffic. Hbr speed limit 4kn. Access HW±2 to drying inner hbr for D, FW.

NAVIGATION WPT 49°44'·23N 02°10'·99W, 035°/215° from/to front ldg lt 215°, 1·05M. The main hazards are strong tidal streams and the many rocks encircling Alderney. The safest appr is from the NE. Take the Swinge and the Race at/near slack water to avoid the dangerous overfalls in certain wind and tide conditions (see 9.14.5). In the Swinge calmest area is often near Corbet Rk. At mid-flood (NE-going) a strong eddy flows SW past the hbr ent. On the S side of the island during the ebb, a strong NE-going eddy runs close inshore of Coque Lihou. Give Brinchetais Ledge (E end) a wide berth to avoid heavy overfalls. An Historic Wreck is 5ca N of Quenard Pt lt ho (see 9.0.3h). Call HM for radar assisted approach if required.

LIGHTS AND MARKS From NW, N side of Ft Albert and end of Admiralty bkwtr 115° clear the Nannels. Iso WR 4s at Château à l'Etoc Pt, E of the hbr, vis R071°-111°, W111°-151°, in line 111° with Quenard Pt lt ho, Fl (4) 15s, clears sunken ruins of bkwtr. Ldg lts, both Q vis 210°-220°, lead 215° into hbr; front 8m 17M; rear 17m 18M. The Admty bkwtr hd has a lt, L Fl 10s 7m 5M. By day, St Anne's church spire on with W bn at Douglas Quay leads 210° to fairway which is marked by a QR and QG buoy and an inner Q (2) G 5s buoy. End of steamer quay has 2 FR (vert) lts. Little Crabby Hbr ent: FG and FR.

RADIO TELEPHONE Call: *Alderney Radio* VHF Ch **74** 16 12 (May to Sept, 0800 -1800, daily; Oct 0800-1700 daily; Nov to Apr, 0800-1700, Mon-Fri: all LT). Note: In fog/limited vis radar assistance and RDF bearings to small craft can be provided by the Hr Mr during above hrs. Outside these hrs call St Peter Port. Mainbrayce Marine Ch 80 M (Apr-mid Sept: 0800-2000LT). Water taxi (£1 a head) call *Mainbrayce* Ch M, 0800-2359.

TELEPHONE (Dial code 01481) Hr Mr & ⊜ 822620, 📠 823699; Marinecall 09068 500 432; Recorded forecasts see 9.14.2; Police 822731; Dr 822077; Ⓗ 822822; ❶ Info 822994 (H24).

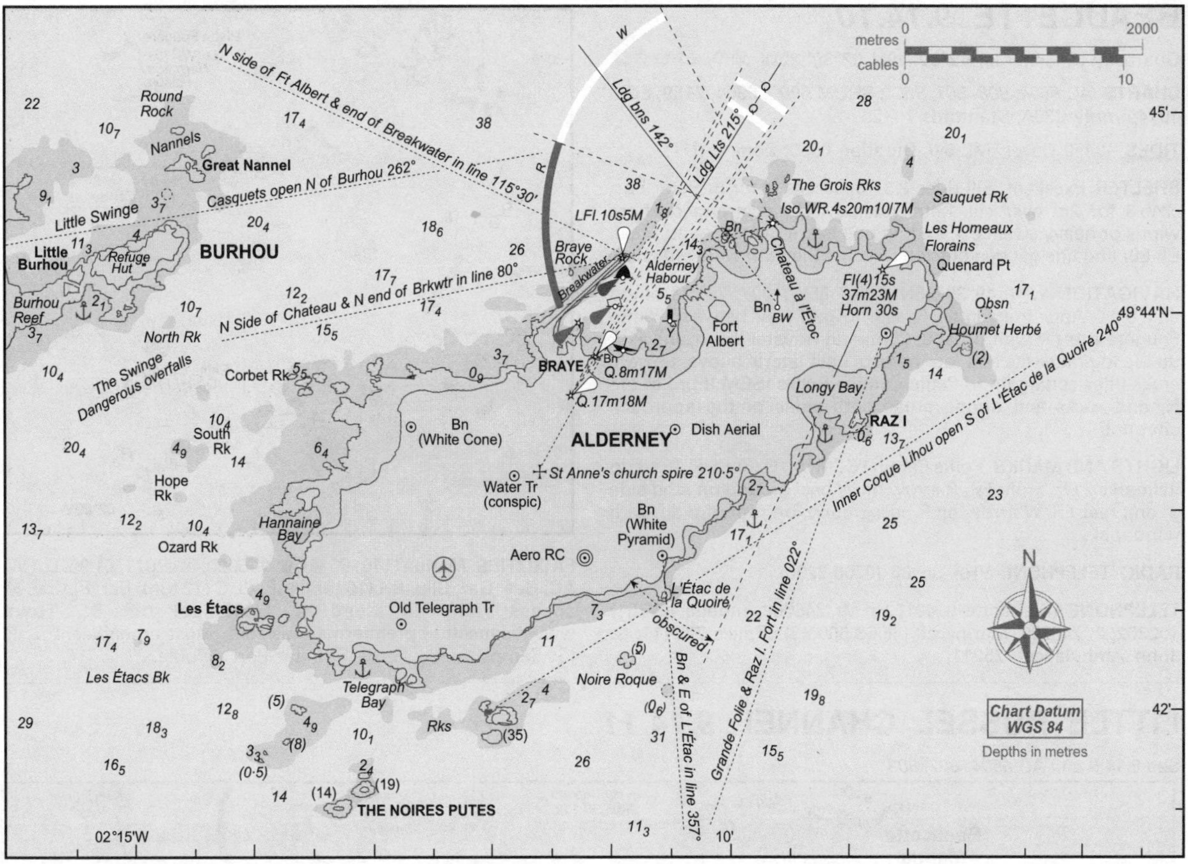

FACILITIES Hbr (£11 flat rate), ⚓ £2 inc shower; **Jetty**, FW, C, ; **Sapper Slip**, FW; **Alderney SC** ☎ 822758, Bar; **Services**: Slip, FW, ME, El, Ⓔ, Gas, SM, Sh, CH, ACA, P (cans), D (Mainbrayce, inner hbr HW±2). **Town** EC Wed; V, R, Bar, ✉, Ⓑ, ✈ to Jersey, Guernsey and Southampton; to Dinard, Gatwick, Manchester and Cherbourg via Guernsey. Ferry: via Guernsey – Poole, Portsmouth, St Malo and Weymouth.

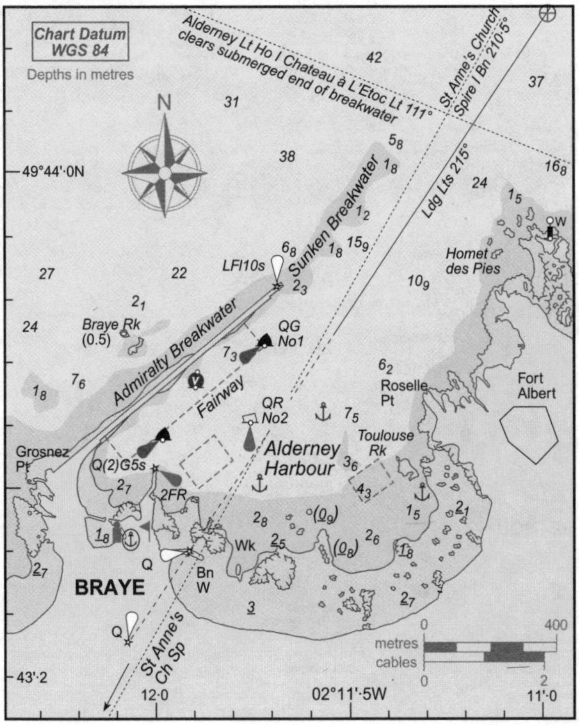

ANCHORAGES AROUND ALDERNEY There are several ⚓s, all picturesque but only safe in off-shore winds. Most ⚓s are very small and many have offlying rocks. Without local knowledge, advice from the Hr Mr and a good Pilot book plus AC 60 and/or 2845, it is not recommended to enter these anchorages. None provide any facilities. Clockwise from Braye they are:

Saye Bay. Small sandy bay 4ca E of ent to Braye Hbr. Appr on transit 142° of ldg bns, opening to the E. Ent is 100m wide between Homet des Pies and Homet des Agneaux. Exposed to N'lies. Château à l'Étoc ☆ is 300m ENE.

Corblets Bay. AC 2845. Appr with BW bn △ (rear ldg mark of 142° transit for Braye) brg 210°. Leave Platte Rk (1·8m) 100m to port. Beware drying reefs closer in. ⚓ in 2·5m when Quenard lt ho and Château à l'Étoc ☆ are in line.

Longy Bay. AC 2845. Wide drying bay with good holding in sand. Appr on N between Queslingue (14m high) and rk 0·6m to stbd. ⚓ in 3·5m closer to Essex Castle than to Raz Island to await fair tide in the Race.

La Tchue. Good holding in small bay surrounded by cliffs. La Rocque Pendante to the E and smoking rubbish tip to the NW are both conspic.

Telegraph Bay. Pleasant sandy bay on SW tip of the island but ringed by rocks. Appr on NNE between Noires Putes and Coupé. Telegraph Twr is conspic until close inshore.

Hannaine Bay. A good place to await the flood tide. Appr on transit 057° of Tourgis Bn △ and SE side of Fort Clonque. Beware rks either side. ⚓ on sand in 3m, 100m S of Fort.

Platte Saline Bay. AC 2845. Good shelter from E winds.

Burhou. Temp'y ⚓ in bay in SSW of Burhou, only on SW stream; exposed at HW on the NE-going stream. Appr on 010° for the gap between Burhou and Little Burhou.

BEAUCETTE *9.14.10*

Guernsey (Channel Is) **49°30'.19N 02°30'·20W**

CHARTS AC *5604, 808, 807, 3654*; SHOM 6903, 6904, 7159; ECM 1014; Imray C33A; Stanfords 16, 26

TIDES –0450 Dover; ML 5·0; Duration 0550; Zone 0 (UT)

SHELTER Excellent. Sill dries 2.37m; access is for St Peter Port HW±3 for 2m over sill. Entry not advised in strong onshore winds or heavy swell. 6 Y waiting buoys are outside (water taxi, Ch 80) and tide gauges outside & inside the 18m wide ent chan.

NAVIGATION WPT 49°30′·15N 02°28′·85W, 097°/277° from/to ent, 8½ca. Appr from Little Russel to mid-way between Platte Fougère lt tr (W with B band, 25m) and Roustel lt tr (ruin). Pick up the ldg marks/lts and four pairs of unlit lateral buoys. Beware cross tides setting on to Petite Canupe Rocks (SCM lt bn) to the N, and rocks and drying areas both sides of the approach channel.

LIGHTS AND MARKS Petite Canupe SCM bn, Q (6) + L Fl 15s. Ldg lts/marks 277°: Front FR, R arrow on W background on stbd side of ent; rear FR, W arrow on R background, on roof of bldg, with windsock.

RADIO TELEPHONE VHF Ch **80** (0700-2200).

TELEPHONE (Dial code 01481) Hr Mr 245000, mobile (07781) 102302; ⊜ 245000; Marinecall 09068 500 432; Police 725111; St John Ambulance 725211.

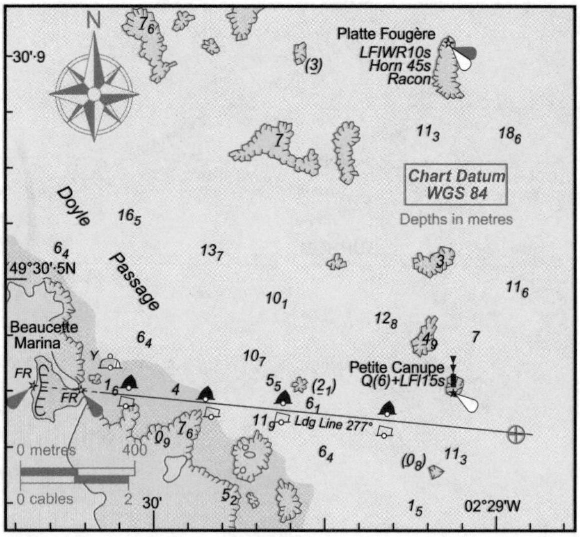

FACILITIES **Marina** (140+50 ⓥ), ☎ 245000, 47071, £1.95, D, FW, AC, Gas, Gaz, Slip, BH (16 ton), ME, El, C (12 ton), Bar, R, V, : access ramp is steep @ LW. Fuel on 'B'. **Town** www.beaucette@premiermarinas.com, Most amenities, ✉, Ⓑ (St Sampson), ✈. Ferry: St Peter Port – Poole.

LITTLE RUSSEL CHANNEL *9.14.11*

See 8.14.5 and AC *5604, 807, 808*

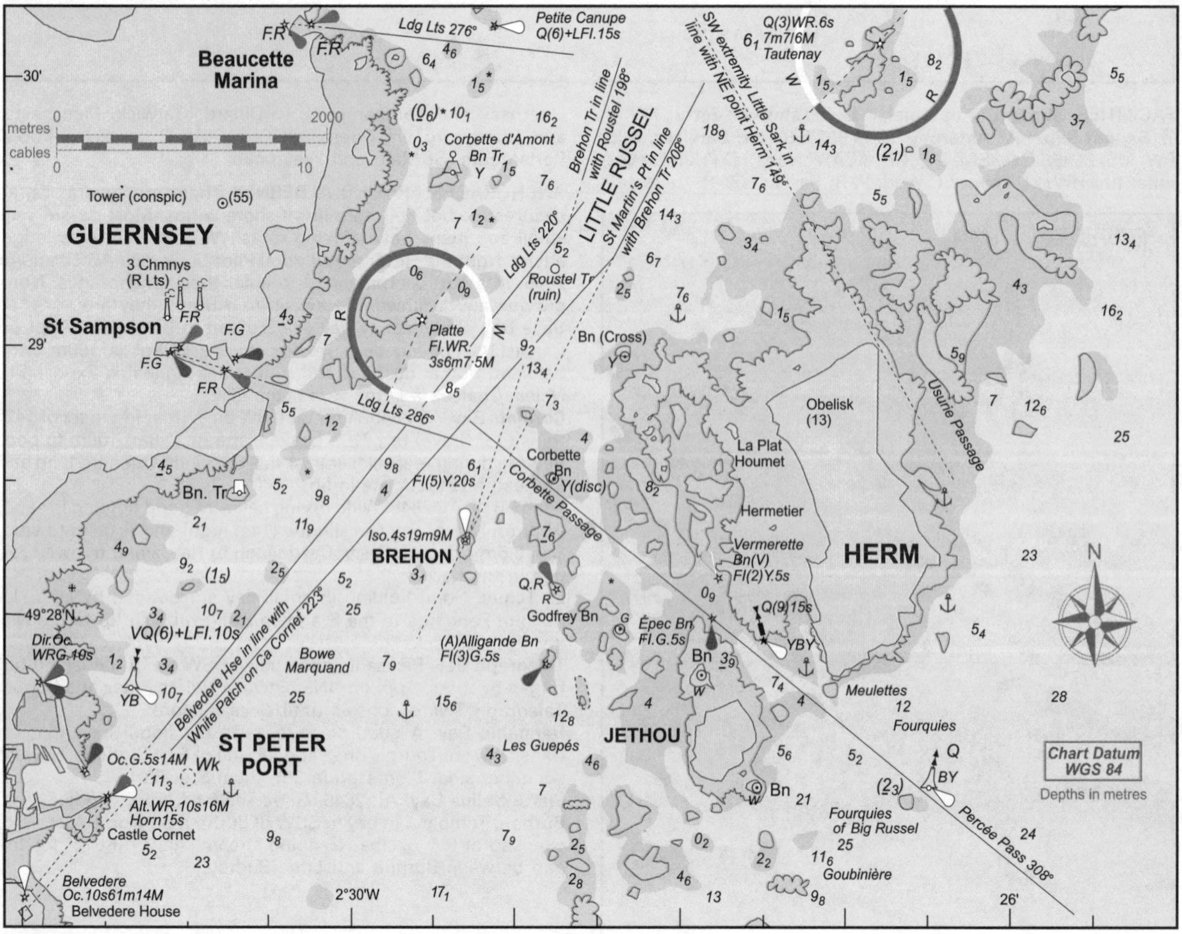

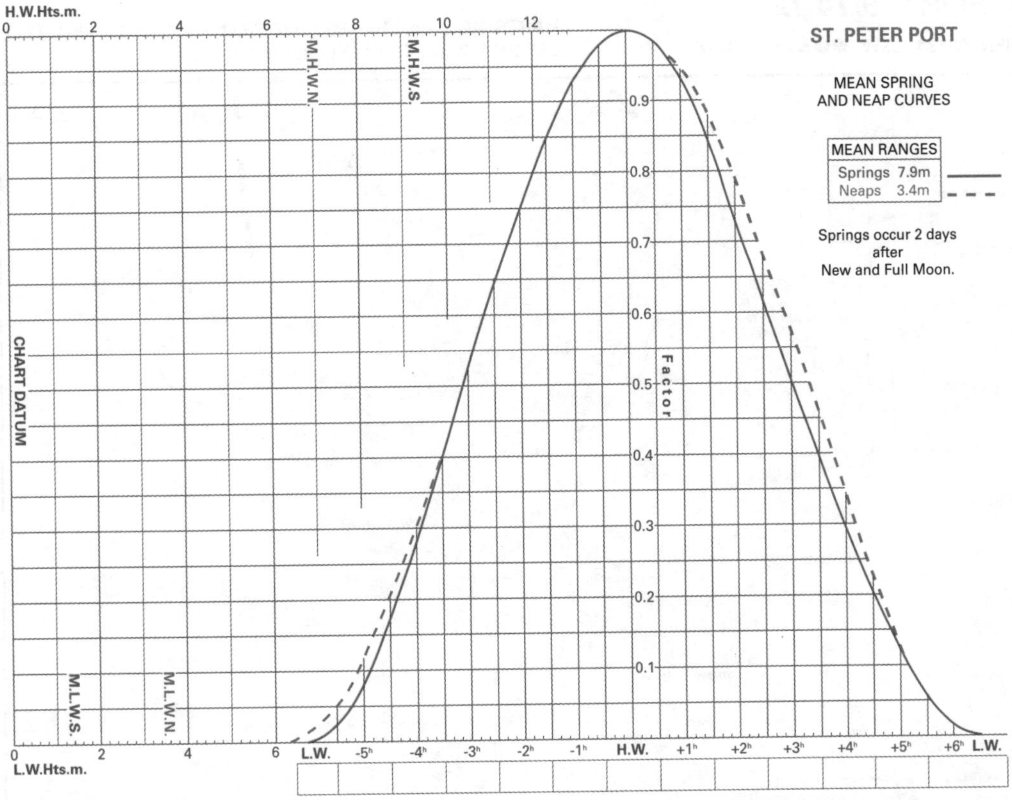
ST. PETER PORT
MEAN SPRING
AND NEAP CURVES
MEAN RANGES
Springs 7.9m
Neaps 3.4m
Springs occur 2 days
after
New and Full Moon.
H.W.Hts.m.
0 2 4 6 8 10 12
M.H.W.N.
M.H.W.S.
CHART DATUM
M.L.W.S.
M.L.W.N.
0 2 4 6
L.W.Hts.m.
Factor
0.9
0.8
0.7
0.6
0.5
0.4
0.3
0.2
0.1
L.W. -5h -4h -3h -2h -1h H.W. +1h +2h +3h +4h +5h +6h L.W.

HARBOURS AND ANCHORAGES AROUND GUERNSEY

Charts 807 and 808 are essential. ⚓s and hbrs are listed clockwise from Beaucette. All have buses to St Peter Port (from cliff-top level on the E and S coasts).

EAST COAST

Bordeaux Harbour. Small drying hbr full of local moorings. Rky appr with strong cross tide. Exposed to E. Café.

St Sampson's Harbour. Hbr dries $\underline{5}$·2m. Official port of entry. Good shelter but the disadvantages of a commercial and fishing hbr. Marina planned for local yachts only. Visiting yachts may only enter by prior arrangement or for commercial services. WPT 49°28'·70N 02°29'·64W, the intersection of St Peter Port and St Sampson ldg lts. 3 chys on N side are conspic. Ldg lts 286°: Front, FR 3m 5M, on S Arm, vis 230°-340°; rear, FG 13m, 390m from front, on clocktower. N pier hd FG 3m 5M, vis 230°-340°. Crocq pier hd, FR 11m 5M, vis 250°-340°, and tfc sigs. A Fl Y on S Arm flashes when petroleum/gas tankers are moving in the hbr; do not obstruct. Speed limit 6kn. No ⚓ in hbr. VHF Ch 12 (H24). Facilities: Call Dockmaster ☎ 720229 for entry, AB, C, FW. No special facilities for yachts, though marina planned for 2002. **Services**: Slip, BY, ME, El, Sh, C.

Havelet Bay. Enter between SHM buoy QG and PHM buoy QR, marking Oyster Rk, bn 'O', and Moulinet Rk, bn 'M'. Unlit SHM and PHM buoy about 100m closer inshore. Crowded ⚓ in summer but sheltered in SW gales; no Øs. Landing slip close W of Castle Cornet. Cable on chartlet normally buried to 1m but caution needed.

Soldier's Bay. Good holding on sand; exposed to E. On appr beware rky spur off Les Terres Point. Anfré Rk ($\underline{3}_3$), bn 'A', is 4ca offshore. Steps to cliff path. No facilities.

Fermain Bay. Good holding on sand; exposed to E. From N beware Gold Fisher Rk ($\underline{2}_1$), drying reefs off NE end of bay. From SE beware Gabrielle Rk ($\underline{2}_1$). Popular tourist beach. R, hotel, Bar.

SOUTH COAST

In the centre of first bight W of St Martin's Pt, beware Mouillière ($\underline{8}_5$). S winds can bring swell above half tide. Within this bight are:

Petit Port. Good holding on sand. Steep steps to cliff-top bar.

Moulin Huet. Good holding on sand. Tea garden and hotel.

Saints Bay. Good holding on sand. Below half tide beware uncharted rock in middle and unburied telephone cable on E side. ⚓ outside moorings with trip line. Café, hotel, bar.

Icart Bay. Beware Fourquie de la Moye ($\underline{3}_3$) in centre of ent between Icart Pt and Pte de la Moye. In Icart Bay are:

Jaonnet. Good holding on sand off small beach or further E off rky shore. Exposed to S. No facilities. Cliff path inland.

Petit Bôt Bay. Beware drying reef on E side. A short swell often works in. Café; up hill to hotel, bar, airport, ✉, V. Better ⚓ close W at:

Portelet. Good holding on sand in small ⚓. Sheltered from N and W. No access inland. Facilities via dinghy/Petit Bôt.

WEST COAST

Good visibility and chart essential; a pilot and E'ly wind desirable. Pass outside Les Hanois, unless bound for:

Portelet Harbour. Good holding on sand. Exposed to W. ⚓ outside moorings and clear of fish farm. Rky appr; local knowledge advised. Best avoid small drying stone quay. Hotel, bar, café.

Lihou Island. ⚓ off NE corner. Sheltered from E. Between Lihou and Guernsey is a drying rocky area and causeway. Tide runs fast. Respect bird sanctuaries on off-lying islets. No facilities.

Perelle Bay. Good holding on sand. Exposed to W; rky appr. Beware Colombelle Rk ($\underline{1}_5$) NE of bay. ⚓ outside moorings. Bar, hotel, D & P (cans).

Vazon Bay. Wide sandy beach for settled conditions, but exposed to the W. Beware Boue Vazon ($\underline{3}$) in appr, many lobster pots, surfers and bathers. Long surf line. Hotel, R.

Cobo Bay. Beware Boue Vazon ($\underline{3}$) in appr and many lobster pots. Rky appr from S of Moulière. Good holding on sand; ⚓ outside local moorings. Facilities: Hotel, Bar, R, B, ✉, V, D & P (cans).

Grande Havre. Very popular, many local moorings. Rky appr, exposed to NW, sheltered from S'lies. ⚓ to W of Hommet de Grève. Stone slip, busy in summer; lying alongside not recommended. Facilities: Hotel, Bar.

L'Ancresse Bay. Good holding on sand. Exposed to the N, but good shelter from S/SW. Hotel, Bar, Café.

Fontenelle Bay. Good holding on sand. Exposed to the N. Beware drying rks on E of ent. No facilities.

ST PETER PORT *9.14.12*

Guernsey **49°27'·35N 02°31'·53W** ❀❀❀⚓⚓⚓✿✿✿

CHARTS AC *5604*, 3140, *808*, *807*, *3654*; SHOM 6903, 6904, 7159; ECM 1014; Imray C33A; Stanfords 16

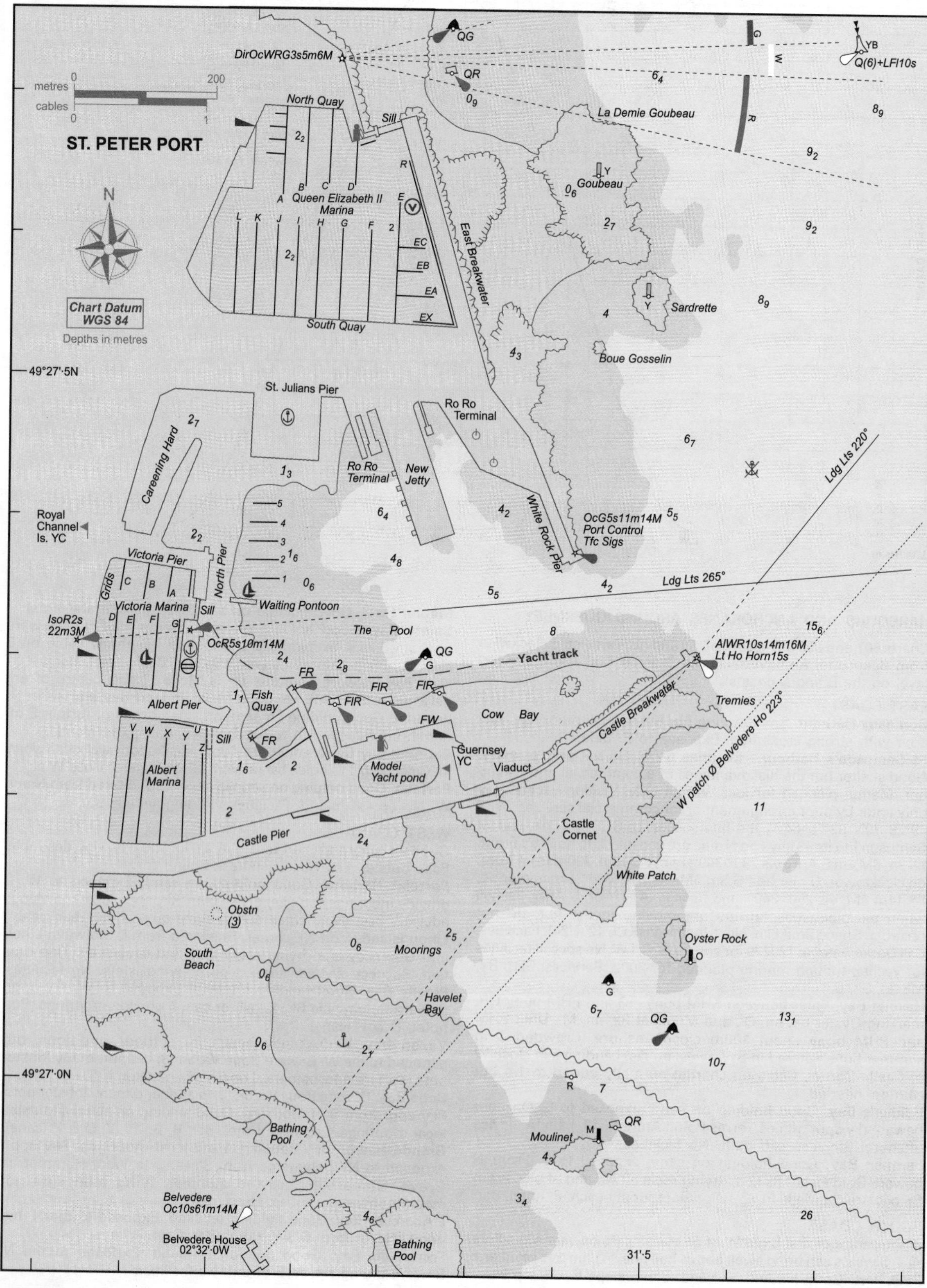

TIDES –0439 Dover; ML 5·2; Duration 0550; Zone 0 (UT) NOTE: Now a Standard Port, predicted times and hts of HW/LW for each day of the year are shown below. To find depth of water over the sill into Victoria marina:

1. Look up predicted time and height of HW St Peter Port.
2. Enter table below on the line for height of HW.
3. Extract depth (m) of water for time before/after HW.

Ht (m) of HW St Peter Port	Depth of Water in metres over the Sill (dries 4·2 m)						
	HW	±1hr	±2hrs	±2½hrs	±3hrs	±3½hrs	±4hrs
6·20	2·00	1·85	1·55	1·33	1·10	0·88	0·65
·60	2·40	2·18	1·75	1·43	1·10	0·77	0·45
7·00	2·80	2·52	1·95	1·53	1·10	0·67	0·25
·40	3·20	2·85	2·15	1·63	1·10	0·57	0·05
·80	3·60	3·18	2·35	1·73	1·10	0·47	0·00
8·20	4·00	3·52	2·55	1·83	1·10	0·37	0·00
·60	4·40	3·85	2·75	1·93	1·10	0·28	0·00
9·00	4·80	4·18	2·95	2·03	1·10	0·18	0·00
·40	5·20	4·52	3·15	2·13	1·10	0·08	0·00
·80	5·60	4·85	3·35	2·23	1·10	0·00	0·00

SHELTER Good, especially in Victoria Marina which has a sill 4·2m above CD, with a gauge giving depth over sill. Access approx HW±2½ according to draft; see Table above. R/G tfc lts control ent/exit. Appr via buoyed/lit chan along S side of hbr. Marina boat will direct yachts to waiting pontoon or a visitors' pontoon with FW (nos 1-5) N of the Waiting Pontoon. Pontoons for tenders are each side of marina ent. Local moorings are in centre of hbr, with a secondary fairway N of them. ⚓ prohib. Queen Elizabeth II and Albert marinas are for local boats only.

NAVIGATION WPT 49°27'·82N 02°30'·78W, 047°/227° from/to hbr ent, 0·68M. Offlying dangers, big tidal range and strong tidal streams demand careful navigation. Easiest appr from N is via Big Russel between Herm and Sark, passing S of Lower Hds SCM lt buoy. The Little Russel is slightly more direct, but needs care especially in poor visibility; see 9.14.5 and 9.14.11 chartlet. From W and S of Guernsey, give Les Hanois a wide berth. Beware ferries and shipping. Hbr speed limits: 6kn from outer pier heads to line from New Jetty to Castle Cornet; 4kn W of that line. The **RDF beacon, GY** 304·50kHz, on Castle breakwater is synchronised with the co-located horn* to give distance finding. The horn blast begins simultaneously with the 27 sec long dash following the four GY ident signals. Time the number of seconds from the start of the long dash until the horn blast is heard, multiply by 0·18 = your distance in M from the horn; several counts are advised.

LIGHTS AND MARKS Appr ldg lts 220°: Front, Castle bkwtr hd Al WR 10s 14m 16M (vis 187°-007°) Horn 15s*; rear, Belvedere Oc 10s 61m 14M, intens 217°-223°. By day, White patch at Castle Cornet in line 223° with Belvedere Ho (conspic). Inner ldg lts 265°: Front, Oc R 5s; rear, Iso R 2s, vis 260°–270° (10°). This ldg line is for the use of ferries berthing at New Jetty. It extends through moorings in The Pool, so must not be used by yachts which should appr Victoria marina via the buoyed/lit S channel (dashed line). **Traffic Signals** on White Rock pierhead:
● (vis from seaward) = No ent
● (vis from landward) = No exit (also at SW corner of New Pier).
These sigs do not apply to boats, <15m LOA, under power and keeping clear of the fairways.

RADIO TELEPHONE St Peter Port Marina Ch M 80 (office hrs). Monitor St Peter Port Control VHF Ch **12** (H24) but call Port Control if necessary when within the pilotage area. Water taxi Ch 10 (0800-2359LT). Call St Peter Port Radio CRS Ch 20 for safety traffic. Link calls Ch 62. St Sampson Ch 12 (H24).

TELEPHONE (Dial code 01481) Hr Mr 720229, Fax 714177; Marina 725987; ⊖ 726911; CG Sig Stn 720672; Marinecall 09068 500 432; Dr 711237 (H24), Pier Steps at Boots; 725211 (St John Ambulance); Police 725111; Forecasts prepared by the Jersey Met Office for the Channel Is area and as far as the adjacent coasts of Normandy and Brittany are available (premium rate) ☎ 0900 665 0022. This number is available throughout the Channel Is, UK and France, (from the latter replace the first 0 by 00 44). Guernsey Met office (from Guernsey only at lowest premium rate) ☎ 0906 713 0111 to discuss local Wx.

FACILITIES Victoria Marina (400, all visitors) ☎ 725987, £5 + £1 per m, special deals outside July/Aug, FW, AC, Slip, ♿, Ⓛ, R, Max LOA/draft = 12·8m/1·8m, Max stay 14 days or longer by arrangement; cranage available by arrangement **Castle Pier** P, D, FW approx HW±3, 0730-1730 Mon-Sat, 0730-1200 Sun; (also fuel pontoon at QE II marina). **Royal Chan Is YC** ☎ 723154 Bar; **Guernsey YC** ☎ 722838; **Services:** CH, Gas, Gaz, ACA, ME, El, SM, BY, Ⓔ. **Town** P, D, V, CH, R, Ⓛ, Bar, ✉, Ⓑ. Fast ferry to Poole, Weymouth, Jersey, St Malo; ferry to Portsmouth, Diélette, Sark, Herm; ✈ (Guernsey Airport).

HERM ISLAND

Access to Herm is not difficult, given adequate planning.

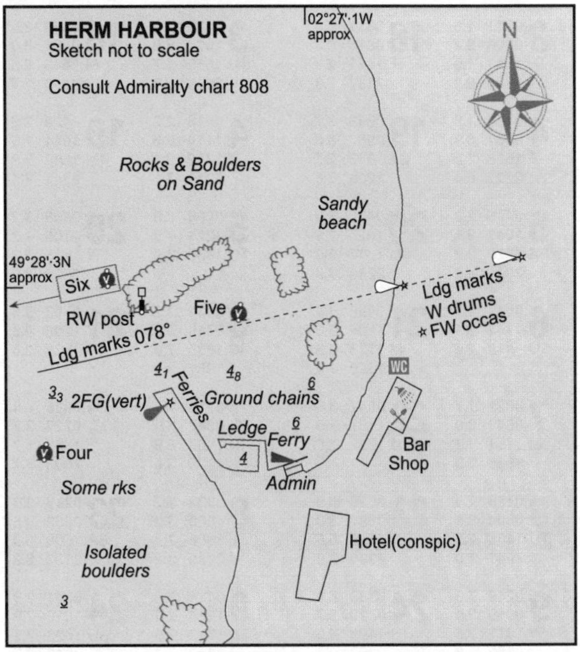

SHELTER Good, safe in all winds. Access HW±2½. Options: a. Lie to mooring lines secured to N and S walls inside hbr. b. Dry out on the beach to the E, below Bar and Shop, moored fore/aft to chains. c. 5 Ⓥs to N and 4 to W of hbr dry out; 6 more to NW: rky bottom to the N; isolated boulders/sand to W.

NAVIGATION Appr from Little Russel to skirt close N of Vermerette bn in line 074° with W patch on Hbr quay. When base of Vermerette bn is awash, there is 1m at hbr ent. The tide will be setting N. See Pilot for details of Corbette, Alligande and other passages from the W.

LIGHTS AND MARKS Ldg lts, both FW (occas) and W drums at 078°. 2FG (vert) on quay hd. Night appr not advised for visitors.

TELEPHONE Island Admin ☎ 722377 for permission to stay overnight.

FACILITIES No fees; donations welcome. Showers, FW, Hotel, Bar, R, limited V. Very congested in season at weekends, but plenty of space Sun to Thurs nights; many ferries by day.

Rosière Steps Access at all tides for landing; do not remain alongside. Caution: From just before HW to HW+2 tide sets hard onto the steps. Easiest appr is from Big Russel via Percée passage; avoid Fourquies (2_3), NCM lt buoy, and Meulettes (1_7) off SW tip of Herm. ⚓ NW of Rosière steps; good holding on sand, but exposed to S and SW. Buoys are for ferries and locals. Facilities: as Herm Hbr, 400m N.
Belvoir Bay and **Shell Beach** on the E coast are good ⚓s on sand, sheltered from W. Easy access from E; from S keep 400m offshore. Beach café or walk 800m to village.
Note: Jethou, Crevichon and Grande Fauconnière islands are private. No landing.

TIME ZONE (UTC)
For Summer Time add ONE hour in **non-shaded areas**

CHANNEL ISLANDS – ST PETER PORT

LAT 49°27′N LONG 2°31′W

TIMES AND HEIGHTS OF HIGH AND LOW WATERS

SPRING & NEAP TIDES
Dates in red are SPRINGS
Dates in blue are NEAPS

YEAR **2002**

JANUARY

Date	Day	Time	m	Time	m	Time	m	Time	m
1	TU	0141	1.4	0739	9.3	1410	1.2	2008	9.1
2	W	0226	1.4	0824	9.4	1455	1.3	2053	9.0
3	TH	0311	1.6	0909	9.2	1541	1.5	2139	8.8
4	F	0357	1.9	0957	8.9	1628	1.8	2227	8.4
5	SA	0446	2.3	1047	8.5	1720	2.2	2321	8.0
6	SU	0542	2.7	1144	8.1	1818	2.6		
7	M	0022	7.7	0647	3.0	1251	7.7	1926	2.9
8	TU	0136	7.5	0804	3.1	1406	7.5	2041	3.0
9	W	0249	7.6	0919	3.0	1517	7.6	2150	2.8
10	TH	0353	7.8	1021	2.7	1618	7.8	2247	2.6
11	F	0447	8.1	1116	2.4	1712	8.0	2338	2.4
12	SA	0536	8.4	1204	2.1	1800	8.3		
13	SU	0024	2.1	0619	8.7	1249	1.9	● 1843	8.5
14	M	0106	2.0	0700	8.9	1330	1.8	1923	8.6
15	TU	0143	1.9	0738	8.9	1406	1.7	2000	8.5
16	W	0217	2.0	0813	8.8	1440	1.8	2034	8.4
17	TH	0248	2.2	0846	8.6	1512	2.1	2106	8.2
18	F	0317	2.4	0918	8.3	1542	2.3	2137	7.9
19	SA	0348	2.7	0950	8.0	1613	2.7	2209	7.6
20	SU	0420	3.0	1025	7.6	1647	3.0	2245	7.3
21	M	0458	3.4	1105	7.3	1728	3.3	2328	7.0
22	TU	0547	3.6	1157	7.0	1822	3.5		
23	W	0026	6.9	0656	3.8	1305	6.8	1935	3.6
24	TH	0143	6.9	0820	3.7	1425	6.9	2053	3.4
25	F	0301	7.1	0933	3.3	1537	7.3	2200	3.0
26	SA	0407	7.6	1036	2.7	1640	7.7	2300	2.5
27	SU	0503	8.2	1133	2.1	1736	8.3	2354	2.0
28	M	0556	8.8	1226	1.6	1827	8.8	○	
29	TU	0045	1.5	0644	9.3	1316	1.1	1915	9.2
30	W	0134	1.1	0731	9.6	1403	0.7	2000	9.4
31	TH	0219	0.8	0816	9.8	1448	0.6	2044	9.5

FEBRUARY

Date	Day	Time	m	Time	m	Time	m	Time	m
1	F	0303	0.8	0900	9.8	1531	0.7	2127	9.3
2	SA	0345	1.1	0943	9.4	1612	1.1	2209	8.9
3	SU	0428	1.6	1027	8.9	1655	1.7	2253	8.3
4	M	0513	2.2	1114	8.2	1742	2.4	2343	7.7
5	TU	0606	2.8	1211	7.5	1838	3.0		
6	W	0048	7.2	0715	3.3	1325	7.0	1955	3.4
7	TH	0213	7.0	0847	3.5	1453	6.9	2125	3.5
8	F	0333	7.2	1006	3.2	1606	7.1	2235	3.2
9	SA	0434	7.6	1106	2.8	1702	7.5	2328	2.8
10	SU	0523	8.0	1154	2.4	1749	7.9		
11	M	0013	2.4	0606	8.4	1237	2.0	1830	8.3
12	TU	0053	2.0	0646	8.7	1315	1.7	● 1908	8.6
13	W	0128	1.8	0722	8.9	1349	1.5	1943	8.7
14	TH	0200	1.7	0755	9.0	1420	1.5	2014	8.7
15	F	0228	1.7	0826	8.9	1449	1.6	2043	8.6
16	SA	0255	1.9	0855	8.6	1515	1.9	2110	8.3
17	SU	0322	2.1	0922	8.3	1542	2.2	2137	8.0
18	M	0350	2.5	0951	8.0	1610	2.6	2206	7.7
19	TU	0420	2.9	1024	7.6	1643	2.9	2241	7.4
20	W	0458	3.2	1106	7.2	1725	3.3	2329	7.0
21	TH	0552	3.6	1206	6.8	1828	3.6		
22	F	0038	6.8	0717	3.7	1333	6.7	2003	3.7
23	SA	0215	6.9	0859	3.5	1509	6.9	2132	3.3
24	SU	0341	7.3	1016	2.9	1623	7.5	2242	2.7
25	M	0447	8.0	1119	2.1	1723	8.2	2341	1.9
26	TU	0542	8.8	1213	1.3	1815	8.9		
27	W	0033	1.2	0631	9.5	1303	0.7	○ 1901	9.5
28	TH	0121	0.6	0718	10.0	1349	0.2	1945	9.8

MARCH

Date	Day	Time	m	Time	m	Time	m	Time	m
1	F	0205	0.3	0801	10.2	1431	0.1	2027	9.9
2	SA	0247	0.3	0842	10.1	1511	0.3	2106	9.7
3	SU	0326	0.6	0922	9.7	1549	0.8	2145	9.2
4	M	0405	1.2	1002	9.0	1627	1.5	2223	8.5
5	TU	0444	1.9	1043	8.2	1707	2.4	2305	7.8
6	W	0530	2.8	1131	7.3	1755	3.2		
7	TH	0000	7.0	0631	3.5	1243	6.6	1906	3.8
8	F	0130	6.6	0811	3.8	1433	6.4	2103	4.0
9	SA	0314	6.7	0953	3.5	1554	6.8	2222	3.5
10	SU	0418	7.2	1052	3.0	1648	7.3	2313	3.0
11	M	0506	7.8	1137	2.4	1732	7.8	2354	2.4
12	TU	0547	8.3	1216	2.0	1810	8.3		
13	W	0032	2.0	0624	8.7	1252	1.6	1845	8.6
14	TH	0106	1.6	0659	9.0	1325	1.4	● 1918	8.9
15	F	0136	1.5	0732	9.1	1354	1.3	1949	8.9
16	SA	0203	1.4	0801	9.0	1421	1.4	2017	8.8
17	SU	0230	1.5	0829	8.8	1447	1.6	2042	8.6
18	M	0256	1.8	0855	8.6	1513	1.9	2107	8.4
19	TU	0322	2.1	0922	8.2	1539	2.3	2134	8.0
20	W	0350	2.5	0953	7.8	1609	2.7	2207	7.6
21	TH	0424	3.0	1033	7.3	1649	3.2	2252	7.2
22	F	0515	3.4	1132	6.9	1750	3.6		
23	SA	0001	6.9	0639	3.7	1301	6.6	1927	3.8
24	SU	0140	6.8	0835	3.5	1449	6.9	2110	3.4
25	M	0319	7.3	0958	2.8	1608	7.5	2224	2.7
26	TU	0428	8.1	1101	1.9	1706	8.3	2323	1.8
27	W	0523	8.9	1154	1.1	1755	9.1		
28	TH	0014	1.0	0612	9.6	1242	0.5	○ 1840	9.7
29	F	0101	0.5	0657	10.1	1327	0.1	1923	10.0
30	SA	0145	0.1	0740	10.2	1408	0.0	2003	10.1
31	SU	0225	0.1	0820	10.1	1447	0.2	2042	9.8

APRIL

Date	Day	Time	m	Time	m	Time	m	Time	m
1	M	0304	0.5	0859	9.6	1524	0.8	2118	9.3
2	TU	0341	1.1	0937	8.9	1559	1.6	2154	8.6
3	W	0418	1.9	1015	8.1	1636	2.5	2233	7.8
4	TH	0501	2.8	1100	7.2	1720	3.4	2321	7.0
5	F	0600	3.5	1205	6.5	1828	4.0		
6	SA	0043	6.5	0731	3.9	1404	6.3	2024	4.2
7	SU	0242	6.6	0924	3.7	1529	6.6	2154	3.7
8	M	0350	7.0	1023	3.1	1621	7.2	2244	3.1
9	TU	0437	7.6	1106	2.6	1703	7.7	2325	2.6
10	W	0518	8.1	1145	2.1	1740	8.2		
11	TH	0001	2.1	0555	8.6	1220	1.7	1815	8.6
12	F	0034	1.7	0630	8.8	1252	1.4	● 1848	8.9
13	SA	0105	1.5	0703	9.0	1322	1.3	1919	9.0
14	SU	0134	1.4	0733	9.0	1351	1.3	1947	8.9
15	M	0203	1.4	0802	8.9	1419	1.5	2014	8.8
16	TU	0231	1.7	0830	8.6	1447	1.8	2041	8.5
17	W	0259	2.0	0859	8.3	1515	2.2	2110	8.2
18	TH	0330	2.4	0933	7.9	1548	2.7	2146	7.8
19	F	0407	2.8	1017	7.4	1630	3.2	2234	7.4
20	SA	0501	3.3	1118	7.0	1734	3.6	2345	7.1
21	SU	0626	3.5	1245	6.8	1909	3.7		
22	M	0118	7.0	0814	3.3	1427	7.1	2048	3.3
23	TU	0253	7.5	0934	2.6	1543	7.7	2200	2.6
24	W	0402	8.2	1035	1.8	1639	8.5	2258	1.8
25	TH	0457	8.9	1128	1.2	1729	9.1	2349	1.1
26	F	0547	9.5	1216	0.6	1815	9.6		
27	SA	0036	0.6	0632	9.8	1301	0.4	○ 1857	9.9
28	SU	0120	0.4	0716	9.9	1343	0.4	1938	9.9
29	M	0202	0.4	0757	9.8	1423	0.6	2017	9.7
30	TU	0241	0.7	0837	9.3	1500	1.2	2054	9.2

Chart Datum: 5·06 metres below Ordnance Datum (Local)

TIME ZONE (UTC)
For Summer Time add ONE hour in **non-shaded areas**

CHANNEL ISLANDS – ST PETER PORT

LAT 49°27′N LONG 2°31′W

TIMES AND HEIGHTS OF HIGH AND LOW WATERS

SPRING & NEAP TIDES
Dates in red are **SPRINGS**
Dates in blue are **NEAPS**

YEAR **2002**

MAY

Date	Day	Time	m	Time	m	Time	m	Time	m
1	W	0319	1.3	0915	8.7	1536	1.9	2130	8.5
2	TH	0357	2.0	0954	7.9	1612	2.7	2209	7.8
3	F	0440	2.8	1038	7.2	1655	3.4	2255	7.2
4	SA	0536	3.4	1138	6.6	1758	4.0		
5	SU	0003	6.7	0652	3.8	1308	6.4	1925	4.2
6	M	0144	6.6	0825	3.7	1441	6.6	2101	3.9
7	TU	0303	6.9	0934	3.3	1538	7.0	2159	3.4
8	W	0356	7.4	1022	2.8	1622	7.6	2242	2.8
9	TH	0439	7.8	1102	2.3	1701	8.0	2320	2.3
10	F	0518	8.2	1139	2.0	1738	8.4	2356	2.0
11	SA	0555	8.5	1214	1.7	1814	8.7		
12	SU ●	0030	1.7	0630	8.7	1248	1.5	1847	8.8
13	M	0104	1.5	0705	8.8	1321	1.5	1919	8.9
14	TU	0137	1.5	0737	8.8	1354	1.6	1949	8.8
15	W	0210	1.6	0810	8.6	1426	1.8	2021	8.7
16	TH	0244	1.9	0845	8.3	1501	2.2	2057	8.4
17	F	0321	2.2	0925	8.0	1539	2.6	2139	8.1
18	SA	0405	2.6	1013	7.6	1627	3.0	2231	7.7
19	SU	0503	2.9	1115	7.3	1731	3.3	2338	7.4
20	M	0620	3.1	1231	7.1	1853	3.4		
21	TU	0057	7.4	0747	2.9	1357	7.4	2019	3.1
22	W	0221	7.7	0903	2.5	1510	7.8	2130	2.5
23	TH	0330	8.2	1005	1.9	1608	8.4	2229	1.9
24	F	0428	8.7	1059	1.5	1700	8.9	2322	1.4
25	SA	0520	9.1	1149	1.1	1747	9.2		
26	SU ○	0011	1.1	0608	9.3	1236	1.0	1832	9.5
27	M	0057	0.9	0654	9.4	1320	1.0	1915	9.5
28	TU	0141	0.9	0737	9.2	1401	1.2	1956	9.3
29	W	0222	1.2	0819	8.9	1440	1.6	2034	9.0
30	TH	0302	1.6	0858	8.5	1518	2.1	2112	8.5
31	F	0341	2.1	0938	7.9	1555	2.7	2151	8.0

JUNE

Date	Day	Time	m	Time	m	Time	m	Time	m
1	SA	0423	2.7	1021	7.4	1636	3.2	2234	7.4
2	SU	0512	3.2	1111	7.0	1727	3.7	2328	7.0
3	M	0611	3.5	1213	6.7	1832	3.9		
4	TU	0036	6.8	0717	3.6	1326	6.7	1944	3.9
5	W	0151	6.8	0824	3.4	1434	6.9	2051	3.6
6	TH	0256	7.1	0922	3.1	1528	7.2	2145	3.2
7	F	0348	7.4	1011	2.8	1615	7.6	2232	2.7
8	SA	0434	7.8	1054	2.4	1657	8.0	2314	2.3
9	SU	0517	8.1	1136	2.1	1738	8.3	2356	2.0
10	M ●	0559	8.4	1216	1.9	1816	8.6		
11	TU	0036	1.8	0638	8.5	1256	1.7	1854	8.8
12	W	0116	1.6	0718	8.6	1335	1.7	1931	8.9
13	TH	0156	1.6	0758	8.6	1414	1.8	2010	8.8
14	F	0237	1.7	0839	8.5	1455	1.9	2052	8.7
15	SA	0320	1.9	0923	8.3	1538	2.2	2137	8.5
16	SU	0407	2.1	1012	8.0	1627	2.5	2228	8.2
17	M	0502	2.4	1108	7.8	1724	2.8	2327	7.9
18	TU	0605	2.6	1212	7.6	1831	2.9		
19	W	0034	7.8	0716	2.7	1323	7.6	1945	2.9
20	TH	0148	7.8	0828	2.5	1434	7.8	2058	2.6
21	F	0259	8.0	0934	2.3	1538	8.1	2202	2.3
22	SA	0401	8.2	1033	2.0	1634	8.4	2258	1.9
23	SU	0458	8.5	1126	1.8	1725	8.7	2350	1.7
24	M ○	0550	8.6	1216	1.7	1813	8.9		
25	TU	0039	1.5	0638	8.8	1302	1.6	1857	9.0
26	W	0125	1.4	0723	8.8	1345	1.7	1939	9.0
27	TH	0208	1.5	0805	8.6	1425	1.8	2019	8.8
28	F	0248	1.7	0845	8.4	1502	2.1	2056	8.6
29	SA	0326	2.0	0922	8.1	1538	2.5	2133	8.2
30	SU	0403	2.4	0959	7.7	1613	2.9	2210	7.8

JULY

Date	Day	Time	m	Time	m	Time	m	Time	m
1	M	0441	2.8	1039	7.4	1651	3.2	2251	7.4
2	TU	0524	3.2	1123	7.1	1736	3.5	2339	7.1
3	W	0616	3.4	1216	6.9	1834	3.7		
4	TH	0037	6.9	0716	3.5	1319	6.8	1940	3.7
5	F	0146	6.9	0818	3.4	1424	6.9	2045	3.5
6	SA	0251	7.0	0917	3.2	1524	7.2	2144	3.2
7	SU	0350	7.3	1011	2.9	1616	7.6	2237	2.7
8	M	0442	7.7	1102	2.5	1705	8.0	2327	2.3
9	TU	0532	8.1	1150	2.2	1751	8.4		
10	W ●	0015	1.9	0619	8.4	1237	1.9	1836	8.8
11	TH	0102	1.6	0705	8.7	1323	1.6	1920	9.0
12	F	0148	1.4	0750	8.8	1407	1.5	2003	9.2
13	SA	0233	1.3	0834	8.9	1451	1.5	2047	9.2
14	SU	0317	1.3	0918	8.8	1535	1.6	2132	9.0
15	M	0402	1.5	1003	8.6	1620	1.9	2218	8.7
16	TU	0449	1.8	1052	8.3	1708	2.2	2309	8.3
17	W	0541	2.2	1145	7.9	1803	2.6		
18	TH	0006	7.9	0641	2.6	1249	7.6	1909	2.9
19	F	0115	7.6	0752	2.9	1401	7.5	2026	3.0
20	SA	0232	7.5	0907	2.9	1513	7.6	2141	2.8
21	SU	0343	7.6	1015	2.7	1616	7.9	2244	2.5
22	M	0445	7.9	1113	2.5	1711	8.2	2339	2.2
23	TU	0539	8.1	1204	2.2	1800	8.5		
24	W ○	0028	1.9	0627	8.4	1251	2.0	1845	8.8
25	TH	0114	1.7	0711	8.6	1333	1.8	1926	8.9
26	F	0154	1.6	0751	8.6	1411	1.8	2003	8.9
27	SA	0231	1.6	0827	8.6	1444	1.9	2038	8.8
28	SU	0304	1.8	0900	8.4	1515	2.1	2110	8.5
29	M	0335	2.1	0932	8.1	1544	2.4	2141	8.2
30	TU	0405	2.5	1003	7.8	1614	2.8	2213	7.8
31	W	0436	2.8	1036	7.4	1646	3.2	2248	7.4

AUGUST

Date	Day	Time	m	Time	m	Time	m	Time	m
1	TH	0512	3.2	1114	7.1	1727	3.5	2332	7.0
2	F	0600	3.5	1204	6.9	1823	3.7		
3	SA	0031	6.8	0708	3.7	1313	6.8	1944	3.8
4	SU	0152	6.8	0827	3.6	1433	6.9	2102	3.5
5	M	0311	7.0	0936	3.3	1542	7.3	2208	3.1
6	TU	0416	7.4	1036	2.9	1641	7.8	2307	2.5
7	W	0514	7.9	1132	2.3	1734	8.4		
8	TH ●	0001	1.9	0605	8.5	1224	1.8	1822	8.9
9	F	0051	1.4	0653	8.9	1312	1.3	1909	9.4
10	SA	0138	1.0	0739	9.3	1357	1.0	1953	9.7
11	SU	0223	0.7	0822	9.4	1440	0.9	2036	9.8
12	M	0305	0.7	0904	9.4	1522	1.0	2118	9.6
13	TU	0346	1.0	0945	9.1	1603	1.3	2200	9.2
14	W	0428	1.5	1028	8.6	1645	1.9	2244	8.5
15	TH	0513	2.1	1115	8.0	1733	2.5	2335	7.9
16	F	0606	2.8	1213	7.5	1834	3.1		
17	SA	0042	7.3	0716	3.4	1331	7.1	1958	3.5
18	SU	0213	7.0	0850	3.5	1459	7.1	2132	3.4
19	M	0338	7.1	1009	3.3	1608	7.5	2240	3.0
20	TU	0441	7.5	1107	2.9	1703	8.0	2333	2.5
21	W	0532	8.0	1155	2.4	1749	8.4		
22	TH ○	0018	2.1	0615	8.4	1238	2.0	1830	8.8
23	F	0059	1.7	0654	8.6	1316	1.8	1908	9.0
24	SA	0135	1.5	0730	8.8	1350	1.7	1942	9.1
25	SU	0208	1.5	0803	8.8	1420	1.7	2014	9.0
26	M	0237	1.6	0832	8.7	1447	1.8	2042	8.8
27	TU	0303	1.9	0900	8.5	1513	2.1	2109	8.5
28	W	0328	2.2	0926	8.1	1538	2.5	2136	8.1
29	TH	0354	2.6	0952	7.8	1605	2.9	2205	7.7
30	F	0423	3.1	1024	7.4	1637	3.3	2242	7.2
31	SA	0501	3.5	1106	7.0	1723	3.7	2334	6.8

Chart Datum: 5·06 metres below Ordnance Datum (Local)

TIME ZONE (UTC)
For Summer Time add ONE hour in **non-shaded areas**

CHANNEL ISLANDS – ST PETER PORT

LAT 49°27′N LONG 2°31′W

TIMES AND HEIGHTS OF HIGH AND LOW WATERS

SPRING & NEAP TIDES
Dates in red are **SPRINGS**
Dates in blue are **NEAPS**

YEAR **2002**

SEPTEMBER

Date	Time	m	Time	m	Time	m	Time	m
1 SU	0600	3.9	1210	6.7	1839	4.0		
2 M	0057	6.6	0738	4.0	1345	6.7	2029	3.8
3 TU	0242	6.8	0910	3.7	1516	7.1	2149	3.3
4 W	0400	7.3	1019	3.0	1623	7.8	2252	2.5
5 TH	0459	8.0	1117	2.3	1718	8.6	2346	1.8
6 F	0550	8.7	1208	1.6	1807	9.2		
7 SA ●	0035	1.1	0636	9.3	1256	1.0	1852	9.8
8 SU	0121	0.6	0720	9.7	1341	0.6	1936	10.1
9 M	0204	0.3	0802	9.9	1422	0.4	2017	10.2
10 TU	0245	0.4	0842	9.8	1502	0.6	2057	9.9
11 W	0323	0.8	0921	9.4	1541	1.1	2136	9.3
12 TH	0402	1.5	1000	8.8	1620	1.8	2217	8.5
13 F	0442	2.3	1043	8.1	1704	2.7	2304	7.7
14 SA	0532	3.2	1137	7.3	1803	3.4		
15 SU	0011	6.9	0645	3.9	1303	6.8	1937	3.9
16 M	0206	6.6	0843	4.0	1449	6.9	2129	3.7
17 TU	0335	6.9	1004	3.6	1558	7.3	2232	3.1
18 W	0432	7.5	1056	3.0	1648	7.9	2318	2.6
19 TH	0515	8.0	1138	2.5	1730	8.4	2358	2.1
20 F	0554	8.5	1216	2.0	1808	8.8		
21 SA ○	0034	1.7	0629	8.8	1252	1.7	1843	9.1
22 SU	0108	1.5	0702	9.0	1323	1.6	1916	9.2
23 M	0138	1.4	0733	9.1	1351	1.5	1946	9.2
24 TU	0205	1.5	0801	8.9	1417	1.7	2013	9.0
25 W	0230	1.8	0827	8.7	1442	2.0	2038	8.7
26 TH	0255	2.1	0851	8.4	1507	2.3	2104	8.3
27 F	0319	2.6	0916	8.0	1532	2.8	2131	7.9
28 SA	0346	3.0	0945	7.6	1602	3.2	2206	7.4
29 SU	0421	3.5	1026	7.2	1645	3.7	2258	6.9
30 M	0518	4.0	1131	6.8	1759	4.0		

OCTOBER

Date	Time	m	Time	m	Time	m	Time	m
1 TU	0023	6.6	0658	4.2	1310	6.7	2003	3.9
2 W	0220	6.8	0848	3.8	1452	7.2	2131	3.3
3 TH	0343	7.5	1000	3.1	1602	7.9	2233	2.4
4 F	0439	8.2	1057	2.2	1656	8.8	2325	1.6
5 SA	0528	9.0	1147	1.4	1745	9.5		
6 SU ●	0013	0.9	0613	9.6	1234	0.8	1830	10.0
7 M	0058	0.5	0656	10.0	1318	0.4	1913	10.3
8 TU	0140	0.3	0737	10.1	1400	0.3	1954	10.2
9 W	0221	0.4	0817	10.0	1440	0.6	2034	9.9
10 TH	0259	0.9	0856	9.5	1519	1.1	2113	9.2
11 F	0337	1.7	0934	8.9	1558	1.9	2153	8.4
12 SA	0416	2.6	1016	8.1	1642	2.8	2239	7.5
13 SU	0504	3.5	1108	7.3	1740	3.6	2345	6.8
14 M	0618	4.2	1233	6.7	1914	4.1		
15 TU	0148	6.5	0824	4.3	1426	6.8	2108	3.8
16 W	0314	6.8	0941	3.8	1533	7.2	2207	3.3
17 TH	0407	7.4	1030	3.2	1621	7.8	2250	2.7
18 F	0448	8.0	1110	2.6	1702	8.3	2328	2.2
19 SA	0524	8.4	1147	2.2	1738	8.7		
20 SU	0003	1.9	0557	8.8	1221	1.8	1813	9.0
21 M ○	0035	1.7	0630	9.0	1251	1.7	1845	9.1
22 TU	0104	1.6	0701	9.1	1319	1.6	1916	9.1
23 W	0132	1.6	0729	9.0	1347	1.7	1944	8.9
24 TH	0159	1.8	0756	8.8	1415	1.9	2011	8.7
25 F	0226	2.1	0821	8.6	1442	2.3	2039	8.4
26 SA	0253	2.5	0849	8.2	1510	2.7	2109	8.0
27 SU	0323	3.0	0922	7.9	1543	3.1	2147	7.5
28 M	0401	3.5	1006	7.4	1630	3.6	2243	7.0
29 TU	0459	3.9	1114	7.0	1745	3.9		
30 W	0006	6.8	0634	4.1	1245	7.0	1936	3.7
31 TH	0151	7.0	0821	3.7	1420	7.4	2103	3.1

NOVEMBER

Date	Time	m	Time	m	Time	m	Time	m
1 F	0313	7.6	0934	3.0	1532	8.1	2206	2.4
2 SA	0410	8.4	1031	2.2	1628	8.8	2258	1.6
3 SU	0500	9.0	1121	1.5	1718	9.4	2346	1.1
4 M ●	0546	9.6	1209	1.0	1805	9.8		
5 TU	0032	0.7	0630	9.9	1255	0.6	1849	10.0
6 W	0116	0.6	0712	10.0	1338	0.6	1932	9.9
7 TH	0158	0.8	0753	9.9	1420	0.8	2014	9.6
8 F	0237	1.3	0833	9.4	1501	1.4	2055	9.0
9 SA	0316	1.9	0913	8.8	1542	2.0	2136	8.3
10 SU	0357	2.7	0956	8.1	1627	2.8	2222	7.5
11 M	0444	3.5	1046	7.4	1722	3.5	2321	6.9
12 TU	0550	4.1	1156	6.9	1837	3.9		
13 W	0053	6.6	0726	4.3	1334	6.8	2013	3.9
14 TH	0228	6.8	0856	4.0	1449	7.1	2121	3.5
15 F	0325	7.2	0950	3.5	1541	7.5	2209	3.1
16 SA	0409	7.7	1033	3.0	1624	7.9	2249	2.6
17 SU	0447	8.1	1110	2.5	1702	8.3	2325	2.3
18 M	0522	8.5	1144	2.2	1739	8.6	2358	2.0
19 TU	0556	8.8	1217	2.0	1814	8.7		
20 W ○	0030	1.9	0629	8.9	1249	1.8	1847	8.8
21 TH	0102	1.8	0701	8.9	1321	1.8	1920	8.8
22 F	0134	1.9	0731	8.9	1354	2.0	1951	8.6
23 SA	0206	2.1	0802	8.7	1426	2.2	2024	8.4
24 SU	0238	2.4	0835	8.4	1501	2.5	2100	8.1
25 M	0314	2.8	0914	8.1	1541	2.8	2144	7.7
26 TU	0358	3.2	1003	7.8	1631	3.2	2240	7.4
27 W	0456	3.6	1106	7.5	1739	3.4	2350	7.2
28 TH	0614	3.7	1221	7.4	1903	3.3		
29 F	0113	7.3	0743	3.5	1343	7.6	2025	3.0
30 SA	0233	7.7	0859	3.0	1456	8.1	2132	2.4

DECEMBER

Date	Time	m	Time	m	Time	m	Time	m
1 SU	0336	8.2	1001	2.4	1557	8.5	2228	1.9
2 M	0430	8.8	1055	1.8	1651	9.0	2320	1.5
3 TU	0520	9.2	1146	1.4	1742	9.3		
4 W ●	0009	1.3	0607	9.5	1234	1.1	1829	9.4
5 TH	0056	1.2	0652	9.6	1321	1.0	1916	9.4
6 F	0140	1.3	0735	9.5	1405	1.2	2000	9.2
7 SA	0222	1.6	0818	9.3	1448	1.5	2042	8.8
8 SU	0303	2.1	0859	8.8	1530	2.0	2124	8.3
9 M	0343	2.6	0940	8.3	1613	2.5	2206	7.7
10 TU	0426	3.2	1025	7.8	1700	3.1	2254	7.2
11 W	0516	3.7	1117	7.3	1754	3.5	2352	6.9
12 TH	0618	4.0	1221	7.0	1857	3.7		
13 F	0103	6.7	0731	4.0	1334	6.9	2004	3.7
14 SA	0216	6.9	0842	3.8	1440	7.0	2106	3.5
15 SU	0314	7.2	0938	3.5	1534	7.3	2157	3.1
16 M	0401	7.6	1024	3.1	1620	7.7	2240	2.8
17 TU	0443	8.0	1105	2.7	1703	8.0	2321	2.5
18 W	0523	8.3	1144	2.3	1744	8.3		
19 TH ○	0000	2.2	0601	8.6	1223	2.1	1823	8.5
20 F	0038	2.0	0638	8.7	1302	1.9	1902	8.6
21 SA	0116	2.0	0715	8.8	1341	1.9	1940	8.6
22 SU	0154	2.0	0752	8.8	1420	1.9	2018	8.5
23 M	0233	2.1	0831	8.7	1500	2.0	2059	8.4
24 TU	0314	2.3	0913	8.5	1543	2.2	2143	8.1
25 W	0358	2.6	1001	8.3	1630	2.5	2232	7.9
26 TH	0449	2.9	1054	8.0	1725	2.7	2329	7.7
27 F	0550	3.1	1155	7.8	1828	2.9		
28 SA	0035	7.5	0701	3.1	1305	7.7	1940	2.9
29 SU	0150	7.6	0819	3.0	1419	7.8	2054	2.7
30 M	0302	7.9	0930	2.7	1528	8.0	2201	2.5
31 TU	0405	8.2	1032	2.3	1630	8.3	2259	2.2

Chart Datum: 5·06 metres below Ordnance Datum (Local)

WGS84 DATUM

SARK 9.14.13

Sark **49°25'·81N 02°20'·45W** Creux ❀❀◊✿✿✿; Maseline ❀❀◊✿

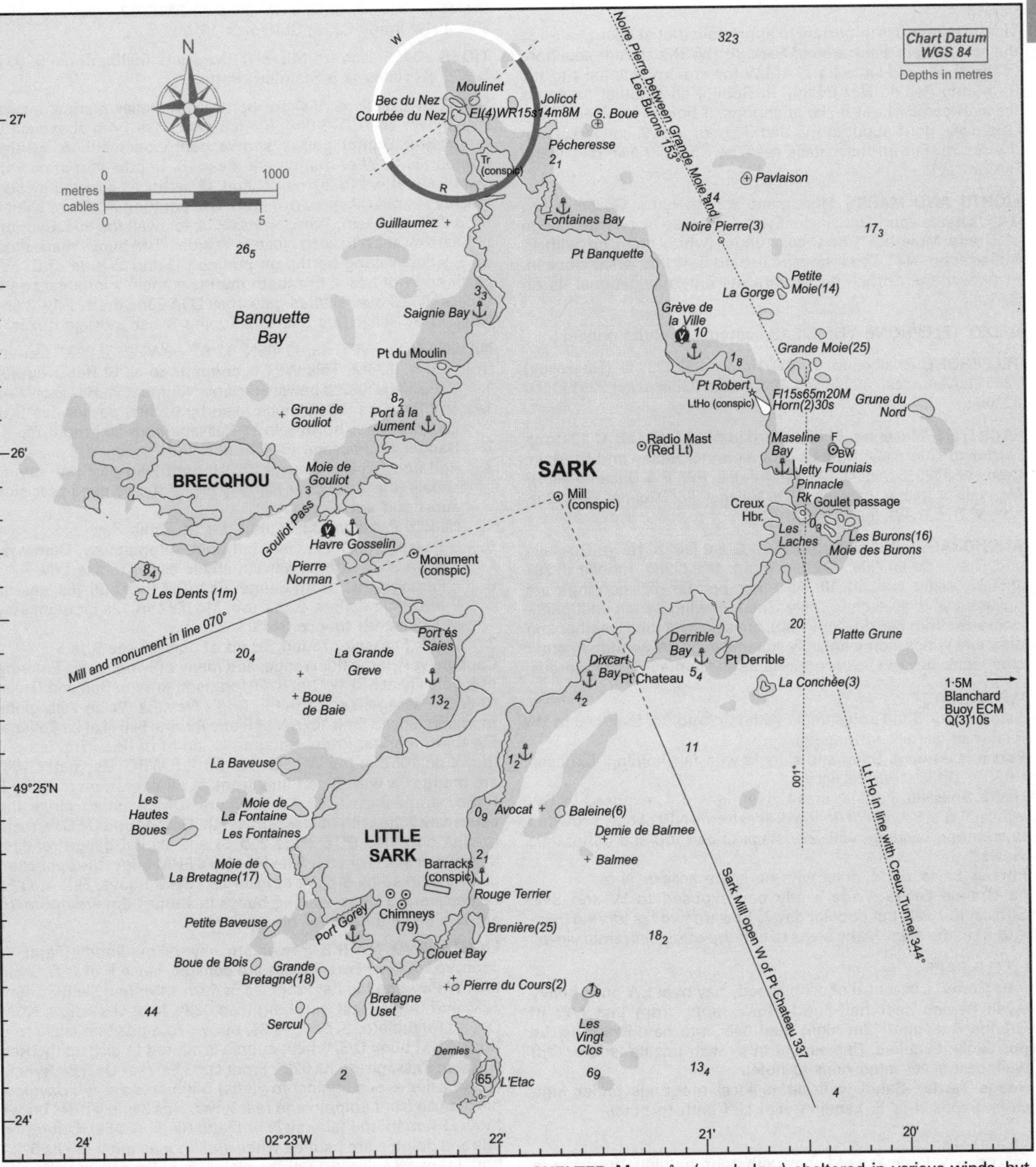

CHARTS AC *5604, 808*; SHOM 6904; ECM 1014; Imray C33A; Stanfords 16, 26

TIDES –0450 Dover; ML 5·3; Duration 0550; Zone 0 (UT)

Standard Port ST HELIER (⟶)

Times				Height (metres)			
High Water		Low Water		MHWS	MHWN	MLWN	MLWS
0300	0900	0200	0900	11·0	8·1	4·0	1·4
1500	2100	1400	2100				
Differences SARK (MASELINE PIER)							
+0005	+0015	+0005	+0010	–2·1	–1·5	–0·6	–0·3

SHELTER Many ⚓s (see below) sheltered in various winds, but may be disturbed, except in settled weather. There are 2 hbrs, both on the E side and prone to surge/swell: **Creux** dries completely, access approx HW±2 in fair weather. Dry out bow to E wall, stern to ⚓, keeping clear of the S pier where there may be some AB at the inner end clear of steps. **Maseline** is a busy ferry hbr with no yacht berths (other than to land people); call Hr Mr Ch 13 for approval to ⚓. Moorings are private. Brecqhou Island is strictly private; landing prohibited.

NAVIGATION Creux WPT 49°25´·24N 02°20´·18W, 164°/344° from/ to ent, 0·57M. Beware large tidal range, strong streams and many lobster pots. The S-bound-only restriction in the Goulet Passage

SARK *continued*

applies to commercial vessels, not yachts. Sark is fringed by rks, but the centres of the bays are mainly clear of dangers. In the extreme SW of Little Sark near Port Gorey the detail in AC 808 is somewhat inaccurate. The tide runs hard here over the HW period.

Tidal streams: It is important to appreciate that at about half-tide the streams are slack around Sark. At HW the stream sets hard to the N, ie onto Little Sark. At LW the stream sets hard to the S, ie onto Bec du Nez (N tip). In Gouliot and Goulet passages these streams run at 6-7kn at springs. If bound for Creux from Guernsey, go N-about at HW and S-about at LW; conversely on the return. For further details see *The Channel Islands* (Heath/RCC/Imray).

LIGHTS AND MARKS Monument above Havre Gosselin brg 070° is a safe appr. Transits for Creux: Pinnacle Rk on with E edge of Grand Moie 001°; or Creux tunnel (white arch) on with Pt Robert lt ho 344°. The lt ho dips behind the cliffs when close in. Pt Robert and Corbée du Nez are the only navigational lts on Sark.

RADIO TELEPHONE VHF Ch 13, summer months only.

TELEPHONE (Dial code 01481) Hr Mr 832323; ⊖ (Guernsey) 726911; Marinecall 09068 500 432; Police (Guernsey) 725111; Dr 832045.

FACILITIES Maseline ☎ 832070 (kiosk), M (free), C (3 ton); Ferries to Guernsey; Condor catamaran to Jersey and St Malo. **Creux** ☎ 832025 (kiosk), Slip, M (free), L, FW, P & D (cans) via Hr Mr; walk or tractor up steep hill to **Village:** P & D (cans), Gas, Gaz, Kos, V, R, Bar, ✉, Ⓑ.

ANCHORAGES AROUND SARK 20 🅥 are laid of Havre Gosselin and Grève de la Ville, £12 per night. ☎ 832260, mobile 07781 106065, water taxi Ch 10. All other permanent moorings are private; use in emergency only. The following ⚓s (all unlit), anti-clockwise from Bec du Nez (N tip), are safe in settled weather and off-shore winds (some are only suitable over LW period). In other conditions they can be uncomfortable and sometimes dangerous:

WEST COAST

Saignie Bay. Sand and shingle with fair holding. Exposed to W. Picturesque rock formations.

Port à la Jument. Sand and shingle with fair holding. Exposed to NW. Difficult shore access.

Havre Gosselin. Popular small, deep (4-9m) ⚓, exposed to SW winds. Y 🅥's. Beware of drying rk at extreme NW of bay. Crowded in summer. Landing, with 299 steps to cliff top and panoramic views.

Port és Saies. Sandy inlet with no shore access. N of:

La Grande Grève. Wide sandy bay exposed to W and SW. Subject to swell, but popular day ⚓. Beware two rks (drying 0·3m and ⊛) in the appr. Many steps to cliff-top and panoramic views.

LITTLE SARK

Port Gorey. ⚓ in centre of deep, weedy bay over LW only; heavy swell begins near half-flood. Rocky appr from just NW of Grande Bretagne (18m high) then 045° into bay. Rks must be positively identified. Remains of quay with unsafe ladder. Cliff walk past silver mine ruins to hotel.

Rouge Terrier. Sandy with some local moorings under high cliffs. Exposed to E. Landing with cliff path to hotel.

EAST COAST

Dixcart Bay. Popular sandy bay with good holding, but open to the S. Drying rocks extend on each side of the the approach but no dangers within the bay. Cliff path and pleasant walk to hotels.

Derrible Bay. Sandy bay with good holding. Exposed to the S. No dangers in the bay, but keep clear of SW tip of Derrible Pt when entering. Picturesque caves and steep climb ashore.

Grève de la Ville. Sand and shingle with fair holding Y🅥's. ⚓ close in out of tide. Exposed to E. Landing and easy walk to village.

Les Fontaines. Sand and shingle with fair holding. Reef drying 4·5m extends 1ca N from shore. ⚓ between reef and Eperquerie headland. Exposed to the E.

With grateful acknowledgements to John Frankland, author of Sark, a Yachtsman's Guide (revised 1998).

ST HELIER *9.14.14*

Jersey (Channel Is) **49°10'·57N 02°06'·98W** ❁❁❁◊◊◊✿✿

CHARTS AC *5604*, 3278, *1137*, *3655*; SHOM 6938, 7160, 7161; ECM 534, 1014; Imray C33B; Stanfords 16, 26

TIDES –0455 Dover; ML 6·1; Duration 0545; Zone 0 (UT) NOTE: St Helier is a Standard Port.

SHELTER Excellent. Visitors berth in **St Helier marina**, access HW±3 over sill (CD+3·6m); hinged gate rises 1·4m above sill to retain 5m. Digital gauge shows depth over sill. A waiting pontoon is to W of marina ent, near LB. Depths in marina vary from 2·8m at ent to 2·1m at N end. 🅥 berths as directed by staff (yachts >12m LOA or >2·1m draft, use pontoon A). Good shelter in **La Collette basin**, 1·8m; access H24, to await the tide. Caution: Ent narrow at LWS; keep close to W side; PHM buoys mark shoal on E side. Waiting berths on pontoon D and W side of C. FVs berth on W of basin. **Elizabeth marina** is mainly for local boats; access HW±3 over sill/flap gate; max LOA 20m, drafts 2·1 – 3·5m. No ⚓ in St Helier Rds due to shipping & fish storage boxes.

NAVIGATION WPT 49°09'·95N 02°07'·38W, 203°/023° from/to front ldg lt, 0·74M. This WPT is common to all St Helier appr's:

1. W Passage (082°); beware race off Noirmont Pt, HW to HW +4.
1A. NW Passage (095°, much used by yachts) passes 6ca S of La Corbière lt ho to join W Passage abm Noirmont Pt.
2. Danger Rk Passage (044°) unlit; and
3. Red and Green Passage (023°); both lead past rky, drying shoals (the latter over Fairway Rk 1·2m) and need precision and good vis.
4. Middle Passage (339°) unlit, for St Aubin Bay.
5. S Passage (341°) is clear but unlit. Alternatively, Demie de Pas on 350° with power stn chy is easier to see D/N.
6. E Passage, 290° from Canger Rk WCM By, Q (9) 15s, passes S of Demie de Pas, B tr/Y top, Mo (D) WR 12s (at night stay in W sector); thence 314°.
7. Violet Passage around SE tip of Jersey, see 9.14.5.

Caution: very large tidal range, and many offlying reefs. Entering hbr, note Oyster Rk (W bn; R 'O' topmark) to W of Red and Green (R & G) Passage; and to the E, Dog's Nest Rk (W bn with globe topmark). Speed limit 10kn N of Platte Rk, and 5kn N of La Collette.

Elizabeth marina: Preferred appr, when ht of tide >7m, is from the W on 106°, in the W sector of Dir lt F WRG. Daymarks 106° are orange □s with B vert line: front, at dir lt; rear, on mast by E RoRo ramp. Pass S of La Vrachère IDM lt bn to cross the causeway 5·0m with at least 2m depth. Oc R 4s and Oc G 4s mark marina ent; also IPTS (sigs 2 & 3) and digital gauge reading depth over sill. From the S (ie N of No 4 PHM buoy) the appr chan 338° is marked by 3 pairs of PHM and SHM buoys, Fl R or G 5s respectively. 3 Y can waiting buoys in about 1·0m are outboard either side of the lateral buoys.

LIGHTS AND MARKS Power stn chy (95m, floodlit) and W concave roofs of Fort Regent are conspic, close E of R & G ldg line. **W Passage** ldg lts: Front Oc 5s 23m 14M; rear Oc R 5s 46m 12M and Dog's Nest bn (unlit) lead 082°, N of Les Fours, NCM Q, and Ruaudière, SHM Fl G 3s, buoys, to a position close to E Rock, SHM buoy QG, where course is altered to pick up the **Red & Green Passage** ldg lts 023°: Front Oc G 5s; rear Oc R 5s, synch; (now easier to see against town lts) Daymarks are red dayglow patches on front dolphin and rear lt twr. Nos 2 and 4 PHM buoys (both QR) mark the fairway N of Platte Rk (Fl R 1·5s). Outer pier hds and dolphin are painted white and floodlit. Inner ldg lts 078°, both FG on W columns; not for yachts. For Elizabeth marina, see under SHELTER.

Entry signals St Helier Port Control shows International Port Traffic Signals (IPTS) in slow occulting format. Lights for small craft will show from the base of the tower and a single long range repeater light will be fitted on top of the tower, these lights will only show during shipping movements. Occ.Y lights = Power-driven craft less than 25m LOA may ent/dep against the main display signals (keep to stbd and well clear of shipping); used whenever possible to expedite ent/dep of small power driven vessels. IPTS will also show at the entrances to St Helier and Elizabeth Marinas with large digital tide gauges showing depth over the sills.

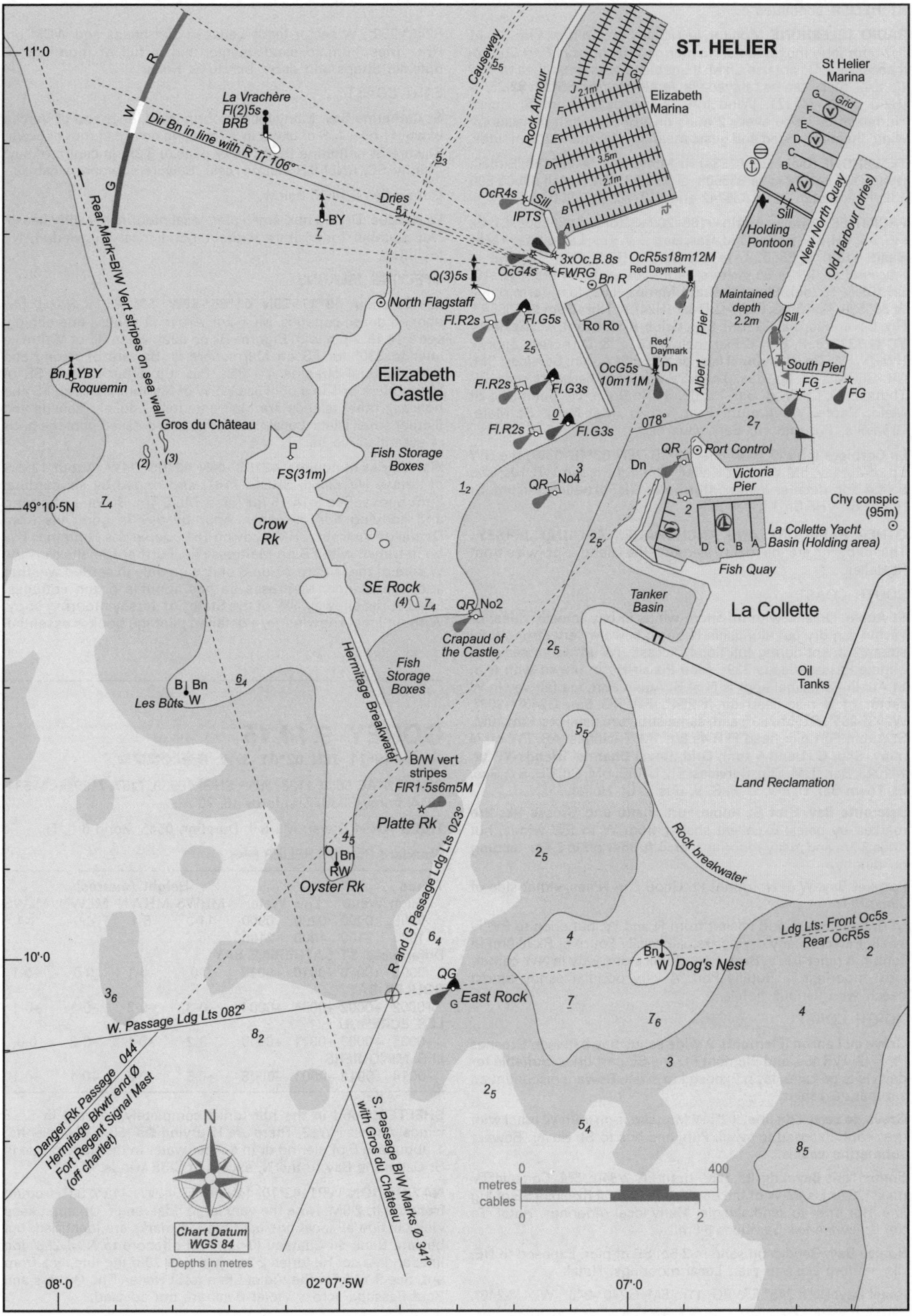
ST. HELIER
Elizabeth Marina
St Helier Marina
Causeway
Rock Armour
La Vrachère
Fl(2)5s
BRB
Dir Bn in line with R Tr 106°
Dries
BY
OcR4s
Sill
IPTS
3xOc.B.8s
FWRG
OcG4s
Bn R
OcR5s18m12M
Red Daymark
Holding Pontoon
New North Quay
Old Harbour (dries)
Maintained depth 2.2m
Q(3)5s
North Flagstaff
Fl.R2s
Fl.G5s
Ro Ro
Albert Pier
South Pier
FG
Rear Mark=B/W Vert stripes on sea wall
Bn YBY
Roquemin
Elizabeth Castle
Fl.G3s
OcG5s 10m11M
Dn
Gros du Château
078°
Fish Storage Boxes
QR
Port Control
Victoria Pier
FS(31m)
No4
Chy conspic (95m)
49°10·5N
Crow Rk
La Collette Yacht Basin (Holding area)
Fish Quay
SE Rock
QR No2
Tanker Basin
La Collette
Crapaud of the Castle
Hermitage Breakwater
Oil Tanks
Les Buts
Land Reclamation
B/W vert stripes
FlR1·5s6m5M
Platte Rk
Rock breakwater
Oyster Rk
R and G Passage Ldg Lts 023°
Ldg Lts: Front Oc5s Rear OcR5s
10'·0
QG
Dog's Nest
East Rock
W. Passage Ldg Lts 082°
Danger Rk Passage 044°
Hermitage Bkwt end Ø
Fort Regent Signal Mast
(off chartlet)
S. Passage B/W Marks Ø 341°
with Gros du Château
metres
cables
Chart Datum WGS 84
Depths in metres
08'·0
02°07'·5W
07'·0
11'·0

ST HELIER *continued*

RADIO TELEPHONE Monitor *St Helier Port Control* VHF Ch 14 (H24) for ferry movements. No marina VHF, but call *Port Control* if necessary. Do not use Ch M. If unable to pass messages to *Port Control*, these can be relayed via *Jersey Radio* CRS, Ch **82** 25 16 (H24) or ☎ 741121. Wind info is broadcast from St Helier Pierheads by voice every 2 mins on VHF Ch 18. It consists of: wind direction, speed and gusts meaned over the last 2 minutes.

TELEPHONE (Dial code 01534) Hr Mr 885588, 📠 885599, E-mail: jsyhbr@itl.net, Marina 885508; ⊖ 833833; Marinecall 09068 500 432; Police 612612; Dr 835742 and 853178; Ⓗ 759000.

FACILITIES **St Helier Marina** (180+200 visitors), ☎ 885508, £1.40, FW, AC, CH, ME, El, Sh, Grid, Gas, Gaz, ⊡, V, Kos; **La Collette Yacht Basin** (130) ☎ 885529, is accessible H24 when marina is inaccessible; it has 50 visitors berths for up to 24 hrs, FW, AC, BH (65 & 16 ton), Slip. **Elizabeth Marina** (589; long term only), ☎ 885530, 📠 885593; FW, AC, D & P (H24), ♂. **Hbrs Dept** ☎ 885588, FW, C (various, max 32 ton), Slip, Grids, BH (65 ton), AC; **St Helier YC** ☎ 732229, R, Bar; **S Pier** (below YC) P & D (Access approx HW±3), FW. **Royal Channel Islands YC**, at St Aubin: **Services**: SM, CH, Sh, ME, El, Ⓔ, Gas. **Town** www.jerseyharbours.com. EC Thurs; P, D, CH, V, R, Bar, ✉, Ⓑ, ✈. Ro Ro Ferry: Guernsey, St Malo, Poole, Weymouth. Fast ferries (Mar-Nov): St Malo, Granville, Portsmouth, Sark, Guernsey.

La Corbiere lt ho (9.14.4) is at 49°10'·79N 02°15'·03W, the SW tip of Jersey, 5M W of St Helier. The light is Iso WR 10s; see 9.14.4 for details. Wind information is broadcast from St Helier on VHF Ch 18; see R/T.

OTHER HARBOURS AND ANCHORAGES AROUND JERSEY
The following are the main ⚓s around the island, clockwise from St Helier:

SOUTH COAST

St Aubin. Quiet ⚓ with off-shore winds in bay (mostly dries) or yachts can dry out alongside N quay; beware very strong tidal streams in ent during full flood. Access HW ±1. From seaward Middle Passage leads 339°, Mon Plaisir Ho in transit with tr at St Aubin Fort. Final appr is N of St Aubin Fort, via fairway in W sector of N pier head dir lt 254°, F WRG 5m, G248° -253°, W253°-255°, R255°-260°; and, same structure, Iso R 4s 12m 10M. St Aubin Fort pier head Fl R 4s 8m 1M. Facilities: AB, FW on N quay, **Slip, C (1 and 5 ton), Grid; Royal Channel Islands YC** ☎ 741023, Bar, R, M, Slip; **Services**: Sh, D, ME, SM, Sh, CH, BY, Gas, El. **Town** Bar, D, FW, ⊡, P, R, V, bus to St. Helier.

Belcroute Bay. S of St Aubin Fort. Platte and Grosse Rks are marked by poles. Excellent shelter from W to SW winds, but dries 3·5m and many moorings; or ⚓ further off in 2·4m, landing by dinghy.

Portelet Bay. W of Noirmont Pt. Good ⚓ in N'lies, either side of Janvrin Tr.

St Brelade Bay. Good shelter from N and W, but open to SW'ly swell. Beware many drying rks, especially Fournier Rk (0·9m) in centre. A quiet ⚓ is in Beau Port. Small stone jetty in NW corner; local moorings in Bouilly Port. A very popular sandy tourist beach with various hotels.

NORTH COAST

Grève au Lancon (Plemont). A wide sandy bay between Grosnez Pt, Fl (2) WR 15s, and Plemont Pt. The SE part dries. Suitable for day visits on calm days. Exposed to swell. Beware discontinued submarine cables.

Grève de Lecq. Ldg line 202°: W Martello tr on with W hotel with grey roof. Exposed to swell. Pub, and bus to St. Helier. Beware submarine cables.

Bonne Nuit Bay. Ldg lts 223°, both FG 7/34m 6M. Conspic TV mast (232m) is ½M W of the bay. Avoid Cheval Rk close SE of ldg line. Hbr dries to sand/shingle. Many local moorings. Hotel. To the E beware Les Sambues 5·5m.

Bouley Bay. Good ⚓ on sand in 2·5m SE of pier. Exposed to NE. Rky bottom close to pier. Local moorings. Hotel.

Rozel Bay. Dir lt 245° F WRG, 11m 5M, G240°-244°, W244°-246°, R246°-250°; W sector leads between pier heads and WCM bn. Hbr, dries 1·5m to sand/shingle, and is full of moorings; ⚓ outside. Shops and pubs, bus to St Helier.

EAST COAST

St Catherine Bay. Many local moorings off inner end of Verclut bkwtr, Fl 1·5s. ⚓ S of bkwtr in 3-7m. Land on slip at root of bkwtr. Beware St Catherine Bank, rocky plateau 3·3m in centre of bay. Dinghy SC, RNLI ILB station, café. Beware submarine cables.

Gorey. See 9.14.15 below.

La Rocque. Drying hbr, small pier, local moorings, sandy beach. Not suitable for visitors without good local knowledge. No facilities.

OFFLYING ISLANDS

Les Ecrehou. 49°17'·39N 01°55'·58W. 5M NE of Rozel, has about a dozen cottages. ML 6·2m. Arrive at about ½ tide ebbing; see 9.14.15. Appr with Bigorne Rk on 022°; when SE of Maître Ile alter to 330° for FS on Marmotière Is. Beware of strong and eddying tidal streams 4 - 8kn. Pick up a buoy close SE of Marmotière or ⚓ in a pool 3ca WSW of Marmotière (with FS and houses); other islands are Maître Ile (one house), Blanche and 5 other small islets. Local knowledge or a detailed pilotage book is essential. No lts.

Plateau des Minquiers. 48°58'·04N 02°03'·74W. About 12M S of Jersey (AC 3656, SHOM 7161) and ringed by six cardinal light buoys. See 9.14.15 for tides. ML 6·4m. Beware of strong and eddying tidal streams. Appr by day in good vis from Demie de Vascelin SHM buoy on 161°, Jetée des Fontaines RW bn in transit with FS on Maîtresse Ile. Further transits skirt the W side of the islet to ⚓ due S of it; safe only in settled weather and light winds. Maîtresse Ile has about a dozen cottages. Land at the slipway NW of the States of Jersey mooring buoy. Without local knowledge, a detailed pilotage book is essential.

GOREY *9.14.15*

Jersey **49°11'·78N 02°01'·37W** ✵✵◊◊✿✿✿

CHARTS AC *5604*, 1138, *3655*; SHOM 6939, 7157, 7160; ECM 534, 1014; Imray C33B; Stanfords 16, 26

TIDES –0454 Dover; ML 6·0; Duration 0545; Zone 0 (UT)

Standard Port ST HELIER (⟶)

Times				Height (metres)			
High Water		Low Water		MHWS	MHWN	MLWN	MLWS
0300	0900	0200	0900	11·0	8·1	4·0	1·4
1500	2100	1400	2100				
Differences ST CATHERINE BAY							
0000	+0010	+0010	+0010	0·0	–0·1	0·0	+0·1
BOULEY BAY							
+0002	+0002	+0004	+0004	–0·3	–0·3	–0·1	–0·1
LES ECREHOU							
+0005	+0009	+0011	+0009	–0·2	+0·1	–0·2	0·0
LES MINQUIERS							
–0014	–0018	–0001	–0008	+0·5	+0·6	+0·1	+0·1

SHELTER Good in the hbr (dries completely), except in S/SE winds. Access HW±3. There are 12 drying ✿s 150m W of pier hd. ⚓ about 2ca E of pier hd or in deeper water in the Roads; also in St Catherine Bay to the N, except in S/SE winds.

NAVIGATION WPT 49°10'·44N 01°57'·42W, 118°/298° from/to front ldg lt, 2·9M. Note the very large tidal range. On appr, keep well outside all local bns until the ldg marks are identified, but beware Banc du Chateau (0·4m), 1M offshore to N of 298° ldg line; and Azicot Rk (dries 2·2m) just S of 298° ldg line, 2ca from ent. See 9.14.5 for the Violet Chan to St Helier. The Gutters and Boat Passage across Violet Bank are not advised.

LIGHTS AND MARKS Mont Orgueil Castle (67m) is conspic from afar. There are at least 3 approaches:

1. Ldg lts 298°: front, Gorey pierhd, Oc RG 5s, W tr, vis R304°-352°, G352°-304°; rear, Oc R 5s 8M, W □ Or border.
2. Front ldg lt on with church spire 304° leads over Road Rk (3·3m), and Azicot Rk (2·2m).
3. Front ldg lt on with white house/R roof 250° leads close to Les Arch bn (B/W with A topmark) and Pacquet Rk (0·3m).

RADIO TELEPHONE *Gorey Hbr* Ch 74 (HW±3 Apr-Oct only).

TELEPHONE (Dial code 01534) Hr Mr 853616, mobile 0979 719336, 🖷 885599; ⊜ 833833; Marinecall 09068 500 432; for Dr contact Hr Mr, or Hr Mr St Helier 885588.

FACILITIES **Hbr** M, AB £6, P, D, FW, C (7 ton), ME, El, Sh, Gas. **Town** EC Thurs; P, CH, V, R, Bar, ✉, Ⓑ, bus to St Helier. Ferry (Mar-Nov) to Portbail, Carteret.

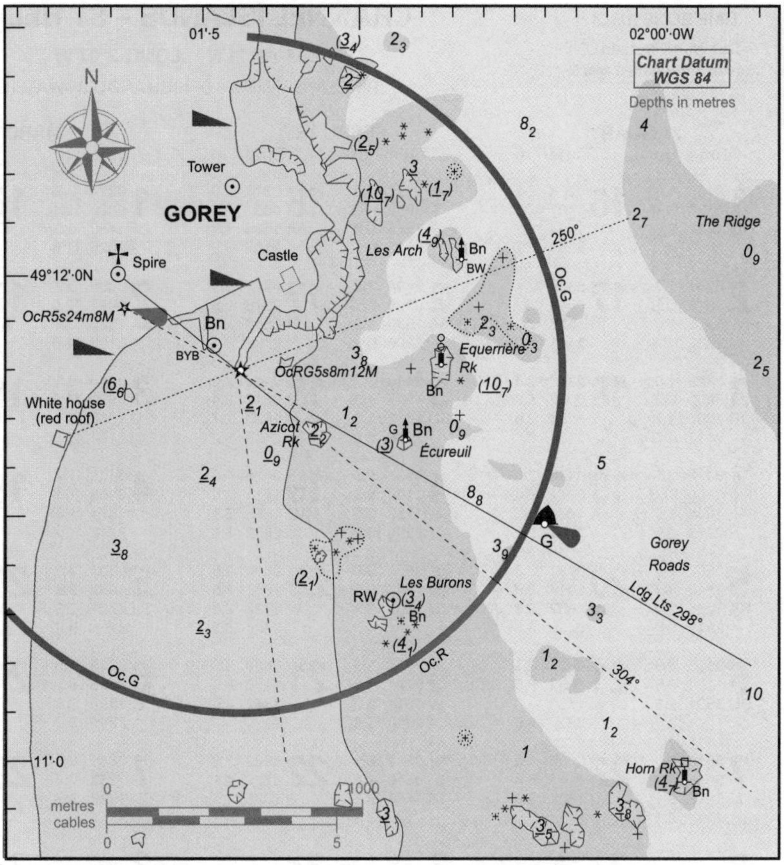

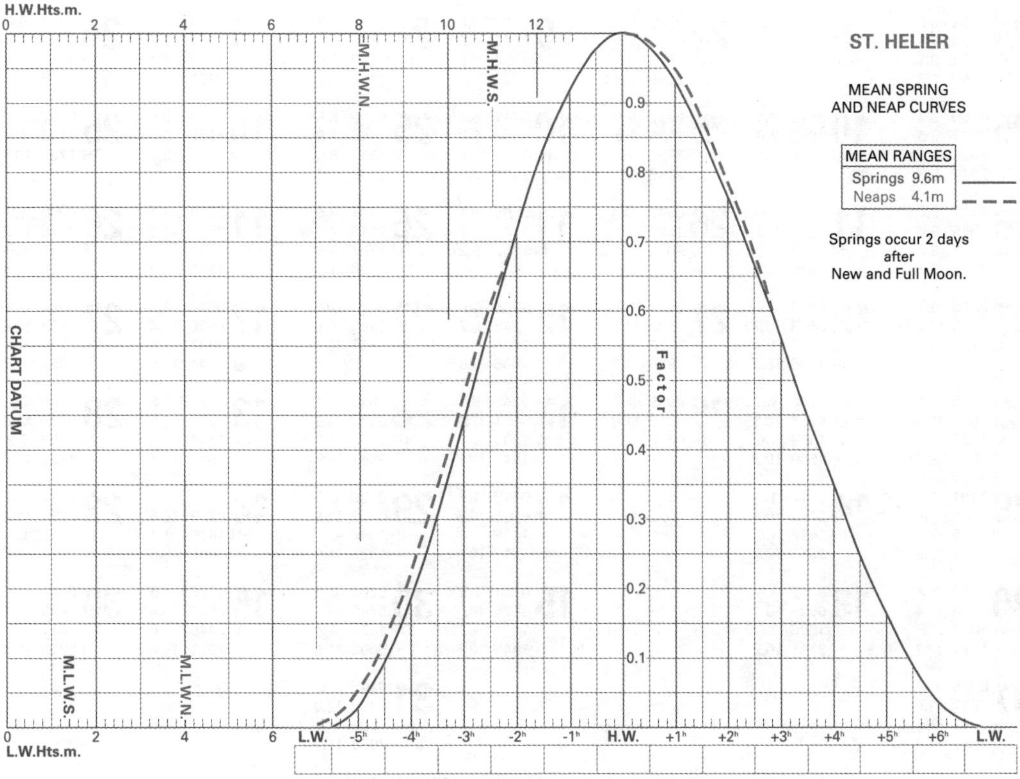

TIME ZONE (UTC)
For Summer Time add ONE hour in **non-shaded areas**

CHANNEL ISLANDS – ST HELIER

LAT 49°11′N LONG 2°07′W

TIMES AND HEIGHTS OF HIGH AND LOW WATERS

SPRING & NEAP TIDES
Dates in red are **SPRINGS**
Dates in blue are **NEAPS**

YEAR **2002**

JANUARY

Date	Day	Time	m	Time	m	Time	m	Time	m
1	TU	0155	1.6	0732	11.0	1422	1.5	2001	10.7
2	W	0241	1.7	0816	11.0	1509	1.6	2046	10.6
3	TH	0326	1.8	0902	10.8	1556	1.7	2133	10.3
4	F	0413	2.1	0950	10.5	1644	2.0	2223	9.9
5	SA	0502	2.5	1042	10.0	1735	2.4	2316	9.4
6	SU	0557	2.9	1139	9.5	1831	2.8		
7	M	0016	9.0	0658	3.2	1246	9.1	1933	3.1
8	TU	0128	8.7	0804	3.4	1400	8.9	2043	3.3
9	W	0245	8.8	0913	3.3	1512	8.9	2154	3.2
10	TH	0351	9.1	1021	3.1	1616	9.2	2256	2.9
11	F	0447	9.5	1121	2.8	1711	9.5	2349	2.6
12	SA	0535	9.9	1214	2.4	1759	9.8		
13	SU	0036	2.4	0617	10.2	1301	2.1	● 1841	10.1
14	M	0118	2.2	0657	10.5	1342	2.0	1921	10.2
15	TU	0155	2.1	0733	10.5	1420	2.0	1957	10.2
16	W	0228	2.2	0807	10.4	1454	2.1	2030	10.0
17	TH	0300	2.4	0840	10.2	1525	2.3	2101	9.7
18	F	0330	2.6	0912	9.8	1554	2.6	2131	9.4
19	SA	0400	2.9	0942	9.4	1624	2.9	2202	9.0
20	SU	0431	3.3	1014	9.0	1657	3.3	2236	8.6
21	M	0507	3.7	1052	8.5	1738	3.6	2320	8.3
22	TU	0556	4.0	1143	8.2	1835	3.9		
23	W	0020	8.0	0707	4.2	1256	7.9	1949	4.0
24	TH	0138	8.0	0830	4.1	1421	8.1	2108	3.8
25	F	0259	8.3	0942	3.6	1536	8.5	2217	3.3
26	SA	0407	9.0	1045	3.0	1638	9.2	2316	2.7
27	SU	0503	9.7	1143	2.4	1733	9.8		
28	M	0010	2.1	0553	10.4	1238	1.7	○ 1824	10.4
29	TU	0101	1.5	0641	11.0	1330	1.2	1911	10.9
30	W	0150	1.2	0728	11.4	1419	0.9	1957	11.2
31	TH	0236	0.9	0812	11.6	1505	0.7	2040	11.3

FEBRUARY

Date	Day	Time	m	Time	m	Time	m	Time	m
1	F	0321	0.9	0856	11.5	1548	0.8	2123	11.1
2	SA	0404	1.2	0939	11.2	1630	1.2	2205	10.6
3	SU	0446	1.7	1022	10.6	1712	1.8	2248	9.9
4	M	0531	2.3	1108	9.8	1758	2.6	2335	9.2
5	TU	0622	3.0	1202	9.0	1852	3.3		
6	W	0035	8.5	0724	3.6	1314	8.3	2000	3.8
7	TH	0204	8.1	0840	3.9	1444	8.1	2125	3.9
8	F	0330	8.3	1003	3.7	1605	8.4	2240	3.6
9	SA	0434	8.8	1111	3.2	1704	8.9	2337	3.1
10	SU	0524	9.4	1203	2.6	1750	9.4		
11	M	0023	2.6	0605	9.9	1247	2.2	1829	9.9
12	TU	0104	2.2	0643	10.3	1327	1.8	● 1906	10.2
13	W	0140	1.9	0718	10.5	1403	1.6	1940	10.3
14	TH	0214	1.8	0752	10.6	1436	1.6	2011	10.3
15	F	0245	1.8	0823	10.4	1506	1.7	2041	10.2
16	SA	0313	2.0	0852	10.2	1534	1.9	2107	9.9
17	SU	0340	2.3	0918	9.8	1558	2.3	2132	9.5
18	M	0403	2.6	0942	9.4	1623	2.7	2158	9.2
19	TU	0429	3.0	1011	9.0	1653	3.1	2232	8.8
20	W	0504	3.5	1051	8.5	1735	3.6	2320	8.3
21	TH	0558	3.9	1150	8.0	1842	4.0		
22	F	0032	7.9	0730	4.1	1328	7.7	2020	4.1
23	SA	0215	7.9	0909	3.8	1509	8.1	2151	3.6
24	SU	0346	8.6	1027	3.1	1625	8.8	2258	2.8
25	M	0450	9.5	1131	2.2	1724	9.7	2356	1.9
26	TU	0543	10.4	1227	1.4	1814	10.6		
27	W	0049	1.2	0632	11.2	1319	0.7	○ 1900	11.3
28	TH	0139	0.6	0717	11.8	1406	0.2	1944	11.7

MARCH

Date	Day	Time	m	Time	m	Time	m	Time	m
1	F	0224	0.2	0800	12.1	1450	0.0	2025	11.8
2	SA	0306	0.2	0841	12.0	1530	0.2	2103	11.6
3	SU	0346	0.5	0920	11.5	1608	0.7	2141	11.0
4	M	0423	1.2	0958	10.8	1644	1.6	2218	10.2
5	TU	0501	2.0	1038	9.8	1722	2.5	2258	9.3
6	W	0545	3.0	1125	8.8	1808	3.5	2349	8.3
7	TH	0645	3.8	1232	7.9	1917	4.3		
8	F	0113	7.7	0808	4.2	1419	7.5	2057	4.4
9	SA	0308	7.8	0948	4.0	1554	7.9	2225	3.9
10	SU	0417	8.4	1056	3.3	1650	8.6	2321	3.3
11	M	0506	9.1	1144	2.7	1732	9.2		
12	TU	0004	2.6	0545	9.7	1225	2.1	1808	9.8
13	W	0042	2.1	0621	10.2	1303	1.7	1842	10.2
14	TH	0118	1.7	0656	10.5	1338	1.4	● 1915	10.5
15	F	0151	1.5	0729	10.7	1411	1.3	1946	10.6
16	SA	0223	1.4	0800	10.6	1441	1.4	2015	10.4
17	SU	0251	1.6	0828	10.3	1508	1.6	2040	10.2
18	M	0316	1.9	0852	10.0	1532	1.9	2103	9.9
19	TU	0338	2.2	0914	9.7	1554	2.4	2127	9.6
20	W	0401	2.6	0942	9.3	1621	2.8	2159	9.1
21	TH	0433	3.1	1020	8.7	1659	3.4	2244	8.6
22	F	0522	3.6	1117	8.1	1800	3.9	2353	8.0
23	SA	0645	4.0	1257	7.6	1940	4.1		
24	SU	0144	7.8	0841	3.8	1449	8.0	2126	3.6
25	M	0325	8.5	1008	3.0	1609	8.8	2239	2.7
26	TU	0431	9.5	1113	2.0	1707	9.8	2338	1.7
27	W	0526	10.5	1209	1.1	1756	10.7		
28	TH	0030	0.9	0613	11.3	1259	0.4	○ 1841	11.5
29	F	0120	0.3	0658	11.9	1346	-0.1	1923	11.9
30	SA	0204	-0.1	0740	12.1	1428	-0.2	2002	12.0
31	SU	0245	0.0	0820	12.0	1506	0.1	2039	11.7

APRIL

Date	Day	Time	m	Time	m	Time	m	Time	m
1	M	0323	0.4	0857	11.5	1542	0.8	2114	11.1
2	TU	0359	1.1	0933	10.7	1615	1.7	2149	10.2
3	W	0433	2.0	1011	9.6	1648	2.7	2227	9.2
4	TH	0512	3.0	1056	8.6	1728	3.7	2315	8.3
5	F	0608	3.9	1201	7.7	1833	4.4		
6	SA	0033	7.6	0736	4.3	1347	7.3	2020	4.6
7	SU	0232	7.6	0917	4.1	1525	7.7	2154	4.1
8	M	0345	8.2	1025	3.4	1619	8.4	2249	3.4
9	TU	0434	8.8	1111	2.7	1700	9.1	2331	2.7
10	W	0514	9.5	1152	2.2	1736	9.7		
11	TH	0010	2.1	0550	10.0	1231	1.7	1811	10.2
12	F	0047	1.7	0626	10.4	1307	1.4	● 1844	10.5
13	SA	0122	1.5	0701	10.5	1341	1.3	1916	10.6
14	SU	0155	1.4	0733	10.5	1412	1.4	1945	10.5
15	M	0225	1.5	0801	10.4	1440	1.6	2011	10.4
16	TU	0251	1.7	0826	10.1	1506	1.9	2036	10.1
17	W	0315	2.1	0851	9.8	1530	2.3	2104	9.8
18	TH	0341	2.4	0923	9.4	1600	2.7	2140	9.3
19	F	0418	2.9	1005	8.8	1643	3.2	2228	8.7
20	SA	0510	3.4	1108	8.2	1745	3.7	2341	8.2
21	SU	0630	3.7	1246	7.9	1919	3.9		
22	M	0125	8.1	0817	3.5	1426	8.2	2059	3.4
23	TU	0258	8.7	0942	2.7	1543	9.0	2212	2.6
24	W	0404	9.6	1047	1.9	1641	9.9	2311	1.7
25	TH	0500	10.4	1143	1.1	1730	10.7		
26	F	0005	1.0	0548	11.2	1233	0.5	1815	11.4
27	SA	0054	0.5	0634	11.6	1320	0.2	○ 1857	11.7
28	SU	0140	0.2	0716	11.8	1403	0.2	1936	11.7
29	M	0222	0.3	0757	11.6	1441	0.6	2014	11.5
30	TU	0300	0.7	0835	11.1	1517	1.2	2050	10.9

Chart Datum: 5·88 metres below Ordnance Datum (Local)

TIME ZONE (UTC)
For Summer Time add ONE hour in **non-shaded areas**

CHANNEL ISLANDS – ST HELIER

LAT 49°11′N LONG 2°07′W

TIMES AND HEIGHTS OF HIGH AND LOW WATERS

SPRING & NEAP TIDES
Dates in red are SPRINGS
Dates in blue are NEAPS

YEAR **2002**

MAY

Date	Time	m	Date	Time	m
1 W	0336	1.4	16 TH	0258	2.0
	0912	10.3		0837	9.9
	1549	2.0		1515	2.3
	2125	10.1		2051	10.0
2 TH	0410	2.2	17 F	0332	2.3
	0950	9.4		0917	9.5
	1621	2.9		1552	2.7
	2203	9.2		2134	9.5
3 F	0448	3.1	18 SA	0414	2.7
	1035	8.5		1006	9.0
	1700	3.7		1639	3.1
	2250	8.4		2227	9.1
4 SA	0540	3.8	19 SU	0511	3.1
	1136	7.8		1112	8.5
	1759	4.3		1743	3.4
				2338	8.7
5 SU	0000	7.8	20 M	0627	3.3
	0657	4.2		1232	8.4
	1303	7.5		1905	3.5
	1928	4.6			
6 M	0139	7.6	21 TU	0104	8.6
	0824	4.1		0753	3.1
	1432	7.7		1355	8.6
	2057	4.2		2029	3.1
7 TU	0254	8.0	22 W	0224	9.0
	0935	3.6		0910	2.6
	1532	8.3		1508	9.1
	2159	3.6		2139	2.6
8 W	0348	8.6	23 TH	0331	9.6
	1026	3.0		1015	2.1
	1617	8.9		1609	9.8
	2246	3.0		2240	1.9
9 TH	0433	9.2	24 F	0430	10.2
	1110	2.5		1113	1.5
	1657	9.5		1701	10.4
	2328	2.5		2336	1.4
10 F	0514	9.6	25 SA	0522	10.7
	1151	2.1		1205	1.2
	1734	9.9		1748	10.9
11 SA	0008	2.1	26 SU	0027	1.1
	0552	10.0		0609	11.0
	1230	1.8		1254	1.0
	1809	10.3		○ 1832	11.2
12 SU	0046	1.8	27 M	0116	0.9
	0628	10.2		0654	11.1
	1306	1.6		1339	1.0
	● 1842	10.4		1913	11.2
13 M	0123	1.7	28 TU	0200	1.0
	0702	10.3		0737	11.0
	1341	1.6		1419	1.3
	1914	10.5		1952	11.0
14 TU	0156	1.7	29 W	0241	1.3
	0733	10.3		0817	10.6
	1413	1.7		1456	1.7
	1944	10.4		2030	10.6
15 W	0228	1.8	30 TH	0319	1.8
	0804	10.1		0856	10.0
	1444	2.0		1529	2.3
	2016	10.3		2106	10.0
			31 F	0355	2.4
				0935	9.4
				1603	3.0
				2145	9.3

JUNE

Date	Time	m	Date	Time	m
1 SA	0432	3.0	16 SU	0422	2.3
	1017	8.7		1010	9.5
	1640	3.5		1642	2.7
	2228	8.7		2227	9.6
2 SU	0516	3.5	17 M	0516	2.6
	1106	8.2		1107	9.2
	1729	4.0		1740	2.9
	2323	8.2		2328	9.3
3 M	0612	3.9	18 TU	0618	2.8
	1208	7.8		1211	8.9
	1833	4.3		1847	3.1
4 TU	0034	7.9	19 W	0037	9.1
	0719	4.0		0725	2.8
	1321	7.8		1321	8.9
	1947	4.2		1957	3.0
5 W	0150	7.9	20 TH	0150	9.1
	0826	3.8		0834	2.8
	1431	8.1		1432	9.1
	2053	3.9		2105	2.8
6 TH	0253	8.3	21 F	0258	9.3
	0926	3.4		0942	2.6
	1526	8.5		1538	9.4
	2150	3.4		2209	2.5
7 F	0345	8.7	22 SA	0401	9.6
	1019	3.0		1045	2.3
	1612	9.0		1635	9.9
	2240	3.0		2310	2.1
8 SA	0432	9.1	23 SU	0459	9.9
	1106	2.6		1141	2.0
	1654	9.5		1726	10.3
	2326	2.5			
9 SU	0515	9.6	24 M	0006	1.8
	1151	2.3		0551	10.2
	1733	9.9		1233	1.8
				○ 1812	10.5
10 M	0010	2.2	25 TU	0058	1.6
	0555	9.9		0638	10.4
	1233	2.0		1320	1.8
	● 1811	10.3		1856	10.7
11 TU	0052	2.0	26 W	0145	1.6
	0634	10.1		0723	10.4
	1313	1.9		1403	1.8
	1848	10.5		1937	10.7
12 W	0133	1.8	27 TH	0228	1.7
	0713	10.2		0804	10.3
	1353	1.9		1441	2.1
	1926	10.5		2015	10.4
13 TH	0212	1.8	28 F	0306	1.9
	0752	10.2		0843	10.0
	1431	2.0		1515	2.4
	2005	10.5		2052	10.1
14 F	0252	1.9	29 SA	0342	2.3
	0833	10.1		0919	9.6
	1510	2.1		1547	2.7
	2047	10.3		2128	9.6
15 SA	0335	2.1	30 SU	0415	2.7
	0919	9.8		0955	9.2
	1553	2.4		1620	3.1
	2134	10.0		2205	9.2

JULY

Date	Time	m	Date	Time	m
1 M	0448	3.1	16 TU	0508	2.0
	1033	8.7		1050	9.8
	1657	3.5		1727	2.4
	2246	8.7		2309	9.9
2 TU	0527	3.4	17 W	0558	2.4
	1116	8.3		1143	9.4
	1742	3.8		1821	2.8
	2334	8.3			
3 W	0615	3.7	18 TH	0006	9.4
	1207	8.1		0654	2.8
	1839	4.1		1244	9.0
				1923	3.1
4 TH	0035	8.0	19 F	0114	9.0
	0714	3.9		0759	3.2
	1310	8.0		1357	8.8
	1947	4.1		2033	3.3
5 F	0144	8.0	20 SA	0228	8.8
	0821	3.8		0913	3.3
	1418	8.1		1512	8.9
	2054	3.9		2147	3.2
6 SA	0250	8.2	21 SU	0341	8.9
	0926	3.6		1024	3.1
	1521	8.5		1618	9.2
	2155	3.5		2256	2.8
7 SU	0349	8.6	22 M	0447	9.2
	1025	3.2		1126	2.8
	1615	9.1		1713	9.6
	2251	3.0		2355	2.4
8 M	0441	9.1	23 TU	0541	9.6
	1118	2.7		1220	2.5
	1703	9.6		1801	10.1
	2342	2.5			
9 TU	0530	9.6	24 W	0046	2.1
	1207	2.3		0628	9.9
	1749	10.1		1308	2.2
				○ 1844	10.4
10 W	0030	2.1	25 TH	0132	1.8
	0616	10.0		0711	10.2
	1254	2.0		1349	2.0
	● 1832	10.5		1924	10.6
11 TH	0119	1.8	26 F	0214	1.7
	0701	10.3		0750	10.3
	1340	1.8		1426	2.0
	1916	10.8		2001	10.5
12 F	0206	1.6	27 SA	0250	1.8
	0746	10.5		0826	10.2
	1425	1.7		1459	2.1
	2000	10.9		2035	10.4
13 SA	0252	1.5	28 SU	0322	2.0
	0831	10.5		0858	10.0
	1509	1.7		1528	2.3
	2045	10.9		2107	10.1
14 SU	0337	1.5	29 M	0351	2.2
	0916	10.4		0929	9.6
	1553	1.8		1556	2.6
	2130	10.7		2139	9.6
15 M	0422	1.7	30 TU	0418	2.6
	1002	10.2		0959	9.3
	1638	2.0		1624	3.0
	2218	10.3		2209	9.2
			31 W	0446	3.0
				1029	8.8
				1656	3.4
				2242	8.7

AUGUST

Date	Time	m	Date	Time	m
1 TH	0520	3.4	16 F	0619	3.1
	1106	8.4		1205	8.8
	1736	3.8		1849	3.4
	2325	8.2			
2 F	0606	3.8	17 SA	0038	8.6
	1157	8.1		0723	3.7
	1834	4.1		1323	8.3
				2005	3.9
3 SA	0028	7.9	18 SU	0204	8.1
	0712	4.1		0850	4.0
	1309	7.9		1456	8.3
	1956	4.2		2136	3.8
4 SU	0154	7.8	19 M	0334	8.2
	0835	4.0		1016	3.8
	1433	8.1		1609	8.7
	2116	3.9		2252	3.3
5 M	0312	8.2	20 TU	0442	8.7
	0951	3.7		1119	3.2
	1545	8.6		1704	9.3
	2224	3.4		2347	2.7
6 TU	0417	8.7	21 W	0533	9.3
	1054	3.1		1209	2.7
	1643	9.3		1750	9.9
	2323	2.7			
7 W	0514	9.4	22 TH	0033	2.2
	1148	2.5		0615	9.8
	1734	10.0		1252	2.2
				○ 1829	10.4
8 TH	0017	2.1	23 F	0115	1.8
	0604	10.1		0653	10.2
	1240	1.9		1331	1.9
	● 1822	10.7		1906	10.7
9 F	0109	1.5	24 SA	0152	1.6
	0652	10.6		0728	10.4
	1329	1.4		1405	1.8
	1908	11.2		1940	10.8
10 SA	0158	1.1	25 SU	0226	1.5
	0738	11.0		0801	10.5
	1416	1.1		1435	1.8
	1953	11.5		2012	10.7
11 SU	0244	0.8	26 M	0256	1.7
	0821	11.2		0831	10.3
	1500	1.0		1503	1.9
	2035	11.5		2043	10.4
12 M	0327	0.8	27 TU	0322	1.9
	0903	11.1		0859	10.0
	1542	1.1		1528	2.2
	2117	11.3		2110	10.0
13 TU	0408	1.1	28 W	0346	2.3
	0944	10.8		0923	9.6
	1622	1.4		1552	2.6
	2159	10.9		2133	9.5
14 W	0448	1.6	29 TH	0409	2.7
	1026	10.3		0946	9.2
	1704	2.0		1617	3.0
	2243	10.2		2156	9.0
15 TH	0530	2.3	30 F	0436	3.2
	1111	9.6		1014	8.8
	1750	2.7		1649	3.5
	2333	9.3		2229	8.5
			31 SA	0514	3.7
				1055	8.3
				1735	4.0
				2321	7.9

Chart Datum: 5·88 metres below Ordnance Datum (Local)

TIME ZONE (UTC)
For Summer Time add ONE hour in **non-shaded areas**

CHANNEL ISLANDS – ST HELIER

LAT 49°11′N LONG 2°07′W

TIMES AND HEIGHTS OF HIGH AND LOW WATERS

SPRING & NEAP TIDES
Dates in red are SPRINGS
Dates in blue are NEAPS

YEAR **2002**

SEPTEMBER

Date	Time	m	Date	Time	m
1 SU	0612	4.2	16 M	0149	7.7
	1202	7.8		0835	4.6
	1853	4.4		1444	7.9
				2133	4.1
2 M	0058	7.6	17 TU	0331	8.0
	0744	4.4		1009	4.1
	1351	7.8		1557	8.5
	2040	4.2		2242	3.5
3 TU	0247	7.9	18 W	0431	8.6
	0923	4.0		1106	3.4
	1524	8.4		1648	9.2
	2204	3.5		2330	2.8
4 W	0402	8.6	19 TH	0514	9.3
	1034	3.2		1150	2.7
	1627	9.2		1728	9.9
	2308	2.7			
5 TH	0500	9.5	20 F	0010	2.2
	1131	2.4		0551	9.9
	1720	10.1		1228	2.2
				1805	10.4
6 F	0003	1.8	21 SA	0048	1.8
	0550	10.3		0626	10.4
	1224	1.6		1303	1.8
	1808	11.0		○ 1839	10.7
7 SA	0054	1.1	22 SU	0123	1.5
	0637	11.0		0659	10.6
	1313	1.0		1336	1.6
	● 1853	11.6		1913	10.9
8 SU	0141	0.6	23 M	0155	1.5
	0720	11.5		0731	10.7
	1359	0.6		1406	1.6
	1936	12.0		1945	10.8
9 M	0225	0.3	24 TU	0225	1.6
	0802	11.7		0800	10.5
	1442	0.4		1434	1.8
	2017	12.0		2014	10.5
10 TU	0306	0.4	25 W	0251	1.8
	0841	11.6		0826	10.3
	1521	0.6		1459	2.1
	2056	11.7		2038	10.1
11 W	0344	0.8	26 TH	0314	2.2
	0919	11.2		0846	9.9
	1559	1.2		1522	2.4
	2135	11.1		2057	9.7
12 TH	0420	1.5	27 F	0336	2.7
	0956	10.4		0907	9.5
	1636	2.0		1546	2.9
	2215	10.2		2120	9.2
13 F	0458	2.5	28 SA	0402	3.2
	1037	9.5		0935	9.1
	1718	2.9		1616	3.4
	2301	9.1		2153	8.7
14 SA	0541	3.5	29 SU	0436	3.7
	1128	8.6		1015	8.5
	1814	3.8		1659	3.9
				2243	8.1
15 SU	0007	8.1	30 M	0532	4.2
	0647	4.3		1118	7.9
	1252	7.9		1811	4.3
	1940	4.3			

OCTOBER

Date	Time	m	Date	Time	m
1 TU	0020	7.5	16 W	0307	7.9
	0703	4.5		0945	4.3
	1316	7.7		1529	8.4
	2006	4.3		2215	3.6
2 W	0225	7.8	17 TH	0402	8.6
	0856	4.1		1038	3.6
	1502	8.4		1617	9.1
	2142	3.5		2259	2.9
3 TH	0343	8.7	18 F	0443	9.3
	1011	3.2		1118	2.9
	1606	9.3		1657	9.7
	2247	2.5		2337	2.4
4 F	0440	9.6	19 SA	0518	9.9
	1109	2.3		1153	2.4
	1659	10.3		1733	10.2
	2341	1.6			
5 SA	0528	10.5	20 SU	0013	2.0
	1201	1.4		0552	10.3
	1746	11.2		1228	2.0
				1808	10.6
6 SU	0030	0.9	21 M	0048	1.7
	0613	11.3		0626	10.6
	1250	0.8		1301	1.8
	● 1831	11.8		○ 1842	10.7
7 M	0117	0.4	22 TU	0120	1.6
	0655	11.8		0657	10.7
	1335	0.4		1333	1.8
	1913	12.1		1914	10.7
8 TU	0200	0.2	23 W	0151	1.7
	0736	11.9		0726	10.6
	1417	0.4		1402	1.9
	1953	12.1		1943	10.5
9 W	0240	0.4	24 TH	0219	2.0
	0814	11.7		0751	10.4
	1456	0.6		1429	2.1
	2032	11.7		2007	10.1
10 TH	0317	1.0	25 F	0244	2.3
	0851	11.2		0814	10.1
	1533	1.3		1455	2.5
	2110	10.9		2029	9.8
11 F	0352	1.8	26 SA	0309	2.7
	0927	10.4		0839	9.7
	1610	2.1		1522	2.9
	2149	9.9		2057	9.4
12 SA	0427	2.8	27 SU	0337	3.2
	1007	9.5		0911	9.3
	1650	3.1		1556	3.3
	2235	8.9		2134	8.8
13 SU	0508	3.8	28 M	0415	3.7
	1057	8.5		0955	8.8
	1745	4.0		1643	3.8
	2342	7.9		2229	8.2
14 M	0614	4.6	29 TU	0513	4.1
	1224	7.8		1101	8.2
	1916	4.5		1753	4.1
15 TU	0130	7.5	30 W	0004	7.8
	0810	4.8		0639	4.3
	1419	7.8		1248	8.0
	2110	4.3		1936	4.0
			31 TH	0154	8.0
				0823	4.0
				1429	8.6
				2109	3.4

NOVEMBER

Date	Time	m	Date	Time	m
1 F	0313	8.8	16 SA	0402	9.0
	0939	3.1		1032	3.3
	1535	9.4		1618	9.3
	2216	2.5		2255	2.8
2 SA	0411	9.7	17 SU	0441	9.5
	1038	2.3		1110	2.8
	1630	10.3		1657	9.8
	2311	1.7		2333	2.4
3 SU	0500	10.6	18 M	0517	10.0
	1131	1.5		1147	2.4
	1719	11.1		1735	10.1
4 M	0001	1.1	19 TU	0009	2.1
	0545	11.2		0551	10.3
	1221	1.0		1224	2.2
	● 1804	11.6		1810	10.3
5 TU	0049	0.7	20 W	0045	2.0
	0628	11.7		0624	10.5
	1308	0.7		1259	2.1
	1848	11.8		○ 1843	10.4
6 W	0133	0.6	21 TH	0119	2.0
	0709	11.8		0654	10.5
	1352	0.7		1333	2.1
	1930	11.7		1914	10.3
7 TH	0214	0.9	22 F	0151	2.1
	0749	11.6		0723	10.4
	1433	1.0		1405	2.2
	2010	11.3		1943	10.1
8 F	0252	1.4	23 SA	0221	2.4
	0827	11.1		0753	10.2
	1512	1.6		1437	2.5
	2049	10.6		2014	9.9
9 SA	0328	2.2	24 SU	0252	2.7
	0904	10.3		0825	10.0
	1550	2.4		1510	2.8
	2130	9.7		2049	9.5
10 SU	0404	3.1	25 M	0325	3.1
	0944	9.5		0904	9.6
	1632	3.2		1549	3.1
	2216	8.8		2133	9.0
11 M	0446	3.9	26 TU	0409	3.4
	1033	8.6		0952	9.1
	1725	3.9		1640	3.4
	2318	8.0		2231	8.6
12 TU	0546	4.5	27 W	0506	3.8
	1148	8.0		1056	8.7
	1841	4.4		1747	3.6
				2348	8.3
13 W	0047	7.7	28 TH	0622	3.9
	0716	4.8		1220	8.6
	1331	7.9		1909	3.6
	2012	4.3			
14 TH	0218	7.9	29 F	0113	8.4
	0847	4.5		0747	3.7
	1442	8.3		1347	8.8
	2124	3.9		2029	3.2
15 F	0318	8.4	30 SA	0232	8.9
	0948	3.9		0900	3.1
	1535	8.8		1457	9.4
	2214	3.3		2138	2.6

DECEMBER

Date	Time	m	Date	Time	m
1 SU	0336	9.6	16 M	0359	8.9
	1003	2.5		1021	3.4
	1557	10.0		1618	9.1
	2238	2.1		2249	3.0
2 M	0430	10.2	17 TU	0440	9.4
	1100	2.0		1107	3.0
	1651	10.6		1700	9.5
	2333	1.6		2332	2.7
3 TU	0520	10.8	18 W	0518	9.8
	1154	1.5		1150	2.6
	1741	11.0		1740	9.8
4 W	0023	1.4	19 TH	0013	2.4
	0605	11.2		0554	10.1
	1245	1.3		1232	2.4
	● 1828	11.2		○ 1818	10.0
5 TH	0110	1.3	20 F	0053	2.2
	0649	11.3		0630	10.4
	1333	1.2		1312	2.2
	1912	11.1		1854	10.2
6 F	0154	1.5	21 SA	0132	2.2
	0730	11.2		0706	10.5
	1418	1.4		1352	2.2
	1955	10.8		1932	10.2
7 SA	0235	1.8	22 SU	0209	2.3
	0810	10.9		0743	10.4
	1500	1.8		1431	2.2
	2036	10.4		2010	10.0
8 SU	0313	2.4	23 M	0247	2.4
	0849	10.3		0822	10.3
	1540	2.4		1511	2.4
	2117	9.7		2051	9.8
9 M	0350	3.0	24 TU	0327	2.6
	0929	9.7		0905	10.1
	1621	3.0		1555	2.5
	2200	9.1		2136	9.6
10 TU	0429	3.6	25 W	0411	2.8
	1013	9.0		0953	9.8
	1705	3.5		1643	2.7
	2248	8.5		2228	9.2
11 W	0517	4.1	26 TH	0502	3.1
	1106	8.5		1047	9.5
	1758	3.9		1738	3.0
	2346	8.0		2326	9.0
12 TH	0617	4.4	27 F	0603	3.3
	1215	8.1		1150	9.2
	1900	4.1		1841	3.1
13 F	0059	7.8	28 SA	0032	8.8
	0725	4.5		0712	3.4
	1334	8.0		1303	9.0
	2005	4.1		1949	3.1
14 SA	0215	8.0	29 SU	0147	8.8
	0832	4.2		0822	3.2
	1438	8.3		1418	9.1
	2107	3.8		2100	3.0
15 SU	0313	8.4	30 M	0301	9.1
	0930	3.8		0930	3.0
	1532	8.6		1527	9.4
	2202	3.4		2209	2.7
			31 TU	0405	9.6
				1035	2.6
				1630	9.7
				2310	2.4

Chart Datum: 5·88 metres below Ordnance Datum (Local)

Fig. 9 (1)

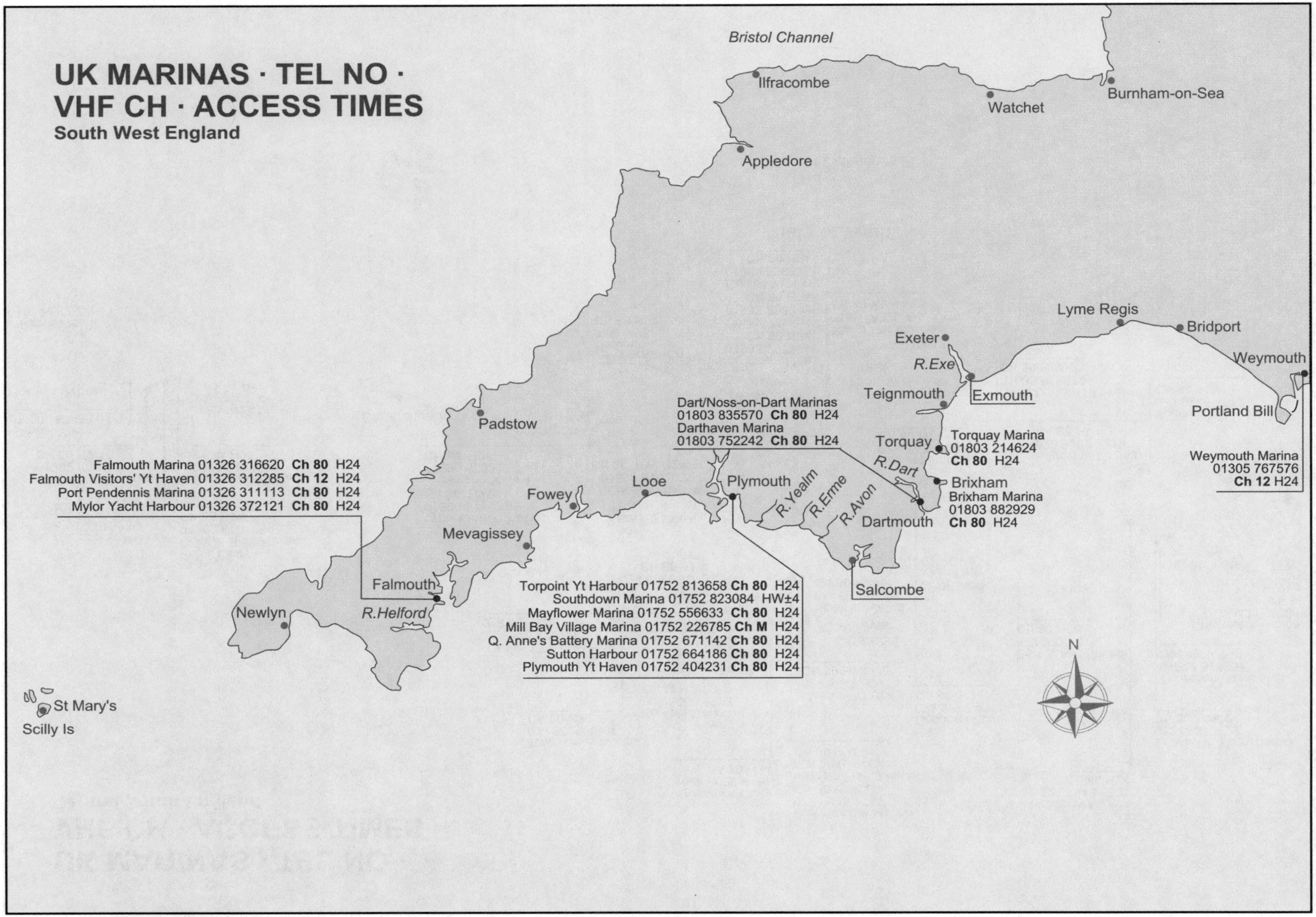
UK MARINAS · TEL NO ·
VHF CH · ACCESS TIMES
South West England
Bristol Channel
Ilfracombe
Watchet
Burnham-on-Sea
Appledore
Padstow
Lyme Regis
Bridport
Exeter
R.Exe
Exmouth
Weymouth
Portland Bill
Teignmouth
Torquay
Torquay Marina
01803 214624
Ch 80 H24
R.Dart
Brixham
Brixham Marina
01803 882929
Ch 80 H24
Dartmouth
Weymouth Marina
01305 767576
Ch 12 H24
Dart/Noss-on-Dart Marinas
01803 835570 Ch 80 H24
Darthaven Marina
01803 752242 Ch 80 H24
Falmouth Marina 01326 316620 Ch 80 H24
Falmouth Visitors' Yt Haven 01326 312285 Ch 12 H24
Port Pendennis Marina 01326 311113 Ch 80 H24
Mylor Yacht Harbour 01326 372121 Ch 80 H24
Fowey
Looe
Plymouth
R.Yealm
R.Erme
R.Avon
Mevagissey
Salcombe
Falmouth
R.Helford
Newlyn
Torpoint Yt Harbour 01752 813658 Ch 80 H24
Southdown Marina 01752 823084 HW±4
Mayflower Marina 01752 556633 Ch 80 H24
Mill Bay Village Marina 01752 226785 Ch M H24
Q. Anne's Battery Marina 01752 671142 Ch 80 H24
Sutton Harbour 01752 664186 Ch 80 H24
Plymouth Yt Haven 01752 404231 Ch 80 H24
N
St Mary's
Scilly Is

C9

Fig. 9 (2)

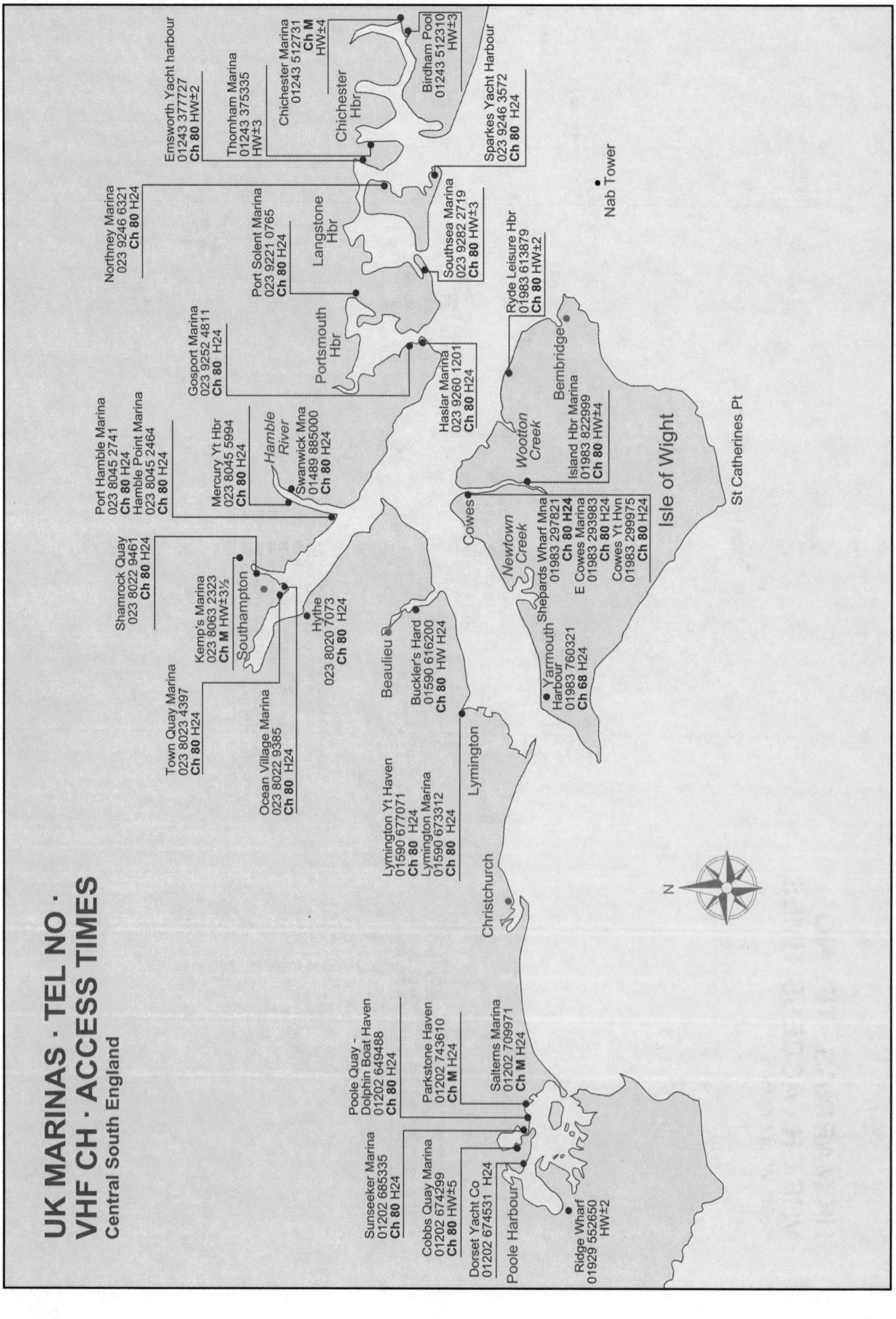
UK MARINAS · TEL NO ·
VHF CH · ACCESS TIMES
Central South England
Sunseeker Marina
01202 685335
Ch 80 H24
Cobbs Quay Marina
01202 674299
Ch 80 HW±5
Dorset Yacht Co
01202 674531 H24
Poole Harbour
Ridge Wharf
01929 552650
HW±2
Poole Quay -
Dolphin Boat Haven
01202 649488
Ch 80 H24
Parkstone Haven
01202 743610
Ch M H24
Salterns Marina
01202 709971
Ch M H24
Christchurch
Lymington Yt Haven
01590 677071
Ch 80 H24
Lymington Marina
01590 673312
Ch 80 H24
Lymington
Ocean Village Marina
023 8022 9385
Ch 80 H24
Town Quay Marina
023 8023 4397
Ch 80 H24
Kemp's Marina
023 8063 2323
Ch M HW±3½
Southampton
Shamrock Quay
023 8022 9461
Ch 80 H24
Hythe
023 8020 7073
Ch 80 H24
Beaulieu
Buckler's Hard
01590 616200
Ch 80 HW H24
Yarmouth
Harbour
01983 760321
Ch 68 H24
Shepards Wharf Mna
01983 297821
Ch 80 H24
E Cowes Marina
01983 293983
Ch 80 H24
Cowes Yt Hvn
01983 299975
Ch 80 H24
Newtown
Creek
Cowes
Port Hamble Marina
023 8045 2741
Ch 80 H24
Hamble Point Marina
023 8045 2464
Ch 80 H24
Mercury Yt Hbr
023 8045 5994
Ch 80 H24
Hamble
River
Swanwick Mna
01489 885000
Ch 80 H24
Wootton
Creek
Island Hbr Marina
01983 822999
Ch 80 HW±4
Isle of Wight
St Catherines Pt
Gosport Marina
023 9252 4811
Ch 80 H24
Portsmouth
Hbr
Haslar Marina
023 9260 1201
Ch 80 H24
Ryde Leisure Hbr
01983 613879
Ch 80 HW±2
Bembridge
Northney Marina
023 9246 6321
Ch 80 H24
Port Solent Marina
023 9221 0765
Ch 80 H24
Langstone
Hbr
Southsea Marina
023 9282 2719
Ch 80 HW±3
Nab Tower
Emsworth Yacht harbour
01243 377727
Ch 80 HW±2
Thornham Marina
01243 375335
HW±3
Chichester Marina
01243 512731
Ch M
HW±4
Chichester
Hbr
Birdham Pool
01243 512310
HW±3
Sparkes Yacht Harbour
023 9246 3572
Ch 80 H24
N

Fig. 9 (3)

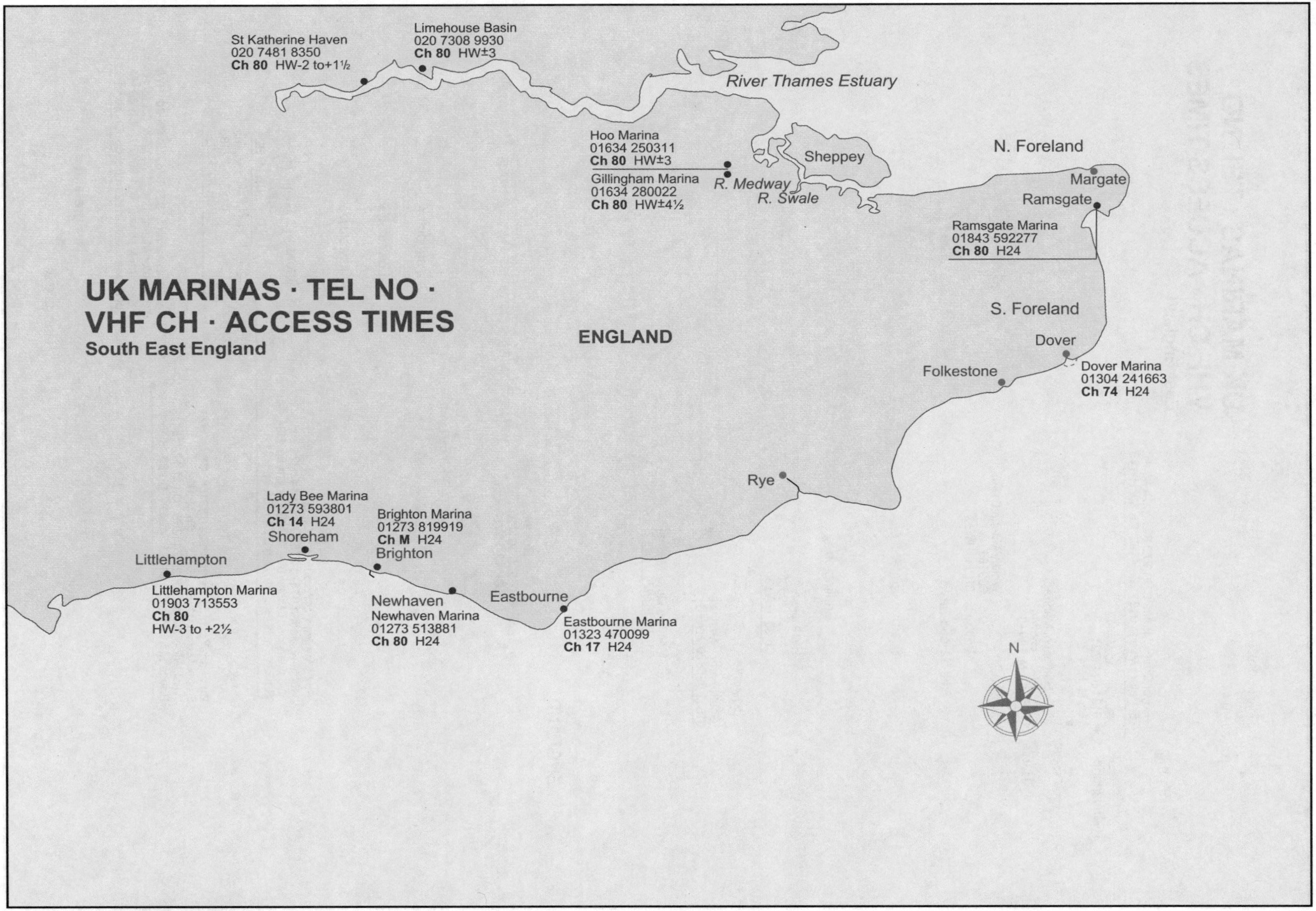
UK MARINAS · TEL NO ·
VHF CH · ACCESS TIMES
South East England
ENGLAND
St Katherine Haven
020 7481 8350
Ch 80 HW-2 to+1½
Limehouse Basin
020 7308 9930
Ch 80 HW±3
River Thames Estuary
Hoo Marina
01634 250311
Ch 80 HW±3
Gillingham Marina
01634 280022
Ch 80 HW±4½
Sheppey
R. Medway
R. Swale
N. Foreland
Margate
Ramsgate
Ramsgate Marina
01843 592277
Ch 80 H24
S. Foreland
Dover
Dover Marina
01304 241663
Ch 74 H24
Folkestone
Rye
Eastbourne
Eastbourne Marina
01323 470099
Ch 17 H24
Newhaven
Newhaven Marina
01273 513881
Ch 80 H24
Brighton Marina
01273 819919
Ch M H24
Brighton
Lady Bee Marina
01273 593801
Ch 14 H24
Shoreham
Littlehampton
Littlehampton Marina
01903 713553
Ch 80
HW-3 to +2½
N

Fig. 9 (4)

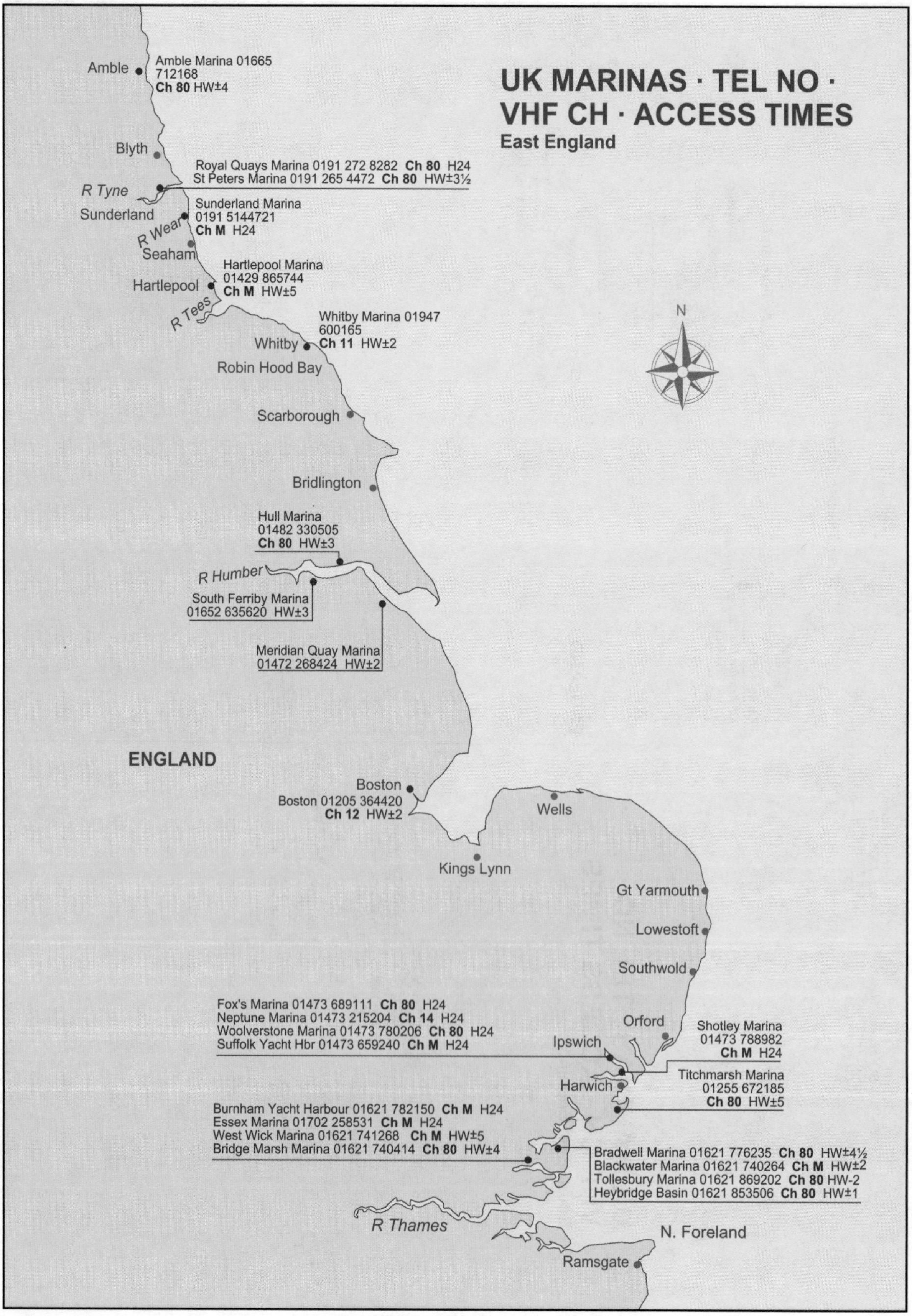
UK MARINAS · TEL NO · VHF CH · ACCESS TIMES
East England
Amble
Amble Marina 01665 712168 Ch 80 HW±4
Blyth
Royal Quays Marina 0191 272 8282 Ch 80 H24
St Peters Marina 0191 265 4472 Ch 80 HW±3½
R Tyne
Sunderland
Sunderland Marina 0191 5144721 Ch M H24
R Wear
Seaham
Hartlepool
Hartlepool Marina 01429 865744 Ch M HW±5
R Tees
Whitby
Whitby Marina 01947 600165 Ch 11 HW±2
Robin Hood Bay
Scarborough
Bridlington
Hull Marina 01482 330505 Ch 80 HW±3
R Humber
South Ferriby Marina 01652 635620 HW±3
Meridian Quay Marina 01472 268424 HW±2
N
ENGLAND
Boston
Boston 01205 364420 Ch 12 HW±2
Wells
Kings Lynn
Gt Yarmouth
Lowestoft
Southwold
Orford
Fox's Marina 01473 689111 Ch 80 H24
Neptune Marina 01473 215204 Ch 14 H24
Woolverstone Marina 01473 780206 Ch 80 H24
Suffolk Yacht Hbr 01473 659240 Ch M H24
Ipswich
Shotley Marina 01473 788982 Ch M H24
Harwich
Titchmarsh Marina 01255 672185 Ch 80 HW±5
Burnham Yacht Harbour 01621 782150 Ch M H24
Essex Marina 01702 258531 Ch M H24
West Wick Marina 01621 741268 Ch M HW±5
Bridge Marsh Marina 01621 740414 Ch 80 HW±4
Bradwell Marina 01621 776235 Ch 80 HW±4½
Blackwater Marina 01621 740264 Ch M HW±2
Tollesbury Marina 01621 869202 Ch 80 HW-2
Heybridge Basin 01621 853506 Ch 80 HW±1
R Thames
N. Foreland
Ramsgate

Fig. 9 (5)

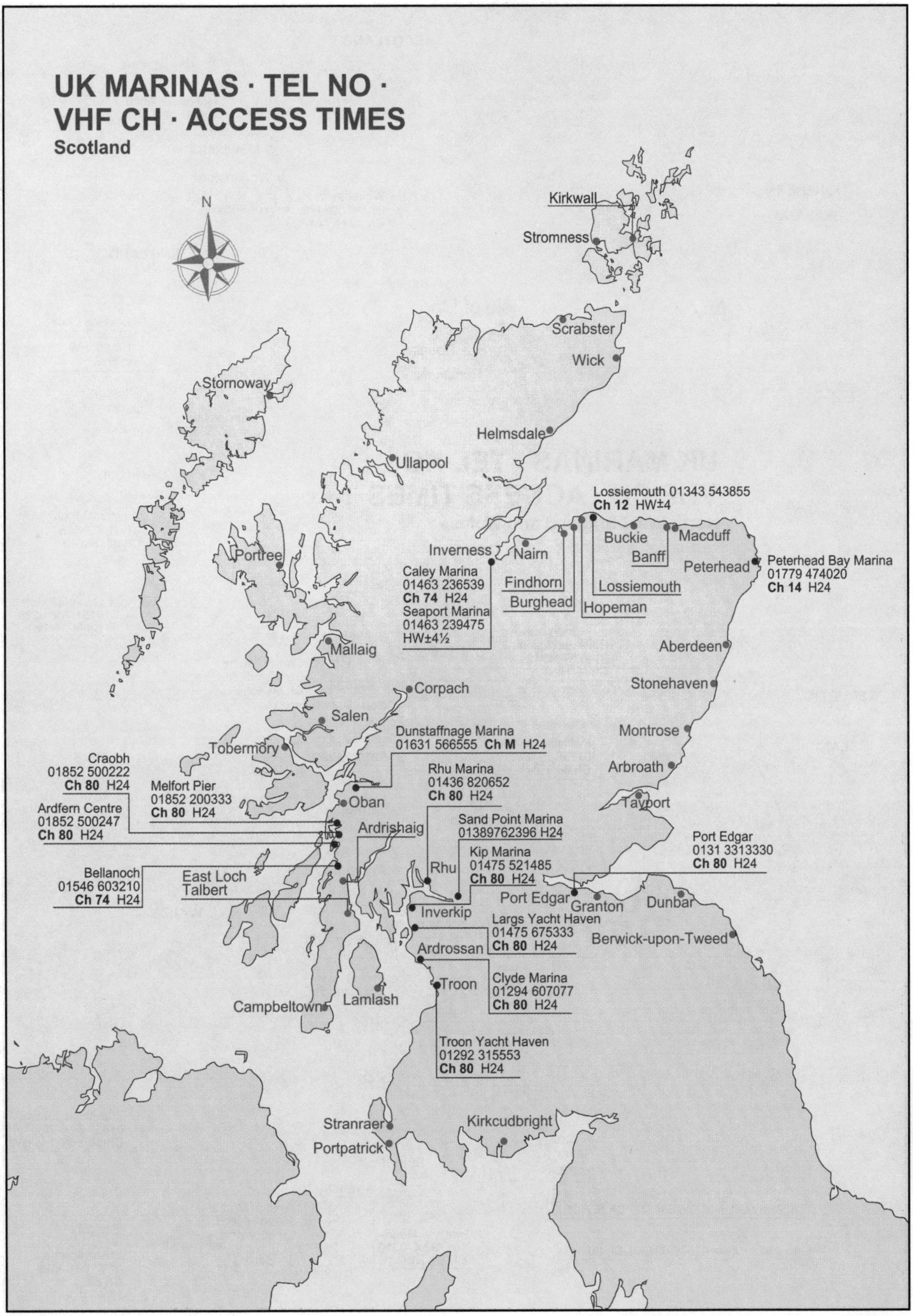
UK MARINAS · TEL NO ·
VHF CH · ACCESS TIMES
Scotland
N
Kirkwall
Stromness
Scrabster
Wick
Stornoway
Helmsdale
Ullapool
Lossiemouth 01343 543855
Ch 12 HW±4
Buckie
Macduff
Banff
Peterhead
Peterhead Bay Marina
01779 474020
Ch 14 H24
Portree
Inverness
Nairn
Caley Marina
01463 236539
Ch 74 H24
Seaport Marina
01463 239475
HW±4½
Findhorn
Burghead
Hopeman
Lossiemouth
Mallaig
Aberdeen
Corpach
Stonehaven
Salen
Montrose
Tobermory
Dunstaffnage Marina
01631 566555 Ch M H24
Craobh
01852 500222
Ch 80 H24
Melfort Pier
01852 200333
Ch 80 H24
Rhu Marina
01436 820652
Ch 80 H24
Arbroath
Tayport
Oban
Ardfern Centre
01852 500247
Ch 80 H24
Ardrishaig
Sand Point Marina
01389762396 H24
Kip Marina
01475 521485
Ch 80 H24
Port Edgar
0131 3313330
Ch 80 H24
Rhu
Bellanoch
01546 603210
Ch 74 H24
East Loch
Talbert
Port Edgar
Granton
Dunbar
Inverkip
Largs Yacht Haven
01475 675333
Ch 80 H24
Berwick-upon-Tweed
Ardrossan
Troon
Clyde Marina
01294 607077
Ch 80 H24
Lamlash
Campbeltown
Troon Yacht Haven
01292 315553
Ch 80 H24
Stranraer
Kirkcudbright
Portpatrick

C9

Fig. 9 (6)

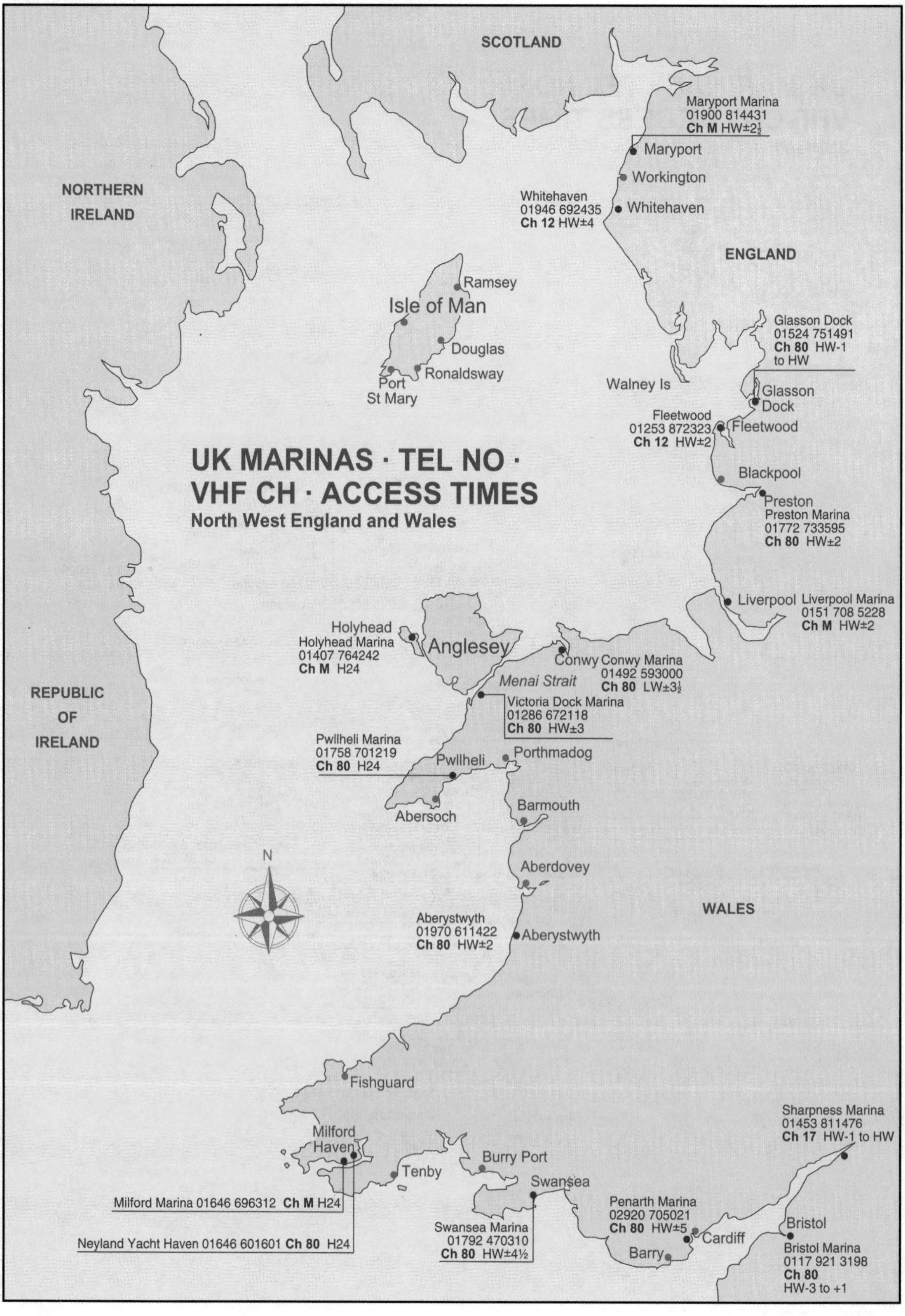
SCOTLAND
NORTHERN IRELAND
ENGLAND
REPUBLIC OF IRELAND
WALES
UK MARINAS · TEL NO · VHF CH · ACCESS TIMES
North West England and Wales
Maryport Marina 01900 814431 Ch M HW±2½
Maryport
Workington
Whitehaven 01946 692435 Ch 12 HW±4
Whitehaven
Ramsey
Isle of Man
Douglas
Ronaldsway
Port St Mary
Walney Is
Glasson Dock 01524 751491 Ch 80 HW-1 to HW
Glasson Dock
Fleetwood 01253 872323 Ch 12 HW±2
Fleetwood
Blackpool
Preston
Preston Marina 01772 733595 Ch 80 HW±2
Liverpool
Liverpool Marina 0151 708 5228 Ch M HW±2
Holyhead
Holyhead Marina 01407 764242 Ch M H24
Anglesey
Conwy
Conwy Marina 01492 593000 Ch 80 LW±3½
Menai Strait
Victoria Dock Marina 01286 672118 Ch 80 HW±3
Pwllheli Marina 01758 701219 Ch 80 H24
Pwllheli
Porthmadog
Abersoch
Barmouth
N
Aberdovey
Aberystwyth 01970 611422 Ch 80 HW±2
Aberystwyth
Fishguard
Milford Haven
Tenby
Burry Port
Swansea
Milford Marina 01646 696312 Ch M H24
Neyland Yacht Haven 01646 601601 Ch 80 H24
Swansea Marina 01792 470310 Ch 80 HW±4½
Penarth Marina 02920 705021 Ch 80 HW±5
Cardiff
Barry
Sharpness Marina 01453 811476 Ch 17 HW-1 to HW
Bristol
Bristol Marina 0117 921 3198 Ch 80 HW-3 to +1

Fig. 9 (7)

N IRELAND MARINAS · TEL NO · VHF CH · ACCESS TIMES

North of Ireland

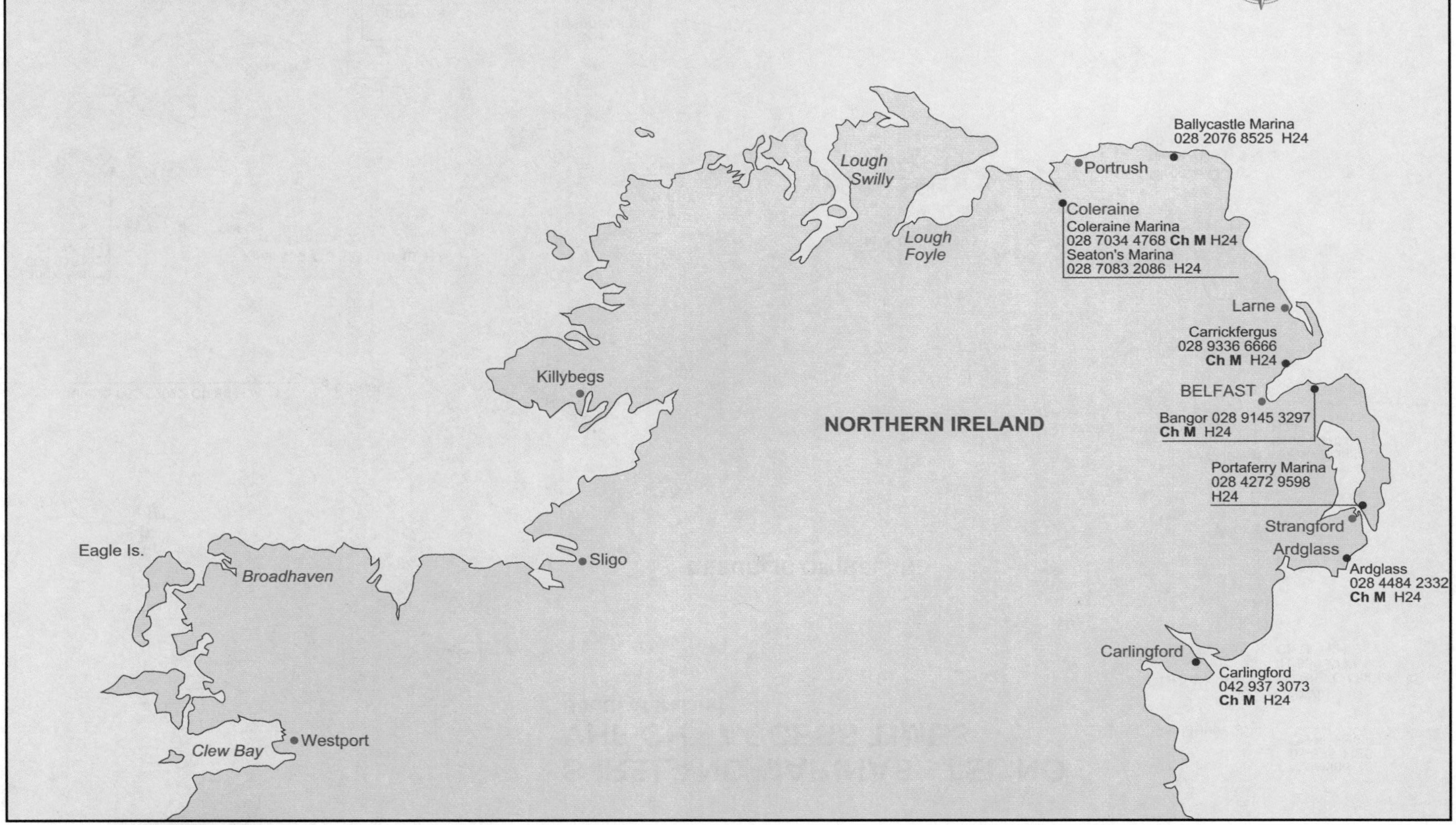
N
Ballycastle Marina
028 2076 8525 H24
Portrush
Lough Swilly
Lough Foyle
Coleraine
Coleraine Marina
028 7034 4768 Ch M H24
Seaton's Marina
028 7083 2086 H24
Larne
Carrickfergus
028 9336 6666
Ch M H24
BELFAST
Bangor 028 9145 3297
Ch M H24
NORTHERN IRELAND
Portaferry Marina
028 4272 9598
H24
Strangford
Ardglass
Ardglass
028 4484 2332
Ch M H24
Carlingford
Carlingford
042 937 3073
Ch M H24
Killybegs
Sligo
Eagle Is.
Broadhaven
Clew Bay
Westport

Fig. 9 (8)

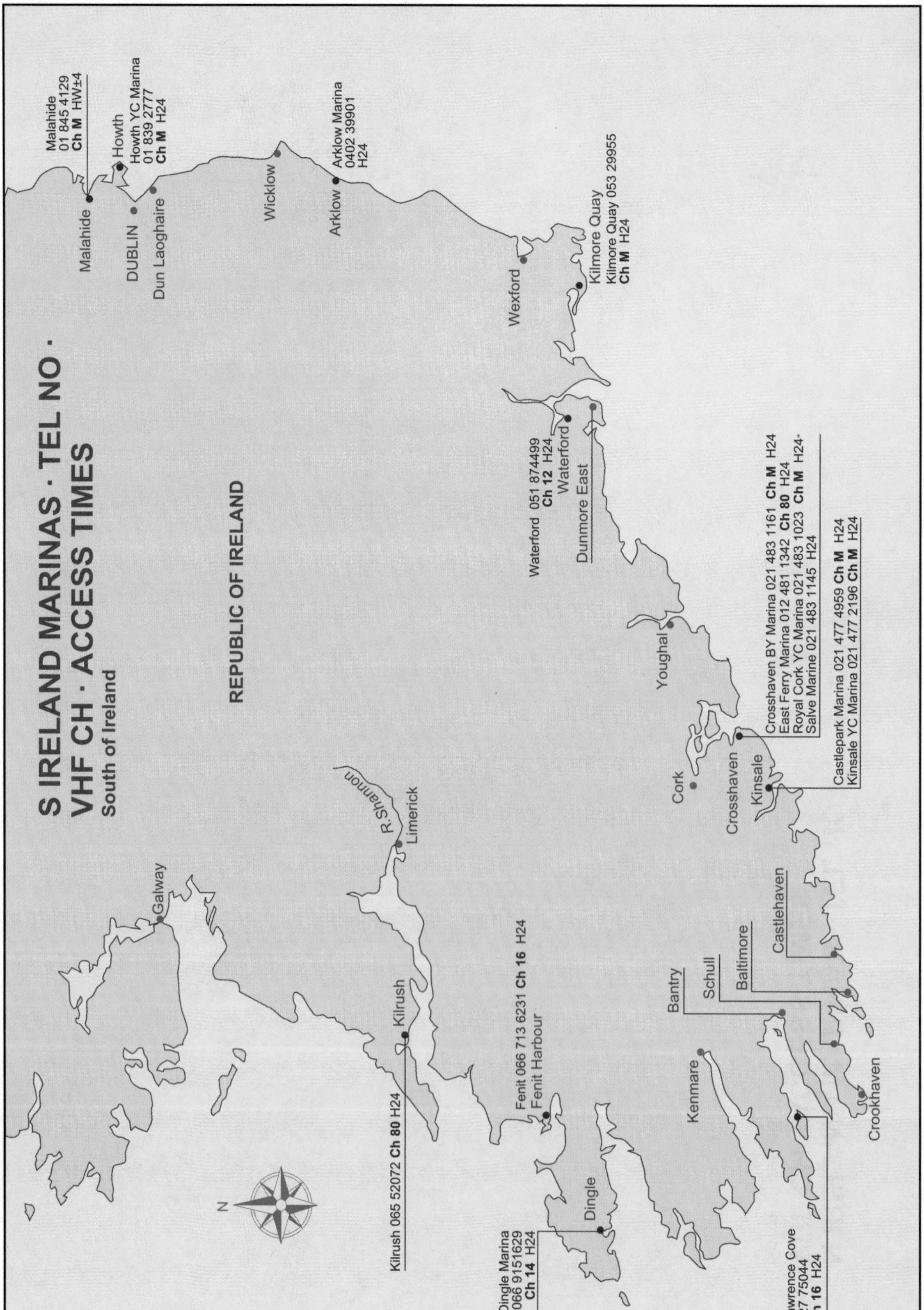
S IRELAND MARINAS · TEL NO · VHF CH · ACCESS TIMES
South of Ireland
REPUBLIC OF IRELAND
Malahide 01 845 4129 Ch M HW±4
Howth
Howth YC Marina 01 839 2777 Ch M H24
Malahide
DUBLIN
Dun Laoghaire
Wicklow
Arklow
Arklow Marina 0402 39901 H24
Wexford
Kilmore Quay
Kilmore Quay 053 29955 Ch M H24
Waterford 051 874499 Ch 12 H24
Waterford
Dunmore East
Youghal
Cork
Crosshaven
Kinsale
Crosshaven BY Marina 021 483 1161 Ch M H24
East Ferry Marina 012 481 1342 Ch 80 H24
Royal Cork YC Marina 021 483 1023 Ch M H24
Salve Marine 021 483 1145 H24
Castlepark Marina 021 477 4959 Ch M H24
Kinsale YC Marina 021 477 2196 Ch M H24
Castlehaven
Baltimore
Schull
Bantry
Kenmare
Crookhaven
Lawrence Cove 027 75044 Ch 16 H24
Fenit 066 713 6231 Ch 16 H24
Fenit Harbour
Kilrush
Kilrush 065 52072 Ch 80 H24
Dingle
Dingle Marina 066 9151629 Ch 14 H24
Galway
R.Shannon
Limerick
N

MAPTECH®
Leading the world in digital navigation
Maptech UK Ltd • +44 (0)1243 389352 • sales@maptech.co.uk

Maptech world class digital chart CDs
Worldwide coverage from over 4,500 charts

Maptech award winning software
Easy to use navigation software
• **Chart Navigator** • **Cruising Navigator** • **Offshore Navigator**

www.maptech.co.uk

Area 15

Central North France
Cherbourg to
St. Quay-Portrieux

9.15.1	Index	Page 737
9.15.2	Area map	738
9.15.3	Tidal stream charts	740
9.15.4	Lights, buoys & waypoints	742
9.15.5	Passage information	745
9.15.6	Distance table	746
9.15.7	Special notes for France	746
9.15.8	Cherbourg, Standard Port, tidal curves Port de Lévi Port du Becquet	748
9.15.9	Omonville-la-Rogue Port Racine Goury	753
9.15.10	Diélette	754
9.15.11	Carteret	754
9.15.12	Portbail	755
9.15.13	Granville	756
9.15.14	Iles Chausey	756
9.15.15	St. Malo (Dinard) Standard Port, tidal curves Cancale Rotheneuf	760
9.15.16	River Rance/Dinan Plouër Lyvet	762
9.15.17	Inland waterways of Brittany	763
9.15.18	Dahouet Saint Cast Erquy Val André	764
9.15.19	Le Légué/St Brieux	764
9.15.20	Binic	765
9.15.21	St. Quay-Portrieux	766

Register for your FREE weekly weather email service from Macmillan Reeds
at www.nauticaldata.com – NOW!
weekend weather reports sent to your email address, every Thursday

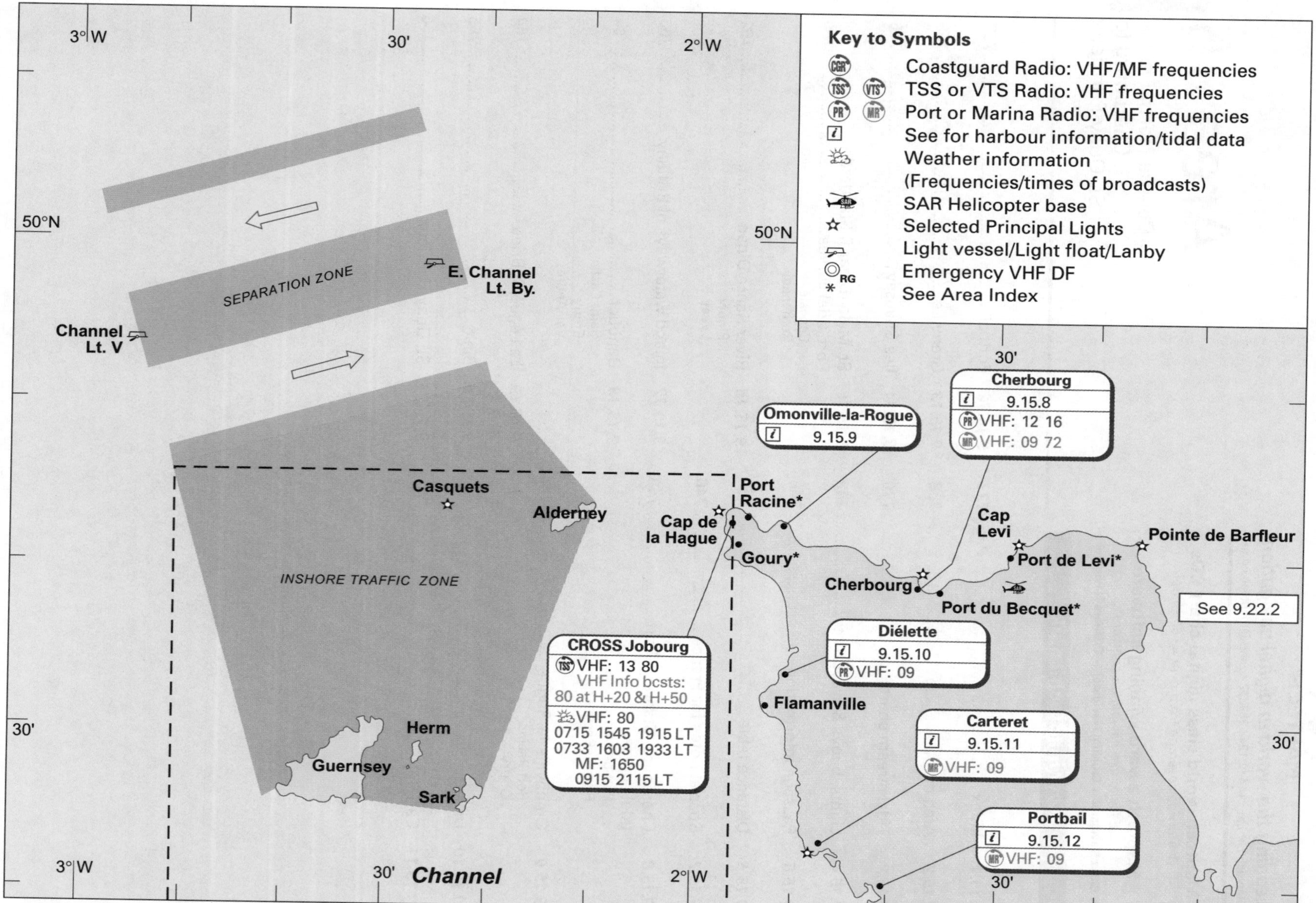
Key to Symbols
Coastguard Radio: VHF/MF frequencies
TSS or VTS Radio: VHF frequencies
Port or Marina Radio: VHF frequencies
See for harbour information/tidal data
Weather information
(Frequencies/times of broadcasts)
SAR Helicopter base
Selected Principal Lights
Light vessel/Light float/Lanby
Emergency VHF DF
See Area Index
3°W
30'
2°W
50°N
30'
SEPARATION ZONE
E. Channel Lt. By.
Channel Lt. V
INSHORE TRAFFIC ZONE
Casquets
Alderney
Guernsey
Herm
Sark
Channel
Cap de la Hague
Port Racine*
Goury*
Omonville-la-Rogue
9.15.9
Cherbourg
9.15.8
VHF: 12 16
VHF: 09 72
Cap Levi
Port de Levi*
Pointe de Barfleur
Cherbourg
Port du Becquet*
See 9.22.2
CROSS Jobourg
VHF: 13 80
VHF Info bcsts:
80 at H+20 & H+50
VHF: 80
0715 1545 1915 LT
0733 1603 1933 LT
MF: 1650
0915 2115 LT
Diélette
9.15.10
VHF: 09
Flamanville
Carteret
9.15.11
VHF: 09
Portbail
9.15.12
VHF: 09

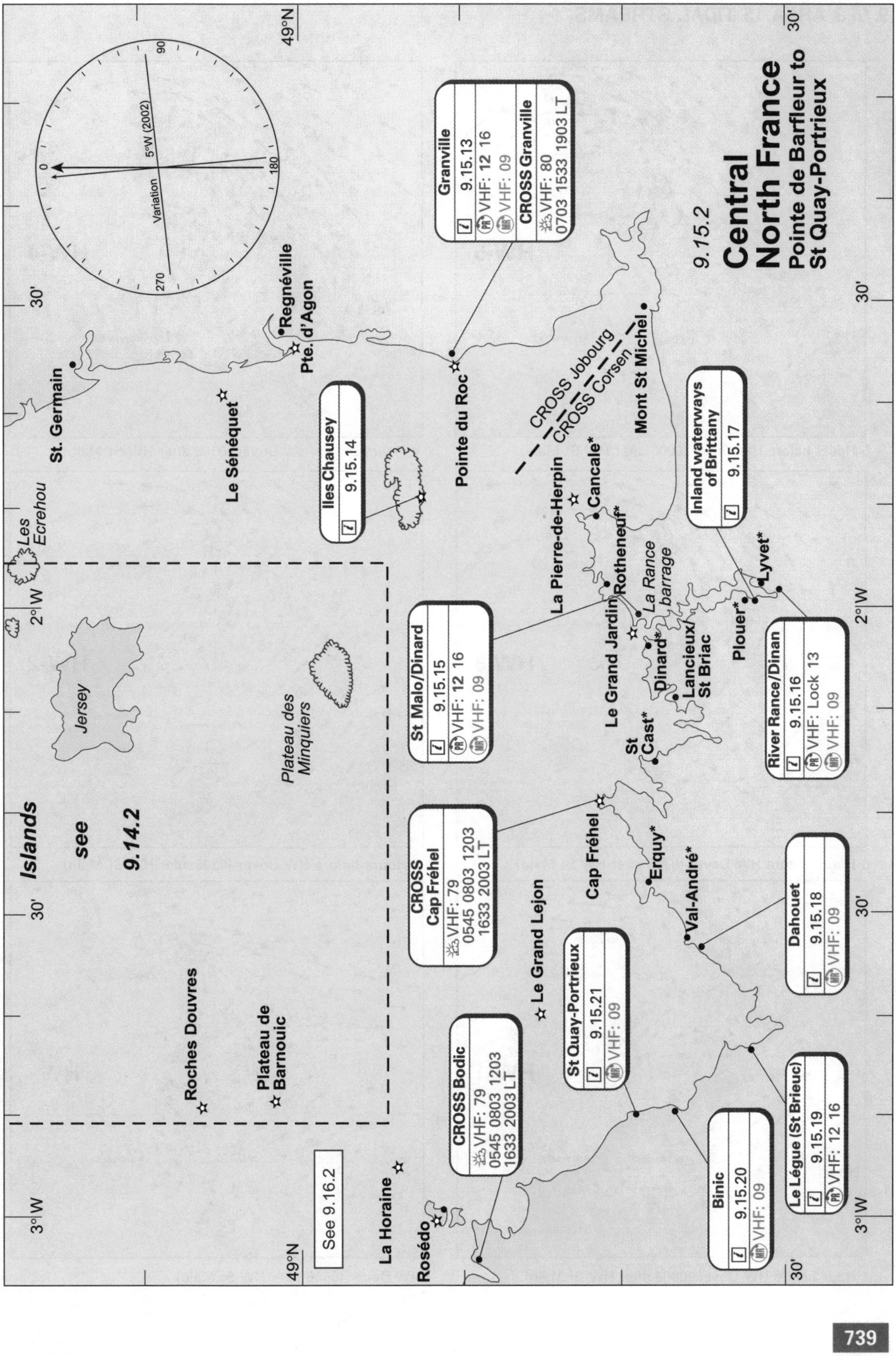
9.15.2
Central
North France
Pointe de Barfleur to
St Quay-Portrieux
Islands
see
9.14.2
See 9.16.2
Variation
5°W (2002)
0
90
180
270
49°N
30'
3°W
2°W
Jersey
Les
Ecrehou
Plateau des
Minquiers
Roches Douvres
Plateau de
Barnouic
La Horaine
Rosédo
Le Grand Lejon
St. Germain
Le Sénéquet
Regnéville
Pte. d'Agon
Pointe du Roc
Granville
9.15.13
VHF: 12 16
VHF: 09
CROSS Granville
VHF: 80
0703 1533 1903 LT
Iles Chausey
9.15.14
CROSS Jobourg
CROSS Corsen
Mont St Michel
Cancale*
La Pierre-de-Herpin
Rotheneuf*
La Rance
barrage
Le Grand Jardin
St Malo/Dinard
9.15.15
VHF: 12 16
VHF: 09
Inland waterways
of Brittany
9.15.17
Lyvet*
Plouer*
Dinard*
Lancieux/
St Briac
River Rance/Dinan
9.15.16
VHF: Lock 13
VHF: 09
St
Cast*
Cap Fréhel
CROSS
Cap Fréhel
VHF: 79
0545 0803 1203
1633 2003 LT
Erquy*
Val-André*
Dahouet
9.15.18
VHF: 09
St Quay-Portrieux
9.15.21
VHF: 09
CROSS Bodic
VHF: 79
0545 0803 1203
1633 2003 LT
Binic
9.15.20
VHF: 09
Le Légue (St Brieuc)
9.15.19
VHF: 12 16

9.15.3 AREA 15 TIDAL STREAMS

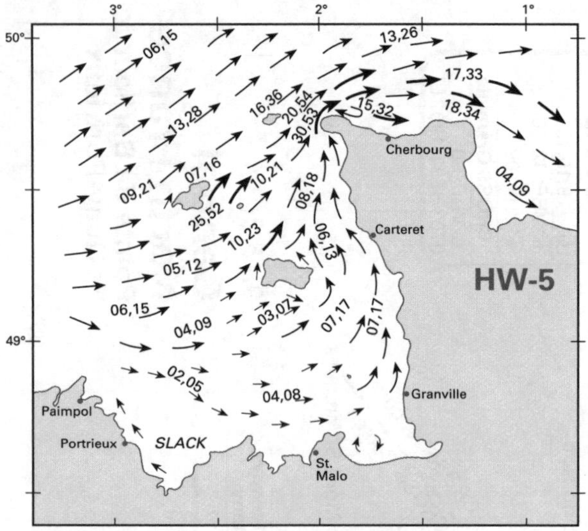

5 Hours before HW Dover (0006 after HW St Malo)

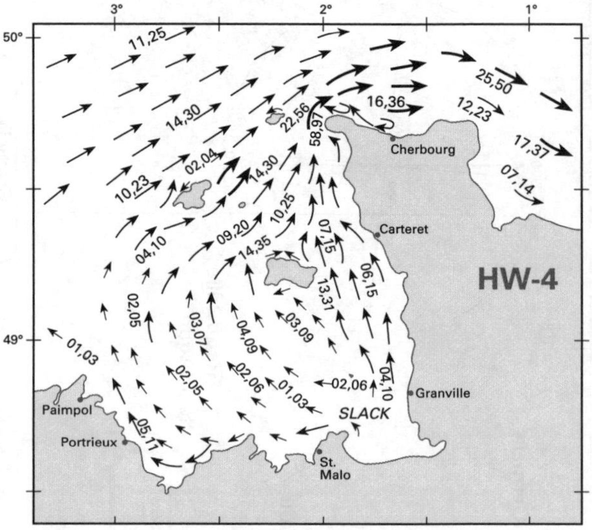

4 Hours before HW Dover (0106 after HW St Malo)

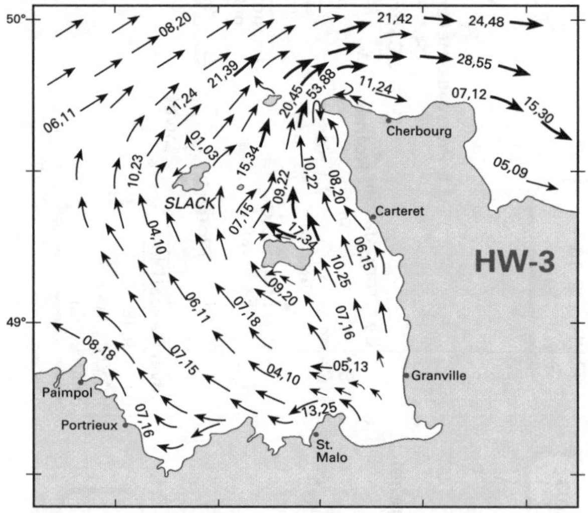

3 Hours before HW Dover (0206 after HW St Malo)

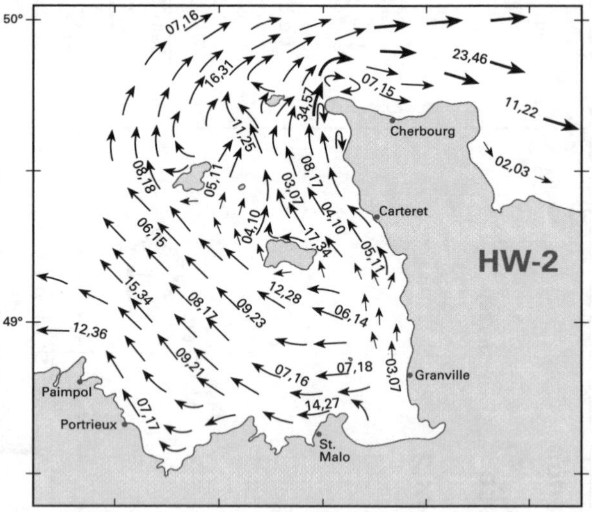

2 Hours before HW Dover (0306 after HW St Malo)

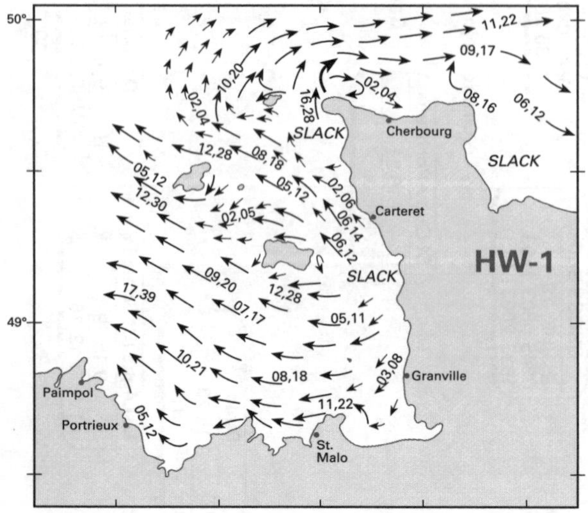

1 Hour before HW Dover (0406 after HW St Malo)

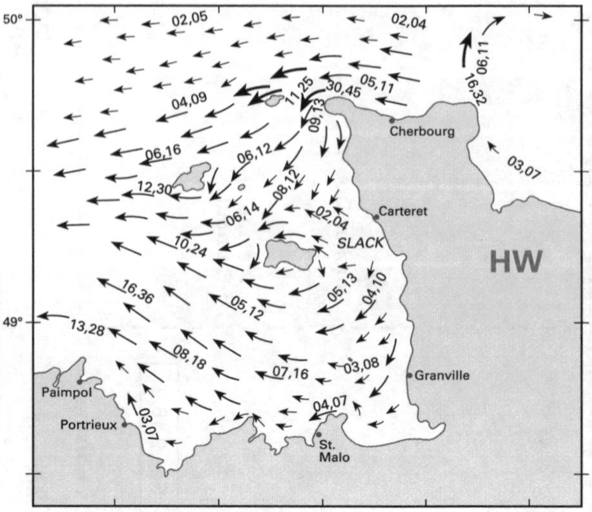

HW Dover (0506 after HW St Malo)

Westward 9.16.3 Channel Islands 9.14.3 Eastward 9.22.3 Northward 9.2.3

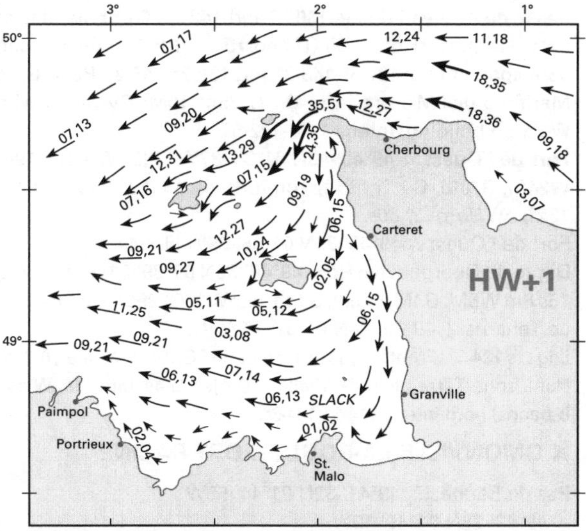

1 Hour after HW Dover (0554 before HW St Malo)

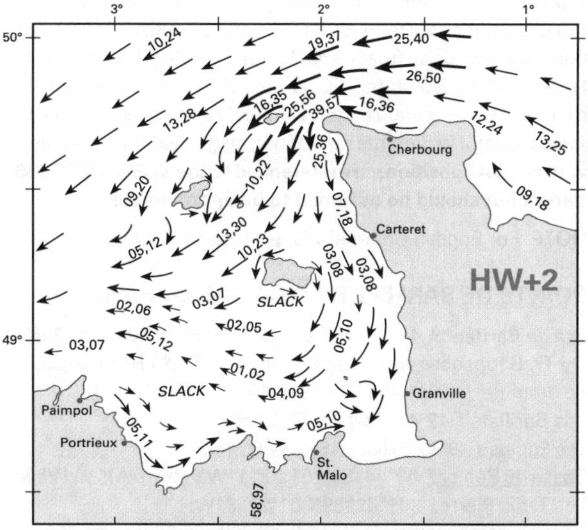

2 Hours after HW Dover (0454 before HW St Malo)

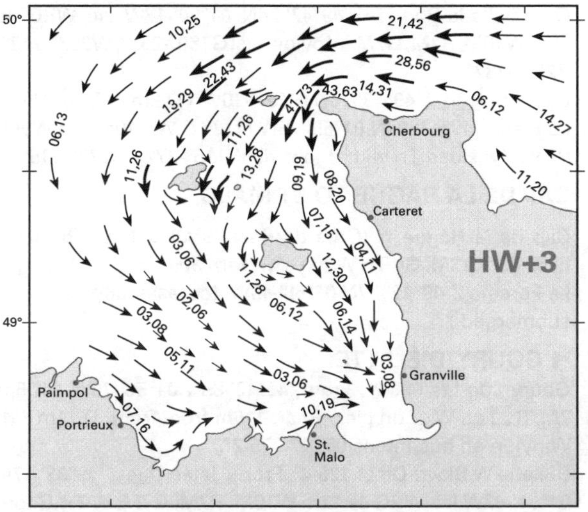

3 Hours after HW Dover (0354 before HW St Malo)

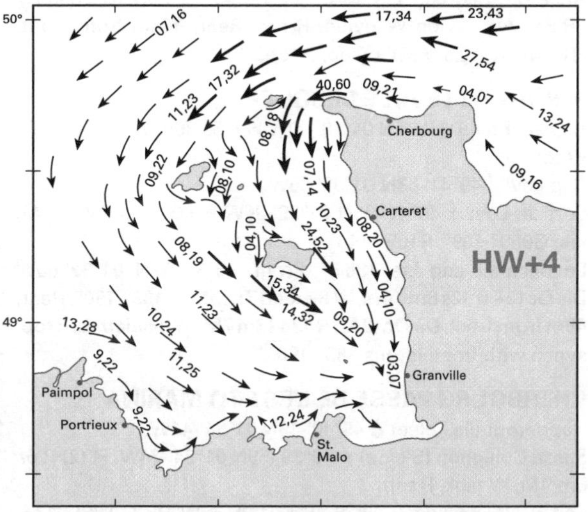

4 Hours after HW Dover (0254 before HW St Malo)

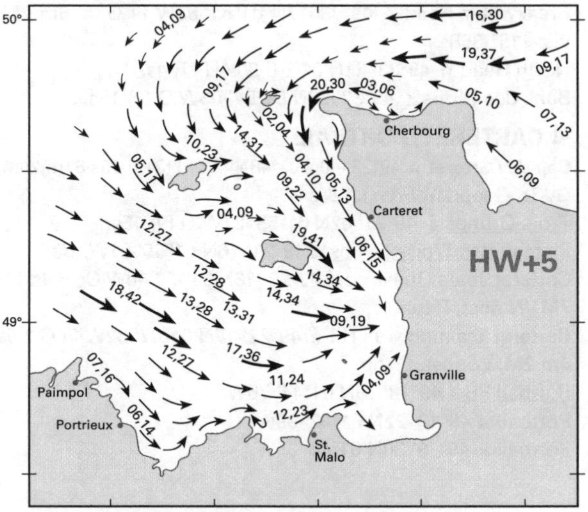

5 Hours after HW Dover (0154 before HW St Malo)

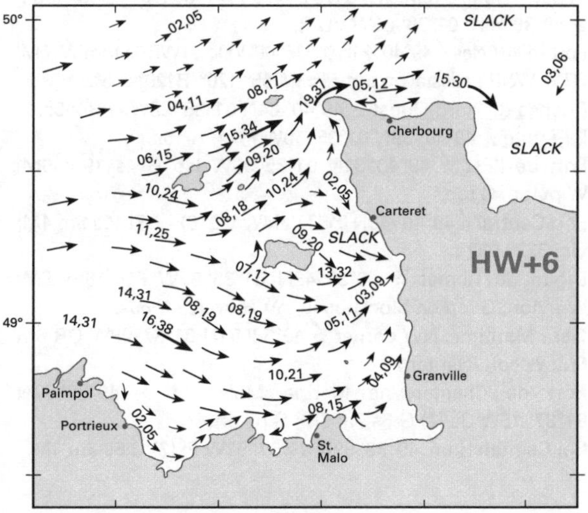

6 Hours after HW Dover (0054 before HW St Malo)

9.15.4 LIGHTS, BUOYS AND WAYPOINTS

Abbreviations used below are given in the Introduction. Principal lights ☆ are in **bold** print, places in CAPITALS, and light-vessels, light floats and Lanbys in *CAPITAL ITALICS*. Unless otherwise stated lights are white. m – elevation in metres; M – nominal range in miles. Fog signals are in *italics*. Useful waypoints are underlined – use those on land with care. **All positions are referenced to the WGS84/ETRS89 datum but should be assumed to be approximate.**

NOTE: For English Channel Waypoints see 9.1.7.

POINTE DE BARFLEUR TO CAP DE LA HAGUE

Pte de Barfleur ☆ 49°41'·78N 01°15'·96W Fl (2) 10s 72m **29M**; Gy Tr, B top; obsc when brg less than 088°; *Horn (2) 60s.*
La Jamette 49°41'·86N 01°15'·59W.
Les Barillets 49°41'·76N 01°16'·77W.
Les Équets 49°43'·61N 01°18'·36W Q 3M.
Basse du Rénier 49°44'·84N 01°22'·11W VQ 8m 4M; *Whis.*
Les Trois Pierres 49°42'·89N 01°21'·81W.
La Pierre Noire 49°43'·53N 01°29'·09W Q (9) 15s 8m 4M.
Anse de Vicq Ldg Lts 158°. Front, 49°42'·20N 01°23'·95W FR 8m 7M; △ on W pylon, R top. Rear, 403m from front, FR 14m 7M; △ on W pylon, R top.

◀ PORT DE LÉVI/LE BECQUET

Cap Lévi ☆ 49°41'·75N 01°28'·40W Fl R 5s 36m **22M**; Gy □ Tr; W top.
Cap Levi 49°41'·53N 01°32'·46W.
Port de Lévi ☆ 49°41'·23N 01°28'·36W F RG 7m,R7M, G7M; vis: G050°-109°, R109°-140°.
Le Becquet Ldg Lts 186·5°. Front, 49°39'·22N 01°32'·86W Dir Oc (2+1) 12s 8m 10M; W 8-sided Tr; intens 183°-190°. Rear, 49m from front, Dir Oc (2+1) R 12s 13m 7M; W 8-sided Tr, R top; synch with front, intens 183°-190°.

CHERBOURG PASSE DE L'EST TO MARINA

Happetout (Ile Pelée) 49°40'·46N 01°34'·41W.
Passe Collignon (S side) ☆ 49°39'·59N 01°34'·24W. Fl (2) R 6s 5m 4M; W tank, R top.
Fort des Flamands ☆ 49°39'·10N 01°35'·65W Dir Q WRG 13m W12M, R10M, G10M; vis: G173·5°-176°, W176°-183°, R183°-193°.
49°39'·44N 01°36'·60W VQ R.
Forte d'Île Pelée ☆ 49°40'·21N 01°35'·08W Oc (2) WR 6s 19m W10M, R7M; W&R pedestal on fort; vis: W055°-120°, R120°-055°.
Roches du Nord-Ouest 49°40'·64N 01°35'·28W Fl R 2·5s.
La Truite 49°40'·39N 01°35'·50W Fl (4) R 15s.
Fort de l'Est ☆ 49°40'·31N 01°35'·93W Iso G 4s 19m 9M; W pylon, G top.
Fort Central ☆ 49°40'·40N 01°37'·04W VQ (6) + L Fl 10s 5m 4M; vis: 322°-032°.
Digue du Homet ☆ 49°39'·48N 01°36'·97W FG 10m 8M; W pylon, G top on blockhouse; *Horn (2+1) 60s.*
Gare Maritime, NW corner ☆ 49°38'·91N 01°37'·08W QR 6m 6M; W col, R lantern.
Port de Chantereyne Marina Môle Hd ☆ 49°38'·87N 01°37'·15W Oc (2) G 6s 7m 6M; G pylon.
Épi Caiman Hd ☆ 49°38'·99N 01°37'·52W Fl (2) G 6s 3m 1M.

◀ CHERBOURG PASSE DE L'OUEST

CH1 49°43'·24N 01°42'·09W L Fl 10s 8m 4M; *Whis.*
Passe de l'Ouest Ldg Lts 140·3° and 142·2°. **Front,** two Lts at root of Digue du Homet Dir Q (2 hor) 5m **17M**; W △ on parapet; 63m apart; intens 137·3°-143·3° and 139·2°-145·2°. Rear, Gare Maritime 0·99M from front Dir Q 35m **19M**; Gy pylon with W △ on building; intens 140°-142·5°.
Fort de l'Ouest ☆ 49°40'·45N 01°38'·87W Fl (3) WR 15s 19m **W24M, R20M**; Gy Tr, R top, on fort; vis: W122°-355°, R355°-122°; *Horn (3) 60s.*
Fort de l'Ouest 49°40'·39N 01°38'·89W Fl R 4s.
Digue de Querqueville Hd ☆ 49°40'·30N 01°39'·81W Fl (4) WG 15s 8m W6M, G4M; W col, G top; vis: W120°-290°, G290°-120°.
Le Tenarde 49°39'·74N 01°37'·75W VQ.
Ldg Lts 124·3°. Front, Digue du Homet Hd FG 10m 8M. Rear, 0·75M from front, Terre-plein de Mielles, Dir Iso G 4s 16m 7M; W col, B bands; both intens 114·3°-134·3°.

◀ OMONVILLE-LA-ROGUE/PORT RACINE

Raz de Bannes 49°41'·32N 01°44'·55W.
49°42'·28N 01°49'·13W.
L'Étonnard 49°42'·32N 01°49'·85W.
Omonville-la-Rogue ☆ 49°42'·24N 01°50'·17W Iso WRG 4s 13m W10M, R7M, G7M; W pylon; vis: G180°-252°, W252°-262°, R262°-287°.
Basse Bréfort 49°43'·76N 01°51'·10W VQ 8m 4M; *Whis.*
La Plate 49°43'·97N 01°55'·75W Fl (2+1) WR 10s 11m W9M, R6M; Y 8-sided Tr, with B top; vis W115°-272°, R272°-115°.

CAP DE LA HAGUE TO ST MALO

Cap de la Hague ☆ (Gros du Raz) 49°43'·31N 01° 57'·28W Fl 5s 48m **23M**; Gy Tr, W top; *Horn 30s.*
La Foraine 49°42'·87N 01°58'·49W; (occasionally submerged.)

◀ GOURY/DIÉLETTE

Goury Ldg Lts 065·2°. Front, 49°42'·89N 01°56'·70W QR 5m 7M; R □ on W □ on pier. Rear, 116m from front, Q 11m 7M; W pylon on hut. Intens 057·2°-075·2°.
Diélette W Bkwtr Dir Lt 125·4°. Front, Jetée Ouest 49°33'·17N 01°51'·83W Iso WRG 4s 12m W10M, R7M, G7M; W Tr, G top; vis: G070°-135°, W135°-145°, R145°-180°.
Breakwater Head ☆ 49°33'·17N 01°51'·83W Fl G 4s 6m 2M; vis: 115°-358°.
North Head ☆ 49°33'·21N 01°51'·80W Fl R 4s.
Banc des Dious 49°32'·56N 01°54'·03W Q (9) 15s.

◀ CARTERET/PORTBAIL

Cap de Carteret ☆ 49°22'·40N 01°48'·44W Fl (2+1) 15s 81m **26M**; Gy Tr, G top; *Horn (3) 60s.*
Trois-Grunes 49°21'·82N 01°55'·21W Q (9) 15s.
Plateau des Trois-Grunes 49°21'·76N 01°55'·01W; *Bell.*
Carteret Jetée Ouest Hd ☆ 49°22'·13N 01°47'·40W Oc R 4s 7m 7M; W post, R top.
Carteret Training wall Hd ☆ 49°22'·17N 01°47'·32W Fl G 2·5s 4m 2M; W post, G top.
Portbail PB 49°18'·39N 01°44'·75W.
Portbail 49°19'·22N 01°42'·99W.
Portbail 49°19'·30N 01°43'·35W.

Portbail Ldg Lts 042°. Front, La Caillourie 49°19'·74N 01°42'·52W Q 14m 10M; W pylon, R top. Rear, 870m from front, Oc 4s 20m 10M; belfry.
Portbail Training wall Hd ☆ 49°19'·43N 01°43'·01W Q (2) R 5s 5m 1M; W mast, R top.
49°19'·50N 01°42'·87W

◀ REGNÉVILLE

Internationale 49°01'·83N 01°48'·84W Q (9)15s.
International E 49°02'·13N 01°47'·18W.
International F 49°02'·25N 01°43'·03W.
Les Nattes 49°03'·52N 01°41'·87W; *Bell.*
La Catheue 48°57'·82N 01°42'·06W Q (6) + L Fl 15s.
No. 5 49°01'·13N 01°38'·21W.
Le Ronquet 49°00'·09N 01°38'·09W Fl (2) WR 6s 6/4M; vis: R100°-293°, W293°-100°.
No. 6 48°59'·37N 01°37'·37W.
Pte d'Agon ☆ 49°00'·25N 01°34'·60W Oc (2) WR 6s 12m W10M, R7M; W Tr, R top, W dwelling; vis: R063°-110°, W110°-063°.
Regnéville Dir Lt 028° 49°00'·69N 01°33'·37W Dir Oc WRG 4s 9m W12M, R9M, G9M; House; vis: G024°-027°, W027°-029°, R029°-033°.

PASSAGE DE LA DÉROUTE

Écrévière 49°15'·25N 01°52'·17W Q (6) + L Fl 15s; *Bell.*
Bas Jourdan 49°06'·83N 01°44'·16W Q (3) 10s; *Whis.*
Les Bœuf 49°06'·53N 01°47'·18W.
Les Bœuftins 49°06'·82N 01°45'·97W.
Le Sénéquet ☆ 49°05'·47N 01°39'·75W Fl (3) WR 12s 18m W13M, R10M; W Tr; vis: R083·5°-116·5°, W116·5°-083·5°.
Le Sénéquet 49°05'·95N 01°41'·21W.
Basse le Marié 49°01'·83N 01°48'·84W Q (9) 15s.
NE Minquiers 49°00'·84N 01°55'·31W VQ (3) 5s; *Bell.*
Les Ardentes 48°57'·77N 01°51'·64W Q (3) 10s.
SE Minquiers 48°53'·43N 02°00'·10W Q (3) 10s; *Bell.*
S Minquiers 48°53'·07N 02°10'·11W Q (6) + L Fl 15s.

◀ ÎLES CHAUSEY

La Petite Entrée 48°54'·53N 01°49'·59W.
Anvers Wk 48°53'·85N 01°40'·95W Q (3) 10s.
Basse du Founet 48°53'·27N 01°42'·33W: *Bell.*
Le Pignon ☆ 48°53'·47N 01°43'·40 W Oc (2) WR 6s 10m W11M, R8M; B Tr, Y band; vis: R005°-150°, W150°-005°.
La Haute Foraine 48°52'·89N 01°43'·70W.

Grande Île ☆ (Pte de la Tour) 48° 52'·17N 01°49'·36W Fl 5s 39m **23M**; Gy □ Tr; *Horn 30s.*
Channel 48°52'·12N 01°49'·09W Fl G 2s.
La Crabière Est 48°52'·47N 01°49'·41W Oc WRG 4s 5m W9M, R6M, G6M; B Tr, Y top; vis: W079°-291°, G291°-329°, W329°-335°, R335°-079°.
La Cancalaise 48°51'·92N 01°51'·16W.
Le Videcoq 48°49'·60N 01°42'·12W VQ (9) 10s; *Whis.*

◀ GRANVILLE

La Fourchie 48°50'·15N 01°37'·00W.
Pointe du Roc ☆ 48°50'·06N 01°36'·78W Fl (4) 15s 49m **23M**; Gy Tr, R top.
Le Loup 48°49'·57N 01°36'·25W Fl (2) 6s 8m 11M.
Jetée Est Head ☆ 48°49'·93N 01°36'·19W Iso G 4s 11m 6M.
Jetée Ouest Hd ☆ 48°49'·86N 01°36'·23W Iso R 4s 12m 6M.
Hérel Marina Head ☆ 48°49'·89N 01°35'·90W Fl R 4s 12m 8M; W ○ Tr, R top; *Horn (2) 40s.*
Hérel Marina Head ☆ 48°49'·93N 01°35'·90W Fl G 4s 4m 4M.

◀ CANCALE/ROTHENEUF

La Fille 48°44'·15N 01°48'·49W.
La Pierre-de-Herpin ☆ 48°43'·77N 01°48'·92W Oc (2) 6s 20m **17M**; W Tr, B top and base; *Siren Mo (N) 60s.*
Ruet 48°43'·38N 01°50'·15W.
Barbe Brûlée 48°42'·10N 01°50'·57W.
Cancale Jetty Hd ☆ 48°40'·08N 01°51'·13W Oc (3) G 12s 12m 7M; W pylon, G top, G hut; obsc when brg less than 223°.
Rothneuf Entrance 48°41'·36N 01°57'·71W.
B. Rochefort 48°42'·63N 01°57'·46W.
Rochefort 48°42'·83N 01°58'·24W.
Les Letruns 48°40'·74N 02°00'·53W.

ST MALO TO ST QUAY PORTRIEUX

◀ APPROACHES TO ST MALO

La St Servantine 48°41'·90N 02°00'·99W *Bell.*
La St Servantine 48°41'·95N 02°01'·02La W Fl (5) Y 20s.
Le Brunel 48°40'·84N 02°05'·28W Q (9) 15s; *Bell.*
La Plate 48°40'·78N 02°01'·92W Fl WRG 4s 11m, W10M, R7M, G7M; vis: W140°-203°, R203°-210°, W210°-225°, G225°-140°.

◀ CHENAL DE LA PETITE PORTE/ RADE DE ST MALO

Ldg Lts 128·7°. Front, **Le Grand Jardin** ☆ 48°40'·19N 02°04'·98W Fl (2) R 10s 24m **15M**; Gy Tr, R top. Rear, **La Balue** ☆, 4·08M from front, Dir FG 69m **25M**; Gy □ Tr; intens 128°-129·5°.
Vieux-Banc E 48°42'·38N 02°09'·12W Q; *Bell.*
View Banc W 48°41'·83N 02°10'·20W VQ (9) 10s.
St Malo Fairway 48°41'·38N 02°07'·28W L Fl 10s; *Whis.*
Les Courtis 48°40'·45N 02°05'·82W Fl (3) G 12s 14m 7M.

◀ CHENAL DE LA BIGNE/RADE DE ST MALO

Le Petite Bigne 48°41'·66N 01°58'·73W.
Les Létruns 48°40'·72N 02°00'·54W; *Bell.*
Les Bouton 48°40'·59N 02°01'·85W.
Roches-aux-Anglais 48°39'·65N 02°02'·27W Fl (2) G 6s.
Les Crapauds-du-Bey 48°39'·37N 02°02'·56W Fl (2) R 6s.

◀ CHENAL DE LA GRANDE PORTE

Ldg Lts 089·1°. **Front, Le Grand Jardin** ☆ 48°40'·19N 02°04'·98W Fl (2) R 10s 24m **15M**. Rear, **Rochebonne** ☆ 4·2M from front 48°40'·32N 01°58'·61W Dir FR 40m **24M**; Gy □ Tr, R top; intens 088·2°-089·7°.
Le Sou 48°40'·11N 02°05'·30W VQ (3) 5s; *Bell.*
Basse du Nord No. 5 48°39'·98N 02°05'·04W.
Les Pierres-Garnier No. 8 48°39'·98N 02°04'·41W.
Clef d'Aval No. 10 48°39'·72N 02°03'·91W.
Bas du Boujaron No. 1 48°40'·16N 02°05'·97W Fl G 4s; *Whis.*
No. 2 48°40'·19N 02°07'·58W Fl (3) R 12s; *Whis.*
Banchenou 48°40'·44N 02°11'·48W Fl (5) G 20s.
Buharats W No. 2 48°40'·22N 02°07'·49W Fl (3) R 12s; *Whis.*
Buharats E No. 4 48°40'·23N 02°07'·20W *Bell.*
Bassee du Boujaron No. 1 48°40'·16N 02°05'·97W Fl G 4s; *Whis.*

Ldg Lts 128·7°. Front, **Les Bas-Sablons** ☆ 48°38'·16N 02°01'·31W Dir FG 20m **22M**; W n Tr, B top; intens 127·5°-130·5°. Common rear, **La Balue** ☆, 0·9M from front Dir FG 69m **25M**; Gy □ Tr; intens 128·2°-129·7°.
Basse du Buron No. 12 48°39'·41N 02°03'·51W L Fl R 10s.
Le Buron 48°39'·32N 02°03'·66W Fl (2) G 6s 15m 7M; G Tr.
Plateau Rance Nord 48°38'·64N 02°02'·35W VQ.
Plateau Rance Sud 48°38'·43N 02°02'·28W Q (6) + L Fl 15s.

◀ ST MALO

Ldg Lts 070·7°. Écluse du Naye Front, 48°38'·58N 02°01'·49W FR 7m 3M. Rear, FR 23m 7M; vis: 030°-120°.
La Grenouille 48°38'·34N 02°02'·00W Fl (4) G 15s.
Môle des Noires Hd ☆ 48°38'·52N 02°01'·91W Fl R 5s 11m 13M; W Tr, R top; *Horn (2) 20s.*
3rd Caisson Jetty Hd ☆ 48°38'·44N 02°01'·76W Fl R 4s 3m 1M; vis: 080°-260°.
Bas-Sablons Marina Môle Head ☆ 48°38'·41N 02°01'·70W Fl G 4s 7m 5M; Gy mast.

◀ LA RANCE

Zl 12 48°37'·47N 02°01'·62W Fl R 4s.
La Jument 48°37'·44N 02°01'·76W Fl (5) G 20s 6m 3M; G Tr.
Tidal barrage, NW wall ☆ 48°37'·06N 02°01'·73W Fl G 4s 6m 5M, G pylon, vis: 191°-291°.
NE dolphin ☆ 48°37'·09N 02°01'·71W Fl (2) R 6s 6m 5M; vis: 040°-200°.
Tidal barrage, SW wall ☆ 48°37'·00N 02°01'·70W Iso G 4s.
SE dolphin ☆ 48°36'·97N 02°01'·66W Oc (2) R 6s.
Zl 20 48°36'·86N 02°01'·57W Fl R 4s.

◀ ST BRIAC/ST CAST

Embouchure du Fremur. Dir Lt 125° 48°37'·07N 02°08'·20W Dir Iso WRG 4s 10m W13M, R11M, G11M; W mast on hut, vis: G121·5°-124·5°, W124·5°-125·5°, R125·5°-129·5°.
Les Bourdinots 48°39'·00N 02°13'·50W.
St Cast Môle Hd ☆ 48°38'·40N 02°14'·63W Iso WG 4s 11m W11M, G8M; G and W structure; vis: W204°-217°, G217°-233°, W233°-245°, G245°-204°.
Cap Fréhel ☆ 48°41'·04N 02°19'·14W Fl (2) 10s 85m **29M**; Gy □ Tr, G lantern; *Horn (2) 60s.*

◀ CHENAL D'ERQUY/ERQUY/VAL-ANDRÉ

Les Justières 48°40'·56N 02°26'·49W Q (6) + L Fl 15s.
Basses du Courant 48°39'·21N 02°29'·17W VQ (6) + L Fl 10s.
Les Chatelets 48°38'·96N 02°28'·99W.
L'Evette 48°38'·50N 02°31'·46W.
Erquy S Môle Hd ☆ 48°38'·06N 02°28'·66W Oc (2+1) WRG 12s 11m W11M, R8M, G8M; W Tr, R top; vis: R055°-081°, W081°-094°, G094°-111°, W111°-120°, R120°-134°.
Erquy Inner Jetty Hd ☆ 48°38'·09N 02°28'·38W Fl R 2·5s 10m 3M; R&W Tr.
Petit Bignon 48°36'·85N 02°35'·01W.

◀ PORT DE DAHOUET

La Dahouet 48°35'·21N 02°35'·37W.
La Petite-Muette 48°34'·85N 02°34'·30W Fl WRG 4s 10m W9M, R6M, G6M; △ on G & W Tr; vis: G055°-114°, W114°-146°, R146°-196°.
Dahouet ent Fl (2) G 6s 5m 1M; vis: 156°-286°.

◀ BAIE DE SAINT BRIEUC

Grand Léjon ☆ 48°44'·90N 02°39'·87W Fl (5) WR 20s 17m **W18M**, R14M; R Tr, W bands; vis: R015°-058°, W058°-283°, R283°-350°, W350°-015°.
Le Rohein 48°38'·80N 02°37'·77W VQ (9) WRG 10s 13m W10M, R7M, G7M; Y Tr, B band; vis: R072°-105°, W105°-180°, G180°-193°, W193°-237°, G237°-282°, W282°-301°. G301°-330°, W330°-072°.

◀ LE LÉGUÉ (St BRIEUC)

Tra-Hillion 48°33'·38N 02°38'·52W.
Le Légué 48°34'·32N 02°41'·16W Mo (A)10s; *Whis.*
No. 1 48°32'·37N 02°42'·39W.
No. 1A 48°32'·23N 02°42'·78W.
No. 2 48°32'·12N 02°42'·51W.
Pointe à l'Aigle Jetty ☆ 48°32'·09N 02°43'·13W VQ G 13m 8M; W Tr, G top; vis: 160°-070°.
Custom House Jetty ☆ 48°31'·89N 02°43'·43W Iso G 4s 6m 2M, W cols, G top.
No. 8 48°31'·87N 02°43'·32W Fl R 2s.
No. 9 48°31'·85N 02°43'·43W Fl G 2s.
No.12 48°31'·69N 02°43'·60W.

◀ BINIC

Binic Môle de Penthièvre Head ☆ 48°36'·06N 02°48'·93W Oc (3) 12s 12m 11M; W Tr, G lantern; unintens 020°-110°.

◀ SAINT-QUAY-PORTRIEUX

Les Hors 48°39'·60N 02°44'·04W; *Bell.*
Caffa 48°37'·81N 02°43'·09W Q (3) 10s.
La Longue 48°37'·89N 02°44'·69W.
La Roselière 48°37'·45N 02°46'·43W VQ (9) 10s.
Herflux Dir Lt 130° 48°39'·06N 02°47'·95W Dir Fl (2) WRG 6s 10m W8M, R6M, G6M; vis: G115°-125°, W125°-135°, R135°-145°.
Elbow ☆ 48°38'·99N 02°49'·09W Dir Iso WRG 4s 16m **W15M**, R11M, G11M; vis: 159°-179°, G179°-316°, W316°-320·5°, R320·5°-159°; Reserve Lt ranges 12/9M.
Madeux 48°40'·40N 02°48'·81W.
Île Harbour Roches de Saint-Quay ☆ 48°39'·99N 02°48'·50W Oc (2) WRG 6s 16m W10M, R8M, G8M; vis: R011°-133°, G133°-270°, R270°-306°, G306°-358°, W358°-011°.
Grandes Moulières 48°39'·76N 02°49'·91W.
Moulières de Portrieux 48°39'·25N 02°49'·21W.
Les Noirs 48°39'·09N 02°48·46W.
NE Môle Hd ☆ 48°38'·83N 02°49'·03W Fl (3) G 12s 10m 2M.
SE Môle Hd ☆ 48°38'·90N 02°48'·84W Fl (3) R 12s 10m 2M.

9.15.5 PASSAGE INFORMATION

Current Pilots for this area include: *N Brittany and CI Cruising Companion* (Macmillan Reeds/Cumberlidge); *Shell Channel Pilot* (Imray/Cunliffe); *Normandy and CI Pilot* (Adlard Coles/ Brackenbury) as far W as St Malo; *N Brittany Pilot* (Imray/RCC) W'ward from St Malo; Admiralty *Channel Pilot.* Charts *2669* and *1106 cover t*he whole area.

Off the French coastline between Pte de Barfleur and Cap Lévi rky shoals extend up to 2·5M seaward. From C. Lévi around C. de la Hague and S to C. de Flamanville the coast is cleaner with few dangers extending more than 1M offshore. Southward to Mont St Michel and W to St Malo the coast changes to extensive offshore shoals, sand dunes studded with rks and a series of drying hbrs. From St Malo to St Quay-Portrieux the coast is characterised by deep bays (often drying), a few rugged headlands and many offlying rks.

The sea areas around this coast, including the Channel Islands, are dominated by powerful tidal streams with an anti-clockwise rotational pattern and a very large tidal range. Across the top of the Cotentin Peninsula and between C. de la Hague and Alderney the main English Channel tidal streams are rectilinear E/W. Neap tides are best, particularly for a first visit, and tidal streams need to be worked carefully. Boats which can take the ground have an advantage for exploring the shallower hbrs. Be careful to avoid lobster pots, and oyster and mussel beds in some rivers and bays.

CROSSING FROM UK TO CHERBOURG OR ALDERNEY The popular cross-Channel route from hbrs between Portland and Chichester to those on the Cotentin peninsula or in the Channel Islands is normally straightforward in summer, but can never be taken for granted. Review the planning guidelines in 9.3.5, especially at the start of the season. Cross-Channel distances are in 9.0.6 and waypoints in 9.1.7. Note any tidal constraints shown under the departure hbr itself. Other local factors to be considered include:

Portland & Weymouth: the Portland Race and Shambles Bank both require a wide berth. Check the tidal streams for possible wind-over-tide conditions.

Poole: leave hbr on the ebb, but at springs with a S/SE wind beware short steep seas in the Swash Channel; off Handfast, Peveril and Anvil Pts overfalls occur with wind against tide.

From **Solent ports** decide whether to leave via the Needles or east of the IOW. The former usually requires a fair tide through Hurst Narrows (HW Portsmouth –1 to +4½), which in turn will dictate your ETD from hbr. The latter has no tidal gate, but is longer and may give a less favourable slant if the wind is in the SW; in W'lies it offers better shelter in the lee of the IOW. In practice the nearer exit may prove to be the obvious choice.

On passage the greatest hazard is likely to be crossing the shipping lanes, especially if fog/poor vis are forecast when it may be safest not to sail. Whether crossing at the Casquets TSS, or further up-Channel, is almost academic; the risk of collision with another ship is the same. Finally, review destination(s) and possible hbrs of refuge:

Braye (Alderney), whilst accessible at all times, presents a slight risk, especially at springs, of being swept past Alderney on a W-going tide. The yacht may then clew up in Guernsey, having unwittingly negotiated the Swinge or the Alderney Race. The moral is to plan and monitor track so as to approach from well up-tide. (For Guernsey, Sark & Jersey see 9.14.5).

French ports on the W side of the Cotentin (Diélette to Granville) are tidally constrained and exposed to the W; they are however in a lee with anticyclonic Easterlies.

Cherbourg is accessible at all times. On closing the coast specially at springs, a very large drift angle may be needed to maintain track. To the E (see Area 22), **Barfleur** dries; **St Vaast** is a safe anch, if awaiting lock opening into marina.

POINTE DE BARFLEUR TO CAP DE LA HAGUE (AC *1106*) The N coast of the Cotentin Peninsula runs E/W for 26M, mostly bordered by rks which extend 2·5M offshore from Pte de Barfleur to C. Lévi, and 1M offshore between Pte de Jardeheu and C. de la Hague. Tidal streams reach 5kn at sp, and raise a steep sea with wind against tide.

Pte de Barfleur has dangers up to 2M offshore, and a race, in which the sea breaks heavily, extends 3-4M NE and E from the lt ho. In bad weather, particularly with winds from NW or SE against the tide, it is necessary to keep at least 6M to seaward to avoid the worst effects; in calmer conditions the Pte can be rounded close inshore.

The inner passage between Pte de Barfleur and C. Lévi, keeping S of three cardinal buoys, is not recommended without local knowledge except in good weather and visibility when the transits shown on chart *1106* can be used. Tidal streams run strongly with considerable local variations.

Off C. Lévi a race develops with wind against tide, and extends nearly 2M to N. Port Lévi and Port de Becquet are two small drying hbrs E of Cherbourg. Off Cherbourg (9.15.8) the stream is E-going from about HW – 0430 and W-going from HW + 0230.

Close inshore between Cherbourg and C. de la Hague a back eddy runs W. As an alternative to Omonville (9.15.9) there is anch in Anse de St Martin, about 2M E of C. de la Hague, open to N, but useful to await the tide in the Alderney Race.

THE ALDERNEY RACE (chart *3653*) The Alderney Race, so called due to very strong tidal streams, runs SW/NE between C. de la Hague and Alderney. The fairway, approx 4M wide, is bounded by Race Rk and Alderney S Banks to the NW, and to the SE by rky banks 4M WSW of C. de la Hague, Milieu and Banc de la Schôle (least depth 2·7m). These dangers which cause breaking seas and heavy overfalls should be carefully avoided. In bad weather and strong wind-against-tide conditions the seas break in all parts of the Race and passage is not recommended. Conditions are exacerbated at sp tides.

In mid-chan the the SW-going stream starts at HW St Helier + 0430 (HW Dover) and the NE-going stream at HW St Helier –0210 (HW Dover + 0530), sp rates both 5·5kn. The times at which the stream turns do not vary much for various places, but the rates do; for example, 1M W of C. de la Hague the sp rates reach 7 to 8kn.

To obtain optimum conditions, timing is of the essence. As a rule of thumb the Race should be entered on the first of the fair tide so as to avoid the peak tidal stream with attendant overfalls/seas. Thus, bound SW, arrrive off C. de la Hague at around HW St Helier + 0430 (HW Dover) when the stream will be slack, whilst just starting to run SW off Alderney. A yacht leaving Cherbourg at HW Dover – 0300 will achieve the above timing by utilising the inshore W-going tidal eddy.

Conversely, NE bound, leave St Peter Port, say, at approx local HW St Helier – 0430 (HWD+3) with a foul tide so as to pass Banc de la Schôle as the first of the fair tide starts to make. A later departure should achieve a faster passage, but with potentially less favourable conditions in the Race. On the NE stream the worst overfalls are on the French side.

CAP DE LA HAGUE TO ST MALO (charts *3659*, 3656, *3655*, *3653*) The Jobourg radar surveillance station (CROSS) and atomic energy station Chy (R lts) are conspic about 3-4M SE of Gros du Raz (lt, fog sig), off C de la Hague. 5M S of C de la Hague beware Les Huquets de Jobourg, an extensive bank of drying and submerged rks, and Les Huquets de Vauville (dry) close SE of them.

The W coast of the Cotentin Peninsula is exposed, and is mostly rky and inhospitable; along much of this coast S of Carteret there is little depth of water, so that a nasty sea can build. Dielette* (9.15.10) has H24 access for 1·5m draught if coefficient is <80; clearing close to Cap de la Hague 2H before the end of the ebb should allow arrival at HW. The drying hbrs/non-tidal marinas* at Goury, Carteret* (9.15.11) and Portbail (9.15.12) are more readily accessible if cruising from S to N on the tide, since all hbrs are restricted by drying approaches.

The two main chans from/to the Alderney Race are Déroute de Terre and, further offshore, Passage de la Déroute. Neither chan are well marked in places, and are not advised at night. The former leads between Plateau des Trois Grunes and Carteret, between Basses de Portbail and Bancs Félés, between Le Sénéquet lt tr and Basse Jourdan, and E of Îles Chausey toward Pte du Roc, off Granville (9.15.13). The S end of this chan, E of Îles Chausey, is very shallow; for detailed directions see *Channel Pilot*.

The Passage de la Déroute passes W of Plateau des Trois Grunes, between Basses de Taillepied and Les Écrehou, between Chaussée de Boeufs and Plateau de l'Arconie, E and SE of Les Minquiers and Les Ardentes, and W of Îles Chausey (9.15.14).

To the S of Granville is the drying expanse of B du Mont St Michel. Proceeding W, the drying hbr of Cancale (9.15.15) with many oyster beds and a fair weather anch SE of Île des Rimains, lies 4M S of Pte du Grouin, off which the many dangers are marked by La Pierre-de-Herpin (lt, fog sig). The large drying inlet of Rothéneuf, with anch off in good weather, is 4M E of St Malo (9.15.15 and chart 2700).

ST MALO TO L'OST PIC (charts *3674, 3659*) In the apprs to St Malo (chart 2700) are many islets, rks and shoals, between which are several chans that can be used in good vis. Tidal streams reach 4kn at sp, and can set across chans. From E and N, with sufficient rise of tide and good vis, Chenal de la Bigne, Chenal des Petits Pointus or Chenal de la Grande Conchée can be used, but they all pass over or near to drying patches. From the W and NW, Chenal de la Grande Porte and Chenal de la Petite Porte are the easiest routes and are well marked/lit. Chenal du Décollé is a shallow, demanding inshore route from the W, and no shorter than Chenal de la Grande Porte.

By passing through the lock at W end of the R. Rance barrage (9.15.16) it is possible to cruise up river to Dinan, via the lock at Châtelier (SHOM chart 4233). At Dinan is the entrance to the Canal d'Ille et Rance to Biscay (9.15.17).

6M NW of St Malo beware Le Vieux-Banc (dries). Here the E-going stream begins at HW St Helier – 0555, and the W-going at HW St Helier – 0015, sp rates 2·5kn. There are W-going eddies very close inshore on the E-going stream. Between St Malo and C. Fréhel is St Cast hbr (9.15.18), and there are anchs S of Île Agot in the apprs to the drying hbr of St Briac, in B de l'Arguenon and B de la Fresnaye. From C. Fréhel to C. d'Erquy there are no worthwhile hbrs.

About 3ca off Cap d'Erquy, and inshore of the various rky patches close to seaward Chenal d'Erquy runs WSW/ENE into the E side of the B de St Brieuc. Erquy is a pleasant, drying hbr, but often crowded with fishing boats. The Plateau du Rohein (lt), at W end of a long ridge, is 6M W of C. d'Erquy. There are several rky shoals within the B itself, some extending nearly 2M offshore.

To seaward of Bay de St Brieuc is Grand Léjon (lt), a rky shoal 9M NE of St Quay-Portrieux. Rks extend 2½ca W and 8ca NNE of the lt ho. Petit Léjon (dries) lies 3·5M SSE of lt ho. From the N/NW, keep W of these dangers via a chan 3-4M wide which gives access to the shallow, partly drying S end of the Bay and the hbrs of Val André, Dahouet (9.15.18), Le Légué/St Brieux (9.15.19), and Binic (9.15.20). On the W side of Bay de St Brieuc, Roches de St Quay and offlying patches extend 4M E from St Quay-Portrieux (9.15.21) which can only be approached from NW or SE.

To the N and NE of L'Ost-Pic extensive offshore shoals guard the approaches to Paimpol (9.16.8), Ile de Bréhat and the Trieux river. Further N, the Plateau de Barnouic and Plateau des Roches Douvres (lt, fog sig, RC) should be avoided. Here the E-going stream begins at about HW St Malo – 0400 and the W-going at about HW St Malo +0100 with Sp rates exceeding 4kn.

9.15.6 DISTANCE TABLE

Approximate distances in nautical miles are by the most direct route, whilst avoiding dangers and allowing for Traffic Separation Schemes. See also 9.19.6 for distances between Barfleur and Grandcamp-Maisy. Places in *italics* are in adjoining areas; places in **bold** are in 9.0.6, Cross-Channel Distances.

1.	Calais	1																			
2.	*Barfleur*	148	2																		
3.	**Cherbourg**	160	20	**3**																	
4.	Omonville	163	27	10	**4**																
5.	Cap de la Hague	167	32	18	6	**5**															
6.	*Braye (Alderney)*	172	41	25	15	9	**6**														
7.	***St Peter Port***	193	60	44	34	28	23	**7**													
8.	*Creux (Sark)*	190	55	37	29	23	22	10	**8**												
9.	***St Helier***	213	77	64	51	45	46	29	24	**9**											
10.	Carteret	192	55	41	29	23	28	31	23	26	**10**										
11.	Portbail	196	59	49	33	27	32	35	27	25	5	**11**									
12.	Iles Chausey	222	87	69	61	55	58	48	43	25	33	30	**12**								
13.	Granville	227	93	75	67	61	66	55	50	30	38	35	9	**13**							
14.	Dinan	250	117	102	91	85	85	66	64	50	62	59	29	35	**14**						
15.	**St Malo**	238	105	90	79	73	73	54	52	38	50	47	17	23	12	**15**					
16.	Dahouet	240	106	88	80	74	72	54	52	41	60	59	37	45	41	29	**16**				
17.	Le Légué/St Brieux	244	110	96	86	78	76	57	56	46	69	69	41	49	45	33	8	**17**			
18.	Binic	244	115	95	84	78	75	56	55	46	70	70	43	51	45	33	10	8	**18**		
19.	**St Quay-Portrieux**	244	106	88	80	74	73	56	51	46	64	64	47	54	47	35	11	7	4	**19**	
20.	***Lézardrieux***	238	106	88	80	74	68	48	38	47	68	71	53	54	61	49	33	32	30	21	**20**

9.15.7 SPECIAL NOTES FOR FRANCE (Areas 15 to 18 & 22)

Some minor differences in the information for French hbrs are: Instead of 'County' the 'Département' is given. French Standard Time is –0100 (ie 1300 Standard Time in France is 1200UT), DST not having been taken into account. For details of documentation apply to the French Tourist Office, 178 Piccadilly, London, W1V 0AL; ☎ 0906 824 4123, 📠 020 7493 6594.

AFFAIRES MARITIMES In every French port there is a representative of the central government, L'Administration Maritime, known as Affaires Maritimes. This organisation watches over all maritime activities (commercial, fishing, pleasure) and helps them develop harmoniously. Information on navigation and other maritime issues can be supplied by a local representative whose ☎ is given under each port. The Head Office is: Ministère Chargé de la Mer, Bureau de la Navigation de Plaisance, 3 Place Fontenoy, 75007 Paris, ☎ 01 44 49 80 00.

CHARTS Two types of French chart are shown: SHOM as issued by the *Service Hydrographique et Oceanographique de la Marine*, the French Navy's Hydrographic Service; ECM *Éditions Cartographiques Maritimes* are charts for sea and river navigation. Notes: Under 'Facilities', SHOM means a chart agent. Any new edition of a SHOM chart receives a new, different chart number. SHOM charts refer elevations of lights, bridges etc to Mean Level (ML), not to MHWS as on Admiralty charts.

TIDAL COEFFICIENTS See 9.16.24 for Coefficients based on Brest, together with explanatory notes and French tidal terms.

PUBLIC HOLIDAYS New Year's Day, Easter Sunday and Monday, Labour Day (1 May), Ascension Day, Armistice Day 1945 (8 May), Whit Sunday and Monday, National (Bastille) Day (14 July), Feast of the Assumption (15 Aug), All Saints' Day (1 Nov), Remembrance Day (11 Nov), Christmas Day.

French Glossary: see introduction.

FACILITIES At some marinas fuel can only be obtained/paid for by using a French credit card (of the smart variety) in a slot machine. If not in possession of such a card, it may be possible to persuade a Frenchman to use his card on your behalf and to reimburse him in cash. The cost shown for a visitor's overnight berth is unavoidably the previous year's figure. It is based on high season rates and is where possible expressed as cost/metre LOA, although beam may be taken into account at some ports. Low season rates and concessions can much reduce costs. The fee usually includes electricity, but rarely showers which range between €1.20 and €2.

TELEPHONES ☎ Nos contain 10 digits, the first 2 digits being Zone codes (01 to 05), as appropriate to location. Mobile ☎ Nos are prefixed 06. Info Nos, eg the recorded weather (Auto) are prefixed 08. The ringing tone is long, equal on/off tones (slower than UK engaged tone). Rapid pips mean the call is being connected. Engaged tone is like that in UK. A recorded message means ☎ No unobtainable.
To telephone France from UK, dial 00 33, followed by the 9 digit number, ie omitting the 0 from the Zone code prefix. To telephone UK from France dial 00 44 followed by the Area Code (omitting the first 0) and the number. **Emergencies**: Dial 18 for Fire, 17 Police, 15 Ambulance; or 112 as used in all EC countries. Phonecards for public 'phones may be bought at the PTT or at many Hr offices, cafés and tabacs. Cheap rates are 2130-0800 Mon-Fri 1330-0800 Sat-Mon.

SIGNALS Standard sets of Traffic, Storm Warning and Tidal signals apply in all French ports unless otherwise stated.

Traffic Signals

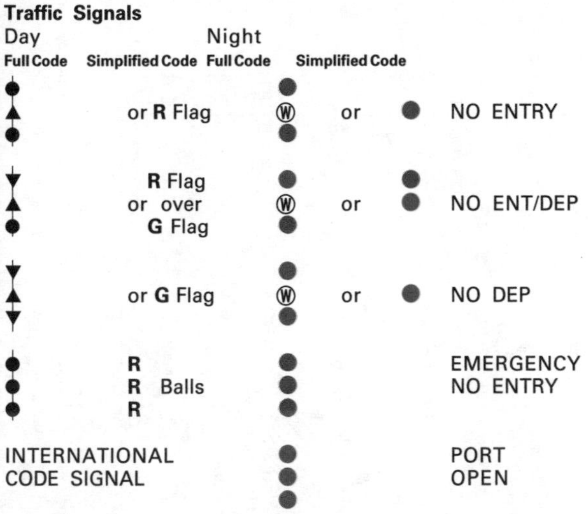
Day
Night
Full Code
Simplified Code
Full Code
Simplified Code
or R Flag
or
NO ENTRY
R Flag
or over
G Flag
or
NO ENT/DEP
or G Flag
or
NO DEP
R
R Balls
R
EMERGENCY
NO ENTRY
INTERNATIONAL
CODE SIGNAL
PORT
OPEN

A Black Flag indicates a shipping casualty in the area. Flag 'P' sometimes indicates that lock or dock gates are open.

Storm Signals (International System)

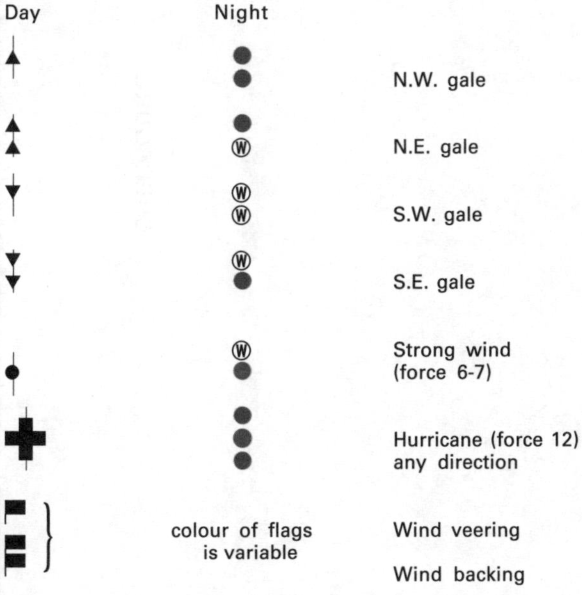
Day
Night
N.W. gale
N.E. gale
S.W. gale
S.E. gale
Strong wind
(force 6-7)
Hurricane (force 12)
any direction
colour of flags
is variable
Wind veering
Wind backing

In France, Ⓦ Lts, Q or IQ, by day only, indicate forecast wind >F6, as follows: Q = within 3 hrs; IQ = within 6 hrs.

Tidal Signals
There are two sets of signals, one showing the state of the tide and the other showing the height of tide.
a. State of the tide is shown by:

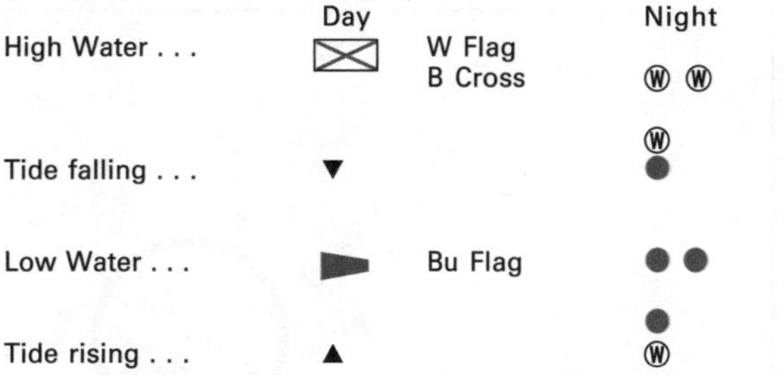
Day
Night
High Water . . .
W Flag
B Cross
Tide falling . . .
Low Water . . .
Bu Flag
Tide rising . . .

b. The height of tide signals show the height above CD by adding together the values of the various shapes.

Day: ▼ = 0·2m; ■ = 1·0m; ● = 5·0m. Night: ● = 0·2m; ● = 1·0m; Ⓦ = 5·0m. The three different shapes are shown horizontally, with ▼s to the left of ■s and ●s to the right, viewed from seaward. Lights are disposed similarly.

The following examples will help to explain:

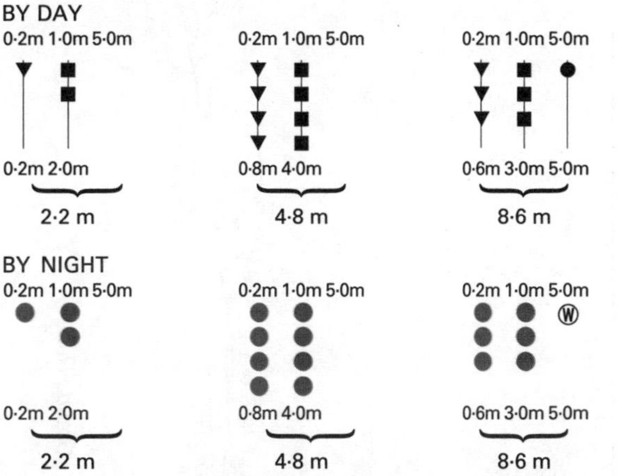
BY DAY
0·2m 1·0m 5·0m
0·2m 1·0m 5·0m
0·2m 1·0m 5·0m
0·2m 2·0m
0·8m 4·0m
0·6m 3·0m 5·0m
2·2 m
4·8 m
8·6 m
BY NIGHT
0·2m 1·0m 5·0m
0·2m 1·0m 5·0m
0·2m 1·0m 5·0m
0·2m 2·0m
0·8m 4·0m
0·6m 3·0m 5·0m
2·2 m
4·8 m
8·6 m

TOLLS AND QUALIFICATIONS ON INLAND WATERWAYS Tolls are due on waterways managed by Voies Navigable de France (VNF), ie those E of a line Le Havre to Bordeaux, plus the R. Loire. See also 9.15.17. In 2000 licences were available for either one year, 30 days (not necessarily consecutive), 16 consecutive days or 1 day. The rates, based on 5 categories of boat area, ie LOA x Beam (m) = m^2, were as follows in French francs:

	<12m²	12-25m²	25-40m²	40-60m²	>60m²
1 Year	469	678	1356	2191	2713
30 days	271	485	855	1330	1649
16 days	104	209	313	417	521
1 day	51	102	153	204	256

Licence stickers (*vignettes*) must be visibly displayed stbd side forward; they are obtainable in person or by post from VNF offices at Le Havre, Rouen, Calais and Dunkerque and at tobacco shops and larger centres on the canals; or from: Librairie VNF, 18 Quai d'Austerlitz, 75013 Paris; ☎ 01.45.84.85.69.
Detailed brochure from: French National Tourist Office, 178 Piccadilly, London W1V 0AL; ☎ 020 7629 2869, 📠 020 7493 6594; Info 0891 244123. Or: VNF Head Office, 175 Rue Ludovic Boutleux, BP 820, 62400 Bethune, France. ☎ 03.21.63.24.24; 📠 03.21.63.24.42. Web site: www.vnf.fr
Helmsmen of craft <15m LOA and not capable of >20 kph (11kn) must have a Helmsman's Overseas Certificate of Competence or International Certificate of Competence, plus a copy of the French CEVNI rules. For larger, faster craft the requirements are under review. On some canals automatic locks are activated by an electronic blipper called *Sesame* which is issued to vessels in transit. Loss of or damage to *Sesame* may incur fines of €150 to 12,200. Specific notification may be required to obtain insurance cover against this risk.

CHERBOURG *9.15.8*

Manche **49°38'·94N 01°37'·11W** (Marina ent)

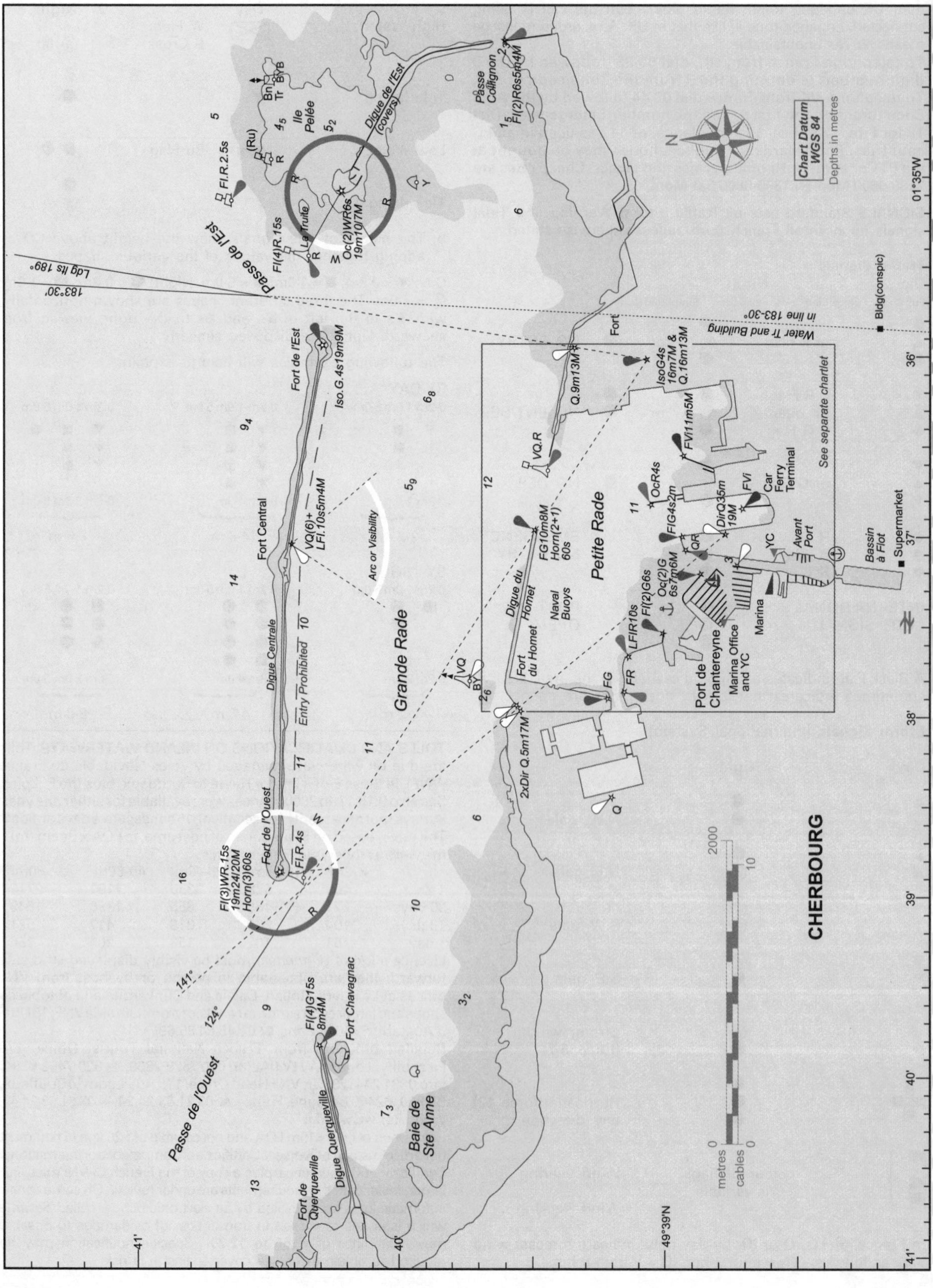

CHERBOURG *continued*

CHARTS AC 2602, *1106*, *2669*; SHOM 7120; ECM 528, 1014; Imray C32, C33A; Stanfords 7, 16, 21.

TIDES –0308 Dover; ML 3·8; Duration 0535; Zone –0100

SHELTER Excellent; hbr accessible in all tides and weather. Visitors berth in 2·6m on pontoons M, N, P & Q, on S side of Chantereyne Marina. There is also a small craft ⚓ N of marina bkwtr. Lock into Bassin à Flot (HW±1) provides10 ⓥ berths; br opens (Ch 06) HW-45m and HW + 45m. Good ⚓ in Baie de Ste Anne

NAVIGATION WPT **Passe de l'Ouest** 49°41´·04N 01°39´·88W, 321°/141° from/to W ent, 0·85M. Note: CH1 SWM spar buoy, L Fl 10s, bears 323° from Fort de l'Ouest 3·5M. WPT **Passe de l'Est** 49°40´·94N 01°35´·78W, 000°/180° from/to E ent, 0·65M. For coastal features from Cap de la Hague to Pte de Barfleur see 9.22.5. There are 3 ents:

1. Passe de l'Ouest (W ent) is the easiest. Rks extend about 80m from each bkwtr. From W, the white sector of Fort de l'Ouest lt (bearing more than 122° by day) keeps clear of offlying dangers E of Cap de la Hague.
2. Passe de l'Est (E ent) carries 6m. Keep to W side of chan (but at least 80m off Fort de l'Est) to avoid dangers W of Ile Pelée marked by PHM buoy, Fl (4) R 15s, and by 2 unlit bn trs on N side which must be given a wide berth.
3. Passe Collignon is a shallow (2m) chan, 93m wide, through Digue de l'Est (covers), near the shore. Not recommended except in good conditions and near HW.

Entry is prohibited in the area S of the Digue Centrale due to fish farms and in the area shown adjacent to the Port Militaire. Anchoring is prohibited in the area of the Passe de L'Ouest and the Passe de L'Est. Speed limits: Grande Rade14kn, Petite Rade 8kn.

LIGHTS AND MARKS There are three powerful lts near Cherbourg:

1. To the E, Cap Levi, Fl R 5s 36m 22M; and further E,
2. Pte de Barfleur, Fl (2) 10s 72m 29M;
3. To the W, Cap de la Hague, Fl 5s 48m 23M;

Further W, the lts of Alderney (Quenard Pt, Fl (4) 15s 37m 28M) and Casquets, Fl (5) 30s 37m 24M, can often be seen. See 9.14.4, 9.15.4 and 9.22.4 for details. Fort de l'Ouest lt, at W end of Digue Centrale, Fl (3) WR 15s 19m 24/20M, vis W122°-355°, R355°-122°, Reed (3) 60s. Close SSW is PHM buoy, Fl R 4s, marking shoal. Passe de l'Ouest ldg lts 140·5°: Gare Maritime lt, Dir Q 35m 21M, in line with centre of 2Q (hor) 5m 15M at base of Digue du Homet. Grande Rade ldg lts 124°: Front FG 10m 9M, W pylon, G top, on blockhouse; rear, 0·75M from front, Iso G 4s 16m 12M, W column, B bands, W top, intens 114°-134°. Passe de l'Est is covered by 189° Ldg Lts as shown on plan. Inside Petite Rade steer 200° for marina ent, QR and Oc (2) G 6s. Shore lights may be confusing and mask nav lts.

RADIO TELEPHONE Marina: call *Chantereyne* Ch 09 72 (0800-2300LT). Cherbourg commercial port: call *Le Homet* Ch 12 16. *Jobourg Traffic* Ch **13** 16 (H24) provides radar surveillance of the Casquets TSS/ITZ and from Mont St Michel to Cap d'Antifer. Radar assistance is available on request, Ch 80, to vessels in the sector from due W to due N, out to 35M, from Jobourg Centre at 49°41'N 01°54'·5W. Jobourg also broadcasts traffic, nav and weather info in English and French on Ch 80 at H+20 & H+50; and at H+05 & H+35, when visibility< 2M.

TELEPHONE Marina 02·33·87·65·70; 📠 02·33·53·21·12; Hr Mr (Port) 02·33·20·41·25; Lock 02·33·44·23·18; Aff Mar 02·33·23·36·12; ⊖ 02·33·23·34·02; CROSS 02·33·52·72·13; Météo 02·33·53·53·44; Auto 08.36.68.08.50; Police 02·33·44·20·22; Ⓗ 02·33·20·70·00; Dr 02·33·53·05·68; Brit Consul 01·33·44·20·13. Lock 02·33·44·23·18.

FACILITIES Port de Plaisance ☎ 02·33·87·65·70, 📠 02·33·53·21·12, access H24, (900+300 ⓥ on N, P, Q pontoons), €2, Slip, AC, FW, ME, El, Sh, BH (30 ton), CH, P & D (0800-1200; 1400-1900), ♿; email: cherbourg.marina@wanadoo.fr and www.ville-cherbourg.fr:**YC de Cherbourg** ☎ 02·33·53·02·83, FW, R, Bar; **Services:** ME, El, Ⓔ, Sh, CH, M, SM, SHOM. **City** P, D, Gaz, V, R, Bar, ✉, Ⓑ, ⓑ, ≈, ✈ (☎ 02·33.22.91.32). Ferry: Portsmouth, Poole.

MINOR HARBOURS TO THE EAST OF CHERBOURG

PORT DU BECQUET, Manche, **49°39´·24N 01°32´·88W**. AC *1106*; SHOM 7120. Tides as 9.15.8. Dries with clean sand bottom. Shelter is good except in winds from N to E when a strong scend occurs. Secure to S of jetty (which lies E/W). Ldg lts 186·5°: Front Dir Oc (2+1) 12s 8m 10M, W 8-sided tr, intens 183·5°-190·5°; rear, 49m from front, Dir Oc (2+1) R 12s 13m 7M, synch, also in W 8-sided tr. Facilities: very few; all facilities at Cherbourg 2·5M.

PORT DE LÉVI, Manche, **49°41´·24 N 01°28´·38W**. AC *1106*; SHOM 7092, 5609; HW –0310 on Dover (UT); +0024 on Cherbourg. HW ht +0·2m on Cherbourg. Dries. Shelter good except in winds SW to N. Secure bows on to NE side below white wall, amongst small FVs. Lt is F RG 7m 7M, G050°-109°, R109°-140°. Keep in G sector. By day keep the white wall and lt between the white marks on each pier hd. Beware lobster pots. Facilities: Peace. Fermanville (1·5M) has V, R, Bar.

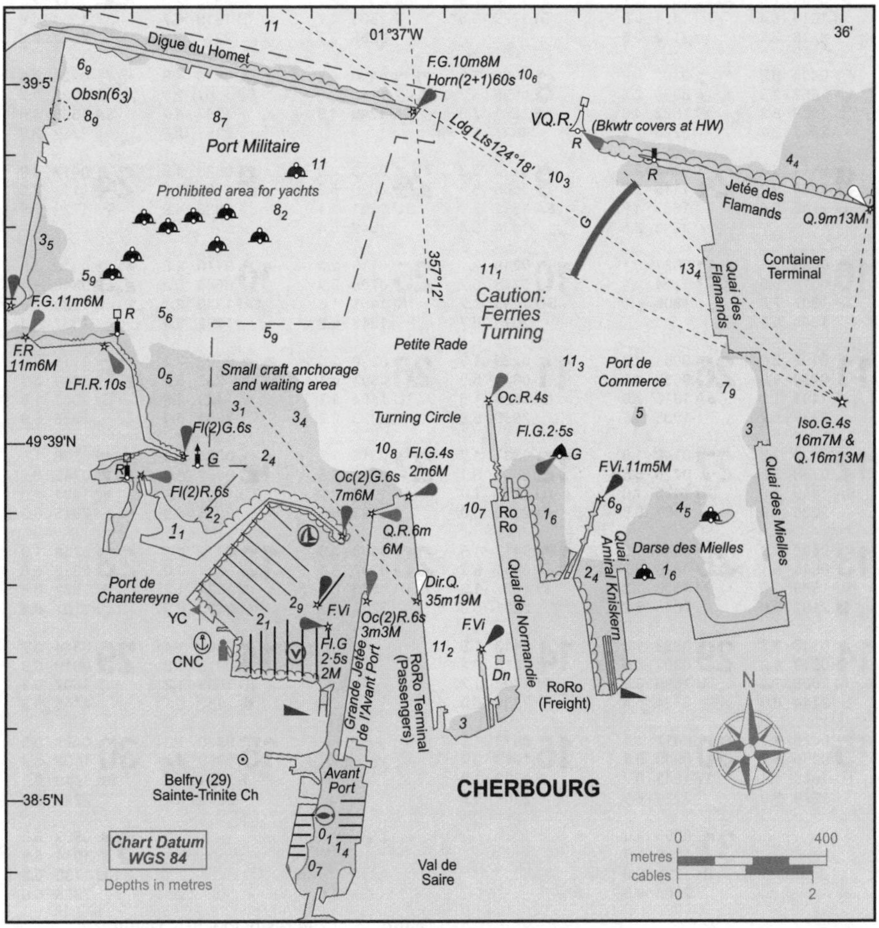

TIME ZONE -0100
(French Standard Time)
Subtract 1 hour for UT
For French Summer Time add ONE hour in **non-shaded areas**

FRANCE – CHERBOURG

LAT 49°39′N LONG 1°38′W

TIMES AND HEIGHTS OF HIGH AND LOW WATERS

SPRING & NEAP TIDES
Dates in red are **SPRINGS**
Dates in blue are **NEAPS**

YEAR **2002**

JANUARY

Date	Day	Time	m	Time	m	Time	m	Time	m
1	TU	0425	1.3	0956	6.5	1651	1.0	2228	6.3
2	W	0510	1.3	1041	6.5	1737	1.1	2315	6.2
3	TH	0557	1.4	1128	6.3	1825	1.2		
4	F	0000	6.0	0646	1.6	1217	6.1	1915	1.4
5	SA	0054	5.8	0738	1.9	1309	5.9	2008	1.6
6	SU	0150	5.6	0835	2.1	1407	5.6	2108	1.9
7	M	0254	5.4	0940	2.3	1515	5.4	2216	2.1
8	TU	0404	5.3	1052	2.3	1628	5.3	2327	2.2
9	W	0513	5.4	1204	2.2	1740	5.4		
10	TH	0036	2.1	0616	5.6	1307	2.0	1844	5.5
11	F	0133	2.0	0710	5.8	1401	1.8	1939	5.7
12	SA	0224	1.8	0758	6.0	1449	1.6	2026	5.8
13	SU	0308	1.7	0840	6.1	1530	1.5	● 2107	5.9
14	M	0348	1.7	0919	6.2	1609	1.4	2144	6.0
15	TU	0425	1.7	0955	6.2	1645	1.4	2218	5.9
16	W	0500	1.7	1030	6.1	1719	1.4	2252	5.9
17	TH	0534	1.8	1104	6.0	1752	1.5	2325	5.7
18	F	0606	1.9	1136	5.8	1825	1.7	2357	5.5
19	SA	0639	2.1	1209	5.6	1858	1.9		
20	SU	0030	5.3	0714	2.3	1244	5.4	1934	2.2
21	M	0108	5.1	0755	2.5	1327	5.1	2017	2.4
22	TU	0157	5.0	0847	2.7	1421	4.9	2112	2.6
23	W	0300	4.9	0955	2.8	1532	4.8	2223	2.7
24	TH	0416	4.9	1113	2.7	1653	4.9	2340	2.5
25	F	0531	5.1	1224	2.4	1805	5.1		
26	SA	0051	2.3	0633	5.5	1325	2.0	1905	5.5
27	SU	0148	1.9	0726	5.8	1418	1.6	1957	5.9
28	M	0240	1.6	0815	6.2	1508	1.2	○ 2046	6.2
29	TU	0329	1.3	0902	6.4	1556	0.9	2134	6.4
30	W	0417	1.1	0949	6.6	1643	0.7	2221	6.5
31	TH	0503	1.0	1035	6.7	1728	0.6	2306	6.5

FEBRUARY

Date	Day	Time	m	Time	m	Time	m	Time	m
1	F	0548	1.0	1120	6.7	1813	0.7	2351	6.4
2	SA	0632	1.1	1204	6.5	1858	1.0		
3	SU	0034	6.1	0718	1.4	1249	6.1	1944	1.4
4	M	0120	5.8	0806	1.8	1336	5.7	2034	1.8
5	TU	0211	5.4	0902	2.2	1434	5.3	2134	2.3
6	W	0317	5.1	1013	2.5	1552	5.0	2251	2.5
7	TH	0438	5.1	1136	2.5	1720	5.0		
8	F	0003	2.5	0555	5.2	1251	2.3	1837	5.1
9	SA	0122	2.3	0658	5.4	1351	2.0	1934	5.4
10	SU	0215	2.1	0748	5.7	1439	1.7	2018	5.7
11	M	0259	1.9	0830	5.9	1520	1.5	2056	5.8
12	TU	0337	1.7	0907	6.1	1555	1.4	● 2129	6.0
13	W	0412	1.5	0941	6.2	1628	1.3	2201	6.0
14	TH	0443	1.5	1013	6.2	1700	1.2	2231	6.0
15	F	0513	1.5	1043	6.2	1729	1.3	2259	5.9
16	SA	0542	1.6	1111	6.0	1757	1.4	2327	5.8
17	SU	0610	1.7	1139	5.9	1825	1.6	2356	5.6
18	M	0640	1.9	1209	5.6	1856	1.9		
19	TU	0024	5.4	0714	2.2	1241	5.3	1931	2.2
20	W	0101	5.2	0756	2.4	1324	5.0	2017	2.5
21	TH	0153	4.9	0854	2.7	1429	4.8	2124	2.7
22	F	0311	4.8	1017	2.7	1605	4.7	2253	2.7
23	SA	0450	4.9	1148	2.5	1740	4.9		
24	SU	0023	2.5	0608	5.2	1301	2.1	1848	5.4
25	M	0130	2.0	0708	5.7	1401	1.6	1943	5.8
26	TU	0226	1.5	0801	6.1	1454	1.1	2033	6.2
27	W	0316	1.1	0850	6.5	1542	0.7	○ 2121	6.5
28	TH	0403	0.8	0937	6.8	1628	0.4	2207	6.7

MARCH

Date	Day	Time	m	Time	m	Time	m	Time	m
1	F	0448	0.6	1022	6.9	1712	0.3	2250	6.7
2	SA	0530	0.6	1105	6.9	1754	0.5	2331	6.6
3	SU	0612	0.8	1145	6.6	1835	0.8		
4	M	0002	6.3	0653	1.2	1225	6.2	1916	1.3
5	TU	0047	5.9	0736	1.7	1306	5.7	2000	1.9
6	W	0131	5.4	0826	2.2	1358	5.1	2054	2.5
7	TH	0232	5.0	0933	2.6	1519	4.7	2214	2.8
8	F	0403	4.8	1107	2.7	1707	4.7	2351	2.8
9	SA	0536	4.9	1234	2.5	1830	4.9		
10	SU	0110	2.5	0644	5.2	1336	2.1	1922	5.3
11	M	0203	2.2	0732	5.5	1423	1.8	2001	5.6
12	TU	0244	1.9	0812	5.8	1501	1.5	2035	5.8
13	W	0319	1.6	0847	6.0	1534	1.3	2107	6.0
14	TH	0351	1.4	0919	6.2	1605	1.2	● 2137	6.1
15	F	0420	1.3	0950	6.2	1634	1.1	2205	6.1
16	SA	0448	1.3	1018	6.2	1701	1.2	2231	6.0
17	SU	0515	1.4	1045	6.1	1728	1.3	2257	6.0
18	M	0543	1.5	1112	6.0	1755	1.5	2324	5.8
19	TU	0611	1.6	1140	5.7	1824	1.7	2352	5.6
20	W	0643	1.9	1210	5.4	1858	2.0		
21	TH	0023	5.3	0723	2.2	1249	5.1	1942	2.4
22	F	0110	5.0	0817	2.5	1350	4.8	2047	2.7
23	SA	0226	4.8	0938	2.7	1536	4.6	2222	2.8
24	SU	0417	4.8	1119	2.5	1723	4.9		
25	M	0010	2.5	0546	5.1	1239	2.0	1832	5.4
26	TU	0111	2.0	0649	5.7	1341	1.5	1926	5.9
27	W	0208	1.5	0743	6.2	1434	1.0	2015	6.3
28	TH	0258	1.0	0832	6.6	1522	0.6	○ 2101	6.6
29	F	0344	0.7	0919	6.8	1607	0.3	2145	6.8
30	SA	0427	0.5	1003	6.9	1649	0.3	2227	6.8
31	SU	0509	0.5	1044	6.8	1730	0.5	2306	6.6

APRIL

Date	Day	Time	m	Time	m	Time	m	Time	m
1	M	0548	0.8	1123	6.5	1808	0.9	2343	6.3
2	TU	0628	1.2	1201	6.1	1847	1.5		
3	W	0017	5.9	0708	1.6	1240	5.6	1929	2.1
4	TH	0058	5.4	0755	2.2	1329	5.0	2020	2.6
5	F	0156	4.9	0858	2.6	1450	4.6	2140	3.0
6	SA	0329	4.7	1031	2.7	1643	4.6	2322	3.0
7	SU	0506	4.8	1201	2.6	1804	4.9		
8	M	0041	2.6	0614	5.1	1304	2.2	1853	5.2
9	TU	0134	2.2	0702	5.4	1351	1.9	1930	5.5
10	W	0215	1.9	0742	5.7	1429	1.6	2004	5.8
11	TH	0250	1.7	0818	5.9	1503	1.4	2037	6.0
12	F	0322	1.5	0851	6.1	1534	1.3	● 2107	6.1
13	SA	0351	1.3	0922	6.2	1603	1.2	2136	6.1
14	SU	0420	1.3	0951	6.2	1631	1.2	2203	6.1
15	M	0449	1.3	1019	6.1	1700	1.3	2231	6.1
16	TU	0518	1.3	1049	6.0	1729	1.4	2300	5.9
17	W	0549	1.5	1121	5.8	1801	1.7	2331	5.7
18	TH	0623	1.7	1155	5.5	1837	2.0		
19	F	0010	5.4	0705	2.0	1239	5.1	1925	2.4
20	SA	0056	5.1	0801	2.3	1343	4.8	2033	2.7
21	SU	0211	4.9	0921	2.5	1525	4.7	2205	2.7
22	M	0353	4.9	1056	2.3	1703	5.0	2335	2.4
23	TU	0520	5.2	1214	1.9	1808	5.5		
24	W	0047	1.9	0624	5.7	1316	1.4	1902	5.9
25	TH	0143	1.4	0718	6.1	1409	1.0	1951	6.3
26	F	0234	1.0	0809	6.5	1457	0.7	2037	6.6
27	SA	0320	0.8	0856	6.7	1542	0.5	○ 2120	6.7
28	SU	0404	0.6	0940	6.7	1625	0.6	2201	6.7
29	M	0446	0.7	1022	6.6	1705	0.8	2240	6.5
30	TU	0526	0.9	1101	6.3	1743	1.2	2317	6.2

Chart Datum: 3·33 metres below IGN Datum

TIME ZONE -0100
(French Standard Time)
Subtract 1 hour for UT
For French Summer Time add ONE hour in **non-shaded areas**

FRANCE – CHERBOURG

LAT 49°39′N LONG 1°38′W

TIMES AND HEIGHTS OF HIGH AND LOW WATERS

SPRING & NEAP TIDES
Dates in red are SPRINGS
Dates in blue are NEAPS

YEAR **2002**

MAY

Day	Time	m	Time	m	Time	m	Time	m
1 W	0605	1.2	1140	5.9	1822	1.7	2355	5.8
2 TH	0646	1.7	1221	5.5	1904	2.2		
3 F	0035	5.4	0731	2.1	1310	5.0	1955	2.6
4 SA	0130	5.0	0829	2.5	1421	4.7	2107	2.9
5 SU	0250	4.7	0948	2.6	1555	4.6	2236	2.9
6 M	0417	4.7	1109	2.6	1712	4.8	2350	2.7
7 TU	0525	4.9	1214	2.3	1806	5.1		
8 W	0048	2.4	0618	5.2	1305	2.0	1848	5.4
9 TH	0133	2.1	0702	5.5	1347	1.8	1926	5.7
10 F	0212	1.8	0742	5.7	1424	1.6	2001	5.9
11 SA	0247	1.6	0818	5.9	1458	1.4	2035	6.0
12 SU	0320	1.4	0852	6.0	1530	1.3	● 2106	6.1
13 M	0352	1.3	0925	6.0	1603	1.3	2137	6.1
14 TU	0425	1.3	0958	6.0	1636	1.4	2209	6.1
15 W	0459	1.3	1033	5.9	1710	1.5	2244	6.0
16 TH	0534	1.4	1111	5.8	1747	1.7	2322	5.8
17 F	0614	1.6	1153	5.5	1830	2.0		
18 SA	0006	5.6	0700	1.9	1242	5.3	1922	2.3
19 SU	0057	5.3	0759	2.1	1346	5.0	2030	2.5
20 M	0206	5.1	0912	2.2	1511	5.0	2150	2.5
21 TU	0330	5.1	1033	2.1	1633	5.2	2308	2.2
22 W	0449	5.4	1145	1.8	1738	5.5		
23 TH	0018	1.9	0554	5.7	1247	1.4	1833	5.9
24 F	0116	1.5	0651	6.0	1342	1.2	1924	6.2
25 SA	0209	1.2	0745	6.2	1432	1.0	2011	6.4
26 SU	0257	1.0	0834	6.4	1518	0.9	○ 2056	6.5
27 M	0343	0.9	0920	6.4	1602	1.0	2138	6.4
28 TU	0426	1.0	1003	6.3	1643	1.2	2218	6.3
29 W	0507	1.1	1043	6.1	1723	1.5	2257	6.1
30 TH	0547	1.3	1124	5.8	1803	1.8	2336	5.8
31 F	0628	1.6	1205	5.5	1845	2.1		

JUNE

Day	Time	m	Time	m	Time	m	Time	m
1 SA	0018	5.5	0711	2.0	1250	5.2	1932	2.5
2 SU	0107	5.2	0801	2.2	1346	4.9	2030	2.7
3 M	0207	5.0	0900	2.4	1453	4.8	2139	2.8
4 TU	0316	4.8	1007	2.5	1603	4.8	2248	2.7
5 W	0423	4.9	1112	2.4	1705	5.0	2349	2.5
6 TH	0522	5.0	1209	2.2	1757	5.2		
7 F	0043	2.3	0615	5.2	1258	2.0	1842	5.4
8 SA	0129	2.0	0701	5.4	1342	1.8	1923	5.7
9 SU	0210	1.8	0744	5.6	1422	1.7	2002	5.9
10 M	0249	1.6	0825	5.8	1501	1.5	2039	6.0
11 TU	0328	1.4	0903	5.9	1540	1.5	● 2116	6.1
12 W	0407	1.3	0942	6.0	1619	1.5	2154	6.1
13 TH	0446	1.3	1022	5.9	1659	1.5	2234	6.1
14 F	0527	1.3	1105	5.9	1742	1.6	2317	6.0
15 SA	0612	1.4	1151	5.7	1829	1.8		
16 SU	0004	5.8	0700	1.5	1242	5.5	1922	2.0
17 M	0055	5.6	0755	1.7	1340	5.4	2022	2.1
18 TU	0155	5.5	0858	1.8	1447	5.3	2129	2.2
19 W	0303	5.4	1005	1.9	1558	5.3	2239	2.1
20 TH	0415	5.4	1114	1.8	1704	5.5	2346	2.0
21 F	0524	5.5	1218	1.7	1804	5.7		
22 SA	0050	1.7	0627	5.7	1317	1.5	1859	5.9
23 SU	0147	1.5	0725	5.9	1410	1.4	1950	6.1
24 M	0239	1.4	0818	6.0	1459	1.4	○ 2037	6.2
25 TU	0327	1.2	0906	6.0	1544	1.4	2120	6.2
26 W	0411	1.2	0949	6.0	1627	1.5	2201	6.2
27 TH	0452	1.3	1029	5.9	1707	1.6	2241	6.1
28 F	0532	1.4	1108	5.8	1746	1.8	2320	5.9
29 SA	0610	1.5	1147	5.6	1825	2.0	2359	5.7
30 SU	0648	1.7	1226	5.4	1906	2.2		

JULY

Day	Time	m	Time	m	Time	m	Time	m
1 M	0040	5.5	0728	2.0	1306	5.2	1949	2.4
2 TU	0123	5.2	0812	2.2	1352	5.0	2040	2.6
3 W	0212	5.0	0903	2.4	1447	4.9	2139	2.7
4 TH	0311	4.9	1002	2.5	1550	4.9	2244	2.7
5 F	0416	4.8	1106	2.5	1656	5.0	2347	2.5
6 SA	0522	4.9	1208	2.4	1755	5.2		
7 SU	0045	2.3	0622	5.2	1302	2.2	1847	5.4
8 M	0136	2.0	0714	5.4	1351	1.9	1933	5.7
9 TU	0223	1.7	0802	5.6	1437	1.7	2017	5.9
10 W	0308	1.5	0846	5.9	1522	1.5	● 2059	6.1
11 TH	0352	1.3	0930	6.0	1607	1.4	2142	6.2
12 F	0437	1.1	1015	6.1	1652	1.3	2226	6.3
13 SA	0521	1.0	1100	6.1	1737	1.3	2311	6.3
14 SU	0606	1.0	1146	6.0	1823	1.4	2358	6.2
15 M	0653	1.2	1233	5.9	1912	1.6		
16 TU	0045	6.0	0741	1.4	1322	5.7	2004	1.8
17 W	0136	5.8	0834	1.6	1416	5.5	2102	2.0
18 TH	0234	5.5	0935	1.9	1519	5.4	2208	2.1
19 F	0343	5.3	1043	2.0	1630	5.3	2319	2.2
20 SA	0459	5.3	1154	2.1	1740	5.4		
21 SU	0031	2.0	0612	5.4	1259	2.0	1842	5.6
22 M	0133	1.8	0717	5.5	1357	1.9	1938	5.8
23 TU	0228	1.6	0811	5.7	1448	1.7	2026	6.0
24 W	0316	1.4	0858	5.9	1533	1.6	○ 2109	6.1
25 TH	0359	1.3	0938	5.9	1614	1.6	2148	6.2
26 F	0437	1.3	1014	5.9	1652	1.6	2225	6.2
27 SA	0514	1.3	1049	5.9	1727	1.6	2300	6.1
28 SU	0547	1.4	1122	5.8	1801	1.8	2334	5.9
29 M	0620	1.5	1154	5.6	1833	1.9		
30 TU	0003	5.7	0652	1.8	1226	5.4	1907	2.2
31 W	0039	5.4	0725	2.0	1259	5.2	1945	2.4

AUGUST

Day	Time	m	Time	m	Time	m	Time	m
1 TH	0117	5.2	0804	2.3	1340	5.0	2032	2.6
2 F	0204	4.9	0853	2.5	1434	4.9	2133	2.8
3 SA	0307	4.7	0959	2.7	1546	4.8	2249	2.8
4 SU	0429	4.7	1117	2.7	1708	4.9		
5 M	0010	2.5	0549	4.9	1228	2.5	1816	5.2
6 TU	0108	2.2	0651	5.2	1327	2.1	1910	5.6
7 W	0201	1.8	0744	5.6	1419	1.8	1958	5.9
8 TH	0251	1.4	0832	5.9	1508	1.5	● 2044	6.2
9 F	0338	1.1	0918	6.2	1555	1.2	2130	6.5
10 SA	0424	0.8	1004	6.4	1640	1.1	2215	6.6
11 SU	0508	0.7	1048	6.4	1724	1.0	2259	6.6
12 M	0551	0.7	1131	6.4	1808	1.1	2343	6.5
13 TU	0634	0.9	1213	6.2	1852	1.3		
14 W	0025	6.3	0718	1.2	1256	5.9	1939	1.6
15 TH	0111	5.9	0806	1.6	1342	5.6	2032	2.0
16 F	0204	5.5	0902	2.1	1441	5.3	2137	2.3
17 SA	0314	5.1	1014	2.4	1600	5.1	2258	2.4
18 SU	0445	5.0	1137	2.5	1724	5.2		
19 M	0021	2.3	0610	5.1	1251	2.4	1835	5.4
20 TU	0127	2.0	0716	5.4	1352	2.1	1930	5.7
21 W	0220	1.7	0805	5.7	1441	1.9	2016	6.0
22 TH	0305	1.5	0845	5.9	1522	1.7	○ 2055	6.1
23 F	0343	1.3	0921	6.0	1558	1.5	2130	6.2
24 SA	0417	1.3	0953	6.0	1631	1.5	2203	6.3
25 SU	0449	1.2	1023	6.0	1702	1.5	2234	6.2
26 M	0519	1.3	1052	6.0	1731	1.6	2303	6.1
27 TU	0547	1.4	1119	5.8	1759	1.7	2331	5.9
28 W	0614	1.6	1145	5.7	1827	2.0	2359	5.6
29 TH	0643	1.9	1212	5.5	1858	2.2		
30 F	0028	5.3	0715	2.2	1245	5.2	1937	2.5
31 SA	0108	5.0	0756	2.6	1331	4.9	2030	2.8

Chart Datum: 3·33 metres below IGN Datum

TIME ZONE -0100
(French Standard Time)
Subtract 1 hour for UT
For French Summer Time add ONE hour in **non-shaded areas**

FRANCE – CHERBOURG

LAT 49°39'N LONG 1°38'W

TIMES AND HEIGHTS OF HIGH AND LOW WATERS

SPRING & NEAP TIDES
Dates in red are SPRINGS
Dates in blue are NEAPS

YEAR **2002**

SEPTEMBER

Date	Day	Time	m	Time	m	Time	m	Time	m
1	SU	0207	4.7	0858	2.8	1442	4.7	2152	2.9
2	M	0341	4.6	1031	2.9	1625	4.8	2327	2.7
3	TU	0525	4.8	1201	2.7	1750	5.1		
4	W	0045	2.3	0633	5.2	1308	2.3	1849	5.5
5	TH	0142	1.8	0726	5.7	1402	1.8	1939	6.0
6	F	0232	1.3	0815	6.1	1451	1.3	2026	6.4
7	SA	0319	0.9	0900	6.4	1537	1.0	● 2112	6.7
8	SU	0404	0.6	0945	6.6	1621	0.8	2157	6.9
9	M	0447	0.5	1027	6.7	1704	0.7	2240	6.9
10	TU	0529	0.5	1108	6.6	1746	0.8	2322	6.7
11	W	0610	0.8	1147	6.4	1827	1.1		
12	TH	0000	6.3	0651	1.3	1226	6.0	1911	1.6
13	F	0044	5.9	0735	1.8	1308	5.6	2002	2.1
14	SA	0135	5.3	0829	2.4	1404	5.2	2108	2.5
15	SU	0251	4.9	0948	2.8	1533	4.9	2241	2.7
16	M	0441	4.8	1128	2.9	1713	5.0		
17	TU	0005	2.5	0611	5.0	1245	2.6	1825	5.3
18	W	0116	2.1	0706	5.4	1341	2.2	1916	5.6
19	TH	0205	1.8	0747	5.7	1424	1.9	1956	6.0
20	F	0244	1.5	0822	5.9	1501	1.7	2032	6.2
21	SA	0319	1.4	0854	6.1	1534	1.5	○ 2105	6.3
22	SU	0350	1.3	0924	6.1	1604	1.4	2135	6.3
23	M	0419	1.3	0952	6.1	1632	1.4	2204	6.3
24	TU	0447	1.3	1018	6.1	1659	1.5	2230	6.1
25	W	0513	1.4	1042	6.0	1726	1.6	2256	6.0
26	TH	0539	1.6	1107	5.8	1753	1.8	2322	5.7
27	F	0606	1.9	1133	5.6	1822	2.1	2351	5.4
28	SA	0637	2.2	1203	5.4	1858	2.4		
29	SU	0027	5.1	0717	2.6	1245	5.1	1948	2.7
30	M	0126	4.8	0817	2.9	1355	4.8	2107	2.9

OCTOBER

Date	Day	Time	m	Time	m	Time	m	Time	m
1	TU	0308	4.6	0954	3.1	1548	4.7	2255	2.8
2	W	0504	4.8	1136	2.8	1724	5.1		
3	TH	0020	2.3	0612	5.3	1245	2.3	1825	5.6
4	F	0118	1.7	0703	5.8	1339	1.7	1915	6.1
5	SA	0208	1.2	0750	6.3	1428	1.2	2003	6.5
6	SU	0255	0.8	0836	6.6	1514	0.9	● 2049	6.8
7	M	0340	0.5	0919	6.8	1558	0.7	2134	7.0
8	TU	0422	0.5	1001	6.8	1640	0.7	2217	6.9
9	W	0503	0.6	1041	6.7	1722	0.8	2258	6.7
10	TH	0544	1.0	1119	6.5	1803	1.2	2339	6.3
11	F	0624	1.5	1157	6.1	1846	1.7		
12	SA	0020	5.7	0707	2.1	1238	5.6	1935	2.2
13	SU	0112	5.2	0801	2.7	1334	5.1	2041	2.6
14	M	0231	4.8	0924	3.1	1505	4.8	2218	2.8
15	TU	0425	4.7	1108	3.0	1648	4.9	2345	2.6
16	W	0548	5.0	1222	2.7	1758	5.2		
17	TH	0048	2.3	0638	5.3	1314	2.3	1846	5.5
18	F	0134	1.9	0715	5.7	1355	2.0	1925	5.9
19	SA	0213	1.7	0749	5.9	1431	1.7	2000	6.1
20	SU	0246	1.5	0821	6.1	1504	1.6	2033	6.2
21	M	0317	1.4	0851	6.2	1533	1.5	○ 2104	6.3
22	TU	0346	1.4	0919	6.2	1602	1.5	2133	6.2
23	W	0414	1.4	0944	6.2	1630	1.5	2200	6.1
24	TH	0442	1.5	1010	6.1	1658	1.6	2227	6.0
25	F	0510	1.7	1037	6.0	1727	1.8	2257	5.8
26	SA	0539	2.0	1107	5.8	1759	2.0	2330	5.5
27	SU	0613	2.3	1140	5.5	1836	2.3		
28	M	0012	5.2	0656	2.6	1225	5.2	1928	2.6
29	TU	0111	4.9	0758	2.9	1335	4.9	2044	2.8
30	W	0248	4.7	0930	3.0	1517	4.9	2223	2.6
31	TH	0433	4.9	1106	2.7	1649	5.2	2345	2.2

NOVEMBER

Date	Day	Time	m	Time	m	Time	m	Time	m
1	F	0541	5.4	1216	2.2	1753	5.6		
2	SA	0049	1.7	0634	5.9	1312	1.7	1846	6.1
3	SU	0140	1.2	0721	6.3	1402	1.3	1936	6.5
4	M	0228	0.9	0807	6.6	1449	1.0	● 2024	6.8
5	TU	0314	0.7	0851	6.8	1534	0.8	2110	6.8
6	W	0357	0.7	0933	6.8	1618	0.8	2154	6.8
7	TH	0439	0.9	1014	6.7	1700	1.0	2237	6.5
8	F	0520	1.3	1053	6.4	1742	1.3	2319	6.1
9	SA	0601	1.7	1133	6.1	1825	1.7	2359	5.7
10	SU	0645	2.3	1216	5.6	1913	2.2		
11	M	0053	5.2	0738	2.7	1310	5.2	2013	2.5
12	TU	0203	4.9	0850	3.0	1428	4.9	2133	2.8
13	W	0335	4.8	1022	3.0	1556	4.9	2255	2.7
14	TH	0454	4.9	1135	2.8	1708	5.0		
15	F	0000	2.5	0550	5.2	1231	2.5	1801	5.3
16	SA	0051	2.2	0632	5.5	1316	2.2	1845	5.6
17	SU	0132	1.9	0710	5.7	1355	2.0	1923	5.8
18	M	0209	1.8	0745	5.9	1430	1.8	2000	6.0
19	TU	0243	1.6	0817	6.1	1502	1.6	2034	6.1
20	W	0315	1.6	0847	6.1	1534	1.5	○ 2106	6.1
21	TH	0346	1.6	0916	6.2	1605	1.5	2137	6.1
22	F	0418	1.6	0947	6.1	1638	1.6	2209	6.0
23	SA	0450	1.8	1019	6.1	1711	1.7	2244	5.8
24	SU	0524	1.9	1055	5.9	1748	1.8	2324	5.6
25	M	0603	2.2	1135	5.7	1830	2.0		
26	TU	0010	5.3	0650	2.4	1224	5.4	1923	2.3
27	W	0109	5.1	0751	2.6	1326	5.2	2030	2.4
28	TH	0226	5.0	0908	2.7	1446	5.1	2150	2.4
29	F	0352	5.1	1030	2.6	1608	5.3	2307	2.1
30	SA	0502	5.4	1141	2.2	1717	5.6		

DECEMBER

Date	Day	Time	m	Time	m	Time	m	Time	m
1	SU	0015	1.8	0600	5.8	1242	1.8	1816	6.0
2	M	0111	1.4	0652	6.2	1336	1.5	1910	6.3
3	TU	0203	1.2	0740	6.4	1427	1.2	2002	6.5
4	W	0251	1.1	0827	6.6	1514	1.0	● 2050	6.5
5	TH	0337	1.1	0911	6.6	1600	1.0	2137	6.5
6	F	0420	1.3	0953	6.5	1644	1.1	2221	6.3
7	SA	0503	1.5	1035	6.3	1727	1.3	2304	6.0
8	SU	0545	1.8	1116	6.1	1809	1.6	2347	5.7
9	M	0628	2.2	1200	5.8	1854	2.0		
10	TU	0032	5.4	0715	2.5	1248	5.4	1942	2.3
11	W	0125	5.1	0809	2.8	1344	5.1	2038	2.5
12	TH	0229	4.9	0914	2.9	1450	5.0	2143	2.6
13	F	0338	4.9	1026	2.9	1558	4.9	2250	2.6
14	SA	0443	5.0	1131	2.7	1701	5.0	2351	2.5
15	SU	0538	5.2	1227	2.5	1756	5.2		
16	M	0045	2.3	0626	5.4	1314	2.3	1844	5.4
17	TU	0129	2.1	0707	5.7	1356	2.0	1928	5.6
18	W	0210	1.9	0746	5.9	1434	1.8	2007	5.8
19	TH	0247	1.8	0822	6.0	1511	1.6	○ 2045	5.9
20	F	0325	1.7	0857	6.1	1548	1.5	2121	6.0
21	SA	0402	1.7	0932	6.2	1625	1.5	2159	6.0
22	SU	0440	1.7	1010	6.2	1704	1.5	2239	5.9
23	M	0520	1.7	1051	6.1	1745	1.5	2322	5.8
24	TU	0602	1.9	1134	6.0	1829	1.6		
25	W	0006	5.6	0649	2.0	1221	5.8	1918	1.8
26	TH	0100	5.5	0742	2.2	1314	5.6	2014	2.0
27	F	0159	5.3	0843	2.3	1416	5.4	2117	2.1
28	SA	0308	5.3	0952	2.4	1527	5.4	2227	2.1
29	SU	0420	5.4	1104	2.2	1641	5.5	2338	2.0
30	M	0526	5.6	1213	2.0	1750	5.6		
31	TU	0045	1.8	0626	5.8	1315	1.7	1852	5.8

Chart Datum: 3·33 metres below IGN Datum

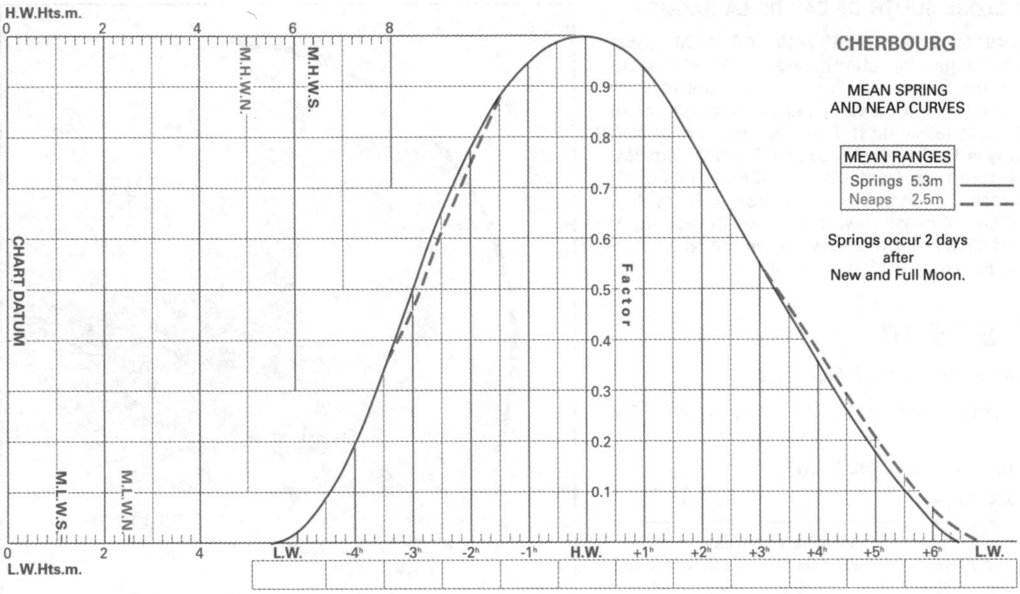

OMONVILLE-LA-ROGUE *9.15.9*

Manche **49°42'·28N 01°49'·86W**

CHARTS AC *1106, 2669*; SHOM 7120, 7158; ECM 528, 1014; Imray C33A; Stanfords 7, 16

TIDES –0330 Dover; ML 3·8; Duration 0545; Zone –0100

Standard Port CHERBOURG (⟵)

Times				Height (metres)			
High Water		Low Water		MHWS	MHWN	MLWN	MLWS
0300	1000	0400	1000	6·4	5·0	2·5	1·1
1500	2200	1600	2200				
Differences OMONVILLE							
–0010	–0010	–0015	–0015	–0·1	–0·1	0·0	0·0
GOURY							
–0100	–0040	–0105	–0120	+1·7	+1·6	+1·0	+0·3

SHELTER Good, except in strong winds from N to SE. There are 4 W conical ◆s or ⚓ S of bkwtr; beware rks off outer end.

NAVIGATION WPT 49°42′·44N 01°48′·68W, 079°/259° from/to Omonville lt, 1·0M. Ent is 100m wide, between rks extending N from Omonville Fort, and running ESE from bkwtr marked by Le Tunard, G bn tr. From W or N, keep clear of Basse Bréfort (depth 1m, marked by NCM buoy, VQ) 0·6M N of Pte de Jardeheu. Appr on 195° transit (below), passing 100m E of Le Tunard and into W sector of lt before turning stbd 290° for old Custom Ho and moorings. From E, appr on 255° transit in W sector of lt, until S of Le Tunard. To ENE of port is a military firing area; when active, a R flag is flown from the bkwtr head.

LIGHTS AND MARKS Omonville lt, Iso WRG 4s 13m 11/8M, on W framework tr with R top, vis G180°-252°, W252°-262°, R262°-287°. Lt in transit 255° with ⊕ steeple, 650m beyond, leads S of Le Tunard. From N, Le Tunard leads 195° in transit with fort. Street lts adequately illuminate the hbr area.

RADIO TELEPHONE None.

TELEPHONE Aff Mar 02·33·53·21·76; ⊖ 02·33·53·05·60; CROSS 02·33·52·72·13; 02·33·52·71·33; Météo 02·33·22·91·77; Auto 08.36.68.08.50; Police 02·33·52·72·02; Dr 02·33·53·08·69; Brit Consul 01·33·44·20·13.

FACILITIES Jetty M, L, FW, AB, V, R, Bar. **Village** V, Gaz, R, Bar, showers at l'Association du Camping in village centre, nearest fuel (cans) at Beaumont-Hague 5km, ✉, Ⓑ, ⇌ (bus to Cherbourg), ✈. Ferry: See Cherbourg.

MINOR HARBOUR 2M EAST OF CAP DE LA HAGUE

PORT RACINE, Manche, **49°42'·72N 01°53'·78W**. AC *1106, 3653;* SHOM 7120. Tides as 9.15.9. Port Racine (said to be the smallest hbr in France) is in the SW corner of Anse de St. Martin. This bay, 2M E of Cap de la Hague, has ⚓s sheltered from all but onshore winds. From N, appr with conspic chy (279m) at atomic stn brg 175°; or from NE via Basse Bréfort NCM buoy, VQ, on with St Germain des Vaux spire brg 240°. Both lines clear La Parmentière rks awash in centre of bay and Les Herbeuses and Le Grun Rks to W and E respectively. ⚓ or moor off the hbr which is obstructed by lines; only accessible by dinghy. R is only facility.

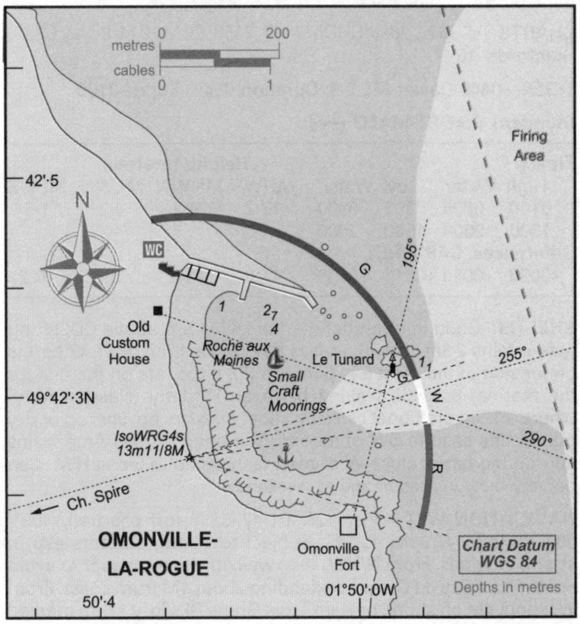

MINOR HARBOUR CLOSE SOUTH OF CAP DE LA HAGUE

GOURY, Manche, **49°42´·94N 01°56´·78W.** AC *1106, 3653*; SHOM 7133 (essential large scale chart) , 5636, 7158. HW –0410 on Dover (UT); ML 5·1m. See 9.15.9. For visitors, appr at slack water nps with no swell and good vis; a fair wx hbr only, dries to flat sand/mud. Cap de la Hague lt, Fl 5s, is 0·5M NW of hbr; La Foraine WCM buoy is 1·1M to the W. Ldg lts: Front QR 4m 7M, on bkwtr hd; rear (110m from front), Q 10m 12M, intens 057°-075°, lead 065° between Charlin to S and Les Grois to N. By day, W patch with R ■ at end of bkwtr on with W pylon of rear ldg lt, 065°. ⚓ W of the 2 LB slips in 1·7m or dry out on the NE side of the bkwtr. Facilities: R, Bar at Auderville (0·5M).

DIÉLETTE *9.15.10*

Manche, **49°33´·24N 01°51´·89W** ❁❁⛵⛵⛵✿✿

CHARTS AC *3653*; SHOM 7158; ECM 528, 1014; Imray C33A; Stanfords 16

TIDES HW –0430 on Dover (UT); ML 5·4m

Standard Port ST-MALO (⟶)

Times				Height (metres)			
High Water		Low Water		MHWS	MHWN	MLWN	MLWS
0100	0800	0300	0800	12·2	9·3	4·2	1·5
1300	2000	1500	2000				
Differences DIÉLETTE							
+0045	+0035	+0020	+0035	–2·5	–1·9	–0·7	–0·3

SHELTER Good in marina, but do not attempt entry in strong W'lies. Outer hbr entr dredged to CD and so accessible on most tides; though significantly less water reported (2000). W side of outer hbr dries approx 5m (local moorings). Entry to marina is limited by a sill with a lifting gate 4·0m above CD; access about HW±3 for 1·5m draft, waiting pontoon outside.

NAVIGATION WPT 49°33'·49N 01°52'·24W, 320°/140° from/to W bkwtr lt, 0·40M. Appr is exposed to W'ly winds/swell. Caution: rky reef dries close NE of appr; cross tides at hbr ent. Prohib area from hbr to C de Flamanville extends 5ca offshore.

LIGHTS AND MARKS Power stn chys (72m) are conspic 1·2M to SW. Dir lt 140°, Iso WRG 4s 12m 10/7M, W tr/G top at hd of West

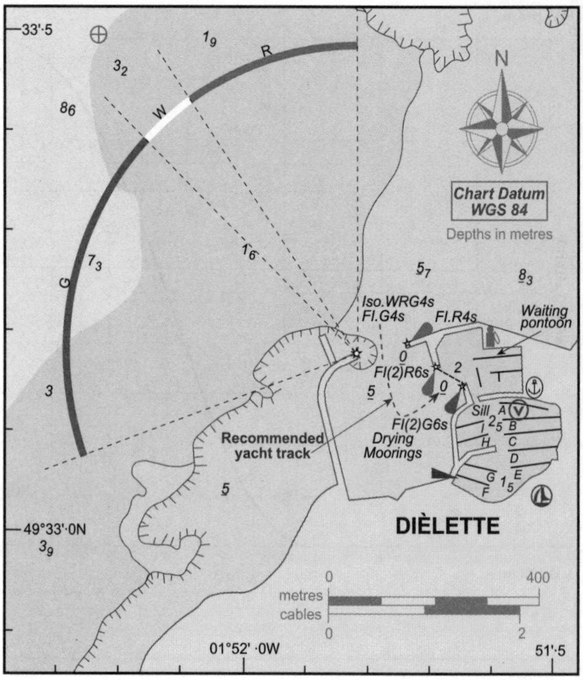

bkwtr, vis G070°-135°, W135°-145° (10°), R145°-180°; on same tr is a lower lt, Fl G 4s 6m 2M. N bkwtr hd, Fl R 4s 8m 5M, W mast/R top. Spur, close SE at ent to new basin, is Fl (2) R 6s 6m 1M. Opposite spur, Fl G 6s 6m 2M, vis 115°-358°.

RADIO TELEPHONE VHF Ch 09; summer 0800-1300, 1400-2000LT; winter 0900-1200, 1330-1800LT.

TELEPHONE Hr Mr 02·33.53.68.78, 🖷 02·33.53.68.79; ⊖ 02·33.23.34.00; Aff Mar 02·33.23.36.10; Météo 08·36·68·08·50; CROSS 02·33.52.72.13; SNSM 02·33.04.93.17; YC ☎ 02·33·93·10·24.

FACILITIES **Marina** (370+70Ⓥ) €2.13, AC, FW, Fuel, Slip, C (30ton); **Village**, Bar, R. Also facilities at Flamanville (1·3M). Ferry to CI.

CARTERET *9.15.11*

Manche **49°22'·16N 01°47'·35W** ❁❁⛵⛵⛵✿✿

CHARTS AC *3655, 2669*; SHOM 7157, 7158; ECM 1014; Imray C33A; Stanfords 16

TIDES –0440 Dover; ML 5·9; Duration 0545; Zone –0100

Standard Port ST-MALO (⟶)

Times				Height (metres)			
High Water		Low Water		MHWS	MHWN	MLWN	MLWS
0100	0800	0300	0800	12·2	9·3	4·2	1·5
1300	2000	1500	2000				
Differences CARTERET							
+0030	+0020	+0015	+0030	–1·6	–1·2	–0·5	–0·2

SHELTER Good in non-tidal marina (sill is 5m above CD; lifting gate retains 2·3m within); access HW±2½ for 1·5m draft. Ⓥ berths on far side of the most E'ly pontoon (F). If too late on the tide for the marina, possible waiting berth on W Jetty (clear of ferry) where a 1·5m draft boat can stay afloat for 6 hrs np, 9hrs sp or dry out on fine sand to SW of marina. The tiny Port des Américains and drying basin, close W of marina, have up to 5m at HW. Can be very busy in season and at weekends.

NAVIGATION WPT 49°21´·12N 01°47´·59W (off chartlet), 189°/009° from/to W Jetty lt, 1M. Subject to strong currents esp in strong W winds. From N/NW, keep well off shore on appr to avoid rks 1M N of Cap de Carteret extending about 1M from coast. From W, about 4M off shore, beware Trois Grune Rks (dry 1·6m) marked by WCM buoy, Q (9) 15s. Appr dries ½M offshore and is exposed to fresh W/SW winds which can make ent rough. There are no safe ⚓s off shore. Best appr at HW–2 to avoid max tidal stream, 4½kn sp. Bar, at right angles to W Jetty, dries 4m; the chan dries progressively to firm sand, and is dredged to drying hts of 4m and 4.5m just W of the marina. Best water is mid-chan keeping inside marks. The outer end of W bkwtr partly cover at springs. No ⚓ in river. Traffic sigs near Capitainerie.

LIGHTS AND MARKS Cap de Carteret, Fl (2+1) 15s 81m 26M, grey tr, G top, Horn (3) 60s, and conspic Sig stn are 8ca WxN of the ent. W Jetty, Oc R 4s 6m 8M, W col, R top; E bkwtr, Fl G 2·5s, W mast G top. These lts in transit lead about 009° to ent. The bend in the chan is marked by a PHM bn, Fl (2) R 6s, & a SHM bn, Fl (2) G 6s. Marina sill is marked by a PHM bn, Fl (3) R 12s, and a SHM bn, Fl (3) G 12s; plus Y poles. Caution: a concrete caisson projects from the PHM bn.

RADIO TELEPHONE Marina Ch 09. Sig stn 10, 16.

TELEPHONE Marina 02·33·52·60·73; CROSS 02·33·52·72·13; ⊖ 02·33·04· 90·08; Météo 02·33·22·91·77; Auto 08.36.68.08.50; Police 02·33·53·80·17; Ⓗ (Valognes) 02·33·40·14·39; Brit Consul 01·33·44·20·13.

FACILITIES **Port de Plaisance "Le Port des Iles"** ☎ 02·33·52·60·73, 🖷 02.33.52.60.98, (260 + 60 visitors), €2.13 (possible discount Mon-Thu), AC, FW, CH; **West Jetty** AB free for 6 hrs, then at 50% of marina rate, Slip, FW, R, Bar; **Yacht Club Barneville-Carteret** ☎ 02·33·52·60·73, 🖷 02·33·52·65·98, Slip, M, Bar. **Town** ME, P & D (cans), V, Gaz, R, Bar, ✉, Ⓑ (Barneville), ≹ (Valognes), ✈ (Cherbourg). Ferry: Cherbourg, Jersey.

CARTERET *continued*

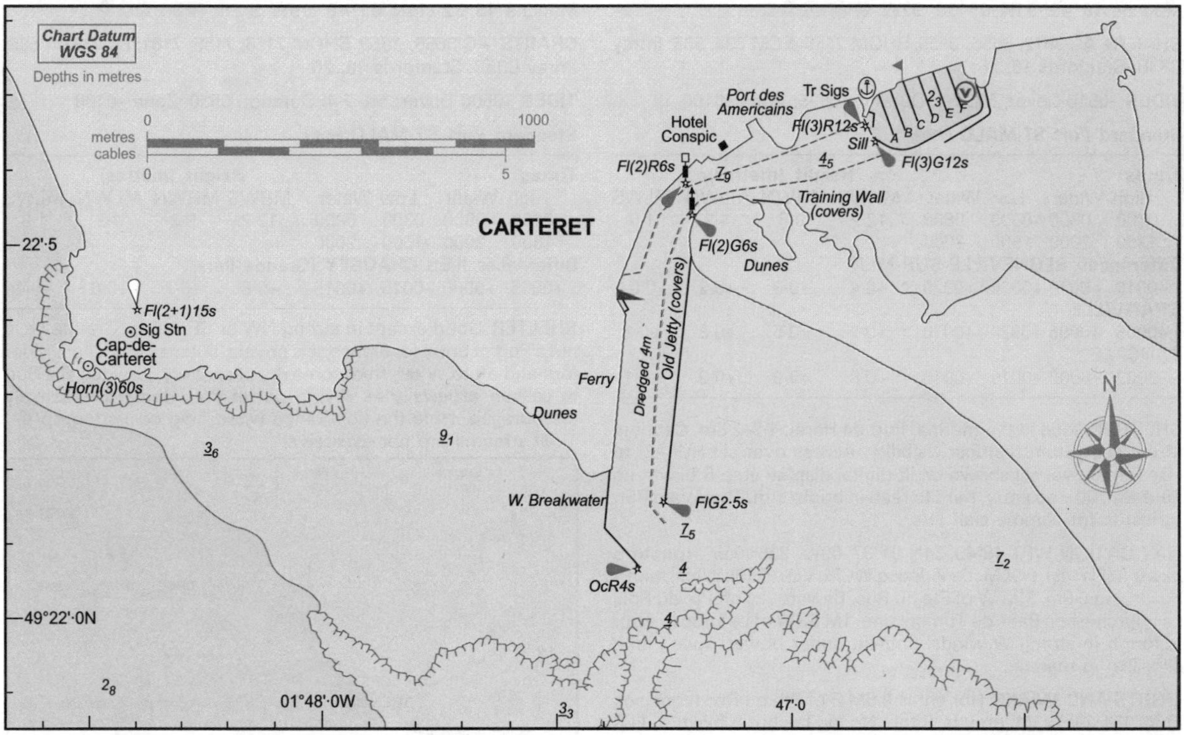
Chart Datum WGS 84
Depths in metres
metres
cables
0
1000
0
5
CARTERET
Port des Americains
Tr Sigs
Hotel Conspic
Fl(3)R12s
Sill
Fl(3)G12s
Fl(2)R6s
Training Wall (covers)
Fl(2)G6s
Dunes
22'·5
Fl(2+1)15s
Sig Stn
Cap-de-Carteret
Horn(3)60s
Ferry
Dredged 4m
Old Jetty (covers)
Dunes
W. Breakwater
FlG2·5s
OcR4s
N
49°22'·0N
01°48'·0W
47'·0

PORTBAIL 9.15.12

Manche **49°19'·40N 01°42'·94W**

CHARTS AC *3655, 2669*; SHOM 7157; ECM 1014; Imray C33A; Stanfords 16

TIDES HW –0440 on Dover (UT); ML 6·3m; Duration 0545

Standard Port ST-MALO (⟶)

Times				Height (metres)			
High Water		Low Water		MHWS	MHWN	MLWN	MLWS
0100	0800	0300	0800	12·2	9·3	4·2	1·5
1300	2000	1500	2000				
Differences PORTBAIL							
+0030	+0025	+0025	+0030	–0·8	–0·6	–0·2	–0·1
ST GERMAIN-SUR-AY							
+0025	+0025	+0035	+0035	–0·7	–0·5	0·0	+0·1
LE SÉNÉQUET							
+0015	+0015	+0023	+0023	–0·3	–0·3	+0·1	+0·1

SHELTER Good. Hbr dries 7·0m, but access HW±½ at np, HW±2½ at sp for 1m draft. Drying basin to E of jetty: visitors berth on pontoon parallel with NW side of basin or moor on first line of buoys parallel to jetty. Portbail is 4M SE of Carteret.

NAVIGATION WPT 49°18'·24N 01°44'·80W (off chartlet, abeam unlit "PB" SWM buoy), 222°/042° from/to chan buoys, 1·4M. Beware very strong tide over bar. Ldg line crosses sand banks (drying about 8ca offshore) to a pair of unlit PHM/SHM buoys. Thence via chan dredged 5·2m; on port side a training wall (covers at HW) is marked by R spar bns, the first Q (2) R 5s.

LIGHTS AND MARKS A Water Tr (43m) is conspic 6ca NNW of ent. Ldg lts 042°: Front (La Caillourie) QW 14m 10M, W pylon, R top; rear, 870m from front, Oc 4s 20m 10M (church spire). Training wall hd, Q (2) R 5s 5m 1M.

RADIO TELEPHONE VHF Ch 09.

TELEPHONE Hr Mr ☎ 02·33·04·90·08 (15 Jun-31 Aug). CROSS 02·33·52·72·13.

FACILITIES Quay (100) €1.22, FW, D, P, AC, C (5 ton); **Club Nautique de Portbail-Denneville** ☎ 02·33·04·86·15, Bar, R; **YC Portbail** ☎ 02·33·04·86·15, AB, C, Slip; **Services:** Sh, ME, El. **Town** (½M by causeway) Bar, Ⓑ, ✉, R, V, D, P, ≹ (Valognes).

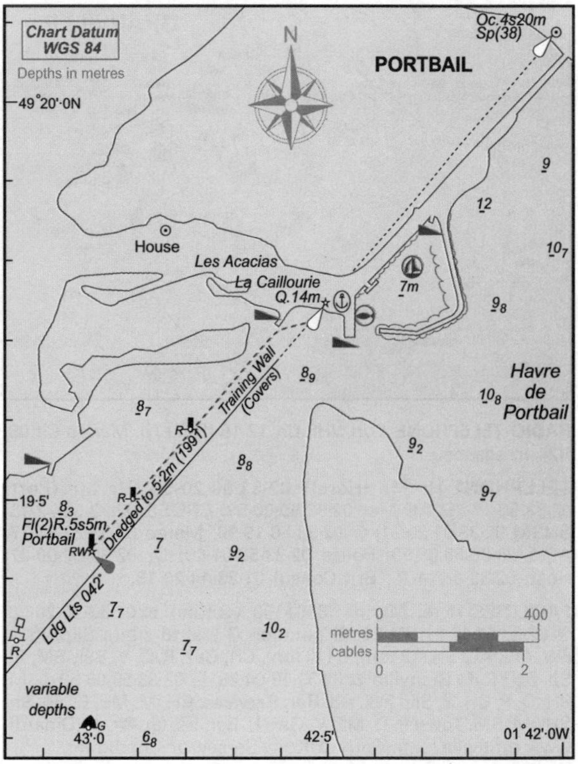
Chart Datum WGS 84
Depths in metres
N
PORTBAIL
Oc.4s20m Sp(38)
49°20'·0N
House
Les Acacias
La Caillourie Q.14m
7m
Havre de Portbail
Training Wall (Covers)
Dredged to 5·2m (1991)
19·5'
Fl(2)R.5s5m Portbail
Ldg Lts 042°
metres
cables
0
400
0
2
variable depths
43'·0
42·5'
01°42'·0W

GRANVILLE *9.15.13*

Manche **48°49'·91N 01°35'·97W** ❁❁◊◊◊✿✿

CHARTS AC 3672, 3656, *3659*; SHOM 7156; ECM 534, 535; Imray C33B; Stanfords 16, 26

TIDES –0510 Dover; ML 7·1; Duration 0525; Zone –0100

Standard Port ST-MALO (⟶)

Times				Height (metres)			
High Water		Low Water		MHWS	MHWN	MLWN	MLWS
0100	0800	0300	0800	12·2	9·3	4·2	1·5
1300	2000	1500	2000				
Differences REGNÉVILLE-SUR-MER							
+0010	+0010	+0030	+0020	+0·4	+0·3	+0·2	0·0
GRANVILLE							
+0005	+0005	+0020	+0010	+0·7	+0·5	+0·3	+0·1
CANCALE							
–0002	–0002	+0010	+0010	+0·8	+0·6	+0·3	+0·1

SHELTER Good in the marina, Port de Hérel, 1·5–2·5m. Caution: at ent sharp turn restricts visibility. Access over sill HW –2½ to +3½. Depth over sill shown on lit digital display atop S bkwtr: eg 76=7·6m; 00 = no entry; hard to read in bright sun. The Avant Port (dries) is for commercial/ FVs.

NAVIGATION WPT 48°49′·34N 01°37′·09W, 235°/055° from/to S bkwtr lt (Fl R 4s), 0·95M. Le Videcoq WCM, VQ (9) 10s Whis, marks rks drying 0·8m, 3¼M W of Pte du Roc. Beware rks off Pte du Roc, La Fourchie and Banc de Tombelaine, 1M SSW of Le Loup lt. Appr is rough in strong W winds. Ent/exit under power; speed limit 4kn, 2kn in marina.

LIGHTS AND MARKS Hbr ent is 0·6M E of Pte du Roc (conspic), Fl (4) 15s 49m 23M, grey tr, R top. No ldg lts, but S bkwtr lt, Fl R 4s, on with TV mast leads 055° to ent. Best appr at night is with Le Loup bearing 085° to avoid pot markers off Pte du Roc; hbr lts are hard to see against town lts. Turn port at bkwtr to cross the sill between R/G piles, Oc R/G 4s. Sill of bathing pool to stbd is marked by 5 R piles, lit Fl Bu 4s.

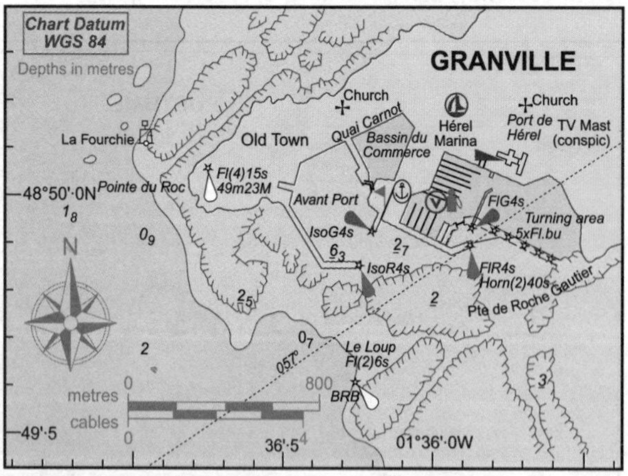

RADIO TELEPHONE Port VHF Ch 12 16 (HW±1½). Marina Ch 09, H24 in season.

TELEPHONE Hr Mr (Hérel) 02·33·50·20·06; Hr Mr (Port) 02·33·50·17·75; Aff Mar 02·33·50·00·59; CROSS 02·33·52·72·13; SNSM 02·33·61·26·51; ⊜ 02·33·50·19·90; Météo 02·33·22·91·77; Auto 08.36.68.08.50; Police 02·33·50·01·00; Dr 02·33·50·00·07; Hosp 02·33·90·74·75; Brit Consul 01·33·44·20·13.

FACILITIES Hérel Marina (850+150 visitors) ☎ 02·33·50·20·06, 📠 02·33·50·17·01, €1·80, ❶ pontoon G (1st to stbd), Slip, P, D, FW, ME, AC, BH (12 ton), C (10 ton), CH, Gaz, R, ⊡, V, Bar, SM, El, Sh, ⓔ; **YC de Granville** ☎ 02·33·50·04·25, 📠 02·33·50·06·59, L, M, BH, D, P, CH, ⊡, Slip FW, AB, Bar; **Services**: CH, M, ME, El, Ⓔ, Sh, SHOM, SM. **Town** P, D, ME, V, Gaz, R, Bar, ✉, Ⓑ, ⇌, ✈ (Dinard), www.granville.cci.fr. Ferry: UK via Jersey or Cherbourg.

ILES CHAUSEY *9.15.14*

Manche **48°52'·14N 01°49'·09W** S ent ❁❁◊✿✿✿

CHARTS AC 3656, *3659*; SHOM 7156, 7155, 7161; ECM 534, 535; Imray C33B; Stanfords 16, 26

TIDES –0500 Dover; ML 7·4; Duration 0530; Zone –0100

Standard Port ST-MALO (⟶)

Times				Height (metres)			
High Water		Low Water		MHWS	MHWN	MLWN	MLWS
0100	0800	0300	0800	12·2	9·3	4·2	1·5
1300	2000	1500	2000				
Differences ILES CHAUSEY (Grande Ile)							
+0005	+0005	+0015	+0015	+0·8	+0·7	+0·6	+0·4

SHELTER Good except in strong NW or SE winds. Grande Ile is not a Port of Entry for France; it is private, but may be visited. Moor fore-and-aft to W ⚓s, free; some dry at sp. Very crowded Sat/Sun in season especially as drying out in Port Homard is actively discouraged. Note the tidal range when ⚓ing or picking up ⚓. Tidal streams are not excessive.

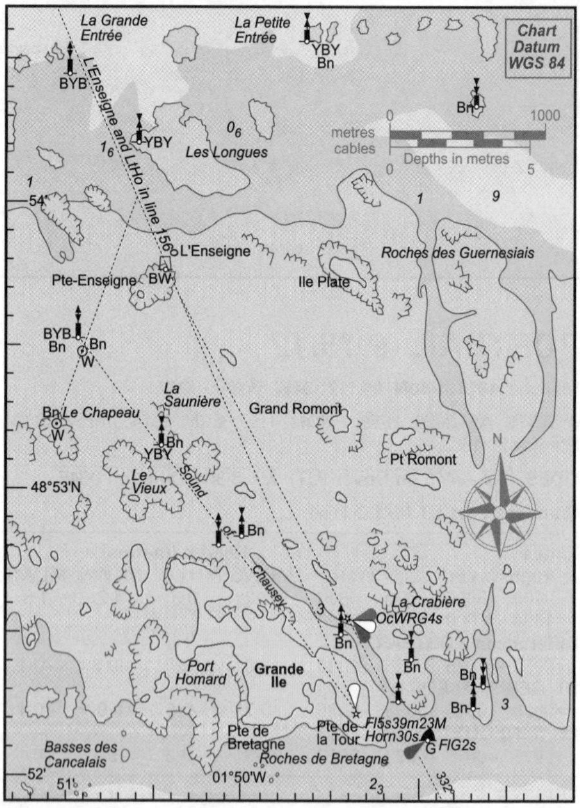

NAVIGATION WPT 48°51′·44N 01°48′·57W, 152°/332° from/to La Crabière lt, 1·2M. The easier route into the Sound is from the S, but beware rks E and S of Pte de la Tour, marked by ECM bns. The N route requires adequate ht of tide, SHOM 7134 or detailed SDs for transits, and/or local knowledge. Dangerous wk reported N of La Petite Entree (off chartlet).

LIGHTS AND MARKS Pte de la Tour, Fl 5s, is conspic. La Crabière, Oc WRG 4s 5m 9/6M, B tr, Y top; W sector leads into sound; see 9.15.4. From N, L'Enseigne bn tr (19m) on with Pte de la Tour lt ho leads 156°. From S, La Crabière on with L'Enseigne leads 332°.

RADIO TELEPHONE None.

TELEPHONE Police 02·33·52·72·02; CROSS 02·33·52·72·13; Auto 08.36.68.08.50; SNSM 02.33.50.28.33.

FACILITIES R. Tourelle L, ⊡. **Village** FW & V (limited), Gaz, R, Bar. See also Granville. Ferry to UK via Granville and Jersey.

TIME ZONE -0100
(French Standard Time)
Subtract 1 hour for UT
For French Summer Time add ONE hour in **non-shaded areas**

FRANCE – ST MALO

LAT 48°38′N LONG 2°02′W

TIMES AND HEIGHTS OF HIGH AND LOW WATERS

SPRING & NEAP TIDES
Dates in red are SPRINGS
Dates in blue are NEAPS

YEAR **2002**

JANUARY

Day		Time	m	Time	m	Time	m	Time	m
1	TU	0253	1.9	0816	12.3	1520	1.7	2046	11.9
2	W	0338	1.9	0901	12.2	1606	1.7	2131	11.8
3	TH	0422	2.1	0946	12.0	1652	2.0	2216	11.5
4	F	0507	2.4	1032	11.6	1738	2.3	2303	11.0
5	SA	0553	2.9	1120	11.1	1825	2.8	2353	10.5
6	SU	0642	3.3	1213	10.5	1917	3.3		
7	M	0053	10.1	0740	3.7	1318	10.1	2017	3.6
8	TU	0203	9.8	0849	3.9	1433	9.9	2129	3.7
9	W	0318	9.9	1006	3.8	1547	10.1	2242	3.6
10	TH	0426	10.3	1116	3.4	1653	10.4	2346	3.2
11	F	0525	10.7	1217	3.0	1750	10.8		
12	SA	0044	3.0	0616	11.1	1309	2.7	1840	11.0
13	SU	0130	2.7	0701	11.4	1353	2.5	● 1923	11.2
14	M	0210	2.6	0740	11.5	1432	2.4	2002	11.3
15	TU	0245	2.6	0816	11.6	1507	2.4	2037	11.3
16	W	0318	2.7	0849	11.5	1540	2.5	2109	11.1
17	TH	0349	2.8	0920	11.3	1610	2.7	2139	10.9
18	F	0417	3.0	0950	11.0	1640	3.0	2209	10.6
19	SA	0445	3.4	1020	10.6	1709	3.4	2239	10.2
20	SU	0514	3.7	1052	10.1	1741	3.7	2313	9.8
21	M	0549	4.1	1129	9.7	1820	4.1		
22	TU	0006	9.4	0636	4.5	1221	9.2	1913	4.5
23	W	0057	9.1	0742	4.7	1334	9.0	2023	4.6
24	TH	0217	9.1	0906	4.7	1500	9.1	2145	4.4
25	F	0337	9.4	1028	4.2	1616	9.6	2258	3.9
26	SA	0444	10.1	1135	3.5	1718	10.2		
27	SU	0008	3.2	0541	10.8	1234	2.8	1813	11.0
28	M	0101	2.6	0633	11.5	1330	2.1	○ 1904	11.6
29	TU	0154	2.0	0722	12.2	1423	1.5	1953	12.1
30	W	0245	1.5	0809	12.6	1513	1.1	2039	12.4
31	TH	0332	1.3	0854	12.8	1600	0.9	2122	12.5

FEBRUARY

Day		Time	m	Time	m	Time	m	Time	m
1	F	0416	1.3	0937	12.7	1643	1.1	2204	12.2
2	SA	0457	1.5	1019	12.4	1724	1.5	2245	11.8
3	SU	0537	2.0	1100	11.8	1803	2.2	2326	11.1
4	M	0617	2.7	1144	11.0	1845	2.9		
5	TU	0014	10.4	0703	3.4	1237	10.1	1935	3.7
6	W	0116	9.7	0804	4.1	1350	9.5	2045	4.3
7	TH	0240	9.3	0930	4.4	1520	9.3	2212	4.3
8	F	0406	9.5	1056	4.1	1641	9.6	2328	4.0
9	SA	0513	10.0	1203	3.5	1742	10.1		
10	SU	0030	3.5	0606	10.6	1256	3.0	1830	10.6
11	M	0117	3.0	0649	11.0	1339	2.7	1910	11.0
12	TU	0156	2.7	0725	11.4	1416	2.4	● 1945	11.3
13	W	0230	2.5	0759	11.6	1449	2.2	2017	11.4
14	TH	0301	2.3	0829	11.7	1520	2.1	2046	11.5
15	F	0331	2.3	0858	11.7	1550	2.1	2114	11.4
16	SA	0358	2.3	0926	11.5	1617	2.3	2141	11.3
17	SU	0424	2.6	0953	11.2	1643	2.7	2208	10.9
18	M	0449	2.9	1021	10.8	1710	3.1	2237	10.5
19	TU	0518	3.4	1051	10.2	1741	3.6	2310	10.0
20	W	0555	3.9	1130	9.6	1823	4.2	2354	9.4
21	TH	0646	4.5	1227	9.0	1923	4.7		
22	F	0108	8.9	0806	4.8	1402	8.7	2052	4.8
23	SA	0249	8.9	0946	4.5	1547	9.0	2224	4.3
24	SU	0419	9.6	1108	3.8	1702	9.9	2337	3.5
25	M	0525	10.5	1215	2.8	1801	10.8		
26	TU	0045	2.5	0620	11.5	1316	1.9	1852	11.7
27	W	0141	1.7	0710	12.4	1411	1.1	○ 1939	12.5
28	TH	0233	1.0	0756	13.0	1501	0.5	2023	12.9

MARCH

Day		Time	m	Time	m	Time	m	Time	m
1	F	0320	0.6	0839	13.3	1545	0.3	2105	13.0
2	SA	0402	0.6	0920	13.3	1626	0.5	2144	12.8
3	SU	0440	0.9	0959	12.8	1703	1.0	2221	12.2
4	M	0516	1.5	1037	12.1	1738	1.9	2258	11.4
5	TU	0551	2.4	1116	11.1	1813	2.9	2339	10.5
6	W	0631	3.4	1203	10.0	1856	3.9		
7	TH	0036	9.5	0725	4.3	1314	9.0	2002	4.7
8	F	0207	8.8	0858	4.8	1501	8.6	2147	4.9
9	SA	0349	8.9	1038	4.5	1632	9.0	2313	4.4
10	SU	0500	9.6	1147	3.8	1729	9.7		
11	M	0012	3.7	0549	10.2	1237	3.1	1812	10.4
12	TU	0058	3.1	0628	10.8	1317	2.6	1847	10.9
13	W	0135	2.6	0702	11.3	1353	2.2	1920	11.3
14	TH	0209	2.2	0734	11.6	1426	1.9	● 1950	11.6
15	F	0240	2.0	0804	11.9	1456	1.8	2019	11.8
16	SA	0309	1.8	0833	11.9	1525	1.7	2047	11.8
17	SU	0336	1.9	0900	11.9	1553	1.9	2114	11.7
18	M	0402	2.1	0928	11.6	1618	2.2	2141	11.4
19	TU	0428	2.5	0955	11.1	1644	2.7	2208	10.9
20	W	0455	3.0	1024	10.5	1713	3.3	2239	10.3
21	TH	0528	3.6	1059	9.8	1751	4.0	2318	9.6
22	F	0614	4.3	1149	9.1	1847	4.6		
23	SA	0025	8.9	0729	4.7	1322	8.5	2018	4.9
24	SU	0216	8.7	0917	4.6	1529	8.8	2200	4.4
25	M	0400	9.4	1047	3.7	1647	9.8	2317	3.5
26	TU	0508	10.4	1156	2.6	1743	10.9		
27	W	0026	2.4	0602	11.5	1257	1.6	1833	11.9
28	TH	0123	1.4	0650	12.5	1352	0.8	○ 1918	12.7
29	F	0214	0.7	0735	13.2	1441	0.2	2001	13.1
30	SA	0300	0.4	0818	13.4	1524	0.1	2041	13.2
31	SU	0341	0.3	0859	13.3	1603	0.4	2119	13.0

APRIL

Day		Time	m	Time	m	Time	m	Time	m
1	M	0419	0.7	0937	12.8	1638	1.1	2156	12.3
2	TU	0453	1.5	1014	11.9	1711	2.0	2232	11.4
3	W	0527	2.4	1052	10.8	1744	3.1	2311	10.4
4	TH	0604	3.4	1137	9.7	1823	4.1		
5	F	0000	9.3	0656	4.4	1246	8.7	1927	5.0
6	SA	0136	8.6	0826	4.9	1436	8.3	2118	5.2
7	SU	0321	8.6	1008	4.6	1607	8.7	2245	4.6
8	M	0431	9.2	1114	4.0	1701	9.5	2341	3.8
9	TU	0518	9.9	1202	3.3	1740	10.2		
10	W	0025	3.1	0556	10.6	1243	2.7	1815	10.8
11	TH	0103	2.6	0631	11.1	1320	2.2	1848	11.3
12	F	0138	2.2	0704	11.5	1355	1.9	● 1920	11.6
13	SA	0212	1.9	0736	11.8	1428	1.7	1950	11.8
14	SU	0243	1.7	0806	11.9	1458	1.6	2019	11.9
15	M	0313	1.7	0835	11.8	1528	1.8	2048	11.8
16	TU	0342	1.9	0905	11.6	1555	2.1	2116	11.6
17	W	0410	2.3	0935	11.2	1624	2.6	2146	11.1
18	TH	0440	2.8	1007	10.5	1655	3.2	2220	10.4
19	F	0515	3.4	1045	9.8	1735	3.9	2303	9.7
20	SA	0603	4.1	1139	9.1	1833	4.5		
21	SU	0015	9.1	0718	4.5	1313	8.6	2002	4.7
22	M	0158	8.9	0858	4.3	1509	9.0	2138	4.2
23	TU	0335	9.5	1023	3.5	1622	9.9	2253	3.3
24	W	0442	10.5	1132	2.5	1718	11.0		
25	TH	0007	2.3	0536	11.5	1232	1.6	1806	11.9
26	F	0058	1.5	0625	12.3	1327	0.9	1852	12.6
27	SA	0150	0.9	0711	12.9	1415	0.5	○ 1935	12.9
28	SU	0236	0.6	0755	13.1	1459	0.5	2016	13.0
29	M	0318	0.7	0836	12.9	1538	0.8	2055	12.7
30	TU	0356	1.0	0916	12.3	1613	1.5	2133	12.1

Chart Datum: 6·29 metres below IGN Datum

TIME ZONE -0100
(French Standard Time)
Subtract 1 hour for UT
For French Summer Time add ONE hour in **non-shaded areas**

FRANCE – ST MALO

LAT 48°38′N LONG 2°02′W

TIMES AND HEIGHTS OF HIGH AND LOW WATERS

SPRING & NEAP TIDES
Dates in red are **SPRINGS**
Dates in blue are **NEAPS**

YEAR **2002**

MAY

Date	Day	Time	m	Time	m	Time	m	Time	m
1	W	0431	1.7	0954	11.5	1646	2.4	2210	11.2
2	TH	0506	2.6	1034	10.5	1718	3.3	2250	10.3
3	F	0543	3.5	1119	9.5	1757	4.2	2341	9.3
4	SA	0632	4.3	1221	8.7	1855	5.0		
5	SU	0057	8.6	0746	4.8	1347	8.3	2029	5.2
6	M	0227	8.5	0913	4.7	1512	8.6	2152	4.8
7	TU	0339	8.9	1020	4.2	1611	9.2	2250	4.1
8	W	0431	9.5	1112	3.5	1656	9.9	2337	3.4
9	TH	0514	10.2	1158	2.9	1734	10.5		
10	F	0022	2.8	0553	10.8	1240	2.4	1811	11.1
11	SA	0102	2.4	0630	11.2	1320	2.1	1846	11.4
12	SU	0139	2.1	0705	11.5	1356	1.9	● 1920	11.7
13	M	0215	1.9	0739	11.6	1431	1.9	1953	11.8
14	TU	0249	1.9	0813	11.6	1504	1.9	2025	11.8
15	W	0323	2.0	0846	11.5	1536	2.2	2058	11.6
16	TH	0356	2.3	0922	11.1	1610	2.6	2134	11.2
17	F	0433	2.7	1001	10.6	1648	3.1	2214	10.6
18	SA	0514	3.2	1046	10.0	1733	3.7	2304	9.9
19	SU	0606	3.7	1145	9.4	1832	4.1		
20	M	0015	9.5	0715	4.0	1306	9.1	1950	4.3
21	TU	0139	9.4	0836	3.8	1436	9.4	2111	3.9
22	W	0302	9.8	0954	3.3	1547	10.0	2223	3.2
23	TH	0409	10.5	1102	2.6	1646	10.8	2327	2.5
24	F	0506	11.3	1203	2.0	1737	11.6		
25	SA	0029	1.9	0558	11.9	1259	1.5	1825	12.1
26	SU	0123	1.4	0647	12.2	1349	1.3	○ 1911	12.4
27	M	0211	1.3	0733	12.3	1433	1.3	1954	12.4
28	TU	0255	1.3	0817	12.1	1513	1.6	2035	12.2
29	W	0334	1.6	0858	11.7	1549	2.1	2114	11.7
30	TH	0411	2.1	0939	11.1	1623	2.7	2153	11.1
31	F	0447	2.7	1019	10.4	1657	3.4	2233	10.4

JUNE

Date	Day	Time	m	Time	m	Time	m	Time	m
1	SA	0524	3.4	1101	9.7	1734	4.0	2318	9.6
2	SU	0606	4.0	1148	9.1	1821	4.6		
3	M	0010	9.0	0659	4.4	1245	8.7	1926	4.9
4	TU	0116	8.7	0805	4.5	1352	8.7	2040	4.8
5	W	0225	8.8	0912	4.3	1459	8.9	2146	4.4
6	TH	0328	9.2	1013	3.9	1558	9.5	2242	3.9
7	F	0422	9.7	1107	3.4	1647	10.1	2333	3.3
8	SA	0510	10.3	1157	2.9	1732	10.6		
9	SU	0022	2.8	0554	10.7	1242	2.6	1813	11.1
10	M	0106	2.5	0636	11.0	1325	2.3	1852	11.4
11	TU	0148	2.2	0716	11.3	1405	2.2	● 1930	11.6
12	W	0228	2.1	0755	11.4	1444	2.1	2008	11.7
13	TH	0308	2.0	0835	11.4	1523	2.2	2048	11.6
14	F	0349	2.1	0917	11.2	1604	2.4	2130	11.4
15	SA	0432	2.4	1001	10.9	1647	2.7	2215	11.0
16	SU	0517	2.7	1049	10.5	1734	3.1	2305	10.6
17	M	0608	3.0	1143	10.1	1828	3.5		
18	TU	0009	10.2	0704	3.3	1245	9.8	1930	3.6
19	W	0111	10.0	0809	3.4	1356	9.8	2038	3.6
20	TH	0224	10.0	0919	3.3	1507	10.0	2149	3.3
21	F	0335	10.3	1029	3.0	1612	10.5	2257	2.9
22	SA	0438	10.8	1134	2.6	1711	11.0	2359	2.5
23	SU	0536	11.1	1233	2.3	1804	11.4		
24	M	0059	2.2	0629	11.4	1325	2.1	○ 1853	11.7
25	TU	0150	2.0	0718	11.5	1411	2.1	1938	11.8
26	W	0235	2.0	0803	11.5	1453	2.2	2020	11.7
27	TH	0315	2.1	0845	11.3	1530	2.4	2059	11.5
28	F	0353	2.3	0924	11.0	1604	2.7	2136	11.2
29	SA	0427	2.6	1000	10.6	1637	3.1	2212	10.7
30	SU	0501	3.1	1035	10.2	1710	3.6	2248	10.2

JULY

Date	Day	Time	m	Time	m	Time	m	Time	m
1	M	0535	3.5	1111	9.7	1745	4.0	2326	9.7
2	TU	0612	3.9	1150	9.4	1827	4.3		
3	W	0014	9.3	0659	4.2	1239	9.1	1922	4.6
4	TH	0109	9.0	0757	4.3	1340	9.0	2030	4.6
5	F	0217	9.0	0905	4.3	1450	9.1	2142	4.3
6	SA	0326	9.3	1012	4.0	1556	9.6	2246	3.9
7	SU	0428	9.7	1113	3.6	1654	10.1	2342	3.4
8	M	0522	10.2	1207	3.1	1744	10.6		
9	TU	0036	2.9	0612	10.6	1257	2.7	1830	11.1
10	W	0125	2.5	0658	11.0	1344	2.4	● 1915	11.5
11	TH	0212	2.1	0744	11.3	1431	2.1	1958	11.8
12	F	0259	1.9	0828	11.6	1516	2.0	2042	11.9
13	SA	0345	1.7	0913	11.6	1601	1.9	2126	11.9
14	SU	0430	1.8	0957	11.5	1645	2.0	2210	11.7
15	M	0514	1.9	1041	11.3	1728	2.3	2255	11.4
16	TU	0558	2.3	1127	10.9	1814	2.7	2343	10.9
17	W	0644	2.7	1217	10.4	1904	3.2		
18	TH	0040	10.4	0737	3.2	1317	10.0	2004	3.5
19	F	0147	10.0	0842	3.5	1429	9.9	2117	3.7
20	SA	0304	9.9	0958	3.6	1544	10.0	2234	3.5
21	SU	0418	10.1	1112	3.4	1653	10.4	2342	3.1
22	M	0523	10.4	1215	3.0	1753	10.8		
23	TU	0045	2.7	0620	10.8	1310	2.7	1843	11.2
24	W	0136	2.5	0709	11.0	1357	2.6	○ 1928	11.5
25	TH	0220	2.3	0752	11.2	1437	2.5	2007	11.6
26	F	0259	2.2	0829	11.2	1513	2.5	2042	11.6
27	SA	0333	2.3	0903	11.2	1545	2.5	2115	11.4
28	SU	0405	2.4	0934	11.0	1614	2.7	2146	11.2
29	M	0435	2.6	1004	10.8	1642	3.0	2215	10.8
30	TU	0502	3.0	1033	10.4	1710	3.3	2245	10.4
31	W	0531	3.4	1104	10.0	1740	3.8	2319	9.8

AUGUST

Date	Day	Time	m	Time	m	Time	m	Time	m
1	TH	0606	3.8	1141	9.6	1820	4.2		
2	F	0009	9.3	0651	4.2	1231	9.2	1916	4.6
3	SA	0107	8.9	0753	4.6	1342	8.9	2035	4.8
4	SU	0230	8.8	0915	4.6	1507	9.1	2200	4.5
5	M	0351	9.1	1033	4.2	1622	9.6	2310	3.8
6	TU	0458	9.7	1138	3.6	1722	10.3		
7	W	0013	3.1	0554	10.4	1236	3.0	1814	11.0
8	TH	0107	2.5	0645	11.1	1329	2.3	● 1902	11.6
9	F	0200	1.9	0732	11.6	1420	1.8	1948	12.2
10	SA	0250	1.4	0818	12.1	1508	1.4	2032	12.5
11	SU	0337	1.1	0901	12.3	1552	1.2	2114	12.7
12	M	0420	1.0	0943	12.3	1634	1.3	2156	12.5
13	TU	0500	1.3	1023	12.0	1714	1.7	2236	12.0
14	W	0539	1.8	1103	11.5	1754	2.3	2318	11.3
15	TH	0618	2.5	1147	10.8	1837	3.0		
16	F	0008	10.5	0704	3.3	1241	10.0	1932	3.7
17	SA	0114	9.7	0806	4.0	1357	9.5	2050	4.2
18	SU	0242	9.3	0935	4.3	1528	9.5	2220	4.0
19	M	0410	9.5	1100	4.0	1647	9.9	2334	3.5
20	TU	0520	10.0	1206	3.5	1747	10.6		
21	W	0036	3.0	0613	10.6	1259	3.0	1833	11.1
22	TH	0124	2.5	0656	11.0	1343	2.6	○ 1913	11.5
23	F	0204	2.3	0733	11.3	1420	2.4	1947	11.7
24	SA	0239	2.1	0806	11.4	1453	2.2	2019	11.8
25	SU	0310	2.0	0836	11.5	1522	2.2	2048	11.8
26	M	0339	2.1	0903	11.5	1549	2.3	2116	11.6
27	TU	0406	2.2	0930	11.3	1615	2.5	2142	11.3
28	W	0431	2.6	0957	11.0	1639	2.9	2209	10.9
29	TH	0456	3.0	1024	10.5	1705	3.4	2237	10.3
30	F	0524	3.6	1054	10.0	1737	4.0	2311	9.6
31	SA	0601	4.2	1134	9.4	1823	4.6		

Chart Datum: 6·29 metres below IGN Datum

TIME ZONE -0100
(French Standard Time)
Subtract 1 hour for UT
For French Summer Time add ONE hour in **non-shaded areas**

FRANCE – ST MALO

LAT 48°38'N LONG 2°02'W

TIMES AND HEIGHTS OF HIGH AND LOW WATERS

SPRING & NEAP TIDES
Dates in red are SPRINGS
Dates in blue are NEAPS

YEAR **2002**

SEPTEMBER

Date	Time	m	Time	m	Time	m	Time	m
1 SU	0010	8.9	0655	4.8	1237	8.8	1936	5.0
2 M	0136	8.5	0822	5.0	1422	8.6	2119	4.9
3 TU	0326	8.7	1002	4.7	1600	9.2	2245	4.1
4 W	0442	9.5	1117	3.8	1706	10.1	2350	3.2
5 TH	0539	10.5	1218	2.9	1759	11.1		
6 F	0051	2.2	0629	11.4	1313	2.1	1847	12.0
7 SA	0145	1.4	0716	12.1	1405	1.3	● 1932	12.7
8 SU	0235	0.8	0759	12.7	1453	0.9	2015	13.1
9 M	0321	0.5	0841	13.0	1537	0.7	2056	13.2
10 TU	0402	0.5	0921	12.9	1617	0.8	2135	13.0
11 W	0440	1.0	0959	12.4	1654	1.3	2214	12.3
12 TH	0516	1.7	1037	11.7	1731	2.2	2253	11.4
13 F	0551	2.7	1118	10.8	1812	3.1	2339	10.3
14 SA	0633	3.7	1210	9.8	1905	4.1		
15 SU	0049	9.3	0736	4.6	1334	9.1	2032	4.6
16 M	0231	8.8	0922	4.9	1521	9.1	2213	4.4
17 TU	0407	9.1	1053	4.4	1640	9.7	2325	3.7
18 W	0511	9.8	1155	3.6	1733	10.4		
19 TH	0020	3.0	0556	10.5	1242	2.9	1813	11.1
20 F	0102	2.5	0633	11.1	1321	2.5	1849	11.5
21 SA	0139	2.2	0706	11.4	1355	2.2	○ 1921	11.8
22 SU	0212	2.0	0736	11.7	1426	2.0	1951	12.0
23 M	0242	1.8	0805	11.8	1455	1.9	2019	12.0
24 TU	0310	1.9	0832	11.8	1522	2.0	2045	11.9
25 W	0337	2.0	0858	11.7	1548	2.3	2111	11.6
26 TH	0401	2.4	0924	11.4	1612	2.7	2137	11.1
27 F	0425	2.9	0950	10.9	1637	3.2	2205	10.5
28 SA	0452	3.5	1018	10.3	1707	3.8	2236	9.7
29 SU	0525	4.2	1053	9.6	1749	4.5	2320	8.9
30 M	0616	4.9	1149	8.8	1858	5.1		

OCTOBER

Date	Time	m	Time	m	Time	m	Time	m
1 TU	0053	8.4	0745	5.3	1346	8.5	2047	5.0
2 W	0307	8.6	0936	4.9	1541	9.1	2222	4.2
3 TH	0424	9.6	1055	3.9	1646	10.1	2329	3.1
4 F	0519	10.7	1156	2.8	1737	11.3		
5 SA	0031	2.0	0607	11.7	1252	1.8	1824	12.2
6 SU	0124	1.1	0652	12.5	1344	1.0	● 1909	13.0
7 M	0213	0.6	0735	13.1	1432	0.6	1952	13.4
8 TU	0258	0.4	0816	13.3	1516	0.5	2033	13.4
9 W	0339	0.5	0856	13.1	1556	0.8	2113	13.0
10 TH	0416	1.1	0934	12.5	1634	1.4	2152	12.2
11 F	0451	2.0	1012	11.7	1711	2.3	2232	11.2
12 SA	0525	3.0	1053	10.7	1751	3.3	2318	10.0
13 SU	0606	4.1	1146	9.6	1845	4.3		
14 M	0030	8.9	0711	5.0	1314	8.9	2014	4.9
15 TU	0214	8.5	0903	5.2	1502	8.9	2152	4.6
16 W	0347	8.9	1031	4.6	1616	9.5	2259	3.9
17 TH	0444	9.7	1127	3.8	1704	10.2	2347	3.2
18 F	0525	10.4	1209	3.1	1742	10.8		
19 SA	0028	2.7	0600	11.0	1247	2.6	1816	11.3
20 SU	0105	2.3	0633	11.4	1322	2.2	1849	11.7
21 M	0139	2.0	0704	11.7	1355	2.0	○ 1920	11.9
22 TU	0211	1.9	0733	11.9	1426	2.0	1949	11.9
23 W	0241	1.9	0801	11.9	1456	2.0	2018	11.8
24 TH	0309	2.1	0829	11.8	1524	2.3	2045	11.6
25 F	0335	2.4	0856	11.5	1551	2.7	2113	11.1
26 SA	0402	2.9	0924	11.1	1618	3.2	2143	10.5
27 SU	0430	3.5	0955	10.5	1651	3.8	2218	9.8
28 M	0506	4.2	1033	9.7	1735	4.4	2306	9.1
29 TU	0559	4.8	1132	9.0	1843	4.9		
30 W	0035	8.6	0725	5.1	1319	8.7	2021	4.8
31 TH	0238	8.8	0907	4.7	1509	9.2	2152	4.1

NOVEMBER

Date	Time	m	Time	m	Time	m	Time	m
1 F	0354	9.7	1026	3.8	1615	10.2	2300	3.0
2 SA	0450	10.8	1129	2.7	1708	11.3		
3 SU	0009	2.0	0538	11.8	1225	1.8	1757	12.2
4 M	0057	1.3	0624	12.5	1318	1.2	● 1843	12.9
5 TU	0147	0.8	0709	13.0	1407	0.8	1928	13.2
6 W	0233	0.7	0751	13.1	1453	0.8	2011	13.1
7 TH	0315	1.0	0833	12.9	1535	1.1	2053	12.6
8 F	0353	1.6	0913	12.3	1614	1.7	2134	11.9
9 SA	0428	2.4	0953	11.6	1653	2.5	2216	10.9
10 SU	0504	3.3	1035	10.6	1734	3.5	2304	9.9
11 M	0545	4.3	1128	9.7	1825	4.3		
12 TU	0001	9.0	0644	5.0	1241	9.0	1938	4.8
13 W	0129	8.6	0815	5.3	1411	8.8	2100	4.8
14 TH	0254	8.7	0939	4.9	1527	9.1	2207	4.3
15 F	0356	9.3	1038	4.2	1619	9.7	2259	3.7
16 SA	0441	9.9	1124	3.6	1701	10.3	2343	3.1
17 SU	0520	10.6	1206	3.0	1738	10.9		
18 M	0025	2.7	0556	11.1	1245	2.6	1814	11.3
19 TU	0103	2.4	0630	11.5	1323	2.4	1849	11.5
20 W	0139	2.2	0703	11.7	1358	2.2	○ 1923	11.6
21 TH	0212	2.2	0735	11.8	1431	2.2	1955	11.6
22 F	0244	2.3	0806	11.7	1503	2.4	2027	11.4
23 SA	0315	2.6	0837	11.5	1536	2.7	2100	11.1
24 SU	0347	2.9	0910	11.2	1610	3.1	2135	10.6
25 M	0421	3.4	0948	10.7	1648	3.5	2217	10.0
26 TU	0503	3.9	1032	10.1	1735	4.0	2309	9.5
27 W	0557	4.4	1131	9.5	1837	4.3		
28 TH	0023	9.1	0708	4.6	1252	9.3	1954	4.3
29 F	0154	9.2	0831	4.4	1423	9.5	2114	3.9
30 SA	0312	9.8	0949	3.8	1535	10.2	2225	3.2

DECEMBER

Date	Time	m	Time	m	Time	m	Time	m
1 SU	0414	10.6	1056	3.0	1635	11.0	2328	2.5
2 M	0508	11.4	1156	2.3	1728	11.8		
3 TU	0029	1.9	0558	12.1	1252	1.7	1819	12.3
4 W	0122	1.5	0646	12.5	1344	1.4	● 1908	12.5
5 TH	0210	1.4	0731	12.6	1432	1.3	1954	12.4
6 F	0253	1.6	0815	12.5	1517	1.5	2039	12.1
7 SA	0333	2.1	0858	12.1	1558	2.0	2122	11.5
8 SU	0410	2.7	0939	11.5	1638	2.6	2204	10.8
9 M	0447	3.3	1021	10.8	1717	3.3	2247	10.1
10 TU	0525	4.0	1105	10.0	1759	3.9	2332	9.4
11 W	0609	4.6	1155	9.4	1848	4.5		
12 TH	0026	8.9	0707	5.0	1255	9.0	1947	4.7
13 F	0129	8.7	0816	5.0	1404	8.9	2051	4.7
14 SA	0238	8.9	0925	4.7	1511	9.1	2153	4.3
15 SU	0340	9.3	1026	4.3	1608	9.6	2249	3.8
16 M	0432	9.9	1119	3.7	1656	10.1	2340	3.4
17 TU	0517	10.5	1207	3.2	1740	10.6		
18 W	0027	3.0	0559	11.0	1251	2.8	1822	11.0
19 TH	0109	2.7	0638	11.3	1331	2.6	○ 1901	11.2
20 F	0148	2.6	0715	11.5	1410	2.4	1939	11.3
21 SA	0226	2.5	0751	11.6	1449	2.4	2017	11.3
22 SU	0303	2.5	0828	11.6	1528	2.5	2055	11.2
23 M	0342	2.7	0907	11.5	1608	2.6	2136	11.0
24 TU	0422	2.9	0949	11.2	1651	2.9	2219	10.6
25 W	0505	3.2	1034	10.8	1736	3.2	2307	10.3
26 TH	0553	3.6	1124	10.4	1827	3.5		
27 F	0009	9.9	0648	3.9	1224	10.0	1925	3.7
28 SA	0110	9.7	0753	4.0	1336	9.9	2031	3.7
29 SU	0225	9.8	0906	3.8	1452	10.1	2145	3.5
30 M	0336	10.2	1021	3.5	1603	10.5	2256	3.1
31 TU	0440	10.8	1130	2.9	1706	11.0		

Chart Datum: 6·29 metres below IGN Datum

ST MALO/DINARD *9.15.15*

Ille et Vilaine **48°38'·48N 02°01'·91W**
Vauban ❀❀⚓⚓✿✿✿ Sablons ❀❀⚓⚓✿✿✿

CHARTS AC 2700, *3659, 2669*; SHOM 7155, 7156, 6966; ECM 535; Imray C33B; Stanfords 16, 26

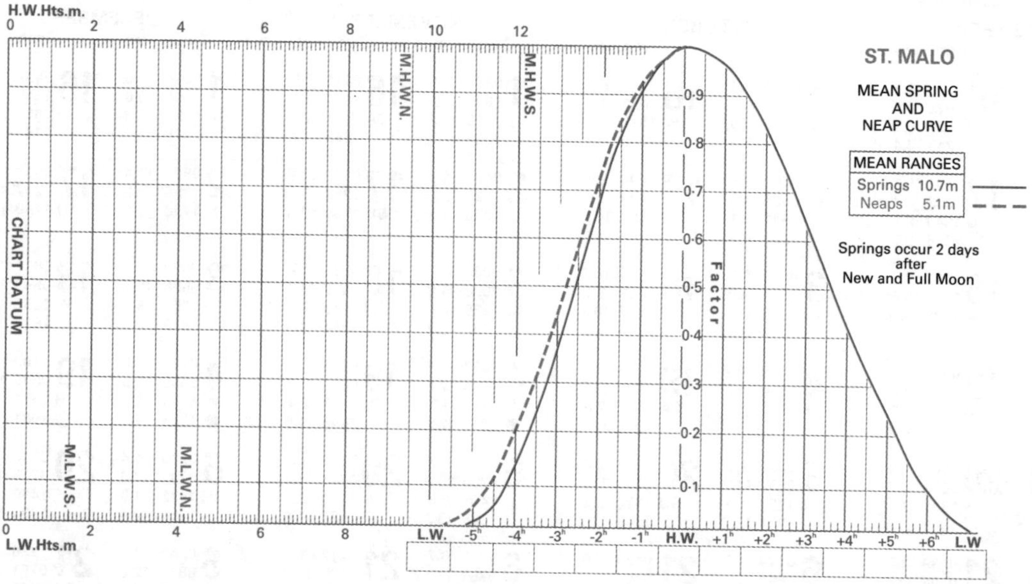

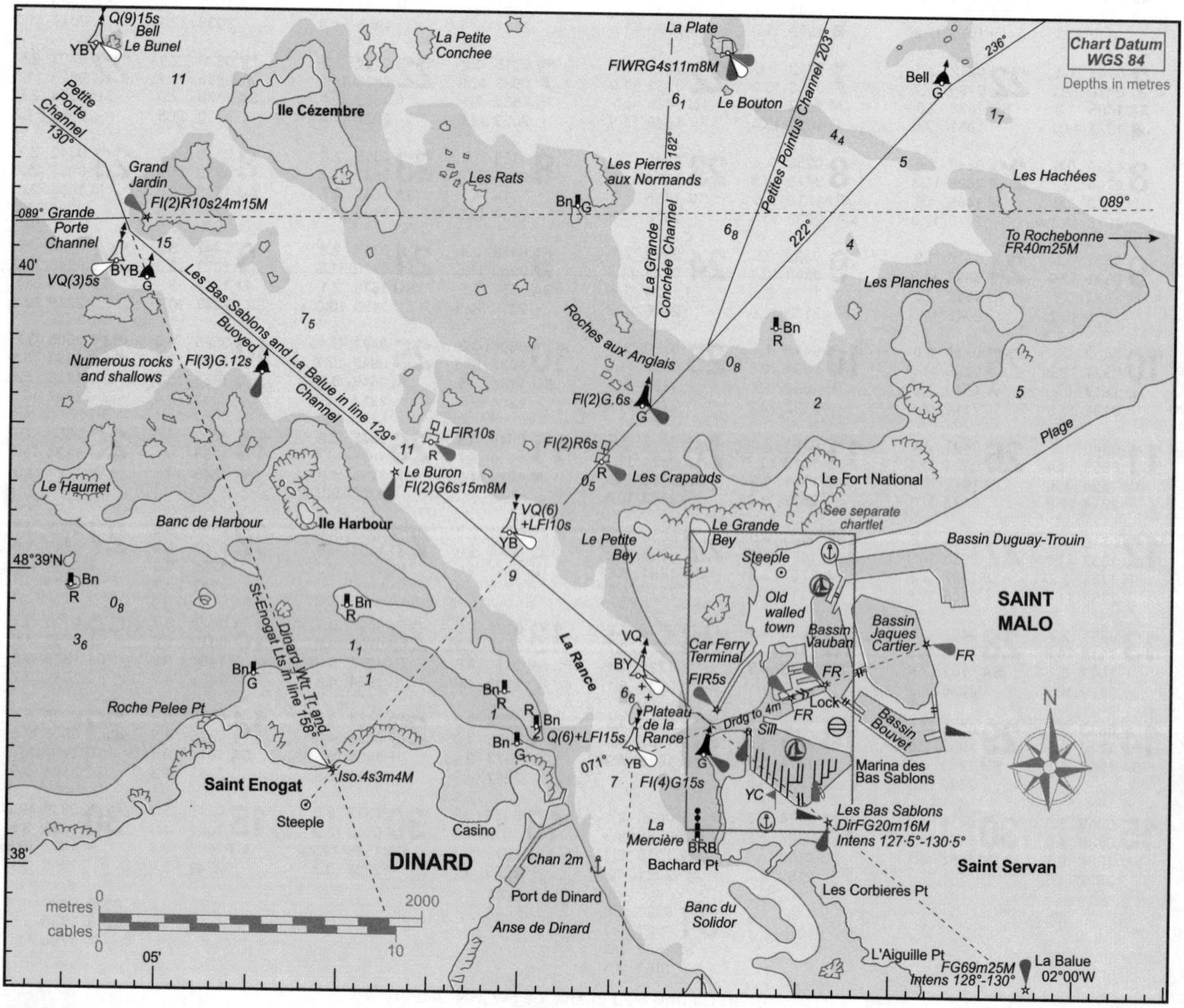

ST MALO/DINARD *continued*

TIDES –0506 Dover; ML 6·8; Duration 0535; Zone –0100.

SHELTER Two options:

1. Lock into the Bassin Vauban, min depth 6m. Excellent shelter near the walled city. Use pontoon appropriate to your length as marked. Bassin Duguay -Trouin, via bridge, is better for long stay. No ⚓ in basins; 3kn speed limit. Outside the lock are 3 waiting buoys N of appr chan; keep clear of vedette and Condor berths. See next column for lock times and signals.
2. Good shelter nearer St Servan in Bas Sablons marina, entered over sill 2m above CD. Ⓥ berths are 32-66 (even side) and 43-75 (odd side) on Pontoon A, and 92-102 and 91-101 on Pontoon B. N end of pontoon 'A' is exposed to NW winds. Caution: marina ent is only 40m wide, close S of ferry pier extending W from N corner of Bas-Sablons basin and beyond marina bkwtr, Fl G 4s 7m 5M. Two W waiting buoys outside. Depth of water over sill is shown on a digital gauge atop the bkwtr, visible only from seaward; inside, a conventional gauge at base of bkwtr shows depths <3m.

At **Dinard** there is a yacht ⚓ and moorings, reached by a beaconed chan, all dredged 2m, but virtually filled by local boats.

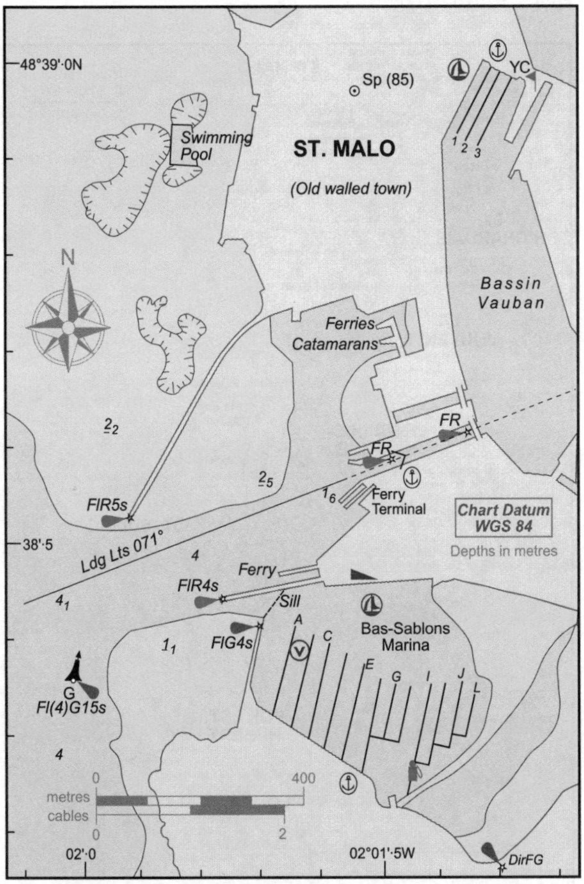

NAVIGATION WPT Fairway SWM buoy, L Fl 10s Whis, 48°41´·38N 02°07´·28W, 307°/127° from/to Grand Jardin lt, 1·9M. Care is needed due to many dangerous rks around the appr chans, plus strong tidal streams. The 3 main chans are:

1. Petite Porte (130°/129°); best from N or NW and at night.
2. Grande Porte (089°/129°); from the W.

These 2 chans meet at Le Grand Jardin lt and continue 129°.

3. La Grande Conchée (182°); most direct from N.

The first two are well lit. In fresh W'lies it can be quite rough in the vicinity of Le Grand Jardin.

LIGHTS AND MARKS Chenal de la Petite Porte: Ldg lts 130°, front, Le Grand Jardin, Fl (2) R 10s 24m 15M, grey tr; rear, La Balue, FG 69m 25M. Chenal de la Grande Porte: Ldg lts 089°, front, Le Grand Jardin; rear, Rochebonne, FR 40m 24M, (off chartlet) 4·2M from front; leads into Chenal de la Petite Porte. Inner ldg lts 129° from Le Grand Jardin lt ho: Front, Les Bas Sablons, FG 20m 16M; rear, La Balue (as above). La Plate lt, Fl WRG 4s 11m 9/6M, W140°-203°, R203°-210°, W210°-225°, G225°-140°.

St Malo lock: Ldg lts, 2 FR, 071° into lock. Lock operates five times in each direction, ie

Inbound: HW –2½, –1½, –½, HW+½, +1½.
Outbound: HW–2, –1, HW, +1, +2.

Freeflow operation is rare due to road traffic over rolling bridge.

Lock sigs:

● Ⓦ ●	No ent to lock without instructions
● ● ●	Boats may enter lock
● ● ●	No ent. Keep 200m from gates

● alongside the top lt shows that both gates are open; instructions are the same, but beware current.

2 ● over ● = all movements prohib, except big ship departure.

RADIO TELEPHONE Call: *St Malo Port* or *Grand Jardin* VHF Ch **12** 16 (H24). Port Vauban and Les Bas Sablons marinas Ch 09.

TELEPHONE

ST MALO: Port Hr Mr 02·99·20·25·01, fax 02·99·40·25·87; Hr Mr (Vauban) 02·99·56·51·91; Hr Mr (Sablons) 02·99·81·71·34; Aff Mar 02·99·56·87·00; CROSS 02·98·89·31·31; SNSM 02·98·89· 31·31; ⊖ 02·99·81·65·90; Météo 02·99·46·10·46; Auto 08.36.68.08.35; Police 02·99·81·52·30; Ⓗ 02·99·56·56·19; Brit Consul 02·99·46·26·64.

DINARD: Hr Mr 02·99·46·65·55; ⊖ 02·99·46·12·42; Météo 02·99·46·10·46; Auto 08.36.68.08.35; Ⓗ 02·99·46·18·68.

FACILITIES

ST MALO: **Bassin Vauban** (250 + 100 Ⓥ) ☎ 02·99·56·51·91, 📠 02.99.56.57.81, €2·58, FW, AC, C (1 ton); **Société Nautique de la Baie de St. Malo** ☎ 02·99·40·84·42, 📠 02.99.56.39.41, Bar (visitors welcome).

ST SERVAN: **Marina Les Bas-Sablons** (1216 + 64 visitors on Pontoon A, berths 43-75 and 32-64) ☎ 02·99·81·71·34, 📠 02.99.81.91.81, €2.13, Slip, C, AC, FW, CH, BH (10 ton), Gaz, R, YC, Bar, P & D at Pontoon I; Note: Fuel may only be paid for by French credit card. **Services:** El, Ⓔ, ME, CH, Sh, C, BY, SM, SHOM. **Town** Slip, P, Gaz, D, ME, El, Sh, C, V, R, Bar, ✉, Ⓑ, ⇌, ✈ (Dinard). Ferry: Portsmouth, Poole or Jersey.

DINARD: **Port de Dinard** ☎ 02·99·46·65·55, Slip, ⚓, M €1.83, P, D, L, FW, temp AB; **YC de Dinard** ☎ 02·99·46·14·32, Bar; **Services:** ME, El, Ⓔ, Sh, M, SM. **Town** P, D, ME, El, CH, V, Gaz, R, Bar, ✉, Ⓑ, ⇌, ✈.

OTHER HARBOURS EAST OF ST MALO

CANCALE, Ille-et-Vilaine, **48°40´·04N 01°51´·19W**. AC *3659*; SHOM 7131, 7155. HW –0510 on Dover (UT); ML 7·2m; Duration 0535. See 9.15.13. A drying hbr just inside Bay of Mont St Michel, 1M SW of Pte de la Chaine. Area dries to about 1M off-shore; ⚓ off Pte de la Chaine in deep water. Drying berths usually available in La Houle, the hbr in Cancale. Exposed to winds SW to SE. Jetty hd lt Oc (3) G 12s 12m 8M, obsc when brg < 223°. Facilities: **Quay** D, P, C (1·5 ton), FW; **Services:** El, M, ME, Sh; **Club Nautique de Cancale** ☎ 02·99·89·90·22. **Town** (famous for oysters), Ⓑ, Bar, D, P, ✉, R, V.

ROTHENEUF, Ille-et-Vilaine, **48°41´·36N 01°57´·65W**. AC *3659*; SHOM 7131, 7155. HW –0510 on Dover (UT); Tides as for St. Malo; ML 7·0m; Duration 0540. Complete shelter in hbr which dries completely. ⚓ outside in 4m just N of spar bn marking ent. Rks on both sides of ent which is less than 170m wide. Safest to enter when rks uncovered. Ldg line at 163°, W side of Pte Benard and old converted windmill. There are no lts. Facilities: FW, Slip. **Village** Bar, D, P, R, V.

RIVER RANCE/DINAN *9.15.16*

Ille-et-Vilaine **48°37'·04N 02°01'·71W** (Barrage) ❁❁◊◊✿✿

CHARTS AC 2700, *3659*; SHOM 4233, 7130; Imray C33B; Stanfords 26

TIDES Standard Port ST MALO (⟵) Zone –0100
Water levels up-river of the Rance hydro-electric tidal barrage are strongly affected by the operation of the sluice gates and occasional use of the turbines as pumps. On most days from 0700 – 2100LT, 4m above CD is maintained. There is generally 8·5m above CD for a period of 4 hours from 0700 – 2000LT. A French language pamphlet, issued by Électricité de France, should be obtained from Hr Mr's at St Malo or Bas Sablons, or from the office at the barrage lock. It gives forecasts for the summer months of when heights of 4m and 8·5m above CD will occur in the period 0700 – 2000LT. The local daily paper *Ouest-France* gives a forecast for the next day of HW and LW up-stream of the barrage, under the heading *Usine Marémotrice de la Rance*.

SHELTER Good shelter up-river dependent on wind direction. The principal ⚓s/moorings on the E bank are at St Suliac and Mordreuc, and at La Richardais, La Jouvente, Le Minihic and La Pommeraie on the W bank. Marinas at Plouër, Lyvet (E bank, beyond Chatelier lock) and Dinan: see opp.

NAVIGATION From St Malo/Dinard, appr the lock at the W end of the barrage between a prohib area to port, marked by PHM buoys and wire cables, and Pointe de La Jument to stbd. 3 white waiting buoys are on the E side of the appr chan, close to the prohibited zone. There is one similar buoy upstream of the barrage. Lock opening by day from seaward on the hour, every hour provided the level is at least 4m above CD on both sides of the barrage. Yachts should arrive at H –20 mins,. The lifting road-bridge across the lock opens only between H and H +15. Boats leaving the lock have priority. Up-river of the lock a further prohib area to port is marked as above.
The 3M chan to St Suliac has min depth of 2m; the next 6M to the Chatelier lock partially dries. The suspension bridge and road bridge at Port St. Hubert have 23m clearance. A viaduct 1M beyond Mordreuc has 19m clearance.
The Chatelier lock and swing bridge operate 0800-2000LT, provided there is at least 8·5m rise of tide. HW Chatelier is 2-3 hours after HW St Malo depending on the barrage. Allow 2-3 hours from the barrage to Chatelier. The final 3M to Dinan has a published min depth in the marked chan of 1·4m; check with lock-keeper. Beware overhead cables 16m air clearance approx 2ca downstream of N end of quay at Port de Dinan. Dinan gives access to Ille et Rance Canal and River Vilaine to Biscay (see 9.15.17).

LIGHTS AND MARKS Approaching the barrage from seaward: Pte de la Jument bn tr, Fl (5) G20s 6m 4M; PHM Prohib Area buoy opposite, Fl R 4s. NW side of lock, Fl G 4s, with G ▲ on W background. First dolphin, Fl R (2) 6s, with R ■ on W background.
Approaching from Dinan:
PHM, Oc R 4s, at S end of Prohib Area.
Last dolphin, Oc R (2) 6s, with R ■ on W background.
SW side of lock, Iso G4s, G ▲ on W background.
Lock entry sigs:

By day	By night	
●	●	= Entry from N prohibited.
▼	●	= Entry from S prohibited.

Additional sigs on the barrage to the E of the lock show the direction of flow through the turbines.The chan up-river is partly buoyed and marked by stakes.

RADIO TELEPHONE Barrage lock: call *Barrage de la Rance* VHF Ch 13.

TELEPHONE Water levels/navigation 02·99·46·14·46; Barrage/lock info 02·99·46·21·87; Hr Mr (Richardais) 02·99·46·24·20; Hr Mr (Plouër) 02·96·86·83·15; Chatelier lock 02·96·39·55·66; Hr Mr (Lyvet) 02·96·83·35·57; Hr Mr (Dinan) 02·96·39·04·67; Météo 02·99·46·10·46; Auto 08.36.68.08.35; Aff Mar 02·96· 39·56·44; Police 02·99·81·52·30; Brit Consul 02·99·46·26·64.

FACILITIES St. Suliac Slip, M, Bar, R, V, Divers (Convoimer); **Mordreuc** Slip, L, M, Bar, R; **La Richardais** El, ME, Sh, Bar, D, P, ✉, R, V, Ⓑ; **La Jouvente** AB, Bar, R; **Le Minihic** M, L, Slip, ME, El, Sh; **La Cale de Plouër** M, L, SC, R.

MARINAS ON THE RIVER RANCE

PLOUËR, Côtes d'Armor, **49°32'N 01°58'W.** ❁❁◊◊✿✿. Marina is on the W bank of the R Rance, 6M above the barrage and 0·5M above the two St Hubert bridges. Access approx HW±3, when tide is 8m above CD, giving at least 1·5m water above rising gate. Approach on about 285°, ent in line with Plouër church spire. Unlit PHM and SHM perches are 30m from ent at S end of bkwtr. Ent is marked by FR and FG lts which are lit, by day or night, whenever access is available. Depth gauge (hard to read) has W flood-light. Facilities: **Marina** (240+ Ⓥ on pontoon B) ☎ 02·96·86·83·15. VHF Ch 09. AB €1·58, Slip, AC, CH, FW, BY, C, ME, BH (10-14 ton), R, Bar, limited V.

LYVET, Hr Mr ☎ 02·96·83·35·57; **Marina** (175 berths) €1·25 AC, FW, R, Bar, limited V. Immediately upstream of Chatelier lock, on the E bank.

DINAN, Hr Mr ☎ 02·96.39.56.44; **Marina** AC, FW, P, D, C for masts, R, Bar. Berths line the W bank of the river, with finger pontoons close to the Port. Low bridge beyond Port has 2·5m headroom, giving access to the Ille et Rance canal. **Town** (75m above water level) V, R, ✉, Ⓑ, ⇌, ✈ (Dinard).

Ille et Rance canal (see opposite): On the Breton canals the tolls charged elsewhere in France (see 9.15.7) are not envisaged. A certificate of competence is not required, unless LOA >15m or speed >20kph/11kn.

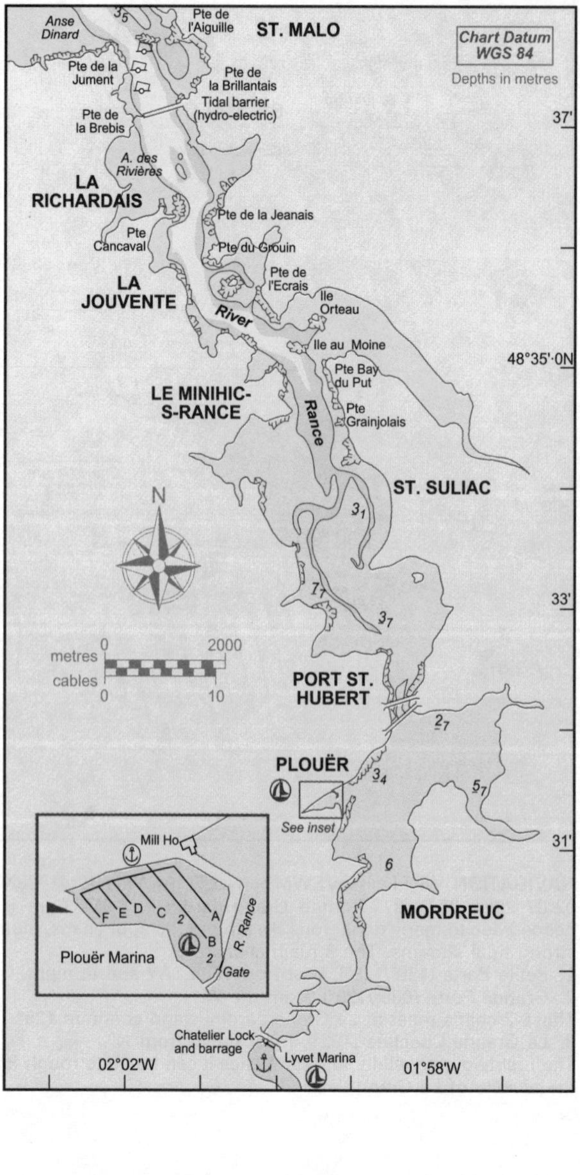

INLAND WATERWAYS OF BRITTANY *9.15.17*

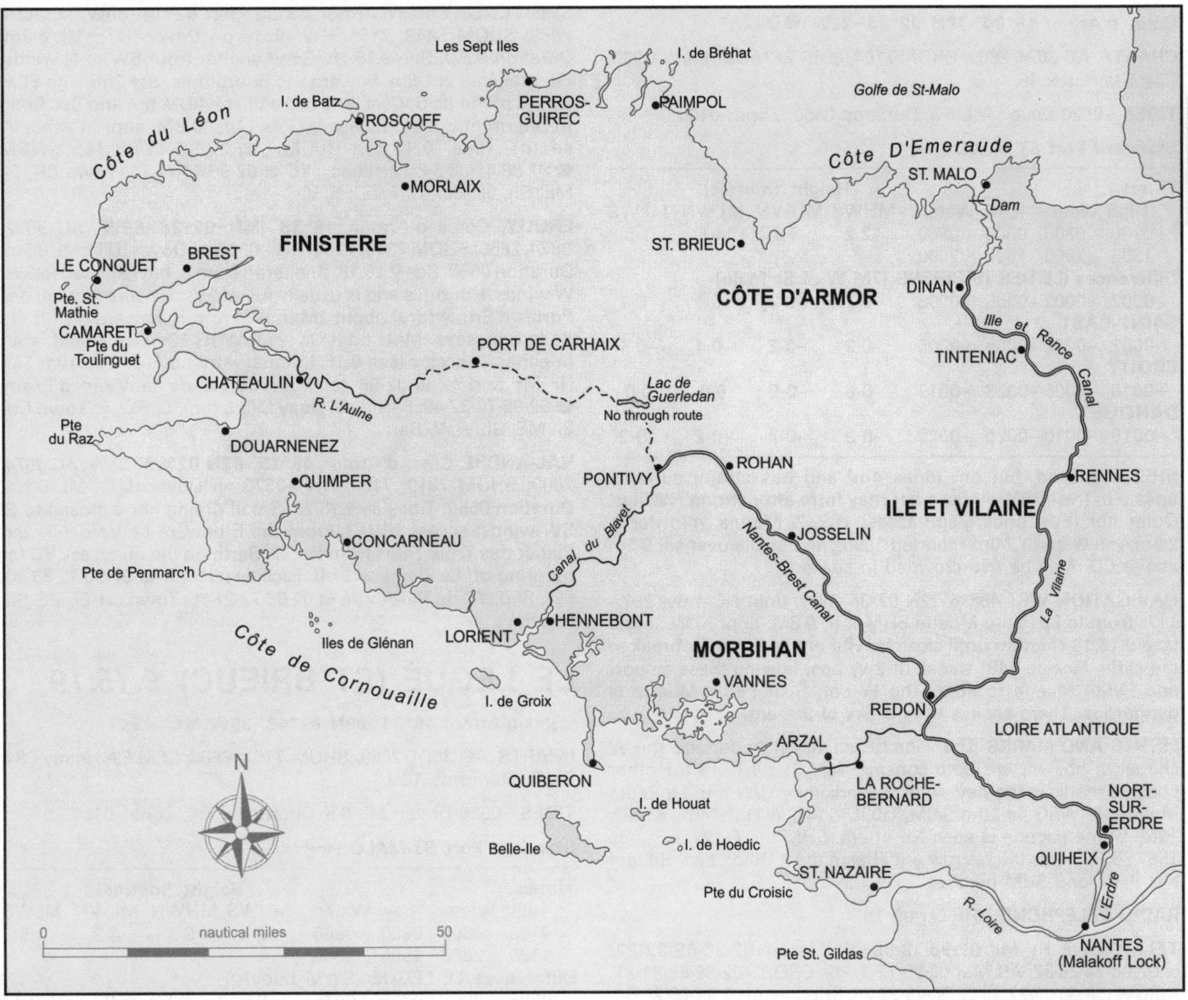

NAVIGATION Canals and rivers across and within Brittany enable boats of limited water and air drafts to go from the Channel to the Bay of Biscay avoiding the passage around Finistere. Dinan to Arzal takes about 5 days. Distances, number of locks, boat size and speed limits are summarised opposite.

LOCKS From Apr to Sept locks are worked 7 days a week 0800-1930LT, closing for lunch 1230-1330 approx. All locks are attended, but a fair measure of self-help is the order of the day. In Jul/Aug, in order to conserve water, locks may open on the hour only (and at H+30 if traffic demands).

ACCESS For prior estimate of max draught possible, write: Equipement, Ille et Vilaine, 1 Avenue de Mail, 35000 Rennes. (☎ 02·99.59.20.60; 📠 02·99.54.03.99); or obtain recorded information update on ☎ 02·99.59.11.12. For latest info on the Ille et Rance Canal/R Vilaine, contact: Rennes ☎ 02·99.59.20.60 or Redon ☎ 02·99.71.03.78. For the Lorient-Nantes Canal, contact: Nantes ☎ 02·40.71.02.00; Hennebont ☎ 02·97.85.15.15; Lorient ☎ 02·97.21.21.54; Pontivy ☎ 02·97.25.55.21. Closures *(Chômages)* for maintenance are scheduled in late autumn and in winter each Wednesday (approx first week in November to last week in March).

INFORMATION *Inland Waterways of France:* D Edwards-May (Imray) and the ECM Carte-Guide No 12 are recommended.

TOLLS may be due on the R Loire only; see 9.15.7 for rates.

SUMMARY	Length km	No of locks	Max draft m	Max air draft m	Max LOA m	Max beam m	Speed limit kn
St MALO-ARZAL (Ille et Rance Canal and La Vilaine)							
R Rance-Dinan	29·0	1	1·3	19	25	–	5·4
Ille et Rance Canal							
Dinan-Rennes	79·0	48	1·2	2·5	25	4·5	4·3
Rennes-Redon	89·0	13	1·2	3·2/2·6*	25	4·5	4·3
Redon-Arzal	42·0	1	1·3	–			
*Depending on water level							
LORIENT - NANTES (See 9.17.14)							
Canal du Blavet							
Lorient-Pontivy	70	28	1·4	2·6	25	4·6	4·3
Nantes-Brest Canal	184·3	106	–	3	25	4·6	4·3
Pontivy-Rohan			0·8 (possible closure)				
Rohan-Josselin			1·0				
Josselin-Redon			1·4				
Redon-Quiheix			1·1				
L'Erdre River	27·6	1	1·4	3·8	400	6·2	13·5
R Loire, above Nantes (9.17.28), may be navigable to Angers.							
R L'AULNE (See 9.16.27)							
Brest-Chateaulin	42	1	3·0	N/A	25	–	–
Chateaulin-Carhaix	72	33	1·1	2·5	25	4·6	4·3

DAHOUET *9.15.18*

Côtes d'Armor **48°34′·79N 02°34′·39W** ❁❁♪♪✿

CHARTS AC *3674*, 2669; SHOM 7154, 6966; ECM 536; Imray C33B, C34; Stanfords 16

TIDES –0520 Dover; ML 6·3; Duration 0550; Zone –0100

Standard Port ST-MALO (⟵)

Times				Height (metres)			
High Water		Low Water		MHWS	MHWN	MLWN	MLWS
0100	0800	0300	0800	12·2	9·3	4·2	1·5
1300	2000	1500	2000				
Differences ÎLE DES HÉBIHENS (7M W of St Malo)							
–0002	–0002	–0005	–0005	–0·2	–0·2	–0·1	–0·1
SAINT CAST							
–0002	–0002	–0005	–0005	–0·2	–0·2	–0·1	–0·1
ERQUY							
–0010	–0005	–0023	–0017	–0·6	–0·5	0·0	0·0
DAHOUET							
–0010	–0010	–0025	–0020	–0·9	–0·7	–0·2	–0·2

SHELTER Good, but ent (dries 4m) and has strong currents unsafe in fresh NW winds; a bar may form after strong NW'lies. Outer hbr (FVs) dries 5·5m; access HW±2. Marina, min depth 2·5m, (on Ⓥ berth 2·0m reported 1998); accessible over sill 5·5m above CD. May be overcrowded in season.

NAVIGATION WPT 48°35′·22N 02°35′·37W, unlit NCM By, 297°/117° from/to La Petite Muette SHM lt tr, 0·8M; appr in W sector (see 9.15.19 chartlet) until close in. Hbr ent is a narrow break in the cliffs. Pick up 148° transit of 2 W bns, leaving these to port and Petite Muette to stbd. The W ent, S of Petite Muette is dangerous. There are rks W and SW of the ent.

LIGHTS AND MARKS The wide beach at Val André and the W chapel at hbr ent are both conspic; see also 9.15.19 for other conspic marks in the bay. Appr is marked by G/W lt tr, La Petite Muette, Fl WRG 4s 10m 9/6M, G055°-114°, W114°-146°, R146°-196°. Stone pagoda is seen NE of ent. SHM bn, Fl (2) G 6s, vis 156°-286°, marks the narrow ent abeam the 2 W ldg bns. Sill ent has PHM and SHM perches.

RADIO TELEPHONE VHF Ch 09 16.

TELEPHONE Hr Mr 02·96·72·82·85; Météo 02·36·65·02·22; ⊜ 02·96·74·75·32; Aff Mar 02·96·72·31·42; CROSS 02·98·89·31·31; Auto 08.36.68.08.22; Ⓗ 02·96·45·23·28; Brit Consul 02·99·46·26·64; Police 02·96·72·22·18.

FACILITIES Marina (318+20) ☎ 02·96·72·82·85, €1·49, FW, AC, BH (10 ton), Slip, C (14 ton); **Quay** P, D (in cans), C (4 ton); **YC du Val-André** ☎ 02·96·72·21·68; **Services:** CH, El, ME, Sh. **Town**, V, R, Bar, ⥱ (Lamballe), ✈ (St. Brieuc). Ferry: St. Malo-Portsmouth.

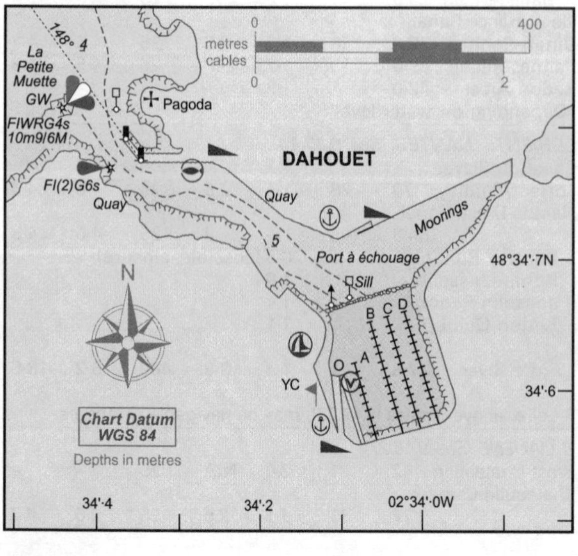

OTHER HARBOURS BETWEEN ST MALO AND DAHOUET

SAINT CAST, Côtes d'Armor, **48°38′·39N 02°14′·60W**. AC *3659*, 2669; SHOM 5646, 7155. HW –0515 on Dover (UT); ML 6·8m; Duration 0550. See 9.15.18. Good shelter from SW to N winds; ⚓s available in 1·8m. Beware Les Bourdinots (dry 2m) with ECM ¾M NE of Pte de St Cast, and La Feuillade (IDM bn) and Bec Rond (R bn) off hbr. Mole hd, Iso WG 4s 11m 11/8M; appr in either W sector (see 9.15.4). Hr Mr ☎ 02·96·41·88·34; SNSM ☎ 02·96·41·88·34; Facilities: **YC** ☎ 02·96·41·71·71. **Town** CH, El, ME, Sh, Ⓑ, Bar, D, P, ✉, R, V.

ERQUY, Côtes d'Armor, **48°38′·04N 02°28′·69W**. AC 3672, *3674*, 2669; SHOM 7310, 7154. HW –0515 on Dover (UT); ML 6·5m; Duration 0550. See 9.15.18. Sheltered from E, but exposed to SW/W winds. Hbr dries and is usually full of FVs. Beware Plateau des Portes d'Erquy (dry) about 2M to W. From S, beware rks off Pte de la Houssaye. Mole hd lt Oc (2+1) WRG 12s 11m 11/8M; appr in either W sector (see 8.15.4). Inner jetty hd Fl R 2·5s 10m 3M. Hr Mr and ⊜ ☎ 02·96·72·19·32; **Cercle de la Voile d'Erquy** ☎ 02·96·72·32·40; Facilities: **Quay** C (3·5 ton), D, FW, P; **Town** CH, El, ME, Sh, R, V, Bar.

VAL-ANDRÉ, Côtes d'Armor, **48°35′·82N 02°33′·33W**. AC *3674*, 2669; SHOM 7310, 7154. HW –0520 on Dover (UT); ML 6·1m; Duration 0550. Tides as 9.15.26. Small drying hbr exposed to S/SW winds; access HW±3. From the E beware Le Verdelet, and Platier des Trois Têtes from the W. Berth on the quay, ask YC for mooring off Le Piegu or ⚓ off. Facilities: Hr Mr ☎ 02·96·72·83·20, FW, Slip; **YC du Val-André** ☎ 02·96·72·21·68; **Town** CH, El, ME, Sh, Bar, R, V.

LE LÉGUÉ (ST BRIEUC) *9.15.19*

Côtes d'Armor **48°31′·89N 02°43′·39W** ❁❁♪♪♪✿

CHARTS AC *3674*, 2669; SHOM 7154, 6966; ECM 536; Imray C34, C33B; Stanfords 16

TIDES –0520 Dover; ML 6·5; Duration 0550; Zone –0100

Standard Port ST-MALO (⟵)

Times				Height (metres)			
High Water		Low Water		MHWS	MHWN	MLWN	MLWS
0100	0800	0300	0800	12·2	9·3	4·2	1·5
1300	2000	1500	2000				
Differences LE LÉGUÉ (SWM buoy)							
–0005	–0005	–0025	–0015	–0·8	–0·5	–0·2	–0·1

SHELTER Very good in Le Légué (the port for St Brieuc), especially in the wet basin. Yachts use Bassin No 2 (min 3m) near viaduct. Lock opens HW –2 to HW+1 sp; HW ±1 nps. The lock sill is 5·0m above CD. Yachts can wait against Le Quai Gilette (N bank), but soft mud slopes very steeply to chan.

NAVIGATION WPT 48°34′·33N 02°41′·18W, Le Légué SWM buoy, Fl Mo (A) 10s, Whis, 030°/210° from/to Pte de l'Aigle lt, 2·6M. Appr via buoyed chan (with some gaps); not advised in strong N/NE winds. The area dries E/SE of conspic Pte du Roselier. Keep close to Pte à l'Aigle to avoid Les Galettes.

LIGHTS AND MARKS Conspic marks: Rohein tr, from N, and Le Verdelet Is from E (beware Plateau des Jaunes). No ldg lines; 2 lts on the NW bank of the river de Gouet ent: Pte de l'Aigle, QG 13m 8M, vis 160°-070°, W tr G top. Jetée de la Douane (W columns with G top), Iso G 4s 6m 2M.

RADIO TELEPHONE Call: *Légué Port* VHF Ch 12 16 (approx HW–2 to +1½).

TELEPHONE Hr Mr 02·96·33·35·41, 🏛 02·96·61·46·94; Aff Mar 02·96·68·30·70; CROSS 02·98·89·31·31; Météo 02·99·46·10·46 and VHF Ch 13; Auto 08·36·68·08·22; SNSM 02·96·88·35·47; ⊜ 02·96·74·75·32; Police 02·96·94·52·25; Dr St Brieuc 02·96·61·49·07; Brit Consul 02·99·46·26·64.

FACILITIES Quai (100+20 visitors), AB €1·48, C (30 ton), P & D (cans on quai or tanker); **Services:** Sh, ME, El, CH, SM, Ⓔ, El, CH. **Town (St Brieuc)** P & D (cans), FW, Gaz, V, R, Bar, ✉, Ⓑ, ⥱, ✈. Ferry: St Malo.

LE LÉGUÉ/ST BRIEUC *continued*

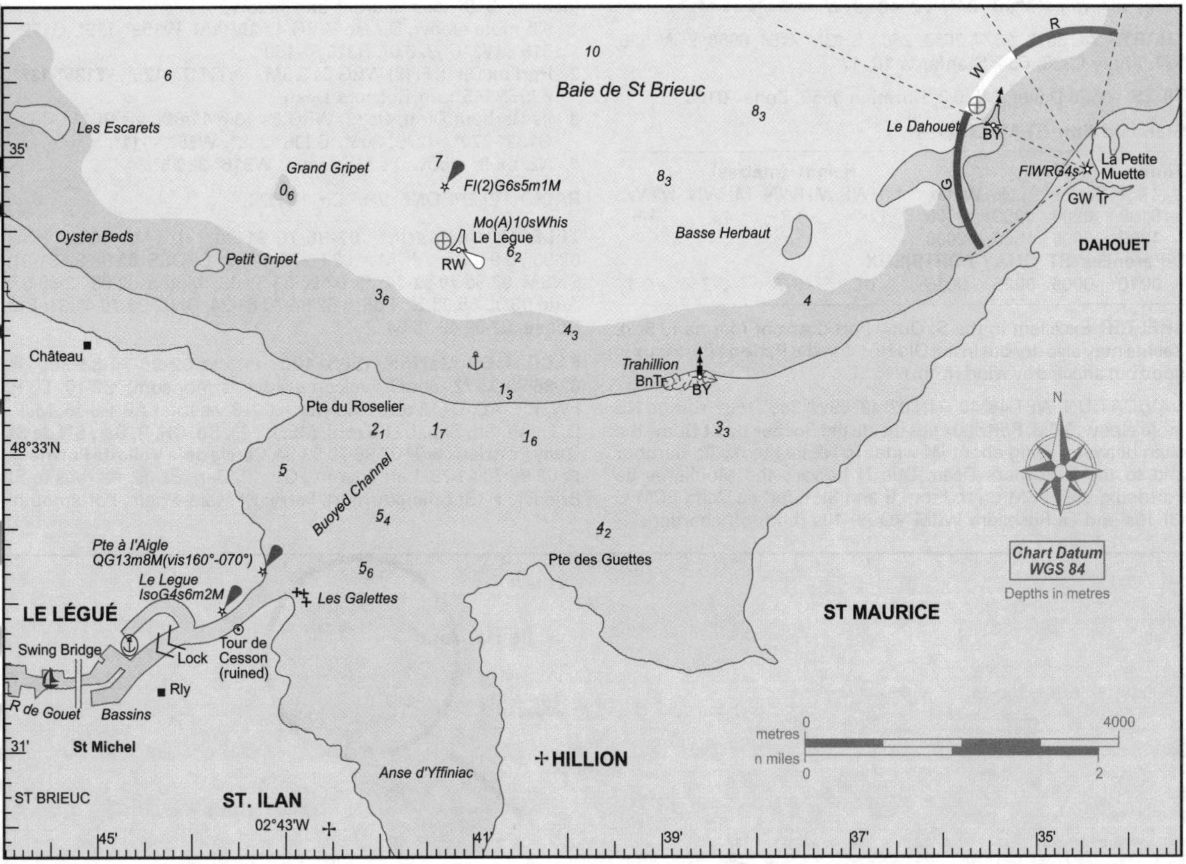

10
6
Baie de St Brieuc
8₃
Les Escarets
Le Dahouet
BY
R
W
G
35'
Grand Gripet
7
Fl(2)G6s5m1M
8₃
FlWRG4s
La Petite Muette
GW Tr
0₆
Mo(A)10sWhis
Le Legue
Oyster Beds
Basse Herbaut
RW
6₂
DAHOUET
Petit Gripet
3₆
4
4₃
Château
Trahillion
BnTr
BY
1₃
Pte du Roselier
2₁
1₇
1₆
3₃
48°33'N
5
Buoyed Channel
5₄
4₂
Pte à l'Aigle
QG13m8M(vis160°-070°)
Pte des Guettes
Chart Datum
WGS 84
Depths in metres
5₆
Le Legue
IsoG4s6m2M
Les Galettes
LE LÉGUÉ
ST MAURICE
Tour de Cesson (ruined)
Swing Bridge
Lock
Rly
R de Gouet
Bassins
metres
0
4000
n miles
0
2
31'
St Michel
HILLION
Anse d'Yffiniac
ST BRIEUC
ST. ILAN
02°43'W
45'
41'
39'
37'
35'

BINIC 9.15.20

Côtes d'Armor **48°36'·06N 02°48'·99W**

CHARTS AC *3674*, 2669; SHOM 7154, 6966; ECM 536; Imray C33B, C34; Stanfords 16

TIDES –0525 Dover; ML 6·3; Duration 0550; Zone –0100

Standard Port ST-MALO (⟵)

Times				Height (metres)			
High Water		Low Water		MHWS	MHWN	MLWN	MLWS
0100	0800	0300	0800	12·2	9·3	4·2	1·5
1300	2000	1500	2000				
Differences BINIC							
–0008	–0008	–0030	–0015	–0·8	–0·7	–0·2	–0·2

SHELTER Good, especially in Bassin à Flot/marina (1·5-3m). Easy access HW±3 by day/night to Avant Port (dries), except in E winds. Lock opens, in working hrs, approx HW–2 to HW, if tide reaches 8·5m; no opening near nps.

NAVIGATION WPT 48°36'·94N 02°42'·09W, 078°/258° from/to ent, 4·7M. Best appr from E, from Baie de St Brieuc (see 9.15.5) keeping E of Caffa ECM, from which ent bears 246°; or from N through Rade de Portrieux. Ent between moles dries 4·2m.

LIGHTS AND MARKS Ldg line 275°, N mole hd lt tr, Oc (3) 12s 12m 12M, W tr, G gallery, on with church spire. Gate and sliding bridge sigs on mast N of gate:

No lights = Gate closed
● = Gate closed and bridge in place
● = Gate open

RADIO TELEPHONE VHF Ch 09.

TELEPHONE Hr Mr 02·96·73·61·86, 02·96·73.72.38; Aff Mar 02·96·70· 42·27; SNSM 02·96·73·74.41; CROSS 02·98·89·31·31; ⊖ 02·96·74·75·32; Météo 02·99·46·10·46; Auto 08·36·68·08·22; Police 02·96·73·60·32; Dr 02·96·42·61·05; Ⓗ 02·96.94.31.71; Brit Consul 02·99·46·26·64.

FACILITIES Bassin (420), AB €1·45 to 11·5 depending on season, FW, AC, C (20 ton), Slip; **Club Nautique de Binic** ☎ 02·96·73·31·67; **Services:** CH, ME, El, Ⓔ, Sh, SM, SHOM. **Town** P, V, Gaz, R, Bar, ✉, Ⓑ, ⇌ (bus to St Brieuc), ✈ (St Brieuc). Ferry: St Malo.

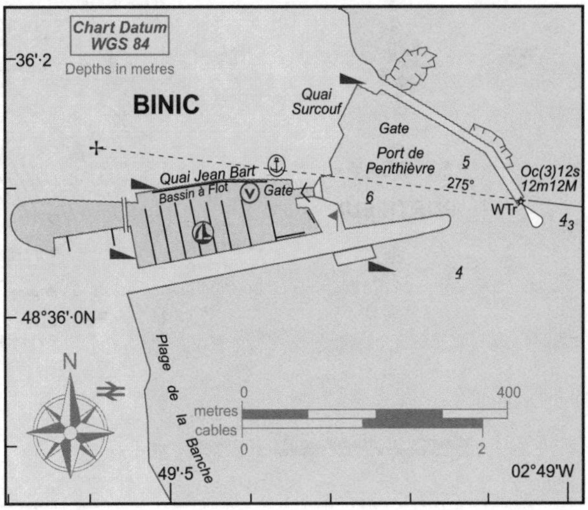

Chart Datum
WGS 84
Depths in metres
36'·2
BINIC
Quai Surcouf
Gate
Port de Penthièvre
5
Quai Jean Bart
Bassin à Flot
Gate
275°
Oc(3)12s 12m12M
6
WTr
4₃
4
48°36'·0N
Plage de la Banche
metres
cables
0
400
0
2
49'·5
02°49'W

ST QUAY-PORTRIEUX *9.15.21*

Côtes d'Armor **48°38´·84N 02°48´·97W**

CHARTS AC 3672, *3674*, 2669, *2668*; SHOM 7154, 6966; ECM 536, 537; Imray C33B, C34; Stanfords 16, 17

TIDES –0520 Dover; ML 6·3; Duration 0550; Zone –0100

Standard Port ST-MALO (⟵)

Times				**Height (metres)**			
High Water		Low Water		MHWS	MHWN	MLWN	MLWS
0100	0800	0300	0800	12·2	9·3	4·2	1·5
1300	2000	1500	2000				
Differences ST QUAY-PORTRIEUX							
–0010	–0005	–0025	–0015	–1·0	–0·7	–0·2	–0·1

SHELTER Excellent in the St Quay Port d'Armor marina (3·5m). Yachts may also dry out in the Old Hbr. ⚓ in the Rade de Portrieux is good but affected by winds from N to SE.

NAVIGATION WPT 48°40´·94N 02°49´·69W, 349°/169° from/to NE mole elbow, 2·0M. Portrieux lies inside the Roches de St Quay, the chan between being about ½M wide. To NE lie the rky Ile Harbour and to the E Rochers Déan. Due N beware the Moulières de Portrieux, unlit ECM bn tr. From E and SE appr via Caffa ECM Q (3) 10s and La Roselière WCM VQ (9) 10s (both off chartlet).

LIGHTS AND MARKS At night, from the N, White sectors of 4 Dir lts lead safely to the marina in sequence 169°, 130°, 005° (astern), 318° (see chartlet and below):

1. NE mole elbow, Dir Iso WRG 4s 15/11M, **W159°-179°**, G179°-316°, W316°-320.5°, R320.5°-159°.
2. Herflux Dir lt, Fl (2) WRG 6s 8/6M, vis G115°-125°, **W125°-135°**, R135°-145°; on Rochers Déan.
3. Ile Harbour Dir lt, Oc (2) WRG 6s 16m 11/8M, vis R011° -133°, G133°-270°, R270°-306°, G306°-358°, **W358°-011°**.
4. NE mole elbow, as (1) above, **W316°-320·5°**.

RADIO TELEPHONE VHF Ch 09 H24.

TELEPHONE Marina 02·96·70·81·30; Hr Mr (Old Hbr) 02·96·70·95·31; Aff Mar 02·96·70·42·27; CROSS 02·98·89·31·31; SNSM 02·96·70·52·04; ⊜ 02·96·33·33·03; Météo 02·98·32·55·57; Auto 08.36.68.08.22; Police 02·96·70·61·24; Dr 02·96·70·41·31; Brit Consul 02·99·46·26·64.

FACILITIES Marina (900+100 Ⓥ) ☎ 02·96·70·81·30, 📠 02·96·70·38·72, email: welcome@port-armor.com, €2·10, D, P, FW, BH, AC, C (12 ton); **Old Hbr** (500+8 visitors) AB €9·15, M, P, D, L, FW, Sh, Slip, C (1·5 ton), ME, El, Ⓔ, Sh, CH, R, Bar; **SN de St Quay Portrieux** ☎/📠 02·96·70·93·34, **Cercle de la Voile de Portrieux** ☎ 02·96·70·41·75, Bar; **Town** V, Gaz, R, Bar, ✉, Ⓑ, ⥈ (bus to St Brieuc), ✈ (St Brieuc/Armor). Ferry: St Malo–Poole, Portsmouth.

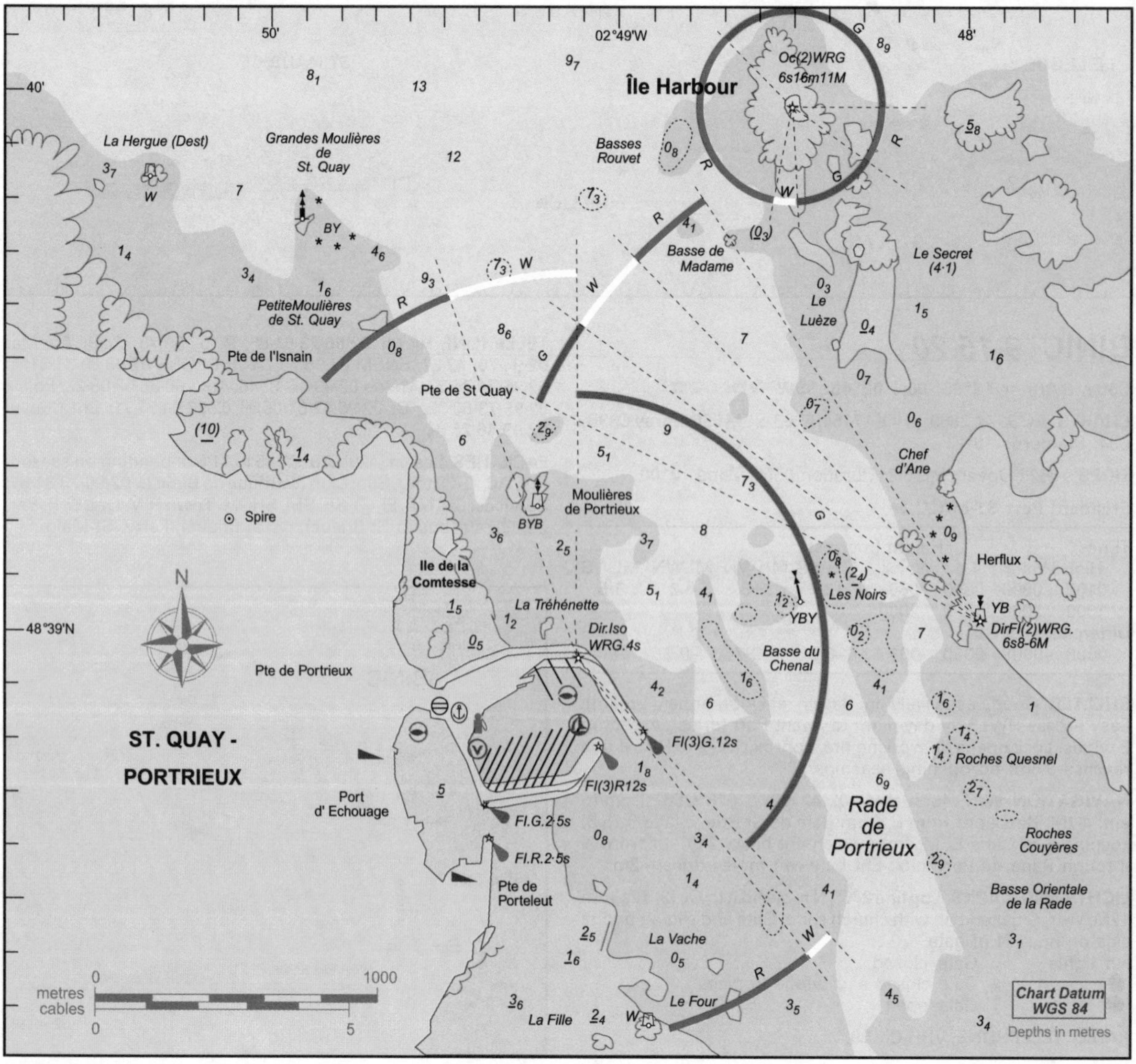

MAPTECH®
Leading the world in digital navigation
Maptech UK Ltd • +44 (0)1243 389352 • sales@maptech.co.uk

Maptech world class digital chart CDs
Worldwide coverage from over 4,500 charts

Maptech award winning software
Easy to use navigation software
• Chart Navigator • Cruising Navigator • Offshore Navigator

www.maptech.co.uk

Area 16

North Brittany
Paimpol to Raz de Sein

9.16.1 Index .... Page 767

9.16.2 Area map 768

9.16.3 Tidal stream charts 770

9.16.4 Lights, buoys & waypoints 772

9.16.5 Passage information 776

9.16.6 Distance table 777

9.16.7 Special notes for France See *9.15.7*

9.16.8 Paimpol 778

9.16.9 Ile de Bréhat 778

9.16.10 Lézardrieux 779

9.16.11 Pontrieux 780

9.16.12 Tréguier 781
Port Blanc

9.16.13 Perros-Guirec 782

9.16.14 Ploumanac'h 782
Trégastel

9.16.15 Trébeurden 783

9.16.16 Lannion 784
Les Sept Iles
Locquemeau
Locquirec
Primel-Trégastel

9.16.17 Morlaix 785
Penzé River
Moguériec
Brignogan (Pontusval)

9.16.18 Roscoff 786
Ile de Batz

9.16.19 L'Aberwrac'h 787

9.16.20 L'Aberbenoit 787

9.16.21 Baie de Lampaul 788
Baie du Stiff

9.16.22 L'Aberildut 788

9.16.23 Chenal du Four 789

9.16.24 Tidal coefficients 790
Portsall
Argenton
Ile de Molène

9.16.25 Le Conquet 791

9.16.26 Brest, Standard Port, tidal curves 792
Anse de Berthaume

9.16.27 Le Rade de Brest 793

9.16.28 Camaret 797

9.16.29 Morgat 797

9.16.30 Douarnenez 798

Register for your FREE weekly weather email service from Macmillan Reeds
›› at www.nauticaldata.com – NOW! ‹‹
weekend weather reports sent to your email address, every Thursday

9.16.2
North Brittany
Paimpol to Raz de Sein

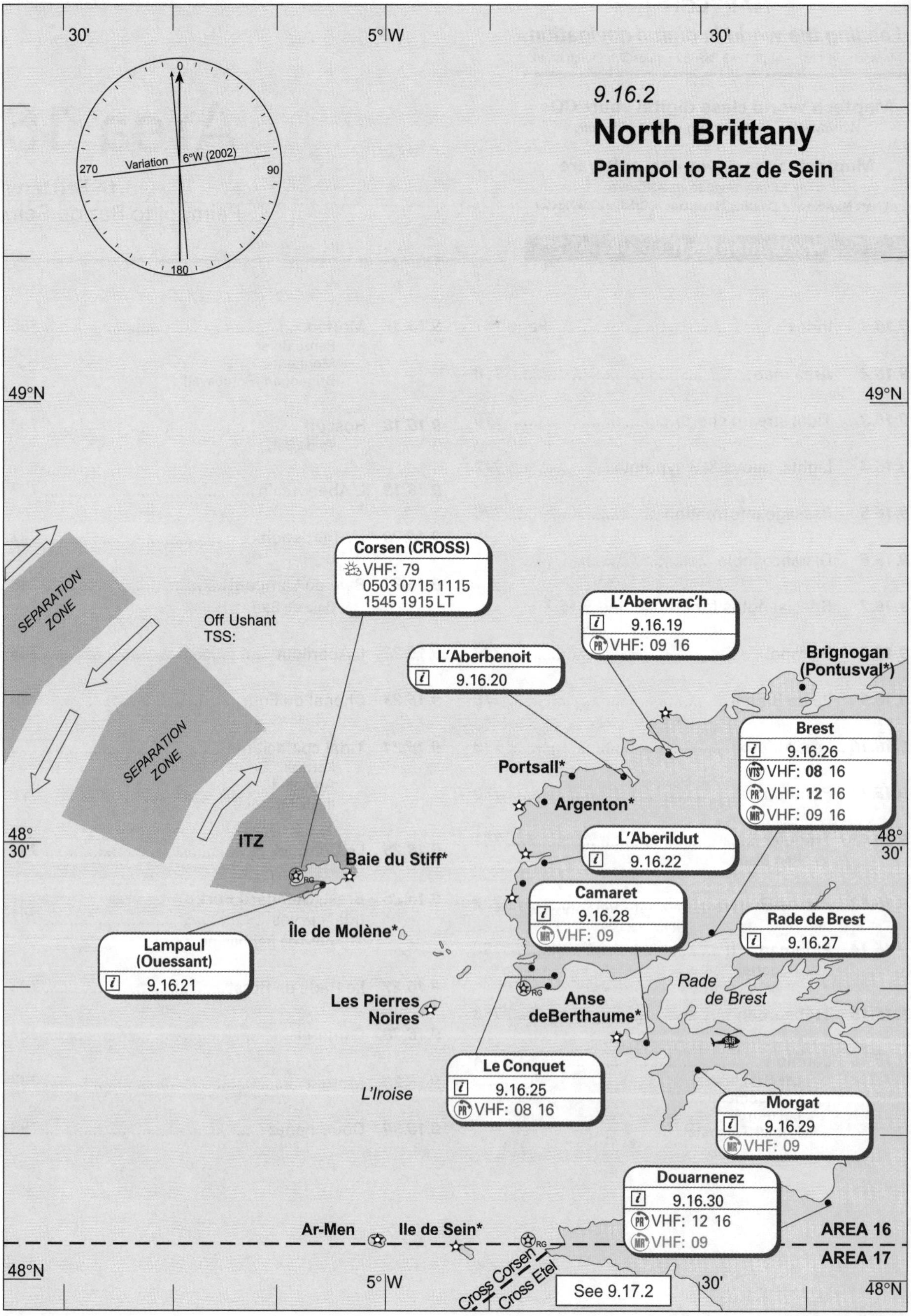
30'
5°W
30'
Variation 6°W (2002)
0
90
180
270
49°N
49°N
48° 30'
48° 30'
48°N
48°N
SEPARATION ZONE
SEPARATION ZONE
Off Ushant TSS:
ITZ
Corsen (CROSS)
VHF: 79
0503 0715 1115
1545 1915 LT
L'Aberwrac'h
9.16.19
VHF: 09 16
L'Aberbenoit
9.16.20
Brignogan (Pontusval*)
Brest
9.16.26
VHF: 08 16
VHF: 12 16
VHF: 09 16
Portsall*
Argenton*
L'Aberildut
9.16.22
Baie du Stiff*
RG
Camaret
9.16.28
VHF: 09
Rade de Brest
9.16.27
Île de Molène*
Lampaul (Ouessant)
9.16.21
Les Pierres Noires
Anse deBerthaume*
Rade de Brest
Le Conquet
9.16.25
VHF: 08 16
L'Iroise
Morgat
9.16.29
VHF: 09
Douarnenez
9.16.30
VHF: 12 16
VHF: 09
Ar-Men
Ile de Sein*
AREA 16
AREA 17
Cross Corsen
Cross Etel
See 9.17.2

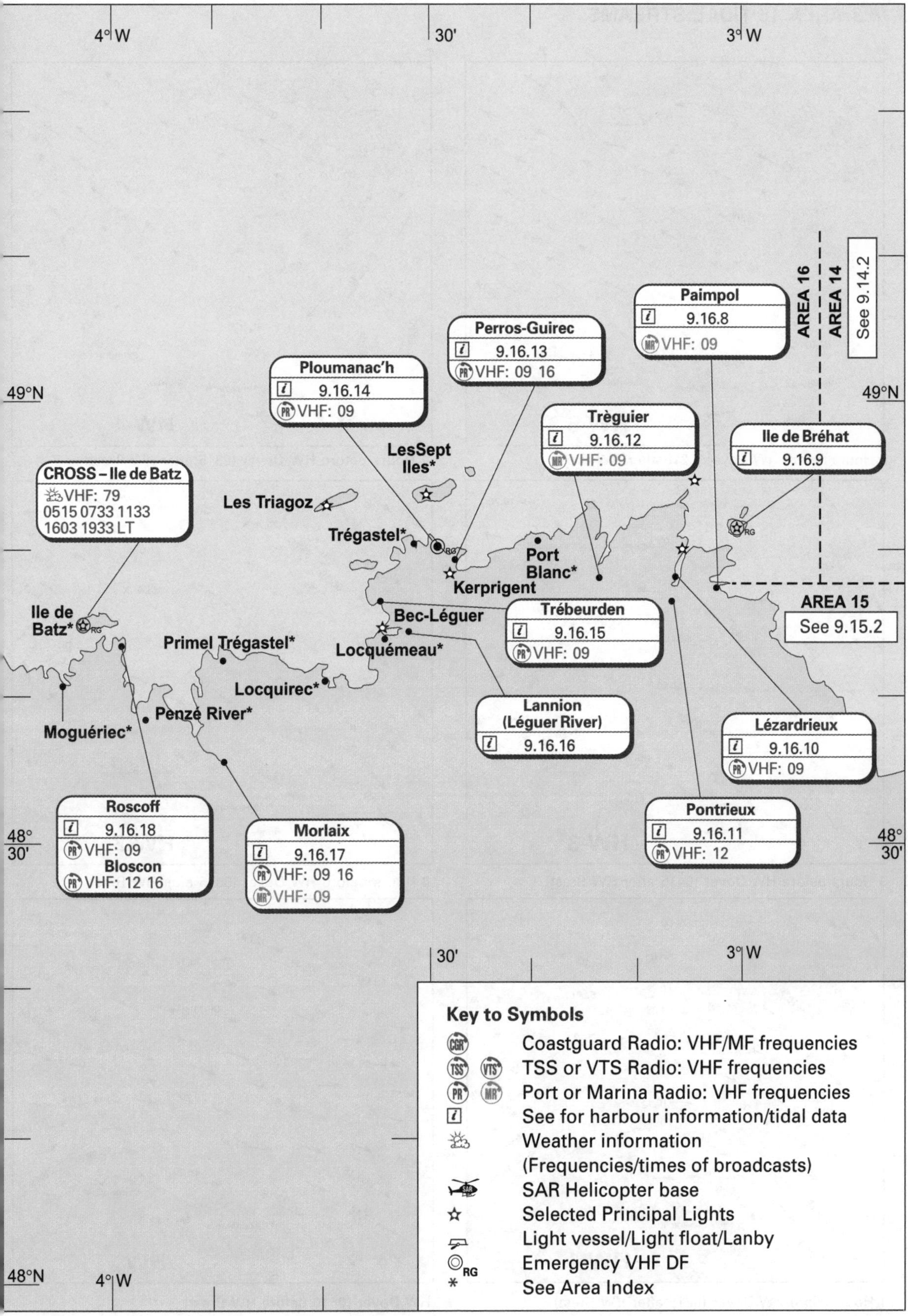
4° W
30'
3° W
49°N
48° 30'
48°N
Paimpol
9.16.8
VHF: 09
AREA 16
AREA 14
See 9.14.2
Perros-Guirec
9.16.13
VHF: 09 16
Ploumanac'h
9.16.14
VHF: 09
Trèguier
9.16.12
VHF: 09
Ile de Bréhat
9.16.9
LesSept Iles*
CROSS – Ile de Batz
VHF: 79
0515 0733 1133
1603 1933 LT
Les Triagoz
Trégastel*
Port Blanc*
Kerprigent
AREA 15
See 9.15.2
Ile de Batz*
Bec-Léguer
Trébeurden
9.16.15
VHF: 09
Primel Trégastel*
Locquémeau*
Locquirec*
Penzé River*
Moguériec*
Lannion (Léguer River)
9.16.16
Lézardrieux
9.16.10
VHF: 09
Roscoff
9.16.18
VHF: 09
Bloscon
VHF: 12 16
Morlaix
9.16.17
VHF: 09 16
VHF: 09
Pontrieux
9.16.11
VHF: 12
Key to Symbols
Coastguard Radio: VHF/MF frequencies
TSS or VTS Radio: VHF frequencies
Port or Marina Radio: VHF frequencies
See for harbour information/tidal data
Weather information
(Frequencies/times of broadcasts)
SAR Helicopter base
Selected Principal Lights
Light vessel/Light float/Lanby
Emergency VHF DF
See Area Index

9.16.3 AREA 16 TIDAL STREAMS

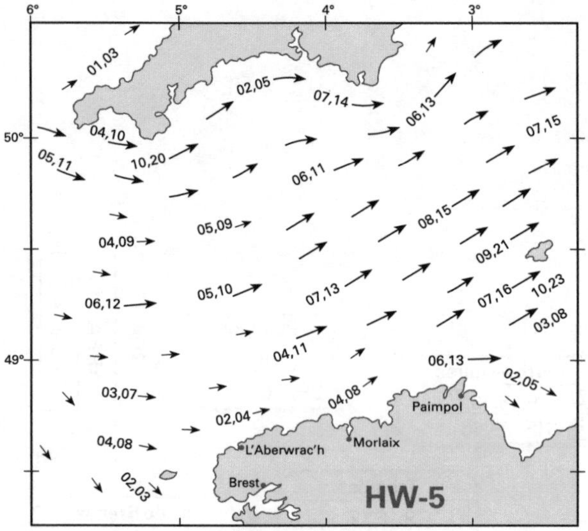

5 Hours before HW Dover (0215 after HW Brest)

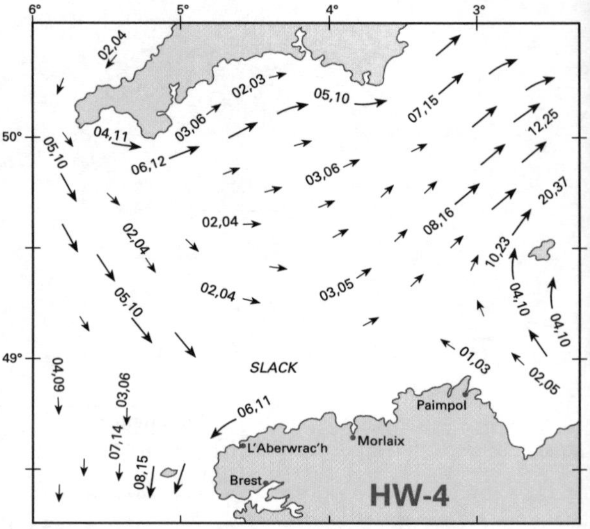

4 Hours before HW Dover (0315 after HW Brest)

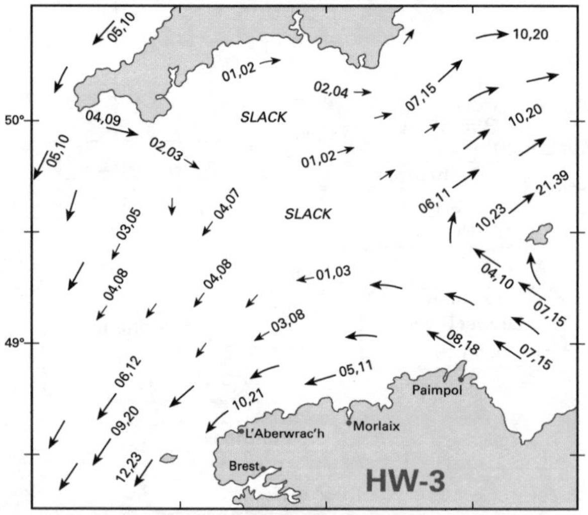

3 Hours before HW Dover (0415 after HW Brest)

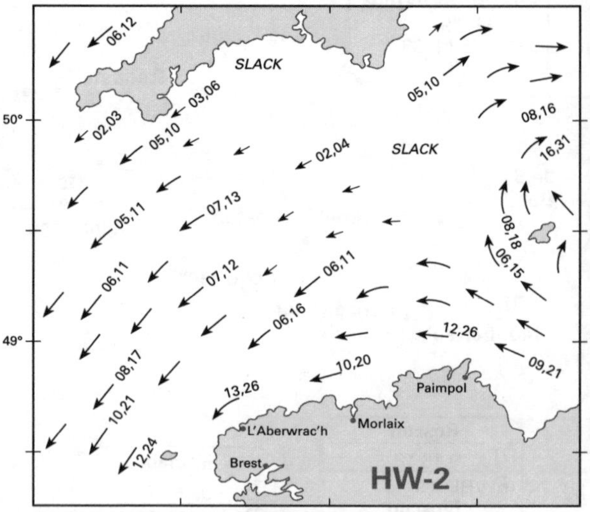

2 Hours before HW Dover (0515 after HW Brest)

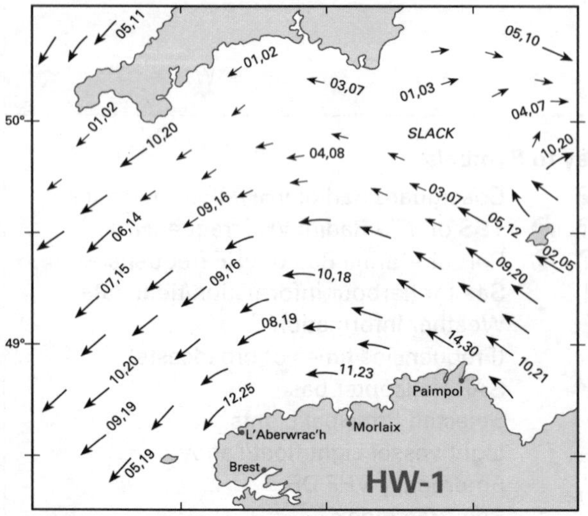

1 Hour before HW Dover (0615 after HW Brest)

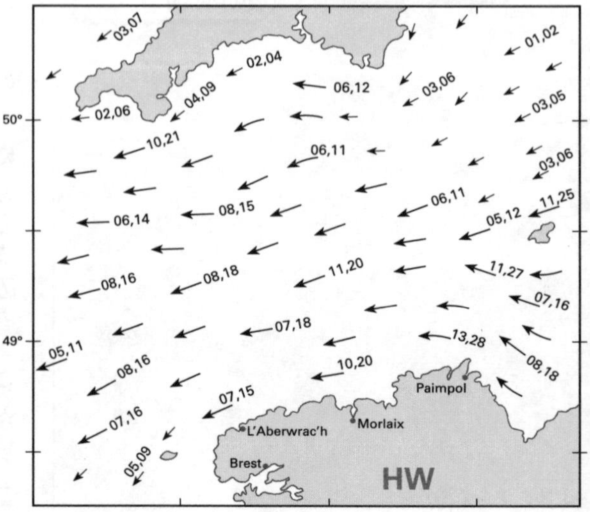

HW Dover (0510 before HW Brest)

Southward 9.17.3 Eastward 9.15.3 Northward 9.1.3

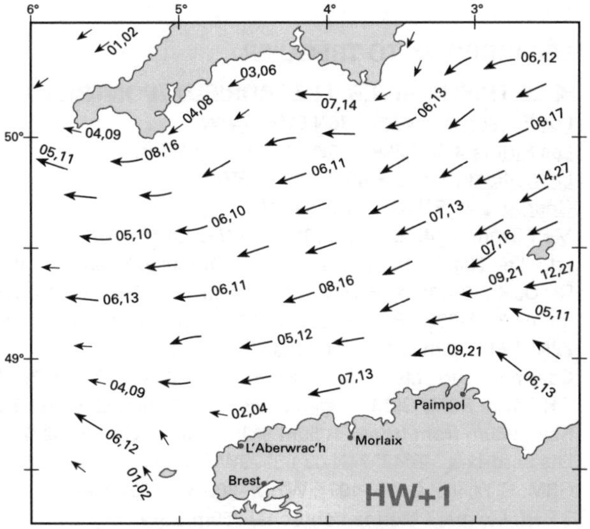

1 Hour after HW Dover (0410 before HW Brest)

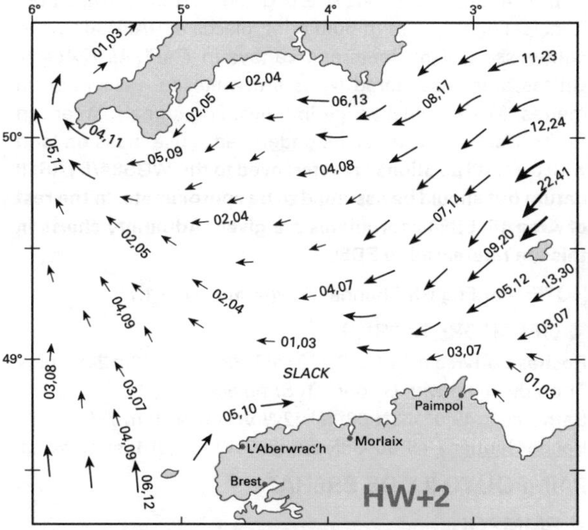

2 Hours after HW Dover (0310 before HW Brest)

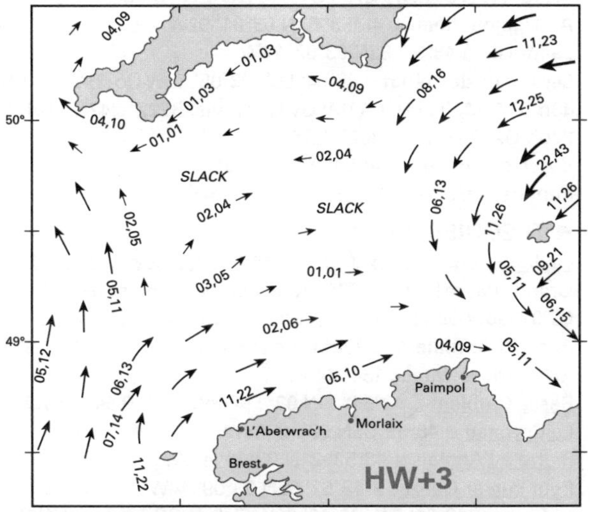

3 Hours after HW Dover (0210 before HW Brest)

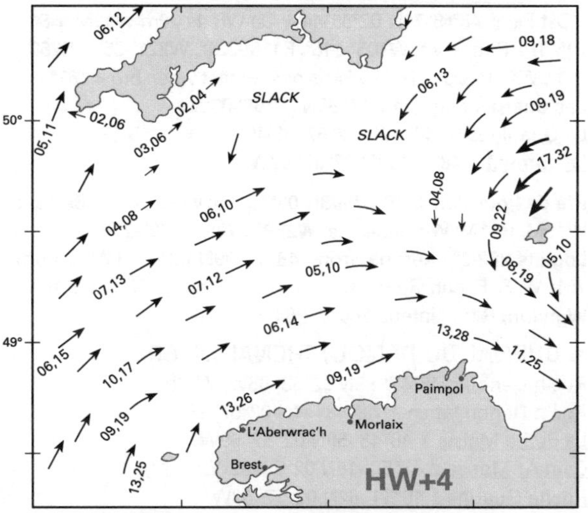

4 Hours after HW Dover (0110 before HW Brest)

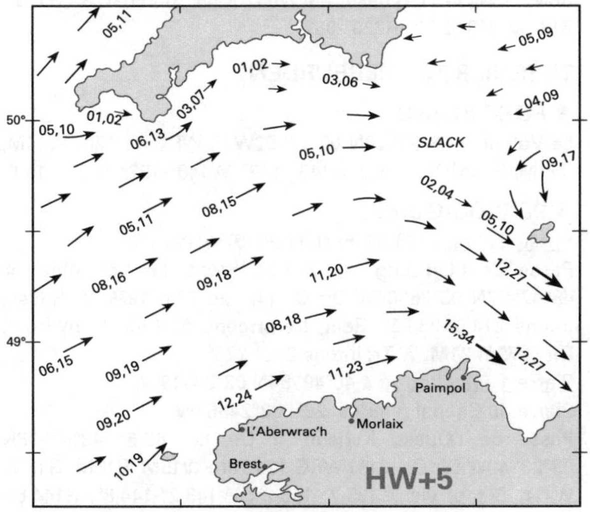

5 Hours after HW Dover (0010 before HW Brest)

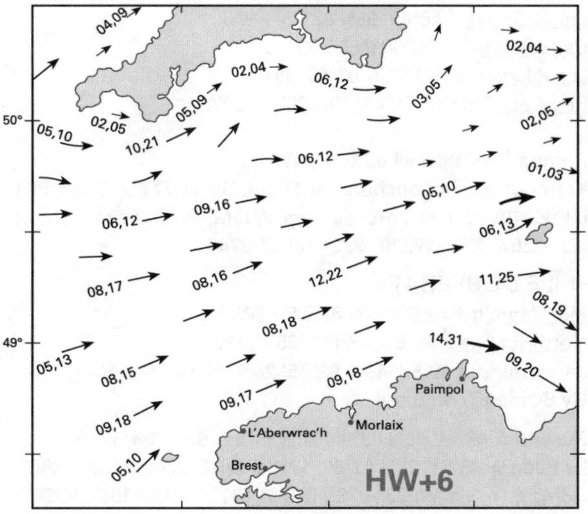

6 Hours after HW Dover (0050 after HW Brest)

9.16.4 LIGHTS, BUOYS AND WAYPOINTS

Abbreviations used below are given in the Introduction. Principal lights ☆ are in **bold** print, places in CAPITALS, and light-vessels, light floats and Lanbys in *CAPITAL ITALICS.* Unless otherwise stated lights are white. m – elevation in metres; M – nominal range in miles. Fog signals are in *italics*. Useful waypoints are underlined – use those on land with care. **All positions are referenced to the WGS84/ETRS89 datum but should be assumed to be approximate. In the rest of Area 16, ED50 coordinates are given. Admiralty charts in this are referenced to ED50.**

NOTE: For English Channel Waypoints see 9.1.7.

◄ OFFSHORE MARKS

Roches Douvres ☆ 49°06'·28N 02°48'·89W Fl 5s 60m **28M**; pink Tr on dwelling with G roof; *Siren 60s.*
Barnouic 49°01'·63N 02°48'·42W VQ (3) 5s 15m 7M.
Roche Gautier 49°00'·38N 02°53'·01W VQ (9) 10s; *Whis.*

PAIMPOL TO ÎLE DE BRÉHAT

◄ PAIMPOL

Les Calemarguiers 48°46'·98N 02°54'·85W.
L'Ost Pic 48°46'·76N 02°56'·44W Oc WR 4s 20m W11M, R8M; 2 W Trs, R tops; vis: W105°-116°, R116°-221°, W221°-253°, R253°-291°, W291°-329°; obsc by islets near Bréhat when brg < 162°.
Les Charpentiers 48°47'·89N 02°56'·03W.
La Gueule 48°47'·42N 02°57'·33W.
La Jument 48°47'·34N 02°57'·97W.

Pte de Porz-Don ☆ 48°47'·48N 03°01'·55W Oc (2) WR 6s 13m **W15M**, R11M; W house; vis: W269°-272°, R272°-279°.
Ldg Lts 262·2°. Kernoa, front, 48°47'·09N 03°02'·44W FR 5m 7M; W & R hut. Rear, 370m from front, Dir FR 12m 14M; W pylon, R top; intens 260·2°-264·2°.

◄ CHENAL DU DENOU/CHENAL DE BRÉHAT

Roc'h Denou 48°47'·85N 02°58'·05W; W Bn.
Roc'h Denou Vihan 48°48'·44N 02°57'·95W.
La Petite Moisie 48°48'·59N 02°57'·69W.
Cain Ar Monse 48°50'·16N 02°56'·82W.
Roche Guarine 48°51'·62N 02°57'·63W.

◄ CHENAL DU FERLAS

Lel Ar Serive 48°49'·98N 02°58'·76W.
Cadenenou 48°49'·81N 02°59'·06W.
Les Piliers 48°49'·77N 02°59'·99W.
Réceveur Bihan 48°49'·70N 03°01'·96W.

Rompa 48°49'·58N 03°02'·75W.
Kermouster, Embouchure du Trieux Dir Lt 271°, 48°49'·54N 03°05'·19W Dir Fl WRG 2s 16m W10M, R8M, G8M; W col; vis: G267°-270°, W270°-272°, R272°-274°.

◄ ÎLE DE BRÉHAT

Men-Marc'h 48°53'·17N 02°51'·83W.
Nord Horaine 48°54'·43N 02°55'·15W.
La Horaine 48°53'·49N 02°55'·24W Fl (3) 12s 13m 11M; Gy 8-sided Tr on B hut.

Rosédo ☆ 48°51'·45N 03°00'·30W Fl 5s 29m **20M**; W Tr.
Le Paon 48°51'·93N 02°59'·17W F WRG 22m W11M, R8M, G8M; Y Tr ; vis: W033°-078°, G078°-181°, W181°-196°, R196°-307°, W307°-316°, R316°-348°.
Men-Joliguet 48°50'·11N 03°00'·20W Iso WRG 4s 6m W13M, R10M, G10M; WCM Bn Tr; vis: R255°-279°, W279°-283°, G283°-175°.

LÉZARDRIEUX TO TRÉGUIER

◄ LE TRIEUX RIVER, LÉZARDRIEUX/PONTRIEUX

Les Echaudés 48°53'·36N 02°57'·34W.
Les Sirlots 48°52'·93N 02°59'·55W; *Whis.*
La Vieille du Tréou 48°51'·99N 03°01'·08W.
Gosrod 48°51'·41N 03°01'·23W.
Men Grenn 48°51'·21N 03°03'·90W Q (9) 15s 7m 7M.
Ldg Lts 224·7°. Front, **La Croix** ☆ 48°50'·22N 03°03'·24W Dir Oc 4s 15m **19M**; two Gy ○ Trs joined, W on NE side, R tops; intens 215°-235°. Rear **Bodic** ☆, 2·1M from front Dir Q 55m **22M**; W ho with G gable; intens 221°-229°.
Coatmer Ldg Lts 218·7°. Front, 48°48'·26N 03°05'·75W F RG 16m R9M, G9M; W gable; vis: R200°-250°, G250°-053°. Rear, 660m from front, FR 50m 9M; W gable; vis: 197°-242°.
Les Perdrix 48°47'·74N 03°05'·79W Fl (2) WG 6s 5m W6M, G3M; G Tr; vis: G165°-197°, W197°-202·5°, G202·5°-040°.
3 F Bu Lts mark Marina pontoons, 750m SSW.

◄ LE TRIEUX RIVER TO TRÉGUIER RIVER

An Ogejou Bihan 48°53'·37N 03°01'·92W.
La Moisie 48°53'·82N 03°02'·24W.
Les Héaux de Bréhat ☆ 48°54'·50N 03°05'·18W Oc (3) WRG 12s 48m **W15M**, R11M, G11M; Gy ○ Tr; vis: R227°-247°, W247°-270°, G270°-302°, W302°-227°.
Basse des Héaux 48°54'·07N 03°05'·29W.
Pont de la Gaîne 48°53'·12N 03°07'·42W.

◄ TRÉGUIER RIVER

La Jument des Héaux 48°55'·36N 03°08'·05W VQ; *Bell.*
Grande Passe Ldg Lts 137°. Front, Port de la Chaîne 48°51'·55N 03°07'·90W Oc 4s 12m 11M; W house; vis: 042°-232°. W house. Rear, **St Antoine** ☆, 0·75M from front, Dir Oc R 4s 34m **15M**; R&W house; intens 134°-140°.
Basse Crublent 48°54'·29N 03°11'·18W Fl (2) R 6s; *Whis.*
Le Corbeau 48°53'·35N 03°10'·28W.
Pierre à l'Anglais 48°53'·21N 03°10'·46W.
Petit Pen ar Guézec 48°52'·52N 03°09'·44W.
La Corne 48°51'·34N 03°10'·63W Fl (3) WRG 12s 14m W11M, R8M, G8M; W Tr, R base; vis: W052°-059°, R059°-173°, G173°-213°, W213°-220°, R220°-052°.

TRÉGUIER TO TRÉBEURDEN

◄ PORT BLANC

Le Voleur 48°50'·20N 03°18'·52W Fl WRG 4s 17m W14M, R11M, G11M; W Tr; vis: G140°-148°, W148°-152°, R152°-160°.

◄ PERROS-GUIREC

Basse Guazer 48°51'·58N 03°20'·97W; *Whis.*
Passe de l'Est Ldg Lts 224·5°. Front, **Le Colombier** ☆ 48°47'·87N 03°26'·66W Dir Oc (4) 12s 28m **18M**; W house; intens 214·5°-234·5°. Rear, **Kerprigent** ☆, 1·5M from front, Dir Q 79m **21M**; W Tr; intens 221°-228°.
Pierre à Jean Rouzic 48°49'·54N 03°24'·19W.
Pierre du Chenal 48°49'·28N 03°24'·67W.
Passe de l'Ouest. **Kerjean** ☆ Dir Lt 143·6° 48°47'·78N 03°23'·40W Dir Oc (2+1) WRG 12s 78m **W15M**, R13M, G13M; W Tr, B top; vis: G133·7°-143·2°, W143·2°-144·8°, R144·8°-154·3°.

Roc'h Hu de Perros 48°48'·82N 03°24'·94W.
Jetée du Linkin Hd 48°48'·20N 03°26'·31W Fl (2) G 6s 4m 7M; W pile, G top.
Roche Bernard 48°49'·43N 03°25'·46W.
La Fronde 48°49'·87N 03°25'·98W.
Bilzic 48°50'·18N 03°25'·75W.
La Horaine 48°49'·88N 03°27'·26W.
Les Couillons de Tomé 48°50'·87N 03°25'·69W.

◀ **PLOUMANAC'H**

Men-Ruz 48°50'·26N 03°29'·03W Oc WR 4s 26m W12M, R9M; pink □ Tr; vis: W226°-242°, R242°-226°; obsc by Pte de Trégastel when brg less than 080°, and part obsc by Les Sept-Îles 156°-207°, and by Île Tomé 264°-278°.

◀ **LES SEPT ILES**

Île-aux-Moines ☆ 48°52'·73N 03°29'·43W Fl (3) 15s 59m **24M**; Gy Tr and dwelling; obsc by Îlot Rouzic and E end of Île Bono 237°-241°, and in Baie de Lannion when brg less than 039°.
Les Dervinis 48°52'·33N 03°27'·32W.

◀ **TRÉGASTEL**

Île Dhu 48°50'·37N 03°31'·24W.
Le Taureau 48°50'·40N 03°31'·63W.

Les Triagoz 48°52'·27N 03°38'·80W Oc (2) WR 6s 31m W14M, R11M; Gy ■ Tr, R lantern; vis: W010°-339°, R339°-010°; obsc in places 258°-268° by Les Sept-Îles.
Bar ar Gall 48°49'·78N 03°36'·23W VQ (9) 10s.
Le Crapaud 48°46'·67N 03°40'·60W Q (9) 15s.

◀ **TRÉBEURDEN**

Ar Gouredec 48°46'·41N 03°36'·60W VQ (6) + L Fl 10s.
An Ervennou 48°46'·48N 03°35'·99W Fl (2) R 6s.
Pt de Lan Kerellec 48°46'·74N 03°35'·07W Iso WRG 4s; W8M, R5M, G5M; vis: G058°-064°, W064°-069°, R069°-130°.
N Breakwater Head 48°46'·34N 03°35'·20W Fl G 2·5s 8m 2M.

TRÉBEURDEN TO ROSCOFF

◀ **LÉGUER RIVER, LANNION**

Kinierbel 48°44'·14N 03°35'·19W; *Bell.*
Beg-Léguer 48°44'·31N 03°32'·93W Oc (4) WRG 12s 60m W12M, R9M, G9M; W face of W house, R lantern; vis: G007°-084°, W084°-098°, R098°-129°.

◀ **LOCQUÉMEAU**

Ldg Lts 121°. Front, 48°43'·41N 03°34'·46W FR 21m 6M; W pylon, R top; vis: 068°-228°. Rear, 484m from front Oc (2+1) R 12s 39m 7M; W gabled house; vis: 016°-232°.
Locquémeau 48°43'·86N 03°35'·93W; *Whis.*

◀ **PRIMEL**

Ldg Lts 152°. Front, 48°42'·45N 03°49'·20W FR 35m 6M; W □, R stripe on pylon; vis: 134°-168°. Rear, 172m from front, FR 56m 6M; W □, R stripe.
Marina Jetty Head 48°42'·77N 03°49'·51W Fl G 4s 6m 7M.

◀ **BAIE DE MORLAIX**

Méloine 48°45'·56N 03°50'·69W; *Whis.*
Chenal du Tréguier Ldg Lts 190·5°. Front, Île Noire 48°40'·34N 03°52'·56W Oc (2) WRG 6s 15m W11M, R8M, G8M; W □ Tr, R top; vis: G051°-135°, R135°-211°, W211°-051°; obsc in places. Common Rear, **La Lande** ☆ 48°38'·19N 03°53'·16W Fl 5s 85m **23M**; W □ Tr, B top; obsc by Pte Annelouesten when brg more than 204°.

La Pierre Noire 48°42'·55N 03°52'·22W.
La Chambre 48°40'·73N 03°52'·54W.
Grande Chenal Ldg Lts 176·4°. Front, **Île Louet** ☆ 48°40'·40N 03°53'·34W Oc (3) WG 12s 17m **W15M**; G10M; W □ Tr, B top; vis: W305°-244°, G244°-305°, vis: 139°-223° from offshore, except when obsc by Is. Common Rear, **La Lande** above.
Pot de Fer 48°44'·24N 03°54'·02W; *Whis.*
Vieille 48°42'·60N 03°54'·11W.
Stolvezen 48°42'·64N 03°53'·41W.
La Noire 48°41'·65N 03°54'·08W.
Ricard 48°41'·54N 03°53'·51W.
Barre de-Flot No.1 48°40'·18N 05°52'·95W.
No. 2 48°39'·88N 05°52'·53W Fl R 2s.
No. 4 48°38'·62N 05°51'·63W Fl R 2s.

◀ **BLOSCON/ROSCOFF**

Le Menk 48°43'·28N 03°56'·71W Q (9) WR 15s 6m W5M, R3M; vis: W160°-188°.
Bloscon Jetty Hd 48°43'·21N 03°57'·69W Fl WG 4s 9m W10M, G7M; W Tr, G top, vis: W200°-210°, G210°-200°. In fog Fl 2s.
Ar Pourven 48°43'·04N 03°57'·71W Q.
Astan 48°44'·91N 03°57'·67W VQ (3) 5s 9m 6M; *Whis.*
Basse de Bloscon 48°43'·72N 03°57'·55W VQ.
Ar-Chaden 48°43'·93N 03°58'·26 W Q (6) + L Fl WR 15s 14m W8M, R6M; vis: R262°-289·5°, W289·5°-293°, R293°-326°, W326°-110°.
Men-Guen-Bras 48°43'·76N 03°58'·07W Q WRG 14m W9M, R6M, G6M; vis: W068°-073°, R073°-197°, W197°-257°, G257°-068°.
Roscoff Ldg Lts 209°. Front, N Môle 48°43'·55N 03°58'·67W Oc (2+1) G 12s 7m 7M; W col, G top; vis 078°-318°. **Rear**, 430m from front, Oc (2+1) 12s 24m **15M**; Gy □ Tr, W on NE side; vis: 062°-242°.
Jetty Hd 48°43'·92N 03°58'·97W F Vi; W & Purple.

ÎLE DE BATZ TO ÎLE VIERGE

◀ **ÎLE DE BATZ**

Lt Ho ☆ 48°44'·71N 04°01'·63W Fl (4) 25s 69m **23M**; Gy Tr; auxiliary Lt FR 65m 7M; same Tr; vis: 024°-059°.

◀ **CANAL DE L'ÎLE DE BATZ**

Perroch 48°44'·10N 03°59'·71W.
Île aux Moutons Ldg stage S end 48°44'·25N 04°00'·53W VQ (6)+ L Fl 10s 3m 7M.
L'Oignon 48°44'·04N 04°01'·36W.
Basse Plate 48°44'·25N 04°02'·54W.

◀ **MOGUÉRIEC.**

Ldg Lts 162°. Front, Jetty Head 48°41'·31N 04°04'·53W Iso WG 4s 9m W11M, G6M; vis: W158°-166°, G166°-158°. Rear, 440m from front, FG 22m 7M; W col, G top; vis: 142°-182°.

◀ **PONTUSVAL**

Pointe de Pontusval 48°41'·42N 04°19'·33W.
Ar Peich 48°40'·90N 04°19'·17W.
An Neudenn 48°40'·66N 04°19'·12W.
Pte de Beg-Pol 48°40'·67N 04°20'·83W Oc (3) WR 12s 16m W10M, R7M; W Tr, B top, W dwelling; vis: W shore-056°, R056°-096°, W096°-shore. QY and FR Lts on towers 2·4M S.

Aman-ar-Ross 48°41'·83N 04°27'·09W Q 9m 7M; *Whis.*
Barr Ar-Skoaz 48°38'·22N 04°30'·08W.
Lizen Ven Ouest 48°40'·47N 04°33'·73W VQ (9) 10s 8m 5M; *Whis.*

16

Île-Vierge ☆ 48°38'·33N 04°34'·06W Fl 5s 77m **27M**; Gy Tr; vis: 337°-325°.

ÎLE VIERGE TO LE FOUR

◀ L'ABERWRAC'H

Libenter 48°37'·50N 04°38'·45W Q (9) 15s 8m 6M; *Whis.*
Ldg Lts 100·1° Front, Île Wrac'h 48°36'·88N 04°34'·56W QR 20m 7M; W □ Tr, Or top, dwelling. Rear, Lanvaon 1·63M from front, Dir Q 55m 12M; W □ Tr, Or △ on top; intens 090°-110°.
Trepied 48°37'·29N 04°37'·56W.
Grand Pot de Beurre 48°37'·21N 04°36'·49W.
Petit Pot de Beurre 48°37'·12N 04°36'·23W.
Basse de la Croix 48°36'·92N 04°35'·99W Fl (3) G 12s.
Breac'h Ver 48°36'·63N 04°35'·38W Fl G 2·5s 6m 3M; △ on Tr.
Dir Lt 128°, N Bkwtr 48°35'·89N 04°33'·82W Dir Oc (2) WRG 6s 5m W13M, R11M, G11M; vis: G125·7°-127·2°, W127·2°-128·7°, R128·7°-130·2°.

◀ L'ABER BENOÎT

Petite Fourche 48°36'·98N 04°38'·75W.
Rusven Est 48°36'·30N 04°38'·64W.
Rusven Ouest 48°36'·07N 04°39'·44W; *Bell.*
Basse de Chenal 48°35'·80N 04°38'·53W.
Poul Orvil 48°35'·51N 04°38'·30W.
La Jument 48°35'·10N 04°37'·42W.
Ar Gazel 48°34'·90N 04°37'·28W.
Le Chien 48°34'·67N 04°36'·88W.
Le Relec 48°35'·99N 04°40'·86W.

◀ PORTSALL/ARGENTON

Corn-Carhai 48°35'·19N 04°43'·94W Fl (3) 12s 19m 9M; W 8-sided Tr, B top.
Grande Basse de Portsall 48°36'·70N 04°46'·14W VQ (9) 10s 9m 4M; *Whis.*
Basse Paupian 48°35'·31N 04°46'·28W.
Bosven Aval 48°33'·82N 04°44'·28W.
Men ar Pic 48°33'·65N 04°44'·03W.
Portsall 48°33'·84N 04°42'·27W Oc (4) WRG 12s 9m W13M, R10M, G10M; W col, R top; vis: G058°-084°, W084°- 088°, R088°-058°.
Île Dolvez Front Ldg Mark 48°31'·25N 04°46'·24W; W Bn.

OUESSANT AND ÎLE DE MOLÈNE

Men-Korn 48°27'·96N 05°01'·33W VQ (3) WR 5s 21m W8M, R8M; vis: W145°-040°, R040°-145°.
Le Stiff ☆ 48°28'·47N 05°03'·41W Fl (2) R 20s 85m **24M**; two adjoining W Trs.
Gorle Vihan 48°28'·32N 05°02'·60W.
Port du Stiff, Môle Est Hd 48°28'·12N 05°03'·26W Dir Q WRG 11m W10M, R7M, G7M; W Tr, G top; vis: G251°-254°, W254°-264°, R264°-267°.

OUESSANT SW LANBY 48°31'·15N 05°49'·24W Fl 4s 10m **20M**; Racon (M).
NE 48°45'·78N 05°11'·76W L Fl 10s; *Whis*; Racon (B).
Créac'h ☆ 48°27'·55N 05°07'·76W Fl (2) 10s 70m **32M**; W Tr, B bands; obsc 247°-255°; Racon (C); *Horn (2) 120s.*
Nividic 48°26'·74N 05°09'·07W VQ (9) 10s 28m 9M; W 8-sided Tr, R bands; obsc by Ouessant 225°-290°. Helicopter platform.
La Jument ☆ 48°25'·34N 05°08'·05W Fl (3) R 15s 36m **22M**; Gy 8-sided Tr, R Top; vis: 241°-199°; *Horn (3) 60s.*

Men ar Froud 48°26'·61N 05°03'·69W.
Kéréon (Men-Tensel) ☆ 48°26'·24N 05°01'·55W Oc (2+1) WR 24s 38m **W17M**, R7M; Gy Tr; vis: W019°-248°, R248°-019°; *Horn (2+1) 120s*; danger sigs.
Pierres-Vertes 48°22'·19N 05°04'·77W VQ (9) 10s 9m 5M; *Whis.*

◀ ÎLE DE MOLÈNE

Les Trois-Pierres 48°24'·70N 04°56'·85W Iso WRG 4s 15m W9M, R6M, G6M; W col; vis: G070°-147°, W147°-185°, R185°-191°, G191°-197°, W197°-213°, R213°-070°.
Molène, Old Môle Head Dir Lt 191° 48°23'·85N 04°57'·29W Dir Fl (3) WRG 12s 6m W9M, R7M, G7M; vis: G183°-190°, W190°-192°, R192°-203°. Chenal des Laz Dir Lt 261°, Dir Fl (2) WRG 6s 9m W9M, R7M, G7M; same structure; vis: G252·5°-259·5°, W259·5°-262·5°, R262·5°-269·5°.

CHENAL DU FOUR

Le Four ☆ 48°31'·38N 04°48'·32W Fl (5) 15s 28m **18M**; Gy ○ Tr; *Horn (3+2) 60s.*

Le Taureau 48°31'·45N 04°47'·34W.

◀ L'ABER-ILDUT

L'Aber-Ildut ☆ 48°28'·26N 04°45'·57W Dir Oc (2) WR 6s 12m **W25M, R20M**; W bldgs; vis: W081°-085°, R085°-087°.
Ldg Lts 158·5°. Front, **Kermorvan** ☆ 48°21'·72N 04°47'·42W Fl 5s 20m **22M.** Rear, **Pte de St Mathieu** ☆ Fl 15s 56m **29M.** Dir F 54m **28M**; same Tr; intens 157·5°-159·5° (see above).
Les Plâtresses 48°26'·28N 04°50'·92W Fl RG 4s 17m 6M; W Tr; vis: R343°-153°, G153°-333°.
La Valbelle 48°26'·43N 04°50'·04W Fl (2) R 6s 8m 5M; *Whis.*
SE Plâtresses 48°25'·96N 04°50'·52W.
Le Tendoc 48°25'·67N 04°49'·44W.
Saint Paul 48°24'·82N 04°49'·16W Oc (2) R 6s.
Pte de Corsen 48°24'·89N 04°47'·63W Dir Q WRG 33m W12M, R8M, G8M; W hut; vis: R008°-012°, W012°-015°, G015°-021°.
Taboga 48°23'·77N 04°48'·08W.
Rouget 48°22'·05N 04°48'·88W Fl G 4s; *Whis.*
La Grande Vinotière 48°21'·93N 04°48'·43W L Fl R 10s 15m 5M; R 8-sided Tr.
Kermorvan ☆ 48°21'·72N 04°47'·42W Fl 5s 20m **22M**; W □ Tr; obsc by Pte de St Mathieu when brg less than 341°.

◀ LE CONQUET

Môle Sainte Barbe 48°21'·58N 04°46'·99W Oc G 4s 5m 6M.
Les Renards 48°21'·00N 04°47'·50W.
Lochrist ☆ 48°20'·55N 04°45'·82W Dir Oc (3) 12s 49m **22M**; W 8-sided Tr, R top; intens 135°-140°.
Tournant et Lochrist 48°20'·64N 04°48'·12W Iso R 4s.
Ar C'hristian Braz 48°20'·67N 04°50'·15W.
Ldg Lts 007°. Front, **Kermorvan** ☆ 48°21'·72N 04°47'·42W Fl 5s 20m **22M.** Rear, **Trézien** ☆ 48°25'·41N 04°46'·74W Dir Oc (2) 6s 84m **20M**; Gy Tr, W on S side; intens 003°-011°.
Pte de St Mathieu ☆ 48°19'·79N 04°46'·27W Fl 15s 56m **29M**; W Tr, R top. Dir F 54m **28M**; same Tr; intens 157·5°-159·5°. 54m 291° from St Mathieu Q WRG 26m, W14M, R11M, G11M; W Tr; vis: G085°-107°, W107°-116°, R116°-134°.
La Fourmi 48°19'·25N 04°47'·97W.
Les Vieux-Moines 48°19'·33N 04°46'·63W Fl R 4s 16m 5M; R 8-sided Tr; vis: 280°-133°.

CHENAL DE LA HELLE

Ldg Lt 137·9°. Front, **Kermorvan** ☆ 48°21'·72N 04°47'·42W Fl 5s 20m **22M**. Rear, **Lochrist** ☆ 48°20·55N 04°45'·82W Dir Oc (3) 12s 49m **22M** (see above).
Luronne 48°26'·61N 04°53'·79W; *Bell.*
Ldg Lts 293·5°. Front, Le Faix 48°25'·73N 04°53'·92W VQ 16m 8M; NCM. Rear, **Le Stiff** ☆ 48°28'·47N 05°03'·41W Fl (2) R 20s 85m **24M** (see below).
Ldg Lt 142·5° for Chenal de La Helle. Front, **Kermorvan** ☆ 48°21'·72N 04°47'·42W Fl 5s 20m **22M** (see above). Rear, two W Bns 48°20'·17N 04°45'·44W.
Pourceaux 48°24'·01N 04°51'·34W Q.
S. Pierre 48°23'·09N 04°49'·10W.

◀ L'IROISE/BREST AND APPROACHES

Pierres Noires 48°18'·47N 04°58'·16W; *Bell.*
Les Pierres Noires ☆ 48°18'·67N 04°54'·88W Fl R 5s 27m **19M**; W Tr, R top; *Horn (2) 60s.*
Basse Royale 48°17'·45N 04°49'·62W Q (6) + L Fl 15s.
Vandrée 48°15'·20N 04°48'·25W VQ (9) 10s; *Whis.*
La Parquette 48°15'·89N 04°44'·30W Fl RG 4s 17m R6M, G6M; W 8-sided Tr, B diagonal stripes; vis: R244°-285°, G285°-244°.

◀ GOULET DE BREST

Charles Martel 48°18'·85N 04°42'·19W Fl (4) R; *Whis.*
Swansea Vale 48°18'·27N 04°38'·84W Fl (2) 6s; *Whis.*
Pte du Petit-Minou ☆ 48°20'·19N 04°36'·87W Fl (2) WR 6s 32m **W19M, R15M**; Gy Tr, R top; vis: Rshore-252°, W252°-260°, R260°-307°, W(unintens) 307°-015°,W015°-065·5°, W070·5°-shore. Same structure, Ldg Lts 068°. **Front** ☆, Dir Q 30m **23M**, intens 067·3°-068·8°. **Rear, Pte du Portzic** ☆, Dir Q 56m **22M**; intens 065°-071°.
Fillettes 48°19'·75N 04°35'·67W VQ (9); *Whis.*
Kerviniou 48°19'·77N 04°35'·25W Fl (2) R 6s.

◀ BREST

Basse Goudron 48°20'·02N 04°34'·87W QR.
Roche Mengam 48°20'·32N 04°34'·57W Fl (3) WR 12s 10m W11M, R8M, R Tr, B bands; vis: R034°-054°, W054°-034°.
Pte du Portzic ☆ 48°21'·49N 04°32'·06W Oc (2) WR 12s 56m **W19M, R15M**; Gy Tr; vis: R219°-259°, W259°-338°, R338°-000°, W000°-065·5°, W070·5°-219°. Same structure Dir Q (6) + L Fl 15s 54m **23M**; intens 045°-050°.
Pénoupèle 48°21'·45N 04°30'·53W Fl (3) R 12s.
Port Militaire, Jetée Sud Hd ☆ 48°22'·10N 04°29'·46W QR 10m 5M; W Tr, R top; vis: 094°-048°.
Jetée Est Hd ☆ 48°22'·15N 04°29'·22W QG 10m 7M; W Tr, G top; vis: 299°-163°.
Port Militaire Ldg Lts 344°. Front, 48°22'·79N 04°29'·63W VQ WRG 24m W10M, R5M, G5M; vis: G 334°-342°, W342°-346°, R346°-024°. Rear, 118m from front, Dir VQ 32m 10; intens 342°-346°.
La Penfeld Ldg Lts 314° Front 48°22'·87N 04°29'·95W Dir Iso R 5s 9m; intens 309°-319°. Rear, 7m from front, Dir Iso R 5s 16m; intens 309°-319°; sync with front.
Port de Commerce Jetée du Sud Ouest Hd ☆ 48°22'·60N 04°29'·12W Fl G 4s 10m 4M; vis: 022°-257°.
Port de Commerce Jeteé du Sud E Hd ☆ 48°22'·69N 04°28'·48W Oc (2) R 6s 8m 5M; W pylon, R top; vis: 018°-301°.
R2 48°22'·01N 04°28'·75W Fl (2) R 6s.
R1 48°21'·83N 04°28'·29W Fl G 4s.
R4 48°22'·22N 04°28'·06W L Fl R 10s.
Water Intake, off St Marc 48°22'·69N 04°26'·54W Fl (4) R 15s.

◀ LE MOULIN BLANC/MARINA

Moulin Blanc 48°22'·79N 04°25'·99W Fl (3) R 12s.
MB2 48°23'·22N 04°25'·84W Fl R 2s.
MB 4 Bkwtr N end ☆ 48°23'·48N 04°25'·80W Fl R 2s 2m 1M.
MB 3 Bkwtr, E side, S end ☆ 48°23'·49N 04°25'·72W Fl G 2s 2m 1M.

16

◀ CAMARET

Môle Nord Hd ☆ 48°16'·85N 04°35'·32W Iso WG 4s 7m W12M, G9M; W pylon, G top; vis: W135°-182°, G182°-027°.
Môle Sud Hd ☆ 48°16'·63N 04°35'·33W Fl (2) R 6s 9m 5M; R pylon.

Pointe du Toulinguet ☆ 48°16'·82N 04°37'·73W Oc (3) WR 12s 49m **W15M**, R11M; W □ Tr on bldg; vis: W shore-028°, R028°-090°, W090°-shore.

◀ L'IROISE/BAIE DE DOUARNENEZ

Mendufa 48°16'·05N 04°39'·43W.
Basse Du Lis 48°12'·99N 04°44'·53W Q (6) + L Fl 15s 9m 6M; *Whis.*
Le Chevreau 48°13'·38N 04°36'·82W.
Le Bouc 48°11'·51N 04°37'·38W Q (9) 15s; *Bell.*
Basse Vieille 48°08'·23N 04°35'·76W Fl (2) 6s 8m 7M; *Whis.*

◀ MORGAT

Pointe de Morgat ☆ 48°13'·17N 04°29'·81W Oc (4) WRG 12s 77m **W15M**, R11M, G10M; W □ Tr, R top, W dwelling; vis: W shore-281°, G281°-301°, W301°-021°, R021°-043°.
Mole Hd ☆ 48°13'·51N 04°29'·97W Oc (2) WR 6s 8m W9M, R6M; W&R Tr; vis: W007°-257°, R257°-007°.
48°13'·57N 04°29'·67W Fl R 4s
Marina ent through wavebreak pontoons marked by Fl G 4s to stbd and Fl R 4s to port.

◀ DOUARNENEZ

Tréboul Pointe Biron Hd ☆ 48°06'·09N 04°20'·47W QG 7m 6M; W col, G top.
Île Tristan ☆ 48°06'·14N 04°20'·25W Oc (3) WR 12s 35m W13M, R10M; Gy Tr, W band, B top; vis: W shore-138°, R138°-153°, W153°-shore.
Bassin Nord, N Mole E Hd ☆ 48°05'·96N 04°19'·28W Iso G 4s 9m 4M; W & G pylon.
S Mole N Hd ☆ 48°05'·91N 04°19'·27W Oc (2) R 6s 6m 6M; W&R pylon.
Elbow, Môle de Rosmeur Head ☆ 48°05'·79N 04°19'·23W Oc G 4s 6m 6M; W pylon, G top; vis: 170°-097°.

Pointe du Millier ☆ 48°05'·92N 04°27'·95W Oc (2) WRG 6s 34m **W16M**, R12M, G11M; W house; vis: G080°-087°, W087°-113°, R113°-120°, W120°-129°, G129°-148°, W148°-251°, R251°-258°.
Basse Jaune 48°04'·67N 04°42'·47W.
Tévennec ☆ 48°04'·27N 04°47'·74W Q WR 28m W9M, R6M; W Tr; vis: W090°-345°, R345°-090°. Dir Fl 4s 24m 12M; same Tr intens 324°-332°.

9.16.5 PASSAGE INFORMATION

NORTH BRITTANY (charts 2643 *2644 2668*) Refer to *North Brittany and CI Cruising Companion* (Macmillan Reeds/ Cumberlidge); *North Brittany Pilot* (Imray/RCC); Admiralty *Channel Pilot* (NP 27); *Brittany and CI Cruising Guide* (Adlard Coles/Jefferson), and *Shell Channel Pilot* (Imray/Cunliffe).

Good landfall marks must be carefully identified before closing this rock-strewn coast. Closer inshore the tidal streams and currents vary, and overfalls are best avoided. In rough weather, low visibility (fog and summer haze are frequent) or if uncertain of position, it may be prudent to lie off and wait for conditions to improve; there are few safe havens. A high degree of planning is needed to achieve safe pilotage. In the W of the area the size of Atlantic swells can much reduce the range at which objects, especially floating marks, are seen.

PAIMPOL TO PLOUMANAC'H (AC 3670) In the offing, between 11M and 18M NNE of Île de Bréhat, are Plateau de Barnouic (lit) and Plateau des Roches Douvres (lt, fog sig, RC), both with drying and submerged rks, to be given a wide berth particularly in poor vis.

Approaching from the SE, keep to seaward of the three ECM buoys off L'Ost-Pic or enter B de Paimpol (9.16.8) from a point about 1M E of the most N'ly ECM (Les Charpentiers). The Ferlas chan (AC 3673) runs S of Île de Bréhat (9.16.9), and is useful if entering/leaving R. Trieux from/to the E. It is well marked and not difficult, but best taken at half tide due to unmarked rks in chan almost awash at or near LW.

For the many yachts approaching from Guernsey, Les Héaux-de-Bréhat lt ho is a conspic landfall day/night for either Tréguier or Lézardrieux. Closer in or from the E, La Horaine (lt bn) is the best landfall for the latter. It marks the Plateaux de la Horaine and des Échaudés and other rks to the SE. In poor visibility it should be closed with caution and left at least 7ca to the SE, as the flood stream sets strongly onto it. The Grand Chenal is the main, lit chan into R. de Trieux for Lézardrieux (9.16.10) and up-river to Pontrieux (9.16.11). From NW the unlit Chenal de La Moisie leads SSE to join the Grand Chenal at Ile de Bréhat (9.16.9).

Between Lézardrieux and Tréguier (9.16.12) the Passage de la Gaine is a useful inshore route, avoiding a detour round Les Heaux. It is unlit and needs good vis, but if taken at above half tide, presents no problem in fair weather. The Grande Passe into R. de Tréguier is well lit, but ldg marks are less easy to see by day. The NE Passage should be used with caution.

Between Basse Crublent lt buoy and Port Blanc unmarked rks extend 2M offshore. Port Blanc (AC 3672) can be difficult to identify by day. Perros-Guirec (9.16.13) is approached either side of Ile Tomé from NE or NW via well lit/marked chans (AC 3672). Ploumanac'h (9.16.14) can only be entered by day.

LES SEPT ÎLES TO BAIE DE MORLAIX (AC 3669) Les Sept Îles (9.16.16 and AC 3670) consist of five main islands and several islets, through which the tide runs strongly. Île aux Moines is lit, and all the islands are bird sanctuaries. Further W, Plateau des Triagoz has offlying dangers WSW and NE of the lt, where the sea breaks heavily. Here the stream turns ENE at HW Brest –0325, and WSW at HW Brest +0245, sp rates both 3·8kn.

Trégastel Ste Anne (9.16.14) is a small anchorage W of Ploumanac'h. To the SW the coast as far as Trébeurden (9.16.15) is not easily approached due to many offlying rks. The radome NE of Trébeurden is conspic. Further S in the B de Lannion is Locquémeau and anchs near the mouth of the drying R. Léguier up to Lannion (9.16.16). Primel (9.16.16), at the E ent to Baie de Morlaix, provides a good deep anch. To the N is the drying Plateau de la Méloine.

The B de Morlaix (9.16.17 and AC 2745) is bestrewn with drying rks and shoals, all marked. Careful pilotage and adequate visibility are needed to negotiate any of the chans which are narrow in parts. The Grand Chenal passes close E of Île Ricard with Île Louet and La Lande (both lit) in transit 176°; abeam Calhic bn tr alter to port to transit between Château du Taureau (conspic) and Île Louet. Continue SSE for the river up to Morlaix. The anchorage NE of Carantec is reached from Chenal Ouest de Ricard.

ÎLE DE BATZ TO LE FOUR (charts 3668, 3669) N of Île de Batz the E-going stream begins at HW Brest –0435, and the W-going stream at HW Brest +0105, sp rates 3·8kn. Approaching Roscoff (9.16.18) from NE, leave Basse Astan ECM lt buoy to stbd steering with Men Guen Bras NCM lt bn in transit 213° with Chapelle St Barbe to round Ar Chaden for Roscoff hbr (dries); or transit W via Canal de L'Île de Batz.

In daylight and above half tide Canal de L'Île de Batz is a useful short cut between the island and the mainland. From near Ar Chaden steer 275° for the Vi bn at end of the conspic Roscoff ferry pier. Pass 30m N of this bn, and at this point alter to 300° for Run Oan SCM. Thence steer 283°, leaving Perroch NCM bn 100m to port. When clear of this rky, drying shoal alter to 270°, leaving

Por Kernock hbr bkwtrs well to stbd and aiming midway between L'Oignon NCM and La Croix SCM. When these are abeam steer 281° for Basse Plate NCM bn; thence West into open waters.

Proceeding W from Île de Batz toward Le Four there are many off-lying dangers, in places 3M offshore. Swell may break on shoals even further to seaward. The tide runs strongly, and in poor vis or bad weather it is a coast to avoid. But in good conditions this is an admirable cruising ground with delightful hbrs such as Moguériec and Pontusval (9.16.17), L'Aberwrac'h (9.16.19), L'Aberbenoit (9.16.20), Portsall and Argenton (9.16.24). N of L'Aberwrac'h is Île Vierge lt ho, reputedly the tallest in the world, and a conspic landmark. Off Le Libenter, at N side of L'Aberwrac'h ent, the E-going stream starts at HW Brest – 0500, sp rate 3·8kn, and the W-going stream at HW Brest + 018.

W of L'Aberwrac'h is an inshore chan leading past Portsall to Le Four (lt bn). This is a sheltered short-cut, but must only be used by day and in good visibility. AC 1432 or SHOM 5772 and full directions, as in *North Brittany Pilot*, are needed.

OUESSANT (USHANT) (chart 2694) Île Ouessant lies 10M off NW Brittany. It is a rky island, with dangers extending 5ca to NE, 7½ca to SE, 1·5M to SW and 1M to NW; here Chaussée de Keller is a dangerous chain of drying and submerged rks running 1M W of Île de Keller and into the ITZ. Apart from Lampaul (9.16.21) the only other anch is B du Stiff which gives some shelter in moderate winds between S and NW. Tidal streams are strong close to the island, and in chans between it and mainland. Off Pte de Créac'h (lt, fog sig) the stream turns NNE at HW Brest – 0550, and SSW at HW Brest + 0045, sp rate 5·5kn.

The route outside Ouessant TSS, has little to commend it. Unless bound to/from Spain/Portugal it adds much to the distance and is exposed to sea and swell. Yachts should round Ouessant via the ITZ or the inshore channels. Besides being an important landfall, Ouessant in thick weather is an unhealthy area, and it is prudent to stay in harbour until the vis improves. But in fair weather and reasonable visibility the pilotage in the chans between it and the mainland is not very demanding. They are well buoyed and marked (see 9.16.23), but the tide runs hard in places, causing overfalls when against wind >Force 5.

The three main chans between the island and mainland are: The Chenal du Four, inshore and most direct and popular; Chenal de la Helle, an alternative to N part of Chenal du Four (partly used for access to Île Moléne), is not so direct but better in bad weather. Passage du Fromveur, close SE of Ouessant, is easiest but longer and can become extremely rough; tidal streams may exceed 8kn.

CHENAL DU FOUR (9.16.23 and AC 3345, 2694) It is imperative to work the tides to best advantage through this passage: 1M W of Le Four the S-going stream begins at HW Brest + 0130; the N-going stream at HW Brest – 0545, sp rates 3·6kn. Further S, off Pte de Corsen, the stream is weaker, max 2·3kn at sp. The tide runs strongest at S end of Chenal du Four, off Le Conquet. Here the S-going stream starts at HW Brest + 0015, max 5kn; the N-going stream begins at HW Brest – 0550, 5·2kn max at sp. Wind-over-tide effects may be considerable.

Yachts are less rigidly tied to transits/dir lts than large ships and the following pilotage sequence can be used day or night, buoy-hopping as necessary if transits are obscured:

From 1·2M W of Le Four, track 180° (04°50'W: clear of Les Liniou reef to port) for 5M to Valbelle PHM lt buoy. Here pick up the transit 158·5°of Pte de Kermorvan on with Pte St Mathieu. Maintain this transit until Pte de Corsen lt bears 012° astern; then alter 192° to pass between La Grande Vinotière lt bn and Roche du Rouget lt buoy. Stand on until Le Faix lt bn is on with Grand Courleau bn 325° astern; alter 145° to maintain this track for 2·3M when open water will be reached with Vieux-Moines lt bn 4ca abeam to port.

Double check all lt/marks; do not confuse St Mathieu with Lochrist. L'Aberildut (9.16.22), 3·5M SSE of Le Four, and Le Conquet (9.16.25), 3ca SE of Pte de Kermorvan are the only ports off the Chenal du Four; but in offshore winds anch can be found in Anse de Porsmoguer and Anse des Blancs-Sablons, both between Corsen and Kermorvan.

Homeward-bound, or along the N coast of France, enter the S end of Chenal du Four at LW Brest; a fair tide can then be carried through the chan and NE past Île Vierge. The reverse sequence of pilotage is followed.

CHENAL DE LA HELLE (9.16.23 and AC 3345, 2694) At N end of Chenal de la Helle the ENE stream starts at HW Brest – 0520 (sp rate 2·8kn), and the SW stream at HW Brest – 0045 (sp rate 3·8kn). The Ch de la Helle converges at a 20° angle with the Ch du Four. From the N, steer SW from Le Four towards Ile de Molène lt to pick up the 138° transit of Pte de Kermorvan and Lochrist close to Luronne unlit WCM buoy. Maintain this transit until Le Faix lt bn and Le Stiff lt ho are in transit 293° astern; steer 113° for 8ca until Pte de Kermorvan is on with 2 W bns (Pignons de Kéravel) at 142°. This transit avoids Basse St Pierre (4·7m) and intercepts the Ch du Four 7ca N of Grande Vinotière.

APPROACHES TO BREST (charts 798, 3427, 3428) The outer approaches lie between Chaussée des Pierres Noires and Pte St Mathieu to the N and Pte du Toulinguet to the S. From the W steer on the 068° transit of Petit Minhou and Portzic on the N shore. From the S steer NNE toward Petit Minhou to pick up the transit, but beware rks 7M W and SW of Pte du Toulinguet. Yachts <25m LOA are exempt from VTM, but should monitor VHF Ch 08 or 16.

Abeam Petit Minhou lt ho the Goulet (Narrows) de Brest narrows to 1M; there are well-marked drying rks almost in mid-stream. A course of 075° through the Passe Nord leaves Roc Mengam lt bn 2ca to stbd. Tidal streams attain 4·5kn in the Goulet. In Passe Sud there is a useful back-eddy close inshore which runs ENE during the ebb. Once beyond Pte du Portzic a buoyed chan leads ENE past the Naval and commercial hbrs to the Moulin Blanc marina (9.16.26). The Rade de Brest (9.16.27) opens to the S and E.

16

L'IROISE/BAIE DE DOUARNENEZ (charts 3427, 798) L'Iroise is the area between Chaussée des Pierres Noires and Chaussée de Sein; the B de Douarnenez lies further E. On the NE side of L'Iroise (chart 3427) a chain of rks extends 7M W from Pte du Toulinguet. There are several chans through these rks, of which the simplest for Brest (9.16.26) and Camaret (9.15.28) is the 3ca wide Chenal du Toulinguet which runs NNW between La Louve bn tr (1ca W of Pte du Toulinguet) on E side and Le Pohen rk on the W side.

Here the N-going stream begins at HW Brest – 0550, and the S-going at HW Brest + 0015, sp rates 2·75kn. 2·5M NW of C. de la Chèvre is Le Chévreau (dries), with La Chèvre 5ca to NE of it (1·25M WSW of Pte de Dinan). 7M W of Pte de Dinan lies Basse du Lis, rky shoals with depth of 2·4m.

The B de Douarnenez is entered between C. de la Chèvre and Raz de Sein. Off C. de la Chèvre various dangers, on which the sea breaks, extend SW for 2·25M to Basse Vieille (dries), lt buoy. Morgat (9.16.29) lies 4M NNE of C. de la Chèvre. Beware group of drying rks, including La Pierre-Profonde and Le Taureau close SSW of Les Verrès (rk 9m high), which lies nearly 2·5M ESE of Morgat.

Approaching Douarnenez (9.16.30) beware Basse Veur and Basse Neuve. The S shore of the B is clear of dangers more than 2ca offshore, except for Duellou Rk (4m high) 5ca offshore, and other rks 1M eastward. Further W beware Basse Jaune, an isolated rk (dries) about 1M N of Pte du Van.

9.16.6 DISTANCE TABLE

Approximate distances in nautical miles are by the most direct route, whilst avoiding dangers and allowing for Traffic Separation Schemes. Places in *italics* are in adjoining areas; places in **bold** are in 9.0.6, Cross-Channel Distances.

1. ***St Quay-Portrieux***	**1**																			
2. Paimpol	24	**2**																		
3. Bréhat (Port Clos)	15	8	**3**																	
4. **Lézardrieux**	21	14	6	**4**																
5. **Tréguier**	46	29	22	22	**5**															
6. Perros-Guirec	37	35	28	28	21	**6**														
7. Ploumanac'h	40	33	27	29	25	6	**7**													
8. Trébeurden	48	44	38	40	32	17	11	**8**												
9. **Lannion**	52	48	42	44	33	21	15	6	**9**											
10. Morlaix	67	64	58	60	46	36	30	23	24	**10**										
11. **Roscoff**	59	58	52	54	41	28	22	17	19	12	**11**									
12. **L'Aberwrac'h**	91	88	82	84	72	60	54	49	51	48	32	**12**								
13. L'Aberbenoit	92	89	83	85	76	61	55	50	52	45	33	7	**13**							
14. Lampaul	114	110	104	106	98	83	77	72	74	67	55	29	28	**14**						
15. **Le Conquet**	114	110	104	106	98	83	77	72	71	68	55	29	23	17	**15**					
16. Brest (marina)	125	119	114	114	107	92	86	83	87	79	67	42	41	31	18	**16**				
17. Camaret	124	120	114	116	108	93	87	82	81	78	65	39	33	27	13	10	**17**			
18. Morgat	134	130	124	126	118	103	97	92	91	88	75	49	43	37	20	24	16	**18**		
19. Douarnenez	139	135	129	131	123	108	102	97	96	93	80	54	48	42	25	29	21	11	**19**	
20. *Audierne*	144	139	133	135	128	113	108	102	101	98	86	55	53	40	30	34	28	27	30	**20**

9.16.7 Special Notes for France: See 9.15.7.

PAIMPOL *9.16.8*

Côtes d'Armor **48°47´·06N 03°02´·47W**

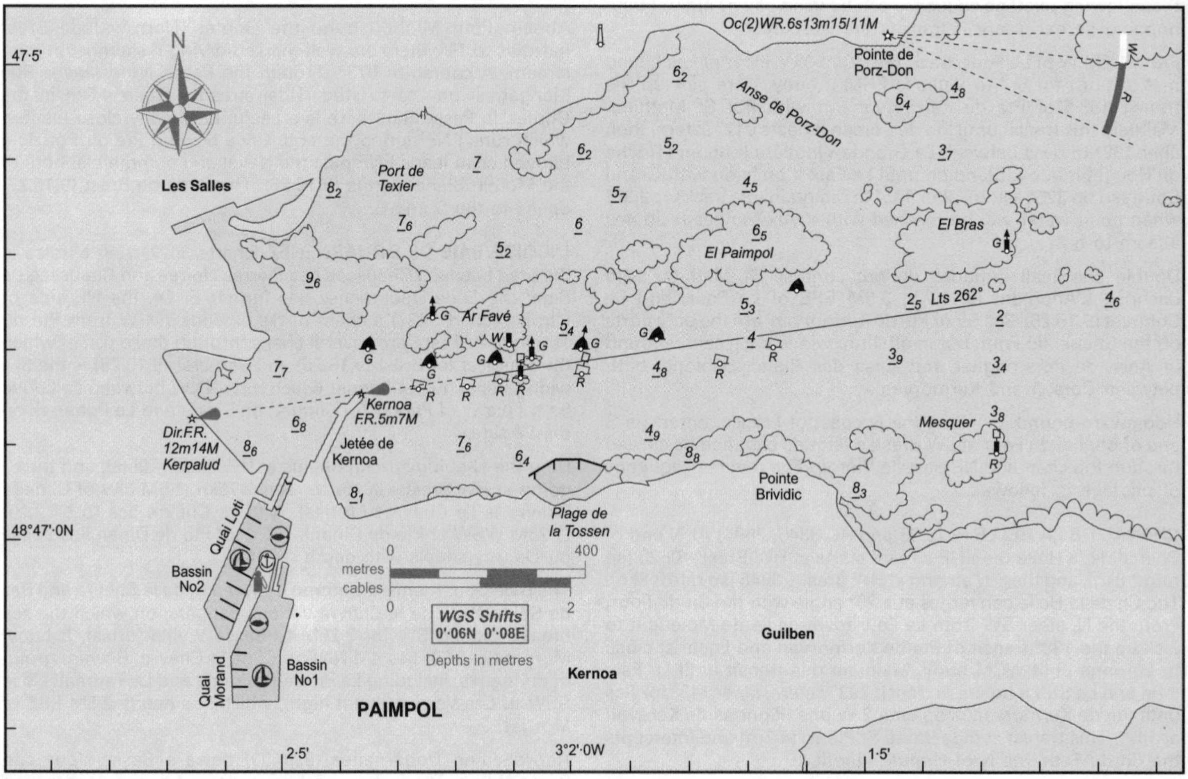

CHARTS AC 3673, 3670, *2668*; SHOM 7152, 7154; ECM 537; Imray C34; Stanfords 17

TIDES Dover –0525; ML 6·1; Duration 0600; Zone –0100

Standard Port ST MALO (⟵)

Times				Height (metres)			
High Water		Low Water		MHWS	MHWN	MLWN	MLWS
0100	0800	0300	0800	12·2	9·3	4·2	1·5
1300	2000	1500	2000				
Differences PAIMPOL							
–0005	–0010	–0035	–0025	–1·4	–0·9	–0·4	–0·1

SHELTER Good shelter from all winds in hbr, but few ⚓s as most of the Anse de Paimpol dries, including the appr chan to hbr. Lock opens HW ±2 when height of HW <10m; HW ±2½ when HW >10m. Visitors' berths at pontoon A, Basin No 2, min depth 3·8m. Larger yachts berth in Basin No 1.

NAVIGATION WPT 48°47´·88N 02°54´·50W, 080°/260° from/to summit of Pte Brividic 4·7M. Chenal de la Jument is the normal appr from the E. After La Jument PHM bn tr, either ⚓ to await the tide; or alter 262° for small unlit buoys/bns marking final 1M of chan; hard to see against a low evening sun. The drying rks (El Paimpol, El Bras and Ar Fav) are close N of the ldg line. An alternative appr from Ile de Bréhat at HW+2 lies E of Les Piliers NCM bn tr, thence S past Pte de la Trinité; or appr from further E via Chenal du Denou 193°. Bearing in mind the large tidal range, there is enough water in the bay from half-flood for most craft.

LIGHTS AND MARKS 4M E is L'Ost-Pic lt, Oc WR 4s 20m 11/8M, conspic □ W tr. Pte de Porz-Don, Oc (2) WR 6s 13m 15/11M, vis W269°-272°, R272°-279°, is 7ca ENE of hbr ent. W sector leads 270° to the inner ldg lts 262°. A conspic tr (52m) is 3ca W of Porz -Don. Outer ldg marks 260° for Chenal de la Jument: Paimpol ✠ spire on with the summit (27m) of Pte Brividic. Inner ldg lts 262°: front, Jetée de Kernoa, FR 5m 7M; rear, Dir FR 12m 14M, intens 260°-264°.

RADIO TELEPHONE VHF Ch 09 (0800-1200LT and lock opening hrs).

TELEPHONE Hr Mr 02·96.20.47.65; Port Mgr 02·96·20·80·77; Lock 02·96·20·90·02; ⊜ 02·96·20·81·87; Aff Mar 02·96·55·35·00; CROSS 02·98·89·31·31; Auto 08·36·68·08·22; Police 02·96·20·80·17; Ⓗ 02·96·20·86·02; Dr 02·96·20·80·04; Brit Consul 02·99·46·26·64.

FACILITIES Basin No 2 (marina 280+20 visitors), €1·68, FW, AC, D (quay), P (cans), ME, El, ♿; **Basin No 1** C (6 and 4 ton); **Quai de Kernoa** P, ME; **Quai neuf** Slip, M, FW, AB; **Services:** Sh, CH, SHOM, Ⓔ. **Town** P, CH, V, R, Bar, Gaz, ☎, ✉, Ⓑ, ⇌, ✈ Dinard, Brest, Rennes. Ferry: Roscoff, St Malo.

ILE DE BRÉHAT *9.16.9*

Côtes d'Armor 48°51'·00N 03°00'·00W

CHARTS AC 3673, 3670, *2668*; SHOM 7152, 7154; ECM 537; Imray C34; Stanfords 17

TIDES –0525 Dover; ML 5·8; Duration 0605; Zone –0100

Standard Port ST MALO (⟵)

Times				Height (metres)			
High Water		Low Water		MHWS	MHWN	MLWN	MLWS
0100	0800	0300	0800	12·2	9·3	4·2	1·5
1300	2000	1500	2000				
Differences LES HEAUX DE BRÉHAT							
–0018	–0017	–0050	–0050	–2·4	–1·7	–0·6	–0·2
ILE DE BRÉHAT							
–0008	–0013	–0040	–0037	–1·8	–1·3	–0·4	–0·2

SHELTER Port Clos: drying main hbr; good shelter, but busy with vedettes. No AB; ⚓ clear of fairway. (Due to cables across the Ferlas Chan, ⚓ is prohib to the SW of Port Clos). Port de la Corderie: hbr dries; get well out of strong tides. Good shelter, except in W winds.

ILE DE BREHAT *continued*

E of Le Bourg there are free drying private moorings near ⚓, but some were reported unsafe due lack of maintenance. La Chambre: ⚓ in upper reaches just S of the moorings area. Slip can be floodlit by pressing button on lamp post at top of slip. Guerzido in the Chenal de Ferlas is good holding, partly out of the strong tides; or ⚓ E of Men Allan and close to the buoys of the boat barrier.

NAVIGATION WPT Ferlas chan 48°49'·45N 02°55'·00W, 098°/278° from/to La Croix lt, 5·5M. See also 9.16.10. On appr, beware La Horaine, Men Marc'h and C'hign Bras closer in.

LIGHTS AND MARKS For the three principal lts on Ile de Bréhat, see 9.16.4.

RADIO TELEPHONE Sémaphore de Bréhat VHF Ch 16 10, Day only.

TELEPHONE Hr Mr none; CROSS 02·98·89·31·31; SNSM 02·96·20·00·14; Auto 08·36·68·08·22; ⊜ 02·96·20·81·87; Police 02·96·20·80·17; Dr 02·96·20·00·99; Brit Consul 02·99·46·26·64.

FACILITIES Hbrs M, FW, P from fuel barge at Port Clos, Slip, full access at HW; CN de Bréhat, FW, Bar; Services: ME. Village V, Gaz, Bar, Y, Q (Paimpol), ⇄ (ferry to Pte de l'Arcouest, bus to Paimpol thence to Paris, Brest, Roscoff and St Malo), ✈ (Dinard, Brest, Rennes to London). Ferry: Plymouth-Roscoff. No cars on island.

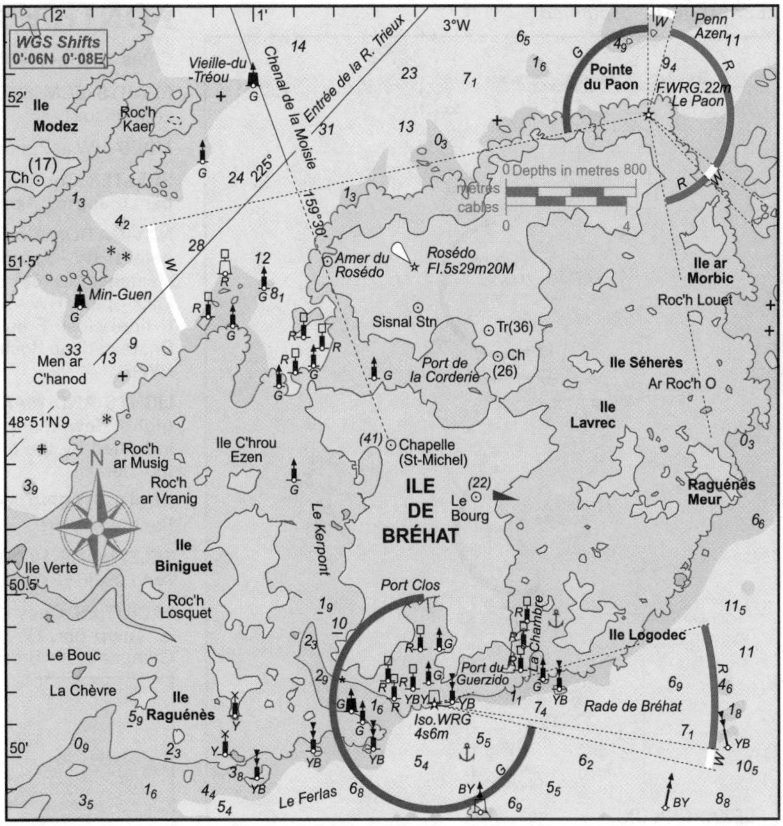

LÉZARDRIEUX 9.16.10

Côtes d'Armor **48°47'·41N 03°05'·83W**

CHARTS AC 3673, 3670, *2668*; SHOM 7152; ECM 537; Imray C34; Stanfords 17

TIDES –0510 Dover; ML 5·9; Duration 0610; Zone –0100

Standard Port ST MALO (⟵)

Times				Height (metres)			
High Water		Low Water		MHWS	MHWN	MLWN	MLWS
0100	0800	0300	0800	12·2	9·3	4·2	1·5
1300	2000	1500	2000				
Differences LÉZARDRIEUX							
–0010	–0010	–0047	–0037	–1·7	–1·3	–0·5	–0·2

SHELTER Very good in all weathers. The Trieux River and marina pontoons are accessible H24. Very close SW, a marina extension (247 berths) has some Ⓥ berths (2·4m inside). Access over sill 4·9m above CD, with automatic flap. As sill covers on the flood to 6·15m CD, flap automatically drops to give 1·25m clearance. A depth gauge shows water over sill. IPTS in use. See chartlet overleaf. Multihulls and boats >12·5m LOA should moor on Ⓥs in the stream. Yachts can go about 12km up river (via bridge, clearance 17m) to lock in at Pontrieux (9.16.11).

NAVIGATION WPT 48°55'·00N 02°56'·20W, 045°/225° from/to front ldg lt 225° (La Croix), 6·7M. Roches Douvres and Barnouic are dangers in the outer apps; closer in, are the Plateau de la Horaine and rky shoals to the W. Off river ent beware strong cross streams. The 3 well-marked ent chans are:

- Ferlas Chan from the E, running S of Ile de Bréhat;
- Grand Chenal, main chan from NE, best for strangers; and
- Moisie, unlit from the NW, which also connects with Passe de la Gaine from/to Tréguier (9.16.12).

LIGHTS AND MARKS Offshore lts: Roches Douvres, Fl 5s 60m 28M, pink tr. Barnouic ECM bn tr, VQ (3) 5s 15m 9M. Les Héaux de Bréhat, Oc (3) WRG 12s 48m 17/12M, gy tr. Pte du Paon and Rosédo, on Bréhat, see 9.16.4 and .9. The ldg marks/lts for the ent chans are:

1. Ferlas chan:
   W sector of Men Joliguet lt bn tr 271° (see 9.16.9).
   W sector of Roche Quinonec Dir Q WRG 257°.
   W sector of Kermouster Dir Fl WRG 2s leads 271° to join Coatmer ldg line.
2. Grand Chenal ldg lts 225°: Front, La Croix Oc 4s 15m 19M; two grey trs joined, W on NE side with R tops, intens 215°-235°; rear, Bodic (2·1M from front) Q 55m 22M (intens 221°-229°).
3. Moisie chan: Amer du Rosédo W obelisk on 159° with St Michael's chapel (both conspic on Ile de Bréhat).

Within the Trieux river:

4. Coatmer ldg lts 219°: front F RG 16m 9/9M, vis R200°-250°, G250°-053°; rear, 660m from front, FR 50m 9M.
5. W sector 200° of Les Perdrix G tr, Fl (2) WG 6s.

Beware, at night, the unlit Roc'h Donan 2½ca S of Perdrix. The only lts beyond Perdrix are F Bu lts at the outboard ends of the 3 tidal marina pontoons, and a Fl R 4s and Fl G 4s buoy 50 - 100m E of the ent to new marina; also unlit perches: PHM/SHM at ent; 1 ECM 50m NE of ent, and 5 Y SPM marking the limits of the marina.

RADIO TELEPHONE VHF Ch 09 (0730-2200 Jul/Aug. 0800-1200 and 1400-1800 rest of year).

TELEPHONE Hr Mr 02·96·20·14·22; Aff Mar at Paimpol 02·96·55·35·00; CROSS 02·98·89·31·31; ⊜ at Paimpol 02·96·20·81·87; Auto 08·36·68·08·22; Police 02·96·20·8·17; Dr 02·96·20·8·30; Brit Consul 02·99·46·26·64.

FACILITIES **Marina** (675 incl 50 Ⓥ as directed by Hr Mr), ☎ 02·96·55·35·00, 📠 02·96.22.10.34, €1·68, Slip, P, D, FW, AC, ME, El, CH, SM, Sh, C (6ton), Gaz, R, ⊡, Bar; **YC de Trieux** ☎ 02·96·20·10·39. **Services:** Divers, Ⓔ; **Town** EC Sun; P, D, V, Gaz, R, Bar, ✉, Ⓑ, ⇄ (occas bus to Paimpol), ✈ Lannion. Ferry: Roscoff.

See **LÉZARDRIEUX** plans overleaf

LÉZARDRIEUX *continued*

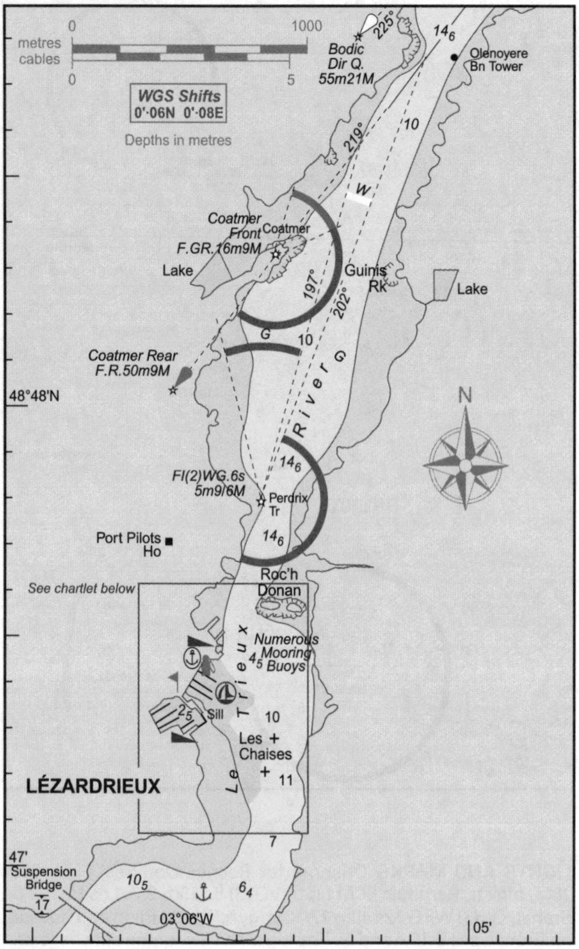

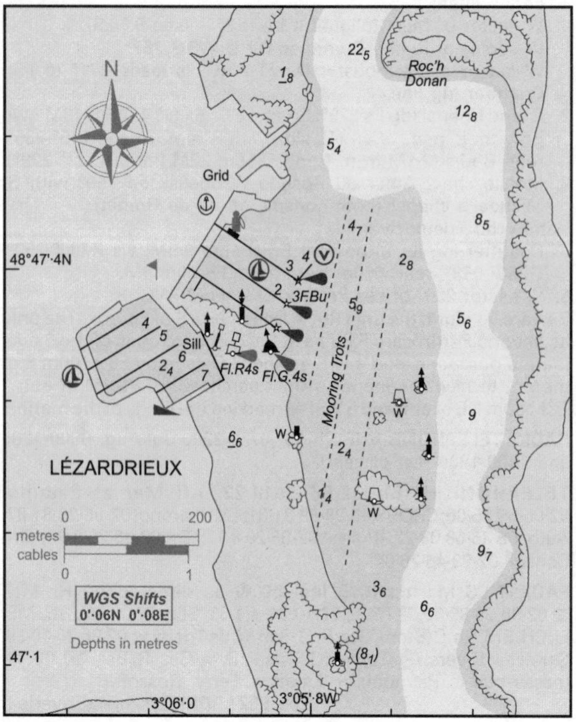

PONTRIEUX 9.16.11

Côtes d'Armor **48°42'·80N 03°08'·90W**

CHARTS ECM 537; AC 3673 and SHOM 7152 downstream of Lézardrieux

TIDES HW at Pontrieux Lock is at HW ST MALO. See also 9.16.10.

SHELTER Complete shelter in 2-4m depth alongside Quay (SE bank), approx 1km above lock.

NAVIGATION See 9.16.10 for approach up to Lézardrieux. Not before HW –3, proceed via suspension bridge (17m at MHWS clearance) for 6M up-river, keeping to high, rky bank on bends. Lock opens HW –2 (–1 at weekends) to HW+1. 2 Waiting buoys (½ tide) close E and slip with FW and AC on the bend. Below Château de la Roche Jagu there is also a waiting buoy available HW±3.

LIGHTS AND MARKS River is unlit (beware sand dredgers at night); few marks. The best water between river bends is indicated by the alignment of reflective posts (1-2m high) near the bends.

RADIO TELEPHONE Lock VHF Ch 12, HW –1½ to +1. [tel] link to Pontrieux Port.

TELEPHONE Hr Mr [tel]/[fax] 02·96·95·34·87; Lock 02·96·95·60·70; Auto 08·36·68·08·22. There is a [tel] at the Château Roche Jagu.

FACILITIES **Quay** (160+40 Ⓥ) AB €1.48, FW, AC, C (6 ton), R, Bar, [disabled]. **Town** Bar, FW, R, Slip, V, Gaz, P, D, [bank], [post], [clock], [train] Paimpol/Guingamp, [airport] Brest, Rennes, Dinard & Paris.

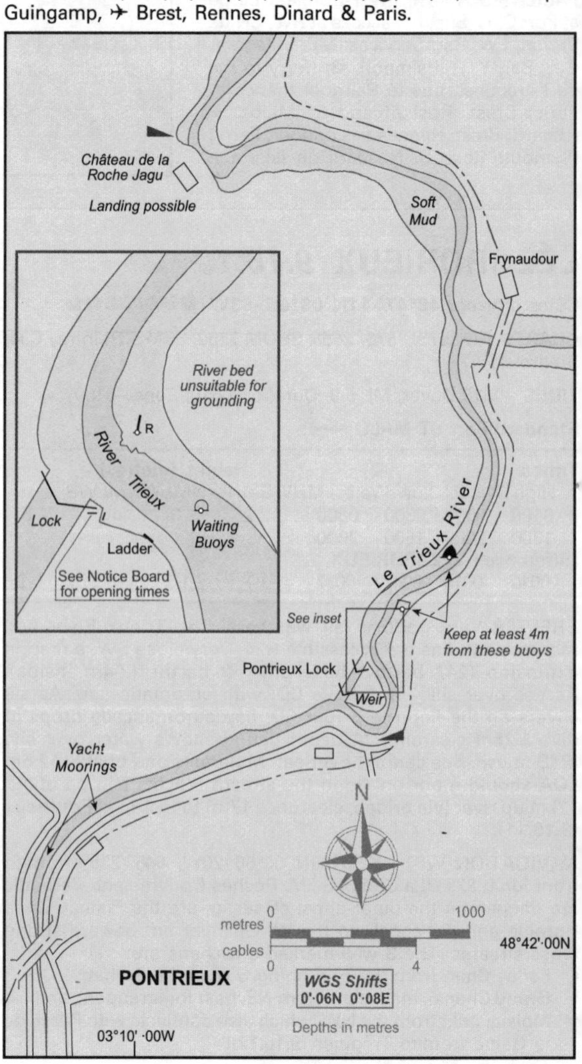

TRÉGUIER *9.16.12*

Côtes d'Armor **48°47'·27N 03°13'·18W** ❁❁❁⚓⚓⚓✿✿✿

CHARTS AC 3672, 3670, *2668*; SHOM 7152; ECM 537; Imray C34; Stanfords 17

TIDES –0540 Dover; ML 5·7; Duration 0600; Zone –0100

Standard Port ST MALO (⟵)

Times				Height (metres)			
High Water		Low Water		MHWS	MHWN	MLWN	MLWS
0100	0800	0300	0800	12·2	9·3	4·2	1·5
1300	2000	1500	2000				
Differences TRÉGUIER							
–0005	–0010	–0055	–0040	–2·3	–1·6	–0·6	–0·2
PORT-BÉNI							
–0017	–0022	–0100	–0045	–2·4	–1·6	–0·5	–0·1

SHELTER Good in marina; but try to arrive/dep at slack water as the tide runs hard through the pontoons. Possible ⚓s, keeping clear of the chan: 7ca SW of La Corne lt tr, but exposed to N'lies; N and S of La Roche Jaune village; in pool 1ca NE of No 10 buoy (1M N of marina).

NAVIGATION WPT 48°55'·25N 03°13'·00W, 317°/137° from/to front ldg lt, 5M (Grande Passe). There are three ent chans:

1. Grande Passe: well marked/lit, but marks are hard to see by day. Caution: strong tidal streams across the chan.
2. Passe de la Gaine: well marked, navigable with care by day in good vis. Unlit short cut to/from Lézardrieux.
3. Passe du Nord-Est: unlit, dangerous with winds from W and NW as sea breaks across the chan.

Within the R Jaudy it is important to heed channel buoys and bns, eg keep E of an unlit SHM buoy 300m SW of La Corne lt ho to avoid the drying bank which it marks. Speed limit is 6kn above La Roche Jaune.

LIGHTS AND MARKS Important marks: La Corne WR lt tr, Fl (3) WRG 12s 11/8M; 6ca to the N is Men Noblance WB bn tr on SE corner of Ile d'Er; and 4ca SW is Skeiviec W bn tr. The spire of Tréguier cathedral is 4·6M SSW of La Corne, but may be obscured by high wooded banks when entering the river estuary in the vicinity of Pen ar Guézec. Ldg lts/marks for the appr chans:

1. For Grande Passe 137°: front, Port de la Chaine, Oc 4s 12m 12M, white ho; rear, St Antoine Dir Oc R 4s 34m 15M, RW ho. At Pen ar Guézec unlit SHM buoy steer 216° in the W sector of La Corne lt. Note: The ldg marks are very hard to identify by day. From Basse Crublent PHM buoy the Pleubian spire and water tower offer a clear transit 154° towards the Pierre à l'Anglais and Le Corbeau lateral buoys.
2. For Passe de la Gaine 242°: Men Noblance bn tr, W with horiz B band, on with rear mark (W wall with B vert stripe) below the skyline and just right of conspic Plougrescant ❁. Hold this transit exactly to stay in narrow, marked chan; but marks hard to see from afar, especially against a low sun or in poor visibility.
3. Passe du Nord-Est, for direct appr to La Corne having cleared W of La Jument NCM By and adjacent rky shoals: Tréguier cathedral spire and Skeiviec at 207°.

RADIO TELEPHONE Marina Ch 09 (In season: Mon-Sat 0800-1200, 1330-2100; Sun 0800-1000, 1600-1800. Out of season: Sun/Mon closed; Tue-Sat 0800-1200, 1330-1700. All LT).

TELEPHONE Hr Mr 02·96·92·42·37; Aff Mar 02·96·92·30·38 (Paimpol); CROSS 02·96·54·11·11; ⊖ 02·96·92·31·44; Auto 08·36·68·08·22; Police 02·96·92·32·17; Dr 02·96·92·32·14; Ⓗ 02·96·05·71·11 (Lannion); Brit Consul 02·99·46·26·64.

FACILITIES Marina (200+130 ⓥ), ☎ 02·96·92·42·37, 📠 02·96.92.29.25 (indicate for Port de Plaisance), €1·67, Slip, FW, ME, C (8 ton), D (on most N'ly pontoon HW±1), CH, El, Sh, AC, Bar, R, Gaz, ⓘ; **Bar des Plaisanciers** ☎ 02·96·92·49·69, excellent facilities, open all year. **Club Nautique de Tréguier** 02.96.92.37.49 Bar, opp marina open Sat eves only. **Services:** BY ☎ 02·96·92·15·15, M, CH; **Town** EC Mon; Market Wed, P, FW, CH, V, Gaz, R, Bar, ✉, Ⓑ, V (small supermarket just W of cathedral delivers to boats), ⇌ (bus to Paimpol, Guingamp, Lannion, ✈ (Brest, Rennes, Dinard). Ferry: Roscoff, St Malo.

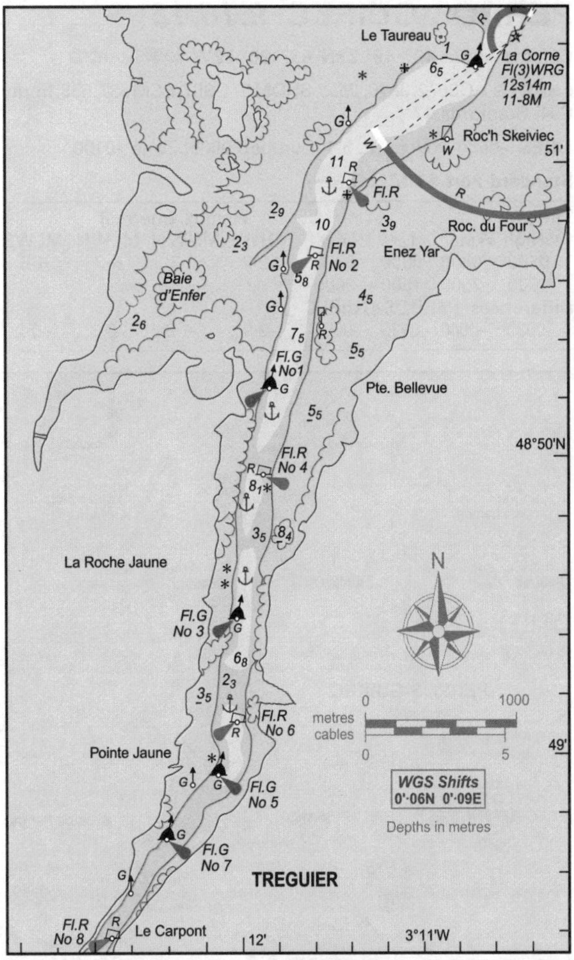

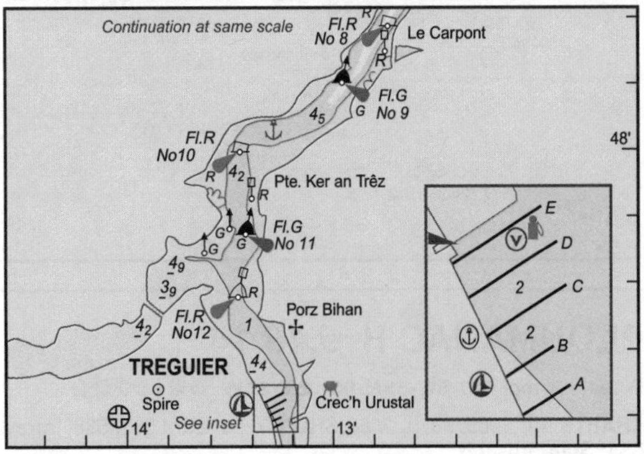

MINOR HARBOUR, approx 8M ENE of PERROS-GUIREC

PORT BLANC, Côte d'Armor, **48°50'·60N 03°18'·80W**, AC 3672, 3670; SHOM 7125, 7152. HW –0545 on Dover (UT); HW–0040 and ht –2·0m on St Malo; ML 5·3m; Duration 0600. Good natural hbr (known as Port Bago), but open to winds between NW and NNE. Appr on 150° toward Le Voleur Dir lt, Fl WRG 4s 17m 14/11M, G140°-148°, W148°-152°, R152°-160°. Note: the former rear ldg mark is reported ruined/obsc'd. The most conspic daymark is a 16m high W obelisk on Ile du Chateau Neuf, to stbd of appr chan; a less obvious W tr is to port on Ile St Gildas. There are 30 W ⓐs (reported 1998 to be poorly marked and almost all occupied by local boats) in the pool or yachts can ⚓ off or dry out alongside quays, 1·3m. Facilities: AB €0·61, FW, AC, C (16 ton), Slip; **Services:** CH, El, ME, Sh. **Town** Bar, R, V.

PERROS-GUIREC *9.16.13*

Côtes d'Armor **48° 48'·23N 03° 26'·12W**

CHARTS AC 3672, 3670, *2668*; SHOM 974, 967; ECM 537, 538; Imray C34; Stanfords 17

TIDES –0550 Dover; ML 5·4; Duration 0605; Zone –0100

Standard Port ST MALO (⟵)

Times				Height (metres)			
High Water		Low Water		MHWS	MHWN	MLWN	MLWS
0100	0800	0300	0800	12·2	9·3	4·2	1·5
1300	2000	1500	2000				
Differences PERROS-GUIREC							
–0030	–0040	–0115	–0055	–2·9	–1·9	–0·8	–0·2

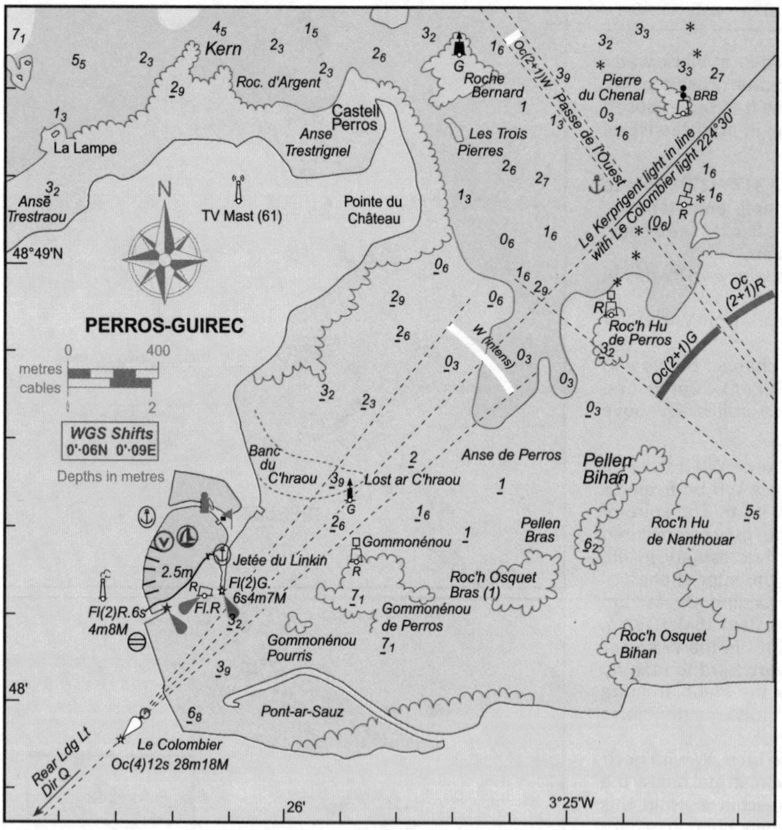

SHELTER Very good in marina (2·5m); Ⓥ on 2 most N'ly pontoons. Access via 6m wide gate, which is opened when rise of tide reaches 7m (there is no lock). Sill under gate is 3·5m above CD, giving 3·5m water inside gateway on first opening. Gate opening times depend mainly on tidal Coefficient (9.16.24), ie: Coeff >70, approx HW±$1\frac{1}{2}$; Coeff 60-70, HW±1; Coeff 50-60, HW–1 to +$\frac{1}{2}$; Coeff 40-50, HW–$\frac{1}{2}$ to HW. Caution: at Coeff <40, gate may not open for up to 4 days (neaped). Gate may open up to 30 mins ahead of published times, depending on weather, but does not close early. Retaining wall is marked by R & W poles. ⚓ prohib in basin. Drying moorings 1ca E of Jetée du Linkin. Off Pte du Chateau in approx 3m good holding and safe ⚓, except in NE'lies, plus 2 W Ⓥs.

NAVIGATION WPT 48°52'·40N 03°20'·00W, 045°/225° from/to front ldg lt (Le Colombier), 6·4M. Beware Ile Tomé in the ent to Anse de Perros; rks extend 7ca off the W side and 6ca E of the N side. Explosive dumping ground is 8ca NNE of the island.

LIGHTS AND MARKS From NE: Ldg lts 225°: front Le Colombier Dir Oc (4) 12s 28m 18M, intens 220°-230°; rear Kerprigent (1·5M from front) Q 79m 22M, intens 221°-228°. Passe de l'Ouest: Kerjean Dir lt 144° Oc (2+1) WRG 12s 78m 15/13M, vis G134°-143°, W143°-144°, R144°-154°. Gate sigs (flags/lts):
● over ● closed;
● = open, priority to enter; ● = open, priority to leave.

RADIO TELEPHONE VHF Ch 09 16.

TELEPHONE Hr Mr 02·96.23.37.82, 📠 02·96.47.40.87; Basin gate 02·96.23.19.03; Aff Mar 02·96.20.81.87; ⊜ 02·96.23.18·12; CROSS 02·98·89.31.31; SNSM 02·96.91.40.10; Auto 08·36.68·08·22; Police 02·96.23.20.17; Dr 02·96.23.20.01; Brit Consul 02·99.46.26.64.

FACILITIES Marina (720+80 Ⓥ) ☎ 02·96·23·37·82, €2.06, P, D, FW, ME, AC, El, Sh, C (7 ton), CH, V, R, SM, Gas, Gaz, Kos, ▣;SR Perros ☎ 02·96·91·12·65 **Services:** Ⓔ, SHOM; **Town** CH, V, Gaz, R, Bar, ✉, Ⓑ, ⇌ (Lannion), ✈ (Brest, Rennes, Dinard). Ferry: Roscoff.

PLOUMANAC'H *9.16.14*

Côtes d'Armor **48° 50'·35N 03° 29'·14W**

CHARTS AC 3669, 3670, *2668*; SHOM 7152; ECM 537, 538; Imray C34; Stanfords 17

TIDES –0550 Dover; ML 5·5; Duration 0605; Zone –0100

Standard Port ST MALO (⟵)

Times				Height (metres)			
High Water		Low Water		MHWS	MHWN	MLWN	MLWS
0100	0800	0300	0800	12·2	9·3	4·2	1·5
1300	2000	1500	2000				
Differences PLOUMANAC'H							
–0023	–0033	–0112	–0053	–2·9	–1·9	–0·6	–0·1

SHELTER Good; Ⓥs are first line of dumbell buoys. A sill, drying 2·55m, retains 1·2m to 2·3m within. Depth gauges are on the 4th (unreliable) and the last PHM stakes. If the concrete base of the 3rd SHM stake is covered, depth over sill is >1·2m. Inside the sill, for best water keep to port and appr moorings from N. FV moorings to stbd of ent. SE and SW sides of hbr are very shallow.

NAVIGATION WPT 48°51'·50N 03°29'·00W, 008°/188°, 1·25M from/to ent between Mean Ruz lt ho and Chateau Costaeres (conspic). Ent is difficult in strong NW'lies. From/to NW, beware An Dreuzinier, unmarked rks (drying 1·4m), 100m N and NE of No 1 SHM stake; not a problem with sufficient rise of tide, but near LW keep very close W of a line through the first two PHM stakes. Chan is marked by unlit stakes.

LIGHTS AND MARKS Mean Ruz lt ho, Oc WR 4s, W 226°-242°, R 242°-226° to E with adjacent sig stn, conspic.

RADIO TELEPHONE VHF Ch 09.

TELEPHONE Hr Mr 02·96.91.44.31; Auto 08·36.68·08·22; SNSM 02·96.20.00.45; Dr 02·96.91.42.00; ME 02·96.23.31.40.

FACILITIES Port de Plaisance (230 + 20 Ⓥ) M, €1·83; **Quai Bellevue** FW, AC, L, Slip, P & D cans; Bus to Lannion & Perros; **YC Société Nautique de Perros Guirec.** Ferry: See Roscoff.

PLOUMANAC'H *continued*

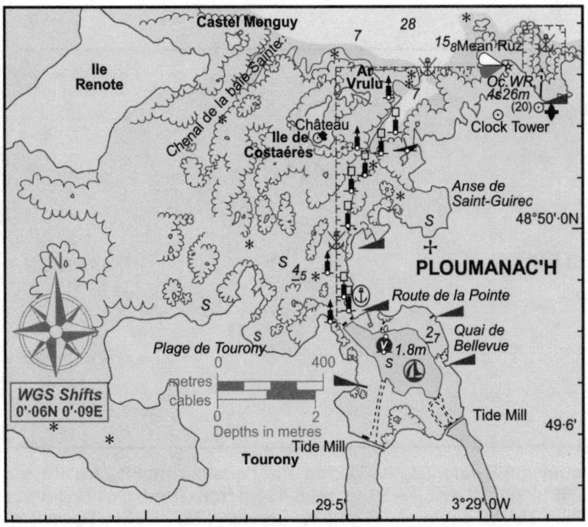

ANCHORAGE 1M WEST OF PLOUMANAC'H

TRÉGASTEL, Côtes d'Armor, **48°50´·10N 03°31´·20W,** AC 3669, 3670; SHOM 7152. HW –0550 on Dover (UT); +0005 and –1·8m on Brest HW; ML 5·1m; Duration 0605. Use 9.16.15 differences. Good ⚓ in 2m, but exposed to winds from W to N. Ent, 2ca W of La Pierre Pendue (conspic rk), is marked by PHM bn on Ile Dhu and SHM buoy off Le Taureau, rk drying 4·5m (bn destroyed). Turreted house, conspic, brg approx 165° leads between Ile Dhu and Le Taureau. Thence after 2 more PHM and 1 SHM bns, turn E to the ⚓ or Orange buoys S of Ile Ronde. Facilities: Slip; **Club Nautique de Trégastel** ☎ 02·96·23·45·05; **Town** (Ste Anne, 0·5M inland) CH, Ⓑ, ✉, Bar, R, V.

TRÉBEURDEN *9.16.15*

Côtes d'Armor 48°46´·35N 03°35´·06W

CHARTS AC 3669; SHOM 7151; ECM 537, 538; Imray C34; Stanfords 17

TIDES –0605 Dover; ML 5·5; Duration 0605; Zone –0100

Standard Port BREST (⟶)

Times				Height (metres)			
High Water		Low Water		MHWS	MHWN	MLWN	MLWS
0000	0600	0000	0600	6·9	5·4	2·6	1·0
1200	1800	1200	1800				
Differences TRÉBEURDEN							
+0100	+0110	+0120	+0100	+2·3	+1·9	+0·9	+0·4

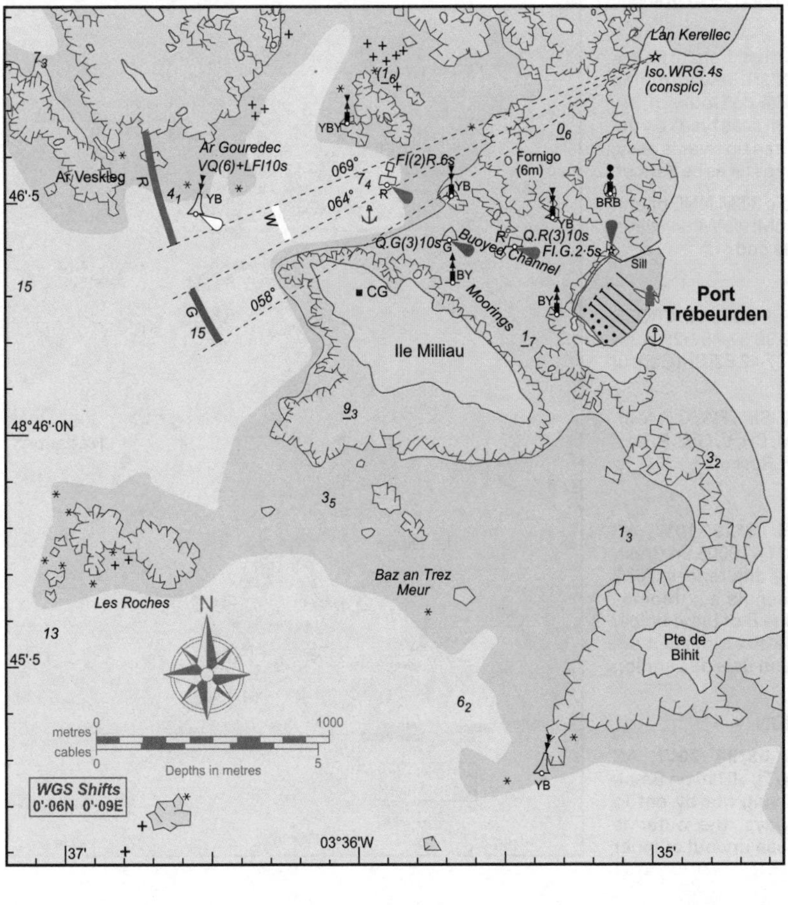

SHELTER Good in marina (1·5m to 3m). Access HW±4½ (±3¾ at sp) over moving sill (2m CD; 15m wide) at stbd side of ent; rest of sill is fixed 3·5m. Tide gauge floodlit, port side of sill. Ⓥ on pontoon F (2nd from ent). Do not manoeuvre within 10 mins of the sill dropping, due to strong underwater inrush. 15 deep-water waiting buoys outside, or ⚓ off NE side of Ile Milliau, but exposed to W'lies.

NAVIGATION WPT 48°45´·13N 03°40´·68W, 246°/066° from/to Lan Kerellec Dir lt, 4·1M. From W, appr is clear. From E and N, round Bar ar Gall and Le Crapaud WCM buoys; continue S for 1·5M, then alter 066° toward Ile Milliau (conspic CG bldg); thence as below to enter the marked chan to marina ent. From Ar Gouredec SCM buoy, VQ (6) + L Fl 10s, ✠ spire (conspic) brg 098° leads to ent via chan buoyed as shown.

LIGHTS AND MARKS Le Crapaud WCM buoy, Q (9) 15s. Lan Kerellec Dir lt, Iso WRG 4s 8/5M, G058°-064°, W064°-069°, R069°-130°, leads 066° past Ile Milliau. IPTS (sigs 2 & 4) on bkwtr and on sill gateway; 4 Y SPM bns mark fixed sill.

RADIO TELEPHONE Call *Port Trébeurden* VHF Ch 09 16.

TELEPHONE Hr Mr ☎ 02·96·23·64·00; Aff Mar 02·96·91·21·28; CROSS 02·98·89·31·31; SNSM 02·96·23·53·82; ⊜ 02·96·92·31·44; Police 02·96·23·51·96 (Jul/Aug); Ⓗ (Lannion) 02.96.05.71.11.

FACILITIES Marina (400 + 100 Ⓥ), ☎ as Hr Mr, 02·96·47·40·87, €2·13, FW, AC, P, D, BY; **YC de Trébeurden** ☎ 02·96·15·45·97 (July-Aug); **Services:** BY, ME, El, Sh, CH. **Town** V, R, Bar, ✉, Ⓑ, ✈ (Brest, Rennes, Dinard). Ferry: Roscoff/St Malo.

LANNION (Léguer River) *9.16.16*

Côtes d'Armor **48°44'·00N 03°33'·50W**

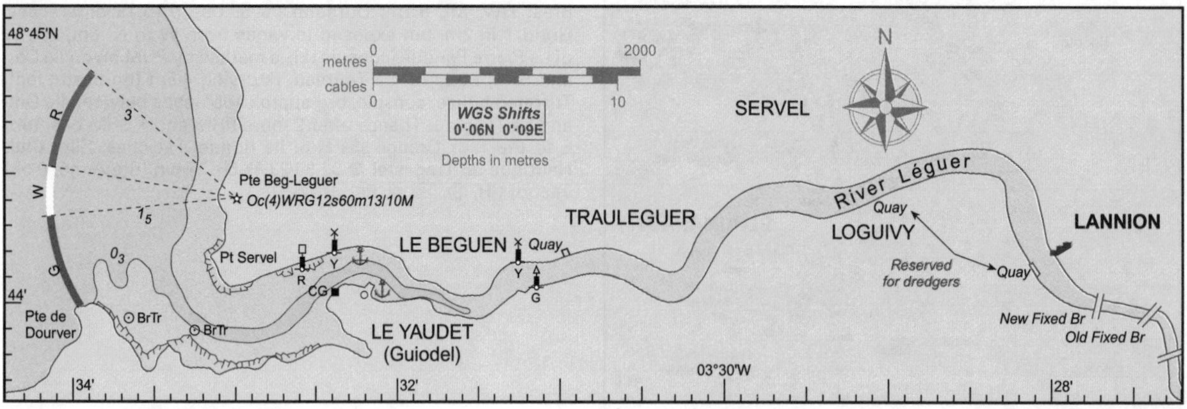

CHARTS AC 3669, *2668*; SHOM 7151; ECM 537, 538; Imray C34; Stanfords 17

TIDES –0605 Dover; ML 5·4; Duration: no data; Zone –0100

Standard Port BREST (⟶)

Times				Height (metres)			
High Water		Low Water		MHWS	MHWN	MLWN	MLWS
0000	0600	0000	0600	6·9	5·4	2·6	1·0
1200	1800	1200	1800				
Differences LOCQUIREC							
+0058	+0108	+0120	+0100	+2·2	+1·8	+0·8	+0·3

SHELTER Good, except in strong W/NW winds. ⚓ in estuary or in non-drying pools off Le Yaudet and Le Beguen. It may be possible to dry out on the N bank just below Lannion town, but a recce by dinghy or on foot is advised.

NAVIGATION WPT 48°44'·40N 03°36'·60W, 284°/104° from/to Pointe de Dourven 1·9M (also on Locquemeau ldg lts 122°). Beware drying sandbank extending approx 2ca N/NE from Pte de Dourven. No access at very LW, esp with strong NW'lies when seas break on the drying bar. Enter chan close to two G bn trs. Chan up river is easy, but narrow, steep-to and marked by trs/bns only as far as Le Yaudet.

LIGHTS AND MARKS Large W radome conspic 3·5M NNE of ent. Pointe Beg-Léguer lt, Oc (4) WRG 12s 60m 13/10M; vis W084°-098°, R098°-129°, G007°-084°; It is on a cottage gable end.

RADIOTELEPHONE None.

TELEPHONE Hr Mr 02·96·37·06·52; Aff Mar 02·96·37·06·52; CROSS 02·98·89·31·31; SNSM 02·96·23·52·07; ⊜ 02·96·37·45·32; Auto 08·36.68·08·22; Police 02·96·37·03·78; Dr 02·96·37·42·52; Brit Consul 02·99·46·26·64.

FACILITIES **Quai de Loguivy** AB in emergency, Slip, FW, C (1 ton). **Services:** M, ME, El, Sh, SHOM, Ⓔ, CH. **Town** M, CH, V, Gaz, R, Bar, ✉, Ⓑ, ⇌, ✈ (Brest, Rennes, Dinard). Ferry: Roscoff.

OFFSHORE ISLANDS

LES SEPT ILES, Côte d'Armor, **48° 52'·80N 03°29'·10W**, AC 3669, 3670; SHOM 7152. HW-0550 on Dover (UT); +0005 on Brest. HW ht –1·8m on Brest. ML 5·2m. Use 9.16.14 differences. All 7 islands form a bird sanctuary. Main ⚓ between Île aux Moines and Ile Bono. Landing on latter is prohib. ⚓ due E of jetty; below the Old Fort, or close to S side of Ile Bono. Île aux Moines lt ho, grey tr, Fl (3) 15s 59m 24M, obsc 237°-241° and in Baie de Lannion when brg < 039°. No facilities.

ADJACENT HARBOURS IN BAIE DE LANNION

LOCQUEMEAU, Côte d'Armor, **48°43'·60N 03°34'·70W**, AC 3669, 2668; SHOM 7124. HW–0600 on Dover (UT); +0110 on Brest; HW ht +1·5m on Brest; ML 5·3m. A small drying hbr by ent to Lannion River (9.16.16). There are two quays: the outer is accessible at LW, but open to W 'lies. Yachts can dry out at inner quay, on S side. Ldg lts 122° to outer quay: front FR 21m 6M, vis 068°-228°, W pylon + R top; rear, 484m from front, Oc (2+1) R 12s 39m 7M, W gable and R gallery. **Services:** ME, El, Sh; **Town** Bar.

LOCQUIREC, Côte d'Armor, **48°41'·50N 03°38'·68W**. AC 3669, 2668; SHOM 7124. Tidal data as for Locquemeau, above. Small drying hbr at mouth of R Le Douron, with good shelter from W/SW winds. The whole estuary dries to shifting sandbanks (2·9m to 6·1m). Access HW±3. No lights, but a NCM buoy is 7ca N of Pte de

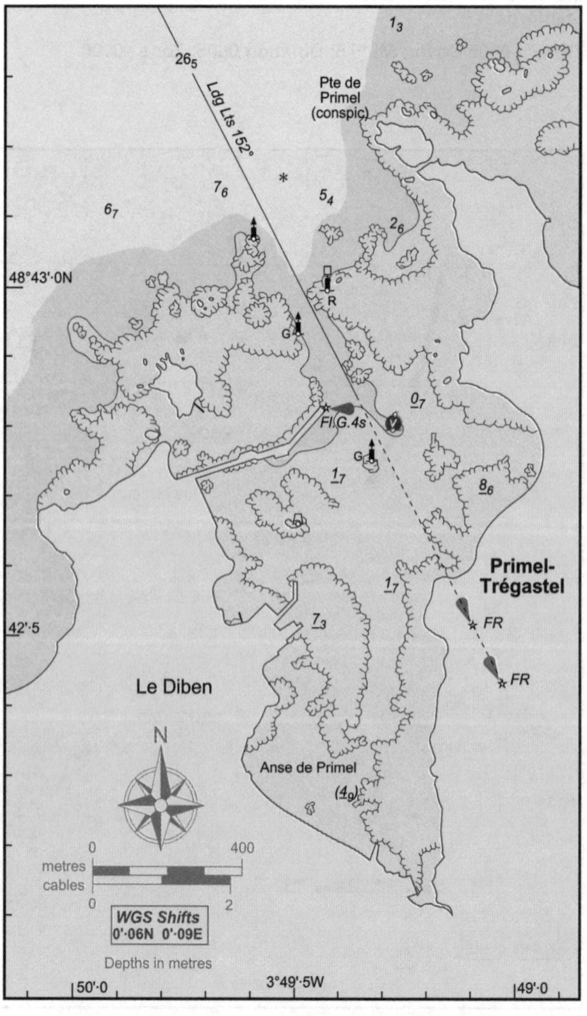

Locqueric and a SHM bn tr (6ca S of the hbr) is conspic as the bay opens up. A pleasant temp ⚓, or overnight if able to take the ground. Many moorings, inc 10 Ⓥs. Land at slip.

PRIMEL-TRÉGASTEL, Finistere, **48°42´·80N 03°49´·30W**, AC 2745, 3669; SHOM 7095, 7151. HW –0610 on Dover (UT); ML 5·3m; Duration 0600. See facing chartlet. All tides access. Good ⚓, but open to N/NW'lies; seas break across ent in strong winds. Beware drying rks off Pte de Primel to E, and off Ar Zammeguez (3m high, SHM bn) to W of ent. Enter exactly on daymarks 152°, both are W □ walls with R vert stripe, on hillside; or co-located ldg lts, both FR 35/56m 6M, front vis 134°-168°. Pass between a PHM and SHM bn, the former quite short. 15 (10 deep water) W Ⓥs or ⚓ to SE or SW of bkwtr hd, Fl G 4s 6m 7M, in 2-9m. Le Diben on W side is FV port. Drying upper reaches are well sheltered. VHF Ch 09 16 (season). Hr Mr ☎ 02·98·62·28·40. **Facilities**: C (25 ton), FW, Slip, CH, El, ME, Sh, Ⓔ, R, Bar.

MORLAIX *9.16.17*

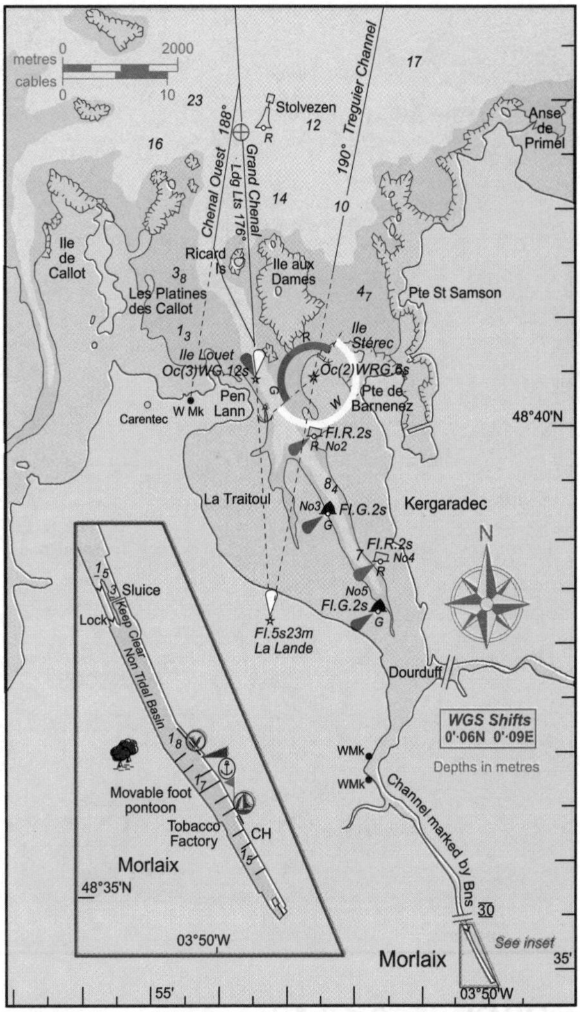

Finistere **48°35´·50N 03°50´·50W** ❁❁🌢🌢🌢✿✿✿

CHARTS AC 2745, 3669; SHOM 7151; ECM 538; Imray C34, C35; Stanfords 17

TIDES –0610 Dover; ML 5·3; Duration 0610; Zone –0100

Standard Port BREST (⟼)

Times				Height (metres)			
High Water		Low Water		MHWS	MHWN	MLWN	MLWS
0000	0600	0000	0600	6·9	5·4	2·6	1·0
1200	1800	1200	1800				
Differences MORLAIX (CHÂTEAU DU TAUREAU)							
+0055	+0105	+0115	+0055	+2·0	+1·7	+0·8	+0·3
ANSE DE PRIMEL							
+0100	+0110	+0120	+0100	+2·1	+1·7	+0·8	+0·3

SHELTER Good in the bay and at Dourduff (dries), clear of extensive oyster beds marked by small orange buoys/stakes. Boats can go 5M up to Morlaix town (though ch. subject to silting) and lock in to the Bassin à Flot; lock opens by day only, at HW –1½, HW and HW+1. Complete shelter at the marina; Ⓥ's pontoon on E bank, just N of slip and YC. A movable footbridge across the marina abeam the YC, is usually open during lock hours.

NAVIGATION WPT 48°42'·71N 03°53'·44W, abeam Stolvezen PHM buoy, 356°/176° from/to Ile Louet lt, 2·25M (Grand Chenal). The three ent channels all have rky dangers:

1. Chenal Ouest 188°, W of Ricard Is. Deepest chan, but unlit.
2. Grand Chenal 176°, E of Ricard Is, shallower but lit.
3. Chenal de Tréguier, 190°, best at night, but almost dries. Strong N'lies can raise a steep sea even in the estuary. The Penzé river lies W of Ile de Callot.

LIGHTS AND MARKS Grand Chenal ldg lts 176°: front Ile Louet, Oc (3) WG 12s; rear La Lande, Fl 5s. Chenal de Tréguier ldg lts 190°: Ile Noire, Oc (2) WRG 6s; rear La Lande, Fl 5s. River up to Morlaix, 3M above Dourduff, is buoyed but unlit.

RADIO TELEPHONE Port and marina VHF Ch 09 16.

TELEPHONE Hr Mr 02·98·62·13·14; 🖷 02·98·88·80·55, Lock 02·98·88·15·10; Aff Mar 02·98·62·10·47; CROSS 02·98·89·31·31; SNSM 02·98·88·00·76; ⊖ 02·98·88·06·31; Auto 08·36·68·02·29; Police 02·98·88·58·13; Ⓗ 02·98·62·61·60; Brit Consul 02·99·46·26·64.

FACILITIES Marina (180+30 visitors) ☎ 02·98·62·13·14, access as lock times, €1·30, AC, FW, C (8 ton), P & D, Slip, ME, El, Sh, CH; **YC de Morlaix** ☎ 02·98·88·38·00; **Town** P, D, SM, Ⓔ, SHOM, V, Gaz, R, Bar, ✉, Ⓑ, ▣. Ferry: Roscoff.

ANCHORAGES N AND NW OF MORLAIX

PENZÉ RIVER, Finistere, Ent **48°42´·00N 03°56´·40W**, AC 2745; SHOM 7095. HW –0610 on Dover (UT), +0105 on Brest; HW ht +1·2m Brest; ML 5·0m; Duration 0605. From NNW appr between Cordonnier and Guerhéon bn trs at mid-flood or, for deeper water, from the ENE between Les Bizeyer reef and Le Paradis bn tr; thence pass W of Ile Callot. A short cut from Morlaix estuary to the Penzé is the drying Passe aux Moutons, between Carantec and Ile Callot, with adequate rise. The ⚓ NE of Carantec is open, especially to NW; landing stage dries about 4·6m. Yachts can dry out inside Pempoul bkwtr off St Pol-de-Léon. Further S the chan narrows and is scantily marked only by oyster withies and local moorings. SW of Pte de Lingos shelter is better; or moor off St Yves where the old ferry slips provide landing places. S of the Pont de la Corde (11m clearance) the river is buoyed and navigable on the tide for 3M to complete shelter at Penzé. There is a Nature Reserve at the head of the river - limited access Mar 1st to Aug 31st. Facilities at Carantec: El, ME, Sh, M, CH, P, D, Ⓔ. **Town** Ⓑ, Bar, ✉, R, V. **Penzé** AB (drying), limited V, R, Bar.

OTHER HARBOURS WEST OF ROSCOFF

MOGUÉRIEC, Finistere, **48°40'·40N 04°04'·40W**, AC 3669, *2668*; SHOM 7151. Tides approx as for Ile de Batz (9.16.18). A small drying fishing hbr, 3M SSW of W ent to Canal de Batz, open to NW swell. Ldg lts 162°: both W trs/G tops, front on jetty, Iso WG 4s 9m, W158°-166°; rear FG 22m. Beware Méan Névez rk, dries 3·3m, to W of appr. ⚓ close SW of Ile de Siec, or 3ca WSW of Ar Skeul WCM bn tr in 4m, or 2ca NNE of Moguériec's drying jetty. Facilities: V, R, Bar, P.

BRIGNOGNAN (Pontusval), Finistere, **48°40´·65N 04°19´·08W**, AC 3668, *2644*; SHOM 7150. HW +0605 on Dover (UT); ML 4·7m; Duration 0600; see 9.16.18. App from ECM buoy (48°41'·51N 04°19'·12W) via ldg marks 178° W bn on with ch spire 1M S. Ent between An Neudenn R bn tr to E and 3 white-topped rks to W. ⚓ here in approx 4m or dry out closer in. Hbr is open to N winds and often full of FVs. Entry at night prohib. Facilities: Bar, FW, R, V, 5 Ⓥ's (free).

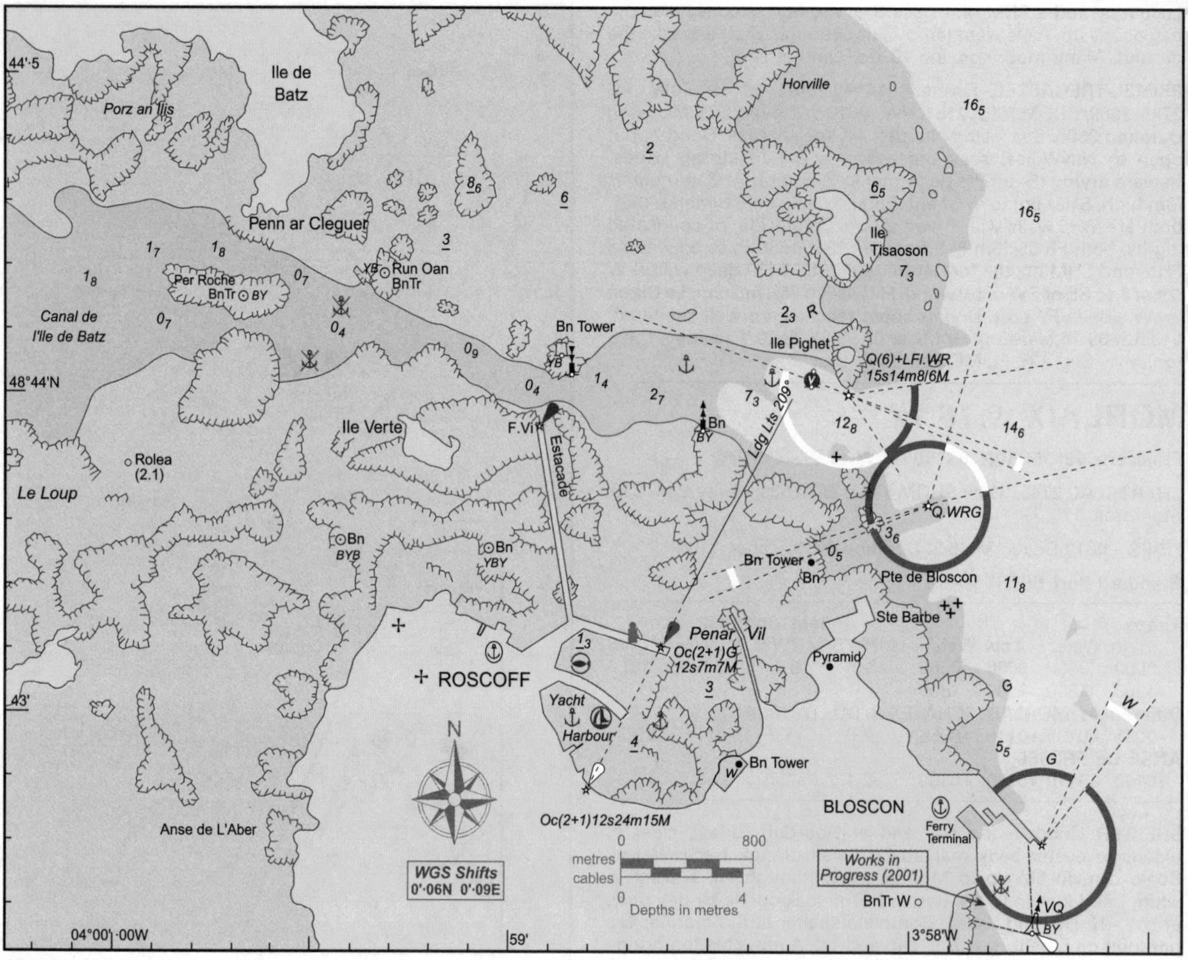

ROSCOFF *9.16.18*

Finistere **48°43'·60N 03°58'·50W** ❀❀⛵✿✿✿

CHARTS AC 2745, 3669; SHOM 7151; ECM 538; Imray C35; Stanfords 17

TIDES –0605 Dover; ML 5·2; Duration 0600; Zone –0100

Standard Port BREST (⟶)

Times				Height (metres)			
High Water		Low Water		MHWS	MHWN	MLWN	MLWS
0000	0600	0000	0600	6·9	5·4	2·6	1·0
1200	1800	1200	1800				
Differences ROSCOFF							
+0055	+0105	+0115	+0055	+1·9	+1·6	+0·8	+0·3
ILE DE BATZ							
+0045	+0100	+0105	+0055	+2·0	+1·6	+0·9	+0·4
BRIGNOGAN							
+0040	+0045	+0058	+0038	+1·5	+1·2	+0·6	+0·2

SHELTER Good in Roscoff (dries 4·9m) except in strong N/E winds. Access HW±2. AB on S side of jetty in Yacht Hbr, but FVs leave little room; or dry out against road wall or secure to ⓥ in SW corner. Close W of Ar Chaden are W ⓥs in 4-5m. Bloscon ferry hbr should only be entered with Hr Mr's approval, but ⓥs or ⚓ to the S, clear of ferries (good for crew change). Beware foul ground inshore and WIP.

NAVIGATION WPT 48°46'·00N 03°55'·80W, 033°/213° from/to Men Guen Bras lt, 2·6M. The ent to Roscoff needs care due to many large rks in the area; best to enter near HW. See 9.16.5 for pilotage in the Canal de l'Ile de Batz. Chans are well marked and must be kept to. Appr to Bloscon is easier.

LIGHTS AND MARKS Ile de Batz lt ho (conspic) Fl (4) 25s 69m 23M. At E end of Canal de l'Ile de Batz are Ar Chaden Q (6)+L Fl WR 15s, SCM bn tr, & Men-Guen-Bras Q WRG, NCM. Ldg lts/marks 209° for Roscoff hbr: both Oc (2+1) G 12s, front 7m 7M, W col, G top, with B/W vert stripes on end of mole; rear conspic W lt ho 24m 15M. Bloscon ferry jetty Fl WG 4s, W200°-210°, G210°-200°, appr in W sector; in fog, Fl W 2s.

RADIO TELEPHONE Roscoff Ch 09. *Bloscon* Ch 12 16; 0830-1200, 1330-1800LT.

TELEPHONE Hr Mr (Port de Plaisance) 02·98·69·76·37, 📠 02·98·69·76·37; Hr Mr (Roscoff) 02·98·61·27·84, 📠 02·98·19·31·87; Aff Mar 02·98·69·70·15; CROSS 02·98·89· 31·31; SNSM 06·82·18·01·34; ⊖ (Roscoff) 02·98·69·70·15; ⊖ (Bloscon) 02·98·69·70·84; Auto 08·36.68·08·29; Police 02·98·69·00·48; Ⓗ 02·98·88·40·22; Dr 02·98·69·71·18; Brit Consul 02·99·46·26·64.

FACILITIES Vieux Port (280+20 visitors) ☎ 02·98·69·76·37, €0·61 AB (with fender board), FW, AC, M; **Quai Neuf** Reserved for FVs, C (5 ton); **Club Nautique de Roscoff** ☎ 02·98·69·72·79, Bar; **Bloscon** M, L, Slip. **Services:** BY, ME, El, Sh, CH. **Town** P, D, ME, El, Sh, CH, Gaz, V, R, Bar, ✉, Ⓑ, ⚌, ✈ (Brest, Rennes, Dinard). Ferry: Plymouth, Rosslare.

HARBOUR/ANCHORAGE CLOSE NORTH

ILE DE BATZ, Finistere, **48°44'·50N 04°00'·50W**, AC 2745, 3669; SHOM 7095; HW +0610 Dover (UT); ML 5·2m. See 9.16.18. Porz-Kernoc'h gives good shelter but dries. E slip is reserved for ferries. ⚓ in E or W parts of the chan depending on wind, but holding ground poor. ⚓ prohib in area W of Roscoff landing slip. Ile de Batz lt ho Fl (4) 25s. Facilities: a few shops.

L'ABERWRAC'H *9.16.19*

Finistere **48°36'·75N 04°35'·30W** ❀❀⛵⛵✿✿✿

CHARTS AC 1432, 2644; SHOM 7150; ECM 539; Imray C35; Stanfords 17

TIDES +0547 Dover; ML 4·5; Duration 0600; Zone –0100

Standard Port BREST (⟶)

Times				Height (metres)			
High Water		Low Water		MHWS	MHWN	MLWN	MLWS
0000	0600	0000	0600	6·9	5·4	2·6	1·0
1200	1800	1200	1800				
Differences L'ABERWRAC'H, ILE CÉZON							
+0030	+0030	+0040	+0035	+0·8	+0·7	+0·2	0·0

SHELTER Good, except in strong NW'lies. At La Palue either berth on the single seasonal pontoon (max LOA = 12m) or pick up one of 30 numbered W ♠s. Free water taxi in summer every H, 0800-2200. Excellent shelter in all winds at Paluden, 1·5M up-river (off chartlet), on dumbell ♠s; plus landing jetty, but ⚓ prohib.

NAVIGATION WPT for Grand Chenal 48°37'·40N 04°38'·40W, 280°/100° from/to front ldg lt 2·6M. Keep clear of Le Libenter bank marked by WCM buoy, Q (9) 15s (Whis), brg 254° from Ile Vierge lt 3·0M; also Basse Trousquennou to S. Two outer appr chans lead to the inner 128° appr line:

1. Grand Chenal 100° (well lit and best for strangers) runs S of Libenter, Grand and Petit Pot de Beurre.
2. Chenal de la Malouine, a narrow short cut from N/E, only by day and in good weather: 176° transit of Petit Pot de Beurre with Petite Ile de la Croix W bn; great precision is required. Caution: breakers and cross-tides.

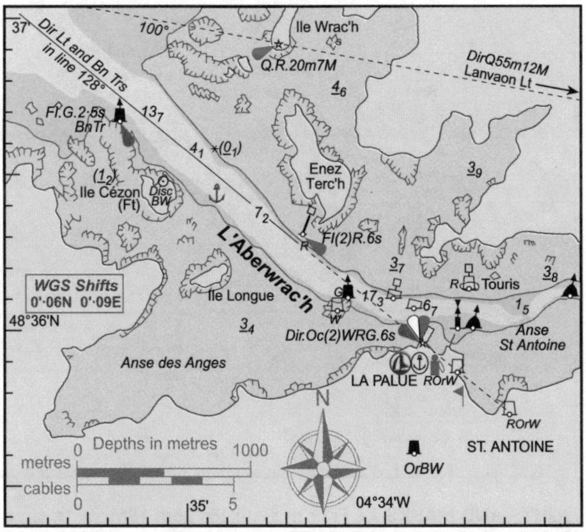

LIGHTS AND MARKS Ile-Vierge lt ho Fl 5s 77m 27M, Gy tr, Horn 60s, RC, vis 337°–325° (348°). For the Grand Chenal the 100° ldg lts/marks are: front QR, Ile Vrac' h, W □ tr orange top; and, 1·63M to the rear, Dir Q, Lanvaon, W □ tr orange △ on top. Then Dir Oc (2) WRG 6s, W127·2°-128·7°, leads 128° almost to the pontoon at La Palue. Unlit up river.

RADIO TELEPHONE VHF Ch 09 16 (0700-2200LT in season).

TELEPHONE Hr Mr 02·98·04·91·62; Aff Mar 02·98·04·90·13; CROSS/SNSM 02·98·89·31·31; ⊜ 02·98·85·07·40; Météo Auto 08·36.68·08·29; Police 02·98·04·00·18; ⊞ 02·98·22·33·33; Dr 02·98·04·91·87; SAMU 15; Brit Consul 02·99·46·26·64.

FACILITIES Pontoon (80 incl 28 ♥) ☎ 02·98·04·91·62, 📠 02·98·04·85·54, €1·54, M, D, (HW ±2, 0800-2000) FW, ME, El, CH, BH (12 ton); **YC des Abers** ☎ 02·98·04·92·60, Bar, ♿, ▣; **Services**: Sh, Ⓔ, Slip, C (3 ton mobile). **Town** P, V, Gaz, R, ▣, P, Bar, ✉, Ⓑ (Landeda, every a.m. except Mon), ⇌, ✈, (bus to Brest). Ferry: Roscoff.

L'ABER BENOIT *9.16.20*

Finistere **48°34'·65N 04°36'·80W** ❀❀⛵⛵✿✿✿

CHARTS AC 1432, 2644; SHOM 7150; ECM 539, 540; Imray C35; Stanfords 17

TIDES +0535 Dover; ML 4·7; Duration 0555; Zone –0100

Standard Port BREST (⟶)

Times				Height (metres)			
High Water		Low Water		MHWS	MHWN	MLWN	MLWS
0000	0600	0000	0600	6·9	5·4	2·6	1·0
1200	1800	1200	1800				
Differences L'ABER BENOIT							
+0022	+0025	+0035	+0020	+1·0	+0·9	+0·4	+0·2
PORTSALL							
+0015	+0020	+0025	+0015	+0·6	+0·5	+0·1	0·0

SHELTER Excellent, but do not enter at night, in poor vis nor in strong WNW winds; best near LW when dangers can be seen. Six ♠s and ⚓ as shown or further up-river. R navigable on the tide to Tréglonou bridge 3M upstream. Beware oyster beds.

NAVIGATION WPT 48°37'·05N 04°38'·75W, close W of Petite Fourche WCM. Thence follow the track shown on the plan.

LIGHTS AND MARKS Unlit. Chan bns and buoys must be carefully identified.

RADIO TELEPHONE None.

TELEPHONE Hr Mr nil; CROSS/SNSM 02·98·89·31·31; ⊜ 02·98·85·07·40; Météo Auto 08·36.68·08·29; Police 02·98·48·10·10; Dr 02·98·89·75·67; Brit Consul 02·99·46·26·64.

FACILITIES Le Passage Slip, M (free), L, FW; **Tréglonou** Slip; **Services:** Sh, ME, El. **Town** P & D (cans-2km)Gaz, ✉, Ⓑ (Ploudalmezeau), ⇌, ✈ (bus to Brest). Ferry: Roscoff.

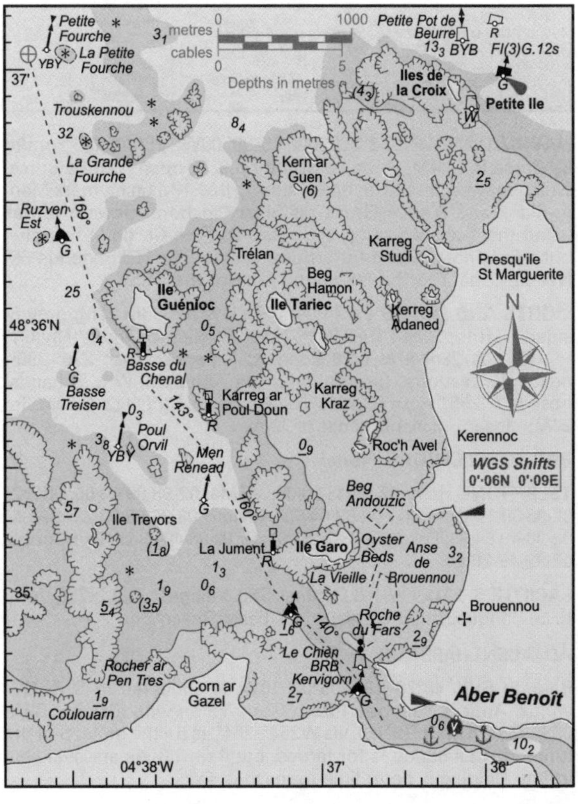

LAMPAUL (OUESSANT) *9.16.21*

Finistere **48°26'·70N 05°07'·40W** ❁❁◊✿✿

CHARTS AC 2694; SHOM 7123, 7149; ECM 540; Imray C36; Stan 17

TIDES +0522 Dover; ML 3·9; Duration 0555; Zone –0100

Standard Port BREST (⟼)

Times				Height (metres)			
High Water		Low Water		MHWS	MHWN	MLWN	MLWS
0000	0600	0000	0600	6·9	5·4	2·6	1·0
1200	1800	1200	1800				
Differences BAIE DE LAMPAUL							
+0005	+0005	–0005	+0003	0·0	–0·1	–0·1	0·0
ILE DE MOLENE							
+0012	+0012	+0017	+0017	+0·4	+0·3	+0·2	+0·1

SHELTER Bay is open to SW winds and swell; only usable in settled weather, prone to poor vis, esp in July. There are approx 14 Øs to S of the small drying hbr to E of pier, ent 15m wide, which normally has no room for visitors. There are fish farms at the N end of the SE shore of the bay.

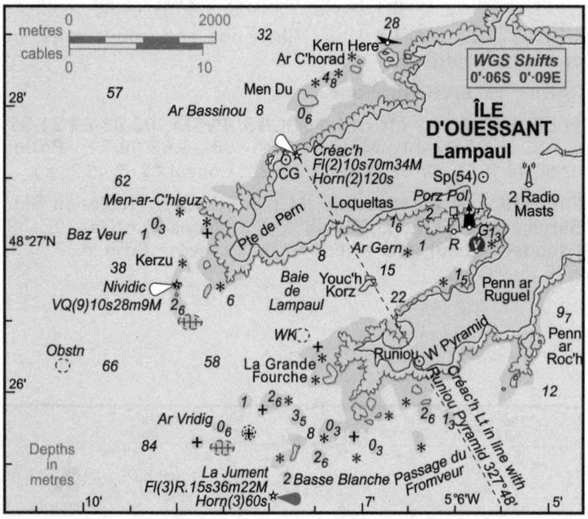

NAVIGATION WPT 48°26'·30N 05°09'·00W, 250°/070° from/to Le Corce Rk, 1·4M. Bring Le Stiff lt ho 055° open N of Le Corce, which may be passed on either side. PHM/SHM bn trs mark Men-ar-Blank and Men-ar-Groas rks closer inshore. Beware ferries using the T-shaped quay; they also use the Ch de la Fourche, but this is not advised for visiting yachts. The ITZ extends 5M NW of Ushant to the NE-bound lane of the TSS.

LIGHTS AND MARKS La Jument Fl (3) R 15s 36m **22**M; grey 8-sided tr, R top; obsc 199°-241°; Horn (3) 60s. An-Ividig (Nividic) VQ (9) 10s 28m 9M; W 8-sided tr, R bands; obsc 225°-290°; helicopter platform. Creac'h Fl (2) 10s 70m **34**M; W tr, B bands; obsc 247°-255°; Horn (2) 120s; RC; Racon. Le Stiff Fl (2) R 20s 85m **24**M; close to conspic radar tr 72m.

RADIO TELEPHONE None.

TELEPHONE Hr Mr 02·98·48·80·09; Aff Mar 02·98·89·00·05; CROSS 02·98·89·31·31; Météo 02·98·84·60·64; Auto 08·36·68·08·29; SNSM 02·98·48·84·33; Police 02·98·48·81·61; Dr 02·98·48·83·22; Brit Consul 02·99·46·26·64.

FACILITIES 20 Ø, FW, P & D (cans), Slip. **Village** R, Gaz, ✉, Ⓑ, ferry to Le Conquet and Brest ⇌, ✈. UK Ferry: Roscoff.

ADJACENT HARBOUR

Baie du Stiff, 48°28'·13N 05°03'·18W, is sheltered in S to NW winds. Appr is clear apart from Gorle Vihan with IDM bn. Dir lt 259°, Q WRG 11m 10/7M, vis W254°-264°, is on the mole. S of the lt ho, Porz Liboudou is for ferries, but 4 or 5 R Øs are available in 5m. Holding is poor; little room to ⚓. FW.

L'ABERILDUT *9.16.22*

Finistere **48°28'·30N 04°45'·72W** ❁❁◊◊✿✿✿

CHARTS AC 3345, 2694, 2644; SHOM 7149; ECM 540; Imray C36; Stanfords 17

TIDES +0520 on Dover (UT); ML 4·2m; Zone –0100

Standard Port BREST (⟼)

Times				Height (metres)			
High Water		Low Water		MHWS	MHWN	MLWN	MLWS
0000	0600	0000	0600	6·9	5·4	2·6	1·0
1200	1800	1200	1800				
Differences L'ABERILDUT							
+0010	+0010	+0023	+0010	+0·4	+0·3	0·0	0·0

SHELTER Very good inside, but appr is open to W winds; access all tides and at night with care. Hbr partly dries, but a narrow chan at the ent has 2m, with pools to 6m inside. Beyond the FV quay (NW side) a pontoon provides landing and fuel. Some 'dumbell' Øs; little room to ⚓, but ⚓s outside as chartlet in good weather. A useful passage hbr to await the tide in the Ch du Four.

NAVIGATION WPT 48°28'·12N 04°48'·13W, 263°/083° from/to Dir lt, 1·6M. From N beware Les Liniou Rks 1·5M NNW of the WPT and Plateau des Fourches 1·2M SSW. Appr is fairly easy in good vis, but beware strong cross tides. At the ent leave both Men Tassin PHM bn and Roche du Crapaud, a large rounded rk, close to port to clear drying spit on S side of the narrow ent. For Chenal du Four see opposite and 9.16.5.

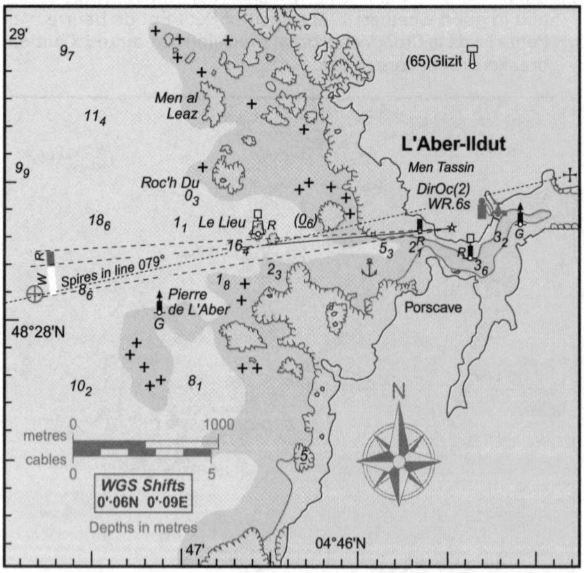

LIGHTS AND MARKS Le Four tr, Fl (5) 15s 28m 18M, gy tr, siren (3+2) 60s, is 3·35M N of the WPT. Pointe de Corsen lt, Dir Q WRG 33m 12/8M, is 3·2M S of the WPT. A stern transit 258° of Kéréon lt, gy tr, Oc (2+1) WR 24s 38m **17**M, with La Jument lt, Fl (3) R 15s 36m **22**M, gy tr + R top, (both off Ouessant) leads to the W sector of a powerful Dir lt 083°, Oc (2) WR 6s 12m **25/20**M, vis W081° - 085°, R085°-087°, on W bldg at hbr ent; good daymark. Ldg marks (difficult to see from afar): front, Lanildut spire on with Brélès spire leads 079° into fairway. Drying rks are marked by Pierre de l'Aber SHM bn and Le Lieu PHM bn tr 5m; the latter is easier to see.

RADIO TELEPHONE None.

TELEPHONE Hr Mr 02·98·04.36.40 (Jun-Sep)and mobile 06·11·66.31.64; Aff Mar 02·98·48·66.54; Auto 08·36.68·08·29; ⊖ 02·98·44.35.20; CROSS 02·98·89.31.31; SNSM 02·98·89·30·31; Police 02·98·48·10·10; Dr 02·98·04.33.08.

FACILITIES Hbr, M (300, inc 12 Øs; €1·14), FW, D, ♿, Slips, AC at FV quay; **Services:** BY, Sh, ME, El, CH, M. **Village** V, R, Bar, ✉. All needs at Brest 25km. Ferry: Roscoff.

CHENAL DU FOUR *9.16.23*

See 9.16.5 for notes on these passages.

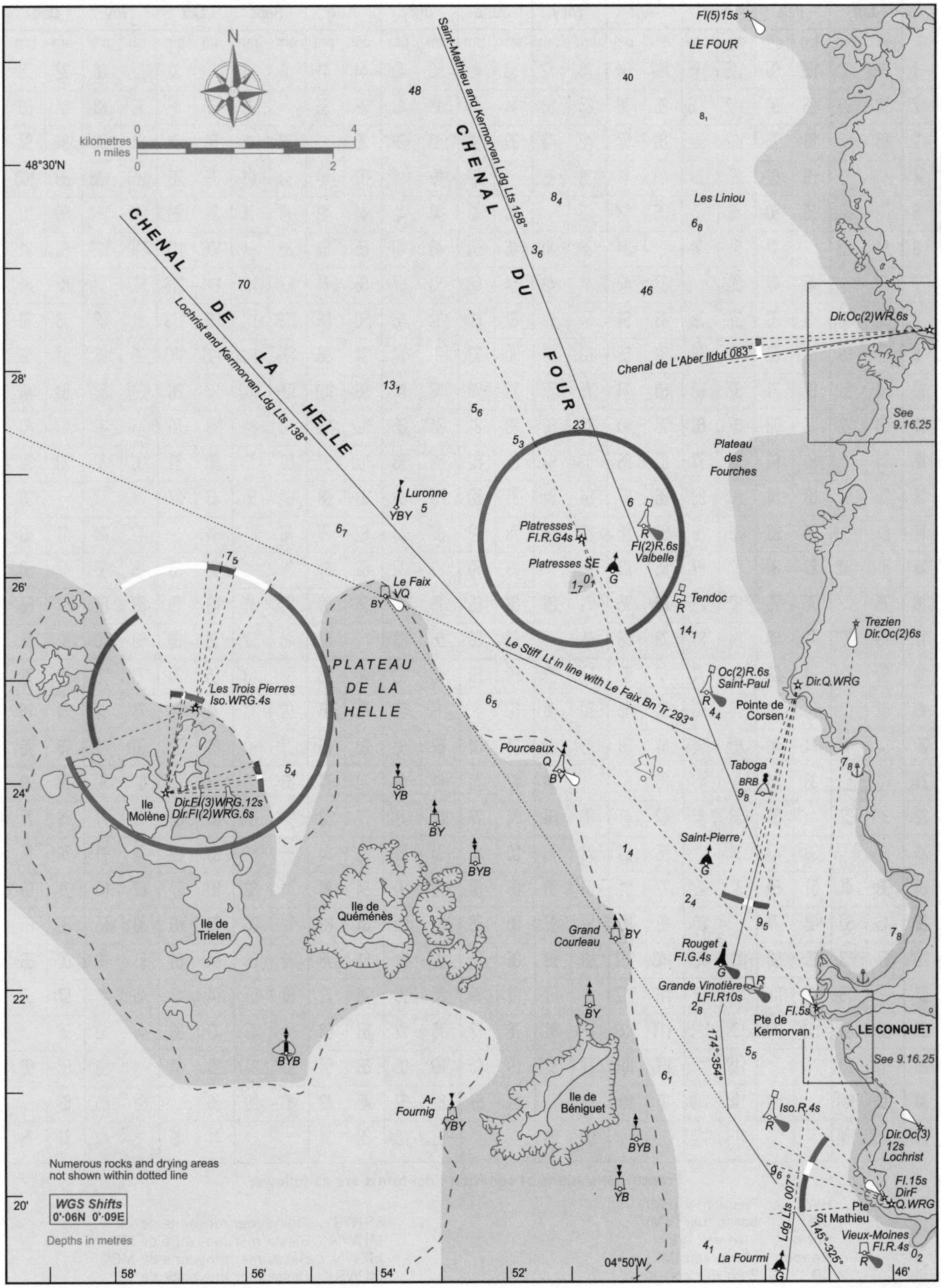

BREST TIDAL COEFFICIENTS 2002

Date	Jan		Feb		Mar		Apr		May		June		July		Aug		Sept		Oct		Nov		Dec	
	am	pm	am	pm	am	pm	am	pm	am	pm	am	pm	am	pm	am	pm	am	pm	am	pm	am	pm	am	pm
1	92	92	102	99	115	115	102	94	80	72	53	49	53	49	44	41	31	31		32	57	66	72	78
2	92	90	95	90	112	108	85	76	64	56	44	41	45	43	38	36		33	37	45	75	83	84	89
3	88	85	83	76	102	95	66	57	49	43	39	38	40	39	35		38	45	54	64	91	98	94	97
4	81	77	69	62	87	79	49	41	38	35		39	39		37	40	53	61	73	83	104	108	99	100
5	72	68	55	50	69	60	36	33	35		40	43	40	42	44	49	70	78	91	99	110	111	99	98
6	64	60		47	51	44		34	36	40	46	50	45	49	55	62	86	94	106	111	110	107	95	91
7	58		45	47	39		37	42	44	49	54	58	53	57	68	74	100	106	114	116	103	98	87	81
8	56	56	49	53	37	38	48	54	54	59	62	66	62	66	80	86	109	112	115	113	91	83	76	70
9	57	59	58	62	41	46	59	65	63	67	70	73	70	74	91	96	113	111	109	103	76	67	64	58
10	62	65	67	71	52	58	69	74	71	75	76	78	78	81	99	101	109	104	96	88	59	51	53	48
11	68	72	75	78	63	68	77	80	77	80	80	81	84	86	102	102	98	91	79	69	45	40	43	40
12	74	77	80	82	73	77	83	85	82	83	82	82	88	88	100	97	83	73	60	51	36	36	38	38
13	79	80	83	84	80	83	86	87	84	84	81	80	89	88	93	88	64	55	43	37		37		39
14	81	81	84	83	85	86	87	86	83	82	78	76	87	84	82	75	48	41	34		40	44	41	43
15	81	80	82	80	87	87	85	83	80	77	73	70	82	78	68	61	38		35	38	49	53	47	50
16	79	77	78	75	87	85	80	76	74	69	68	65	75	70	55	50	38	41	43	49	58	62	54	58
17	75	72	72	68	84	81	73	68	65	61	62	60	66	63		47	46	52	55	60	66	70	62	65
18	69	65	64	59	78	74	63	57	57	53	59	59	60	58	46	48	58	63	66	70	73	75	69	71
19	62	57	54	49	70	65	51	46	50	48	60			57	51	55	69	73	74	77	78	79	74	76
20	54	49	44	40	60	54	41	39	48	51	61	64	57	59	60	65	77	80	80	82	80	81	78	79
21	46	42	36	34	49	43	38			54	67	70	61	64	70	74	83	85	84	85	81	80	79	79
22	39	37		35	38	34	42	47	60	66	74	77	68	71	77	80	86	86	85	84	79	77	79	77
23	37		38	43	34		55	63	72	78	80	83	74	77	82	84	86	85	83	82	74	71	76	74
24	38	41	51	59	37	42	72	81	84	89	85	86	79	80	84	84	84	82	80	77	67	64	71	69
25	45	50	68	77	51	60	89	96	93	97	86	86	82	82	84	83	79	76	73	69	59	55	66	63
26	57	63	85	93	70	79	103	107	99	99	85	84	82	81	81	78	72	68	64	59	51	48	60	58
27	70	76	101	106	89	97	110	112	99	97	82	79	80	78	75	72	62	57	54	48	45	45	57	56
28	83	89	111	114	105	111	111	109	95	91	76	73	75	72	68	63	51	45	43	38	46	48	56	
29	94	98			115	117	106	101	87	82	69	65	69	65	58	54	39	34	35	34		53	58	60
30	102	104			118	116	95	88	76	71	61	57	61	57	48	43	30	29	36		59	65	63	67
31	105	104			113	108			65	59			52	48	38	34			41	49			71	76

French translations of common tidal terms are as follows:

HW	Pleine mer (PM)
LW	Basse mer (BM)
Springs	Vive eau (VE)
Neaps	Morte eau (ME)
CD	Zero des cartes
MHWS	Pleine mer moyenne de VE
MHWN	Pleine mer moyenne de ME
MLWN	Basse mer moyenne de ME
MLWS	Basse mer moyenne de VE

TIDAL COEFFICIENTS *9.16.24*

These indicate at a glance the magnitude of the tide on any particular day by assigning a non-dimensional coefficient to the twice-daily range of tide. The coefficient is based on a scale of 45 for mean neap (morte eau) and 100 for mean spring (vive eau) ranges at Brest. The coefficient is 70 for an average tide. A very small np tide may have a coefficient of only 20, whilst a very big sp tide might be as high as 120. The ratio of the coefficients of different tides equals the ratio of their ranges; the range, for example, of the largest sp tide (120) is six times that of the smallest np tide (20).

The table opposite is for Brest, but holds good elsewhere along the Channel and Atlantic coasts of France.

French tide tables, similar to Admiralty tide tables as in this Almanac, show for Secondary ports their time and height differences against the appropriate standard port for vive eau (springs) and for morte eau (neaps). The tidal coefficient for the day may be used to decide which correction(s) to apply. In general it is satisfactory to use the vive eau corrections for coefficients over 70 and the morte eau corrections for the others. Where it is necessary to obtain more accurate corrections (in estuaries for example) this can be done by interpolating or extrapolating.

Coefficients may also be used to determine rates of tidal streams on a given day, using a graph similar in principle to that shown in Fig 7 (7). On the vertical axis plot tidal coefficients from 20 at the bottom to 120 at the top. The horizontal axis shows tidal stream rates from zero to (say) five knots. From the tidal stream atlas or chart, plot the np and sp rates against coefficient 45 and 95 respectively; join these two points. Entering with the tidal coefficient for the day in question, go horizontally to the sloping line, then vertically to read the required rate on the horizontal axis.

ADJACENT HARBOURS

PORTSALL, Finistere, **48°33´·85N 04°42´·95W**. AC 1432, 3688; SHOM 7094, 7150. HW +0535 on Dover (UT); ML 4·4m; Duration 0600. See 9.16.20. Small drying hbr at head of bay. Access HW±3. Good shelter except in strong N winds. Ldg marks: Le Yurc'h rk (7m) on with Ploudalmézeau spire leads 109°; thence 085° on W & RW marks. By night use W sector 084°-088° of lt Oc (4) WRG 12s 9m 13/10M, W col/R top. Appr marked by 5 bn trs. Beware many rks for about 2M off-shore. ⚓ to W of ent, or go alongside quay in hbr. Facilities: Aff Mar ☎ 98·48·66·54; SNSM ☎ 02·98·48·77·44; Dr ☎ 02·98·48·8·46; **Quay** C (0·5 ton), D, FW, P, Slip; **Club Naut** ☎ 02·98·48·63·10; **Coop de Pêcheurs** ☎ 02·98·48·63·26, CH. **Town** Bar, ✉, R, V.

ARGENTON, Finistere, **48°31´·32N 04°46´·25W.** AC 3347, 2694; SHOM 7122. HW +0535 on Dover (UT); ML 4·6m; Duration 0600; use PORTSALL diffs 9.16.20. Small drying hbr; good shelter except in W winds when a swell comes up the bay into the hbr. Access HW±3. Appr 086° on 2 W bns & RW wall. Le Four lt Fl (5) 15s is 1·4M to W. Beware strong E-W tides. ⚓ in deep water off hbr ent. 10 Ⓥs. Facilities: FW, P on quay; **SC** ☎ 02·98·89·54·04. **Town** Bar, R, V.

ILE DE MOLENE, Finistere, **48°24´·13N 04°57´·26W.** AC 2694; SHOM 7123, 7122, 7149. HW +0520 on Dover (UT); ML 4·6m; see 9.16.21. Hbr, part-drying, is easier at nps, good wx/vis. Beware strong tidal streams. Best appr is via Ch de la Helle, twixt Le Faix bn tr, VQ 16m, and Luronne WCM buoy. Track W to pick up ldg marks 215°: front, Trois Pierres bn, Iso WRG 4s, 15m; rear, RW N. Mill bn tr. Nearing front mark, alter stbd to align spire 199° between ECM bn tr and WCM buoy. ⚓ S of N bkwtr hd in about 1·5m; 10 Ⓥs in inner hbr, €4·57. Dir lt 191°, Fl (3) WRG 12s, W190°-192°, is on old S pier; same lt, but Fl (2) WRG 6s, also covers Chenal des Las (W259·5°-262·5°). Facilities: FW, V, CH, R, Bar, ✉.

LE CONQUET *9.16.25*

Finistere **48°21'·60N 04°47'·15W** ✽✽◇◇✿✿

CHARTS AC 3345, 2694; SHOM 7149, 7148; ECM 540; Imray C36; Stanfords 17

TIDES +0535 Dover; ML 3·9; Duration 0600; Zone –0100

Standard Port BREST (⟶)

Times				Height (metres)			
High Water		Low Water		MHWS	MHWN	MLWN	MLWS
0000	0600	0000	0600	6·9	5·4	2·6	1·0
1200	1800	1200	1800				
Differences LE CONQUET							
–0005	0000	+0007	+0007	–0·1	–0·1	–0·1	0·0

SHELTER Good except in strong W winds. A busy fishing port with some new yacht facilities. ⚓ prohib in Avant Port. Yachts can ⚓ further up hbr but it dries and may be foul.

NAVIGATION WPT 48°21´·50N 04°48´·50W, 263°/083° from/to Mole Ste Barbe lt, 1M. From the NW, beware the Grande Vinotière rks. Also note strong cross streams in the Chenal du Four.

LIGHTS AND MARKS Ldg line 095° lt on Mole Ste Barbe, Oc G 4s in line with spire of Le Conquet church. La Louve R bn tr and end of Mole St Christophe in line at 079°.

RADIO TELEPHONE Le Conquet Port (Hr Mr) VHF 08 16.

TELEPHONE Hr Mr 02·98·89·08·07; Aff Mar 02·98·89·00·05; Météo 02·98·84·60·64; Auto 08·36.68·08·08; CROSS 02·98·89·31·31; SNSM 02·98·89·02·07; Police 02·98·89·00·13; Dr 02·98·89·01·86; Brit Consul 02·99·46·26·64.

FACILITIES Hbr Slip, M, L, D; **Services:** ME, El, P (cans), CH. **Town** P, D, FW, ME, El, V, Gaz, R, Bar, ✉, Ⓑ, ⇌ (bus to Brest), ✈ (Brest). Ferry: Roscoff.

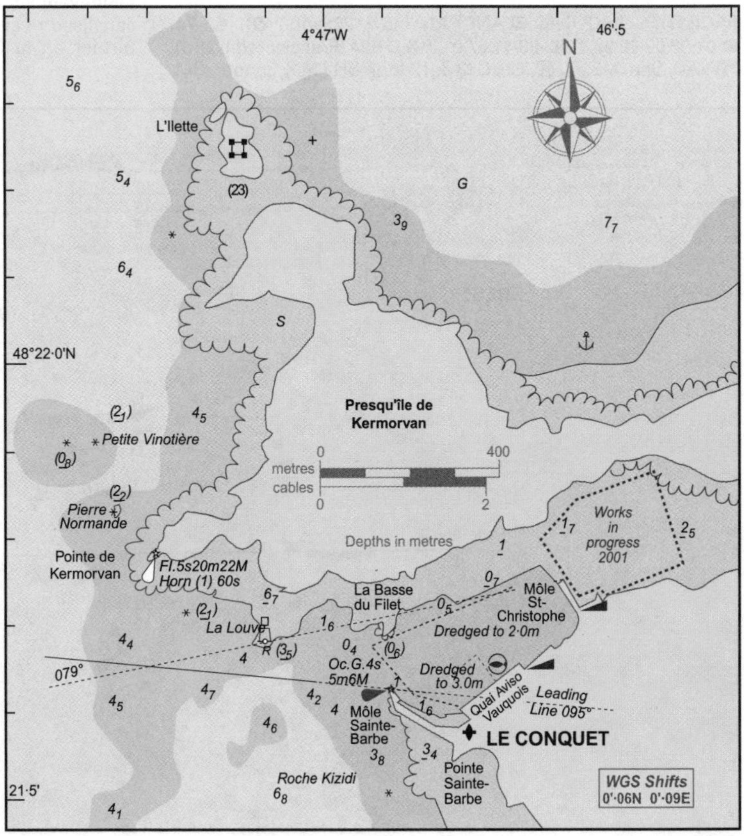

BREST *9.16.26*

Finistere **48°21'·30N 04°25·70W** (Moulin Blanc) ❀❀❀◊◊◊✿✿

CHARTS AC 3428, 3427, 3429; SHOM 7397, 7398, 7399, 7400, 7401, 7149, 7172; ECM 542; Imray C36; Stanfords 17

TIDES +0520 Dover; ML 4·0; Duration 0605; Zone –0100. NOTE: Brest is a Standard Port. Daily tidal predictions are given on pages (⟷); tidal coefficients are in 9.16.24.

SHELTER Excellent in Brest, and at many ⚓s in the Rade de Brest (50 sq miles). Access at any tide H24. Yachts should use Moulin Blanc marina, not the Port du Commerce. Brest is a busy commercial, naval and fishing port. The Port Militaire and a zone round Ile Longue are prohib areas.

NAVIGATION WPT 48°18´·30N 04°44´·00W, 248°/068° from/to front ldg lt (Pte du Petit Minou), 5·3M. Tidal streams run hard in the Goulet de Brest. In mid-chan beware rks, well marked; pass either side. As WPT to Marina, use Moulin Blanc PHM buoy, Fl (3) R 12s, 48°22´·85N 04°25´·90W, 207°/027° from/to MB1 and MB2 chan buoys, 0·55M.

LIGHTS AND MARKS Apprs marked by lts at Pte St Mathieu, Pte du Petit Minou and Pte du Portzic. Oceanopolis bldg, W roof, is conspic. Marina, 2M E of the Port de Commerce, has buoyed chan; MB4 lt and the ECM lt By can be obsc'd by berthed craft.

RADIO TELEPHONE Monitor *Brest Port* (at Pte du Portzic) VHF Ch 08 16 (controls apprs to Brest). All vessels entering keep watch on Ch 16. Marina Ch 09 16 (office hrs). **Corsen-Ouessant**, callsign *Ouessant Traffic* on Ch **13** 79, operates a VTS reporting system which is mandatory for vessels > 300grt within a circle radius 35M centred on Le Stiff, including Ouessant TSS. Position and navigational help can be given to any craft, if necessary; monitor Ch 16 whilst in the area.

TELEPHONE Hr Mr Brest 02·98·33·41·47; Moulin Blanc 02·98·02·20·02; Aff Mar 02·98·80·62·25; CROSS 02·98·89·31·31; ⊜ 02·98·44·35·20; Auto 08·36.68·08·29; Météo 02·98·32·55·55; Police 02·98·43·77·77; Dr 02·98·44·38·70; Ⓗ 02·98·22·33·33; Brit Consul 02·99·46·26·64.

FACILITIES (MOULIN BLANC) Marina (1225+100 Ⓥ), €1·74, ☎ 02·98·02·20·02, 📠 02·98·41.67.91, P & D H24 (French credit card), FW, AC, Slip, ME, El, Ⓔ, Sh, C (3 & 12 ton), BH (14 & 35 ton), SM, CH, SHOM, Gaz, R, ⊡, Ⓛ, V, Bar; **Sté des Régates de Brest** ☎ 02·98·02·53·36, R.
BREST Services: CH, SM, ME, El, Sh, Ⓔ, SHOM. City all facilities, Gaz, ✉, Ⓑ, ⇌, ✈. Ferry: Roscoff.

ADJACENT ANCHORAGE TO THE WEST

ANSE DE BERTHAUME, 48°20'·50N 04°41'·75W. AC 3427. A useful passage ⚓ if awaiting the tide E into Goulet de Brest; N into Ch du Four, or S toward Raz de Sein. Good shelter in W'lies. ⚓ in 5m off slip N of Fort de Berthaume (conspic); 1ca NE, beware Le Chat rk, dries 6·8m. No lts.

RADE DE BREST *9.16.27*

Finistere

TIDES In most of the bays in the Rade de Brest tidal streams are weak, but in the main rivers they can exceed 2kn at sp.

SHELTER AND NAVIGATION The Rade de Brest offers a sheltered cruising ground, useful in bad weather, with many attractive ⚓s.
To the NE, ½M beyond Pont Albert-Louppe (29m) and Pont de l'Iroise (25m clearance), is good ⚓ at Le Passage. The drying port of Landerneau, 6M up R L'Elorn, can be reached on the tide, lifting br ☎ 02·11·03·31·20; keep well inboard of chan buoys. On the S side of Rade de Brest are various naval sites with prohib ⚓ and landing around Ile Longue. There are however ⚓s at Le Fret, on SE side of Ile Longue, and at Roscanvel on E side of the Quelern Peninsula.
To the SE, L'Aulne is a lovely river with steep wooded banks. Near the mouth of its estuary, on the N shore, is a good ⚓ and W Ⓥs in 3m in Anse de l'Auberlach. Further E, 3 small drying rivers run into the Aulne from the north: R Daoulas, R de l'Hôpital and R du Faou and offer shelter for boats which can dry out. Up the Aulne there are ⚓s near Landévennec, below Térénez bridge (27m), and also 1½M above that bridge. At Guily-Glaz, 14M above Landévennec, a lock (open HW Brest –2 to +1½) opens into the canalised river to Port Launay (AB on quay, AC, FW, R), and 3M further on to Chateaulin, AB on pontoons; most facilities.

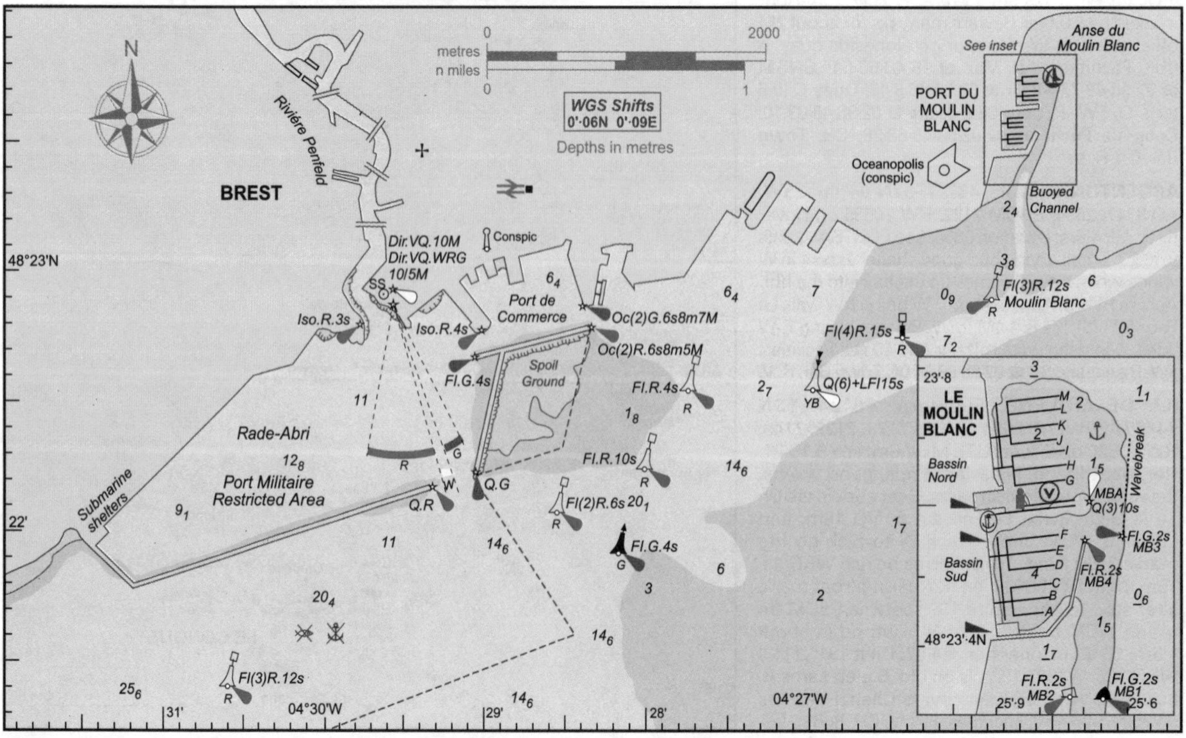

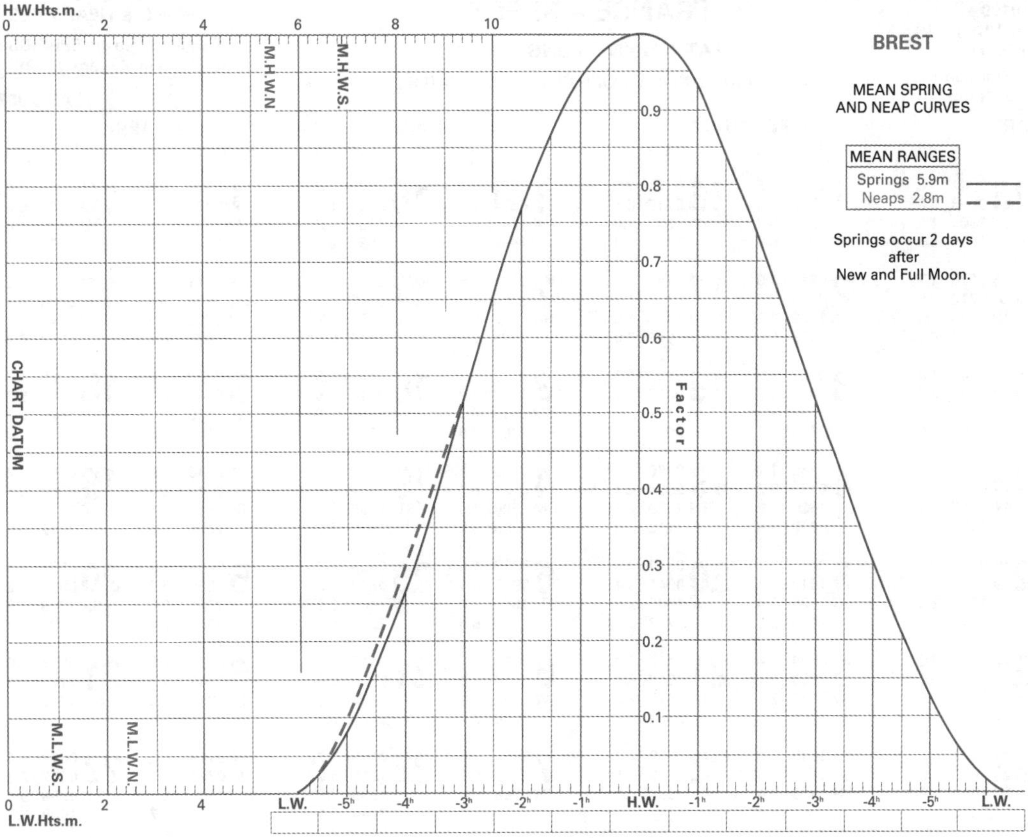

RADE DE BREST *continued*

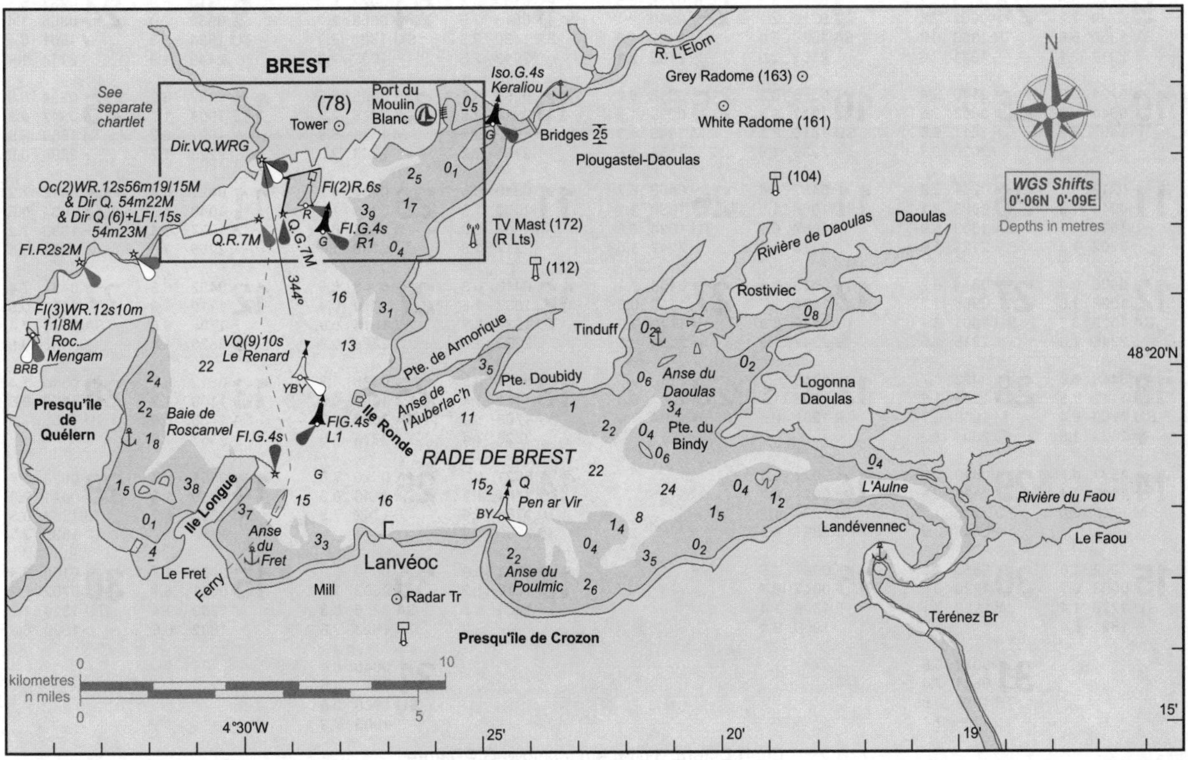

TIME ZONE -0100
(French Standard Time)
Subtract 1 hour for UT
For French Summer Time add ONE hour in **non-shaded areas**

FRANCE – BREST

LAT 48°23′N LONG 4°30′W

TIMES AND HEIGHTS OF HIGH AND LOW WATERS

SPRING & NEAP TIDES
Dates in red are **SPRINGS**
Dates in blue are **NEAPS**

YEAR **2002**

JANUARY

Date	Day	Time	m	Time	m	Time	m	Time	m
1	TU	0004	1.2	0605	7.0	1230	1.0	1830	6.8
2	W	0050	1.2	0651	7.0	1317	1.0	1917	6.7
3	TH	0137	1.3	0738	6.9	1406	1.2	2006	6.5
4	F	0226	1.5	0828	6.7	1457	1.4	2058	6.3
5	SA	0319	1.7	0922	6.4	1552	1.7	2155	6.0
6	SU	0417	2.0	1022	6.1	1653	2.0	2258	5.8
7	M	0521	2.2	1128	5.9	1758	2.2		
8	TU	0005	5.7	0629	2.3	1240	5.8	1907	2.2
9	W	0120	5.8	0739	2.2	1350	5.8	2013	2.1
10	TH	0224	6.0	0844	2.0	1451	6.0	2112	1.9
11	F	0319	6.2	0940	1.8	1543	6.2	2202	1.8
12	SA	0406	6.4	1028	1.6	1629	6.3	2246	1.6
13	SU	0448	6.6	1111	1.5	1709	6.4	● 2327	1.6
14	M	0527	6.7	1149	1.4	1746	6.4		
15	TU	0002	1.5	0603	6.7	1226	1.4	1821	6.4
16	W	0041	1.6	0638	6.6	1301	1.5	1854	6.3
17	TH	0115	1.7	0712	6.5	1335	1.6	1927	6.1
18	F	0148	1.9	0746	6.3	1408	1.8	2000	5.9
19	SA	0223	2.1	0820	6.0	1443	2.1	2035	5.7
20	SU	0259	2.3	0857	5.8	1522	2.3	2115	5.5
21	M	0342	2.6	0941	5.5	1607	2.6	2205	5.2
22	TU	0434	2.8	1038	5.3	1703	2.7	2310	5.1
23	W	0539	2.9	1147	5.2	1811	2.8		
24	TH	0028	5.2	0652	2.8	1303	5.3	1923	2.6
25	F	0140	5.4	0803	2.5	1411	5.6	2028	2.3
26	SA	0241	5.8	0903	2.1	1509	5.9	2124	1.9
27	SU	0334	6.2	0956	1.7	1601	6.3	2215	1.5
28	M	0423	6.7	1046	1.2	1649	6.7	○ 2303	1.2
29	TU	0510	7.0	1133	0.9	1735	7.0	2349	0.9
30	W	0555	7.3	1220	0.6	1820	7.1		
31	TH	0039	0.8	0641	7.4	1306	0.6	1905	7.1

FEBRUARY

Date	Day	Time	m	Time	m	Time	m	Time	m
1	F	0125	0.8	0726	7.3	1352	0.7	1950	6.9
2	SA	0211	1.0	0811	7.1	1439	1.0	2036	6.6
3	SU	0259	1.3	0858	6.7	1527	1.4	2124	6.2
4	M	0349	1.7	0949	6.2	1620	1.9	2219	5.8
5	TU	0447	2.1	1049	5.7	1721	2.3	2325	5.5
6	W	0554	2.4	1203	5.4	1832	2.6		
7	TH	0048	5.4	0712	2.5	1328	5.4	1951	2.5
8	F	0207	5.6	0829	2.4	1441	5.5	2058	2.3
9	SA	0308	5.9	0929	2.1	1535	5.8	2151	2.0
10	SU	0356	6.2	1017	1.8	1619	6.1	2235	1.8
11	M	0437	6.4	1058	1.6	1657	6.3	2313	1.6
12	TU	0513	6.6	1134	1.4	1730	6.4	● 2347	1.5
13	W	0545	6.7	1206	1.3	1801	6.5		
14	TH	0020	1.4	0617	6.7	1237	1.3	1831	6.5
15	F	0051	1.5	0647	6.7	1308	1.4	1900	6.4
16	SA	0121	1.6	0717	6.5	1337	1.6	1929	6.2
17	SU	0151	1.7	0747	6.3	1408	1.8	1958	6.0
18	M	0223	2.0	0818	6.1	1441	2.0	2031	5.8
19	TU	0300	2.3	0854	5.7	1520	2.3	2112	5.5
20	W	0344	2.5	0941	5.4	1609	2.6	2207	5.2
21	TH	0442	2.8	1047	5.2	1713	2.8	2323	5.1
22	F	0558	2.9	1213	5.1	1834	2.8		
23	SA	0058	5.2	0725	2.7	1342	5.3	1957	2.6
24	SU	0216	5.6	0840	2.2	1450	5.8	2103	2.1
25	M	0316	6.2	0938	1.6	1545	6.3	2158	1.5
26	TU	0408	6.7	1030	1.1	1634	6.8	2247	1.0
27	W	0455	7.2	1118	0.6	1720	7.2	○ 2334	0.6
28	TH	0540	7.5	1204	0.3	1804	7.4		

MARCH

Date	Day	Time	m	Time	m	Time	m	Time	m
1	F	0023	0.4	0624	7.7	1248	0.3	1846	7.4
2	SA	0107	0.5	0706	7.5	1332	0.5	1928	7.2
3	SU	0150	0.7	0748	7.2	1415	0.9	2009	6.8
4	M	0235	1.1	0831	6.7	1500	1.4	2053	6.3
5	TU	0322	1.6	0917	6.1	1548	2.0	2143	5.8
6	W	0415	2.2	1013	5.5	1645	2.5	2246	5.4
7	TH	0521	2.6	1129	5.1	1758	2.9		
8	F	0005	5.2	0646	2.8	1309	5.0	1929	2.8
9	SA	0150	5.3	0813	2.6	1430	5.3	2043	2.5
10	SU	0253	5.7	0914	2.2	1522	5.7	2135	2.2
11	M	0340	6.0	1000	1.9	1603	6.0	2217	1.8
12	TU	0418	6.3	1037	1.6	1637	6.2	2253	1.6
13	W	0451	6.5	1111	1.4	1708	6.4	2325	1.4
14	TH	0521	6.7	1141	1.3	1736	6.6	● 2356	1.3
15	F	0551	6.8	1210	1.2	1804	6.6		
16	SA	0025	1.3	0620	6.8	1239	1.3	1831	6.6
17	SU	0053	1.4	0648	6.7	1307	1.4	1859	6.5
18	M	0122	1.5	0716	6.5	1336	1.6	1927	6.3
19	TU	0153	1.7	0747	6.2	1408	1.9	1959	6.0
20	W	0229	2.0	0822	5.9	1446	2.2	2037	5.7
21	TH	0312	2.4	0906	5.5	1534	2.5	2129	5.4
22	F	0408	2.7	1010	5.2	1636	2.8	2244	5.1
23	SA	0523	2.8	1142	5.0	1801	2.9		
24	SU	0027	5.2	0658	2.7	1320	5.3	1932	2.6
25	M	0153	5.6	0818	2.2	1431	5.8	2043	2.0
26	TU	0256	6.2	0919	1.5	1526	6.4	2138	1.4
27	W	0348	6.8	1010	0.9	1614	6.9	2228	0.9
28	TH	0435	7.3	1058	0.5	1659	7.3	○ 2314	0.5
29	F	0520	7.6	1143	0.3	1742	7.5		
30	SA	0000	0.3	0603	7.7	1226	0.3	1823	7.5
31	SU	0045	0.4	0644	7.5	1308	0.5	1903	7.3

APRIL

Date	Day	Time	m	Time	m	Time	m	Time	m
1	M	0128	0.7	0724	7.1	1350	1.0	1943	6.9
2	TU	0211	1.1	0805	6.6	1432	1.5	2025	6.4
3	W	0256	1.7	0849	6.0	1519	2.1	2112	5.8
4	TH	0348	2.2	0943	5.4	1614	2.6	2215	5.3
5	F	0451	2.7	1059	5.0	1726	3.0	2340	5.1
6	SA	0615	2.9	1241	4.9	1859	3.0		
7	SU	0119	5.2	0744	2.7	1404	5.2	2016	2.7
8	M	0224	5.5	0845	2.3	1455	5.6	2108	2.3
9	TU	0310	5.9	0930	2.0	1534	5.9	2148	1.9
10	W	0347	6.2	1007	1.7	1607	6.2	2223	1.7
11	TH	0421	6.4	1040	1.5	1637	6.4	2255	1.5
12	F	0452	6.6	1110	1.3	1706	6.6	● 2326	1.4
13	SA	0522	6.7	1140	1.3	1735	6.6	2357	1.3
14	SU	0551	6.7	1210	1.3	1803	6.7		
15	M	0026	1.3	0621	6.7	1239	1.4	1832	6.6
16	TU	0057	1.4	0651	6.5	1310	1.6	1903	6.4
17	W	0130	1.6	0724	6.2	1344	1.8	1937	6.2
18	TH	0208	1.9	0802	5.9	1424	2.1	2018	5.8
19	F	0254	2.2	0850	5.5	1514	2.5	2112	5.5
20	SA	0351	2.5	0957	5.2	1618	2.7	2227	5.3
21	SU	0507	2.6	1127	5.1	1742	2.8		
22	M	0012	5.4	0637	2.5	1258	5.4	1909	2.5
23	TU	0128	5.7	0755	2.0	1406	5.9	2018	2.0
24	W	0231	6.3	0855	1.4	1501	6.4	2114	1.4
25	TH	0324	6.8	0947	0.9	1550	6.9	2204	0.9
26	F	0412	7.2	1034	0.6	1635	7.2	2251	0.6
27	SA	0457	7.4	1119	0.5	1718	7.4	○ 2336	0.5
28	SU	0540	7.4	1202	0.5	1759	7.3		
29	M	0023	0.6	0621	7.2	1244	0.8	1839	7.1
30	TU	0106	0.9	0702	6.9	1326	1.2	1920	6.8

Chart Datum: 3·64 metres below IGN Datum

TIME ZONE -0100
(French Standard Time)
Subtract 1 hour for UT
For French Summer Time add ONE hour in **non-shaded areas**

FRANCE – BREST

LAT 48°23'N LONG 4°30'W

TIMES AND HEIGHTS OF HIGH AND LOW WATERS

SPRING & NEAP TIDES
Dates in red are **SPRINGS**
Dates in blue are **NEAPS**

YEAR **2002**

MAY

Date	Day	Time	m	Time	m	Time	m	Time	m
1	W	0149	1.3	0743	6.4	1408	1.7	2002	6.3
2	TH	0234	1.7	0827	5.9	1454	2.2	2050	5.8
3	F	0324	2.2	0920	5.4	1547	2.6	2149	5.4
4	SA	0423	2.6	1028	5.0	1653	2.9	2303	5.2
5	SU	0535	2.8	1153	4.9	1813	3.0		
6	M	0028	5.2	0654	2.7	1314	5.1	1929	2.8
7	TU	0136	5.4	0759	2.5	1410	5.4	2024	2.4
8	W	0226	5.7	0847	2.2	1452	5.7	2108	2.1
9	TH	0307	6.0	0927	1.9	1529	6.0	2146	1.9
10	F	0344	6.2	1003	1.7	1602	6.3	2221	1.6
11	SA	0419	6.4	1037	1.5	1634	6.4	2255	1.5
12	SU	0452	6.5	1110	1.4	1706	6.6	● 2328	1.4
13	M	0524	6.6	1142	1.4	1738	6.6		
14	TU	0002	1.4	0557	6.6	1215	1.4	1810	6.6
15	W	0037	1.4	0632	6.4	1250	1.6	1846	6.5
16	TH	0115	1.6	0711	6.2	1329	1.8	1926	6.3
17	F	0158	1.8	0755	5.9	1414	2.0	2012	6.0
18	SA	0247	2.0	0848	5.6	1506	2.3	2109	5.7
19	SU	0345	2.2	0954	5.4	1610	2.5	2220	5.6
20	M	0457	2.3	1113	5.4	1726	2.5	2340	5.6
21	TU	0615	2.2	1230	5.6	1842	2.3		
22	W	0059	5.9	0727	1.9	1337	6.0	1949	1.9
23	TH	0202	6.3	0827	1.5	1433	6.4	2048	1.5
24	F	0258	6.6	0921	1.2	1524	6.7	2140	1.1
25	SA	0348	6.9	1010	1.0	1611	6.9	2229	0.9
26	SU	0435	7.0	1056	0.9	1655	7.1	○ 2316	0.8
27	M	0520	7.0	1141	1.0	1738	7.0		
28	TU	0000	0.9	0602	6.8	1223	1.1	1820	6.9
29	W	0047	1.1	0644	6.5	1305	1.4	1902	6.6
30	TH	0130	1.4	0725	6.2	1348	1.8	1944	6.3
31	F	0214	1.7	0809	5.8	1432	2.1	2030	5.9

JUNE

Date	Day	Time	m	Time	m	Time	m	Time	m
1	SA	0300	2.1	0856	5.5	1520	2.5	2121	5.6
2	SU	0351	2.4	0951	5.2	1614	2.7	2220	5.4
3	M	0448	2.6	1055	5.0	1717	2.8	2325	5.2
4	TU	0551	2.7	1204	5.1	1825	2.8		
5	W	0032	5.3	0655	2.6	1308	5.2	1927	2.6
6	TH	0131	5.5	0752	2.4	1400	5.5	2019	2.4
7	F	0221	5.7	0840	2.2	1445	5.8	2104	2.1
8	SA	0305	5.9	0923	1.9	1525	6.0	2145	1.9
9	SU	0345	6.1	1002	1.7	1603	6.3	2225	1.7
10	M	0424	6.3	1041	1.6	1640	6.4	2303	1.5
11	TU	0502	6.4	1119	1.5	1717	6.5	● 2342	1.4
12	W	0541	6.4	1157	1.5	1756	6.6		
13	TH	0024	1.4	0622	6.4	1238	1.5	1837	6.6
14	F	0107	1.4	0705	6.3	1321	1.6	1921	6.5
15	SA	0152	1.5	0753	6.1	1409	1.8	2010	6.3
16	SU	0243	1.7	0846	5.9	1501	1.9	2105	6.1
17	M	0338	1.8	0945	5.8	1559	2.1	2206	5.9
18	TU	0441	2.0	1050	5.7	1705	2.2	2314	5.9
19	W	0549	2.0	1158	5.7	1813	2.1		
20	TH	0027	5.9	0656	1.9	1304	5.9	1920	1.9
21	F	0133	6.0	0759	1.7	1405	6.1	2022	1.7
22	SA	0234	6.2	0857	1.6	1501	6.4	2120	1.5
23	SU	0329	6.4	0950	1.4	1552	6.6	2212	1.3
24	M	0419	6.5	1039	1.3	1639	6.7	○ 2301	1.2
25	TU	0505	6.5	1124	1.3	1723	6.7	2346	1.2
26	W	0548	6.5	1207	1.4	1805	6.7		
27	TH	0031	1.3	0629	6.4	1248	1.5	1846	6.6
28	F	0112	1.4	0708	6.2	1328	1.7	1926	6.4
29	SA	0152	1.6	0747	5.9	1408	1.9	2006	6.1
30	SU	0232	1.9	0826	5.7	1448	2.2	2048	5.9

JULY

Date	Day	Time	m	Time	m	Time	m	Time	m
1	M	0314	2.1	0909	5.5	1532	2.4	2133	5.6
2	TU	0359	2.4	0957	5.2	1622	2.6	2224	5.4
3	W	0450	2.6	1054	5.1	1719	2.8	2323	5.2
4	TH	0548	2.7	1158	5.1	1821	2.8		
5	F	0028	5.3	0650	2.6	1302	5.2	1924	2.6
6	SA	0130	5.4	0750	2.5	1359	5.5	2021	2.4
7	SU	0226	5.6	0843	2.2	1450	5.8	2111	2.1
8	M	0315	5.8	0931	2.0	1535	6.1	2158	1.8
9	TU	0401	6.1	1016	1.7	1619	6.3	2242	1.6
10	W	0445	6.3	1100	1.5	1702	6.6	● 2326	1.3
11	TH	0529	6.5	1144	1.4	1745	6.7		
12	F	0013	1.2	0613	6.6	1228	1.3	1829	6.8
13	SA	0058	1.1	0658	6.6	1313	1.2	1914	6.8
14	SU	0144	1.1	0744	6.5	1400	1.3	2001	6.7
15	M	0232	1.2	0833	6.3	1449	1.5	2051	6.5
16	TU	0323	1.5	0924	6.1	1541	1.7	2144	6.2
17	W	0418	1.7	1021	5.9	1640	1.9	2244	6.0
18	TH	0519	2.0	1125	5.7	1744	2.1	2351	5.8
19	F	0625	2.1	1233	5.7	1853	2.2		
20	SA	0108	5.7	0734	2.1	1343	5.8	2003	2.1
21	SU	0218	5.8	0840	2.0	1446	6.0	2107	1.9
22	M	0319	6.0	0937	1.8	1541	6.3	2202	1.6
23	TU	0410	6.1	1027	1.7	1629	6.5	2251	1.5
24	W	0455	6.3	1112	1.5	1712	6.6	○ 2334	1.3
25	TH	0535	6.3	1152	1.5	1751	6.7		
26	F	0013	1.3	0612	6.3	1230	1.5	1828	6.6
27	SA	0051	1.4	0646	6.3	1305	1.6	1903	6.5
28	SU	0126	1.5	0719	6.2	1340	1.7	1936	6.3
29	M	0200	1.7	0752	6.0	1414	1.9	2010	6.1
30	TU	0234	1.9	0826	5.7	1449	2.2	2046	5.8
31	W	0310	2.2	0902	5.5	1529	2.4	2126	5.5

AUGUST

Date	Day	Time	m	Time	m	Time	m	Time	m
1	TH	0352	2.5	0947	5.3	1616	2.7	2216	5.3
2	F	0443	2.7	1046	5.1	1715	2.8	2321	5.1
3	SA	0547	2.8	1159	5.1	1826	2.9		
4	SU	0038	5.1	0659	2.8	1314	5.2	1939	2.7
5	M	0151	5.3	0808	2.5	1418	5.5	2042	2.3
6	TU	0252	5.6	0906	2.2	1513	5.9	2136	1.9
7	W	0343	6.0	0956	1.8	1602	6.3	2225	1.5
8	TH	0431	6.4	1044	1.4	1647	6.7	● 2311	1.1
9	F	0516	6.7	1129	1.1	1732	7.0		
10	SA	0001	0.8	0600	6.9	1214	0.9	1816	7.2
11	SU	0044	0.7	0643	7.0	1258	0.8	1859	7.2
12	M	0128	0.7	0726	6.9	1343	0.9	1943	7.1
13	TU	0213	0.9	0811	6.7	1429	1.2	2029	6.8
14	W	0300	1.3	0857	6.4	1518	1.5	2118	6.4
15	TH	0351	1.7	0949	6.0	1613	1.9	2214	5.9
16	F	0449	2.2	1052	5.6	1716	2.3	2322	5.5
17	SA	0557	2.5	1207	5.5	1831	2.5		
18	SU	0051	5.3	0716	2.5	1329	5.5	1952	2.4
19	M	0213	5.5	0831	2.4	1439	5.8	2101	2.1
20	TU	0315	5.8	0930	2.1	1533	6.1	2155	1.8
21	W	0403	6.0	1017	1.8	1618	6.4	2239	1.5
22	TH	0443	6.3	1058	1.6	1657	6.6	○ 2318	1.4
23	F	0518	6.4	1135	1.5	1732	6.7	2353	1.3
24	SA	0550	6.5	1208	1.4	1804	6.7		
25	SU	0026	1.3	0619	6.5	1239	1.5	1834	6.7
26	M	0056	1.4	0648	6.4	1309	1.6	1904	6.5
27	TU	0126	1.6	0717	6.2	1339	1.8	1933	6.3
28	W	0155	1.8	0745	6.0	1410	2.0	2004	6.0
29	TH	0227	2.1	0816	5.8	1444	2.3	2037	5.7
30	F	0303	2.4	0854	5.5	1525	2.6	2120	5.4
31	SA	0349	2.7	0945	5.2	1619	2.9	2221	5.1

Chart Datum: 3·64 metres below IGN Datum

TIME ZONE -0100
(French Standard Time)
Subtract 1 hour for UT
For French Summer Time add ONE hour in **non-shaded areas**

FRANCE – BREST

LAT 48°23′N LONG 4°30′W

TIMES AND HEIGHTS OF HIGH AND LOW WATERS

SPRING & NEAP TIDES
Dates in red are SPRINGS
Dates in blue are NEAPS

YEAR **2002**

SEPTEMBER

Date	Day	Time	m	Time	m	Time	m	Time	m
1	SU	0451	2.9	1100	5.0	1732	3.0	2348	4.9
2	M	0612	3.0	1233	5.1	1902	2.9		
3	TU	0124	5.2	0738	2.7	1353	5.4	2019	2.5
4	W	0233	5.6	0844	2.3	1453	6.0	2117	1.9
5	TH	0326	6.1	0937	1.8	1543	6.5	2206	1.3
6	F	0413	6.6	1025	1.2	1629	7.0	2252	0.9
7	SA	0457	7.0	1111	0.8	1713	7.4	● 2337	0.5
8	SU	0540	7.3	1155	0.6	1756	7.6		
9	M	0024	0.4	0622	7.4	1239	0.5	1839	7.6
10	TU	0107	0.5	0703	7.2	1322	0.7	1921	7.3
11	W	0150	0.8	0745	6.9	1407	1.0	2004	6.9
12	TH	0235	1.3	0829	6.5	1454	1.5	2050	6.3
13	F	0323	1.9	0919	6.0	1548	2.0	2145	5.7
14	SA	0420	2.4	1023	5.5	1652	2.5	2259	5.2
15	SU	0533	2.8	1147	5.3	1814	2.7		
16	M	0043	5.1	0703	2.8	1320	5.4	1944	2.6
17	TU	0209	5.4	0821	2.5	1429	5.8	2050	2.2
18	W	0304	5.7	0916	2.2	1519	6.1	2139	1.8
19	TH	0346	6.1	1000	1.8	1559	6.4	2219	1.6
20	F	0422	6.3	1037	1.6	1635	6.6	2255	1.4
21	SA	0453	6.5	1110	1.5	1706	6.8	○ 2326	1.3
22	SU	0522	6.6	1141	1.4	1736	6.8	2356	1.3
23	M	0549	6.6	1210	1.4	1804	6.8		
24	TU	0024	1.4	0617	6.6	1238	1.5	1832	6.6
25	W	0052	1.5	0643	6.4	1306	1.7	1900	6.4
26	TH	0120	1.7	0711	6.3	1336	1.9	1928	6.2
27	F	0151	2.0	0740	6.0	1409	2.2	2001	5.8
28	SA	0226	2.4	0816	5.7	1450	2.5	2042	5.4
29	SU	0312	2.7	0905	5.3	1543	2.9	2142	5.1
30	M	0413	3.0	1020	5.1	1655	3.0	2314	4.9

OCTOBER

Date	Day	Time	m	Time	m	Time	m	Time	m
1	TU	0537	3.1	1200	5.1	1832	2.9		
2	W	0102	5.2	0711	2.8	1328	5.5	1955	2.4
3	TH	0211	5.7	0821	2.3	1429	6.1	2054	1.8
4	F	0304	6.3	0915	1.7	1520	6.7	2143	1.2
5	SA	0350	6.8	1003	1.1	1607	7.2	2229	0.7
6	SU	0434	7.2	1048	0.7	1651	7.5	● 2314	0.4
7	M	0516	7.5	1133	0.5	1734	7.7	2358	0.4
8	TU	0557	7.5	1217	0.4	1816	7.6		
9	W	0043	0.5	0638	7.4	1300	0.7	1858	7.3
10	TH	0126	0.9	0720	7.0	1345	1.1	1940	6.8
11	F	0210	1.5	0803	6.5	1432	1.6	2027	6.2
12	SA	0258	2.1	0854	6.0	1526	2.2	2123	5.6
13	SU	0355	2.6	0959	5.5	1630	2.6	2239	5.1
14	M	0509	3.0	1125	5.3	1753	2.8		
15	TU	0025	5.0	0641	3.0	1257	5.4	1922	2.7
16	W	0147	5.3	0758	2.7	1404	5.7	2025	2.3
17	TH	0238	5.7	0850	2.3	1452	6.0	2111	2.0
18	F	0318	6.0	0932	2.0	1531	6.3	2150	1.7
19	SA	0352	6.3	1008	1.7	1605	6.5	2224	1.5
20	SU	0423	6.5	1041	1.5	1636	6.7	2255	1.4
21	M	0451	6.6	1111	1.5	1706	6.7	○ 2324	1.4
22	TU	0519	6.7	1141	1.5	1735	6.7	2353	1.4
23	W	0547	6.7	1210	1.5	1803	6.6		
24	TH	0022	1.6	0615	6.6	1240	1.7	1832	6.5
25	F	0052	1.8	0644	6.4	1311	1.9	1903	6.2
26	SA	0124	2.0	0716	6.2	1346	2.1	1938	5.9
27	SU	0202	2.3	0754	5.8	1429	2.4	2022	5.5
28	M	0250	2.6	0845	5.5	1523	2.7	2125	5.2
29	TU	0351	2.9	0959	5.3	1634	2.9	2254	5.0
30	W	0513	3.0	1132	5.3	1804	2.8		
31	TH	0033	5.3	0642	2.7	1257	5.6	1925	2.3

NOVEMBER

Date	Day	Time	m	Time	m	Time	m	Time	m
1	F	0142	5.8	0752	2.2	1400	6.2	2025	1.8
2	SA	0236	6.4	0848	1.6	1453	6.7	2116	1.2
3	SU	0324	6.9	0938	1.1	1541	7.2	2204	0.8
4	M	0409	7.2	1025	0.8	1627	7.4	● 2249	0.6
5	TU	0452	7.4	1111	0.6	1712	7.5	2334	0.6
6	W	0534	7.5	1156	0.6	1755	7.4		
7	TH	0020	0.8	0617	7.3	1241	0.8	1838	7.1
8	F	0104	1.2	0659	7.0	1326	1.2	1922	6.6
9	SA	0148	1.7	0744	6.5	1414	1.7	2009	6.1
10	SU	0236	2.2	0834	6.0	1505	2.2	2103	5.6
11	M	0331	2.6	0935	5.6	1605	2.6	2211	5.2
12	TU	0438	2.9	1049	5.3	1717	2.8	2334	5.0
13	W	0557	3.0	1210	5.3	1836	2.7		
14	TH	0059	5.2	0713	2.8	1319	5.5	1941	2.5
15	F	0156	5.5	0810	2.5	1411	5.8	2031	2.2
16	SA	0239	5.8	0855	2.2	1453	6.1	2112	2.0
17	SU	0316	6.1	0933	2.0	1530	6.3	2148	1.8
18	M	0349	6.3	1008	1.8	1604	6.4	2222	1.6
19	TU	0421	6.5	1042	1.6	1637	6.5	2254	1.6
20	W	0452	6.6	1114	1.6	1709	6.6	○ 2326	1.6
21	TH	0523	6.6	1147	1.6	1741	6.5	2359	1.6
22	F	0554	6.6	1220	1.6	1814	6.4		
23	SA	0033	1.7	0627	6.5	1255	1.8	1850	6.2
24	SU	0109	1.9	0704	6.3	1334	2.0	1930	6.0
25	M	0151	2.2	0747	6.0	1419	2.2	2018	5.7
26	TU	0240	2.4	0840	5.8	1513	2.4	2118	5.4
27	W	0339	2.6	0945	5.6	1618	2.5	2232	5.3
28	TH	0450	2.7	1103	5.6	1734	2.5	2352	5.5
29	F	0608	2.5	1220	5.8	1848	2.2		
30	SA	0106	5.8	0718	2.2	1326	6.1	1952	1.8

DECEMBER

Date	Day	Time	m	Time	m	Time	m	Time	m
1	SU	0204	6.3	0818	1.7	1425	6.5	2048	1.4
2	M	0257	6.7	0913	1.3	1517	6.8	2139	1.1
3	TU	0345	7.0	1004	1.0	1607	7.1	2228	1.0
4	W	0432	7.2	1052	0.9	1654	7.1	● 2314	1.0
5	TH	0517	7.2	1139	0.9	1739	7.0	2359	1.1
6	F	0601	7.1	1225	1.0	1824	6.8		
7	SA	0046	1.4	0645	6.9	1311	1.3	1908	6.5
8	SU	0131	1.7	0729	6.6	1356	1.6	1952	6.1
9	M	0216	2.0	0815	6.2	1443	2.0	2040	5.7
10	TU	0304	2.4	0905	5.8	1533	2.3	2132	5.4
11	W	0357	2.7	1001	5.5	1628	2.6	2233	5.2
12	TH	0458	2.9	1105	5.4	1730	2.7	2342	5.1
13	F	0605	2.9	1212	5.3	1836	2.7		
14	SA	0051	5.2	0710	2.8	1314	5.4	1936	2.6
15	SU	0148	5.5	0806	2.6	1406	5.6	2027	2.4
16	M	0234	5.7	0853	2.3	1452	5.9	2110	2.1
17	TU	0315	6.0	0935	2.1	1533	6.1	2150	1.9
18	W	0352	6.2	1014	1.9	1611	6.3	2228	1.8
19	TH	0429	6.4	1052	1.7	1649	6.4	○ 2304	1.7
20	F	0505	6.5	1129	1.6	1726	6.4	2341	1.6
21	SA	0541	6.6	1207	1.5	1804	6.4		
22	SU	0021	1.6	0619	6.6	1246	1.5	1844	6.4
23	M	0101	1.7	0700	6.5	1328	1.6	1926	6.2
24	TU	0145	1.8	0745	6.4	1413	1.7	2013	6.1
25	W	0232	2.0	0833	6.2	1503	1.9	2106	5.9
26	TH	0325	2.1	0928	6.0	1559	2.1	2205	5.7
27	F	0424	2.3	1031	5.9	1702	2.2	2312	5.7
28	SA	0532	2.3	1140	5.8	1811	2.2		
29	SU	0025	5.8	0642	2.2	1251	5.9	1919	2.0
30	M	0132	6.0	0750	2.0	1358	6.1	2022	1.8
31	TU	0233	6.3	0852	1.7	1459	6.3	2120	1.6

Chart Datum: 3·64 metres below IGN Datum

CAMARET *9.16.28*

Finistere **48°16'·80N 04°35'·19W**

CHARTS AC 3427, ; SHOM 7401, 7148, 7149; Imray C36; ECM 540, 542; Stanfords 17

TIDES +0500 Dover; ML 3·8; Duration 0610; Zone –0100

Standard Port BREST (⟵)

Times				Height (metres)			
High Water		Low Water		MHWS	MHWN	MLWN	MLWS
0000	0600	0000	0600	6·9	5·4	2·6	1·0
1200	1800	1200	1800				
Differences CAMARET							
–0010	–0010	–0013	–0013	–0·3	–0·3	–0·1	0·0

SHELTER Good, except in strong winds. Plaisance La Pointe (5m) is mainly for visitors with 80 Ⓥ, but Styvel also has visitors berths for smaller craft and is nearer town.

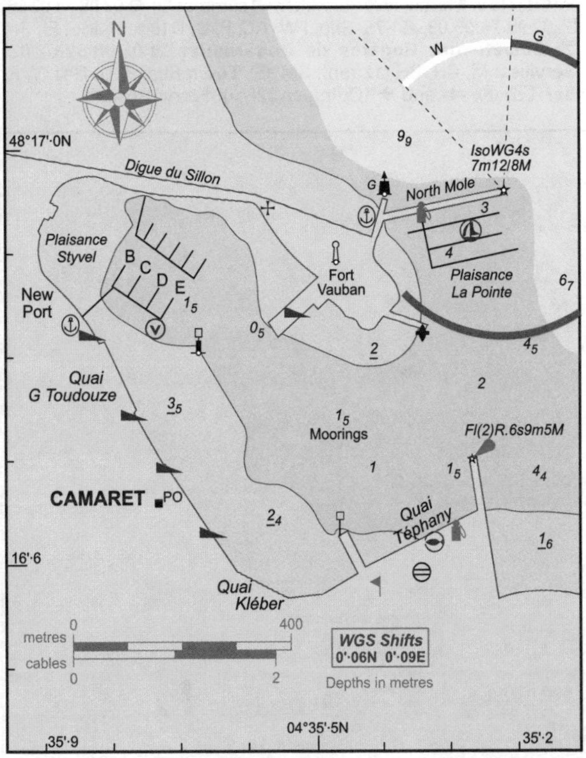

NAVIGATION WPT 48°18'·00N 04°36'·00W, 335°/155° from/to N mole lt, 1·2M. Beware rks W of Pte du Grand Gouin. ⚓ in hbr prohib.

LIGHTS AND MARKS Lt ho at E end of N mole, Iso WG 4s, W135°-182°, G182°-027°; appr in W sector. The G SHM bn tr at the W end of the N mole is very conspic; also Tour Vauban and chapel close SW.

RADIO TELEPHONE VHF Ch 09.

TELEPHONE Hr Mr 02·98·27·81·31; Aff Mar 02·98·27·93·28; CROSS 02·98·89·31·31; ⊖ 02·98·27·93·02; Auto 08·36.68·08·29; Police 02·98·27·00·22; Dr 02·98·57·91·35; Brit Consul 01·40·63·16·02.

FACILITIES **Plaisance La Pointe** (100+80 visitors) ☎ 02·98·27·95·99, €1·38, FW, AC, C (8 ton), D, Access H24; **Plaisance 'Styvel'** (200+50 visitors), ☎ 02·98·27·89·31, 📠 02·98·27.96.45, FW, AC, ♿, Access H24, dredged 1·5m; **Services:** M, ME, El, Ⓔ, Sh, CH, P, C (5 ton), SM, SHOM. **Town** P, V, Gaz, R, Bar, ✉, Ⓑ, ⇌ (Brest), ✈ (Brest or Quimper). Ferry: Roscoff.

MORGAT *9.16.29*

Finistere **48°13'·62N 04°29'·69W**

CHARTS AC 2349; SHOM 7171, 7172; Imray C36; ECM 541, 542; Stanfords 17

TIDES +0500 Dover; ML 3·8; Duration No data; Zone –0100

Standard Port BREST (⟵)

Times				Height (metres)			
High Water		Low Water		MHWS	MHWN	MLWN	MLWS
0000	0600	0000	0600	6·9	5·4	2·6	1·0
1200	1800	1200	1800				
Differences MORGAT							
–0008	–0008	–0020	–0010	–0·4	–0·4	–0·2	0·0

SHELTER The port is exposed to winds from the W and N, but the marina is protected by floating concrete wavebreaks. There are pleasant day ⚓s between Morgat and Cap de la Chèvre in the bays of St Hernot, St Norgard & St Nicolas; sheltered from the W. Also 2·5M to E in lee of Is de l'Aber.

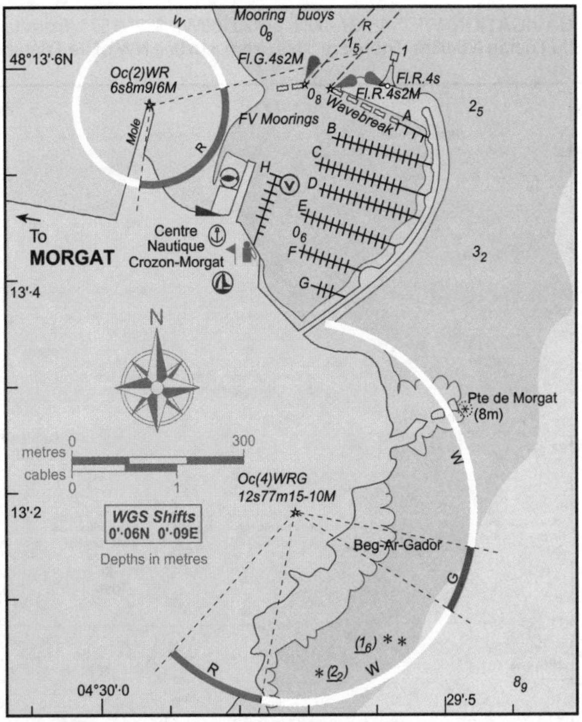

NAVIGATION WPT 48°12'·00N 04°28'·00W, 147°/327° from/to E bkwtr hd, 1·9M. There are rks close under the cliffs S of Pte de Morgat, and Les Verres 2M ESE of ent. Ent chan, dredged 1·5m, is marked by PHM buoy Fl R 4s, close SE of which is depth of 1m. Fl R/G 4s lts are at end of wavebreaks.

LIGHTS AND MARKS Pte de Morgat lt, Oc (4) WRG 12s 77m 15/10M, is 4ca S of hbr; G sector covers Les Verres. Appr in W sector, 007°-257°, of inner Mole lt, Oc (2) WR 6s 8m 9/6M.

RADIO TELEPHONE Marina VHF Ch 09.

TELEPHONE Hr Mr 02·98·27·01·97; Aff Mar 02·98·27·09·95; CROSS 02·98·89·31·31; Auto 08·36.68·08·29; SNSM 02·98·10·51·41; ⊖ 02·98·27·93·02; Police 02·98·27·00·22; Ⓗ 02·98·27·05·33; Brit Consul 01·40·63·16·02.

FACILITIES **Marina** (550+32 Ⓥ), ☎ 02·98·27·01·97, 📠 02·98·27.19.76, €1·37, AC, FW, C (8 ton), Slip, CH, D, P, ME, ♿, Access H24; **YC du Crozon-Morgat** ☎ 98·27·01·98; **Services:** M, C (6 ton), El, Sh, Ⓔ. **Town** (Crozon), V, Gaz, R, Bar, ✉, Ⓑ, ⇌, ✈ (Brest or Quimper). Ferry: Roscoff.

DOUARNENEZ *9.16.30*

Finistere **48°06'·17N 04°20'·32W**

CHARTS AC 2349; SHOM 7171; Imray C36; ECM 542; Stnfrds 17

TIDES +0500 Dover; ML 3·7; Duration 0615; Zone –0100

Standard Port BREST (⟵)

Times				Height (metres)			
High Water		Low Water		MHWS	MHWN	MLWN	MLWS
0000	0600	0000	0600	6·9	5·4	2·6	1·0
1200	1800	1200	1800				
Differences DOUARNENEZ							
–0010	–0015	–0018	–0008	–0·5	–0·5	–0·3	–0·1

SHELTER Very good; access H24, all weathers and tides to visitors' berths in the marina (1·5m) at Tréboul, or in the river outside (subject to wash from passing traffic). About 2ca S of the marina the river has been dammed to form a non-tidal basin (3·2m), Port Rhu, as a museum for classic craft; limited access via a sill usually open. The Fishing hbr is prohib to yachts and Port du Rosmeur is full of moorings.

NAVIGATION WPT 48°07'·00N 04°20'·68W, 337°/157° from/to Ile Tristan lt 0·88m. There are 3 rks, from 3 to 9ca NW of Ile Tristan lt (in R sector), Basse Veur, Petite Basse Neuve and Basse Neuve, least depth 1·8m also a rocky ledge La Tête de Pierre, 3ca NW of Le Poulain which should be given a wide berth.

LIGHTS AND MARKS Approx 5M to W is Pte du Milier lt, Oc (2) WRG 6s 34m 16/11M, G080°-087°, W087°-113°, R113°-120°, W120°-129°, G129°-148°, W148°-251°, R 251°-258°. Ile Tristan Oc (3) WR 12s 33m 13/10M, vis R138°-153°, W elsewhere; R sector covers Basse Veur and Basse Neuve, least depth 1·8m. On the high road bridge at S end of Port Rhu, Dir lt 157°, Fl (5) WRG 20s 16m 5/4M, covers the Grande Passe and river; vis G154°-156°, W156°-158°, R158°-160°. Port Rhu lock ent is marked by a Fl R 5s and a Fl G 5s.

RADIO TELEPHONE Marina VHF Ch 09 (0700-1200 and 1330-2100LT in season; out of season 0830-1200, 1330-1730LT). Port Ch 12 16.

TELEPHONE Hr Mr (Plaisance) 02·98·74·02·56; Aff Mar 02·98·75·31·30; CROSS 02·98·89·31·31; SNSM 02·98·89·63·16; ⊜ 02·98·52·87·40; Météo 02·98·84·60·64; Auto 08·36.68·08·29; Police 02·98·92·01·22; Ⓗ 02·98·92·25·00; Brit Consul 01·40·63·16·02.

FACILITIES Marina (390+10 winter, 60 summer Ⓥ) ☎ 02·98·74·02·56, 📠 02·98·74.05.08, €1·75, Slip, FW, AC, P, D, C (6 ton), ME, El, Sh, ⊡; **Société des Regates de Douarnenez** ☎ 02·98·92·02·03; **Services:** M, CH, BH (12 ton), SM, Ⓔ. **Town** Slip, P, D, Gaz, V, R, Bar, ✉, Ⓑ, ⇌ and ✈ (Quimper 22km). Ferry: Roscoff.

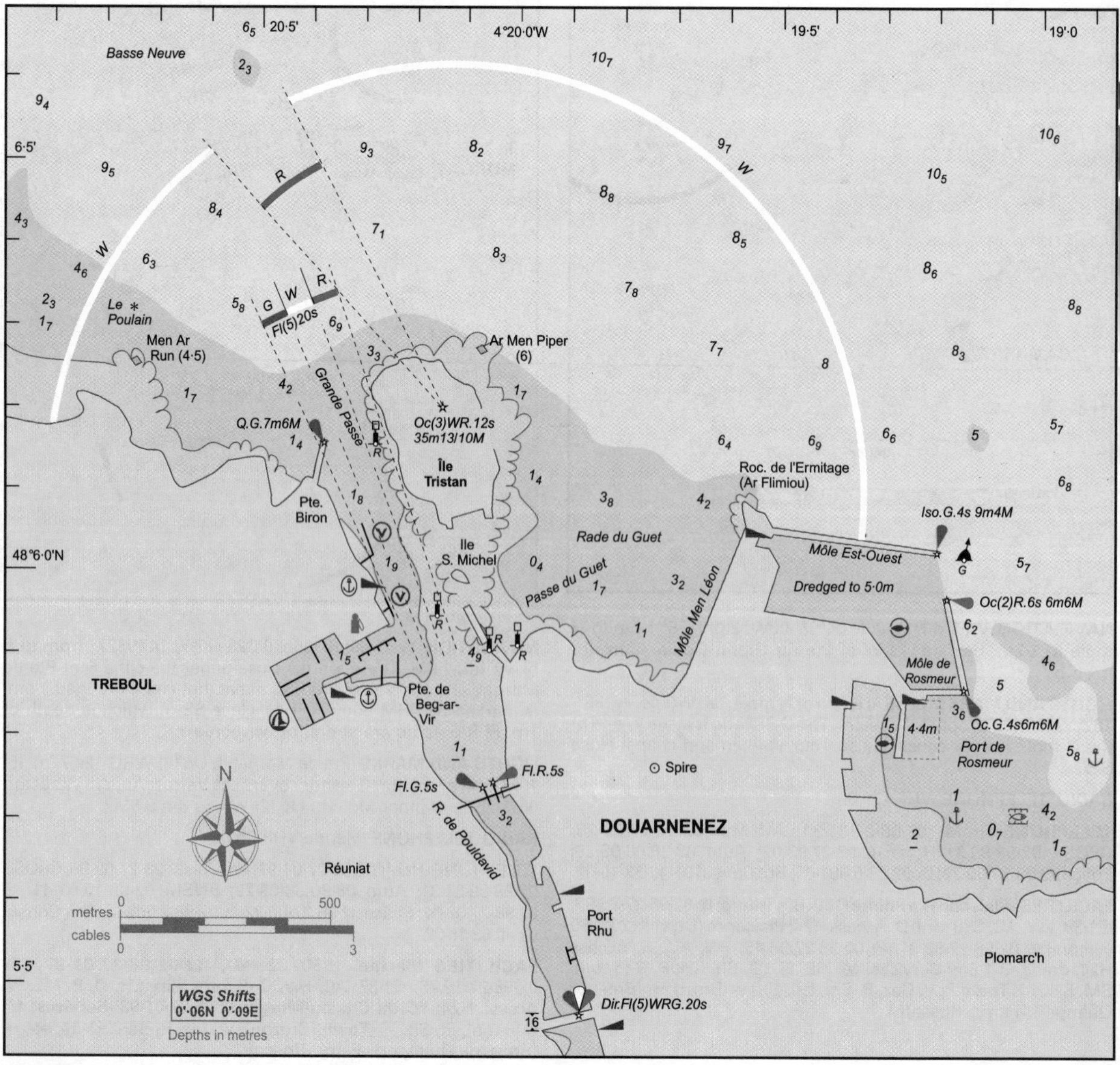

MAPTECH®
Leading the world in digital navigation
Maptech UK Ltd • +44 (0)1243 389352 • sales@maptech.co.uk

Maptech world class digital chart CDs
Worldwide coverage from over 4,500 charts

Maptech award winning software
Easy to use navigation software
• Chart Navigator • Cruising Navigator • Offshore Navigator

www.maptech.co.uk

Area 17

South Brittany
Raz de Sein to River Loire

9.17.1 Index .... Page 799

9.17.2 Area map 800

9.17.3 Tidal stream charts 802

9.17.4 Lights, buoys & waypoints 804

9.17.5 Passage information 810

9.17.6 Distance table 811

9.17.7 Special notes for France See *9.15.7*

9.17.8 Audierne 812
Ile de Sein
St Guénolé
Le Guilvinec
Lesconil

9.17.9 Loctudy 813

9.17.10 Bénodet 813

9.17.11 Port-la-Forêt 814

9.17.12 Concarneau 815
Iles de Glénan
Aven and Bélon Rivers
Brigneau
Merrien
Doëlan
Le Pouldu

9.17.13 Port Tudy (Ile de Groix) 816
Loc Maria

9.17.14 Lorient 817

9.17.15 River Etel 818

9.17.16 Le Palais (Belle Ile) 819
Sauzon

9.17.17 Port Haliguen 819
Port Maria

9.17.18 La Trinité-sur-Mer 820

9.17.19 Crouesty 820
Ile Houat

9.17.20 Golfe du Morbihan 821

9.17.21 Vannes 823

9.17.22 Vilaine River 824
Penerf

9.17.23 Piriac 825
Ile Dumet

9.17.24 La Turballe 825

9.17.25 Le Croisic 826

9.17.26 Le Pouliguen 826

9.17.27 Pornichet 827

9.17.28 River Loire and St Nazaire 828
Port de Comberge
Port de la Gravette
Saint-Gildas

Register for your FREE weekly weather email service from Macmillan Reeds
at www.nauticaldata.com – NOW!
weekend weather reports sent to your email address, every Thursday

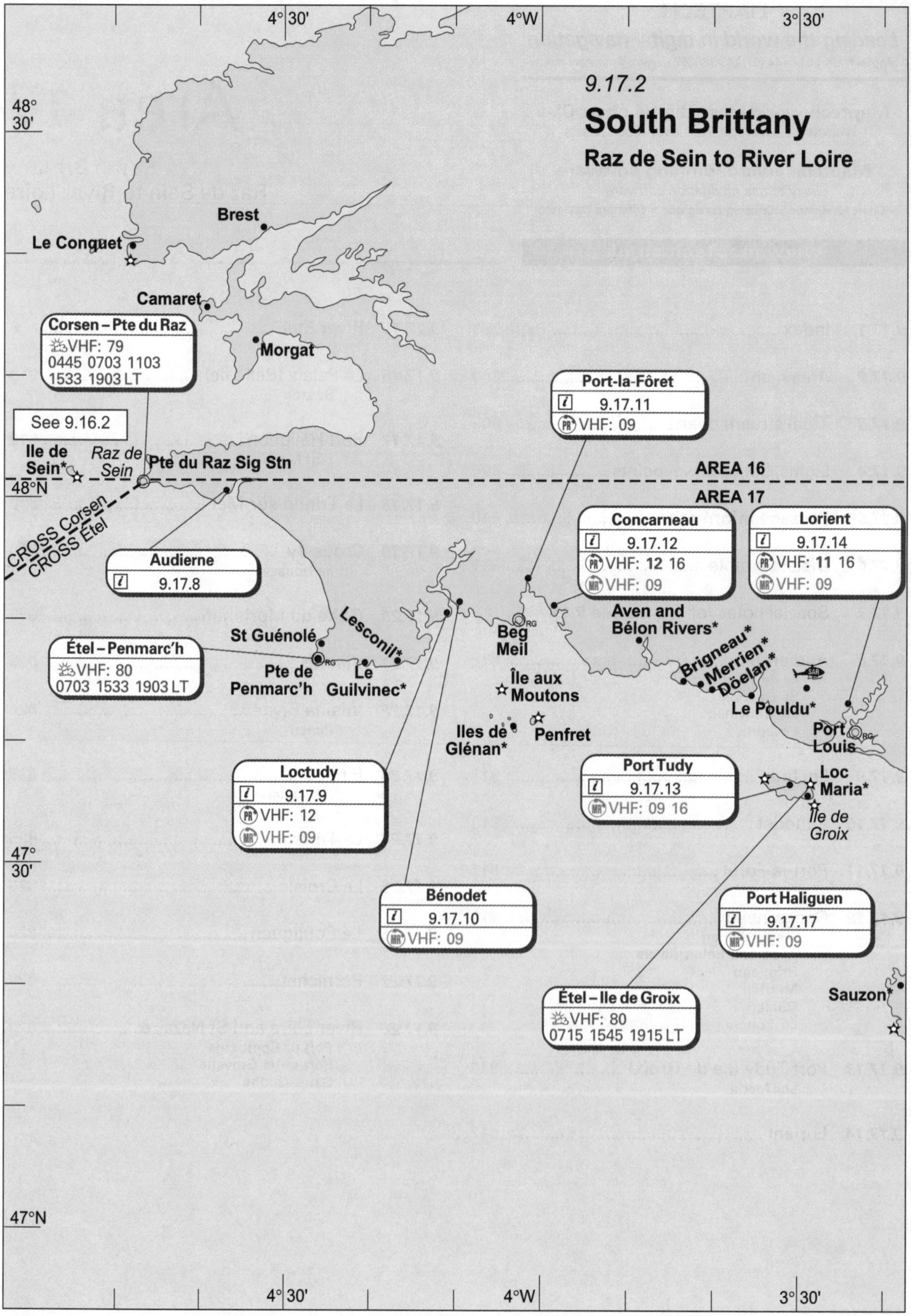
9.17.2
South Brittany
Raz de Sein to River Loire
4° 30'
4°W
3° 30'
48° 30'
48°N
47° 30'
47°N
Brest
Le Conquet
Camaret
Morgat
Corsen – Pte du Raz
VHF: 79
0445 0703 1103
1533 1903 LT
See 9.16.2
Ile de Sein*
Raz de Sein
Pte du Raz Sig Stn
CROSS Corsen
CROSS Étel
AREA 16
AREA 17
Port-la-Fôret
9.17.11
VHF: 09
Audierne
9.17.8
Concarneau
9.17.12
VHF: 12 16
VHF: 09
Lorient
9.17.14
VHF: 11 16
VHF: 09
Lesconil*
St Guénolé
Étel – Penmarc'h
VHF: 80
0703 1533 1903 LT
Pte de Penmarc'h
Le Guilvinec*
Beg Meil
Aven and Bélon Rivers*
Brigneau*
Merrien*
Döelan*
Le Pouldu*
Île aux Moutons
Iles de Glénan*
Penfret
Port Louis
Port Tudy
9.17.13
VHF: 09 16
Loc Maria*
Île de Groix
Loctudy
9.17.9
VHF: 12
VHF: 09
Bénodet
9.17.10
VHF: 09
Port Haliguen
9.17.17
VHF: 09
Étel – Ile de Groix
VHF: 80
0715 1545 1915 LT
Sauzon*

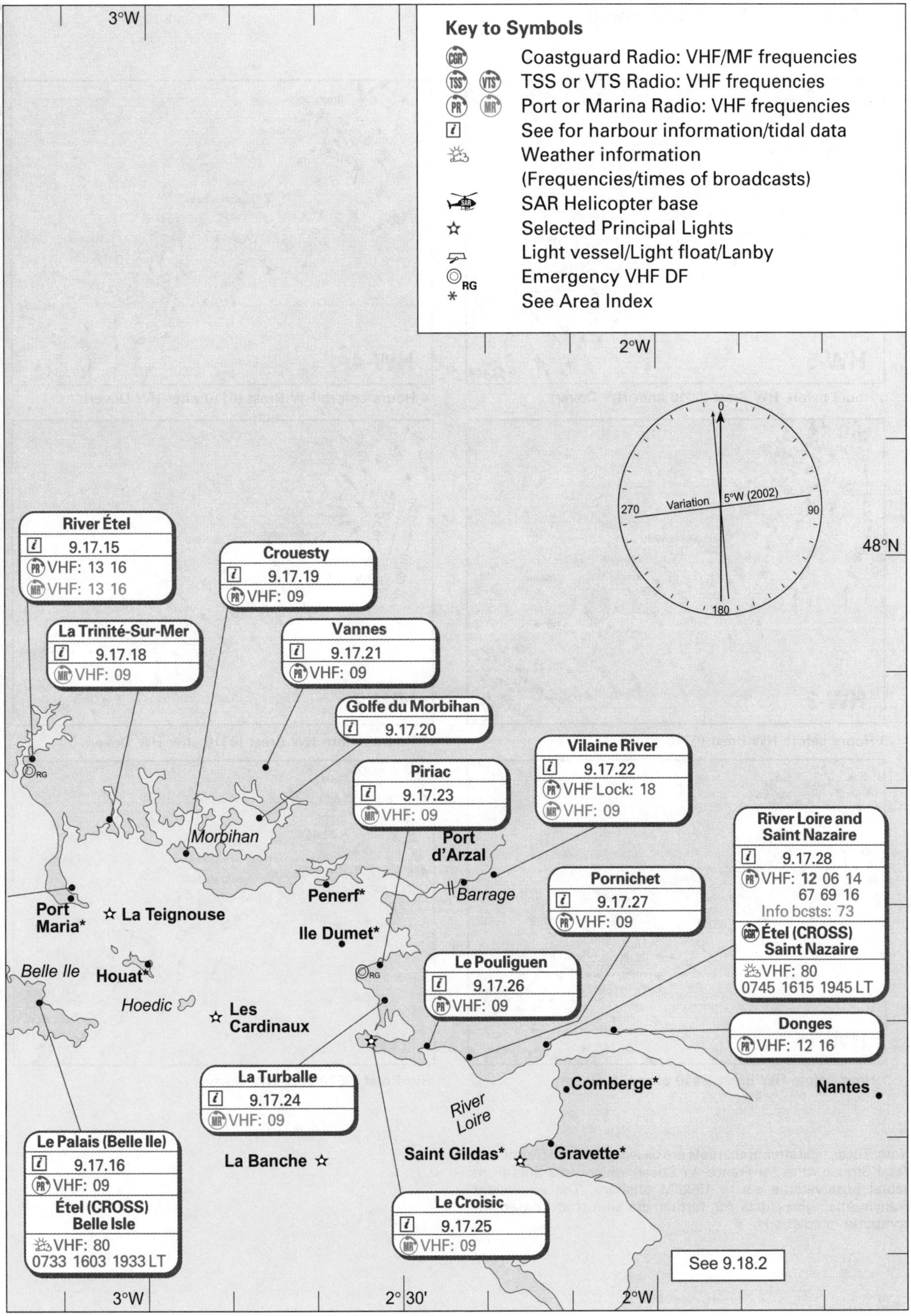
3°W
Key to Symbols
CGR Coastguard Radio: VHF/MF frequencies
TSS VTS TSS or VTS Radio: VHF frequencies
PR MR Port or Marina Radio: VHF frequencies
i See for harbour information/tidal data
Weather information (Frequencies/times of broadcasts)
SAR Helicopter base
☆ Selected Principal Lights
Light vessel/Light float/Lanby
RG Emergency VHF DF
* See Area Index
2°W
0
270
Variation 5°W (2002)
90
180
48°N
River Étel
i 9.17.15
PR VHF: 13 16
MR VHF: 13 16
Crouesty
i 9.17.19
PR VHF: 09
La Trinité-Sur-Mer
i 9.17.18
MR VHF: 09
Vannes
i 9.17.21
PR VHF: 09
Golfe du Morbihan
i 9.17.20
Vilaine River
i 9.17.22
PR VHF Lock: 18
MR VHF: 09
Piriac
i 9.17.23
MR VHF: 09
River Loire and Saint Nazaire
i 9.17.28
PR VHF: 12 06 14 67 69 16
Info bcsts: 73
CGR Étel (CROSS) Saint Nazaire
VHF: 80
0745 1615 1945 LT
Pornichet
i 9.17.27
PR VHF: 09
Morbihan
Port d'Arzal
Barrage
Penerf*
Port Maria*
☆ La Teignouse
Ile Dumet*
Belle Ile
Houat*
Hoedic
☆ Les Cardinaux
RG
Le Pouliguen
i 9.17.26
PR VHF: 09
Donges
PR VHF: 12 16
Comberge*
Nantes
River Loire
La Turballe
i 9.17.24
MR VHF: 09
Saint Gildas* ☆
Gravette*
La Banche ☆
Le Palais (Belle Ile)
i 9.17.16
PR VHF: 09
Étel (CROSS) Belle Isle
VHF: 80
0733 1603 1933 LT
Le Croisic
i 9.17.25
MR VHF: 09
See 9.18.2
3°W
2° 30'
2°W

9.17.3 AREA 17 TIDAL STREAMS

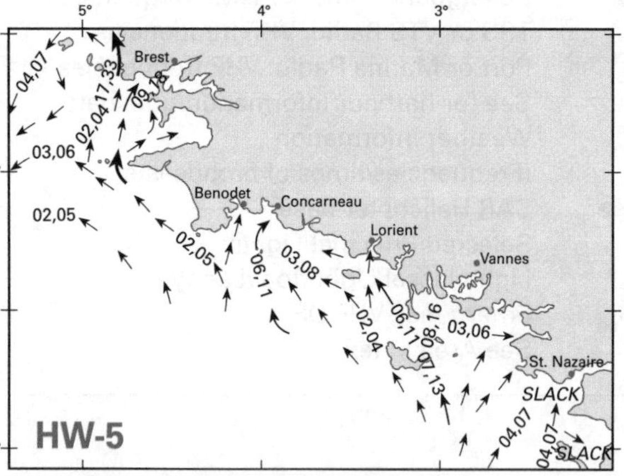

5 Hours before HW Brest (0010 after HW Dover)

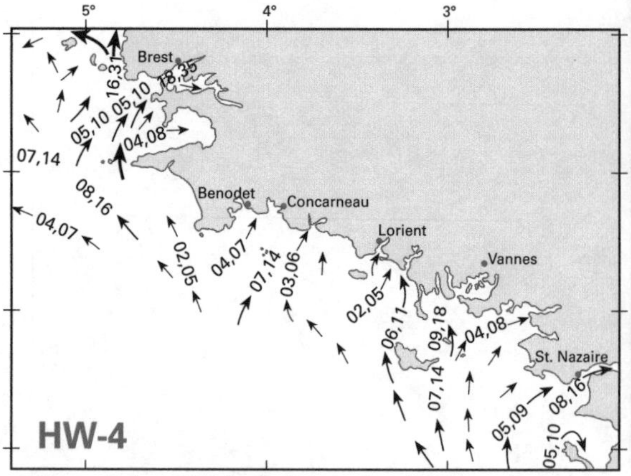

4 Hours before HW Brest (0110 after HW Dover)

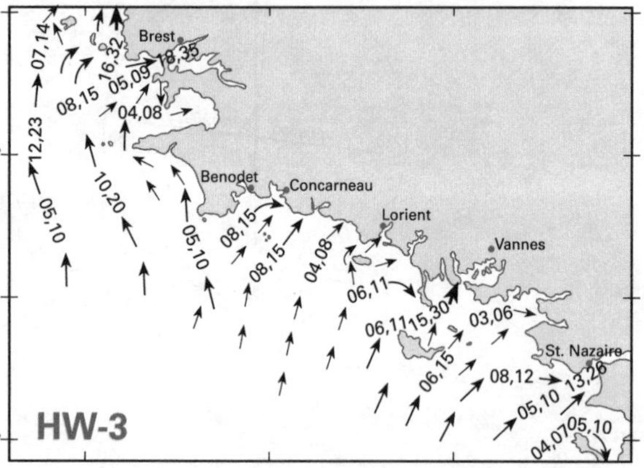

3 Hours before HW Brest (0210 after HW Dover)

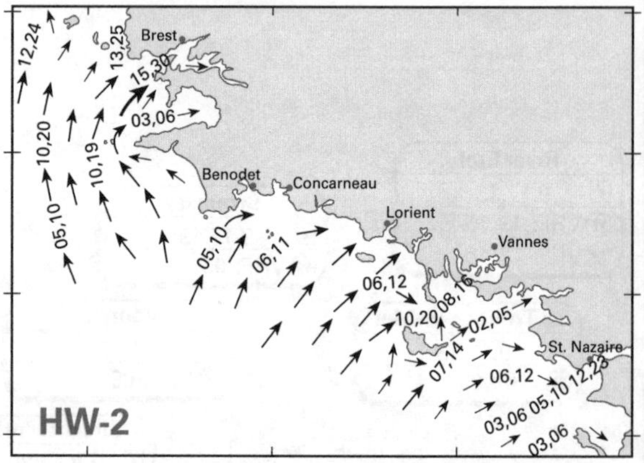

2 Hours before HW Brest (0310 after HW Dover)

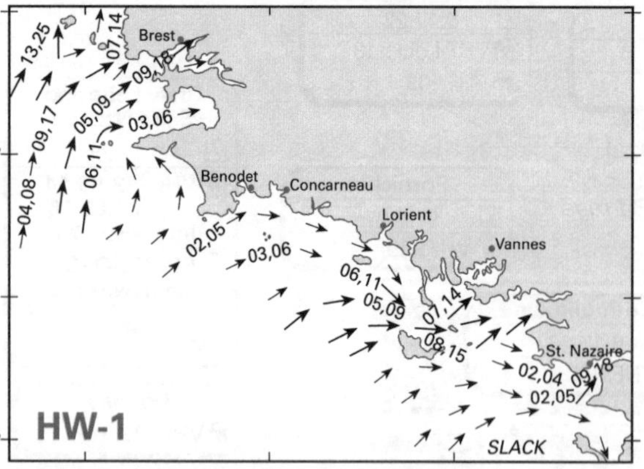

1 Hour before HW Brest (0410 after HW Dover)

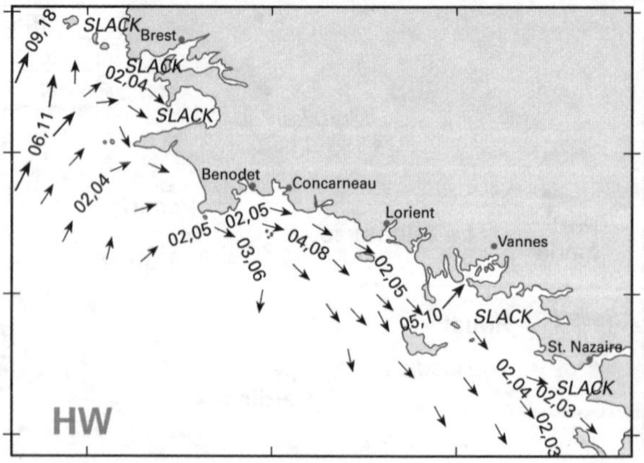

HW Brest (0510 after HW Dover)

Note: These tidal stream chartlets are based on NP 265 (Admiralty Tidal Stream Atlas for France, W Coast) which uses data from actual observations out to 15-25M offshore. The equivalent French Atlas gives data for further offshore, but based on computer predictions.

Northward 9.16.3 Souhward 9.18.3

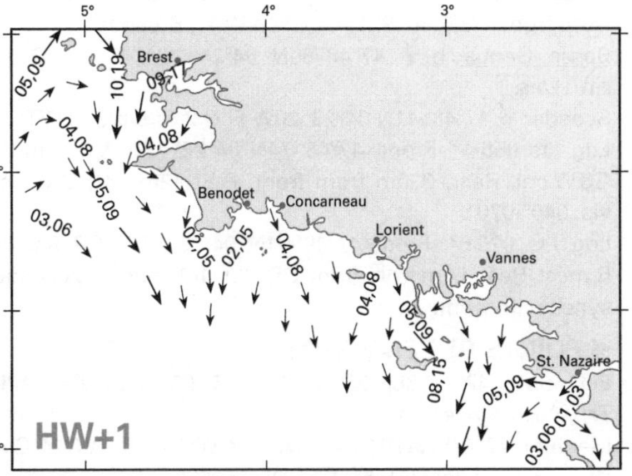

1 Hour after HW Brest (0610 after HW Dover)

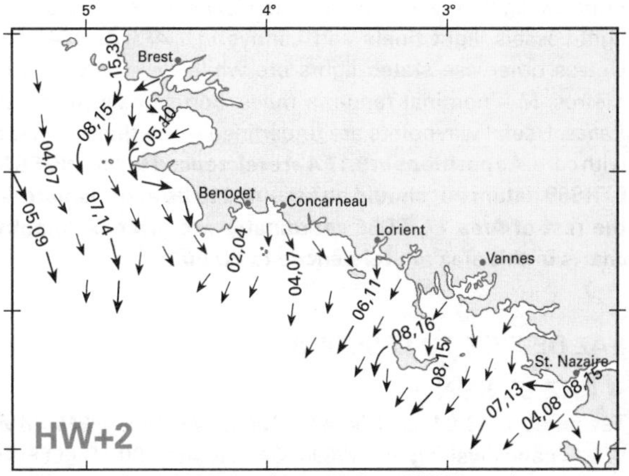

2 Hours after HW Brest (0515 before HW Dover)

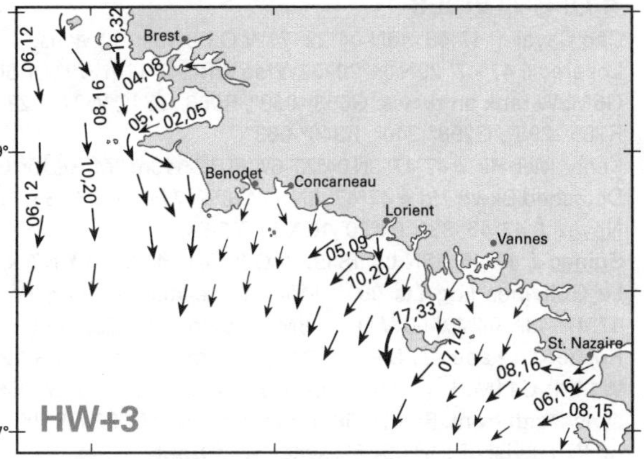

3 Hours after HW Brest (0415 before HW Dover)

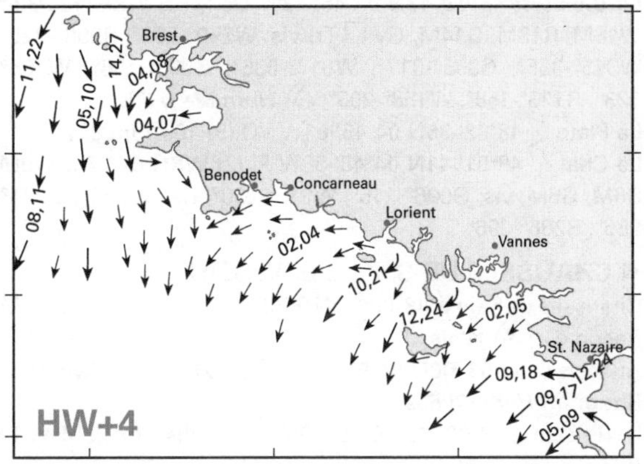

4 Hours after HW Brest (0315 before HW Dover)

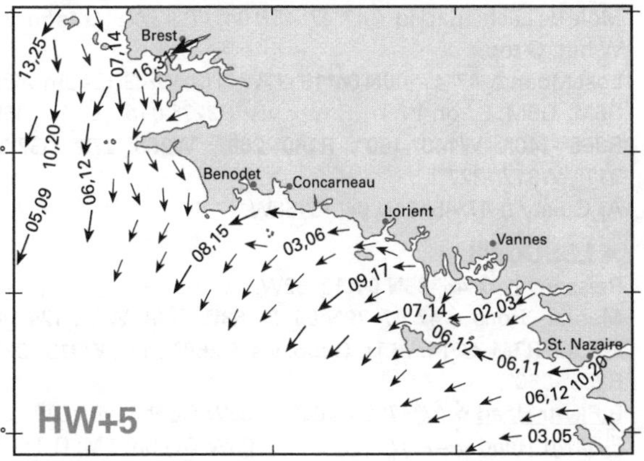

5 Hours after HW Brest (0215 before HW Dover)

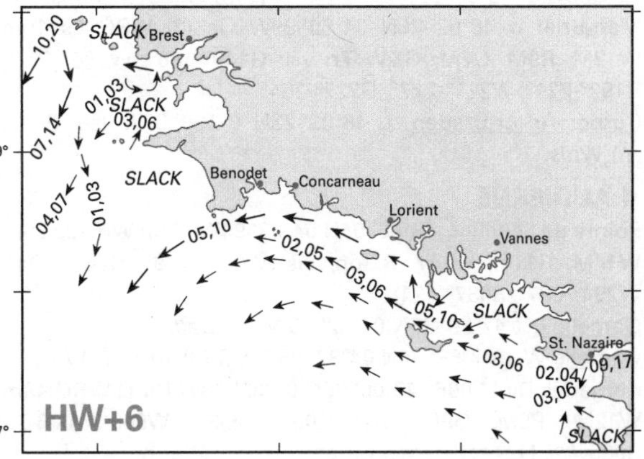

6 Hours after HW Brest (0115 before HW Dover)

Note: These tidal stream chartlets are based on NP 265 (Admiralty Tidal Stream Atlas for France, W Coast) which uses data from actual observations out to 15-25M offshore. The equivalent French Atlas gives data for further offshore, but based on computer predictions.

9.17.4 LIGHTS, BUOYS AND WAYPOINTS

Abbreviations used below are given in the Introduction. Principal lights ☆ are in **bold** print, places in CAPITALS, and light-vessels, light floats and Lanbys in *CAPITAL ITALICS*. Unless otherwise stated lights are white. m – elevation in metres; M – nominal range in miles. Fog signals are in *italics*. Useful waypoints are underlined – use those on land with care. **All positions in 9.17.4 are referenced to the WGS84/ ETRS89 datum but should be assumed to be approximate. In the rest of Area 17, ED50 coordinates are given. Admiralty charts in this area are referenced to ED 50.**

RAZ DE SEIN TO LESCONIL

◄ RAZ DE SEIN

Tévennec ☆ 48°04'·28N 04°47'·76W Q WR 28m W9M R6M; W □ Tr and dwelling; vis: W090°-345°, R345°-090°; Dir Lt Fl 4s 24m 12M; same Tr; intens 324°-332°.

La Vieille ☆ 48°02'·43N 04°45'·43W Oc (2+1) WRG 12s 33m **W18M**, R13M, G14M; Gy □ Tr; vis: W290°-298°, R298°-325°, W325°-355°, G355°-017°, W017°-035°, G035°-105°, W105°-123°, R123°-158°, W158°-205°; *Horn (2+1) 60s.*

La Plate 48°02'·35N 04°45'·61W VQ (9) 10s 19m 8M.

Le Chat 48°01'·41N 04°48'·88W Fl (2) WRG 6s 27m W9M, R6M, G6M; vis: G096°-215°, W215°-230°, R230°-271°, G271°-286°, R286°-096°.

◄ CHAUSSÉE DE SEIN/ÎLE DE SEIN

Chaussée de Sein 48°03'·75N 05°07'·79W VQ (9) 10s 9m 6M; Racon (O); *Whis.*

Ar-Men ☆ 48°03'·00N 04°59'·92W Fl (3) 20s 29m **23M**; W Tr, B top; *Horn (3) 60s.*

Île de Sein ☆ 48°02'·63N 04°52'·06W Fl (4) 25s 49m **29M**; W Tr, B top.

Ar Guéveur 48°01'·92N 04°51'·42W 20m; W Tr; *Whis.*

Men-Brial ☆ 48°02'·26N 04°50'·99W Oc (2) WRG 6s 16m W12M, R9M, G7M; G&W Tr; vis: G149°-186°, W186°-192°, R192°-221°, W221°-227°, G227°-254°.

Cornoc-An-Ar-Braden 48°03'·23N 04°50'·87W Iso G 4s; *Whis.*

◄ AUDIERNE

Pointe de Lervily ☆ 48°00'·04N 04°33'·94W Fl (3) WR 12s 20m W14M, R11M; W Tr, R top; vis: W211°-269°, R269°-294°, W294°-087°, R087°-121°.

Gamelle E 47°59'·45N 04°32'·05W; *Bell.*

Gamelle W 47°59'·46N 04°32'·85W VQ (9) 10s; *Whis.*

Kergadec Dir Lt 006° 48°00'·95N 04°32'·78W Dir Q WRG 43m W12M, R9M, G9M; vis: G000°-005·3°, W005·3°-006·7°, R006·7°-017°.

Jetée de Sainte-Évette ☆ 48°00'·31N 04°33'·07W Oc (2) R 6s 2m 7M; R lantern; vis: 090°-270°.

Passe de l'Est Ldg Lts 331°. Front, Jetée de Raoulic 48°00'·54N 04°32'·45W Fl (3) WG 12s 11m W14M, G9M; W ○ Tr; vis: Wshore-034°, G034°-shore, but may show W037°-055°. Rear, Kergadec, 0·5M from front, Dir FR 44m 9M; W 8-sided Tr, R top; intens 321°-341°.

◄ PORS POULHAM

W side of ent ☆ 47°59'·09N 04°27'·89W QR 14m 9M.

◄ SAINT GUÉNOLÉ

Chenal de Groumilli Ldg Lts 123°. Front, 47°48'·12N 04°22'·70W FG 9m 9M; Or ○ on W Tr, B bands. Rear, 300m from front, FG 13m 9M ; Or ○ on W Tr, B bands.

Basse Gaouac'h 47°48'·60N 04°24'·25W Fl (3) G 12s; *Whis.*

Scoedec ☆ 47°48'·41N 04°23'·20W Fl G 2·5s 6m 3M; G Tr.

Ldg Lts 055·4°. Front, 47°48'·74N 04°22'·72W VQ 5m 2M; G&W col. Rear, 320m from front, F Vi 12m 1M; G&W col; vis: 040°-070°.

Ldg Lts 026·5°. Front 47°49'·01N 04°22'·71W QR 8m 4M; R mast. Rear, 51m from front, QR 12m 4M; mast, R&W bands; synch with front.

◄ POINTE DE PENMARC'H

Eckmühl ☆ 47°47'·88N 04°22'·39W Fl 5s 60m **23M**; Gy 8-sided Tr; *Horn 60s.*

Menhir ☆ 47°47'·73N 04°24'·03W Fl (2) WG 6s 19m W7M, G4M; W Tr, B band; vis: G135°-315°, W315°-135°.

◄ LE GUILVINEC

Cap Caval 47°46'·46N 04°22'·71W Q (9) 15s; *Whis.*

Locarec ☆ 47°47'·29N 04°20'·33W Iso WRG 4s 11m W9M, R6M, G6M; W tank on rk; vis: G063°-068°, R068°-271°, W271°-285°, R285°-298°, G298°-340°, R340°-063°.

Kérity. Men Hir ☆ 47°47'·3N 04°20'·6W Fl R 2·5s 6m 2M; R □ on Bn.

Detached Bkwtr Hd ☆ 47°47'·6N 04°20'·9W Fl (2) G 6s 5m 1M.

Névez 47°45'·83N 04°20'·10W Fl G 2·5s.

Spinec 47°45'·18N 04°18'·92W Q (6) + L Fl 15s; *Whis.*

Le Guilvinec Ldg Lts 053°. Môle de Léchiagat, spur, Front 47°47'·43N 04°17'·08W Q 7m 8M; W pylon; vis: 233°-066°.

Rocher Le Faoutés, Middle, 210m from front, Q WG 12m W14M, G11M; R □ on R col; vis: W006°-293°, G293°-006°; synch with front. Rear, 0·58M from front, Dir Q 26m 8M; R □ on W Tr; vis: 051·5°-054·5°; synch with front.

Capelan 47°47'·14N 04°17'·55W Fl (2) G 6s.

Môle de Léchiagat Hd ☆ 47°47'·45N 04°17'·17W Fl G 4s 5m 7M; W hut, G top.

Lost Moan 47°47'·00N 04°16'·77W Fl (3) WRG 12s 8m W9M, R6M, G6M; □ on W Tr, R top; vis: R327°-014°, G014°-065°, R065°-140°, W140°-160°, R160°-268°, W268°-273°, G273°-317°, W317°-327°.

Ar Guisty 47°45'·61N 04°15'·58W.

◄ LESCONIL

Reissant 47°46'·38N 04°13'·52W.

Men-ar-Groas ☆ 47°47'·79N 04°12'·68W Fl (3) WRG 12s 14m W10M, R7M, G7M; W Tr, G top; vis: G268°-313°, W313°-333°, R333°-050°.

S Bkwtr Head ☆ 47°47'·68N 04°12'·65W Oc R 4s 5m 6M

E Bkwtr Head ☆ 47°47'·70N 04°12'·65W QG 5m 5M; G Tr.

Karek Greis 47°46'·04N 04°11'·40W Q (3) 10s; *Whis.*

LOCTUDY TO CONCARNEAU

◄ LOCTUDY

Rostolou 47°46'·65N 04°07'·33W.

Roc'h Hélou 47°47'·12N 04°08'·12W.

Bas Boulanger 47°47'·36N 04°09'·16W VQ (6) + L Fl 10s.

Basse Malvic 47°48'·46N 04°06'·65W.

Bas du Chenal 47°48'·53N 04°07'·07W.

Bilien 47°49'·08N 04°08'·13W VQ (3) 5s; *Whis.*

Pointe de Langoz ☆, S side 47°49'·87N 04°09'·59W Fl (4) WRG 12s 12m **W15M**, R11M, G11M; W Tr, R top; vis: W115°-257°, G257°-284°, W284°-295°, R295°-318°, W318°-328°, R328°-025°.
Men Audierne 47°50'·31N 04°09'·06W.
Karek-Saoz 47°50'·02N 04°09'·38W Fl R 2·5s 3m 1M; R Tr.
47°50'·19N 04°09'·49W Fl (2) R 6s.
No. 1 47°50'·28N 04°09'·65W Fl (2) G 6s.
No. 3 47°50'·28N 04°09'·91W Fl (3) G 12s.
47°50'·17N 04°10'·37W Fl G.
Le Blas ☆ 47°50'·28N 04°10'·23W Fl (4) G 15s 5m 1M; G △ on truncated col.

◀ BENODET

Ldg Lts 345·5°. Front, **Pte du Coq** ☆ 47°52'·31N 04°06'·70W, Dir Oc (2+1) G 12s 11m **17M**; W ○ Tr, G stripe; intens 345°-347°. Common rear Pyramide, 336m from front, Oc (2+1) 12s 48m 11M; W Tr, G top; vis: 338°-016°, synch with front.
Ldg Lts 000·5°. Front, Pte de Combrit 47°51'·86N 04°06'·78W, Oc (3+1) WR 12s 19m W12M , R9M; W □ Tr, Gy corners; vis: W325°-017°, R017°-325°. Common rear, Pyramide, 0·63M from front.
Les Verrés 47°51'·55N 04°06'·14W.
La Rousse 47°51'·56N 04°06'·47W.
La Potée 47°51'·75N 04°06'·56W.
Le Four 47°51'·79N 04°06'·41W.
Pte du Toulgoët ☆ 47°52'·29N 04°06'·86W Fl R 2s 2m 1M.
Le Taro 47°50'·51N 04°04'·83W
La Vache 47°49'·54N 04°02'·62W.
La Voleuse 47°48'·76N 04°02'·49W Q (6) + L Fl 15s; *Whis.*
Men Vras 47°49'·66N 04°01'·58W.
Men Déhou 47°48'·11N 04°04'·71W.
Les Poulains 47°47'·69N 04°03'·48W.

◀ BEG-MEIL

Linuen 47°50'·65N 03°57'·76W.
Chaussée de Beg'Meil 47°50'·76N 03°57'·31W Q (3) 10s.
Laouen Pod 47°51'·23N 03°58'·00W.
Quay Hd ☆ 47°51'·66N 03°58'·94W Fl R 2s 6m 1M; R&W col.

◀ PORT-LA-FORÊT

Le Scoré 47°52'·75N 03°57'·56W.
Les Ormeaux 47°53'·27N 03°58'·34W.
Channel 47°53'·39N 03°58'·13W Fl G 2·5s.
Channel 47°53'·38N 03°58'·22W Fl R 2·5s.
Channel 47°53'·44N 03°58'·24W.
Channel 47°53'·48N 03°58'·20W.
Cap Coz Mole Head ☆ 47°53'·48N 03°58'·28W Fl (2) WRG 6s 5m W7M, R5M, G5M; Rshore-335°, G335°-340°, W340°-346°, R346°-shore.
Kerleven Mole Head ☆ 47°53'·60N 03°58'·37W Fl G 4s 8m 6M.
Port-la-Forêt Marina Bkwtr Head ☆ 47°53'·90N 03°58'·57W Iso G 4s 5m 1M.

◀ CONCARNEAU

47°51'·40N 03°55'·75W.
Le Cochon 47°51'·47N 03°55'·54W Fl (3) WRG 12s 5m W9M, R6M, G6M; G Tr; vis: G048°-205°, R205°-352°, W352°-048°.
Basse du Chenal 47°51'·52N 03°55'·68W QR.
La Medée 47°52'·06N 03°54'·80W Fl R 4s 4M.
Ldg Lts 028·5°. Front, La Croix 47°52'·15N 03°55'·08W Oc (3) 12s 14m 13M; R&W Tr; vis: 006·5°-093°. **Rear, Beuzec** ☆, 1·34M from front, Dir Q 87m **23M**; Belfry; intens 026·5°-030·5°.

Men Fall 47°51'·76N 03°55'·29W Fl G 4s.
Lanriec ☆ 47°52'·00N 03°54'·64W QG 13m 8M; vis: 063°-078°.
Marina Hd ☆ 47°52'·20N 03°54'·72W Fl (3) R 12s; R □ on post.
Kersos 47°51'·80N 03°54'·94W.

◀ BAIE DE POULDOHAN

Petit Taro 47°51'·10N 03°55'·29W.
Pouldohan ☆ 47°50'·97N 03°53'·70W Fl G 4s 7m 8M; W □ Tr, G top; vis: 053°-065°.
Roché Tudy 47°50'·52N 03°54'·49W.

ÎLES DE GLENAN

◀ ÎLES DE GLÉNAN/ÎLE AUX MOUTONS

Basse Pérennès 47°41'·06N 04°06'·17W Q (9) 15s 8m 5M; *Whis.*
Jument de Glénan 47°38'·75N 04°01'·43W Q (6) + L Fl 15s 10m 4M; *Whis.*
Penfret ☆ 47°43'·26N 03°57'·17W Fl R 5s 36m **21M**; W □ Tr, R top; auxiliary Lt Dir Q 34m 12M; same Tr; vis: 295°-315°.
Les Bluniers 47°43'·35N 04°03'·81W.
Broc'h 47°43'·16N 04°01'·40W.
La Pie 47°43'·75N 03°59'·75W; Fl (2) 6s 9m 3M.
Île de Bananec 47°43'·26N 03°59'·21W.
Rouge de Glénan 47°45'·48N 04°04'·00W VQ (9) 10s 8m 8M; *Whis.*
Île-aux-Moutons ☆ 47°46'·48N 04°01'·70W Oc (2) WRG 6s 18m **W15M**, R11M, G11M; W □ Tr and dwelling; vis: W035°-050°, G050°-063°, W063°-081°, R081°-141°, W141°-292°, R292°-035°; **auxiliary** ☆ Dir Oc (2) 6s 17m **24M**; same Tr; synch with main Lt, intens 278·5°-283·5°.
Grand Pourceaux 47°45'·97N 04°00'·84W Q.
Rochers Leuriou 47°45'·13N 03°59'·97W.
Jaune de Glénan 47°42'·54N 03°49'·87W Q (3) 10s; *Whis.*
Cor-Loch 47°42'·17N 03°52'·34W.
Basse an Ero 47°40'·40N 03°55'·49W.
Laoennou 47°39'·64N 03°54'·70W.

CONCARNEAU TO ÎLE DE GROIX

◀ TRÉVIGNON TO PORT MANECH

Les Soldats 47°47'·87N 03°53'·44W VQ (9) 10s.
Trévignon Mole Hd ☆ 47°47'·67N 03°51'·30W Fl G 4s 5m 8M.
Trévignon Bkwtr root ☆ 47°47'·59N 03°51'·34W Oc (3+1) WRG 12s 11m W14M, R11M, G11M; W □ Tr, G top; vis: W004°-051°, G051°-085°, W085°-092°, R092°-127°, R322°-351°.
Men Du 47°46'·35N 03°50'·49W.
Corn Vas 47°45'·86N 03°50'·26W.
Men ar Tréas 47°45'·76N 03°49'·69W.
Île Verte 47°46'·31N 03°48'·04W.
Île de Raguénès 47°46'·89N 03°47'·75W.

◀ PORT MANECH/AVEN AND BÉLON RIVERS

Pointe de Beg-ar-Vechen ☆ 47°47'·98N 03°44'·35W Oc (4) WRG 12s 38m W10M, R7M, G7M; W & R Tr; vis: W (unintens) 050°-140°, W140°-296°, G296°-303°, W303°-311°, R311°-328° over Les Verrès, W328°-050°; obsc when brg less than 299°.
Les Verrès 47°46'·63N 03°42'·72W.

◀ BRIGNEAU/MERRIEN/DOËLAN

Brigneau Mole Hd ☆ 47°46'·89N 03°40'·19W Oc (2) WRG 6s 7m W12M, R9M, G9M; W col, R top; vis: G280°-329°, W329°-339°, R339°-034°.

Brigneau 47°46'·09N 03°40'·08W; *Whis.*
Merrien ☆ 47°47'·01N 03°38'·95W QR 26m 7M; W□Tr, R top; vis: 004°-009°.
Port de la Merrien ent 47°46'·44N 03°38'·93W.
Roc Bali 47°46'·27N 03°38'·54W.
Bas La Croix 47°45'·98N 03°36'·85W.
Bas La Croix 47°46'·08N 03°36'·45W.
Doëlan Ldg Lts 013·8°. Front, 47°46'·47N 03°36'·51W Oc (3) WG 12s 20m W13M, G10M; W Tr, G band and top; vis: W shore-305°, G305°-314°, W314°-shore. Rear, 326m from front, QR 27m 9M; W Tr, R band and top.

◀ LE POULDU TO LOMENER/RIVIÈRE DE QUIMPERLÉ

Le Pouldu Ent 47°45'·71N 03°32'·24W.
Grand Cochon 47°43'·01N 03°30'·85W.
Kerroc'h ☆ 47°41'·94N 03°27'·64W Oc (2) WRG 6s 22m W11M, R8M, G8M; W Tr, R top; vis: R096·5°-112°·5, G112·5°-132°, R132°-302°, W302°-096·5°.
Lomener Anse de Stole Dir Lt 357·2° 47°42'·29N 03°25'·63W Dir Q WRG 13m W10M, R8M, G8M; W Tr, R top; vis: G349·2°-355·2°, W355·2°-359·2°, R359·2°-005·2°.

◀ ÎLE DE GROIX/PORT TUDY/LOCMARIA

Pen Men ☆ 47°38'·86N 03°30'·54W Fl (4) 25s 59m **29M**; W□Tr, B top; vis: 309°-275°.
Port Tudy Môle N Head ☆ 47°38'·70N 03°26'·74W Iso G 4s 12m 6M; W Tr, G top.
Port Tudy Môle E Head ☆ 47°38'·65N 03°26'·78W Fl (2) R 6s 11m 6M; W Tr R top vis: 112°-226°.
Bas Melité 47°38'·86N 03°25'·56W.
Pointe de la Croix ☆ 47°38'·03N 03°25'·00W Oc WR 4s 16m W12M, R9M; W pedestal, R lantern; vis: W169°-336°, R336°-345°, W345°-353°.
Edouard de Cougy 47°37'·91N 03°23'·91W.
Pointe des Chats ☆ 47°37'·21N 03°25'·31W Fl R 5s16m **19M**; W□ Tr and dwelling.
Les Chats 47°35'·69N 03°23'·58W Q (6) + L Fl 15s; *Whis.*

LORIENT

◀ PASSE DE L'OUEST

Ldg Lts 057°. Front, Les Sœurs 47°42'·13N 03°21'·83W Dir Q 11m 13M, R Tr, W bands; vis: intens 042·5°-058·5°, (4M) 058·5°-042·5°. Rear **Port Louis** ☆, 740m from front, Dir Q 22m **18M**.
'L' Banc des Truies 47°40'·76N 03°24'·48W Q (9) 15s.
A2 Locqueltas 47°40'·94N 03°24'·98W Fl R 2·5s.
A4 47°41'·18N 03°24'·12W Fl (3) R 12s.
A5 47°41'·50N 03°23'·11W Fl (2) G 6s.
Paté du Cheval 47°41'·42N 03°22'·94W.
A7 47°41'·70N 03°22'·66W Fl G 2·5s.
Les Trois Pierres 47°41'·53N 03°22'·47W Q RG 11m R6M, G6M; B Tr, W bands; vis: G060°-196°, R196°-002°.

◀ PASSE DU SUD

Ldg Lts 008·5°. **Front** ☆, Fish Market 47°43'·76N 03°21'·74W Dir QR 16m **17M**; R □, G bands on Gy Tr; intens 006°-011°. **Rear** ☆, Kergroise-La Perrière, 515m from front, Dir QR 34m **16M**; R □, W ▮ on Gy Tr; synch with front; intens 006°-011°.
Bastresse Sud 47°40'·77N 03°22'·09W QG; *Bell.*
Les Errants 47°41'·10N 03°22'·38W Fl (2) R 6s.
Bastresse Nord 47°41'·11N 03°22'·20W.
Goëland 47°41'·59N 03°22'·09W.

◀ ENTRANCE CHANNEL

Île Saint Michel Passe de la Citadelle Ldg Lts 016·5°. **Front** ☆, 47°43'·47N 03°21'·62W Dir Oc (3) G 12s 8m **16M**; W Tr, G top. **Rear** ☆, 306m from front, Dir Oc (3) G 12s 14m **16M**; W Tr, G top; synch with front; both intens 014·5°-017·5°.
Écrevisse 47°42'·13N 03°22'·37W.
Toulhars 47°42'·25N 03°22'·27W.
La Potée de Beurre 47°42'·24N 03°21'·98W.
Chan W side, La Petite Jument 47°42'·58N 03°22'·07W Oc R 4s 5m 6M; R Tr; vis: 182°-024°.
Chan E side, Tourelle de la Citadelle 47°42'·59N 03°21'·94W Oc G 4s 6m 6M; G Tr; vis: 009°-193°.
Chan W side Le Cochon 47°42'·80N 03°22'·00W Fl R 4s 5m 5M; R Tr, G band.

◀ KERNEVEL

Le Pot 47°42'·72N 03°22'·02W.
No. 1 47°42'·80N 03°21'·84W.
No. 2 47°43'·04N 03°21'·87W Fl R 2·5s.
Banc du Turc 47°43'·33N 03°21'·85W Fl (3) G 12s.
Port de Kernevel Marina ent 47°43'·41N 03°22'·09W Fl Y 2·5s 3m 2M; SPM with can topmark. Also Fl (4) Y 15s.
Ldg Lts 217° **Front, Kernevel** ☆ 47°43'·02N 03°22'·32W Dir QR 10m **15M**; R&W Tr; intens 215°-219°. **Rear** ☆, 290m from front, Dir QR 18m **15M**; W□Tr, R top; synch with front; intens 215°-219°.

◀ PORT LOUIS

La Paix 47°41'·97N 03°21'·87W.
La Paix 47°41'·84N 03°21'·92W Fl G 2·5s.
Île aux Souris ☆ 47°42'·15N 03°21'·52W Dir Q WG 6m W3M, G2W; G Tr; vis: W041·5°-043·5°, G043·5°-041·5°.
Jetty ☆ 47°42'·76N 03°21'·29W Iso G 4s 7m 6M; W Tr, G top.

◀ KÉROMAN/FISHING HBR/RADE DE PENMANÉ

Submarine base Ldg Lts 350°. **Front** ☆, 47°43'·60N 03°22'·02W Dir Oc (2) R 6s 25m **15M**. **Rear** ☆, 91m from front, Dir Oc (2) R 6s 31m **15M**; R&W topmark on Gy pylon, R top; Lts synch and intens 349°-3513°.
Fishing Hbr Môle Central, E side of ent, ☆ 47°43'·62N 03°21'·87W Fl RG 4s 7m 6M; W Tr, G top; vis: G000°-235°, R235°-360°.
Pengarne 47°43'·88N 03°21'·22W Fl G 2·5s 3m 3M; G Tr.
Pointe de l'Espérance Dir Lt 037° 47°44'·51N 03°20'·66W Dir Q WRG 8m W10M, R8M, G8M; W Tr, G top; vis: G034·2°-036·7°, W036·7°-037·2°, R037·2°-047·2°.
Ro-Ro Terminal ☆ 47°44'·42N 03°20'·96W Oc (2) R 6s 7m 6M.
Marina ent Lt By No. 8 47°44'·55N 03°20'·98W Fl R 2·5s.
No. 11 47°44'·04N 03°21'·01W QG.
Pen-Mané Bwtr elbow ☆ 47°44'·11N 03°20'·86W Fl (2) G 6s 4M.
Sainte Catherine Marina ☆ 47°43'·51N 03°21'·08W QG 6s 2M.

LORIENT TO BELLE ÎLE

◀ RIVIÈRE D'ÉTEL

Roheu 47°38'·52N 03°14'·77W.
Barre d'Etel 47°38'·54N 03°12'·91W.
W side ent ☆ 47°38'·70N 03°12'·91W Oc (2) WRG 6s 13m W9M, R6M, G6M; R Tr; vis: W022°-064°, R064°-123°, W123°-330°, G330°-022°; 2 FR on radio mast 2·3M NW; FR and F on radio masts 2·4M NW.
Les Pierres Noires 47°35'·48N 03°13'·39W.

◀ PORT MARIA
Le Pouilloux 47°27'·88N 03°08'·02W.
Ldg Lts 006·5°. **Front**, 47°28'·63N 03°07'·19W Dir QG 5m **16M**; W Tr, B band. **Rear**, 230m from front, Dir QG 13m **17M**; W Tr, B band; both intens 005°-008°.
Main light 47°28'·78N 03°07'·46W Q WRG 28m W14M, R10M, G10M; W Tr, G lantern; vis: W246°-252°, W291°-297°, G297°-340°, W340°-017°, R017°-051°, W051°-081°, G081°-098°, W098°-143°.
Bas An Tréac'h 47°27'·91N 03°07'·20W.
Les Deux Freres 47°28'·34N 03°07'·30W Fl R 2·5s.
S Bkwtr Head 47°28'·54N 03°07'·32W Oc (2) R 6s 9m 7M; W Tr, R top.
Mole E Head 47°28'·58N 03°07'·37W Iso G 4s 9m 7M.

PLATEAU DES BIRVIDEAUX
Tower 47°29'·13N 03°17'·50W Fl (2) 6s 24m 10M; B Tr, R bands; IDM.

BELLE ÎLE/SAUZON/LE PALAIS
N Poulains 47°23'·62N 03°14'·97W.
Les Poulains 47°23'·34N 03°16'·76W.
Pte des Poulains ☆ 47°23'·28N 03°15'·17W Fl 5s 34m **23M**; W ☐ Tr and dwelling; vis: 023°-291°.
B1 47°17'·01N 03°16'·54W.
Goulphar ☆ 47°18'·64N 03°13'·69W Fl (2) 10s 87m **26M**; Gy Tr.
La Truie 47°17'·05N 03°11'·72W.
Bas Gareau 47°22'·76N 03°13'·06W.
Sauzon Jetée NW Hd 47°22'·51N 03°13'·10W Fl G 4s 8m 8M.
Jetée SE Head 47°22'·43N 03°13'·10W Fl R 4s 8m 8M; W Tr, R top; vis: 315°-272°.
Le Palais Jetée Nord 47°20'·82N 03°09'·08W Fl (2+1) G 12s 11m 7M; W Tr; obsc 298°-170°.
Le Palais Jetée Sud 47°20'·80N 03°09'·12W Oc (2) R 6s 11m 11M; Obscd by Pte de Kerdonis and de Taillefer 298°-170°.
La Truie du Bugul 47°19'·53N 03°06'·59W.
Pointe de Kerdonis ☆ 47°18'·59N 03°03'·61W Fl (3) R 15s 35m **15M**; W ☐ Tr and dwelling; obsc by Pointes d'Arzic and de Taillefer 025°-129°.
Les Galères 47°18'·75N 03°02'·82W.

BAIE DE QUIBERON AND MORBIHAN

◀ CHAUSSÉE AND PASSAGE DE LA TEIGNOUSE
Le Four 47°27'·80N 03°06'·44W.
Bas Cariou 47°26'·94N 03°06'·44W; *Bell.*
Bas du Chenal 47°26'·66N 03°05'·83W.
Goué Vaz N 47°26'·20N 03°05'·49W.
Goué Vaz S 47°25'·79N 03°04'·87W Q (6) + L Fl 15s; *Whis.*
Basse du Milieu 47°25'·93N 03°04'·18W Fl (2) G 6s 9m 2M.
Goué Vaz E 47°26'·24N 03°04'·30W Fl (3) R 12s.
La Teignouse ☆ 47°27'·45N 03°02'·79W Fl WR 4s 19m **W15M**, R11M; W ○ Tr, R top vis: W033°-039°, R039°-033°.
NE Teignouse 47°26'·57N 03°01'·89W Fl (3) G 12s.
Basse Nouvelle 47°26'·97N 03°01'·95W Fl R 2·5s.
Quiberon S 47°28'·03N 03°02'·38W Q (6) + L Fl 15s.
Quiberon N 47°29'·63N 03°02'·63W.

◀ PORT HALIGUEN
New Bkwtr Head 47°29'·30N 03°05'·99W Oc (2) WR 6s 10m W11M, R8M; W Tr, R top; vis: W233°-240·5°, R240·5°-299°, W299°-306°, R306°-233°.
NW Bkwtr Head 47°29'·36N 03°06'·00W Fl G 2·5s 9m 6M.
Bugalet Wreck 47°31'·19N 03°05'·45W.
Men er Roue 47°32'·25N 03°06'·06W.

◀ RIVIÈRE DE CRAC'H/LA TRINITÉ-SUR-MER
Ldg Lts 347°. Front, 47°34'·08N 03°00'·42W Q WRG 11m W10M, R7M, G7M; W Tr, G top; vis: G321°-345°, W345°-013·5°, R013·5°-080°. **Rear** ☆, 560m from front, Dir Q 21m **15M**; W ○ Tr, G top; synch with front, intens 337°-357°.
Roche Souris 47°31'·95N 03°01'·25W.
Roche Rat 47°32'·81N 03°01'·81W.
Petit Trého 47°33'·47N 03°00'·77W Fl (4) R 15s.
La Trinité-sur-Mer Dir Lt 347° 47°35'·01N 03°01'·01W Dir Oc WRG 4s 9m W13M, R11M, G11M; W Tr; vis: G345°-346°, W346°-348°, R348°-349°.
S Pier Hd 47°35'·09N 03°01'·52W Oc (2) WR 6s 6m W10M, R7M; W Tr, R top; vis: R090°-293·5°, W293·5°-300·5°, R300·5°-329°.
Marina Jetty Head 47°35'·27N 03°01'·47W Iso R 4s 8m 5M.
Buissons de Méaban 47°31'·64N 02°58'·51W.
Le Petit Buissons 47°32'·13N 02°58'·50W.
Méaban 47°30'·76N 02°56'·23W.

17

◀ MORBIHAN
Auray No. 13 47°39'·54N 02°58'·55W.
César 47°38'·36N 02°58'·22W.
Port du Parun 47°36'·77N 02°57'·09W.
Catis 47°36'·13N 02°57'·23W.
Grégan 47°33'·90N 02°55'·05W Q (6) + L Fl 3m 8M.
Grand Mouton 47°33'·70N 02°54'·85W QG.
Jument 47°34'·27N 02°53'·46W.
Gavrinis 47°34'·21N 02°54'·10W.
Creizic S 47°34'·62N 02°52'·84W.
Creizic N 47°34'·93N 02°52'·21W.
Les Rechauds 47°36'·17N 02°51'·30W; 2 x.
Truie d'Arradon 47°36'·57N 02°50'·27W.
Logoden 47°36'·69N 02°49'·91W.
Drenec 47°36'·84N 02°48'·39W.
Roguédas 47°37'·12N 02°47'·28W Fl G 2·5s 4m 4M; G Tr.

◀ PLATEAU DU GRAND MONT
Basse de S Gildas 47°29'·78N 02°52'·91W.
Roc de l'Epieu 47°29'·49N 02°52'·99W.
Chimère 47°28'·84N 02°54'·04W.
Basse du Grand Mont 47°28'·98N 02°51'·16W.

◀ CHAUSSÉE DU BÉNIGUET
Les Esclassiers 47°25'·68N 03°03'·09W.
Le Grand Coin 47°24'·43N 03°00'·29W.
Bonnenn Vraz 47°24'·24N 02°59'·91W.

◀ ÎLE DE HOUAT
Le Rouleau 47°23'·68N 03°00'·33W.
Port de Saint-Gildas Môle Nord 47°23'·55N 02°57'·40W Fl (2) WG 6s 8m W9M, G6M; W Tr, G top; vis: W168°-198°, G198°-210°, W210°-240°, G240°-168°.
Men Grouiz 47°22'·76N 02°55'·05W.
Er Rouzez 47°22'·00N 02°54'·39W.
Pot de Feu 47°21'·68N 02°59'·84W.

◀ ÎLE DE HÖEDIC
Er Palaire 47°20'·12N 02°55'·21W.
Les Sœurs 47°21'·13N 02°54'·81W.
La Chèvre 47°21'·09N 02°52'·63W.

Port de l'Argol Bkwtr Hd ☆ 47°20'·69N 02°52'·56W Fl WG 4s 10m W9M , G6M ; W Tr, G top; vis: W143°-163°, G163°-183°, W183°-203°, G203°-143°.
Le Chariot 47°18'·87N 02°53'·00W.
Les Grands Cardinaux ☆ 47°19'·29N 02°50'·19W Fl (4) 15s 28m 13M; R and W Tr.
Cohfournik 47°19'·39N 02°49'·83W.
Er Guéranic 47°20'·50N 02°50'·52W.

CROUESTY TO LE CROISIC

◀ PORT NAVALO/CROUESTY EN ARZON

Pte de Port-Navalo ☆ 47°32'·86N 02°55'·13W Oc (3) WRG 12s 32m **W15M**, R11M , G11M ; W Tr and dwelling; vis: W155°-220°, G317°-359°, W359°-015°, R015°-105°.
Grand Mouton 47°33'·70N 02°54'·85W QG. 4m 3M.
Grégan 47°33'·90N 02°55'·05W Q (6) + L Fl 15s 3m 3M.
Port du Crouesty Ldg Lts 058°. **Front** ☆, 47°32'·54N 02°53'·94W Dir Q 10m **19M**; R panel with W vert stripe; intens 056·5°-059·5°. **Rear** ☆, 315m from front, Dir Q 27m **19M**; W Tr; intens 056·5°-059·5°
No. 1 47°32'·15N 02°54'·72W.
No. 2 47°32'·25N 02°54'·76W.
N Jetty Head ☆ 47°32'·47N 02°54'·14W Oc (2) R 6s 9m 7M; R&W □ Tr, R top.
S Jetty Hd ☆ 47°32'·44N 02°54'·10W Fl G 4s 9m 7M; G&W □ Tr.

◀ PLATEAU DE S JACQUES/SAINT-JACQUES-EN-SARZEAU

Le Bozec 47°28'·86N 02°49'·49W.
Plateau de S Jacques 47°28'·15N 02°47'·58W.
Saint-Jacques-en-Sarzeau ☆ 47°29'·17N 02°47'·55W Oc (2) R 6s 5m 6M; W 8-sided Tr, R top.

◀ PLATEAU DE LA RECHERCHE

Recherche 47°25'·58N 02°50'·41W Q (9) 15s.
Locmariaquer 47°25'·80N 02°47'·42W.

◀ PÉNERF

Penvins 47°28'·89N 02°40'·16W.
Borenis 47°29'·15N 02°38'·40W.
Le Pignon 47°30'·01N 02°38'·95W Fl (3) WR 12s 6m W9M, R6M; R □ on Tr; vis: R028·5°-167°, W167°-175°, R175°-349·5°, W349·5°-028·5°.

◀ VILAINE RIVER

Les Mâts 47°29'·13N 02°34'·97W.
Basse de Kervoyal 47°30'·36N 02°32'·66W Dir Q WR W8M, R5M; vis: W269°-271°, R271°-269°.
Basse Bertrand 47°31'·04N 02°30'·74W Iso WG 4s 6m W9M, G6M; G Tr; vis: W040°-054°, G054°-227°, W227°-234°, G234°-040°.
Penlan ☆ 47°30'·98N 02°30'·15W Oc (2) WRG 6s 26m **W15M**, R11M, G11M; W Tr, R bands; vis R292·5°-025°, G025°-052°, W052°-060°, R060°-138°, G138°-180°.
Bas de Prières No. 2 47°30'·39N 02°28'·75W Fl R.
Bas de Prières No. 1 47°30'·29N 02°28'·67W Fl G.
Petit Sécé 47°30'·07N 02°28'·79W.
Pointe du Scal ☆ 47°29'·67N 02°26'·87W QG 12s 8m 4M.

◀ ÎLE DUMET

Fort ☆ 47°24'·71N 02°37'·23W Fl (3) WRG 15s 14m W7M, R4M, G4M; W col, G top on fort; vis: G090°-272°, W272°-285°, R285°-335°, W335°-090°.
E Île Dumet 47°25'·12N 02°35'·11W Q (3) 10s.

◀ MESQUER

Laronesse 47°25'·94N 02°29'·53W.
Basse Normande 47°25'·44N 02°29'·82W.
Bas de Beaulieu 47°25'·01N 02°29'·31W.
Jetty Head ☆ 47°25'·27N 02°28'·08W Oc (3+1) WRG 12s 7m W10M, R7M, G7M; W col and bldg; vis: W067°-072°, R072°-102°, W102°-118°, R118°-293°, W293°-325°, G325°-067°.

◀ PIRIAC-SUR-MER

Grand Norven 47°23'·54N 02°32'·91W VQ (on trial).
Le Rohtres 47°23'·36N 02°33'·45W.
Inner Mole Hd ☆ 47°22'·94N 02°32'·75W Oc (2) WRG 6s 8m W10M, R7M, G7M; W col; vis: R066°-148°, G148°-194°, W194°-201°, R201°-221°; *Siren 120s (ocas).*
Bkwtr E Hd ☆ Fl R 4s 4m 5M.
Les Bayonnelles 47°22'·50N 02°35'·00W Q (9) 15s; *Whis.*
Oil Pipeline ☆ 47°22'·10N 02°32'·78W Oc (2+1) WRG 12s 14m W12M, R9M, G9M; W □, R stripe on R Tr; vis: G300°-036°, W036°-068°, R068°-120°.

◀ LA TURBALLE/LE CROISIC

La Turballe Ldg Lts 006·5° both Dir F Vi 11/19m 3M, both intens 004°-009°.
Jetée de Garlahy ☆ 47°20'·69N 02°30'·94W Fl (4) WR 12s 13m W10M, R7M; W pylon, R top; vis: R060°-315°, W315°-060°.
Basse Hergo 47°18'·62N 02°31'·62W Fl G 2·5s 5m 3M.
Le Croisic Jetée de Tréhic Head ☆ 47°18'·49N 02°31'·44W Iso WG 4s 12m W14M, G11M; Gy Tr, G top; vis: G042°-093°, W093°-137°, G137°-345°; F Bu Fog Det Lt.
Le Grand Mabon 47°18'·04N 02°31'·03W Fl R 2·5s 6m 2M, R pedestal.
Le Croisic Ldg Lts 156°. **Front** ☆ 47°18'·02N 02°30'·92W Dir Q 10m **19M. Rear** ☆, 116m from front, Dir Q 14m **19M**; both intens 154°-158°.
Le Croisic Ldg Lts 174°. Front 47°18'·06N 02°31'·07W QG 5m 11M. Rear, 48m from front, QG 8m 11M. Both vis: 170·5°-177·5°.

LE CROISIC TO PTE DE ST GILDAS

◀ PLATEAU DU FOUR/BANC DE GUÉRANDE

Bonen du Four 47°18'·53N 02°39'·30W Q; *Whis.*
Le Four ☆ 47°17'·87N 02°38'·07W Fl 5s 23m **18M**; W Tr, B stripes, G top.
W Basse Capella 47°15'·65N 02°44'·75W Q (9) 15s; *Whis.*
Goué-Vas-du-Four 47°14'·91N 02°38'·24W Q (6) + L Fl 15s.
Sud Banc Guérande 47°08'·79N 02°42'·82W VQ (6) + L Fl 10s; *Whis.*

◀ PLATEAU DE LA BANCHE

NW Banche 47°12'·85N 02°31'·03W Q 8m 4M; *Bell.*
W Banche 47°11'·58N 02°32'·45W VQ (9) 10s; *Whis.*
La Banche ☆ 47°10'·62N 02°28'·06W Fl (2+1) WR 15s 22m **W15M**, R11M; B Tr, W bands; vis: R266°-280°, W280°-266°.
SE Banche 47°10'·39N 02°26'·10W.

BAIE DU POULIGUEN APPROACHES (Baie de la Baule)

Penchateau 47°15'·24N 02°24'·35W Fl R 2·5s.
Les Guérandaises 47°15'·03N 02°24'·29W Fl G 2·5s.
47°15'·24N 02°23'·52W.
NNW Pierre Percée 47°13'·59N 02°20'·63W.
La Vieille 47°14'·03N 02°19'·53W.

Sud de la Vieille 47°13'·74N 02°19'·56W.
Le Caillou 47°13'·65N 02°19'·19W.
Le Petit Charpentier 47°13'·33N 02°18'·95W.

◀ LE POULIGUEN

Les Petits Impairs 47°15'·98N 02°24'·61W Fl (2) G 6s 6m 2M; G △, on Tr.
S Jetty 47°16'·39N 02°25'·40W QR 13m 9M; W col; vis: 171°-081°.

◀ PORT DE PORNICHET

La Baule S Bkwtr Head 47°15'·49N 02°21'·15W Iso WG 4s 11m W10M, G7M; W Tr; vis: G084°-081°, W081°-084°.
South Breakwater QG 3m 1M.
North Breakwater QR 4m 1M.
Le Grand Charpentier 47°12'·82N 02°19'·15W Q WRG 22m W14M, R10M, G10M, Gy Tr, G lantern; vis: G020°-049°, W049°-111°, R111°-310°, W310°-020°; Sig Stn 1·5M NE.
Euler 47°11'·60N 02°18'·38W VQ (6) + L Fl 10s.

◀ LOIRE APPROACHES

Loire Approach SN1 47°00'·07N 02°39'·84W L Fl 10s 8m 5M; *Whis*; Racon (Z).
Loire Approach SN2 47°02'·08N 02°33'·49W Iso 4s 8m 5M.
Thérésia 47°04'·83N 02°27'·29W Fl R 2·5s.
Les Chevaux 47°03'·52N 02°26'·39W Fl G 2·5s.
La Couronnée 47°07'·59N 02°20'·05W QG 8m 6M; Racon.
Lancastria 47°08'·88N 02°20'·37W VQ R 8m 2M.

◀ PLATEAU DE LA LAMBARDE

SE Lambarde 47°10'·03N 02°20·81W Q (6) + L Fl 15s; *Bell.*
NW Lambard 47°10'·84N 02°22'·94W.

◀ PASSE DES CHARPENTIERS

Portcé ☆ Ldg Lts 025·5°. **Front**, 47°15'·23N 02°15'·00W Dir Q 6m **22M** ; W col. **Rear** ☆, 0·75M from front, Q 36m **24M**; B □ Tr, W stripe; both intens 024·7°-026·2° (H24).
47°09'·94N 02°18'·40W Iso R 4s
No. 1 47°09'·94N 02°18'·40W VQ G.
No. 2 47°10'·05N 02°18'·73W VQ R.
No. 8 47°12'·75N 02°16'·86W QR.
No. 7 47°13'·30N 02°16'·12W VQ G.
Pointe d'Aiguillon ☆ 47°14'·54N 02°15'·78W Oc (4) WR 12s 27m **W13M**, R10M; W Tr; vis: W(unintens)207°-233°; W233°-293°, W297°-300°, R300°-327°, W327°-023°, W027°-089°.

◀ VILLE-ES-MARTIN

Jetty Hd 47°15'·33N 02°13'·66W Fl (2) 6s 10m 10M; W Tr.
Morées 47°15'·00N 02°13'·02W Fl (3) WR 12s 11m W6M, R4M; G Tr; vis: W058°-224°, R300°-058°.

◀ SAINT-NAZAIRE

W Jetty 47°15'·97N 02°12'·25W Oc (4) R 12s 11m 8M; W Tr, R top.
East Jetty 47°15'·99N 02°12'·14W Oc (4) G 12s 11m 11M; W Tr, G top.
Old Môle Head 47°16'·27N 02°11'·82W Oc (2+1) 12s 18m 11M; W Tr, R top; vis: 153·5°-063·5°; weather signals.
Basse Nazaire S 47°16'·23N 02°11'·62W Q (6) + L Fl 15s.

◀ POINTE DE MINDIN

No.19 47°16'·49N 02°10'·69W Iso G 4s.
W Môle 47°16'·17N 02°10'·16W Fl G 2·5s 6m 3M. Removed (T) 1996.

◀ LE POINTEAU/PORT DE COMBERGE/PORT DE LA GRAVETTE

Le Pointeau Digue S Head 47°14'·08N 02°10'·89W Fl WG 4s 4m W10M, G6M; G&W ○ hut; vis: G050°-074°, W074°-149°, G149°-345°, W345°-050°.
La Truie 47°12'·12N 00°13'29W
Port de Comberge S Jetty 47°10'·60N 02°09'·95W Oc WG 4s 7m W9M, G5M; W Tr, G top; vis: W123°-140°, G140°-123°.
La Gravette 47°09'·87N 02°12'·99W.
Port de la Gravette Jetty Head 47°09'·70N 02°12'·64W Fl (3) WG 12s 7m W8M, G5M; W structure, G top; vis: G224°-124°, W124°-224°.

◀ SAINT GILDAS (Anse de Boucau)

Pte de Saint Gildas 47°08'·10N 02°14'·67W Q WRG 20m W14M, R10M, G10M; framework tower on W house; vis: R264°-308°, G308°-078°, W078°-088°, R088°-174°, W174°-180°, G180°-264°.

RIVER LOIRE TO NANTES

No. 24 47°17·12N 02°10'·43W VQ R.
Bridge (Chan centre) 47°17·10N 02°10'·25W Iso 4s 55m.
MA 47°17·49N 02°09'·23W Iso G 4s.
MB 47°17·95N 02°07'·54W VQ G.
Fernais 47°18·10N 02°06'·60W Iso G 4s.

◀ DONGES

SW dolphin 47°18'·06N 02°04'·97W Fl G 2·5s 12m 5M; Gy col.
NE dolphin (close ENE) 47°18'·10N 02°04'·80W Iso G 4s 12m 4M; G col.
Jetty Head 47°18'·29N 02°04'·20W Fl (2) R 6s 9m 9M.
Donges Sud 47°18·02N 02°03'·84W QG.

◀ PAIMBŒUF

Brillantes No. 29 47°17'·95N 02°03'·06W VQ (3) G 5s.
Môle Hd 47°17'·42N 02°01'·96W Oc (3) WG 12s 9m W10M, G7M; W Tr, G top; vis: G shore-123°, W123°-shore.
Île du Petit Carnet 47°17'·23N 02°00'·36W Fl G 2·5s 8m 3M; W framework Tr, G top.
From Paimbœuf to Nantes Lts on S side are G, and N Red.

PORT DE TRENTE MOULT/NANTES

Trente Moult 47°11'·78N 01°34'·70W.
Quai du Président Wilson Hd 47°11'·95N 01°34'·46W Fl R 2·5s.

17

9.17.5 PASSAGE INFORMATION

SOUTH BRITTANY (charts 2643, 2646) *West France Cruising Companion* (Macmillan Reeds/Featherstone). The Admiralty *Bay of Biscay Pilot*. The *French Pilot* (Vol 3) (Nautical/Robson - out of print), although out of print, contains many unique almost timeless sketches and transits. French charts (SHOM) are often larger scale than Admiralty charts, and hence more suitable for inshore waters. The following Breton words have navigational significance: *Aber*: estuary. *Aven*: river, stream. *Bann*: hill. *Bian*: small. *Bras*: great. *Du*: black. *Enez, Inis*: island. *Garo*: rough, hard. *Glas*: green. *Goban*: shoal. *Gwenn*: white. *Karreg*: rock. *Ker*: house. *Men, mein*: rock, stone. *Morlenn*: creek. *Penn*: strait. *Porz*: harbour. *Raz*: tide race. *Ruz*: red. *Trez*: sand.

Mist and haze are quite common in the summer, fog less so. Winds are predominantly from SW to NW, often light and variable in summer, but in early and late season N or NE winds are common. Summer gales are infrequent, and are usually related to passing fronts. In summer the sea is often calm or slight, but swell, usually from W or NW, can severely affect exposed anchorages. When crossing B of Biscay, allow for a likely set to the E, particularly after strong W winds.

A particular feature of this coast during the summer is the sea and land breeze cycle, known locally as the *vent solaire*. After a quiet forenoon, a W'ly sea breeze sets in about midday, blowing onshore. It slowly veers to the NW, almost parallel to the coast, reaching Force 4 by late afternoon; it then veers further to the N, expiring at dusk. Around midnight a land breeze may pipe up from the NE and freshen sufficiently to kick up rough seas – with consequent disruption to moorings and anchs open to the NE. By morning the wind has abated.

Tidal streams are weak offshore, but can be strong in estuaries, channels and around headlands, especially nearer the English Chan. The tidal stream chartlets at 9.17.3 are based on NP 265 (Admiralty Tidal Stream Atlas for France, W Coast) which uses data from actual observations out to 15-25M offshore. The equivalent French Atlas gives more data, but based on computer predictions.

Inland waterways (9.15.17) can be entered from Lorient (9.17.14), Vilaine R (9.17.22) and the R. Loire (9.17.28).

RAZ DE SEIN TO BENODET (chart 2351) Chaussée de Sein (chart 798) is a chain of islands, rks and shoals extending 15M W from the Pte du Raz. A WCM lt buoy marks the seaward end. For directions on Île de Sein (9.17.8) and Raz de Sein see *North Biscay Pilot* (RCC/Imray).

Raz de Sein (chart 798) is the chan between Le Chat bn tr (at E end of Chaussée de Sein) and the dangers extending 8ca off Pte du Raz, the extremity of which is marked by La Vieille lt ho and La Plate lt tr. The Plateau de Tévennec is 2M N of Raz de Sein; it consists of islets, rks and shoals which extend 5ca in all directions from the lt ho thereon. Other dangers on the N side of the Raz are rks and shoals extending nearly 1M W and WSW from Pte du Van, and Basse Jaune (dries) 1M to N. On the S side the main dangers, all 1·5M off La Vieille, are: to the SW, Kornog Bras, a rk with depth of 3m; to the S, Masklou Greiz, rky shoals on which sea can break heavily; and to the SE, Roche Moulleg.

In the middle of Raz de Sein the NE-going (flood) stream begins at HW Brest +0550, sp rate 6·5kn; the SW-going (ebb) stream begins at HW Brest –0030, sp rate 5·5kn. There are eddies near La Vieille on both streams. In good weather, near np, and with wind and tide together, the Raz presents no difficulty, but in moderately strong winds it should be taken at slack water, which lasts for about ½ hour at end of flood stream. In strong winds the chan must not be used with wind against tide, when there are overfalls with a steep breaking sea. The B des Trépassés (1·5M ENE of La Vieille) is possible anch to await the S-going tide. Port Bestrée or Anse du Loc'h (1M and 4M E of Pte du Raz) may be suitable anchs if N-bound.

Audierne (9.17.8) lies between Raz de Sein and Pte de Penmarc'h (lt, fog sig, RC) off which dangers extend 1M to NW, W and S, and 3M to SE, and breaking seas occur in strong winds. The fishing hbrs of St Guénolé, Le Guilvinec (9.17.8) and Lesconil provide excellent shelter, but have difficult ents. Loctudy (9.17.9) is well sheltered from W/SW.

BENODET TO LORIENT (chart 2352) Îles de Glénan (chart 3640, SHOM 6648, 9.17.12), lie to seaward of Loctudy and Concarneau. With offlying dangers they stretch 5M from W to E and 4M from N to S. The islands are interesting to explore, but anchs are rather exposed. Between Îles de Glénan and Bénodet lie Les Pourceaux, reefs which dry, and Île aux Moutons which has dangers extending SW and NW.

Along the coast the larger ports are Bénodet (9.17.10), Port-la-Forêt (9.17.11) and Concarneau (9.17.12). Anse de Bénodet has rky shoals on both sides but is clear in the middle.The coast from Pte de Mousterlin to Beg Meil is fringed by rks, many of which dry, extending 1M offshore. Chaussée de Beg Meil extends 8½ca SE, where Linuen rk (dries) is marked by bn. From Concarneau to Pte de Trévignon rks extend nearly 1·5M offshore in places.

Between Pte de Trévignon and Lorient are rky cliffs and several interesting lesser hbrs and anchs, delightful in fair weather; but most dry and are dangerous to approach in strong onshore winds. These include the Aven and Bélon rivers, Brigneau, Merrien (mostly dries), Doëlan (but most of hbr dries) and Le Pouldu (Rivière de Quimperlé). All are described in 9.17.12 and the *North Biscay Pilot*.

Hazards SE and E of Pte de Trévignon include: Men Du, a rk 0·3m high, marked by IDM bn, about 1·25M SE of the same pt. Corn Vas, depth 1·8m, and Men ar Tréas, a rk which dries, are close S, both buoyed. Île Verte lies 6ca S of Ile de Raguénès, with foul ground another 2ca to S. The approaches to Aven and Bélon Rivers are clear, except for Le Cochon and Les Verrés (IDM bn) to the SE. Between Le Pouldu and Lorient, Grand Cochon (SCM buoy) and Petit Cochon lie about 1M offshore.

LORIENT TO QUIBERON (charts 2352, 2353) The great seaport of Lorient (9.17.14) has sheltered apprs and 4 marinas. Île de Groix lies 4M SW. Its main offlying dangers are to the E and SE: shoals off Pte de la Croix; Les Chats which extend 1M SE from Pte des Chats; and shoals extending 7½ca S of Loc Maria. Port Tudy (9.17.13), on N coast, is the main hbr, and is easy of access and well sheltered except from NE.

7M SE of Lorient, River Étel (9.17.15) is an attractive hbr with a difficult ent which must only be approached in good weather and on the last of the flood. Further S do not appr the isthmus of the Quiberon peninsula closely due to rky shoals. 6M W of Quiberon lies Plateau des Birvideaux (lt), a rky bank (depth 4·6m) on which the sea breaks in bad weather.

Belle Île has no dangers more than 2½ca offshore, apart from buoyed rks which extend 7½ca W of Pte des Poulains, and La Truie rk marked by IDM bn tr 5ca off the S coast. The S coast is much indented and exposed to swell from W. In good settled weather (only) and in absence of swell there is an attractive anch in Port du Vieux Château (Ster Wenn), 1M S of Pte des Poulains; see *North Biscay Pilot*. On the NE coast lie Le Palais (9.17.16) and Sauzon, which partly dries but has good anch off and is sheltered from S and W. Off Le Palais the ESE-going (flood) stream begins at HW Brest –0610, and the WNW- going at HW Brest +0125, sp rates 1·5kn.

BAIE DE QUIBERON (chart 2353) B de Quiberon is an important and attractive yachting area, with centres at Port Haliguen (9.17.17), La Trinité (9.17.18), Crouesty (9.17.19) and the Morbihan (9.17.20). The S side of the bay is enclosed by a long chain of islands, islets, rks and shoals from Presqu'île de Quiberon to Les Grands Cardinaux 13M SE. This chain includes the attractive islands of Houat (9.17.19) and Hoëdic, well worth visiting, preferably mid-week. The Bay is open to the E and SE.

From W or S, enter the B via Passage de la Teignouse in W sector (033°-039°) of La Teignouse lt ho; thence 068° between Basse Nouvelle lt buoy and NE Teignouse lt buoy. In this chan the NE-going (flood) stream begins at HW Brest – 0610, and the SW-going at HW Brest – 0005, sp rates 3·75 kn; in strong winds it is best to pass at slack water. Good alternative chans are Passage du Béniguet, NW of Houat, and Passage des Soeurs, NW of Hoëdic.

The Golfe du Morbihan, on the N side of B de Quiberon, is an inland sea containing innumerable islands and anchs. Port Navalo anch is on the E side of the ent with Port du Crouesty close SE. Inside, River Auray flows in from the NW and the city of Vannes (9.17.21) is on the N side. Sp stream rates in the vicinity of Grand Mouton achieve 8kn and elsewhere in the ent can exceed 4kn. Flood commences HW Brest – 0400 and turns at HW Brest + 0200.

CROUESTY TO LE CROISIC (chart 2353) Eastwards from the Morbihan, dangers extend 1M seaward of Pte de St Jacques, and 3M offshore lies Plateau de la Recherche with depths of 1·8m. SE of Penerf (9.17.22), which provides good anch, Plateau des Mats is an extensive rky bank, drying in places, up to 1·75M offshore.

Approaching the R. Vilaine (9.17.22) beware La Grande Accroche, a large shoal with least depth 1m, astride the ent. The main lit chan keeps NW of La Grande Accroche, to the bar on N side thereof. Here the flood begins at HW Brest – 0515, and the ebb at HW Brest + 0035, sp rates 2·5kn. In SW winds against tide the sea breaks heavily; when the Passe de la Varlingue, 5ca W of Pte du Halguen, is better, but beware La Varlingue (dries). At Arzal/Camoël yachts can lock into the non-tidal river for canal to Dinan/St Malo (see 9.15.15/16).

S of Pte du Halguen other dangers, close inshore, are the rky shoals, depth 0·6m, of Basse de Loscolo and Basse du Bile. Off Pte du Castelli, the Plateau de Piriac extends about 1·75M NW with depths of 2·3m and drying rks closer inshore. The small hbr of Piriac (9.17.23) lies on the N side of Pointe du Castelli and Les Bayonelles (dry) extend 5ca W. A chan runs between Plateau de Piriac and Île Dumet (lt), which is fringed by drying rks and shoals particularly on N and E sides.

In the Rade du Croisic are the hbrs of La Turballe (9.17.24) and Le Croisic (9.17.25). Off Pte du Croisic dangers extend 1M to N and W. Plateau du Four, a dangerous drying bank of rks, lies about 4M W and WSW of Pte du Croisic, marked by buoys and lt ho near N end. Between Pte du Croisic and Pte de Penchâteau, Basse Lovre is a rky shoal with depths of 1m, 5ca offshore.

LE CROISIC TO R. LOIRE (chart 2353, 3216) From Chenal du Nord, B du Pouliguen (9.17.26) is entered between Pte de Penchâteau and Pte du Bec, 3M to E. In SE corner of bay is the yacht hbr of Pornichet (9.17.27). The B is partly sheltered from S by rks and shoals extending SE from Pte de Penchâteau to Le Grand Charpentier, but a heavy sea develops in strong S-SW winds. The W chan through these rks runs between Penchâteau and Les Guérandaises lateral buoys; other chans lie further E.

The River Loire estuary (chart 3216), which carries much commercial tfc, is entered via either the Chenal du Nord or the Chenal du Sud. The former runs ESE between the mainland and two shoals, Plateau de la Banche and Plateau de la Lambarde; these lie about 4M S of B du Pouliguen. Chenal du Sud, the main DW chan, leads NE between Plateau de la Lambarde and Pte de St Gildas. Here the in-going stream begins at HW Brest – 0500, and the out-going at HW Brest + 0050, sp rates about 2·75kn.

In the near apprs to St Nazaire (9.17.28 and charts 2985, 2989) beware Le Vert, Les Jardinets and La Truie (all dry) which lie close E of the chan. The river is navigable as far as Nantes. On the E side of the estuary, between the Loire bridge and Pte de St Gildas, are the small drying hbrs of Comberge, La Gravette and St Gildas (9.17.28).

17

9.17.6 DISTANCE TABLE

Approximate distances in nautical miles are by the most direct route, whilst avoiding dangers and allowing for Traffic Separation Schemes. Places in *italics* are in adjoining areas; places in **bold** are in 9.0.6, Cross-Channel Distances.

1.	***Le Conquet***	**1**																			
2.	*Camaret*	13	**2**																		
3.	*Morgat*	22	16	**3**																	
4.	*Douarnenez*	29	21	11	**4**																
5.	Audierne	30	28	27	30	**5**															
6.	Loctudy	55	55	53	55	30	**6**														
7.	Bénodet	58	58	57	60	33	4	**7**													
8.	Port-la-Forêt	65	64	63	66	36	12	12	**8**												
9.	Concarneau	63	62	61	64	37	12	11	4	**9**											
10.	Lorient	84	86	85	88	61	38	36	33	32	**10**										
11.	Le Palais (Belle Ile)	95	99	98	101	74	54	52	48	47	26	**11**									
12.	Port Haliguen	100	105	104	107	80	59	57	55	53	32	11	**12**								
13.	La Trinité	108	110	109	112	85	64	62	60	58	37	16	8	**13**							
14.	Crouesty	108	110	109	112	85	64	62	60	58	37	16	9	8	**14**						
15.	Vannes	120	121	120	123	96	75	73	71	69	48	27	20	19	12	**15**					
16.	Arzal/Camöel	131	130	129	132	105	84	82	80	78	57	36	31	31	28	37	**16**				
17.	Le Croisic	124	125	124	127	100	79	77	75	73	48	27	26	26	22	33	18	**17**			
18.	La Baule/Pornichet	134	131	130	133	106	85	82	80	78	55	34	35	36	30	40	30	13	**18**		
19.	St Nazaire	145	138	137	140	113	95	91	90	87	66	41	42	45	40	50	39	24	12	**19**	
20.	*Pornic*	146	149	148	151	124	105	101	100	97	72	45	47	49	43	55	42	24	18	16	**20**

9.17.7 Special notes for France: See 9.15.7.

AUDIERNE *9.17.8*

Finistere **48°00'·61N 04°32'·33W**

CHARTS AC 2819; SHOM 7147, 7148; Imray C36, C37; ECM 541

TIDES +0440 Dover; ML 3·1; Duration 0605; Zone 0100

Standard Port BREST (⟵)

Times				Height (metres)			
High Water		Low Water		MHWS	MHWN	MLWN	MLWS
0000	0600	0000	0600	6·9	5·4	2·6	1·0
1200	1800	1200	1800				
Differences AUDIERNE							
−0035	−0030	−0035	−0030	−1·7	−1·3	−0·6	−0·2
ILE DE SEIN							
−0005	−0005	−0010	−0005	−0·7	−0·6	−0·2	−0·1
LE GUILVINEC							
−0010	−0025	−0025	−0015	−1·8	−1·4	−0·6	−0·1
LESCONIL							
−0008	−0028	−0028	−0018	−1·9	−1·4	−0·6	−0·1

SHELTER Good in marina, 3 pontoons 2ca SW of the bridge. Access HW–2 to +1 for 2m draft, except in strong SE-SW winds when seas break at the ent. Chan dredged about 1m, but may be less. Drying banks close to stbd. Quays reserved for FVs. At **Ste Evette** a long bkwtr, Oc (2) R 6s, gives good shelter, except in SE-SW winds when swell enters. Many unmarked W ⚓s to the N leave no room to ⚓ in lee of bkwtr. Keep clear of slip area as vedettes enter with much verve.

NAVIGATION WPT 47°59'·54N 04°32'·91W, 186°/006° from/to Kergadec lt, 1·5M. Appr between La Gamelle, rks drying 0·9m in the middle of the bay, and Le Sillon de Galets rks to the W. From the SE, leave La Gamelle to port. Appr is difficult in strong SE-SW winds. Inside the ent, dredged chan initially favours the W bank with ldg marks, vert R/W chevrons, in line 359°. At root of bkwtr chan turns NE, with 2nd set of R/W chevrons on fish shed in transit 045°; cross river to abeam fish market on stbd side, then alter 90° port to marina. Keep close to FV quays and yacht pontoons; banks dry to stbd.

LIGHTS AND MARKS By day from the WPT, Kergadec, W 8-sided lt tr, R top, on with old lt ho (hard to see) leads 006°. At night stay in the W sector (005°-007°) of Kergadec, Dir Q WRG 43m 12/9M. From SE, ldg marks/lts at 331°: Front Fl (3) WG 12s 11m 14/9M, W / tr on hbr bkwtr; rear FR 44m 9M (Kergadec).

RADIO TELEPHONE None. Adjacent sig stn at Pte du Raz Ch 16.

TELEPHONE Hr Mr 02·98·75·04·93; Aff Mar 02·98·70·03·33; CROSS 02·98·89·31·31; SNSM 02·98·70·03·31; ⊜ 02·98·94·68·67; Auto 08.36.68.08.29; Police 02·98·70·04·38; ⊞ 02·98·75·10·10; Brit Consul 01·40·63·16·02.

FACILITIES Port de Plaisance (100 + 20 ⓥ), ☎ 02.98.75.04.93, €1·52, AC, FW, CH, ME, El, Ⓔ, Sh, Bar, R, V; **Poulgoazec** C (15 ton), Slip. **Town** P & D (cans), V, Gaz, R, Bar, ✉, Ⓑ, bus to Quimper ⇌, ✈. Ferry: Roscoff. **Ste Evette**, Hr Mr ☎ 02·98.70.00.28, access H24, M, P & D (cans), ⊡, Showers.

ADJACENT HARBOURS AND ANCHORAGES

ILE DE SEIN, Finistere, **48°02'·40N 04°50'·80W**. AC 798, 2819; SHOM 5252, 7148. Tides, see above; ML 3·8m. Ile de Sein is the only inhabited Is in the Chausée de Sein, a chain of islands, rks and shoals extending 15M W from the Pte du Raz. The outer end has a WCM lt buoy and 5M E is Ar-Men lt tr, Fl (3) 20s 29m, horn (3) 60s. The E end is separated from the mainland by the Raz de Sein; see 9.17.5. Ile de Sein is worth visiting in fair weather, with good vis and preferably near nps. Best appr is from the N, 187° via Chenal d'Ezaudi, with Men-Brial lt ho, Oc (2) WRG 6s, on with third house (W with B stripe) from left (close S of lt ho). Chan between drying rks is entered at Cornoc-An- Ar-Braden SHM buoy, Iso G 4s and tide sets across the chan, which is marked by bn trs. There are also chans from NE and E. ⚓ off or inside the mole, but open to N and E. Hbr partly dries. See *North Biscay Pilot* (RCC/Imray) for more detailed directions. Facilities: limited V, R, CH, Sh.

ST GUÉNOLÉ, Finistere, **47°48'·70N 04°22'·90W**. AC 2819; SHOM 6645, 7146; ECM 543. Strictly a fishing port; yachts not welcomed. Access difficult in fresh W'lies, impossible in heavy weather. 3 sets of ldg marks/lts. Lts as 9.17.4. Pilot book & SHOM 6645 essential. Hr Mr ☎ 02.98.58.60.43.

LE GUILVINEC, Finistere, **47°47'·52N 04°17'·10W**. AC 2819, 2351; SHOM 6646, 7146. HW + 0447 on Dover (UT); ML 3·0m. See 9.17.8. Good shelter and useful passage port; hbr (3m) accessible H24 for <2·5m draft €1·30, but total priority to FVs; no ent/exit 1600-1830. Good ⚓ off ent in lee of reef but stay clear of fairway. Beware Lost Moan Rks SE of ent marked by RW bn tr, Fl (3) WRG 12s 8m 9/6M. Ent is easy if vis adequate to see ldg lts/marks. Three ldg lts, all synch, in line 053°: front, Mole de Lechiagat Q 7m 8m, W pylon, vis 233°-066°; middle, Rocher Le Faoutés, 210m from front, QWG 12m 14/11M, R □ on W pylon, vis W006°-293°, G293°-006°; rear, 0·58M from front, Dir Q 26m 8M, R □ on W pylon with R stripe, vis 051·5°-054·5°. VHF Ch 12. Facilities: Hr Mr ☎ 02.98·58·05·67; Aff Mar ☎ 02.98·58·13·13; ⊜, C, FW, D, P, El, ME, Sh, CH, Ⓔ.

LESCONIL, Finistere, **47°47'·76N 04°12'·57W**. AC 2819; SHOM 6646, 7146; ECM 543. Tides, see 9.17.8; ML 3m. Fishing port 3M SW of Loctudy; yachts not welcome. Do not enter/leave 1630-1830LT due to FV inrush. Appr from Karek Greis ECM buoy, Q (3) 10s, on ldg line 325°, belfry just open W of Men ar Groas lt ho, Fl (3) WRG 12s 14m 10/7M; at night in W sector 313°-333°. Bkwtr lts are QG and Oc R 4s. Possible drying mooring inside S bkwtr; no ⚓s, no AB on quays. Hr Mr ☎ 02.98.82.22.97. Facilities of fishing port.

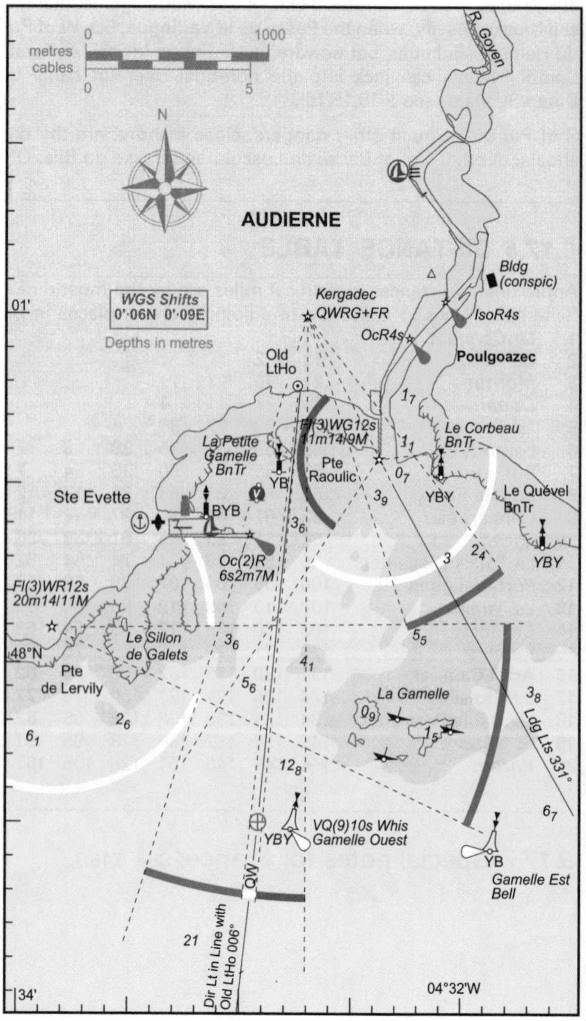

LOCTUDY 9.17.9

Finistere **47°50´·30N 04°10´·50W**

CHARTS AC 3641, 2820; SHOM, 7146; ECM 543; Imray C37, 38

TIDES +0505 Dover (UT); ML 3·0; Duration 0615; Zone –0100

Standard Port BREST (⟵)

Times				Height (metres)			
High Water		Low Water		MHWS	MHWN	MLWN	MLWS
0000	0600	0000	0600	6·9	5·4	2·6	1·0
1200	1800	1200	1800				
Differences LOCTUDY							
–0013	–0033	–0035	–0025	–1·9	–1·5	–0·7	–0·2

SHELTER Excellent in marina and hbr, except in strong ESE winds. The many Øs and moorings in the river leave little space to ⚓. Keep clear of FVs, esp 17-1900LT daily when yachts are discouraged from entering/leaving hbr.

NAVIGATION WPT 47°50´·12N 04°08´·86W, 105°/285° from/to Les Perdrix tr, 0·73M. From S and W, leave Bas Bilien ECM, VQ (3), to port, thence to WPT. From E/NE, give Men Audierne SHM bn a wide berth - note new (2000) buoyage . Bar has least depth 0·9m, deeper to the N. Sp ebb runs at 3½kn; enter under power only. Appr 285° (to clear Karek Croisic rk) ; when 300m short, alter course to port onto 274° to marina. Beware rky ledges close S of Les Perdrix and SHM bn, Fl (4) G 15s. Pont l'Abbé (3M up-river) dries about 2m, but is accessible to shoal draft boats on the flood; chan marked by perches.

LIGHTS AND MARKS Pte de Langoz Fl (4) WRG 12s 12m 15/11M (see 8.15.4) and as plan.

RADIO TELEPHONE Marina VHF Ch 09 (Office hrs); Port Ch 12.

TELEPHONE Hr Mr 02·98·87·51·36; 🕮 02·98.87.96.77; Météo ☎ 08·36·68·08·29, Aff Mar 02·98·58·13·13; CROSS 02·97·55·35·35; SNSM 02·98·87·41·12; ⊖ 02·98·58·28·80; Auto 08·36·68·08·29; Dr 02·98·87·41·80; Ⓗ (6km) 02·98·82·40·40; Brit Consul 01·40.63.16.02.

FACILITIES Marina (657 + 65 visitors;) ☎ 02·98·87·51·36, €2.13, FW, AC, Slip, P, C (9 tons), CH, Sh, ME, El; ♿. **Town** Bar, V, R, Dr, ✉, Ⓑ.

BÉNODET 9.17.10

Finistere **47°51'·80N 04°06'·40W**

CHARTS AC 3641, 2820; SHOM 6679, 6649, 7146; ECM 543; Imray C37

TIDES +0450 Dover; ML 3·1; Duration 0610; Zone –0100

Standard Port BREST (⟵)

Times				Height (metres)			
High Water		Low Water		MHWS	MHWN	MLWN	MLWS
0000	0600	0000	0600	6·9	5·4	2·6	1·0
1200	1800	1200	1800				
Differences BÉNODET							
0000	–0020	–0023	–0013	–1·7	–1·3	–0·5	–0·1
CORNIGUEL							
+0015	+0010	–0015	–0010	–2·0	–1·6	–1·0	–0·7

SHELTER Marinas at Ste Marine (W bank, town of Combrit) and at Anse de Penfoul (E bank, Bénodet), both accessible H24 at any tide. Caution: In both marinas, best to arr/dep near slack water to avoid the strong stream, esp 4kn ebb, through the pontoons with risk of damage. Some Øs available. ⚓ in Anse du Trez in offshore winds. Speed limit 3kn in hbr.

R Odet is navigable near HW to Quimper, but masted vessels must ⚓ at Poulguinan bridge (5·8m clearance), 1M beyond Corniguel and 0·5M below the city; pleasant ⚓s at Anse de Combrit, Anse de Kérautret, Porz Keraign, Porz Meilou, Anse de Toulven and SW of Lanroz. N of Lanroz the river shoals progressively to 0·5m in places. SHOM 6679 is recommended.

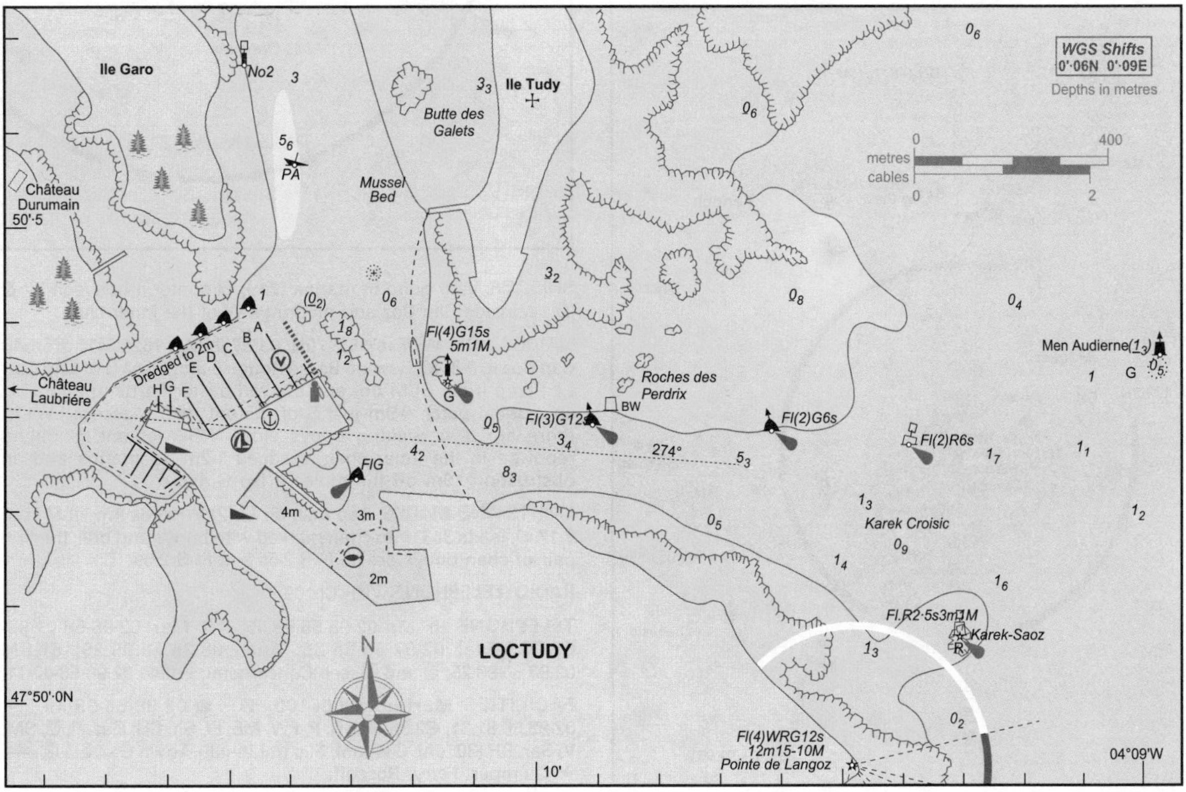

BÉNODET *continued*

NAVIGATION WPT 47°51'·00N 04°06'·10W, 166°/346° from/to front ldg lt, 1·43M. The centre of the bay is clear for small craft, but beware Roches de Mousterlin at the SE end of the bay and various rks off Loctudy to the SW. There is a tanker chan past the Ile aux Moutons, 6M SSE of hbr.

LIGHTS AND MARKS Ldg lts/daymarks 346°: Front, Oc (2+1) G 12s 11m 17M, intens 345°-347°, W ○ tr, G vert stripe, G top (hard to see until close); rear Oc (2+1) 12s 48m 11M, conspic W tr, G top, synch. Ile-aux-Moutons (6M SSE), Oc (2) WRG 6s 18m 15/11M + Dir Oc (2) 6s 17m 24M, intens 278°-283°.

RADIO TELEPHONE Marinas VHF Ch 09 (0800-2000LT in season).

TELEPHONE Hr Mr (Ste Marine)02·98·56·38·72, 📠 02·98.51.95.17, Hr Mr (Pen Foul)02·98·57·05·78, 📠 02·98.57.00.21; Aff Mar 02·98·57·03·82; CROSS 02·97·55·35·35; SNSM 02·98·57·02·00; ⊜ 02·98·55·04·19; Météo 02·98·94·03·43; Dr 02·98·57·22·21; Brit Consul 01·40·63·16·02.

FACILITIES
BENODET: **Anse de Penfoul Marina** (510+40 Ⓥ AB €2·29; also 175 buoys +15 Ⓥ) ☎ 02·98·57·05·78, 📠 02·98.57.00.21, AC, FW, ⊡, R, CH, ME, V, P, D, M, El, Ⓔ, Sh, C, SM, Divers. **Quay** C (10 ton). **Town** All facilities, Gaz, ⊠, Ⓑ, bus to Quimper ⇌, ✈.

COMBRIT: **Sainte Marine Marina** (350+70 Ⓥ), €2·29 or €1·52 for Ⓥ, ☎ 02·98·56·38·72, 📠 02·98.51.95.17, AC, CH, FW. **Town** V, R, Bar, ⊡, Ⓔ. Pedestrian ferry to Bénodet.

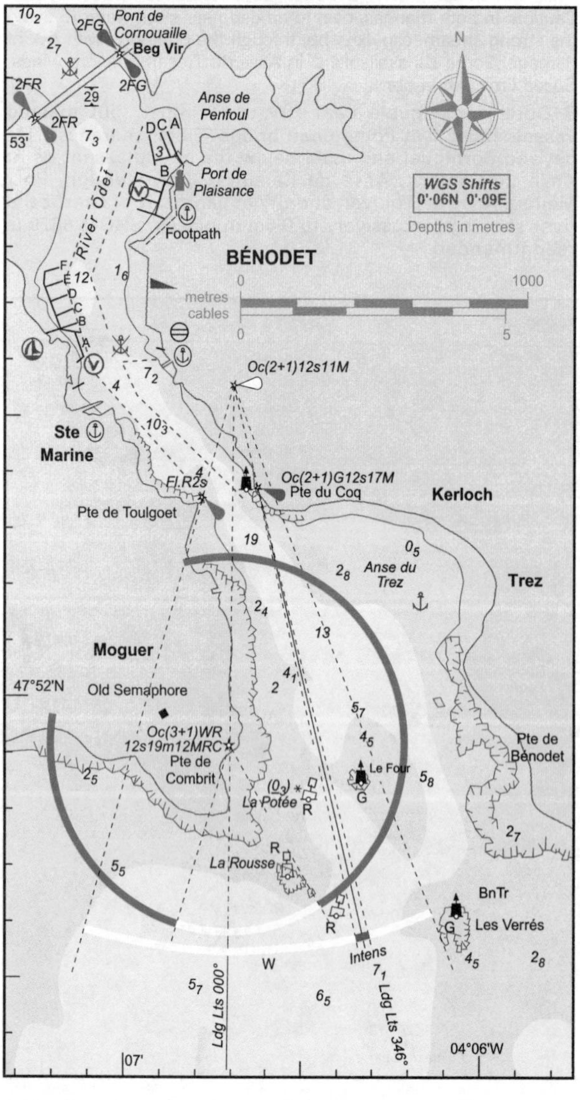

PORT-LA-FORÊT *9.17.11*

Finistere **47°53'·55N 03°58'·17W**

CHARTS AC 3641, 2820; SHOM 6650, 7146; ECM 543, 544; Imray C38

TIDES +0450 Dover; ML 2·9; Duration 0615; Zone –0100
Use Differences CONCARNEAU 9.17.12

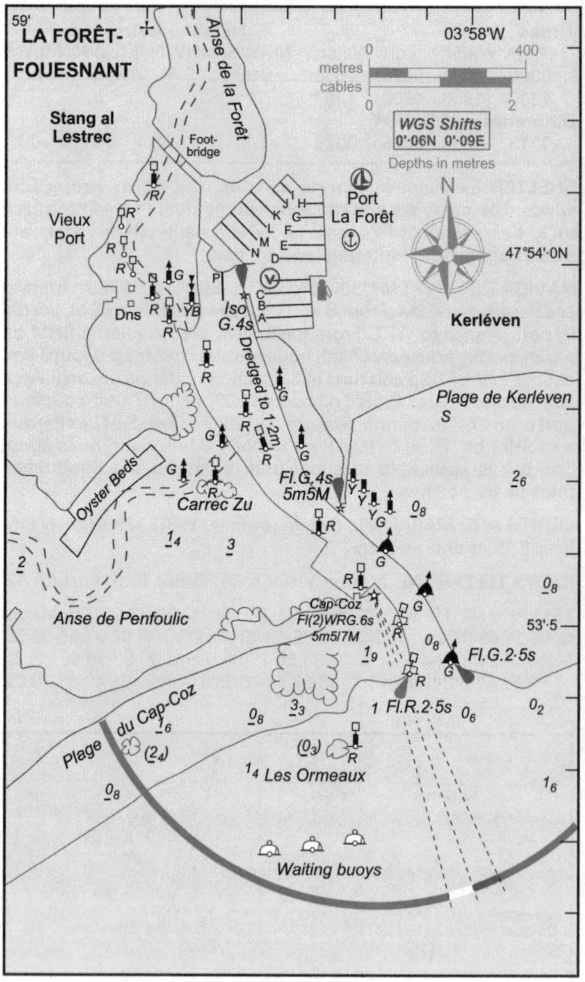

SHELTER Very good in marina (2m); Ⓥ pontoon between 'C' & 'D'. ⚓ inside Cap Coz and moorings W of the inner chan.

NAVIGATION WPT 47°52'·70N 03°57'·80W, 162°/342° from/to Cap Coz lt, 0·89M. Beware Basse Rouge 0·8m, 6·5ca S of Cap Coz; Le Scoré (unlit SCM bn) and buoyed oyster farms in apprs. At sp a shoal patch 0·9m just S of the ent denies access LW±1½; there are 3 W waiting buoys close WSW of ent. Shoaling reported in the inner chan, dredged 1·2m, to marina and an obstruction 10m off the mole (☆ Iso G 4s).

LIGHTS AND MARKS Cap Coz, dir Fl (2) WRG 6s 5m 7/5M (see 9.17.4), leads 343° into chan marked with buoys and bns; the first pair of chan buoys are lit, Fl R 2·5s and Fl G 2·5s.

RADIO TELEPHONE VHF Ch 09.

TELEPHONE Hr Mr 02·98·56·98·45; Aff Mar 02·98·56·01·98; CROSS-Etel 02·97·55·35·35; Auto 08.36.68.08.29; SNSM 02·98·56·98·25; ⊜ and Ⓗ see Concarneau; Police 02·98·56·00·11.

FACILITIES **Marina** (900+100 Ⓥ) ☎ 02·98·56·98·45, 📠 02·98.56.81.31, €2·36, AC, D, P, FW, ME, El, Sh, CH, Gaz, R, ⊡, SM, V, Bar, BH (30 ton), C (4 ton), Slip (multihull). **Town** Gaz, ⊠, Ⓑ, ⇌, ✈ Quimper. Ferry: Roscoff.

CONCARNEAU 9.17.12

Finistere **47°52'·10N 03°54'·68W** ❁❁❁◊◊◊✿✿✿

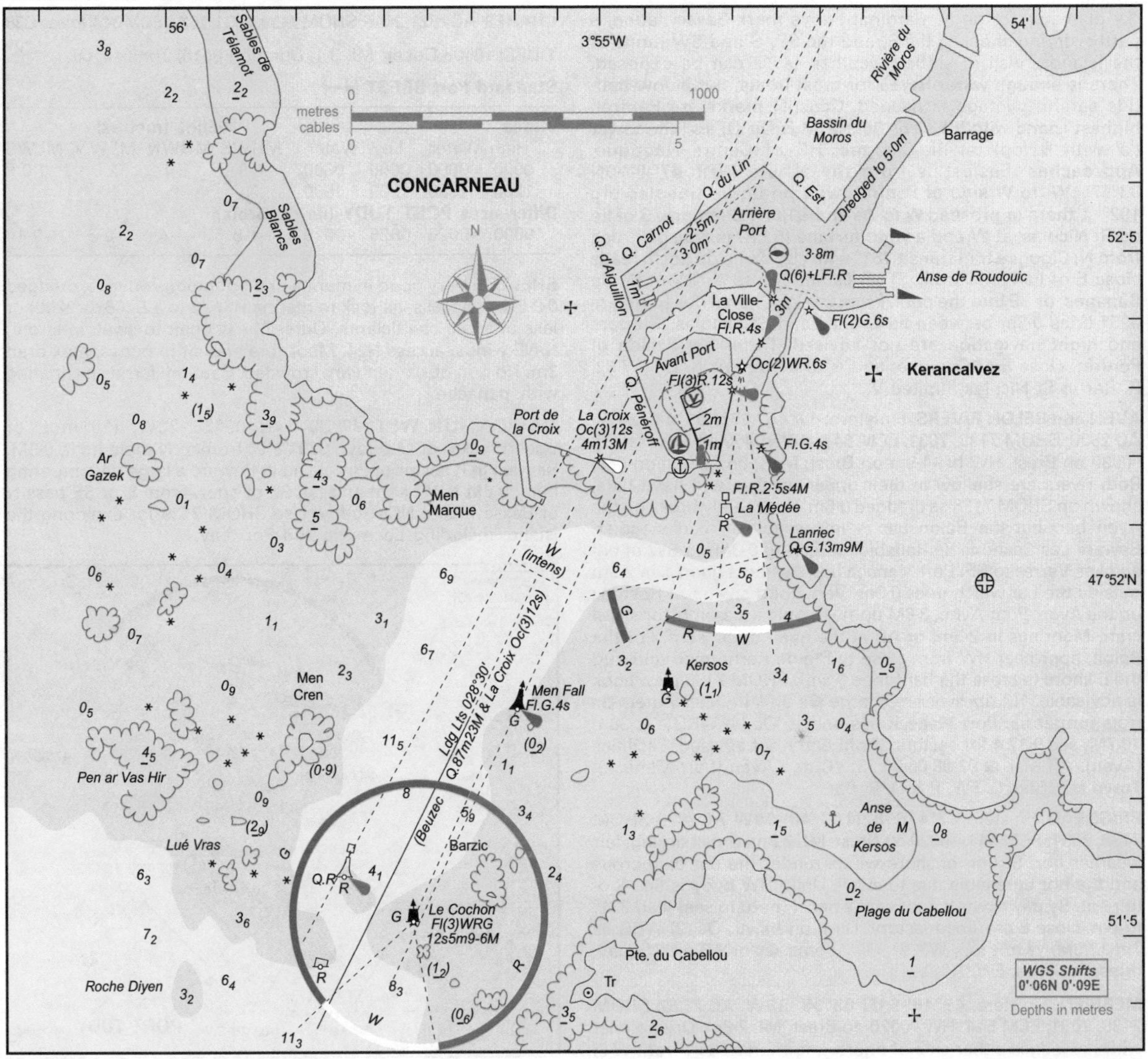

CHARTS AC 3641, 2820; SHOM 6650, 7146; ECM 543/4; Imray C38

TIDES +0455 Dover; ML 3·0; Duration 0615; Zone –0100

Standard Port BREST (⟵)

Times				Height (metres)			
High Water		Low Water		MHWS	MHWN	MLWN	MLWS
0000	0600	0000	0600	6·9	5·4	2·6	1·0
1200	1800	1200	1800				
Differences CONCARNEAU							
–0010	–0030	–0030	–0020	–1·9	–1·5	–0·7	–0·2
ILE DE PENFRET (Iles de Glénan)							
–0005	–0030	–0028	–0018	–1·9	–1·5	–0·7	–0·2

SHELTER Good, except in strong S'lies. The marina (2m) has an anti-wash barrier. The Arrière Port is solely for FVs; yacht pontoon on NE corner of La Ville Close is only for locals.

NAVIGATION WPT 47°50'·75N 03°56'·18W, 209°/029° from/to front ldg lt 028°, 1·67M. Beware rks around Men Cren and Le Cochon. Speed limit 5kn between le Cochon and Men Fall, 4kn above Men Fall.

LIGHTS AND MARKS Ldg lts 028°: front Oc (3) 12s 14m 13M, RW tr which is hard to see against bldgs behind; rear, 1·35M from front, Q 87m 23M, spire on skyline. Steer between Le Cochon G bn tr, Fl WRG 12s, and Basse du Chenal PHM buoy, QR; the former is easier to see than the ldg marks. Past Men Fall SHM buoy Fl G 4s, steer 070° for Lanriec lt, QG 13m 8M, vis 063°-078°, G window on W gable.

RADIO TELEPHONE Marina Ch 09 (0700-2100LT in season). FV hbr Ch **12** 16 (H24).

TELEPHONE Marina 02·98·97·57·96; Hr Mr (FV hbr) 02·98·60·51·18; Aff Mar 02·98·60·55·56; CROSS 02·97·55·35·35; Météo 02·98·32·55·57; Auto 08.36.68.08.08; ⊜ 02·98·97·01·73; Police 17; Fire 18; Ⓗ 02·98·52·60·02; Brit Consul 01·40·63·16·02; Dr 02·98·97·85·95.

FACILITIES **Marina** (336 + 52 visitors; pontoon 'D'), €2·26 (Jul, Aug) €1·98 for remainder of year, P, D, FW, M, AC, Slip, C (17 ton), Sh, ME, El, CH, SHOM, ACA, SM. **Town** Ⓔ, Gaz, V, R, Bar, ✉, Ⓑ, bus to Quimper ⇌ and ✈. Ferry: Roscoff.

OTHER HARBOURS AND ANCHORAGES BETWEEN CONCARNEAU AND LORIENT

ILES DE GLÉNAN, 47°43'·04N 03°59'·51W (twr on Île Cigogne). A good Pilot and large-scale chart are essential: AC 3640; SHOM 6648 (larger scale than AC 3640), 7146, 7313; ECM 243.

continued on next page

ILES DE GLÉNAN *continued*

Tides see 9.17.12. A low-lying archipelago, 10M SSW of Concarneau, with Ile aux Moutons and Les Pourceaux, both rky plateaux, to the N. Cardinal buoys mark Basse Jaune, a partly drying shoal to the E, and the SE, S and SW limits of the Islands. Visit in settled weather as ⚓s can be exposed. There is enough water HW±3 for most boats, but below half-tide careful pilotage is needed. **Conspic marks** are Penfret, highest island with lt Fl R 5s 36m 21M & Dir Q; and the tower (W with B top) on Ile Cigogne, HQ of Centre Nautique. **Approaches**: Easiest is from the N, via WPT 47°44'·0N 03°57'·5W, to W side of Penfret, with bn on Ile Guéotec brg 192°. ⚓ there or proceed W to Ⓥs and ⚓ in La Chambre, S of Ile de St Nicolas; at W end a wind turbine (5 FR) is conspic. Also from N, Cigogne tr in transit 181° with chy on Ile du Loc'h leads close E of La Pie IDM bn, Fl (2) 6s 9m 3M, to ⚓ NW of Ile de Bananec; or SE into the pool. From the W, Chenal des Bluiniers 095° dries 0·8m between Ile Drénec and St Nicolas. S apprs and night navigation are not advised. Other ⚓s: E side of Penfret; close E of Cigogne; and N of Ile du Loc'h. Ⓥs €7·62. R, Bar in St Nicolas, limited V.

AVEN and BELON RIVERS, Finistere, **47°48′·05N 03°44′·20W**, AC 2820; SHOM 7138, 7031; ECM 544. HW +0450 on Dover (UT), –0030 on Brest. HW ht –1·9m on Brest; ML 2·8m; Duration 068. Both rivers are shallow in their upper reaches and have bars, shown on SHOM 7138 as dredged 0·6m. Seas rarely break on the Aven bar, but the Belon bar is impassable in bad weather. Beware Les Cochons de Rousbicout (drying 0·3m) to SW of ent and Les Verres to SE. Port Manech has Ⓥs and a good ⚓ in 2·5m outside the bar which dries 0·9m. Very good shelter at Rosbras up the **Aven**; Pont-Aven, 3·6M up-river, only accessible for shoal craft. Moorings in 2·5m; or AB at the quay dries 2·5m. For the **Belon**, appr near HW from close to Pte de Kerhermen and hug the E shore to cross the bar (dries 0·3m); SHOM 7138/pilot book is advisable. 1M up-river are 3 large Ⓥs or ⚓ in deep water; Ⓥs trots further up. Port Manech has only lt, Oc (4) WRG 12s 38m 10/7M, see 9.17.4 for sectors. Night entry not advised. Facilities (Aven): Aff Mar ☎ 02·98·06·00·73; **YC de l'Aven** (Port Manech). **Town** ME, Slip, C, FW, P & D, R, Bar.

BRIGNEAU, Finistere, **47°476'·82N 03°40'·00W**. AC 2820; SHOM 7138, 7031; ECM 544. –0020 on Brest; ML 2·8m. Small drying, fair weather hbr. Strong onshore winds render the ent dangerous and the hbr untenable due to swell. Unlit RW buoy is 8ca S of hbr ent. By day bkwtr lt and rear W panel (hard to see) lead 331° to ent, close E of ruined factory. Dir lt on bkwtr, Oc (2) WRG 6s 7m 12/9M, W tr/R top, W329°-339°. Some Ⓥs or AB on W quay, dries. Facilities: FW, AC, V.

MERRIEN, Finistere, **47°46'·51N 03°38'·98W**. AC 2820; SHOM 7138, 7031; ECM 544. HW –0020 on Brest; ML 2·8m. Drying inlet with rky ledges either side of apprs. Ldg marks 005°: front W □ lt tr/R top; rear, house gable. Dir lt QR 26m 7M, vis 004°-009°. ⚓ outside ent or moor to Ⓥ or AB on quay SE side. Avoid oyster beds beyond quay. Facilities: FW, AC, R.

DOËLAN, Finistere, **47°46′·20N 03°36′·45W**. AC 2820; SHOM 7138, 7031; ECM 544. HW +0450 on Dover (UT), –0035 on Brest; HW ht –2·2m on Brest; ML 3·1m; Duration 0607. Fair weather only, open to onshore winds. Drying AB at quays; or afloat on W buoys just N and S of bkwtr, €6·86 <12m. Conspic factory chy E of front ldg lt. Daymark, W bn/B stripe, (about 1km NNE of rear ldg lt) on with ldg lts 014°: front Oc (3) WG 12s 20m 13/10M, W tr/G band & top, W shore -305°, G305°-314°, W314° -shore; rear QR 27m 9M, W tr/R band & top. Facilities: Aff Mar ☎ 02·98·96·62·38; **Services:** CH, El, Ⓔ, ME, Sh. **Town** D, P, FW, Dr, ✉, R, V, Bar.

LE POULDU (La Laïta or Quimperlé River), Finistere, **47°45'·70N 03°32'·20W**. AC 2820; SHOM 7138, 7031; ECM 544. HW –0020 on Brest; ML 2·8m. Strictly a fair weather hbr, but once inside a small marina on the E bank provides adequate shelter for small yachts; or ⚓ in deeper pools upstream. At HW appr the estuary ent close E of a W ○ tr on low cliffs. The ent favours the W side, but chan shifts often and local advice is needed. In onshore winds the bar is dangerous on the ebb. Tides reach 6kn at sp. No lights. Facilities: FW, V, R, Bar.

PORT TUDY *9.17.13*

Morbihan (Ile de Groix) **47°38'·74N 03°26'·63W** ❁❁❁◊◊✿✿

CHARTS AC 2821, 2646; SHOM 7139, 7031, 7032; ECM 544; Imray C38

TIDES +0505 Dover; ML 3·1; Duration 0610; Zone –0100

Standard Port BREST (⟵)

Times				Height (metres)			
High Water		Low Water		MHWS	MHWN	MLWN	MLWS
0000	0600	0000	0600	6·9	5·4	2·6	1·0
1200	1800	1200	1800				
Differences PORT TUDY (Ile de Groix)							
0000	–0025	–0025	–0015	–1·8	–1·4	–0·6	–0·1

SHELTER Very good in marina or on pontoons outside, dredged 0·9-2·4m. Access via lock to marina HW –2 to +2, (0630–2200) or less at small coefficients. Outer hbr is open to swell in strong N/NE winds, access H24. Moor fore and aft to buoys; max draft 3m. No ⚓ in hbr, often very crowded. Caution: ferries navigating with panache.

NAVIGATION WPT 47°39'·14N 03°26'·28W, (100m E of Speerbrecker ECM buoy), 039°/219° from/to N mole hd lt, 0·5M. Remain in R sector of E mole hd lt. Beware a large unlit mooring buoy 0·6M NW of ent and rks SE of appr. From E or SE pass N of Basse Melite NCM buoy. Use SHOM 7139 for exploring the island, including Locmaria and Port Lay.

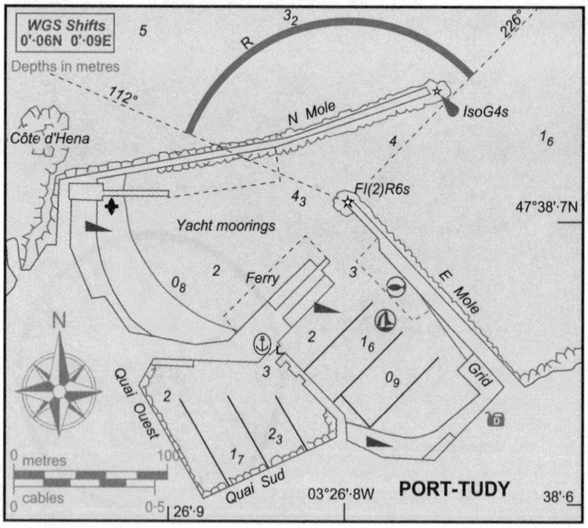

LIGHTS AND MARKS Pen-Men lt ho (at NW end of island), Fl (4) 25s 59m 29M, W □ tr, B top. Pte de la Croix lt (at E end of island), Oc WR 4s 16m 12/9M. Ldg line at 220°, church spire in line with W end of N mole. By night, mole hd lts in transit 219° clear offlying rks to the NE.

RADIO TELEPHONE VHF Ch 09 16 during lock opening times.

TELEPHONE Hr Mr 02·97·86·54·62, 📠 02·98.27.19.76; Aff Mar 02·97·37·16·22; CROSS 02·97·55·35·35; SNSM 02·97·86·82·87; ⊜ 02·97·86·80·93; Auto 08·36·68·08·56; Police 02·97·86·81·17; Ⓗ (Lorient) 02·97·83·04·02.

FACILITIES **Marina** (104 plus 100 in E Hr and 120 moorings), €0·76 Ⓥ, €2·29 AB, FW, AC; **Quay** P & D (cans, 0800–1200 & 1400–1900, ☎ 02·97·86·80·96), ME, El, Sh, C (3 ton), CH. **Town** V, R, ⓘ, ✉, Bar. Ferry to Lorient.

OTHER HARBOUR ON ILE DE GROIX

LOCMARIA, Morbihan, **47°37'·85N 03°26'·28W**. AC 2820/1, SHOM 7139; –0020 Brest; ML 2·8m. Appr is open to the S, but tiny drying hbr gives shelter in offshore winds. Steer N for G bn tr initially; then ldg line 350°, W bn on with conspic Ho. Close in, 2 PHM bns and a SCM and NCM bn mark the unlit chan. Limited space inside to dry out; or ⚓ outside the hbr W of the ldg line. Facilities in village, V, R.

LORIENT *9.17.14*

Morbihan **47°42'·64N 03°21'·92W**

CHARTS AC 304, 2821; SHOM 7140, 7139, 7031, 7032; ECM 544, 545; Imray C38

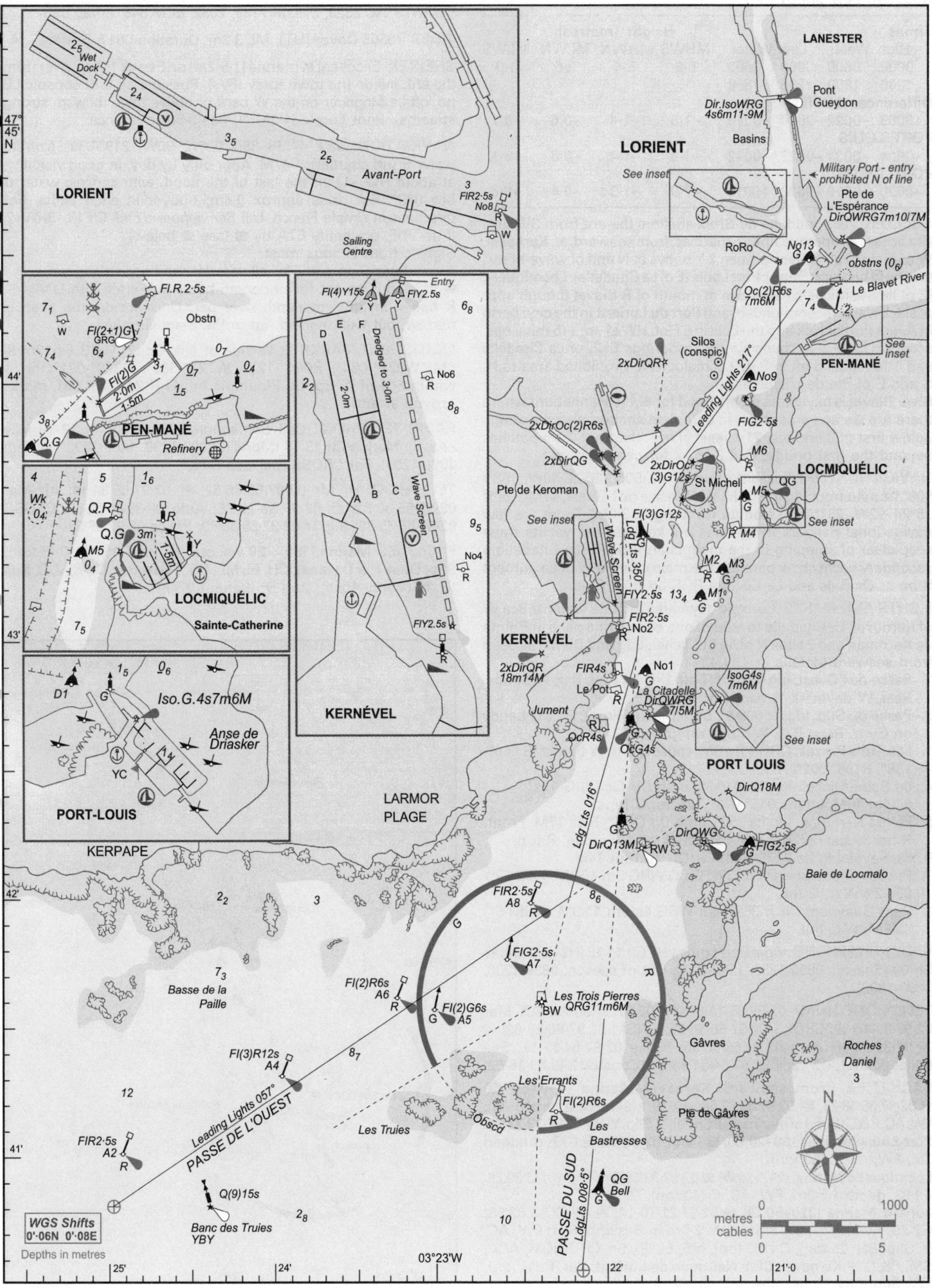

LORIENT *continued*

TIDES +0455 Dover; ML 3·1; Duration 0620; Zone –0100

Standard Port BREST (⟵)

Times				Height (metres)			
High Water		Low Water		MHWS	MHWN	MLWN	MLWS
0000	0600	0000	0600	6·9	5·4	2·6	1·0
1200	1800	1200	1800				
Differences LORIENT							
+0003	–0022	–0020	–0010	–1·8	–1·4	–0·6	–0·2
PORT LOUIS							
+0004	–0021	–0022	–0012	–1·8	–1·4	–0·6	–0·1
PORT D'ETEL							
+0020	–0010	+0030	+0010	–2·0	–1·3	–0·4	+0·5

SHELTER Very good. Ile de Groix shelters the ent from SW'lies. Hbr access all tides/weather. 5 marinas, from seaward, at: **Kernével**, W of main chan (enter between 2 Y buoys at N end of wave-break, thence Ⓥ berths at S end); **Port Louis** (E of La Citadelle); **Locmiquélic** (E of Ile Ste Michel); **Pen Mané** at mouth of R Blavet though appr at slack water recommended; and **Port du Lorient** in the city: berth in Avant Port or lock into the Bassin à Flot, HW±1 sp, ±15 mins nps; access HJ. No ⚓ in chans/hbr, but moorings ENE of La Citadelle and ⚓ for shoal draft in B de Locmalo. Note prohibited area to N, S and E of Pte de L'Espérance.

River Blavet is navigable on the flood for 6M to Hennebont where there are Ⓥs and a pontoon in complete shelter; also moorings below first of 3 bridges, 21m least cl'nce. Caution: 0.3m patches beyond the first bridge. See 9.15.17 for canal access.

NAVIGATION WPT Passe du Sud 47°40′·50N 03°22′·40W, 188°/008° from/to front ldg lt, 3·35M. WPT Passe de l'Ouest, 47°40′·80N 03°24′·92W, 237°/057° from/to front ldg lt, 3·0M. There are few navigational dangers if ldg lines are kept to, but yachts must keep clear of shipping in the main chan. Abeam La Citadelle a secondary yacht chan parallels the main chan to W of La Jument R bn tr, Oc R 4s and Le Cochon RGR bn tr, Fl R 4s.

LIGHTS AND MARKS Conspic daymarks include water tr 8ca W of Kernevel, La Citadelle to stbd of ent, submarine pens at Pointe de Keroman and 2 silos N of Ile St Michel. Ldg and Dir lts, as seen from seaward (details in 9.17.4):

1. Passe de l'Ouest: ldg lts 057°, both Dir Q; Front, R tr, W bands. Rear, W daymark, R bands on bldg.
2. Passe du Sud: ldg lts 008·5°, both Dir QR; Front, R □, G bands on Gy tr. Rear, R □, W stripe on grey tr.
3. Les Trois Pierres: QRG 11m 6M; conspic B tr, W bands; G 060°-196°, R196°-002°.
4. Île Saint-Michel: ldg lts 016·5°, both Dir Oc (3) G 12s 8/14m 16M, intens 015°-018°; W trs, G tops.
5. Pte de Keroman: ldg lts 350°, both Dir Oc (2) R 6s 17M. Front, R ho, W bands; Rear, RW topmark on Gy pylon, R top.
6. Kernével: ldg lts 217°, both Dir QR 10/18m 14M.
7. Pte de l'Esperance: Dir lt 037°: Dir Q WRG 8m 10/7M, W036·7°-037·2°; W tr, G top.
8. Pont Gueydon: Dir lt 352°: Iso WRG 4s 6m 11/9M, W351·5°-352·5°; W □ hut.

RADIO TELEPHONE *Vigie Port Louis* VHF Ch 11 16 (H24). Marinas Ch 09 (Season: 0800-1230, 1330-2000. Out of season: 0830-1200, 1400-1800).

TELEPHONE Hr Mr 02·97·37·11·86, 🖷 02.97.37.90.73; Aff Mar 02·97·37·16·22; CROSS 02·97·55·35·35; SNSM 02·97·86·29·62; ⊜ 02·97·37·34·66; Auto 08.36.68.08.56; Police 02·97·64·27·17; Sea Police 02·97·12·12·12; ⊞ 02·97·64·81·58; Brit Consul 01·40·63·16·02.

FACILITIES (from seaward) **Kernével Marina** (410+60 Ⓥ) ☎ 02·97·65·48·25, 🖷 02·97.33.63.56; €2·29. H24 access, depth 3m; FW, AC, P & D (S end of marina; call Ch 09), ⊡, Slip, YC ☎ 02·97·33·77·78.
Port-Louis Marina (160+20 Ⓥ), ☎ 02·97·82·59·55, €1·77, dredged 2m, FW, AC, C (50 ton).
Locmiquélic Marina, (217+10 Ⓥ) ☎ 02·97.33.59.51, 🖷 02·97.33.89.25, €1·83, depth 1·5-3m, FW, AC, C (40 ton), ⊡.
Lorient Marina (320+50 Ⓥ) ☎ 02·97·21·10·14, 🖷 02·97.33.63.56; €2·29, Avant Port 2·5-3m depth, 2·5m in Bassin à Flot; FW, AC, ⊡, Slip, BH (25 ton), C (100 ton), ME, El, Ⓔ, Sh, CH, SHOM, ACA, SM, P& D @ Kernevel; **Club Nautique de Lorient**, Bar, C (1½ ton), FW, Slip. **City** All facilities, ✉, Ⓑ, ≹, ✈.

RIVER ÉTEL *9.17.15*

Morbihan **47°39′·60N 03°12′·38W** ✿✿✿✿✿

CHARTS AC 2822; SHOM 7138, 7032; ECM 545; Imray C38

TIDES +0505 Dover (UT); ML 3·2m; Duration 0617. See 9.17.14

SHELTER Excellent at marina (1·5-2m) on E bank 1M up-river from the ent, inside the town quay (FVs). Possible ⚓s S of conspic LB ho, off Le Magouër on the W bank or above town (beware strong streams). Pont Lorois (1·3M N) has 9·5m clearance.

NAVIGATION WPT 47°38'·38N 03°12'·90W, 219°/039° from/to water tr (off chartlet), 1·47M. Appr only by day, in good visibility, at about HW –1½ on the last of the flood, with conspic water tr brg 039°. Bar dries approx 0·4m; buoyed/lit chan shifts. For directions in simple French, call *Semaphore d'Etel* Ch 13, -3HW+2. If no VHF, pre-notify ETA by ☎ (see ☎ below).
Signals from Fenoux mast:
Arrow horiz = no entry for all vessels; conditions dangerous.
● hoisted = no ent for undecked boats and craft <8m LOA.
R flag = insufficient depth over bar. Once inside, the chan is narrow, but well marked, up to Pte Saint-Germain.

LIGHTS AND MARKS Lt W side of ent, Oc (2) WRG 6s 13m 9/6M, W022°-064°, R064°-123°, W123°-330°, G330°-022°; no ⚓ within 5ca of it. Épi de Plouhinic bn, Fl R 2·5s 7m 2M, marks groyne at ent.

RADIO TELEPHONE Call *Semaphore d'Etel* VHF Ch 13 16 (see above). Marina Ch 13 16 (Mon/Fri 0800-1200, 1400-1800. Sat/Sun 1000-1200). For CROSS Étel, see 6.15.1.

TELEPHONE Hr Mr 02·97·55·46·62, 🖷 02·97.55.34.14; Aff Mar 02·97·55·30·32; ⊜ 02·97·36·20·76; Auto 08·36·65·02·56; CROSS 02·97·55·35·35; Sig Tr 02·97·55·35·59; Police 02·97·55·32·11.

FACILITIES Marina (180 + 20 visitors) €1·52, FW, AC, C (6 ton), Slip; **Quay** P & D (cans), CH, El, ME, Sh. **Town** Bar, Dr, R, V, ⊡, Bus to ≹ (Auray 15km) and ✈ (Lorient 32km).

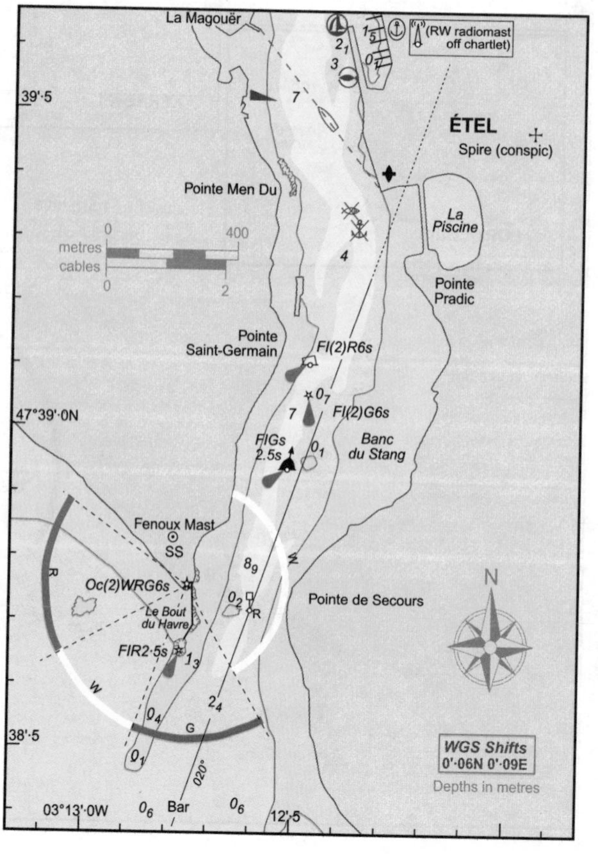

LE PALAIS (BELLE ILE) *9.17.16*

Morbihan **47°20'·89N 03°08'·98W** ✽✽✽◊◊◊✿✿✿

CHARTS AC 2822; Imray C39; SHOM 7142, 7032; ECM 545

TIDES +0458 Dover; ML 3·1; Duration 0615; Zone –0100

Standard Port BREST (⟵)

Times				Height (metres)			
High Water		Low Water		MHWS	MHWN	MLWN	MLWS
0000	0600	0000	0600	6·9	5·4	2·6	1·0
1200	1800	1200	1800				
Differences LE PALAIS							
+0007	–0028	–0025	–0020	–1·8	–1·4	–0·7	–0·3
ILE DE HOUAT							
+0010	–0025	–0020	–0015	–1·7	–1·3	–0·6	–0·2
ILE DE HÖEDIC							
+0010	–0035	–0027	–0022	–1·8	–1·4	–0·7	–0·3

SHELTER Good, except in strong E'lies which cause marked swell. Very crowded in season. Deep draft yachts moor on 3 trots of Ⓥs inside Mole Bourdelle; shallow draft on Ⓥs to port. Inner hbr mostly dries. Lock into the Bassin à Flot opens HW –1½ to +1 (0600-2200LT), for berths on S side in 2·5m; thence via lifting bridge into marina (1·7m).

NAVIGATION WPT 47°21'·20N 03°08'·00W, 065°/245° from/to Jetée Nord lt, 0·80M. No navigational dangers, but beware fast ferries. ⚓ between Sauzon (see below) and Le Palais is prohib.

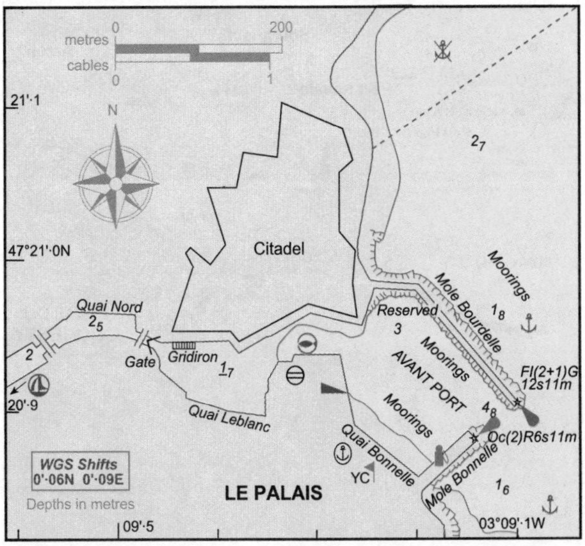

LIGHTS AND MARKS Lts as chartlet. La Citadelle is conspic on N side of hbr.

RADIO TELEPHONE VHF Ch 09 (Season: 0800-1200, 1400-2000. Out of season 0800-1200, 1500-1800).

TELEPHONE Hr Mr 02·97·31·42·90; Aff Mar 02·97·31·80·16 (open Tues am); SNSM 02·97·31·54·07; CROSS 02·97·55·35·35; ⊖ 02·97·31·85·95; Auto 08.36.68.08.56; Police 02·97·31·80·22; Dr 02·97·31·40·90; Ⓗ 02·97·31·48·48; Brit Consul 01·40·63·16·02.

FACILITIES **Marina** (100 buoys Avant Port, 100 Bassin á Flot) ☎ 02·97·31·42·90, €1·28, P, D, AC, FW, ME, El, Sh, Access HW–1½ to +1, HJ; **Avant Port** M, AB, P, D, Slip, FW, C (10 & 5 ton). **Town** V, Gaz, R, Bar, ✉, Ⓑ, ⇌ (ferry to Quiberon), ✈. Ferry: Roscoff.

OTHER HARBOUR ON BELLE ILE

SAUZON, Belle Ile, **47°22'·53N 03°12'·93W**. AC 2822; SHOM 7142, 7032; ECM 545; HW +0450 on Dover (UT); ML 3·0m; Duration 0615. Small attractive hbr, 4M WNW of Le Palais. Good shelter except in E winds. 12 Ⓥs in about 1·5m on W side of Avant Port €1·10 (FVs moor on E side), or dry out in inner hbr, or ⚓ N of the NW Jetée, €0·91. Main lt QG 9m 6M. NW Jetée Fl G 4s. SE Jetée Fl R 4s. Facilities: FW on quay; V, R, Bar in village. Hr Mr for Jul/Aug only.

PORT HALIGUEN *9.17.17*

Morbihan **47°29'·40N 03°06'·00W** ✽✽✽◊◊◊✿✿

CHARTS AC 2822; Imray C38, 39; SHOM 7141, 7032, 7033; ECM 545

TIDES +0500 Dover; ML 3·1; Duration 0615; Zone –0100

Standard Port BREST (⟵)

Times				Height (metres)			
High Water		Low Water		MHWS	MHWN	MLWN	MLWS
0000	0600	0000	0600	6·9	5·4	2·6	1·0
1200	1800	1200	1800				
Differences PORT HALIGUEN							
+0015	–0020	–0015	–0010	–1·7	–1·3	–0·6	–0·3
LA TRINITÉ							
+0020	–0020	–0015	–0005	–1·5	–1·1	–0·5	–0·2

SHELTER Good, but uncomfortable in strong NW to NE winds. Access H24 at all tides. Marina boat will meet. Visitors usually berth alongside on pontoon 'V' to stbd of ent.

NAVIGATION WPT 47°29'·80N 03°05'·00W, 060°/240° from/to bkwtr lt, 0·75M. From W or S, appr via Passage de la Teignouse. Banc de Quiberon, marked by NCM and SCM buoys, is shoal (1·5m) at S end. 500m ENE of bkwtr lt in R sector 240°-299°, beware 1·8m shoal, with unlit SCM buoy.

LIGHTS AND MARKS W sector 246°-252° of Port-Maria main lt, Q WRG 28m 14/10M, leads N of Banc de Quiberon; W sector 299°-306° of bkwtr lt, Oc (2) WR 6s 10m 12/9M, leads S of it.

RADIO TELEPHONE VHF Ch 09.

TELEPHONE Hr Mr 02·97·50·20·56; ⊖ 02·97·55·73·46; CROSS 02·97·55· 35·35; SNSM 02·97·50·14·39; Météo 02·97·64·34·86; Auto 08.36.68.08.56; Police 02·97·50·07·39; Dr 02·97·50·13·94.

FACILITIES **Marina** (860+100Ⓥ) ☎ 02·97·50·20·56, 📠 02·97·50·50·50, €1·98, Slip, P, D, C (2 ton), BH (13 ton), ME, El, Sh, AC, CH, FW, ⊡, SM, Bar, R, V. **Town** (Quiberon) V, Gaz, R, Ice, Bar, ✉, Ⓑ, ⇌, ✈.

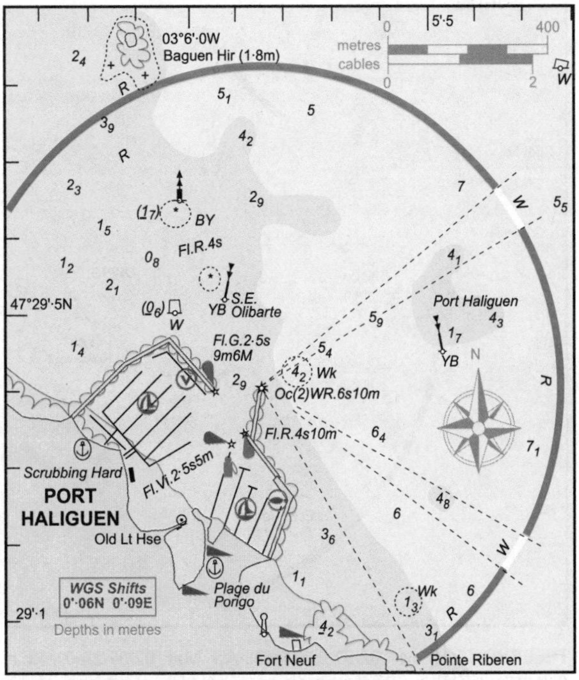

PORT MARIA, Morbihan, **47°28'·65N 03°07'·25W**. AC 2822; SHOM 5352, 7032. Tides as 9.17.17. Shelter good in all winds, but busy ferry/FV port; only suitable for yachts as a refuge or in emergency. Access dangerous in strong SE–SW winds. N half hbr dries. E mole reserved for ferries. ⚓ in SW of hbr in approx 2m. Hr Mr/Aff Mar ☎ 02·97·50·08·71; Facilities: ⊖, C (6 ton), FW at E quay, El, ME, Sh, SHOM.

LA TRINITÉ-SUR-MER *9.17.18*

Morbihan **47°34'·06N 03°00'·60W** ❁❁❁◊◊◊✿✿

CHARTS AC 2358, 2823; Imray C39; SHOM 7141, 7033, 7034; ECM 545, 546

TIDES +0455 Dover; ML 3·2; Duration 0610; Zone –0100
Standard Port BREST (⟵). Differences see 9.17.17.

SHELTER Very good, except in strong SE/S winds near HW when La Vaneresse sandbank is covered. Access H24 at all tides. Marina boat will meet. No ⚓/fishing in river. Speed limit 5kn.

NAVIGATION WPT 47°33′·38N 03°00′·30W, 167°/347° from/to front ldg lt, 1·75M. No navigational dangers; the river is well marked by buoys and perches. Best water close to E bank. Beware many oyster beds, marked with perches. The channel is buoyed on both W sectors.

LIGHTS AND MARKS Conspic daymarks include: Mouskerrk, off-white top; and ✠ spire at La Trinité. Ldg marks (below) are difficult to see by day. Pte de Kernevest ldg lts 347°: Front Q WRG 11m 10/7M (W345°-013°); rear Dir Q 21m 15M, synch, intens 337°-357°. 1M up-river: Dir lt 347°, Oc WRG 4s 9m 13/11M (W346°-348°). S Pier, Oc (2) WR 6s (W293°-300°). Ⓥ pontoon is first beyond ☆ Iso R 4s.

RADIO TELEPHONE Marina VHF Ch 09.

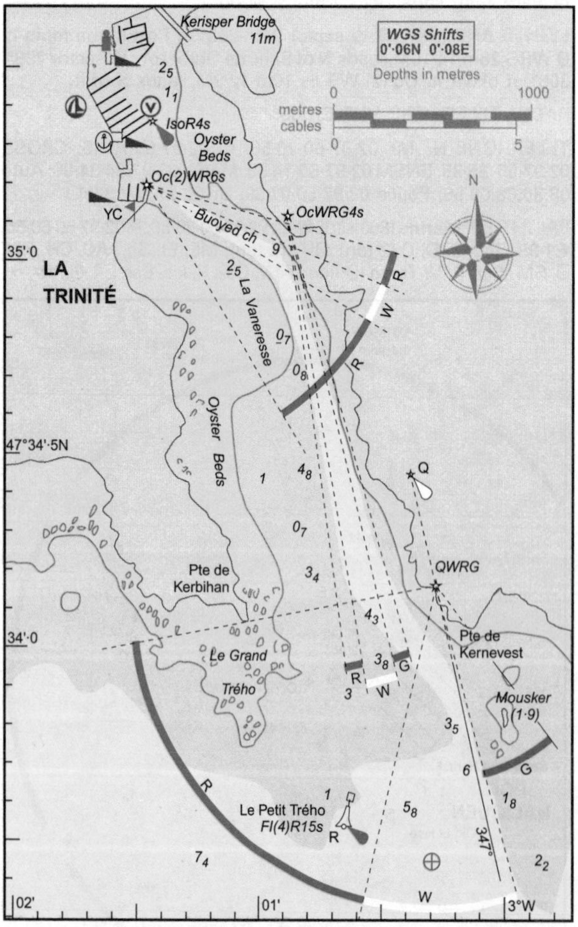

TELEPHONE Hr Mr 02·97·52·71·49; Aff Mar 02·97·24·01·43 at Auray; CROSS 02·97·55·35·35; SNSM 02·97·55·01·15; ⊜ 02·97·55·73·46; Météo 02·97·64·34·86; Auto 08.36.68.08.56; Police 02·97·55·71·62; Dr 02·97·55·74·03; Brit Consul 01·40·63·16·02.

FACILITIES **Marina** (900+100Ⓥ) ☎ 02·97·52·71·49, 📠 02·97.55.86.89, €2·29, AC, P, D, FW, BH (36 ton), Gridiron, M, ME, El, CH, SHOM, Ⓔ, SM, Sh; **Club Nautique** ☎ 02·97·55·73·48. **Town** V, Gaz, R, Bar, Ice, ✉, Ⓑ, ⇌ (Auray), ✈ (Lorient). Ferry: Roscoff or St Malo.

CROUESTY *9.17.19*

Morbihan **47°32'·52N 02°54'·03W** ❁❁❁◊◊◊✿✿

CHARTS AC 2823, 2353; Imray C39; SHOM 6992, 7034, 7033; ECM 546

TIDES +0505 Dover; ML 3·0; Duration 0555; Zone –0100

Standard Port BREST (⟵)

Times				Height (metres)			
High Water		Low Water		MHWS	MHWN	MLWN	MLWS
0000	0600	0000	0600	6·9	5·4	2·6	1·0
1200	1800	1200	1800				
Differences PORT NAVALO							
+0030	–0005	–0010	–0005	–2·0	–1·5	–0·8	–0·3

SHELTER Good, protected from W'lies by Quiberon Peninsula; additional shelter in very large marina which contains 5 (7 planned for 2001) large separate basins. Ⓥ pontoons on S side of fairway.

NAVIGATION WPT 47°32′·04N 02°55′·21W, 238°/058° from/to front ldg lt, 1·1M. There are no navigational problems, the ent being well marked and dredged 1·8m through strong onshore winds can raise dangerous seas in the entrance. See also Morbihan 9.17.20.

LIGHTS AND MARKS Ldg lts 058°: both Dir Q 10/27m 19M, intens 056·5°-059·5°. By day, front W vert stripe on R panel; rear grey lt ho. Bkwtr hds: N = Oc (2) R 6s, S = Fl G 4s, plus lead-in buoys.

RADIO TELEPHONE VHF Ch 09.

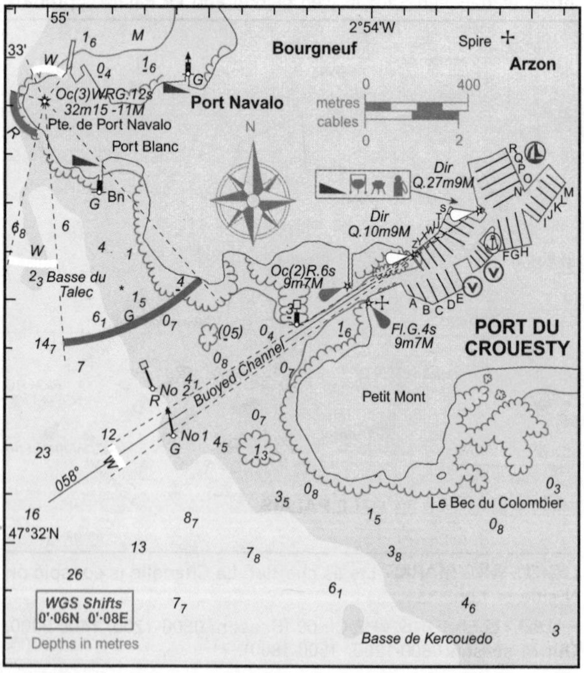

TELEPHONE Hr Mr 02·97·53·73·33; Aff Mar 02·97·41·84·10; ⊜ 02·97·01·36·00; CROSS 02·97·55·35·35; Auto 08·36·68·08·56; SNSM 02·97·41·35·35; Police 02·97·53·71·65; Dr 02·97·53·71·61; Brit Consul 01·40·63·16·02.

FACILITIES **Marina** (1400+120 Ⓥ) ☎ 02·97·53·73·33, 📠 02·97.53.90.22, €2·29, P, D, AC, FW, ME, El, Sh, Slip, BH (45 ton), C (10 ton), CH, Bar, M, Ⓔ, SM. **Town** V, Gaz, R, Bar, ✉ & Ⓑ (Arzon), ⇌ (Vannes), ✈ (Vannes, Lorient, St Nazaire).

ISLAND HARBOUR IN THE BAIE DE QUIBERON

ÎLE HOUAT, 47°23′·60N 02°57′·25W. AC 2353; SHOM 7033. HW +0505 on Dover (UT); ML 3·1m; Duration 0605; See 9.17.16. Good shelter, except from N/NE'lies, at Port St Gildas, near E end of the N coast. Appr from N or NE passing abeam La Vieille rk (conspic 14m). Avoid rks 6m inboard of bkwtr and 15m off lt tr. Moor on double trots; no ⚓ in hbr. S part of hbr dries. Keep clear of ferries and FVs on W and N quays. Lts as 8.17.4. Few facilities.

GOLFE DU MORBIHAN *9.17.20*

Morbihan **47°32'·92N 02°55'·26W**

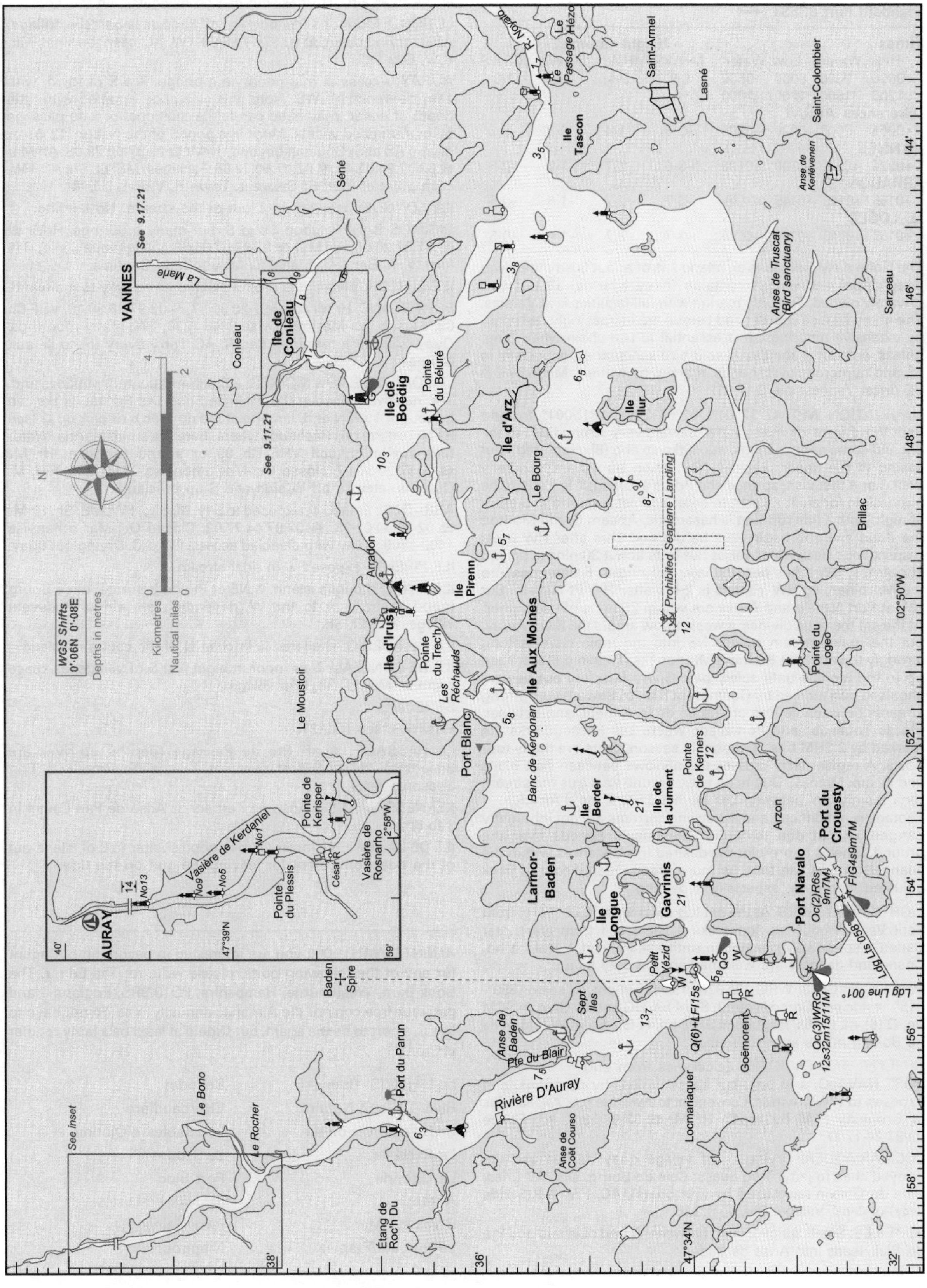

CHARTS AC 2358, 2823; Imray C39; SHOM 6992, 7034, 7033; ECM 546

TIDES +0515 Dover; ML 3·0; Zone –0100

Standard Port BREST (⟵)

Times				Height (metres)			
High Water		Low Water		MHWS	MHWN	MLWN	MLWS
0000	0600	0000	0600	6·9	5·4	2·6	1·0
1200	1800	1200	1800				
Differences AURAY							
+0055	0000	+0020	+0005	–2·0	–1·4	–0·8	–0·2
VANNES							
+0220	+0200	+0200	+0125	–3·6	–2·7	–1·6	–0·5
ARRADON							
+0155	+0145	+0145	+0130	–3·7	–2·7	–1·6	–0·5
LE LOGEO							
+0155	+0140	+0145	+0125	–3·7	–2·7	–1·6	–0·5

The Golfe du Morbihan is an inland sea of about 50sq miles with deep apprs and ent. It contains many islands, all but two privately owned. The only marina with full facilities is at Vannes. The many ⚓s (see chartlet and below) are increasingly restricted by extensive moorings. It is essential to use chain when ⚓ing, unless well out of the tide. Avoid bird sanctuaries, especially in SE and numerous oyster beds, marked by withies. Much of E & SE dries. Vannes, see 9.17.21.

NAVIGATION WPT 47°32′·04N 02°55′·21W, 181°/001° from/to Petit Vézid front ldg mark, 2·2M. Beware very strong tides in the ent and some narrow chans, max 5$\frac{3}{4}$kn sp ebb (8kn reported), but easing in the upper reaches. Navigation buoys are generally unlit. For a first visit, springs should be avoided; it is likely to be impossible for an aux yacht to enter against a sp ebb and entry at night with a tide running is hazardous. Abeam Grand Mouton the flood and ebb begin 3hrs before and 3hrs after HW Brest respectively; slack water varies but lasts about 30mins at sp and 1hr at nps. HW times become later the further E one goes into the Morbihan, eg HW Vannes is 2 hrs after HW Pt Navalo. But HW at Port Navalo and Auray are within 25 mins of each other. At the ent the flood divides: a weaker flow enters the River Auray; but the major stream rushes NE into the main chan, setting strongly toward Petit & Grand Mouton rks. To avoid these, keep up to the ldg line until safely past Grand Mouton, but beware shoals to port marked by Goémorent R bn tr. Beware very strong streams between Île Berder and Île de la Jument, and between Pte de Toulindac and Port Blanc where Les Réchauds rks are marked by 2 SHM bns. Caution: In season, there are many tour boats. A regular ferry crosses the narrows between Port Blanc and Île aux Moines. Due to an eddy around Île d'Irus the stream runs mainly SW between Les Réchauds and Pte d'Arradon.

Pilotage is not difficult and the strong currents are not inherently dangerous, but due to higher than usual speeds over the ground, it helps to pre-plot the desired trks/distances within the channels; marks can then be more readily identified and track adjusted with ease, especially if beating.

LIGHTS AND MARKS At the ent ldg daymarks on 001° are: front Petit Vézid W obelisk (looks like a yacht sail from afar), rear Baden ✠ spire (3·3M); maintain until abeam Port Navalo lt ho. Chans and dangers are well marked; the only lts are:

Port Navalo Oc (3) WRG 12s 32m 15/11M at ent, W sector 359°-015°. Inside ent: Grand Mouton SHM bn, QG and Le Grégan SCM bn, Q (6) + L Fl 15s. Roguédas SHM bn, Fl G 2·5s, at W end of Île de Boëdig marks appr to Vannes.

SHELTER AND FACILITIES (clockwise from ent)

PORT NAVALO: ⚓ in bay, but space limited by moorings, and exposed to W/NW winds. Convenient to await the tide. All facilities at Crouesty (½M by road). Hr Mr ☎ 02·97·53·82·12; Police 02·97·24·17·17.

LOCMARIAQUER: Drying ⚓ off village quay; ferries use the buoyed chan to jetty. Two quays: Cale de Bourg, slip, AB dries; Cale du Guilvin (also used by tour boats), AC, FW, AB (S side only) or ⚓ off. Village: Bar, V, R, ME.

SEPT ÎLES: Small, quiet ⚓; chan between W end of island and Pte du Blair leads into Anse de Baden.

PORT DU PARUN: No mooring but boatyard with quay, slip and all facilities. ☎ 02·97·57·00·15.

LE ROCHER: Good shelter, but almost full of moorings. Further N the river almost dries, but can be navigated on the tide.

LE BONO: Moor or ⚓ (rky bottom) off Banc de la Sarcelle. **Village**, AB in drying basin, ☎ 02·97·57·88·98, FW, AC, cash terminal, ME, R, V, Gaz, ✉.

AURAY: Access at mid-flood via a bridge, 3ca S of town, with 14m clearance MHWS. Note: this clearance, coupled with little depth of water, may need careful calculations for safe passage by high-masted yachts. Moor in a pool S of the bridge; 12 Ⓥs or drying AB at St Goustan beyond. HrMr ☎ 02.97.56.29.08, Aff Mar ☎ 02.97.24.01.43, 📠 02.97.50.72.66. Facilities: ME, El, Sh, AC, FW, cash point at Pont St Sauveur. **Town** R, V, Bar, ✉, ⇌.

ILE LONGUE: near SE tip ⚓ out of the stream. No landing.

LARMOR BADEN: good ⚓s to S, but many moorings, HrMr ☎ 02.97.57.20.86. Aff Mar ☎ 02·97·57·05·66. Village: quay, slip, C (5 ton), V, R, Bar, ✉. In season ferry to I. de Gavrinis.

ILE BERDER: pleasant ⚓ E of the island; causeway to mainland.

PORT BLANC: Hr Mr ☎ 02·97·26·30·57, 📠 02.97.26.30.16. VHF Ch 09. Closed Oct-Mar otherwise 0845-1230, FW; many moorings. Quay, slip, cash terminal, Bar, R, AC. Ferry every ½hr to Île aux Moines.

LE PORT D'ILE AUX MOINES: a much-frequented, public island. The narrows between the mainland and Les Réchauds rks can be rough. ⚓ off N end, landing at Pte du Trec'h or pick up Ⓥ (see Hr Mr) off Pte des Réchauds where there is a small marina. Water taxi available; call VHF Ch 09 or sound foghorn. Hr Mr ☎ 02·97·26·30·57, closed Oct-Mar otherwise 0845-1230, FW, M. Other quieter ⚓s off W side and S tip of island.

ARRADON: limited ⚓, exposed to S'ly. M, Slip, FW, ME, Sh. Hr Mr ☎ 02·97·44·01·23, 📠 02.97.44.77.03. Closed Oct-Mar otherwise 1400-1700. Quay with disabled access, FW, AC. Drying out quay.

ILE PIRENN: exposed ⚓ in tidal stream.

ILE D'ARZ: a public island. ⚓ NE of Pte du Béluré; E of Le Bourg (good shelter), or to the W, depending on winds. Rudevent village: ME, El, Sh.

ILE DE BOËDIG: sheltered ⚓ in chan N of the centre of island.

ILE DE CONLEAU: ⚓ or moor in bight just S of village, as space permits. ME, El, Sh, R in village.

SÉNÉ: ME.

VANNES: see 9.17.21.

LE PASSAGE: ⚓ off Pte du Passage (depths up-river are uncertain), 2M to SW of river ent. Village (St Armel): V, Bar. Seasonal ferry.

KERNERS: ⚓ off the Anse de Kerners or Anse de Pen Castel in 3 to 6m.

ILE DE LA JUMENT (or Ar Gazek): good shelter to E of island out of the tide; convenient for leaving the gulf on the tide.

AGENTS WANTED If you are interested in becoming our agent for any of the following ports, please write to: The Editor, The Book Barn, Westbourne, Hampshire, PO10 8RS, England – and get your free copy of the Almanac annually. You do not have to live in a port to be the agent, but should at least be a fairly regular visitor.

Le Légué (St Brieuc)	Bénodet
River Loire/St Nazaire	L'Herbaudière
St Gilles-Croix-de-Vie	Les Sables d'Olonne
La Rochelle	La Seudre
La Gironde	Port Bloc
Anglet	St Jean-de-Luz
Dives-sur-Mer	River Seine
Le Touquet/Étaples	Nieupoort

VANNES *9.17.21*

Morbihan **47°38'·45N 02°45'·62W**

CHARTS AC 2358, 2823; Imray C39; SHOM 7034; ECM 546

TIDES See GOLFE DU MORBIHAN 9.17.20. ML 2·0m; Zone –0100

SHELTER Very good, protected from all winds. Access by day only. Waiting pontoons are upstream (nearly dries) or downstream of **swing bridge**, which only opens whilst lock gate into wet basin is open, ie HW±2½. Bridge opens at H and H+30 in season (15 Jun – 15 Sep) and at weekends; but only at H out of season. Outbound craft have priority over arrivals. NB: during the first and final ½ hour periods when the lock is open, the bridge will open on request VHF Ch 09. There is an intercom to Hr Mr on downstream waiting pontoon. The narrow **lock gate**, remotely-controlled by the Hr Mr, opens HW±2½ (in season 0800-2100LT and 0800-1900 Sun; out of season 0900-1200 1330-1800 Mon-Fri; 0900-1200, 1400-1800 Sat; 0830-1200 Sun). Lock sill, 0·4m above CD, retains 2·4m inside wet basin.
Note: HW Vannes –2½ just happens to be HW Port Tudy (9.17.13) which is used by the Hr Mr to determine when the lock opens. *Horaires d'Ouverture du Bassin* (a free annual schedule of lock hrs) is available from: Bureau du Port de Plaisance, La Rabine, 56000 Vannes.
Berths: Marina boat may indicate a vacant finger pontoon; otherwise visitors berth N/S on pontoons D and G just S of movable inner foot-bridge (*passerelle*).

NAVIGATION WPT: see 9.17.20. After Roguédas SHM lt bn do not cut the corner. Where the chan turns N can be identified by a pink house on the E bank. Thereafter passage past Ile de Conleau is easy and well marked. Beacon'd appr chan to Vannes is narrow, least depth 0·7m.

LIGHTS AND MARKS Bridge sigs (vert) on bridge's central pier are:
2 ● = no passage; 2 Oc ● = standby; 2 ● = proceed;
2 Oc ● = only transit if committed;
● = unmasted boats may transit.
Lock sigs: ● and ● = Lock closed; No lts = Lock open.

RADIO TELEPHONE VHF Ch 09.

TELEPHONE Hr Mr 02·97·54·16·08, 02·97·54·00·47, Fax 02·97·42·48·80; Aff Mar 02·97·63·40·95, Fax 02.97.63.46.77; ⊖ 02·97·63·33·28; CROSS 02·97·55·35·35, Fax 02.97.63.71.75; SNSM 02·97·26·00·56; Météo 02·97·42·49·49; Auto 08.36.65.08.56; Police 02·97·47·19·20; Dr 02·97·47·47·25; Ⓗ 02·97·01·41·41, Fax 02.97.01.40.07; Brit Consul 01·40·63·16·02.

FACILITIES **Marina** (240+60 Ⓥ), ☎ 02·97·54·16·08, Fax 02·97.42.48.80, €1·83, Slip, Ⓓ, FW, AC, ME, C (12 ton); P & D @ HW±2½ from pontoon on E side of canal, just S of lock. **City** V, R, Sh, CH, El, Ⓔ, SM, SHOM, ✉, Ⓑ, ⇌, ✈

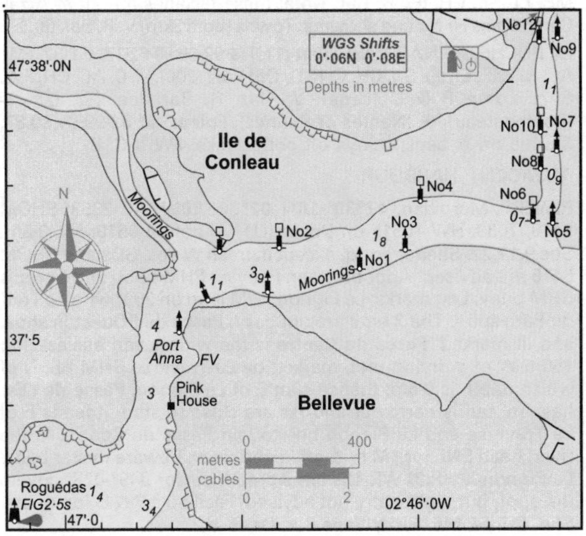

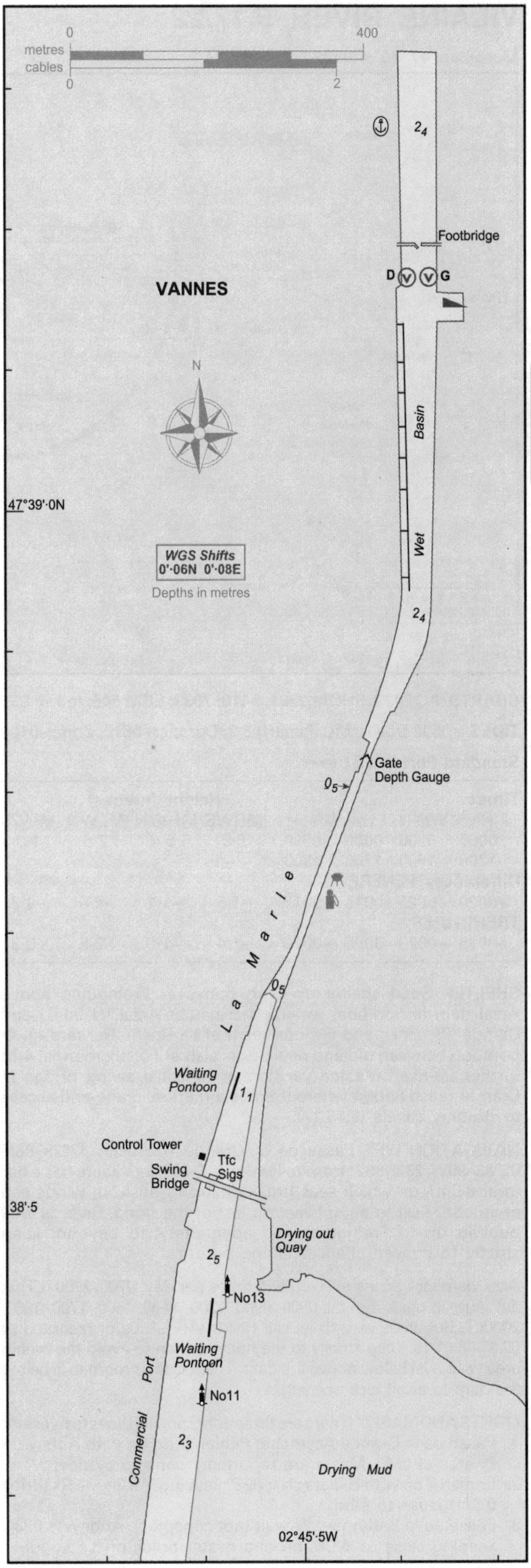

VILAINE RIVER *9.17.22*

Morbihan **47°30'·40N02°28'·60W**

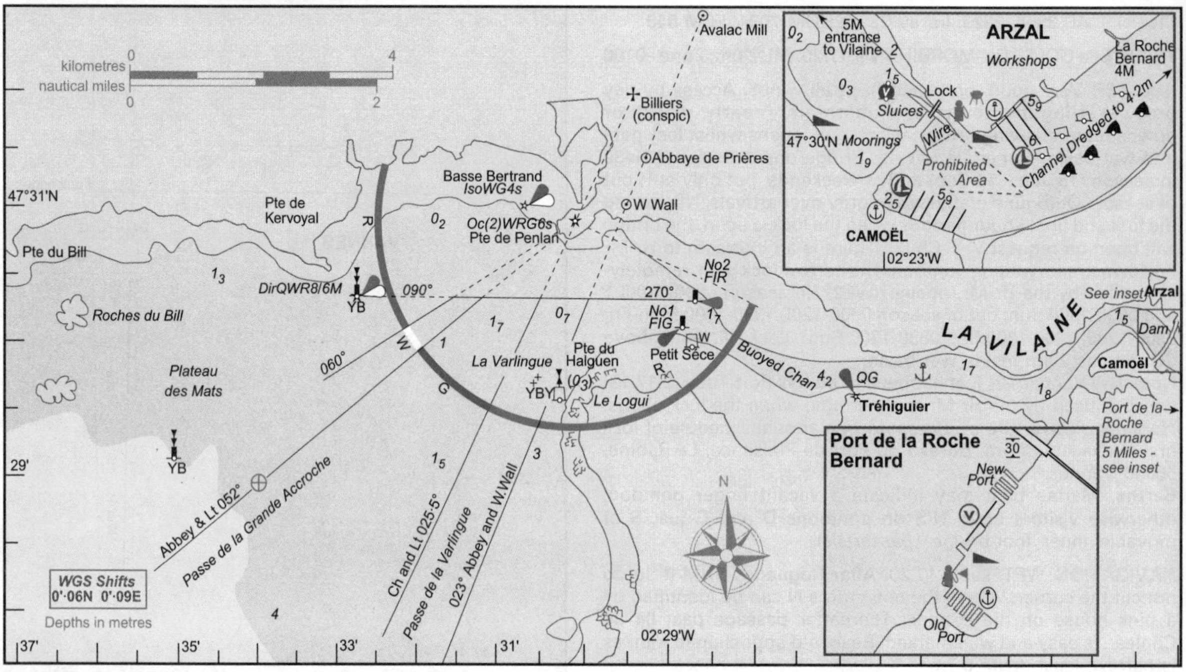

CHARTS AC 2823; SHOM 2381, 5418, 7033; ECM 546; Imray C39

TIDES +0500 Dover; ML (Penerf) 3·3; Duration 0610; Zone –0100

Standard Port BREST (⟵)

Times				Height (metres)			
High Water		Low Water		MHWS	MHWN	MLWN	MLWS
0000	0600	0000	0600	6·9	5·4	2·6	1·0
1200	1800	1200	1800				
Differences PENERF							
+0020	–0025	–0015	–0015	–1·5	–1·1	–0·6	–0·3
TRÉHIGUIER							
+0035	–0020	–0005	–0010	–1·4	–1·0	–0·5	–0·3

SHELTER Good shelter up-river: buoys at Tréhiguier; above Arzal dam in non-tidal waters, marinas at Arzal (N bank) and Camoël (S bank); and 5M upstream at La Roche Bernard on Ⓥ pontoon between old and new ports; also at Foleux marina, 4½M further up-river. Masted yachts can transit a swing bridge at Cran to reach Redon where there is a marina, crane and access to Brittany canals (9.15.17).

NAVIGATION WPT Passe de la Grande Accroche 47°29'·00N 02°33'·90W, 232°/052° from/to Penlan lt, 3·3M. La Vilaine has a bar (min 0·5m), on which seas break in strong onshore winds esp at sp ebb. Best to enter/leave on last of the flood. River is well buoyed up to Tréhiguier and adequately so beyond; keep strictly to buoyed chan as silting occurs.

Arzal dam lock opens at H, up to 9 times per day, 0700–2200 (LT) in Jul/ Aug; in other months 0800, 0900, 1200, 1400, 1600, 1700, 1900, 2000LT. But times vary daily; call Hr Mr VHF Ch 09 or recorded ☎ 02·97·45·01·15. Keep strictly to the buoyed chan to avoid the prohib area (Y buoys) below/above the dam. There is Ⓥ or room to ⚓ below the dam to await lock opening.

LIGHTS AND MARKS There are three apprs and ldg lines to river ent:

1. Passe de la Grande Accroche: Penlan lt ho on with Abbey de Prières at 052°. Marks are reportedly conspic by day.
2. Penlan lt on with Billiers ch tr 023°, leaving Varlingue Rk (dries 0·3m) close to stbd.
3. Passe de la Varlingue: W wall (not conspic) ⌡ Abbey Tr 023°, keeping close to WCM bn and oyster poles off Le Logui.

Two principal lights are visible in the approaches:

1. Basse Bertrand G tr, Iso WG 4s 6m 9/6M, W040°-054°, G054°-227°, W227°-234°, G234°-040°.
2. Penlan, W tr, R bands Oc (2) WRG 6s 26m 15/11M, R292°-025°, G025°-052°, W052°-060°, R060°-138°, G138°-180°.

At river ent Petit Sécé W bn tr is easier to see than Nos 1 + 2 ch buoys.

RADIO TELEPHONE Lock VHF Ch 18 (HX); Arzal-Camoël marina Ch 09 (French); no VHF at La Roche Bernard.

TELEPHONE
ARZAL/CAMOËL: Hr Mr 02·99·90·05·86; Lock 02·97·45·02·85; Aff Mar 02·99·90·32·62; CROSS 02·97·55·35·35; ⊖ 02·97·63·18·71 at Vannes; Auto 08·36·68·08·56; Brit Consul 01·40·63·16·02; Dr 02·97.45.01.21; Ⓗ 02·99.90.61.20.
LA ROCHE BERNARD: Hr Mr 02·99·90·62·17.

FACILITIES
ARZAL/CAMOËL: **Marina** (630 total, inc 25Ⓥ on each bank) ☎ 02·99·90·05·86, €1·37, FW, AC, ⊡, BH (35 ton), P, D, Gaz, SM, ME, El, Sh, CH, Ⓔ, R, Bar. Note: these facilities are all at Arzal. Camoël has Hr Mr and showers. **Towns** (both 3km) V, R, Bar, Ⓑ, ✉.

LA ROCHE BERNARD: **New Port** (110) ☎ 02·99·90·62·17, €1·37, FW, AC, M, ME, El, Ⓔ, Sh, CH, C(13T); **Old Port** (200), ⊡, C, AC, CH, FW, Slip. **Town** P & D (cans), V, Gaz, R, Bar, Ice, ✉, Ⓑ, ⇌ (Pontchateau), ✈ (Nantes or Rennes). **Foleux:** ☎ 02·99.91.80.87. Marina on N bank; buoys off both banks. FW, AC, R.

ADJACENT HARBOUR

PENERF, Morbihan, **47°30'·10N 02°38'·80W**, AC 2353; SHOM 5418, 7033. HW +0515 on Dover (UT); Duration 0610; ML 3·3m. See 9.17.22. Shelter good, except in fresh W'lies. SDs and SHOM 5418 are advised. Appr between Penvins PHM buoy and Borenis SHM buoy. Ldg marks: Le Pignon PHM lt bn on 359° with Le Tour du Parc spire. The 3 ents are not easy: **Passe de l'Ouest** is shoal and ill marked. **Passe du Centre** is the widest and easiest, ldg 150m W of a drying reef, marked by La Traverse SHM bn, N of which depth is 0·5m; thence 40m E of Le Pignon. **Passe de l'Est** has 4m, but is narrower and rks are close to stbd. It leads E of La Traverse and Le Pignon bns to join Passe du Centre. In the river, head ENE for 1M to Ⓥ off Penerf quay. Beware oyster beds. Le Pignon lt, Fl (3) WR 12s 6m 9/6M, W sector 349°-028° covers the appr, but night entry not advised. Facilities: P & D (on quay), Slip, CH, El, ME, Sh. **Village** Bar, Dr, R, V.

PIRIAC 9.17.23

Loire Atlantique **47°23´·00N 02°32´·63W** ❀❀◇◇✿✿

CHARTS AC 2823; Imray C39, 40; SHOM 7033; ECM 546

TIDES As for Le Croisic 9.17.25. Zone –0100. HW +0505 on Dover (UT); ML 3·1m; Duration 0605.

SHELTER Good in new marina on the E side of the drying FV hbr in small resort village. May be exposed to N'lies. Access HW±3 over sill 2·4m above CD; flap gate is marked by traffic lts (GGW open > 1·5m RRR no entry), a PHM and a SHM perch and by 4 Y SPM perches.

NAVIGATION WPT 47°24´·30N 02°32´·10W, 017°/197° from/to hbr ent, 1·25M. From S and SW keep clear of Plateau de Piriac extending about 1M W and N from the hbr; to the W it is marked by a WCM buoy, Q (9) 15s, and to the NNW by 2 unlit NCM bns. Ile Dumet lies 3.5M WNW with lt, Fl (3) WRG 15s 14m 7/4M; at night its W sector (272° -285°) used in conjunction with the W sector (067°-072°) of Pte de Mesquer lt, Oc (3+1) WRG 12s 7m 10/7M, helps to position within the W sector of Piriac lt, see below; night appr requires care.

LIGHTS AND MARKS Piriac church belfry is conspic daymark, approx aligned 197° with chan. Inner mole hd lt on W bcn tr, Dir Oc (2) WRG 6s 8m 10/7M, R066°-148°, G148°-194°, W194°-201°, R201°-221°; W sector leads 197° through hbr ent. Bkwtr lts are Fl G 4s 5m 5M and Fl R 4s 4m 5M. IPTS at sill.

RADIO TELEPHONE VHF Ch 09.

TELEPHONE Hr Mr ☎ 02·40·23·52·32 , 📠 02·40·15·51·78. Aff Mar 02·40·23·33·35; ⊜ 02·40·23·32·51; CROSS 02·97· 55·35·35; Auto 08·36·68·08·44; SNSM 02·40·23·55·74 (Jul-Aug only).

FACILITIES Marina (480+20 visitors), €1·98, FW, AC, D, P (cans) on quay, Slip, C (15 tons), CH, Ⓔ, El, ME, Sh; drying M, in FV hbr. **Ile Dumet**, 3·5M WNW of Piriac, has pleasant ⚓ on NE side in 2m, clear of mussel beds. Appr with lt ho, Fl (2+1) WRG 15s 14m 7/4M, bearing 215°.

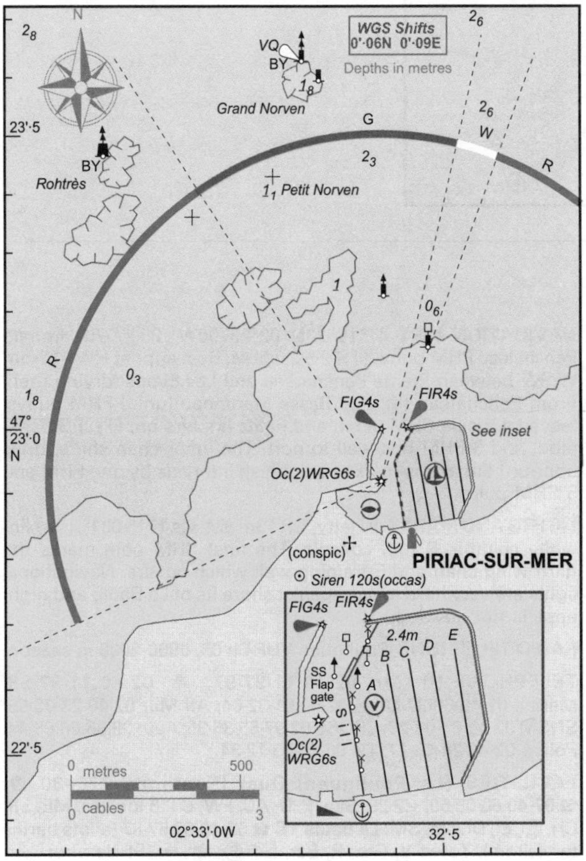

LA TURBALLE 9.17.24

Loire Atlantique **47°20´·78N 02°30´·80W** ❀❀◇◇✿✿

CHARTS AC 2823; Imray C39, 40; SHOM 6826, 7033; ECM 546

TIDES As for Le Croisic 9.17.25

SHELTER Good in all winds, but in strong SSW'lies heavy swell can close the hr. Access H24. Inside ent, turn smartly stbd into marina (1·5-2m) in SE corner. There is an active FV fleet. In Jul/Aug the marina is sometimes closed to new arrivals due to overcrowding. Call before entering; see RT below. In winds N to E it is possible to ⚓ S of the hbr.

NAVIGATION WPT 47°20´·25N 02°32´·35W, 245°/065° from/to W bkwtr lt, 1·15M. Appr from S or W avoiding Plateau du Four, which is well marked/lit.

LIGHTS AND MARKS Plateau du Four, Fl 5s 23m 19M, is 5M SW. Hbr is in G sector (136°-345°) of Le Croisic, Iso WG 4s, 2M to S. (Note: WPT is also on Le Croisic ldg line 156°). Appr in W sector (315°-060°) of W bkwtr lt, Fl (4) WR 12s, to pick up ldg lts 006·5°, both Dir F Vi 11/19m 3M, intens 004°-009°. By day Trescalan ✠ and water tr (conspic), 1M ENE of hbr, lead 070° to just S of ent. R bn tr is 80m off W bkwtr.

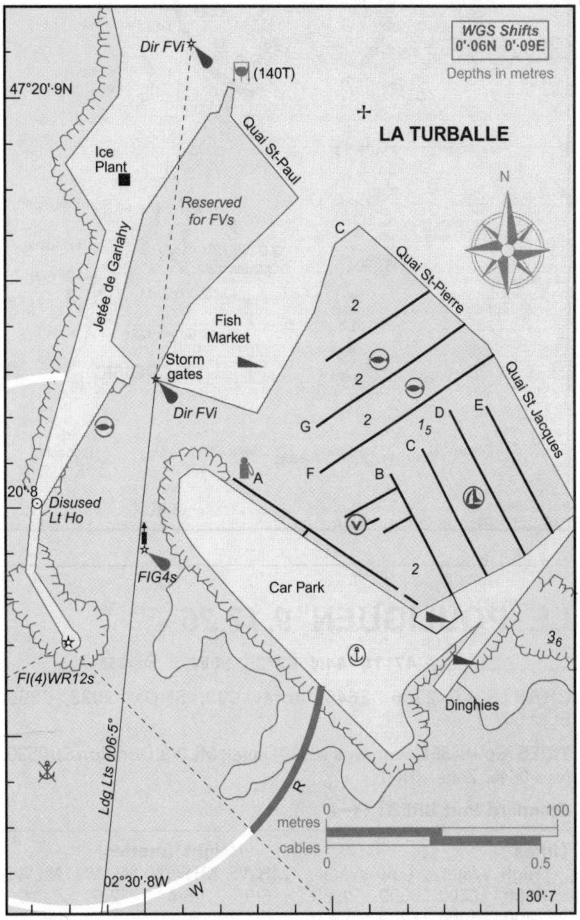

RADIO TELEPHONE Call Marina VHF Ch 09 before entering. If full in Jul/Aug due to overcrowding, an announcement is made on Ch 09.

TELEPHONE Hr Mr 02·40·62·80·40, 📠 02.40.23.47.64; Aff Mar 02·40·23·33·35; ⊜ 02·40·23·32·51; Auto 08·36·68·08·44; SNSM 02·40·23·42·67.

FACILITIES Marina (290+20 visitors, pontoon B), ☎ 02·40·62·80·40, €1·77, FW, AC, Slip, M, C (16 tons), BH (140 tons), D (H24), P at garage 500m, ME, El, Ⓔ, Sh, CH, ♿ in Master Hbr House (Capitainerie), Gaz, R, SM, YC, SHOM, Ice. **Town** V, R, Ⓑ, ✉, 🅟, Dr, Bus to St Nazaire and Nantes.

LE CROISIC *9.17.25*

Loire Atlantique **47°18'·56N 02°31'·27W** ❁❁◊◊◊✿✿✿

CHARTS AC 2823, 2986, 2646; Imray C39; SHOM 6826, 7033, 7395; ECM 546, 547

TIDES +0450 Dover; ML 3·3; Duration 0605; Zone –0100

Standard Port BREST (⟵)

Times				Height (metres)			
High Water		Low Water		MHWS	MHWN	MLWN	MLWS
0000	0600	0000	0600	6·9	5·4	2·6	1·0
1200	1800	1200	1800				
Differences LE CROISIC							
+0015	–0040	–0020	–0015	–1·5	–1·1	–0·6	–0·3

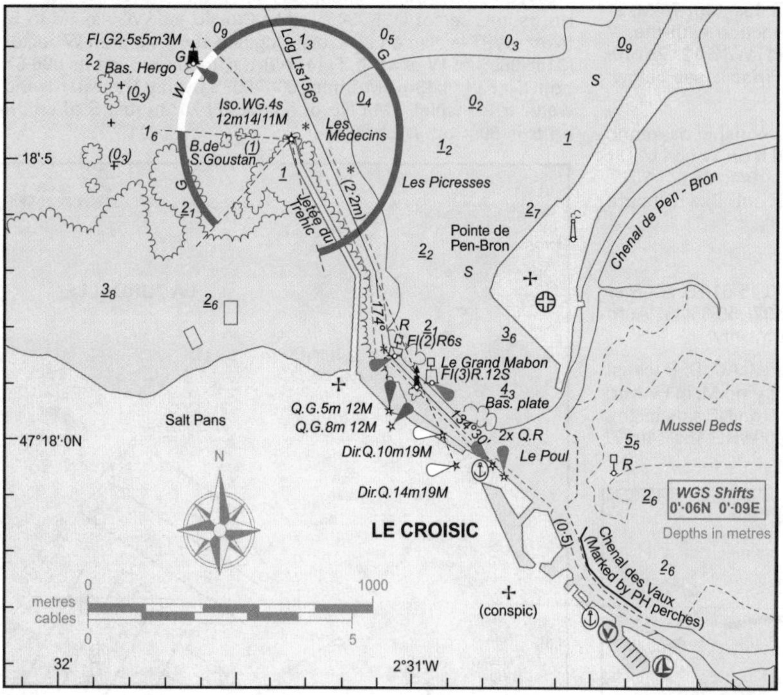

SHELTER Five drying (1·7m) basins, called *Chambres* are formed by islands *(Jonchères)*. Berth in the last *Chambre,* bows to pontoon or against the wall, access HW±1. See Hr Mr for mooring. ⚓ not advised.

NAVIGATION WPT 47°19'·00N 02°31'·55W, 336°/156° from/to front ldg lt, 1·08M. Sp tides reach 4kn. Safest ent is HW±1 sp, HW±2 np. Beware the rks at Hergo Tr, SHM, Fl G 2·5s. Note: the W sector (093°-137°) of Tréhic lt, Iso WG 4s, which leads clear of distant dangers, will lead onto close-in dangers. Keep to the ldg lines as appr and hbr dry extensively to the E.

LIGHTS AND MARKS The hospital and ch belfry are conspic. Outer ldg lts 156°: both Dir Oc (2+1) 12s 10/14m 18M; intens 154°-158°, synch; R □s on W pylons, rear has G top. Middle ldg lts 174°: both QG 5/8m 11M; vis 170°-177°; Y □s with G stripe on G & W pylons, almost obsc'd by trees. Inner ldg lts QR 134°; R/W chequered □s on Fish market roof.

RADIO TELEPHONE VHF Ch 09 (0800-1200; 1330-2000 in season).

TELEPHONE Hr Mr 02·40·23·10·95, 📠 02·40.15·75·92; Aff Mar 02·40·23·06·56; CROSS 02·97·55·35·35; SNSM 02·40·23·01·17; ⊜ 02·40·23·05·38; Météo 08·36·68·08·08; Police 02·40·23·00·19; Dr 02·40·23·01·70; Ⓗ 02·40·23·01·12; Brit Consul 01·40·63·16·02; Marina 02·40·60·37·40.

FACILITIES **Marina** (5th Chambre; 220+15 Ⓥ), €1·00, FW, ME, El, Sh; **Quai** Slip, C (8 & 180 ton), CH, Ⓔ, YC, Divers, ♿. **Town** P & D (cans), V, Gaz, R, Bar, ✉, Ⓑ, ⇌, ✈ (St Nazaire).

LE POULIGUEN *9.17.26*

Loire Atlantique **47°16'·44N 02°25'·30W** ❁❁◊◊✿✿✿

CHARTS AC 2986, 2646; Imray C39; SHOM 7033, 7395; ECM 547

TIDES Sp +0435 Dover, Nps +0530 Dover; ML 3·3; Duration Sp 0530, Nps 0645; Zone –0100

Standard Port BREST (⟵)

Times				Height (metres)			
High Water		Low Water		MHWS	MHWN	MLWN	MLWS
0000	0600	0000	0600	6·9	5·4	2·6	1·0
1200	1800	1200	1800				
Differences LE POULIGUEN							
+0020	–0025	–0020	–0025	–1·5	–1·1	–0·6	–0·3

SHELTER Very good, except in SE winds. 30 Ⓥ berths on pontoon A, to stbd at ent. Yachts up to 2m draft can stay afloat but entrance may dry. Beware strong ebb tide. Fixed bridge up-river has 3m clearance MHWS. Le Pornichet, 3M to the E, is an easier approach and ent. Reefs running 4M SE towards Grand Charpentier lt ho, Q WRG, form a barrier across the Baie du Pouliguen which may be entered through any of 4 passes. In strong S winds, beware swell and breakers.

NAVIGATION WPT 47°15'·20N 02°25'·00W, 250°/070° from/to Penchâteau PHM buoy, Fl R 2·5s, 0·58M. Best appr at HW –1 from W/SW between Pte de Penchateau and Les Evens (drying reef). From Penchâteau (lit) and Basse Martineau (unlit) PHM buoys, leave La Vieille SHM perch and Petits Impairs bn, Fl (2) G 6s, to stbd, and 3 PHM bns well to port. The inner chan shifts, dries approx 1·5m and is marked at longish intervals by one PHM and 5 SHM poles.

LIGHTS AND MARKS W jetty, QR 13m 9M, vis 171°-081°, is a slim white column, R top, conspic. The final SHM pole marks the narrowing chan and E training wall which covers. Navigational lights are very hard to see against shore lts of La Baule and night appr is not advised.

RADIO TELEPHONE Pouliguen VHF Ch 09, 0900-2000 in season.

TELEPHONE Hr Mr 02·40·11·97·97, 📠 02·40.11·97·98; Marina 02·40·60·37·40; ⊜ 02·40·61·32·04; Aff Mar 02·40·23·06·56; SNSM 02·40·61·03·20; CROSS 02·97·55·35·35; Auto 08.36.68.08.44; Police 02·40·24·48·17; Dr 08·36·69·12·34.

FACILITIES **(Le Pouliguen) Quai** (Pontoons 720+30 Ⓥ) ☎ 02·40·60·03·50, €2·29, Slip, P, D, AC, FW, C (18 ton), M, ME, Sh, CH, Ⓔ, El, Divers, SM; **La Baule YC** ☎ 02·40·60·57·87 (allots berths to visitors). **Town** V, Gaz, R, Bar, ✉, Ⓑ, ⇌, ✈ (St Nazaire).

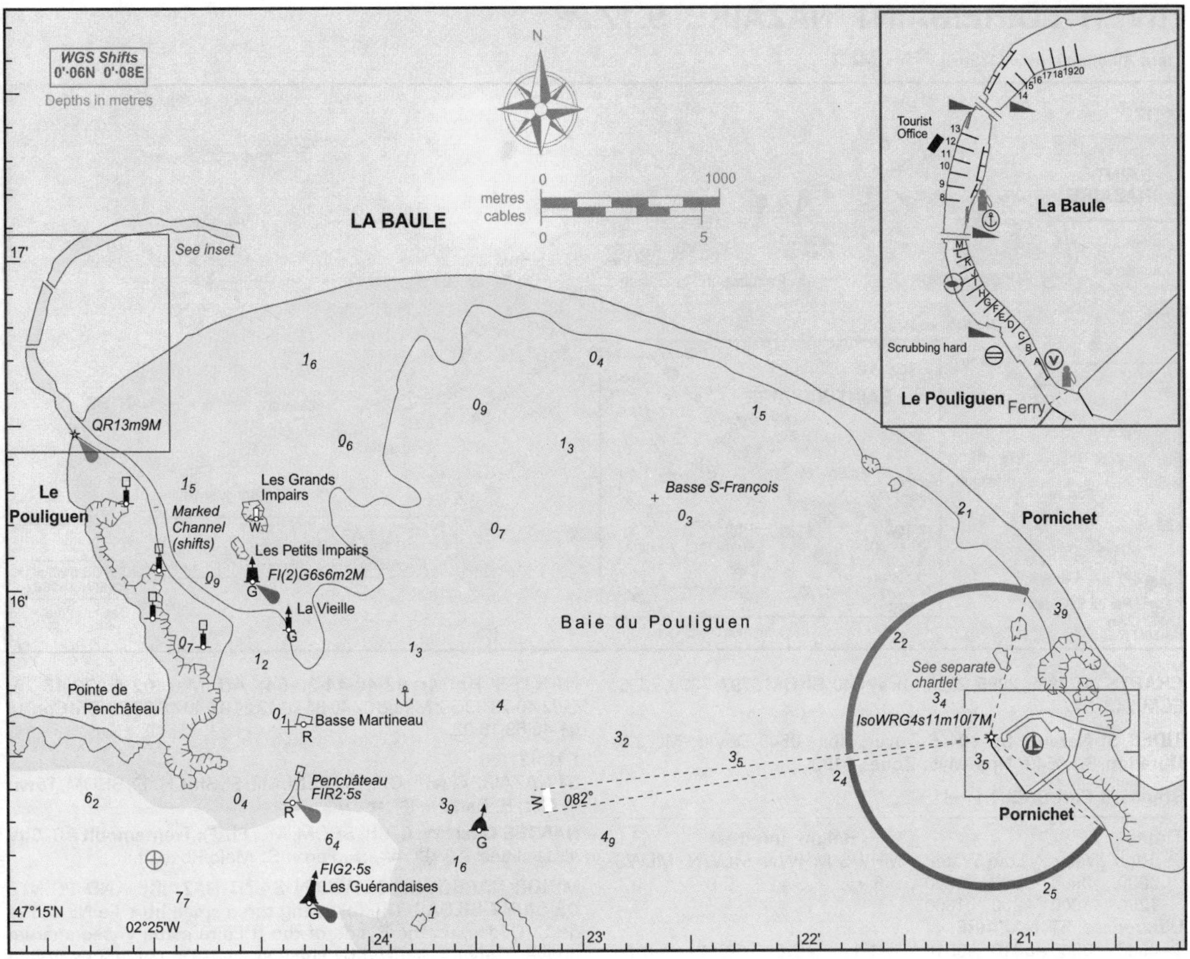
WGS Shifts
0'·06N 0'·08E
Depths in metres
N
metres
cables
0
1000
5
LA BAULE
See inset
17'
16'
QR13m9M
Le Pouliguen
Marked Channel (shifts)
Les Grands Impairs
Les Petits Impairs
Fl(2)G6s6m2M
La Vieille
Pointe de Penchâteau
Basse Martineau
Penchâteau
FlR2·5s
FlG2·5s
Les Guérandaises
Basse S-François
Baie du Pouliguen
See separate chartlet
IsoWRG4s11m10/7M
082°
Pornichet
47°15'N
02°25'W
24'
23'
22'
21'
Tourist Office
La Baule
Scrubbing hard
Le Pouliguen
Ferry

PORNICHET *9.17.27*

Loire Atlantique **47°15´·55N 02°21´·05W**

CHARTS AC 2986, 2989; Imray C39; SHOM 6797, 7395; ECM 547

TIDES Sp +0435 Dover, Nps +0530 Dover; ML 3·3; Duration Sp 0530, Nps 0645; Zone –0100

Standard Port BREST (⟵)

Times				Height (metres)			
High Water		Low Water		MHWS	MHWN	MLWN	MLWS
0000	0600	0000	0600	6·9	5·4	2·6	1·0
1200	1800	1200	1800				
Differences PORNICHET							
+0020	–0045	–0022	–0022	–1·4	–1·0	–0·5	–0·2

SHELTER A very large artificial marina at the E end of the B de la Baule, with excellent shelter and facilities. Access at all tides for up to 2·5m draft. Best to call ahead for berth.

NAVIGATION Appr from the W, as for Le Pouliguen (3M), then direct via W sector (082°) of Iso WG 4s bkwtr lt; also from SW, track 035° between Les Evens PHM and Les Troves SHM unlit bns; or from SSE track 335° from Grand Charpentier lt.

LIGHTS AND MARKS Navigational lts are very hard to see against shore lts of La Baule. S bkwtr Iso WG 4s 11m 10/7M, W081°-084° (3°), G084°-081° (357°). Inside ent, QR 4m 1M and QG 3m 1M on perches define the channel.

RADIO TELEPHONE VHF Ch 09.

TELEPHONE Hr Mr 02·40·61·03·20, 📠 02·40·61·87·18; Aff Mar 02·40·23·06·56; CROSS 02·97·55·35·35; ⊜ 02·40·45·88·78; Météo 02·40·90·08·80; Auto 08·36·68·08·44; Ⓗ (St Nazaire) 02·40·90·60·60; Dr (La Baule) 02·40·60·17·20; Brit Consul 01·40·63·16·02.

FACILITIES Marina (1000+150 visitors) ☎ 02·40·61·03·20, €1·91, AC, Slip, FW, P, D, BH (24 ton), V, R, Bar, ⓛ, ME, El, Ⓔ, Sh, CH, SHOM. **Town** Bar, Dr, R, V, Ⓑ, ✉, ⇄, ✈ (St Nazaire).

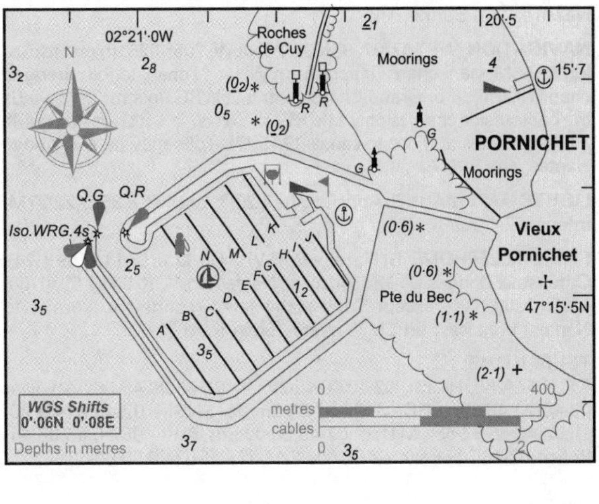
02°21'·0W
20'·5
15'·7
N
Roches de Cuy
Moorings
PORNICHET
Moorings
Q.G
Q.R
Iso.WRG.4s
Vieux Pornichet
Pte du Bec
47°15'·5N
WGS Shifts
0'·06N 0'·08E
Depths in metres
metres
cables
400

RIVER LOIRE/SAINT NAZAIRE *9.17.28*

Loire Atlantique (St Nazaire) ❁❁◊◊✿✿

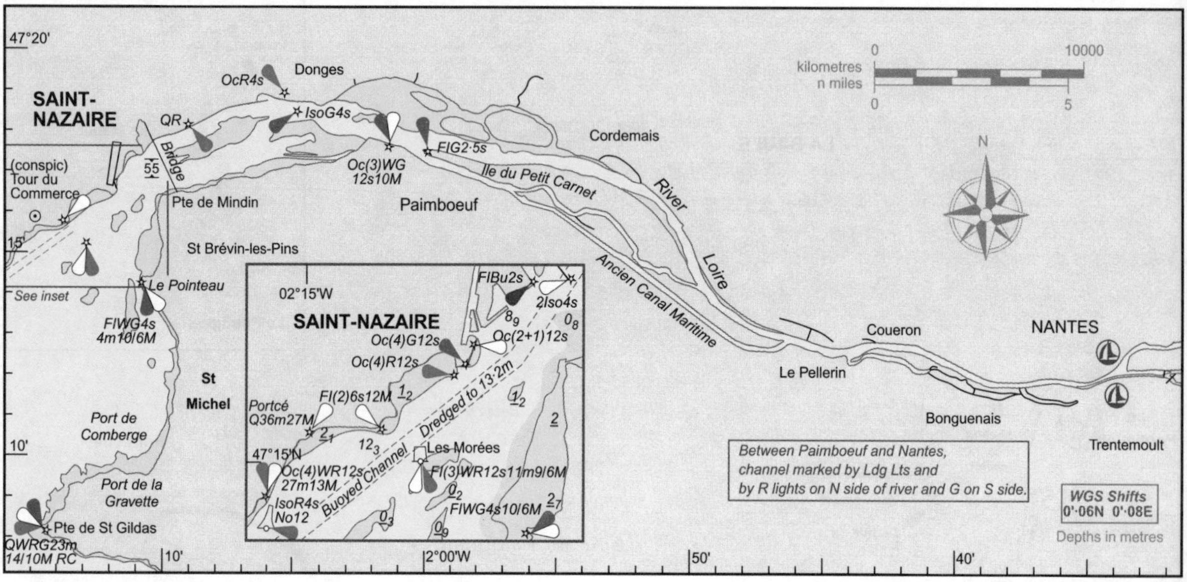

CHARTS AC 2989, 2985, 2986; Imray C40; SHOM 6797, 7396, 7395; ECM 248, 547

TIDES St Nazaire: Sp +0445 Dover, Nps –0540 Dover; ML 3·6; Duration Sp 0640, Nps 0445; Zone –0100

Standard Port BREST (⟵)

Times				Height (metres)			
High Water		Low Water		MHWS	MHWN	MLWN	MLWS
0000	0600	0000	0600	6·9	5·4	2·6	1·0
1200	1800	1200	1800				
Differences ST NAZAIRE							
+0030	–0040	–0010	–0010	–1·1	–0·8	–0·4	–0·2
LE GRAND CHARPENTIER							
+0015	–0045	–0025	–0020	–1·5	–1·1	–0·6	–0·3
DONGES							
+0035	–0035	+0005	+0005	–1·0	–0·7	–0·5	–0·4
CORDEMAIS							
+0055	–0005	+0105	+0030	–0·7	–0·5	–0·7	–0·4
LE PELLERIN							
+0110	+0010	+0145	+0100	–0·7	–0·5	–0·9	–0·4
NANTES (Chantenay)							
+0135	+0055	+0215	+0125	–0·6	–0·3	–0·8	–0·1

SHELTER Hbr is mainly naval and commercial, but yachts can berth at S end of Bassin Penhoet; ent via E lock and Bassin de St Nazaire. ⚓ in Bonne Anse.

NAVIGATION WPT 47°07'·95N 02°20'·00W, 205°/025° from/to front ldg lt, 7·3M, via S chan. Or appr from W, via N chan, to join dredged chan (13·2m) SE of Grand Charpentier lt Q WRG. In strong W winds the bar (outside chan) is only safe HW–3 to HW. R Loire navigable 28M to Nantes and ent to canals (9.15.17). Tolls may be due above Nantes; see 9.15.7.

LIGHTS AND MARKS Appr ldg lts 025½°: both Q 6/36m 22/27M, intens 024°-027°.

RADIO TELEPHONE St Nazaire Port VHF Ch **12** 16 06 14 67 69 (H24). Other stns: Donges Ch 12 16 (occas); Nantes Ch 12 16 06 67 69 (0700-1100, 1300-1700, except Sun); water level reports (St Nazaire to Nantes) broadcast on Ch 73 every 15min from H+00.

TELEPHONE
ST NAZAIRE Hr Mr 02·40·00·45·20, 📠 02.40.00·45·66; Aff Mar 02·40·22·46·32; CROSS 02·97·55·35·35; SNSM 02·40·61·03·20; ⊖ 02·40·66·82·65; Météo 02·40·90·00·80; Auto 08.36.68.08.44; Police 02·40·70·55·00; Dr 02·40·22·15·32; Ⓗ 02·40·90·60·60.

NANTES Hr Mr 02·40·44·20·54; Aff Mar 02·40·73·18·70; ⊖ 02·40·73·39·55; Météo 02·40·84·80·19; Ⓗ 02·40·48·33·33; Brit Consul 01·40·63·16·02.

FACILITIES
ST NAZAIRE **Quai** P, D, L, FW, C, M, ME, El, Sh, CH, Ⓔ, SHOM. **Town** V, Gaz, R, Bar, ✉, Ⓑ, ⇌, ✈.

NANTES **Quai** FW, C, CH, SHOM, ME, El, Ⓔ; **Trentemoult** AB. **City** all facilities: ✉, Ⓑ, ⇌, ✈. Ferry: St Malo/Roscoff.

MINOR HARBOURS BETWEEN SAINT-NAZAIRE AND POINTE DE SAINT-GILDAS The following three small hbrs lie NE of Pte de St-Gildas, on the E side of the R Loire estuary; see chartlet above. They are flanked by shellfish beds on rky ledges drying to about 4ca offshore; they are sheltered from W'lies but open to N'lies. Charts are AC 2986, 2981, 3216; SHOM 7395, 6797; ECM 547. Tidal data may be interpolated from Le Grand Charpentier, St-Nazaire (9.17.28) and Pornic (9.18.8). The bay is shallow. Note: 4M N of Pte de St-Gildas is La Truie rk, drying 2·6m and marked by unlit IDM bn; 1·3M SSW of it is a shoal patch 0·7m.

PORT DE COMBERGE, Loire Atlantique, **47°10'·60N 02°09'·50W**; this is position of S bkwtr lt, Oc WG 4s 7m 9/5M, W tr with G top, W123°-140°, G elsewhere. Appr in the W sector or by day on 136° with the bkwtr lt in transit with the disused lt ho beyond. Beware Les Moutons, rk drying 0·4m, 7½ca NW of the bkwtr lt, close to the approach track. The ent is narrow; tiny hbr dries about 2m, access from half-flood. Hr Mr ☎ 02.40.27.82.85; Facilities: M, FW, YC, Slip, C (6 ton), L. Other facilities at nearby town of St Michel-Chef-Chef.

PORT DE LA GRAVETTE, Loire Atlantique, **47°09'·71N 02°12'·60W**; this is position of the lt on end of the bkwtr, Fl (3) WG 12s 7m 8/5M, W sector 124°-224°, G elsewhere. The hbr is 2·2M NE of Pte de St-Gildas. Daymarks are bkwtr lt in transit 130° with La Treille water tr, 2M inland. Shellfish beds to the W and E are marked by unlit NCM bns. On rounding the 600m long bkwtr, turn stbd between lateral buoys; there is about 1·2m water in the N part of the hbr which dries closer in. Many local moorings, few facilities.

SAINT-GILDAS (Anse du Boucau), Loire Atlantique, **47°08'·45N 02°14'·65W**. The hbr is 5ca N of Pte de St Gildas lt ho, Q WRG 23m 14/10M (see 9.17.4). The hbr bkwtr extends 3ca N, with a large automatic tide gauge and ☆ Fl (2) G 6s at its N end. An unlit SHM bn, and a SHM buoy, Fl G 2·5s (May-Sept), lie 1ca and 2ca NW of bkwtr hd. Appr from about 1M N of Pte de St-Gildas on a brg of 177° or at night in its W sector 174°-180°. L'Ilot rky ledge is marked by a PHM bn. Pick up a mooring in 1·5m in the N part of the hbr or dry out further S. Hr Mr ☎ 02.40.21.60.07. VHF Ch 09. Facilities: Slips, YC, FW, C (5 ton), V at Préfailles 1M to E.

MAPTECH®
Leading the world in digital navigation
Maptech UK Ltd • +44 (0)1243 389352 • sales@maptech.co.uk

Maptech world class digital chart CDs
Worldwide coverage from over 4,500 charts

Maptech award winning software
Easy to use navigation software
• Chart Navigator • Cruising Navigator • Offshore Navigator

www.maptech.co.uk

Area 18

South Biscay
River Loire to Spanish Border

9.18.1	Index	Page 829
9.18.2	Area map	830
9.18.3	Tidal stream charts	832
9.18.4	Lights, buoys & waypoints	834
9.18.5	Passage information	838
9.18.6	Distance table	840
9.18.7	Special notes for France See *9.15.7*	840
9.18.8	Pornic	840
9.18.9	L'Herbaudière (Ile de Noirmoutier) Noirmoutier-en-l'Ile Fromentine	841
9.18.10	Port Joinville, Ile d'Yeu Port de la Meule	842
9.18.11	St Gilles-Croix-de-Vie	843
9.18.12	Les Sables d'Olonne	844
9.18.13	Bourgenay Jard-sur-Mer L'Aiguillon/La Faute-sur-Mer Marans La Flotte, Ile de Ré	844
9.18.14	St Martin, Ile de Ré	846
9.18.15	Ars-en-Ré	846
9.18.16	La Rochelle	847
9.18.17	Ile d'Oléron (Le Douhet, Port St Denis, Boyardville) Le Chateau	848
9.18.18	Rochefort Ile d'Aix	849
9.18.19	Seudre River (Marennes, La Tremblade)	850
9.18.20	La Gironde & Canals (Pointe de Grave, Standard Port, tidal curves)	850
9.18.21	Royan Meschers-sur-Gironde Mortagne-sur-Gironde Pauillac Blaye Bordeaux	852
9.18.22	Port Bloc	853
9.18.23	Arcachon La Vigne Andernos Fontainevieille Audenge	857
9.18.24	Landes range	858
9.18.25	Capbreton	859
9.18.26	Anglet/Bayonne	859
9.18.27	St Jean-de-Luz	860
9.18.28	Hendaye & Hondarribia	861
Fig.9(9)	Marinas in France	862

18

Register for your FREE weekly weather email service from Macmillan Reeds
at www.nauticaldata.com – NOW!
weekend weather reports sent to your email address, every Thursday

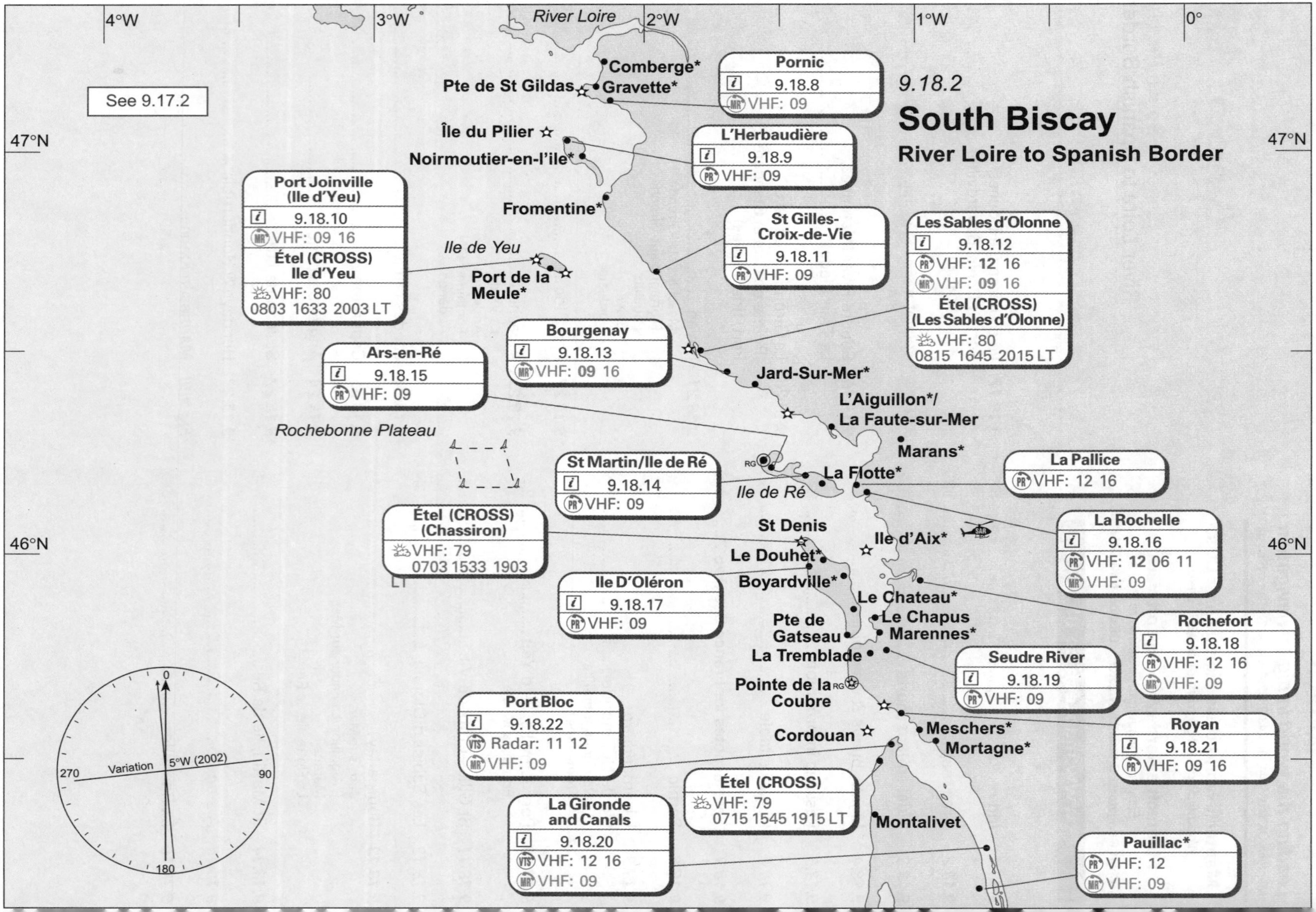
9.18.2
South Biscay
River Loire to Spanish Border
See 9.17.2
4°W
3°W
2°W
1°W
0°
47°N
46°N
River Loire
Comberge*
Gravette*
Pte de St Gildas
Île du Pilier
Noirmoutier-en-l'ile*
Fromentine*
Ile de Yeu
Port de la Meule*
Jard-Sur-Mer*
L'Aiguillon*/ La Faute-sur-Mer
Marans*
La Flotte*
Ile de Ré
Rochebonne Plateau
St Denis
Ile d'Aix*
Le Douhet*
Boyardville*
Le Chateau*
Le Chapus
Marennes*
Pte de Gatseau
La Tremblade
Pointe de la Coubre
Cordouan
Meschers*
Mortagne*
Montalivet
RG
LT
Pornic 9.18.8 VHF: 09
L'Herbaudière 9.18.9 VHF: 09
Port Joinville (Ile d'Yeu) 9.18.10 VHF: 09 16
Étel (CROSS) Ile d'Yeu VHF: 80 0803 1633 2003 LT
St Gilles-Croix-de-Vie 9.18.11 VHF: 09
Les Sables d'Olonne 9.18.12 VHF: 12 16 VHF: 09 16
Étel (CROSS) (Les Sables d'Olonne) VHF: 80 0815 1645 2015 LT
Bourgenay 9.18.13 VHF: 09 16
Ars-en-Ré 9.18.15 VHF: 09
St Martin/Ile de Ré 9.18.14 VHF: 09
La Pallice VHF: 12 16
La Rochelle 9.18.16 VHF: 12 06 11 VHF: 09
Étel (CROSS) (Chassiron) VHF: 79 0703 1533 1903
Ile D'Oléron 9.18.17 VHF: 09
Rochefort 9.18.18 VHF: 12 16 VHF: 09
Seudre River 9.18.19 VHF: 09
Royan 9.18.21 VHF: 09 16
Port Bloc 9.18.22 Radar: 11 12 VHF: 09
Étel (CROSS) VHF: 79 0715 1545 1915 LT
La Gironde and Canals 9.18.20 VHF: 12 16 VHF: 09
Pauillac* VHF: 12 VHF: 09
Variation 5°W (2002)
0
90
180
270

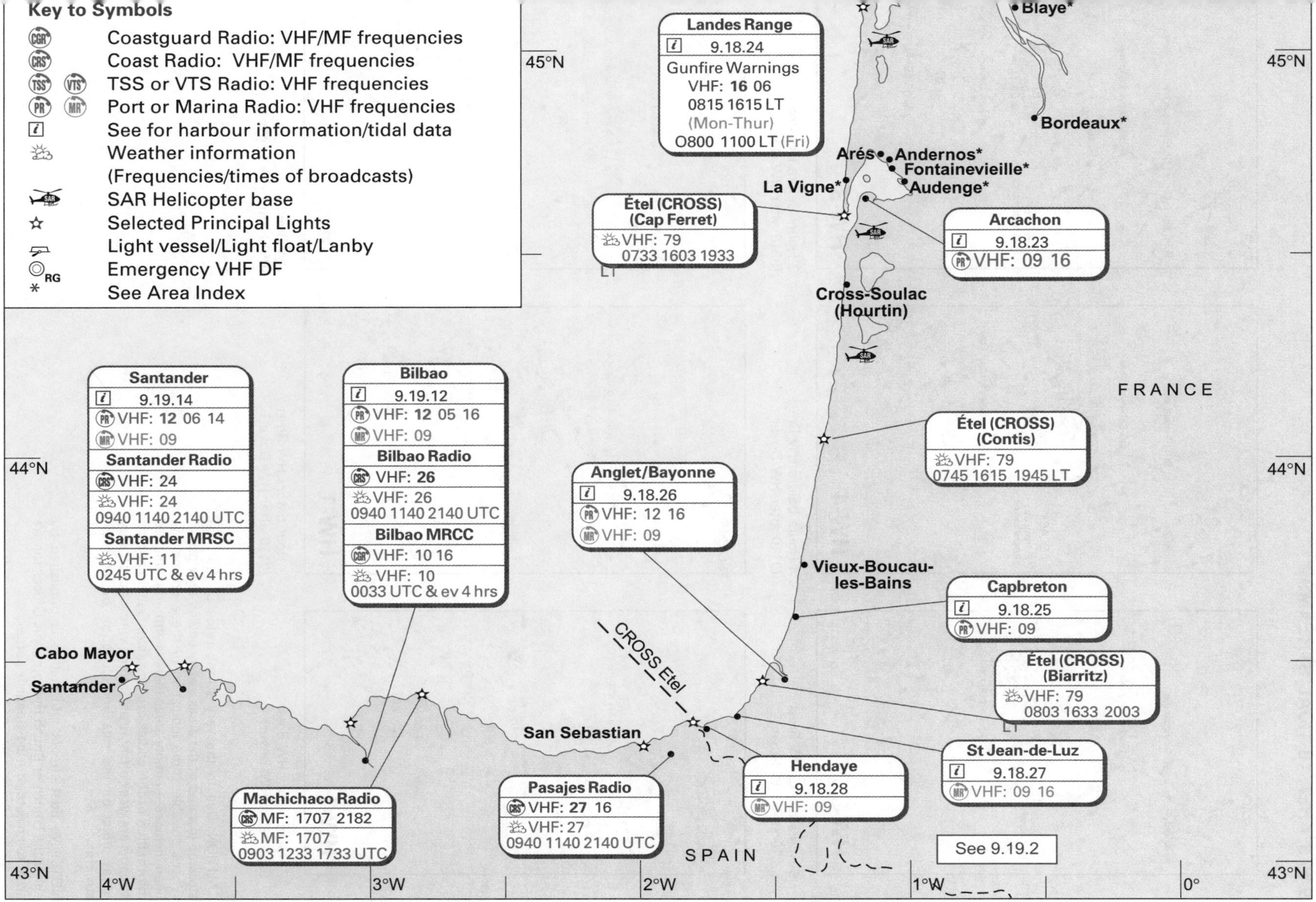
Key to Symbols
CGR Coastguard Radio: VHF/MF frequencies
CRS Coast Radio: VHF/MF frequencies
TSS VTS TSS or VTS Radio: VHF frequencies
PR MR Port or Marina Radio: VHF frequencies
i See for harbour information/tidal data
Weather information
(Frequencies/times of broadcasts)
SAR Helicopter base
Selected Principal Lights
Light vessel/Light float/Lanby
RG Emergency VHF DF
* See Area Index
45°N
44°N
43°N
4°W
3°W
2°W
1°W
0°
Landes Range
9.18.24
Gunfire Warnings
VHF: 16 06
0815 1615 LT
(Mon-Thur)
0800 1100 LT (Fri)
Blaye*
Bordeaux*
Arés
Andernos*
Fontainevieille*
Audenge*
La Vigne*
Étel (CROSS)
(Cap Ferret)
VHF: 79
0733 1603 1933
Arcachon
9.18.23
PR VHF: 09 16
Cross-Soulac
(Hourtin)
FRANCE
Étel (CROSS)
(Contis)
VHF: 79
0745 1615 1945 LT
Santander
9.19.14
PR VHF: 12 06 14
MR VHF: 09
Santander Radio
CRS VHF: 24
VHF: 24
0940 1140 2140 UTC
Santander MRSC
VHF: 11
0245 UTC & ev 4 hrs
Bilbao
9.19.12
PR VHF: 12 05 16
MR VHF: 09
Bilbao Radio
CRS VHF: 26
VHF: 26
0940 1140 2140 UTC
Bilbao MRCC
CGR VHF: 10 16
VHF: 10
0033 UTC & ev 4 hrs
Anglet/Bayonne
9.18.26
PR VHF: 12 16
MR VHF: 09
Vieux-Boucau-
les-Bains
Capbreton
9.18.25
PR VHF: 09
Étel (CROSS)
(Biarritz)
VHF: 79
0803 1633 2003
CROSS Etel
Cabo Mayor
Santander
San Sebastian
Machichaco Radio
CRS MF: 1707 2182
MF: 1707
0903 1233 1733 UTC
Pasajes Radio
CRS VHF: 27 16
VHF: 27
0940 1140 2140 UTC
Hendaye
9.18.28
MR VHF: 09
St Jean-de-Luz
9.18.27
MR VHF: 09 16
SPAIN
See 9.19.2

18

9.18.3 AREA 18 TIDAL STREAMS

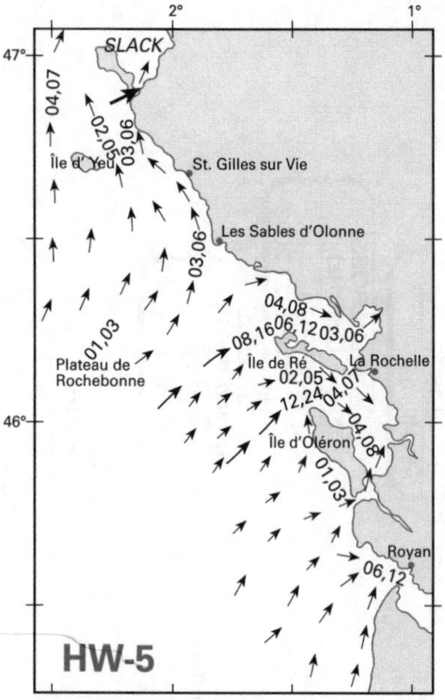

5 Hours before HW Brest
(0010 after HW Dover)

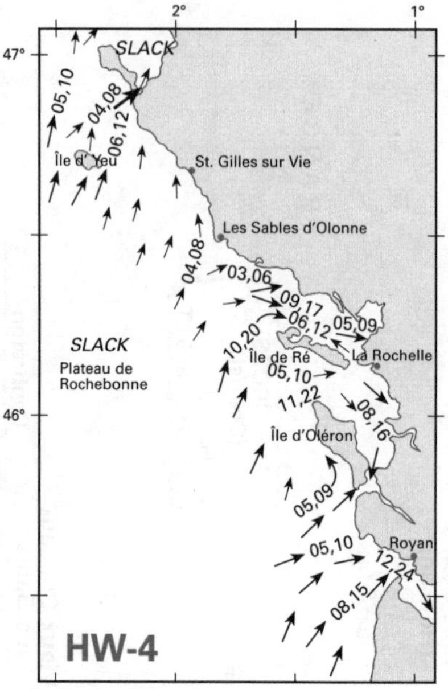

4 Hours before HW Brest
(0110 after HW Dover)

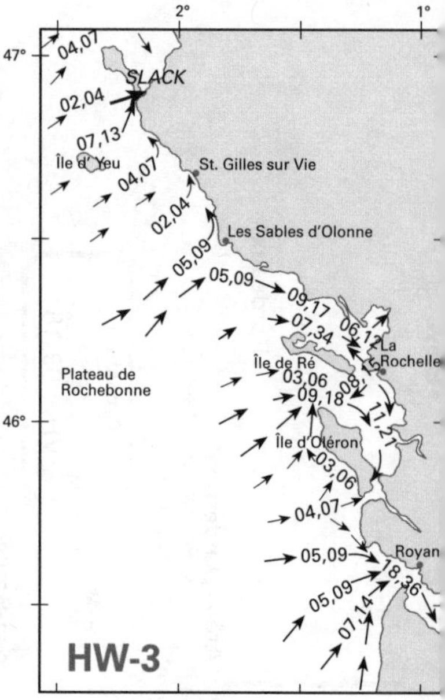

3 Hours before HW Brest
(0210 after HW Dover)

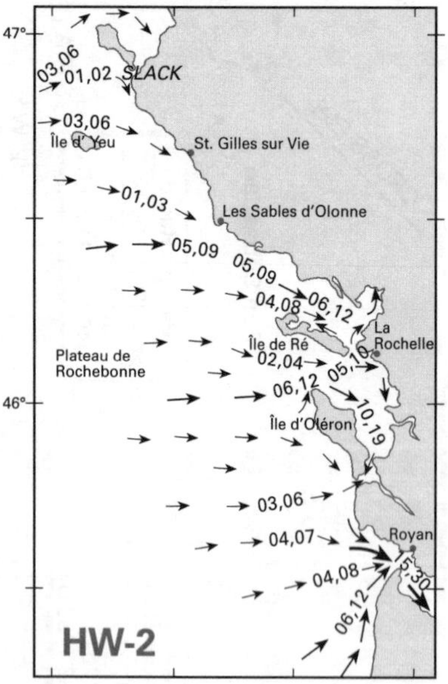

2 Hours before HW Brest
(0310 after HW Dover)

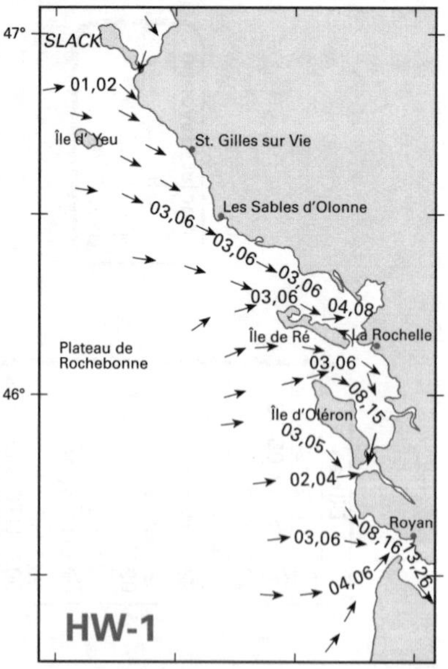

1 Hour before HW Brest
(0410 after HW Dover)

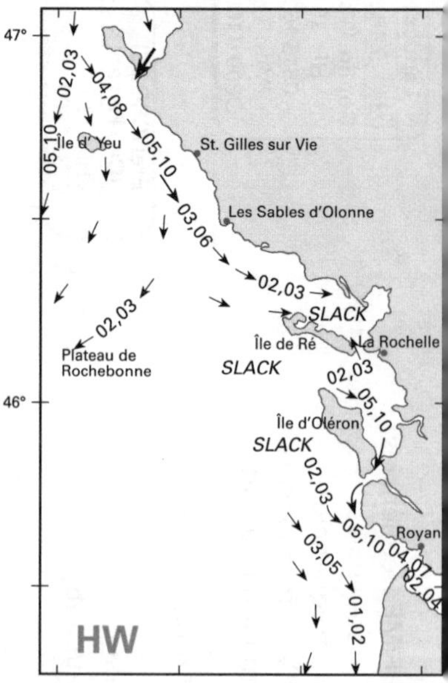

HW Brest
(0510 after HW Dover)

CAUTION: Due to the very strong rates of the tidal streams in some of the areas, many eddies may occur. Where possible some indication of these eddies has been included. In many areas there is either insufficient information or the eddies are unstable. Generally tidal streams are weak offshore and strong winds have a very great effect on the rate and direction of the tidal streams.

NOTE: No tidal stream information is published by either the French or British Hydrographic Offices for the area southwards to the Spanish border.

Northward 9.17.3

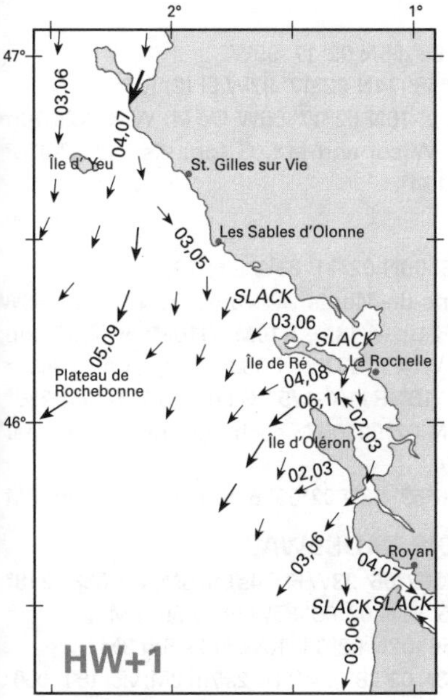

1 Hour after HW Brest
(0610 after HW Dover)

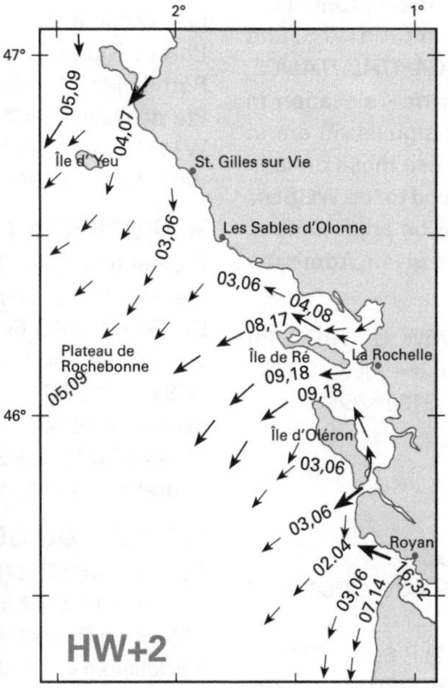

2 Hours after HW Brest
(0515 before HW Dover)

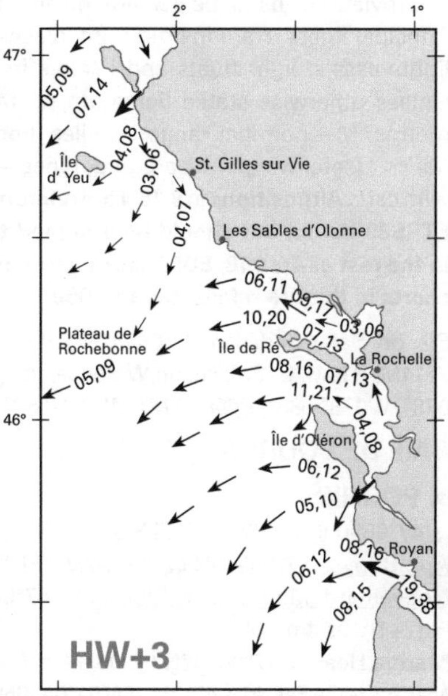

3 Hours after HW Brest
(0415 before HW Dover)

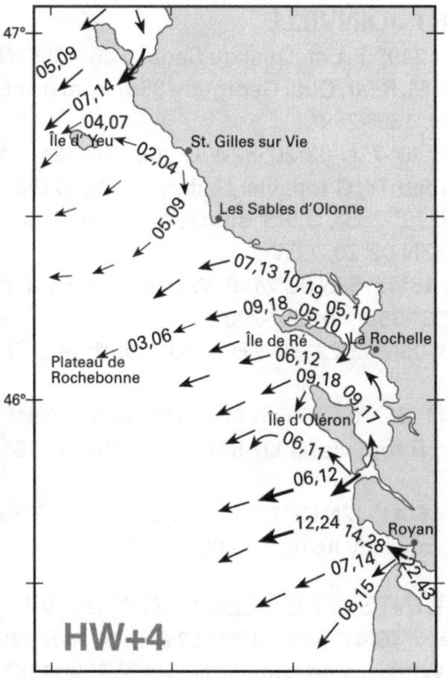

4 Hours after HW Brest
(0315 before HW Dover)

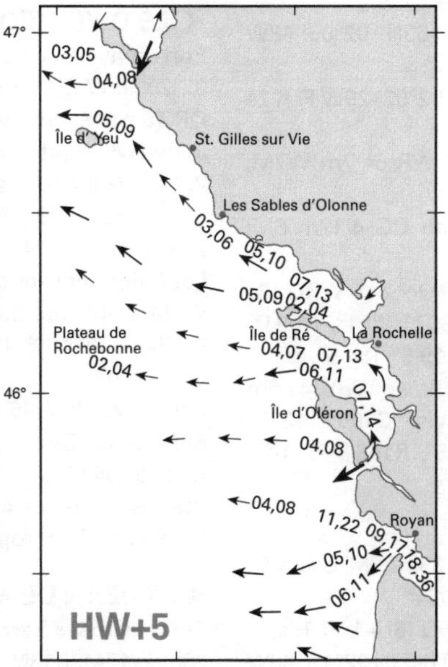

5 Hours after HW Brest
(0215 before HW Dover)

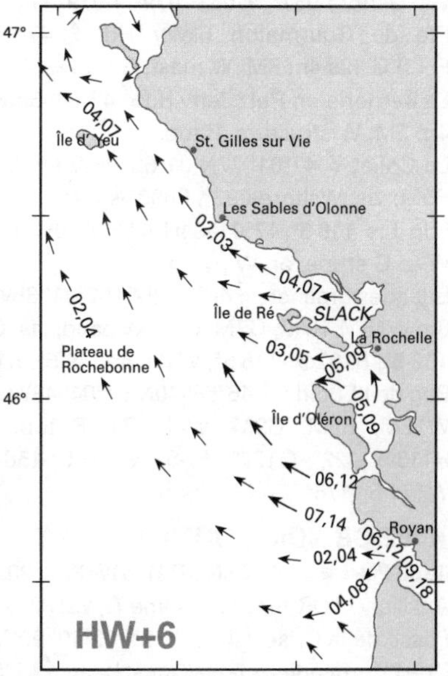

6 Hours after HW Brest
(0115 before HW Dover)

CAUTION: Due to the very strong rates of the tidal streams in some of the areas, many eddies may occur. Where possible some indication of these eddies has been included. In many areas there is either insufficient information or the eddies are unstable. Generally tidal streams are weak offshore and strong winds have a very great effect on the rate and direction of the tidal streams.

NOTE: No tidal stream information is published by either the French or British Hydrographic Offices for the area southwards to the Spanish border.

9.18.4 LIGHTS, BUOYS AND WAYPOINTS

Abbreviations used below are given in the Introduction. Principal lights ☆ are in **bold** print, places in CAPITALS, and light-vessels, light floats and Lanbys in *CAPITAL ITALICS*. Unless otherwise stated lights are white. m – elevation in metres; M – nominal range in miles. Fog signals are in *italics*. Useful waypoints are underlined – use those on land with care. **All positions in 9.18.4 are referenced to the WGS84/ ETRS89 datum but should be assumed to be approximate. In the rest of Area 18, ED50 coordinates are given. Admiralty charts in this are referenced to ED50.**

Pte de Saint-Gildas 47°08'·02N 02°14'·76W Q WRG 23m W14M, R10M, G10M; col on W house; vis: R264°-308°, G308°-078°, W078°-088°, R088°-174°, W174°-180°, G180°-264°.

BAIE DE BOURGNEUF

◀ PORNIC

47°06'·00N 02°07'·47W Fl Y 2·5s.
App Buoy 47°06'·45N 02°06'·64W L Fl 10s.
Noëveillard Marina SW Elbow 47°06'·44N 02°06'·97W Fl (2+1) 10s 4m 3M.
Marina Head 47°06'·47N 02°06'·68W Fl (2) R 6s 4m 2M.
Marina Jetée Est Hd 47°06'·48N 02°06'·66W Fl (2) G 6s 4m 2M.
Pte de Noëveillard 47°06'·62N 02°06'·92W Oc (4) WRG 12s 22m W13M, R9M, G9M; W □ Tr, G top, W dwelling; vis: Gshore-051°, W051°-079°, R079°-shore.
Pte de Gourmalon Bkwtr Hd 47°06'·63N 02°06'·48W Fl (3) G 12s 4m 8M; W mast, G top.
La Bernerie-en-Retz Jetty Hd 47°04'·56N 02°02'·29W Fl R 2s 4m 5M; W structure, R top.
Le Collet 47°01'·77N 01°58'·95W Oc (2) WR 6s 7m W7M, R5M; vis: Wshore-093°, R093°-shore.
Ldg Lts 118·5° 47°01'·34N 01°59'·10W both QG 4/12m 6M; W □ G stripe, on W pylon.
Étier des Brochets 46°59'·87N 02°01'·85W Oc (2+1) WRG 12s 8m W10M, R7M, G7M; G Tr, W band; vis: G071°-091°, W091°-102·5°, R102·5°-116·5°, W116·5°-119·5°, R119·5°-164·5°.
Bec de l'Époids 46°56'·40N 02°04'·48W Dir Iso WRG 4s 6m W12M, R9M, G9M; W □ Tr, R top; vis: G106°-113·5°, R113·5°-122°, G122°-157·5°, W157·5°-158·5°, R158·5°-171·5°, W171·5°-176°.

◀ ÎLE DE NOIRMOUTIER

Île du Pilier ☆ 47°02'·55N 02°21'·61W Fl (3) 20s 33m **29M**; Gy △ Tr. Auxiliary Lt QR 10m 11M, same Tr; vis: 321°-034°.
Passe de la Grise 47°01'·72N 02°19'·99W Q (6) + L Fl 15s.
P de l'Herbaudière Jetée Ouest Head 47°01'·63N 02°17'·86W Oc (2+1) WG 12s 9m W10M, G7M; W col and hut, G top; vis: W187·5°-190°, G190°-187·5°.
Ldg Lts 187·5°. Front, 47°01'·59N 02°17'·85W Q 5m 7M; Gy mast. Rear, 310m from front, Q 26m 7M; Gy mast.
Basse du Martroger 47°02'·60N 02°17'·12W Q WRG 11m W9M, R6M, G6M; vis: G033°-055°, W055°-060°, R060°-095°, G095°-124°, W124°-153°, R153°-201°, W201°-240°, R240°-033°.
Pierre Moine 47°03'·35N 02°12'·36W Fl (2) 6s 14m 7M.
Notre Dame 47°05'·42N 02°08'·27W Fl (2) 6s 7m 3M.
Pte des Dames ☆ 47°00'·66N 02°13'·27W Oc (3) WRG 12s 34m **W19M, R15M, G15M**; W □ Tr; vis: G016·5°-057°, R057°-124°, G124°-165°, W165°-191°, R191°-267°, W267°-357°, R357°-016·5°.
La Chaise 46°01'·21N 02°13'·14W.
Noirmoutier Jetty Hd 46°59'·27N 02°13'·14W Oc (2) R 6s 6m 6M; W col, R top.
Port de Morin 46°58'·65N 02°17'·95W.
Port de Morin 46°58'·74N 02°17'·97W Fl (2) R 6s.
Pte de Devin 46°59'·15N 02°17'·60W Oc (4) WRG 12s 10m W11M, R8M, G8M; W col and hut, G top; vis: G314°-028°, W028°-035°, R035°-134°.

◀ FROMENTINE

Fromentine 46°53'·06N 02°11'·63W L Fl 10s.
Pte de Notre Dame-de-Monts 46°53'·33N 02°08'·56W Dir Oc (2) WRG 6s 21m W13M, R10M, G10M; W Tr, B top; vis: G000°-043°, W043°-063°, R063°-073°, W073°-094°, G094°-113°, W113°-116°, R116°-175°, G175°-196°, R196°-230°.
Bridge ☆ 46°53'·52N 02°09'·00W each side on centre span Iso 4s 32m **18M**; H24.
Tourelle Milieu 46°53'·58N 02°09'·63W Fl (4) R 12s 6m 5M.

◀ ROUTE DU GOIS CAUSEWAY

E shore 46°55'·27N 02°06'·23W Fl R 4s 6m 6M; vis: 038°-218°.
E turning Pt 46°55'·65N 02°06'·87W Fl 2s 5m 5M.
W turning Pt 46°56'·02N 02°08'·10W Fl 2s 5m 3M.
Bassotière 46°56'·03N 02°08'·89W Fl G 2s 7m 2M; vis: 180°-000°.
Les Boeufs 46°55'·04N 02°28'·02W VQ (9) 10s; *Bell.*

ILE D'YEU TO BOURGENAY

◀ ÎLE D'YEU/PORT JOINVILLE

Port Joinville Ldg Lts 219°. Front, Quai du Canada 46°43'·61N 02°20'·95W QR 11m 5M. Rear, Quai Georgette 85m from front QR 16m 5M; both vis: 169°-269°.
Jetty NW Head 46°43'·77N 02°20'·82W Oc (3) WG 12s 9m W11M, G8M; W 8-sided Tr, G top; vis: G shore-150°, W150°-232°, G232°-279°, W279°-285°, G285°-shore; *Horn (3) 30s.*
La Galiote 46°43'·73N 02°20'·71W.
Les Chiens Perrins 46°43'·58N 02°24'·61W Q (9) WG 15s 16m W8M, G5M; vis: G330°-350°, W350°-200°.
Petite Foule ☆ 46°43'·05N 02°22'·96W Fl 5s 56m **24M**; W □ Tr, G lantern.
P de la Meule 46°41'·66N 02°20'·75W Oc WRG 4s 9m W9M, R6M, G5M; Gy □ Tr, R top; vis: G007·5°-018°, W018°-027·5°, R027·5°-041·5°.
Pte des Corbeaux ☆ 46°41'·42N 02°17'·11W Fl (2+1) R 15s 25m **20M**; W □ Tr, R top; obsc by Île de Yeu 083°-143°.

◀ ST JEAN DE MONTS/ST GILLES-CROIX-DE-VIE

Pte de Grosse Terre ☆ 46°41'·54N 01°57'·92W Fl (4) WR 12s 25m **W17M**, R13M; W truncated conical Tr; vis: W290°-125°, R125°-145°.
St Jean de Monts 46°46'·90N 02°04'·91W Fl R.
St Jean de Monts Jetty Hd 46°47'·07N 02°05'·13W Fl (2) R 6s 10m 1M; W mast, R top.
Pilours 46°40'·98N 01°58'·10W Q (6) + L Fl 15s; *Bell.*
Ldg Lts 043·5°. Front, 46°41'·85N 01°56'·67W Dir Oc (3+1) R 12s 7m 13M; W □ Tr, R top. Rear, 260m from front, Dir Oc (3+1) R 12s 28m 13M; W □ Tr, R top; synch with front; both intens 033·5°-053·5°.
Jetée de la Garenne Head 46°41'·45N 01°57'·26W Q WG 8m W8M, G6M; vis: G045°-335°, W355°-045°; *Horn 20s.*
Jetée de Boisvinet 46°41'·62N 01°57'·16W Fl (2) WR 6s 8m W8M, R5M; vis: R045°-225°, W225°-045°.

◀ LES SABLES D'OLONNE

Les Barges ☆ 46°29'·70N 01°50'·50W Fl (2) R 10s 25m 13M; Gy Tr.

La Petite Barge 46°28'·90N 01°50'·61W Q (6) + L Fl 15s 8m 7M; *Whis.*

L'Armandèche ☆ 46°29'·40N 01°48'·29W Fl (2+1) 15s 42m **24M**; W 6-sided Tr, R top; vis: 295°-130°.

Nouch Sud 46°28'·55N 01°47'·42W Q (6) + L Fl 15s.

Ldg Lts 033°. **Front** ☆, 46°29'·42N 01°46'·37W Iso 4s 14m **16M**; mast; H24. **Rear** ☆, **La Potence**, 330m from front, Iso 4s 33m **16M**; W □ Tr; H24.

Ldg Lts 320°, Jetée des Sables Head Front ☆, 46°29'·44N 01°47'·51W QG 11m 8M; W Tr, G top. Rear, Tour d'Arundel, 465m from front, Oc (2+1) 12s 33m 13M; large Gy □ Tr.

Ldg Lts 328·1°, Front 46°29'·66N 01°47'·75W, FR 6m 11M; R line on W hut. Rear, 65m from front, FR 9m 11M; R line on W Tr.

Jetée St Nicolas Head ☆ 46°29'·23N 01°47'·52W UQ (2) R 1s 16m 10M; W Tr, R top; vis: 143°-094°.

◀ BOURGENAY

Ldg Lts 040°. Front, 46°26'·37N 01°40'·61W QG 8M; vis: 020°-060°. Rear, QG 8M; vis: 010°-070°.

Roches du Joanne 46°25'·28N 01°41'·91W L Fl 10s.

Digue W Head ☆ 46°26'·43N 01°40'·51W Fl R 4s 9M.

◀ PLATEAU DE ROCHEBONNE (Offshore shoal) (Area to be avoided)

Rochbonne NO 46°12'·96N 02°31'·63W Q (9) 15s; *Whis.*

Rochbonne NE 46°12'·69N 02°24'·84W Iso G 4s.

Rochbonne SE 46°09'·18N 02°21'·21W Q (3) 10s; *Bell.*

Rochbonne SO 46°10'·06N 02°27'·05W Fl (2) R 6s.

PERTUIS BRETON/ÎLE DE RÉ

◀ JARD-SUR-MER/LA TRANCHE-SUR-MER

Jard App 46°23'·68N 01°35'·03W.

Jard App 46°23'·73N 01°34'·93W.

Jard-sur-Mer S Bkwtr Head 46°24'·37N 01°34'·86W.

La Tranche Pier Head ☆ 46°20'·55N 01°25'·60W Fl (2) R 6s 6m 6M; R col.

Pte du Grouin-du-Cou ☆ 46°20'·67N 01°27'·83W Fl WRG 5s 29m **W20M, R16M, G16M**; W 8-sided Tr, B top; vis: R034°-061°, W061°-117°, G117°-138°, W138°-034°.

◀ L'AIGUILLON/LA FAUTE-SUR-MER

Le Lay 46°16'·10N 01°16'·53W Q (6) + L Fl 15s.

No. 1 46°16'·59N 01°16'·29W.

No. 2 46°16'·90N 01°16'·28W.

◀ ANSE DE L'AIGUILLON/MARANS

Pte de L'Aiguillon 46°15'·32N 01°11'·53W L Fl 10s.

No. 9 46°15'·56N 01°12'·24W.

No. 10 46°15'·11N 01°11'·44W.

Anse de L'Aiguillon 46°17'·18N 01°09'·68W.

Port du Pavé ent ☆ 46°18'·15N 01°08'·01W Fl G 4s 9m 7M; W col, G top.

◀ PORT DU PLOMB

W Môle ☆ 46°12'·11N 01°12'·23W Fl R 4s 9m 7M; W col, R top.

◀ LA FLOTTE

La Flotte N Bkwtr Hd ☆ 46°11'·32N 01°19'·34W Fl WG 4s 10m W12M, G9M; W ○ Tr, G top; vis: G130°-205°, W205°-220°, G220°-257°; *Horn (3) 30s* (by day HW–2 to HW+2). Moiré effect Dir Lt 212·5°.

Rivedoux-Plage Ldg Lts 194·5°. Front, N Pier Head 46°09'·78N 01°16'·65W QG 6m 6M; W Tr, G top. Rear, 100m from front, QG 9m 6M; W and G chequered col; synch with front.

◀ ST MARTIN DE RÉ

Pointe du Couronneau 46°12'·78N 01°20'·91W.

Bkwtr West Head ☆ 46°12'·51N 01°21'·91W Fl R 2·5s 7m 2M; W post, R top.

On ramparts, E of ent ☆ 46°12'·44N 01°21'·91W Oc (2) WR 6s 18m W10M, R7M; W Tr, R top; vis: Wshore-245°, R245°-281°, W281°-shore.

Mole Head ☆ 46°12'·48N 01°21'·95W Iso G 4s 10m 6M; W tripod, G top; obsc by Pte de Loix when brg less than 124°.

◀ PORT D'ARS-EN-RÉ

46°14'·30N 01°26'·02W.

Le Fier d'Ars Ldg Lts 265°. Front, 46°14'·07N 01°28'·76W Iso 4s 5m 11M; □ on W hut; vis: 141°-025°. **Rear**, 370m from front, Dir Iso G 4s 13m **15M**; G □ on dwelling; synch with front, intens 264°-266°.

Ldg Lts 232°. Front, 46°12'·76N 01°30'·60W Q 5m 9M; W hut, R lantern. Rear, 370m from front, Q 13m 11M; B stripe on W framework Tr, G top; vis: 142°-322°.

Les Baleines ☆ 46°14'·64N 01°33'·69W Fl (4) 15s 53m **27M**; Gy 8-sided Tr, R lantern.

Les Baleineaux ☆ 46°15'·81N 01°35'·22W Oc (2) 6s 23m 11M; pink Tr, R top.

ÎLE DE RÉ SOUTH/PERTUIS D'ANTIOCHE/ ÎLE D'OLÉRON

◀ ÎLE DE RÉ (SOUTH COAST)

Chanchardon ☆ 46°09'·73N 01°28'·42W Fl WR 4s 15m W11M, R8M; B 8-sided Tr, W base; vis: R118°-290°, W290°-118°.

Chauveau ☆ 46°08'·09N 01°16'·33W Oc (3) WR 12s 27m **W15M**, R11M; W ○ Tr, R top; vis: W057°-094°, R094°-104°, W104°-342°, R342°-057°.

Pte de Sablanceaux ☆ 46°09'·75N 01°15'·18W VQ (3) 5s 10m 5M; W mast and hut, G top.

PERTUIS D'ANTIOCHE

◀ PERTUIS D'ANTIOCHE/LA ROCHELLE

Chauveau 46°06'·56N 01°16'·09W VQ (6) + L Fl 10s; *Whis.*

Roche du Sud 46°06'·36N 01°15'·25W Q (9) 15s.

Le Lavardin 46°08'·09N 01°14'·54W Fl (2) WG 6s 14m W11M, G8M; vis: G160°-169°, W169°-160°.

Plateau du Lavardin 46°07'·63N 01°14'·19W.

La Pallice, Môle d'Escale ☆ 46°09'·75N 01°14'·35W Dir Lt 016°. Dir Q WRG 33m W14M, R13M, G13M; Gy Tr; vis: G009°-014·7°, W014·7°-017·3°, R017·3°-031°. Sig Stn.

Les Minimes 46°08'·01N 01°11'·56W Q(9) 15s.

Tour Richelieu ☆ 46°08'·89N 01°10'·36W Fl (4) R 15s 10m 9M; R Tr; *Siren (4) 60s* (HW–1 to HW+1).

La Rochelle Ldg Lts 059°. Front, 46°09'·35N 01°09'·16W Dir Q 15m 13M; R ○ Tr, W bands; intens 056°-062°; by day Fl 4s. Rear, 235m from front, Q 25m 14M; W 8-sided Tr, G top; synch with front, vis: 044°-074°, obsc 061°-065° by St Nicolas Tr; by day Fl 4s.

PA 46°05'·62N 01°42'·45W Iso 4s 8m 7M; *Whis.*

◀ ÎLE D'AIX/PASSAGE DE L'EST

Île d'Aix ☆ 46°00'·60N 01°10'·72W Fl WR 5s 24m **W24M, R20M**; two W ○ Trs; vis: R103°-118°, W118°-103°.

Fort Boyard Tr ☆ 45°59'·96N 01°12'·87W Q (9) 15s.

◀ FOURAS
Port Sud Bkwtr Hd ☆ 45°59'·04N 01°05'·74W Fl WR 4s 6m 9/6M; vis: R115°-177°, W177°-115°.
Port Nord Pier Hd ☆ 45°59'·88N 01°05'·68W Oc (3+1) WG 12s 9m W11M, G8M; W&G Tr; vis: G084°-127°, W127°-084°.

◀ LA CHARENTE/ROCHEFORT
Les Palles 45°59'·52N 01°09'·62W Q.
Sablière 45°58'·97N 01°07'·62W.
Ldg Lts 115°. Front, **Fort de la Pointe** ☆ 45°57'·96N 01°04'·40W Dir QR 8m **19M**; W □ Tr, R top. **Rear** ☆, 600m from front, Dir QR 21m **20M**; W □ Tr, R top; both intens 113°-117°. QR 21m 8M; same Tr; vis: 322°-067° over Port-des-Barques anchorage.
Fontenelles 45°58'·57N 01°06'·59W.
Moucliere 45°58'·24N 01°06'·14W.
Port-des-Barques Ldg Lts 134·3°. Front, 45°56'·95N 01°04'·16W Iso G 4s 5m 9M. Rear, 490m from front, Iso G 4s 13m 11M; synch with front; both intens 125°-145°.

◀ ÎLE D'OLÉRON
Chassiron ☆ 46°02'·77N 01°24'·67W Fl 10s 50m, **28M**; W ○ Tr, B bands; part obsc 297°-351°; Sig Stn.
Rocher d'Antioche 46°03'·92N 01°24'·67W Q 20m 11M.

◀ ST DENIS
Les Palles 46°03'·03N 01°22'·34W.
E Jetty Hd ☆ 46°02'·10N 01°22'·07W Fl (2) WG 6s 6m W9M G6M, □ hut; vis: G205°-277°, W277°-292°, G292°-165°.
S Jetty Hd ☆ 46°02'·11N 01°22'·21W Fl (2) R 6s 3m 6M.
Dir Lt 205° 46°01'·61N 01°21'·96W Dir Iso WRG 4s 14m W11M, R8M, G8M; vis: G190°-204°, W204°-206°, R206°-220°.

◀ PORT DU DOUHET/PASSAGE DE L'OUEST
N ent 46°00'·10N 01°19'·19W.
46°01'·58N 01°17'·09W.
Chan 46°00'·48N 01°17'·71W Q.
Chan 46°00'·22N 01°15'·35W Q.
Chan 45°59'·84N 01°14'·80W Q (3) 10s.

◀ LE CHÂTEAU D'OLÉRON
Ldg Lts 319°. Front, 45°53'·11N 01°11'·37W QR 11m 7M; R line on W Tr; vis: 191°-087°. Rear, 240m from front, QR 24m 7M; W Tr, R top; synch with front.
Tourelle Juliar 45°54'·16N 01°09'·37W Q (3) WG 10s 12m W11M; G8M; vis: W147°-336°, G336°-147°.

◀ BOYARDVILLE (LA PÉRROTINE)
Longe Botard S 45°58'·65N 01°11'·93W.
La Pérrotine 45°58'·30N 01°13'·30W.
Mole Hd ☆ 45°58'·24N 01°13'·86W Fl (2) R 6s 8m 5M; W Tr, R top; obsc by Pte des Saumonards when brg less than 150°.

◀ LA SEUDRE
Pont de la Seudre ☆ 45°48'·06N 01°08'·17W Q 20m 9M each side, vis: 054°-234° and 234°-054°.
Pte de Mus de Loup ☆ 45°47'·96N 01°08'·42W Oc G 4s 8m 6M; vis: 118°-147°.

◀ LA COTINIÈRE
Dir Lt 048° 45°54'·35N 01°18'·67W Dir Oc WRG 4s 13m W11M, R9M, G9M; W stripe with B border on W col; vis: G033°-046°, W046°-050°, R050°-063°.
Ent Ldg Lts 339°. 45°54'·72N 01°19'·79W Front, Dir Oc (2) 6s 6m 13M; W Tr, R top; vis: 329°-349°. Rear, 425m from front, Dir Oc (2) 6s 14m 12M; W Tr, R bands; synch with front; intens 329°-349°.
ATT Maumusson 45°46'·89N 01°17'·89W L Fl 10s.
Banc de Gatseau 45°47'·65N 01°16'·34W.
Banc des Mattes 45°47'·23N 01°16'·61W.

LA GIRONDE AND APPROACHES

◀ LA GIRONDE, GRANDE PASSE DE L'OUEST
BXA 45°37'·53N 01°28'·69W Iso 4s 8m 7M; Racon (B); *Whis.*
No. 1 45°38'·00N 01°21'·90W QG.
No. 2 45°38'·32N 01°17'·51W Q (9) 15s.
No. 6 45°38'·56N 01°18'·24W Iso R 4s.
No. 7 45°38'·17N 01°17'·51W Q (9) 15s.
No. 11 45°39'·07N 01°10'·59W Iso G 4s.
Pte de la Coubre ☆ 45°41'·78N 01°13'·99W Fl (2) 10s 64m **28M**; W Tr, R top; Sig Stn. F RG 42m R12M, G10M; same Tr; vis: R030°-043°, G043°-060°, R060°-110°.
Ldg Lts 081·5°. **Front** ☆, 1·1M from rear, Dir Iso 4s 21m **20M**; W mast on dolphin; intens 080·5°-082·5°; Q (2) 5s 10m 3M; same structure. **La Palmyre, common rear** ☆, 45°39'·71N 01°07'·22W Dir Q 57m **27M**; W radar Tr; intens 080·5°-082·5°. Dir FR 57m **17M**; same Tr; intens 325·5°-328·5°.
Ldg Lts 327°. **Terre-Nègre** ☆, Front, 1·1M from rear, Oc (3) WRG 12s 39m **W18M**, R14M, G14M; W Tr, R top on W side; vis: R304°-319°, W319°-327°, G327°-000°, W000°-004°, G004°-097°, W097°-104°, R104°-116°.
Pte de Grave Jetée Nord Hd 45°34'·42N 01°03'·68W, Q 6m 2M.
Spur 45°34'·32N 01°03'·66W Iso G 4s 5m 2M; vis: 190°-045°.

◀ LA GIRONDE, PASSE SUD
G1 45°31'·18N 01°11'·33W.
G2 45°32'·07N 01°10'·07W.
G3 45°32'·78N 01°07'·72W.
No. 13A 45°35'·68N 01°04'·21W Fl (3) G 12s.
Cordouan ☆ 45°35'·16N 01°10'·39W Oc (2+1) WRG 12s 60m **W22M, R18M, G18M**; W △ Tr, Gy band; vis: W014°-126°, G126°-178·5°, W178·5°-250°, W(unintens) 250°-267°, R(unintens) 267°-294·5°, R294·5°-014°; obsc in est when brg more than 285°.
Ldg Lts 063°. **St Nicolas Front** ☆, 45°33'·72N 01°05'·03W Dir QG 22m **16M**; W □ Tr; intens 061·5°-064·5°. **Rear, Pte de Grave** ☆, 0·84M from front, Oc WRG 4s 26m **W19M, R15M, G15M**; W □ Tr, B corners and top; vis: W(unintens) 033°-054°, W054°-233·5°, R233·5°-303°, W303°-312°, G312°-330°, W330°- 341°, W(unintens) 341°-025°.
Ldg Lts 041°, **Le Chay Front** ☆, 45°37'·30N 01°02'·40W Dir QR 33m **18M**; W Tr, R top; intens 039·5°-042·5°. **Rear, St Pierre** ☆, 0·97M from front, Dir QR 61m **18M**; R water Tr; intens 039°-043°.

◀ ROYAN
R1 45°36'·56N 01°01'·96W Iso G 4s.
Royan Jetée Sud ☆ 45°37'·01N 01°01'·82W VQ (2) R 1s 11m 12M; vis: 199°-116°; *Horn (2) 20s.*
Royan Harbour Nouvelle Jetée Head ent ☆ 45°37'·13N 01°01'·64W Oc (2) R 6s 8m 6M.

◀ PORT BLOC

No. 13B 45°34'·60N 01°02'·98W QG.
Port Bloc Ent N side ☆ 45°34'·14N 01°03'·74W Fl G 4s 9m 3M.
S Pier Hd ☆ 45°34'·11N 01°03'·71W Iso R 4s 8m 4M.

◀ PAUILLAC/BLAYE

No. 43 45°12'·44N 00°44'·27W Fl (2) G 6s.
Pauillac NE Bkwtr ☆ 45°11'·96N 00°44'·61W Fl G 4s 7m 5M.
Ent E side ☆ 45°11'·86N 00°44'·60W QG 7m 4M.
No. 52A 45°06'·96N 00°41'·50W QR.
D6 45°06'·90N 00°39'·94WFl (2) R 6s.
Blaye Ent N side ☆ 45°07'·49N 00°40'·01W Q (3) R 5s 6m 3M.

◀ LA GARONNE/BORDEAUX

Pont d'Aquitaine ☆ 44°52'·82N 00°32'·31W 4 F Vi.

LA GIRONDE TO L'ADOUR

Hourtin ☆ 45°08'·48N 01°09'·67W Fl 5s 55m **23M**; R □ Tr.

◀ BASSIN D'ARCACHON

ATT-ARC 44°34'·60N 01°18'·56W L Fl 10s 8m 5M; (frequently shifted).
Cap Ferret ☆ 44°38'·76N 01°14'·95W Fl R 5s 53m **27M**; W ○ Tr, R top. Oc (3) 12s 46m 14M; same Tr; vis: 045°-135°.
La Salie 44°30'·43N 01°17'·76W Fl (2) 6s.
La Salie Wharf Hd 44°30'·89N 01°15'·68W Q (9) 15s 19m 10M.
No. 15 44°39'·83N 01°12'·04W.
Arcachon Marina West Breakwater Head ☆ 44°39'·77N 01°09'·15W QG 6m 6M.
Arcachon Marina East Bkwtr Head ☆ 44°39'·76N 01°09'·07W QR 6m 6M.
Port de La Vigne ☆ 44°40'·43N 01°14'·36W Iso R 4s 7m 5M; (occas).

SM 44°20'·32N 01°28'·73W Fl (3) Y 12s.
ZDL 44°12'·88N 01°22'·14W Fl Y 4s.
Contis ☆ 44°05'·59N 01°19'·05W Fl (4) 25s 50m **23M**; W ○ Tr, B diagonal stripes.

◀ CAPBRETON

Digue Nord Hd ☆ 43°39'·38N 01°27'·01W Fl (2) R 6s 13m 12M; W ○ Tr, R top; *Horn 30s*.
Estacade Sud ☆ 43°39'·25N 01°26'·89W Fl G 4s 7m 12M.

L'ADOUR TO BAIE DE FONTARABIE

◀ ANGLET/BAYONNE

BA 43°32'·55N 01°32'·79W L Fl 10s.
Digue du large Head 43°31'·88N 01°31'·99W QR 11m 8M; W Tr, R top.
Digue extérieure Sud 43°31'·60N 01°31'·77W, Q (9) 15s 7M.
Adour-Sud Head ☆ 43°31'·73N 01°31'·48W ☆ Iso G 4s 9m 10M; W □ Tr, G top.
Jetée Nord Head ☆ 43°31'·82N 01°31'·42W Oc (2) R 6s 12m 8M; W pylon, R top.
Digue exterieure Sud 43°31'·53N 01°31'·77W Q (9) 15s 15m 6M; WCM Bn.
Ent Ldg Lts 111·5° (moved as necessary and lit when chan practicable). Front 43°31'·63N 01°30'·94W Dir FG 6m 14M; W hut, G band. Rear,149m from front, Dir FG 10m 14M; both intens 109°-114°.
Boucau ☆ Ldg Lts 090°. Front, 43°31'·81N 01°31'·23W Dir Q 9m **19M**. Rear, 250m from front, Dir Q 15m 19M; both W Trs, R tops, both intens 086·5°-093·5°.
Anglet Marina ent ☆ 43°30'·92N 01°30'·51W Fl G 2s 5m 2M.
Pte de Blanc- Pignon ☆ 43°30'·92N 01°29'·61W Fl (2) G 6s 8m 9M; W col, G top.
La Forme de Radoub (Blanc-Pignon) ☆ 43°30'·51N 01°29'·81W VQ G 17m **16M**.
Pont de L'Aveugle ☆ 43°30'·05N 01°29'·53W Dir Q WRG W3M, R2M, G2M; vis: G165°-170°, W170°-175°, R175°-180°.

◀ BIARRITZ

Pointe Saint-Martin ☆ 43°29'·62N 01°33'·24W Fl (2) 10s 73m **29M**; W Tr, B top.
Biarritz Ldg Lts 174° Front 43°29'·00N 01°33'·96W Fl R 2s 7m 3M. Rear, 83m from front, Fl R 2s 19m 3M.
Aero Mo (L) 43°28'·38N 01°31'·99W 7·5s 80m.
Guethary Ldg Lts 133°. Front, 43°25'·59N 01°36'·53W QR 11m 6M; W mast. Rear, 66m from front, QR 33m 6M; W Tr.

18

◀ ST JEAN DE LUZ

Passe D'illarguitia Ldg Lts 138·5°. Front, Le Socoa, 43°23'·70N 01°41'·20W Q WR 36m W12M, R8M; W □ Tr, B stripe; vis: Wshore-264°, R264°-282°, W282°-shore. **Rear, Bordagain**, 0·77M from front, Dir Q 67m **20M**; intens 134·5°-141·5°.
Ste Barbe ☆ Ldg Lts 101°. **Front** ☆, 43°23'·96N 01°39'·88W Dir Oc (4) R 12s 30m **18M**; W △ on W building; intens 095°-107°. **Rear** ☆, 340m from front, Dir Oc (4) R 12s 47m **18M**; B △, W □ W Tr; synch with front; intens 095°-107°.
Digue des Criquas Head ☆ 43°23'·84N 01°40'·67W Iso G 4s 11m 6M; G □ Tr; *Horn 15s*.
Groyne Head ☆ 43°23'·33N 01°40'·15W Fl Bu 4s
Ldg Lts 150·7°, **Front Jetée Est** ☆, 43°23'·25N 01°40'·15W Dir QG 18m **16M**; W □ Tr, R stripe. **Rear** ☆, 410m from front, Dir QG 27m **16M**; W □ Tr, G stripe. Both intens 149·75°-152·2°.

◀ HENDAYE

Cabo Higuer ☆ 43°23'·51N 01°47'·53W Fl (2) 10s 63m **23M**; Tr, W lantern; vis: 072°-340°.
Fuenterrabia Breakwater Corner ☆ 43°23'·17N 01°47'·29W Fl G 3s 12m 3M
Hendaye Epi Socoburu Hd ☆ 43°22'·66N 01°47'·24W L Fl R 10s 8m 5M.
Training Wall Hd ☆ 43°22'·82N 01°47'·36W Fl (3) G 9s 9m 5M.
Pte des Dunes ☆ 43°22'·38N 01°47'·37W Fl R 2·5s 6m 4M.
43°22'·33N 01°47'·49W Fl (4) G 11s.
43°22'·10N 01°47'·29W VQ (3) G 5s 3m 3M; G mast.
Marina Digue Coude ☆ 43°22'·07N 01°47'·18W Fl (2) R 6s 6m 2M; vis: 294°-114°.
Marina Jetée Sud ☆ 43°22'·05N 01°47'·07W Fl Y 4s 5m 4M.
43°21'·99N 01°47'·09W L Fl G 10s 4M; G mast.

9.18.5 PASSAGE INFORMATION

BAY OF BISCAY (charts 1104, 20, 2664, 1102), *West France Cruising Companion* (Macmillan Reeds/Featherstone) covers from Brittany to the Spanish border and *South Biscay Pilot* (Adlard Coles), the R Gironde to La Coruna; the Admiralty *Bay of Biscay Pilot*. Larger scale French charts are more suitable for inshore waters.

Despite its reputation, weather in the S part of the Bay is often warm and settled in summer when the Azores high and Spanish heat low are the dominant weather features. NE'lies prevail in sea area Finisterre in summer and gales may occur twice monthly, although forecast more frequently. Atlantic lows can bring W'ly spells at any time together with long swells which are dangerous inshore. SE or S winds are rare, but wind direction and speed often vary from day to day. Sea and land breezes can be well developed in the summer. Off N Spain *Galernas* are dangerous squally NW winds which blow with little warning. Rainfall is moderate, increasing in the SE, where thunder is more frequent. Sea fog occurs May-Oct, but is less common in winter. Japanese seaweed has been reported as a nuisance.

Tidal streams are weak offshore, but can be strong in estuaries and channels, and around headlands. The tidal stream chartlets at 9.18.3 are based on NP 265 (Admiralty Tidal Stream Atlas for France, W Coast) which uses data from actual observations out to 15-25M offshore. The equivalent French Atlas gives more data, but based on computer predictions.

The general direction and rate of the surface current much depends on wind: in summer it is SE, towards the SE corner of B of Biscay, where it swings W along N coast of Spain. In winter with W gales, the current runs E along N coast of Spain, sometimes at 3kn or more. When crossing B of Biscay, allow for a likely set to the E, particularly after strong W winds.

BAIE DE BOURGNEUF (charts 3216, 2646) B de Bourgneuf is entered between Pte de St Gildas and Pte de l'Herbaudière, the NW tip of Île de Noirmoutier. Within the B the only yacht hbrs are Pornic (9.18.8) and L'Herbaudière (9.18.9). There are minor drying hbrs at La Bernerie-en-Retz, Le Collet, Port des Brochets and Bec de l'Epoids; with a good anch 5ca NE of Pte des Dames. The E and S sides of the B are encumbered with shoals, rks and oyster or mussel fisheries. The Bay is sheltered except in W winds, which can raise a heavy sea on the ebb stream.

From the NW (chart 3216) the approach is simple, but beware La Couronnée (dries 1·8m; buoyed) a rky bank about 2M WSW of Pte de St Gildas. Adjacent to it, Banc de Kerouars (least depth 1m; breaks) extends 3M further E. Approach Pornic in the W sector of Pte de Noveillard lt, ie S of Banc de Kerouars and NW of Notre Dame IDM bn tr, which lies 2M SW of Pornic and marks end of a line of rks extending ESE to La Bernerie. Pierre du Chenal is an isolated rk about 1M SSE of Notre Dame.

At the N end of Île de Noirmoutier, Chenal de la Grise, between Île du Pilier and Pte de l'Herbaudière and in the W sector of Martroger NCM bn lt, carries 3m, and gives access to L'Herbaudière marina. If heading E to Pornic, pass N of Martroger, and clear of Roches des Pères about 1M ENE. Extending 6M to seaward off the NW end of the island, beware Chaussée des Boeufs, buoyed rks, some drying on to which the tide sets. The S ent via Goulet de Fromentine (SHOM 5039; ECM 549) is difficult due to a shifting bar and 8 hrs of W-going stream; the conspic bridge has 24m clearance. Once inside, further progress to NNE is restricted to shoal draft at sp HW±1 by Route du Gois, causeway drying 3m.

ILE D'YEU TO PERTUIS BRETON (AC 2663) Les Marguerites, rky shoals, lie SSW of Goulet de Fromentine, with the part-drying reef, Pont d'Yeu (SCM buoy), extending midway between the mainland and the Île d'Yeu; here anch is prohib due to underwater cables. The passage along the NE of the island carries 6-7m nearer to the island. The low-lying, wooded Côte de la Vendée continues 40M SE to Pte du Grouin Cou with few dangers more than 1·5M offshore, except near Les Sables-d'Olonne.

Île d'Yeu, 30m high, has the main lt ho near the NW end and on the NE coast a very conspic water tr close to Port Joinville (9.18.10), crowded in season . Pte des Courbeaux lt ho is at the low SE end of the island and a lesser lt is at the NW end. The SW coast is steep-to and rky, with a tiny drying hbr at Port de la Meule (best to anch outside) and, further E, anch at Anse des Vieilles, both only tenable in settled conditions.

14M to the E of Île d'Yeu lies St Gilles-Croix-de-Vie (9.18.11). Thence 14M further SE is Les Sables-d'Olonne (9.18.12), with Les Barges drying reef (lt) 2·5M W of the ent. Bourgenay (9.18.13) is 6M further SE. The approaches to these secure hbrs are exposed to onshore winds from SE to NW, and susceptible to swell. Jard-sur-Mer is a small drying hbr midway between Bourgenay and Pte du Grouin Cou.

PERTUIS BRETON (chart 2641) Pertuis Breton is entered between Pte du Grouin du Cou and Pte des Baleines on Île de Ré, (both lit). Beware rky ledges (dry) extending 2·5M NW from Les Baleines. It gives access to the hbrs of Ars-en-Ré (9.18.15), St Martin (9.18.14) and La Flotte on the N shore of Île de Ré which is surrounded by shallows and drying areas. From St Martin to Pte de Sablanceaux there are extensive oyster beds.

On the mainland side, in fresh NW winds against tide a bad sea builds on the bank which extends 8M W of Pte du Grouin du Cou. 1M S of the Pte is Roche de l'Aunis (depth 0·8m). From the Pte sand dunes and mussel beds, with seaward limits marked by SPM buoys, run 8M ESE to the drying ent to Rivière Le Lay, which is fronted by a bar (dries 1m), dangerous in bad weather. The chan to L'Aiguillon/La Faute-sur-Mer (9.18.15) is marked by bns and buoys. 4M further E is entrance to Anse de l'Aiguillon, in which are extensive mussel beds. In NE corner is entrance to Sèvre Niortaise which, after 3·5M, gives access to the canal leading to the port of Marans. Further S is a sheltered route to La Rochelle and Pertuis d'Antioche via Coureau de la Pallice and the road bridge (30m clearance) from the mainland to Île de Ré.

PERTUIS D'ANTIOCHE (chart 2746) A SWM buoy marks the W approach to Pertuis d'Antioche which runs between Île de Ré and Île d'Oléron, giving access to La Rochelle (9.18.16), Ile d'Aix, La Charente and Rochefort (9.18.18). Its shores are low-lying. Île de Ré forms the N side, fringed by rky ledges extending 2·5M SE from Pte de Chanchardon (lt) and nearly 1M from Pte de Chauveau (marked by lt tr and two bns). Off Pte de Chassiron (lt ho, Sig Stn), at the N tip of Île d'Oléron, reefs extend 5ca W, 1·5M N to Rocher d'Antioche (lit), and 1·5M E, and there is often a nasty sea.

Well offshore, 34-40M W of Île de Ré, Plateau de Rochebonne is a large rky plateau on which the sea breaks dangerously. It is steep-to on all sides, has least depth 3·3m and is buoyed.

ÎLE D'OLERON (charts 2746, 2663) On the NE coast of Ile d'Oléron (9.18.17) there are marinas at Port St Denis and Le Douhet at the N end; further S are yacht and fishing hbrs at Boyardville and Le Château. All are sheltered from the prevailing W'lies.

From Pertuis d'Antioche, Grande Rade des Trousses is entered via either Passage de l'Est close to Île d'Aix (9.18.18) or Passage de l'Ouest, which run each side of La Longe le Boyard, an extensive sandbank on which stands Ft Boyard tr. From Grande Rade, where good anch is found except in fresh NW winds, the narrow and shallow Coureau d'Oléron winds between ledges,oyster beds and constantly changing shoals, with buoys moved to conform. About 2M SE of Le Chateau it is crossed by a bridge, clearance 15m; the bridge arch for the navigable chan is marked at road level by W □ boards, with G ▲ or R ■ superimposed, illuminated at night. Just N of bridge is Fort du Chapus, connected to mainland by causeway. SHOM 6335 is needed. S-going stream starts at HW Pte de Grave – 0230, N-going at HW Pte de Grave + 0500, sp rates 2kn. Up the Seudre River (9.18.19) there are anchs and yacht facilities at Marennes.

The W coast, from Pte de Chassiron 15M SSE to Pte de Gatseau, is bounded by drying rks and shoals. In bad weather the sea breaks 4 or 5M offshore. La Cotinière, the only hbr, is much used by fishing boats and is exposed to the Atlantic. Tidal streams are weak, sp rate 1kn, starting NW at HW Pte de Grave + 0300 and SE at HW Pte de Grave – 0505, but often overcome by current due to prevailing wind. The rate however increases towards Pte de Gatseau.

Here Pertuis de Maumusson separates the island from the mainland. Its ent is marked by a SWM buoy about 3M WSW of Pte de Gatseau. Banc de Gatseau and Banc des Mattes, both of which dry in places, lie N and S of the chan, and are joined by a sand bar which usually has a depth of about 1·5m. Depth and position vary, and buoys may not mark the best water. Any swell speedily forms breakers, and the chan is very dangerous then or in any onshore winds, especially on the ebb (sp rate 4kn). In calm weather with no swell, a stout craft and reliable engine, and having gained local advice, enter about HW – 1; ideally follow a local FV with deeper draught.

APPROACHES TO LA GIRONDE (chart 2910) The Gironde (9.18.20) is formed from the Garonne and Dordogne, which join at Bec d'Ambès, 38M above Pte de Grave. BXA lt buoy is moored off the mouth of the estuary, about 11M WSW of Pte de la Coubre. Banc de la Mauvaise, the S end of which dries extends 5M seaward. Cordouan lt ho is on a large sand spit in the middle of the estuary. Grande Passe de l'Ouest starts about 4M E of BXA buoy and is dredged through Grand Banc, the outer bar of La Gironde. Enter to seaward of buoys Nos. 1 and 2, and keep in buoyed chan with ldg lts. Off Terre-Nègre lt the SE-going stream begins at HW – 0500 (sp 1·5kn), and the NW-going at HW+0130 (sp 2·5kn).

Passe Sud, a lesser chan, is entered at the SWM lt buoy, 9M SW of Pte de Grave, and runs NE past Pte de Grave. There are two sets of ldg lts; the second lead over Platin de Grave, but it is better to pass NW of this shoal. Both entrance chans are dangerous in strong onshore winds, due to breakers and also the mascaret (bore) on the outgoing stream. Westerly swell breaks on La Mauvaise and around Cordouan, and sandbanks shift constantly. In places tidal streams run 4kn or more, and with wind against tide a dangerous sea can build.

LA GIRONDE TO CAPBRETON (charts 1102, 2664) From Pte de la Négade to Capbreton, the coast is a featureless stretch of 107M broken only by the entrance to Arcachon (9.18.23). It is bordered by sand dunes and pine trees, and is often a lee shore with no shelter from W winds. 5M offshore a current usually sets N at about 0·5kn, particularly with a S wind; in winter this may be stronger after W winds. Within 1M of the coast there may be a S'ly counter-current.

A missile range, operated by Centre d'Essais des Landes, lies between Pointe de la Négade and Capbreton and extends up to 45M offshore. For details of boundaries, activity and sources of information, see 9.18.24.

The Fosse (or Gouf) de Capbreton, a submarine canyon, runs at right angles to the coast. The 50m depth contour is 3ca W of Capbreton hbr bkwtr and the 100m line is 4ca further W. In strong W winds a dangerous sea breaks along the N and S edges of it. Strong N or W winds and swell make the ent to the large marina at Capbreton (9.18.25) impassable. Anglet/Bayonne may then be a safer option; or stay at sea.

CAPBRETON TO SPANISH BORDER (charts 1343, 1102) There is a marina at Anglet (9.18.26), but few facilities for yachts further up the R. Adour at Bayonne. At L'Adour ent the flood runs E and SE, sp rate 2-4kn; the ebb runs W, sp rate 3-5kn. S of Pte St Martin the coast has mostly sandy beaches and rky cliffs, with offlying rky shoals and Pyrenees mountains inland. In strong W winds the sea breaks over Loutrou shoal; and on Plateau de St Jean-de-Luz, a chain of rky shoals lying 1-4M offshore.

St Jean-de-Luz (chart 1343 and 9.18.27) is best approached first time or in bad weather through Passe d'Illarguita (between Illarguita and Belhara Perdun shoals): follow the 138° transit (Le Socoa lt on with Bordagain lt) until the Ste Barbe ldg lts (101°) are in transit; thence enter by Passe de l'Ouest on the 151° transit of the inner hbr ldg lts.

Baie de Fontarabie, in Spanish Rada de Higuer, lies on the border of France and Spain, and is entered between Pte Ste Anne and Cabo Higuer (a bare, rugged cape with lt ho) 1·75M WNW. Les Briquets (dry) lie 1M N of Pte Ste Anne. Keep to W of Banc Chicharvel and Bajo Iruarri in ent to B. Entry should not be attempted with strong onshore winds or heavy swell. R La Bidassoa is entered between breakwaters in SW corner of the B, giving access to marina at Hendaye-Plage (9.18.28). In the middle of the bay is a neutral area, marked by beacons and shown on chart 1181. To seaward of this area the boundary line (approximately 01°46'·2W) runs N from a white pyramid on the S shore, about 1M SW of Pte Ste Anne.

AGENTS WANTED If you are interested in becoming our agent for any of the following ports, please write to: The Editor, The Book Barn, Westbourne, Hampshire, PO10 8RS, England – and get your free copy of the Almanac annually. You do not have to live in a port to be the agent, but should at least be a fairly regular visitor.

Portbail	Le Légué
Lampaul (Ile d'Ouessant)	La Forêt
River Etel	River Loire/Saint Nazaire
St Gilles-Croix-de-Vie	Les Sables d'Olonne
La Rochelle	Seudre River
La Gironde	Port-Bloc
Anglet	St Jean-de-Luz
Pasajes	San Sebastián
Guetaria	Lequeitio
Elanchove	Bilbao
Castro Urdiales	Santander
Ribadesella	Gijón
Cudillero	Luarca
Ria de Ribadeo	Ría de Vivero
Ría de Cedeira	El Ferrol
La Coruña	Ría de Camariñas
Ría de Muros	Ría de Arosa
Ría de Pontevedra	Ría de Vigo
Bayona	Viana do Castelo
Leixões	Figueira da Foz
Nazaré	Peniche
Cascais	Lisboa
Sesimbra	Setúbal
Sines	Lagos
Portimão	Vilamoura
Vila Real de Santo-António	Ayamonte
Isla Cristina	Mazagón
Chipiona	Sevilla
Bahia de Cádiz	Sancti-Petri
Barbate	Algeciras
Gibraltar	

9.18.6 DISTANCE TABLE

Approximate distances in nautical miles are by the most direct route, whilst avoiding dangers and allowing for Traffic Separation Schemes. Places in *italics* are in adjoining areas; places in **bold** are in 9.0.6, Cross-Channel Distances.

1.	***Le Conquet***	**1**																			
2.	*St Nazaire*	145	**2**																		
3.	Pornic	146	16	**3**																	
4.	L'Herbaudière	144	16	10	**4**																
5.	Port Joinville	147	35	30	20	**5**															
6.	St Gilles-C-de-Vie	166	45	40	29	18	**6**														
7.	Sables d'Olonne	181	65	55	40	31	16	**7**													
8.	Bourgenay	190	74	64	49	40	25	9	**8**												
9.	St Martin (I de Ré)	208	92	75	67	55	44	27	20	**9**											
10.	La Rochelle	218	101	92	76	66	51	36	29	12	**10**										
11.	Rochefort	242	126	116	102	84	75	61	54	36	26	**11**									
12.	R La Seudre	242	125	116	100	89	71	58	52	33	24	30	**12**								
13.	Port St Denis	220	103	94	78	59	48	33	30	21	13	26	22	**13**							
14.	Port Bloc/Royan	234	122	115	107	97	85	71	60	56	52	68	27	42	14						
15.	Bordeaux	289	177	170	162	152	140	126	115	111	107	123	82	97	55	**15**					
16.	Cap Ferret	274	168	160	153	138	130	113	110	102	98	114	75	88	68	123	**16**				
17.	Capbreton	316	220	215	211	192	186	169	166	165	156	172	131	145	124	179	58	**17**			
18.	Anglet/Bayonne	328	232	223	223	200	195	181	178	177	168	184	143	157	132	187	70	12	**18**		
19.	*Santander*	300	243	237	229	212	210	204	204	206	202	218	184	192	180	235	133	106	103	**19**	
20.	*Cabo Finisterre*	382	404	399	390	377	395	393	394	406	407	423	399	397	401	456	376	370	373	274	**20**

9.18.7 Special notes for France: See 9.15.7.

PORNIC *9.18.8*

Loire Atlantique **47°06´·55N 02°06´·59W** ❁❁⛵⛵⛵✿✿✿

CHARTS AC 2981, 2986, 2646; Imray C40; SHOM 7394, 7395; ECM 547, 549

TIDES +0515 Dover; ML 3·6; Duration 0540; Zone –0100

Standard Port BREST (⟵)

Times				Height (metres)			
High Water		Low Water		MHWS	MHWN	MLWN	MLWS
0500	1100	0500	1100	6·9	5·4	2·6	1·0
1700	2300	1700	2300				
Differences PORNIC							
–0050	+0030	–0010	–0010	–1·1	–0·8	–0·4	–0·2

SHELTER Very good in large marina (2m); access HW±5. But no access LW±1 when Coeff >75, nor in winds >F7 from SE to SW. Leave the SWM buoy to stbd, especially near LWS. Do not cut the corner round the S bkwtr head due to rky spur. Enter between the SHM pile and 2 PHM piles, on which the ☆s are mounted. A rky spur also extends SW from the head of the E jetty. Visitors berths are on P1 (for LOA >12m), P2 and P3 pontoons (first to stbd). Old hbr dries $\underline{1}$·8m; access HW±2½ via marked, lit drying chan.

NAVIGATION WPT 47°06´·10N 02°08´·70W, 253°/073° from/to jetty hd, 1·5M. 4-6M WSW of hbr beware Banc de Kerouars, least depth 1m, on which seas break; it is unmarked, but the W sector of Pte de Noëveillard lt clears it by night. From the NW pass between this bank and the mainland. All other hazards are well marked. The S end of B de Bourgneuf is full of oyster beds, and many obstructions.

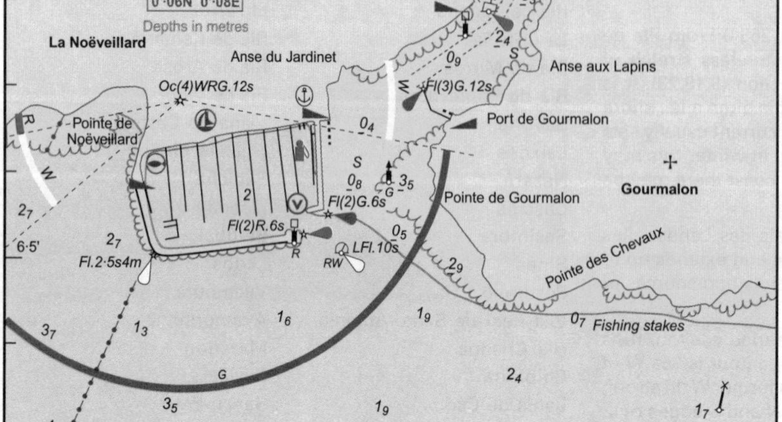

LIGHTS AND MARKS Pte de Noëveillard Oc (4) WRG 12s 22m 13/9M; G shore-051°, W051°-079°, R079°-shore; the W sector lies between Notre-Dame rk, IDM bn tr Fl(2)6s, and the E end of Banc de Kerouars. Also as plan. Entry sigs (simplified).

RADIO TELEPHONE VHF Ch 09 (H24).

TELEPHONE Hr Mr 02·40·82·05·40; Aff Mar 02·40·82·01·69; CROSS 02·97·55·35·35; ⊖ 02·40·82·03·17; SNSM 02·40·82·00·47; Auto 08·36·68·08·44; Police 02·40·82·01·54; Dr 02·40·82·01·80; Brit Consul 01·40·63·16·02.

FACILITIES Port-la-Noëveillard Marina (754+165 Ⓥ) ☎ 02·40·82·05·40, 📠 02.40.82·55·37, €1·80, P, D (on pontoon), FW, ME, AC, El, Sh, BH (50 ton), C (6 ton) CH, 🗟; **CN de Pornic** ☎ 02·40·82·34·72; **Services:** ME, El, Ⓔ, Sh, CH, SM. **Town** Market Sun am. V, Gaz, R, Bar, ✉, Ⓑ, ⇌, ✈ (Nantes). Ferry: Roscoff/St Malo.

L'HERBAUDIÈRE *9.18.9*

Vendée **47°01´·70N 02°17´·77W** (Ile de Noirmoutier)

CHARTS AC 2981, 2986, 2646; Imray C40; SHOM 7394, 7395; ECM 547, 549

TIDES +0500 Dover; ML 3·4; Zone −0100

Standard Port BREST (⟵)

Times				**Height (metres)**			
High Water		Low Water		MHWS	MHWN	MLWN	MLWS
0500	1100	0500	1100	6·9	5·4	2·6	1·0
1700	2300	1700	2300				
Differences L'HERBAUDIERE							
−0047	+0023	−0020	−0020	−1·4	−1·0	−0·5	−0·2
FROMENTINE							
−0050	+0020	−0020	+0010	−1·6	−1·2	−0·7	0·0

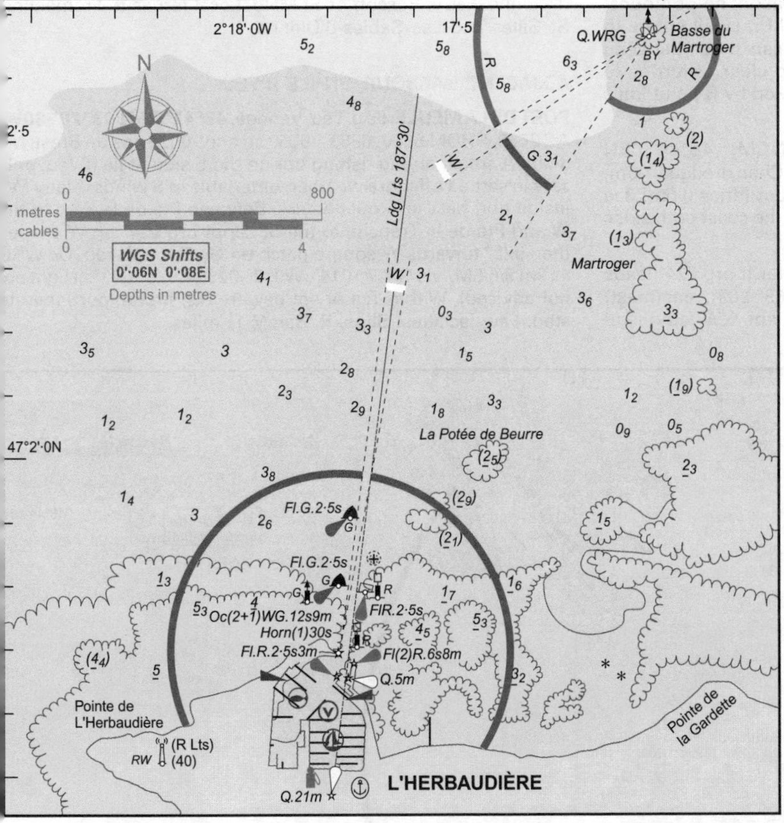

SHELTER Good in marina (E side) except in winds E of N, dredged 1·5m; Ⓥs berth on pontoon F. FV hbr (W side); NB early morning departures. The ⚓ off Pte des Dames lt, Oc (3) WRG 12s, is exposed to N and E winds.

NAVIGATION WPT 47°03´·05N 02°17´·5W, 009°/189° from/to W jetty lt, 1·4M. There are rks and banks to the SW, NW and NE of Pte de l'Herbaudière. Ldg lts and white sector (187·5°-190°) of the W jetty lt both lead into ent chan, dredged to 1·3m and passing close W of two 0·3m patches; care is needed at LWS. Two SHM buoys, both Fl G 2·5s, and a PHM buoy, Fl R 2·5s, mark the last 2ca of the chan. W bkwtr obscures vessels leaving.

LIGHTS AND MARKS Visibility in summer is often poor. Conspic daymarks are R/W radio mast 500m W of hbr and water tr about 1M SE. Ile du Pilier, Fl (3) 20s 33m 29M, is 2·5M WNW of hbr. Appr in any of the 3 W sectors of Basse de Martroger, NCM bn, Dir Q WRG 11m 9/6M, G033°-055°, W055°-060°, R060°-095°, G095°-124°, W124°-153°, R153°-201°, W201°-240°, R240°-033°. Ldg lts 188°, both grey masts, Q 5/26m 7M, vis 098°-278°, lead over Banc de la Blanche (1·8m) approx 2M N of hbr. L'Herbaudière W jetty, Oc (2+1) WG 12s 9m 10/7M, W187·5°-190° (2½°), G elsewhere. E jetty head Fl (2) R 6s 8m 4M; inner head Fl R 2·5s 3m 1M.

RADIO TELEPHONE Hr Mr VHF Ch 09 (HO).

TELEPHONE Hr Mr 02·51·39·05·05; Aff Mar 02·51·39·94·03; SNSM 02·51·39·33·90; CROSS 02·97·55·35·35; Météo 02·40·84·80·19; Auto 08·36·68·08·85; ⊖ 02·51·39·06·80; Police 02·51·39·04·36; Dr 02·51·39·05·64; Brit Consul 01·40·63·16·02.

FACILITIES Marina (442+50 Ⓥ), ☎ 02·51.39.05.05, 📠 02·51.39.75.97; €2·07, FW, P, D, AC, C (25 ton), Slip, ME, SM, ▣, Gas, Gaz, V, R, Bar (July, Aug), Sh, SC; **Quay** Bar, R, ME, Sh, V; **Services:** El, Ⓔ, CH.

ADJACENT HARBOUR ON ILE DE NOIRMOUTIER

NOIRMOUTIER-EN-L'ILE 46°59´·40N 02°13´·10W. AC 2981; SHOM 7394. Tides as above. Good shelter and AB, 4M SE of L'Herbaudiere, but FV hbr dries up to 3·0m on mud/gravel. Appr HW±1 across extensive drying rock ledges to the N and E of ent. The E'ly of 2 chans runs SSW from approx 47°00´·50N 02°11´·10W, then doglegs WNW to the ent. It is marked by 5 unlit PHM bns. An inshore chan runs S from off Pte des Dames lt ho, Oc (3) WRG12s 34m. It is more easily followed, keeping about 400m off 5 unlit SHM bns along the shore. Both chans meet at the ent where the flood tide sets S. S jetty hd has ☆ Oc (2) R 6s. Follow the jetty on N side for about 1M to hbr. A prior recce (3M overland from L'Herbaudiere) is advised. Hr Mr ☎ 02.51.39.08.39. **Quay** AB, FW, C (4 ton); **Services:** ME, El, Ⓔ, Sh, CH, SM. **Town** P, D, V, Gaz, R, Bar, ▣, ✉, Ⓑ, ⇌ ✈ at Nantes, via ferry to Pornic and bus. Ferry: Roscoff or St Malo.

ADJACENT HARBOUR

FROMENTINE, Vendée, 46°53´·60N 02°08´·60W. AC 2981, SHOM 7394, 6853. HW +0550 on Dover (UT); ML 3·2m; Duration 0540. Tides above. Do not appr from Baie de Bourgneuf as there is a road causeway, dries 3m, from Ile de Noirmoutier to the mainland. Enter through Goulet de Fromentine, under the bridge (clearance 24m). The chan is buoyed, moved as necessary, but is very shallow, so dangerous in bad weather. At sp the ebb can reach 8kn, the flood 5kn. Do not attempt night entry. ⚓ W of pier. Coming from N, beware Les Boeufs. Tourelle Milieu lies on the N side of Le Goulet de Fromentine, Fl (4) R 12s 6m 5M, R tr. Pte de Notre Dames-de-Monts Dir lt, Oc (2) WRG 6s 21m 13/10M, G000°-043°, W043°-063°, R063°-073°, W073°-094°, G094°-113°, W113°-116°, R116°-175°, G175°-196°, R196°-230°. Fromentine SWM lt buoy, L Fl 10s+bell, 46°53´·10N 02°11´·50W, is about 1·5M WSW of Pte du Notre Dames-de-Monts. Bridge, two x Iso 4s 32m 18M. Facilities: Aff Mar at Noirmoutier; ⊖ at Beauvois-sur-Mer; **Quay** Slip, C (3 ton), FW; **Cercle Nautique de Fromentine-Barfatre** (CNFB); **Services:** ME, El, Sh, CH.

PORT JOINVILLE, Ile d'Yeu *9.18.10*

Vendée 46°43'·80N 02°20'·75W ❁❁◊◊◊✿✿✿

CHARTS AC 3640, 2663; Imray C40; SHOM 7410; ECM 549, 1022

TIDES +0550 Dover; ML 3·1; Duration 0600; Zone –0100

Standard Port BREST (⟵)

Times				Height (metres)			
High Water		Low Water		MHWS	MHWN	MLWN	MLWS
0500	1100	0500	1100	6·9	5·4	2·6	1·0
1700	2300	1700	2300				
Differences PORT JOINVILLE (Ile d'Yeu)							
–0040	+0015	–0030	–0035	–1·9	–1·4	–0·7	–0·3

SHELTER Good in enlarged marina, but very crowded in season; best to pre-book as it is the only secure hbr on the island. The wet basin (3·7m) access HW±1½, is mainly for FVs, but possible overflow for yachts in high season; no pontoons; tfc lts R & G, just S of lock. No ⚓ in outer hbr; swell enters in N/NE winds. If the marina is full, yachts can moor between Gare Maritime and the ice factory, keeping clear of ferries to W. A grid to the W of the ice factory is marked by R paint lines on quay wall.

NAVIGATION WPT Basse Mayence NCM, 46°44´·65N 02°19´·10W, 055°/235° from/to bkwtr lt, 1·3M. Chan dredged 1·5m, appr with care at LW. Beware Basse du Bouet (dries 0·6m) 3ca NW, La Sablaire shoal to the E and rks along the coast both sides of hbr ent.

LIGHTS AND MARKS Very conspic high water tr brg 224° leads to hbr. Ldg lts 219°, both QR 11/16m 6M, vis 169°-269°; rear (mast) 85m from front. Conspic chimney W of hbr ent. NW jetty head Oc (3) WG 12s 9m 11/8M; G shore-150°, W150°-232°, G232°-279° W279°-285°, G285°-shore; horn (3) 30s, tidal sigs. Quai du Canada hd Iso G 4s 7m 6M unintens 337°-067°. Galiote jetty roo Fl R 2·5s 1M.

RADIO TELEPHONE Marina VHF Ch 09 16 (HO).

TELEPHONE Hr Mr 02·51·58·38·11; Locks 02·51·58·37·01; Af Mar 02·51·59·42·60; ⊖ 02·51·39·06·80; CROSS 02·97·55·35·35 Météo 02·51·36·10·78; Auto 08·36·68·08·85; SNSM 02·51·58·32·01 Police 02·51·58·30·05; Dr 02·51·59·30·00/02·51·58·30·58 🄷 02·51·68·30·23; Brit Consul 01·40·63·16·02. Note: There are phone-card telephones only.

FACILITIES Marina (390+170 ♥), ☎ 02·51·58·38·11, 🖷 02.51.26.03.49, €1·45 (€2·44 in Jul/Aug), FW, AC, P, D, El, ME, Sh **Wet Basin** Slip, FW, C (18 ton); **CN Ile d'Yeu** ☎ 02·51·58·31·50 **Services:** ME, El, Sh, CH, Ⓔ. **Town** V, Gaz, R, Bar, ✉, Ⓑ ≹ (St Gilles-Croix-de-Vie), ✈ (Nantes). Flights from airfield 2M west of Port Joinville to Nantes and (summers only) to Les Sables d'Olonne. Ferry: Roscoff or St Malo. Local ferries to Fromentine St Gilles and Les Sables-d'Olonne.

ADJACENT HARBOUR ON ILE D'YEU

PORT DE LA MEULE, Ile d'Yeu, Vendée, **46°41'·75N 03°20'·60W** AC 2663; SHOM 6890, 6853. –0050 sp and –0020 nps on Brest; ML 3·0m. A small, drying fishing hbr on the S side of Ile d'Yeu, only safe in settled offshore weather; untenable in S winds. Many FVs inside hbr; best to ⚓ outside ent. Between Pte de la Père to the W and Pte de la Tranche to the SE, appr brg 034° on W chapel then 022° towards W square patch on Gy □ lt tr, R top, Oc WRG 4s 9m 9/6/5M, vis G007°-018°, W018°-028°, R028°-042°. (Night ent not advised). Within 1ca of ent beware rks, first to port, then to stbd. Few facilities: Slips, R, Bar; V 1½ miles.

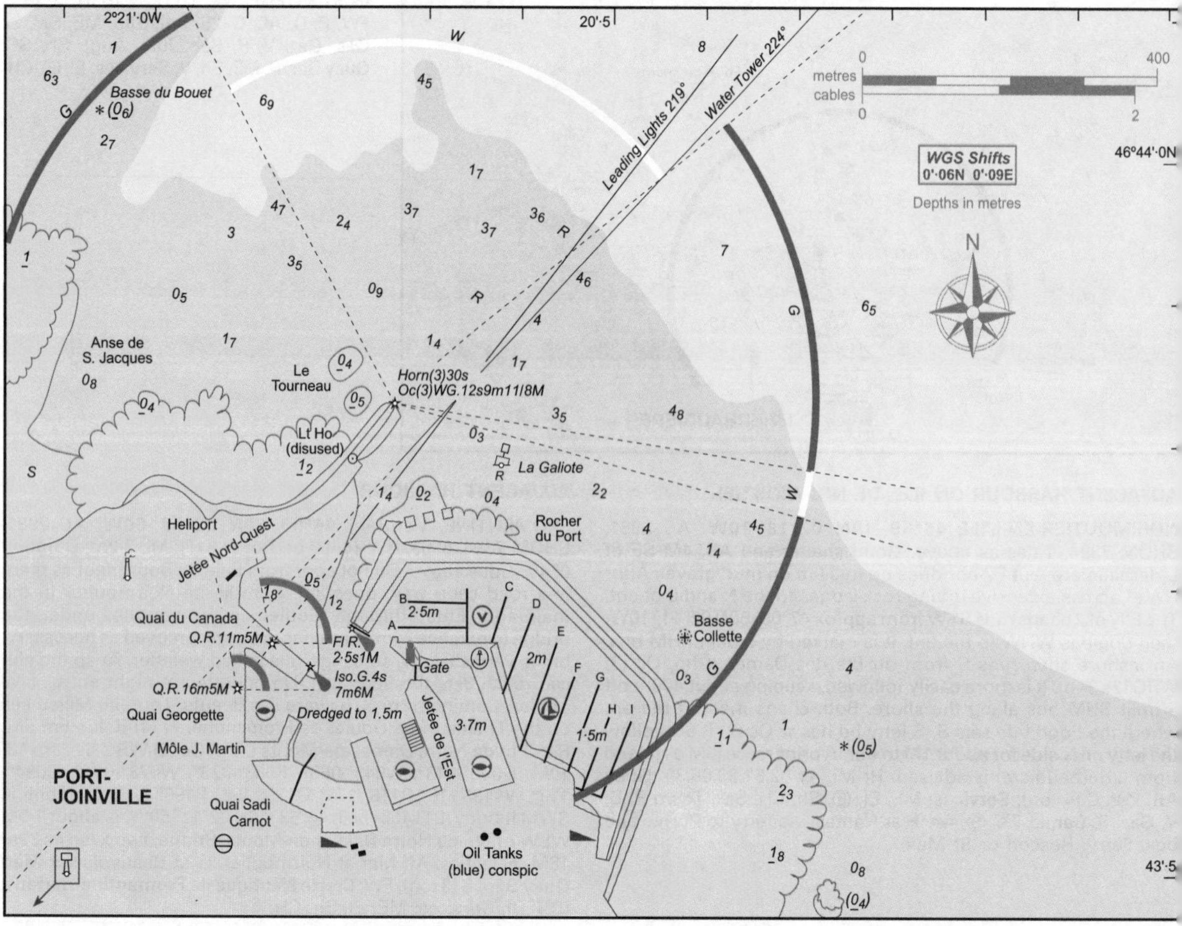

ST GILLES-CROIX-DE-VIE *9.18.11*

Vendée **46°41'·60N 01°57'·05W** ❀❀❀⚓⚓⚓✿✿

CHARTS AC 3640, 2663; Imray C40; SHOM 7402; ECM 1022, 549

TIDES +0500 Dover; ML 3·2; Duration 0600; Zone –0100

Standard Port BREST (⟵)

Times				Height (metres)			
High Water		Low Water		MHWS	MHWN	MLWN	MLWS
0500	1100	0500	1100	6·9	5·4	2·6	1·0
1700	2300	1700	2300				
Differences ST GILLES-CROIX-DE-VIE							
–0030	+0015	–0032	–0032	–1·8	–1·3	–0·6	–0·3

SHELTER Good shelter, and easy access except in strong SW'lies or swell when breakers form off ent. Silting persists and despite dredging, depths may be reduced. On N bank: a small drying yacht basin inside Grand Môle; 2 tidal FV basins; beyond them the marina nominally dredged to 1·5m. Or pick up ⚓ opposite marina; or AB on drying quay on E bank below bridge. In settled weather ⚓ off ent, close SE of ldg line in 3·5m.

NAVIGATION WPT Pill'Hours SCM, Q (6) + L Fl 15s, Bell, 46°41'·04N 01°58'·01W, 231°/051° from/to Jetée de la Garenne lt, 0·75M. From W & NW, beware Rocher Pill'Hours (2·8m) and drying reefs extending 1ca (180m) SE. Best arr/dep HW –2 to HW, to avoid strong ebb, up to 6kn in ent at springs. Do not arr/dep LW±2 if >1·5m draft. Ent chan (⚓ prohib) is dredged 1·5m, but narrow and very shallow near bkwtr hds due to silting. Keep well off the first two chan buoys which are laid outboard of drying rks. The 043·5° ldg line inside the bkwtrs is tangential to drying banks on the E side; tfc permitting, keep slightly W of ldg line. A dangerous wreck is located just S of the S edge of the Intens R rear ldg lt at 46°38'·07N 02°00'·80W

LIGHTS AND MARKS Daymarks are Pte de Grosse-Terre (rky hdland) with lt ho, W truncated conical tr; the rear ldg lt structure; and two spires NE of the marina. Lights: Pte de Grosse Terre Fl (4) WR 12s 25m 17/13M, vis W290°-125°, R125°-145°. Ldg lts 043·5°: both Dir Oc (3+1) R 12s 7/28m 13M; W □ trs, R top; intens 033·5°-053·5°, synch. SE mole hd, QWG 8m 9/6M, vis G045°-335°, W335°-045°, Reed 20s. NW mole hd, Fl (2) WR 6s 8m 10/7M, R045°-225°, W225°-045°.

RADIO TELEPHONE VHF Ch 09 (season 0600-2200; out of season 0800-1200, 1400-1800LT).

TELEPHONE Hr Mr Port de Plaisance 02·51·55·30·83; Aff Mar 02·51·55·10·58; ⊖ 02·51·55·10·18; CROSS 02·97·55·35·35; SNSM 02·51·55·01·19; Météo 02·51·36·10·78; Auto 08·36·68·08·85; Police 02·51·55·01·19; Dr 02·51·55·11·93; Brit Consul 01·40·63·16·02.

FACILITIES **Port la Vie Marina** (800+80 visitors) ☎ 02·51·55·30·83, 🖷 02·51.55.31.43, €2·04, Access H24, P, D, FW, AC, ME, El, CH, Gaz, SM, BH (26 ton), Slip, R, V, Bar; **Quay** Slip, FW, C (6 ton); **CN de Havre de Vie** ☎ 02·51·55·87·91; **Services:** ME, El, Sh, CH, Ⓔ, C (15 ton), SM, SHOM. **Town** V, Gaz, R, Bar, ✉, Ⓑ, ⇌. A ferry runs to Ile d'Yeu. Ferry: Roscoff or St Malo.

18

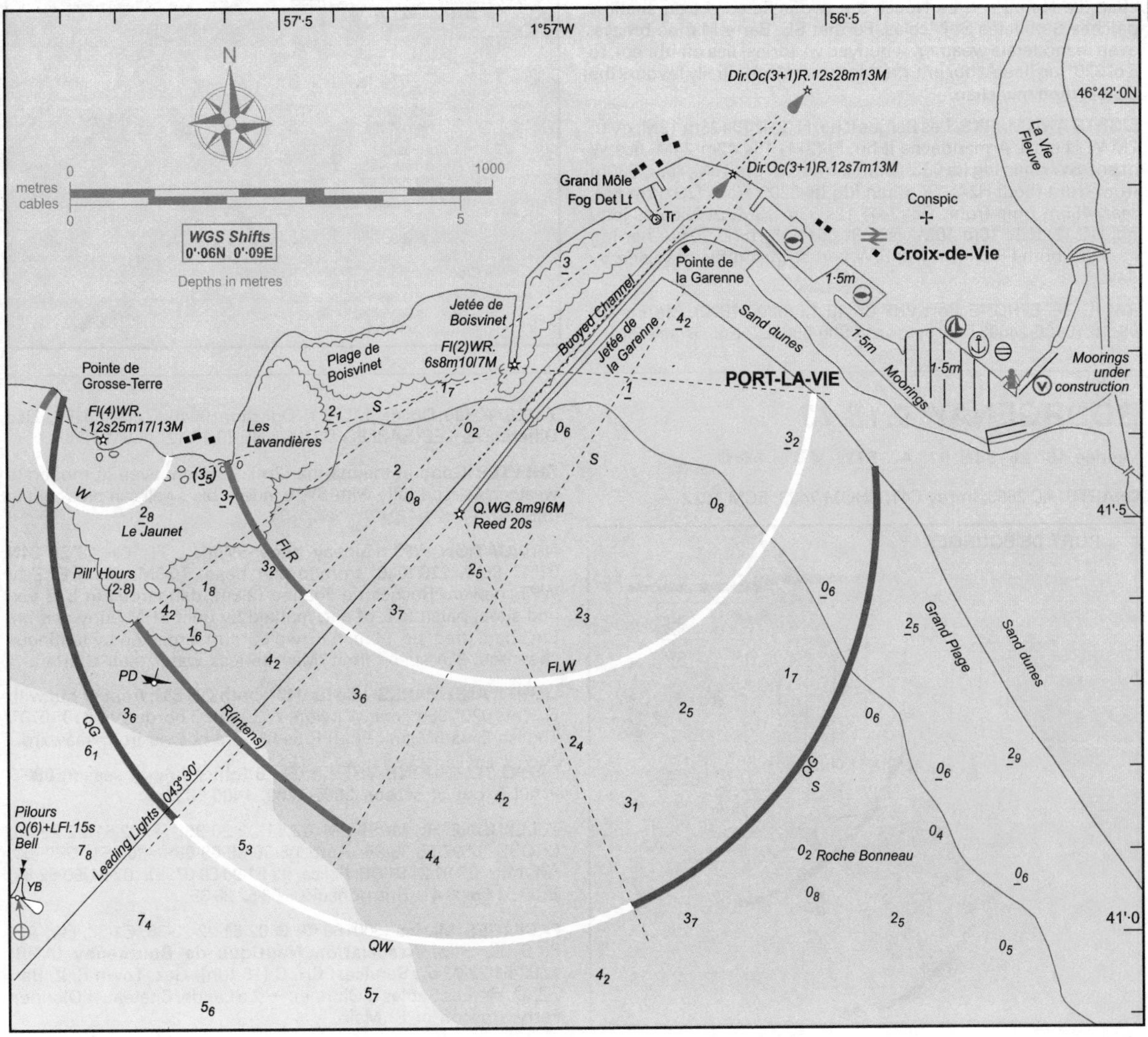

LES SABLES D'OLONNE *9.18.12*

Vendée **46°29'·40N 01°47'·40W**

CHARTS AC 3640, 2663; Imray C40, C41; SHOM 7403, 7411; ECM 1022

TIDES +0530 Dover; ML 3·2; Duration 0640; Zone –0100

Standard Port BREST (⟵)

Times				**Height (metres)**			
High Water		Low Water		MHWS	MHWN	MLWN	MLWS
0500	1100	0500	1100	6·9	5·4	2·6	1·0
1700	2300	1700	2300				
Differences LES SABLES D'OLONNE							
–0030	+0015	–0035	–0035	–1·7	–1·3	–0·6	–0·3

SHELTER Access at all tides; entry is easy except in winds from SE to SW when apprs get rough. Sailing is prohib in the entry chan to hbr. Commercial and FV Basins prohib to yachts. Access to marina (1·5 - 3·5m) H24. Visitors check in at pontoon port side, by Capitainerie. Pontoon L, at NE end, is for visitors and multihulls; or berth as directed.

NAVIGATION WPT Nouch Sud SCM, Q (6)+L Fl 15s, 46°28'·61N 01°47'·35W, 220°/040° from/to front ldg lt 033°, 1·2M. To the W, beware Les Barges d'Olonne, extending 3M W of Pte de Aiguille. There are 2 appr chans: the SW chan with La Potence ldg lts 033°, which lead into SE chan on ldg line 320°. In bad weather use the SE chan. Le Noura and Le Nouch are two isolated rks on shallow patches S of Jetée St Nicolas. Further SE, Barre Marine breaks, even in moderate weather. A buoyed wk (dries) lies off hbr ent, to E of 320° ldg line. At hbr ent, dredged chan (2m) initially favours the E side, then mid-chan.

LIGHTS AND MARKS Les Barges lt ho, Fl (2) R 10s 25m 13M, gy tr, 2M W of ent. L'Armandèche lt ho, Fl (2+1) 15s 42m 24M, 6ca W of ent. SW Chan ldg lts 033°: both Iso 4s 14/33m 16M; rear, 330m from front (both H24). SE Chan ldg lts 320°: front QG 11m 8M; rear, 465m from front, Oc (2+1) 12s 33m 13M. St Nicolas jetty hd, UQ (2) R 1s 16m 10M vis 143°-094°; Horn (2) 30s. Inner ldg lts 328°, both FR 6/9m 11M; R/W vert stripes difficult to see by day.

RADIO TELEPHONE Port VHF Ch 12 16 (0800-1800). Marina Ch 09 16 (0600-2400LT in season; 0800-2000LT out of season).

TELEPHONE Hr Mr 02·51·95·11·79, 📠 02·51·21·40·04; Marina 02·51·32·51·16; Aff Mar 02·51·28·81·91; CROSS 02·97·55·35·35; Météo 02·51·36·10·78; Auto 08·36·68·08·85; ⊖ 02·51·23·58·00; SNSM 02·51·21·20·55; Police 02·51·33·69·91; Dr 02·51·95·14·47; Ⓗ 02·51·21·06·33; Brit Consul 05·56·52·28·35.

FACILITIES Port Olona Marina (990+110 Ⓥ), ☎ 02·51·32·51·16, 📠 02·51·32·37·13, €1.66 (Jun & Sep), €2.36 (Jul + Aug), Slip, P, D, FW, ME, El, AC, Sh, ⊡; **Services:** El, Sh, CH, BH (27 ton), Ⓔ, SHOM, SM, Divers. **Town** P, D, V, Gaz, R, Bar, ⌧, Ⓑ, ⇌, ✈. Ferry: Roscoff or St Malo.

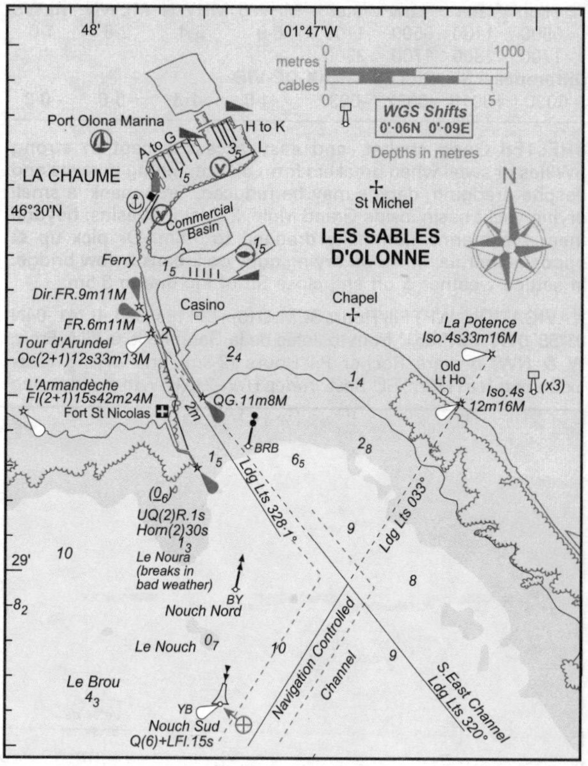

BOURGENAY *9.18.13*

Vendée **46° 26'·38N 01° 40'·57W**

CHARTS AC 2663; Imray C41; SHOM 7403; ECM 1022

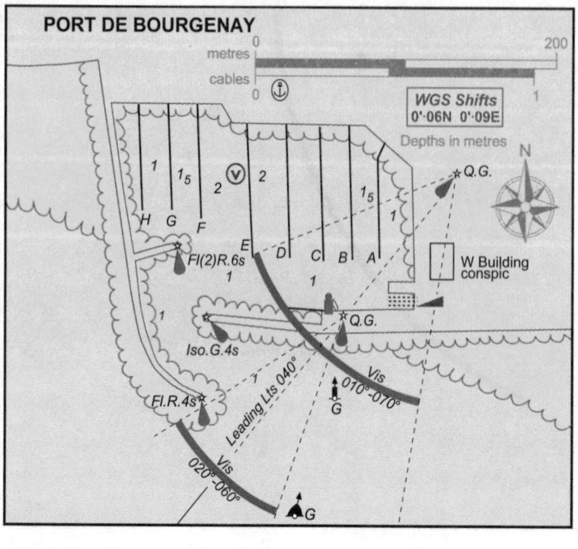

TIDES +0600 Dover; ML 3·1; Duration 0640; Zone –0100. Use Differences LES SABLES D'OLONNE (9.18.12), 5·5M NW.

SHELTER Good in the marina (2m). Caution: even in moderate weather, & especially with SW winds, a big swell can break at the ent.

NAVIGATION WPT Fairway buoy SWM, L Fl 10s, 46°25'·34N 01°41'·86W, 220°/040° from/to pier head, 1·35M. 600m ENE of WPT, beware Roches de Joanne (2·9m; dangerous in bad wx) and shoal patch to E of ent, marked by unlit SHM buoy and bn. Ent chan, dredged 1·0m, has two 90° turns marked by luminous chevrons; 3kn speed limit. May be less water than charted.

LIGHTS AND MARKS Ldg lts 040°: both QG 8M; front W hut with G□, vis 020°-060°; rear W pylon, W□ with G border, vis 010°-070°. The Iso G 4s 5M and Fl (2) R 6s 5M are not vis from seaward.

RADIO TELEPHONE VHF Ch 09 16 (office hrs; in season 0800-2100LT, out of season 0900-1200, 1400-1800).

TELEPHONE Hr Mr/SNSM 02·51·22·20·36, 📠 02·51·22·29·45; CROSS 02·97·55·35·35; Auto 08·36·68·08·85; ⊖ 02·51·23·58·00; Aff Mar 02·51·21·81·81; Police 02·51·90·60·07; Dr 02·51·90·62·68; Ⓗ 02·51·96·00·41; Brit Consul 05·56·52·28·35.

FACILITIES Marina (500+60 Ⓥ) ☎ 02·51·22·20·36, €1·86, FW, AC, P, D, ⊡, Slip; **Association Nautique de Bourgenay** (ANB) ☎ 02·51·22·02·57; **Services:** CH, C (15 ton), Gaz. **Town** R, V, Bar, ⌧, Ⓑ, ⇌ (Les Sables d'Olonne), ✈ (La Lande, Chateau d'Olonne). Ferry: Roscoff or St Malo.

MINOR HARBOURS IN PERTUIS BRETON

JARD-SUR-MER, Vendée, **46°24´·45N 01°34´·75W**. AC 2641, 2663; SHOM 6522. HW +0600 on Dover (UT); HW–0010 & ht –2·0m on Brest; ML 3·1m; Duration 0640. Small drying hbr, access HW±2, 4·5m max at HW. Moorings inside bkwtr, inc 7 Y Ⓥs. Hr Mr's office with blue roof and adjacent bldgs are conspic from afar. W daymarks 4ca (740m) E of hbr lead 038° via narrow ent between the drying Roches de l'Islatte and Roches de la Brunette, marked by buoys. Then pick up 293° transit of RW marks on W side of hbr, ldg to ent. There are no lights. Hr Mr (occas) ☎ 02·51·33·40·17; ⊖ ☎ 02·51·95·11·33; Facilities: **Jetty** FW, C (5 ton); **Services:** CH, Divers.

L'AIGUILLON/LA-FAUTE-SUR-MER, Vendée, **46°20´·00N 01°18´·60W**. AC 2641, 2663; SHOM 6521. HW +0535 on Dover (UT), HW –0030, ht +0·6m on Pte de Grave (Zone –0100); ML 3·4m. Shelter good in two yacht hbrs, but avoid in strong S or W winds; ent only safe in fine weather with off-shore winds. Access HW±2½. Beware mussel beds with steel piles which cover at HW; also oyster beds. The area is very flat and, being shallow, waves build up quickly in any wind. The bar to seaward dries and is dangerous in bad weather. Ent can best be identified by a conspic transformer on a hill, La Dive, opposite side of chan to Pointe d'Arcay. Enter at Le Lay SCM buoy, Q (6) + L Fl 15s, with transformer brg 033°. ⚓ in R Lay or berth at L'Aiguillon (NE bank); or in drying tidal basin at La Faute (SW bank). Hr Mrs (L'Aiguillon) ☎ 05.51.97.06.57; (La Faute) ☎ 05.51·56·45·02; Aff Mar ☎ 05.51·56·45·35; CROSS ☎ 05.56·09·82·00; Dr ☎ 05.51·56·46·17; Facilities: **Club Nautique Aiguillonais et Fautais** (CNAF) ☎ 05.51·97·04·60; **Services:** ME, CH.

MARANS, Vendée, **46°19'·00N 01°00'·00W**. AC 2641, 2663; SHOM 6521; ECM 551. Tides: see L'Aiguillon above; HW at Brault lock = HW La Rochelle + 0020. Good shelter in non-tidal hbr approx 10M from SWM buoy, L Fl 10s, (46° 15'·40N 01°11'·42W) abeam Pte de l'Aiguillon with 10m high B bn. Buoyed chan, dries 1·0m, leads NE past Pavé jetty, Fl G 4s, thence 3½M up-river to Brault lifting bridge and 5ca to lock, open yachts leaving HW -1, entering HW. Waiting pontoons before bridge; pontoon inside vast lock which has small swing bridge at far end. Straight 3M canal to stbd side pontoon. Brault lock ☎ 05.46.01.53.77; Facilities: **Quay** ☎ 05.46.01.02.99, AB (40+10 Ⓥ), €3·35, FW, C (3 tons), P & D (cans); BY, ME, Sh, SM. **Town** V, R, Bar.

OTHER HARBOUR ON ILE DE RÉ

LA FLOTTE, Charente Maritime, **46°11´·35N 01°19´·25W**. AC 2641, 2746; SHOM 6668, 6521. HW +0535 on Dover (UT). La Flotte is 2M SE of St Martin (9.18.14). From NW keep clear of Le Couronneau; from E, keep N of bn off Pte des Barres. Appr on 215° in W sector of La Flotte lt ho, W tr with G top, Fl WG 4s 10m 12/9M; vis G130°-205°, W205°-220°, G220°-257°; horn (3) 30s by day HW±2. Moiré indicator shows vert B line when on course 215°, or chevrons to regain course. 5 waiting Bys outside; or ⚓ off in 3m, sheltered from S & W. Outer hbr sheltered by mole and dries 2·4m; access HW±3. 3 pontoons in outer hbr for 8 visitors; pre-booking advised. Inner hbr dries 2·7m. Hr Mr ☎ 05.46.09.67.66; ⊖ at St Martin; Facilities: **Quay** €1·68, Slip, FW, Ⓥ berth on mole, Grid; **Cercle Nautique de la Flotte-en-Ré** (CNLF) (open Jul-15 Sep) ☎ 05·46.09.97.34, Bar; **Services:** P & D (cans), CH, ME, SM, ⊡.

18

ILE-DE-RÉ *9.18.14 & 9.18.15*

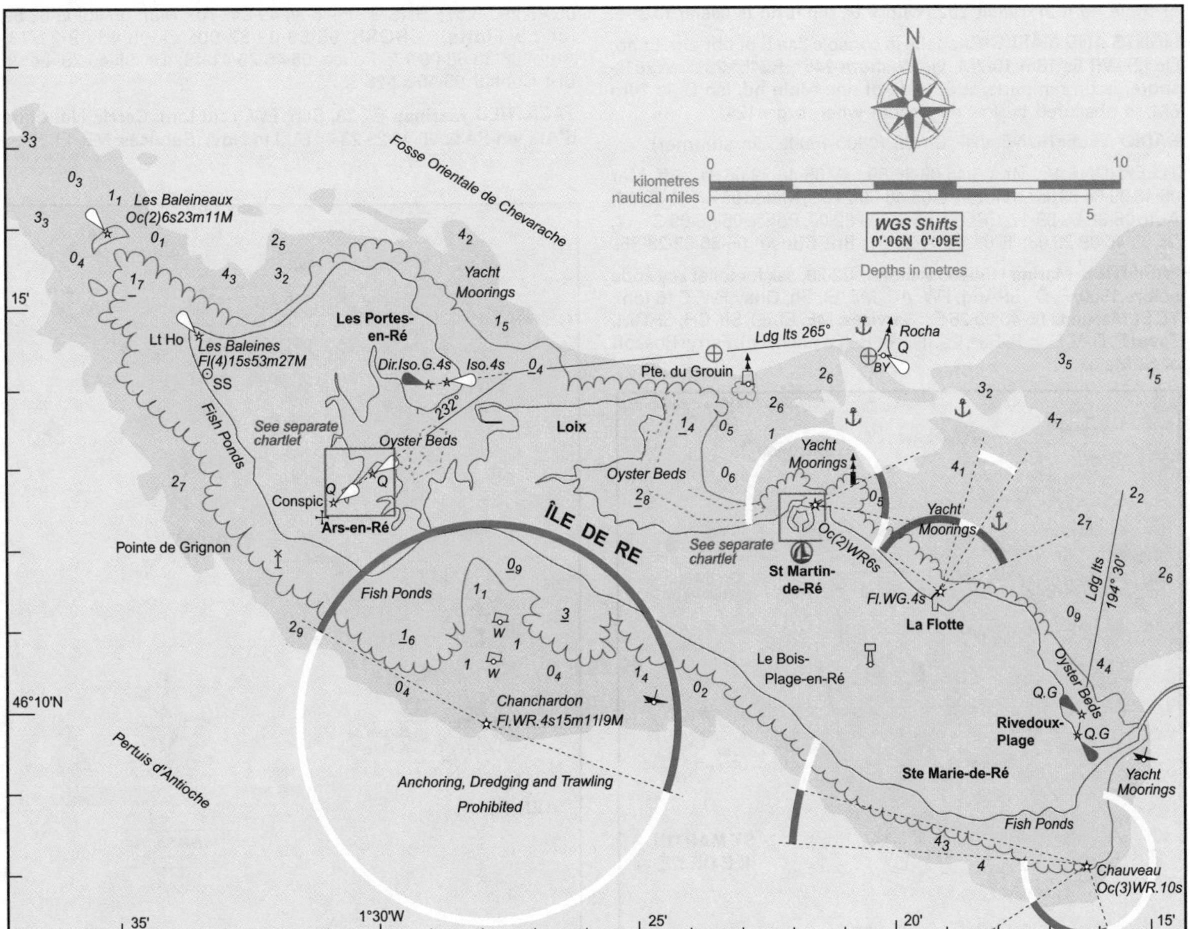

ST MARTIN, Ile de Ré *9.18.14*

Charente Maritime **46°12'·56N 01°21'·84W**

CHARTS AC 2641, 2746; Imray C41; SHOM 7404, 7412; ECM 551, 1022

TIDES +0535 Dover; ML 3·7; Zone –0100

Standard Port POINTE DE GRAVE (⟶)

Times				Height (metres)			
High Water		Low Water		MHWS	MHWN	MLWN	MLWS
0000	0600	0500	1200	5·4	4·4	2·1	1·0
1200	1800	1700	2400				
Differences ST MARTIN, Ile de Ré							
+0015	–0030	–0025	–0020	+0·6	+0·5	+0·3	–0·1

SHELTER Complete shelter in non-tidal marina (depth 3m); often very crowded with queue to enter. 4 W waiting buoys off ent. Avant port is protected by bkwtr close to the NE and mole on NW side. Inside mole a waiting pontoon (season only) is dredged 2·3m; can be disturbed in fresh NW to NE winds. Access HW–3 to +2 via chan (dries 1·5m) to drying basin for FVs. Marina gates open about HW–2 and close HW+2½, depending on coefficient (sill is 0·8m above CD), 0630-2200LT May, Jun and Sept; 0500-2300 Jul and Aug. Berth as directed by Hr Mr.

NAVIGATION WPT Rocha NCM By, Q, 46°14'·75N 01°20'·80W, 020°/200° from/to St Martin mole hd, 2·4M. From the NW, pass N and E of Le Rocha, a rky bank extending 2½M ENE from Pte du Grouin. Beware: Explosives reported (Feb 1999) on seabed at 46°13'·2N 01°21'·8W, 6ca N of hbr ent, near to moorings. From SE, pass well N of unlit NCM bn, about ¾M NE of ent, marking Le Couronneau drying ledge in R sector (245°-281°) of St Martin lt ho Oc (2) WR 6s. By day appr with lt ho and ✠ □ tr in line 210°, or mole hd lt in transit 202° with ✠ tr; the lt ho is easier to see.

LIGHTS AND MARKS Citadelle is conspic 3ca E of hbr ent. Lt ho, Oc (2) WR 6s 18m 10/7M, vis W shore-245°, R245°-281°, W281°-shore, is on ramparts at SE side of ent. Mole hd, Iso G 4s 10m 6M, is obscured by Pte du Grouin when brg <124°.

RADIO TELEPHONE VHF Ch 09 (0800-1900LT in summer).

TELEPHONE Hr Mr 05·46·09·26·69, ✉ 05·46·29·66·91; Aff Mar 05·46·09·68·89 (in La Flotte); ⊖ 05·46·09·21·78; Météo 05·46·41·29·14; Auto 08·36·68·08·17; CROSS 05·56·09·82·00; Police 05·46·09·21·17; Dr 05·46·09·20·08; ⊞ 05·46·09·20·01; Brit Consul 05·56·52·28·35.

FACILITIES **Marina** (135+50 visitors), €2·29, ask for toilet key code before 1900, P, D Jul-Aug, FW, AC, ME, El, Sh; **Quay** FW, C (6 ton); **YC St Martin** ☎ 05·46·09·26·69; **Services:** ME, El, Ⓔ, Sh, CH, SHOM. **Town** P, D, V, Gaz, R, Bar, ✉, Ⓑ, ⇌, ✈ (La Rochelle). Ferry: Roscoff or St Malo.

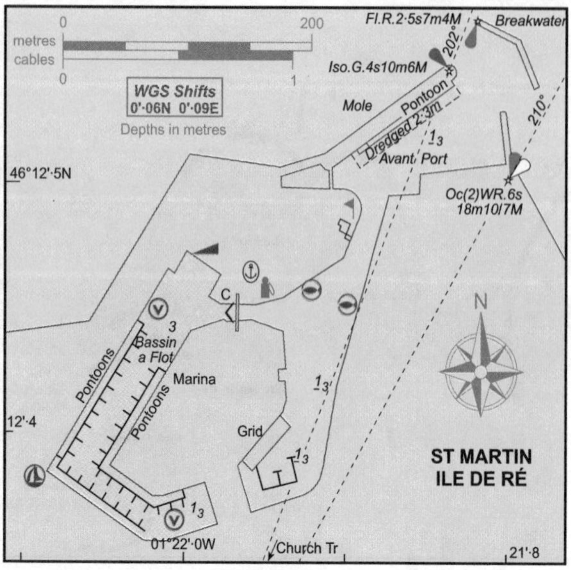

ARS-EN-RÉ *9.18.15*

Charente Maritime **46°12'·70N 01°30'·62W**

CHARTS AC 2641; Imray C41; SHOM 7404, 7412; ECM 551, 1022

TIDES +0540 Dover; ML 3·7m; Zone –0100; See 9.18.16

SHELTER Two sheltered marinas:

a. Bassin de la Criée (2m), is on NW side of chan approx 600m NE of town; access HW±2 over sill 2.5m CD, Ⓥ berths on pontoon H, to port.
b. Bassin Prée, at head of chan, access HW ±2 over sill, dries 2·9m; Ⓥ berths to stbd. Or AB outside on NW quay drying to mud. Note: draught, tidal coefficient and wind/barometer dictate access times.

NAVIGATION WPT 46°14'·45N 01°23'·55W, 087°/267° from/to first SHM chan buoy, 1·66M. Beware shoal ground close S of outer ldg line. The appr chan is restricted by rky ledges drying 0·4m and 1·5m; access HW±3. Chan is marked by 2 sets of ldg lts, buoys and bns. There is ⚓ in a pool (2m) close S of Pte du Fier. Port d'Ars is at the head of a chan in the SW corner of the bay, Le Fier d'Ars, which dries to salt pans & oyster beds.

LIGHTS AND MARKS Conspic ✠ spire, white with black top, is in the town, about 1ca SE of the 232° ldg line. Outer ldg lts 265° (from near Le Rocha NCM buoy, Q): front, Iso 4s 5m 11M, W □ on hut, vis 141°-025°; rear, 370m from front, Dir Iso G 4s 13m 15M, G □ tr on house (synch, intens 264°-266°). Port d'Ars ldg lts, hard to see by day, lead 232° across Fiers d'Ars into hbr: front, Q 5m 9M, W □ with R lantern; rear, 370m from front, Q 13m 11M, B □ on W framework tr, G top, vis 142°-322°.

RADIO TELEPHONE VHF Ch 09.

TELEPHONE Hr Mr (La Criée) 05·46·29·25·10, (La Prée) 05·46.29.08.52; SNSM 05·46·34·49·84; Aff Mar 05·46·09·68·89 (at La Flotte); CROSS 05·56·09·82·00; ⊖ 05·46·09·21·78; Auto 08·36·68·08·17; Police 05·46·29·41·48; Dr 05·46·29·44·19; Brit Consul 05·56·52·28·35.

FACILITIES **Marinas** €2·29, Slip, FW, C (6 ton); **Cercle Nautique d'Ars -en-Ré** ☎ 05·46·29·23·04 (Apl to Nov); **Services:** ME, El, Sh.

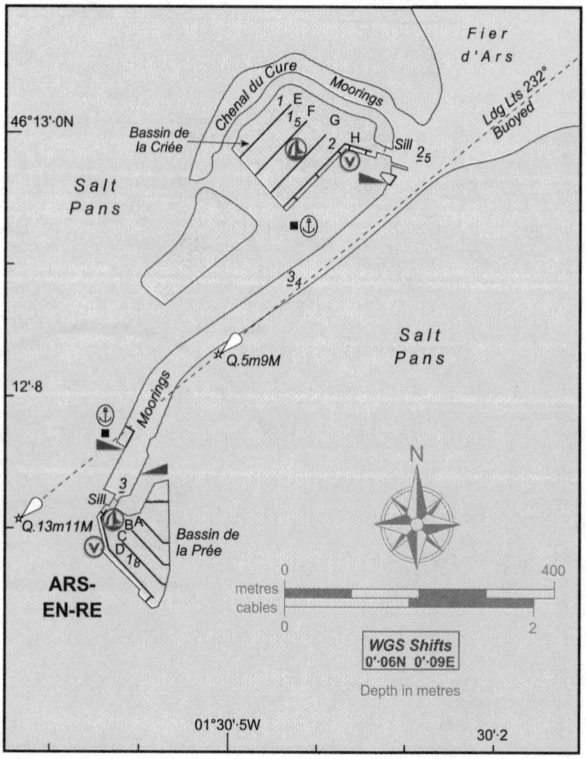

LA ROCHELLE *9.18.16*

Charente Maritime **46°09'·40N 01° 09'·15W** ❀❀◊◊◊✿✿✿

CHARTS AC 2743, 2746, 2641; Imray C41; SHOM 7404, 7413; ECM 551, 1022

TIDES +0515 Dover; ML 3·8; Zone –0100

Standard Port POINTE DE GRAVE (⟶)

Times				Height (metres)			
High Water		Low Water		MHWS	MHWN	MLWN	MLWS
0000	0600	0500	1200	5·4	4·4	2·1	1·0
1200	1800	1700	2400				
Differences LA ROCHELLE and LA PALLICE							
+0015	–0030	–0025	–0020	+0·6	+0·5	+0·3	–0·1

SHELTER Excellent in **Port des Minimes**, a very large marina with 3·5m depth (max LOA 25m); in the Vieux Port, and in the Inner Basin. The large non-tidal **Bassin des Chalutiers** has pontoons on the N/NE sides for visitors >16m LOA. **Vieux Port**, in the old town, is entered beyond the two trs of St Nicolas and La Chaine. It has a tidal basin (dredged 1·3m) with 100+ berths for smaller yachts. On the E side a non-tidal **Inner Basin** (3m) is entered by a lock with sill 1·2m above CD, opens HW–2 to HW+½; night ent by prior arrangement ☎ 46.41.32.05. Note: La Pallice is strictly a commercial/FV port 3M W, with no yacht facilities.

NAVIGATION WPT 46°08'·23N 01°11'·88W, 237°/057° from/to Tour Richelieu, 1·34M. Appr from about 1M S of Le Lavardin lt tr on ldg line 059°. Off Pte des Minimes (SW of marina) drying rks extend ¼M offshore; further S there is a firing danger area marked by 5 SPM buoys. Shallow appr chan needs care at MLWS. Tour Richelieu (with tide gauge) marks a drying rky spit to the N of the chan; least depth in chan 0·2m. Ent to Port des Minimes is 1ca past Tour Richelieu, marked by WCM and 2 PHM buoys, all unlit; but mole heads are lit. For Vieux Port stay on 059° ldg line in chan (35m wide), leaving 4 PHM buoys well to port. Caution: many ferries. Note: The bridge (30m clearance) from the mainland to Ile de Ré is lit and buoyed for big ships: between piers Nos 13 and 14 = N-bound; between piers Nos 10 and 11 = S-bound. Yachts may transit other spans, subject to air and water clearances.

LIGHTS AND MARKS Ldg lts 059°: Front, Q 15m 14M (Fl 4s by day), R○ tr, W bands; rear, Q 25m 14M (Fl 4s by day), W octagonal tr, G top; synch, obsc 061°-065° by St Nicolas tr. Le Lavardin, rky shoal 3M WSW of Tr Richelieu, Fl (2) WG 6s 14m 11/8M, B tr, R band, vis G160°-169°, W169°-160°. Tour Richelieu, Fl (4) R 12s 10m 9M, conspic R tr, RC, siren (4) 60s. Port des Minimes: W mole hd Fl G 4s; E mole hd Fl (2) R 6s.

RADIO TELEPHONE Port des Minimes Ch 09 (H24). Hbr Ch 06 11 12. Vieux Port Ch 09.

TELEPHONE Port des Minimes Hr Mr 05·46·44·41·20, Vieux Port Hr Mr 05·46·41·32·05; Aff Mar 05·46·41·43·91; ⊜ 05·46·42·64·64; CROSS 05·56·09·82·00; Météo 05·46·41·29·14; Auto 08·36·68·08·17; Dr 05·46·42·19·22; Police 05·46·34·67·55; Ⓗ 05·46·27·33·33; Brit Consul 05·56·52·28·35.

FACILITIES

PORT DES MINIMES **Marina** (3,200+350 Ⓥs on pontoons 13-15 in SW basin), €1·68, ☎ 05·46·44·41·20, 📠 05.46.44.36.49, AC, Slip, C (10 ton), P & D (Jul/Aug 0800-2000), FW, BH (50 ton), R, Ice, Bar, Ⓑ, ✉, ♿, 🅾. Water bus to the town every H, 1000-2000, except 1300; Jul/Aug H and H+30, 0900-2330, except 1300. **Société des Régates Rochellaises** ☎ 05·46·44·62·44; **Services:** ME, Sh, CH, Ⓔ, El, SHOM, SM, Gaz.

VIEUX PORT **Quay** €14·48, Slip, FW, C (10 ton), BH (300 ton), SM, ME, Sh, CH, no toilets/showers, may be noisy. **Inner Basin** or **Bassin des Chalutiers** ☎ 05·46·41·32·05 (3m), €1·68, Access HW –2 to HW+½, FW, AC. **Town** P, D, V, Gaz, R, Bar, ✉, Ⓑ, ⇌, ✈. Ferry to Ile de Ré; internal air services (and to London in season) from Laleu airport (2½km N of port). Ferry: Roscoff or St Malo.

18

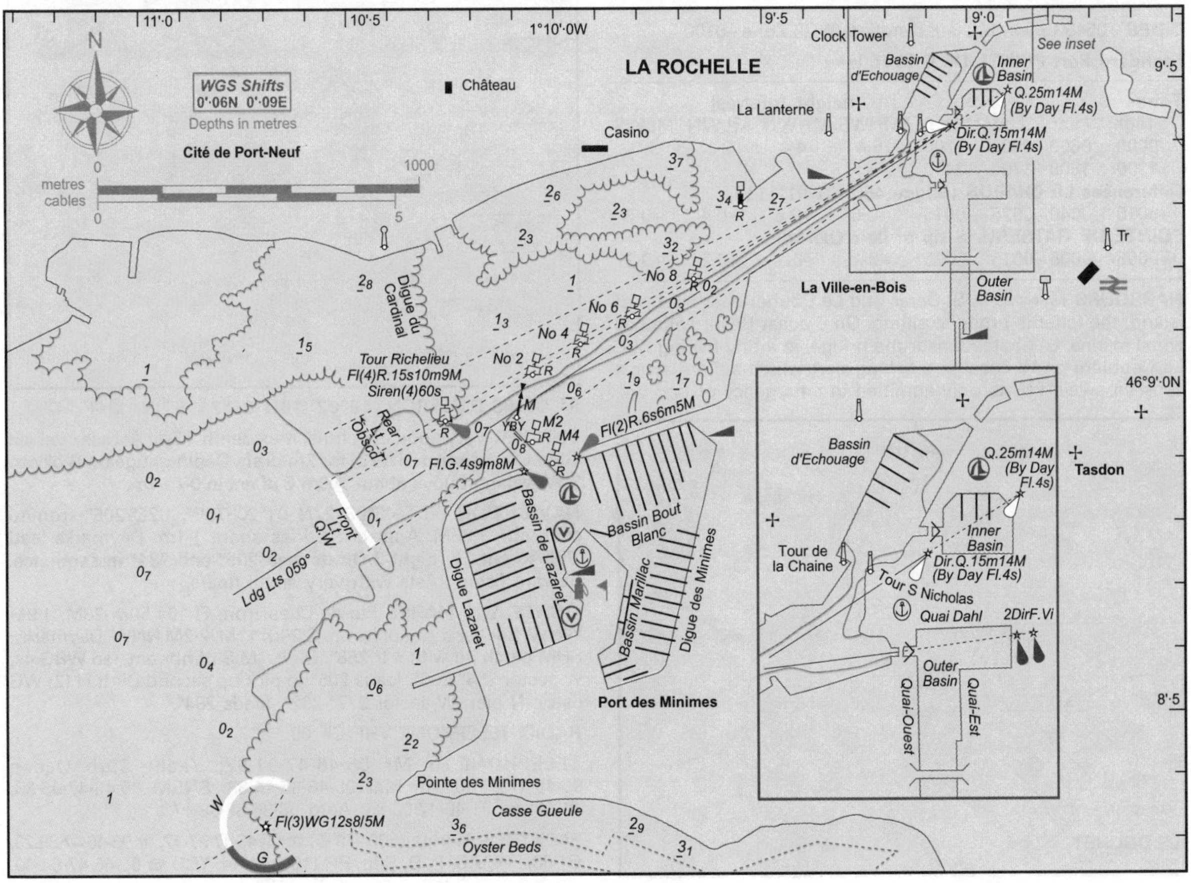

ILE D'OLÉRON *9.18.17*

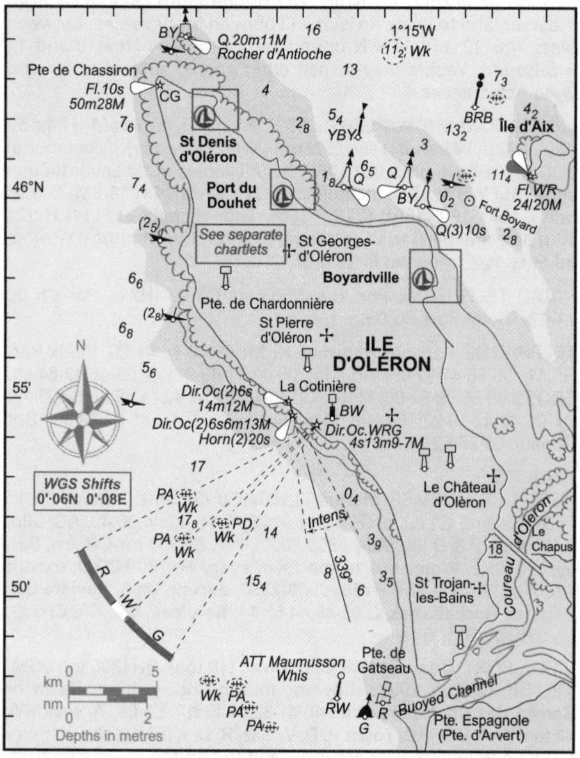

CHARTS AC 2746, 2663; Imray C41; SHOM 6914, 7414, 6335, 7404; ECM 552

TIDES +0545 Dover; ML 3·9; Duration 0540; Zone –0100

Standard Port POINTE DE GRAVE (⟶)

Times				Height (metres)			
High Water		Low Water		MHWS	MHWN	MLWN	MLWS
0000	0600	0500	1200	5·4	4·4	2·1	1·0
1200	1800	1700	2400				
Differences LE CHAPUS (Bridge 45°51'N 01°11'W)							
+0015	–0040	–0025	–0015	+0·6	+0·6	+0·4	+0·2
POINTE DE GATSEAU (S tip of Île d'Oléron)							
+0005	–0005	–0015	–0025	–0·1	–0·1	+0·2	+0·2

HARBOURS Marinas at St Denis and Le Douhet near NE tip of island; the latter is prone to silting. On E coast Boyardville has small marina. Le Chateau, near the bridge, is a tiny fishing hbr. La Cotinière on W coast is a fishing port which suffers almost constant swell; yachts only admitted in emergency or bad wx.

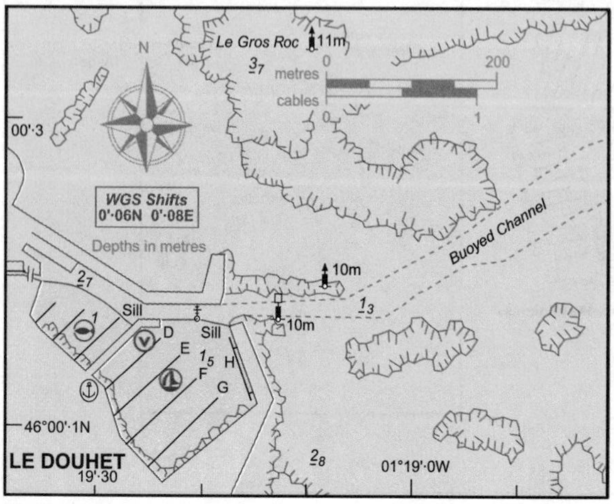

LE DOUHET 46°00'·15N 01°19'·18W

SHELTER Very good in marina on SE side of hbr; FVs use NW part. Ent difficult in fresh NE'lies against ebb; beware swell and overfalls. Access HW±2 for 1·5m draft, over sill 1·8m CD. Sill is marked by SHM bn. Beware: sandbanks encroach on appr chan, reducing access times and needing frequent dredging, sometimes closing hbr completely.

NAVIGATION WPT 46°00'·54N 01°17'·61W, NCM buoy Q, 068°/248° from/to ent 1·1M. Unlit, buoyed appr chan dries about 1·5m to approx 0·35M offshore. Note: the WPT buoy is the W'ly of two NCM lt buoys, both Q, marking a fish farm. Further E, La Longe le Boyard, a rocky/sandy shoal, is marked by Fort Boyard, conspic tr 27m, Q (9) 15s. The Passage de l'Ouest (toward Boyardville) is marked by an ECM buoy, Q (3) 10s.

LIGHTS AND MARKS No lts, ldg marks or conspic features other than yacht masts. Bkwtrs marked by perches.

RADIO TELEPHONE VHF Ch 09.

TELEPHONE Hr Mr 05·46·76·71·13, 📠 05·46.76.78.26.

FACILITIES Marina (305+45 visitors), €1·68, FW, AC, Max LOA 15m, ♿; V at St Georges d'Oléron and La Brée.

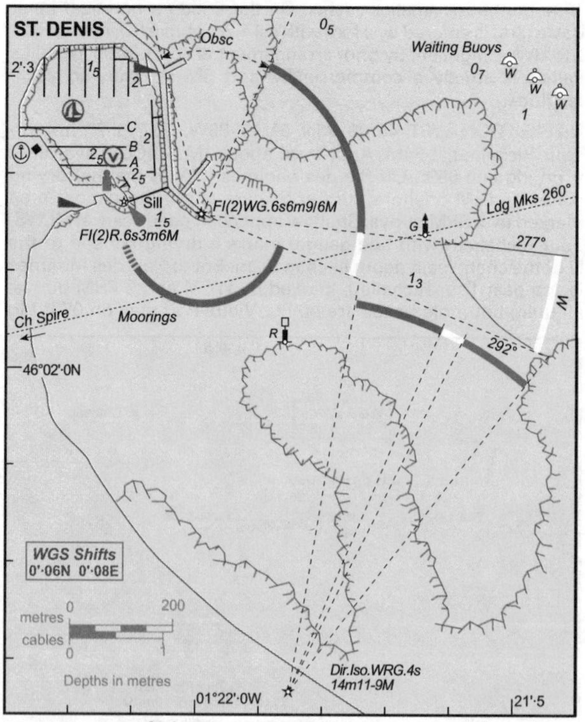

ST DENIS D'OLÉRON 46°02'·16N 01°21'·97W

SHELTER Very good in marina, max depth 2·5m. Access over sill 1·5m CD is approx HW±2½ for 2m draft. Depth gauge on S bkwtr. 3 W waiting buoys about 700m E of ent in 0·7 - 1m.

NAVIGATION WPT 46°03'·27N 01°20'·75W, 025°/205° from/to chan ent, 1·35M. Appr chan dries about 1·1m. Daymarks lead 258° to ent. By night 2 Dir lts lead 205° and 284° in sequence. Beware fishing nets with very small floats.

LIGHTS AND MARKS Pte de Chassiron, Fl 10s 50m 28M, 1·9M WNW. Rocher d'Antioche bn, Q 20m 11M, 2·2M NNW. Daymarks: SHM perch on with ⊕ tr 258°. Dir lt, ½M S of hbr ent, Iso WRG 4s, W sector 204°-206°, leads 205° to pick up second Dir lt Fl (2) WG 6s on N pier; W sector 277°-292°, leads 284°.

RADIO TELEPHONE VHF Ch 09.

TELEPHONE Hr Mr 05·46·47·97·97; Yacht Club Océan 05·46·47·84·40; Aff Mar 05·46·85·14·33; SNSM 05·46·47·06·33; Ⓗ (12km) 05·46·47·00·86; Auto 08·36·68·08·17.

FACILITIES Marina (600+70 Ⓥ) ☎ 05·46·47·97·97, 📠 05·46.47.88.23, €1·68, FW, AC, P, D, Slip, BH (10 ton), ♿; **YCO** ☎ 05·46·47·84·40.

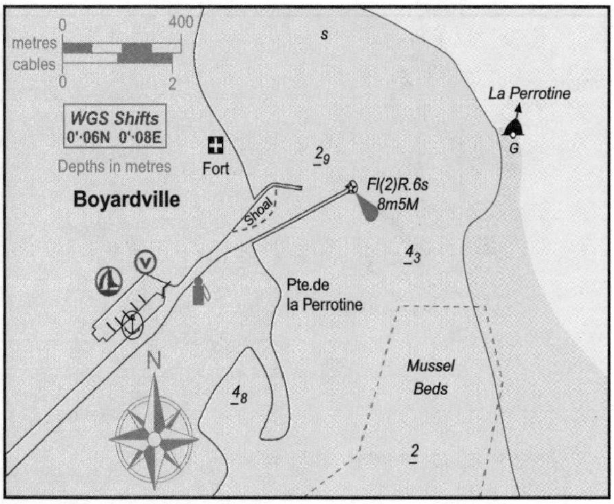

BOYARDVILLE 45°58´·30N 01°13´·76W ❀❀⚓⚓✿✿

TIDES HW +0545 on Dover (UT); use Ile d'Aix (9.18.18).

SHELTER Very good in non-tidal marina (2m). Visitors berths are on quay to stbd; multiple rafting is the norm. Access HW±2 to drying appr chan and into marina to stbd via automatic lock. This opens H24, approx HW±1½ @ nps and HW±2½ @ sp. FVs berth further up-river. Six W waiting buoys ½M N of chan or ⚓ in 3m.

NAVIGATION WPT 45°58'·50N 01°13'·28W, La Perrotine SHM buoy, 080°/260° from/to S bkwtr head 4ca. The appr chan leads direct to ent chan where best water is close to S bkwtr. Strong river current, 2kn @ sp. Stand on beyond the lock to avoid a bank, then turn 120° stbd for the lock; best to allow all departing boats to get clear first. To the N, La Longe le Boyard, a rocky/ sandy shoal, is marked by Fort Boyard, conspic tr 27m, Q (9) 15s. The Passage de l'Ouest (toward Le Douhet) is marked by an ECM buoy, Q (3) 10s.

LIGHTS AND MARKS No lts/ldg marks. S bkwtr lt, Fl (2) R 6s 8m 5M. A ● lt indicates movement of the ent gate.

RADIO TELEPHONE VHF Ch 09.

TELEPHONE Hr Mr 05·46·47·23·71; 🌤 05·46.75.06.13; ⊖ 05·46.47.72.30; Aff Mar 05·46.47.00.18; Auto 08.36.68.08.17.

FACILITIES **Marina** (165+30 Ⓥ) €1·68, AC, FW, Slip, C (10 ton), P & D on opposite bank; **YCB** ☎ 05·46·47·10·28. **Services:** ME, El, Sh, CH, ♿.

MINOR HARBOUR ON ILE D'OLÉRON

LE CHATEAU, Ile d'Oléron, Charente Maritime, **45°52´·95N 01°11´·30W**. AC 2663; SHOM 6913, 6334, 6335; ECM 552. HW +0545 on Dover (UT); tides as for Ile d'Aix (9.18.18), ML 3·8m, duration 0540. Mainly occupied by oyster FVs; not recommended for yachts, except temporary visit. Possible drying berth on NE quay. Access HW±2. From N, appr via Chenal Est, to SCM bn marking Grand Montanne and ent to appr chan. From S, appr via Coureau d'Oléron, under mainland bridge (clnce 18m), thence 1M to ent chan. Ldg lts 319°, QR 11/24m 7M synch; chan is marked by SHM withies. Hr Mr ☎ 05·46·47·00·01. Facilities: Slip, L, FW, C (25 ton).

18

ROCHEFORT *9.18.18*

Charente Maritime **45°56'·60N 00°57'·20W** ❀❀⚓⚓⚓✿✿✿

CHARTS AC 2748, 2746; Imray C41; SHOM 4333, 7414; ECM 552

TIDES +0610 Dover; Zone –0100

Standard Port POINTE DE GRAVE (⟶)

Times				Height (metres)			
High Water		Low Water		MHWS	MHWN	MLWN	MLWS
0000	0600	0500	1200	5·4	4·4	2·1	1·0
1200	1800	1700	2400				
Differences ROCHEFORT							
+0035	–0010	+0030	+0125	+1·1	+0·9	+0·1	–0·2
ILE D'AIX							
+0015	–0040	–0030	–0025	+0·7	+0·5	+0·3	–0·1

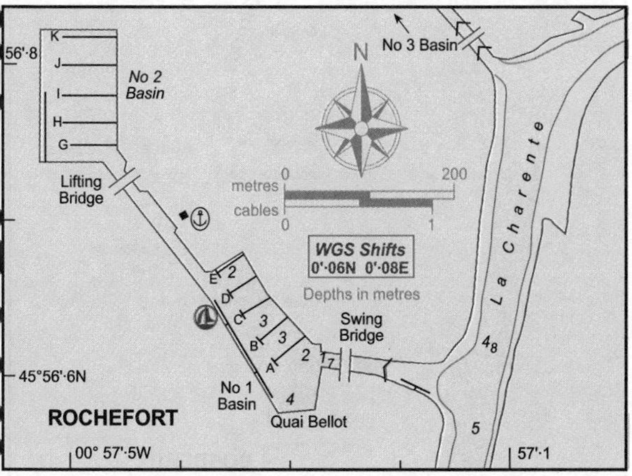

SHELTER Excellent. Rochefort is about 10M up-river from Port-des-Barques. Appr advised on late flood, as bar breaks on ebb. Lock gate is open from HW La Rochelle +¼ to +¾; wise to call Hr Mr day before. Waiting pontoon, just outside gate, dries to soft mud. Fuel not in commission (1999). If late, ⚓ out of chan at Soubise or Martrou. Beware very strong currents here, except at HW or LW. Bridge between Bassin Nos 1 and 2 lifts when gate open. (No 3 Bassin, 400m N, is for commercial craft). A 36m pontoon, 120m S of lock, is short stay foc + AC, FW.

NAVIGATION WPT Les Palles NCM, Q, 45°59´·58N 01°09´·53W, 293°/113° from/to front ldg lt 115°, 4·0M. Stream in river runs about 2kn (4kn in narrows), and at sp there is a small bore. Beware wk just S of WPT. When WSW of Fouras pick up second (Port-des-Barques) ldg line (135°). The bar at Fouras carries about 0·5m. Lettered pairs (RR to AA) of unlit ldg bns are mainly for Big Ships. Fixed bridge, 32m cl'nce, is 2M before Rochefort. The river is navigable 3·5M on to Tonnay-Charente.

LIGHTS AND MARKS Ile d'Aix Fl WR 5s 24m 24/20M; twin W trs with R tops; vis R103°-118°, W118°-103°. Ldg lts 115°, both QR, intens 113°-117°, W □ trs with R tops. Port Sud de Fouras, pier hd, Fl WR 4s 6m, 9/6M, vis R115°-177°, W177°-115°. Port-des-Barques ldg lts 135°, both Iso G 4s synch, intens 125°-145°, W □ trs; rear has B band on W side.

RADIO TELEPHONE Port VHF Ch 12 16. Marina Ch 09 (HW±1).

TELEPHONE Hr Mr/🌤 05·46·99·44·93, 🌤 05·46·99·44; Aff Mar 05·46·84·22·67; CROSS 05·56·09·82·00; Météo 05·46·41·11·11; Auto 08.36.68.08.17; ⊖ 05·46·99·03·90; Dr 05·46·99·61·11; Police 05·46·87·26·12; Brit Consul 05·56·52·28·35.

FACILITIES **Marina** (280+20 Ⓥ) in Basins 1 & 2 ☎ 05·46·83·99·96, 🌤 05·46·99·80·56, €1·08, FW, AC, ME, El, Sh, C (30 ton), D & P (outside lock) but not working (1999), ♿; **Port Neuf** Slip, FW; **Club Nautique Rochefortais** ☎ 05·46·87·34·61, Slip; **Services:** ME, El, Ⓔ, Sh, CH. **Town** P, D, V, Gaz, R, Bar, ✉, Ⓑ, ⇌, ✈ (La Rochelle). Ferry: Roscoff or St Malo.

ADJACENT ANCHORAGE AT MOUTH OF LA CHARENTE

ILE D'AIX, Charente Maritime, **46°01´·00N 01°10´·00W**. AC 2746, 2748; SHOM 6914, 6334. HW +0545 on Dover (UT); ML 3·9m. Tides see 9.18.18. Only a fine weather ⚓ or pick up a buoy off the landing jetty at St Catherine's Pt, Fl WR 5s 24m 24/20M, the S tip of the island. Moorings E of St Catherine's Pt (depths shoal rapidly); four W buoys to west (deeper) and five SE of the Pt. On W side of island, near LW keep 3ca off the two WCM perches. **Facilities:** €7·62 for mooring, C (1·5 ton), Slip, AB (SE jetty), V, R.

LA SEUDRE *9.18.19*

CHARTS AC 2663; Imray C41, C42; SHOM 6335; ECM 552

TIDES +0545 Dover; ML 3·6; Duration Sp 0545, Np 0700

Standard Port POINTE DE GRAVE (⟶)

Times				Height (metres)			
High Water		Low Water		MHWS	MHWN	MLWN	MLWS
0000	0600	0500	1200	5·4	4·4	2·1	1·0
1200	1800	1700	2400				
Differences LA CAYENNE							
+0030	–0015	–0010	–0005	+0·2	+0·2	+0·3	0·0

SHELTER Good in the yacht basin (2m) at Marennes. Lock opens about HW±2 sp, HW±1 np; or secure ⚓s at La Cayenne, La Grève (½M upstream), and at ent to Chenal de la Tremblade.

NAVIGATION WPT 45°55'·88N 01°08'·65W, Chenal Est-Nord WCM buoy, for Chenal Est and Coureau d'Oléron. Best to appr La Seudre from N, through Coureau d'Oléron, and thence via Chenal de la Soumaille (dries about 0·7m). Chenal de la Garrigue carries slightly more water. Both are marked by bns and buoys. Beware oyster beds. Pont de Seudre has clearance of 18m. Overhead power cables (24m) span Canal de Marennes. La Seudre is navigable to lock at Riberou. Beware: Pertuis de Maumusson is usable only in good weather, at about HW –1; see 9.18.5. In even moderate weather it is **extremely dangerous**, especially with out-going stream or any swell.

LIGHTS AND MARKS There are no ldg lts/marks. Lights: Pte de Mus de Loup, Oc G 4s 8m 6M, vis 118°-147°. On bridge, between piers 6 and 7, Q 20m 10M, vis up/downstream. Chan marked by W boards.

RADIO TELEPHONE VHF Ch 09.

TELEPHONE **Marennes**: Hr Mr 05·46·85·02·68; Aff Mar 05·46·85·14·33; Police 05·46·85·00·19; Dr 05·46·85·23·06. **La Tremblade**: Hr Mr 05·46·36·00·22; ⊜ 05·46·47·62·53; Auto 08.36.68.08.17; Dr 05·46·36·16·35; Brit Consul 05·56·36·16·35.

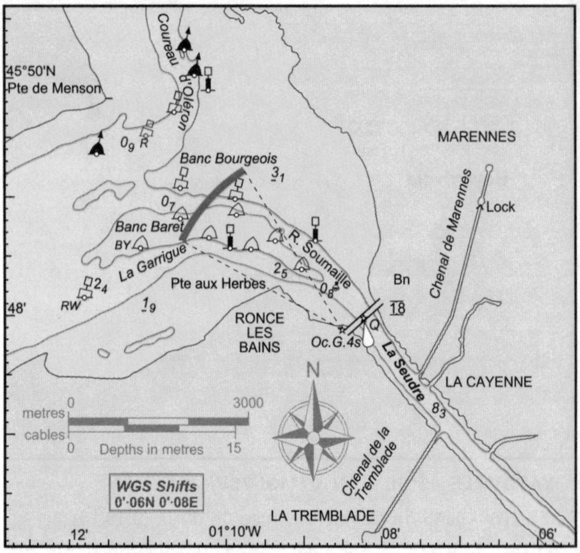

FACILITIES

MARENNES **Basin** ☎ 05·46·85·02·68, FW, AC, C (6 ton), ME, CH; **Services**: Sh, ME, CH. **Town** Slip, M, P, D, L, FW, V, R, Bar.

LA TREMBLADE **Quay** Slip, P, D, FW, C (5 ton); **Services**: ME, Sh, SM, CH. **Town** Slip, P, D, L, FW, Gaz, V, R, Bar, ✉, Ⓑ, ⇌, ✈ (La Rochelle). Ferry: Roscoff or St Malo.

LA GIRONDE & CANALS *9.18.20*

CHARTS AC 2910, 2916, 2663; Imray C41, C42; SHOM 7028, 7029, 7030

NAVIGATION **La Gironde estuary** is a substantial waterway. The mouth of the estuary is 9M wide between Pointe de la Coubre and Pointe de Grave. From Royan to Bordeaux (55M) the river narrows from 6M wide to 2.5M at Pauillac. The outer apprs can be dangerous due to Atlantic swell, very strong tidal streams and currents, extensive shoals and shifting sandbanks, see 9.18.5. Swell, strong W'lies and an ebb tide raises dangerous, breaking seas some 5m high; in these conditions do not attempt entry. Be alert for ferries and shipping. In the Gironde and the Dordogne the sp flood reaches 3kn and the ebb 4kn. In the Garonne the sp flood starts with a small bore and runs at 3kn, ebb reaches 5kn. AC 2910 and 2916, or SHOM 7028 and 7029, are essential.

SHELTER Yacht hbrs from Royan (9.18.21 to Bordeaux* include Port Bloc (9.18.22), St Georges-de-Didonne, Meschers, Mortagne, Pauillac*, Lamarque, Blaye* and Port de Bourg. For *hbrs, see 9.18.21.

NAVIGATION WPT BXA SWM buoy, Iso 4s, Whis, Racon, 45°37'·60N 01°28'·62W, 261°/081° from/to Grande Passe de l'Ouest Nos 1 & 2 buoys, 4·8M. Do not cut corners. The estuary is entered via two approach channels:

1. **Grande Passe de l'Ouest**. Leave No 1 buoy at LW. 081° on La Palmyre ldg lts; thence 100° to enter the river on astern transit of 327° (see below). The chan is deep and well marked/lit. Give the Mauvaise bank, Banc de la Coubre and shoals around Cordouan a wide berth.
2. **Passe du Sud**. From 'G' unlit SWM buoy track 063° on the ldg lts at St Nicolas/Pte de Grave until 3M abeam Cordouan lt ho; thence 041° on Le Chay/St Pierre ldg lts to pick up the 327° astern transit (see below). The chan carries approx 5m through shoals; not advised in poor vis or heavy swell. Platin de Grave, between G4 and G7 Bys, has only 1·8m. The 6 lateral buoys are not lit.

The astern transit 327° of Terre-Nègre lt with La Palmyre, FR 57m 17M, leads NE of Pte de Grave and up-river.

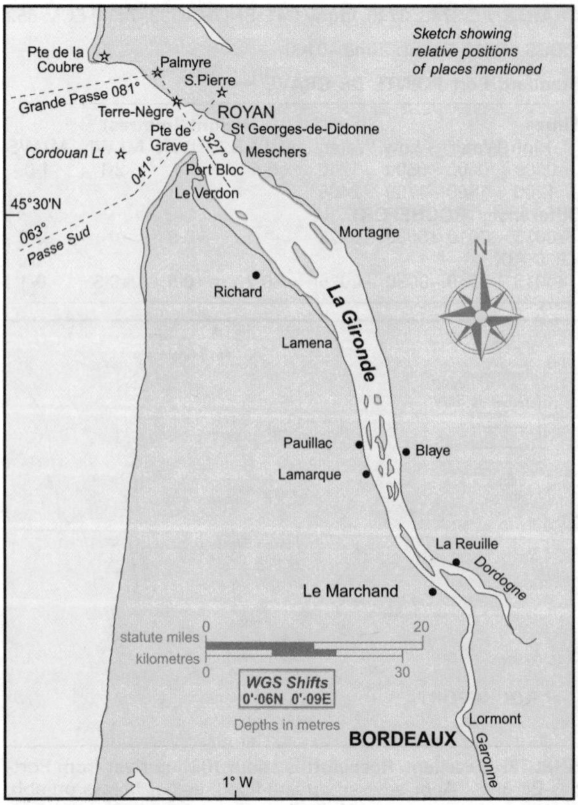

LIGHTS AND MARKS

1. **Grande Passe de l'Ouest** ldg lts 081°, both intens 080·5°-082·5°: Front Dir Iso 4s 21m 22M, and Q (2) 5s 10m 3M same structure, W pylon on dolphin; rear, La Palmyre Dir Q 57m

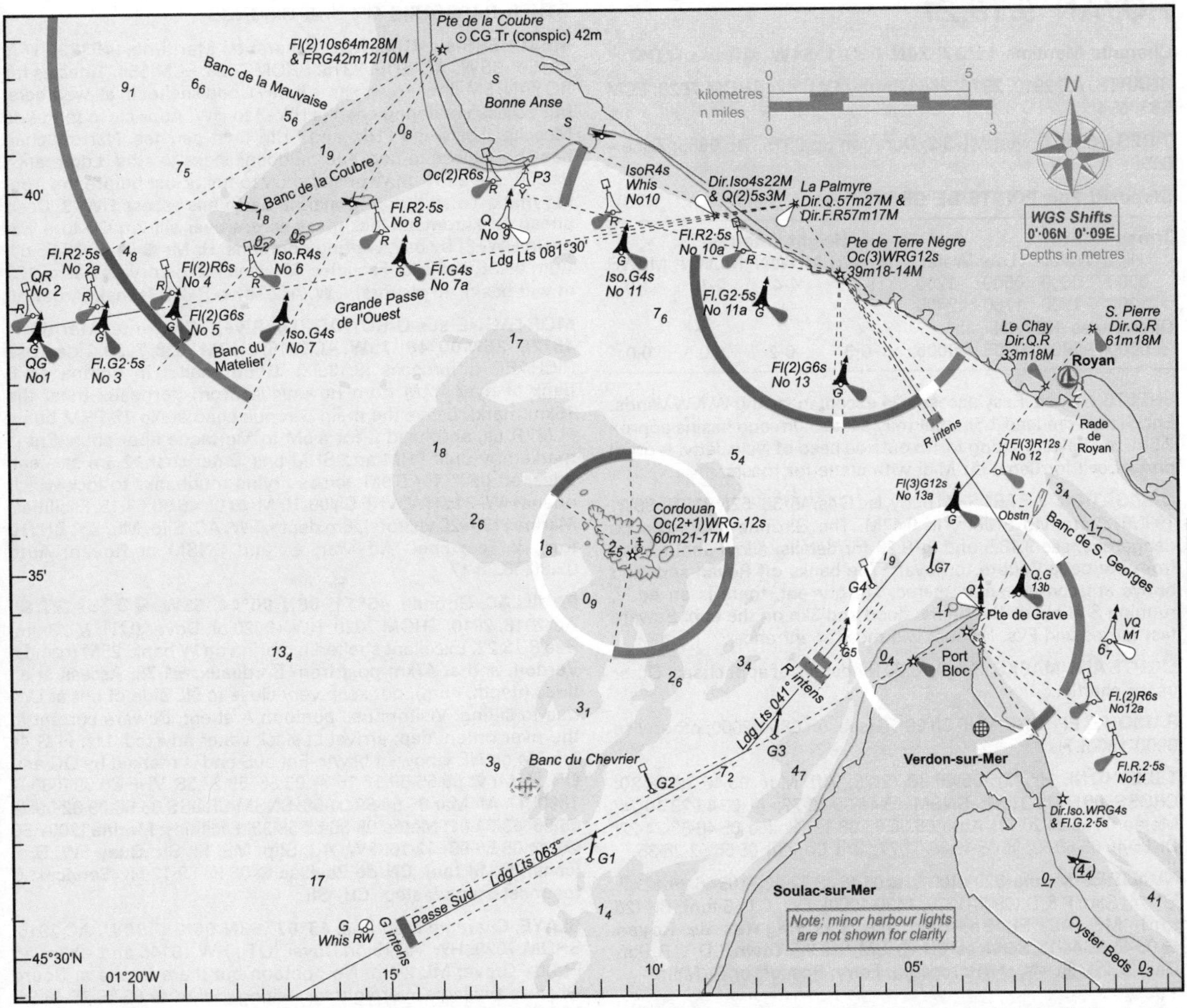
Pte de la Coubre
CG Tr (conspic) 42m
Fl(2)10s64m28M
& FRG42m12/10M
Banc de la Mauvaise
Bonne Anse
kilometres
n miles
Banc de la Coubre
Oc(2)R6s
P3
IsoR4s
Whis
No10
Dir.Iso4s22M
& Q(2)5s3M
La Palmyre
Dir.Q.57m27M &
Dir.F.R57m17M
WGS Shifts
0'·06N 0'·09E
Depths in metres
Fl.R2·5s
No 8
Q
No 9
Fl.R2·5s
No 10a
Pte de Terre Négre
Oc(3)WRG12s
39m18-14M
Fl.R2·5s
No 2a
QR
No 2
Fl(2)R6s
No 4
Iso.R4s
No 6
Ldg Lts 081°30'
Fl.G4s
No 7a
Iso.G4s
No 11
Fl.G2·5s
No 11a
Fl(2)G6s
No 5
Grande Passe de l'Ouest
Iso.G4s
No 7
Banc du Matelier
QG
No1
Fl.G2·5s
No 3
Le Chay
Dir.Q.R
33m18M
S. Pierre
Dir.Q.R
61m18M
Royan
Fl(2)G6s
No 13
R intens
Rade de Royan
Fl(3)R12s
No 12
Fl(3)G12s
No 13a
Obstn
Banc de S. Georges
Cordouan
Oc(2+1)WRG.12s
60m21-17M
G7
G4
Q.G
13b
Pte de Grave
VQ
M1
G5
Port Bloc
R intens
Ldg Lts 041°
Fl.(2)R6s
No12a
G3
Verdon-sur-Mer
Banc du Chevrier
G2
Fl.R.2·5s
No14
Dir.Iso.WRG4s
& Fl.G.2·5s
G1
Ldg Lts 063°
Passe Sud
Soulac-sur-Mer
Note: minor harbour lights are not shown for clarity
Whis RW
G intens
Oyster Beds
40'
35'
45°30'N
01°20'W
15'
10'
05'

27M, W radar tr. From No 9 SHM buoy, use W sector 097°- 104° of Pte de Terre-Nègre, Oc (3) WRG 12s 39m 18/14M.

2. **Passe du Sud**, Outer ldg lts 063°: Front St Nicolas Dir QG 22m 16M, intens 061·5°-064·5°, W □ tr; rear, Pte de Grave Oc WRG 4s 26m 19/15M. Inner ldg lts 041°, both QR 33/61m 18M, intens 039°-043°: Front, Le Chay; rear, Ste Pierre 0·97M from front.

Other major lts in estuary: La Coubre lt ho, Fl (2) 10s 64m 28M RC, also FRG 42m 12/10M R030°-043°, G043°-060°, R060°-110°. Courdouan lt Oc (2+1) WRG 12s 60m 22/18M, W014°-126°, G126°-178·5°, W178·5°-250°, W (unintens) 250°-267°, R (unintens) 267°-294·5°, R294·5°-014°; obscured in estuary when brg > 285°.

RADIO TELEPHONE A VTS, (compulsory), provides radar surveillance from BXA buoy to Bordeaux. Call *Bordeaux Traffic* or *Radar Verdon* on VHF Ch 12 16 (H24). In poor vis or on request *Radar Verdon* provides radar information between BXA and Verdon roads. Height of water is broadcast on Ch 17 every 5 mins, plus a weather bulletin and nav info on request.

Canal Latéral à la Garonne and Canal du Midi provide a popular route to the Mediterranean, despite some 120 locks. The transit can be done in about a week, but 12 days is more relaxed. Masts can be unstepped at Royan, Pauillac or Bordeaux. Leave Bordeaux at LW Pointe de Grave for the 30M leg up river to the first lock at Castets. Commercial traffic and W-bound boats have right of way. Most of the locks on the Canal Latéral à la Garonne are automatic. On the Canal du Midi there are many hire cruisers in summer. Garonne Canal depths reported 1·4m and Canal du Midi 1·5m. Fuel is available by hose at Mas d'Agenais, Agen, Port Sud (Toulouse), Castelnaudary, Port la Robine, and by can elsewhere. V and FW are readily obtained. Tolls are listed in 9.15.7. *Guide Vagnon No 7* or *Navicarte No 11* are advised. Further info from: Service de la Navigation de Toulouse, 8 Port St Etienne, 31079 Toulouse Cedex, ☎ 05·61·80·07·18.

SUMMARY

Canal	*From*	*To*	*Km/ Locks*	*Min Dpth(m)*	*Min Ht(m)*
Latéral à la Garonne	Castets	Toulouse	193/53	2·2	3·5
Du Midi	Toulouse	Sete	240/65	1·6	3·0
De la Nouvelle	Salleles	Port la Nouvelle	37/14	1·5	3·1

Notes: Max LOA 30m; draft 1·5m (varies with season); max beam 5·5m. Headroom of 3·3m is to centre of arch; over a width of 4m, clearance is about 2·40m. Speed limit 8km/hr (about 4½kn), but 3km/hr under bridges/over aqueducts.

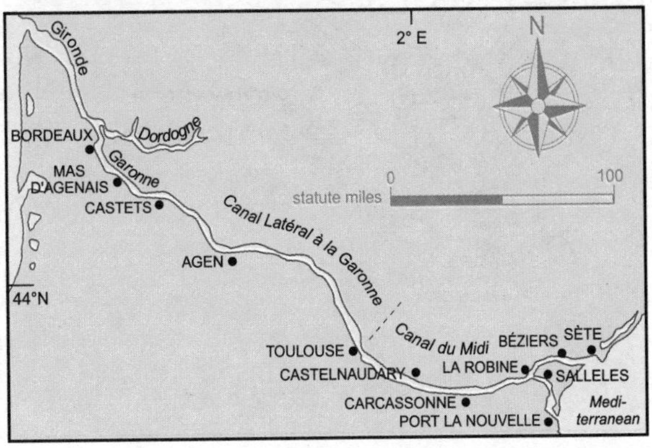
Gironde
2° E
N
BORDEAUX
Dordogne
MAS D'AGENAIS
Garonne
CASTETS
statute miles
0
100
Canal Latéral à la Garonne
AGEN
44°N
Canal du Midi
BÉZIERS
SÈTE
TOULOUSE
CASTELNAUDARY
LA ROBINE
SALLELES
CARCASSONNE
PORT LA NOUVELLE
Medi-terranean

ROYAN *9.18.21*

Charente Maritime **45°37'·20N 01°01'·54W** ❁❁◇◇◇✿✿✿

CHARTS AC 2910, 2916, 2664; Imray C41, 42; SHOM 7028; ECM 553, 554

TIDES +0530 Dover; ML 3·2; Duration Sp 0615, Np 0655; Zone –0100

Standard Port POINTE DE GRAVE (⟶)

Times				Height (metres)			
High Water		Low Water		MHWS	MHWN	MLWN	MLWS
0000	0600	0500	1200	5·4	4·4	2·1	1·0
1200	1800	1700	2400				
Differences ROYAN							
0000	–0005	–0005	–0005	–0·3	–0·2	0·0	0·0

SHELTER Good. Easy access H24 except in strong W/NW winds. Ent chan is dredged 1·5m, but may silt to 1.0m and basins approx 2·5m, but beware silting to 1m outside head of New Jetty. A good port of call for Canal du Midi with crane for masts.

NAVIGATION WPT R1 SHM buoy, Iso G 4s, 45°36´·62N 01°01´·90W, 193°/013° from/to S Jetty lt, 0·47M. The Gironde apprs can be dangerous; see 9.18.5 and 9.18.20 for details; allow about 2 hrs from Pte de la Coubre to Royan. The banks off Royan shift and buoys are consequently altered. Off hbr ent, there is an eddy, running S at about 1kn on the flood and 3kn on the ebb. Beware fast ferries and FVs. Hr boat will meet at entrance

LIGHTS AND MARKS See 9.18.20 for details of appr chans. Other lts as chartlet.

RADIO TELEPHONE VHF Ch 09 16 (season 0800-2000; otherwise 0900-1800LT).

TELEPHONE Hr Mr 05·46·38·72·22; Aff Mar 05·46·39·26·30; CROSS 05·56·73·31·31; SNSM 05·46·38·75·79; ⊖ 05·46·23·10·24; Météo 05·56·34·20·11; Auto 08.36.68.08.17; Police 05·46·38·34·22; Dr 05·46·05·68·69; Ⓗ 05·46·38·01·77; Brit Consul 05·56·52·28·35.

FACILITIES **Marina** (920+100 Ⓥ) ☎ 05·46·38·72·22, 📠 05·46.39.42.47, €1·74, Slip, P & D (0900-1230, 1430-1900), FW, C (1·5 ton), BH (26 ton), ME, AC, El, Sh, Grid, Ice; **Les Régates de Royan** ☎ 05·46·05·44·13; **Services:** CH, Ⓔ, SM, SHOM. **Town** P, D, V, R, Bar, Gaz, ✆, ✉, Ⓑ, ⇌, ✈ (Bordeaux). Ferry: Roscoff or St Malo.

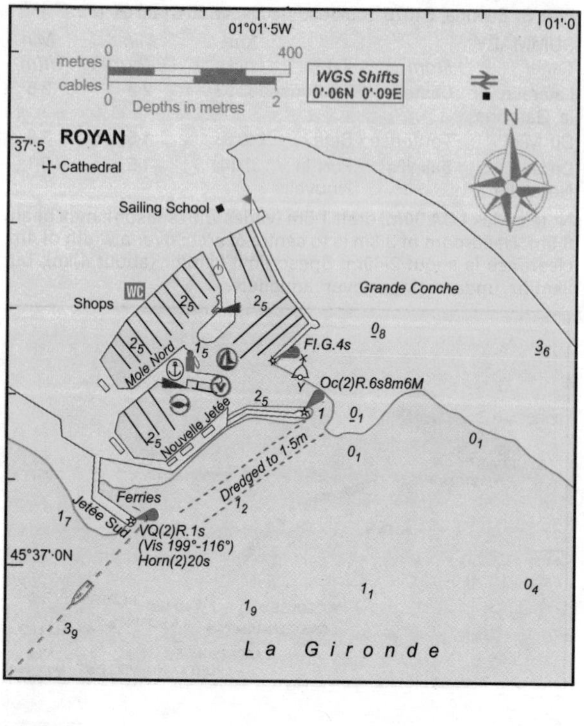

OTHER HARBOURS ON THE GIRONDE

MESCHERS-sur-GIRONDE, Charente Maritime, **45°33'·15N 00°56'·55W**. AC 2910, 2916; SHOM 7028; ECM 554. Tides as for ROYAN, 5M down-river same bank. Good shelter in all weathers, but access via drying chan is HW–3 to HW. Appr close to Pte de Meschers between PHM and SHM unlit perches. Narrow chan has shore close to port and mudbank close to stbd. Ldg marks/lts 000° are 2 FW on W posts; entry to hbr is just before the front ldg mark. To stbd drying marina basin has access HW±3. Dead ahead an automatic lock gives access over sill 2m CD to a wet basin HW±2½ by day; waiting pontoons. Hr Mr ☎ 05.46.02.56.89; Auto 05.36.68.08.17. Facilities: **Marinas** (125 in drying basin, 123 in wet basin, 18 visitors), FW, AC. **Town** P & D (cans), R, Bar, V.

MORTAGNE-sur-GIRONDE (La Rive), Charente Maritime, **45°28'·25N 00°48'·75W**. AC 2916; SHOM 7028, 7029. Tides, use RICHARD differences (9.18.22). Good shelter in marina on E bank of river, 14M from Royan/40M from Bordeaux (near the 75km mark). Leave the main Gironde chan at No 18 PHM buoy, Fl (2) R 6s, and head E for 4·5M to Mortagne appr chan. Ent is marked by unlit PHM and SHM bns. Enter chan, 2·5m at mean tides, on 063°, for 0·9M across drying mudbanks to lock which opens HW–2 to HW. VHF Ch 09. Hr Mr ☎ 05.46.90.63.15. Facilities: **Marina** (130+20 visitors), 6m depth, FW, AC, Slip, ME, BY, BH (10 ton), V, Ice; Fuel, Aff Mar, ⊖, and SNSM at Royan; Auto 05.36.68.08.17.

PAUILLAC, Gironde, **45°11´·88N 00°44´·53W**. ❁❁◇◇◇✿✿✿. AC 2916, 2910; SHOM 7029; HW +0620 on Dover (UT); ML 3·0m. See 8.18.22. Excellent shelter in marina on W bank, 25M from Le Verdon, and at 47km post from Bordeaux, €1·75. Access at all tides (depth 1·5m), but keep very close to NE side of ent at LW, due to silting. Visitors use pontoon A at ent. Beware current in the river on ent/dep; arrival at slack water advised. Lts: Fl G 4s 7m 5M on NE elbow of bkwtr. Ent at S end is marked by QG and QR. Hr Mr ☎ 05·56·59·12·16, 📠 05.56. 59.23.38; VHF Ch 09 (0800–1800LT). Aff Mar 05·56·59·01·58; SNSM/CROSS 05·56·09·82·00; ⊖ 05·56 ·59·04·01; Météo 05·36·68·08·33. Facilities: **Marina** (200+ 50 Ⓥ), ☎ 05·56·59· 12·16, FW, AC, Slip, ME, El, Sh; **Quay** FW, D, P (cans), C (14 ton); **CN de Pauillac** ☎ 05·56·59·12·58; **Services:** C for mast step/un-step, CH, Sh.

BLAYE, Charente Maritime, **45°07´·53N 00°39´·90W**. AC 2916; SHOM 7029. HW +0715 on Dover (UT); HW +0145 and –0·3m on Pte de Grave; ML 2·4m. No pontoon but there is one at Bourg which is available overnight for visiting yachts. ☎ 05·56·75·46·54. FW, AC.

BORDEAUX, Gironde, **44°52´·80N 00°32´·30W**. AC 2916; SHOM 7029, 7030. HW +0715 on Dover (UT); ML 2·4m. See 9.18.22. Bordeaux is about 55M from Royan up the Gironde estuary and R Garonne. Beware big ships, strong currents (up to 5kn when river in spate) and large bits of flotsam. The chan is well marked and lit. De-masting crane at Lormont YC on E bank. Berths may also be available, by arrangement with Hr Mr, 1½M above bridge in No 2 Basin, access HW –½ to HW+½; crane available. Or berth on wharves between No 1 Basin and Pont de Pierre, but stream is strong. VHF Ch 12. Hr Mr ☎ 05·56·31·58·64; Hr Mr Lormont YC ☎ 05·56·38·27·53; Hr Mr No 2 Basin ☎ 06·13·79·10·75 or 05·56·90·59·57; Aff Mar ☎ 05·56·52·26·23; ⊖ ☎ 05·56·44·47·10; Météo ☎ 05·56·90·91·21; Facilities: **Marina** ☎ 05·56·50·84·14 VHF Ch 09; **Sport Nautique de la Gironde** ☎ 05·56·50·84·14; **Services:** Slip, C (5 ton), ME, El, Sh, CH, Ⓔ, SHOM.

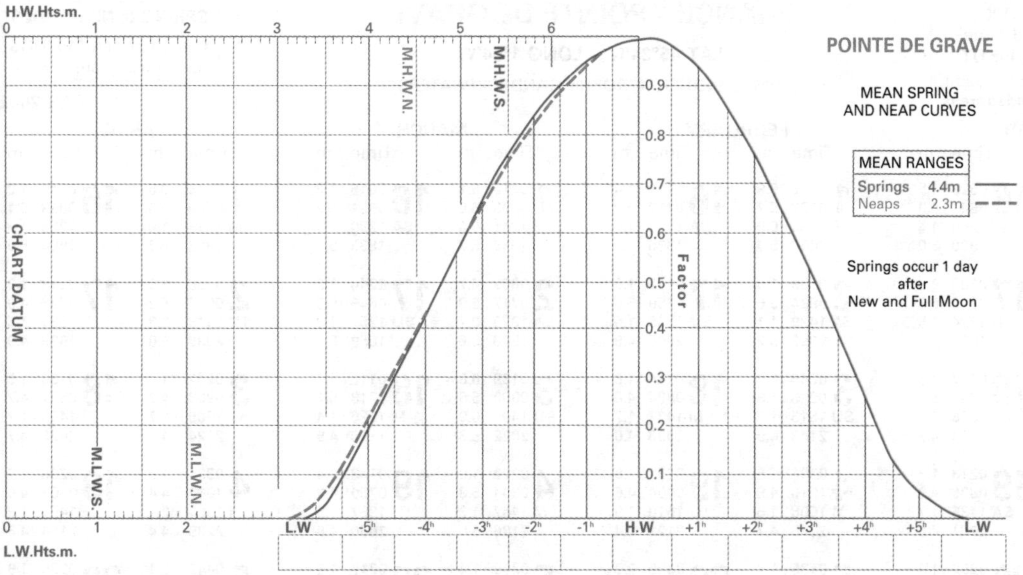
H.W.Hts.m.
POINTE DE GRAVE
MEAN SPRING
AND NEAP CURVES
MEAN RANGES
Springs 4.4m
Neaps 2.3m
Springs occur 1 day
after
New and Full Moon
CHART DATUM
M.H.W.N.
M.H.W.S.
M.L.W.S.
M.L.W.N.
Factor
L.W.Hts.m.
L.W
H.W
L.W

PORT BLOC *9.18.22*

Gironde **45°34'·18N 01°03'·64W** ❁❁⚓⚓✿✿

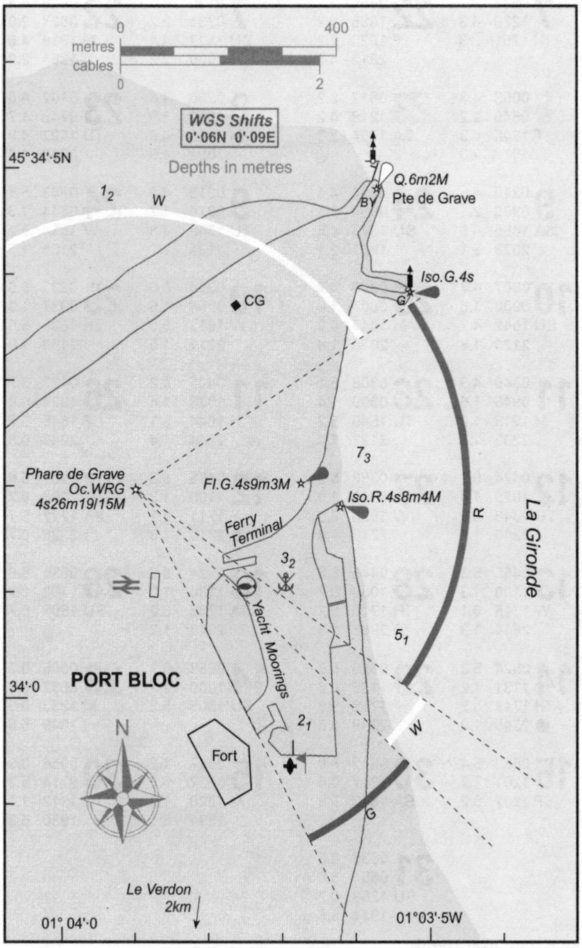
metres
cables
0
400
0
2
WGS Shifts
0'·06N 0'·09E
45°34'·5N
Depths in metres
Q.6m2M
Pte de Grave
Iso.G.4s
CG
Phare de Grave
Oc.WRG
4s26m19/15M
Fl.G.4s9m3M
Iso.R.4s8m4M
Ferry
Terminal
Yacht Moorings
La Gironde
PORT BLOC
34'·0
Fort
N
Le Verdon
2km
01° 04'·0
01°03'·5W

CHARTS AC 2910, 2664, 2916; Imray C42; ECM 553, 554; SHOM 7028. Note: 7029 & 7030 cover to Bordeaux/Libourne

TIDES (Pauillac) +0720 Dover; ML 3·0; Duration: Sp 0615; Np 0655; Zone –0100 NOTE: Pointe de Grave is a Standard Port; these predictions apply to Port Bloc

Standard Port POINTE DE GRAVE (⟶)

Times				Height (metres)			
High Water		Low Water		MHWS	MHWN	MLWN	MLWS
0000	0600	0500	1200	5·4	4·4	2·1	1·0
1200	1800	1700	2400				
Differences RICHARD							
+0018	+0018	+0028	+0033	–0·1	–0·1	–0·4	–0·5
LAMENA							
+0035	+0045	+0100	+0125	+0·2	+0·1	–0·5	–0·3
PAUILLAC							
+0100	+0100	+0135	+0205	+0·1	0·0	–1·0	–0·5
LA REUILLE							
+0135	+0145	+0230	+0305	–0·2	–0·3	–1·3	–0·7
LE MARQUIS							
+0145	+0150	+0247	+0322	–0·3	–0·4	–1·5	–0·9
BORDEAUX							
+0200	+0225	+0330	+0405	–0·1	–0·2	–1·7	–1·0
LIBOURNE (La Dordogne)							
+0250	+0305	+0525	+0540	–0·7	–0·9	–2·0	–0·4

SHELTER Good, but mainly a ferry hbr, dredged 3m and 4ca S of Pte de Grave. Space for yachts is limited; possible AB on pontoons on W side of the hbr. Royan is a better option.

NAVIGATION WPT 13b SHM buoy, QG, 45°34'·65N 01°02'·91W, 047°/227° from/to hbr ent, 7ca. Caution strong tidal streams. Ent is 30m wide; ferries have priority.

LIGHTS AND MARKS Pte de Grave lt ho, Oc WRG 4s 26m 19/15M, W □ tr, B corners and top. Hbr ent: NW quay Fl G 4s 9m 3M, SE bkwtr Iso R 4s 8m 4M. Le Verdon oil jetty is 1.5M SSE.

RADIO TELEPHONE Radar Verdon Ch 11 12 (H24).

TELEPHONE Hr Mr 05·56·09·63·91; Aff Mar 05·56·09·60·23; CROSS 05·56·73·31·31; Météo 05·56·34·20·11; Auto 08.36.68.08.17; ⊖ 05·56·09·65·14; Police 05·56·09·80·29; Dr 05·56·09·60·37; Brit Consul 05·56·52·28·35.

FACILITIES Moto Yachting Club de la Pte de Grave ☎ 05·56·09·84·02, D, FW, C (10 ton), ME, El, Sh, CH. Town P, Gaz, V, R, ✉ & Ⓑ (Verdon), ≹, ✈ (Bordeaux). Ferry: Local to Royan.

TIME ZONE -0100
(French Standard Time)
Subtract 1 hour for UT
For French Summer Time add ONE hour in **non-shaded areas**

FRANCE – POINTE DE GRAVE

LAT 45°34′N LONG 1°04′W

TIMES AND HEIGHTS OF HIGH AND LOW WATERS

SPRING & NEAP TIDES
Dates in red are SPRINGS
Dates in blue are NEAPS

YEAR **2002**

JANUARY

Date	Time	m
1 TU	0612	5.5
	1223	1.1
	1842	5.4
2 W	0039	1.2
	0659	5.5
	1309	1.1
	1931	5.3
3 TH	0125	1.3
	0749	5.4
	1357	1.2
	2022	5.1
4 F	0213	1.4
	0841	5.3
	1446	1.3
	2118	5.0
5 SA	0305	1.5
	0939	5.1
	1540	1.5
	2219	4.8
6 SU	0403	1.7
	1045	4.9
	1640	1.7
	2327	4.7
7 M	0507	1.8
	1157	4.8
	1747	1.8
8 TU	0039	4.7
	0616	1.9
	1310	4.8
	1856	1.8
9 W	0143	4.8
	0726	1.8
	1416	4.8
	2001	1.8
10 TH	0240	4.9
	0830	1.7
	1513	4.9
	2058	1.7
11 F	0330	5.0
	0927	1.6
	1602	5.0
	2148	1.5
12 SA	0414	5.2
	1016	1.5
	1644	5.1
	2233	1.5
13 SU	0454	5.3
	1100	1.4
	1722	5.1
●	2314	1.4
14 M	0532	5.3
	1139	1.3
	1757	5.1
	2352	1.4
15 TU	0608	5.3
	1216	1.3
	1829	5.0
16 W	0028	1.5
	0641	5.3
	1250	1.4
	1900	5.0
17 TH	0103	1.5
	0715	5.2
	1324	1.5
	1931	4.8
18 F	0137	1.6
	0749	5.0
	1358	1.6
	2004	4.7
19 SA	0213	1.7
	0826	4.9
	1435	1.7
	2041	4.5
20 SU	0252	1.9
	0907	4.7
	1514	1.9
	2127	4.4
21 M	0336	2.1
	0957	4.5
	1601	2.1
	2226	4.2
22 TU	0430	2.2
	1059	4.4
	1659	2.2
	2342	4.2
23 W	0537	2.3
	1212	4.3
	1809	2.3
24 TH	0058	4.3
	0648	2.2
	1325	4.4
	1918	2.1
25 F	0202	4.5
	0753	2.0
	1429	4.6
	2018	1.9
26 SA	0256	4.8
	0851	1.8
	1524	4.9
	2113	1.7
27 SU	0345	5.1
	0946	1.5
	1614	5.2
	2204	1.4
28 M	0432	5.4
	1037	1.2
	1701	5.4
○	2253	1.2
29 TU	0518	5.6
	1126	1.0
	1747	5.5
	2340	1.0
30 W	0604	5.7
	1214	0.8
	1833	5.6
31 TH	0030	0.9
	0650	5.8
	1259	0.8
	1918	5.6

FEBRUARY

Date	Time	m
1 F	0115	0.9
	0737	5.7
	1344	0.9
	2004	5.4
2 SA	0159	1.0
	0824	5.5
	1429	1.1
	2052	5.2
3 SU	0246	1.2
	0913	5.3
	1515	1.3
	2143	4.9
4 M	0336	1.5
	1010	4.9
	1608	1.6
	2245	4.7
5 TU	0435	1.7
	1122	4.7
	1710	1.9
	2358	4.5
6 W	0545	2.0
	1245	4.5
	1824	2.1
7 TH	0119	4.5
	0703	2.0
	1402	4.5
	1940	2.1
8 F	0227	4.6
	0816	1.9
	1507	4.6
	2044	1.9
9 SA	0321	4.8
	0916	1.7
	1556	4.8
	2137	1.7
10 SU	0406	5.0
	1005	1.6
	1636	4.9
	2221	1.5
11 M	0443	5.2
	1047	1.4
	1709	5.0
	2301	1.4
12 TU	0517	5.3
	1124	1.3
	1739	5.1
●	2336	1.3
13 W	0549	5.3
	1157	1.3
	1808	5.1
14 TH	0008	1.3
	0619	5.3
	1228	1.3
	1835	5.1
15 F	0041	1.3
	0649	5.3
	1258	1.3
	1902	5.0
16 SA	0111	1.4
	0719	5.2
	1328	1.4
	1930	4.9
17 SU	0142	1.5
	0750	5.0
	1359	1.5
	2000	4.8
18 M	0214	1.6
	0824	4.8
	1431	1.7
	2036	4.6
19 TU	0251	1.8
	0904	4.6
	1510	1.9
	2121	4.4
20 W	0335	2.0
	0958	4.4
	1558	2.1
	2227	4.2
21 TH	0436	2.2
	1114	4.2
	1706	2.3
22 F	0008	4.2
	0557	2.3
	1245	4.3
	1831	2.3
23 SA	0126	4.4
	0718	2.1
	1405	4.5
	1948	2.1
24 SU	0233	4.7
	0828	1.8
	1507	4.8
	2052	1.8
25 M	0328	5.1
	0929	1.4
	1559	5.2
	2148	1.4
26 TU	0417	5.4
	1022	1.1
	1647	5.5
	2238	1.1
27 W	0504	5.7
	1111	0.8
	1732	5.7
○	2325	0.8
28 TH	0549	5.9
	1157	0.6
	1815	5.8

MARCH

Date	Time	m
1 F	0013	0.7
	0633	6.0
	1241	0.6
	1858	5.7
2 SA	0057	0.7
	0717	5.9
	1323	0.7
	1940	5.6
3 SU	0139	0.8
	0800	5.6
	1405	0.9
	2022	5.3
4 M	0222	1.0
	0844	5.3
	1447	1.3
	2106	5.0
5 TU	0309	1.4
	0934	4.9
	1535	1.7
	2201	4.6
6 W	0403	1.7
	1043	4.5
	1634	2.0
	2320	4.4
7 TH	0513	2.1
	1220	4.3
	1751	2.3
8 F	0053	4.3
	0640	2.2
	1348	4.3
	1918	2.3
9 SA	0210	4.5
	0800	2.1
	1455	4.5
	2028	2.1
10 SU	0307	4.7
	0900	1.8
	1542	4.7
	2120	1.8
11 M	0349	4.9
	0946	1.6
	1618	4.9
	2203	1.6
12 TU	0424	5.1
	1025	1.4
	1648	5.0
	2240	1.4
13 W	0455	5.3
	1100	1.3
	1715	5.1
	2314	1.3
14 TH	0524	5.3
	1131	1.2
	1741	5.2
●	2345	1.2
15 F	0553	5.4
	1201	1.2
	1807	5.2
16 SA	0015	1.2
	0621	5.3
	1230	1.2
	1833	5.1
17 SU	0044	1.2
	0649	5.3
	1257	1.3
	1859	5.1
18 M	0112	1.3
	0718	5.1
	1326	1.4
	1928	4.9
19 TU	0143	1.4
	0750	4.9
	1357	1.5
	2000	4.8
20 W	0217	1.6
	0828	4.7
	1433	1.7
	2041	4.5
21 TH	0259	1.8
	0919	4.4
	1519	2.0
	2141	4.3
22 F	0355	2.1
	1036	4.2
	1623	2.2
	2312	4.2
23 SA	0517	2.2
	1218	4.2
	1754	2.3
24 SU	0054	4.4
	0650	2.1
	1343	4.5
	1921	2.1
25 M	0209	4.7
	0807	1.8
	1447	4.9
	2030	1.8
26 TU	0308	5.1
	0909	1.4
	1540	5.2
	2127	1.4
27 W	0358	5.5
	1002	1.0
	1626	5.5
	2218	1.0
28 TH	0445	5.8
	1050	0.7
	1710	5.7
○	2305	0.8
29 F	0529	5.9
	1135	0.6
	1752	5.8
	2349	0.6
30 SA	0612	6.0
	1217	0.6
	1833	5.8
31 SU	0035	0.6
	0654	5.8
	1258	0.7
	1914	5.6

APRIL

Date	Time	m
1 M	0116	0.8
	0736	5.5
	1338	1.0
	1953	5.3
2 TU	0158	1.0
	0817	5.2
	1419	1.3
	2035	5.0
3 W	0242	1.4
	0903	4.7
	1505	1.7
	2124	4.7
4 TH	0334	1.8
	1007	4.4
	1601	2.1
	2239	4.4
5 F	0442	2.1
	1149	4.1
	1718	2.4
6 SA	0003	4.3
	0609	2.3
	1322	4.2
	1848	2.4
7 SU	0138	4.4
	0731	2.2
	1427	4.4
	2000	2.2
8 M	0236	4.6
	0831	1.9
	1513	4.6
	2052	1.9
9 TU	0319	4.8
	0916	1.7
	1548	4.8
	2134	1.7
10 W	0354	5.0
	0954	1.5
	1617	5.0
	2211	1.5
11 TH	0425	5.2
	1028	1.4
	1644	5.1
	2244	1.4
12 F	0455	5.3
	1100	1.3
	1711	5.2
●	2316	1.3
13 SA	0524	5.3
	1130	1.2
	1738	5.2
	2347	1.2
14 SU	0553	5.3
	1200	1.2
	1805	5.2
15 M	0017	1.2
	0622	5.2
	1228	1.3
	1834	5.1
16 TU	0047	1.2
	0653	5.1
	1258	1.3
	1904	5.0
17 W	0119	1.3
	0727	4.9
	1331	1.5
	1939	4.9
18 TH	0155	1.5
	0807	4.7
	1409	1.7
	2023	4.7
19 F	0238	1.7
	0903	4.5
	1457	1.9
	2124	4.5
20 SA	0335	1.9
	1022	4.3
	1602	2.2
	2249	4.4
21 SU	0456	2.1
	1158	4.3
	1730	2.2
22 M	0026	4.5
	0627	2.0
	1319	4.6
	1854	2.0
23 TU	0142	4.8
	0743	1.7
	1422	4.9
	2003	1.7
24 W	0243	5.1
	0844	1.3
	1514	5.2
	2101	1.3
25 TH	0335	5.5
	0937	1.0
	1601	5.5
	2153	1.0
26 F	0422	5.7
	1024	0.8
	1645	5.7
	2241	0.8
27 SA	0507	5.8
	1109	0.7
	1727	5.7
○	2326	0.7
28 SU	0550	5.8
	1152	0.7
	1809	5.7
29 M	0005	0.7
	0632	5.6
	1233	0.9
	1849	5.5
30 TU	0054	0.9
	0714	5.3
	1312	1.1
	1930	5.3

Chart Datum: 2·83 metres below IGN Datum

TIME ZONE -0100
(French Standard Time)
Subtract 1 hour for UT
For French Summer Time add ONE hour in **non-shaded areas**

FRANCE – POINTE DE GRAVE

LAT 45°34′N LONG 1°04′W

TIMES AND HEIGHTS OF HIGH AND LOW WATERS

SPRING & NEAP TIDES
Dates in red are SPRINGS
Dates in blue are NEAPS

YEAR **2002**

MAY

Date	Day	Time	m	Time	m	Time	m	Time	m
1	W	0135	1.1	0754	5.0	1353	1.5	2011	5.0
2	TH	0219	1.4	0839	4.6	1438	1.8	2059	4.7
3	F	0309	1.8	0936	4.3	1532	2.1	2203	4.5
4	SA	0410	2.1	1101	4.1	1641	2.4	2326	4.3
5	SU	0526	2.2	1233	4.1	1803	2.4		
6	M	0045	4.3	0644	2.2	1341	4.3	1915	2.3
7	TU	0148	4.5	0747	2.0	1429	4.5	2010	2.0
8	W	0236	4.7	0835	1.8	1507	4.7	2055	1.8
9	TH	0316	4.9	0915	1.6	1540	4.9	2134	1.6
10	F	0351	5.0	0951	1.5	1610	5.0	2210	1.5
11	SA	0424	5.1	1025	1.4	1640	5.1	2244	1.4
12	SU	0456	5.2	1059	1.3	1711	5.2	● 2318	1.3
13	M	0528	5.2	1131	1.3	1742	5.2	2352	1.2
14	TU	0602	5.2	1204	1.3	1814	5.2		
15	W	0027	1.3	0637	5.1	1238	1.4	1850	5.1
16	TH	0103	1.3	0716	4.9	1314	1.5	1931	5.0
17	F	0142	1.4	0803	4.7	1357	1.7	2020	4.8
18	SA	0230	1.6	0901	4.5	1448	1.8	2121	4.6
19	SU	0329	1.8	1015	4.4	1554	2.0	2236	4.6
20	M	0443	1.9	1137	4.5	1710	2.0		
21	TU	0000	4.6	0602	1.8	1251	4.6	1825	1.9
22	W	0113	4.8	0714	1.6	1353	4.9	1933	1.6
23	TH	0216	5.1	0815	1.3	1447	5.1	2033	1.4
24	F	0311	5.3	0910	1.1	1536	5.3	2127	1.1
25	SA	0401	5.4	0959	1.0	1621	5.4	2218	1.0
26	SU	0447	5.5	1045	0.9	1705	5.5	○ 2305	0.9
27	M	0532	5.4	1128	1.0	1748	5.5	2350	0.9
28	TU	0615	5.3	1210	1.1	1830	5.4		
29	W	0035	1.1	0656	5.1	1250	1.3	1912	5.2
30	TH	0116	1.2	0737	4.9	1331	1.5	1953	5.0
31	F	0159	1.5	0818	4.6	1415	1.8	2038	4.8

JUNE

Date	Day	Time	m	Time	m	Time	m	Time	m
1	SA	0244	1.7	0905	4.4	1504	2.0	2129	4.6
2	SU	0336	1.9	1006	4.2	1602	2.2	2230	4.4
3	M	0436	2.1	1120	4.1	1708	2.3	2339	4.3
4	TU	0543	2.1	1233	4.2	1816	2.2		
5	W	0046	4.4	0648	2.1	1332	4.3	1916	2.1
6	TH	0143	4.5	0743	1.9	1419	4.5	2007	2.0
7	F	0231	4.6	0830	1.8	1459	4.7	2052	1.8
8	SA	0313	4.8	0912	1.6	1536	4.8	2134	1.6
9	SU	0353	4.9	0951	1.5	1611	5.0	2213	1.5
10	M	0431	5.0	1030	1.4	1647	5.1	2253	1.3
11	TU	0509	5.1	1108	1.3	1723	5.2	● 2332	1.3
12	W	0548	5.1	1146	1.3	1802	5.2		
13	TH	0014	1.2	0630	5.0	1225	1.3	1844	5.1
14	F	0055	1.3	0714	5.0	1307	1.4	1929	5.1
15	SA	0139	1.3	0803	4.8	1353	1.5	2019	5.0
16	SU	0228	1.4	0858	4.7	1445	1.6	2116	4.9
17	M	0324	1.5	1002	4.6	1544	1.7	2221	4.8
18	TU	0427	1.6	1111	4.6	1649	1.8	2331	4.8
19	W	0535	1.6	1220	4.6	1757	1.7		
20	TH	0044	4.8	0643	1.6	1324	4.8	1904	1.6
21	F	0150	4.9	0747	1.5	1422	4.9	2008	1.5
22	SA	0250	5.0	0845	1.3	1515	5.1	2106	1.3
23	SU	0344	5.1	0938	1.3	1603	5.2	2200	1.2
24	M	0433	5.1	1026	1.2	1649	5.3	○ 2249	1.1
25	TU	0519	5.1	1111	1.2	1733	5.3	2335	1.1
26	W	0601	5.1	1153	1.3	1814	5.3		
27	TH	0019	1.2	0641	5.0	1233	1.3	1854	5.2
28	F	0059	1.3	0718	4.8	1313	1.5	1933	5.0
29	SA	0139	1.4	0754	4.7	1352	1.6	2012	4.9
30	SU	0219	1.6	0832	4.5	1434	1.8	2053	4.7

JULY

Date	Day	Time	m	Time	m	Time	m	Time	m
1	M	0301	1.7	0915	4.3	1521	2.0	2140	4.5
2	TU	0348	1.9	1009	4.2	1613	2.1	2235	4.4
3	W	0441	2.0	1115	4.1	1713	2.2	2337	4.3
4	TH	0542	2.1	1224	4.2	1816	2.2		
5	F	0042	4.3	0644	2.1	1326	4.3	1916	2.1
6	SA	0143	4.4	0742	2.0	1418	4.5	2010	1.9
7	SU	0237	4.5	0833	1.8	1504	4.7	2059	1.7
8	M	0325	4.7	0920	1.6	1546	4.8	2146	1.6
9	TU	0411	4.9	1005	1.5	1628	5.0	2232	1.4
10	W	0455	5.0	1049	1.3	1709	5.2	● 2317	1.2
11	TH	0539	5.1	1133	1.2	1752	5.3		
12	F	0006	1.1	0623	5.1	1217	1.2	1837	5.3
13	SA	0050	1.1	0709	5.1	1302	1.2	1923	5.3
14	SU	0135	1.1	0756	5.1	1347	1.2	2012	5.2
15	M	0221	1.2	0845	4.9	1435	1.3	2103	5.1
16	TU	0310	1.3	0939	4.8	1526	1.5	2200	4.9
17	W	0404	1.4	1040	4.6	1624	1.6	2305	4.8
18	TH	0505	1.6	1149	4.6	1729	1.7		
19	F	0018	4.6	0613	1.7	1259	4.6	1840	1.7
20	SA	0131	4.6	0723	1.7	1405	4.7	1950	1.7
21	SU	0239	4.7	0828	1.6	1503	4.8	2054	1.5
22	M	0337	4.8	0924	1.5	1554	5.0	2150	1.4
23	TU	0427	4.9	1014	1.4	1639	5.1	2239	1.3
24	W	0510	4.9	1059	1.3	1720	5.2	○ 2323	1.2
25	TH	0548	4.9	1140	1.3	1758	5.2		
26	F	0001	1.2	0622	4.9	1218	1.3	1833	5.2
27	SA	0041	1.3	0654	4.9	1253	1.4	1907	5.1
28	SU	0115	1.3	0724	4.8	1327	1.5	1940	5.0
29	M	0149	1.4	0755	4.6	1402	1.6	2015	4.8
30	TU	0224	1.6	0829	4.5	1439	1.7	2053	4.6
31	W	0300	1.7	0910	4.3	1520	1.9	2138	4.4

AUGUST

Date	Day	Time	m	Time	m	Time	m	Time	m
1	TH	0342	1.9	1001	4.2	1609	2.1	2233	4.2
2	F	0434	2.1	1109	4.1	1712	2.2	2340	4.1
3	SA	0541	2.2	1228	4.1	1824	2.2		
4	SU	0056	4.2	0654	2.2	1338	4.3	1931	2.1
5	M	0205	4.3	0758	2.0	1435	4.5	2031	1.9
6	TU	0303	4.6	0854	1.8	1525	4.8	2124	1.6
7	W	0354	4.8	0945	1.5	1611	5.1	2215	1.3
8	TH	0441	5.0	1034	1.3	1655	5.3	● 2303	1.1
9	F	0526	5.2	1120	1.1	1740	5.5	2349	0.9
10	SA	0610	5.3	1205	1.0	1824	5.6		
11	SU	0037	0.8	0654	5.4	1249	0.9	1909	5.6
12	M	0121	0.8	0738	5.3	1333	1.0	1955	5.4
13	TU	0204	1.0	0823	5.1	1417	1.1	2043	5.2
14	W	0248	1.2	0911	4.9	1504	1.3	2136	4.9
15	TH	0337	1.4	1007	4.6	1558	1.6	2240	4.6
16	F	0435	1.7	1119	4.5	1703	1.8	2357	4.4
17	SA	0545	2.0	1241	4.4	1821	1.9		
18	SU	0124	4.4	0705	2.0	1356	4.5	1941	1.9
19	M	0237	4.5	0818	1.9	1458	4.7	2048	1.7
20	TU	0335	4.6	0916	1.7	1548	4.9	2142	1.5
21	W	0420	4.8	1004	1.5	1629	5.1	2227	1.4
22	TH	0456	4.9	1046	1.4	1704	5.2	○ 2307	1.3
23	F	0528	5.0	1123	1.3	1736	5.2	2343	1.2
24	SA	0557	5.0	1157	1.3	1807	5.2		
25	SU	0016	1.2	0624	4.9	1229	1.3	1836	5.2
26	M	0047	1.3	0650	4.9	1259	1.4	1905	5.1
27	TU	0116	1.4	0717	4.8	1328	1.5	1935	4.9
28	W	0145	1.5	0745	4.7	1359	1.6	2007	4.7
29	TH	0216	1.6	0818	4.5	1433	1.8	2045	4.5
30	F	0251	1.9	0859	4.3	1513	2.0	2134	4.2
31	SA	0335	2.1	0959	4.1	1608	2.2	2245	4.1

Chart Datum: 2·83 metres below IGN Datum

18

TIME ZONE -0100
(French Standard Time)
Subtract 1 hour for UT
For French Summer Time add ONE hour in **non-shaded areas**

FRANCE – POINTE DE GRAVE

LAT 45°34′N LONG 1°04′W

TIMES AND HEIGHTS OF HIGH AND LOW WATERS

SPRING & NEAP TIDES
Dates in red are SPRINGS
Dates in blue are NEAPS

YEAR **2002**

SEPTEMBER

Date	Time	m	Date	Time	m
1 SU	0438	2.3	16 M	0120	4.2
	1129	4.0		0651	2.3
	1729	2.4		1347	4.5
				1933	2.1
2 M	0018	4.0	17 TU	0232	4.4
	0606	2.3		0806	2.1
	1301	4.2		1449	4.7
	1857	2.2		2038	1.8
3 TU	0140	4.2	18 W	0324	4.6
	0726	2.2		0901	1.8
	1410	4.5		1534	4.9
	2007	2.0		2126	1.6
4 W	0243	4.6	19 TH	0403	4.8
	0831	1.9		0946	1.6
	1504	4.8		1610	5.1
	2105	1.6		2207	1.4
5 TH	0336	4.9	20 F	0433	4.9
	0925	1.5		1025	1.4
	1552	5.2		1640	5.2
	2157	1.3		2243	1.3
6 F	0423	5.2	21 SA	0500	5.0
	1015	1.2		1059	1.3
	1637	5.5		1709	5.3
	2244	1.0		○ 2316	1.3
7 SA	0507	5.4	22 SU	0526	5.1
	1102	1.0		1131	1.3
	1721	5.7		1736	5.3
	● 2330	0.8		2346	1.3
8 SU	0549	5.6	23 M	0551	5.1
	1147	0.8		1200	1.3
	1805	5.8		1804	5.3
9 M	0017	0.7	24 TU	0014	1.3
	0632	5.6		0616	5.0
	1230	0.7		1229	1.3
	1849	5.8		1831	5.2
10 TU	0059	0.7	25 W	0042	1.4
	0714	5.5		0641	4.9
	1312	0.8		1256	1.4
	1933	5.6		1859	5.0
11 W	0140	0.9	26 TH	0109	1.5
	0756	5.3		0708	4.8
	1355	1.0		1325	1.6
	2020	5.3		1929	4.8
12 TH	0223	1.2	27 F	0139	1.6
	0841	5.0		0738	4.7
	1440	1.3		1356	1.7
	2111	4.9		2003	4.6
13 F	0309	1.6	28 SA	0213	1.8
	0936	4.7		0815	4.5
	1533	1.7		1435	2.0
	2217	4.5		2050	4.3
14 SA	0406	2.0	29 SU	0256	2.1
	1053	4.4		0911	4.2
	1639	2.0		1525	2.2
	2347	4.3		2206	4.1
15 SU	0521	2.2	30 M	0355	2.3
	1227	4.3		1044	4.1
	1806	2.2		1643	2.4
				2348	4.1

OCTOBER

Date	Time	m	Date	Time	m
1 TU	0526	2.4	16 W	0210	4.4
	1227	4.2		0741	2.2
	1826	2.3		1423	4.7
				2013	2.0
2 W	0118	4.3	17 TH	0258	4.6
	0656	2.3		0835	1.9
	1343	4.6		1507	4.9
	1943	2.0		2059	1.7
3 TH	0221	4.7	18 F	0333	4.8
	0804	1.9		0918	1.7
	1440	5.0		1541	5.1
	2042	1.6		2137	1.5
4 F	0312	5.0	19 SA	0401	5.0
	0901	1.5		0956	1.6
	1530	5.3		1610	5.2
	2133	1.2		2212	1.4
5 SA	0358	5.4	20 SU	0427	5.1
	0951	1.2		1030	1.4
	1615	5.7		1638	5.3
	2220	0.9		2244	1.4
6 SU	0442	5.6	21 M	0454	5.1
	1038	0.9		1101	1.4
	1659	5.9		1707	5.3
	● 2305	0.7		○ 2313	1.3
7 M	0524	5.7	22 TU	0520	5.2
	1124	0.7		1131	1.4
	1743	5.9		1735	5.3
	2348	0.7		2342	1.4
8 TU	0606	5.7	23 W	0546	5.1
	1207	0.7		1200	1.4
	1826	5.8		1803	5.2
9 W	0034	0.8	24 TH	0011	1.4
	0648	5.6		0613	5.1
	1250	0.8		1229	1.5
	1911	5.6		1832	5.0
10 TH	0115	1.0	25 F	0040	1.5
	0730	5.3		0642	5.0
	1333	1.1		1259	1.6
	1957	5.2		1903	4.9
11 F	0157	1.4	26 SA	0112	1.7
	0815	5.0		0714	4.8
	1418	1.4		1333	1.7
	2049	4.8		1940	4.6
12 SA	0243	1.8	27 SU	0148	1.9
	0910	4.7		0754	4.6
	1510	1.8		1412	1.9
	2158	4.4		2031	4.4
13 SU	0340	2.1	28 M	0233	2.1
	1029	4.4		0853	4.4
	1616	2.1		1504	2.2
	2333	4.2		2149	4.2
14 M	0456	2.4	29 TU	0334	2.3
	1205	4.4		1019	4.3
	1744	2.3		1619	2.3
				2326	4.2
15 TU	0104	4.2	30 W	0459	2.4
	0627	2.4		1155	4.4
	1324	4.5		1755	2.2
	1911	2.2			
			31 TH	0051	4.5
				0624	2.2
				1312	4.7
				1912	1.9

NOVEMBER

Date	Time	m	Date	Time	m
1 F	0153	4.8	16 SA	0253	4.7
	0733	1.9		0841	1.9
	1412	5.1		1503	4.9
	2013	1.6		2100	1.7
2 SA	0245	5.1	17 SU	0325	4.9
	0831	1.5		0920	1.7
	1504	5.4		1537	5.1
	2105	1.2		2136	1.6
3 SU	0332	5.4	18 M	0355	5.0
	0924	1.2		0956	1.6
	1552	5.7		1609	5.2
	2153	1.0		2210	1.5
4 M	0416	5.6	19 TU	0424	5.1
	1013	1.0		1030	1.5
	1637	5.8		1640	5.2
	● 2239	0.8		2242	1.5
5 TU	0459	5.7	20 W	0453	5.2
	1100	0.8		1104	1.5
	1722	5.8		1712	5.2
	2323	0.8		○ 2314	1.5
6 W	0542	5.7	21 TH	0524	5.2
	1146	0.8		1136	1.4
	1807	5.7		1744	5.2
				2346	1.5
7 TH	0003	1.0	22 F	0555	5.2
	0625	5.6		1210	1.5
	1230	0.9		1817	5.0
	1852	5.5			
8 F	0051	1.2	23 SA	0020	1.6
	0710	5.4		0628	5.1
	1313	1.2		1244	1.5
	1939	5.1		1853	4.9
9 SA	0134	1.5	24 SU	0056	1.7
	0756	5.1		0706	5.0
	1359	1.5		1321	1.7
	2030	4.8		1936	4.7
10 SU	0220	1.9	25 M	0136	1.8
	0849	4.8		0751	4.8
	1449	1.8		1404	1.8
	2134	4.4		2030	4.5
11 M	0315	2.2	26 TU	0223	2.0
	0957	4.6		0849	4.7
	1550	2.1		1457	2.0
	2258	4.2		2139	4.4
12 TU	0424	2.4	27 W	0323	2.1
	1120	4.5		1002	4.6
	1706	2.3		1605	2.1
				2300	4.4
13 W	0022	4.2	28 TH	0436	2.2
	0544	2.4		1123	4.6
	1237	4.5		1723	2.0
	1826	2.3			
14 TH	0127	4.4	29 F	0018	4.6
	0658	2.3		0551	2.1
	1338	4.6		1238	4.8
	1930	2.1		1836	1.9
15 F	0216	4.6	30 SA	0121	4.8
	0755	2.1		0659	1.8
	1426	4.8		1342	5.1
	2019	1.9		1940	1.6

DECEMBER

Date	Time	m	Date	Time	m
1 SU	0216	5.1	16 M	0247	4.7
	0801	1.6		0840	2.0
	1439	5.3		1503	4.8
	2036	1.4		2059	1.8
2 M	0306	5.3	17 TU	0324	4.9
	0858	1.3		0922	1.8
	1531	5.5		1542	4.9
	2127	1.2		2138	1.7
3 TU	0353	5.5	18 W	0359	5.0
	0951	1.1		1002	1.7
	1620	5.6		1619	5.0
	2215	1.1		2215	1.6
4 W	0439	5.6	19 TH	0433	5.1
	1041	1.0		1040	1.5
	1707	5.6		1655	5.1
	● 2302	1.1		○ 2252	1.5
5 TH	0524	5.6	20 F	0508	5.2
	1128	1.0		1119	1.5
	1753	5.5		1732	5.1
	2347	1.2		2329	1.5
6 F	0610	5.6	21 SA	0544	5.2
	1214	1.1		1157	1.4
	1839	5.3		1810	5.1
7 SA	0033	1.3	22 SU	0009	1.5
	0655	5.4		0623	5.2
	1258	1.2		1237	1.4
	1924	5.1		1851	5.0
8 SU	0116	1.5	23 M	0049	1.5
	0740	5.2		0704	5.2
	1343	1.5		1318	1.5
	2010	4.8		1935	4.9
9 M	0201	1.8	24 TU	0131	1.6
	0826	5.0		0750	5.1
	1429	1.7		1402	1.6
	2059	4.5		2025	4.8
10 TU	0250	2.0	25 W	0218	1.7
	0917	4.8		0842	5.0
	1519	2.0		1451	1.7
	2158	4.3		2122	4.7
11 W	0346	2.2	26 TH	0311	1.8
	1017	4.6		0942	4.9
	1617	2.2		1547	1.8
	2309	4.2		2227	4.6
12 TH	0449	2.3	27 F	0412	1.9
	1125	4.5		1050	4.8
	1723	2.3		1651	1.8
				2338	4.6
13 F	0019	4.3	28 SA	0518	1.9
	0557	2.4		1204	4.8
	1232	4.5		1759	1.8
	1829	2.2			
14 SA	0118	4.4	29 SU	0048	4.7
	0700	2.3		0627	1.8
	1331	4.6		1314	4.9
	1928	2.1		1907	1.7
15 SU	0206	4.5	30 M	0150	4.9
	0754	2.1		0734	1.7
	1420	4.7		1419	5.0
	2017	2.0		2010	1.6
			31 TU	0247	5.1
				0838	1.5
				1517	5.2
				2107	1.5

Chart Datum: 2·83 metres below IGN Datum

ARCACHON *9.18.23*

Gironde **44°39´·83N 01°09´·04W** ☸⚓⚓⚓✿✿✿

TIDES +0620 Dover; ML 2·5; Zone –0100
Standard Port POINTE DE GRAVE (⟵)

Times				Height (metres)			
High Water		Low Water		MHWS	MHWN	MLWN	MLWS
0000	0600	0500	1200	5·4	4·4	2·1	1·0
1200	1800	1700	2400				
Differences ARCACHON							
+0010	+0025	0000	+0020	–1·1	–1·0	–0·8	–0·6
CAP FERRET							
–0015	+0005	–0005	+0015	–1·4	–1·2	–0·8	–0·5

CHARTS AC 2750, 2664; Imray C42; SHOM 6766, 7070; ECM 255, 1024

SHELTER Good in marina (max LOA 15m), but it is impossible to ent Bassin d'Arcachon in strong SW-N winds or at night. Visitors' berths in the marina are very scarce in season. If marina full, there is a good ⚓ N of it, except in strong N'lies. Around the Bassin are many small drying hbrs worth exploring by shoal draft boats: On the W, La Vigne*, Le Canon, Piquey and Claouey; on the NE, Port de Lège, Arès, Andernos*, Fontainevieille*, Lanton (Cassy) and Audenge*; and on the S, La Teste and Gujan. *see over for notes.

NAVIGATION WPT 44°34´·66N 01°18´·66W, ATT ARC (SWM) buoy, 260°/080° from/to N Passe first chan buoys, 0·78M. Only appr is the well buoyed, unlit N Passe which runs E, NE then

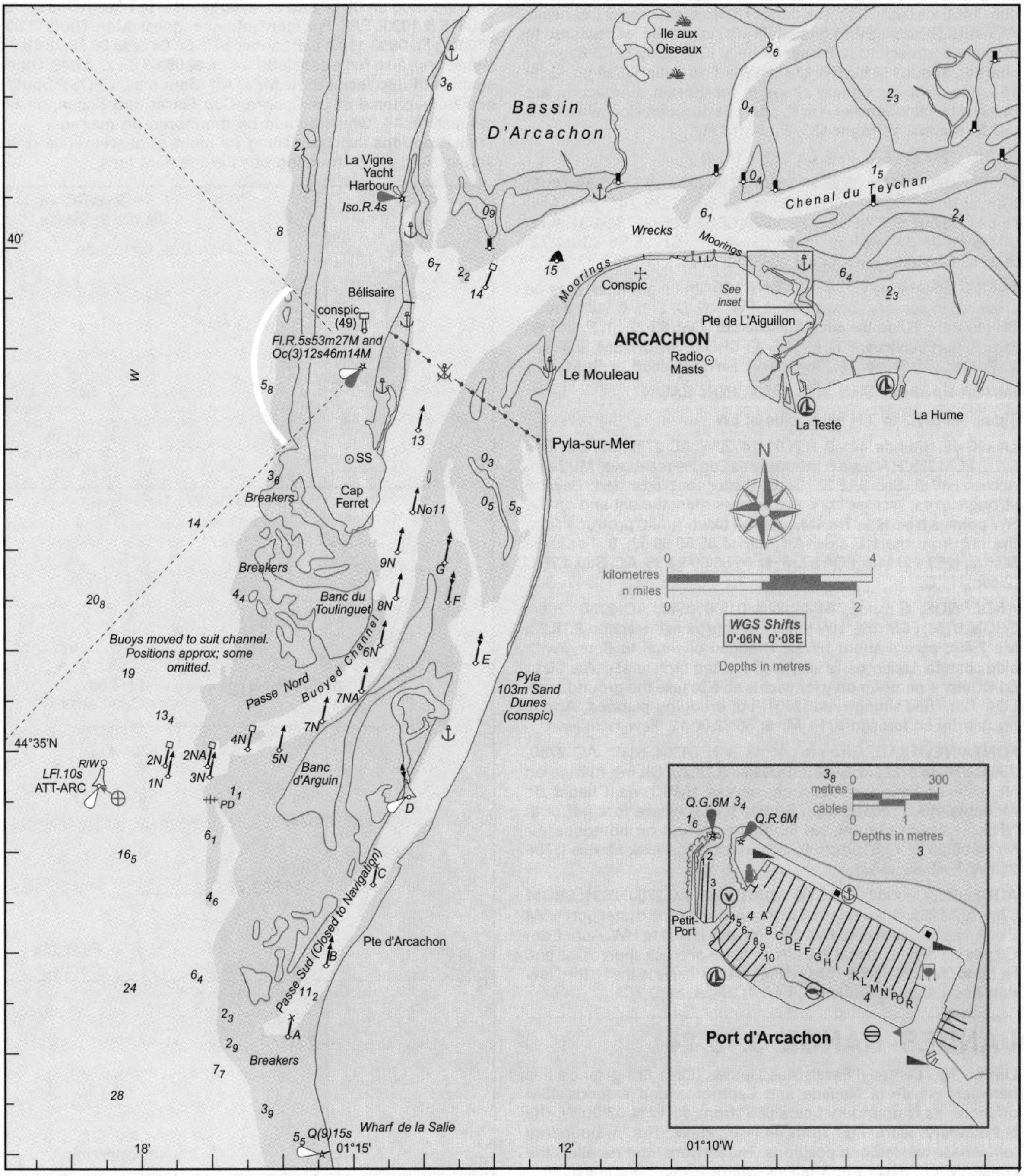

N between Banc d'Arguin and Banc du Toulinguet towards Cap Ferret where it meets the longer S Passe. The latter, although used by a few local FVs, is closed to navigation. Between Cap Ferret and Wharf de la Salie the sea breaks in any wind on the shifting sand banks; the chan can be seen between the breakers. Buoys are moved frequently, or may be missing.
Best time to start appr is HW–1 and no later than HW+1. Due to the ebb (6kn sp) the chan bar (mean depth 4·5m) is impassable from HW+1 until LW, and it is best to wait until LW+3. When swell is higher than 1m, bar may be dangerous. Best to leave on the last of the flood. For navigation update call *Cap Ferret Semaphore* Ch 16 10 (HJ); or Service de la Marine Gironde ☎ 05·56·82·32·97. Beware firing ranges between Arcachon and Capbreton, out to 45M offshore; see 9.18.25, next page.

LIGHTS AND MARKS Cap Ferret Fl R 5s 53m 27M and Oc (3) 12s 46m 14M, vis 045°-135°. The dunes (103m high) are very conspic. ATT-ARC (landfall/SWM buoy, L Fl 10s) is moved as required to indicate approach to N Passe. La Salie IDM buoy Fl (2) 6s is off chartlet, about 1·5M WSW of the Wharf de Salie WCM bn, Q (9) 15s 19m 10M. Secondary chans in the Bassin d'Arcachon are marked by piles lettered A to K, plus pile number, clockwise from the N. **Marina**: W bkwtr QG, E bkwtr QR.

RADIO TELEPHONE VHF Ch 09 16 (H24).

TELEPHONE Hr Mr 05·56·22·36·75 0730-2030, 📠 05.56.83.26.19; Semaphore 05·56·60·60·03 ⊖ 05·56·72·29·24; Aff Mar 05·57·52·57·07; SNSM 05·56·22·36·75; CROSS 05·56·73·31·31; Auto 08·36·68·08·33; Police 05·56·83·04·63; Dr 05·56·83·04·72; Ⓗ 05·56·83·39·50; Brit Consul 05·56·52·28·35.

FACILITIES Marina (2245+200 Ⓥ), €2·90 (2nd night free), may be crowded in season, access HW±3, FW, AC, D, Slip, C (10/20 ton), BH (45 ton); **YC du Bassin d'Arcachon** ☎ 05·56·83·22·11, P, D, FW, Slip, R, Bar; **Services:** P, D, ME, El, Ⓔ, SHOM, Sh, CH, SM, ⓢ. **Town** V, R, Gaz, ✉, Ⓑ, ≷, ✈ (Bordeaux). Ferry: Roscoff or St Malo.

MINOR HARBOURS IN THE ARCACHON BASIN

Tides. All dry 2 to 3 H either side of LW.

LA VIGNE, Gironde, 44°40′·50N 01°14′·20W. AC 2750, 2664; SHOM 6766; ECM 255. HW time & ht approx as Cap Ferret above; ML 2·4m. Access HW±2. See 9.18.23. Good shelter, but crowded; beware strong currents across hbr ent. 2 perches mark the ent and on the SW point, a lt Iso R 4s 7m 4M. A small bkwtr (unlit) protrudes into the ent from the NE side. Aff Mar ☎ 05.56·60·52·76. Facilities: **Marina** (268 + 2) Max LOA 8·5m, ☎ 05·56·60·54·36, AC, Slip, CH, C (2 ton), P, D.

ANDERNOS, Gironde, 44°44'·32N 01°06'·05W. AC 2750, 2664; SHOM 6766; ECM 255. HW time & ht approx as Arcachon 9.18.23; ML 2·4m; access about HW±2. Dredged channel to Bétey, with side chan to Andernos, is very well marked by lateral poles D0 to D14. Jetty + pontoon only for yachts able to take the ground, max LOA 12m. Bad silting repd (2001) but dredging planned. Also ⚓ on flat drying foreshore. Hr Mr ☎ 56.82.00.12. Few facilities.

FONTAINEVIEILLE, Gironde, 44°43'·36N 01°04'·51W. AC 2750, 2664; SHOM 6766; ECM 255. Tides as 9.18.23. Drying marina on NE side of Bassin d'Arcachon, access HW±3 via Chenal de Mouchtalette. Proceed from E0 pile to E8, where fork left onto NNE for 7ca to hbr ent. No lts. Boats dry out on pontoons. Hr Mr ☎ 05.56.82.17.31; Auto 05.36.65.08.33. Facilities: **Marina** (178+ 2), FW, Fuel, Slip, ME.

AUDENGE, Gironde, 44°40'·65N01°01'·50W. AC 2750, 2664; SHOM 6766; ECM 255. Tides as 9.18.23. Drying marina and oyster port 5·5M E of Arcachon, access sp HW–2 to HW, nps HW–1 to HW. Appr from G0 pile via drying Chenal d'Audenge to G8 pile, 5ca short of the ent. Hr Mr ☎ 05.56.26.88.97. The Old Port (84 berths) is to the N; the New Port has 130 pontoon berths, FW, AC, Fuel, Slip, YC.

LANDES RANGE *9.18.24*

Limits: The Centre d'Essais des Landes (CEL) firing range lies between Pte de la Negade and Capbreton and extends 45M offshore. Its N boundary bears 065° from 45°12'N 02°00'W; the S boundary bears 115° from 44°N 02°25'W. The W boundary joins these two lat/long positions. The inshore limit parallels the coast 3M off, except in 3 places where it joins the coast:
a. at Sector 31H, off Hourtin, between 45°14'N and 45°09'N;
b. at Sector 31K, between 44°31'N and 44°28'N; and
c. at Sector 31A, between 44°28'N and 44°13'N, which itself extends 12M offshore. (This is the most often used sector).
Sector designations: The range is split into blocks 31N and 31S, to the N and S of a clear corridor (31B) 8M wide bearing 270° from Arcachon. 31N and 31S are sub-divided into N/S sectors delineated by distance off the coast. Thus, 31S 27.45 means the S block, in a sector 27-45M offshore.
Range activity: Various sectors are active from 0830-1800 LT Mon-Fri; but never on Sun, rarely on a Sat. The range is not active in August. Navigation through active sectors is prohib from the coast to the 12M territorial limit; beyond 12M it is strongly discouraged.
Information: Landes broadcasts range activity on VHF Ch 06, after warning on Ch 06 and 16, at 0815 & 1615LT Mon-Thurs, and at 0815 & 1030LT Fri. For more info on request (Mon-Thurs 0800-1700LT; Fri 0800-1100) call Landes VHF Ch 06 or ☎ 05.58.78.18.00 (same hrs); also recorded data H24 on ☎ 05.58.82.22.42/43. Other sources of info include: Hr Mr's, Aff Maritimes, CROSS Soulac and Sémaphores at La Coubre, Cap Ferret and Socoa; all on request Ch 16, which should be monitored on passage.
Transit options include: sailing by night or at weekends or in July or August; or routeing outside the 45M limit.

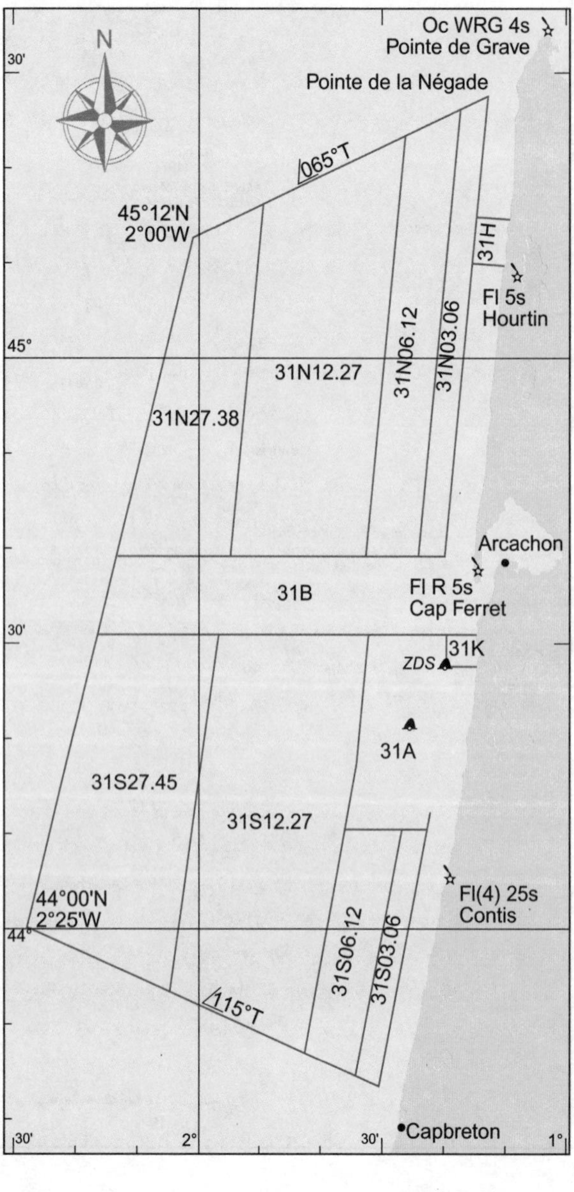

CAPBRETON *9.18.25*

Landes **43°39'·42N 01°26'·82W**

CHARTS AC 1102; SHOM 6586, 6557, 6786; ECM 555, 1024

TIDES +0450 Dover; ML 2·3; Zone –0100

Standard Port POINTE DE GRAVE (⟵)

Times				Height (metres)			
High Water		Low Water		MHWS	MHWN	MLWN	MLWS
0000	0600	0500	1200	5·4	4·4	2·1	1·0
1200	1800	1700	2400				
Differences CAPBRETON							
–0030	–0035	–0025	–0040	–1·2	–1·1	–0·4	–0·3

SHELTER Good. Appr advised HW–3 to +1; not before LW+2½. Narrow canalised ent dangerous in strong winds from W to N. Keep S of mid channel. Do not enter if swell or seas break in mid-chan; they often break on either side. Hbr and chan dredged 1·5m. Visitors' pontoon 'B' (first to stbd of marina ent). There are 3 basins.

NAVIGATION WPT 43°39'·69N 01°27'·41W, 303°/123° from/to N pier lt, ½M. Bkwtr lts in line 123° lead to hbr ent. Depths shoal rapidly in last 3ca from 50m to 3m; see 9.18.5 for Gouf de Capbreton. No ⚓ off ent. Inside Canal de Boucarot best water is close to N bkwtr initially; from abeam small statue of Virgin Mary, move to mid-chan or just S of mid-chan. Marina ent is via obvious gap in training wall on SE side of chan, abeam conspic Capitainerie.

LIGHTS AND MARKS N pier hd, Fl (2) R 6s 13m 12M, Horn 30s. S bkwtr hd, Fl (2) G 6s 7m 12M; the former lt, now disused, is close E. (Silting occurs around head of S bkwtr). Fl R 4s and Fl G 4s lts at marina ent. Casino is conspic S of ent.

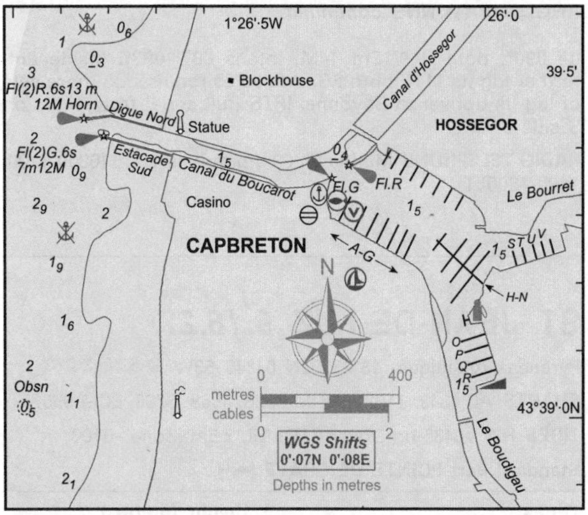

RADIO TELEPHONE VHF Ch 09 (0800-1900 in season).

TELEPHONE Hr Mr 05·58·72·21·23; Aff Mar 05·58·72·10·43; CROSS 05·56·73·31·31; ⊜ 05·59·46·68·80; SNSM 05·58·72·47·44; Auto 08.36.68.08.40; ⊞ (Bayonne) 05·59·44·35·35; Police 05·58·72·01·18; Brit Consul 05·56·52·28·35.

FACILITIES Marina (950+60 Ⓥ), ☎ 05·58·72·21·23, 📠 05·58.72.40.35, €2·15, Slip, BH (30 ton), AC, P & D (0830-1200, 1400-1800 or ☎ 05.58.72.15.66), FW, ME, El, C (30 ton), Sh, ⓪; **CN Capbreton-Hossegor-Seignosse** ☎ 05·58·72·03·39; **Services:** Sh, CH, SM, Ⓔ; ⇌ Bayonne (17km); ✈ Biarritz (25km).

18

ANGLET *9.18.26*

Pyrénées Atlantique **43°31´·95N 01°31´·92W**

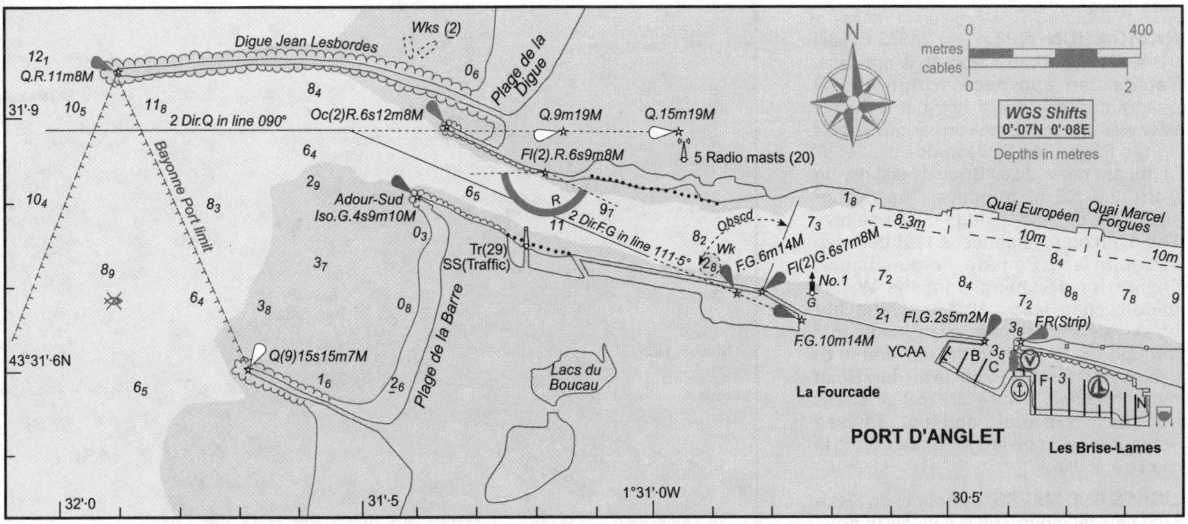

CHARTS AC 1343, 1102; SHOM 6536, 6557, 6786; ECM 555

TIDES +0450 Dover (UT); ML 2·5; Zone –0100

Standard Port POINTE DE GRAVE (⟵)

Times				Height (metres)			
High Water		Low Water		MHWS	MHWN	MLWN	MLWS
0000	0600	0500	1200	5·4	4·4	2·1	1·0
1200	1800	1700	2400				
Differences L'ADOUR (BOUCAU)							
–0030	–0035	–0025	–0040	–1·2	–1·1	–0·4	–0·3

SHELTER Very good in Anglet marina, 0·70M from ent, on S bank of R Adour. But cement dust from N bank can be a problem. Possible berths at Bayonne, 3M up river, on S bank below bridge (5·2m clearance). River is well marked, but ⚓ prohib due to commercial tfc.

NAVIGATION WPT 43°32´·66N 01°32´·68W, BA SWM buoy, 322°/142° from/to N bkwtr lt, 0·9M. Access good except in strong W winds. Strong tidal stream, max 5kn at sp ebb.

LIGHTS AND MARKS BA HFP buoy, L Fl 10s (WPT), is NW of ent. Pte St Martin Fl (2) 10s 73m 29M is 2·45M SSW of hbr. Ldg

ANGLET/BAYONNE *continued*

lts 090°, both Q 9/15m 14M, intens 087°-093°. Inside ent, further ldg lts 111°, both FG, moved as required. 3 more sets of ldg lts upriver to Bayonne. IPTS (full code) from sig tr on S side of ent.

RADIO TELEPHONE Marina Ch 09. Port/pilots 12 16 (0800-1200; 1400-1800LT).

TELEPHONE Marina 05·59·63·05·45; Hr Mr Bayonne 05·59·63·11·57; CROSS 05·56·09·82·00; ⊖ 05·59·59·08·29; Aff Mar 05·59·55·06·68; SNSM 05·59·83·40·50; Ⓗ 05·59·44·35·35; Météo 05·59·23·84·15; Auto 08·36·65·08·64.

FACILITIES **Marina** (425+50 ♥), ☎ 05·59·63·05·45; €1·78, P, D, FW, ME, El, AC, C (1·3 ton), ⊡, BH (13 ton), Slip, Sh; (New marina planned to W of existing marina). **YC Adour Atlantique** ☎ 05·59·63·16·22; **Port** C (30 ton), Slip, FW, P, D; **Services:** CH, Ⓔ, SHOM. **Town** ⇌, ✈ (Biarritz). Ferry: Bilboa-Portsmouth.

ST JEAN-DE-LUZ *9.18.27*

Pyrénées Atlantique, 43°23'·92N 01°40'·53W ✿✿✿✿✿✿

CHARTS AC 1343, 1102; SHOM 6526, 6558, 6786; ECM 555

TIDES HW +0435 on Dover (UT); ML 2·5m; Zone –0100

Standard Port POINTE DE GRAVE (⟵)

Times				Height (metres)			
High Water		Low Water		MHWS	MHWN	MLWN	MLWS
0000	0600	0500	1200	5·4	4·4	2·1	1·0
1200	1800	1700	2400				
Differences ST JEAN DE LUZ (SOCOA)							
–0040	–0045	–0030	–0045	–1·1	–1·1	–0·6	–0·4

SHELTER Except in strong NW winds, the bay can be entered at all times and good ⚓s found in approx 4m on the W and SE sides. Beware antipollution booms off the beaches and a submerged jetty in SE corner of bay. There are 2 hbrs:

St Jean-de-Luz in S of bay with a very small marina (2·5m) at Ciboure, close to rear QG ldg lt. Sailing in the port is prohib. Unmasted craft may ⚓ in La Nivelle River via fixed bridge 1·9m clearance.

Socoa hbr (dries about 0·5m) on the NW side of the bay, close S of conspic fort. Tide gauge at ent.

NAVIGATION WPT 43°24'·16N 01°40'·71W, 331°/151° from/to W ent, 2½ca. Yachts can approach within the N quadrant direct to hbr ent, but in heavy W'ly weather seas break on various shoals on the Plateau de St Jean-de-Luz. 3M W of hbr ent beware Les Briquets rks, drying 0·4m, 2M NE of Hendaye. The 3 appr chans are defined by ldg lts (see below): The main outer chan leads 138° between Illarguita and Belhara Perdun banks. Thence, or if coming from the W, the middle chan leads 101° past the hbr breakwaters. The inner chan leads 151° through the W ent into the bay and to St Jean de Luz hbr. The E ent to the bay is not recommended. There are other chans but these are unlit and not advised without local knowledge. Speed limit in the bay is 7kn.

LIGHTS AND MARKS La Rhune, an 898m high conical mountain, is conspic in good vis 5·5M SSE of hbr. Digue d'Artha is a detached unlit bkwtr across the middle of the bay.

Outer 138° ldg lts:

Front, Socoa lt, QWR 36m 12/8M, W □ tr, B stripe, vis W shore-264°, R264°-282°, W282°-shore; R sector covers Socoa hbr ent. Rear Q 67m 20M, hard to see by day, but nearby Bordagain tr, 100m, is more conspic.

Ste Barbe ldg lts 101°:

Both Oc (4) R 12s 30/47m 18M; front, W bldg with △ gable; rear B ▲ on W tr.

Inner 151° ldg lts:

Both Dir QG 18/27m 16M intens 149·5°-152°; front, W tr, R stripe; rear, W tr, G stripe. Digue des Criquas hd, Iso G 4s 11m 7M.

RADIO TELEPHONE Marina VHF Ch 09 16.

TELEPHONE

ST JEAN-DE-LUZ: Hr Mr 05·59·47·26·81; ⊖ 05·59.47.18.61; Aff Mar 05·59·47·14·55; CROSS 05·56.73.31.31; Météo 05·59·22·03·30; Auto 08.36.68.08.64; SNSM 05·59.47.22.98; Police 05·59.26.01.55;

SOCOA: As for St Jean de Luz.

FACILITIES

ST JEAN-DE-LUZ: €1·86, FW, AC, P, C (6 ton), Slip; **Services:** Ⓔ, ME, El, Sh, CH.

SOCOA **Jetty** C (1 ton), FW, P, D, AC, Slip, BY; **YC Basque** ☎ 05·59·47·18·31; **Services:** ME, CH, El, Sh. **Town** V, R, Bar, ⊡, ✉, Ⓑ, ⇌.

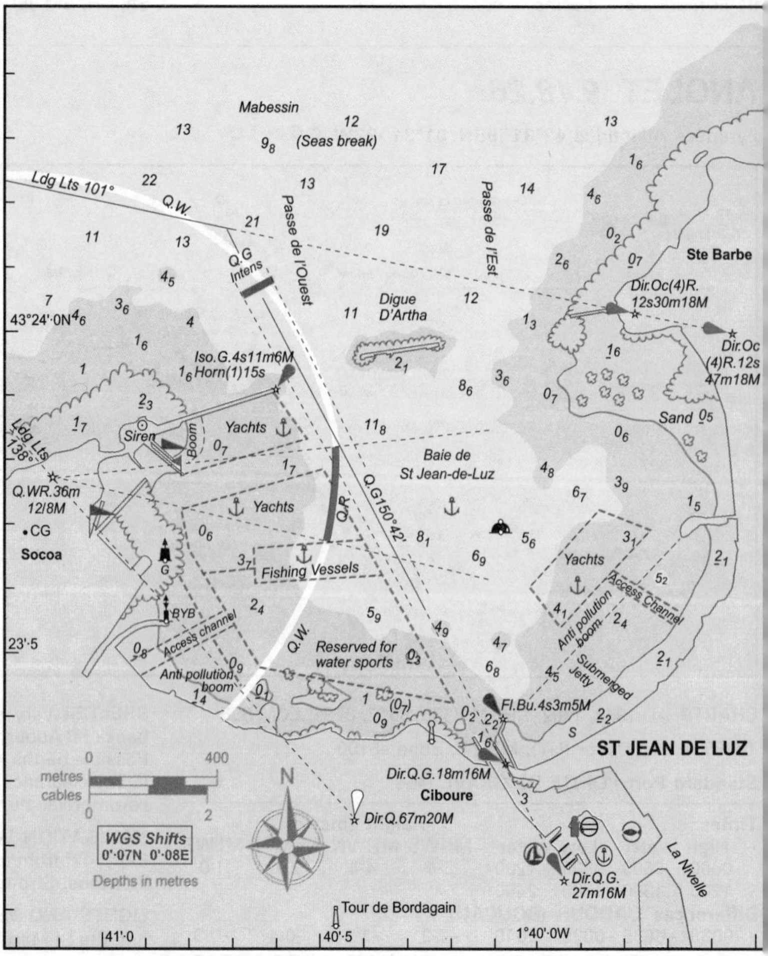

HENDAYE & HONDARRIBIA *9.18.28*

Pyrénées Atlantique **43°22'·91N 01°47'·25W** ❁❁❁◊◊◊✿✿✿

CHARTS AC 1181, 1102; SHOM 6556, 6558, 6786; ECM 555

TIDES HW +0450 on Dover (UT); ML 2·3m; Zone –0100
Use differences ST JEAN DE LUZ (SOCOA) 9.18.27

SHELTER Excellent in marina (3m); access H24. Or in Port of Refuge (S of C Higuer) in 2-3m. Good ⚓ in river off Fuenterrabia. Moorings in the B de Chingoudy are exposed to N/NE and S/SW gales. NB: Hendaye is on the French bank of the Rio Bidassoa; Fuenterrabia on the Spanish side. A neutral area lies in the Baie de Fontarabie.

NAVIGATION WPT 43°24'·00N 01°46'·50W, 025°/205° from/to W bkwtr hd 1·25M. Beware Les Briquets 8ca N of Pte Ste Anne at E end of the Baie and, near centre of B, keep clear of Bajo Iruarri. River ent is easy except in heavy N'ly swell; sp ebb is very strong. Inshore of Pte des Dunes lt, Fl R 2·5s, hug the E training wall for best water. A spit drying 1·3m (SHM bn, VQ (3) G 5s) off Hondarrabia narrows the chan to about 100m before marina ent opens up.

LIGHTS AND MARKS On W end of bay, Cabo Higuer lt ho, Fl (2) 10s 63m 23M. River ent bkwtrs: East L Fl R 10s 7m 5M; West Fl (3) G 9s 9m 5M. River dredged to 2m. Marina ent between Fl (2) R 6s 6m 2M on elbow of W bkwtr (hd marked by FR strip lt) and Fl Y 4s 5m 3M at E side; near the latter is a conspic RW TV relay mast (40m).

RADIO TELEPHONE Marinas VHF Ch 09 (H24).

TELEPHONE Hr Mr 05·59·48·06·10; Aff Mar 05·59·20·77·67; ⊖ 05·59·20·70·82; CROSS 05·59.09.82.00; SNSM 05·59.20.60.33; Météo 05·59.24.58.80; Auto 08.36.68.08.64; Police 05·59·20.65.52; H 05·59.20.08.22.

FACILITIES **Hendaye Marina** (600 + 120) ☎ 05·59.48.06.10, €2·90, AC, FW, P, D, C (30 ton), Slip; **Hondarrabia Marina** Hr Mr ☎ 34(9) 450·9739, fax 34(9) 450·19·786; AB 650 max LOA 15m, FW, E, BH, C, D. Boats > 17m LOA should moor in Baie de Chingoudy; **Club Maritime Hendayais** ☎ 05·59·20·03·02, Bar; **Services:** CH, Sh, El, Ⓔ, ME. **Town** V, R, Bar, Gaz, ✉, Ⓑ, ⇌, ✈ (Fuenterrabia or Biarritz). Local ferry from marina to Fuenterrabia. UK ferry from Bilbao/Santander.

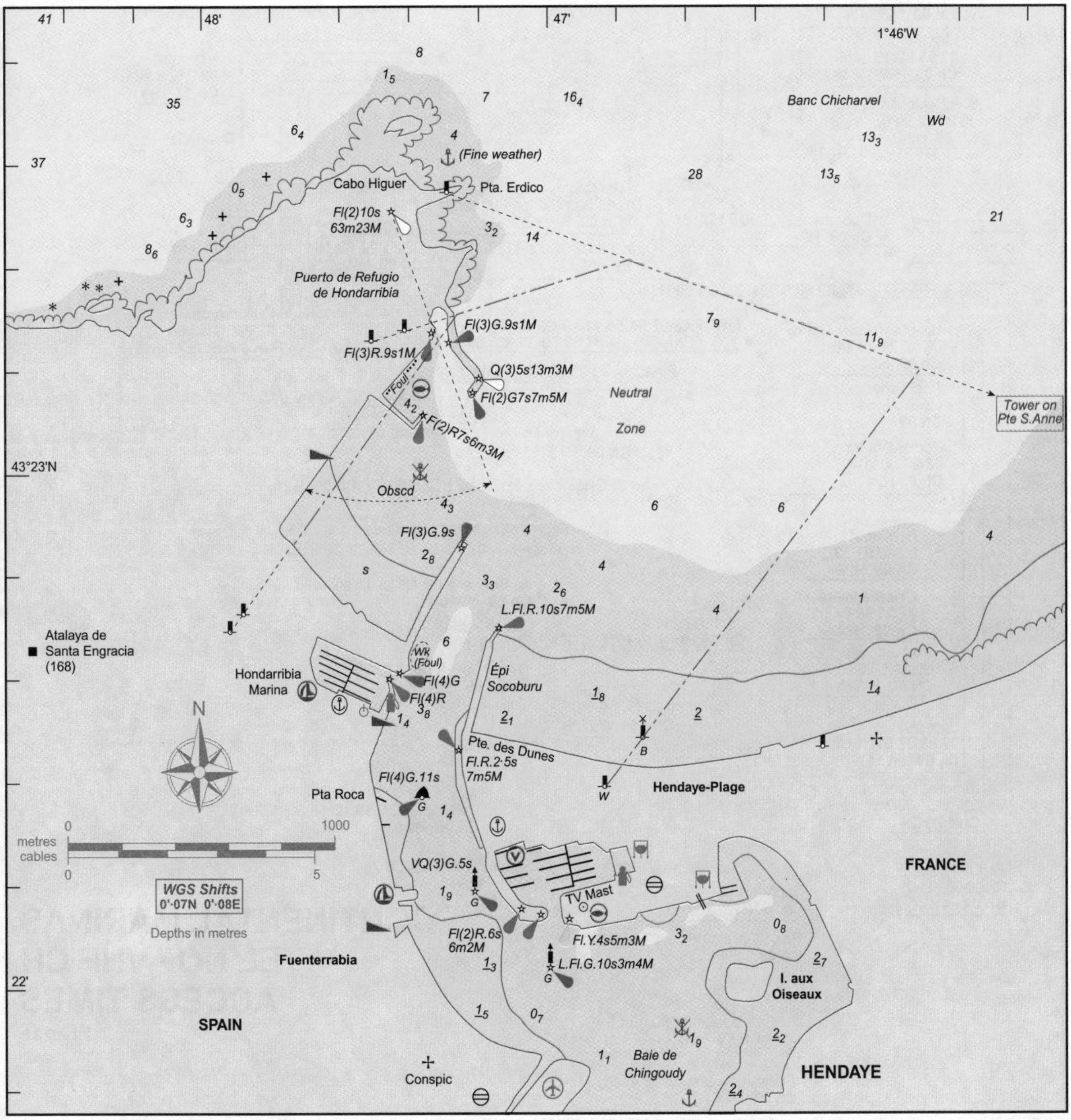

Fig. 9 (9)

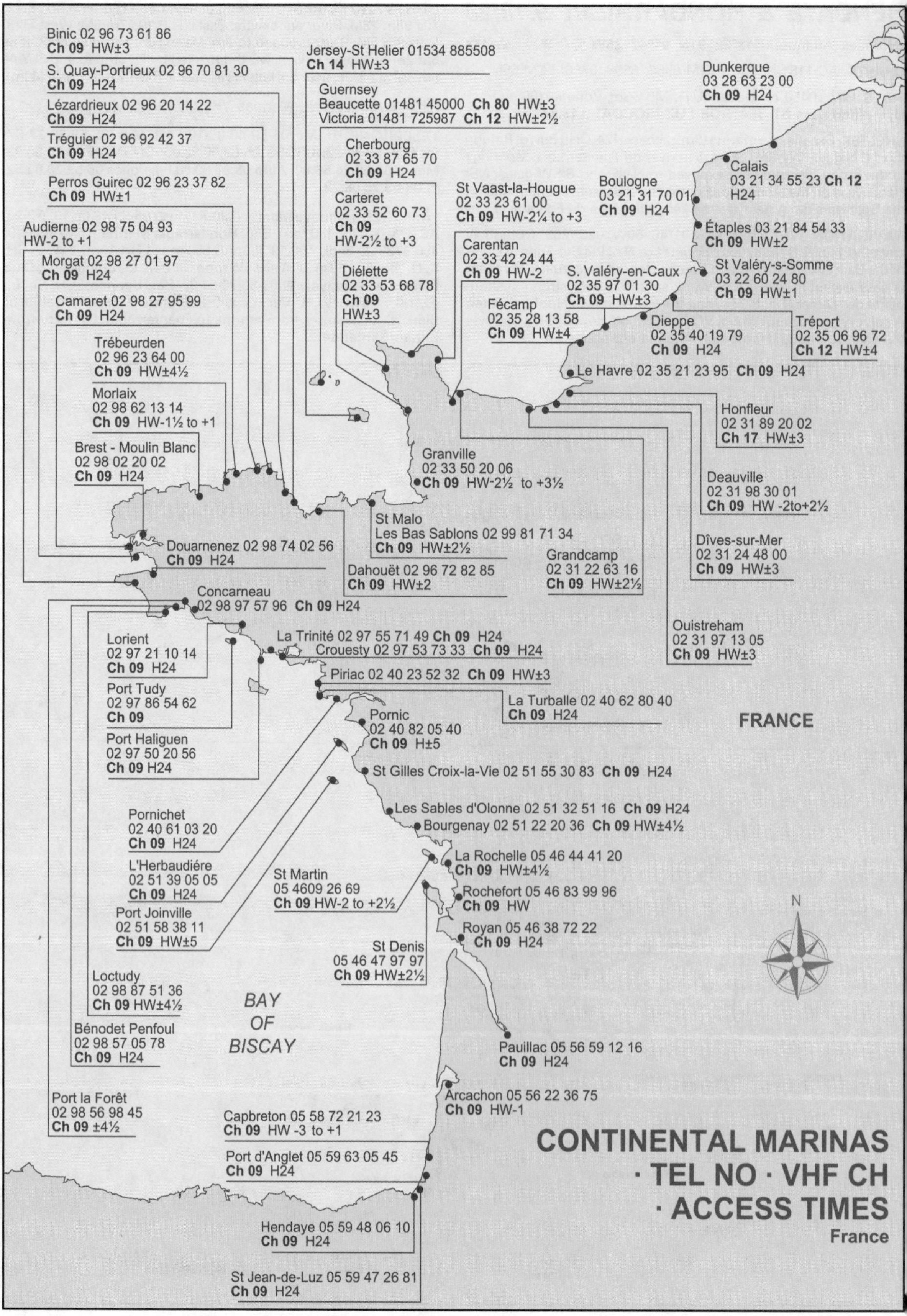
Binic 02 96 73 61 86
Ch 09 HW±3
S. Quay-Portrieux 02 96 70 81 30
Ch 09 H24
Lézardrieux 02 96 20 14 22
Ch 09 H24
Tréguier 02 96 92 42 37
Ch 09 H24
Perros Guirec 02 96 23 37 82
Ch 09 HW±1
Audierne 02 98 75 04 93
HW-2 to +1
Morgat 02 98 27 01 97
Ch 09 H24
Camaret 02 98 27 95 99
Ch 09 H24
Trébeurden
02 96 23 64 00
Ch 09 HW±4½
Morlaix
02 98 62 13 14
Ch 09 HW-1½ to +1
Brest - Moulin Blanc
02 98 02 20 02
Ch 09 H24
Jersey-St Helier 01534 885508
Ch 14 HW±3
Guernsey
Beaucette 01481 45000 Ch 80 HW±3
Victoria 01481 725987 Ch 12 HW±2½
Cherbourg
02 33 87 65 70
Ch 09 H24
Carteret
02 33 52 60 73
Ch 09
HW-2½ to +3
Diélette
02 33 53 68 78
Ch 09
HW±3
St Vaast-la-Hougue
02 33 23 61 00
Ch 09 HW-2¼ to +3
Carentan
02 33 42 24 44
Ch 09 HW-2
Boulogne
03 21 31 70 01
Ch 09 H24
Dunkerque
03 28 63 23 00
Ch 09 H24
Calais
03 21 34 55 23 Ch 12
H24
Étaples 03 21 84 54 33
Ch 09 HW±2
St Valéry-s-Somme
03 22 60 24 80
Ch 09 HW±1
S. Valéry-en-Caux
02 35 97 01 30
Ch 09 HW±3
Fécamp
02 35 28 13 58
Ch 09 HW±4
Dieppe
02 35 40 19 79
Ch 09 H24
Tréport
02 35 06 96 72
Ch 12 HW±4
Le Havre 02 35 21 23 95 Ch 09 H24
Honfleur
02 31 89 20 02
Ch 17 HW±3
Granville
02 33 50 20 06
Ch 09 HW-2½ to +3½
Deauville
02 31 98 30 01
Ch 09 HW -2to+2½
St Malo
Les Bas Sablons 02 99 81 71 34
Ch 09 HW±2½
Dîves-sur-Mer
02 31 24 48 00
Ch 09 HW±3
Douarnenez 02 98 74 02 56
Ch 09 H24
Grandcamp
02 31 22 63 16
Ch 09 HW±2½
Dahouët 02 96 72 82 85
Ch 09 HW±2
Concarneau
02 98 97 57 96 Ch 09 H24
Ouistreham
02 31 97 13 05
Ch 09 HW±3
Lorient
02 97 21 10 14
Ch 09 H24
La Trinité 02 97 55 71 49 Ch 09 H24
Crouesty 02 97 53 73 33 Ch 09 H24
Port Tudy
02 97 86 54 62
Ch 09
Piriac 02 40 23 52 32 Ch 09 HW±3
La Turballe 02 40 62 80 40
Ch 09 H24
Port Haliguen
02 97 50 20 56
Ch 09 H24
Pornic
02 40 82 05 40
Ch 09 H±5
FRANCE
St Gilles Croix-la-Vie 02 51 55 30 83 Ch 09 H24
Les Sables d'Olonne 02 51 32 51 16 Ch 09 H24
Bourgenay 02 51 22 20 36 Ch 09 HW±4½
Pornichet
02 40 61 03 20
Ch 09 H24
La Rochelle 05 46 44 41 20
Ch 09 HW±4½
L'Herbaudiére
02 51 39 05 05
Ch 09 H24
St Martin
05 4609 26 69
Ch 09 HW-2 to +2½
Rochefort 05 46 83 99 96
Ch 09 HW
Port Joinville
02 51 58 38 11
Ch 09 HW±5
Royan 05 46 38 72 22
Ch 09 H24
N
St Denis
05 46 47 97 97
Ch 09 HW±2½
Loctudy
02 98 87 51 36
Ch 09 HW±4½
BAY
OF
BISCAY
Bénodet Penfoul
02 98 57 05 78
Ch 09 H24
Pauillac 05 56 59 12 16
Ch 09 H24
Port la Forêt
02 98 56 98 45
Ch 09 ±4½
Arcachon 05 56 22 36 75
Ch 09 HW-1
Capbreton 05 58 72 21 23
Ch 09 HW -3 to +1
CONTINENTAL MARINAS
· TEL NO · VHF CH
· ACCESS TIMES
France
Port d'Anglet 05 59 63 05 45
Ch 09 H24
Hendaye 05 59 48 06 10
Ch 09 H24
St Jean-de-Luz 05 59 47 26 81
Ch 09 H24

MAPTECH®
Leading the world in digital navigation
Maptech UK Ltd • +44 (0)1243 389352 • sales@maptech.co.uk

Maptech world class digital chart CDs
Worldwide coverage from over 4,500 charts

Maptech award winning software
Easy to use navigation software
• Chart Navigator • Cruising Navigator • Offshore Navigator

www.maptech.co.uk

Area 19

North and Northwest Spain
Pasajes to Bayona

9.19.1 Index ..... **Page 863**
9.19.2 Area map **864**
9.19.3 Lights, buoys & waypoints **866**
9.19.4 Passage information **869**
9.19.5 Special notes for Spain **870**
9.19.6 Distance table (Biscay/N Spain) **870**
9.19.7 Pasajes (Pasaia) **871**
9.19.8 San Sebastián **871**
9.19.9 Guetaria **872**
Zumaya
Motrico
9.19.10 Lequeitio **872**
9.19.11 Elanchove **873**
Bermeo
9.19.12 Bilbao **873**
9.19.13 Castro Urdiales **874**
Ría de Santoña
9.19.14 Santander **875**
San Vicente de la Barquera
9.19.15 Ribadesella **876**
9.19.16 Gijon **876**
Avilés
9.19.17 Cudillero **877**
9.19.18 Luarca **877**
9.19.19 Ría de Ribadeo **878**
9.19.20 Ría de Vivero **878**
9.19.21 Ría de Cedeira **879**
Ría del Barquero
Ensenada de Santa Marta
9.19.22 Ría de El Ferrol **879**
Sada
9.19.23 La Coruña **880**
9.19.24 Ría de Camariñas **880**
9.19.25 Ría de Muros **881**
9.19.26 Ría de Arosa **882**
9.19.27 Ría de Pontevedra **883**
9.19.28 Ría de Vigo **884**
9.19.29 Bayona **885**

19

Register for your **FREE** weekly weather email service from Macmillan Reeds
at **www.nauticaldata.com – NOW!**
weekend weather reports sent to your email address, every Thursday

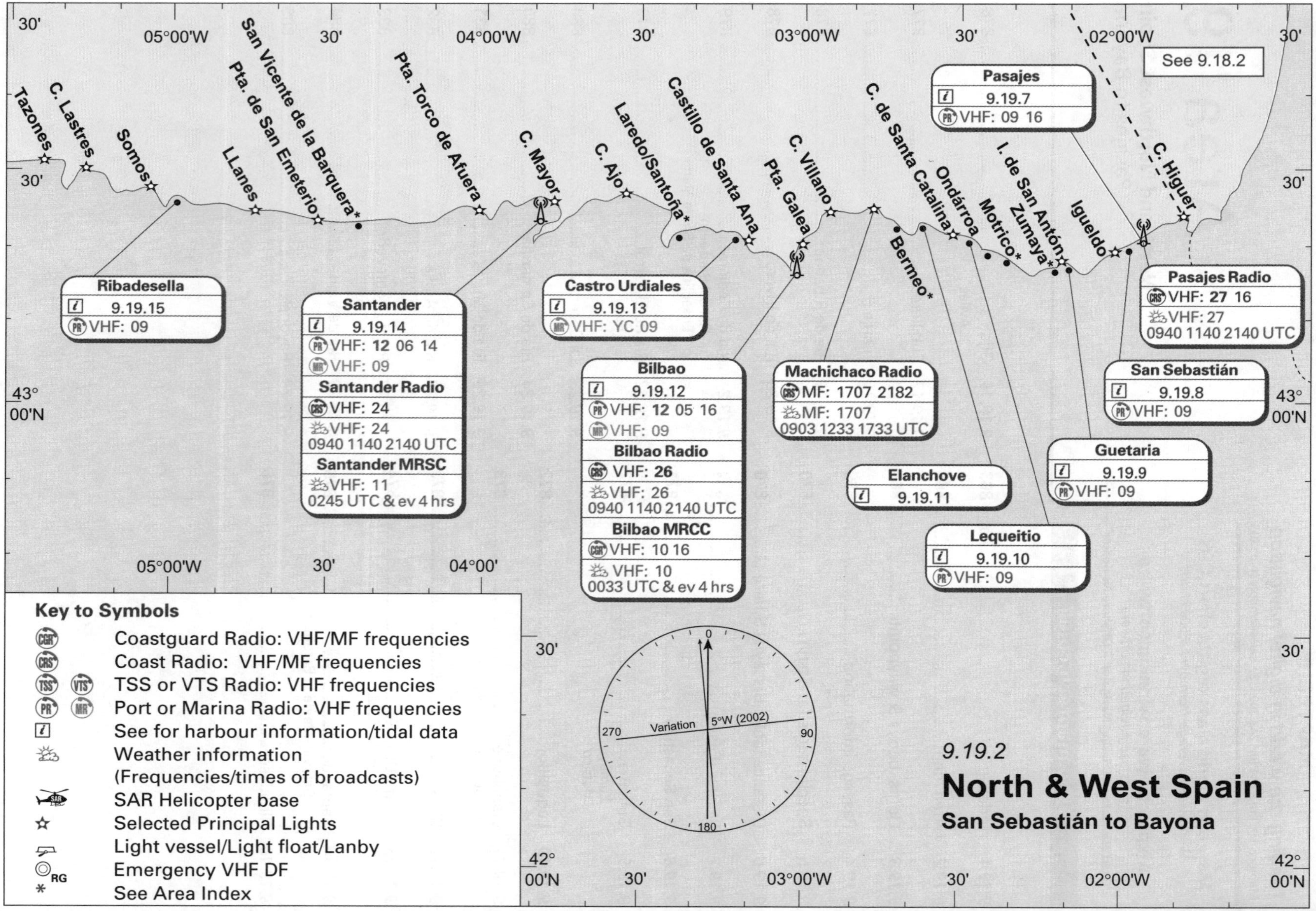
9.19.2
North & West Spain
San Sebastián to Bayona
See 9.18.2
Tazones
C. Lastres
Somos
LLanes
Pta. de San Emeterio
San Vicente de la Barquera*
Pta. Torco de Afuera
C. Mayor
C. Ajo
Laredo/Santoña*
Castillo de Santa Ana
Pta. Galea
C. Villano
C. de Santa Catalina
Bermeo*
Ondárroa
Motrico*
Zumaya*
I. de San Antón
Igueldo
C. Higuer
Ribadesella
9.19.15
VHF: 09
Santander
9.19.14
VHF: 12 06 14
VHF: 09
Santander Radio
VHF: 24
VHF: 24
0940 1140 2140 UTC
Santander MRSC
VHF: 11
0245 UTC & ev 4 hrs
Castro Urdiales
9.19.13
VHF: YC 09
Bilbao
9.19.12
VHF: 12 05 16
VHF: 09
Bilbao Radio
VHF: 26
VHF: 26
0940 1140 2140 UTC
Bilbao MRCC
VHF: 10 16
VHF: 10
0033 UTC & ev 4 hrs
Machichaco Radio
MF: 1707 2182
MF: 1707
0903 1233 1733 UTC
Elanchove
9.19.11
Lequeitio
9.19.10
VHF: 09
Guetaria
9.19.9
VHF: 09
San Sebastián
9.19.8
VHF: 09
Pasajes
9.19.7
VHF: 09 16
Pasajes Radio
VHF: 27 16
VHF: 27
0940 1140 2140 UTC
30'
05°00'W
30'
04°00'W
30'
03°00'W
30'
02°00'W
30'
43°
00'N
42°
00'N
Variation 5°W (2002)
0
90
180
270
Key to Symbols
Coastguard Radio: VHF/MF frequencies
Coast Radio: VHF/MF frequencies
TSS or VTS Radio: VHF frequencies
Port or Marina Radio: VHF frequencies
See for harbour information/tidal data
Weather information
(Frequencies/times of broadcasts)
SAR Helicopter base
Selected Principal Lights
Light vessel/Light float/Lanby
Emergency VHF DF
See Area Index

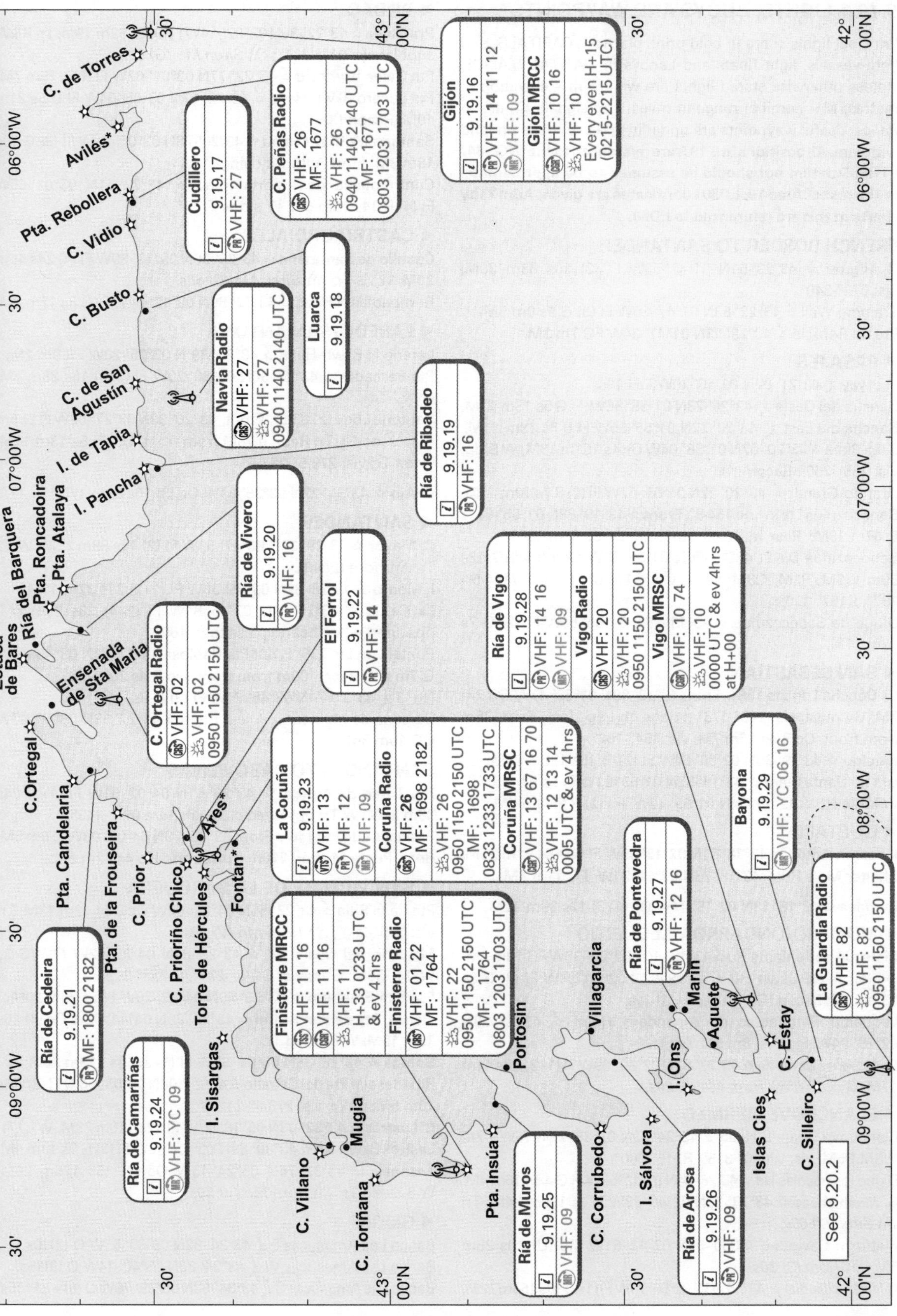
06°00'W
30'
07°00'W
30'
08°00'W
30'
09°00'W
30'
43°00'N
30'
42°00'N
30'
C. de Torres
Avilés*
Pta. Rebollera
C. Vidio
C. Busto
C. de San Agustín
I. de Tapia
I. Pancha
Pta. Atalaya
Pta. Roncadoira
Ría del Barquera
Estaca de Bares
Ensenada de Sta Maria
C.Ortegal
Pta. Candelaria
Pta. de la Frouseira
C. Prior
C. Prioriño Chico
Ares*
Torre de Hércules
Fontan*
I. Sisargas
C. Villano
Mugia
C. Toriñana
Pta. Insúa
Portosin
C. Corrubedo
Villagarcia
I. Sálvora
I. Ons
Marin
Aguete
Islas Cies
C. Estay
C. Silleiro
Gijón
9.19.16
VHF: 14 11 12
VHF: 09
Gijón MRCC
VHF: 10 16
VHF: 10
Every even H+15
(0215-2215 UTC)
C. Peñas Radio
VHF: 26
MF: 1677
VHF: 26
0940 1140 2140 UTC
MF: 1677
0803 1203 1703 UTC
Cudillero
9.19.17
VHF: 27
Luarca
9.19.18
Navia Radio
VHF: 27
VHF: 27
0940 1140 2140 UTC
Ría de Ribadeo
9.19.19
VHF: 16
Ría de Vivero
9.19.20
VHF: 16
El Ferrol
9.19.22
VHF: 14
C. Ortegal Radio
VHF: 02
VHF: 02
0950 1150 2150 UTC
La Coruña
9.19.23
VHF: 13
VHF: 12
VHF: 09
Coruña Radio
VHF: 26
MF: 1698 2182
VHF: 26
0950 1150 2150 UTC
MF: 1698
0833 1233 1733 UTC
Coruña MRSC
VHF: 13 67 16 70
VHF: 12 13 14
0005 UTC & ev 4 hrs
Ría de Vigo
9.19.28
VHF: 14 16
VHF: 09
Vigo Radio
VHF: 20
VHF: 20
0950 1150 2150 UTC
Vigo MRSC
VHF: 10 74
VHF: 10
0000 UTC & ev 4hrs
at H+00
Ría de Cedeira
9.19.21
MF: 1800 2182
Finisterre MRCC
VHF: 11 16
VHF: 11 16
VHF: 11
H+33 0233 UTC
& ev 4 hrs
Finisterre Radio
VHF: 01 22
MF: 1764
VHF: 22
0950 1150 2150 UTC
MF: 1764
0803 1203 1703 UTC
Ría de Pontevedra
9.19.27
VHF: 12 16
Bayona
9.19.29
VHF: YC 06 16
La Guardia Radio
VHF: 82
VHF: 82
0950 1150 2150 UTC
Ría de Camariñas
9.19.24
VHF: YC 09
Ría de Muros
9.19.25
VHF: 09
Ría de Arosa
9.19.26
VHF: 09
See 9.20.2

19

9.19.3 LIGHTS, BUOYS AND WAYPOINTS

Principal lights ☆ are in bold print, places in CAPITALS, and light-vessels, light floats and Lanbys in *CAPITAL ITALICS*. Unless otherwise stated lights are white. m – elevation in metres; M – nominal range in miles. Fog signals are in *italics*. Useful waypoints are underlined – use those on land with care. **All positions in 9.19.3 are referenced to the WGS84/ ETRS89 datum but should be assumed to be approximate. In the rest of Area 19, ED50 coordinates are given. Admiralty charts in this are referenced to ED50.**

FRENCH BORDER TO SANTANDER

C. Higuer ☆ 43°23'·51N 01°47'·53W Fl (2) 10s 63m **23M**; vis: 072°-340°.
Training Wall 43°22'·83N 01°47'·36W Fl (3) G 9s 9m 5M.
Pto de Refugio 43°23'·13N 01°47'·34W FG 7m 3M.

◀ PASAJES

Fairway 43°21'·07N 01°56'·20W L Fl 10s.
Bancha del Oeste 43°20'·23N 01°55'·86W Fl G 5s 18m 11M.
Bancha del East 43°20'·22N 01°55'·65W Fl R 5s 18m 11M.
C. La Plata 43°20'·07N 01°56'·04W Oc 4s 151m 13M; W Bldg; vis: 285°-250°; Racon (K).
Arando-Grande 43°20'·22N 01°55'·67W Fl (2) R 7s 10m 11M.
Senocozulúa Lts in line 154·8°. **Front** ☆ 43°19'·88N 01°55'·61W Q 67m **18M**. **Rear** ☆, 45m from front, Oc 3s 86m **18M**.
Senocozulúa Dir Lt 43°19'·90N 01°55'·60W Oc (2) WRG 12s 50m W6M, R3M, G3M; W Tr; vis: G129·5°-154·5°, W154·5°-157°, R157°-190°.
Dique de Senocozulúa 43°19'·96N 01°55'·58W Fl (2) G 7s 12m 11M.

◀ SAN SEBASTIÁN

La Concha Ldg Lts 158°. Front 43°18'·89N 01°59'·47W QR 7m 7M; Gy mast; vis: 143°-173° (intens on Ldg Line). Rear, 25m from front, Oc R 4s 16m 7M; vis: 154°-162°.
Igueldo ☆ 43°19'·35N 02°00'·64W Fl (2+1) 15s 132m **26M**.
Isla de Santa Clara 43°19'·32N 01°59'·91W Fl 5s 51m 9M.
W Mole Hd 43°19'·34N 01°59'·42W F l (2) R 8s 8m 5M.

◀ GUETARIA

I. de San Antón ☆ 43°18'·61N 02°12'·09W Fl (4) 15s 91m **21M**.
Shelter Mole Hd 43°18'·26N 02°11'·91W FG 11m 3M.

Zumaya 43°18'·18N 02°15'·14W Oc (1+3) 12s 39m 12M.

◀ MOTRICO/ONDÁRROA/LEQUEITIO

Malecón de Poniente Hd 43°18'·44N 02°22'·98W FG 10m 2M.
Ondárroa NE Bkwtr Hd 43°19'·53N 02°24'·94W Fl (3) G 8s 13m 12M; Racon (G); *Siren (3) 20s.*
Lequeitio Rompeolas de Amandarri Head 43°21'·99N 02°29'·94W Fl G 4s 8m 5M; Gy Tr.
C. de Santa Catalina ☆ 43°22'·67N 02°30'·69W Fl (1+3) 20s 44m **17M**; Gy ○ Tr; *Horn Mo (L) 20s.*

◀ ELANCHOVE/BERMEO

Elanchove Digue S Head 43°24'·23N 02°38'·27W F WR 7m W8M,R5M; vis: W000°-315°, R315°-000°.
Digue Rompeolas Hd 43°25'·34N 02°42'·62W Fl G 4·5s 16m 4M.
C. Machichaco ☆ 43°27'·36N 02°45'·22W Fl 7s 120m **24M**; Tr; *Siren (2) 60s.*
Platform Gaviota 43°30'·04N 02°41'·61W Mo (U) 10s 25m 5M; *Horn (3) 30s.*
C. Villano (Gorliz) ☆ 43°25'·93N 02°56'·74W Fl (1+2) 16s 163m **22M**.

◀ BILBAO

Pta Galea ☆ 43°22'·30N 03°02'·14W Fl (3) 8s 82m **19M**; Tr, R&W cupola; vis: 011°-227°; *Siren Mo (G) 30s.*
Pta Galea bkwtr Hd 43°22'·77N 03°04'·67W Fl R 5s 19m 7M.
Pta Lucero Bkwtr Head 43°22'·67N 03°05'·04W Fl G 5s 21m 10M; Racon (X).
Santurce W Bkwtr Head 43°20'·78N 03°01'·92W Fl (3) G 10s 18m 3M. (Port Authority bldg).
Contramuelle de Algorta Head 43°20'·51N 03°01'·65W Fl (4) R 14s 18m 6M, W stone Tr.

◀ CASTRO URDIALES

Castillo de Santa Ana ☆ 43°23'·06N 03°12'·89W Fl (4) 24s 46m **20M**; W △ Tr; *Siren Mo (C) 60s.*
Rompeolas N Head 43°22'·86N 03°12'·54W Fl G 3s 12m 6M.

◀ LAREDO/SAN ANTOÑA

Laredo N Bkwtr Head 43°24'·89'N 03°25'·20W FR 9m 2M.
Pta Pescador 43°27'·90N 03°26'·20W Fl (3+1) 15s 38m 9M; Gy ○ Tr.
Santoña Ldg Lts 283·5°. Front, 43°26'·33N 03°27'·62W Fl 2s 6m 8M; ▽ on Gy Tr. Rear, 0·75M from front, Oc (2) 5s 13m 11M; ○ on Tr; vis: 279·5°-287·5°.

C. Ajo ☆ 43°30'·77N 03°35'·31W Oc (3) 16s 69m **17M**; ○ Tr.

◀ SANTANDER

C. Mayor ☆ 43°29'·37N 03°47'·51W Fl (2) 10s 89m **21M**; W ○ Tr; *Horn (2) 40s.*
I. Mouro 43°28'·39N 03°45'·36W Fl (1+2) 21s 37m 11M.
La Cerda 43°26'·01N 03°45'·84W Fl (1+4) 20s 22m 8M; obscured when bearing less than 160°.
Puntal Ldg Lts 236° Front Pta Rabiosa 43°27'·51N 03°46'·43W Q 7m 6M. Rear, 100m from front, Iso R 4s 10m 6M.
No. 3 43°27'·71N 03°46'·21W Fl (3) G 9s.
Dársena de Molnedo, Mole E Head 43°27'·68N 03°47'·47W QG 10m 3M.

SANTANDER TO CABO PEÑAS

Pta Torco de Afuera ☆ 43°26'·51N 04°02'·61W Fl (1+2) 24s 33m **22M**; W Tr; obscured close inshore 091°-113°.
Suances Ldg Lts 146°. Front 43°26'·19N 04°02'·08W Q 8m 5M. Rear, Punta Marzán 210m from front, Iso 4s 12m 5M.

◀ SAN VICENTE DE LA BARQUERA

Pta de la Silla 43°23'·56N 04°23'·62W Oc 3·5s 42m 13M; Tr; vis: 115°-250°; *Horn Mo (V) 30s.*
Malecón del Oeste Hd 43°23'·80N 04°23'·02W Fl WG 2s W7M, G6M; G Tr; vis: G175°-235°, W235°-045°.
Pta San Emeterio ☆ 43°23'·90N 04°32'·20W Fl 5s 66m **20M**.
Llanes, Pta de San Antón ☆ 43°25'·09N 04°44'·99W Oc (4) 15s 16m **15M**; W 8-sided Tr.
Somos ☆ 43°28'·36N 05°04'·98W Fl (1+2) 12s 113m **25M**; Tr.
Ribadesella Pta del Caballo 43°28'·08N 05°03'·98W Fl (2) R 6s 10m 5M; ○ Tr; vis: 278·4°-212·9°.
C. Lastres ☆ 43°32'·03N 05°18'·07W Fl 12s 116m **23M**. W ○ Tr.
Lastres Bkwtr Hd 43°30'·89N 05°15'·90W Fl (3) G 9s 13m 4M.
Tazones ☆ 43°32'·74N 05°24'·13W Oc (3) 15s 125m **20M**; W 8-sided Tr; *Horn Mo (V) 30s.*

◀ GIJÓN

Banco Las Amasucas E 43°34'·82N 05°39'·53W Q (3)10s.
Banco Las Amasucas W 43°34'·83N 05°40'·14W Q (9)15s.
Banco Las Amasucas S 43°34'·53N 05°39'·79W Q (6) + L Fl 15s.

C. de Torres ☆ 43°34'·29N 05°41'·97W Fl (2) 10s 80m **18M**.
Dique Principe de Asturias ☆ 43°34'·25N 05°40'·58W Fl G 3s 12m 6M; G Tr.
Candás Punta del Cuerno ☆ 43°35'·71N 05°45'·56W Oc (2)10s 38m **15M**; R Tr, W Ho; *Horn Mo (C) 60s.*
Luanco Ldg Lts 255°. Front, Mole Hd, 43°36'·91N 05°47'·35W Fl R 3s 4m 4M. Rear, 240m from front, Oc R 8s 8m 4M.
C. Peñas ☆ 43°39'·31N 05°50'·90W Fl (3) 15s 115m **35M**; Gy 8-sided Tr; *Siren Mo (P) 60s.*

CABO PEÑAS TO PUNTA DE LA ESTACA DE BARES

Ría de Avilés 43°35'·73N 05°57'·69W Fl G 5s.
Avilés ☆ 43°35'·72N 05°56'·72W Oc WR 5s 38m **W20, R17M**; W □ Tr; vis: R091·5°-113°, W113°-091·5°; *Siren Mo (A) 30s.*
Avilés Ent Chan S side ☆ 43°35'·57N 05°56'·49W Fl (2) G 7s 12m 5M; vis: 106°-280°; W ○ Tr, G band.
Puerto de S. Estaban ☆ West Breakwater elbow 43°34'·20N 06°04'·64W Fl (2) 12s 19m **15M**; W ▮, B bands; *Horn* Mo (N) 30s.
San Esteban de Pravia Ldg Lts 182·2° Front 43°33'·47N 06°04'·66W FR 6m 3M. Rear, 160m from front, FR 10m 3M.
Pta Rebollera ☆ 43°33'·96N 06°08'·68W Oc (4) 16s 42m **16M**; W 8-sided Tr; *Siren Mo (D) 30s.*
C. Vidio ☆ 43°35'·60N 06°14'·79W Fl 5s 99m **25M**; ○ Tr; Siren *Mo (V) 60s.*
C. Busto ☆ 43°34'·13N 06°28'·23W Fl (4) 20s 84m **25M**.

◀ LUARCA

Pta Focicón (Blanca) ☆ 43°33'·03N 06°31'·85W Oc (3) 15s 63m 14M; W □ Tr; *Siren Mo (L) 30s.*
Ldg Lts 170°. Front 43°32'·83N 06°32'·02W Fl 5s 18m 2M. Rear, 41m from front, Oc 4s 25m 2M.
Dique del Canouco Hd ☆ 43°32'·97N 06°32'·05W Fl (3) R 9s 22m 5M.
Ría de Navia Outfall 43°34'·18N 06°43'·64W Fl Y 10s.
C. de San Agustín ☆ 43°33'·83N 06°44'·07W Oc (2) 12s 70m **25M**; W ○ Tr, B bands.
C. de Tapia ☆ 43°34'·43N 06°56'·78W Fl (2+1) 19s 22m **18M**.

◀ RÍA DE RIBADEO

I. Pancha ☆ 43°33'·39N 07°02'·53W Fl (3+1) 20s 26m **21M**; W ○ Tr, B bands; *Siren Mo (R) 30s.*
Pta de la Cruz ☆ 43°33'·40N 07°01'·75W Fl (2) 7s 16m 5M.
Ldg Lts 140°. Front, Pta Aerojo, 43°32'·83N 07°01'·53W QR 18m 5M. Rear, 228m from front, Oc R 4s 24m 5M. R ◇, W Trs.
Ldg Lts 205°. Front, Muelle de García, 43°32'·49N 07°02'·24W Q R 8m 3M R ◇ W Tr. Rear, 178m from front, Oc R 2s 18m 3M W □ on structure.
Ría de Foz Trg Wall Hd ☆ 43°34'·43N 07°14'·67W Fl G 3s 3m 10M.
Piedra Burela 43°39'·80N 07°20'·90W Q (3) 10s 11m 7M.
Pta Atalaya (Cabo de S. Ciprian) ☆ 43°42'·03N 07°26'·21W Fl (5) 20s 39m **20M**; W ○ Tr, B band.
Alúmina Port N Breakwater Head ☆ 43°42'·98N 07°27'·59W Fl (2) WG 8s 18m 4M; vis: W110°-180°, G180°-110°.
Pta Roncadoira ☆ 43°43'·94N 07°31'·65W Fl 7·5s 92m **21M**; W ○ Tr.

◀ RÍA DE VIVERO/RÍA DEL BARQUERO

Pta Socastro ☆ 43°43'·08N 07°36'·42W Fl G 7s 18m 5M; W Tr.
Pta de Faro ☆ 43°42'·74N 07°35'·03W Fl (2) R 14s 18m 5M.
Cillero dique Head ☆ 43°40'·93N 07°36'·16W Fl (2) R 8m 5M.
I. Coelleira ☆ 43°45'·51N 07°37'·77W Fl (4) 24s 87m 8M.
Pta del Castro ☆ 43°44'·46N 07°40'·48W Fl (2) 7s 14m 5M.
Vicedo, N Pier Hd ☆ 43°44'·34N 07°40'·65W Fl (4) R 11s 9m 5M.
S Pier Hd ☆ 43°44'·37N 07°40'·64W Fl (4) G 11s 9m 3M.
Pta de la Barra ☆ 43°44'·51N 07°41'·31W Fl WRG 3s 15m 5M; vis: 213°-240°, R240°-255°, G255°-213°; W △ Tr.

PUNTA DE LA ESTACA DE BARES TO CABO VILLANO

Pta de la Estaca de Bares ☆ 43°47'·21N 07°41'·14W Fl (2) 7·5s 99m **25M**; 8-sided Tr & house; *Siren Mo (B) 60s.*
Espasante Outer Bkwtr ☆ 43°43'·36N 07°48'·91W Fl R 5s 11m 3M.
43°46'·36N 07°49'·51W Q (9) 15s.
Carino Bkwtr Head ☆ 43°44'·05N 07°51'·73W Fl G 2s 12m 3M.
C. Ortegal ☆ 43°46'·22N 07°52'·30W Oc 8s 122m **18M**.
Pta Candelaria ☆ 43°42'·65N 08°02'·98W Fl (3+1) 24s 87m **21M**.

◀ RÍA DE CEDEIRA

Punta del Sarridal ☆ 43°39'·65N 08°04'·53W Oc WR 6s 39m 11M; vis: W145°-172°, R172°-145°.
Piedra de Media Mar ☆ 43°39'·37N 08°04'·80W Fl (2) 5s 12m 4M; W ○ Tr.
Dique de Abrigo Hd ☆ 43°39'·30N 08°04'·20W Fl (2) R 7s 10m 4M.
Pta Promontorio ☆ 43°39'·05N 08°04'·21W Oc (4) 10s 24m 11M.
Pta de la Frouxeira ☆ 43°37'·02N 08°11'·31W Fl (5) 15s 73m **20M**.
C. Prior ☆ 43°34'·05N 08°18'·87W Fl (1+2) 15s 105m **22M**; 6-sided Tr; vis: 055·5°-310°.

◀ RÍA DE EL FERROL

C. Prioriño Chico ☆ 43°27'·52N 08°20'·40W Fl 5s 34m **23M**; W 8-sided Tr.
Muela del Segaño 43°27'·42N 08°18'·81W Fl G 2s.
Ldg Lts 085·4° Front, Pta de San Martín 43°27'·57N 08°17'·06W Fl 1·5s 10m 3M. Rear, 701m from front Oc 4s 5M.
No. 3 43°27'·62N 08°17'·05W Fl (2) G 7s.
Dársena de Curuxeiras Mole Head ☆ 43°28'·53N 08°14'·66W Fl (4) R 11s 5m 3M; W ▮.
Sada. Dique de Abrigo Hd ☆ 43°21'·76N 08°14'·54W Fl (3) G 9s 9m 4M; G Tr.

◀ LA CORUÑA

Torre de Hércules ☆ 43°23'·15N 08°24'·39W Fl (4) 20s 104m **23M**; □ Tr; *Siren Mo (L) 30s.*
Banco Yacentes 43°24'·70N 08°23'·02W Fl (5) Y 20s.
Ldg Lts 108·5°. Front, Pta Mera 43°23'·00N 08°21'·28W Oc WR 4s 54m W8M R3M; vis: R000°-023°, R100·5°-105·5°, W105·5°-114·5°, R114·5°-153°; Racon (M).
Ldg Lts 182°. Front, Pta Fiaiteira 43°20'·59N 08°22'·25W Iso WRG 2s 28m W4M, R3M, G3M; vis: G146·4°-180°, W180°-184°, R184°-217·6°. Rear, 380m from front, Oc R 4s 52m 3M.
Dique d'Abrigo Hd ☆ 43°21'·90N 08°22'·48W Fl G 3s 16m 6M.
Malpica Shelter Mole Hd ☆ 43°19'·34N 08°48'·31W Fl G 3s 18m 4M.
I. Sisargas ☆ 43°21'·53N 08°50'·77W Fl (3) 15s 108m **23M**; W cupola on Tr, on W bldg; *Siren (3) 30s.*
Punta Nariga ☆ 43°19'·24N 08°54'·72W Fl (3+1) 20s 53m **22M**; W ○ Tr.
Pta del Roncudo ☆ 43°16'·42N 08°59'·53W Fl 6s 36m 10M.
Pta Lage ☆ 43°13'·88N 09°00'·83W Fl (5) 20s 64m **20M**; W Tr.
Corme Mole Hd ☆ 43°15'·70N 08°57'·89W Fl (2) R 5s 13m 3M.
Puerto de Lage dique N Hd ☆ 43°13'·34N 08°59'·96W Fl G 3s 16m 4M; G ○ Tr.
C. Villano ☆ 43°09'·60N 09°12'·70W Fl (2) 15s 102m **28M** Y/Gy 8-sided Tr; Racon (M); *Siren Mo (V) 60s.*

CABO VILLANO TO PORTUGUESE BORDER

◀ RÍA DE CAMARIÑAS/MUGIA

Ldg Lts 079·7° Front, Pta Villueira 43°07'·37N 09°11'·56W Fl 5s 14m 9M; W ○ Tr, R ◇. Rear, 610m from front, Pta del Castillo Iso 4s 25m 11M; W ○ Tr, R bands; vis: 078·2°-081·2°.
Pta de Lago ☆ 43°06'·60N 09°10'·01W Oc (2) WRG 6s 15m W6M, R4M, G4M; vis: W029·5°-093°,G093°-107·8°, W107·8°-109·1°, R109·1°-139·3°, W139·3°-213·5°; ○ Tr.
Camariñas Outer Bkwtr Head ☆ 43°07'·43N 09°10'·83W FR 1M.
Pier Head ☆ 43°07'·63N 09°10'·93W Fl (3) R 8s 9m 4M FR (T) 1996.
Pta de la Barca ☆ 43°06'·79N 09°13'·19W Oc 4s 13m 7M.
Mugia Bkwtr Hd ☆ 43°06'·35N 09°12'·75W Fl (2) G 10s 12m 4M.

C. Toriñana ☆ 43°03'·17N 09°18'·01W Fl (2+1) 15s 63m **24M**.
C. Finisterre ☆ 42°52'·93N 09°16'·29W Fl 5s 141m 23M; 8-sided Tr; Racon (O); obscd when brg >149°.
Finisterre Bkwtr Hd ☆ 42°54'·56N 09°15'·38W Fl R 2s 12m 4M.
I. Lobeira Grande ☆ 42°52'·84N 09°11'·22W Fl (3) 15s 16m 9M.
Carrumeiro Chico ☆ 42°54'·37N 09°10'·80W Fl (2) 7s 6m 6M.
C. Cée ☆ 45°55'·00N 09°11'·07W Fl (5) 13s 25m 7M; Gy Tr.
Corcubión Bkwtr Hd ☆ 42°56'·69N 09°11·39W Fl (2) R 8s 9m 4M.

Puertocubelo Bkwtr Hd ☆ 42°48'·40N 09°08'·15W Fl G 2s 9m 4M.
Pta Insúa ☆ 42°46'·29N 09°07'·56W Fl (3) WR 25m 9s; **W15M**, R14M; vis: R020°-045°, W045°-070°, R070°-090°, W090°-125°, R125°-152°, W152°-·020°.

◀ RÍA DE MUROS

Pta Queixal ☆ 42°44'·36N 09°04'·75W Fl (2+1) 12s 25m 9M.
C. Reburdiño ☆ 42°46'·20N 09°02'·91W Fl (2) R 6s 16m 7M.
Muros Outer Mole Head ☆ 42°46'·64N 09°03'·31W Fl (4) R 13s 8m 4M; W ○ Tr.
El Freijo Mole Hd ☆ 42°47'·62N 08°56'·63W Fl (2) R 5s 7m 4M.
Portosin Bkwtr Hd ☆ 42°45'·89N 08°56'·90W Fl (2) G 5s 7m 3M.
Pta Cabeiro ☆ 42°44'·41N 08°59'·42W Fl WRG 5s 35m W9M, R6M, G6M; W Tr; vis: R054·4°-058·5°, G058·5°-099·5°, W099·5°-189·5°.
El Son Bkwtr Head ☆ 42°43'·73N 08°00'·07W Fl G 5s 4m 6M.
Pta Sofocho ☆ 42°41'·89N 09°01'·71W Fl 5s 27m 4M; ○ Tr.

C. Corrubedo ☆ 42°34'·59N 09°05'·39W Fl (2+3) WR 20s 30m **W15M, R15M**; dangerous sector 347°-040°; *Siren (3) 60s*; Racon (K).
Corrubedo Bkwtr Hd ☆ 42°34'·34N 09°04'·19W Iso WRG 3s 10m W6M, R4M, G3M; ○ Tr; vis: R000°-016°, G016°-352°, W352°-000°.

◀ RÍA DE AROSA

I Sálvora ☆ 42°27'·82N 09°00'·80W Fl (3+1) 20s 38m **21M**; clear sector 217°-126°. Fl (3) 20s dangerous sector 126°-160°.
Uslas de Sagres ☆ 42°30'·48N 09°03'·00W Fl 5s 23m 8M.
Piedras del Sargo E Rk ☆ 42°30'·30N 09°00'·50W QG 11m 8M; W △ Tr, G band.
Puerto de Aguiño Breakwater Head ☆ 42°31'·09N 09°00'·90W Fl R 2s 12m 3M.
Santa Eugenia Breakwater Head ☆ 42°33'·58N 08°59'·24W Fl (2) R 7s 7m 4M; R ○ Tr.
Isla Rúa ☆ 42°32'·95N 08°56'·36W Fl (2+1) WR 21s 24m 13M.
Puebla del Caramiñal E Bkwtr Head ☆ 42°36'·28N 08°55'·87W Oc G 2s 8m 4M; ○ Tr G band.
Rianjo Outer Bkwtr Hd ☆ 42°39'·06N 08°49'·44W Fl G 3s 9m 5M
Villagarcia de Arosa Muelle del Ramal Head ☆ 42°36'·11N 08°46'·33W Iso 2s 2m 10M; ○ Tr.
I. de Arosa, St Julian N Bay Mole Head ☆ 42°33'·96N 08°52'·18W FR 7m 1M; R masonry ▮.
Pta Caballo ☆ 42°34'·33N 08°53'·03W Fl (4) 11s 11m 10M.
San Martin del Grove Mole Head ☆ 42°29'·85N 08°51'·51W Oc G 2·5s 9m 3M; B & W chequered ○ Tr.
Bajo Pombeiriño ☆ 42°28'·88N 08°56'·80W Fl (2) G 12s 13m 8M; G △ Tr, G band.

◀ RÍA DE PONTEVEDRA

I. Ons ☆ 42°22'·94N 08°56'·17W Fl (4) 24s 126m **25M**; 8-sided Tr
Playa del Curro Pier ☆ 42°22'·63N 08°55'·78W Fl R 4s 7m 2M R ○ Tr
Bajo Camouco ☆ 42°23'·70N 08°54'·75W Fl (3) R 18s 10m 8M.
Bajo Picamillo ☆ 42°24'·37N 08°53'·37W Fl G 5s 10m 8M; Tr.
Portonovo Mole Hd ☆ 42°23'·65N 08°49'·13W Fl (3) R 6s 8m 4M
Sangenjo Mole Hd ☆ 42°23'·76N 08°48'·11W QR 5m 4M.
Cabezo de Morrazan ☆ 42°22'·36N 08°47'·04W Iso R 5s.
Rajo Mole Hd ☆ 42°24'·10N 08°45'·26W Fl (2) R 8s 9m 3M R ○ Tr
Combarro Mole Hd ☆ 42°25'·77N 08°42'·26W Fl (2) R 8s 7m 3M
I. Tambo ☆ 42°24'·48N 08°42'·48W Oc (3) 8s 33m 11M; W ○ Tr
Marin Bkwtr Hd ☆ 42°23'·93N 08°42'·32W Fl (3) G 7s 7m 6M.
Bueu N Mole Hd ☆ 42°19'·77N 08°47'·11W Fl G 3s 7m 4M G Tr
Bajo Mourisca ☆ 42°20'·90N 08°49'·17W Fl (2) G 7s 10m 5M
Aldán Mole Hd ☆ 42°16'·95N 08°49'·39W Fl (2) R 10s 5m 5M.
Pta Couso ☆ 42°18'·56N 08°51'·33W Fl (3) WG 10.5s 18m W10M, G8M G060°-096°, W096°-190°, G190°-000°.

◀ ISLAS CÍES

Monte Agudo ☆ 42°14'·60N 08°54'·19W Fl G 5s 24m 9M; W Tr
No. 2 (Roca Omear) ☆ 42°14'·56N 08°51'·91W Fl (4) R 10s *Bell*.
Monte Faro ☆ 42°12'·85N 08°54'·91W Fl (2) 8s 185m **22M** ○ Tr
Pta Canabal ☆ 42°12'·73N 08°54'·78W Fl (3) 20s 63m 9M; W Tr
C. Vicos ☆ 42°11'·51N 08°53'·49W Fl (3) R 9s 92m 7M; W Tr.
Islote Boiero ☆ 42°10'·75N 08°54'·61W Fl (2) R 8s 22m 6M. W Tr

◀ RÍA DE VIGO

C. Home Ldg Lts 129° Front 42°15'·15N 08°52'·37W Fl 3s 36m 9M; W Tr. Rear Pta Subrido, 815m from front, Oc 6s 52m 11M W Tr; both vis: 090°-180°.
Cangas Outer Mole Hd ☆ 42°15'·61N 08°46'·83W Fl (1+2) R 12s 8m 3M; R ○ Tr.
Pta Areiño. **La Guia** ☆ 42°15'·56N 08°42'·15W Oc (2+1) 20s 35m **15M**; W ○ Tr.
C. Estay Ldg Lts 069·3°. **Front** ☆, 42°11'·12N 08°48'·89W Iso 2s 16m **18M**; *Horn Mo (V) 60s*. Rear ☆, 660m from front Oc 4s 48m **18M**. Both R △ Trs, W bands; vis: 066·3°-072·3°.
Pta Lameda ☆ 42°09'·39N 08°50'·98W Fl (2) G 8s 27m 5M; W Tr

◀ BAYONA

Las Serralleiras ☆ 42°08'·77N 08°52'·67W Fl G 4s 10m 6M.
Ldg Lts 084° Front Cabezo de San Juan ☆ 42°08'·24N 08°50'·09W Q (2) 4s 7m 4M; W △ Tr. Rear Panjón, 1·05M from front, Oc W 3·8s 17m 9M; W ▽ Tr.
Bayona Dique de Abrigo Head ☆ 42°07'·49N 08°50'·58W QG 12m 6M. B and W chequered ○ Tr.
C. Silleiro ☆ 42°06'·27N 08°53'·80W Fl (2+1) 15s 83m **24M**.
La Guardia ☆ 41°54'·01N 08°52'·94W Fl R 5s 11m 5M; R △ Tr

9.19.4 PASSAGE INFORMATION

BIBLIOGRAPHY The *North Spain Cruising Companion* (Macmillan Reeds/Jens) covers from the French Border to Bayona, *South Biscay Pilot* (Adlard Coles) covers from the Gironde to La Coruña. The *Atlantic Spain and Portugal* guide (Imray/RCC, 3rd edition 1995) covers from El Ferrol to Gibraltar. The *Bay of Biscay Pilot* (Admiralty, NP 22) covers from Pte de Penmarc'h to Cabo Ortegal, whence The *W coasts of Spain and Portugal Pilot* (Admiralty, NP 67) continues south to Gibraltar. *Portos de Galicia* (English/Spanish) has good photographs. *Guia del Navegante*, also in English, has fair cover of SW Spain, but is limited elsewhere.

BAY OF BISCAY (S): WIND, WEATHER AND SEA Despite its reputation, the S part of the Bay is often warm and settled in summer when the Azores high and Spanish heat low are the dominant weather features. NE'lies prevail in sea area Finisterre in summer and gales may occur twice monthly, although forecast more frequently. Atlantic lows can bring W'ly spells at any time. SE or S winds are rare, but wind direction and speed often vary from day to day. Sea and land breezes can be well developed in the summer. Off N Spain *Galernas* are dangerous squally NW winds which blow with little warning. Coastal winds are intensified by the Cordillera Cantábrica (2615m mountains). Rainfall is moderate, increasing in the SE, where thunder is more frequent. Sea fog, which may mean imminent strong winds, occurs May-Oct, but is less common in winter.

No tidal stream atlases are published; streams are weak offshore, but can be strong in narrow channels and around headlands. Surface current much depends on wind: in summer it sets SE ½ - ¾kn, towards the SE corner of B of Biscay, thence W along N coast of Spain. When crossing the Bay, allow for some set to the E, particularly after strong W winds.

CROSSING THE BAY OF BISCAY (chart 1104) From the English Channel to Cabo Villano, the track (210°/365M) from Ushant lies close to busy shipping lanes, but a track (213°/355M) from, say, Raz de Sein to Cabo Villano is offset from the shipping route. From Scilly or Eire the direct track lies in about 7°-8°W. Within the Bay itself, sailing down the French coast is attractive and allows a 200M passage from, say, La Rochelle to Santander. S of the Gironde a missile range (9.18.24) may inhibit coastal passage. The Continental Shelf where depths plummet from 150m to over 4000m in only 30M, can cause dangerous seas in swell and bad weather. It trends SE from about 60M SW of Ile de Sein and is clearly depicted on AC 1104. Loran-C (chain 6731) covers N Spain well and extends down to about 40°N and westward to 15°W.

The Atlantic swell, rarely experienced in UK waters except off the W coasts of Ireland and Scotland, runs in mainly from W or NW. It is not a problem well offshore, except over the Continental Shelf in bad weather. Considerable rolling is probable and other yachts may be lost to view in the troughs. Closer inshore swell will exacerbate the sea state and render entry to, and exit from, lee shore hbrs dangerous. For example, with a 2m swell running, crossing a bar with 4m depth over it and breaking seas would be foolhardy. In winter some hbrs are closed for weeks at a time, more particularly along the Portuguese coast.

FRENCH BORDER TO CABO ORTEGAL (charts 1102, 1105, 1108) The N coast of Spain is bold and rocky. In clear visibility the peaks of the Cordillera Cantábrica may be seen from well offshore. Although the coast is mostly steep-to, it is best to keep 2-3M offshore (beyond the 50m contour) to avoid short, steep seas breaking on isolated shoals. Many major lights are sited so high as to be obscured by low cloud/mist in onshore weather. Of the many small rivers, most are obstructed by bars and none are navigable far inland.

Between the French border and Santander are several interesting fishing hbrs: Motrico, Lequeitio (9.19.10), Elanchove (9.19.11) and Laredo/Santoña offer anchorage or AB. Marinas are still the exception rather than the rule. Pasajes is a port of refuge, but also a large, commercial/fishing port. 3M to the W, San Sebastián (9.19.8) is an attractive ⚓ but exposed to the NW. Bilbao (9.19.12) and Santander (9.19.14) are major cities and ferry ports for the UK, with marinas. In NW gales ports of refuge for yachts are Guetaria (9.19.9), Bermeo, Bilbao (9.19.12), Castro Urdiales (9.19.13) and Santander (9.19.14).

Beyond Santander hbrs are increasingly far apart. Gijón (9.19.16) with a modern marina and San Ciprian offer refuge only within their vast commercial ports. Cudillero (9.19.17) and Luarca (9.19.18) are small fishing hbrs worth visiting, but beware swell particularly at Cudillero. Ría de Ribadeo (9.19.19) at 7°W is the first of the rías altas (upper or northern), sunken estuaries not unlike a Scottish sea loch. The Ría de Vivero (9.19.20), Ría del Barquero and the Ensenada de Santa Marta, to E and W of Pta de la Estaca de Bares, offer many attractive ⚓s sheltered from all but N/NE winds; but beware S/SW winds off the mountains being accelerated by funnelling effects through the valleys.

CABO ORTEGAL TO CABO FINISTERRE (charts 1111, 3633) Cabo Ortegal should be rounded at least 2M off due to the offlying needle rks, Los Aguillones. Most of the major headlands should be given a good offing to avoid fluky winds and, in some cases, pinnacle rocks. The deeply indented coast begins to trend WSW, with 600m high mountains rising only 5M inland. Here also many major lights are sited so high as to be obscured by low cloud/mist in onshore weather. Tidal streams set SW on the ebb and NE on the flood. Any current tends to run SW, then S.

The Ría de Cedeira (9.19.21) is entered 3M SSW of Pta Candelaria lt ho. This small attractively wooded ría offers refuge by day/night to yachts unable to round Cabo Ortegal in strong NE'lies. Several banks along this stretch break in heavy weather when they should be passed well to seaward. About 20M further SW, having passed Pta de la Frouseira, Cabo Prior, Pta del Castro and C. Prioriño Chico, all lit, is the ent to Ría de El Ferrol (9.19.22), a well sheltered commercial and naval port. La Coruña (9.19.23), 5M SSW, can be entered in all weathers and has far better yacht facilities. Between these two large ports are the quiet and little frequented rías de Ares and Betanzos, the latter with a marina at Fontan/Sada. W of the conspic Torre de Hércules lt ho a wide bight is foul as far as Islas Sisargas, three islets 2M offshore. 8M SW of Pta Nariga (43°19'·3N 08°54'·6W), between Pta del Roncudo and Pta de Lage, is the attractive Ría de Corme y Lage.

Cabo Villano, a rky headland with lt ho and conspic wind generators, is a possible landfall after crossing Biscay. A pinnacle rk awash at CD, lurks 4ca NW of it. The ent to Ría de Camariñas (9.19.24), the last of the rías altas and a safe refuge, is close S. 20M W/NW of Cabo Villano and Finisterre is a TSS; see 9.19.23 for Maritime Traffic Service. Cabo Toriñana and Cabo Finisterre both have charted dangers, mostly pinnacle rks, lying up to 1M offshore; hence the popular name *Costa del Morte* for this wild, magnificentand sometimes forbidding coast.

CABO FINISTERRE TO RIO MIÑO (chart 3633) NE of Cabo Finisterre the Ensenada del Sardineiro and Ría de Corcubión are sheltered ⚓s except in S'lies. From 5 to 11M south, beware various islets, reefs and shoals N and W of Pta Insua, notably Las Arrosas and Bajo de los Meixidos; the latter can be passed inshore if making for Ría de Muros (9.19.25).

The 40M stretch to Cabo Silleiro embraces an impressive cruising ground in its own right, namely the four major rías bajas (lower or southern), from N to S: Muros, Arosa (9.19.26), Pontevedra (9.19.27) and Vigo (9.19.28). The last three rías are sheltered from onshore winds by coastal islands at their mouth, but in summer NE winds can blow strongly down all rías, usually without raising any significant sea. Arosa, the largest ría, runs 12M inland and is up to 6M wide; Villagarcia is the principal hbr and marina. All resemble large and scenic Scottish sea lochs with interesting pilotage to fishing hbrs and many sheltered anchorages. Ría de Vigo is notable for the beautiful Islas Cies, the port of Vigo and the pleasant passage hbr of Bayona (9.19.29).

The Río Miño (*Minho* in Portuguese), 15M S of Cabo Silleiro, forms the N border between Spain and Portugal. The river ent is difficult and best not attempted.

9.19.5 SPECIAL NOTES FOR SPAIN

Regions/Provinces: Spain is divided into 17 autonomous regions, ie in this Almanac, the Basque Country, Cantabria, Asturias, Galicia and Andalucía. Most of the regions are subdivided into provinces, eg in Galicia: Lugo, La Coruña, Pontevedra and Orense (inland). The province is shown below the name of each main port.

Language: This Almanac recognises the significant regional differences (eg Basque, Gallego), but in the interests of standardisation uses the spelling of Castilian Spanish where practicable.

Charts: Spanish charts (SC) are obtainable from Instituto Hidrográfico de la Marina, Tolosa Latour 1, 11007 Cádiz, ☎ (956) 599412, 🖷 275358; order from Seccion Economica by post/bank transfer or in person for cash. Also from Centro Nacional de Informacion Geografica, 6 Calle Lopez Doriga, Santander. Hbrs are often charted at larger scale than British Admiralty charts.

Courtesy Ensign: Until W of Bilbao it may be politic not to fly a courtesy ensign in view of Basque sensitivity.

Time: Spain keeps UTC+1 as standard time; DST (Daylight Saving Time) is kept from the last Sunday in March until the Saturday before the 4th Sunday in October, as in other EU nations. Note: Portugal keeps UTC as standard time and UTC+1 as DST.

Secondary Spanish Ports Related to Lisboa: A number of Spanish ports in Areas 19 and 21 are related to Lisboa as the Standard Port and it is important to realise that time differences for these ports when applied to the printed times of HW and LW for Lisboa (UT) will give HW and LW times in the Zone Time for Spain (UT –0100) and no further correction is required, other tha for Daylight Saving Time, when this applies.

Telephone: To call Spain from UK dial 00-34, then the area code, followed by the ☎ number. To call UK from Spain, dial 07-44, then area code, less the initial 0, then the ☎ number.

Emergencies: ☎ 900 202 202 for Fire, Police and Ambulance.

Rioja Cruz (Red Cross) operate LBs.

Public Holidays: Jan 1, 6; Apr 10 (Good Friday); 1 May (Labou Day); June 11 (Corpus Christi); Aug 15 (Assumption); Oct 1 (National Day); Nov 1 (All Saints Day); Dec 6, 8 (Immaculate Conception), 25.

Representation: Spanish National Tourist Office, 57 St James St, London SW1A 1LD; ☎ 020 7486 8077, 🖷 020 7186 8034.

British Embassy, Calle de Fernando el Santo 16, 28010 Madrid ☎ (91) 700 8200, 🖷 700 8311. There are British Consuls at Bilbao Santander, Vigo, Seville and Algeciras (qv).

Buoyage: IALA Region A system is used. However buoys may lack topmarks, be unpainted (or wrongly painted) more ofter than in N Europe. Preferred chan buoys (RGR, Fl (2+1) R and GRG, Fl (2+1) G) are quite widely used.

Documents: Spain, although an EU member, still asks to check paperwork. This can be a time-consuming, repetitive and inescapable process. The only palliatives are courtesy, patience and good humour. Organise your papers to include:

Personal – Passports; crew list, ideally on headed paper with the yacht's rubber stamp, giving DoB, passport nos, where joined intended departure. Certificate of Competence (Yachtmaste Offshore, ICC/HOCC etc). Radio Operator's certificate. Form E111 (advised for medical treatment).

Yacht – Registration certificate, Part 1 or SSR. Proof of VAT status. Marine insurance. Ship's Radio licence. Itinerary, backed up by ship's log.

Access: Ferries sail from UK to Santander and Bilbao . There are flights from UK to Bilbao, Santiago de Compostela and Jerez also Sevilla, Madrid, Malaga and Gibraltar. Internal flights via Madrid to Asturias, La Coruña and Vigo. Bus services are usually good and trains adequate, except in the more remote regions.

9.19.6 DISTANCE TABLE: BAY OF BISCAY AND N/NW COASTS OF SPAIN

Approximate distances in nautical miles are by the most direct route, whilst avoiding dangers and allowing for Traffic Separation Schemes. Places in *italics* are in Ireland, England and West coast of France. See also Distance Table at 9.20.6.

1.	*Crosshaven (Cork)*	**1**																			
2.	*Tuskar Rk*	85	**2**																		
3.	*Longships*	144	130	**3**																	
4.	*Ushant (Créac'h)*	235	230	100	**4**																
5.	*Bénodet*	303	298	168	68	**5**															
6.	*Belle Ile*	409	336	206	106	52	**6**														
7.	*Ile d' Yeu*	460	387	257	157	102	51	**7**													
8.	*La Rochelle*	526	453	323	223	168	117	66	**8**												
9.	*Arcachon*	515	510	380	280	227	187	138	98	**9**											
10.	San Sebastián	572	567	437	337	290	246	203	177	87	**10**										
11.	Cabo Machichaco	550	549	419	319	272	233	195	177	101	34	**11**									
12.	Bilbao (ent)	549	550	420	320	273	238	201	187	116	50	16	**12**								
13.	Santander	534	541	411	311	266	236	206	198	133	82	48	36	**13**							
14.	Gijón	508	528	391	298	267	254	237	248	205	162	128	116	90	**14**						
15.	Cabo Peñas	500	523	385	293	264	252	237	249	211	170	136	126	96	10	**15**					
16.	Ría de Ribadeo	499	520	391	308	308	279	271	288	252	223	189	179	149	63	53	**16**				
17.	Cabo Ortegal	484	510	388	307	307	290	289	313	285	258	224	214	184	98	88	40	**17**			
18.	La Coruña	508	538	418	338	327	326	326	351	323	296	262	252	222	136	126	78	38	**18**		
19.	Cabo Villano	523	556	439	365	356	358	359	383	355	328	294	284	254	168	158	110	70	43	**19**	
20.	Bayona	594	627	510	436	427	429	430	454	426	399	365	355	325	239	229	181	141	114	71	**20**

PASAJES (Pasaia) *9.19.7*

Guipúzcoa **43°20'·21N 01°55'·69W**

CHARTS AC 1181, 1102; SC 9440; SHOM 6375, 6558

TIDES See 9.19.8

SHELTER A port of refuge, 3·5M E of San Sebastián, but also a busy FV and commercial hbr with no yacht facilities. Yachts may ⚓: on E side of fairway, in bay to NE of Dir lt; E or W of fairway if space allows, but subject to wash. Basins further S are commercial/FV. Space for 60 yachts in San Pedro and Dársena Herrera.

NAVIGATION WPT 43°21'·16N 01°56'·12W, SWM buoy, L Fl 10s, 340°/160° from/to hbr ent 1·0M. Hbr ent is a 200m wide cleft in the cliffs, marked by trs Fl R 5s and G 5s and ☆ Oc 4s high on the W cliff. Enter on 155° transit of Dir lt, Oc (2) WRG 12s (W 154·5°-157°) with ldg lts: front Q 67m 18M, rear Oc 3s 86m 18M. Inner chan, dredged 10m, is only 100m wide, but well marked/lit; do not impede large vessels/FVs.

LIGHTS AND MARKS Tfc sigs, 3 vert lts, high on E cliff show: ● Ⓦ ● = no entry; ● Ⓦ ● = no exit; ● Ⓦ ● = port closed.

RADIO TELEPHONE VHF Ch 09 16 (H24).

TELEPHONE Hr Mr ☎ (943) 351816, 📠 351348.

FACILITIES **Services:** Sh, El, Ⓔ, ME (Big Ship orientated). **Town** V, R, Bar, ✉, Ⓑ. UK ferry from Bilbao/Santander.

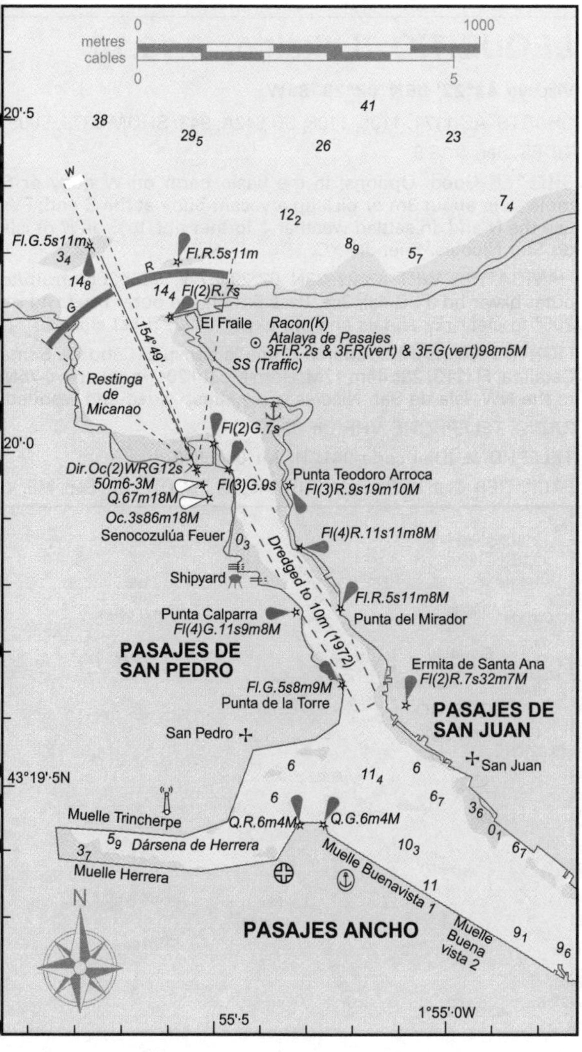

SAN SEBASTIÁN (Donostia) *9.19.8*

Guipúzcoa **43°19'·42N 01°59'·32W**

CHARTS AC 1181, 1102; SC 19B, 944, 945; SHOM 6558, 6786

TIDES

Standard Port PTE DE GRAVE (⟵); Zone –0100

Times				Height (metres)			
High Water		Low Water		MHWS	MHWN	MLWN	MLWS
0000	0600	0500	1200	5·4	4·4	2·1	1·0
1200	1800	1700	2400				
Differences PASAJES							
–0050	–0030	–0015	–0045	–1·2	–1·3	–0·5	–0·5
SAN SEBASTIÁN							
–0110	–0030	–0020	–0040	–1·2	–1·2	–0·5	–0·4

SHELTER Fair; the ⚓ becomes lively or dangerous in any NW/N'lies when heavy swell enters. Launch from Real Club Nautico will meet and direct (VHF Ch 09). Options: ⚓ S of Isla Santa Clara or SW of YC, in both cases clear of moorings and with ⚓ buoyed; or pick up a vacant mooring. Possible temp AB on pontoon at ent to the over-crowded Dársena de la Concha basins (no berths).

NAVIGATION WPT 43°19'·85N 01°59'·90W, 338°/158° from/to narrows (between Isla de Santa Clara and Monte Urgull), 0·5M. Avoid La Bancha on which the sea breaks in swell and heavy weather. Open up the bay before standing in.

LIGHTS AND MARKS Monte Urgull (huge statue of Virgin Mary) prominent from all directions; from E it looks like an island. Monte Igueldo on W side of entr Fl(2+1) 15s 132m 26M is only slightly less obvious. Isla de Santa Clara is low and inconspicuous and not seen until the nearer appr. Ldg marks (grey masts) are hard to see, but a large R & W Palladian-styled villa is conspic on 158°. Ldg lts, although intens, may be masked by shore lts.

RADIO TELEPHONE Real Club Nautico VHF Ch 09 (H24).

TELEPHONE (Dial code 943) Hr Mr 423574; CG Emerg'y 900 202 202; LB 94 483 9286; Met 274030; Auto 906 365320; Ⓗ 945 454000; Police 092; Brit Consul 94 415 7600.

FACILITIES **Darsena de la Concha** (Yacht/FV basins, both solid with local boats). **Real Club Náutico** ☎ 423575, 📠 431365, R, Bar, Ice. **City:** Gaz, V, R, Bar, Ⓑ, ✉, Ⓗ; ⇌ & ✈ Fuenterrabia (25km); ✈ also at Bilbao (92km) and ferry to UK. The city's elegance is not matched by facilities for visiting yachts.

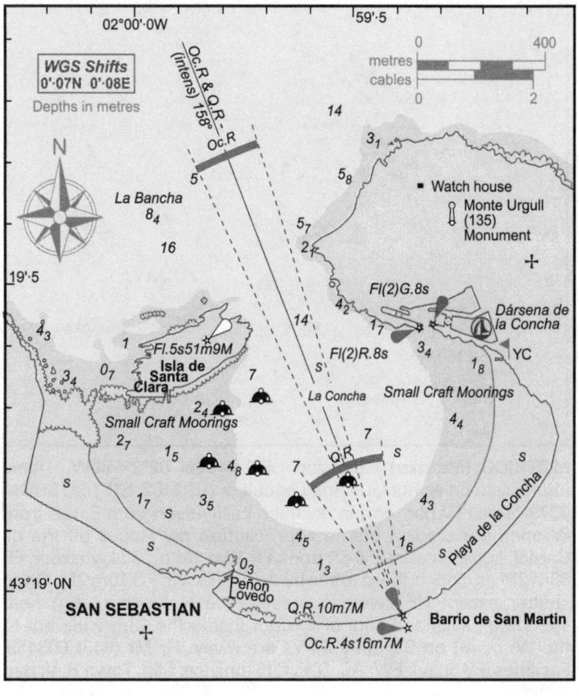

GUETARIA (Getaria) *9.19.9*

Guipúzcoa **43°18'·30N 02°11'·80W**

CHARTS AC 1171, 1102; SC 303A, 944, 943, 128; SHOM 6379, 6786

TIDES

Standard Port PTE DE GRAVE (⟵); Zone –0100

Times				**Height (metres)**			
High Water		Low Water		MHWS	MHWN	MLWN	MLWS
0000	0600	0500	1200	5·4	4·4	2·1	1·0
1200	1800	1700	2400				
Differences GUETARIA							
–0110	–0030	–0020	–0040	–1·0	–1·0	–0·5	–0·4
LEQUEITIO							
–0115	–0035	–0025	–0045	–1·2	–1·2	–0·5	–0·4

SHELTER The only good shelter between Pasajes and Bilbao from winds S to NW - pontoons to port on entry. FVs fill the inner hbr and also berth on N and W sides of outer hbr. No ⚓ in hbr which is generally foul. In fair weather ⚓ on sand or pick up a buoy close S of hbr ent, but exposed to E'lies.

NAVIGATION WPT 43°18'·90N 02°11'·00W, 045°/225° from/to hbr ent, 8½ca. Appr is straightforward day/night in fair visibility.

LIGHTS AND MARKS Lts as chartlet.

RADIO TELEPHONE VHF Ch 09 H24.

TELEPHONE (Dial code 943) Hr Mr 140213, 🖷 140201; ⊖ via Hr Mr; Met 906 365 320; Auto 906 365365; LB 900 202 202.

FACILITIES Marina (270), ☎ 140201, FW, AC, BH (30 ton); **Club Náutico y Pesca** ☎ 140201, R, Bar. **Services:** Slip, D, Sh, CH, SM, ME, El, C (5 ton); **Town:** V, R, Bar, Gaz, ☎, ✉, ⇌; ✈ Bilbao (UK ferry).

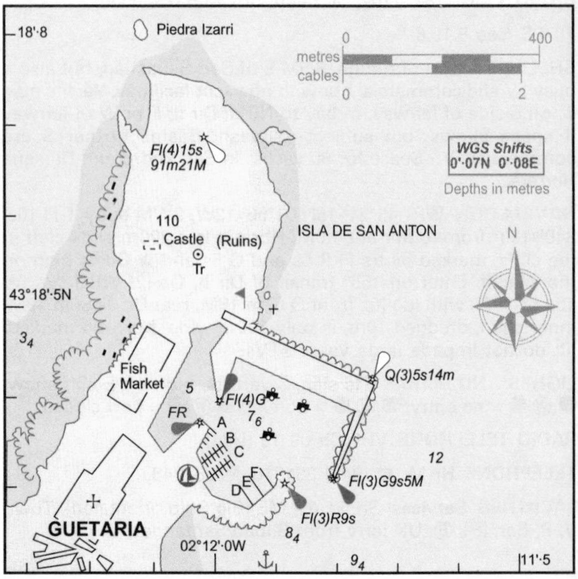

ADJACENT HARBOURS

ZUMAYA 43°18'N 02°15'W. Tides: as 9.19.9. AC 1102. New marina welcomes visitors. Easy appr from NE with rocks on both sides. Zumaya Lt Oc (3+1) 12s 39m 12M. 8 sided tower. Breakwaters lit FlG 5s and Fl (2) R 10s. All facilities. ☎ 943 862592, 🖷 943 862078. VHF Ch 09.

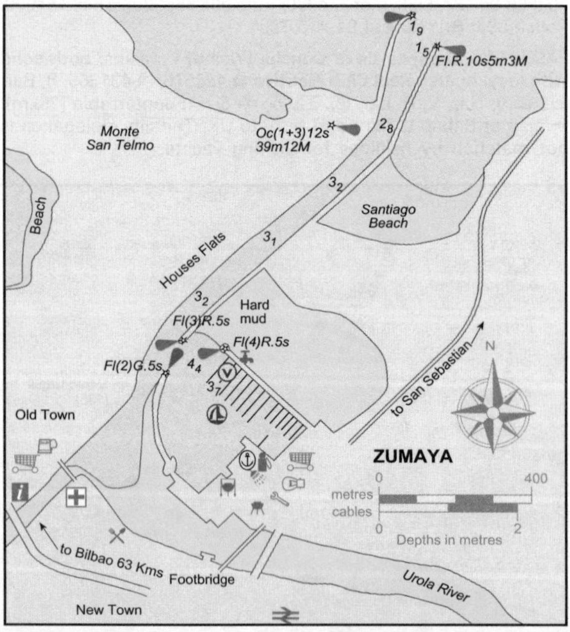

MOTRICO (Mutriku) Guipúzcoa **43°18'·80N 02°22'·80W.** Tides: interpolate times/hts Guetaria/Lequeitio. AC 1102; SC 16a; SHOM 6379. Small FV hbr (4m) in rky inlet. Easily seen from E, but from W open hbr & town before appr; caution rky ledges off Pta de Cardal. Ldg lts/marks 236·5°: front, FR 10m 2M on S bkwtr; rear, FR 63m 2M on clock tr (hard to see by day). N bkwtr, FG 10m 2M. Good shelter except NE swell. ⚓ outside the N bkwtr in 5m near spending beach and slip; or ⚓/moor inside the 23m wide ent to the W; or AB on SE quay if FVs are away. Hr Mr (943) 603459. **Facilities** (FV quay): FW, AC, D, P, C (5 ton), Ice; Slip. **Town** R, V, Bar.

LEQUEITIO (Lekeitio) *9.19.10*

Vizcaya **43°22'·06N 02°29'·85W**

CHARTS AC 1171, 1105, 1108; SC 642A, 943; SHOM 6379, 5009

TIDES See 9.19.9

SHELTER Good. Options: In the basin berth on W quay or S mole. ⚓ in about 3m or pick up a vacant buoy at the S end; FVs use the N end. In settled weather ⚓ further out, to E or W of Isla de San Nicolas. Friendly YC.

NAVIGATION WPT 43°22'·33N 02°29'·67W, 026°/206° from/to outer bkwtr hd (Fl G 4s), 3ca. Pass 5m off the outer bkwtr hd on 206° to clear rky shoals and old bkwtr (Fl (2) R 8s) close E.

LIGHTS AND MARKS Church dome is conspic. Cabo de Santa Catalina, Fl (1+3) 20s 44m 17M, Horn Mo (L) 20s, is conspic 0·75M to the NW. Isla de San Nicolas is rky, steep-sided and wooded.

RADIO TELEPHONE VHF Ch 09.

TELEPHONE (Dial code 941) Hr Mr 6840500.

FACILITIES Club de Pesca ☎ (94) 6840500; FW, D, P, CH, Slip, ME, V.

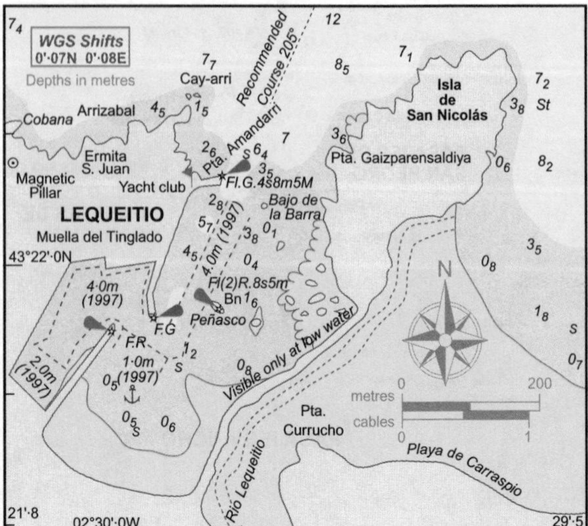

ELANCHOVE (Elantxobe) *9.19.11*

Vizcaya **43°24'·30N 02°38'·18W**

CHARTS AC 1171, 1105, 1108; SC 321A, 942, 943; SHOM 6380, 6991

TIDES Interpolate between Lequeitio and Bermeo.
Standard Port PTE DE GRAVE (⟵); Zone –0100

Times				**Height (metres)**			
High Water		Low Water		MHWS	MHWN	MLWN	MLWS
0000	0600	0500	1200	5·4	4·4	2·1	1·0
1200	1800	1700	2400				
Differences BERMEO							
–0055	–0015	–0005	–0025	–0·8	–0·7	–0·5	–0·4

SHELTER Sheltered from W in lee of Cabo Ogoño, but exposed to N/E. Tiny hbr in spectacular setting at foot of steep cliffs. The N part of outer hbr and all the inner hbr dry. At ent turn hard port into S part of outer hbr to ⚓ (buoy the ⚓) or pick up buoy in about 3m. AB on S mole is feasible, but a 1m wide underwater ledge requires holding-off line to kedge ⚓. In calm weather tempy ⚓ to E of hbr ent in 5m.

NAVIGATION WPT 43°22'·33N 02°29'·67W, 045°/225° from/to N mole hd, 6ca. From the W, hbr is not visible until bearing >205°.

LIGHTS AND MARKS N Mole, Fl G 3s 8m 4M; S Mole, F WR 7m 8/5M, W000°-315°, R 315°-000° showing over inshore dangers to the SE.

RADIO TELEPHONE Nil

TELEPHONE (Dial code 94) Hr Mr ☎ 6555119.

FACILITIES **Village:** FW, Basic V, R, Bar; Bus to Bilbao for ⇶, ✈.

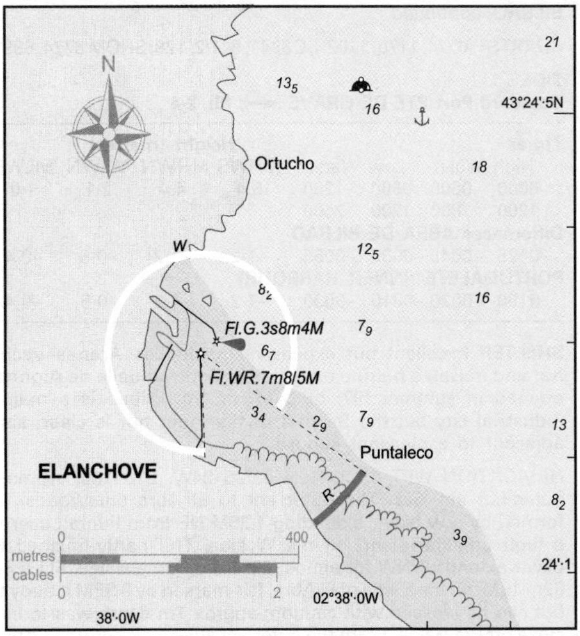

BILBAO (Bilbo) *9.19.12*

Vizcaya **43°22'·80N 03°04'·80W** (outer entrance)

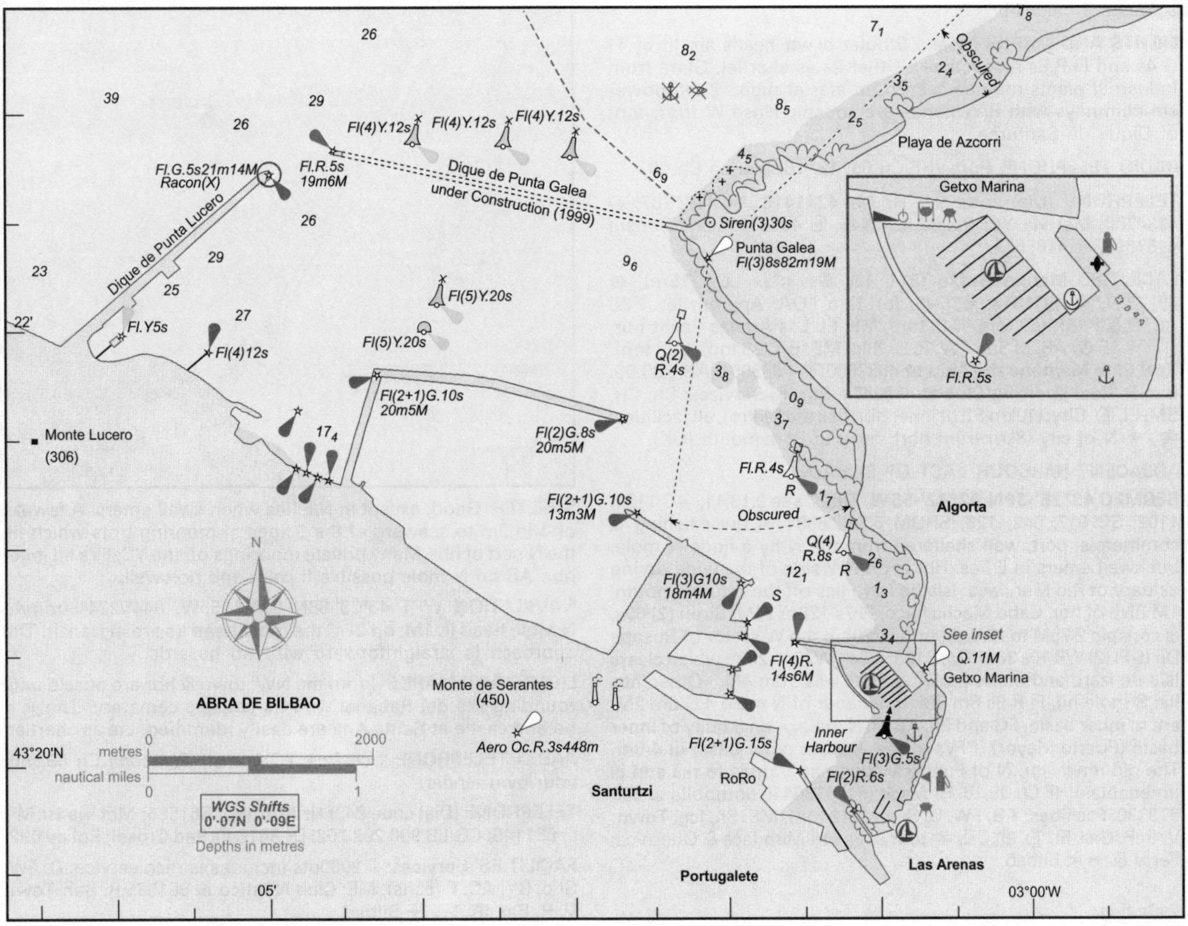

BILBAO *continued*

CHARTS AC 74, 1170, 1102; SC 3941, 941/2, 128; SHOM 6774, 6991

TIDES

Standard Port PTE DE GRAVE (⟵); ML 2·4

Times				**Height (metres)**			
High Water		Low Water		MHWS	MHWN	MLWN	MLWS
0000	0600	0500	1200	5·4	4·4	2·1	1·0
1200	1800	1700	2400				
Differences ABRA DE BILBAO							
−0125	−0045	−0035	−0055	−1·2	−1·2	−0·5	−0·4
PORTUGALETE (INNER HARBOUR)							
−0100	−0020	−0010	−0030	−1·2	−1·2	−0·5	−0·4

SHELTER Excellent but expensive inside Las Arenas yacht hbr and in Getxo marina on S side of Contramuelle de Algorta opened in summer '97; or ⚓ off in 4m. Bilbao is a major industrial city but the SE part of the inner hbr is clean and adjacent to a pleasant suburb.

NAVIGATION WPT 43°23'·10N 03°05'·34W, 310°/130° from/to outer hbr ent, 5ca. The outer ent to El Abra (inlet/roads) is formed by a W bkwtr extending 1.25M NE from Punta Lucero, a high unlit headland on the W side. The partly-finished E bkwtr extends WNW for almost 2M from Punta Galea, Fl (3) 8s 82m 19M, on the E side of El Abra. It is marked by 3 SPM lt buoys, but can be crossed with caution; approx 7m depth was found close off Pta Galea. From the outer ent steer 127° across El Abra for 3M to round the Dique de Santurce, Fl (2) G 12s. In 1998/9 much construction work in progress on the SW side of El Abra. The head of a new bkwtr extending E from the SW shore was recorded by GPS at 43°21'·52N 03°02'·66W, not far from the fairway. After passing Contramuelle de Algorta head, Fl (4) R 14s, turn ESE for the new marina; or SE for Las Arenas yacht hbr across the inner hbr.

LIGHTS AND MARKS W and E outer bkwtr heads are lit by Fl G 4s and Fl R 6s respectively. Other lts as chartlet. Glare from industrial plants may be seen from afar at night. 2 tall power stn chimneys with R/W bands are conspic close W from root of Dique de Santurce.

RADIO TELEPHONE Port VHF Ch 05, **12**, 16. Marina Ch 09.

TELEPHONE (Dial code 94) Hr Mr 4241416, 📠 4871207; ⊖ 4234700; Met via YC; Police 4246445; ⊞ 4903100; Brit Consul 4157600, 📠 4167632.

FACILITIES **Marina Getxo** (821, inc Ⓥs; max LOA 15m), ☎ 4912367, 📠 4911818; €35·46, for 12m LOA. Approx 3m. FW, AC, D & P, BH (50 ton), C (5 ton), ME, El. **Las Arenas Yacht hbr**, (125 + 15 Ⓥ) AB, M 3m, FW, P, D, Slip, ME, BH (25 ton), C (3 ton). **Real Club Maritimo del Abra** ☎ 4637600, 📠 4638061, AB €30.05, Bar, R; **Real Sporting Club** ☎ 4162411, Bar, R. **Services:** Sh, CH, SM, El, Ⓔ. **City:** (10km SE of inner hbr; use the Metro), all facilities; ≷, ✈ N of city (8km from hbr); ferry to Portsmouth (UK).

ADJACENT HARBOUR EAST OF BILBAO

BERMEO 43°25'·38N 02°42'·55W. Tides: see 9.19.11. AC 1171, 1102; SC 917, 942, 128; SHOM 6380, 6991. A busy fishing & commercial port, well sheltered from the N by a huge N mole, but swell enters in E'lies. Hbr is on NW side of the wide drying estuary of Rio Mundaca. Isla de Izaro lies off the estuary mouth, 1M ENE of hbr. Cabo Machichaco, Fl 7s 120m 24M, Siren (2) 60s, is conspic 2·75M to NW. Appr on 220° in the W sector of Rosape Dir lt, Fl (2) WR 10s 36m 7M, R108°-204°, W204°-232°, which clears Isla de Izaro and the N mole hd, Fl G 4·5s 16m 4M. Other hbr lts: S mole hd, Fl R 3s 6m 3M; inner spur of N mole, FG 5m 2M; ent to inner basin, FG and FR. AB on N mole or on S quay of inner basin (Puerto Mayor) if FVs at sea. Or ⚓ in outer basin in 4-6m. The old inner hbr, N of Puerto Mayor, partly dries to rks and is untenable. VHF Ch 09,16. Hr Mr ☎ (94) 6186445 or mobile ☎ 908 873330. **Facilities**: AB, FW, D, Slip, C (12 ton), ME, Sh, Ice. **Town:** V, R, P, Gaz, El, Ⓔ, Ⓑ, ✉, ≷ tourist line to Mundaca & Guernica; Ferry & ✈ at Bilbao.

CASTRO URDIALES *9.19.13*

Cantabria **43°22'·87N 03°12'·50W**

CHARTS AC 1171, 1170, 1102; SC 165A, 941, 128; SHOM 3542, 6991

TIDES

Standard Port PTE DE GRAVE (⟵); Zone −0100

Times				**Height (metres)**			
High Water		Low Water		MHWS	MHWN	MLWN	MLWS
0000	0600	0500	1200	5·4	4·4	2·1	1·0
1200	1800	1700	2400				
Differences CASTRO URDIALES							
−0040	−0120	−0020	−0110	−1·4	−1·5	−0·6	−0·6
RIA DE SANTOÑA (03°28'W)							
−0005	−0045	+0015	−0035	−1·4	−1·4	−0·6	−0·6

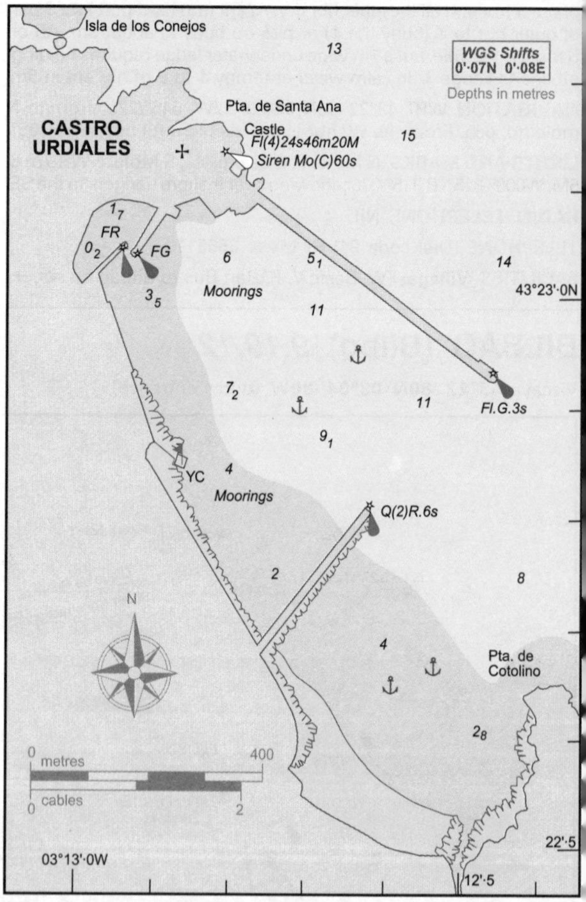

SHELTER Good, except in N/E'lies when swell enters. A few Ⓐs or ⚓ in 9m to seaward of the 6 lines of mooring trots which fill the N part of hbr. Many private moorings off the YC; FVs fill inner hbr. AB on N mole possible if calm and no swell.

NAVIGATION WPT 43°23'·68N 03°11'·55W, 044°/224° from/to N Mole head lt, 1M; on 224° the mole head lts are in transit. The approach is straightforward with no hazards.

LIGHTS AND MARKS From the NW, town & hbr are obsc'd until rounding Pta del Rabanal with its conspic cemetery. The ✠, lt ho and castle at Santa Ana are easily identified. Lts as chartlet.

RADIO TELEPHONE Use free YC launch *Blancona* Ch 09, not your own tender.

TELEPHONE (Dial code 942) Hr Mr/Club 861585; Met via Hr Mr; ⊖ 861146; CG/LB 900 202 202; Dr 861640(Red Cross); Police 092.

FACILITIES **Services:** ⚓ 2000pts includes launch service, D, FW, Slip, BY, AC, P (cans), ME; **Club Náutico** ☎ 861585 R, Bar. **Town** V, R, Bar, Ⓑ, ✉; ✈ Bilbao.

ADJACENT HARBOUR/ANCHORAGE

RÍA DE SANTOÑA Cantabria. **43°25'·90N 03°24'·67W**. AC 1171, 1102; SC 24B, 940/1; SHOM 3542. Tide: see 9.19.13. The Lat/Long given is WPT off river mouth and on ldg lts 283·5°. The sandy estuary is dominated by Monte Ganzo (374m) on N side and is exposed to E and S. Laredo, small FV hbr, is on S side. The river narrows off Pta del Pasaje: Santoña is to the NW with 2 small, dirty basins both lit; to the S, yacht ⚓, pontoons, moorings and CN are on the W tip of Pta del Pasaje. A shallow chan runs 2M S to Colindres. Lts: Pta Pescador, Fl (3+1) 15s, is on N side of Monte Ganzo. Ldg lts 283·5°: front, Fl 2s 6m 8M; rear, Oc (2) 5s 13m 11M. Laredo, N mole FR 9m 2M. CN de Laredo ☎ (942) 605812/16, M, Slip, C (6 ton), R, Bar.

SANTANDER *9.19.14*

Cantabria **43°27'·75N 03°47'·42W** (Darsena de Molnedo)

CHARTS AC 1155, 1102/5; SC 4011/2, 940, 127; SHOM 7365, 6991

TIDES Standard Port PTE DE GRAVE (⟵); ML 2·3

Times				Height (metres)			
High Water		Low Water		MHWS	MHWN	MLWN	MLWS
0000	0600	0500	1200	5·4	4·4	2·1	1·0
1200	1800	1700	2400				
Differences SANTANDER							
−0020	−0100	0000	−0050	−1·3	−1·4	−0·6	−0·6
RÍA DE SUANCES (04°03'W)							
0000	−0030	+0020	−0020	−1·5	−1·5	−0·6	−0·6
SAN VICENTE DE LA BARQUERA							
−0020	−0100	0000	−0050	−1·5	−1·5	−0·6	−0·6
RÍA DE TINA MAYOR (04°31'W)							
−0020	−0100	0000	−0050	−1·4	−1·5	−0·6	−0·6

SHELTER Access in all weather/tides. There are three facilities for yachts in Santander; CN La Horadada (CNH), CM de Santander (CMS) and the Marina de Santander (MS). To stbd on entering the CNH provides ⚓ for 100 craft, 7–10m (☎ 942 273013); the CMS, further along in the Dársena de Puerto Chico, has 250 berths to 12m(☎ 942 214050, 📠 361972) with water, electricty and fuel. You may also moor to the CMS buoys just outside the dock. Both these facilities are near the city and its services. The MS is in the SW quadrant of the port near the airport.

NAVIGATION From the E, WPT 43°29'·00N 03°43'·80W, bears 055°/235° from/to Nos 2/3 chan buoys, 2M; appr between Isla de Santa Maria and Bajo Santoñuca (16·7m; breaks). From the W, WPT 43°29'·55N 03°46'·50W (4ca E of Cabo Mayor). Thence in fair weather head SE between Isla de Mouro and Peninsula de la Magdalena (min depth 7·3m); in heavy weather keep NE of Isla de Mouro. Punta Rabiosa ldg lts lead 236° into the well-buoyed/lit DW chan. Second ldg lts 259·5°. Lt buoys Nos 4, 5, 6 and 7 omitted for clarity. No 14 bcn tr, Fl (4) R 11s, is easily identified. Beyond the conspic oil terminal/jetty pass a SHM buoy, Fl G 4s, and an inflatable ECM buoy; **after** a small preferred chan buoy, Fl (2+1) G 10s, turn WSW for marina ent. The ldg marks/lts (hard to see) to marina lead 235·5° across a drying sandbank. Note: marina advises against a night entry unless already visited by day.

LIGHTS AND MARKS The former Royal Palace, now a university, is conspic on top of Peninsula de la Magdalena. A glazed pyramid-shaped bldg about 400m W of Marina del Cantabrico is a good daymark. Lts and buoys as chartlet.

RADIO TELEPHONE Port Authority *Santander Prácticos* VHF Ch 06, **12**, 14, 16; Marinas Ch 09 (06). Local weather is broadcast on Ch 11 at 0045 and every 4 hrs until 2045, plus 0715 and 1115.

TELEPHONE (Dial code 942) Hr Mr 223900, 📠 362413; ⊖ and Met via Hr Mr; Brit Consul 220000.

FACILITIES Darsena de Molnedo (1·7m; 108 berths; apply at YC for berth), ☎ 223900, 📠 362413, Slip, AC, D, FW, C (1·5 ton); **Real Club Maritimo de Santander** ☎ 273750, ⚓ and ⚓ 50-100m off YC, Bar, R; **Marina del Cantabrico** (2·2-3·1m; AB 700+, max LOA 20m; still under construction), €7·37, ☎ 369288, FW, C, P, D, Slip, BH (27 ton), CH, ME, Sh, El, Ⓔ, Gaz, R, Bar. Plenty of berths and adequate security to leave a yacht. The adjacent airport generates few flights and little noise. **City:** www.puertosantander.com, all amenities; ⇌ & bus; Brittany ferry terminal to Plymouth is 6ca W of Darsena de Molnedo; ✈ (Parayas).

19

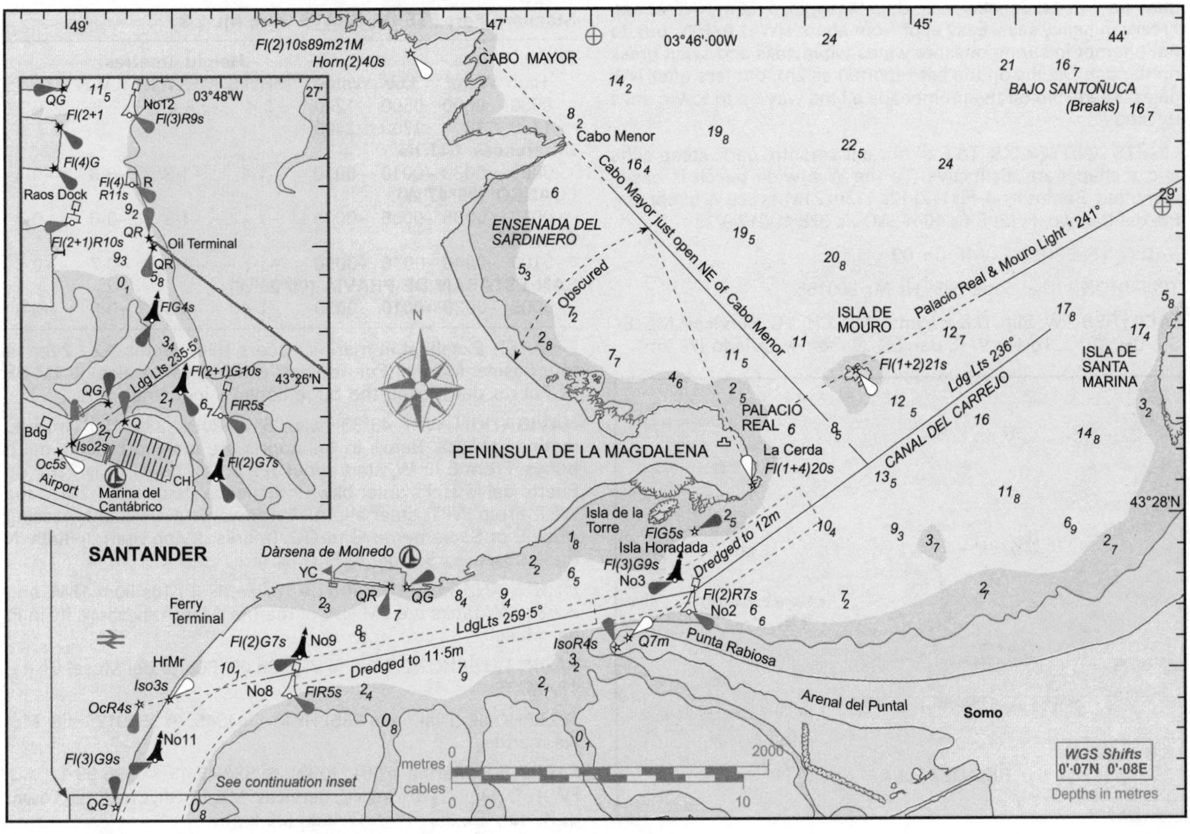

MINOR HARBOUR BETWEEN SANTANDER AND RIBADESELLA

SAN VICENTE DE LA BARQUERA, Cantabria. **43°23'·72N 04°23'·07W**. AC 1150, 1105; SHOM 6381, 6991; SC 4021, 938. Tides see 9.19.14. Fishing hbr with good shelter in large shallow estuary, access HW±3; but HW±1 is advised if there is any swell at the entrance. Beware shallow bar and tidal streams 3-4kn. Appr on 225° to enter between Isla Peña Menor to stbd and hd of training wall to port. Beyond hotel and ☆ FG on post among pine trees keep to the NW bank; drying areas to the SE have encroached on the chan. AB on fish quay is possible or ⚓ near ship mooring buoy close to root of trng wall. Moorings by the rebuilt bridge and castle are awkward and subject to traffic noise H24. Lights: Punta de Silla, Oc 3·5s 42m 13M; Horn Mo (V) 30s. Isla Peña Menor, Fl WG 2s 7m 7/6M, G175°-235°, W235°-045°. Hd of trng wall, Fl (2) R 8s 8m 5M. Hr Mr ☎ (942) 710009; CG 900 202 202; Met 232405; Dr 712450; Police 710288. **Facilities**: Fish quay FW, ME, C, SM, D pump is for FVs only. **Town**: R, V, Bar, P & D (cans), Ⓑ, ✉; ✈ (Santander 62km).

RIBADESELLA *9.19.15*

Asturias 43°28'·16N 05°04'·00W

CHARTS AC 1150, 1105; SC 4031, 937, 127; SHOM 6381, 6691

TIDES

Standard Port PTE DE GRAVE (⟵); Zone –0100

Times				Height (metres)			
High Water		Low Water		MHWS	MHWN	MLWN	MLWS
0000	0600	0500	1200	5·4	4·4	2·1	1·0
1200	1800	1700	2400				
Differences RIBADESELLA							
+0005	–0020	+0020	–0020	–1·4	–1·3	–0·6	–0·4

SHELTER Good. AB, clear of FVs, on the NE/E quays in 2-3m, well short of the low bridge, fender board needed. Limited space to ⚓.

NAVIGATION WPT 43°28'·55N 05°04'·00W, 349°/1169° from/to quay hd (Pta del Caballo), 6ca. Bajo Serropio, 1100m NNE of ent, breaks in heavy seas. Easy appr from about HW–1 to HW, but do not attempt in strong onshore winds when seas and swell break on the bar. Depths on the bar reported as 2m, but less after NW gales. Keep 25m off the promenade all the way up to town; dries to stbd.

LIGHTS AND MARKS To E of hbr ent smooth, dark, steep cliffs and a chapel are distinctive. To the W a wide beach is easily identified. Somos lt ho, Fl (1+2) 12s 113m 21M, is 8ca W of hbr ent. Pta del Caballo, Fl (2) R 6s 10m 5M, vis 278·4°-212·9°.

RADIO TELEPHONE VHF Ch 09 occas.

TELEPHONE (Dial code 985) Hr Mr 860155.

FACILITIES FW, Slip, D & P (cans), ME, CH, YC. **Services:** ME, El, Sh, CH, Ⓔ, ⊡. **Town:** V, R, Bar, ✉, Ⓑ, ⇌; ✈ Oviedo (78 km).

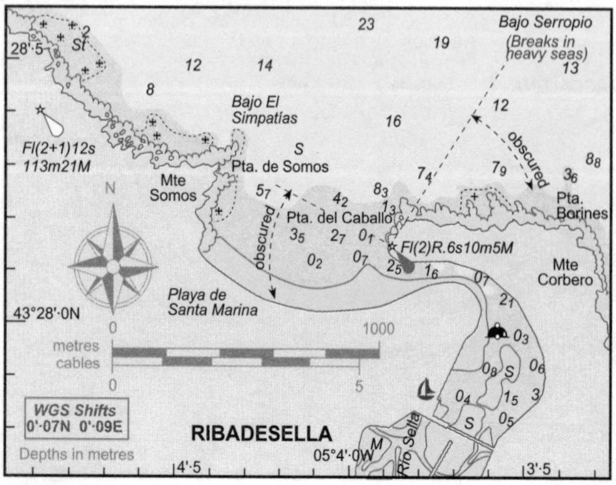

GIJÓN *9.19.16*

Asturias 43°32'·82N 05°40'·06W

CHARTS AC 1154, 1153, 1105, 1108; SC 4042, 935, 127; SHOM 6381, 5009

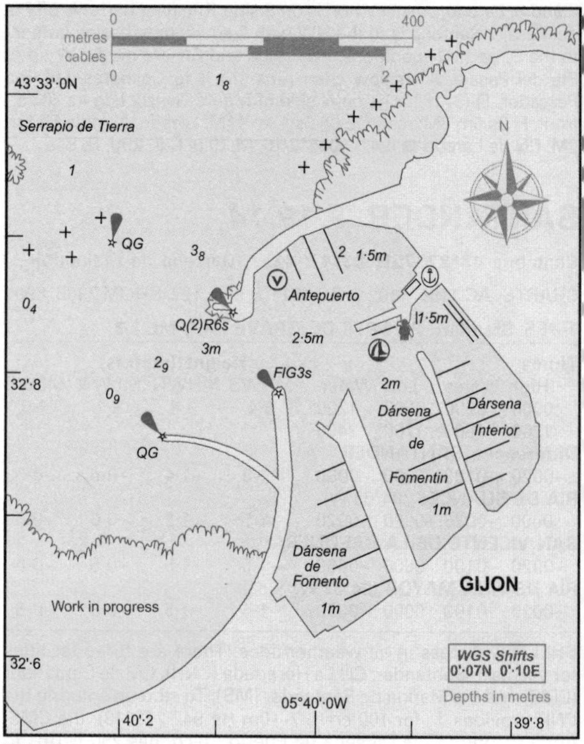

TIDES

Standard Port PTE DE GRAVE (⟵); ML 2·3

Times				Height (metres)			
High Water		Low Water		MHWS	MHWN	MLWN	MLWS
0000	0600	0500	1200	5·4	4·4	2·1	1·0
1200	1800	1700	2400				
Differences GIJON							
–0005	–0030	+0010	–0030	–1·4	–1·3	–0·6	–0·4
LUANCO (05°47'W)							
–0010	–0035	+0005	–0035	–1·4	–1·3	–0·6	–0·4
AVILÉS							
–0100	–0040	–0015	–0050	–1·5	–1·4	–0·7	–0·5
SAN ESTABAN DE PRAVIA (06°05'W)							
–0005	–0030	+0010	–0030	–1·4	–1·3	–0·6	–0·4

SHELTER Excellent in marina, access H24, depths 1·2 - 2·8m in four basins. Marina (Puerto Local or Muelles Locales) is 1M SE of Puerto del Musel, the huge conspic industrial port.

NAVIGATION WPT 43°33'·08N 05°40'·30W, 330°/150° from/to marina ent, 3ca. Banks in the appr's are marked by cardinal lt buoys. From E or W, start about 1ca E of lt ho, Fl G 3s 22m, on Puerto del Musel's outer bkwtr hd; thence steer 180°/1·2M to the WPT. From WPT, steer about 150° towards marina ent, passing close E of Sacramento G tr, QG, (marks drying reef). Initially N mole obscures S mole lt, Fl G 3s.

LIGHTS AND MARKS Cabo de Torres, Fl (2) 10s 80m 18M, and conspic W tanks are 2M NW of marina. Many nav/shore lts in P. del Musel.

RADIO TELEPHONE Marina VHF Ch 09. Puerto del Musel Ch 11, 12, **14**, 16.

TELEPHONE (Dial code 985) Hr Mr 394945, 📠 359917; ⊖ & Met via marina.

FACILITIES **Marina** (750+120 ♥), ☎ 534 45 43, 📠 535 99 17, AC, FW, P, D, Slip, C (10 ton), YC; **Services:** ME, El, Sh, CH, Ⓔ, ⊡. **Town:** V, R, Bar, ✉, Ⓑ, ⇌; ✈ Oviedo (26 km).

ADJACENT HARBOUR EAST OF CUDILLERO

AVILÉS, Asturias. **43°35'·80N 05°57'·00W**. AC 1133, 1151; SC 4052, 935; SHOM 7361, 5009. Tides: 9.19.16. A port of refuge, except in >F9 W/NW'lies, but also an industrial, commercial and fishing hbr. The ent, S of Pta del Castillo lt (Oc WR 5s 38m 20/17M) and N of conspic white beach, is open to W/NW but well sheltered from N'lies. The ent chan runs ExS for 7ca then turns S for 2M. Best ⚓ is in 5-6m on E side of chan, just S of the bend. The chan is well marked/lit all the way up-hbr. Port VHF Ch 06, 09, 12, **14**, 16. Hr Mr ☎ (985) 563013. No yacht facilities per se, but usual FV supplies and domestics. Club Náutico at Salinas.

CUDILLERO *9.19.17*

Asturias **43°33'·90N 06°08'·80W**

CHARTS AC 1108; SC 934/5, 126a; SHOM 5009.

TIDES Use San Estaban de Pravia; see 9.19.16.

SHELTER Good in large modern basin, NW of hbr ent and village, but N'ly swell can make entry/exit difficult and can work into the basin. AB on N'ly of 3 pontoons on N wall, or ⚓ off these pontoons in 8-9m. FVs occupy the NW end of the basin. The old hbr, S of ent, is exposed to swell, but convenient for dinghies; a yacht can dry out on slip.

NAVIGATION WPT 43°34'·40N 06°08'·30W, 020°/200° from/to hbr ent, 6½ca. From the W keep 5ca offshore until clear of Islotes las Colinas, small islets NW of ent. Appr with Punta Rebollera lt ho on initial bearing of 200°. The rocky ent, marked by FR and FG lts, opens up only when close to. Turn 90° stbd through narrow inlet into basin.

LIGHTS AND MARKS Punta Rebollera lt ho, Oc (4) 16s 42m 16M.

RADIO TELEPHONE Hr Mr Ch 27.

TELEPHONE (Dial code 985) Hr Mr 591114.

FACILITIES FW, D (gasoleo B) from FV quay, P (cans), ME, Slip, small commercial shipyard. **Village**: 5 mins by dinghy, 25 mins on foot; V, R, Bar, ✉.

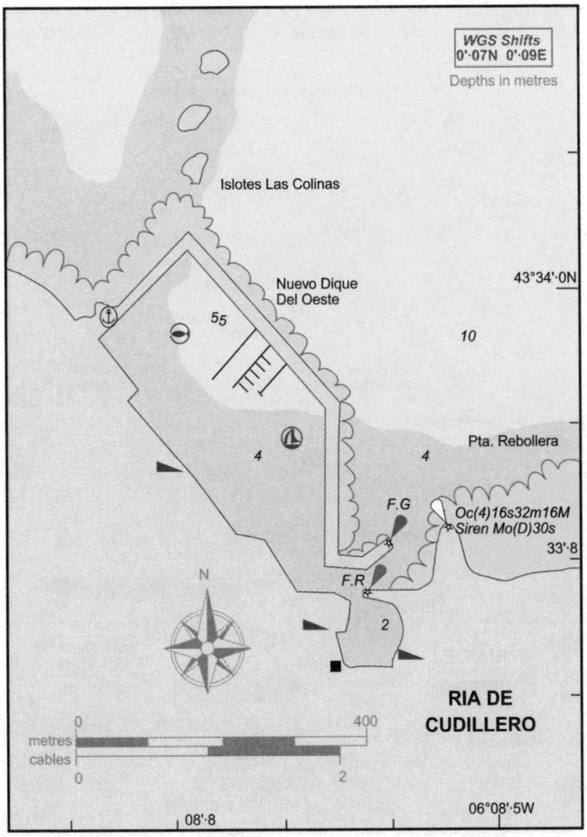

LUARCA *9.19.18*

Asturias **43°33'·00N 06°32'·10W**

CHARTS AC 1133, 1108; SC 933, 934, 126a; SHOM 6381, 5009

TIDES
Standard Port PTE DE GRAVE (⟵); Zone –0100

Times				Height (metres)			
High Water		Low Water		MHWS	MHWN	MLWN	MLWS
0000	0600	0500	1200	5·4	4·4	2·1	1·0
1200	1800	1700	2400				
Differences LUARCA							
+0010	–0015	+0025	–0015	–1·2	–1·1	–0·5	–0·3

SHELTER Good shelter in the outer hbr protected from all but N'lies; moor fore and aft to the E bkwtr or alongside if no swell. No room to ⚓ except outside the E bkwtr in settled weather. Narrow chan leads SE to inner hbr dredged 2m (prone to silting). Little chance of a berth; pontoons in SE corner are full of local craft; temp'y AB on NW side may be possible.

NAVIGATION WPT 43°33'·59N 06°32'·26W, 350°/170° from/to E bkwtr hd, 6ca. Appr on the ldg lts/marks 170° to clear rky shoals either side. The E bkwtr lt ho is conspic and almost in transit with the ldg marks.

LIGHTS AND MARKS Cabo Busto, Fl (4) 20s 84m 25M, is 3M ENE of hbr ent. Pta Blanca, Oc (3) 15s 63m 14M, siren Mo (L) 30s, W □ tr and house on prominent headland 300m ENE of hbr ent; also conspic ✠. Ldg lts 170°: front, Fl 5s 18m 2M; rear, Oc 4s 25m 2M; both on thin W pylons, R bands. W bkwtr hd, Fl (3) G 9s 7m 5M. E bkwtr hd, Fl (3) R 9s 22m 5M, ○ concrete tr. Inner spur, Fl (4) G 11s 6m 1M.

RADIO TELEPHONE None

TELEPHONE (Dial code 985) Hr Mr 5640176

FACILITIES FW, AC, D from FV quay, P (cans), ME, CH, Slip, C (8 ton). **Town**: YC, V, R, Bar, Ⓑ, ✉, ⇄.

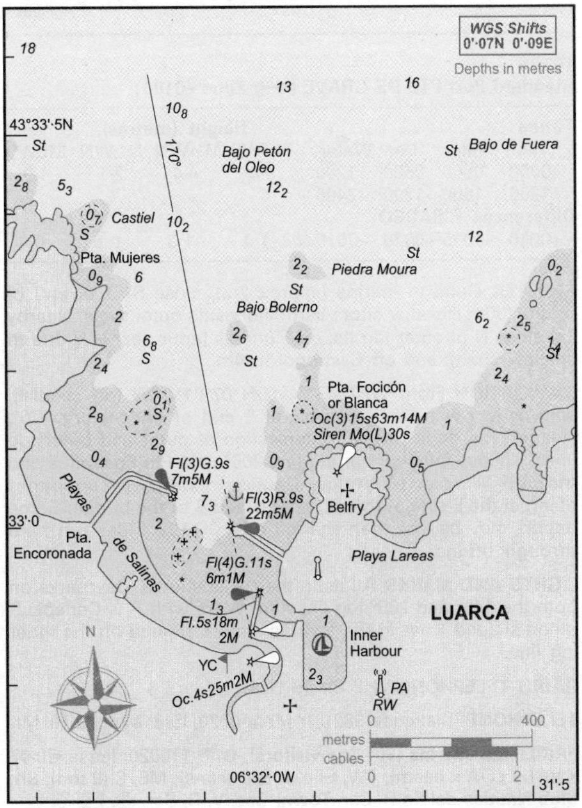

RÍA DE RIBADEO *9.19.19*

Lugo **43°32'·53N 07°02'·10W**

CHARTS AC 1122, 1108; SC 550A, 932, 126; SHOM 5009

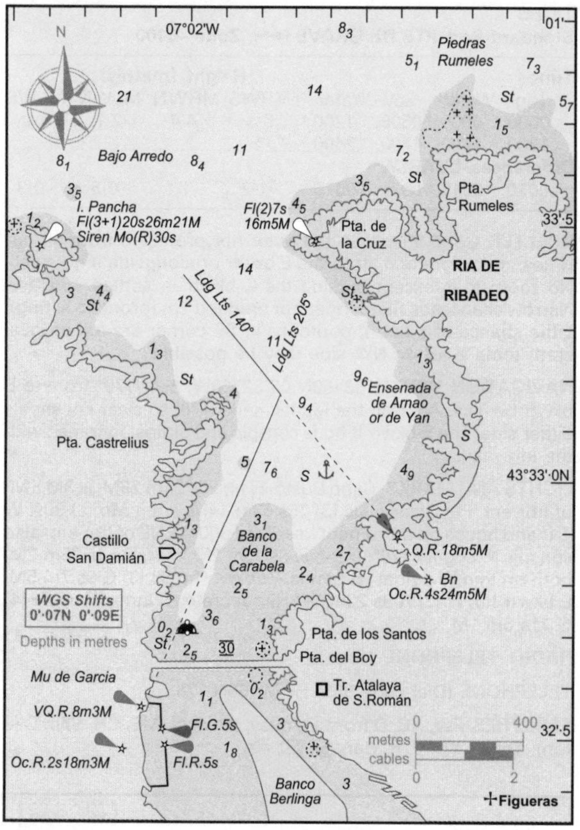

TIDES

Standard Port PTE DE GRAVE (⟵); Zone –0100

Times				Height (metres)			
High Water		Low Water		MHWS	MHWN	MLWN	MLWS
0000	0600	0500	1200	5·4	4·4	2·1	1·0
1200	1800	1700	2400				
Differences RIBADEO							
+0010	–0015	+0025	–0015	–1·4	–1·3	–0·6	–0·4

SHELTER Good in marina (approx 2m), close S of W end of bridge (30m clnce). Visitors berth alongside outer mole. Nearby ⚓s: close N of outer ldg lts; off Figueras (appr near HW due to shallow chan); and off Castropol in 4m.

NAVIGATION From WPT 43°34'·00N 07°01'·93W (off chartlet), appr by day with W tr (conspic at E end of bridge) brg 170°, clearing Pta de la Cruz, to intersection of outer and inner ldg lines. Thence follow inner ldg line 205° past Pta Castrelius and through W span of bridge. Caution: extensive sandbanks obstruct the E side of the ría, both N and S of the bridge. Some depths may be less than charted on AC 1122. Tides run hard through bridge.

LIGHTS AND MARKS All lts in the ría as shown. Daymarks on both the 140° and 205° ldg lines are W trs with R ◊. Conspic R onion-shaped ✠ twr in the town is almost aligned on the inner ldg line.

RADIO TELEPHONE VHF Ch 16 H24.

TELEPHONE (Dial code 982) Hr Mr 110020; ⊜ & Met via Hr Mr.

FACILITIES Marina (30+ few visitors), ☎/📠 110020; fee is €0·07 x m² (ie LOA x beam); FW, Slip, P & D (cans), ME, C (8 ton), Sh; **Club Náutico del Eo** R, Bar. **Town:** Gas, V, R, Bar, Ⓑ, ✉, ▣.

RÍA DE VIVERO *9.19.20*

Lugo **43°41'·00N 07°36'·06W** (Cillero bkwtr ☆ FR)

CHARTS AC 1122, 1108; SC 4082, 931, 126a; SHOM 5009

TIDES

Standard Port PTE DE GRAVE (⟵); Zone –0100

Times				Height (metres)			
High Water		Low Water		MHWS	MHWN	MLWN	MLWS
0000	0600	0500	1200	5·4	4·4	2·1	1·0
1200	1800	1700	2400				
Differences RÍA DE VIVERO							
+0010	–0015	+0025	–0015	–1·4	–1·3	–0·6	–0·4
SANTA MARTA DE ORTIGUEIRA (07°51'W)							
–0020	0000	+0020	–0010	–1·3	–1·2	–0·6	–0·4

SHELTER Good, except in N'lies. ⚓ in E'lies inside Isla Insua d'Area, 1·3M NE of Cillero. In S-W winds ⚓ at the head of the ria off Playa de Covas in 6-7m. Cillero is a major FV hbr; keep clear of the N and E quays. AB on rough quay on SSW of hbr. Marina (3m) lies 6ca up-river.

NAVIGATION WPT 43°43'·00N 07°35'·40W (mouth of the ria), 195°/015° from/to bkwtr hd at Cillero. Easy ent, 7ca wide, between Pta Socastro and Pta de Faro.

LIGHTS AND MARKS Pta Socastro, Fl G 7s; Pta de Faro, Fl (2) R14s; both 18m 5M.

RADIO TELEPHONE Cillero Port VHF Ch 16.

TELEPHONE (Dial code 982) Hr Mr ☎ 561040, 📠 560410; YC ☎ 561014; Dr 561202; Police 562922;

FACILITIES Cillero: D & P, FW, ME, Bar. **Marina:** ⓥ, YC, FW, AC; **Vivero**: V, R, Bar, Ⓑ, ✉, ⇄, Ⓗ (Burela 20km, ☎ 982-589900).

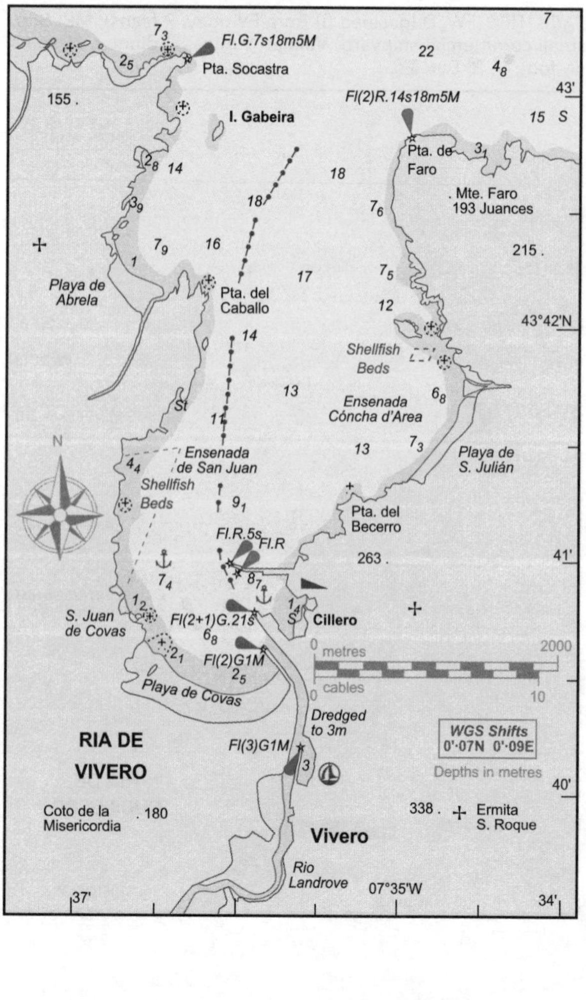

ADJACENT HARBOURS

RÍA DEL BARQUERO. 43°45'·00N 07°40'·50W. AC 1122; SC 18A; SHOM 6383. Tides: 9.19.20. A delightful ría, but no shelter from NE'lies. Small hbrs at Bares and El Barquero (☎ 981-414002) on the W side; and on the E side, close S of Pta del Castro, at Vicedo; piers Fl (4) G 11s & Fl (4) R 11s. Lts: Isla Coelleira (islet between this ría and Ría de Vivero), Fl (4) 24s 87m 8M; Pta de la Barra, Fl WRG 3s, see 9.19.3 for sectors; Pta del Castro, Q (2) R 6s.

ENSENADA DE SANTA MARTA. 43°45'·00N 07°50'·00W. AC 1122, 1108; SC 18A; SHOM 6383. Tides: 9.19.20. From the above position Puerto de Carino bears 233°/1·5M; or head approx 188°/2·3M for the ent to Ría de Santa Marta leading up to Santa Marta de Ortigueira. The latter is a tricky river with variable sandbanks and little charted data, but a rewarding experience and town. Puerto Carino is less appealing due to a coaling wharf, but ⚓ in 6m within the bay, sheltered from all W'lies.

RÍA DE CEDEIRA *9.19.21*

La Coruña **43°39'·50N 08°03'·80W**

CHARTS AC 1122, 1111; SC 930, 41A; SHOM 5009, 3007

TIDES Interpolate between Santa Marta de Ortigueira (9.19.20) and El Ferrol (9.19.22). ML No data; Zone –0100.

SHELTER Very good; a pleasant refuge for yachts trying to weather Cabo Ortegal in a NE'ly. ⚓ about 500m E of the modern FV port in 3-4m, clear of the fairway. The E/SE end of the bay shoals rapidly toward the drying river mouth.

NAVIGATION WPT 43°41'·25N 08°05'·60W (7½ca off chartlet), 335°/155° from/to Pta Promontorio lt ho, 2·35M. From N keep about 1M off Pta Candelaria until the ría ent opens. From the S a similar offing will clear rks off Pta Chirlateira. Appr on 155° transit of Pta Promontorio lt ho and Pta del Sarridal; when abeam Pta Chirlateira alter 161° to pass midway between Pta del Sarridal and Piedras de Media Mar, W lt tr conspic in centre of ría. Then steer E past bkwtr head.

LIGHTS AND MARKS Pta Candelaria, Fl (3+1) 24s, is 2·6M NE of the WPT. Pta de la Frouxeira, Fl (5) 15s, is 6M to SW. Pta del Sarridal, Oc WR 6s, on E side of ent. Piedras de Media Mar, Fl (2) 5s 12m 4M, commands the ría and can be passed either side.

RADIO TELEPHONE No VHF. MF *Cedeira Cofradia* 1800kHz, 2182.

TELEPHONE (Dial code 981) Hr Mr 480389; ⊖ & Met via Hr Mr.

FACILITIES **Hbr**: FW, Slip, ME, El, Sh, L just N of ⚓ symbol. **Town:** Ⓔ, D & P (cans), V, R, Bar, Ⓑ, ✉, ⓟ, ⇌ & ✈ La Coruña.

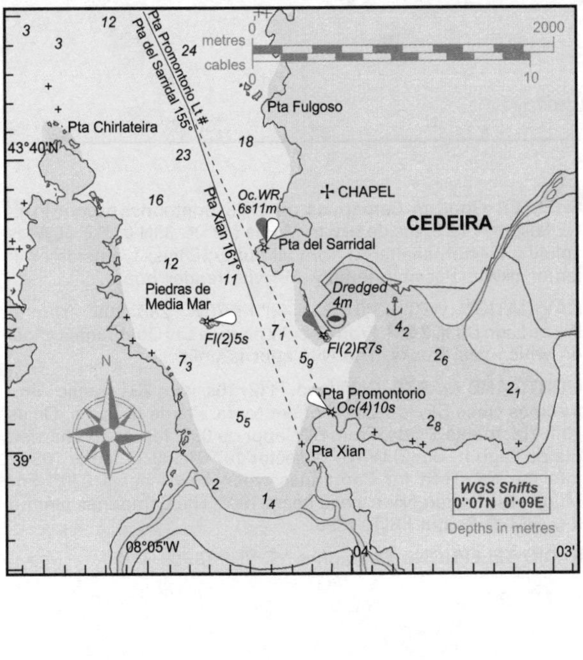

EL FERROL *9.19.22*

La Coruña 43°28'·62N 08°14'·50W (Curuxeiras)

CHARTS AC 1115, 1111; SC 4122/3/4, 412A, 929; SHOM 3007

TIDES

Standard Port PTE DE GRAVE (⟵); Zone –0100

Times				Height (metres)			
High Water		Low Water		MHWS	MHWN	MLWN	MLWS
0000	0600	0500	1200	5·4	4·4	2·1	1·0
1200	1800	1700	2400				
Differences EL FERROL							
–0045	–0100	–0010	–0105	–1·6	–1·4	–0·7	–0·4

SHELTER Good inside the narrow, but straightforward ent to ría. El Ferrol is a naval and commercial port with limited yacht facilities. Be aware of strong tides and occasional squalls in the narrows. Caution: New Spanish charts show depths up to 2m less than charted in some areas. A small marina at La Graña may have AB or ⚓/moor off. Dársena de Curuxeiras is central: AB in 2m on NE side on stone walls and prone to ferry wash; 3 pontoons at the head of this inlet are not available to visitors. ⚓s, from seaward: off Cariño (poor holding) and Pereiro on N shore of ent chan and at Baño and Mugardos inside the ría (see chartlet).Good ⚓ at Ensenada de Ares in 2·5m.

NAVIGATION WPT 48°27'·15N 08°20'·00W, 238°/058° from/to S. Cristobal Dir lt, Oc (2) WR 10s, 1·6M. In bad weather avoid the outer banks (Tarracidos, Cabaleiro and Leixiñas) to the N and W.

LIGHTS AND MARKS C. Priorino Chico, Fl 5s 34m 23M, marks N side of ría ent. Inner ldg lts 085° to the narrows; front Fl 1·5s, rear Oc 4s; both W trs. Chan is deep and adequately buoyed/lit.

RADIO TELEPHONE Port Control *Ferrol Prácticos* VHF Ch **14** (H24).

TELEPHONE (Dial Code 981) Hr Mr 352945, 🕮 353174; ⊖ & Met via Hr Mr.

FACILITIES **Marina Terramar** at La Graña (approx 50), FW, Slip, AC, ME, P & D (cans), El, C (1·5 ton), Sh; bus every ½hr to the city (20 mins); **Club Náutico. Curuxeiras** ☎ 321594; Slip, FW, D, P (cans), ME, El, CH, C (8 ton). **City:** All needs, ⇌; ✈ (La Coruña).

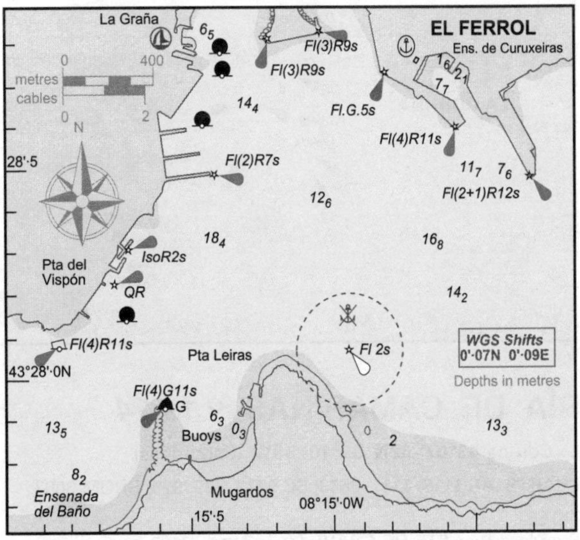

ADJACENT HBRS IN RÍAS DE ARES AND DE BETANZOS

ARES 43°25'·50N 08°14'·00W. AC 1114, 1111; SC 4125, 412A. Wide, sheltered bay with modern FV basin in SW corner, bkwtr hd Fl (3) R 9s. Possible AB in basin or ⚓ off in 3m or to E of Pta Modias, clear of mussel beds.

FONTAN 43°21'·70N 08°14'·35W. Charts as above. Good shelter; Marina in SE corner of hrb. FW, E. FVs berth inside N mole. ⚓ in 3m inside bkwtrs, clear of fairway and La Pulgueira rk, Fl (4) R 11s. Good CH. VHF: Hr Mr Ch 09, ☎ 981 620895.

LA CORUÑA *9.19.23*

La Coruña **43°22'·13N 08°23'·10W** (marina)

CHARTS AC 1114, 1111; SC 4126, 412A, 929; SHOM 3007

TIDES

Standard Port PTE DE GRAVE (⟵); Zone –0100

Times				Height (metres)			
High Water		Low Water		MHWS	MHWN	MLWN	MLWS
0000	0600	0500	1200	5·4	4·4	2·1	1·0
1200	1800	1700	2400				
Differences LA CORUÑA							
–0110	–0050	–0030	–0100	–1·6	–1·6	–0·6	–0·5

SHELTER Good at marinas, protected from wash by unlit floating wavebreak close NE of Cas S. Anton. Two N'ly pontoons are Sporting Club (Casino); S'ly 2 are Real Club Náutico. Speed limit 3kn. Both YCs offer Ⓥs; or ⚓ further out on possible foul ground. At Dársena de la Marina, 2 small pontoons close W of old RCN bldg may be negotiable.

NAVIGATION WPT 43°23'·28N 08°22'·03W, 011°/191° from/to head of Dique de Abrigo, Fl G 5s, 1·35M. Note the 108° & 182° ldg lines meet at this WPT. Avoid Banco Yacentes, about 1M NW of WPT, between the ldg lines (off chartlet).

LIGHTS AND MARKS Conspic marks: Torre de Hércules, Fl (4) 20s; 5·3M SW of which is power stn chy (218m); twin white twrs (85m, R lts, hbr control) at root of Dique de Abrigo, next to marina. Pta Fiaiteira ldg lts 182°: front, Iso WRG 2s; rear, Oc R 4s. Storm signals are displayed from Cas de S. Anton

RADIO TELEPHONE Port Control *Dársena Radio Torre Hércules* VHF Ch 12; VTS 13; Marinas 09; LB 73.

TELEPHONE (Dial code 981) Hr Mr 226001, ℻ 205862; Sporting Club (Casino) ☎ 209007, ℻ 213953; Real Club Náutico ☎ 203265; ℻ 203008; Hr Mr 226001, ℻ 205862; ⊖ & Met via YCs; Ⓗ 277905; Dr 287477.

FACILITIES **Marinas:** (250+ some Ⓥ), €15·02, AB (F&A), FW, AC, P, D, M, Slip, BH (30 ton), ME, El, C (1 ton), Sh, ▣, CH, SM, Ⓔ. **City:** all amenities; ⇌, ✈ (international via Santiago).

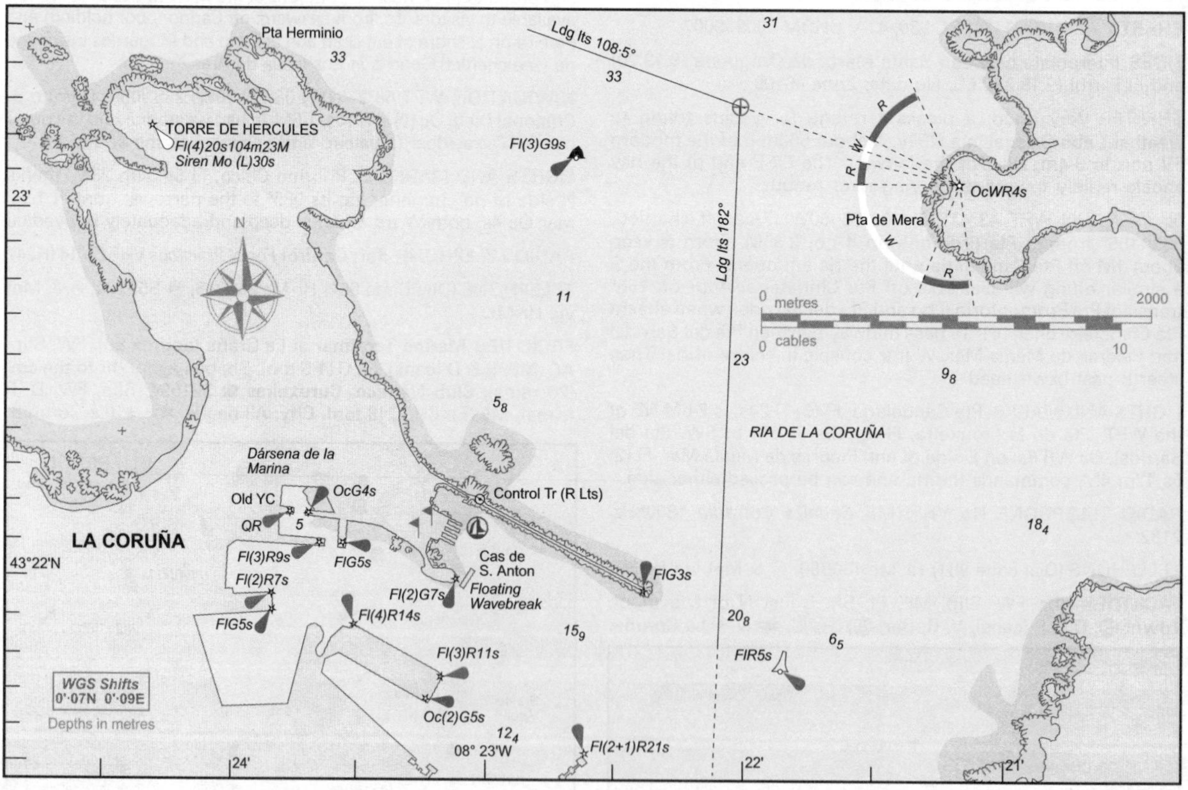

RÍA DE CAMARIÑAS *9.19.24*

La Coruña **43°07'·62N 09°10'·88W** (Camariñas)

CHARTS AC 1113, 1111, 3633; SC 9272, 927, 928; SHOM 3007

TIDES

Standard Port PTE DE GRAVE (⟵); Zone –0100

Times				Height (metres)			
High Water		Low Water		MHWS	MHWN	MLWN	MLWS
0000	0600	0500	1200	5·4	4·4	2·1	1·0
1200	1800	1700	2400				
Differences RÍA DE CORME (43°16'N 08°58'W)							
–0025	–0005	+0015	–0015	–1·7	–1·6	–0·6	–0·5
RÍA DE CAMARIÑAS							
–0115	–0055	0000	–0105	–1·6	–1·6	–0·6	–0·5

SHELTER Good in Camariñas on 2 YC pontoons, except in E/NE'lies; or ⚓ to S, inside bkwtr. Mugia (43°06'·39N 09°12'·60W) is solely a FV hbr, sheltered from all but E/SE'lies; ⚓ outside or in lee of bkwtr. Possible temp'y AB with fender board.

NAVIGATION WPT 43°07'·60N 09°13'·75W, 288°/108° from/to Pta de Lago Dir lt, 2·9M. From N or W beware Las Quebrantes shoal on which sea breaks. The N'ly appr is unlit.

LIGHTS AND MARKS C. Villano, Fl (2) 15s, with 23 conspic wind turbines close SE, is 2·2M N of ent to ría. Pta de la Barca, Oc 4s 13m 7M, marks S side. From SW, appr on 080° ldg lts, as chartlet. Pta de Lago lt, Oc (2) WRG, W sector 107·8°-109·1°, leads 108·5° into the ría. Turn for Camariñas when bkwtr bears 030°. For Mugia, turn when bkwtr head bears 190°. The Camarinas pier hd lt is Fl(3) R 8s but FR(T) 1996).

RADIO TELEPHONE Camariñas YC VHF Ch 09.

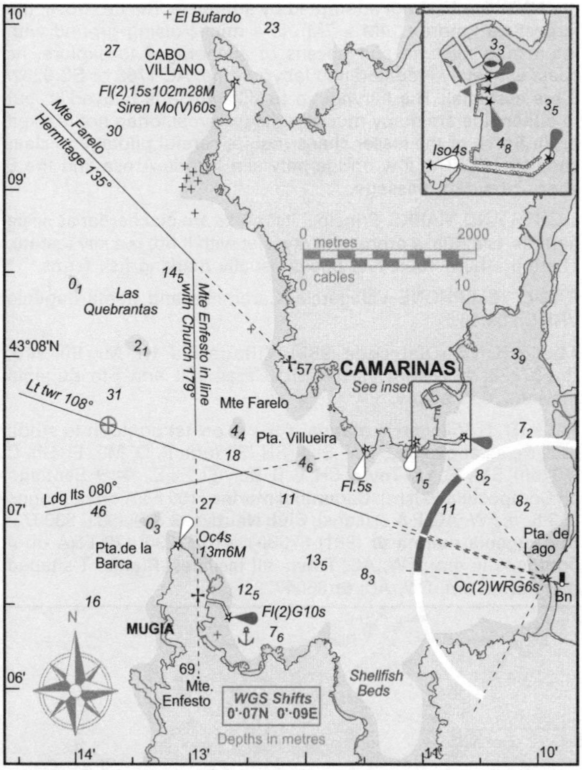

TELEPHONE (Dial code 981) CNC 736002; ⊜ & Met via CNC; Mugia Hr Mr 742030.

FACILITIES Club Náutico Camariñas (60 + Ⓥ), ☎ 737130, 📠 736325; F&A, €6·97. **Services** (both hbrs): Slip, AC, D & P (cans), FW, ME, C, Sh. **Villages**: V, R, Bar, ✉, Ⓑ; Bus to La Coruña, ✈ Santiago de Compostela.

RÍA DE MUROS *9.19.25*

La Coruña **42°43'·50N 09°04'·00W** (Ent WPT)

CHARTS AC 1756; SC 9264, 9260, 926; SHOM 3007

TIDES

Standard Port LISBOA (⟶); Zone –0100

Times				Height (metres)			
High Water		Low Water		MHWS	MHWN	MLWN	MLWS
0500	1000	0300	0800	3·8	3·0	1·5	0·5
1700	2200	1500	2000				
Differences CORCUBION (42°57'N 09°12'W)							
+0055	+0110	+0120	+0135	–0·5	–0·4	–0·3	0·0
MUROS							
+0050	+0105	+0115	+0130	–0·3	–0·3	–0·2	0·0

SHELTER Good at Muros (42°46'·71N 09°03'·25W), but 2 pontoons in the inner hbr are full of locals. ⚓ off on weedy holding (2 or 3 shots may be needed) or at Ens de San Francisco. Noya, at the head of the ría, is only accessible to shoal draft. Portosín marina (3·5-8m) is at 42°45'·96N 08°56'·77W. El Son has difficult access and no yacht facilities. Extensive shellfish beds.

NAVIGATION WPT 42°43'·50N. 09°04'·00W, 1M SSE of Pta Queixal lt and 2·3M NW of Pta Castro lt, Fl 5s (off chartlet). From the N keep to seaward of Bajo de los Meixidos and Los Bruyos which lie up to 6M WNW of Pta Queixal. The ría is mostly deep and clear, but beware mussel rafts off the N shore.

LIGHTS AND MARKS Mte Louro is a conspic conical hill at the W side of ent. At the head of the ría Isla Quiebra is a good mark. At night Pta Queixal and Cabo Reburdino light the NW shore and Pta Castro and Pta Cabeiro the SE.

RADIO TELEPHONE *Club Náutico Portosín* VHF Ch 09.

TELEPHONE (Dial code 981) Hr Mr Muros 826005, Hr Mr Portosin 820505, Marina Portosin 826140.

FACILITIES Muros: FW, D (not near LW), P (cans), V, R, Bar, Ⓑ, ✉; ⇌ and ✈ Santiago de Compostela (40 km by bus via Noya). **Club Náutico Portosín marina** (200+ some Ⓥ), F&A €12·17, Slip, BH (32 ton), AC, D, P, FW, ME, El, C (3 ton), Sh, R, Bar, ▣; **Portosín:** CH, V, R, Bar, ✉.

19

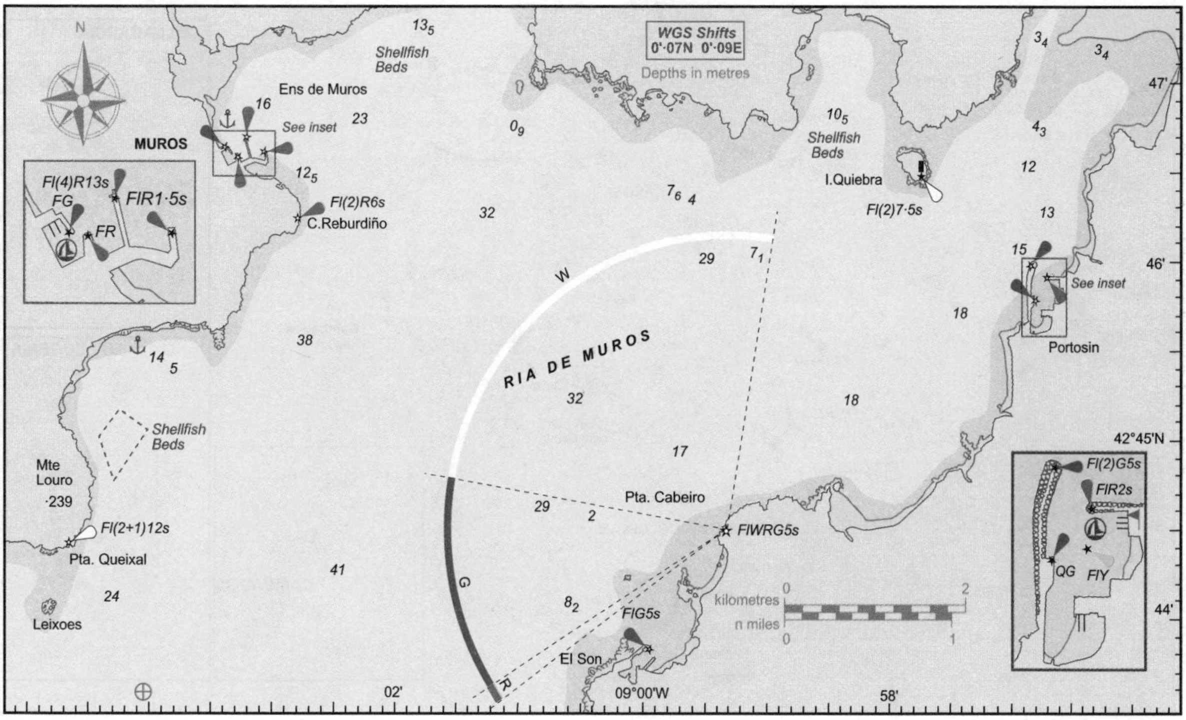

RÍA DE AROSA *9.19.26*

La Coruña (NW)/Pontevedra (SE). ⊕ **42°26'·50N 08°59'·00W**

CHARTS AC 1764, 1768, 1755, 1757, 3633; SC 9262/3, 4153; SHOM 5536, 3007

TIDES

Standard Port LISBOA (⟶); ML 2·05; Zone –0100

Times				**Height (metres)**			
High Water		Low Water		MHWS	MHWN	MLWN	MLWS
0500	1000	0300	0800	3·8	3·0	1·5	0·5
1700	2200	1500	2000				
Differences VILLAGARCIA							
+0040	+0100	+0110	+0120	–0·3	–0·2	–0·2	0·0

SHELTER Shelter can be found from most winds. Santa Eugenia and Caramiñal on the NW shore and Villagarcia, principal hbr/town, at the NE corner have marinas (see insets). At the head of the ría, Rianjo has a yacht pontoon in about 3m inside the hbr. FV hbrs (clockwise from ent) include: Aguino, Puerto Cruz, Carril, Villanueva, S. Julian (Isla Arosa), Cambados (N'ly of two hbrs) and San Martin del Grove (2 pontoons for very small craft).

NAVIGATION WPT 42°26'·50N 08°59'·00W, 198°/018° from/to Is Rua (lt), 6·8M. Isla Sálvora (lt) at the mouth of the ría should be left to port; the rocky chans between it and C. Corrubedo 7M to the NNW are best not attempted by strangers. Ría de Arosa, the largest ría (approx 14M x 7M), is a mini-cruising ground with interesting pilotage and dozens of anchorages to explore. Its coast is heavily indented and labyrinthine. AC 1768 or SC 9262/3 are essential. The fairway up to Villagarcia is buoyed/lit, but to either side are many mussel rafts (*viveros*), often not marked or lit. Some of the lesser chans require careful pilotage to clear shoals/rocks. The low bridge between Isla de Arosa and the E shore prevents passage.

LIGHTS AND MARKS Principal lts/marks are on chartlet as scale permits. Isla Rúa, a prominent rky islet with lt ho, is a key feature. There are numerous Y Lt buoys usually marking fish farms.

RADIO TELEPHONE Villagarcia, Caramiñal and Santa Eugenia VHF Ch 09 16.

TELEPHONE (Dial code 982) Villagarcia Hr Mr 501340, 📠 507923; ⊜ & Met via Hr Mr; Caramiñal and Sta Eugenia marinas, see below.

FACILITIES **Villagarcia marina** (416+ Ⓥ on 1st pontoon to stbd); ☎ & 📠, as above; AC, FW, Slip, BH (35 ton), P, D, ME, El, Sh, C (70 ton), SM, Ⓔ, YC. **Town**: CH, V, R, Bar, Ⓑ, ✉, ◙, ⇌; ✈ Santiago de Compostela (53km). **Caramiñal marina** (150 F&A on pontoons in 3·5m); FW, AC, P & D (cans); **Club Náutico** ☎ & 📠 (981) 830970; **Sta Eugenia marina** ☎ (981) 873801, 📠 873290; (70 F&A on 4 pontoons in 4m); FW, AC. **Town**: all facilities. **Rianjo**: T-shaped pontoon in 3m, FW, AC; ☎ 860477.

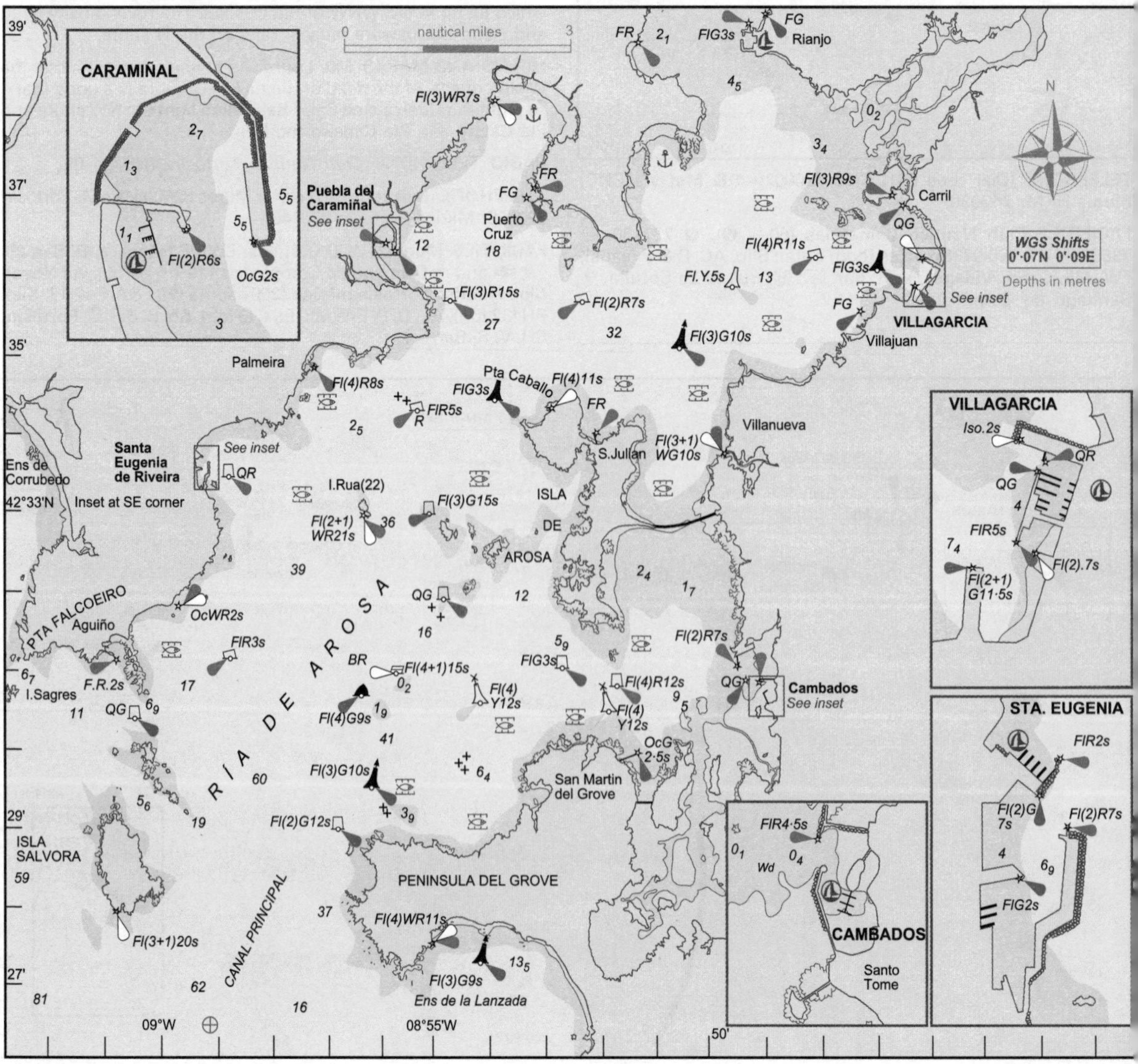

ꟾÍA DE PONTEVEDRA *9.19.27*

ontevedra **42°22'·00N 08°50'·00W** (centre of ría)

HARTS AC 1758, 3633; SC 9251, 4161/2/3, 925; SHOM 3007

IDES

Standard Port LISBOA (⟶); ML 1·9; Zone –0100

imes				Height (metres)			
High Water		Low Water		MHWS	MHWN	MLWN	MLWS
0500	1000	0300	0800	3·8	3·0	1·5	0·5
1700	2200	1500	2000				
ifferences MARIN (42°24'N 08°42'W)							
+0050	+0110	+0120	+0130	–0·5	–0·4	–0·3	0·0

HELTER Good shelter can be found from any wind. Islas Ons nd Onza off the mouth of the ría offer a barrier to wind and swell. angenjo has new marina. Aguete marina is not yet fully ompleted. Other hbrs and ⚓s, clockwise from NW ent, include, n the N shore: Porto Novo, Rajó and Combarro, and on the S hore: Bueu and Aldán. Anchorage on E side of Isla Ons. See ACILITIES. Access to Pontevedra, the provincial capital, is estricted by a shallow chan and low bridge. Marin is a naval ase and commercial port of little interest to yachts.

AVIGATION From WPT 42°18'·00N 08°56'·88W, (which also es on the 129° ldg lts for Ria de Vigo) track 053° to enter via the ain chan, Boca del Sudoeste, into centre of ria between C. de dra and Pta Cabicastro. From N, transit Paso de la Fagilda on 30°, or Canal de Los Camoucos on 175°; both chans need care. la Tambo is a restricted military area; landing prohib.

IGHTS AND MARKS Lts and marks as chartlet. Isla Ons is a teep, rky island with conspic lt ho, Fl (4) 24s 126m 25M, ctagonal tr.

ADIO TELEPHONE Marin VHF Ch 12 16.

ELEPHONE (Dial code 986). See below for ☎ numbers.

FACILITIES (Clockwise from N entrance)

Porto Novo: Full of moorings, no space to ⚓ inside the hbr. Find a vacant ⚲ or ⚓ NE of ent in about 6m. Small pontoon on the N mole is suitable for landing only. Keep clear of FVs and ferries on S mole, Fl (3) R 6s. CN ☎ 723266, FW, D, CH, ME, V, R, Bar, Ⓑ. Ferry to Isla Ons.

Sangenjo: Marina lies inside new L-shaped bkwtr which extends S, then E from near original molehd, Fl (4) R 12s. ☆ QR at hd of new bkwtr, 42°23'·84N 08°48'·01W. Small inner hbr is full of FVs; unlit W tr, G top, marks shoal. Marina ☎ +(34) 986 720517, 📠 720578; 500 AB, D, BH, FW, AC. CN ☎ 720517, 📠 720578, FW, C (5 ton), ME, V, R, Bar, Ⓑ, ✉.

Rajó: Temp'y ⚓ in about 5m off the bkwtr hd, Fl (2) R 8s.

Combarro: ⚓ in about 3m to SE of bkwtr hd, Fl (2) R 8s. A new mole 1ca S of the old bkwtr gives added shelter; the lt on hd is inop. The bay is generally shallow; the village is noted for *horreos* and tourists. Possible security risk.

Pontevedra: Enter by dinghy near HW between training walls, Fl G/R 5s. The N side of chan avoids shoals and old bridge foundations in mid-channel between overhead cables and motorway bridge (both 12m clearance). Small private marina in Rio Lérez beyond. Town: all facilities.

Aguete: New marina in pleasant bay, but the 2 pontoons S of floating wavebreak were not in use July '98; many ⚲s. The YC bldg resembles superstructure of a liner. Do not round mole hd lt too close due to offlying rks to SW/W. **Marina** (approx 100 F&A, inc Ⓥ), ☎ 702373, 📠 702708, Slip, BH (28 ton), AC, P, D, FW, ME, M, El, C (8 ton), Sh; **Club de Mar** R, Bar. Village: few shops.

Bueu: essentially a FV hbr, but possible AB outside the E mole, or ⚓ to W of hbr in about 5m. Caution: mussel rafts to NNW and NNE. Hbr ent is lit, Fl G 3s and Fl (2) R 6s. Hr Mr ☎ 320253. P & D (cans), CH, V, R, Bar. Ferry to Isla Ons.

Ria de Aldán: Worth exploring in settled weather; beware mussel rafts on W side. Temp'y ⚓s may be found on E side and at head of ría; uncomfortable in fresh N'lies.

Isla Ons: Ferry jetty at Almacen. Fair weather ⚓ in 5m off the beach at Melide. Almost uninhabited, but tourist trap in season. Bar, R at Almacen. No landing on Isla Onza.

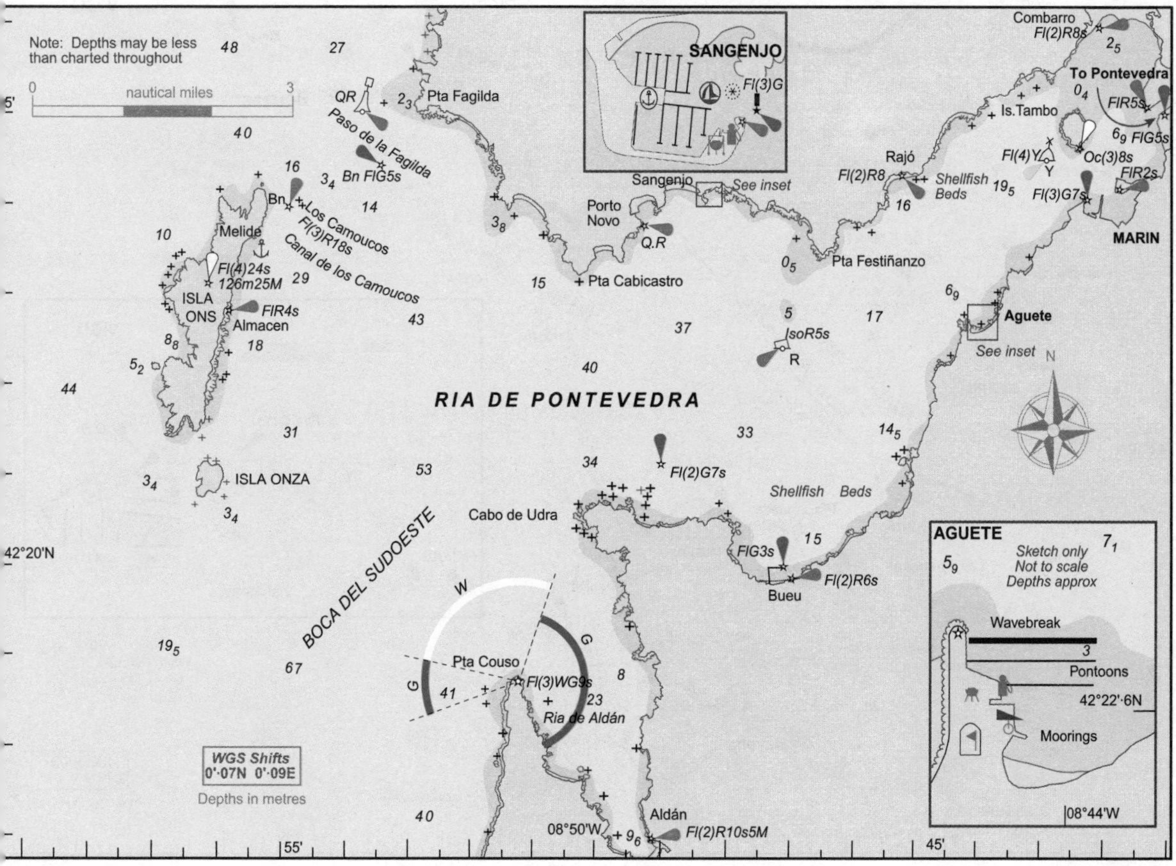

RÍA DE VIGO *9.19.28*

Galicia **42°14'·63N 08°43'·35W** (Ent to Vigo marina)

CHARTS AC 1757, 2548, 3633; SC 9240/1, 4165/6; SHOM 7595, 7596, 3007

TIDES

Standard Port LISBOA (⟶); ML 1·96; Zone –0100

Times				Height (metres)			
High Water		Low Water		MHWS	MHWN	MLWN	MLWS
0500	1000	0300	0800	3·8	3·0	1·5	0·5
1700	2200	1500	2000				
Differences VIGO							
+0040	+0100	+0105	+0125	–0·4	–0·3	–0·2	0·0

SHELTER The ent to ría is protected by Islas Cies with easy appr chans from N and S. Good shelter in Vigo marina, unless a NW'ly scend enters. Narrow ent to marina, marked by PHM/SHM lt twrs, is close E of the most E'ly of 4 conspic blue cranes. The old YC bldg, like a liner's superstructure, is in centre of marina. Cangas on the N shore is a sizable town with FV hbr; ⚓ inside or to the E. Very attractive ⚓s on E side of Islas Cies off Isla del Norte, Isla del Faro and Isla de S. Martin, all of which form a Nature Reserve. Ensenada de San Simón, beyond motorway suspension bridge, is shallow but scenic with ⚓s on W, E and S sides.

NAVIGATION North Chan WPT 42°16'·62N 08°54'·58W, 309 129° from/to Cabo del Home front ldg lt, 2·2M. Isla del Nort (Cies) lies SW; the chan is 1·4M wide and clear. South Chan WP 42°09'·42N 08°55'·00W, 249°/069° from/to Cabo Estay front ld lt, 5·0M. Caution: on N side of 1·5M wide chan, Castros d Agoeiro shoal (4·1m) lies 5ca S of Isla Boeiro lt ho. A WCM buoy defines SE side of chan and marks Las Serralleiras, rk islets NW of Bayona. Inside the ría beware extensive unl mussel rafts along the N shore. The docks and city of Vigo lin the SE shore.

LIGHTS AND MARKS Islas Cies are readily identified by the high, rugged bare slopes and white beaches on the E side. Ld lts/marks for the appr chans are as per the chartlet. The buoye inner fairway lies between brgs of 066° and 077° on the consp Hermitage (chapel) tower on Monte de la Guía.

RADIO TELEPHONE Port Control *Vigo Prácticos* VHF Ch 14 1 Marina Ch 09.

TELEPHONE (Dial code 986) Hr Mr 449694, 📠 449695; ⊖ & M via marina; British Consul 437133.

FACILITIES **Vigo marina** (413 F&A + few Ⓥ), ☎ 224003, 📠 22351 P & D, Slip, BH (32 ton), AC, FW, ME, El, Ⓔ, CH, C (3 ton), Sh, **Real Club Náutico** ☎ 433588, R, Bar. CN de Bouzas ☎ 232442. **Cit** all amenities; ⇄ ; ✈ (national).

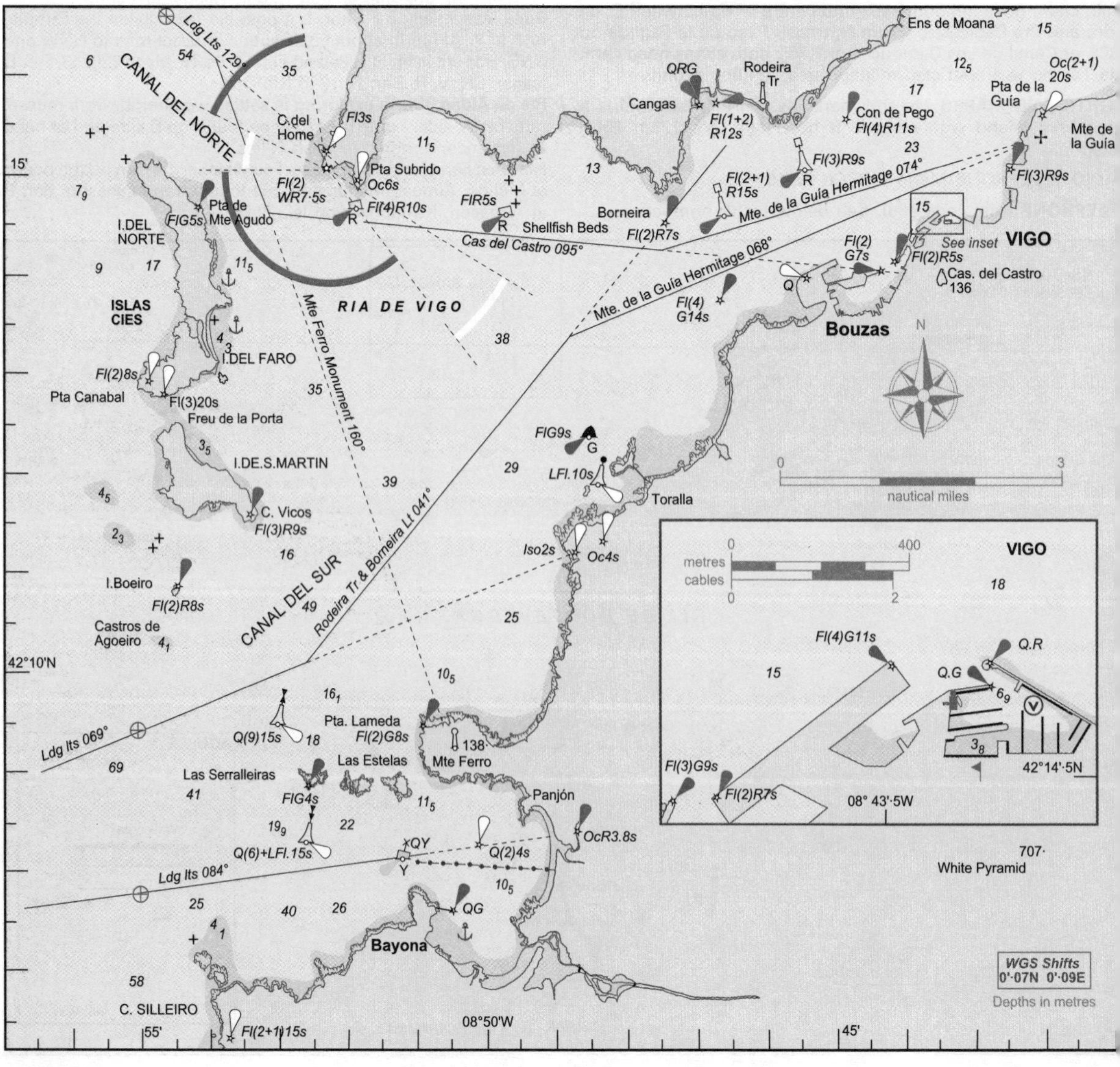

BAYONA *9.19.29*

Galicia **42°07'·45N 08°50'·55W**

CHARTS AC 2548, 3633; SC 4167, 9241, 924/5; SHOM 3007

TIDES

Standard Port LISBOA (⟶); Zone –0100

Times				Height (metres)			
High Water		Low Water		MHWS	MHWN	MLWN	MLWS
0500	1000	0300	0800	3·8	3·0	1·5	0·5
1700	2200	1500	2000				
Differences BAYONA							
+0035	+0050	+0100	+0115	–0·3	–0·3	–0·2	0·0
LA GUARDIA (41°54'N 08°53'W)							
+0040	+0055	+0105	+0120	–0·5	–0·4	–0·3	–0·1

SHELTER Excellent; berth in marina, run by YC or on their Ⓜs. Or ⚓ E of marina, but clear of fairway to FV jetty.

NAVIGATION WPT 47°07'·80N 08°55'·00W, 264°/084° from/to SPM buoy QY, 2·8M. From S keep 1M off Cabo Silleiro to clear reefs. To the N of ldg line, 4 islets and outliers are marked by SCM and WCM lt buoys. The Canal de la Porta, between Monte Ferro and Las Estelas is a useful shortcut to/from Ría de Vigo, but keep W of 0·9m patch in mid-channel.

LIGHTS AND MARKS Ldg lts 084° as chartlet, hard-to-see white conical twrs, the front on a tiny rky islet. At bkwtr head (Dique de Abrigo) ☆, QG 12m 6M, is on a B/W chequered ○ tower. N of the bay, a prominent white monument is on Monte Ferro, near Pta Lameda. Other conspic daymarks are: castle walls (parador), white wall of Dique de Abrigo and flag-mast in marina. FV jetty has white crane.

RADIO TELEPHONE *Monte Real Club de Yates* VHF Ch 06, 16.

TELEPHONE (Dial code 986) Hr Mr 355234; ⊜ & Met via YC; Ⓗ 352011; Police 355027.

FACILITIES Marina, run by Monte Real Club de Yates, (200+ some ⓥ in 6m), ☎ 355576, 📠 355061, €10·52, AB, F&A, M, AC, P, D, FW, Slip, BH (20 ton), C (1·5 ton), ME, El, Ⓔ, CH, SM, Sh, Bar, Ice, R. **Town:** most facilities inc ⊠; ⇌, ✈ Vigo (21 km).

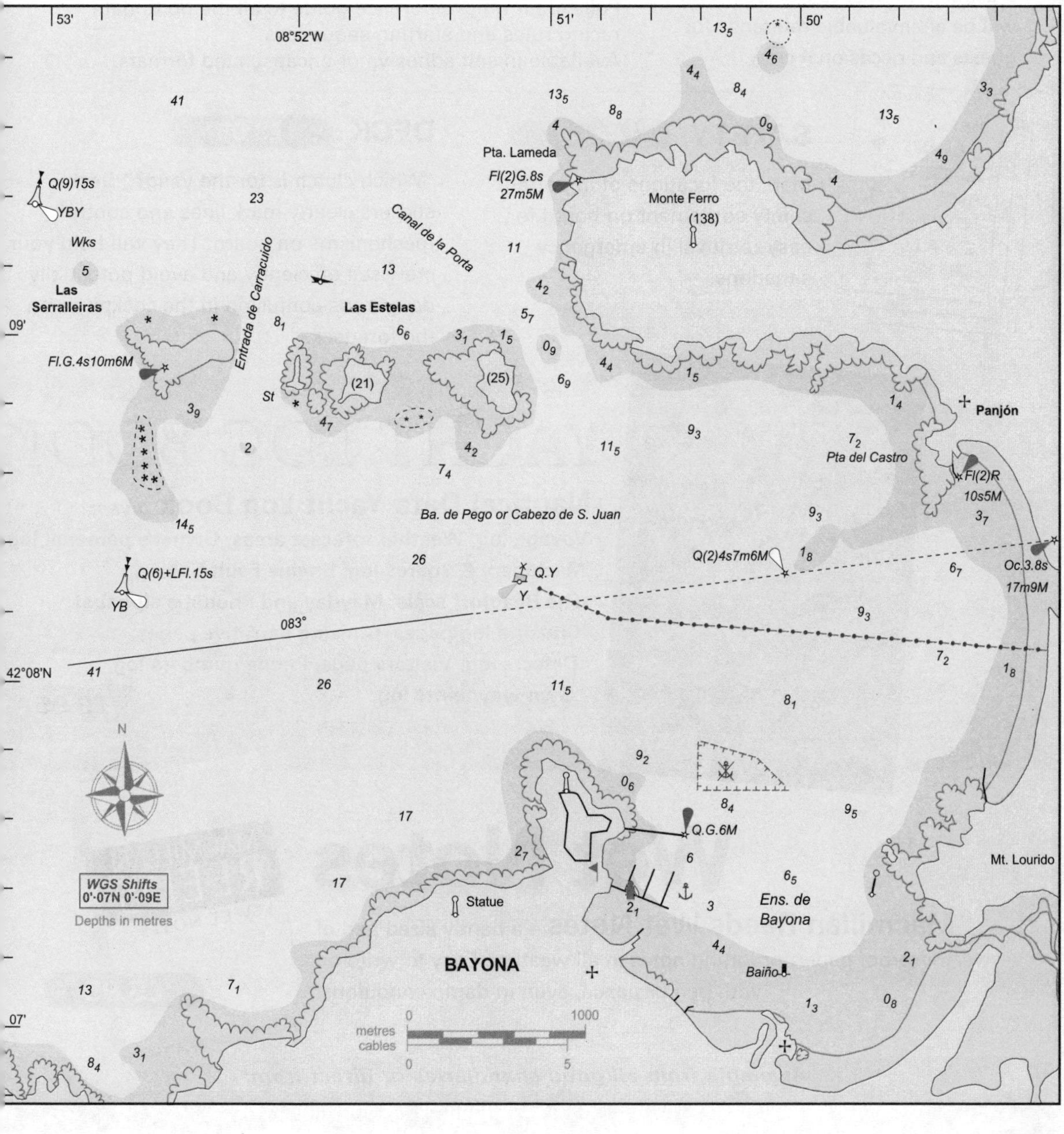

MACMILLAN·REEDS PRODUCTS

NAVIGATORS **Aids**

Stickers

Macmillan Reeds self-adhesive stickers

are a convenient way of highlighting important information aboard your boat. Durable, waterproof and colour-fast, these stickers may be placed just where they're needed, either above or below decks. These stickers provide a useful reminder to a skipper and will be an invaluable reference for guests and occasional crew.

RACING SIGNALS **£3.95**

Full colour quick reference guide to all the up to date racing rules and starting sequences.
Available in self adhesive or encapsulated formats.

SAFETY **£3.95**

Mark the locations of important safety equipment on board for easy retrieval in emergency situations.

DECK **£3.95**

"Which clutch is for the vang?" Deck stickers clearly mark lines and control mechanisms on board. They will help your crew sail efficiently and avoid potentially dangerous confusion in the cockpit or on the foredeck.

YACHT LOG BOOK

Nautical Data Yacht Log Book *gives:*

Voyage log, Weather forecast areas, Owner's personal log, Machinery & spares log, Engine Fault finding, The Beaufort scale, Mayday and Phonetic alphabet, Cruising log pages, Cruising narrative pages, Defects log, Visitors page, Phone numbers log, Own waypoints log.

£9.95

Wet Notes

Macmillan Reeds Wet Notes – a handy sized pad of weatherproof paper for jotting notes in all weather. Easy to write on with pen or pencil, even in damp conditions.

£5.95

Available from all good chandleries or direct from:

Nautical Data Limited • The Book Barn • Westbourne • Hampshire PO10 8RS • UK
tel: +44 (0)1243 389352 • fax: +44 (0)1243 379136 • email: sales@nauticaldata.com • web: www.nauticaldata.com

Prices include UK VAT at 17.5% where applicable, but exclude delivery

e&oe

Area 20

Portugal
Viana do Castelo to Santo Antonio

9.20.1 Index .... **Page 887**

9.20.2 Area map **888**

9.20.3 Lights, buoys & waypoints **890**

9.20.4 Passage information **892**

9.20.5 Special notes for Portugal **892**

9.20.6 Distance table (Portugal/S Spain) **893**

9.20.7 Viana do Castelo **893**
Põvoa de Varzim

9.20.8 Leixões (Pôrto) **894**

9.20.9 Figueira da Foz **894**

9.20.10 Nazaré **895**

9.20.11 Peniche **895**

9.20.12 Cascais **896**

9.20.13 Lisboa, tidal predictions/curves **896**

9.20.14 Sesimbra **899**

9.20.15 Setúbal **899**
Arrábida

9.20.16 Sines **903**
Baleeira

9.20.17 Lagos **903**

9.20.18 Portimão **904**

9.20.19 Vilamoura **904**
Faro/Olhão
Tavira

9.20.20 Vila Real de Santo Antonio **905**

20

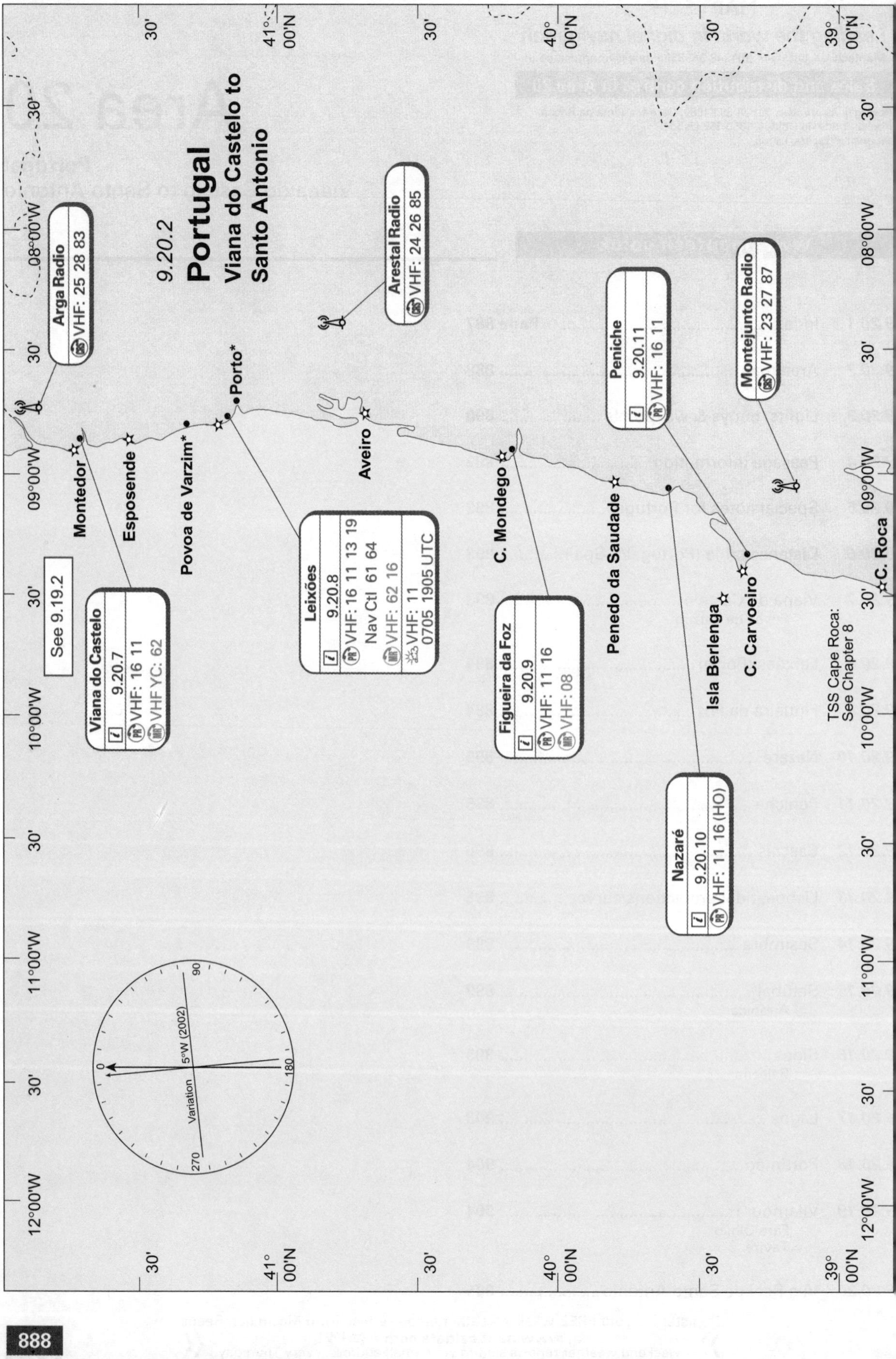
9.20.2
Portugal
Viana do Castelo to
Santo Antonio
Arga Radio
VHF: 25 28 83
Arestal Radio
VHF: 24 26 85
Montedor
Esposende
Povoa de Varzim*
Porto*
Aveiro
See 9.19.2
Viana do Castelo
9.20.7
VHF: 16 11
VHF YC: 62
Leixões
9.20.8
VHF: 16 11 13 19
Nav Ctl 61 64
VHF: 62 16
VHF: 11
0705 1905 UTC
C. Mondego
Figueira da Foz
9.20.9
VHF: 11 16
VHF: 08
Penedo da Saudade
Peniche
9.20.11
VHF: 16 11
Montejunto Radio
VHF: 23 27 87
Isla Berlenga
C. Carvoeiro
C. Roca
TSS Cape Roca:
See Chapter 8
Nazaré
9.20.10
VHF: 11 16 (HO)
Variation
5°W (2002)
0
90
180
270
12°00'W
30'
11°00'W
30'
10°00'W
30'
09°00'W
30'
08°00'W
30'
41°
00'N
40°
00'N
39°
00'N

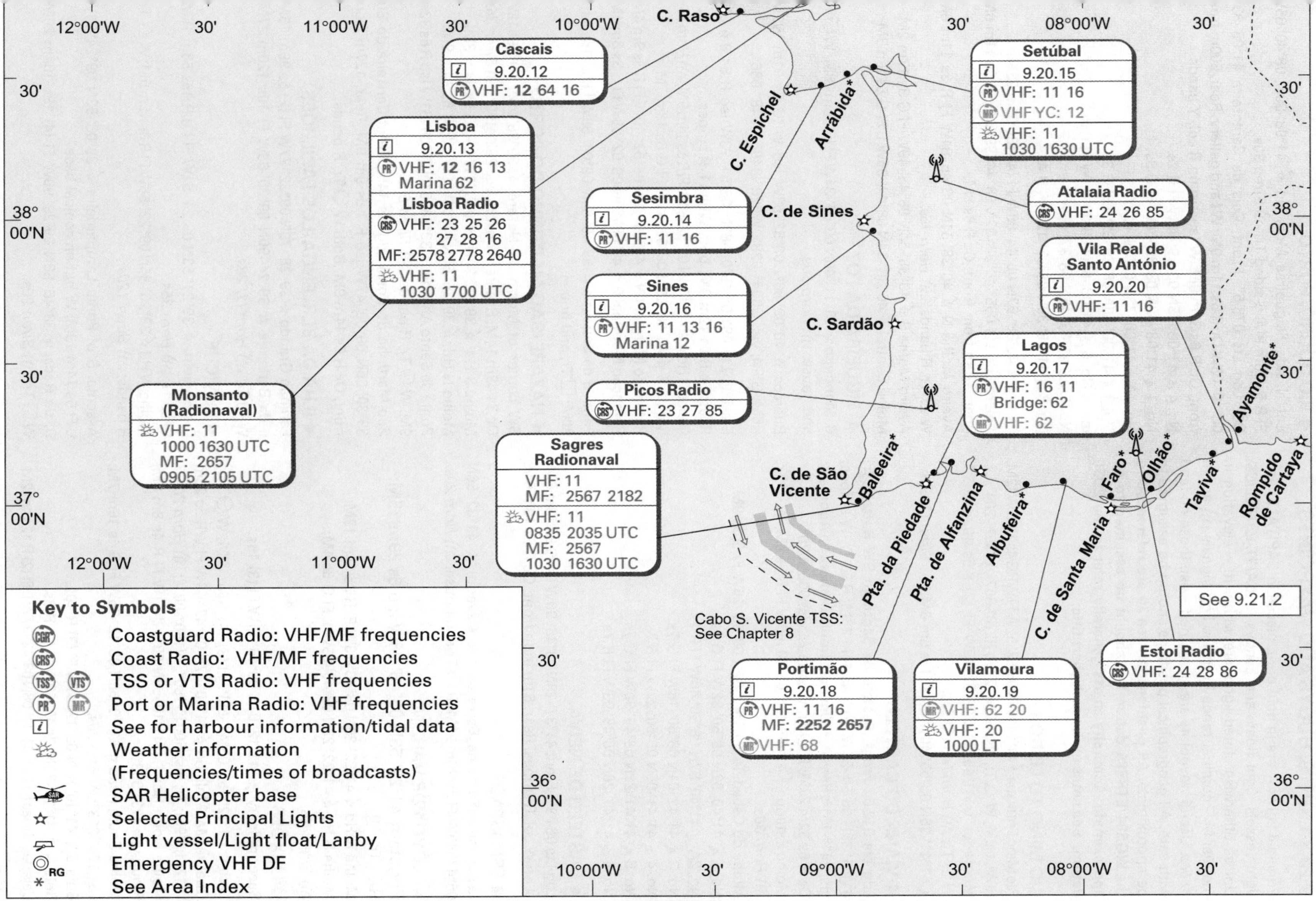
12°00'W
30'
11°00'W
30'
10°00'W
30'
08°00'W
30'
38° 00'N
37° 00'N
36° 00'N
09°00'W
C. Raso
Cascais
9.20.12
VHF: 12 64 16
Lisboa
9.20.13
VHF: 12 16 13
Marina 62
Lisboa Radio
VHF: 23 25 26
27 28 16
MF: 2578 2778 2640
VHF: 11
1030 1700 UTC
Monsanto (Radionaval)
VHF: 11
1000 1630 UTC
MF: 2657
0905 2105 UTC
C. Espichel
Arrábida*
Setúbal
9.20.15
VHF: 11 16
VHF YC: 12
VHF: 11
1030 1630 UTC
Sesimbra
9.20.14
VHF: 11 16
C. de Sines
Atalaia Radio
VHF: 24 26 85
Sines
9.20.16
VHF: 11 13 16
Marina 12
C. Sardão
Vila Real de Santo António
9.20.20
VHF: 11 16
Picos Radio
VHF: 23 27 85
Lagos
9.20.17
VHF: 16 11
Bridge: 62
VHF: 62
Ayamonte*
Sagres Radionaval
VHF: 11
MF: 2567 2182
VHF: 11
0835 2035 UTC
MF: 2567
1030 1630 UTC
C. de São Vicente
Baleeira*
Pta. da Piedade
Pta. de Alfanzina
Albufeira*
C. de Santa Maria
Faro*
Olhão*
Taviva*
Rompido de Cartaya
See 9.21.2
Cabo S. Vicente TSS: See Chapter 8
Portimão
9.20.18
VHF: 11 16
MF: 2252 2657
VHF: 68
Vilamoura
9.20.19
VHF: 62 20
VHF: 20
1000 LT
Estoi Radio
VHF: 24 28 86
Key to Symbols
Coastguard Radio: VHF/MF frequencies
Coast Radio: VHF/MF frequencies
TSS or VTS Radio: VHF frequencies
Port or Marina Radio: VHF frequencies
See for harbour information/tidal data
Weather information (Frequencies/times of broadcasts)
SAR Helicopter base
Selected Principal Lights
Light vessel/Light float/Lanby
Emergency VHF DF
See Area Index

20

9.20.3 LIGHTS, BUOYS AND WAYPOINTS

Principal lights ☆ are in **bold** print, places in CAPITALS, and light-vessels, light floats and Lanbys in *CAPITAL ITALICS*. Unless otherwise stated lights are white. m – elevation in metres; M – nominal range in miles. Fog signals are in *italics*. Useful waypoints are underlined – use those on land with care. All geographical positions should be assumed to be approximate. **All positions in Area 20 are referenced to the WGS84/ETRS89 datum but should be assumed to be approximate. Admiralty charts generally refer to the ED50 datum. See notes under each chart title.**

RIO MIÑO TO LISBOA

Río Miño Ent Ínsua 41°51'·55N 08°52'·52W Fl WRG 4s 15m W12M, R8M, G9M; W △ Tr; vis: G204°-270°, R270°-357°, W357°-204°.
Montedor ☆ 41°45'·09N 08°52'·49W Fl (2) 9·5s 102m **22M**; W □ Tr; *Horn Mo (S) 25s.*
41°41'·35N 08°55'·40W Fl (3) 15s 6m 6M; *Siren (3) 30s.*

◀ VIANA DO CASTELO

Ldg Lts 012·5°. **Front, Castelo de Santiago SW Battery** ☆, 41°41'·33N 08°50'·35W Iso R 4s 14m **23M**; R ○ Tr, W stripes; vis: 241°-151°. **Rear** ☆, 500m from front, **Senhora da Agonia** ☆ Oc R 6s 32m **23M**; R ○ Tr, W stripes: vis: 005°-020°.
Molhe Exterior 41°40'·45N 08°50'·66W Fl R 3s 9M; W ○ Tr; *Horn 30s.*
Molhe do Cabedelo 41°40'·67N 08°50'·25W Fl G 3s 9M.
No. 1 41°40'·82N 08°50'·32W Fl G 7s.
No. 2A 41°40'·87N 08°50'·40W Fl R 7s.
No. 3 41°41'·01N 08°50'·18W Fl G 7s.
No. 4 41°41'·05N 08°50'·22W Fl R 7s.
No. 5 41°41'·22N 08°49'·90W Fl G 7s.
No. 6 41°41'·26N 08°49'·93W Fl R 7s.

◀ CASTELO DE NEIVA

Ldg Lts 064·9°. Front 41°37'·29N 08°48'·90W Oc G 6s 13m 6M; ◇ on W col, R stripes. Rear, 61m from front, Oc G 6s 19m 6M.

◀ ESPOSENDE

Esposende (Forte da Barra do Río Cávado) ☆ 41°32'·56N 08°47'·49W Fl 5s 20m **21M**; R ○ Tr and house; *Horn 20s.*

◀ PÓVOA DE VARZIM

Regufe ☆ 41°22'·53N 08°45'·28W Iso 6s 29m 15M; R ○ Tr.
Molhe N Hd 41°22'·29N 08°46'·23W Fl R 3s 14m 12M;
Molhe S Hd 41°22'·23N 08°46'·03W L Fl G 6s 4M; *Siren 40s.*

◀ LEIXÕES

Sacor refinery 41°12'·07N 08°45'·11W Fl (3) 15s.
Leça ☆ 41°12'·15N 08°42'·65W Fl (3) 14s 56m **28M**; W ○ Tr.
Quebra Mar Mole Hd 41°10'·37N 08°42'·49W Fl WR 5s 23m W12M, R9M; Tr; vis: R001°-180°, W180°-001°; *Horn 20s.*
Molhe North Head 41°10'·69N 08°42'·51W Fl R 4s 8m 6M; R hut; vis: 173°-353°.
Molhe South Head 41°10'·68N 08°42'·35W Fl G 4s 16m 7M; vis: 175°-363°; *Horn 30s.*
Bóia S 41°10'·81N 08°42'·51W Fl (3) R 10s.
Bóia N 41°10'·86N 08°42'·60W Fl (2) R 6s.
Cais das Gruas E Hd 41°11'·08N 08°42'·27W L Fl (2) R 12s 4m 2M.

◀ RIO DOURO, PORTO

Ent N side Felgueiras Mole Hd 41°08'·80N 08°40'·65 Fl R 5s 16m 9M; 6-sided Tr; *Siren 30s.*
Bar Ldg Lts 078·5°. Front, Cais da Cantareira 41°08'·83 08°40'·03W Oc R 6s 11m 9M; W ▮ and gallery. Rear, 500m fro front, Oc R 6s 32m 9M; W lantern on R col, Y bands.
No. 4 41°08'·73N 08°39'·85W Fl R 2s.
No. 1 41°08'·68N 08°39'·66W Fl G 3s.
No. 4A 41°08'·73N 08°39'·42W.
No. 3 41°08'·69N 08°39'·32W Fl G 3s.
Insua No. 6 41°08'·80N 08°39'·11W Fl R 3s.
No. 6A 41°08'·45N 08°37'·26W.
No. 8 41°08'·39N 08°37'·12W Fl R 4s.

Aveiro ☆ 40°38'·57N 08°44'·88W Fl (4) 13s 65m **23M**.
Aviero Ldg Lts 065° 40°38'·82N 08°44'·99W Oc R 3s 11m 8 Rear, 320m from front, Oc R 6s 8M.
Aveiro Molhe N 40°38'·61N 08°45'·81W Fl R 3s 11m 8 W △ Tr, R bands; *Horn 15s.*
Aveiro Molhe S 40°38'·54N 08°45'·49W Fl G 3s 17m 2M.
Molhe Central 40°38'·64N 08°44'·95W L Fl G 5s 8m 3M.

◀ FIGUEIRA DA FOZ

C. Mondego ☆ 40°11'·46N 08°54'·34W Fl 5s 96m **28M**; W □ T and house; *Horn 30s.*
Buarcos 40°09'·86N 08°52'·53W Iso WRG 6s 11m W9 R6M, G5M; vis: G004°-028°, W028°-048°, R048°-086°.
Ent Ldg Lts 081·5° 40°08'·83N 08°51'·23W Iso R 5s 8m 8 Rear, Oc R 6s 12m 8M; both White ▮, R stripes.
Molhe N Hd 40°08'·74N 08°52'·50W Fl R 6s 14m 9M; *Horn 35*
Molhe S 40°08'·59N 08°52'·41W Fl G 6s 13m 7M.
Retançao Marginal N 40°08'·78N 08°52'·10W Fl R 3s 9m 4M
Retançao Marginal S 40°08'·69N 08°52'·08W Fl G 3s 8m 4M
Penedo da Saudade ☆ 39°45'·84N 09°01'·89W Fl (2) 15s 54 **30M**; □ Tr, and house.

◀ NAZARÉ/SÃO MARTINHO DO PORTO

SW corner of Morro da Nazaré 39°36'·25N 09°05'·18 Oc 3s 49m 14M; R lantern on fort; vis: 282°-192°; *Siren 35*
Molhe S Hd 39°35'·34N 09°04'·76W L Fl G 5s 14m 8M.
Molhe N Hd 39°35'·50N 09°04'·59W L Fl R 5s 14m 9M.
Ponta de Santo António 39°30'·61N 09°08'·61W Iso R 6s 32 9M; W ○ Tr, R bands; *Siren 60s.*
São Martinho do Porto Ldg Lts 145°. Front Carrreira do Su 39°30'·05N 09°08'·47W Iso R 1·5s 9m 9M. Rear, 127m fro front, Oc R 6s 11m 9M. Both W ○ Tr, R bands.

◀ ILHA DA BERLENGA/LOS FARILHÕES

Farilhão Grande 39°28'·73N 09°32'·77W Fl (2) 5s 99m 13M
I. da Berlenga ☆ 39°24'·90N 09°30'·63W Fl 10s 120m **27M** W □ Tr; *Horn (1) 28s.*

◀ PENICHE

C. Carvoeiro ☆ 39°21'·63N 09°24'·51W Fl (3) R 15s 56m **15M** W □ Tr; *Horn 35s.*
Molhe W Hd 39°20'·85N 09°22'·56W Fl R 3s 12m 9M; W △ T R bands; *Siren 120s.*
Assenta. S of Ponta Lampardeira 39°03'·53N 09°24'·91 L Fl 5s 74m 13M; W hut on conical base.
C. da Roca ☆ 38°46'·88N 09°29'·90W Fl (4) 18s 164m **26M** W □ Tr; *Siren 20s.*

C. Raso (Forte de São Brás) ☆ 38°42'·55N 09°29'·20W Fl (3)15s 22m **20M**; R ○ Tr; vis: 324°-189°; Horn *Mo (I) 60s.*

C1 38°40'·22N 09°28'·41W Fl Y 4s.

C2 38°40'·00N 09°27'·97W Fl Y 5s.

C3 38°40'·68N 09°27'·97W Fl Y 6s.

C4 38°40'·88N 09°27'·50W Fl Y 7s.

LISBOA TO SPANISH BORDER

◄ CASCAIS

Ldg Lts 284·7° Front, **Pta do Salmodo, Forte de Santa Marta** 38°41'·42N 09°25'·27W Oc WR 6s 24m **W18M**, R14M; W □ Tr, Bu bands; vis: R233°-334°, W334°-098°; *Horn 10s*. Rear, **Nossa Senhora de Guia**, 2280m from front, Iso WR 2s **W19M**, **R16M**, W Tr; vis: W326°-092°, R278°-292°.

Praia da Ribeira ☆ 38°41'·80N 09°25'·22W Oc R 4s 5m 6M; W col, R bands; vis: 251°-309°.

No. 2 38°41'·69N 09°24'·99W Fl R 10s (May-Oct).

Albatroz ☆ 38°41'·98N 09°25'·03W Oc R 6s 12m 5M.

◄ LISBOA, RIO TEJO AND APPROACHES

Ldg Lts 047°. Front, **Gibalta** 38°41'·95N 09°15'·98W Oc R 3s 30m **21M**; W ○ Tr. Rear, **Esteiro**, 760m from front, Oc R 6s 81m **21M**; W □ Tr, R bands; both vis: 039·5°-054·5°; Racon (Q).

Mama Sul ☆ 38°43'·65N 09°13'·65W Iso 6s 154m **21M**; vis: 045·5°-048·5°.

No. 2 38°37'·29N 09°23'·29W Fl R 10s.

No. 1 38°39'·55N 09°18'·78W Fl G 2s.

Forte de São Julião ☆ 38°40'·46N 09°19'·53W Oc R 5s 38m 14M.

Forte Bugio ☆ 38°39'·63N 09°17'·94W Fl G 5s 27m 9M; ○ Tr on fort; *Horn Mo (B) 30s* (TD 1999).

No. 3 38°40'·04N 09°18'·25W Fl G 3s.

Lage 38°40'·74N 09°18'·61W Fl Y 12s.

No. 5 38°40'·43N 07°17'·66W Fl G 4s.

No. 7 38°40'·64N 09°16'·91W Fl G 5s.

C. Espichel ☆ 38°24'·92N 09°13'·05W Fl 4s 167m **26M**; W 6-sided Tr; *Horn 31s.*

◄ SESIMBRA/SETÚBAL, RIO SADO

Cavalo ☆ 38°26'·06N 09°07'·08W Oc 5s 34m 14M; R ○ Tr.

Sesimbra Ldg Lts 004°. Front 38°26'·56N 09°06'·16W L Fl R 5s 9m 7M. Rear, L Fl R 5s 21m 6M.

Setúbal Ldg Lts 039·8°. Front, Doca Pesca 38°31'·15N 08°53'·95W Oc R 3s 12m 14M; R structure, W stripes. Rear, **Azêda**, 1·7M from front, Iso R 6s 61m **20M**; R hut; vis: 038·3°-041·3°.

No. 1 38°26'·98N 08°58'·18W Fl G 3s 5M.

No. 2 38°27'·21N 08°58'·45W Fl (2) R 10s 13m 9M; R Bn; Racon (B).

No. 4 38°27'·92N 08°57'·71W Fl R 4s 13m 4M.

No. 3 38°28'·33N 08°56'·78W Fl G 3s.

Forte de Outão ☆ 38°29'·31N 08°56'·06W Oc R 6s 33m 12M.

Pinheiro da Cruz ☆ 38°15'·46N 08°46'·34W Fl 3s 66m11M: W ○ col, R stripes.

◄ SINES

C. de Sines ☆ 37°57'·56N 08°52'·83W Fl (2) 15s 55m **26M**.

Molhe Oeste ☆ 37°56'·46N 08°53'·33W Fl 3s 20m 12M.

37°56'·12N 08°53'·25W Fl R 3s.

Mohle Leste Hd ☆ 37°56'·33N 08°51'·96W L Fl G 8s 16m 6M.

Marina Bkwtr Head ☆ 37°57'·04N 08°52'·04W Fl G 4s 4M.

Ponta de Gaivota ☆ 37°51'·10N 08°47'·79W L Fl 7s 19m 13M.

Porto Covo ☆ 37°51'·03N 08°47'·37W Fl R 4s 31m 5M.

Rio Mira Entrance ☆ 37°43'·13N 08°47'·43W Fl 3s 21m 10M.

C. Sardão ☆ 37°35'·94N 08°49'·02W Fl (3) 15s 66m **23M**.

◄ CAP ST VINCENT/SAGRES

C. de São Vicente ☆ 37°01'·37N 08°59'·82W Fl 5s 84m **32M**; W ○ Tr; *Horn Mo (I) 30s.*

Pta de Sagres ☆ 36°59'·64N 08°56'·97W Iso R 2s 52m 11M.

Baleeira Mole Hd ☆ 37°00'·67N 08°55'·50W Fl WR 4s 12m W14M, R11M; W Tr; vis: W254°-355°, R355°-254°.

◄ LAGOS/PORTIMÃO

Pta da Piedade ☆ 37°04'·81N 08°40'·20W Fl 7s 49m **20M**.

Lagos Mole E Hd ☆ 37°05'·93N 08°39'·98W Mo (A) G 10s 6M.

Ponta do Altar ☆ 37°06'·34N 08°31'·17W L Fl R 5s 31m 14M; W □ Tr; vis: 290°-170°.

Portimão Mole E Hd ☆ 37°06'·50N 08°31'·59W Fl G 5s 8m 7M.

Portimão Mole W Hd ☆ 37°06'·52N 08°31'·77W Fl R 5s 8m 7M.

No. 2 37°06'·96N 08°31'·54W Fl R 4s.

No. 4 37°07'·29N 08°31'·54W Fl (2) R 4s.

No. 1 37°07'·34N 08°31'·44W Fl G 4s.

Ferragudo Ldg Lts 020·9°. Front 37°07'·35N 08°31'·32W Oc R 5s 17m 8M. Rear, 90m from front, Oc R 7s 31m 8M

Praia do Carvoeiro ☆ 37°05'·81N 08°28'·21W L Fl R 7s 11m 6M.

Pta de Alfanzina ☆ 37°05'·22N 08°26'·59W Fl (2) 15s 62m **29M**.

Ponta da Baleeira ☆ 37°04'·84N 08°15'·88W Oc 6s 30m 11M.

Praia da Albufeira, E Pt of Bay ☆ 37°05'·24N 08°14'·94W Iso R 3s 21m 8M; W △ Tr, R bands.

Olhos de Água ☆ 37°05'·47N 08°11'·40W L Fl 5s 28m 7M.

◄ VILAMOURA

Vilamoura ☆ 37°04'·50N 08°07'·42W Fl 10s 17m **19M**.

Marina W Mole Hd ☆ 37°04'·19N 08°07'·49W Fl R 4s 13m 5M.

E Mole Hd ☆ 37°04'·22N 08°07'·42W Fl G 4s 13m 5M.

◄ FARO/OLHÃO/TAVIRA

Ldg Lts 021°. Front Barra Nova 37°58'·22N 07°52'·00W Oc 4s 8m 6M. Rear, **C. de Santa Maria** ☆ 36°58'·48N 07°51'·88W Fl (4) 17s 49m **25M**; W ○Tr.

Mole W Head ☆ 37°57'·84N 08°52'·26W Fl R 4s 9m 6M.

Barra Nova Mole E Hd ☆ 36°57'·79N 07°52'·14W Fl G 4s 9m 6M.

Canal de Faro Ldg Lts 101·5°. Front, Mar Santo 36°58'·50N 07°52'·04W Oc R 5s 9m 5M. Rear, **C. de Santa Maria** ☆ 36°58'·48N 07°51'·88W Fl (4) 17s 49m **25M**; W ○ Tr.

Cais Ldg Lts 043·8° 37°01'·43N 07°50'·62W Iso R 6s 9m 7M. Rear, Igreja 390m from front, 37°01'·57N 07°50'·44W Oc R 4s 20m 6M; Church Belfry.

Barra ☆ 37°02'·98N 07°43'·01W Fl 8s 6m 7M.

Tavira W Mole Hd ☆ 37°06'·79N 07°37'·10W Fl R 2·5s 8m 7M.

◄ RIO GUADIANA

Rio Guadiana Channel 37°08'·90N 07°23'·44W Q (3) G 6s.

37°09'·14N 07°23'·82W Fl R 4s.

W Trng Wall Head ☆ 37°09'·75N 07°24'·03W Fl R 5s 4M.

Ayamonte Dique de Levant, S end ☆ 37°09'·93N 07°23'·63W Fl G 3s 4M.

Vila Real de Santo António ☆ 37°11'·23N 07°25'·00W Fl 6·5s 51m **26M**; W ○ Tr, B bands.

9.20.4 PASSAGE INFORMATION

BIBLIOGRAPHY The *SW Spain & Portugal Cruising Companion* (Macmillan Reeds/Jens) covers from Viano do Costello to Gibraltar, *W coasts of Spain and Portugal Pilot* (Admiralty, NP 67) covers from Cabo Ortegal to Gibraltar, and the *Atlantic Spain and Portugal* guide (Imray/RCC, 3rd edition 1995) covers from El Ferrol to Gibraltar. *Guia del Navegante* has fair cover, in English, of SW Spain, but is limited elsewhere. Passage information for the coasts of NW and N Spain is in 9.19.4.

RÍO MIÑO TO CABO CARVOEIRO (AC 3634, 3635) The Río Miño (*Minho* in Portuguese), 15M S of Cabo Silleiro, forms the N border between Spain and Portugal. The river ent is difficult and best not attempted.

In summer the Portuguese Trades (*Nortada*) are N'ly F4-6 and the Portugal Current runs S at $\frac{1}{2}$-$\frac{3}{4}$kn. Tidal streams appear to set N on the flood and S on the ebb, but are ill documented. In summer gales are rare; coastal fog is common in the mornings. If N-bound, especially if lightly crewed, it is worth making daily passages between about 0400 and 1200 to avoid the stronger winds in the afternoon, which may be increased by a fresh onshore sea breeze.

The 150M long coastline is hilly as far S as Pôrto, then generally low and sandy, backed by pine forests, to Cabo Carvoeiro; there are few prominent features. Coasting yachts should keep about 3M offshore. Viana do Castelo (9.20.7) is a commercial and fishing port, with a marina at the NE end. Except for Leixões (9.20.8), an industrial port 2M N of the mouth of the R. Douro, other hbrs can be closed in bad weather due to heavy swell breaking on the bar. The R. Douro is not easily entered; but Oporto can be visited by road from Leixões. Aveiro and Figueira da Foz (9.20.9) are both exposed to the west; the latter has a marina and can be identified from N or S by the higher ground (257m) of Cabo Mondego. 34M further SSW Nazaré (9.20.10) is an artificial fishing hbr and port of refuge with easy ent and a marina. Cabo Carvoeiro, the W tip of Peniche peninsula, looks like an island from afar (do not confuse with Ilha Berlenga). Peniche fishing port and marina (9.20.11) on the S side of the peninsula are well sheltered from N'lies, but always prone to SW swell.

Ilha da Berlenga and Os Farilhões, both lit, are respectively 6 and 9·5M NW of Cabo Carvoeiro, 14M W of which is a N/S orientated TSS. The normal coastal route is between Cabo Carvoeiro and Berlenga; this chan is deep, clear and 5M wide, although it appears narrower until opened up.

CABO CARVOEIRO TO SINES (charts 3635, 3636) The coastline rises steadily to the high (527m) ridge of Sintra, inland of Cabo da Roca, S of which it drops steeply to the low headland of Cabo Raso. A TSS lies 10M W of Cabo da Roca, the most W'ly point of Europe. Cascais (9.20.12), about 3·5M E of Cabo Raso,has a new marina and is a favoured anch for yachts on passage or not wishing to go 12M further E to Lisboa. From Cascais to the Rio Tejo (Tagus) use the Barra Norte (least depth 5m) which joins the main Barra Sul abeam São Julião lt. In Lisboa (9.20.13) there are 6 marinas along the N bank of R Tejo which is 1M wide and clear. If S-bound from Lisboa, stand on about 1M SW of Forte Bugio lt before altering toward Cabo Espichel.

E from this flattish cape the coast rises to 500m high cliffs nearing the ent to Rio Sado. The fishing hbr of Sesimbra (9.20.14) is well sheltered from the N, or anchor in a shallow bay at Arrábida. The port of Setúbal (9.20.15) has limited yacht facilities. Unbroken beach stretches 35M from R Sado to Cabo de Sines, lt ho and 3 conspic chimneys to the E. At Sines (8.20.16), a strategically placed commercial port, a small marina has limited facilities.

SINES TO RIO GUADIANA (AC 89, 90) The 56M rky coast to Cabo São Vicente offers no shelter except at Punta da Arrifana (37°17'·5N), a tiny bay protected from N'lies by high cliffs. 5M off Cabo São Vicente a TSS is orientated NW/SE. There are passage anchs, sheltered from N'lies, at Enseada de Belixe, E of C. São Vicente, and at Enseadas de Sagres and da Baleeira, NE of Pta da Sagres. E of C. São Vicente the summer weather becomes more Mediterranean, ie hotter, clearer and winds more from the NW to SW. Swell may decrease, tidal streams are slight and the current runs SE. Hbrs along the coasts of the Algarve and SW Andalucía are sheltered from all but S'lies (infrequent).

The choice of routes to Gibraltar is between a direct track (Cabo São Vicente to Tarifa is 110°/175M) or a series of coastal legs. There is a good marina at Lagos (9.20.17) and pontoons at Portimão (9.20.18), 20M and 25M E of C. São Vicente. Vilamoura (9.20.19) is a large, established marina about 10M W of Faro. At Cabo de Santa Maria a gap in the low-lying dunes gives access to the lagoons and chans leading to Faro and Olhão, where some peaceful anchs may be found, although yacht facilities are limited. On the Portuguese bank of the Rio Guadiana there is a marina at Vila Real de Santo António (9.20.20).

9.20.5 SPECIAL NOTES FOR PORTUGAL

Districts/Provinces: Mainland Portugal is divided into 18 a dministrative districts. However the names of the former provinces (on the coast: Minho, Douro, Beira Litoral, Estremadura, Alentejo and Algarve) are still used and are shown below the name of each main port.

Charts: There are 2 folios, the new F94 (very few charts; 5 digit chart nos) and the old FA (*antigo*). Navigação de Recreio are coastal charts available on a scale of 1:150 000 in A2 format in a ring binder. Two excellent guides are also published: Lisbon and Ports of the Central Zone (1998) and Southern West Coast and Algarve (1999). Portuguese charts (PC) and publications are available from: Instituto Hidrográfico, Rua das Trinas 49, 1296 Lisboa Codex; ☎ (01) 3955119, 🖷 3960515.

Time: Portugal keeps UTC as Standard time and UTC+1 as DST, from the last Sunday in March until the Saturday before the 4th Sunday in October, as in other EU nations.

Representation: Portuguese Trade and Tourism Office, 22-25A Sackville St, London W1X 1DE; ☎ 020 7494 1441, 🖷 020 7494 1868. British Embassy, Rua de S. Bernardo 33, 1200 Lisbon; ☎ (01) 392 4000, 🖷 392 4185. There are Brit Consuls at Porto & Portimão (qv).

Telephone: To telephone Portugal from UK dial 00-351, followed by the area code, less the initial 0, then the ☎ number. To call UK from Portugal, dial 00-44, followed by the area code, less the initial 0, then the ☎ number.

Access: There are daily flights in season to/from the UK via Porto, Lisbon and Faro. These airports are quite well connected by bus and some trains to other towns. See also 9.19.5 for Spanish flights.

Currency: The € is the unit of currency. Credit cards are widely accepted; cash dispensers are available in most medium-sized towns.

Public Holidays: Jan 1; Shrove Tues; Good Friday; April 25 (Liberation Day); May 1 (Labour Day); Jun 6 (Corpus Christi); Jun 10 (Camões Day); Aug 15 (Assumption); Oct 5 (Republic Day); Nov 1 (All Saints Day); Dec 1 (Independence Day), 8 (Immaculate Conception), 25 (Christmas). Also every town has a local *festa.*

Buoyage conforms to the IALA Region A system.

Documents: Portugal is no different to any other EC country and formalities are simple, however, organise your papers to include:

Personal – Passports; crew list, ideally on headed paper with the yacht's rubber stamp, giving DoB, passport nos, where joined/ intended departure. Certificate of Competence (Yachtmaster Offshore, ICC/HOCC etc). Radio Operator's certificate. Form E111 (advised for medical treatment).

Yacht – Registration certificate, Part 1 or SSR. Proof of VAT status. Marine insurance. Ship's Radio licence. Itinerary, backed up by ship's log.

Storm signals: a black cylinder by day or a single ● at night signifies that a Levante is probable in the Strait of Gibraltar and wave heights of 2m or more may be expected from the SE.

9.20.6 DISTANCE TABLE: COASTS OF NW SPAIN, PORTUGAL AND SW SPAIN

Approximate distances in nautical miles are by the most direct route, whilst avoiding dangers and allowing for Traffic Separation Schemes. Places in *italics* are off UK and North West coast of France. See also Distance Table at 9.19.6.

1.	*Longships*	**1**																			
2.	*Ushant (Créac'h)*	100	**2**																		
3.	La Coruña	418	338	**3**																	
4.	Cabo Villano	439	365	43	**4**																
5.	Bayona	510	436	114	71	**5**															
6.	Viana do Castelo	537	468	141	98	32	**6**														
7.	Leixões (Pôrto)	565	491	169	126	63	33	**7**													
8.	Nazaré	659	585	263	220	156	127	97	**8**												
9.	Cabo Carvoeiro	670	596	274	231	171	143	114	22	**9**											
10.	Cabo Raso	710	636	314	271	211	183	154	62	40	**10**										
11.	Lisboa (bridge)	686	652	330	287	227	199	170	78	56	16	**11**									
12.	Cabo Espichel	692	658	336	293	233	205	176	84	62	22	23	**12**								
13.	Sines	726	692	370	327	267	239	210	118	96	54	57	34	**13**							
14.	Cabo São Vicente	777	743	421	378	318	290	261	169	147	104	108	85	57	**14**						
15.	Lagos	797	763	441	398	338	310	281	189	167	124	128	105	77	20	**15**					
16.	Vilamoura	820	786	464	421	361	333	304	212	190	147	151	128	100	43	27	**16**				
17.	Cádiz	911	877	555	512	452	424	395	303	281	238	242	219	191	134	120	95	**17**			
18.	Cabo Trafalgar	928	894	572	529	469	441	412	320	298	255	259	236	208	151	139	115	28	**18**		
19.	Tarifa	952	918	596	553	493	465	436	344	322	279	283	260	232	175	163	139	52	24	**19**	
20.	Gibraltar	968	934	612	569	509	481	450	360	338	295	299	276	248	191	179	155	68	40	16	**20**

VIANA DO CASTELO *9.20.7*

Miñho **41°41'·68N 08°49'·21W** (Marina ent)

CHARTS AC 3254, 3633/4; PC 53, 31, 1; SC 4110, 41B

TIDES

Standard Port LISBOA (⟶); ML 2·0; Zone 0 (UT)

Times				Height (metres)			
High Water		Low Water		MHWS	MHWN	MLWN	MLWS
0400	0900	0400	0900	3·8	3·0	1·5	0·5
1600	2100	1600	2100				
Differences VIANA DO CASTELO							
−0020	0000	+0010	+0015	−0·3	−0·3	−0·1	0·0
ESPOSENDE (41°32'N)							
−0020	0000	+0010	+0015	−0·6	−0·5	−0·2	0·0
PÕVOA DE VARZIM (41°22'N)							
−0020	0000	+0010	+0015	−0·3	−0·3	−0·1	0·0

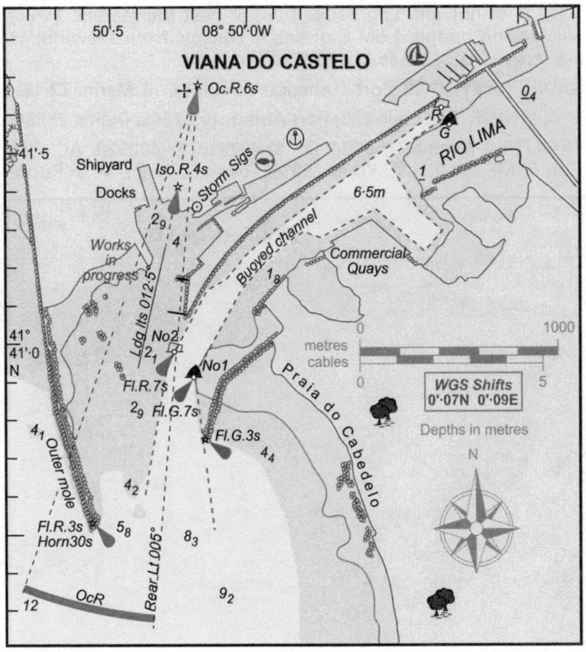

SHELTER Excellent in marina (3m), 1·5M up R. Lima, 200m short of low and noisy road/rail bridge; possible strong cross current when entering marina. Moor on outside of first pontoon, fore and aft. No other yacht berths; no ⚓ in river.

NAVIGATION WPT 41°40'·05N 08°50'·33W, 185°/005° from/to No 1 SHM lt buoy, 8½ca. From WPT keep rear ldg lt on brg 005° to enter the chan, dredged 8m, which curves to NE and is marked by 14 lateral buoys, all Fl R 7s or G 7s. The outer mole hd should be given a wide clearance; best water lies further E. Night entry not advised if any swell.

LIGHTS AND MARKS Montedor, Fl (2) 9·5s, is 4M NNW. ✠ dome on Monte Santa Luzia is conspic in transit with ldg lts. But ignore front ldg lt, Iso R 4s; its transit 012·5° passes too close to the outer mole hd (Fl R 3s), and leads into shipyard and FV area. Storm signals are displayed as shown.

RADIO TELEPHONE Call *Porto de Viana* VHF Ch 16; 11 (0900-1200; 1400-1700LT), Yacht Club VHF Ch 62.

TELEPHONE (Dial code 258) Hr Mr 829096; ⊖ 823346; Met, via marina; Police 822345.

FACILITIES Marina (150+ some Ⓥ; F&A on D pontoon), €11·97, ☎ 359546, 📠 359535, Slip, AC, P, D, FW, C (56 ton), YC; **Services:** ME, El, Sh, CH, BY, SM, Gaz, Ⓔ. **Town:** V, R, Bar, ✉, Ⓗ, Ⓑ, ⥂ (1km); ✈ Porto (50 km).

ADJACENT HARBOUR

PÕVOA DE VARZIM, **41°22'·20N 08°46'·00W**. AC 3634. Tides above. Busy FV hbr and new marina (VHF Ch 62)☎ 25 2688121, 📠 25 2688123, with good shelter in all winds, but in heavy swell ent is rough. Regufe lt ho, Iso 6s 29m 15M, overlooks the hbr; N and S moles: Fl R 3s and L Fl G 6s. Facilities: D, FW, ME, El, Gaz, ✉, Ⓑ, ⥂.

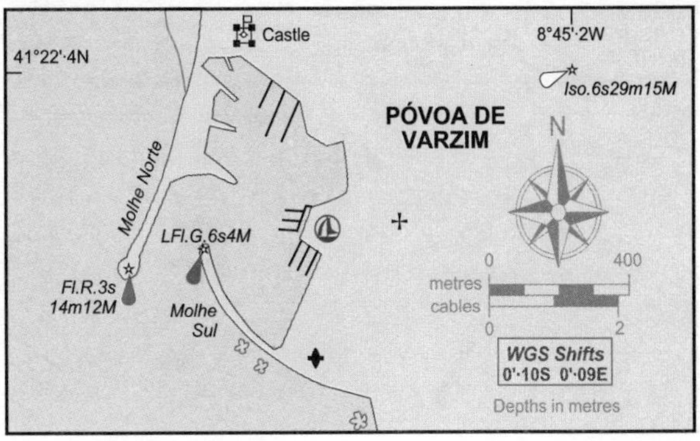

LEIXÕES *9.20.8*

Douro **41°11'·17N 08°42'·18W** (Marina ent)

CHARTS AC 3254, 3634; PC 58, 21, 22, 16; SC 4210, 42A

TIDES

Standard Port LISBOA (⟶); ML 2·0; Zone 0 (UT)

Times				Height (metres)			
High Water		Low Water		MHWS	MHWN	MLWN	MLWS
0400	0900	0400	0900	3·8	3·0	1·5	0·5
1600	2100	1600	2100				
Differences LEIXÕES							
−0025	−0010	0000	+0010	−0·3	−0·3	−0·2	0·0
RIO DOURO ENT							
−0010	+0005	+0015	+0025	−0·6	−0·5	−0·2	0·0
RIO PORTO							
+0002	+0002	+0040	+0040	−0·5	−0·4	−0·2	+0·1

SHELTER Very good in rather dirty marina (4m), or ⚓ outside in about 4m; no swell once inside N mole. Outer ⚓ is for medium vessels.

NAVIGATION WPT 41°10'·20N 08°42'·11W, 170°/350° from/to inner mole hds, 6ca. Ent is simple; keep at least 150m off the N mole hd, due to wreck/sunken bkwtr to S & W of it. Leça lt brg 350° leads into inner hbr, thence steer 015° to marina.

LIGHTS AND MARKS Lts as chartlet. Leça lt, Fl (3) 14s 57m 28M, W tr/B bands, is 1·7M N of hbr ent. N of it is oil refinery with many R/W banded chy's. From the S, bldgs of Pōrto are conspic.

RADIO TELEPHONE Marina *Pōrto Atlântico* VHF Ch 62, 16.

TELEPHONE (Dial code 22) Hr Mr 995 3000; ⊖ 995 1476; Met 948 4527 (Pōrto airport); LB 617 0091; Police 938 0774; Brit Consul 6184789.

FACILITIES **Marina Pōrto Atlântico** (200 + 40 ♥, F&A), €,9.38 ☎ 996 4895, 📠 996 4899, AC, FW, P, D, ME, El, C (6·5 ton), CH, SM, Ⓔ, Sh, ▣; **Clube de Vela Atlântico** ☎ 995 2725; **Clube Naval de Leça** ☎ 995 1700. **Town:** V, Bar, R, Ⓑ, ✉; ⇌ and ✈ Pōrto (5km).

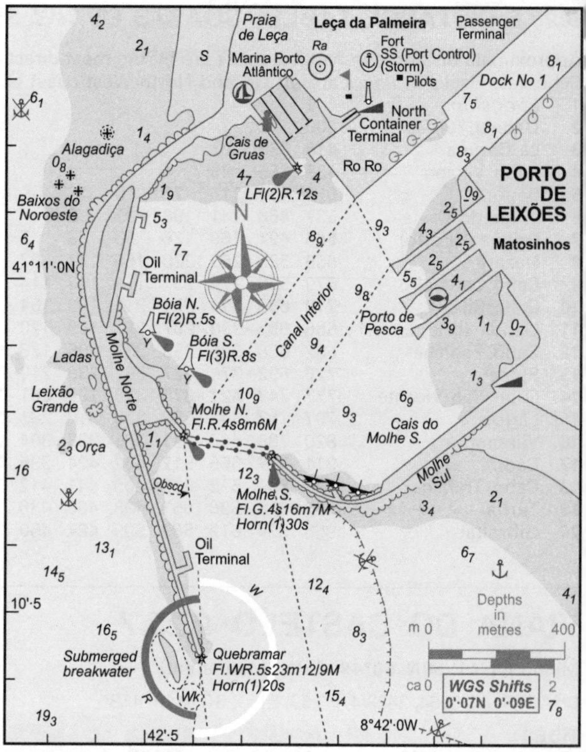

ADJACENT HARBOUR

PŌRTO, 41°08'·80N 08°40'·55W. Tides, see above. Difficult river ent, prone to swell and fast current; dangerous in strong W'lies. Limited AB at Cais de Estiva, N bank. Easy to visit by land from Leixões and pre-recce the R. Douro.

FIGUEIRA DA FOZ *9.20.9*

Beira Litoral **40°08'·75N 08°52'·40W**

CHARTS AC 3253, 3634, 3635; PC 64, 2, 22, 34; SC 42A

TIDES **See Nazaré, 9.20.10; ML 2·0; Zone 0 (UT)**

SHELTER Excellent in marina (2·5-3m) on N bank, ¾M from hbr ent. Strong ebb tide can affect pontoons nearest marina ent. Shipyards, repair basins and fishing harbour on S bank.

NAVIGATION WPT 40°08'·72N 08°52'·70W, 261°/081° from/to hbr ent, 500m. No offshore dangers. Bar at ent is dredged 5m, but shifts/shoals constantly and can be dangerous in swell, especially Nov-Mar with strong S/SW winds. Conditions on the bar may be broadcast on VHF Ch 11 and shown by light/day sigs from Forte de Santa Catarina:

GRG fixed lts (vert) or ● at masthead = Bar closed;
GRG flashing lts (vert) or ● at halfmast = Bar dangerous.

LIGHTS AND MARKS Lts as chartlet. Cabo Mondego, Fl 5s 101m 28M, is 3M NW of hbr ent. Buarcos, Iso WRG 6s, is on the beach 1·1M N of hbr ent. Ldg lts lead 081·5° past marina ent. White suspension bridge, 1·5M E of ent, is conspic from seaward; as are extensive beaches N and S of hbr ent.

RADIO TELEPHONE Port *Postradfoz* VHF Ch 11, 16. Marina Ch 08.

TELEPHONE (Dial code 233) Port Authority 22945; Police 28881.

FACILITIES **Marina** (150+ 50 ♥), ☎ 402910, 📠 402920, AC, FW, Gaz, C, ME, Sh, CH, ▣; **YC** ☎ 28019. **Town:** R, V, Ⓑ, ⇌; ✈ Pōrto.

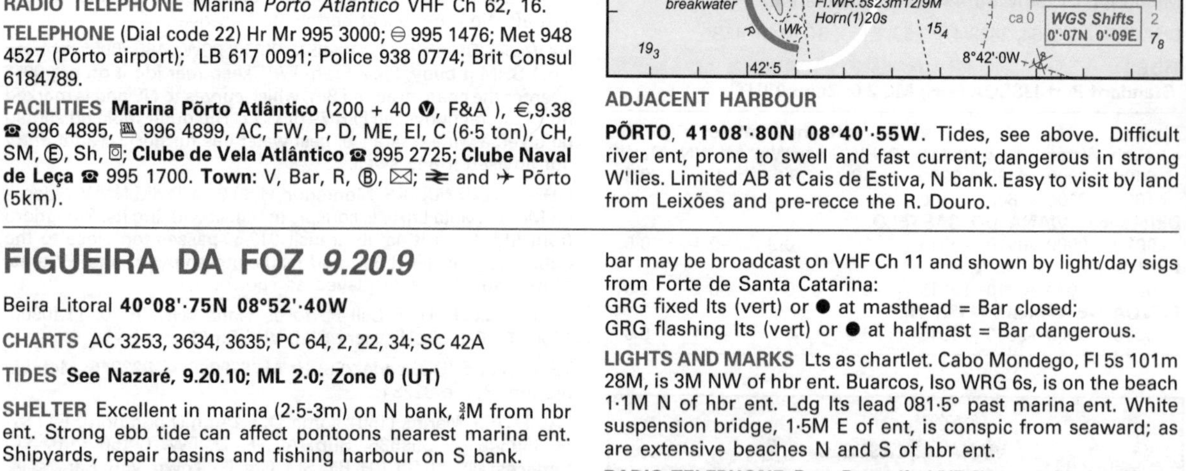

NAZARÉ *9.20.10*

Estremadura **39°35'·50N 09°04'·57W**

CHARTS AC 3635; PC 65, 34, 35, 22; SC 42B

TIDES
Standard Port LISBOA (⟶); ML 2·0; Zone 0 (UT)

Times				Height (metres)			
High Water		Low Water		MHWS	MHWN	MLWN	MLWS
0400	0900	0400	0900	3·8	3·0	1·5	0·5
1600	2100	1600	2100				
Differences BARRA DE AVEIRO							
+0005	+0010	+0010	+0015	−0·5	−0·4	−0·1	+0·1
FIGUEIRA DA FOZ							
−0015	0000	+0010	+0020	−0·3	−0·3	−0·2	0·0
NAZARÉ (Pederneira)							
−0030	−0015	−0005	+0005	−0·5	−0·4	−0·1	+0·1

SHELTER All-weather access to this man-made fishing hbr. Marina is in the SW corner of the inner hbr; visitors should berth on the hammerheads or outer pontoons. The pontoons in the NE corner are for local craft. No ⚓ in outer harbour.

NAVIGATION WPT 39°35'·60N 09°04'·70W, 310°/130° from/to hbr ent, 290m. Due to an underwater canyon there are depths of 150m and 452m 4ca and 5M offshore respectively.

LIGHTS AND MARKS Hbr lts as chartlet. Pontal da Nazaré, Oc 3s 49m 14M, siren 35s, is 1M NNW of hbr ent on a low headland which should be cleared by at least 2ca due to offlying rks.

RADIO TELEPHONE VHF Ch 11, 16 (HO).

TELEPHONE (Dial code 262) Hr Mr 561255; ⊖ & Met via Hr Mr; H 561116.

FACILITIES **Marina** (41 + 12 visitors), 3·5m, ☎ 561402, 📠 561402, AC, FW, Slip, D & P in NE corner, ME, C, Sh, 🗟; **Club Naval de Nazaré. Town:** (1½M to the N), V, R, Bar, Ⓑ, ✉; ≉ Valado dos Frades (7km); ✈ Lisbon (125km).

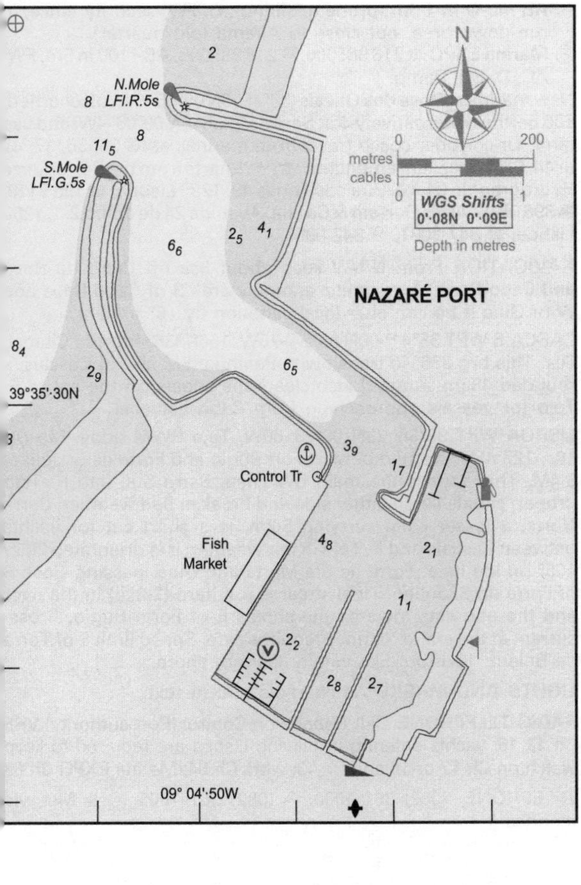

PENICHE *9.20.11*

Estremadura **39°20'·80N 09°22'·43W**

CHARTS AC 3635; PC 69, 36, 35, 22; SC 42B

TIDES
Standard Port LISBOA (⟶); ML 2·0; Zone 0 (UT)

Times				Height (metres)			
High Water		Low Water		MHWS	MHWN	MLWN	MLWS
0400	0900	0400	0900	3·8	3·0	1·5	0·5
1600	2100	1600	2100				
Differences PENICHE							
−0035	−0015	−0005	0000	−0·3	−0·4	−0·2	0·0
ERICEIRA (38°58'N)							
−0040	−0025	−0010	−0010	−0·4	−0·3	−0·1	+0·1

SHELTER A good but rather uncomfortable hbr with all-weather access, but SW swell may work in. Inside W mole berth on outer pontoon of small marina (2·4-3·5m) which is prone to FV wash. Possible moorings or ⚓ in SE part of hbr; holding is good, but ground may be foul. 3kn speed limit in hbr. The ⚓ in 4m on N side of peninsula is open to swell, even in S'lies. On the SE side of Ilha Berlenga there is ⚓ below the lt ho. Storm sigs are displayed from the root of the W mole.

NAVIGATION WPT 39°20'·50N 09°22'·45W, 180°/000° from/to W mole hd, 5ca. The 5M wide chan between Cabo Carvoeiro and

Continued overleaf

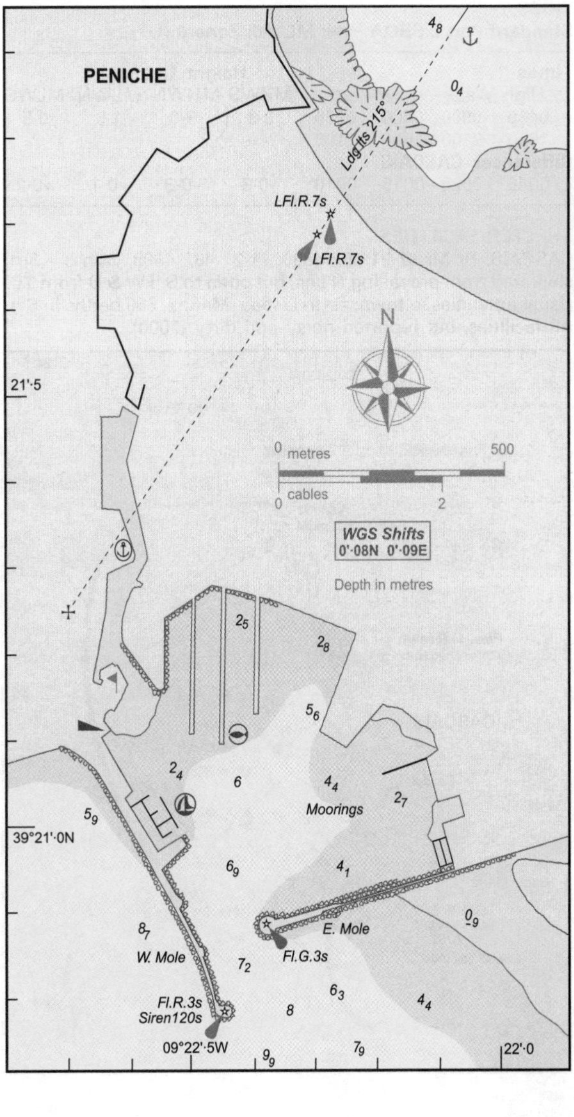

20

PENICHE *continued*

Ilha da Berlenga is often rough. Os Farilhões lies 4·5M further to theNW. The E edge of the N/S TSS is 14M W of Cabo Carvoeiro; the ITZ embraces Peniche and the offshore islands.

LIGHTS AND MARKS Ilha da Berlenga, Fl (3) 20s 120m 27M. Farilhão Grande, Fl 5s 99m 13M. Cabo Carvoeiro, Fl (3) R 15s 57m 15M, is 2M WNW of hbr ent and steep-to apart from Nau dos Carvos, a conspic high rk close-in. Other lts as chartlet. Peniche looks like an island from afar, with conspic water tr in town centre.

RADIO TELEPHONE VHF Ch 16 (H24), 11.

TELEPHONE (Dial code 262) Hr Mr 781153, 784767; ⊖ & Met via Hr Mr; Ⓗ 781702; Emergency 115 or 789666; LB 789629.

FACILITIES **Marina** (130+ 20 Ⓥ), ☎ 781153, 784225, AC, FW; **Clube Náutico; Services:** P & D (cans or tanker), CH, BY, ME, El, Ⓔ, C, Gaz, Slip. **Town**: V, R, Bar, Ⓑ, ✉; ≷ Obidos (30km), ✈ Lisbon (80km).

CASCAIS *9.20.12*

Estremadura **38°41'·50N 09°24'·93W**

CHARTS AC 3263/4, 3635; PC 45, 46, 48, 263 03/05/06/07; SC 4310, 42B

TIDES
Standard Port LISBOA (⟶); ML 2·0; Zone 0 (UT)

Times				Height (metres)			
High Water		Low Water		MHWS	MHWN	MLWN	MLWS
0400	0900	0400	0900	3·8	3·0	1·5	0·5
1600	2100	1600	2100				
Differences CASCAIS							
−0040	−0025	−0015	−0010	−0·3	−0·3	−0·1	+0·2

SHELTER/FACILITIES
CASCAIS: Hr Mr ☎ 21 482 4800, 21 482 4899, ⚓ in 3 – 5m, sheltered from prevailing N'lies, but open to S. FW & D from YC. Usual amenities in town; ≷ to Lisboa. Marina, 660 berths in 6m. All facilities, but reported noisy and dirty (2000)

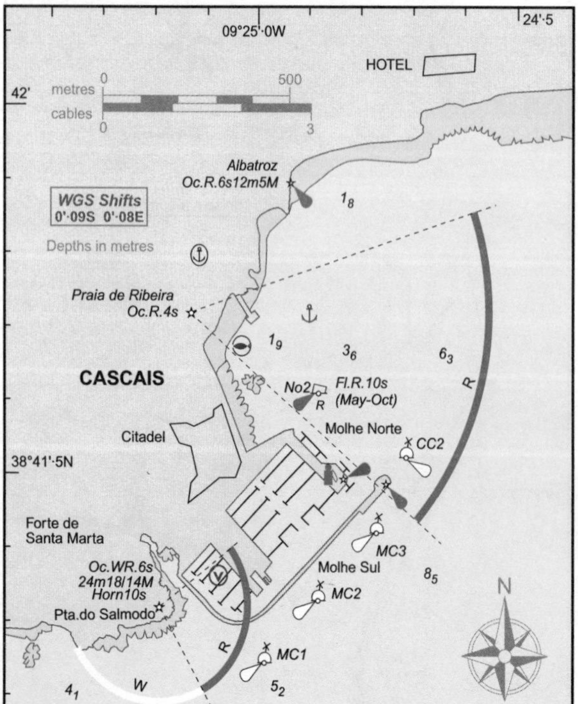

LISBOA *9.20.13*

Estremadura **38°41'·30N 09°10'·55W** (Ponte 25 de Abril)

CHARTS AC 3263/4, 3635; PC 45, 46, 48, 263 03/05/06/07; SC 4310, 42B

TIDES
Standard Port LISBOA (⟶); ML 2·0; Zone 0 (UT)

Times				Height (metres)			
High Water		Low Water		MHWS	MHWN	MLWN	MLWS
0400	0900	0400	0900	3·8	3·0	1·5	0·5
1600	2100	1600	2100				
Differences PACO DE ARCOS (5·5M W of Tejo bridge)							
−0020	−0030	−0005	−0005	−0·4	−0·4	−0·2	0·0

SHELTER/FACILITIES
LISBOA: (Dial code 2139) The 5 marinas, Ⓐ to Ⓔ on chartlet below, are:

Ⓐ **Doca de Bom Successo**, close E of the ornate Torre de Belém (conspic) and red Pilots bldg. Almost full of local yachts. 100 F&A, 3m, ☎ 22011 22038, AC, FW, C, CH, R, Slip, D & P (cans), ≷, bus to Lisbon.

Ⓑ **Doca de Belém**, 150m E of Monument to the Discoveries (conspic). Almost full of local yachts; 200 F&A, 3m, ☎ 22011 22038 AC, FW, D (hose), BH, C, R; ≷, bus to Lisbon.

Ⓒ **Doca de Santo Amaro**, almost below the suspension bridge (road traffic "hums" overhead, plus night life noise). 330 AB (few Ⓥ), 4m, ☎ 22011, 22038, AC, FW, R, Bar, V; ≷, bus 2M to city centre.

Ⓓ **Doca de Alcântara**, ent is E of the container/cruise ship terminal; chan doubles back W, via swing bridge, toward marina at W end of dock. Swing bridge is reported permanently open. Marina: 180 AB inc Ⓥ (best for foreign yachts), 8m, ☎ 22011, 22038, security fencing, AC, FW, R, Bar, V; ≷; bus 2M to city centre.

Ⓔ **Doca do Terreiro do Trigo** (also known as *APORVELA* Portuguese STA), approx 700m ENE of the ferry terminal, beyond naval Doca de Marinha. ☎ 218 876854, 218 873885, AB inc Ⓥ in 1·5m (prone to silting), D, FW, security fence; in run-down area, but close to Alfama (old quarter).

Ⓕ **Marina EXPO** ☎ 218 985000, 218 985008, AB 1100 in 5m, FW, AC, D, BH, Ramp.

New marina at **Doca dos Olivais** (38°45'·8N 09°05'·5W, off chartlet), 500 berths . Alternatively ⚓ at Seixal (38°38'·6N 09°06'·4W) and use ferry. Or consider coach travel from marinas at IG 35, 36, 37, 42 or 44. **City**: Excellent amenities; ≷, ✈. Charts from the Portuguese Hydrographic Office, Rua das Trinas 49, 1296 Lisboa; ☎ 395 5119, 396 0515. ACA: Garraio & Ca Lda, Avenida 24 de Julho 2-1, 1200 Lisboa; ☎ 347 3081, 342 8950.

NAVIGATION From N/NW keep about 5ca off Cabo da Roca and Cabo Raso. A magnetic anomaly area S of Cabo Raso and W of Guia lt ho can alter local variation by +5° to −3°.

CASCAIS WPT 38°41'·00N 09°24'·73W, 156°/336° from/to Citadel, 6ca. This brg 336° in transit with Peninha (5M NW of Cascais; a rounded 485m summit) also clears the shoals off the ent to R. Tejo for vessels approaching from Cabo Espichel.

LISBOA WPT 38°36'·23N 09°23'·60W, Tejo SWM buoy, Mo (A) 10s, 227°/047° from/to betwixt Fort Bugio and Forte de S. Juliao, 5·4M. This appr is the main DW chan, Barra Sul, into R. Tejo proper; shoals lie on either side and break in bad weather. Barra Norte, a lesser chan carrying 5·2m, is a short cut for yachts between Cascais and R. Tejo in fair weather; it is orientated 285°/105° on ldg lts at Forte de Sta Marta and Guia, passing close S of Forte de S. Juliao. Tidal streams run hard (2-3kn) in the river and the ebb sets towards the shoals E of Forte Bugio. Cross-current at the ent to marinas requires care. Speed limit E of Torre de Belém: 10kn but 5kn within 300m of shore.

LIGHTS AND MARKS As chartlets and in text.

RADIO TELEPHONE Call *Lisboa Port* Control (Port authority) VHF Ch **12** 16; yachts entering or leaving Lisboa are required to keep watch on Ch 12 or 16 and Ch 13; work Ch 64; Marina EXPO Ch 62

TELEPHONE (082) 361 1000, (082) 361 1005, ⊖ & Met, via marinas.

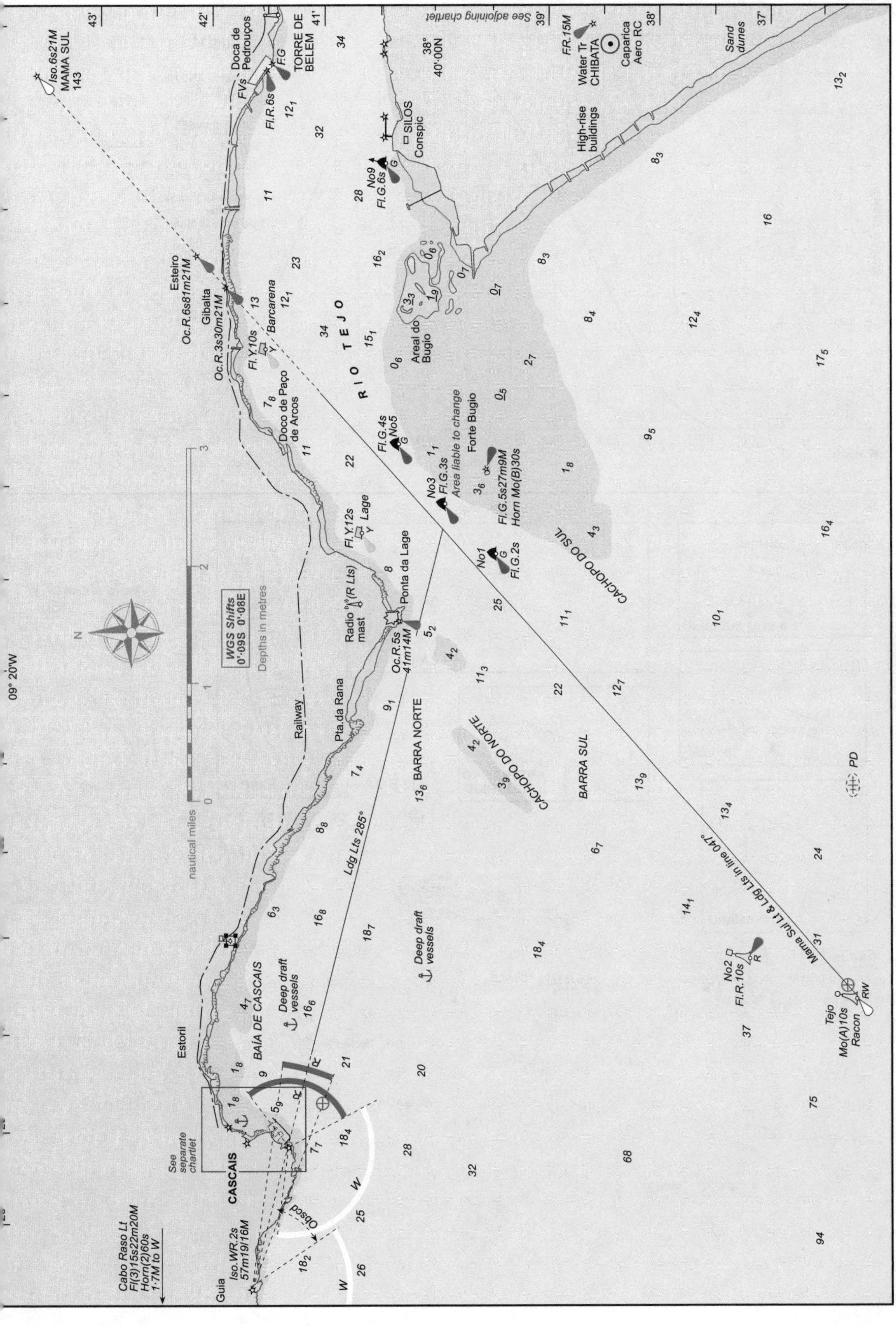
09° 20'W
43'
42'
41'
39'
38'
37'
Iso.6s21M
MAMA SUL
143
Doca de Pedrouços
FVs
F.G
Fl.R.6s
TORRE DE BELEM
38° 40'·00N
See adjoining chartlet
FR.15M
Water Tr CHIBATA
Caparica Aero RC
Sand dunes
High-rise buildings
SILOS Conspic
No9
Fl.G.6s
Esteiro
Oc.R.6s81m21M
Gibalta
Oc.R.3s30m21M
Fl.Y.10s
Barcarena
RIO TEJO
Areal do Bugio
Doco de Paço de Arcos
Fl.G.4s
No5
No3
Fl.G.3s
Area liable to change
Forte Bugio
Fl.G.5s27m9M
Horn Mo(B)30s
Fl.Y.12s
Lage
No1
Fl.G.2s
CACHOPO DO SUL
Radio mast
(R Lts)
Ponta da Lage
Oc.R.5s
41m14M
WGS Shifts
0'·09S 0'·08E
Depths in metres
nautical miles
Railway
Pta.da Rana
BARRA NORTE
CACHOPO DO NORTE
BARRA SUL
PD
Ldg Lts 285°
Mama Sul Lt & Ldg Lts in line 047°
Deep draft vessels
Estoril
BAÍA DE CASCAIS
Deep draft vessels
No2
Fl.R.10s
Tejo
Mo(A)10s
Racon
RW
See separate chartlet
CASCAIS
Cabo Raso Lt
Fl(3)15s22m20M
Horn(2)60s
1·7M to W
Guia
Iso.WR.2s
57m19/16M
Obscd
W

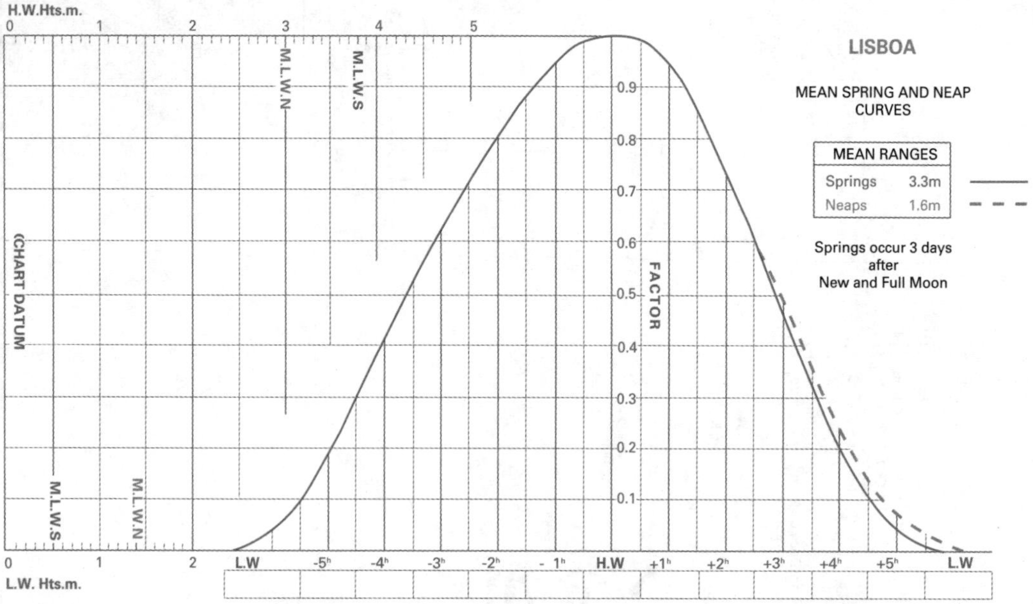
H.W.Hts.m.
M.L.W.N
M.L.W.S
(CHART DATUM
FACTOR
L.W. Hts.m.
L.W
-5h
-4h
-3h
-2h
- 1h
H.W
+1h
+2h
+3h
+4h
+5h
L.W
LISBOA
MEAN SPRING AND NEAP CURVES
MEAN RANGES
Springs 3.3m
Neaps 1.6m
Springs occur 3 days after New and Full Moon

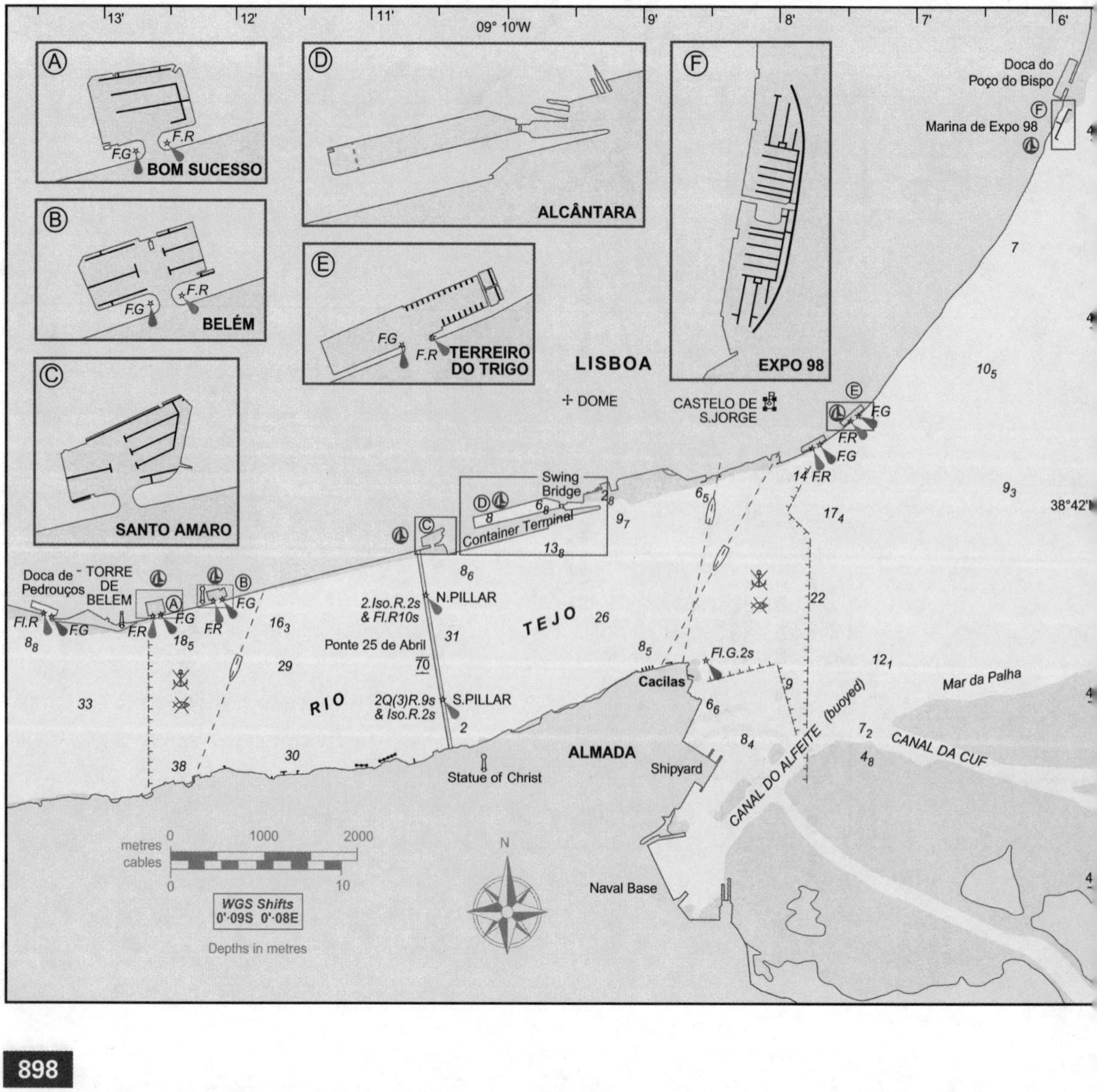
13'
12'
11'
09° 10'W
9'
8'
7'
6'
38°42'
BOM SUCESSO
BELÉM
SANTO AMARO
ALCÂNTARA
TERREIRO DO TRIGO
EXPO 98
LISBOA
DOME
CASTELO DE S.JORGE
Doca do Poço do Bispo
Marina de Expo 98
Swing Bridge
Container Terminal
Doca de Pedrouços
TORRE DE BELEM
N.PILLAR
S.PILLAR
2.Iso.R.2s & Fl.R10s
2Q(3)R.9s & Iso.R.2s
Ponte 25 de Abril
TEJO
RIO
Cacilas
Fl.G.2s
ALMADA
Shipyard
Statue of Christ
Naval Base
CANAL DO ALFEITE (buoyed)
CANAL DA CUF
Mar da Palha
metres
cables
WGS Shifts
0'·09S 0'·08E
Depths in metres

SESIMBRA *9.20.14*

Baixo Alentejo **38°26'·20N 09°06'·40W**

CHARTS AC 3635, 3636; PC 79; SC42B

TIDES

Standard Port LISBOA (⟼); ML 2·0; Zone 0 (UT)

Times				Height (metres)			
High Water		Low Water		MHWS	MHWN	MLWN	MLWS
0400	0900	0400	0900	3·8	3·0	1·5	0·5
1600	2100	1600	2100				
Differences SESIMBRA							
−0045	−0030	−0020	−0010	−0·4	−0·4	−0·1	+0·1

SHELTER A substantial outer bkwtr encloses this FV hbr. Sesimbra is not a yachting harbour though NW of ☆ Fl R 3s, yachts may find free AB in an inlet with slip; or ⚓ in about 5m to N of ent and clear of fairway. Caution: strong N'lies blow down from high ground late pm/evening.

NAVIGATION WPT 38°24'·68N 09°06'·22W, 174°/354° 1·63M from/to Breakwater Head Lt.

LIGHTS AND MARKS Ldg lts 004°, both L Fl R 5s 9/21m 7/6M. Outer bkwtr hd, Fl R 3s 8M, W tr, R bands; root, Oc 5s 34m 14M, R ○ tr (Forte de Cavalo).

RADIO TELEPHONE VHF Ch 11

TELEPHONE (Dial code 021) YC 2233451 📠 2281039.

FACILITIES FW, D from fish market; tourist amenities. Bus to Lisboa or, to avoid tfc jams, local bus to Cacilhas and ferry across the Tejo. **Town:** (1½M to the N), V, R, Bar, Ⓑ, ✉; ⇌ Valado dos Frades (7km); ✈ Lisbon (125km).

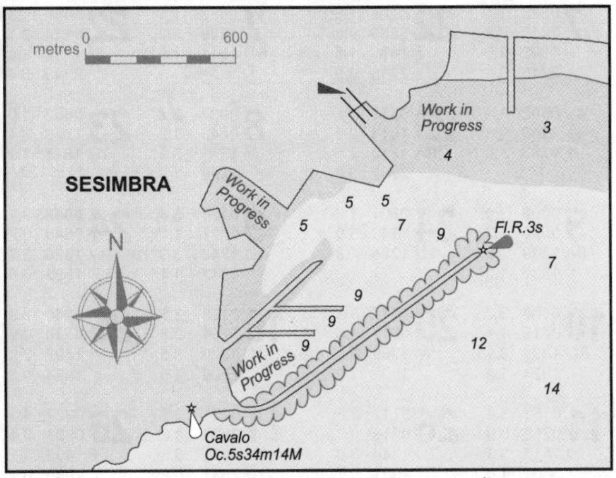

SETÚBAL *9.20.15*

Baixo Alentejo **38°31'·32N 08°53'·04W** (Marina)

CHARTS AC 3270, 3635/6; PC 82, 263 08/09; SC42B

TIDES

Standard Port LISBOA (⟼); ML 2·0; Zone 0 (UT)

Times				Height (metres)			
High Water		Low Water		MHWS	MHWN	MLWN	MLWS
0400	0900	0400	0900	3·8	3·0	1·5	0·5
1600	2100	1600	2100				
Differences SETUBAL							
−0020	−0015	−0005	+0005	−0·3	−0·3	−0·2	0·0

SHELTER New marina in W half of Doca de Comercio. Local boats only in small Doca de Recreio. Industrial quays to ESE.

NAVIGATION WPT 38°26'·65N 08°58'·68W, 220°/040° from/to front ldg lt, 6M. Rio Sado is shoal on both sides until past Forte de Outão, Oc R 6s.

LIGHTS AND MARKS Ldg lts 040°: front, Oc R 3s, R structure + W stripes; rear, Iso R 6s, R hut on piles. No 1 buoy, Fl G 3s, and No 2 bn, Fl (2)R 10s, mark the start of the chan.

RADIO TELEPHONE VHF Ch 11, 16, YC Ch 12

TELEPHONE (Dial code 265) Hr Mr 542075 📠 230992; ⊖ & Met via Hr Mr; Ⓗ 561116.

FACILITIES **Marina** (155 AB) 3·8m, AC, FW, Slip, D & P in NE corner, ME, C, Sh, ⊡; **Club Naval de Nazaré. Town:** (1½M to the N), V, R, Bar, Ⓑ, ✉; ⇌ Valado dos Frades (7km); ✈ Lisbon (125km).

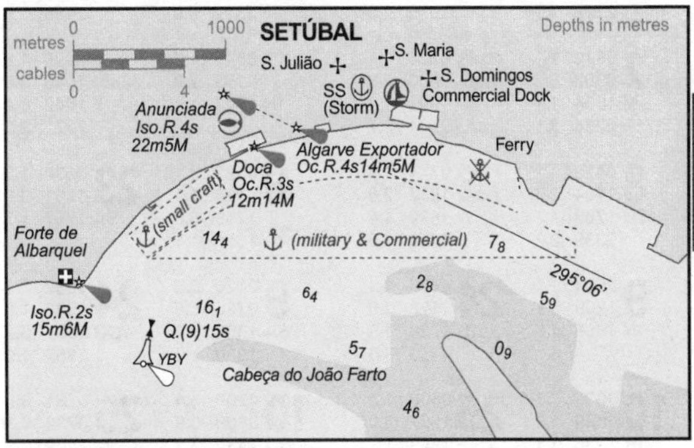

ADJACENT ANCHORAGE

ARRÁBIDA 38°28'·5N 08°58'·75W, 1·4M N of ent to Rio Sado. Popular but shallow ⚓ (3·7m) sheltered from N by high ground. Appr from SSW to avoid Baixo de Alpertuche (0·7m) close offshore and rks at NE end of bay.

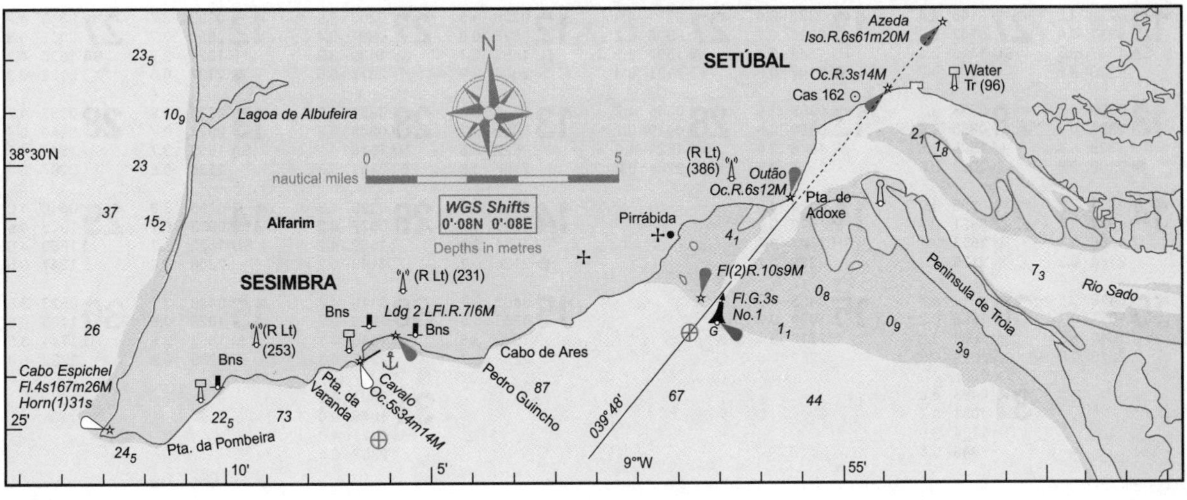

20

TIME ZONE (UTC)
For Summer Time add ONE hour in **non-shaded areas**

PORTUGAL – LISBOA

LAT 38°42′N LONG 9°08′W

TIMES AND HEIGHTS OF HIGH AND LOW WATERS

SPRING & NEAP TIDES
Dates in red are SPRINGS
Dates in blue are NEAPS

YEAR **2002**

JANUARY

Date	Time	m	Time	m	Time	m	Time	m
1 TU	0423	3.8	1016	0.4	1650	3.6	2230	0.6
2 W	0509	3.8	1103	0.5	1738	3.6	2317	0.6
3 TH	0557	3.8	1152	0.6	1828	3.5		
4 F	0007	0.8	0648	3.7	1244	0.7	1921	3.3
5 SA	0101	0.9	0743	3.5	1341	0.9	2019	3.2
6 SU	0201	1.0	0844	3.3	1445	1.0	2125	3.1
7 M	0310	1.1	0953	3.2	1554	1.1	2234	3.1
8 TU	0423	1.1	1104	3.2	1703	1.1	2339	3.2
9 W	0534	1.1	1209	3.2	1805	1.0		
10 TH	0039	3.3	0636	1.0	1308	3.3	1900	0.9
11 F	0132	3.4	0730	0.9	1400	3.3	1947	0.9
12 SA	0220	3.5	0817	0.8	1447	3.3	2030	0.8
13 SU	0303	3.6	0859	0.7	1529	3.3	● 2109	0.8
14 M	0343	3.6	0937	0.7	1606	3.3	2144	0.8
15 TU	0419	3.6	1011	0.7	1640	3.3	2218	0.8
16 W	0451	3.5	1045	0.7	1712	3.3	2251	0.9
17 TH	0522	3.5	1117	0.8	1742	3.2	2325	0.9
18 F	0554	3.4	1152	0.9	1815	3.1		
19 SA	0000	1.0	0629	3.3	1229	1.0	1853	3.0
20 SU	0040	1.2	0709	3.1	1312	1.1	1938	2.9
21 M	0128	1.3	0758	3.0	1405	1.3	2035	2.8
22 TU	0228	1.4	0900	2.9	1509	1.4	2144	2.7
23 W	0341	1.5	1012	2.8	1620	1.4	2255	2.8
24 TH	0455	1.4	1123	2.9	1726	1.3	2359	3.0
25 F	0600	1.2	1227	3.0	1823	1.1		
26 SA	0056	3.2	0656	1.0	1324	3.2	1915	0.9
27 SU	0148	3.4	0747	0.7	1416	3.4	2003	0.7
28 M	0238	3.7	0835	0.5	1505	3.6	○ 2050	0.5
29 TU	0325	3.9	0921	0.3	1553	3.7	2135	0.4
30 W	0412	4.0	1006	0.2	1639	3.8	2220	0.3
31 TH	0458	4.0	1051	0.2	1724	3.8	2305	0.4

FEBRUARY

Date	Time	m	Time	m	Time	m	Time	m
1 F	0543	4.0	1136	0.3	1809	3.7	2350	0.5
2 SA	0629	3.8	1222	0.5	1856	3.5		
3 SU	0038	0.7	0718	3.6	1311	0.7	1947	3.3
4 M	0130	0.9	0812	3.3	1407	1.0	2045	3.1
5 TU	0233	1.1	0918	3.1	1513	1.2	2156	3.0
6 W	0350	1.2	1035	3.0	1631	1.3	2312	3.0
7 TH	0515	1.2	1153	2.9	1747	1.3		
8 F	0022	3.1	0629	1.1	1259	3.0	1850	1.1
9 SA	0120	3.3	0725	1.0	1352	3.1	1938	1.0
10 SU	0209	3.4	0809	0.9	1436	3.3	2019	0.9
11 M	0250	3.5	0847	0.8	1514	3.3	2055	0.8
12 TU	0326	3.6	0920	0.7	1548	3.4	● 2127	0.8
13 W	0359	3.6	0950	0.6	1618	3.4	2158	0.7
14 TH	0429	3.6	1020	0.6	1647	3.4	2228	0.7
15 F	0458	3.6	1050	0.7	1716	3.4	2259	0.8
16 SA	0528	3.5	1121	0.7	1746	3.3	2330	0.9
17 SU	0600	3.4	1153	0.9	1818	3.2		
18 M	0004	1.0	0635	3.3	1228	1.0	1855	3.1
19 TU	0042	1.1	0715	3.1	1308	1.2	1941	2.9
20 W	0130	1.3	0806	2.9	1402	1.4	2041	2.8
21 TH	0238	1.5	0915	2.8	1517	1.5	2158	2.8
22 F	0406	1.5	1040	2.8	1642	1.4	2321	2.9
23 SA	0530	1.3	1201	3.0	1757	1.2		
24 SU	0032	3.2	0637	1.0	1307	3.2	1857	1.0
25 M	0131	3.5	0732	0.7	1402	3.5	1949	0.7
26 TU	0223	3.8	0820	0.4	1451	3.7	2036	0.5
27 W	0311	4.0	0906	0.2	1537	3.9	○ 2121	0.3
28 TH	0356	4.2	0949	0.1	1621	4.0	2204	0.2

MARCH

Date	Time	m	Time	m	Time	m	Time	m
1 F	0440	4.2	1032	0.1	1704	4.0	2246	0.2
2 SA	0524	4.2	1114	0.3	1746	3.9	2329	0.4
3 SU	0607	4.0	1156	0.5	1829	3.7		
4 M	0013	0.6	0652	3.7	1240	0.8	1915	3.5
5 TU	0102	0.9	0742	3.3	1331	1.1	2009	3.2
6 W	0202	1.2	0845	3.0	1435	1.4	2119	3.0
7 TH	0323	1.4	1010	2.8	1602	1.5	2246	3.0
8 F	0502	1.4	1140	2.8	1733	1.5		
9 SA	0006	3.0	0620	1.3	1249	3.0	1837	1.3
10 SU	0105	3.2	0712	1.1	1338	3.1	1924	1.2
11 M	0151	3.4	0752	0.9	1417	3.3	2001	1.0
12 TU	0229	3.5	0825	0.8	1451	3.4	2034	0.9
13 W	0302	3.6	0855	0.7	1522	3.5	2104	0.8
14 TH	0333	3.7	0924	0.6	1551	3.6	● 2134	0.7
15 F	0403	3.8	0953	0.6	1620	3.6	2203	0.7
16 SA	0433	3.7	1022	0.7	1648	3.6	2233	0.7
17 SU	0503	3.7	1051	0.7	1718	3.5	2303	0.8
18 M	0534	3.5	1121	0.9	1749	3.4	2335	0.9
19 TU	0607	3.4	1152	1.0	1824	3.3		
20 W	0010	1.1	0644	3.2	1229	1.2	1905	3.1
21 TH	0055	1.3	0731	3.0	1318	1.4	2000	3.0
22 F	0200	1.5	0839	2.8	1433	1.5	2118	2.9
23 SA	0333	1.5	1013	2.8	1610	1.5	2252	3.0
24 SU	0507	1.3	1143	3.0	1735	1.3		
25 M	0011	3.3	0617	1.0	1250	3.3	1838	1.0
26 TU	0112	3.6	0713	0.7	1344	3.6	1931	0.7
27 W	0203	3.9	0801	0.4	1432	3.9	2017	0.5
28 TH	0251	4.2	0845	0.3	1516	4.1	○ 2101	0.3
29 F	0335	4.3	0927	0.2	1559	4.2	2143	0.2
30 SA	0419	4.3	1008	0.2	1640	4.1	2225	0.3
31 SU	0501	4.2	1049	0.4	1721	4.0	2307	0.4

APRIL

Date	Time	m	Time	m	Time	m	Time	m
1 M	0544	4.0	1129	0.6	1803	3.8	2351	0.7
2 TU	0628	3.6	1212	0.9	1847	3.5		
3 W	0039	1.0	0717	3.3	1300	1.2	1938	3.3
4 TH	0138	1.3	0818	3.0	1402	1.5	2046	3.0
5 F	0259	1.5	0945	2.8	1532	1.7	2216	3.0
6 SA	0438	1.5	1118	2.8	1706	1.7	2338	3.0
7 SU	0553	1.4	1225	3.0	1811	1.5		
8 M	0037	3.2	0643	1.2	1311	3.2	1856	1.3
9 TU	0121	3.4	0721	1.1	1348	3.3	1933	1.1
10 W	0158	3.5	0754	0.9	1420	3.5	2006	1.0
11 TH	0231	3.7	0824	0.8	1451	3.6	2037	0.8
12 F	0303	3.7	0854	0.7	1521	3.7	● 2107	0.8
13 SA	0335	3.8	0924	0.7	1552	3.7	2138	0.8
14 SU	0406	3.8	0953	0.7	1622	3.7	2208	0.8
15 M	0438	3.7	1023	0.8	1653	3.6	2239	0.9
16 TU	0510	3.6	1053	0.9	1726	3.5	2313	0.9
17 W	0545	3.4	1126	1.0	1802	3.4	2351	1.1
18 TH	0625	3.3	1205	1.2	1844	3.3		
19 F	0039	1.3	0715	3.1	1257	1.4	1940	3.1
20 SA	0145	1.4	0825	2.9	1413	1.5	2058	3.1
21 SU	0316	1.4	0958	2.9	1549	1.5	2231	3.2
22 M	0444	1.3	1124	3.1	1712	1.4	2348	3.4
23 TU	0553	1.0	1228	3.4	1815	1.1		
24 W	0048	3.7	0648	0.7	1320	3.7	1907	0.8
25 TH	0140	3.9	0736	0.5	1407	3.9	1954	0.6
26 F	0227	4.1	0821	0.4	1452	4.1	2039	0.4
27 SA	0313	4.2	0903	0.3	1535	4.2	○ 2122	0.3
28 SU	0357	4.2	0944	0.4	1617	4.1	2204	0.4
29 M	0440	4.0	1025	0.5	1659	4.0	2247	0.5
30 TU	0523	3.8	1105	0.8	1741	3.8	2332	0.8

TIME ZONE (UTC)
For Summer Time add ONE hour in **non-shaded areas**

PORTUGAL – LISBOA

LAT 38°42′N LONG 9°08′W

TIMES AND HEIGHTS OF HIGH AND LOW WATERS

SPRING & NEAP TIDES
Dates in red are SPRINGS
Dates in blue are NEAPS

YEAR **2002**

MAY

Date	Time	m	Date	Time	m
1 W	0607 1147 1824	3.5 1.0 3.6	16 TH	0532 1110 1749 2342	3.4 1.0 3.5 1.0
2 TH	0020 0655 1234 1912	1.0 3.2 1.3 3.3	17 F	0617 1155 1836	3.3 1.2 3.4
3 F	0116 0752 1332 2012	1.3 2.9 1.6 3.1	18 SA	0034 0711 1251 1934	1.1 3.1 1.3 3.3
4 SA	0228 0909 1452 2131	1.5 2.8 1.7 3.0	19 SU	0140 0820 1403 2047	1.2 3.0 1.4 3.2
5 SU	0352 1035 1618 2251	1.5 2.8 1.7 3.0	20 M	0259 0942 1527 2208	1.3 3.1 1.4 3.3
6 M	0504 1141 1725 2352	1.5 2.9 1.6 3.1	21 TU	0417 1057 1643 2320	1.2 3.2 1.3 3.4
7 TU	0557 1230 1815	1.3 3.1 1.4	22 W	0524 1200 1747	1.0 3.4 1.1
8 W	0039 0640 1309 1856	3.3 1.1 3.3 1.2	23 TH	0021 0620 1253 1841	3.6 0.8 3.6 0.8
9 TH	0119 0716 1344 1932	3.4 1.0 3.5 1.1	24 F	0114 0710 1342 1931	3.8 0.6 3.8 0.6
10 F	0156 0750 1417 2006	3.5 0.9 3.6 0.9	25 SA	0204 0756 1428 2018	3.9 0.5 3.9 0.5
11 SA	0231 0822 1450 2039	3.6 0.8 3.7 0.9	26 SU	0251 0840 1513 ○ 2103	3.9 0.5 4.0 0.5
12 SU	0306 0854 1523 ● 2112	3.7 0.8 3.7 0.8	27 M	0337 0922 1557 2148	3.9 0.6 4.0 0.5
13 M	0340 0926 1557 2146	3.7 0.8 3.7 0.8	28 TU	0422 1004 1640 2232	3.8 0.7 3.9 0.6
14 TU	0416 0958 1632 2221	3.6 0.8 3.7 0.9	29 W	0506 1045 1722 2316	3.6 0.9 3.7 0.8
15 W	0452 1032 1709 2259	3.5 0.9 3.6 0.9	30 TH	0550 1126 1804	3.4 1.1 3.5
			31 F	0001 0633 1210 1847	1.0 3.1 1.3 3.3

JUNE

Date	Time	m	Date	Time	m
1 SA	0050 0721 1300 1935	1.2 3.0 1.5 3.1	16 SU	0030 0707 1245 1927	0.9 3.2 1.1 3.4
2 SU	0146 0819 1402 2033	1.4 2.8 1.6 3.0	17 M	0129 0808 1348 2031	1.0 3.2 1.2 3.4
3 M	0251 0928 1514 2143	1.4 2.8 1.6 3.0	18 TU	0236 0916 1459 2140	1.0 3.1 1.2 3.3
4 TU	0358 1037 1623 2250	1.4 2.8 1.6 3.0	19 W	0345 1025 1610 2250	1.0 3.2 1.2 3.4
5 W	0459 1135 1722 2347	1.3 3.0 1.5 3.1	20 TH	0452 1129 1717 2353	1.0 3.3 1.1 3.5
6 TH	0550 1222 1812	1.2 3.1 1.3	21 F	0552 1226 1817	0.9 3.5 0.9
7 F	0035 0634 1303 1855	3.2 1.1 3.3 1.1	22 SA	0051 0646 1319 1912	3.5 0.8 3.6 0.8
8 SA	0117 0713 1342 1934	3.3 1.0 3.4 1.0	23 SU	0145 0735 1409 2003	3.6 0.7 3.7 0.7
9 SU	0158 0750 1419 2012	3.4 0.9 3.5 0.9	24 M	0235 0821 1456 ○ 2050	3.6 0.7 3.8 0.6
10 M	0237 0826 1457 ● 2049	3.5 0.9 3.6 0.8	25 TU	0323 0905 1541 2135	3.6 0.7 3.8 0.6
11 TU	0317 0902 1536 2128	3.5 0.8 3.7 0.8	26 W	0408 0947 1624 2218	3.5 0.8 3.7 0.7
12 W	0358 0939 1616 2208	3.5 0.8 3.7 0.8	27 TH	0450 1027 1704 2258	3.4 0.9 3.7 0.8
13 TH	0440 1019 1658 2251	3.5 0.8 3.7 0.8	28 F	0530 1105 1741 2337	3.3 1.0 3.5 0.9
14 F	0525 1102 1743 2338	3.4 0.9 3.6 0.8	29 SA	0607 1144 1818	3.2 1.1 3.4
15 SA	0613 1150 1832	3.3 1.0 3.5	30 SU	0017 0645 1225 1856	1.0 3.0 1.2 3.2

JULY

Date	Time	m	Date	Time	m
1 M	0101 0727 1312 1940	1.2 2.9 1.4 3.1	16 TU	0109 0745 1326 2008	0.8 3.3 1.0 3.5
2 TU	0151 0818 1408 2034	1.3 2.8 1.5 3.0	17 W	0206 0845 1428 2111	0.9 3.2 1.1 3.3
3 W	0249 0920 1514 2139	1.3 2.8 1.5 2.9	18 TH	0311 0951 1538 2220	1.0 3.2 1.1 3.3
4 TH	0353 1027 1621 2245	1.4 2.8 1.5 3.0	19 F	0420 1059 1652 2330	1.1 3.2 1.1 3.2
5 F	0455 1127 1723 2345	1.3 3.0 1.4 3.0	20 SA	0527 1204 1801	1.1 3.3 1.0
6 SA	0549 1219 1816	1.2 3.1 1.3	21 SU	0035 0629 1303 1903	3.3 1.0 3.4 0.9
7 SU	0038 0636 1306 1904	3.1 1.1 3.2 1.1	22 M	0134 0722 1356 1955	3.3 0.9 3.6 0.8
8 M	0127 0719 1350 1948	3.2 1.0 3.4 0.9	23 TU	0226 0810 1444 2042	3.4 0.9 3.7 0.7
9 TU	0213 0801 1434 2031	3.3 0.9 3.5 0.8	24 W	0312 0852 1528 ○ 2123	3.4 0.8 3.7 0.7
10 W	0259 0843 1519 ● 2114	3.4 0.8 3.7 0.7	25 TH	0353 0931 1607 2200	3.4 0.8 3.7 0.7
11 TH	0344 0926 1603 2157	3.5 0.7 3.8 0.6	26 F	0431 1007 1643 2235	3.4 0.8 3.7 0.7
12 F	0430 1009 1649 2242	3.6 0.7 3.8 0.5	27 SA	0504 1041 1715 2308	3.4 0.9 3.6 0.8
13 SA	0516 1054 1734 2328	3.6 0.7 3.8 0.6	28 SU	0536 1115 1746 2342	3.3 0.9 3.5 0.9
14 SU	0603 1141 1822	3.5 0.7 3.8	29 M	0607 1150 1819	3.2 1.0 3.4
15 M	0017 0652 1231 1912	0.6 3.4 0.8 3.6	30 TU	0017 0642 1228 1856	1.0 3.1 1.2 3.2
			31 W	0058 0723 1312 1940	1.1 3.0 1.3 3.1

AUGUST

Date	Time	m	Date	Time	m
1 TH	0145 0814 1407 2035	1.3 2.9 1.5 2.9	16 F	0237 0919 1511 2156	1.2 3.2 1.2 3.1
2 F	0245 0917 1516 2143	1.4 2.8 1.5 2.9	17 SA	0352 1034 1636 2316	1.3 3.1 1.3 3.1
3 SA	0354 1028 1632 2256	1.5 2.8 1.5 2.9	18 SU	0512 1149 1757	1.3 3.2 1.2
4 SU	0502 1135 1740	1.4 3.0 1.4	19 M	0029 0621 1253 1900	3.1 1.2 3.4 1.1
5 M	0003 0602 1234 1837	3.0 1.3 3.2 1.2	20 TU	0127 0715 1346 1948	3.2 1.1 3.5 0.9
6 TU	0101 0654 1326 1928	3.1 1.1 3.4 1.0	21 W	0216 0759 1431 2029	3.4 1.0 3.7 0.8
7 W	0154 0742 1416 2014	3.3 0.9 3.6 0.7	22 TH	0257 0838 1510 ○ 2104	3.5 0.9 3.7 0.7
8 TH	0243 0828 1503 ● 2059	3.5 0.7 3.8 0.5	23 F	0333 0912 1545 2136	3.5 0.8 3.8 0.7
9 F	0330 0912 1549 2143	3.7 0.6 4.0 0.4	24 SA	0405 0944 1616 2206	3.5 0.8 3.8 0.7
10 SA	0415 0956 1634 2227	3.8 0.5 4.1 0.3	25 SU	0435 1015 1646 2236	3.5 0.8 3.7 0.7
11 SU	0500 1040 1719 2311	3.8 0.5 4.1 0.4	26 M	0503 1045 1715 2307	3.5 0.9 3.6 0.8
12 M	0544 1124 1804 2355	3.8 0.5 4.0 0.5	27 TU	0532 1117 1746 2338	3.4 0.9 3.5 0.9
13 TU	0630 1210 1851	3.7 0.7 3.8	28 W	0604 1150 1819	3.3 1.1 3.4
14 W	0043 0718 1301 1942	0.7 3.5 0.9 3.5	29 TH	0012 0640 1227 1858	1.1 3.2 1.3 3.2
15 TH	0135 0813 1359 2042	0.9 3.3 1.1 3.3	30 F	0051 0723 1312 1946	1.3 3.0 1.4 3.0
			31 SA	0141 0818 1416 2050	1.5 2.9 1.6 2.9

TIME ZONE (UTC)
For Summer Time add ONE hour in **non-shaded areas**

PORTUGAL – LISBOA

LAT 38°42′N LONG 9°08′W

TIMES AND HEIGHTS OF HIGH AND LOW WATERS

SPRING & NEAP TIDES
Dates in red are SPRINGS
Dates in blue are NEAPS

YEAR 2002

SEPTEMBER

Date	Day	Time	m	Time	m	Time	m	Time	m
1	SU	0252	1.6	0933	2.9	1543	1.6	2213	2.8
2	M	0418	1.6	1055	3.0	1709	1.5	2336	3.0
3	TU	0534	1.4	1207	3.2	1815	1.2		
4	W	0042	3.2	0633	1.2	1306	3.5	1909	0.9
5	TH	0137	3.5	0724	0.9	1357	3.8	1956	0.7
6	F	0226	3.7	0811	0.7	1445	4.0	2041	0.4
7	SA	0311	3.9	0855	0.5	1530	4.2	● 2124	0.3
8	SU	0355	4.0	0938	0.4	1614	4.3	2206	0.3
9	M	0438	4.1	1020	0.3	1658	4.3	2248	0.3
10	TU	0521	4.0	1103	0.4	1742	4.1	2330	0.5
11	W	0604	3.9	1147	0.6	1827	3.9		
12	TH	0015	0.8	0650	3.6	1236	0.9	1917	3.6
13	F	0105	1.1	0743	3.4	1334	1.1	2018	3.2
14	SA	0207	1.4	0850	3.2	1452	1.4	2138	3.0
15	SU	0331	1.6	1015	3.1	1629	1.5	2308	3.0
16	M	0503	1.5	1137	3.2	1753	1.3		
17	TU	0022	3.1	0613	1.4	1240	3.4	1850	1.2
18	W	0115	3.3	0702	1.2	1329	3.5	1932	1.0
19	TH	0157	3.4	0742	1.1	1410	3.7	2007	0.9
20	F	0233	3.6	0816	0.9	1445	3.8	2038	0.8
21	SA	0305	3.7	0848	0.9	1517	3.8	○ 2107	0.8
22	SU	0335	3.7	0918	0.8	1547	3.8	2136	0.7
23	M	0404	3.7	0947	0.8	1616	3.8	2205	0.8
24	TU	0432	3.7	1017	0.8	1646	3.7	2234	0.9
25	W	0501	3.6	1047	0.9	1716	3.6	2303	1.0
26	TH	0532	3.5	1118	1.1	1749	3.5	2334	1.1
27	F	0605	3.3	1152	1.2	1825	3.3		
28	SA	0009	1.3	0645	3.2	1234	1.4	1910	3.1
29	SU	0055	1.5	0737	3.0	1335	1.6	2013	2.9
30	M	0204	1.7	0851	3.0	1506	1.7	2143	2.9

OCTOBER

Date	Day	Time	m	Time	m	Time	m	Time	m
1	TU	0342	1.7	1023	3.0	1642	1.5	2315	3.0
2	W	0509	1.5	1143	3.3	1753	1.3		
3	TH	0023	3.3	0612	1.2	1244	3.6	1847	0.9
4	F	0117	3.6	0704	0.9	1336	3.9	1934	0.6
5	SA	0204	3.9	0750	0.6	1423	4.2	2018	0.4
6	SU	0248	4.1	0834	0.4	1508	4.3	● 2100	0.3
7	M	0332	4.2	0916	0.3	1552	4.4	2142	0.3
8	TU	0414	4.2	0959	0.3	1636	4.3	2223	0.4
9	W	0456	4.1	1042	0.4	1720	4.1	2305	0.6
10	TH	0540	4.0	1127	0.6	1805	3.8	2349	0.9
11	F	0626	3.7	1216	0.9	1856	3.5		
12	SA	0038	1.2	0718	3.5	1315	1.2	1957	3.2
13	SU	0140	1.5	0825	3.2	1435	1.5	2120	3.0
14	M	0308	1.7	0951	3.1	1613	1.5	2252	3.0
15	TU	0442	1.7	1114	3.2	1731	1.4		
16	W	0001	3.1	0550	1.5	1215	3.3	1823	1.3
17	TH	0050	3.3	0637	1.3	1302	3.5	1903	1.1
18	F	0129	3.5	0715	1.2	1340	3.6	1936	1.0
19	SA	0203	3.6	0749	1.0	1415	3.7	2007	0.9
20	SU	0234	3.7	0820	0.9	1447	3.8	2037	0.8
21	M	0305	3.8	0851	0.8	1518	3.8	○ 2107	0.8
22	TU	0334	3.8	0921	0.8	1548	3.8	2136	0.8
23	W	0404	3.7	0951	0.9	1619	3.7	2205	0.9
24	TH	0434	3.7	1022	0.9	1651	3.6	2234	1.0
25	F	0506	3.6	1054	1.0	1725	3.4	2306	1.1
26	SA	0541	3.5	1130	1.2	1803	3.3	2342	1.3
27	SU	0621	3.3	1214	1.4	1849	3.1		
28	M	0029	1.5	0713	3.2	1315	1.5	1954	2.9
29	TU	0138	1.6	0826	3.1	1441	1.6	2123	2.9
30	W	0313	1.6	0957	3.1	1613	1.4	2251	3.1
31	TH	0440	1.5	1117	3.3	1724	1.2	2358	3.4

NOVEMBER

Date	Day	Time	m	Time	m	Time	m	Time	m
1	F	0545	1.2	1218	3.6	1820	0.9		
2	SA	0051	3.7	0639	0.9	1311	3.9	1909	0.6
3	SU	0139	3.9	0726	0.6	1359	4.1	1953	0.4
4	M	0224	4.1	0811	0.5	1445	4.2	● 2037	0.4
5	TU	0308	4.2	0856	0.4	1530	4.2	2119	0.4
6	W	0352	4.2	0939	0.4	1615	4.1	2201	0.5
7	TH	0435	4.1	1024	0.5	1701	3.9	2243	0.7
8	F	0519	3.9	1110	0.7	1747	3.7	2327	1.0
9	SA	0605	3.7	1200	0.9	1837	3.4		
10	SU	0015	1.3	0656	3.5	1256	1.2	1935	3.1
11	M	0113	1.5	0756	3.2	1407	1.4	2049	2.9
12	TU	0230	1.7	0912	3.1	1529	1.5	2211	2.9
13	W	0355	1.7	1030	3.1	1644	1.5	2320	3.0
14	TH	0505	1.6	1134	3.2	1740	1.3		
15	F	0011	3.2	0558	1.4	1223	3.3	1824	1.2
16	SA	0052	3.3	0640	1.2	1304	3.4	1901	1.0
17	SU	0129	3.5	0717	1.1	1341	3.5	1935	0.9
18	M	0202	3.6	0751	1.0	1416	3.6	2007	0.9
19	TU	0235	3.6	0824	0.9	1449	3.6	2039	0.8
20	W	0307	3.7	0857	0.9	1523	3.6	○ 2110	0.8
21	TH	0339	3.7	0930	0.9	1557	3.6	2141	0.9
22	F	0413	3.7	1003	0.9	1633	3.5	2213	0.9
23	SA	0448	3.6	1039	0.9	1710	3.4	2249	1.0
24	SU	0527	3.5	1119	1.0	1752	3.3	2329	1.2
25	M	0610	3.4	1206	1.2	1841	3.1		
26	TU	0019	1.3	0703	3.3	1305	1.3	1943	3.0
27	W	0124	1.4	0809	3.2	1419	1.3	2100	3.0
28	TH	0244	1.5	0928	3.2	1538	1.3	2219	3.1
29	F	0405	1.4	1044	3.3	1650	1.1	2326	3.3
30	SA	0513	1.1	1149	3.5	1749	0.9		

DECEMBER

Date	Day	Time	m	Time	m	Time	m	Time	m
1	SU	0023	3.5	0611	0.9	1245	3.7	1842	0.7
2	M	0114	3.7	0703	0.7	1336	3.9	1930	0.6
3	TU	0201	3.9	0752	0.5	1425	3.9	2015	0.5
4	W	0248	4.0	0839	0.4	1513	3.9	● 2100	0.5
5	TH	0334	4.0	0925	0.4	1600	3.8	2143	0.6
6	F	0419	4.0	1011	0.5	1647	3.7	2226	0.7
7	SA	0504	3.8	1057	0.7	1732	3.5	2310	0.9
8	SU	0548	3.7	1143	0.9	1818	3.3	2354	1.1
9	M	0633	3.4	1232	1.1	1906	3.0		
10	TU	0043	1.3	0721	3.2	1325	1.2	2000	2.9
11	W	0140	1.5	0817	3.0	1427	1.4	2105	2.8
12	TH	0248	1.6	0923	3.0	1534	1.4	2214	2.8
13	F	0400	1.5	1031	3.0	1638	1.4	2316	2.9
14	SA	0504	1.5	1131	3.0	1734	1.3		
15	SU	0007	3.1	0558	1.3	1221	3.1	1821	1.1
16	M	0050	3.2	0643	1.2	1305	3.3	1901	1.0
17	TU	0129	3.3	0723	1.0	1345	3.3	1938	0.9
18	W	0206	3.4	0801	0.9	1424	3.4	2013	0.9
19	TH	0243	3.5	0837	0.9	1502	3.4	○ 2048	0.8
20	F	0320	3.6	0914	0.8	1541	3.4	2124	0.8
21	SA	0358	3.6	0951	0.7	1621	3.4	2201	0.8
22	SU	0438	3.6	1031	0.7	1702	3.4	2240	0.8
23	M	0519	3.6	1113	0.8	1746	3.3	2324	0.9
24	TU	0604	3.5	1200	0.9	1834	3.2		
25	W	0012	1.0	0654	3.4	1252	0.9	1929	3.1
26	TH	0108	1.1	0751	3.3	1353	1.0	2032	3.1
27	F	0214	1.2	0857	3.2	1501	1.1	2142	3.1
28	SA	0326	1.2	1009	3.2	1611	1.0	2251	3.2
29	SU	0438	1.1	1118	3.3	1718	0.9	2354	3.3
30	M	0545	0.9	1221	3.4	1817	0.8		
31	TU	0051	3.5	0645	0.8	1319	3.5	1911	0.7

SINES *9.20.16*

Baijo Alentejo **37°56'·95N 08°52'·06W** (marina ent)

CHARTS AC 3276, 3636; PC 84, 39; SC 4311, 43A

TIDES

Standard Port LISBOA (⟵); ML 2·0; Zone 0 (UT)

Times				Height (metres)			
High Water		Low Water		MHWS	MHWN	MLWN	MLWS
0400	0900	0400	0900	3·8	3·0	1·5	0·5
1600	2100	1600	2100				
Differences SINES							
−0050	−0030	−0020	−0010	−0·4	−0·4	−0·1	+0·1
MILFONTES (37°43'·0N 08°47'·0W)							
−0040	−0030	No data		−0·1	−0·1	0·0	+0·2
ARRIFANA (37°17'·5N 08°52'·0W)							
−0030	−0020	No data		−0·1	0·0	−0·1	+0·2

SHELTER Good in small marina protected by new mole at E end of Praia Vasco de Gama (FVs are at W end); or ⚓ NW of the marina in 4m. Nearby Old town is pleasant, away from commercial terminals in NW and SE parts of the large hbr. Sines is a strategically located haven, 51M SSE of Cascais and Lisbon and 57M N of Cape St Vincent.

NAVIGATION WPT 37°56'·03N 08°53'·18W, PHM buoy (Fl R 3s) 225°/045° from/to ent to ⚓ or marina, 1·25M. From the NW, caution: the southern 800m section of the W mole is derelict and partly covers. The ☆ (Fl 3s 20m 12M) on it is 400m N of the unlit mole end; the WPT buoy is 270m S of the mole end and must be rounded; no short cuts! In strong S'lies swell may enter, causing turbulence off the W mole.

LIGHTS AND MARKS From afar, an oil refinery flare in the town and several tall chy's/masts 3-4M to the E (all with R lts) help to locate the port. Cabo de Sines lt ho, Fl (2) 15s 50m 26M, is 8ca NW of the marina; it is obsc'd by oil tanks 001°-003° and 004°-007°.

RADIO TELEPHONE Call *Porto de Sines* (Port Authority) VHF Ch 11, 13, 16, Marina Ch 12

TELEPHONE (Dial code 269) Hr Mr 860600, 📠 860690.

FACILITIES Marina (250, inc some ♥ 4m); contact via Hr Mr; AC, FW; (planned to expand); **Club Náutico** close SE of marina; **Services:** D & P from FV dock near HW; ME, El. **Town:** R, V, Bar, Gaz, Ⓑ, ✉, ⇌, ✈ Lisboa or Faro.

BALEEIRA, Algarve 37°00'·06N 08°55'·50W. Useful ⚓, 5M E of C St Vincent, 2M NE of Pta de Sagres. Shelter from W, but open to E'lies, when Ensenada de Belixe is better. ⚓ N of the 2 jetties in 6m, see 9.20.3 for lts.

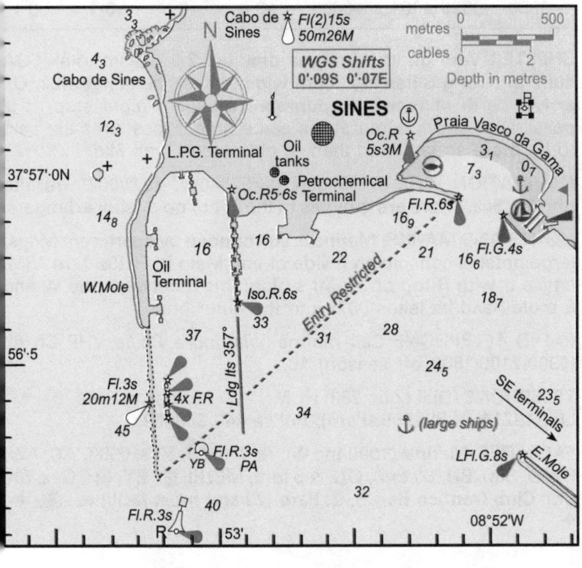

LAGOS *9.20.17*

Algarve **37°05'·84N 08°39'·90W**

CHARTS AC 3636, 89; PC 88, 40, 41, 7, 24; SC 43A, 44A

TIDES

Standard Port LISBOA (⟵); ML 2·0; Zone 0 (UT)

Times				Height (metres)			
High Water		Low Water		MHWS	MHWN	MLWN	MLWS
0400	0900	0400	0900	3·8	3·0	1·5	0·5
1600	2100	1600	2100				
Differences LAGOS							
−0100	−0040	−0030	−0025	−0·4	−0·4	−0·1	+0·1
ENSEADA DE BELIXE (Cape St. Vincent)							
−0050	−0030	−0020	−0015	+0·3	+0·2	+0·2	+0·3

SHELTER Very good in marina (dredged 3m) on E bank, 7ca up-river from hbr ent, access H24 all tides. 3kn speed limit in hbr. The ⚓ close NE of the E Mole in 3-5m is exposed only to E and S winds and possible SW swell.

NAVIGATION WPT 37°05'·76N 08°39'·58W, 104°/284° from/to hbr ent, 2½ca. Fishing nets may extend up to 1M offshore. From Ponta da Piedade, Fl 7s 49m 20M, 1·2M to the S, keep 5ca offshore to clear rocks; otherwise there are no offshore dangers. Final appr is on 284°, W mole head lt, Fl R 6s, in transit with Santo António church. Shoaling possible in entrance. Berth at arrival pontoon stbd side just before lifting foot-bridge which opens on request 0800-2200 June to mid-Sept (0900-1900 winter), except for some ¼hr spells for train passengers. R/G tfc lts, but unmasted craft may transit when bridge is down.

LIGHTS AND MARKS Lts as chartlet. The river chan is unlit, apart from shore lts. Alvor lt, L Fl R 6s 31m 7M, is 3·5M to ENE; Ponta do Altar (Portimão), L Fl R 5s 30m 14M, is 7M E.

RADIO TELEPHONE Call *Marina de Lagos* VHF Ch 62 for bridge opening.

TELEPHONE (Dial code 282) Hr Mr 770210, 📠 770219, ⊖, Met: 417714; Ⓗ 763034; Police 762930; Fire 760115; Brit Consul 417800.

FACILITIES Marina (462+ ♥, max LOA 20m), €9.06, P, D, AC, FW, Slip, BY, ME, El, Sh, V, R, Bar, CH, Ⓑ, ▣; **Club de Vela** ☎ 762256; **Services:** usual amenities, ⇌; ✈ Faro (75 km) ☎ (089) 818281.

20

PORTIMÃO *9.20.18*

Algarve **37°06'·60N 08°31'·64W**

CHARTS AC 83, 3636, 89, 92; PC 26321, 41, 7, 24; SC 43A, 44A

TIDES

Standard Port LISBOA (⟵); ML 2·0; Zone 0 (UT)

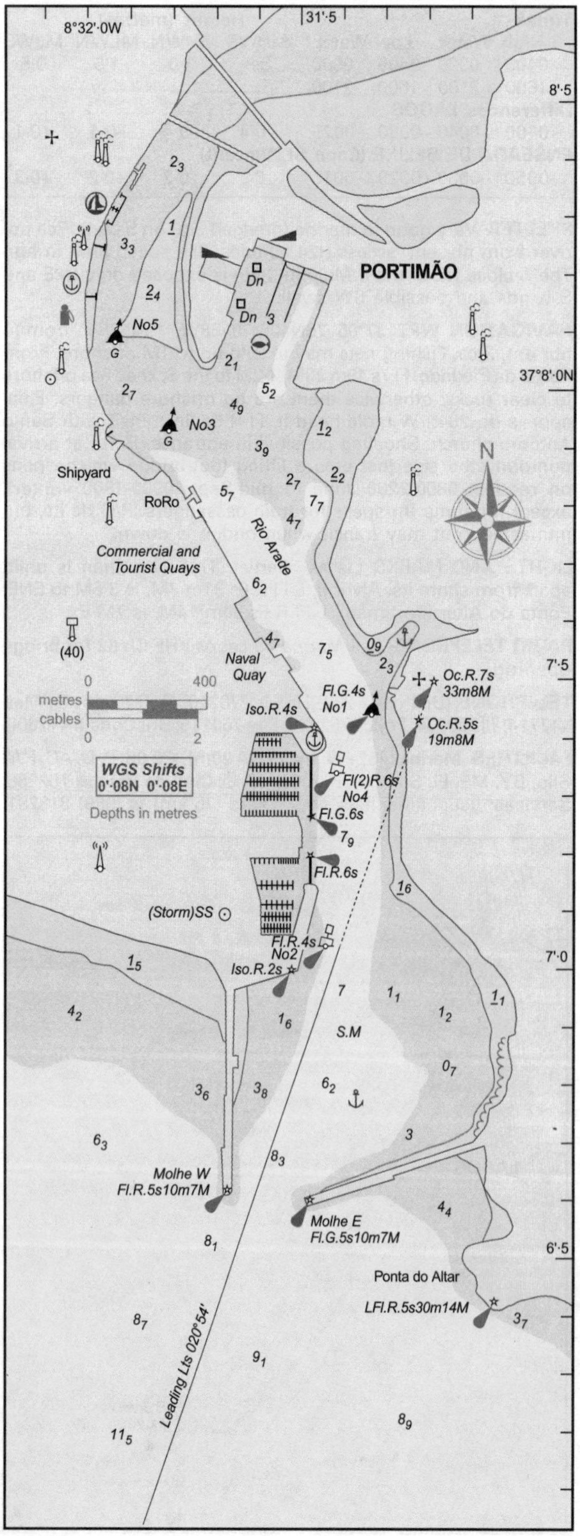

TIDES *continued*

Times				Height (metres)			
High Water		Low Water		MHWS	MHWN	MLWN	MLWS
0400	0900	0400	0900	3·8	3·0	1·5	0·5
1600	2100	1600	2100				
Differences PORTIMÃO							
−0100	−0040	−0030	−0025	−0·5	−0·4	0·0	+0·2
PONTA DO ALTAR (Lt ho E of ent)							
−0100	−0040	−0030	−0025	−0·3	−0·3	0·0	+0·1

SHELTER Good in new marina on W bank, 2M up-river from hb ent, just before 2 low road/rail bridges. Caution: flood & eb streams run hard; berth bows to the stream. Good ⚓ inside mole in about 4m, but prone to wash from FVs and swel possible.

NAVIGATION WPT 37°06'·40N 08°31'·73W, 201°/021° from/to hbr ent, 2ca. There are no offshore hazards; entrance and rive are straightforward.

LIGHTS AND MARKS Pta do Altar lt ho is on low cliffs to E o ent. The R-roofed church at Ferragudo is conspic by day, almos on ldg line 021°. Ldg lts: front Oc R 5s 17m 8M; rear, Oc R 7s 33m 8M; both on R/W banded columns, moved to suit chan.

RADIO TELEPHONE Port VHF Ch 11 16. Marina VHF Ch 68

TELEPHONE (Dial code 282) Hr Mr 400680 📠 400681; ⊖ 24239 Police 22440; Consul 417800.

FACILITIES Marina (620 AB); **Services:** CH, El, ME, BY, Gaz, R, V Bar, Ⓑ, ✉; ⇄, ✈ Faro (65 km). BY with 40T hoist up river.

HARBOUR BETWEEN PORTIMÃO AND VILAMOURA

ALBUFEIRA 37°05'N 08°15'W. A new marina (620 AB) unde construction (2001).

VILAMOURA *9.20.19*

Algarve **37°04'·10N 08°07'·35W**

VILAMOURA *continued*

CHARTS AC 89, 92; PC 8, 24, 42; SC 44A; SHOM 3388

TIDES

Standard Port LISBOA (⟵); ML 2·0; Zone 0 (UT)

Times				Height (metres)			
High Water		Low Water		MHWS	MHWN	MLWN	MLWS
0400	0900	0400	0900	3·8	3·0	1·5	0·5
1600	2100	1600	2100				
Differences ENSEADA DE ALBUFEIRA (6M to the W)							
−0035	+0015	−0005	0000	−0·2	−0·2	0·0	+0·2
CABO DE SANTA MARIA (Faro/Olhão, 14M to the ESE)							
−0050	−0030	−0015	+0005	−0·4	−0·4	−0·1	+0·1

SHELTER Very good in marina dredged 2·0 – 3·3m, max LOA 40m. In strong S'lies the 100m wide ent can be dangerous. On arrival berth at reception pontoon (⛵); for a night stop, it is possible to check in/out at the same time. Procedures are said to be more streamlined than of old. Speed limit 3kn.

NAVIGATION WPT 37°03'·60N 08°07'·40W, 187°/007° from/to hbr ent, 5ca. There are groynes to the E, but no offshore dangers.

LIGHTS AND MARKS Marina is surrounded by apartment bldgs; large hotel is conspic on E side of ent. Main lt, Fl 10s 17m 19M, lattice tr with R top on Hr Mr's bldg; this lt between the W and E mole head lts leads 007° into the outer hbr.

RADIO TELEPHONE Call marina *Vilamoura Radio* VHF Ch 62 (0900-2100/1800 off season) 16.

TELEPHONE (Dial code 289) Hr Mr, ⊖ & Met: as marina, below; LB 313214; Ⓗ 802555 (Faro); Police 440 388989.

FACILITIES **Marina** (1000 inc Ⓥ), ☎ 310560, 📠 310580, AC, FW, P & D, Slip, BH (60 ton), C (2 & 6 ton), ME, El, Ⓔ, BY, CH, Gaz, Sh SM; **Club Náutico** Bar, R, ⊡; **Faro** (20 km) most facilities; Ⓑ, ⇄, ✈.

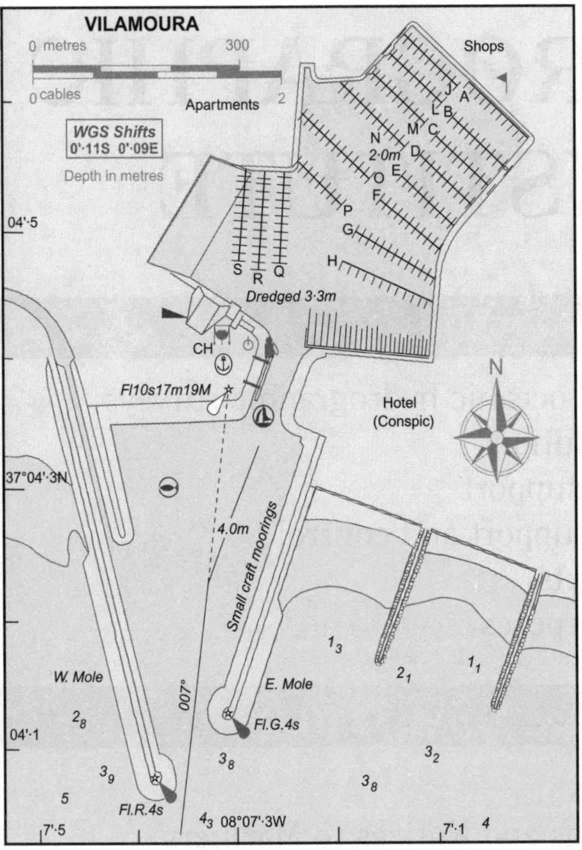
VILAMOURA
0 metres 300
0 cables 2
WGS Shifts
0'·11S 0'·09E
Depth in metres
Shops
Apartments
2·0m
Dredged 3·3m
CH
Fl10s17m19M
Hotel
(Conspic)
N
37°04'·3N
04'·5
4.0m
Small craft moorings
W. Mole
E. Mole
007°
Fl.G.4s
04'·1
Fl.R.4s
08°07'·3W
7'·5
7'·1

OTHER HARBOURS AND ANCHORAGES EASTWARD TO THE PORTUGUESE/SPANISH BORDER

FARO and OLHÃO. Ent **36°57'·90N 07°52'·11W**. AC 83; PC 26311, 91, 92; SC 44A/B. Tide, see above (Cabo de Santa Maria). The narrow ent through sand dunes leads into lagoons amongst salt marshes. Appr on 352° to clear shoals W of ent between moles, Fl R and G 4s respectively. Cabo de Santa Maria lt ho at root of long E mole is conspic, Fl (4) 17s 49m 25M. It is also rear ldg lt 021° once inside ent; front ldg lt, Barra Nova Oc 4s 8m 6M. Abeam Cabo de Santa Maria, fork WNW to Faro or NE to Olhão. The **Faro** chan carries 5·4m, but depths change; it is buoyed/lit for the 4M to the Commercial quay (unsuitable for AB). Appr near HW to ⚓ in 3m, 3ca SW of Doca de Recreio (low bridge across ent). Some noise from airport, but not after 2100LT. The chan to **Olhão** (5M) is shallower, 2·4m. ⚓ off Ponte Cais (Ilha da Culatra) or off Olhão yacht hbr, for small craft only. Both towns are sizeable with usual facilities, inc ⇄, ✈.

TAVIRA. 37°06'·75N 07°37'·00W. AC 89; PC 91, 92; SC 44A/B. Tide, see above (Cabo de Santa Maria). The narrow (about 70m) ent between I de Tavira and sand dunes to the E is lit with Fl G and R lts 2·5s and has ldg lts over the bar, front Fl R 3s and rear Iso R 6s. The ent should only be only be attempted near HW and in settled weather. Local knowledge is desirable. The town is 1½M NW of the bar and, apart from a small craft shipyard and diesel supply, has little to offer a visiting yacht, being essentially a working fishing port. AB maybe possible in 2m alongside a pier on W side of the river which is connected to the town by a causeway. Hospital and usual small town amenities.

VILA REAL DE SANTO ANTÓNIO *9.20.20*

Algarve **37°11'·60N 07°24'·70W** (Marina)

CHARTS AC 89, 92; PC 26312, 97; SC 4411

TIDES

Standard Port LISBOA (⟵); ML 2·0; Zone 0 (UT)

Times				**Height (metres)**			
High Water		Low Water		MHWS	MHWN	MLWN	MLWS
0400	0900	0400	0900	3·8	3·0	1·5	0·5
1600	2100	1600	2100				
Differences VILA REAL DE SANTO ANTÓNIO							
−0050	−0015	−0010	0000	−0·4	−0·4	−0·2	+0·2

SHELTER Good in the new marina but streams are very strong; aim for slack water. Vila Real de Santo Antonio is on the W bank (Portugal) of Rio Guadiana and Ayamonte on E bank (Spain). The river is navigable for about 20M to Alcoutim and Pomerão (27M).

NAVIGATION WPT 37°09'·00N 07°23'·35W (No 1 SHM buoy, Q (3) G 6s), 160°/340° from/to hd of W trng wall, 9ca. The bar (2·5m) is marked by the 2nd pair of P/SHM lt buoys. Enter the river between training walls between HW–3 and HW. Upriver the better water is off the W bank. Caution: Extensive drying areas to W and E of the training walls stretch 2M east, almost to Isla Cristina (9.21.8).

LIGHTS AND MARKS High bldgs, FR lts, are 3M WNW of ent. White suspension bridge 2M inland is visible from seaward. Other lts: Vila Real lt ho, Fl 6·5s 51m 26M, W / tr, B bands. E trng wall (partly covers) bn, Fl G 3s; W trng wall hd, Fl R 5s.

RADIO TELEPHONE *Porto de Vilareal* VHF Ch 11, 16; Marina Ch 12

TELEPHONE (Dial code 281) Marina 541571, 🏥 511140

FACILITIES **Marina** (357AB), 2m, FW, D on pontoon just N of marina, YC, R, Slip; **Town** V, R, Bar, Ⓑ, ✉, ✈ (Faro).

20

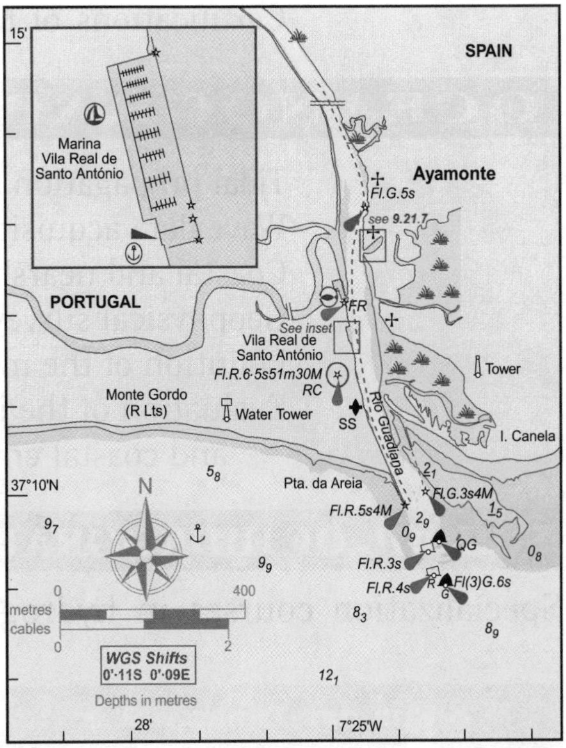
15'
Marina
Vila Real de
Santo António
SPAIN
Ayamonte
Fl.G.5s
see 9.21.7
PORTUGAL
FR
See inset
Vila Real de
Santo António
Fl.R.6·5s51m30M
RC
Tower
Monte Gordo
(R Lts)
Water Tower
SS
Rio Guadiana
I. Canela
Pta. da Areia
37°10'N
N
Fl.G.3s4M
Fl.R.5s4M
QG
Fl.R.3s
Fl.R.4s
Fl(3)G.6s
metres 0 400
cables 0 2
WGS Shifts
0'·11S 0'·09E
Depths in metres
28'
7°25'W

MAPTECH®
Leading the world in digital navigation
Maptech UK Ltd • +44 (0)1243 389352 • sales@maptech.co.uk

Maptech world class digital chart CDs
Worldwide coverage from over 4,500 charts
Maptech award winning software
Easy to use navigation software
• Chart Navigator • Cruising Navigator • Offshore Navigator

www.maptech.co.uk

Area 21

South West Spain

Ayamonte to Gibraltar

9.21.1	Index	Page 907
9.21.2	Area map	908
9.21.3	Lights, buoys & waypoints	909
9.21.4	Passage information	911
9.21.5	Special notes for Spain	911
9.21.6	Distance table See *9.20.6*	
9.21.7	Ayamonte	912
9.21.8	Isla Cristina Rio de las Piedras Punta Umbria	912
9.21.9	Mazagón	913
9.21.10	Chipiona Rio Guadalquivir	913
9.21.11	Sevilla	914
9.21.12	Bay of Cádiz: Rota, Puerto Sherry, P'to Santa Maria, P'to America	915
9.21.13	Sancti-Petri	916
9.21.14	Barbate	916
9.21.15	Strait of Gibraltar Tarifa	917
9.21.16	Algeciras	917
9.21.17	Gibraltar, tidal predictions/curves	918
Fig.9(10)	Marinas in Spain, Portugal and Gibraltar	922

21

Register for your FREE weekly weather email service from Macmillan Reeds
at www.nauticaldata.com – NOW!
weekend weather reports sent to your email address, every Thursday

9.21.2 South West Spain
Ayamonte to Gibraltar

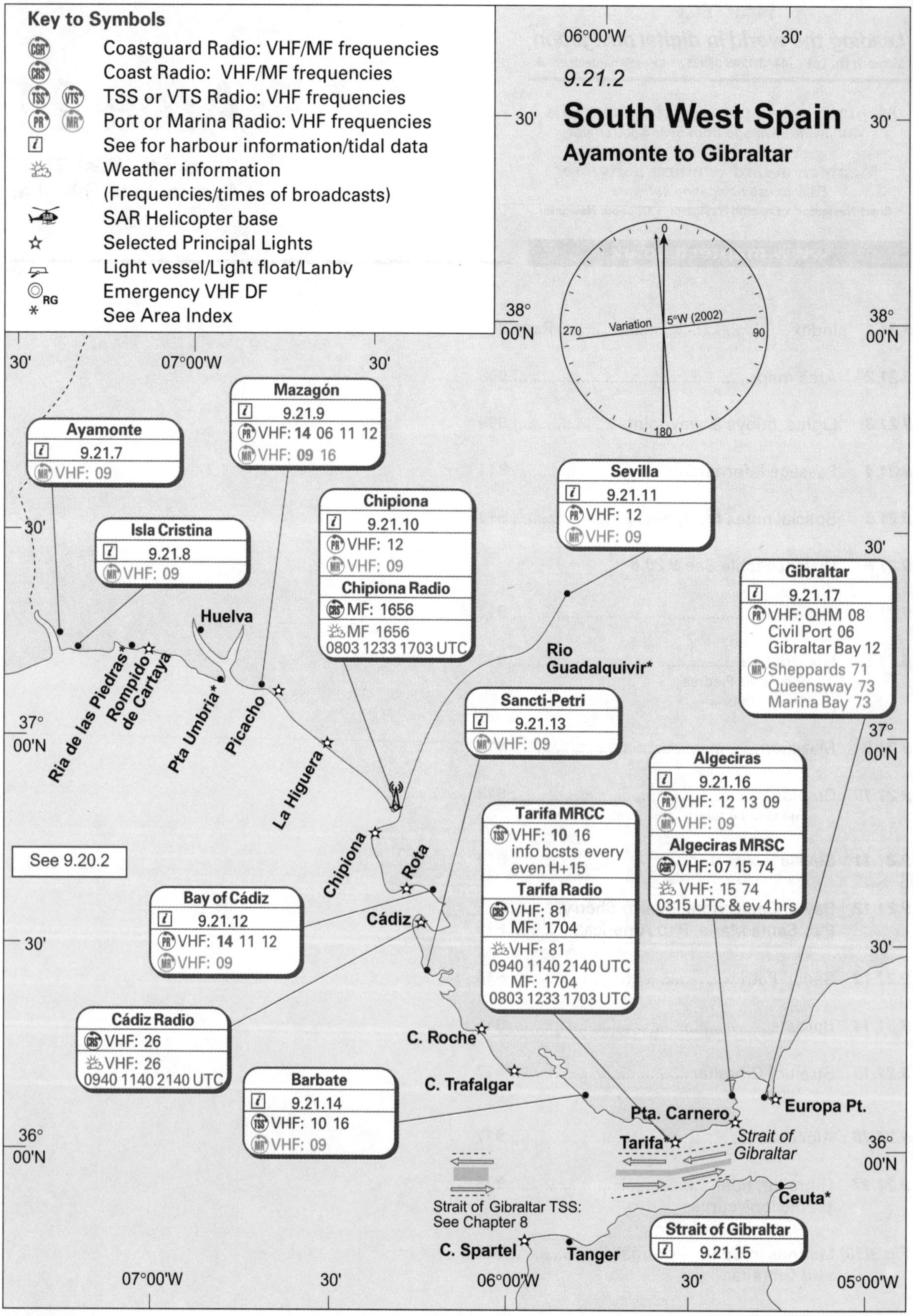
Key to Symbols
Coastguard Radio: VHF/MF frequencies
Coast Radio: VHF/MF frequencies
TSS or VTS Radio: VHF frequencies
Port or Marina Radio: VHF frequencies
See for harbour information/tidal data
Weather information
(Frequencies/times of broadcasts)
SAR Helicopter base
Selected Principal Lights
Light vessel/Light float/Lanby
Emergency VHF DF
RG
See Area Index
06°00'W
30'
38° 00'N
37° 00'N
36° 00'N
07°00'W
05°00'W
Variation 5°W (2002)
0
90
180
270
Ayamonte
9.21.7
VHF: 09
Isla Cristina
9.21.8
VHF: 09
Mazagón
9.21.9
VHF: 14 06 11 12
VHF: 09 16
Chipiona
9.21.10
VHF: 12
VHF: 09
Chipiona Radio
MF: 1656
MF 1656
0803 1233 1703 UTC
Sevilla
9.21.11
VHF: 12
VHF: 09
Gibraltar
9.21.17
VHF: QHM 08
Civil Port 06
Gibraltar Bay 12
Sheppards 71
Queensway 73
Marina Bay 73
Sancti-Petri
9.21.13
VHF: 09
Algeciras
9.21.16
VHF: 12 13 09
VHF: 09
Algeciras MRSC
VHF: 07 15 74
VHF: 15 74
0315 UTC & ev 4 hrs
Tarifa MRCC
VHF: 10 16
info bcsts every even H+15
Tarifa Radio
VHF: 81
MF: 1704
VHF: 81
0940 1140 2140 UTC
MF: 1704
0803 1233 1703 UTC
Bay of Cádiz
9.21.12
VHF: 14 11 12
VHF: 09
Cádiz Radio
VHF: 26
VHF: 26
0940 1140 2140 UTC
Barbate
9.21.14
VHF: 10 16
VHF: 09
Strait of Gibraltar
9.21.15
See 9.20.2
Huelva
Ria de las Piedras*
Rompido de Cartaya
Pta Umbria*
Picacho
La Higuera
Chipiona
Rota
Cádiz
Rio Guadalquivir*
C. Roche
C. Trafalgar
Pta. Carnero
Tarifa*
Strait of Gibraltar
Europa Pt.
Ceuta*
Tanger
C. Spartel
Strait of Gibraltar TSS:
See Chapter 8

9.21.3 LIGHTS, BUOYS AND WAYPOINTS

Principal lights ☆ are in **bold** print, places in CAPITALS, and light-vessels, light floats and Lanbys in *CAPITAL ITALICS*. Unless otherwise stated lights are white. m – elevation in metres; M – nominal range in miles. Fog signals are in *italics*. Useful waypoints are underlined – use those on land with care. All geographical positions should be assumed to be approximate. **All positions in 9.21.3 are referenced to the WGS84/ETRS89 datum but should be assumed to be approximate. In the rest of Area 21, ED50 coordinates are given. Admiralty charts of this area are generally referenced to ED50.**

SOUTH-WEST SPAIN

Rio Guadiana Chan No. 1 37°08'·90N 07°23'·44W Q (3) G 6s.
No. 2 37°09'·14N 07°23'·82W Fl R 4s.
No. 3 37°09'·56N 024'·42W QG.
Molhe W 37°09'·76N 07°24'·00W Fl R 5s 4M.
Vila Real de Santo Antònio ☆ 37°11'·23N 07°25'·00W Fl 6·5s 51m **26M**.
Dique de Levant S End 37°09'·93N 07°23'·63W Fl G 3s 4M.

◀ ISLA CRISTINA, RÍA DE LA HIGUERITA

No. 1 Appr 37°10'·90N 07°19'·60W L Fl 10s.
W Mole Head 37°10'·84N 07°19'·68W VQ (2) R 5s 7m 4M.
Rompido de Cartaya N bank ☆ 37°13'·12N 07°07'·69W Fl (2) 10s 41m **24M**; W ▌, B bands.

◀ HUELVA, MAZAGÓN

Pta. Umbria 37°09'·75N 06°56'·92W VQ (6) + L Fl 10s 3M.
Off Pta Unbria 37°09'·56N 06°57'·18W VQ (6) + L Fl 10s.
Yacht Club Pier 37°10'·49N 06°57'·07W Fl (3) G 15s 5m 3M.
Hbr Works Pier 37°10'·76N 06°57'·35W Fl (2) G 10s 6m 3M.
Tanker mooring 37°04'·77N 06°55'·61W Fl (4) Y 20s 8M; *Siren 30s.*
Picacho ☆ 37°08'·10N 06°49'·56W Fl (2+4) 30s 50m **25M**.
Canal del Padre Santo Ldg Lts 339·2°. Front, 37°08'·46N 06°50'·64W Q 49m 8M; □ on R&W Tr. Rear, 158m from front Fl R 2s 55m 8M; □ on R&W Tr.
37°05'·54N 06°49'·11W Q (9) 15s.
No. 1 37°06'·26N 06°49'·46W Fl G 5s.
No. 2 37°06'·33N 06°49'·72W Fl R 5s.
Ría de Huelva Dique Hd 37°06'·47N 06°49'·94W Fl (3+1) WR 20s 30m W12M, R9M; vis: W165°-100°, R100°-125°; Racon (K).
No. 3 37°06'·87N 06°49'·77W Fl (2) G 10s.
No. 4 37°06'·82N 06°49'·97W Fl (2) R 10s.
No. 5 37°07'·38N 06°50'·03W Fl (3) G 15s.
No. 6 37°07'·44N 06°50'·27W Fl (3) R 15s.
No. 7 37°07'·77N 06°50'·29W Fl (4) G 20s.
Porto Deportivo (Marina) Dique Hd 37°07'·85N 06°50'·11W QG 7m 2M.
Porto Deportivo (Marina) Dique Hd 37°07'·91N 06°50'·03W QR 5m 2M.
No. 8 37°07'·76N 06°50'·50W Fl(4) R 20s.
No.10 37°07'·91N 06°50'·83W Fl R 5s.
No.11 37°08'·35N 06°51'·48W Fl (2) G 10s.
No.12 37°08'·35N 06°51'·74W Fl (2) R 10s.
No.15 37°08'·99N 06°52'·90W Fl (4) G 12s.
No. 19 37°09'·66N 06°54'·01W Fl (2) G 7s.
No. 20 37°09'·64N 06°54'·25W Q (2) R 4s.
Off Torre del Oro (Ruins) 37°04'·22N 06°43'·67W Fl (2) 10s.
La Higuera ☆ 37°00'·47N 06°34'·16W Fl (3) 20s 46m **20M**; Tr.

◀ RÍO GUADALQUIVIR, SEVILLA

New Canal Ldg Lts 068·9°. Front 36°47'·84N 06°20'·24W Q 27m 10M; R △. Rear, 0·6M from front, Iso 4s 60m 10M.
No. 1 36°45'·74N 06°27'·03W L Fl 10s; Racon (M).
No. 2 36°47'·37N 06°26'·82W Q (9) 10s.
No. 4 36°47'·33N 06°25'·40W Fl R 5s.
No. 3 36°46'·16N 06°25'·36W Fl G 5s.
No. 6 36°46'·50N 06°24'·81W Fl (2) R 6s.
No. 7 36°46'·61N 06°24'·01W Fl (3) G 10s.
No. 11 36°46'·96N 06°22'·90W Fl G 5s.
No.13 36°47'·12N 06°22'·36W Fl (2) G 6s.
No.17 36°47'·46N 06°21'·23W Fl (4) G 12s.
No.20 36°47'·81N 06°20'·70W Fl (4) G 12s.
Shelter Mole S end 36°48'·14N 06°20'·29W Fl (2+1) G 21s 6m 5M.
Chipiona No. 2 36°45'·14N 06°25'·59W Fl (2) R 6s.
No. 4 36°45'·05N 06°25'·52W Fl (4) R 11s.
Marina Breakwater Head 36°44'·96N 06°25'·70W Fl (2) G 10s 6m 5M.
Marina Jetty 36°44'·89N 06°25'·78W Fl (3) G 9s 2m 1M.
Marina 36°44'·89N 06°25'·71W Fl (2) R 10s 4m 3M.
Chipiona Pta del Perro ☆ 36°44'·26N 06°26'·53W Fl 10s 67m **25M**; Racon (M).
Bajo Salmedina 36°44'·32N 06°28'·68W Q (9) 15s 9m 5M.
36°44'·28N 06°28'·54W Fl (5) Y 20s.
Bajo Salmedina 36°44'·27N 06°28'·64W Q (9) 15s 9m 5M; Racon (M).
Bajo El Quemado 36°35'·88N 06°23'·95W Fl (2) R 9s.

◀ BAY OF CADIZ: ROTA/PUERTO SHERRY

Rota ☆ 36°38'·13N 06°20'·84W Aero Alt Fl WG 9s 79m **17M**.
Rota 36°36'·96N 06°21'·44W Oc 4s 33m 13M; W ○ Tr, R band.
Las Cabezuelas 36°35'·21N 06°19'·96W Q (4) R 10s.
Rota Marina Mole Hd 36°36'·86N 06°21'·05W Fl (3) R 10s 8m 9M.
Rota Ldg Lts 345·5°. Front, 36°37'·54N 06°19'·73W Q 14m 9M; vis: 335·5°-355·5°. Rear, 272m from front, Oc 3s 26m 11M; vis: 335·5°-355·5°.
Naval Base Breakwater Head 36°36'·63N 06°19'·57W Oc (2) R 6s 16m 4M.
SE Bkwtr Head 36°36'·78N 06°19'·35W Q (3) G 7s 13m 6M.
Puerto Sherry Breakwater Head 36°34'·64N 06°15'·25W Oc R 4s 4M.
Antedarsena Ent 36°34'·69N 06°15'·22W Oc G 5s 3M.

◀ PUERTO DE SANTA MARIA

Santa María Bkwtr Hd 36°34'·34N 06°14'·96W Fl R 5s 10m 3M.
Ldg Lts 040°. Front, 36°35'·77N 06°13'·36W QG 16m 4M. Rear, 253m from front, Iso G 4s 20m 4M.
Escollera Head 36°34'·66N 06°14'·41W Fl (2) G 7s 9m 3M.
Escollera de Levante 36°34'·45N 06°14'·36W VQ (9) 15s 3M.
Escollera de Poniente 36°35'·10N 06°14'·12W QR 5m 2M.

◀ CÁDIZ

Castillo de San Sebastián ☆ 36°31'·70N 06°18'·97W Fl (2) 10s 38m **25M**; Tr on castle; *Horn Mo (N) 20s.*
Los Cochinos No.1 36°33'·12N 06°19'·07W Fl G 3s.
No. 4 El Diamante 36°33'·53N 06°17'·93W Fl (2) R 4s.
No. 6 36°33'·38N 06°17'·18W Fl (3) R 10s.

El Fraile No. 5 36°33'·03N 06°17'·38W Fl (3) G 13s.
Off Dique S. Filepe 36°32'·74N 06°16'·75W QG.
Malecón de San Felipe Head ☆ 36°32'·56N 06°16'·77W Fl G 3s 10m 5M; G mast on hut.
Malecón de Levante Hd ☆ 36°32'·44N 06°16'·63W Fl R 2s 11m 5M.
Real Club Nautico Pier ☆ 36°32'·34N 06°17'·13W FG.
Bajos de San Sebastián 36°31'·30N 06°20'·36W Q (9) 15s.

◄ SANCTI PETRI

I de Sancti Petri N Head ☆ 36°22'·75N 06°13'·33W Fl 3s 44m 18m 9M; □ Tr.
C. Roche ☆ 36°17'·70N 06°08'·59W Fl (4) 24s 44m **20M**.
C. Trafalgar ☆ 36°10'·92N 06°02'·29W Fl (2+1) 15s 50m **22M**.

◄ BARBATE

Ldg Lts 297·5°. Front 36°10'·82N 05°53'·37W Q 2m 1M Rear, 70m from front, Q 7m 1M; both vis: 280·5°-310·5°.
Barbate ☆ 36°11'·21N 05°55'·42W Fl (2) WR 7s 22m W10M, R7M; W281°-015°, R015°-095°.
Dique de Poniente Head ☆ 36°10'·75N 05°55'·53W Fl (2) R 6s 11m 5M.
Contradique Head ☆ 36°10'·95N 05°55'·79W Fl G 3s 7m 2M.

◄ STRAIT OF GIBRALTAR

Pta de Gracia ☆ 36°05'·42N 05°48'·63W Oc (2) 5s 74m 13M.
Pta Paloma ☆ 36°03'·86N 05°43'·24W Oc WR 5s 44m W10M, R7M; W010°-340°, R340°-010°.

◄ TARIFA

Tarifa ☆ 36°00'·06N 05°36'·58W Fl (3) WR 10s 40m **W26M**, **R18M**; W Tr; vis: W113°-089°, R089°-113°; Racon (C); *Siren (3) 60s.*
Lado E ☆ 36°00'·23N 05°36'·40W Fl R 5s 12m 3M.
Dique del Sagrado Corazón Head ☆ 36°00'·38N 05°36'·22W Fl G 5s 10m 5M.
Mole No. 1 corner ☆ 36°00'·51N 05°36'·17W Fl (2) R 6s 7m 1M.
Pta Carnero ☆ 36°04'·61N 05°25'·57W Fl (4) WR 20s 42m **W18M**, R9M; vis: W018°-325°, R325°-018°; *Siren Mo (K) 30s.*

◄ ALGECIRAS

Off San Garcia 36°06'·73N 05°24'·76W Q (3).
36°07'·07N 05°25'·73W Q (2) R 7s.
36°07'·19N 05°25'·97W Q (3) G 9s.
Marina S Outer Jetty Hd ☆ 36°07'·10N 05°26'·13W Q (3) R 9s 7m 3M.
North Jetty Head ☆ 36°07'·13N 05°26'·23W Q (4) G 11s 2m 1M.
S Inner Jetty Hd ☆ 36°07'·14N 05°26'·28W Fl (3) R 11s 2m 3M.
App 36°08'·86N 05°25'·22W Mo (A) 4s.
36°09'·93N 05°24'·91W Fl (3) Y; Siren Mo (U).
Muelle de Interior ☆ 36°10'·40N 05°25'·19W Fl (2) G 10s 9m 4M.
Muelle de I.Verde ☆ 36°07'·59N 05°26'·50W Fl (3) R 5s 6m 2M.

◄ LA LÍNEA

36°09'·56N 05°22'·00W Fl (3) R 6s.
36°09'·51N 05°22'·03W Fl (3) G 6s.
Dique de Abrigo ☆ 36°09'·51N 05°22'·05W Fl (2) G 6s 8m 4M.
Marina ent ☆ 36°09'·56N 05°21'·67W QR 7m 2M.
Jetty de San Felipe ☆ 36°09'·56N 05°21'·57W Fl R 5s 5m 2M.

◄ GIBRALTAR

Aero Lt 36°08'·57N 05°20'·60W Mo (GB) R 10s 405m **30M**.
S Mole 'A' Head ☆ 36°08'·03N 05°21'·85W Fl 2s 18m **15M** *Horn 10s.*
'B' Mole Head ☆ 36°08'·14N 05°21'·85W QR 9m 5M.
'C' Mole Head ☆ 36°08'·54N 05°22'·04W QG 10m 5M.
'D' Mole Head ☆ 36°08'·65N 05°21'·95W QR 18m 5M.
'E' Mole Head ☆ 36°08'·90N 05°21'·95W FR 28m 5M.
Europa Pt Victoria Tr ☆ 36°06'·58N 05°20'·69W Iso 10s 49m **19M**; vis: 197°-042°; intens 067°-125°. Same structure Oc R 10s **15M**; vis: 042°-067° and FR 44m **15M**; vis: 042°-067° W ○ Tr, R band; *Horn 20s.*

MOROCCO

C. Spartel ☆ 35°47'·45N 05°55'·43W Fl (4) 20s 95m **30M**; Y □ Tr; *Dia (4) 90s.*
Monte Dirección (Le Charf) ☆ 35°46'·01N 05°47'·40W Oc (3) WRG 12s 88m **W16M**, R12M, G11M; vis: G140°-174·5° W174·5°-200°, R200°-225°.

◄ TANGIER

35°47'·73N 05°47'·00W L Fl 10s.
Roche Bourée 35°47'·52N 05°46'·53W Oc (2) Y 6s.
Bkwtr Head ☆ 35°47'·55N 05°47'·52W Fl (3) W 12s 20m 14M.
S. Mole Head Quai No. 2 ☆ 35°47'·39N 05°47'·77W Oc (2) R 6s 7m 6M.
Yacht Club Jetty Hd ☆ 35°47'·31N 05°48'·06W Iso G 4s 6m 6M.
Basse des Almirantes 35°49'·73N 05°45'·71W VQ.
Pta Malabata ☆ 35°49'·08N 05°44'·86W Fl 5s 77m **22M**. W □ Tr
Ksar es Srhir ☆ 35°50'·90N 05°33'·66W Fl (4) 12s 16m 8M.
Punta Círes ☆ 35°54'·52N 05°28'·96W Fl (3) 12s 44m **18M**, vis: 060°-330°.

◄ CEUTA

Dique de Levante Hd ☆ 35°53'·73N 05°18'·47W Fl R 5s 13m 5M
Digue de Poniente Hd ☆ 35°53'·75N 05°18'·68W Fl G 5s 13m 10M; Racon (O); *Siren 15s.*
E Corner Spur ☆ 35°53'·72N 05°18'·72W 7m 1M.
Muelle España W Hd ☆ 35°53'·61N 05°18'·90W Fl (2+1) R 12s 7m 1M.
Muelle del Comercio Bkwtr Head ☆ 35°53'·61N 05°18'·90W Fl (4) R 11s 8m 1M.
Marina Bkwtr Hd ☆ 35°53'·41N 05°18'·91W Fl (4) G 11s 5m 1M.
Pta Almina ☆ 35°53'·90N 05°16·86W Fl (2) 10s 148m **22M**; W Tr; *Siren (2) 45s.*

9.21.4 PASSAGE INFORMATION

BIBLIOGRAPHY The *SW Spain and Portugal* (Macmillan Reeds/ Jens) covers from Viano do Costello to Gibraltar, *W Coasts of Spain and Portugal Pilot* (Admiralty, NP 67) covers from Cabo Ortegal to Gibraltar. The *Atlantic Spain and Portugal* guide (Imray/RCC, 3rd edition 1995) covers from El Ferrol to Gibraltar. *Guia del Navegante* has fair cover, in English, of SW Spain, but is limited elsewhere. *Yacht Scene, Gibraltar and Surrounding Areas* (DM Sloma, PO Box 555, Gibraltar, £6.50) is useful for that area. Passage information for the coasts of NW and N Spain is in 9.19.4.

RIO GUADIANA TO CAPE TRAFALGAR On the Spanish bank Ayamonte has a new marina. 4M to the E, Isla Cristina (9.21.8) is the most W'ly of seven modern marinas in SW Andalucía. 13M further E, Rio de las Piedras requires care on entry but is a peaceful river with yacht facilities at El Rompido. In the apps to Huelva there are pontoons at Punta Umbria and a marina at Mazagón (9.21.9). About 30M SE is the mouth of Rio Guadalquivir (9.21.10 and chart 85), navigable 54M to Sevilla (9.21.11). Caution: NW of the river mouth large fish havens in shoal waters extend 5M offshore. There is a marina at Chipiona (9.21.10) on the SE side of the ent. Around Cádiz Bay (9.21.12) there are marinas at Rota, Puerto Sherry, Santa Maria and in the hbr of Cádiz itself. S of Cádiz keep about 4M offshore on the 20m line to clear inshore banks. Sancti-Petri marina (9.21.13) lies on a remote and interesting river. Cabo Trafalgar may be rounded within 100m of the lt ho, inshore of a tidal race, or about 4M off to clear foul ground/shoals lying from SW to NW of the cape. Tunny nets up to 7M offshore are a hazard, Apr-Oct, especially off Barbate (9.21.14). See also AC 90 for details of artificial reefs which may reduce charted depths by approx 2·5m

THE GIBRALTAR STRAIT (charts 142, 1448) 9.21.15 shows the timing of tidal streams with notes on surface flow. Hbrs include Barbate (9.21.14), Tarifa (9.21.15), Algeciras (9.21.16) and Gibraltar (9.21.17). Yachts bound to/from Gibraltar will usually use the northern ITZ.

Levantes are E'lies common in the Strait when pressure is high to the N and low to the S. A persistent *Levante* produces the roughest seas. The *Poniente* is a W'ly wind, slightly less common in summer. The *Vendavale* is a moist SW'ly with rain/ drizzle.

9.21.6 Distance Table see 9.20.6.

9.21.5 SPECIAL NOTES FOR SPAIN

Regions/Provinces: Spain is divided into 17 autonomous regions, ie in this Almanac, the Basque Country, Cantabria, Asturias, Galicia and Andalucía. Most of the regions are sub-divided into provinces, eg in Galicia: Lugo, La Coruña, Pontevedra and Orense (inland). The province is shown below the name of each main port.

Language: This Almanac recognises the significant regional differences (eg Basque, Gallego), but in the interests of standardisation uses the spelling of Castilian Spanish where practicable.

Charts: Spanish charts (SC) are obtainable from Instituto Hidrográfico de la Marina, Tolosa Latour 1, 11007 Cádiz, ☎ (956) 599412, 📠 275358; order from Seccion Economica by post/bank transfer or in person for cash. Also from Centro Nacional de Informacion Geografica, 6 Calle Lopez Doriga, Santander. Hbrs are often charted at larger scale than British Admiralty charts.

Courtesy Ensign: Until W of Bilbao it may be politic not to fly a courtesy ensign in view of Basque sensitivity.

Time: Spain keeps UTC+1 as standard time; DST (Daylight Saving Time) is kept from the last Sunday in March until the Saturday before the 4th Sunday in October, as other EU nations. Note: Portugal keeps UTC as standard time and UTC+1 as DST.

Secondary Spanish Ports Related to Lisboa: A number of Spanish ports in Areas 19 and 21 are related to Lisboa as the Standard Port and it is important to realise that time differences for these ports when applied to the printed times of HW and LW for Lisboa (UT) will give HW and LW times in the Zone Time for Spain (UT –0100) and no further correction is required, other tha for Daylight Saving Time, when this applies.

Telephone: To call Spain from UK dial 00-34, then the area code, followed by the ☎ number. To call UK from Spain, dial 07-44, then area code, less the initial 0, then the ☎ number.

Emergencies: ☎ 900 202 202 for Fire, Police and Ambulance. *Rioja Cruz* (Red Cross) operate LBs.

Public Holidays: Jan 1, 6; Apr 10 (Good Friday); 1 May (Labour Day); June 11 (Corpus Christi); Aug 15 (Assumption); Oct 12 (National Day); Nov 1 (All Saints Day); Dec 6, 8 (Immaculate Conception), 25.

Representation: Spanish National Tourist Office, 57 St James St, London SW1A 1LD; ☎ 020 7486 8077, 📠 020 7486 8034.

British Embassy, Calle de Fernando el Santo 16, 28010 Madrid; ☎ (91) 700 8200, 📠 700 8311. There are British Consuls at Bilbao, Santander, Vigo, Seville and Algeciras.

Buoyage: IALA Region A system is used. However buoys may lack topmarks, be unpainted (or wrongly painted) more often than in N Europe. Preferred chan buoys (RGR, Fl (2+1) R and GRG, Fl (2+1) G) are quite widely used.

Documents: Spain, although an EU member, still asks to check paperwork. This can be a time-consuming, repetitive and inescapable process. The only palliatives are courtesy, patience and good humour. Organise your papers to include:

Personal – Passports; crew list, ideally on headed paper with the yacht's rubber stamp, giving DoB, passport nos, where joined/ intended departure. Certificate of Competence (Yachtmaster Offshore, ICC/HOCC etc). Radio Operator's certificate. Form E111 (advised for medical treatment).

Yacht – Registration certificate, Part 1 or SSR. Proof of VAT status. Marine insurance. Ship's Radio licence. Itinerary, backed up by ship's log.

Marina charges: Most marinas now have a uniform tariff - approx €1·00 in the high season, €0·50 in the low season (2001).

Access: Ferries sail from UK to Santander and Bilbao. There are flights from UK to Bilbao, Santiago de Compostela and Jerez; also Sevilla, Madrid, Malaga and Gibraltar. Internal flights via Madrid to Asturias, La Coruña and Vigo. Bus services are usually good and trains adequate, except in the more remote regions.

AYAMONTE *9.21.7*

Huelva **37°12'·70N 07°24'·50W**

CHARTS AC 89; SC 4411, 441; PC 97

TIDES

Standard Port LISBOA (⟵); ML 1·8; Zone –0100

Times				**Height (metres)**			
High Water		Low Water		MHWS	MHWN	MLWN	MLWS
0500	1000	0500	1100	3·8	3·0	1·5	0·5
1700	2200	1700	2300				
Differences AYAMONTE							
+0005	+0015	+0025	+0045	–0·7	–0·6	–0·1	–0·1
RÍA DE HUELVA, BAR							
0000	+0015	+0035	+0030	–0·6	–0·5	–0·3	–0·1

SHELTER Good in marina on Spanish bank of Rio Guadiana, 1·5M NNE of Vila Real. Marina is dredged 1·5m to 2·0m. Fuel pontoon is just inside ent. Sanlucar, about 20M up the river, is accessible.

NAVIGATION WPT 37°09'·00N 07°23'·35W (No 1 SHM buoy, Q (3) G 6s), 160°/340° from/to hd of W trng wall, 9ca. Least depth over bar 2·5m. See 9.20.20 for directions into Rio Guadiana.

LIGHTS AND MARKS High bldgs, FR lts, are 3M WNW of ent. White suspension bridge 2M inland is visible from seaward. Other lts: Vila Real lt ho, Fl 6·5s 51m 26M, W ○ tr, B bands, is 1·5M S. E trng wall (partly covers), Fl G 3s; W trng wall hd, Fl R 5s. ☆ Fl G 5s is near ferry berths, about 350m N of marina ent.

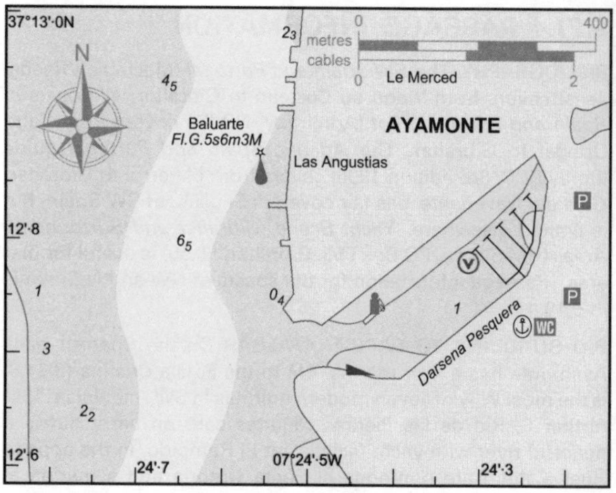

RADIO TELEPHONE Marina VHF Ch 09 (H24).

TELEPHONE (Dial code 959) Hr Mr ☎/📠 321694; ⊖, Met: via marina.

FACILITIES **Marina** ☎/📠 321694, 174 AB, inc Ⓥ in 3m, €1·03; FW, AC, D & P pontoon, Slip, ME, El, Sh, R, YC, Bar, YC, ⊡. Ayamonte is first (E-bound) of 8 modern marinas run by Junta de Andalucía. **Town:** V, R, Bar, Ⓑ, ✉; Ferry to Vila Real de S'to Antonio; Bus Huelva (60 km); ✈ Faro (48 km).

ISLA CRISTINA *9.21.8*

Huelva **37°11'·88N 07°19'·65W**

CHARTS AC 89; SC 4411, 441, 44B

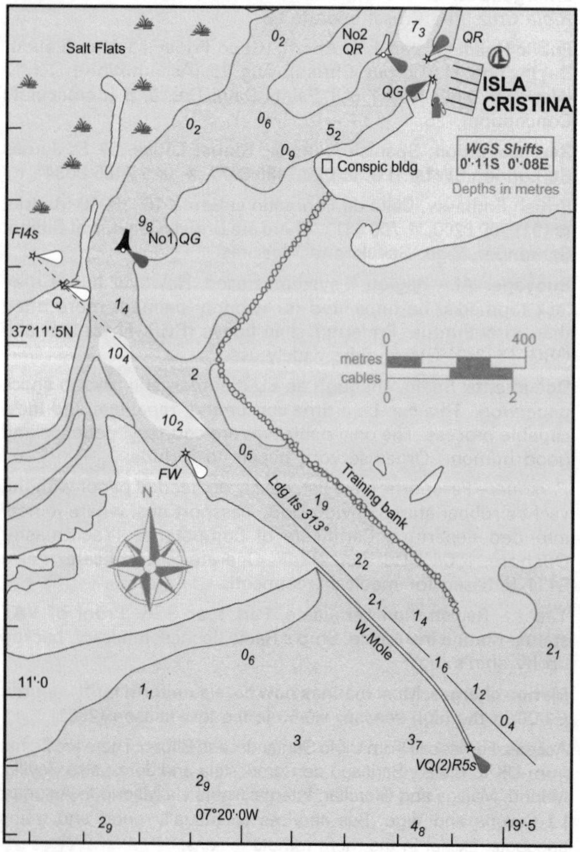

TIDES Use Differences AYAMONTE (9.21.7)

SHELTER Good once inside marina (2·0); the river ent is open to SE winds (like many hbrs on the Algarve). FVs berth at quays to the N of marina. There is little space to ⚓.

NAVIGATION WPT 37°10'·75N 07°19'·25W (off chartlet), 133°/313° from/to chan ent lts, 3ca. Chan runs NW for nearly 1M, then curves to stbd, past No 1 SHM lt buoy. Stand on until tall conspic W bldg (looks like a lt ho) bears about 100°, then alter for it. At a small W buoy (uncharted) just short of this bldg, turn NE for No 2 PHM lt buoy, close W of marina. Best appr at half-flood, to see drying sandbanks. Chan beyond ldg lts is prone to change depth/direction.

LIGHTS AND MARKS Ldg lts (front Q 7m 5M; rear Fl 4s 12m 5M) lead approx 313°, between the W mole head VQ (2) R 5s 7m 4M and bn, Fl G 2s 4m 5M, on head of drying trng bank to stbd. The powerful lt, Fl 6·5s 51m 26M, W tr + B bands, at Vila Real de Santo António is 4M to the W.

RADIO TELEPHONE Marina VHF Ch 09.

TELEPHONE (Dial code 959) Hr Mr 343501, 📠 343501, ⊖, Met: via marina.

FACILITIES **Marina** (203 AB, inc Ⓥ), ☎/📠 343501, €1·03, FW, AC, D, Slip, BH (32 ton), ME, El, Sh, R, Bar, Ice, ⊡.**Town:** V, R, Bar, Ⓑ, ✉; Bus Ayamonte (17 km); ✈ Faro (65 km).

HARBOURS CLOSE WEST OF RIA DE HUELVA

RIO DE LAS PIEDRAS. SC 4412. SWM buoy, L Fl 10s, at **37°11'·82N 07°02'·35W** marks ent; thence steer NW past SHM buoy, Fl G 5s, and PHM buoy, Fl (2) R 6s, into river. Buoys are moved to suit shifting chan (0·6m) and shoals. ⚓ in river is sheltered by long spit. El Rompido, lt ho Fl (2) 10s, is 4M to W with YC, ☎ (959) 399349, 📠 399217; BY.

PUNTA UMBRIA. AC 83. SC 4413. SCM buoy, VQ (6)+L Fl 10s, at **37°09'·64N 06°57'·09W** marks chan ent (1·1m). NB: the oil pipe line described under IG 46 is close E. Bkwtr head, also VQ (6)+L Fl 10s, is to port. YC, dark R bldg, and pontoon is 1M up-river, Fl (3) G. Note: all 3 lts on SW side are G. Temp'y AB, M or ⚓ if any room. YC ☎ (959) 311899.

MAZAGÓN *9.21.9*

luelva **37°08'·00N 06°50'·00W**

:HARTS AC 83, 90, 92; SC 4413, 441, 442; SHOM 6862, 7300

IDES See 9.21.7 (Ría de Huelva, Bar); ML 1·8; Zone –0100

HELTER Good in large, modern marina, ent facing WNW up-iver. Inner approach is sheltered by training wall on SW side.

JAVIGATION WPT 37°05'·65N 06°49'·05W, WCM buoy, Q (9) 5s, 159°/339° from/to marina, 2·5M. From the W, be aware of an il pipe line running N/S, ending about 5M W of the WPT; it is narked by 4 SPM buoys, each Fl (4) Y 20s. The appr is traightforward via well lit, buoyed, dredged (10m) chan 339°, vhich bears away NW to Huelva industrial complex. After the irst pair of chan buoys, the very long training wall lies to port; ts seaward end has lt twr, Fl (3+1) WR 20s 30m 12/9M. Keep clear f merchant ships.

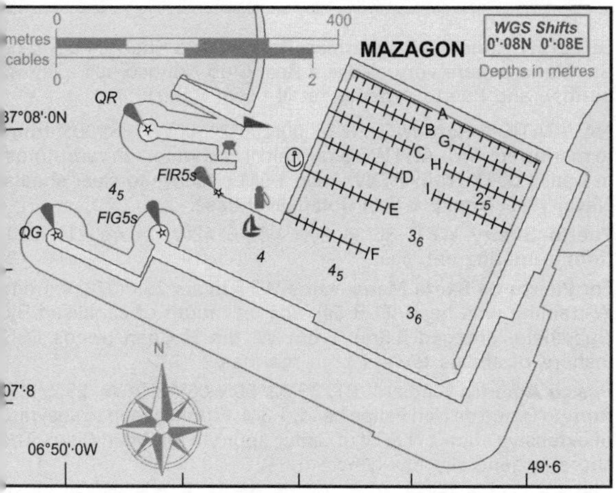

IGHTS AND MARKS Ldg lts 339°: front, Q 49m 8M; rear, Fl R 2s 5m 8M, both on R/W chequered trs. After No 7 SHM buoy, Fl 4) G 20s, alter stbd for the marina ent. Picacho lt ho, Fl (2+4) 30s 1m 25M, W tr with R corners, is 5ca NE of marina ent.

ADIO TELEPHONE Marina VHF Ch 09 16. Huelva Port Ch 06 11 2 **14** 16.

ELEPHONE (Dial code 959) Marina, ☎ 536 251, 📠 376 237; ⊖ & Aet via marina.

ACILITIES **Marina** (497 AB in 4m, inc Ⓥ), €1·03, FW, P, D, AC, lip, BH (32 ton), ME, El, Sh, Ice, YC, Bar, R.⇶ Huelva (24km); ✈ evilla (130km).

CHIPIONA *9.21.10*

ádiz **36°45'·00N 06°25'·63W**

:HARTS AC 85; SC 4421, 4422 (18 sheets)

IDES

Standard Port LISBOA (⟵); ML 1·9; Zone –0100

Times				Height (metres)			
High Water		Low Water		MHWS	MHWN	MLWN	MLWS
0500	1000	0500	1100	3·8	3·0	1·5	0·5
1700	2200	1700	2300				
)ifferences RIO GUADALQUIVIR, BAR							
–0005	+0005	+0020	+0030	–0·6	–0·5	–0·2	–0·1
ONANZA (36°48'N 06°20'W)							
+0025	+0040	+0100	+0120	–0·8	–0·6	–0·4	0·0
ORTA DE LOS JERONIMOS (37° 08'N 06°05'W)							
+0210	+0230	+0255	+0345	–1·2	–0·9	–0·5	0·0
EVILLA							
+0400	+0430	+0510	+0545	–1·7	–1·2	–0·6	0·0

SHELTER Good in modern marina, but swell intrudes in NW gales. Yachts berth on SE side in 3·5m, larger yachts in first basin on port side. FVs berth against the NW bkwtr.

NAVIGATION WPT 36°45'·82N 06°26'·95W, No 1 SWM buoy, L Fl 10s (Racon T), 308°/128° from/to marina ent, 1·33M. Caution: extensive fish havens with obstructions 2·5m high lie from 3·5M to 7·5M NW of the WPT. Same WPT is on ldg line 069° for buoyed chan into Rio Guadalquivir (below).

LIGHTS AND MARKS Chipiona lt ho, Fl 10s 68m 25M, is conspic 1M SW of marina. 1·7M W of this lt ho, the drying Bajo Salmedina (off chartlet) which must be rounded if coming from S, is marked by WCM bn tr, Q (9) 15s, and WCM buoy, also Q (9) 15s. Inside hbr bkwtr, ☆ Fl (3) G 9s, near FV berths, is not visible from seaward.

RADIO TELEPHONE Marina VHF Ch 09. Port and Rio Guadalquivir Ch 12.

TELEPHONE (Dial code 956) Marina ☎ 373844, 📠 370037, ⊖ and Met: via marina.

FACILITIES **Marina** (355 AB inc Ⓥ in 3·5m), €1·03, AC, P, D, FW, Slip, BH (32 ton), CH, ME, El, Sh, Bar, R, ⊡; **Town:** V, R, Bar, Ⓑ, ✉; ⇶ and ✈ Jerez (32 km).

RIO GUADALQUIVIR

Huelva/Cádiz **36°45'·82N 06°26'·95W** (No 1 SWM buoy)

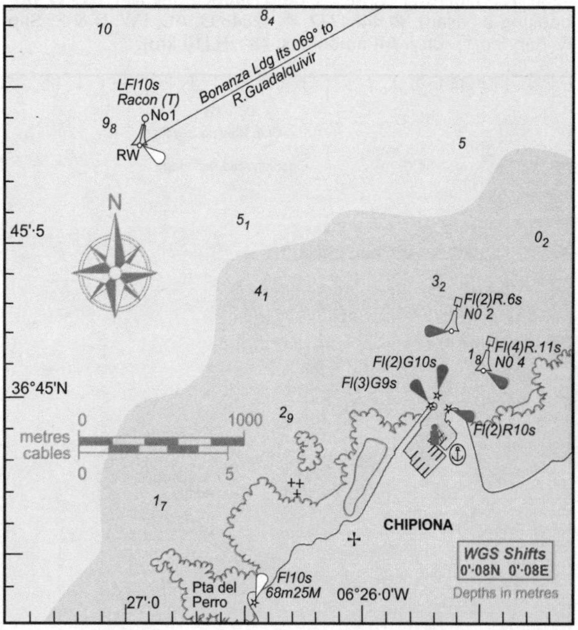

Charts Updated AC 85 or SC 4422 essential as buoys/bns liable to change.

Navigation The river is not difficult to navigate but can be hot and uninspiring, through the flat and almost featureless terrain of the Doñana National Park. From No 1 SWM buoy (shown above and as WPT for CHIPIONA, 9.21.10) the Bonanza ldg lts (front Q 27m 10M; rear Iso 4s 60m 10M) lead 068·9° for 5M through lit, buoyed chan. From No 1 SWM buoy to a lock 2M S of Sevilla is about 49M. At Bonanza (36°48'N 06°20'W) the channel becomes truly riverine, 750m wide; 250m nearer Sevilla. The banks are well marked throughout by lt beacons. Depths are rarely less than 5m, best water usually being on the outside of bends, which are often buoyed in the broader lower reaches.

Tidal streams The flood makes for about 7hrs (3kn sp, 1kn nps), the ebb for 5½ hrs; so it should be possible to reach the lock on one tide, passing Bonanza at LW–½hr.

Shelter There are no recognised stopping places and any ⚓ is vulnerable to passing traffic; monitor VHF Ch 12. The lock, 2M S of Sevilla (9.21.11), is below HT cables (44m clearance) between conspic R/W pylons; see overleaf.

SEVILLA *9.21.11*

Sevilla **37°20'·00N 05°59'·65W** (Lock)

CHARTS & TIDES See 9.21.10. ML Sevilla 1·3M; Zone –0100

SHELTER The 3 marinas are: **Gelves**, 1·5M N of Bn 52 on the W arm of the river. It is badly silted and approx 3M from the city. **Marina Yachting Sevilla**, 300m E of the lock almost below HT cables, one long pontoon in quiet creek 3M from city; useful stopover prior to transiting road/rail bridge 2M N. **Club Náutico de Sevilla**, excellent facilities close to city.

NAVIGATION See Rio Guadalquivir (9.21.10). The lock, 2M S of city centre, opens H24 approx every 3 hrs (check at Chipiona); secure to ladders/rubber strips. After conspic high suspension bridge (ring road), negotiate a road/rail bridge, opening 0800 & 2000 in season (0800 & 1800 winter); check times at lock. Beyond that, bascule bridge is permanently open.

RADIO TELEPHONE Marinas VHF Ch 09. Port, lock and road/rail bridge Ch 12.

TELEPHONE (Dial code 95; see below. Brit Consul 4228875).

FACILITIES **Gelves marina** (150+ Ⓥ), 650pta ☎ 5760 728, about 1·5m, waiting pontoon in river, AC, FW, CH, ME, BH (25 ton), ⊡, R, V, Bar; **Marina Yachting Sevilla** (400+ Ⓥ), 6m, ☎ 4230326, 📠 4230172, Slip, AC, FW, ME, ⊡; **Club Náutico Sevilla** (100+ Ⓥ, pre-booking advised), ☎ 4454777, 📠 4284693, AC, FW, D & P, Slip, R, Bar, Ice, ⊡. **City**: All amenities; ⇌; ✈ (10 km).

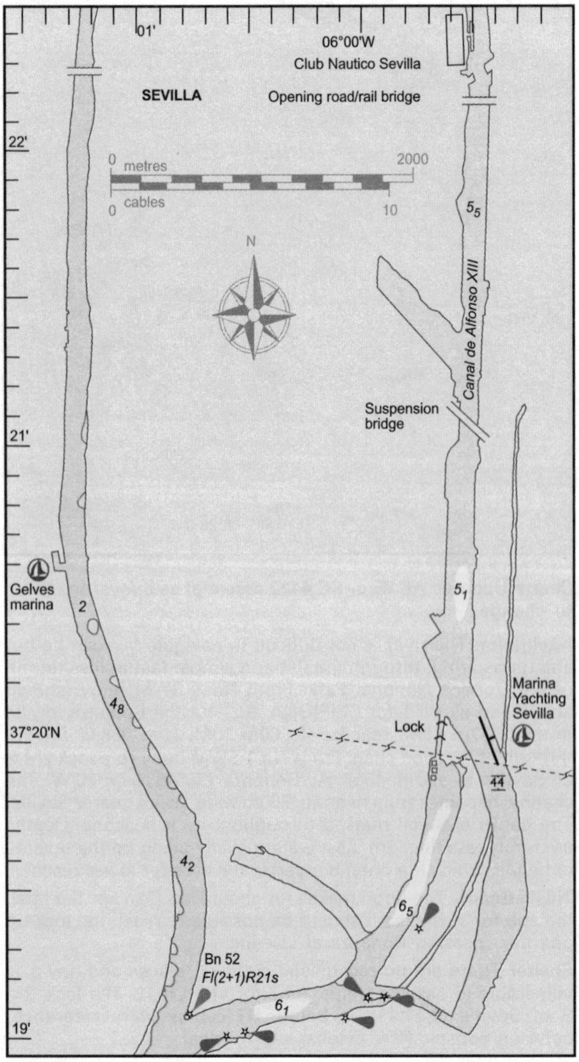

BAY OF CÁDIZ *9.21.12*

Cádiz **36°33'·50N 06°18'·70W**

CHARTS AC 86, 90; SC 443A, 443B, 443

TIDES
Standard Port LISBOA (⟵); ML 1·8; Zone –0100

Times				Height (metres)			
High Water		Low Water		MHWS	MHWN	MLWN	MLWS
0500	1000	0500	1100	3·8	3·0	1·5	0·5
1700	2200	1700	2300				
Differences ROTA							
–0010	+0010	+0025	+0015	–0·7	–0·6	–0·4	–0·1
PUERTO DE SANTA MARIA							
+0006	+0006	+0027	+0027	–0·6	–0·4	–0·4	–0·1
PUERTO CÁDIZ							
0000	+0020	+0040	+0025	–0·5	–0·5	–0·3	0·0

SHELTER Good in all 4 marinas: Rota, Puerto Sherry, Puerto de Sta Maria (where very pleasant Real Club Náutico has a few Ⓥ berths), and Puerto America (at N tip of Cádiz).

NAVIGATION **Rota** WPT, 36°36'·00N 06°21'·00W, 185°/005° from/to marina ent, 1M. Al Fl WG 9s airfield lt and water tank are almost in transit 005°. From W/NW keep 1·5M offshore to clear shoals. Naval vessels may ⚓ S of Rota Naval base.

Puerto Sherry WPT, 36°34'·30N 06°15'·42W, bears 210°/030° from/to marina ent, 5ca.

For **Puerto de Santa Maria**, same WPT bears 258°/078° from/to W training wall head (Fl R 5s), 5ca (at mouth of canalised Rio Guadalete, dredged 4·5m). From W, the N Chan trends ESE inshore of shoals toward both marinas.

Puerto America (Cádiz) WPT, 36°33'·50N 06°18'·70W, 297°/117° from/to Dique de San Felipe head, 1·8M. From S, keep to seaward of extensive shoals N & W of Cádiz; appr via the Main Chan. The shore is generally low-lying.

LIGHTS AND MARKS Lts/buoys as shown; Rota lt ho, Oc 4s, W tr + R band, overlooks marina. Conspic daymarks include:
Puerto Sherry, W bkwtr hd ○ twr. Cádiz city, golden-domed cathedral and radio twr (113m) close SE. Two cable pylons (154m) and shipyard cranes in docks area. W bldg on Dique de San Felipe near Puerto America.

RADIO TELEPHONE Marinas VHF Ch 09. Cádiz port 11, 12, **14**, 16

TELEPHONE (Dial code 956) Hr Mr 224011, 📠 240476; ⊖ & Met via marinas (see below).

FACILITIES **Rota Marina** (496 AB, inc Ⓥ in 4·5m), €1·03, ☎ 840069, 📠 813811, AC, P, D, FW, Slip, BH (32 ton), ME, El, C (5 ton). Average charge per m (LOA) is €1·31 for 1st 3 days if staying <15 days.

Puerto Sherry Marina (753 AB, inc Ⓥ; 3·0-4·5m), ☎ 870303, 📠 873902, AC, P, D, FW, Slip, BH (50 ton), ME, El, C, SM, Ⓔ, CH, Sh, ⊡, R, Bar, YC; Arrivals berth to port inside the ent.

Real Club Náutico de Puerto de Santa Maria (175 AB+few Ⓥ 3·0-8·0m); 10 hammerhead pontoons (A-K) on NW bank plus two mid-stream pontoons. ☎ 854400, 📠 871399; €6, AC, P, D, FW, Sh, ME, C (5 ton), BH (25 ton), Slip, R, Bar;

Puerto America Marina (152 AB, inc Ⓥ; 7·5m), €1.03, ☎ 224240, 📠 224240, AC, P, D, FW, Slip, ME, El, C (10 ton). Average charge per m (LOA) is €6 for 1st 3 days if staying <15 days.

Real Club Náutico de Cádiz (182 AB; 5m) ☎ 253903; R, Bar, D (Close SW of Puerto America).

City: all amenities, ⇌; ✈ Jerez (25 km). Spanish Hydrographic Office is at Tolosa Latour 1, Cadiz.

BAY OF CÁDIZ *including marinas at:* ROTA, PUERTO SHERRY, PUERTO DE SANTA MARIA and PUERTO AMERICA

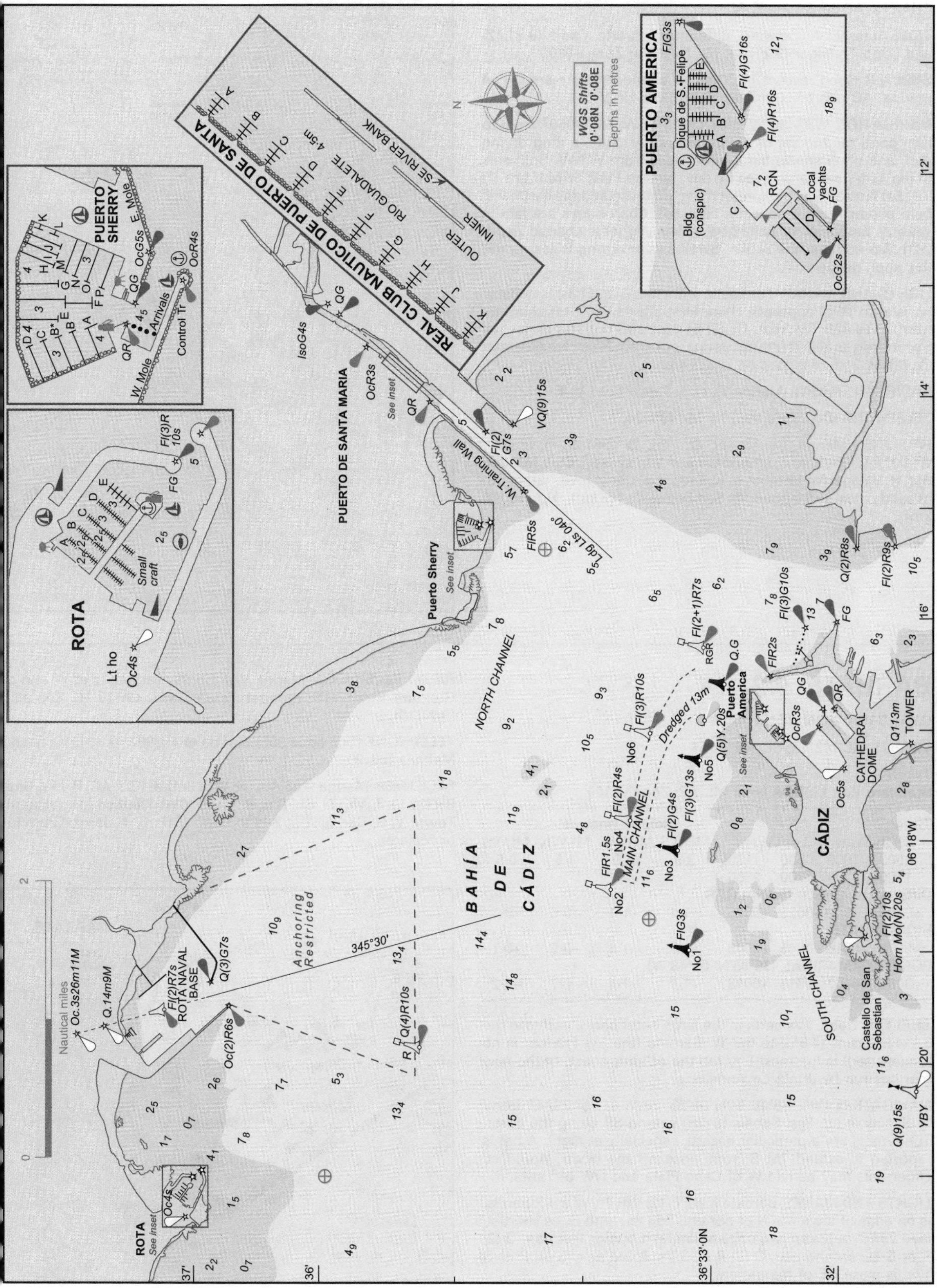

SANCTI-PETRI *9.21.13*

Cádiz **36°23'·80N 06°12'·50W**

CHARTS AC 90; SC 4438, 443

TIDES Interpolate between differences Puerto Cádiz (9.21.12) and Cabo Trafalgar (9.21.14); ML No data; Zone –0100

SHELTER Good, except in S'lies. ⚓ or moor in stream, W of marina; AB pontoons in 2·5m depth; see Hr Mr.

NAVIGATION WPT 36°22'·40N 06°13'·05W, 230°/050° from/to turn point for 2nd set of ldg lts, 5ca. El Arrecife, a long drying reef, and other shoals bar a direct appr from W/NW. Both sets of ldg lts/trs are hard to see by day, but the PHM/SHM lt bns (Fl R/G 5s) are easily seen; careful fixing on these and the castle will help pilotage (night appr not advised). Chan buoys are laid in season. Best appr at half-flood in fair vis; least charted depth 2·2m. Sp tide reaches 2½-3kn. Swell and/or strong S'lies render the appr dangerous.

LIGHTS AND MARKS The castle with 16m □ tr, Fl 3s, is conspic on islet to W of approach chan. First ldg lts 050° (off chartlet): front, Fl 5s 12m 6M; rear, Oc (2) 6s 16m 6M, both on lattice trs. Second ldg lts 346·5° (Pta del Boquerón): front Fl 5s 11m 6M; rear, Oc (2) 6s 21m 6M, both on lattice trs.

RADIO TELEPHONE Marina *Puerto Sancti-Petri* VHF Ch 09.

TELEPHONE (Dial code 956) Hr Mr 495434.

FACILITIES **Marina** (88 AB, inc Ⓥ; 5m), ☎ 496169, 📠 495434, €1·03, AC, FW, Slip, C, limited CH and V in season. **Club Náutico** Bar, R. **Village:** No facilities in abandoned "ghost town" at mouth of sandy, peaceful lagoon; ⇌ San Fernando (18 km); ✈ Jerez (50 km).

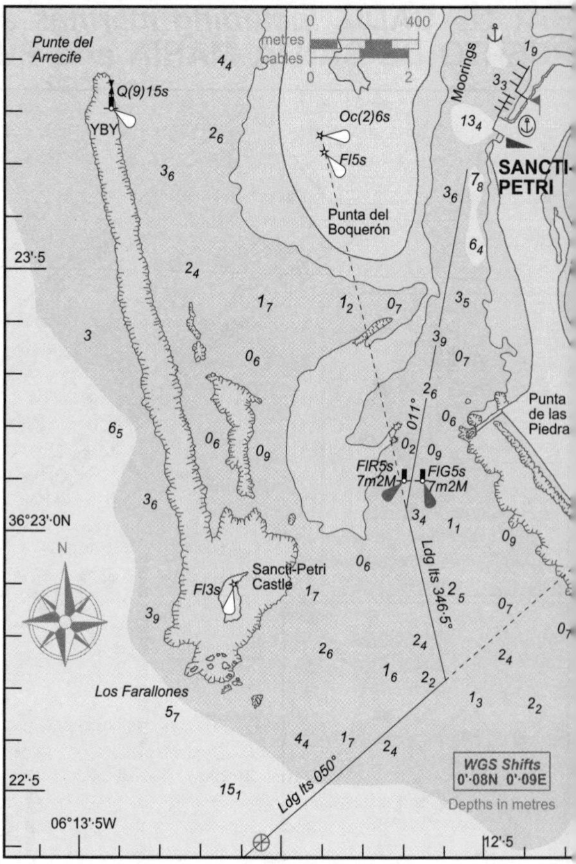

BARBATE *9.21.14*

Cádiz **36°10'·89N 05°55'·50W**

CHARTS AC 142, 92; SC 4441, 444

TIDES

Standard Port LISBOA (⟵); ML 1·2; Zone –0100

Times				Height (metres)			
High Water		Low Water		MHWS	MHWN	MLWN	MLWS
0500	1000	0500	1100	3·8	3·0	1·5	0·5
1700	2200	1700	2300				
Differences CABO TRAFALGAR							
–0003	–0003	+0026	+0026	–1·4	–1·1	–0·6	–0·1
RIO BARBATE							
+0016	+0016	+0045	+0045	–1·9	–1·5	–0·5	+0·1
PUNTA CAMARINAL (36°05'N 05°48'W)							
–0007	–0007	+0013	+0013	–1·7	–1·4	–0·7	–0·2

SHELTER Good. FVs berth in the large outer basin, yachts in the 3 inner basins (4·5m) to the W. Barbate (the "de Franco" is no longer used) is the most E'ly (on the Atlantic coast) of the new marinas run by Junta de Andalucía.

NAVIGATION WPT 36°10'·50N 05°55'·20W, 117·5°/297·5° from/ to SW mole hd, 2ca. Shoals (6·6m) extend SE along the coast. Tunny nets are a particular hazard, especially at night. A net is reported to extend 2M S from close off the bkwtr, April-Oct. Other nets may be laid W of Cabo Plata and NW of Tarifa.

LIGHTS AND MARKS Barbate lt ho, Fl (2) WR 7s, W tr + R bands, is on edge of town 4ca N of hbr ent. Ldg lts, both Q, as chartlet, lead 297·5° between two pairs of lateral lt buoys: first pair, Q (2) R or G 5s; second pair, Q (3) R or G 7s. A 3rd pair, Q (4) R or G 12s, is close NE of marina ent.

RADIO TELEPHONE Marina VHF Ch 09. Barbate is at W end of Gibraltar Strait VTS; monitor *Tarifa Traffic* Ch 10 16. See also (9.21.15).

TELEPHONE (Dial code 956) Marina ☎ 431907, 📠 431918; ⊖ and Met: via marina.

FACILITIES **Marina** (256 AB, inc Ⓥ in 3m), €1·03, AC, P, FW, Slip, BH (32 ton), ME, El, Sh, Bar, R, Ice, ⊡; **Club Náutico** (portakabin). **Town:** V, R, Bar, Ⓑ, ✉; Bus to Cádiz (61km); ✈ Jerez, Gibraltar or Malaga.

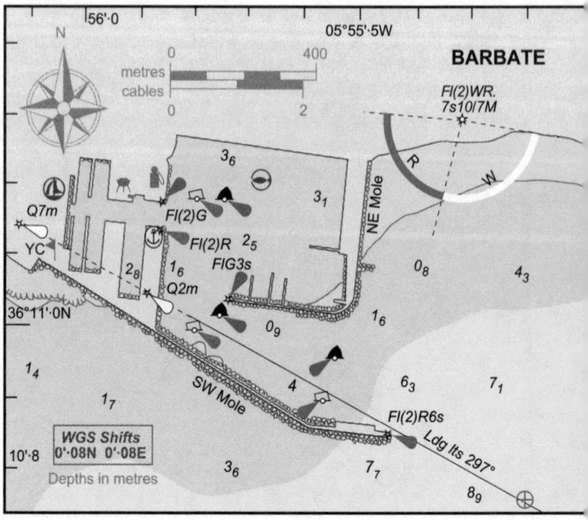

STRAIT OF GIBRALTAR *9.21.15*

SURFACE FLOW IN THE GIBRALTAR STRAIT

Surface flow is the net effect of the prevailing E-going current from the Atlantic into the Med (further influenced by recent E or W winds) and tidal streams. Max surface flows are about 2kn W-going and 5kn E-going. Max surface current is about 2kn E-going in the middle of the Strait. Max tidal stream rates are about 3kn in either direction, usually to be found close inshore around headlands. Thus as surface current decreases away from mid-Strait, tidal streams increase closer inshore.

Tidal streams are insufficiently observed and are therefore approximate, although generally accurate. Near the middle of the Strait the E-going stream starts at HW Gib and the W-going at HWG+6. Closer inshore, streams start to make progressively earlier.

Tidal races on the Spanish side form: off Cape Trafalgar, usually up to 2M SW, but 5-12M in heavy weather; near Bajo de Los Cabezos (2-4M S of Pta Paloma); and off Tarifa. As ever the position and violence of these races depends on wind, especially over tide, springs/neaps and the state of the tide.

For more information, see W Coasts of Spain and Portugal Pilot (NP 67) and Strait of Gibraltar: surface and sub-surface water movements (NP 629).

MINOR HARBOURS ON THE GIBRALTAR STRAIT

TARIFA 36°00'·40N 05°36'·20W. AC 142; SC 4450, 445B; SHOM 7619, 7042. Inset chartlet is opposite. Tides, see 9.21.16. A FV, naval and ferry hbr with no yacht berths. Ferries berth on the outboard end of the outer mole and on S side of the hbr; FVs fill the S and W sides of the hbr; naval pens and *Guardia Civil* craft use the N side. Best options for yachts are the N end of outer mole or, by agreement, the naval pens. ⚓ off hbr ent in 5m. If a *levanter* is blowing ⚓ NW of Isla de Tarifa (prohib military area joined by causeway to mainland). Lts: Lt ho, Fl (3) WR 10s 40m 26/18M, W113-089°, R089°-113°; Siren (3) 60s; Racon, RDF bn. E side of Isla de Tarifa, Fl R 5s 12m 3M. Outer mole hd, Fl G 5s 10m 5M. Inner mole hd, Fl (2) R 6s 6m 1M. Inner spur Fl (2) G 6s 5m 2M. **Tarifa VTS**, c/s *Tarifa Trafico* VHF Ch **10** 16, provides a reporting service (voluntary for yachts).

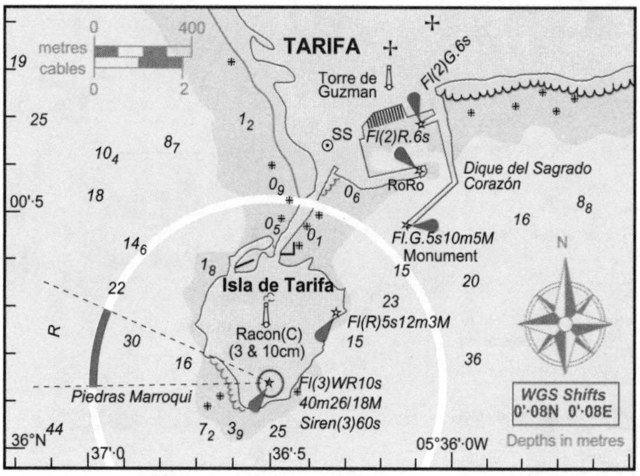

ALGECIRAS *9.21.16*

Cádiz **36°07'·20N 05°26'·15W**

CHARTS AC 1448, 142, 3578; SC 4451, 445A, 445; SHOM 7026, 7042

TIDES

Standard Port GIBRALTAR (⟶); ML 0·66; Zone –0100

Times				**Height (metres)**			
High Water		Low Water		MHWS	MHWN	MLWN	MLWS
0000	0700	0100	0600	1·0	0·7	0·3	0·1
1200	1900	1300	1800				
Differences TARIFA							
–0038	–0038	–0042	–0042	+0·4	+0·3	+0·3	+0·2
PUNTA CARNERO							
–0010	–0010	0000	0000	0·0	+0·1	+0·1	+0·1
ALGECIRAS							
–0010	–0010	–0010	–0010	+0·1	+0·2	+0·1	+0·1

SHELTER Good, except perhaps in strong SE'lies. A new marina is now open at Darsena del Saladillo, S of the docks.

NAVIGATION WPT 36°06'·80N 05°24'·68W, ECM buoy, Q (3) 10s, (off chartlet) 109°/289° from/to new marina ent, 1·25M. From S, keep 5ca off Pta de San García. From N/E, beware drying reefs close N of ent; also big ships at ⚓ in the bay.

LIGHTS AND MARKS Conspic Hbr Control twr leads 289° by day from WPT to new marina.

RADIO TELEPHONE Marina VHF Ch 09 16. Port Ch 09, 12, 13, 16.

TELEPHONE (Dial code 956) Hr Mr 572620, 📠 585443; Port Authority 585400, 📠 585445; ⊖ and Met via marina; Brit Vice-Consul 661600/04.

FACILITIES Marina ☎ 572503, AC, D, FW, ME, Slip; **Real Club Náutico ☎** 572503, R, Bar; **New marina**: no details available; contact Port Authority. **Town:** V, R, Bar, Ⓑ, ✉, ≠; ✈ Jerez, Gibraltar, Malaga.

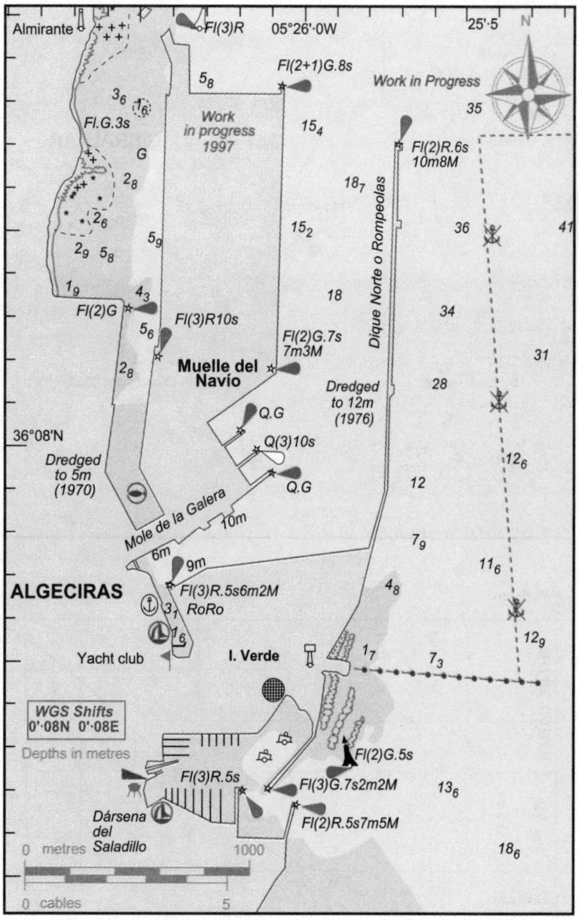

GIBRALTAR *9.21.17*

36°08'·50N 05°22'·00W

CHARTS AC 45, 144, 1448, 142; SC 4451/2, 445A

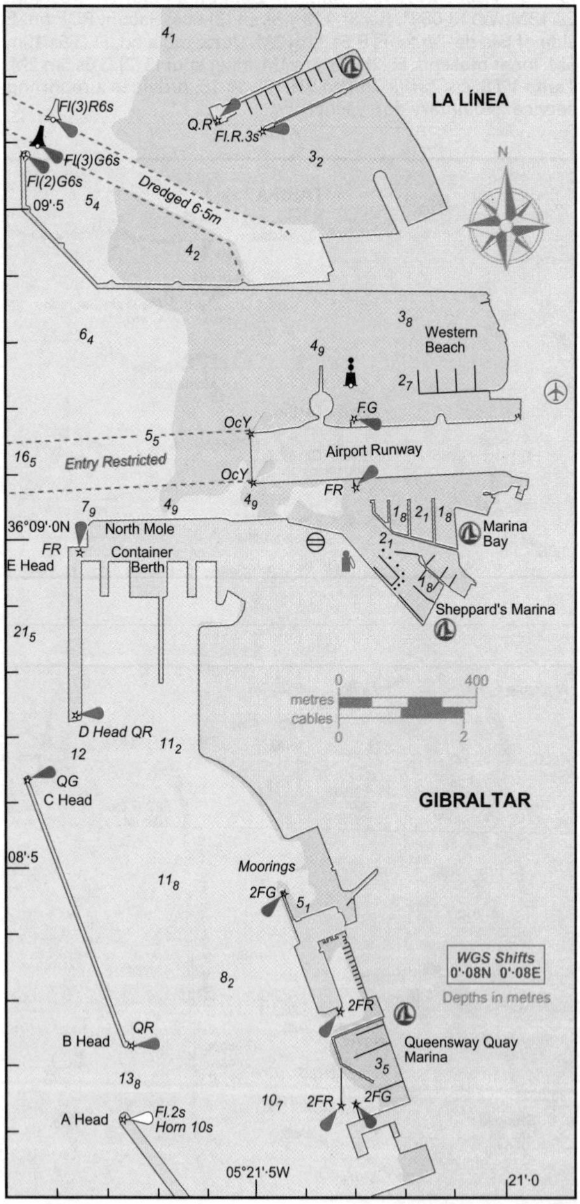

TIDES

Standard Port GIBRALTAR (⟶); ML 0·5; Zone –0100

Times				Height (metres)			
High Water		Low Water		MHWS	MHWN	MLWN	MLWS
0000	0700	0100	0600	1·0	0·7	0·3	0·1
1200	1900	1300	1800				
Differences SANDY BAY (E side of the Rock)							
–0011	–0011	–0016	–0016	–0·2	–0·1	0·0	0·0

SHELTER Good in 3 marinas, from S to N: Queensway Quay, close to town centre; Sheppards at N end of town; and adjacent Marina Bay, close to airport runway. Advisable to pre-book. All can be affected by swell in W'lies and by fierce gusts in the E'ly *levanter*. ⚓ in 4m, to NW of runway (well clear of flight path); pontoons are for small local craft only.

NAVIGATION WPT 36°06'·00N 05°23'·00W, 250°/070° from/to Europa Point, 2M. The Rock is steep-to all round; from the SW, beware shoals to S of Pta Carnero. From the E, yachts may round Europa Pt 3ca off. In the Bay commercial vessels at ⚓ and navigational lights may be hard to see at night. Customs: Yacht arrivals for Sheppards and Marina Bay **must** clear in at adjacent conspic Customs berth (Waterport); Queensway Quay will clear yachts by fax. Visiting RIBs (Rigid Inflatable Boats) must obtain prior written permission to enter from Collector of Customs, Customs House, Waterport, Gibraltar, 📠 78362; entry may otherwise be refused.

LIGHTS AND MARKS The Rock (423m) is not easily missed, but from the W is not seen until rounding Pta Carnero, 5M to SW. On top of Rock is powerful Aero lt, Mo (GB) R 10s 405m 30M. Europa Pt, less obvious, has 3 sectored lts; see 9.21.3. At N end of bay, industrial plants are conspic day/night.

RADIO TELEPHONE Marina Bay VHF Ch 73; Queensway Quay and Sheppards Ch 71. Civil port Ch 06; Gibraltar Bay Ch 12; QHM Ch 08.

TELEPHONE (International code 350, no Area code); from Spain dial 956 7 + 5 digit tel no). Port Captain (Hr Mr) 77254; QHM via HM Naval Base; Marinas, see below; ⊖ 78879, 📠 78362; Met 53416; Ⓗ 79700; Ambulance/Police 199; Fire 190; ✈ 75984.

FACILITIES Queensway Quay Marina, PO Box 19. (120+ Ⓥ), ☎ 44700, 📠 44699, AB/F&A £6.75 < 12m in 3·5m least depth, AC, FW, CH, D & P (min 200ltrs from tanker) by arrangement, ◙;

Sheppards Marina, Waterport, Gib. (150, inc Ⓥ on F & G pontoons), ☎ 75148, 📠 42535, AB £0·70/m stern-to £0.38/m, AC, FW, BH (40 ton), C (10 ton), ME, El, BY, Sh, CH, Ⓔ;

Marina Bay Marina, PO Box 80. (209 inc Ⓥ) ☎ 73300, 📠 42656, AB £6.25 (up to 12m LOA, max draft 4·5m), AC, FW, CH, R, V, ◙; **Services**: ACA, SM; D & P, Gaz, Ice from Fuel berth (near Customs); **Royal Gibraltar YC. Town:** V, R, Bar, ✉, Ⓗ, Ⓑ, ✈.

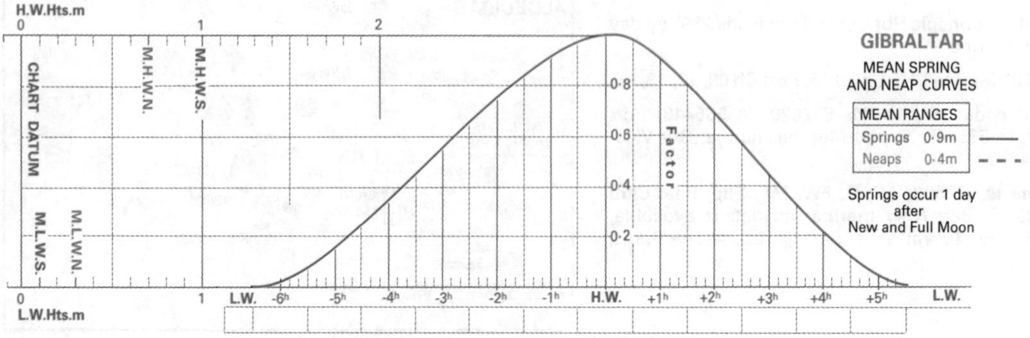

TIME ZONE -0100
(French Standard Time)
Subtract 1 hour for UT
For French Summer Time add ONE hour in **non-shaded areas**

GIBRALTAR

LAT 36°08'N LONG 5°21'W

TIMES AND HEIGHTS OF HIGH AND LOW WATERS

SPRING & NEAP TIDES
Dates in red are SPRINGS
Dates in blue are NEAPS

YEAR **2002**

JANUARY

Day	Time	m	Time	m	Time	m	Time	m
1 TU	0419	1.0	0953	0.1	1636	1.0	2218	0.1
2 W	0504	1.0	1040	0.1	1723	1.0	2303	0.1
3 TH	0552	1.0	1130	0.2	1812	0.9	2352	0.1
4 F	0643	0.9	1226	0.2	1905	0.9		
5 SA	0047	0.2	0740	0.9	1331	0.2	2004	0.8
6 SU	0152	0.2	0843	0.9	1443	0.2	2109	0.8
7 M	0306	0.3	0951	0.8	1558	0.2	2223	0.7
8 TU	0425	0.3	1102	0.8	1712	0.2	2338	0.8
9 W	0536	0.2	1206	0.8	1814	0.2		
10 TH	0041	0.8	0630	0.2	1301	0.9	1904	0.1
11 F	0134	0.8	0716	0.2	1349	0.9	1948	0.1
12 SA	0220	0.8	0758	0.1	1435	0.9	2029	0.1
13 SU	0303	0.9	0837	0.1	1518	0.9	● 2107	0.1
14 M	0343	0.9	0915	0.1	1558	0.9	2143	0.1
15 TU	0420	0.9	0952	0.1	1637	0.9	2218	0.1
16 W	0454	0.9	1027	0.1	1713	0.8	2251	0.1
17 TH	0528	0.8	1103	0.2	1748	0.8	2324	0.1
18 F	0602	0.8	1138	0.2	1824	0.8	2358	0.2
19 SA	0639	0.8	1217	0.2	1903	0.7		
20 SU	0036	0.2	0720	0.7	1302	0.3	1946	0.7
21 M	0122	0.3	0808	0.7	1357	0.3	2037	0.6
22 TU	0223	0.3	0904	0.7	1505	0.3	2139	0.6
23 W	0343	0.3	1009	0.7	1627	0.3	2256	0.6
24 TH	0503	0.3	1119	0.7	1739	0.2		
25 F	0007	0.7	0602	0.2	1221	0.8	1832	0.2
26 SA	0104	0.8	0649	0.2	1315	0.8	1918	0.1
27 SU	0153	0.8	0733	0.1	1405	0.9	2002	0.1
28 M	0240	0.9	0817	0.1	1454	0.9	○ 2046	0.0
29 TU	0326	1.0	0903	0.0	1542	1.0	2130	0.0
30 W	0410	1.0	0948	0.0	1628	1.0	2213	0.0
31 TH	0454	1.0	1034	0.0	1714	1.0	2255	0.0

FEBRUARY

Day	Time	m	Time	m	Time	m	Time	m
1 F	0539	1.0	1121	0.0	1801	1.0	2338	0.0
2 SA	0627	1.0	1209	0.1	1850	0.9		
3 SU	0024	0.1	0718	0.9	1303	0.1	1943	0.8
4 M	0117	0.2	0815	0.8	1405	0.2	2041	0.8
5 TU	0220	0.2	0918	0.8	1520	0.2	2150	0.7
6 W	0345	0.3	1033	0.7	1653	0.2	2314	0.7
7 TH	0522	0.3	1150	0.7	1810	0.2		
8 F	0032	0.7	0627	0.2	1255	0.8	1902	0.2
9 SA	0131	0.7	0714	0.2	1346	0.8	1944	0.1
10 SU	0218	0.8	0754	0.1	1431	0.8	2022	0.1
11 M	0257	0.8	0830	0.1	1511	0.8	2057	0.1
12 TU	0332	0.8	0905	0.1	1547	0.9	● 2130	0.0
13 W	0404	0.9	0939	0.1	1621	0.9	2201	0.0
14 TH	0434	0.9	1010	0.1	1652	0.9	2231	0.1
15 F	0503	0.9	1041	0.1	1723	0.8	2259	0.1
16 SA	0532	0.8	1111	0.1	1754	0.8	2327	0.1
17 SU	0602	0.8	1141	0.1	1826	0.8	2356	0.2
18 M	0638	0.8	1215	0.2	1905	0.7		
19 TU	0029	0.2	0720	0.7	1257	0.2	1951	0.7
20 W	0113	0.3	0812	0.7	1356	0.3	2050	0.6
21 TH	0223	0.3	0917	0.7	1527	0.3	2206	0.6
22 F	0418	0.3	1039	0.7	1716	0.2	2336	0.6
23 SA	0544	0.3	1159	0.7	1821	0.2		
24 SU	0045	0.7	0638	0.2	1301	0.8	1909	0.1
25 M	0139	0.8	0725	0.1	1354	0.9	1953	0.0
26 TU	0226	0.9	0809	0.0	1443	0.9	2036	0.0
27 W	0311	1.0	0854	0.0	1530	1.0	○ 2118	-0.1
28 TH	0355	1.0	0938	-0.1	1615	1.0	2159	-0.1

MARCH

Day	Time	m	Time	m	Time	m	Time	m
1 F	0438	1.0	1022	-0.1	1700	1.0	2239	-0.1
2 SA	0522	1.0	1104	0.0	1745	1.0	2318	0.0
3 SU	0606	1.0	1147	0.0	1831	0.9	2359	0.1
4 M	0654	0.9	1234	0.1	1921	0.8		
5 TU	0044	0.2	0747	0.8	1329	0.2	2016	0.8
6 W	0140	0.2	0848	0.7	1442	0.3	2121	0.7
7 TH	0306	0.3	1005	0.7	1634	0.3	2248	0.7
8 F	0513	0.3	1137	0.7	1801	0.3		
9 SA	0020	0.7	0624	0.3	1248	0.7	1851	0.2
10 SU	0120	0.7	0707	0.2	1338	0.8	1929	0.2
11 M	0203	0.8	0742	0.2	1419	0.8	2003	0.1
12 TU	0238	0.8	0814	0.1	1454	0.8	2036	0.1
13 W	0310	0.9	0846	0.1	1527	0.9	2107	0.1
14 TH	0338	0.9	0917	0.1	1557	0.9	● 2136	0.1
15 F	0406	0.9	0947	0.1	1627	0.9	2204	0.1
16 SA	0433	0.9	1015	0.1	1656	0.9	2231	0.1
17 SU	0501	0.9	1043	0.1	1725	0.8	2258	0.1
18 M	0531	0.8	1111	0.1	1757	0.8	2325	0.2
19 TU	0605	0.8	1142	0.2	1835	0.8	2357	0.2
20 W	0645	0.8	1219	0.2	1922	0.7		
21 TH	0037	0.3	0736	0.7	1312	0.3	2020	0.7
22 F	0141	0.3	0842	0.7	1446	0.3	2135	0.6
23 SA	0346	0.3	1008	0.7	1655	0.3	2309	0.7
24 SU	0527	0.3	1139	0.7	1804	0.2		
25 M	0024	0.7	0624	0.2	1246	0.8	1852	0.1
26 TU	0119	0.8	0711	0.1	1338	0.9	1935	0.0
27 W	0206	0.9	0755	0.0	1426	0.9	2016	0.0
28 TH	0251	1.0	0839	-0.1	1512	1.0	○ 2057	0.0
29 F	0334	1.0	0921	-0.1	1557	1.0	2137	-0.1
30 SA	0417	1.1	1003	-0.1	1641	1.0	2216	0.0
31 SU	0500	1.0	1043	0.0	1725	1.0	2254	0.0

APRIL

Day	Time	m	Time	m	Time	m	Time	m
1 M	0543	1.0	1124	0.0	1810	0.9	2333	0.1
2 TU	0629	0.9	1206	0.1	1859	0.8		
3 W	0016	0.2	0721	0.8	1256	0.2	1953	0.8
4 TH	0108	0.3	0821	0.7	1405	0.3	2056	0.7
5 F	0231	0.3	0936	0.7	1556	0.3	2217	0.7
6 SA	0448	0.4	1111	0.7	1729	0.3	2348	0.7
7 SU	0602	0.3	1225	0.7	1820	0.3		
8 M	0048	0.7	0642	0.2	1314	0.8	1857	0.2
9 TU	0130	0.8	0715	0.2	1352	0.8	1931	0.2
10 W	0204	0.8	0747	0.1	1426	0.8	2003	0.1
11 TH	0234	0.9	0818	0.1	1457	0.9	2034	0.1
12 F	0304	0.9	0848	0.1	1528	0.9	● 2104	0.1
13 SA	0333	0.9	0918	0.1	1558	0.9	2133	0.1
14 SU	0402	0.9	0948	0.1	1629	0.9	2202	0.1
15 M	0433	0.9	1017	0.1	1700	0.9	2231	0.1
16 TU	0505	0.9	1046	0.1	1735	0.8	2301	0.2
17 W	0540	0.8	1119	0.2	1815	0.8	2336	0.2
18 TH	0622	0.8	1157	0.2	1903	0.8		
19 F	0020	0.3	0715	0.7	1252	0.3	2003	0.7
20 SA	0130	0.3	0822	0.7	1429	0.3	2116	0.7
21 SU	0324	0.3	0946	0.7	1624	0.3	2242	0.7
22 M	0500	0.3	1116	0.7	1734	0.2	2356	0.8
23 TU	0601	0.2	1223	0.8	1824	0.1		
24 W	0051	0.9	0649	0.1	1316	0.9	1908	0.1
25 TH	0139	0.9	0734	0.0	1403	0.9	1949	0.0
26 F	0224	1.0	0817	0.0	1449	1.0	2030	0.0
27 SA	0309	1.0	0900	-0.1	1534	1.0	○ 2111	0.0
28 SU	0352	1.0	0941	0.0	1619	1.0	2151	0.0
29 M	0436	1.0	1021	0.0	1703	1.0	2230	0.1
30 TU	0520	0.9	1101	0.1	1749	0.9	2310	0.1

21

Chart Datum: 0·25 metres below Alicante Datum (Mean Sea Level, Alicante)

TIME ZONE -0100
(French Standard Time)
Subtract 1 hour for UT
For French Summer Time add ONE hour in **non-shaded areas**

GIBRALTAR

LAT 36°08′N LONG 5°21′W

TIMES AND HEIGHTS OF HIGH AND LOW WATERS

SPRING & NEAP TIDES
Dates in red are **SPRINGS**
Dates in blue are **NEAPS**

YEAR **20**

MAY

Day	Time	m	Day	Time	m
1 W	0606 1142 1837 2352	0.9 0.1 0.8 0.2	16 TH	0524 1104 1800 2324	0.9 0.2 0.8 0.2
2 TH	0657 1229 1931	0.8 0.2 0.8	17 F	0609 1148 1850	0.8 0.2 0.8
3 F	0044 0755 1334 2030	0.3 0.7 0.3 0.7	18 SA	0015 0702 1247 1949	0.3 0.8 0.3 0.8
4 SA	0159 0903 1503 2138	0.3 0.7 0.3 0.7	19 SU	0127 0808 1412 2057	0.3 0.7 0.3 0.8
5 SU	0342 1024 1630 2254	0.4 0.7 0.3 0.7	20 M	0258 0924 1542 2212	0.3 0.7 0.3 0.8
6 M	0510 1140 1730 2357	0.3 0.7 0.3 0.7	21 TU	0423 1045 1654 2323	0.3 0.7 0.2 0.8
7 TU	0600 1232 1813	0.3 0.7 0.3	22 W	0530 1154 1750	0.2 0.8 0.2
8 W	0042 0637 1313 1850	0.8 0.2 0.8 0.2	23 TH	0020 0623 1250 1837	0.9 0.1 0.9 0.1
9 TH	0119 0711 1349 1924	0.8 0.2 0.8 0.2	24 F	0110 0710 1339 1921	0.9 0.1 0.9 0.1
10 F	0152 0744 1422 1957	0.9 0.2 0.9 0.2	25 SA	0157 0755 1425 2004	1.0 0.0 0.9 0.1
11 SA	0225 0816 1455 2029	0.9 0.1 0.9 0.2	26 SU	0243 0839 1512 ○ 2047	1.0 0.0 0.9 0.1
12 SU	0258 0849 1529 ● 2101	0.9 0.1 0.9 0.2	27 M	0329 0921 1558 2128	1.0 0.0 0.9 0.1
13 M	0332 0921 1603 2134	0.9 0.1 0.9 0.2	28 TU	0414 1002 1643 2210	1.0 0.0 0.9 0.1
14 TU	0407 0953 1639 2207	0.9 0.1 0.9 0.2	29 W	0459 1042 1729 2251	0.9 0.1 0.9 0.2
15 W	0444 1027 1717 2243	0.9 0.1 0.9 0.2	30 TH	0545 1123 1816 2334	0.9 0.1 0.8 0.2
			31 F	0635 1207 1906	0.8 0.2 0.8

JUNE

Day	Time	m	Day	Time	m
1 SA	0023 0728 1302 1959	0.3 0.7 0.3 0.8	16 SU	0010 0652 1237 1932	0.2 0.8 0.2 0.9
2 SU	0124 0826 1409 2054	0.3 0.7 0.3 0.7	17 M	0115 0753 1345 2033	0.3 0.8 0.2 0.8
3 M	0237 0928 1520 2152	0.3 0.7 0.3 0.7	18 TU	0228 0859 1458 2139	0.3 0.8 0.2 0.8
4 TU	0352 1036 1625 2252	0.3 0.7 0.3 0.7	19 W	0342 1012 1610 2247	0.2 0.8 0.2 0.9
5 W	0459 1138 1720 2344	0.3 0.7 0.3 0.8	20 TH	0456 1124 1716 2350	0.2 0.8 0.2 0.9
6 TH	0551 1227 1806	0.3 0.7 0.3	21 F	0559 1225 1812	0.2 0.8 0.2
7 F	0028 0632 1308 1844	0.8 0.2 0.8 0.2	22 SA	0044 0652 1318 1901	0.9 0.1 0.9 0.2
8 SA	0108 0709 1346 1921	0.8 0.2 0.8 0.2	23 SU	0135 0739 1407 1946	0.9 0.1 0.9 0.1
9 SU	0146 0745 1423 1956	0.9 0.2 0.9 0.2	24 M	0223 0824 1456 ○ 2030	0.9 0.1 0.9 0.1
10 M	0225 0821 1501 2033	0.9 0.1 0.9 0.2	25 TU	0311 0907 1542 2113	0.9 0.1 0.9 0.1
11 TU	0305 0857 1540 ● 2111	0.9 0.1 0.9 0.2	26 W	0357 0947 1626 2155	0.9 0.1 0.9 0.1
12 W	0347 0935 1620 2150	0.9 0.1 0.9 0.2	27 TH	0442 1026 1709 2235	0.9 0.1 0.9 0.2
13 TH	0429 1014 1702 2232	0.9 0.1 0.9 0.2	28 F	0525 1104 1751 2315	0.9 0.1 0.9 0.2
14 F	0512 1055 1747 2318	0.9 0.2 0.9 0.2	29 SA	0609 1143 1834 2358	0.8 0.2 0.8 0.2
15 SA	0559 1141 1837	0.9 0.2 0.9	30 SU	0655 1225 1918	0.8 0.2 0.8

JULY

Day	Time	m	Day	Time	m
1 M	0044 0742 1314 2003	0.3 0.7 0.3 0.8	16 TU	0053 0733 1313 2006	0.2 0.9 0.2 0.9
2 TU	0138 0832 1410 2050	0.3 0.7 0.3 0.7	17 W	0156 0834 1417 2107	0.2 0.8 0.2 0.9
3 W	0237 0927 1512 2142	0.3 0.7 0.3 0.7	18 TH	0305 0942 1529 2214	0.2 0.8 0.3 0.8
4 TH	0343 1030 1618 2239	0.3 0.7 0.3 0.7	19 F	0425 1056 1648 2324	0.2 0.8 0.3 0.8
5 F	0452 1133 1719 2335	0.3 0.7 0.3 0.8	20 SA	0543 1207 1757	0.2 0.8 0.3
6 SA	0552 1226 1809	0.3 0.7 0.3	21 SU	0027 0642 1307 1851	0.9 0.2 0.8 0.2
7 SU	0026 0638 1313 1851	0.8 0.2 0.8 0.3	22 M	0123 0731 1359 1938	0.9 0.1 0.9 0.2
8 M	0113 0719 1356 1931	0.9 0.2 0.8 0.2	23 TU	0213 0814 1446 2021	0.9 0.1 0.9 0.2
9 TU	0159 0759 1439 2012	0.9 0.2 0.9 0.2	24 W	0300 0854 1530 ○ 2101	0.9 0.1 0.9 0.1
10 W	0245 0839 1522 ● 2054	0.9 0.1 0.9 0.2	25 TH	0344 0931 1609 2140	0.9 0.1 0.9 0.1
11 TH	0331 0920 1604 2138	1.0 0.1 1.0 0.1	26 F	0424 1006 1646 2216	0.9 0.1 0.9 0.1
12 F	0416 1002 1648 2222	1.0 0.1 1.0 0.1	27 SA	0502 1039 1721 2252	0.9 0.1 0.9 0.2
13 SA	0501 1044 1732 2309	1.0 0.1 1.0 0.1	28 SU	0538 1112 1755 2327	0.9 0.2 0.9 0.2
14 SU	0548 1129 1819 2358	1.0 0.1 1.0 0.2	29 M	0615 1145 1829	0.8 0.2 0.8
15 M	0638 1217 1910	0.9 0.2 0.9	30 TU	0003 0652 1222 1906	0.2 0.8 0.2 0.8
			31 W	0042 0735 1302 1947	0.3 0.7 0.3 0.8

AUGUST

Day	Time	m	Day	Time	m
1 TH	0128 0823 1354 2035	0.3 0.7 0.3 0.8	16 F	0230 0914 1452 2143	0. 0. 0. 0.
2 F	0226 0921 1503 2132	0.3 0.7 0.4 0.7	17 SA	0400 1033 1630 2305	0. 0. 0. 0.
3 SA	0344 1032 1628 2240	0.3 0.7 0.4 0.7	18 SU	0536 1157 1753	0. 0. 0.
4 SU	0512 1146 1738 2349	0.3 0.7 0.3 0.8	19 M	0021 0637 1303 1847	0. 0. 0. 0.
5 M	0614 1244 1830	0.3 0.8 0.3	20 TU	0120 0722 1353 1930	0. 0. 0. 0.
6 TU	0048 0659 1334 1914	0.8 0.2 0.9 0.2	21 W	0208 0800 1435 2008	0. 0. 0. 0.
7 W	0140 0741 1419 1957	0.9 0.1 0.9 0.2	22 TH	0249 0835 1512 ○ 2044	0. 0. 0. 0.
8 TH	0229 0822 1504 ● 2040	1.0 0.1 1.0 0.1	23 F	0326 0908 1546 2118	0. 0. 1. 0.
9 F	0316 0904 1547 2125	1.0 0.1 1.1 0.1	24 SA	0401 0939 1616 2151	0. 0. 1. 0.
10 SA	0402 0946 1630 2209	1.0 0.1 1.1 0.1	25 SU	0433 1009 1645 2222	0. 0. 1. 0.
11 SU	0447 1027 1713 2253	1.1 0.1 1.1 0.1	26 M	0503 1038 1714 2253	0. 0. 0. 0.
12 M	0532 1109 1757 2339	1.0 0.1 1.1 0.1	27 TU	0533 1107 1742 2323	0. 0. 0. 0
13 TU	0619 1152 1845	1.0 0.1 1.0	28 W	0605 1136 1814 2355	0. 0. 0. 0.
14 W	0027 0711 1241 1937	0.2 0.9 0.2 1.0	29 TH	0641 1209 1852	0. 0. 0.
15 TH	0123 0808 1338 2035	0.2 0.9 0.3 0.9	30 F	0032 0727 1249 1939	0. 0. 0. 0.
			31 SA	0122 0826 1353 2038	0. 0. 0. 0.

Chart Datum: 0·25 metres below Alicante Datum (Mean Sea Level, Alicante)

Register for your **FREE** weekly weather email service from Macmillan Reeds
at **www.nauticaldata.com – NOW!**
weekend weather reports sent to your email address, every Thursday

TIME ZONE -0100
(French Standard Time)
Subtract 1 hour for UT
For French Summer Time add ONE hour in **non-shaded areas**

GIBRALTAR

LAT 36°08'N LONG 5°21'W

TIMES AND HEIGHTS OF HIGH AND LOW WATERS

SPRING & NEAP TIDES
Dates in red are **SPRINGS**
Dates in blue are **NEAPS**

YEAR **2002**

SEPTEMBER

Date	Time	m	Date	Time	m
1 SU	0241	0.4	**16** M	0527	0.4
	0940	0.7		1148	0.8
	1541	0.4		1748	0.4
	2153	0.7			
2 M	0441	0.4	**17** TU	0018	0.8
	1109	0.7		0624	0.3
	1715	0.4		1252	0.9
	2320	0.8		1836	0.3
3 TU	0555	0.3	**18** W	0113	0.9
	1220	0.8		0703	0.3
	1812	0.3		1336	0.9
				1913	0.3
4 W	0029	0.8	**19** TH	0154	0.9
	0642	0.2		0737	0.2
	1313	0.9		1412	1.0
	1857	0.2		1946	0.2
5 TH	0124	0.9	**20** F	0229	0.9
	0723	0.1		0808	0.2
	1359	1.0		1444	1.0
	1940	0.1		2018	0.2
6 F	0212	1.0	**21** SA	0301	1.0
	0803	0.1		0838	0.2
	1443	1.1		1514	1.0
	2023	0.1		○ 2050	0.2
7 SA	0259	1.1	**22** SU	0331	1.0
	0844	0.1		0907	0.1
	1526	1.1		1542	1.0
	● 2107	0.0		2121	0.1
8 SU	0343	1.1	**23** M	0400	1.0
	0924	0.0		0936	0.2
	1608	1.2		1609	1.0
	2150	0.0		2151	0.1
9 M	0427	1.1	**24** TU	0428	1.0
	1005	0.0		1005	0.2
	1650	1.2		1636	1.0
	2232	0.0		2219	0.2
10 TU	0511	1.1	**25** W	0456	1.0
	1045	0.1		1032	0.2
	1733	1.1		1704	1.0
	2315	0.1		2248	0.2
11 W	0557	1.0	**26** TH	0526	0.9
	1125	0.2		1100	0.3
	1819	1.1		1735	0.9
	2359	0.2		2317	0.2
12 TH	0646	1.0	**27** F	0602	0.9
	1209	0.2		1131	0.3
	1909	1.0		1812	0.9
				2351	0.3
13 F	0049	0.3	**28** SA	0648	0.8
	0742	0.9		1208	0.4
	1303	0.3		1859	0.8
	2006	0.9			
14 SA	0155	0.3	**29** SU	0035	0.4
	0848	0.8		0747	0.8
	1420	0.4		1307	0.4
	2117	0.8		2001	0.8
15 SU	0339	0.4	**30** M	0156	0.4
	1013	0.8		0903	0.7
	1619	0.4		1509	0.5
	2253	0.8		2119	0.8

OCTOBER

Date	Time	m	Date	Time	m
1 TU	0418	0.4	**16** W	0554	0.4
	1035	0.8		1223	0.9
	1652	0.4		1810	0.4
	2255	0.8			
2 W	0533	0.3	**17** TH	0050	0.9
	1154	0.8		0632	0.3
	1751	0.3		1305	0.9
				1844	0.3
3 TH	0011	0.9	**18** F	0128	0.9
	0620	0.2		0704	0.3
	1249	0.9		1339	1.0
	1837	0.2		1916	0.2
4 F	0106	1.0	**19** SA	0200	0.9
	0701	0.2		0735	0.2
	1334	1.0		1409	1.0
	1920	0.1		1947	0.2
5 SA	0152	1.0	**20** SU	0230	1.0
	0740	0.1		0805	0.2
	1418	1.1		1437	1.0
	2002	0.1		2019	0.2
6 SU	0237	1.1	**21** M	0259	1.0
	0819	0.1		0835	0.2
	1501	1.2		1506	1.0
	● 2045	0.0		○ 2050	0.2
7 M	0321	1.1	**22** TU	0328	1.0
	0859	0.1		0905	0.2
	1543	1.2		1535	1.0
	2127	0.0		2120	0.2
8 TU	0405	1.1	**23** W	0357	1.0
	0939	0.1		0934	0.2
	1626	1.2		1605	1.0
	2208	0.0		2150	0.2
9 W	0448	1.1	**24** TH	0427	1.0
	1019	0.1		1003	0.2
	1709	1.1		1636	1.0
	2249	0.1		2219	0.2
10 TH	0533	1.0	**25** F	0459	1.0
	1059	0.2		1033	0.3
	1753	1.0		1709	0.9
	2331	0.2		2250	0.2
11 F	0621	1.0	**26** SA	0537	0.9
	1141	0.3		1106	0.3
	1843	0.9		1748	0.9
				2324	0.3
12 SA	0017	0.3	**27** SU	0623	0.9
	0716	0.9		1146	0.4
	1233	0.4		1836	0.8
	1940	0.9			
13 SU	0121	0.4	**28** M	0009	0.4
	0823	0.8		0722	0.8
	1352	0.5		1249	0.4
	2054	0.8		1938	0.8
14 M	0310	0.4	**29** TU	0130	0.4
	0946	0.8		0836	0.8
	1556	0.5		1445	0.4
	2232	0.8		2055	0.8
15 TU	0458	0.4	**30** W	0344	0.4
	1120	0.8		1002	0.8
	1723	0.4		1621	0.4
	2359	0.8		2227	0.8
			31 TH	0501	0.3
				1122	0.9
				1724	0.3
				2346	0.9

NOVEMBER

Date	Time	m	Date	Time	m
1 F	0552	0.2	**16** SA	0053	0.9
	1219	0.9		0628	0.3
	1813	0.2		1258	0.9
				1844	0.2
2 SA	0042	0.9	**17** SU	0128	0.9
	0634	0.2		0702	0.2
	1307	1.0		1331	0.9
	1856	0.1		1917	0.2
3 SU	0129	1.0	**18** M	0159	0.9
	0714	0.1		0734	0.2
	1351	1.1		1402	1.0
	1939	0.1		1950	0.2
4 M	0214	1.1	**19** TU	0230	1.0
	0754	0.1		0806	0.2
	1434	1.1		1434	1.0
	● 2022	0.0		2023	0.2
5 TU	0258	1.1	**20** W	0301	1.0
	0834	0.1		0838	0.2
	1518	1.1		1507	1.0
	2104	0.0		○ 2055	0.2
6 W	0342	1.1	**21** TH	0333	1.0
	0915	0.1		0909	0.2
	1602	1.1		1541	1.0
	2146	0.1		2127	0.2
7 TH	0426	1.1	**22** F	0407	1.0
	0956	0.1		0942	0.2
	1646	1.1		1617	1.0
	2227	0.1		2200	0.2
8 F	0511	1.0	**23** SA	0443	0.9
	1037	0.2		1016	0.3
	1732	1.0		1655	0.9
	2308	0.2		2234	0.2
9 SA	0559	0.9	**24** SU	0523	0.9
	1121	0.3		1053	0.3
	1822	0.9		1736	0.9
	2354	0.3		2312	0.3
10 SU	0653	0.9	**25** M	0609	0.9
	1213	0.4		1139	0.3
	1920	0.8		1825	0.8
11 M	0054	0.4	**26** TU	0001	0.3
	0756	0.8		0705	0.8
	1328	0.4		1244	0.4
	2027	0.8		1924	0.8
12 TU	0225	0.4	**27** W	0114	0.3
	0909	0.8		0812	0.8
	1508	0.4		1416	0.4
	2148	0.7		2033	0.8
13 W	0400	0.4	**28** TH	0255	0.3
	1029	0.8		0927	0.8
	1633	0.4		1542	0.3
	2313	0.8		2153	0.8
14 TH	0506	0.4	**29** F	0416	0.3
	1135	0.8		1043	0.9
	1728	0.4		1650	0.3
				2312	0.8
15 F	0012	0.8	**30** SA	0517	0.2
	0551	0.3		1147	0.9
	1222	0.9		1746	0.2
	1808	0.3			

DECEMBER

Date	Time	m	Date	Time	m
1 SU	0014	0.9	**16** M	0053	0.8
	0607	0.2		0632	0.3
	1239	1.0		1255	0.9
	1834	0.1		1851	0.2
2 M	0106	0.9	**17** TU	0131	0.8
	0651	0.1		0709	0.2
	1326	1.0		1332	0.9
	1920	0.1		1928	0.2
3 TU	0153	1.0	**18** W	0206	0.9
	0733	0.1		0743	0.2
	1412	1.0		1409	0.9
	2005	0.0		2003	0.2
4 W	0239	1.0	**19** TH	0241	0.9
	0816	0.1		0817	0.2
	1458	1.0		1447	0.9
	● 2048	0.0		○ 2038	0.1
5 TH	0325	1.0	**20** F	0318	0.9
	0858	0.1		0852	0.2
	1544	1.0		1527	0.9
	2131	0.1		2114	0.1
6 F	0411	1.0	**21** SA	0355	0.9
	0941	0.1		0929	0.2
	1631	1.0		1607	0.9
	2213	0.1		2151	0.1
7 SA	0456	0.9	**22** SU	0434	0.9
	1024	0.2		1008	0.2
	1717	0.9		1648	0.9
	2255	0.2		2229	0.2
8 SU	0543	0.9	**23** M	0515	0.9
	1109	0.2		1050	0.2
	1806	0.9		1731	0.9
	2339	0.2		2309	0.2
9 M	0633	0.9	**24** TU	0600	0.9
	1159	0.3		1137	0.2
	1858	0.8		1818	0.9
				2356	0.2
10 TU	0030	0.3	**25** W	0651	0.9
	0727	0.8		1235	0.3
	1300	0.3		1911	0.8
	1955	0.8			
11 W	0136	0.3	**26** TH	0054	0.2
	0826	0.8		0749	0.8
	1413	0.4		1345	0.3
	2057	0.7		2011	0.8
12 TH	0250	0.4	**27** F	0207	0.3
	0928	0.8		0854	0.8
	1527	0.4		1500	0.3
	2205	0.7		2120	0.8
13 F	0402	0.3	**28** SA	0325	0.3
	1031	0.8		1005	0.8
	1633	0.3		1614	0.2
	2314	0.7		2236	0.8
14 SA	0503	0.3	**29** SU	0440	0.2
	1128	0.8		1115	0.9
	1728	0.3		1723	0.2
				2348	0.8
15 SU	0010	0.8	**30** M	0544	0.2
	0551	0.3		1215	0.9
	1215	0.8		1821	0.1
	1812	0.3			
			31 TU	0048	0.8
				0637	0.2
				1309	0.9
				1912	0.1

Chart Datum: 0·25 metres below Alicante Datum (Mean Sea Level, Alicante)

Register for your **FREE** weekly weather email service from Macmillan Reeds
at **www.nauticaldata.com – NOW!**
weekend weather reports sent to your email address, every Thursday

Fig. 9 (10)

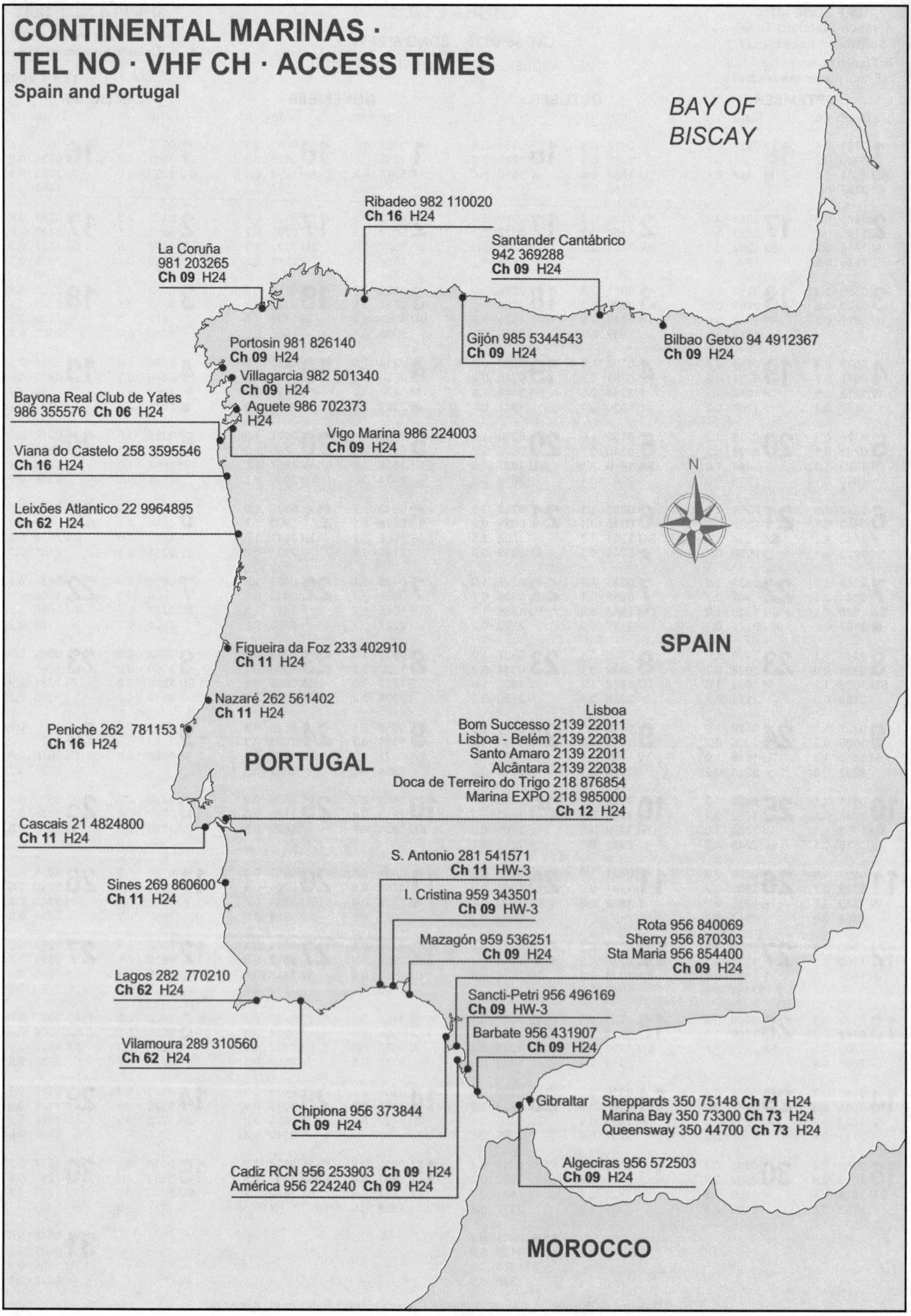
CONTINENTAL MARINAS · TEL NO · VHF CH · ACCESS TIMES
Spain and Portugal
BAY OF BISCAY
Ribadeo 982 110020 Ch 16 H24
Santander Cantábrico 942 369288 Ch 09 H24
La Coruña 981 203265 Ch 09 H24
Gijón 985 5344543 Ch 09 H24
Bilbao Getxo 94 4912367 Ch 09 H24
Portosin 981 826140 Ch 09 H24
Villagarcia 982 501340 Ch 09 H24
Bayona Real Club de Yates 986 355576 Ch 06 H24
Aguete 986 702373 H24
Vigo Marina 986 224003 Ch 09 H24
Viana do Castelo 258 3595546 Ch 16 H24
Leixões Atlantico 22 9964895 Ch 62 H24
N
SPAIN
Figueira da Foz 233 402910 Ch 11 H24
Nazaré 262 561402 Ch 11 H24
Peniche 262 781153 Ch 16 H24
PORTUGAL
Lisboa
Bom Successo 2139 22011
Lisboa - Belém 2139 22038
Santo Amaro 2139 22011
Alcântara 2139 22038
Doca de Terreiro do Trigo 218 876854
Marina EXPO 218 985000
Ch 12 H24
Cascais 21 4824800 Ch 11 H24
S. Antonio 281 541571 Ch 11 HW-3
Sines 269 860600 Ch 11 H24
I. Cristina 959 343501 Ch 09 HW-3
Rota 956 840069
Sherry 956 870303
Sta Maria 956 854400
Ch 09 H24
Mazagón 959 536251 Ch 09 H24
Lagos 282 770210 Ch 62 H24
Sancti-Petri 956 496169 Ch 09 HW-3
Barbate 956 431907 Ch 09 H24
Vilamoura 289 310560 Ch 62 H24
Gibraltar
Sheppards 350 75148 Ch 71 H24
Marina Bay 350 73300 Ch 73 H24
Queensway 350 44700 Ch 73 H24
Chipiona 956 373844 Ch 09 H24
Algeciras 956 572503 Ch 09 H24
Cadiz RCN 956 253903 Ch 09 H24
América 956 224240 Ch 09 H24
MOROCCO

MAPTECH®
Leading the world in digital navigation
Maptech UK Ltd • +44 (0)1243 389352 • sales@maptech.co.uk

Maptech world class digital chart CDs
Worldwide coverage from over 4,500 charts

Maptech award winning software
Easy to use navigation software
• Chart Navigator • Cruising Navigator • Offshore Navigator

www.maptech.co.uk

Area 22

North-East France
Barfleur to Dunkerque

9.22.1 Index .... Page 923

9.22.2 Area map 924

9.22.3 Tidal stream charts 926

9.22.4 Lights, buoys & waypoints 928

9.22.5 Passage information 932

9.22.6 Distance table 933

9.22.7 Special notes for France See *9.15.7*

9.22.8 Barfleur 934

9.22.9 St Vaast-la-Hougue 934

9.22.10 Carentan and Isigny 935
Iles St Marcouf

9.22.11 Grandcamp-Maisy 936

9.22.12 Port-en-Bessin 936
Arromanches

9.22.13 Courseulles-sur-Mer 937

9.22.14 Ouistreham 938
Caen

9.22.15 Dives-sur-Mer 939

9.22.16 Deauville and Trouville 940

9.22.17 Honfleur 941

9.22.18 River Seine 942
Rouen

9.22.19 Routes to the Mediterranean 942

9.22.20 Le Havre, Standard Port, tidal curves 943

9.22.21 Fécamp 947

9.22.22 St Valéry-en-Caux 947

9.22.23 Dieppe, Standard Port, tidal curves 948

9.22.24 Le Tréport 949

9.22.25 St Valéry-sur-Somme/Le Crotoy 953

9.22.26 Le Touquet and Etaples 953

9.22.27 Boulogne 954

9.22.28 Calais 955
Gravelines

9.22.29 Dunkerque (Port Est), Standard Port, tidal curves 956

Register for your **FREE** weekly weather email service from Macmillan Reeds
›› at **www.nauticaldata.com – NOW!** ‹‹
weekend weather reports sent to your email address, every Thursday

9.22.2

North-East France

Barfleur to Dunkerque

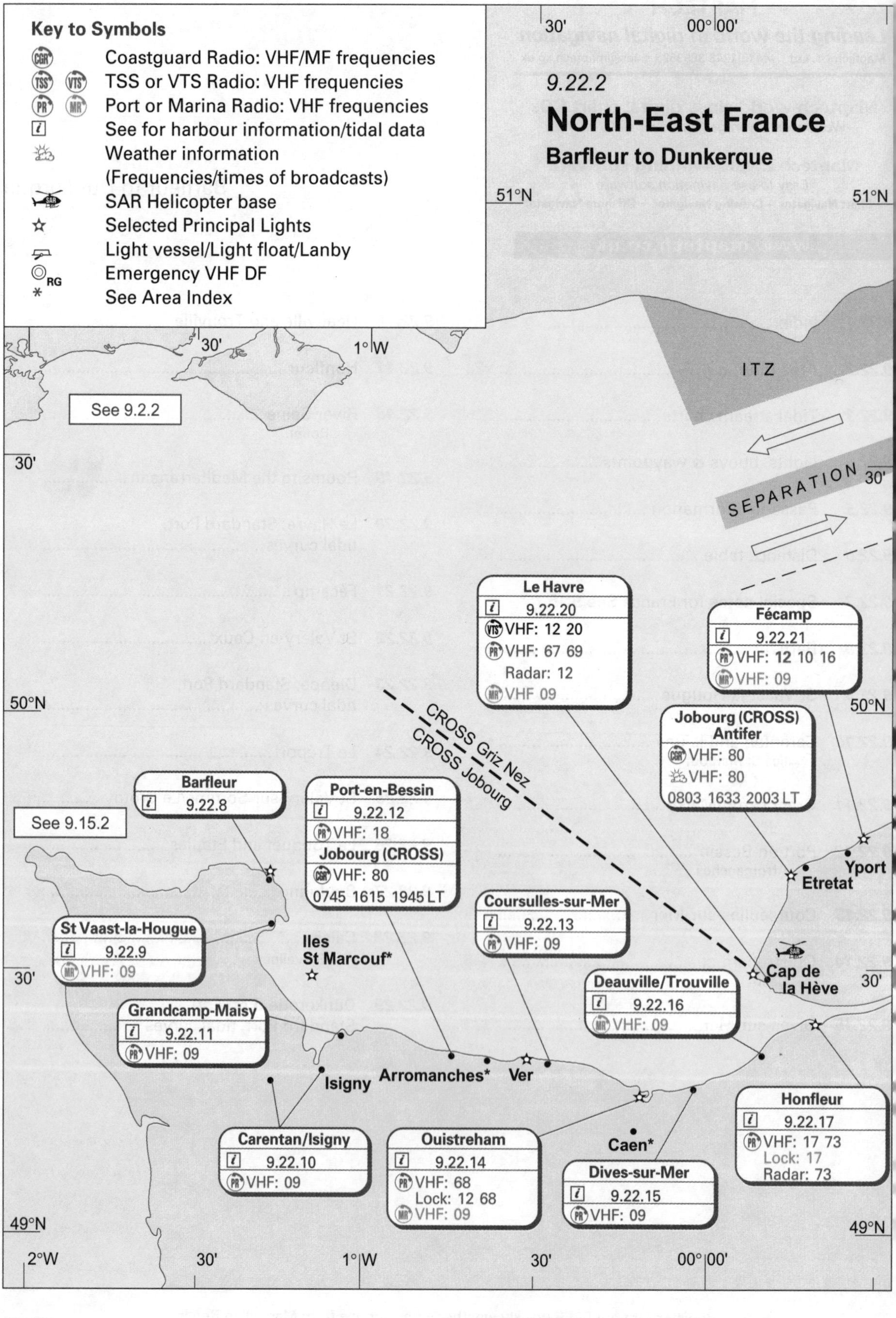

Key to Symbols
Coastguard Radio: VHF/MF frequencies
TSS or VTS Radio: VHF frequencies
Port or Marina Radio: VHF frequencies
See for harbour information/tidal data
Weather information
(Frequencies/times of broadcasts)
SAR Helicopter base
Selected Principal Lights
Light vessel/Light float/Lanby
Emergency VHF DF
See Area Index
30'
00° 00'
51°N
51°N
30'
1° W
See 9.2.2
30'
ITZ
SEPARATION
30'
Le Havre
9.22.20
VHF: 12 20
VHF: 67 69
Radar: 12
VHF 09
Fécamp
9.22.21
VHF: 12 10 16
VHF: 09
50°N
50°N
Jobourg (CROSS) Antifer
VHF: 80
VHF: 80
0803 1633 2003 LT
CROSS Griz Nez
CROSS Jobourg
Barfleur
9.22.8
See 9.15.2
Port-en-Bessin
9.22.12
VHF: 18
Jobourg (CROSS)
VHF: 80
0745 1615 1945 LT
Yport
Etretat
Coursulles-sur-Mer
9.22.13
VHF: 09
St Vaast-la-Hougue
9.22.9
VHF: 09
Iles St Marcouf*
Cap de la Hève
30'
30'
Deauville/Trouville
9.22.16
VHF: 09
Grandcamp-Maisy
9.22.11
VHF: 09
Isigny
Arromanches*
Ver
Honfleur
9.22.17
VHF: 17 73
Lock: 17
Radar: 73
Caen*
Carentan/Isigny
9.22.10
VHF: 09
Ouistreham
9.22.14
VHF: 68
Lock: 12 68
VHF: 09
Dives-sur-Mer
9.22.15
VHF: 09
49°N
49°N
2°W
30'
1° W
30'
00° 00'

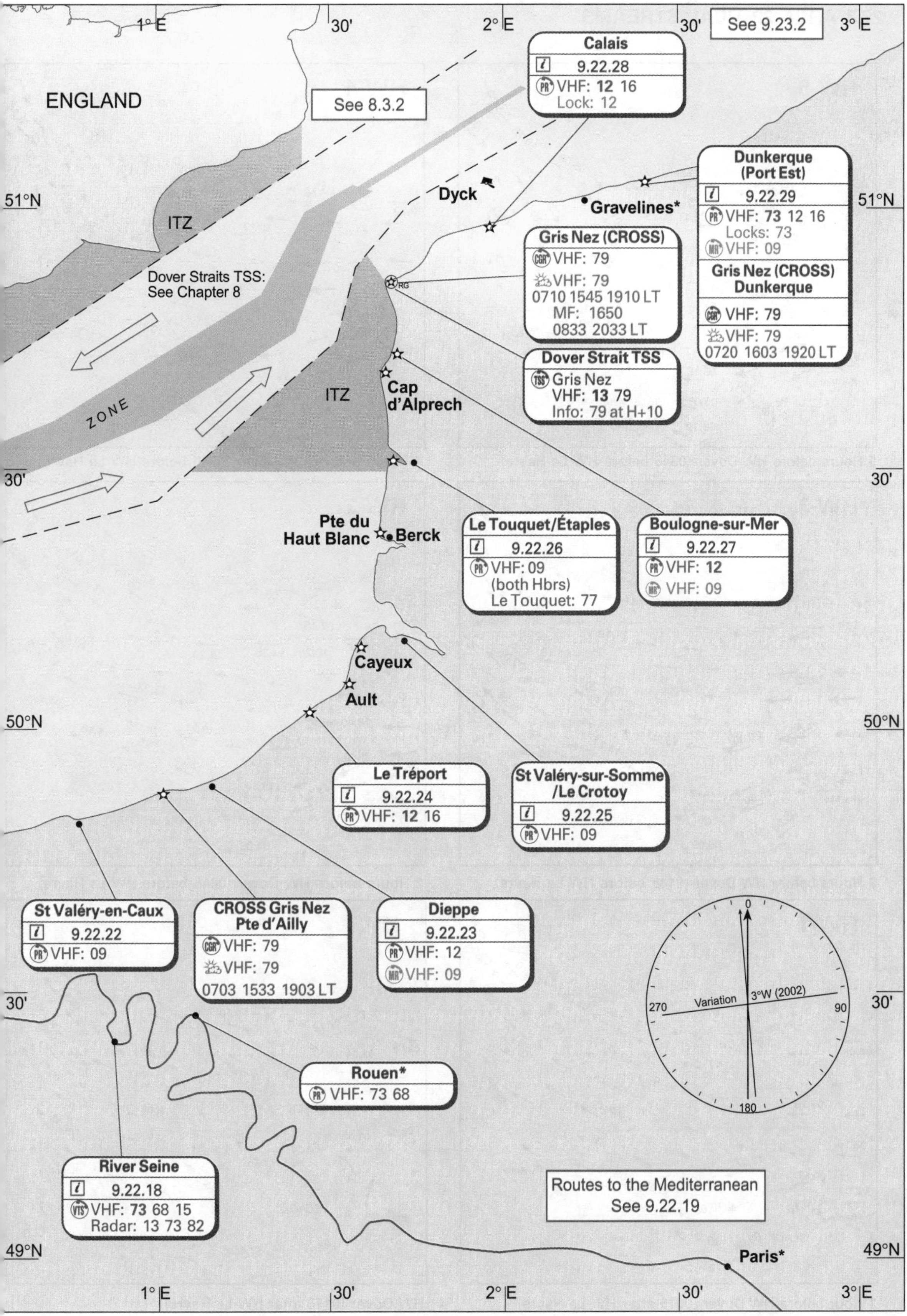
1°E
30'
2°E
30'
See 9.23.2
3°E
ENGLAND
See 8.3.2
Calais
9.22.28
VHF: 12 16
Lock: 12
Dunkerque (Port Est)
9.22.29
VHF: 73 12 16
Locks: 73
VHF: 09
Gris Nez (CROSS) Dunkerque
VHF: 79
VHF: 79
0720 1603 1920 LT
Dyck
Gravelines*
51°N
ITZ
Gris Nez (CROSS)
VHF: 79
VHF: 79
0710 1545 1910 LT
MF: 1650
0833 2033 LT
Dover Straits TSS: See Chapter 8
RG
Dover Strait TSS
Gris Nez
VHF: 13 79
Info: 79 at H+10
ZONE
ITZ
Cap d'Alprech
30'
Pte du Haut Blanc
Berck
Le Touquet/Étaples
9.22.26
VHF: 09
(both Hbrs)
Le Touquet: 77
Boulogne-sur-Mer
9.22.27
VHF: 12
VHF: 09
Cayeux
Ault
50°N
Le Tréport
9.22.24
VHF: 12 16
St Valéry-sur-Somme /Le Crotoy
9.22.25
VHF: 09
St Valéry-en-Caux
9.22.22
VHF: 09
CROSS Gris Nez Pte d'Ailly
VHF: 79
VHF: 79
0703 1533 1903 LT
Dieppe
9.22.23
VHF: 12
VHF: 09
0
270
Variation
3°W (2002)
90
180
Rouen*
VHF: 73 68
River Seine
9.22.18
VHF: 73 68 15
Radar: 13 73 82
Routes to the Mediterranean
See 9.22.19
49°N
Paris*
22

9.22.3 AREA 22 TIDAL STREAMS

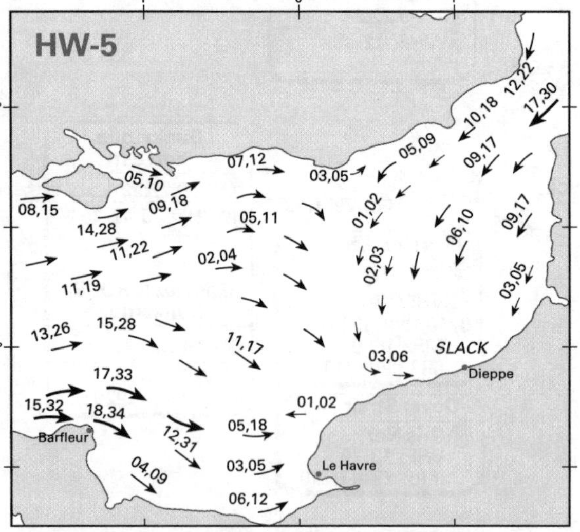

5 Hours before HW Dover (0345 before HW Le Havre)

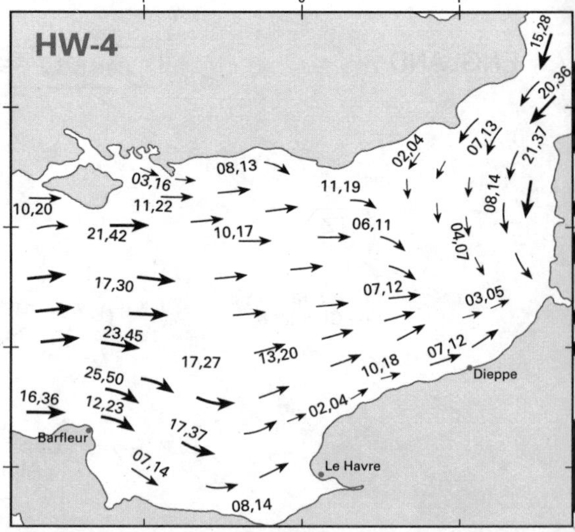

4 Hours before HW Dover (0245 before HW Le Havre)

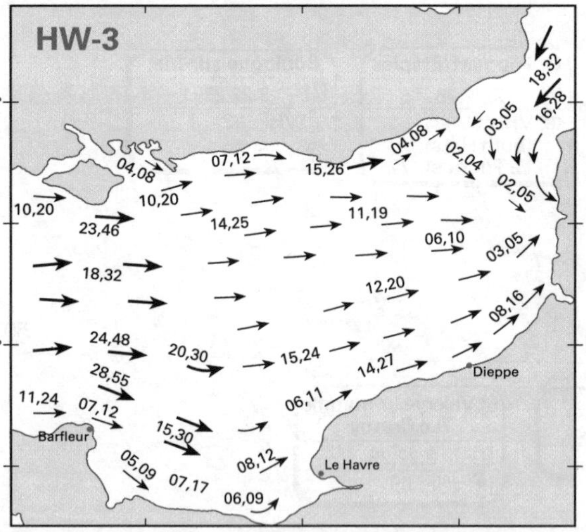

3 Hours before HW Dover (0145 before HW Le Havre)

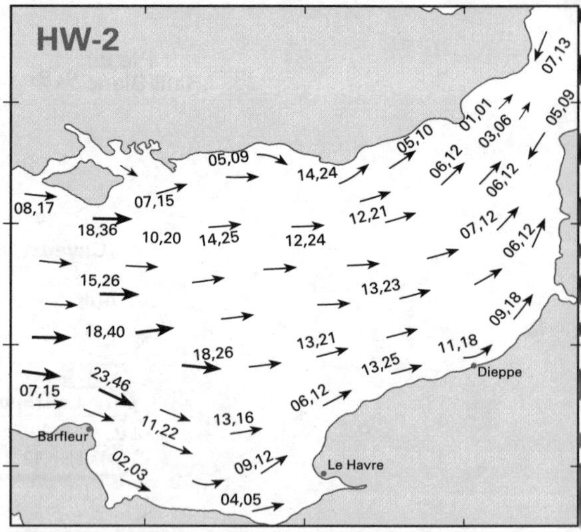

2 Hours before HW Dover (0045 before HW Le Havre)

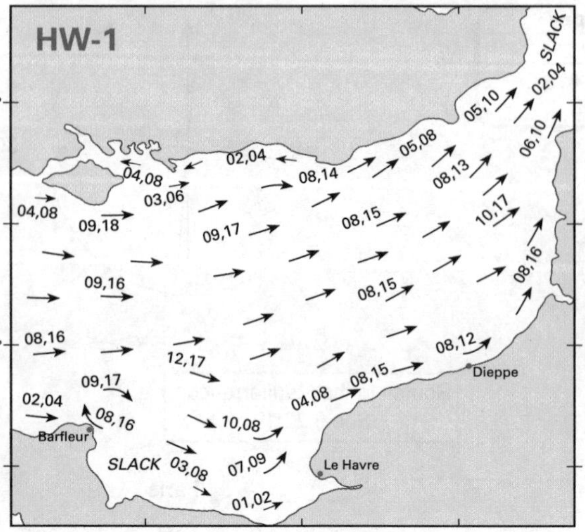

1 Hour before HW Dover (0015 after HW Le Havre)

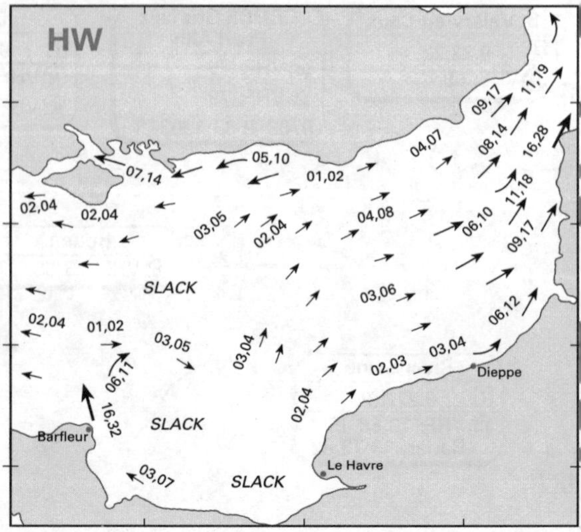

HW Dover (0115 after HW Le Havre)

Westward 9.15.3 Northward 9.2.3 North-eastward 9.3.3 Eastward 9.23.3

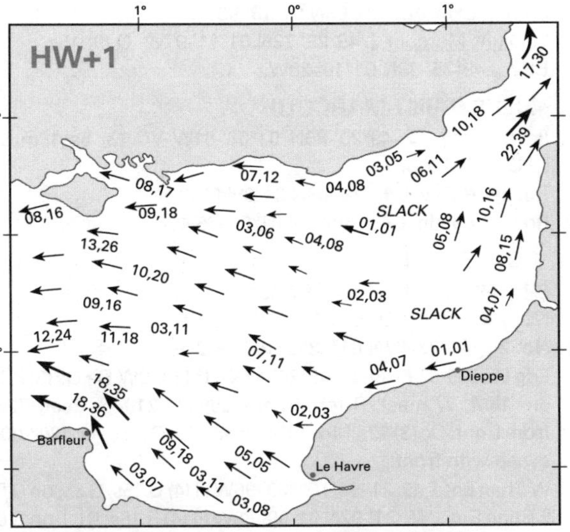

1 Hour after HW Dover (0215 after HW Le Havre)

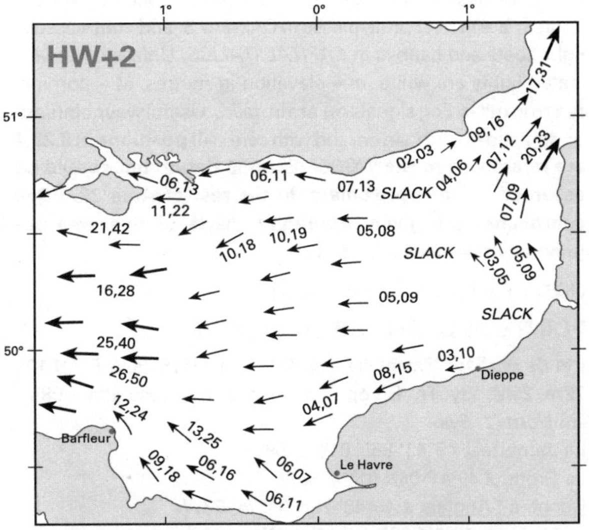

2 Hours after HW Dover (0315 after HW Le Havre)

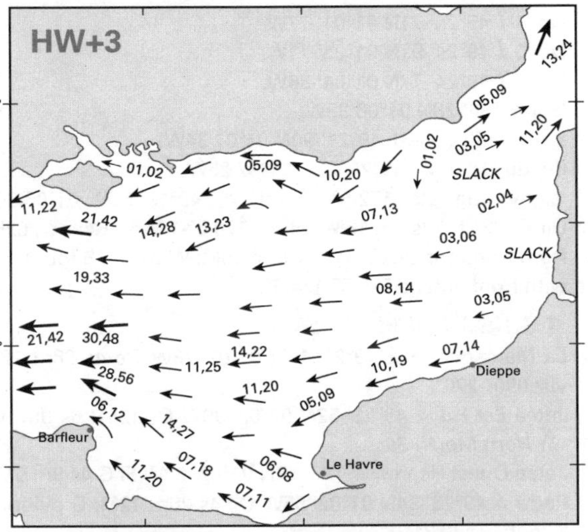

3 Hours after HW Dover (0415 after HW Le Havre)

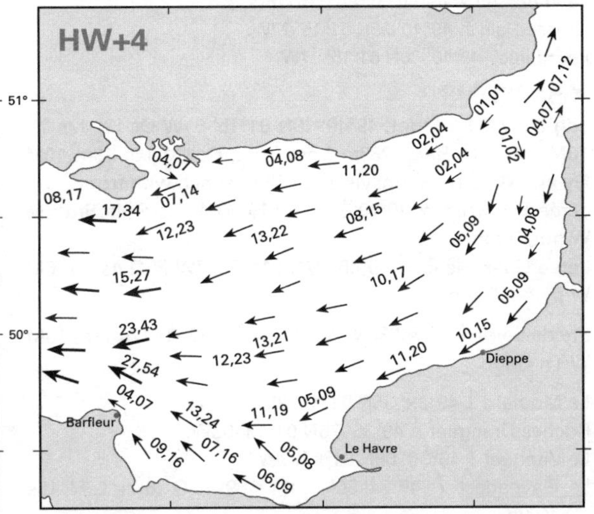

4 Hours after HW Dover (0515 after HW Le Havre)

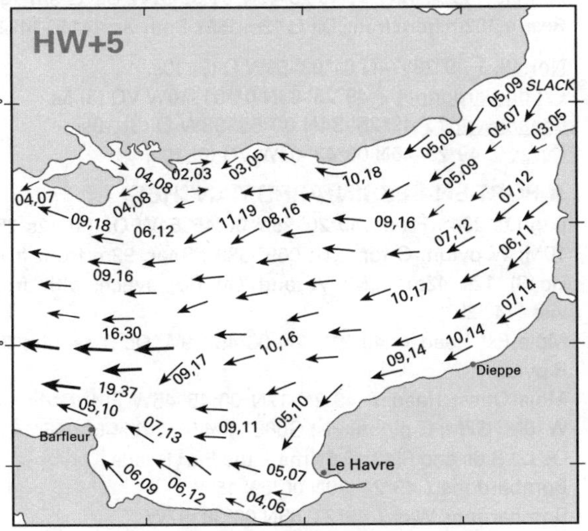

5 Hours after HW Dover (0615 after HW Le Havre)

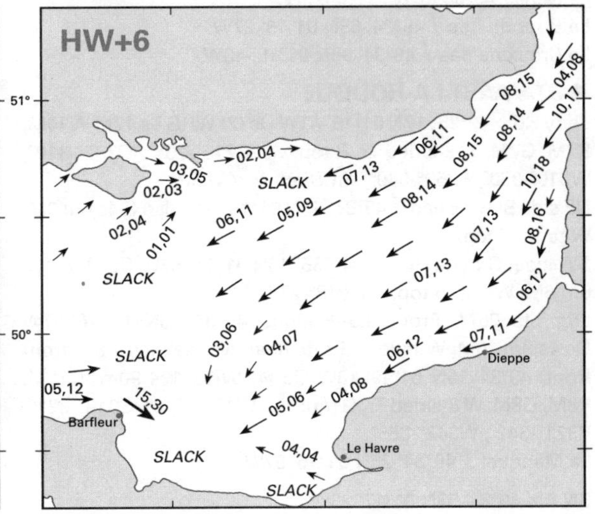

6 Hours after HW Dover (0510 before HW Le Havre)

22

9.22.4 LIGHTS, BUOYS AND WAYPOINTS

Abbreviations used below are given in the Introduction. Principal lights ☆ are in **bold** print, places in CAPITALS, and light-vessels, light floats and Lanbys in *CAPITAL ITALICS*. Unless otherwise stated lights are white. m – elevation in metres; M – nominal range in miles. Fog signals are in *italics*. Useful waypoints are underlined – use those on land with care. **All positions in 9.22.4 are referenced to the WGS84/ETRS89 datum but should be assumed to be approximate. In the rest of Area 22, ED50 coordinates are given. Admiralty charts of this area are generally referenced to ED50.**

NOTE: For English Channel Waypoints see 9.1.7.

POINTE DE BARFLEUR TO DEAUVILLE

Pte de Barfleur-Gatteville ☆ 49°41'·78N 01°15'·96W Fl (2) 10s 72m **29M**; Gy Tr, B top; obsc when brg less than 088°; *Horn (2) 60s.*
La Jamette 49°41'·86N 01°15'·59W.
La Grotte 49°41'·06N 01°14'·86W.
Roche-à-l'Anglais 49°40'·78N 01°14'·93W.
Le Hintar 49°40'·69N 01°14'·85W.
La Vimberge 49°40'·54N 01°15'·26W.
Grosse-Haie 49°40'·38N 01°15'·27W.
Fourquie 49°40'·30N 01°15'·17W.

◀ BARFLEUR

Ldg Lts 219·5°. Front, 49°40'·18N 01°15'·61W Oc (3) 12s 7m 10M; W □ Tr. Rear, 288m from front, Oc (3) 12s 13m 10M; Gy and W □ Tr, G top; vis: 085°-355°; synch with front.
Jetée Est Head 49°40'·31N 01°15'·47W Oc R 4s 5m 6M; W hut, R top.
Jetée Ouest Head 49°40'·32N 01°15'·57W Fl G 4s 8m 6M; W pylon, G top.

Pte de Saire 49°36'·36N 01°13'·79W Oc (2+1) 12s 11m 10M; W Tr, G top.

Le Moulard 49°39'·35N 01°13'·95W.
Roches Dranguet 49°36'·75N 01°13'·03W.
Le Vitéquet 49°36'·08N 01°13'·38W.
Le Gavendest 49°34'·36N 01°13'·89W; Q (6) + L Fl 15s; *Whis.*
La Dent 49°34'·57N 01°14'·22W.
Le Bout du Roc 49°34'·68N 01°15'·27W.
Le Creux de Bas 49°34'·99N 01°15'·40W.

◀ ST VAAST-LA-HOUGUE

Jetty Hd 49°35'·17N 01°15'·41W Oc (2) WRG 6s 12m W10M, R7M, G7M; W 8-sided Tr, R top; vis: R219°-237°, G237°-310°, W310°-350°, R350°-040°; *Siren Mo(N) 30s.*
NE side Bkwtr Head 49°35'·18N 01°15'·64W Iso G 4s 6m 3M; W tank, G top.
SW side, Groyne Head 49°35'·16N 01°15'·66W Oc (4) R 12s 6m 6M; W hut, R top; vis: 018°-278°.
Ldg Lts 267°. Front, La Hougue 49°34'·25N 01°16'·37W Oc 4s 9m 10M; W pylon, G top. Rear, Morsalines 1·8M from front, 49°34'·16N 01°19'·10W Oc (4) WRG 12s 90m W11M, R8M, G8M; W 8-sided Tr, G top; vis: W171°-316°, G316°-321°, R321°-342°, W342°-355°.
Le Manquet 49°34'·25N 01°15'·57W.

BN 4 49°33'·53N 01°17'·28W.
BN1 49°31'·83N 01°16'·98W.
Quineville Wk 49°31'·79N 01°12'·39W Q (9) 10s.
Saint Floxel 49°30'·63N 01°13'·93W.
W Saint-Marcouf 49°29'·73N 01°11'·97W Q (9) 15s.
BS2 49°25'·33N 01°10'·28W.

◀ ÎLES SAINT-MARCOUF

Île du Large 49°29'·86N 01°08'·81W VQ (3) 5s 18m 8M; □ Gy Tr, G top.
Rocher d'Ovy 49°29'·83N 01°09'·08W.
Rocher Bastin 49°29'·55N 01°09'·65W.

◀ CARENTAN

C-I 49°25'·44N 01°07'·09W Iso 4s.
No. 1 49°23'·92N 01°08'·53W Fl G 2·5s.
No. 2 49°23'·87N 01°08'·38W Fl R 2·5s.
Ldg Lts 209·5°. **Front** ☆, 49°20'·47N 01°11'·19W Dir Oc (3) R 12s 6m **18M**; W mast, R top; intens 208·2°°-210·7°. Rear, 723m from front, Oc (3) 12s 14m 10M; W gantry, G top; vis: 120°-005°, synch with front.
W Chan Ent 49°21'·94N 01°09'·96W Fl (4) G 15s; G △, on G Bn.
E Chan Ent 49°21'·92N 01°09'·88W Fl (4) R 15s; R □, on R Bn.

◀ ISIGNY-SUR-MER

No. 1 49°24'·71N 01°01'·77W.
No. 3 49°24'·91N 01°03'·71W.
No. 5 49°24'·77N 01°04'·86W.
IS 49°24'·28N 01°06'38W.
Banc de Rouelle 49°21'·90N 01°07'34W.
Pte du Grouin 49°21'·42N 01°07'25W.
Isigny Ldg Lts 172·5°. **Front** ☆, 49°19'·55N 01°06·80W Dir Oc (2+1) 12s 7m **18M**; intens 170·5°-174·5°. **Rear** ☆, 625m from front, Dir Oc (2+1) 12s 19m **18M**; W pylon, B top; synch with front; intens 170·5°-174·5°.

◀ GRANDCAMP-MAISY

La Maresquerie 49°23'·16N 01°02'·78W Oc 4s 28m 12M; vis: 090°-270°.
Jetée Est Hd 49°23'·52N 01°02'·98W Oc (2) R 6s 9m 9M; *Horn Mo(N) 30s.*
Jetée Ouest Head 49°23'·47N 01°02'·98W Fl G 4s 9m 6M.
Perré 49°23'·34N 01°02'·55W Oc 4s 28m 12M; G pylon on W hut; vis: 083°-263°.
Ldg Lts 146°. **Front** ☆, 49°23'·42N 01°02'·92W Dir Q 9m **15M**. **Rear** ☆,102m from front, Dir Q 12m **15M**. Both vis: 144·5°-147·5°.

Norfalk 49°28'·74N 01°03'·69W Q (3) 10s.
Est du Cardonnet 49°26'·83N 01°01'·10W VQ (3) 5s.
Broadsword 49°25'·34N 00°52'·98W Q (3) 10s.
Cussy 49°29'·45N 00°43'·04W VQ (9) 10s.

◀ PORT-EN-BESSIN/ARROMANCHES

Ldg Lts 204°. Front, 49°20'·95N 00°45'·54W Oc (3) 12s 25m 10M; W pylon, G top; vis: 069°-339°; Rear, 93m from front, Oc (3) 12s 42m 11M; W and Gy Ho; synch with front; vis: 114°-294°.
Môle Est Head 49°21'·12N 00°45'·39W Oc R 4s 14m 7M; R pylon.
Môle Ouest Head 49°21'·17N 00°45'·45W Fl WG 4s 14m W10M, G7M; G pylon; vis: G065°-114·5°, W114·5°-065°.
Oc (2) R 6s and Fl (2) G 6s mark the Pier Heads.
Bombardons 49°21'·70N 00°39'·15W.
Bombardons Wks 49°21'·65N 00°38'·97W.

Harpagas 49°22'·14N 00°37'·58W.
Port Winston (Arromanches) 49°21'·35N 00°37'·27W.
Port Winston (Arromanches) 49°21'·24N 00°37'·31W.
Roseberry 49°23'·09N 00°36'·49W.

Ver ☆ 49°20'·39N 00°31'·15W Fl (3) 15s 42m **26M**; W Tr, Gy top; obsc by cliffs of St Aubin when brg more than 275°.

◄ COURSEULLES-SUR-MER

Courseulles 49°21'·28N 00°27'·69W Iso 4s.
Jetée Ouest Head ☆ 49°20'·41N 00°27'·38W Iso WG 4s 7m W9M, G6M; brown pylon on Dn, G top; vis: W135°-235°, G235°-135°; *Horn 30s* sounded from HW±2 hours.
Jetée Est Head ☆ 49°20'·25N 00°27'·40W Oc (2) R 6s 9m 7M.
Essarts de Langrune 49°22'·58N 00°21'·37W; *Bell.*
Luc 49°20'·76N 00°18'·43W.
Lion 49°20'·70N 00°15'·97W.

◄ OUISTREHAM/CAEN

Ouistreham 49°20'·42N 00°14'·82W VQ (3) 5s.
W-SRCO 49°19'·30N 00°15'·25W.
No. 1 49°19'·19N 00°14'·67W QG.
No. 2 49°19'·17N 00°14'·43W QR.
No. 3 49°18'·76N 00°14'·70W Fl G 4s.
No. 4 49°18'·75N 00°14'·49W Fl R 4s.
No. 5 49°18'·41N 00°14'·73W QG.
No. 6 49°18'·40N 00°14'·55W QR.
Ouistreham Main Lt ☆ 49°16'·85N 00°14'·80W Oc WR 4s 37m **W17M**, R13M; W Tr, R top; vis: R115°-151°, W151°-115°.
Ldg Lts 184·5°. **Front** ☆, 49°17'·09N 00°14'·80W Jetée Est Hd Dir Oc (3+1) R 12s 10m **17M**; W pylon, R top. **Rear** ☆, 610m from front, Dir Oc (3+1) R 12s 30m **17M**; Tripod, R top; synch with front; intens 183·5°-186·5°.
Barnabé ☆ 49°18'·02N 00°14'·76W Iso G 4s 7m 3M.
St-Médard ☆ 49°18'·02N 00°14'·62W Oc (2) R 6s 7m 8M.
Viaduc de Calix, Caen 49°11'·18N 00°19'·77W Iso 4s on E and W sides; FG on N side, FR on S side.

Merville 49°19'·65N 00°13'·40W VQ.

◄ DIVES

D1 49°18'·85N 00°05'·83W L Fl 10s.
No. 1 49°18'·49N 00°05'·69W.
No. 2 49°18'·50N 00°05'·57W.
Dives-sur-Mer ☆ 49°17'·80N 00°05'·24W Oc (2+1) WRG 12s 6m W12M, R9M, G9M, R hut; vis: G125°-157°, W157°-162°, R162°-194°.
No. 3 ☆ 49°18'·30N 00°05'·56W QG 7m 4M (Destroyed (T)).

◄ DEAUVILLE/TROUVILLE

Semoy 49°24'·14N 00°02'·35E VQ (3) 5s.
Trouville SW 49°22'·54N 00°02'·56E VQ (9) 10s.
West Jetty ☆ 49°22'·37N 00°04'·10E Fl WG 4s 10m W9M, G6M; B pylon, G top; vis: W005°-176°, G176°-005°.
Trouville East Jetty ☆ 49°22'·22N 00°04'·33E Fl (4) WR 12s 8m W7M, R4M; W pylon, R top; vis: W131°-175°, R175°-131°.
Ldg Lts 148°. Front, Pointe de la Cahotte, 49°22'·03N 00°04'·48E Oc R 4s 11m 12M; W Tr, R top; vis: 330°-150°; *Horn (2) 30s.* Rear, 217m from front, Oc R 4s 17m 10M; W pylon, R top; synch with front; vis: 120°-170°.
Roches Noires 49°22'·76N 00°04'·89E.

◄ ESTUAIRE DE LA SEINE/LE HAVRE

Ratelets 49°25'·29N 00°01'·71E Q (9) 15s.
Ratier S 49°25'·15N 00°07'·12E VQ (6) + L Fl 10s.

◄ CHENAL DE ROUEN

Ratier NW 49°26'·82N 00°02'·50E VQ G.
No. 4 49°26'·97N 00°02'·60E QR.
Ducan-L-Clinch 49°27'·18N 00°02'·50E VQ (9) 10s.
S Carosse 49°27'·17N 00°02'·80E Q.
No. 5 49°26'·50N 00°03'·59E Fl (2) G 6s.
Amfard SW 49°26'·30N 00°04'·82E QR.
Tide Gauge A 49°25'·94N 00°06'·58E VQ.
No. 7 49°26'·19N 00°04'·74E QG.
No. 10 49°26'·10N 00°06'·39E QR.
No. 11 49°25'·92N 00°07'·75E QG.
No. 14 49°26'·00N 00°09'·19E QR.
Digue du Ratier Hd 'A' ☆ 49°25'·93N 00°06'·58E VQ 10m 4M; NCM tide gauge.
St Simeon ☆ 49°25'·72N 00°12'·71E VQ (9) 10s 8m 7M.

◄ HONFLEUR

Falaise des Fonds ☆ 49°25'·47N 00°12'·85E Fl (3) WRG 12s 15m, **W17M**, R13M, G13M; W □ Tr, G top; vis: G040°-080°, R080°-084°, G084°-100°, W100°-109°, R109°-162°, G162°-260°.
No. 19 ☆ 49°25'·73N 00°13'·51E QG.
La Risberne ☆ 49°25'·67N 00°13'·94E Q 9m 9M.
Digue Ouest ☆ 49°25'·68N 00°13'·81E QG 10m 6M.
Digue Est Head ☆ 49°25'·68N 00°13'·93E Q 9m 8M; *Horn (5) 40s.* (Km 356 from Paris.)

◄ LA SEINE MARITIME

No. 24 49°25'·85N 00°16'·41E QR; (Km 353).
La Risle, Digue Sud ☆ 49°26'·30N 00°21'·97E Iso G 4s 11m 6M; W pylon, G top; (Km 346 from Paris).
Épi de la Roque ☆ 49°27'·11N 00°25'·22E QG 8m 6M.
Marais-Vernier ☆ 49°27'·71N 00°26'·80E Fl G 4s 8m 5M.
Digue Nord, Tancarville ☆ 49°28'·76N 00°28'·22E QR 9m 6M; R&W col; (Km 337·4).
Quillebeuf 49°28'·84N 00°31'·24E QG 12m 8M (Km 332·4).
Caudebec-en-Caux ☆ 49°31'·45N 00°43'·66E VQ R (Km 309·5).
Duclair ☆ 49°28'·73N 00°52'·24E QR (Km 278·5 from Paris).

◄ ROUEN

Rouen ☆ 49°26'·42N 01°02'·68E Oc (2) R 6s 10m (Km 245·5).
Tide Gauge ☆ 49°26'·20N 01°02'·42E (Km 246).

◄ APPROACHES TO LE HAVRE

LHA Lanby 49°31'·38N 00°09'·88W Mo (A) 12s 10m 9M; R&W; Racon.
RNA 49°28'·64N 00°05'·54E Iso 4s.
HP 49°29'·56N 00°03'·83E Fl Y 4s; *Whis.*
LH5 49°30'·55N 00°02'·34E Fl G 4s.
LH7 49°30'·25N 00°00'·82E Iso G 4s.
RP 49°28'·61N 00°01'·19E Fl (2) 6s.
LH11 49°29'·64N 00°02'·25E VQ (9) 10s.
N du Mouillage 49°28'·59N 00°01'·27E Fl (4) Y 15s.
Ldg Lts 106·8°. Front, **Quai Roger Meunier** ☆ 49°28'·91N 00°06'·49E Dir F 36m **25M**; Gy Tr, G top; intens 106°-108°; (H24). Rear, 0·73M from front, **Quai Joannes Couvert** ☆ Dir F 78m **25M**; Gy Tr, G top; intens 106°-108° (H24); Ra refl.

22

◄ LE HAVRE

Cap de la Hève ☆ 49°30'·74N 00°04'·15E Fl 5s 123m **24M**; W 8-sided Tr, R top; vis: 225°-196°.

Digue Sud Head ☆ 49°29'·05N 00°05'·38E VQ (3) G 2s 15m 11M; W Tr, G top.

Digue Nord Head ☆ 49°29'·19N 00°05'·44E Fl R 5s 15m **21M**; W ○ Tr, R top; *Horn 15s.*

Yacht Harbours, (Anse de Joinville & Anse des Régates) Digue Augustin Normand Breakwater ☆ 49°29'·26N 00°05'·56E Fl (2) G 6s 5m 2M.

Yacht Hbr Breakwater Head ☆ 49°29'·21N 00°05'·53E Fl (2) R 6s.

◄ LE HAVRE TO CAP D'ANTIFER

Grande Rade S 49°31'·11N 00°00'·33E VQ (3) 5s.

Octeville W 49°31'·61N 00°01'·75E VQ (6) + L Fl 10s.

Général Metzinger 49°32'·73N 00°02'·00E VQ.

Port du Havre-Antifer ☆ 49°39'·51N 00°09'·18E Dir Oc WRG 4s 24m **W15M**, R13M, G13M; W pylon, B top; vis: G068·5°-078·5°, W078·5°-088·5°, R088·5°-098·5°.

A17 49°41'·52N 00°01'·74E Iso G 4s.

DA 49°40'·97N 00°01'·71E Fl (2) 6s.

A18 49°42'·01N 00°02'·17E QR.

A23 49°39'·87N 00°05'·58E Iso G 4s.

A24 49°40'·13N 00°05'·84E QR.

A25 49°39'·13N 00°07'·04E Iso G 4s.

A26 49°39'·70N 00°06'·71E QR.

Port d'Antifer Ldg Lts 127·5°. **Front** ☆, 49°38'·32N 00°09'·11E Dir Oc 4s 113m **22M**; W pylon, G top vis: 127°-128°. **Rear** ☆, 430m from front, Dir Oc 4s 135m **22M**; vis: 127°-128°; W mast, G top. By day both show FW Lts **33M**; vis: 126·5°-128·5°; (occas.)

◄ CAP D'ANTIFER TO POINTE DU HAUT BLANC

Cap d'Antifer ☆ 49°41'·01N 00°09'·90E Fl 20s 128m **29M**; Gy 8-sided Tr, G top; vis: 021°-222°.

Yport Ldg Lts 166°. Front, 49°44'·36N 00°18'·62E Oc 4s 10m, W mast, G top. Rear, 30m from front, Oc 4s 14m, W pylon, G top on house.

◄ FÉCAMP

Jetée Nord ☆ 49°45'·93N 00°21'·78E Fl (2) 10s 15m **16M**; Gy Tr, R top; *Horn (2) 30s.*

Jetée Sud Head ☆ 49°45'·88N 00°21'·80E QG 14m 9M; Gy Tr, G top; vis: 072°-217°.

Jetée root ☆ 49°45'·90N 00°21'·99E QR 10m 4M.

Paluel 49°52'·22N 00°38'·00E Q.

◄ SAINT VALÉRY-EN-CAUX

Jetée Ouest ☆ 49°52'·41N 00°42'·51E Fl (2) G 6s 13m 14M; W Tr, G top.

Jetée Est Head ☆ 49°52'·32N 00°42'·67E Fl (2) R 6s 8m 4M; W mast.

Roches d'Ailly 49°56'·58N 00°56'·72E VQ; *Whis.*

Pointe d'Ailly ☆ 49°54'·96N 00°57'·50E Fl (3) 20s 95m **31M**; W □ Tr, G top; *Horn (3) 60s.* (TD 1997).

Daffodils Wk 50°02'·46N 01°04'·01E VQ (9) 10s.

◄ DIEPPE

D1 49°57'·05N 01°01'·25E VQ (3) 5s; *Bell.*

Jetée Est Hd ☆ 49°56'·16N 01°05'·06E Iso R 4s 12m 8M; R col.

Jetée Ouest ☆ 49°56'·27N 01°04'·95E Iso G 4s 11m 8M, W □ Tr, G top; *Horn 30s.*

Falaise du Pollet ☆ 49°55'·92N 01°05'·30E Q 35m 11M; R & W structure; vis: 105·5°-170·5°.

Berneval Wk 50°03'·41N 01°06'·53E.

Penly No. 1 49°59'·03N 01°11'·38E Fl (3) Y 12s.

Penly No. 2 49°59'·45N 01°12'03E Fl Y 4s.

◄ LE TRÉPORT

Jetée Ouest Head ☆ 50°03'·87N 01°22'·13E Fl (2) G 10s 15m **20M**; W Tr, G top; *Horn Mo(N) 30s.*

Jetée Est ☆ 50°03'·86N 01°22'·21E Oc R 4s 8m 6M; W col, R top.

Ault ☆ 50°06'·28N 01°27'·23E Oc (3) WR 12s 95m **W18M**, R14M, W Tr, R top; vis: W040°-175°, R175°-220°.

◄ BAIE DE SOMME/LE CROTOY/ST VALÉRY-SUR-SOMME

Cayeux-sur-Mer ☆ 50°11'·65N 01°30'·67E Fl R 5s 32m **22M**; W Tr, R top.

AT-SO 50°14'·23N 01°28'·55E VQ.

Pte du Hourdel ☆ 50°12'·90N 01°33'·96E Oc (3) WG 12s 19m W12M, G9M; W Tr, G top; vis: W053°-248°, G248°-323°; tidal sigs; *Reed (3) 30s.*

Le Crotoy ☆ 50°12'·89N 01°37'·55E Oc (2) R 6s 19m 8M; W pylon; vis: 285°-135°.

Yacht Hbr, E side ☆ 50°12'·98N 01°38'·20E Fl G 2s 4m 2M.

Yacht Hbr, W side ☆ Fl R 2s 4m 2M.

St Valéry-sur-Somme, Embankment Head ☆ 50°12'·25N 01°36'·02E Iso G 4s 9m 9M; W pylon, G top; W pylon, G top; vis: 347°-222°.

La Ferté Môle Head ☆ 50°11'·16N 01°38'·80E Fl R 4s 9m 9M; W pylon, R top; vis: 000°-250°.

◄ SOMME TO LE TOUQUET

Pointe de Haut-Blanc (Berck-Plage) ☆ 50°23'·89N 01°33'·62E Fl 5s 44m **23M**; W Tr, R bands, G top.

Vergoyer SW 50°26'·98N 01°00'·00E VQ (9) 10s.

Bassurelle 50°32'·74N 00°57'·69E Fl (4) R 15s 6M; Racon (B); *Whis.*

Vergoyer W 50°34'·63N 01°13'·54E Fl G 4s.

Vergoyer E 50°35'·74N 01°19'·65E VQ (3) 5s.

Vergoyer NW 50°37'·13N 01°17'·85E Fl (2) G 6s.

Vergoyer N 50°39'·64N 01°22'·18E VQ; Racon (C).

LE TOUQUET TO DUNKERQUE

◄ LE TOUQUET

Le Touquet (La Canche) ☆ 50°31'·42N 01°35'·50E Fl (2) 10s 54m **25M**; Or Tr, brown band; W and G top.

Mérida Wk 50°32'·76N 01°33'·40E.

Camiers, Rivière Canche ent, N side ☆ 50°32'·76N 01°36'·50E Oc (2) WRG 6s 17m W10M, R7M, G7M; R pylon; vis: G015°-090°, W090°-105°, R105°-141°.

Cap d'Alprech ☆ 50°41'·90N 01°33'·75E Fl (3) 15s 62m **23M**; W Tr, B top; FR Lts on radio mast 600m ENE.

Ophélie 50°43'·85N 01°30'·84E Fl G 4s.

◄ BOULOGNE

Boulogne Approaches 50°45'·31N 01°31'·07E VQ (6) + L Fl 10s 8m 6M; *Whis.*

Digue (Carnot) ☆ 50°44'·44N 01°34'·05E Fl (2+1) 15s 25m **19M**; W Tr, G top; *Horn (2+1) 60s.*

Digue Nord Head ☆ 50°44'·71N 01°34'·18E Fl (2) R 6s 10m 7M.

Rade Carnot RC1 50°43'·93N 01°34'·43E Fl G 4s.

tée NW ☆ 50°43'·67N 01°34'·50E Iso G 4s 8m 5M.
rse Sarraz-Bournett Jetée NW ☆ 50°43'·90N 01°35'·11E
c (2) R 6s 8m 6M.
2 50°43'·89N 01°34'·73E Fl (2) R 6s.
tée SW ☆ 50°43'·90N 01°35'·11E FG 17m 5M; W col, G top;
Horn 30s.
tée NE Head ☆ 50°43'·65N 01°34'·66E FR 11m 9M.

1 50°44'·99N 01°27'·21E Fl (4) Y 15s.
ssure de Baas 50°48'·53N 01°33'·04E VQ; *Bell.*
p Gris-Nez ☆ 50°52'·09N 01°34'·94E Fl 5s 72m **29M**; W Tr,
top; vis: 005°-232°; *Horn 60s.*
2 50°53'·53N 01°30'·88E Fl (2+1) Y 15s.
obeville Wk 50°56'·05N 01°37'·56E VQ (9) 10s.
3 50°56'·82N 01°41'·12E Fl G 4s; *Whis.*
4 50°58'·89N 01°45'·11E VQ (9) 10s 8m 8M; *Whis.*
6 50°58'·24N 01°45'·63E VQ R.
5 50°57'·64N 01°46'·10E QG.
ngatte ☆ 50°57'·19N 01°46'·47E Oc WG 4s 12m W8M, G5M;
pylon, B top; vis: G065°-089°, W089°-152°, G152°-245°.
8 50°58'·38N 01°48'·65E QR; *Bell.*
10 50°58'·63N 01°49'·92E Fl (2) R 6s.
W 51°01'·23N 01°45'·34E VQ.
2 51°00'·87N 01°48'·69E Q.
ck 51°02'·98N 01°51'·76E Fl 3s; Racon (B).
E 51°02'·44N 01°53'·22E Iso G 4s.

CALAIS

tée Ouest Head ☆ 50°58'·24N 01°50'·40E Iso G 3s 12m 9M;
fog Fl 5s); W Tr, G top; *Bell (1) 5s.*
tée Est Head ☆ 50°58'·40N 01°50'·45E Fl (2) R 6s 12m **17M**;
Tr, R top; *Horn (2) 40s;* (in fog 2 Fl (2) 6s (vert).
lais ☆ 50°57'·68N 01°51'·21E Fl (4) 15s 59m **22M**; W 8-sided
, B top; vis: 073°-260°.

PC 51°06'·11N 01°38'·21E Fl Y 2·5s 10m 6M.
NDETTIÉ 51°09'·36N 01°47'·12E Fl 5s 12m **15M**; R hull;
Horn 30s; Racon (T).
ndettié SW 51°09'·72N 01°45'·60E Q (9) 15s.
ytingen SW 51°04'·98N 01°46'·83E Fl (3) G 12s; *Bell.*
ytingen W 51°06'·91N 01°50'·43E VQ.
ytingen NW 51°09'·08N 01°57'·29E Fl G 4s.
ytingen N 51°13'·10N 02°10'·28E VQ.
ytingen SE 51°09'·20N 02°08'·92E VQ (3) 15s.
ytingen E 51°14'·55N 02°17'·92E VQ.
rgues S 51°15'·10N 02°19'·42E Q (6) + L Fl 15s.
rgues 51°17'·15N 02°18'·62E Fl G 4s.
ck W 51°17'·15N 02°26'·32E Q (9) 15s.
rgues N 51°19'·92N 02°24'·50E Q.

DUNKERQUE APPROACHES – PASSE DE L'OUEST

A 51°02'·54N 01°56'·95E L Fl 10s.
V5 51°02'·19N 02°00'·91E QG.
V7 51°02'·53N 02°02'·52E Fl G 4s.
V9 51°02'·65N 02°03'·97E Fl (2) G 6s.
ck E 51°05'·62N 02°05'·63E Q (3) 10s.
Gravavelines 51°04'·03N 02°05'·03E VQ (9) 10s.
V13 51°03'·03N 02°07'·09E QG.
V15 51°02'·64N 02°08'·86E Fl (2) G 6s.

◄ GRAVELINES

51°01'·50N 02°06'·74E Fl (5) Y 20s.
51°01'·37N 02°06'·73E Fl (5) Y 20s.
Jetée Ouest ☆ 51°00'·93N 02°05'·46E Fl (2) WG 6s 9m W8M, G8M; Y ○ Tr, G top; vis: W317°-327°, G078°-085°, W085°-244°.
Gravelines 51°00'·98N 02°05'·54E VQ 6m 4M.
Jetée Est ☆ 51°00'·93N 02°05'·62E Fl (3) R 12s 5m 4M.

◄ DYCK CENTRAL

DY1 51°08'·96N 02°14'·92E Fl G 4s.
DY2 51°09'·45N 02°19'·41E Fl (2) R 6s.
DY3 51°11'·45N 02°22'·42E Q.

◄ DUNKERQUE PORT OUEST

DKB 51°02'·95N 02°09'·26E VQ (9) 10s.
Port Ouest Ldg Lts 120°. **Front** ☆, 51°01'·66N 02°11'·91E Dir FG 16m **21M**; W col, G top; intens 119°-121°. **Rear** ☆, 600m from front, Dir FG 30m **21M**; W col, G top; intens 119°-121°. By day both show F **28M**; intens 119°-121°.
Jetée Clipon Head ☆ 51°02'·64N 02°09'·77E Fl (4) R 15s 24m **16M**; W col, R top; vis: 278°-243°; In fog Fl (4) 15s **20M**.
Jetée du Dyck Head ☆ 51°02'·26N 02°09'·78E Fl (4) G 15s 24m **16M**.

DW11 51°02'·85N 02°05'·77E Fl (3) G 12s.
DW12 51°03'·17N 02°05'·54E Fl (3) R 12s.
DW13 51°03'·05N 02°07'·10E QG.
DW15 51°02'·67N 02°08'·85E Fl (2) G 6s.
DW16 51°03'·30N 02°08'·98E Fl (2) R 6s.
DW17 51°03'·10N 02°10'·38E Fl (3) G 12s.
DW18 51°03'·47N 02°10'·38E Fl (3) R 12s.
DW19 51°03'·22N 02°11'·97E Fl G 4s.
DW20 51°03'·61N 02°11'·97E Fl R 4s.
DW21 51°03'·35N 02°13'·54E Fl (2) G 6s.
DW23 51°03'·54N 02°15'·18E QG; *Bell.*
DW25 51°03'·58N 02°16'·72E Fl G 4s.
DW26 51°03'·91N 02°16'·73E Fl R 4s.
DW29 51°03'·85N 02°20'·21E Fl (3) G 12s.
DW30 51°04'·14N 02°20'·18E Fl (3) R 12s.

DUNKERQUE PORT EST

Dunkerque ☆ 51°02'·91N 02°21'·86E Fl (2) 10s 59m **26M**.
Jetée Ouest Head ☆ 51°03'·62N 02°20'·97E Oc (2+1) G 12s 35m 11M; W Tr, brown top.
Jetée Est Head ☆ 51°03'·59N 02°21'·17E Fl (2) R 10s 12m **16M**; R □ on W pylon, R top. (Fl (2) 10s in fog).

◄ DUNKERQUE – PASSE DE L'EST

W 51°04'·86N 02°21'·22E Fl Y 4s.
E2 51°04'·35N 02°22'·30E Fl (2) R 6s.
E1 51°04'·12N 02°23'·04E Fl (2) G 6s.
E4 51°04'·58N 02°24'·52E Fl R 4s.
E6 51°04'·86N 02°27'·08E QR.
E7 51°05'·18N 02°28'·50E Fl (3) G 12s.
E8 51°05'·37N 02°28'·49E Fl (3) R 12s; *Whis.*
E10 51°05'·90N 02°29'·62E Fl (2) R 6s.
E11 51°07'·25N 02°30'·62E Fl G 4s.
E12 51°07'·92N 02°30'·61E VQ (6) + L Fl 10s.

22

9.22.5 PASSAGE INFORMATION

For detailed sailing directions refer to: *North France and Belgium Cruising Companion* (Macmillan Reeds/Featherstone), *Normandy and Channel Islands Pilot* (Adlard Coles/ Brackenbury), The *Shell Channel Pilot* (Imray/Cunliffe). Also the Admiralty *Channel Pilot* and *Dover Strait Pilot.*

The coasts of Normandy and Picardy are convenient to hbrs along the S Coast of England – the distance from (say) Brighton to Fécamp being hardly more than an overnight passage. It should be noted however that many of the hbrs dry, so that a boat which can take the ground is an advantage. For details of TSS in the Dover Strait, see Fig 8 (29). Notes on the English Channel and on cross-Channel passages appear in 9.3.5 and 9.15.5; see 9.0.6 for cross-Channel distances. For French glossary, see the Introduction. The coast and ports westward from Pte de Barfleur are covered in Area 15.

The inland waterways system can be entered via the Seine (9.22.19), St Valéry-sur-Somme (9.22.25), Calais, Gravelines (9.22.28), and Dunkerque (9.22.29). See 9.15.7 for tolls.

POINTE DE BARFLEUR TO GRANDCAMP (chart 2135) Raz de Barfleur must be avoided in bad weather. In calm weather it can be taken at slack water (HW Cherbourg –4½ and +2) or the inshore passage used, passing 5ca E of La Jamette ECM bn. Pte de Barfleur marks the W end of B de Seine, which stretches 55M east to C d'Antifer, 12M N of Le Havre. There are no obstructions on a direct course across the Bay, but a transhipment area for large tankers is centred about 10M ESE of Pte de Barfleur. A feature of the Baie de Seine is the stand of tide at HW. Caution: The W end of the Baie de Seine is affected by floating Sargassum weed; in hbrs from Grandcamp to St Vaast propeller fouling is commonplace.

Approach St Vaast-la-Hougue (9.22.9) S of Île de Tatihou, but beware drying rks: La Tourelle, Le Gavendest and La Dent, which lie near the approaches and are buoyed. 2M N is Pte de Saire with rks and shoals up to 1M offshore. From Pte de Saire the coast runs 4M NNW to Barfleur (9.22.8).

Îles St Marcouf (9.15.10) lie 7M SE of St Vaast-la-Hougue, about 4M offshore, and consist of Île du Large (lt) and Île de Terre about ¼M apart. The Banc du Cardonnet, with depths of 5·2m and many wks, extends for about 5M ESE from the islands. Banc de St Marcouf, with depths of 2·4m and many wks, extends 2·5M NW from the islands, and the sea breaks on this in strong N or NE winds.

At the head of B du Grand Vey, about 10M S of Îles St Marcouf, are the (very) tidal hbrs of Carentan and Isigny (9.22.10); entry is only possible near HW. The Carentan chan is well buoyed and adequately lit. It trends SSW across sandbanks for about 4M, beyond which it runs between two breakwaters leading to a lock gate, and thence into canal to Carentan. The Isigny chan is deeper, but the hbr dries. Neither chan should be attempted in strong onshore winds.

On E side of B du Grand Vey, Roches de Grandcamp (dry) extend more than 1M offshore, N and W of Grandcamp (9.22.11), but they are flat and can be crossed from the N in normal conditions HW±1½. Three NCM buoys mark the N edge of the shoal. Heavy kelp can give false echo soundings.

PORT-EN-BESSIN TO DEAUVILLE (chart 2136, *2613*) Between Pte de la Percée and Port-en-Bessin (9.22.12) a bank lies offshore, with drying ledges extending 3ca. A race forms over this bank with wind against tide. Off Port-en- Bessin the E-going stream begins about HW Le Havre –0500, and the W-going at about HW Le Havre +0050, sp rates 1·25kn.

From Port-en-Bessin the coast runs east 4M to C Manvieux, beyond which lie remnants of the wartime hbr of Arromanches, where there is occas anch. Between C Manvieux and Langrune, 10M E, Plateau du Calvados lies offshore. Rocher du Calvados (dries 1·6m) lies on the W part of this bank. There are numerous wrecks and obstructions in the area.

Roches de Ver (dry) lie near centre of Plateau du Calvado extending 8ca offshore about 1M W of Courseulles-sur-M (9.22.13). The approach to this hbr is dangerous in stron onshore winds. Les Essarts de Langrune (dry) lie E of Courseulle sur-Mer, and extend up to 2·25M seaward of Langrune. At the E end lie Roches de Lion (dry), which reach up to 1·5M offsho in places and extend to a point 2·5M W of Ouistreham ferry h and marina (9.22.14). Here a canal leads 7M inland to a marin in the centre of Caen.

6M E of Ouistreham is River Dives (9.22.15) with marina.Th banks dry for 1M to seaward, and entry is only possible from H ± 2½, and not in fresh onshore wind conditions.

Deauville/Trouville (9.22.16), 8M ENE of Dives, is an importa yachting hbr. The sands dry more than 5ca offshore; strong W or N winds the entrance is dangerous and the se breaks between the jetties. In such conditions it is be attempted within 15 mins of HW, when the stream is slac To the NE beware Banc de Trouville (dries 2m), and sho water to the N where Les Ratelets dries at the mouth of th Seine.

ESTUAIRE DE LA SEINE/LE HAVRE (charts 2146, 2990) Th Seine est is entered between Deauville and Le Havre, and encumbered by shallow and shifting banks which exten seawards to Banc de Seine, 15M W of Le Havre. With win against tide there is a heavy sea on this bank. Here the SW-goin stream begins at HW Le Havre + 0400, and the NE-going at H Le Havre –0300, sp rates 1·5kn. Between Deauville and Le Hav the sea can be rough in W winds.

Chenal du Rouen is the main chan into R. Seine, and carrie much commercial tfc. The S side of the chan is contained b Digue du Ratier, a training wall which extends E to Honfleu (9.22.17). With almost 24 hours access/exit, Honfleur is a usef starting port when bound up-river. See 9.22.18/19 for notes o R. Seine, Rouen and Paris; and canals to the Med.

Le Havre (9.22.20) is a large commercial port, as well as yachting centre. From the NW, the most useful mark is the L Havre Lanby 9M W of C de la Hève (lt). The appr chan, which ru 6M WNW from the hbr ent, is well buoyed and lit.

Strong W winds cause rough water over shoal patches eith side of the chan. Coming from the N or NE, there is deep wat close off C de la Hève, but from here steer S to join the main e chan. Beware Banc de l'Éclat (depth 0·1m), which lies on N sid of main chan and about 1·5M from harbour ent.

9M N of C de la Hève is Port d'Antifer, a VLCC harbour. A hug breakwater extends about 1·5M seaward, and should be give a berth of about 1·5M, or more in heavy weather when there ma be a race with wind against tide. Commercial vessels in th buoyed app chan have priority. Yachts should cross the ap chan to the NW of A17/A18 lt buoys; at 90° to its axis; as quick as possible, and well clear of ships in the chan. Crossing vesse should contact *Vigie Port d'Antifer* and any priority vessel o VHF Ch 16. Off Cap d'Antifer the NE-going stream begins abo HW Le Havre – 0430, and the SW-going at about HW Le Hav + 0140. There are eddies close inshore E of Cap d'Antifer on bo streams.

CAP D'ANTIFER TO DIEPPE (chart *2451*) From C d'Antifer t Fécamp (9.22.21) drying rks extend up to 2½ca offshore. A Fécamp pierheads the E-going stream begins about HW L Havre – 0500, and the W-going at about HW Le Havre + 0025, s rates 2·75kn. Off Pte Fagnet, close NE of Fécamp, lie Le Charpentiers (rks which dry, to almost 2ca offshore).

From Fécamp to St Valéry-en-Caux (9.22.22), 15M ENE, (an beyond to Le Treport and Ault) the coast consists of chalk clif broken by valleys. There are rky ledges, extending 4ca offsho in places. The nuclear power station at Paluel 3M W of St Valér en-Caux (prohibited area marked by lt buoy) is conspi Immediately E of St Valéry-en-Caux shallow sandbanks, Le Ridens, with a least depth of 0·6m, extend about 6ca offshor At St Valéry-en-Caux ent the E-going stream begins about H

Dieppe – 0550, and the W-going stream begins about HW Dieppe – 0015, sp rates 2·75kn. E of the ent a small eddy runs W on the E-going stream.

Between St Valéry-en-Caux and Pte d'Ailly (lt, fog sig, RC) there are drying rks 4ca offshore in places. About 1·5M E of Pte de Sotteville a rky bank (depth 4·2m) extends about 1M NNW; a strong eddy causes a race over this bank.

Drying rks extend 5ca off Pte d'Ailly, including La Galère, a rk which dries 6·8m, about 3ca N of the Pte. Dangerous wks lie between about 1·2M WNW and 1·5M NNW of the lt ho. About 3M N of Pte d'Ailly, Les Ecamias are banks with depths of 11m, dangerous in a heavy sea.

From Pte d'Ailly to Dieppe (9.22.23) the coast is fringed by a bank, drying in places, up to 4ca offshore. E of Pte d'Ailly an eddy runs W close inshore on first half of E-going stream. Off Dieppe the ENE-going stream begins about HW Dieppe –0505, and the WSW-going at about HW Dieppe +0030, sp rates 2kn.

DIEPPE TO BOULOGNE Between Dieppe and Le Tréport (9.22.24), 14M NE, rky banks, drying in places, extend 5ca offshore. A prohib area extends 6ca off Penly nuclear power station and is marked by lt Bys. About 3M NW of Le Tréport, Ridens du Tréport (depth 5·1m) should be avoided in bad weather. Banc Franc-Marqué (depth 3·6m) lies 2M offshore, and about 3M N of Le Tréport.

N of Ault (lt) the coast changes from medium cliffs to low sand dunes. Offshore there are two shoals, Bassurelle de la Somme and Quémer, on parts of which the sea breaks in bad weather. 4·5M NW of Cayeux-sur-Mer the stream is rotatory anti-clockwise. The E-going stream begins about HW Dieppe –0200, and sets 070° 2·5kn at sp : the W-going stream begins about HW Dieppe + 0600, and sets 240° 1·5kn at sp.

B de Somme, between Pte du Hourdel and Pte de St Quentin, is a shallow, drying area of shifting sands. The chan, which runs close to Pte du Hourdel, is buoyed, but the whole est dries out 3M to seaward, and should not be approached in strong W or NW winds. For St Valéry-sur-Somme and Le Crotoy, see 9.22.25.

From Pte de St Quentin the coast runs 17M N to Pte du Touquet, with a shallow coastal bank which dries to about 5ca offshore, except in the approaches to the dangerous and constantly changing Embouchure de l'Authies (about 7M north), where it dries up to 2M offshore.

Le Touquet/Étaples (9.22.26) lies in the Embouchure de la Canche, entered between Pte du Touquet and Pte de Lornel, and with a drying bank which extends 1M seaward of a line joining these two points. Le Touquet-Paris-Plage lt is shown from a conspic tr, 1M S of Pte du Touquet. Off the entrance the N-going stream begins about HW Dieppe – 0335, sp rate 1·75kn; and the S-going stream begins about HW Dieppe + 0240, sp rate 1·75kn.

In the approaches to Pas de Calais a number of shoals lie offshore: La Bassurelle, Le Vergoyer, Bassure de Baas, Le Battur, Les Ridens, and The Ridge (or Le Colbart). In bad weather, and particularly with wind against tide in most cases, the sea breaks heavily on all these shoals. From Pte de Lornel to Boulogne (9.22.27; chart 438) the coast dries up to 5ca offshore. Off Digue Carnot the N-going stream begins HW Dieppe – 0130, and the S-going at HW Dieppe + 0350, sp rates 1·75kn.

BOULOGNE TO DUNKERQUE (charts *2451*, *1892*, *323*) Between Boulogne and C Gris Nez (lt, fog sig) the coastal bank dries about 4ca offshore. The NE-bound traffic lane of the Dover Strait TSS lies only 3M off C Gris Nez. Keep a sharp lookout not only for coastal traffic in the ITZ, but also cross-Channel ferries, particularly very fast hovercraft and catamarans. 1M NW of C Gris Nez the NE-going stream begins at HW Dieppe – 0150, and the SW-going at HW Dieppe + 0355, sp rates 4kn.

In bad weather the sea breaks heavily on Ridens de Calais, 3M N of Calais (9.22.28 and chart 1352), and also on Ridens de la Rade about 1·5M NE of the hbr. The drying hbr of Gravelines (9.22.28), which should not be used in strong onshore winds, is about 3M SW of Dunkerque Port Ouest; this is a commercial/ferry port which yachts should not enter. The old port, Dunkerque Port Est (9.22.29), has good yacht facilities and is 7·5M further E. If E-bound, the Passe de Zuydcoote (3·3m) is an inshore link to West Diep.

Offshore a series of banks lie roughly parallel with the coast: Sandettié bank (about 14M to N), Outer Ruytingen midway between Sandettié and the coast, and the Dyck banks which extend NE'wards for 30M from a point 5M NE of Calais. There are well-buoyed channels between some of these banks, but great care is needed in poor visibility. In general the banks are steep-to on the inshore side, and slope seaward. In bad weather the sea breaks on the shallower parts.

22

9.22.6 DISTANCE TABLE

Approximate distances in nautical miles are by the most direct route, whilst avoiding dangers and allowing for Traffic Separation Schemes. Places in *italics* are in adjoining areas; places in **bold** are in 9.0.6, Cross-Channel Distances; places underlined are in 9.0.8, Distances across the North Sea.

1.	***Cherbourg***	**1**																			
2.	Barfleur	20	**2**																		
3.	**St Vaast**	26	10	**3**																	
4.	Carentan	41	26	20	**4**																
5.	Grandcamp-Maisy	39	21	16	13	**5**															
6.	Courseulles	54	39	35	37	25	**6**														
7.	**Ouistreham**	66	46	46	46	35	11	**7**													
8.	Dives-sur-Mer	69	53	49	51	38	17	8	**8**												
9.	**Deauville/Trouville**	76	56	53	56	43	21	14	7	**9**											
10.	Honfleur	82	62	69	62	50	28	24	17	10	**10**										
11.	**Le Havre**	70	56	53	56	45	23	19	13	8	11	**11**									
12.	**Fécamp**	80	64	63	72	64	40	39	39	32	34	25	**12**								
13.	St Valéry-en-Caux	82	77	78	88	80	55	58	55	44	45	38	15	**13**							
14.	**Dieppe**	108	94	95	105	94	75	68	67	61	63	54	29	16	**14**						
15.	St Valéry-sur-Somme	130	120	120	132	125	103	103	97	95	95	85	62	45	35	**15**					
16.	Étaples	134	124	130	140	130	110	110	117	100	100	90	70	58	50	19	**16**				
17.	**Boulogne**	142	128	133	145	135	118	115	108	108	110	101	76	61	54	30	12	**17**			
18.	**Calais**	160	148	157	170	168	140	138	129	128	130	121	96	81	74	50	32	20	**18**		
19.	Dunkerque	182	170	179	192	190	162	160	151	150	152	143	118	103	96	69	51	42	22	**19**	
20.	*Nieuwpoort*	197	185	194	207	205	177	175	166	165	167	158	133	118	111	84	66	57	37	15	**20**

9.22.7 Special notes for France: See 9.15.7.

BARFLEUR 9.22.8

Manche **49°40'·34N 01°15'·48W** ❀❀◊◊✿✿✿

CHARTS AC 1349, *2135*, 1106, *2613*; SHOM 7120, 6864, 7120; ECM 528; Imray C32; Stanfords 1, 7, 21

TIDES –0208 Dover; ML 3·9; Duration 0550; Zone –0100

Standard Port CHERBOURG (⟵)

Times				Height (metres)			
High Water		Low Water		MHWS	MHWN	MLWN	MLWS
0300	1000	0400	1000	6·4	5·0	2·5	1·1
1500	2200	1600	2200				
Differences BARFLEUR							
+0110	+0055	+0052	+0052	+0·1	+0·3	0·0	0·0

SHELTER Excellent, but ent difficult in fresh E/NE winds. Hbr dries; access HW ±2½. Yachts may berth at SW end of quay but very limited space due to FVs. Beware rks/shoals in SE of hbr. Safe to ⚓ outside hbr in off-shore winds. See Hr Mr for moorings.

NAVIGATION WPT 49°41'·44N 01°14'·16W, 037°/217° from/to front ldg lt, 1·59M. In rough weather, esp wind against tide, keep 5M off Pte de Barfleur to clear the Race; see 9.22.5. From the N, identify La Jamette ECM bn and La Grotte SHM buoy. From the S, keep seaward of Pte Dranguet and Le Moulard, both ECM bns. Beware cross currents and Le Hintar rks (buoyed) and La Raie (bn) to E of ldg line. The chan may not be clearly identified until close in. A new spur bkwtr (55m long) is still planned from the ☆ Fl G 4s, halfway across the ent, toward the ☆ Oc R 4s.

LIGHTS AND MARKS Pte de Barfleur lt ho is conspic 1½M NNW of hbr, Fl (2) 10s 72m 29M, grey tr, B top, Reed (2) 60s. The church tr is a conspic daymark. Ldg lts 219°: both Oc (3) 12s 7/13m 10M, W □ trs, synch; not easy to see by day. Buoys are small. Jetée Est Oc R 4s 5m 6M. Jetée Ouest Fl G 4s 8m 6M.

RADIO TELEPHONE None.

TELEPHONE Hr Mr 02.33.54.08.29; Aff Mar 02.33.23.36.00; CROSS 02.33.52.72.13; SNSM 02.33.23.10.10; ⊖ 02.33.44.19.20; Météo 02.33.53.53.44; Auto 08.36.68.08.50; Police 17; SAMU 15; Dr 02.33.54.00.02; Brit Consul 02.99.46.26.64.

FACILITIES NW Quay (125 + 20 visitors), AB €0.64, M, Slip, L, FW, AC (long cable needed); **SC** ☎ 02.33.43.16.62. **Town** Gaz, ME (Montfarville: 1km S), V, R, Bar, ✉, Ⓑ, bus to Cherbourg for ⇌, ✈, Ferry.

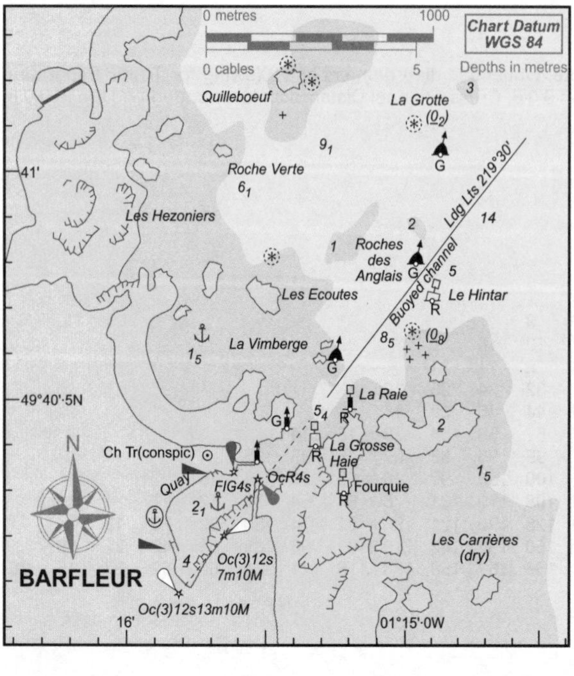

ST VAAST-LA-HOUGUE 9.22.9

Manche **49°35'·19N 01°15'·43W** ❀❀◊◊✿✿✿

CHARTS AC 1349, *2135*, *2613*; SHOM 7090, 6864, 7056, 7120; ECM 527, 528; Imray C32; Stanfords 1, 7, 21

TIDES –0240 Dover; ML 4·1; Duration 0530; Zone –0100

Standard Port CHERBOURG (⟵)

Times				Height (metres)			
High Water		Low Water		MHWS	MHWN	MLWN	MLWS
0300	1000	0400	1000	6·4	5·0	2·5	1·1
1500	2200	1600	2200				
Differences ST VAAST-LA-HOUGUE							
+0120	+0050	+0120	+0115	+0·3	+0·5	0·0	–0·1

SHELTER Excellent in marina, 2·3m; lock open HW–2¼ to HW+3. Crowded in season. If full, or awaiting lock, ⚓ off in White sector of jetty lt between brgs of 330° and 350°, but this ⚓ becomes untenable in strong E-S winds.

NAVIGATION WPT 49°34'·34N 01°13'·86W, 130°/310° from/to main jetty lt (Oc 6s) 1·3M. Appr in W sector, leaving le Gavendest SCM By to stbd and Le Bout du Roc ECM By and Le Creux de Bas ECM bn to port. The ent is wide and well marked. Beware boats at ⚓, cross currents and oyster beds. "Le Run" appr is not advised and should not be attempted >1·2m draft.

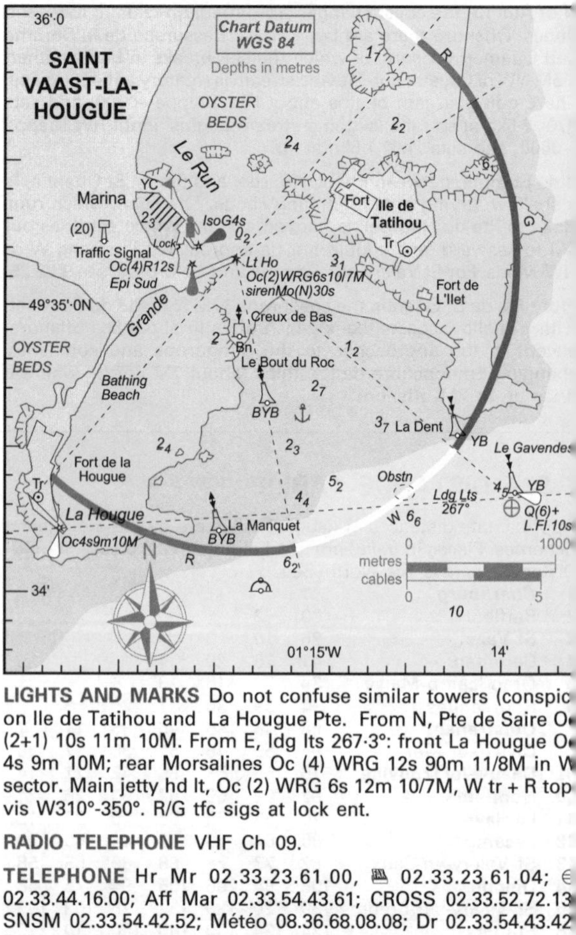

LIGHTS AND MARKS Do not confuse similar towers (conspic) on Ile de Tatihou and La Hougue Pte. From N, Pte de Saire Oc (2+1) 10s 11m 10M. From E, ldg lts 267·3°: front La Hougue Oc 4s 9m 10M; rear Morsalines Oc (4) WRG 12s 90m 11/8M in W sector. Main jetty hd lt, Oc (2) WRG 6s 12m 10/7M, W tr + R top, vis W310°-350°. R/G tfc sigs at lock ent.

RADIO TELEPHONE VHF Ch 09.

TELEPHONE Hr Mr 02.33.23.61.00, 📠 02.33.23.61.04; ⊖ 02.33.44.16.00; Aff Mar 02.33.54.43.61; CROSS 02.33.52.72.13; SNSM 02.33.54.42.52; Météo 08.36.68.08.08; Dr 02.33.54.43.42; Police 02.33.54.12.11; Brit Consul 02.33.44.20.13.

FACILITIES Marina (655 + 150 Ⓥ) ☎ 02.33.23.61.00, €1.59 Access HW –2¼ to +3, FW, C (25 ton), AC, D, P, BY, ME, El, Sh, Gaz, CH, Bar, R, ⊡, V, Slip; **Cercle Nautique de la Hougue** ☎ 02.33.54.55.73, Bar, R, C (3 ton), P, D, CH, FW, V. **Town** www.saint-vaast-reville.com, P, D, V, Gaz, R, Bar, ⊡, ✉, Ⓑ, ⇌ (bus to Valognes), Cherbourg: ✈, Ferry. Tourist Office 02.33.54.41.37.

CARENTAN/ISIGNY *9.22.10*

Manche ❁❁✿✿✿❀❀❀ Calvados ❁❁✿✿❀

CHARTS AC *2135, 2613*; SHOM 7056; ECM 527; Imray C32; Stanford 1, 21

TIDES –0225 Dover; ML Rade de la Chapelle 4·4; Duration 0510; Zone –0100

Standard Port CHERBOURG (⟵)

Use differences RADE DE LA CAPELLE 9.22.11.
HW Carentan is HW Cherbourg +0110. See tidal graph for Carentan appr chan.

SHELTER Temp ⚓ N of buoyed chans in winds <F5. Entry protected from prevailing S to W winds, but is not to be attempted in onshore winds >F5. Drying out on the hard sands of the estuary is not advised; nor is an early approach, as a bore (*mascaret*) may occur in the river channels between HW–3 and HW –2½ particularly at springs. At **Carentan** complete shelter in the canal/river and in the locked marina (max/min depths 3·5/2·9m). At **Isigny** drying pontoons on SW bank ¼M N of town. In emergency the Iles St Marcouf, conspic 5M N, provide some shelter from NNE, N and W winds (see next col).

NAVIGATION WPT CI SWM buoy, Iso 4s, 49°25'·45N 01°07'·07W.
For **Carentan**: leave WPT at HW–2 to –1½, tracking 214° to ent to drying chan, 1·6M. Chan is liable to vary in both depth and direction. Graph gives approx access times, using draft and tidal range at Cherbourg. There is a margin under the keel of 0·4 - 1·0m. All buoys have R or G reflective panels; 6 are lit, Fl 1, 2 or 3 R or G. After about 4M the chan enters between 2 bkwtrs, marked by bns. 3·5M further on the chan divides into three, forming a small pool. Enter the lock ahead (opens HW –2 to HW +3, tfc sigs); waiting pontoons are on E side above and below lock. Lock keeper will assign ⓥ berth, usually pontoon K.
For **Isigny**: leave WPT at HW –2½ heading about 159°/1·25M for IS unlit NCM buoy and ent to buoyed chan which is deeper than Carentan's, but unlit. From IS buoy track about 212° for 1·25M to first chan buoys. Pairs of buoys are spaced at approx 3ca intervals, but between Nos 9/10 and 11/12 the interval is 6ca, with a SHM perch midway.

LIGHTS AND MARKS **Carentan**: Bkwtr outer bns are lit, Fl (4)R 15s and Fl (4)G 15s. Ldg lts: Front Oc (3)R 12s 6m 18M and rear Oc (3) 12s 14m 10M, lead 209°30' for 1·6M from the ends of the bkwtrs and immediately outside (not valid within the buoyed chan). Lock sigs: FG = lock open, FR = lock closed.

Isigny: Ldg lts, both Oc (2+1) 12s 7/19m 18M synch & intens 171°-175°, lead 173° for 1·9M between bkwtrs to front ldg lt. Here turn port into R l'Aure for ½M to town.

RADIO TELEPHONE VHF Carentan, Call *Écluse de Carentan,* Ch 09 (0800-1200, 1400-1600LT & in lock opening hrs). Ch 09 also at Isigny (0900-1200 & 1400-1800LT).

TELEPHONE Hr Mr Carentan 02.33.42.24.44; Lockmaster 02.33.71.10.85; Hr Mr Isigny 02.31.22.10.67; Aff Mar 02.33.44.00.13; Auto 08.36.68.08.50; ⊖ 02.33.44.16.00; CROSS 02.33.52.72.13; Police 02.33.42.00.17; Ⓗ 02.33.42.14.12; Dr 02.33.42.33.21; Brit Consul 02.33.44.20.13.

FACILITIES

CARENTAN **Marina** (270 + 50 ⓥ) ☎ 02.33.42.24.44, 📠 02.33.42.00.03, €1.52; Access HW –2 to HW +3, FW, AC, P & D (0900-1000 Mon-Sat), Slip, C (50 ton), BH (16 ton); **YC Croiseurs Côtiers de Carentan** ☎ 02.33.42.28.53, Bar; **Services:** ME, El, Sh, CH, BY. **Town** Bar, Ⓑ, D, P, ✉, ⇌, R, V, ✈ (Cherbourg). Ferry: Cherbourg.

ISIGNY **Quay** AB (55+5), FW, AC, P, D, C (8 ton), Slip; **Club Nautique** AB, C, R, Bar; **Services:** ME, El, Sh. **Town** www.sctelfrance.com/portcarentan, R, V, Bar, Ⓑ, ✉.

ADJACENT ANCHORAGE

ILES ST MARCOUF, Manche, **49°29'·64N 01°08'·78W**. AC 2135, *2613*; SHOM 7056. Tides,9.22.12. The two islands, Île de Terre and to the N, Île du Large, look from afar like ships at ⚓. The former is a bird sanctuary and is closed to the public; the latter has a small dinghy hbr on the W side. ⚓ SW or SE of Ile du Large or SE or NE of the Ile de Terre. Holding is poor on pebbles and kelp; no shelter in S'lies. Ile du Large lt, VQ (3) 5s 18m 8M. Both islands are surrounded by drying rks, uninhabited and lack facilities.

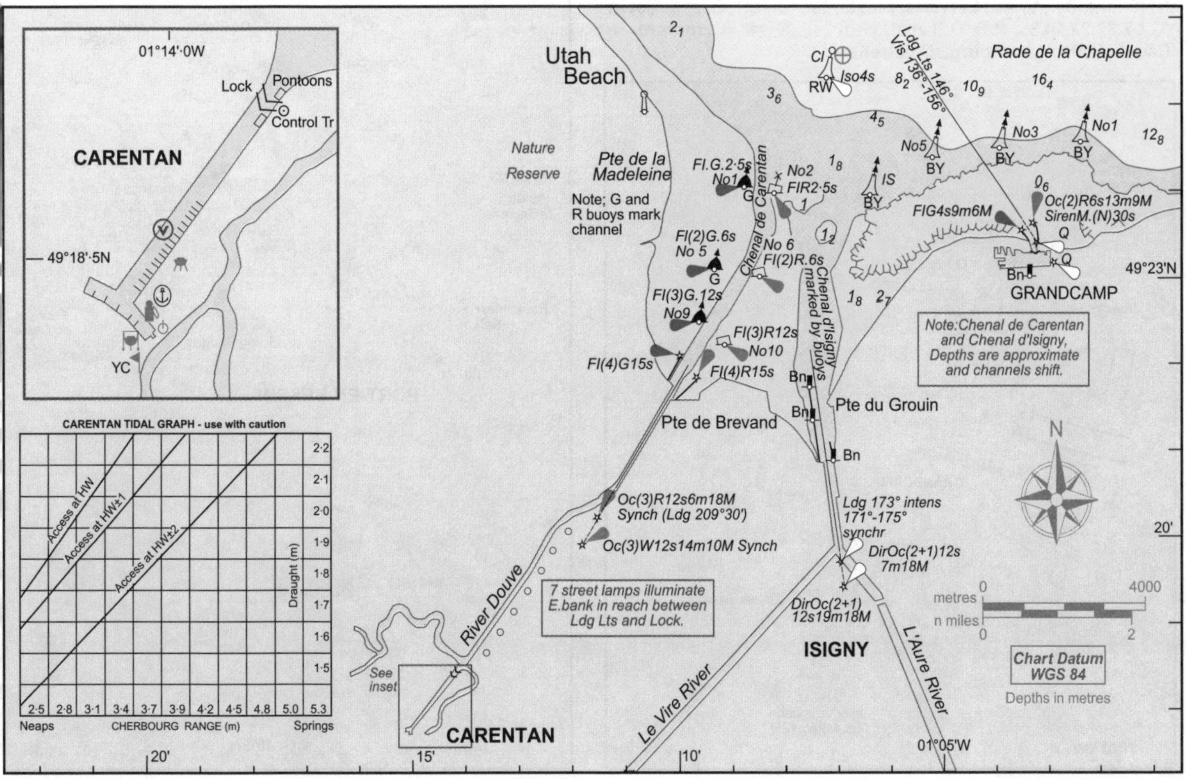

GRANDCAMP-MAISY *9.22.11*

Calvados **49°23'·44N 01°02'·95W**

CHARTS AC *2135*, *2613*; SHOM 7420, 6874, 7421; ECM 527; Imray C32; Stanford 1, 21

TIDES –0220 Dover; ML Rade de la Chapelle 4·4; Duration 0510; Zone –0100

Standard Port CHERBOURG (⟵)

Times				Height (metres)			
High Water		Low Water		MHWS	MHWN	MLWN	MLWS
0300	1000	0400	1000	6·4	5·0	2·5	1·1
1500	2200	1600	2200				
Differences RADE DE LA CAPELLE (3M to NW)							
+0115	+0050	+0130	+0117	+0·8	+0·9	+0·1	+0·1
ILES SAINT MARCOUF							
+0118	+0052	+0125	+0110	+0·6	+0·7	+0·1	+0·1

SHELTER Access day & night, but difficult in NW to NE winds > F6. Safe appr sp HW ±2, nps HW ±1.5. Gate into wet basin, with marina to the W, opens approx local HW ±2½. Ⓥ on N pontoon at E end.

NAVIGATION WPT 49°25'·10N 01°04'·62W, 326°/146° from/to front ldg lt 2·0M. Large flat rks, Les Roches de Grandcamp, extend about 1½M out from the hbr and dry approx 1·5m; heavy kelp cover can cause echosounders to under-read.

LIGHTS AND MARKS 3 NCM Bys, numbered 1, 3 and 5, mark the seaward limit of Les Roches de Grandcamp. Appr between Nos 3 & 5. E pier hd lt, Oc (2) R 6s, on a RW col. Ldg lts 146°: both Dir Q 9/12m 15M (vis 144·5°-147·5°). Two other ldg lts: Oc 4s 8/28m 12M, to E and S of hbr, lead 221°.

RADIO TELEPHONE VHF Ch 09.

TELEPHONE Hr Mr 02.31.22.63.16; Aff Mar 02.31.22.60.65; CROSS 02.33.52.72.13; SNSM 02.31.22.67.12; Météo 02.21.33.25.26; Auto 08.36.68.08.14; Police 02.31.22.00.18; Dr 02.31.22.60.44; Ⓗ Bayeux 02.31.51.51.51; Brit Consul 02.35.42.27.47.

FACILITIES Marina (240 + 10 Ⓥ) ☎ 02.31.22.63.16, €1.52, El, FW, BH (5 ton), Bar, V, AC; **Services:** ME, El, ✉, Sh, CH, Gaz, C. **Town** YC 02.31.22.14.35, P & D (cans), Gaz, ✉, Ⓑ, ⇌ (Carentan), ✈ (Caen). Ferry: Cherbourg, Ouistreham.

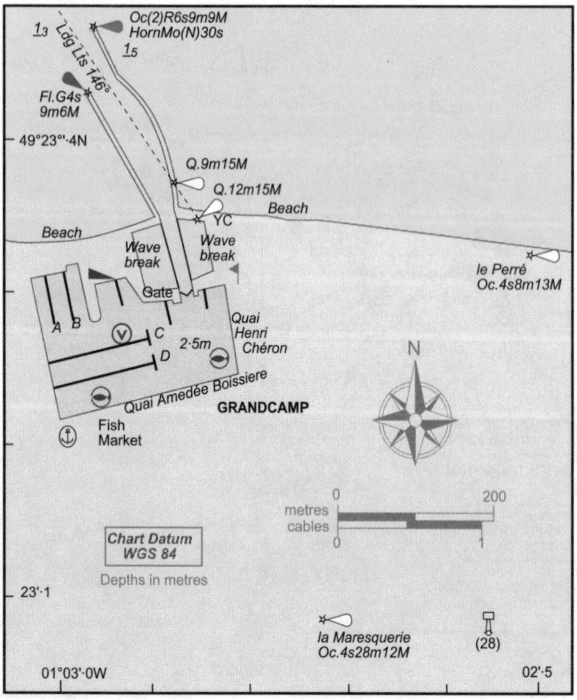

PORT-EN-BESSIN *9.22.12*

Calvados **49°21'·16N 00°45'·48W**

CHARTS AC 2136, *2613*; SHOM 7420, 6874, 7421; ECM 527; Imray C32; Stan'd 1, 21

TIDES –0215 Dover; ML 4·4; Duration 0520; Zone –0100

Standard Port LE HAVRE (⟶)

Times				Height (metres)			
High Water		Low Water		MHWS	MHWN	MLWN	MLWS
0000	0500	0000	0700	7·9	6·6	2·8	1·2
1200	1700	1200	1900				
Differences PORT-EN-BESSIN							
–0055	–0030	–0030	–0035	–0·7	–0·7	–0·2	–0·1
ARROMANCHES							
–0055	–0025	–0027	–0035	–0·6	–0·6	–0·2	–0·2

SHELTER Good in 2nd basin; outer hbr dries completely. Busy FV port. Yachts may stay for 24 hrs, but are not encouraged; there is little room. Basins accessible HW ±2. Contact Hr Mr on arrival. Waiting berths on Quai de L'Epi.

NAVIGATION WPT 49°21'·94N 00°44'·88W, 024°/204° from/to front ldg lt 204°, 1·1M. ⚓ prohib in outer hbr and 1ca either side of 204° transit. Ent is difficult with strong N/NE winds and >F8 it is dangerous. Beware submerged jetty (marked by R bn) to E of ent chan. Keep out of G sector of W mole lt.

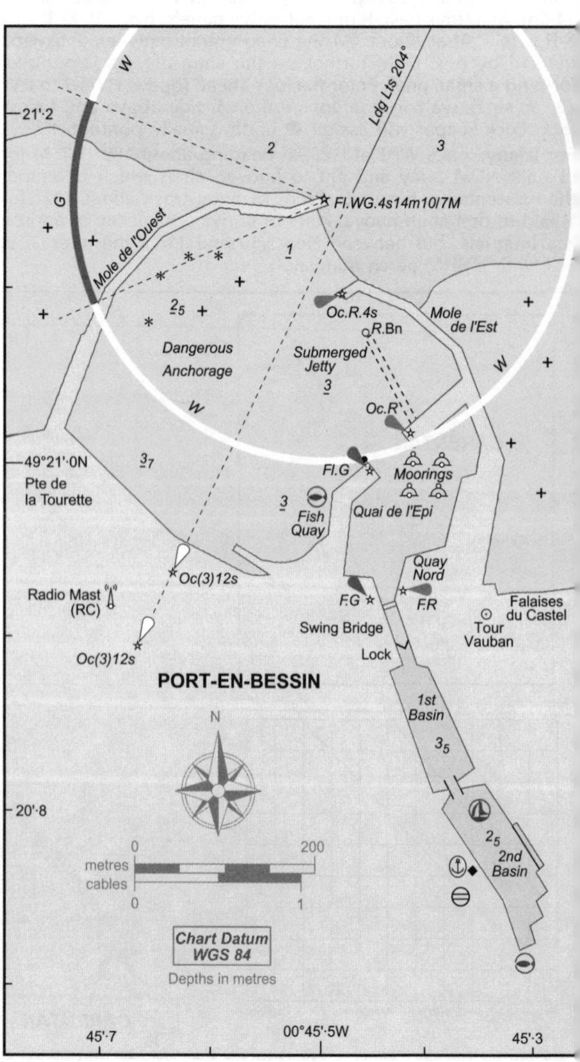

PORT-EN-BESSIN *continued*

LIGHTS AND MARKS Ldg lts 204°: Front Oc (3) 12s 25m 10M, W pylon, G top, vis 069°-339°; Siren 20s (sounded over 90° each side of ldg line, continuous in W sector, interrupted in E sector) TD 1997; rear, Oc (3) 12s 42m 11M, W and grey house; vis 114°-294°, synch with front; RC. Other lts as chartlet; inner pier hds are Oc (2) R 6s and Fl (2) G 6s. **Entry sigs:** ● over ●, or R over G flags = basins closed. Bridge has FR lt each side, and FR in the middle when shut. Lock opens HW ±2. When lock open, bridge opens whenever possible to suit yachts and FVs.

RADIO TELEPHONE VHF Ch 18 (HW ±2) for lock opening.

TELEPHONE Hr Mr 02.31.21.70.49; Aff Mar 02.31.21.71.52; Lock and br 02.31.21.71.77 HW ±2 ⊜ 02.31.21.71.09; CROSS 02.33.52.72.13; Semaphore/SNSM 02.31.21.81.51; Auto 08.36.68.08.14; Police 02.31.21.70.10; Dr 02.31.21.74.26; Ⓗ 02.31.51.51.51; Brit Consul 02.35.42.27.47.

FACILITIES **Outer Hbr** Slip, L; **Bassin II** €3.05 for 7m, Slip, M, L, FW, AB, C (4 ton); **Services:** CH, El, Ⓔ, ME, Sh. **Town** P, AB, V, Gaz, R, Bar, ⊠, Ⓑ, ⇌ (bus to Bayeux), ✈ (Caen, ☎ 02.31.26.58.00). Ferry: See Ouistreham.

ANCHORAGE BETWEEN PORT-EN-BESSIN AND COURSEULLES-SUR-MER

ARROMANCHES, Manche, **49°21'·74N 00°37'·28W**. AC *2135*, *2613*; SHOM 6927. HW is –0040 on Le Havre; see Port-en-Bessin (9.22.12). Strictly a fair weather ⚓, with little shelter from the WW II Mulberry caissons which are conspic esp at LW. Rochers du Calvados dries 1·6m, 7ca ENE of ent. There are many wrecks offshore; 3 to the W and N are marked by a WCM and two ECM buoys. The most N'ly ECM buoy (Roseberry, 49°23'·1N 00°36'·5W) bears approx 025°/1·5M from the ent (lat/long as line 1) which is marked by a small unlit PHM and SHM buoy. Enter on about 245° for ⚓ in 3m to S of the caissons, or sound closer inshore. Caution rky plateau off the beach and obstructions to SE of ent, marked by four W buoys. Facilities: YC Port Winston ☎ 02.31.22.31.01, 2 slips (dinghies).

COURSEULLES-SUR-MER *9.22.13*

Calvados **49°20'·42N 00°27'·35W** ❁❁⚓⚓⚓✿✿

CHARTS AC *1349*, 2136, *2613*; SHOM 7420, 7421; ECM 526, 527; Imray C32; Stanfords 1, 21

TIDES –0145 Dover; ML 4·6; Duration No data; Zone –0100

Standard Port LE HAVRE (⟶)

Times				Height (metres)			
High Water		Low Water		MHWS	MHWN	MLWN	MLWS
0000	0500	0000	0700	7·9	6·6	2·8	1·2
1200	1700	1200	1900				
Differences COURSEULLES-SUR-MER							
–0045	–0015	–0020	–0025	–0·5	–0·5	–0·1	–0·1

SHELTER Good in **Bassin Joinville** (3m), but appr becomes difficult in strong N to NE winds. Avant Port dries 2·5m; best ent at HW –1. Swing bridge/lock into Bassin Joinville opens on request, HW ±2. Fair weather ⚓ (3-5m) at Anneau de la Marguerite, 134°/0·4M from landfall buoy.

NAVIGATION WPT 49° 21'.28N 00° 27'.69W, 314°/134° landfall By Iso 4s, 1.0M 350° from E jetty. RW Bys lead 134° on tr of Bernières-sur-mer church tower and La Delivrande twin spires (partly obsc'd by trees). Maintain 134° for 0.55M until ent bears 198°. Plateau du Calvados extends 2M seaward and banks dry for 0.6M. Beware rks awash at CD either side of ldg line.

LIGHTS AND MARKS Pte de Ver lt ho 40° 20'.40N 00° 31'.10W, is 2·5M W of hbr and obsc'd by cliffs when brg >275°, but from the N provides useful distance-to-go bearings. W Bkwtr is marked by ☆, Iso WG 4s 14m 9/5M (stay in W sector), and by 2 SHM perches and conspic crucifix at root. E Bkwtr is marked by 2 PHM perches and ☆ Oc (2) R 6s 9m 7M at root on E jetty. This lt in transit with Chateau (conspic) leads 194° to hbr ent.

RADIO TELEPHONE VHF Ch 09: Control Tr HW±2. Hr Mr & Office only open:

Mon-Sat	Sun	Daytime
0900-1200	0900-1200	HW±2
All year	Apr-Jun	Jul-Aug

TELEPHONE Hr Mr 02.31.37.51.69; Control tr 02.31.37.46.03; Aff Mar @ Caen 02.31.85.40.55; CROSS 02.33.52.72.13; ⊜ @ Port-en-Bessin 02.31.21.71.09; SNSM 02.31.37.45.47; Météo 08.36.68.12.34; Auto 08.36.68.08.14; Police @ Ouistreham 02.31.97.13.15; Dr 02.31.37.45.28; Ambulance 15; Fire 18; Brit Consul Cherbourg 02.33.88.65.70.

FACILITIES **Bassin Joinville** ☎ 02.31.37.51.69, report to pontoon X on E Quay unless otherwise directed by Control Tr, €2.18, Slip, FW, AC, C (25 ton). **Services:** P & D (cans 600m), BY, ME, El, Ⓔ, Sh, CH, SM. **Société des Régates de Courseulles** ☎ 02.31.37.47.42, Bar. **Bassin Île Plaisance** FW, AC, no Ⓥ; local shoal draft boats. **Town** V, Gaz, R, Bar, ⊠, ⓘ, Ⓑ, ⇌ (via bus to Caen), ✈ (Caen-Carpiquet). Taxi ☎ 02.31.37.46.00. Ferry: See Ouistreham.

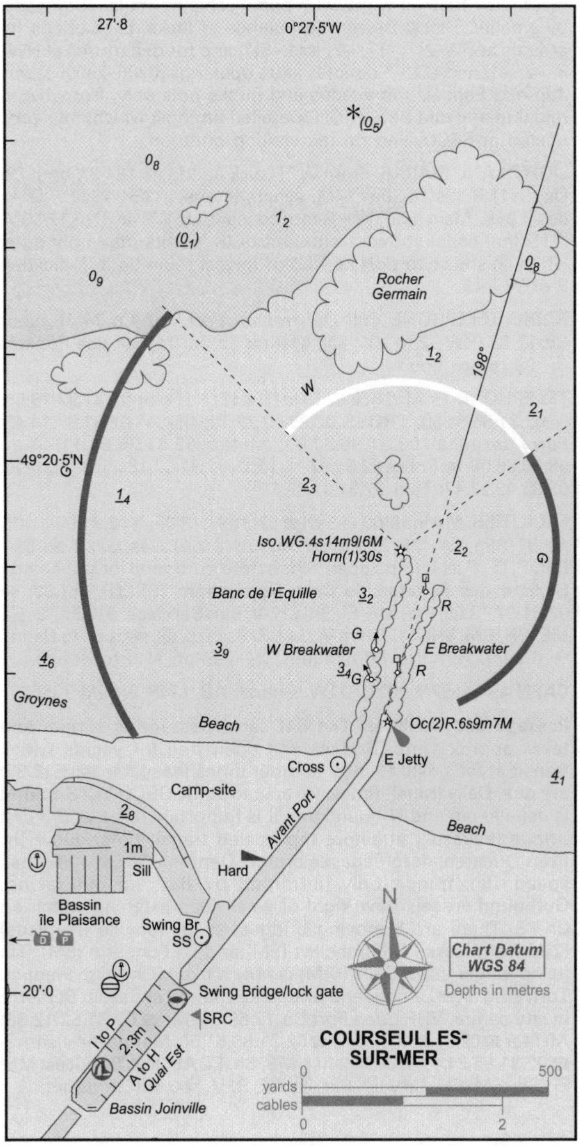
27'·8
0°27·5'W
49°20·5'N
20'·0
Rocher Germain
198°
W
G
Iso.WG.4s14m9/6M Horn(1)30s
Banc de l'Equille
W Breakwater
E Breakwater
Groynes
Beach
Oc(2)R.6s9m7M
E Jetty
Cross
Camp-site
Avant Port
1m
Sill
Hard
Bassin Île Plaisance
Swing Br SS
Swing Bridge/lock gate
SRC
1 to P
2.3m
A to H
Quai Est
Bassin Joinville
N
Chart Datum WGS 84
Depths in metres
COURSEULLES-SUR-MER
yards
cables
0
500
2

OUISTREHAM 9.22.14

Calvados **49°16'·82N 00°14'·89W** (E lock) ❁❁◊◊◊✿✿

CHARTS AC 1349, 2136, *2613*; SHOM 7420, 7421, 7418; ECM 526; Imray C32; Stanfords 1, 21

TIDES –0118 Dover; ML 4·6; Duration 0525; Zone –0100

Standard Port LE HAVRE (⟶)

Times				Height (metres)			
High Water		Low Water		MHWS	MHWN	MLWN	MLWS
0000	0500	0000	0700	7·9	6·6	2·8	1·2
1200	1700	1200	1900				
Differences OUISTREHAM							
–0045	–0010	–0005	0000	–0·3	–0·3	–0·2	–0·3

Note: There is a double HW at Ouistreham. The HW time differences, when referred to the start of the stand at Le Havre, give the time of the first HW.

SHELTER Very good in marina (depth 3·5m and access HW±3), 1ca S of locks on E side. Waiting pontoon in 3m on E of Avant Port.

NAVIGATION WPT ECM buoy, VQ (3) 5s, 49° 20'·42N 00° 14'·81W, 352°/172° from/to No 1 & 2 buoys, 1·26M. Ent chan is marked by training walls, with bns. Yachts normally enter canal by smaller E lock. Beware turbulence in locks. Lock opens for arrivals at HW–2½*, –1½, +2¼ and +3¼*; and for departures at HW–3, –2, +1¾ and +2¾*. * denotes extra openings (0700–2000LT) mid Jun-mid Sep; also at w/ends and public hols only, from 1 Apr-mid Jun and mid Sep-31 Oct. Detailed timings, which may vary, posted at SRCO, and on the waiting pontoon.

LIGHTS AND MARKS From WPT, pick up ldg lts 184·5°, both Dir Oc (3+1) R 12s 10/30m 17M, synch, intens 183·5°–186·5°. Chan has lt bys. Main lt ho, W + R top, conspic, Oc WR 4s 37m 17/13M. IPTS (full code) shown from control tr. Yachts may only enter when Ⓦ shows to port or stbd of lowest main tfc lt, indicating E or W lock.

RADIO TELEPHONE Call *Ouistreham Port* VHF Ch **74** 16; Lock Ch 12 68 (HW –2 to HW +3); Marina Ch 09, 74; Sté des Régates Ch 09 (office hours).

TELEPHONE Hr Mr/Lock 02.31.97.14.43; Aff Mar 02.31.97.18.65; ⊖ 02.31.86.61.50; CROSS 02.33.52.72.13; SNSM 02.31.97.14.43; Ferry terminal 02.31.96.80.80; Météo 02.31.26.68.11; Auto 08.36.68.08.14; Police 02.31.97.13.15; Dr 02.31.97.18.45; Brit Consul 02.35.42.27.47; Taxi 02.31.97.35.67.

FACILITIES Marina (600 + 65 Ⓥ) ☎ 02.31.97.13.05, 📠 02.31.96.31.25, €2.01, Slip, FW, ME, El, Sh, CH, AC, BH (8 ton), Gas, Gaz, Kos, SM, Bar, P, D, (Fuel pumps open ¾ hr before outbound lock opening); **Société des Régates de Caen-Ouistreham** (SRCO), €1.39, ☎ 02.31.97.13.05, FW, ME, El, Sh, CH, V, Bar; **Services:** BY, Sh, El, Ⓔ, ME, CH, SM, SHOM. **Town** V, Gaz, R, Bar, ✉, Ⓑ, ⇌ (bus to Caen), ✈ (Caen). Ferry: to Portsmouth. (May-Sept, also to Poole).

CAEN 49°11'·97N 00°21'·21W. Charts: AC *1349*, SHOM 7055.

Passage and Facilities: The 8M canal passage is simple and takes approx 1¾hrs. Bridges will open free for yachts which transit at the posted times; at other times fees (at least €12.35) are due. Daily transit times are posted at the SRCO YC: S-bound is usually pm and N-bound am. It is important to be *at the first bridge* (Pegasus) at/before the posted transit time; allow ½hr from Ouistreham to Pegasus bridge. Depths 2·5m to 10m; max speed 7kn; transit only permitted by day; no overtaking. Outbound vessels have right of way. Keep listening watch on Ch 68. There are 3 moving bridges, at: Bénouville (Pegasus) (2½M from locks), Colombelles (5M) and La Fonderie (8M). Tfc lts no longer used. Calix (6½M) is now a fixed 33m high viaduct. Turn stbd after La Fonderie bridge for marina at Bassin St Pierre in city centre. VHF *Caen Port* Ch 12 68. Hr Mr ☎ 02.31.52.12.88; Aff Mar ☎ 02.31.85.40.55; ⊖ ☎ 02.31.86.61.50; **Marina** (64 visitors) ☎ 02.31.95.24.47, P & D (cans), ME, Sh, El, AB, FW; **Services:** ME, El, Sh, SM, CH. **City** Ⓑ, Bar, Ⓗ, ✉, R, V, ⇌, ✈ (Carpiquet).

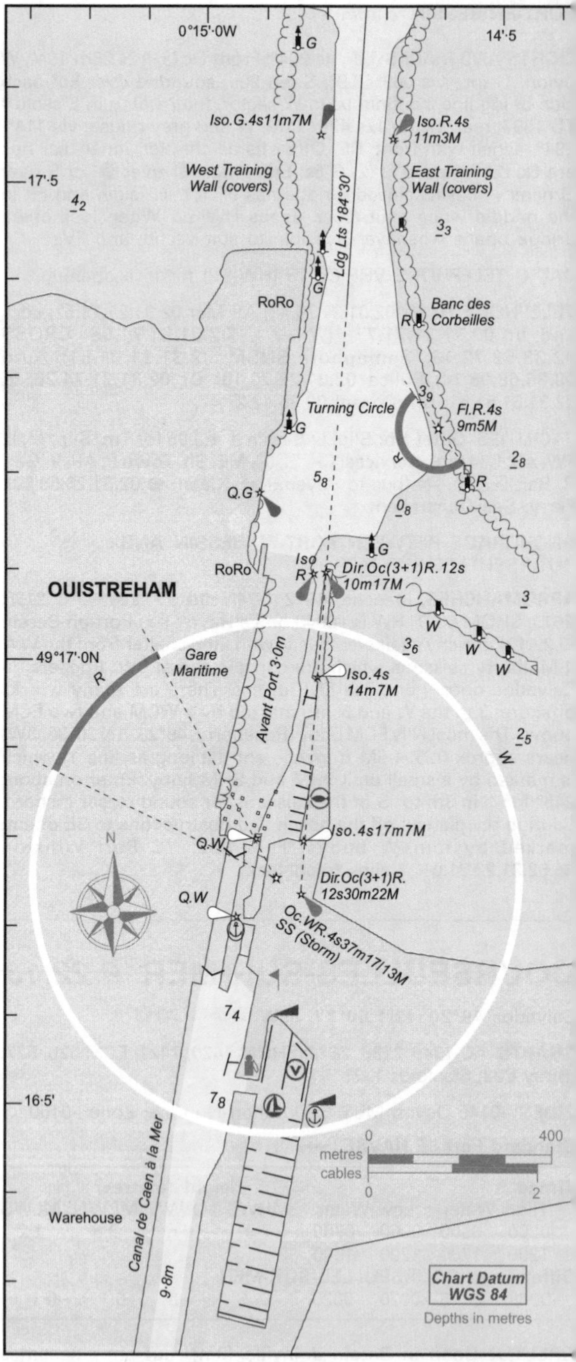

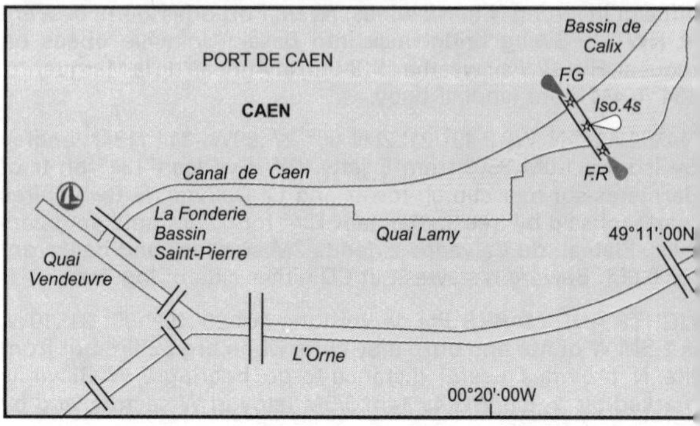

DIVES-SUR-MER *9.22.15*

Calvados **49°17'·92N 00°05'·29W** ✽✽◊◊◊✿✿

CHARTS AC 2146; SHOM 7420, 7418; ECM 526; Imray C32; Stanfords 1, 21

TIDES –0135 Dover; ML 5·1m; Duration; Zone –0100

Standard Port LE HAVRE (⟶)

Times				Height (metres)			
High Water		Low Water		MHWS	MHWN	MLWN	MLWS
0000	0500	0000	0700	7·9	6·6	2·8	1·2
1200	1700	1200	1900				
Differences DIVES-SUR-MER							
–0100	–0010	0000	0000	+0·3	+0·2	+0·2	+0·1

Note: There is a double HW at Dives. HW time differences, referred to the start of the stand at Le Havre, give times of the first HW.

SHELTER Excellent in marina. Appr dries to 1M offshore and can be difficult in NW/NE > F5. Marina ent 400m W of Dir lt, off shallow R La Dives. Access HW±3 (HW±2½ for draft >1·5m) via single gate. Sill below gate is 2·5m above CD; gate opens when tide 4·5m above CD and may create a 4-5kn current for the first 45 mins at springs. In low season it is advised to pre-check marina opening hours. Alternatively follow river chan to berth on YC pontoon (2 Ⓥ) below footbridge (max draft 1·5m).

NAVIGATION WPT 49°18'·86N 00°05'·83W, Landfall buoy "DI", L Fl 10s, 339°/159° from/to Nos 1/2 buoys, 4ca. (Note: buoy "DI" is off chartlet). 2 waiting buoys (untenable in WNW F4) are reported close to WPT in 3m. Beware sandbanks (drying 4·2m) each side of buoyed chan; keep well clear of two large SHM bns on W side. After last chan buoys, hug the shore to GRG buoy and 2 G perches marking submerged training wall leading to marina ent.

LIGHTS AND MARKS Densely wooded hills E of Houlgate locate the ent. 4 PHM and 2 SHM unlit buoys are moved to suit shifting chan; Nos 3 and 5 SHMs are bns, QG 12m 4M and Fl G 4s 13m 4M respectively. Dir lt 159° Oc (2+1) WRG 12s 7m 12/9M, R hut opposite Pte de Cabourg, vis G125°-157°, W157°-162°, R162°-194°. W sector covers chan only up to Nos 3/4 marks; thence follow the chan buoys/bns. Close E of marina a preferred-chan-to-port GRG buoy, IQG (2+1), marks shoals to N and R La Dives. Caution: Buoys/bns may not be numbered.

RADIO TELEPHONE VHF Ch 09, H24.

TELEPHONE Hr Mr 02.31.24.48.00, ℻ 02.31.24.73.02; CROSS 02.35.52.72.13; Météo = via Hr Mr; Auto 08.36.68.08.14; Police 02.31.24.85.00; Dr 02.31.91.05.44.

FACILITIES Marina (Port Guillaume) (545+55 Ⓥ) ☎ 02.31.24.48.00, ℻ 02.31.24.73.02, €1.83, AC, FW, P, D, ⊡, Slip, BH (30 ton), C (1·5 ton), mast lowering; **Cabourg YC** ☎ 02.31.91.23.55, Bar; **Services**: BY, ME, El, CH, Sh. **Town** V, R, Bar, Ⓑ, ✉, ✈ (Deauville). Ferry: Ouistreham.

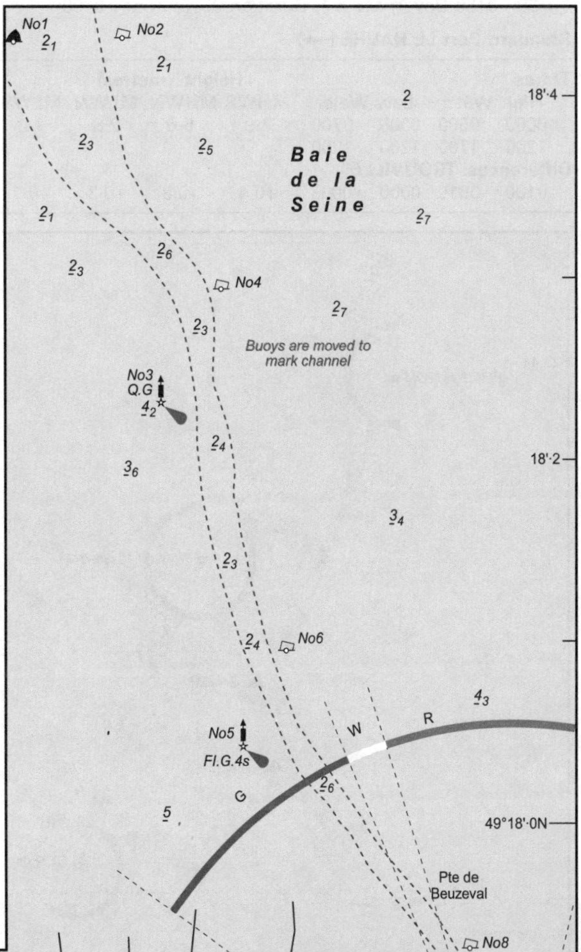

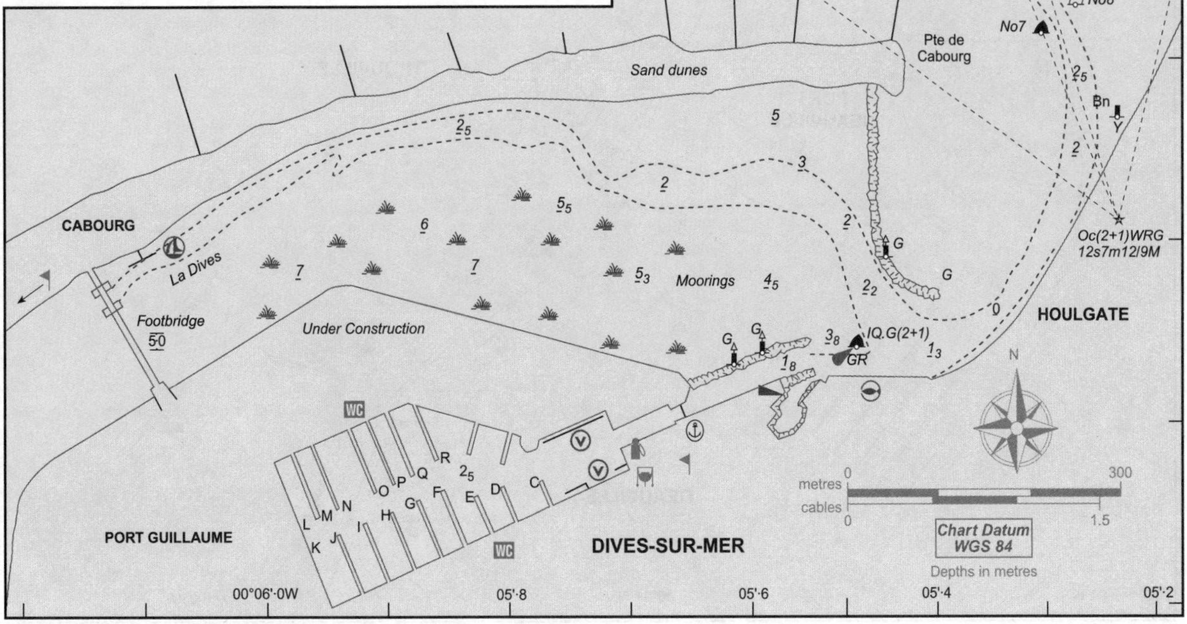

DEAUVILLE/TROUVILLE *9.22.16*

Calvados **49° 22'·38N 00° 04'·15E**

CHARTS AC *1349*, 2146, *2613*; SHOM 7420, 7418; ECM 526, 1012; Imray C32; Stanfords 1, 21

TIDES –0130 Dover; ML 5·1; Duration 0510; Zone –0100

Standard Port LE HAVRE (⟶)

Times				Height (metres)			
High Water		Low Water		MHWS	MHWN	MLWN	MLWS
0000	0500	0000	0700	7·9	6·6	2·8	1·2
1200	1700	1200	1900				
Differences TROUVILLE							
–0100	–0010	0000	+0005	+0·4	+0·3	+0·3	+0·1

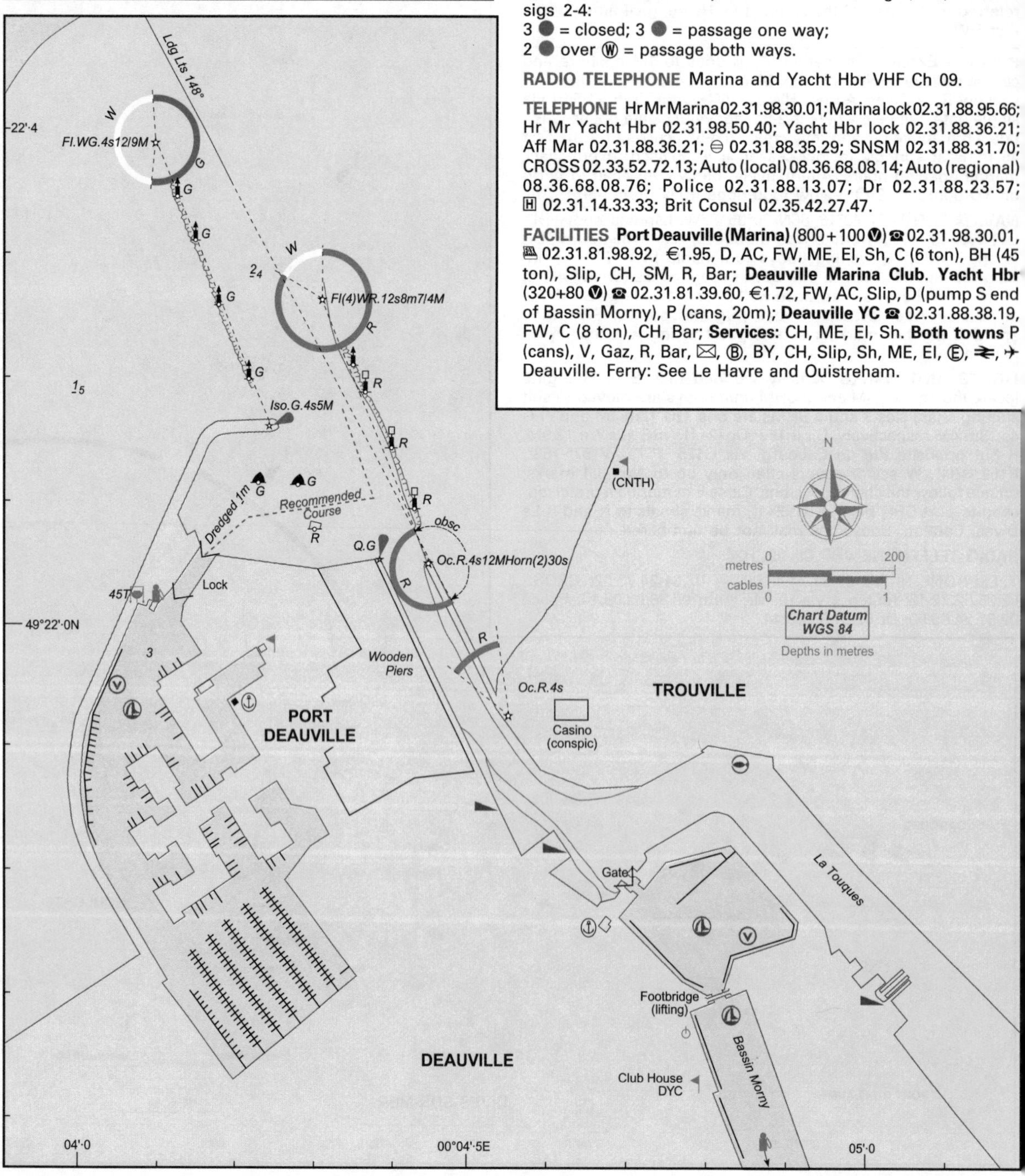

Note: There is a double HW at Trouville. The HW time differences, when referred to the start of the stand at Le Havre, give the time of the first HW.

SHELTER Good in marina and Yacht Hbr, but ent to chan difficult in NW/N winds > force 6. Chan and river dry 2·4m; no access LW±2½, for 2m draft. Marina lock opens H24, if enough water outside. Yacht Hbr gate open HW –2 to HW +2½.

NAVIGATION WPT 49°22'·94N 00°03'·62E, 331°/151° from/to W bkwtr lt Fl WG 4s, 0·65M. Semoy ECM, VQ (3) 5s, marks wreck 2·2M from ent, on ldg line. Do not appr from E of N due to Les Ratelets and Banc de Trouville. Trouville SW buoy, WCM, VQ (9) 10s, is 1M WNW of ent.

LIGHTS AND MARKS Casino is conspic on Trouville side. Ldg lts 148°, both Oc R 4s synch. Yacht Hbr ent sigs (vert) are IPTS sigs 2-4:
3 ● = closed; 3 ● = passage one way;
2 ● over Ⓦ = passage both ways.

RADIO TELEPHONE Marina and Yacht Hbr VHF Ch 09.

TELEPHONE Hr Mr Marina 02.31.98.30.01; Marina lock 02.31.88.95.66; Hr Mr Yacht Hbr 02.31.98.50.40; Yacht Hbr lock 02.31.88.36.21; Aff Mar 02.31.88.36.21; ⊜ 02.31.88.35.29; SNSM 02.31.88.31.70; CROSS 02.33.52.72.13; Auto (local) 08.36.68.08.14; Auto (regional) 08.36.68.08.76; Police 02.31.88.13.07; Dr 02.31.88.23.57; Ⓗ 02.31.14.33.33; Brit Consul 02.35.42.27.47.

FACILITIES Port Deauville (Marina) (800 + 100 Ⓥ) ☎ 02.31.98.30.01, Fax 02.31.81.98.92, €1.95, D, AC, FW, ME, El, Sh, C (6 ton), BH (45 ton), Slip, CH, SM, R, Bar; **Deauville Marina Club. Yacht Hbr** (320+80 Ⓥ) ☎ 02.31.81.39.60, €1.72, FW, AC, Slip, D (pump S end of Bassin Morny), P (cans, 20m); **Deauville YC** ☎ 02.31.88.38.19, FW, C (8 ton), CH, Bar; **Services:** CH, ME, El, Sh. **Both towns** P (cans), V, Gaz, R, Bar, ✉, Ⓑ, BY, CH, Slip, Sh, ME, El, Ⓔ, ⇌, ✈ Deauville. Ferry: See Le Havre and Ouistreham.

HONFLEUR *9.22.17*

Calvados **49° 25'·69N 00° 13'·90E**

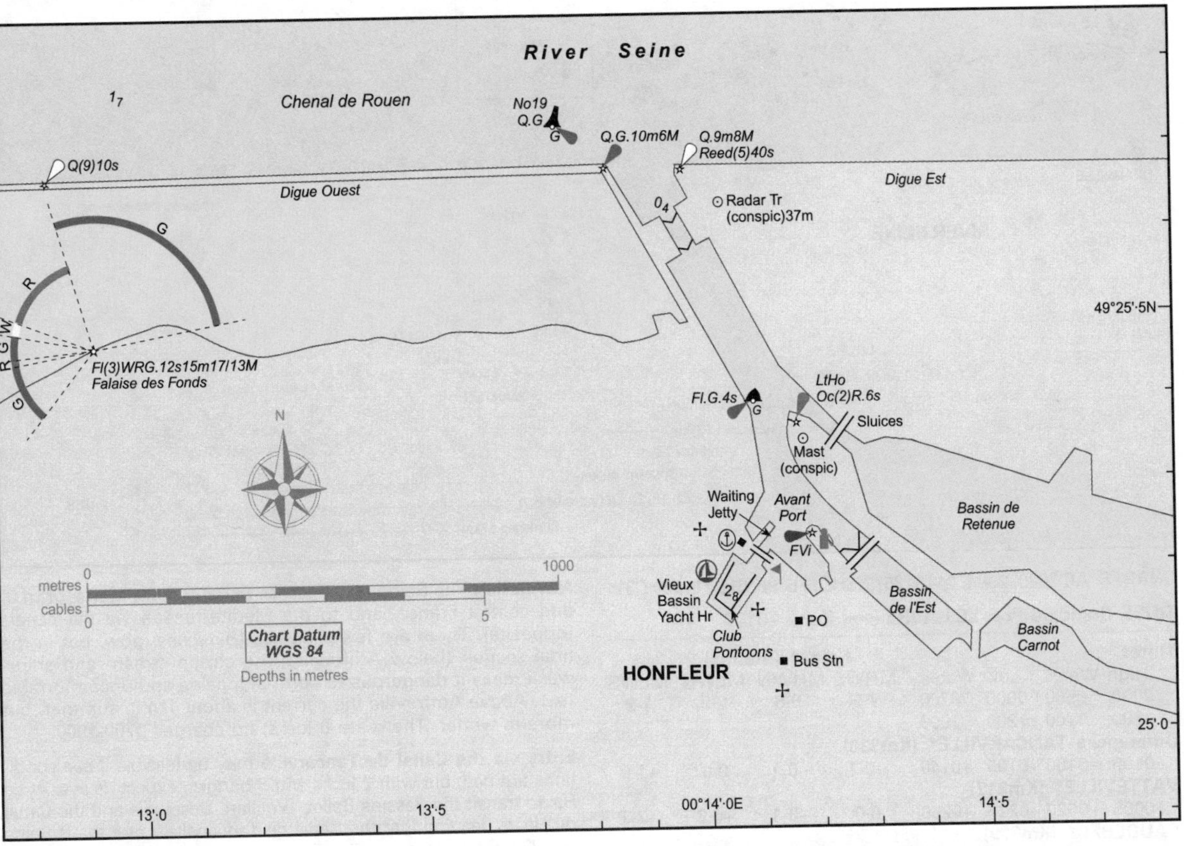

CHARTS AC 2994, 2146, *2613*; SHOM 7420, 6683, 7418; ECM 1012; Imray C31; Stanfords 1, 21

TIDES –0135 Dover; ML 5·0; Duration 0540; Zone –0100

Standard Port LE HAVRE (⟵)

Times				Height (metres)			
High Water		Low Water		MHWS	MHWN	MLWN	MLWS
0000	0500	0000	0700	7·9	6·6	2·8	1·2
1200	1700	1200	1900				
Differences HONFLEUR							
–0135	–0135	+0015	+0040	+0·1	+0·1	+0·1	+0·3
ANTIFER							
+0025	+0015	+0005	–0007	+0·1	0·0	0·0	0·0

In the Seine there is a HW stand of about 2hrs 50 mins. The HW time differences refer to the beginning of the stand.

SHELTER Excellent in the Vieux Bassin where visitors raft up on a pontoon on NW side but no multi-hulls. Or ask YC for possible vacant berth on YC finger pontoons. Immediately outside the Vieux Bassin yachts can wait on E side of the jetty. There are also berths on the W side of Avant Port, close N of the waiting jetty. There are no yacht berths elsewhere in the Avant Port. Larger yachts can enter Bassin de l'Est; see Hr Mr.

NAVIGATION WPT Ratier NW SHM buoy, VQG, 49°26'·84N, 00°02'·50E, at ent to buoyed/lit Chenal de Rouen. Appr at HW ±3, keeping between the Digue Nord, marked by posts, and the PHM chan buoys to avoid shipping. Ent between No 19 SHM buoy and conspic radar tr. Beware strong stream across ent. Rouen is 60M and Paris 192M up-river.

LOCK AND BRIDGE The **lock** (fitted with recessed bollards and ladders, but no pontoons) operates H24, but NOT LW±2 due to silting. It opens at H, every hour for arrivals; and every H+30 for departures. IPTS are in force. At the Vieux Bassin the old lock gate is permanently open. The **road bridge** lifts as shown below (LT). Yachts leaving have priority over arrivals.

2 Jan to 30 April and 10 Oct to 2 Jan
Weekdays: 0830, 1130, 1430, 1730.
Sat/Sun/Hols: 0830, 0930, 1030, 1130, 1430, 1530, 1630, 1730.
1 May to 30 Sept
Every day: 0730, 0830, 0930, 1030, 1730, 1830, 1930, 2030.

LIGHTS AND MARKS Falaise des Fonds lt, 0·75M W of ent Fl (3) WRG 12s 15m, 17/13M, W □ tr, vis G040°-080°, R080°-084°, G0084°-100°, W100°-109°, R109°-162°, G162°-260°. E mole Q 9m 9M, Y metal framework tr with B top, Reed (5) 40s. W mole QG 10m 6M, G framework tr. **IPTS** are in force at the lock. Note: The Pont de Normandie, 1·7M E of Honfleur ent, has 52m clearance and a pile lt, Fl Y 2·5s 3m, on N side of chan.

RADIO TELEPHONE Hr Mr VHF Ch 17 73 16; Lock 17 16 (H24); Radar tower Ch **73** 16 (H24).

TELEPHONE Hr Mr ☎ 02.31.89.20.02, 📠 02.31.89.42.10; Lock 02.31.98.72.82; CROSS 02.33.52.72.13; Aff Mar 02.31.89.20.67; ⊖ 02.31.14.44.30; SNSM 02.31.89.16.49; Auto (regional) 08.36.68.08.76; Auto (offshore) 08.36.68.08.08; Police 02.31.89.11.26; Dr 02.31.89.34.05; Ⓗ 02.31.89.04.74; Cercle Nautique ☎/📠 02.31.98.87.13; Brit Consul 02.35.42.27.47.

FACILITIES **Vieux Bassin Yacht Hbr** (120 + 30 Ⓥ, max LOA 20m), €1.68 AB, FW, AC; **Cercle Nautique d'Honfleur** ☎ & 📠 02.31.89.87.13, M; **Services:** BY, Sh, Ⓔ, C (10 ton), Slip. **Town** P & D (cans), V, R, Bar, Ⓞ, Gaz, ✉, Ⓑ, ⇌, ✈ Deauville. Ferry: Le Havre.

RIVER SEINE *9.22.18*

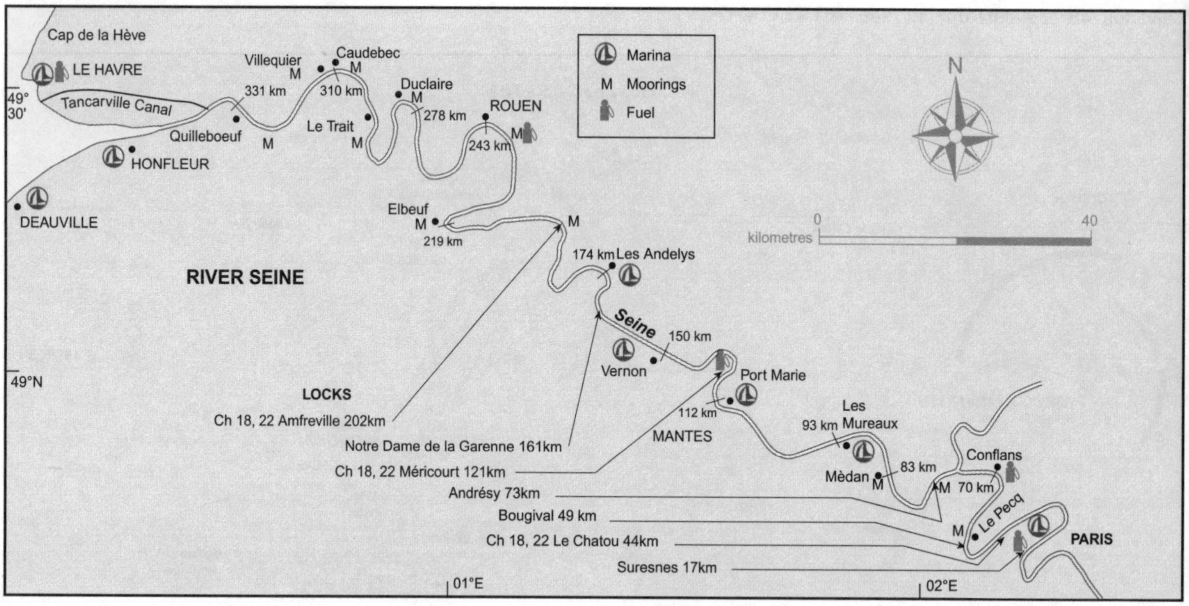

CHARTS AC 2880, 2994, 2146, *2613*; SHOM 6796, 6117; Imray C31

TIDES Standard Port LE HAVRE (⟵) Zone –0100

Times				**Height (metres)**			
High Water		Low Water		MHWS	MHWN	MLWN	MLWS
0000	0500	0000	0700	7·9	6·6	2·8	1·2
1200	1700	1200	1900				
Differences TANCARVILLE* (Km338)							
–0105	–0100	+0105	+0140	–0·1	–0·1	0·0	+1·0
VATTEVILLE* (Km317)							
+0005	–0020	+0225	+0250	0·0	–0·1	+0·8	+2·3
CAUDEBEC* (Km309)							
+0020	–0015	+0230	+0300	–0·3	–0·2	+0·9	+2·4
HEURTEAUVILLE* (Km295)							
+0110	+0025	+0310	+0330	–0·5	–0·2	+1·1	+2·7
DUCLAIR* (Km278)							
+0225	+0150	+0355	+0410	–0·4	–0·3	+1·4	+3·3
ROUEN (Km245)							
+0440	+0415	+0525	+0525	–0·2	–0·1	+1·6	+3·6

*HW time differences refer to the start of a stand lasting about 2¾ hrs up to Vatteville and about 1¾hrs at Duclair.

INFO: *Paris by Boat* (Jefferson/A Coles). *R Seine Cruising Guide* (Bowskill/Imray). *Carte-Guide Navicarte No 1.*

SHELTER/FACILITIES: Marinas/moorings/fuel, see above. Masts can be lowered at Dives, Deauville, Le Havre (marina qv; also storage) or Rouen.

TIDAL STREAMS require careful study; see the Admiralty *Channel Pilot.* At Ratier NW SHM buoy the flood starts at LW Le Havre +1 and at La Roque (Km342) at LW+2, and progressively later further up-river. So even a 4kn boat which left Le Havre at LW and passed the W end of the Digue du Ratier at LW+1½, can carry the flood for the next 65M/120km to Rouen; or leave Honfleur asap after LW Le Havre +2. Caudebec is a good half-way stop, if delayed. Going down-river on the ebb a boat will meet the flood. In a fast boat it is worth continuing, rather than ⚓ for about 4 hrs, because the ebb starts sooner the further down-river one gets.

Entry is usually via the dredged/buoyed Chenal de Rouen, which can be rough in a strong W'ly wind and ebb tide. Care is needed, especially near the mouth where there are shifting banks and often morning fog. Monitor Ch 73. From No 4 buoy to Tancarville bridge yachts must keep out of the Chenal de Rouen, ie outboard of the PHM chan buoys, whether going up or downstream. Yacht navigation is prohib at night, and ⚓s are few. A radar reflector, VHF aerial and ⚓ Ⓦ lt are needed, even with mast down.

Navigation The Seine gives access to Paris (Pont Marie = Km 0) and central France, and to the Mediterranean via the canals (opposite). There are fewer barges (*péniches*) now, but in the tidal section (below Amfreville) the strong stream and ships' wash make it dangerous to berth alongside and uncomfortable to ⚓. Above Amfreville the current is about 1kn in summer, but more in winter. There are 6 locks; no charges 0700-1900.

Entry via the Canal de Tancarville may be feasible if sea conditions are bad, but with 2 locks and 8 bridges, expect delays. At Le Havre transit the Bassins Bellot, Vétillart, Despujols and the Canal du Havre, leading into the Canal de Tancarville. Enter the R Seine (Km338) via locks close E of Tancarville suspension bridge (50m).

ROUEN, Seine Maritime, **49°26'·63N 01°03'·00E**. AC 2880, 2994; SHOM 6117. Yacht navigation prohib SS+½ to SR–½. Mast down/up @ pontoon SE side Bassin St Gervais (N bank, Km245) cost €122 in 1998; max stay 48 hrs. Berth in La Halte de Plaisance, NE side of Ile Lacroix, Km241. *Rouen Port* VHF Ch **73** 68. Hr Mr 02.35.52.54.56; Aff Mar 02.35.98.53.98; ⊜ 02.35.98.27.60; Météo 02.35.80.11.44; Facilities: **Bassin St Gervais** C (3 to 25 ton); **Halte de Plaisance** (50) ☎ 02.35.88.00.00, FW, AC, Slip, D, C (30 ton), BH (4 ton); **Rouen YC** ☎ 02.35.66.52.52; **Services:** ME, El, Sh, CH, Ⓔ, P (cans), D barge at Km239.

ROUTES TO THE MEDITERRANEAN *9.22.19*

The quickest route is Le Havre-Paris-St Mammès-canal du Loing-canal de Briare-canal Latéral à la Loire-canal du Centre-Saône-Rhône, approx 1318km (824M), 182 locks; allow 4 weeks. Max dimensions: LOA 38·5m, beam 5m, draft 1·8m, air draft 3·5m. Alternatives above St Mammès: R Yonne-Laroche, then either canal de Bourgogne-Saône; or canal du Nivernais-canal du Centre-Saône. Both slowed by many locks. There are other routes via R Oise/Aisne or R Marne, both continuing via canal de la Marne à la Saône. The Saône can also be accessed via the canals of N France, entered at Calais, Dunkerque; or via Belgian and Dutch ports.

Useful reading: *Inland waterways of France* (Edwards-May/ Imray); *Notes on French inland waterways* (Cruising Association); *Vagnon Cartes Guides de Plaisance.* More info, inc dates of closures (*chomages*), from the French Tourist Office, 178 Piccadilly, London, W1V 0AL, ☎ 020 629-2869, 📠 020 493-6594. Tolls are due; see 9.15.7.

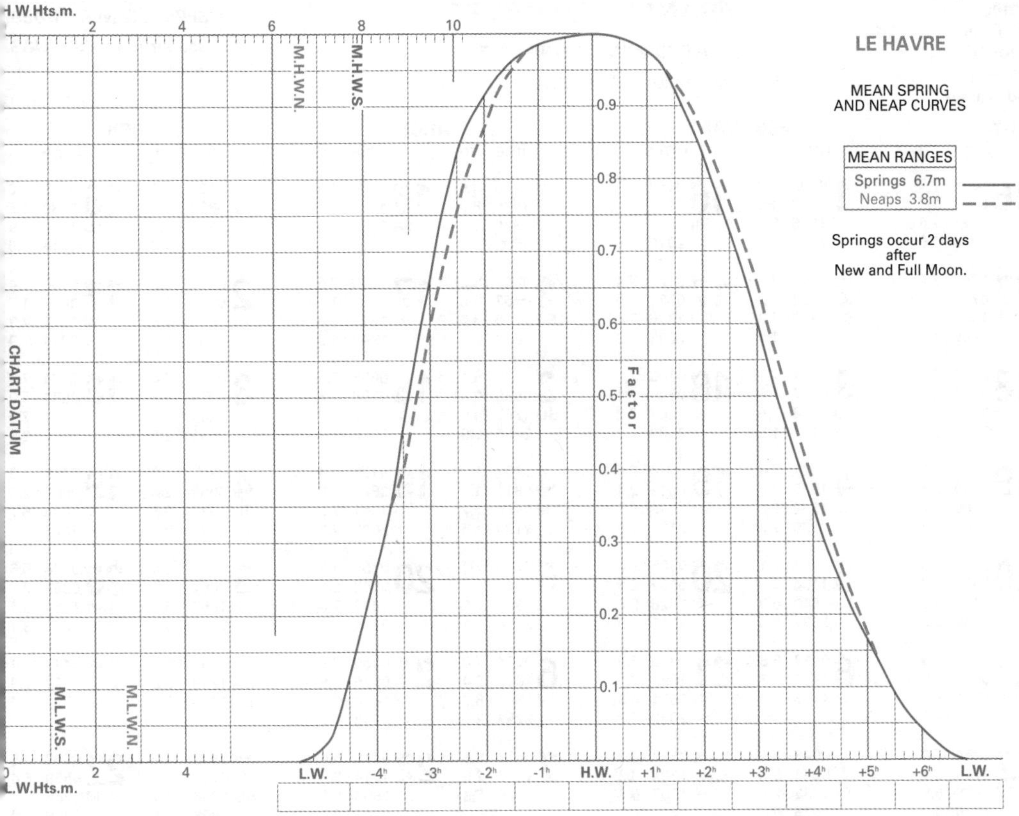

LE HAVRE *9.22.20*

Seine Maritime **49°29'·12N 00°05·43E**

CHARTS AC 2990, 2146, *2613*; SHOM 6683, 7418; ECM 526, 1012; Imray C31; Stanfords 1, 21

TIDES –0103 Dover; ML 4·9; Duration 0543; Zone –0100. Le Havre is a Standard Port. There is a stand at HW of about 3 hrs.

SHELTER Excellent in marina, access H24. Ⓥ pontoon 'O', first to stbd. Or request Hr Mr for long stay in Bassin Vauban.

NAVIGATION WPT 49°30'·99N 00°04'·08W, 287°/107° from/to bkwtrs, 6·4M. ⚓ prohib in and to the N of the fairway; it is also prohib to cross the fairway E of buoys LH7 and LH8. Banc de l'Éclat, awash at LW, lies N of appr chan and lobster pots close each side. Obey IPTS at end of Digue Nord.

LIGHTS AND MARKS Ldg lts 107° both Dir FW 36/78m 25M; grey trs, G tops; intens 106°-108° (H24). 2 chys, RW conspic, on ldg line.

RADIO TELEPHONE Call: Havre Port Control tr VHF Ch 12 20 (or 2182 kHz). Port Ops Ch 67 69 (H24). Radar Ch 12. Marina Ch 09.

TELEPHONE Hr Mr 02.32.74.74.00; Marina 02.35.21.23.95; Aff Mar 02.35.19.29.99; CROSS 02.33.52.72.23; ⊜ 02.35.41.33.51; SNSM 02.35.22.41.03; Météo 02.35.42.21.06; Auto 08.36.68.08.76; Dr 02.35.41.23.61; Ⓗ 02.35.73.32.32.

FACILITIES **Marina** (973 + 60 Ⓥ) ☎ 02.35.21.23.95, 📠 02.35.22.72.72, €1.98, AC, BH (16 ton), C (6 ton), CH, Slip, P & D (cash in HO; credit card OT), El, FW, Gas, Gaz, R, ⊡, ♿, V; De-mast @ marina or de-mast/store to await return: Chantier Naval de la Baie de Seine ☎ 02.35.25.30.51; 📠 02.35.24.44.18. **YC Sport Nautique (SNH)** ☎ 02.35.21.01.41, Bar; **Sté des Régates du Havre (SRH)** ☎ 02.35.42.41.21, R, Bar (closed Aug); **Services:** Ⓔ, ME, Sh, SHOM, ACA. Ferry: Portsmouth.

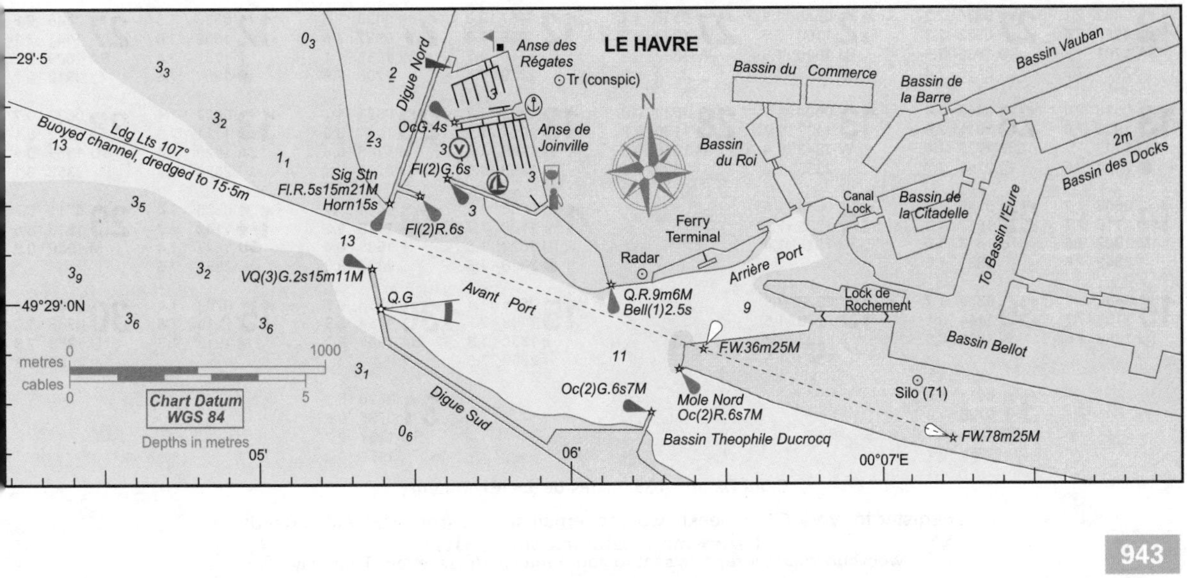

TIME ZONE -0100
(French Standard Time)
Subtract 1 hour for UT
For French Summer Time add ONE hour in **non-shaded areas**

FRANCE – LE HAVRE

LAT 49°29′N LONG 0°07′E

TIMES AND HEIGHTS OF HIGH AND LOW WATERS

SPRING & NEAP TIDES
Dates in red are SPRINGS
Dates in blue are NEAPS

YEAR **2002**

JANUARY

Date	Day	Time	m	Time	m	Time	m	Time	m
1	TU	0643	1.5	1153	7.9	1912	1.2		
2	W	0026	7.8	0730	1.5	1239	7.9	1958	1.2
3	TH	0114	7.7	0816	1.6	1327	7.8	2044	1.3
4	F	0203	7.6	0902	1.8	1417	7.6	2130	1.6
5	SA	0255	7.4	0950	2.0	1510	7.4	2218	1.9
6	SU	0353	7.2	1042	2.3	1611	7.1	2312	2.2
7	M	0455	7.1	1142	2.5	1719	7.0		
8	TU	0015	2.4	0604	7.0	1252	2.6	1832	6.9
9	W	0128	2.5	0712	7.1	1408	2.5	1944	7.0
10	TH	0239	2.4	0816	7.2	1514	2.3	2048	7.1
11	F	0340	2.2	0910	7.4	1611	2.0	2140	7.3
12	SA	0432	2.1	0957	7.5	1701	1.8	2226	7.5
13	SU	0518	2.0	1039	7.6	1743	1.7	● 2306	7.5
14	M	0559	1.9	1116	7.7	1822	1.6	2343	7.6
15	TU	0637	1.8	1152	7.7	1858	1.5		
16	W	0018	7.5	0713	1.8	1227	7.6	1933	1.6
17	TH	0052	7.4	0747	1.9	1301	7.5	2005	1.8
18	F	0125	7.3	0819	2.1	1334	7.3	2035	2.0
19	SA	0158	7.1	0849	2.3	1406	7.2	2104	2.2
20	SU	0230	7.0	0920	2.6	1441	6.9	2136	2.5
21	M	0307	6.8	0957	2.8	1523	6.7	2217	2.8
22	TU	0354	6.6	1045	3.1	1618	6.5	2310	3.0
23	W	0457	6.5	1145	3.2	1730	6.4		
24	TH	0016	3.1	0617	6.5	1300	3.2	1856	6.4
25	F	0136	3.0	0731	6.7	1423	2.8	2010	6.7
26	SA	0254	2.7	0830	7.0	1532	2.3	2105	7.1
27	SU	0356	2.2	0922	7.3	1630	1.8	2155	7.4
28	M	0453	1.8	1011	7.6	1725	1.4	○ 2243	7.7
29	TU	0548	1.4	1057	7.9	1818	1.0	2330	7.9
30	W	0639	1.2	1144	8.1	1908	0.8		
31	TH	0017	8.0	0728	1.0	1231	8.1	1954	0.7

FEBRUARY

Date	Day	Time	m	Time	m	Time	m	Time	m
1	F	0102	8.0	0812	1.0	1316	8.1	2037	0.8
2	SA	0148	7.9	0854	1.2	1402	7.9	2117	1.1
3	SU	0234	7.7	0934	1.5	1448	7.6	2157	1.5
4	M	0321	7.4	1015	2.0	1538	7.2	2239	2.0
5	TU	0414	7.1	1104	2.4	1640	6.9	2332	2.5
6	W	0517	6.8	1208	2.8	1758	6.6		
7	TH	0045	2.9	0641	6.7	1332	2.9	1926	6.6
8	F	0209	2.9	0759	6.8	1451	2.7	2038	6.8
9	SA	0322	2.7	0859	7.0	1558	2.3	2132	7.0
10	SU	0423	2.4	0946	7.2	1652	2.0	2215	7.3
11	M	0510	2.1	1025	7.4	1734	1.7	2251	7.4
12	TU	0549	1.9	1100	7.6	1810	1.5	● 2324	7.5
13	W	0624	1.7	1132	7.7	1843	1.4	2355	7.6
14	TH	0658	1.6	1205	7.7	1915	1.4		
15	F	0026	7.5	0728	1.6	1237	7.7	1943	1.5
16	SA	0057	7.5	0756	1.7	1307	7.6	2010	1.6
17	SU	0126	7.4	0822	1.9	1336	7.4	2035	1.9
18	M	0155	7.2	0849	2.1	1407	7.2	2102	2.1
19	TU	0226	7.0	0919	2.4	1443	6.9	2134	2.5
20	W	0305	6.8	0957	2.8	1528	6.6	2218	2.9
21	TH	0356	6.5	1050	3.1	1631	6.3	2320	3.2
22	F	0511	6.3	1204	3.2	1807	6.2		
23	SA	0047	3.2	0650	6.4	1343	3.0	1944	6.5
24	SU	0224	2.9	0805	6.8	1506	2.4	2045	7.0
25	M	0336	2.3	0904	7.2	1612	1.8	2140	7.4
26	TU	0440	1.7	0956	7.6	1713	1.2	2228	7.8
27	W	0538	1.2	1044	8.0	1808	0.8	○ 2314	8.0
28	TH	0630	0.8	1130	8.2	1856	0.5	2359	8.2

MARCH

Date	Day	Time	m	Time	m	Time	m	Time	m
1	F	0715	0.6	1215	8.3	1940	0.4		
2	SA	0043	8.2	0757	0.6	1259	8.2	2019	0.5
3	SU	0126	8.1	0835	0.9	1342	8.0	2056	0.9
4	M	0207	7.8	0911	1.3	1424	7.7	2130	1.5
5	TU	0248	7.4	0947	1.8	1508	7.2	2206	2.1
6	W	0334	7.0	1029	2.4	1604	6.7	2253	2.7
7	TH	0437	6.6	1127	2.9	1726	6.3		
8	F	0003	3.2	0608	6.3	1255	3.1	1910	6.3
9	SA	0141	3.3	0740	6.4	1427	2.9	2025	6.5
10	SU	0308	2.9	0843	6.7	1546	2.5	2117	6.8
11	M	0414	2.5	0929	7.0	1638	2.1	2156	7.1
12	TU	0457	2.0	1005	7.3	1716	1.7	2229	7.4
13	W	0533	1.7	1037	7.5	1750	1.5	2258	7.5
14	TH	0605	1.5	1108	7.7	1822	1.3	● 2328	7.6
15	F	0636	1.4	1139	7.7	1850	1.3	2358	7.6
16	SA	0704	1.4	1210	7.7	1917	1.3		
17	SU	0028	7.6	0730	1.5	1240	7.6	1942	1.5
18	M	0056	7.5	0756	1.6	1310	7.5	2008	1.7
19	TU	0125	7.4	0823	1.8	1341	7.3	2035	2.0
20	W	0155	7.2	0852	2.1	1416	7.0	2104	2.4
21	TH	0230	6.9	0926	2.5	1458	6.6	2143	2.8
22	F	0318	6.6	1014	2.9	1600	6.3	2243	3.2
23	SA	0432	6.3	1127	3.1	1739	6.2		
24	SU	0016	3.3	0620	6.3	1315	3.0	1920	6.5
25	M	0202	2.9	0743	6.7	1444	2.4	2026	7.0
26	TU	0317	2.2	0845	7.2	1553	1.7	2120	7.5
27	W	0423	1.6	0937	7.6	1655	1.1	2208	7.9
28	TH	0521	1.1	1024	8.0	1748	0.6	○ 2253	8.1
29	F	0611	0.7	1110	8.2	1835	0.4	2337	8.3
30	SA	0655	0.5	1154	8.3	1917	0.4		
31	SU	0020	8.3	0735	0.6	1237	8.2	1955	0.6

APRIL

Date	Day	Time	m	Time	m	Time	m	Time	m
1	M	0100	8.1	0812	0.8	1319	8.0	2030	1.0
2	TU	0140	7.8	0846	1.3	1400	7.6	2102	1.6
3	W	0219	7.4	0920	1.8	1444	7.1	2136	2.3
4	TH	0302	7.0	0958	2.4	1537	6.6	2220	2.9
5	F	0401	6.5	1054	2.9	1658	6.2	2331	3.4
6	SA	0533	6.2	1219	3.2	1840	6.2		
7	SU	0108	3.4	0708	6.2	1348	3.0	1958	6.4
8	M	0233	3.0	0815	6.5	1503	2.6	2049	6.8
9	TU	0337	2.5	0900	6.9	1558	2.2	2126	7.1
10	W	0423	2.1	0936	7.2	1641	1.8	2157	7.3
11	TH	0502	1.7	1008	7.4	1718	1.6	2227	7.5
12	F	0536	1.5	1039	7.6	1751	1.4	● 2257	7.6
13	SA	0607	1.4	1111	7.6	1820	1.4	2328	7.6
14	SU	0635	1.4	1143	7.7	1847	1.4	2359	7.6
15	M	0703	1.4	1215	7.6	1915	1.5		
16	TU	0029	7.6	0732	1.5	1247	7.5	1944	1.6
17	W	0100	7.4	0802	1.7	1323	7.3	2014	1.9
18	TH	0134	7.2	0834	2.0	1402	7.0	2046	2.3
19	F	0213	7.0	0909	2.3	1448	6.7	2127	2.7
20	SA	0304	6.6	0958	2.7	1551	6.4	2228	3.1
21	SU	0417	6.4	1112	2.9	1727	6.4		
22	M	0002	3.1	0559	6.4	1255	2.7	1856	6.7
23	TU	0139	2.7	0718	6.8	1419	2.2	2001	7.1
24	W	0253	2.1	0820	7.2	1526	1.6	2055	7.6
25	TH	0357	1.5	0913	7.6	1627	1.1	2143	7.9
26	F	0455	1.1	1001	7.9	1721	0.8	2229	8.1
27	SA	0546	0.8	1047	8.1	1809	0.6	○ 2312	8.2
28	SU	0630	0.7	1132	8.1	1851	0.7	2355	8.1
29	M	0711	0.7	1216	8.0	1929	0.9		
30	TU	0035	8.0	0748	1.0	1259	7.8	2004	1.3

Chart Datum: 4·38 metres below IGN Datum

TIME ZONE -0100
(French Standard Time)
Subtract 1 hour for UT
For French Summer Time add ONE hour in **non-shaded areas**

FRANCE – LE HAVRE

LAT 49°29'N LONG 0°07'E

TIMES AND HEIGHTS OF HIGH AND LOW WATERS

SPRING & NEAP TIDES
Dates in red are SPRINGS
Dates in blue are NEAPS

YEAR **2002**

MAY

Date	Day	Time	m	Time	m	Time	m	Time	m
1	W	0116	7.7	0822	1.4	1341	7.5	2037	1.8
2	TH	0156	7.3	0857	1.8	1425	7.0	2112	2.4
3	F	0239	6.9	0935	2.4	1516	6.6	2157	2.9
4	SA	0334	6.5	1028	2.8	1626	6.3	2304	3.3
5	SU	0448	6.2	1142	3.1	1750	6.2		
6	M	0026	3.3	0615	6.2	1258	3.0	1907	6.4
7	TU	0140	3.0	0726	6.4	1405	2.7	2004	6.7
8	W	0242	2.6	0818	6.7	1503	2.3	2045	7.0
9	TH	0334	2.2	0858	7.0	1554	2.0	2119	7.2
10	F	0420	1.9	0933	7.3	1637	1.8	2153	7.4
11	SA	0459	1.7	1008	7.4	1714	1.6	2226	7.5
12	SU	0534	1.6	1043	7.5	1746	1.6	● 2259	7.6
13	M	0605	1.5	1118	7.5	1817	1.5	2331	7.6
14	TU	0638	1.4	1153	7.5	1850	1.6		
15	W	0005	7.6	0712	1.5	1230	7.5	1924	1.7
16	TH	0042	7.5	0747	1.6	1310	7.3	1959	1.9
17	F	0122	7.3	0823	1.8	1354	7.1	2037	2.2
18	SA	0206	7.1	0903	2.1	1444	6.9	2123	2.6
19	SU	0259	6.8	0956	2.4	1548	6.7	2227	2.8
20	M	0409	6.6	1108	2.6	1711	6.7	2351	2.8
21	TU	0536	6.7	1233	2.4	1828	6.9		
22	W	0112	2.5	0649	6.9	1348	2.1	1931	7.2
23	TH	0223	2.0	0751	7.2	1455	1.7	2027	7.5
24	F	0327	1.6	0848	7.5	1556	1.4	2117	7.8
25	SA	0425	1.3	0939	7.7	1651	1.2	2204	7.9
26	SU	0518	1.1	1027	7.8	1740	1.1	○ 2249	8.0
27	M	0604	1.0	1113	7.9	1823	1.2	2332	7.9
28	TU	0646	1.0	1158	7.8	1903	1.3		
29	W	0014	7.8	0724	1.2	1242	7.6	1940	1.6
30	TH	0054	7.6	0801	1.5	1324	7.4	2016	2.0
31	F	0136	7.3	0837	1.8	1407	7.1	2054	2.4

JUNE

Date	Day	Time	m	Time	m	Time	m	Time	m
1	SA	0219	7.0	0916	2.2	1454	6.7	2137	2.7
2	SU	0307	6.7	1002	2.6	1549	6.5	2232	3.0
3	M	0407	6.4	1100	2.8	1654	6.4	2336	3.2
4	TU	0517	6.3	1203	2.9	1801	6.4		
5	W	0041	3.1	0623	6.4	1306	2.8	1902	6.6
6	TH	0143	2.8	0723	6.6	1406	2.6	1953	6.8
7	F	0241	2.5	0813	6.8	1501	2.3	2037	7.1
8	SA	0332	2.3	0857	7.0	1550	2.1	2117	7.3
9	SU	0418	2.0	0938	7.2	1634	1.9	2155	7.4
10	M	0459	1.8	1017	7.3	1713	1.8	2232	7.5
11	TU	0538	1.6	1057	7.4	1752	1.7	● 2309	7.6
12	W	0617	1.5	1136	7.5	1832	1.6	2348	7.6
13	TH	0658	1.4	1218	7.5	1913	1.7		
14	F	0029	7.6	0739	1.5	1302	7.4	1955	1.8
15	SA	0114	7.5	0822	1.6	1349	7.3	2039	2.0
16	SU	0201	7.3	0908	1.8	1440	7.1	2128	2.2
17	M	0254	7.1	0959	2.0	1539	7.0	2226	2.4
18	TU	0356	7.0	1059	2.1	1646	7.0	2331	2.4
19	W	0508	6.9	1205	2.2	1756	7.0		
20	TH	0040	2.3	0618	7.0	1315	2.1	1859	7.2
21	F	0151	2.2	0724	7.1	1423	1.9	2000	7.4
22	SA	0257	1.9	0826	7.3	1526	1.8	2055	7.5
23	SU	0357	1.7	0923	7.5	1622	1.7	2146	7.7
24	M	0452	1.5	1014	7.6	1713	1.6	○ 2232	7.7
25	TU	0541	1.4	1101	7.6	1759	1.6	2316	7.7
26	W	0624	1.3	1145	7.6	1841	1.6	2357	7.7
27	TH	0705	1.4	1227	7.5	1921	1.7		
28	F	0037	7.6	0743	1.5	1307	7.4	1959	1.9
29	SA	0116	7.4	0820	1.7	1346	7.2	2036	2.2
30	SU	0156	7.2	0855	2.0	1426	7.0	2113	2.4

JULY

Date	Day	Time	m	Time	m	Time	m	Time	m
1	M	0236	6.9	0932	2.3	1507	6.8	2153	2.7
2	TU	0319	6.7	1012	2.6	1553	6.6	2238	2.9
3	W	0410	6.5	1059	2.8	1649	6.5	2331	3.1
4	TH	0512	6.4	1154	2.9	1753	6.5		
5	F	0032	3.1	0621	6.4	1257	2.9	1856	6.6
6	SA	0138	2.9	0726	6.5	1404	2.8	1952	6.8
7	SU	0243	2.6	0821	6.7	1505	2.5	2042	7.0
8	M	0338	2.3	0910	7.0	1558	2.2	2127	7.2
9	TU	0428	2.0	0956	7.2	1647	2.0	2210	7.4
10	W	0516	1.7	1040	7.4	1734	1.8	● 2252	7.6
11	TH	0604	1.4	1124	7.5	1822	1.6	2335	7.7
12	F	0651	1.3	1208	7.6	1910	1.5		
13	SA	0020	7.8	0738	1.2	1254	7.6	1956	1.5
14	SU	0106	7.7	0824	1.2	1340	7.6	2041	1.6
15	M	0153	7.6	0907	1.3	1429	7.5	2126	1.7
16	TU	0242	7.5	0952	1.6	1519	7.3	2212	1.9
17	W	0335	7.3	1039	1.8	1615	7.2	2304	2.2
18	TH	0436	7.1	1133	2.1	1718	7.0		
19	F	0007	2.4	0546	6.9	1240	2.4	1828	7.0
20	SA	0120	2.4	0701	6.9	1354	2.4	1938	7.1
21	SU	0232	2.3	0814	7.0	1502	2.3	2041	7.3
22	M	0336	2.1	0915	7.2	1602	2.1	2135	7.4
23	TU	0434	1.8	1007	7.4	1656	2.0	2222	7.6
24	W	0526	1.7	1052	7.5	1745	1.9	○ 2303	7.6
25	TH	0610	1.5	1132	7.5	1827	1.8	2341	7.7
26	F	0650	1.5	1209	7.5	1905	1.7		
27	SA	0018	7.6	0725	1.5	1244	7.5	1941	1.8
28	SU	0053	7.6	0759	1.6	1319	7.4	2013	1.9
29	M	0128	7.4	0829	1.8	1352	7.2	2043	2.1
30	TU	0201	7.2	0857	2.0	1425	7.0	2112	2.4
31	W	0234	7.0	0926	2.3	1457	6.9	2144	2.7

AUGUST

Date	Day	Time	m	Time	m	Time	m	Time	m
1	TH	0311	6.8	1000	2.6	1537	6.7	2225	2.9
2	F	0358	6.5	1046	2.9	1631	6.5	2320	3.2
3	SA	0503	6.3	1147	3.2	1745	6.4		
4	SU	0031	3.2	0630	6.3	1306	3.2	1906	6.5
5	M	0156	3.0	0750	6.5	1428	2.9	2011	6.8
6	TU	0307	2.5	0847	6.8	1532	2.5	2105	7.1
7	W	0405	2.1	0938	7.2	1628	2.1	2153	7.4
8	TH	0500	1.6	1025	7.5	1723	1.7	● 2238	7.7
9	F	0554	1.3	1111	7.7	1816	1.4	2323	7.9
10	SA	0645	1.0	1156	7.9	1904	1.2		
11	SU	0008	8.0	0731	0.8	1240	8.0	1949	1.1
12	M	0053	8.0	0814	0.8	1324	7.9	2030	1.1
13	TU	0138	7.9	0854	1.0	1409	7.8	2110	1.4
14	W	0223	7.7	0932	1.3	1454	7.5	2150	1.7
15	TH	0310	7.4	1013	1.8	1542	7.2	2236	2.2
16	F	0406	7.0	1101	2.3	1643	6.9	2334	2.6
17	SA	0519	6.7	1206	2.8	1801	6.7		
18	SU	0054	2.8	0649	6.6	1332	2.9	1925	6.8
19	M	0216	2.6	0811	6.8	1449	2.7	2035	7.0
20	TU	0327	2.3	0911	7.0	1557	2.4	2127	7.2
21	W	0431	2.0	0958	7.3	1654	2.1	2210	7.5
22	TH	0520	1.7	1038	7.5	1737	1.9	○ 2247	7.6
23	F	0558	1.5	1113	7.6	1813	1.7	2321	7.7
24	SA	0631	1.4	1145	7.6	1846	1.6	2353	7.7
25	SU	0703	1.4	1216	7.6	1917	1.6		
26	M	0025	7.7	0732	1.5	1247	7.5	1945	1.7
27	TU	0057	7.6	0758	1.6	1317	7.4	2011	1.9
28	W	0126	7.4	0822	1.9	1344	7.3	2036	2.2
29	TH	0155	7.2	0847	2.2	1413	7.1	2104	2.5
30	F	0228	6.9	0917	2.5	1448	6.8	2138	2.8
31	SA	0310	6.6	0956	2.9	1535	6.5	2226	3.1

Chart Datum: 4·38 metres below IGN Datum

TIME ZONE -0100
(French Standard Time)
Subtract 1 hour for UT
For French Summer Time add ONE hour in **non-shaded areas**

FRANCE – LE HAVRE

LAT 49°29′N LONG 0°07′E

TIMES AND HEIGHTS OF HIGH AND LOW WATERS

SPRING & NEAP TIDES
Dates in red are SPRINGS
Dates in blue are NEAPS

YEAR **2002**

SEPTEMBER

Date	Time	m	Date	Time	m
1 SU	0409	6.3	16 M	0033	3.1
	1052	3.3		0642	6.4
	1643	6.3		1318	3.3
	2335	3.4		1914	6.5
2 M	0540	6.1	17 TU	0205	2.9
	1216	3.5		0804	6.6
	1824	6.3		1444	2.9
				2023	6.8
3 TU	0117	3.2	18 W	0321	2.4
	0724	6.3		0859	7.0
	1400	3.2		1552	2.5
	1945	6.6		2112	7.1
4 W	0244	2.7	19 TH	0419	2.0
	0827	6.8		0941	7.3
	1513	2.6		1641	2.1
	2045	7.1		2151	7.4
5 TH	0347	2.0	20 F	0501	1.7
	0920	7.3		1015	7.5
	1613	2.0		1718	1.8
	2135	7.5		2224	7.6
6 F	0445	1.5	21 SA	0534	1.5
	1007	7.7		1046	7.6
	1710	1.5		1750	1.6
	2221	7.8		○ 2254	7.8
7 SA	0540	1.0	22 SU	0605	1.4
	1051	7.9		1115	7.7
	1802	1.1		1820	1.5
	● 2305	8.1		2325	7.8
8 SU	0629	0.7	23 M	0635	1.4
	1135	8.1		1144	7.7
	1849	0.8		1849	1.6
	2350	8.2		2355	7.8
9 M	0713	0.5	24 TU	0701	1.5
	1219	8.2		1214	7.6
	1931	0.8		1915	1.7
10 TU	0034	8.3	25 W	0025	7.6
	0754	0.6		0726	1.6
	1301	8.1		1242	7.5
	2011	0.9		1940	1.8
11 W	0117	8.1	26 TH	0054	7.5
	0832	0.9		0751	1.9
	1344	7.9		1308	7.4
	2049	1.2		2006	2.0
12 TH	0200	7.8	27 F	0122	7.2
	0908	1.4		0816	2.2
	1426	7.6		1336	7.2
	2126	1.7		2033	2.3
13 F	0245	7.4	28 SA	0155	6.9
	0945	2.0		0844	2.6
	1511	7.2		1410	6.9
	2207	2.3		2105	2.7
14 SA	0339	6.9	29 SU	0237	6.6
	1030	2.6		0921	3.0
	1610	6.8		1456	6.5
	2304	2.8		2149	3.1
15 SU	0458	6.5	30 M	0337	6.3
	1138	3.2		1014	3.4
	1739	6.5		1605	6.3
				2256	3.4

OCTOBER

Date	Time	m	Date	Time	m
1 TU	0509	6.1	16 W	0140	3.0
	1140	3.6		0742	6.6
	1751	6.2		1420	3.0
				1959	6.7
2 W	0047	3.3	17 TH	0249	2.6
	0659	6.4		0835	6.9
	1338	3.2		1520	2.5
	1920	6.6		2046	7.0
3 TH	0221	2.7	18 F	0342	2.2
	0804	6.9		0913	7.3
	1452	2.5		1606	2.1
	2021	7.1		2123	7.3
4 F	0325	2.0	19 SA	0423	1.9
	0857	7.4		0945	7.5
	1553	1.9		1643	1.8
	2112	7.6		2155	7.6
5 SA	0423	1.4	20 SU	0459	1.6
	0943	7.8		1014	7.6
	1649	1.3		1718	1.7
	2158	8.0		2225	7.7
6 SU	0516	0.9	21 M	0533	1.5
	1027	8.1		1042	7.7
	1740	1.0		1750	1.6
	● 2243	8.2		○ 2255	7.7
7 M	0605	0.6	22 TU	0603	1.5
	1111	8.3		1112	7.7
	1826	0.7		1819	1.6
	2327	8.3		2327	7.7
8 TU	0649	0.5	23 W	0630	1.6
	1154	8.3		1141	7.7
	1908	0.7		1846	1.7
				2357	7.6
9 W	0011	8.3	24 TH	0656	1.7
	0729	0.7		1210	7.6
	1236	8.2		1913	1.8
	1948	0.9			
10 TH	0055	8.1	25 F	0028	7.5
	0807	1.1		0724	1.9
	1317	7.9		1238	7.5
	2025	1.3		1942	2.0
11 F	0138	7.7	26 SA	0100	7.3
	0842	1.6		0753	2.2
	1359	7.6		1311	7.3
	2102	1.8		2013	2.2
12 SA	0224	7.3	27 SU	0138	7.0
	0918	2.3		0824	2.6
	1444	7.1		1348	7.0
	2142	2.4		2046	2.6
13 SU	0319	6.8	28 M	0223	6.7
	1003	2.9		0902	3.0
	1543	6.7		1437	6.6
	2239	3.0		2130	2.9
14 M	0439	6.4	29 TU	0323	6.4
	1115	3.4		0956	3.3
	1713	6.3		1545	6.4
				2236	3.2
15 TU	0008	3.2	30 W	0450	6.3
	0621	6.3		1122	3.5
	1258	3.4		1723	6.4
	1848	6.4			
			31 TH	0021	3.1
				0630	6.6
				1309	3.1
				1849	6.7

NOVEMBER

Date	Time	m	Date	Time	m
1 F	0150	2.6	16 SA	0250	2.5
	0734	7.0		0833	7.1
	1424	2.4		1519	2.4
	1952	7.2		2046	7.1
2 SA	0256	1.9	17 SU	0338	2.2
	0828	7.5		0907	7.3
	1525	1.8		1603	2.1
	2045	7.6		2121	7.3
3 SU	0354	1.4	18 M	0420	1.9
	0915	7.9		0939	7.5
	1621	1.4		1643	1.9
	2133	8.0		2155	7.5
4 M	0448	1.0	19 TU	0457	1.8
	1001	8.1		1010	7.6
	1714	1.0		1718	1.8
	● 2220	8.2		2228	7.6
5 TU	0538	0.8	20 W	0530	1.8
	1045	8.3		1042	7.7
	1801	0.9		1750	1.7
	2305	8.2		○ 2302	7.6
6 W	0623	0.8	21 TH	0601	1.8
	1129	8.3		1114	7.7
	1845	0.9		1820	1.7
	2351	8.2		2335	7.6
7 TH	0704	1.0	22 F	0631	1.8
	1211	8.1		1145	7.7
	1925	1.0		1852	1.7
8 F	0036	8.0	23 SA	0009	7.5
	0743	1.4		0704	2.0
	1254	7.9		1219	7.6
	2004	1.4		1926	1.8
9 SA	0121	7.6	24 SU	0047	7.3
	0820	1.9		0738	2.2
	1337	7.5		1257	7.4
	2041	1.9		2001	2.1
10 SU	0207	7.2	25 M	0129	7.1
	0858	2.4		0815	2.5
	1422	7.1		1340	7.1
	2122	2.4		2039	2.3
11 M	0301	6.8	26 TU	0216	6.9
	0944	3.0		0857	2.7
	1518	6.7		1429	6.9
	2215	2.9		2126	2.6
12 TU	0411	6.4	27 W	0313	6.7
	1050	3.3		0952	3.0
	1631	6.4		1531	6.7
	2329	3.1		2229	2.8
13 W	0534	6.3	28 TH	0429	6.6
	1213	3.4		1109	3.1
	1758	6.3		1653	6.6
				2351	2.8
14 TH	0047	3.1	29 F	0557	6.8
	0652	6.5		1232	2.9
	1327	3.2		1813	6.8
	1911	6.5			
15 F	0154	2.8	30 SA	0111	2.5
	0751	6.8		0658	7.1
	1428	2.8		1347	2.4
	2005	6.8		1918	7.1

DECEMBER

Date	Time	m	Date	Time	m
1 SU	0221	2.0	16 M	0248	2.6
	0755	7.5		0824	7.0
	1453	2.0		1520	2.5
	2016	7.5		2045	7.0
2 M	0323	1.7	17 TU	0338	2.4
	0847	7.8		0904	7.2
	1553	1.6		1606	2.3
	2110	7.8		2126	7.2
3 TU	0419	1.4	18 W	0421	2.2
	0936	8.0		0941	7.4
	1647	1.3		1646	2.0
	2200	7.9		2204	7.3
4 W	0511	1.2	19 TH	0500	2.1
	1023	8.1		1017	7.5
	1737	1.1		1724	1.9
	● 2249	8.0		○ 2242	7.4
5 TH	0558	1.2	20 F	0537	1.9
	1108	8.1		1053	7.6
	1823	1.1		1801	1.7
	2336	8.0		2319	7.5
6 F	0641	1.4	21 SA	0614	1.9
	1153	8.0		1129	7.7
	1905	1.2		1839	1.6
				2358	7.5
7 SA	0022	7.8	22 SU	0653	1.9
	0722	1.6		1207	7.7
	1235	7.8		1919	1.6
	1945	1.4			
8 SU	0107	7.6	23 M	0038	7.5
	0802	1.9		0733	2.0
	1319	7.6		1249	7.6
	2025	1.8		2000	1.7
9 M	0151	7.3	24 TU	0122	7.4
	0842	2.3		0815	2.1
	1403	7.2		1333	7.4
	2105	2.2		2042	1.9
10 TU	0238	7.0	25 W	0209	7.2
	0925	2.7		0900	2.3
	1451	6.9		1421	7.3
	2149	2.6		2128	2.1
11 W	0331	6.7	26 TH	0301	7.1
	1016	3.0		0950	2.5
	1548	6.6		1515	7.1
	2241	2.9		2220	2.3
12 TH	0433	6.5	27 F	0401	7.0
	1115	3.2		1048	2.6
	1653	6.4		1620	7.0
	2341	3.0		2320	2.4
13 F	0539	6.5	28 SA	0510	7.0
	1218	3.3		1153	2.6
	1802	6.4		1733	6.9
14 SA	0045	3.0	29 SU	0028	2.4
	0643	6.6		0621	7.1
	1324	3.1		1306	2.5
	1906	6.5		1844	7.0
15 SU	0149	2.9	30 M	0142	2.3
	0738	6.8		0724	7.2
	1426	2.8		1421	2.3
	2000	6.8		1952	7.2
			31 TU	0253	2.1
				0824	7.5
				1527	2.0
				2054	7.4

Chart Datum: 4·38 metres below IGN Datum

FÉCAMP *9.22.21*

ɜeine Maritime **49°45'·91N 00°21'·76E** ❀❀◊◊◊✿✿

CHARTS AC 1352; SHOM 7207, 7417; ECM 1012; Imray C31; ɜtanfords 1

TIDES –0044 Dover; ML 4·9; Duration 0550; Zone –0100

Standard Port DIEPPE (⟶)

Times				Height (metres)			
High Water		Low Water		MHWS	MHWN	MLWN	MLWS
0100	0600	0100	0700	9·3	7·4	2·5	0·8
1300	1800	1300	1900				
Differences FÉCAMP							
–0015	–0010	–0030	–0040	–1·0	–0·6	+0·3	+0·4
ÉTRETAT							
–0020	–0020	–0045	–0050	–1·2	–0·8	+0·3	+0·4

SHELTER Excellent in basins, but in even moderate W/NW winds a considerable surf runs off the ent and the Avant Port (Ⓥ at 'V' pontoon) can be uncomfortable. Bassin Bérigny is entered via lock, HW –2 to HW +½; pontoons at E end.

NAVIGATION WPT 49°46'·04N 00°21'·03E, 282°/102° from/to Jetée Nord lt, 0·50M. Beware the Charpentier Rks off Pte Fagnet and strong cross currents, depending on tides. Access best at HW +1. Ent chan dredged 1·5m, but prone to silting; best water is close to N jetty. Boats < 1·2m draft can enter at any tide and in most weathers.

LIGHTS AND MARKS Ent lies SSW of conspic ✠, sig stn and TV mast on Pte Fagnet cliff. N jetty Fl (2) 10s 15m 16M, grey tr, R top; horn (2) 30s sounded HW –2½ to HW +2; root QR 10m 4M. Jetée Sud hd, QG 14m 9M; obscd by cliff when brg more than 217°. QR and QG in transit 082° lead towards hbr ent. IPTS on tr by Avant Port show when Bassin Bérigny lock is open.

RADIO TELEPHONE VHF Ch **12** 10 16 (HW –3 to HW + 1). Ch 09 Marina and Écluse Bérigny (0800-1200; 1400-2000LT).

TELEPHONE Hr Mr 02.35.28.13.58; CROSS 03.21.87.21.87; SNSM 02.35.28.00.91; ⊜ 02.35.28.19.40; Auto 08.36.68.08.76; Police 02.35.28.16.69; Ⓗ 02.35.28.05.13; British Consul 02.35.42.27.47.

FACILITIES **Marina** (600 + 75 Ⓥ) ☎ 02.35.28.13.58, €1.68, FW, AC, D, C (mobile 36 ton), ♿; **Bassin Bérigny lock** ☎ 02.35.28.23.76, AB, M, D, FW, Slip; **Sté des Régates de Fécamp** ☎ 02.35.28.08.44, AB, FW; **Services:** Slip, M, ME, El, Ⓔ, Sh, CH, Gaz, C (30 ton). **Town** EC Mon; P, D, V, Gaz, R, Bar, ✉, Ⓑ, ⇌, ✈ (Le Havre).

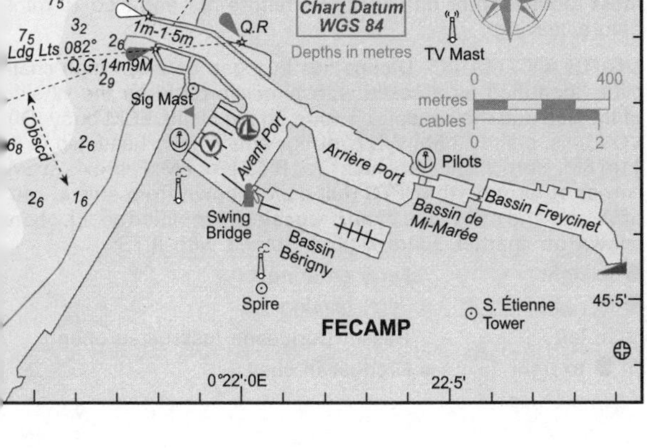

ST VALÉRY-EN-CAUX *9.22.22*

Seine Maritime **49°52'·48N 00°42'·64E** ❀❀◊◊◊✿✿

CHARTS AC *2451*; SHOM 7417; ECM 1012; Imray C31; Stanfords 1

TIDES –0044 Dover; ML 4·6; Duration 0530; Zone –0100

Standard Port DIEPPE (⟶)

Times				Height (metres)			
High Water		Low Water		MHWS	MHWN	MLWN	MLWS
0100	0600	0100	0700	9·3	7·4	2·5	0·8
1300	1800	1300	1900				
Differences ST VALÉRY-EN-CAUX							
–0005	–0005	–0015	–0020	–0·5	–0·4	–0·1	–0·1

SHELTER Good. Avant Port dries 3m; access from HW –3. Lock opens HW ±2¼ by day; by night, at HW±½ (bridge opens H and H+30 during these periods). Ⓥ pontoon to stbd, past lock.

NAVIGATION WPT 49°52'·96N 00°42'·40E, 000°/180° from/to Jetée Ouest lt, 0·60M. Coast dries to approx 150m off the pier hds. Ent is easy, but in fresh W to NE winds there are confused breaking seas and strong tidal streams across ent. Shingle builds up against W wall; hug the E side. Inside the pier hds, wave-breaks (marked by posts each side) dampen the swell. 6 W waiting buoys N of lock.

LIGHTS AND MARKS Hbr is hard to see between high chalk cliffs. From N or W the nuclear power stn at Paluel is conspic 3M W of ent. From E a white bldg is conspic E of ent, as is a vert white stripe in the cliffs close W of ent. Lts as on chartlet. Tfc sigs at the bridge/lock are coordinated to seaward/inland: ● = ent/exit; ● = no ent/ exit; ● + ● = no movements.

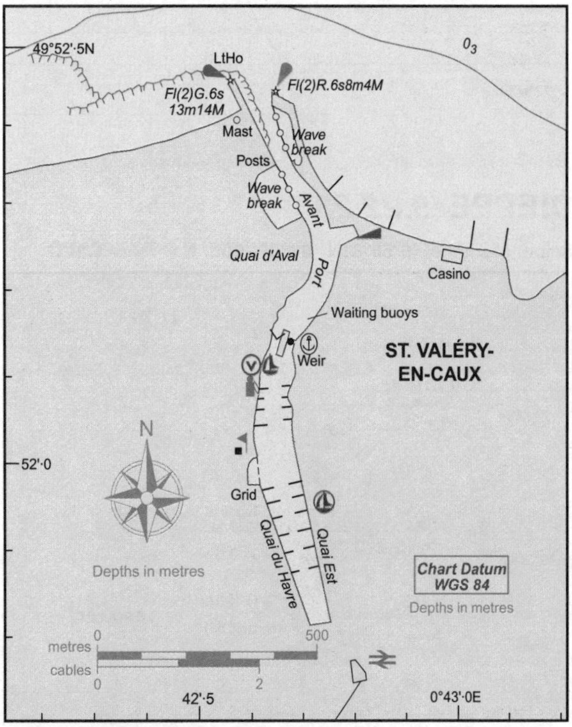

RADIO TELEPHONE VHF Ch 09 (French only).

TELEPHONE Hr Mr 02.35.97.01.30; Aff Mar 02.35.10.34.34; CROSS 03.21.87.21.89; SNSM 02.35.97.09.03; ⊜ 02.32.14.06.80; Météo Auto 08.36.68.08.76; Police 02.35.97.00.17; Dr 02.35.97.05.99; Ⓗ 02.35.97.00.11; Brit Consul 02.35.42.27.47.

FACILITIES **Marina** (580 + 20 Ⓥ) ☎ 02.35.97.01.30, 📠 02.35.97.79.81, €1.98, AC, FW, C (5/10 ton), CH, El, Gaz, ME, Sh, V, Bar; **Club Nautique Valeriquais** ☎ 02.35.97.25.49, C (8 ton), Bar; **Services:** Ⓔ. **Town** EC Mon (all day); P, D, CH, V, Gaz, R, Bar, ✉, Ⓑ, bus to ⇌ at Yvetot; ✈ & Ferry Dieppe.

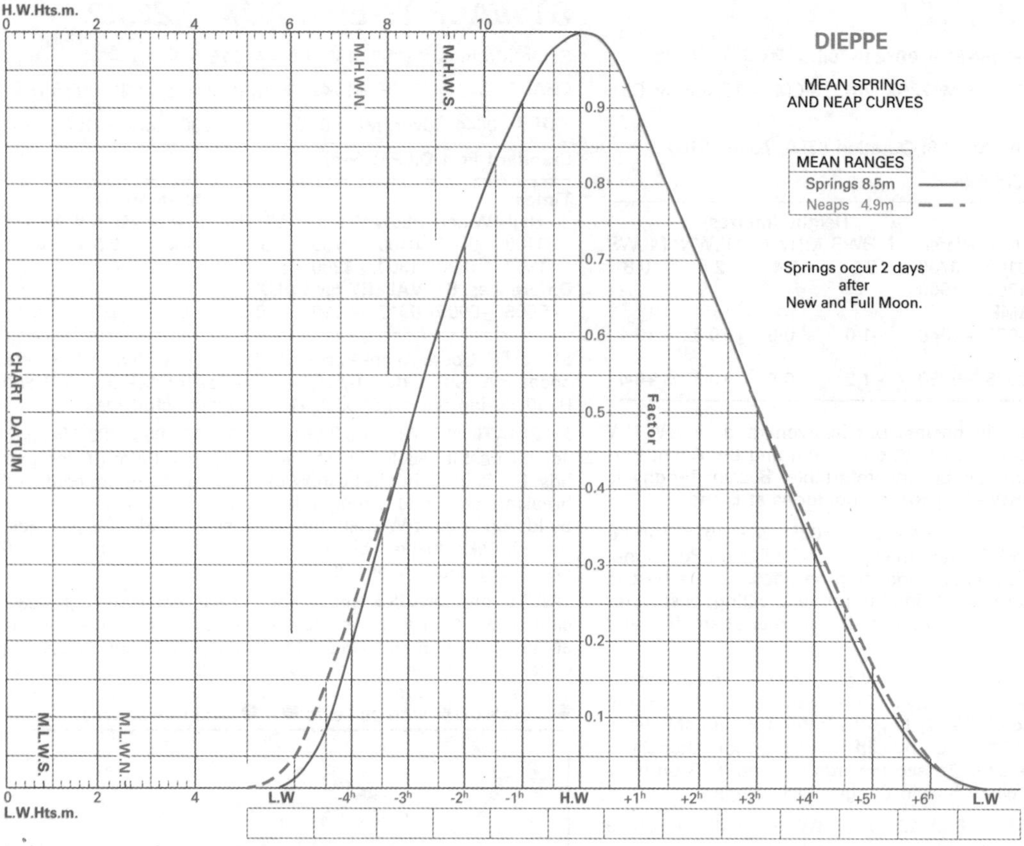

DIEPPE *9.22.23*

Seine Maritime **49°56'·31N 01°05'·00E**

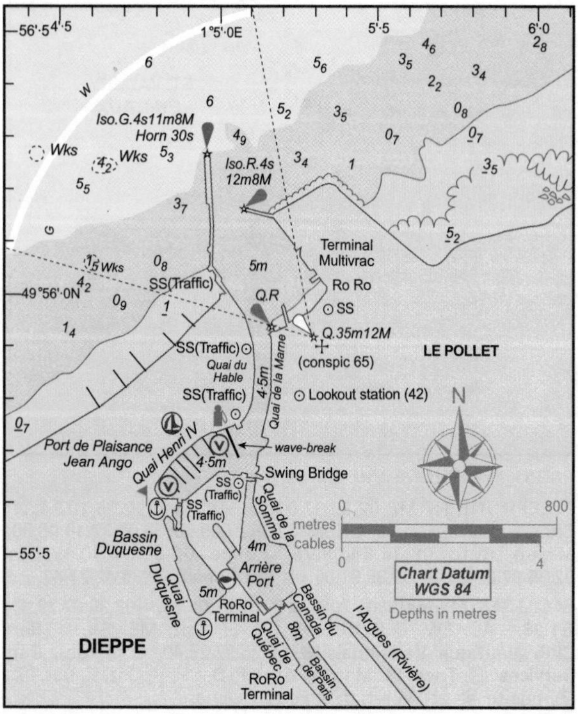

CHARTS AC 2147, *2451*; SHOM 7317, 7417; ECM 1011, 1012; Imray C31; Stanfords 1

TIDES –0011 Dover; ML 4·9; Duration 0535; Zone –0100
NOTE: Dieppe is a Standard Port (⟶).

SHELTER Very good. Access all tides, but ent is exposed to winds from NW to NE, causing a heavy scend. An effective fixed wavebreak across the narrowest part of the chan protects and gives access (about 30m wide) at its E end to marina Jehan Ango (8 pontoons) in the Avant Port at Quai Henri IV. Berth on either first or last pontoon but not on the outer end of either. The new ferry terminal is at the E side of port ent. Yachts prohib in Arrière Port.

NAVIGATION WPT 49°56'·43N 01°04'·52E, 298°/118° from/to W jetty extension, 0·35M. Ent to hbr is simple, but beware strong stream across ent. ⚓ is prohib in a zone 5ca off pierhead. Ent chan and Avant Port are dredged 5m. Entry/exit are controlled during ferry movements. Due to restricted visibility, yachts **must** request entry on Ch 12, 2M before hbr ent; also 10 mins before leaving.

LIGHTS AND MARKS Dieppe lies in a gap between high chalk cliffs, identified by a castle with pinnacle roofs on the W side of the gap and the conspic ch spire on the E cliff. ECM buoy (DI), VQ (3) 5s, bell, is 2·5M WNW of hbr ent. W jetty head, Iso G 4s 11m 8M, Horn 30s. E jetty head, Iso R 4s 12m 8M. Fl Vio 4s at SW corner of ferry berths. **IPTS** (full code) shown from stns at root of W jetty and on W side of hbr; repeated (simplified code) where shown on chartlet. Extra sigs combined with IPTS:

● to right	= Ferry entering;
● to right	= Ferry leaving.
Ⓦ to left	= Bassin Duquesne lock gates open.
● ● to right	= Dredger in chan.

DIEPPE *continued*

RADIO TELEPHONE *Dieppe Port* VHF Ch **12** (HO) 16 (H24) for entry/depart; see **NAVIGATION**. Ch 09 for marina which also monitors Ch 12 and operates (1/6 to 15/9) 0700–2200 else 0900–1900.

TELEPHONE Hr Mr 02.35.84.10.55, 📠 02.35.06.12.56; Marina 02.35.40.19.79; Aff Mar 02.35.06.96.70; CROSS 03.21.87.21.87; ⊖ 02.35.82.24.47; SNSM 02.35.84.8.55; Météo 03.21.31.52.23; Auto 08.36.68.08.76; Police 02.35.06.96.74; Ⓗ 02.35.06.76.76; Brit Consul 02.35.42.27.47.

FACILITIES Port de Plaisance (Jehan Ango) ☎ 02.35.40.19.79 (450 inc 50 Ⓥ) €2.32, FW, AC, D by credit card-operated pumps H24, call VHF Ch 09 if not manned (P by cans), C (12 ton), access by magnetic card; **Cercle de la Voile de Dieppe** ☎ 02.35.84.32.99, FW, R, Bar, access to showers/toilets by same magnetic card; **Services:** ME, El, Ⓔ, Sh, CH, Sh. **Town** P, D, FW, V, Gaz, R, Bar, ✉, ⌧, Ⓑ, ≷, ✈. Ferry: Dieppe - Newhaven (seasonal).

LE TRÉPORT *9.22.24*

Seine Maritime **50°03'·89N 01°22'·20E** ❁❁◊◊◊✿✿

CHARTS AC 1352, 2147, 2612, *2451*; SHOM 7207, 7416, 7417; ECM 1011; Imray C31; Stanfords 1

TIDES –0025 Dover; ML 5·0; Duration 0530; Zone –0100

Standard Port DIEPPE (⟶)

Times				Height (metres)			
High Water		Low Water		MHWS	MHWN	MLWN	MLWS
0100	0600	0100	0700	9·3	7·4	2·5	0·8
1300	1800	1300	1900				
Differences LE TRÉPORT							
+0005	0000	+0007	+0007	+0·1	+0·1	0·0	+0·1
CAYEUX							
0000	+0005	+0015	+0010	+0·4	+0·5	+0·5	+0·5

SHELTER Good in marina at S side of first S Basin (3·7m), E of FVs. But ent chan and most of Avant Port dry; S side is dredged 1·5m, but prone to silting. Lock opens HW±4 1 Mar-1 Dec; other months HW ±3. E of the marina a lifting bridge gives access to extra berths in 2nd basin dredged 2m. Port de Commerce is only used by yachts on passage as an overflow. Strong cross-current at entrance 5kn speed limit.

NAVIGATION WPT 50°04'·24N 01°21'·61E, 315°/135° from/to ent, 0·52M. Coast dries to approx 300m off the pier hds. Shingle spit extends NW from E pier hd; keep well to the W. Entry difficult in strong on-shore winds which cause scend in Avant Port.

LIGHTS AND MARKS Le Tréport is identified between high chalk cliffs, with crucifix (lit) above town and conspic church S of hbr. No ldg lts/marks. IPTS were installed 1996, as shown. W jetty Fl (2) G 10s 15m 20M. E jetty Oc R 4s 8m 6M. Lock sigs shown from head of dredged/piled chan to S Basin:
3 ● (vert) = enter lock; 3 ● (vert) = no entry.

RADIO TELEPHONE Call: *Capitainerie Le Tréport* VHF Ch 12 72 16 (HW ±3).

TELEPHONE Hr Mr 02.35.86.17.91, 📠 02.35.86.60.11; Marina 02.35.06.96.72; Lock (to marina) 02.35.86.27.67; Aff Mar 02.35.06.96.70; SNSM 02.35.86.8.91; Auto 08.36.68.08.76; CROSS 03.21.87.21.87; ⊖ 02.35.86.15.34; Police 02.35.86.12.11; Dr 02.35.86.16.23; Brit Consul 03.21.96.33.76.

FACILITIES Marina (115+15) **€1.81**, AC, FW; **Avant Port** M; **Port de Commerce** C (10 ton); **YC de la Bresle** ☎ 02.35.86.19.93, C, Bar; **Services:** ME, CH, El, Ⓔ, P, D, Gaz. **Town** P, D, V, Gaz, R, Bar, ✉, Ⓑ, ≷, ✈ (Dieppe). Ferry: Le Havre.

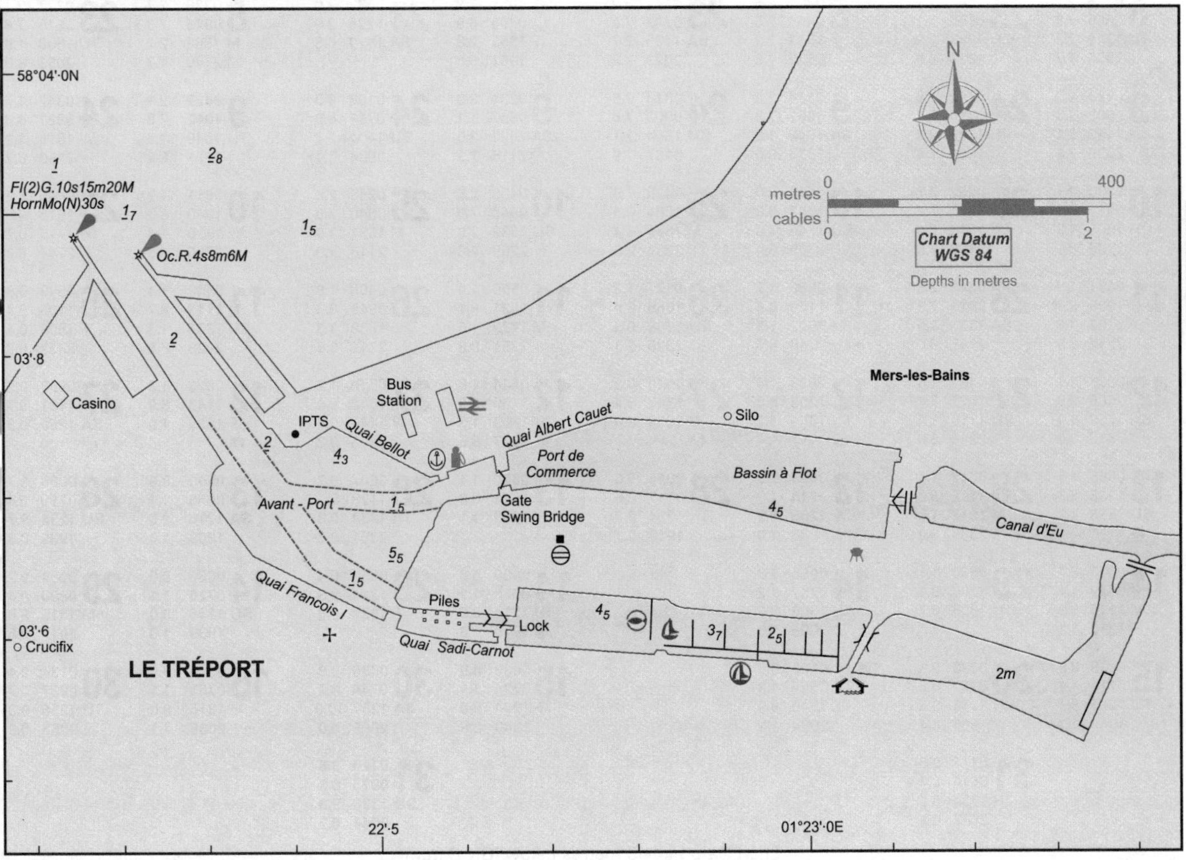

TIME ZONE -0100
(French Standard Time)
Subtract 1 hour for UT
For French Summer Time add ONE hour in **non-shaded areas**

FRANCE – DIEPPE

LAT 49°56′N LONG 1°05′E

TIMES AND HEIGHTS OF HIGH AND LOW WATERS

SPRING & NEAP TIDES
Dates in red are **SPRINGS**
Dates in blue are **NEAPS**

YEAR 200.

JANUARY

Date	Day	Time	m	Time	m	Time	m	Time	m
1	TU	0039	9.2	0732	1.1	1256	9.3	2000	0.8
2	W	0125	9.2	0818	1.1	1342	9.3	2046	0.8
3	TH	0212	9.1	0905	1.2	1429	9.1	2132	1.0
4	F	0300	8.9	0952	1.4	1518	8.8	2219	1.2
5	SA	0351	8.6	1042	1.6	1611	8.5	2309	1.5
6	SU	0445	8.3	1136	1.9	1708	8.1	2359	1.8
7	M	0546	8.0	1238	2.1	1813	7.8		
8	TU	0108	2.1	0655	7.8	1348	2.2	1925	7.7
9	W	0220	2.2	0807	7.9	1459	2.1	2035	7.8
10	TH	0330	2.1	0912	8.1	1605	1.8	2138	8.1
11	F	0431	1.9	1008	8.4	1702	1.6	2232	8.3
12	SA	0523	1.7	1056	8.6	1750	1.4	2318	8.6
13 ●	SU	0608	1.5	1138	8.8	1833	1.2		
14	M	0000	8.7	0649	1.4	1216	8.9	1912	1.2
15	TU	0039	8.8	0728	1.4	1253	8.9	1949	1.1
16	W	0115	8.8	0804	1.4	1328	8.8	2024	1.2
17	TH	0149	8.7	0837	1.6	1403	8.7	2056	1.4
18	F	0223	8.5	0907	1.8	1437	8.4	2125	1.6
19	SA	0255	8.3	0937	2.0	1510	8.1	2155	1.9
20	SU	0327	8.0	1010	2.2	1544	7.8	2229	2.2
21	M	0404	7.7	1051	2.5	1625	7.4	2312	2.5
22	TU	0450	7.4	1141	2.7	1717	7.1		
23	W	0002	2.7	0550	7.1	1243	2.9	1828	6.9
24	TH	0112	2.9	0710	7.1	1358	2.8	1951	7.1
25	F	0232	2.7	0827	7.4	1516	2.4	2100	7.5
26	SA	0346	2.3	0929	7.9	1621	1.9	2157	8.0
27	SU	0447	1.8	1022	8.4	1718	1.4	2249	8.6
28	M	0542	1.4	1112	8.9	1812	1.0	○ 2339	9.0
29	TU	0636	1.1	1200	9.3	1905	0.7		
30	W	0030	9.3	0727	0.8	1248	9.5	1955	0.4
31	TH	0117	9.5	0816	0.7	1334	9.6	2042	0.3

FEBRUARY

Date	Day	Time	m	Time	m	Time	m	Time	m
1	F	0202	9.5	0901	0.7	1419	9.6	2125	0.4
2	SA	0246	9.4	0944	0.8	1504	9.3	2207	0.7
3	SU	0330	9.0	1025	1.1	1549	8.9	2248	1.1
4	M	0416	8.6	1109	1.5	1638	8.3	2333	1.7
5	TU	0508	8.1	1200	2.0	1736	7.8		
6	W	0025	2.2	0613	7.6	1306	2.4	1849	7.3
7	TH	0138	2.6	0733	7.4	1426	2.5	2012	7.3
8	F	0301	2.6	0854	7.5	1543	2.2	2127	7.6
9	SA	0414	2.3	0957	7.9	1648	1.9	2224	8.0
10	SU	0513	2.0	1047	8.3	1740	1.5	2309	8.4
11	M	0559	1.7	1128	8.6	1822	1.3	2348	8.6
12 ●	TU	0638	1.4	1203	8.8	1859	1.1		
13	W	0023	8.8	0714	1.3	1236	8.9	1933	1.0
14	TH	0055	8.9	0747	1.2	1309	9.0	2005	1.0
15	F	0127	8.9	0817	1.3	1340	8.9	2034	1.1
16	SA	0157	8.8	0845	1.4	1410	8.8	2100	1.2
17	SU	0225	8.6	0910	1.5	1439	8.5	2126	1.5
18	M	0253	8.4	0939	1.8	1509	8.2	2154	1.8
19	TU	0324	8.1	1012	2.1	1543	7.8	2229	2.1
20	W	0401	7.7	1053	2.4	1626	7.4	2314	2.6
21	TH	0450	7.3	1148	2.8	1725	7.0		
22	F	0016	2.9	0603	7.0	1302	2.9	1856	6.8
23	SA	0141	3.0	0743	7.0	1435	2.7	2029	7.2
24	SU	0314	2.5	0903	7.6	1554	2.1	2137	7.9
25	M	0425	1.9	1004	8.3	1659	1.4	2234	8.5
26	TU	0527	1.3	1058	8.9	1758	0.9	2325	9.1
27 ○	W	0625	0.9	1147	9.4	1853	0.4		
28	TH	0016	9.5	0717	0.5	1234	9.8	1943	0.1

MARCH

Date	Day	Time	m	Time	m	Time	m	Time	m
1	F	0101	9.8	0804	0.3	1318	9.9	2027	0.0
2	SA	0144	9.8	0847	0.3	1401	9.9	2108	0.1
3	SU	0225	9.6	0926	0.5	1442	9.6	2145	0.5
4	M	0305	9.3	1002	0.9	1524	9.1	2221	1.1
5	TU	0345	8.7	1040	1.4	1608	8.4	2259	1.7
6	W	0430	8.0	1125	2.0	1701	7.6	2348	2.4
7	TH	0531	7.3	1226	2.6	1814	7.0		
8	F	0059	2.9	0700	6.9	1352	2.8	1951	6.8
9	SA	0234	3.0	0837	7.1	1522	2.5	2114	7.3
10	SU	0400	2.6	0943	7.6	1632	2.0	2209	7.8
11	M	0500	2.0	1031	8.1	1723	1.6	2251	8.3
12	TU	0544	1.6	1109	8.5	1803	1.3	2327	8.6
13	W	0620	1.4	1143	8.8	1838	1.1		
14	TH	0000	8.8	0653	1.2	1214	8.9	● 1910	1.0
15	F	0030	8.9	0724	1.1	1244	9.0	1940	0.9
16	SA	0100	9.0	0753	1.1	1314	9.0	2007	0.9
17	SU	0128	9.0	0820	1.1	1343	9.0	2033	1.1
18	M	0155	8.9	0845	1.3	1411	8.8	2058	1.3
19	TU	0223	8.7	0912	1.5	1440	8.5	2125	1.6
20	W	0253	8.4	0942	1.8	1513	8.1	2157	2.0
21	TH	0328	8.0	1019	2.2	1554	7.6	2240	2.5
22	F	0413	7.4	1112	2.6	1650	7.1	2341	2.9
23	SA	0523	7.0	1226	2.9	1820	6.8		
24	SU	0108	3.0	0711	6.9	1404	2.7	2004	7.1
25	M	0249	2.6	0840	7.5	1531	2.0	2118	7.9
26	TU	0405	1.9	0945	8.3	1639	1.3	2215	8.6
27	W	0510	1.2	1040	9.0	1740	0.7	2305	9.2
28	TH	0607	0.7	1128	9.5	1834	0.3	○ 2351	9.7
29	F	0659	0.4	1214	9.8	1922	0.0		
30	SA	0039	9.9	0744	0.2	1257	10.0	2005	0.0
31	SU	0120	9.8	0825	0.3	1339	9.9	2044	0.2

APRIL

Date	Day	Time	m	Time	m	Time	m	Time	m
1	M	0159	9.6	0902	0.5	1419	9.5	2119	0.6
2	TU	0237	9.2	0936	0.9	1459	9.0	2153	1.2
3	W	0316	8.6	1012	1.4	1541	8.3	2229	1.9
4	TH	0359	7.9	1055	2.1	1631	7.5	2316	2.6
5	F	0456	7.2	1153	2.7	1742	6.8		
6	SA	0027	3.1	0623	6.7	1317	2.9	1921	6.7
7	SU	0203	3.1	0807	6.8	1447	2.7	2046	7.1
8	M	0328	2.7	0915	7.3	1558	2.2	2140	7.7
9	TU	0427	2.1	1002	7.9	1649	1.7	2221	8.2
10	W	0511	1.7	1040	8.3	1730	1.4	2256	8.5
11	TH	0549	1.4	1113	8.7	1806	1.2	2328	8.8
12 ●	F	0623	1.2	1145	8.9	1839	1.0		
13	SA	0000	8.9	0655	1.1	1216	9.0	1909	1.0
14	SU	0030	9.0	0725	1.1	1246	9.0	1939	1.0
15	M	0059	9.0	0753	1.1	1316	9.0	2006	1.1
16	TU	0128	8.9	0822	1.2	1346	8.8	2034	1.3
17	W	0158	8.8	0851	1.4	1418	8.5	2104	1.6
18	TH	0231	8.5	0923	1.7	1454	8.2	2139	2.0
19	F	0308	8.0	1002	2.0	1538	7.7	2224	2.4
20	SA	0356	7.5	1055	2.4	1636	7.2	2325	2.7
21	SU	0507	7.1	1209	2.7	1805	7.0		
22	M	0051	2.8	0650	7.1	1344	2.5	1941	7.3
23	TU	0227	2.4	0815	7.6	1508	1.9	2053	8.0
24	W	0342	1.7	0921	8.3	1615	1.2	2150	8.7
25	TH	0445	1.2	1016	9.0	1715	0.7	2241	9.2
26	F	0543	0.8	1105	9.4	1808	0.4	2327	9.6
27 ○	SA	0633	0.5	1151	9.7	1856	0.3		
28	SU	0008	9.7	0719	0.4	1234	9.7	1939	0.3
29	M	0054	9.7	0800	0.4	1315	9.6	2017	0.5
30	TU	0134	9.4	0837	0.7	1356	9.3	2053	0.9

Chart Datum: 4·43 metres below IGN Datum

TIME ZONE -0100
(French Standard Time)
Subtract 1 hour for UT
For French Summer Time add ONE hour in **non-shaded areas**

FRANCE – DIEPPE

LAT 49°56′N LONG 1°05′E

TIMES AND HEIGHTS OF HIGH AND LOW WATERS

SPRING & NEAP TIDES
Dates in red are SPRINGS
Dates in blue are NEAPS

YEAR **2002**

MAY

Date	Day	Time	m	Time	m	Time	m	Time	m
1	W	0213	9.1	0912	1.0	1436	8.8	2128	1.4
2	TH	0252	8.5	0949	1.5	1519	8.2	2205	2.0
3	F	0335	7.9	1030	2.1	1607	7.5	2251	2.6
4	SA	0429	7.2	1125	2.6	1711	7.0	2356	3.0
5	SU	0543	6.8	1237	2.8	1831	6.8		
6	M	0119	3.1	0711	6.7	1355	2.7	1953	7.0
7	TU	0235	2.8	0825	7.1	1503	2.4	2054	7.5
8	W	0335	2.3	0918	7.6	1558	2.0	2139	7.9
9	TH	0425	1.9	1000	8.1	1645	1.6	2217	8.3
10	F	0507	1.6	1037	8.4	1725	1.4	2253	8.6
11	SA	0546	1.4	1112	8.6	1802	1.2	2326	8.8
12	SU	0622	1.3	1146	8.8	1837	1.2	●	
13	M	0000	8.9	0656	1.2	1219	8.8	1910	1.1
14	TU	0032	8.9	0729	1.1	1252	8.9	1942	1.2
15	W	0105	8.9	0802	1.1	1327	8.8	2016	1.3
16	TH	0140	8.8	0837	1.3	1404	8.6	2051	1.5
17	F	0218	8.5	0915	1.5	1445	8.3	2131	1.9
18	SA	0300	8.1	0958	1.8	1533	7.9	2220	2.2
19	SU	0353	7.7	1052	2.1	1635	7.5	2321	2.4
20	M	0504	7.4	1202	2.3	1754	7.4		
21	TU	0039	2.5	0629	7.4	1325	2.1	1913	7.7
22	W	0202	2.1	0746	7.8	1441	1.7	2022	8.2
23	TH	0313	1.7	0852	8.3	1546	1.3	2121	8.6
24	F	0416	1.3	0950	8.8	1646	1.0	2214	9.0
25	SA	0513	1.0	1041	9.1	1739	0.8	2301	9.3
26	SU	0605	0.8	1128	9.3	1828	0.7	○ 2346	9.4
27	M	0652	0.7	1212	9.3	1911	0.8		
28	TU	0031	9.3	0735	0.7	1255	9.2	1952	0.9
29	W	0112	9.2	0814	0.9	1337	9.0	2030	1.2
30	TH	0152	8.9	0852	1.1	1418	8.7	2107	1.6
31	F	0233	8.5	0930	1.5	1500	8.2	2146	2.0

JUNE

Date	Day	Time	m	Time	m	Time	m	Time	m
1	SA	0316	8.0	1010	1.9	1546	7.8	2229	2.4
2	SU	0404	7.5	1056	2.3	1637	7.3	2321	2.7
3	M	0501	7.1	1152	2.6	1737	7.1		
4	TU	0024	2.9	0608	6.9	1256	2.7	1844	7.0
5	W	0132	2.8	0717	7.0	1401	2.5	1950	7.3
6	TH	0235	2.5	0820	7.3	1500	2.3	2046	7.6
7	F	0331	2.2	0912	7.7	1554	2.0	2133	8.0
8	SA	0421	1.9	0958	8.0	1642	1.7	2215	8.3
9	SU	0506	1.6	1039	8.3	1725	1.5	2254	8.5
10	M	0548	1.4	1118	8.5	1806	1.4	2331	8.7
11	TU	0629	1.3	1156	8.7	1845	1.3	●	
12	W	0010	8.8	0708	1.2	1235	8.8	1924	1.3
13	TH	0049	8.9	0749	1.1	1315	8.8	2004	1.3
14	F	0129	8.8	0830	1.2	1358	8.7	2046	1.4
15	SA	0213	8.7	0914	1.3	1444	8.5	2131	1.6
16	SU	0300	8.4	1000	1.5	1534	8.3	2220	1.8
17	M	0353	8.1	1053	1.7	1630	8.0	2317	2.0
18	TU	0455	7.9	1152	1.8	1734	7.9		
19	W	0021	2.1	0603	7.8	1259	1.8	1842	7.9
20	TH	0132	2.0	0715	7.9	1409	1.7	1949	8.1
21	F	0242	1.8	0823	8.1	1516	1.6	2052	8.4
22	SA	0347	1.5	0925	8.4	1617	1.4	2149	8.6
23	SU	0446	1.3	1020	8.6	1713	1.3	2240	8.8
24	M	0540	1.2	1110	8.8	1803	1.2	○ 2328	8.9
25	TU	0629	1.1	1157	8.9	1849	1.2		
26	W	0010	9.0	0714	1.0	1240	8.9	1931	1.2
27	TH	0056	8.9	0756	1.1	1321	8.8	2012	1.3
28	F	0136	8.8	0836	1.2	1401	8.7	2050	1.5
29	SA	0216	8.5	0913	1.4	1441	8.4	2127	1.8
30	SU	0255	8.2	0948	1.7	1520	8.1	2203	2.1

JULY

Date	Day	Time	m	Time	m	Time	m	Time	m
1	M	0335	7.9	1024	2.0	1600	7.8	2242	2.4
2	TU	0418	7.5	1104	2.3	1645	7.5	2328	2.6
3	W	0507	7.2	1153	2.5	1737	7.2		
4	TH	0022	2.7	0606	7.0	1250	2.6	1839	7.1
5	F	0125	2.8	0715	7.0	1355	2.6	1946	7.3
6	SA	0232	2.6	0821	7.3	1500	2.4	2046	7.6
7	SU	0334	2.3	0918	7.6	1600	2.1	2138	7.9
8	M	0429	1.9	1008	8.0	1652	1.8	2225	8.2
9	TU	0519	1.6	1054	8.3	1740	1.6	2309	8.5
10	W	0607	1.4	1138	8.6	1826	1.4	● 2352	8.8
11	TH	0654	1.1	1222	8.8	1912	1.2		
12	F	0038	9.0	0741	1.0	1307	9.0	1959	1.1
13	SA	0123	9.1	0828	0.9	1352	9.0	2044	1.1
14	SU	0209	9.0	0914	0.9	1438	9.0	2130	1.2
15	M	0256	8.9	0958	1.0	1524	8.8	2216	1.3
16	TU	0343	8.7	1044	1.2	1613	8.5	2304	1.5
17	W	0435	8.3	1133	1.5	1706	8.2	2357	1.8
18	TH	0534	8.0	1229	1.8	1808	8.0		
19	F	0059	2.0	0643	7.8	1335	2.0	1917	7.9
20	SA	0211	2.1	0757	7.7	1447	2.0	2028	7.9
21	SU	0323	1.9	0908	7.9	1555	1.9	2133	8.2
22	M	0428	1.7	1010	8.2	1655	1.7	2229	8.4
23	TU	0525	1.5	1102	8.4	1748	1.5	2318	8.6
24	W	0615	1.3	1148	8.7	1835	1.4	○	
25	TH	0000	8.8	0700	1.2	1229	8.8	1917	1.3
26	F	0043	8.9	0741	1.1	1306	8.8	1956	1.3
27	SA	0120	8.8	0818	1.1	1342	8.8	2031	1.4
28	SU	0155	8.7	0851	1.3	1416	8.7	2103	1.6
29	M	0229	8.5	0921	1.5	1449	8.4	2133	1.8
30	TU	0302	8.3	0949	1.7	1522	8.2	2202	2.0
31	W	0334	7.9	1020	2.0	1555	7.8	2237	2.3

AUGUST

Date	Day	Time	m	Time	m	Time	m	Time	m
1	TH	0411	7.6	1058	2.3	1634	7.5	2321	2.6
2	F	0457	7.2	1146	2.7	1725	7.2		
3	SA	0017	2.9	0600	6.9	1247	2.9	1836	7.0
4	SU	0128	2.9	0725	6.9	1404	2.9	1959	7.1
5	M	0249	2.7	0842	7.2	1522	2.6	2106	7.5
6	TU	0358	2.2	0943	7.7	1624	2.1	2201	8.0
7	W	0456	1.7	1035	8.2	1719	1.7	2251	8.5
8	TH	0551	1.3	1124	8.7	1812	1.3	● 2338	8.9
9	F	0644	1.0	1210	9.1	1903	1.0		
10	SA	0028	9.2	0735	0.7	1255	9.3	1951	0.8
11	SU	0113	9.4	0821	0.5	1339	9.5	2037	0.7
12	M	0157	9.5	0905	0.5	1422	9.4	2120	0.7
13	TU	0240	9.3	0945	0.6	1505	9.2	2201	1.0
14	W	0324	9.0	1024	1.0	1549	8.9	2243	1.3
15	TH	0409	8.6	1106	1.5	1636	8.4	2330	1.8
16	F	0503	8.0	1156	2.0	1734	7.8		
17	SA	0028	2.2	0612	7.5	1303	2.4	1849	7.5
18	SU	0145	2.4	0738	7.3	1426	2.6	2013	7.5
19	M	0308	2.3	0902	7.5	1544	2.3	2127	7.8
20	TU	0420	2.0	1006	8.0	1649	2.0	2224	8.2
21	W	0520	1.6	1055	8.4	1742	1.6	2310	8.6
22	TH	0607	1.3	1137	8.7	1825	1.4	○ 2349	8.8
23	F	0647	1.2	1213	8.9	1902	1.3		
24	SA	0025	8.9	0722	1.1	1245	9.0	1936	1.2
25	SU	0058	9.0	0755	1.1	1316	8.9	2007	1.3
26	M	0129	8.9	0824	1.1	1347	8.9	2035	1.4
27	TU	0159	8.8	0850	1.3	1416	8.7	2101	1.6
28	W	0227	8.5	0914	1.5	1443	8.4	2126	1.8
29	TH	0255	8.2	0940	1.8	1511	8.1	2155	2.1
30	F	0327	7.8	1012	2.2	1544	7.7	2232	2.5
31	SA	0406	7.4	1054	2.7	1628	7.3	2322	2.9

Chart Datum: 4·43 metres below IGN Datum

TIME ZONE -0100
(French Standard Time)
Subtract 1 hour for UT
For French Summer Time add ONE hour in **non-shaded areas**

FRANCE – DIEPPE

LAT 49°56′N LONG 1°05′E

TIMES AND HEIGHTS OF HIGH AND LOW WATERS

SPRING & NEAP TIDES
Dates in red are SPRINGS
Dates in blue are NEAPS

YEAR **2002**

SEPTEMBER

Date	Day	Time	m	Time	m	Time	m	Time	m
1	SU	0501	6.9	1152	3.1	1732	6.8		
2	M	0033	3.1	0628	6.6	1315	3.2	1912	6.8
3	TU	0208	3.0	0811	7.0	1450	2.9	2039	7.3
4	W	0333	2.4	0921	7.6	1602	2.2	2141	8.0
5	TH	0437	1.7	1017	8.3	1701	1.6	2233	8.6
6	F	0535	1.2	1106	9.0	1756	1.1	2321	9.2
7	SA	0630	0.7	1152	9.4	1848	0.7	●	
8	SU	0010	9.6	0719	0.4	1236	9.7	1936	0.5
9	M	0054	9.8	0804	0.3	1318	9.8	2020	0.4
10	TU	0137	9.8	0845	0.3	1400	9.7	2101	0.5
11	W	0218	9.6	0922	0.6	1440	9.4	2140	0.8
12	TH	0300	9.2	0958	1.1	1521	8.9	2218	1.3
13	F	0343	8.6	1037	1.7	1606	8.3	2302	1.9
14	SA	0434	7.8	1125	2.3	1703	7.6	2358	2.5
15	SU	0546	7.2	1235	2.9	1825	7.1		
16	M	0124	2.8	0725	7.0	1410	3.0	2002	7.1
17	TU	0257	2.6	0855	7.4	1536	2.5	2118	7.6
18	W	0412	2.1	0953	8.0	1639	2.0	2210	8.2
19	TH	0506	1.6	1038	8.5	1727	1.6	2251	8.6
20	F	0548	1.3	1115	8.8	1806	1.3	2327	8.9
21	SA	0624	1.2	1148	9.0	1839	1.2	○	
22	SU	0000	9.0	0655	1.1	1218	9.0	1909	1.2
23	M	0030	9.1	0725	1.1	1246	9.1	1938	1.2
24	TU	0100	9.0	0753	1.1	1315	9.0	2005	1.3
25	W	0128	8.9	0818	1.3	1342	8.9	2030	1.5
26	TH	0155	8.7	0842	1.5	1408	8.6	2055	1.7
27	F	0223	8.4	0907	1.8	1436	8.3	2122	2.0
28	SA	0254	8.0	0935	2.3	1508	7.9	2156	2.4
29	SU	0331	7.5	1014	2.7	1550	7.4	2244	2.8
30	M	0424	7.0	1113	3.2	1652	6.9	2353	3.2

OCTOBER

Date	Day	Time	m	Time	m	Time	m	Time	m
1	TU	0550	6.6	1239	3.4	1834	6.7		
2	W	0135	3.1	0743	7.0	1423	3.0	2012	7.2
3	TH	0309	2.4	0857	7.7	1539	2.2	2117	8.0
4	F	0415	1.7	0953	8.5	1639	1.5	2211	8.8
5	SA	0513	1.0	1042	9.2	1735	0.9	2259	9.3
6	SU	0607	0.6	1128	9.6	1826	0.6	● 2344	9.7
7	M	0656	0.3	1212	9.9	1914	0.4		
8	TU	0031	9.9	0740	0.3	1254	9.9	1958	0.4
9	W	0114	9.9	0820	0.4	1334	9.8	2038	0.5
10	TH	0155	9.6	0857	0.8	1414	9.4	2116	0.9
11	F	0236	9.1	0932	1.3	1455	8.9	2154	1.4
12	SA	0319	8.4	1010	1.9	1540	8.2	2237	2.1
13	SU	0410	7.7	1059	2.6	1637	7.4	2334	2.7
14	M	0522	7.0	1211	3.1	1759	6.9		
15	TU	0058	3.0	0702	6.8	1348	3.2	1938	7.0
16	W	0231	2.8	0829	7.3	1511	2.7	2052	7.5
17	TH	0342	2.3	0926	7.8	1610	2.1	2142	8.0
18	F	0434	1.8	1008	8.4	1656	1.7	2223	8.5
19	SA	0515	1.5	1044	8.7	1733	1.4	2257	8.8
20	SU	0550	1.3	1116	8.9	1807	1.3	2329	8.9
21	M	0622	1.2	1146	9.0	1838	1.2	○	
22	TU	0000	9.0	0652	1.2	1215	9.0	1908	1.2
23	W	0030	9.0	0721	1.2	1243	9.0	1937	1.3
24	TH	0059	8.9	0748	1.4	1311	8.9	2004	1.4
25	F	0128	8.8	0814	1.6	1339	8.7	2031	1.6
26	SA	0158	8.5	0842	1.9	1410	8.4	2101	1.9
27	SU	0232	8.1	0913	2.3	1446	8.0	2137	2.3
28	M	0312	7.7	0955	2.7	1530	7.5	2225	2.7
29	TU	0406	7.2	1054	3.1	1633	7.0	2332	3.0
30	W	0531	6.9	1217	3.2	1808	6.9		
31	TH	0107	2.9	0713	7.2	1355	2.8	1940	7.4

NOVEMBER

Date	Day	Time	m	Time	m	Time	m	Time	m
1	F	0239	2.3	0826	7.9	1511	2.1	2047	8.1
2	SA	0347	1.6	0924	8.6	1612	1.4	2143	8.8
3	SU	0445	1.1	1015	9.2	1708	0.9	2233	9.3
4	M	0539	0.7	1101	9.6	1800	0.6	● 2319	9.6
5	TU	0628	0.5	1146	9.8	1849	0.5		
6	W	0003	9.8	0712	0.5	1228	9.8	1933	0.5
7	TH	0051	9.7	0753	0.7	1310	9.7	2014	0.7
8	F	0133	9.4	0832	1.0	1352	9.3	2054	1.0
9	SA	0216	8.9	0909	1.5	1434	8.8	2133	1.5
10	SU	0300	8.4	0949	2.1	1519	8.1	2216	2.1
11	M	0351	7.7	1038	2.7	1614	7.5	2309	2.6
12	TU	0455	7.2	1143	3.1	1725	7.0		
13	W	0020	3.0	0614	6.9	1304	3.2	1847	6.9
14	TH	0140	2.9	0736	7.1	1420	2.8	2004	7.2
15	F	0249	2.6	0840	7.5	1521	2.4	2100	7.7
16	SA	0344	2.2	0926	8.0	1610	2.0	2144	8.1
17	SU	0430	1.8	1005	8.4	1652	1.7	2221	8.4
18	M	0510	1.6	1040	8.7	1731	1.5	2256	8.6
19	TU	0546	1.5	1113	8.8	1806	1.4	2329	8.8
20	W	0620	1.4	1145	8.9	1839	1.3	○	
21	TH	0001	8.8	0652	1.4	1216	8.9	1911	1.3
22	F	0035	8.8	0723	1.5	1247	8.9	1943	1.4
23	SA	0108	8.7	0755	1.6	1320	8.8	2016	1.5
24	SU	0143	8.6	0828	1.8	1356	8.5	2051	1.8
25	M	0222	8.3	0906	2.1	1436	8.2	2131	2.1
26	TU	0306	7.9	0951	2.4	1524	7.8	2220	2.3
27	W	0401	7.5	1048	2.7	1625	7.4	2322	2.5
28	TH	0515	7.3	1200	2.8	1744	7.3		
29	F	0040	2.5	0637	7.5	1322	2.5	1903	7.6
30	SA	0202	2.2	0749	8.0	1437	2.1	2012	8.1

DECEMBER

Date	Day	Time	m	Time	m	Time	m	Time	m
1	SU	0312	1.7	0851	8.5	1542	1.6	2113	8.6
2	M	0414	1.3	0946	9.0	1640	1.2	2207	9.0
3	TU	0509	1.1	1036	9.3	1734	0.9	2257	9.3
4	W	0600	0.9	1123	9.5	1824	0.7	● 2344	9.4
5	TH	0646	0.9	1208	9.5	1911	0.7		
6	F	0033	9.3	0730	1.0	1251	9.4	1954	0.8
7	SA	0117	9.2	0812	1.2	1334	9.2	2036	1.1
8	SU	0201	8.9	0852	1.6	1417	8.8	2116	1.4
9	M	0244	8.4	0932	2.0	1502	8.3	2157	1.9
10	TU	0330	8.0	1016	2.4	1550	7.8	2242	2.3
11	W	0420	7.5	1107	2.7	1643	7.4	2333	2.6
12	TH	0517	7.2	1206	3.0	1745	7.1		
13	F	0033	2.8	0622	7.1	1311	3.0	1852	7.0
14	SA	0138	2.8	0730	7.2	1416	2.8	1958	7.2
15	SU	0242	2.6	0830	7.5	1516	2.5	2054	7.5
16	M	0339	2.3	0920	7.9	1608	2.1	2142	7.9
17	TU	0428	2.0	1003	8.2	1654	1.8	2223	8.2
18	W	0511	1.8	1042	8.5	1735	1.6	2302	8.4
19	TH	0551	1.7	1119	8.7	1814	1.5	○ 2340	8.6
20	F	0629	1.6	1155	8.8	1852	1.3		
21	SA	0018	8.7	0706	1.5	1232	8.9	1930	1.3
22	SU	0056	8.8	0744	1.5	1310	8.9	2009	1.3
23	M	0136	8.7	0824	1.6	1351	8.7	2049	1.4
24	TU	0219	8.6	0906	1.7	1434	8.5	2132	1.6
25	W	0305	8.3	0951	1.9	1522	8.3	2219	1.8
26	TH	0355	8.1	1042	2.1	1615	8.0	2311	2.0
27	F	0452	7.9	1140	2.2	1716	7.8		
28	SA	0004	2.1	0559	7.8	1246	2.3	1825	7.8
29	SU	0119	2.1	0710	7.9	1400	2.1	1938	7.9
30	M	0233	2.0	0819	8.2	1511	1.8	2045	8.2
31	TU	0343	1.8	0921	8.5	1616	1.5	2146	8.5

Chart Datum: 4·43 metres below IGN Datum

ST VALÉRY-SUR-SOMME/ LE CROTOY *9.22.25*

Somme **50°11'·34N 01°38'·90E** ❁❁◊◊✿✿

CHARTS AC *2451*; SHOM 7416; ECM 1011; Imray C31; Stanfords 1

TIDES LE HOURDEL –0010 Dover; ML —; Zone –0100

Standard Port DIEPPE (⟵)

Times				Height (metres)			
High Water		Low Water		MHWS	MHWN	MLWN	MLWS
0100	0600	0100	0700	9·3	7·4	2·5	0·8
1300	1800	1300	1900				
Differences ST VALÉRY-SUR-SOMME							
+0035	+0035	No data		+0·9	+0·7	No data	
LE HOURDEL							
+0020	+0020	No data		+0·8	+0·6	No data	

SHELTER The B de Somme is open to W and can be dangerous in onshore winds >F6. Silting is a major problem. All 3 very well sheltered hbrs (ie Le Hourdel, Le Crotoy and St Valéry-sur-Somme) are FV ports; Options:

1. Dry out on hard sand at Le Hourdel; access HW±1½.
2. Enter Le Crotoy marina when tidal range at Dover >4·4m (approx Coefficient 85) with max. draft 1·5m.
3. Enter (HW ±1) St Valéry marina (max. draft 2·0m). Usually met and guided to berth.
4. Enter Abbeville Canal at St Valéry (max. draft 2·0m up to Abbeville) by prior arrangement and daylight only.

NAVIGATION WPT 'ATSO' NCM By, VQ, 50°14'·25N 01°28'·57E, about 1·6M NW of buoyed chan (shifts). From N, beware being set by the flood onto shoals off Pte St Quentin. The whole estuary dries up to 3M seaward of Le Hourdel. The sands build up in ridges offshore, but inside Pte du Hourdel are generally flat, except where R Somme and minor streams scour their way to the sea. If Dover tidal range >4·4m, at HW ±1 there is sufficient water over the sands inside Pte du Hourdel for vessels <1·5m draft. Start appr from 'ATSO' at HW St Valéry –2. Buoys are moved to suit ever-shifting chans. Follow chan with lateral buoys numbered S1 to S50 (some lit), in strict order (no corner-cutting!) to small unlit WCM Division buoy, in variable position N or E of Pte du Hourdel; then see below. Departure from Le Hourdel/Le Crotoy is not possible before HW–2; St Valéry HW–2, for a fair tide if N-bound. Navigation of the Abbeville Canal was suspended (2001) due to flooding.

LIGHTS AND MARKS Only landmark is Cayeux-sur-Mer lt ho (W with R top) Fl R 5s 32m 22M (off chartlet to SSW). Pte du Hourdel lt ho Oc (3) WG 12s 19m 12/9M. Le Crotoy Oc (2) R 6s 19m 9M.

LE HOURDEL: Chan unmarked; follow 'S' buoys, then head SW toward end of shingle spit; hug the shingle.

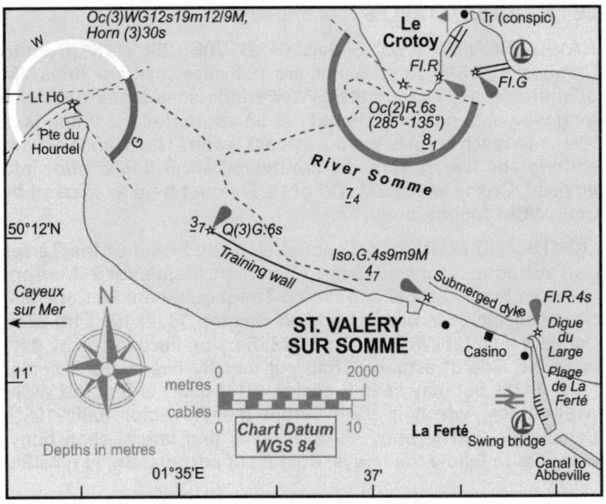

LE CROTOY: From Division By chan runs N & E with lateral Bys C1 to C8. Enter hbr very close to FV stages (port-side). Little used by yachts. Secure at last FV stage and ask YC for berth. Tidal hbr badly silted, with 2 drying pontoons.

ST VALÉRY-SUR-SOMME: From Division buoy, buoyed chan continues with SHMs becoming bns on submerged training wall, the seaward end of which is lit, Fl (3) G 6s 2m 2M; then four bns on end of groynes. Iso G 4s 9m 9M marks beginning of tree-lined promenade; submerged dyke opposite marked with PHM bns. W tr on head of Digue du Large, Fl R 4s 9m 9M, leads into marina, dredged 2m, and town quay.

RADIO TELEPHONE VHF Ch 09 (St Valéry HW ±2; Le Crotoy YC Jul/Aug only).

TELEPHONE St Valéry Hr Mr 03.22.60.24.80; Le Crotoy (Port de plaisance) 03.22.27.83.11; Aff Mar 03.22.27.81.44; ⊜ 03.22.24.04.75; Lock (canal) 03.22.60.80.23; CROSS 03.21.87.21.87; Auto 08.36.68.08.80; Police 03.22.60.82.08; Dr 03.22.26.92.25; Brit Consul 03.21.96.33.76.

FACILITIES

ST VALÉRY **Marina and YC Sport Nautique Valéricain** (250 + 30 Ⓥ) ☎ 03.22.60.24.80, 📠 03.22.60.24.82, €1.60, FW, AC, C (9ton), Slip, R, ⊡, Bar; Access HW ±1; **Services:** ME, El, CH, Ⓔ. **Town** EC Mon; P, D, CH, V, Gaz, R, Bar, ✉, Ⓑ, ⇌ and ✈ (Abbeville). Ferry: See Dieppe or Calais.

LE CROTOY **Marina** (280) ☎ 03.22.27.83.11, FW, C (6 ton), Slip; **YC Nautique de la Baie de Somme** ☎ 03.22.27.83.11, Bar. **Town** EC Mon; Ⓑ, Bar, D, P, ✉, R, ⇌, V.

LE TOUQUET/ÉTAPLES *9.22.26*

Pas de Calais **50°33'·10N 01°33'·37E** ❁❁◊◊✿✿

CHARTS AC *2451*; SHOM 7416; ECM 1011; Imray C31; Stanfords 1, 9

TIDES –0010 Dover; ML 5·3; Duration 0520; Zone –0100

Standard Port DIEPPE (⟵)

Times				Height (metres)			
High Water		Low Water		MHWS	MHWN	MLWN	MLWS
0100	0600	0100	0700	9·3	7·4	2·5	0·8
1300	1800	1300	1900				
Differences LE TOUQUET (ÉTAPLES)							
+0007	+0017	+0032	+0032	+0·2	+0·3	+0·4	+0·4
BERCK							
+0007	+0017	+0028	+0028	+0·5	+0·5	+0·4	+0·4

SHELTER Good, except in strong W'lies. Drying moorings to stbd off Le Touquet YC. At Étaples, access HW±2 to small marina (1.2m) close downstream of low bridge; beware strong 5kn current.

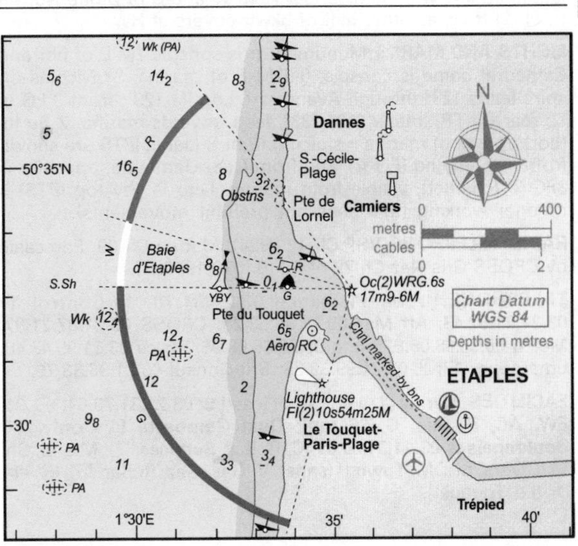

LE TOUQUET/ETAPLES *continued*

NAVIGATION WPT 50°35'·04N 01°31'·70E, 308°/128° from/to Camiers lt, 3·8M. Appr & ent are not easy; estuary dries 2M offshore. In even moderate SW/W winds seas break heavily a long way out and entry should not be attempted. Best app is at HW –1 to reach Étaples marina at slack water. The chan is always shifting and buoys, some lit, are moved accordingly; prior info advised. Drying wreck 2M NW of Le Touquet lt ho, is marked by unlit WCM Mérida buoy.

LIGHTS AND MARKS Le Touquet is at the S end of the Terres de Tourmont, a conspic range 175m high, visible for 25M. Appr between Pte de Lornel and Pte du Touquet, where La Canche lt ho is conspic Or tr, brown band, W & G top, Fl (2) 10s 54m 25M. Camiers lt Oc (2) WRG 6s 17m 9/6M (R pylon hard to see by day) is on NE side of estuary. Chan ent usually lies in lt's R sector (105°-141°), but may lie in G sector, (015°-090°) ie S of the WCM wreck buoy, which is itself within the W sector (090°-105°). Canche No 2 PHM buoy, Fl (2) R 6s, is first lateral chan buoy; essential to follow the buoys; do not cut corners. Bn, Fl R 4s 8m 2M, approx 4ca SW of Camiers Lt, marks the seaward end of sunken training wall defining NE side of River Canche to marina; wall also marked by posts.

RADIO TELEPHONE VHF Ch 09 (both hbrs), 77 (Le Touquet only).

TELEPHONE Hr Mr Le Touquet 03.21.05.12.77; Hr Mr Étaples 03.21.84.54.33, 🖷 03.21.09.76.96; Aff Mar Étaples 03.21.94.61.50; Auto 08.36.68.08.62; ⊖ 03.21.05.01.72; CROSS 03.21.87.21.87; Police 03.21.94.60.17; Dr 03.21.05.14.42; Brit Consul 03.21.96.33.76.

FACILITIES
LE TOUQUET **Cercle Nautique du Touquet** ☎ 03.21.05.12.77, M, P, Slip, ME, D, FW, C, CH, R, Bar; **Services:** BY, Sh, SM. **Town** P, D, V, Gaz, R, Bar, ✉, Ⓑ, ≹, ✈.

ÉTAPLES **Marina** (115 + 15 visitors), €1.37, FW, C (8 ton), AC, P, D; **Quay** BH (130 ton), FW, Slip; **Centre Nautique de la Canche** ☎ 03.21.94.74.26, Bar, Slip; **Services:** CH, El, Ⓔ, M, ME, Sh, D.
Town Ⓑ, Bar, D, P, ✉, R, ≹, V. ✈ Le Touquet. Ferry: Boulogne-Folkestone.

BOULOGNE-SUR-MER *9.22.27*

Pas de Calais **50°44'·67N 01°34'·05E** ❁❁◊◊✿✿

CHARTS AC 438, *1892, 2451*; SHOM 7247,7323, 7416; ECM 1010, 1011; Imray C8, C31; Stanfords 1, 9, 20

TIDES 0000 Dover; ML 4·9; Duration 0515; Zone –0100

Standard Port DUNKERQUE (⟶)

Times				Height (metres)			
High Water		Low Water		MHWS	MHWN	MLWN	MLWS
0200	0800	0200	0900	6·0	5·0	1·5	0·6
1400	2000	1400	2100				
Differences BOULOGNE							
–0045	–0100	–0045	–0025	+2·8	+2·2	+1·1	+0·5

SHELTER Good, except in strong NW'lies. Ent possible at all tides and in most weather. Very busy ferry and FV port; beware wash from FVs. Marina pontoons (2·9m) are on SW side of tidal basin alongside Quai Chanzy; max LOA 10m. If >10m, pre-arrange. No yacht berths on Quai Gambetta; FVs only. When R Liane in spate beware turbulent water.

NAVIGATION WPT 50°44'·45N 01°32'·92E, 270°/090° from/to S bkwtr (Digue Carnot) lt, 0·72M. Fairway buoy SCM, VQ (6) + L Fl 10s, is 295°/2·1M from S bkwtr lt. Cap d'Alprech lt ho, Fl (3) 15s 62m 23M, is 2·5M S of hbr ent. E side of hbr dries. Obey IPTS from SW jetty (see below). No navigational dangers and ent is easily identified and well marked, but keep W and S of Digue Nord lt tr, Fl (2) R 6s, as outer half of bkwtr covers at HW.

LIGHTS AND MARKS Monument tr is conspic 2M E of hbr ent. Cathedral dome is conspic, 0·62M E of marina. St Nicolas Ch spire leads 123° through Avant Port. Ldg lts 123°: front 3 FG in ▽; rear Dir FR, intens 113°-133°, lead towards marina. 2 Bu lts (hor) upriver of marina = sluicing from R Liane. **IPTS** are shown from SW jetty hd (FG ☆), and from Quai Gambetta, opposite ☆ 3FG ▽ (chartlet), visible from marina. One ● (by top IPTS) = dredger working (this does not prohibit movements).

RADIO TELEPHONE VHF Ch **12** (H24). Marina Ch 09. Forecasts by CROSS Gris Nez Ch 79 at H+10 (078-1910LT).

TELEPHONE Hr Mr Plaisance 03.21.31.70.01; Control Tr 03.21.31.52.43; Aff Mar 03.21.30.53.23; CROSS 03.21.87.21.87; Météo 08.36.68.08.62; Auto 08.36.65.08.08; Police 03.21.99.48.48; Emergency 17; Ⓗ 03.21.99.33.33; Brit Consul 03.21.96.33.76.

FACILITIES Marina (114 + 17 Ⓥ, at least) ☎ 03.21.31.70.01, €1.91, FW, AC, D, Slip, C (20 ton); **Quai Gambetta** FVs only; **YC Boulonnais** ☎ 03.21.31.80.67, C, R, Bar; **Services:** Ⓔ, ME, El, Sh, M, Divers, SHOM; **Town** P (cans), V, Gas, Gaz, R, Bar, ✉, Ⓑ, ≹, ✈ (Le Touquet).

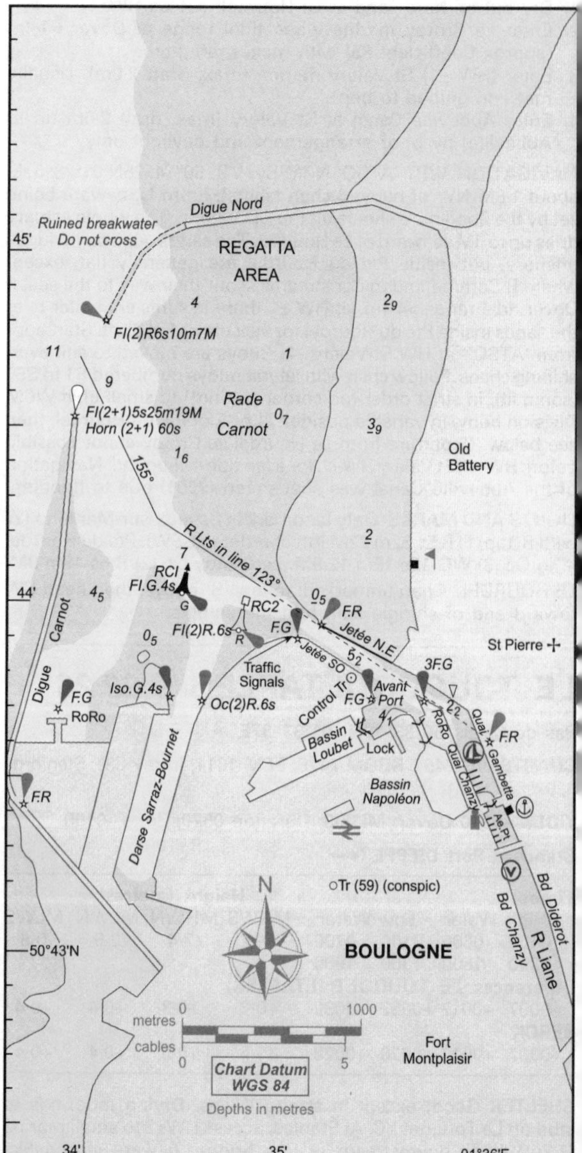

CALAIS *9.22.28*

Pas de Calais **50°58'·33N 01°50'·42E** ❁❁⚓⚓✿✿

CHARTS AC 1351, *1892, 323*; SHOM 7258, 6651; ECM 1010; Imray C8; Stanfords 1, 20

TIDES +0048 Dover; ML 4·0; Duration 0525; Zone –0100

Standard Port DUNKERQUE (⟶)

Times				Height (metres)			
High Water		Low Water		MHWS	MHWN	MLWN	MLWS
0200	0800	0200	0900	6·0	5·0	1·5	0·6
1400	2000	1400	2100				
Differences CALAIS							
–0020	–0030	–0015	–0005	+1·2	+0·9	+0·6	+0·3

SHELTER Very good, especially in the marina at Bassin de l'Ouest (3-6m). R waiting buoys outside tidal gate (see times below). ⓥ pontoon is first to stbd. In strong NW to NE winds hbr ent is rough with heavy swell; access H24. Enter lock into Bassin Carnot only if bound for the canals. Works are planned to start 15 Sep 2001 which may interrupt operation of marina.

NAVIGATION WPT 50°58'·45N 01°49'·82E, 298°/118° from/to Jetée Ouest lt, 0·43M. Beware the Ridens de la Rade, about 4ca N of ent, a partly drying (0·6m) sandbank on which seas break. From the E it may be best to keep seaward of this bank until able to round CA8 PHM lt buoy and appr from 1M W of hbr. Byelaws require yachts to have engine running (even if sailing) and not to impede commercial vessels/ferries. Speed limits: Avant-Port and Bassin Est 10kn; Arrière-Port 8kn; other basins 5kn.

LIGHTS AND MARKS Cap Blanc-Nez and Dover Patrol monument are conspic 5·5M WSW of hbr ent. Several churches and bldgs in the town are conspic. From a position ¼M SE of CA 10 PHM buoy, Fl (2) R 6s, the main lt ho (conspic), Fl (4) 15s, leads 141° through ent. The intens sector (115·5°-121·5°) of Dir FR 14m 14M at Gare Maritime leads close past the W jetty Iso G 3s. Hbr Control is conspic, pyramidal bldg on port-side as Arrière Port is entered. **IPTS** (full code), shown from Hbr Control, must be obeyed. If no sigs are shown (ie no ferries under way), yachts may enter/leave. Or they may follow a ferry entering/leaving, keeping to the stbd side of the fairway. Supplementary traffic sigs, shown alongside the top IPTS lt, are:

● = ferry leaving; no movements.
● = ferry entering; no movements.
One ● (alongside lower IPTS lt) = dredger working, (this does not prohibit movements).

Bassin de l'Ouest: Tidal gate and bridge open HW –1½, HW and HW +½. (Sat/Sun, Hols: HW –2, HW and HW +1). Times may vary.

●	= 10 mins before gate opens.
●	= All movements prohib.
●	= Movement authorised.
4 blasts	= Request permission to enter.

Prior to leaving, best to tell bridge operator your ETD.

Bassin Carnot: Gates open HW –1½ to HW +¾. Lock sigs:

● ● (hor)	= Enter.
●● (hor)	= Do not enter.
●	= Exit from basin permitted.
●	= Do not exit from basin.
2 blasts	= Request permission to enter.

RADIO TELEPHONE Whilst underway in appr's and hbr, keep a close listening watch on Ch **12** 16 (H24) *Calais Port Traffic* and marina. Carnot lock Ch 12 (occas). Hoverport Ch 20 (occas). Cap Gris Nez, Channel Navigation Info Service (CNIS), call: *Gris Nez Traffic* Ch **13** 79 16 (H24). Info broadcasts in English and French on Ch 79, at H + 10, and also at H + 25 when vis is < 2M. *CROSS Gris Nez* Ch 15, 67, **68**, 73.

TELEPHONE Hr Mr (Marina) 03.21.34.55.23; Hr Mr (Port) 03.21.96.31.20; Aff Mar 03.21.34.52.70; CROSS 03.21.87.21.87; SNSM 03.21.96.31.20; ⊖ 03.21.34.75.40; Météo 03.21.33.24.25; Auto 08.36.68.08.62; Police 03.21.96.74.17; Ⓗ 03.21.46.33.33; Brit Consul 03.21.96.33.76.

FACILITIES Marina (350 + 400 ⓥ) ☎ 03.21.34.55.23, 📠 03.21.96.10.78. e-mail: calais-marina@calais-port.com, €0.91, Access HW –1½ to HW +½. AB pontoon: €0.91 summer; D, P (cans), FW, C (3 ton), AC, Bar; **YC de Calais** ☎ 03.21.97.02.34, M, P, Bar; **Town** D, P (cans), ▣, Sh, SM, V, Gaz, R, Bar, ✉, Ⓑ, ⇌, ✈. Ferry: Dover.

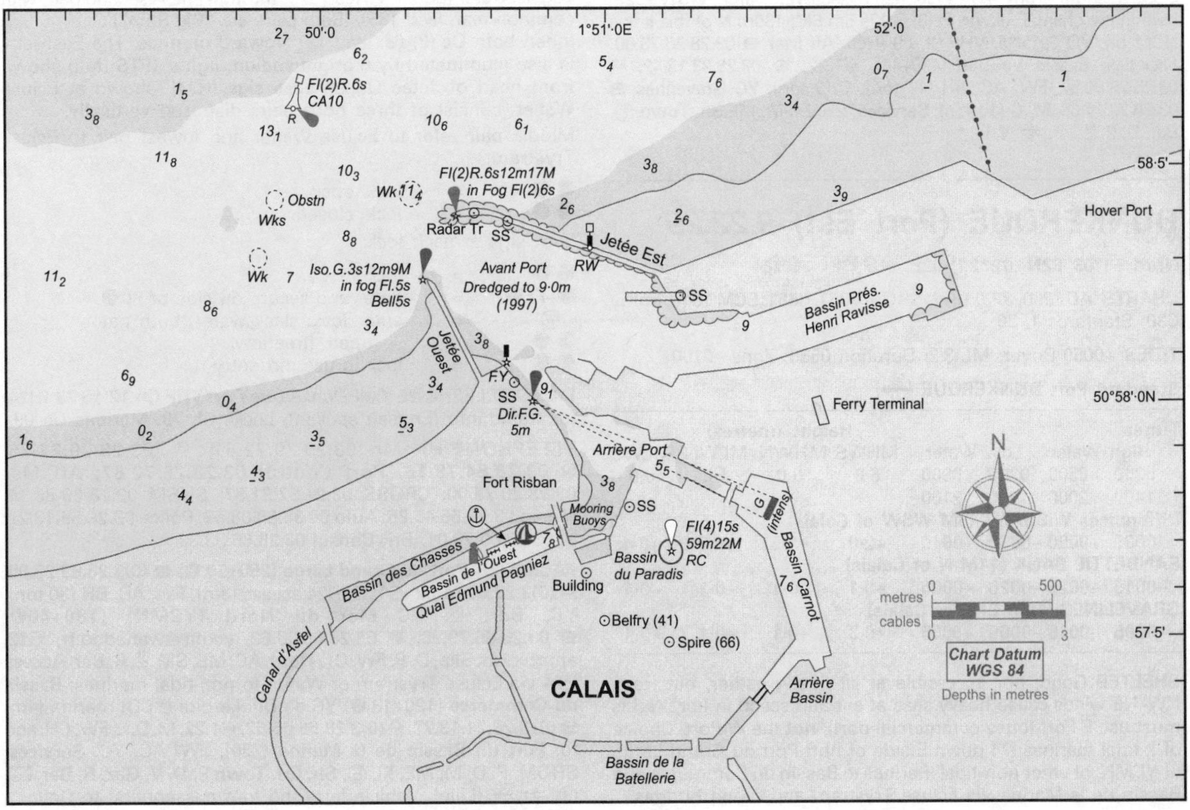

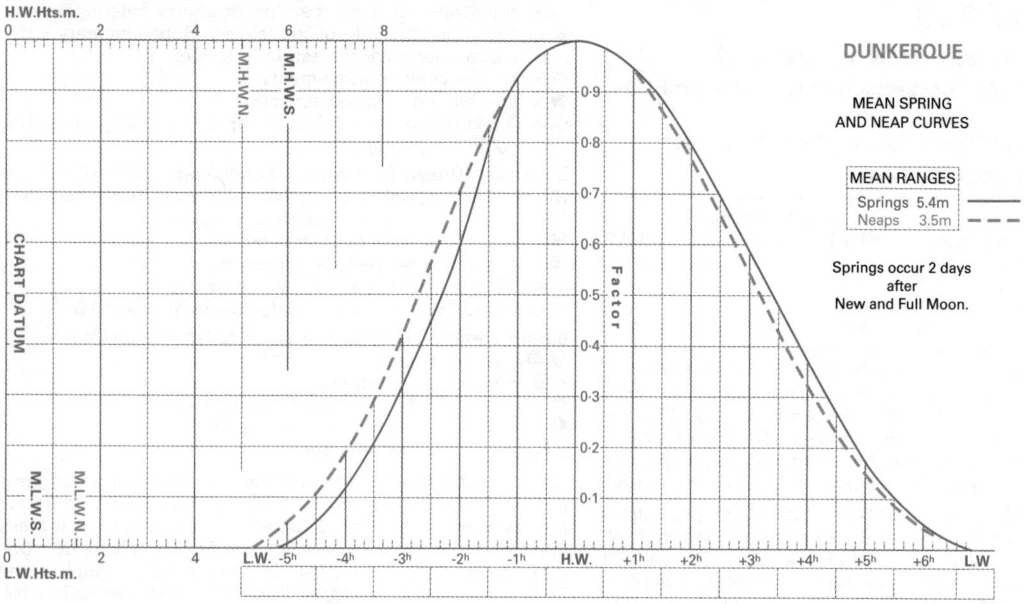
H.W.Hts.m.
0
2
4
6
8
M.H.W.N.
M.H.W.S.
CHART DATUM
M.L.W.S.
M.L.W.N.
L.W.Hts.m.
0.9
0.8
0.7
0.6
0.5
0.4
0.3
0.2
0.1
Factor
L.W.
-5h
-4h
-3h
-2h
-1h
H.W.
+1h
+2h
+3h
+4h
+5h
+6h
L.W
DUNKERQUE
MEAN SPRING AND NEAP CURVES
MEAN RANGES
Springs 5.4m
Neaps 3.5m
Springs occur 2 days after New and Full Moon.

MINOR HARBOUR (10M W of Dunkerque Est)

GRAVELINES, Nord, **51°00'·85N 02°05'·67E**, AC 1350, *323;* SHOM 7057, 6651. HW +0045 on Dover (UT); ML 3·3m; Duration 0520. See 9.22.29. Good shelter, but chan only has 0·5m at LWS; do not attempt it in strong onshore winds. Appr to bkwtrs, with old lt ho (unlit, conspic B/W spiral) in transit with wtr tr 142°. Nuclear power stn 1M NE. Beware strong E-going stream across ent at HW. Keep to W on entry and to E when inside. Hbr dries (soft mud). Yachts may take the ground or enter Bassin Vauban which also dries. Lts: W bkwtr, Fl (2) WG 6s 9m 8M, vis G078°-085° (very close inshore from W), W085°-244° (seaward arc), W317°-327° (within ent chan); E bkwtr, Fl (3) R 12s 5m 6M; 130m N of this lt is a NCM bn, VQ 6m 4M. VHF Ch 09 (HO). Aff Mar ☎ 03.28.26.73.00. Facilities: **Bassin Vauban** (410+40), €1.22, ☎ 03.28.23.13.42, 📠 03.28.23.00.57, FW, AC, BH (12 ton), C (3 ton); **YC Gravelines** ☎ 03.28.23.14.68, M, C (10 ton); **Services:** CH, El, M, ME,Sh. **Town** Ⓑ, Bar, D, P, ✉, R, ⇌, V, ⊡.

DUNKERQUE (Port Est) *9.22.29*

Nord **51°03'·62N 02°21'·02E** ❁❁❁◊◊◊✿✿

CHARTS AC 1350, *323*, 1872; SHOM 7057, 6651; ECM 1010; Imray C30; Stanfords 1, 20

TIDES +0050 Dover; ML 3·2; Duration 0530; Zone –0100

Standard Port DUNKERQUE (⟶)

Times				Height (metres)			
High Water		Low Water		MHWS	MHWN	MLWN	MLWS
0200	0800	0200	0900	6·0	5·0	1·5	0·6
1400	2000	1400	2100				
Differences WISSANT (8M WSW of Calais)							
–0035	–0050	–0030	–0010	+2·0	+1·5	+0·8	+0·4
SANDETTIE BANK (11M N of Calais)							
–0015	–0025	–0020	–0005	+0·1	–0·1	–0·1	–0·1
GRAVELINES (10M ENE of Calais)							
–0005	–0015	–0005	+0005	+0·3	+0·1	–0·1	–0·1

SHELTER Good; hbr accessible at all tides/weather, but fresh NW–NE winds cause heavy seas at ent and scend in hbr. Yachts must use E Port (busy commercial port), **not** the W Port. Choice of 2 tidal marinas ¾M down E side of hbr: Port du Grand Large or YCMN; or enter non-tidal marinas in Bassin du Commerce and Bassin de la Marine via Ecluse Trystram and swing bridges.

NAVIGATION WPT (E Port) 51°03'·85N 02°20'·92E, 355°/175° from/to Jetée Ouest lt, 0·20M. From the W, fetch the Dyke PHM buoy (Fl 3s), 5M N of Calais, thence to DKA SWM buoy (L Fl 10s), and then via series of DW lt buoys past W Port to DW 29 SHM buoy, ½M WNW of ent. From the E, via Nieuwpoort Bank WCM buoy, Q (9) 15s, the E1-12 buoys (8.19.4) lead S of Banc Hills but shore lights obscure navigation lights and lights of other vessels. Streams reach about 3½kn.

LIGHTS AND MARKS Two power stn chimneys (113m) are conspic 1M WSW of hbr ent. Main lt ho Fl (2) 10s 59m 28M, W tr with B top. Ldg lts: Outer (both F Vi) lead 179° through ent. A second pair, with common rear, lead 185°. (Both pairs are "Big Ship").
Inner, both Oc (2) 6s, lead 137° toward marinas. The East jetty is also illuminated by 6 bright sodium lights. **IPTS** (full) shown from head of Jetée Ouest. **Lock sigs** (H24), shown at Ecluse Watier, consist of three horiz pairs disposed vertically.
Middle pair refer to Ecluse Watier and lowest pair to Ecluse Trystram:

●● = lock open.
●● = lock closed.

Lock sigs at each lock:

●● = lock ready.
●+Fl ● = enter and secure on side of Fl ●.
Ⓦ = enter lock; slack water, both gates open (freeflow).
●●
●● = lock in use, no entry.

RADIO TELEPHONE Call *Dunkerque Port* VHF Ch 12 16 **73** (H24) for traffic info (English spoken). Locks Ch 73. Marinas Ch 09.

TELEPHONE Hr Mr 03.28.29.72.61, 📠 03.28.29.72.75; ⊖ 03.28.64.78.16; Port Control 03.28.29.72.87; Aff Mar 03.28.26.73.00; CROSS 03.21.87.21.87; SNSM 03.28.66.86.14; Météo 03.28.66.45.25; Auto 08.36.68.08.59; Police 03.28.59.13.22; Ⓗ 03.28.66.70.01; Brit Consul 03.28.66.33.33.

FACILITIES Port du Grand Large (250+50 Ⓥ) ☎ (0)3.28.63.23.00, 📠 (0)3.28.66.66.62, €1.83, H24 access (3m), FW, AC, BH (30 ton), YC, Bar, ⊡; **YC Mer du Nord** (YCMN) (180+40Ⓥ) ☎ 03.28.66.79.90, 📠 03.28.66.36.62, ycmn@wanadoo.fr, €12, approx 2m, Slip, D, P, FW, C (7½ ton), AC, ME, SM, ⊡, R, Bar; Access H24 via Ecluse Trystram or Watier to non-tidal marinas: **Bassin du Commerce** (120+13 Ⓥ) YC de Dunkerque (YCD) marina (4m) ☎ (0) 3.28.21.13.77, 📠 (0)3.28.66.66.62, €1.22, M, D, L, FW, CH; and to: **Port du Bassin de la Marine** (250), FW, AC, YC. **Services:** SHOM, P, D, M, ME, El, Ⓔ, Sh, CH. **Town** P, D, V, Gaz, R, Bar, ✉, Ⓑ, ⇌, ✈ (Lille). Vehicle ferry (no foot passengers) to Dover.

AGENTS WANTED If you are interested in becoming our agent for any of the following ports, please write to: The Editor, The Book Barn, Westbourne, Hampshire, PO10 8RS, England – and get your free copy of the Almanac annually. You do not have to live in a port to be the agent, but should at least be a fairly regular visitor.

Le Légué (St Brieuc)	Bénodet
River Loire/St Nazaire	L'Herbaudière
St Gilles-Croix-de-Vie	Les Sables d'Olonne
La Rochelle	La Seudre
La Gironde	Port Bloc
Anglet	St Jean-de-Luz
Dives-sur-Mer	River Seine
Le Touquet/Étaples	Nieupoort
Oostend	Stellendam & Hellevoetsluis
Norderney	Spiekeroog

WGS SHIFT Since so many yachts use GPS receivers for navigation, it is important to realise that care should be taken in plotting the instrument reading directly on the chart. Some British Admiralty and foreign charts now have a WGS84 base but most still have Ordnance Survey or appropriate foreign bases. It is important therefore to read the title of the chart in use to check the base and to plot any GPS readings in conformity. A number of sections in editions of the Macmillan Reeds range of almanacs have been converted to WGS84 - generally in line with the British Hydrographic Office's chart conversion programme - these are clearly marked at the head of each page. For example:

GPS reading	50°20′·00N	04°08′·00W
WGS shift	00′·03S	00′·07E
Position applied to chart	50°19′·97N	04°07′·93W

The usual rule applies, viz **add** similar headings, **subtract** dissimilar ones. At first sight this may seem academic but failure to apply the shift may easily give a plotted position on the wrong side of a narrow passage.

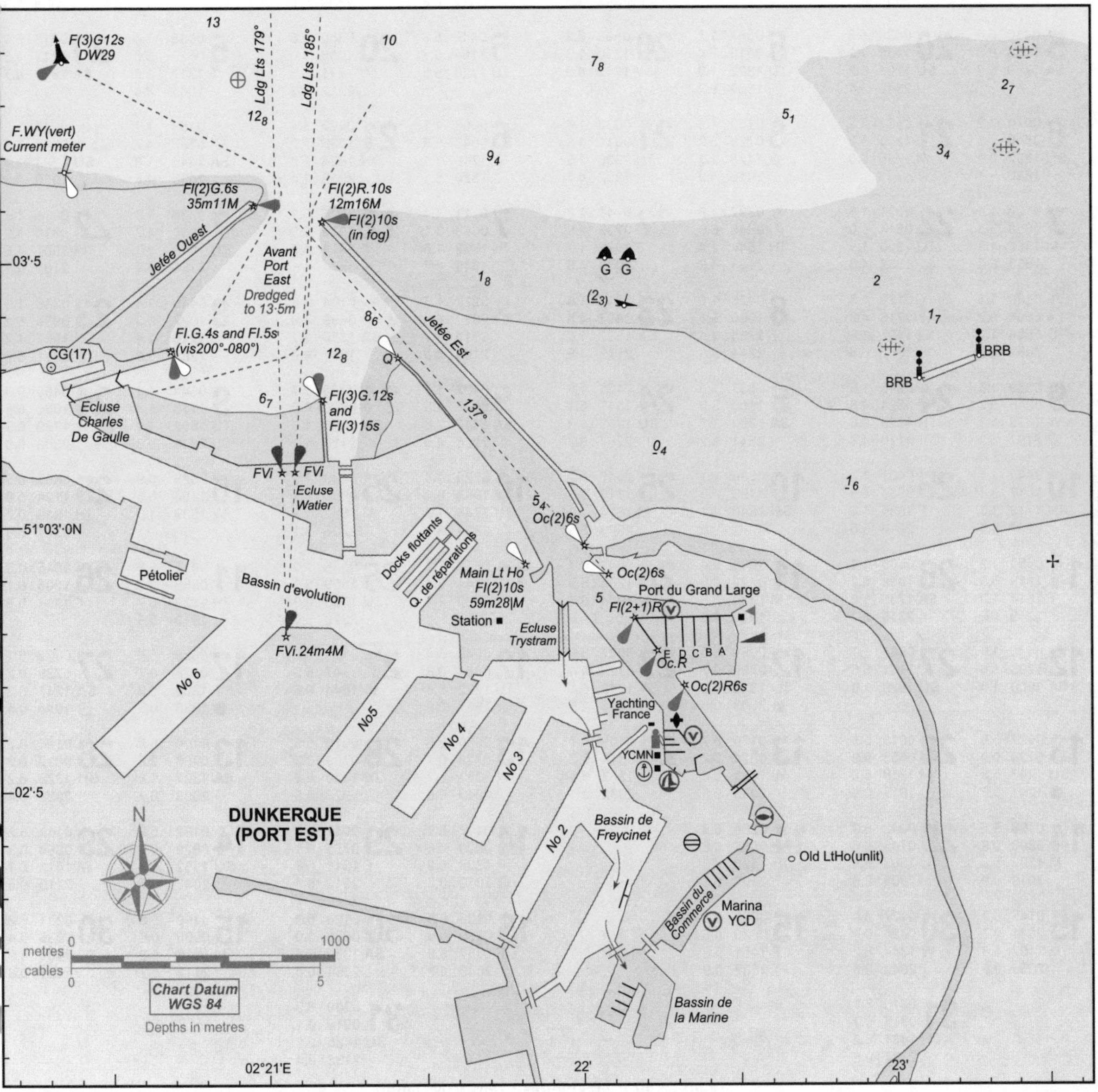

TIME ZONE -0100
(French Standard Time)
Subtract 1 hour for UT
For French Summer Time add ONE hour in **non-shaded areas**

FRANCE – DUNKERQUE

LAT 51°03'N LONG 2°22'E

TIMES AND HEIGHTS OF HIGH AND LOW WATERS

SPRING & NEAP TIDES
Dates in red are **SPRINGS**
Dates in blue are **NEAPS**

YEAR 200

JANUARY

Date	Day	Time	m	Time	m	Time	m	Time	m
1	TU	0138	6.0	0839	0.6	1358	6.1	2059	0.7
2	W	0223	6.0	0926	0.6	1446	6.1	2146	0.8
3	TH	0310	5.9	1013	0.6	1536	6.0	2233	0.9
4	F	0359	5.8	1101	0.7	1627	5.8	2322	1.1
5	SA	0450	5.6	1153	0.8	1723	5.6		
6	SU	0020	1.2	0546	5.5	1252	0.9	1826	5.4
7	M	0122	1.4	0650	5.3	1356	1.0	1939	5.3
8	TU	0230	1.5	0804	5.2	1504	1.1	2052	5.2
9	W	0339	1.5	0915	5.2	1613	1.1	2157	5.3
10	TH	0449	1.4	1017	5.4	1719	1.1	2257	5.4
11	F	0550	1.2	1113	5.5	1814	1.0	2349	5.5
12	SA	0640	1.0	1203	5.6	1900	1.0		
13	SU	0027	5.6	0724	0.9	1247	5.8	● 1941	0.9
14	M	0108	5.7	0803	0.8	1328	5.8	2019	0.9
15	TU	0145	5.7	0841	0.7	1407	5.8	2055	0.9
16	W	0219	5.7	0917	0.8	1443	5.8	2129	1.0
17	TH	0252	5.7	0951	0.8	1516	5.7	2201	1.1
18	F	0326	5.6	1023	0.9	1550	5.5	2234	1.2
19	SA	0401	5.5	1055	1.0	1626	5.4	2308	1.3
20	SU	0439	5.3	1130	1.2	1707	5.2	2345	1.4
21	M	0521	5.2	1210	1.3	1755	5.0		
22	TU	0031	1.6	0614	5.0	1300	1.5	1852	4.8
23	W	0128	1.8	0716	4.8	1407	1.6	1957	4.8
24	TH	0245	1.8	0824	4.8	1526	1.6	2110	4.8
25	F	0401	1.7	0935	4.9	1635	1.4	2219	5.0
26	SA	0506	1.4	1039	5.2	1735	1.2	2315	5.3
27	SU	0604	1.1	1131	5.5	1829	1.0		
28	M	0010	5.6	0655	0.9	1218	5.8	○ 1917	0.8
29	TU	0043	5.9	0743	0.6	1303	6.1	2003	0.6
30	W	0127	6.0	0829	0.4	1348	6.2	2049	0.6
31	TH	0210	6.1	0915	0.3	1434	6.2	2134	0.6

FEBRUARY

Date	Day	Time	m	Time	m	Time	m	Time	m
1	F	0255	6.1	1001	0.2	1521	6.1	2218	0.6
2	SA	0339	6.0	1047	0.3	1609	6.0	2303	0.8
3	SU	0426	5.9	1134	0.5	1658	5.8	2350	1.0
4	M	0517	5.7	1224	0.7	1753	5.5		
5	TU	0047	1.2	0615	5.4	1322	1.0	1858	5.2
6	W	0150	1.5	0726	5.2	1428	1.3	2016	4.9
7	TH	0302	1.6	0846	5.0	1544	1.4	2133	4.9
8	F	0426	1.6	1000	5.1	1704	1.4	2244	5.0
9	SA	0537	1.3	1106	5.2	1803	1.2	2341	5.2
10	SU	0630	1.1	1158	5.5	1848	1.1		
11	M	0019	5.4	0712	0.9	1239	5.6	1927	1.0
12	TU	0056	5.6	0750	0.7	1316	5.8	● 2003	0.9
13	W	0130	5.7	0824	0.7	1351	5.8	2035	0.8
14	TH	0200	5.8	0857	0.6	1422	5.8	2107	0.8
15	F	0229	5.8	0928	0.6	1451	5.8	2137	0.9
16	SA	0259	5.8	0957	0.7	1520	5.7	2207	0.9
17	SU	0329	5.7	1025	0.8	1550	5.6	2236	1.0
18	M	0358	5.6	1055	0.9	1621	5.4	2307	1.2
19	TU	0428	5.4	1129	1.1	1656	5.2	2343	1.3
20	W	0509	5.2	1210	1.3	1747	4.9		
21	TH	0033	1.6	0611	4.9	1306	1.5	1902	4.7
22	F	0141	1.8	0732	4.8	1428	1.7	2023	4.6
23	SA	0312	1.8	0857	4.8	1557	1.6	2149	4.8
24	SU	0435	1.5	1017	5.1	1713	1.3	2257	5.2
25	M	0545	1.1	1117	5.5	1814	1.0	2349	5.5
26	TU	0641	0.7	1205	5.9	1904	0.7		
27	W	0027	5.9	0729	0.4	1249	6.1	○ 1949	0.5
28	TH	0109	6.1	0814	0.2	1333	6.3	2032	0.4

MARCH

Date	Day	Time	m	Time	m	Time	m	Time	m
1	F	0151	6.2	0858	0.1	1416	6.3	2115	0.4
2	SA	0233	6.2	0942	0.0	1500	6.2	2157	0.5
3	SU	0316	6.2	1025	0.2	1544	6.1	2239	0.6
4	M	0401	6.0	1108	0.4	1630	5.8	2322	0.8
5	TU	0449	5.8	1154	0.7	1720	5.5		
6	W	0003	1.1	0543	5.5	1246	1.1	1820	5.1
7	TH	0111	1.4	0653	5.1	1352	1.5	1940	4.7
8	F	0227	1.7	0820	4.8	1516	1.7	2109	4.6
9	SA	0402	1.7	0944	4.8	1645	1.6	2226	4.8
10	SU	0520	1.4	1053	5.1	1745	1.3	2324	5.1
11	M	0612	1.1	1144	5.4	1830	1.1		
12	TU	0006	5.4	0654	0.8	1222	5.6	1907	0.9
13	W	0036	5.6	0728	0.7	1257	5.7	1940	0.8
14	TH	0107	5.7	0800	0.6	1328	5.8	● 2010	0.8
15	F	0135	5.8	0830	0.6	1357	5.8	2040	0.7
16	SA	0202	5.8	0900	0.6	1422	5.8	2110	0.7
17	SU	0229	5.8	0929	0.6	1449	5.8	2139	0.8
18	M	0256	5.8	0956	0.7	1515	5.7	2207	0.8
19	TU	0322	5.7	1024	0.8	1541	5.5	2236	1.0
20	W	0350	5.6	1056	1.0	1611	5.3	2311	1.2
21	TH	0429	5.4	1135	1.2	1654	5.0	2359	1.4
22	F	0525	5.1	1229	1.5	1814	4.7		
23	SA	0104	1.6	0655	4.8	1350	1.7	1951	4.6
24	SU	0236	1.7	0830	4.8	1528	1.6	2125	4.7
25	M	0409	1.5	0958	5.1	1652	1.3	2236	5.1
26	TU	0525	1.0	1059	5.5	1755	0.9	2328	5.5
27	W	0621	0.6	1147	5.9	1844	0.6		
28	TH	0013	5.9	0709	0.3	1230	6.2	○ 1928	0.5
29	F	0047	6.1	0753	0.1	1311	6.3	2010	0.4
30	SA	0128	6.2	0836	0.0	1353	6.3	2051	0.4
31	SU	0209	6.3	0918	0.1	1435	6.2	2133	0.4

APRIL

Date	Day	Time	m	Time	m	Time	m	Time	m
1	M	0252	6.2	1000	0.2	1518	6.0	2214	0.5
2	TU	0337	6.1	1042	0.5	1603	5.8	2256	0.8
3	W	0424	5.8	1124	0.8	1651	5.4	2341	1.1
4	TH	0518	5.4	1214	1.3	1749	5.0		
5	F	0038	1.4	0625	5.0	1317	1.6	1905	4.6
6	SA	0153	1.7	0753	4.7	1444	1.8	2038	4.5
7	SU	0330	1.7	0920	4.7	1613	1.7	2156	4.7
8	M	0449	1.4	1027	5.0	1716	1.4	2252	5.0
9	TU	0544	1.1	1116	5.3	1802	1.1	2333	5.3
10	W	0625	0.9	1154	5.5	1839	1.0		
11	TH	0010	5.5	0658	0.7	1229	5.7	1910	0.9
12	F	0038	5.7	0728	0.7	1300	5.8	● 1939	0.8
13	SA	0106	5.8	0758	0.6	1327	5.8	2009	0.7
14	SU	0132	5.8	0829	0.6	1352	5.8	2041	0.7
15	M	0159	5.8	0900	0.6	1418	5.8	2112	0.7
16	TU	0227	5.8	0929	0.7	1446	5.7	2142	0.8
17	W	0256	5.8	0959	0.8	1514	5.6	2214	0.9
18	TH	0329	5.6	1033	1.0	1548	5.4	2252	1.1
19	F	0411	5.4	1115	1.2	1635	5.1	2339	1.3
20	SA	0513	5.1	1212	1.5	1803	4.7		
21	SU	0049	1.5	0642	4.9	1333	1.6	1930	4.6
22	M	0216	1.5	0810	4.9	1507	1.5	2101	4.8
23	TU	0346	1.3	0935	5.2	1627	1.2	2211	5.2
24	W	0459	0.9	1036	5.6	1729	0.9	2303	5.6
25	TH	0557	0.5	1124	5.9	1819	0.7	2347	5.8
26	F	0645	0.3	1206	6.1	1904	0.5		
27	SA	0022	6.1	0729	0.2	1247	6.2	○ 1946	0.5
28	SU	0104	6.2	0812	0.2	1328	6.2	2028	0.4
29	M	0146	6.2	0854	0.3	1412	6.1	2110	0.5
30	TU	0231	6.2	0936	0.4	1456	5.9	2151	0.6

Chart Datum: 2·69 metres below IGN Datum

Register for your **FREE** weekly weather email service from Macmillan Reeds
❯❯ at **www.nauticaldata.com – NOW!** ❮❮
weekend weather reports sent to your email address, every Thursday

TIME ZONE -0100
(French Standard Time)
Subtract 1 hour for UT
For French Summer Time add ONE hour in **non-shaded areas**

FRANCE – DUNKERQUE

LAT 51°03'N LONG 2°22'E

TIMES AND HEIGHTS OF HIGH AND LOW WATERS

SPRING & NEAP TIDES
Dates in red are **SPRINGS**
Dates in blue are **NEAPS**

YEAR **2002**

MAY

Date	Day	Time	m	Time	m	Time	m	Time	m
1	W	0317	6.0	1017	0.7	1542	5.7	2234	0.8
2	TH	0405	5.7	1059	1.0	1630	5.3	2318	1.0
3	F	0458	5.4	1146	1.3	1723	5.0		
4	SA	0003	1.3	0559	5.0	1244	1.7	1829	4.7
5	SU	0119	1.6	0716	4.7	1402	1.8	1955	4.5
6	M	0244	1.6	0841	4.7	1525	1.7	2111	4.6
7	TU	0401	1.4	0946	4.9	1631	1.5	2207	4.9
8	W	0459	1.2	1036	5.2	1721	1.3	2252	5.2
9	TH	0543	1.0	1118	5.4	1801	1.1	2331	5.4
10	F	0619	0.9	1155	5.6	1834	0.9		
11	SA	0004	5.6	0652	0.8	1227	5.7	1906	0.9
12	SU	0033	5.7	0725	0.7	1255	5.7	● 1939	0.8
13	M	0102	5.7	0759	0.7	1322	5.8	2014	0.7
14	TU	0133	5.8	0834	0.7	1354	5.8	2049	0.7
15	W	0207	5.8	0908	0.8	1428	5.7	2125	0.7
16	TH	0243	5.8	0944	0.9	1505	5.6	2203	0.8
17	F	0324	5.6	1023	1.0	1549	5.3	2245	1.0
18	SA	0414	5.4	1110	1.2	1650	5.1	2336	1.1
19	SU	0520	5.2	1208	1.4	1759	4.9		
20	M	0044	1.3	0631	5.1	1323	1.5	1910	4.9
21	TU	0202	1.2	0747	5.1	1445	1.4	2031	5.0
22	W	0321	1.1	0907	5.3	1557	1.2	2140	5.3
23	TH	0430	0.8	1009	5.6	1659	1.0	2234	5.5
24	F	0529	0.6	1058	5.8	1752	0.8	2320	5.8
25	SA	0620	0.5	1143	5.9	1840	0.7		
26	SU	0011	6.0	0706	0.4	1226	6.0	○ 1925	0.6
27	M	0044	6.1	0750	0.5	1309	6.0	2008	0.6
28	TU	0130	6.1	0833	0.5	1355	5.9	2051	0.6
29	W	0216	6.0	0916	0.7	1441	5.8	2134	0.6
30	TH	0304	5.9	0957	0.9	1527	5.6	2217	0.8
31	F	0351	5.6	1039	1.1	1612	5.4	2300	1.0

JUNE

Date	Day	Time	m	Time	m	Time	m	Time	m
1	SA	0438	5.4	1122	1.3	1658	5.1	2346	1.2
2	SU	0530	5.1	1211	1.6	1750	4.9		
3	M	0041	1.4	0629	4.9	1312	1.7	1854	4.7
4	TU	0148	1.5	0741	4.8	1424	1.7	2009	4.7
5	W	0259	1.5	0851	4.8	1531	1.6	2113	4.8
6	TH	0401	1.3	0947	5.0	1627	1.4	2205	5.0
7	F	0452	1.2	1034	5.2	1715	1.2	2250	5.2
8	SA	0536	1.0	1116	5.4	1756	1.1	2330	5.4
9	SU	0616	1.0	1152	5.5	1834	1.0		
10	M	0009	5.5	0655	0.9	1226	5.6	1913	0.9
11	TU	0037	5.7	0734	0.8	1300	5.7	● 1952	0.8
12	W	0114	5.8	0814	0.8	1338	5.7	2033	0.7
13	TH	0155	5.8	0855	0.8	1420	5.7	2115	0.7
14	F	0238	5.8	0937	0.9	1506	5.6	2158	0.7
15	SA	0326	5.7	1022	1.0	1556	5.5	2244	0.8
16	SU	0417	5.6	1110	1.1	1648	5.3	2335	0.9
17	M	0513	5.5	1204	1.2	1743	5.2		
18	TU	0036	1.0	0614	5.4	1308	1.3	1845	5.2
19	W	0144	1.0	0721	5.3	1418	1.3	1956	5.2
20	TH	0254	0.9	0834	5.3	1526	1.2	2106	5.3
21	F	0400	0.9	0940	5.5	1630	1.1	2206	5.5
22	SA	0503	0.8	1036	5.6	1729	1.0	2300	5.6
23	SU	0559	0.7	1127	5.6	1822	0.9	2350	5.7
24	M	0650	0.7	1215	5.7	1910	0.8	○	
25	TU	0033	5.9	0736	0.7	1301	5.7	1955	0.7
26	W	0120	5.9	0819	0.8	1346	5.8	2039	0.6
27	TH	0207	5.9	0900	0.8	1430	5.7	2121	0.6
28	F	0251	5.8	0940	0.9	1511	5.6	2201	0.7
29	SA	0334	5.6	1018	1.1	1550	5.5	2240	0.9
30	SU	0414	5.5	1057	1.2	1629	5.3	2319	1.0

JULY

Date	Day	Time	m	Time	m	Time	m	Time	m
1	M	0456	5.3	1137	1.4	1710	5.1		
2	TU	0001	1.2	0542	5.1	1222	1.5	1758	5.0
3	W	0051	1.3	0634	4.9	1318	1.6	1854	4.9
4	TH	0150	1.4	0734	4.8	1425	1.7	1958	4.8
5	F	0257	1.5	0839	4.8	1529	1.6	2105	4.9
6	SA	0358	1.4	0941	4.9	1627	1.5	2204	5.0
7	SU	0454	1.3	1035	5.1	1720	1.3	2255	5.2
8	M	0544	1.2	1122	5.3	1807	1.1	2341	5.4
9	TU	0630	1.0	1204	5.5	1852	1.0		
10	W	0019	5.6	0715	0.9	1245	5.6	● 1936	0.8
11	TH	0101	5.8	0800	0.8	1326	5.8	2020	0.6
12	F	0144	5.9	0845	0.8	1410	5.8	2105	0.5
13	SA	0229	6.0	0930	0.8	1455	5.8	2151	0.5
14	SU	0316	5.9	1015	0.8	1541	5.7	2237	0.5
15	M	0404	5.9	1101	0.9	1629	5.6	2324	0.6
16	TU	0455	5.7	1149	1.0	1719	5.5		
17	W	0020	0.7	0550	5.6	1244	1.2	1815	5.4
18	TH	0119	0.8	0652	5.4	1347	1.3	1921	5.3
19	F	0225	1.0	0802	5.3	1455	1.3	2034	5.2
20	SA	0333	1.1	0915	5.2	1604	1.3	2145	5.3
21	SU	0443	1.1	1021	5.3	1714	1.2	2249	5.4
22	M	0548	1.0	1121	5.4	1812	1.0	2346	5.6
23	TU	0641	1.0	1213	5.5	1902	0.8		
24	W	0029	5.7	0726	0.9	1256	5.6	○ 1946	0.7
25	TH	0114	5.8	0807	0.9	1336	5.7	2027	0.6
26	F	0155	5.8	0845	0.9	1414	5.7	2106	0.6
27	SA	0234	5.8	0921	0.9	1449	5.7	2142	0.7
28	SU	0310	5.7	0955	1.0	1522	5.6	2216	0.8
29	M	0345	5.6	1028	1.1	1555	5.5	2248	0.9
30	TU	0420	5.5	1101	1.2	1630	5.4	2322	1.0
31	W	0458	5.3	1136	1.3	1710	5.2		

AUGUST

Date	Day	Time	m	Time	m	Time	m	Time	m
1	TH	0000	1.2	0541	5.1	1217	1.5	1758	5.0
2	F	0045	1.4	0633	4.9	1309	1.7	1855	4.9
3	SA	0145	1.6	0735	4.8	1422	1.8	2003	4.7
4	SU	0300	1.7	0845	4.7	1538	1.8	2117	4.8
5	M	0412	1.6	0957	4.9	1645	1.6	2225	5.0
6	TU	0517	1.4	1057	5.2	1745	1.3	2320	5.4
7	W	0612	1.2	1146	5.4	1836	1.0		
8	TH	0012	5.7	0701	1.0	1230	5.7	● 1922	0.7
9	F	0046	5.9	0747	0.8	1311	5.9	2006	0.5
10	SA	0129	6.1	0831	0.7	1352	6.0	2051	0.4
11	SU	0212	6.2	0915	0.6	1434	6.0	2135	0.3
12	M	0257	6.2	0958	0.7	1516	6.0	2219	0.3
13	TU	0343	6.1	1041	0.8	1601	5.9	2304	0.4
14	W	0431	5.9	1126	0.9	1649	5.8	2352	0.6
15	TH	0523	5.7	1215	1.1	1743	5.6		
16	F	0049	0.9	0622	5.4	1315	1.4	1849	5.3
17	SA	0154	1.2	0733	5.1	1426	1.5	2009	5.1
18	SU	0309	1.4	0855	4.9	1546	1.5	2133	5.1
19	M	0433	1.4	1013	5.0	1705	1.3	2245	5.3
20	TU	0542	1.3	1117	5.2	1804	1.1	2342	5.5
21	W	0632	1.1	1206	5.5	1851	0.8		
22	TH	0022	5.7	0713	1.0	1244	5.6	○ 1932	0.7
23	F	0101	5.8	0750	0.9	1318	5.8	2009	0.6
24	SA	0137	5.9	0823	0.9	1350	5.8	2043	0.6
25	SU	0210	5.9	0856	0.9	1421	5.8	2116	0.6
26	M	0241	5.8	0927	0.9	1449	5.8	2146	0.7
27	TU	0310	5.8	0957	1.0	1517	5.7	2215	0.8
28	W	0340	5.6	1025	1.1	1548	5.6	2243	1.0
29	TH	0410	5.5	1055	1.2	1620	5.4	2314	1.2
30	F	0442	5.3	1129	1.4	1656	5.2	2351	1.4
31	SA	0526	5.0	1213	1.7	1753	4.9		

Chart Datum: 2·69 metres below IGN Datum

Register for your FREE weekly weather email service from Macmillan Reeds
at www.nauticaldata.com – NOW!
weekend weather reports sent to your email address, every Thursday

TIME ZONE -0100
(French Standard Time)
Subtract 1 hour for UT
For French Summer Time add ONE hour in **non-shaded areas**

FRANCE – DUNKERQUE

LAT 51°03′N LONG 2°22′E

TIMES AND HEIGHTS OF HIGH AND LOW WATERS

SPRING & NEAP TIDES
Dates in red are **SPRINGS**
Dates in blue are **NEAPS**

YEAR **200**

SEPTEMBER

Day	Time	m	Day	Time	m
1	0044	1.7	16	0250	1.8
	0638	4.7		0837	4.7
SU	1315	1.9	M	1531	1.7
	1913	4.7		2123	5.0
2	0201	1.9	17	0422	1.7
	0800	4.6		1001	4.9
M	1445	1.9	TU	1653	1.4
	2038	4.7		2236	5.2
3	0333	1.8	18	0528	1.4
	0925	4.7		1104	5.2
TU	1613	1.7	W	1750	1.1
	2200	5.0		2330	5.5
4	0453	1.5	19	0615	1.2
	1035	5.1		1149	5.5
W	1724	1.3	TH	1834	0.8
	2301	5.4			
5	0556	1.2	20	0009	5.7
	1128	5.5		0653	1.0
TH	1819	0.9	F	1222	5.7
	2350	5.8		1912	0.7
6	0645	0.9	21	0041	5.9
	1211	5.8		0726	1.0
F	1905	0.6	SA	1252	5.8
			○	1945	0.7
7	0027	6.1	22	0113	5.9
	0729	0.7		0756	0.9
SA	1249	6.0	SU	1322	5.9
●	1948	0.4		2015	0.7
8	0108	6.3	23	0141	5.9
	0811	0.6		0826	0.9
SU	1327	6.1	M	1349	5.9
	2031	0.2		2044	0.7
9	0150	6.3	24	0207	5.9
	0853	0.6		0856	0.9
M	1407	6.2	TU	1415	5.9
	2113	0.2		2113	0.8
10	0232	6.3	25	0233	5.9
	0935	0.6		0925	1.0
TU	1448	6.2	W	1441	5.8
	2156	0.2		2141	0.9
11	0317	6.2	26	0300	5.8
	1017	0.7		0952	1.1
W	1532	6.1	TH	1508	5.7
	2239	0.4		2208	1.0
12	0403	6.0	27	0325	5.6
	1059	0.9		1020	1.2
TH	1619	5.9	F	1535	5.6
	2324	0.7		2237	1.2
13	0454	5.7	28	0353	5.4
	1146	1.2		1053	1.4
F	1715	5.6	SA	1607	5.4
				2312	1.4
14	0018	1.1	29	0431	5.1
	0553	5.3		1135	1.6
SA	1244	1.5	SU	1651	5.0
	1823	5.2			
15	0125	1.5	30	0004	1.7
	0707	4.9		0536	4.8
SU	1400	1.7	M	1235	1.9
	1950	4.9		1832	4.7

OCTOBER

Day	Time	m	Day	Time	m
1	0119	2.0	16	0357	1.8
	0724	4.6		0935	4.8
TU	1403	2.0	W	1628	1.5
	2007	4.7		2211	5.1
2	0259	1.9	17	0502	1.6
	0855	4.7		1034	5.1
W	1541	1.7	TH	1725	1.1
	2135	5.0		2303	5.4
3	0429	1.6	18	0549	1.3
	1011	5.1		1117	5.4
TH	1658	1.3	F	1808	0.9
	2239	5.5		2342	5.7
4	0534	1.2	19	0626	1.1
	1104	5.5		1151	5.6
F	1755	0.8	SA	1844	0.8
	2327	5.9			
5	0623	0.9	20	0014	5.8
	1145	5.9		0657	1.0
SA	1842	0.5	SU	1223	5.8
				1915	0.8
6	0012	6.2	21	0043	5.9
	0706	0.7		0725	1.0
SU	1222	6.1	M	1252	5.9
●	1925	0.3	○	1943	0.8
7	0044	6.4	22	0110	5.9
	0747	0.6		0755	0.9
M	1259	6.3	TU	1318	5.9
	2007	0.2		2012	0.8
8	0125	6.4	23	0134	5.9
	0828	0.6		0826	0.9
TU	1339	6.3	W	1343	5.9
	2049	0.2		2042	0.8
9	0207	6.3	24	0201	5.9
	0910	0.6		0856	1.0
W	1421	6.3	TH	1410	5.9
	2131	0.4		2111	0.9
10	0252	6.2	25	0228	5.8
	0952	0.7		0924	1.0
TH	1506	6.2	F	1439	5.8
	2214	0.6		2140	1.1
11	0338	5.9	26	0256	5.7
	1034	0.9		0955	1.2
F	1555	5.9	SA	1509	5.6
	2258	0.9		2211	1.3
12	0428	5.6	27	0328	5.5
	1121	1.2		1030	1.3
SA	1652	5.6	SU	1544	5.4
	2348	1.4		2249	1.5
13	0526	5.2	28	0409	5.2
	1217	1.5		1114	1.5
SU	1801	5.2	M	1633	5.1
				2340	1.7
14	0056	1.8	29	0515	4.8
	0640	4.8		1216	1.7
M	1334	1.8	TU	1812	4.8
	1929	4.9			
15	0226	2.0	30	0057	1.9
	0813	4.6		0654	4.7
TU	1508	1.8	W	1337	1.8
	2102	4.9		1939	4.8
			31	0231	1.9
				0820	4.8
			TH	1510	1.6
				2105	5.1

NOVEMBER

Day	Time	m	Day	Time	m
1	0358	1.6	16	0507	1.5
	0938	5.1		1035	5.3
F	1627	1.2	SA	1730	1.1
	2211	5.5		2304	5.5
2	0503	1.2	17	0548	1.3
	1032	5.5		1115	5.5
SA	1726	0.8	SU	1809	1.0
	2301	5.9		2340	5.6
3	0555	0.9	18	0622	1.1
	1115	5.9		1150	5.6
SU	1816	0.5	M	1841	0.9
	2344	6.1			
4	0640	0.8	19	0011	5.7
	1154	6.1		0653	1.1
M	1900	0.4	TU	1222	5.7
●				1910	0.9
5	0020	6.3	20	0039	5.8
	0723	0.7		0726	1.0
TU	1234	6.3	W	1249	5.8
	1943	0.3	○	1942	0.9
6	0102	6.3	21	0107	5.8
	0805	0.6		0759	1.0
W	1316	6.3	TH	1318	5.9
	2026	0.4		2015	0.9
7	0146	6.3	22	0136	5.9
	0847	0.6		0833	1.0
TH	1401	6.3	F	1349	5.9
	2109	0.6		2049	1.0
8	0231	6.1	23	0209	5.8
	0931	0.7		0907	1.0
F	1449	6.1	SA	1424	5.8
	2152	0.8		2123	1.1
9	0318	5.8	24	0244	5.7
	1015	0.9		0942	1.1
SA	1539	5.9	SU	1501	5.7
	2237	1.1		2159	1.3
10	0407	5.5	25	0322	5.5
	1101	1.2		1022	1.2
SU	1635	5.5	M	1544	5.5
	2325	1.5		2241	1.4
11	0502	5.2	26	0409	5.2
	1154	1.5		1109	1.3
M	1738	5.2	TU	1642	5.2
				2332	1.6
12	0026	1.8	27	0514	5.0
	0606	4.8		1207	1.5
TU	1302	1.7	W	1756	5.1
	1857	4.9			
13	0144	2.0	28	0041	1.7
	0730	4.7		0626	4.9
W	1426	1.7	TH	1317	1.5
	2024	4.8		1909	5.1
14	0308	2.0	29	0201	1.7
	0850	4.7		0740	5.0
TH	1543	1.6	F	1438	1.4
	2130	5.0		2028	5.2
15	0416	1.7	30	0321	1.6
	0949	5.0		0855	5.2
F	1643	1.3	SA	1552	1.1
	2221	5.3		2137	5.5

DECEMBER

Day	Time	m	Day	Time	m
1	0428	1.3	16	0500	1.5
	0956	5.5		1034	5.2
SU	1654	0.8	M	1724	1.3
	2232	5.8		2302	5.3
2	0525	1.1	17	0544	1.3
	1046	5.8		1116	5.4
M	1749	0.7	TU	1805	1.2
	2320	5.9		2341	5.5
3	0616	0.9	18	0623	1.2
	1131	6.0		1153	5.5
TU	1838	0.6	W	1842	1.1
4	0011	6.1	19	0015	5.6
	0702	0.8		0701	1.1
W	1216	6.1	TH	1227	5.7
●	1924	0.6	○	1918	1.0
5	0046	6.1	20	0047	5.7
	0747	0.7		0739	1.0
TH	1302	6.2	F	1301	5.8
	2009	0.6		1956	1.0
6	0131	6.1	21	0122	5.8
	0832	0.7		0818	0.9
F	1350	6.2	SA	1338	5.8
	2053	0.7		2035	1.0
7	0218	6.0	22	0159	5.8
	0917	0.7		0857	0.9
SA	1440	6.0	SU	1418	5.9
	2137	0.9		2115	1.0
8	0304	5.8	23	0239	5.7
	1001	0.9		0938	0.9
SU	1529	5.8	M	1501	5.8
	2220	1.2		2156	1.1
9	0350	5.5	24	0321	5.6
	1045	1.0		1020	0.9
M	1619	5.5	TU	1546	5.7
	2304	1.4		2239	1.2
10	0436	5.3	25	0407	5.5
	1131	1.3		1106	1.0
TU	1710	5.2	W	1637	5.5
	2352	1.7		2326	1.3
11	0527	5.0	26	0459	5.3
	1224	1.5		1157	1.1
W	1810	5.0	TH	1734	5.4
12	0050	1.8	27	0023	1.4
	0626	4.8		0558	5.2
TH	1327	1.6	F	1256	1.2
	1922	4.8		1837	5.3
13	0159	1.9	28	0128	1.5
	0740	4.7		0702	5.2
F	1436	1.6	SA	1406	1.2
	2032	4.8		1948	5.2
14	0308	1.8	29	0242	1.5
	0850	4.8		0813	5.2
SA	1540	1.5	SU	1517	1.1
	2129	5.0		2102	5.3
15	0408	1.7	30	0352	1.4
	0946	5.0		0923	5.4
SU	1636	1.4	M	1624	1.0
	2219	5.2		2207	5.5
			31	0458	1.3
				1024	5.6
			TU	1727	0.9
				2305	5.6

Chart Datum: 2·69 metres below IGN Datum

Register for your **FREE** weekly weather email service from Macmillan Reeds
at **www.nauticaldata.com – NOW!**
weekend weather reports sent to your email address, every Thursday

Area 23

Belgium and the Netherlands
Nieuwpoort to Delfzijl

.23.1 Index .... **Page 961**

.23.2 Area map **962**

.23.3 Tidal stream charts **964**

.23.4 Lights, buoys and waypoints **966**

.23.5 Passage information **972**

.23.6 Distance table **973**

.23.7 Special notes for Belgium and the Netherlands **974**

.23.8 Southern North Sea waypoints **975**

.23.9 Nieuwpoort (Nieuport) **976**

.23.10 Oostende (Ostend) **977**

.23.11 Blankenberge **977**

.23.12 Zeebrugge **978**

.23.13 Breskens **978**

.23.14 Westerschelde **979**
- Ellewoutsdijk
- Houede Kenskerke
- Hansweert
- Walsoorden
- Paal
- Doel
- Lillo

.23.15 Terneuzen **980**

.23.16 Antwerpen (Antwerp) **980**

9.23.17 Vlissingen (Flushing), Standard Port, tidal curves **981**

9.23.18 Oosterschelde **985**

9.23.19 Stellendam & Hellevoetsluis **987**

9.23.20 Hoek van Holland Standard Port, tidal curves **991**

9.23.21 Rotterdam **992**

9.23.22 Scheveningen **993**

9.23.23 IJmuiden **994**

9.23.24 Amsterdam **995**

9.23.25 IJsselmeer **995**

9.23.26 Den Helder **997**

9.23.27 Oudeschild **998**

9.23.28 Harlingen **998**
- Nes (Ameland)

9.23.29 Vlieland **999**

9.23.30 West Terschelling **999**

9.23.31 Zeegat van Terschelling **1000**

9.23.32 Lauwersoog **1000**
- Oostmahorn
- Zoutkamp

9.23.33 Delfzijl **1001**
- Schiermonnikoog
- Eemshaven
- Termunterzijl

Fig.9(11) Marinas in Belgium, Netherlands and Germany **1002**

9.23.2

Belgium and the Netherlands

Nieuwpoort to Delfzijl

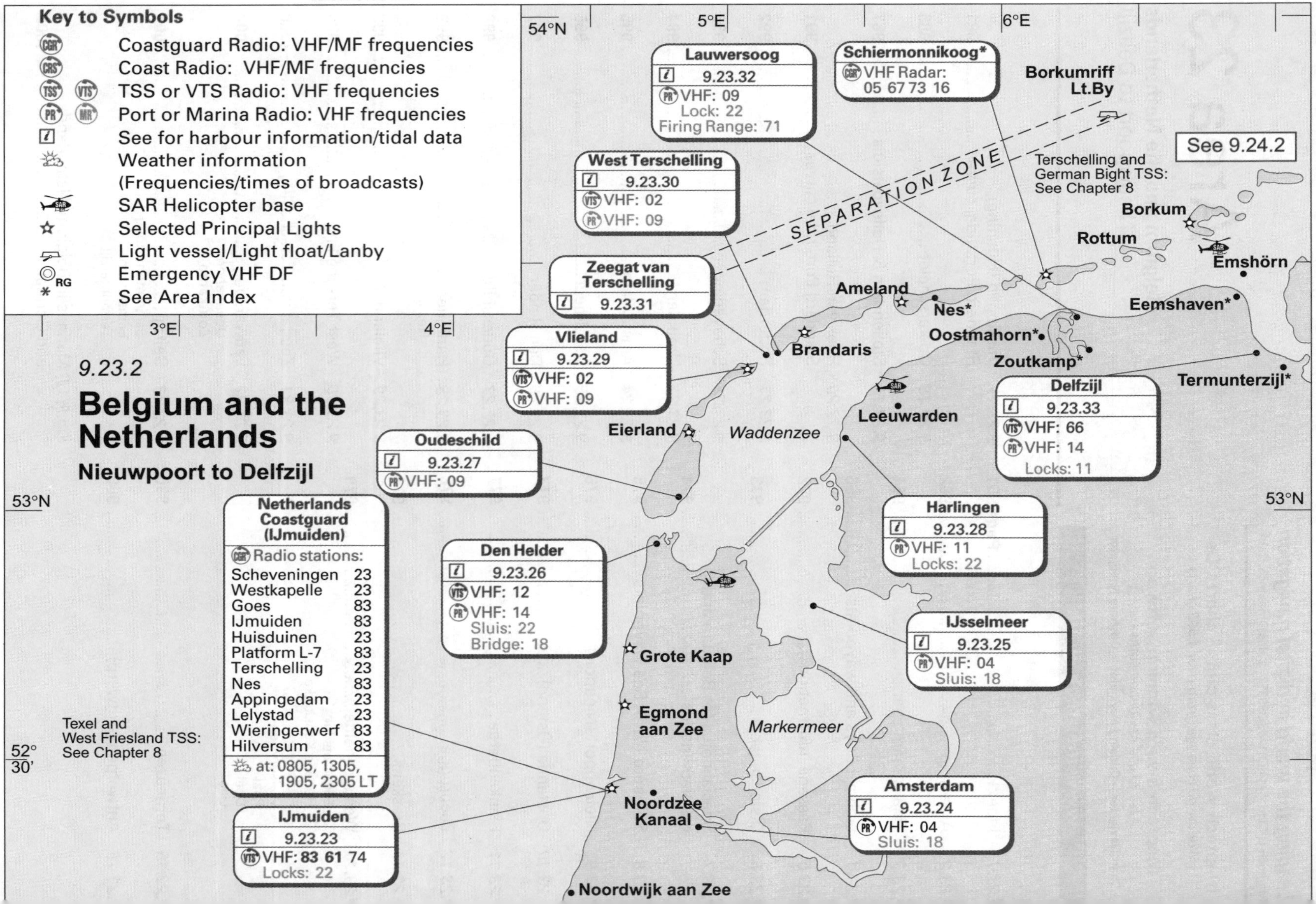

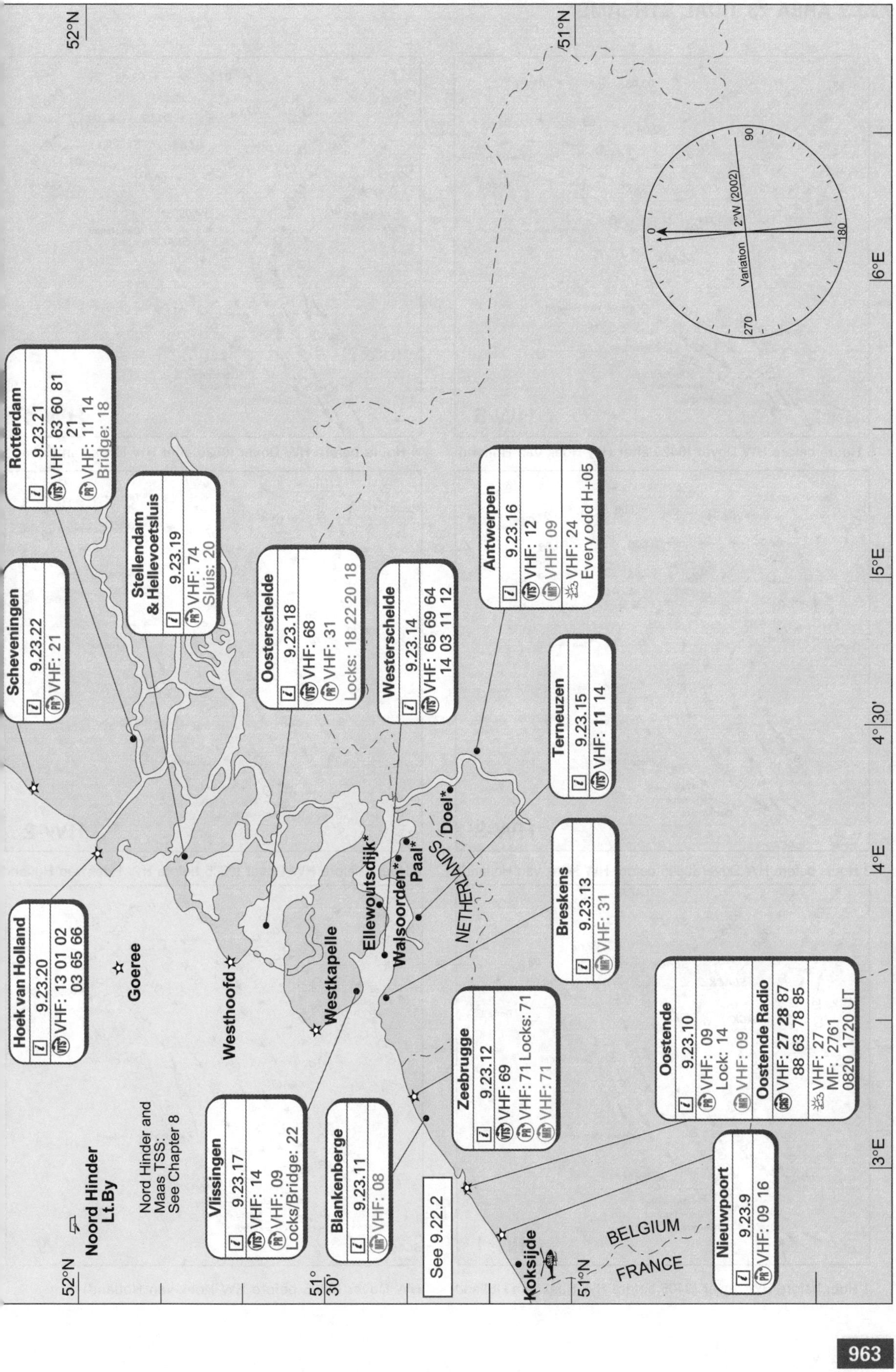
52°N
51°N
4°30'
4°E
3°E
5°E
6°E
51° 30'
Variation 2°W (2002)
0
90
180
270
Noord Hinder Lt.By
Nord Hinder and Maas TSS: See Chapter 8
Goeree
Westhoofd
Westkapelle
Ellewoutsdijk*
Walsoorden*
Paal*
Doel*
NETHERLANDS
BELGIUM
FRANCE
Koksijde
SAR
See 9.22.2
Hoek van Holland
9.23.20
VHF: 13 01 02 03 65 66
Scheveningen
9.23.22
VHF: 21
Rotterdam
9.23.21
VHF: 63 60 81 21
VHF: 11 14
Bridge: 18
Stellendam & Hellevoetsluis
9.23.19
VHF: 74
Sluis: 20
Oosterschelde
9.23.18
VHF: 68
VHF: 31
Locks: 18 22 20 18
Westerschelde
9.23.14
VHF: 65 69 64 14 03 11 12
Antwerpen
9.23.16
VHF: 12
VHF: 09
VHF: 24
Every odd H+05
Terneuzen
9.23.15
VHF: 11 14
Breskens
9.23.13
VHF: 31
Vlissingen
9.23.17
VHF: 14
VHF: 09
Locks/Bridge: 22
Blankenberge
9.23.11
VHF: 08
Zeebrugge
9.23.12
VHF: 69
VHF: 71 Locks: 71
VHF: 71
Oostende
9.23.10
VHF: 09
Lock: 14
VHF: 09
Oostende Radio
VHF: 27 28 87 88 63 78 85
VHF: 27
MF: 2761
0820 1720 UT
Nieuwpoort
9.23.9
VHF: 09 16

23

9.23.3 AREA 23 TIDAL STREAMS

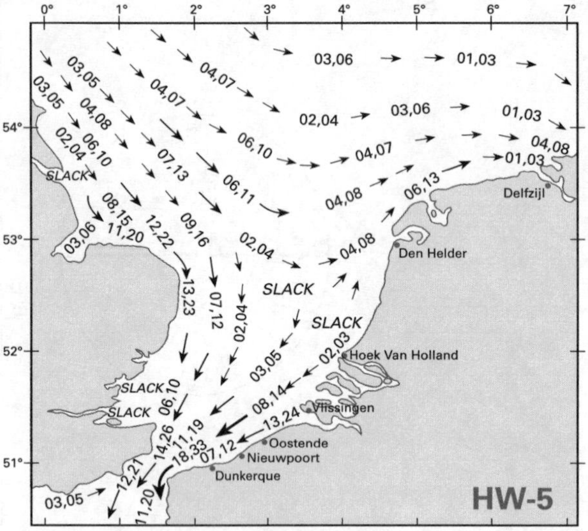

5 Hours before HW Dover (0420 after HW Hoek van Holland)

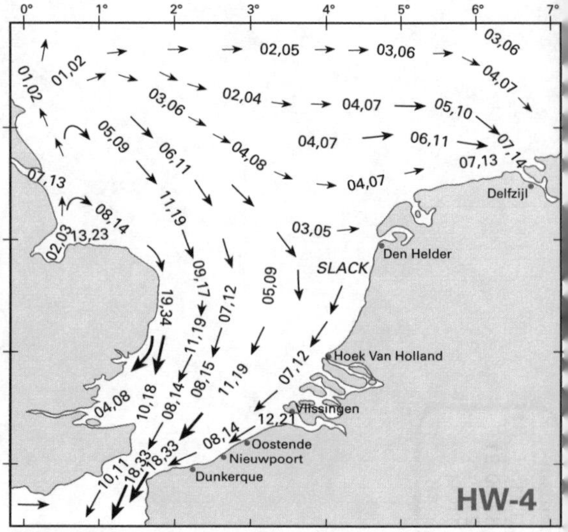

4 Hours before HW Dover (0520 after HW Hoek van Holland

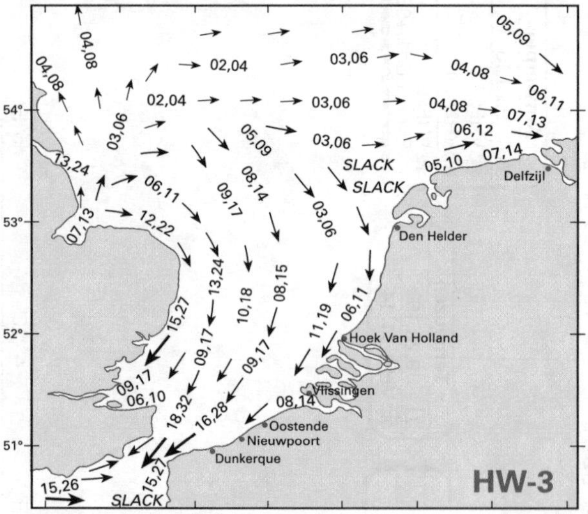

3 Hours before HW Dover (0605 before HW Hoek van Holland)

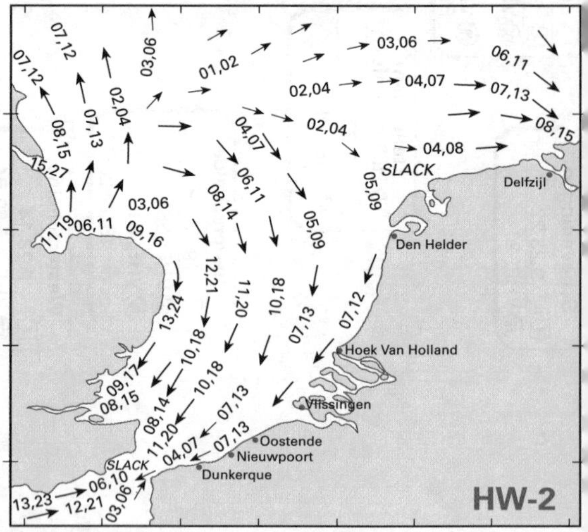

2 Hours before HW Dover (0505 before HW Hoek van Holland

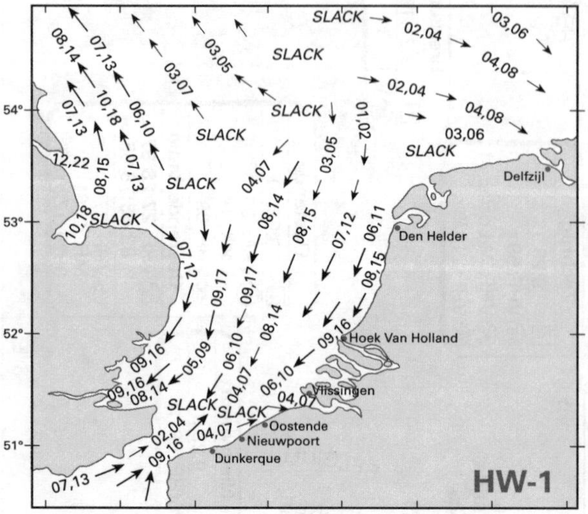

1 Hour before HW Dover (0405 before HW Hoek van Holland)

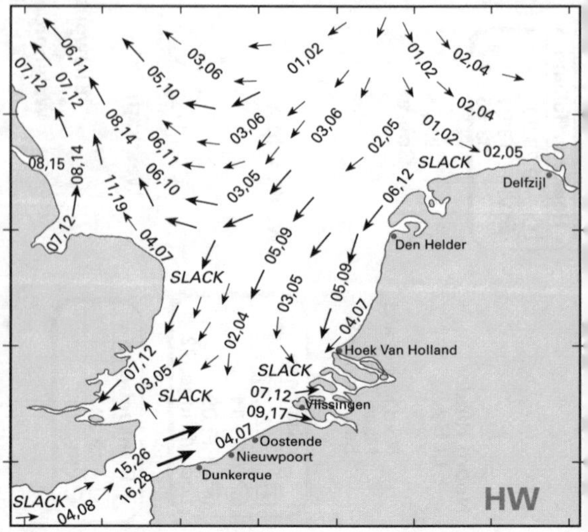

HW Dover (0305 before HW Hoek van Holland)

South-westward 9.19.3 North-westward 9.4.3 North-eastward 9.21.3

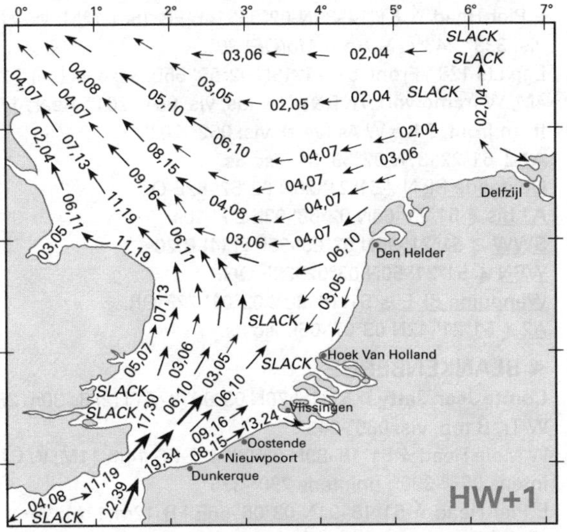

1 Hour after HW Dover (0205 before HW Hoek van Holland)

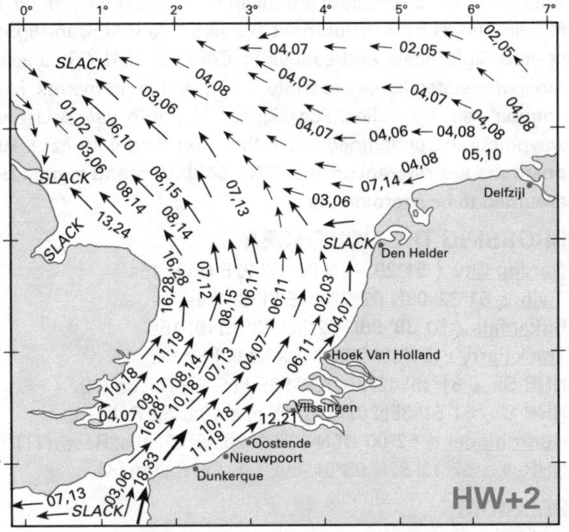

2 Hours after HW Dover (0105 before HW Hoek van Holland)

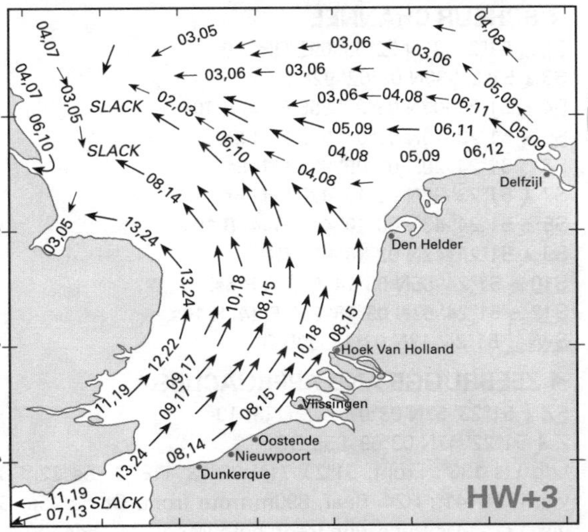

3 Hours after HW Dover (0005 after HW Hoek van Holland)

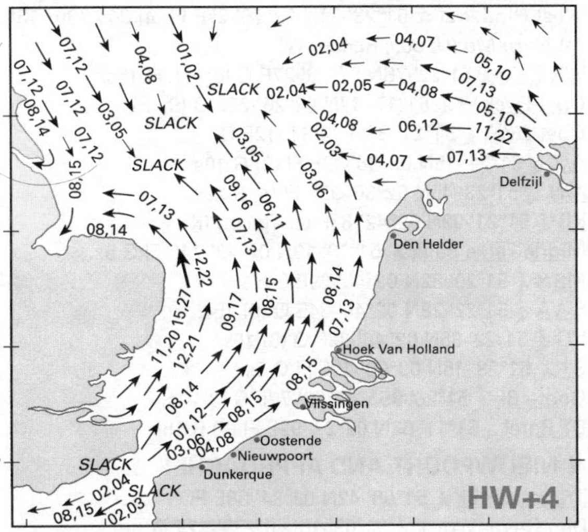

4 Hours after HW Dover (0055 after HW Hoek van Holland)

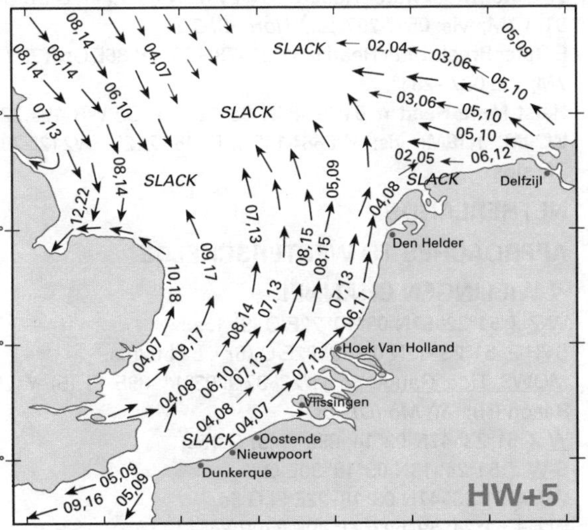

5 Hours after HW Dover (0155 after HW Hoek van Holland)

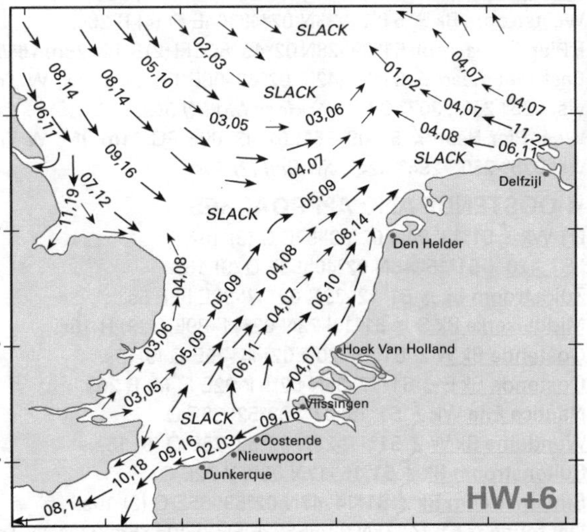

6 Hours after HW Dover (0255 after HW Hoek van Holland)

9.23.4 LIGHTS, BUOYS AND WAYPOINTS

Abbreviations used below are given in the Introduction 1.4.1. Principal lights ☆ are in **bold** print, places in CAPITALS, and light-vessels, light floats and Lanbys in *CAPITAL ITALICS.* Unless otherwise stated lights are white. m – elevation in metres; M – nominal range in miles. Fog signals are in *italics.* Useful waypoints are underlined – use those on land with care. **All positions are referenced the WGS 84 datum and should be assumed to be approximate.**

CROSSING THE NORTH SEA

Garden City 51°29'·12N 02°17'·92E Q (9) 15s.
Twin 51°32'·05N 02°22'·62E Fl (3) Y 9s.
Birkenfels 51°38'·96N 02°32'·03E Q (9) 15s.
Track Ferry 51°33'·78N 02°36'·33E Fl Y 5s.
NHR-SE 51°45'·42N 02°39'·92E Fl G 5s; Racon (N).
NHR-S 51°51'·35N 02°28'·71E Fl Y 10s; *Bell.*
Noordhinder 52°00'·15N 02°51'·20E Fl (2) 10s; Racon (T)
NHR-N 52°10'·82N 03°04'·69E L Fl 8s; Racon (K).

BELGIUM

◀ WEST HINDER TO SCHEUR CHANNEL

West Hinder Lt ☆ 51°23'·31N 02°26'·27E Fl (4) 30s 23m 13M; *Horn Mo (U) 30s*; Racon (W).
WH Zuid 51°22'·78N 02°26'·27E Q (6) + L Fl 15s.
Oost-Dyck W 51°17'·17N 02°26'·22E Q (9) 15s.
Oost-Dyck 51°21'·38N 02°31'·12E Q.
A/Z 51°21'·15N 02°36'·92E Fl (3) G 10s.
A/N 51°23'·45N 02°36'·92E Fl (4) R 20s.
KB 51°21'·03N 02°42'·83E Q; Racon (K).
Middelkerke Bank 51°18'·19N 02°42'·74E Fl G 5s.
MBN 51°20'·82N 02°46'·29E Q.
SWA 51°22'·28N 02°46'·34E Q (9) 15s.
VG 51°22'·95N 02°46'·32E Q (9) 15s.
S1 51°23'·15N 03°00'·12E Fl G 5s.
Goote Bk 51°26'·95N 02°52'·72E Q (3)10s.
BT Ratel 51°11'·62N 02°27'·92E Fl (4) R 15s.

◀ NIEUWPOORT AND APPROACHES

Trapegeer Bk 51°08'·42N 02°34'·38E Fl G 10s.
Den Oever Wreck 51°09'·15N 02°39'·42E Q.
Nieuwpoort Bk 51°10'·17N 02°36'·09E Q (9) 15s.
Weststroom Bk 51°11'·33N 02°43'·04E Fl (4) R 20s.
E Pier ☆, near root, 51°09'·28N 02°43'·80E Fl (2) R 14s 28m **16M.**
East Pier Head ☆ 51°09'·42N 02°43'·08E FR 11m 9M; W Tr; vis: 025°-250°, 307°-347°; *Horn Mo (K) 30s.*
West Pier Head ☆ 51°09'·35N 02°43'·00E FG 11m 9M; W Tr; vis: 025°-250°, 284°-324°; *Bell (2) 10s.*

◀ OOSTENDE AND APPROACHES

D1 Wk 51°13'·94N 02°38'·57E Q (3) 10s.
LST 420 51°15'·46N 02°40'·58E Q (9) 15s.
Zuidstroom Bk 51°12'·29N 02°47'·38E Fl R 5s.
Middelkerke Bk S 51°14'·73N 02°41'·89E Q (9) R 15s.
Oostende Bk W 51°16'·20N 02°44'·75E Q (9)15s.
Oostende Bk E 51°17'·35N 02°51'·92E Fl (4) R 20s.
Nautica Ena Wk 51°18'·07N 02°52'·80E Q.
Wenduine Bk W 51°17'·23N 02°52'·75E Q (9) 15s.
Buitenstroom Bk 51°15'·17N 02°51'·72E Q.
Binnenstroom Bk 51°14'·47N 02°53'·65E Q (3) 10s.
Oostende ☆ 51°14'·18N 02°55'·83E Fl (3) 10s 65m **27M**; W Tr; obsc 069·5°-071°.
W Pier Head ☆ 51°14'·31N 02°55'·03E FG 14m 10M; W Tr; vis: 057°-327°; *Bell (1) 4s.*
E Pier Head ☆ 51°14'·39N 02°55'·14E FR 15m 12M; W ○ Tr, vis: 333°-243°; *Horn Mo(OE) 30s.*
Ldg Lts 128°, Front, 51°14'·13N 02°55'·55E. 3 Iso 4s (vert) 22m 4M; W framework Tr, R&W bands; vis: 051°-201°. Rear, 175m from front, 3 Iso W 4s (vert); vis: 052°-201°.
A1 51°22'·37N 02°53'·34E Iso 8s.
Oostende Bk N 51°21'·20N 02°52'·82E Q.
A1 bis 51°21'·68N 02°58'·02E L Fl 10s.
SWW 51°21'·95N 03°00'·95E Fl (4) R 20s.
WBN 51°21'·50N 03°02'·59E QG.
Wenduine Bk E 51°18'·88N 03°01'·72E QR.
A2 51°21'·42N 03°07'·05E Iso 8s.

◀ BLANKENBERGE

Comte Jean Jetty ☆ 51°18'·76N 03°06'·87E Fl (2) 8s 30m **20M**; W Tr, B top; vis: 065°-245°.
W Mole Head ☆ 51°18'·89N 03°06'·43E FG 14m 11M; W ○ Tr; intens 065°-290°, unintens 290°-335°.
E Pier Head ☆ 51°18'·91N 03°06'·56E FR 12m 11M; W ○ Tr; vis: 290°-245°; *Bell (2) 15s.*

◀ SCHEUR CHANNEL

S2 51°23'·37N 02°58'·09E QR.
S3 51°24'·30N 03°02'·92E Q.
S4 51°25'·03N 03°02'·85E Fl (4) R 10s.
S5 51°23'·70N 03°05'·92E Fl G 5s.
S6 51°24'·20N 03°05'·92E Fl R 5s.
S7 51°23'·98N 03°10'·42E Fl G 5s.
S8 51°24'·43N 03°10'·42E Fl (4) R 10s.
S9 51°24'·42N 03°14'·98E QG.
S10 51°24'·85N 03°14'·98E Fl R 5s.
S12 51°24'·67N 03°18'·21E Fl (4) R 10s.
S-W 51°24'·13N 03°18'·30E Q.

◀ ZEEBRUGGE AND APPROACHES

SZ 51°23'·67N 03°07'·57E Q (3) 10s.
Z 51°22'·47N 03°09'·95E QG.
Ldg Lts 136°. Front, 51°20'·71N 03°13'·11E Oc 5s 22m 8M; vis: 131°-141°; H24. Rear, 890m from front, Oc 5s 45m 8M; vis: 131°-141°; sync with front; both W col, R bands.
W Outer Breakwater Head ☆ 51°21'·73N 03°11'·17E Oc G 7s 31m 7M; vis: 057°-267°; *Horn (3) 30s.*
E Outer Breakwater Head ☆ 51°21'·78N 03°11'·86E Oc R 7s 31m 7M; vis: 087°-281°.
Heist Mole Head ☆ 51°20'·86N 03°12'·18E Oc WR 15s 22m, **W20M, R18M**; vis: W068°-145°, R145°-212°, W212°-296°; Tfc sigs.

NETHERLANDS

APPROACHES TO WESTERSCHELDE

◀ WIELINGEN CHANNEL

W-Z 51°22'·57N 03°10'·72E Q (9) 15s.
BVH 51°23'·12N 03°12'·02E Q (6) + L Fl R 15s.
MOW3 Tide Gauge ☆ 51°23'·37N 03°11'·89E Fl (5) Y 20s; Racon (H); *Mo (U) 30s.*
W 51°23'·47N 03°14'·89E Fl (3) G 15s.
S-W 51°24'·13N 03°18'·30E Q.
W1 51°23'·47N 03°18'·22E Fl G 5s.
W2 51°24'·59N 03°21'·49E Iso R 8s.
Fort Maisonneuve 51°24'·19N 03°21'·46E VQ (9) 10s.

W3 ▲ 51°23'·97N 03°21'·50E Iso G 8s.
Wave observation post ☆ 51°22'·77N 03°22'·74E Fl (5) Y 20s.
W4 ▭ 51°24'·87N 03°24'·40E Iso R 4s.
W5 ▲ 51°24'·27N 03°24'·39E Iso G 4s.
W6 ▭ 51°25'·12N 03°27'·23E Iso R 8s.
W7 ▲ 51°24'·60N 03°27'·22E Iso G 8s.
W8 ▭ 51°25'·42N 03°30'·07E Iso R 4s.
W9 ▲ 51°24'·91N 03°30'·04E Iso G 4s.
W10 ▭ 51°25'·73N 03°32'·90E QR.
Nieuwe Sluis ☆ 51°24'·41N 03°31'·27E Oc WRG 10s 27m W14M, R11M, G10M; B 8-sided Tr, W bands; vis: R055°-086°, W086°-091·5°, G091·5°-134°, W134-140·5°, G140·5°-144·5°, W144·5°-236·5°, G236·5°-243°, R243°-260°, G260°-263·5, R263·5-292°, W292°-055°; *Horn (3) 30s.*

◀ APPROACHES TO BRESKENS

Songa ▲ 51°25'·31N 03°33'·67E QG.
SS-VH 51°24'·71N 03°33'·93E Q.

◀ BRESKENS FERRY HARBOUR

W Mole Head ☆ 51°24'·36N 03°33'·09E FG 8m 4M; B&W mast; in fog FY; Fog Det Lt.

◀ BRESKENS

W Mole Head ☆ 51°24'·03N 03°34'·06E F WRG 6m; Gy mast; vis: R090°-128°, W128°-157°, G157°-169·5°, W169·5°-173°, R173°-194°, G194°-296°, W296°-300°, R300°-320°, G320°-090°; in fog FY; *Horn Mo (U) 30s.*

WESTKAPELLE TO VLISSINGEN

OG-GR 51°32'·74N 03°24'·71E VQ (3) 5s.
Noorderhoofd Ldg Lts 149·5°. Front 51°32'·40N 03°26'·20E, 0·73M from rear, Oc WRG 10s 20m W13M, R10M, G10M; R ○ Tr, W band; vis: R353°-008°, G008°-029°, W029°-169°.
Westkapelle ☆, Common rear, 51°31'·75N 03°26'·80E Fl 3s 50m **28M**; □ Tr, R top; obsc on certain brgs.
Zoutelande Ldg Lts 326°, Front, 51°30'·26N 03°28'·39E, 1·8M from rear, FR 21m 12M; R □ Tr; vis: 321°-352°.
Molenhoofd ☆ 51°31'·58N 03°26'·03E Oc WRG 6s 9m; W mast R bands; vis: R306°-329°, W329°-349°, R349°-008°, G008°-034·5°, W034·5°-036·5°, G036·5°-144°, W144°-169°, R169°-198°.
OG5 ▲ 51°31'·12N 03°25'·50E QG.
Kaapduinen, Ldg Lts 130°. Front, 51°28'·46N 03°30'·96E Oc 5s 25m 13M; Y □ Tr, R bands; vis: 115°-145°. Rear, 220m from front, Oc 5s 36m 13M; synch with front; vis: 107·5°-152·5°.
Fort de Nolle ☆ 51°26'·94N 03°33'·11E Oc WRG 9s 11m W6M, R4M, G4M; W col, R bands; vis: R293°-309°, W309°-324·5°, G324·5°-336·5°, R336·5°-027°, G027°-044°, R044°-090°, G090°-110·5°, W110·5°-114·5°, G114·5°-119°, R119-130°.

◀ VLISSINGEN (FOR KANAAL DOOR WALCHEREN)

Ldg Lts 117°. Leugenaar, Front, 51°26'·43N 03°34'·12E Oc R 5s 6m 7M; W&R pile; intens 108°-126°. Rear Sardijngeul, 550m from front, 51°26'·34N 03°34'·63E Oc WRG 5s 8m W12M, R9M, G8M; R △ with W bands on R&W mast; synch; vis: R245°-271°, G271°-285°, W285°-123°, R123°-147°.
Koopmanshaven, W Mole root ☆ 51°26'·30N 03°34'·55E Iso WRG 3s 15m W12M, R10M, G9M; R pylon; vis: R253°-270°, W270°-059°, G059°-071°, W071°-077°, R077°-101°, G101°-110°, W110°-114°.
Buitenhaven W Mole Head ☆ 51°26'·38N 03°36'·05E FR 10m 5M; also Iso WRG 4s; B mast; vis: W072°-021°, G021°-042°, W042°-056°, R056°-072°; Tfc sigs; *Horn 15s.*
Buitenhaven E Mole Head ☆ 51°26'·41N 03°36'·36E FG 7m 4M.
Schone Waardin ☆ 51°26'·54N 03°37'·90E Oc WRG 9s 10m W13M, R10M, G9M; R mast, W bands; vis: R248°-260·5°, G260·5°-269°, W269°-287·5°, G287·5°-326°, R326°-341°, G341°-023°, W023°-024°, G024°-054°, R054°-065°, W065°-075·5°, G075·5°-079·5°, R079·5°-083°.

◀ VLISSINGEN OOST

W Mole Head ☆ 51°26'·88N 03°40'·08E FR 8m 5M; W col; in fog FY; *Horn (2) 20s.*
Ldg Lts 023°. Front, 51°27'·876N 03°40'·99E Oc R 8s 6m 8M; G mast. Rear, 100m from front, Oc R 8s 11m 8M; G mast; synch with front, both vis: 015°-031°.
Flushing E Hbr Dir Lt 305° 51°27'·88N 03°40'·53E Dir F WRG; vis: 303·5°-304·9°; W304·9°-305·1°, G305·1°-306·5°.

WESTERSCHELDE

◀ BORSSELE-NOORDNOL

Pier Head ☆ 51°25'·50N 03°42'·75E Oc WRG 5s; 9m; R mast, W bands; vis: R305°-336°, W336°-341°, G341°-001·5°, W001·5°-007·5°, R007·5°-022°, G022°-054°, W054°-057°, G057°-109·5°, W109·5°-128°, R128°-155°, W155°-305°.
Borssele, Total Jetty, NW end ☆ 51°24'·79N 03°43'·59E Oc WR 10s 10m; vis: R133°-159°, W159°-133°.
Borssele-Everingen ☆ 51°24'·68N 03°44'·08E Iso WRG 4s 9m; vis: G028°-076°, W076°-094°, W094°-134°, W134°-270°, R270°-313°, W313°-345°, G345°-359°, W359°-028°.

◀ ELLEWOUTSDIJK

W Pier Head (unlit) 51°23'·09N 03°49'·02E (ent to ⊕).

◀ TERNEUZEN (FOR GENT)

Nieuw Neuzenpolder Ldg Lts 125°. Front, 51°20'·97N 03°47'·24E Oc 5s 6m 13M; W col, B bands; intens 117°-133°. Rear, 365m from front, Oc 5s 16m 13M; B&W Tr; synch with front; intens 117°-133°.
West Buitenhaven E Mole Head ☆ (for Westsluis and Middensluis) 51°20'·56N 03°48'·85E FR 5M; tfc sigs.
Oost Buitenhaven E Mole Head ☆ (Oostsluis) 51°20'·56N 03°49'·19E FR 5M; Tfc sigs.
Jacht Haven W Jetty ☆ 51°20'·53N 03°49'·57E Oc WRG 5s 14m W9M, R7M, G6M; B&W Tr; vis: R090°-115°, W115°-238·5°, G238·5°-248°, W248°-279°, R279°-004°.
W Mole Head ☆ 51°20'·57N 03°49'·63E FG 6m; Gy mast; in fog FY.

◀ HANSWEERT (FOR KANAAL DOOR ZUID BEVELAND

W Mole Head ☆ 51°26'·41N 04°00'·53E Oc WRG 10s 9m W9M, R7M, G6M; R Tr, W band; vis: R288°-310°, W310°-334°, G334°-356·5°, W356·5°-042·5°, R042·5°-061·5°, W061·5°-082·5°, G082·5°-102·5°, W102·5°-114·5°, R114·5°-127·5°, W127·5°-288°; in fog FY.

◀ WALSOORDEN

S Mole Head Ent ☆ 51°22'·90N 04°02'·12E FR 5m; Gy col.

◀ PAAL APPROACHES

Speelmansgat Lt Bn ☆ 51°21'·94N 04°06'·13E Fl (5) Y 20s.

◀ ZANDVLIET

Dir Lt 118·38°. Front, 51°20'·68N 04°16'·28E Dir WRG 20m W4M, R3M, G3M; vis: Oc G116·63°-117·17°, FG117·18°-117·58°, AlGW117·58°-118·63°, F 118·13°-118·63°, AlRW118·63°-119·18°, FR119·18°-119·58°, Oc R 119·58°-120·13°.

◀ DOEL/LILLO/ANTWERPEN (Belgium)

Ldg Lts 185·5°. Front, 51°18'·45N 04°16'·17E Fl WRG 3s 5m W9M, R7M, G6M; vis: Rshore-175°, W175°-202°, G202°-306·5°, W306·5°-330·9°, R330·9°-shore. Rear, 260m from front, Fl 3s 14m 9M; synch with front. By day vis: 183°-185°.

Doel Jetty Head 51°18'·68N 04°16'·08E Oc WR 5s 9m W9M, R7M; Y □, B stripes on Tr; vis: Rdownstream-185°, W185°-334°, R334°-upstream shore.

Lillo Pier SE end 51°18'·15N 04°17'·21E Oc WRG 10s 5m W9M, R7M, G6M; R □ W on B Bn; vis: Rshore-303·1°, W303·1°-308·2°, G308·2°-096·5°, W096·5°-148°, R148°-shore.

No. 109 (off Imalso) 51°13'·89N 04°23'·87E Iso G 8s.

Jachthaven Antwerp 51°13'·91N 04°23'·70E F WR 9m 3M; B ⊙, R lantern. vis: Wshore-283°, R283°-shore.

OOSTERSCHELDE AND APPROACHES

◀ OUTER APPROACHES

Wave observation post ⊙ VR 51°30'·28N 03°14'·45E Fl Y 5s.

SW Thornton 51°30'·95N 02°50'·92E Iso 8s.

TB 51°34'·38N 02°59'·10E Q.

ZSB 51·36'·59N 03°15'·69E VQ (9) 10s.

Westpit 51°33'·65N 03°09'·92E Iso 8s.

Rabsbank 51°38'·25N 03°09'·90E Iso 4s.

Middelbank 51°40'·83N 03°18'·21E Iso 8s.

MD 3 51°42'·71N 03°26'·97E Fl G5s.

Schouwenbank 51°44'·94N 03°14'·31E Mo (A) 8s; Racon (O).

◀ OUDE ROOMPOT (selected marks)

OG-WG 51°37'·18N 03°23'·81E VQ (9) 10s.

WG1 51°38'·00N 03°26'·23E Iso G 8s.

WG4 51°38'·60N 03°28'·77E L Fl R 8s.

WG7 51°39'·40N 03°32'·65E Iso G 4s.

WG-GB 51°39'·70N 03°32'·67E.

OR2 51°39'·48N 03°33'·70E QR.

OR5 51°38'·71N 03°35'·51E Iso G 8s.

OR6 51°38'·71N 03°36'·29E Iso R 8s.

OR8 51°38'·23N 03°37'·35E.

OR11 51°36'·97N 03°38'·38E Iso G 4s.

OR12 51°37'·26N 03°39'·25E Iso R 8s.

Roompotsluis Ldg Lts 073·5°. Front, 51°37'·33N 03°40'·74E Oc G 5s. Rear, 280m from front, Oc G 5s; synch.

N Bkwtr Head 51°37'·30N 03°40'·09E FR 6m; *Horn(2) 30s.*

◀ SOPHIAHAVEN/COLIJNSPLAAT

Roompot Marina N Mole Head 51°35'·62N 03°43'·20E FR.

Colijnsplaat E Head 51°36'·22N 03°51'·07E FR 3m 3M; *Horn.*

Zeeland Bridge. N and S passages marked by FY Lts 14m.

◀ KATS/GOESSCHE SAS (GOES)/WEMELDINGE

Marina Kats S Jetty Head 51°34'·37N 03°53'·61E Oc WRG 8s 5m 5M; vis: W344°-153°, R153°-165°, G165°-200°, W200°-214°, G214°-258°, W258°-260°, G260°-313°, W313°-331°.

Goessche Sas S Mole Head 51°32'·23N 03°55'·90E FR.

Galgeplaat 51°32'·60N 03°58'·95E Q (6) + L Fl 15s.

Wemeldinge W Jetty Head 51°31'·34N 04°00'·17E FG 7M.

W Head new ent 51°31'·17N 04°00'·84E Oc WRG 5s 7m W9M, R7M, G7M; vis: R105·5°-114°, W114°-124°, G124°-140·5°, W140·5°-144°, G144°-192°, W192°-205°, R205°-233·5°, W233·5°-258·5°, R258·5°-296·5°. R&G Lts mark canal.

◀ YERSEKE/THOLENSCHE GAT/GORISHOEK

O25/Sv 12 51°31'·35N 04°02'·36E QG.

Ldg Lts 155° (through Schaar van Yerseke). Front 51°30'·02N 04°03'·38E Iso 4s 8m; in fog FY. Rear, 180m from front, Iso 4s 13m; synch; in fog 2 FY. FG and FR mark mole heads.

Tholensche Gat. Strijenham 51°31'·35N 04°08'·83E Oc WRG 5s 9m W8M, R5M, G5M; vis: Wshore-268°, R268°-281·5°, W281·5°-297°, G297°-310°, R310°-060·5°, G060·5°-068°, W068°-082°. R082°-115°, W115°-shore.

Werkhaven (Bergsediepsluis) W Mole Head 51°30'·88N 04°09'·68W FG.

Gorishoek 51°31'·52N 04°04'·59E Iso WRG 8s 7m W6M, R4M, G4M; R pedestal, W bands; vis: R260°-278°, W278°-021°, G021°-025°, W025°-071°, G071°-085°, W085°-103°, R103°-120°, W120°-260°.

◀ STAVENISSE/ST ANNALAND

Hoek Van Ouwerkerk Ldg Lts 009·2° Front, 51°36'·86N 03°58'·26E Iso WRG 6s; vis: R267°-306°, W306°-314°, G314°-007·5°, W007·5°-011·5°, G011·5°-067°, W067°-068·5°, G068·5°-085°, W085°-102·°5, G102·5°-112·5°, R112·5°-121·5°. Rear, 340m from front, Iso 6s.

Keeten B 51°36'·35N 03°58'·05E Mo (A) 8s; Racon (K).

Stavenisse E Mole Head 51°35'·68N 04°00'·26E Oc WRG 5s 10m W12M, R9M, G8M; B pylon; vis: R090°-106°, W106°-109°, G109°-116°, W116°-123°, G123°-155°, W155°-157°, G157°-215°, W215°-219°, G219·5°-230°, W230°-236, R236°-249°.

St Annaland Entrance W side 51°36'·26N 04°06'·53E FG.

◀ ZIJPE/ANNA JACOBAPOLDER

Zipje N Mole Head 51°38'·63N 04°06'·02E Iso G 4s.

St Philipsland, on dyke 51°39'·11N 04°07'·07E Oc WRG 4s 9m W8M, R5M, G4M; pylon on B ○ col; vis: W051°-100°, R100°-144°, W144°-146°, G146°-173°.

Zijpsche Bout 51°38'·79N 04°05'·67E Oc WRG 10s 9m W12M, R9M, G8M; mast on R col; vis: R208°-211°, W211°-025°, G025°-030°, W030°-040°, R040°-066°.

Tramweghaven S Mole 51°38'·85N 04°05'·77E Iso R 4s 7m.

◀ KRAMMER/BRUINISSE/KRAMMERSLUIZEN

Stoofpolder 51°39'·48N 04°06'·29E Iso WRG 4s 10m W12M, R9M, G8M; B Tr, W bands; vis: W147°-154°, R154°-226·5°, G226·5°-243°, W243°-253°, G253°-259°, W259°-263°, G263°-270°, R270°-283°, W283°-008°.

Bruinisse N Mole Head 51°39'·90N 04°05'·94E FG 3M; Gy Bn.

Krammersluizen N Bkwtr Head 51°39'·78N 04°08'·35E FR.

DE VAL/ZIERIKZEE

Engelsche Vaarwater Ldg Lts 019°. Front, 51°37'·68N 03°55'·50E Iso WRG 3s 7m W6M, R4M, G4M; R pedestal, W band; vis: R290°-306°, W306°-317·5°, G317·5°-334°, W334°-336·5°, G336·5°-017·5°, W017·5°-026°, G026°-090°, R090°-108°, W108°-290°. Rear, 300m from front, Iso 3s 15m 6M.

Zierikzee W Jetty Head 51°37'·89N 03°53'·38E Oc WRG 6s 10m W6M, R4M, G4M; R pedestal, W band; vis: G063°-100°, W100°-133°, R133°-156°, W156°-278°, R278°-306°, G306°-314°, W314°-333°, R333°-350°, W350°-063°.

◀ FLAUWERSPOLDER/SCHELPHOEK/ BURGHSLUIS

Flauwerspolder W Mole Head 51°40'·63N 03°50'·79E Iso WRG 4s 7m W6M, R4M, G4M; W daymark, B band on pylon; vis: R303°-344°, W344°-347°, G347°-083°, W083°-086°, G086°-103°, W103°-110°, R110°-128°, W128°-303°.

Schelphoek E Bkwtr Head ☆ 51°41'·22N 03°48'·71E Fl (2) 10s 8m.
Hammen. Burghsluis S Mole Head ☆ 51°40'·53N 03°45'·49E F WRG 9m W8M, R5M, G4M; mast on R col; vis: W218°-230°, R230°-245°, W245°-253·5°, G253·5°-293°, W293°-000°, G000°-025·5°, W025·5°-032°, G032°-041°, R041°-070°, W070°-095°.

◄ HARINGVLIET AND APPROACHES

Buitenbank 51°51'·14N 03°25'·69E Iso 4s.
Bollen 51°49'·99N 03°32'·98E VQ (9) 10s.
MW 51°44'·25N 03°23'·66E Q (9) 15s.
MN 51°47'·65N 03°29'·90E Q.
BG2 51°46'·05N 03°37'·00E Fl Y 5s; Y pile.
West Schouwen ☆ 51°42'·53N 03°41'·48E Fl (2+1)15s 58m **30M**; Gy Tr, R diagonal stripes on upper part.
Ooster 51°47'·89N 03°41'·27E Q (9) 15s.
SH 51°49'·47N 03°45'·77E VQ (9) 10s.
Ha10 51°51'·76N 03°51'·59E Fl Y 5s; Y pile.
SG 51°51'·93N 03°51'·40E Iso 4s.
SG 2 51°51'·75N 03°53'·42E Iso R 2s.
SG 5 51°50'·87N 03°55'·35E L Fl G 8s.
SG 9 51°50'·75N 03°57'·30E L Fl G 8s.
SG 17 51°51'·30N 04°00'·00E L Fl G 8s.
P3 51°51'·23N 04°01'·06E L Fl G 5s.
P5 51°50'·85N 04°01'·86E Iso G 2s.
G1 51°50'·05N 04°02'·18E L Fl G 8s.

◄ STELLENDAM

N Mole Head ☆ 51°49'·87N 04°02'·01E FG; *Horn (2) 15s.*

◄ HELLEVOETSLUIS/HELIUSHAVEN

Hellevoetsluis W side ☆ 51°49'·18N 04°07'·66E Iso WRG 10s 16m W11M, R8M, G7M; W Tr, R cupola; vis: G shore-275°, W275°-294°, R294°-316°, W316°-036°, G036°-058°, W058°-095°, R095°-shore.
Tramhaven E Mole Head ☆ 51°49'·18N 04°07'·91E FG 6m.
Heliushaven W Jetty ☆ 51°49'·24N 04°07'·16E FR 7m 4M.
Hoornsche Hoofden, watchhouse on dyke ☆ 51°48'·28N 04°10'·96E Oc WRG 5s 7m W7M, R5M, G4M; vis: W288°-297°, G297°-313°, W313°-325°, R325°-335°, G335°-344·5°, W344·5°-045°, G045°-055°, W055°-131°, R131°-shore.

◄ MIDDELHARNIS/NIEUWENDIJK

Middelharnis West Pier Head ☆ 51°46'·60N 04°11'·72E F WRG 5m W8M, R5M, G4M; vis: W144°-164·5°, R164·5°-176·5°, G176·5°-144°.
Nieuwendijk Ldg Lts 303·5°. Front, 51°45'·04N 04°19'·38E Iso WRG 6s 8m W9M, R7M, G6M; B framework Tr; vis: G093°-100°, W100°-103·5°, R103·5°-113°, W113°-093°. Rear, 450m from front, F 11m 9M; B framework Tr.

◄ VOLKERAKSLUIZEN/WILLEMSTAD

Jachtensluis W side, S ent ☆ 51°41'·91N 04°24'·29E FG.
Jachtensluis E side, E ent ☆ 51°41'·91N 04°25'·44E FR.
Noorder Voorhaven, W Mole Head ☆ 51°42'·03N 04°25'·77E FG 6m 4M; R lantern on pedestal; in fog FY.
Willemstad HD 9 51°41'·81N 04°26'·62E Iso G 4s.

◄ HOEK VAN HOLLAND AND APPROACHES

Noord Hinder 52°00'·04N 02° 51'·03E Fl (2) 10s: Racon (T); *Horn (2) 30s.*
Europlatform 51°59'·75N 03°16'·42E Mo (U) 15s; W structure, R bands; helicopter platform; *Horn Mo(U) 30s.*
Goeree ☆ 51°55'·42N 03°40'·03E Fl (4) 20s 32m **28M**; R and W chequered Tr on platform; helicopter platform; Racon (T); *Horn (4) 30s.*
Westhoofd ☆ 51°48'·78N 03°51'·82E Fl (3) 15s 56m **30M**; R ☐ Tr.
Kwade Hoek ☆ 51°50'·17N 03°58'·95E Iso WRG 4s 10m W12M, R9M, G8M; B mast, W bands; vis: W 235°-068°, R068°-088°, G088°-107°, W107°-113°, R113°-142°, W142°-228°, R228°-235°.
MC 52°01'12N 03°53'·46E Iso 4s; Racon (M).
Hinder 51°54'·53N 03°55'·40E Q (9) 15s.
MV 51°57'·44N 03°58'·40E Q (9) 15s.
MVN 51°59'·59N 04°00'·19E VQ.
Indusbank N 52°02'·89N 04°03'·57E Q.

◄ HOEK VAN HOLLAND/ROTTERDAM

Maasvlakte ☆ 51°58'·19N 04°00'·84E Fl (5) 20s 67m **28M**; B 8-sided Tr, Y bands; vis: 340°-267°; H24.
Nieuwe Noorderdam Head ☆ 51°59'·65N 04°02'·82E FR 25m 10M; Or Tr, B bands; in fog Al Fl WR 6s; vis: 278°-255°.
Nieuwe Zuiderdam Head ☆ 51°59'·13N 04°02'·47E FG 25m 10M; Or Tr, B bands; helicopter platform; in fog Al Fl WG 6s; vis: 330°-307°; *Horn 10s.*
Maasmond Ldg Lts 107° **Front** ☆, 51°58'·55N 04°07'·53E Iso R 6s 29m **18M**; R Tr, W bands; vis: 099·5°-114·5°, synch.
Rear ☆, 450 m from front, Iso R 6s 43m **18M**; R Tr, W bands: vis: 099·5°-114·5°; synch. By day, 7M.
Maassluis Buitenhaven E Ent ☆ 51°54'·93N 04°14'·81E FG.
Vlaardingen Buitenhaven E Ent ☆ 51°53'·99N 04°20'·95E FG.
Spuihaven W Ent ☆ 51°53'·98N 04°23'·98E FR.
Veerhaven E Ent ☆ 51°54'·40N 04°28'·74E FG.

HOEK VAN HOLLAND TO DEN HELDER

◄ SCHEVENINGEN

SCH 52°07'·75N 04°14'·11E Iso 4s.
Scheveningen ☆ 52°06'·24N 04°16'·09E Fl (2) 10s 49m **29M**; brown Tr; vis: 014°-244°.
Ldg Lts 156°. Front, 52°05'·78N 04°15'·60E Iso 4s 17m 14M. Rear, 100m from front, Iso 4s 21m 14M; synch with front.
SW Mole Head ☆ 52°06'·23N 04°15'·16E FG 11m 9M; G 6-sided Tr, W bands, R lantern; *Horn (3) 30s.*
Noordwijk-aan-Zee ☆ 52°14'·90N 04°26'·01E Oc (3) 20s 32m **18M**; W ☐ Tr.
Survey platform ☆ 52°16'·35N 04°17'·81E Mo (U) 15s 42m and FR; R&W check; *Horn Mo (U) 20s.*
Eveline Wk 52°25'·49N 04°25'·00E VQ (9) 10s.

IJMUIDEN

A-NE 52°27'·93N 03°48'·60E L Fl Y 10s.
IJ 3 52°29'·69N 04°11'·94E Fl (3) Y 10s.
IJmuiden(IJM) 52°28'·44N 04°23'·78E Mo (A) 8s; Racon (Y).
Ldg Lts 100·5°. **Front** ☆, 52°27'·70N 04°34'·46E F WR 30m **W16M**, R13M; dark R Tr; vis: W050°-122°, R122°-145°, W145°-160°. By day F 4m vis: 090·5-110·5°. **Rear** ☆, 570m from front, Fl 5s 52m **29M**; dark R Tr; vis: 019°-199°.
S Breakwater Head ☆ 52°27'·81N 04°31'·91E FG 14m 10M; in fog Fl 3s; *Horn (2) 30s.*

◄ NOORDZEE KANAAL/AMSTERDAM/ IJSSELMEER

Ø Km mark 52°27'·81N 04°35'·55E.
20 Km mark 52°24'·72N 04°51'·85E.
Sixhaven Yacht Hbr ☆ 52°22'·99N 04°53'·69E F & FR.
Oranjesluizen (to IJsselmeer) 52°22'·90N 04°57'·63E.

◀ IJMUIDEN TO TEXEL

BSP 52°30'·72N 04°29'·88E Fl (4) Y 10s.
CP-Q8-A Platform 52°35'·71N 04°31'·79E Mo (U) 15s.
Egmond-aan-Zee ☆ 52°37'·13N 04°37'·27E Iso WR 10s 36m **W18M**, R14M; W ○ Tr; vis: W010°-175°, R175°-188°.
Petten 52°47'·33N 04°36'·68E VQ (9) 10s.

◀ ZEEGAT VAN TEXEL

Vinca G 52°45'·93N 04°12'·35E Q (9) 15s; Racon (D).
TX1 52°48'·00N 04°15'·48E Fl G 5s.
ZH 52°54'·65N 04°34'·71E VQ (6) + L Fl 10s.
MR 52°56'·76N 04°33'·81E Q (9) 15s.
NH 53°00'·26N 04°35'·43E VQ.
Grote Kaap ☆ 52°52'·85N 04°42'·88E Oc WRG 10s 31m W11M, R8M, G8M; vis: G041°-088°, W088°-094°, R094°-131°.

◀ SCHULPENGAT

Schulpengat. Ldg Lts 026·5°. **Front** ☆, 53°00'·85N 04°44'·42E Iso 4s **18M**; vis: 024·5°-028·5°. Rear, **Den Hoorn** ☆ 0·83M from front, Oc 8s **18M**; church spire; vis: 024·5°-028·5°.
SG 52°52'·90N 04°37'·90E Mo (A) 8s; Racon (Z).
S1 52°53'·51N 04°38'·84E Iso G 4s.
S2 52°53'·81N 04°37'·93E Iso R 4s.
S3 52°54'·43N 04°39'·52E Iso G 8s.
S4 52°54'·62N 04°38'·78E Iso R 8s.
S5 52°55'·33N 04°40'·23E Iso G 4s.
S7 52°56'·25N 04°40'·91E QG.
S6A 52°56'·52N 04°40'·51E QR.
S8 52°57'·06N 04°41'·01E.
S9 52°56'·85N 04°42'·07E.
S10 52°57'·59N 04°41'·56E Iso R 8s.
Huisduinen ☆ 52°57'·13N 04°43'·29E F WR 27m W14M, R11M; □ Tr; vis: W070°-113°, R113°-158°, W158°-208°.
Kijkduin ☆, Rear, 52°57'·33N 04°43'·58E Fl (4) 20s 56m **30M**; brown Tr; visible except where obsc by dunes on Texel.
S11 52°57'·55N 04°43'·25E Iso G 8s.
S14/MG17 52°58'·45N 04°43'·51E VQ (6) + L Fl 10s.

◀ MOLENGAT

MG 53°03'·90N 04°39'·37E Mo (A) 8s.
MG1 53°02'·89N 04°40'·84E Iso G 4s.
MG2 53°03'·10N 04°41'·29E Iso R 4s.
MG6 53°01'·26N 04°41'·86E Iso R 4s.
MG5 53°01'·27N 04°41'·69E Iso G 4s.
MG9 53°00'·17N 04°41'·54E QG.
MG10 53°00'·18N 04°41'·87E QR.
MG13 52°59'·16N 04°42'·29E Iso G 8s.
MG16 52°58'·86N 04°43'·12E QR.
MG20 52°58'·71N 04°44'·30E Iso R 8s.

◀ MARSDIEP/DEN HELDER

T1 52°57'·99N 04°44'·61E Fl (3) G 10s.
T3 52°58'·06N 04°46'·41E Iso G 8s.
Marinehaven, W Breakwater Head (Harssens I) ☆ 52°57'·95N 04°47'·07E QG 12m 8M; *Horn 20s*.
MH6, E of ent ☆ 52°57'·94N 04°47'·39E Iso R 4s 9m 4M; R pile.
Ent West side, ☆ 52°57'·77N 04°47'·08E Fl G 5s 9m 4M; vis: 180°-067° (H24).
Ent East side, ☆ 52°57'·77N 04°47'·37E QR 9m 4M; (H24).
Ldg Lts 191°. Front, 52°57'·37N 04°47'·08E Oc G 5s 16m 14M; B △ on bldg; vis: 161°-221°. Rear, 275m from front, Oc G 5s 25m 14M; B ▽ on bldg; vis: 161°-247°, synch.

Schilbolsnol ☆ 53°00'·50N 04°45'·68E F WRG 27m **W15M** R12M, G11M; G Tr; vis: W338°-002°, G002°-035°, W035°-038° (leading sector for Schulpengat), R038°-051°, W051°-068°.
Mok ☆ 53°00'·17N 04°46'·79E Oc WRG 10s 10m W10M, R7M, G6M; vis: R229°-317°, W317°-337°, G337°-112°.

WADDENZEE

◀ DEN OEVER/STEVINSLUIZEN

M13 52°59'·32N 04°52'·51E Iso G 8s.
LW 52°59'·51N 04°55'·90E L Fl 10s.
VG1/W2 52°58'·98N 04°56'·83E Fl (2+1) G 10s.
W9 52°57'·24N 04°57'·51E.
O3 52°56'·89N 05°01'·57E QG.
Ldg Lts 131° 52°56'·32N 05°02'·98E Front and Rear both Oc 10s 7M; vis: 127°-137°.
Detached Breakwater North Head ☆ 52°56'·76N 05°02'·29E L Fl R 10s.
Stevinsluizen W wall, 80m from Head ☆ 52°56'·22N 05°02'·15E Iso WRG 2s; vis: G195°-213°, W213°-227°, R227°-245°.

◀ TEXELSTROOM/OUDESCHILD

T17 53°01'·71N 04°52'·32E Iso G 8s.
T12 53°02·23N 04°51'·53E Iso R 8s.
Oudeschild S Mole Head ☆ 53°02'·33N 04°51'·17E FR 7m; *Horn (2) 30s* (sounded 0600-2300).
Ldg Lts 291°. Front, 53°02'·40N 04°50'·94E, Oc 6s 14m Lt seen between FR and FG leads into hbr; intens 291°.
T23 53°03'·53N 04°55'·68E QG.
T27 53°03'·59N 04°59'·41E Iso G 4s.

◀ DOOVE BALG/KORNWERDERZAND/LORENTZ-SLUIZEN

D4 53°02'·55N 05°03'·64E Iso R 8s.
D3A/J2 53°01'·92N 05°07'·76E Fl (2+1) G 10s; G post, R band.
D16 53°02'·79N 05°10'·70E Iso R 8s.
D24 53°03'·78N 05°15'·55E Iso R 8s.
BO11/KZ2 53°04'·95N 05°20'·25E Q.
Kornwerderzand Buitenhaven, W Mole Head ☆ 53°04'·70N 05°20'·03E FG 9m 7M; *Horn Mo(N) 30s*.
Spuihaven Noord, W Mole Hd ☆ 53°04'·76N 05°19'·61E L Fl G 10s 7m 7M.

◀ BOONTJES/APPROACHES TO HARLINGEN

BO11/KZ/2 53°04'·94N 05°20'·25E Q.
BO15 53°05'·59N 05°21'·76E Iso G 2s.
BO28 53°07'·81N 05°22'·49E Iso R 8s.
BO34 53°08'·84N 05°22'·93E Iso R 2s.
BO40 53°09'·87N 05°23'·26E Iso R 4s.

◀ VLIESTROOM (selected marks)

VL 2/SG 1 53°19'·60N 05°09'·12E.
VL1 53°18'·91N 05°08'·73E QG.
VL4 53°19'·25N 05°09'·67E QR.
VL 5 53°18'·37N 05°09'·89E L Fl G 8s.
VL9 53°17'·23N 05°09'·89E Fl G 5s.
VL11 53°16'·06N 05°09'·69E Iso G 4s.

◀ APPROACH TO HARLINGEN/BLAUWE SLENK/ POLLENDAM (selected marks)

BS1/IN2 53°14'·85N 05°09'·56E VQ.
BS3 53°14'·51N 05°09'·99E L Fl G 5s.
BS7 53°13'·63N 05°12'·97E Iso G 4s.
BS13 53°13'·31N 05°17'·13E QG.

S19 53°11'·89N 05°18'·26E VQ G.
S23 53°11'·52N 05°19'·66E L Fl G 8s.
1 53°11'·38N 05°20'·31E Iso G 2s.
2 53°11'·47N 05°20'·37E Iso R 2s.
3 53°11'·10N 05°21'·49E Iso G 4s.
7 53°10'·68N 05°23'·44E VQ G.

◀ HARLINGEN

9/BO44 53°10'·59N 05°23'·88E VQ.
dg Lts 112°. Front, 53°10'·51N 05°24'·19E Iso 6s 8m 13M; is: 097°-127°; and FG 9m 7. Rear, 500m from front, Iso 6s 19m 3M; both on B masts, W bands; vis: 104·5°-119·5° (H24).
Mole Hd 53°10'·59N 05°24'·32E FR 9m 4M; R pedestal.

TEXEL TO AMELAND

◀ APPROACHES TO EIERLANDSE GAT

ierland ☆ (N Pt of Texel) 53°10'·93N 04°51'·30E Fl (2) 10s 52m 9M; R ○ Tr.
X 3 52°58'·58N 04°22'·29E Fl (3) G 10s.
L-South 53°08'·86N 04°26'·50E L Fl Y 10s.
L1 53°10'·95N 04°35'·30E Fl (2) G 10s.
aden 53°13'·58N 04°41'·23E Q (9) 15s.
G 53°13'·35N 04°47'·08E VQ (9) 10s.

◀ ZEEGAT VAN TERSCHELLING AND APPROACHES

L-C 53°26'·93N 04°39'·85E Fl 5s 12M; Racon (C); *Horn(2) 30s.*
lieland ☆ 53°17'·69N 05°03'·46E Iso 4s 53m **20M.**
L3 53°16'·89N 04°39'·58E Fl (3) G 9s.
L5 53°22'·83N 04°43'·88E QG.
L7 53°25'·46N 04°53'·85E Fl (3) G 10s.

◀ ZUIDER STORTEMELK (selected marks)

S 53°19'·78N 04°55'·88E Iso 4s.
S1 53°19'·22N 04°57'·56E VQ.
S5 53°18'·63N 05°01'·61E L Fl G 8s.
S11/VS2 53°18'·64N 05°05'·73E Q; leave to port for Vlieland nd to stbd for Terschelling and Harlingen.

◀ VLIELAND

S3 53°18'·27N 05°06'·23E VQ G.
S5 53°18'·03N 05°06'·12E L Fl G 5s.
S14 53°17'·58N 05°05'62E Iso R 4s.
Mole Hd 53°17'·68N 05°05'·51E FG.
V Mole Hd 53°17'·68N 05°05'·48E FR.

◀ WEST TERSCHELLING

Ent via Schuitengat (Buoys changed frequently).
L 2/SG 1 53°19'·61N 05°09'·12E.
G 9/S2 53°20'·47N 05°11'·71E Q (9) 15s.
G 17 53°21'·17N 05°13'·26E L Fl G 8s.
Brandaris Tr ☆ 53°21'·61N 05°12'·84E Fl 5s 55m **29M**; Y □ Tr; vis: except where obsc by dunes on Vlieland and Terschelling.
W Hbr Mole Hd, 53°21'·25N 05°13'·09E FR 5m 5M; R post, W bands; *Horn 15s.*
W Terschelling E Pier Hd 53°21'·26N 05°13'·19E FG 5m 4M.

◀ ZEEGAT VAN AMELAND AND APPROACHES

TG 53°24'·17N 05°02'·32E Q (9) 15s.
Otto 53°24'·54N 05°06'·41E VQ (3) 5s.
TE 1 53°29'·97N 05°13'·46E Fl (3) G 10s.
TE 3 53°31'·74N 05°22'·70E L Fl G 10s.
TE 5 53°33'·66N 05°32'·50E Fl (3) G 9s.
TS 53°28'·16N 05°21'·51E VQ.
Ameland ☆ W end 53°26'·92N 05°37'·52E Fl (3) 15s 57m **30M.**
BR 53°30'·64N 05°33'·51E Q.
Ballumerbocht 53°25'·85N 05°43'·87E Iso R 4s 5m 4M.

◀ NES

MG28-R1 53°25'·71N 05°45'·88E VQ.
Reegeul R3 53°25'·80N 05°45'·93E Iso G 4s.
Reegeul R5 53°25'·86N 05°46'·01E QG.
Reegeul R7 53°25'·90N 05°46'·21E L Fl G 8s.
Nieuwe Veerdam Mole Head 53°25'·97N 05°46'·45E Iso 6s 2m 8M.

AMELAND TO DELFZIJL

◀ AMELAND TO SCHIERMONNIKOOG

TE9 53°37'·35N 05°51'·74E Fl (3) G 9s.
TE13 53°41'·06N 06°11'·01E QG.
AM 53°30'·94N 05°44'·69E VQ.
NAM21 53°31'·34N 05°55'·69E Fl Y 5s.
WRG 53°32'·83N 06°03'·14E Q.
WG 53°32'·96N 06°09'·68E Iso 8s; Racon (N).
Schiermonnikoog ☆ 53°29'·19N 06°08'·78E Fl (4) 20s 43m **28M**; dark R ○ Tr. F WR 29m **W15M**, R12M; (same Tr); vis: W210°-221°, R221°-230°.
Ferry Pier Head 53°28'·09N 06°12'·10E 2 F.

◀ LAUWERSOOG/OOSTMAHORN/ZOUTKAMP

Lauwersoog E Mole Head 53°24'·65N 06°12'·06E FR 4M.
Lauwersoog W Mole Head 53°24'·68N 06°12'·00E FG 3M; in fog FY; *Horn (2) 30s.*
Oostmahorn Ent 53°22'·96N 06°09'·64E FG.
Zoutkamp Ent (unlit) 53°20'·42N 06°17'·66E.

◀ DELFZIJL ENTRANCE

PS3/BW26 53°19'·25N 07°00'·31E Fl (2+1) G 12s.
W Mole Head E Ent 53°19'·01N 07°00'·26E FG; Ra refl.
Ldg Lts 203°. Front, 53°18'·62N 07°00'·16E Iso 4s. Rear, 310m from front; Iso 4s.
Zeehavenkanaal, N side (odd numbered posts Fl G. S side (even numbered posts Fl R).

◀ TERMUNTERZIJL

BW 13 53°18'·63N 07°02'·31E Fl G 5s.

For Die Ems see also 9.24.4.

9.23.5 PASSAGE INFORMATION

North France and Belgium Cruising Companion (Macmillan Reeds/Featherstone) and *Netherlands Cruising Companion* (Macmillan Reeds/Cumberlidge), *North Sea Passage Pilot* (Imray/ Navin) - North Sea and Belgian/Dutch coasts to Den Helder. Refer also to *Havengids Nederland* (Vetus) in Dutch, well illustrated.

BELGIUM (chart 1872) Features of this coast are the long shoals lying roughly parallel to it. Mostly the deeper, buoyed chans run within 3M of shore, where the outer shoals can give some protection from strong W or SW winds. Strong W to NE winds can equally create dangerous conditions especially in wind against tide situations. Approaching from seaward it is essential to fix position from one of the many marks, so that the required chan is correctly identified before shoal water is reached. Shipping is a hazard, but it helps to identify the main routes.

From the SW/W, the natural entry to the buoyed chans is at Dunkerque Lanby. From the Thames, bound for Oostende (9.23.10) or the Westerchelde (9.23.14), identify W Hinder lt. From the N, route via NHR-S and NHR-SE buoys or the N Hinder lt buoy.

Off the Belgian coast the E-going stream begins at HW Vlissingen – 0320 (HW Dover – 0120), and the W-going at HW Vlissingen + 0240 (HW Dover + 0440), sp rates 2kn. Mostly the streams run parallel with the coast. Nieuwpoort (9.23.9) is 8M from the French border. From the W, approach through Passe de Zuydcoote (buoyed with least depth 3·3m) and West Diep. From ENE app through Kleine Rede, the inner road off Oostende which carries a depth of 6m. There are other apprs through the chans and over the banks offshore, but they need care in bad weather.

Sailing E from Oostende, leave about HW Vlissingen – 0300 to carry the E-going stream. If bound for Blankenberge (9.23.11) it is only necessary to keep a mile or two offshore, but if heading E of Zeebrugge (9.23.12) it is advisable to clear the hbr extension by 1M or more. The main route to Zeebrugge for commercial shipping is through Scheur (the deep water chan of the Westerschelde) as far as Scheur-Zand lt buoy, about 3M NW of hbr ent. There is much commercial traffic, and yachts should keep clear (S of) the buoyed chan so far as possible. Beware strong tidal stream and possibly dangerous seas in approaches to Zeebrugge.

NETHERLANDS (charts 325, 110, 2322) While British Admiralty charts are adequate for through passages, coastal navigation, and entry to the main ports, larger scale Dutch charts are essential for any yacht exploring the cruising grounds along this coast or using any of the smaller hbrs. The folding chart Staande-Mastroute door Nederland (Fixed Mast Route through the Netherlands), free to visitors, is invaluable.

Numerous wrecks and obstructions lie offshore and in coastal areas; those that could be hazardous are marked. The Off Texel TSS extends NNE from the TX 1 lt buoy: the separation zone incorporates the Helder gas field. Some 20–30M N lie the Placid and Petroland fields with production platforms. For general notes on N Sea oil and gas installations, see 9.5.5. The shoals of the North Sea coast and Waddenzee are liable to change due to gales and tidal streams. Sea level may also be affected by barometic pressure; wise to take advice from the Coastguard.

TO WESTERSCHELDE AND DEN HELDER The main approach chans to Westerschelde are Scheur/Wielingen and Oostgat, but yachts are required to keep clear of these. From Zeebrugge keep close to S side of estuary until past Breskens (9.23.13) when, if proceeding to Vlissingen (9.23.17), cross close W of By H-SS. From N, use Deurloo/Spleet chans to S side of estuary. The tide runs hard in the estuary, causing a bad sea in chans and overfalls on some banks in strong winds. Vessels under 20m must give way to larger craft; and yachts under 12m are requested to stay just outside the main buoyed chans, including those betwee Walsoorden and Antwerpen (9.23.16) if navigation permits.

The Oosterschelde (9.23.18 and chart 192) is entered via th Roompotsluis, in the South half of the barrage. Coming from the S Oostgat runs close to the Walcheren shore. Westkapelle lt ho i conspic near the W end of Walcheren. There are two lesser lts nearby Molenhoofd 5ca WSW and Noorderhoofd 7ca NNW. Having passe the latter the coast runs NE past Domburg but becomes shallowe as the Roompot is approached, so it is necessary to keep near th Roompot chan which here is marked by unlit buoys. It is importar to have updated information on the buoyage and the chans.

The Schaar, Schouwenbank, Middelbank and Steenbanken li off the W approaches to Oosterschelde. Westgat and Oud Roompot are the main channels, both well marked. From th north, Geul van de Banjaard (unlit) leads to Oude Roompo Further north, the Slijkgat (lit) is the approach chan to Stellendar (9.23.19 and entry to the Haringvliet.

Shipping is very concentrated off Hoek van Holland (9.23.20) a the ent to Europoort and Rotterdam (9.23.21). Maas TSS mus be noted and regulations for yachts obeyed.

The coast N to Den Helder is low, and not easily visible fron seaward, like most of the Dutch coast. Conspic landmark include: Scheveningen light house and big hotels, Noordwij aan Zee light, big hotels at Zandvoort, two lt ho's at IJmuiden chys of steelworks N of IJmuiden, Egmond aan Zee lt, and chy of nuclear power station 1·5M NNE of Petten. 3M W of IJmuide (9.23.23) the N-going stream begins at HW Hoek van Holland - 0120, and the S-going at HW Hoek van Holland + 0430, sp rate about 1·5kn. Off ent to IJmuiden the stream turns about 1h earlier and is stronger, and in heavy weather there may be a dangerous sea. At IJmuiden the Noordzeekanaal leads to Amsterdam (9.23.24) and the IJsselmeer (9.23.25).

THE WEST FRISIAN ISLANDS (charts 2593) N from Den Helde (9.23.26), thence E for nearly 150M along the Dutch and Germar coasts, lies the chain of Frisian Is. They have similar characteristic – being low, long and narrow, with the major axis parallel to th coast. Texel is the largest and, with Vlieland and Terschelling, lie further offshore.

Between the islands, narrow chans (*zeegat* in Dutch, *Seegat* ir German) give access to/from the North Sea. Most of these chans are shallow for at least part of their length, and in these shoal areas a dangerous sea builds up in a strong onshore winc against the outgoing (ebb) tide. The zeegaten between De Helder and Texel, between Vlieland and Terschelling and th zeegat of the Ems are safe for yachts up to force 8 winds betweer SW and NE. All the others are unsafe in strong onshore winds

The flood stream along this coast is E-going, so it starts to rur in through the zeegaten progressively from W to E. Where th tide meets behind each island, as it flows in first at the W enc and a little later at the E end, is formed a bank called a *wac* (Dutch) or *Watt* (German). These banks between the islands and the coast are major obstacles to E/W progress inside the islands. The chans are narrow and winding, marked by buoys and/or withies (‡ ‡) in the shallower parts, and they mostly dry, so that it is essential to time the tide correctly.

This is an area most suited to shallow-draft yachts, particularly flat bottomed or with bilge keels, centreboards or legs, that car take the ground easily. Whilst the zeegaten are described briefly below, the many chans inside the islands and across the Waddenzee are mentioned only for orientation.

TEXEL TO TERSCHELLING Zeegat van Texel (chart 191) lies between Den Helder and the Is of Texel, and gives access to the Waddenzee, the tidal part of the former Zuider Zee. Haaksgronden shoals extend 5M seaward, with three chans: Schulpengat or S side, leading into Breewijd; Westgat through centre of shoals, where the stream sets across the chan, is only suitable for passage in good weather and in daylight; and Molengat near the

Texel shore. Schulpengat is the well marked main chan, buoys being prefixed with letter 'S'; but strong SW winds cause rough sea against the SW-going (ebb) stream which begins at HW Helgoland – 0330, while the NE-going (flood) stream begins at HW Helgoland + 0325, sp rates 1·5kn. Molengat is marked by buoys prefixed by letters 'MG', but strong winds between W and N cause a bad sea. When coming from the NW or NE the Molengat is always the best route unless the weather is exceptionally bad. Routeing via the Schulpengat involves a southerly deviation of approx 15M and leads W of the very dangerous Zuider Haaks which should be avoided in bad weather. In Molengat the N-going (ebb) stream begins at HW Helgoland – 0145, and the S-going (flood) stream at HW Helgoland + 0425, sp rates 1·25kn. For Oudeschild, see 9.23.27.

E of Den Helder and the **Marsdiep**, the flood makes in three main directions through the SW Waddenzee:

a. to E and SE through Malzwin and Wierbalg to Den Oever (where the lock into IJsselmeer is only available during daylight hours on working days); thence NE along the Afsluitdijk, and then N towards Harlingen (9.23.28);
b. to NE and E through Texelstroom and Doove Balg towards the Pollen flats; and (c) from Texelstroom, NE and N through Scheurrak, Omdraai and Oude Vlie, where it meets the flood stream from Zeegat van Terschelling. The ebb runs in reverse. The Kornwerderzand locks (available H24), near NE end of Afsluitdijk, also give access to the IJsselmeer (9.23.25).

Eierlandsche Gat, between Texel and Vlieland, consists of dangerous shoals between which run very shallow and unmarked chans, only used by fishermen.

Zeegat van Terschelling (chart 112 and 9.23.31), between Vlieland (9.23.29) and Terschelling, gives access to the hbrs of Vlieland, West Terschelling (9.23.30) and Harlingen (9.23.28); also to the locks at Kornwerderzand. Shallow banks extend more than 5M seaward; the main chan (buoyed) through them is Zuider Stortemelk passing close N of Vlieland. In this chan the buoys are prefixed by letters 'ZS', and the E-going (flood) stream begins at HW Helgoland + 0325, while the W-going (ebb) stream begins at HW Helgoland – 0230, sp rates 2·5kn. Vliesloot leads to Oost Vlieland hbr. Approach West Terschelling via West Meep and Slenk. From Zuider Stortemelk the Vliestroom, a deep well buoyed chan (buoys prefixed by letters 'VL'), runs S about 4M until its junction with Blauwe Slenk and Inschot. Blauwe Slenk runs ESE to Harlingen; and Inschot SE to Kornwerderzand.

AMELAND TO DELFZIJL (charts 2593, 3509, 3510) **Zeegat van Ameland**, between Terschelling and Ameland, is fronted by the sandbank of Bornrif extending 3M seaward. Westgat is the main entrance, with buoys prefixed by letters 'WG'. The chan runs close N of Terschelling, and divides into Boschgat and Borndiep. For Nes (Ameland), see 9.23.28. In Westgat the flood stream begins at HW Helgoland + 0425, and the ebb stream at HW Helgoland –0150, sp rates 2kn. A dangerous sea develops in strong onshore winds.

Friesche Zeegat, between Ameland and Schiermonnikoog (9.23.23), has a main chan also called Westgat and buoys marked 'WG'. In strong winds the sea breaks across the whole passage. Westgat leads S through Wierumer Gronden, past Engelsmanplaat (a prominent sandbank) and into Zoutkamperlaag which is the main chan (marked by buoys prefixed 'Z') to Lauwersoog (9.23.32), where locks give access to the Lauwersmeer and inland waterways.

Further E, the estuary of R Ems (chart 3509) runs seaward past the SW side of the German island of Borkum (9.24.10). It leads to Delfzijl and Termunterzijl (9.23.33), or Emden (9.24.8), see 9.24.5. Hubertgat, which runs parallel to and S of the main Westerems chan, is slightly more direct when bound to/from the W, but in both these well lit chans there is a dangerous sea in strong NW winds over the ebb. The E-going (flood) stream begins at HW Helgoland + 0530, and the W-going (ebb) stream begins at HW Helgoland –0030, sp rates 1·5kn.

CROSSING NORTH SEA FROM BELGIUM AND SCHELDE (charts *1406*, *323*) Avoid major traffic areas and cross TSS at 90° to take departure from either Dyck PHM buoy or W Hinder lt depending on destination. From Dyck PHM buoy make good Ruytingen SW buoy, thence CS4 buoy and S Goodwin lt F (on W-going stream) or E Goodwin lt F (on N-going stream). From W Hinder lt for N Thames Estuary, make good Garden City buoy (on E-going stream) or Twin buoy (on W-going stream) in order to make N or S Galloper buoys and thence Long Sand Head buoy. Avoid shallower patches over W Hinder, Fairy, N Falls and Galloper Banks, particularly in rough weather when under-keel clearance may be reduced. For distances across the North Sea, see 9.0.8.

CROSSING NORTH SEA FROM THE NETHERLANDS Charts *1406*, *1408*, 1872, *2449*, 3371) From ports S of Hoek van Holland proceed westward across banks avoiding shallower patches to pick up Birkenfels buoy, across N Hinder W TSS and thence to N Galloper buoy (for N Thames estuary) or Outer Gabbard buoy (for Lowestoft and North). For ports N of Hoek van Holland passages can be made from coast to coast avoiding TSS areas and crossing DW routes with care.

9.23.6 DISTANCE TABLE

23

Approximate distances in nautical miles are by the most direct route, whilst avoiding dangers and allowing for Traffic Separation Schemes. Places in *italics* are in adjoining areas; places in **bold** are in 9.0.8, Distances across the North Sea.

1. ***Dunkerque***	**1**																			
2. **Nieuwpoort**	15	**2**																		
3. **Oostende**	26	9	**3**																	
4. Blankenberge	35	18	9	**4**																
5. **Zeebrugge**	40	23	13	5	**5**															
6. **Vlissingen**	55	39	29	21	16	**6**														
7. **Roompotsluis**	68	51	40	33	28	24	**7**													
8. Stellendam	90	83	72	55	50	45	32	**8**												
9. Hook of Holland	92	77	67	59	54	47	48	16	**9**											
10. Rotterdam	112	97	87	79	74	67	68	36	20	**10**										
11. **Scheveningen**	106	91	81	73	68	61	50	30	14	34	**11**									
12. **IJmuiden**	131	116	106	98	93	86	87	55	39	59	25	**12**								
13. Amsterdam	144	129	110	111	106	99	100	68	52	72	38	13	**13**							
14. **Den Helder**	169	154	131	136	131	120	125	93	77	97	63	38	51	**14**						
15. Den Oever	180	165	142	147	142	131	136	104	88	108	74	49	*62	11	**15**					
16. Harlingen	199	184	161	166	161	150	155	123	107	127	93	68	81	30	21	**16**				
17. Vlieland	202	187	164	169	164	153	158	126	110	130	96	71	84	33	33	18	**17**			
18. Terschelling	201	186	163	168	163	152	157	125	109	129	95	70	83	39	34	19	7	**18**		
19. **Delfzijl**	277	262	239	244	239	228	233	201	185	205	171	146	159	115	110	102	92	85	**19**	
20. *Borkum*	257	242	219	224	219	208	213	181	165	185	151	126	139	95	90	80	72	65	22	**20**

9.23.7 SPECIAL NOTES FOR BELGIUM AND THE NETHERLANDS

CURRENCY The Euro (€) is now used exclusively in Belgium and the Netherlands.

BELGIUM

PROVINCES are given for ports in lieu of UK 'counties'.

CHARTS Those most widely used are the *'Vlaamse Banken'* issued by the Hydrografische Dienst der Kust. Imray C30 is also popular amongst Belgian yachtsmen.

TIME ZONE is –0100, which is allowed for in tidal predictions but no provision is made for daylight saving schemes.

HARBOURS: Although the Hr Mr ☎ is given for Belgian hbrs, he is not the key figure for yachtsmen that he is in UK hbrs. Berths and moorings are administered by the local YCs. The prefix VVW = *Vlaamse Vereniging voor Watersport* ≅ Association of Flemish Watersports. Diesel fuel coloured red, where available, is duty free.

SIGNALS IPTS are used at Nieuwpoort, Oostende and Zeebrugge, which are the Ports of entry. In season (early April to late Sept) Blankenberge is also a Port of entry with Customs. Small craft wind warnings (onshore wind >F3; offshore wind >F4) apply to craft <6m LOA and are shown at these 3 ports and Blankenberge as follows: Day: 2 black ▼s, points together. By night: Lt Fl Bu.

TELEPHONE To call UK from Belgium, dial 00-44 then the UK area code minus the prefix 0, followed by the number required. To call Belgium from UK, dial 00-32 then the code and number. Dial codes are incorporated in the nine digit subscriber No.

Emergencies: Police 101; Fire, Ambulance and Marine 100. 112 (EC emergency number) is also operational.

MRCC Oostende, ☎ (059) 70.10.00, coordinates SAR operations. In emergency call *Oostende Radio* VHF Ch 16 (☎ 70.24.38) or ☎ 100. For medical advice call *Radiomédical Oostende* on Ch 16.

PUBLIC HOLIDAYS New Year's Day, Easter Mon, Labour Day (1 May), Ascension Day, Whit Mon, National Day (21 July), Feast of the Assumption (15 Aug), All Saints' Day (1 Nov), Armistice Day (11 Nov), King's Birthday or Fete de la Dynastie (15 Nov), Christmas Day.

RULES: Hbr police are strict about yachts using their engines entering hbr. If sails are used as well, hoist a ▼. Yachts may not navigate within 200m of shore (MLWS).

INLAND WATERWAYS: *Immatriculatieplaat* (licence plates) are required for all yachts on the Flemish waterways. These plates cost are obtainable from: 2000 ANTWERPEN, Markgravestraat 16. ☎ 03/232.98.05; or from offices in Brussels and other cities. Boats should fly the 'drapeau de navigation', a R flag with W □ in centre. Belgian Competence requirements for helmsmen are the same as the Dutch (RH col). **Note:** More info from Belgian Tourist Office, 255 Marshwall, London E14 9FW, ☎ 0906 302 0245, 📠 020 7531 0393; or Federation Royale Belge du Yachting, FRYB/KBJV, PB 241 Bouchoutlaan, 1020 Brussels, Belgium.

NETHERLANDS

PROVINCES are given in lieu of 'counties' in the UK.

CHARTS The following Dutch charts are quoted:

a. Zeekaarten (equivalent to AC); issued by the Royal Netherlands Navy Hydrographer, and updated by Dutch Notices to Mariners; available from chart agents.
b. Dutch Yacht Charts (DYC) "Kaarten voor Kust-en Binnenwateren"; issued every March by the Hydrographer in 8 sets, booklet format (54 x 38cm), covering coastal and inland waters.
c. ANWB Waterkaarten (ANWB); 18 charts of inland waterways (lettered A to S, excluding Q) .

TIME ZONE is –0100, which is allowed for in tidal predictions, but no provision is made for daylight saving schemes.

HARBOURS Most yacht hbrs are private clubs or Watersport Associations (WSV or WV): *Gem (Gemeentelijke)* = municipal. Sometimes (in Belgium also) berth-holders show a green tally if a berth is free, or a red tally if returning same day, but check with Hr Mr. Duty-free fuel (coloured red) is not available for pleasure craft and may only be carried in the tank, NOT in cans. A tourist tax of between €0.45 and €1.82/person/night is often levied.

CUSTOMS Main customs/ports of entry are Breskens, Vlissingen, Roompotsluis*, Hoek van Holland, Maassluis, Vlaardingen, Schiedam, Rotterdam, Scheveningen, IJmuiden, Den Helder, Harlingen, Vlieland*, West Terschelling, Lauwersoog and Delfzijl. No entry/customs at Stellendam, Den Oever or Kornwerderzand. *Summer only.

BUOYAGE Buoys are often named by the abbreviations of the banks or chans which they mark (eg VL = Vliestroom). A division buoy has the abbreviations of both chans meeting there, eg VL2-SG2 = as above, plus Schuitengat. Some chans are marked by withies: SHM bound ⇞; PHM unbound ⇡. On tidal flats (eg Friesland) where the direction of main flood stream is uncertain, bound withies are on the S side of a chan and unbound on the N side; the banks thus marked are steep-to. In minor chans the buoyage may be moved without notice to accommodate changes. The SIGNI buoyage system is used on inland waters, including the IJsselmeer (see 9.23.25), but not on the Westerschelde, Waddenzee, Eems and Dollard.

HIGH SPEED FERRIES operate between Hook of Holland and Harwich (40kn).

SIGNALS Traffic signals The standard French/Belgian system is not used in the Netherlands. Where possible the local system is given.

Sluicing signals The following signals may be shown:

By day: A blue board, with the word 'SPUIEN' on it; often in addition to the night signal of 3 ● in a △.

Visual storm signals Lt sigs only are shown day and night, as per the International System (see 9.15.7), at IJmuiden and Terschelling.

Inland waterways (Most bridges and locks work VHF Ch 18)

Bridge and lock signals (shown on each side):

To request bridges to open sound 'K' (–•–).

● = Bridge open.
● = Bridge closed (opens on request).
● over ● = Bridge about to open.
2 ● (vert) = Bridge out of use.
2 ● (vert) = Bridge open but not in use (you may pass).
1 ○ or 1 ◊ = Pass under this span, two-way traffic.
2 ○ or 2 ◊s = Pass under this span, one-way traffic.

Railway bridges Opening times of railway bridges are in a free annual leaflet *'Openingstijden Spoorwegbruggen'* available from ANWB, L & A/Wat, Postbus 93200, 2509 BA, Den Haag; (send A5 SAE with international reply coupon).

RADIO TELEPHONE Use low power setting (1 watt) throughout inland waters, except for emergencies. Monitor TSS info broadcasts and make contact on VTS sector channels. Note: Do not use Ch M in Dutch waters, where it is a salvage frequency; Ch 31 is for Dutch marinas. In emergency call Ch 16 for IJmuiden CG, VHF sector ch or VHF ch of nearest lock or br. VHF Ch 10 for commercial ship-ship.

TELEPHONE To call UK from the Netherlands, dial 00-44; then the UK area code minus the prefix 0, followed by the number required. To call the Netherlands from UK dial 00-31 then the area code minus the prefix 0 followed by two or three digits, followed by a seven or six subscriber no. **Emergencies**: Fire, Police, Ambulance, dial 112 (free); **Non-emergencies** 0900 8844.

PUBLIC HOLIDAYS New Year's Day, Easter Sun and Mon, Queen's Birthday (30 April), Liberation Day (5 May), Ascension Day, Whit Mon, Christmas and Boxing Days.

INLAND WATERWAYS: All craft must carry a copy of the waterway regulations, *Binnenvaart Politiereglement (BPR)*, as given in the current ANWB publication *Almanak voor Watertoerisme, Vol 1* (written in Dutch). Craft >15m LOA or capable of more than 20kph (11kn) must be commanded by the holder of either an RYA Yacht Master Certificate (Coastal) or (Offshore) or Coastal Skipper's Certificate plus a Helmsman's Certificate.

9.23.8 SOUTHERN NORTH SEA WAYPOINTS

Southern North Sea waypoint and major light positions south of 54°N are listed alphabetically below. **They are all referenced to the WGS84 Datum.**

Areas 23 and 24

A1 Lt By	51°22′·36N	02°53′·32E
A1 bis Lt By	51°21′·68N	02°58′·02E
A2 Lt By	51°21′·42N	03°07′·05E
Akkaert NE Lt By	51°27′·28N	02°59′·32E
Ameland Lt	53°26′·95N	05°37′·42E
A/N Lt By	51°23′·45N	02°36′·92E
A/Z Lt By	51°21′·15N	02°36′·92E
Bergues Bk N Lt By	51°19′·92N	02°24′·50E
BG 2 Lt By	53°58′·42N	03°17′·50E
Binnenstroom Bk Lt By	51°14′·47N	02°53′·65E
Birkenfels Lt By	51°38′·96N	02°32′·03E
Bollen Lt By	51°49′·99N	03°32′·98E
Borkumriff Lt By	53°47′·44N	06°22′·05E
BR Lt By	53°30′·65N	05°33′·46E
Buitenbank Lt By	51°51′·14N	03°25′·69E
Buitenstroom Bk Lt By	51°15′·17N	02°51′·72E
BVH Lt By	51°23′·12N	03°12′·02E
Dovetief Lt By	53°45′·23N	07°08′·97E
Eierland Lt	53°10′·93N	04°51′·30E
Elbe Lt By	53°59′·95N	08°06′·49E
Eveline Lt By	52°25′·49N	04°25′·00E
Fairy W Lt By	51°23′·88N	02°09′·28E
Garden City Lt By	51°29′·12N	02°17′·92E
Goeree Lt	51°55′·42N	03°40′·03E
Goote Bank Lt By	51°26′·95N	02°52′·72E
GW/Ems Lt F	54°09′·96N	06°20′·72E
GZ Lt By	51°24′·25N	02°44′·51E
Harle Lt By	53°49′·29N	07°48′·99E
Hinder Lt By	51°54′·53N	03°55′·40E
Hubert Gat Lt By	53°34′·84N	06°14′·19E
IJM (IJmuiden) Lt By	52°28′·44N	04°23′·78E
Indusbank N Lt By	52°02′·88N	04°03′·57E
Juist-N Lt By	53°43′·77N	06°55′·36E
Kaloo Lt By	51°35′·55N	03°23′·24E
KB Lt By	51°21′·03N	02°42′·83E
Kijkduin Lt	52°57′·33N	04°43′·58E
LST '420' Lt By	51°15′·46N	02°40′·58E
MC Lt By	52°01′·12N	03°53′·46E
MBN Lt By	51°20′·82N	02°46′·29E
MD 3 Lt By	51°42′·71N	03°26′·97E
MG (Verkenningston)	53°03′·90N	04°39′·37E
Middelbank Lt By	51°40′·83N	03°18′·21E
Middelkerke Bk S Lt By	51°14′·73N	02°41′·89E
Middelkerke Bk Lt By	51°18′·19N	02°42′·74E
MSB Lt By	51°38′·67N	03°20′·39E
MV Lt By	51°57′·44N	03°58′·40E
MW Lt By	51°44′·25N	03°23′·66E
Nautica Ena Lt By	51°18′·07N	02°52′·80E
NHR-N	52°10′·82N	03°04′·69E
Nieuwpoort E Pier Lt	51°09′·42N	02°43′·08E
Nieuwpoort Bk Lt By	51°10′·17N	02°36′·09E
Nippon Wk Lt By	51°22′·56N	03°05′·14E
Noordhinder Lt By	52°00′·15N	02°51′·20E
Norderney N Lt By	53°46′·07N	07°17′·13E
Oost Dyck Lt By	51°21′·38N	02°31′·12E
Oost Dyck W Lt By	51°17′·17N	02°26′·22E
Oostendebank N Lt By	51°21′·20N	02°52′·82E
Oostendebank E Lt By	51°17′·35N	02°51′·92E
Oostendebank W Lt By	51°16′·20N	02°44′·75E
Ooster Lt By	51°47′·89N	03°41′·27E
Osterems Lt By	53°41′·88N	06°36′·14E
Rabsbank Lt By	51°38′·25N	03°09′·90E
Riffgat Lt By	53°38′·93N	06°27′·03E
S 3 Lt By	51°24′·30N	03°02′·92E
S 4 Lt By	51°25′·03N	03°02′·85E
Sandettie N Lt By	51°18′·35N	02°04′·73E
SBZ Lt By	51°42′·43N	03°16′·60E
SCH Lt By	52°07′·75N	04°14′·11E
Schiermonnikoog Lt	53°29′·19N	06°08′·78E
Schlucter Lt By	53°44′·45N	07°02′·20E
Schlusseltone Lt By	53°56′·25N	07°54′·76E
Schouwenbank Lt By	51°44′·94N	03°14′·31E
SG (Haringvliet) Lt By	51°51′·93N	03°51′·40E
SG (Schulpengat) Lt By	52°52′·90N	04°37′·90E
S-W Lt By	51°24′·13N	03°18′·30E
SWA Lt By	51°22′·28N	02°46′·34E
SWW Lt By	51°21′·95N	03°00′·95E
SZ Lt By	51°23′·67N	03°07′·57E
TB Lt By	51°34′·38N	02°59′·10E
TG1/Ems Lt By	53°43′·27N	06°22′·24E
TG3 Lt By	53°44′·62N	06°31′·09E
TG5 Lt By	53°45′·81N	06°39′·99E
TG7 Lt By	53°47′·24N	06°49′·65E
TG9 Lt By	53°48′·35N	06°57′·66E
TG11 Lt By	53°49′·58N	07°06′·48E
TG13 Lt By	53°50′·92N	07°15′·37E
TG15 Lt By	53°52′·13N	07°24′·27E
TG17/Weser1 Lt By	53°53′·43N	07°33′·13E
TG19/Weser 2 Lt By	53°54′·99N	07°44′·66E
Thornton SW Lt By	51°30′·95N	02°50′·92E
Track Ferry Lt By	51°33′·78N	02°36′·33E
Trapegeer Lt By	51°08′·42N	02°34′·38E
Trawl Lt By	51°26′·27N	03°28′·22E
Twin Lt By	51°32′·05N	02°22′·62E
TX 1 Lt By	52°48′·00N	04°15′·48E
TX 3 Lt By	52°58′·58N	04°22′·29E
VG Lt By	51°22′·95N	02°46′·32E
VL 1 (Eierland) Lt By	53°10′·95N	04°35′·30E
VL 9 (Ameland)	53°28′·11N	05°03′·89E
Vlieland Lt	53°17′·69N	05°03′·46E
WBN Lt By	51°21′·50N	03°02′·59E
W Hinder Lt	51°23′·31N	02°26′·27E
Wenduine Bk E Lt By	51°18′·88N	03°01′·72E
Wenduine Bk W Lt By	51°17′·23N	02°52′·75E
Weser Lt By	53°54′·25N	07°50′·00E
Weser 1/Jade 2 Lt By	53°52′·12N	07°47′·35E
Westerems Lt By	53°36′·88N	06°19′·38E
Westpit Lt By	51°33′·65N	03°09′·92E
Weststroom Bk Lt By	51°11′·33N	02°43′·04E
WG (Schiermonnikoog) Lt By	53°32′·96N	06°09′·68E
WG-OG (Westgat) Lt By	51°37′·18N	03°23′·81E
W-Z Lt By	51°22′·57N	03°10′·72E
Z (Zand) Lt By	51°22′·47N	03°09′·95E
ZS Lt By (Vlieland)	53°19′·78N	04°55′·88E
ZSB Lt By	51°36′·59N	03°15′·69E
Zuidstroombank Lt Buoy	51°12′·29N	02°47′·35E

NIEUWPOORT (NIEUPORT) *9.23.9*

Belgium, West Flanders **51°09'·40N 02°43'·23**

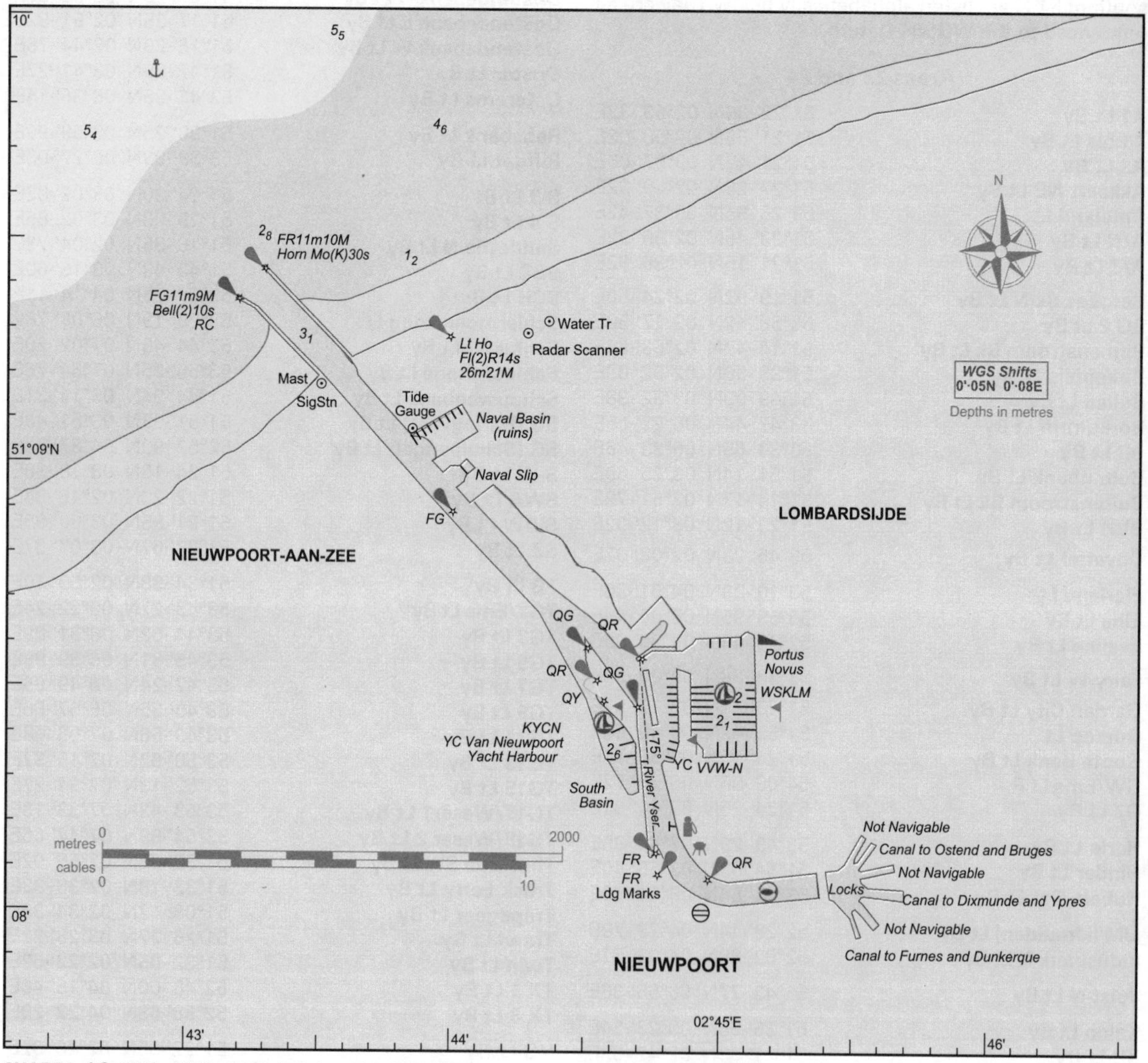

CHARTS AC 1873, 1872, *2449*; Belgian 101, D11; DYC 1801.2; SHOM 7214; ECM 1010; Imray C30; Stanfords 1, 19, 20

TIDES +0105 Dover; ML 2·7; Duration 0515; Zone –0100

Standard Port VLISSINGEN (⟶)

Times				Height (metres)			
High Water		Low Water		MHWS	MHWN	MLWN	MLWS
0300	0900	0400	1000	4·8	3·9	0·9	0·3
1500	2100	1600	2200				
Differences NIEUWPOORT							
–0110	–0050	–0035	–0045	+0·6	+0·5	+0·4	+0·1

SHELTER Good except in strong NW'lies. There are two yacht hbrs, access H24, run by three YCs: Royal YC of Nieuwpoort (**KYCN**) to the SW gets very full; but there is always room in the Portus Novus, run by the Air Force YC (**WSKLM**) at the N and E side; and **VVW-N**ieuwpoort to the S and centre.

NAVIGATION WPT 51°10'·00N 02°42'·00E, 308°/128° from/to ent, 0·90M. The bar (1·5m) is liable to silt up but there is usually sufficient water for yachts. At sp the stream reaches 2kn across the ent. The 1M long ent chan to both yacht hbrs is dredged, although levels can drop to about 2m. Note: For activity at firing range E of Nieuwpoort, call range officer on Ch 67; range is not used mid-June to end Sept. See notice boards for speed limits.

LIGHTS AND MARKS Lt ho Fl (2) R 14s 26m 21M; conspic R tr, W bands. E pier head FR 11m 10M, W tr, vis 025°-250°, 307°-347°, Horn Mo (K) 30s. W pier head, FG 11m 9M, W tr, vis 025°-250°, 284°-324°, Bell (2) 10s, RC. IPTS from root of W pier, plus: 2 cones, points together or Fl Bu lt = No departure for craft < 6m LOA. Watch out for other tfc sigs, especially STOP sign near exit from Novus Portus, shown in conjunction with IPTS.

RADIO TELEPHONE VHF Ch 09 16 (H24).

TELEPHONE (Dial code 058) Hr Mr/Pilots 233000, ℻ 231575; Lock 233050; CG/Marine Police 233045; Marine Rescue Helicopter 311714; ⊜ 233451; Duty Free Store 233433; Ⓗ (Oostende) 707631; Dr 233089; Brit Consul (02) 2179000; Police 234246.

FACILITIES **KYCN** (420 + 80 Ⓥ) ☎ 234413, €14.87, M, FW, C (10 ton), Slip, CH, Gas, ME, El, Sh, V, D, Ⓟ, R, Bar; **WSKLM** (500 + Ⓥ) ☎ 233641, ℻ 239845, €0.87, M, L, FW, C (2 ton mobile), CH, R, Bar; **VVW-N** (950 + Ⓥ) ☎ 235232, ℻ 234058, €1.24, Slip, FW, El, Ⓔ, Ⓟ, BH (45 & 10 ton), AC (meters), CH, P, D, ♂, Sh, SM, R, Bar, Free bicycles for shopping; **Services**: D, L, ME, El, Sh, C (15 ton), Gaz, CH, SM. **Town** P, D, V, R, Bar, ✉, Ⓑ, ⇌, ✈ (Ostend). Ferry: See Ostend. (Fuel can be bought at the hbr by arrangement).

)OSTENDE *9.23.10*

elgium, West Flanders **51°14'·30N 02°55'·18E** ❁❁❁♁♁♁✿✿✿

HARTS AC 1873, 1874, 1872, *2449*; SHOM 7214; ECM 1010; YC 1801.2; Imray C30; Stanfords 1, 19, 20

IDES +0120 Dover; ML 2·6; Duration 0530; Zone –0100

tandard Port VLISSINGEN (⟶)

imes				Height (metres)			
High Water		Low Water		MHWS	MHWN	MLWN	MLWS
0300	0900	0400	1000	4·8	3·9	0·9	0·3
1500	2100	1600	2200				
ifferences OOSTENDE							
–0055	–0040	–0030	–0045	+0·4	+0·4	+0·3	+0·1

HELTER Very good, esp in the Mercator Yacht Hbr (5·0m); ent a Montgomery Dock and lock. NSYC (2·7m) and ROYC may be ncomfortable due ferries and/or strong W/NW winds.

AVIGATION WPT 51°15'·00N 02°53'·97E, 308°/128° from/to ent, 98M. Avoid the offshore banks esp in bad weather; appr via Vest Diep inside Stroombank or from the NW via Kwintebank nd buoyed chan. Busy ferry/commercial hbr with high speed erries operating in the area.

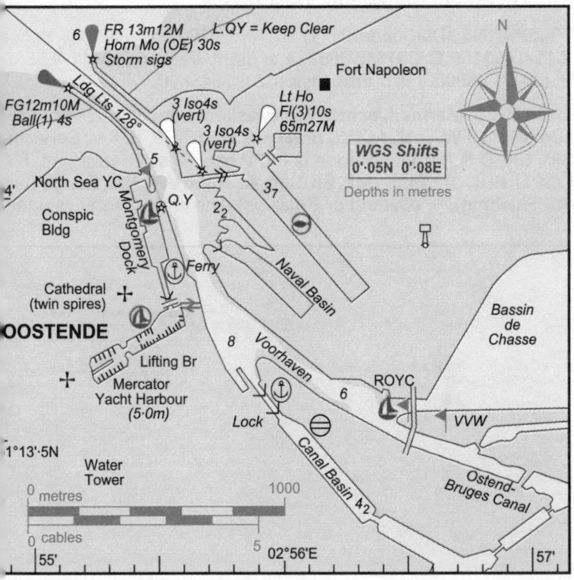

IGHTS AND MARKS Europa Centrum bldg (105m) is conspic 3ca SW of ent. Lt ho Fl (3) 10s 63m 27M, conspic W tr with 2 sinusoidal lue bands. Ldg lts 128°, both 3 Iso 4s (vert) 18/32m 4M, X on W ylons, R bands, vis 051°-201°. W pier, FG 12m 10M, W tr, vis 057°-27°, Bell 4s. E pier FR 13m 12M, W tr, vis 333°-243°, horn Mo (OE) 0s. IPTS shown from E pier, plus QY lts = keep clear of ent and chan, or ferry arrival/departure. 2 ▼, points together or Fl Bu lt = No eparture for craft < 6m LOA; (shown at ent to Montgomery dock).

ADIO TELEPHONE Port VHF Ch 09 16 (H24). All vessels inc achts, call *Signal Post* Ch 09 to ent/dep. Mercator lock/yacht hbr Ch 4 (H24).

ELEPHONE (Dial code 059) Hr Mr 330905, 🖷 330387; Life Saving 01100; ⊖ 322009; Police 500925; Ⓗ 707637; Weather (no code eeded): 1603 (Dutch), 1703 (French); Brit Consul (02) 2179000.

ACILITIES Berthing dues: Hbr and lock dues in € in cash to be paid n lock outbound. **Montgomery Dock** (70+50 Ⓥ) YC, Bar, R, FW, Slip; **orth Sea YC** (N end of Montgomery Dock) ☎ 505912, FW, AB, R, ar; **Mercator Yacht Hbr** (450+50 Ⓥ) ☎ 705762, FW, D, AC, C, Slip; **Royal)ostende YC** (1M SE up Voorhaven, 160 + 40 Ⓥ) ☎ 321452, Slip, M, W, AB, C (½ ton), R, Bar; Access via Achterhaven to the Belgian, Dutch nd French canals. **Services:** ME, CH, Sh, El, SM. D at FV hbr or by anker ☎ 500874. **Town** All amenities, ⇌, ✈. Ferry: Dover. A frequent ram service runs between Knokke and De Panne.

BLANKENBERGE *9.23.11*

Belgium, West Flanders **51°18'·95N 03°06'·60E** ❁❁♁♁♁✿✿

CHARTS AC 1874, 1872, *2449*; DYC 1801.3; Imray C30; Stanfords 1, 19

TIDES +0130 Dover; ML 2·5; Duration 0535; Zone –0100

Standard Port VLISSINGEN (⟶)

Times		Height (metres)			
High Water	Low Water	MHWS	MHWN	MLWN	MLWS
All times	All times	4·7	3·9	0·8	0·3
Differences BLANKENBERGE					
–0040	–0040	–0·3	–0·1	+0·3	+0·1

SHELTER Good. Keep to port, past the FV hbr, to the old Yacht Hbr (2·4m); VNZ pontoons are on N side and SYCB to the E. Or turn stbd into new Hbr and marina (2·4m) with 15 pontoons, numbered clockwise I - XV from the N; these are controlled by VNZ, SYCB and VVW. From early Apr to late Sept Blankenberge is a Port of Entry, with Customs.

NAVIGATION WPT 51°19'·60N 03°05'·40E, 314°/134° from/to piers, 1M. Do not attempt entry in strong NW'lies. Beware strong tides (& fishing lines) across ent. Access HW ±2 but up to ±4 in season due to dredging; ent chan between piers silts, only dredged 1·5m in season otherwise dries at LW. Do not try to enter/depart LW±1½, especially at sp. Oct-end May, only ent/leave HW±1, unless depth is pre-checked.

LIGHTS AND MARKS Conspic high-rise blocks E of lt ho, Fl (2) 8s 30m 20M, W tr B top. Ldg lts 134°, both FR 5/8m 3M, (Red X on mast) show the best water. A Water tr is conspic on E side of new Hbr. FS by lt ho shows 2 ▼, points inward, or Fl Bu lt = No departure for craft < 6m LOA (small craft warning). Caution: 3 unlit Y SPM buoys and one Fl (4) Y 20s lie about 400m off hbr ent and to E and W.

RADIO TELEPHONE Marinas VHF Ch 08. *Blankenberge Rescue* Ch 08; or relay Zeebrugge Traffic Centre Ch 69.

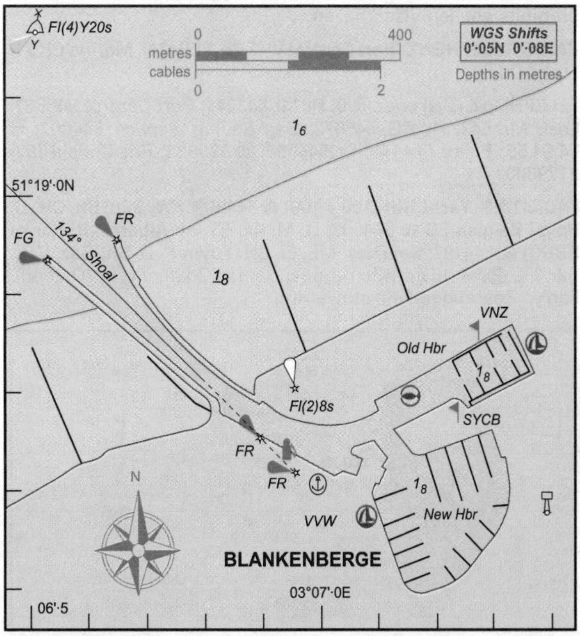

TELEPHONE (Dial code 050) Hr Mr: use VNZ, SYCB or VVW Tel Nos; ⊖ 544223; Police 429842; Dr 333668; Ⓗ 413701; Brit Consul (02) 2179000.

FACILITIES Fees: Based on beam, <3m = €9.92; <3.5m = €12.39; <4m = €14.87; plus €2.48 for every additional 0·25m. **Old Yacht Hbr** (mainly locals): **YC Vrije Noordzeezeilers (VNZ)** ☎ 429150, AC, FW, Bar, R; **Scarphout YC (SYCB)** ☎ 411420, C (10/2½ ton), CH, FW, AC, Slip, Bar, R, ♿; **Marina (VVW)** ☎ 417536, AC, FW, ⚓, Bar, 🗑, Slip, P, D (hose, duty free), ME, Sh, Ⓔ, El, SM, CH, C (20 ton). **Town** Gaz, R, Bar, ✉, Ⓑ, ⇌, ✈ Ostend.

23

ZEEBRUGGE *9.23.12*

Belgium, West Flanders **51°21'·80N 03°11'·60E** ✿✿✿◊◊◊✿✿

CHARTS AC 1874, 1872, *2449*; Zeekaart 1441; DYC 1801.3, 1803; Imray C30; Stanfords 1, 19

TIDES +0110 Dover; ML 2·4; Duration 0535; Zone –0100

Standard Port VLISSINGEN (⟶)

Times				Height (metres)			
High Water		Low Water		MHWS	MHWN	MLWN	MLWS
0300	0900	0400	1000	4·8	3·9	0·9	0·3
1500	2100	1600	2200				
Differences ZEEBRUGGE							
–0035	–0015	–0020	–0035	+0·1	+0·1	+0·3	+0·1

SHELTER Very good in the Yacht Hbr, access H24. Caution on ent/dep due to limited vis and fast FVs; give all jetties a wide berth. Brugge is 6M inland by canal.

NAVIGATION WPT Scheur-Zand ECM By, Q (3) 10s, 51°23'·72N 03°07'·67E, 309°/129° from/to ent, 3·1M. Beware strong currents in hbr apprs (up to 4kn at HW–1) and major WIP on container terminal in outer hbr N of Leopold Dam. Zeebrugge is the main Belgian fishing port and a ferry terminal, so keep clear of FVs and ferries.

LIGHTS AND MARKS Heist (W inner bkwtr hd) Oc WR 15s 22m 20/18M, Gy ○ tr. Ldg lts toward Vissershaven for marina at W end:

1. 136°: Both Oc 5s 22/45m 8M H24, vis 131°-141°, synch.
2. 154°: Front Oc WR 6s 20m 3M H24, R △, W bands; rear Oc 6s 34m 3M, R ▽, W bands, synch.
3. 220°: Front 2FW neon (vert) 30/22m; rear FW neon 30m. Both W concrete columns, B bands.
4. 193°: Both FR 22/30m; W concrete cols, R bands.

IPTS are shown at hds of W outer and inner bkwtrs. When LNG-Gas tanker is under way, 3 FY (vert) lts next to IPTS Nos 2 and 5 prohibit all movements in hbr/apprs unless special permission to move has been given. At S side of Visserhaven a QY lt prohibits ent/dep Visserhaven.

RADIO TELEPHONE Port Control VHF Ch 71 (H24). Marina Ch 71. Locks Ch 68.

TELEPHONE (Dial code 050) Hr Mr 543241; Port Control 546867; Lock Mr 543231; CG 545072; Sea Saving Service 544007; ⊖ 54.54.55; Police 544148; Dr 544590; Ⓗ 320832; Brit Consul (02) 2179000.

FACILITIES **Yacht Hbr** (100 + 100) ☎ 544903, FW, Slip, Sh, CH, D; **Royal Belgian SC** ☎ 544903, D, M, AB €2.04; **Alberta** (R, Bar of RBSC) ☎ 544197; **Services:** ME, El, CH. **Town** P, D, Sh, Gaz, V, R, Bar, ✉, Ⓑ, ⇌ 15 mins to Brugge, tram to Oostende, ✈ (Ostend). Ferry: Zeebrugge-Felixstowe/Hull.

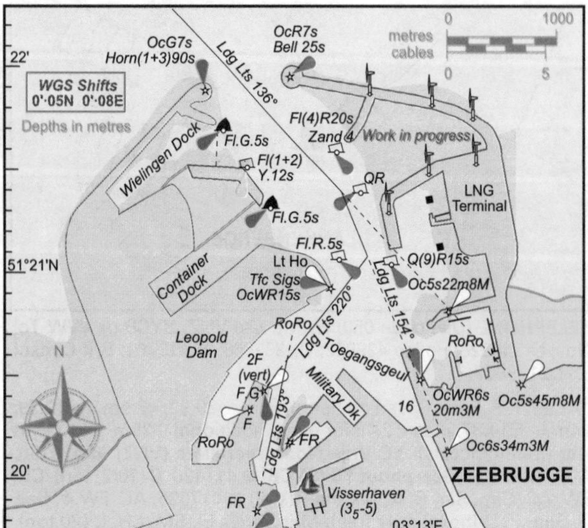

BRESKENS *9.23.13*

Zeeland **51°24'·02N 03°34'·15E** ✿✿✿◊◊◊✿✿✿

CHARTS AC 120, 1874, 1872; Zeekaart 120, 101; DYC 1801.4, 1803.2; Imray C30; Stanfords 1, 19

TIDES +0210 Dover; ML no data; Duration 0600; Zone –0100

Standard Port VLISSINGEN (⟶)

SHELTER Good in all winds; access H24, 5m at ent. Enter marina between two wave break barges. Moor to first pontoon and ☎ H Mr from end of pontoon. ⚓ off Plaat van Breskens, in fine weather not in commercial/fishing hbr. Beware fast ferries.

NAVIGATION WPT SS-VH NCM By, Q, 51°24'·75N 03°34'·00E 353°/173° from/to W mole lt (within W sector), 0·69M. Beware strong tides across the ent. Do not confuse the ent with the ferry port ent, 0·7M WNW, where yachts are prohib.

LIGHTS AND MARKS Large bldg/silo on centre pier in hbr and two apartment blocks (30m) SE of marina are conspic. W mole hd F WRG 6m; vis R090°-128°, W128°-157°, G157°-169·5°, W169·5°-173°, R173°-194°, G194°-296°, W296°-300°, R300°-320°, G320°-090°; Horn Mo (U) 30s. E mole hd FR 5m. Nieuwe Sluis lt, Oc WRG 10s 28m 14/10M, B 8-sided tr, W bands, is 1·2M W of ferry hbr.

RADIO TELEPHONE Marina VHF Ch 31.

TELEPHONE (Dial code 0117) Hr Mr 381902; ⊖ 382610; Police (0117) 453156; Dr 381566/389284, at night/weekends 0117 455565; Ⓗ (0117) 459000; Brit Embassy (070) 3645800.

FACILITIES **Marina (Jachthaven Breskens)** ☎ 381902, €0.15 for 10m yacht, FW, ⊡, ⚡, AC; **YC Breskens** ☎ 383278, R, Bar; **Services** SM, CH, D & P (fuel pontoon is in FV hbr), Gaz, chart agent, BY, C(30T), BH(70T), El, Ⓔ, ME, Sh, Slip, ♿. **Town** V, R, Bar, ✉, Ⓑ, Gas, ⇌ (Flushing), ✈ (Ostend or Brussels). Ferry: local to Vlissingen.

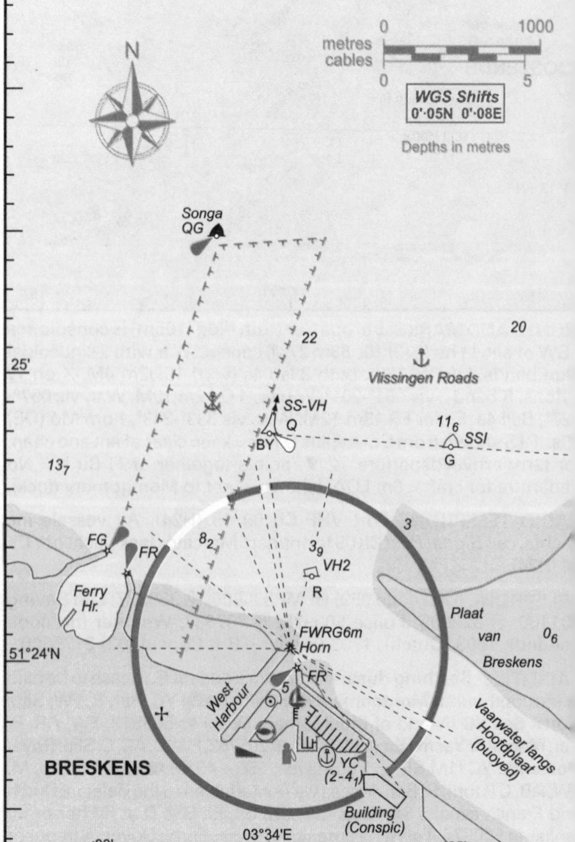

VESTERSCHELDE *9.23.14*

eeland

HARTS AC 1874, 120, 139; Zeekaart 1443; DYC 1803; Imray C30

IDES +0200 Dover; ML Hansweert 2·7, Westkapelle 2·0, Bath 8; Duration 0555; Zone –0100

tandard Port VLISSINGEN (⟶)

imes				Height (metres)			
High Water		Low Water		MHWS	MHWN	MLWN	MLWS
0300	0900	0400	1000	4·8	3·9	0·9	0·3
1500	2100	1600	2200				
ifferences WESTKAPELLE							
–0025	–0015	–0010	–0025	–0·6	–0·5	–0·1	0·0
ANSWEERT							
+0100	+0050	+0040	+0100	+0·6	+0·6	0·0	0·0
ATH							
+0125	+0115	+0115	+0140	+1·0	+0·9	0·0	0·0

HELTER AND FACILITIES Some hbrs for yachts between erneuzen and Antwerpen (38M) are listed below in sequence om seaward:

LLEWOUTSDIJK, 51°23'·00N 03°49'·00E. DYC 1803.2. HW 0200 and +0·3m on Vlissingen; ML 2·6m, €0.45. Small, safe hbr ut strong cross eddy on ebb; unlit. Dries, easy access HW ±3; ·5m at MLWS. Hr Mr ☎ (0113) 548248 FW, D, Gaz; **YC llewoutsdijk.**

OEDEKENSKERKE, 51°25'·25N 03·55'·00E. DYC 1803.3. Dissed ferry hbr (dries) on N bank, abeam ☆ Iso WRG 2s R □ tr, W and. Access HW–2½ to +3 for 1m draft, €4.54 per night. **YC WV oedekenskerke** ☎ (0113) 63x259; Ⓥ berths, P, D, Gaz, FW, ME. **own** ✉, Ⓑ, ⇌ (Goes).

ANSWEERT, 51°26'·40N 04°00'·75E. DYC 1803.3. Tidal differnces above. Can be used temporarily, but it is the busy ent to uid Beveland canal. Lt Oc WRG 10s, R lattice tr, W band, at ent. Vaiting berths outside lock on E side. Ⓥ berths in inner hbr, W de; **no smoking or naked flames in, or near lock. Services:** ME, Y, P, D, C (17 ton), CH, R. **Town** ✉, Ⓑ, ⇌ (Kruiningen-Yerseke).

VALSOORDEN, 51°23'·00N 04°02'·00E. DYC 1803.3. HW is 0110 and +0·7m on Vlissingen; ML 2·6m, €0.32/m (€3.22 min), ax stay H24. Prone to swell. SHM buoy 57A, L Fl G 8s, is 1ca of ent. Ldg lts 220° both Oc 3s. Hbr ent marked with FG and R. Unmarked stone pier just outside E hbr pier, dries partly at W. Yacht basin dead ahead on ent to hbr, depths 2 to 2·8m. *andvliet Radio* VHF Ch 12. Hr Mr ☎ (0114) 681235, FW, Slip; **ervices:** Gas, P, D, BY, ME, El. **Town** R, Bar, ✉.

AAL, 51°21'·30N 04°06'·70E. DYC 1803.3. HW +0120 and +0·8m n Vlissingen; ML 2·7m. Unlit, drying yacht hbr on W side at ver mouth, ent marked by withy. Appr from No. 63 SHM buoy, Fl G 8s, and Tide gauge, Fl (5) Y 20s across drying peelmansgat. *Zandvliet Radio* VHF Ch 12. Hr Mr ☎ (0114) 15548; **Jachthaven** AC, FW; **Services:** V, P, D, Gaz, ME, El, R.

OEL, Antwerpen, 51°18'·70N 04°16'·15E. DYC 1803.5. HW +0100 nd +0·7m on Vlissingen. Small drying hbr on W bank. Ldg lts 185·5°: front Fl WRG 3s; rear Fl 3s, synch. N pier hd lt, Oc WR 5s. Hr Mr ☎ (03) 7733072; **YC de Noord** ☎ 7733669, R, Bar, FW.

LILLO, Antwerpen, 51°18'·24N 04°17'·40E. DYC 1803.5. 1M SE of Doel on opp bank; small drying hbr for shoal-draft only; HW±3. Landing stage in river has Oc WRG 10s. Hr Mr (035) 686456; **YC Scaldis.**

NAVIGATION WPTs: See Breskens (9.23.13), Terneuzen (9.23.15) and Vlissingen (9.23.17). The approaches into the estuary from seaward are described in detail under 9.23.17; also the busy junction area between Vlissingen and Breskens. The Westerschelde chan winds through a mass of well marked sand-banks. It is the waterway to Antwerpen and Gent (via canal), very full of shipping and barges . It is necessary to work the tides, which average 2½kn, more at springs. Yachts should keep to the edge of main chan. Alternative chans must be used with caution, particular going downstream on the ebb.

LIGHTS AND MARKS The apprs to Westerschelde are well lit by lt ho's: on the S shore at Kruishoofd and Nieuwe Sluis, and on the N shore at Westkapelle. See 9.23.4. The main fairways are, for the most part, defined by ldg lts and by the W sectors of the many Dir lts.

COMMUNICATIONS AND CONTROL (VTS) Commercial traffic in the Westerschelde must comply with a comprehensive VTS which covers from the North Sea Outer Approaches up-river to Antwerp.

7 Traffic Centres control the following areas:
In offshore approaches:
1. *Wandelaar* Ch 65 (NW of Oostende);
2. *Zeebrugge* Ch 69 (W, N and E of Zeebrugge);
3. *Steenbank* Ch 64 (NW of Vlissingen).

Within the Westerschelde:
4. *Vlissingen* Ch 14 (Vlissingen to E2A/PvN SPR buoys at approx 51°24'N 03°44'E);
5. *Terneuzen* Ch 03 (thence to Nos 32/35 buoys at approx 51°23'N 03°57'E);

Also *Terneuzen* Ch 11 covers the Terneuzen-Gent Canal.

6. *Hansweert* Ch 65 (thence to Nos 46/55 buoys at approx 51°24'N 04°02'E);
7. *Zandvliet* Ch 12 (thence to Antwerpen).

Radar: In addition, within the 7 Traffic areas above, 16 unmanned Radar stns, as shown in brackets in the diagram opposite, provide radar, weather and hbr info on separate VHF Channels.

Broadcast reports of visibility, met, tidal data and ship movements are made in Dutch and on request only in English at:
Every H+55 on Ch 14 by *Vlissingen*;
Every H+00 on Ch 11 by *Terneuzen*;
Every H+35 on Ch 12 by *Zandvliet*.

Yachts should listen at all times on the VHF Ch for the area in which they are, so as to be aware of other shipping and to be contactable if required. Do not transmit, unless called. If you have a problem and need help, state vessel's name, position and the nature of the problem. Dutch is the primary language, English secondary. If you have an **emergency**, call initially on the working/channel in use; you may then be switched to *Schelde Cordination Centre* (SCC at Vlissingen) Ch 67.

23

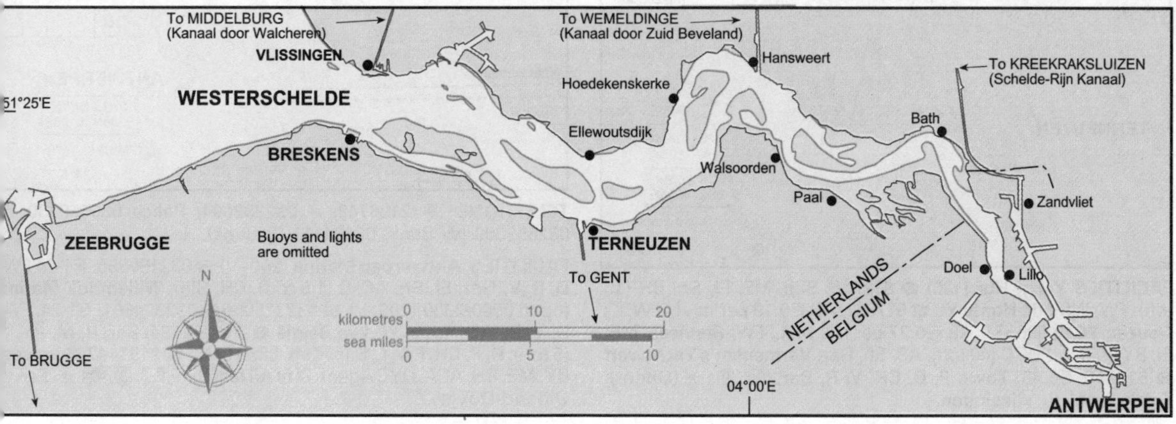

TERNEUZEN *9.23.15*

Zeeland **51°20'·62N 03°49'·75E** ❀❀❀◊◊◊✿✿

CHARTS AC 120; Zeekaart 1443; DYC 1803.2; Imray C30

TIDES +0230 Dover; ML 2·5; Duration 0555; Zone –0100

Standard Port VLISSINGEN (⟶)

Times				Height (metres)			
High Water		Low Water		MHWS	MHWN	MLWN	MLWS
0300	0900	0400	1000	4·8	3·9	0·9	0·3
1500	2100	1600	2200				
Differences TERNEUZEN							
+0020	+0020	+0020	+0030	+0·3	+0·3	0·0	0·0

SHELTER Very good except in strong NW winds. Marina in the Veerhaven is tidal and exposed to NE. Or enter the E lock (Oostsluis) and see Lockmaster for berth as on chartlet. Yachts are prohib in W Hbr and lock (Westsluis).

NAVIGATION WPT No 18 PHM Buoy, Iso R 8s, 51°20'·95N 03°48'·83E, 299°/119° from/to Veerhaven ent, 0·65M. The Terneuzen-Gent canal is 17M long with 3 bridges, min clearance 6·5m when closed.

LIGHTS AND MARKS The Dow Chemical works and storage tanks are conspic 2M W of hbr. For the Veerhaven, the water tr to SE and the Oc WRG lt on W mole are conspic. When entry prohib, a second R lt is shown below FR on E mole. Sigs for Oostsluis: R lts = entry prohib; G lts = entry permitted.

RADIO TELEPHONE Call: *Havendienst Terneuzen* VHF Ch 11 (H24); also info broadcasts every H+00 for vessels in the basins & canal. East lock Ch 18. For Terneuzen-Gent canal call on Ch 11 and keep watch during transit. Contact Zelzate Bridge (call: *Uitkijk Zelzate*) direct on Ch 11, other bridges through Terneuzen or, at the S end, *Havendienst Gent* Ch 05 11 (H24). See also 9.23.14.

TELEPHONE (Dial code 0115) Hr Mr 612161; Marina Jacht Haven 612716; CG (0255) 534344 (H24); ⊜ 612377; Police 613017; Ⓗ 688000; Dr 112; Brit Consul (020) 6764343.

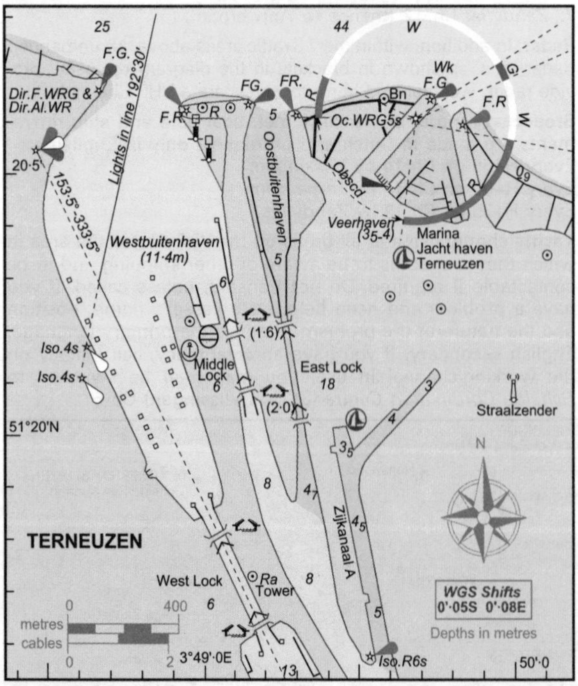

FACILITIES **Yacht Hbr** (120) ☎ 612716, Slip, ME, El, Sh, BH (15 ton), FW; **WSV de Honte YC** ☎ 617633, AB €0.19 per m², L, FW, ▣; **Neuzen YC** ☎ 696331, AB €0.27 per m², M, L, FW; **Services:** ME, El, BY, P, D, L, FW, C (40 ton), AB, Sh, Gaz. **Vermeulen's Yachtwerf** ☎ 612716, €0.45. **Town** P, D, CH, V, R, Bar, ✉, Ⓑ, ✈ (Ghent). Ferry: local to Vlissingen.

ANTWERPEN *9.23.16*

Antwerpen **51°13'·85N 04°23'·77E** ❀❀◊◊✿✿✿

CHARTS AC 139; Zeekaart 1443; DYC 1803.5

TIDES +0342 Dover; ML 2·9; Duration 0605; Zone –0100

Standard Port VLISSINGEN (⟶)

Times				Height (metres)			
High Water		Low Water		MHWS	MHWN	MLWN	MLW
0300	0900	0400	1000	4·8	3·9	0·9	0·3
1500	2100	1600	2200				
Differences ANTWERPEN							
+0128	+0116	+0121	+0144	+1·1	+0·9	0·0	0·0

SHELTER Excellent in (1) Antwerpen Marina on W bank, 4ca SV of Kattendijksluis and ½M from city centre (via two tunnels Access by lock HW ±1 (H24, 1 Apr-31 Oct)). In winter lock open only by arrangement. (2) Willemdok Marina, H24 access vi Royerssluis, Siberiabrug, Londenbrug, very close to city centre A T-shaped ferry pontoon is 2½ca N of ent, with waiting berth on inshore side; also a waiting buoy (IMALSO) is off ent.

NAVIGATION Before entering Antwerp Hbr an FD number i required. ☎ 3 219 27 84, 🖷 3 219 67 48. For Westerschelde se 9.23.14. It is advised to check off the buoys coming up-rive After No 116 PHM buoy, Iso R 8s, there is a gap of 1.5M befor reaching No. 107 SHM buoy, Iso G 8s, which marks a 90° ben in the river onto S and is close to the pontoon (see SHELTER No 109 SHM buoy, Iso G 8s, is 250m NE of marina ent.

RADIO TELEPHONE Call *Jachthaven Antwerpen* VHF Ch 0 (HW±1). Call Port Operations *Antwerpen Havendienst* Ch 7 (H24) and for Safety; VTS Ch 18; Radar Ch 02 60; Bridges Ch 62

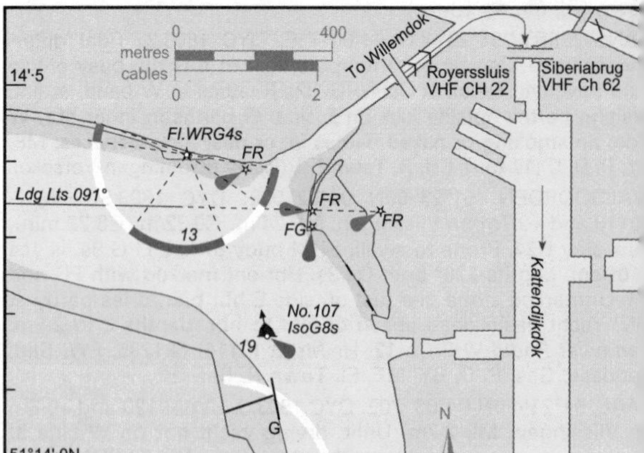

TELEPHONE 🖷 2196748; ⊜ 032292004; Police 035460730; 032852000 (W Bank) 03234111 (E Bank).

FACILITIES **Antwerpen Marina** (200+V) ☎ 032190895, €1·24 FW D, R, V, Gaz, El, Sh, AC, C (1·5 ton), CH, Slip; **Willemdok Marin** (open 0500-2300)(200+V), ☎ 032315066 🖷 032324601, €1·24, FW D, V, El, AC, **Royal YC van België** ☎ 3 219 2784, Bar, R, M, BY, (5 ton), D, P, CH, FW, L, Slip; **Kon. Liberty YC** ☎ 2191147; **Service** BY, ME, BH, ACA, DYC Agent. **City** All facilities, ✉, Ⓑ, ⇌, ✈. Ferry Ostend-Dover.

VLISSINGEN (FLUSHING) *9.23.17*

Zeeland **51°26'·36N 03°34'·70E**
(Koopmanshaven) ❁❁❁◊◊◊✿✿✿

CHARTS AC 120, 1872, 1874; Zeekaart 1442, 1443, 1533; DYC 1801.3, 1803.8; Imray C30; Stanfords 1, 19

TIDES +0215 Dover; ML 2·3; Duration 0555; Zone –0100 NOTE: Vlissingen is a Standard Port.

SHELTER Very good in both yacht hbrs:

1. **Michiel de Ruyter** marina (2·9m) in the Vissershaven has 6m wide ent, approached from the Koopmanshaven. Storm barrier is open 1 Apr-1 Nov. Sill with 1·0m water at MLWS; check depth gauge on barrier wall. Small swing bridge (pedestrian) is operated by Hr Mr 0800-2000LT, with R/G tfc lts. The bridge is open 2000-0800LT, but only for yachts to leave; ● ● (vert) tfc lts prohibit arrival from sea, because the marina is not lit.
2. **VVW Schelde** (3m) is near the ent to the Walcheren Canal. Entering the Buitenhaven beware ferries. Keep to port and S of ferry terminal for the locks, which operate H24; yachts use smallest, most N'ly lock. Waiting possible on piles to SE. Marina is to NW, past both Binnenhaven.

NAVIGATION WPT H-SS NCM buoy, Q, 51°25'·97N 03°37'·54E, 125°/305° from/to Buitenhaven ent, 0·95M. **Commercial Shipping**: Yachts should keep clear of the busy shipping chans, ie Wielingen from the SW, Scheur from the W, and Oostgat from the NW. To the E of where Wielingen and Scheur merge (NCM buoy S-W), be aware of the major ship anchorages: Wielingen Noord and Zuid either side of the fairway as defined by buoys W6, 7, 9, 10 and Songa. Close to the E, Vlissingen Roads are also a major anchorage (N of buoys SS-VH to SS7, and SW of H-SS). There is a precautionary TSS area between this anch and Vlissingen itself. Yachts are forbidden to sail in the TSS fairways. Ocean-going ships often manoeuvre off the town to transfer pilots. Fast ferries frequently enter/leave the Buitenhaven terminal.

Recommended Yacht routes:
From the SW there are few dangers. After Zeebrugge, keep S of the Wielingen chan buoys (W1-9). Off Breskens be aware of the fast ferries to/from Vlissingen; continue E to SS3 buoy, then cross to Vlissingen on a N'ly track, keeping W of H-SS buoy. From the W, keep clear of the Scheur chan by crossing to the S of Wielingen as soon as practicable.
From N, by day, in vicinity of Kaloo or DR1 buoys, follow the Geul van de Rassen, Deurloo and Spleet chans to SP4 buoy. Turn S to cross Wielingen at 90° between buoys W6 and W8; thence via W9 as per the SW approach. A variation after Deurloo is to use the Nollegeul channel (NG1-15), crossing quickly to the Vlissingen shore as and when traffic in Oostgat permits. Another route, slightly further offshore, is to skirt the NW side of Kaloo bank to Botkil-W buoy, thence SE via Geul van de Walvischstaart to SP5 and 4 buoys. None of these N'ly routes is lit. By night the Oostgat can be used with caution keeping outside the SW edge of the buoyed chan.

LIGHTS AND MARKS From NW, Oostgat ldg lts 117°: Front Leugenaar, Oc R 5s 5m 7M; rear Sardijngeul, 550m from front, Oc WRG 5s 10m 12/8M, R △, W bands on R and W mast. Note: Conspic Radar Tr (close NW of Koopmanshaven) shows a Fl Y lt to warn if ships are approaching from the NW, ie around the blind arc from Oostgat/Sardijngeul. The lt ho at the root of the W bkwtr of Koopmanshaven is brown metal framework tr, Iso WRG 3s 15m 12/9M. On S side of de Ruyter marina is a conspic W metal framework tr (50m), floodlit. Buitenhaven tfc sigs from mole W side of ent: R flag or extra ● near FR on W mole hd = Entry prohib.

RADIO TELEPHONE *Zeeland Seaports* Ch 09. Lock Ch 18; bridges info Ch 22. See also Westerschelde (9.23.14) for VTS.

TELEPHONE (Dial code 0118) Hr Mr 0115 647400; East Hbr Port Authority 478741; Schelde Tfc Coordination Centre 424790; Buitenhaven Lock 412372; ⊜ 484600; Police 424400; 🅷 425000; Dr 412233; Brit Consul (020) 6764343.

FACILITIES **Michiel de Ruyter** (100 + 40 visitors) ☎ 414498, €1.60, D, FW, AC, Bar, R, YC, ⊡; **Jachthaven 'VVW Schelde'** (90 + 50 visitors) ☎ 465912, €0.91, AC, Bar, C (10 ton), CH, D, FW, R, ⊡, ⚓, M, Slip, (Access H24 via lock), approx 1km by road from ferry terminal; **Services:** BY, ME, Sh, SM, bikes for hire. **Town** P, D, CH, V, R, Bar, ✉, Ⓑ, ⇌, ✈ (Antwerpen). Ferry: local to Breskens/Terneuzen.

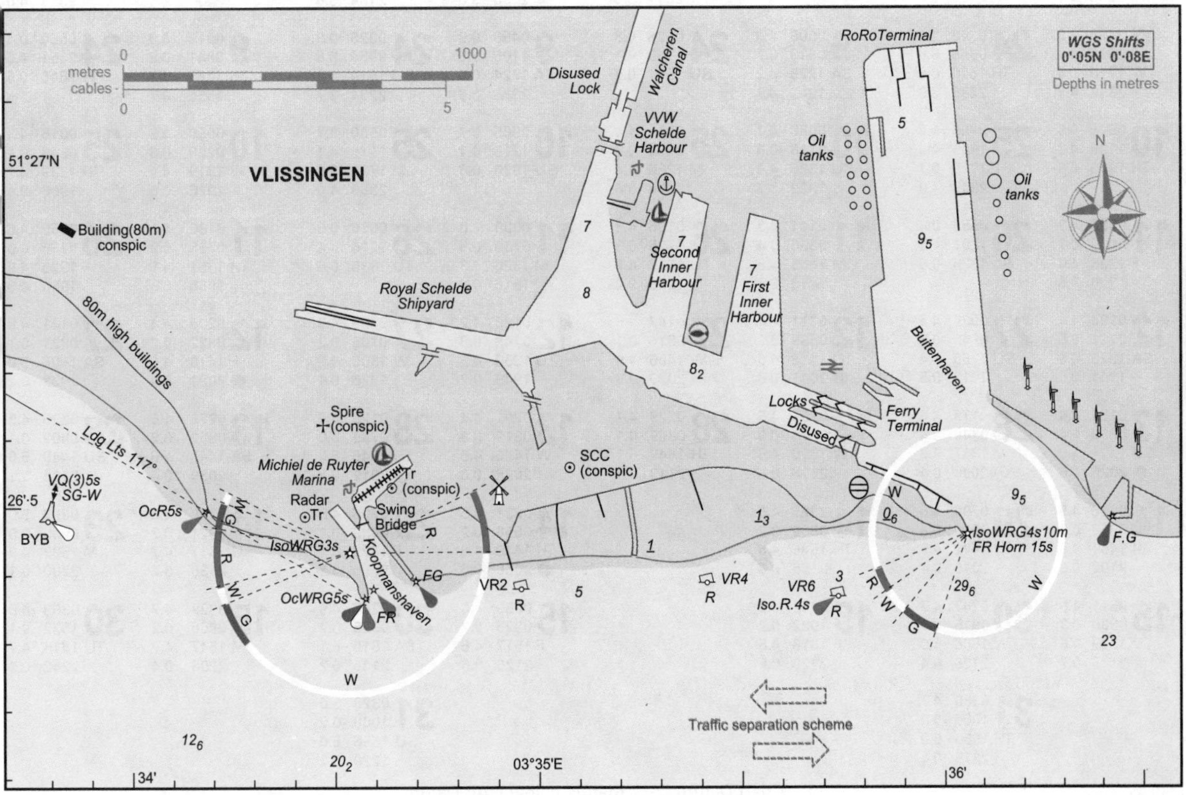

TIME ZONE -0100
(Dutch Standard Time)
Subtract 1 hour for UT
For Dutch Summer Time add ONE hour in **non-shaded areas**

NETHERLANDS – VLISSINGEN

LAT 51°27′N LONG 3°36′E

TIMES AND HEIGHTS OF HIGH AND LOW WATERS

SPRING & NEAP TIDES
Dates in red are **SPRINGS**
Dates in blue are **NEAPS**

YEAR **2002**

JANUARY

Date	Day	Time	m	Time	m	Time	m	Time	m
1	TU	0302	4.7	0928	0.3	1519	4.9	2146	0.4
2	W	0345	4.7	1016	0.2	1606	4.9	2230	0.5
3	TH	0429	4.6	1105	0.2	1650	4.8	2318	0.6
4	F	0517	4.5	1151	0.2	1742	4.6		
5	SA	0006	0.7	0611	4.3	1246	0.2	1846	4.5
6	SU	0100	0.8	0709	4.2	1346	0.3	1948	4.3
7	M	0154	0.9	0816	4.1	1445	0.5	2055	4.2
8	TU	0310	1.0	0925	4.1	1606	0.6	2205	4.1
9	W	0425	1.0	1036	4.1	1710	0.6	2312	4.2
10	TH	0545	0.9	1136	4.2	1816	0.6		
11	F	0008	4.3	0635	0.7	1236	4.4	1900	0.5
12	SA	0105	4.4	0721	0.5	1325	4.5	1941	0.5
13	SU	0151	4.4	0809	0.4	1411	4.6	● 2026	0.6
14	M	0236	4.5	0856	0.3	1451	4.6	2102	0.6
15	TU	0311	4.5	0936	0.3	1529	4.6	2135	0.7
16	W	0346	4.5	1009	0.3	1606	4.6	2216	0.7
17	TH	0421	4.5	1048	0.3	1638	4.5	2248	0.7
18	F	0457	4.4	1126	0.4	1715	4.4	2320	0.8
19	SA	0529	4.3	1156	0.5	1749	4.3	2349	0.8
20	SU	0610	4.2	1226	0.5	1835	4.1		
21	M	0036	0.9	0649	4.1	1306	0.6	1920	4.0
22	TU	0116	1.0	0745	3.9	1355	0.7	2021	3.9
23	W	0215	1.1	0850	3.8	1506	0.8	2126	3.8
24	TH	0340	1.1	0955	3.8	1620	0.8	2235	3.9
25	F	0455	1.0	1105	4.0	1719	0.7	2340	4.0
26	SA	0555	0.8	1201	4.2	1826	0.6		
27	SU	0035	4.2	0645	0.7	1256	4.4	1912	0.5
28	M	0119	4.4	0740	0.4	1337	4.7	○ 2000	0.4
29	TU	0206	4.6	0830	0.3	1422	4.9	2046	0.4
30	W	0247	4.7	0915	0.1	1506	5.0	2129	0.4
31	TH	0330	4.7	1005	0.0	1550	5.0	2215	0.4

FEBRUARY

Date	Day	Time	m	Time	m	Time	m	Time	m
1	F	0415	4.8	1052	-0.1	1636	4.9	2306	0.4
2	SA	0501	4.7	1135	-0.1	1726	4.8	2348	0.5
3	SU	0548	4.6	1226	0.1	1819	4.6		
4	M	0035	0.6	0641	4.4	1316	0.2	1916	4.3
5	TU	0125	0.7	0742	4.3	1410	0.4	2020	4.1
6	W	0224	0.9	0850	4.1	1526	0.7	2129	3.9
7	TH	0350	0.9	1006	3.9	1640	0.8	2250	3.8
8	F	0516	0.9	1119	4.0	1756	0.8		
9	SA	0000	4.0	0619	0.7	1225	4.2	1845	0.7
10	SU	0056	4.1	0716	0.5	1326	4.4	1929	0.7
11	M	0141	4.3	0806	0.4	1405	4.5	2010	0.7
12	TU	0221	4.4	0839	0.3	1438	4.6	● 2041	0.5
13	W	0255	4.5	0916	0.3	1515	4.6	2118	0.6
14	TH	0325	4.5	0950	0.2	1546	4.6	2156	0.6
15	F	0357	4.6	1022	0.2	1616	4.6	2226	0.6
16	SA	0427	4.6	1052	0.3	1646	4.5	2256	0.6
17	SU	0459	4.5	1120	0.3	1716	4.4	2315	0.6
18	M	0531	4.4	1151	0.4	1748	4.4	2350	0.6
19	TU	0605	4.3	1226	0.4	1826	4.2		
20	W	0030	0.7	0646	4.2	1305	0.5	1916	4.0
21	TH	0120	0.8	0751	3.9	1406	0.7	2031	3.8
22	F	0223	1.0	0905	3.8	1526	0.9	2148	3.7
23	SA	0406	1.0	1030	3.8	1645	0.8	2311	3.8
24	SU	0526	0.8	1140	4.1	1801	0.7		
25	M	0016	4.0	0630	0.6	1236	4.4	1856	0.6
26	TU	0106	4.3	0725	0.3	1322	4.7	1945	0.4
27	W	0147	4.6	0816	0.1	1406	4.9	○ 2030	0.3
28	TH	0229	4.7	0859	-0.1	1449	5.1	2113	0.3

MARCH

Date	Day	Time	m	Time	m	Time	m	Time	m
1	F	0310	4.9	0946	-0.2	1533	5.1	2158	0.2
2	SA	0353	4.9	1029	-0.2	1616	5.0	2242	0.3
3	SU	0438	4.9	1115	-0.1	1703	4.9	2325	0.3
4	M	0522	4.8	1156	0.0	1751	4.6		
5	TU	0005	0.4	0611	4.6	1246	0.2	1846	4.3
6	W	0056	0.6	0708	4.3	1329	0.5	1941	4.0
7	TH	0200	0.7	0819	4.0	1435	0.8	2100	3.7
8	F	0315	0.9	0934	3.8	1604	1.0	2230	3.6
9	SA	0456	0.9	1105	3.8	1724	0.9	2338	3.8
10	SU	0605	0.7	1215	4.1	1829	0.8		
11	M	0039	4.0	0706	0.5	1306	4.3	1916	0.7
12	TU	0128	4.2	0748	0.3	1350	4.5	1949	0.7
13	W	0201	4.4	0819	0.3	1426	4.5	2026	0.6
14	TH	0231	4.5	0856	0.2	1449	4.6	● 2056	0.5
15	F	0259	4.6	0925	0.2	1517	4.6	2125	0.5
16	SA	0329	4.6	0955	0.2	1548	4.6	2200	0.4
17	SU	0357	4.6	1025	0.2	1615	4.6	2228	0.4
18	M	0429	4.6	1052	0.3	1642	4.6	2252	0.5
19	TU	0500	4.6	1116	0.3	1716	4.5	2326	0.5
20	W	0532	4.5	1150	0.4	1751	4.4		
21	TH	0000	0.5	0609	4.3	1236	0.5	1838	4.1
22	F	0051	0.6	0702	4.1	1325	0.7	1946	3.8
23	SA	0155	0.8	0826	3.8	1445	0.9	2104	3.6
24	SU	0323	0.9	0954	3.8	1614	0.9	2234	3.7
25	M	0500	0.7	1115	4.1	1736	0.8	2350	4.0
26	TU	0616	0.5	1216	4.4	1836	0.6		
27	W	0039	4.3	0708	0.2	1305	4.7	1926	0.4
28	TH	0126	4.6	0755	0.0	1346	5.0	○ 2012	0.3
29	F	0206	4.8	0839	-0.1	1428	5.1	2056	0.2
30	SA	0247	4.9	0925	-0.2	1510	5.1	2135	0.2
31	SU	0328	5.0	1006	-0.2	1556	5.0	2220	0.2

APRIL

Date	Day	Time	m	Time	m	Time	m	Time	m
1	M	0413	5.0	1051	-0.1	1639	4.8	2259	0.2
2	TU	0456	4.8	1130	0.1	1726	4.6	2346	0.3
3	W	0545	4.6	1209	0.3	1816	4.2		
4	TH	0029	0.4	0640	4.3	1300	0.6	1915	3.9
5	F	0124	0.6	0746	3.9	1405	0.9	2025	3.6
6	SA	0256	0.8	0916	3.7	1546	1.1	2206	3.5
7	SU	0426	0.8	1046	3.8	1655	1.0	2320	3.7
8	M	0540	0.6	1149	4.0	1805	0.9		
9	TU	0015	3.9	0641	0.5	1239	4.3	1855	0.7
10	W	0058	4.2	0720	0.3	1319	4.4	1926	0.6
11	TH	0136	4.3	0755	0.3	1351	4.5	1956	0.5
12	F	0206	4.4	0822	0.2	1418	4.6	● 2031	0.4
13	SA	0228	4.5	0852	0.2	1446	4.6	2059	0.4
14	SU	0259	4.6	0921	0.2	1517	4.7	2136	0.4
15	M	0329	4.7	0956	0.2	1547	4.7	2206	0.4
16	TU	0401	4.7	1026	0.3	1617	4.6	2236	0.4
17	W	0433	4.6	1059	0.3	1652	4.5	2306	0.4
18	TH	0507	4.5	1130	0.4	1727	4.4	2347	0.4
19	F	0545	4.4	1216	0.5	1815	4.1		
20	SA	0036	0.5	0639	4.2	1310	0.7	1920	3.8
21	SU	0146	0.7	0805	3.9	1425	0.9	2050	3.6
22	M	0316	0.7	0938	3.9	1555	0.9	2212	3.7
23	TU	0446	0.6	1051	4.1	1716	0.8	2321	4.0
24	W	0550	0.4	1151	4.5	1816	0.6		
25	TH	0016	4.3	0648	0.1	1239	4.7	1906	0.4
26	F	0059	4.6	0735	0.0	1326	4.9	1950	0.3
27	SA	0141	4.8	0821	-0.1	1406	5.0	○ 2033	0.2
28	SU	0226	4.9	0902	-0.1	1449	5.0	2115	0.1
29	M	0307	5.0	0943	0.0	1533	4.9	2200	0.1
30	TU	0353	4.9	1022	0.1	1616	4.7	2242	0.2

Chart Datum: 2·32 metres below NAP Datum

TIME ZONE -0100
(Dutch Standard Time)
Subtract 1 hour for UT
For Dutch Summer Time add ONE hour in **non-shaded areas**

NETHERLANDS – VLISSINGEN

LAT 51°27′N LONG 3°36′E

TIMES AND HEIGHTS OF HIGH AND LOW WATERS

SPRING & NEAP TIDES
Dates in red are **SPRINGS**
Dates in blue are **NEAPS**

YEAR **2002**

MAY

Date	Day	Time	m	Time	m	Time	m	Time	m
1	W	0435	4.8	1105	0.3	1702	4.5	2326	0.3
2	TH	0522	4.5	1146	0.5	1749	4.2		
3	F	0016	0.4	0616	4.2	1235	0.8	1841	3.9
4	SA	0116	0.5	0719	3.9	1346	1.0	1945	3.6
5	SU	0226	0.7	0846	3.7	1500	1.1	2127	3.5
6	M	0340	0.7	1010	3.7	1625	1.1	2234	3.6
7	TU	0454	0.6	1115	3.9	1715	0.9	2336	3.8
8	W	0555	0.5	1201	4.1	1804	0.8		
9	TH	0018	4.1	0640	0.4	1245	4.3	1844	0.6
10	F	0057	4.2	0715	0.4	1316	4.4	1925	0.5
11	SA	0126	4.4	0745	0.3	1348	4.5	2001	0.4
12	SU	0157	4.5	0815	0.3	1417	4.6	● 2036	0.4
13	M	0227	4.6	0856	0.2	1447	4.7	2108	0.3
14	TU	0302	4.7	0928	0.3	1521	4.6	2146	0.3
15	W	0337	4.7	1006	0.3	1555	4.6	2220	0.3
16	TH	0410	4.6	1041	0.4	1632	4.4	2258	0.3
17	F	0451	4.6	1116	0.5	1712	4.3	2346	0.4
18	SA	0536	4.4	1206	0.6	1806	4.1		
19	SU	0036	0.4	0636	4.2	1254	0.8	1909	3.8
20	M	0145	0.5	0756	4.0	1404	0.9	2024	3.7
21	TU	0255	0.5	0916	4.1	1536	0.9	2146	3.8
22	W	0416	0.4	1026	4.2	1656	0.8	2251	4.0
23	TH	0525	0.3	1126	4.4	1756	0.6	2345	4.3
24	F	0626	0.2	1218	4.6	1842	0.5		
25	SA	0035	4.5	0715	0.1	1305	4.7	1930	0.3
26	SU	0123	4.7	0757	0.0	1347	4.8	○ 2015	0.2
27	M	0205	4.8	0839	0.1	1433	4.8	2100	0.2
28	TU	0249	4.8	0926	0.2	1515	4.7	2146	0.1
29	W	0335	4.8	1006	0.3	1602	4.6	2230	0.2
30	TH	0421	4.7	1041	0.5	1646	4.4	2316	0.2
31	F	0505	4.5	1126	0.7	1731	4.2	2355	0.3

JUNE

Date	Day	Time	m	Time	m	Time	m	Time	m
1	SA	0600	4.3	1205	0.8	1814	4.0		
2	SU	0044	0.5	0656	4.0	1306	1.0	1909	3.8
3	M	0150	0.6	0755	3.8	1416	1.1	2016	3.6
4	TU	0255	0.6	0916	3.7	1514	1.1	2141	3.6
5	W	0355	0.7	1025	3.8	1619	1.0	2246	3.7
6	TH	0500	0.6	1118	4.0	1714	0.8	2332	3.9
7	F	0545	0.5	1206	4.2	1805	0.7		
8	SA	0016	4.1	0636	0.5	1238	4.3	1845	0.6
9	SU	0052	4.3	0705	0.4	1312	4.5	1928	0.5
10	M	0128	4.4	0745	0.4	1349	4.5	2006	0.4
11	TU	0205	4.5	0826	0.3	1425	4.6	● 2046	0.4
12	W	0242	4.6	0906	0.4	1500	4.6	2125	0.3
13	TH	0316	4.7	0946	0.4	1541	4.5	2208	0.3
14	F	0356	4.7	1026	0.5	1621	4.4	2252	0.3
15	SA	0441	4.6	1111	0.5	1705	4.3	2339	0.3
16	SU	0528	4.5	1156	0.7	1758	4.2		
17	M	0035	0.3	0626	4.3	1250	0.8	1859	4.0
18	TU	0136	0.3	0740	4.2	1356	0.8	2010	4.0
19	W	0240	0.3	0850	4.2	1506	0.9	2116	4.0
20	TH	0346	0.4	0956	4.2	1615	0.8	2226	4.1
21	F	0506	0.4	1059	4.3	1726	0.7	2321	4.3
22	SA	0600	0.3	1156	4.4	1826	0.6		
23	SU	0016	4.4	0649	0.3	1247	4.5	1915	0.4
24	M	0106	4.6	0735	0.3	1336	4.6	○ 1959	0.3
25	TU	0155	4.7	0822	0.3	1420	4.6	2045	0.2
26	W	0241	4.7	0901	0.4	1505	4.6	2132	0.2
27	TH	0325	4.7	0945	0.5	1548	4.5	2216	0.2
28	F	0408	4.6	1021	0.6	1631	4.4	2255	0.2
29	SA	0456	4.5	1102	0.7	1716	4.3	2334	0.3
30	SU	0536	4.3	1146	0.8	1756	4.2		

JULY

Date	Day	Time	m	Time	m	Time	m	Time	m
1	M	0026	0.4	0626	4.1	1236	0.9	1835	4.0
2	TU	0105	0.5	0705	4.0	1315	1.0	1928	3.9
3	W	0200	0.6	0805	3.8	1425	1.0	2025	3.8
4	TH	0301	0.7	0905	3.8	1536	1.0	2130	3.7
5	F	0355	0.7	1004	3.8	1625	1.0	2236	3.8
6	SA	0449	0.7	1116	4.0	1725	0.9	2329	4.0
7	SU	0550	0.6	1202	4.1	1812	0.7		
8	M	0016	4.1	0635	0.6	1245	4.3	1900	0.6
9	TU	0058	4.3	0718	0.5	1326	4.4	1946	0.5
10	W	0143	4.5	0800	0.5	1406	4.5	● 2026	0.4
11	TH	0222	4.7	0846	0.4	1447	4.6	2112	0.3
12	F	0302	4.7	0928	0.4	1527	4.6	2158	0.2
13	SA	0346	4.8	1012	0.5	1609	4.5	2245	0.1
14	SU	0431	4.8	1058	0.5	1657	4.5	2336	0.1
15	M	0518	4.7	1145	0.6	1746	4.4		
16	TU	0026	0.1	0612	4.5	1236	0.7	1839	4.3
17	W	0116	0.2	0716	4.4	1329	0.8	1942	4.2
18	TH	0216	0.3	0819	4.3	1435	0.8	2049	4.1
19	F	0316	0.4	0925	4.2	1539	0.9	2151	4.1
20	SA	0436	0.5	1036	4.1	1706	0.8	2302	4.2
21	SU	0541	0.5	1139	4.2	1806	0.7		
22	M	0001	4.3	0635	0.5	1238	4.3	1906	0.5
23	TU	0101	4.5	0726	0.5	1325	4.4	1952	0.3
24	W	0151	4.6	0805	0.5	1416	4.5	○ 2038	0.2
25	TH	0236	4.6	0845	0.6	1455	4.5	2120	0.2
26	F	0316	4.7	0925	0.6	1535	4.5	2200	0.2
27	SA	0355	4.6	1002	0.7	1608	4.5	2238	0.2
28	SU	0431	4.6	1040	0.7	1646	4.5	2316	0.3
29	M	0508	4.4	1116	0.8	1718	4.4	2351	0.4
30	TU	0546	4.3	1150	0.8	1758	4.3		
31	W	0026	0.5	0626	4.2	1225	0.9	1840	4.1

AUGUST

Date	Day	Time	m	Time	m	Time	m	Time	m
1	TH	0106	0.6	0706	4.0	1305	1.0	1925	4.0
2	F	0134	0.7	0800	3.9	1359	1.1	2026	3.8
3	SA	0250	0.8	0854	3.8	1530	1.1	2136	3.7
4	SU	0400	0.9	1015	3.8	1635	1.0	2246	3.8
5	M	0506	0.8	1119	3.9	1746	0.9	2345	4.0
6	TU	0606	0.7	1220	4.1	1835	0.7		
7	W	0042	4.3	0655	0.6	1305	4.3	1926	0.5
8	TH	0125	4.6	0746	0.5	1347	4.5	● 2012	0.3
9	F	0207	4.8	0828	0.5	1429	4.7	2055	0.2
10	SA	0246	4.9	0909	0.4	1510	4.7	2142	0.0
11	SU	0330	5.0	0955	0.4	1553	4.8	2230	0.0
12	M	0415	5.0	1039	0.5	1636	4.7	2315	0.0
13	TU	0501	4.9	1125	0.5	1726	4.6		
14	W	0002	0.1	0551	4.7	1215	0.6	1810	4.5
15	TH	0050	0.2	0645	4.5	1301	0.7	1909	4.4
16	F	0146	0.4	0748	4.2	1405	0.8	2011	4.2
17	SA	0245	0.6	0855	4.0	1516	0.9	2126	4.0
18	SU	0400	0.8	1016	3.9	1646	0.9	2246	4.0
19	M	0526	0.8	1130	4.0	1755	0.7	2354	4.2
20	TU	0626	0.7	1229	4.2	1855	0.5		
21	W	0055	4.4	0709	0.7	1318	4.4	1942	0.4
22	TH	0146	4.6	0755	0.7	1406	4.5	○ 2025	0.3
23	F	0225	4.7	0832	0.7	1442	4.6	2101	0.2
24	SA	0258	4.7	0905	0.7	1516	4.6	2138	0.2
25	SU	0331	4.7	0940	0.7	1546	4.6	2209	0.3
26	M	0406	4.6	1015	0.7	1617	4.6	2246	0.3
27	TU	0436	4.6	1046	0.7	1646	4.6	2309	0.4
28	W	0508	4.5	1116	0.7	1719	4.5	2335	0.5
29	TH	0538	4.4	1140	0.8	1751	4.3		
30	F	0008	0.6	0616	4.2	1216	0.8	1829	4.2
31	SA	0045	0.7	0656	4.1	1300	0.9	1920	4.0

Chart Datum: 2·32 metres below NAP Datum

Register for your FREE weekly weather email service from Macmillan Reeds
at www.nauticaldata.com – NOW!
weekend weather reports sent to your email address, every Thursday

TIME ZONE -0100
(Dutch Standard Time)
Subtract 1 hour for UT
For Dutch Summer Time add ONE hour in **non-shaded areas**

NETHERLANDS – VLISSINGEN

LAT 51°27′N LONG 3°36′E

TIMES AND HEIGHTS OF HIGH AND LOW WATERS

SPRING & NEAP TIDE
Dates in red are SPRING
Dates in blue are NEAPS

YEAR 20

SEPTEMBER

Day	Time	m	Day	Time	m
1	0140	0.9	16	0335	1.0
	0800	3.8		0952	3.7
SU	1359	1.1	M	1615	0.9
	2046	3.8		2236	3.9
2	0305	1.0	17	0505	1.0
	0920	3.7		1116	3.9
M	1556	1.1	TU	1745	0.7
	2206	3.8		2344	4.2
3	0430	1.0	18	0615	0.9
	1046	3.8		1218	4.1
TU	1705	1.0	W	1846	0.5
	2319	4.0			
4	0546	0.9	19	0045	4.5
	1155	4.0		0706	0.8
W	1810	0.7	TH	1305	4.4
				1930	0.4
5	0015	4.3	20	0129	4.6
	0635	0.7		0740	0.7
TH	1246	4.3	F	1345	4.5
	1905	0.5		2006	0.3
6	0106	4.7	21	0206	4.7
	0722	0.6		0809	0.7
F	1327	4.6	SA	1418	4.6
	1955	0.3		○ 2040	0.3
7	0147	4.9	22	0238	4.7
	0808	0.5		0846	0.7
SA	1406	4.8	SU	1445	4.7
	● 2041	0.1		2110	0.3
8	0226	5.1	23	0306	4.7
	0852	0.4		0916	0.6
SU	1448	4.9	M	1516	4.7
	2126	0.0		2139	0.3
9	0309	5.2	24	0332	4.7
	0935	0.4		0946	0.6
M	1530	5.0	TU	1546	4.7
	2207	-0.1		2212	0.4
10	0353	5.1	25	0400	4.7
	1018	0.4		1019	0.6
TU	1612	5.0	W	1616	4.7
	2252	0.0		2235	0.5
11	0436	5.0	26	0431	4.6
	1102	0.5		1040	0.7
W	1655	4.9	TH	1643	4.6
	2335	0.1		2306	0.5
12	0525	4.8	27	0502	4.5
	1148	0.5		1108	0.7
TH	1746	4.7	F	1716	4.5
				2330	0.6
13	0015	0.3	28	0536	4.4
	0616	4.5		1135	0.7
F	1235	0.7	SA	1749	4.4
	1838	4.5			
14	0106	0.6	29	0008	0.7
	0715	4.2		0616	4.2
SA	1336	0.8	SU	1226	0.8
	1945	4.2		1836	4.1
15	0204	0.8	30	0055	0.9
	0826	3.9		0705	3.9
SU	1443	0.9	M	1325	1.0
	2106	3.9		1951	3.9

OCTOBER

Day	Time	m	Day	Time	m
1	0210	1.1	16	0445	1.2
	0835	3.7		1049	3.8
TU	1454	1.1	W	1726	0.7
	2130	3.8		2325	4.1
2	0356	1.1	17	0550	1.0
	1010	3.7		1156	4.1
W	1636	1.0	TH	1826	0.5
	2255	4.0			
3	0504	1.0	18	0019	4.4
	1125	4.0		0635	0.9
TH	1745	0.7	F	1235	4.3
	2355	4.4		1906	0.4
4	0609	0.8	19	0106	4.6
	1217	4.3		0716	0.8
F	1846	0.4	SA	1318	4.5
				1940	0.4
5	0045	4.8	20	0138	4.7
	0700	0.6		0745	0.7
SA	1303	4.6	SU	1350	4.6
	1929	0.2		2010	0.4
6	0123	5.0	21	0206	4.7
	0747	0.5		0816	0.6
SU	1342	4.9	M	1415	4.7
	● 2016	0.0		○ 2041	0.4
7	0205	5.2	22	0237	4.7
	0831	0.4		0848	0.6
M	1426	5.0	TU	1446	4.7
	2100	0.0		2111	0.4
8	0246	5.2	23	0306	4.7
	0912	0.3		0915	0.6
TU	1506	5.1	W	1515	4.8
	2143	0.0		2140	0.4
9	0329	5.1	24	0332	4.7
	0957	0.3		0951	0.6
W	1546	5.1	TH	1546	4.7
	2226	0.1		2208	0.5
10	0413	5.0	25	0403	4.6
	1040	0.4		1016	0.6
TH	1632	5.0	F	1617	4.7
	2305	0.2		2235	0.6
11	0459	4.7	26	0432	4.6
	1126	0.5		1046	0.6
F	1717	4.8	SA	1648	4.6
	2348	0.5		2306	0.6
12	0547	4.4	27	0507	4.4
	1210	0.6		1114	0.7
SA	1812	4.5	SU	1726	4.5
				2346	0.7
13	0038	0.7	28	0547	4.3
	0646	4.1		1206	0.7
SU	1305	0.8	M	1816	4.3
	1915	4.1			
14	0135	1.0	29	0035	0.9
	0755	3.8		0646	4.0
M	1425	0.9	TU	1305	0.9
	2046	3.9		1920	4.0
15	0304	1.2	30	0146	1.1
	0930	3.6		0810	3.7
TU	1600	0.9	W	1424	0.9
	2215	3.9		2106	3.9
			31	0320	1.2
				0941	3.7
			TH	1606	0.8
				2226	4.1

NOVEMBER

Day	Time	m	Day	Time	m
1	0440	1.0	16	0605	1.0
	1049	4.0		1201	4.2
F	1726	0.6	SA	1830	0.6
	2325	4.4			
2	0546	0.8	17	0028	4.4
	1148	4.3		0635	0.8
SA	1818	0.4	SU	1238	4.3
				1906	0.5
3	0016	4.7	18	0106	4.5
	0636	0.7		0716	0.7
SU	1235	4.6	M	1316	4.4
	1908	0.2		1936	0.5
4	0056	5.0	19	0136	4.6
	0722	0.5		0746	0.6
M	1318	4.9	TU	1346	4.6
	● 1952	0.1		2006	0.5
5	0141	5.1	20	0205	4.6
	0808	0.4		0815	0.6
TU	1359	5.0	W	1416	4.7
	2036	0.0		○ 2038	0.5
6	0226	5.1	21	0236	4.7
	0852	0.3		0852	0.5
W	1443	5.1	TH	1447	4.7
	2120	0.1		2110	0.5
7	0308	5.0	22	0307	4.7
	0937	0.3		0926	0.5
TH	1526	5.1	F	1521	4.7
	2202	0.2		2146	0.5
8	0353	4.9	23	0338	4.6
	1019	0.3		1000	0.5
F	1612	4.9	SA	1555	4.7
	2242	0.4		2219	0.6
9	0439	4.6	24	0416	4.5
	1106	0.4		1035	0.6
SA	1658	4.7	SU	1631	4.6
	2326	0.6		2256	0.7
10	0527	4.4	25	0453	4.4
	1156	0.5		1111	0.6
SU	1755	4.5	M	1711	4.5
				2336	0.8
11	0010	0.9	26	0538	4.2
	0619	4.1		1200	0.6
M	1245	0.7	TU	1802	4.4
	1856	4.1			
12	0110	1.1	27	0026	0.9
	0728	3.8		0636	4.0
TU	1400	0.8	W	1300	0.7
	2016	3.9		1910	4.1
13	0225	1.3	28	0130	1.0
	0845	3.7		0748	3.9
W	1515	0.9	TH	1416	0.7
	2146	3.8		2029	4.1
14	0355	1.3	29	0245	1.1
	1016	3.7		0906	3.9
TH	1640	0.8	F	1537	0.7
	2256	4.0		2148	4.2
15	0510	1.1	30	0359	1.0
	1116	3.9		1015	4.0
F	1745	0.7	SA	1646	0.6
	2346	4.2		2251	4.4

DECEMBER

Day	Time	m	Day	Time	m
1	0516	0.9	16	0544	1.
	1116	4.3		1159	4.
SU	1750	0.4	M	1820	0.
	2347	4.6			
2	0615	0.7	17	0025	4.
	1207	4.5		0638	0
M	1846	0.3	TU	1240	4.
				1901	0.
3	0037	4.8	18	0106	4
	0702	0.6		0716	0.
TU	1256	4.8	W	1316	4.
	1930	0.2		1936	0.
4	0126	4.8	19	0137	4.
	0750	0.4		0752	0.
W	1340	4.9	TH	1348	4.
	● 2016	0.2		○ 2005	0.
5	0208	4.9	20	0212	4.
	0837	0.3		0830	0.
TH	1425	5.0	F	1428	4.
	2058	0.3		2046	0.
6	0253	4.8	21	0247	4.
	0922	0.3		0905	0.
F	1512	4.9	SA	1502	4.
	2142	0.4		2126	0.
7	0339	4.7	22	0326	4.
	1008	0.3		0948	0.
SA	1557	4.9	SU	1539	4.
	2222	0.5		2200	0.
8	0426	4.6	23	0402	4.
	1049	0.3		1030	0.
SU	1648	4.7	M	1619	4.
	2306	0.7		2239	0.
9	0511	4.4	24	0442	4.
	1135	0.4		1112	0.
M	1735	4.5	TU	1706	4.
	2348	0.9		2327	0.
10	0559	4.2	25	0529	4.
	1230	0.5		1206	0.
TU	1829	4.2	W	1750	4.
11	0036	1.0	26	0016	0.
	0656	4.0		0626	4.
W	1314	0.7	TH	1256	0.
	1930	4.0		1856	4.
12	0140	1.2	27	0110	0.
	0756	3.8		0725	4.
TH	1426	0.8	F	1356	0.
	2034	3.8		2006	4.
13	0250	1.2	28	0209	1.
	0906	3.7		0836	4.
F	1525	0.8	SA	1500	0.
	2155	3.8		2111	4.
14	0406	1.2	29	0326	1.
	1020	3.8		0946	4.
SA	1634	0.8	SU	1604	0.
	2301	3.9		2219	4.
15	0455	1.1	30	0435	0.
	1117	3.9		1045	4.
SU	1735	0.8	M	1727	0.
	2346	4.1		2325	4.
			31	0551	0.
				1145	4.
			TU	1826	0.

Chart Datum: 2·32 metres below NAP Datum

Register for your FREE weekly weather email service from Macmillan Reeds
at www.nauticaldata.com – NOW!
weekend weather reports sent to your email address, every Thursday

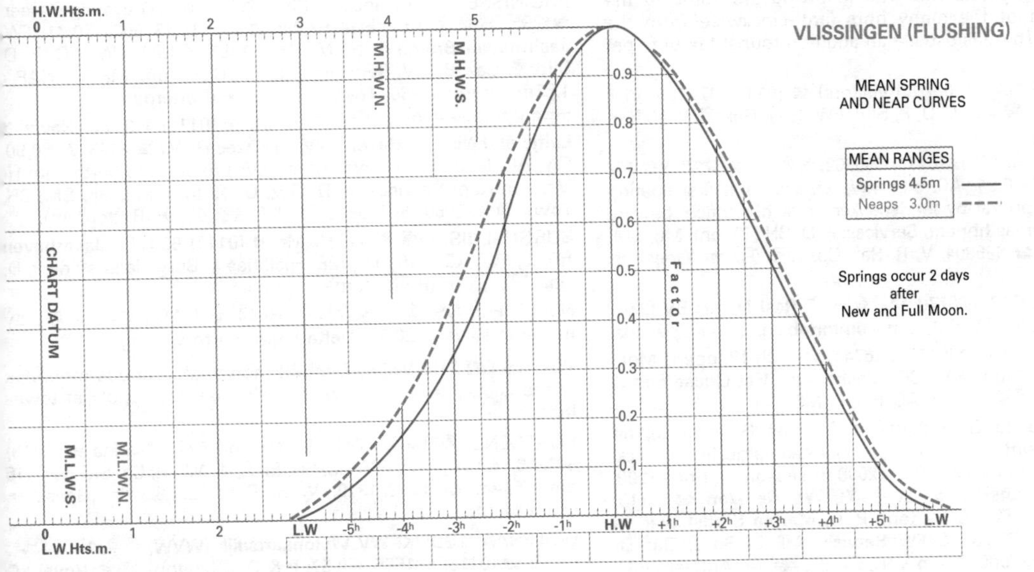

OOSTERSCHELDE *9.23.18*

Zeeland **51°37'·30N 03°40'·20E** (Roompotsluis)

CHARTS AC 110, 120, 3371; Zeekaart 1448; DYCs 1805.8, 1801.5; Imray C30; Stanfords 19

TIDES +0230 Dover Zone –0100; ML Sas van Goes 2·0, Zierikzee 1·8; Duration Sas van Goes 0615, Zierikzee 0640

Standard Port VLISSINGEN (⟵)

Times				Height (metres)			
High Water		Low Water		MHWS	MHWN	MLWN	MLWS
0300	0900	0400	1000	4·8	3·9	0·9	0·3
1500	2100	1600	2200				
Differences ROOMPOT BUITEN							
–0015	+0005	+0005	–0020	–1·2	–1·0	–0·3	0·0
STAVENISSE							
+0150	+0120	+0055	+0115	–1·3	–0·9	–0·5	0·0
LUDIJKSE GAT							
+0145	+0125	+0105	+0115	–0·7	–0·4	–0·3	0·0

SHELTER Good shelter in many hbrs at any tide. Veerse Meer is a non-tidal waterway with moorings; enter from Oosterschelde via Zandkreekdam lock. The Schelde-Rijn Canal can be entered at Bergsediepsluis near Tholen; and the S Beveland Canal at Wemeldinge.

NAVIGATION WPT WG1 SHM buoy, LFl.G 5s, 51°38'·05N 03°26'·30E at ent to Westgat/Oude Roompot buoyed chan. There are several offshore banks, see 9.23.5. Not advised to enter in strong W/NW'lies, and only from HW –6 to HW +1½ Zierikzee. All vessels must use the Roompotsluis (lock), fixed br 18.1m clearance. Lock ☎ 0111 659265. The areas each side of the barrier are very dangerous due to strong tidal streams and many obstructions. Passage is prohib W of Roggenplaat. Zeelandbrug has 12·2m clearance at centre of arch in buoyed chans. Clearance (m) is indicated on some of bridge supports. If wind < F 7, bascule bridge near N end lifts at H & H+30, Mon-Fri 0700-2130; Sat/Sun from 0900.

LIGHTS AND MARKS See 9.23.4. Roompotsluis ldg lts 073·5° both Oc G 5s; Ent: N side FR, S side FG; depth 5m.

RADIO TELEPHONE VHF-fitted craft must monitor Ch 68 in the Oosterschelde. Ch 68 broadcast local forecasts at H+15. *Verkeerspost Wemeldinge* Ch 68 MUST be called if entering canal; also for radar guidance in poor vis. Call *Zeelandbrug* Ch 18 for opening times and clearance. Locks: *Roompotsluis* Ch 18. *Krammersluizen* Ch 22 (H24). Zandreek *Sluis Kats* Ch 18; *Sluis Grevelingen* Ch 20; Bergse Diepsluis Ch 18.

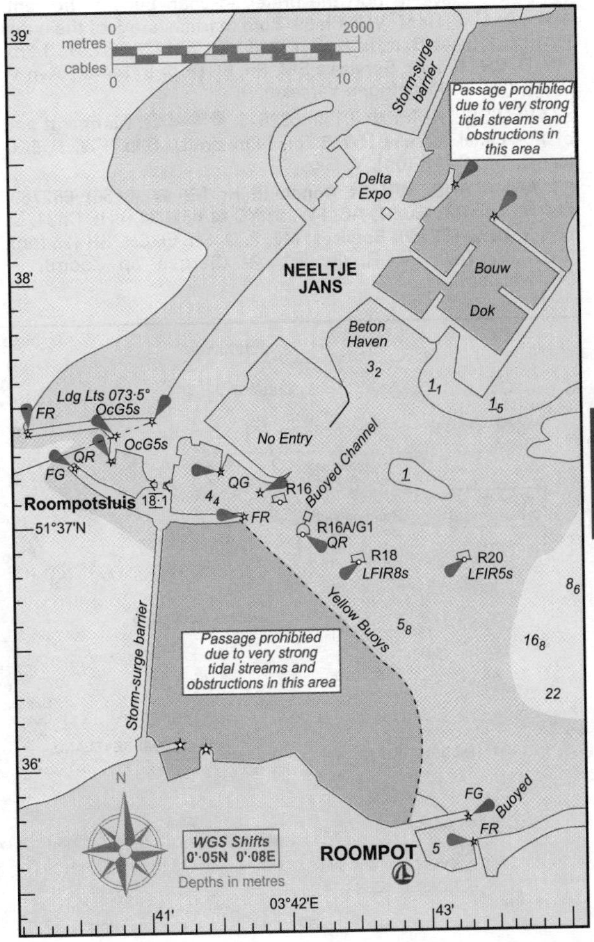

HARBOURS AND FACILITIES The following are some of the more important of the many hbrs (anti-clockwise from the Roompotsluis). There is usually an addition tourist tax of f1 per person:

ROOMPOT MARINA: (150 + 80 visitors) ☎ (0113) 374125, VHF Ch 31, ☸☸☸◊◊◊✿✿, AC, D, P, Slip, FW, Gas, Gaz, ▣, R, V, Bar, Ⓑ, Dr ☎ 372565.

COLIJNSPLAAT: Hr Mr ☎ (0113) 695762; ☸☸☸◊◊◊✿✿, **YC WV Noord Beveland** €0.91, AC, Slip, FW, ▣; secure at first floating jetty and report arrival by loudspeaker or at hbr office; beware strong current across hbr ent; **Services:** P, D, BH (40 ton), ME, SM, Sh, ⛢. **Town** Dr ☎ 695304, V, R, Bar, Gaz, ⊠, Ⓑ, ⇌ (Goes), ✈ (Rotterdam).

KATS: Hr Mr ☎ (0113) 600270; ☸☸☸◊◊✿, **Rest Nautic BV** f2.00, AC, ME, BH (35 ton), FW, SM, ▣; uncomfortable in strong E winds.

SAS VAN GOES: Lock ☎ (0113) 216744, VHF Ch 18; opens Mon-Fri 0600-2200, Sat/Sun 0800-2000. **Jachthaven Het Goese Sas** ☎ 223944, €0.79, ☸☸☸◊◊✿✿, AC, FW, D, ME, Slip, BH (12 ton), ▣.

GOES: The canal to Goes starts at Sas van Goes (lock); no facilities at Wilhelminadorp; bridge operates same hrs as lock. Town bridges open every H 0800-2000 in season, but not 1200. ☸☸☸◊◊✿✿✿. Outskirts of Goes: **YC WV De Werf** ☎ (0113) 216372, f1.75, AC, FW, C (3½ ton), P, D; **Marina Stadshaven** in centre: ☎ 216136, €0.79, AC, FW; **Services**: ME, El, Sh, ▣, Gaz, Dr ☎ 227451, Ⓗ ☎ 227000. **Town** V, R, ⊠, Ⓑ, ⇌, ✈ (Antwerpen).

WEMELDINGE: Hr Mr ☎ (0113) 622022. ☸☸☸◊◊✿. Yachts transit the Kanaal door Zuid Beveland via a section 1km E of the town. Use the former ent (via R/G tfc lts) to berth at the yacht hbrs in the Voorhaven or Binnenhaven. SHM buoy O21 to N of the E mole marks a shoal. **Services:** €1.13, ME, SM, AC, C (6·5 ton) ME, FW, P, D, ⛢, Dr ☎ 6227451, Ⓗ ☎ 6227000. **Town** V, R, ⊠, Ⓑ, ⇌ (Goes), ✈ (Antwerpen).

YERSEKE: Leave to port the preferred chan buoy at hbr ent. ☸☸☸◊◊✿✿. Hr Mr VHF Ch 09. Both marinas are S of the outer FV hbr: **Prinses Beatrix Haven** ☎ (0113) 571726, €1.07, 1·6m, FW, D, BH (10 ton); **Services:** SM, Sh, El, Dr ☎ 571444. **Town** V, R, ⊠, Ⓑ, ⇌ (Kruiningen-Yerseke), ✈ .

STAVENISSE: Hr Mr ☎ (0166) 692815. ☸☸◊◊✿. **Marina** at end of hbr canal (access HW±3 for 1·8m draft), Slip, FW, P & D (cans), Sh, C (4 5 ton), V, Gaz.

ST ANNALAND: **WV St Annaland** Hr Mr ☎ (0166) 652783, ☸☸☸◊◊◊✿✿, €0.91, AC, FW, ⛢; **YC** ☎ 652634, VHF Ch31, ▣, Bar, R; Dr ☎ 652400. **Services:** ME, P, D, Sh, El, CH, BH (25 ton), Gaz, BY. **Town** V, R, Ⓑ, ⊠, ⇌ (Bergen op Zoom), ✈ (Antwerpen).

BRUINISSE: via lock (Ch 20) to Grevelingenmeer ☸☸☸◊◊◊✿✿. **WV 'Bru'** Hr Mr ☎ (0111) 481506, €0.91, FW **Jachthaven Bruinisse** Hr Mr ☎ 481485, €1.00, FW, AC, P, D Slip, ▣, Gaz, Bar, V; **Services:** ME, Sh, C (16 ton). MHW = NAP + 1.53m; Dr ☎ 481280. **Town** ⊠, Ⓑ, ✈ (Rotterdam).

ZIERIKZEE: ☸☸☸◊◊◊✿✿✿. Hr Mr ☎ (0111) 413174; **Haven 't Luitje** and **Nieuwe Haven: WV Zierikzee** Hr Mr ☎ 414877, €0.90 FW, AC; Note: For yachts >15m LOA pre-arrange berth with H Mr, Jun-Aug; **Services:** P, D, Gaz, C (18 ton), ME, Sh, SM, CH **Town** Dr 412080, Ⓗ 416900, ▣, V, R, ⊠, Ⓑ, ✈ (Rotterdam).

BURGHSLUIS: ☸☸☸◊✿. Hr Mr ☎ (0111) 653114; **Jachthave**n €0.65, FW, AC, C (6 ton), ME. Facilities at Burg-Haamstede P, D Gaz, ⊠, Ⓑ, ✈ (Rotterdam).

NEELTJE JANS: ☸☸☸◊✿✿✿. Hr Mr ☎ (0113) 374225. Ⓥ jetty in Beton Haven, €0.54. **Delta Expo** worth visiting.

TOWNS ON THE VEERSE MEER (non-tidal). Various moorings at the islets/jetties are now free. Normal dues apply at towns below:

KORTGENE: ☸☸☸◊◊◊✿✿. Hr Mr and **Delta Marina** ☎ (0113 301315, €1.25, P, D, FW, AC, CH, El, ▣, ⛢, ME, R, Sh, SM, V, C (16 ton). **Town** Dr ☎ 301319, V, R, Bar, ⊠, Ⓑ, ⇌ (Goes), ✈ (Rotterdam).

WOLPHAARTSDIJK: **WV Wolphaartsdijk (WVW)** ☸☸☸◊◊◊✿✿ Hr Mr ☎ (0113) 581565, €0.57, P & D, C (20 ton), ▣, ⛢; **Royal YC Belgique (RYCB)** ☎ 581496, f1.50, P & D, Sh.

DE PIET: ☸☸☸◊✿✿✿. There are 72m of pontoons for small craft; 4 other little havens around De Omloop.

ARNEMUIDEN: ☸☸☸◊✿✿. **Jachthaven Oranjeplaat** Hr Mr ☎ (0118) 501248, €0.68, Slip, P & D, C (12 ton), ⇌.

VEERE: ☸☸☸◊◊◊✿✿✿. Yacht berths at: **Jachtclub Veere** in the Stadshaven, very busy, ☎ (0118) 501246, €0.91, FW, AC; **Marina Veere** on canal side, ☎ 501553, €0.91, FW, AC; **Jachtwerf Oostwatering,** ☎ 501665, €0.82, FW, AC, ▣; **WV Arne**, at Oostwatering – report at Ⓥ jetty, ☎ 501484, €0.64 FW, AC. **Town** Dr ☎ 501271, V, R, Bar, ⊠, Ⓑ, ⇌ (Middelburg), ✈ (Rotterdam).

MIDDELBURG: (This town is about 3M S of Veere on the Walcheren canal to Vlissingen). ☸☸☸◊◊✿✿✿. No mooring in Kanaal door Walcheren. All bridges & Veere lock: Ch 22. **WV Arne** fronts onto 1st Binnenhven (visitors) and backs onto the Dockhaven, ☎ (0118) 627180, €0.88, R, FW, AC, ME, El, Sh, SM, ▣; **Services:** D, Gaz, CH, BY, AC, Sh, Slip. **Town** Dr ☎ 612637; Ⓗ ☎ 625555; V, R, Bar, ⊠, Ⓑ, ⇌, ✈ (Rotterdam).

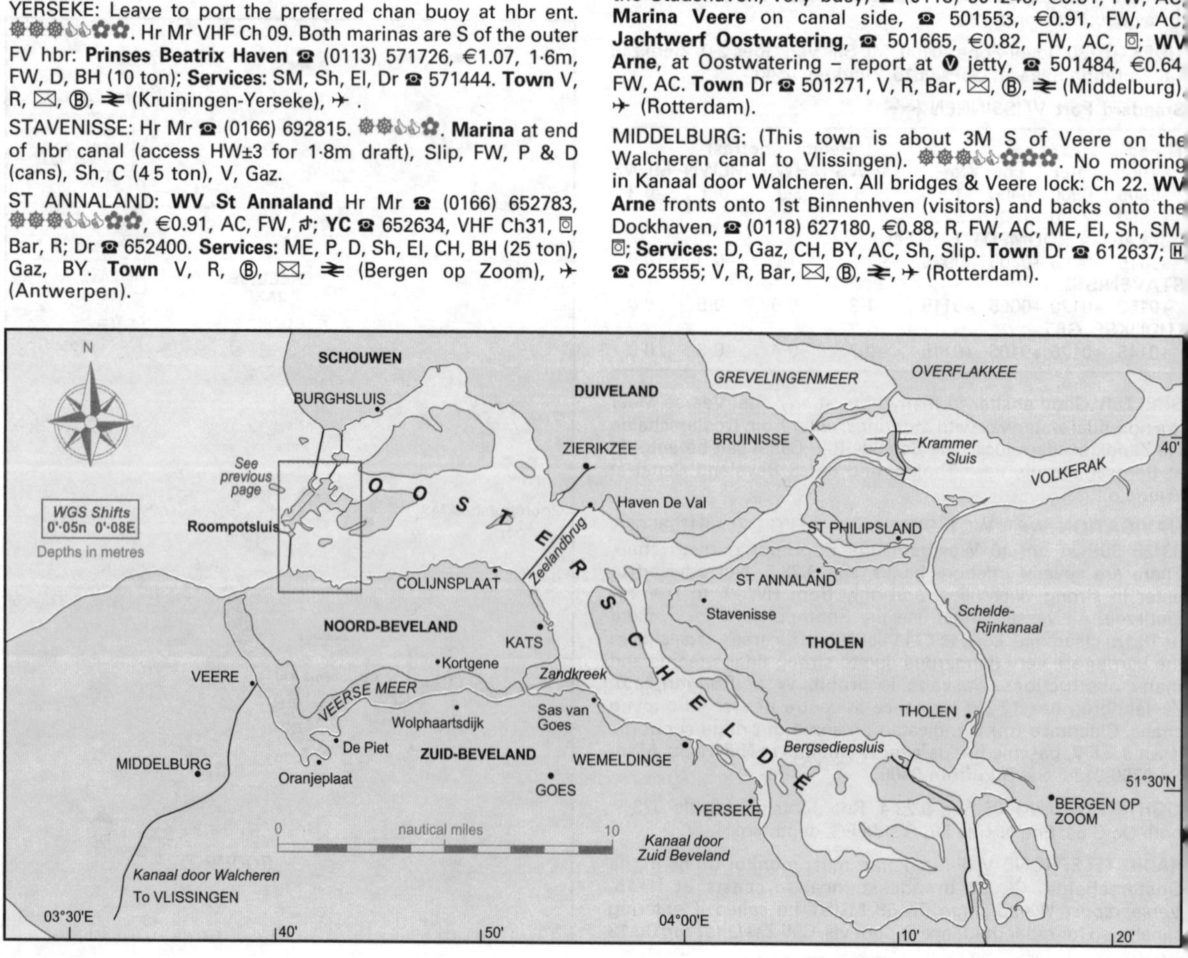

;TELLENDAM & HELLEVOETSLUIS *9.23.19*

uid Holland **51°49'·88N 04°02'·10E**
;tellendam) ✿✿◊✿; (Hellevoetsluis) ✿✿✿◊◊◊✿✿✿

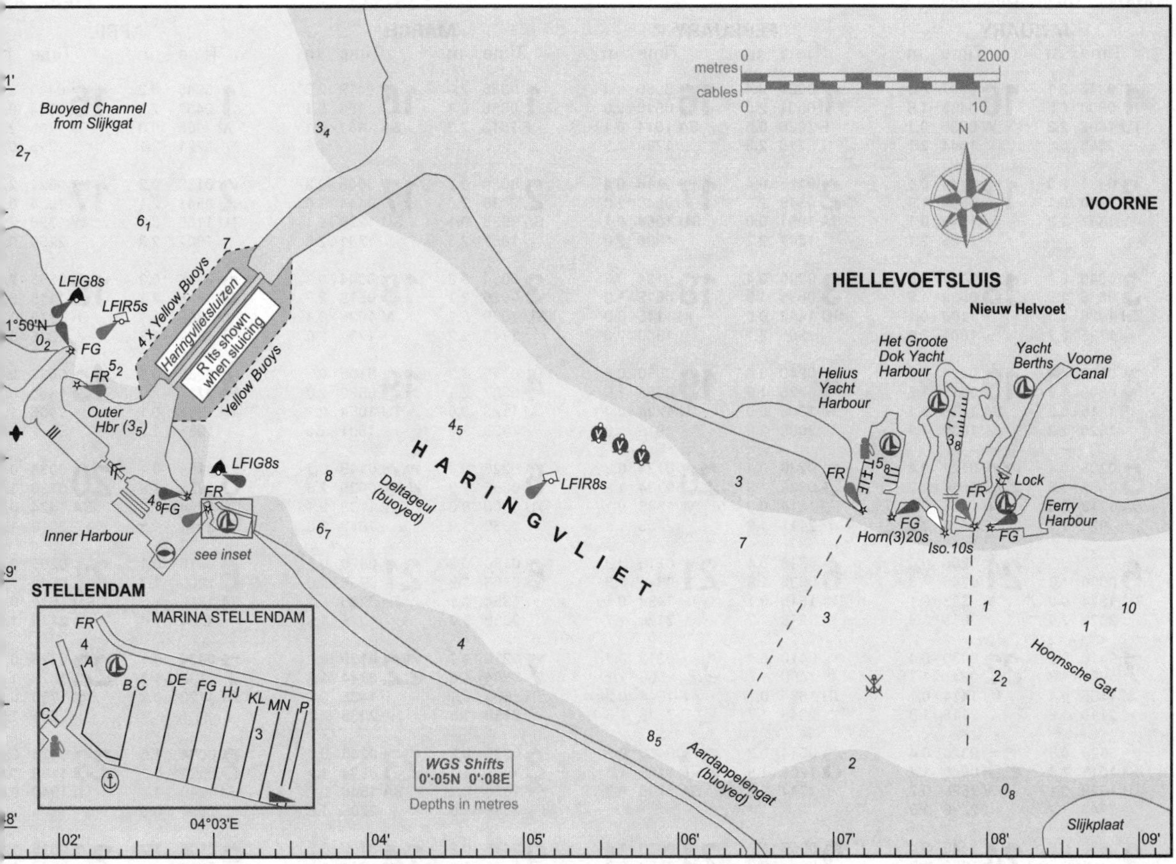

HARTS AC 2322; Zeekaart 1447, 1448; DYC 1801.6, 1807.6; nray C30; Stanfords 19

IDES +0300 Dover; ML 1·2; Duration 0510; Zone –0100

tandard Port VLISSINGEN (⟵)

imes				Height (metres)			
High Water		Low Water		MHWS	MHWN	MLWN	MLWS
0300	0900	0400	1000	4·8	3·9	0·9	0·3
1500	2100	1600	2200				
ifferences HARINGVLIETSLUIZEN							
+0015	+0015	+0015	–0020	–1·8	–1·6	–0·5	0·0

IOTE: Double LWs occur. The rise after the 1st LW is called the gger. Water levels on this coast are much affected by weather. rolonged NW gales can raise levels by up to 3m.

HELTER Good in Stellendam marina, beyond the lock and the ner hbr; or go 3M to Hellevoetsluis for one of the 3 yacht hbrs: leliushaven (1·9-5m); via swing bridge into Het Groote Dok (2-4m); nd via lock into the Voorne canal (2·8-4·8m). In the Haringvliet there re about 6 large pontoons (*vlot* on the DYC) equipped for barbecue icnics; but they are prone to wash and only useable in calm onditions. Within 10M upstream of Hellevoetsluis there are good acht facilities on the S bank at Middelharnis, Stad aan't Haringvliet nd Den Bommel; on the N bank at YC De Put (Vuile Gat) and Hitsertse ade. If bound for Rotterdam, proceed via Spui or Dordrecht.

IAVIGATION WPT Slijkgat SG SWM buoy, Iso 4s, 51°52'·00N 3°51'·50E, 290°/110° from/to Kwade Hoek lt, 5·0M. From the N, the iat van de Hawk chan to Stellendam lock is no longer buoyed nd is dangerous due to long-term WIP south of Maasvlakte. It s therefore best to take the well buoyed/lit Slijkgat chan along he Goeree shore, but it is dangerous to enter Slijkgat in strong W/NW winds. Beware a shoal about 5ca from the lock, marked by SHM buoys. Keep clear of dam during sluicing.

Lock and lifting bridge operate H24 throughout the year. Within the Haringvliet the 3M leg to Hellevoetsluis is well marked by 10 PHM buoys (DG2 to DG18 and HV2); only DG16 is lit as on chartlet. The SW side of the Haringvliet has 6 SHM buoys (DG1-11) leading to the well buoyed, but unlit Aardappelengat chan (S of Slijkplaat) and the ent to Middelharnis.

LIGHTS AND MARKS Haringvlietsluizen sluicing sigs: 3 ● in △, shown from pier heads on dam; danger area marked by small Y buoys. Hellevoetsluis lt Iso WRG 8s 16m 11/7M, W stone tr, R cupola. G shore-275°, W275°-294°, R294°-316°, W316°-036°, G036°-058°, W058°-095°, R096°-shore.

RADIO TELEPHONE For lock call: *Goereese Sluis* VHF Ch 20. Hellevoetsluis Hr Mr and Middelharnis Hr Mr: Ch 74.

TELEPHONE (Dial codes: 0187 Stellendam; 0181 Hellevoetsluis) Hr Mr Stellendam 491000, Hellevoetsluis 330911; ⊖ Rotterdam (010) 4298088 or Vlissingen (0118) 484600; Police, Fire, Ambulance 112; Brit Consul (020) 6764343.

FACILITIES

STELLENDAM (0187) **Stellendam Marina** ☎ 493769, 📠 493807, €1.36 (70/175 berths inc Ⓥ, eventually 400). FW, AC, Fuel, Slip, C, Bar, R, V. **Town** V, R, Bar, ✉ (2½ km), ✈ (Rotterdam).

HELLEVOETSLUIS (0181) **Marina, Het Groote Dok** ☎ 312166, €0.79, swing bridge opens every H in daylight from 0800 in summer; waiting pontoons are downstream. El, Gaz, FW, ME, CH, R, Bar, V; **Helius Haven YC** ☎ 315868, AB €0.79, P, D, FW; **Voorne Canal YC** ☎ 315476, AB f1.75, P, D, FW; **Services:** CH, El, ME. **Town** P, D, V, R, Bar, ✉, Ⓑ, ✈ (Rotterdam). Ferry: Hook of Holland-Harwich; or Rotterdam-Hull. Bus to Vlissingen and Spijkenisse.

23

Note - Double LWs often occur. The predictio
are for the lower LW which is usually the first.

TIME ZONE -0100
(Dutch Standard Time)
Subtract 1 hour for UT
For Dutch Summer Time add ONE hour in **non-shaded areas**

NETHERLANDS – HOEK VAN HOLLAND

LAT 51°59′N LONG 4°06′E

TIMES AND HEIGHTS OF HIGH AND LOW WATERS

SPRING & NEAP TIDES
Dates in red are **SPRINGS**
Dates in blue are **NEAPS**

YEAR 20

JANUARY

Day	Time	m	Day	Time	m
1	0346	2.1	16	0007	0.5
	0900	0.2		0435	1.9
TU	1602	2.3	W	0939	0.1
	2345	0.4		1644	2.1
2	0431	2.0	17	0044	0.5
	0940	0.1		0504	1.9
W	1647	2.3	TH	1015	0.1
				1725	2.1
3	0046	0.4	18	0124	0.5
	0515	1.9		0539	1.9
TH	1026	0.1	F	1100	0.1
	1735	2.2		1801	2.0
4	0136	0.4	19	0124	0.5
	0605	1.9		0615	1.9
F	1115	0.0	SA	1135	0.1
	1825	2.2		1839	1.9
5	0205	0.4	20	0127	0.4
	0655	1.8		0656	1.9
SA	1213	0.0	SU	1225	0.1
	1925	2.1		1925	1.9
6	0307	0.5	21	0200	0.4
	0800	1.8		0740	1.8
SU	1324	0.0	M	1325	0.1
	2025	2.0		2015	1.8
7	0410	0.5	22	0230	0.4
	0905	1.8		0847	1.7
M	1435	0.1	TU	1414	0.1
	2145	1.9		2116	1.8
8	0524	0.5	23	0324	0.4
	1015	1.8		0945	1.7
TU	1539	0.1	W	1520	0.2
	2244	1.9		2226	1.8
9	0630	0.5	24	0440	0.4
	1115	1.8		1056	1.7
W	1650	0.2	TH	1625	0.2
	2355	1.9		2319	1.8
10	0740	0.4	25	0540	0.4
	1220	1.9		1156	1.7
TH	2000	0.2	F	1740	0.3
11	0056	1.9	26	0025	1.8
	0850	0.4		0620	0.3
F	1311	2.0	SA	1245	1.9
	2040	0.3		1825	0.3
12	0145	1.9	27	0120	1.9
	0937	0.3		0644	0.3
SA	1405	2.0	SU	1335	2.0
	2130	0.4		1904	0.3
13	0234	1.9	28	0205	1.9
	1030	0.3		0724	0.3
SU	1449	2.1	M	1421	2.1
	● 2240	0.4		○ 1945	0.3
14	0325	2.0	29	0249	2.0
	0824	0.2		0754	0.2
M	1531	2.1	TU	1505	2.2
	2330	0.4		2255	0.4
15	0405	2.0	30	0330	2.0
	0859	0.2		0840	0.1
TU	1615	2.1	W	1547	2.3
				2350	0.4
			31	0415	2.0
				0919	0.0
			TH	1636	2.3

FEBRUARY

Day	Time	m	Day	Time	m
1	0035	0.4	16	0050	0.4
	0501	2.0		0518	2.0
F	1006	0.0	SA	1014	0.1
	1718	2.3		1736	2.0
2	0115	0.4	17	0116	0.4
	0545	2.0		0545	2.0
SA	1051	0.0	SU	1054	0.1
	1807	2.2		1806	2.0
3	0200	0.4	18	0134	0.3
	0635	1.9		0619	1.9
SU	1144	0.0	M	1145	0.0
	1906	2.1		1840	2.0
4	0240	0.4	19	0050	0.3
	0725	1.9		0655	1.9
M	1305	0.0	TU	1224	0.0
	2005	2.0		1915	1.9
5	0230	0.4	20	0134	0.3
	0830	1.9		0734	1.8
TU	1414	0.0	W	1345	0.1
	2111	1.9		2003	1.8
6	0310	0.4	21	0215	0.3
	0936	1.8		0845	1.8
W	1515	0.1	TH	1434	0.1
	2213	1.7		2126	1.7
7	0410	0.4	22	0315	0.3
	1050	1.8		1006	1.7
TH	1634	0.2	F	1544	0.2
	2346	1.7		2246	1.6
8	0514	0.3	23	0450	0.3
	1205	1.8		1125	1.7
F	1744	0.3	SA	1705	0.3
9	0056	1.7	24	0000	1.6
	0604	0.3		0550	0.3
SA	1305	1.9	SU	1230	1.8
	2125	0.3		1820	0.3
10	0135	1.8	25	0059	1.7
	0940	0.2		0625	0.2
SU	1354	2.0	M	1326	2.0
	2210	0.3		2115	0.3
11	0234	1.9	26	0149	1.8
	1030	0.2		0655	0.2
M	1445	2.0	TU	1405	2.1
	2255	0.4		2214	0.3
12	0320	1.9	27	0236	1.9
	0814	0.2		0735	0.1
TU	1519	2.1	W	1447	2.2
	● 2320	0.4		○ 2245	0.3
13	0349	1.9	28	0315	2.0
	0845	0.1		0818	0.0
W	1556	2.1	TH	1531	2.3
	2355	0.4		2335	0.3
14	0415	1.9			
	0915	0.1			
TH	1629	2.1			
15	0030	0.4			
	0445	2.0			
F	0945	0.1			
	1706	2.1			

MARCH

Day	Time	m	Day	Time	m
1	0355	2.0	16	0419	2.0
	0856	-0.1		1154	0.1
F	1613	2.3	SA	1631	2.1
2	0026	0.3	17	0005	0.3
	0438	2.0		0444	2.0
SA	0939	-0.1	SU	1224	0.1
	1657	2.3		1701	2.0
3	0054	0.3	18	0044	0.3
	0525	2.1		0519	2.0
SU	1029	-0.1	M	1026	0.1
	1746	2.2		1731	2.0
4	0145	0.3	19	0105	0.3
	0607	2.1		0550	2.0
M	1123	0.0	TU	1054	0.1
	1835	2.0		1801	2.0
5	0225	0.3	20	0145	0.2
	0655	2.0		0625	2.0
TU	1300	0.0	W	1133	0.1
	1930	1.9		1842	2.0
6	0130	0.3	21	0000	0.2
	0756	1.9		0705	2.0
W	1354	0.1	TH	1235	0.1
	2030	1.7		1925	1.8
7	0230	0.2	22	0120	0.2
	0854	1.8		0744	1.8
TH	1504	0.1	F	1436	0.1
	2150	1.6		2035	1.7
8	0335	0.2	23	0245	0.2
	1025	1.7		0904	1.7
F	1624	0.2	SA	1546	0.2
	2319	1.5		2205	1.5
9	0445	0.2	24	0400	0.2
	1144	1.7		1044	1.7
SA	1724	0.3	SU	1700	0.3
				2336	1.5
10	0036	1.6	25	0504	0.2
	0555	0.2		1203	1.8
SU	1300	1.9	M	2006	0.3
	2104	0.3			
11	0130	1.7	26	0040	1.6
	0914	0.1		0555	0.1
M	1356	2.0	TU	1305	2.0
	2200	0.3		2110	0.2
12	0213	1.8	27	0125	1.7
	1005	0.1		0636	0.1
TU	1429	2.0	W	1345	2.1
	2225	0.3		2206	0.2
13	0255	1.9	28	0215	1.9
	1055	0.1		0716	0.0
W	1459	2.0	TH	1427	2.2
	2257	0.3		○ 2225	0.3
14	0325	1.9	29	0250	2.0
	0830	0.1		0749	-0.1
TH	1529	2.1	F	1507	2.3
	● 2336	0.3		2315	0.3
15	0344	1.9	30	0332	2.0
	0843	0.1		0836	-0.1
F	1558	2.1	SA	1552	2.3
	2350	0.3			
			31	0000	0.3
				0416	2.1
			SU	0918	-0.1
				1636	2.2

APRIL

Day	Time	m	Day	Time	m
1	0045	0.2	16	0449	2.
	0457	2.1		1234	0.
M	1005	0.0	TU	1705	2.
	1721	2.1		2215	0.
2	0135	0.2	17	0521	2.
	0541	2.1		1024	0.
TU	1105	0.1	W	1738	2.
	1807	2.0		2250	0.
3	0215	0.2	18	0555	2.
	0625	2.1		1115	0.
W	1300	0.1	TH	1815	1.
	1855	1.8		2335	0.
4	0035	0.1	19	0636	2.
	0725	2.0		1350	0.
TH	1354	0.1	F	1906	1.
	1955	1.6			
5	0154	0.1	20	0034	0.
	0823	1.8		0730	1.
F	1454	0.2	SA	1424	0.
	2114	1.5		2010	1.
6	0315	0.1	21	0205	0.
	1005	1.7		0844	1.
SA	1616	0.3	SU	1530	0.
	2254	1.4		2145	1.
7	0434	0.1	22	0325	0.
	1135	1.7		1023	1.
SU	1720	0.3	M	1750	0.
				2305	1.
8	0004	1.5	23	0424	0.
	0524	0.1		1139	1.
M	1240	1.8	TU	1940	0.
	2020	0.3			
9	0106	1.7	24	0015	1.
	0613	0.1		0526	0.
TU	1325	1.9	W	1235	2.
	2115	0.2		2056	0.
10	0155	1.8	25	0101	1.
	0945	0.1		0606	0.
W	1405	2.0	TH	1321	2.1
	2216	0.2		2125	0.
11	0223	1.8	26	0148	1.
	0739	0.1		0648	0.
TH	1436	2.0	F	1406	2.2
	2240	0.3		2216	0.3
12	0256	1.9	27	0229	2.
	0810	0.1		0725	0.
F	1458	2.0	SA	1447	2.2
	● 2304	0.3		○ 2255	0.3
13	0319	1.9	28	0309	2.1
	1030	0.1		0812	0.
SA	1531	2.1	SU	1531	2.2
	2310	0.3		2031	0.2
14	0349	2.0	29	0350	2.1
	1115	0.1		0855	0.
SU	1606	2.1	M	1615	2.1
	2335	0.2		2118	0.2
15	0419	2.0	30	0436	2.1
	1205	0.1		1306	0.1
M	1631	2.0	TU	1658	2.0
	2135	0.2		2205	0.1

Chart Datum: 0·84 metres below NAP Datum

Register for your **FREE** weekly weather email service from Macmillan Reeds
at **www.nauticaldata.com – NOW!**
weekend weather reports sent to your email address, every Thursday

Note - Double LWs often occur. The predictions are for the lower LW which is usually the first.

TIME ZONE -0100
(Dutch Standard Time)
Subtract 1 hour for UT
For Dutch Summer Time add ONE hour in **non-shaded areas**

NETHERLANDS – HOEK VAN HOLLAND

LAT 51°59′N LONG 4°06′E

TIMES AND HEIGHTS OF HIGH AND LOW WATERS

SPRING & NEAP TIDES
Dates in red are SPRINGS
Dates in blue are NEAPS

YEAR **2002**

MAY

Day	Time	m	Time	m	Time	m	Time	m
1 W	0519	2.1	1334	0.1	1745	1.9	2300	0.1
2 TH	0606	2.1	1425	0.2	1835	1.7		
3 F	0005	0.0	0654	1.9	1344	0.2	1925	1.6
4 SA	0115	0.0	0805	1.8	1435	0.3	2035	1.5
5 SU	0257	0.0	0930	1.7	1550	0.3	2215	1.4
6 M	0404	0.0	1054	1.7	1650	0.3	2336	1.5
7 TU	0510	0.0	1159	1.8	1830	0.3		
8 W	0024	1.6	0554	0.0	1250	1.9	2030	0.3
9 TH	0115	1.7	0634	0.1	1325	1.9	2115	0.2
10 F	0144	1.8	0730	0.1	1354	2.0	2215	0.2
11 SA	0215	1.8	0830	0.2	1429	2.0	2240	0.2
12 SU	0248	1.9	1000	0.2	1459	2.0	● 2250	0.2
13 M	0320	2.0	1047	0.2	1531	2.0	2320	0.2
14 TU	0356	2.0	1125	0.2	1605	2.0	2354	0.2
15 W	0425	2.0	1215	0.2	1641	2.0	2155	0.2
16 TH	0459	2.0	1244	0.2	1720	1.9	2229	0.1
17 F	0538	2.1	1315	0.2	1759	1.8	2319	0.0
18 SA	0626	2.0	1400	0.2	1849	1.7		
19 SU	0025	0.0	0716	1.9	1440	0.3	1955	1.5
20 M	0144	0.0	0840	1.8	1557	0.3	2125	1.5
21 TU	0255	0.0	1006	1.9	1737	0.3	2240	1.5
22 W	0345	0.0	1116	1.9	1855	0.3	2346	1.6
23 TH	0450	0.0	1204	2.0	2005	0.3		
24 F	0038	1.7	0534	0.0	1256	2.1	2105	0.3
25 SA	0125	1.9	0626	0.0	1345	2.1	2145	0.3
26 SU	0205	2.0	0709	0.1	1427	2.1	○ 1936	0.2
27 M	0248	2.1	0755	0.1	1512	2.0	2015	0.2
28 TU	0336	2.1	1134	0.2	1558	2.0	2059	0.1
29 W	0417	2.1	1235	0.2	1645	1.9	2150	0.1
30 TH	0501	2.1	1335	0.2	1725	1.8	2239	0.0
31 F	0545	2.0	1416	0.3	1815	1.7	2334	0.0

JUNE

Day	Time	m	Time	m	Time	m	Time	m
1 SA	0634	1.9	1455	0.3	1906	1.6		
2 SU	0045	0.0	0740	1.8	1430	0.4	1955	1.5
3 M	0220	0.0	0846	1.7	1517	0.4	2106	1.5
4 TU	0334	0.0	0955	1.7	1620	0.3	2245	1.4
5 W	0435	0.0	1105	1.7	1710	0.3	2346	1.5
6 TH	0524	0.1	1206	1.8	1744	0.3		
7 F	0025	1.6	0620	0.1	1256	1.9	1824	0.3
8 SA	0105	1.7	0700	0.1	1326	1.9	1915	0.2
9 SU	0135	1.8	0730	0.2	1354	1.9	1940	0.2
10 M	0215	1.9	0734	0.2	1428	2.0	1955	0.2
11 TU	0249	2.0	0805	0.3	1509	2.0	● 2029	0.2
12 W	0325	2.0	1107	0.3	1548	2.0	2105	0.2
13 TH	0406	2.1	1145	0.3	1625	1.9	2134	0.1
14 F	0445	2.1	1224	0.3	1705	1.8	2225	0.1
15 SA	0526	2.1	1326	0.3	1749	1.8	2315	0.0
16 SU	0611	2.0	1410	0.3	1845	1.7		
17 M	0005	0.0	0705	2.0	1457	0.3	1945	1.6
18 TU	0120	0.0	0826	1.9	1557	0.3	2100	1.6
19 W	0215	0.0	0935	1.9	1705	0.3	2210	1.6
20 TH	0325	0.0	1035	1.9	1835	0.3	2316	1.7
21 F	0425	0.0	1145	2.0	1930	0.3		
22 SA	0005	1.8	0525	0.1	1238	2.0	2030	0.3
23 SU	0102	1.9	0614	0.1	1329	2.0	2120	0.3
24 M	0149	2.0	0704	0.2	1416	2.0	○ 1925	0.2
25 TU	0235	2.0	1020	0.3	1505	1.9	2004	0.2
26 W	0318	2.1	1125	0.3	1548	1.9	2056	0.1
27 TH	0406	2.1	1226	0.3	1635	1.9	2135	0.1
28 F	0449	2.1	1316	0.4	1715	1.8	2225	0.0
29 SA	0531	2.0	1355	0.4	1751	1.8	2314	0.0
30 SU	0614	1.9	1435	0.4	1836	1.7		

JULY

Day	Time	m	Time	m	Time	m	Time	m
1 M	0004	0.0	0705	1.9	1420	0.4	1926	1.7
2 TU	0110	0.0	0800	1.8	1450	0.4	2005	1.6
3 W	0230	0.1	0856	1.7	1534	0.3	2104	1.6
4 TH	0406	0.1	0944	1.7	1624	0.3	2215	1.6
5 F	0445	0.1	1100	1.7	1704	0.3	2315	1.6
6 SA	0544	0.2	1205	1.8	1755	0.3		
7 SU	0015	1.7	0620	0.2	1246	1.8	1835	0.3
8 M	0101	1.8	0650	0.3	1325	1.9	1914	0.3
9 TU	0146	1.9	0715	0.3	1405	1.9	1939	0.2
10 W	0226	2.0	0745	0.3	1449	1.9	● 2010	0.2
11 TH	0305	2.1	0824	0.4	1528	1.9	2045	0.1
12 F	0347	2.1	1140	0.4	1611	1.9	2114	0.1
13 SA	0429	2.2	1230	0.3	1655	1.9	2159	0.0
14 SU	0515	2.2	1304	0.3	1738	1.8	2245	0.0
15 M	0601	2.1	1354	0.3	1829	1.8	2339	0.0
16 TU	0656	2.1	1456	0.4	1925	1.7		
17 W	0049	0.0	0755	2.0	1525	0.4	2030	1.7
18 TH	0154	0.0	0905	1.9	1627	0.4	2136	1.7
19 F	0255	0.0	1004	1.9	1730	0.4	2246	1.7
20 SA	0409	0.1	1120	1.9	1844	0.4	2348	1.8
21 SU	0520	0.2	1226	1.8	2000	0.3		
22 M	0046	1.9	0814	0.3	1319	1.9	1835	0.3
23 TU	0139	2.0	0920	0.3	1415	1.9	1924	0.2
24 W	0224	2.0	1030	0.4	1459	1.9	○ 2005	0.2
25 TH	0315	2.1	1105	0.4	1545	1.9	2045	0.1
26 F	0350	2.1	1154	0.5	1614	1.9	2119	0.1
27 SA	0435	2.1	1256	0.5	1655	1.9	2200	0.1
28 SU	0508	2.1	1336	0.5	1729	1.9	2235	0.1
29 M	0549	2.0	1405	0.5	1805	1.9	2325	0.1
30 TU	0629	1.9	1400	0.5	1845	1.8		
31 W	0015	0.1	0709	1.9	1400	0.4	1925	1.8

AUGUST

Day	Time	m	Time	m	Time	m	Time	m
1 TH	0104	0.1	0806	1.8	1440	0.4	2026	1.7
2 F	0154	0.1	0845	1.8	1520	0.4	2115	1.7
3 SA	0255	0.2	0950	1.7	1640	0.4	2226	1.6
4 SU	0430	0.3	1055	1.7	1734	0.3	2329	1.7
5 M	0550	0.3	1205	1.7	1814	0.3		
6 TU	0031	1.8	0630	0.3	1306	1.8	1845	0.3
7 W	0125	1.9	0700	0.3	1349	1.9	1915	0.3
8 TH	0208	2.0	0729	0.4	1431	1.9	● 1945	0.2
9 F	0249	2.2	0805	0.4	1515	2.0	2019	0.1
10 SA	0332	2.2	1130	0.4	1555	2.0	2058	0.0
11 SU	0412	2.3	1204	0.4	1635	2.0	2139	0.0
12 M	0455	2.3	1255	0.4	1721	2.0	2225	0.0
13 TU	0541	2.2	1334	0.4	1808	1.9	2315	0.0
14 W	0635	2.1	1415	0.4	1855	1.9		
15 TH	0025	0.0	0725	2.0	1510	0.4	1956	1.9
16 F	0145	0.1	0830	1.9	1450	0.4	2100	1.8
17 SA	0255	0.1	0940	1.8	1540	0.4	2215	1.8
18 SU	0405	0.2	1054	1.7	1650	0.4	2325	1.8
19 M	0514	0.3	1216	1.7	1745	0.3		
20 TU	0035	1.9	0850	0.4	1313	1.8	2116	0.3
21 W	0140	2.0	0945	0.4	1409	1.9	2205	0.2
22 TH	0223	2.1	1034	0.4	1455	1.9	○ 1955	0.2
23 F	0305	2.1	1055	0.5	1524	1.9	2025	0.2
24 SA	0339	2.1	1145	0.5	1606	2.0	2100	0.1
25 SU	0411	2.1	1220	0.5	1635	2.0	2124	0.1
26 M	0445	2.1	1245	0.5	1705	2.0	2159	0.1
27 TU	0519	2.1	1320	0.5	1735	2.0	2239	0.2
28 W	0555	2.0	1340	0.5	1808	2.0	2325	0.2
29 TH	0626	2.0	1200	0.4	1839	1.9		
30 F	0004	0.2	0700	1.9	1304	0.4	1913	1.9
31 SA	0114	0.2	0739	1.9	1400	0.4	2010	1.8

Chart Datum: 0·84 metres below NAP Datum

Register for your FREE weekly weather email service from Macmillan Reeds
» at www.nauticaldata.com – NOW! «
weekend weather reports sent to your email address, every Thursday

Note - Double LWs often occur. The predictions are for the lower LW which is usually the first.

TIME ZONE -0100
(Dutch Standard Time)
Subtract 1 hour for UT
For Dutch Summer Time add ONE hour in **non-shaded areas**

NETHERLANDS – HOEK VAN HOLLAND

LAT 51°59′N LONG 4°06′E

TIMES AND HEIGHTS OF HIGH AND LOW WATERS

SPRING & NEAP TIDES
Dates in red are **SPRINGS**
Dates in blue are **NEAPS**

YEAR 200

SEPTEMBER

Day	Time	m	Day	Time	m
1 SU	0220	0.2	16 M	0345	0.4
	0856	1.8		1050	1.6
	1455	0.4		1630	0.3
	2124	1.7		2326	1.8
2 M	0325	0.3	17 TU	0640	0.4
	1010	1.7		1206	1.7
	1700	0.4		1724	0.3
	2255	1.7			
3 TU	0510	0.4	18 W	0035	1.9
	1124	1.6		0827	0.4
	1754	0.4		1306	1.8
				2045	0.2
4 W	0010	1.8	19 TH	0123	2.1
	0620	0.4		0945	0.4
	1240	1.7		1356	1.9
	1815	0.3		2155	0.2
5 TH	0105	2.0	20 F	0204	2.1
	0905	0.4		1024	0.4
	1324	1.8		1433	2.0
	1844	0.3		2234	0.2
6 F	0145	2.1	21 SA	0245	2.2
	1006	0.4		1050	0.5
	1408	1.9		1504	2.0
	1919	0.2		○ 2004	0.2
7 SA	0225	2.3	22 SU	0315	2.2
	1025	0.4		1114	0.5
	1451	2.0		1535	2.0
	● 1955	0.1		2035	0.2
8 SU	0308	2.4	23 M	0348	2.2
	1105	0.5		1150	0.5
	1536	2.1		1605	2.1
	2031	0.0		2054	0.2
9 M	0351	2.4	24 TU	0419	2.2
	1155	0.5		1220	0.5
	1613	2.1		1635	2.1
	2116	0.0		2124	0.2
10 TU	0436	2.3	25 W	0449	2.1
	1246	0.5		1250	0.4
	1657	2.1		1705	2.1
	2159	0.0		2206	0.3
11 W	0517	2.3	26 TH	0520	2.1
	1314	0.5		1019	0.4
	1741	2.1		1731	2.1
	2249	0.1		2240	0.2
12 TH	0605	2.1	27 F	0545	2.1
	1355	0.4		1100	0.4
	1826	2.1		1801	2.1
	2355	0.2		2315	0.2
13 F	0655	2.0	28 SA	0619	2.0
	1420	0.4		1134	0.3
	1919	2.0		1840	2.0
14 SA	0145	0.2	29 SU	0004	0.3
	0800	1.9		0659	2.0
	1400	0.4		1240	0.3
	2026	1.9		1925	1.9
15 SU	0240	0.3	30 M	0154	0.3
	0910	1.7		0756	1.8
	1505	0.4		1407	0.4
	2155	1.8		2024	1.8

OCTOBER

Day	Time	m	Day	Time	m
1 TU	0310	0.4	16 W	0625	0.5
	0915	1.6		1146	1.7
	1525	0.4		1704	0.3
	2214	1.7			
2 W	0440	0.4	17 TH	0004	2.0
	1106	1.6		0750	0.5
	1710	0.4		1234	1.8
	2334	1.9		2007	0.2
3 TH	0630	0.5	18 F	0105	2.1
	1215	1.7		0916	0.4
	1746	0.3		1330	1.9
				2125	0.2
4 F	0039	2.1	19 SA	0146	2.1
	0837	0.4		0956	0.4
	1305	1.8		1404	2.0
	1816	0.2		2216	0.2
5 SA	0125	2.2	20 SU	0215	2.2
	0946	0.4		1015	0.4
	1348	2.0		1439	2.0
	1856	0.1		1945	0.3
6 SU	0205	2.3	21 M	0249	2.2
	1026	0.5		1047	0.5
	1427	2.1		1505	2.1
	● 1930	0.1		○ 2004	0.3
7 M	0246	2.4	22 TU	0319	2.2
	0755	0.5		1126	0.5
	1509	2.2		1535	2.1
	2010	0.0		2035	0.3
8 TU	0328	2.4	23 W	0345	2.2
	0829	0.5		0855	0.4
	1549	2.2		1605	2.1
	2049	0.1		2059	0.3
9 W	0410	2.4	24 TH	0419	2.2
	0915	0.4		1210	0.4
	1632	2.3		1635	2.1
	2135	0.1		2136	0.3
10 TH	0455	2.2	25 F	0449	2.1
	0955	0.4		0953	0.4
	1716	2.3		1705	2.1
	2230	0.2		2210	0.3
11 F	0541	2.1	26 SA	0522	2.1
	1049	0.4		1036	0.3
	1801	2.2		1738	2.1
	2334	0.3		2245	0.3
12 SA	0629	2.0	27 SU	0555	2.0
	1145	0.3		1104	0.3
	1855	2.1		1816	2.1
				2324	0.4
13 SU	0136	0.3	28 M	0638	1.9
	0725	1.8		1155	0.3
	1320	0.3		1900	2.0
	2006	1.9			
14 M	0214	0.4	29 TU	0147	0.4
	0834	1.6		0730	1.8
	1444	0.3		1334	0.3
	2115	1.8		1959	1.9
15 TU	0334	0.5	30 W	0245	0.5
	1025	1.6		0906	1.6
	1605	0.3		1456	0.3
	2315	1.8		2156	1.8
			31 TH	0440	0.5
				1025	1.6
				1606	0.3
				2316	2.0

NOVEMBER

Day	Time	m	Day	Time	m
1 F	0654	0.5	16 SA	0029	2.0
	1139	1.7		0807	0.4
	1644	0.3		1256	1.8
				1830	0.2
2 SA	0015	2.1	17 SU	0116	2.1
	0825	0.4		0910	0.4
	1235	1.8		1336	1.9
	1739	0.2		1920	0.3
3 SU	0055	2.2	18 M	0150	2.1
	0904	0.4		0945	0.4
	1322	2.0		1406	2.0
	1825	0.1		1957	0.3
4 M	0142	2.3	19 TU	0214	2.1
	0956	0.5		1036	0.4
	1400	2.1		1435	2.0
	● 1905	0.1		2120	0.3
5 TU	0226	2.4	20 W	0249	2.1
	0729	0.4		0815	0.4
	1445	2.2		1501	2.1
	1945	0.1		○ 2220	0.4
6 W	0307	2.3	21 TH	0326	2.1
	0809	0.4		0834	0.4
	1527	2.3		1535	2.1
	2032	0.2		2310	0.4
7 TH	0351	2.3	22 F	0355	2.1
	0855	0.3		0905	0.4
	1611	2.3		1608	2.2
	2118	0.3		2356	0.4
8 F	0435	2.2	23 SA	0425	2.1
	0939	0.3		0945	0.3
	1656	2.3		1641	2.2
				2150	0.4
9 SA	0126	0.4	24 SU	0501	2.0
	0521	2.0		1014	0.3
	1029	0.3		1718	2.2
	1738	2.2		2235	0.4
10 SU	0157	0.4	25 M	0539	2.0
	0605	1.9		1055	0.2
	1125	0.2		1758	2.1
	1828	2.1			
11 M	0110	0.5	26 TU	0140	0.4
	0706	1.8		0626	1.9
	1234	0.2		1155	0.2
	1935	2.0		1845	2.1
12 TU	0155	0.5	27 W	0207	0.5
	0804	1.6		0720	1.8
	1355	0.2		1254	0.2
	2054	1.8		1949	2.0
13 W	0320	0.6	28 TH	0310	0.5
	0956	1.6		0835	1.6
	1540	0.2		1426	0.2
	2235	1.8		2126	1.9
14 TH	0537	0.5	29 F	0450	0.5
	1105	1.6		0955	1.6
	1634	0.2		1515	0.2
	2335	1.9		2235	2.0
15 F	0700	0.5	30 SA	0617	0.5
	1205	1.7		1110	1.7
	1746	0.2		1620	0.2
				2340	2.1

DECEMBER

Day	Time	m	Day	Time	m
1 SU	0735	0.5	16 M	0029	1.9
	1206	1.8		0614	0.4
	1709	0.2		1249	1.8
				1850	0.3
2 M	0029	2.2	17 TU	0116	2.0
	0846	0.4		0654	0.4
	1256	2.0		1330	1.9
	1755	0.2		1950	0.3
3 TU	0117	2.2	18 W	0149	2.0
	0915	0.4		0724	0.4
	1338	2.1		1406	1.9
	1845	0.2		2050	0.3
4 W	0205	2.2	19 TH	0226	2.0
	0715	0.4		0804	0.4
	1426	2.2		1435	2.0
	● 1935	0.2		○ 2150	0.4
5 TH	0251	2.2	20 F	0255	2.1
	0756	0.3		0824	0.3
	1509	2.3		1511	2.1
	2014	0.3		2240	0.4
6 F	0335	2.1	21 SA	0335	2.1
	0835	0.3		0855	0.3
	1556	2.3		1549	2.2
				2330	0.4
7 SA	0005	0.4	22 SU	0408	2.0
	0421	2.1		0925	0.2
	0925	0.2		1626	2.2
	1638	2.3			
8 SU	0106	0.4	23 M	0010	0.4
	0509	2.0		0449	2.0
	1015	0.2		1006	0.2
	1728	2.2		1706	2.2
9 M	0156	0.5	24 TU	0044	0.4
	0556	1.9		0529	1.9
	1115	0.1		1045	0.1
	1815	2.1		1745	2.2
10 TU	0227	0.5	25 W	0146	0.4
	0639	1.8		0616	1.8
	1205	0.1		1136	0.1
	1916	2.0		1838	2.1
11 W	0140	0.5	26 TH	0230	0.4
	0735	1.7		0710	1.8
	1324	0.1		1246	0.1
	2014	1.9		1934	2.0
12 TH	0235	0.5	27 F	0307	0.5
	0835	1.6		0816	1.7
	1450	0.2		1335	0.1
	2124	1.8		2055	2.0
13 F	0350	0.5	28 SA	0407	0.5
	1000	1.6		0919	1.7
	1610	0.2		1456	0.1
	2244	1.8		2205	2.0
14 SA	0435	0.5	29 SU	0527	0.5
	1125	1.6		1030	1.8
	1716	0.2		1556	0.1
	2350	1.9		2305	2.0
15 SU	0524	0.5	30 M	0650	0.5
	1205	1.7		1136	1.8
	1755	0.2		1650	0.2
			31 TU	0010	2.0
				0800	0.5
				1229	1.9
				1750	0.2

Chart Datum: 0·84 metres below NAP Datum

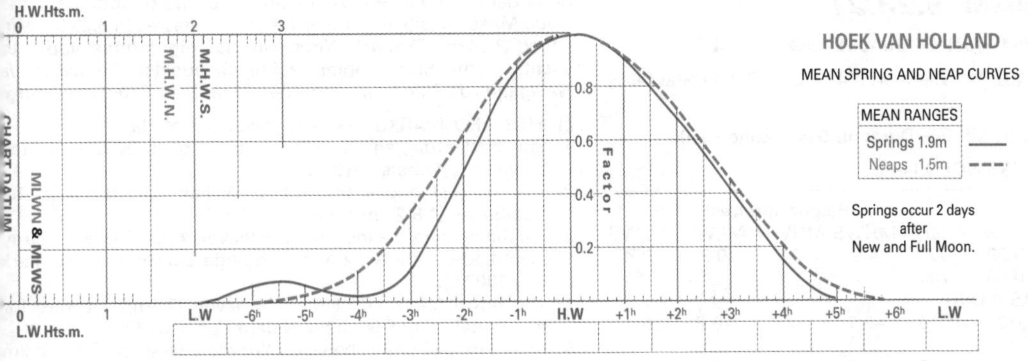

IOEK VAN HOLLAND *9.23.20*

'uid Holland **51°59'·50N 04°02'·78E** (Ent) ❀❀❀⚓⚓✿✿

:HARTS AC 132, 122; Zeekaart 1540, 1349, 1350, 1449; DYC 1809, 801; Imray C30, Y5; Stanfords 19

'IDES +0251 Dover; ML 0·9; Duration 0505; Zone –0100.
IOEK VAN HOLLAND is a Standard Port. Double LWs occur, nore obviously at sp; in effect a LW stand. Predictions are for the *ower* LW. The 1st LW is about 5½ hrs after HW and the 2nd LW bout 4¾ hrs before the next HW. The slight rise after the first LW s called the Agger. Water levels on this coast are much affected y the weather. Prolonged NW gales can raise the levels by up o 3m.

;HELTER Ent safe except in strong on-shore winds when eavy seas/swell develop. Berghaven hbr is closed to yachts; etter shelter at Maassluis (3m), 6M up river (km 1019).

NAVIGATION WPTs From S: MV-N NCM lt By, Q, 51°59'·66N)4°00'·29E, 288°/108° from/to Nieuwe Zuiderdam lt, 1·5M. From N: Indusbank NCM lt By, Q, 52°02'·93N 04°03'·72E, 010°/190° 'rom/to Nieuwe Noorderdam lt, 3·2M. There are no real navigational dangers but it is a very busy waterway with a constant stream of ocean-going and local ships. Keep clear of ships manoeuvering whilst transferring pilots.

Crossing the Entrance: To cross the Maasgeul (seaward of the okwtrs), yachts should call *Maas Ent* Ch 03, with position and course, and keep watch on Ch 03. Cross under power on a track,)30°/210°, close W of line joining buoys MV (51°57'·50N 03°58'·50E), MV-N (51°59'·65N 04°00'·30E) and Indusbank N (52°02'·93N)4°03'·72E). Beware the strong tidal set across the ent.

Rules for Yachts (in Nieuwe Waterweg): Comply with VTS (see R/T). Keep to extreme stbd limit of buoyed line avoiding debris between buoy and bank. No tacking/beating; no ⚓. Eng ready for instant start. Able to motor at 3.24kn (6km/hr). Hoist a radar reflector, esp in poor vis or at night. Cross chan quickly at 90°. Docks, inc the Calandkanaal/Beerkanaal (Europoort), are prohib to yachts, except for access to a marina.

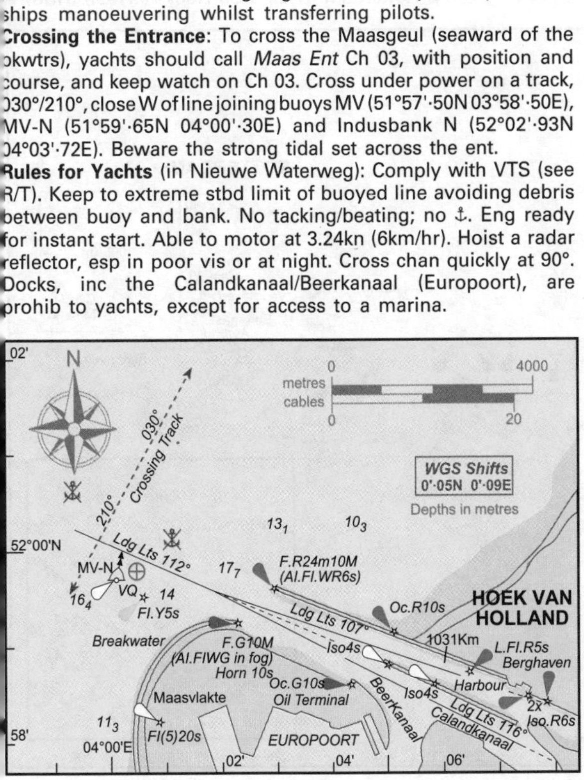

Note: An anti-flood barrier across the Nieuwe Waterweg at km 1026·5 (4°10'E), is approx 2·5M up-stream from the conspic ldg lts (Iso R 6s) at Berghaven. The barrier will close when a water height of at least 3·2m is predicted. After 4 hrs warning, only 2 hrs will be available to transit.

LIGHTS AND MARKS Maasvlakte Fl (5) 20s 66m 28M; B 8-sided tr, W bands; vis 340°-267° (H24). Nieuwe Noorderdam, hd FR 24m 10M; Or tr, B bands, helipad; in fog Al Fl WR 6s. Nieuwe Zuiderdam, hd FG 24m 10M; Or tr, B bands, helipad; in fog Al Fl WG 6s; Horn 10s. Ldg lts 107° (for Nieuwe Waterweg): Both Iso R 6s 29/43m 18M; R trs, W bands; vis 100°-114° (H24); synch.

Traffic Sigs from Pilot/Sig Stn, which has RDF bn HH 288, (N side of Nieuwe Waterweg, close W of Berghaven):

●●● Ⓦ ●●● = No entry to, or exit from, Maas Estuary

Nieuwe Waterweg:

●● Ⓦ ●● = No entry. ●● Ⓦ ●● = No exit

Patrol vessels show a Fl Bu lt. If such vessels show a Fl R lt, it means 'Stop'.

RADIO TELEPHONE 3 main **Traffic Centres**, each on Ch 13, with their radar stn sub-sectors *(italics)* on a dedicated VHF Ch, are as follows:

1. **Traffic Centre Hoek van Holland (VCH)**
   Maas Approach Ch 01, (Outer apps, from 38M W of Hook);
   Pilot Maas Ch 02, (from approx 11M in to 4M W of Hook);
   Maas Ent (Maasmond) Ch 03, (from 4M in to km 1031);
   Rozenburg Ch 65, (Nieuwe Waterweg to km 1023);

Note: **English** language spoken on Ch 01, 02 and 03.

2. **Traffic Centre Botlek (VCB)**
   Maassluis Ch 80, (km 1023 to km 1017);
   Botlek Ch 61, (km 1017 to km 1011);
3. **Traffic Centre Stad (VCS)**
   Eemhaven Ch 63, (km 1011 to km 1007);
   Waalhaven Ch 60, (km 1007 to km 1003);

Note: Hartel and Maasboulevard Tfc Centres, and their radar sectors, have been omitted because yachts would not usually enter their areas. The Hbr Coordination Centre (HCC) administers Rotterdam port on Ch 11 14.

Yachts should **first report** to *Maas Approach* or *Pilot Maas* (or to *Maas Ent* if using the ITZ), stating name/type of vessel, position & destination; then obey instructions, listening on the appropriate VHF Ch's as shown by W □ signboards on the river banks. (Km signs are similar).

Info broadcasts (weather, vis, tfc and tidal) are made by Traffic Centres and radar stns on request.

Other stations: Oude Maas Ch 62; Spijkenisserbrug and Botlekbrug Ch 18; Brienenoordbrug Ch 20; Bridge at Alblasserdam Ch 22; Dordrecht Ch 19 04 71 (H24).

TELEPHONE (Dial code 010) Port Authority (HCC) 4251400; Pilot (Hook) 4251422; Police 4141414; ⊞ 4112800; Brit Consul (020) 6764343.

FACILITIES **Maasluis** ☎ 5912277, AB, CH, El, FW, BY, ME, Sh. **Town** P, D, V, R, Bar, ✉, Ⓑ, ⇌, ✈ (Rotterdam).Ferry: Hook-Harwich (HSS); Rotterdam Europoort-Hull.

ROTTERDAM *9.23.21*

Zuid Holland **51°54'·00N 04°28'·00E** ❁❁❁⛵⛵⛵✿✿

CHARTS AC 133, 132, 122; Zeekaart 1540/1/2; DYC 1809; Stanfords 19

TIDES +0414 Dover; ML 0·9; Duration 0440; Zone –0100

Standard Port VLISSINGEN (⟵)

Times				Height (metres)			
High Water		Low Water		MHWS	MHWN	MLWN	MLWS
0300	0900	0400	1000	4·8	3·9	0·9	0·3
1500	2100	1600	2200				
Differences MAASSLUIS							
+0155	+0115	+0100	+0310	–2·7	–2·1	–0·6	0·0
VLAARDINGEN							
+0150	+0120	+0130	+0330	–2·7	–2·1	–0·6	–0·1

NOTE 1: Maasluis and Vlaardingen are both referenced to Vlissingen, as shown above, in British Admiralty Tables. The Dutch *Guide to the Netherlands and Belgian coasts* (HP11) shows the following time differences relative to HW and the first LW at Hoek van Holland: HW
LW
Maasluis +0113 +0038
Vlaardingen and Schiedam +0114 +0112
Rotterdam +0123 +0352
These figures, plus the tidal curves, take account of local river conditions. The Dutch Tables (HP33) do not include Secondary Port differences; in effect all the major ports, including Rotterdam, are regarded as Standard Ports and full daily predictions are published.
NOTE 2: Double LWs occur. The rise after the first LW is called the Agger. See 9.23.17.

SHELTER Good in the yacht hbrs (see FACILITIES), but in the river there is always a considerable sea and swell due to constant heavy traffic; Europoort/Rotterdam is the world's largest port complex. All but local yachts are discouraged from using the Nieuwe Maas.

NAVIGATION See 9.23.20. There are no navigational dangers other than the amount of heavy sea-going traffic. Berghaven to Rotterdam is about 19M. 7M before the centre of Rotterdam, the Oude Maas joins (km 1013); same rules apply as in 9.23.20. Min speed 3.24kn (6km/hr). **Note:** Special regulations apply to yachts in the Rhine; obtain a French booklet *Service de la Navigation du Rhin* from 25 Rue de la Nuée Bleu, 6700 Strasbourg.

LIGHTS AND MARKS Marks to locate Yacht Havens:

1. Ent to Vlaardingen YC (2·7m) is on N bank by Delta Hotel, between km posts 1010-1011.
2. 2M on, just above the ent to Wilhelmina Haven is the Spuihaven (1·8-2·3m); N bank by km 1007.
3. Parkhaven and the lock into Coolhaven Yacht Hbr are clearly identified on the N bank by the huge Euromast in the park (km 1002·5).
4. The Royal Maas YC at the Veerhaven (3·3m), a centre for traditional yachts, is on the N bank (km 1001·5).
5. City Marina (4·0m) is between Noordereiland and S bank; km post 1000 is on NW bank. Transit the eye-catching Erasmus bridge (11m clearance below fixed span; lifting section at SE end through which ldg lts, both Iso 2s, lead 056·7°); then 2nd ent to stbd, via lifting bridge.

RADIO TELEPHONE The VTS Ch's for central Rotterdam are 63, 60, 81 and 21; see 8.2.5 and related diagram. The Hbr Coordination Centre (HCC) administers Rotterdam port on Ch 11 14. Call HCC Ch 11 for emergencies. English is official second language. Erasmus bridge Ch 18.

TELEPHONE (Dial code 010) Hbr Coordination Centre (HCC) 4251400, also Emergency; ⊖ 4298088; Police 4141414; 🅗 4112800; Brit Consul (020) 6764343.

FACILITIES Vlaardingen YC (Oude Haven via lock/bridge), M, BY, ME, SM, FW, P, D, Gaz, ⇄; **Hr Mr** ☎ 4346786. **Schiedam YC** (Spuihaven) ☎ 4267765, D, L, FW, ME, El, Sh, CH, AB, ⇄; **Coolhaven Yacht Hbr** ☎ 4738614, Slip, M, P, D, L, FW, ME, El, Sh, C, CH, AB, V, R, Bar; **Royal Maas YC** ☎ 4137681, D, L, FW, ME, El, SH, CH, AB; home of the "Brown Fleet", traditional Dutch barges. **City Marina** (51°54'·68N 04°29'·82E, S bank close to Noordereiland). ☎ via (0187) 493769, 📠 493807, 110 AB in 4m, FW, AC, YC, Water taxi. **YC IJsselmonde** ☎ 482833, AB (1·2-1·8m), AC, FW; on S bank at km 994, opposite the Hollandsche IJssel fork (off chartlet). **Services:** P, D, ME; Gaz, ACA, DYC Agent. **City** all facilities, ✉, Ⓑ, ⇄, ✈, Ferry: Rotterdam - Hull, also Hook-Harwich (HSS).

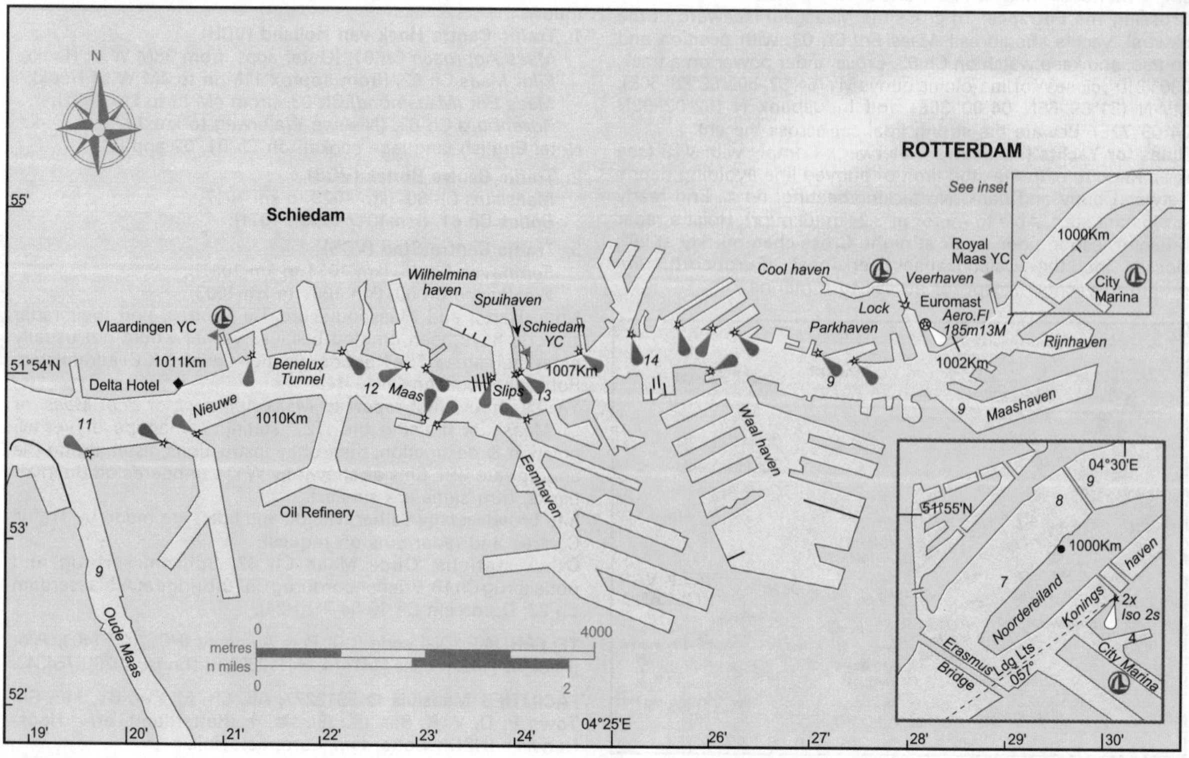

;CHEVENINGEN *9.23.22*

'uid Holland **52°06'·28N 04°15'·35E** ❁❁❁⚓⚓⚓✿✿

:HARTS AC 122, 2322; Zeekaart 1035, 1349, 1350, 1449; DYC 801.7; ANWB H/J; Imray C25; Stanfords 19

'IDES +0320 Dover; ML 0·9; Duration 0445; Zone −0100

;tandard Port VLISSINGEN (⟵)

'imes				Height (metres)			
High Water		Low Water		MHWS	MHWN	MLWN	MLWS
0300	0900	0400	1000	4·8	3·9	0·9	0·3
1500	2100	1600	2200				
)ifferences SCHEVENINGEN							
+0105	+0100	+0220	+0245	−2·6	−2·1	−0·6	−0·1

NOTE: Double LWs occur. The rise after the 1st LW is called the Agger. Water levels on this coast can be much affected by winds: Prolonged NW gales can raise levels by up to 3m, whilst strong : winds can lower levels by 1m.

;HELTER Very good at marina in the Second Hbr; access H24. The :han from 1st to 2nd Hbrs is narrow with limited vis, so sound horn.

NAVIGATION WPT SCH (SWM) buoy, Iso 4s, 52°07'·80N)4°14'·20E, 336°/156° from/to ent, 1·6M. Strong tidal streams setting NE/SW across the ent can cause problems. Winds >F6 from SW to N cause scend in the outer hbr, when ent can be difficult. Beware large ships entering and leaving.

LIGHTS AND MARKS Outer ldg lts, both Iso 4s, 156°; Inner, both Oc G 5s, 131°. **Tfc signals** (from Semaphore mast):

● over Ⓦ = Entry prohib. Ⓦ over ● = Exit prohib.
Fl ● = entry difficult due to vessels leaving.
Q ● is shown by ent to First Hbr (W side) when vessels are entering or leaving port.

Tide signals:
● over Ⓦ = tide rising. Ⓦ over ● = tide falling.

RADIO TELEPHONE Call: *Scheveningen Haven* VHF Ch 21 (H24) prior to entry/dep to avoid ferries and FVs. Radar also Ch 21.

TELEPHONE (Dial code 070) Marina Hr Mr mobile 06-53293137; Port Hr Mr 3527701; Traffic Centre 3527721; ⊖ 3514481; Police 3103048; Dr 3450650/4550963; Ambulance 112; Brit Consul (020) 6764343.

FACILITIES YC Scheveningen (223 + 100 visitors) ☎ 3520017, €0.51 plus tourist tax €0.98 per adult, €0.39 per child, AC, Bar, C (15 ton), CH, D, El, FW, ME, R, ⊡, Sh, SM; **Clubhouse** ☎ 3520308; **Hbr** Slip, FW, ME, Sh, CH, R, Bar; **Services:** ME, El, Sh, CH, SM, DYC Agent. **Town** P, D, V, R, Bar, ✉, Ⓑ, ⇌, ✈ Rotterdam/Amsterdam. Ferry: See Rotterdam or Hoek van Holland.

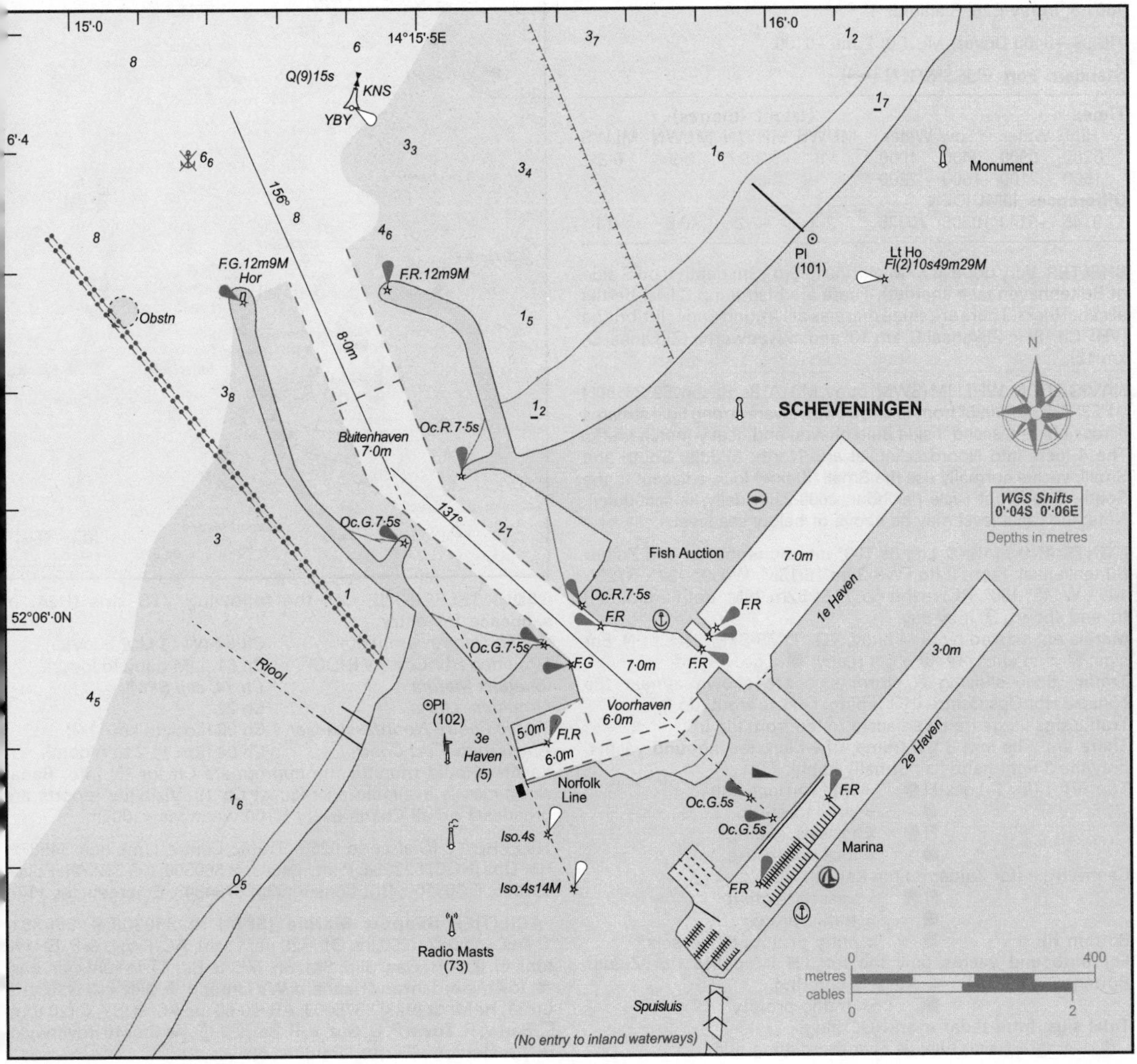

IJMUIDEN *9.23.23*

Noord Holland 52°28'·03N 04°32'·00E Rtgs: see Facilities

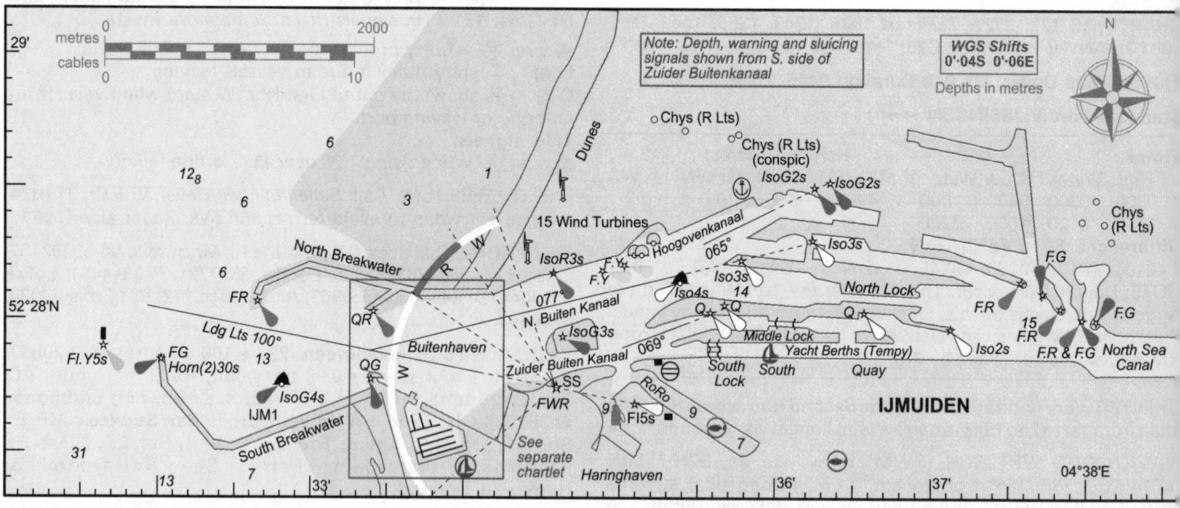

CHARTS AC 124, 2322; Zeekaart 1450, 1543, 1035, 1350; DYC 1801.8; Imray C25; Stanfords 19

TIDES +0400 Dover; ML 1·0; Zone –0100

Standard Port VLISSINGEN (⟵)

Times				Height (metres)			
High Water		Low Water		MHWS	MHWN	MLWN	MLWS
0300	0900	0400	1000	4·8	3·9	0·9	0·3
1500	2100	1600	2200				
Differences IJMUIDEN							
+0145	+0140	+0305	+0325	–2·7	–2·2	–0·6	–0·1

SHELTER Very good at SPM marina (5·5m - 3m depths) on S side of Buitenhaven (see chartlet). There are also temp (2hrs) berths at canal locks. There are small marinas at IJmond under lift-bridge (VHF Ch 18) in Zijkanaal C, km 10; and at Nauwerna (Zijkanaal D, km 12).

NAVIGATION WPT IJM (SWM) buoy, Mo (A) 8s, Racon, 52°28'·50N 04°23'·87E, 275°/095° from/to ent, 5·0M. Beware strong tidal streams across hbr ent, scend inside Buitenhaven and heavy merchant tfc. The 4 locks into Noordzeekanaal are: North, Middle, South and Small; yachts normally use the Small (Kleine) lock, adjacent to the South. One in/out cycle per hour, 0600-2100 daily, is scheduled. Note: the canal level may be above or below sea level.

LIGHTS AND MARKS Ldg lts 100° into Buitenhaven and Zuider Buitenkanaal: Front lt ho FWR 30m 16/13M, W050°-122°, R122°-145°, W145°-160°, RC; rear lt ho, Fl 5s 52m 29M. Both are dark R trs and show a Ⓦ lt by day.
Marina ent marked by SPM buoy, VQ, "IJM3-SPM", 1ca to N. Ent sigs: ● = no entry; ●+● = get ready; ● = go.
Traffic, tidal, sluicing & storm sigs are shown at/near the conspic Hbr Ops Centre (HOC) bldg, next to front ldg lt.
Traffic sigs (large frame adjacent to the front ldg lt):
There are 9 lts in a 3 x 3 frame, of which, for **inbound** yachts, only the 3 right-hand lts normally apply:
Top RH lt (for S Lock) Fl ● = wait for lock entry.
● = clear to enter.
Fl ● = vessels exiting.
● = lock not in use.
Centre RH lt (for Zuider Buiten Kanaal)
Fl ● = vessels exiting.
● = traffic prohib.
Bottom RH lt ● = entry prohib, all vessels.
For **outbound yachts** only the top LH lt applies (for Zuider Buitenkanaal) Fl ● = vessels entering.
● = traffic prohib.
Tidal sigs, from radar tr on HOC bldg:
● over Ⓦ = rising tide; Ⓦ over ● = falling tide.

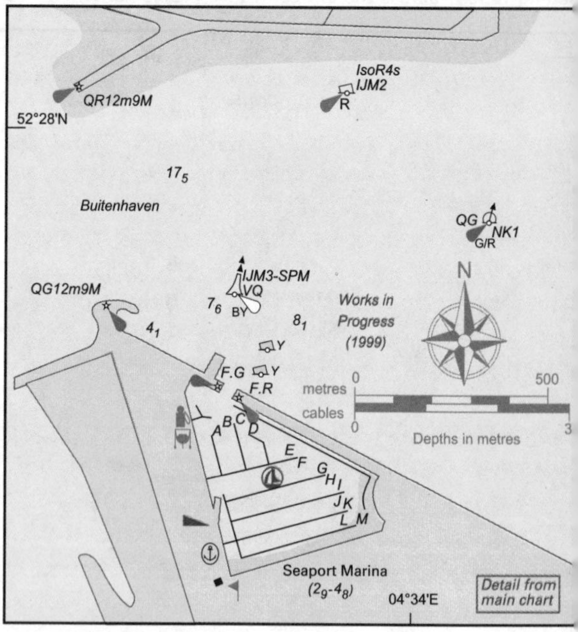

RADIO TELEPHONE Call the following VTS stns (H24) in sequence for entry:

Traffic Centre IJmuiden	Ch 07 (W of IJM buoy).
IJmuiden Hbr Control (HOC)	Ch 61 (IJM buoy to locks).
(***Seaport Marina***	***Ch 74; call SPM***).
IJmuiden Locks	Ch 22.
Traffic Centre Noordzeekanaal	Ch 03 (Lock to km 11·2).
Amsterdam Port Control	Ch 04 (Km 11·2 to A'dam).

Yachts should monitor the appropriate Ch for tfc info. Radar assistance is available on request Ch 19. Visibility reports are broadcast on all Chans every H+00 when vis <1000m.

TELEPHONE (Dial code 0255) Traffic Centre IJmuiden 545875; Hbr Ops (HOC) 523934; Pilot 564503; ⊜ 560800; CG 537644; Police 535035; E 565100; Brit Consul (020) 6764343; Emergencies 112.

FACILITIES Seaport Marina (SPM) ☎ 560300/📠 560301. ⚓⚓⚓⚓⚓⚓⚓. (600 inc Ⓥ), €20 per yacht, AC, FW, D & P, BH (70 ton), El, Ⓔ, CH, Gas, Slip, SM, Sh, ME, R, Bar, ▣, in summer, bus/ ⇌ to Amsterdam and Haarlem; **WV IJmond** ⚓⚓⚓⚓⚓⚓⚓. VHF Ch 31, Hr Mr ☎ (023) 5375003, AB €0.60 inc AC, D, BY, C (20 ton), ▣, Bar, V, R. **Town** P, D, Gaz, V, R, Bar, ✉, Ⓑ, ⇌ (bus to Beverwijk), ✈ Amsterdam. Ferry: IJmuiden-Newcastle.

AMSTERDAM *9.23.24*

oord Holland 52°23'·00N 04°54'·00E Rtgs: see Facilities

HARTS AC 124; Zeekaart 1543; DYC 1801, 1810; ANWB G, I

IDES Amsterdam is between the Noordzeekanaal and the sselmeer, both of which are non-tidal; Zone –0100.

HELTER Complete in any of 4 yacht hbrs/marinas (see chartlet Facilities). The main one is Sixhaven, on the N bank, NE of the ⇌ (conspic); it is small, pleasant and well located, so mostly full y 1800. WV Aeolus is a good alternative. Aquadam is more for e larger yacht; bus to city centre. There is a small marina, WV uiderzee, on N bank immediately E of Oranjesluizen.

AVIGATION See 9.23.23. The 13·5M transit of the oordzeekanaal is simple, apart from the volume of commercial affic. The speed limit is 9kn. Schellingwoude bridge (9m), at 500m of Oranjesluizen, opens: all year H24 but closed Mon-Fri 0600-900 and 1600-1800. After 2200 call VHF Ch 18. There are waiting ontoons both sides of Oranjesluizen. Amsterdam gives access to canals running to N & S and also, via the Oranjesluizen (H24), into the IJsselmeer.

LIGHTS AND MARKS Both banks of the canal and the ents to branch canals and basins are lit. The chan E towards the Oranjesluizen and the Amsterdam-Rijn canal is lit/buoyed.

RADIO TELEPHONE VHF Ch 04 14. See also 9.23.23. Oranjesluizen Ch 18.

TELEPHONE (Dial code 020) Port Control 6221515; ⊖ 5867511; Emergency 112; Police 0900 8844; Dr 5555555; Brit Consul: 6764343.

FACILITIES **Marinas: Sixhaven** (60 + some Ⓥ) ☎ 6370892, ❁❁❁⛵⛵✿✿✿, €1.00 inc AC, FW, Bar (weekends); **ZV Aeolus** ☎ 6360791, ❁❁❁⛵⛵✿✿✿, €0.80 inc AC, YC, FW; **Aquadam** ☎ 6320616, Rtg 1-2-2, €1.40, AC, FW, Sh, P, C (30 ton); **WV Zuiderzee** ☎ 4904590, ❁❁❁⛵✿✿✿, €0.6, YC, AC, FW. **City**: All facilities, Gaz, Ⓔ, ACA, DYC Agent, Ⓑ, ✉, ⇌, ✈. Ferries: IJmuiden-Newcastle. See also Hoek van Holland.

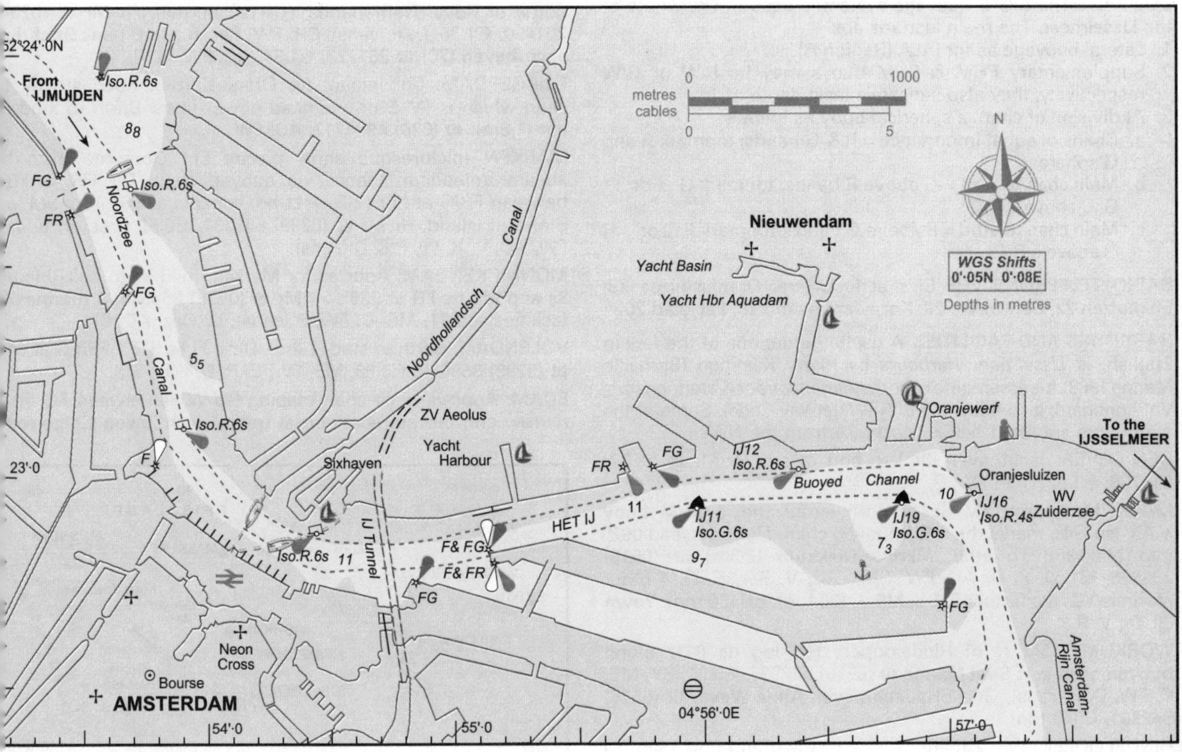

IJSSELMEER *9.23.25*

CHARTS AC *1408*, 2593; Zeekaart 1351, 1454; DYC 1810: up to late copy is essential to avoid live firing ranges, fishing areas and other hazards; it also has many hbr chartlets.

TIDES The IJsselmeer is non-tidal. Tides at locks at Den Oever and Kornwerderzand: –0230 Dover; ML 1·2; Zone –0100

Standard Port HELGOLAND (⟶)

Times				Height (metres)			
High Water		Low Water		MHWS	MHWN	MLWN	MLWS
0200	0700	0200	0800	2·7	2·3	0·4	0·0
1400	1900	1400	2000				
Differences KORNWERDERZAND							
–0210	–0315	–0300	–0215	–0·5	–0·4	0·0	+0·2
DEN OEVER							
–0245	–0410	–0400	–0305	–0·8	–0·6	0·0	+0·2

SHELTER Excellent in the many marinas, some of which are listed below. Most berths are bows on to a pontoon, stern lines to piles; there are few ⚓s.

NAVIGATION The IJsselmeer is the un-reclaimed part of the former Zuiderzee; it is separated from the Waddenzee by the 20M long Afsluitdijk, completed in 1932. It is divided into two parts by the Houtribdijk, with locks at Enkhuizen to the NW and Lelystad in the SE. The SW part is the Markermeer (20M x 15M, 2-4·5m deep); the rest of the IJsselmeer is 30M x 20M, 7m max. Three ents via locks:

1. IJmuiden, Noordzeekanaal to Oranjesluizen (9.23.23).
2. Den Oever (SW end of the Afsluitdijk): Appr from Waddenzee via well marked/lit chan; ldg lts 131°, both Oc 10s to ent, thence follow Dir Iso WRG 2s, 220° to wait in Buitenhaven. 2 bridges and locks operate in unison HO. From IJsselmeer, wait in Binnenhaven; FR/G at ent.
3. Kornwerderzand lock (NE end of the Afsluitdijk) H24. From Waddenzee, via W, NW or NE chans. Ent has FR/G and Iso G 6s. Wait in Buitenhaven; yachts use the smaller E lock. From IJsselmeer, ldg lts Iso 4s 348° to FR/G at ent; wait in Binnenhaven (3·6m).

Standard lock sigs (vert): ● ● = not in service; ● = no entry; ● ● = stand by; ● = enter.

23

IJSSELMEER *continued*

Speed limits: in buoyed chans and <250m from shore 10·5kn. Hbr limits vary; see ANWB Almanak Vol 2.
Strong winds get up very quickly and often cause short seas; they can also raise the water level on a lee shore, or lower it on a weather shore, by 1m or more. Most hbrs have water level gauges which should be checked in bad weather. In non-tidal waters CD usually refers to the level at which the water is kept. In the Netherlands, this may be Kanaalpeil, which is related to Normaal Amsterdams Peil (NAP), which in turn is approx Mean Sea Level.The chartered levels refer to summer; in winter, to allow for flooding, the level is kept 0·5m lower.
A firing range, operational Tues to Thurs 1000 - 1900LT, extends S from Breezanddijk (53°01'·0N 05°12'·5E) to 3M N of Medemblik then NNW to Den Oever (DYC 188.3). Call the range control on Ch 71 *Schietterrein Breezanddijk.* Scheveningen Radio broadcasts firing times on the day of firing after Dutch forecasts, at even hours; also at 1900 the previous day in English Ch 25, 27, 83 after the weather.

BUOYAGE The SIGNI buoyage system is used in the whole of the IJsselmeer. The main features are:

1. Lateral buoyage as for IALA (Region A).
2. Supplementary PHM & SHM buoys may be R/W or G/W respectively; they also indicate a least depth of 2m.
3. At division of chan, a spherical buoy as follows:
   a. Chans of equal importance = R & G bands; topmark R and G sphere;
   b. Main chan to port = G above R bands; topmark G △ or G △ above a G ○;
   c. Main chan to stbd = R above G bands; topmark R □ or R □ above a R ○.

RADIO TELEPHONE VHF Ch's at locks are: Oranjesluizen 18; Enkhuizen 22; Den Oever 20; Kornwerderzand 18; Lelystad 20.

HARBOURS AND FACILITIES A useful guide, one of the few in English, is *IJsselmeer Harbours* by Hilary Keatinge (Barnacle Marine 1988). It is essential to have the *Almanac voor Watertoerisme*, Vol I onboard; it contains the BPR (Waterway Code). Some of the many hbrs are listed below (clockwise from the NW):

DEN OEVER: Jachthaven (3m) to port of ent; Hr Mr ☎ (0227) 511798, €1.02, D, P, FW, ▣.

MAKKUM: Approx 1M SE of Kornwerderzand, a SHM buoy MA5, Iso G4s, marks the 4·1M buoyed chan. FR/FG lts lead 092° into Makkum. To stbd, **Marina Makkum** (2·5m) ☎ (0515) 232828, €1.00, P, D, AC, FW, SM, Gaz, V, Bar, R, ▣. 4 other marinas/YCs are further E; BY, ME, C (30 ton), BH (30 ton). **Town** Ⓑ, Dr, V, R.

WORKUM: 2·5M N of Hindeloopen; FW ldg lts 081° along buoyed chan to **It Soal Marina** ☎ (0515) 542937, €0.91, BY, ME, C, FW, D, P (cans), Gaz, BH; **Jachthaven Anne Wever** ☎ (0515) 542361, C (40 ton).

HINDELOOPEN: has 2 marinas, one in town and one 180m to N. **Jachthaven Hindeloopen** (500) Hr Mr ☎ (0514) 521866, €1.09, P, D, FW, AC, ▣, BH (30 ton), CH, R, Bar; **Old Hbr** €0.57, D, P, FW, ME, El, Sh; **W.V Hylper Haven** Hr Mr ☎ (0514) 522009, €0.57, P, D, FW, ME, El, Sh.

STAVOREN: Ent Buitenhaven 048° on Dir lt Iso 4s between FR/G. Marina, €0.45, E of ent in Oudehaven; ☎ (0514) 681216, VHF Ch 74. Or, 1km S, ent Nieuwe Voorhaven (FR/G & Fl 5s Dir lt) then via lock to **Stavoren Marina** (3m) ☎ 681566, €1.13, BY, ME, C, FW, P, D, SM, Gaz, BH (20 ton); **Outer Marina** (3·5m) close S of Nieuwe Voorhaven, €1.25. Also 3 other marinas. **Town** Ⓑ, Dr, V, R, ⇌.

LEMMER: Appr on ldg lts 038°, Iso 8s, to KL5/VL2 By; then ldg lts 083°, Iso 8s, through Lemstergeul. Lastly FG and Iso G 4s lead 065° into town and some 14 marinas. **Gem. Jachthaven** Hr Mr ☎ (0514) 561331, €0.86; **Services**: BY, ME, C, FW, P, D, Gaz, SM. **Town** Ⓑ, Dr, V, R, ✉.

URK: Hbr ent ½M SE of lt ho, Fl 5s 27m 18M. Dir lt Iso G 4s to hbr ent, FR/G. Hbr has 4 basins; keep NNW to berth in Nieuwe Haven, Westhaven or Oosthaven (3·3m), €0.59. Hr Mr ☎ (0527) 689970. **Westhaven** P & D (cans), SM; **Oosthaven** ME, El, Sh, Ⓔ, CH. **Town** EC Tues; Ⓑ, ✉, Dr.

KETELHAVEN: Ent Ketelmeer via bridge (12·9m) which lifts at : end; after 4M to By WK1 Iso G 4s, ldg lts Iso 8s 101°/0·7M i buoyed chan. Turn S for unlit marina ent (2·2m). **Marina** (200 €0.77, FW, AC, R. Hr Mr ☎ (0321) 312271. W ent has FG/R lts t Ketelsluis: Hr Mr ☎ 318237 D, P (cans).

LELYSTAD: has 3 marinas: 2M NNE of lock is **Flevo** (550) ☎ (0320) 279803, €1.13, BY, ME, C, FW, AC, P, D, Gaz, ▣, BH (5 ton), R, Bar, V. Close N of the lock is **Houtribhaven** (560) Hr M ☎ 260198, €0.82, D, CH, V, R, Bar, C (12 ton). Radio mast, R lts (140m) is conspic; marinas are lit, S of lock **Marin Lelystadhaven** 0320 260326, €1.00, AC, FW, D, P, G, R.

MARKERMEER

MUIDERZAND: Ent 1M N of Hollandsebrug at buoys IJM5 JH2/IJM3. **Marina** ☎ (036) 5365151, €1.20, FW, AC, D, P, C, ME R, CH.

NAARDEN: 1M SE of Hollandsebrug (12·9m), ent at GM5 buoy. **Gem Jachthaven** (1000) ☎ (036) 6942106, €0.91, D, P, AC FW, El, BH, C, CH, V, R, Bar, ⇌ (Naarden-Bussum).

MUIDEN: Ldg lts Q 181° into **KNZ & RV Marina** (2·6m), W of en home of Royal Netherlands YC (150 berths). Hr Mr ☎ (0294 261450, €1.36, D, P (cans), CH, FW, Bar, R. On E bank **Stichtin Jachthaven** (70) ☎ 261223, €1.34, AC, FW, D, P.

DURGERDAM: Convenient for Oranjesluizen. Keep strictly t chan which is ½M E of overhead power lines. Berth to stbd c ent (1·8m). ☎ (020) 4904717, AC, FW.

MARKEN (picturesque show piece): Ent Gouwzee from N abeam Volendam, thence via buoyed chan; Dir FW lt 116 between FR/G at hbr (2·2m). Lt ho, conspic, Oc 8s 16m 9M, o E end of island. Hr Mr ☎ (0299) 603231, €0.59 (free on quay FW, AC, V, R, Ⓑ, P & D (cans).

MONNICKENDAM: Appr as for Marken, then W to MO10 Iso 8s and ldg lts FR at 236°. Hr Mr ☎ (0299) 658585. 4 marinas & facilities: €0.91, ME, C, FW, P (cans), D, Gaz, AC, CH.

VOLENDAM: Berth to stbd (2·4m). Dir lt Fl 5s 313°. FR/FG at en ☎ (0299) 369620, €0.68, ME, FW, C, P, D, Gaz, SM.

EDAM: Appr via unlit chan keeping Iso W 8s between FG /R a narrow ent; beware commercial traffic. **Jachthaven Galgenvel**

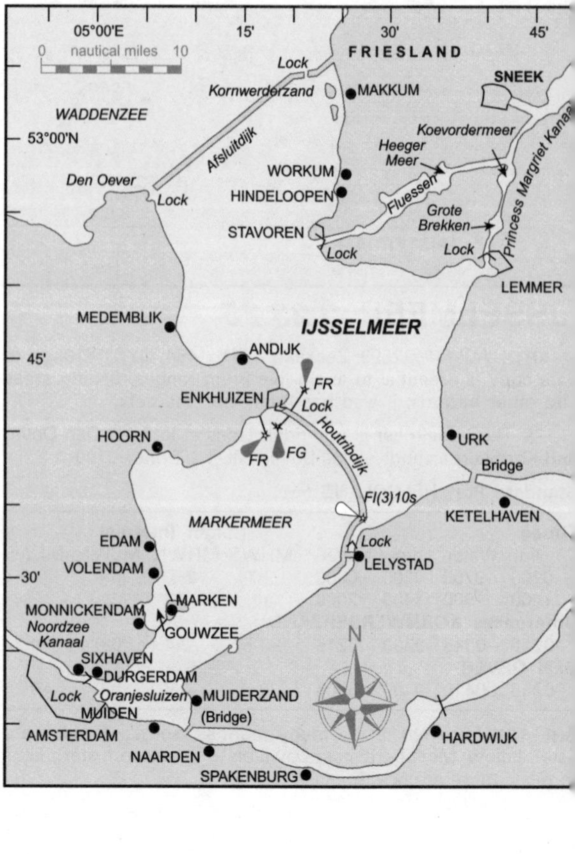

SSELMEER (WEST) *Continued*

·5m) S side pf outer hbr, €0.73. Or lock into the Oorgat and via canal to Nieuwe Haven. Hr Mr ☎ (0299) 371092, €0.79, ME, El, h. **Town** Bar, ⊡, ✉, Gaz, Ⓑ.

OORN: Radio tr (80m) 1·5M ENE of hbr. Iso 4s 15m 10M and R/G at W Hbr ent. Four options: to port **Stichting Jachthaven oorn** (700) Hr Mr ☎ (0299) 215208, €0.77, FW, AC, ⊡, CH, V, IE, El, Sh, C; to stbd ⚓ in **Buitenhaven** (2m); ahead & to stbd **luchthaven Marina** €0.82, (100) ☎ 213540 FW; ahead to **innenhaven** (2·7m) via narrow lock (open H24) AB €0.77, P, W. **Town** V, CH, ✉, R, Dr, P & D (cans), Ⓑ, Gaz, ⇌.

NKHUIZEN: From SW, appr via buoyed chan and ldg lts Iso s at 036°; from NE, ldg lts Iso 8s at 230° and FR /G at bkwtrs ad to Krabbersgat lock and hbr. Call lock Ch 22. The 2 narinas and Buitenhaven are NE of the lock: **ompagnieshaven** (500) Hr Mr ☎ (0228) 313353 €0.94, P, D, W, AC, CH, BH (12), Gaz; **Buyshaven** (195) ☎ 315660, €1.25, W, AC; **Buitenhaven** ☎ 312444 €0.70, FW. **Town** EC Mon; larket Wed; C, Slip, CH, SM, ME, El, Sh, Ⓑ, Bar, P & D (cans), Dr, ✉, ⇌.

NDIJK: Visitors use **Stichting Jachthaven Andijk,** the first of marinas; (600) ☎ (0228) 593075, €0.91, narrow ent with tight turn between FR/G lts. ME, C (20), SM, Gaz, ⊡, D, CH.

MEDEMBLIK: Ent on Dir lt Oc 5s 232° between FR/G. Go via Oosterhaven (P & D) into Middenhaven (short stay), then via bridge to Westerhaven. **Pekelharinghaven** (120) Hr Mr ☎ (0227) 542175, €0.86; ent is to port by Castle, CH, Bar, R; **Middenhaven** Hr Mr ☎ 541686, €0.68, FW; **Stichting Jachthaven** Hr Mr ☎ 541681 in Westerhaven, €0.86, FW, AC, ⊡, C. **Town** Ⓑ, CH, ME, El, SM, Sh, ✉, Dr, Bar, ⊡, R, V. **Regatta Centre** (0·5M S of Medemblik hbr entr. Hr Mr ☎ (0227) 547781, AB 450, €1.36, C, Slip, CH, R.

INLAND ROUTE TO RIVER EMS (DELFZIJL 9.23.33)

As an alternative to the shallow tidal route inshore of the Frisian Islands, or as a bad weather option, masted yachts can transit the canals/lakes from the IJsselmeer to Delfzijl without lowering masts. From Lemmer to Delfzijl is about 100M/180km, via Prinses Margrietkanaal, Leeuwarden, Dokkumer Ee, Dokkum, Lauwersmeer, Zoutkamp, Reit Diep, Groningen and Eemskanaal. Leeuwarden can also be reached from Harlingen via the Van Harinxma Kanaal or from Stavoren via the Johan Friso Kanaal. Minimum depths approx 1·8m. ANWB charts A and B are needed.

DEN HELDER *9.23.26*

Noord Holland **52°58'·00N 04°47'·35E**

CHARTS AC 191, 2322, 2593; Zeekaart 1454, 1546; DYC 1811.2, 801.10; ANWB F; Imray C25; Stanfords 19

TIDES –0430 Dover; ML 1·1; Duration No data; Zone –0100

Standard Port HELGOLAND (⟶)

Times				Height (metres)			
High Water		Low Water		MHWS	MHWN	MLWN	MLWS
0200	0700	0200	0800	2·7	2·4	0·4	0·0
1400	1900	1400	2000				
Differences DEN HELDER							
–0410	–0520	–0520	–0430	–1·0	–0·9	0·0	+0·2

SHELTER Good in the Naval Hbr, the yacht hbr (KMYC) being hard to stbd on entering. Den Helder is the main base of the Royal Netherlands Navy which owns and runs the KMYC and the Marinehaven Willemsoord. Caution: many FVs, ferries and off-shore service vessels. 2 other YCs/marinas both of which can only be reached via the Rijkszeehaven, Moorman bridge, Nieuwe Diep and lock, offer AB in or near the Binnenhaven: MWV and YC Den Helder; see below under FACILITIES for details.

NAVIGATION WPT Schulpengat SG (SWM) buoy, Mo (A) 8s, 52°52'·95N 04°38'·00E, 206·5°/026·5° from/to Kaap Hoofd, 6·0M. Two chans lead via the Marsdiep to the hbr ent:

1. From N, the Molengat is good except in strong NW winds when seas break heavily.
2. From S, the Schulpengat is well marked and lit.

Beware fast ferries to/from Texel and strong tidal streams across the hbr ent. Speed limit 6kn.

LIGHTS AND MARKS Schulpengat: Ldg lts 026·5° on Texel; front Iso 4s 18M; rear Oc 8s 18M, Ch spire, both vis 025°-028°. Kijkduin lt ho Fl (4) 20s 56m 30M, R tr, is conspic 2·3M WSW of hbr. Molengat: ldg lts 141·5°; front Iso 5s 13m 8M; rear, 650m from front, FW 22m 8M; tr on Ⓗ; both vis 124°-157°. Hbr ldg lts 191°. Both Oc G 5s 16/25m 14M (synch); front B ▲ on bldg; rear B ▼ on B framework tr. A 60m radar tower is conspic on the E side of hbr ent. **Entry sigs**, from Harssens hbr office on W side of ent: ●● (vert) = No entry/exit; no traffic allowed within hbr. **Bridges**: Moorman bridge operates 7 days a week H24. Access to the North Holland Canal via the Nieuwe Diep and Koopvaardersschutsluis.Van Kinsbergen bridge operated by Hr Mr, 0500-2300 Mon-Fri; 0700-1400 Sat. All bridges remain closed 0715-0810, 1200-1215, 1245-1300, Mon-Fri. Also 0830-0910 Mon and 1545-1645 Fri. All LT.

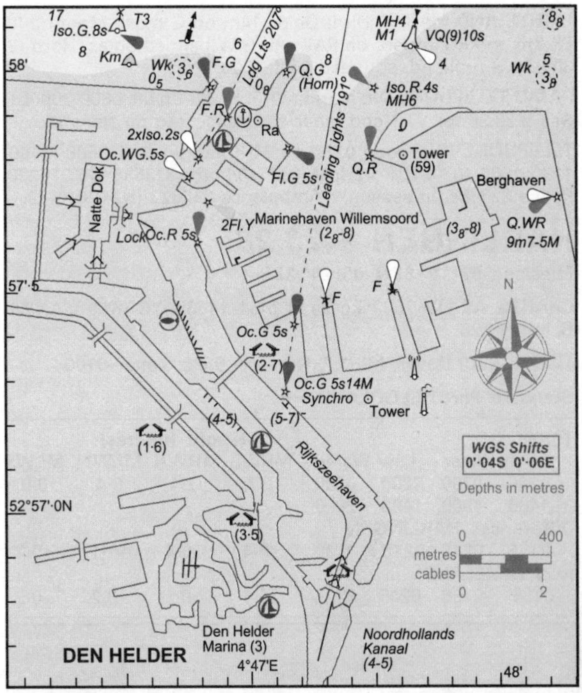

RADIO TELEPHONE Monitor VTS Ch 12 *Den Helder Traffic* in the Schulpengat, Molengat and Marsdiep; weather forecast available on request. Port Ch 14 (H24); also Ch 14 for van Kinsbergen bridge (remote control). Koopvaardersschutsluis Ch 22 (H24), which also operates Burgemeester Vissersbrug by remote control. Moormanbridge Ch 18 (H24).

TELEPHONE (Dial code 0223) Municipal Hr Mr 613955, 📠 627780, mobile ☎ 0652 97 94 80; Hr Mr (Yacht Haven) 637444; Pilot 617424; Vessel Traffic Centre 652770; Naval Base Commander 657522; Emergency 112; Police 655700; Ⓗ 611414; Water Police 616767; Immigration 657515; Brit Consul (020) 6764343.

FACILITIES In naval hbr: **KMYC** ☎ 652645, €0.64, FW, D, AC, Bar, R; In or near Binnenhaven: **MWV YC** ☎ 617076, €0.54, P (at garage), D, L, FW, AB; **Yacht Haven Den Helder** ☎ 637444, €0.73, ME, El, Sh, C, CH, Slip, FW, R, Bar; **YC WSOV** ☎ 652173; **YC HWN** ☎ 624422; **Services:** CH, SM, Floating dock, Gaz. **Town** P, CH, V, R, Bar, ✉, Ⓑ, ⇌, ✈ (Amsterdam). Ferry: Hook of Holland-Harwich; Rotterdam-Hull.

23

OUDESCHILD 9.23.27

Texel, **53°02'·39N 04°51'·26E** ❁❁❁◊◊◊✿✿

CHARTS AC 191, 2593; Zeekaart 1546, 1454; DYC 1811·3

TIDES –0355 Dover; ML 1·1m; Duration 0625; Zone –0100

Standard Port HELGOLAND (⟶)

Times				**Height (metres)**			
High Water		Low Water		MHWS	MHWN	MLWN	MLWS
0200	0700	0200	0800	2·7	2·4	0·4	0·0
1400	1900	1400	2000				
Differences OUDESCHILD							
–0310	–0420	–0445	–0400	–1·0	–0·9	0·0	+0·2

SHELTER Very good in marina (2·1m) in NE basin. ⚓ prohib. Hr Mr is only available in season. Yachts are advised not to ent/dep Mon and Fri mornings when all FVs sail/return.

NAVIGATION WPT 53°02'·28N 04°51'·72E, 111°/291° from/to hbr ent, 3ca. From seaward, app via Schulpengat or Molengat into Marsdiep (see 9.23.26). Thence from abeam ferry hbr of 't Horntje (Texel) steer NE via Texelstroom for 3·5M to hbr ent, marked by PHM buoy (T14), Iso R 8s. Enter on course 291° with dir lt, Oc 6s, midway between S mole hd FR and N mole hd FG. Speed limit 5kn (9kph).

LIGHTS AND MARKS Dir lt Oc 6s 14m on G mast. Mole hd lts FR 7m and FG 7m are on R/W and G/W banded poles. Horn (2) 30s on S mole hd, sounded 0600-2300.

RADIO TELEPHONE No marina VHF. Hr Mr Ch 09, 0800-2000LT. See 9.23.26 for VTS and radar assistance/info on request.

TELEPHONE (Dial code 0222) Hr Mr (marina) ☎ 313608 (1100-1130; 1800-1930LT); Port Hr Mr 312710/home 313538; CG 316270; Police 322188 (in season); Ambulance 312323 (H24) or 112.

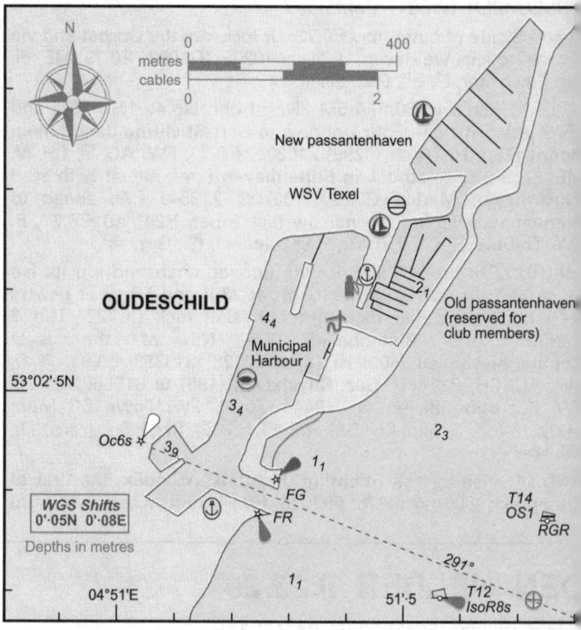

FACILITIES Marina (Schoeiershoek-Passantenhaven) 200 berths ☎ 313608, €1.13, D, FW, AC, Slip, ▣, Bar, R, ♿; **YC WV Texel**, C **Services:** ME, BY, Sh, ⚒, Dry dock, C, SM, V by mobile shop in season. **Village** (walking distance), CH, P, Gaz, V (supermarket) Ⓑ, ✉, R. Ferry from 't Horntje to Den Helder. UK ferries from Hook Rotterdam. ✈ Amsterdam.

HARLINGEN 9.23.28

Friesland **53°10'·63N 05°24'·22E**

CHARTS AC 112, 2593; Zeekaart 1454, 1456; DYC 1811·5; ANWB B; Imray C26

TIDES –0210 Dover; ML 1·2; Duration 0520; Zone –0100

Standard Port HELGOLAND (⟶)

Times				**Height (metres)**			
High Water		Low Water		MHWS	MHWN	MLWN	MLWS
0200	0700	0200	0800	2·7	2·4	0·4	0·0
1400	1900	1400	2000				
Differences HARLINGEN							
–0155	–0245	–0210	–0130	–0·4	–0·4	–0·1	+0·2
NES (AMELAND)							
–0135	–0150	–0245	–0225	+0·1	+0·1	+0·2	+0·2

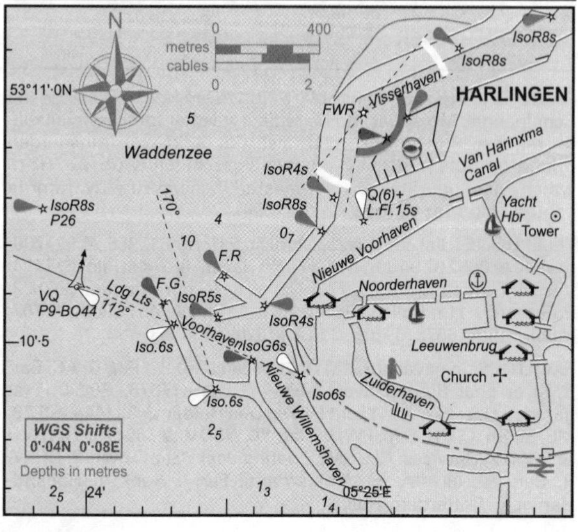

SHELTER Very good once in Noorderhaven, but main hbr en can be rough at HW with W/NW winds. Entering on the flood beware strong stream across ent. Note: Access to/from Noorderhaven is restricted by N/S bridges into the Oude Buitenhaven and Noorderhaven; these open in unison 2 x per hr 0600-2200 in season (on request in winter) and are shut at times of boat trains/ferries and at HW springs. Van Harinxma yacht hbr only advised if going via the canal to the lakes.

NAVIGATION WPT SM buoy from seaward (see 9.23.27). Then follow the buoyed Vliestroom and Blauwe Slenk chans which is narrow for the last 2½M, and is bordered on the NE by a dam Beware of ferries passing very close. Caution: When training wall is covered, tidal stream sweeps across the Pollendam marked by lateral lt bns.

LIGHTS AND MARKS Ldg lts 112°, Iso 6s 8/19m 13M, H24; B masts, W bands.

RADIO TELEPHONE VHF Ch 11 (Mon 0000 to Sat 2200LT) Harinxma Canal locks Ch 22.

TELEPHONE (Dial code 0517) Hr Mr 492300; CG (Brandaris) (0562) 442341; ⊜ 418750; Police 413333; ⊞ 499999; Brit Consu (020) 6764343.

FACILITIES Noorderhaven Yacht Hbr ☎ 415666, FW, El, CH, V, R, Bar, ▣; **Yacht Hbr Van Harinxma Canal** ☎ 416898, FW, ▣, C (6 ton); **Services:** CH, El, E, Gaz, Diving/salvage, El, ME (by arrangement), D, P. **Town** EC Mon; LB, D, P, V, R, Bar, SM, ✉, Ⓑ, ⇌, ✈ (Amsterdam). Ferry: See Hook.

NES, AMELAND, Friesland, 53°26'·28N 05°46'·62E. AC 2593, Zeekaart 1458, DYC 1811.6, 1812.2. HW –0055 on Dover; ML 1·6m, Duration 0625. See 9.23.28. Shelter from all but E/S winds. Yacht pontoons at N end of hbr (0·8m) beyond ferry terminal; W side dries to soft mud. Beware sandbanks in the Zeegat van Ameland. Enter from Molengat at MG28-R1 SCM By, VQ(6) + L Fl 10s. Lts: Ameland (W end), Fl (3) 15s 57m 30M, RC. Ferry pier hd Iso 6s 2m 8M. L Fl R 8s and L Fl G 8s piles at ent to yacht hbr ('t Leye Gat, 140 berths), €0.73. Facilities: Gaz, YC. Hr Mr ☎ (0515) 32159.

'LIELAND 9.23.29

·EST FRISIAN ISLANDS
·iesland **53°17'·73N 05°05'·57E**

·HARTS AC 112, 2593; Zeekaart 1456; DYC 1811.4/.5; Imray C26

·DES –0300 Dover; ML 1·4; Duration 0610; Zone –0100

:andard Port HELGOLAND (⟶)

·mes				**Height (metres)**			
High Water		Low Water		MHWS	MHWN	MLWN	MLWS
0200	0700	0200	0800	2·7	2·4	0·4	0·0
1400	1900	1400	2000				
·ifferences VLIELAND-HAVEN							
-0250	–0320	–0355	–0330	–0·3	–0·3	+0·1	+0·2

·HELTER Good; yacht hbr (2m) is crowded in season. Visitors' ·rths are on pontoons nos 4-10. ⚓ in 4-9m, about 0·5M W of the ·r (and nearer the village), except in strong SE/SW winds; but do ·t ⚓ in buoyed chan between hbr and ferry pier (no berthing). ·om the S a safe ⚓ is in Fransche Gaatje, SE of Richel, 6M from hbr.

·AVIGATION WPT SM (SWM) By, Iso 4s, 53°19'·29N 04°55'·71E, ·4°/094° from/to ZS1 and ZS2 Bys, 2·3M (via ZS Bank NCM). See ·20.37. In fresh W/NW winds a heavy ground swell can raise ·angerous seas from the WPT to ZS1/2 Bys. The Zuider Stortemelk · deep, well marked/lit and leads to the Vliestroom. Vliesloot, which ·rks off to the S, is narrow and in places has only 2· 5m at LW sp; ·ep in mid-chan.

·GHTS AND MARKS Main lt ho Iso 4s 53m 20M; R tr, W lantern, · top; RC. Tfc sigs: R Flag or ●● at ent = hbr closed (full).

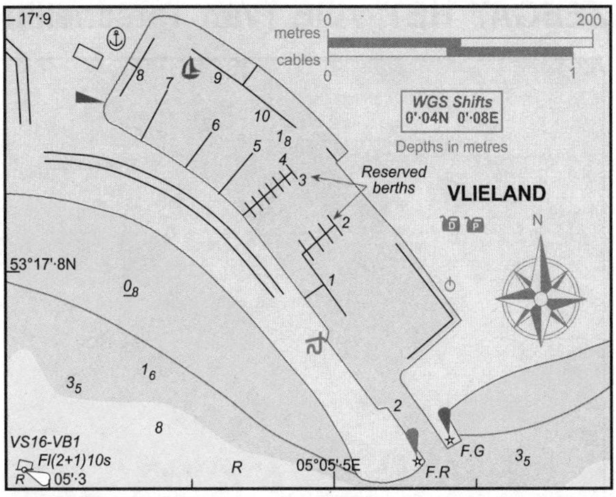

RADIO TELEPHONE Hr Mr Ch 09; CG Ch 02 (Brandaris, W. Terschelling). All vessels in the Zeegat van Terschelling and N Waddenzee must monitor Ch 02 for the *Brandaris Traffic Centre VTS.*

TELEPHONE (Dial code 0562) Hr Mr 451729; CG (0562) 442341; ⊖ 451522; Police 451312; Dr 451307; Brit Consul (020) 6764343.

FACILITIES Yacht Hbr (300) ☎ 451729, €0.41 per m² + €0.84 per person, FW, AC, dinghy slip, ⊡; **Hbr** C (10 ton), P & D (cans, 10 mins); D by hose at Harlingen, ♿. **Village** El, Gaz, V, R, ✉, Ⓑ, ⇌ (ferry to Harlingen), ✈ (Amsterdam). Ferry: Hook of Holland-Harwich.

'VEST TERSCHELLING 9.23.30

'EST FRISIAN ISLANDS
·iesland **53°21'·40N 05°13'·23E**

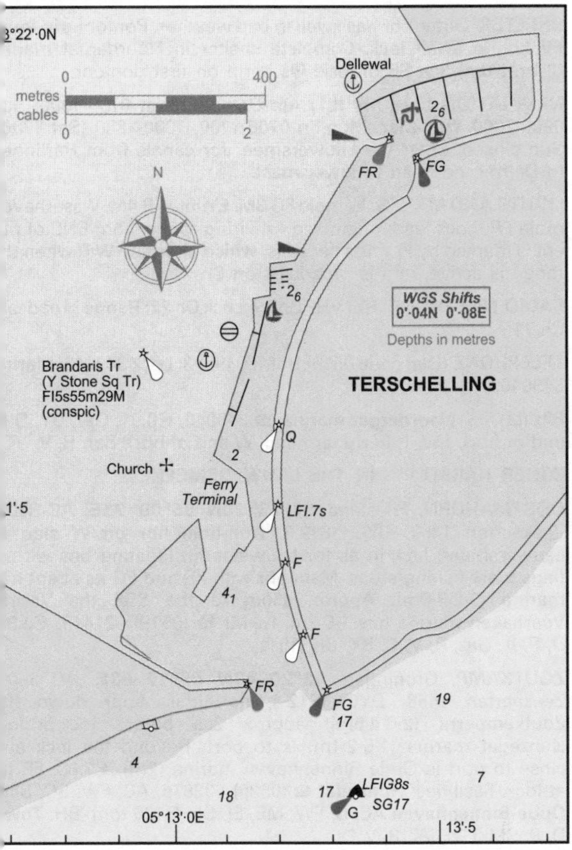

CHARTS AC 112, 2593; Zeekaart 1456; DYC 1811.4/.5; Imray C25

TIDES –0300 Dover; ML 1·4; Duration No data; Zone –0100

Standard Port HELGOLAND (⟶)

Times				**Height (metres)**			
High Water		Low Water		MHWS	MHWN	MLWN	MLWS
0200	0700	0200	0800	2·7	2·4	0·4	0·0
1400	1900	1400	2000				
Differences WEST TERSCHELLING							
–0220	–0250	–0335	–0310	–0·4	–0·3	+0·1	+0·2

SHELTER Good, especially in marina in NE corner of hbr beyond ferry and FV quays. Very crowded in season; considerable commercial traffic and ferries in confined waters.

NAVIGATION WPT: SM buoy from all directions (see 9.23.29 and .31). Thence via Stortemelk, but first call *Brandaris* for the latest nav/tidal info before deciding the better route:

a. Vliestroom into West Meep. At NOM4-S13 ECM buoy, VQ (3) 5s, 53°19'·15N 05°15'·65E, enter Slenk chan ldg WNW into the Schuitengat. Best timing = HW±2 .
b. Schuitengat, shorter and safer than (a) but the ent is narrow/shallow (2·5m at HW±2). Inside the ent follow the chan buoys to hbr ent. Call Ch 02 for latest information.

LIGHTS AND MARKS Brandaris tr (conspic Y □ tr), Fl 5s 55m 29M, storm sigs, dominates the town and hbr.

RADIO TELEPHONE Hr Mr Ch 09. CG Ch 02 04 16 67. *Brandaris* (VTS) Ch 02 broadcasts wx, vis, tfc, tidal info at odd H+30 in Dutch and English on request. Yachts in the area must monitor Ch 02 (see 9.23.29); visitors can get update on nav/chans.

TELEPHONE (Dial code 0562) Hr Mr 442910/442919; CG 442341; ⊖ 442884.

FACILITIES Marina: Stichting Passantenhaven (500) ☎ 443337, f24.00 (€1.04/metre + €0.45 per head + €0.45), C, FW; **Hbr** Slip; **Services:**Gaz, ME, SM, Chart agent, ♿. **Village** EC Wed; CH, V, R, Bar, ✉, P & D (cans, see Hr Mr; nearest D by hose is at Harlingen), Ⓑ, ⇌ (ferry to Harlingen), ✈ (Amsterdam). Ferry: Hook-Harwich; Europoort-Hull.

23

ZEEGAT HET VLIE (Van Terschelling) *9.23.31*

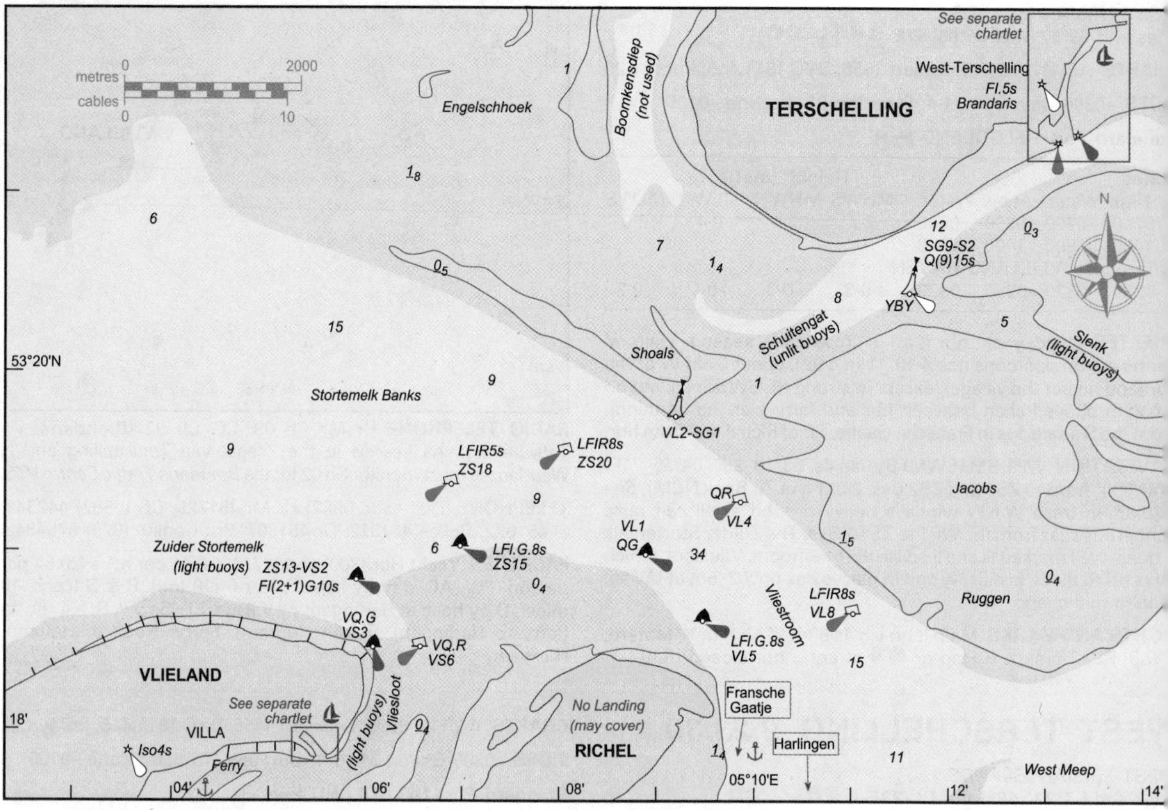

See separate chartlet
West-Terschelling
Fl.5s Brandaris
TERSCHELLING
Engelschhoek
Boomkensdiep (not used)
metres
cables
Stortemelk Banks
Shoals
Schuitengat (unlit buoys)
SG9-S2 Q(9)15s
YBY
Slenk (light buoys)
VL2-SG1
LFIR5s ZS18
LFIR8s ZS20
QR VL4
VL1 QG
Jacobs
Zuider Stortemelk (light buoys)
ZS13-VS2 Fl(2+1)G10s
LFl.G.8s ZS15
LFIR8s VL8
Ruggen
Vliestroom
LFl.G.8s VL5
VQ.G VS3
VQ.R VS6
VLIELAND
See separate chartlet
VILLA
Iso4s
Ferry
Vliesloot (light buoys)
No Landing (may cover)
RICHEL
Fransche Gaatje
Harlingen
West Meep
53°20'N
05°10'E

LAUWERSOOG *9.23.32*

Friesland, **53°24'·72N 06°12'·10E**

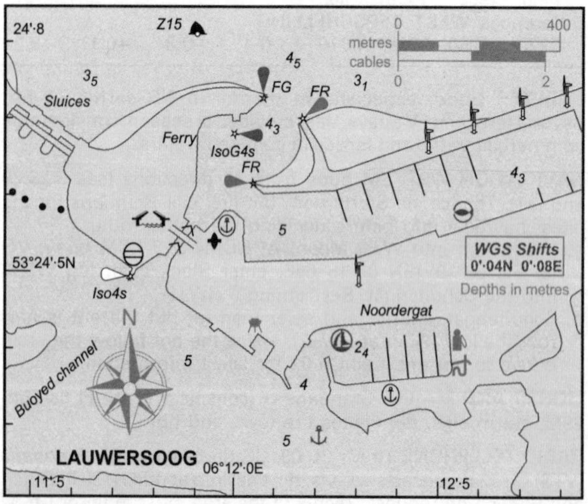

Z15
metres
cables
Sluices
FG
FR
Ferry
IsoG4s
FR
WGS Shifts 0'·04N 0'·08E
Depths in metres
Iso4s
Noordergat
Buoyed channel
LAUWERSOOG
53°24'·5N
06°12'·0E

CHARTS AC 3509, 3761; Imray C26; Zeekaart 1458; DYC 1812.3

TIDES HW –0150 on Dover; ML 1·7m; Zone –0100

Standard Port HELGOLAND (⟶)

Times				Height (metres)			
High Water		Low Water		MHWS	MHWN	MLWN	MLWS
0200	0700	0200	0800	2·7	2·4	0·4	0·0
1400	1900	1400	2000				
Differences LAUWERSOOG							
–0130	–0145	–0235	–0220	+0·2	+0·2	+0·3	+0·3

SHELTER Outer hbr has swell in bad weather. Pontoons in inne FV hbr to await lock. Complete shelter in Noordergat marin (2·4m-2·8m) 3ca SE of lock; ♥s berth on first pontoon.

NAVIGATION Lock hrs (LT) **Apr-Oct**: Mon-Sat 0700-1900; Su 0900-2000. **Nov-Mar**: Mon-Fri 0700-1200, 1300-1800 (Sat 1700 Sun closed. Enter the Lauwersmeer for canals from Harlinge to Delfzijl; no need to lower mast.

LIGHTS AND MARKS W mole FG 3M. E mole FR 4M. Visserhave mole FR. Lock lead-in jetty Iso 4s. Firing range 1·5m ENE of hb ent is marked by Fl Y 10s beacons, which alternate W/R when th range is active; info is broadcast on Ch 71.

RADIO TELEPHONE Hbr VHF Ch 09; Lock Ch 22; Range broadcas Ch 71.

TELEPHONE (Dial code 0519) Hr Mr 349023; Lock 349043; Marin 349040.

FACILITIES **Noordergat marina**, ☎ 349040, €0.91, Gaz, BY, D (end of hbr), FW; P (ferry terminal, W end of hbr), Bar, R, V, YC

OTHER HARBOURS IN THE LAUWERSMEER

OOSTMAHORN, Friesland, **53°22'·90N 06°09'·71E**. AC 350 Zeekaarten 1458, DYC 1812·3. Non-tidal hbr on W side c Lauwersmeer; lock in as for Lauwersoog. Floating bns with flags mark fishing areas. Main hbr with FR and FG lts at ent ha marina (2·2-3·0m). Approx 450m to the SSE the Voor Veerhaven marina has 1·5-2m. Hr Mr ☎ (0519) 321445; €0.9 D, P, ⚓, Gaz, R, V, C, BY, BH (15T)

ZOUTKAMP, Groningen, **53°20'·43N 06°17'·63E**. AC 350 Zeekaarten 1458, DYC 1812·3; non-tidal. Appr down th Zoutkamperril (2·6-4·5m); approx 2ca before lock/bridg Hunzegat marina (1·5-2·1m) is to port. Beyond the lock an close to port is Oude Binnenhaven marina (2m), €3.63. FR l at lock. Facilities: **Hunzegat** ☎ (0595) 402875, AC, FW, SC, Slip **Oude-Binnenhaven** AC, C, FW, ME, El, Sh, C (20 ton), BH. **Tow** D, P, SM, Gaz, ✉, R, V, Dr.

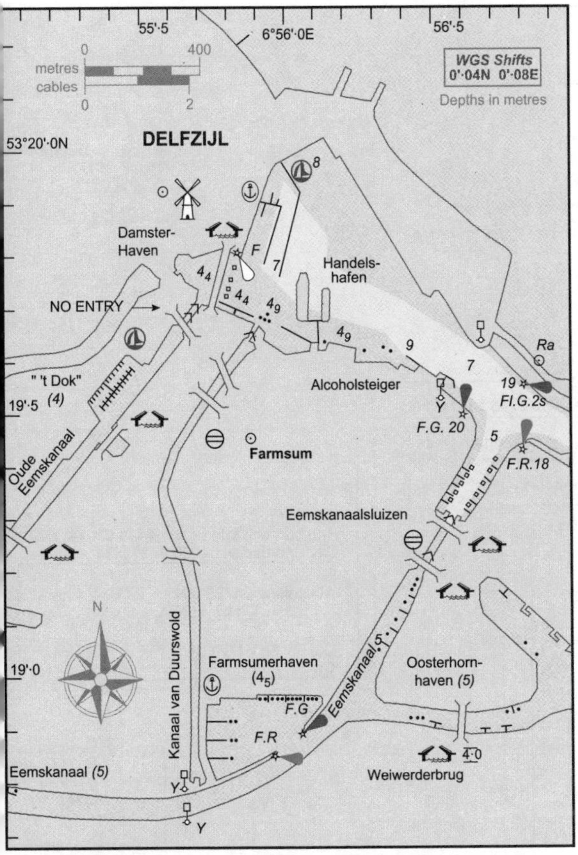

OTHER HARBOUR ON THE WEST FRISIAN ISLANDS

SCHIERMONNIKOOG, Friesland, **53°28'·12N 06°10'·10E**. AC3509, 3761, Zeekaart 1458, DYC 1812.3. HW –0150 on Dover. See 9.23.33. Appr via Westgat, buoyed/lit, but in bad weather dangerous due to shoals (3·8m) at seaward end. Leave Zoutkamperlaag via Glinder chan (1·5m) to enter Gat van Schiermonnikoog (buoyed). From GVS16-R1 buoy a drying chan, marked by perches/withies, runs 1M N to small yacht hbr (1·3-1·5m) about 1M W of the ferry pier. Access HW –2 to +1, with 1·5m max depth at HW in apprs. Picturesque, but very full in high season; not cheap, ie €1.27. Lts: at W end of island, lt ho Fl (4) 20s 43m 28M, R tr; Ferry pier hd lt FW and Fl (5) Y 20s tide gauge. Hr Mr ☎ (0519) 51544 (May-Sept); Facilities: FW, AC. Note: The CG station at the lt ho provides radar surveillance of the Terschelling/German Bight TSS out to 48M radius and coordinates local SAR operations. It keeps watch on VHF Ch 00, 05, 16, 67 and 73 (all H24); ☎ 0519 531247, 📠 0519 531000.

ADJACENT HARBOUR AT MOUTH OF THE EMS

EEMSHAVEN, Groningen, **53°27'·75N 06°50'·40E**. AC 3509, 3510, Zeekaart 1555, DYC 1812.5/.6. HW –0100 (approx) on Dover. Tides as for Borkum 9.24.10. Eemshaven is a modern commercial port, but may be used by yachts as a port of refuge. Easy appr via Randzelgat and Doekegat or via the buoyed/lit Oude Westereems (Alte Ems), passing the outer anchorage for merchant ships. The last buoy, 1·5M before the hbr ent, is A16 PHM Fl (4) R. Call *Eemshaven Radar* Ch 19 (H24) for VTS info; and *Eemshaven Port Control* Ch 14 for clearance to enter. There are many wind turbines to the NW and N of the port. A large power stn and chy (128m) are 2M ESE of the port. White roofed bldgs at the port are conspic. Enter on Iso 4s ldg lts 175°, between mole hds, FG and FR. Inner ldg lts, both Iso R 4s, leads 195° to S end of port. Yachts turn stbd here into Emmahaven, marked by FG and FR, and berth on floating jetty on the S bank. Hr Mr ☎ (Delfzijl Port Authority) 640400, 📠 630424; other ☎ numbers see Delfzijl. Facilities: No special facilities for yachts.

DELFZIJL *9.23.33*

Groningen **53°19'·00N 07°00'·50E** ❀❀❀◊◊✿✿

CHARTS AC 3510, 3509; Imray C26; Zeekaart 1555; DYC 1812.6; ANWB A

TIDES –0025 Dover; ML 2·1; Duration 0605; Zone –0100

Standard Port HELGOLAND (⟶)

Times				Height (metres)			
High Water		Low Water		MHWS	MHWN	MLWN	MLWS
0200	0700	0200	0800	2·7	2·4	0·4	0·0
1400	1900	1400	2000				
Differences DELFZIJL							
+0020	–0005	–0040	0000	+0·9	+0·8	+0·3	+0·3
SCHIERMONNIKOOG							
–0120	–0130	–0240	–0220	+0·2	+0·2	+0·3	+0·3
KNOCK (R. Ems)							
+0018	+0005	–0028	+0004	+0·6	+0·6	0·0	0·0

SHELTER Good in Neptunus Marina (3·5m) on W of Handelshaven. The Floating Jetty acts as a wavebreak. Berthing (4·5m) also in Farmsumerhaven (24hr only) via the Eemskanaal lock; or at the N end of the Old Eemskanaal in Yacht Hbr 't Dok (4m).

NAVIGATION WPT Huibertgat SWM buoy, Iso 8s, Whis, 53°34'·90N 06°14'·32E, 270°/090° from/to Borkum Kleiner lt, 15·5M, in W sector. Chan buoys unlit for first 10M. WPT Westereems SWM buoy, Iso 4s, Racon, 53°36'·97N, 06°19'·48E, 272°/092° from/to Nos 1 and 2 Westereems chan buoys, 1·6M. WPT from N & E: Riffgat SWM buoy, Iso 8s, 53° 38'·90N 06° 27'·10E, 312°/132° from/to Westereems chan buoys, 3·2M; and 8·75M to Borkum Kleiner lt (See 9.24.10). Thence via Randzelgat and Doekegat (well buoyed/lit) to enter 3M ESE of the city of Delfzijl. Beware strong cross tides at the ent.

INLAND ROUTE TO IJSSELMEER: ***See 9.23.25.***

LIGHTS AND MARKS From the river, appr ldg lts 203°, both Iso 4s. Hbr ent, FG on W arm and FR on E arm (in fog, Horn 15s and FY). Zeehavenkanaal has Fl G lts to N and Fl R to S. Entry sigs on both piers: 2 ● = No entry, unless cleared by Hbr office on VHF Ch 14.

RADIO TELEPHONE All vessels, except recreational craft, must call *Delfzijl Radar* VHF Ch 66 (H24) for VTS, co-ordinated with Ems Traffic. *Port Control* is Ch 14; Sea Locks Ch 11. Traffic, wx and tidal info is broadcast every even H+10 on Ch 14 in Dutch and English on request. *Ems Traffic* Ch 15 18 20 21 (H24) broadcasts every H + 50 weather and tidal info in German, including gale warnings for coastal waters between Die Ems and Die Weser.

TELEPHONE (Dial code 0596) Hr Mr (Delfzijl Port Authority) 640400, 📠 630424; Neptunus Hr Mr 615004; Hr Mr 't Dok 616560; Sea locks 613293; CG (Police) 613831; ⊖ 615060; Police 112; Ⓗ 644444; Brit Consul (020) 6764343.

FACILITIES **Neptunus Yacht Hbr** ☎ 615004, f1.60, D, Bar, M, L, FW; **Yacht Hbr 't Dok** AB €0.41, D, FW; **Ems Canal** L, FW, AB; **Motor Boat Club Abel Tasman** ☎ 616560 Bar, M, D, FW, L, ⓢ, V. **Services:** CH, ACA, DYC Agent, ME, El, Gaz. **Town** P, D, V, R, Bar, ✉, Ⓑ, ⥈, ✈ (Groningen/Eelde). Ferry: See Hook of Holland.

ADJACENT HARBOURS

TERMUNTERZIJL Groningen, **53°18'·21N 07°02'·30E**. AC 3510; Zeekaart 1555; DYC 1812. HW –0025 on Dover (UT); use Differences Delfzijl. Ent (1·3M ESE of Delfzijl ent) is close to BW13 SHM buoy Fl G 5s (53°18' 70N 07°02' 40E); thence chan marked by 7 R and 7 G unlit bns. Yachts berth in Vissershaven (0·9m), stbd of ent, or on pontoons (1m) to port of ent, €0.36. Hr Mr ☎ (0596) 601891 (Apr-Sept), VHF Ch 09, FW, AC, Bar, R.

Fig. 9 (11)

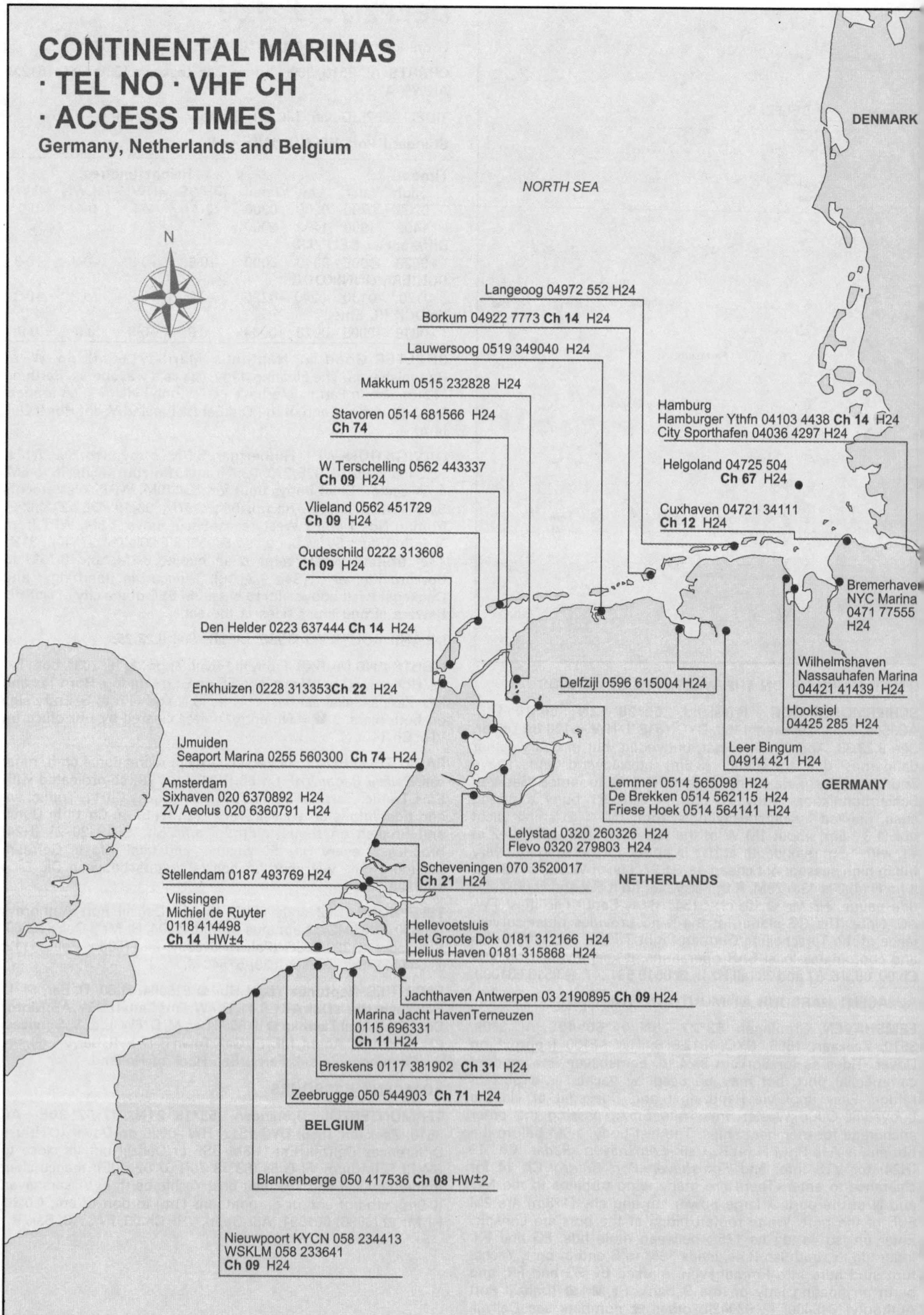
CONTINENTAL MARINAS
· TEL NO · VHF CH
· ACCESS TIMES
Germany, Netherlands and Belgium
N
NORTH SEA
DENMARK
GERMANY
NETHERLANDS
BELGIUM
Langeoog 04972 552 H24
Borkum 04922 7773 Ch 14 H24
Lauwersoog 0519 349040 H24
Makkum 0515 232828 H24
Stavoren 0514 681566 H24 Ch 74
W Terschelling 0562 443337 Ch 09 H24
Vlieland 0562 451729 Ch 09 H24
Oudeschild 0222 313608 Ch 09 H24
Den Helder 0223 637444 Ch 14 H24
Enkhuizen 0228 313353Ch 22 H24
IJmuiden
Seaport Marina 0255 560300 Ch 74 H24
Amsterdam
Sixhaven 020 6370892 H24
ZV Aeolus 020 6360791 H24
Scheveningen 070 3520017 Ch 21 H24
Stellendam 0187 493769 H24
Vlissingen
Michiel de Ruyter
0118 414498
Ch 14 HW±4
Hellevoetsluis
Het Groote Dok 0181 312166 H24
Helius Haven 0181 315868 H24
Jachthaven Antwerpen 03 2190895 Ch 09 H24
Marina Jacht HavenTerneuzen
0115 696331
Ch 11 H24
Breskens 0117 381902 Ch 31 H24
Zeebrugge 050 544903 Ch 71 H24
Blankenberge 050 417536 Ch 08 HW±2
Nieuwpoort KYCN 058 234413
WSKLM 058 233641
Ch 09 H24
Hamburg
Hamburger Ythfn 04103 4438 Ch 14 H24
City Sporthafen 04036 4297 H24
Helgoland 04725 504 Ch 67 H24
Cuxhaven 04721 34111 Ch 12 H24
Bremerhaven
NYC Marina
0471 77555
H24
Wilhelmshaven
Nassauhafen Marina
04421 41439 H24
Hooksiel
04425 285 H24
Leer Bingum
04914 421 H24
Delfzijl 0596 615004 H24
Lemmer 0514 565098 H24
De Brekken 0514 562115 H24
Friese Hoek 0514 564141 H24
Lelystad 0320 260326 H24
Flevo 0320 279803 H24

MAPTECH®
Leading the world in digital navigation
Maptech UK Ltd • +44 (0)1243 389352 • sales@maptech.co.uk

Maptech world class digital chart CDs
Worldwide coverage from over 4,500 charts

Maptech award winning software
Easy to use navigation software
• Chart Navigator • Cruising Navigator • Offshore Navigator

www.maptech.co.uk

Area 24

Germany
Emden to Danish border

9.24.1 Index .... Page 1003

9.24.2 Area map 1004

9.24.3 Tidal stream charts 1006

9.24.4 Lights, buoys & waypoints 1008

9.24.5 Passage information 1013

9.24.6 Distance table 1014

9.24.7 Special notes for Germany 1015

9.24.8 Emden 1016
Greetsiel
Norddeich
Nessmersiel
Bensersiel
Neuharlingersiel
Harlesiel

9.24.9 East Frisian Islands 1017
Juist
Baltrum

9.24.10 Borkum 1018

9.24.11 Norderney 1018

9.24.12 Dornumer-Accumersiel 1019

9.24.13 Langeoog 1019

9.24.14 Spiekeroog 1020

9.24.15 Wangerooge 1020

9.24.16 Hooksiel 1021
Wangersiel
Rüstersiel

9.24.17 Wilhelmshaven, Standard Port, tidal curves 1025
Dangast

9.24.18 Bremerhaven 1026

9.24.19 Cuxhaven, Standard Port, tidal curves 1027
Otterndorf

9.24.20 River Elbe and Hamburg 1031

9.24.21 Brunsbüttel 1032

9.24.22 Nord-Ostsee Kanal 1033

9.24.23 Helgoland, Standard Port, tidal curves 1034

9.24.24 Büsum 1038
Tönning
Husum
Pellworm
Wittdün (Amrum)
Wyk (Föhr)

9.24.25 Sylt 1039
Hörnum

Register for your FREE weekly weather email service from Macmillan Reeds
at www.nauticaldata.com – NOW!
» weekend weather reports sent to your email address, every Thursday «

9.24.2
Germany
Emden to Danish Border

Key to Symbols

- CGR — Coastguard Radio: VHF/MF frequencies
- CRS — Coast Radio: VHF/MF frequencies
- TSS VTS — TSS or VTS Radio: VHF frequencies
- PR MR — Port or Marina Radio: VHF frequencies
- i — See for harbour information/tidal data
- Weather information (Frequencies/times of broadcasts)
- SAR Helicopter base
- ☆ Selected Principal Lights
- Light vessel/Light float/Lanby
- RG — Emergency VHF DF
- * See Area Index

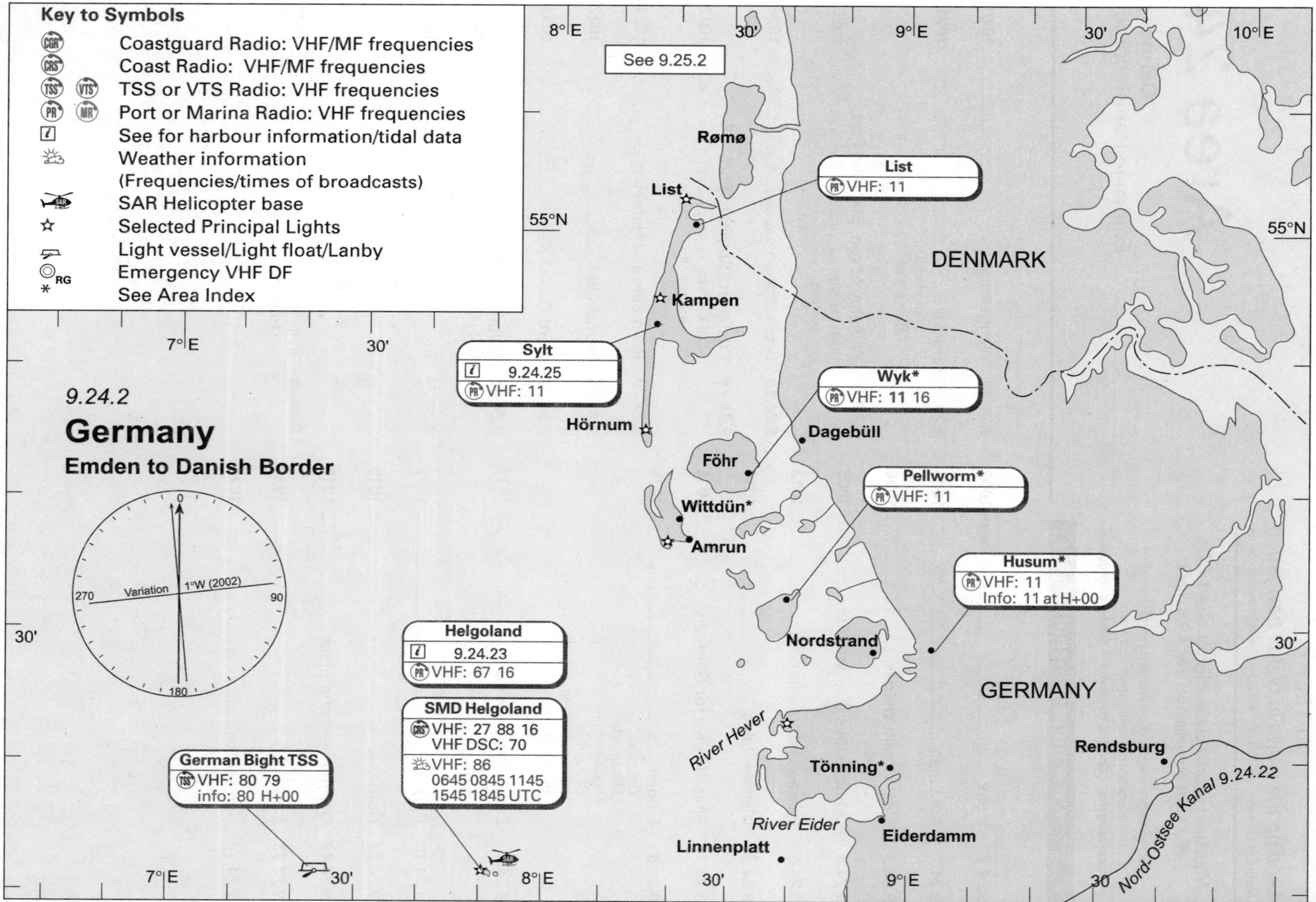

See 9.25.2
8°E
30'
9°E
10°E
7°E
55°N
Rømø
List
List
VHF: 11
DENMARK
Kampen
Sylt
9.24.25
VHF: 11
Wyk*
VHF: 11 16
Hörnum
Dagebüll
Föhr
Pellworm*
VHF: 11
Wittdün*
Amrun
Variation
1°W (2002)
0
90
180
270
Husum*
VHF: 11
Info: 11 at H+00
Helgoland
9.24.23
VHF: 67 16
Nordstrand
GERMANY
SMD Helgoland
VHF: 27 88 16
VHF DSC: 70
VHF: 86
0645 0845 1145
1545 1845 UTC
River Hever
Rendsburg
German Bight TSS
VHF: 80 79
info: 80 H+00
Tönning*
Nord-Ostsee Kanal 9.24.22
River Eider
Eiderdamm
Linnenplatt

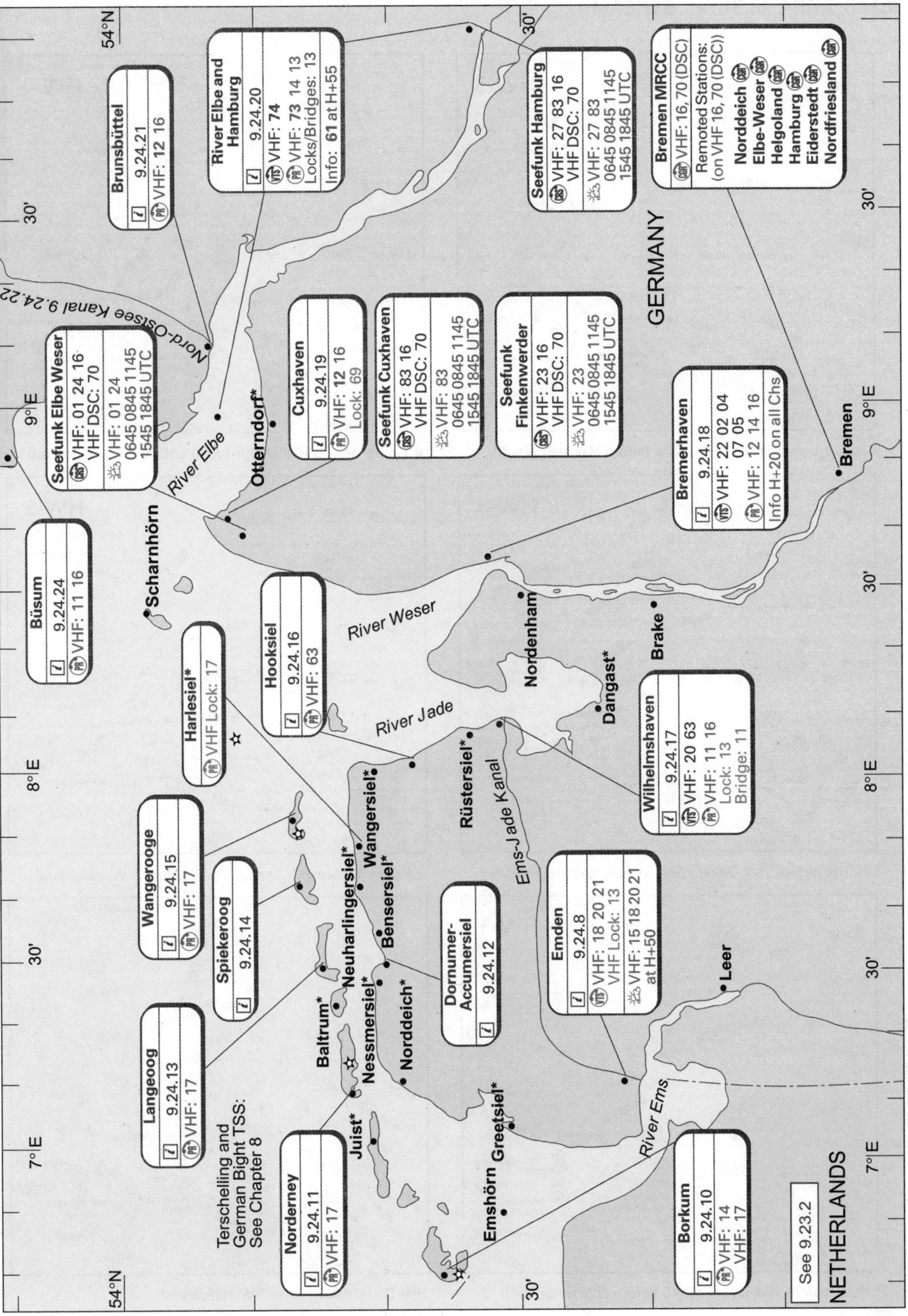
54°N
30'
9°E
8°E
7°E
Brunsbüttel
9.24.21
VHF: 12 16
River Elbe and Hamburg
9.24.20
VHF: 74
VHF: 73 14 13
Locks/Bridges: 13
Info: 61 at H+55
Seefunk Hamburg
VHF: 27 83 16
VHF DSC: 70
VHF: 27 83
0645 0845 1145
1545 1845 UTC
Bremen MRCC
VHF: 16, 70 (DSC)
Remoted Stations:
(on VHF 16, 70 (DSC))
Norddeich
Elbe-Weser
Helgoland
Hamburg
Eiderstedt
Nordfriesland
Nord-Ostsee Kanal 9.24.22
Seefunk Elbe Weser
VHF: 01 24 16
VHF DSC: 70
VHF: 01 24
0645 0845 1145
1545 1845 UTC
Cuxhaven
9.24.19
VHF: 12 16
Lock: 69
Seefunk Cuxhaven
VHF: 83 16
VHF DSC: 70
VHF: 83
0645 0845 1145
1545 1845 UTC
Seefunk Finkenwerder
VHF: 23 16
VHF DSC: 70
VHF: 23
0645 0845 1145
1545 1845 UTC
GERMANY
Otterndorf*
River Elbe
Scharnhörn
Büsum
9.24.24
VHF: 11 16
Bremerhaven
9.24.18
VHF: 22 02 04
07 05
VHF: 12 14 16
Info H+20 on all Chs
Bremen
Hooksiel
9.24.16
VHF: 63
River Weser
Nordenham
Brake
Harlesiel*
VHF Lock: 17
River Jade
Dangast*
Wilhelmshaven
9.24.17
VHF: 20 63
VHF: 11 16
Lock: 13
Bridge: 11
Wangerooge
9.24.15
VHF: 17
Wangersiel*
Rüstersiel*
Ems-Jade Kanal
Spiekeroog
9.24.14
Neuharlingersiel*
Bensersiel*
Dornumer-Accumersiel
9.24.12
Emden
9.24.8
VHF: 18 20 21
VHF Lock: 13
VHF: 15 18 20 21
at H+50
Langeoog
9.24.13
VHF: 17
Baltrum*
Nessmersiel*
Norddeich*
Leer
Terschelling and German Bight TSS:
See Chapter 8
Juist*
Greetsiel*
River Ems
Norderney
9.24.11
VHF: 17
Emshörn
Borkum
9.24.10
VHF: 14
VHF: 17
See 9.23.2
NETHERLANDS

24

9.24.3 AREA 24 TIDAL STREAMS

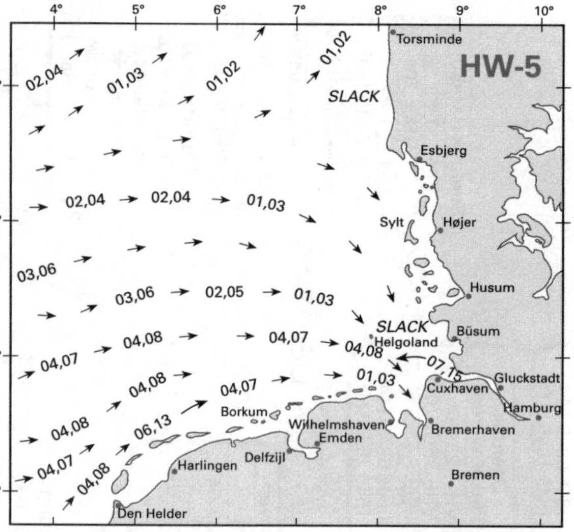

5 Hours before HW Dover (0440 before HW Helgoland)

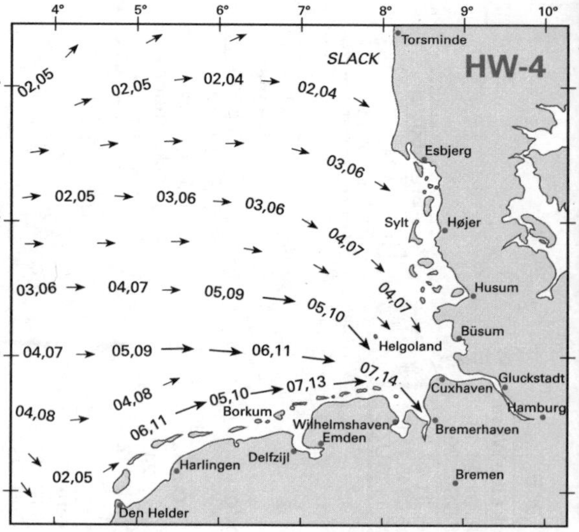

4 Hours before HW Dover (0340 before HW Helgoland)

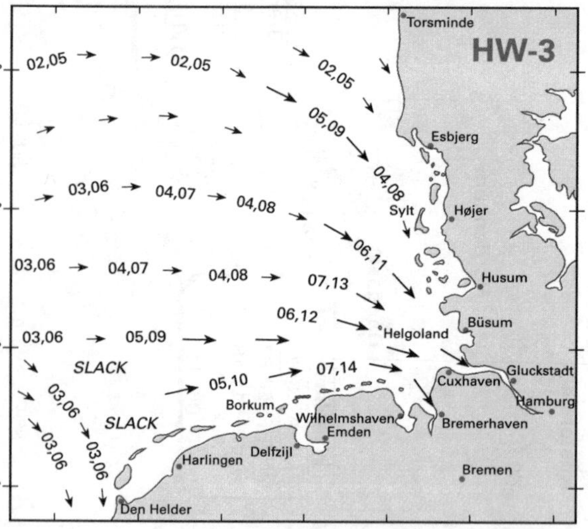

3 Hours before HW Dover (0240 before HW Helgoland)

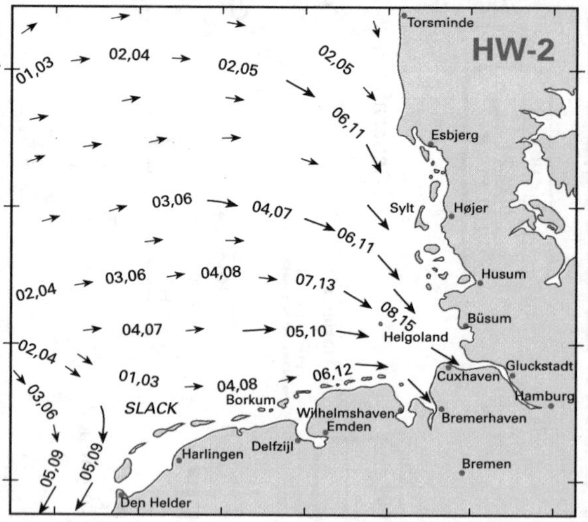

2 Hours before HW Dover (0140 before HW Helgoland)

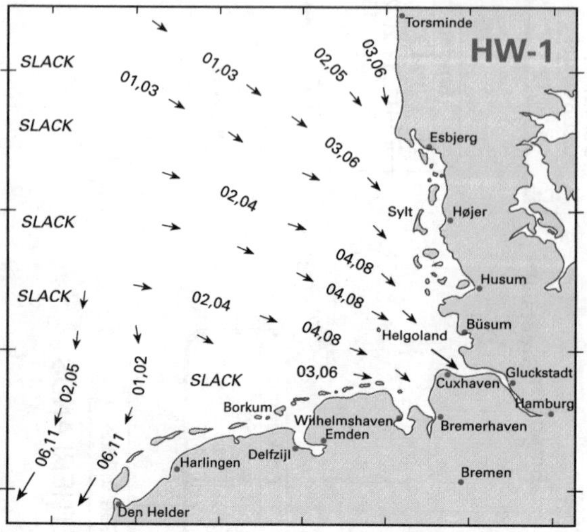

1 Hour before HW Dover (0040 before HW Helgoland)

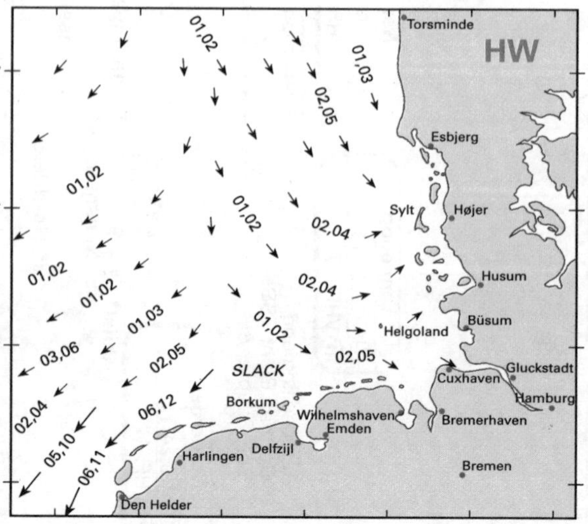

HW Dover (0020 after HW Helgoland)

outh-westward 9.23.3

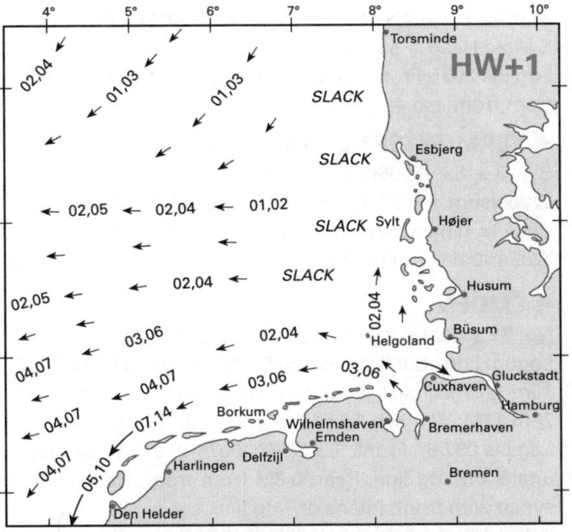

1 Hour after HW Dover (0120 after HW Helgoland)

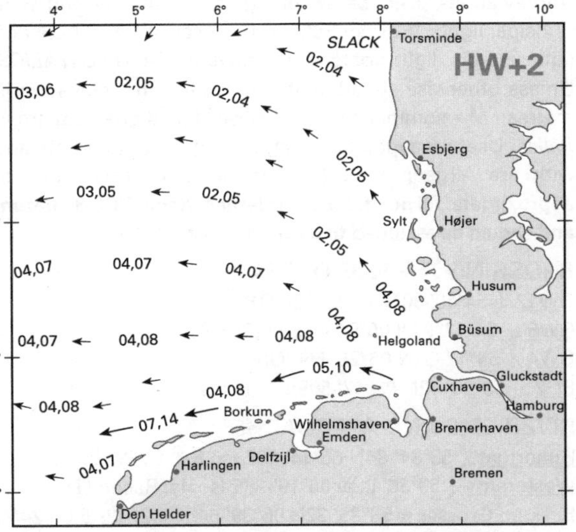

2 Hours after HW Dover (0220 after HW Helgoland)

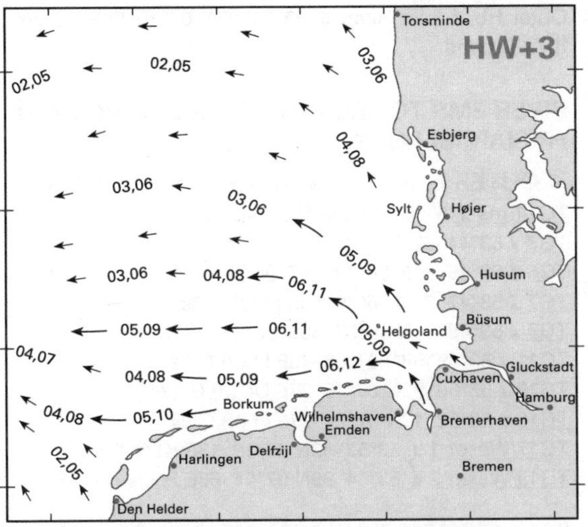

3 Hours after HW Dover (0320 after HW Helgoland)

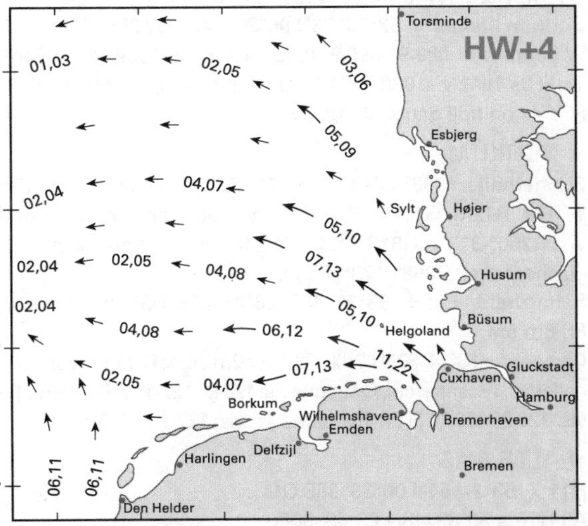

4 Hours after HW Dover (0420 after HW Helgoland)

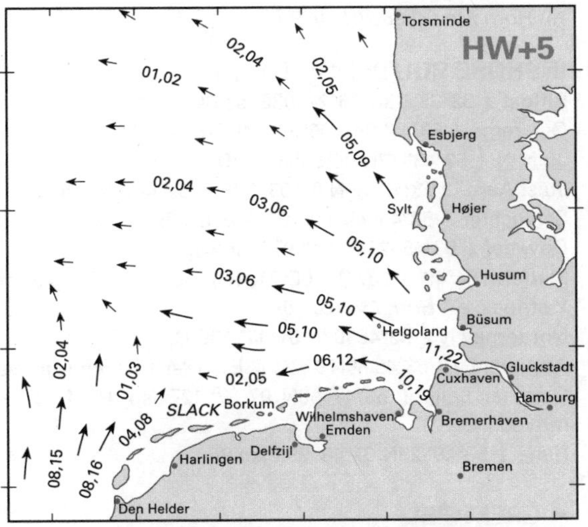

5 Hours after HW Dover (0520 after HW Helgoland)

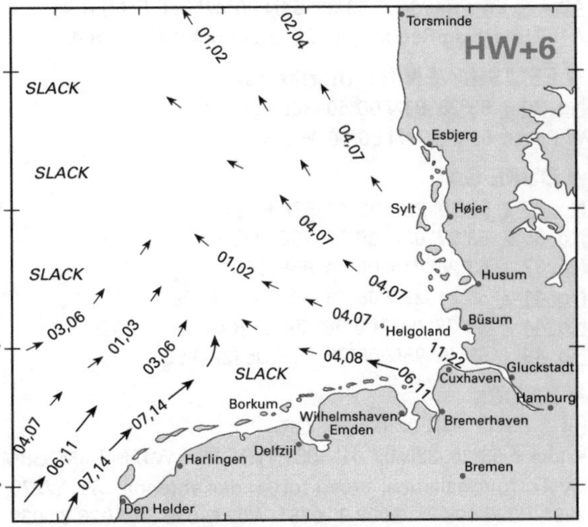

6 Hours after HW Dover (0620 after HW Helgoland)

24

9.24.4 LIGHTS, BUOYS AND WAYPOINTS

Abbreviations used below are given in the Introduction. Principal lights ☆ are in **bold** print, places in CAPITALS, and light vessels, light floats and Lanbys in *CAPITAL ITALICS*. Unless otherwise stated lights are white. m – elevation in metres; M – nominal range in miles. Fog signals are in *italics*. Useful waypoints are underlined – use those on land with care. All geographical positions should be assumed to be approximate. **All positions are referenced the WGS 84 datum and should be assumed to be approximate.**

CROSSING THE NORTH SEA

GW12 54°13'·30N 07°22'·43E QR.
GW8 54°12'·97N 06°51'·46E Fl (2) R 9s.
GW4 54°12'·54N 06°20'·56E QR.
BG2 53°58'·42N 03°17'·50E L Fl R 10s.

RIVER EMS AND APPROACHES

Hubertgat 53°34'·84N 06°14'·19E Iso 8s; *Whis.*
Westerems 53°36'·88N 06°19'·38E Iso 4s; Racon (T).
Borkum Grosser ☆ 53°35'·32N 06°39'·64E Fl (2) 12s 63m **24M**; Brown ○ Tr. Same structure, F WRG 46m **W19M**, R15M, G15M; vis: G107·4°-109°, W109°-111·2°, R111·2°-112·6°.
Borkum Kleiner ☆ 53°34'·73N 06°39'·94E FW 32m **30M**; R Tr, W bands; vis: 089·9°-090·9° (Ldg sector for Hubertgat); Same Tr Fl 3s **16M**; vis: 088°-089·9°; Q (4) 10s **16M**; vis: 090·9°-093°; Fl Y 4s on tide gauge 420m SW.

◄ BORKUM

Fischerbalje ☆ 53°33'·16N 06°42'·86E Oc (2) WRG 16s 15m **W16M**, R12M, G11M; W ○ Tr, R top and lantern, on tripod; vis: R260°-313°, G313°-014°, W014°-068°, (Ldg sector to Fischerbalje); R068°-123°. Fog Det Lt.
Schutzhafen Ent ☆ 53°33'·48N 06°45'·02E FG 10m 4M, and FR 8m 5M.
Campen ☆ 53°24'·33N 07°00'·92E F 62m **30M**; R framework Tr, 2 galleries, W central col, G cupola; vis: 126·8°-127·1°. Fl 5s (same Tr); vis: 126·3°-126·8°. Fl (4) 15s (same Tr) vis: 127·1°-127·6°.

◄ ALTE EMS

H11 53°34'·61N 06°33'·38E QG.
A3/H16 53°33'·48N 06°38'·50E.
A5/H15 53°33'·21N 06°38'·55E.
A8/Alte Ems Reede 53°30'·54N 06°42'·50E Fl (2) R 9s.
A16/Umschlag-Reede 53°28'·87N 06°48'·45E Fl R 4s.

◄ EEMSHAVEN (Netherlands)

No. 30 53°28'·81N 06°50'·38E Fl (2) R 9s.
W Pier ☆ 53°27'·74N 06°50·06E FG 8m 3M.

◄ DUKE GAT

No. 27 53°30'·24N 06°47'·52E Fl G 4s.
No. 35 53°27'·03N 06°52'·79E Fl G 4s.
No. 37 53°26'·01N 06°54'·85E QG.
No. 41 53°24'·25N 06°56'·68E Fl (2) G 9s.
No. 44 53°22'·07N 06°58'·69E Fl R 4s.
No. 49 53°19'·95N 06°59'·71E Oc (2) G 9s.

◄ KNOCK

K4 53°19'·84N 07°00'·76E QR.
Knock ☆ 53°20'·32N 07°01'·40E F WRG 28m W12M, R9M, G8M; Gy Tr, four galleries, broad top, radar antenna; vis: W270°-299°, R299-008·3°, G008·3°-023°, W023°-026·8°, R026·8°-039°, W039°-073°, R073°-119°, W119°-154°; Fog Det Lt.

◄ DELFZIJL ENTRANCE (Netherlands)

PS3/BW26 53°19'·22N 07°00'·35E Fl (2+1) G 12s.
W Mole Head, E ent ☆ 53°19'·02N 07°00'·26E FG.
E Mole Head ☆ 53°18'·94N 07°00'·60E FR, in fog FY.
Ldg Lts 203°. Front, 53°18'·64N 07°00'·16E Iso 4s. Rear, 310m from front, Iso 4s.

◄ TERMUNTERZIJL (Netherlands)

BW13 53°18'·65N 07°02'·28E Fl G 5s.
Wybelsum ☆ 53°20'·17N 07°06'·48E F WR 16m W6M, R5M, W ○ Tr, R bands; radar antenna; vis: W295°-320°, R320°-024°, W024°-049°; Fog Det Lt.

◄ EMDEN

No. 71 53°19'·91N 07°09'·75E Oc (2) G 9s.
Logum Ldg Lts 075·2°. Front, 53°20'·12N 07°07'·96E Oc (2) 12s 16m 12M; W mast, R bands. Rear, 630m from front, Oc (2) 12s 28m 12M; W mast, R bands; synch with front.
Ldg Lts 087·6°. Front, 53°20'·03N 07°12'·07E Oc 5s 14m 14M, intens on Ldg line. Rear, 0·8M from front, Oc 5s 30m 14M, synch with front, intens on Ldg line.
W Pier Head ☆ 53°20'·06N 07°10'·49E FR 10m 4M; R 8-sided Tr; *Horn Mo (ED) 30s.*
Outer Hbr E pier Head ☆ 53°20'·05N 07°10'·84E FG 7m 5M; R Tr, B band.

RIVER EMS TO RIVER JADE, INCLUDING EAST FRISIAN ISLANDS.

◄ OUTER LIMIT OF INSHORE TRAFFIC ZONE

TG1/Ems 53°43'·27N 06°22'·24E IQ. G 13s.
TG3 53°44'·62N 06°31'·09E Fl (2) G 9s.
TG5 53°45'·81N 06°39'·99E Oc (3) G 12s.
TG7 53°47'·24N 06°49'·65E Fl (2) G 9s.
TG9 53°48'·35N 06°57'·66E Oc (3) G 12s.
TG11 53°49'·58N 07°06'·48E Fl (2) G 9s.
TG13 53°50'·92N 07°15'·37E Oc (3) G 12s.
TG15 53°52'·13N 07°24'·27E Fl (2) G 9s.
TG17/Weser 1 53°53'·43N 07°33'·13E IQ G 13s.
TG19/Weser 2 53°54'·99N 07°44'·66E Fl (2+1) G 15s.

Borkumriff 53°47'·44N 06°22'·05E Oc 4s; Racon (T).
GW/EMS 54°09'·96N 06°20'·72E Iso 8s 12m **17M**; *Horn Mo (R) 30s (H24)*; Racon (T).

INSHORE ROUTE EMS TO JADE

Riffgat 53°38'·93N 06°27'·03E Iso 8s.
Osterems 53°41'·88N 06°36'·14E Iso 4s.
Juist-N 53°43'·77N 06°55'·36E VQ.
Juist Aero Lt 53°40'·85N 07°03'·37E Fl 5s 14m (occas).
Schluchter 53°44'·45N 07°02'·20E Iso 8s.
Dovetief 53°45'·23 07°08'·97E Iso 4s.
Platform 54°42'·1N 07°10'·0E; Mo (U) 15s 24m 9M; R platform, Y stripes; *Horn Mo (U) 30s.*
Norderney N 53°46'·07N 07°17'·13E Q.
Accumer Ee 53°46·80N 07°24·43E Iso 8s; (frequently moved).
Otzumer Balje 53°47'·98N 07°37'·12E Iso 4s; (frequently moved.)
Harle 53°49'·29N 07°48'·99E Iso 8s.

◄ GREETSIEL

Meßstation Lt Bn 53°32'·97N 07°02'·22E Fl Y 4s 15m 3M.

◀ JUIST
Training Wall, S end 53°39'·70N 06°59'·92E; pile.
Juist 53°41'·9N 07°03'·5E Aero Fl 5s 14m.
Schluchter 53°44'·45N 07°02'·20E Iso 8s.

◀ NORDDEICH
W Training Wall, Head 53°38'·7N 07°09'·0E FG 8m 4M; framework Tr, W lantern; vis: 021°-327°.
Training Wall Head FR 8m 4M; R & W △ on R Tr; vis: 327°-237°.
Ldg Lts 144°. Front, Iso WR 6s 6m W6M, R4M; B mast; vis: R078°-122°, W122°-150°. Rear, 140m from front, Iso 6s 9m 6M; B mast; synch with front.

◀ NORDERNEY
Norderney ☆ 53°42'·58N 07°13'·83E Fl (3) 12s 59m **23M**; R 8 sided Tr; unintens 067°-077° and 270°-280°.
Fish Hbr W Mole Head 53°41'·9N 07°09'·9E Oc (2) R 9s 13m 4M.
Norderney N 53°46'·10N 07°17'·22E Q.

◀ BALTRUM
Baltrum Groyne Head 53°43'·3N 07°21'·7E Oc WRG 6s 7m W6M, R4M, G3M; vis: G074·5°-090°, W090°-095°, R095°-074·5°.

◀ NESSMERSIEL
Mole N Head 53°41'·9N 07°21'·7E Oc 4s 6m 5M; G mast.
Accumer Ee 53°46·80N 07°24·43E Iso 8s; (frequently moved).

◀ LANGEOOG
W Mole Head 53°43'·42N 07°30'·13E Oc WRG 6s 8m W7M, R5M, G4M; R basket on R mast; vis: G064°-070°, W070°-074°, R074°-326°, W326°-330°, G330°-335°, R335°-064°; *Horn Mo (L) 30s* (0730-1800LT).

◀ DORNUMER-ACCUMERSIEL
W Bkwtr Head 53°41'·25N 07°29'·40E.

◀ BENSERSIEL
E Training Wall Head 53° 41'·84N 07°32'·90E Oc WRG 6s 6m W5M, R3M, G2M; vis: G110°-119°, W119°-121°, R121°-110°.
Ldg Lts 138°. Front, Iso 6s 7m 9M. Rear, 167m from front, Iso 6s 11m 9M. Both intens on Ldg line.
Otzumer Balje 53°47'·98N 07°37'·12 Iso 4s (frequently moved.)

◀ SPIEKEROOG
Spiekeroog 53°45'·0N 07°41'·3E FR 6m 4M; R mast; vis: 197°-114°.

◀ NEUHARLINGERSIEL
Training Wall Head 53°43'·22N 07°42'·30E Oc 6s 6m 5M.

◀ HARLESIEL
Harle 53°49'·28N 07°49'·00E Iso 8s.
Carolinensieler Balje, Leitdamm 53°44'·13N 07°50'·10E L Fl 8s 7m 6M; G mast.
N Mole Head 53°42'·63N 07°48'·70E Iso R 4s 6m 7M.

◀ WANGEROOGE
Wangerooge ☆, W end 53°47'·40N 07°51'·41E Fl R 5s 60m **23M**; R ◯ Tr, 2 W bands; same Tr; Same structure F WR 24m **W15M**, R11M, vis: W055°-060·5°, R060·5°-065·5°, W065·5°-071°. Same structure Dir F WRG 24m **W22M, G18M, R17M**; vis: G119·4°-138·8°, W138·8°-152·2° Ldg sector, R152·2°-159·9°.
Buhne W Bkwtr Head 53°46'·33N 07°51'·93E FR 3m 4M.

◀ RIVER JADE AND APPROACHES
JW5/Jade 1 53°52'·47N 07°44'·10E Oc G 4s.
Weser 1/Jade 2 53°52'·12N 07°47'·35E Fl (2+1) G 15s; Racon (T).
Mellumplate ☆ 53°46'·28N 08°05'·51E F 28m **24M**; R □ Tr, W band; vis: 116·1°-116·4°; Ldg sector for outer part of Wangerooger Fahrwasser. The following Lts are shown from the same Tr over sectors indicated. Fl 4s **23M**; vis: 114°-115·2°. Fl (4) 15s vis: 117·2°-118·4°. Mo (A) 7·5s; vis 115·2°-116·1° Ldg sector. Mo (N) 7·5s; vis: 116·4°-117·2°.
No. 7 53°50'·31N 07°51'·30E Oc (3) G 12s.
No.11 53°49'·19N 07°55'·20E Fl G 4s.
No.15/Blaue Balje 53°48'·07N 07°59'·10E IQ. G 13s.
No.19 53°47'·14N 08°01'·85E QG.
No.23 53°45'·20N 08°02'·79E Oc (3) G 12s.
No. 31/P-Reede/W Siel 1 53°41'·59N 08°04'·51E Oc (3) G 12s.

◀ HOOKSIEL
No. 37/Hooksiel 1 53°39'·37N 08°06'·58E IQ G 13s.
H3 53°38'·65N 08°05'·63E Fl G 4s.
Hooksiel Marina Ent 53°38'·63N 08°05'·25E L Fl R 6s 4m 3M.
Voslapp ☆ Ldg Lts 164·5°. **Front**, 53°37'·18N 08°06'·87E Iso 6s 15m **24M**; R ○ Tr, W bands, R lantern; intens on Ldg line. **Rear** ☆, 2·35M from front Iso 6s 60m **27M**; W ◯ Tr, R bands.
Tossens ☆ Ldg Lts 146°. **Front**, 53°34'·55N 08°12'·42E Oc 6s 15m **20M**; W ◯ Tr, R band, R lantern. **Rear**, 2M from front, Oc 6s 51m **20M**; R ◯ Tr, W stripes, 3 galleries.

◀ WILHELMSHAVEN
Eckwarden Ldg Lts 154°. **Front, Solthörner Watt** ☆ 53°32'·40N 08°13'·00E Iso WRG 3s 15m **W19M**, W12M, R9M, G8M; R ◯ Tr, W bands; vis: R346°-348°, W348°-028°, R028°-052°; W (intens) 052°-054° Ldg sector, G054°-067·5°, W067·5°-110°, G110°-152·6°; W (intens) 152·6° across fairway, with undefined limit on E side of Ldg line. **Rear** ☆, 1·27M from front, Iso 3s 41m **21M**; R Tr & lantern; synch with front.
Neuer Vorhaven Ldg Lts 207·8°. Front, 53°31'·82N 08°09'·60E Iso 4s 17m 11M; B mast, R lantern. Rear, 180m from front, Iso 4s 23m 11M; Y bldg; intens on Ldg line.
W Mole Head 53°32'·48N 08°10'·08E Oc G 6s 15m 4M.
E Mole Head 53°32'·43N 08°10'·24E Oc R 6s 5M.
Fluthaffen N Mole Hd 53°30'·86N 08°09'·32E F WG 9m W6M, G3M; G Tr; vis: W216°-280°, G280°-010°, W010°-020°, G020°-130°.
Flutmole Head 53°30'·80N 08°09'·17E FR 6m 5M.
Arngast ☆ Dir Lt 53°28'·88N 08°10'·89E F WRG 30m **W21M**, W10, **R16M**, **G17M**, G7M; R ○ Tr, W bands; vis: W135°-142°, G142°-150°, W150°-152°, G152°-174·6°, R180·5°-191°, W191°-213°, R213°-225°, W(10M) 286°-303°, G(7M) 303°-314°. Same structure Fl WG 3s, vis: G174·6°-175·5°, W175·5°-176·4°. Same structure Fl (2) 9s; vis: 177·4°-180·5°. Same structure Oc 6s **20M**; vis: 176·4°-177·4°.

◀ DANGAST
Lock 53°26'·73N 08°06'·47E.

◀ VARELER SIEL
Lock 53°24'·57N 08°11'·28E.

◀ RIVER WESER AND APPROACHES
Weser 53°54'·25N 07°50'·00E Iso 5s 12m **17M**; Racon.
Schlüsseltonne 53°56'·25N 07°54'·76E Iso 8s.
Alte Weser ☆ 53°51'·79N 08°07'·65E F WRG 33m **W23M**, **R19M**, **G18M**; R ◯ Tr, 2 W bands, B base, floodlit; vis: W288°-352°, R352°-003°, W003°-017°, Ldg sector for Alte Weser, G017°-045°, W045°-074°, G074°-118°, W118°-123°, Ldg sector for Alte Weser, R123°-140°, G140°-175°, W175°-183°, R183°-196°, W196°-238°; Fog Det Lt; *Horn Mo (AL) 60s*.

24

Tegeler Plate ☆, N end 53°47'·87N 08°11'·45E Oc (3) WRG 12s 21m **W21M, R17M, G16M**; R ○ Tr, gallery, W lantern, R roof; vis: W329°-340°, R340°-014°, W014°-100°, G100°-116°, W116°-119°; Ldg sector for Neue Weser, R119°-123°, G123°-144°, W144°-147°; Ldg sector for Alte Weser R147°-264°; Fog Det Lt.

Hohe Weg ☆, NE part 53°42'·74N 08°14'·57E F WRG 29m **W19M, R16M, G15M**; R 8-sided Tr, 2 galleries, G lantern; vis: W102°-138·5°, G138·5°-142·5°, W142·5°-145·5°, R145·5°-184°, W184°-278·5°; Fog Det Lt.

Robbennordsteert ☆ 53°42'·13N 08°20'·37E F WR 11m W10M, R7M; R col; vis: W324°-004°, R004°-090°, W090°-121°.

Robbenplate Ldg Lts 122·3°. **Front** ☆, 53°40'·89N 08°22'·99E Oc 6s 15m **17M**; R tripod; intens on Ldg line. **Rear** ☆, 0·54M from front, Oc 6s 37m **18M**; R □ Tr, 3 galleries, G lantern; vis: 116°-125·5°; synch with front; Fog Det Lt.

Wremerloch Ldg Lts 140·1°. Front, 53°38'·42N 08°25'·07E Iso 6s 15m 13M. Rear, 0·57M from front, Iso 6s 31m 14M; synch with front.

Dwarsgat ☆ Ldg Lts 320·1°. Front, 53°43'·12N 08°18'·44E Iso 6s 16m **15M**. **Rear** ☆, 0·75M from front, Iso 6s 35m **17M**; synch with front (same Ldg Line as Wremer Loch).

Langlütjen Ldg Lts 305·2°. Front, 53°39'·62N 08°22'·79E Oc 6s 15m 13M; B mast, B & W gallery; vis: 288°-310°. Rear, 930m from front, Oc 6s 31m 14M; synch with front.

Imsum Ldg Lts 125·2°. Front 53°36'·38N 08°30'·53E Oc 6s 15m 13M; R tripod with gallery; **Rear** ☆, 1·02M from front, Oc 6s 39m **16M**; synch with front.

Solthorn Ldg Lts 320·6°. Front 53°38'·29N 08°27'·32E Iso 4s 15m 13M; R&W mast. **Rear** ☆, 700m from front, Iso 4s 31m **17M**; synch with front.

Fischeriehafen ☆ Ldg Lts 150·8°. **Common front**, 53°31'·88N 08°34'·52E Oc 6s 17m **18M**, R △ on W mast. **Rear** ☆ , 0·68M from front, Oc 6s 45m **18M** 2 R ▽ on W mast, R bands; synch with front.

No. 61 53°32'·26N 08°33'·93E QG; (Km 66·0).

◀ BREMERHAVEN

Vorhafen N Pier ☆ 53°32'·15N 08°34'·50E FR 15m 5M.

S Pier Hd ☆ 53°32'·09N 08°34'·50E FG 15m 5M; vis: 355°-265°.

Nordenham Hafen N ent ☆ 53°28'·06N 08°29'·05E FG 11m 2M.

Nordenham Ldg Lts 355·9°. Front, 53°27'·87N 08°29'·29E Iso 4s 15m **16M**; on R mast, W bands. Rear, 1M from front, Iso 4s 41m **19M**; sync with front.

No.99/Hunte 53°15'·45N 08°28'·86E IQ G; Km 32·7.

◀ BREMEN

Hasenbüren Sporthafen ☆ 53°07'·51N 08°40'·03E 2 FY (vert); Km 11·6.

GERMAN BIGHT

GW/EMS 54°10'·00N 06°20'·80E Iso 8s 12m **17M**; R hull marked GW/EMS; Racon (T); .))) *Horn Mo (R) 30s*.

D-B Weser 54°02'·42N 07°43'·05E Oc (3) R 12s; Racon.

◀ HELGOLAND

Helgoland-W 54°10'·61N 07°48'·20E (Restricted area).

Helgoland-O 54°08'·96N 07°53'·48E Q (3) 10s; .))) *Whis*.

Helgoland ☆ 54°10'·91N 07°52'·93E Fl 5s 82m **28M**; Brown □ Tr, B lantern, W balcony. FR on radio masts 180m SSE and 740m NNW.

Vorhafen. Ostmole, S elbow ☆ 54°10'·31N 07°53'·94E Oc WG 6s 5m W6M, G3M; G post; vis: W203°-250°, G250°-109°; Fog Det Lt.

Ostmole Head ☆ 54°10'·33N 07°53'·88E FG 7m 4M; vis: 289° 180°; .))) *Horn (3) 30s*.

Sudmole Hd ☆ 54°10'·24N 07°53'·94E Oc (2) R 12s 7m 4M R post; vis: 101°-334°.

Binnenhafen Ldg Lts 302·2° W Pier, Front ☆ 54°10'·78N 07°53'·36E Oc R 6s 8m 6M. Rear, 50m from front ☆, Oc R 6 10m 6M; synch with front.

DÜNE

Düne -S 54°09'·57N 07°56'·01E Q (6) + L Fl 15s.

Ldg Lts 020°. Front 54°10'·87N 07°54'·80E ☆ Iso 4s 11m 8M intens on Ldg line. Rear, 120m from front, Iso WRG 4s 17m W11M, R10M, G10M; synch with front; vis: G010°-018·5° W018·5°-021°, R021°-030, G106°-125°, W125°-130°, R130°144°

Sellebrunn W 54°14'·43N 07°49'·83E Q (9) 15s; .))) *Whis*.

Nathurn-N 54°13'·40N 07°49'·05E.

RIVER WESER TO RIVER ELBE

Nordergründe N 53°57'·10N 08°00'·14E VQ.

Elbe 53°59'·95N 08°06'·49E Iso 10s; Racon (T).

Westertill N 53°58'·14N 08°06'·71E Q.

Scharnhörnriff W 53°58'·49N 08°08'·72E Q (9) 15s.

Scharnhörnriff N 53°58'·95N 08°11'·15E Q.

RIVER ELBE AND APPROACHES

No.1 53°59'·21N 08°13'·20E QG.

No.5 53°59'·31N 08°18'·93E QG.

No.11 53°58'·65N 08°26'·02E Fl G 4s.

Grosser Vogelsand 53°59'·74N 08°28'·59E .))) *Horn Mo (VS) 30s*.

No.19 53°57'·71N 08°34'·33E QG.

No.25 53°56'·62N 08°38'·25E QG.

Neuwerk ☆, S side 53°54'·92N 08°29'·73E L Fl (3) WRG 20s 38m **W16M**, R12M, G11M; vis: G165·3°-215·3°, W215·3°-238·8° R238·8°-321°, R343°-100°.

◀ CUXHAVEN

Ldg Lts 151·2°. **Baumrönne** ☆, front, 53°51'·19N 08°44'·15E 1·55M from rear, Fl 3s 25m **17M**; W ○ Tr, B band on gallery vis: 143·8°-149·2°. Same Tr, Iso 4s **17M**; vis: 149·2°-154·2° Fl (2) 9s **17M**; vis: 154·2°-156·7°. **Altenbruch, common rear** ☆ 53°49'·81N 08°45'·43E Iso 4s 58m **21M**; intens on Ldg line synch with front. Same structure, Iso 8s 51m **22M**; synch with front.

Altenbruch Ldg Lts 261°. **Common front** ☆, 53°50'·02N 08°47'·66E Iso 8s 19m **19M**; W ○ Tr, B bands. Same structure Iso WRG 8s W8M, R9M, G8M; vis: G117·5°-124°, W124°-135° R135°-140°. Rear, Wehldorf 53°49'·82N 08°48'·09E Iso 8s 31m 11M; W ○ Tr, B bands; synch with front.

No. 35 53°50'·67N 08°45'·77E Oc (2) G 9s.

No. 43 53°50'·23N 08°52'·24E Oc (2) G 9s.

◀ OTTERNDORF

No. 45 Ottewrndorf 53°50'·39N 08°54'·24E Fl G 4s.

Medem, Hadelner Kanal ent ☆ 53°50'·15N 08°53'·85E Fl (3) 12s 6m 5M; B △, on B col.

Balje ☆ Ldg Lts 081°. **Front**, 53°51'·29N 09°02'·63E Iso 8s 24m **17M**; W ○ Tr, R bands. **Rear**, 1·35M from front, Iso 8s 54m **21M**; W ○ Tr, R bands; intens on Ldg line; synch with front.

Zweidorf ☆ 53°53'·38N 09°05'·60E Oc R 5s 9m 3M; R □ on W pylon; vis: 287°-107°.

Jo. 51 53°51'·03N 09°00'·15E QG.
Jo. 57 53°52'·50N 09°06'·30E QG.

◀ BRUNSBÜTTEL

dg Lts 065·5°'. Front, **Schleuseninsel** ☆ 53°53'·32N 09°08'·47E so 3s 24m **16M**; R Tr, W bands; vis: North of 063·3°. Rear, **ndustriegebiet** ☆, 0·9M from front, Iso 3s 46m **21M**; R ◯ Tr, V bands; synch with front.

ılterhaven N Mole (Mole 4) Hd ☆ 53°53'·25N 09°07'·53E F WR vert) 13m W10M, R8M; vis: R275·5°-079°, W079°-084°.

ɴORD-OSTSEE KANAL (KIEL CANAL),

◀ RENDSBURG/KIEL-HOLTENAU

Jo. 2/Obereider 1 54°18'·91N 09°42'·64E Fl (2+1) R 15s.
‹iel Nordmole ☆ 54°21'·79N 10°09'·10E Oc (2) WR 9s 23m.
iessenkal ☆ Oc (3) WG 12s 22m.

◀ FRIEBURG

Entrance Bn (unlit) 53°50'·25N 09°18'·90E; SHM.
Rhinplatte Nord ☆ 53°48'·09N 09°23'·36E Oc WRG 6s 11m V6M, R4M, G3M; vis: G122°-144°, W144°-150°, R150°-177°, V177°-122°; Ra refl.

◀ STÖRLOCH/BORSFLETH, STÖR/BEIDENFLETH

Stör Ldg Lts 093·8°. Front, 53°49'·29N 09°23'·91E Fl 3s 7m 6M; △ on R ◯ Tr. Rear, 200m from front, Fl 3s 12m 6M; synch with ront.

◀ GLÜCKSTADT

Glückstadt Ldg Lts 131·8° Front ☆, 53°48'·31N 09°24'·24E so 8s 15m **19M**; W Tr, R bands; intens on Ldg line. **Rear** ☆, ·68M from front, Iso 8s 30m **21M**; W Tr, R bands; intens on .dg line.

ı Mole ☆ 53°47'·12N 09°24'·53E Oc WRG 6s 9m W9M R7M, G6M; W Tr with gallery; vis R330°-343°, W343°-346°, G346°008°, G123°-145°, W145°-150°, R150°-170°.

ı Pier Hd ☆ 53°47'·10N 09°24'·50E FR 5m 5M. (FG on South Mole Hd.)

Pagensand Ldg Lts 135° 53°41'·76N 09°30'·51E. Front, Iso 4s 20m 13M; W Tr, R bands. Rear, 880m from front, Iso 4s 32m 13M.

◀ STADE

No. 103 53°37'·96N 09°31'·50E Oc (2) G 9s.
Stadersand ☆ 53°37'·69N 09°31'·64E Iso 8s 20m 14M.

HAMBURG

◀ HAMBURGER YACHT HAFEN, WEDEL

No.119/HN1 53°34'·04N 09°39'·42E QG.
No. 122 53°34'·15N 09°40'·62E Oc (2) R 9s.
Hamburger Jachthafen E Ent E Pier Hd ☆ 53°34'·25N 09°40'·79E FG 5m 3M. (Both ent show FR & FG May to Oct.).

◀ SCHULAU

No. 123 53°33'·85N 09°41'·97E Fl G 4s.
Hafen Schulau E Pier Head ☆ 53°34'·09N 09°41'·95E FG 5m 3M.
HN3 53°33'·41N 09°40'·01E.
Neuenschleuse Yacht Hbr 53°33'·24N 09°40'·19E.

◀ MÜHLENBERG

Ent E Pier Head 53°33'·19N 09°49'·40E (unmarked).
No.130 53°33'·01N 09°50'·16E Oc R 4s.

◀ RÜSCHKANAL

No. 133 53°32'·86N 09°49'·95E Oc (2) G 9s.
East Ent ☆ 53°32'·59N 09°51'·02E FR 9m 3M.

◀ TEUFELSBRÜCK

Ent W Breakwater Hd 53°32'·83N 09°52'·04E (unmarked).

◀ CITY SPORTHAFEN

Brandenburger Hafen Ent ☆ 53°32'·52N 09°58'·81E Iso Or 2s.

RIVER ELBE TO DANISH BORDER

◀ INSHORE ROUTE RIVER ELBE TO SYLT

Süderpiep 54°05'·93N 08°21'·89E Iso 8s; *Whis.*
Hever 54°20'·46N 08°18'·87E Oc 4s; *Whis.*
Rütergat 54°30'·28N 08°12'·12E Iso 8s.
Amrum Bank S 54°31'·94N 08°04'·84E Q (6) + L Fl 15s.
Vortrapptief 54°34'·87N 08°12'·97E Iso 4s.
Amrum Bank W 54°37'·93N 07°54'·85E Q (9) 15s.
Theeknobs W 54°43'·48N 08°09'·81E Q (9) 15s.
Amrum Bank N 54°44'·93N 08°06'·85E Q.
Lister Tief 55°05'·32N 08°16'·67E Iso 8s; *Whis.*

◀ BÜSUM

Süderpiep 54°05'·93N 08°21'·89E Iso 8s; *Whis.*
Büsum ☆ 54°07'·62N 08°51'·41E Iso WRG 16s 22m **W17M**, R14M, G13M; vis: W248°-317°, R317°-024°, W024°-084°, G084°-092·5°, W092·5°-094·5° Ldg sector for Süder Piep, R094·5°-097°, W097°-148°.
W Mole Hd ☆ 54°07'·19N 08°51'·52E Oc (3) R 12s 10m 4M; R Tr; vis: 186°-120°.
E Mole Head ☆ 54°07'·19N 08°51'·65E Oc (3) G 12s 10m 4M; G Tr; vis: 260°-168°.
Ldg Lts 355·1°. Front, 54°07'·53N 08°51'·58E Iso 4s 9m 13M; B mast, W bands. Rear, 110m from front, Iso 4s 12m 13M; synch with front.

◀ RIVER EIDER

Eider 54°14'·53N 08°27'·54E Iso 4s.
St Peter ☆ 54°17'·24N 08°39'·10E L Fl (2) WR 15s 23m **W15M**, R12M; R Tr, B lantern; vis: R271°-294°, W294°-325°, R325°-344°, W344°-035°, R035°-055°, W055°-068°, R068°-091°, W091°-120°.
Eiderdamm Lock, N Mole, W end ☆ Oc (2) R 12s 8m 5M; W Tr.
S Mole, W end ☆ Oc G 6s 8m 6M: W Tr, Gy top.

◀ TÖNNING

W Mole Head ☆ 54°18'·93N 08°57'·09E FR 5m 4M; R col.
Quay ☆ 54°18'·95N 08°57'·12E FG 5m 4M; G col.

RIVER HEVER

Hever 54°20'·42N 08°18'·82E Oc 4s; *Whis.*
No. 3 54°20'·69N 08°23'·12E Fl G 4s.
No. 8 54°21'·39N 08°27'·11E Fl R 4s.
Norderhever 54°22'·46N 08°30'·83E Fl (2+1) R 15s.
Westerheversand ☆ 54°22'·37N 08°38'·36E Oc (3) WRG 15s 14m **W21M, R17M, G16M**; R Tr, W bands; vis: W012·2°-069°, G069°-079·5°°, W079·5°-080·5°; Ldg sector for Hever, R080·5°-107°, W107°-157°, R157°-169°, W169°-206·5°, R206·5°-218·5°, W218·5°-233°, R233°-248°.

◀ HUSUM

Husumer Au Outer Ldg Lts 106·5°. Front, 54°28'·57N 09°00'·78E Iso R 8s 8m 5M; R mast, W bands; intens on Ldg line. Rear, 0·52M from front, Iso R 8s 17m 6M; Y mast; synch with front.

Inner Ldg Lts 090°. Front, 54°28'·79N 09°00'·32E Iso G 8s 7m 3M; R mast, W bands; intens on Ldg line. Rear, 40m from front, Iso G 8s 9m 3M; intens on Ldg line; synch with front.

◀ NORDSTRAND

Strucklahnungshörn, W Mole Head ☆ 54°29'·91N 08°48'·29E Oc G 6s 8m 2M.

◀ PELLWORM

Pellworm ☆ S side Ldg Lts 041°. Front, 54°29'·82N 08°40'·05E Oc WR 5s 14m **W20M**, W11M, R8M. Intens on Ldg line; vis: W303·5°-313·5°, R313.5°-316·5°. **Rear** ☆, 0·8M from front, Oc 5s 38m **20M**; R Tr, W band; synch with front. Same Tr as rear Lt, Cross Light ☆ Oc WR 5s 38m W14M, W9M, R11M, R6M; vis: R11M 122·6°-140°, W14M 140°-161·5°, R11M 161·5°-179·5°, W14M 179·5°-210·2°, R6M 255°-265·5°, W9M 265·5°-276°, R6M 276°-297°, W9M 297°-307°.

◀ WITTDÜN, AMRUM

Rütergat ⛯ 54°30'·28N 08°12'·12E Iso 8s.

Amrum Hafen Ldg Lts 272°. Front, 54°37'·88N 08°22'·92E Iso R 4s 11m 10M; W mast, R stripe; intens on Ldg Line. **Rear** ☆, 0·9M from front, Iso R 4s 33m **15M**.

Amrum ☆ 54°37'·84N 08°21'·23E Fl 7·5s 63m **23M**; R Tr, W bands.

Wriakhorn Cross Lt ☆ 54°37'·62N 08°21'·22E L Fl (2) WR 15s 26m W9M, R7M; vis: W297·5°-319·5°, R319·5°-330°, W330°-005·5°, R055·5°-034°.

Nebel ☆ 54°38'·75N 08°21'·75E Oc WRG 5s 16m **W20M, R15M, G15M**; R Tr, W band; vis R255·5°-258·5°, W258·5°-260·5°, G260·5°-263·5°.

Norddorf ☆ 54°40'·13N 08°18'·46E Oc WRG 6s 22m **W15M**, R12M, G11M; W ○ Tr, R lantern; vis: W009-036·8°, R036·8-099°, W099°-146°, R146°-176·5°, W176·5°-178·5°, G178·5°-188°, G(unintens) 188°-202°, W(partially obscd) 202°-230°.

◀ LANGENESS

Nordmarsch ☆ 54°37'·58N 08°31'·85E L Fl (3) WR 20s 13m W14M, R11M; Dark Brown Tr; vis: W268°-279°, R279°-306°, W306°-045°, R045°-070°, W070°-218°.

◀ OLAND

Near W Point ☆ 54°40'·51N 08°41'·28E F WRG 7m W13M, R10M, G9M; R Tr; G086°-093°, W093°-160°, R160°-172°.

◀ SCHLÜTTSIEL

Schl No. 20 ⛯ 54°40'·83N 08°44'·60E.

Harbour ent, S side ▲ 54°40'·89N 08°45'·10E.

◀ WYK, FÖHR

Nieblum ☆ 54°41'·10N 08°29'·20E Oc (2) WRG 10s 11m **W19M R15M, G15M**; R Tr, W band; vis: G028°-031°, W031°-032·5° R032·5°-035·5°.

◀ DAGEBÜLL

Dagebüll ☆ 53°43'·82N 08°41'·43E Iso WRG 8s 22m **W15M** R12M, G11M; G mast; vis: G042°-043°, W043°-044·5°, R044·5° 047°. FW Lts shown on N and S Mole Hd.

◀ SYLT

Theeknobs W ⛯ 54°43'·49N 08°09'·72E Q (9) 15s.

Hörnum ☆ 54°45'·23N 08°17'·47E Fl (2) 9s 48m **20M**.

N Pier ☆ Head FG 6m 4M; vis: 024°-260°.

South Mole Head ☆ 54°45'·57N 08°17'·97E FR 7m 4M.

Kampen, Rote Kliff ☆ 54°56'·76N 08°20'·38E L Fl WR 15s 62m **W20M, R16M**; W Tr, B band; vis: W193°-260°, W(unintens) 260°-339°, W339°-165°, R165°-193°.

Lister Tief ⛯ 55°05'·32N 08°16'·67E Iso 8s; ·))) *Whis.*

List West (Ellenbogen) ☆ 55°03'·15N 08°24'·00E Oc WRG 6s 19m W14M, R11M, G10M; W Tr, R lantern; vis: R040°-133° W133°-227°, R227°-266·4°, W266·4°-268°, G268°-285°, W285°-310°, W(unintens) 310°-040°.

List Ost (N side), ☆ 55°02'·93N 08°26'·58E Iso WRG 6s 22m W14M, R11M, G10M; W Tr, R band; vis: W(unintens) 010·5°-098°, W098°-262°, R262°-278°, W278°-296°, R296°-323·3° W323·3°-324·5°, G324·5°-350°, W350°-010·5°, Q 4M on Tr 9·4M NNE, shown when firing takes place.

List Land ☆ 55°01'·03N 08°26'·47E Oc WRG 3s 14m W13M, R10M, G9M; W mast, R band; vis: W170°-203°, G203°-212°, W212°-215·5°, R215·5°-232·5°, W232·5°-234°, G234°-243°, W243°-050°.

List Hafen N Mole Head ☆ 55°01'·03N 08°26'·52E FG 5m 3M; G mast; vis: 218°-038°.

S Mole Head ☆ 55°01'·01N 08°26'·51E FR 5m 4M; R mast, vis: 218°-353°.

9.24.5 PASSAGE INFORMATION

Refer to: Admiralty Pilot *North Sea (East); Cruising Guide to Germany and Denmark* (Imray/Navin) and *Frisian Pilot* (Adlard Coles/Brackenbury - out of print).

RIVER EMS (charts 3509, 3510) The River Ems forms the boundary between Netherlands and Germany, and is a major waterway leading to Eemshaven, Delfzijl (9.23.33), Emden (9.24.8), Leer and Papenburg. Approach through Hubertgat or Westerems, which join W of Borkum; the latter is advised at night. Both are well buoyed but can be dangerous with an ebb stream and a strong W or NW wind. The flood begins at HW Helgoland + 0530, and the ebb at HW Helgoland – 0030, sp rates 1·5kn.

From close SW of Borkum the chan divides: Randzel Gat to the N and Alte Ems running parallel to it to the S – as far as Eemshaven on the S bank. About 3M further on the chan again divides. Bocht van Watum is always varying so keep in main chan, Ostfriesisches Gatje, for Delfzijl and beyond. Off Eemshaven the stream runs 2-3kn.

Osterems is the E branch of the estuary of R. Ems, passing between Borkum and Memmert. It is poorly marked, unlit and much shallower than Westerems. It also gives access to the Ley chan, leading to the hbr of Greetsiel (9.24.8). But it is not advised without local knowledge and in ideal weather.

RIVER EMS TO RIVER JADE (chart 3761) The route to seaward of the Frisian Is from abeam Borkum to the E end of Wangerooge is about 50 miles. This is via the ITZ, S of the Terschellinger-German Bight TSS, the E-going lane of which is marked on its S side by SHM buoys lettered DB1, DB3, DB5 etc. About 4M S of this line of buoys the landward side of the ITZ is marked by landfall buoys showing the apprs to the eight main seegaten between the East Frisian Is. There are major lts on Borkum, Norderney and Wangerooge. Near the TSS the E-going stream begins at HW Helgoland – 0500, and the W-going at HW Helgoland + 0100, sp rates 1·2kn. Inshore the stream is influenced by the flow through the seegaten.

THE EAST FRISIAN ISLANDS (9.24.9 and chart 3761) The East Frisian Islands have fewer facilities for yachtsmen than the Dutch Islands to the W, and most of them are closer to the mainland. For general notes, see 9.23.5 and 9.24.9. For navigating inside the islands, in the *wattfahrenwassern* or so-called watt chans, it is essential to have the large scale pleasure craft charts (BSH) and to understand the system of channel marking. Withies, unbound (‡ with twigs pointing up) are used as PHMs, and withies which are bound (‡ with twigs pointing down) as SHMs. Inshore of the islands the *conventional direction of buoyage is always from West to East*, even though this may conflict with the actual direction of the flood stream in places.

The general tactic, whether E or W-bound, is to leave as early as possible on the flood (dependent on distance) so as to reach your destination or negotiate the shallowest part of the *wattfahrenwassern* near HW. Springs occur around midday and give approx 0·5m more water than neaps.

Borkum (9.24.10 and chart 3509) lies between Westerems and Osterems, with high dunes each end so that at a distance it looks like two separate islands. Round the W end of Borkum are unmarked groynes, some extending 2¾ca offshore. Conspic landmarks include Grosse bn and Neue bn, a water tr, Borkum Grosser lt ho, Borkum Kleiner lt ho, and a disused lt ho; all of which are near the W end of the island.

Memmert on the E side of Osterems is a bird sanctuary, and landing is prohibited. There are Nature Reserves (entry prohibited) inshore of Baltrum, Langeoog and the W end of Spiekeroog (chart 1875). **Juist** (9.24.9) is the first of the chain of similar, long, narrow and low-lying islands. Most have groynes and sea defences on their W and NW sides. Their bare sand dunes are not easy to identify, so the few conspic landmarks must be carefully selected. Shoals extend seaward for 2M or more in places. The seegaten between the islands vary in position and depth, and all of them are dangerous on the ebb tide, even in a moderate onshore wind.

Norderneyer Seegat is a deep chan close W of **Norderney**, but it is approached across dangerous offshore shoals, through which lead two shallow buoyed channels, Dovetief and Schluchter. Dovetief is the main chan, but Schluchter is more protected from the NE. Depths vary considerably and at times the chans silt up. Neither should be used in strong winds. Further inshore, Norderneyer Seegat leads round the W end of the island to the harbour of Norderney (9.24.11). Beware groynes and other obstructions along the shore.

SW of Norderney, Busetief leads in a general S direction to the tidal hbr of Norddeich (9.24.8), which can also be approached with sufficient rise of tide from Osterems through the Norddeich Wattfahrwasser with a depth of about 2m at HW. Busetief is deeper than Dovetief and Schluchter, and is buoyed. The flood begins at HW Helgoland – 0605, and the ebb at HW Helgoland – 0040, sp rates 1kn.

Baltrum (9.24.9) is about 2·5M long, very low in the E and rising in the W to dunes about 15m high. With local knowledge and only in good weather it could be approached through Wichter Ee, a narrow unmarked channel between Norderney and Baltrum; but it is obstructed by drying shoals and a bar and is not advised. A small pier and groyne extend about 2ca from the SW corner of Baltrum. The little hbr dries, and is exposed to the S and SW. Southwards from Wichter Ee, the Nessmersiel Balje, with buoys on its W side prefixed by 'N', leads to the sheltered hbr of Nessmersiel (9.24.8).

Proceeding E, the next major chan through the islands is Acummer Ee between Baltrum and **Langeoog**. Shoals extend 2M offshore, depths in chan vary considerably and it is prone to silting; it is marked by buoys prefixed with 'A', moved as necessary. In onshore winds the sea breaks on the bar and the chan should not be used. Apart from Langeoog (9.24.13), Accumer Ee gives access to the mainland hbrs of Dornumer-Accumersiel (9.24.12) and Bensersiel (9.24.8).

Between Langeoog and **Spiekeroog** (9.24.14), the buoyed Westerbalje and Otzumer Balje chans lead inward. The latter is usually the deeper (0·7m–2·0m) but both chans may silt up and should be used only in good weather and on a rising tide.

Harle chan (buoys prefixed by 'H') leads W of **Wangerooge** (9.24.15), but beware Buhne H groyne which extends 7½ca WSW from end of island to edge of fairway. Dove Harle (buoys prefixed by 'D') leads to the hbr. In bad weather Harlesiel, 4M S on the mainland, is a more comfortable berth.

Blau Balje leads between the E end of Wangerooge and **Minsener Oog**. Although marked by buoys (prefixed 'B' and moved as necessary) this chan is dangerous in N winds. A prohib area (15 May–31 Aug) S of the E end of Wangerooge is for the protection of seals.

RIVER JADE (charts 3368, 3369) To the E of Wangerooge and Minsener Oog lie the estuaries of R. Jade and R. Weser. Although not so hazardous as R. Elbe, the outer parts of both rivers can become very rough with wind against tide, and are dangerous on the ebb in strong NW winds.The Jade is entered from Jade 1 buoy via the Wangerooger Fahrwasser (buoyed) which leads SSE past Wangersiel and the yachting centre of Hooksiel (9.24.16) to Wilhelmshaven (9.24.17). To the S of Wilhelmshaven, the Jadebusen is a large, shallow area of water, through which chans run to the small hbrs of Dangastersiel and Vareler Siel.

RIVER WESER (charts 3368, 3405, 3406, 3407) The R Weser is a major waterway leading to Bremerhaven, Nordenham, Brake and Bremen which connect with the inland waterways. The upper reaches, *Unterweser*, run from Bremen to Bremerhaven (9.24.18) and below Bremerhaven the *Aussenweser* flows into a wide estuary split by two main chans, Neue Weser and Alte Weser. The position and extent of sandbanks vary: on the W side they tend to be steep-to, but on the E side there are extensive shoals (eg Tegeler Plate).

Weser lt buoy marks the approach from NW to Neue Weser (the main fairway) and Alte Weser which are separated by Roter Sand and Roter Grund, marked by the disused Roter Sand lt tr (conspic). Both chans are well marked and they join about 3M S of Alte Weser lt tr (conspic). From this junction Hohewegrinne (buoyed) leads inward in a SE direction past Tegeler Plate lt tr (conspic) on the NE side and Hohe Weg lt tr (conspic) to the SW; here it is constrained by training walls. In the Aussenweser the stream, which runs over 3kn at sp, often sets towards the banks and the branch chans which traverse them.

The Weser-Elbe Wattfahrwasser is a demanding, but useful inshore passage between R. Weser and R. Elbe. It leads NNE from the Wurster Arm (E of Hohe Weg), keeping about 3M offshore; SE of Neuwerk and around Cuxhaven training wall. It normally requires two tides, but there are suitable anchs.

RIVER ELBE (charts 3619, 3625, 3266, 3268) Yachts entering the Elbe are probably bound for the Nord-Ostsee Kanal ent at Brunsbüttel (9.24.21). See 9.24.19 for Cuxhaven and 9.24.20 for the River Elbe and Hamburg. From E end of TSS the chan is well marked by buoys and beacon trs. Commercial traffic is very heavy. At Elbe 1 lt Float the E-going (flood) stream begins at HW Helgoland – 0500, and the W-going (ebb) stream at HW Helgoland + 0500, sp rates 2kn. The stream runs harder N of Scharnhörn, up to 3·5kn on the ebb, when the Elbe estuary is dangerous in strong W or NW winds.

ELBE TO NORTH FRISIAN ISLANDS (charts 1875, 3767) The W coast of Schleswig-Holstein is flat and marshy, with partly-drying banks extending 5 - 10M offshore. Between the banks and islands, the chans change frequently. Süderpiep and Norderpiep lead to Büsum (9.24.24) and Meldorfer Hafen, joining S of Blauort. Norderpiep has a bar (depth 3m) and is unlit; Süderpiep is deeper and preferable in W'lies. Landmarks from seaward are Tertius bn and Blauortsand bn, and a conspic silo at Büsum.

Approaching R. Eider from seaward, find the Ausseneider lt buoy, about 6M W of the buoyed ent chan. The ent can be rough in W winds, and dangerous in onshore gales. St Peter lt ho is conspic on N shore. Here the estuary winds up to the Eiderdamm a storm barrage with a lock (H24) and sluices. Tönning is abou 5M up-river. The upper Eider parallels the Nord-Ostsee Kana which it joins at Gieselau.

The R. Hever consists of several chans on the N side o Eiderstedt Peninsula, and S of the North Frisian Islands o **Süderoogsand** and **Pellworm**. Mittelhever is the most importan of the three buoyed chans through the outer grounds, all o which meet SE of Süderoogsand before they separate onc more into Heverstrom leading to Husum (9.24.24), an Norderhever which runs NE between Pellworm and Nordstran into a number of watt channels. Schmaltief and Rütergat giv access to **Amrum** (hbr on SE side), to Wyk on the E side of **Foh** and to Dagebüll.

Sylt (9.24.25) is the largest of the N Frisian Islands, almost 20M long from S to N. It has a straight seaward coast, and a peninsul on its E side connects by Hindenburgdamm to the mainland Vortrapptief is the chan inward between Amrum and Sylt leading to Hörnum Hafen. It has a depth of about 4m (subjec to frequent change) and is buoyed and lit. The area should no be approached in strong W winds. The flood (ESE-going stream begins at HW Helgoland – 0350, and the ebb (WNW going) at HW Helgoland + 0110, sp rates 2·5kn.

Lister Tief is the chan between the N end of Sylt and th Danish island of **Rømø**; it gives access to List Roads and hb as well as to Danish hbrs. Lister Tief is well buoyed, with a least depth over the bar of about 4m. In relative terms it is th safest chan on this coast (after Süderpiep), available fo yachts seeking anch under the lee of Sylt in strong W winds (when however there would be a big swell over the bar on th ebb). Beware buoyed obstructions (ODAS), 18M WSW of Lis West lt ho.

FROM GERMAN BIGHT TO UK (charts 2182A, 1405, 3761, 2593 1505) From the Elbe, Weser and Jade estuaries, skirt the E ends of TSS to take departure from Helgoland (9.24.23). Thenc parallel the N side of TSS, towards Botney Ground (BG2 buoy if heading to ports north of the Humber. If bound for the Thames Estuary or down Channel, it is advisable to follow the ITZ westwards until well S of Texel (TX 1 lt buoy); thence take departure westward from the Netherlands (see 9.23.5). The edges of the TSS are well marked by lt buoys. Avoid areas o offshore industrial activity (9.5.5). West of German Bigh streams run approx E/W, spring rates under 1kn. For distances across the North Sea, see 9.0.8.

9.24.6 DISTANCE TABLE

Approximate distances in nautical miles are by the most direct route, whilst avoiding dangers and allowing for Traffic Separatio Schemes. Places in *italics* are in adjoining areas; places in **bold** are in 9.0.8, Distances across the North Sea.

1.	***Den Helder***	1																			
2.	***Delfzijl***	115	2																		
3.	Borkum	95	22	3																	
4.	Emden	125	10	32	4																
5.	Norderney	115	41	31	47	5															
6.	Langeoog	130	56	46	63	18	6														
7.	Wangerooge	148	65	55	80	29	21	7													
8.	**Helgoland**	153	81	67	85	44	35	24	8												
9.	Hooksiel	150	83	71	97	44	34	19	35	9											
10.	**Wilhelmshaven**	159	89	80	106	53	43	27	43	9	10										
11.	**Bremerhaven**	180	100	88	115	62	47	38	44	36	45	11									
12.	Cuxhaven	175	105	95	120	69	60	42	38	47	56	58	12								
13.	**Brunsbüttel**	192	120	110	137	84	77	55	51	64	70	78	17	13							
14.	Kiel/Holtenau	245	173	163	190	137	130	108	104	117	123	131	70	53	14						
15.	Hamburg	229	159	104	174	81	114	61	88	101	110	81	54	37	90	15					
16.	Husum	198	127	105	137	85	77	52	47	73	82	82	66	76	129	113	16				
17.	**Hörnum Lt (Sylt)**	192	119	97	129	77	72	60	38	69	78	80	63	75	128	112	48	17			
18.	***Esbjerg***	187	155	133	165	123	119	109	83	116	125	127	110	126	179	163	95	47	18		
19.	*Thyboron*	322	222	200	232	186	204	178	154	301	310	201	200	196	249	233	163	120	90	19	
20.	***Skagen***	378	327	305	337	291	308	283	259	405	414	306	304	301	231	338	268	225	195	104	20

9.24.7 SPECIAL NOTES FOR GERMANY

LANDS are given in lieu of 'counties' in the UK.

CHARTS: German charts are issued by the Bundesamt für Seeschiffahrt und Hydrographie (BSH), Hamburg. In this Almanac those prefixed 'D' are standard German nautical charts. The BSH prefix refers to the 3000 Series of charts for pleasure craft. These are a convenient size (42 x 59cm) and are stowed in a large clear polythene envelope; each set has up to 16 sheets at medium/large scale. All charts are corrected by *Nachrichten für Seefahrer* (NfS) = Notices to Mariners. Where possible the AC, Imray and Dutch chart numbers are also quoted.

LIGHTS: In coastal waters particular use is made of light sectors. A leading or directional sector (usually W, and often intens) may be flanked by warning sectors to show the side on which the vessel has deviated: If to port, a FR lt or a Fl W lt with an even number of flashes; if to starboard, a FG lt or a Fl W lt with an odd number of flashes. Crossing lts with R, W and G sectors may indicate the limits of roadsteads, turning points in chans etc.

SIGNALS: Local port, tidal, distress and traffic signals are given where possible:

Lights on movable bridges and locks

● ●	= Passage/entry prohib.
●	= Be prepared to pass or enter.
Ⓦ ● ●	= Bridge closed or down; vessels which can pass under the available clearance may proceed, but beware of oncoming tfc which has right of way.
ⓌⓌ ● ●	= Lift bridge will remain at first step; vessels which can pass under the available vertical clearance may proceed.
● ●	= Passage/entry permitted; oncoming tfc stopped.
Ⓦ ● ●	= Passage permitted, but beware of oncoming traffic which may have right of way.
● ●	= Bridge, lock or barrage closed to navigation.
●	= Exit from lock prohib.
●	= Exit from lock permitted.

Signals hoisted at masts

By day	*By night*	*Meaning*
R cylinder	Ⓦ ● Ⓦ	= Reduce speed to minimize wash.
● ● ▼	● ● ●	= Fairway obstructed.
● ▼ ▲ (or R board with W band)	● ● Ⓦ	= Chan permanently closed.

When motoring under sail, always display a motoring ▼. Rule 25e is strictly enforced and non-compliance will incur a fine.

HARBOURS: There are no commercially run marinas. Most yacht hbrs are owned by the state or community and run by a local Yacht Club (as in Belgium and the Netherlands).

TRAFFIC SEPARATION SCHEMES: The extensive TSS (off Terschelling, in the German Bight and in the approaches to the Rivers Jade and Elbe) link up with the various Dutch TSS. Information broadcasts by VTS centres and their associated communications are also shown in Area 23.

Caution: When in the ITZ to the south of the E-bound lane of the Terschelling-German Bight TSS, it is forbidden to cross the TSS between the Rivers Ems and Jade. Nor should the S edge of the E-bound lane (well marked by buoys TG1 to TG17) be approached closer than 1M, except in emergency or stress of weather. The German Water Police can impose on-the-spot fines or confiscate equipment to the value of €1023, pending payment of the fine. Skippers are, therefore, advised to:

- Make note of positions with times, courses, wind, weather, seastate, other traffic and use of sail or engine. These data can be of importance in any litigation and also makes the skipper realise what he is doing. In addition, it can show that the skipper is navigating in a responsible manner.
- Always listen out on the appropriate VTS channel. If a deviation from the rules is necessary, inform the VSS.
- Beware of deep draught vêssels proceeding from the German Bight pilot station to the Jade and eastgoing traffic crossing in the VSS. These have right of way over eastgoing traffic. Yachts either east-or westbound must take this into account.
- Any course changes made by a yacht must be timely and clear to other shipping.

HIGH SPEED CRAFT: High Speed Craft ply between Emden and Borkum; and Hamburg to Stadersand, Cuxhaven and Helgoland. Keep a good lookout.

TELEPHONES: To call UK from Germany: dial 00 44; then the UK area code, minus the initial zero; followed by the number required. To call Germany from UK: dial 00-49; then area code minus initial zero; then desired number.

EMERGENCIES: Police: dial 110. Fire, Ambulance: dial 112.

PUBLIC HOLIDAYS: New Year's Day, Good Friday, Easter Monday, Labour Day (1 May), Ascension Day, Whit Monday, Day of German Unity (3 Oct), Christmas Day and Boxing Day.

National Water Parks exist in the Wadden Sea areas (tidal mud flats) of Lower Saxony, (excluding the Jade and Weser rivers and the Ems-Dollart estuary), and along the west coast of Schleswig-Holstein. Conservation of the ecology is the prime aim. The Parks (shown on AC & BSH charts) are divided into 3 zones with certain rules:

Zone 1 comprises the most sensitive areas (about 30%) where yachts must keep to buoyed chans, except HW±3. Speed limit 8kn.
Zone 2 is a buffer zone.
Zone 3 is the remainder. No special constraints exist in Zones 2 and 3.

CUSTOMS: Ports of entry are: Borkum, Norderney, Norddeich, Wilhelmshaven, Bremerhaven, Cuxhaven. Not Helgoland.

GAS: Sometimes Calor gas bottles can be re-filled. German 'Flussig' gas can be used with Calor regulators.

CURRENCY: Euro (€)

VISITORS' TAX: of up to €2·56 per person per day may be payable.

USEFUL ADDRESSES: German National Tourist Office, PO Box 2695, London W1A 3TN; ☎ 020 7317 0908; 📠 020 7495 6129. German Embassy, 23 Belgrave Sq, Chesham Place, London SW1X 8PX (☎ 020 7824 1300).

EMDEN *9.24.8*

Niedersachsen, Ostfriesland **53°20'·10N 07°10'·80E**

CHARTS AC 3510; Imray C26; BSH 90, 91, 3012 sheets 5 & 6

TIDES HW +0022 on Dover (UT); ML 1·9m; Zone – 0100

Standard Port HELGOLAND (⟶)

Times				Height (metres)			
High Water		Low Water		MHWS	MHWN	MLWN	MLWS
0200	0700	0200	0800	2·7	2·4	0·4	0·0
1400	1900	1400	2000				
Differences EMDEN							
+0041	+0028	–0011	+0022	+0·8	+0·8	0·0	0·0
EMSHÖRN							
–0037	–0041	–0108	–0047	+0·1	+0·1	0·0	0·0
KNOCK (R Ems)							
+0018	+0005	–0028	+0004	+0·6	+0·6	0·0	0·0

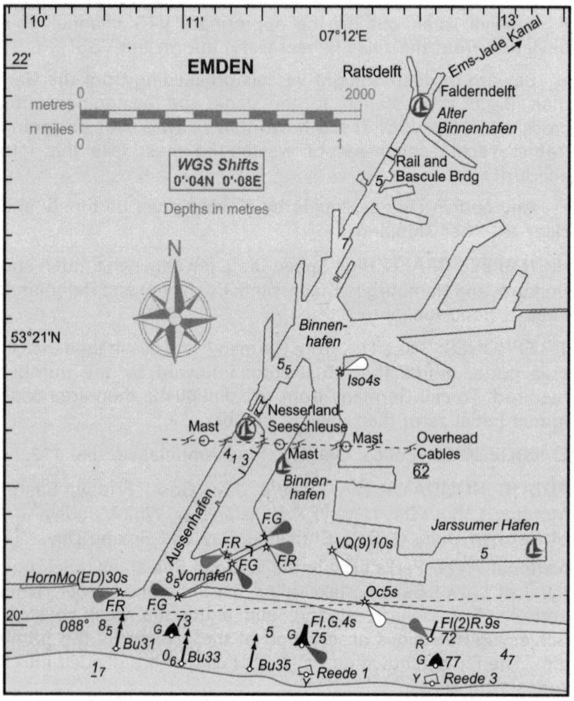

SHELTER Good shelter, except in SW winds, in Außenhafen (3m) at yacht hbr on E side just before Nesserlander Lock. If full, lock into Binnenhafen, sheltered in all winds; Binnenhafen (4-5m), Ratsdelft (3m) and Falderndelft (3m). Rlybridge opens 0650,0912,1128,1317,1410,1516,1724,1830 and 2106 on request. For opening sound M (- -). Inland bound: lock opens every ½ hour 0730-1730 (Sun 0730-1430). Seaward bound every H 0700-1800 (Sun 0700-1500). For opening sound M (- -). Sun: Enter Binnenhafen via Vorhafen 1700,2000, depart 1730,2030 or H24 with commercial traffic. Jarßumer Hafen (5m) in SE corner is mainly for locals and far from city.

NAVIGATION See Delfzijl (9.23.33) and Borkum (9.24.10) for outer approaches via well buoyed/lit R Ems to abeam Knock lt ho. Thence 6M via Emder Fahrwasser which has drying banks and training walls close outboard of chan buoys. 3 conspic HT pylons (101m) help identify Außenhafen.

LIGHTS AND MARKS Fahrwasser ldg lts 075°, both Oc (2) 12s 16/28m 12M (off chartlet). Ldg lts 088°, both Oc 5s 14/30m 12M, lead to hbr ent, marked by FR and FG lts. City centre bears 030°/2M.

RADIO TELEPHONE Radar cover of the Ems is as follows:

Borkum Radar	Ch 18	Buoys 1 - 35;
Knock Radar	Ch 20	Buoys 35 - 57;
Wybelsum Radar	Ch 21	Buoys 57 - Emden Hbr ent;

Ems Traffic broadcasts safety & weather info in German H+50 on Ch 15, 18, 20 and 21. Emden locks Ch 13 (H24).

TELEPHONE (Dial code 04921) Hr Mr ☎ 897260 (H24); Nesserlander lock ☎ 897-270; Tourist Info 97400; Police 110; Fire Ambulance 112; ⊜ ☎ 929285.

FACILITIES YC ☎ 997147, AC, FW, ⛽, C, €0·77/m, Mariners Club ☎ 996943, AC, FW, €0·51/mEms-Jade GmbH ☎ 97400, AC, FW, ⛽, ◙ ⚓, €0·66/m, D 0171 3244337/92750.; all amenities in city (1M). Ferry to Borkum. Note: The Ems-Jade canal, 39M to Wilhelmshaven, can be used by yachts with lowering masts & max draft 1·7m. Min bridge clearance 3·75m. It has 6 locks. Speed limit 4kn.

OTHER MAINLAND HARBOURS BETWEEN R. EMS AND JADE

GREETSIEL, Niedersachsen, **53°32'·90N 07°02'·15E**. AC 3509, 3761 BSH 89, 3012, 3015.5 & .2. HW –0400 on Dover (UT), –0010 on Helgoland (zone –0100); ML 2·6m. Leave Osterems O18/M2 PHM buoy heading ExS for 1·5M to O19 SHM buoy, marking the start of the Ley chan. This trends SxE for 6M to O30/L2 buoy where it turns NE for 2½M to L9 SHM buoy and Ley bn, Fl Y 4s, tide gauge. Here alter 165° for 7ca, between bkwtrs to lock (dir lt 165°, F WRG 8M). Lock opens HW–3 to +3, thence 4M chan in 3m depths to Greetsiel, FV hbr and AB on marina pontoons (2m). A canal links Greetsiel to Emden. Hr Mr ☎ (04926) 990371; ⊜ ☎ (04931) 2764 **Village** YC, Bar, R, V, ⇌.

NORDDEICH, Niedersachsen, **53°38'·75N 07°08'·98E**. AC 3761, BSH 3012.1, 3015.5. HW –0030 on Dover (UT); See 9.24.11 Very good shelter in hbr, reached by chan 50m wide, 2m deep and over 1M long between two training walls which cover at HW and are marked by stakes. Hr divided by central mole; yachts berth in W hbr. Lts on W training wall hd FG 8m 4M, vis 021°-327°. On E training wall hd FR 8m 4M, vis 327°-237°. Ldg lts 144° front, Iso WR 6s 6m 6/4M; rear, 140m from front, Iso W 6s 9m 6M synch. Ldg lts 350°: front Iso WR 3s 5m 6/4M; rear, 95m from front, Iso W 3s 8m 6M. Ldg lts 170°: front Iso W 3s 12m 10M; rear 420m from front, Iso W 3s 23m 10M, synch. Hr Mr VHF Ch 17, ☎ (04931) 81317; ⊜ ☎ (04931) 8435; YC ☎ 3560; Facilities: AB, C (5 ton), D ☎ 2721, FW, Slip, CH, BSH agent. **Town** Ⓑ, Bar, Dr, ✉, R ⇌, V, Gaz. Ferry to Juist and Norderney.

NESSMERSIEL, Niedersachsen, **53°41'·80N 07°21'·73E**. AC 1875, 3761; BSH 3015.6, D89; HW –0040 on Dover (UT); –0020 on Helgoland (zone –0100); HW ht –0·2m on Helgoland. Good shelter in all weathers. Appr down the Nessmersieler Balje chan marked by SHM buoys and bns leading to end of Leitdamm. Here, a lt bn, Oc 4s 5M, together with unlit bns mark the course of the Leitdamm on W; ⸸ mark the E side of chan. Leitdamm covers at HW. Beyond ferry berth is a Yachthafen (1½M); secure to pontoons S of Ferry Quay. Hbr dries (2m at HW). Hr Mr ☎ 2095, 0171 7121198. Facilities: **Nordsee YC Nessmersiel**; no supplies except FW. **Village** (1M to S) has limited facilities. Ferry to Baltrum.

BENSERSIEL, Niedersachsen, **53°41'·80N 07°32'·90E**. AC 1875, 3761; BSH 3015.7. HW –0024 on Dover (UT); +0005 on Helgoland (zone –0100); HW ht +0·4m on Helgoland. Very good shelter in the yacht hbr (dries). Ent chan from Rute 1·5M between training walls with depth of 1·5m. Walls cover at HW. Yacht hbr to SW just before hbr ent (2m); also berths on the SW side of main hbr. Lights: E training wall hd Oc WRG 6s 6m 5/2M, G110°-119°, W119°-121°, R121°-110°. W mole hd FG; E mole hd FR. Ldg lts 138°, both Iso W 6s 7/11m 9M (intens on line), synch. Hr Mr VHF Ch 17, ☎ (04971) 2502; Facilities: FW, C (8 ton), D (on E pier), P (cans), El, Slip, ME, Sh. **Town** Ⓑ, Bar, ✉, R, ⇌, V, Gaz. Ferry to Langeoog.

NEUHARLINGERSIEL, Niedersachsen, **53°43'·20N 07°42'·40E** AC 3368, 1875, 3761; BSH 3015.8. HW 0000 on Dover (UT); see differences under 8.24.13. Appr chan well marked from Bakledge N end of Leitdamm, Oc 6s. Beware strong tidal streams across the ent. Chan runs close E of Leitdamm which is marked by stakes with ⸸. It covers at HW. Yachts lie in NE corner of hbr; where there are many poles. Visitors berths very limited. Hr Mr ☎ (04974) 289. Facilities: **Quay** FW, D. **Village** (picturesque) V, R, Bar. Ferry to Spiekeroog (35 mins).

HARLESIEL, Niedersachsen, **53°44'·10N 07°50'·10E**. AC 3369, 3368; BSH 3015.8. HW –0100 on Dover (UT); HW (zone –

100) –0005 and ht +0·5m on Helgoland. Excellent shelter S of ock which opens approx HW ±1. 120 yacht berths on pontoons to W by village or at BY to E after passing through lock on W side of dyke. River navigable up to Carolinensiel. Lock, VHF Ch 17, 0700-2100. Hr Mr ☎ (04464) 472, berthing fees similar to Wangerooge; ⊖ ☎ (04462) 6154; YC ☎ 1473; Facilities: BY, C, V, R, Slip, P, D, FW. **Town** El, ME, Gaz, ✉, V, ✈ and ferry to Wangerooge.

EAST FRISIAN ISLANDS *9.24.9*

The East Frisian Islands off the North Sea coast of Germany and the North Frisian Islands off Schleswig-Holstein and Denmark together comprise the German Frisian Islands. The East Frisian Islands run from the Ems estuary to the Jade Bay with two small islands in the Elbe estuary. They lie between 3 and 20M off-shore and were, at one time, the north coast. The area between the low-lying islands and the present coastline which is now flooded by the sea is called the Watten. The islands are known locally as the Ostfriesischen and the inhabitants speak a patois known as Fries, a language with a close resemblance to English.

TIDES: *Seegats* are the gaps between the islands and *Watten* are the watersheds or watts between the islands and the mainland (where the tide meets having swept both ways round the island, usually about ⅓ of the way from the E end). Tidal streams are very slack over the watts but very strong in the Seegats, especially on the sp ebb. Persistent strong W/NW winds may raise the sea level by over 0.25m (exceptionally by 3m); against the ebb they cause steep dangerous seas over the bars near the entrance to the Seegats. Strong E/SE winds can lower sea level by more than 0.25m, dangerously reducing clearances. Caution: All the Seegats are dangerous in winds >F4 with any N in them.

DEPTHS: Cruising between the islands and the mainland is generally only for bilge-keelers, lifting keelers and other shoal draft boats able to take the ground. Fin keelers with a draft >1·4m are likely to be constrained by their draft.

BUOYAGE: Deep water chans are buoyed, but shoal chans (*wattfahrenwassern*) are marked by withies (*pricken*). Withies the natural way up ⸸ are to be taken as PHMs and withies bound or inverted thus ⸸ as SHMs. The conventional direction of buoyage is always from West to East inside the islands, so leave PHMs to the N whichever way the stream is flowing.

BRIEF NOTES ON HARBOURS:

BORKUM (14 sq miles): The largest island, see 9.24.10.

LUTJEHORN: Bird sanctuary; landing prohib.

MEMMERT: Bird sanctuary; landing prohib. Lt on stone tr with G cupola, Oc (2) WRG 14s 15m 17/12M.

JUIST (6½ sq miles): No yacht hbr. See below.

NORDERNEY (10 sq miles): Lt on R octagonal tr, Fl (3) W 12s 59m 23M. See 9.24.11

BALTRUM (3 sq miles): Pretty island with small town and hbr at W end. See below.

LANGEOOG (7 sq miles): See 9.24.13.

SPIEKEROOG (5 sq miles): See 9.24.14.

WANGEROOGE (2 sq miles): See 9.24.15.

MINSENER OOG: Large bn. Beware groynes and overfalls in strong NW winds.

ALTE MELLUM: Bird sanctuary; landing prohib.

SCHARHÖRN (2 sq miles): Between Alte Mellum and Neuwerk; (off chartlet, in Elbe estuary). Uninhabited.

GROSSES KNECHTSAND: Between Alte Mellum and Neu Werk; Bird sanctuary; landing prohib; (off chartlet).

NEUWERK (off chartlet, in Elbe estuary): Island only inhabited by LB crew and lt ho men. Lt in □ brick tr with B cupola, L Fl (3) WRG 20s 38m 16/12M. On W side there is a conspic W radar tr and landing stage. Ferry to Cuxhaven.

OTHER HARBOURS IN THE EAST FRISIAN ISLANDS

JUIST, Niedersachsen, **53°39'·70N 07°00'·00E**. AC 3509; BSH 90, 3015.4. HW –0105 on Dover (UT); HW –0035 and +0·1 on Helgoland (zone –0100); both differences valid at Memmert (see 9.24.11). Easiest approach is via Norderney (9.24.11) and past the E end of the island into Juister Wattfahrwasser. Entry is through a narrow chan running N into the centre of the S side of island, marked by withies to port. To the W of these is the long (5ca) landing pier. Off the W end of Juist the unmarked Haaksgat leads into the Juister Balje which runs E for about 6M to Juist. Conspic marks are: West bn, on Haakdünen at W end of island, Juist water tr in centre and East bn, 1M from E end of island. Aero lt Fl W 5s 14m (occas) at the airfield. There is no yacht hbr, but yachts can dry out on soft mud alongside quay in ferry hbr. ⚓ 1ca S of W part of town ½M E of steamer pier or at E end of island. Hr Mr ☎ 724; ⊖ ☎ 1321. Facilities: FW, Slip, C; villages of Oosdorp, Westdorp and Loog in centre of island have limited facilities, V, R, Bar, Gaz. Ferry to Norddeich.

BALTRUM, Niedersachsen, **53°43'·30N 07°21'·80E**. AC 1875, 3761; BSH 3015.6/7. HW –0040 on Dover (UT); Use differences Langeoog 9.24.13. Shelter is good except in SW winds. The appr from seaward via the unmarked, drying Wichter Ee Seegat is not recommended without detailed local knowledge and ideal conditions. Better appr is at HW via the Norderneyer Wattfahrwasser running S of Norderney (which also gives access to Neßmersiel). Lt at the groyne head Oc WRG 6s 7m 6/3M G082·5°-098°, W098°-103°, R103°-082·5°. Hbr partly dries. Yacht moorings in the Bootshafen at the E end of hbr. Hr Mr ☎ (04939) 448; ⊖ ☎ (04939) 668. Facilities: Hbr AB, FW; **Baltrumer Bootsclub YC. Village** (¼M NNE) V, R, Bar. No fuel. Ferry from Neßmersiel.

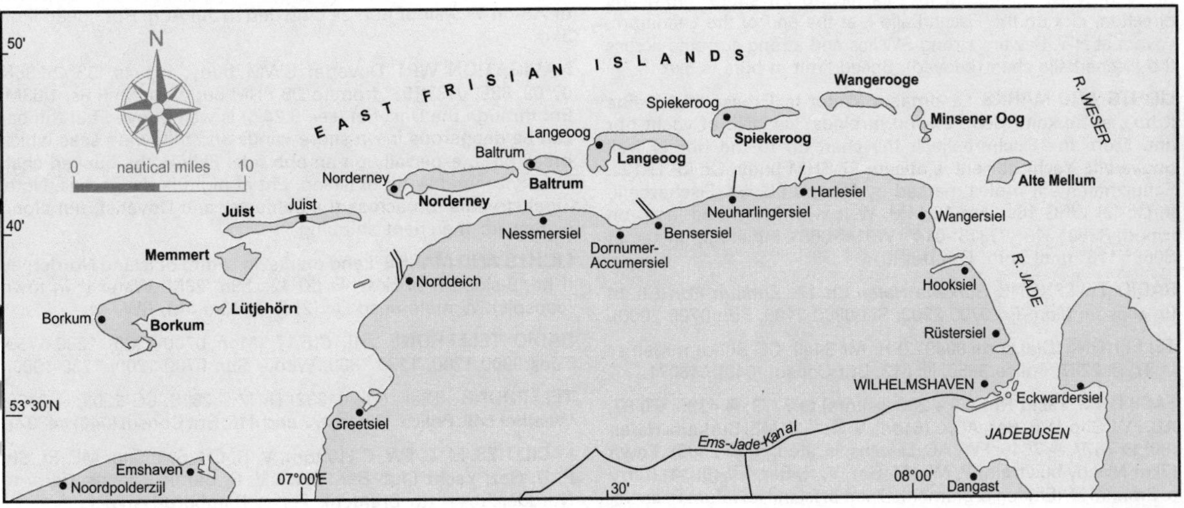

BORKUM *9.24.10*

EAST FRISIAN ISLANDS
Niedersachsen **53°33'·50N 06°45'·10E**

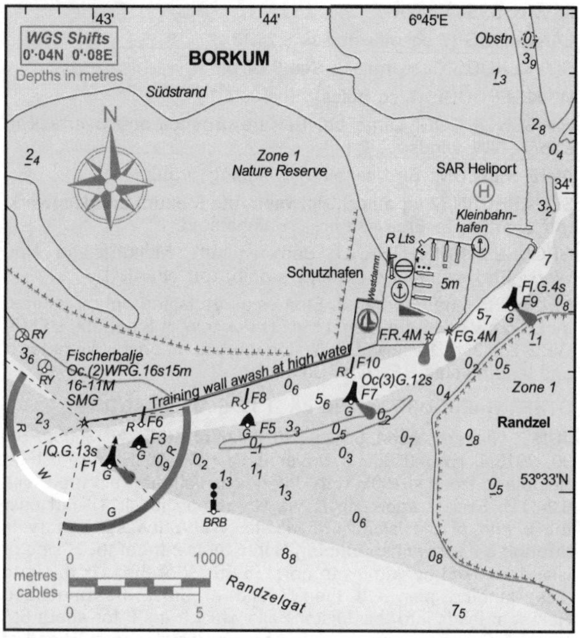

CHARTS AC 3509, 3761; Imray C26; BSH 3015/2, D90; DYC 1812; ANWB A

TIDES –0105 Dover; ML 1·4; Duration 0610; Zone –0100

Standard Port HELGOLAND (⟶)

Times				Height (metres)			
High Water		Low Water		MHWS	MHWN	MLWN	MLWS
0200	0700	0200	0800	2·7	2·4	0·4	0·0
1400	1900	1400	2000				
Differences BORKUM (FISCHERBALJE)							
–0048	–0052	–0124	–0105	0·0	0·0	0·0	0·0

SHELTER Good in both yacht hbr (2 - 2·5m) and at Burkana Hafen (pontoons IV - VI in 5 - 6m) in NE part of the Schutzhafen; access to both H24. Pontoons I-III on W side are for YC members and boats <8m LOA. The ferry hbr (*fährhafen*) is prohib to yachts.

NAVIGATION WPT Riffgat (SWM) buoy, Iso 8s, 53°38'·90N 06°27'·10E, 302°/122° from/to Fischerbalje lt, 11M. See also 9.23.33. Many groynes extend up to 2¾ca (500m) off shore. From any direction, pick up the Fischerbalje lt at the end of the Leitdamm, covers at HW. Beware strong SW'lies and strong currents across the Fischerbalje chan (buoyed). Speed limit in hbrs is 5kn.

LIGHTS AND MARKS Landmarks: Water tr, Grosse and Kleine lt ho's at Borkum town; 2 wind turbines 3ca NNE of yacht hbr ent. From the Fischerbalje lt the chan up to the hbr is well buoyed/lit. Yacht hbr ent is abeam F7 SHM buoy, Oc (3) G 12s. Schutzhafen ent moles marked by FR and FG ☆s. Fischerbalje lt, Oc (2) WRG 16s 15m 16/11M, W tr with R top and lamp on tripod; R260°-313°, G313°-014°, W014°-068°. Initial app in sector R068°-123° until abm. Fog det lt.

RADIO TELEPHONE *Burkana Hafen* Ch 17. *Borkum Port* Ch 14 (In season: Mon -Fri 0700-2200; Sat 0800-2100; Sun 0700-2000).

TELEPHONE (Dial code 004922) Hr Mr 3440; CG Borkum Kleiner Lt Tr; ⊖ 2287; Police 3950; H 813; Brit Consul (040) 446071.

FACILITIES **Yacht Hbr** (50 + 200 visitors) ☎ 7773, 📠 4399, €0·87, AB, FW, Slip, D, R, Bar, AC, C (6 ton), V, ⊡, ♿, P, ME; **Burkana Hafen** (80) ☎ 7877, 📠 7646; FW, AC, D (cans, limited; or ☎ 2483). **Town** (7km NW by bus/train) P, ME, El, Gaz, V, R, Bar, ✉, Ⓑ, ⇌ (ferry to Emden), ✈ (Emden & Bremen). S part of island is Nature Reserve.

NORDERNEY *9.24.11*

EAST FRISIAN ISLANDS
Niedersachsen **53°41'·94N 07°09'·93E**

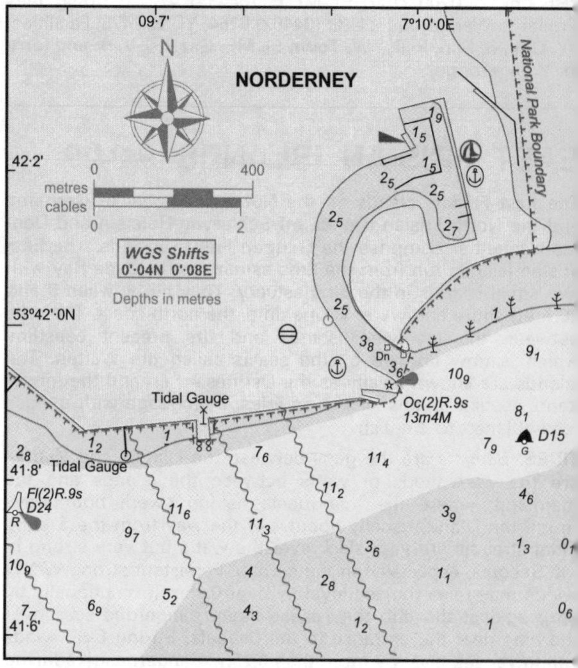

CHARTS AC 3761; Imray C26; DYC 1812; Zeekarten 1353; BSH 3015, 3012, D89

TIDES –0042 Dover; ML 1·4; Duration 0605; Zone –0100

Standard Port HELGOLAND (⟶)

Times				Height (metres)			
High Water		Low Water		MHWS	MHWN	MLWN	MLWS
0200	0700	0200	0800	2·7	2·4	0·4	0·0
1400	1900	1400	2000				
Differences NORDERNEY (RIFFGAT)							
–0024	–0030	–0056	–0045	+0·1	0·0	0.0	0·0
NORDDEICH HAFEN							
–0018	–0017	–0029	–0012	+0·2	+0·1	0·0	0·0
MEMMERT							
–0032	–0038	–0114	–0103	+0·1	+0·1	0·0	0·0

SHELTER Good; the hbr is accessible H24. Yacht hbr is at the NE of the hbr, where yachts lie bow to pontoon, stern to posts; or AB on W wall of hbr, as crowded in Jul/Aug. Hbr speed limit 3kn.

NAVIGATION WPT Dovetief SWM buoy, Iso 4s, 53°45'·35N 07°09'·83E, 013°/193° from/to D8 PHM buoy, Oc (2) R 9s, 1·63M. Ent through the Dovetief (see 9.24.5) is well buoyed but the bar can be dangerous in on-shore winds and following seas which break on it, especially on an ebb tide. Follow the buoyed chan closely around W tip of island. Ent at night is dangerous. Note: Tidal streams run across the Schlucter and Dovetief, not along it. Beware merchant shipping.

LIGHTS AND MARKS Land marks: in centre of island Norderney lt ho, 8-sided R brick tr, Fl (3) 12s 59m 23M. Water tr in town (conspic). W mole head Oc (2) R 9s 13m 4M, RW ○ tr.

RADIO TELEPHONE VHF Ch 17 (Mon 0700-1200, 1230-1730; Tues 0900-1200, 1230-1900; Wed – Sun 0700-1200, 1230-1900).

TELEPHONE (Dial code 04932) Hr Mr 82826; CG 2293; ⊖ 2386; Weather 549; Police 788; H 477 and 416; Brit Consul (040) 446071.

FACILITIES M, L, FW, C (10 ton), V, R, CH, SM, Slip, ME, El, Sh, P, D, Gaz; **Yacht Club** Bar. **Town** V, R, Bar, ✉, Ⓑ, ⇌ (ferry to Norddeich), ✈ (to Bremen). Ferry: Hamburg-Harwich.

ORNUMER-ACCUMERSIEL *9.24.12*

iedersachsen **53°41'·40N 07°29'·40E**

HARTS AC 1875, 3761; Imray C26; BSH 3015/7, D89

IDES –0040 Dover; ML 1·4; Duration 0600; Zone –0100

tandard Port HELGOLAND (⟶)

se Differences LANGEOOG (9.24.13)

HELTER The marina provides complete shelter in all winds; epth 3m, access HW ±4. Ent is narrow; keep to W of chan on ntering. Marina is fenced so obtain a key before leaving.

AVIGATION Appr through Accumer Ee (see 9.24.5 and 9.24.13) eading into Accumersieler Balje and to AB3 SHM buoy, IQ G 13s. rom here keep four withies ⍏ to stbd, clear of the Leitdamm. Note arnings on German chart D89.

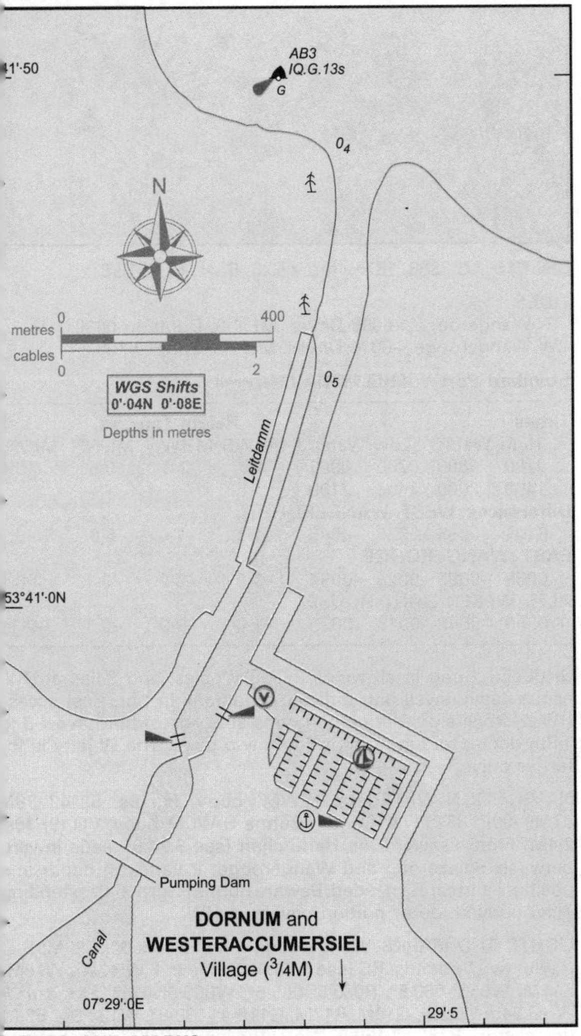

LIGHTS AND MARKS None.

RADIO TELEPHONE None.

TELEPHONE (Dial code 04933) Hr Mr 2510; Deputy Hr Mr 441; ⊜ (04971) 7184; Lifeboat (04972) 247; Weather 0190 116048; Police 2218; Ⓗ 04941-940; Brit Consul (040) 446071.

FACILITIES **Dornumer Yacht Haven** (250) **YC** ☎ 2240; All facilities; FW, R, Slip, Gaz, D, ME, El, Sh; pontoons are lifted out of season. **Town** V, R, Bar, ✉, Ⓑ, ⇌ (Harlesiel), ✈ (Bremen or Hamburg). Ferry: Hamburg-Harwich.

LANGEOOG *9.24.13*

EAST FRISIAN ISLANDS
Niedersachsen **53°43'·42N 07°30'·20E**

CHARTS AC 1875, 3761; Imray C26; BSH 3015, Sheet 7, D89

TIDES –0010 Dover; ML No data; Duration 0600; Zone –0100

Standard Port HELGOLAND (⟶)

Times				Height (metres)			
High Water		Low Water		MHWS	MHWN	MLWN	MLWS
0200	0700	0200	0800	2·7	2·4	0·4	0·0
1400	1900	1400	2000				
Differences LANGEOOG							
+0003	–0001	–0034	–0018	+0·4	+0·2	0·0	0·0
NEUHARLINGERSIEL							
+0014	+0008	–0024	–0013	+0·6	+0·5	+0·1	+0·1

SHELTER Hbr is well sheltered (1·5m) by 20m high sand dunes, but it is open to the S. The E side of hbr dries; chan to yacht pontoons is marked by ⍏ withies.

NAVIGATION All buoys subject to frequent changes. WPT Accumer Ee SWM buoy, Iso 8s, 53°46'·80N 07°24'·43E, thence to A1 chan buoy Oc (2) G 9s; thence via buoyed chan to A9/B26 SHM lt buoy. W sector of W mole lt leads 072° to ent. Ice protectors extend about 40m E of E mole, awash at HW, marked by withies.

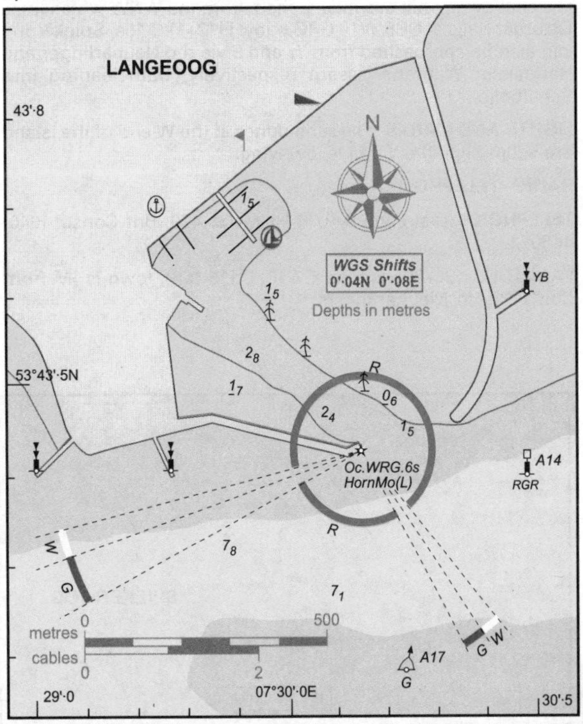

LIGHTS AND MARKS Lt bn on W mole, Oc WRG 6s 8m 7/4M; G064°-070°, W070°-074°, R074°-326°, W326°-330°, G330°-335°, R335°-064°, Horn Mo (L) 30s (sounded 0730-1800LT). Daymarks: Langeoog ch and water tr 1·5M to NNW.

RADIO TELEPHONE Hr Mr VHF Ch 17, 0700-1700.

TELEPHONE (Dial code 04972) Hr Mr 301; Lifeboat CG 247; ⊜ 275; Weather 0190 116048; Police 810; Dr 589; Brit Consul (040) 446071.

FACILITIES **Langeoog Marina** (70 + 130 visitors) ☎ 552, Slip, FW, C, (12 ton), El, Bar, R; **Segelverein Langeoog YC**. **Village** (1½ M) V, R, Gaz, Bar, ✉, Ⓑ, ⇌ (ferry to Norddeich), ✈ (to Bremen). Ferry: Hamburg-Harwich. NOTE: Motor vehicles are prohib on the island. Village is 1½M away; go by foot, pony and trap or train. Train connects with ferries to Bensersiel.

SPIEKEROOG *9.24.14*

EAST FRISIAN ISLANDS
Niedersachsen **53°45'·00N 07°41'·40E** (ent to inner chan)

CHARTS AC 3368, 1875, 3761; Imray C26; BSH 89, D2, 3015/8

TIDES HW –0008 on Dover (UT); ML 1·3m; Duration 0555.

Standard Port HELGOLAND (⟶)

Times				Height (metres)			
High Water		Low Water		MHWS	MHWN	MLWN	MLWS
0200	0700	0200	0800	2·7	2·4	0·4	0·0
1400	1900	1400	2000				
Differences SPIEKEROOG							
+0003	–0003	–0031	–0012	+0·4	+0·3	0·0	0·0

SHELTER Good shelter except in S/SW winds which cause heavy swell. 3 yacht pontoons to the E of ferry berth almost dry to soft mud.

NAVIGATION WPT Otzumer Balje SWM buoy, Iso 4s, 53°48'·01N 07°37'·38E, 350°/170° from/to OB1 SHM buoy, Oc (2) G 9s, 0·5M. Least depth here on the bar is about 2·2m. The appr from seaward via Otzumer Balje is well buoyed, but only 5 buoys are lit. The chan curves past the SW end of island into Schillbalje and to ☆ FR 6m 4M, vis 197°-114°, R mast (see lat/long at head of page). This mast marks ent to inner chan, marked by withies, which leads 020°/1M to small ferry hbr (1.6m) on S side of Spiekeroog Island. Westerbalje is a shallower, unlit secondary chan from the WNW which joins Otzumer Balje at OB5/W10 GRG buoy, Fl (2+1) G 15s. Spiekeroog can also be approached from W and E via the Neuharlinger and Harlesieler Wattfahrwassern respectively, both leading into Schillbalje.

LIGHTS AND MARKS The sand dunes at the W end of the island are >20m high; the E end is low-lying.

RADIO TELEPHONE None.

TELEPHONE (Dial code 04976) Hr Mr ☎ 470; Brit Consul (040) 446071.

FACILITIES 120+80 visitors, €7·16, C (15 ton), town is ½M from hbr. Ferry to Nieuharlingersiel.

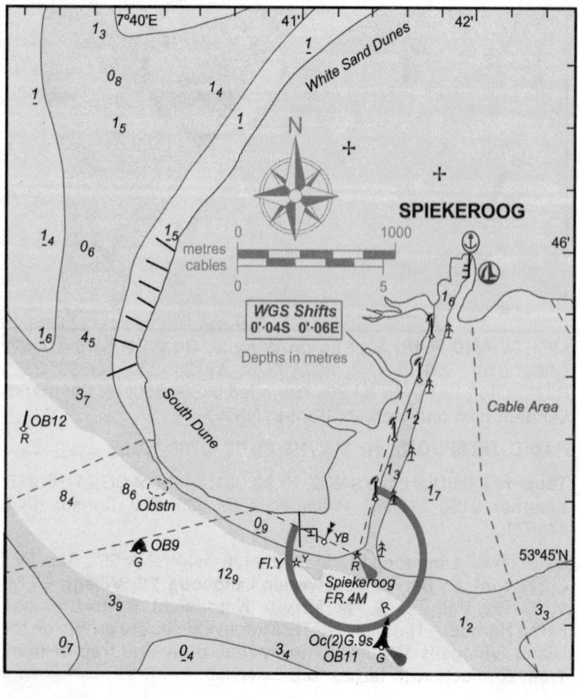

WANGEROOGE *9.24.15*

EAST FRISIAN ISLANDS
Niedersachsen **53° 46'·50N 07° 52'·18E**

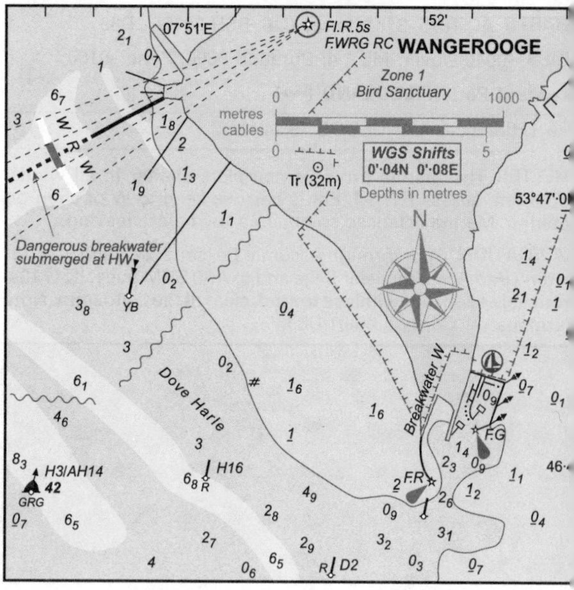

CHARTS AC 3368, 1875; Imray C26; BSH D2, 3015/8

TIDES
E Wangerooge, –0009 Dover; ML 1·9. Duration 0600
W Wangerooge, –0014 Dover; ML 1·5. Zone –0100

Standard Port WILHELMSHAVEN (⟶)

Times				Height (metres)			
High Water		Low Water		MHWS	MHWN	MLWN	MLWS
0200	0800	0200	0900	4·3	3·8	0·5	0·0
1400	2000	1400	2100				
Differences WEST WANGEROOGE							
–0101	–0058	–0035	–0045	–1·1	–1·0	0·0	0·0
EAST WANGEROOGE							
–0058	–0053	–0024	–0034	–1·0	–0·9	–0·1	0·0
ALTE WESER LIGHT HOUSE							
–0055	–0048	–0015	–0029	–1·0	–0·9	–0·1	–0·1

SHELTER Good in all winds, but SW gales, and S'lies at HW cause heavy swell and difficult conditions in hbr. Best access HW±2. Yachts on marina pontoons at E side of hbr have 1·3 to 1·8m depth; rafting no more than two deep. The W jetty is for ferries only.

NAVIGATION WPT Harle (SWM) buoy, Iso 8s, 53°49'·28N 07°49'·00E, 351°/171° from/to Buhne H WCM buoy, VQ (9) 10s 2·4M. From seaward the Harle chan (see 9.24.5) leads inward between Spiekeroog and Wangerooge; it varies in depth and position, and care is needed. Beware Buhne H (groyne), extending 7½ca, buoyed; outer portion covers at HW.

LIGHTS AND MARKS Wangerooge lt ho Fl R 5s 60m 23M; R C tr with two W bands; RC (see 9.24.4). Same tr: F WR 24m W15M R11M, W055°-060·5°, R060·5°-065·5°, W065·5°-071°. Same tr: F WRG 24m W22M, G18M, R17M, G119·4°-138·8°, W138·8°-152·2° (ldg sector), R152·2°-159·9°. Note: the last 3 GWR sectors above lead in from seaward; they are not shown on the chartlet.

RADIO TELEPHONE Hr Mr VHF Ch 17, 0700-1700.

TELEPHONE (Dial code 04469) Hr Mr 630; ⊜ 519; Weather Bremerhaven 72220; Police 205; Ambulance 112; Brit Consul (040) 446071; Dr 1700.

FACILITIES **Wangerooge YC** ☎ 1697, €7·92, L, M, Gaz. **Village** El, V, CH, ✉, Ⓑ, ⇌ (ferry to Harlesiel), ✈ (to Harle and Helgoland). Ferry: Hamburg-Harwich.

HOOKSIEL *9.24.16*

Niedersachsen 53°38'·85N 08°05'40E

CHARTS AC 3369; Imray C26; BSH 3015 Sheet 10, D7

TIDES +0034 Dover; ML no data; Duration 0605; Zone –0100

Standard Port WILHELMSHAVEN (⟶)

Times				Height (metres)			
High Water		Low Water		MHWS	MHWN	MLWN	MLWS
0200	0800	0200	0900	4·3	3·8	0·5	0·0
1400	2000	1400	2100				
Differences HOOKSIEL							
–0023	–0022	–0008	–0012	–0·5	–0·4	0·0	0·0
SCHILLIG							
–0031	–0025	–0006	–0014	–0·7	–0·7	0·0	0·0

SHELTER Temp AB in the Vorhafen (approx 1m at MLWS) but it is very commercial and uncomfortable in E winds. Beyond the lock there is complete shelter in the Binnentief, 2M long and approx 2·8m deep. Best berths for visitors in Alter Hafen Yacht Hbr in the town. Max draught 2m; bigger yachts go to YCs; see lockmaster.

NAVIGATION WPT No 37/Hooksiel 1 SHM buoy, IQ G 13s, 53°39'·38N 08°06'·63E 227°/047° from/to ent 1·1M. Ent is marked by small H3 SHM buoy, approx 350m E, and by withies. Caution: strong cross tide, tanker pier and restricted area to SE of ent. Appr to lock through Vorhafen, enclosed by two moles. Depth in chan 2·5m. Lock hrs Mon - Fri 0800-1900, Sat/Sun 0900-2000 (LT); exact times on noticeboard. Secure well in lock. Do not enter Watersports Area due to water-ski cables. Dredging may take place at LW.

LIGHTS AND MARKS Ldg lts 164·5°, both Iso 6s 15/24m 24/27M, synch/intens, lead W of the WPT. Conspic chys of oil refinery 1·7M S of lock. ☆ L Fl R 6s on dayglo R pile on S mole and a street lamp on N mole. R/G tfc sigs at lock.

RADIO TELEPHONE Port VHF Ch 63. VTS Centre, *German Bight Traffic* broadcasts safety and weather info Ch 80 every H in German/English; *Jade Traffic* broadcasts info in German every H+10 Ch 20 63. Radar cover of the Jade is as follows:
Jade Radar I Ch 63 Buoys 1 - 33;
Jade Radar II Ch 20 Buoys 33 - 58.

TELEPHONE (Dial code 04425) Hr Admin 958012; Lockmaster 430; ⊜ 1302; CG (0421) 5550555; Weather (0190) 116047; Police 269; 🄷 (04421) 2080; Dr 1080; Brit Consul (040) 446071.

FACILITIES Visitors Yacht Hr (50) AB, €4·60 (at €0·51/metre LOA). AC, FW, Bar; **Whf** (Werft BY) ☎ 95850, BH (25 ton), Slip; **Alter Hafen** AB, FW, V, R, Bar; **Wilhelmshaven YC** ☎ 285. **Town** BY, SM, ME, El, CH, P, D, Gaz, V, R, Bar, Ⓑ, ✉, ⇌ (Wilhelmshaven), ✈ (Wilhelmshaven or Bremen).

ADJACENT HARBOURS ON THE RIVER JADE

WANGERSIEL, Niedersachsen, **53°41'·00N 08°01'·60E**. AC 3369; BSH 3015.9/8. HW –0100 on Dover (UT); use SCHILLIG differences 9.24.16; ML 3·3m. From spar buoy W2 (PHM) besom perches mark the N side of the chan to the hbr. Best water 10 to 20m from perches. Depth at ent, 1·3m. Chan keeps shifting especially at E end. Boats drawing 1·5m can cross the bar HW ±2½. Most of hbr dries. Berth on N quay. YC and FW are in the NW corner. Hr Mr ☎ 238. Facilities: No fuel. At Horumersiel (¼M) V, R, Bar.

RÜSTERSIEL, Niedersachsen, **53°33'·74N 08°09'·33E**. AC 3369; BSH 3015.12. Tides approx as Wilhelmshaven, 3M to the S. Appr from No 47 SHM buoy, IQ G 13s; SW for 9ca to Maadesiel, close N of NWO oil pier and tanks. A conspic factory chy (275m) is 4ca N of ent. The outer hbr dries; access HW±2 via sluice gate. The small marina (3m) is 8ca up the Maade river; or continue 1M, via opening bridge (0700-1700 Mon-Fri), to berth on N quay at Rüstersiel.

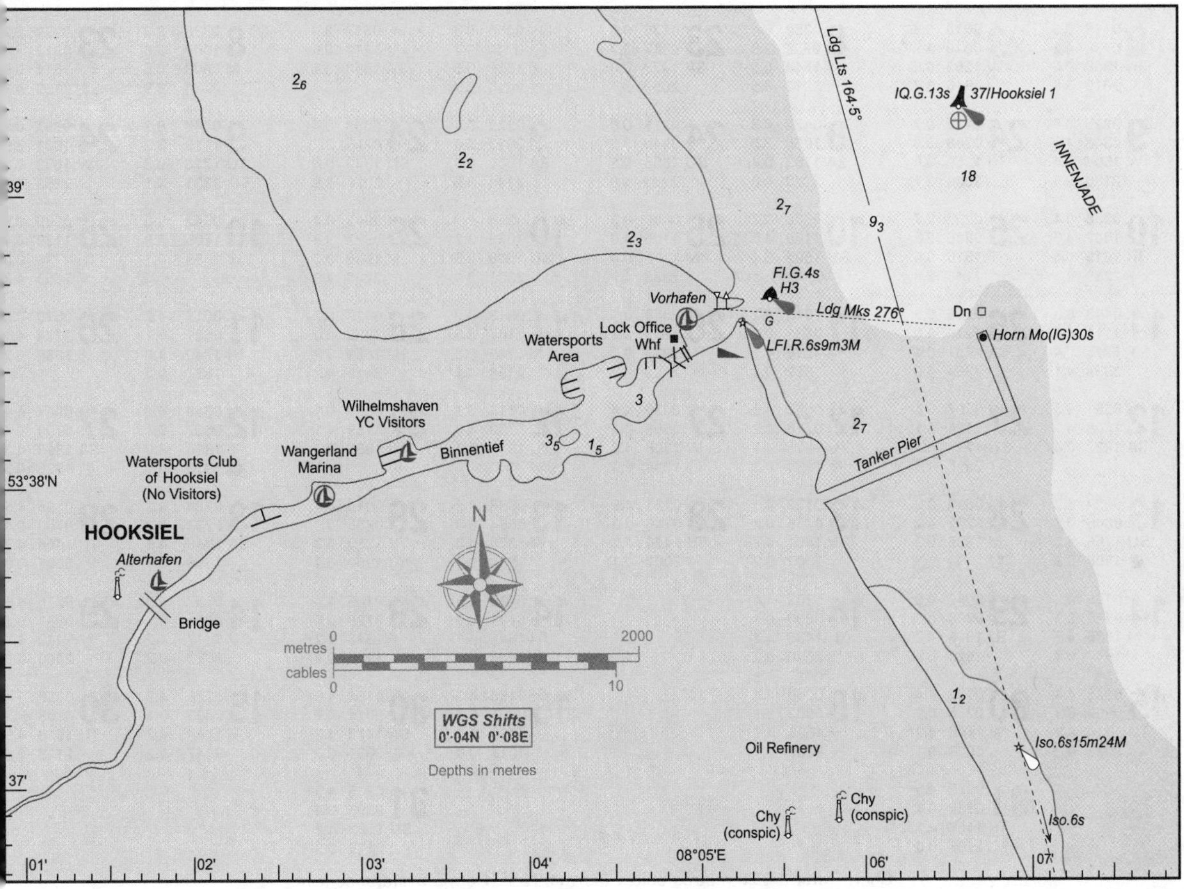

TIME ZONE -0100
(German Standard Time)
Subtract 1 hour for UT
For German Summer Time add ONE hour in **non-shaded areas**

GERMANY – WILHELMSHAVEN

LAT 53°31'N LONG 8°09'E

TIMES AND HEIGHTS OF HIGH AND LOW WATERS

SPRING & NEAP TIDES
Dates in red are **SPRINGS**
Dates in blue are **NEAPS**

YEAR 200

JANUARY

Day	Time	m	Day	Time	m
1 TU	0145	4.4	16 W	0221	4.4
	0807	0.1		0847	0.3
	1414	4.2		1450	4.2
	2026	0.2		2058	0.3
2 W	0231	4.4	17 TH	0257	4.5
	0856	0.0		0923	0.3
	1504	4.1		1524	4.1
	2112	0.1		2129	0.3
3 TH	0316	4.4	18 F	0331	4.4
	0941	0.0		0955	0.2
	1551	4.1		1556	4.0
	2155	0.2		2158	0.3
4 F	0400	4.4	19 SA	0405	4.3
	1024	0.0		1026	0.3
	1639	4.0		1629	3.9
	2239	0.3		2228	0.3
5 SA	0448	4.4	20 SU	0440	4.2
	1112	0.1		1058	0.3
	1730	3.9		1703	3.8
	2328	0.4		2300	0.4
6 SU	0540	4.4	21 M	0515	4.1
	1204	0.2		1129	0.4
	1822	3.9		1737	3.8
				2333	0.5
7 M	0021	0.5	22 TU	0551	4.0
	0636	4.3		1203	0.4
	1257	0.3		1819	3.7
	1917	3.8			
8 TU	0118	0.5	23 W	0016	0.6
	0738	4.2		0640	3.9
	1358	0.4		1252	0.6
	2019	3.8		1916	3.7
9 W	0225	0.5	24 TH	0119	0.7
	0848	4.1		0748	3.8
	1507	0.4		1359	0.6
	2130	3.8		2030	3.7
10 TH	0338	0.4	25 F	0237	0.7
	1002	4.0		0906	3.9
	1619	0.4		1516	0.5
	2239	3.9		2146	3.8
11 F	0448	0.3	26 SA	0356	0.5
	1111	4.1		1020	4.0
	1725	0.4		1631	0.4
	2338	4.1		2254	4.0
12 SA	0551	0.3	27 SU	0507	0.4
	1209	4.1		1124	4.1
	1822	0.4		1738	0.4
				2352	4.2
13 SU	0027	4.2	28 M	0610	0.2
	0645	0.2		1222	4.2
	1256	4.2		1836	0.3
	● 1908	0.3		○	
14 M	0108	4.3	29 TU	0043	4.3
	0730	0.3		0705	0.0
	1336	4.2		1316	4.2
	1947	0.3		1929	0.2
15 TU	0145	4.4	30 W	0133	4.4
	0809	0.3		0758	-0.1
	1414	4.2		1408	4.2
	2023	0.3		2020	0.1
			31 TH	0222	4.5
				0850	-0.1
				1458	4.2
				2107	0.0

FEBRUARY

Day	Time	m	Day	Time	m
1 F	0309	4.5	16 SA	0311	4.4
	0936	-0.2		0931	0.1
	1545	4.1		1534	4.0
	2149	-0.1		2136	0.1
2 SA	0353	4.5	17 SU	0343	4.3
	1019	-0.2		1000	0.1
	1629	4.1		1604	4.0
	2229	0.0		2206	0.1
3 SU	0438	4.5	18 M	0416	4.3
	1101	0.0		1030	0.1
	1712	4.0		1634	4.0
	2312	0.2		2234	0.1
4 M	0524	4.4	19 TU	0445	4.2
	1144	0.1		1055	0.1
	1754	4.0		1700	3.9
	2354	0.3		2257	0.2
5 TU	0610	4.3	20 W	0511	4.0
	1225	0.3		1116	0.2
	1838	3.9		1728	3.8
				2322	0.3
6 W	0039	0.3	21 TH	0547	3.8
	0704	4.1		1149	0.4
	1313	0.4		1815	3.7
	1935	3.8			
7 TH	0139	0.4	22 F	0013	0.5
	0813	3.9		0649	3.7
	1421	0.5		1254	0.6
	2049	3.7		1930	3.6
8 F	0258	0.4	23 SA	0135	0.6
	0936	3.8		0817	3.7
	1544	0.5		1423	0.6
	2211	3.8		2059	3.7
9 SA	0422	0.3	24 SU	0311	0.5
	1056	3.9		0948	3.9
	1703	0.4		1555	0.5
	2320	4.0		2223	4.0
10 SU	0535	0.2	25 M	0440	0.3
	1159	4.0		1106	4.0
	1805	0.4		1716	0.4
				2333	4.2
11 M	0013	4.2	26 TU	0553	0.1
	0631	0.2		1211	4.2
	1246	4.1		1823	0.2
	1852	0.3			
12 TU	0055	4.3	27 W	0030	4.4
	0716	0.2		0653	-0.1
	1325	4.1		1308	4.2
	● 1931	0.3		○ 1918	0.0
13 W	0133	4.4	28 TH	0121	4.5
	0755	0.2		0746	-0.3
	1401	4.2		1400	4.2
	2007	0.2		2007	-0.1
14 TH	0208	4.4			
	0830	0.1			
	1435	4.2			
	2040	0.2			
15 F	0240	4.4			
	0903	0.1			
	1505	4.1			
	2109	0.1			

MARCH

Day	Time	m	Day	Time	m
1 F	0209	4.5	16 SA	0221	4.3
	0835	-0.3		0836	-0.1
	1446	4.2		1443	4.1
	2053	-0.2		2046	-0.1
2 SA	0256	4.5	17 SU	0250	4.3
	0921	-0.4		0904	-0.1
	1530	4.2		1510	4.1
	2134	-0.2		2113	-0.1
3 SU	0340	4.5	18 M	0320	4.3
	1002	-0.3		0931	-0.1
	1610	4.1		1538	4.1
	2212	-0.2		2140	-0.1
4 M	0422	4.5	19 TU	0350	4.2
	1040	-0.1		0958	0.0
	1647	4.1		1606	4.0
	2248	0.0		2207	-0.1
5 TU	0503	4.4	20 W	0418	4.1
	1116	0.1		1021	0.0
	1723	4.0		1629	4.0
	2323	0.1		2228	0.0
6 W	0544	4.2	21 TH	0442	4.0
	1149	0.2		1040	0.1
	1802	3.9		1654	3.8
				2250	0.1
7 TH	0002	0.2	22 F	0516	3.8
	0633	3.9		1110	0.3
	1230	0.4		1738	3.7
	1856	3.8		2336	0.3
8 F	0059	0.3	23 SA	0617	3.6
	0741	3.7		1214	0.5
	1338	0.5		1853	3.7
	2014	3.7			
9 SA	0222	0.4	24 SU	0059	0.5
	0910	3.6		0748	3.7
	1509	0.6		1349	0.6
	2144	3.8		2028	3.8
10 SU	0358	0.3	25 M	0243	0.4
	1039	3.7		0927	3.8
	1639	0.5		1530	0.5
	2303	3.9		2200	4.0
11 M	0518	0.2	26 TU	0418	0.2
	1147	3.8		1052	4.0
	1745	0.3		1656	0.3
	2358	4.1		2315	4.2
12 TU	0613	0.1	27 W	0534	-0.1
	1232	4.0		1159	4.1
	1831	0.2		1805	0.1
13 W	0038	4.2	28 TH	0014	4.4
	0654	0.0		0635	-0.3
	1308	4.0		1255	4.2
	1908	0.1		○ 1900	-0.1
14 TH	0115	4.3	29 F	0106	4.4
	0731	0.0		0728	-0.4
	1342	4.1		1345	4.2
	● 1944	0.0		1948	-0.3
15 F	0150	4.3	30 SA	0154	4.5
	0805	-0.1		0814	-0.5
	1414	4.1		1428	4.2
	2017	0.0		2031	-0.3
			31 SU	0238	4.5
				0858	-0.4
				1507	4.2
				2112	-0.3

APRIL

Day	Time	m	Day	Time	m
1 M	0321	4.5	16 TU	0255	4.2
	0937	-0.3		0900	-0.1
	1544	4.2		1511	4.1
	2148	-0.3		2114	-0.2
2 TU	0402	4.4	17 W	0325	4.1
	1012	-0.2		0927	-0.1
	1619	4.1		1540	4.1
	2222	-0.2		2142	-0.1
3 W	0442	4.2	18 TH	0356	4.1
	1044	0.0		0954	0.0
	1654	4.1		1608	4.0
	2256	-0.1		2210	-0.1
4 TH	0522	4.0	19 F	0429	4.0
	1117	0.2		1022	0.1
	1733	4.0		1641	4.0
	2335	0.1		2242	0.0
5 F	0609	3.8	20 SA	0511	3.8
	1157	0.4		1100	0.2
	1826	3.8		1729	3.9
				2331	0.2
6 SA	0031	0.2	21 SU	0613	3.7
	0714	3.5		1204	0.5
	1301	0.5		1841	3.9
	1941	3.7			
7 SU	0151	0.3	22 M	0050	0.3
	0840	3.5		0738	3.7
	1430	0.6		1335	0.6
	2111	3.8		2011	3.9
8 M	0326	0.3	23 TU	0227	0.2
	1009	3.6		0912	3.8
	1603	0.5		1511	0.5
	2234	3.9		2139	4.1
9 TU	0448	0.2	24 W	0357	0.0
	1119	3.7		1034	3.9
	1713	0.3		1633	0.2
	2331	4.1		2253	4.2
10 W	0542	0.0	25 TH	0509	-0.2
	1205	3.9		1139	4.1
	1759	0.1		1739	0.0
				2353	4.3
11 TH	0011	4.2	26 F	0610	-0.4
	0621	-0.1		1234	4.1
	1240	4.0		1836	-0.2
	1837	0.0			
12 F	0048	4.2	27 SA	0047	4.4
	0657	-0.1		0704	-0.4
	1315	4.0		1323	4.2
	● 1915	0.0		○ 1925	-0.3
13 SA	0124	4.2	28 SU	0135	4.5
	0733	-0.2		0750	-0.4
	1348	4.1		1404	4.3
	1950	-0.1		2007	-0.3
14 SU	0157	4.3	29 M	0218	4.5
	0805	-0.1		0831	-0.3
	1417	4.2		1440	4.3
	2020	-0.2		2045	-0.3
15 M	0226	4.3	30 TU	0259	4.4
	0833	-0.1		0908	-0.2
	1444	4.2		1516	4.3
	2047	-0.2		2123	-0.3

Chart Datum: 2·26 metres below Normal Null (German reference level)

TIME ZONE -0100
(German Standard Time)
Subtract 1 hour for UT
For German Summer Time add ONE hour in **non-shaded areas**

GERMANY – WILHELMSHAVEN

LAT 53°31′N LONG 8°09′E

TIMES AND HEIGHTS OF HIGH AND LOW WATERS

SPRING & NEAP TIDES
Dates in red are SPRINGS
Dates in blue are NEAPS

YEAR **2002**

MAY

Day		Time	m	Time	m	Time	m	Time	m
1	W	0341	4.2	0943	-0.1	1553	4.2	2200	-0.2
2	TH	0422	4.1	1018	0.0	1631	4.1	2238	-0.1
3	F	0503	3.9	1053	0.2	1712	4.1	2320	0.0
4	SA	0549	3.7	1135	0.4	1803	4.0		
5	SU	0012	0.2	0648	3.6	1230	0.5	1908	3.9
6	M	0120	0.3	0801	3.5	1346	0.6	2027	3.9
7	TU	0241	0.3	0921	3.5	1511	0.5	2146	3.9
8	W	0359	0.2	1031	3.7	1624	0.3	2248	4.0
9	TH	0457	0.0	1123	3.9	1717	0.1	2334	4.1
10	F	0540	-0.1	1203	4.0	1800	0.1		
11	SA	0013	4.2	0620	-0.1	1241	4.1	1842	0.0
12	SU	0052	4.2	0658	-0.1	1317	4.2	● 1919	-0.1
13	M	0128	4.2	0732	-0.1	1348	4.2	1952	-0.1
14	TU	0200	4.2	0802	-0.1	1417	4.3	2022	-0.2
15	W	0232	4.2	0834	-0.1	1448	4.2	2054	-0.2
16	TH	0307	4.1	0906	-0.1	1522	4.2	2128	-0.1
17	F	0345	4.0	0941	0.0	1559	4.2	2205	-0.1
18	SA	0428	4.0	1020	0.1	1641	4.1	2249	0.0
19	SU	0519	3.8	1108	0.3	1734	4.1	2343	0.0
20	M	0620	3.8	1209	0.4	1840	4.1		
21	TU	0053	0.1	0734	3.8	1327	0.4	1957	4.1
22	W	0214	0.1	0854	3.9	1450	0.3	2116	4.2
23	TH	0333	0.0	1008	4.0	1605	0.2	2226	4.3
24	F	0440	-0.2	1111	4.0	1709	0.0	2328	4.3
25	SA	0540	-0.3	1206	4.1	1807	-0.2		
26	SU	0024	4.3	0637	-0.3	1256	4.2	○ 1900	-0.2
27	M	0114	4.4	0726	-0.3	1338	4.3	1943	-0.2
28	TU	0158	4.4	0806	-0.2	1415	4.4	2023	-0.2
29	W	0239	4.3	0843	0.0	1452	4.4	2104	-0.1
30	TH	0322	4.2	0921	0.0	1532	4.3	2145	-0.1
31	F	0405	4.0	0959	0.1	1613	4.3	2226	0.0

JUNE

Day		Time	m	Time	m	Time	m	Time	m
1	SA	0446	3.9	1036	0.2	1654	4.2	2308	0.1
2	SU	0529	3.8	1116	0.3	1739	4.1	2353	0.2
3	M	0617	3.7	1201	0.5	1832	4.1		
4	TU	0045	0.3	0714	3.6	1259	0.5	1935	4.0
5	W	0147	0.3	0820	3.6	1410	0.5	2044	4.0
6	TH	0256	0.3	0927	3.7	1523	0.4	2151	4.0
7	F	0359	0.2	1027	3.9	1625	0.3	2246	4.1
8	SA	0452	0.1	1117	4.0	1717	0.2	2333	4.1
9	SU	0538	0.0	1202	4.1	1804	0.1		
10	M	0016	4.2	0622	0.0	1241	4.2	1846	0.0
11	TU	0057	4.2	0700	0.0	1318	4.3	● 1924	-0.1
12	W	0136	4.2	0738	0.0	1354	4.3	2004	-0.1
13	TH	0216	4.2	0818	0.0	1433	4.3	2045	-0.1
14	F	0259	4.1	0859	0.0	1513	4.3	2125	-0.1
15	SA	0342	4.1	0940	0.0	1555	4.3	2208	-0.1
16	SU	0430	4.0	1024	0.1	1642	4.3	2257	0.0
17	M	0523	3.9	1115	0.2	1736	4.3	2352	0.0
18	TU	0621	3.9	1212	0.3	1835	4.3		
19	W	0052	0.0	0722	3.9	1315	0.3	1939	4.3
20	TH	0157	0.1	0827	3.9	1424	0.3	2048	4.2
21	F	0304	0.0	0934	4.0	1534	0.2	2157	4.2
22	SA	0410	0.0	1038	4.0	1639	0.0	2303	4.2
23	SU	0513	0.0	1136	4.1	1741	-0.1		
24	M	0003	4.3	0613	0.0	1229	4.2	○ 1838	-0.1
25	TU	0056	4.3	0706	0.0	1315	4.3	1926	-0.1
26	W	0142	4.3	0749	0.0	1355	4.4	2009	0.0
27	TH	0224	4.3	0828	0.1	1434	4.5	2052	0.0
28	F	0306	4.2	0908	0.2	1515	4.5	2135	0.0
29	SA	0347	4.1	0945	0.2	1555	4.4	2215	0.1
30	SU	0425	4.0	1019	0.2	1633	4.4	2252	0.2

JULY

Day		Time	m	Time	m	Time	m	Time	m
1	M	0503	3.9	1054	0.3	1713	4.3	2330	0.3
2	TU	0542	3.8	1132	0.4	1754	4.2		
3	W	0009	0.3	0625	3.8	1214	0.5	1840	4.1
4	TH	0052	0.4	0714	3.7	1308	0.5	1936	4.0
5	F	0148	0.4	0814	3.8	1414	0.5	2042	4.0
6	SA	0252	0.4	0920	3.8	1524	0.5	2149	4.0
7	SU	0356	0.3	1023	3.9	1628	0.3	2248	4.1
8	M	0454	0.2	1119	4.1	1725	0.2	2341	4.2
9	TU	0548	0.2	1207	4.2	1816	0.1		
10	W	0030	4.2	0637	0.1	1252	4.3	● 1905	0.0
11	TH	0118	4.2	0724	0.1	1337	4.4	1953	0.0
12	F	0206	4.2	0811	0.1	1422	4.5	2041	-0.1
13	SA	0253	4.2	0858	0.0	1506	4.5	2125	-0.2
14	SU	0339	4.1	0940	0.0	1549	4.5	2207	-0.2
15	M	0425	4.1	1022	0.0	1635	4.4	2254	-0.1
16	TU	0515	4.0	1110	0.1	1726	4.4	2346	0.0
17	W	0605	4.0	1201	0.2	1818	4.4		
18	TH	0037	0.1	0655	4.0	1252	0.3	1913	4.3
19	F	0130	0.2	0750	3.9	1351	0.3	2016	4.2
20	SA	0231	0.3	0856	3.9	1500	0.3	2129	4.1
21	SU	0342	0.3	1007	4.0	1614	0.2	2243	4.1
22	M	0453	0.2	1114	4.1	1723	0.1	2349	4.2
23	TU	0557	0.2	1210	4.2	1824	0.1		
24	W	0044	4.2	0652	0.2	1257	4.4	○ 1916	0.1
25	TH	0130	4.2	0737	0.2	1340	4.4	2000	0.1
26	F	0212	4.3	0817	0.2	1420	4.5	2042	0.1
27	SA	0250	4.2	0855	0.2	1457	4.5	2121	0.1
28	SU	0326	4.2	0928	0.2	1533	4.5	2155	0.1
29	M	0358	4.1	0957	0.2	1608	4.4	2227	0.2
30	TU	0431	4.0	1028	0.2	1642	4.4	2259	0.3
31	W	0504	3.9	1101	0.3	1717	4.3	2331	0.3

AUGUST

Day		Time	m	Time	m	Time	m	Time	m
1	TH	0537	3.9	1133	0.4	1750	4.1		
2	F	0000	0.4	0612	3.8	1210	0.5	1831	4.0
3	SA	0040	0.5	0701	3.8	1303	0.6	1932	3.9
4	SU	0140	0.6	0809	3.8	1417	0.6	2048	3.9
5	M	0256	0.5	0926	3.8	1537	0.5	2204	3.9
6	TU	0412	0.4	1038	4.0	1650	0.4	2312	4.1
7	W	0520	0.4	1138	4.2	1755	0.2		
8	TH	0011	4.2	0621	0.3	1232	4.3	● 1851	0.1
9	F	0105	4.3	0715	0.2	1321	4.5	1944	0.0
10	SA	0156	4.3	0804	0.1	1408	4.5	2033	-0.1
11	SU	0243	4.3	0851	0.0	1453	4.6	2118	-0.2
12	M	0328	4.2	0932	-0.1	1535	4.5	2159	-0.2
13	TU	0410	4.1	1012	-0.1	1619	4.5	2240	-0.1
14	W	0453	4.1	1053	0.1	1705	4.5	2325	0.1
15	TH	0536	4.1	1137	0.2	1752	4.4		
16	F	0008	0.3	0619	4.0	1220	0.3	1841	4.2
17	SA	0053	0.4	0709	3.9	1314	0.4	1944	4.0
18	SU	0154	0.5	0819	3.9	1428	0.4	2105	3.9
19	M	0315	0.6	0942	3.9	1555	0.4	2231	3.9
20	TU	0439	0.5	1059	4.1	1715	0.2	2342	4.0
21	W	0548	0.4	1158	4.2	1817	0.2		
22	TH	0035	4.1	0640	0.3	1243	4.4	○ 1906	0.2
23	F	0117	4.2	0722	0.3	1324	4.4	1947	0.2
24	SA	0155	4.2	0801	0.2	1402	4.5	2024	0.1
25	SU	0229	4.2	0836	0.2	1436	4.5	2058	0.1
26	M	0300	4.2	0906	0.2	1507	4.5	2128	0.1
27	TU	0328	4.1	0932	0.1	1538	4.4	2155	0.2
28	W	0355	4.1	0959	0.2	1609	4.3	2223	0.2
29	TH	0424	4.0	1028	0.2	1639	4.2	2250	0.3
30	F	0451	4.0	1054	0.3	1704	4.1	2312	0.4
31	SA	0518	3.9	1119	0.4	1736	3.9	2340	0.5

Chart Datum: 2·26 metres below Normal Null (German reference level)

TIME ZONE -0100
(German Standard Time)
Subtract 1 hour for UT
For German Summer Time add ONE hour in **non-shaded areas**

GERMANY – WILHELMSHAVEN

LAT 53°31′N LONG 8°09′E

TIMES AND HEIGHTS OF HIGH AND LOW WATERS

SPRING & NEAP TIDES
Dates in red are SPRINGS
Dates in blue are NEAPS

YEAR 2002

SEPTEMBER

Date	Day	Time	m	Time	m	Time	m	Time	m
1	SU	0559	3.8	1202	0.6	1831	3.8		
2	M	0036	0.7	0707	3.7	1318	0.8	1955	3.7
3	TU	0202	0.8	0835	3.8	1453	0.7	2127	3.8
4	W	0335	0.7	1002	4.0	1623	0.5	2249	4.0
5	TH	0458	0.5	1113	4.2	1737	0.3	2354	4.2
6	F	0606	0.4	1211	4.4	1837	0.1		
7	SA	0050	4.2	0702	0.2	1302	4.5	● 1929	-0.1
8	SU	0140	4.3	0750	0.1	1349	4.6	2016	-0.2
9	M	0225	4.3	0834	0.0	1433	4.6	2100	-0.2
10	TU	0307	4.3	0915	-0.1	1516	4.6	2140	-0.2
11	W	0347	4.2	0952	-0.1	1558	4.5	2218	0.0
12	TH	0424	4.2	1029	0.0	1640	4.4	2255	0.2
13	F	0501	4.1	1106	0.2	1722	4.2	2332	0.4
14	SA	0541	4.0	1146	0.3	1811	4.0		
15	SU	0014	0.6	0632	3.9	1240	0.4	1915	3.8
16	M	0118	0.8	0746	3.8	1359	0.5	2042	3.7
17	TU	0246	0.8	0917	3.8	1536	0.5	2215	3.7
18	W	0421	0.7	1043	4.0	1704	0.4	2330	3.9
19	TH	0534	0.5	1144	4.2	1804	0.2		
20	F	0020	4.0	0621	0.4	1225	4.3	1846	0.2
21	SA	0055	4.1	0658	0.3	1300	4.4	○ 1922	0.1
22	SU	0129	4.1	0734	0.2	1336	4.4	1956	0.1
23	M	0201	4.1	0809	0.2	1410	4.4	2028	0.1
24	TU	0230	4.2	0839	0.2	1439	4.4	2055	0.2
25	W	0255	4.2	0904	0.1	1506	4.3	2119	0.2
26	TH	0320	4.1	0928	0.1	1535	4.2	2144	0.2
27	F	0346	4.1	0953	0.2	1602	4.1	2208	0.3
28	SA	0411	4.0	1017	0.3	1628	4.0	2230	0.4
29	SU	0437	3.9	1041	0.4	1700	3.8	2259	0.6
30	M	0517	3.8	1123	0.6	1754	3.7	2354	0.8

OCTOBER

Date	Day	Time	m	Time	m	Time	m	Time	m
1	TU	0625	3.7	1239	0.8	1919	3.6		
2	W	0123	0.9	0757	3.8	1420	0.7	2058	3.8
3	TH	0305	0.9	0930	4.0	1557	0.5	2226	3.9
4	F	0434	0.6	1047	4.2	1714	0.2	2334	4.1
5	SA	0544	0.4	1147	4.4	1814	0.0		
6	SU	0029	4.2	0640	0.2	1239	4.5	● 1906	-0.1
7	M	0118	4.3	0728	0.0	1325	4.5	1952	-0.2
8	TU	0201	4.3	0810	0.0	1409	4.6	2035	-0.1
9	W	0240	4.3	0850	-0.1	1452	4.6	2114	-0.1
10	TH	0317	4.3	0927	0.0	1534	4.4	2150	0.1
11	F	0353	4.2	1003	0.0	1616	4.3	2224	0.2
12	SA	0429	4.1	1039	0.2	1658	4.1	2259	0.5
13	SU	0510	4.0	1120	0.3	1746	3.8	2342	0.7
14	M	0602	3.9	1215	0.5	1849	3.6		
15	TU	0043	0.9	0714	3.8	1331	0.6	2012	3.5
16	W	0209	0.9	0843	3.8	1505	0.6	2143	3.6
17	TH	0344	0.8	1010	4.0	1633	0.5	2259	3.7
18	F	0501	0.6	1115	4.1	1734	0.3	2349	3.9
19	SA	0550	0.4	1156	4.2	1813	0.2		
20	SU	0024	4.0	0626	0.3	1230	4.3	1848	0.1
21	M	0056	4.1	0702	0.3	1305	4.3	○ 1922	0.2
22	TU	0128	4.1	0739	0.2	1339	4.3	1953	0.2
23	W	0157	4.2	0809	0.2	1408	4.3	2020	0.2
24	TH	0222	4.2	0835	0.2	1435	4.2	2044	0.2
25	F	0247	4.2	0900	0.1	1504	4.1	2109	0.2
26	SA	0314	4.1	0925	0.2	1533	4.0	2135	0.3
27	SU	0342	4.1	0952	0.3	1605	3.9	2204	0.5
28	M	0415	4.0	1024	0.4	1644	3.8	2241	0.6
29	TU	0459	3.9	1110	0.5	1740	3.6	2337	0.8
30	W	0604	3.8	1221	0.6	1859	3.6		
31	TH	0100	0.9	0729	3.9	1354	0.6	2031	3.7

NOVEMBER

Date	Day	Time	m	Time	m	Time	m	Time	m
1	F	0236	0.9	0859	4.0	1527	0.5	2157	3.9
2	SA	0403	0.6	1015	4.2	1642	0.2	2306	4.0
3	SU	0512	0.4	1118	4.3	1743	0.0		
4	M	0001	4.1	0610	0.2	1212	4.4	● 1837	-0.1
5	TU	0050	4.2	0700	0.1	1300	4.5	1925	-0.1
6	W	0132	4.3	0743	0.0	1345	4.5	2006	0.0
7	TH	0209	4.3	0822	0.0	1428	4.4	2045	0.1
8	F	0246	4.3	0902	0.0	1512	4.3	2123	0.2
9	SA	0326	4.3	0942	0.1	1556	4.1	2200	0.3
10	SU	0406	4.2	1022	0.2	1639	3.9	2237	0.4
11	M	0448	4.1	1105	0.3	1725	3.7	2318	0.6
12	TU	0538	4.0	1155	0.5	1821	3.6		
13	W	0011	0.8	0640	3.9	1259	0.6	1931	3.5
14	TH	0122	0.9	0756	3.9	1418	0.7	2050	3.5
15	F	0247	0.9	0917	3.9	1538	0.6	2204	3.6
16	SA	0405	0.7	1025	4.0	1643	0.4	2301	3.8
17	SU	0504	0.5	1114	4.1	1729	0.3	2342	4.0
18	M	0548	0.4	1153	4.2	1808	0.2		
19	TU	0018	4.1	0628	0.4	1230	4.2	1845	0.2
20	W	0052	4.2	0705	0.3	1306	4.2	○ 1918	0.2
21	TH	0123	4.2	0738	0.2	1338	4.2	1947	0.2
22	F	0152	4.3	0808	0.2	1409	4.1	2016	0.2
23	SA	0222	4.2	0839	0.2	1443	4.1	2048	0.2
24	SU	0255	4.2	0910	0.2	1519	4.0	2120	0.3
25	M	0329	4.2	0944	0.2	1558	3.9	2156	0.4
26	TU	0408	4.1	1022	0.3	1643	3.8	2239	0.6
27	W	0455	4.1	1111	0.3	1738	3.7	2333	0.7
28	TH	0555	4.0	1213	0.4	1845	3.7		
29	F	0043	0.7	0707	4.0	1329	0.5	2002	3.7
30	SA	0204	0.7	0824	4.1	1450	0.4	2119	3.9

DECEMBER

Date	Day	Time	m	Time	m	Time	m	Time	m
1	SU	0324	0.6	0939	4.2	1604	0.2	2228	4.0
2	M	0433	0.4	1045	4.3	1707	0.1	2326	4.1
3	TU	0535	0.2	1144	4.3	1806	0.1		
4	W	0018	4.2	0631	0.1	1237	4.3	● 1858	0.0
5	TH	0103	4.2	0718	0.1	1324	4.4	1941	0.1
6	F	0143	4.3	0800	0.1	1409	4.3	2022	0.2
7	SA	0222	4.4	0843	0.1	1455	4.2	2104	0.3
8	SU	0305	4.4	0929	0.1	1541	4.1	2144	0.3
9	M	0349	4.3	1012	0.2	1624	3.9	2222	0.4
10	TU	0431	4.3	1053	0.3	1705	3.8	2258	0.5
11	W	0514	4.2	1136	0.4	1750	3.7	2340	0.7
12	TH	0604	4.1	1223	0.5	1842	3.5		
13	F	0032	0.8	0702	3.9	1319	0.6	1944	3.5
14	SA	0138	0.8	0808	3.9	1426	0.7	2051	3.6
15	SU	0253	0.8	0918	3.9	1534	0.6	2155	3.8
16	M	0403	0.7	1020	4.0	1633	0.5	2251	3.9
17	TU	0501	0.5	1110	4.1	1723	0.4	2337	4.1
18	W	0549	0.4	1153	4.1	1807	0.3		
19	TH	0017	4.2	0631	0.3	1234	4.2	○ 1846	0.3
20	F	0053	4.2	0709	0.2	1313	4.2	1922	0.3
21	SA	0130	4.3	0748	0.2	1353	4.1	2000	0.3
22	SU	0208	4.3	0829	0.2	1433	4.1	2040	0.2
23	M	0246	4.3	0907	0.1	1514	4.0	2117	0.2
24	TU	0324	4.3	0944	0.1	1556	3.9	2155	0.3
25	W	0405	4.3	1024	0.1	1643	3.9	2239	0.4
26	TH	0453	4.2	1112	0.2	1734	3.8	2329	0.4
27	F	0546	4.2	1204	0.2	1828	3.8		
28	SA	0025	0.5	0643	4.2	1303	0.3	1928	3.8
29	SU	0129	0.6	0749	4.1	1410	0.4	2035	3.8
30	M	0241	0.5	0901	4.1	1522	0.3	2146	3.9
31	TU	0354	0.4	1014	4.1	1632	0.3	2252	4.0

Chart Datum: 2·26 metres below Normal Null (German reference level)

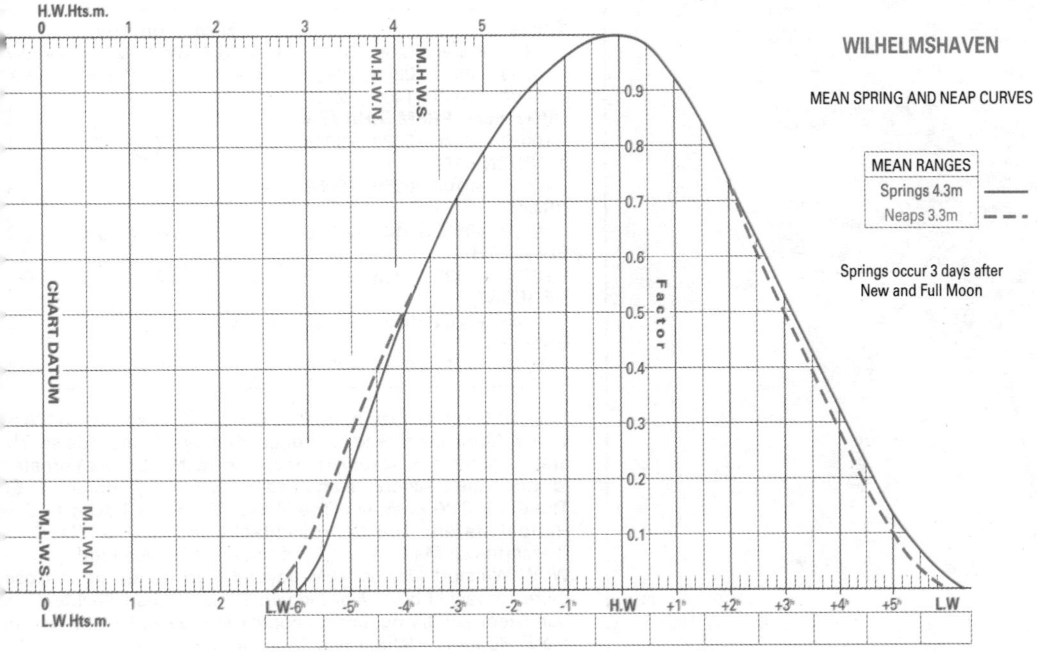

WILHELMSHAVEN *9.24.17*

Niedersachsen **53°31'·00N 08°09'·00E**

CHARTS AC 3369; Imray C26; BSH 3015/12, D7

TIDES +0050 Dover; ML 2·3; Duration 0615; Zone –0100
WILHELMSHAVEN is a Standard Port. (⟵).

SHELTER Good in the yacht hbrs at Großer Hafen and Nordhafen, inside the sea lock, the latter rather remote. Sea lock operates Mon-Thur: 0600-1830; Fri: 0600-1700; Sat, Sun and hols: 0800-1600 (all LT). Nassauhafen in the tidal hbr (*Fluthafen*) has yacht pontoons in about 1·7m.

NAVIGATION WPT JW5/Jade 1 SHM buoy, Oc G 4s, 53°52'·47N 07°44'·10E, 296°/116° from/to Mellumplate lt, 14·2M. From abeam this lt, it is approx 15M to Wilhelmshaven, a busy commercial port, via the deep, wide and well marked fairway. Note: The Ems-Jade canal, 39M to Emden, is usable by yachts with lowering masts and max draft 1·7m. Min bridge clearance 3·75m. It has 6 locks. Speed limit 4kn.

LIGHTS AND MARKS R Jade is well marked/lit; for principal lts see 9.24.4. Ldg lts 208° into Neuer Vorhafen both Iso 4s. Fluthafen N mole FWG 9m 6/3M (sectors on chartlet); S arm, hd FR.

RADIO TELEPHONE Port Ch 11 16 (H24). Sea lock Ch 13. Bridge opening Ch 11. See 9.24.16 for VTS, broadcast info and radar assistance.

TELEPHONE (Dial code 04421) Hr Mr 291256; Port Authority 48000; Naval base/Port Captain 684923 (operator); Sea Lock 186480; VTS 489381; ⊜ 480723; Weather Bremerhaven 72220; Water Police 942358; Ⓗ 8011; Brit Consul (040) 446071.

FACILITIES **Nassauhafen Marina** (28 + 100 Ⓥ) ☎ 41439, €6·14, AC, P, D, BY, Slip, ME, Bar, FW, SM, R; **Wiking Sportsboothafen** (30) ☎ 41301 AC, Bar, CH, El, FW, Gaz, ME, R, SM, V, Sh; **Hochsee YC Germania** ☎ 44121. There are 16 YCs in the area. **City** BY, SM, ME, CH, El, P, D, Gaz, V, ✉, Ⓑ, ⇌, ✈. Ferry: Hamburg-Harwich.

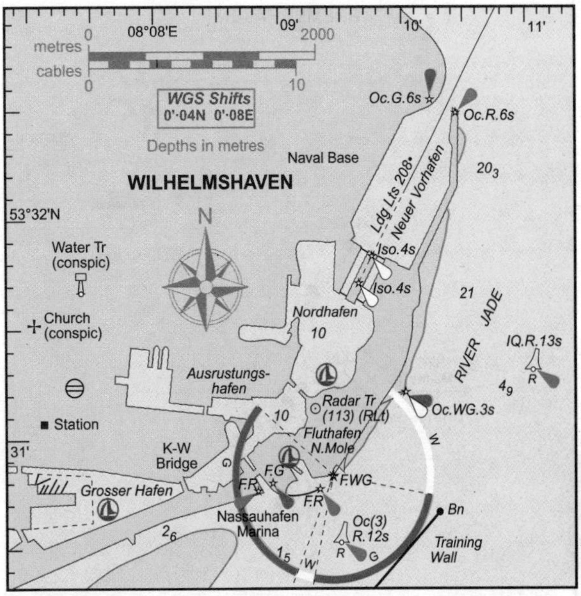

24

ADJACENT HARBOUR IN JADEBUSEN

DANGAST, Niedersachsen, 53°27'·00N 08°07'·00E. AC 3369; BSH 3015.13. HW +0055 on Dover (UT). 4M S of Wilhelmshaven, drying hbr in the wide Jadebusen bay, which mostly dries. Appr via Stenkentief, marked on NW side by stakes, thence SW into Dangaster Aussentief (0·5m at LWS). Unlit, other than Arngast lt, F WRG (not visible from SW), R tr, W bands, in the middle of Jadebusen. Yacht hbr (dries) on W side just before lock into Dangaster Tief, access HW ±2. Facilities: usual amenities can be found in the seaside town of Dangast.

BREMERHAVEN *9.24.18*

Federal State of Bremen **53°32'·16N 08°34'·57E**

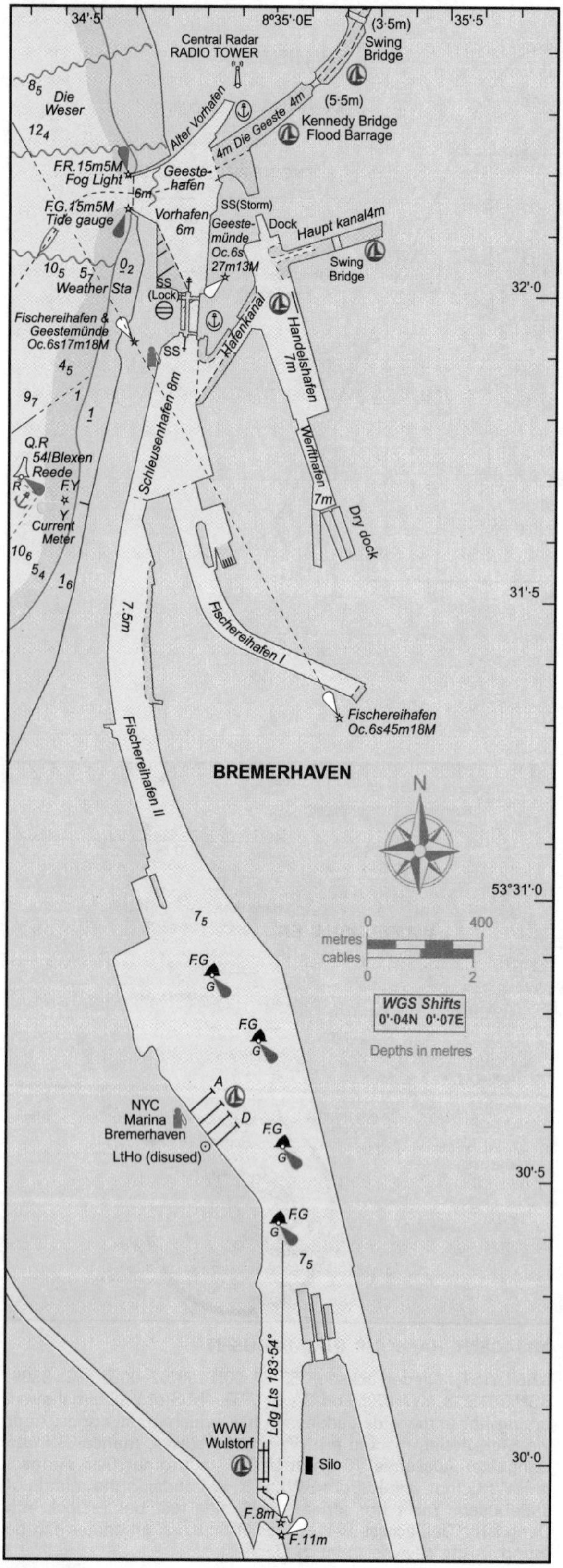

CHARTS AC 3406, 3621; Imray C26; BSH 3011/7, 8 & 10, D4

TIDES +0051 Dover; ML 2·0; Duration 0600; Zone –0100

Standard Port WILHELMSHAVEN (⟵)

Times				**Height (metres)**			
High Water		Low Water		MHWS	MHWN	MLWN	MLWS
0200	0800	0200	0900	4·3	3·8	0·5	0·0
1400	2000	1400	2100				
Differences BREMERHAVEN							
+0029	+0046	+0033	+0038	–0·2	–0·2	–0·1	–0·1
NORDENHAM							
+0051	+0109	+0055	+0058	–0·2	–0·2	–0·3	–0·3
BRAKE							
+0120	+0119	+0143	+0155	–0·3	–0·3	–0·4	–0·3
ELSFLETH							
+0137	+0137	+0206	+0216	–0·2	–0·2	–0·3	–0·1
VEGESACK							
+0208	+0204	+0250	+0254	–0·3	–0·3	–0·4	–0·2
BREMEN							
+0216	+0211	+0311	+0314	–0·2	–0·2	–0·5	–0·3

SHELTER Yachts may berth in R Geeste, but exposed to SW/W winds. All yachts able to pass under Kennedy Br must do so. The area W of the br is reserved for sailing yachts. Or, via Vorhafen lock into the Fischereihafen II; sound Q (—-•—) and ent on ●. There are 3 YC/marinas: The Weser YC Yacht Haven to E of Handelshafen; the Nordseeyachting Marina (NYC or Bremerhaven Marina), 1·3M S of locks on W side (3m); and the WVW Wulstorf Marina 0·5M beyond. Further up the R Weser there are yacht hbrs at Nordenham, Rodenkirchen, Rechtenfleth, Sandstedt (all drying; access approx HW±2) and Brake; and on the R Hunte at Elsfleth and Oldenburg.

NAVIGATION WPT Alte Weser: Schlüsseltonne (SWM) buoy Iso 8s, 53°56'·30N 07°54'·87E, 300°/120° from/to Alte Weser lt, 9M. For R Weser (very well marked) see 9.24.5. Leave R Weser at SHM lt buoy 61. Beware much commercial shipping; also ferries using R Geeste. Note: The Geeste and Hadelner Kanals (1·5m depth; air draft 2·7m) link Bremerhaven to Otterndorf (32M).

LIGHTS AND MARKS Ldg lts, both Oc 6s 17/45m 18M, synch lead 151° down main chan (R Weser). Vorhafen ent, FR & FG 15m 5M, is close SW of conspic 112m radar tr.

RADIO TELEPHONE Radar cover and info in the outer Weser is as follows:

Alte Weser Radar	Ch 22	Neue Weser: buoys 3a -19H;
ditto	ditto	Alte Weser: buoys A1 - 16a;
Hohe Weg Radar I & II	Ch 02	Buoys 21 - 37;
Robbenplate Rdr I & II	Ch 04	Buoys 37 - 53;
Blexen Radar	Ch 07	Buoys 53 - 63;
Luneplate Radar I	Ch 05	Buoys 63 - 58;

Bremerhaven Weser Traffic broadcasts info in German at H+20 on all the above chans. *Bremerhaven Port* & locks Ch 12 16 (H24). *Brake Lock* Ch 10 (H24). *Bremen-Weser Traffic* broadcasts at H+30 on Ch 19 78 81; *Oslebshausen Lock Radio* Ch 12. *Bremen Port Radio* Ch 03 14 16 (H24). *Hunte Traffic* broadcasts at H+30 on Ch 17. *Hunte Bridge Radio* Ch 10 (HJ). *Oldenburg Bridge Radio* Ch 69 (H24).

TELEPHONE (Dial code 0471) Hr Mr 9474625; Fischereihafen Lock 9474628; Weather 72220; Police 94667; Ⓗ 2991; Brit Consul (040) 4480320.

FACILITIES About €0·77. **Weser YC** ☎ 23531 C, AC, FW, R, Bar; **NYC Marina** ☎ 77555 P, D, C, Slip, AC, FW; **WVW Marina** ☎ 73268, FW, Slip, C, El; At Boot Bremerhaven (W bank of Fischereihafen II) BY, SM, ME. **City** all facilities: ACA, Gaz, ⇌, ✈.

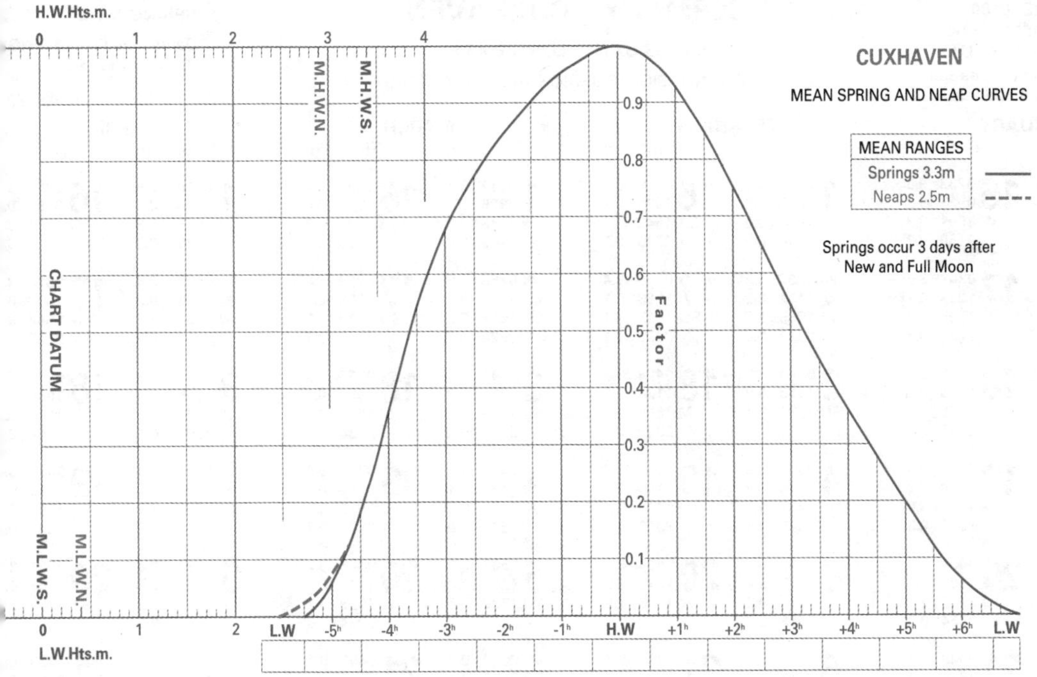

;UXHAVEN *9.24.19*

Jiedersachsen **53°52'·48N 08°42'·56E** (Marina ent)

:HARTS AC 3619; Imray C26; BSH 3010 Sheet 1

IDES +0103 Dover; ML 1·7; Duration 0535; Zone –0100

:UXHAVEN predictions (⟶)

HELTER Good in the YC marina (4m; closed in winter) NW of adar tr. Marina Cuxhaven, close S of radio mast, is entered from lter Hafen via bridge which opens (0600-2100) H and H+30, equested by 2 long blasts, not at night or in winds > F7 Yachts 20m LOA may berth in the Alter Hafen or Alter Fischereihafen.

IAVIGATION WPT No 31 SHM buoy, Fl G 4s, 53°53'·97N 8°41'·27E, 332°/152° from/to marina ent, 1·7M. From No 23 SHM uoy, appr is in W sector (144°-149°) of Baumrönne ldg lt Fl 3s. :han well marked/lit, see 9.24.4. Ebb runs up to 5kn off Cuxhaven. luch commercial shipping.

IGHTS AND MARKS Ent to YC Marina is close NW of conspic adar tr, and N of main lt ho (dark R with copper cupola) FWR, l (4) 12s, Oc 6s and Fl (5) 12s (for sectors see chartlet). YC marina nt, N side FWG; S side FWR, shown 1 Apr-31 Oct.

ADIO TELEPHONE Radar cover of the outer Elbe is as follows:

:lbe West Radar	Ch 65	G. Bight lt float - buoy 1;
:lbe East Radar	Ch 19	Elbe lt float - buoy 5;
Scharhörn Radar	Ch 18	Buoys 3 - 15;
Neuwerk Radar	Ch 05	Buoys 13 - 29;
Cuxhaven Radar	Ch 21	Buoys 27 - 41;
Belum Radar	Ch 03	Buoys 39 - 53.

Cuxhaven Elbe Traffic broadcasts nav/weather info for the outer :lbe on Ch 71 in German & English every H + 55. CG & LB: Ch 16. *Cuxhaven Elbe Port* Ch **12** 16 (H24). Port/lock work Ch 69.

TELEPHONE (Dial code 04721) Hr Mr 34111 (Apr-Oct); LB 34622 nd Ch 16; Weather 36400; Port Authority 501450; ⊖ 21085; British Cruising Ass'n and Little Ship Club 57270, 📠 572757; Police 110; Waterway Police 745930; CG and MRCC 0421 536870, Ch16; Dr & Fire 112; Brit Consul (040) 446071.

FACILITIES Cuxhaven YC Marina (Segler-Vereinigung) ☎ 34111 (summer only), €10·22, Slip, FW, P & D (cans), C (10 ton), AC (free up to 500 watts, then €0·36/kilowatt), BY, ME, El, Sh, CH, SM, Gaz, chart agent, Ⓔ, R, Bar, ⊡, ⊖, bikes available foc; **Cuxhaven Marina** ☎ 37363, open all year, 90 berths inc approx 45 for Ⓥ, €10·22, usual facilities. Swing bridge opens every H and H+30 during daytime. **City** All facilities, ⇌, ✈ (Bremen, Hamburg, Hanover). Ferry: Hamburg -Harwich.

HARBOUR 7m ESE of CUXHAVEN, on S bank of ELBE

OTTERNDORF, Niedersachsen, **53°50'·20N 08°54'·00E.** AC 3619, 3625; BSH 3014.11. HW +0100 on Dover (UT); ML 2·9m; Duration 0525; interpolate between Cuxhaven and Brunsbüttel. Ent marked by Medem lt bn Fl (3) 12s 6m 5M & perches. Appr chan (0·8m) from Elbe divides: yachts can take the W branch to Kutterhafen (0·9m); or to E, through lock for the Hadelner Kanal and turn sharp stbd to yacht hbr. Lockmaster ☎ (04751) 2190; Yacht hbr ☎ 13131 C, AC, FW, Bar. **Town** (3km) ME, Gaz, V, ✉.

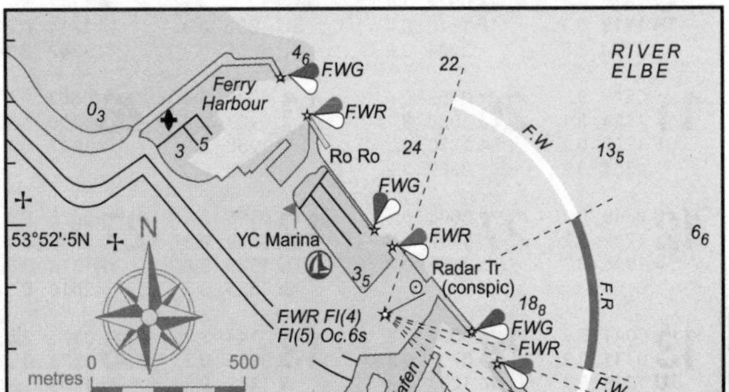

TIME ZONE -0100
(German Standard Time)
Subtract 1 hour for UT
For German Summer Time add ONE hour in **non-shaded areas**

GERMANY – CUXHAVEN

LAT 53°52′N LONG 8°43′E

TIMES AND HEIGHTS OF HIGH AND LOW WATERS

SPRING & NEAP TIDES
Dates in red are **SPRINGS**
Dates in blue are **NEAPS**

YEAR 20

JANUARY

Date	Day	Time	m	Time	m	Time	m	Time	m
1	TU	0156	3.4	0901	0.1	1425	3.3	2119	0.2
2	W	0241	3.5	0951	0.0	1514	3.2	2205	0.1
3	TH	0325	3.5	1037	0.0	1602	3.1	2248	0.2
4	F	0409	3.5	1120	0.0	1650	3.1	2333	0.3
5	SA	0457	3.5	1207	0.1	1742	3.1		
6	SU	0024	0.4	0551	3.5	1259	0.2	1836	3.0
7	M	0117	0.4	0648	3.4	1355	0.3	1933	3.0
8	TU	0216	0.4	0750	3.3	1457	0.3	2036	2.9
9	W	0324	0.4	0901	3.2	1608	0.3	2145	3.0
10	TH	0438	0.3	1015	3.1	1719	0.3	2253	3.0
11	F	0548	0.2	1124	3.1	1822	0.3	2352	3.2
12	SA	0649	0.2	1222	3.2	1915	0.3		
13	SU	0041	3.3	0741	0.2	1309	3.3	● 2000	0.3
14	M	0122	3.4	0823	0.3	1348	3.3	2039	0.3
15	TU	0158	3.5	0900	0.3	1425	3.3	2115	0.3
16	W	0233	3.5	0937	0.3	1501	3.3	2150	0.3
17	TH	0308	3.5	1013	0.2	1535	3.2	2221	0.3
18	F	0342	3.5	1046	0.2	1608	3.1	2249	0.3
19	SA	0416	3.4	1119	0.2	1642	3.0	2321	0.3
20	SU	0452	3.3	1153	0.3	1717	3.0	2354	0.3
21	M	0528	3.2	1225	0.3	1754	2.9		
22	TU	0028	0.4	0607	3.1	1258	0.4	1837	2.8
23	W	0113	0.5	0658	3.0	1348	0.5	1937	2.8
24	TH	0219	0.5	0806	2.9	1458	0.5	2049	2.9
25	F	0340	0.5	0922	3.0	1616	0.4	2204	3.0
26	SA	0459	0.4	1035	3.1	1730	0.3	2309	3.2
27	SU	0608	0.3	1137	3.2	1835	0.3		
28	M	0004	3.3	0707	0.2	1233	3.3	○ 1931	0.2
29	TU	0054	3.4	0800	0.0	1326	3.3	2021	0.1
30	W	0141	3.5	0852	-0.1	1416	3.3	2111	0.0
31	TH	0228	3.5	0943	-0.1	1505	3.3	2158	0.0

FEBRUARY

Date	Day	Time	m	Time	m	Time	m	Time	m
1	F	0313	3.5	1029	-0.2	1551	3.2	2240	0.0
2	SA	0357	3.5	1111	-0.2	1635	3.1	2322	0.0
3	SU	0443	3.5	1153	0.0	1721	3.1		
4	M	0006	0.2	0530	3.5	1237	0.1	1806	3.1
5	TU	0049	0.2	0619	3.4	1320	0.2	1853	3.0
6	W	0136	0.2	0713	3.2	1411	0.3	1950	2.9
7	TH	0238	0.3	0824	3.0	1520	0.3	2104	2.9
8	F	0359	0.2	0947	2.9	1644	0.3	2224	2.9
9	SA	0524	0.2	1108	3.0	1801	0.3	2334	3.1
10	SU	0634	0.1	1212	3.1	1900	0.3		
11	M	0027	3.3	0727	0.2	1258	3.2	1946	0.3
12	TU	0108	3.4	0809	0.2	1335	3.2	● 2024	0.2
13	W	0144	3.4	0845	0.2	1409	3.3	2059	0.2
14	TH	0217	3.5	0919	0.1	1442	3.3	2131	0.1
15	F	0248	3.5	0952	0.1	1512	3.2	2200	0.1
16	SA	0319	3.5	1022	0.1	1542	3.1	2228	0.1
17	SU	0350	3.4	1053	0.1	1613	3.1	2258	0.1
18	M	0424	3.3	1124	0.1	1645	3.0	2328	0.1
19	TU	0455	3.3	1149	0.1	1713	3.0	2352	0.1
20	W	0524	3.1	1210	0.2	1743	2.9		
21	TH	0020	0.3	0602	3.0	1245	0.3	1832	2.8
22	F	0114	0.4	0705	2.9	1352	0.4	1947	2.8
23	SA	0240	0.4	0832	2.9	1524	0.5	2115	2.9
24	SU	0417	0.4	1001	3.0	1656	0.4	2236	3.1
25	M	0543	0.2	1117	3.2	1814	0.3	2342	3.3
26	TU	0652	0.1	1220	3.3	1917	0.1		
27	W	0036	3.4	0749	-0.1	1314	3.3	○ 2010	0.0
28	TH	0125	3.5	0839	-0.3	1403	3.3	2057	-0.1

MARCH

Date	Day	Time	m	Time	m	Time	m	Time	m
1	F	0211	3.6	0926	-0.3	1448	3.3	2142	-0.2
2	SA	0256	3.6	1011	-0.3	1532	3.2	2224	-0.2
3	SU	0340	3.6	1053	-0.3	1613	3.2	2303	-0.2
4	M	0423	3.5	1132	-0.1	1653	3.2	2342	0.0
5	TU	0507	3.4	1208	0.0	1732	3.1		
6	W	0019	0.0	0550	3.3	1243	0.2	1814	3.0
7	TH	0059	0.1	0641	3.0	1326	0.3	1909	2.9
8	F	0158	0.1	0752	2.8	1435	0.4	2026	2.8
9	SA	0324	0.2	0921	2.7	1608	0.4	2156	2.9
10	SU	0500	0.2	1049	2.8	1738	0.3	2314	3.1
11	M	0618	0.1	1156	3.0	1843	0.2		
12	TU	0009	3.2	0710	0.0	1241	3.1	1926	0.2
13	W	0048	3.3	0748	0.0	1315	3.1	2002	0.1
14	TH	0122	3.4	0823	0.0	1348	3.2	● 2037	0.0
15	F	0156	3.4	0855	-0.1	1419	3.2	2109	0.0
16	SA	0226	3.4	0926	0.0	1447	3.2	2138	-0.1
17	SU	0254	3.4	0955	-0.1	1514	3.2	2205	-0.1
18	M	0323	3.3	1024	-0.1	1543	3.1	2234	-0.1
19	TU	0355	3.3	1053	-0.1	1613	3.1	2302	-0.1
20	W	0425	3.2	1117	0.0	1639	3.1	2324	0.0
21	TH	0453	3.1	1136	0.1	1707	3.0	2349	0.1
22	F	0529	2.9	1207	0.2	1752	2.9		
23	SA	0038	0.2	0631	2.8	1313	0.4	1907	2.8
24	SU	0204	0.3	0801	2.8	1450	0.5	2041	3.0
25	M	0349	0.3	0938	2.9	1630	0.4	2210	3.2
26	TU	0522	0.1	1100	3.1	1753	0.2	2320	3.4
27	W	0633	-0.1	1203	3.2	1858	0.0		
28	TH	0016	3.4	0729	-0.3	1256	3.3	○ 1951	-0.2
29	F	0105	3.5	0819	-0.4	1343	3.3	2037	-0.3
30	SA	0152	3.5	0904	-0.4	1427	3.3	2120	-0.3
31	SU	0236	3.6	0946	-0.3	1507	3.3	2200	-0.3

APRIL

Date	Day	Time	m	Time	m	Time	m	Time	m
1	M	0319	3.5	1026	-0.3	1545	3.3	2239	-0.3
2	TU	0402	3.4	1103	-0.2	1623	3.2	2316	-0.2
3	W	0444	3.3	1136	0.0	1701	3.1	2352	-0.1
4	TH	0527	3.1	1209	0.1	1742	3.1		
5	F	0032	0.0	0617	2.9	1251	0.3	1837	2.9
6	SA	0129	0.1	0724	2.7	1357	0.4	1952	2.8
7	SU	0251	0.2	0850	2.6	1528	0.4	2121	2.9
8	M	0427	0.2	1018	2.7	1702	0.3	2243	3.0
9	TU	0548	0.0	1127	2.9	1811	0.2	2339	3.2
10	W	0640	-0.1	1212	3.0	1855	0.1		
11	TH	0018	3.2	0716	-0.1	1246	3.1	1931	0.0
12	F	0053	3.3	0751	-0.2	1319	3.1	● 2007	-0.1
13	SA	0128	3.3	0825	-0.2	1352	3.2	2042	-0.1
14	SU	0200	3.3	0857	-0.1	1420	3.3	2112	-0.1
15	M	0228	3.4	0925	-0.1	1446	3.3	2140	-0.2
16	TU	0257	3.	0953	-0.	1514	3.	2208	-0.
17	W	0328	3.	1022	-0.	1544	3.	2237	-0.
18	TH	0402	3.	1050	0.	1616	3.	2306	-0.
19	F	0437	3.	1118	0.	1651	3.	2341	0.
20	SA	0521	2.	1157	0.	1739	3.		
21	SU	0033	0.	0624	2.	1302	0.	1852	3.
22	M	0153	0.	0749	2.	1433	0.4	2020	3.1
23	TU	0329	0.1	0920	2.9	1609	0.3	2146	3.2
24	W	0458	0.0	1039	3.1	1728	0.1	2256	3.4
25	TH	0606	-0.2	1141	3.2	1831	-0.1	2353	3.4
26	F	0703	-0.3	1233	3.2	1926	-0.2		
27	SA	0044	3.5	0754	-0.4	1320	3.3	○ 2014	-0.3
28	SU	0132	3.5	0839	-0.4	1402	3.3	2055	-0.3
29	M	0216	3.5	0918	-0.3	1440	3.4	2135	-0.3
30	TU	0259	3.5	0956	-0.2	1518	3.4	2214	-0.2

Chart Datum: 1·66 metres below Normal Null (German reference level)

TIME ZONE -0100
(German Standard Time)
Subtract 1 hour for UT
For German Summer Time add ONE hour in **non-shaded areas**

GERMANY – CUXHAVEN

LAT 53°52′N LONG 8°43′E

TIMES AND HEIGHTS OF HIGH AND LOW WATERS

SPRING & NEAP TIDES
Dates in red are SPRINGS
Dates in blue are NEAPS

YEAR **2002**

MAY

Day	Time m	Time m	Time m	Time m
1 W	0342 3.3	1033 -0.1	1556 3.3	2254 -0.2
2 TH	0425 3.2	1109 0.0	1636 3.2	2333 -0.1
3 F	0509 3.0	1145 0.2	1720 3.2	
4 SA	0016 0.0	0558 2.8	1227 0.3	1812 3.1
5 SU	0108 0.1	0657 2.7	1325 0.4	1918 3.0
6 M	0217 0.2	0811 2.6	1443 0.4	2036 3.0
7 TU	0340 0.2	0930 2.7	1609 0.3	2153 3.0
8 W	0458 0.1	1039 2.8	1721 0.2	2254 3.1
9 TH	0554 -0.1	1129 2.9	1812 0.1	2339 3.2
10 F	0634 -0.1	1209 3.1	1853 0.0	
11 SA	0018 3.2	0713 -0.2	1245 3.2	1933 0.0
12 SU	0056 3.3	0750 -0.1	1320 3.2	● 2010 -0.1
13 M	0131 3.3	0823 -0.1	1350 3.3	2042 -0.1
14 TU	0202 3.3	0854 -0.1	1419 3.3	2114 -0.1
15 W	0234 3.3	0926 -0.1	1451 3.3	2147 -0.2
16 TH	0310 3.2	1000 -0.1	1526 3.3	2222 -0.1
17 F	0350 3.1	1035 0.0	1604 3.2	2301 -0.1
18 SA	0435 3.1	1115 0.1	1648 3.2	2346 0.0
19 SU	0527 3.0	1203 0.2	1742 3.2	
20 M	0042 0.0	0629 2.9	1305 0.3	1848 3.2
21 TU	0151 0.1	0743 2.9	1423 0.3	2005 3.2
22 W	0312 0.0	0901 3.0	1546 0.3	2121 3.3
23 TH	0429 -0.1	1013 3.1	1659 0.1	2229 3.3
24 F	0535 -0.2	1113 3.2	1801 -0.1	2328 3.4
25 SA	0633 -0.2	1206 3.2	1858 -0.2	
26 SU	0023 3.4	0727 -0.3	1255 3.3	○ 1949 -0.2
27 M	0114 3.4	0814 -0.2	1338 3.3	2032 -0.2
28 TU	0159 3.5	0853 -0.1	1417 3.4	2113 -0.2
29 W	0241 3.4	0931 0.0	1455 3.5	2155 -0.1
30 TH	0325 3.3	1010 0.0	1536 3.4	2237 -0.1
31 F	0409 3.2	1049 0.1	1618 3.4	2319 0.0

JUNE

Day	Time m	Time m	Time m	Time m
1 SA	0452 3.0	1127 0.2	1701 3.3	
2 SU	0001 0.1	0537 2.9	1207 0.3	1747 3.2
3 M	0046 0.2	0626 2.8	1254 0.4	1841 3.2
4 TU	0139 0.2	0724 2.7	1353 0.4	1944 3.1
5 W	0243 0.2	0830 2.8	1504 0.4	2052 3.1
6 TH	0352 0.2	0937 2.8	1617 0.3	2157 3.1
7 F	0454 0.1	1036 3.0	1719 0.2	2252 3.1
8 SA	0544 0.0	1125 3.1	1810 0.1	2339 3.2
9 SU	0630 0.0	1208 3.2	1855 0.1	
10 M	0022 3.3	0713 0.0	1247 3.3	1936 0.0
11 TU	0101 3.3	0752 0.0	1322 3.3	● 2014 0.0
12 W	0139 3.3	0829 0.0	1358 3.4	2053 -0.1
13 TH	0219 3.3	0909 0.0	1436 3.4	2136 -0.1
14 F	0303 3.2	0950 0.0	1516 3.4	2218 -0.1
15 SA	0347 3.2	1031 0.0	1559 3.4	2301 -0.1
16 SU	0436 3.1	1116 0.1	1647 3.4	2351 0.0
17 M	0529 3.0	1208 0.2	1742 3.4	
18 TU	0046 0.0	0628 3.0	1305 0.2	1842 3.4
19 W	0145 0.0	0731 3.0	1409 0.3	1946 3.4
20 TH	0250 0.1	0836 3.0	1518 0.2	2054 3.3
21 F	0359 0.0	0942 3.1	1628 0.1	2202 3.3
22 SA	0505 0.0	1044 3.1	1732 0.0	2306 3.3
23 SU	0606 0.0	1140 3.2	1832 -0.1	
24 M	0006 3.3	0702 0.0	1232 3.3	○ 1928 -0.1
25 TU	0100 3.4	0753 0.0	1319 3.4	2015 0.0
26 W	0146 3.4	0835 0.1	1400 3.5	2058 0.0
27 TH	0229 3.4	0915 0.1	1440 3.5	2141 0.1
28 F	0311 3.3	0955 0.2	1521 3.6	2224 0.1
29 SA	0352 3.2	1033 0.2	1600 3.5	2303 0.1
30 SU	0432 3.1	1108 0.2	1639 3.4	2341 0.2

JULY

Day	Time m	Time m	Time m	Time m
1 M	0511 3.0	1143 0.3	1720 3.4	
2 TU	0020 0.2	0552 3.0	1222 0.4	1803 3.3
3 W	0100 0.3	0636 2.9	1306 0.4	1851 3.2
4 TH	0144 0.3	0728 2.9	1400 0.4	1947 3.1
5 F	0240 0.3	0828 2.9	1506 0.4	2052 3.1
6 SA	0344 0.3	0934 3.0	1617 0.3	2158 3.1
7 SU	0447 0.2	1035 3.1	1721 0.2	2257 3.1
8 M	0545 0.1	1129 3.2	1817 0.2	2349 3.2
9 TU	0639 0.1	1216 3.3	1907 0.1	
10 W	0037 3.3	0727 0.1	1259 3.4	● 1954 0.1
11 TH	0124 3.3	0814 0.1	1343 3.5	2042 0.0
12 F	0211 3.3	0900 0.1	1426 3.5	2131 -0.1
13 SA	0258 3.3	0946 0.0	1509 3.5	2216 -0.1
14 SU	0343 3.2	1028 0.0	1551 3.5	2258 -0.1
15 M	0429 3.1	1111 0.0	1638 3.5	2345 -0.1
16 TU	0520 3.1	1201 0.1	1731 3.5	
17 W	0036 0.0	0613 3.1	1253 0.2	1825 3.5
18 TH	0128 0.1	0706 3.1	1345 0.2	1921 3.4
19 F	0222 0.2	0803 3.0	1445 0.3	2025 3.3
20 SA	0325 0.2	0907 3.0	1556 0.2	2138 3.2
21 SU	0436 0.2	1017 3.1	1709 0.1	2252 3.2
22 M	0545 0.2	1122 3.2	1817 0.0	2358 3.2
23 TU	0647 0.2	1218 3.3	1915 0.1	
24 W	0052 3.3	0739 0.2	1306 3.4	○ 2004 0.1
25 TH	0137 3.3	0824 0.2	1348 3.5	2047 0.1
26 F	0218 3.4	0904 0.2	1427 3.6	2128 0.2
27 SA	0257 3.4	0941 0.2	1505 3.6	2207 0.2
28 SU	0333 3.3	1015 0.2	1540 3.6	2241 0.2
29 M	0406 3.2	1044 0.2	1614 3.5	2314 0.2
30 TU	0440 3.1	1116 0.2	1650 3.4	2348 0.3
31 W	0515 3.1	1150 0.3	1726 3.4	

AUGUST

Day	Time m	Time m	Time m	Time m
1 TH	0021 0.3	0550 3.0	1224 0.4	1802 3.2
2 F	0050 0.4	0628 3.0	1301 0.5	1846 3.1
3 SA	0130 0.5	0719 2.9	1356 0.5	1947 3.0
4 SU	0232 0.5	0828 2.9	1512 0.5	2102 3.0
5 M	0349 0.4	0943 3.0	1633 0.4	2218 3.1
6 TU	0505 0.4	1052 3.1	1745 0.3	2323 3.2
7 W	0613 0.3	1150 3.3	1847 0.2	
8 TH	0020 3.3	0712 0.3	1241 3.4	● 1942 0.1
9 F	0113 3.3	0804 0.2	1328 3.5	2033 0.0
10 SA	0202 3.4	0852 0.1	1413 3.6	2121 -0.1
11 SU	0248 3.3	0937 0.0	1456 3.6	2206 -0.1
12 M	0331 3.3	1019 0.0	1537 3.6	2247 -0.2
13 TU	0414 3.2	1059 0.0	1622 3.6	2329 -0.1
14 W	0459 3.2	1143 0.1	1710 3.5	
15 TH	0015 0.1	0545 3.2	1229 0.2	1759 3.5
16 F	0059 0.3	0632 3.1	1314 0.3	1852 3.3
17 SA	0146 0.4	0725 3.0	1410 0.3	1957 3.1
18 SU	0248 0.4	0834 2.9	1526 0.3	2119 3.0
19 M	0409 0.5	0955 3.0	1654 0.2	2244 3.0
20 TU	0533 0.4	1112 3.1	1811 0.2	2355 3.1
21 W	0639 0.4	1211 3.3	1909 0.2	
22 TH	0047 3.2	0730 0.3	1255 3.4	○ 1954 0.2
23 F	0126 3.3	0811 0.3	1334 3.5	2033 0.2
24 SA	0202 3.3	0849 0.2	1410 3.5	2110 0.2
25 SU	0237 3.3	0923 0.2	1444 3.6	2144 0.2
26 M	0309 3.3	0953 0.2	1515 3.6	2215 0.2
27 TU	0337 3.2	1020 0.2	1545 3.5	2244 0.2
28 W	0406 3.2	1048 0.2	1617 3.4	2314 0.3
29 TH	0437 3.1	1118 0.2	1649 3.3	2341 0.3
30 F	0506 3.1	1146 0.3	1719 3.2	
31 SA	0003 0.4	0536 3.0	1212 0.4	1754 3.0

Chart Datum: 1·66 metres below Normal Null (German reference level)

TIME ZONE -0100
(German Standard Time)
Subtract 1 hour for UT
For German Summer Time add ONE hour in **non-shaded areas**

GERMANY – CUXHAVEN

LAT 53°52′N LONG 8°43′E

TIMES AND HEIGHTS OF HIGH AND LOW WATERS

SPRING & NEAP TIDES
Dates in red are SPRINGS
Dates in blue are NEAPS

YEAR 200

SEPTEMBER

	Time	m		Time	m
1	0033	0.5	16	0213	0.6
	0619	2.9		0803	2.9
SU	1258	0.6	M	1500	0.4
	1851	2.9		2059	2.8
2	0131	0.6	17	0343	0.6
	0729	2.9		0934	2.9
M	1416	0.6	TU	1638	0.4
	2013	2.9		2232	2.8
3	0259	0.7	18	0517	0.6
	0856	2.9		1058	3.1
TU	1553	0.5	W	1803	0.3
	2144	3.0		2346	3.0
4	0433	0.6	19	0629	0.4
	1020	3.1		1159	3.3
W	1722	0.4	TH	1900	0.2
	2303	3.1			
5	0553	0.5	20	0034	3.1
	1128	3.3		0715	0.3
TH	1832	0.3	F	1238	3.4
				1937	0.2
6	0006	3.3	21	0107	3.2
	0658	0.4		0750	0.3
F	1222	3.5	SA	1312	3.4
	1929	0.1	○	2011	0.2
7	0058	3.3	22	0139	3.2
	0751	0.2		0825	0.2
SA	1309	3.6	SU	1346	3.4
●	2018	0.0		2045	0.2
8	0146	3.4	23	0211	3.3
	0837	0.1		0859	0.2
SU	1354	3.6	M	1419	3.5
	2104	-0.1		2117	0.2
9	0230	3.4	24	0240	3.3
	0921	0.0		0929	0.2
M	1437	3.6	TU	1448	3.5
	2148	-0.1		2145	0.2
10	0311	3.4	25	0305	3.3
	1002	0.0		0955	0.2
TU	1519	3.6	W	1515	3.4
	2228	-0.1		2212	0.2
11	0351	3.3	26	0331	3.2
	1040	0.0		1020	0.2
W	1601	3.6	TH	1544	3.3
	2307	0.0		2238	0.2
12	0431	3.2	27	0359	3.2
	1119	0.1		1046	0.2
TH	1646	3.5	F	1614	3.2
	2345	0.2		2303	0.3
13	0512	3.2	28	0427	3.1
	1159	0.2		1112	0.3
F	1732	3.3	SA	1643	3.1
				2325	0.4
14	0024	0.4	29	0456	3.0
	0556	3.1		1139	0.4
SA	1242	0.3	SU	1719	3.0
	1824	3.1		2355	0.6
15	0108	0.5	30	0538	2.9
	0649	3.0		1224	0.5
SU	1338	0.3	M	1815	2.8
	1932	2.9			

OCTOBER

	Time	m		Time	m
1	0053	0.7	16	0309	0.7
	0647	2.9		0902	2.9
TU	1342	0.6	W	1609	0.5
	1940	2.8		2202	2.7
2	0224	0.8	17	0444	0.7
	0818	3.0		1027	3.1
W	1524	0.6	TH	1736	0.4
	2117	2.9		2317	2.9
3	0405	0.7	18	0600	0.5
	0949	3.2		1130	3.2
TH	1659	0.4	F	1834	0.2
	2242	3.1			
4	0531	0.5	19	0005	3.0
	1102	3.3		0647	0.4
F	1812	0.2	SA	1210	3.3
	2346	3.2		1909	0.2
5	0637	0.4	20	0038	3.1
	1158	3.5		0721	0.3
SA	1908	0.0	SU	1242	3.3
				1941	0.1
6	0038	3.3	21	0109	3.2
	0730	0.2		0756	0.2
SU	1246	3.5	M	1317	3.4
●	1957	-0.1	○	2014	0.2
7	0123	3.3	22	0140	3.2
	0817	0.1		0831	0.2
M	1332	3.6	TU	1350	3.4
	2041	-0.1		2045	0.2
8	0205	3.4	23	0208	3.3
	0858	0.0		0901	0.2
TU	1415	3.6	W	1418	3.4
	2123	-0.1		2113	0.2
9	0245	3.4	24	0233	3.3
	0938	0.0		0928	0.2
W	1457	3.6	TH	1445	3.3
	2203	0.0		2139	0.2
10	0323	3.4	25	0259	3.3
	1018	0.0		0953	0.2
TH	1540	3.5	F	1515	3.2
	2241	0.1		2206	0.2
11	0402	3.3	26	0327	3.2
	1056	0.1		1020	0.2
F	1624	3.4	SA	1547	3.1
	2316	0.2		2233	0.3
12	0442	3.2	27	0359	3.2
	1135	0.2		1050	0.3
SA	1710	3.2	SU	1622	3.0
	2353	0.4		2302	0.4
13	0525	3.1	28	0433	3.1
	1218	0.3		1124	0.4
SU	1801	2.9	M	1703	2.9
				2339	0.6
14	0037	0.6	29	0519	3.0
	0620	3.0		1213	0.4
M	1314	0.4	TU	1800	2.8
	1907	2.7			
15	0141	0.7	30	0037	0.7
	0733	2.9		0625	3.0
TU	1433	0.5	W	1325	0.5
	2031	2.6		1919	2.8
			31	0201	0.8
				0749	3.0
			TH	1458	0.5
				2050	2.9

NOVEMBER

	Time	m		Time	m
1	0337	0.7	16	0507	0.6
	0917	3.2		1040	3.1
F	1629	0.4	SA	1745	0.3
	2213	3.0		2319	2.9
2	0501	0.5	17	0604	0.4
	1031	3.3		1129	3.2
SA	1742	0.2	SU	1828	0.2
	2318	3.2		2359	3.1
3	0608	0.3	18	0645	0.3
	1130	3.4		1207	3.2
SU	1839	0.0	M	1904	0.2
4	0011	3.3	19	0033	3.2
	0703	0.2		0722	0.3
M	1221	3.5	TU	1244	3.3
●	1930	0.0		1939	0.2
5	0057	3.3	20	0106	3.2
	0751	0.1		0759	0.2
TU	1308	3.5	W	1318	3.3
	2016	-0.1	○	2012	0.2
6	0138	3.3	21	0136	3.3
	0834	0.0		0831	0.2
W	1353	3.5	TH	1349	3.3
	2056	0.0		2042	0.2
7	0217	3.4	22	0205	3.3
	0913	0.0		0902	0.2
TH	1437	3.5	F	1421	3.2
	2136	0.1		2113	0.2
8	0256	3.4	23	0235	3.3
	0955	0.1		0934	0.2
F	1521	3.4	SA	1455	3.2
	2215	0.2		2145	0.2
9	0337	3.4	24	0308	3.3
	1038	0.1		1007	0.2
SA	1607	3.2	SU	1533	3.1
	2254	0.3		2218	0.3
10	0419	3.3	25	0344	3.2
	1119	0.2		1042	0.2
SU	1652	3.0	M	1613	3.0
	2331	0.4		2254	0.4
11	0503	3.2	26	0424	3.2
	1203	0.3		1123	0.3
M	1741	2.9	TU	1700	2.9
				2338	0.5
12	0014	0.5	27	0512	3.2
	0555	3.1		1213	0.3
TU	1255	0.4	W	1755	2.9
	1839	2.7			
13	0110	0.7	28	0032	0.5
	0658	3.0		0612	3.1
W	1400	0.5	TH	1316	0.3
	1950	2.6		1903	2.8
14	0223	0.7	29	0143	0.6
	0815	3.0		0724	3.2
TH	1521	0.5	F	1432	0.4
	2110	2.6		2020	2.9
15	0348	0.7	30	0304	0.6
	0934	3.0		0841	3.2
F	1642	0.5	SA	1552	0.3
	2223	2.8		2136	3.0

DECEMBER

	Time	m		Time	m
1	0423	0.5	16	0503	0.
	0953	3.3		1035	3.
SU	1704	0.2	M	1732	0.
	2242	3.1		2310	3.0
2	0532	0.3	17	0559	0.4
	1057	3.3		1126	3.1
M	1806	0.1	TU	1820	0.3
	2338	3.2		2354	3.2
3	0631	0.2	18	0644	0.3
	1155	3.4		1209	3.2
TU	1901	0.0	W	1902	0.1
4	0028	3.2	19	0032	3.2
	0725	0.1		0725	0.3
W	1247	3.4	TH	1248	3.4
●	1950	0.0	○	1941	0.2
5	0113	3.3	20	0107	3.3
	0811	0.1		0803	0.2
TH	1335	3.4	F	1326	3.2
	2033	0.1		2017	0.2
6	0153	3.4	21	0142	3.3
	0853	0.1		0841	0.1
F	1420	3.4	SA	1405	3.2
	2113	0.2		2056	0.2
7	0234	3.4	22	0220	3.4
	0938	0.1		0923	0.1
SA	1507	3.3	SU	1446	3.2
	2157	0.3		2136	0.2
8	0317	3.5	23	0258	3.4
	1025	0.1		1004	0.1
SU	1553	3.2	M	1527	3.1
	2238	0.3		2213	0.2
9	0401	3.4	24	0336	3.3
	1108	0.2		1041	0.1
M	1636	3.0	TU	1609	3.0
	2316	0.4		2252	0.2
10	0444	3.3	25	0418	3.3
	1149	0.3		1122	0.1
TU	1720	2.9	W	1656	3.0
	2354	0.4		2337	0.3
11	0529	3.3	26	0506	3.3
	1232	0.4		1210	0.1
W	1806	2.8	TH	1748	2.9
12	0037	0.5	27	0027	0.3
	0619	3.2		0559	3.3
TH	1321	0.4	F	1303	0.2
	1900	2.7		1844	2.9
13	0131	0.6	28	0123	0.4
	0718	3.1		0657	3.3
F	1419	0.5	SA	1403	0.2
	2003	2.7		1945	2.9
14	0238	0.6	29	0228	0.5
	0825	3.0		0803	3.2
SA	1527	0.5	SU	1511	0.3
	2111	2.7		2052	3.0
15	0354	0.6	30	0341	0.4
	0934	3.0		0914	3.2
SU	1635	0.5	M	1623	0.3
	2215	2.9		2202	3.0
			31	0454	0.3
				1026	3.2
			TU	1732	0.2
				2306	3.1

Chart Datum: 1·66 metres below Normal Null (German reference level)

ɪIVER ELBE/HAMBURG *9.24.20*

ɪiedersachsen/Schleswig-Holstein ❁❁❁◊◊◊✿✿

ɪHARTS AC 3625, 3266, 3268; Imray C26; BSH 3010/1 to 12, D46, 47, D48

ɪDES

ɪückstadt	ML 1·2	Duration 0515	Zone -0100
ɪunshausen	ML 1·1	Duration 0510	
amburg	ML 1·3	Duration 0435	

ɪtandard Port CUXHAVEN (⟵)

ɪmes				Height (metres)			
High Water		Low Water		MHWS	MHWN	MLWN	MLWS
0200	0800	0200	0900	3·4	2·9	0·4	0·0
1400	2000	1400	2100				
ɪifferences SCHARHÖRN (11M NW of Cuxhaven)							
–0045	–0047	–0101	–0103	0·0	0·0	0·0	–0·1
ɪROßER VOGELSAND							
–0044	–0046	–0101	–0103	0·0	0·0	0·0	0·0
ɪLÜCKSTADT							
+0205	+0214	+0220	+0213	–0·3	–0·2	–0·2	0·0
TADERSAND							
+0241	+0245	+0300	+0254	–0·1	0·0	–0·2	0·0
CHULAU							
+0304	+0315	+0337	+0321	0·0	+0·1	–0·3	–0·1
AMBURG							
+0338	+0346	+0422	+0406	+0·2	+0·3	–0·4	–0·2

ɪAVIGATION Distances: Elbe lt float to Cuxhaven = 24M; uxhaven to Wedel Yacht Haven = 45M; Wedel to City Sport Hafen 11·5M. The river has 13m up to Hamburg and is tidal to ɪeesthacht, 24M above Hamburg. Strong W winds can raise the ɪvel by as much as 4m. Entry should not be attempted with strong ɪ/NW winds against the ebb. It is a very busy waterway and at ɪight the many lights can be confusing. Yachts should keep to ɪtbd, preferably just outside the marked chan. Elbe VTS (not ɪandatory for yachts) offers radar guidance and broadcasts met, av & tidal info.

SHELTER AND FACILITIES Some of the better hbrs are listed below, but it is not a particularly salubrious yachting area:

FREIBURG: 7M above Brunsbüttel on the SW bank. Small vessels can enter at HW and there is excellent shelter at Freiburg Reede. ML 2·2m. Hr Mr ☎ (04779) 8314. Facilities: ME, El, Sh, C, FW, Slip, YC; **Jugendheim & YC Klubheim** V, R, Bar. (Sheet 4).

STÖRLOCH/BORSFLETH: Ent approx 600m above locks on E bank. ML 2·8m. Hr Mr ☎ (04124) 71437. Facilities: FW, YC. Stör Bridge VHF Ch 09, 16. (Sheet 4).

STÖR/BEIDENFLETH: ML 2·8m (Sheet 4). **Langes Rack YC.**

GLÜCKSTADT: on the NE bank, 2½M above mouth of R Stör. Good shelter; inner and outer hbrs have 2m depth. Lock into inner hbr opens HW –2 to +½. VHF Ch 11. Hr Mr ☎ (04124) 2087; ⊖ ☎ 2171. YC, FW, C, D, V, R, ⊠, Bar. (Sheet 5).

WISCHHAFEN: Hr Mr ☎ (04770) 334; ⊖ 3014 FW, M, Slip, P, D, ML 2·7m. (Sheet 5).

RUTHENSTROM: Ldg marks into hbr, two bns with △ topmarks on 197°. ML 2·6m. Hr Mr ☎ (04143) 5282; C, Slip, FW, ME, El, Sh. (Sheet 6).

KRÜCKAUMÜNDUNG JACHTHAFEN: ☎ (04125) 1521 Slip, FW. ML 2·7m. ⊖ ☎ 20551. (Sheet 6).

PINNAUMÜNDUNG JACHTHAFEN: Ent via lock gate on N bank after passing through main locks. ML 2·5m. Hr Mr ☎ (04101) 22447 Slip, M, FW, YC, C. (Sheet 10).

PINNAU-NEUENDEICH: Marina 1⅓M up the Pinnau from main locks and another at approx 2M. (Sheet 6).

ABBENFLETH: Ent marked by two bns in line 221° with △ topmarks. (Sheets 6/7).

HASELDORF Hafen: Hr Mr ☎ (04129) 268 Slip, FW, V, YC.

R. SCHWINGE on SW bank, 12M up-river from Glückstadt: BRUNSHAUSEN (04141) 3085

HÖRNE/WÖHRDEN ML 2·8m

STADE (04141) 101275 C, YC, V; Access HW ±2. Very good shelter in scenic town. ⊖ ☎ 3014. (Sheets 7/8).

LÜHE: Hafen in town of Lühe. (Sheet 8).

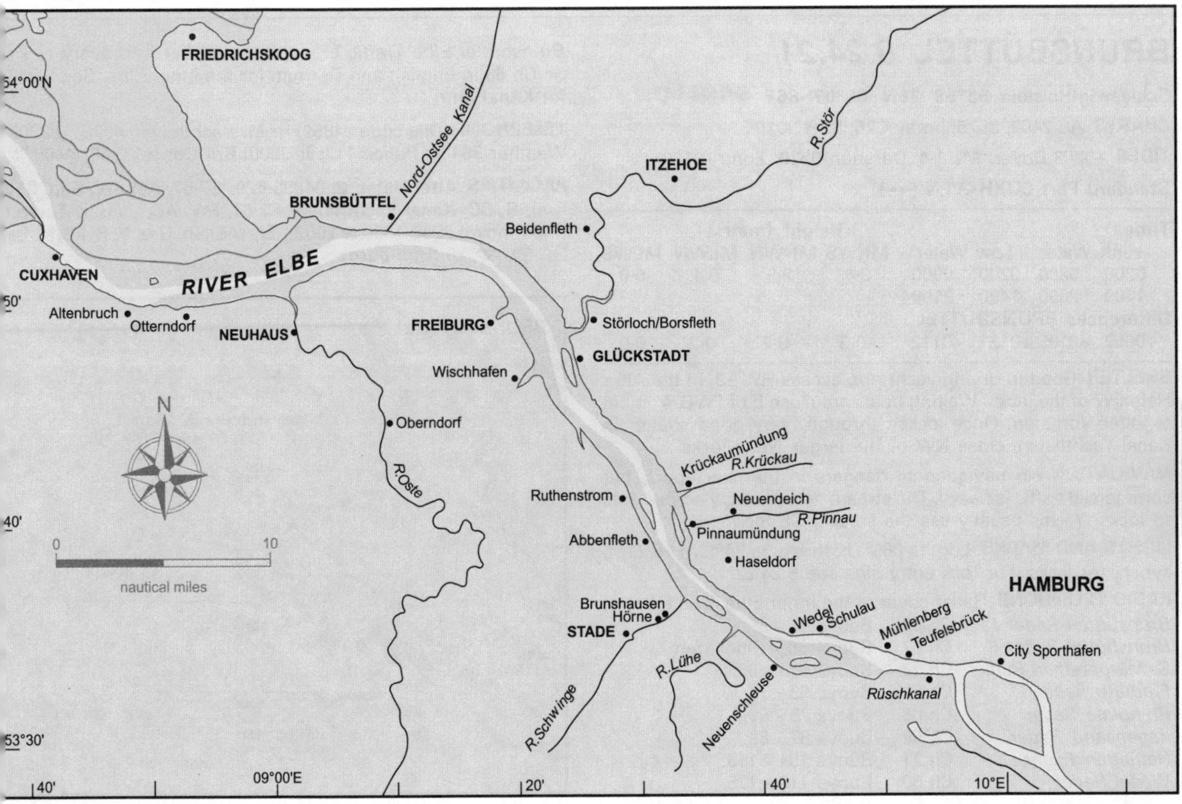

HAMBURG A busy commercial port with several marinas. Visitors berth at Wedel in Hamburger Yachthafen or in the City Sporthafen, in city centre esp for visitors (see below).

WEDEL: on N bank, 12M downstream from Hamburg, very good shelter H24; **Hamburger Yachthafen**, €1·02, (2000 berths) with 2 ents marked by FR and FG lts. A conspic 50m tall radar tr is at W corner of hbr. Hr Mr ☎ (04103) 4438 (office), 5632 (Hr Mr east), 7751 (Hr Mr west); ⊜ ☎ 0171-2766300; D & P (closed Tues), Bar, BH (16 ton), BY, C, CH, El, Ⓔ, FW, ME, SC, Sh, Slip, SM. (Sheets 8/9).

SCHULAU: Good shelter, 7ca E of Wedel. Beware strong tidal streams across ent, marked by FR and FG lts. Hr Mr ☎ 2422, Slip, C, P, D, ME, Ⓗ, CH, SC. (Sheet 8/9).

NEUENSCHLEUSE: opposite Wedel. (Sheet 9).

MÜHLENBERG: N bank, (250), Slip, FW, SC. Small boats only; 0·6m above CD. (Sheets 9/10).

TEUFELSBRÜCK: small hbr on N bank. Good shelter, sandbar at ent. Bar, FW, SC. (Sheets 9/10).

RÜSCHKANAL: on S bank in Finkenwerder, C, CH, El, FW, ME, Slip, Sh, with 4 SCs and nearby resort area.

CITY SPORTHAFEN: (80+50) ☎ 364297, €1·02, D, P, FW, AC; Ent on N bank beyond St Pauli-Landungsbrücken.

RADIO TELEPHONE Elbe VTS: see 9.24.19 for radar cover up to buoy No 53. See 9.24.21 for buoys 51 - 125. Then *Hamburg Radar:*

Ch 19	Buoys 123 - 129;
Ch 03	Buoys 129 - Seemanshöft;
Ch 63	Seemanshöft - Vorhafen (outer hbr);
Ch 07	Parkhafen - Kuhwerder Vorhafen;
Ch 05	Kuhwerder Vorhafen - Norderelbbrücke;
Ch 80	Köhlbrand - Hamburger Häfen.

Hamburg Port Traffic and Hbr Control vessel Ch 13 14 **73** (H24). Süderelbe: Rethe and Kattwyk bridges and Harburg lock Ch 13 (H24). All stns monitor Ch 16.

TELEPHONE (Dial code 040) Met 3190 8826/7; Auto 0190 116456; Brit Consul 446071.

FACILITIES **City** all facilities, ACA, ✉, Ⓑ, ≹, ✈. Ferry: Hamburg-Harwich.

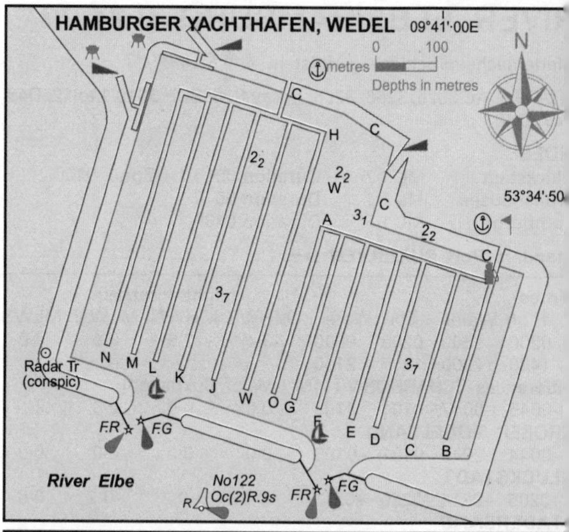

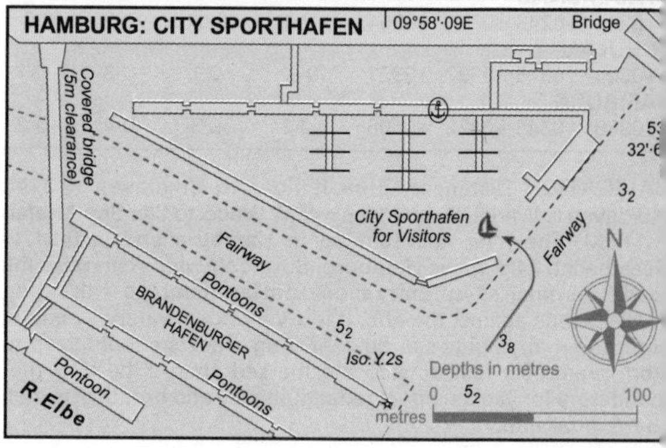

BRUNSBÜTTEL 9.24.21

Schleswig-Holstein **53°53'·28N 09°07'·85E** ❁❁❁◊◊✿✿

CHARTS AC 2469, 3625; Imray C26; BSH 3010/3

TIDES +0203 Dover; ML 1·4; Duration 0520; Zone –0100

Standard Port CUXHAVEN (⟵)

Times				Height (metres)			
High Water		Low Water		MHWS	MHWN	MLWN	MLWS
0200	0800	0200	0900	3·4	2·9	0·4	0·0
1400	2000	1400	2100				
Differences BRUNSBÜTTEL							
+0057	+0105	+0121	+0112	–0·3	–0·2	–0·2	0·0

SHELTER Good in drying yacht hbr, access HW ±3, in the Alter Hafen W of the locks. Waiting posts are close E of FWG ☆ at ent to Alter Vorhafen. Once locked through, very good shelter in Kanal-Yachthafen, close NW of the larger Neue locks.

NAVIGATION No navigational dangers in the near apprs, but commercial traffic is heavy. The stream sets strongly across ents to locks. Yachts usually use the smaller SE locks.

LIGHTS AND MARKS Ldg lts 065°, both Iso 3s 24/46m 16/21M, synch, for locks. For lock entry sigs see 9.24.22.

RADIO TELEPHONE Radar cover of the inner Elbe is as follows:

Brunsbüttel Radar I	Ch 62	Buoys 51 - 59;
Brunsbüttel Radar II	Ch 67	Buoys 60 - Elbehafen;
S. Margarethen Radar	Ch 18	Buoys 57a - 65;
Freiburg Radar	Ch 61	Buoys 63 - 77;
Rhinplate Radar	Ch 05	Buoys 75 - 89;
Pagensand Radar	Ch 66	Buoys 87 - 89;
Hetlingen Radar	Ch 21	Buoys 101 - 115;
Wedel Radar	Ch 60	Buoys 113 - 125.

Brunsbüttel Elbe Traffic broadcasts weather info every H + 0 on Ch 68 in English and German for the inner Elbe. See 9.24.2 for Kanal entry.

TELEPHONE (Dial code 04852) Hr Mr Yachthaven 4276; ⊜ 8300 Weather 36400; Police 112; Ⓗ 9800; Brit Consul (040) 446071.

FACILITIES **Alter Hafen** ☎ 04855-629, €7·67, AC, FW, Slip, C (2 ton), R, SC; **Kanal-Yachthafen**, €7·67, FW, AC, ⊜, Bar. **Town** F D (as shown 0800-1800 ☎ 2002), El, ME, Sh, Gaz, V, R, LB, Ⓗ, Bar ✉, Ⓑ, ≹, ✈ (Hamburg).

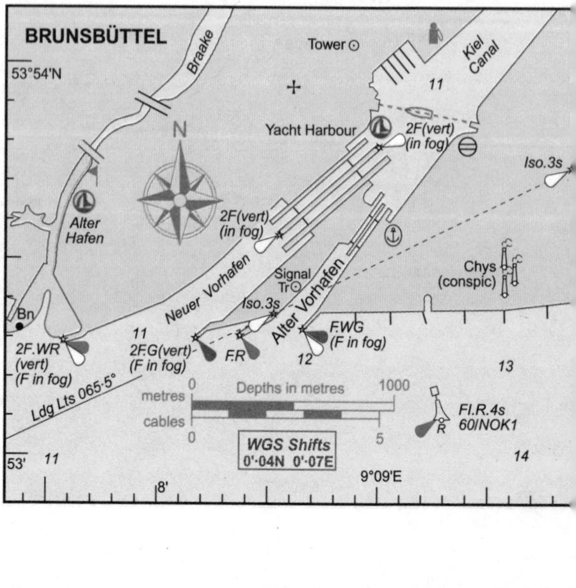

NORD-OSTSEE KANAL (Kiel Canal) *9.24.22*

Schleswig-Holstein

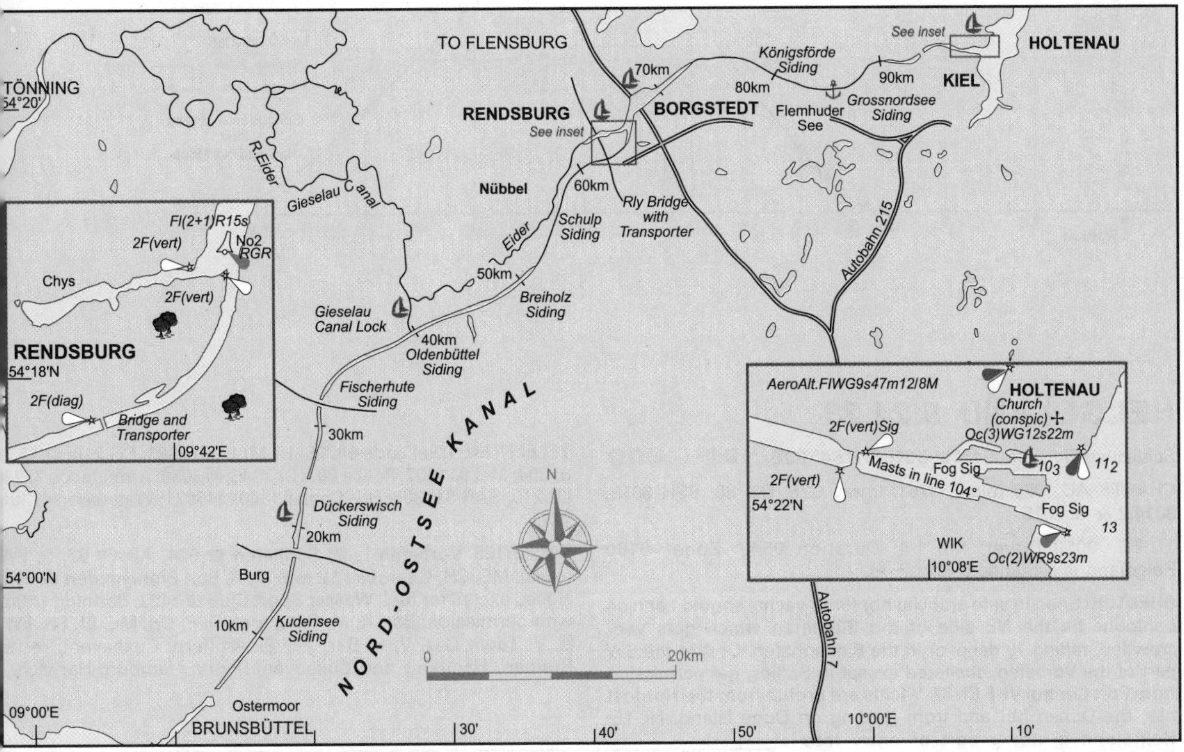

CHARTS AC 2469, 696 (Kieler Förde); BSH 3009/1-4

NAVIGATION The Canal runs from Brunsbüttel (9.24.21) to Kiel-Holtenau, 53·3M (98·7 km). Km posts start from Brunsbüttel. Width is 103 to 162m on the surface, and depth 11m. Yachts may only use the Canal and its ents by day and good vis. (This does not apply to craft going to the Inner or Old Hbrs at Brunsbüttel, or to the yacht berths at Holtenau). Speed limit is 8kn. All 6 bridges have 40m clearance. Fly flag 'N' (no pilot). Sailing, except motor sailing is prohib; yachts must then display a B ▼, or a B pennant. Canal dues are paid at the Holtenau locks at the 'Dues Office' (N bank). Yachts purely in transit are not usually troubled by the Customs Authority; they should fly the third substitute of the International Code.

SHELTER The principal port along the canal is Rensburg, between km posts 60 and 67, with all facilities including 3 yacht hbrs in the Obereidersee. Rensburg is linked to Tönning (see under 9.24.24) by the R Eider and Gieselau Canal. There are 9 passing places (sidings or *weichen*). Yachts are to regulate their passage so as to reach their planned berthing places during daylight. These may be at:

1. Brunsbüttel (km 0);
2. Kudensee siding (km 9·5);
3. Dückerswisch siding (km 20·7);
4. Fischerhütte siding (km 35);
5. Oldenbüttel siding (km 40), at ent to Gieselau Canal;
6. Breiholz siding (km 48);
7. Schülp siding (km 57);
8. The Obereidersee (Rendsburg), ent at km 66;
9. The Borgstedter See, ent at km 70;
10. Königsförde siding (km 80);
11. Grossnordsee siding (km 85), or ⚓ in Flemhuder See;
12. Schwartenbek siding (km 92);
13. Kiel-Holtenau (km 98·7).

Kiel-Holtenau, at the Baltic end of the canal, is a major port with a Yacht Hbr on the N bank (E of locks); all usual facilities. Two pairs of locks (yachts usually use the N pair) lead into the Kieler Förde which is practically tideless and at almost the same level as the canal.

SIGNALS Lock signals (shown at signal tr and centre pier of lock):

●	= no entry.
Ⓦ over ●	= prepare to enter.
Ⓦ	= yachts may enter (berth on pontoons).
Ⓦ over ●	= enter without pilot (yachts follow ships flying Flag N); secure to middle wall.
●	= enter with pilot; secure to middle wall.
Ⓦ over Ⓦ and ●	= enter with pilot and secure by Ⓦ lt.

In the canal, the only traffic sig applicable to yachts is:
3 ● (vert) = STOP. Keep to stbd; give way to large vessel approaching.

RADIO TELEPHONE Before entering/leaving, yachts should request a lock:
at Brunsbüttel to *Kiel Kanal I* on Ch 13;
or at Holtenau to *Kiel Kanal IV* on Ch 12.
Ports: Ostermoor (Brunsbüttel to Burg) Ch 73;
Breiholz (Breiholz to Audorf) Ch 73.
Canal. Maintain listening watch as follows:

Kiel Kanal I	Ch 13	Brunsbüttel ent and locks;
Kiel Kanal II	Ch 02	Brunsbüttel to Breiholz;
Kiel Traffic	Ch 22	Breiholz to Holtenau;
Kiel Kanal IV	Ch 12	Holtenau ent and locks.

Info broadcasts by *Kiel Kanal II* on Ch 02 at H+15, H+45; and by *Kiel Kanal III* on Ch 03 at H+20, H+50. Vessels should monitor these broadcasts and not call the station if this can be avoided.

FACILITIES A BP fuel barge is on the N bank, close E of the Holtenau locks. At Wik (S side of locks) **Nautischer Dienst** (Kapt Stegmann & Co) ☎ 0431 331772 are ACA & BSH Agents. The **British Kiel YC** is 5ca NNW of Stickenhörn ECM buoy, Q (3) 10s, 1M NNE of the locks. It is part of a military centre with no commercial facilities; but AB (about €10·23) may be available for visitors to whom a friendly welcome is extended. Call *Sailtrain* VHF Ch 67 or ☎ (0431) 397921.

24

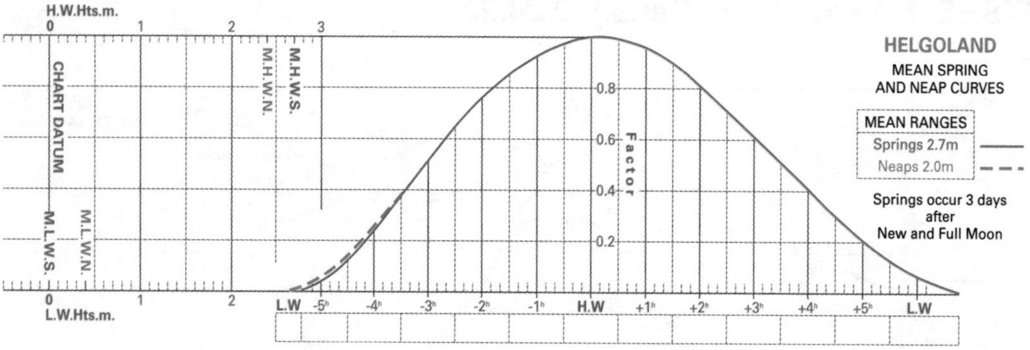

HELGOLAND *9.24.23*

Schleswig-Holstein **54°10'·30N 07°54'·00E** ❁❁❁⚓⚓⚓✿✿✿

CHARTS AC 1875 (plan), 3761; Imray C26; D3, 88; BSH 3013, 3014.2 & .3, 3015

TIDES –0030 Dover; ML 1·4; Duration 0540; Zone –0100

Helgoland is a Standard Port (⟶).

SHELTER Good in safe artificial hbr (5m); yachts should berth on pontoons on the NE side of the Südhafen which gets very crowded, rafting 10 deep; or in the Binnenhafen. Or ⚓ in the SW part of the Vorhafen, sheltered except in SE'lies; get permission from Port Control VHF Ch 67. Yachts are prohib from the Nordost hbr, the Dünen hbr and from landing on Düne Island. NOTE: Helgoland is not a port of entry into Germany. Customs in Helgoland are for passport control. Duty free goods are obtainable; hence many day-trippers by ferry. There is a visitors' tax of €2·56 per person per night.

NAVIGATION WPT Helgoland ECM buoy, Q (3) 10s, Whis, 55°09'·00N 07°53'·57E, 202°/022° from/to Düne front ldg lt, 2·1M. Beware the Hogstean shoal, 4ca S of Sudmole head lt, and other rky shoals either side of chan. The S chan and ent are used by ferries. Beware lobster pots around Düne Is. Caution: Entry is prohib at all times into Nature Reserves close either side of the appr chans from SSW and NW. These Reserves extend about 2M NE and SW of Helgoland; their limits are marked by Cardinal buoys. Marine police are active in this respect. A smaller Reserve, lying to the N, E and S of Düne, is a prohib ⚓, with other restrictions. See BSH 3014.2 and AC 3761 and 1875 (plan) for limits.

LIGHTS AND MARKS Helgoland lt ho, Fl 5s 82m 28M; brown □ tr, B lantern, W balcony. Düne ldg lts 020°: front Iso 4s 11m 8M; rear Dir Iso WRG 4s 17m 11/10M synch, W sector 018·5°-021°. Binnenhafen ldg lts 302°: both Oc R 6s, synch.

RADIO TELEPHONE *Helgoland Port Radio* Ch 67 16 (**1/5 – 31/8.** Mon-Thur: 0700-1200,1300-2000; Fri/Sat 0700-2000; Sun 0700-1200LT. **1/9–30/4.** Mon-Thur 0700-1200, 1300-1600; Fri 0700-1200). Coast Radio Ch 03 16 27 88 (H24). Bremen (MRCC) maintains a distress watch via Helgoland on Ch 16 and Ch 70 DSC.

TELEPHONE (Dial code 04725) Hr Mr 8159 3583; CG 210; ⊖ 1537 or 304; Met 811007; Police 607; Dr 7345; Ⓗ 8030; Ambulance 7723 LB 210; SAR 811305; Brit Consul (040) 446071; Watersports Club 7211.

FACILITIES Vorhafen L, ⚓; **Südhafen** ☎ 504, AB €1·02, D, FW (cans), ME, CH, C (mobile 12 ton), V, R, Bar; **Binnenhafen** ☎ 504, closed except for fuel; **Wasser Sport Club** ☎ 7422, Berthing <10m with permission; Bar, R, M, C (12 ton), D, P, CH, ME, El, Sh, FW, ⊡, V. **Town** Gaz, V, R, Bar, ✉, Ⓑ, ⇌ (ferry Cuxhaven), ✈ (to Bremen, Hamburg and Cuxhaven). Ferry: Hamburg-Harwich.

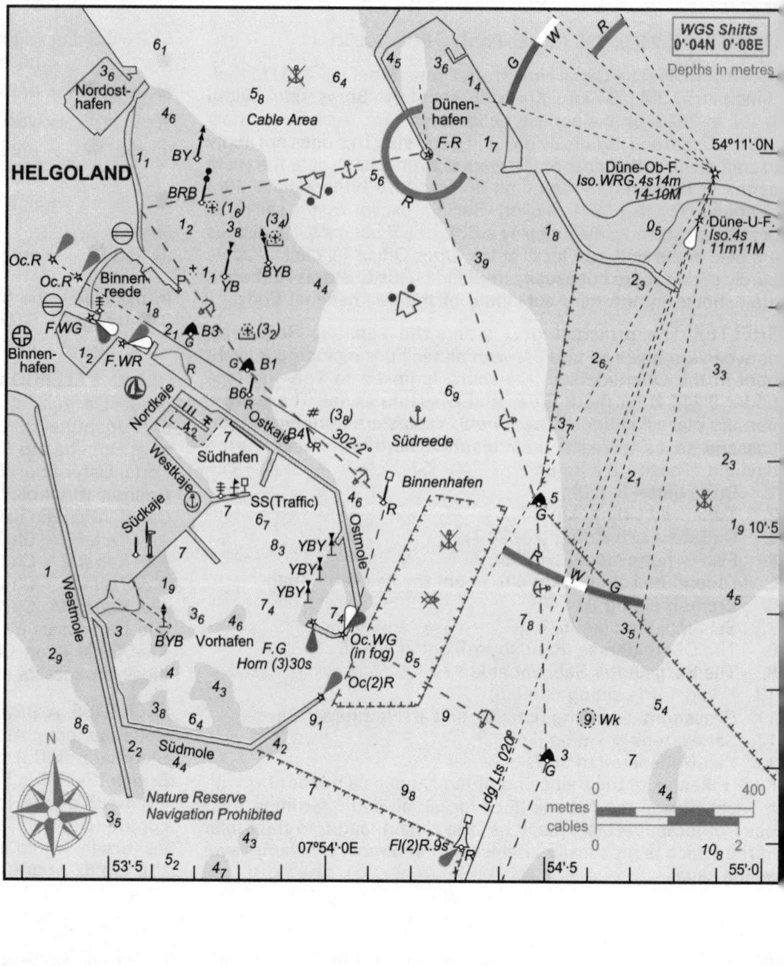

TIME ZONE -0100
(German Standard Time)
Subtract 1 hour for UT
For German Summer Time add ONE hour in **non-shaded areas**

GERMANY – HELGOLAND

LAT 54°11′N LONG 7°53′E

TIMES AND HEIGHTS OF HIGH AND LOW WATERS

SPRING & NEAP TIDES
Dates in red are SPRINGS
Dates in blue are NEAPS

YEAR **2002**

JANUARY

Date	Day	Time	m	Time	m	Time	m	Time	m
1	TU	0040	2.8	0734	0.0	1310	2.7	1950	0.1
2	W	0128	2.8	0824	0.0	1359	2.7	2035	0.1
3	TH	0214	2.9	0910	0.0	1447	2.6	2119	0.1
4	F	0258	2.9	0957	0.0	1535	2.5	2206	0.2
5	SA	0345	2.9	1047	0.1	1628	2.5	2259	0.3
6	SU	0438	2.9	1139	0.1	1725	2.5	2354	0.4
7	M	0537	2.8	1234	0.2	1822	2.4		
8	TU	0055	0.4	0640	2.7	1337	0.3	1925	2.4
9	W	0206	0.3	0751	2.6	1448	0.3	2032	2.4
10	TH	0322	0.3	0904	2.6	1557	0.2	2139	2.5
11	F	0430	0.2	1012	2.6	1657	0.3	2239	2.6
12	SA	0527	0.2	1109	2.7	1747	0.3	2329	2.7
13	SU ●	0616	0.2	1155	2.7	1830	0.3		
14	M	0012	2.8	0656	0.2	1234	2.8	1908	0.3
15	TU	0049	2.9	0733	0.2	1312	2.8	1944	0.3
16	W	0124	2.9	0810	0.2	1349	2.7	2019	0.3
17	TH	0158	2.9	0846	0.2	1424	2.6	2051	0.2
18	F	0232	2.8	0919	0.2	1457	2.5	2122	0.2
19	SA	0305	2.8	0953	0.2	1531	2.5	2156	0.3
20	SU	0341	2.8	1029	0.3	1606	2.4	2231	0.3
21	M	0419	2.7	1102	0.3	1642	2.4	2308	0.4
22	TU	0500	2.6	1139	0.4	1726	2.3	2356	0.5
23	W	0550	2.5	1232	0.4	1825	2.3		
24	TH	0104	0.5	0656	2.4	1343	0.4	1938	2.3
25	F	0223	0.4	0811	2.4	1459	0.4	2052	2.4
26	SA	0338	0.4	0922	2.5	1609	0.3	2156	2.6
27	SU	0443	0.2	1025	2.6	1710	0.2	2250	2.7
28	M	0541	0.1	1121	2.7	1804	0.2	○ 2339	2.8
29	TU	0634	0.0	1212	2.7	1854	0.1		
30	W	0027	2.9	0726	-0.1	1301	2.7	1942	0.0
31	TH	0117	2.9	0816	-0.2	1349	2.6	2029	0.0

FEBRUARY

Date	Day	Time	m	Time	m	Time	m	Time	m
1	F	0204	2.9	0903	-0.2	1436	2.6	2112	-0.1
2	SA	0247	2.9	0946	-0.2	1522	2.6	2156	0.0
3	SU	0331	2.9	1030	-0.1	1608	2.5	2241	0.1
4	M	0418	2.9	1114	0.1	1655	2.5	2327	0.2
5	TU	0508	2.8	1158	0.2	1743	2.5		
6	W	0018	0.2	0604	2.6	1253	0.3	1840	2.4
7	TH	0126	0.2	0714	2.4	1406	0.3	1952	2.3
8	F	0250	0.2	0837	2.4	1527	0.3	2112	2.4
9	SA	0412	0.2	0956	2.4	1639	0.3	2222	2.5
10	SU	0516	0.1	1059	2.5	1734	0.3	2316	2.7
11	M	0605	0.1	1145	2.6	1817	0.3	2358	2.8
12	TU ●	0645	0.1	1222	2.7	1855	0.2		
13	W	0034	2.8	0721	0.1	1256	2.7	1931	0.1
14	TH	0107	2.8	0754	0.1	1330	2.7	2003	0.1
15	F	0138	2.8	0826	0.1	1401	2.6	2032	0.1
16	SA	0208	2.8	0856	0.1	1431	2.5	2101	0.1
17	SU	0240	2.8	0928	0.1	1502	2.5	2132	0.1
18	M	0312	2.7	0959	0.1	1532	2.5	2203	0.1
19	TU	0344	2.7	1026	0.1	1600	2.4	2229	0.1
20	W	0414	2.6	1049	0.2	1630	2.4	2302	0.2
21	TH	0453	2.4	1129	0.3	1719	2.3		
22	F	0001	0.4	0556	2.3	1240	0.4	1835	2.3
23	SA	0127	0.4	0721	2.3	1411	0.4	2005	2.3
24	SU	0300	0.3	0850	2.4	1537	0.4	2126	2.5
25	M	0422	0.2	1007	2.5	1651	0.3	2231	2.7
26	TU	0529	0.0	1108	2.6	1751	0.1	2324	2.8
27	W ○	0625	-0.2	1200	2.6	1843	0.0		
28	TH	0013	2.8	0715	-0.3	1247	2.6	1930	-0.1

MARCH

Date	Day	Time	m	Time	m	Time	m	Time	m
1	F	0100	2.9	0802	-0.3	1332	2.6	2015	-0.2
2	SA	0147	2.9	0846	-0.3	1417	2.6	2058	-0.2
3	SU	0230	2.9	0927	-0.2	1500	2.6	2138	-0.2
4	M	0312	2.9	1006	-0.1	1540	2.6	2218	-0.1
5	TU	0355	2.8	1044	0.0	1620	2.6	2258	0.0
6	W	0439	2.6	1122	0.2	1702	2.5	2345	0.1
7	TH	0530	2.4	1212	0.3	1758	2.3		
8	F	0050	0.1	0641	2.2	1326	0.4	1915	2.3
9	SA	0219	0.2	0810	2.2	1457	0.4	2044	2.3
10	SU	0352	0.2	0938	2.2	1620	0.3	2203	2.5
11	M	0503	0.1	1045	2.4	1719	0.2	2258	2.6
12	TU	0550	0.0	1128	2.5	1801	0.1	2337	2.7
13	W	0627	0.0	1202	2.5	1837	0.1		
14	TH	0012	2.7	0702	-0.1	1234	2.6	● 1911	0.0
15	F	0045	2.7	0733	-0.1	1306	2.6	1942	0.0
16	SA	0115	2.7	0802	-0.1	1335	2.6	2011	-0.1
17	SU	0144	2.8	0830	-0.1	1403	2.5	2039	-0.1
18	M	0213	2.7	0900	-0.1	1431	2.5	2108	-0.1
19	TU	0243	2.6	0929	-0.1	1500	2.5	2137	-0.1
20	W	0313	2.6	0954	0.0	1525	2.5	2200	0.0
21	TH	0341	2.5	1015	0.1	1553	2.4	2229	0.1
22	F	0419	2.4	1051	0.2	1639	2.3	2325	0.2
23	SA	0521	2.3	1201	0.4	1755	2.3		
24	SU	0054	0.3	0650	2.2	1338	0.4	1931	2.4
25	M	0236	0.2	0827	2.3	1514	0.4	2101	2.5
26	TU	0405	0.1	0949	2.4	1631	0.2	2211	2.7
27	W	0514	-0.1	1051	2.5	1733	0.0	2306	2.8
28	TH	0610	-0.3	1142	2.6	1826	-0.1	○ 2354	2.8
29	F	0658	-0.4	1228	2.6	1913	-0.2		
30	SA	0040	2.9	0741	-0.4	1309	2.6	1956	-0.3
31	SU	0124	2.9	0823	-0.3	1350	2.7	2037	-0.3

APRIL

Date	Day	Time	m	Time	m	Time	m	Time	m
1	M	0207	2.8	0902	-0.2	1431	2.6	2116	-0.3
2	TU	0249	2.8	0939	-0.1	1509	2.6	2154	-0.2
3	W	0331	2.7	1014	0.0	1547	2.5	2233	-0.1
4	TH	0414	2.5	1051	0.1	1630	2.5	2320	0.0
5	F	0505	2.3	1140	0.3	1726	2.4		
6	SA	0022	0.1	0612	2.1	1250	0.4	1841	2.3
7	SU	0147	0.2	0738	2.1	1421	0.4	2009	2.3
8	M	0321	0.1	0906	2.1	1548	0.3	2130	2.4
9	TU	0435	0.0	1015	2.3	1651	0.2	2228	2.5
10	W	0523	-0.1	1059	2.4	1733	0.1	2307	2.6
11	TH	0558	-0.1	1133	2.4	1809	0.0	2342	2.6
12	F ●	0632	-0.2	1206	2.5	1845	-0.1		
13	SA	0017	2.6	0705	-0.2	1238	2.6	1917	-0.1
14	SU	0048	2.7	0734	-0.1	1306	2.6	1946	-0.1
15	M	0116	2.7	0802	-0.1	1333	2.6	2015	-0.2
16	TU	0145	2.6	0830	-0.1	1400	2.6	2044	-0.2
17	W	0216	2.6	0859	-0.1	1430	2.5	2114	-0.1
18	TH	0248	2.5	0928	0.0	1502	2.5	2145	-0.1
19	F	0324	2.5	0958	0.1	1537	2.5	2222	0.0
20	SA	0409	2.3	1039	0.2	1626	2.4	2320	0.1
21	SU	0512	2.2	1147	0.3	1739	2.4		
22	M	0044	0.2	0636	2.2	1319	0.4	1908	2.5
23	TU	0220	0.1	0807	2.3	1452	0.3	2035	2.6
24	W	0345	-0.1	0925	2.4	1608	0.1	2145	2.7
25	TH	0450	-0.2	1026	2.5	1709	0.0	2242	2.7
26	F	0545	-0.3	1117	2.5	1804	-0.2	2333	2.8
27	SA ○	0634	-0.4	1203	2.6	1852	-0.3		
28	SU	0019	2.8	0717	-0.3	1244	2.7	1934	-0.3
29	M	0101	2.8	0756	-0.2	1322	2.7	2013	-0.3
30	TU	0143	2.8	0833	-0.1	1401	2.7	2053	-0.2

Chart Datum: 1·68 metres below Normal Null (German reference level)

Register for your **FREE** weekly weather email service from Macmillan Reeds
at **www.nauticaldata.com – NOW!**
weekend weather reports sent to your email address, every Thursday

24

TIME ZONE -0100
(German Standard Time)
Subtract 1 hour for UT
For German Summer Time add ONE hour in **non-shaded areas**

GERMANY – HELGOLAND

LAT 54°11′N LONG 7°53′E

TIMES AND HEIGHTS OF HIGH AND LOW WATERS

SPRING & NEAP TIDES
Dates in red are SPRINGS
Dates in blue are NEAPS

YEAR **2002**

MAY

Date	Day	Time	m	Time	m	Time	m	Time	m
1	W	0226	2.7	0911	-0.1	1442	2.7	2133	-0.2
2	TH	0310	2.5	0947	0.0	1523	2.6	2215	-0.1
3	F	0355	2.4	1027	0.2	1607	2.5	2302	0.0
4	SA	0445	2.3	1114	0.3	1700	2.5	2358	0.1
5	SU	0545	2.1	1216	0.4	1806	2.4		
6	M	0110	0.2	0659	2.1	1335	0.4	1924	2.4
7	TU	0232	0.2	0818	2.1	1457	0.3	2041	2.4
8	W	0346	0.1	0926	2.2	1605	0.2	2143	2.5
9	TH	0438	-0.1	1016	2.3	1653	0.1	2228	2.5
10	F	0517	-0.1	1055	2.4	1733	0.0	2306	2.6
11	SA	0554	-0.1	1131	2.5	1812	0.0	2343	2.6
12	SU ●	0630	-0.1	1205	2.6	1847	-0.1		
13	M	0017	2.6	0702	-0.1	1234	2.6	1918	-0.1
14	TU	0048	2.6	0732	-0.1	1303	2.7	1950	-0.1
15	W	0120	2.6	0804	-0.1	1335	2.6	2024	-0.1
16	TH	0156	2.6	0837	-0.1	1411	2.6	2100	-0.1
17	F	0235	2.5	0913	0.0	1450	2.6	2142	-0.1
18	SA	0319	2.4	0954	0.1	1534	2.6	2230	0.0
19	SU	0411	2.4	1044	0.2	1628	2.6	2329	0.0
20	M	0514	2.3	1147	0.3	1734	2.6		
21	TU	0041	0.0	0628	2.3	1306	0.3	1850	2.6
22	W	0201	0.0	0745	2.4	1429	0.2	2007	2.6
23	TH	0317	-0.1	0856	2.4	1541	0.1	2115	2.7
24	F	0420	-0.2	0956	2.5	1642	-0.1	2214	2.7
25	SA	0515	-0.3	1048	2.5	1738	-0.1	2309	2.7
26	SU	0607	-0.2	1137	2.6	1829	-0.2	○ 2358	2.8
27	M	0651	-0.2	1221	2.7	1912	-0.2		
28	TU	0041	2.8	0729	-0.1	1259	2.8	1951	-0.2
29	W	0122	2.7	0807	0.0	1339	2.8	2033	-0.1
30	TH	0207	2.6	0847	0.0	1422	2.8	2117	-0.1
31	F	0253	2.5	0927	0.1	1505	2.7	2159	0.0

JUNE

Date	Day	Time	m	Time	m	Time	m	Time	m
1	SA	0338	2.4	1007	0.2	1548	2.7	2243	0.1
2	SU	0424	2.3	1050	0.3	1634	2.6	2331	0.2
3	M	0514	2.3	1141	0.4	1728	2.6		
4	TU	0026	0.2	0612	2.2	1241	0.4	1832	2.5
5	W	0131	0.2	0717	2.2	1353	0.4	1941	2.5
6	TH	0239	0.2	0823	2.2	1503	0.3	2046	2.5
7	F	0339	0.1	0922	2.3	1603	0.2	2139	2.5
8	SA	0427	0.0	1010	2.4	1651	0.1	2224	2.6
9	SU	0511	0.0	1052	2.5	1734	0.1	2305	2.6
10	M	0552	0.0	1129	2.6	1814	0.0	2344	2.6
11	TU ●	0630	0.0	1203	2.7	1851	-0.1		
12	W	0023	2.6	0707	0.0	1239	2.7	1931	-0.1
13	TH	0103	2.6	0746	0.0	1319	2.7	2013	-0.1
14	F	0146	2.6	0826	0.0	1400	2.7	2057	-0.1
15	SA	0230	2.5	0907	0.0	1444	2.7	2143	-0.1
16	SU	0318	2.5	0953	0.1	1532	2.7	2234	-0.1
17	M	0412	2.4	1047	0.1	1627	2.7	2331	0.0
18	TU	0512	2.4	1145	0.2	1726	2.7		
19	W	0030	0.0	0614	2.4	1249	0.2	1831	2.7
20	TH	0135	0.0	0719	2.4	1400	0.2	1938	2.7
21	F	0243	0.0	0823	2.5	1511	0.1	2046	2.7
22	SA	0348	-0.1	0925	2.5	1615	0.0	2150	2.7
23	SU	0446	-0.1	1022	2.6	1714	-0.1	2249	2.7
24	M	0540	0.0	1115	2.7	1808	-0.1	○ 2342	2.7
25	TU	0628	0.0	1203	2.8	1854	-0.1		
26	W	0027	2.7	0709	0.1	1244	2.8	1936	0.0
27	TH	0109	2.7	0749	0.1	1325	2.9	2018	0.0
28	F	0152	2.7	0830	0.2	1406	2.9	2101	0.1
29	SA	0236	2.6	0908	0.2	1447	2.8	2141	0.1
30	SU	0317	2.5	0945	0.2	1525	2.8	2219	0.2

JULY

Date	Day	Time	m	Time	m	Time	m	Time	m
1	M	0357	2.4	1023	0.3	1606	2.7	2259	0.2
2	TU	0439	2.4	1104	0.3	1650	2.7	2341	0.3
3	W	0523	2.3	1149	0.4	1739	2.6		
4	TH	0027	0.3	0613	2.3	1245	0.4	1835	2.5
5	F	0125	0.3	0713	2.3	1353	0.4	1939	2.5
6	SA	0230	0.3	0817	2.4	1502	0.3	2043	2.5
7	SU	0331	0.2	0918	2.4	1603	0.2	2139	2.5
8	M	0426	0.1	1011	2.5	1656	0.2	2230	2.6
9	TU	0518	0.1	1057	2.6	1744	0.1	2319	2.7
10	W ●	0605	0.1	1139	2.7	1831	0.0		
11	TH	0006	2.7	0650	0.1	1223	2.8	1919	0.0
12	F	0052	2.7	0734	0.1	1308	2.8	2007	-0.1
13	SA	0139	2.6	0819	0.0	1353	2.8	2053	-0.1
14	SU	0224	2.6	0902	0.0	1436	2.8	2137	-0.2
15	M	0311	2.5	0947	0.0	1522	2.8	2226	-0.1
16	TU	0402	2.5	1038	0.1	1615	2.8	2317	0.0
17	W	0456	2.5	1130	0.2	1710	2.8		
18	TH	0008	0.1	0550	2.5	1224	0.2	1806	2.7
19	F	0102	0.1	0645	2.5	1327	0.2	1909	2.7
20	SA	0207	0.2	0749	2.5	1441	0.2	2021	2.6
21	SU	0319	0.2	0858	2.5	1555	0.1	2133	2.6
22	M	0425	0.2	1004	2.6	1659	0.0	2238	2.6
23	TU	0522	0.2	1101	2.7	1754	0.1	2333	2.7
24	W ○	0611	0.2	1150	2.8	1842	0.1		
25	TH	0018	2.7	0655	0.2	1233	2.9	1924	0.1
26	F	0059	2.7	0735	0.2	1311	2.9	2004	0.1
27	SA	0138	2.7	0814	0.2	1348	2.9	2042	0.2
28	SU	0215	2.7	0848	0.2	1424	2.9	2116	0.2
29	M	0249	2.6	0919	0.2	1459	2.8	2149	0.2
30	TU	0324	2.5	0953	0.2	1534	2.8	2223	0.3
31	W	0400	2.5	1028	0.3	1612	2.7	2256	0.3

AUGUST

Date	Day	Time	m	Time	m	Time	m	Time	m
1	TH	0436	2.4	1102	0.3	1649	2.6	2329	0.4
2	F	0513	2.4	1143	0.4	1733	2.5		
3	SA	0013	0.4	0602	2.4	1241	0.5	1832	2.4
4	SU	0118	0.4	0709	2.3	1357	0.5	1945	2.4
5	M	0234	0.4	0825	2.4	1514	0.4	2058	2.5
6	TU	0346	0.3	0934	2.5	1623	0.3	2204	2.6
7	W	0450	0.3	1032	2.7	1723	0.2	2301	2.7
8	TH	0546	0.2	1122	2.8	1818	0.1	● 2353	2.7
9	F	0636	0.2	1209	2.9	1908	0.0		
10	SA	0041	2.7	0723	0.1	1255	2.9	1956	-0.1
11	SU	0127	2.7	0808	0.0	1340	2.9	2041	-0.2
12	M	0212	2.7	0851	-0.1	1422	2.9	2123	-0.2
13	TU	0256	2.6	0933	0.0	1505	2.9	2206	-0.1
14	W	0341	2.6	1018	0.1	1554	2.9	2251	0.1
15	TH	0428	2.6	1105	0.2	1644	2.8	2335	0.2
16	F	0515	2.5	1152	0.2	1737	2.7		
17	SA	0025	0.3	0608	2.5	1253	0.3	1842	2.5
18	SU	0132	0.4	0716	2.4	1413	0.3	2002	2.4
19	M	0254	0.4	0837	2.5	1541	0.2	2125	2.4
20	TU	0412	0.4	0954	2.6	1653	0.1	2235	2.5
21	W	0513	0.3	1053	2.7	1747	0.1	2327	2.6
22	TH ○	0600	0.3	1138	2.8	1830	0.1		
23	F	0007	2.7	0641	0.3	1218	2.9	1909	0.1
24	SA	0044	2.7	0719	0.2	1254	2.9	1945	0.2
25	SU	0118	2.7	0754	0.2	1327	2.9	2017	0.2
26	M	0150	2.7	0824	0.2	1359	2.9	2047	0.2
27	TU	0220	2.6	0852	0.2	1429	2.8	2116	0.2
28	W	0249	2.6	0922	0.2	1501	2.8	2146	0.2
29	TH	0321	2.6	0953	0.2	1533	2.7	2214	0.3
30	F	0350	2.5	1021	0.3	1604	2.6	2238	0.4
31	SA	0420	2.5	1051	0.4	1640	2.5	2312	0.5

Chart Datum: 1·68 metres below Normal Null (German reference level)

Register for your FREE weekly weather email service from Macmillan Reeds
at www.nauticaldata.com – NOW!
weekend weather reports sent to your email address, every Thursday

TIME ZONE -0100
(German Standard Time)
Subtract 1 hour for UT
For German Summer Time add ONE hour in **non-shaded areas**

GERMANY – HELGOLAND

LAT 54°11′N LONG 7°53′E

TIMES AND HEIGHTS OF HIGH AND LOW WATERS

SPRING & NEAP TIDES
Dates in red are **SPRINGS**
Dates in blue are **NEAPS**

YEAR **2002**

SEPTEMBER

Date	Time	m	Date	Time	m
1 SU	0502 1141 1736	2.4 0.5 2.4	16 M	0058 0648 1349 1944	0.6 2.4 0.3 2.3
2 M	0015 0611 1301 1857	0.6 2.3 0.6 2.4	17 TU	0229 0817 1525 2115	0.6 2.4 0.3 2.3
3 TU	0143 0739 1435 2026	0.6 2.4 0.5 2.4	18 W	0357 0940 1644 2228	0.5 2.6 0.2 2.4
4 W	0313 0903 1600 2145	0.5 2.5 0.4 2.5	19 TH	0502 1041 1735 2315	0.4 2.7 0.2 2.6
5 TH	0428 1011 1708 2247	0.4 2.7 0.2 2.6	20 F	0545 1121 1811 2348	0.3 2.8 0.1 2.6
6 F	0529 1105 1804 2339	0.3 2.8 0.0 2.7	21 SA ○	0620 1156 1845	0.2 2.8 0.1
7 SA ●	0620 1152 1853	0.2 2.9 -0.1	22 SU	0021 0655 1231 1918	2.6 0.2 2.8 0.1
8 SU	0025 0706 1238 1938	2.7 0.1 3.0 -0.1	23 M	0053 0729 1303 1948	2.7 0.2 2.8 0.1
9 M	0109 0750 1322 2021	2.7 0.0 3.0 -0.1	24 TU	0123 0758 1332 2015	2.7 0.1 2.8 0.2
10 TU	0151 0832 1404 2101	2.7 0.0 3.0 -0.1	25 W	0149 0825 1359 2041	2.7 0.1 2.8 0.2
11 W	0233 0913 1445 2140	2.7 0.0 2.9 0.0	26 TH	0215 0852 1428 2108	2.6 0.1 2.7 0.2
12 TH	0313 0953 1529 2219	2.7 0.0 2.9 0.2	27 F	0242 0919 1458 2134	2.6 0.2 2.6 0.3
13 F	0354 1035 1615 2300	2.6 0.1 2.7 0.3	28 SA	0310 0946 1529 2158	2.6 0.2 2.6 0.4
14 SA	0439 1122 1709 2349	2.6 0.2 2.5 0.5	29 SU	0340 1015 1606 2232	2.5 0.4 2.5 0.5
15 SU	0534 1223 1817	2.5 0.3 2.4	30 M	0423 1104 1702 2333	2.4 0.5 2.3 0.7

OCTOBER

Date	Time	m	Date	Time	m
1 TU	0533 1226 1825	2.4 0.6 2.3	16 W	0155 0746 1455 2048	0.7 2.4 0.4 2.2
2 W	0105 0705 1406 2000	0.7 2.4 0.5 2.4	17 TH	0326 0911 1616 2202	0.6 2.5 0.3 2.3
3 TH	0244 0836 1538 2124	0.6 2.6 0.4 2.5	18 F	0435 1015 1709 2249	0.4 2.6 0.2 2.5
4 F	0405 0948 1648 2228	0.5 2.8 0.2 2.6	19 SA	0519 1055 1742 2321	0.3 2.7 0.1 2.6
5 SA	0507 1043 1744 2319	0.3 2.9 0.0 2.7	20 SU	0552 1128 1814 2352	0.3 2.8 0.1 2.6
6 SU ●	0559 1131 1831	0.2 2.9 -0.1	21 M ○	0627 1203 1847	0.2 2.8 0.1
7 M	0004 0645 1217 1915	2.7 0.1 3.0 -0.1	22 TU	0024 0700 1235 1916	2.7 0.2 2.8 0.1
8 TU	0045 0727 1300 1955	2.7 0.0 3.0 -0.1	23 W	0053 0730 1303 1942	2.7 0.1 2.8 0.2
9 W	0124 0809 1342 2035	2.8 0.0 3.0 0.0	24 TH	0119 0757 1330 2009	2.7 0.1 2.7 0.2
10 TH	0204 0849 1423 2112	2.8 0.0 2.9 0.1	25 F	0144 0824 1400 2036	2.7 0.1 2.6 0.2
11 F	0244 0929 1506 2149	2.7 0.0 2.8 0.2	26 SA	0212 0852 1432 2104	2.7 0.2 2.6 0.3
12 SA	0325 1010 1552 2229	2.7 0.1 2.6 0.4	27 SU	0242 0924 1507 2135	2.6 0.2 2.5 0.4
13 SU	0410 1059 1645 2319	2.6 0.2 2.4 0.5	28 M	0318 1001 1550 2214	2.6 0.3 2.4 0.5
14 M	0506 1200 1753	2.5 0.3 2.2	29 TU	0405 1053 1648 2314	2.5 0.4 2.3 0.6
15 TU	0027 0619 1321 1918	0.6 2.4 0.4 2.2	30 W	0512 1209 1805	2.5 0.5 2.3
			31 TH	0040 0637 1342 1935	0.7 2.5 0.4 2.4

NOVEMBER

Date	Time	m	Date	Time	m
1 F	0214 0805 1510 2057	0.6 2.6 0.3 2.5	16 SA	0345 0930 1622 2206	0.5 2.6 0.3 2.4
2 SA	0335 0918 1620 2201	0.5 2.7 0.1 2.6	17 SU	0438 1018 1702 2245	0.4 2.6 0.2 2.5
3 SU	0438 1016 1715 2252	0.3 2.8 0.0 2.6	18 M	0518 1055 1736 2319	0.3 2.7 0.2 2.6
4 M ●	0533 1107 1804 2338	0.1 2.9 -0.1 2.7	19 TU	0555 1130 1811 2352	0.3 2.7 0.2 2.7
5 TU	0621 1154 1848	0.0 2.9 -0.1	20 W ○	0629 1204 1843	0.2 2.7 0.2
6 W	0019 0704 1237 1928	2.7 0.0 2.9 0.0	21 TH	0022 0700 1234 1912	2.7 0.2 2.7 0.2
7 TH	0057 0744 1320 2007	2.8 0.0 2.9 0.1	22 F	0050 0731 1306 1943	2.7 0.1 2.7 0.2
8 F	0138 0827 1404 2046	2.8 0.0 2.8 0.2	23 SA	0121 0804 1341 2015	2.7 0.1 2.6 0.2
9 SA	0221 0910 1449 2125	2.8 0.0 2.7 0.2	24 SU	0154 0839 1418 2048	2.7 0.1 2.6 0.2
10 SU	0304 0954 1535 2206	2.7 0.1 2.5 0.4	25 M	0229 0917 1458 2126	2.7 0.2 2.5 0.3
11 M	0350 1042 1626 2254	2.7 0.2 2.4 0.5	26 TU	0310 1001 1545 2212	2.7 0.2 2.4 0.4
12 TU	0442 1138 1726 2354	2.6 0.3 2.2 0.6	27 W	0359 1054 1643 2308	2.6 0.2 2.3 0.5
13 W	0546 1246 1839	2.5 0.4 2.2	28 TH	0459 1159 1750	2.6 0.3 2.3
14 TH	0109 0702 1405 1959	0.7 2.5 0.5 2.2	29 F	0020 0612 1315 1906	0.6 2.6 0.3 2.4
15 F	0231 0822 1523 2111	0.6 2.5 0.4 2.3	30 SA	0142 0730 1433 2021	0.5 2.7 0.2 2.5

DECEMBER

Date	Time	m	Date	Time	m
1 SU	0300 0842 1543 2125	0.4 2.7 0.1 2.5	16 M	0342 0927 1609 2158	0.5 2.5 0.3 2.5
2 M	0406 0945 1642 2221	0.3 2.8 0.0 2.6	17 TU	0435 1015 1654 2241	0.4 2.6 0.3 2.6
3 TU	0505 1041 1735 2311	0.1 2.8 0.0 2.7	18 W	0519 1055 1735 2318	0.3 2.7 0.2 2.7
4 W ●	0558 1132 1822 2356	0.0 2.8 0.0 2.7	19 TH ○	0558 1134 1813 2352	0.2 2.7 0.2 2.7
5 TH	0643 1218 1903	0.0 2.9 0.1	20 F	0634 1211 1849	0.2 2.7 0.2
6 F	0037 0725 1303 1944	2.8 0.0 2.8 0.2	21 SA	0027 0713 1249 1927	2.7 0.1 2.6 0.2
7 SA	0119 0810 1350 2027	2.9 0.1 2.7 0.3	22 SU	0106 0754 1330 2006	2.8 0.1 2.6 0.2
8 SU	0204 0857 1437 2109	2.9 0.1 2.6 0.3	23 M	0145 0836 1412 2044	2.8 0.1 2.6 0.1
9 M	0249 0942 1521 2149	2.8 0.1 2.5 0.3	24 TU	0223 0916 1454 2124	2.8 0.0 2.5 0.2
10 TU	0332 1025 1606 2231	2.8 0.2 2.4 0.4	25 W	0304 1001 1541 2211	2.8 0.1 2.4 0.2
11 W	0417 1111 1654 2318	2.7 0.3 2.3 0.5	26 TH	0352 1051 1635 2303	2.7 0.1 2.4 0.3
12 TH	0508 1202 1749	2.6 0.4 2.2	27 F	0446 1144 1732	2.7 0.1 2.4
13 F	0014 0609 1302 1853	0.6 2.6 0.5 2.2	28 SA	0000 0545 1243 1833	0.4 2.7 0.2 2.4
14 SA	0122 0717 1409 2001	0.6 2.5 0.5 2.3	29 SU	0106 0652 1351 1939	0.4 2.7 0.2 2.4
15 SU	0236 0827 1515 2105	0.6 2.5 0.4 2.4	30 M	0221 0804 1503 2047	0.3 2.6 0.2 2.5
			31 TU	0334 0915 1610 2151	0.2 2.6 0.1 2.5

Chart Datum: 1·68 metres below Normal Null (German reference level)

BÜSUM *9.24.24*

Schleswig-Holstein **54°07'·20N 08°51'·60E**

CHARTS AC 1875, 3767; BSH 44, 105, 3014/4

TIDES HW +0036 on Dover (UT); ML 1·9m; Duration 0625
Standard Port HELGOLAND (⟵)

Times				Height (metres)			
High Water		Low Water		MHWS	MHWN	MLWN	MLWS
0100	0600	0100	0800	2·7	2·4	0·4	0·0
1300	1800	1300	2000				
Differences BÜSUM							
+0054	+0049	–0001	+0027	+0·9	+0·8	0·0	0·0
LINNENPLATE							
+0047	+0046	+0034	+0046	+0·7	+0·6	0·0	0·0
SÜDERHÖFT							
+0103	+0056	+0051	+0112	+0·7	+0·6	0·0	0·0
EIDERSPERRWERK							
+0120	+0115	+0130	+0155	+0·7	+0·6	0·0	0·0

SHELTER Very good. For lock opening (H24), call VHF Ch 11 or give 1 long blast in appr chan; 2 long blasts on reaching lock if not already open; obey R/G lts. Turn 90° stbd into yacht hbr (1·8m LW) Basin IV. Basin II is deeper; berth on FVs. Meldorf yacht hbr is 4M ESE with full yacht facilities.

NAVIGATION WPT 54°05'·97N 08°21'·98E, SWM buoy Iso 8s, 270°/090° from/to Süderpiep No 2 PHM buoy, 5M. Süderpiep or Norderpiep (unlit; beware bar if wind-over-tide) are well-buoyed chans, approx 15M long; night appr not advised. Beware strong cross-tides and sudden winds over moles.

LIGHTS AND MARKS Lt ho Iso WRG 6s; W092·5°-094·5° leads 093·5° for last 4M of Süderpiep. Hbr lts as chartlet. A high bldg is conspic 9ca NW of hbr; silo is conspic in hbr.

RADIO TELEPHONE VHF call *Büsum Port* Ch 11 16.

TELEPHONE (Dial code 04834) Hr Mr 2183; CG 2246; ⊖ 2376; Dr 2088; YC 2997.

FACILITIES Yacht hbr AB €9·20, AC, FW, M, BY, El, ME, C, P, D, ⓛ. Town CH, V, R, Bar, ✉, Ⓑ, ⇌, Ⓗ, ✈ (Hamburg).

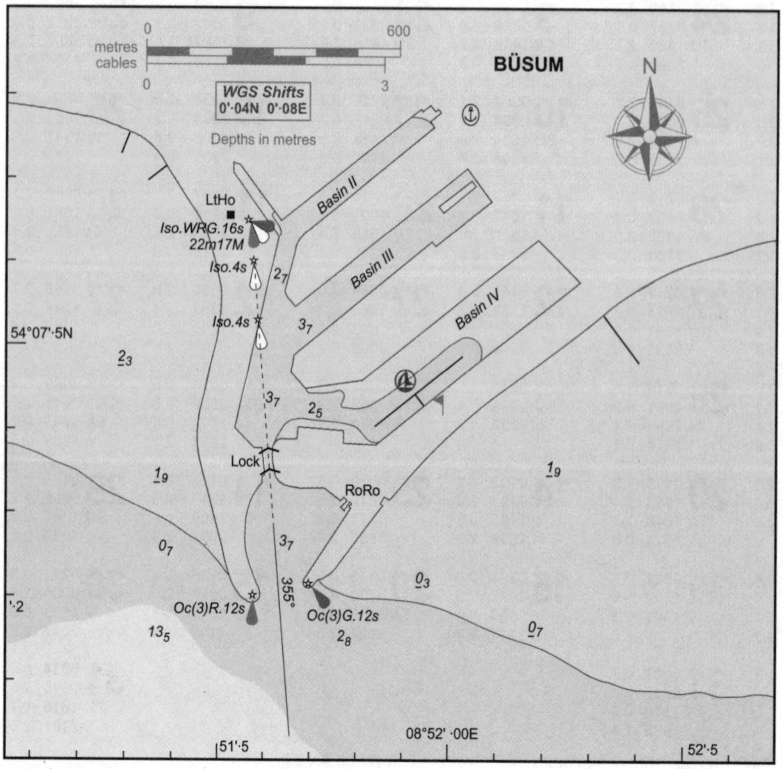

OTHER HBRS ON W COAST OF SCHLESWIG-HOLSTEIN

TÖNNING, Schleswig-Holstein, **54°18'·92N 08°57'·11E**. AC 3767; BSH 104, 3014/8. Eiderdamm lock, 5·5M seawards, operates H24; VHF Ch 14 16. Lts, see 9.24.4. R Eider and the Gieselau Kanal (BSH 3009) link Tönning to the Kiel Canal (9.24.22). Above the dam, R Eider is tidal when sluices are operated HW +3 to HW+½, (beware strong currents). AB on drying S quay in Tonning marina, or on river quays. Up river, bridge (clnce 5·6m) opens on request Mon-Sat 0600-SS. Hr Mr ☎ (04861) 1400; Dr ☎ 389; Ⓗ ☎ 706; Facilities: **Quay** €0·72, FW, P, D, BY, C (5 ton), Slip; **YC** ☎ 754 (all welcome). **Town** Ⓑ, ✉, ⇌, Gaz.

HUSUM, Schleswig-Holstein, **54°28'·78N 09°00'·00E**. AC 3767; BSH 105, 3013/12. HW + 0036 on Dover (UT); ML 1·9m; Duration 0555. See 9.24.25. A sluice/lock, 7ca W of rly bridge, is shut when level > 0·3m over MHW, as shown by ●. Beware the canal effect when passing big ships in the narrow appr chan. In the outer hbr yachts should turn stbd just before rly bridge for pontoons on S bank, or pass through bridge (clnce 5m when shut) to inner hbr by SC Nordsee; both dry. VHF call *Husum Port* Ch 11. Tfc reports broadcast on Ch 11 every H +00 from HW –4 to HW +2. Outer ldg lts 106° both Iso R 8s, synch & intens on ldg line. Inner ldg lts 090° both Iso G 8s, synch & intens on ldg line. Night entry not advised. Hr Mr ☎ (04841) 667218; Sluice ☎ 2565; **Husum YC** ☎ 65670; **SC Nordsee** ☎ 3436; ⊖ ☎ 61759. AB €0·72, P, D, at hbr.

HARBOURS IN THE NORTH FRISIAN ISLANDS

PELLWORM, 54°31'·31N 08°41'·24E. AC 3767; BSH 3013/11. Tides: see Suderoogsand/Husum, 9.24.25. Outer appr via Norderhever; ldg lts 041° Oc 5s. Ent chan from NH18 PHM buoy, Fl (2+1) R 15s, has 0·2m; access near HW. VHF Ch 11. Small yacht hbr 2·8m at MHW; drying on soft mud.

WITTDÜN, Amrum, **54°37'·85N 08°24'·65E**. AC 3767; BSH 107, 3013/6. HW +0107 on Dover (UT); +0137 on Helgoland (zone –0100); ML 2·7m; Duration 0540. See 9.24.25. Wittdün is the main hbr of Amrum. Yachts berth S of stone quay, lying bows to pontoon, stern to posts. Good shelter except in E winds. The quay 800m to the E is reserved for ferries only. Chan has 2m and is marked by PHM withies ⸸. Ldg lts 272°: Both Iso R 4s 11/33m 10/15M; W masts, R bands; intens on ldg line. Lt ho Fl 7·5s 63m 23M; R tr, W bands; same location as rear ldg lt. It is not advisable to enter at night. Wriakhörn, Cross lt, is 1M WSW of hbr, L Fl (2) WR 15s 26m 9/7M; W297·5°-319·5°, R319·5°-330°, W330°-005·5°, R005·5°-034°. Hr Mr ☎ (04682) 2294; ⊖ ☎ 2026; Dr ☎ 2612; Facilities: AB €0·97, P & D (cans) at Nebel; **Amrum YC** ☎ 2054.

WYK, Island of Föhr, **54°41'·70N 08°34'·80E**. AC 3767; BSH107, 3013/6. HW +0107 on Dover (UT); +0137 on Helgoland (zone –0100); ML 2·8. Good yacht hbr (1·5m) to N of ent, sheltered in all winds; visitors berth W side of pontoon 1. Access H24. Also berths on E quay of inner hbr. Ferry hbr (4m). Lts: Oldenhorn (SE point of Föhr), R tr, Oc (4) WR 15s 10m 13/10M; W208°-245°, R245°-298°, W298°-333°, R333°-080°. S mole, FR 9m 4M, R mast. E mole, FG 7m 4M, G mast. Port VHF Ch **11** 16. Yacht hbr Hr Mr ☎ (04681) 3030; Commercial Hr Mr ☎ 2852; **YC** ☎ 1280; Dr ☎ 8998; ⊖ ☎ 2594; Facilities: **Hbr road** (500m), CH, ⓛ, P & D (cans); **Yacht Hbr** €9·20, R, V; **W Quay** D.

SYLT *9.24.25*

Schleswig-Holstein **54°45'·54N 08°17'·86E** (Hörnum)
Hörnum ❀❀◊◊✿✿✿; List ❀❀◊◊✿✿✿

CHARTS AC 3767; BSH D107, D108, 3013/3 List, 3013/5 Hörnum

TIDES +0110 Dover; ML 1·8; Duration 0540; Zone –0100

Standard Port HELGOLAND (⟵)

Times				Height (metres)			
High Water		Low Water		MHWS	MHWN	MLWN	MLWS
0100	0600	0100	0800	2·7	2·4	0·4	0·0
1300	1800	1300	2000				
Differences LIST							
+0252	+0240	+0201	+0210	–0·8	–0·6	–0·2	0·0
HÖRNUM							
+0223	+0218	+0131	+0137	–0·5	–0·4	–0·2	0·0
AMRUM-HAFEN							
+0138	+0137	+0128	+0134	+0·2	+0·2	–0·1	0·0
DAGEBÜLL							
+0226	+0217	+0211	+0225	+0·5	+0·5	–0·1	0·0
SUDEROOGSAND							
+0116	+0102	+0038	+0122	+0·4	+0·3	0·0	0·0
HUSUM							
+0205	+0152	+0118	+0200	+1·1	+1·0	0·0	0·0

SHELTER The island of Sylt, about 20M long, has Westerland (the capital) in the centre, List in the N and Hörnum in the S. The Hindenburgdamm connects it to the mainland.

LIST: The small hbr is sheltered except in NE/E winds. Ent is 25m wide; marina at S end has 2·6m.

HÖRNUM: Good in the small hbr, approx 370m x 90m, protected by outer mole on SE side and by 2 inner moles. Yacht haven at the N end. Good ⚓ in Hörnum Reede in W and N winds and in Hörnumtief in E and S winds.

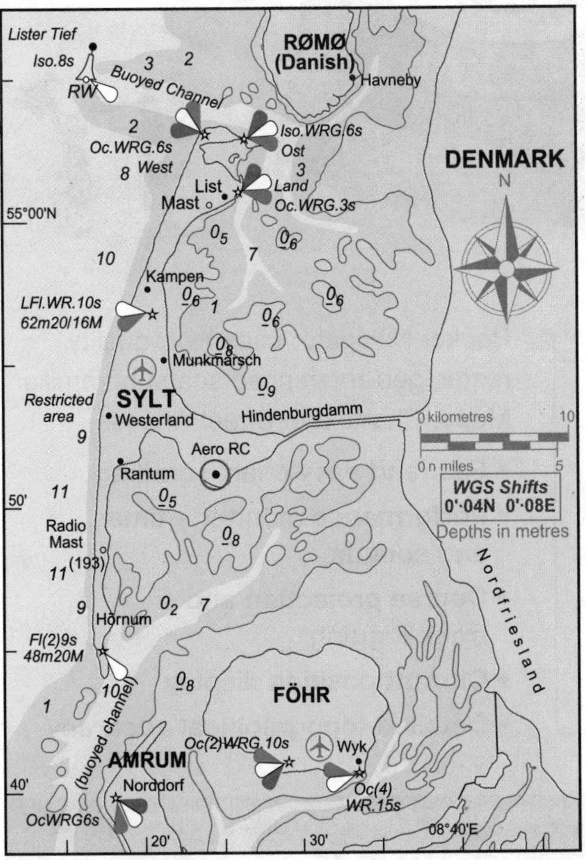

There are two other hbrs; Rantum (€6·60) and Munkmarsch (€6·90) which both dry; access HW ±3. Large areas of Sylt are nature reserves; landing prohib.

NAVIGATION

LIST WPT: Lister Tief SWM buoy, Iso 8s, 55°05'·37N 08°16'·87E, 292°/112° from/to List Ost lt, 6·1M. Lister Tief (see 9.24.4) is well marked. In strong W/NW winds expect a big swell on the bar (depth 4m) on the ebb, which sets on to Salzsand. NE quay is open construction, unsuitable for yachts. Chan buoys through roadstead lead to hbr. Access at all tides, but not in darkness and beware strong cross streams.

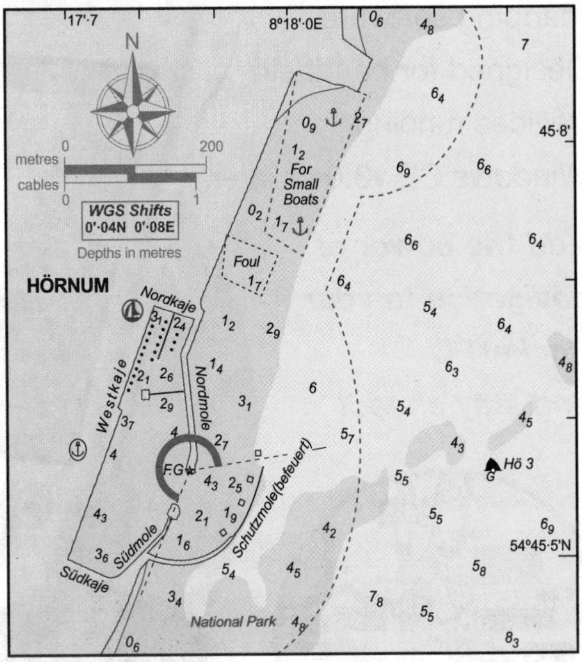

HÖRNUM WPT: Vortrapptief SWM buoy, Iso 4s, 54°35'·00N 08°12'·20E, 215°/035° from/to Norddorf lt (Amrum), 6·35M. Appr in W009°-036·8° sector of Norddorf lt, Oc WRG 6s; Hörnum lt, Fl (2) 9s, bearing 012° leads through buoyed Vortrapptief inside drying banks. In strong W winds the sea breaks on off-lying banks and in the chan. Final appr into hbr from NE, keeping mid-chan in hbr ent. Access at all tides but not in darkness. Hörnum lt is 3½ca SSW of hbr ent.

LIGHTS AND MARKS

LIST: See 9.24.4 for List West lt Oc WRG 6s, List Ost Iso WRG 6s, List Land Oc WRG 3s (overlooks List hbr) and Kampen L Fl WR 10s. Rømø church, 7M NE, is conspic. N mole hd FG, vis 218°-038°. S mole hd FR, vis 218°-353°.

HÖRNUM: Outer mole hd FR. N pier hd FG, vis 024°-260°. Conspic radio mast (5 Fl R lts) 3M N of hbr.

RADIO TELEPHONE List VHF Ch 11 (0800-1200, 1600-1800).

TELEPHONE (Dial code 04651)

LIST: Hr Mr 870374; Police 870510; Ⓗ (Westerland) 04651 8410; ⊖ 870413, CG 870365; Dr 870350.

HÖRNUM: Hr Mr 881027; Dr 881016; Police 881510; CG 881256.

FACILITIES

LIST: **Hbr** AB €0·77, FW, ⊖, Slip, SC. **Village** V, R, Bar, P & D (cans), Ferry to Römö (Denmark).

WESTERLAND: CG 85199; Police 70470. **Town** V, R, Bar, P & D (cans), Gaz, ⊖, ✉, Ⓑ, ≵, ✈.

HÖRNUM: Sylter YC ☎ 880274, AB €10·22, Bar, AC, FW, ⊡. **Town** V, R, Bar, ME, ✉, Ⓑ.

24

MAPTECH®
Leading the world in digital navigation
Maptech UK Ltd • +44 (0)1243 389352 • sales@maptech.co.uk

Maptech world class digital chart CDs
Worldwide coverage from over 4,500 charts

Maptech award winning software
Easy to use navigation software
• **Chart Navigator** • **Cruising Navigator** • **Offshore Navigator**

www.maptech.co.uk

Area 25

Denmark
Rømø to Skagen

9.25.1 Index .... Page 1041

9.25.2 Area map 1042

9.25.3 Tidal stream charts see *9.24.3*

9.25.4 Lights, buoys & waypoints 1043

9.25.5 Passage information 1046

9.25.6 Distance Table 1046

9.25.7 Rømø 1047

9.25.8 Fanø 1047

9.25.9 Esbjerg, Standard Port, tidal curves 1048

9.25.10 Hvide Sande 1052

9.25.11 Torsminde 1052

9.25.12 Thyborøn 1053

9.25.13 Hantsholm 1054

9.25.14 Hirtshals 1054

9.25.15 Skagen 1055

Register for your **FREE** weekly weather email service from Macmillan Reeds
» at **www.nauticaldata.com – NOW!** «
weekend weather reports sent to your email address, every Thursday

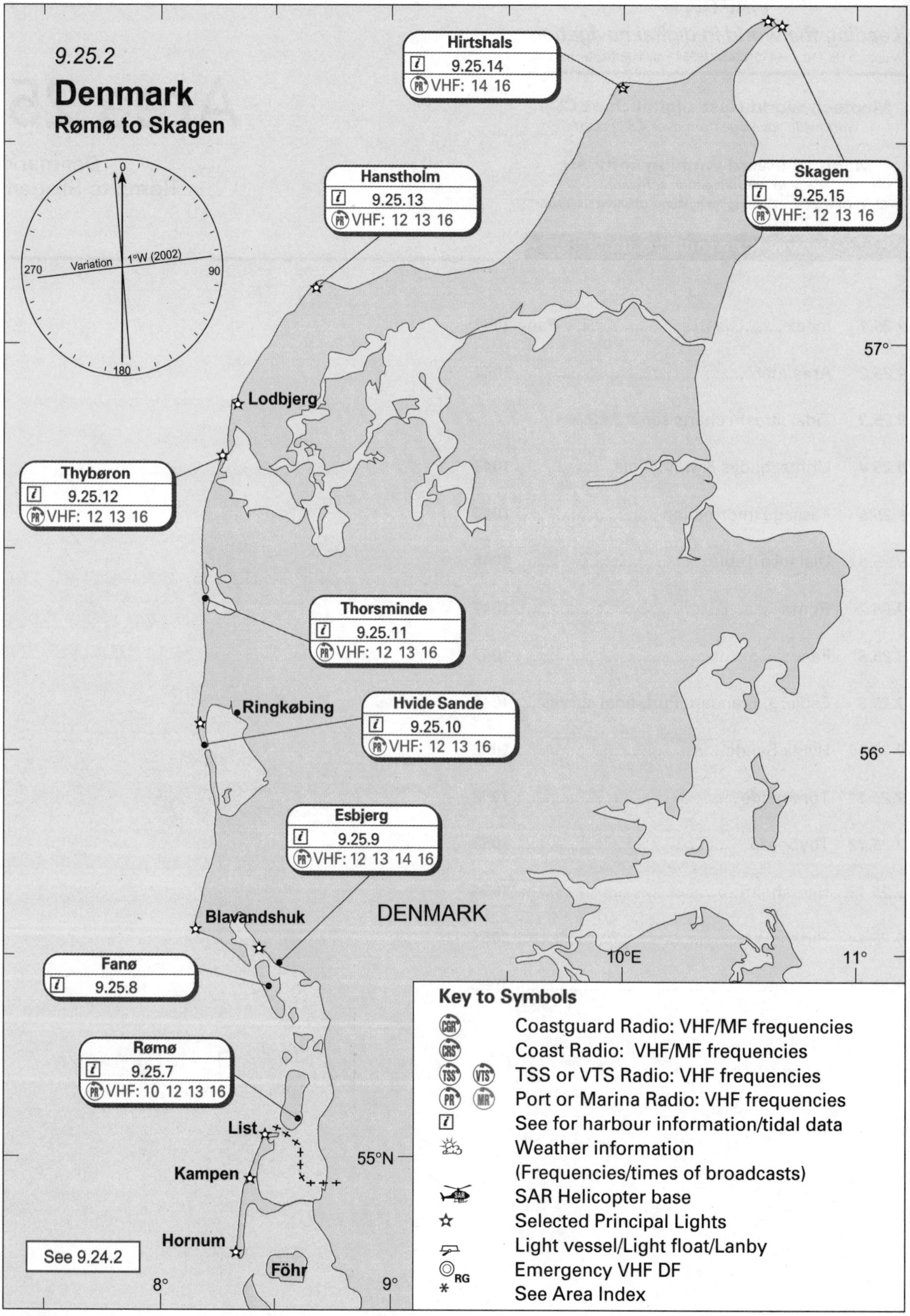
9.25.2
Denmark
Rømø to Skagen
Variation 1°W (2002)
0
90
180
270
Hirtshals
9.25.14
VHF: 14 16
Hanstholm
9.25.13
VHF: 12 13 16
Skagen
9.25.15
VHF: 12 13 16
Lodbjerg
Thybøron
9.25.12
VHF: 12 13 16
Thorsminde
9.25.11
VHF: 12 13 16
Ringkøbing
Hvide Sande
9.25.10
VHF: 12 13 16
Esbjerg
9.25.9
VHF: 12 13 14 16
DENMARK
Blavandshuk
Fanø
9.25.8
Rømø
9.25.7
VHF: 10 12 13 16
List
Kampen
Hornum
Föhr
See 9.24.2
57°
56°
55°N
8°
9°
10°E
11°
Key to Symbols
Coastguard Radio: VHF/MF frequencies
Coast Radio: VHF/MF frequencies
TSS or VTS Radio: VHF frequencies
Port or Marina Radio: VHF frequencies
See for harbour information/tidal data
Weather information
(Frequencies/times of broadcasts)
SAR Helicopter base
Selected Principal Lights
Light vessel/Light float/Lanby
Emergency VHF DF
See Area Index

WGS84 DATUM

9.25.4 LIGHTS, BUOYS AND WAYPOINTS

Abbreviations used below are given in the Introduction. Principal lights ☆ are in **bold** print, places in CAPITALS, and light-vessels, light floats and Lanbys in *CAPITAL ITALICS*. Unless otherwise stated lights are white. m – elevation in metres; M – nominal range in miles. Fog signals are in *italics*. Useful waypoints are underlined – use those on land with care. **All positions in 9.25.4 are referenced to the WGS84/ETRS89 datum but should be assumed to be approximate. In the rest of Area 25, ED50 coordinates are given. Admiralty charts for this area are referenced to ED50.**

APPROACHES TO RØMØ

Lister Tief 55°05'·32N 08°16'·68E Iso 8s; *Whis.*
No 1 55°04'·88E 08°17'·88E.
No 3 55°04'·84E 08°19'·17E Fl G 4s.
No 2 55°04'·22N 08°22'·50E Fl (3) R 10s.
No 9 55°04'·22N 08°22'·50E Fl (2) G 9s.
Lister Landtief No 5 55°03'·76N 08°24'·81E.
No 4 55°03'·92N 08°24'·45E FL (2) R 5s.
L1 55°03'·35N 08°28'·50E Fl Y 4s.

◄ RØMØ HAVN

No. 1 55°03'·26N 08°30'·46E Fl (2) G 10s.
No. 3 55°03'·34N 08°32'·102E.
No. 5 55°03'·93N 08°330'·66E.
No. 7 55°04'·46N 08°34'·32E.
No. 9 55°04'·86N 08°34'·29E.
No. 11 55°05'·25N 08°34'·81E.
S Mole Hd ☆ 55°05'·29N 08°34'·47E Fl R 3s 6m 2M; Gy Tr.
N Mole Hd ☆ 55°05'·32N 08°34'·48E Fl G 3s 6m 2M; Gy Tr.
Inner S Mole ☆ 55°05'·3N 08°34'·2E FR 3m IM.
Inner N Mole ☆ 55°05'·3N 08°34'·2E FG 3m IM.

Rode Klit Sand 55°11'·11N 08°04'·95E Q (9) 15s.

◄ KORE SAND CHANNEL

Juvre J 55°15'·34N 08°20'·43E.
No.2 55°14'·10N 08°22'·88E.
No.4 55°13'·76N 08°24'·73E.
No.6 55°13'·41N 08°26'·60E.
No. 8 55°12'·69N 08°26'·83E.
No. 10 55°12'·55N 08°28'·72E.
Rejsby Stjært 55°13'·15N 08°30'·55E.

◄ KNUDE/PETER MEYERS SAND CHANNEL

Knude K 55°18'·92N 08°20'·06E.
No.2 55°18'·82N 08°21'·33E.
No. 4 55°18'·81N 08°22'·21E.
No. 6 55°18'·38N 08°24'·63E.
No. 10 55°18'·68N 08°28'·50E.
Knoben 55°18'·71N 08°30'·60E.
Juvre G 55°20'·50N 08°24'·28E.

◄ APPROACHES TO ESBJERG

Grådyb 55°24'·63N 08°11'·59E L Fl 10s; Racon (G).
No. 1 55°25'·49N 08°13'·89E Q.
No. 2 55°25'·60N 08°13'·75E Fl (3) R 10s.
No. 3 55°25'·93N 08°14'·84E Fl G 3s.
No. 4 55°26'·02N 08°14'·72E Fl R 3s.
Tide Gauge ☆ 55°26'·05N 08°15'·93E Fl (5) Y 20s 8m 4M
No. 5 55°26'·32N 08°15'·83E Fl G 5s.
No. 6 55°26'·43N 08°15'·70E Fl R 5s.
No. 7 55°26'·76N 08°16'·91E Q.
No. 8 55°26'·89N 08°16'·81E Fl (2) R 5s.
No. 9 55°27'·04N 08°18'·21E Fl (2) G 10s.
No.10 55°27'·20N 08°18'·04E Fl (2) R 10s.
No. 11 55°27'·71N 08°19'·59E Fl G 3s.
No. 12 55°27'·88N 08°19'·39E Fl R 3s.
No. 13 55°28'·40N 08°20'·99E Fl G 5s.
No. 14 55°28'·57N 08°20'·73E Fl R 4s.
Jerg ☆ 55°28'·88N 08°22'·00E Q 7m 5M; B Tr, Y base.
No. 16 55°29'·04N 08°21'·80E Q (6) + L Fl 15s.
Sædding Strand Ldg lts 053·8°. **Front** 55°29'·74N 08°23'·87E Iso 2s 12m **21M**; R bldg; vis: 051·8°-055·8°; H24.
Middle, 630m from front, 55°29'·94N 08°24'·35E Iso 4s 26m **21M**; R Tr, W bands; vis: 051°-057°; (H24).
Rear, 0·75M from front, 55°30'·18N 08°24'·92E F 36m **18M**, R Tr, vis: 052°-056°; (H24).
North Ldg lts 049° Front 55°29'·87N 08°23'·68E F R 16m **16M**; W mast; Rear 55°30'·06N 08°24'·05E FR 27m 16M; Gy T; H24.
No. 15A 55°29'·01N 08°22'·47E Fl (2) G 5s.
No 18 55°29'·19N 08°22'·71E Fl (2) R 5s.
Fovrfelt N ☆ 55°29'·29N 08°23'·79E Oc (2) WRG 6s 6m 5M; Y Tr; vis: G066-5°-073°, W073°-077°, R077°-085, G327°-331°, W331°-333·5°, R333·5°-342°.
Fovrfelt ☆ 55°29'·03N 08°23'·75E Fl (2) R 10s 9m 3M; R Tr.
No 15B 55°28'·83N 08°23'·65E Fl (2) G 10s.
South Ldg lts 067°. **Front** ☆ 55°28'·71N 08°24'·62E FG 10m **16M**; Gy ☐ Tr; H24. Rear FG 25m **16M**; Gy Tr; H24.

◄ ESBJERG HAVN

Strandby, shelter mole, NW corner ☆ 55°28'·76N 08°24'·63E Oc WRG 5s 5m W13M, R9M, G9M; W bldg R band; vis: G101 7°-105·5°, W105·5°-109· 5°, R109·5°-111·7°.
Industrifiskerihavn, W Mole Hd ☆ 55°28'·52N 08°24'·96E Fl R 5s 6m 4M; R △ structure.
E Mole ☆ 55°28'·52N 08°25'·03E Fl G 5s 6m 4M; G △ structure.
Nordsøkai 55°28'·45N 08°25'·04E Q (9) 15s 5M; Y Tr, B band.
Konsumfiskerihavn, West Mole Hd ☆ 55°28'·31N 08°25'·33E FlR 3s 4m; R tr; vis: 203°-119°.
East Mole Head ☆ 55°28·31N 08°25·40E Fl G 3s 4m; G tr; vis: 023°-256°
Trafikhavn, NW corner, ☆ 55°28·22N 08°25·43E Oc (2) WRG 12s 5m W13M, R9M, G9M; W bldg R band; vis: G118°-124·5°, W124·5-129°, R129°-131°.
N Mole Hd ☆ 55°28'·13N 08°25'·46E FR 7m 5M; R conical bldg; vis: 232°-135°.
S Mole Hd ☆ 55°28'·08N 08°25'·51E FG 7m 4M; G conical bldg; vis: 045°-276°.
No. 22 55°27'·62N 08°25'·49E Fl R 5s.
Sønderhavn, W Mole Hd ☆ 55°27'·49N 08°26'·12E FR 8m 4M.
East Mole Hd ☆ 55°27'·43N 08°26'·31E FG 8m 4M.
Slunden Ldg Lts 242°. Front, 55°27'·20N 08°24'·53E Iso 2s 6m 3M; vis: 227°-257°. Rear, 106m from front, Iso 2s 8m 3M; vis: 227°-257°.
Nordby Marina 55°26'·65N 08°24'·53E.

Aero ☆ 55°27'·27N 08°27'·32 3 Fl 1·5s (vert) 251m 12M; on chimney.

◀ SLUGEN CHANNEL

Blavands Huk ☆ 55°33'·46N 08°04'·95E Fl (3) 20s 54m **23M**; W □ Tr.

Oskbøl Firing Range ☆ 55°33'·6N 08°04'·7E AlFl WR 4s 35m **16M**, R13M, (by day Q 10M); Tr; shown when firing is in progress; 55°37'·3N 08°07'·IE Al Fl WR 4s 35m **W16M**, R13M (by day Q 10M); Tr; shown when firing is in progress.

Slugen Chan 55°29'·42N 08°02'·56E Fl (3) R 10s.

Slugen Chan 55°30'·52N 07°59'·20E Fl (2) G 5s.

Slugen Chan 55°31'·46N 07°52'·88E Fl (2) R 5s.

Slugen Chan 55°32'·26N 07°53'·65E Fl G 3s.

Slugen Chan 55°33'·99N 07°49'·38E L Fl G 10s.

Soren Bovbjergs Dyb 55°31'·24N 07°57'·46E.

Soren Bovbjergs Dyb 55°32'·19N 07°56'·29E.

Soren Bovbjergs Dyb 55°32'·82N 07°55'·30E.

Soren Bovbjergs Dyb 55°33'·57N 07°55'·55E

Vyl 55°26'·22N 07°49'·99E Q (6) + L Fl 15s.

Mast (60m) ☆ 55°31'·32N 07°47'·31E 2 Mo (U) 15s 8m 3M.

No. 2 55°26'·22N 07°49'·95E Q (6) + L Fl 15s.

Tuxen 55°28'·7N 07°42'·05E Fl (5) Y 20s.

Tuxen 55°34'·22N 07°41'·90E Q.

Horns Rev W 55°34'·47N 07°26'·05E Q (9) 15s.

55°36'·02N 08°02'·49E.

55°37'·35N 07°56'·98E Fl Y 3s.

55°38'·63N 07°50'·91E Fl Y 3s.

55°42'·32N 08°06'·92E Fl Y 5s.

55°48'·43N 07°56'·29E Fl (5) Y 20s.

◀ HVIDE

Hvide Sande 55°48'·49N 07°56'·27E Fl (5) Y 20s.

Hvide Sande ☆ 56°00'·00N 08°07'·20E F 27m 14M; Gy Tr.

Lee Mole Hd ☆ 55°56'·20N 08°06'·71E Fl R 3s 7m 8M; R hut.

N Mole Hd ☆ 56°00'·04N 08°06' 98E Fl R 5s 10m 6M; R structure; TE 1999; *Horn 15s.*

S Mole Hd ☆ 55°54'·18N 08°06'·52E Fl G 5s 10m 6M.

Nordhavn Pier Head ☆ 56°00'·16N 08°07'·42E FG 4m 4M; galvanised pipe.

Industrihavn, Shelter Mole ☆ 56°00'·07N 08°07'·12E 2 FR 3m 2M; W posts; vis: 060°-035°.

N Inner mole Head ☆ 56°00'·06N 08°07'·22E FR 5m 3M; Gy col.

S Inner mole Hd ☆ 56°00'·06N 08°07'·32E FG 5m 2M; Gy col.

Mole Hd ☆ 56°00'·06N 08°07'·52E FG 4m 2M; Galvanised pipe.

E basin, E pier ☆ 56°00'·06N 08°07'·53E FR 4m 2M; Gy post

Lock entrance Ldg lts 293·5° Front 56°00'·0N 08°07'·8E FR 11m 2M; R △ on gy tr; vis: 201·6°-021·6°. Rear, 72m from front, FR 14m 2M; R ▽ on gy Tr; vis: 201·6°-021·6°.

Fjordhavn Ldg lts 246·6° Front 56°00'·5N 08°07'·9E FR 4m 4M. Rear, 128m from front, Iso G 2s 6m 4M.

Lyngvig (Holmlands Klit) ☆ 56°02'·91N 08°06'·17E Fl 5s 53m **22M**; W ◯ Tr.

SÆDDING STRAND

◀ FANØ

Kremer Sand ☆ 55°27'·3N 08°24'·9E FG 4m 3M; G dolphin.

Slunden W Ldg Lts 242°. Front 55°27'·20N 08°24'·53E Iso 2s 6m 3M; Tr; vis: 227°-257°. Rear Iso 2s 8m 3M; Tr; vis: 227°-257°.

E Ldg Lts 062° Front 55°27'·65N 08°26'·01E FR 7m 3M; Tr; vis: 047°-077°. Rear. FR 9m 3M; Tr; vis: 047°-077°.

Næs Søjord ☆ 55°27'·27N 08°24'·86E FR 5m 3M; R pile.

No. 1 ☆ 55°27'·45N 08°25'·28E Fl (2) G l0s 5m 3M; G pile.

No. 2 ☆ 55°27'·42N 08°25'·32E Fl (4) Y 15s 5m 3M; Y pile.

No. 3 ☆ 55°27'·39N 08°25'·07E Fl G 3s 5m 3M; G pile.

No. 4 ☆ 55°27'·35N 08°25'·10E Fl R 3s 5m 3M; R pile.

Nordby Ldg Lts 213·7° Front 55°26'·94N 08°24'·44E FR 7m 4M W mast; vis: 123·7°-303·7°. Rear, 73m from front, FR 9m 4M Gy Tr; vis: 123·7°-303·7°.

◀ TORSMINDE HAVN

(*All positions below are approximate)

*☆ 56°22'·34N 08°06'·99E F 30m 14M; Gy Tr.

*N Mole Hd ☆ 56°22'·36N 08°06'·62E Iso R 2s 9m 4M; R hut

*S Mole Hd ☆ 56°22'·26N 08°06'·92E Iso G 2s 9m 4M; G hut

*Groyne, N Hd ☆ 56°22'·46N 08°06'·82E Fl 5s 8m 5M; gy hut

*West Hbr, W Mole Hd ☆ 56°22'·36N 08°07'·12E F G 5m 2M Gy post.

*E Mole Hd ☆ 56°22'·26N 08°07'·18E F R 5m 2M; Gy post.

*NW dolphin ☆ 56°22'·26N 08°07'·22E F G 5m 4M; Gy post.

*SE dolphin ☆ 56°22' 26N 08°07' 26E F G 5m 4M; Gy post.

*Lock, E side ☆ 56°22'·36N 08°07'·22E Iso 4s 12m 4M; Gy mast vis: 020°-160°.

*Road Bridge ☆ 56°22'·36N 08°07'·26E Iso 4s 5m 4M: vis: 200°-340°

Bovbjerg ☆ 56°30'·74N 08°07'·16E L Fl (2) 15s 62m **16M**; R ◯ Tr

◀ THYBORØN

Thyboron Landfall 56°42'·52N 08°08'·68E L Fl 10s; Racon (T

Off Havmolen 56°43'·25N 08°12'·51E.

Approach ☆ 56°42'·49N 08°12'·90E Fl (3) 10s 24m **16M**; Tr intens 023·5°-203·5°.

Havrevlen 56°42'·77N 08°12'·88E.

Havrevlen 56°42'·79N 08°13'·36E.

Havrevlen 56°42'·76N 08°13'·71E.

Havrevlen 56°42'·55N 08°13'·75E Fl (2) G 5s.

Agger Tange Ldg Lts 082° Front 56°42'·97N 08°14'·11E Oc WRG 5s 8m W11M, R8M, G8M; R △ on bn; vis: G074·5°-079·5°, W079·5°-084·5°, R084·5°-089·5°. Rear 804m from front Iso 4s 17m 12M; R ▽ on Gy Tr; vis: 080°-084°.

Langholm Ldg lts 120° Front 56°42'·45N 08°14'·53E Iso 2s 7m 11M; R △ on R hut; vis: 115°-125°. Rear, Iso 4s 13m 11M; R ▽ on Gy Tr; vis: 115°-125°.

Thyborøn 56°42'·35N 08°13'·39E Oc (2) WRG 12s 6m W12M R9M, G9M; W Tr R band; vis: G122·5°-146·5°, W146·5°-150° R150°-211·3°, G211·3°-337·5°, W337·5°-340°, R340°-344°.

Yderhavn, N Mole Hd ☆ 56°42'·02N 08°13'·52E Fl G 3s 6m 4M G pedestal.

S Mole Hd ☆ 56°41'·97N 08°13'·53E Fl R 3s 6m 4M; R pedestal

Thisted Bredning ☆ 56°58'·52N 08°41'·15E Aero 3 Fl 1·5s(vert) 183m 10M; TV mast; 45m apart.

◀ THYBORØN KANAL

No. 1 56°41'·14N 08°14'·17E Fl (2) G 5s.

No. 3 56°40'·75N 08°13'·79E Fl G 3s.

No. 7 56°40'·31N 08°13'·52E Fl G 3s.

No. 11 56°39'·83N 08°13'·59E Fl G 3s.

No. 16 56°38'·51N 08°13'·89E Fl R 3s.

No. 18 56°38'·20N 08°14'·36E Fl R 3s.

No. 21 56°38'·98N 08°14'·71E Fl (2) R 5s.

No. 26 56°38'·71N 08°15'·38E Fl R 3s.

No. 29 56°38'·40N 08°15'·94E Fl G 3s.

56°38'·06N 08°16'·70E Q.

Lodbjerg ☆ 56°49'·39N 08°15'·74E Fl (2) 20s 48m **23M** granite

◄ APPROACHES TO LEMVIG/EMVIG HAVN

isum Bredning 56°36'·71N 08°21'·74E Fl (3) G 3s.
ogard Mark Ldg Lts 56°34'·39N 08°17'·29E FR 20m; R △ on V Bn. Rear, 235m from front, FR 30m; R ▽ on W mast; vis: on dg line only.
ppr 56°35'·58N 08°21'·62E L Fl 10s
onnen Spit 56°35'·34N 08°20'·70E.
han 56°33'·25N 08°18'·33E.
)stre Havn 56°33'·17N 08°18'·40E.
V of Hbr Ldg Lts 177·7° 56°33'·04N 08°18'·16FR 8m; R △ on r; vis: 153°-203°. Rear, 190m from front, FR 20m.
Marina S Mole Hd ☆ 56°33'·09N 08°18'·40E FR 3m 4M.
Mole Hd ☆ 56°33'·09N 08°18'·33E FG 3m 5M.

◄ NØRRE VORUPER

Mole Hd ☆ 57°57'·73N 08°21'·64E Fl G 5s 6m 4M.
dg Lts Front 57°57'·44N 08°22'·08E Iso R 4s 20m 9M; vis: 22·5° ither side of alignment. Ldg Lts to safest landing place. Rear, 0m from front, Iso R 4s 30m 9M.

◄ THISTED HAVN (MARINA)

V Mole Hd ☆ 56°57'·10N 08°41'·90E Fl R 3s 4m 2M.
)uter E Mole Hd ☆ 56°57'·10N 08°41'·95E Fl G 3s 4m 2M.

◄ HANSTHOLM

lanstholm 57°07'·95N 08°34'·65E LFl 10s.
lanstholm ☆ 57°06'·65N 08°35'·74E Fl (3) 20s 65m **26M**; V 8-sided Tr.
'estmole Hd ☆ 57°07'·54N 08°35'·46E Fl G 3s 11m 9M; G pillar.
stmole Hd ☆ 57°07'·60N 08°35'·58E Fl R 3s 11m 9M; R pillar.
dg lts 142·6 Front 57°07'·12N 08°36'·15E Iso 2s 37m 13M; R △ n mast; vis: 127·6°-157·6°. Rear, 170m from front, Iso 2s 45m 3M; R ▽ on mast; synch with front.
'estre Tvæmole Hd ☆ 57°07'·41N 08°35'·58E F G 6m 6M; G col.
)stre Tværmole Hd ☆ 57°07'·35N 08°35'·64E F R 6m 6M; R col.
oshage ☆ 57°07'·76N 08°37'·22E Fl 5s 7m 6M.
57°10'·72N 08°56'·16E Fl G 5s.
ildstrand Ldg lts 138° Front 57°09'·21N 08°57'·628E F 12m 7M; nast; vis: 127°-149°. Middle F 12m 7M; mast; vis: 127°-149°. ear F 22m 8M; vis: 127°-149°.

◄ LILD STRAND

ragerne 57°10'·68N 08°56'·20E Fl G 5s.
ild Strand Ldg Lts. Front, 57°09'·13N 08°57'·74E 3 F 12m 7M: is: 127°-149°; fishing (occas).

◄ TRANUM STRAND

57°10'·87N 09°20'·86E; Y By.
57°12'·03N 09°20'·86E; Y By.
ranum No. 1 ☆ 57°10'·68N 09°26'·56E Al WR 4s 20m **W16M** 13M; Tr; by day Fl; shown when firing is taking place.
Tranum No. 2 ☆ 57°12'·42N 09°30'·14E Al WR 4s by day Fl; shown when firing is taking place.
57°15'·39N 09°28'·16E; Y By.

◄ LØKKEN

Lee Bkwtr ☆ 57°22'·47N 09°41'·85E Fl 5s 5m 5M.

◄ HIRTSHALS

Appr Buoys 57°36'·18N 09°56·95E Fl (3) G 10s.
Appr Buoys 57°36'·12N 09°57·15E Fl G 5s.
57°36'·44N 09°57'·68E Fl R 3s.
57°36'·43N 09°57'·72E Fl (5) Y 20s.
57°36'·15N 09°57'·72E Fl (5) Y 20s.
Hirtshals ☆ 57°35'·07N 09°56'·44 F Fl 30s 57m **F 18M; Fl 25M**; W ○ Tr; works in progress (T) 1996.
Ldg lts 166° Front 57°35'·69N 09°57'·64E Iso R 2s 10m 11M; R △ on Tr; vis: 156°-176°. Rear, 330m from front, Iso R 4s 18m 11M; R ▽ on Tr; vis: 156°-176°.
Outer Shelter Mole Hd ☆ 57°35'·97N 09°57'·36E Fl G 3s 14m 6M; G mast; *Horn 15s.*
W Mole Hd ☆ 57°35'·79N 09°57'·55E Fl G 5s 9m 4M; G mast.
E Mole Hd ☆ 57°35'·85N 09°57'·60E Fl R 5s 9m 6M; G mast.
Inner Hbr ☆ 57°35'·71N 09°57'·77E FG 6m 4M; G mast.

◄ SKAGEN

Skagen W ☆ 57°44'·89N 10°35·63E Fl(3)WR 10s 31m **W17M**/R12M; W ○ tr; vis: W053°-248°, R248°-323°.
Skagen ☆ 57°44'·11N 10°37'·75E Fl 4s 44m **23M**; Gy ○ Tr; Racon (G).
Skagen No 1 57°47'·08N 10°45'·93E Iso 4s; Racon (T).
Appr 57°45'·91N 10°43'·66E Q.
Skagen No 1A 57°43'·37N 10°53'·53E L Fl 10s 4s; Racon (N).
57°43'·80N 10°42'·21E Q (3) 10s.
E Bkwtr knuckle ☆ 57°43'·25N 10°36'·44E F 4m 2M; Gy lantern.
Ldg lts 334·5° Front 57°43'·06N 10°35'·45E Iso R 4s 13m 8M; mast. Rear, 57°43'·2N 10°35'·4E Iso R 4s 22m 8M; Tr.
E Bkwtr SW end ☆ 57°42'·88N 10°35'·66E Fl G 3s 8m 5M; G Tr; *Horn (2) 30s.*
W Bkwtr E end ☆ 57°42'·84N 10°35'·59E Fl R 3s 8m 5M; R Tr.
Forhavns SW Mole Hd ☆ 57°42'·94N 10°35'·51 FR 5m 2M; Gy col.
Forhavens NE Mole Hd ☆ 57°42'·96N 10°35'·56E FG 5m 2M; Gy col.
Østhavn, SE side ☆ 57°42'·97N 10°35'·80E FG 4m 4M; Gy col.
Østhavn, NW side ☆ 57°43'·00N 10°35'·76E FR 4m 4M; Gy col.
Inner W Mole Hd ☆ 57°43'·08N 10°35'·51E FR 6m; post; vis: only over the hbr.
Inner E Mole Hd ☆ 57°43'·08N 10°35'·55E FG 6m; post.

25

9.25.5 PASSAGE INFORMATION

Reference books include Admiralty *North Sea (East) Pilot, Cruising Guide to Germany and Denmark* (Imray/Navin), and the *Cruising Association Handbook.* See 9.0.8 for distances across the North Sea.

The W coast of Denmark provides no harbours of refuge in strong onshore winds except for Esbjerg and even this is made difficult by a bar which develops heavy breaking seas in strong W or SW winds. Thyborøn should not be approached on the ebb with winds over Force 5. The only offshore danger of note is Horns Rev which extends some 21M W of Blaavandshuk and which has a navigable buoyed passage some 3½M SW of Blaavandshuk. There are many coastal nature reserves, the areas of which are marked on the charts and into which entry is affected by restrictions and prohibitions. These do not, however, affect the entry to ports and harbours.

Tidal streams are negligible N of Helgoland but considerable off and in the Elbe. Leading beacons have triangular daymarks; that on the rear beacon, point down and that on the front beacon, point up. English and German are commonly spoken. There is much fishing activity and pair trawling is common.

RØMØ TO ESBJERG (Chart 3768) The ingoing tidal stream abreast Rømø Havn begins at -0215 HW Helgoland and runs NNE across the hbr entrance; the outgoing stream begins at +0345 HW Helgoland and runs SSW across the entrance. The maximum rate in each direction is about 2kn. Tidal streams in the Fanø Bugt are shown in tables on chart *3768*. In the open sea the flood is SE going and the ebb is NW going. In calm weather the stream changes about every 6 hrs; there is no slack water, merely a turning of the stream, usually anti-clockwise. The rate is 1½kn at the change; the ebb is often stronger than the flood. Gales often make the stream irregular. In Esbjerg Roads the stream sets ESE at -0305 HW Helgoland and WSW at +0315 HW Helgoland. Firing practice takes place up to 12M seaward of Rømø.

Clear Rømø via the buoyed channel and the Lister Tief SW pillar buoy Iso 8s in posn 55°05'·4N 08°16'·9E and steer 351° 19·8M for the Grådyb Andurning SW pillar buoy Lfl 10s in posn 55°24'·7N 08°11'·7E. Enter Esbjerg via the buoyed channel.

ESBJERG TO HVIDE SANDE (Charts *3768, 1404, Danish 99*) Firing practice takes place in the following areas: in a sector lying between Blaavandshuk Lt Ho and posns 9M W and 10M NNW; to seaward of Nyminde Gab 55°49'N 08°12'E. Charts covering the area are marked with warnings about anchoring and fishing due to wrecks and underwater explosives. 2M W of Hvide Sande tidal stream sets 155° at -0455 HW Helgoland and 335° at +0120 HW Helgoland.

Leave Esbjerg by the Grådyb Andurning SW pillar buoy and steer 314° 6.5M for the PHM Fl(3)R 10s which marks the entrance to Slugen, a buoyed, deep water channel leading NW through the shallow banks. At the SHM LFl.G 10s in posn 55°34'·0N 07°49'·5E which marks the NE end of Normands Byb, the extension of Slugen, steer 020° 27·3M for the entrance to Hvide Sande. Entrance to Hvide Sande can be dangerous, see Port Plan and Notes 9.25.10. Also note the possibility of strong currents in the entranc which are similarly mentioned. Entry to Ringkøbing Fjord is via a lock There are a number of attractive hbrs and anchs but also shallows an conservation areas with prohibited access - see Danish chart *99*.

HVIDE SANDE TO THYBORØN (chart *1404, 2496*) Other than dangerous wreck 316° 7M from the entrance to Hvide Sande an prohibited areas 1M to seaward from the shore there are n problems on this passage. The entrance to Thyborøn Kanal i marked with a SWM Lfl 10s Racon (T) in posn 56°42'·6N 08°08'·6E

Limfjord (charts *2496, 2497, 598* and www.kms.dk), entered fror Thyborøn, offers a large area of sheltered cruising water wit many harbours, not covered here, and gives access to the Balti via Hals Egense. Some of the marinas are only suitable for cra drawing less than 1·5m, but there are plenty of ⚓.

THYBORØN TO HANSTHOLM (chart *1404, 2496, 2671*). O Hanstholm very strong currents may be caused by the wind; wit S and W winds an ingoing flow and with N and E winds an outgoin flow up to 7 kn in each direction. Other than underwater obstruction and explosives making anch and fishing dangerous there are n problems in this passage. The seaward end of Øst Mole at Hanstholn may be difficult to see at HW, so keep close the the West Mole.

HANSTHOLM TO SKAGEN (chart *2671*) From the SWM o Hanstholm to the entrance buoys (PHM and SHM) in pos 57°36'·4N 09°47'·5E off Hirtshals is 058° 52·8M. A course of 065 21·7M from these entrance buoys brings you to a point 1M NN of Skagen W Lt Ho. From thence 087° 5·1M reaches the NCM in pos 57°46'·0N 10°43'·8E. ECMs then bring you the Skagen hbr entrance Other than firing practices which may take place around 57°11'N 09°25'E to seaward of Tranum Sound and the dangerous stat of the sea bed there are no problems on this passage.

CROSSING THE NORTH SEA (charts *2182A, 2182B, 2182C*) Th important considerations when planning a passage are:

1. The distances are considerable, eg Harwich to Esbjerb i 330M and Harwich to Skagen is 483M, so a strong crew use to night passages and a well found yacht are essential.
2. There are large numbers of oil and gas rigs to be avoided
3. South of Lat 54°14', ie about Helgoland, there is an extensive TS system which must be treated with extreme caution.

Since there is only Esbjerg as an all weather port, and even that i doubtful in strong W or SW winds, it may be thought prudent t make Helgoland the first port of call or to wriggle along the Friesia Islands via Holland so that options are open dependent on weathe

From Dover the S Galloper SCM Q6+LFl in posn 51°44'N 01°57' and Smiths Knoll SCM Q6+LFl in posn 52°43'N 02°18'E mak suitable departure points. Course can then be set N of th Botney Ground TSS for Helgoland passing S of BR/S SWM Mo(A) 8s in posn 52°55'N 03°18'E to clear the TSS N of this buoy

9.25.6 DISTANCE TABLE

Approximate distances in nautical miles are by the most direct route, whilst avoiding dangers and allowing for Traffic Separatio Schemes. Places in *italics* are in adjoining areas. Places in **bold** are in 9.0.8 Distances across the North Sea.

1. *Hamburg*	**1**																			
2. *Wangerooge*	61	**2**																		
3. *Cuxhaven*	54	42	**3**																	
4. Helgoland	88	24	38	**4**																
5. Wilhelmshaven	110	27	56	43	**5**															
6. Bremerhaven	81	38	58	44	45	**6**														
7. *Kiel/Holtenau*	90	108	70	104	123	123	**7**													
8. *Husum*	113	52	66	47	82	82	129	**8**												
9. *Hörnum*	99	68	56	39	82	83	126	45	**9**											
10. *Föhr*	110	66	56	40	83	84	126	44	14	**10**										
11. *List*	136	90	82	60	103	104	186	65	26	40	**11**									
12. **Rømø**	139	94	85	63	106	107	189	68	29	43	8	**12**								
13. **Fanø**	167	112	113	85	128	129	183	98	73	87	30	33	**13**							
14. **Esbjerg**	163	109	110	83	125	127	180	95	70	84	27	30	3	**14**						
15. **Hvide Sande**	192	147	138	119	162	163	208	131	86	100	70	73	57	54	**15**					
16. **Torsminde**	216	168	162	141	184	185	232	152	108	122	91	94	79	76	24	**16**				
17. **Thyborøn**	233	178	200	154	310	201	249	163	131	155	113	116	93	90	45	24	**17**			
18. **Hanstholm**	265	210	232	186	242	233	281	195	163	187	145	148	125	122	77	56	32	**18**		
19. **Hirtshals**	317	262	284	238	296	285	233	247	215	239	197	200	177	174	179	108	84	52	**19**	
20. Skagen	338	283	304	259	414	306	261	275	248	272	230	233	210	200	162	141	114	85	33	**20**

RØMØ 9.25.7

55°05′·25N 08°34′·39E

CHARTS AC 3768, 3767, BSH 3013/2 & 3

TIDES +0315 Dover; ML 0·9; Duration 0620; Zone -0100

Standard Port ESBJERG (⟶)

Times				Height (metres)			
High Water		Low Water		MHWS	MHWN	MLWN	MLWS
0300	0700	0100	0800	1·8	1·4	0·4	0·0
1500	1900	1300	2000				
Differences RØMØ							
-0040	-0005	0000	-0020	+0·2	+0·2	-0·1	0·0

SHELTER Good, access at all tides. Yachts berth on the N side of the inner hbr alternatively ⚓ outside the hbr N of the entrance.

NAVIGATION WPT Lister Tief SWM 55°05′·40N 08°16′·75E thence by buoyed channel passing into Rømø Dyb at G1 Pillar buoy Fl.Y 4s, ie not turning to stbd into the channel to List. Rømø Dyb is lit to port by a series of three dolphins and to stbd by a lit SHM at the entrance and then five SHMs to the hbr entrance.

LIGHTS AND MARKS Lister Tief as above. List West Oc.WRG 6s, W tr, R lantern and List Ost Iso.WRG 6s, W tr, R band, R lantern mark the N end of Sylt. The former provides a narrow W sector to mark the first part of Rømø Dyb and a second part is marked by a further narrow W sector from List Land lt Oc.WRG 3s, W mast, R band. S Mole Head Fl.G 3s, Gy metal frame, floodlit. N Mole Head Fl.G 3s, Gy metal frame, floodlit.

RADIO TELEPHONE VHF Ch 16; 10 12 13, HX.

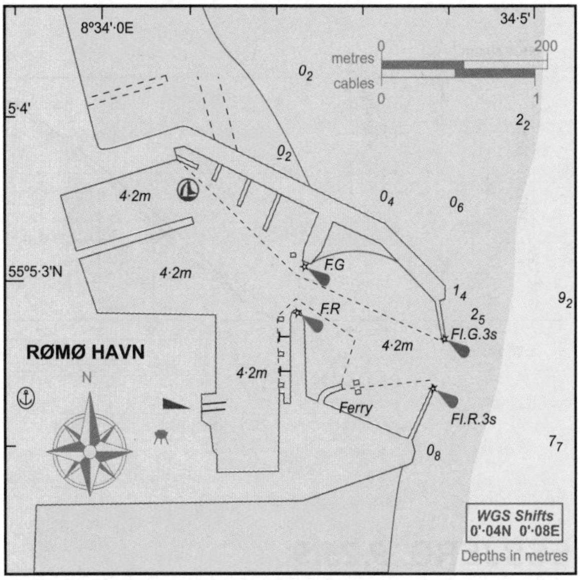

TELEPHONE (Dial code 00 45) Hr Mr 74 75 55 92; CG 74 75 22 22; Hosp (Esbjerg) 75 18 19 00; Pol (Emergency) 112; Taxi 74 75 11 00, 74 75 53 94.

FACILITIES Jetties, D in fishing hbr, FW; **Services**: ME, Sh, CH, Showers & toilets at SC on N pier. **Town**: V, Rail at Vibe, Airport at Esbjerg.

FANØ 9.25.8

55°27′·50N 08°24′·80E

CHARTS AC 417, 3768

TIDES +0340 Dover; ML 0·7; Duration 0605; Zone -0100

Times and heights: as ESBJERG

SHELTER Good, access at all tides. Yachts berth in Nordby Marina in 1·9m via an approach ch with about 1m.

NAVIGATION As Esbjerg until off Sønderhaven, then turn to 242° on Slunden Ldg lts Iso 2s between No 1 Bn Fl(2)G 10s, G pile and No 2 Bn Fl(4)Y 15s, Y pile. Thence between No 3 Bn Fl.G 3s, G pile and No 4 Bn Fl.R 3s, R pile to Næs Søjord Bn F R, R pile, then turning to 213°42′ for F R Ldg lts at Nordby. The final appr is on 161°36′.

LIGHTS AND MARKS As Esbjerg and above. The final ldg line is marked with WR bns.

RADIO TELEPHONE N/A

TELEPHONE (Dial code 00 45) Hr Mr 75 16 31 00, CG 75 16 36 66, Hosp (Esbjerg) 75 18 19 00, Customs (Esbjerg) 75 12 25 00, Pol (Emergency) 112

FACILITIES Pontoons with FW; **Services**: Showers and WC at SC; **Town**: limited V at Nordby, R, Bar. For full services, try Esbjerg.

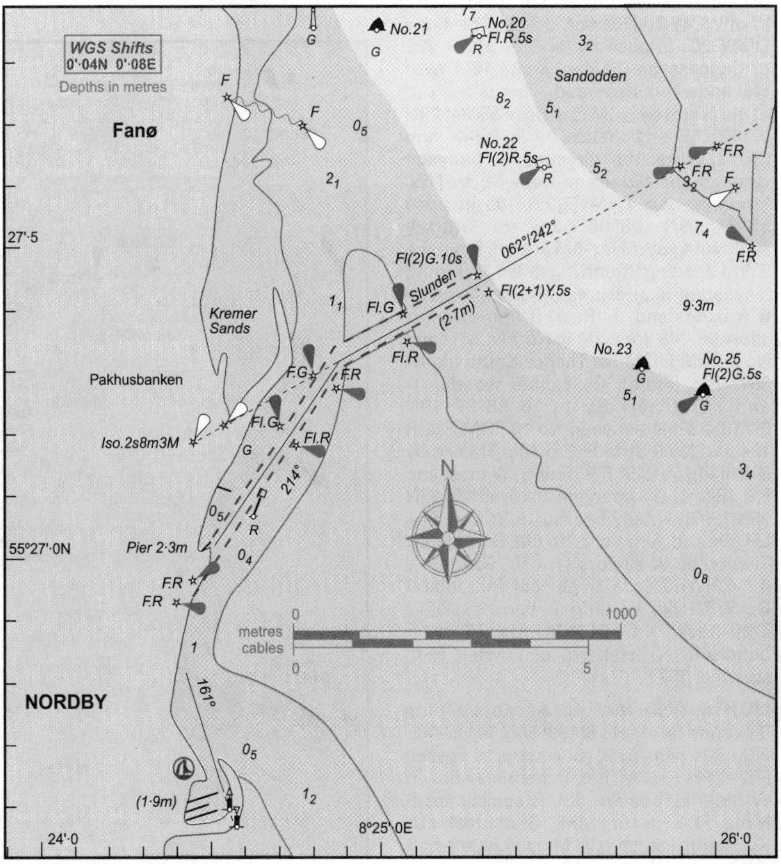

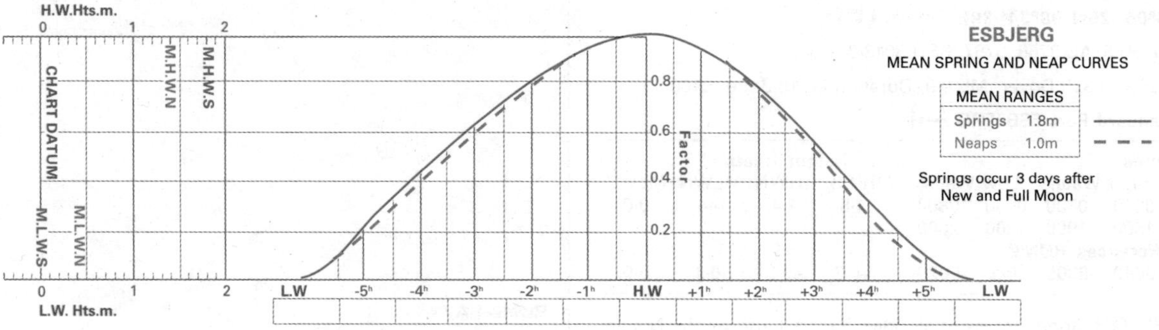

ESBJERG *9.25.9*

55°28'·16N 08°25'·59E (Entrance to Trafikhaven)

CHARTS AC 417, 3768

TIDES +0340 Dover; ML 0·7; Duration 0605; Zone -0100
ESBJERG is a Standard Port (⟶)

SHELTER Good access at all tides. Yachts berth in the new marina as shown or across the channel in Nordby Marina, Fanø.

NAVIGATION From the S or W, the approach is clear to Grådyb Anduvning SWM Lfl 10s Racon G in posn 55°24'·67N 08°11'·72E. From the N sector, Horns Rev which extends some 21M from Blåvands Huk lt must either be cleared to seaward by passing W of WCM Q(9)15s and ODAS Pillar buoy Fl(5)Y 20s in posn 55°34'·55N 07°26'·23E or the passage (Slugen) some 10M W of Blåvands Huk traversed. This is marked at the N end by NCM Q in posn 55°34'·29N 07°42'·00E and thence by lit PHMs and SHMs. **Note: the direction of buoyage through the Slugen is from SE to NW.** From the last PHM Fl(3)R 10s in posn 55°29'·19N 08°03'·53E to Grådyb Anduvning SWM is 6·5M at 134°. From the SWM, Sæding Strand ldg lts Iso 2s (Front), R wooden bldg, Iso 4s (Middle), R metal tr R bands and F (Rear) R framework tr show 053°48' for 3.7M to No 7 NCM Q and No 8 PHM Fl(2)R 5s. Thence South ldg lts 067° F.G (Front), Gy square wooden tr and F.G (Rear) Gy tr, to 55°27'·19N 08°18'·23E, ie between No 10 PHM Fl(2)R 10s and No 9 SHM Fl(2)G 10s. Thence by North ldg lts 049° F.R (Front), W mast and F.R (Rear), Gy concrete tr to 55°29'·03N 08°21'·97E ie between No 16 SCM Q(6) + LFl 15s and Jerg bn Q 7m 6M, B tr Y base. Thence by W sectors (1) 075° Fovrfelt N lt Oc(2)WRG 6s, Y tr (2) 108° Strandby lt Oc WRG 5s, W bldg R band (3) 127° Trafikhaven lt Oc(2) WRG 12s, W bld R band and (4) back brg of Fovrfelt N lt, steering 152°

LIGHTS AND MARKS As above plus Blåvands Huk Lt Ho 55°33'·50N 08°05'·06E Fl(3) 20s 54m 23M; W square tr. Fovrelt Fl(2)R 10s 9m 3M, R tr; Industrifiskerihavn W Mole Fl.R 5s 6m 4M, R conical str; E Mole Fl.G 5s 6m 4M, G conical str; Konsumfiskerihavn W Mole Fl.R 3s 4m, R metal frame tr; E Mole Fl.G 3s 4m, G metal frame tr; Trafikhav N Mole F.R 7m 5M, R conical metal bldg; S Mole F.G 7m 4M, G conical metal bldg.

RADIO TELEPHONE VHF Ch 16: 12 13 14, H24

TELEPHONE (Dial code 00 45) Hr Mr 75 12 92 00, Coastguard 7 12 82 99, Hosp 75 18 19 00, Customs 75 12 25 00, Pol (Emergency 112, Taxi 75 12 69 88

FACILITIES Marina, 60 Kr, D, FW, AC; **Services:** Showers and W at Esbjerg Søsport (YC) ☎ 75 14 47 47, Sh A-Z Snedkeriet ☎ 7 12 65 99, SM Vase As ☎ 75 12 33 33, Diver Bjarnes Dykkerservic ☎ 75 12 04 44, ME; **Town:** V, R, Bar, PO, Rail, Airport

TIME ZONE -0100
(Danish Standard Time)
Subtract 1 hour for UT
For Danish Summer Time add ONE hour in **non-shaded areas**

DENMARK – ESBJERG

LAT 55°28′N LONG 8°27′E

TIMES AND HEIGHTS OF HIGH AND LOW WATERS

SPRING & NEAP TIDES
Dates in red are SPRINGS
Dates in blue are NEAPS

YEAR **2002**

JANUARY

Date	Day	Time	m	Time	m	Time	m	Time	m
1	TU	0357	1.9	0957	0.2	1627	1.8	2210	0.3
2	W	0438	1.9	1043	0.1	1711	1.8	2255	0.2
3	TH	0518	2.0	1128	0.1	1757	1.7	2341	0.3
4	F	0602	2.0	1216	0.1	1845	1.7		
5	SA	0028	0.3	0651	2.0	1308	0.1	1936	1.7
6	SU	0118	0.3	0745	2.0	1403	0.2	2033	1.6
7	M	0214	0.3	0847	1.9	1503	0.3	2137	1.6
8	TU	0316	0.4	0955	1.9	1607	0.3	2244	1.7
9	W	0424	0.4	1106	1.9	1712	0.3	2348	1.7
10	TH	0533	0.3	1214	1.9	1813	0.3		
11	F	0048	1.8	0637	0.3	1316	1.9	1909	0.3
12	SA	0143	1.8	0735	0.2	1412	1.8	2000	0.3
13	SU	0233	1.9	0826	0.2	1503	1.8	● 2046	0.3
14	M	0317	1.9	0914	0.2	1547	1.7	2126	0.3
15	TU	0356	1.9	0958	0.2	1623	1.7	2204	0.3
16	W	0430	1.9	1036	0.2	1654	1.6	2240	0.3
17	TH	0458	1.9	1111	0.3	1720	1.6	2311	0.3
18	F	0524	1.8	1146	0.3	1746	1.6	2345	0.3
19	SA	0554	1.9	1218	0.3	1817	1.6		
20	SU	0020	0.3	0629	1.8	1255	0.3	1857	1.6
21	M	0100	0.3	0712	1.8	1336	0.3	1944	1.6
22	TU	0146	0.3	0802	1.8	1423	0.3	2037	1.6
23	W	0239	0.4	0859	1.8	1519	0.4	2138	1.6
24	TH	0341	0.4	1004	1.7	1623	0.4	2248	1.6
25	F	0452	0.4	1118	1.7	1733	0.4		
26	SA	0001	1.6	0604	0.4	1233	1.7	1839	0.4
27	SU	0107	1.7	0708	0.3	1340	1.7	1935	0.3
28	M	0205	1.7	0805	0.2	1438	1.7	○ 2024	0.2
29	TU	0256	1.8	0856	0.1	1530	1.7	2111	0.2
30	W	0343	1.9	0944	0.0	1617	1.7	2156	0.1
31	TH	0425	1.9	1027	0.0	1701	1.7	2241	0.1

FEBRUARY

Date	Day	Time	m	Time	m	Time	m	Time	m
1	F	0508	2.0	1113	-0.1	1744	1.7	2323	0.1
2	SA	0551	2.0	1159	0.0	1825	1.7		
3	SU	0008	0.1	0637	1.9	1247	0.0	1911	1.6
4	M	0057	0.1	0726	1.9	1337	0.1	2001	1.6
5	TU	0150	0.1	0823	1.8	1431	0.2	2059	1.6
6	W	0249	0.2	0929	1.8	1533	0.3	2205	1.6
7	TH	0357	0.3	1043	1.7	1643	0.3	2315	1.6
8	F	0511	0.3	1154	1.7	1751	0.3		
9	SA	0022	1.6	0621	0.2	1259	1.7	1852	0.3
10	SU	0121	1.7	0722	0.1	1357	1.7	1944	0.2
11	M	0214	1.8	0815	0.1	1448	1.7	2028	0.2
12	TU	0301	1.8	0902	0.1	1530	1.6	● 2109	0.2
13	W	0342	1.8	0942	0.1	1606	1.6	2147	0.2
14	TH	0413	1.8	1015	0.1	1635	1.6	2217	0.2
15	F	0440	1.8	1048	0.1	1658	1.5	2249	0.2
16	SA	0503	1.8	1116	0.2	1719	1.6	2318	0.1
17	SU	0528	1.8	1147	0.2	1747	1.6	2352	0.1
18	M	0559	1.8	1218	0.2	1820	1.6		
19	TU	0029	0.1	0639	1.8	1256	0.2	1902	1.6
20	W	0110	0.1	0723	1.7	1341	0.2	1951	1.6
21	TH	0159	0.2	0817	1.7	1432	0.3	2048	1.5
22	F	0257	0.3	0921	1.6	1535	0.3	2156	1.5
23	SA	0410	0.3	1039	1.5	1651	0.4	2315	1.5
24	SU	0534	0.3	1206	1.5	1807	0.3		
25	M	0035	1.6	0647	0.2	1320	1.6	1910	0.2
26	TU	0140	1.7	0747	0.1	1421	1.6	2004	0.1
27	W	0236	1.8	0838	-0.1	1513	1.7	○ 2053	0.0
28	TH	0323	1.8	0923	-0.1	1600	1.7	2138	0.0

MARCH

Date	Day	Time	m	Time	m	Time	m	Time	m
1	F	0408	1.9	1009	-0.2	1641	1.7	2219	-0.1
2	SA	0451	1.9	1053	-0.2	1720	1.7	2303	-0.1
3	SU	0533	1.9	1136	-0.1	1800	1.6	2348	-0.1
4	M	0616	1.9	1219	-0.1	1840	1.6		
5	TU	0033	-0.1	0703	1.8	1306	0.1	1925	1.6
6	W	0122	0.0	0757	1.7	1358	0.2	2018	1.5
7	TH	0219	0.1	0901	1.6	1458	0.3	2125	1.5
8	F	0330	0.2	1018	1.5	1610	0.4	2241	1.5
9	SA	0453	0.2	1134	1.5	1725	0.3	2353	1.6
10	SU	0606	0.2	1239	1.5	1829	0.3		
11	M	0056	1.6	0707	0.1	1336	1.5	1922	0.2
12	TU	0152	1.7	0758	0.0	1425	1.6	2008	0.1
13	W	0239	1.7	0841	0.0	1508	1.6	2049	0.1
14	TH	0318	1.7	0917	0.0	1543	1.6	● 2122	0.1
15	F	0352	1.7	0951	0.0	1611	1.5	2155	0.0
16	SA	0417	1.7	1018	0.0	1634	1.5	2223	0.0
17	SU	0440	1.7	1047	0.0	1655	1.5	2253	0.0
18	M	0503	1.7	1114	0.0	1719	1.6	2325	0.0
19	TU	0534	1.7	1148	0.0	1751	1.6		
20	W	0001	0.0	0609	1.7	1224	0.1	1830	1.6
21	TH	0043	0.0	0655	1.6	1306	0.1	1914	1.6
22	F	0131	0.1	0749	1.5	1357	0.2	2009	1.5
23	SA	0229	0.2	0854	1.5	1459	0.3	2116	1.5
24	SU	0344	0.2	1015	1.4	1618	0.3	2238	1.5
25	M	0510	0.2	1146	1.4	1741	0.3		
26	TU	0004	1.5	0625	0.1	1300	1.5	1847	0.2
27	W	0113	1.6	0724	-0.1	1400	1.6	1942	0.0
28	TH	0211	1.7	0815	-0.2	1452	1.6	○ 2029	-0.1
29	F	0301	1.8	0902	-0.3	1536	1.6	2113	-0.2
30	SA	0348	1.9	0947	-0.3	1616	1.6	2158	-0.2
31	SU	0430	1.9	1027	-0.2	1654	1.6	2242	-0.2

APRIL

Date	Day	Time	m	Time	m	Time	m	Time	m
1	M	0511	1.8	1109	-0.2	1730	1.6	2323	-0.2
2	TU	0554	1.7	1152	-0.1	1808	1.6		
3	W	0009	-0.1	0638	1.6	1236	0.1	1851	1.5
4	TH	0059	0.0	0728	1.5	1323	0.2	1940	1.5
5	F	0156	0.1	0831	1.4	1420	0.3	2043	1.5
6	SA	0306	0.2	0947	1.3	1534	0.4	2202	1.4
7	SU	0430	0.2	1103	1.3	1654	0.3	2320	1.5
8	M	0544	0.1	1209	1.4	1800	0.3		
9	TU	0025	1.6	0642	0.0	1305	1.4	1854	0.2
10	W	0119	1.6	0729	0.0	1355	1.5	1941	0.1
11	TH	0207	1.7	0811	-0.1	1438	1.5	2019	0.0
12	F	0249	1.7	0849	-0.1	1513	1.6	● 2056	0.0
13	SA	0323	1.7	0919	-0.1	1544	1.6	2127	0.0
14	SU	0352	1.6	0950	0.0	1609	1.5	2158	0.0
15	M	0416	1.6	1016	0.0	1632	1.5	2230	0.0
16	TU	0443	1.6	1048	0.0	1657	1.6	2302	-0.1
17	W	0512	1.6	1120	0.0	1728	1.6	2341	-0.1
18	TH	0551	1.6	1158	0.0	1804	1.6		
19	F	0023	0.0	0636	1.5	1243	0.1	1850	1.5
20	SA	0112	0.0	0730	1.4	1335	0.2	1945	1.5
21	SU	0212	0.1	0836	1.4	1437	0.3	2052	1.5
22	M	0327	0.1	1000	1.3	1554	0.3	2213	1.5
23	TU	0450	0.1	1128	1.4	1712	0.2	2338	1.5
24	W	0601	0.0	1238	1.4	1818	0.1		
25	TH	0047	1.6	0700	-0.1	1336	1.5	1914	0.0
26	F	0147	1.7	0751	-0.2	1425	1.6	2004	-0.1
27	SA	0238	1.8	0837	-0.3	1510	1.6	○ 2052	-0.2
28	SU	0325	1.8	0920	-0.3	1551	1.6	2137	-0.3
29	M	0409	1.8	1003	-0.2	1627	1.6	2219	-0.3
30	TU	0451	1.7	1045	-0.1	1704	1.6	2304	-0.2

Chart Datum: 0·69 metres below Dansk Normal Null

Register for your FREE weekly weather email service from Macmillan Reeds
at www.nauticaldata.com – NOW!
weekend weather reports sent to your email address, every Thursday

TIME ZONE -0100
(Danish Standard Time)
Subtract 1 hour for UT
For Danish Summer Time add ONE hour in **non-shaded areas**

DENMARK – ESBJERG

LAT 55°28′N LONG 8°27′E

TIMES AND HEIGHTS OF HIGH AND LOW WATERS

SPRING & NEAP TIDES
Dates in red are SPRINGS
Dates in blue are NEAPS

YEAR 2002

MAY

Day	Time	m	Time	m	Time	m	Time	m
1 W	0532	1.6	1124	0.0	1741	1.6	2350	-0.1
2 TH	0614	1.5	1207	0.1	1820	1.5		
3 F	0038	0.0	0703	1.4	1253	0.2	1907	1.5
4 SA	0133	0.1	0759	1.3	1347	0.3	2005	1.5
5 SU	0239	0.2	0909	1.3	1452	0.3	2118	1.5
6 M	0356	0.2	1023	1.3	1608	0.3	2235	1.5
7 TU	0506	0.1	1129	1.3	1717	0.3	2342	1.5
8 W	0605	0.1	1225	1.4	1814	0.2		
9 TH	0039	1.6	0654	0.0	1315	1.5	1904	0.1
10 F	0129	1.6	0736	0.0	1400	1.5	1947	0.1
11 SA	0212	1.6	0813	0.0	1441	1.6	2024	0.0
12 SU	0251	1.6	0848	0.0	1514	1.6	● 2100	0.0
13 M	0324	1.6	0918	0.0	1545	1.6	2134	0.0
14 TU	0356	1.6	0952	0.0	1612	1.6	2208	0.0
15 W	0426	1.5	1024	0.0	1641	1.6	2246	-0.1
16 TH	0501	1.5	1100	0.0	1712	1.6	2326	-0.1
17 F	0541	1.5	1142	0.0	1751	1.6		
18 SA	0011	0.0	0627	1.4	1227	0.1	1837	1.6
19 SU	0103	0.0	0721	1.4	1318	0.2	1931	1.6
20 M	0203	0.0	0827	1.3	1420	0.2	2036	1.6
21 TU	0312	0.0	0945	1.3	1532	0.2	2153	1.6
22 W	0425	0.0	1102	1.4	1644	0.2	2311	1.6
23 TH	0533	0.0	1209	1.4	1750	0.1		
24 F	0021	1.7	0632	-0.1	1307	1.5	1849	0.0
25 SA	0122	1.7	0723	-0.2	1359	1.6	1942	-0.1
26 SU	0216	1.7	0812	-0.2	1446	1.6	○ 2030	-0.2
27 M	0306	1.7	0858	-0.1	1527	1.6	2116	-0.2
28 TU	0352	1.7	0942	-0.1	1606	1.6	2203	-0.2
29 W	0435	1.6	1021	0.0	1644	1.6	2249	-0.1
30 TH	0514	1.5	1102	0.1	1719	1.6	2333	-0.1
31 F	0555	1.4	1144	0.1	1757	1.6		

JUNE

Day	Time	m	Time	m	Time	m	Time	m
1 SA	0019	0.0	0636	1.3	1226	0.2	1839	1.6
2 SU	0109	0.1	0723	1.3	1312	0.3	1927	1.6
3 M	0205	0.2	0819	1.3	1406	0.3	2026	1.5
4 TU	0307	0.2	0924	1.3	1510	0.3	2133	1.5
5 W	0411	0.2	1031	1.3	1619	0.3	2242	1.5
6 TH	0512	0.2	1133	1.4	1723	0.3	2345	1.5
7 F	0606	0.1	1229	1.4	1818	0.2		
8 SA	0042	1.6	0654	0.1	1318	1.5	1908	0.2
9 SU	0133	1.6	0736	0.1	1403	1.6	1953	0.1
10 M	0217	1.6	0814	0.0	1445	1.6	2033	0.1
11 TU	0300	1.6	0853	0.0	1521	1.6	● 2112	0.0
12 W	0339	1.6	0929	0.0	1556	1.6	2153	0.0
13 TH	0417	1.5	1007	0.0	1629	1.6	2234	0.0
14 F	0457	1.5	1048	0.1	1704	1.7	2316	0.0
15 SA	0539	1.5	1130	0.1	1745	1.7		
16 SU	0004	-0.1	0624	1.5	1215	0.1	1830	1.7
17 M	0055	0.0	0716	1.4	1306	0.1	1922	1.7
18 TU	0151	0.0	0815	1.4	1402	0.2	2023	1.7
19 W	0253	0.0	0922	1.4	1505	0.2	2133	1.7
20 TH	0358	0.0	1032	1.4	1612	0.2	2246	1.7
21 F	0503	0.0	1139	1.5	1720	0.1	2357	1.7
22 SA	0605	0.0	1240	1.5	1822	0.1		
23 SU	0101	1.7	0701	0.0	1335	1.6	1920	0.0
24 M	0200	1.7	0752	0.0	1424	1.6	○ 2014	-0.1
25 TU	0253	1.7	0839	0.0	1510	1.7	2104	-0.1
26 W	0341	1.6	0922	0.1	1552	1.7	2152	-0.1
27 TH	0423	1.6	1004	0.1	1630	1.7	2236	0.0
28 F	0501	1.5	1045	0.1	1704	1.7	2317	0.0
29 SA	0536	1.4	1122	0.2	1738	1.7		
30 SU	0000	0.1	0609	1.4	1200	0.2	1813	1.7

JULY

Day	Time	m	Time	m	Time	m	Time	m
1 M	0042	0.2	0646	1.4	1242	0.2	1854	1.7
2 TU	0124	0.2	0727	1.4	1325	0.3	1940	1.6
3 W	0211	0.3	0818	1.4	1414	0.3	2032	1.6
4 TH	0303	0.3	0917	1.4	1511	0.3	2132	1.6
5 F	0402	0.3	1022	1.4	1616	0.4	2239	1.6
6 SA	0503	0.3	1129	1.5	1723	0.3	2346	1.6
7 SU	0602	0.3	1231	1.5	1825	0.3		
8 M	0049	1.6	0656	0.2	1325	1.6	1919	0.2
9 TU	0146	1.6	0745	0.2	1414	1.6	2009	0.2
10 W	0238	1.6	0828	0.2	1459	1.7	● 2056	0.1
11 TH	0325	1.6	0910	0.1	1541	1.7	2140	0.0
12 F	0409	1.6	0953	0.1	1619	1.8	2222	0.0
13 SA	0452	1.6	1035	0.1	1658	1.8	2307	0.0
14 SU	0533	1.6	1116	0.1	1739	1.8	2353	-0.1
15 M	0616	1.6	1202	0.1	1822	1.8		
16 TU	0041	0.0	0703	1.5	1250	0.1	1911	1.8
17 W	0131	0.0	0755	1.5	1343	0.1	2007	1.8
18 TH	0225	0.1	0852	1.5	1440	0.2	2111	1.8
19 F	0326	0.2	0957	1.5	1545	0.2	2223	1.7
20 SA	0432	0.2	1105	1.5	1654	0.2	2337	1.7
21 SU	0539	0.2	1212	1.6	1804	0.2		
22 M	0046	1.7	0640	0.2	1313	1.7	1907	0.1
23 TU	0148	1.7	0735	0.2	1408	1.7	2004	0.1
24 W	0243	1.7	0823	0.2	1457	1.8	○ 2055	0.0
25 TH	0330	1.6	0908	0.2	1541	1.8	2141	0.1
26 F	0411	1.6	0950	0.2	1618	1.8	2221	0.1
27 SA	0447	1.6	1026	0.2	1651	1.8	2300	0.1
28 SU	0515	1.5	1101	0.2	1719	1.8	2335	0.2
29 M	0541	1.5	1136	0.2	1748	1.8		
30 TU	0008	0.2	0609	1.5	1209	0.2	1819	1.8
31 W	0044	0.3	0644	1.5	1247	0.2	1859	1.8

AUGUST

Day	Time	m	Time	m	Time	m	Time	m
1 TH	0120	0.3	0725	1.6	1329	0.3	1945	1.7
2 F	0203	0.3	0815	1.6	1417	0.3	2038	1.7
3 SA	0255	0.4	0913	1.5	1514	0.4	2139	1.6
4 SU	0356	0.4	1020	1.5	1624	0.4	2252	1.6
5 M	0506	0.4	1134	1.6	1742	0.4		
6 TU	0009	1.6	0615	0.4	1244	1.6	1850	0.3
7 W	0119	1.6	0714	0.3	1345	1.7	1948	0.2
8 TH	0218	1.7	0806	0.3	1437	1.8	● 2038	0.1
9 F	0310	1.7	0853	0.2	1522	1.9	2122	0.0
10 SA	0357	1.7	0936	0.1	1605	1.9	2207	0.0
11 SU	0439	1.7	1017	0.1	1646	2.0	2251	0.0
12 M	0518	1.7	1100	0.1	1726	2.0	2334	0.0
13 TU	0559	1.7	1145	0.1	1809	2.0		
14 W	0018	0.0	0641	1.7	1230	0.1	1856	2.0
15 TH	0106	0.1	0725	1.7	1317	0.1	1948	1.9
16 F	0157	0.2	0818	1.6	1412	0.2	2049	1.8
17 SA	0255	0.3	0920	1.6	1516	0.3	2202	1.7
18 SU	0402	0.4	1034	1.6	1633	0.3	2321	1.7
19 M	0514	0.4	1148	1.7	1751	0.3		
20 TU	0033	1.7	0621	0.4	1254	1.7	1858	0.2
21 W	0135	1.7	0718	0.4	1352	1.8	1954	0.2
22 TH	0228	1.7	0808	0.3	1443	1.9	○ 2043	0.1
23 F	0315	1.7	0853	0.3	1526	1.9	2123	0.1
24 SA	0355	1.7	0930	0.2	1603	1.9	2203	0.2
25 SU	0426	1.7	1006	0.2	1633	1.9	2236	0.2
26 M	0452	1.7	1039	0.2	1657	1.9	2306	0.3
27 TU	0512	1.7	1108	0.2	1720	1.9	2335	0.3
28 W	0536	1.7	1140	0.2	1749	1.9		
29 TH	0004	0.3	0605	1.7	1212	0.3	1822	1.9
30 F	0039	0.3	0644	1.7	1252	0.3	1904	1.8
31 SA	0117	0.4	0728	1.7	1338	0.3	1955	1.8

Chart Datum: 0·69 metres below Dansk Normal Null

Register for your FREE weekly weather email service from Macmillan Reeds
at www.nauticaldata.com – NOW!
weekend weather reports sent to your email address, every Thursday

TIME ZONE -0100
(Danish Standard Time)
Subtract 1 hour for UT
For Danish Summer Time add ONE hour in **non-shaded areas**

DENMARK – ESBJERG

LAT 55°28′N LONG 8°27′E

TIMES AND HEIGHTS OF HIGH AND LOW WATERS

SPRING & NEAP TIDES
Dates in red are SPRINGS
Dates in blue are NEAPS

YEAR **2002**

SEPTEMBER

Date	Time	m	Date	Time	m
1	0205	0.4	16	0331	0.6
	0821	1.7		1002	1.7
SU	1431	0.4	M	1616	0.4
	2056	1.7		2303	1.7
2	0303	0.5	17	0451	0.6
	0924	1.7		1123	1.8
M	1539	0.5	TU	1738	0.4
	2209	1.7			
3	0416	0.6	18	0014	1.7
	1041	1.7		0602	0.6
TU	1703	0.5	W	1232	1.8
	2336	1.7		1843	0.3
4	0539	0.5	19	0115	1.8
	1203	1.7		0700	0.5
W	1822	0.4	TH	1330	1.9
				1936	0.3
5	0053	1.7	20	0208	1.8
	0647	0.5		0749	0.4
TH	1313	1.8	F	1420	2.0
	1923	0.3		2021	0.2
6	0157	1.8	21	0253	1.8
	0743	0.4		0830	0.3
F	1410	1.9	SA	1504	2.0
	2015	0.2		○ 2103	0.2
7	0250	1.8	22	0330	1.8
	0830	0.3		0908	0.3
SA	1500	2.0	SU	1541	2.0
	● 2102	0.1		2137	0.2
8	0336	1.9	23	0401	1.8
	0913	0.2		0943	0.3
SU	1545	2.1	M	1609	2.0
	2147	0.0		2207	0.3
9	0417	1.9	24	0425	1.8
	0957	0.1		1012	0.3
M	1626	2.1	TU	1633	1.9
	2227	0.0		2235	0.3
10	0457	1.9	25	0446	1.8
	1040	0.1		1043	0.3
TU	1708	2.1	W	1655	1.9
	2310	0.0		2301	0.3
11	0534	1.9	26	0507	1.8
	1122	0.1		1111	0.3
W	1751	2.1	TH	1720	1.9
	2354	0.1		2332	0.3
12	0612	1.8	27	0536	1.8
	1206	0.1		1146	0.3
TH	1835	2.0	F	1754	1.9
13	0039	0.2	28	0004	0.4
	0655	1.8		0609	1.9
F	1255	0.2	SA	1223	0.3
	1925	1.9		1835	1.9
14	0126	0.4	29	0044	0.4
	0745	1.8		0653	1.9
SA	1350	0.3	SU	1307	0.4
	2026	1.8		1924	1.8
15	0222	0.5	30	0131	0.5
	0846	1.7		0745	1.8
SU	1455	0.4	M	1401	0.4
	2142	1.7		2023	1.7

OCTOBER

Date	Time	m	Date	Time	m
1	0227	0.6	16	0421	0.7
	0846	1.8		1051	1.8
TU	1509	0.5	W	1716	0.5
	2139	1.7		2348	1.7
2	0340	0.6	17	0533	0.6
	1001	1.8		1200	1.9
W	1636	0.5	TH	1818	0.4
	2309	1.7			
3	0504	0.6	18	0047	1.8
	1127	1.8		0631	0.5
TH	1756	0.4	F	1259	2.0
				1910	0.3
4	0029	1.8	19	0138	1.8
	0616	0.5		0719	0.4
F	1241	1.9	SA	1351	2.0
	1858	0.3		1955	0.3
5	0132	1.8	20	0221	1.9
	0713	0.4		0803	0.4
SA	1342	2.0	SU	1435	2.0
	1951	0.2		2032	0.3
6	0223	1.9	21	0300	1.9
	0804	0.3		0842	0.3
SU	1434	2.1	M	1511	2.0
	● 2037	0.1		○ 2107	0.3
7	0310	2.0	22	0333	1.9
	0851	0.2		0915	0.3
M	1520	2.2	TU	1543	2.0
	2120	0.1		2137	0.3
8	0352	2.0	23	0359	1.9
	0934	0.1		0948	0.3
TU	1605	2.2	W	1608	1.9
	2203	0.1		2204	0.4
9	0429	2.0	24	0421	1.9
	1016	0.1		1016	0.3
W	1648	2.1	TH	1632	1.9
	2246	0.1		2233	0.4
10	0507	2.0	25	0445	1.9
	1101	0.1		1049	0.3
TH	1729	2.1	F	1659	1.9
	2327	0.2		2303	0.4
11	0545	1.9	26	0511	1.9
	1147	0.1		1123	0.3
F	1814	2.0	SA	1733	1.9
				2339	0.4
12	0010	0.4	27	0546	1.9
	0626	1.9		1202	0.3
SA	1235	0.2	SU	1813	1.8
	1905	1.9			
13	0058	0.5	28	0018	0.4
	0714	1.9		0628	1.9
SU	1329	0.4	M	1250	0.4
	2006	1.8		1904	1.8
14	0153	0.6	29	0106	0.5
	0814	1.8		0717	1.9
M	1437	0.5	TU	1345	0.4
	2122	1.7		2005	1.7
15	0301	0.7	30	0203	0.6
	0932	1.8		0818	1.9
TU	1559	0.5	W	1453	0.5
	2240	1.7		2118	1.7
			31	0314	0.6
				0930	1.9
			TH	1611	0.5
				2243	1.7

NOVEMBER

Date	Time	m	Date	Time	m
1	0434	0.6	16	0005	1.7
	1053	1.9		0553	0.6
F	1726	0.4	SA	1219	1.9
	2359	1.8		1834	0.4
2	0545	0.5	17	0058	1.8
	1208	2.0		0646	0.5
SA	1828	0.3	SU	1311	2.0
				1918	0.3
3	0101	1.8	18	0145	1.9
	0645	0.4		0730	0.4
SU	1311	2.1	M	1358	2.0
	1921	0.2		2000	0.3
4	0155	1.9	19	0226	1.9
	0737	0.3		0811	0.4
M	1407	2.1	TU	1439	2.0
	● 2010	0.1		2035	0.4
5	0242	2.0	20	0302	1.9
	0824	0.2		0849	0.4
TU	1458	2.1	W	1514	1.9
	2056	0.1		○ 2107	0.4
6	0324	2.0	21	0334	1.9
	0911	0.1		0922	0.4
W	1545	2.1	TH	1546	1.9
	2140	0.2		2139	0.4
7	0405	2.0	22	0401	1.9
	0957	0.1		0956	0.4
TH	1628	2.1	F	1615	1.9
	2220	0.2		2209	0.4
8	0443	2.0	23	0427	1.9
	1043	0.1		1031	0.4
F	1712	2.0	SA	1647	1.8
	2303	0.3		2244	0.4
9	0521	2.0	24	0457	1.9
	1128	0.2		1108	0.3
SA	1757	1.9	SU	1721	1.8
	2348	0.4		2320	0.4
10	0602	1.9	25	0532	1.9
	1217	0.3		1151	0.3
SU	1846	1.8	M	1804	1.8
11	0033	0.5	26	0003	0.4
	0649	1.9		0612	2.0
M	1312	0.4	TU	1240	0.3
	1942	1.7		1854	1.7
12	0125	0.6	27	0052	0.5
	0746	1.9		0702	2.0
TU	1415	0.5	W	1334	0.4
	2049	1.6		1953	1.7
13	0227	0.7	28	0148	0.5
	0855	1.9		0801	2.0
W	1529	0.5	TH	1437	0.4
	2201	1.6		2101	1.7
14	0341	0.7	29	0252	0.5
	1010	1.9		0909	1.9
TH	1642	0.5	F	1547	0.4
	2307	1.7		2215	1.7
15	0452	0.7	30	0402	0.5
	1120	1.9		1025	1.9
F	1743	0.4	SA	1655	0.3
				2327	1.7

DECEMBER

Date	Time	m	Date	Time	m
1	0510	0.5	16	0008	1.7
	1139	2.0		0601	0.5
SU	1758	0.3	M	1226	1.8
				1837	0.4
2	0030	1.8	17	0100	1.8
	0613	0.4		0654	0.5
M	1245	2.0	TU	1317	1.9
	1854	0.2		1921	0.4
3	0125	1.9	18	0149	1.8
	0710	0.3		0740	0.4
TU	1345	2.0	W	1404	1.9
	1946	0.2		2002	0.4
4	0216	1.9	19	0232	1.9
	0803	0.2		0821	0.4
W	1439	2.0	TH	1448	1.8
	● 2032	0.2		○ 2040	0.4
5	0302	1.9	20	0309	1.9
	0854	0.2		0902	0.4
TH	1528	2.0	F	1527	1.8
	2117	0.3		2115	0.4
6	0345	2.0	21	0344	1.9
	0942	0.2		0941	0.3
F	1615	1.9	SA	1604	1.8
	2201	0.3		2152	0.4
7	0425	2.0	22	0415	1.9
	1028	0.2		1018	0.3
SA	1700	1.8	SU	1641	1.8
	2245	0.4		2230	0.3
8	0504	2.0	23	0449	1.9
	1115	0.2		1059	0.2
SU	1743	1.7	M	1718	1.7
	2326	0.4		2308	0.3
9	0545	1.9	24	0524	1.9
	1203	0.3		1143	0.2
M	1826	1.7	TU	1800	1.7
				2352	0.3
10	0010	0.5	25	0605	2.0
	0628	1.9		1229	0.2
TU	1254	0.4	W	1847	1.7
	1913	1.6			
11	0058	0.5	26	0040	0.3
	0717	1.9		0653	2.0
W	1349	0.4	TH	1320	0.2
	2007	1.6		1939	1.7
12	0151	0.6	27	0132	0.4
	0813	1.9		0747	2.0
TH	1448	0.5	F	1416	0.3
	2107	1.6		2037	1.7
13	0251	0.6	28	0229	0.4
	0917	1.8		0849	1.9
F	1550	0.5	SA	1517	0.3
	2210	1.6		2143	1.6
14	0356	0.6	29	0333	0.4
	1025	1.8		0958	1.9
SA	1652	0.5	SU	1622	0.3
	2311	1.7		2252	1.7
15	0501	0.6	30	0441	0.4
	1129	1.8		1112	1.9
SU	1748	0.5	M	1726	0.3
				2358	1.7
			31	0548	0.3
				1223	1.9
			TU	1827	0.3

Chart Datum: 0·69 metres below Dansk Normal Null

HVIDE SANDE *9.25.10*

Note: The positions given below and the Port Plan are taken from Danish Chart No 99 which has a WGS-80 base but which has a warning that there may be inaccuracies.

55°59′·93N 08°06′·68E

CHARTS AC 1404, Danish 99

TIDES +0345 Dover, ML 0·2, Duration 0550, Zone -0100

Standard Port ESBJERG (⟵)

Times				**Height (metres)**			
High Water		Low Water		MHWS	MHWN	MLWN	MLWS
0300	0700	0100	0800	1·8	1·4	0·4	0·0
1500	1900	1300	2000				
Differences Hvide Sande							
0000	+0010	-0015	-0025	-1·0	-0·7	-0·3	0·0

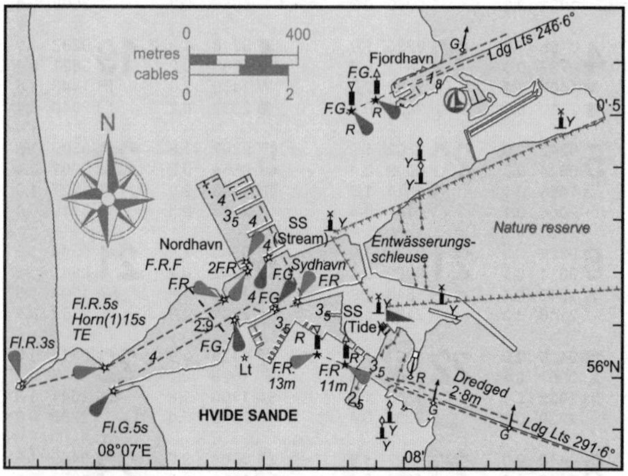

SHELTER Subject to the approach, see below, shelter is good, once inside. Yachts berth in the marina, as shown on the port plan, which is approached through the lock to the Østhavn or in the Nordhavn as allocated by the Hr Mr.

NAVIGATION Strong W winds can cause breakers over bar rendering the entrance dangerous. There is usually 2·5m below MSL in the channel over two sand ridges, the outer of which is about 3ca offshore. However sea level is subject to fluctuations due to wind - W winds can raise the level by up to 3·5m and E winds lower it by up to 2·0m. Water levels relative to MSL are signalled by lights and shapes from the mast near the Hr Mr's office as shown on the plan: zero or above MSL: 2 horiz W lts, 2 long cyinders side by side; -0·25m: W lt, 1 cone; -0·5m: 2 vert W lts, 2 cones; -0·75: 3 vert W lts, 3 cones; -1·0m: R lt, 1 short cylinder; -1·25m: RW vert lts, 1 short cylinder with 1 cone; -1·5m: R/W/W vert lts, 2 cones; -1·75m: R/W/W/W vert lts, 3 cones. The vertical W lts are shown immediately N of the single R lt.
A strong in-going current is signalled from the mast on the N side of the sluice by a N cone, by day and G lt over W lt by night, a strong out-going current is signalled by a S cone by day and a W lt over G lt by night. In case of doubt, check with the Hr Mr by VHF or telephone. The Lee (outer) Mole Fl.R 3s 7m 8M, R hut; N Mole Fl.R 5s 10m 6M, R structure, TE 1996; S Mole Fl.G 5s 10m 6M, G structure. There is 24m clearance beneath the power cable in the outer hbr.

LIGHTS AND MARKS As above, plus Hvide Sande Lt Ho 56°00′·00N 08°07′·26E F 27m 14M, gy frame tr.

RADIO TELEPHONE VHF Ch 16; 12 13, HX

TELEPHONE (Dial code 00 45) Hr Mr 97 31 16 33, Lock 97 31 10 93, Customs 97 32 22 22, Hospital (Esbjerg) 75 18 19 00, Police (Emergency) 112, Taxi 97 32 32 32,

FACILITIES AB, FW, AC, D in fishing hbr; **Services**: Showers, WC, ME, Ch ☎ 97 31 15 22; **Town**: R, V, PO, Rail at Ringkøping, Airport at Esbjerg

TORSMINDE *9.25.11*

56°22′·36N 08°06′·90E

CHARTS AC 1404

TIDES +0425 Dover; ML 0·1; Duration 0605; Zone -0100

Standard Port ESBJERG (⟵)

Times				**Height (metres)**			
High Water		Low Water		MHWS	MHWN	MLWN	MLWS
0300	0700	0100	0800	1·8	1·4	0·4	0·0
1500	1900	1300	2000				
Differences Torsminde							
+0045	+0050	+0040	+0010	-1·2	-0·9	-0·3	0.0

SHELTER Conditions are similar to Hvide Sande. Shelter is good, once inside, but see the notes below. Yachts berth in the Vesthavn on pontoons. Entry into Nissum Fjord is limited by the 3m clearance below the road bridge.

NAVIGATION Even moderate winds can cause breakers over the bar which has normally less than 2·7m below MSL and the hbr may have less water than charted due to silting. Strong winds can cause the same variation in height as at Hvide Sande and there is the same problem with currents into and out of the hbr. The same signals are used from masts shown on the Port Plan. **You are advised to check conditions and to request a berth with the Hr Mr before approaching.** Approach directly from seaward and do not be confused by the light Fl 5s on the groyne to the N of the hbr entrance. N Mole Iso.R 2s 9m 4M, R hut; S Mole Iso.G 2s 9m 4M, G hut. After entry turn hard to stbd into Vesthavn, W Mole F.G 5m 2M, gy post; E Mole F.R 5m 2M, gy post.

LIGHTS AND MARKS As above, plus Torsminde Lt Ho 56°22′·5N 08°07′·2E F.W 30m 14M, gy frame tr; Groyne N Head 56°22′·5N 08°06′·9E Fl 5s 8m 5M, gy hut.

RADIO TELEPHONE VHF Ch 16; 12 13, 0300-1300 1400-2400 LT

TELEPHONE (Dial code 00 45) Hr Mr 97 49 70 44, CG 97 41 22 22, Hospital (Holstebro) 97 41 42 00, Police (Emergency) 112, Taxi 97 82 14 15

FACILITIES FW, AC, D; **Services**: ME; **Town**: R, V at campsite, Rail at Ramme, Holstebro or Ringkøping, Airport at Karup, ☎ 97 10 12 18

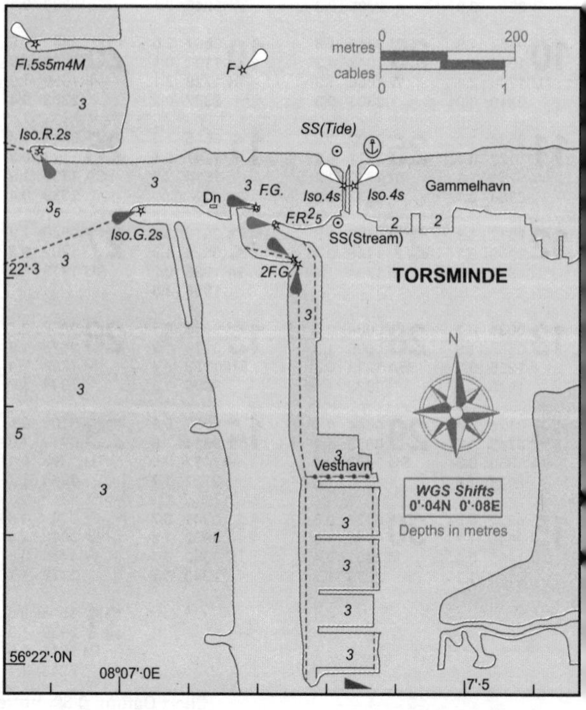

THYBØRON *9.25.12*

56°43'·00N 08°12'·80E

CHARTS AC 426, Danish 108S, German 81

TIDES +0530 Dover; ML 0·0; Duration 0620; Zone -0100

Standard Port ESBJERG (⟵)

Times				**Heights (metres)**			
High Water		Low Water		MHWS	MHWN	MLWN	MLWS
0300	0700	0100	0800	1·8	1·4	0·4	0·0
1500	1900	1300	2000				
Differences Thybøron							
+0120	+0230	+0410	+0210	-1·4	-1·1	-0·3	0.0

SHELTER Subject to the approach, see below, shelter is good, once inside. Yachts berth in the Nordre Inderhavn by arrangement with the Hr Mr.

NAVIGATION Caution: light sectors and buoys are moved to conform to changes in depths. Entry can be dangerous in near gale force onshore winds which can cause breaking seas and violent eddies. The minimum depth is normally about 6m on approach and between 5m and 8m within the bar. The SWM Lfl 10s in posn 56°42'·57N 08°08'·75E is in the W sector of Agger Tange lt Oc.WRG 5s 8m 11/8M, R north triangle on bn which is the front ldg lt 082°; the rear is Iso.W 4s 17m 12M, R south triangle on gy frame tr. At the SHM Fl(2)G 5s bear off onto 120° using the Langholm ldg lts, Front Iso.W 2s 7m 11M, R north triangle on R hut; Rear Iso.W 4s 13m 11M, R south triangle on gy frame tr. At the PHM Fl(2)R 5s turn S until the hr entrance, N Mole Fl.G 3s 6m 4M, G pedestal; S Mole Fl.R 3s 6m 4M, R pedestal. Inside the entrance turn sharp to stbd and proceed to the N head of the hbr.

LIGHTS AND MARKS As above plus Thybøron Approach lt 56°42'·52N 08°12'·98E Fl(3) 10s 24m 16M, frame tr; sectored lt showing outward from entr to Nordre Inderhavn 56°42'·38N 08°13'·46E Oc(2)WRG 12s 6m 12/9/9M, W tr, R band, G122·5°-146·5°, W146·5°-150°, R150°-211·3°, G211·3°-337·5°, W337·5°-340°, R340°-344°. Conspicuous marks on approach are: to S of entrance Nørre Nissum Ch (56°33'N 08°25'E), W with dark spire and to N of entrance Vestervig Ch (56°46'N 08°19'E) with nearby windmill.

RADIO TELEPHONE VHF Ch Ch 16; 12 13, H24

TELEPHONE (Dial code 00 45) Hr Mr 97 83 10 50, Coastguard 97 82 13 22, Hospital (Thisted) 97 92 44 00, Police (Emergency) 112, Taxi 97 83 25 11

FACILITIES 60Kr any lengthAB, FW, AC, D; **Services**: WC, showers, ME, Sh Thybøron Bådebyggeri ☎ 97 83 11 26, SM Thyøron Sejlmageri ☎ 97 83 11 25; **Town**: R, V, PO, Rail, Airport at Thisted ☎ 97 96 51 66.

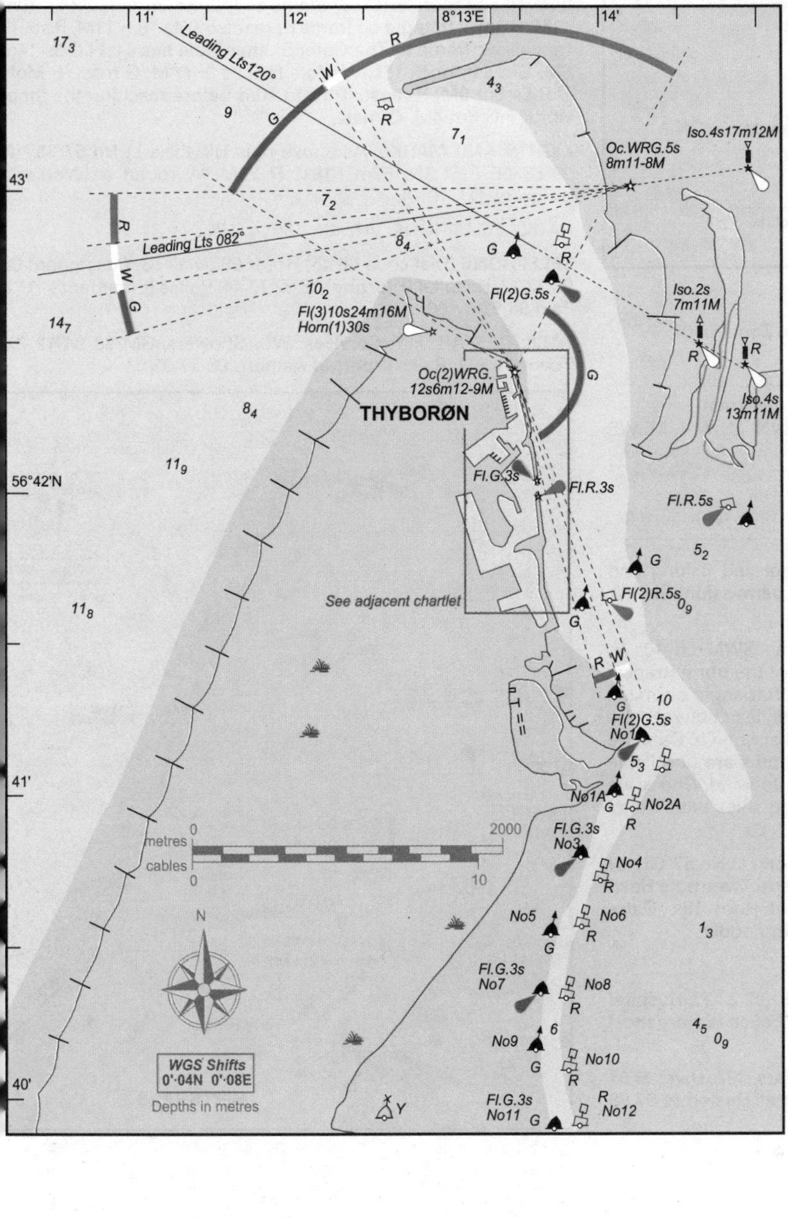

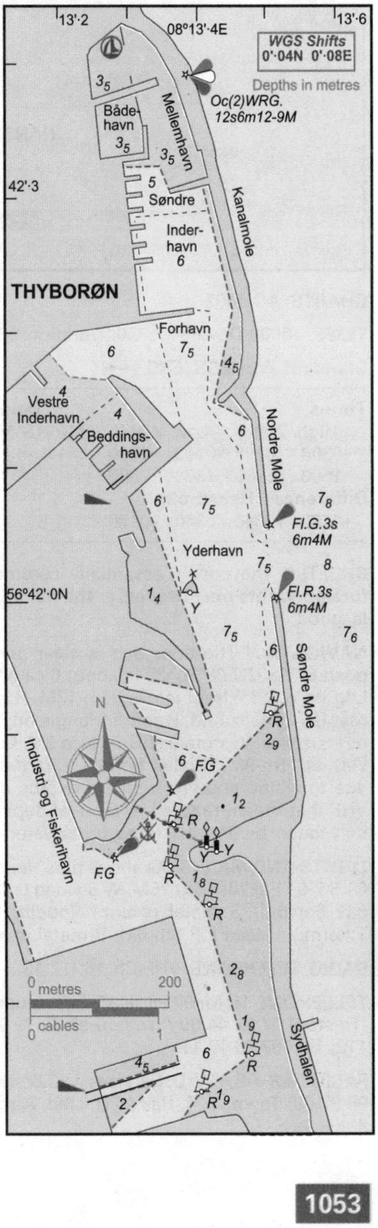

HANSTHOLM *9.25.13*

57°07'·62N 08°35'·58

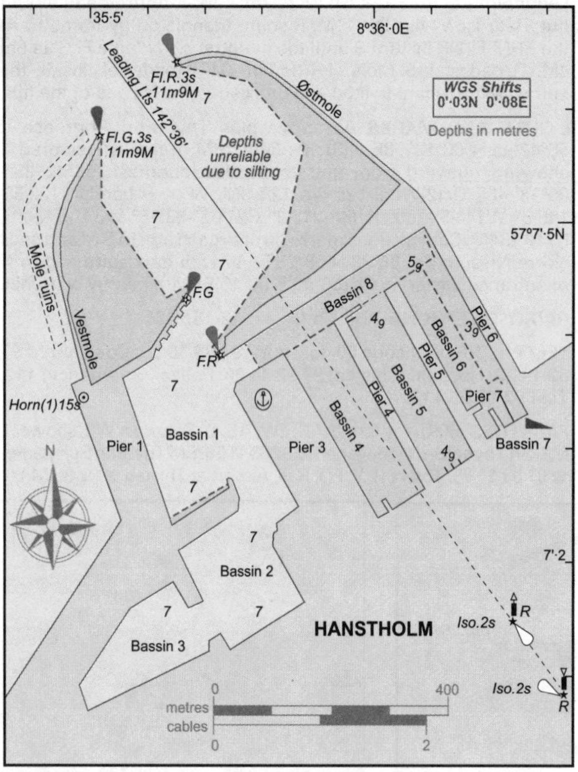

CHARTS AC 1402

TIDES +0600 Dover, ML 0.0, Duration 0630, Zone -0100

Standard Port ESBJERG (⟵)

Times				Height (metres)			
High Water		Low Water		MHWS	MHWN	MLWN	MLWS
0300	0700	0100	0800	1·8	1·4	0·4	0·0
1500	1900	1300	2000				
Differences Hanstholm							
+0100	+0340	+0340	+0130	-1·5	-1·1	-0·3	0·0

SHELTER The port is essentially commercial and fishing and **foreign yachts may only enter the hbr with permission**. Shelter is good.

NAVIGATION The approach is clear and the SWM Lfl 10s in posn 57°08'·2N 08°35'·0E is about 6 ca NW of the hbr entrance. Ldg lts 142°36' front Iso 2s 37m 13M, R north triangle on mast; rear Iso 2s 45m 13M, R south triangle on mast, lead between the outer moles; Vestmole Fl.G 3s 11m 9M, G pillar floodlit; Østmole Fl.R 3s 11m 9M, R pillar floodlit. Charted depths are unreliable due to silting and variations in depths due to wind. Check via VHF that the entrances are clear of departing ships which may be hidden behind the large breakwaters.

LIGHTS AND MARKS As above plus Hanstholm Lt Ho 57°06'·8N 08°36'·0 Fl(3) 20s 65m 26M, W 8-sided tr. Vestre Tværmole Head F.G 6m 6M, G metal column floodlit, Root Horn 15s. Østre Tværmole Head F.R 6m 6M, R metal column floodlit.

RADIO TELEPHONE VHF Ch 16; 12 13, HX

TELEPHONE Hr Mr 97 96 18 33, Coastguard 97 92 22 22, Hospital (Thisted) 97 92 44 00 (Skagen) 99 79 79 79, Police (Emergency) 112, Taxi 97 96 17 11

FACILITIES AB, FW, D; **Services**: WC & showers, ME, Diver ☎ 97 96 27 00; **Town**: V, R, Rail at Thisted, Airport at Thisted ☎ 97 96 51 66

HIRTSHALS *9.25.14*

57°35'·95N 09°57'·62E

CHARTS AC 1402

TIDES +0600 Dover, ML 0·0, Duration 0625, Zone -0100

Standard Port ESBJERG (⟵)

Times				Height (metres)			
High Water		Low Water		MHWS	MHWN	MLWN	MLWS
0300	0700	0100	0800				
1500	1900	1300	2000				
Differences Hirtshals							
+0055	+0320	+0340	+0100	-1·5	-1·1	-0·3	0·0

SHELTER Like Hansholm, Hirtshals is essentially a commercial and fishing hbr and **foreign yachts may only enter with permission.** It is **not advisable to attempt entrance in strong onshore winds** from the N to NW due to heavy seas and currents. Shelter is good. Yachts berth in a small marina in the SW corner of the Forhavnsbassin.

NAVIGATION The PHM Fl.R 3s and SHM Fl(3)G 10s in posn 57°36'·4N 09°57'·5E which mark the entrance may be approached safely subject to weather (above). From thence, the fairway is buoyed and there are 166° ldg lts as follows: front Iso.R 2s 10m 11M, R north triangle on frame tr; rear Iso.R 4s 18m 11M, R south triangle on frame tr. The Outer Shelter Mole has a lt Fl.G 3s 14m 6M, G mast, Horn 15s; W Mole Fl.G 5s 9m 4M, G mast; E Mole Fl.R 5s 9m 6M, R mast. Turn to stbd before reaching the Inner Hbr lt F.G 6m 4M, G mast.

LIGHTS AND MARKS As above plus Hirtshals Lt Ho 57°35'·1N 09°56'·6E F Fl 30s 57m F18M Fl 25M, W round tr (Works in progress (T) 1996).

RADIO TELEPHONE VHF Ch 16; 14, HX

TELEPHONE (Dial code 00 45) Hr Mr 98 94 42 93, Coastguard 98 92 22 22, Hospital (Hjørring) 98 92 72 44, Police (Emergency) 112, Taxi 98 92 47 00

FACILITIES AB, FW; **Services**: WC, Showers, SM 98 94 12 27; **Town**: R, PO, Rail, Airport at Aalborg 98 17 33 11

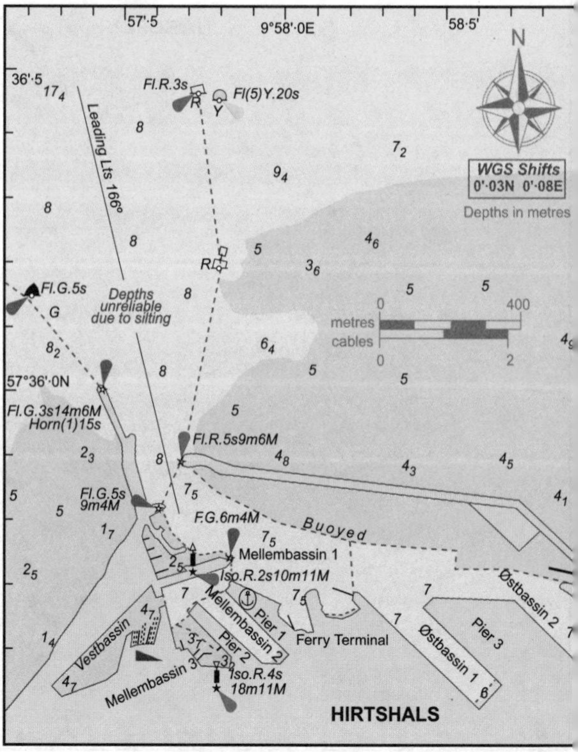

;KAGEN *9.25.15*

7°42'·90N 10°35'·70E ❀❀❀◊◊◊✿

HARTS AC 2114, 1402

DES As variations in heights are so small and largely generated y wind, no published figures are available. Purists may calculate mes and heights using harmonic constants (ref ATT Vol 2).

HELTER Shelter is good and there are no problems in entering any state of tide or weather. Yachts berth W of Gamle Pier.

AVIGATION The SWM Skagen No 1 buoy 57°47'·19N 10°46'·14E o 4s Racon (T) is the turning mark for large vessels leaving The attegat and so is best avoided. SW of this is NCM Q in posn 7°46'·0N 10°43'·8E which makes a good landfall and clear of anger. From this, steer 200° 2·2M to an ECM Q(3) in posn 7°43'·95N 10°42'·33E and thence steer 258° 3·6M to the hbr ntrance. There are ldg lts 334° front Iso.R 4s 13m 8M, mast, rear o.R 4s 22m 8M, metal frame tr and the entrance is marked W reakwater Fl.R 3s 8m 5M, R tower; E breakwater Fl.G 3s 8m 5M, tower, Horn (2) 30s. From the hbr entrance pass between two airs of F.G and F.R lights, then turn half to port for the yacht erths.

GHTS AND MARKS As above plus Skagen W 57°45'·0N)°35'·8E Fl(3)WR 10s 31m 17/12M, W round tr, W053°-248°, 248°-323°, note that the intersection of the R and W sectors asses through the SWM Skagen No 1 buoy; Skagen 57°44'·2N)°35'·8E Fl 4s 44m 23M, gy round tr, Racon (G).

ADIO TELEPHONE VHF Ch 16; 12 13, HX.

ELEPHONE (Dial code 00 45) Hr Mr 98 44 10 60/98 44 13 46/98 4 14 66, Coastguard 98 44 12 22, Hospital 99 79 79 79, Police :mergency) 112, Taxi 98 92 47 00.

ACILITIES AB, FW, AC, D; **Services**: WC, Showers, YC Skagen ejl Klub 98 45 06 79, ME, Sh, SM; **Town**: R, PO, Rail, Airport alborg 98 17 33 11.

AGENTS WANTED If you are interested in becoming our agent for any of the following ports, please write to: The Editor, The Book Barn, Westbourne, Hampshire, PO10 8RS, England – and get your free copy of the Almanac annually. You do not have to live in a port to be the agent, but should at least be a fairly regular visitor.

Keyhaven	Lerwick
Rothesay	Malahide
Le Légué (St Brieuc)	Bénodet
River Loire/St Nazaire	L'Herbaudière
St Gilles-Croix-de-Vie	Les Sables d'Olonne
La Rochelle	La Seudre
La Gironde	Port Bloc
Anglet	St Jean-de-Luz
Dives-sur-Mer	River Seine
Le Touquet/Étaples	Nieupoort
Oostend	Stellendam & Hellevoetsluis
Nordeney	Spiekeroog

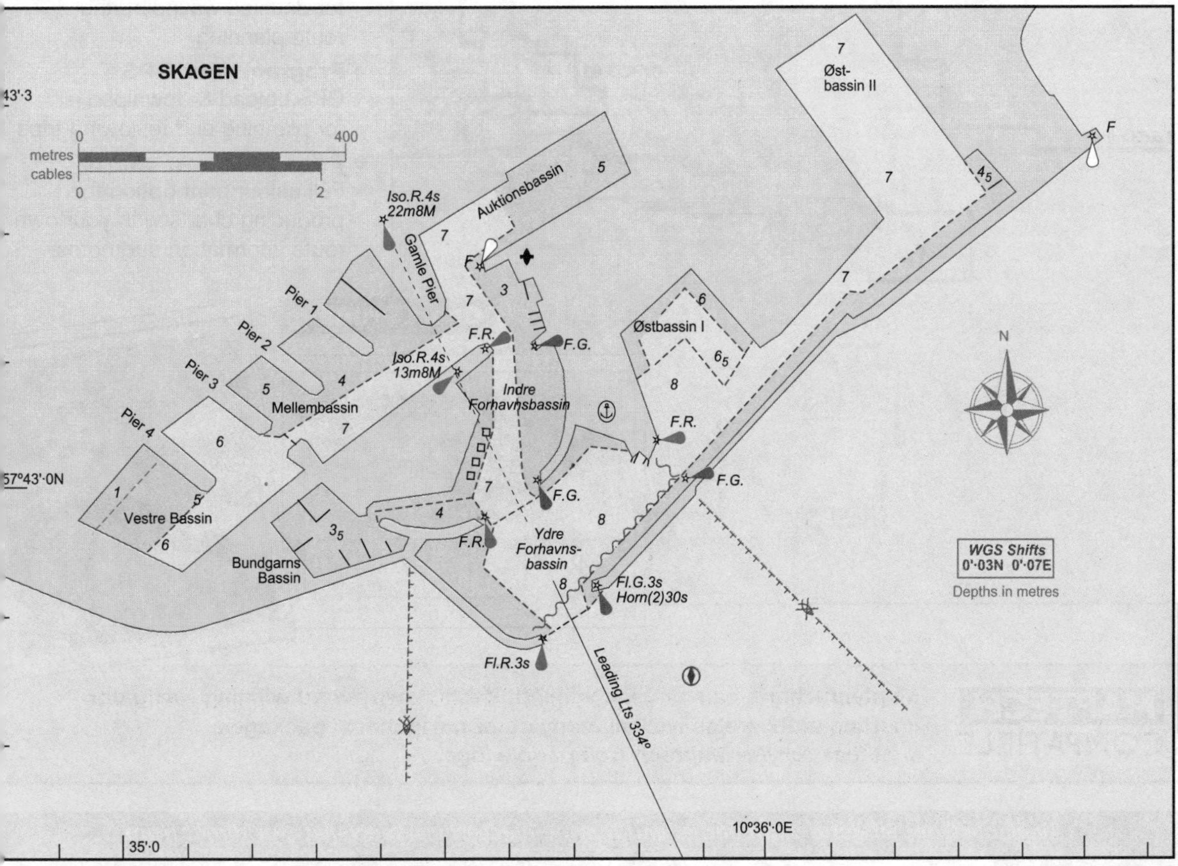

25

A

A'bhodaich 547
Abandon ship 117
Abbenfleth 1031
Abbreviations and symbols 3
Abdominal pain 144
Aberaeron 598, 606
Aberdaron 604
Aberdeen Tides 456-458
Aberdeen 455
Aberdour 446
Aberdovey 598, 606
Aberporth 606
Abersoch 604
Aberystwyth 598, 606
Acairseid Mhór 505
Achill Sound 677
Achillbeg I S Point 677
Adstow 601
Aguete 883
Ailsa Craig Lt 538
Airway, Breathing, Circulation (Resuscitation) 142
Albert Bridge 372
Aldeburgh 394
Alderney 708, 710, 712, 745
Alderney, anchorages around 713
Algeciras 910, 917
Allington Lock 366
Alloa 445
Alt, River 581
Altacarry Head Rathlin East 675
Alte Ems 1008
Alte Mellum 1017
Alte Weser Light House 1020
Alte Weser 1009
Altenbruch 1010
Althorne 381
Alum Bay 288
Amble 408, 430
Ameland 971, 973, 998
Amlwch 568, 588
Amrum 1012
Amrum-Hafen 1039
Amsterdam 970, 995
Andernos 858
Anglesey 568, 570
Anglet 837, 859
Anna Jacobapolder 968
Annalong Hbr 681
Annalong 674
Annan Waterfoot 571
Anse de Penfoul 813
Anse de Primel 785
Anstey's Cove 250
Anstruther Easter 451
Anstruther 451
Antifer 941
Antwerpen 968, 980
Anvil Pt Lt 260
Appledore 626
Aran Islands 698
Aran 676
Aranmore, Rinrawros Point 676
Arbroath 440, 453
Arcachon 857
Ardglass 674, 682
Ardgroom 664
Ardinamar 527
Ardnakinna Pt 636
Ardnamurchan Pt 502
Ardnamurchan Lt 501
Ardnave Point 541
Ardrishaig 536, 543
Ardrossan 538, 555
Area contents:
- Area 1 209
- Area 2 255
- Area 3 321
- Area 4 345
- Area 5 401
- Area 6 433
- Area 7 461
- Area 8 493
- Area 9 531
- Area 10 561
- Area 11 593
- Area 12 629
- Area 13 669
- Area 14 703
- Area 15 737
- Area 16 767
- Area 17 799
- Area 18 829
- Area 19 863
- Area 20 887
- Area 21 907
- Area 22 923
- Area 23 961
- Area 24 1003
- Area 25 1041

Areas, map of 192
Ares 879
Arinagour 501, 518
Arisaig 500, 517
Arklow Lanby 634
Arklow Roadstone Hbr 648
Arklow 634, 648
Armadale Bay 515
Ar-Men 804
Arnemuiden 986
Arngast 1009
Arnish Point 498
Arnside 574
Arrábida 899
Arradon 822
Arran 540
Arrifana 903
Arrival from a non-EU country 23
Arrival from an EU country 23
Arrochar 550
Arromanches 928, 936, 937
Ars-En-Ré 846
Arun, River 330
Arundel 330
Arzal 824
Ashlett Creek 267, 305
Ashore 8
Audenge 858
Audierne 804, 812
Auray 822
Auskerry 485
Auskerry Lt 467
Aust 618
Authority 117
Autolink RT 66
Aveiro 890
Aven River 805
Aveton Gifford 243
Avilés 867, 876, 877
Avoch 476
Avon, River (Bristol) 600
Avon, River (Devon) 243, 287
Avonmouth Tides 619-621
Avonmouth 600, 603
Axmouth 216, 253
Ayamonte 912
Ayr 538, 556

B

B.1D Plaform Dowsing 407
Babbacombe Bay 250
Backaland Bay 484
Badcall Bay 510
Baginbun Head 651
Baie de Bourgneuf 834,838
Baie de Douarnenez 777
Baie de Lampaul 788
Baie de Morlaix 776
Baie de Quiberon 810
Baily 634
Balbriggan 680, 681
Balcombe Creek 244
Baleeira 903
Balivanich 504
Balje 1010
Ballinskelligs Bay 664
Ballycastle 690
Ballycotton 635,657
Ballycrovane Harbour 664
Ballycrovane 636,664
Ballyholme Bay 684
Ballynakill 697
Ballysadare Bay 696
Ballywater 674
Balta Sound 469, 491, 492
Baltimore 636, 661
Baltrum 1009, 1017
Bamburgh Black Rocks Pt Lt 408
Banff 466, 472
Bangor 568, 675
Banjo Pier Hd Lt (Looe) 215
Bann, River 675, 692
Bantham 243
Bantry Bay 636, 663
Bantry 636
Barbate 910, 916
Bardsey I 568, 598
Bardsey Island 568, 570, 588
Barfleur 928, 934
Barmouth 598, 605
Barnstaple 626
Barometer and temperature conversion scales 85
Barometric pressure changes 85
Barometric pressure 156
Barra de Aveiro 895

Barra Hd ... 498, 504
Barra ... 499
Barra ... 504
Barrow Deep ... 352
Barrow ... 569
Barrow-in-Furness ... 566
Barry ... 599, 616
Bartlett Creek ... 366
Bassin d'Arcachon ... 837
Basta Voe ... 490
Bath ... 979
Battlesbridge ... 381
Baumrönne ... 1010
Bawden Rks ... 603
Bayona ... 868, 885
Bayonne ... 837
BBC general (land) forecasts ... 86
BBC Radio 4 Shipping forecast ... 86
Beachley ... 618
Beachy Head ... 326, 328
Beaucette ... 714
Beaufort scale ... 84
Beaulieu River ... 297
Beaulieu ... 261
Beaumaris ... 568, 585, 586
Bee Ness ... 366
Beer ... 253
Beidenfleth ... 1011, 1031
Belcroute Bay ... 724
Belfast Harbour ... 684
Belfast Lough ... 674, 684
Belfast Tides ... 686-688
Belgium:
- Coast radio stations ... 73
- Inland waterways ... 974
- Maritime Rescue Centres ... 974
- Passage Information ... 972
- Public Holidays ... 974
- Special notes ... 974
- Weather information ... 106

Belle Île ... 806, 819
Bélon River ... 805
Belvoir Bay ... 717
Bembridge ... 263, 310
Benodet ... 805, 810, 813
Bensersiel ... 1009, 1016
Berghaven ... 991
Berkeley ... 601, 618
Bermeo ... 866, 874
Berneray ... 498
Berwick-Upon-Tweed ... 408, 410, 432
Biarritz ... 837
Bideford ... 601, 626
Big Russe ... 708
Bilbao ... 866, 873
Bilbo. See Bilbao
Binic ... 744, 765
Bishop Rock Lt ... 214
Bishops ... 602
Black Ball Harbour ... 663
Black Deep ... 352
Black Head ... 677
Black Nore Point ... 600
Black Rock ... 677
Blackpool ... 566, 575
Blacksod Bay ... 677
Blacksod Quay ... 697
Blacktoft ... 418
Blackwater, River ... 385
Blakeney Bar ... 412
Blakeney ... 406, 412
Blankenberge ... 966, 977
Blasket Islands ... 639
Blauwe Slenk ... 971
Blavands Huk ... 1044
Blaye ... 837, 852
Blind Man's Cove ... 639
Bloody Foreland ... 678
Blue Mull Sound ... 491
Blue Mull ... 490
Blyth ... 429
Blyth E Pier Hd ... 408
Boddam ... 459
Bodic ... 772
Bognor Regis ... 330
Bonanza ... 913
Bonawe ... 525
Bonne Nuit Bay ... 724
Boontjes ... 970
Bordeaux Harbour ... 715
Bordeaux ... 837, 852, 853
Borkum Grosser ... 1008
Borkum Kleiner ... 1008
Borkum ... 1008, 1018
Borsfleth ... 1031
Borsfleth, Stör ... 1011
Borssele-Noordnol ... 967
Boscastle ... 627, 628
Bosham Channel ... 319
Bosham ... 319
Boston ... 407, 414
Boucau ... 837
Bouley Bay ... 724
Boulmer ... 430
Boulogne ... 930, 933
Boulogne-sur-Mer ... 954
Bound Skerry Lt ... 468
Bourgenay ... 844
Bournemouth ... 287
Bovbjerg ... 1044
Bovisand Pier ... 236
Bowling ... 551
Boyardville (La Pérrotine) ... 836
Boyne Bar, River ... 681
Bradwell ... 385
Brake ... 1026
Brandon Bay ... 636, 665
Braye ... 708, 712
Breakwater Hd Lt (Folkestone) ... 327
Brehon ... 708
Bremen ... 1010, 1026
Bremerhaven ... 1010, 1026
Brentford Dock Marina ... 375
Breskens ... 967, 978
Bressay ... 468
Bressay, Kirkabister Ness Lt ... 468
Brest Tides ... 794-796
Brest ... 775, 777, 792
Bridgwater ... 624
Bridlington ... 407, 421
Bridport ... 216, 254
Brightlingsea ... 386
Brighton ... 326, 335
Brigneau ... 805
Brignogan ... 786
Bristol Channel ... 599
Bristol Deep ... 60
Bristol ... 62
British Forces Broadcasting Service
- (BFBS) Gibraltar ... 10

Brixham ... 216, 25
Broad Haven Bay ... 67
Broadhaven ... 69
Broadstairs ... 32
Brodick Bay ... 54
Brodick ... 54
Brough Haven ... 42
Brough of Birsay ... 46
Brownsea Is ... 28
Bruckless Hbr ... 69
Bruichladdich ... 541
Bruinisse ... 968, 98
Brunsbüttel ... 1011, 103
Brunshausen ... 1031
Buchan Ness Lt ... 44
Buckie ... 466, 47
Buckler's Hard ... 261, 297
Bude ... 601, 627, 628
Bueu ... 88
Bull Point ... 601
Bull Rock ... 636
Bull Sand Fort ... 418
Bull's Mouth ... 697
Bunbeg ... 676
Buncrana ... 675
Bunessan ... 519
Bunowen Bay ... 698
Buoys and Beacons ... 7
Bur Wick ... 485
Burford Bank ... 638
Burgee ... 68
Burghead ... 466, 475
Burghsluis ... 969, 986
Burhou ... 713
Burnham Overy Staithe ... 413
Burnham ... 381
Burnham-on-Crouch Tides ... 382-384
Burnham-on-Crouch ... 352, 381
Burnham-on-Sea ... 601, 624
Burns, Scalds, Friction Burns ... 144
Burnt Islands ... 546
Burntisland ... 441
Burra Voe ... 491
Burray Ness ... 485
Burry Inlet ... 599, 614
Burton Stather ... 418
Burtonport ... 676, 695
Büsum ... 1011, 1038
Bute ... 540
Butt of Lewis ... 498

C

C. Ajo ... 866
C. Busto ... 867
C. Carvoeiro ... 890
C. Corrubedo ... 868
C. da Roca ... 891
C. de San Agustín ... 867
C. de Santa Catalina ... 866
C. de Santa Maria ... 891

de São Vicente ... 891
de Sines ... 891
de Torres ... 867
Espichel ... 891
Finisterre ... 868
Higuer ... 866
Lastres ... 866
Machichaco ... 866
Mayor ... 866
Mondego ... 890
Ortegal ... 867
Peñas ... 867
Prior ... 867
Prioriño Chico ... 867
Raso (Forte de São Brás) ... 891
Roche ... 910
Sardão ... 891
Silleiro ... 868
Spartel ... 910
Toriñana ... 868
Trafalgar ... 910
Vidio ... 867
Villano ... 868
Villano (Gorliz) ... 866
abo Carvoeiro ... 892
abo de Santa Maria ... 905
abo Finisterre ... 869
abo Higuer ... 837
abo Ortegal ... 869
abo Peñas ... 866
abourg ... 939
adgwith ... 227
adiz ... 909
ádiz, Bay of ... 914, 915
aen ... 929, 938
aernarfon ... 568, 585
aister-on-Sea ... 399
aladh Harbour ... 546
alais ... 931, 955
alculating intermediate times and heights of ... 152
alculations of clearances under bridges ... 154
alculations of times and heights of high and low ... 151
aldey Is ... 602
aledonian Canal ... 466, 477, 501, 521
alf of Man ... 567
alf Sound ... 583
alshot Spit ... 261
amaret ... 775, 797
amoël ... 824
ampbeltown Loch ... 537
ampbeltown ... 544
ampen ... 1008
ancale ... 756, 761
ancelling radio silence ... 119
andás Punta del Cuerno ... 867
angas ... 884
anna ... 500, 503, 517
antick Head Lt ... 467
anvey Is ... 371, 379
ap d'Alprech ... 930
ap d'Antifer ... 930, 932
ap de Carteret ... 742
ap de la Hague ... 742, 745
ap de la Hève ... 930
ap Ferret ... 837
Cap Fréhel ... 744
Cap Gris-Nez ... 931
Cap Lévi ... 742
Capbreton ... 837, 839, 859
Cape Cornwall ... 628
Cape Trafalgar ... 911
Cape Wrath ... 470, 498, 502
Cape Wrath Lt ... 467
Cardiff ... 599, 602, 616
Cardigan Bay ... 598
Cardigan ... 598, 607
Cardinal marks ... 33
Carentan ... 928, 935
Cargreen ... 236
Carlingford Lough ... 674, 681
Carloway ... 504
Carmarthen Bay ... 599
Carmarthen ... 613, 614
Carna ... 635
Carnlough Harbour ... 690, 675
Carnsore Point ... 651
Carradale Bay ... 544
Carrickmannanon Rk ... 678
Carrickarory ... 693
Carrickfergus ... 675, 684
Carrigaholt Bay ... 666
Carsaig Bay ... 519, 520, 542
Carteret ... 742, 754
Cascais ... 891, 896
Cashla Bay ... 677, 698
Casquets, The ... 708, 710
Castelo de Neiva ... 890
Castelo de Santiago SW Battery ... 890
Castillo de San Sebastián ... 909
Castillo de Santa Ana ... 866
Castle Haven ... 636, 660
Castlebay ... 499, 504, 505
Castlemartin Range ... 614
Castletown Bay ... 582
Castletown Bearhaven ... 636
Castletown ... 567, 663
Castletownshend ... 660
Castro Urdiales ... 866, 874
Cat Firth ... 490
Caudebec ... 942
Cayeux ... 949
Cayeux-sur-Mer ... 930
Cemaes Bay ... 588
Ceuta ... 910, 918
CH1 ... 742
Channel ... 216, 708
Channel Islands:
  Coast radio stations ... 70
  Radar Beacons ... 57
  Special notes ... 712
  Weather information ... 98
Chanonry Lt ... 466
Chapman's Pool ... 276
Charlestown ... 234
Chart datum ... 150
Charted depth ... 150
Chassiron ... 836
Chatham ... 366
Chauveau ... 835
Cheek Point ... 652
Chelsea Harbour ... 375
Chenal de la Helle ... 777, 789
Chenal de Rouen ... 929
Chenal du Four ... 774
Chenal Du Four ... 776, 789
Chepstow ... 616
Cherbourg Tides ... 750-752
Cherbourg ... 742, 745, 748
Chesil Beach ... 254
Chesil Cove ... 254
Chester ... 580
Chichester Channel ... 263, 319
Chichester Harbour entrance ... 319
Chichester Harbour ... 318
Chichester ... 263, 319
Chipiona Pta del Perro ... 909
Chipiona ... 913
Choice of burgee ... 69
Christchurch Bay ... 266
Christchurch ... 287
Church Ope Cove ... 276
Clacton-on-Sea ... 386
Clare Island ... 697
Cleanderry ... 664
Clear Island ... 661
Cleavel Point ... 280
Clevedon ... 624
Clew Bay ... 677, 697
Clifden Bay ... 677, 697
Clonakilty Bay ... 660
Clovelly ... 626
Clyde Area Waypoints ... 559
Clyth Ness Lt ... 467
Coast and cliff rescue services ... 129
Coast Radio stations – Hamburg/ Cuxhaven (SMD – S ... 111
Coast radio stations ... 65
Coastal reports (Marinecall Select) ... 90
Coastal station weather reports ... 92
Coastguard MSI navigation warning broadcasts ... 70
Coastguard co-ordination centres ... 131
Coastguard weather forecasts ... 97
Cobh Tides ... 654-656
Cobo Bay ... 715
Cockenzie ... 445
Codling Lanby ... 634
Colchester ... 386
Coleraine ... 675, 693
Colijnsplaat ... 968, 986
Coll ... 501
Colne, River ... 355, 386
Colonsay ... 536
Colwyn Bay ... 580
Combarro ... 883
Combrit ... 813
Common Injuries ... 143
Common medical conditions ... 143
Communications ... 120
Compass variation and deviation ... 32
Computation of tidal stream rates ... 156
Comte Jean Jetty ... 966
Concarneau ... 805, 815
Condition of Casualty – monitoring chart ... 147
Coningbeg ... 635
Connah's Quay ... 567, 580
Connel ... 525
Contentin Peninsula ... 745
Contents of shipping forecast ... 86
Contis ... 837
Control of MAYDAY traffic ... 118

Conversion tables 28
Conwy 568, 569, 584
Copinsay Lt 467
Coquet Lt 408
Coquet Island 410
Corblets Bay 713
Corcubion 881
Cordouan 836
Cork City 657
Cork Harbour 657
Cork 635
Corniguel 813
Corpach 501, 520
Corran Narrows 520
Corryvreckan 539
Corsewall Point Lt 538
Corta de los Jeronimos 913
Coryton 379
Cospas/Sarsat 121
Cotehele Quay 236
Courseulles-sur-Mer 929, 937
Courtesy ensign 69
Courtmacsherry 636, 659
Courtown 648, 648
Cove, The 225
Coverack 227
Covesea Skerries Lt 466
Cowes 262, 298
Craighouse 541
Craignure 519
Crail 446
Cramond 446
Cranfield Point 681
Craobh Haven 501
Craobh Marina 528
Craster 430
Créac'h 774
Creux 721
Criccieth 604
Crinan Canal 536, 542
Crinan 539
Cromarty Firth 466, 478
Cromarty 476
Cromer 412
Cromer Lt 406
Crookhaven 636, 662
CROSS and sous-Cross centres 135
CROSS MF broadcasts 102
CROSS stations 134
CROSS VHF broadcasts 102
Crossing the North Sea 966, 1008
Crouch, River 352
Crouesty en Arzon 808
Crouesty 808
Crouesty 811, 820
Crowlin Islands 500, 515
Crow Rk 602
CRS availability 66
CRS in NW and SE Ireland 72
CRS in SW Ireland 72
CS 1 326
CS 2 326
CS 3 326
Cuan Sound 527
Cudillero 877
Cullen 473
Cullercoats 425
Culmore Bay 693
Cultra 684
Cumberland Basin 622
Cushendall 690
Cushendun Bay 689
Customs regulations 22
Cuxhaven Tides 1028-1030
Cuxhaven 1010, 1027

D

Dagebüll 1012, 1039
Dahouet 764
Dale Roads 608
Dangast 1009, 1025
Darnett Ness 366
Darrynane 636, 664
Dartmouth Tides 245-247
Dartmouth 215, 248
De Piet 986
De Val 968
Deal 338
Deauville 929, 932, 940
Deben, River 393
Dee, River 566, 567
Deer Sound 484, 486
Definitions of emergency 117
Definitions 150
Delfzijl entrance (Netherlands) 1008
Delfzijl 973, 1001
Dell Quay 319
Den Helder 970, 972, 997
Den Hoorn 970
Den Oever 970, 995, 996
Denmark:
  Radar beacons 57
  Coastal radio stations 78
  Weather information 113
  Forecast areas 113
  MSI broadcasts 113
  Coastal nature reserves 1044
  Firing practice areas 1044
  Leading beacons 1044
Depth 33
Derby Haven 583
Derrible Bay 722
Derwent, River 572
Description 57
Devonport 236
DGPS Station locations 53
Diélette 742, 754
Dieppe Tides 950-952
Dieppe 930, 932, 948
Differential GPS beacons 52
Differential GPS 51
Digital Selective Calling 120
Dilution of precision 50
Dinan 762
Dinan, Pte de 777
Dinard 760
Dingle Bay 636, 639
Dingle 636, 665
Dingwall 476
Directing signals by aircraft 127
Direction 32
Distance for a given speed and time 36
Distance of horizon 3
Distance off by Vertical Sextant Angle 3
Distance 3
Distance Tables:
  Across English Channel 20
  Across Irish Sea 20
  Across North Sea 20
  Area 1 21
  Area 2 26
  Area 3 32
  Area 4 35
  Area 5 41
  Area 6 44
  Area 7 47
  Area 8 50
  Area 9 54
  Area 10 57
  Area 11 60
  Area 12 64
  Area 13 68
  Area 14 71
  Area 15 74
  Area 16 77
  Area 17 81
  Area 18 83
  Area 19 87
  Area 20 89
  Area 21 89
  Area 22 93
  Area 23 97
  Area 24 101
  Area 25 104
Distress alerting 12
Distress signals and emergencies 6
Distress signals 22, 117, 11
Distress 11
Distress, Urgency and Safety traffic
  by radiotelephone 6
Dittisham 24
Dives 92
Dives-sur-Mer 93
Dixcart Bay 72
Doca de Alcântara 89
Doca de Belém 89
Doca de Bom Successo 89
Doca de Santo Amaro 89
Doca do Terreiro Do Trigo 89
Doca dos Olivais 89
Dodman Pt 23
Doel 968, 97
Doëlan 80
Donaghadee 674, 684, 68
Donegal Bay 67
Donegal Harbour 69
Donges 80
Donostia. See San Sebastián
Doove Balg 97
Dornie Bridge 51
Dornoch Firth 466, 47
Dornumer-Accumersiel 1009, 101
Douarnenez 775, 79
Double lift: 12
Douglas Head 56
Douglas 567, 58
Douro, Rio 890, 89
Dover Strait TSS 18
Dover Strait 34
Dover Tides 340-34

Dover ... 327, 338
Drogheda ... 674
Drug smuggling ... 24
Drummore ... 571
Drying height ... 150
Dubh Artach Lt ... 501
Dublin Bar ... 643
Dublin Tides ... 645-647
Dublin ... 643
Duclair ... 942
Duddon Bar ... 573
Duke Gat ... 1008
Dumbarton ... 551
Dun Laoghaire ... 634, 643
Dunaff Hd ... 679
Dunany Point ... 681
Dunbar ... 444
Dunbeacon Harbour ... 662
Duncansby Head ... 479
Duncansby Head Lt ... 467
Dundalk ... 674, 681
Dundee ... 452
Dundrum Bay ... 674, 681
Düne ... 1010
Dungarvan Bay ... 657
Dungarvan Harbour ... 635, 653
Dungeness ... 328
Dungeness Lt ... 327
Dunkerque Port Est ... 931
Dunkerque Tides ... 958-960
Dunkerque ... 930, 933, 956
Dunkerron Harbour ... 664
Dunmanus Bay ... 662
Dunmanus Harbour ... 662
Dunmore East ... 635, 653
Dunnet Head Lt ... 467
Dunoon ... 537, 548
Dunstaffnage Bay ... 501, 525
Duration ... 150
Durdle Door ... 276
Durgan Bay ... 227
Durgerdam ... 996
Dury Voe ... 491
Dwarsgat ... 1010
Dyck Central ... 931
Dymchurch ... 337

E

E Goodwin Lt V ... 327
E Weddel Sound ... 484
Eagle I, W end ... 677
Eagle Island ... 676, 679
East Anglian Waypoints ... 357
East Channel ... 708
East Frisian Islands ... 1013, 1017
East Loch Roag ... 499
East Loch Tarbert ... 498, 504, 505, 536, 543
East Pier Head ... 635
East Usk ... 600
East Yell ... 469
Eastbourne ... 336
Eastern Solent Marks ... 262
Eastham ... 580
Eastney ... 314
EC 2 ... 708
Eckmühl ... 804
Edam ... 996
Eday ... 468
Eddystone Lt ... 215
Eemshaven (Netherlands) ... 1001, 1008
Eeragh, Rock Is ... 677
Egilsay ... 468
Egmond-aan-Zee ... 970
Eider, River ... 1011
Eidersperrwerk ... 1038
Eierland ... 971
Eierlandsche Gat ... 971, 973
Eigg Harbour ... 517
Eigg ... 500
Eilean Glas Lt ... 498
El Ferrol ... 879
Elanchove ... 866, 873
Elantxobe. *See* Elanchove
Elbe, River ... 1010, 1014, 1031
Elberry Cove ... 250
Elie ... 446
Elie Nes Lt ... 439
Ellewoutsdijk ... 967, 979
Elsfleth ... 1026
Emden ... 1008, 1016
Emergency VHF DF ... 130
Ems, River ... 1008, 1013
Emshörn ... 1016
Emsworth Channel ... 319
Emsworth ... 319
Endsburg ... 1011
Engine and machinery ... 8
England – East Coast ... 58
England – South Coast ... 58
England – West Coast ... 59
English and Welsh Grounds ... 624
English Channel Waypoints ... 220
Enkhuizen ... 997
Enseada de Albufeira ... 905
Enseada de Belixe ... 903
Ensenada de Santa Marta ... 879
Ensenada de Tetouan ... 918
Ensign ... 68
EPIRBs (Emergency Position Indicating Radio Beacon ... 122
Ericeira ... 895
Eriskay ... 499
Erme, River ... 243
Erquy ... 764
Esbjerg Tides ... 1049-1051
Esbjerg ... 1043, 1048
Esha Ness ... 469
Esposende (Forte da Barra do Río Cávado) ... 890
Esposende ... 890, 893
Esteiro ... 891
Estuaire de la Seine ... 932
Étaples ... 953
Étel, River ... 818
Etretat ... 947
Europa Pt Victoria Tr ... 910
European Ports VTS listening watch ... 167
Exe, River ... 252
Exeter ... 253
Exmouth Dock ... 253
Exmouth ... 216, 253
Eyemouth ... 443

F

F radio ... 65
Fair Head ... 678
Fair Isle ... 468, 491, 492
Fal, River ... 228
Falaise des Fonds ... 929
Falmouth Tides ... 230-232
Falmouth ... 214, 229
Fanad Head ... 675, 694
Fanø ... 1044, 1047
Fareham ... 314
Farne Islands ... 410, 431
Faro ... 891, 905
Faslane ... 550
Fastnet Rock TSS ... 182
Fastnet ... 636
Fawley ... 302
Fécamp ... 930, 947
Fenit Harbour ... 666
Fenit Pier ... 665
Fermain Bay ... 715
Fermanville ... 749
Ferryside ... 614
Fersness ... 484
Fiddler's Ferry ... 580
Fidra ... 444
Fidra Lt ... 438
Fife Ness Lt ... 440
Figueira da Foz ... 890, 894, 895
Filey Bay ... 421
Findhorn ... 466, 475
Findochty ... 473
Fire ... 116
First aid at sea ... 142
First aid equipment ... 146
Firth of Clyde ... 537, 540, 549
Firth of Forth ... 444
Firths Voe ... 469
Fischerbalje ... 1008
Fischeriehafen ... 1010
Fishbourne ... 319
Fishcombe Cove ... 250
Fisherman's Hotline ... 559
Fisherrow ... 446
Fishguard ... 598, 607
Flag etiquette ... 68
Flag Officer's flag ... 68
Flamborough Hd ... 407
Flannan Isles ... 509
Flannan I Lt ... 499
Flat Holm ... 599, 616
Flauwerspolder ... 969
Fleetwood ... 566, 575
Flushing ... 229
Föhr ... 1012, 1038
Folkestone ... 327, 338
Folly Inn ... 298
Folly Reach ... 299
Fontainevieille ... 858
Fontan ... 879
Fontenelle Bay ... 715
Ford ... 330
Forecaster direct (MetCALL Direct) ... 93
Forecasters ... 93

Foreland 310
Formby 580
Fort (Cromwell) Point 636
Fort Belan 585
Fort Blockhouse 314
Fort de l'Ouest 742
Fort de la Pointe 836
Fort William 501, 520
Forth and Clyde Canal 446
Fortrose 476
Foula 469, 491, 492
Fouras 836
Fowey 214, 234
Foynes 637
France:
  Affaires Maritimes 746
  Charts 746
  CROSS 134
  CROSS MSI broadcasts 137
  Facilities 746
  Forecast areas 104
  Inland waterways 747
  Meteo 746
  Public Holidays 746
  Radar beacons 60
  SafetyNET forecast areas Metarea II 105
  Storm signals 747
  Tidal signals 747
  Tourist Office 746
  Traffic signals 747
Fraserburgh 466, 472
Freiburg 1031
Fremington 626
French weather forecasts 103
Freshwater Bay 267, 287, 288
Frieburg 1011
Fromentine 834, 841

G

Gale warnings 85
Galley Head 636
Gallions Point Marina 373
Galway Bay 677, 698
Galway Harbour 699
Galway Tides 700-702
Galway 677
Gardenstown 472
Gareloch 537, 550
Garelochhead 550
Garlieston 566, 571
Garnish Bay 664
Garvan Islands 678
General yachting terms 9
German Bight 1010
Germany:
  Charts 1013
  Coastguard radio stations 139
  Coast radio stations
    (SMD – Schiffsmeldedi 75
  Maritime Rescue Centres 74
  MRCC Coastguard Radio Stations 74
  MSI broadcasts 107
  National Water Parks 1013
  Public Holidays 1013
  Special notes for 1013
  Radar beacons 61
  Special notes 1015
  Storm signals 1013
  Telephone Forecasts 112
  Tourist Office 1013
  TSS 189
  Traffic signals 1013
  Weather forecasts 111
  Weather information 138
Getaria. See Guetaria
Gibalta 891
Gibraltar Strait 911
Gibraltar Strait, Surface Flow 917
Gibraltar:
  Weather information 109
  Passage information 910
  Pilotage information 918
  Tides 919-921
Gigha Island 541
Gigha Sound 541
Gigha 539
Gijón 876
Gilkicker Pt 289
Gills Bay 483
Girdle Ness Lt 440
Girvan 538, 556
Gladstone Dock 580
Glandore 636, 660
Glasgow 548
Glassgorman Banks 638
Glasson Dock 566, 574
Glengariff 636, 663
Glengarrisdale Bay 541
Glin 666
Global Positioning System (GPS) 50
Glossary of foreign terms 8
Glückstadt 1011, 1031
Gluss Is Lt 469
GMDSS 122
Godrevy Is 603
Goeree 969
Goes 986
Goessche Sas (Goes) 968
Goleen 662
Golfe du Morbihan 821
Golspie 478
Gometra 520
Goole 418
Gorey 709
Gorey 724
Gorishoek 968
Gorleston 399
Gorran Haven 233
Gosport 314
Gott Bay 517, 518
Goulphar 807
Gourdon Harbour 440
Gourdon 454
Gourock 548
Goury 742, 754
GPS integrity monitoring 51
Graemsay Is Hoy Sound Low 467
Grand Léjon 744
Grandcamp-Maisy 928, 932, 936
Grande Havre 715
Grande Île 743
Grangemouth 439, 445
Granton 445
Granville 743, 756
Graphical method for interpolating
  time and height 152
Grassholm 602
Gravelines 931, 956
Gravesend 371
Great Blasket 639
Great Foze Rk 639
Great Skellig 639
Great Yarmouth 354, 356, 399, 406
Greatman Bay 698
Greencastle 693
Greenock Tides 552-554
Greenock 538, 548
Greenway Quay 248
Greenwich Lt Shp 326
Greetsiel 1008, 1016
Grève Au Lancon 724
Grève de la Ville 722
Grève de Lecq 724
Greystones 643
Gribbin Head 234, 218
Griminish 499
Grimsay 499
Grimsaey Is Hoy Sound Low Lt 467
Grimsby 418, 420
Grosnez Point 709
Großer Vogelsand 1031
Grosses Knechtsand 1017
Grunna Voe 490
Grutness Voe 490
Guadalquivir, Rio 909, 913
Guadiana, Rio 891, 892, 911
Guernsey 710
Guernsey, anchorages around 715
Guetaria 866, 872
Gunfacts 129
Gurnard Bay 267
GW/Ems 1008
Gweedore Hbr 695
Gwennap Head 218

H

Hale Hea 580
Hamble, River 261, 304
Hamburg 1011, 1031, 1032
Hamburger Yacht Hafen 1011
Hammersmith Bridge 372
Hamna Voe 490
Hamworthy 280
Handbook for Marine Radio
  Communication 64
Hannaine Bay 713
Hanstholm 1045, 1054
Hansweert 967, 979
Haringvliet 969
Haringvlietsluizen 987
Harlesiel 1009, 1016
Harlingen 970, 998
Harmonic Constants 155
Harrington 572
Harris, Sound of 498, 505

Hartland Point 601, 603
Hartlepool 408, 410, 423
Harwich 353, 356
Haseldorf 1031
Haskeir I Lt 499
Hastings 337
Haulbowline 674
Havelet Bay 708, 715
Havengore 380
Haverfordwest 608
Havre Gosselin 722
Hayle 601, 628
Hayling Island 319
Hazards 128
Health regulations 22
Height difference 152
Height of tide 150
Heights of lights, bridges, etc 150
Heist Mole Head 966
Helford River 227
Helgoland Tides 1035-1037
Helgoland 1010, 1034
Helicopter rescue 127
Heliushaven 969
Hellevoetsluis 969, 987
Helmsdale 467, 479
Helvick Hbr 638
Hendaye 837, 861
Hengistbury Hd 287
Herm Island 709, 710, 717
Herne Bay 362
Hestan Islet 571
Heugh, The 408
Heurteauville 942
Hever, River 1011
Heysham 566, 574
HF Radio facsimile broadcasts 93
High Lt Ho (River Tay) 440
Hilbre Island 580
Hi-line: 128
Hill Head 305
Hillhead 262
Hillswick 491
Hindeloopen 996
Hinkley Point 625
Hirtshals 1045, 1054
HM Coastguard MRCCs and MRSCs 124
HM Coastguard 94, 123
HM Customs 23
Hoedekenskerke 967, 979
Hoek van Holland Tides 988-990
Hoek van Holland 969, 991
Hohe Weg 1010
Holburn (Little) Head Lt 467
Holehaven 371
Holliwell Point 381
Holy Island 408, 410, 431
Holyhead Tides 589-591
Holyhead 568, 587
Hondarribia 861
Honfleur 929, 941
Hook Head 635
Hooksiel 1009, 1021
Hope Cove 243
Hopeman 474
Horizontal chart datum 51
Hörne 1031
Horn Head 679
Hörnum 1012, 1039
Horse Sand Fort 314
Horseshoe Harbour 661
Hourtin 837
House flag 69
Houton Bay 485
How to use SMS 91
Howth 634, 642
Hoy Sound 467
Huelva 909
Hugh Town 225
Hull 418, 420
Hullbridge 381
Humber Bridge 418
Humber, River 407, 409, 418
Hunda Sound 484
Hunstanton 413
Hurst Point 287
Hurst Point Ldg Lt 261
Husum 1011, 1038, 1039
Hvide Sande 1044, 1052
Hyperbolic systems 54
Hythe Firing Ranges 337
Hythe 262, 302

I

I Sálvora 868
I. de San Antón 866
I. de Tapia 867
I. Ons 868
I. Pancha 867
I. Sisargas 867
IALA Buoyage System (Region A) 33
Icart Bay 715
Igueldo 866
IJmuiden 969, 994
IJsselmeer 970, 995, 996, 997
Ile Berder 822
Île d'Aix 835, 849
Ile d'Arz 822
Île d'Oléron 835, 836, 838, 848
Île d'Yeu 834
Île de Batz 773, 776, 786
Ile de Boëdig 822
Île de Bréhat 772, 778
Ile de Conleau 822
Île de Groix 805
Île de Höedic 807, 819
Île de Houat 807, 819
Ile de la Jument 822
Île de Molène 774, 788
Île de Noirmoutier 834
Ile de Penfret 815
Île de Ré 835
Île de Sein 804, 812
Île des Hébihens 764
Île du Pilier 834
Île Dumet 808
Île Harbour 744
Île Houat 820
Ile Longue 822
Ile Pirenn 822
Île-aux-Moutons 805
Ile-de-Ré 845
Îles Chausey 743, 756
Îles de Glenan 805, 816
Iles Saint Marcouf 936, 928, 935
Ilfracombe 601, 626
Ilha da Berlenga 890
Immigration 24
Immingham Tides 415-417
Inchcolm 446
Inchkeith Lt 438
Industriegebiet 1011
Inishbofin Harbour 697
Inishbofin 677
Inisheer 677
Inishkeel 695
Inishmore 677
Inishowen 675
Inishraher 697
Inishtearaght 636, 675
Inishtrahull 675
Inishvickillane 639
Inland Waterways of Brittany 763
Inmarsat 66, 121
Inner Dowsing Light Tower 414
Inner Dowsing Lt 407
Inner Sound 500
Inshore route Ems to Jade 1008
Inshore waters forecast, BBC Radio 4 86
Instow 601
Insurance 22
International Certificate of Competence 23
International code 64
International Regulations for Preventing Collision 18
Internet (MetWEB) 94
Inter-ship: 65
Interval 150
Inveraray 543
Invergordon 466, 476
Inverie Bay 517
Inverkip 537, 548
Inverness Firth 466
Inverness 466, 476
Inward Rocks 618
Iona 519
Iona, Sound of 520
Ireland:
    Coastguard 129
    Coast Radio Stations 98
    Coast Rescue Service 704
    Kosan gas 640
    Marine Emergency Service 129
    Northern Ireland Coastguard 129
    Radar beacons 60
    Special Notes 640
Irvine 538, 556
Isigny 935
Isigny-sur-Mer 928
Isla Cristina 909, 912
Isla Ons 883
Islas Cíes 868
Islay 539
Islay, Sound of 536
Isle of Man 567, 569, 582
Isle of May 446
Isle of May Lt 440
Isle of Walney 566
Isle of Whithorn 566, 571
Isles of Scilly 224, 217

Isolated danger marks 33
Itchen, River 262
Itchenor Reach 319
Itchenor 319

J

Jade, River 1008, 1009, 1013
Jaonnet 715
Jard-sur-Mer 835
Jard-Sur-Mer 845
Jersey 709, 711
Jersey, anchorages around 724
Jethou 710
Johnshaven 454
Juist 1009, 1017
Jupiter Point 236
Jura, Sound of 539
Jurby 567

K

Kallin 505
Kames Bay 546
Kampen, Rote Kliff 1012
Kats 968, 986
Kells Bay 665
Kenmare River 636, 664
Kenmare 664
Kéréon (Men-Tensel) 774
Kerjean 772
Kermorvan 774
Kerners 822
Kernével 818
Ketelhaven 996
Kettletoft Pier 486
Kettletoft 484
Kew Bridge 372
Keyhaven 287
Kiel Canal 1011, 1033
Kiel-Holtenau 1011
Kiggaul Bay 677, 698
Kijkduin 970
Kilchattan Bay 546
Kildalloig Bay 544
Kilkeel 674, 681, 682
Kilkieran Bay 698
Kilkieran Cove 698
Killadysert 666
Killala Bay 696
Killala 676
Killantringan 538
Killard Point 682
Killary Harbour 697
Killeany Bay 698
Killough Harbour 682
Killybegs 676, 695
Killyleagh 682
Kilmakilloge 664
Kilmokea Point 652
Kilmore 635, 651
Kilrush 637, 667
Kincardine 445
King's Lynn 406, 413
Kingsbridge 243, 244
Kinlochbervie 510
Kinlochbervie Lt 498
Kinnaird Hd Lt 466
Kinsale 636, 659
Kippford 566, 571
Kirk Sound 484
Kirkcaldy 451
Kirkcudbright Bay 571
Kirkcudbright 566, 571
Kirkwall 468, 486
Kish Bank 634
Knock 1001, 1016
Knock 1008
Knude 1043
Kornwerderzand 970, 995
Kortgene 986
Krammer 968
Krammersluizen 968
Krückaumündung 1031
Kyle Akin 500
Kyle of Bute 537
Kyle of Durness 483
Kyle of Loch Alsh 500
Kyle of Tongue 484

L

L'Aber Benoît 774, 787
L'Aber-Ildut 774
L'Aberwrac'h 774, 787
L'Adour 837, 859
L'Aiguillon 835, 845
L'Ancresse Bay 715
L'Armandèche 835
L'Herbaudière 841
L'Iroise 777
L'ost Pic 746
La Charente 836
La Corbière 709
La Coruña 867, 880
La Cotinière 836
La Croix 772
La Faute-sur-Mer 835
La Flotte 845
La Forme de Radoub 837
La Garonne 837
La Gironde 836, 837, 839, 850
La Grande Grève 722
La Guia 868
La Higuera 909
La Jouvente 762
La Jument 774
La Lande 773
La Línea 910
La Palmyre 836
La Pierre-de-Herpin 743
La Pommeraie 762
La Rance 744
La Reuille 853
La Richardais 762
La Roche Bernard 824
La Rochelle 835, 847
La Rocque 724
La Seine 929
La Seudre 836, 850
La Tchue 713
La Teignouse 80
La Tranche-sur-Mer 835
La Trinité 819
La Trinité-sur-Mer 807, 820
La Turballe 808, 825
La Vigne 858
Labasheeda 666
L'Aberildut 788
Lagos 891
Lagos 903
Laig, Bay of 517
Lambay Island 634, 674, 678
Lamena 853
Lamlash 546
Lampaul 788
Lancaster 574
Land area forecasts – Visibility 86
Land area forecasts – Wind strength 86
Land's End 217, 603
Langeness 1012
Langeoog 1009
Langstone Harbour 317
Langstone 263
Lannion 784
Laredo 866
Largs 538, 547
Larne 675, 689
Lateral marks 33
Lauwersoog 971, 1000
Lavernock Pt 603
Laxey 567, 582
Le Bono 822
Le Chapus 848
Le Château d'Oléron 836
Le Chateau 849
Le Conquet 774, 791
Le Croisic 808, 811, 826
Le Crotoy 930, 953
Le Douhet 848
Le d'Yeu 838
Le Four 774, 776
Le Grand Jardin 743
Le Guilvinec 804, 812
Le Havre Tides 944-946
Le Havre 929, 930, 932, 943
Le Hourdel 953
Le Légué 744, 764
Le Logeo 822
Le Marquis 853
Le Minihic 762
Le Palais 807, 819
Le Passage 822
Le Pointeau 809
Le Port d'Ile aux Moines 822
Le Pouldu 806
Le Pouliguen 809, 826, 827
Le Rocher 822
Le Stiff 774
Le Touquet 930, 953
Le Tréport 930, 949
Le Trieux River 772
Le-aux-Moines 773
Leça 890
Leeds & Liverpool Canal 580

Lee-on-the-Solent 314
Léguer River 784
Leigh-on-Sea 379
Leith Tides 448-450
Leixões 890, 894
Lekeitio. See Lequeitio
Lelystad 996
Lemmer 996
Lemvig 1045
Lequeitio 866, 872
Lerwick Tides 487-489
Lerwick 468, 491
Les Baleines 835
Les de Glénan 815
Les Ecrehou 724
Les Fontaines 722
Les Héaux de Bréhat 772
Les Sables d'Olonne 835, 844
Les Sept Iles 773, 776, 784
Lesconil 804, 812
Leverburgh 498
Lézardrieux 772, 779
Libenter 774
Libourne 853
Life Threatening Conditions 143
Lifeboats 136
Light characteristics 34
Light sectors, arcs of visibility 34
Lights – rising or dipping distance 36
Lights and shapes 20
Lihou Island 715
Lild Strand 1045
Lillo 968, 979
Limeburner Rk 679
Limehouse Basin 374
Limerick Dock 637
Link calls 66
Linklet 484
Linnenplate 1038
Lisboa Tides 900-902
Lisboa 890, 891, 896
Liscannor Bay 639, 679
Liscannor 698
Lismore Lt 501
List 1039
Little Bernera 504
Little Foz Rk 639
Little Haven 607
Little Killary Bay 697
Little Russel Channel 714
Little Samphire I 636
Little Skellig 639
Littlehampton 326, 330
Liverpool Tides 577-579
Liverpool 567, 580
Lizard Point 218
Lizard Lt 214
Llanddwyn Island 585
Llandudno 568, 580
Llanelli 614
Llanes, Pta de San Antón 866
Llangwm 608
Loch A'bhraige 500, 515
Loch Aline 501, 519
Loch Alsh 516
Loch Beag 528
Loch Bervie 510
Loch Boisdale 499, 504, 505
Loch Carnan 499, 504, 505
Loch Carron 500, 516
Loch Craignish 501, 528
Loch Creran 520
Loch Dunvegan 500, 515
Loch Eatharna 517
Loch Eil 520
Loch Eport 505
Loch Eriboll 483, 484
Loch Erisort 498
Loch Etive 525
Loch Ewe 498, 511
Loch Eynort 505
Loch Feochan 527
Loch Fyne 540, 543
Loch Gairloch 498
Loch Gairloch 511
Loch Goil 537
Loch Harport 500, 515
Loch Hourn 515, 517
Loch Indaal 536
Loch Inver 498, 510
Loch Lathaich 501, 520
Loch Laxford 510
Loch Leven 520
Loch Linnhe 501, 520
Loch Long 537
Loch Maddy 499, 504, 505
Loch Melfort 501, 527
Loch Moidart 517
Loch Na Keal 520
Loch Nedd 510
Loch Nevis 517
Loch Ranza 546
Loch Riddon 546
Loch Rodel 505
Loch Ryan 556, 557
Loch Shell 498, 504, 505
Loch Skipport 504, 505
Loch Sligachan 500
Loch Snizort 515
Loch Spelve 520
Loch Sunart 501, 518
Loch Sween 541
Loch Tarbert 541
Loch Torridon 502, 515
Lochgoilhead 550
Lochrist 774
Locmaria 816
Locmariaquer 822
Locquemeau 784
Locquirec 784
Loctudy 804, 813
Loire, River 809, 811, 828
London Bridge Tides 376-378
London Bridge 355
London Bridge, time differences on 372
Londonderry 693
Long Hope 484
Longships 214
Longstone Lt 408
Longy Bay 713
Looe 215, 235
Loop Head 636, 637
Loran-C 55
Lorentz-Sluizen 970
Lorient 806, 810, 817
Lossiemouth 466, 474
Lostwithiel 234
Loth 484, 486
Lough Foyle 675, 693
Lough Swilly 675, 694
Lowestoft Tides 396-398
Lowestoft 395
Lowestoft Lt 354
Luanco 876
Luarca 867, 877
Lucifer Banks 638
Ludaig 499
Ludijkse Gat 985
Lühe 1031
Lulworth Cove 268, 276
Lulworth Firing Ranges 275
Lundy Island 601, 626, 627
Lune, River 566
Lutjehorn 1017
Lybster 467, 479
Lydd Firing Ranges 337
Lydd 337
Lyme Bay 219
Lyme Regis 216, 254
Lymington 261, 295
Lyness 484
Lyngvig (Holmlands Klit) 1044
Lynher, River 238
Lynmouth Foreland 601
Lynmouth 601, 625
Lynn of Lorn 501, 520

M

Maas Centre 969
Maasmond 969
Maassluis 991, 992
Maasvlakte 969
Macduff 466, 472
Machrihanish 541
Making a call 66
Makkum 996
Malahide 634, 638, 641
Maldon 385
Mallaig 500, 517
Malin Beg Head 679
Malpas 229
Mama Sul 891
Man overboard 116
Manchester Ship Canal 580
Map of UK shipping forecast areas 82
Marans 835, 845
Marazion 226
Marchwood 302
Margate 350, 362
Marin 883
Marinecall 89
Marino Point 657
Maritime Safety Information (MSI) 122
Marken 996
Marsdiep 970
Martin's Haven 607
Maryport 566, 572
Maseline 721
Maughold Head Lt 567
MAYDAY acknowledgement 118

MAYDAY calls 118
Maylandsea 385
Mazagón 909, 913
Mcdermott Base 476
Mean High Water and Low Water
Springs/Neaps 150
Mean Level 150
Meavie Pt 470
Medemblik 997
Medical help by RT 121
Medicines 146
Medina, River 298
Mediterranean, Routes to 942
Medway 351
Medway, River 365
Meikle Ferry 478
Mellumplate 1009
Memmert 1017, 1018
Menai Bridge 585, 586
Menai Strait 568, 569, 585
Merrien 805
Mersey, River 566, 567
Meschers-Sur-Gironde 852
Message categories 89
Meteorological conditions 156
MetFAX area planners 91
MetFAX planning forecast areas 90
Methil 451
Mevagissey 214, 233
Mew I 674
MF calls to Coast Radio Stations 66
MF radio 65
Mid Channel 58
Mid Yell Voe 490
Middelburg 986
Middelharnis 969, 987
Middlesbrough 422, 423
Milfontes 903
Milford Haven Tides 610-612
Milford Haven 598, 602, 608
Millport 547
Mine Head 635
Minehead 601, 625
Miño, Rio 869, 892
Minsener Oog 1017
Minsmere 394
Miscellaneous 119
Misery Pt 243
Mizen Head 636
Mizen Head 638
Mobile telephones 119
Mochras Lagoon 598
Mochras 604
Moclett 484
Moelfre 588
Moguériec 785
Molengat 970
Monach Islands 509
Monnickendam 996
Monte Dirección (Le Charf) 910
Monte Faro 868
Montedor 890
Montrose 440, 453
Moray Firth 470
Morbihan 807
Mordreuc 762
Morecambe 566, 574
Morgat 775
Morgat 797
Morlaix 773, 785
Mortagne 852
Mostyn Quay 580
Mostyn 567
Motrico 866, 872
Mousehole 214
Mouth 445
Moville 693
Muck 517
Muckle Flugga Lt 469
Muckle Skerry 485
Mudeford 287
Mugia 868
Mühlenberg 1011, 1032
Muiden 996
Muiderzand 996
Mull of Galloway 540
Mull of Galloway Lt 538
Mull of Kintyre 536, 539
Mull, Sound of 501, 519
Mullaghdoo 676
Mullaghmore 696
Mullion Cove 227
Mulroy Bay 676, 694, 695
Mumbles Head 602
Mumbles 599, 615
Munkmarsch 1039
Mupe Bay 268
Mylor 229

N

N Bank 634
N Bull 634
N Ronaldsay 468
Naarden 996
Nab Tower 263
Nairn 466, 476
Nantes 809
Narlwood Rocks 618
Nash 599
National Coastwatch Institution (NCI) 126
National ensign 22
Naval Radio weather broadcasts 108
Navareas 67
Navas Creek 227
Navigation tables 36
Navigation warnings 67, 136
Navigation 10
Navigation 116
Navigational displays 54
Navtex areas – UK and NW Europe 89
Navtex 67, 88
Nazaré 890, 895
Neath, River 599, 615
Nebel 1012
Needles Channel 261, 288
Needles Fairway 261
Needles Lt 261
Neeltje Jans 986
Neist Point Lt 500
Nes 971, 998
Ness, The 466
Nessmersiel 1009, 1016
Netherlands:
Coastguard (IJmuiden) 110
Coastguard (IJmuiden) radio stations . 74
Coastguard information 138
Coastguard radio stations 139
Maritime Rescue Coordination 120
MSI broadcasts 110
Inland waterways 974
Passage Info 972
Public Holidays 974
Radar beacons 61
Special notes 974
Storm signals 974
Tourist Office 974
Traffic signals 974
TSS 188
Weather information 110
Netley 302
Neuenschleuse 1032
Neuharlingersiel 1009, 1016, 1019
Neuwerk 1010, 1017
New Grimsby 225
New Hythe 366
New Quay 598, 606
New Ross 652
Newarp 406
Newbiggin 429
Newburgh 452
Newcastle 682
Newcastle-upon-Tyne 425
Newhaven 326, 336
Newlyn 214, 226
Newport (IOW) 298, 299,
Newport (Wales) 600, 616, 617
Newport Deep 600
Newquay 601, 628
Newry River 674
Newry 681
Newton Haven 430
Newtown River 296
Neyland 608
Nieblum 1012
Nieuwendijk 969
Nieuwpoort 966, 976
Noirmoutier-en-L'île 841
Noordwijk-aan-Zee 969
Noordzee Kanaal 970
Norddeich Hafen 1018
Norddeich 1009, 1016
Norddorf 1012
Nordenham 1010, 1026
Norderney 1009, 1017, 1018
Nord-Ostsee Kanal 1011, 1033
Nordstrand 1012
Nørre Voruper 1045
North Bay 505
North Berwick 446
North Channel TSS 183
North Channel 262
North Edinburgh Channel 350
North Fambridge 381
North Foreland 328, 355
North Foreland Lt 327
North Harbour 661
North Light 674
North Rona Lt 467
North Ronaldsay 468
North Shields 425
North Spain 60
North Sunderland 431

orth Uist 500
orthern Ireland 60
orthfleet Lower Lt (Gravesend) 351
orthfleet Upper Lt (Gravesend) 351
orthney 319
oss Head Lt 467
otice of departure 23
otification of errors 2
oup Head Lt 468
P 159 Harmonic Method 155
umbering system 1
W European Loran-C chains (NELS) 55

O

ban Tides 522-524
ban 501, 525
btaining Subfacts and Gunfacts 559
det, River 813
ff Cape Roca TSS 190
ff Cape St Vincent TSS 190
ff Casquets TSS 185
ff Finisterre TSS 190
ff Ilha da Berlenga TSS 190
Off Skerries Tss 183
Off Smalls Tss 182
Officialdom 11
Òigh Sgeir 500
Oil and Gas Installations 411
Oland 1012
Old Grimsby 225
Old Head of Kinsale 635, 636, 638
Olhão 891
Olhão 905
Olna Firth 490
Omonville-la-Rogue 742, 753
Ondárroa 866, 872
Önning 1038
Oostende 966, 977
Oosterschelde 968, 985
Oostmahorn 971, 1000
Ore, River 354, 393
Orford Ness 356, 394
Orford Ness Lt 354
Organisation 123
Orkney Islands 467, 484
Ormond's Hbr 664
Ornsay Lt 500
Orsay Island 541
Ortac Rock 710
Ortpatrick 538
Orwell, River 392
Os Farilhões 890
Osea Island 385
Oskbøl Firing Range 1044
Other maritime radio services 68
Otterndorf 1010, 1027
Oude Roompot 968
Oudeschild 970, 998
Ouessant SW Lanby 774
Ouessant 776, 788
Ouistreham 929, 938
Our supplements 2
Ourock 537
Out Skerries 490
Outer Approaches 968
Outer Hebrides 499
Owers 328
Owey Sound 676
Oyster Haven 636, 659

P

Paal 968, 979
Paco de Arcos 896
Padstow 628
Pagham 330
Paignton 216, 250
Paimbœuf 809
Paimpol 772, 776, 778
Pan-Pan – Urgency signal 121
Papa Sound 468
Par 234
Pasajes 866, 871
Passage de la Déroute 743
Passage Information:
- Area 1 217
- Area 2 266
- Area 3 328
- Area 4 355
- Area 5 409
- Area 6 441
- Area 7 470
- Area 8 502
- Area 9 539
- Area 10 569
- Area 11 602
- Area 12 638
- Area 13 678
- Area 14 710
- Area 15 745
- Area 16 776
- Area 17 810
- Area 18 838
- Area 19 869
- Area 20 893
- Area 21 911
- Area 22 932
- Area 23 972
- Area 24 1013
- Area 25 1046

Passage planning check list 36
Passage planning 36
Pauillac 837, 852, 853
Paying for a link call 66
Peel 567, 582
Pegal 484
Pellworm 1012, 1038
Pen Mané 818
Penarth 599, 616
Pendeen 601
Penedo da Saudade 890
Pénerf 808, 824
Penfret 805
Peniche 890, 895
Peninnis Hd Lt 214
Penlan 808
Pennan Bay 472
Penryn 229
Pentland Firth 470
Pentland Skerries Lt 467
Penzance 214, 226
Perelle Bay 715
Perranporth 628
Perros-Guirec 772, 782
Person 64
Personal documents 22
Personal safety 116
Perth 452
Pertuis Breton 835, 838
Pertuis d'Antioche 835, 838
Peterhead 440, 459
Petit Bôt Bay 715
Petit Port 715
Petite Foule 834
Picacho 909
Piedras, Rio de las 912
Pierowall 468, 485, 486
Pierres Noires 775
Pile Light 674
PillarRk Pt Lt 538
Pinnaumündung 1031
Pinnau-Neuendeich 1031
Piriac 825
Pittenweem 439, 446
Pladda Lt 538
Plateau de Rochebonne 835
Plateau des Minquiers 709, 724
Platte Fougère 708
Platte Saline Bay 713
Platte 708
Plemont 724
Plockton 515, 516
Ploumanac'h 773, 776, 782
Plymouth Tides 239-241
Plymouth 215, 236
Point de Grave Tides 856
Point Lynas 568
Point of Ayre 567
Point Robert 709
Pointe d'Ailly 930
Pointe de Barfleur 742, 932
Pointe de Gatseau 848
Pointe de Graves Tides 854-856
Pointe de Haut-Blanc (Berck-Plage) 930
Pointe de Kerdonis 807
Pointe de Morgat 775
Pointe de Penmarc'h 804
Pointe des Chats 806
Pointe du Millier 775
Pointe du Roc 743
Pointe du Toulinguet 775
Pointe Saint-Martin 837
Pollendam 971
Polperro 215, 235
Ponta do Altar 904
Pontevedra 883
Pontrieux 772, 780
Pontusval 773, 785
Poolbeg 634
Poole Bar (No. 1) 260
Poole Harbour Entrance 280
Poole Harbour Tides 284-286
Poole Harbour 280
Poole 260
Poplar Dock Marina 373
Porlock Bay 625
Porlock Weir 601
Pornic 834, 840
Pornichet 827

Pors Poulham 804
Port á la Jument 722
Port Askaig 541
Port Blanc 781,822
Port Bloc 837, 853
Port Cardigan 607
Port Clos 778
Port Crannaich 544
Port d'Ars-en-Ré 835
Port de Comberge 809, 828
Port de Dahouet 744
Port de la Corderie 778
Port de la Gravette 809, 828
Port de la Meule 842
Port de Lévi 742, 749
Port de Pornichet 809
Port des Minimes 847
Port d'Etel 818
Port Dinorwic 568, 585
Port du Becquet 749
Port du Douhet 836
Port du Havre-Antifer 930
Port du Parun 822
Port du Plomb 835
Port Edgar 439
Port Ellen 536, 541
Port Erin 567, 582, 583
Port És Saies 722
Port Glasgow 551
Port Gorey 722
Port Guillaume 939
Port Haliguen 807, 819
Port Isaac 628
Port Joinville 834, 842
Port Louis 806, 818
Port Manech 805
Port Maria 807, 819
Port Navalo 808, 820, 822
Port of Dublin 634
Port Operations: 65
Port Racine 753
Port St Mary 567, 583
Port Talbot 599, 615
Port Traffic signals 67
Port Tudy 806, 816
Port William 571
Portavogie 674, 682, 685
Portbail 742, 755
Port-Béni 781
Portcé 809
Portchester Lake 314
Portchester 316
Portelet Bay 724
Portelet Harbour 708, 715
Portelet 715
Port-en-Bessin 928, 932, 936
Porth Conger 225
Porth Cressa 225
Porth Dinlläen 568, 588
Porth Mellin 227
Porth Trecastell 588
Porth Ysgaden 588
Porthcawl 599, 615
Porthgain 607
Porthleven 214, 227
Porthmadog 598, 605
Portimão 891, 904
Portishead Point 600
Portishead 600, 624
Portknockie 473
Port-la-Forêt 805, 814
Portland Bill Lt 260
Portland Harbour 260, 268
Portland Race 266
Portland Tides 269-271
Portland 266
Portmagee 636, 665
Portmahomack 478
Portmellon 233
Portmore 693
Portnafrankagh 697
Porto Novo 883
Pōrto 890, 894
Porto, Rio 894
Portpatrick 557
Portreath 628
Portree 500, 515
Portrush 675, 692
Portsall 787
Portscatho 233
Portsmouth Harbour 263
Portsmouth hourly height predictions 158
Portsmouth Tides 311-313
Portsmouth 263, 314
Portsoy 466, 472
Portugal:
  Coast radio stations 76
  Coastguard radio stations 141
  CRS MSI broadcasts 108
  Forecast areas 105, 108
  Glossary 14
  MRCC/MRSC 140
  Public Holidays 892
  Radar beacons 60
  Special notes 892
  Weather information 108
Position 30
Pottery Pier 280
Pouldohan 805
Póvoa de Varzim 890, 893
Predicted heights 150
Press forecasts 94
Preston 576
Primel 773, 785
Princes Channel 350
Prowords 65
Pt of Fethaland 469
Pta Almina 910
Pta Atalaya (Cabo de S. Ciprian) 867
Pta Candelaria 867
Pta Carnero 910
Pta da Piedade 891
Pta de Alfanzina 891
Pta de la Estaca de Bares 867
Pta de la Frouxeira 867
Pta Galea 866
Pta Insúa 868
Pta Lage 867
Pta Malabata 910
Pta Rebollera 867
Pta Roncadoira 867
Pta San Emeterio 866
Pta Torco de Afuera 866
Pte de Barfleur 742
Pte de Barfleur-Gatteville 928
Pte de Grosse Terre 834
Pte de la Coubre 8
Pte de Port-Navalo 8
Pte de Porz-Don 7
Pte de St Mathieu 7
Pte des Corbeaux 8
Pte des Dames 8
Pte des Poulains 8
Pte du Grouin-du-Cou 8
Pte du Portzic 7
Public correspondence: ....
Puerto America 914, 9
Puerto Cádiz 9
Puerto de S. Estaban 8
Puerto de Santa Maria 909, 914, 9
Puerto Sherry 909, 914, 9
Puilladobhrain 5
Punta Carnero 9
Punta Nariga 8
Punta Umbria 9
Pwllheli 598, 6

Q

Quai Joannes Couvert 9
Quai Roger Meunier 9
Queenborough 3
Quiberon 807, 8
Quimper 8
Quoile Barrier 6

R

Raasay, Sound of 5
Racons – Europe ....
Racons (Radar Beacons) ....
Radar as a navigation aid ....
Radar beacon listing ....
Radar for collision avoidance ....
Radar in yachts ....
Radar ....
Rade de Brest 7
Rade de la Capelle 9
Radio broadcasting ....
Radio broadcasts – Danmarks Radio 1
Radio communications ....
Radio Gibraltar 1
Radio Licences ....
Radio Telephony (R/T) ....
Radio time signals ....
Radio weather information ....
Raising the alarm 1
Rajó 8
Ramsey Sound 602, 6
Ramsey 568, 5
Ramsgate 327, 3
Rance, River 7
Range 1
Rantum 10
Rapness 4
Rathlin Island 675, 6
Rathlin O'Birne 6
Rathlin O'Birne, W side 6
Rathlin W 6

Rathmullan ... 675, 694
Rattray Hd Lt ... 440
Rattray Head ... 466
Ravenglass ... 566, 573
Raz de Sein ... 804, 810
Recommended Safety equipment for sea-going yachts ... 116
Record of amendments ... 2
Recorded forecasts by telephone ... 101
Red Bay ... 675, 690
Redbridge ... 302
Redkirk ... 571
Registration and false alerts ... 124
Registration ... 22
Regnéville-sur-Mer ... 756
Regufe ... 890
Relaxing radio silence ... 120
Renfrew ... 551
Reports of present weather ... 95
Restricted visibility ... 20
Restronguet ... 229
Rhinns of Islay ... 536
Rhoose Pt ... 603
Rhu Narrows ... 537
Rhu ... 550
Rhubh' a Mháil (Ruvaal) ... 536
Rhum ... 500, 517
Rhyl ... 568
Ria de Aldán ... 883
Ría de Arosa ... 868, 882
Ría de Camariñas ... 868, 880
Ría de Cedeira ... 867, 879
Ría de Corme ... 880
Ría de El Ferrol ... 867
Ría de Huelva ... 912
Ría de La Higuerita ... 909
Ría de Muros ... 868, 881
Ría de Pontevedra ... 868, 883
Ría de Ribadeo ... 867, 878
Ria de Santoña ... 874, 875
Ría de Suances ... 875
Ría de Tina Mayor ... 875
Ría de Vigo ... 868, 884
Ría de Vivero ... 867, 878
Ría del Barquero ... 867, 879
Ribadesella ... 876
Ribble, River ... 567, 576
Richard ... 853
Richborough ... 344
Richmond Lock ... 372
Ringaskiddy ... 657
Ringstead Bay ... 276
Rinmeasa Point ... 679
Rinnafaghla Point ... 679
Rise/Fall of tide ... 150
Rising and Setting ... 44
Rising, Setting and Twilights ... 44
Rivière d'Étel ... 806
Rivière de Crac'h ... 807
Roach, River ... 352, 380
Roancarrigmore ... 636
Roaring Water Bay ... 661
Roberts Cove ... 657
Roche's Point ... 635
Rochebonne ... 743
Rochefort ... 836, 849
Roches Douvres ... 772
Rochester ... 366
Rochford ... 380
Rockabill ... 674
Rockall ... 509
Rømø Havn ... 1043, 1047
Rompido de Cartaya ... 909
Rona ... 483, 500
Roompot Buiten ... 985
Roompot ... 986
Rosbeg Bank ... 638
Roscoff ... 773, 786
Rosehearty ... 472
Rosière Steps ... 717
Rosneath ... 550
Rosslare Harbour ... 650
Rosslare ... 634
Rota ... 909, 914, 915
Rotheneuf ... 761
Rother, River ... 337
Rothesay ... 537, 547
Rotten I ... 676
Rotterdam ... 969, 992
Rouen ... 929, 942
Rouge Terrier ... 722
Round I ... 214
Roundstone Bay ... 698
Roustel ... 708
Route du Gois Causeway ... 834
Royal National Lifeboat Institution (RNLI) 123
Royal Sovereign ... 326
Royan ... 836, 852
Rozel Bay ... 724
RT procedures ... 64
Rubha A'mhàil ... 541
Rubha nan Gall ... 501
Rubha Reidh Lt ... 498
Rue Pt ... 678
Rule 10 ... 181
Runswick Bay ... 422
Rüschkanal ... 1011, 1032
Rüstersiel ... 1021
Ruthenstrom ... 1031
Rutland North Channel ... 676
Ryde ... 262, 309
Rye ... 326, 337

S

S Gare Bkwtr Hd Lt (River Tees) ... 408
S Goodwin Lt V ... 327
Sado, Rio ... 891
Safe water marks ... 34
Safety equipment – legal requirements ... 116
Safety equipment ... 116
Safety ... 67, 117
Safety/Distress ... 11
Sagres ... 891
Saignie Bay ... 722
Saint Aubin ... 709
Saint Bees Hd ... 566
Saint Brieuc ... 744
Saint Cast ... 764
Saint Gildas ... 809
Saint Guénolé ... 804
Saint Valéry-en-Caux ... 930
Saint-Gildas ... 828
Saint-Nazaire ... 809
Saint-Quay-Portrieux ... 744
Saints Bay ... 715
Salcombe ... 215, 244
Salen ... 518, 519
Saltash ... 236
Salutes ... 69
San Antoña ... 866
San Estaban de Pravia ... 876
San Sebastián ... 866, 871
San Vicente de la Barquera ... 866, 875, 876
Sancti Petri ... 910, 916
Sanda Sound ... 539
Sanday Island ... 468
Sandend Bay ... 472
Sandettie Bank ... 956
Sandettié ... 931
Sandown ... 310
Sandpoint ... 551
Sandwich ... 344
Sandy Bay ... 918
Sangatte ... 931
Sangenjo ... 883
Santa Marta de Ortigueir ... 878
Santander ... 866, 875
São Martinho do Porto ... 890
SAR resources ... 129
Sark ... 709, 710, 721
Sark, anchorages around ... 722
SART ... 122
Sas van Goes ... 986
Satellite communications ... 66
Satellite systems ... 50
Saundersfoot ... 599, 613
Sauzon ... 807, 819
Saye Bay ... 713
Scalasaig ... 541
Scalloway ... 469, 491, 492
Scapa Bay ... 484
Scapa Flow ... 467
Scarborough ... 407, 421
Scarinish ... 501
Scharhörn ... 1017, 1031
Schedule of selected UK Fax broadcasts . 93
Schelphoek ... 969
Scheur Channel ... 966
Scheveningen ... 969, 993
Schiermonnikoog ... 971, 1001
Schilbolsnol ... 970
Schillig ... 1021
Schleuseninsel ... 1011
Schlüttsiel ... 1012
Schulau ... 1011, 1031, 1032
Schull ... 636, 662
Schulpengat ... 970
Schwinge, River ... 1031
Scolpaig ... 504
Scotland – East and North Coast ... 59
Scotland – West Coast ... 59
Scotland, ferries on the west coast ... 529
Scrabster ... 467, 483
Scurdie Ness Lt ... 440
Sea Areas ... 121
Sea Mills ... 622
Seaham ... 424
Search and Rescue (SAR) – UK ... 123
Seasickness ... 145
Secondary Ports ... 151, 153
Sécurité – Safety signal ... 119

Seil Sound ... 527
Seine, River ... 942
Selected UK Local Radio Stations ... 87
Sella Ness ... 469
Selsey Bill ... 319, 328
Semaphore (Signal) stations ... 135
Semaphore stations ... 136
Sending a MAYDAY call ... 118
Séné ... 822
Senhora da Agonia ... 890
Sept Îles ... 822
Sesimbra ... 891, 899
Setúbal ... 891, 899
Seven Stones ... 214
Severn Bridges ... 600, 618
Severn Estuary ... 600, 603
Sevilla ... 909, 913, 914
Shaldon Bridge ... 251
Shambles Bank ... 266
Shannon Estuary ... 637, 639, 666
Shannon, River ... 637
Shapinsay ... 485
Sharfleet Creek ... 366
Sharpness Dock ... 618
Sharpness ... 601, 618
Sheep Haven ... 694, 695
Sheep's Head ... 636
Sheephaven ... 676
Sheerness Tides ... 367-369
Shell Beach ... 717
Shetland Islands ... 468, 490
Shiant Islands ... 505
Shieldaig ... 515
Shillay ... 504
Shingles Bank ... 266
Ship Radio Licence ... 64
Shipping Forecast Record ... 83
Shipping forecast Sea Areas ... 92
Shirehampton ... 622
Soe Rk ... 602
Shoeburyness ... 355, 379
Shoots, The ... 600
Shoreham Tides ... 332-334
Shoreham ... 331
Shornmead Lt ... 351
Short Message Service (SMS)
– introduction ... 91
Sidmouth ... 216
Signals used by SAR aircraft ... 127
Signals used in distress situations ... 127
Signs and warnings ... 12
Silloth ... 566, 572
Sines ... 892, 903
Skadan South Lt ... 468
Skagen W ... 1045
Skagen ... 1045, 1055
Skegness ... 414
Skelligs Rock ... 636
Skerries Bank ... 219
Skerries, The ... 468, 568, 680
Skerryvore ... 501
Skokholm I ... 598
Skomer Is ... 607
Skroo Lt ... 468
Skye ... 500, 502
Sleat, Sound of ... 500, 517
Sligo ... 676, 696
Slugen Channel ... 1044
Slyne Head ... 677, 679, 697
Smalls, The ... 598, 602
Smerwick Harbour ... 665
SMS areas ... 91
SMS Inshore waters forecast areas ... 91
Sneem ... 664
Soay ... 515
Soldiers Bay ... 708, 715
Solent Area Waypoints ... 292
Solent Bank ... 296
Solent Marks ... 261
Solent, E ... 262
Solent, The ... 266, 289
Solthörner Watt ... 1009
Solva ... 607
Solway Firth ... 566, 569
Somos ... 866
Sophiahaven ... 968
Sound signals ... 21
Sources of weather information ... 86
South Bishop ... 598
South Channel ... 466
South Dock Marina ... 373
South Ferriby ... 420
South Ness ... 469
South Queensferry ... 445
South Rock ... 674
South Rock ... 682
South Stack ... 568
South Uist ... 499, 500
South Wick ... 484
Southampton Tides ... 306-308
Southampton Water ... 261
Southampton ... 262, 302
Southend ... 544
Southend-on-Sea ... 379
Southern North Sea TSS ... 187
Southerness Point ... 571
Southport ... 580
Southsea ... 314
Southwold ... 394
Southwold Lt ... 354
Sovereign Hbr ... 326
Spain:
Coast radio stations ... 76
Coastguard radio stations ... 141
CRS MSI broadcasts ... 106
Forecast areas ... 105, 107
MRCC/MRSC ... 140
Radar beacons ... 60
Safety services ... 138
Special Notes ... 870, 911
Weather information ... 109
Special ensigns ... 68
Special marks ... 34
Special Tidal Problems from Swanage
to Selsey ... 277
Speed of movement of pressure
systems ... 85
Speed ... 32
Spiddle ... 677
Spiekeroog ... 1009, 1020
Spit Sand Fort ... 314
Spurn ... 407
St Abb's Hd ... 438
St Alban's Head ... 266
St Andrews ... 452
St Ann's Head ... 598
St Annaland ... 968, 986
St Anthony Hd Lt ... 214
St Aubin ... 724
St Brelade Bay ... 724
St Briac ... 744
St Brides Bay ... 607
St Cast ... 744
St Catherine Bay ... 724
St Catherine's Point ... 263
St Denis ... 836
St Germans ... 236, 238
St Gilles-Croix-de-Vie ... 834, 843
St Guénolé ... 812
St Helen's Fort ... 263, 310
St Helen's Pool ... 225
St Helier Tides ... 726-728
St Helier ... 709, 722
St Hernot ... 797
St Ives ... 601
St Ives ... 628
St Jean de Luz ... 837, 860
St Jean de Monts ... 834
St Katharine Haven ... 374
St Kilda ... 500, 509
St Malo Tides ... 757-759
St Malo ... 743, 745, 760
St Margaret's Hope ... 484
St Martin de Ré ... 835
St Martin ... 846
St Mary's ... 214, 225
St Mawes ... 229
St Monance ... 439
St Monans ... 446
St Nazaire ... 828
St Nicolas ... 797
St Ninian's Bay ... 546
St Norgard ... 797
St Peter Port Tides ... 718-720
St Peter Port ... 708, 716
St Peter ... 1011
St Quay-Portrieux ... 766
St Sampson ... 708, 715
St Serva ... 761
St Suliac ... 762
St Thomas Head ... 624
St Tudwal's Roads ... 604
St Vaast-la-Hougue ... 928, 934
St Valéry-en-Caux ... 947
St Valéry-sur-Somme ... 930, 953
Stackpole Quay ... 613
Stade ... 1011, 1031
Stadersand ... 1031
Staffa ... 520
Standard Ports ... 151, 152, 158
Stansore Point ... 297
Starcross ... 253
Start Point ... 218, 244
Start Point Lt ... 215
Start Point Lt (Sanday) ... 468
State of Consciousness ... 143
Stavenisse ... 968, 985, 986
Stavoren ... 996
Ste Evette ... 812
Ste Marine ... 813
Steep Holm ... 616
Stellendam ... 969, 987
Stevinsluizen ... 970
Stirling ... 445
Stoer Head ... 498
Stokes Bay ... 267
Stonehaven ... 440, 454

ör 1031
ores 23
örloch 1011, 1031
orm Tide Warning Service 158
ornoway Tides 506-508
ornoway 498
ornoway 504
our, River (Christchurch) 287
our, River (Harwich) 391
our, River (Sandwich) 344
raight Point 219
rait of Gibraltar 910, 917
raits of Gibraltar TSS 191
rangford Lough 674, 682
ranraer 538
rathy Point Lt 467
raw Is 677
roma 483
roma Lt 467
romness 467, 485
rong wind warnings 85
ronsay 468, 486
rumble Head 598
udland Bay 276
ıbfacts 128
ubfacts 241, 320, 529, 558
ıbmarine exercise areas,
Central English Channel 320
NW Scotland 529
SW Scotland/Irish Sea 559
W English Channel 241
ıbmarines 128
ıdbrook 618
ıderoogsand 1039
ıggestions for improvements 2
ıle Skerry 483
ıle Skerry Lt 467
ıllom Voe 469, 490, 491
ımburgh Head Lt 468
ımburgh 491
ımmer Isles 498, 511
ın's declination 34
ınderland 424
ınderland Roker Pier Hd Lt 408
ınk Head 385
wale, River 350, 363
wanage 260, 276
wansea Bay 599
wansea Vale 775
wansea 599, 615
warbacks Minn 490
wellies, The 586
wilkie Pt 470
winge, The 710
ybil Pt 639
ylt 1012, 1039
ymbols 7

T

ıbs Head 414
ıin 466
ımar, River 238
ıncarville 942
ınger 918
Tangier 910
Tarbat Ness Lt 466
Tarbert Is 666
Tarbert 543
Tarifa 910, 917
Tarn Point 573
Tater-du 214
Tautenay 708
Tavira 891, 905
Taw, River 601, 626
Taylor's Rk 219
Tay, River 440, 452
Tazones 866
Tean Sound 225
Tearaght Rks 639
Teelin Harbour 695
Teelin 676
Tees, River 422
Tegeler Plate 1010
Teignmouth 216, 251
Tejo, Rio 891
Telegraph Bay 713
Television forecasts 94
Temporary importation (TI) 24
Tenby 599, 613
Terms used in weather bulletins 85
Termunterzijl 971, 1001, 1008
Terneuzen 967, 980
Terre-Nègre 836
Terschelling 972
Test, River 262
Teufelsbrück 1011, 1032
Texel 972
Texelstroom 970
Thames Estuary 359
Thames Tidal Barrier 371
Thames, River 351, 370
Thisted Havn 1045
Tholensche Gat 968
Thorney Channel 319
Thorney 319
Three Stone Oar 217
Thurso 467
Thyborøn Kanal 1044
Thyborøn 1044, 1053
Tidal Coefficients 151
Tidal Coefficients 791
Tidal prediction by computer 154
Tidal stream atlases 155
Tidal streams in rivers 156
Tidal streams 155
Tidal stream charts:
Area 1 212
Area 2 258
Area 3 324
Area 4 348
Area 5 404
Area 6 436
Area 7 464
Area 8 496
Area 9 534
Area 10 564
Area 11 596
Area 12 632
Area 13 672
Area 14 706
Area 15 740
Area 16 770
Area 17 802
Area 18 832
Area 22 926
Area 23 964
Area 24 1006
Tidecalc 154
Tighnabruaich 547
Tilbury 372
Time difference 152
Times 150
Timing of gale warnings 85
Tingwall 486
Tinker's Hole 520
Tiree 501
Tiumpan Head Lt 498
Tobermory 501, 519
Todhead Lt 440
Tollesbury 385
Tönning 1011
Topsham 253
Torduff Point 571
Torquay 216, 250
Torr Pt 678
Torre de Hércules 867
Torridge 626
Torridge, River 601
Torsminde Havn 1044, 1052
Tory Island 676
Tossens 1009
Totland Bay 287, 288
Totnes 249
Touquet, Pte de 933
Traffic Centres 111
Traffic Separation Schemes (TSS) 18, 181
Tralee Bay 636, 665
Tranum Strand 1045
Trawbreaga Bay 693
Trawbeaga Lough 679
Trearddur Bay 588
Trébeurden 773, 783
Tréboul 798
Trefor 588
Trégastel 773, 783, 785
Tréguier River 772
Tréguier 781
Tréhiguier 824
Treshnish Isles 520
Trévignon 805
Trevose Head 601
Trézien 774
Trieux River 779
Troon 538, 556
Trouville 929, 940
True bearing of sun at sunrise and sunset 36
Truro 229
Trwyn Dinmor 588
TSS Western Approaches 184
Tuckton 287
Turnberry Point Lt 538
Turnchapel 236
Tuskar Rock TSS 183, 650
Tuskar Rock 634,635, 638, 650
Tuskar 635
Twelfths rule 154
Tyne, River 408, 425
Tyne, River, Tides 426-428
Types and installation 122
Types of systems 50

U

Uig 500
UK Coastguard stations 98
UK HF Fax stations 93
UK Navigation warnings broadcasts 70
UK Ports VTS listening watch 166
Ullapool Tides 512-514
Ullapool 498, 502, 511
Ulva Sound 519
Ulverston 574
Unst 469
Upnor 366
Ura Firth 490
Urgency and safety 119
Urgency 117
Urk 996
Use of factors 153
Useful addresses 24
Ushenish Lt 499
Using the International Code 64
Usk, River 600

V

Vaila Sound 490, 492
Val-André 764
Valentia Harbour 664, 665
Valentia 636
Vannes 822, 823
Vareler Siel 1009
Varne 327
VAT and the single market 24
Vatersay Sound 499
Vatteville 942
Vazon Bay 715
Veere 986
Vegesack 1026
Ventnor 310
Ventry 636
Ver 929
Vessel Traffic Services (VTS) 166
VHF calls to coast radio stations 66
VHF radio 65
Viana Do Castelo 893
Vila Real de Santo António 891, 905, 909
Vilaine River 808, 824
Vilamoura 891, 904
Village Bay 509
Ville-es-Martin 809
Visibility 85
Visual and audible distress signals 117
Visual signals, shore to ships 126
Vlaardingen 992
Vlieland 971, 999
Vliestroom 971
Vlissingen OOST 967
Vlissingen Tides 982-984
Vlissingen 967, 981
Volendam 996
Volkeraksluizen 969
Volmet 94
Voslapp 1009

W

W Burra Firth Inner Lt 469
Waddenzee 970
Wadebridge 628
Wallasea 381
Wallet 352
Walsoorden 968, 979
Walton Backwaters 353, 387
Walton-on-the-Naze Tides 388-390
Wangerooge 1009, 1020
Wangersiel 1021
Wareham 280, 281
Warren Pt 243
Warrenpoint 681
Warsash 304
Wash, The 406
Watchet 601
Watchet 625
Waterfoot 690
Waterford 635, 652
Watermill Cove 225
Watermouth 601, 625
Watwick Point 598
Waypoint navigation 54
Waypoints 54
Weather by FAX (MetFAX marine) 90
Weather Centres 93
Weather information 67
Weather messages 96
Weather systems 86
Weather 13
Wedel 1011, 1032
Wellhouse Rock 618
Wells Bar 412
Wells-next-the-Sea 406, 412
Welsh Channel 567
Wembury Bay 215
Wembury Firing Range 238
Wemeldinge 968, 986
Wemyss Bay 548
Weser, River 1009, 1010, 1013
West Cove 664
West Frisian Islands 972
West Kyle 546
West Loch Tarbert 504, 536, 541
West Mersea 385
West Schouwen 969
West Stones 413
West Terschelling 971, 999
Westerheversand 1011
Westerland 1039
Westerschelde 966, 972, 979
Westhoofd 969
Westkapelle 967, 979
Weston 302
Weston-super-Mare 601, 624
Westport 677, 697
Westray 468
Wexford 634, 649
Weymouth 260, 274
Whalsay 468, 490
Whiddy Isle 636
Whitaker Beacon 381
Whitaker Channel 352
Whitby 422
Whitby High Lt 407
White House 61
Whitehaven 566, 57
Whitehills 466, 47
Whitsand Bay 23
Whitstable 350, 36
Wick Tides 480-48
Wick 467, 479
Wicklow Head 634
Wicklow 634, 648
Wide Firth 468
Widewall Bay 485
Widnes 580
Wielingen Channel 96
Wilhelmshaven Tides 1022-1024
Wilhelmshaven 1009, 1025
Willemstad 969
Wind 156
Wind 85
Winteringham Haven 420
Winterton-on-Sea 399
Wisbech Cut 413
Wisbech 413
Wischhafen 1031
Wissant 956
Wittdün 1012, 1038
Wöhrden 1031
Wolf Rock Lt 214
Wolphaartsdijk 986
Woolwich Reach 371
Woolwich 372
Wootton Creek 309
Wootton 262
Worbarrow Bay 276
Workington 566, 572
Workum 996
Worthing 331
Wouldham 366
Wyk 1012, 1038
Wyre Lighthouse 575
Wyre Sound 484

Y

Yacht and Boat Safety Scheme 126
Yacht documents 22
Yare, River 399
Yarmouth 261, 294
Yealm Entrance 243
Yealm, River 215, 243
Yell Sound 469, 490
Yelland Marsh 626
Yerseke 968, 986
Youghal 635, 653

Z

Zandvliet 968
Zeebrugge 966, 978
Zeegat van Ameland 971
Zeegat van Terschelling 971, 1000
Zeegat van Texel 970
Zierikzee 968, 986
Zijpe 968
Zoutkamp 971, 1000
Zumaya 872